Stanley Gibbons
Simplified Catalogue

# Stamps of the World

Stanley Gibbons Simplified Catalogue

# Stamps of the World

2012 Edition

Countries **Abu Dhabi – Charkhari**

1

**Stanley Gibbons Ltd**
London and Ringwood

By Appointment to
Her Majesty The Queen
Stanley Gibbons Limited
London
Philatelists

77th Edition
Published in Great Britain by
Stanley Gibbons Ltd
Publications Editorial, Sales Offices and Distribution Centre
7, Parkside, Christchurch Road,
Ringwood, Hampshire BH24 3SH
Telephone +44 (0) 1425 472363

British Library Cataloguing in
Publication Data.
A catalogue record for this book is available
from the British Library.

Volume 1
ISBN 10: 0-85259-832-7
ISBN 13: 978-0-85259-832-0

Published as Stanley Gibbons Simplified Catalogue from 1934 to 1970, renamed Stamps of the World in 1971, and produced in two (1982-88), three (1989-2001), four (2002-2005) five (2006-2010) and six from 2011 volumes as Stanley Gibbons Simplified Catalogue of Stamps of the World.



Item No. 2881– Set12

Printed and bound in Wales by Stephens & George

# Contents – Volume 1

# About Us

**Our History**

Edward Stanley Gibbons started trading postage stamps in his father's chemist shop in 1856. Since then we have been at the forefront of stamp collecting for over 150 years. We hold the Royal Warrant, offer unsurpassed expertise and quality and provide collectors with the peace of mind of a certificate of authenticity on all of our stamps. If you think of stamp collecting, you think of Stanley Gibbons and we are proud to uphold that tradition for you.

**399 Strand**

Our world famous stamp shop is a collector's paradise, with all of our latest catalogues, albums and accessories and, of course, our unrivalled stockholding of postage stamps.
www.stanleygibbons.com shop@stanleygibbons.com +44 (0)20 7836 8444

**Specialist Stamp Sales**

For the collector that appreciates the value of collecting the highest quality examples, Stanley Gibbons is the only choice. Our extensive range is unrivalled in terms of quality and quantity, with specialist stamps available from all over the world.
www.stanleygibbons.com/stamps shop@stanleygibbons.com +44 (0)20 7836 8444

**Stanley Gibbons Auctions and Valuations**

Sell your collection or individual rare items through our prestigious public auctions or our regular postal auctions and benefit from the excellent prices being realised at auction currently. We also provide an unparalleled valuation service.
www.stanleygibbons.com/auctions auctions@stanleygibbons.com +44 (0)20 7836 8444

**Stanley Gibbons Publications**

The world's first stamp catalogue was printed by Stanley Gibbons in 1865 and we haven't looked back since! Our catalogues are trusted worldwide as the industry standard and we print countless titles each year. We also publish consumer and trade magazines, Gibbons Stamp Monthly and Philatelic Exporter to bring you news, views and insights into all things philatelic. Never miss an issue by subscribing today and benefit from exclusive subscriber offers each month.
www.stanleygibbons.com/shop orders@stanleygibbons.com +44 (0)1425 472 363

**Stanley Gibbons Investments**

The Stanley Gibbons Investment Department offers a unique range of investment propositions that have consistently outperformed more traditional forms of investment, from capital protected products with unlimited upside to portfolios made up of the world's rarest stamps and autographs.
www.stanleygibbons.com/investment investment@stanleygibbons.com +44 (0)1481 708 270

**Fraser's Autographs**

Autographs, manuscripts and memorabilia from Henry VIII to current day. We have over 60,000 items in stock, including movie stars, musicians, sport stars, historical figures and royalty. Fraser's is the UK's market leading autograph dealer and has been dealing in high quality autographed material since 1978.
www.frasersautographs.com sales@frasersautographs.com +44 (0)20 7557 4404

**stanleygibbons.com**

Our website offers the complete philatelic service. Whether you are looking to buy stamps, invest, read news articles, browse our online stamp catalogue or find new issues, you are just one click away from anything you desire in the world of stamp collecting at stanleygibbons.com. Happy browsing!
www.stanleygibbons.com

# Introduction

**The ultimate reference work for all stamps issued around the world since the very first Penny Black of 1840, now with an improved layout.**

*Stamps of the World* provides a comprehensive, illustrated, priced guide to postage stamps, and is the standard reference tool for every collector. It will help you to identify those elusive stamps, to value your collection, and to learn more about the background to issues. *Stamps of the World* was first published in 1934 and has been updated every year since 1950.

The helpful article 'Putting on a Good Show' provides expert advice on starting and developing a collection, then making the most of its presentation. Also included is a guide to stamp identification so that you can easily discover which country issued your stamp.

Re-designed to provide more colourful, clearer, and easy-to-navigate listings, these volumes continue to present you with a wealth of information to enhance your enjoyment of stamp collecting.

**Features:**

- Current values for every stamp in the world from the experts
- Easy-to-use simplified listings
- World-recognised Stanley Gibbons catalogue numbers
- A wealth of historical, geographical and currency information
- Indexing and cross-referencing throughout the volumes
- Worldwide miniature sheets listed and priced
- Thousands of new issues since the last edition

For this edition, prices have been thoroughly reviewed for Great Britain up to date, and all Commonwealth countries up to 1970, with further updates for Commonwealth countries which have appeared in our recently-published or forthcoming comprehensive catalogues under the titles *Cyprus, Gibraltar and Malta, Eastern Pacific and St Helena, Ascension and Tristan da Cunha*. Other countries with complete price updates from the following comprehensive catalogues are: *China, Germany, Portugal and Spain and United States of America*. New issues received from all other countries have been listed and priced. The first *Gibbons Stamp Monthly* Catalogue Supplement to this edition is September 2011.

# Information for users

## Scope of the Catalogue

*Stamps of the World* contains listings of postage stamps only. Apart from the ordinary definitive, commemorative and air-mail stamps of each country there are sections for the following, where appropriate. Noted below are the Prefixes used for each section (see Guide to Entries for further information):

- postage due stamps – Prefix in listing D
- parcel post or postcard stamps – Prefix P
- official stamps – Prefix O
- express and special delivery stamps - Prefix E
- frank stamps – Prefix F
- charity tax stamps – Prefix J
- newspaper and journal stamps – Prefix N
- printed matter stamps – Prefix
- registration stamps - Prefix R
- acknowledgement of receipt stamps – Prefix AR
- late fee and too late stamps – Prefix L
- military post stamps- Prefix M
- recorded message stamps – Prefix RM
- personal delivery stamps – Prefix P
- concessional letter post – Prefix CL
- concessional parcel post – Prefix CP
- pneumatic post stamps – Prefix PE
- publicity envelope stamps – Prefix B
- bulk mail stamps – Prefix BP
- telegraph used for postage – Prefix PT
- telegraph (Commonwealth Countries) – Prefix T
- obligatory tax – Prefix T
- Frama Labels and Royal Mail Postage Labels No Prefix-

As this is a simplified listing, the following are NOT included:

**Fiscal or revenue stamps:** stamps used solely in collecting taxes or fees for non-postal purposes. For example, stamps which pay a tax on a receipt, represent the stamp duty on a contract, or frank a customs document. Common inscriptions found include: Documentary, Proprietary, Inter. Revenue and Contract Note.

**Local stamps:** postage stamps whose validity and use are limited in area to a prescribed district, town or country, or on certain routes where there is no government postal service. They may be issued by private carriers and freight companies, municipal authorities or private individuals.

**Local carriage labels and Private local issues:** many labels exist ostensibly to cover the cost of ferrying mail from one of Great Britain's offshore islands to the nearest mainland post office. They are not recognised as valid for national or international mail. Examples: Calf of Man, Davaar, Herm, Lundy, Pabay, Stroma.

**Telegraph stamps:** stamps intended solely for the prepayment of telegraphic communication.

**Bogus or "phantom" stamps:** labels from mythical places or non-existent administrations. Examples in the classical period were Sedang, Counani, Clipperton Island and in modern times Thomond and Monte Bello Islands. Numerous labels have also appeared since the War from dissident groups as propaganda for their claims and without authority from the home governments. Common examples are the numerous issues for Nagaland.

**Railway letter fee stamps:** special stamps issued by railway companies for the conveyance of letters by rail. Example: Talyllyn Railway. Similar services are now offered by some bus companies and the labels they issue likewise do not qualify for inclusion in the catalogue.

**Perfins ("perforated initials"):** stamps perforated with the initials or emblems of firms as a security measure to prevent pilferage by office staff.

**Labels:** Slips of paper with an adhesive backing. Collectors tend to make a distinction between stamps, which have postal validity and anything else, which has not.

However, Frama Labels and Royal Mail Postage Labels are both classified as postage stamps and are therefore listed in this catalogue.

**Cut-outs:** Embossed or impressed stamps found on postal stationery, which are cut out if the stationery has been ruined and re-used as adhesives.

Further information on a wealth of terms is in *Philatelic Terms Illustrated*, published by Stanley Gibbons, details are listed under Stanley Gibbons Publications. There is also a priced listing of the postal fiscals of Great Britain in our *Commonwealth & British Empire Stamps 1840-1970* Catalogue and in Volume 1 of the *Great Britain Specialised Catalogue* (5th and later editions). Again, further details are listed under the Stanley Gibbons Publications section (see p.xii).

## Organisation of the Catalogue

The catalogue lists countries in alphabetical order with country headers on each page and extra introductory information such as philatelic historical background at the beginning of each section. The Contents list provides a detailed guide to each volume, and the Index has full cross-referencing to locate each country in each volume.

Each country lists postage stamps in order of date of issue, from earliest to most recent, followed by separate sections for categories such as postage due stamps, express stamps, official stamps, and so on (see above for a complete listing).

### "Appendix" Countries

Since 1968 Stanley Gibbons has listed in an appendix stamps which are judged to be in excess of true postal needs. The appendix also contains stamps which have not fulfilled all the normal conditions for full catalogue listing. Full catalogue listing requires a stamp to be:

- issued by a legitimate postal authority
- recognised by the government concerned
- adhesive
- valid for proper postal use in the class of service for which they are inscribed
- available to the general public at face value with no artificial restrictions being imposed on their distribution (with the exception of categories as postage dues and officials)

Only stamps issued from component parts of otherwise united territories which represent a genuine political, historical or postal division within the country concerned have a full catalogue listing. Any such issues which do not fulfil this stipulation will be recorded in the Catalogue Appendix only.

Stamps listed in the Appendix are constantly under review in light of newly acquired information about them. If we are satisfied that a stamp qualifies for proper listing in the body of the catalogue it will be moved in the next edition.

### "Undesirable Issues"

The rules governing many competitive exhibitions are set by the Federation Internationale de Philatelie and stipulate a downgrading of marks for stamps classed as "undesirable issues".

This catalogue can be taken as a guide to status. All stamps in the main listings are acceptable. Stamps in the Appendix are considered, "undesirable issues" and should not be entered for competition.

### Correspondence

We welcome information and suggestions but we must ask correspondents to include the cost of postage for the return of any materials, plus registration where appropriate. Letters and emails should be addressed to Michelle Briggs, 7 Parkside, Christchurch Road, Ringwood, Hampshire BH24 3SH, UK. mrbriggs@stanleygibbons.co.uk. Where information is solicited purely for the benefit of the enquirer we regret we are seldom able to reply.

### Identification of Stamps

We regret we do not give opinion on the authenticity of stamps, nor do we identify stamps or number them by our Catalogue.

### Thematic Collectors

Stanley Gibbons publishes a range of thematic catalogues (see page xxxix for details) and *Stamps of the World* is ideal to use with these titles, as it supplements those listings with extra information.

### Type numbers

Type numbers (in bold) refer to illustrations, and are not the Stanley Gibbons Catalogue numbers.

A brief description of the stamp design subject is given below or beside the illustrations, or close by in the entry, where needed. Where a design is not illustrated, it is usually the same shape and size as a related design, unless otherwise indicated.

### Watermarks

Watermarks are not covered in this catalogue. Stamps of the same issue with differing watermarks are not listed separately.

### Perforations

Perforations – all stamps are perforated unless otherwise stated. No distinction is made between the various gauges of perforation but early stamp issues which exist both imperforate and perforated are usually listed separately. Where a heading states, "Imperf or perf"or "Perf. or rouletted" this does not necessarily mean that all values of the issue are found in both conditions

### *Se-tenant* Pairs

Se-tenant Pairs – Many modern issues are printed in sheets containing different designs or face values. Such pairs, blocks, strips or sheets are described as being "*se-tenant*" and they are outside the scope of this catalogue, although reference to them may occur in instances where they form a composite design.

Miniature Sheets are now fully listed.

# Guide to Entries

**Ⓐ Country of Issue**

**Ⓑ Part Number** – shows where to find more detailed listings in the Stanley Gibbons Comprehensive Catalogue. Part 6 refers to France and so on – see p. xli for further information on the breakdown of the Catalogue.

**Ⓒ Country Information** – Brief geographical and historical details for the issuing country.

**Ⓓ Currency** – Details of the currency, and dates of earliest use where applicable, on the face value of the stamps. Where a Colony has the same currency as the Mother Country, see the details given in that country.

**Ⓔ Year Date** – When a set of definitive stamps has been issued over several years the Year Date given is for the earliest issue, commeorative sets are listed in chronological order. As stamps of the same design or issue are usually grouped together a list of King George VI stamps, for example, headed "1938" may include stamps issued from 1938 to the end of the reign.

**Ⓕ Stanley Gibbons Catalogue number** – This is a unique number for each stamp to help the collector identify stamps in the listing. The Stanley Gibbons numbering system is universally recognized as definitive. The majority of listings are in chronological order, but where a definitive set of stamps has been re-issued with a new watermark, perforation change or imprint date, the cheapest example is given; in such cases catalogue numbers may not be in numerical order.

Where insufficient numbers have been left to provide for additional stamps to a listing, some stamps will have a suffix letter after the catalogue number. If numbers have been left for additions to a set and not used they will be left vacant.

The separate type numbers (in bold) refer to illustrations (see **M**).

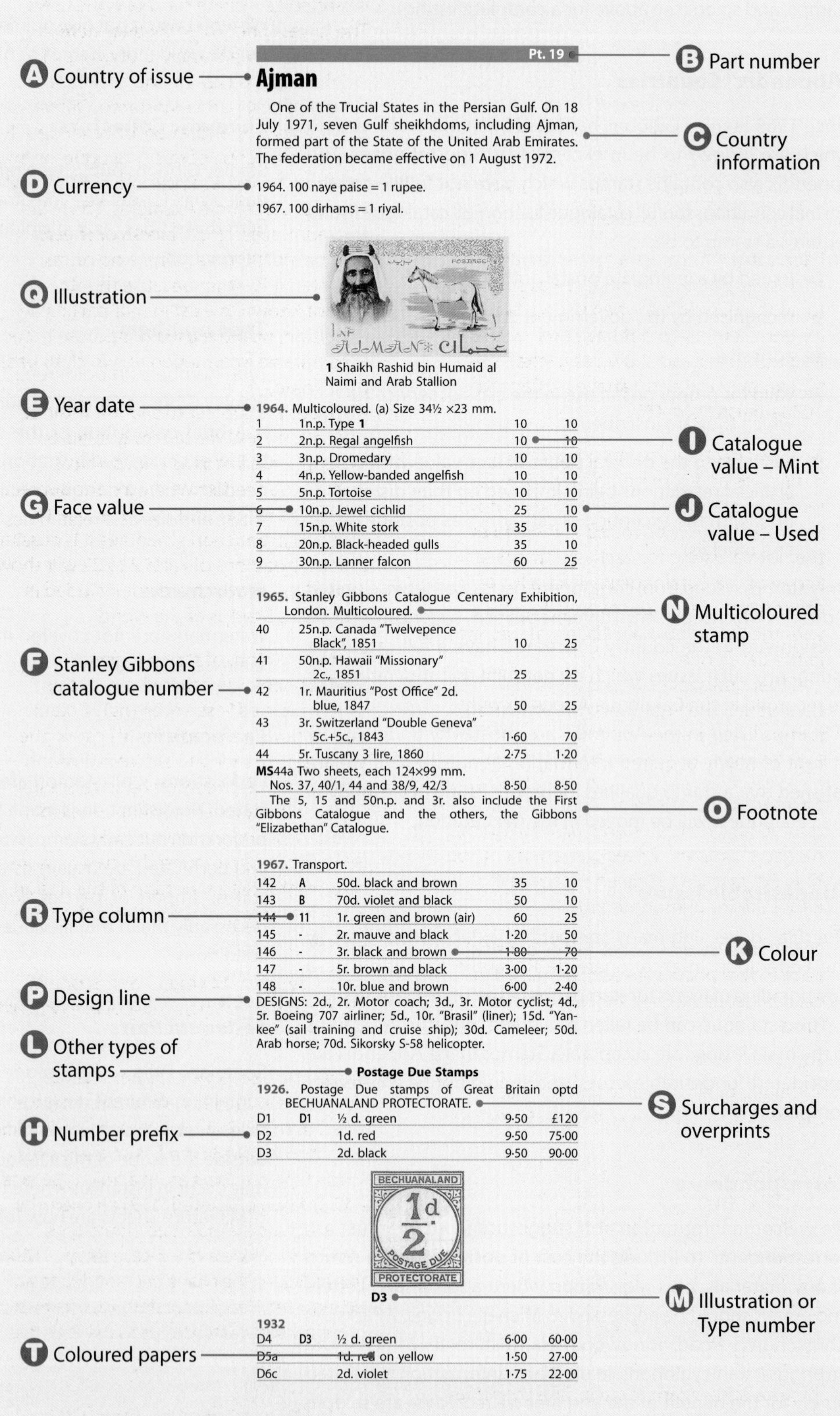


Pt. 19

**Ajman**

One of the Trucial States in the Persian Gulf. On 18 July 1971, seven Gulf sheikhdoms, including Ajman, formed part of the State of the United Arab Emirates. The federation became effective on 1 August 1972.

1964. 100 naye paise = 1 rupee.
1967. 100 dirhams = 1 riyal.

**1** Shaikh Rashid bin Humaid al Naimi and Arab Stallion

**1964.** Multicoloured. (a) Size 34½ ×23 mm.

| | | | |
|---|---|---|---|
| 1 | 1n.p. Type **1** | 10 | 10 |
| 2 | 2n.p. Regal angelfish | 10 | 10 |
| 3 | 3n.p. Dromedary | 10 | 10 |
| 4 | 4n.p. Yellow-banded angelfish | 10 | 10 |
| 5 | 5n.p. Tortoise | 10 | 10 |
| 6 | 10n.p. Jewel cichlid | 25 | 10 |
| 7 | 15n.p. White stork | 35 | 10 |
| 8 | 20n.p. Black-headed gulls | 35 | 10 |
| 9 | 30n.p. Lanner falcon | 60 | 25 |

**1965.** Stanley Gibbons Catalogue Centenary Exhibition, London. Multicoloured.

| | | | |
|---|---|---|---|
| 40 | 25n.p. Canada "Twelvepence Black", 1851 | 10 | 25 |
| 41 | 50n.p. Hawaii "Missionary" 2c., 1851 | 25 | 25 |
| 42 | 1r. Mauritius "Post Office" 2d. blue, 1847 | 50 | 25 |
| 43 | 3r. Switzerland "Double Geneva" 5c.+5c., 1843 | 1·60 | 70 |
| 44 | 5r. Tuscany 3 lire, 1860 | 2·75 | 1·20 |
| **MS**44a | Two sheets, each 124×99 mm. Nos. 37, 40/1, 44 and 38/9, 42/3 | 8·50 | 8·50 |

The 5, 15 and 50n.p. and 3r. also include the First Gibbons Catalogue and the others, the Gibbons "Elizabethan" Catalogue.

**1967.** Transport.

| | | | | |
|---|---|---|---|---|
| 142 | A | 50d. black and brown | 35 | 10 |
| 143 | B | 70d. violet and black | 50 | 10 |
| 144 | 11 | 1r. green and brown (air) | 60 | 25 |
| 145 | - | 2r. mauve and black | 1·20 | 50 |
| 146 | - | 3r. black and brown | 1·80 | 70 |
| 147 | - | 5r. brown and black | 3·00 | 1·20 |
| 148 | - | 10r. blue and brown | 6·00 | 2·40 |

DESIGNS: 2d., 2r. Motor coach; 3d., 3r. Motor cyclist; 4d., 5r. Boeing 707 airliner; 5d., 10r. "Brasil" (liner); 15d. "Yankee" (sail training and cruise ship); 30d. Cameleer; 50d. Arab horse; 70d. Sikorsky S-58 helicopter.

**Postage Due Stamps**

**1926.** Postage Due stamps of Great Britain optd BECHUANALAND PROTECTORATE.

| | | | | |
|---|---|---|---|---|
| D1 | D1 | ½ d. green | 9·50 | £120 |
| D2 | | 1d. red | 9·50 | 75·00 |
| D3 | | 2d. black | 9·50 | 90·00 |

BECHUANALAND ½d POSTAGE DUE PROTECTORATE

D3

**1932**

| | | | | |
|---|---|---|---|---|
| D4 | D3 | ½ d. green | 6·00 | 60·00 |
| D5a | | 1d. red on yellow | 1·50 | 27·00 |
| D6c | | 2d. violet | 1·75 | 22·00 |

**462** Canadian Maple Leaf Emblem

1981

1030a **462** A (30c.) red 20 40

No. 1030a was printed before a new first class domestic letter rate had been agreed, "A" representing the face value of the stamp, later decided to be 30c.

**G Face value** – This refers to the value of each stamp and is the price it was sold for at the Post Office when issued. Some modern stamps do not have their values in figures but instead shown as a letter, see for example the entry above for Canada 1030a/Illustration 462.

**H Number Prefix** – Stamps other than definitives and commemoratives have a prefix letter before the catalogue number. Such stamps may be found at the end of the normal listing for each country. (See Scope of the Catalogue p.viii for a list of other types of stamps covered, together with the list of the main abbreviations used in the Catalogue).

Other prefixes are also used in the Catalogue. Their use is explained in the text: some examples are A for airmail, E for East Germany or Express Delivery stamps.

**I Catalogue Value** – Mint/Unused. Prices quoted for pre-1945 stamps are for lightly hinged examples. Prices quoted of unused King Edward VIII to Queen Elizabeth II issues are for unmounted mint.

**J Catalogue Value** – Used. Prices generally refer to fine postally used examples. For certain issues they are for cancelled-to-order.

*Prices*

Prices are given in pence and pounds. Stamps worth £100 and over are shown in whole pounds:

| Shown in Catalogue as | Explanation |
|---|---|
| 10 | 10 pence |
| 1.75 | £1.75 |
| 15.00 | £15 |
| £150 | £150 |
| £2300 | £2300 |

Prices assume stamps are in 'fine condition'; we may ask more for superb and less for those of lower quality. The minimum catalogue price quoted is 10p and is intended as a guide for catalogue users. The lowest price for individual stamps purchased from Stanley Gibbons is £1.

Prices quoted are for the cheapest variety of that particular stamp. Differences of watermark, perforation, or other details, outside the scope of this catalogue, often increase the value. Prices quoted for mint issues are for single examples. Those in *se-tenant* pairs, strips, blocks or sheets may be worth more. Where no prices are listed it is either because the stamps are not known to exist in that particular condition, or, more usually, because there is no reliable information on which to base their value.

All prices are subject to change without prior notice and we cannot guarantee to supply all stamps as priced. Prices quoted in advertisements are also subject to change without prior notice. Due to differing production schedules it is possible that new editions of Parts 2 to 22 will show revised prices which are not included in that year's Stamps of the World.

**K Colour** – Colour of stamp (if fewer than four colours, otherwise noted as "multicoloured"– see N below). Colour descriptions are simple in this catalogue, and only expanded to aid identification – see other more comprehensive Stanley Gibbons catalogues for more detailed colour descriptions (see p.xxxix).

Where stamps are printed in two or more colours, the central portion of the design is the first colour given, unless otherwise stated.

**L Other Types of Stamps** – See Scope of the Catalogue p.viii for a list of the types of stamps included.

**M Illustration or Type Number** – These numbers are used to help identify stamps, either in the listing, type column, design line or footnote, usually the first value in a set. These type numbers are in a bold type face – **123**; when bracketed (**123**) an overprint or a surcharge is indicated. Some type numbers include a lower-case letter – **123a**, this indicates they have been added to an existing set. New cross references are also normally shown in bold, as in the example below.

**1990.** Small Craft of Canada (2nd series). Early Work Boats. As T **563**. Multicoloured.

**N Multicoloured** – Nearly all modern stamps are multicoloured; this is indicated in the heading, with a description of the stamp given in the listing.

**O Footnote** – further information on background or key facts on issues

**P Design line** – Further details on design variations

**Q Illustration** – Generally, the first stamp in the set. Stamp illustrations are reduced to 75%, with overprints and surcharges shown actual size.

**R Key Type** – indicates a design type (see p. xii for further details) on which the stamp is based. These are the bold figures found below each illustration. The type numbers are also given in bold in the second column of figures alongside the stamp description to indicate the design of each stamp. Where an issue comprises stamps of similar design, the corresponding type number should be taken as indicating the general design. Where there are blanks in the type number column it means that the type of the corresponding stamp is that shown by the number in the type column of the same issue. A dash ( – ) in the type column means that the stamp is not illustrated. Where type numbers refer to stamps of another country, e.g. where stamps of one country are overprinted for use in another, this is always made clear in the text.

**S Surcharges and Overprints** – usually described in the headings. Any actual wordings are shown in bold type. Descriptions clarify words and figures used in the overprint. Stamps with the same overprints in different colours are not listed separately. Numbers in brackets after the descriptions are the catalogue numbers of the non-overprinted stamps. The words "inscribed" or "inscription" refer to the wording incorporated in the design of a stamp and not surcharges or overprints.

**T Coloured Papers** – stamps printed on coloured paper are shown – e.g. "brn on yell" indicates brown printed on yellow paper. No information on the texture of paper, e.g. laid or wove, is provided in this catalogue.

# Key-Types

Standard designs frequently occuring on the stamps of the French, German, Portuguese and Spanish colonies are illustrated below together with the descriptive names and letters by which they are referred to in the lists to avoid repetition. Please see the Guide to Entries for further information.

## French Group

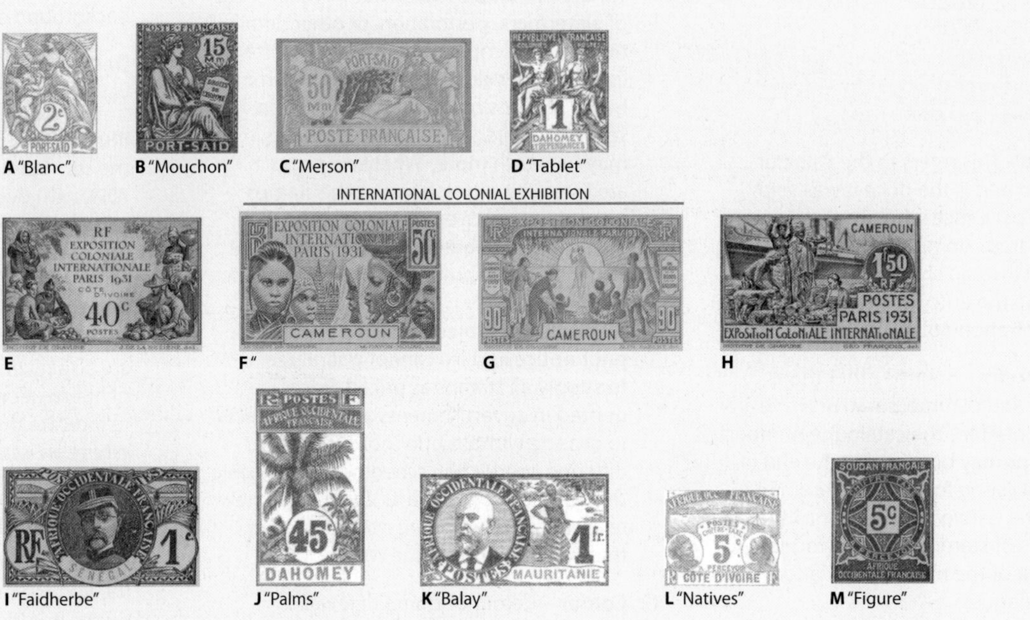

**A** "Blanc" **B** "Mouchon" **C** "Merson" **D** "Tablet"

INTERNATIONAL COLONIAL EXHIBITION

**E** **F** " **G** **H**

**I** "Faidherbe" **J** "Palms" **K** "Balay" **L** "Natives" **M** "Figure"

## German Group

**N** "Yacht" **O** "Yacht"

## Spanish Group

**X** "Alfonso XII" **Y** "Baby" **Z** "Curly Head"

## Portuguese Group

**P** "Crown" **Q** "Embossed" **R** "Figures" **S** "Carlos" **T** "Manoel" **U** Ceres" **V** "Newspaper" **W** "Due"

# Glossary of terms

| *English* | *French* | *German* | *Spanish* | *Italian* |
|---|---|---|---|---|
| Agate | Agate | Achat | Agata | Agata |
| Air stamp | Timbre de la poste aérienne | Flugpostmarke | Sello de correo aéreo | Francobollo per posta aerea |
| Apple Green | Vert-pomme | Apfelgrün | Verde manzana | Verde mela |
| Barred | Annulé par barres | Balkenentwertung | Anulado con barras | Sbarrato |
| Bisected | Timbre coupé | Halbiert | Partido en dos | Frazionato |
| Bistre | Bistre | Bister | Bistre | Bistro |
| Bistre-brown | Brun-bistre | Bisterbraun | Castaño bistre | Bruno-bistro |
| Black | Noir | Schwarz | Negro | Nero |
| Blackish Brown | Brun-noir | Schwärzlichbraun | Castaño negruzco | Bruno nerastro |
| Blackish Green | Vert foncé | Schwärzlichgrün | Verde negruzco | Verde nerastro |
| Blackish Olive | Olive foncé | Schwärzlicholiv | Oliva negruzco | Oliva nerastro |
| Block of four | Bloc de quatre | Viererblock | Bloque de cuatro | Bloco di quattro |
| Blue | Bleu | Blau | Azul | Azzurro |
| Blue-green | Vert-bleu | Blaugrün | Verde azul | Verde azzuro |
| Bluish Violet | Violet bleuâtre | Bläulichviolett | Violeta azulado | Violtto azzurrastro |
| Booklet | Carnet | Heft | Cuadernillo | Libretto |
| Bright Blue | Bleu vif | Lebhaftblau | Azul vivo | Azzurro vivo |
| Bright Green | Vert vif | Lebhaftgrün | Verde vivo | Verde vivo |
| Bright Purple | Mauve vif | Lebhaftpurpur | Púrpura vivo | Porpora vivo |
| Bronze Green | Vert-bronze | Bronzegrün | Verde bronce | Verde bronzo |
| Brown | Brun | Braun | Castaño | Bruno |
| Brown-lake | Carmin-brun | Braunlack | Laca castaño | Lacca bruno |
| Brown-purple | Pourpre-brun | Braunpurpur | Púrpura castaño | Porpora bruno |
| Brown-red | Rouge-brun | Braunrot | Rojo castaño | Rosso bruno |
| Buff | Chamois | Sämisch | Anteado | Camoscio |
| Cancellation | Oblitération | Entwertung | Cancelación | Annullamento |
| Cancelled | Annulé | Gestempelt | Cancelado | Annullato |
| Carmine | Carmin | Karmin | Carmín | Carminio |
| Carmine-red | Rouge-carmin | Karminrot | Rojo carmín | Rosso carminio |
| Centred | Centré | Zentriert | Centrado | Centrato |
| Cerise | Rouge-cerise | Kirschrot | Color de ceresa | Color Ciliegia |
| Chalk-surfaced paper | Papier couché | Kreidepapier | Papel estucado | Carta gessata |
| Chalky Blue | Bleu terne | Kreideblau | Azul turbio | Azzurro smorto |
| Charity stamp | Timbre de bienfaisance | Wohltätigkeitsmarke | Sello de beneficenza | Francobollo di beneficenza |
| Chestnut | Marron | Kastanienbraun | Castaño rojo | Marrone |
| Chocolate | Chocolat | Schokolade | Chocolate | Cioccolato |
| Cinnamon | Cannelle | Zimtbraun | Canela | Cannella |
| Claret | Grenat | Weinrot | Rojo vinoso | Vinaccia |
| Cobalt | Cobalt | Kobalt | Cobalto | Cobalto |
| Colour | Couleur | Farbe | Color | Colore |
| Comb-perforation | Dentelure en peigne | Kammzähnung, Reihenzähnung | Dentado de peine | Dentellatura e pettine |
| Commemorative stamp | Timbre commémoratif | Gedenkmarke | Sello conmemorativo | Francobollo commemorativo |
| Crimson | Cramoisi | Karmesin | Carmesí | Cremisi |

| *Arabic* | *English* |
|---|---|
| عقيقي | Agate |
| طابع بريد جوي | Air stamp |
| أخضر تفاحي | Apple Green |
| | Barred |
| مقسوم الى شطرين | Bisected |
| الذهبي المطفي - بيج | Bistre |
| بيج غامق | Bistre-brown |
| أسود | Black |
| بني مسود | Blackish Brown |
| أخضر مسود | Blackish Green |
| زيتي مسود | Blackish Olive |
| أربعة قطعة واحدة | Block of four |
| أزرق | Blue |
| أخضر مزرق | Blue-green |
| بنفسجي مزرق | Bluish Violet |
| دفتر طوابع | Booklet |
| أزرق فاتح | Bright Blue |
| أخضر فاتح | Bright Green |
| بنفسجي فاتح | Bright Purple |
| أخضر برونزي | Bronze Green |
| بني | Brown |
| بني قرميدي | Brown-lake |
| البنفسجي الغامق | Brown-purple |
| أحمر غامق | Brown-red |
| أصفر داكن | Buff |
| الإلغاء | Cancellation |
| ملغى | Cancelled |
| قرمزي | Carmine |
| أحمر قرمزي | Carmine-red |
| متوسط | Centred |
| أحمر فاتح | Cerise |
| ورق سطحه طباشيري | Chalk-surfaced paper |
| أزرق طباشيري | Chalky Blue |
| طابع خيري | Charity stamp |
| بني فاتح - كستناوي | Chestnut |
| شوكولا | Chocolate |
| بني فاتح جدا - بيج | Cinnamon |
| أحمر داكن | Claret |
| أزرق سماوي | Cobalt |
| لون | Colour |
| تخريم مشطي | Comb-perforation |
| طابع تذكاري | Commemorative stamp |
| أحمر داكن ـ قرزي | Crimson |

| English | French | German | Spanish | Italian | Arabic | English |
|---|---|---|---|---|---|---|
| Deep Blue | Blue foncé | Dunkelblau | Azul oscuro | Azzurro scuro | كحلي ـ أزرق غامق | Deep Blue |
| Deep bluish Green | Vert-bleu foncé | Dunkelbläulichgrün | Verde azulado oscuro | Verde azzurro scuro | أخضر غامق | Deep bluish Green |
| Design | Dessin | Markenbild | Diseño | Disegno | التصميم | Design |
| Die | Matrice | Urstempel. Type Platte, | Cuño | Conio, Matrice | قالب حديد يستخدم للصك | Die |
| Double | Double | Doppelt | Doble | Doppio | ضعف الكمية | Double |
| Drab | Olive terne | Trüboliv | Oliva turbio | Oliva smorto | لون كاكي | Drab |
| Dull Green | Vert terne | Trübgrün | Verde turbio | Verde smorto | أخضر باهت | Dull Green |
| Dull purple | Mauve terne | Trübpurpur | Púrpura turbio | Porpora smorto | بنفسجي باهت | Dull purple |
| Embossing | Impression en relief | Prägedruck | Impresión en relieve | Impressione a relievo | نافر - بارز | Embossing |
| Emerald | Vert-eméraude | Smaragdgrün | Esmeralda | Smeraldo | الزمرد | Emerald |
| Engraved | Gravé | Graviert | Grabado | Inciso | منقوش ـ طباعة بالحفر | Engraved |
| Error | Erreur | Fehler, Fehldruck | Error | Errore | خطأ | Error |
| Essay | Essai | Probedruck | Ensayo | Saggio | تجارب طباعية | Essay |
| Express letter stamp | Timbre pour lettres par exprès | Eilmarke | Sello de urgencia | Francobollo per espresso | طابع رسالة سريعه | Express letter stamp |
| Fiscal stamp | Timbre fiscal | Stempelmarke | Sello fiscal | Francobollo fiscale | طابع مالي | Fiscal stamp |
| Flesh | Chair | Fleischfarben | Carne | Carnicino | زهري غامق | Flesh |
| Forgery | Faux, Falsification | Fälschung | Falsificación | Falso, Falsificazione | تزييف | Forgery |
| Frame | Cadre | Rahmen | Marco | Cornice | إطار | Frame |
| Granite paper | Papier avec fragments de fils de soie | Faserpapier | Papel con filamentos | Carto con fili di seta | ورق الجرانيت | Granite paper |
| Green | Vert | Grün | Verde | Verde | أخضر | Green |
| Greenish Blue | Bleu verdâtre | Grünlichblau | Azul verdoso | Azzurro verdastro | أخضر مزرق | Greenish Blue |
| Greenish Yellow | Jaune-vert | Grünlichgelb | Amarillo verdoso | Giallo verdastro | أخضر مصفر | Greenish Yellow |
| Grey | Gris | Grau | Gris | Grigio | رمادي | Grey |
| Grey-blue | Bleu-gris | Graublau | Azul gris | Azzurro grigio | رمادي مزرق | Grey-blue |
| Grey-green | Vert gris | Graugrün | Verde gris | Verde grigio | رمادي مخضر | Grey-green |
| Gum | Gomme | Gummi | Goma | Gomma | صمغ | Gum |
| Gutter | Interpanneau | Zwischensteg | Espacio blanco entre dos grupos | Ponte | فراغ أبيض يفصل بين طابعين | Gutter |
| Imperforate | Non-dentelé | Geschnitten | Sin dentar | Non dentellato | غير مثقب ـ بدون تخريم | Imperforate |
| Indigo | Indigo | Indigo | Azul indigo | Indaco | نيلي ـ أزرق غامق | Indigo |
| Inscription | Inscription | Inschrift | Inscripción | Dicitura | النقش | Inscription |
| Inverted | Renversé | Kopfstehend | Invertido | Capovolto | معكوس ـ مقلوب | Inverted |
| Issue | Émission | Ausgabe | Emisión | Emissione | اصدار | Issue |
| Laid | Vergé | Gestreift | Listado | Vergato | | Laid |
| Lake | Lie de vin | Lackfarbe | Laca | Lacca | أحمر غامق جداً ـ أحمر دموي | Lake |
| Lake-brown | Brun-carmin | Lackbraun | Castaño laca | Bruno lacca | أحمر أجري | Lake-brown |
| Lavender | Bleu-lavande | Lavendel | Color de alhucema | Lavanda | لون الموف | Lavender |
| Lemon | Jaune-citron | Zitrongelb | Limón | Limone | ليموني | Lemon |
| Light Blue | Bleu clair | Hellblau | Azul claro | Azzurro chiaro | أزرق فاتح | Light Blue |
| Lilac | Lilas | Lila | Lila | Lilla | لون نهدي | Lilac |
| Line perforation | Dentelure en lignes | Linienzähnung | Dentado en linea | Dentellatura lineare | ثقب الخط | Line perforation |
| Lithography | Lithographie | Steindruck | Litografía | Litografia | طباعة حجرية | Lithography |
| Local | Timbre de poste locale | Lokalpostmarke | Emisión local | Emissione locale | محلي | Local |
| Lozenge roulette | Percé en losanges | Rautenförmiger Durchstich | Picadura en rombos | Perforazione a losanghe | تخريم ناعم | Lozenge roulette |
| Magenta | Magenta | Magentarot | Magenta | Magenta | قرمزي | Magenta |
| Margin | Marge | Rand | Borde | Margine | هامش | Margin |
| Maroon | Marron pourpré | Dunkelrotpurpur | Púrpura rojo oscuro | Marrone rossastro | بنفسجي غامق | Maroon |
| Mauve | Mauve | Malvenfarbe | Malva | Malva | بنفسجي | Mauve |
| Multicoloured | Polychrome | Mehrfarbig | Multicolores | Policromo | متعدد الألوان | Multicoloured |
| Myrtle Green | Vert myrte | Myrtengrün | Verde mirto | Verde mirto | أخضر غامق | Myrtle Green |

| English | French | German | Spanish | Italian | Arabic | English |
|---|---|---|---|---|---|---|
| New Blue | Bleu ciel vif | Neublau | Azul nuevo | Azzurro nuovo | أزرق جديد | New Blue |
| Newspaper stamp | Timbre pour journaux | Zeitungsmarke | Sello para periódicos | Francobollo per giornali | طابع جريدة | Newspaper stamp |
| Obliteration | Oblitération | Abstempelung | Matasello | Annullamento | طمس | Obliteration |
| Obsolete | Hors (de) cours | Ausser Kurs | Fuera de curso | Fuori corso | لايستخدم | Obsolete |
| Ochre | Ocre | Ocker | Ocre | Ocra | بيج | Ochre |
| Official stamp | Timbre de service | Dienstmarke | Sello de servicio | Francobollo di | طابع حكومي | Official stamp |
| Olive-brown | Brun-olive | Olivbraun | Castaño oliva | Bruno oliva | بني زيتوني | Olive-brown |
| Olive-green | Vert-olive | Olivgrün | Verde oliva | Verde oliva | أخضر زيتوني | Olive-green |
| Olive-grey | Gris-olive | Olivgrau | Gris oliva | Grigio oliva | رمادي زيتوني | Olive-grey |
| Olive-yellow | Jaune-olive | Olivgelb | Amarillo oliva | Giallo oliva | أصفر زيتوني | Olive-yellow |
| Orange | Orange | Orange | Naranja | Arancio | برتقالي | Orange |
| Orange-brown | Brun-orange | Orangebraun | Castaño naranja | Bruno arancio | بني برتقالي | Orange-brown |
| Orange-red | Rouge-orange | Orangerot | Rojo naranja | Rosso arancio | أحمر برتقالي | Orange-red |
| Orange-yellow | Jaune-orange | Orangegelb | Amarillo naranja | Giallo arancio | أصفر برتقالي | Orange-yellow |
| Overprint | Surcharge | Aufdruck | Sobrecarga | Soprastampa | توشيح | Overprint |
| Pair | Paire | Paar | Pareja | Coppia | زوج | Pair |
| Pale | Pâle | Blass | Pálido | Pallido | شطب على القيمة أو | Pale |
| Pane | Panneau | Gruppe | Grupo | Gruppo | لوح | Pane |
| Paper | Papier | Papier | Papel | Carta | ورقة | Paper |
| Parcel post stamp | Timbre pour colis postaux | Paketmarke | Sello para paquete postal | Francobollo per pacchi postali | رزمة طوابع البريد | Parcel post stamp |
| Pen-cancelled | Oblitéré à plume | Federzugentwertung | Cancelado a pluma | Annullato a penna | ملغي بالقلم ـ مشطوب بالقلم | Pen-cancelled |
| Percé en arc | Percé en arc | Bogenförmiger Durchstich | Picadura en forma de arco | Perforazione ad arco | ثقب | Percé en arc |
| Percé en scie | Percé en scie | Bogenförmiger Durchstich | Picado en sierra | Foratura a sega | تخريم | Percé en scie |
| Perforated | Dentelé | Gezähnt | Dentado | Dentellato | صوة أبيض واسود | Perforated |
| Perforation | Dentelure | Zähnung | Dentar | Dentellatura | ثقب دبوس | Perforation |
| Photogravure | Photogravure, Heliogravure | Rastertiefdruck | Fotograbado | Rotocalco | صفحة لتحديد مكان الطبع | Photogravure |
| Pin perforation | Percé en points | In Punkten durchstochen | Horadado con alfileres | Perforato a punti | لون خوخي | Pin perforation |
| Plate | Planche | Platte | Plancha | Lastra, Tavola | طابع أجرة بريد مستحق | Plate |
| Plum | Prune | Pflaumenfarbe | Color de ciruela | Prugna | لون خوخي | Plum |
| Postage Due stamp | Timbre-taxe | Portomarke | Sello de tasa | Segnatasse | طابع مالي بريدي | Postage Due stamp |
| Postage stamp | Timbre-poste | Briefmarke, Freimarke, Postmarke | Sello de correos | Francobollo postale | طابع بريدي | Postage stamp |
| Postal fiscal stamp | Timbre fiscal-postal | Stempelmarke als Postmarke verwendet | Sello fiscal-postal | Fiscale postale | طابع مالي بريدي | Postal fiscal stamp |
| Postmark | Oblitération postale | Poststempel | Matasello | Bollo | ختم البريد | Postmark |
| Printing | Impression, Tirage | Druck | Impresión | Stampa, Tiratura | طباعة | Printing |
| Proof | Épreuve | Druckprobe | Prueba de impresión | Prova | بروفا | Proof |
| Provisionals | Timbres provisoires | Provisorische Marken. Provisorien | Provisionales | Provvisori | مؤقت ـ طابع محلي | Provisionals |
| Prussian Blue | Bleu de Prusse | Preussischblau | Azul de Prusia | Azzurro di Prussia | أزرق مسود | Prussian Blue |
| Purple | Pourpre | Purpur | Púrpura | Porpora | أرجواني | Purple |
| Purple-brown | Brun-pourpre | Purpurbraun | Castaño púrpura | Bruno porpora | بني ارجواني | Purple-brown |
| Recess-printing | Impression en taille douce | Tiefdruck | Grabado | Incisione | طباعة زاحفة | Recess-printing |
| Red | Rouge | Rot | Rojo | Rosso | أحم | Red |
| Red-brown | Brun-rouge | Rotbraun | Castaño rojizo | Bruno rosso | بني محمر | Red-brown |
| Reddish Lilac | Lilas rougeâtre | Rötlichlila | Lila rojizo | Lilla rossastro | أحمر زهري | Reddish Lilac |
| Reddish Purple | Poupre-rouge | Rötlichpurpur | Púrpura rojizo | Porpora rossastro | أرجواني محمر | Reddish Purple |
| Reddish Violet | Violet rougeâtre | Rötlichviolett | Violeta rojizo | Violetto rossastro | بنفسجي محمر | Reddish Violet |
| Red-orange | Orange rougeâtre | Rotorange | Naranja rojizo | Arancio rosso | برتقالي محمر | Red-orange |
| Registration stamp | Timbre pour lettre chargée (recommandée) | Einschreibemarke | Sello de certificado lettere | Francobollo per raccomandate | طابع تسجيل ـ مسجل | Registration stamp |
| Reprint | Réimpression | Neudruck | Reimpresión | Ristampa | إعادة طبع | Reprint |

| English | French | German | Spanish | Italian | Arabic | English |
|---|---|---|---|---|---|---|
| Reversed | Retourné | Umgekehrt | Invertido | Rovesciato | معكوس ـ مقلوب | Reversed |
| Rose | Rose | Rosa | Rosa | Rosa | وردي | Rose |
| Rose-red | Rouge rosé | Rosarot | Rojo rosado | Rosso rosa | أحمر وردي | Rose-red |
| Rosine | Rose vif | Lebhaftrosa | Rosa vivo | Rosa vivo | وردي غامق | Rosine |
| Roulette | Percage | Durchstich | Picadura | Foratura | تخريم ناعم | Roulette |
| Rouletted | Percé | Durchstochen | Picado | Forato | تخريم ناعم | Rouletted |
| Royal Blue | Bleu-roi | Königblau | Azul real | Azzurro reale | أزرق ملكي | Royal Blue |
| Sage green | Vert-sauge | Salbeigrün | Verde salvia | Verde salvia | أخضر معتدل | Sage green |
| Salmon | Saumon | Lachs | Salmón | Salmone | برتقالي فاتح قريب للزهري | Salmon |
| Scarlet | Écarlate | Scharlach | Escarlata | Scarlatto | قرمزي | Scarlet |
| Sepia | Sépia | Sepia | Sepia | Seppia | بني داكن | Sepia |
| Serpentine roulette | Percé en serpentin | Schlangenliniger Durchstich | Picado a serpentina | Perforazione a serpentina | | Serpentine roulette |
| Shade | Nuance | Tönung | Tono | Gradazione de colore | | Shade |
| Sheet | Feuille | Bogen | Hoja | Foglio | صفحة | Sheet |
| Slate | Ardoise | Schiefer | Pizarra | Ardesia | لون رصاصي | Slate |
| Slate-blue | Bleu-ardoise | Schieferblau | Azul pizarra | Azzurro ardesia | أزرق رمادي | Slate-blue |
| Slate-green | Vert-ardoise | Schiefergrün | Verde pizarra | Verde ardesia | أخضر مسود | Slate-green |
| Slate-lilac | Lilas-gris | Schierferlila | Lila pizarra | Lilla ardesia | نهدي مزرق | Slate-lilac |
| Slate-purple | Mauve-gris | Schieferpurpur | Púrpura pizarra | Porpora ardesia | | Slate-purple |
| Slate-violet | Violet-gris | Schieferviolett | Violeta pizarra | Violetto ardesia | | Slate-violet |
| Special delivery stamp | Timbre pour exprès | Eilmarke | Sello de urgencia | Francobollo per espressi | خدمة البريد السريعة | Special delivery stamp |
| Specimen | Spécimen | Muster | Muestra | Saggio | نموذج ـ عينة | Specimen |
| Steel Blue | Bleu acier | Stahlblau | Azul acero | Azzurro acciaio | أزرق فولاذي | Steel Blue |
| Strip | Bande | Streifen | Tira | Striscia | شريط | Strip |
| Surcharge | Surcharge | Aufdruck | Sobrecarga | Soprastampa | الضريبة الاضافية | Surcharge |
| Tête-bêche | Tête-bêche | Kehrdruck | Tête-bêche | Tête-bêche | | Tête-bêche |
| Tinted paper | Papier teinté | Getöntes Papier | Papel coloreado | Carta tinta | ورق لون خفيف | Tinted paper |
| Too-late stamp | Timbre pour lettres en retard | Verspätungsmarke | Sello para cartas retardadas | Francobollo per le lettere in ritardo | طابع متأخر جداً | Too-late stamp |
| Turquoise-blue | Bleu-turquoise | Türkisblau | Azul turquesa | Azzurro turchese | أزرق تركوازي | Turquoise-blue |
| Turquoise-green | Vert-turquoise | Türkisgrün | Verde turquesa | Verde turchese | أخضر تركوازي | Turquoise-green |
| Typography | Typographie | Buchdruck | Tipografia | Tipografia | نوع من الطباعة | Typography |
| Ultramarine | Outremer | Ultramarin | Ultramar | Oltremare | أزرق لازوردي | Ultramarine |
| Unused | Neuf | Ungebraucht | Nuevo | Nuovo | غير مستخدم | Unused |
| Used | Oblitéré, Usé | Gebraucht | Usado | Usato | مستخدم | Used |
| Venetian Red | Rouge-brun terne | Venezianischrot | Rojo veneciano | Rosso veneziano | لون بندقي ـ بني محمر | Venetian Red |
| Vermilion | Vermillon | Zinnober | Cinabrio | Vermiglione | لون برتقالي محمر ( قمرديني ) | Vermilion |
| Violet | Violet | Violett | Violeta | Violetto | بنفسج | Violet |
| Violet-blue | Bleu-violet | Violettblau | Azul violeta | Azzurro violetto | أزرق بنفسجي | Violet-blue |
| Watermark | Filigrane | Wasserzeichen | Filigrana | Filigrana | علامة مائية | Watermark |
| Watermark sideways | Filigrane couché liegend | Wasserzeichen | Filigrana acostado | Filigrana coricata | | Watermark sideways |
| Wove paper | Papier ordinaire, Papier uni | Einfaches Papier | Papel avitelado | Carta unita | ورقة منسوجه | Wove paper |
| Yellow | Jaune | Gelb | Amarillo | Giallo | أصفر | Yellow |
| Yellow-brown | Brun-jaune | Gelbbraun | Castaño amarillo | Bruno giallo | بني مصفر | Yellow-brown |
| Yellow-green | Vert-jaune | Gelbgrün | Verde amarillo | Verde giallo | أخضر مصفر | Yellow-green |
| Yellow-olive | Olive-jaunâtre | Gelboliv | Oliva amarillo | Oliva giallastro | زيتوني مصفر | Yellow-olive |
| Yellow-orange | Orange jaunâtre | Gelborange | Naranja amarillo | Arancio giallastro | برتقالي مصفر | Yellow-orange |
| Zig-zag roulette | Percé en zigzag | Sägezahnartiger Durchstich | Picado en zigzag | Perforazione a zigzag | تخريم ناعم متعرج | Zig-zag roulette |

# Abbreviations

**Printers**

| | |
|---|---|
| A.B.N. Co. | American Bank Note Co, New York. |
| B.A.B.N. | British American Bank Note Co. Ottawa |
| B.W. | Bradbury Wilkinson & Co, Ltd. |
| C.B.N. | Canadian Bank Note Co, Ottawa. |
| Continental B.N. Co. | Continental Bank Note Co. |
| Courvoisier | Imprimerie Courvoisier S.A., La-Chaux-de-Fonds, Switzerland. |
| D.L.R. | De La Rue & Co, Ltd, London. |
| Enschedé | Joh. Enschedé en Zonen, Haarlem, Netherlands. |
| Harrison | Harrison & Sons, Ltd. London |
| P.B. | Perkins Bacon Ltd, London. |
| Waterlow | Waterlow & Sons, Ltd, London. |

**General Abbreviations**

| | |
|---|---|
| Alph | Alphabet |
| Anniv | Anniversary |
| Comp | Compound (perforation) |
| Des | Designer; designed |
| Diag | Diagonal; diagonally |
| Eng | Engraver; engraved |
| F.C. | Fiscal Cancellation |
| H/S | Handstamped |
| Horiz | Horizontal; horizontally |
| Imp, Imperf | Imperforate |
| Inscr | Inscribed |
| L | Left |
| Litho | Lithographed |
| mm | Millimetres |
| MS | Miniature sheet |
| N.Y. | New York |
| Opt(d) | Overprint(ed) |
| P or P-c | Pen-cancelled |
| P, Pf or Perf | Perforated |
| Photo | Photogravure |
| Pl | Plate |
| Pr | Pair |
| Ptd | Printed |
| Ptg | Printing |
| R | Right |
| R. | Row |
| Recess | Recess-printed |
| Roto | Rotogravure |
| Roul | Rouletted |
| S | Specimen (overprint) |
| Surch | Surcharge(d) |
| T.C. | Telegraph Cancellation |
| T | Type |
| Typo | Typographed |
| Un | Unused |
| Us | Used |
| Vert | Vertical; vertically |
| W or wmk | Watermark |
| Wmk s | Watermark sideways |

(†) = Does not exist

(–) (or blank price column) = Exists, or may exist, but no market price is known.

/ between colours means "on" and the colour following is that of the paper on which the stamp is printed.

**Colours of Stamps**

| | |
|---|---|
| Bl | (blue) |
| blk | (black) |
| brn | (brown) |
| car, carm | (carmine) |
| choc | (chocolate) |
| clar | (claret); |
| emer | (emerald) |
| grn | (green) |
| ind | (indigo) |
| mag | (magenta) |
| mar | (maroon) |
| mult | (multicoloured) |
| mve | (mauve) |
| ol | (olive) |
| orge | (orange) |
| pk | (pink) |
| pur | (purple) |
| scar | (scarlet) |
| sep | (sepia) |
| turq | (turquoise) |
| ultram | (ultramarine) |
| verm | (vermilion) |
| vio | (violet) |
| yell | (yellow). |

**Colour of Overprints and Surcharges**

(B.) = blue
(Blk.) = black
(Br.) = brown,
(C.) = carmine
(G.) = green
(Mag.) = magenta
(Mve.) = mauve
(Ol.) = olive
(O.) = orange,
(P.) = purple
(Pk.) = pink,
(R.) = red,
(Sil.) = silver
(V.) = violet
(Vm.) or (Verm.) = vermilion,
(W.) = white
(Y.) = yellow.

**Arabic Numerals**

As in the case of European figures, the details of the Arabic numerals vary in different stamp designs, but they should be readily recognised with the aid of this illustration:

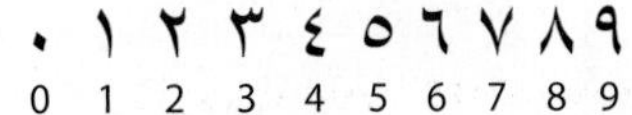

# How to Identify Stamps

*From top to bottom:* Stamps of Switzerland, Japan, Austria, Scandinavia (Denmark) and Latin America (Argentine Republic)

## INTRODUCTION

Identification is the key to the catalogue as you must be able to recognise the country which has issued a stamp before you can look up a stamp in the catalogue. This guide will help you to do just that.

The main elements of a stamp design which provide clues to identity are:

- the country name,
- subordinate or secondary inscriptions,
- national emblems or symbols, such as a coat of arms or monarch's head
- currency or face value.

'Helvetia', for example, is the Latin name for Switzerland and it is used regularly on Swiss stamps. The chrysanthemum emblem appeared on Japanese stamps from 1872 to about 1947, while the modern issues are additionally inscribed 'Nippon', the Japanese name for Japan. Sometimes the actual design of a stamp indicates a particular country or at least the region of its location. The heraldic eagle relates to central Europe and as a design subject it will lead (supported by the inscriptions) to the identification of the early stamps of Austria ('KKPOST' or 'KREUZER'), Germany ('Deutsches Reich' or 'Reichpost'), Poland ('Poczta Polska') and possibly Albania, Finland and Russia. Centimes and Francs indicate a French-speaking country; Ore and Krone (or Krona) are Scandinavian; Centavos and Pesetas or Pesos appear on Spanish and Latin-American stamps.

Brazil

Finland

Spain

Some stamps without a country name

## KEY INSCRIPTIONS

Inscriptions are all the words and figures appearing on the stamp in addition to the design. For purposes of identification the most important words are those representing the country of issue, which may appear in the Roman alphabet; in the Cyrillic or Greek alphabets; or in other alphabets and scripts such as Arabic, Chinese, Korean and Japanese, Hindi (the Devanagari script of India), and Urdu and Bengali (Pakistan). Urdu has many Arabic and Persian words, while Persian, with Pushtu, is also the written language of Afghanistan. Malay is the language of the natives of the Malay Archipelago and islands of South-east Asia (Malaysia) and has Arabic elements infused. The Siamese language (of the inhabitants of Thailand) is derived from a form of Sanskrit, and has affinities with Chinese. Hebrew is the official language of modern Israel, and Amharic is the official tongue of Ethiopia.

Fortunately many of these countries additionally inscribe their stamps in the Roman alphabet, while some use English versions, such as 'Israel' and 'Thailand'. Great Britain is the only country in the world which enjoys the privilege, granted by universal accord as the inventor of the postage stamp, of omitting the country name. Since the famous Penny Black of 1840, British stamps have borne a portrait of the reigning sovereign. New collectors will soon become familiar with the heads of Queen Victoria, King Edward VII, King George V, King Edward VIII, King George VI and Queen Elizabeth II, which also appear on many of the stamps of the Commonwealth territories. In recent times the head of the Queen has been shown in simplified form on GB special stamps, often just as a silhouette.

Chinese

Hebrew

Malay

Korean

Japanese

Thai

Hindi

Amharic

Arabic

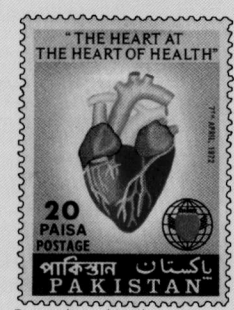

Bengali and Urdu

In early days, before the Universal Postal Union was founded, other countries sometimes omitted their names. These include Austria, Bosnia and Herzegovina, Brazil, Finland, Hungary, the Papal States, Portugal, Sardinia and Spain. The early postage dues of Switzerland comprised figures of value only. On the other stamps the principal clues are the figures of value and/or the portraits depicted on them. Examples are illustrated above and others will be found on pages 39 and 40. Modern stamps of Saudi Arabia use a palm tree emblem instead of a country name.

## USING THE CATALOGUE

The *Stanley Gibbons Simplified Catalogue of Stamps of the World* is extremely simple to use. The countries are arranged in alphabetical order by the name of the stamp issuing country, so North Borneo, for example, will be found under 'N'. The index contains cross-referencing to help locate countries. Each country title is followed by a reference indicating the part of the comprehensive 22-part catalogue which contains the full detailed listing, and by summarised notes of the country's location, status and currency.

The Tristan da Cunha stamp below has a modern look and also depicts Queen Elizabeth II in silhouette in the top right-hand corner. Reference to the catalogue tells you that the stamp is the first or lowest value in a set of 'Bird' definitives issued in 1977. There are twelve stamps in the set and the style of listing is as follows:

**83** Great-winged Petrel

**1977.** Birds. Multicoloured.

| | | |
|---|---|---|
| 220 | 1p. | Type **83** |
| 221 | 2p. | White-faced storm petrel |
| 222 | 3p. | Hall's giant petrel |
| 223 | 4p. | Soft-plumaged petrel |
| 224 | 5p. | Wandering albatross |
| 225 | 10p. | Kerguelen petrel |
| 226 | 15p. | Swallow-tailed tern |
| 227 | 20p. | Greater shearwater |
| 228 | 25p. | Broad-billed prion |
| 229 | 50p. | Great skua |
| 230 | £1 | Common diving petrel |
| 231 | £2 | Yellow-nosed albatross |

The 3p. to £2 designs are vert.

As all the above stamps are multicoloured there was no need to repeat the colours against each stamp, those spaces being used for the design details. A little further on in your catalogue you will find a set of 'Fishes' with a slightly different arrangement:

**31** Two-spined Thornfish

**1978.** Fishes

| | | | |
|---|---|---|---|
| 246 | **31** | 5p. | black, brown and green |
| 247 | | 10p. | black, brown and green |
| 248 | | 15p. | multicoloured |
| 249 | | 20p. | multicoloured |

DESIGNS: 10p. Five-fingered morwong; 15p. Concha wrasse, 20p. Tristan jacopever.

Knowing the country obviously eases the task of locating a particular stamp in the catalogue – look for similarities of design, subject and style. And, of course, you will then know exactly which stamps you need to complete a set, while the detailed information about the stamps and their designs will assist you in writing-up your collection. Just browsing through the catalogue will help you enormously in getting to know the 'look' of a stamp and its various inscriptions. Most countries maintain a distinctive style of design which is easily recognizable and many of the stamps you want to identify will be illustrated. If the actual stamp is not shown you should be able to track down similar characteristics of design. Once you establish the country the rest should be straightforward.

This stamp was intended for use in the Channel Islands, but was also valid in the rest of the United Kingdom

### Non Postage Stamps

*Collectors will frequently find 'stamps' that are not listed in the* Stamps of the World *catalogue. These are usually fiscal or revenue stamps, locals, telegraph stamps or souvenir labels of one kind or another. Some information about them can be found in the 'Information for Users' section of the catalogue. Such 'stamps' are normally referred to as 'cinderellas' and can form the basis of another collection.*

*The Gibbons catalogue only lists stamps issued for postal purposes by official postal administrations.*

## THE ROMAN ALPHABET

A list of country names as they appear on stamps, subordinate inscriptions (including provisional overprints and surcharges, occupation issues and special-purpose inscriptions) and abbreviations.

The names in capital letters are those of the appropriate country in that catalogue. Where items are not listed in *Stamps of the World* the country name is followed by the appropriate part number of the main Stanley Gibbons catalogue.

French Equatorial Africa

Belgian Occupation of Germany

**A**. Overprint on stamps of Colombia for Avianca Air Company. COLOMBIA – Private Air Companies.
**A & T**. Overprint/surcharge on French Colonies 'Commerce' stamps for ANNAM AND TONGKING.
**Açores**. AZORES.
**Admiralty Official**. Overprint on British stamps 1903. GREAT BRITAIN – Official Stamps.
**A.E.F.** 'Afrique Equatoriale Française'. Inscription on 'Centenaire du Gabon' issue of 1938. FRENCH EQUATORIAL AFRICA.
**Afghanes, Postes**. AFGHANISTAN.
**Africa**. PORTUGUESE COLONIES, 1898. General issue.
**Africa Occidental Española**. SPANISH WEST AFRICA.
**Africa Orientale Italiana**. ITALIAN EAST AFRICA.
**Afrique Equatoriale Française**. FRENCH EQUATORIAL AFRICA.
**Afrique Française Libre**. Overprint on stamp of Middle Congo. FRENCH EQUATORIAL AFRICA.
**Afrique Occidentale Française**. FRENCH WEST AFRICA.
**Albania**. With surcharge in para currency. ITALIAN P.O.s IN THE LEVANT.
**Alexandrie**. ALEXANDRIA. French Post Office.
**Algérie**. ALGERIA.

Bavaria

Belgium – Railway Official

Belgium

Trieste

Bohemia and Moravia

Bosnia and Herzegovina

**Allemagne Duitschland**. Belgian stamps overprinted for Rhineland. BELGIAN OCCUPATION OF GERMANY.

**A.M.G. F.T.T.** 'Allied Military Government – Free Territory of Trieste'. Overprint on Italian stamps. TRIESTE.

**A.M.G. V.G.** 'Allied Military Goverment – Venezia Giulia'. Overprint on Italian stamps. VENEZIA GIULIA AND ISTRIA.

**A.M. Post Deutschland**. GERMANY (ALLIED OCCUPATION) – Anglo-American Zone, 1945.

**Amtlicher Verkehr K. Württ. Post**. WURTTEMBERG – Official Stamps.

**Andorre**. ANDORRA (French Post Offices).

**Anna(s)**. Surcharged on British Stamps. BRITISH POSTAL AGENCIES IN EASTERN ARABIA. Also on French stamps for FRENCH P.O.s IN ZANZIBAR.

**Antananarivo, British Consular Mail**. MADACASGAR (*Part 1*).

**A.O.** 'Afrique Orientale'. Overprint on Belgian Congo Red Cross stamps for Belgian Occupation of RUANDA-URUNDI.

**AOF**. 'Afrique Occidentale Française'. Overprint on French stamp. FRENCH WEST AFRICA.

**A.O.I.** 'Africa Orientale Italiana'. Overprint on Italian Postage Due stamps. ITALIAN EAST AFRICA.

**A payer te betalen**. BELGIUM – Postage Dues.

**A percevoir**. 'To collect'. Postage Due stamps of BELGIUM, FRANCE, GUADELOUPE, CANADA, EGYPT, MONACO.

**A percevoir timbre taxe**. FRENCH COLONIES – Postage Dues.

**Archipel des Comores**. COMORO ISLANDS.

**Army Official**. Overprint on British stamps, 1896–1902. GREAT BRITAIN – Official Stamps. Also overprint on Sudan stamps. SUDAN – Army Service Stamps.

**Army Service**. Overprint on Sudan stamps, 1906. SUDAN – Army Service Stamps.

**Arriba España as part of overprint on stamps of Spain**. SPAIN – Civil War issues (*Part 9*).

**Assistência D.L. no. 72**. Educational Tax overprint. PORTUGUESE TIMOR, 1936–37.

**Aunus**. Overprint on Finnish stamps. FINNISH OCCUPATION OF AUNUS.

**Autopaketti.** For parcels carried by road. FINLAND, 1949 onwards.

**Avila por España**. Overprint on stamps of Spain. SPAIN – Civil War issues (*Part 9*).

**Avion Nessre Tafari**. Airmail stamps. ETHIOPIA, 1931.

**Avisporto Maerke**. DENMARK, 1907–15 – Newspaper Stamps.

**Azarbaycan**. AZERBAIJAN.

**B**. 'Bangkok'. Overprint on Straits Settlements stamps for BRITISH POST OFFICES IN SIAM.

**B**. Within oval. Overprint and inscription on Railway Official stamps of BELGIUM.

**B**. As part of overprint/surcharge on stamps of Nicaragua. NICARAGUA – Zelaya (*Part 15*).

**B.A. Eritrea, B.A. Somalia** or **B.A. Tripolitania**. Overprints/ surcharges on British stamps. BRITISH OCCUPATION OF ITALIAN COLONIES.

**Baden**. German State until 1871, listed under BADEN. French zone of occupation 1947–9, listed under GERMANY (ALLIED OCCUPATION).

**Baena por España**. Overprint on stamps of Spain. SPAIN – Civil War issues (*Part 9*).

**Bánát Bacska**. Overprint on Hungarian stamps. ROMANIAN OCCUPATION OF HUNGARY.

**Bani and lei**. Surcharges for K.u.K.Feldpost. AUSTRO-HUNGARIAN MILITARY POST – Issues for Romania.

**Baranya**. Overprint/surcharge on Hungarian stamps. SERBIAN OCCUPATION OF HUNGARY.

**Basel, Stadt Post**. Basel Town Post. SWITZERLAND – Cantonal Administrations (*Part 8*).

**Bayern**. BAVARIA. Now part of Germany.

**B.C.A.** Overprint on Rhodesian stamps for British Central Africa Protectorate. NYASALAND PROTECTORATE, 1891–95.

**B.C.M.** British Consular Mail. MADAGASCAR, 1884–86 (*Part 1*).

**B.C.O.F. Japan 1946**. 'British Commonwealth Occupation Forces'. Overprint on Australian stamps. BRITISH OCCUPATION OF JAPAN.

**België/Belgique**. BELGIUM. Flemish/French inscriptions.

**Belgien**. Overprint/surcharge on German stamps. GERMAN OCCUPATION OF BELGIUM.

**Belgisch Congo**. BELGIAN CONGO.

**Benadir**. SOMALIA, 1903–05.

**Bengasi**. Overprint/surcharge on Italian stamps. ITALIAN P.O.s IN THE LEVANT.

**Berlin**. Overprint on Allied Occupation stamps (1947) for GERMANY (WEST BERLIN).

**Berlin, Notopfer**. GERMANY (ALLIED OCCUPATION) – Obligatory Tax Stamp.

**Berlin, Stadt**. Berlin – Brandenburg. ALLIED OCCUPATION OF GERMANY – Russian Zone (*Part 7*).

**Beyrouth**. Overprint on Russian stamps. RUSSIAN POST OFFICES IN THE TURKISH EMPIRE (*Part 10*).

**B.I.E.** 'Bureau International d'Education' (International Education Office). Overprint on Swiss stamp. SWITZERLAND – International Organizations.

**B L C I (one letter in each corner)**. BHOPAL.

**B.M.A. Malaya**. Overprint on Straits Settlements stamps. MALAYA – British Military Administration.

**B.M.A. Eritrea, B.M.A. Somalia** or **B.M.A. Tripolitania**. Overprints/ surcharges on British stamps. BRITISH OCCUPATION OF ITALIAN COLONIES.

**B.N.F. Castellorizo**. As overprint. See O.N.F. Castellorizo.

**Board of Education**. Overprint on British stamps 1902. GREAT BRITAIN – Official Stamps.

**Böhmen und Mähren**. BOHEMIA AND MORAVIA. German protectorate issues.

**Boka Kotorska**. Overprint/surcharge on stamps of Yugoslavia. GERMAN OCCUPATION OF DALMATIA.

**Bollo Postale**. 'Postage Stamp'. SAN MARINO, 1877–1935.

**Bosna i Hercegovina**. BOSNIA AND HERZEGOVINA – Sarajevo Government. Additionally inscribed 'Hrvatska Republika (or H.R.) Herceg Bosna' – Croatian Posts.

**Bosnien Hercegovina (or Herzegowina)**. BOSNIA AND HERZEGOVINA. Military Post.

**Brasil**. BRAZIL.

**Braunschweig**. BRUNSWICK. Now part of Germany.

**British Bechuanaland**. Overprint and inscription. BECHUANALAND, 1885–91.

**British Central Africa**. NYASALAND PROTECTORATE, 1891–1903.

**British New Guinea**. Former name of PAPUA.

**British Occupation**. Overprint/ surcharge on Russian and Batum stamps. BATUM, 1919–20.

**British Somaliland**. Overprint on Indian stamps for the SOMALILAND PROTECTORATE.

**British South Africa Company**. Former name of RHODESIA.

**Brunei Darussalam**. BRUNEI since 1984.

**Buchanan**. Registration stamp of LIBERIA 1893.

**Bureau International d'Education, also with Courrier du**. 'International Education Office'. Overprint/ inscription on Swiss stamps. SWITZERLAND – International Organizations.

**Bureau International du Travail, also with Courrier du**. 'International Labour Office'. Overprint/inscription on Swiss stamps. SWITZERLAND – International Organizations.

**C**. As part of overprint on stamps of Nicaragua. NICARAGUA – Zelaya (*Part 15*).

**Cabo**. Overprint on stamps of Nicaragua. NICARAGUA – Zelaya (*Part 15*).

**Cabo Jubi/Cabo Juby**. Overprint on stamps of Rio de Oro, Spain or Spanish Morocco. CAPE JUBY.

**Cabo Verde**. CAPE VERDE ISLANDS.

**Cache(s)**. (Unit of currency). Surcharge on Postage Due stamps of France. FRENCH INDIAN SETTLEMENTS.

**Calchi/Karki**. Overprint on Italian stamps for Khalki. DODECANESE ISLANDS.
**Calimno/Calino**. Overprint on Italian stamps for Kalimnos. DODECANESE ISLANDS.
**Camb. Aust. Sigillum Nov.** NEW SOUTH WALES.

**Cambodge**. CAMBODIA.
**Cameroons U.K.T.T.** 'United Kingdom Trust Territory'. Overprint on Nigerian stamps. CAMEROON.
**Campione, Comune de**. CAMPIONE (*Part 8*).
**Canal Maritime de Suez**. SUEZ CANAL COMPANY (*Part 19*).
**Canarias**. As part of surcharge on stamps of Spain. SPAIN – Civil War issues (*Part 9*).

**Caso**. Overprint on Italian stamps for Kasos. DODECANESE ISLANDS.
**Castellorizo/Catelloriso**. CASTELROSSO.
**Cavalle**. CAVALLA (KAVALLA). French Post Office.
**C. CH.** with figure '5' on French Colonies stamps. COCHIN-CHINA.
**Čechy a Morava**. BOHEMIA AND MORAVIA. German protectorate issues.
**C.E.F.** Overprint on Indian stamps for CHINA EXPEDITIONARY FORCE; also with surcharge on German 'Kamerun' stamps for Cameroons Expeditionary Force. CAMEROON.
**Cefalonia e Itaca.** Part of overprint on Greek stamps. ITALIAN OCCUPATION OF CEPHALONIA AND ITHACA.
**Cent (s)**. Also **F** for franc. Surcharges for Belgium and Northern France. GERMAN COMMANDS. Surcharges on stamps of Russia. RUSSIAN P.O.s IN CHINA.
**Centesimi and lire**. Surcharges for K.u.K. Feldpost. AUSTRO-HUNGARIAN MILITARY POST – Issues for Italy.
**Centesimo (or centesimi) di corona**. Surcharge on Italian stamps for AUSTRIAN TERRITORIES ACQUIRED BY ITALY.
**Centimes**. Surcharge on German stamps for GERMAN P.O.s IN THE TURKISH EMPIRE. Also on stamps of Austria for AUSTRO-HUNGARIAN P.O.s IN THE TURKISH EMPIRE.
**Centimos**. Surcharge on French stamps for FRENCH P.O.s IN MOROCCO.
**Centrafricaine, République**. CENTRAL AFRICAN REPUBLIC.

**Česká Republika**. CZECH REPUBLIC. Former part of Czechoslovakia.
**Československe Armady Siberske or Československe Vojsko Na Rusi**. CZECHOSLOVAK ARMY IN SIBERIA.
**Československo(a)**. CZECHOSLOVAKIA.
**Česk´ych Skatu**. CZECHOSLOVAKIA.
**CFA 'Communaute Financielle Africaine'**. Overprint/surcharge on French stamps for REUNION.

**C.G.H.S.** 'Commission de Gouvernement Haute Silésie'. Overprint on German Official stamps for plebiscite in UPPER SILESIA.
**Chemins de Fer Spoorwegen**. Railway Parcels stamps. BELGIUM.
**Chiffre Tax**. Postage Due stamps. FRANCE and FRENCH COLONIES. On stamps denominated in paras and piastres, TURKEY.
**China**. CHINA (PEOPLE'S REPUBLIC), from 1992.
**China**. Overprint on Hong Kong stamps for BRITISH POST OFFICES IN CHINA. Also on German stamps for GERMAN P.O.s IN CHINA.
**China, Republic of**. CHINA, 1913–29 and CHINA (TAIWAN), from 1953.
**Chine**. Overprint, surcharge and inscription for FRENCH P.O.s IN CHINA.
**C.I.H.S.** in circle. Overprint on German stamps for plebiscite in UPPER SILESIA.
**Cilicie**. CILICIA.
**Cinquantenaire 24 Septembre 1853–1903 and eagle overprint on French stamps for 50th anniversary of French occupation**. NEW CALEDONIA.
**Cirenaica**. CYRENAICA.
**Città Del Vaticano**. VATICAN CITY.
**C.M.T.** in box with value. 'Comandamentul Militar Territorial'. Surcharge on stamps of Austria. WEST UKRAINE – Romanian Occupation (*Part 10*).
**Coamo**. Type-set provisional. PUERTO RICO (*Part 22*).
**Co. Ci.** 'Commissariato Civile'. Overprint on Yugoslav stamps for the Italian Occupation of SLOVENIA.
**Cocuk Esirgeme (or C.E.) Kurumu**. Inscription on Child Welfare stamps of TURKEY.
**Colombia**. COLOMBIA. Also inscribed on stamps of PANAMA, 1887–92.
**Coloniale Italiane, R.R. Poste**. ITALIAN COLONIES. General issues, 1932–34.
**Colonie Italiane**. Overprint on Italian 'Dante' stamps of 1932 for ITALIAN COLONIES.
**Colonies de l'Empire Français**. FRENCH COLONIES. 'Eagle' issue, 1859.
**Colonies Postes**. FRENCH COLONIES. French 'Commerce' type, 1881. NOTE. French stamps without special distinction or inscription were also issued for the French Colonies up to 1877. For details see under FRANCE in the Catalogue.
**Comité Français de la Liberation Nationale**. With 'RF' or 'République Française'. FRENCH COLONIES.
**Comité International Olympique**. 'International Olympic Committee'. Inscription on Swiss stamps. SWITZERLAND – International Organizations.
**Comores, Archipel des.** or **Republique Federale Islamique des.** COMORO ISLANDS.
**Communicaciones**. SPAIN.
**Companhia de Mozambique**. MOZAMBIQUE COMPANY.
**Companhia do Nyassa**. NYASSA COMPANY.
**Compañia Colombiana de Navegacíon Aérea**. Private Air Company stamps. COLOMBIA (*Part 20*).
**Confed. Granadina**. COLOMBIA, 1859.
**Confœderatio Helvetica**. SWITZERLAND. 'National Fete' issues, etc. 1938–52.
**Congo**. CONGO (BRAZZAVILLE) 1991–. CONGO (KINSHASA) 1960. On key-types of Portuguese Group – PORTUGUESE CONGO.
**Congo Belge**. BELGIAN CONGO.
**Congo Française Gabon**. GABON.
**Congo Française**. FRENCH CONGO.
**Congo, République Démocratique du**. CONGO DEMOCRATIC REPUBLIC (EX ZAIRE). CONGO (KINSHASA), 1964–71.
**Congo, République du**. CONGO (BRAZZAVILLE), 1959–70, 1993; CONGO (KINSHASA), 1961–64.
**Congo, République Populaire du**. CONGO (BRAZZAVILLE), 1970–91.
**Congreso de los Diputados**. SPAIN – Official Stamps, 1895.
**Congreso Internacional de Ferrocarriles**. Inscription on stamps of SPAIN, 1930.
**Constantinopol Posta Romana**. Circular overprint on Romanian stamps. ROMANIAN P.O.s IN THE TURKISH EMPIRE.

Vatican City

Slovenia

Mozambique Company

Switzerland

Spain

Austrian Territories acquired by Italy

**Constantinople**. Overprint on stamps of Russia. RUSSIAN POST OFFICES IN THE TURKISH EMPIRE (*Part 10*).
**Constantinopoli**. Overprint and surcharge on Italian stamps. ITALIAN P.O.s IN THE TURKISH EMPIRE. For Constantinople.
**Cordoba**. ARGENTINE REPUBLIC – Cordoba (*Part 20*).
**Corfu**. Overprint on Italian stamps. ITALIAN OCCUPATION OF CORFU. Also overprint on Greek stamps. ITALIAN OCCUPATION OF CORFU AND PAXOS.
**Corée, Postes de**. KOREA, 1902–03.
**Corona(e)**. Surcharge on Italian stamps for AUSTRIAN TERRITORIES ACQUIRED BY ITALY.
**Corrientes**. ARGENTINE REPUBLIC – Corrientes (*Part 20*).
**Correspondencia Urgente**. SPAIN – Express Letter Stamps.
**Cos or Coo**. Overprint on Italian stamps for Kos, DODECANESE ISLANDS.

**Côte d'Ivoire**. IVORY COAST.
**Côte Française des Somalis**. FRENCH SOMALI COAST.
**Cour Internationale de Justice or Cour Permanente, etc.** Overprint/ inscription on special stamps for the Court of International Justice, The Hague. NETHERLANDS – International Court of Justice.
**Crete**. Overprint and surcharge on French stamps. FRENCH P.O.s IN CRETE.
**Crna Gora**. MONTENEGRO.
**C.S.** or **C.S.A.** CONFEDERATE STATES OF AMERICA.
**Dai Nippon**. Overprint/surcharge on Malayan States stamps. MALAYA (JAPANESE OCCUPATION OF).
**Danmark**. DENMARK.
**Dansk Vestindiske Öer/Dansk Vestindien**. DANISH WEST INDIES.
**Dardanelles**. Overprint on stamps of Russia. RUSSIAN POST OFFICES IN THE TURKISH EMPIRE (*Part 10*).
**Datia**. DUTTIA. A state of central India.
**DBP**. 'Dalni-Vostochnaya Respublika' (Far Eastern Republic). Overprint in fancy letters on stamps of Russia or Siberia. SIBERIA.
**D de A**. 'Departmento de Antioquia'. Inscription on issue of 1890. ANTIOQUIA.

**DDR**. 'Deutsche Demokratische Republik' (German Democratic Republic). GERMANY (EAST GERMANY).
**Dédéagh**. DEDEAGATZ.
**Deficit**. Overprint/inscription on Postage Due stamps. PERU.
**Demokratska Federativna Jugoslavija**. Overprint/surcharge on Croatian stamps. YUGOSLAVIA (Democratic Federation). Regional issues.
**Denda**. Inscription on Postage Due stamps of MALAYSIA.
**Deutsche Besetzung Zara**. Overprint on stamps of Italy. GERMAN OCCUPATION OF DALMATIA.
**Deutsche Bundespost**. GERMANY (FEDERAL REPUBLIC).
**Deutsche Bundespost Berlin**. GERMANY (WEST BERLIN).
**Deutsche Demokratische Republik**. GERMANY (EAST GERMANY).
**Deutsche Feldpost**. GERMANY. Military Fieldpost stamps, 1944.
**Deutsche Flugpost/Deutsche Luftpost**. GERMANY. Airmail stamps, 1919–38.
**Deutsche Militär-verwaltung Kotor.** Overprint/surcharge on stamps of Italy. GERMAN OCCUPATION OF DALMATIA.
**Deutsche Post.** GERMANY (FEDERAL REPUBLIC) and (ALLIED OCCUPATION) – British and American Zone and Russian Zone.
**Deutsche Post Osten**. Overprint/ surcharge on German stamps for Nazi Occupation. POLAND, 1939.
**Deutsche Reichspost/Deutsches Reich**. GERMANY. 'Empire' issues, 1872–87 and 1902–43.
**Deutschland**. GERMANY (FEDERAL REPUBLIC) from 1995.
**Deutsch-Neu-Guinea**. GERMAN NEW GUINEA.
**Deutsch-Ostafrika**. GERMAN EAST AFRICA.

**Deutschösterreich**. AUSTRIA. Issues of 1918–20.
**Deutsch-Sudwestafrika**. GERMAN SOUTH WEST AFRICA.
**Dienstmarke**. GERMANY. Official stamps from 1920.
**Diligencia**. URUGUAY. 'Mailcoach' issue of 1856.
**Dios Patria Libertad**. DOMINICAN REPUBLIC. Inscription on early issues.
**Dios, Patria, Rey.** SPAIN – Carlist issues (*Part 9*). As overprint on stamps of Spain. SPAIN – Civil War issues (*Part 9*).
**DJ**. Overprint on Obock stamp for DJIBOUTI, 1893.

**Dollar(s)**. Surcharge on stamps of Russia. RUSSIAN P.O.s IN CHINA.
**Dominicana, República**. DOMINICAN REPUBLIC.
**Donau Dampfschiffahrt Gesellshaft, Erste k.k.pr.** DANUBE STEAM NAVIGATION COMPANY (*Part 2*).

**D.P.R.K.** 'Democratic People's Republic of Korea'. KOREA (NORTH KOREA), 1977–80.
**DPR Korea**. KOREA (NORTH KOREA). Issues since 1980 (stamps inscribed DPR of Korea in 1976).
**Drzava S.H.S.** (also **with Bosna i Hercegovina**). YUGOSLAVIA – Issues for Bosnia and Herzegovina, or Slovenia.

**Drzavna Posta Hrvatska**. YUGOSLAVIA – Issues for Croatia, 1918–19.
**Duc. di Parma Piac. Ecc.** PARMA.
**Durango**. As part of overprint on stamps of Spain. SPAIN – Civil War issues (*Part 9*).
**Durazzo**. Overprint/surcharge on Italian stamps. ITALIAN P.O.s IN THE TURKISH EMPIRE.
**EA**. Overprint on stamps of France. ALGERIA.
**E.A.F.** 'East Africa Forces'. Overprint on British stamps. BRITISH OCCUPATION OF ITALIAN COLONIES – Somalia.
**East Africa and Uganda Protectorates**. Listed under KENYA, UGANDA AND TANGANYIKA.
**East India Postage**. INDIA. Stamps of 1860. Also, surcharged with a crown and value in cents – STRAITS SETTLEMENTS first issue of 1867.

**EE. UU. De C., E.S. DEL T.** 'Estados Unidos de Colombia, Estado Soberano del Tolima'. First issue of TOLIMA.
**E.E.F.** 'Egyptian Expeditionary Force'. Inscription on stamps of PALESTINE, 1918–22.

**Eesti**. ESTONIA.
**Egeo**. Overprint on Italian stamps. DODECANESE ISLANDS, 1912.
**Egypte**, **Royaume d'Egypte**, **Postes Egyptiennes** or **Poste Khedevie Egiziane**. EGYPT.

**Eire**. IRELAND (REPUBLIC).
**Eireann, Poblacht na h**. IRELAND (REPUBLIC).
**Elsass**. Overprint on German stamps. GERMAN OCCUPATION OF ALSACE.
**Elua Keneta**. 'Two Cents'. HAWAII.
**E.R.I. 6d.** Surcharge on 6d. stamp of ORANGE FREE STATE.
**Escuelas**. 'Schools'. Fiscals valid for postal use. VENEZUELA.
**España** or **Española**. SPAIN.
**España Valencia**. SPAIN – Carlist issues (*Part 9*).
**Estado da India**. PORTUGUESE INDIA.
**Estados Unidos de Nueva Granada**. COLOMBIA, 1861.
**Est Africain Allemand Occupation Belge** or **Duitsch Oost Afrika Belgische Bezetting** (Flemish). Overprint on Belgian Congo stamps for Belgian Occupation of RUANDA-URUNDI.
**Estensi, Poste**. MODENA, 1852.
**Estero**. 'Foreign'. Overprint on modified Italian stamps for ITALIAN P.O.s IN THE TURKISH EMPIRE.
**Estland Eesti**. GERMAN OCCUPATION OF ESTONIA.
**Etablissements Française dans l'Inde**. FRENCH INDIAN SETTLEMENTS.

**Etablissements** (or **Ets.**) **Française de l'Océanie**. OCEANIC SETTLEMENTS.
**Etat Comorien**. COMORO ISLANDS.
**Etat Indépendant du Congo**. BELGIAN CONGO – Independent State.
**Ethiopie/Postes Ethiopiennes**. ETHIOPIA.
**Eupen & Malmédy**. Overprint/ surcharge on Belgian stamps. BELGIAN OCCUPATION OF GERMANY.
**Expossicion Gral. Sevilla Barcelona**. SPAIN 1929.
**Fanon(s)**. (Unit of currency). Surcharge on Postage Due stamps of France. FRENCH INDIAN SETTLEMENTS.
**Fdo. Poo**. Inscription on surcharged fiscal stamps. FERNANDO POO.
**Filipinas** (or **Filipas**). PHILIPPINES.

**Fiume Rijeka**. Overprint with date 3-V-1945 and surcharge on Italian stamps. VENEZIA GIULIA AND ISTRIA – Yugoslav Occupation.
**Florida**. With picture of heron. URUGUAY. Air stamp of 1925.
**Forces Françaises Libres Levant** with Lorraine Crosses. Overprint/surcharge on Syrian and Lebanese stamps. FREE FRENCH FORCES IN THE LEVANT.

**Føroyar**. FAROE ISLANDS.
**Franc**. Surcharge on Austrian stamps. AUSTRO-HUNGARIAN P.O.s IN THE TURKISH EMPIRE.
**Franc (with Empire or Repub.)**. FRANCE, FRENCH COLONIES.
**France d'Outre-Mer**. FRENCH COLONIES.
**Franco**. 'Helvetia' seated. SWITZERLAND, 1854.
**Franco Bollo**. 'Postage Stamp'. First issues of ITALY, NEAPOLITAN PROVINCES and SARDINIA. With 'Postale' added to crossed keys design, PAPAL STATES.
**Francobollo di Stato**. ITALY – Official Stamps.
**Franco Marke**. BREMEN, 1856.
**Franco Scrisorei**. ROMANIA, 1862.
**Freimarke**. 'Postage Stamp'. With portrait, PRUSSIA, 1850. With large numerals, THURN AND TAXIS.

**Frimaerke (with 4 Skilling)**. First issue of NORWAY.
**Frimaerke Kgl. Post** or **Kgl. Post. Frm.** DENMARK/DANISH WEST INDIES. Kgl. or Kongeligt means 'Royal'.
**G**. Overprint on Cape of Good Hope stamps for GRIQUALAND WEST, 1877.
**G**. Overprint on stamps of CANADA for government use, 1950–63.
**GAB**. Overprint and surcharge on French Colonial stamp for GABON, 1886.
**Gabonaise, République**. GABON.
**G.E.A.** 'German East Africa'. Overprint on Kenya and Uganda stamps for British Occupation of TANGANYIKA.
**Gen.-Gouv. Warschau**. Overprint on German stamps. GERMAN OCCUPATION OF POLAND.

**General Gouvernement**. POLAND – German Occupation, 1940–44.
**Genève, Post de**. Geneva. SWITZERLAND – Cantonal Administrations (*Part 8*).
**Georgie (La) or République Georgienne**. GEORGIA, 1919–21.
**Gerusalemme**. Overprint/surcharge on Italian stamps for Jerusalem. ITALIAN P.O.s IN THE TURKISH EMPIRE.
**G et D (or G & D)**. Overprint/surcharge on Guadeloupe stamps for Guadeloupe and Dependencies. GUADELOUPE.
**G.F.B.** 'Gaue Faka Buleaga' (On Government Service). Overprint on Tonga stamps, 1893. TONGA – Official Stamps.
**G.K.C.A.** Within dotted circle. Overprint on Yugoslav stamps for the Carinthian plebiscite, 1920. YUGOSLAVIA.
**G.N.R.** 'Guardia Nazionale Repubblicana'. Overprint on stamps of Italy. ITALY – Italian Social Republic.
**Golfo de Guinea, Territorios (or Terrs.) del**. Overprint on Spanish stamps for SPANISH GUINEA.
**Govt. Parcels**. Overprint on British stamps, 1883–1902. GREAT BRITAIN – Official Stamps.
**G.P.E.** Overprint/surcharge on French Colonies for GUADELOUPE.
**Graham Land Dependency of**. FALKAND ISLANDS DEPENDENCIES.

Italy – Italian Social Republic

**Granadina, Confed.** COLOMBIA, 1859.
**Grande Comore**. GREAT COMORO.
**Grand Liban**. 'Greater Lebanon'. LEBANON, 1924–26.
**Grenada Carriacou & Petite Martinique**. GRENADINES OF GRENADA.
**Grenville**. Registration stamp of LIBERIA, 1893.
**G.R.I.** 'Georgius Rex Imperator'. Overprint and surcharge in British currency on stamps and registration labels of German New Guinea and Marshall Islands during Australian Occupation of NEW GUINEA; also on German Cameroons stamps for New Zealand administration of SAMOA.
**G.R. Post Mafia**. Overprint on stamps of Indian Expeditionary Force. TANGANYIKA.
**Grønland**. GREENLAND.
**Grossdeutsches Reich**. GERMANY. Issues of 1943–45.
**Gruzija**. GEORGIA.
**Guiné**. PORTUGUESE GUINEA.
**Guinea Ecuatorial, Republica de**. EQUATORIAL GUINEA.
**Guinea Española**. SPANISH GUINEA.
**Guiné-Bissau**. GUINEA-BISSAU.
**Guinée, also Republique de**. FRENCH GUINEA.
**Guinée, République de**. GUINEA.
**Gultig 9. Armee**. Overprint on stamps of Germany. GERMAN OCCUPATION OF ROMANIA.
**Guyane Française**. FRENCH GUIANA.
**G.W.** Overprint on Cape of Good Hope stamps for GRIQUALAND WEST. 1877.
**Harper**. Registration stamp of LIBERIA, 1893.
**Haut (or Ht.) Sénégal-Niger**. UPPER SENEGAL AND NIGER.
**Haute-Silésie**. UPPER SILESIA. Plebiscite issues, 1920–22.

Georgia

**Haute-Volta**. UPPER VOLTA.
**H.E.H. The Nizam's Government/ Silver Jubilee**. HYDERABAD.
**Hellas**. GREECE.
**Helvetia**. SWITZERLAND.
**Herzogth.** (or **Herzogthum**) **Holstein** or **Schleswig**. SCHLESWIG-HOLSTEIN.
**H.H. Nawab Shah Jahan Begam**. BHOPAL.
**H.I. (& U.S.) Postage**. 'Hawaiian Islands'. HAWAII.
**Holkar State**. INDORE.
**Homenaje General Varela**. As part of overprint on stamps of Spain. SPAIN – Civil War issues (*Part 9*).

**Hrvatska (with ND, Nezavisna Drzava or Republika)**. CROATIA.
**Hrvatska (with SHS, Drzavna Posta or DRZ SHS)**. YUGOSLAVIA – Issues for Croatia, 1918–19.
**Hrvatska Republika (with Bosna i Hercegovina)**. BOSNIA AND HERZGOVINA – Croatian Posts.
**Hrzgl. Frm(rk)**. SCHLESWIG-HOLSTEIN.
**I.B.** 'Irian Barat'. WEST IRIAN. Now part of Indonesia.
**I.E.F.** Overprint on Indian stamps for INDIAN EXPEDITIONARY FORCES.
**I.E.F. 'D'**. Overprint/surcharge in annas on Turkish fiscal stamps for Indian forces in Mesopotamia. MOSUL.
**Ierusalem**. Overprint on stamps of Russia. RUSSIAN POST OFFICES IN THE TURKISH EMPIRE (*Part 10*).
**Ile de la Réunion**. REUNION.
**Ile Rouad**. Overprint and surcharge on French stamps for ROUAD ISLAND (ARWAD).
**Iles Wallis et Futuna**. WALLIS AND FUTUNA ISLANDS.
**Imperial British East Africa Company**. BRITISH EAST AFRICA.
**Imperio Colonial Portugues**. Postage Due stamps. PORTUGUESE COLONIES.
**Impuesto (or Impto.) de Guerra**. SPAIN – War Tax Stamps.
**India/India Portugueza (or Port.** or **Portugesa), Estado da**. PORTUGUESE INDIA.
**Inde Française (or Fçaise)**. FRENCH INDIAN SETTLEMENTS.
**Independence 11th November 1965**. Overprint on stamps of Southern Rhodesia. RHODESIA.
**Indo-Chine/Indochine**. INDO-CHINA.
**Instruçao D.L. no. 7 de 3-2-1934**. Educational Tax overprint. TIMOR, 1934.

**Instruccion**. 'Instruction' or 'Teaching'. Fiscals valid for postage. VENEZUELA.
**Insufficiently Prepaid**. Postage Due. No country name. ZANZIBAR, 1929–33.
**Irian Barat**. WEST IRIAN. Formerly Netherlands New Guinea and West New Guinea.
**I.R. Official**. Overprint on British stamps, 1882–1902. GREAT BRITAIN – Official Stamps (Inland Revenue).
**Isla de Menorca**. As part of overprint on stamps of Spain. SPAIN – Civil War issues (*Part 9*).

**Island**. ICELAND.
**Islas Galapagos**. GALAPAGOS ISLANDS.
**Isole Italiani dell'Egeo**. Overprint on Italian stamps. DODECANESE ISLANDS.
**Isole Jonie**. Overprint on Italian stamps. ITALIAN OCCUPATION OF IONIAN ISLANDS.

**Istra**. Overprint and surcharge on Italian stamps. VENEZIA GIULIA AND ISTRIA.

**Itä-Karjala Sot. hallinto**. Overprint on Finnish stamps. FINNISH OCCUPATION OF EASTERN KARELIA.
**Italia/Poste Italiane**. ITALY.
**Jaffa**. Overprint on stamps of Russia. RUSSIAN POST OFFICES IN THE TURKISH EMPIRE (*Part 10*).
**Jam. Dim. Soomaaliya**. SOMALIA, 1974–75.
**Janina**. Overprint and surcharge on Italian stamps. ITALIAN P.O.s IN THE TURKISH EMPIRE.
**J.D. Soomaaliya**. SOMALIA. 1976–77.
**J.D. Soomaaliyeed**. SOMALIA. 1977–.
**Jeend (Jhind or Jind) State**. Overprint on Indian stamps for JIND.
**Jubilé de l'Union Postale Universelle**. SWITZERLAND, 1900.
**Jugoslavija**. YUGOSLAVIA.

**Julio 1936**. Inscription on stamp of Spain. SPAIN – Civil War issues (*Part 9*).

**K(ais). K(ön). Zeitungs-Stempel**. 'Imperial/Royal Newspaper Stamp'. AUSTRIA or LOMBARDY AND VENETIA.

**Kalayaan nang Pilipinas**. JAPANESE OCCUPATION OF PHILIPPINES.

**Kamerun**. CAMEROUN. The former German colony.

**Karabakh, Republic of Mountainous**. NAGORNO-KARABAKH.

**Karjala**. KARELIA (*Part 10*).

**Karki**. Overprint on Italian stamps for Khalki. DODECANESE ISLANDS.

**Karnten Abstimmung**. Overprint on modified Austrian stamps for Carinthian plebiscite, 1920. AUSTRIA.

**Karolinen**. CAROLINE ISLANDS. The former German protectorate.

**Kazahstan**. KAZAKHSTAN.

**Keneta**. 'Cent' or 'cents'. HAWAII.

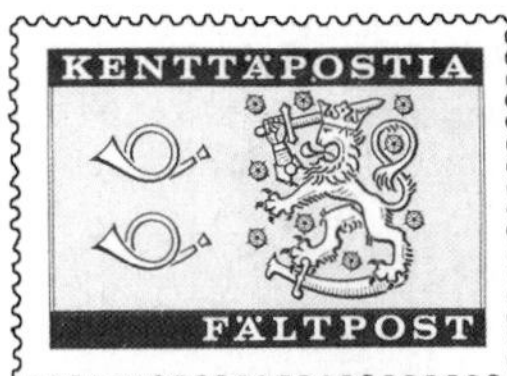


**Kenttäpostia Fältpost**. FINLAND – Military Field Post.

**Kenya and Uganda**. KENYA, UGANDA AND TANGANYIKA.

**Kerassunde**. Overprint on stamps of Russia. RUSSIAN POST OFFICES IN THE TURKISH EMPIRE (*Part 10*).

**KGCA**. Part of surcharge on Yugoslav Newspaper stamp for 1920 Carinthia Plebiscite. YUGOSLAVIA – Issues for Slovenia.

**Kgl. Post. Frm.** See 'Frimaerke Kgl'.

**Kibris Türk Yonetimi/Kibris Türk Federe Devleti Postalari**. CYPRUS (TURKISH CYPRIOT POSTS).

**Kizilay Dernegi**. (Red Crescent). Inscription on Obligatory Tax stamps of TURKEY.

**K.K. Post-Stempel**. 'Imperial/Royal Postage Stamp'. AUSTRIA (denominated in Kreuzer); LOMBARDY AND VENETIA (denominated in centes).

**Klaipeda**. Overprint, surcharge or inscription for MEMEL – Lithuanian Occupation.

**Korea/Republic of Korea**. KOREA (SOUTH KOREA).

**Kosovo, United Nations Interim Administration in**. UNITED NATIONS – Kosovo.

**Kraljevstvo (or Kraljevina) Srba, Hrvata i Slovenaca**. YUGOSLAVIA, 1921–31.

**K.S.A.** Kingdom of SAUDI ARABIA. Stamps so inscribed 1975–82, since when inscription in Arabic only. Stamps identifiable by palm tree and crossed swords emblem.

**K.u.K. Feldpost**. 'Imperial and Royal Field Post'. AUSTRO-HUNGARIAN MILITARY POST.

**K.u.K. Milit. Verwaltung Montenegro**. Overprint on K.u.K. Feldpost stamps for the AUSTRO-HUNGARIAN MILITARY POST – Montenegro issues.

**K.u.K. Militärpost**. BOSNIA AND HERZEGOVINA. Austro-Hungarian Military Post.

**Kurland**. Overprint/surcharge on stamps of Germany. GERMAN OCCUPATION ISSUES, 1939–45 – Latvia (Courland) (*Part 7*).

**Kuzey Kibris Türk Cumhuriyeti**. CYPRUS (TURKISH CYPRIOT POSTS), since 1983.

**K. Wurtt. Post**. WURTTEMBERG.

**La Canea**. Overprint and surcharge on Italian stamps. ITALIAN P.O.s IN CRETE.

**La Guaira**. VENEZUELA – La Guaira (*Part 20*).

**Läibäch, Provinz**. Overprint/surcharge on stamps of Italy or inscription. SLOVENIA – German Occupation, 1943–45.

**Land-Post Porto-Marke**. BADEN – Rural Postage Due Samps.

**LANSA (Lineas Aéreas Nacionales Sociedad Anonima)**. COLOMBIA – Private Air Companies.

**Lao (Postes)**. LAOS since 1976.

**L.A.R.** 'Libyan Arab Republic'. LIBYA, 1969–77.

**Lattaquie**. Overprint on Syrian stamps for LATAKIA (formerly Alaouites).

**Latvija (or Latwija)**. LATVIA.

**Latvija 1941·I·VII**. Overprint on Russian stamps for GERMAN OCCUPATION OF LATVIA.

**Latvijas Aizsargi**. 'Latvian Militia'. Overprint and surcharge. LATVIA.

**Latvijas PSR**. Issue inscribed for absorption of Latvia by Soviet Union, 1940. LATVIA.

**Lero or Leros**. Overprint on Italian stamps for Leros. DODECANESE ISLANDS.

**Levant**. Overprint on British stamps for Middle East post offices. BRITISH LEVANT. Also overprint on Polish stamps for POLISH P.O. IN TURKEY.

**Levante**. Overprint and surcharge on Italian Express Letter stamps. ITALIAN P.O.s IN THE TURKISH EMPIRE.

**Liban/République Libanaise**. LEBANON.

**Libia or Libye**. LYBIA.

**Libra**. (Unit of weight). SPAIN – Official Stamps.

**Lietuva or Lietuvos**. LITHUANIA.

**Lignes Aeriennes F.A.F.L.** Overprint and surcharge on Syrian Air stamps of 1931. FREE FRENCH FORCES IN THE LEVANT, 1942.

**Lima**. Inscription and overprint on early issues of PERU (Lima is the capital).

**Limbagan 1593–1943**. Overprint on stamp of Philippines. JAPANESE OCCUPATION OF PHILIPPINES.

**Linja Autorahti Bussfrakt**. FINLAND – Parcel Post Stamps.

**Lipso or Lisso**. Overprint on Italian stamps for Lipso. DODECANESE ISLANDS.

**Litwa Srodkowa**. CENTRAL LITHUANIA. Independence issues of 1920–22.

**L. Marques**. Overprint on Mozambique stamps for LOURENCO MARQUES.

Lebanon

Lithuania

North West Russia

**Logroño**. As part of overprint on stamps of Spain. SPAIN – Civil War issues (*Part 9*).

**Lokalbref**. Local issue for Stockholm. SWEDEN (*Part 11*).

**Lösen**. Inscription on postage due stamps for SWEDEN, 1874.

**Lothringen**. Overprint on German stamps for GERMAN OCCUPATION OF LORRAINE, 1940.

**LP 'Latwija Pashparwalac' (Independent Latvia) and cross of Russia**. NORTH WEST RUSSIA.

**Lubiana, R. Commissariato Civile**, etc. Overprint on Yugoslav stamps for the Italian Occupation of SLOVENIA.

**Luftfeldpost**. Inscription on Nazi Air stamp of 1942. GERMANY – Military Fieldpost.

**Macau**. MACAO.

**Madagascar, British Inland Mail**. MADAGASCAR (*Part 1*).

**Mafia, G.R. Post**. Overprint on Indian Expeditionary Force stamps for TANGANYIKA – British Occupation, 1915.

**Magyar Kir. Posta/Magyar Posta/Magyarország**. HUNGARY.

**Makedonija**. MACEDONIA.

**Malgache, République/Malagasy, Repoblika**. MALAGASY REPUBLIC.

**Malmédy**. See Eupen & Malmedy.

**Marianen**. Inscription and overprint on German stamps for the MARIANA ISLANDS.

Spanish Morocco

**Maroc**. FRENCH MOROCCO.

**Maroc, Royaume du**.'Kingdom of Morocco'. MOROCCO.

**Marocco or Marokko**. Overprint and surcharge on German stamps for GERMAN P.O.s IN MOROCCO.

**Marruecos, etc**. SPANISH MOROCCO, SPANISH P.O.s IN TANGIER.

**Marschall (or Marshall) Inseln**. MARSHALL ISLANDS.

**Mauritanie**. MAURITANIA.

**M.B.D.** in oval. Overprint for Official stamps of NANDGAON.

**Mecklenb. Schwerin**. MECKLENBURG-SCHWERIN.

**Mecklenb. Strelitz**. MECKLENBURG-STRELITZ.

**Mecklenburg-Vorpomm(ern)**. Mecklenburg-Vorpommern. ALLIED OCCUPATION OF GERMANY – Russian Zone (*Part 7*).

**Medellin**. ANTIOQUIA (Colombia). Issue of 1888.

**M.E.F.** 'Middle East Forces'. Overprint on British stamps. BRITISH OCCUPATION OF ITALIAN COLONIES.

**Mejico, Correos**. MEXICO. Issues of 1856 and 1864.

**Melaka Malaysia**. MALACCA. Issues from 1965.

British Postal Agencies in Eastern Arabia

**Memelgebiet**. Overprint and surcharge on German stamps for MEMEL.

**Memento Avdere Semper L1 Bvccari**. Surcharge on Yugoslav stamp. FIUME AND KUPA ZONE.

**Metelin**. Overprint on stamps of Russia. RUSSIAN POST OFFICES IN THE TURKISH EMPIRE (*Part 10*).

**Militärpost Eilmarke**. BOSNIA AND HERZEGOVINA – Newspaper Stamps.

Norway

**Militärpost Portomarke**. BOSNIA AND HERZEGOVINA – Postage Due Stamps.

**Milliemes/Mill**. Surcharges on French Colonial stamps. ALEXANDRIA AND PORT SAID.

**Moçambique**. MOZAMBIQUE.

**Moçambique, Companhia (or Comp.) de**. MOZAMBIQUE COMPANY.

**Modonensi, Provincie**. MODENA.

**Monrovia**. Registration stamp of LIBERIA, 1893.

**Mont-Athos**. Overprint on stamps of Russia. RUSSIAN POST OFFICES IN THE TURKISH EMPIRE (*Part 10*).

**Montevideo**. URUGUAY. Issues of 1858–59 and Air stamp of 1925.

**Moyen Congo**. MIDDLE CONGO.

**MQE**. Surcharge on French Colonies 'Commerce' type for MARTINIQUE.

**M.V.i.R.** Within frame. 'Militärverwaltung in Rumänien' (Military Administration in Romania). Overprint/surcharge in 'bani' on German stamps for the GERMAN OCCUPATION OF ROMANIA.

**Nandgan**. NANDGAON.

**Napoletana, Bollo della Posta**. NAPLES.

**Nationaler Verwaltungsausschus 10·XI·1943**. Overprint on Italian occupation stamps for MONTENEGRO – German Occupation.

**Nations Unies**. UNITED NATIONS – Geneva Headquarters. Overprint/inscription on Swiss stamps (1950–63). SWITZERLAND – International Organizations.

**Naxçivan Poçt**. NAKHICHEVAN.

**N.C.E.** or **N.-C.E.** Overprint/surcharge on French Colonies stamps for NEW CALEDONIA.

**Negeri Sembilan**. NEGRI SEMBILAN. Malaysia.

**Nederland**. NETHERLANDS.

**Nederlands (or Ned.) Nieuw-Guinea**. NETHERLANDS NEW GUINEA.

**Nederlandsch (Ned.** or **Nederl**) **Indië**. NETHERLANDS INDIES.

**Nederlandse (or Ned.) Antillen**. NETHERLANDS ANTILLES.

**Nepriklausoma Lietuva 1941·VI·23**. Overprint on Russian stamps for GERMAN OCCUPATION OF LITHUANIA.

**Nezavisna Drzava (or N.D.) Hrvatska**. Inscription or overprint on Yugoslav stamps for CROATIA.

**N.F.** Overprint on Nyasaland stamps for Nyasa-Rhodesian Force during British Occupation of TANGANYIKA, 1916. Sometimes erroneously ascribed to '(Gen.) Northey's Force'.

**Nieuwe Republiek**. NEW REPUBLIC. South Africa.

**Nippon**. JAPAN.

**Nisiro or Nisiros**. Overprint on Italian stamps for Nisiros. DODECANESE ISLANDS.

**Nlle. Caledonie**. Inscription or overprint on French stamps. NEW CALEDONIA.

**Norddeutscher Postbezirk**. NORTH GERMAN CONFEDERATION.

**Norge/Noreg**. NORWAY.

**Nouvelle (or Nlle.) Caledonie et Dependances**. NEW CALEDONIA.

**Nouvelles Hebrides, Condominium des**. NEW HEBRIDES.

**NP**. 'Naye paise' (Indian currency). Surcharge on British stamps for BRITISH POSTAL AGENCIES IN EASTERN ARABIA.

**NSB**. Overprint/surcharge on French Colonies stamps for NOSSI-BE.

**N. Sembilan**. NEGRI SEMBILAN. Malaysia.

**N.S.W.** NEW SOUTH WALES.

**Nueva Granada, etc**. See Estados Unidos.

**N.W. Pacific Islands**. 'North-West Pacific Islands'. Overprint on Australian stamps. NEW GUINEA.

**N.Z.** Inscription on Postage Due stamps (1899), Express Delivery stamp (1903) and Life Insurance Department stamps of NEW ZEALAND.

**O.B.** Overprint for 'Official Business' mail. PHILIPPINES.

**Occupation Française**. Overprint and surcharge on Hungarian stamps for FRENCH OCCUPATION OF HUNGARY – Arad.

**Océanie**. OCEANIC SETTLEMENTS.

**Oesterreich(ische)/Oesterr. Post**. AUSTRIA.

**O.F. Castellorisio**. 'Occupation Française'. Overprint on French stamps for occupation of CASTELROSSO.

**Offentlig Sak/Off. Sak./O.S.** Official stamps of NORWAY.

**Office des Postes et Telecommunications**. FRENCH WEST AFRICA.

**Official**. Overprint or inscription on stamps for use by government departments, e.g. BRITISH GUIANA, NEW ZEALAND.

**O.H.M.S.** 'On His/Her Majesty's Service'. Overprint on stamps for government use, e.g. CANADA, COOK ISLANDS, MONTSERRAT, NIUE (**O.K.G.S.** KIRIBATI).

**Oil Rivers, British Protectorate**. Overprint/surcharge on British stamps for Oil Rivers Protectorate. NIGER COAST PROTECTORATE.

**Olsztyn Allenstein**. Overprint on stamps of Germany. ALLENSTEIN.

**Oltre Giuba**. JUBALAND.

**O.M.F. Cilicie**. 'Occupation Militaire Française'. Overprint/surcharge on French stamps for French Military Occupation of CILICIA. Also, in full, on Turkish fiscal stamps.

**O.M.F. Syrie**. 'Occupation Militaire Française'. Overprint/surcharge on French stamps for French Military Occupation of SYRIA.

**O.N.F.** (or **B.N.F.**) **Castellorizo**. 'Occupation (or Base) Navale Française'. Overprint/surcharge on French/French Levant stamps for French Occupation of CASTELROSSO.

**Onza**. (Unit of weight). SPAIN – Official Stamps.

**O.P.S.O.** 'On Public Service Only'. Overprint on NEW ZEALAND stamps, 1891–1906.

**Orange River Colony**. Overprint on Cape of Good Hope stamps, or inscription, for ORANGE FREE STATE.

**Oranje Vrij Staat**. ORANGE FREE STATE.

**Organisation Internationale pour les Réfugiés**.'International Refugees Organisation'. Overprint on Swiss stamps. SWITZERLAND – International Organizations.

**Organisation Météorologique Mondiale**. 'World Meteorological Organization'. Inscription on Swiss stamps. SWITZERLAND – International Organizations.

**Organisation Mondiale de la Propriete Intellectuelle**. 'World Intellectual Property Organization'. Inscription on Swiss stamps. SWITZERLAND – International Organizations.

**Organisation Modiale de la Santé**. 'World Heath Organisation'. Overprint/inscription on Swiss stamps. SWITZERLAND – International Organizations.

**Orts-Post**. 'Local Post'. SWITZERLAND, 1850.

**O.S.** Overprint on Australian stamps. AUSTRALIA – Official Stamps. Also PAPUA, TRINIDAD. Also see 'Offentlig Sak', etc.

**O.S.G.S.** 'On Sudan Government Service'. Overprint on Sudanese stamps. SUDAN – Official Stamps.

**Österreich(ische)**. AUSTRIA.

**Ostland**. Overprint on German stamps for GERMAN OCCUPATION OF RUSSIA, 1941.

**Ottomanes, Postes**. TURKEY, 1914.

**Oubangui-Chari/Oubangui-Chari-Tchad**. UBANGI-SHARI.

**O.V.S.** 'Oranje Vrij Staat'. Inscription on Military Frank and Police Frank stamps of ORANGE FREE STATE.

**O.W. Official**. Overprint on British stamps. GREAT BRITAIN – Official Stamps (Office of Works).

**O'zbekiston**. UZBEKISTAN,

**P (in oval with crescent and star)**. Overprint on Straits Settlements stamp. PERAK.

**Pacchi Postali**. 'Parcel Post'. ITALY. Also, inscribed 'R.S. Marino', SAN MARINO.

**Packhoi**. Overprint and Chinese surcharge on Indo-Chinese stamps for PAKHOI.

**Pakke-Porto**. 'Parcel Post'. GREENLAND.

**Palestine**. Overprint on E.E.F. stamps of PALESTINE. Overprint on Egyptian stamps. GAZA – Egyptian Occupation.

German Occupation of Russia

**Para(s)**. Currency inscription on first issues of EGYPT. Also surcharge on stamps for AUSTRIAN P.O.s IN TURKEY, BRITISH LEVANT, FRENCH LEVANT, GERMAN P.O.s IN TURKEY, ITALIAN P.O.s IN THE TURKISH EMPIRE, ROMANIAN P.O.s IN THE TURKISH EMPIRE, RUSSIAN P.O.s IN THE TURKISH EMPIRE.

**Parm, Stati, Parma, Duc. di** or **Parmensi, Stati**. PARMA.

**Parlamento a Cervantes, El**. Cervantes commemorative. Official stamps of SPAIN, 1916.

**Patmo or Patmos**. Overprint on Italian stamps for Patmos. DODECANESE ISLANDS.

**P D and numeral**. 'Payé à Destination'. Overprint on plain paper. ST PIERRE ET MIQUELON (*Part 6*).

**Pechino**. Overprint/surcharge on Italian stamps for Peking. ITALIAN P.O.s IN CHINA.

**Pentru Cultura**. Inscription on Postal Tax stamps of ROMANIA, 1932.

**Persanes, Postes**. IRAN. Formerly 'Persia'.

**Persekutuan Tanah Melayu**. MALAYAN FEDERATION.

**Peruana, Republica**. PERU.

**Pesa**. Surcharge on German stamps for GERMAN EAST AFRICA.

**Peseta(s)**. Surcharge on French stamps for FRENCH P.O.s IN MOROCCO.

**P.G.S.** 'Perak Government Service'. Overprint on Straits Settlements stamps. PERAK – Official Stamps.

**Piaster**. Surcharge on Austrian stamps for AUSTRIAN P.O.s IN THE TURKISH EMPIRE. Also on German stamps for GERMAN P.O.s IN THE TURKISH EMPIRE.

**Piastra**. Surcharge on Italian stamp. ITALIAN P.O.s IN CRETE.

**Piastre(s)**. Surcharge on stamps for BRITISH LEVANT, FRENCH LEVANT, ITALIAN P.O.s IN THE TURKISH EMPIRE, RUSSIAN P.O.s IN THE TURKISH EMPIRE.

**Pilgrim Tercentenary**. Inscription on UNITED STATES commemorative set of 1920.

**Pilipinas**. PHILIPPINES. Inscription since 1962.

**Pilipinas, Republika ng**. JAPANESE OCCUPATION OF THE PHILIPPINES.

**Piscopi**. Overprint on Italian stamps for Tilos (Piskopi). DODECANESE ISLANDS.

**Plebiscite Olsztyn Allenstein**. Overprint on German stamps for plebiscite in ALLENSTEIN, 1920.

**Pohjois Inkeri**. NORTH INGERMANLAND. Part of Russia.

**Polska/Poczta Polska**. POLAND.

**Polynesie Française**. FRENCH POLYNESIA.

**Porteado Correio**. PORTUGAL – Postage Due Stamps.

**Porte de Mar**. MEXICO (*Part 15*).

**Porte Franco**. PERU.

Great Britain – Postage Due

Ireland – Postage Due

**Port Gdansk**. Overprint on Polish stamps for POLISH POST IN DANZIG.

**Porte Franco**. Inscription on early issues of PERU.

**Porto Gazetei (Moldavian 'Bulls') or Porto Scrisorei**. Earliest issues of ROMANIA.

**Porto Rico**. Overprint on U.S. stamps. PUERTO RICO–US OCCUPATION.

**Portuguesa, Republica**. PORTUGAL.

**Portzegel**. Overprint and surcharge for Postage Dues. NETHERLANDS.

**Postage Due**. No country name. GREAT BRITAIN or AUSTRALIA.

**Postal Charges**. Overprint for Postage Due stamps. PAPUA NEW GUINEA.

**Post & Receipt or Post Stamp**. Inscriptions on 'annas' stamps of HYDERABAD.

**Postas le híoc**. IRELAND – Postage Dues.

**Poste Khedivie e Giziane/Postes Egyptiennes**. EGYPT, 1872–88.

**Poste Locale**. SWITZERLAND – Transitional Period (*Part 8*) or Federal Administration.

**Postgebeit Ob. Ost.** Overprint on stamps of Germany. GERMAN COMMANDS.

**Postzegel**. Inscription on first issues of NETHERLANDS.

**P.P.** in box. Overprint on French Postage Due stamps. FRENCH MOROCCO.

**Preussen**. PRUSSIA.

**P.R.G.** 'People's Revolutionary Government', overprint on stamps of GRENADA for official use, 1982. Also Grenadines.

**Pro Juventute**. 'For the Children'. Charity stamps of SWITZERLAND.

**Pro Patria**. 'For the Fatherland'. National culture fund stamps of SWITZERLAND.

**Pro (Plebiscito) Tacna y Arica**. Obligatory Tax stamps of PERU, 1927–28.

**Protectorado Español en Marruecos**. SPANISH MOROCCO.

**Protectorat Français**. Overprint on French 'Maroc' key-types for FRENCH MOROCCO.

**Pro Tuberculosis Probres**. Inscription on stamp of SPAIN, 1937.

**Pro Union Iberoamericana**. Inscription on stamps of SPAIN, 1930.

**Provinz Laibach/Ljubljanska Pokrajina**. Inscription/overprint on Italian stamps for German Occupation of SLOVENIA.

**Pto. Rico**. PUERTO RICO.

**P S N C (one letter in each in corner)**. 'Pacific Steam Navigation Company'. Provisional issue of PERU (*Part 20*).

**Pulau Pinang Malaysia**. PENANG. Issues from 1965.

**Puolustusvoimat Kenttäpostia**. FINLAND – Military Field Post.

**Puttialla State**. Overprint on Indian stamps for first issues of PATIALA.

**R.** Overprint/surcharge on French Colonies stamps for REUNION, 1885.

**Raj Shahpura**. SHAHPURA.

**Rarotonga**. Overprint/surcharge on New Zealand stamps, also inscription. COOK ISLANDS.

**Rayon**. SWITZERLAND, 1850–54.

**Recargo/Recargo Transitorio de Guerra**. SPAIN – War Tax Stamps.

**Recuerdo del 1 de Febrero 1916 and portrait of Francisco Bertrand**. HONDURAS.

**Regatul Romaniei**. Overprint with values in bani, leu or lei on Hungarian stamps for ROMANIA – Transylvania, 1919.

**Regno d'Italia Trentino 3 nov 1918/Venezia Giulia 3·XI·18.** Overprint on Austrian stamps. AUSTRIAN TERRITORIES ACQUIRED BY ITALY.
**Reichspost**. GERMANY. Empire issues, 1889–1901.
**R.E.P.** (or **Republika**) **Shqiptare**. ALBANIA, 1925–30, 1939–43.
**Repub. Franc.** (Republique Française). Abbreviation on early stamps of FRANCE and FRENCH COLONIES.
**Repubblica Sociale (or Rep. Soc.) Italiana**. Overprint on stamps of Italy. ITALY – Italian Social Republic.
**Républica Oriental**. URUGUAY.
**Republika Popullore e or R.P.S.E. Shqiperise**. ALBANIA, 1946–91.
**République Française**. FRANCE, FRENCH COLONIES.
**République Khmere**. KHMER REPUBLIC. Cambodia, 1971–75.
**Retymno**. Rethymnon Province – RUSSIAN POST OFFICES IN CRETE.

**R.F.** 'République Française'. FRANCE, FRENCH COLONIES.
**R.H.** 'République d'Haiti'. Abbreviation on Postage Due stamps. HAITI, 1898.
**R.H. Official**. Overprint on British stamps. GREAT BRITAIN – Official Stamps (Royal Household).
**Rheinland-Pfalz**. GERMANY. Allied Occupation, 1947–49.
**Rialtar Sealadac na Héireann 1922**. 'Provisional Government of Ireland'. Overprint on British stamps for IRELAND (REPUBLIC).
**Rizeh**. Overprint on stamps of Russia. RUSSIAN POST OFFICES IN THE TURKISH EMPIRE (*Part 10*).
**R.O.** Overprint on stamps of Turkey. EASTERN ROUMELIA AND SOUTH BULGARIA.
**Robertsport**. Registration stamp of LIBERIA, 1893.

**Rodi**. Overprint on Italian stamps, or inscription, for Rhodes. DODECANESE ISLANDS.
**Romagne, Franco Bollo Postale**. ROMAGNA.
**Romana/Romina**. ROMANIA.
**Rossija**. RUSSIA – Russian Federation.
**Roumelie Orientale**. Overprint on stamps of Turkey, or inscription. EASTERN ROUMELIA AND SOUTH BULGARIA.
**Royaume de l'Arabie Soudite (or Saoudite)**. SAUDI ARABIA.
**R P SH**. 'Republika Popullore e Shqiperise'. On stamp depicting dove with olive branch. ALBANIA.

**RSA**. 'Republic of South Africa'. SOUTH AFRICA.
**R.S.M.** 'Repubblica di San Marino'. SAN MARINO.
**Ruanda**. Overprint on stamps of Belgian Congo. RUANDA-URUNDI.
**Rumänien**. Overprint and value in 'bani' surcharged on German stamps. GERMAN OCCUPATION OF ROMANIA.
**Rupee(s)**. Surcharge on British stamps for BRITISH POSTAL AGENCIES IN EASTERN ARABIA.
**Russisch-Polen**. Overprint on German stamps for GERMAN OCCUPATION OF POLAND.
**Rwandaise, République**. RWANDA, 1962–76.
**Ryukus**. RYUKU ISLANDS.
**S.** Overprint on Straits Settlements 2c. stamp for SELANGOR, 1882.
**S.A.** SAUDI ARABIA.

**Saargebeit/Saarland**. SAAR. Now part of Germany.
**Sachsen**. SAXONY.
**Sachsen, Bundesland**. East Saxony. ALLIED OCCUPATION OF GERMANY – Russian Zone (*Part 7*).

**Sachsen, Provinz**. Saxony. ALLIED OCCUPATION OF GERMANY – Russian Zone (*Part 7*).
**Sahara Español**. SPANISH SAHARA.
**Sahara Occidental, Posesiones Españolas del**. SPANISH SAHARA.
**Salonicco**. Overprint/surcharge on Italian stamps for Salonika (Thessaloniki). ITALIAN P.O.s IN THE TURKISH EMPIRE.
**Salonique**. Overprint on stamps of Russia. RUSSIAN POST OFFICES IN THE TURKISH EMPIRE (*Part 10*).
**Salvador**. EL SALVADOR.
**Samoa i Sisifo**. SAMOA.
**Sandjak d'Alexandrette**. Overprint/surcharge on Syrian stamps. ALEXANDRETTA.
**Saorstát Eireann 1922**. 'Irish Free State'. Overprint on British stamps for IRELAND (REPUBLIC).
**S.A.R.** 'Syrian Arab Republic'. SYRIA.
**Sarkari**. Overprint on Official stamps of SORUTH.
**Sarre**. Overprint on stamps of Germany and Bavaria. SAAR.
**Saurashtra**. SORUTH (Indian state).
**Scarpanto**. Overprint on Italian stamps for Karpathos. DODECANESE ISLANDS.
**Scinde District Dawk**. INDIA, 1852.
**Scutari di Albania**. Overprint/ surcharge on Italian stamps for ITALIAN P.O.s IN THE TURKISH EMPIRE.
**Segnatasse**. ITALY – Postage Due Stamps.
**Sello 10Ϸ/25c. de Peso**. Inscription on surcharged fiscal stamp. FERNANDO POO.
**Senegambie et Niger**. SENEGAMBIA AND NIGER.

**Serbien**. Overprint/surcharge on Yugoslav stamps for German Occupation of SERBIA; also overprint on Bosnian stamps for Serbian Issues of AUSTRO-HUNGARIAN MILITARY POST.
**Sevilla**. As part of overprint on stamps of Spain. SPAIN – Civil War issues (*Part 9*).
**S H (one letter in each upper corner)**. SCHLESWIG-HOLSTEIN.
**Shanghai China**. Overprint/surcharge on U.S. stamps for UNITED STATES POSTAL AGENCY IN SHANGHAI.
**Shqipenia**. ALBANIA, 1913–20, 1995–.
**Shqipenie**. ALBANIA, 1920–22.
**Shqiperia**. ALBANIA, 1962–91.
**Shqiperise**. ALBANIA, 1948–62.
**Shqipni**. ALBANIA, 1937–38.

Albania

Slovakia

**Shqipnija**. ALBANIA, 1944, 1947.
**Shqiptare**. ALBANIA, 1991–95.
**Shqyptare**. ALBANIA, 1922–25, 1930.
**Shri Lanka**. SRI LANKA, issues of 1992–93.
**S.H.S.** 'Srba (Serbs), Hrvata (Croats), Slovena (Slovenes)'. Early issues of YUGOSLAVIA.
**Siam**. THAILAND, 1887–1939.
**Sicilia, Bollo della Posta**. SICILY.
**Simi**. Overprint on Italian stamps for Simi. DODECANESE ISLANDS.
**Slesvig**. SCHLESWIG. Plebiscite issues, 1920.
**Slovenija**. SLOVENIA.
**Slovensko/Slovanska Posta**. SLOVAKIA.
**Slovenský Stat**. Overprint on stamps of Czechoslovakia. SLOVAKIA.
**Slova Posta**. CZECHOSLOVAKIA – Postage Due stamps, 1919.
**S. Marino, Repubblica** (or **Rep.**) **di**. SAN MARINO.
**Smirne**. Overprint/surcharge on Italian stamps for Smyrna (Izmir). ITALIAN P.O.s IN THE TURKISH EMPIRE.
**Smyrne**. Overprint on stamps of Russia. RUSSIAN POST OFFICES IN THE TURKISH EMPIRE (*Part 10*).

**S.O. 1920**. 'Silesie Orientale'. Overprint on Czech and Polish stamps for EAST SILESIA.
**Sobreporte**. Special Fee stamp of COLOMBIA, 1865.
**Socialist People's Libyan Arab Jamahiriya**. LIBYA since 1977.
**Sociedad Colombo-Alemana de Transportes Aéreos**. Private Air Company stamps. SCADTA (*Part 20*), COLOMBIA (*Part 20*) and ECUADOR (*Part 20*).
**Societé des Nations, also with Courrier de la or Service de la**. Overprints on Swiss stamps for League of Nations. SWITZERLAND – International Organizations.
**Soomaaliya (Soomaaliyeed or Somaliya)**. SOMALIA.
**Soudan**. Overprint on Egyptian stamps. SUDAN.
**Soudan Français**. FRENCH SUDAN.
**South Georgia Dependency of**. FALKAND ISLANDS DEPENDENCIES.
**South Orkneys Dependency of**. FALKAND ISLANDS DEPENDENCIES.
**South Shetlands Dependency of**. FALKAND ISLANDS DEPENDENCIES.
**Sowjetische Besatzungs Zone**. Overprint on German stamps for GERMANY (ALLIED OCCUPATION) – Russian Zone.

**SPM or St-Pierre M-on**. Overprint/surcharge on French Colonies stamps, or inscription. ST PIERRE ET MIQUELON.
**Srbija**. SERBIA.
**Srbija i Crna Gora**. SERBIA AND MONTENEGRO.
**Srodkowa Litwa**. CENTRAL LITHUANIA.
**Stampalia**. Overprint on Italian stamps for Astipalaia. DODECANESE ISLANDS.
**S. Thomeé** (or **Tomé**) **e Principe**. ST THOMAS AND PRINCE ISLANDS.
**S.T. Trsta Vuja**. TRIESTE – Zone B Yugoslav Military Government.
**STT Vuja (or Vujna)**. Overprints on Yugoslav stamps. TRIESTE – Zone B Yugoslav Military Government.
**Sud Kasai, Etat Autonome du**. Overprint and inscription. SOUTH KASAI.
**Sul Bolletino or Sulla Ricevuta**. Inscriptions on left and right halves of Parcel Post stamps. ITALY. With star and crescent SOMALIA.
**S.U./S. Ujong**. SUNGEI UJONG.
**Suidafrika (Suid-Afrika or Republiek van Suid-Afrika)**. SOUTH AFRICA.
**Suidwes-Afrika**. SOUTH WEST AFRICA.
**Suomi**. FINLAND.
**Suriname**. SURINAM.

**Sverige**. SWEDEN.

**S.W.A**. (or **SWA**). Overprints on South African stamps, also abbreviated inscription on stamps, for SOUTH WEST AFRICA.
**Syrie/République Syrienne**. SYRIA.
**Syrie Grand Liban**. Surcharge on French stamps. SYRIA – French Mandated Territory.
**T with monetary unit in f(rancs)**. BELGIUM – Postage Due Stamps.
**Tadzikistan**. TAJIKISTAN.
**Takse Pulu**. Inscription on Postage Due stamps of TURKEY.
**Tanganyika & Zanzibar, Republic of**. TANZANIA.
**Tanger**. Overprint on French/French Morocco stamps for FRENCH P.O.s in TANGIER. Also overprint on Spanish stamps, or inscription, for SPANISH P.O.s IN TANGIER.
**Tangier**. Overprint on British stamps for MOROCCO AGENCIES – Tangier International Zone.
**Tassa Gazette**. MODENA – Newspaper Stamp.
**Taxa de Guerra**. War Tax surcharge. Distinguished by currencies. PORTUGUESE COLONIES ($), PORTUGUESE GUINEA (reis), PORTUGUESE INDIA (Rps), MACAO (avos).
**Taxa Porto Pentru Cultura**. Postal Tax Postage Due stamp of ROMANIA.
**Te Betalen Port**. Postage Due stamps of NETHERLANDS, CURAÇAO, SURINAM.
**T.-C.** Overprint on stamp of Cochin. TRAVANCORE-COCHIN.
**T.C.E.K.** 'Turkiye Cocuk Esirgeme Kurumu'. Inscription on Child Welfare stamps of TURKEY.
**Tchad**. CHAD.
**T.C. Postalari**. TURKEY.
**T.E.O.** 'Territoires Ennemis Occupés'. Overprint with surcharge in milliemes or piastres on French stamps for French Military Occupation of SYRIA. Also in paras on French Levant stamps for CILICIA.
**T.E.O. Cilicie**. Overprint on Turkish stamps for French Occupation of CILICIA.
**Terres Australes et Antarctiques Françaises**. FRENCH SOUTHERN AND ANTARCTIC TERRITORIES.
**Territoire Français des Afars et des Issas**. FRENCH TERRITORY OF THE AFARS AND THE ISSAS.
**Territorios Espanoles del Golfo de Guinea**. Inscription or overprint on Spanish stamps for SPANISH GUINEA.
**Tetuan**. Handstamp on Spanish stamps for SPANISH MOROCCO – Spanish P.O.s in Morocco.

**Thailand, with value in cents**. MALAYA (THAI OCCUPATION).
**Thirty Two Cents**. With sailing ship. LIBERIA, 1886.
**Thuringen**. Thuringia. ALLIED OCCUPATION OF GERMANY – Russian Zone (*Part 7*).
**Tientsin**. Overprint/surcharge on Italian stamps for ITALIAN P.O.s IN CHINA.
**Timor-Leste**. EAST TIMOR.
**Timor Lorosae**. UNITED NATIONS – East Timor (UN Transitional Administration).

**Tjeneste Frimaerke**. DENMARK – Official Stamps.
**Tjenestefrimerke**. NORWAY – Official Stamps, 1925.

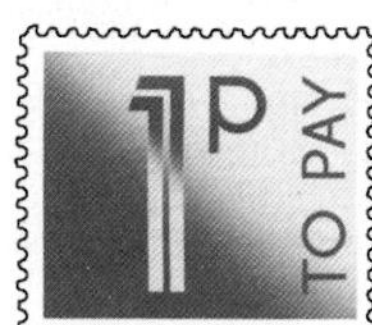


**To Pay**. No country name. GREAT BRITAIN – Postage Due Stamps.

**Toga**. TONGA, 1897–1944.
**Togolaise, République**. TOGO.
**Toscano, Francobollo Postale**. TUSCANY.
**Touva**. TUVA.
**Traité de Versailles**. Overprint on stamps of Germany. ALLENSTEIN.
**Transjordan**. JORDAN.
**Trebizonde**. Overprint on stamps of Russia. RUSSIAN POST OFFICES IN THE TURKISH EMPIRE (*Part 10*).
**Trieste Trst in surcharge with date 1**.V.1945 on Italian stamps. VENEZIA GIULIA AND ISTRIA – Yugoslav Occupation.
**Tripoli di Barberia**. Overprint on Italian stamps for ITALIAN P.O.s IN THE TURKISH EMPIRE.
**Tripoli, Fiera Campionaria**. On stamps inscribed Poste Italiane, R.R. Poste Coloniali or Posta Aerea with date 1935. TRIPOLITANIA. On stamps with dates 1936, 1937, 1938. LIBYA.
**T.Ta.C.** Inscription on Aviation Fund stamp of TURKEY.
**T T T T**. In corners of stamps with large numerals. DOMINICAN REPUBLIC – Postage Due Stamps.
**Tunis, Tunisie or République Tunisienne**. TUNISIA.
**Türkiye Cumhuriyeti (or T.C.) Postalari**. TURKEY.
**Türkiye (or Turk) Postalari**. TURKEY.
**Türkmenpoçta**. TURKMENISTAN.
**Two Pence**. Denomination on stamps showing Queen Victoria on throne. VICTORIA, 1852.
**U.A.E.** UNITED ARAB EMIRATES.
**U.A.R.** 'United Arab Republic'. Inscription on issues of EGYPT (value in milliemes), 1958–71, and SYRIA (value in piastres), 1958–61.
**U.G.** Typewritten inscription on first 'Missionary' stamps for UGANDA, 1895.
**Ukraina**. UKRAINE.
**Ukraine**. Overprint on German stamps for GERMAN OCCUPATION OF RUSSIA, 1941.
**Ultramar**. 'Beyond the Seas'. Inscription with year dates on stamps of CUBA, also overprinted for PUERTO RICO. Appears also on postal-fiscals of MACAO (values in avos) and PORTUGUESE GUINEA (values in reis).
**UNEF**. Overprint on Indian stamp for INDIAN U.N. FORCE IN GAZA (PALESTINE).
**UN Force (India) Congo**. Overprint on stamps of India, 1962. INDIAN U.N. FORCE IN CONGO.
**Union Internationale des Télécommunications**. 'International Telecommunications Union'. Inscription on Swiss stamps. SWITZERLAND – International Organizations.
**Union Postale Universelle**. 'Universal Postal Union'. Inscription on Swiss stamps. SWITZERLAND – International Organizations.
**Union Postale Universelle, Jubile de l'**. SWITZERLAND, 1900.
**UNTEA**. 'United Nations Temporary Executive Authority'. Overprint on stamps of Netherlands New Guinea for WEST NEW GUINEA.
**Urundi**. Overprint on stamps of Belgian Congo. RUANDA-URUNDI.
**U.S.** or **U.S.A.** UNITED STATES OF AMERICA.
**U.S.T.C.** Overprint on stamp of Cochin. TRAVANCORE-COCHIN.
**Vallées d'Andorre**. ANDORRA (French Post Offices), 1932–37.
**Valona**. Overprint/surcharge on Italian stamps. ITALIAN P.O.s IN THE TURKISH EMPIRE.
**Vancouver Island**. BRITISH COLOMBIA AND VANCOUVER ISLAND.
**Van Diemen's Land**. First issues of TASMANIA.
**Vaticane, Poste**. VATICAN CITY, to 1993. (Posta Aerea Vaticana – Air stamps).
**Venezia Giulia**. Overprint/surcharge on Italian stamps. AUSTRIAN TERRITORIES ACQUIRED BY ITALY.
**Venezia Tridentina**. Overprint/ surcharge on Italian stamps. AUSTRIAN TERRITORIES ACQUIRED BY ITALY.

**Vereinte Nationen**. UNITED NATIONS – Vienna Centre.
**VII Congreso U.P.U. Madrid 1920**. Inscription on stamps of SPAIN.
**VIII Världspost-Kongressen i Stockholm**. SWEDEN, 1924.
**Vilnius**. Overprint on Russian stamps for GERMAN OCCUPATION OF LITHUANIA.
**Virgin Islands**. BRITISH VIRGIN ISLANDS.
**Viva España as part of overprint on stamps of Spain**. SPAIN – Civil War issues (*Part 9*).
**Vojna Uprava Jugoslavenske Armije**. Overprint/surcharge on Yugoslav stamps for VENEZIA GIULIA AND ISTRIA – Yugoslav Military Government.
**Vojenska Posta**. CZECHOSLOVAK ARMY IN SIBERIA.
**Vom Empfänger Einzuziehen**. DANZIG – Postage Due Stamps.
**Vom Empfänger Zahlbar**. BAVARIA – Postage Due Stamps.
**V R in top corners**. FIJI.
**V.R.I.** 'Victoria Regina Imperatrix'. Overprint with values in British currency on stamps of ORANGE FREE STATE.
**W or West Australia**. WESTERN AUSTRALIA.
**Wilayah Persekutuan**. MALAYSIA – Federal Territory issues.
**Wendenschen Kreises, Briefmarke des/Packenmarke des**. WENDEN.
**Western Samoa**. SAMOA.
**Württemberg**. WURTTEMBERG. Independent Kingdom. Also GERMANY (ALLIED OCCUPATION).
**Y.A.R.** 'Yemen Arab Republic'. YEMEN.
**Yemen PDR**. YEMEN PEOPLE'S DEMOCRATIC REPUBLIC.
**Yemen, Republic of**. YEMEN REPUBLIC (Combined).
**Yunnansen/Yunnanfou**. Overprint/surcharge on Indo-Chinese stamps. YUNNANFU.
**Z. Afr. Rep(ubliek)**. TRANSVAAL.
**Zanzibar**. Overprint/surcharge on French stamps for FRENCH P.O.s IN ZANZIBAR.
**Zara**. Overprint on Italian stamps. GERMANY OCCUPATION OF DALMATIA.
**Zelaya, Dpto**. NICARAGUA – Zelaya (*Part 15*).
**Zeitungs Stempel**. 'Newspaper Stamp'. AUSTRIA or LOMBARDY AND VENETIA.
**Zil Eloigne Sesel Seychelles**. 'Seychelles Outer Islands'. ZIL EL WANNYEN SESEL, 1980–82.
**Zil Elwagne Sesel Seychelles**. See above, 1982–84.
**Zona de Ocupatie Romana in small oval**. Overprint on Hungarian stamps for Debrecen. ROMANIAN OCCUPATION OF HUNGARY.
**Zona Occupata Fiumano Kupa**. Overprint on Yugoslav stamps. FIUME AND KUPA ZONE.
**Zona (de) Protectorado Español/en Marruecos**. SPANISH MOROCCO.

**Zone Française**. GERMANY (ALLIED OCCUPATION) – French Zone, 1945–46.
**Zuid Afrika**. SOUTH AFRICA.
**Zuid Afrikaansche (or Z. Afr.) Republiek**. TRANSVAAL.
**Zuidwest Afrika**. SOUTH WEST AFRICA.
**Zurich, Local Taxe**. Zurich. SWITZERLAND – Cantonal Administrations (*Part 8*).

Czechoslovak Army in Siberia

Yemeni Arab Republic

Turkey

United Arab Emirates

The first Greek stamp showing Hermes

## OTHER ALPHABETS AND SCRIPTS

### *The Greek Alphabet*

Greek is one of the classic languages – its alphabet was 'borrowed' from the Phoenicians whose extinct Semitic language was allied to Carthaginian and akin to Hebrew, and was, perhaps, the first tongue written in an alphabet proper. The word 'alphabet' itself is derived from *alpha*, *beta*, the first two Greek letters. Greek stamps have the country name 'Hellas' expressed (in Greek), a word which can be spelled out from the table below as *Ellas*. In fact since 1966 the version 'Hellas' has been printed alongside the Greek characters on the stamps.

Aerospresso Co issue of 1926

Greek stamp marking the cession of the Ionian Islands

Modern Greek stamp inscribed 'ΕΛΛΑΣ ΔΗΜΟΚΡΑΤΙΑ'

Look out for the distinctive currency inscription – 100 lepta = 1 drachma. *Lepta* (singular, *lepton*) is expressed in a word which looks like 'ΛΕΝΤΑ' (although the first letter is an inverted 'V'), while *drachmai* (plural) appears at first glance as 'ΑΡΑΧΜΑΙ', though again the first letter is a triangle, the equivalent for 'D'. Sometimes these words are abbreviated. You may encounter overprints on Greek stamps and once you have decoded them it should be an easy matter to locate them in the catalogue. *Ellenike Dioikesis* ('Greek Administration') may be found on the Greek stamps of 1912 (provisionals for Balkan territories), or the Greek Occupation of Albania in 1940. The initials *S.D.D.* adjoining a surcharge within a scroll can be pinpointed to the Greek Occupation of the Dodecanese Islands. Thrace suffered various occupations in 1920, and a typical overprint reads, when decoded, *Diokesis Dutikes Frakes* or 'Administration of Western Thrace'. Stamps for the Greek island of Crete bear the inscription ΚΡΗΤΗ which translates as *Krete*.

Anti Tuberculosis Fund

**SIMPLIFIED GREEK TABLE** *with English equivalents*

| *Greek* | *English* | *Greek* | *English* |
|---|---|---|---|
| Αα | A | Ξξ | X |
| Ββ | B | Οο | O |
| Γγ | G | Ππ | P |
| Δδ | D | Ρρ | R |
| Εε | E | Σσ | S |
| Ζζ | Z | ς | (final) |
| Ηη | E | Ττ | T |
| Θθ | TH | Υυ | U |
| Ιι | I | Φφ | F |
| Κκ | K | Χχ | KH |
| Λλ | L | Ψψ | PS |
| Μμ | M | Ωω | O |
| Νν | N | | |

*Conventional English equivalents are given. The actual pronunciation of some letters differs in modern spoken Greek.*

Greece – Administration of (Western) Thrace

A list of inscriptions in the Greek alphabet as they appear on stamps.

**ΒΟΗΘΕΙΤΕ ΤΟΝ**. Inscription on Charity Tax stamps. GREECE.

**ΔΙΟΙΚΗΣΙΣ ΔΥΤΙΚΗΣ ΘΡΑΚΗΣ or Διοίκησις (Δυτικής) Θράκης**. 'Administration of (Western) Thrace'. Overprint on stamps of Greece. THRACE.

**Ε*Δ**. Overprint on stamps of Greece for Khios. GREECE – Balkan War Issues (*Part 3*).

**ΕΛΛΑΣ 2-Χ-43 in box**. Handstamp on stamps for the Italian Occupation of Ionian Islands. GERMAN OCCUPATION OF ZANTE.

**ΕΛΛΑΣ, ΕΛΛΑC or ΕΛΛ**. GREECE.

**ΕΛΛ. ΔΙΟΙΚ. ΓΚΙΟΥΜΟΥ ΛΤΖΙΝΑΣ**. Overprint/surcharge on stamps of Turkey. THRACE – Greek Occupation, 1913, Issue for Gumultsina (*Part 3*).

**ΕΛΛΗΝΙΚΗ ΧΕΙΜΑΡΡΑ**. EPIRUS (*Part 3*).

**ΕΛΛΗΝΙΚΗ ΔΗΜΟΚΡΑΤΙΑ**. GREECE.

**ΕΛΛΗΝΙΚΗ ΔΙΟΙΚΗCΙC**. Overprint on stamps of Greece. GREEK OCCUPATION OF ALBANIA.

**ΕΛΛΗΝΙΚΗ ΔΙΟΙΚΗΣΙΣ**. Overprint on stamps of Greece, 1912. GREECE. Also on stamps of Greece (Ikaria) and Bulgaria (Kavalla). GREECE – Balkan War Issues (*Part 3*).

**ΕΛΛΗΝΙΚΗ ΔΙΟΙΚΗΣΙΣ ΔΕΔΕΑΓΑΤΣ**. 'Greek Administration Dedeagtz'. THRACE – Greek Occupation, 1913. Issue for Dedeagatz (*Part 3*).

**Ελληνική Κατοχή Μυτιλήνης**. 'Greek Possession Mytilene'. Overprint on stamps of Turkey for Lesvos. GREECE – Balkan War Issues (*Part 3*).

**ΕΝΑΡΙΘΜΟΝ ΓΡΑΜΜΑΤΟΣΗΜΟΝ**. Postage Due. GREECE.

**ΕΘΝΙΚΗ ΠΕΡΙΘΑΛΨΙΣ**. Inscription on 1914 Charity Tax stamp. GREECE.

**ΕΠΑΝΑΣΤΑΣΙΣ 1922**. 'Revolution 1922'. Overprint on stamps of Crete (and Greece). GREECE.

**ΗΠΕΙΡΟΣ**. EPIRUS (*Part 3*).

**ΙΚΑΡΙΑΣ**. Ikaria. GREECE – Balkan War Issues (*Part 3*).

**ΙΟΝΙΚΟΝ ΚΡΑΤΟΣ**. IONIAN ISLANDS.

**ΙΤΑΛΙΑΣ–ΕΛΛΑΔΟΣ–ΤΟΥΡΚΙΑΣ**. Inscription on Aerospresso Co issue of 1926. GREECE.

**ΚΟΙΝΟΝ ΝΗΣΙΩΤΩΝ**. Island Committee for Union with Greece. DODECANESE ISLANDS (*Part 3*).

**Κ. Π.** Overprint on Fiscal stamps (inscribed ΧΑΡΤΟΣΗΜΟΝ) of GREECE.

**ΚΡΗΤΗ**. CRETE.

**Λ(or Α)ΗΜΝΟΣ**. Overprint on stamps of Greece for Limnos. GREECE – Balkan War Issues (*Part 3*).

**ΟΛΥΜΠ. ΑΓΩΥΕΣ** or **ΟΛΥΜΠΙΑΚΟΙ ΑΓΩΝΕΣ**. Olympic Games issue of 1906. GREECE.

**Π.Ι.Π.** (P.I.P. 'Patriotic Charity League'). Overprint on Red Cross stamp. GREECE.

**ΠΡΟΣΤΑΣΙΑ ΦΥΜΑΤΙΚΩΝ**. Anti-Tuberculosis Fund. GREECE.

**ΠΡΟΣΩΡΙΝΗ ΚΥΒΕΡΝΗΣΙΣ**. CRETE – Revolutionary Assembly.

**ΠΡΟΣΩΡΙΝΟΝ ΤΑΧΥΔΡΟΜΕΙΟΝ ΗΡΑΚΛΕΙΟΥ**. Candia Province – BRITISH P.O.s IN CRETE.

**ΡΕΘΥΜΝΗΣ**. Rethymnon Province – RUSSIAN POST OFFICES IN CRETE.

**ΣΑΜΟΥ**. Samos. GREECE – Balkan War Issues (*Part 3*).

**Σ.Δ.Δ.** Overprint on stamps of Greece. Greek Military Administration. DODECANESE ISLANDS (*Part 3*).

**Ύάτη Αρμοστεία Θράκης**. 'High Commission of Thrace'. Overprint/surcharge on stamps of Turkey. THRACE.

Greek Occupation of Albania

Greek Administration

Greek Postage Due

Epirus

Ikaria

### *The Cyrillic Group*

Saint Cyril, creator of the Cyrillic alphabet, and his brother St. Methodius depicted on a Bulgarian stamp of 1975

Cyril and his brother Methodius were 9th century saints, apostles of the Slavs and natives of Salonika (now Thessalonica). They worked as Christian missionaries among the Slav peoples, and it was in an effort to unify the Slavonic languages that Cyril, nicknamed 'the philosopher', created what became known as the Cyrillic alphabet, a modification of the Greek alphabet with marked individual characteristics, comprising 33 letters. Cyril set down his alphabet in AD 855, and it can be seen from the tables of Greek and Cyrillic letters that several Cyrillic characters are identical to those of the Greek alphabet: some, indeed, have the same English equivalents.

Despite these similarities, the Cyrillic letters are quite distinctive and mark out that the stamp belongs to Russia (or one of its former districts or regional governments and post offices) or to Mongolia, Yugoslavia (including the ancient kingdoms of Montenegro and Serbia), or Bulgaria, which was once the territory of a great empire.

### *RUSSIA*

The language of the peoples of Central Russia – which is also the official and literary language of the Russian nation – has a great many dialects, but in the main these are phonetic variations. The basic Cyrillic alphabet is universal throughout the country. Prior to the Revolution of 1917, Russian stamps were simply inscribed *mapka*, which translates as 'marka' or 'stamp', or with a word which looks like *noyta*, meaning 'pochta' or 'post'. Clues to identification are also provided by the currency denominations – the word which looks like *kon* is easily decoded as 'kop', short for 'kopeck', the unit of Russian currency. A hundred kopecks equal one 'rouble', a word which again is abbreviated on Russian stamps – the word, which looks like *pye*, is decoded as 'roob' or 'rouble'. Immediately following the Revolution, Russian stamps bore an inscription which looked something like 'P.C.I.C.P.'. This is interpreted as 'R.S.F.S.R.', an abbreviation for the provisional country name of 'Russian Socialist Federal Soviet Republic'. From 1923 to 1991 Russian stamps were inscribed CCCP, which translates as 'SSSR', the initial letters for the four Russian words meaning 'Union of Soviet Socialist Republics' (*Soyuz Sovyetskikh Sotsialisticheskikh Respublik*), familiar to us as 'U.S.S.R.'. Also familiar on Russian stamps until 1991 was the word *noyta* which meant 'post'. Since 1991 the country name has also appeared in the western alphabet as 'ROSSIJA'.

Stamps were issued in Batum (or Batoum), a town in Georgia on the eastern shore of the Black Sea, in 1919 during the British occupation following the War of 1914–18, the inscription in the scroll at the top of the stamps translates to *Batoomskaya pochta*, which means 'Batum post'. Stamps issued for the Russian Post Offices in Turkey in 1868 and 1879 can be identified by the inscription around the value numeral which may be decoded as *Vostochnaya korrespondentsia* or 'Oriental correspondence'. The penultimate letter 'I' in this inscription is now obsolete.

Various anti-Bolshevik governments existed in Siberia for some years after the Revolution – the Cyrillic inscriptions and overprints are similar to those on Russian stamps and positive identification is best obtained by reference to the catalogue. South Russia also had temporary post-Revolution governments and here again reference to the catalogue illustrations is advised.

The Ukraine is a vast territory of the U.S.S.R. which issued stamps during its temporary independence after the Revolution, between 1918 and 1923 and again from 1992. The 'trident' emblem on overprints and in designs is a clue to identity, while reference to the Cyrillic chart decodes the main inscription as *Ookrains'ka*, or Ukraine. For West Ukraine, Austrian stamps were overprinted with a trident in 1919 and letters which translate to *Z.Oo.N.R.*, meaning 'West Ukraine People's Republic'. Wenden, the 'Land of the Wends', now part of Latvia, issued its own stamps up to 1901 – the principal word in the inscription emerges as *Vendenskaya*. Earlier issues are inscribed in German – *Wendensche Kries Briefmarke*.

Ukraine

Russian stamps were overprinted/surcharged for Armenia – mostly new-value surcharges and distinctive monogram devices; Georgia – surcharges, including the hammer and sickle, in 1923; and for the Russian Post Offices in China – note that the overprinted country name (which looks like the Greek name for 'Crete'), which translates as *Kitai*, is the Russian word for 'China'. Mongolia, the republic in Central Asia located between Russia and China, is largely under Russian influence.

The Mongolian language used to be written in a vertical script and this is found on early stamps; the Cyrillic alphabet was introduced on stamps in 1943 and has continued since. The common inscription translates as *Mongol shoodan*, or 'Mongolian post', while the Cyrillic initials *BNMAU* stand for 'All-in-agreement Mongol People's Country'. Mongolian stamps from 1959 have been additionally inscribed 'Mongolia' in the normal alphabet, thus making identification an easy matter.

Left to Right: Macedonia, Uzbekistan and Mongolia

The splitting of the former Soviet Union into separate states has resulted in new stamps from Russian Federation, Armenia, Azerbaijan, Belarus, Estonia, Georgia, Kazakhstan, Kyrgyzstan, Latvia, Lithuania, Moldovia, Tajikistan, Turkmenistan, Ukraine and Uzbekistan. The stamps of the three Baltic States and Moldovia are inscribed in the normal alphabet and Azerbaijan as 'Az3rbaycan'; Georgia has its own script. Most stamps of the other states are inscribed in both alphabets.

Yugoslavia

### *YUGOSLAVIA*

The Socialist Federal Republic of Yugoslavia – the land of the southern Slavs – was proclaimed in 1945. It was, however, established in 1918 as the kingdom of the Serbs, Croats and Slovenes, comprising Montenegro, Serbia, Bosnia, Herzegovina and parts of pre-war Hungary, with separate stamp issues for the various states. In 1931, when the new country title of 'Jugoslavija' was officially adopted, definitive stamps appeared inscribed in Serbo-Croat (the *lingua franca* of Yugoslavia) and in the Cyrillic alphabet. Occasionally, since that time, Yugoslav stamps have been issued bearing only the Cyrillic inscription, but these are readily identifiable on reference to any of the dual-language stamps.

The former monarchy of Montenegro issued its own stamps from 1874 until 1913, and the country name – in Cyrillic characters – is rather misleading. It decodes in the native tongue as *Tsrna* (or *Tsr.*) *Gora*, or

Serbia and Montenegro

Stamps of Russia (left to right): Empire, Russian Socialist Federal Soviet Republic, Union of Soviet Socialist Republics and Russian Federation

Finland (denominated in markka)

Top: Kingdom of Bulgaria, an Express stamp of 1939
Above: A modern stamp of Bulgaria

*Tsrne Gore* – in modern parlance, *Grna Gora*, in other words, Montenegro or 'Black mountain'. *Poshte* is another version of the word for 'post'. The former kingdom of Serbia first issued stamps in 1866 and used the Cyrillic alphabet consistently, even through the German occupation of 1941–43. The country name readily translates as *Srbija*, *Srbska* or *Srpska*. Note that the 'j' is one of the Serbian special letters. The word for 'post' is *poshta*, and the currency is another clue – 100 para equalling 1 dinar. The Cyrillic for 'para' looks like *napa*.

The division of Yugoslavia in the 1990s has led to separate issues for Bosnia and Herzegovina, Croatia, Macedonia and Slovenia. Since 2003 the country has become Srbija i Crna Gora (Serbia and Montenegro), in Roman or Cyrillic alphabets.

### BULGARIA

A Balkan republic, Bulgaria adjoins the Black Sea on the east, and is bounded by Romania, former Yugoslavia (Serbia), Greece and Turkey. Formerly a Turkish province, it became a principality under Turkish suzerainty in 1878, Eastern Roumelia was incorporated with it in 1885. Bulgaria's first stamps were issued in 1879, establishing the country name in Cyrillic letters which can be deduced as 'B'lgariya' (the second letter is silent and is thus represented by an apostrophe). With the accession of Tsar Ferdinand in 1907, the word for 'kingdom' – 'Tsarstvo' – was added. The currency – 100 stotinki = 1 lev (plural, leva) – is also easily identified: 'stotinki' is expressed as 'ctot…'. After Bulgaria became a republic in 1946, until 1989, stamps bore the Cyrillic letters 'HP' before the country name, translated as 'NR' or 'Narodna Republika' or 'People's Republic'. Since 1989 Bulgarian stamps have also been inscribed 'Bulgaria'.

Some inscriptions in the Cyrillic alphabet as they appear on stamps.

Bulgarian Sunday delivery stamp

Serbia

Batum

**А.С.С.Р. 'A.S.S.R'** (Azerbaijan Soviet Socialist Republic). AZERBAIJAN.
**АЭ ИДЖАНСКАЯ**. AZERBAIJAN.
**АМЖРСКАЯ ОБЛСТИАЯ ПОЧТОВАЯ МАРКА**. 'Amur Province Postage Stamp'. SIBERIA.
**БАНЛЕРОЛЬНОЕ ОТПРАВЛЕНIЕ НА ВОСТОКЪ**. 'Dispatch under wrapper to the East'. RUSSIAN POs IN THE TURKISH EMPIRE.
**БАТУМСАЯ ПОЧТА, БАТУМ(Ъ) or БАТУМ. ОБЛ. BATUM. БЪЛ**(orΛ) **ГАРИЯ**. BULGARIA.
**БЪЛГАРСКА**. BULGARIA.
**ВЕНДЕНКАЯ**. WENDEN.
**ВОСТОЧНАЯ КОРРЕСПОНДЕНЦІЯ**. 'Eastern Correspondence'. RUSSIAN POs INTHE TURKISH EMPIRE.
**В П26П V 1921–1922** in oval. Overprint on stamps of SIBERIA.
**Г.С.С.Р.** in circle with star 'G.S.S.R.' (Gorskaya Soviet Socialist Republic). Overprint on stamps of Russia. SOUTH RUSSIA (Part 10).
**Д.В.** Overprint on Russian stamps. SIBERIA.
**ДРЖВА СХС**. YUGOSLAVIA –Issues for Bosnia and Herzegovina.
**ЕДИНАЯ РОССІЯ**. SOUTH RUSSIA.
**Э.А.** and cross of Russia in circle. 'Zapadnaya Armiya' (Western Army). Overprint on stamps of Latvia. NORTH WEST RUSSIA.
**ЗСФСР**. TRANSCAUCASIAN FEDERATION.
**З.У.Н.Р.** Overprint in corners of Austrian stamps. WEST UKRAINE.
**КАЗАКСТАН**. KAZAKHSTAN.
**КИТАЙ**. Overprint on stamps of Russia. RUSSIAN POs IN CHINA.
**КРАЉЕВСТВО СХС**. YUGOSLAVIA – Issues for Bosnia and Herzegovina.
**КРЫМСКАГО КРАЕВОГО ПРАВИТЕПЬСТВА**. 'Crimean Regional Government'. Inscription on postage and currency stamp. SOUTH RUSSIA.
**К. С. or К.** СРБСКА ПОШТА. SERBIA.
**КЫРГЫЗСТАН**. KYRGYSTAN.
**КЊ**. СРП. ПОШТА. SERBIA.
**МАКЕДОНИЯ**. Overprint on stamps of Bulgaria. MACEDONIA – German Occupation.
**МАКЕДОНИЈА**. MACEDONIA.
**Н НА А В. П. П.** Handstamp on stamps of Russia. SIBERIA (Part 10).
**ОКСА**. 'Osobiy Korpus Severnoy Armiy' (Special Corps Northern Army). NORTH WEST RUSSIA.
**П.З.К.** below three horizontal bars, all in frame. Handstamp on stamps of SIBERIA.
**ПОЧТОВАЯ МАРКА**. 'Postage Stamp'. Inscription on early stamps of FINLAND, RUSSIA, SERBIA, SIBERIA and SOUTH RUSSIA.
**ПОШТЕЦРНЕГОЕ**.MONTENEGRO.
**ПОРТО СКРИСОРИ**. ROMANIA – Moldavia.
**Прпам. ЗЕМСКЇЙ Край.** 'Priam Zemskiye Kraye' (Primur Territory). SIBERIA.
**ПЯТЬ**. Overprint on stamps of Russia. SOUTH RUSSIA.
**РЕРУБЛИКА СРПСКА КРАЈИНА**. CROATIA – Serbian Posts (Republic of Srpska Krajina).
**РЕПУБЛИКА СРПСА**. 'Republika Srpska'. Serbian administration in BOSNIA AND HERZEGOVINA.
**РОПИТ**. 'Russian Company for Steam Shipping and Trade'. RUSSIAN POs IN THE TURKISH EMPIRE.
**РОССІЯ**. RUSSIA, SOUTH RUSSIA.
**РСФСР**. 'RSFSR' (Russian Socialist Federal Soviet Republic). RUSSIA.
**РУССКОЙ АРМІИ**. Overprint on stamps of Russia, South Russia andRussian POs in the Turkish Empire. RUSSIAN REFUGEES POST (Part 10).
**СБЕРЕГАТЕЛЬНАЯ МАРКА**.Inscription on Postal Savings Bankstamps authorised for postage. RUSSIA.
**СРБИЈА**. SERBIA.
**СРЬИЈА И ЦОРА**.'Serbia and Montenegro'. SERBIA.
**СРЕМСКО-БАРАІЬСКА ОБЛАСТ**.CROATIA – Serbian Posts (Sremsko Braanjska Oblast).
**СССР**. 'USSR' (Union of Soviet Socialist Republics). RUSSIA.
**ТЬВА or ТЫВА**. TUVA.
**УКРАЇНСЬКА, УКРАЇНИ or УКРАЇНА**. UKRAINE.
**УКР. Н. Р.** or **УКР. Н. РЕП.** Overprint on stamps of Austria, Austro-Hungarian Military Post and Bosnia and Herzegovina. WEST UKRAINE.
**У.С.С.Р.** UKRAINE.
**ФОНД(Ъ) САНАТОРИУМЪ**. 'Sanatorium Fund'. Inscription on Sunday Delivery stamps of BULGARIA.
**ЦР. ГОРЕ, ЦРНЕ ГОРЕ** or **ЦРНА ГОРЕ**. MONTENEGRO.
**ЮГЪ РОССИИ**. Overprint on stamps of Russia. SOUTH RUSSIA.
**ЮЖНА БЪЛАРИЯ**. Overprint on stamps of Bulgaria. EASTERN ROUMELIA AND SOUTH BULGARIA.
**JУГОСЛАВИЈА**. YUGOSLAVIA.

**SIMPLIFIED CYRILLIC TABLE** *with English equivalents*

| Russian | English | Russian | English | Obsolete | |
|---|---|---|---|---|---|
| **А а** | A | **П п** | P | **І і** | I |
| **Б б** | B | **Р р** | R | **Ѣ ѣ** | YE |
| **В в** | V | **С с** | S | **Ѳ ѳ** | F |
| **Г г** | G | **Т т** | T | **Ѵ ѵ** | I |
| **Д д** | D | **У у** | OO | **Ѫ ѫ** | U |
| **Е е** | E | **Ф ф** | F | *Ukranian* | |
| **Ё ё** | YO | **Х х** | KH | **Є ε** | YE |
| **Ж ж** | ZH | **Ц ц** | TS | *Macedonian* | |
| **З з** | Z | **Ч ч** | CH | S s | DZ |
| **И и** | I | **Ш ш** | SH | *Serbian* | |
| **Й й** | I | **Щ щ** | SHCH | **Ђ ђ** | DJ |
| **К к** | K | **Ъ ъ** | (silent) | **Ћ ћ** | C |
| **Л л** | L | **Ы ы** | I | *Serbian & Macedonian* | |
| **М м** | M | **Ь ь** | (silent) | J j | J |
| **Н н** | N | **Э э** | E | **Љ љ** | LJ |
| **О о** | O | **Ю ю** | YU | **Њ њ** | NJ |
| | | **Я я** | YA | **Џ џ** | DZ |
| | | | | *Mongolian* | |
| | | | | Y y | Ü |
| | | | | **Ѳ ѳ** | Ö* |

*Obsolete letter revived with new sound

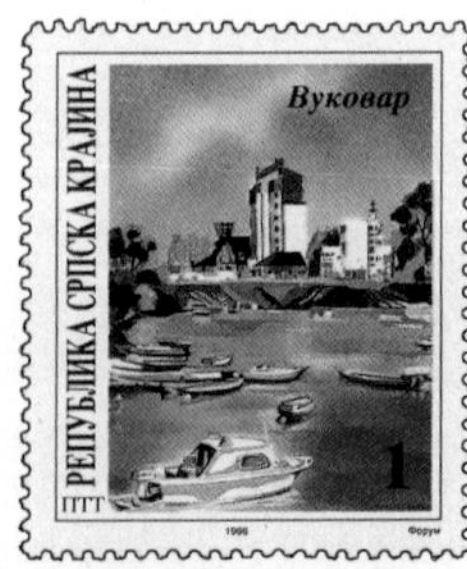

Croatia – Serbian Posts (Srpska Krajina)

## INDIAN NATIVE STATES

Prior to independence in 1947, India embraced numerous princely states, some of which issued stamps. For convenience, philatelists divide them into two groups – the so-called Convention States and the Indian Feudatory States. The Convention States, which, under a series of postal conventions established by the Imperial Government, used Indian stamps overprinted with their various names (usually in English and thus easily identified), were: Chamba; Faridkot after 1887; Gwalior; Jind (Jhind or Jeend) from 1885; Nabha; and Patiala (also spelled Puttialla). The exceptional overprint of Gwalior official stamps is illustrated. These stamps were valid for postage within the state of issue, to other Convention states and to destinations in British India.

Stamps in a wide variety of often primitive designs were issued by the Indian Feudatory States – these could only be used within the borders of their respective states. Some issues are extremely rare and the whole group has become quite popular with collectors seeking a novel and complex subject for philatelic study. Some typical designs are illustrated from each Feudatory State. With the exception of the 'Anchal' stamps of Travancore-Cochin (1951), all these stamps were replaced by those of the Republic of India on 1 May 1950.

### *Indian Feudatory States*

Alwar

Bahawalpur

Bamra

Barwani

Bhopal

Bhor

Bijawar

Bundi

Bussahir

Charkhari

Cochin

Dhar

Duttia

Faridkot pre –1887

Hyderabad

Idar

Indore (Holkar)

Jaipur

Jammu & Kashmir

Jasdan

'Official' overprint on Indian stamp for the Convention State of Gwalior

Jhalawar

Jind pre-1885

Kishangarh

Las Bela

Morvi

Nandgaon

Nawanagar

Orcha

Poonch

Rajasthan

Rajpipla

Sirmoor

Soruth

Travancore

Travancore - Cochin

Wadhwan

## FAR EAST SCRIPTS

Some difficult stamps for the new collector to identify are those from the countries of the Far East – China, Japan, Manchukuo, Ryukyu Islands and North and South Korea. China is further complicated because of the several different governments which have been in control (on the mainland and on the island of Taiwan, also known as Formosa). Parts of China have also been occupied by the Japanese and there are innumerable overprints and surcharges among China's prolific stamp issues. A preliminary study of the historical notes and the illustrations listed under China in the catalogue is recommended.

### *CHINA*

Chinese provinces Top: Kirin and Heilungkiang, Sinkiang and below Szechwan and Yunnan

A distinguishing emblem – the twelve-rayed sun – was used on Chinese stamps in pre-Communist times (up to 1949): note that it was also used on stamps listed under the Japanese Occupation of China. In the Chinese language each character is a complete word: the various symbols are not letters of an alphabet. At one time the characters read downwards, one below the other, but nowadays sentences are more often written horizontally, though from right to left. In modern times – particularly under the Communist regime – the tendency is to write from left to right as in English. Look for the character *chung* (it is rather like a double-sided flag) at the beginning of the sentence (whether it is first or last) and count up to the third character – if it resembles a letter 'R' then the stamp is a pre-Communist issue. In the same location on stamps of the Communist People's Republic the character looks like an inverted 'V'. Most China (People's Republic) commemorative stamps have a serial number at the foot of the design, for example 'T. 108. (6-4) 1986'. This helps to aid rapid identification of Chinese issues.

Stamps of Imperial China and the Chinese People's Republic and on the far right Taiwan (Republic of China)

From 1992 People's Republic stamps have included the name 'CHINA' in the Western alphabet.

The same rule applies to the stamps of Taiwan from 1949 – the birth of the Chinese Nationalist Republic. Modern Taiwan stamps are inscribed 'Republic of China'.

## JAPAN

Japan. Design with Chrysanthemum emblem, stamp with name in Japanese characters only and issue including the name 'Nippon'

Japanese is written in ideographic (picture-symbol) characters, acquired from China. Indeed, through constant contact with the Chinese people down the centuries (in peace and war), the Japanese language has enriched itself with Chinese words and expressions. Japanese stamps up to 1947 often had an emblem representing a chrysanthemum included in the design. From 1966 the word 'Nippon' in the Roman alphabet has been added to Japanese stamp designs. Inscriptions in the native language include the country name which comprises a standard group of four characters. The first of these (which may be last depending in which direction the sentence has been written) is easily recognizable – it resembles a box with a horizontal line through the middle.

In 1930 Japan alleged that her interests in Manchuria were being jeopardized by the Chinese and began the military occupation of the area, setting up a new puppet state of Manchukuo, consisting of the former provinces of Fegtien, Kirin, Heilungchiang and Jehol. Pu Yi, who later became Emperor Kang-teh (of *The Last Emperor* film fame), was appointed Head of State. The stamps, identified by the orchid crest and by the currency – 100 fen = 1 yuan – are listed in the catalogue under Manchukuo.

## RYUKYU ISLANDS

Ryukyu stamps, first issued in 1948, closely resembled those of Japan in style, inscriptions and currency – 100 sen = 1 yen. The main inscription, however, lacks the box-like character noted above for Japan. Under United States administration the stamps were issued in American cents and dollars from 1958 – note the distinctive '¢' for cents. From 1961 the word 'Ryukyus' appeared on the stamps, which ceased in 1972 when the islands were handed back to Japan.

## KOREA

Korea. US military Government surcharge on Japanese stamp, issues of South and North Korea

The divided nation. Emblems and inscriptions help to distinguish the stamps of South and North Korea. Unlike Chinese, each sign in the Korean language is a separate letter of the alphabet – these are combined in groups to form complete characters. North Korean inscriptions have four such characters, those of South Korea have six, the first one resembling 'CH'. South Korean stamps additionally bear the *yin yang* symbol – a circle part light and part dark – and have been inscribed 'Republic of Korea' in English since 1966.

Japanese occupation of Malaya

## OTHER SCRIPTS

Unfamiliar scripts and alphabets may present a problem if there is no other clue to a stamp's origins. Some are illustrated here as a general guide. Note the appearance and 'look' of an inscription, and observe particularly whether the script comprises separate characters (like the Amharic language from Ethiopia, or the Siamese language of Thailand

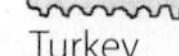

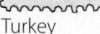

Turkey

Afganistan

which is derived from a form of Sanskrit and has affinities with Chinese), or in flowing style like Arabic or Persian, which is a version of Arabic. Most Arab countries inscribe their stamps additionally in English or French, but remember that Arabic is written from right to left and that there are six chief dialects – Algerian, Moroccan, Syrian, Egyptian,

Manchukuo

Ryukyu Islands

Iran

Saudi Arabia

Malaya (Perak)

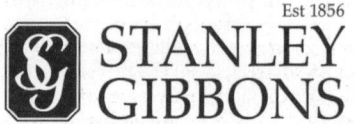

Left to right: Different scripts on stamps of Georgia, Nepal, Burma and Tuva

Alsace and Lorraine

Austria

Austria – Postage Due

Austria – Newspaper stamps

Bosnia and Herzegovina

Belgium

Bahrain – War tax

Iraqi and Arabian. The Turkish language, formerly written in Arabic characters, was changed to Roman by the order of Ataturk in 1928. Note also that Israel stamps, following the first 'Coins' issue of 1948, have been inscribed not only in Hebrew and Arabic, but in English as well.

Some of the Malay States are easy to identify with the names shown in English – Johore, Kedah, Malacca (or Melaka), Penang (or Pulau Pinang) and Sungei Ujong. But some have the state's name only in Malay script – which contains 'dots and dashes' and has Arabic elements. These include Kelantan, Negri Sembilan (or Negeri Sembilan), Pahang, Perak, Perlis, Selangor and Trengganu. Look for a similar sultan's portrait or state arms in the catalogue. The Afghan languages are Persian or Pushtu (or Pashtu), but the stamps are usually inscribed in French – Postes Afghanes – as well as the native script. Nepali is the spoken language of the Gurkha peoples of Nepal, but all except the earliest stamps have been additionally inscribed 'Nepal' in English. Burmese, the language of the people of Burma (also known as Myanmar), is allied to Chinese and is written in an alphabet derived from India, the characters of which are more or less circular and thereby easily identifiable on Burmese stamps in addition to the 'Burma Postage' or 'Union of Burma' inscriptions. The stamps of Sri Lanka (Ceylon) are unusual in that they are inscribed trilingually – Sinhalese, Tamil and English.

United States of America

## 'No-name' Stamps

As mentioned in the beginning of this book, Great Britain is the only country in the world whose stamps do not bear the name of the issuing country, although all of them bear the likeness of the ruling monarch. In early days – before the foundation of the Universal Postal Union, other countries sometimes did not include their names either. Three stamps which apparently defied the U.P.U. convention were issued by the United States in 1920, marking the tercentenary of the Landing of the Pilgrim Fathers – they omitted the customary 'U.S. Postage'.

Some 'difficult' countries are listed below with a number of the stamps illustrated.

**Austria**. Check the currencies on early issues because, although the designs are similar, your stamps might be from Austrian Post Offices in Turkey, or from Lombardy and Venetia. The head of Mercury, messenger of the gods, appears on Austrian newspaper stamps.

**Bahrain**. Arabic inscription with 'key'-like word under circle – 1974 War Tax Stamp. (Also 1973 issue, without 'key'.)

**Bosnia and Herzegovina**. The Austrian coat-of-arms is prominent.

**Brazil**. The early 'numeral' stamps represented 'Bull's-eyes', 'Goat's-eyes' and 'Snake's-eyes' respectively. A 'Bull's-eye' is shown on page 5.

**Finland**. Circles in the designs distinguish the 1891 issue from the similar issues of Russia. Also issues between 1901 and 1911 bear the face value in Finnish *penni* and *markkaa*.

**Hungary**. 1871–88. Similar to Austria, but the designs are distinctive.

**Papal States**. The crossed keys are the main clue. Cf. First issue of Vatican City.

**Portugal**. 'Correio', the 'reis' currency and the Royal heads suggest Portugal.

**Sardinia**. Compare with very similar stamps of Italy, 1862.

**Saudi Arabia**. Palm tree emblem only on stamps from 1982.

**Spain**. Stamps with various portraits, often inscribed Communicaciones, sometimes dated, and with currencies in cuartos, centimos and pesetas, indicate 19th century Spain, but should be checked with contemporary issues of Cuba, Puerto Rico or the Philippines, particularly if the inscription includes Ultramar.

**Switzerland**. Early postage dues were unnamed, being regarded as of internal significance only.

Emblems on stamps can also aid identification. Shown below are Yin yang (South Korea), Chrysanthemum (Japan), Orchid (Manchukuo), Star and crescent (Turkey, Pakistan, Bahawalpur, Hyderabad), Toughra (Turkey, Saudi Arabia, Afghanistan), Palm tree and crossed scimitar (Saudi Arabia) and Trident (Ukraine)

# Putting on a Good Show

**Paul Brittain looks at the question of mounting and presentation**

It's only natural—having acquired some stamps, you want to be able to enjoy them in the best possible way. And what better way than placing them on pages. Most collectors start by using a stamp album whose pages have been specifically designed, usually with large or small squares, making it easy to arrange the stamps neatly. Such albums normally have the names of countries printed at the tops of the pages, so that the correct stamps can be affixed to each page.

## Mounting

It is the method of affixing that is key, however. Many try various ways—using glue; if the stamp is gummed, simply licking the back and using the stamp's own adhesive; using clear sticky tape; perhaps using the blank white paper that normally surrounds stamps in a sheet. None of these should be tried. In the initial stages, when putting stamps on a page, always use stamp hinges. These are small pieces of opaque paper, gummed on one side. You fold the piece of paper over about one third down its length (some are ready-folded), with the gummed side on the outside. The smaller portion is gently moistened, and affixed to the back of the stamp, at the top centrally, just below the perforations. A small portion of the part not affixed to the stamp is similarly moistened. By holding both stamp and hinge with a pair of stamp tweezers, it is now possible to position the stamp where required on the album page. With a little bit of pressure with a finger (some like to use a piece of paper between finger and stamp for this purpose), the stamp can be made secure on the page. If the hinge has been used correctly, it should be possible to lift the stamp up to examine the back. As long as the hinge has been gently moistened, no damage should occur to stamp or album page if the hinge is subsequently removed. However, do not be in a hurry to remove the hinge. If you find you have made a mistake, such as putting the stamp in the wrong place, leave the hinge to dry for a while before attempting to remove it.

Returning to the idea of pressing the stamp in place with a piece of paper, I recall seeing one collector, so keen to mount a new acquisition into his album, that he did not bother to wash his hands after coming in from gardening. When pressing the stamps in place with his finger, he left a lovely fingerprint on each.

Stamp mounts welded at top and bottom (left) and at bottom only

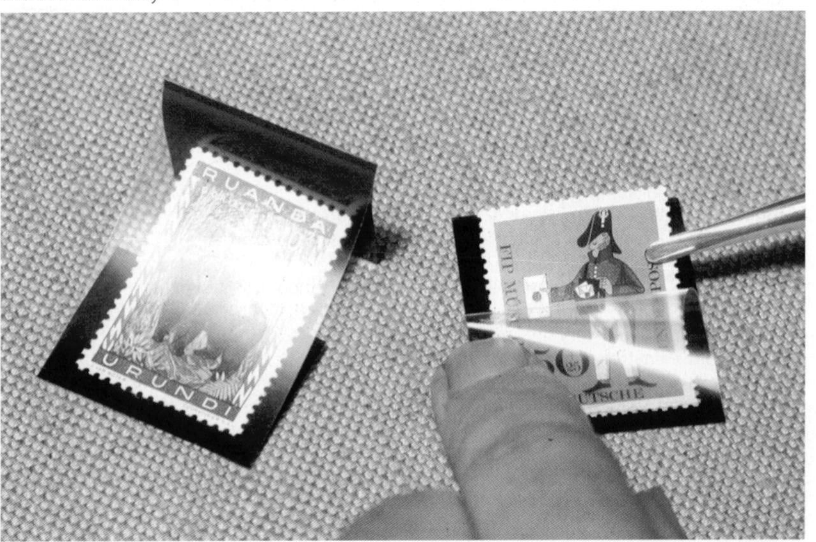


## Mounted or unmounted?

Over the years there have been concerns about even affixing a hinge to a stamp. When you buy a stamp from a post office, it has all its gum on the back. Once you fix a hinge to the back, you damage part of that gum. For many stamps, especially the rarer ones, there can be a great difference in price between a stamp which has all its original gum intact (known as mint, unmounted, or unmounted mint) compared with one to which a hinge has been attached (known as mounted, or sometimes as mounted mint). Of course, generally speaking a stamp that still has its gum has not been on an item sent through the post, and therefore is regarded as unused. (Some countries deliberately postmark unused stamps for sale to collectors, and these may still have their gum, in addition to a post-mark.) If a stamp has been through the post, it will not normally still retain its gum: it is therefore known as used. It could be argued that it does not matter if you affix a hinge to a used stamp, as there is no gum to disturb. However, there are collectors who are concerned about leaving the marks where a stamp hinge has been, even on a used stamp.

The answer has been to use what are known as stamp mounts. These comprise two pieces of clear material, welded together, between which the stamp is placed. The front is always clear, so that the stamp is clearly visible. The back is sometimes clear, but can be dark coloured (virtually black) to highlight the stamp. Such mounts invariably come in strips of different heights, designed to accommodate various sizes of stamp. The strips can be cut into the required length for each stamp. Such strips are either welded just along the bottom edge, or along both the top and bottom edges. The latter tend to hold stamps more securely in place, but make it more difficult to remove stamps for closer inspection once mounted. Similar mounts are available for larger items, such as blocks of stamps or miniature sheets.

Such mounts are not cheap, especially when compared with the price of stamp hinges, while unmounted stamps will cost more to buy in the first place. Whether to use mounts must therefore be a personal choice. However, it must be added that over the years there has been growing concern that some mounts, especially those manufactured in the early years, inflict harm on material, and cannot be recommended for the long-term safety of your stamps. I have seen stamps which have been in such mounts for some years, and where the design of the stamp has migrated on to the mount itself. If you are going to use mounts, therefore, do ensure you buy the best conservation quality.

By the way, if you are mounting larger items, an alternative is to use photo corners, especially those with a clear face that enable the item to be fully viewed.

Some collectors adopt a variety of methods, putting their more precious stamps in mounts, using photo corners for larger items, and stamp hinges for the rest. The trouble is that this can look a mess, so might be best avoided, although the visual impact can be improved, as we shall see later.

## Planning

Before any start is made designing your pages, it will first be necessary to plan your collection. If you are collecting the stamps of just one country, this can be fairly straightforward. Most choose a chronological approach, putting the stamps and sets in the date order they are issued. Since the stamp catalogues list the stamps for each country in this way, it becomes quite easy to arrange the stamps in order. The only decision that might need to be made is which stamps you are likely to acquire, and which, probably because of their cost, you might have to forget for a while. It is not ideal to see a collection with lots of gaps for stamps not yet obtained, especially if there is really no chance of being able to acquire the missing stamps in the foreseeable future. Much better therefore to arrange your collection as though those stamps do not

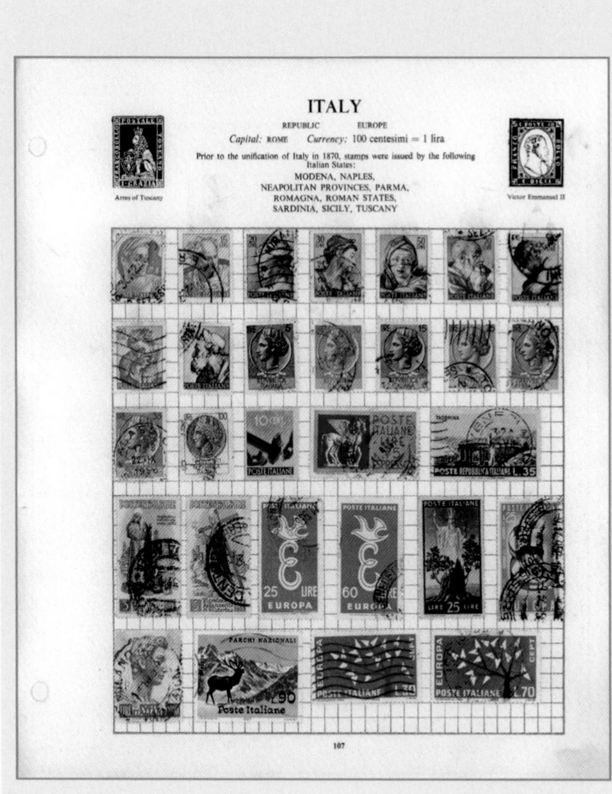


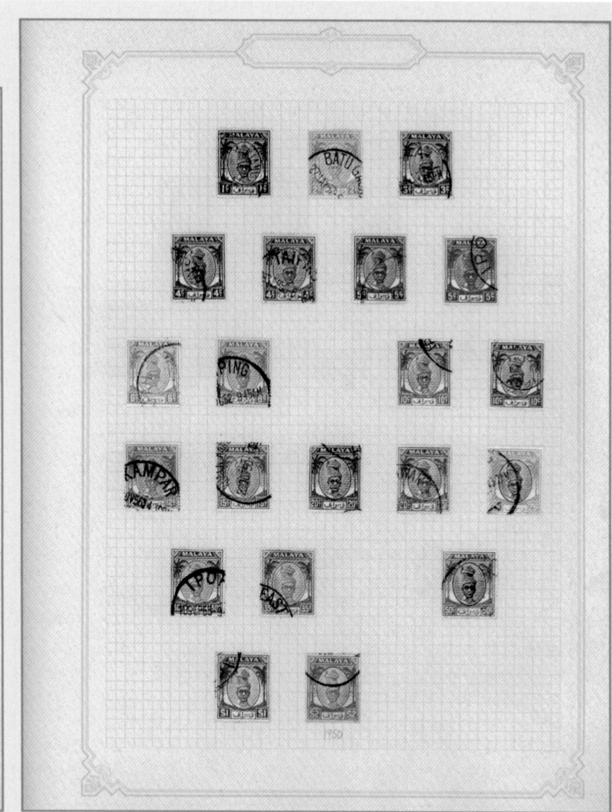

Album page with printed heading (left). Page with gaps left for stamps not yet obtained

exist: do not leave spaces for them. If, later on, some of these stamps come your way, you will be so pleased, you will not mind having to redesign a page or two of your collection.

With thematic collecting, life is a little more difficult. You will want to tell a `story' with your material, and therefore need to sort out that story before you start to plan your pages. In this case, it is often better to use a stockbook initially to arrange your stamps. You can easily move the material around until it is in the sequence in which you want it to appear finally on your album pages. Once again, there may be items you would still like to add for your theme: the joy of collecting is always finding new items. However, you cannot wait indefinitely before you start to put your collection on to pages: when more material comes along, you might need to redesign some pages.

### Choosing your album pages

A question to be asked now is exactly what sort of paper you are going to use on which to mount your material. The obvious answer is to use the pages of a loose-leaf stamp album. However, the majority are not of a standard paper size. As will be discussed more fully later, many collectors are now designing their pages on a computer screen, often adding the written information at the same time. While printers attached to computers can accommodate various sizes of paper, many will only take a maximum paper size of A4. Increasingly therefore, collectors are turning to using blank A4 sheets of paper for their collections. As with the standard album pages, the paper used must be strong enough to take the material, and should also be of conservation quality. While pale shades can be attractive, white paper is still preferable. Also try to ensure that all the collection uses the same shade of paper (even white can vary), although this is not always easy to achieve. At one time black paper was popular, but is far less used these days.

Once you have decided what is going to be put on to each page, whether it be stamps, blocks, covers, miniature sheets, or whatever, the first thing is to arrange the items in the most attractive, yet still logical, way. While each page you prepare should look pleasing, it would lose its point if an item is simply out of place. Starting with a blank page, move the items around until the preferred layout is achieved. Some now indicate the positioning of each item with feint pencil marks, ready for mounting the material later. Those who have opted to use the help of a computer can design their pages on screen. By measuring each item to appear on a page, it is possible to create a 'box' of the correct size. The boxes can then be moved around until a pleasing layout is achieved. It is, in fact, a good idea to make such boxes slightly smaller than the item concerned: once the item is mounted, the actual box will then be obscured.

An alternative however is to make the boxes fractionally bigger than the items: that way the boxes become an effective border. It is also possible to scan each item, so that a better impression of the final layout can be gleaned. A border can still be added. (Another advantage of scanning is that it does provide a good record of the items in the collection—however, again for conservation reasons, it is best only to scan an item once.)

### Writing up

Having 'designed' your page, it is invariably best to add any 'write up' before mounting your material. However, even before you start, you must decide what information is going to accompany your stamps. The advice usually given is to keep it to a minimum. Write out what you think should appear—then precis it, and precis it again. The point is, of course, that this is your collection, and you should include the information that you feel is interesting and relevant. If you want to show your collection to others then the extent of any writing up is important—you want to interest, even enthuse, the viewer, not bore them to tears. The key aspect is that whatever you include should be there to enhance the material you are showing, not detract from it.

Again, today many prefer to produce the writing up on computer. It allows you to position it in the best place in relation to the items you are showing, and to edit or correct as necessary. You can vary the type-face, type size, add italics or underlining as appropriate. The key is not to become carried away by all the computer can provide. Never forget that what should impress the viewer is your material, it should not be overwhelmed by the writing up. Clearly if designing and writing up your pages on computer, once you are satisfied on screen, then the page can be printed off on your chosen paper, and the items are ready to be mounted as previously described.

If you feel the computer does not provide the right 'personal' touch to the writing up, there are always the more traditional methods. For years collectors used their skills with a pen: some would demonstrate the fine art of calligraphy. The quality of pen, and thickness of nib are all important: ball-point pens don't produce the same effect. Some are quite content with pencil. You must be your own judge as to whether

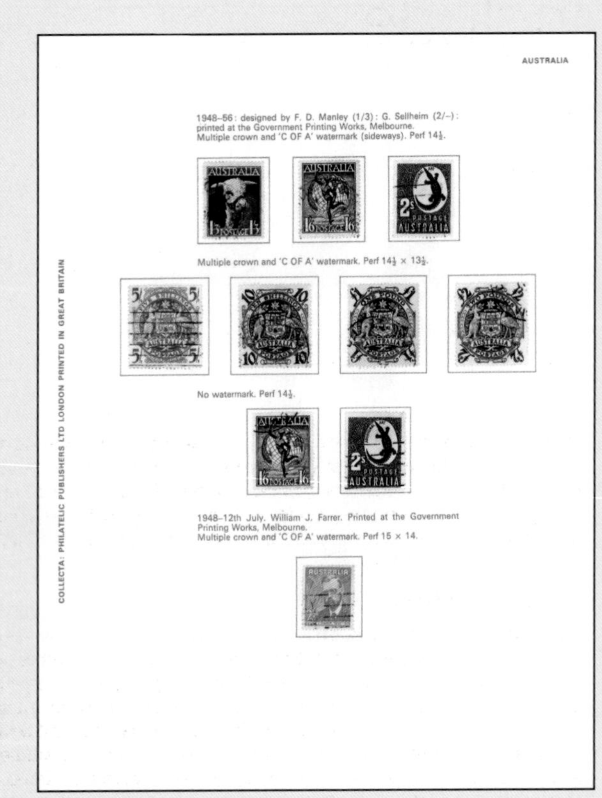

A printed page from a one-country album (left) and a type-written album page

your writing is sufficiently neat. Other methods that have been used include press-down dry lettering, such as the once famous Letraset brand, stencils, even cut-out labels. These have now been largely superseded. Some still use typewriters, perhaps typing directly on to the album page. Others prefer to type on to blank sheets of paper, which are then carefully cut out and positioned on the page. (The same principle can easily be used with a computer.) If using a more conventional method, it is better to complete the writing up before mounting: a mistake can occur, resulting in the page having to be rewritten, or in an item being damaged.

Having designed and written up each page, the material can be mounted. Even if various methods are used (hinges, mounts, photo corners), the final page should look uniform. For example, if your mounts have a black backing, ensure that covers, etc, even if mounted with photo corners, are on a similar, thin, black backing. Don't have some items with a backing, others without. If you prefer a black line to border each item, and do not wish to undertake this using a computer, ensure that these are drawn neatly, especially keeping the corners tidy.

There can be no doubt that a well presented collection, carefully arranged and neatly written up, is a joy to behold—for both its owner and others. It enhances not only the look but also the interest gained from the material. You are proud of your stamps, so you should do them proud.

## Using a stamp hinge

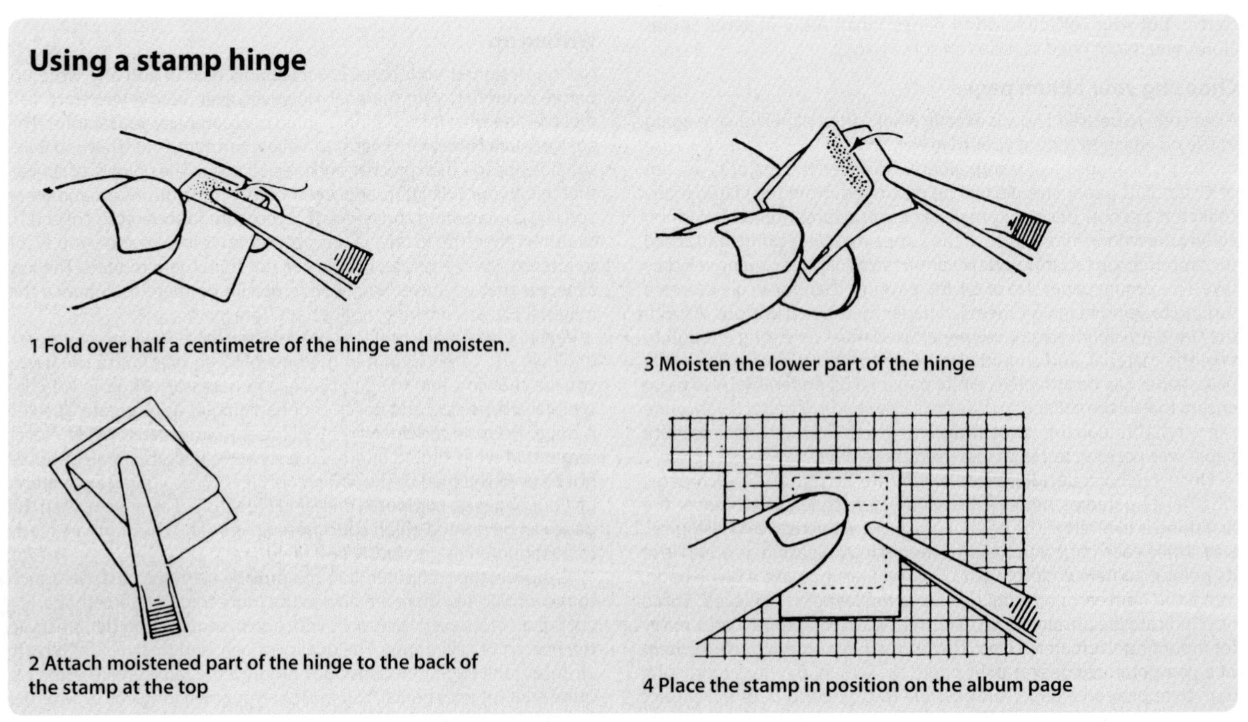

**1 Fold over half a centimetre of the hinge and moisten.**

**2 Attach moistened part of the hinge to the back of the stamp at the top**

**3 Moisten the lower part of the hinge**

**4 Place the stamp in position on the album page**

# To include, or not to include, that is the question

**Paul Brittain explores the question of what is acceptable in a collection**

What to include in a stamp collection is a matter that many ponder. The basic answer is that anything goes; for it is your personal collection, there to bring you pleasure. However, such an answer might be a little too simplistic. It really depends on how you intend to use the collection. Is it purely for personal enjoyment, or do you intend to share it with others? Are those others going to be stamp-collecting friends, perhaps fellow members of a stamp dub, or might they be non-collectors who you would like to see equally enthused by the hobby? Perhaps you intend to enter competitions, whether at local, regional, national or even international level. In each case a different approach might be needed.

There are many who develop several collections simultaneously, using each in different ways. In the days when thematic collecting was less established than today, there were several collectors I knew who would be very open about their more 'traditional' material, while secretly enjoying putting together a theme.

So let us consider from the outset what might be included in a collection that is for you to enjoy alone. In such cases, as stated, anything goes. If you want to include postcards, maps, newspaper cuttings, letters and so on, who is going to stop you, and who can say that you are wrong? Probably the only limit will be what can physically be mounted on an album page. If items are too large to fit on to a standard size page, they might prove more difficult to handle. That said, there are many collectors who put two album pages together in order to accommodate a larger piece. There needs to be a word of warning in such cases, however: odd-sized items are far more prone to damage, and therefore need special care at all times. Bulky or heavy items are also going to prove difficult, so do ensure that the quality of paper on which you mount items can stand their weight. At times thin card might be more appropriate.

The result could be that your collection looks more like a scrap book; at the other extreme it might appear more like a drawing exercise as you illustrate every nuance for your extensive study of a single stamp.

In addition to the material included comes the question of the amount of information you provide, the write-up. Again, for personal use what you include is up to you, and if it ends up looking like a book with a few illustrations, so be it.

### Showing to others

Such points need to be addressed if you are going to show your collection to others, especially to those who may not be quite so absorbed by the subject as you are. If you are going to share your collection with those who do not collect, you must ensure you maintain their interest, hopefully creating such a fascination that they will want to know more and start exploring for themselves. It means that studies will not be appropriate, and a much lighter diet should be offered. I recall that when I started collecting, back in my primary school days, my next door neighbour was an avid collector. I was enthralled by his collection, and seeing it, and chatting with him, certainly encouraged me in my collecting. It was some years later when I came to see his collection again that I realised it was fairly straightforward.

Nothing wrong in that, of course, but the fact remains that had it been more specialised it might not have acted as such a catalyst for me.

The same can apply if showing part of the collection to members of a stamp club. If it is to members of a specialist society, then a fairly detailed study might be appropriate, but for a general audience, it is far better to keep it simple. We all have areas of collecting that we find particularly fascinating, but should never assume that others will derive the same satisfaction. It is equally true that some collectors are so blinkered they do not view displays, or read magazine articles, on anything other than their own particular interest. By adopting such a

### Stockbooks

There are collectors who never venture as far as mounting their material. They are quite content with arranging their stamps in stockbooks. This does have the advantage of making it easy if you want to rearrange the order, or add new items, but is not really so dynamic visually. The majority prefer to see the material on pages in albums, even though most will admit that they are way behind with the process.

As a youngster you begin with a printed album and probably place the stamps in rows on each page. (There are also albums produced, notably for a few countries particularly popular with collectors, which have the pages ready designed for the stamps to be added.) However, once you have decided that you want to be more specialised in your interest, perhaps concentrating on a particular country or a certain theme, you will want to be more adventurous. the next move will be to albums supplied with the pages blank. In such cases it is left to the individual to arrange the layout of the stamps on each page. In addition, most prefer to add some information about the stamps.

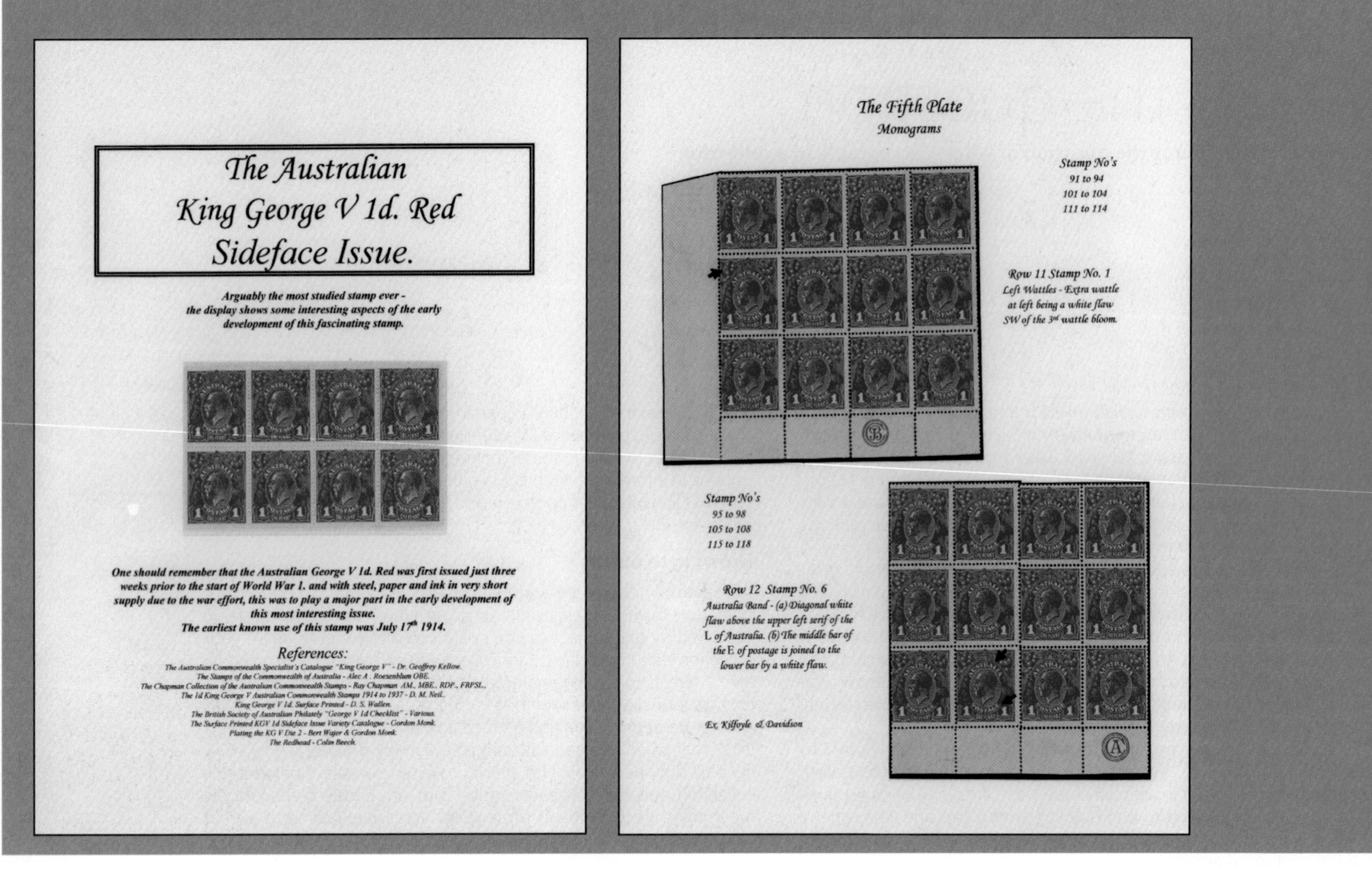


narrow-minded approach much useful information can be missed—it is surprising how the results of someone else's research can have a bearing on your own collecting..

The basic rule if showing to a more general audience, such as the members of a local stamp club, is to keep it interesting for all, irrespective of what they personally collect. Generally speaking such audiences will expect the material you show to be reasonably `conventional'. While you might include a great deal of ephemera or periphery material in your personal collection, those in your audience are stamp collectors, and expect primarily to see philatelic material. Equally, do not bore by including such minutiae that few can enjoy what you are showing. The point to re-member at any stamp club meeting is that, at best, the audience will only be able to glance at most of what you show, perhaps focusing on the one or two items that particularly catch the attention. There is simply not the time for a careful perusal of all you are showing, while the conditions may not make close inspection at all easy. By the same token, the writing up should be short and to the point. Long descriptions will simply not be read. One leading collector, sadly no longer with us, offered the advice that the write-up should be prepared, then edited to about half, then precised to half again: only then might it be of an acceptable length.

While not strictly on the theme of this article, remember if talking to any audience, not only should you not bore by your material, equally do not turn your audience off by your delivery. Speak to the audience, and keep what you say brief and stimulating.

Many collectors are invited to give talks and displays to societies other than of stamp collectors. With the right material and a fascinating tale to tell these can prove absorbing for the audience, but clearly the right balance is crucial in terms of material, the write up and the spoken word.

There are many collectors who, for whatever reason, are reluctant to show their material to others. Perhaps they feel that what they collect is not of sufficient interest, that it is poorly presented, or that they will not be able to convey their enthusiasm. Once someone starts to show, all such fears quickly prove unfounded. It becomes a great thrill to share your passion, and to discover that others really do enjoy what you have to say and show.

## Competitions

The same reluctance is very evident when it comes to competitions. Some will use the argument that they do not approve of competitions, and the fact that to achieve the best result it is necessary to specially to prepare the required number of pages, usually from eight upwards. Would it not be fairer simply to take pages straight from the collection? There was a time when at competitions at events such as Stampex, the collection had to be submitted to support the pages that actually went on display, to demonstrate that what was shown was a true reflection of the entire collection. Today it is different, and there are many who exhibit who prepare the particular pages specifically for competition.

This is not the occasion to discuss the rights and wrongs of competitions: perhaps that can be the subject for a future article. However, I do not subscribe to the view that what goes into competition should necessarily be of the same standard as the rest of the collection, unless the entire collection is maintained to a high standard.

All competitions have their rules and regulations, which in the case of our hobby will include what material is acceptable and how it is presented. If you are entering any serious competition, whether a dog show, a flower or vegetable show, or a major sporting event, you know that you must abide by the rules. You would never dream of entering your pet dog into a major show without ensuring that all its features were exactly as looked for by the judges, and that it had been meticulously groomed. You would not expect to achieve the highest standards in a particular sport without years of practice and adopting all the correct techniques, gradually progressing from the lowest to the highest levels. So why should it be any different with a stamp competition?

You should expect to adhere to the rules, and to work up from local club level to as far as you personally aspire. So study the rules, particularly in relation to what can or should not be included. Most local/regional competitions are divided into the basic classes of traditional (often postal stationery is included within traditional), postal history, aerophilately, thematics, and Cinderellas and revenues.

Traditional philately is essentially the study of the stamps, and so would not include items that relate to postal history, although could well include covers to show the correct usage of the stamps

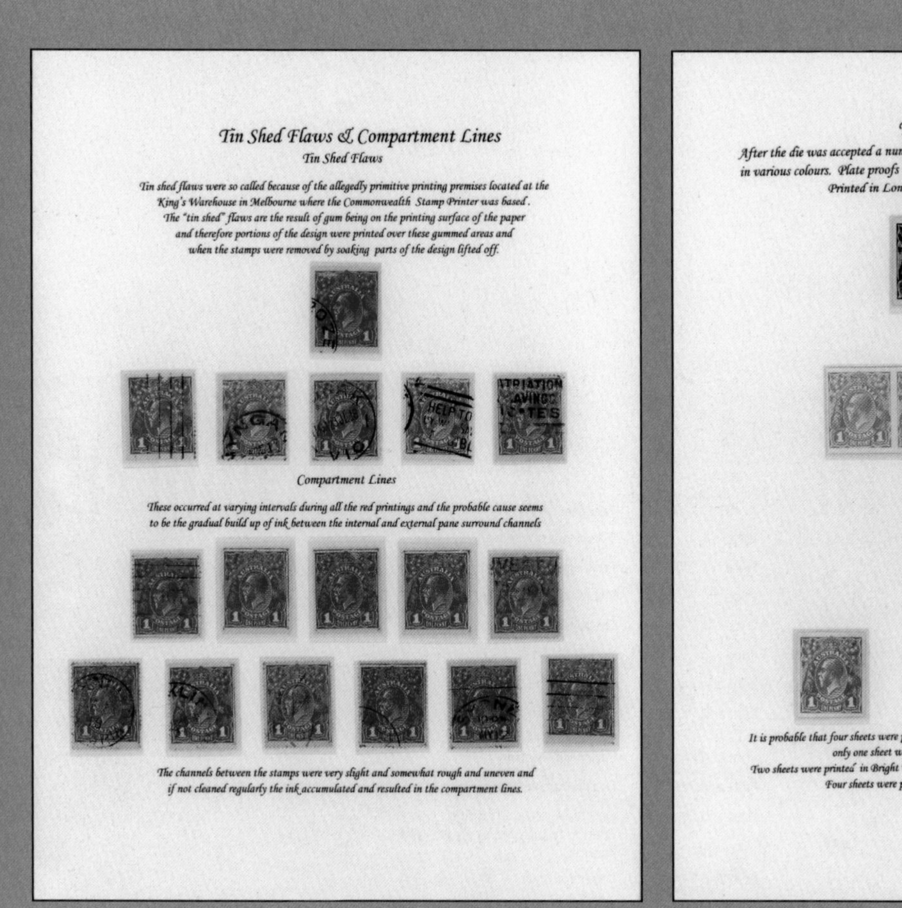


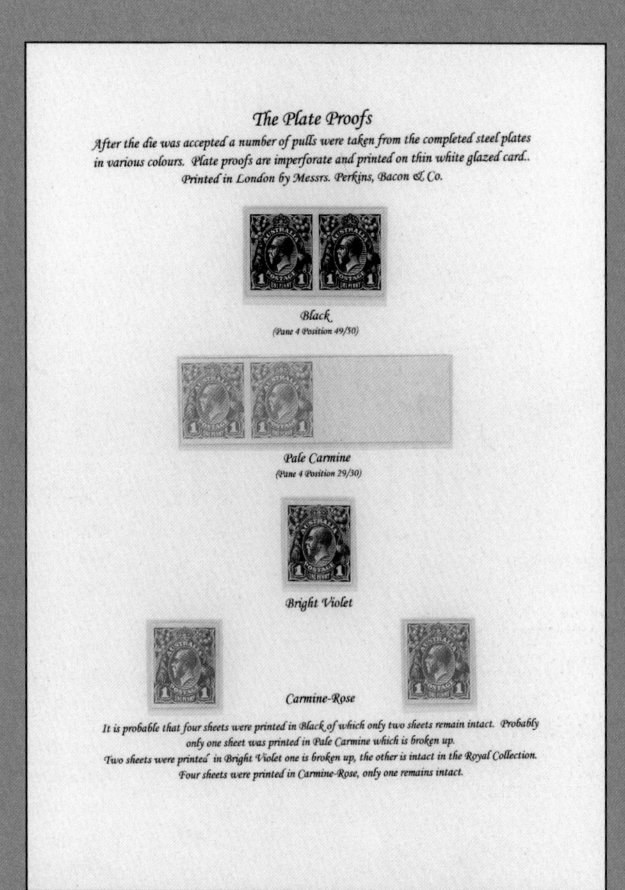


Pages from a traditional collection devoted to a specialised study of the King George V 1d. red stamp of Australia. Illustrations courtesy of Colin Mount.

in question. Covers are needed as they show not only the stamp and the service provided, but also that it was used during the valid period and to the right destination. A traditional exhibit will encompass the stamps, perhaps in plate blocks, with printings, shade, perforation or watermark variations, errors and varieties, 'Specimen' overprints, even proofs and essays. The stamps can be unused or used, although there is some debate as to whether mint and used should be mixed on the same page: in some cases this might be unavoidable if certain items are only known either unused or used. Postal history naturally relates to the development of the postal service, and thus will concentrate on the rates charged and the routes taken, although postal markings are usually also included in this class. Items will usually be covers, or perhaps fronts of covers, although stamps on piece are acceptable if sufficient to show the marking being demonstrated. Aerophilately of course relates to mail carried by air, and thus will normally involve covers, but can also include airmail stamps. Cinderellas and revenues are clearly less easy to define, but fascinating displays can be assembled which might involve local postage services, such as those on places such as Herm and Lundy islands, postal orders, railway letter stamps, the college stamps of Oxford and Cambridge, or stamps produced for fiscal purposes: these are, however, just a few examples. It is when it comes to thematics that the greatest confusion often arises. This is understandable, for what is regarded as acceptable has changed over the years. Again the whole question of thematics is a subject for another article, but suffice to say that these days it is expected that a far wider range of philatelic material will be included rather than just stamps. The material shown must however be relevant in some way to the chosen theme: there is often the temptation to stretch a point simply to include a prized item. It is also easy with thematics to become carried away by including interesting items that nevertheless should not have a place in a competitive exhibit: such items might include photographs, postcards and similar ephemera with no postal or philatelic relevance. Again these are fine in, and will often enhance, a personal collection, or even one used purely for showing to others, but not in competition.

It is because there is the realisation that many like to include additional items to add interest to the collection that in recent years new classes have been tested, such as the Open Class and Social Philately, which permit say up to 50 per cent of non-philatelic, yet still relevant, material to be included. A good example is the display of Supermarket Philately that has been developed by Dr Jean Alexander. Her focus is the many 'on-pack' offers where on offer are postally related items, such as first day covers, presentation packs or books of stamps. Her display includes the special packaging, such as cereal boxes, any promotional leaflets that were produced, perhaps the envelope in which the offered item arrived, plus of course the item itself. Such items would never have found a place within a conventional competitive entry a few years ago, although there is no doubt it would have delighted many a society audience. However, today Jean is able to include such material as part of a Social Philately exhibit.

I must repeat, however, that while non-philatelic material can be included, it must be relevant to the story being told, and certainly in the case of Social Philately should have a connection with the postal service in some way. This might take the form of letters, postal notices and documents, telegrams, packaging material used by Post Offices, and so on.

At an international exhibition in Amsterdam a few years ago special frames were created in which to display the Open Class entries. In the centre of the frame was a clear 'bubble' so that three-dimensional objects could be shown: I recall one exhibit on railway letter posts featured model locomotives. This, however, was unusual, and generally speaking the non-philatelic items will still be two-dimensional.

At the end of the day, what is important is that the collection becomes special to you, and brings you pleasure and pride. Without offending, hopefully, the many who are absorbed by the intricacies of a single issue, if you find it tedious to keep adding the new denominations, colour changes, booklets, and so on, to your collection, then why continue? If the collection has now become a bore, perhaps it is time to explore new ground.

Include what you find interesting, and in the early stages worry only about what pleases you. If later you decide to embark on the competition trail, then take a look at what others do, to see just what is acceptable for inclusion. Start at a modest level, and never be put off, even if you don't win straight away. Never forget: it is quite simply a hobby.

# Features listing

| Area | Feature | Collect British Stamps | Stamps of the World | Thematic Catalogues | Comprehensive Catalogue, Parts 1-22 (including Commonwealth and British Empire Stamps and one country catalogues) | Great Britain Concise | Specialised catalogues |
|---|---|---|---|---|---|---|---|
| General | SG number | √ | √ | √ | √ | √ | √ |
| General | Specialised Catalogue number | | | | | | √ |
| General | Year of issue of first stamp in design | √ | √ | √ | √ | √ | √ |
| General | Exact date of issue of each design | | | | √ | √ | √ |
| General | Face value information | √ | √ | √ | √ | √ | √ |
| General | Historical and geographical information | √ | √ | √ | √ | √ | √ |
| General | General currency information, including dates used | √ | √ | √ | √ | √ | √ |
| General | Country name | √ | √ | √ | √ | √ | √ |
| General | Booklet panes | | | | √ | √ | √ |
| General | Coil stamps | | | | √ | | √ |
| General | First Day Covers | √ | | | | √ | √ |
| General | Brief footnotes on key areas of note | √ | √ | √ | √ | √ | √ |
| General | Detailed footnotes on key areas of note | | | | √ | √ | √ |
| General | Extra background information | | | | √ | √ | √ |
| General | Miniature sheet information (including size in mm) | √ | √ | √ | √ | √ | √ |
| General | Sheetlets | | | | √ | | |
| General | Stamp booklets | | | | √ | √ | √ |
| General | Perkins Bacon "Cancelled" | | | | √ | | |
| General | PHQ Cards | √ | | | | √ | √ |
| General | Post Office Label Sheets | | | | | √ | |
| General | Post Office Yearbooks | √ | | | | √ | √ |
| General | Presentation and Souvenir Packs | √ | | | | √ | √ |
| General | Se-tenant pairs | √ | | | √ | √ | √ |
| General | Watermark details - errors, varieties, positions | | | | √ | √ | √ |
| General | Watermark illustrations | √ | | | √ | √ | √ |
| General | Watermark types | √ | | | √ | √ | √ |
| General | Forgeries noted | | | | √ | | √ |
| General | Surcharges and overprint information | √ | √ | √ | √ | √ | √ |
| Design and Description | Colour description, simplified | | √ | √ | | | |
| Design and Description | Colour description, extended | √ | | | √ | √ | √ |
| Design and Description | Set design summary information | √ | √ | √ | √ | √ | √ |
| Design and Description | Designer name | | | | √ | √ | √ |
| Design and Description | Short design description | √ | √ | √ | √ | √ | √ |
| Design and Description | Shade varieties | | | | √ | √ | √ |
| Design and Description | Type number | √ | √ | | √ | √ | √ |
| Illustrations | Multiple stamps from set illustrated | √ | | | √ | √ | √ |
| Illustrations | A Stamp from each set illustrated in full colour (where possible, otherwise mono) | √ | √ | √ | √ | √ | √ |
| Price | Catalogue used price | √ | √ | √ | √ | √ | √ |
| Price | Catalogue unused price | √ | √ | √ | √ | √ | √ |
| Price | Price - booklet panes | | | | √ | √ | √ |
| Price | Price - shade varieties | | | | √ | √ | √ |
| Price | On cover and on piece price | | | | √ | √ | √ |
| Price | Detailed GB pricing breakdown | √ | | | √ | √ | √ |
| Print and Paper | Basic printing process information | √ | √ | √ | √ | √ | √ |
| Print and Paper | Detailed printing process information, e.g. Mill sheets | | | | √ | | √ |
| Print and Paper | Paper information | | | | √ | | √ |
| Print and Paper | Detailed perforation information | √ | | | √ | √ | √ |
| Print and Paper | Details of research findings relating to printing processes and history | | | | | | √ |
| Print and Paper | Paper colour | √ | √ | | √ | √ | √ |
| Print and Paper | Paper description to aid identification | | | | √ | √ | √ |
| Print and Paper | Paper type | | | | √ | √ | √ |
| Print and Paper | Ordinary or chalk-surfaced paper | | | | √ | √ | √ |
| Print and Paper | Embossing omitted note | | | | | | √ |
| Print and Paper | Essays, Die Proofs, Plate Descriptions and Proofs, Colour Trials information | | | | | | √ |
| Print and Paper | Glazed paper | | | | √ | √ | √ |
| Print and Paper | Gum details | | | | √ | | √ |
| Print and Paper | Luminescence/Phosphor bands - general coverage | √ | | | √ | √ | √ |
| Print and Paper | Luminescence/Phosphor bands - specialised coverage | | | | | | √ |
| Print and Paper | Overprints and surcharges - including colour information | √ | √ | √ | √ | √ | √ |
| Print and Paper | Perforation/Imperforate information | √ | √ | | √ | √ | √ |
| Print and Paper | Perforation errors and varieties | | | | √ | √ | √ |
| Print and Paper | Print quantities | | | | √ | | √ |
| Print and Paper | Printing errors | | | | √ | √ | √ |
| Print and Paper | Printing flaws | | | | | | √ |
| Print and Paper | Printing varieties | | | | √ | √ | √ |
| Print and Paper | Punctured stamps - where official | | | | √ | | |
| Print and Paper | Sheet positions | | | | √ | √ | √ |
| Print and Paper | Specialised plate number information | | | | | | √ |
| Print and Paper | Specimen overprints (only for Commonwealth & GB) | | | | √ | √ | √ |
| Print and Paper | Underprints | | | | | √ | √ |
| Print and Paper | Visible Plate numbers | √ | | | √ | √ | √ |
| Print and Paper | Yellow and Green paper listings | | | | √ | | √ |
| Index | Design index | √ | | | √ | √ | |

# Stanley Gibbons Stamp Catalogue Complete list of parts

## 1 Commonwealth & British Empire Stamps 1840–1970
(114th edition, 2012)

## Commonwealth Country Catalogues

***Australia and Dependencies*** (6th edition, 2010)
***Bangladesh, Pakistan & Sri Lanka*** (2nd edition, 2011)
***Belize, Guyana, Trinidad & Tobago*** (1st edition, 2009)
***Brunei, Malaysia & Singapore*** (3rd edition, 2009)
***Canada*** (4th edition, 2011)
***Central Africa*** (2nd edition, 2008)
***Cyprus, Gibraltar & Malta*** (3rd edition, 2011)
***East Africa with Egypt and Sudan*** (2nd edition, 2010)
***Eastern Pacific*** (2nd edition, 2011)
***Falkland Islands*** (4th edition, 2010)
***Hong Kong*** (3rd edition, 2010)
***India (including Convention and Feudatory States)*** (3rd edition, 2009)
***Indian Ocean*** (1st edition, 2006)
***Ireland*** (4th edition, 2008)
***Leeward Islands*** (1st edition, 2007)
***New Zealand*** (4th edition, 2010)
***Northern Caribbean, Bahamas & Bermuda*** (2nd edition, 2009)
***St. Helena & Dependencies*** (4th edition, 2011)
***Southern Africa*** (2nd edition, 2007)
***West Africa*** (1st edition, 2009)
***Western Pacific*** (2nd edition, 2009)
***Windward Islands and Barbados*** (1st edition, 2007)

## Stamps of the World 2011

***Volume 1*** ***Abu Dhabi – Charkhari***
***Volume 2*** ***Chile – Georgia***
***Volume 3*** ***German Commands – Jasdan***
***Volume 4*** ***Jersey – New Republic***
***Volume 5*** ***New South Wales – Singapore***
***Volume 6*** ***Sirmoor – Zululand***

## Foreign Countries

*2* ***Austria & Hungary*** (7th edition, 2009)
*3* ***Balkans*** (5th edition, 2009)
*4* ***Benelux*** (6th edition, 2010)
*5* ***Czechoslovakia & Poland*** (6th edition, 2002)
*6* ***France*** (7th edition, 2010)
*7* ***Germany*** (9th edition, 2011)
*8* ***Italy & Switzerland*** (7th edition, 2010)
*9* ***Portugal & Spain*** (6th edition, 2011)
*10* ***Russia*** (6th edition, 2008)
*11* ***Scandinavia*** (6th edition, 2008)
*12* ***Africa since Independence A-E*** (2nd edition, 1983)
*13* ***Africa since Independence F-M*** (1st edition, 1981)
*14* ***Africa since Independence N-Z*** (1st edition, 1981)
*15* ***Central America*** (3rd edition, 2007)
*16* ***Central Asia*** (4th edition, 2006)
*17* ***China*** (8th edition, 2011)
*18* ***Japan & Korea*** (5th edition, 2008)
*19* ***Middle East*** (7th edition, 2009)
*20* ***South America*** (4th edition, 2008)
*21* ***South-East Asia*** (4th edition, 2004)
*22* ***United States of America*** (7th edition, 2010)

## Great Britain Catalogues

***Collect British Stamps*** (62nd edition, 2011)
***Great Britain Concise Stamp Catalogue*** (26th edition, 2011)
***Volume 1*** ***Queen Victoria*** (15th edition, 2008)
***Volume 2*** ***King Edward VII to King George VI*** (13th edition, 2009)
***Volume 3*** ***Queen Elizabeth II Pre-decimal issues*** (12th edition, 2011)
***Volume 4*** ***Queen Elizabeth II Decimal Definitive Issues – Part 1*** (10th edition, 2008)
***Queen Elizabeth II Decimal Definitive Issues – Part 2*** (10th edition, 2010)
***Volume 5*** ***Queen Elizabeth II Decimal Special Issues*** (3rd edition, 1998 with 1998-99 and 2000/1 Supplements)

## Thematic Catalogues

Stanley Gibbons Catalogues for use with ***Stamps of the World.***
***Collect Aircraft on Stamps*** (2nd edition, 2009)
***Collect Birds on Stamps*** (5th edition, 2003)
***Collect Chess on Stamps*** (2nd edition, 1999)
***Collect Fish on Stamps*** (1st edition, 1999)
***Collect Motor Vehicles on Stamps*** (1st edition 2004)

## Other publications

***Africa Simplified*** (1st edition, 2011)
***Asia Simplified*** (1st edition, 2010)
***Antarctica (including Australian and British Antarctic Territories, French Southern and Antarctic Territories and Ross Dependency)*** (1st edition, 2010)
***Collect Channel Islands and Isle of Man Stamps*** (26th edition, 2010)
***Commonwealth Simplified*** (4th edition, 2010)
***Enjoy Stamp Collecting*** (7th edition, 2006)
***Great Britain Numbers Issued*** (3rd edition, 2008)
***How to Identify Stamps*** (4th edition, 2007)
***North America Combined*** (1st edition, 2010)
***Philatelic Terms Illustrated*** (4th edition, 2003)
***United Nations (also including International Organizations based in Switzerland and UNESCO)*** (1st edition, 2010)
***Western Europe Simplified*** (2005)

For other titles, and further details on the above, please see *www.stanleygibbons.com*

# The Stanley Gibbons Group plc - About us

## Our History

Edward Stanley Gibbons started trading postage stamps in his father's chemist shop in Plymouth in 1856; we have been at the forefront of stamp collecting for more than 150 years, making us the world's oldest philatelic company.

As Royal Warrant holders since 1914 we offer unsurpassed expertise and provide collectors worldwide with peace of mind that all stamps purchased from us come with our certified lifetime guarantee of authenticity*.

If you think of stamp collecting, you think of Stanley Gibbons and we are proud to uphold that tradition for you.

## 399 Strand

Our world famous stamp shop is a collector's paradise, with all of our latest catalogues, albums and accessories and of course, our unrivalled stockholding of postage stamps.

www.stanleygibbons.com
shop@stanleygibbons.co.uk
+44 (0)20 7836 8444

## Specialist Stamp Sales

For the collector that appreciates the value of collecting the highest quality examples, Stanley Gibbons is the only choice. Our extensive range is unrivalled in terms of quality and quantity, with specialist stamps available from all over the world.

www.stanleygibbons.com/stamps
shop@stanleygibbons.co.uk
+44 (0)20 7836 8444

## Mail order

Stamp collecting made easy! Order anything you need to enhance your collection, from our world famous catalogues to brand new supplements, from our long-running range of albums to cutting edge accessories, all available via telephone, email or post.

orders@stanleygibbons.com
FREEPHONE (UK only) 0800 611 622
+44 (0) 1425 472363

## Stanley Gibbons Auctions and Valuations

Sell your collection or individual rare items through our prestigious public auctions and regular postal auctions. You too can benefit from the excellent prices being realised at auction currently.

We also provide an unparalleled valuation service-drop your collection or rare items into us at 399 Strand, call us about our collection service or make an appointment at one of our valuation days held at venues across the UK.

www.stanleygibbons.com/auctions
auctions@stanleygibbons.co.uk
+44 (0)20 7836 8444

## Stanley Gibbons Investments

The Stanley Gibbons Investment Department offers a unique range of investment propositions that have consistently outperformed more traditional forms of investment, from guaranteed minimum return products with unlimited upside to portfolios made up of the world's rarest stamps and autographs.

www.stanleygibbons.com/investment
investment@stanleygibbons.co.uk
+44 (0)1481 708 270

## Stanley Gibbons Publications

The world's first stamp catalogue was printed by Stanley Gibbons in 1865 and we haven't looked back since! Our catalogues are trusted worldwide as the industry standard and we print countless titles each year. We also publish the consumer and trade magazines, Gibbons Stamp Monthly and Philatelic Exporter; bringing you news, views and insights into all things philatelic. For more information see 'Stanley Gibbons Publications Information.'

www.stanleygibbons.com/shop
orders@stanleygibbons.co.uk
+44 (0)1425 472 363

## stanleygibbons.com

Our website offers the complete philatelic service. Whether you are looking to buy stamps, invest, read news articles, browse our online stamp catalogue or find new issues, you are just one click away from anything you desire in the world of stamp collecting at stanleygibbons.com. Happy browsing!

www.stanleygibbons.com

## Fraser's Autographs

Autographs, manuscripts and memorabilia from Henry VIII to current day. We have over 60,000 items in stock, including movie stars, musicians, sport stars, historical figures and royalty. Fraser's is the UK's market leading autograph dealer and has been dealing in high quality autographed material since 1978.

www.frasersautographs.com
sales@frasersautographs.co.uk
+44 (0)20 7557 4404

## The Stanley Gibbons Lifetime Guarantee of Authenticity

Stanley Gibbons sells stamps and philatelic items on the basis that they are genuine originals; if they are proved not to fit the description as represented by us, you may return them at any time and we will refund you the original purchase price.

All stamps supplied by Stanley Gibbons are guaranteed originals under the following terms:

If not as described, and returned by the purchaser, we undertake to refund the price paid in the original transaction.

If any stamp is certified as genuine by the Expert Committee of the Royal Philatelic Society, London, or by B.P.A. Expertising Ltd., the purchaser shall not be entitled to make any claim against us for any error, omission or mistake in such certificate.

Consumers' statutory rights are not affected by the above guarantee.

## Stanley Gibbons Group plc- Contact us

### The Stanley Gibbons Group plc

### Stanley Gibbons Auctions

399 Strand, London WC2R OLX
Telephone + 44 (0)20 7836 8444
Fax + 44 (0) 20 7836 7342
enquires@stanleygibbons.co.uk
www.stanleygibbons.com for all departments

### Auction and Specialist Stamp Departments

Open Monday–Friday 9.30am to 5pm
Shop open Monday–Friday 9am to 5.30pm and Saturday 9.30am to 5.30pm

### Fraser's

(a division of Stanley Gibbons Group plc)
399 Strand, London WC2R OLX
Autographs, photographs, letters and documents
Telephone + 44 (0) 20 7836 8444
Fax +44 (0) 20 7836 7342,
info@frasersautographs.co.uk
www.frasersautographs.com
Monday–Friday 9 a.m. to 5.30 p.m. and Saturday 10 a.m. to 4 p.m.

### Stanley Gibbons Publications

7 Parkside, Christchurch Road, Ringwood, Hampshire BH24 3SH.
Telephone + 44 (0)1425 472363 (24 hour answer phone service)
UK FREEPHONE 0800611 622
Fax +44 (0) 1425 470247
info@stanleygibbons.co.uk

### Publications Mail Order

FREEPHONE 0800 611622
Monday–Friday 8.30 am to 5pm

### Stanley Gibbons (Guernsey) Limited

### Investments

18-20 Le Bordage, St Peter Port, Guernsey, Channel Islands, GY1 1DE
+44 (0) 1481 708 270
Toll free from USA +1 866 644 6146
investment@stanleygibbons.co.uk
www.stanleygibbons.com/investment

### Gibbons Stamp Monthly and Philatelic Exporter

7 Parkside, Christchurch Road, Ringwood, Hampshire BH24 3SH.
Subscriptions. 01425 472363
Fax 01425 470247
gsm@stanleygibbons.co.uk

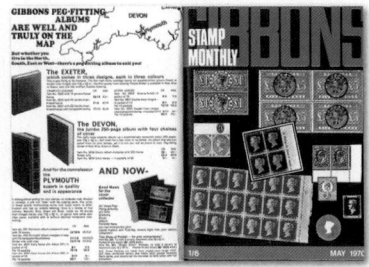

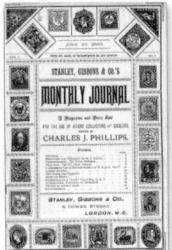

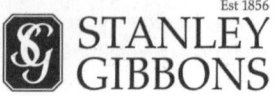

Pt. 1, Pt. 19

# ABU DHABI

The largest of the Trucial States in the Persian Gulf. Treaty relations with Great Britain expired on 31 December 1966, when Abu Dhabi took over the postal services. On 18 July 1971, seven of the Gulf sheikhdoms, including Abu Dhabi, agreed to form the State of the United Arab Emirates. The federation came into being on 1 August 1972.

1964. 100 naye paise = 1 rupee.
1966. 1,000 fils = 1 dinar.

**1** Shaikh Shakhbut bin Sultan

**3** Ruler's Palace

**1964**

| | | | | |
|---|---|---|---|---|
| 1 | **1** | 5n.p. green | 4·00 | 4·25 |
| 2 | **1** | 15n.p. brown | 3·50 | 1·75 |
| 3 | **1** | 20n.p. blue | 4·25 | 1·75 |
| 4 | **1** | 30n.p. orange | 4·25 | 1·50 |
| 5 | - | 40n.p. violet | 5·50 | 1·25 |
| 6 | - | 50n.p. bistre | 7·50 | 2·75 |
| 7 | - | 75n.p. black | 9·00 | 5·50 |
| 8 | **3** | 1r. green | 4·25 | 2·75 |
| 9 | **3** | 2r. black | 8·50 | 4·00 |
| 10 | - | 5r. red | 21·00 | 12·00 |
| 11 | - | 10r. blue | 27·00 | 14·00 |

DESIGNS: As Type **1**: 40 to 75n.p. Mountain gazelle; As Type **3**: 5, 10r. Oil rig and camels.

**5** Saker Falcon

**1965.** Falconry.

| | | | | |
|---|---|---|---|---|
| 12 | **5** | 20n.p. brown and blue | 15·00 | 2·25 |
| 13 | - | 40n.p. brown and blue | 18·00 | 3·00 |
| 14 | - | 2r. sepia and turquoise | 32·00 | 15·00 |

DESIGNS: 40n.p., 2r. Other types of Saker falcon on gloved hand.

**1966.** Nos. 1/11 surch in new currency ("Fils" only on Nos. 5/7) and ruler's portrait obliterated with bars.

| | | | | |
|---|---|---|---|---|
| 15 | **1** | 5f. on 5n.p. green | 11·00 | 5·50 |
| 16 | **1** | 15f. on 15n.p. brown | 16·00 | 9·50 |
| 17 | **1** | 20f. on 20n.p. blue | 16·00 | 8·00 |
| 18 | **1** | 30f. on 30n.p. orange | 15·00 | 19·00 |
| 19 | - | 40f. on 40n.p. violet | 14·00 | 1·00 |
| 20 | - | 50f. on 50n.p. bistre | 50·00 | 50·00 |
| 21 | - | 75f. on 75n.p. black | 50·00 | 50·00 |
| 22 | **3** | 100f. on 1r. green | 18·00 | 4·50 |
| 23 | **3** | 200f. on 2r. black | 18·00 | 13·00 |
| 24 | - | 500f. on 5r. red | 30·00 | 38·00 |
| 25 | - | 1d. on 10r. blue | 55·00 | 65·00 |

**9** Shaikh Zaid bin Sultan al Nahayyan

**10**

**1967**

| | | | | |
|---|---|---|---|---|
| 26 | | 5f. red and green | 55 | 20 |
| 27 | | 15f. red and brown | 65 | 20 |
| 28 | | 20f. red and blue | 1·00 | 20 |
| 29 | | 35f. red and violet | 1·10 | 35 |
| 30 | **9** | 40f. green | 1·60 | 35 |
| 38 | **10** | 40f. green | 4·75 | 2·40 |
| 31 | **9** | 50f. brown | 1·90 | 55 |
| 39 | **10** | 50f. brown | 5·75 | 1·70 |
| 32 | **9** | 60f. blue | 2·20 | 55 |
| 40 | **10** | 60f. blue | 21·00 | 4·00 |
| 33 | **9** | 100f. red | 3·25 | 80 |
| 41 | **10** | 100f. red | 30·00 | 10·50 |
| 34 | - | 125f. brown and green | 6·75 | 2·50 |
| 35 | - | 200f. brown and blue | 36·00 | 11·00 |
| 36 | - | 500f. violet and orange | 17·00 | 7·75 |
| 37 | - | 1d. blue and green | 40·00 | 22·00 |

DESIGNS—As Types **9&10**—VERT: 5f. to 35f. National flag. HORIZ: (47×27 mm); 125f. Mountain gazelle; 200f. Lanner falcon; 500f., 1d. Palace. Each with portrait of Ruler.

**11** Human Rights Emblem and Shaikh Zaid

**1968.** Human Rights Year.

| | | | | |
|---|---|---|---|---|
| 42 | **11** | 35f. multicoloured | 2·20 | 90 |
| 43 | **11** | 60f. multicoloured | 3·50 | 1·30 |
| 44 | **11** | 150f. multicoloured | 9·00 | 3·25 |

**12** Arms and Shaikh Zaid

**1968.** Anniv of Shaikh Zaid's Accession.

| | | | | |
|---|---|---|---|---|
| 45 | **12** | 5f. multicoloured | 3·25 | 65 |
| 46 | **12** | 10f. multicoloured | 3·25 | 90 |
| 47 | **12** | 100f. multicoloured | 8·75 | 2·20 |
| 48 | **12** | 125f. multicoloured | 13·00 | 4·00 |

**13** New Construction

**1968.** 2nd Anniv of Shaikh's Accession. "Progress in Abu Dhabi". Multicoloured.

| | | | | |
|---|---|---|---|---|
| 49 | | 5f. Type **13** | 2·75 | 55 |
| 50 | | 10f. Airport buildings (46½×34 mm) | 5·25 | 1·20 |
| 51 | | 35f. Shaikh Zaid, bridge and Northern goshawk (59×34 mm) | 24·00 | 9·50 |

**14** Petroleum Installations

**1969.** 3rd Anniv of Shaikh's Accession. Petroleum Industry. Multicoloured.

| | | | | |
|---|---|---|---|---|
| 52 | | 35f. Type **14** | 2·00 | 70 |
| 53 | | 60f. Marine drilling platform | 5·25 | 1·60 |
| 54 | | 125f. Separator platform, Zakum field | 8·75 | 3·25 |
| 55 | | 200f. Tank farm | 14·50 | 7·75 |

**15** Shaikh Zaid

**1970**

| | | | | |
|---|---|---|---|---|
| 56 | - | 5f. multicoloured | 70 | 20 |
| 57 | **15** | 10f. multicoloured | 1·00 | 20 |
| 58 | - | 25f. multicoloured | 1·90 | 20 |
| 59 | **15** | 35f. multicoloured | 2·50 | 35 |
| 60 | **15** | 50f. multicoloured | 3·50 | 55 |
| 61 | - | 60f. multicoloured | 4·00 | 65 |
| 62 | **15** | 70f. multicoloured | 6·75 | 80 |
| 63 | - | 90f. multicoloured | 8·50 | 1·50 |
| 64 | - | 125f. multicoloured | 12·50 | 2·00 |
| 65 | - | 150f. multicoloured | 12·50 | 2·50 |
| 66 | - | 500f. multicoloured | 38·00 | 13·50 |
| 67 | - | 1d. multicoloured | 65·00 | 22·00 |

DESIGNS: Nos. 56, 58, 61 and 63 as Type **15**, but frames changed, and smaller country name; 125f. Arab stallion; 150f. Mountain gazelle; 500f. Fort Jahili; 1d. Great Mosque.

No. 67 has face value in Arabic only.

**17** Shaikh Zaid and "Mt. Fuji" (T. Hayashi)

**1970.** "Expo 70" World Fair, Osaka, Japan.

| | | | | |
|---|---|---|---|---|
| 68 | **17** | 25f. multicoloured | 3·25 | 1·20 |
| 69 | **17** | 35f. multicoloured | 4·75 | 1·90 |
| 70 | **17** | 60f. multicoloured | 8·75 | 2·75 |

**18** Abu Dhabi Airport

**1970.** 40th Anniv of Shaikh's Accession. Completion of Abu Dhabi Airport. Mult.

| | | | | |
|---|---|---|---|---|
| 71 | | 25f. Type **18** | 3·25 | 90 |
| 72 | | 60f. Airport entrance | 7·25 | 2·10 |
| 73 | | 150f. Aerial view of Abu Dhabi (vert) | 17·00 | 5·25 |

**19** Pres. G. A. Nasser

**1971.** Gamal Nasser (President of Egypt) Commemoration.

| | | | | |
|---|---|---|---|---|
| 74 | **19** | 25f. black on pink | 6·00 | 3·75 |
| 75 | **19** | 35f. black on lilac | 8·25 | 5·50 |

**20** Military Land Rover Series II 88

**1971.** 5th Anniv of Shaikh's Accession. Defence Force. Multicoloured.

| | | | | |
|---|---|---|---|---|
| 76 | | 35f. Type **20** | 6·00 | 1·60 |
| 77 | | 60f. Patrol-boat "Baniyas" | 8·00 | 2·20 |
| 78 | | 125f. Armoured car | 17·00 | 3·50 |
| 79 | | 150f. Hawker Hunter FGA.76 jet fighters | 22·00 | 6·75 |

**1971.** No. 60 surch.

| | | | | |
|---|---|---|---|---|
| 80 | **15** | 5f. on 50f. multicoloured | 95·00 | 80·00 |

**22** Dome of the Rock

**1972.** Dome of the Rock, Jerusalem. Multicoloured.

| | | | | |
|---|---|---|---|---|
| 81 | | 35f. Type **22** | 25·00 | 5·00 |
| 82 | | 60f. Mosque entrance | 43·00 | 9·00 |
| 83 | | 125f. Mosque dome | 80·00 | 22·00 |

**1972.** Provisional Issue. Nos. 56/67 optd UAE and arabic inscr.

| | | | | |
|---|---|---|---|---|
| 84 | - | 5f. multicoloured | 2·50 | 2·50 |
| 85 | **15** | 10f. multicoloured | 2·50 | 1·50 |
| 86 | - | 25f. multicoloured | 3·25 | 3·25 |
| 87 | **15** | 35f. multicoloured | 5·00 | 4·50 |
| 88 | **15** | 50f. multicoloured | 7·75 | 7·75 |
| 89 | - | 60f. multicoloured | 9·00 | 9·00 |
| 90 | **15** | 70f. multicoloured | 11·00 | 11·00 |
| 91 | - | 90f. multicoloured | 17·00 | 17·00 |
| 92 | - | 125f. multicoloured | 55·00 | 55·00 |
| 93 | - | 150f. multicoloured | 65·00 | 65·00 |
| 94 | - | 500f. multicoloured | £150 | £150 |
| 95 | - | 1d. multicoloured | £300 | £300 |

For later issues see **UNITED ARAB EMIRATES**.

Pt. 1

# ADEN

Peninsula on southern coast of Arabia. Formerly part of the Indian Empire. A Crown Colony from 1 April 1937 to 18 January 1963, when Aden joined the South Arabian Federation, whose stamps it then used.

1937. 16 annas = 1 rupee.
1951. 100 cents = 1 shilling.

**1** Dhow

**1937**

| | | | | |
|---|---|---|---|---|
| 1 | **1** | ½a. green | 3·75 | 2·75 |
| 2 | **1** | 9p. green | 3·75 | 3·25 |
| 3 | **1** | 1a. brown | 3·75 | 1·75 |
| 4 | **1** | 2a. red | 5·00 | 3·00 |
| 5 | **1** | 2½a. blue | 6·50 | 2·00 |
| 6 | **1** | 3a. red | 10·00 | 8·50 |
| 7 | **1** | 3½a. blue | 7·50 | 5·50 |
| 8 | **1** | 8a. purple | 24·00 | 9·50 |
| 9 | **1** | 1r. brown | 50·00 | 11·00 |
| 10 | **1** | 2r. yellow | 95·00 | 32·00 |
| 11 | **1** | 5r. purple | £200 | £120 |
| 12 | **1** | 10r. olive | £550 | £500 |

**2** King George VI and Queen Elizabeth

**1937.** Coronation.

| | | | | |
|---|---|---|---|---|
| 13 | **2** | 1a. brown | 65 | 1·25 |
| 14 | **2** | 2½a. blue | 75 | 1·40 |
| 15 | **2** | 3½a. blue | 1·00 | 2·75 |

**3** Aidrus Mosque, Crater

**1939**

| | | | | |
|---|---|---|---|---|
| 16 | **3** | ½a. green | 1·75 | 60 |
| 17 | - | ¾a. brown | 2·50 | 1·25 |
| 18 | - | 1a. blue | 60 | 40 |
| 19 | - | 1½a. red | 2·75 | 60 |
| 20 | **3** | 2a. brown | 1·00 | 25 |
| 21 | - | 2½a. blue | 1·75 | 30 |
| 22 | - | 3a. brown and red | 1·75 | 25 |
| 23 | - | 8a. orange | 2·00 | 40 |
| 23a | - | 14a. brown and blue | 3·75 | 1·00 |
| 24 | - | 1r. green | 4·50 | 2·50 |
| 25 | - | 2r. blue and mauve | 9·00 | 2·50 |
| 26 | - | 5r. brown and olive | 27·00 | 15·00 |
| 27 | - | 10r. brown and violet | 42·00 | 16·00 |

DESIGNS: ¾a., 5r. Adenese Camel Corps; 1a., 2r. The Harbour; 1½a., 1r. Adenese dhow; 2½, 8a. Mukalla; 3, 14a., 10r. "Capture of Aden, 1839" (Capt. Rundle).

**9** Houses of Parliament, London

**1946.** Victory.

| | | | | |
|---|---|---|---|---|
| 28 | **9** | 1½a. red | 20 | 1·75 |
| 29 | **9** | 2½a. blue | 60 | 1·00 |

**10**

**11** King George VI and Queen Elizabeth

**1949.** Royal Silver Wedding.

| | | | | |
|---|---|---|---|---|
| 30 | **10** | 1½a. red | 40 | 2·25 |
| 31 | **11** | 10r. purple | 38·00 | 48·00 |

**1949.** 75th Anniv of U.P.U. As T **20/23** of Antigua surch with new values.

| | | | |
|---|---|---|---|
| 32 | 2½a. on 20c. blue | 50 | 1·50 |
| 33 | 3a. on 30c. red | 2·00 | 1·50 |
| 34 | 8a. on 50c. orange | 1·40 | 2·00 |
| 35 | 1r. on 1s. blue | 1·60 | 5·00 |

**1951.** Stamps of 1939 surch in cents or shillings.

| | | | |
|---|---|---|---|
| 36 | 5c. on 1a. blue | 25 | 40 |
| 37 | 10c. on 2a. brown | 15 | 45 |
| 38 | 15c. on 2½a. blue | 30 | 1·25 |
| 39 | 20c. on 3a. brown and red | 30 | 40 |
| 40 | 30c. on 8a. orange | 50 | 65 |
| 41 | 50c. on 8a. orange | 1·25 | 35 |
| 42 | 70c. on 14a. brown and blue | 2·25 | 1·50 |
| 43 | 1s. on 1r. green | 2·00 | 30 |
| 44 | 2s. on 2r. blue and mauve | 15·00 | 3·75 |
| 45 | 5s. on 5r. brown and olive | 26·00 | 15·00 |
| 46 | 10s. on 10r. brown and violet | 38·00 | 16·00 |

**13** Queen Elizabeth II

**1953.** Coronation.

| | | | | |
|---|---|---|---|---|
| 47 | **13** | 15c. black and green | 1·25 | 1·25 |

**14** Minaret

**15** Camel Transport

**1953**

| | | | | |
|---|---|---|---|---|
| 48 | **14** | 5c. green | 20 | 10 |
| 49a | **14** | 5c. turquoise | 10 | 1·25 |
| 50 | **15** | 10c. orange | 40 | 10 |
| 51 | **15** | 10c. red | 20 | 30 |
| 52 | - | 15c. turquoise | 1·25 | 60 |
| 79 | - | 15c. grey | 70 | 4·00 |
| 80 | - | 25c. red | 2·50 | 40 |
| 56 | - | 35c. blue | 2·50 | 1·50 |
| 58 | - | 50c. blue | 20 | 10 |
| 60 | - | 70c. grey | 20 | 10 |
| 61a | - | 70c. black | 1·25 | 20 |
| 62 | - | 1s. brown and violet | 30 | 10 |
| 63 | - | 1s. black and violet | 1·50 | 10 |
| 64 | - | 1s.25 blue and black | 7·50 | 60 |
| 65 | - | 2s. brown and red | 1·50 | 50 |
| 66 | - | 2s. black and red | 11·00 | 50 |
| 67 | - | 5s. brown and blue | 1·50 | 1·00 |
| 68 | - | 5s. black and blue | 11·00 | 1·25 |
| 69 | - | 10s. brown and green | 1·75 | 8·00 |
| 70 | - | 10s. black and bronze | 17·00 | 1·75 |
| 71 | - | 20s. brown and lilac | 6·50 | 10·00 |
| 72 | - | 20s. black and lilac | 65·00 | 17·00 |

DESIGNS—HORIZ: 15c. Crater; 25c. Mosque; 1s. Dhow building; 20s. (38×27 mm); Aden in 1572. VERT: 35c. Dhow; 50c. Map; 70c. Salt works; 1s.25, Colony's badge; 2s. Aden Protectorate Levy; 5s. Crater Pass; 10s. Tribesmen.

**1954.** Royal Visit. As No. 62 but inscr "ROYAL VISIT 1954".

| | | | |
|---|---|---|---|
| 73 | 1s. sepia and violet | 60 | 60 |

**1959.** Revised Constitution. Optd **REVISED CONSTITUTION 1959** (in Arabic on No. 74).

| | | | |
|---|---|---|---|
| 74 | 15c. green (No. 53) | 30 | 2·00 |
| 75 | 1s.25 blue and black (No. 64) | 1·00 | 1·00 |

**28** Protein Foods

**1963.** Freedom from Hunger.

| | | | | |
|---|---|---|---|---|
| 76 | **28** | 1s.25 green | 1·25 | 1·75 |

For later issues see **SOUTH ARABIAN FEDERATION**.

Pt. 16

# AFGHANISTAN

An independent country in Asia, to N.W. of Pakistan. Now a republic, the country was formerly ruled by monarchs from 1747 to 1973.

1871. 60 paisa = 12 shahi = 6 sanar = 3 abasi = 2 kran = 1 rupee.
1920. 60 paisa = 2 kran = 1 rupee.
1926. 100 poul (pul) = 1 afghani (rupee).

The issues from 1860 to 1892 (Types **1** to **16**) are difficult to classify because the values of each set are expressed in native script and are generally all printed in the same colour. As it is not possible to list these in an intelligible simplified form we would refer users to the detailed list in the Stanley Gibbons Part 16 (Central Asia) Catalogue.

**1**

**4**

**5**

**6** **8**

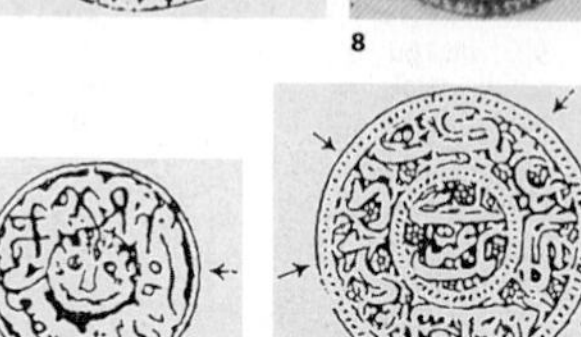
**10** **12**

**16**

**17** National Coat of Arms

**1893.** Dated "1310".

| | | | | |
|---|---|---|---|---|
| 147 | **17** | 1a. black on green | 3·25 | 3·25 |
| 148 | **17** | 1a. black on red | 3·75 | 3·25 |
| 149a | **17** | 1a. black on purple | 3·75 | 3·50 |
| 150 | **17** | 1a. black on yellow | 3·50 | 3·25 |
| 151 | **17** | 1a. black on orange | 4·00 | 4·00 |
| 152 | **17** | 1a. black on blue | 6·25 | 5·25 |

**18** 2 Abasi

**1894.** Undated.

| | | | | |
|---|---|---|---|---|
| 153 | **18** | 2a. black on green | 12·50 | 8·25 |
| 154 | **18** | 1r. black on green | 15·00 | 13·00 |

**20** 1 Abasi

**1907.** Imperf, roul or perf.

| | | | | |
|---|---|---|---|---|
| 156a | **20** | 1a. green | 17·00 | 21·00 |
| 157 | - | 2a. blue | 6·50 | 8·25 |
| 158 | - | 1r. green | 45·00 | 23·00 |

The 2a. and 1r. are in similar designs.

**23**

**24** 1 Abasi

**1909.** Perf.

| | | | | |
|---|---|---|---|---|
| 165 | **23** | 2 paisa brown | 13·00 | 4·50 |
| 166 | **24** | 1a. blue | 5·25 | 2·10 |
| 168 | **24** | 1a. red | 1·20 | 1·00 |
| 169 | - | 2a. green | 3·00 | 2·50 |
| 170a | - | 2a. bistre | 2·75 | 3·00 |
| 171 | - | 1r. brown | 5·00 | 5·25 |
| 172 | - | 1r. olive | 7·75 | 7·75 |

The frames of the 2a. and 1r. differ from Type **24**.

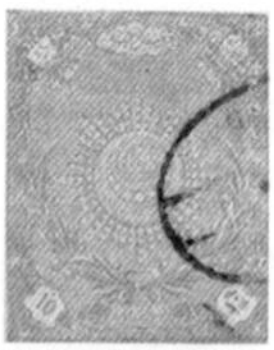
**27** Royal Star of Order of Independence

**1920.** 1st Anniv of End of War of Independence. Size 39×47 mm.

| | | | | |
|---|---|---|---|---|
| 173 | **27** | 10p. red | 49·00 | 33·00 |
| 174 | **27** | 20p. purple | 80·00 | 55·00 |
| 175 | **27** | 30p. green | £160 | £160 |

**1921.** Size 23×29 mm.

| | | | |
|---|---|---|---|
| 177 | 10p. red | 2·10 | 95 |
| 178 | 20p. purple | 4·50 | 2·75 |
| 180b | 30p. green | 6·50 | 3·00 |

**(28)**

**1923.** 5th Independence Day. Optd with T **28**.

| | | | |
|---|---|---|---|
| 181 | 10p. red | 41·00 | 41·00 |
| 181a | 20p. brown | 49·00 | 49·00 |
| 182 | 30p. green | 60·00 | 60·00 |

**29** Crest of King Amanullah

**1924.** 6th Independence Day.

| | | | | |
|---|---|---|---|---|
| 183 | **29** | 10p. brown (24×32 mm) | 37·00 | 37·00 |

**29a**

**1924**

| | | | | |
|---|---|---|---|---|
| 183b | **29a** | 5k. blue | 41·00 | 41·00 |
| 183c | **29a** | 5r. mauve | 16·00 | 25·00 |

**1925.** 7th Independence Day.

| | | | | |
|---|---|---|---|---|
| 184 | **29** | 10p. brown (29×37 mm) | 60·00 | 45·00 |

**1926.** 7th Anniv of Independence.

| | | | |
|---|---|---|---|
| 185 | 10p. blue (26×33 mm) | 6·50 | 8·25 |

**30** Crest of King Amanullah

**1927.** 8th Anniv of Independence.

| | | | | |
|---|---|---|---|---|
| 186 | **30** | 10p. mauve | 18·00 | 13·00 |

Types **31/3**, **36/37** and **41**, National Seal.

**31** **32**

**33**

**1927.** Perf or imperf.

| | | | | |
|---|---|---|---|---|
| 188A | **31** | 15p. red | 1·30 | 1·30 |
| 189A | **32** | 30p. green | 2·75 | 1·20 |
| 190B | **33** | 60p. blue | 3·00 | 2·10 |

See also Nos. 207A/13A.

**34** Crest of King Amanullah

**1928.** 9th Anniv of Independence.

| | | | | |
|---|---|---|---|---|
| 191 | **34** | 15p. red | 5·00 | 5·00 |

**36** **37**

**1928**

| | | | | |
|---|---|---|---|---|
| 193 | **36** | 10p. green | 1·10 | 40 |
| 194 | **37** | 25p. red | 1·20 | 80 |
| 195 | - | 40p. blue | 1·20 | 80 |
| 196 | - | 50p. red | 1·50 | 1·00 |

The frames of the 40 and 50p. differ from Type **37**.
See also Nos. 207A/13A.

**41**

**1929**

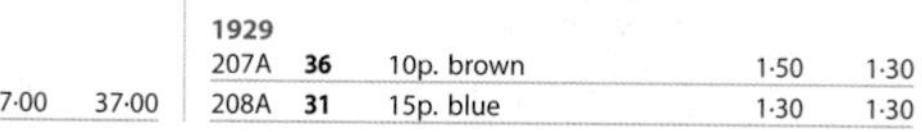

| | | | | |
|---|---|---|---|---|
| 207A | **36** | 10p. brown | 1·50 | 1·30 |
| 208A | **31** | 15p. blue | 1·30 | 1·30 |

| | | | | |
|---|---|---|---|---|
| 209A | 37 | 25p. blue | 1·30 | 1·20 |
| 210A | 41 | 30p. green | 1·30 | 1·20 |
| 211A | - | 40p. red | 1·60 | 1·50 |
| 212A | - | 50p. blue | 2·10 | 1·50 |
| 213A | 33 | 60p. black | 3·25 | 2·30 |

**42** Independence Memorial

**1931.** 13th Independence Day.

| | | | | |
|---|---|---|---|---|
| 214 | 42 | 20p. red | 2·50 | 1·20 |

**46** National Assembly Building

**1932.** Inauguration of National Council.

| | | | | |
|---|---|---|---|---|
| 215 | - | 40p. brown (31×24 mm) | 65 | 40 |
| 216 | - | 60p. violet (29×26 mm) | 1·10 | 80 |
| 217 | 46 | 80p. red | 1·50 | 1·20 |
| 218 | - | 1a. black (24×27 mm) | 10·50 | 7·75 |
| 219 | - | 2a. blue (36×25 mm) | 5·25 | 4·00 |
| 220 | - | 3a. green (36×24 mm) | 5·50 | 3·75 |

DESIGNS: Nos. 215/16, 218/19, Council Chamber; 3a. National Assembly Building (different).

**50** Mosque at Balkh

**1932**

| | | | | |
|---|---|---|---|---|
| 221 | 50 | 10p. brown | 60 | 25 |
| 222 | - | 15p. brown | 40 | 35 |
| 223 | - | 20p. red | 65 | 25 |
| 224 | - | 25p. green | 80 | 25 |
| 225 | - | 30p. red | 80 | 25 |
| 226 | - | 40p. orange | 1·00 | 50 |
| 227 | - | 50p. blue | 1·50 | 1·30 |
| 228 | - | 60p. blue | 1·30 | 90 |
| 229 | - | 80p. violet | 2·50 | 2·10 |
| 230 | - | 1a. blue | 4·50 | 80 |
| 231 | - | 2a. purple | 5·00 | 2·30 |
| 232 | - | 3a. red | 5·75 | 3·00 |

DESIGNS—32×23 mm: 15p. Kabul Fortress; 20, 25p. Parliament House, Darul Funun, Kabul; 40p. Memorial Pillar of Knowledge and Ignorance, Kabul; 1a. Ruins at Balkh; 2a. Minarets at Herat. 32×16 mm: 30p. Arch of Paghman. 23×32 mm: 60p. Minaret at Herat. 23×25 mm: 30p. Arch at Qalai Bust, near Kandahar; 50p. Independence Memorial, Kabul. 16×32 mm: 3a. Great Buddha at Bamian.

See also Nos. 237/51.

**62** Independence Memorial

**1932.** 14th Independence Day.

| | | | | |
|---|---|---|---|---|
| 233 | 62 | 1a. red | 5·00 | 3·25 |

**63** National Liberation Monument, Kabul

**1932.** Commemorative Issue.

| | | | | |
|---|---|---|---|---|
| 234 | 63 | 80p. red | 2·10 | 1·50 |

**64** Arch of Paghman

**1933.** 15th Independence Day.

| | | | | |
|---|---|---|---|---|
| 235 | 64 | 50p. blue | 2·10 | 1·50 |

**65** Independence Memorial

**1934.** 16th Independence Day.

| | | | | |
|---|---|---|---|---|
| 236 | 65 | 50p. green | 3·25 | 2·75 |

**1934.** As Nos. 219/20 and 221/30, but colours changed and new values.

| | | | | |
|---|---|---|---|---|
| 237 | 50 | 10p. violet | 25 | 15 |
| 238 | - | 15p. green | 40 | 15 |
| 239 | - | 20p. mauve | 40 | 15 |
| 240 | - | 25p. red | 50 | 25 |
| 241 | - | 30p. orange | 60 | 35 |
| 242 | - | 40p. black | 65 | 35 |
| 243 | - | 45p. blue | 2·10 | 1·60 |
| 244 | - | 45p. red | 40 | 15 |
| 245 | - | 50p. red | 75 | 25 |
| 246 | - | 60p. violet | 80 | 40 |
| 247 | - | 75p. red | 3·00 | 2·10 |
| 248 | - | 75p. blue | 80 | 65 |
| 248b | - | 80p. brown | 1·30 | 80 |
| 249 | - | 1a. mauve | 2·10 | 1·60 |
| 250 | - | 2a. grey | 4·00 | 2·50 |
| 251 | - | 3a. blue | 4·50 | 3·00 |

DESIGNS (new values)—34×23 mm: 45p. Royal Palace, Kabul. 20×34 mm: 75p. Hunters Canyon Pass, Hindu Kush.

**68** Independence Memorial

**1935.** 17th Independence Day.

| | | | | |
|---|---|---|---|---|
| 252 | 68 | 50p. blue | 3·00 | 2·50 |

**69** Firework Display

**1936.** 18th Independence Day.

| | | | | |
|---|---|---|---|---|
| 253 | 69 | 50p. mauve | 3·25 | 2·75 |

**70** Independence Memorial and Mohamed Nadir Shah

**1937.** 19th Independence Day. Perf or imperf.

| | | | | |
|---|---|---|---|---|
| 254 | 70 | 50p. brown and violet | 7·25 | 2·20 |

**71** Mohamed Nadir Shah

**1938.** 20th Independence Day. Perf or imperf.

| | | | | |
|---|---|---|---|---|
| 255 | 71 | 50p. brown and blue | 2·50 | 2·50 |

**72** Aliabad Hospital

**1938.** Obligatory Tax. Int Anti-cancer Fund.

| | | | | |
|---|---|---|---|---|
| 256 | 72 | 10p. green | 3·25 | 5·00 |
| 257 | - | 15p. blue | 3·25 | 5·00 |

DESIGN—44×28 mm: 15p. Pierre and Marie Curie.

**74** Mohamed Nadir Shah

**1939.** 21st Independence Day.

| | | | | |
|---|---|---|---|---|
| 258 | 74 | 50p. red | 2·30 | 1·50 |

**76** Darul Funun Parliament House, Kabul

**79** Independence Memorial

**82** Mohamed Zahir Shah

**83** Sugar Mill, Baghlan

**1939**

| | | | | |
|---|---|---|---|---|
| 259 | 76 | 10p. purple (36½×24 mm) | 25 | 20 |
| 260 | 76 | 15p. green (34×21 mm) | 35 | 20 |
| 261 | 76 | 20p. purple (34×22½ mm) | 40 | 25 |
| 262 | - | 25p. red | 50 | 35 |
| 263 | - | 25p. green | 35 | 25 |
| 264 | - | 30p. orange | 40 | 25 |
| 265 | - | 35p. orange | 1·50 | 1·00 |
| 266 | - | 40p. grey | 80 | 50 |
| 267 | 79 | 45p. red | 80 | 40 |
| 268 | 79 | 50p. orange | 65 | 25 |
| 269 | 79 | 60p. violet | 80 | 25 |
| 270 | - | 70p. violet | 2·10 | 1·00 |
| 271 | - | 70p. purple | 2·10 | 1·00 |
| 272 | - | 75p. blue | 2·30 | 80 |
| 273 | - | 75p. purple | 1·80 | 1·60 |
| 274 | - | 75p. red | 3·00 | 3·00 |
| 275 | - | 80p. brown | 1·50 | 1·00 |
| 276 | 82 | 1a. purple | 1·60 | 80 |
| 277 | - | 1a. purple | 1·60 | 1·00 |
| 278d | 83 | 1a.25 blue | 2·10 | 70 |
| 279a | - | 2a. red | 2·50 | 1·20 |
| 280 | - | 3a. blue | 3·75 | 2·50 |

DESIGNS—31×19 mm: 25, 30p. Royal Palace, Kabul. 30×18 mm: 40p. Royal Palace, Kabul. 30×21 mm: 70p. Ruins at Qalai Bust, near Kandahar. 35½×21½ mm: 75p. Independence Memorial and Mohamed Nadir Shah. 34½×21 mm: 80p. As 75p. 35×20 mm: 1a. (No. 277), 2a. Mohamed Zahir Shah; 3a. As Type **82** but head turned more to left. 19×31 mm: 35p. Minarets at Herat.

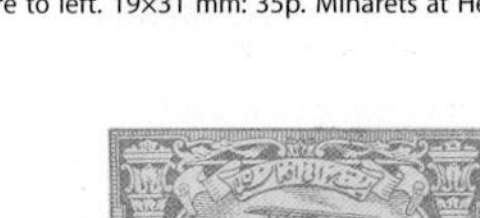
**85** Potez 25A2 over Kabul

**1939.** Air.

| | | | | |
|---|---|---|---|---|
| 280a | 85 | 5a. orange | 5·75 | 4·50 |
| 280b | 85 | 10a. blue | 5·75 | 4·50 |
| 280c | 85 | 20a. green | 11·50 | 7·75 |

See also Nos. 300/2.

**86** Mohamed Nadir Shah

**1940.** 22nd Independence Day.

| | | | | |
|---|---|---|---|---|
| 281 | 86 | 50p. green | 2·10 | 1·50 |

**87** Arch of Paghman

**1941.** 23rd Independence Day.

| | | | | |
|---|---|---|---|---|
| 282 | - | 15p. green | 9·00 | 5·75 |
| 283 | 87 | 50p. brown | 2·50 | 2·10 |

DESIGN: (19×29½ mm): 15p. Independence Memorial.

**87b** Mohamed Nadir Shah and Arch of Paghman

**1942.** 24th Independence Day.

| | | | | |
|---|---|---|---|---|
| 284 | - | 35p. green | 3·75 | 3·75 |
| 285 | 87b | 125p. blue | 3·00 | 2·10 |

DESIGN—VERT: 35p. Independence Memorial in medallion.

**88** Independence Memorial and Mohamed Nadir Shah

**1943.** 25th Independence Day.

| | | | | |
|---|---|---|---|---|
| 286 | - | 35p. red | 14·00 | 12·50 |
| 287 | 88 | 1a.25 blue | 3·25 | 2·50 |

DESIGN—HORIZ: 35p. Independence Memorial seen through archway and Mohamed Nadir Shah in oval frame.

**89** Arch of Paghman

**90** Independence Memorial and Mohamed Nadir Shah

**1944.** 26th Independence Day.

| | | | | |
|---|---|---|---|---|
| 288 | 89 | 35p. red | 1·30 | 75 |
| 289 | 90 | 1a.25 blue | 2·30 | 2·00 |

**91** Mohamed Nadir Shah and Independence Memorial

**92** Arch of Paghman and Mohamed Nadir Shah

**1945.** 27th Independence Day.

| | | | | |
|---|---|---|---|---|
| 290 | 91 | 35p. red | 2·30 | 80 |
| 291 | 92 | 1a.25 blue | 3·75 | 2·10 |

**93** Independence Memorial

**1946.** 28th Independence Day. Dated "1946".

| | | | | |
|---|---|---|---|---|
| 292 | - | 15p. green | 1·20 | 75 |
| 293 | **93** | 20p. mauve | 2·10 | 90 |
| 294 | - | 125p. blue | 3·25 | 2·10 |

DESIGNS—HORIZ: 15p. Mohamed Zahir Shah. VERT: 125p. Mohamed Nadir Shah.

**94** Mohamed Nadir Shah and Independence Memorial

**1947.** 29th Independence Day. Dated "1947".

| | | | | |
|---|---|---|---|---|
| 295 | | 15p. green | 1·20 | 60 |
| 296 | | 35p. mauve | 1·30 | 80 |
| 297 | **94** | 125p. blue | 3·25 | 2·00 |

DESIGNS—HORIZ: 15p. Mohamed Zahir Shah and ruins of Kandahar Fort; 35p. Mohamed Zahir Shah and Arch of Paghman.

**95** Hungry Boy

**1948.** Child Welfare Fund.

| | | | | |
|---|---|---|---|---|
| 298 | **95** | 35p. green | 5·00 | 4·00 |
| 299 | - | 125p. blue | 5·00 | 4·00 |

DESIGN—26×33½ mm: 125p. Hungry boy in vert frame.
See also No. 307.

**1948.** Air. As T **85** but colours changed.

| | | | | |
|---|---|---|---|---|
| 300 | **85** | 5a. green | 23·00 | 23·00 |
| 301 | **85** | 10a. orange | 23·00 | 23·00 |
| 302 | **85** | 20a. blue | 23·00 | 23·00 |

**96** Independence Memorial

**1948.** 30th Independence Day. Dated "1948".

| | | | | |
|---|---|---|---|---|
| 303 | - | 15p. green | 80 | 35 |
| 304 | **96** | 20p. mauve | 1·00 | 40 |
| 305 | - | 125p. blue | 2·20 | 1·10 |

DESIGNS—VERT: 15p. Arch of Paghman. HORIZ: 125p. Mohamed Nadir Shah.

**97** U.N. Symbol

**1948.** 3rd Anniv of U.N.O.

| | | | | |
|---|---|---|---|---|
| 306 | **97** | 1a.25 blue | 11·00 | 9·00 |

**98** Hungry Boy

**1949.** Obligatory Tax. Child Welfare Fund.

| | | | | |
|---|---|---|---|---|
| 307 | - | 35p. orange | 3·25 | 2·10 |
| 308 | **98** | 125p. blue | 4·00 | 2·10 |

DESIGN—HORIZ: 35p. As Type **98** but 29×22½ mm.

**99** Victory Monument

**1949.** 31st Independence Day. Dated "1949" (Nos. 310/11).

| | | | | |
|---|---|---|---|---|
| 309 | **99** | 25p. green | 1·00 | 50 |
| 310 | - | 35p. mauve | 1·20 | 65 |
| 311 | - | 1a.25 blue | 2·30 | 1·30 |

DESIGNS—HORIZ: 35p. Mohamed Zahir Shah and ruins of Kandahar Fort; 1a.25, Independence Memorial and Mohamed Nadir Shah.

**100** Arch of Paghman

**1949.** Obligatory Tax. 4th Anniv of U.N.O.

| | | | | |
|---|---|---|---|---|
| 312 | **100** | 125p. green | 15·00 | 9·00 |

**101** King Mohamed Zahir Shah and Map of Afghanistan

**1950.** Obligatory Tax. Return of King Mohamed Zahir Shah from Visit to Europe.

| | | | | |
|---|---|---|---|---|
| 313 | **101** | 125p. green | 3·25 | 1·50 |

**102** Hungry Boy

**1950.** Obligatory Tax. Child Welfare Fund.

| | | | | |
|---|---|---|---|---|
| 314 | **102** | 125p. green | 4·50 | 2·50 |

**103** Mohamed Nadir Shah

**1950.** 32nd Independence Day.

| | | | | |
|---|---|---|---|---|
| 315 | **103** | 35p. brown | 65 | 40 |
| 316 | **103** | 125p. blue | 1·80 | 60 |

**104**

**1950.** Obligatory Tax. 5th Anniv of U.N.O.

| | | | | |
|---|---|---|---|---|
| 317 | **104** | 1a.25 blue | 9·00 | 3·00 |

**106**

**1950.** 19th Anniv of Faculty of Medicine, Kabul.

| | | | | |
|---|---|---|---|---|
| 318 | **106** | 35p. green (postage) | 1·20 | 75 |
| 319 | - | 1a.25 blue | 4·25 | 2·30 |
| 320 | **106** | 35p. red (obligatory tax) | 1·00 | 50 |
| 321 | - | 1a.25 black | 7·00 | 2·30 |

DESIGN: Nos. 319 and 321, Sanatorium. Nos. 318 and 320 measure 38½×25½ mm and Nos. 319 and 321, 45×30 mm.

**107** Minaret at Herat

**109** Mohamed Zahir Shah

**110** Mosque at Balkh

**118**

**1951**

| | | | | |
|---|---|---|---|---|
| 322 | **107** | 10p. brown and yellow | 50 | 15 |
| 323 | **107** | 15p. brown and blue | 50 | 15 |
| 324 | - | 20p. black | 9·75 | 5·25 |
| 325 | **109** | 25p. green | 50 | 15 |
| 326 | **110** | 30p. red | 60 | 15 |
| 327 | **109** | 35p. violet | 65 | 15 |
| 328 | - | 40p. brown | 65 | 15 |
| 329 | - | 45p. blue | 65 | 15 |
| 330 | - | 50p. black | 1·90 | 25 |
| 331 | - | 60p. black | 1·50 | 25 |
| 332 | - | 70p. black, red and green | 80 | 25 |
| 333 | - | 75p. red | 1·20 | 50 |
| 334 | - | 80p. black and red | 2·10 | 90 |
| 336 | **118** | 125p. black and purple | 1·80 | 1·00 |
| 335 | - | 1a. violet and green | 1·50 | 65 |
| 337 | **118** | 2a. blue | 2·75 | 80 |
| 338 | **118** | 3a. blue and black | 5·75 | 1·20 |

DESIGNS—19×29 mm: 20p. Buddha of Bamian; 45p. Maiwand Victory Monument; 60p. Victory Towers, Ghazni. 22×28 mm: 75, 80p., 1a. Mohamed Zahir Shah. 28×19 mm: 40p. Ruins at Qalai Bust; 70p. Flag. 30×19 mm: 50p. View of Kandahar.
See also Nos. 425/425k.

**119** Douglas DC-3 over Kabul

**1951.** Air.

| | | | | |
|---|---|---|---|---|
| 339 | **119** | 5a. red | 3·25 | 65 |
| 339a | **119** | 5a. green | 1·80 | 40 |
| 340 | **119** | 10a. grey | 7·50 | 1·80 |
| 341 | **119** | 20a. blue | 10·50 | 3·00 |

See also Nos. 415a/b.

**120** Shepherdess

**1951.** Obligatory Tax. Child Welfare Fund.

| | | | | |
|---|---|---|---|---|
| 342 | **120** | 35p. green | 1·50 | 90 |
| 343 | - | 125p. blue | 1·50 | 90 |

DESIGN—34½×44 mm: 125p. Young shepherd.

**121** Arch of Paghman (122)

**1951.** 33rd Independence Day. Optd with T **122**.

| | | | | |
|---|---|---|---|---|
| 344 | **121** | 35p. black and green | 1·20 | 65 |
| 345 | - | 125p. blue | 3·00 | 1·40 |

DESIGN (34×18½ mm): 125p. Mohamed Nadir Shah and Independence Memorial.
See also Nos. 360/1b and 418/19.

**IMPERF STAMPS.** From 1951 many issues were made available imperf from limited printings.

**124** Flag of Pashtunistan

**1951.** Obligatory Tax. Pashtunistan Day.

| | | | | |
|---|---|---|---|---|
| 346 | **124** | 35p. brown | 1·50 | 80 |
| 347 | - | 125p. blue | 3·00 | 2·10 |

DESIGN—42½×21½ mm: 125p. Afridi tribesman.

**125** Dove and Globe

**1951.** Obligatory Tax. United Nations Day.

| | | | | |
|---|---|---|---|---|
| 348 | **125** | 35p. mauve | 80 | 40 |
| 349 | - | 125p. blue | 2·10 | 1·60 |

DESIGN—VERT: 125p. Dove and globe.

**126** Avicenna (physician)

**1951.** Obligatory Tax. 20th Anniv of Faculty of Medicine.

| | | | | |
|---|---|---|---|---|
| 350 | **126** | 35p. mauve | 7·75 | 1·50 |
| 351 | **126** | 125p. blue | 3·00 | 4·00 |

**127** Amir Sher Ali and First Stamp

**1951.** Obligatory Tax. 76th Anniv of U.P.U.

| | | | | |
|---|---|---|---|---|
| 352 | **127** | 35p. brown | 65 | 40 |
| 353 | - | 35p. mauve | 65 | 40 |
| 354 | **127** | 125p. blue | 1·20 | 80 |
| 355 | - | 125p. blue | 1·20 | 80 |

DESIGN: Nos. 353 and 355, Mohamed Zahir Shah and first stamp.

**128** Children and Postman

**1952.** Obligatory Tax. Child Welfare Fund.

| | | | | |
|---|---|---|---|---|
| 356 | **128** | 35p. brown | 80 | 65 |
| 357 | - | 125p. violet | 1·60 | 1·00 |

DESIGN—HORIZ: 125p. Girl dancing (33×23 mm).

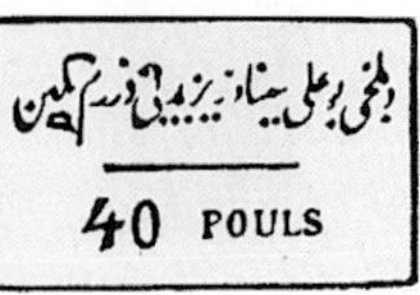

**(129)**

**1952.** Obligatory Tax. Birth Millenary of Avicenna (physician and philosopher). (a) Surch with T **129**.

| | | | | |
|---|---|---|---|---|
| 358 | **110** | 40p. on 30p. red | 5·25 | 3·00 |

(b) Surch **MILLIEME ANNIVERSAIRE DE BOALI SINAI BALKI 125 POULS** in frame.

| | | | |
|---|---|---|---|
| 359 | 125p. on 30p. red | 7·50 | 3·50 |

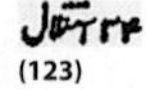
**(123)**

**1952.** 34th Independence Day. As Nos. 344/5. (a) Optd with T **123**.

| | | | |
|---|---|---|---|
| 360 | 35p. black and green | 3·25 | 2·30 |
| 361 | 125p. blue | 3·25 | 2·30 |

(b) Without opt.

| | | | |
|---|---|---|---|
| 361a | 35p. black and green | 1·40 | 60 |

| | | | | |
|---|---|---|---|---|
| 361b | | 125p. blue | 3·00 | 1·20 |

**131** Soldier and Flag of Pashtunistan

**1952.** Obligatory Tax. Pashtunistan Day.

| | | | | |
|---|---|---|---|---|
| 362 | **131** | 35p. red | 80 | 80 |
| 363 | **131** | 125p. blue | 1·20 | 1·20 |

**132** Orderly and Wounded Soldier

**1952.** Obligatory Tax. Red Crescent Day.

| | | | | |
|---|---|---|---|---|
| 364 | **132** | 10p. green | 80 | 65 |

**133**

**1952.** Obligatory Tax. United Nations Day.

| | | | | |
|---|---|---|---|---|
| 365 | **133** | 35p. red | 80 | 65 |
| 366 | **133** | 125p. turquoise | 1·60 | 1·20 |

**134** Staff of Aesculapius

**1952.** Obligatory Tax. 21st Anniv of Faculty of Medicine.

| | | | | |
|---|---|---|---|---|
| 367 | **134** | 35p. brown | 75 | 50 |
| 368 | **134** | 125p. blue | 2·00 | 1·30 |

**135** Stretcher Bearers and Wounded

**1953.** Obligatory Tax. Red Crescent Day.

| | | | | |
|---|---|---|---|---|
| 369 | **135** | 10p. green and brown | 80 | 80 |
| 370 | - | 10p. brown and orange | 80 | 80 |

DESIGN: No. 370, Wounded soldier, orderly and eagle.

**136** Prince Mohamed Nadir

**1953.** Obligatory Tax. Children's Day.

| | | | | |
|---|---|---|---|---|
| 371 | **136** | 35p. orange | 40 | 25 |
| 372 | **136** | 125p. blue | 80 | 60 |

**137** Mohamed Nadir Shah and Flag-bearer

**1953.** 35th Year of Independence. Inscr "1953".

| | | | | |
|---|---|---|---|---|
| 373 | **137** | 35p. green | 40 | 25 |
| 374 | - | 125p. violet | 80 | 60 |

DESIGN—VERT: 125p. Independence Memorial and Mohamed Nadir Shah.

**138** Flags of Afghanistan and Pashtunistan

**1953.** Obligatory Tax. Pashtunistan Day. Inscr "1953".

| | | | | |
|---|---|---|---|---|
| 375 | **138** | 35p. red | 40 | 15 |
| 376 | - | 125p. blue | 80 | 65 |

DESIGN—HORIZ: 125p. Badge of Pashtunistan (26×20 mm).

**139** U.N. Emblem

**1953.** Obligatory Tax. United Nations Day.

| | | | | |
|---|---|---|---|---|
| 377 | **139** | 35p. mauve | 1·00 | 80 |
| 378 | **139** | 125p. blue | 2·10 | 1·50 |

**140** Mohamed Nadir Shah

**1953.** Obligatory Tax. 22nd Anniv of Faculty of Medicine.

| | | | | |
|---|---|---|---|---|
| 379 | **140** | 35p. orange | 1·50 | 1·50 |
| 380 | - | 125p. blue | 3·00 | 3·00 |

DESIGN: 125p. As Type **140** but inscribed "1953" and with French inscription.

No. 379 was wrongly inscribed "23rd" in Arabic (the extreme right-hand figure in the second row of the inscription) and No. 380 was wrongly inscr "XXIII" and had the words "ANNIVERSAIRE" and "MEDECINE" wrongly spelt "ANNIVERAIRE" and "MADECINE". These mistakes were subsequently corrected but the corrected stamps are much rarer than the original issue.

**141** Children's Band and Map of Afghanistan

**1954.** Obligatory Tax. Child Welfare Fund.

| | | | | |
|---|---|---|---|---|
| 381 | **141** | 35p. violet | 65 | 40 |
| 382 | **141** | 125p. blue | 1·80 | 80 |

**142** Mohamed Nadir Shah and Cannon

**1954.** 36th Independence Day.

| | | | | |
|---|---|---|---|---|
| 383 | **142** | 35p. red | 65 | 40 |
| 384 | **142** | 125p. blue | 1·80 | 80 |

**143** Hoisting the Flag

**1954.** Obligatory Tax. Pashtunistan Day.

| | | | | |
|---|---|---|---|---|
| 385 | **143** | 35p. orange | 65 | 40 |
| 386 | **143** | 125p. blue | 1·80 | 80 |

**144**

**1954.** Red Crescent Day.

| | | | | |
|---|---|---|---|---|
| 387 | **144** | 20p. red and blue | 60 | 35 |

**145** U.N. Flag and Map

**1954.** United Nations Day and 9th Anniv of U.N.O.

| | | | | |
|---|---|---|---|---|
| 388 | **145** | 35p. red | 1·20 | 1·20 |
| 389 | **145** | 125p. blue | 3·25 | 2·20 |

**146** Globe and Clasped Hands

**1955.** 10th Anniv of Signing of U.N. Charter.

| | | | | |
|---|---|---|---|---|
| 390 | **146** | 35p. green | 1·00 | 60 |
| 391 | - | 125p. blue | 1·80 | 1·10 |

DESIGN—28½×36 mm. 125p. U.N. emblem and flags.

See also Nos. 403/4.

**147** Amir Sher Ali and Mohamed Zahir Shah

**1955.** 85th Anniv of Postal Service.

| | | | | |
|---|---|---|---|---|
| 392 | **147** | 35p.+15p. red | 1·00 | 60 |
| 393 | **147** | 125p.+25p. grey | 1·90 | 1·10 |

**148** Children on Swing

**1955.** Child Welfare Fund.

| | | | | |
|---|---|---|---|---|
| 394 | **148** | 35p.+15p. green | 1·20 | 75 |
| 395 | **148** | 125p.+25p. violet | 2·50 | 1·20 |

**149** Mohamed Nadir Shah (centre) and brothers

**1955.** 37th Year of Independence.

| | | | | |
|---|---|---|---|---|
| 396 | **149** | 35p. blue | 65 | 40 |
| 397 | **149** | 35p. mauve | 65 | 40 |
| 398 | - | 125p. violet | 1·40 | 90 |
| 399 | - | 125p. purple | 1·40 | 90 |

DESIGN: 125p. Mohamed Zahir Shah and battle scene.

**150**

**1955.** Obligatory Tax. Pashtunistan Day.

| | | | | |
|---|---|---|---|---|
| 400 | **150** | 35p. brown | 60 | 25 |
| 401 | **150** | 125p. green | 1·90 | 60 |

**151** Red Crescent

**1955.** Obligatory Tax. Red Crescent Day.

| | | | | |
|---|---|---|---|---|
| 402 | **151** | 20p. red and grey | 60 | 35 |

**152** U.N. Flag

**1955.** Obligatory Tax. 10th Anniv of United Nations.

| | | | | |
|---|---|---|---|---|
| 403 | **152** | 35p. brown | 90 | 60 |
| 404 | **152** | 125p. blue | 1·80 | 1·10 |

**153** Child on Slide

**1956.** Children's Day.

| | | | | |
|---|---|---|---|---|
| 405 | **153** | 35p.+15p. blue | 90 | 40 |
| 406 | **153** | 140p.+15p. brown | 2·30 | 80 |

**154** Independence Memorial and Mohamed Nadir Shah

**1956.** 38th Year of Independence.

| | | | | |
|---|---|---|---|---|
| 407 | **154** | 35p. green | 60 | 35 |
| 408 | **154** | 140p. blue | 2·30 | 90 |

**155** Exhibition Building

**1956.** International Exhibition, Kabul.

| | | | | |
|---|---|---|---|---|
| 409 | **155** | 50p. brown | 80 | 40 |
| 410 | **155** | 50p. blue | 80 | 40 |

**156** Pashtun Square, Kabul

**1956.** Pashtunistan Day.

| | | | | |
|---|---|---|---|---|
| 411 | **156** | 35p.+15p. violet | 40 | 25 |
| 412 | **156** | 140p.+15p. brown | 1·10 | 75 |

**157** Mohamed Zahir Shah and Crescent

**1956.** Obligatory Tax. Red Crescent Day.

| | | | | |
|---|---|---|---|---|
| 413 | **157** | 20p. green and red | 40 | 25 |

158 Globe and Sun

1956. U.N. Day and 10th Anniv of Admission of Afghanistan into U.N.O.

| | | | | |
|---|---|---|---|---|
| 414 | 158 | 35p.+15p. blue | 1·20 | 1·10 |
| 415 | 158 | 140p.+15p. brown | 2·10 | 1·80 |

1957. Air. As Nos. 339/40, but colours changed.

| | | | | |
|---|---|---|---|---|
| 415a | 119 | 5a. blue | 2·10 | 60 |
| 415b | 119 | 10a. violet | 3·00 | 1·10 |

159 Children on See-saw

1957. Child Welfare Fund.

| | | | | |
|---|---|---|---|---|
| 416 | 159 | 35p.+15p. red | 80 | 60 |
| 417 | 159 | 140p.+15p. blue | 1·60 | 1·50 |

1957. 39th Independence Day. As Nos. 344/5 but 35p. has longer Arabic opt (19 mm) and 125p. optd **39 em Anv**.

| | | | | |
|---|---|---|---|---|
| 418 | 121 | 35p. black and green | 65 | 35 |
| 419 | 121 | 125p. blue | 1·00 | 75 |

162 Pashtu Flag

1957. Pashtunistan Day.

| | | | | |
|---|---|---|---|---|
| 420 | 162 | 50p. red | 1·00 | 60 |
| 421 | 162 | 155p. violet | 1·50 | 1·10 |

No. 421 is inscr "JOURNEE DU PASHTUNISTAN" beneath flag instead of Pushtu characters.

163 Red Crescent Headquarters, Kabul

1957. Obligatory Tax. Red Crescent Day.

| | | | | |
|---|---|---|---|---|
| 422 | 163 | 20p. blue and red | 90 | 60 |

164 U.N. Headquarters, New York

1957. U.N. Day.

| | | | | |
|---|---|---|---|---|
| 423 | 164 | 35p.+15p. brown | 60 | 40 |
| 424 | 164 | 140p.+15p. blue | 1·10 | 1·10 |

165 Buzkashi Game

1957. As stamps of 1951, but colours changed and new value.

| | | | | |
|---|---|---|---|---|
| 425 | 110 | 30p. brown | 40 | 15 |
| 425a | - | 40p. red | 60 | 15 |
| 425b | - | 50p. yellow | 65 | 15 |
| 425c | - | 60p. blue | 80 | 15 |
| 425d | - | 75p. violet | 1·00 | 15 |
| 425e | - | 80p. brown and violet | 1·10 | 15 |
| 425g | 165 | 140p. purple and green | 2·75 | 65 |
| 425f | - | 1a. blue and red | 1·80 | 15 |
| 425k | 118 | 2a. blue | 5·75 | 80 |
| 425h | 118 | 3a. black and orange | 2·75 | 90 |

166 Children Bathing

1958. Child Welfare Fund.

| | | | | |
|---|---|---|---|---|
| 426 | 166 | 35p.+15p. red | 65 | 40 |
| 427 | 166 | 140p.+15p. brown | 80 | 65 |

167 Mohamed Nadir Shah and Old Soldier

1958. 40th Independence Day.

| | | | | |
|---|---|---|---|---|
| 428 | 167 | 35p. green | 40 | 25 |
| 429 | 167 | 140p. brown | 1·20 | 1·00 |

168 Exhibition Buildings

1958. International Exhibition, Kabul.

| | | | | |
|---|---|---|---|---|
| 430 | 168 | 35p. green | 50 | 25 |
| 431 | 168 | 140p. red | 1·20 | 1·00 |

169

1958. Pashtunistan Day.

| | | | | |
|---|---|---|---|---|
| 432 | 169 | 35p.+15p. turquoise | 40 | 25 |
| 433 | 169 | 140p.+15p. brown | 1·00 | 65 |

170 President Bayar

1958. Visit of Turkish President.

| | | | | |
|---|---|---|---|---|
| 434 | 170 | 50p. blue | 35 | 15 |
| 435 | 170 | 100p. brown | 65 | 35 |

171 Red Crescent and Map of Afghanistan

1958. Obligatory Tax. Red Crescent Day.

| | | | | |
|---|---|---|---|---|
| 436 | 171 | 25p. red and green | 40 | 15 |

172

1958. "Atoms for Peace".

| | | | | |
|---|---|---|---|---|
| 437 | 172 | 50p. blue | 60 | 50 |
| 438 | 172 | 100p. purple | 90 | 65 |

173 Flags of U.N. and Afghanistan

1958. U.N. Day.

| | | | | |
|---|---|---|---|---|
| 439 | 173 | 50p. multicoloured | 65 | 65 |
| 440 | 173 | 100p. multicoloured | 1·40 | 1·20 |

174 UNESCO Headquarters, Paris

1958. Inauguration of UNESCO Headquarters Building, Paris.

| | | | | |
|---|---|---|---|---|
| 441 | 174 | 50p. green | 80 | 65 |
| 442 | 174 | 100p. brown | 80 | 80 |

175 Globe and Torch

1958. 10th Anniv of Declaration of Human Rights.

| | | | | |
|---|---|---|---|---|
| 443 | 175 | 50p. mauve | 50 | 50 |
| 444 | 175 | 100p. purple | 1·00 | 1·20 |

176 Tug-of-War

1959. Child Welfare Fund.

| | | | | |
|---|---|---|---|---|
| 445 | 176 | 35p.+15p. purple | 60 | 35 |
| 446 | 176 | 165p.+15p. mauve | 1·20 | 50 |

177 Mohamed Nadir Shah and Flags

1959. 41st Independence Day.

| | | | | |
|---|---|---|---|---|
| 447 | 177 | 35p. red | 60 | 50 |
| 448 | 177 | 165p. violet | 1·50 | 65 |

178 Tribal Dance

1959. Pashtunistan Day.

| | | | | |
|---|---|---|---|---|
| 449 | 178 | 35p.+15p. green | 60 | 35 |
| 450 | 178 | 165p.+15p. orange | 1·20 | 75 |

179 Badge-sellers

1959. Obligatory Tax. Red Crescent Day.

| | | | | |
|---|---|---|---|---|
| 451 | 179 | 25p. red and violet | 40 | 15 |

180 Horseman

1959. United Nations Day.

| | | | | |
|---|---|---|---|---|
| 452 | 180 | 35p.+15p. orange | 35 | 25 |
| 453 | 180 | 165p.+15p. green | 65 | 40 |

181 "Uprooted Tree"

1960. World Refugee Year.

| | | | | |
|---|---|---|---|---|
| 454 | 181 | 50p. orange | 25 | 25 |
| 455 | 181 | 165p. blue | 35 | 25 |

**MS**455a 108×80 mm. Nos. 454/5. Imperf 5·75 7·75

**MS**455b As last, colours transposed 7·50 9·00

182 Buzkashi Game

183 Buzkashi Game

1960

| | | | | |
|---|---|---|---|---|
| 456 | 182 | 25p. pink | 60 | 25 |
| 457 | 182 | 25p. violet | 1·00 | 25 |
| 458 | 182 | 25p. olive | 2·75 | 25 |
| 459 | 182 | 50p. turquoise | 1·40 | 60 |
| 460 | 182 | 50p. blue | 50 | 35 |
| 460a | 182 | 50p. orange | 50 | 35 |
| 461 | 183 | 100p. olive | 80 | 25 |
| 462 | 183 | 150p. orange | 65 | 35 |
| 463 | 183 | 175p. brown | 2·50 | 50 |
| 464 | 183 | 2a. green | 1·50 | 1·10 |

184 Children receiving Ball

1960. Child Welfare Fund.

| | | | | |
|---|---|---|---|---|
| 465 | 184 | 75p.+25p. blue | 90 | 35 |
| 466 | 184 | 175p.+25p. green | 1·80 | 50 |

185 Douglas DC-6 over Mountains

1960. Air.

| | | | | |
|---|---|---|---|---|
| 467 | 185 | 75p. violet | 65 | 25 |
| 468 | 185 | 125p. blue | 80 | 40 |
| 469 | 185 | 5a. olive | 1·50 | 90 |

186 Independence Monument, Kabul

1960. 42nd Independence Day.

| | | | | |
|---|---|---|---|---|
| 470 | 186 | 50p. blue | 40 | 25 |
| 471 | 186 | 175p. mauve | 1·10 | 40 |

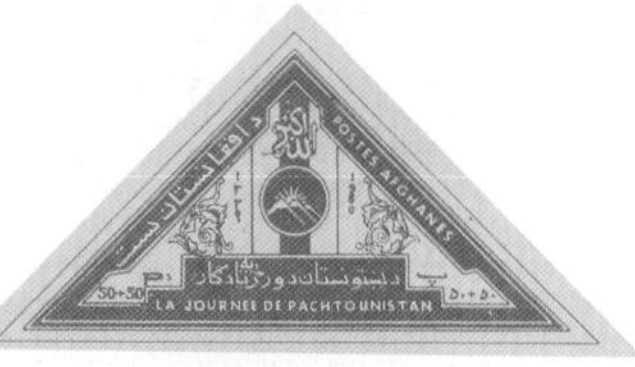
187

1960. Pashtunistan Day.

| | | | | |
|---|---|---|---|---|
| 472 | 187 | 50p.+50p. red | 60 | 30 |
| 473 | 187 | 175p.+50p. blue | 1·40 | 1·10 |

188 Insecticide Sprayer

**1960.** Anti-Malaria Campaign Day.

474 **188** 50p.+50p. orange 1·30 1·20
475 **188** 175p.+50p. brown 3·50 2·75

**189** Mohamed Zahir Shah

**1960.** King's 46th Birthday.

476 **189** 50p. brown 65 25
477 **189** 150p. red 1·60 60

**190** Ambulance

**1960.** Red Crescent Day.

478 **190** 50p.+50p. violet & red 65 50
479 **190** 175p.+50p. blue & red 1·60 1·00

**191** Teacher with Globe and Children

**1960.** Literacy Campaign.

480 **191** 50p. mauve 40 35
481 **191** 100p. green 1·10 50

**192** Globe and Flags

**1960.** U.N. Day.

482 **192** 50p. purple 25 15
483 **192** 175p. blue 1·00 65
**MS**483a 128×86 mm. Nos. 482/3. Imperf 6·25 4·50

**1960.** Olympic Games, Rome. Optd **1960** in figures and in Arabic and Olympic Rings.

484 **183** 175p. brown 1·80 2·10
**MS**484a 86×62 mm. No. 484. Imperf 6·25 8·25

**1960.** World Refugee Year. Nos. 454/5 surch **+25 Ps.**

485 **181** 50p.+25p. orange 1·80 1·80
486 **181** 165p.+25p. blue 1·80 1·80
**MS**486a 108×80 mm. Nos. 485/6. Imperf 6·25 6·50

**195** Mir Wais Nika (patriot)

**1960.** Mir Wais Nika Commemoration.

487 **195** 50p. mauve 65 40
488 **195** 175p. blue 1·20 50
**MS**488a 108×78 mm. Nos. 487/8. Imperf 3·75 3·75

The very numerous issues of Afghanistan which we do not list appeared between 21 April 1961 and 15 March 1964 (both dates inclusive), and were made available to the philatelic trade by an agency acting under the authority of a contract granted by the Afghanistan Government.

It later became evident that token supplies were only placed on sale in Kabul for a few hours and some of these sets contained stamps of very low denominations for which there was no possible postal use.

When the contract for the production of these stamps expired in 1963 it was not renewed and the Afghanistan Government set up a Philatelic Advisory Board to formulate stamp policy. The issues from No. 489 onwards were made in usable denominations and placed on sale without restriction in Afghanistan and distributed to the trade by the Philatelic Department of the G.P.O. in Kabul.

Issues not listed here will be found recorded in the Appendix at the end of this country. It is believed that some of the higher values from the agency sets were utilised for postage in late 1979.

**196** Band Amir Lake

**1961**

489 **196** 3a. blue 50 25
490 **196** 10a. purple 1·30 1·20

**197** Independence Memorial

**1963.** 45th Independence Day.

491 **197** 25p. green 15 15
492 **197** 50p. orange 35 25
493 **197** 150p. mauve 50 35

**198** Tribesmen

**1963.** Pashtunistan Day.

494 **198** 25p. violet 15 15
495 **198** 50p. blue 25 25
496 **198** 150p. brown 65 40

**199** Assembly Building

**1963.** National Assembly.

497 **199** 25p. brown 15 15
498 **199** 50p. red 15 15
499 **199** 75p. brown 25 15
500 **199** 100p. olive 25 15
501 **199** 125p. lilac 40 15

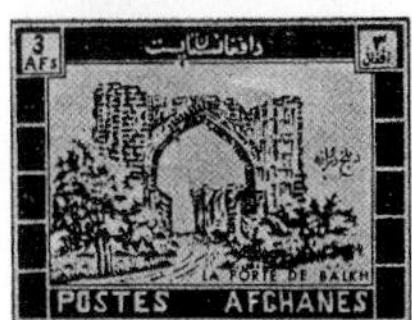


**200** Balkh Gate

**1963**

502 **200** 3a. brown 1·00 25

**201** Kemal Ataturk

**1963.** 25th Death Anniv of Kemal Ataturk.

503 **201** 1a. blue 15 15
504 **201** 3a. violet 65 50

**202** Mohamed Zahir Shah

**1963.** King's 49th Birthday.

505 **202** 25p. green 15 15
506 **202** 50p. grey 25 15
507 **202** 75p. red 35 25
508 **202** 100p. brown 50 25

**203** Afghan Stamp of 1878

**1964.** "Philately". Stamp Day.

509 **203** 1a.25 black, green & gold 25 15
510 **203** 5a. black, red and gold 60 40

**204** Kabul International Airport

**1964.** Air. Inauguration of Kabul Int Airport.

511 **204** 10a. green and purple 80 25
512 **204** 20a. purple and green 1·00 40
513 **204** 50a. turquoise and blue 2·75 1·20

**205** Kandahar International Airport

**1964.** Air. Inauguration of Kandahar Int Airport.

514 **205** 7a.75 brown 65 40
515 **205** 9a.25 blue 90 80
516 **205** 10a.50 green 1·20 1·00
517 **205** 13a.75 red 1·40 1·10

**206** Unisphere and Flags

**1964.** New York World's Fair.

518 **206** 6a. black, red and green 25 15

**207** "Flame of Freedom"

**1964.** 1st U.N. Human Rights Seminar, Kabul.

519 **207** 3a.75 multicoloured 25 15

**208** Snow Leopard

**1964.** Afghan Wildlife.

520 **208** 25p. blue and yellow 1·80 25
521 - 50p. green and red 2·10 25
522 - 75p. purple and blue 2·50 25
523 - 5a. brown and green 2·75 90

ANIMALS—VERT: 50p. Ibex. HORIZ: 75p. Argali; 5a. Yak.

**209** Herat

**1964.** Tourist Publicity. Inscr "1964".

524 **209** 25p. brown and blue 15 15
525 - 75p. blue and ochre 25 15
526 - 3a. black, red and green 50 25

DESIGNS—VERT: 75p. Tomb of Gowhar Shad, Herat. HORIZ: 3a. Map and flag.

**210** Hurdling

**1964.** Olympic Games, Tokyo.

527 **210** 25p. sepia, red and bistre 15 10
528 - 1a. sepia, red and blue 15 15
529 - 3a.75 sepia, red and green 40 25
530 - 5a. sepia, red and brown 50 35
**MS**530a 95×95 mm. Nos. 527/30. Imperf. (sold at 15a.) 1·20 1·20

DESIGNS—VERT: 1a. Diving. HORIZ: 3a.75, Wrestling; 5a. Football.

**211** Afghan Flag

**1964.** 46th Independence Day.

531 **211** 25p. multicoloured 15 15
532 **211** 75p. multicoloured 35 15

On the above the Pushtu inscription "33rd Anniversary" is blocked out in gold.

**212** Pashtu Flag

**1964.** Pashtunistan Day.

533 **212** 100p. multicoloured 25 15

**213** Mohamed Zahir Shah

**1964.** King's 50th Birthday.

534 **213** 1a.25 green and gold 25 15
535 **213** 3a.75 red and gold 40 40
536 **213** 50a. black and gold 3·50 2·30

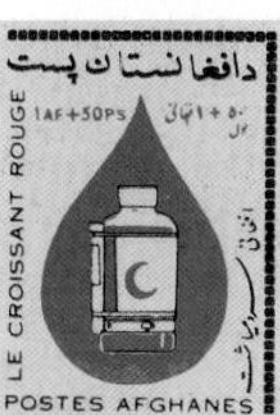


**214** "Blood Transfusion"

**1964.** Red Crescent Day.

537 **214** 1a.+50p. red and black 35 25

**215** Badges of Afghanistan and U.N.

**1964.** U.N. Day.

538 **215** 5a. blue, black and gold 25 15

**216** Doves with Necklace

**1964.** Women's Day.

| | | | | |
|---|---|---|---|---|
| 539 | **216** | 25p. blue, green and pink | 60 | 35 |
| 540 | **216** | 75p. blue, green & lt blue | 90 | 40 |
| 541 | **216** | 1a. blue, green and silver | 1·20 | 60 |

**217** M. Jami

**1964.** 550th Birth Anniv of Mowlana Jami (poet).

| | | | | |
|---|---|---|---|---|
| 542 | **217** | 1a.50 cream, green & blk | 1·00 | 80 |

**218** Scaly-bellied Green Woodpecker

**1965.** Birds. Multicoloured.

| | | | |
|---|---|---|---|
| 543 | 1a.25 Type **218** | 3·00 | 40 |
| 544 | 3a.75 Lanceolated jay (vert) | 5·25 | 90 |
| 545 | 5a. Himalayan monal pheasant (vert) | 6·25 | 2·00 |

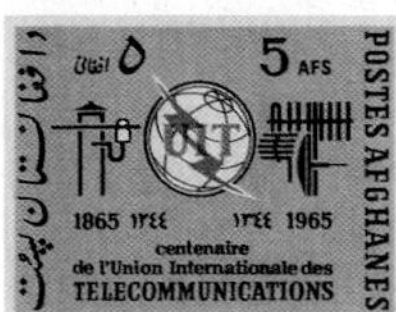


**219** I.T.U. Emblem and Symbols

**1965.** Centenary of I.T.U.

| | | | | |
|---|---|---|---|---|
| 546 | **219** | 5a. black, red and blue | 50 | 35 |

**220** "The Red City"

**1965.** Tourist Publicity. Inscr "1965". Mult.

| | | | |
|---|---|---|---|
| 547 | 1a. Type **220** | 25 | 10 |
| 548 | 3a.75 Bami Yan (valley and mountains) | 40 | 15 |
| 549 | 5a. Band-E-Amir (lake and mountains) | 60 | 25 |

**221** I.C.Y. Emblem

**1965.** International Co-operation Year.

| | | | | |
|---|---|---|---|---|
| 550 | **221** | 5a. multicoloured | 50 | 35 |

**222** Douglas DC-3 and Emblem

**1965.** 10th Anniv of Afghan Airlines (ARIANA).

| | | | | |
|---|---|---|---|---|
| 551 | **222** | 1a.25 multicoloured | 35 | 10 |
| 552 | - | 5a. black, blue & purple | 90 | 15 |
| 553 | - | 10a. multicoloured | 1·60 | 60 |
| **MS**553a | | 90×90 mm. Nos. 551/3. Imperf | 3·00 | 3·00 |

DESIGNS: 5a. Convair CV 240; 10a. Douglas DC-6A.

**223** Mohamed Nadir Shah

**1965.** 47th Independence Day.

| | | | | |
|---|---|---|---|---|
| 554 | **223** | 1a. brown, black & green | 40 | 15 |

**224** Pashtu Flag

**1965.** Pashtunistan Day.

| | | | | |
|---|---|---|---|---|
| 555 | **224** | 1a. multicoloured | 40 | 15 |

**225** Promulgation of New Constitution

**1965.** New Constitution.

| | | | | |
|---|---|---|---|---|
| 556 | **225** | 1a.50 black and green | 40 | 15 |

**226** Mohamed Zahir Shah

**1965.** King's 51st Birthday.

| | | | | |
|---|---|---|---|---|
| 557 | **226** | 1a.25 brown, blue & pink | 25 | 15 |
| 558 | **226** | 6a. indigo, purple & blue | 40 | 35 |

See also Nos. 579/80, 606/7 and 637/8.

**227** First Aid Post

**1965.** Red Crescent Day.

| | | | | |
|---|---|---|---|---|
| 559 | **227** | 1a.50+50 brn, grn & red | 35 | 25 |

**228** U.N. and Afghan Flags

**1965.** U.N. Day.

| | | | | |
|---|---|---|---|---|
| 560 | **228** | 5a. multicoloured | 25 | 15 |

**229** Fat-tailed Gecko

**1966.** Reptiles. Multicoloured.

| | | | |
|---|---|---|---|
| 561 | 3a. Type **229** | 1·00 | 25 |
| 562 | 4a. "Agama caucasica" (lizard) | 1·20 | 35 |
| 563 | 8a. "Testudo horsfieldi" (tortoise) | 2·00 | 65 |

**230** Cotton

**1966.** Agriculture Day. Multicoloured.

| | | | |
|---|---|---|---|
| 564 | 1a. Type **230** | 90 | 25 |
| 565 | 5a. Silkworm moth (caterpillar) | 1·80 | 35 |
| 566 | 7a. Oxen | 2·75 | 50 |

**231** Footballer

**1966.** World Cup Football Championship, England.

| | | | | |
|---|---|---|---|---|
| 567 | **231** | 2a. black and red | 75 | 25 |
| 568 | **231** | 6a. black and blue | 1·30 | 35 |
| 569 | **231** | 12a. black and brown | 2·75 | 75 |

**232** Independence Memorial

**1966.** Independence Day.

| | | | | |
|---|---|---|---|---|
| 570 | **232** | 1a. multicoloured | 35 | 25 |
| 571 | **232** | 3a. multicoloured | 90 | 35 |

**233** Pashtu Flag

**1966.** Pashtunistan Day.

| | | | | |
|---|---|---|---|---|
| 572 | **233** | 1a. blue | 60 | 25 |

**234** Founding Members

**1966.** Red Crescent Day.

| | | | | |
|---|---|---|---|---|
| 573 | **234** | 2a.+1a. green and red | 35 | 25 |
| 574 | **234** | 5a.+1a. brown & mve | 75 | 35 |

**235** Map of Afghanistan

**1966.** Tourist Publicity. Multicoloured.

| | | | |
|---|---|---|---|
| 575 | 2a. Type **235** | 25 | 25 |
| 576 | 4a. Bagh-i-Bala, former Palace of Abdur Rahman | 50 | 35 |
| 577 | 8a. Tomb of Abdur Rahman, Kabul | 75 | 75 |
| **MS**578 | 111×80 mm. Nos. 575/7. Imperf | 2·10 | 2·10 |

DESIGN: 6a. I.T.Y. emblem on map of Afghanistan.

**1966.** King's 52nd Birthday. Portrait similar to T **226** but with position of inscr changed. Dated "1966".

| | | | |
|---|---|---|---|
| 579 | 1a. green | 25 | 25 |
| 580 | 5a. brown | 60 | 35 |

**236** Mohamed Zahir Shah and U.N. Emblem

**1966.** U.N. Day. Inscr "20TH ANNIVERSAIRE DES REFUGIES".

| | | | | |
|---|---|---|---|---|
| 581 | **236** | 5a. green, brown & emer | 40 | 15 |
| 582 | **236** | 10a. red, green & yellow | 80 | 15 |

**237** Children Dancing

**1966.** Child Welfare Day.

| | | | | |
|---|---|---|---|---|
| 583 | **237** | 1a.+1a. red and green | 15 | 10 |
| 584 | **237** | 3a.+2a. brown & yell | 35 | 15 |
| 585 | **237** | 7a.+3a. green & purple | 55 | 35 |

**238** Construction of Power Station

**1967.** Afghan Industrial Development. Mult.

| | | | |
|---|---|---|---|
| 586 | 2a. Type **238** | 25 | 25 |
| 587 | 5a. Handwoven carpet (vert) | 25 | 25 |
| 588 | 8a. Cement works | 50 | 35 |

**239** UNESCO Emblem

**1967.** 20th Anniv (1966) of UNESCO.

| | | | | |
|---|---|---|---|---|
| 589 | **239** | 2a. multicoloured | 25 | 15 |
| 590 | **239** | 6a. multicoloured | 40 | 15 |
| 591 | **239** | 12a. multicoloured | 1·00 | 25 |

**240** I.T.Y. Emblem

**1967.** International Tourist Year.

| | | | | |
|---|---|---|---|---|
| 592 | **240** | 2a. black, blue and yellow | 25 | 25 |
| 593 | - | 6a. black, blue and brown | 50 | 25 |
| **MS**594 | | 110×70 mm. Nos. 592/3. Imperf. (sold at 10a.) | 1·20 | 1·20 |

DESIGN: 6a. I.T.Y. emblem on map of Afghanistan.

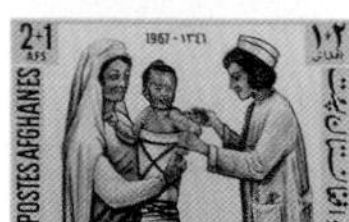


**241** Inoculation

**1967.** Anti-tuberculosis Campaign.

| | | | | |
|---|---|---|---|---|
| 595 | **241** | 2a.+1a. black & yellow | 25 | 25 |
| 596 | **241** | 5a.+2a. brown & pink | 65 | 35 |

**242** Hydroelectric Power Station, Doruntа

**1967.** Development of Electricity for Agriculture.

| | | | | |
|---|---|---|---|---|
| 597 | **242** | 1a. lilac and green | 15 | 15 |
| 598 | - | 6a. turquoise and brown | 40 | 25 |
| 599 | - | 8a. blue and purple | 60 | 40 |

DESIGNS—VERT: 6a. Dam. HORIZ: 8a. Reservoir, Jalalabad.

**243** Rhesus Macaque

**1967.** Wildlife.

| | | | | |
|---|---|---|---|---|
| 600 | **243** | 2a. blue and buff | 75 | 25 |
| 601 | - | 6a. sepia and green | 1·30 | 35 |
| 602 | - | 12a. brown and blue | 2·10 | 80 |

ANIMALS—HORIZ: 6a. Striped hyena; 12a. Goitred gazelles.

**244** "Saving the Guns at Maiwand" (after R. Caton Woodville)

**1967.** Independence Day.

| | | | | |
|---|---|---|---|---|
| 603 | **244** | 1a. brown and red | 35 | 25 |
| 604 | **244** | 2a. brown and mauve | 60 | 25 |

**245** Pashtu Dancers

**1967.** Pashtunistan Day.

| | | | | |
|---|---|---|---|---|
| 605 | **245** | 2a. violet and purple | 60 | 25 |

**1967.** King's 53rd Birthday. Portrait similar to T **226** but with position of inscr changed. Dated "1967".

| | | | |
|---|---|---|---|
| 606 | 2a. brown | 15 | 15 |
| 607 | 8a. blue | 65 | 35 |

**246** Red Crescent

**1967.** Red Crescent Day.

| | | | | |
|---|---|---|---|---|
| 608 | **246** | 3a.+1a. red, blk & ol | 25 | 25 |
| 609 | **246** | 5a.+1a. red, blk & blue | 40 | 25 |

**247** U.N. Emblem and Fireworks

**1967.** U.N. Day.

| | | | | |
|---|---|---|---|---|
| 610 | **247** | 10a. multicoloured | 75 | 35 |

**248** Wrestling

**1967.** Olympic Games, Mexico City.

| | | | | |
|---|---|---|---|---|
| 611 | **248** | 4a. purple and green | 50 | 25 |
| 612 | - | 6a. brown and red | 1·00 | 25 |
| **MS**613 | | 100×65 mm. Nos. 611/12 | 2·10 | 2·10 |

DESIGN: 6a. Wrestling throw.

**249** Said Jamal-ud-Din Afghan

**1967.** 70th Death Anniv of Said Afghan.

| | | | | |
|---|---|---|---|---|
| 614 | **249** | 1a. purple | 25 | 25 |
| 615 | **249** | 5a. brown | 40 | 25 |

**250** Bronze Vase

**1967.** Archaeological Treasures (11th–12th century Ghasnavide era).

| | | | | |
|---|---|---|---|---|
| 616 | **250** | 3a. brown and green | 35 | 15 |
| 617 | - | 7a. green and yellow | 65 | 25 |
| **MS**618 | | 65×100 mm. Nos. 616/17. Imperf | 3·00 | 3·00 |

DESIGN: 7a. Bronze jar.

**251** W.H.O. Emblem

**1968.** 20th Anniv of W.H.O.

| | | | | |
|---|---|---|---|---|
| 619 | **251** | 2a. blue and bistre | 25 | 25 |
| 620 | **251** | 7a. blue and red | 50 | 35 |

**252** Karakul Sheep

**1968.** Agricultural Day.

| | | | | |
|---|---|---|---|---|
| 621 | **252** | 1a. black and yellow | 25 | 25 |
| 622 | **252** | 6a. brown, black and blue | 1·00 | 35 |
| 623 | **252** | 12a. brown, sepia & blue | 1·60 | 50 |

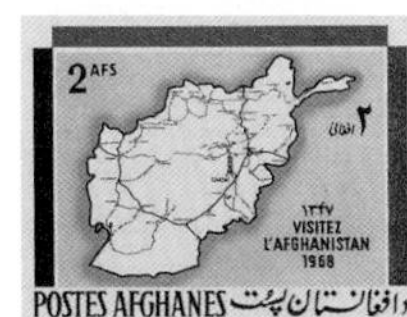

**253** Road Map of Afghanistan

**1968.** Tourist Publicity. Multicoloured.

| | | | |
|---|---|---|---|
| 624 | 2a. Type **253** | 25 | 25 |
| 625 | 3a. Victory Tower, Ghazni (21×31 mm) | 35 | 25 |
| 626 | 16a. Mausoleum, Ghazni (21×31 mm) | 1·20 | 60 |

**254** Queen Humaira

**1968.** Mothers' Day.

| | | | | |
|---|---|---|---|---|
| 627 | **254** | 2a.+2a. brown | 35 | 25 |
| 628 | **254** | 7a.+2a. green | 90 | 60 |

**255** Cinereous Vulture

**1968.** Wild Birds. Multicoloured.

| | | | |
|---|---|---|---|
| 629 | 1a. Type **255** | 1·80 | 65 |
| 630 | 6a. Eagle owl | 4·25 | 2·00 |
| 631 | 7a. Greater flamingos | 6·25 | 2·30 |

**256** "Pig-sticking"

**1968.** Olympic Games, Mexico. Multicoloured.

| | | | |
|---|---|---|---|
| 632 | 2a. Olympic flame and rings (21×31 mm) | 35 | 15 |
| 633 | 8a. Type **256** | 65 | 40 |
| 634 | 12a. Buzkashi game | 1·10 | 65 |

**257** Flowers on Army Truck

**1968.** Independence Day.

| | | | | |
|---|---|---|---|---|
| 635 | **257** | 6a. multicoloured | 50 | 25 |

**258** Pashtu Flag

**1968.** Pashtunistan Day.

| | | | | |
|---|---|---|---|---|
| 636 | **258** | 3a. multicoloured | 45 | 25 |

**1968.** King's 54th Birthday. Portrait similar to T **226** but differently arranged and in smaller size (21×31 mm).

| | | | |
|---|---|---|---|
| 637 | 2a. blue | 25 | 25 |
| 638 | 8a. brown | 60 | 35 |

**259** Red Crescent

**1968.** Red Crescent Day.

| | | | | |
|---|---|---|---|---|
| 639 | **259** | 4a.+1a. multicoloured | 60 | 25 |

**260** Human Rights Emblem

**1968.** U.N. Day and Human Rights Year.

| | | | | |
|---|---|---|---|---|
| 640 | **260** | 1a. brown, bistre & green | 25 | 25 |
| 641 | **260** | 2a. black, bistre & violet | 25 | 25 |
| 642 | **260** | 6a. violet, bistre & purple | 50 | 25 |
| **MS**643 | | 101×65 mm. **260** 10a. orange, bistre and purple. Imperf | 1·80 | 1·80 |

**261** Maolala Djalalodine Balkhi

**1968.** 695th Death Anniv of Maolala Djalalodine Balkhi (historian).

| | | | | |
|---|---|---|---|---|
| 644 | **261** | 4a. mauve and green | 35 | 25 |

**262** Temple Painting

**1969.** Archaeological Treasures (Bagram era).

| | | | | |
|---|---|---|---|---|
| 645 | **262** | 1a. red, yellow and green | 35 | 25 |
| 646 | - | 3a. purple and violet | 90 | 25 |
| **MS**647 | | 101×66 mm. Nos. 6545/6. Imperf. (sold at 10a.) | 1·60 | 1·60 |

DESIGN: 3a. Carved vessel.

**263** I.L.O. Emblem

**1969.** 50th Anniv of I.L.O.

| | | | | |
|---|---|---|---|---|
| 648 | **263** | 5a. black and yellow | 35 | 25 |
| 649 | **263** | 8a. black and blue | 60 | 35 |

**264** Red Cross Emblems

**1969.** 50th Anniv of League of Red Cross Societies.

| | | | | |
|---|---|---|---|---|
| 650 | **264** | 3a.+1a. multicoloured | 65 | 35 |
| 651 | **264** | 5a.+1a. multicoloured | 80 | 35 |

On Nos. 650/1 the commemorative inscr in English and Pushtu for the 50th anniv of the League of Red Cross Societies has been obliterated by gold bars.

**266** Mother and Child

**1969.** Mothers' Day.

| | | | | |
|---|---|---|---|---|
| 654 | **266** | 1a.+1a. brown & yell | 25 | 25 |
| 655 | **266** | 4a.+1a. violet & mve | 40 | 35 |
| **MS**656 | | 121×81 mm. Nos. 654/5. Imperf. (sold at 10a.) | 2·10 | 2·10 |

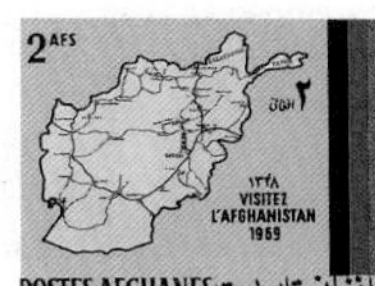

**267** Road Map of Afghanistan

**1969.** Tourist Publicity. Badakshan and Pamir Region. Multicoloured.

| | | | | |
|---|---|---|---|---|
| 657 | **266** | 2a. Type **267** | 60 | 25 |
| 658 | **266** | 4a. Pamir landscape | 65 | 35 |
| 659 | **266** | 7a. Mountain mule transport | 1·10 | 65 |
| **MS**660 | | 136×90 mm. Nos. 657/9. Imperf (sold at 15a.) | 2·50 | 2·50 |

**268** Bust (Hadda era)

**1969.** Archaeological Discoveries. Multicoloured.

| | | | |
|---|---|---|---|
| 661 | 1a. Type **268** | 15 | 10 |
| 662 | 5a. Vase and jug (Bagram period) | 40 | 15 |
| 663 | 10a. Statuette (Bagram period) | 65 | 35 |

**269** Mohamed Zahir Shah and Queen Humaira

**1969.** Independence Day.

| | | | | |
|---|---|---|---|---|
| 664 | **269** | 5a. red, blue and gold | 40 | 25 |
| 665 | **269** | 10a. green, purple & gold | 75 | 40 |

**270** Map and Rising Sun

**1969.** Pashtunistan Day.

| | | | | |
|---|---|---|---|---|
| 666 | **270** | 2a. red and blue | 25 | 15 |

**271** Mohamed Zahir Shah

**1969.** King's 55th Birthday.

| | | | | |
|---|---|---|---|---|
| 667 | **271** | 2a. multicoloured | 25 | 10 |
| 668 | **271** | 6a. multicoloured | 60 | 25 |

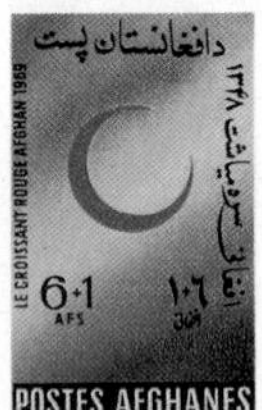

**272** Red Crescent

**1969.** Red Crescent Day.

| | | | | |
|---|---|---|---|---|
| 669 | **272** | 6a.+1a. multicoloured | 80 | 25 |

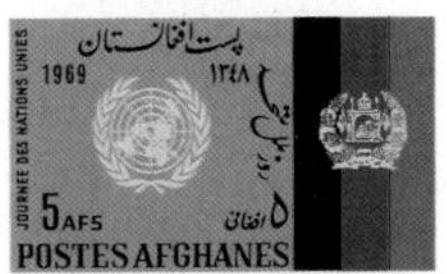

**273** U.N. Emblem, Afghan Arms and Flag

**1969.** United Nations Day.

| | | | | |
|---|---|---|---|---|
| 670 | **273** | 5a. multicoloured | 80 | 25 |

**274** I.T.U. Emblem

**1969.** World Telecommunications Day.

| | | | | |
|---|---|---|---|---|
| 671 | **274** | 6a. multicoloured | 35 | 25 |
| 672 | **274** | 12a. multicoloured | 75 | 40 |

**275** Indian Crested Porcupine

**1969.** Wild Animals. Multicoloured.

| | | | | |
|---|---|---|---|---|
| 673 | **274** | 1a. Type **275** | 50 | 35 |
| 674 | **274** | 3a. Wild boar | 1·20 | 40 |
| 675 | **274** | 8a. Bactrian red deer | 1·60 | 50 |

**276** Footprint on the Moon

**1969.** 1st Man on the Moon.

| | | | | |
|---|---|---|---|---|
| 676 | **276** | 1a. multicoloured | 25 | 25 |
| 677 | **276** | 3a. multicoloured | 35 | 25 |
| 678 | **276** | 6a. multicoloured | 50 | 25 |
| 679 | **276** | 10a. multicoloured | 75 | 40 |

**277** "Cancer the Crab"

**1970.** W.H.O. "Fight Cancer" Day.

| | | | | |
|---|---|---|---|---|
| 680 | **277** | 2a. red, dp green & green | 25 | 25 |
| 681 | **277** | 6a. red, deep blue & blue | 50 | 25 |

**278** Mirza Bedel

**1970.** 250th Death Anniv of Mirza Abdul Quader Bedel (poet).

| | | | | |
|---|---|---|---|---|
| 682 | **278** | 5a. multicoloured | 40 | 15 |

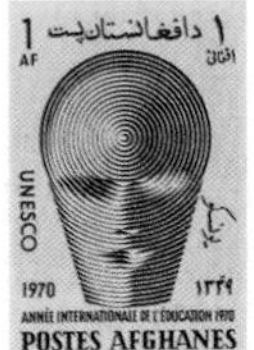

**279** I.E.Y. Emblem

**1970.** International Education Year.

| | | | | |
|---|---|---|---|---|
| 683 | **279** | 1a. black | 25 | 25 |
| 684 | **279** | 6a. red | 40 | 25 |
| 685 | **279** | 12a. green | 90 | 40 |

**280** Mother and Child

**1970.** Mothers' Day.

| | | | | |
|---|---|---|---|---|
| 686 | **280** | 6a. multicoloured | 35 | 25 |

**281** U.N. Emblem, Scales and Satellite

**1970.** 25th Anniv of United Nations.

| | | | | |
|---|---|---|---|---|
| 687 | **281** | 4a. blue, dp blue & yellow | 25 | 25 |
| 688 | **281** | 6a. blue, deep blue & red | 40 | 25 |

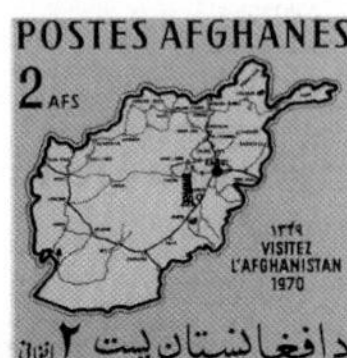

**282** Road Map of Afghanistan with Location of Sites

**1970.** Tourist Publicity. Inscr "1970". Mult.

| | | | | |
|---|---|---|---|---|
| 689 | **282** | 2a. black, green and blue | 15 | 15 |
| 690 | - | 3a. multicoloured | 25 | 15 |
| 691 | - | 7a. multicoloured | 60 | 25 |

DESIGNS (36×26 mm): 3a. Lakeside mosque, Kabul; 7a. Arch of Paghman.

**283** Common Quail

**1970.** Wild Birds. Multicoloured.

| | | | |
|---|---|---|---|
| 692 | 2a. Type **283** | 2·10 | 65 |
| 693 | 4a. Golden eagle | 4·00 | 1·00 |
| 694 | 6a. Common pheasant | 5·25 | 1·60 |

**284** Shah Reviewing Troops

**1970.** Independence Day.

| | | | | |
|---|---|---|---|---|
| 695 | **284** | 8a. multicoloured | 40 | 25 |

**285** Group of Pashtus

**1970.** Pashtunistan Day.

| | | | | |
|---|---|---|---|---|
| 696 | **285** | 2a. blue and red | 40 | 25 |

**286** Mohamed Zahir Shah

**1970.** King's 56th Birthday.

| | | | | |
|---|---|---|---|---|
| 697 | **286** | 3a. violet and green | 25 | 25 |
| 698 | **286** | 7a. purple and blue | 75 | 35 |

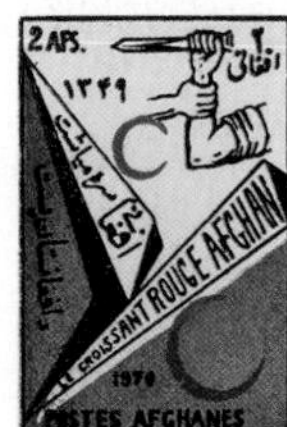

**287** Red Crescent Emblems

**1970.** Red Crescent Day.

| | | | | |
|---|---|---|---|---|
| 699 | **287** | 2a. black, red and gold | 25 | 15 |

**288** U.N. Emblem and Plaque

**1970.** United Nations Day.

| | | | | |
|---|---|---|---|---|
| 700 | **288** | 1a. multicoloured | 25 | 25 |
| 701 | **288** | 5a. multicoloured | 25 | 25 |

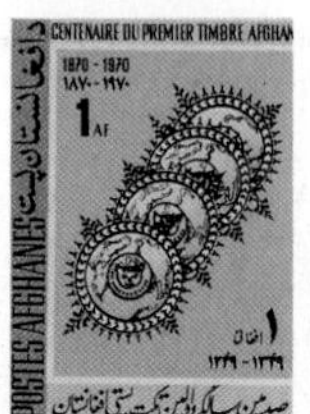

**289** Afghan Stamps of 1871

**1970.** Centenary of First Afghan Stamps.

| | | | | |
|---|---|---|---|---|
| 702 | **289** | 1a. black, blue & orange | 35 | 25 |
| 703 | **289** | 4a. black, yellow & blue | 60 | 25 |
| 704 | **289** | 12a. black, blue and lilac | 1·00 | 40 |

**290** Global Emblem

**1971.** World Telecommunications Day.

| | | | | |
|---|---|---|---|---|
| 705 | **290** | 12a. multicoloured | 65 | 40 |

**291** "Callimorpha principalis"

**1971.** Butterflies and Moths. Multicoloured.

| | | | |
|---|---|---|---|
| 706 | 1a. Type **291** | 1·30 | 60 |
| 707 | 3a. "Epizygaenella afghana" | 2·75 | 1·20 |
| 708 | 5a. "Parnassius autocrator" | 4·00 | 1·80 |

**292** Lower half of old Kushan Statue

**1971.** UNESCO Kushan Seminar.

| | | | | |
|---|---|---|---|---|
| 709 | **292** | 6a. violet and yellow | 50 | 25 |
| 710 | **292** | 10a. purple and blue | 80 | 35 |

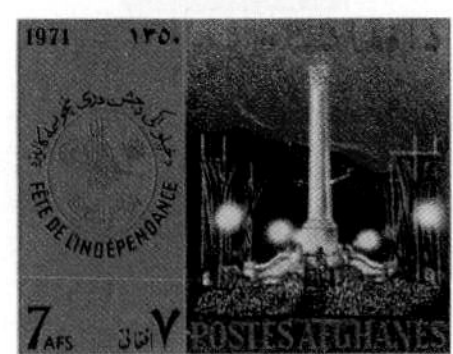

**293** Independence Memorial

**1971.** Independence Day.

| | | | | |
|---|---|---|---|---|
| 711 | **293** | 7a. multicoloured | 60 | 25 |
| 712 | **293** | 9a. multicoloured | 90 | 35 |

**294** Pashtunistan Square, Kabul

**1971.** Pashtunistan Day.

| | | | | |
|---|---|---|---|---|
| 713 | **294** | 5a. purple | 50 | 25 |

**295** Mohamed Zahir Shah and Kabul Airport

**1971.** Air. Multicoloured.

| | | | |
|---|---|---|---|
| 714 | 50a. Type **295** | 4·50 | 4·50 |
| 715 | 100a. King, airline emblem and Boeing 727 airplane | 5·75 | 3·50 |

**296** Mohamed Zahir Shah

**1971.** King's 57th Birthday.
716 **296** 9a. multicoloured 60 35
717 **296** 17a. multicoloured 1·20 65

**297** Map, Nurse and Patients

**1971.** Red Crescent Day.
718 **297** 8a. multicoloured 50 35

**298** Emblem of Racial Equality Year

**1971.** United Nations Day.
719 **298** 24a. blue 1·50 80

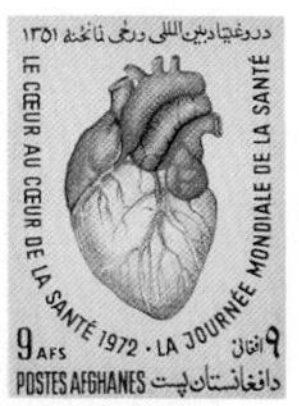


**299** Human Heart

**1972.** World Health Day and World Heart Month.
720 **299** 9a. multicoloured 90 35
721 **299** 12a. multicoloured 1·80 40

**300** "Tulipa lanata"

**1972.** Afghan Flora and Fauna. Multicoloured.
722 7a. Type **300** 1·30 75
723 10a. Chukar partridge (horiz) 7·75 1·60
724 12a. Lynx (horiz) 2·50 1·20
725 18a. "Allium stipitatum" 2·50 1·30

**301** Buddha of Hadda

**1972.** Tourist Publicity.
726 **301** 3a. blue and brown 60 25
727 - 7a. green and red 90 35
728 - 9a. purple and green 1·30 40
DESIGNS: 7a. Greco-Bactrian seal, 250 B.C.; 9a. Greek temple, Ai-Khanum, 3rd–2nd century B.C.

**302** King with Queen Humaira at Independence Parade

**1972.** Independence Day.
729 **302** 25a. multicoloured 4·50 1·20

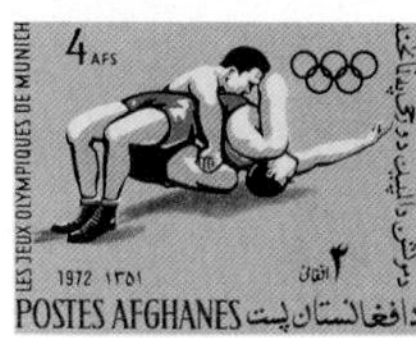


**303** Wrestling

**1972.** Olympic Games, Munich. Various Wrestling Holds as T 303.
730 4a. multicoloured 35 15
731 8a. multicoloured 60 25
732 10a. multicoloured 65 35
733 19a. multicoloured 1·50 50
734 21a. multicoloured 1·60 60
**MS**735 160×110 mm. Nos. 730/4. Imperf (sold at 60a.) 3·25 3·25

**304** Pathan and Mountain View

**1972.** Pashtunistan Day.
736 **304** 5a. multicoloured 60 25

**305** Mohamed Zahir Shah

**1972.** King's 58th Birthday.
737 **305** 7a. blue, black and gold 75 25
738 **305** 14a. brown, black & gold 1·20 40

**306** Ruined Town and Refugees

**1972.** Red Crescent Day.
739 **306** 7a. black, red and blue 65 25

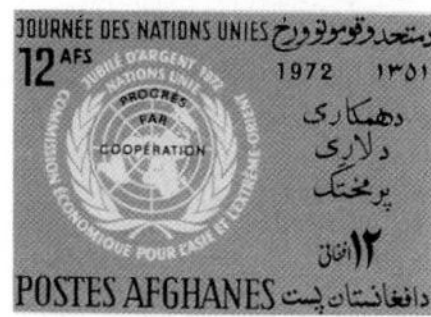


**307** E.C.A.F.E. Emblem

**1972.** U.N. Day. 25th Anniv of U.N. Economic Commission for Asia and the Far East.
740 **307** 12a. black and blue 60 35

**308** Ceramics

**1973.** Afghan Handicrafts. Multicoloured.
741 7a. Type **308** 40 25
742 9a. Embroidered coat (vert) 50 35
743 12a. Coffee set (vert) 75 40
744 16a. Decorated boxes 1·10 50
**MS**745 110×110 mm. Nos. 741/4. Imperf (sold at 45a.) 3·75 3·75

**309** W.M.O. and Afghan Emblems

**1973.** Cent of World Meteorological Organization.
746 **309** 7a. green and mauve 60 25
747 **309** 14a. red and blue 1·40 40

**310** Emblems and Harvester

**1973.** 10th Anniv of World Food Programme.
748 **310** 14a.+7a. purple & blue 1·40 90

**311** Al-Biruni

**1973.** Birth Millenary of Abu-al Rayhan al-Biruni (mathematician and philosopher).
749 **311** 10a. multicoloured 65 40

**312** Association Emblem

**1973.** Family Planning Week.
750 **312** 9a. purple and orange 65 25

**313** Himalayan Monal Pheasant

**1973.** Birds. Multicoloured.
751 8a. Type **313** 3·00 2·10
752 9a. Great crested grebe 3·75 2·50
753 12a. Himalayan snowcock 4·50 3·25

**314** Buzkashi Game

**1973.** Tourism.
754 **314** 8a. black 60 35

**315** Firework Display

**1973.** Independence Day.
755 **315** 12a. multicoloured 65 35

**316** Landscape and Flag

**1973.** Pashtunistan Day.
756 **316** 9a. multicoloured 65 15

**317** Red Crescent

**1973.** Red Crescent.
757 **317** 10a. multicoloured 1·00 25

**318** Kemal Ataturk

**1973.** 50th Anniv of Turkish Republic.
758 **318** 1a. blue 25 25
759 **318** 7a. brown 1·20 25

**319** Human Rights Flame

**1973.** 25th Anniv of Declaration of Human Rights.
760 **319** 12a. blue, black and silver 60 40

**320** Asiatic Black Bears

**1974.** Wild Animals. Multicoloured.
761 5a. Type **320** 65 15
762 7a. Afghan hound 1·10 40
763 10a. Goitred gazelle 1·40 50
764 12a. Leopard 1·80 60
**MS**765 120×100 mm. Nos. 761/4. Imperf 10·50 10·50

**321** "Workers"

**1974.** Labour Day.
766 **321** 9a. multicoloured 50 35

**322** Arch of Paghman and Independence Memorial

**1974.** Independence Day.
767 **322** 4a. multicoloured 40 10
768 **322** 11a. multicoloured 60 25

**323** Arms of Afghanistan and Hands clasping Seedling

**1974.** 1st Anniv of Republic. Multicoloured.
769 4a. Type **323** 40 10
770 5a. Republican flag (36×26 mm) 60 15
771 7a. Gen. Mohammed Daoud (26×36 mm) 65 25
772 15a. Soldiers and arms 1·20 35
**MS**773 Two sheets. Imperf (a) 120×80 mm. Nos. 769 and 772. (b) 100×100 mm. Nos. 770/1 3·75 3·75

**324** Lesser Spotted Eagle

**1974.** Afghan Birds. Multicoloured.
774 1a. Type **324** 2·10 50
775 6a. White-fronted goose, ruddy shelduck and greylag goose 4·50 80
776 11a. Black crane and common coots 7·50 1·30

**325** Flags of Pashtunistan and Afghanistan

**1974.** Pashtunistan Day.
777 **325** 5a. multicoloured 35 25

**326** Republic's Coat of Arms

**1974**
778 **326** 100p. green 80 25

**327** Pres. Daoud

**1974**
779 **327** 10a. multicoloured 65 25
780 **327** 16a. multicoloured 2·50 90
781 **327** 19a. multicoloured 90 50
782 **327** 21a. multicoloured 1·40 60
783 **327** 22a. multicoloured 3·75 2·00
784 **327** 30a. multicoloured 5·00 2·75

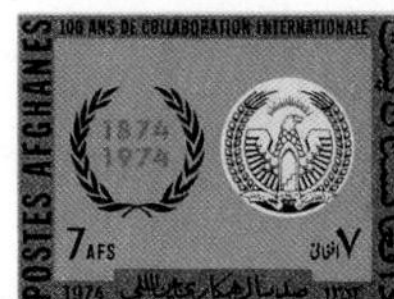

**328** Arms and Centenary Years

**1974.** Centenary of U.P.U.
785 **328** 7a. green, black and gold 35 25

**329** "UN" and U.N. Emblem

**1974.** United Nations Day.
786 **329** 5a. blue and ultramarine 40 15

**330** Pres. Daoud

**1975**
787 **330** 50a. multicoloured 2·75 1·40
788 **330** 100a. multicoloured 5·75 2·50

**331** Minaret, Jam

**1975.** South Asia Tourist Year. Multicoloured.
789 7a. Type **331** 35 15
790 14a. "Griffon and Lady" (2nd century) 65 40
791 15a. Head of Buddha (4th–5th century) 80 40
**MS**792 130×90 mm. Nos. 789/91. Imperf 3·75 3·75

**332** Afghan Flag

**1975.** Independence Day.
793 **332** 16a. multicoloured 80 25

**333** Rejoicing Crowd

**1975.** 2nd Anniv of Revolution.
794 **333** 9a. multicoloured 50 15
795 **333** 12a. multicoloured 65 25

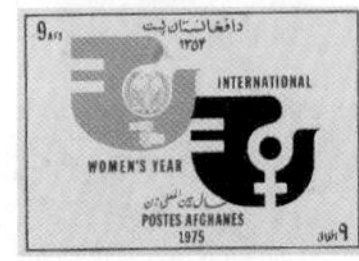

**334** I.W.Y. Emblem

**1975.** International Women's Year.
796 **334** 9a. black, blue and purple 50 15

**335** Rising Sun and Flag

**1975.** Pashtunistan Day.
797 **335** 10a. multicoloured 40 15

**336** Wazir M. Akbar Khan

**1976.** 130th Death Anniv of Akbar Khan (resistance leader).
798 **336** 15a. multicoloured 60 40

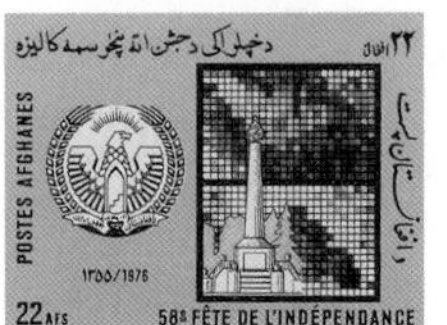

**337** Independence Monument and Arms

**1976.** Independence Day.
799 **337** 22a. multicoloured 75 50

**338** Pres. Daoud raising Flag

**1976.** 3rd Anniv of Republic.
800 **338** 30a. multicoloured 80 60

**339** Mountain

**1976.** Pashtunistan Day.
801 **339** 16a. multicoloured 65 50

**340** Arms

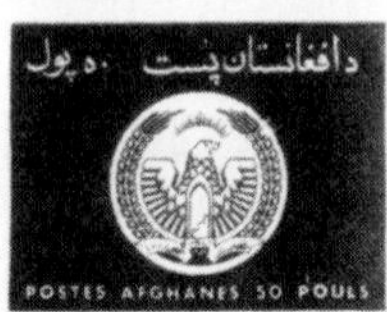

**340a**

**1976**
802 - 25p. salmon 50 35
803 **340** 50p. green 60 25
803a **340a** 50p. rosine 60 25
804 **340** 1a. blue 65 10

DESIGN: 25p. As Type **340** but with Arms on left and inscription differently arranged.

**341** Flag and Monuments on Open Book

**1977.** Independence Day.
805 **341** 20a. multicoloured 75 65

**342** Presidential Address

**1977.** Election of First President and New Constitution. Multicoloured.
806 7a. President Daoud and Election (45×27 mm) 80 60
807 8a. Type **342** 90 75
808 10a. Inaugural ceremony 1·20 90
809 18a. Promulgation of new constitution (45×27 mm) 2·00 1·60
**MS**810 136×106 mm. Nos. 806/9. Imperf 3·75 3·75

**343** Medal

**1977.** 80th Death Anniv of Sayed Jamaluddin (Afghan reformer).
811 **343** 12a. black, blue & gold 40 15

**344** Crowd with Afghan Flag

**1977.** Republic Day.
812 **344** 22a. multicoloured 75 40

**345** Dancers around Fountain

**1977.** Pashtunistan Day.
813 **345** 30a. multicoloured 1·20 90

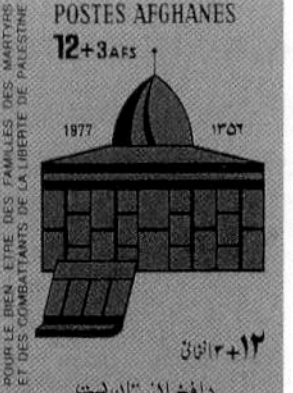

**346** Dome of the Rock

**1977.** Palestinian Welfare.
814 **346** 12a.+3a. black, gold and pink 2·10 60

**347** Arms and Carrier Pigeon

**1977**

| | | | | |
|---|---|---|---|---|
| 815 | **347** | 1a. blue and black | 40 | 15 |

**348** President Daoud acknowledging Crowd

**1978.** 1st Anniv of Presidential Election.

| | | | | |
|---|---|---|---|---|
| 816 | **348** | 20a. multicoloured | 2·10 | 1·20 |

**349** U.P.U. Emblem on Map of Afghanistan

**1978.** 50th Anniv of Admission to U.P.U.

| | | | | |
|---|---|---|---|---|
| 817 | **349** | 10a. gold, green & black | 40 | 15 |

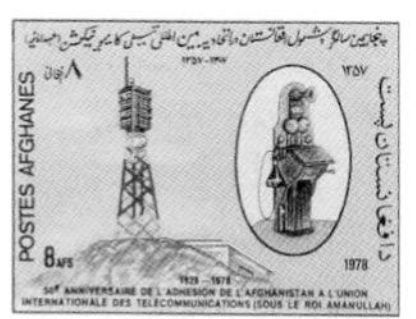
**350** Transmitting Aerial and Early Telephone

**1978.** 50th Anniv of Admission to I.T.U.

| | | | | |
|---|---|---|---|---|
| 818 | **350** | 8a. multicoloured | 40 | 15 |

**351** Red Crescent, Red Cross and Red Lion Emblems

**1978.** Red Crescent.

| | | | | |
|---|---|---|---|---|
| 819 | **351** | 3a. black | 1·20 | 65 |

**352** Arms

**1978**

| | | | | |
|---|---|---|---|---|
| 820 | **352** | 1a. red and gold | 1·60 | 65 |
| 821 | **352** | 4a. red and gold | 2·10 | 90 |

**353** Ruin, Qalai Bust

**1978.** Independence Day. Multicoloured.

| | | | |
|---|---|---|---|
| 822 | 16a. Buddha, Bamian | 1·20 | 50 |
| 823 | 22a. Type **353** | 1·60 | 75 |
| 824 | 30a. Women in national costume | 2·10 | 1·20 |

**354** Afghans with Flag

**1978.** Pashtunistan Day.

| | | | | |
|---|---|---|---|---|
| 825 | **354** | 7a. red and blue | 50 | 15 |

**355** Crest and Symbols of the Five Senses

**1978.** International Literacy Day.

| | | | | |
|---|---|---|---|---|
| 826 | **355** | 20a. red | 90 | 40 |

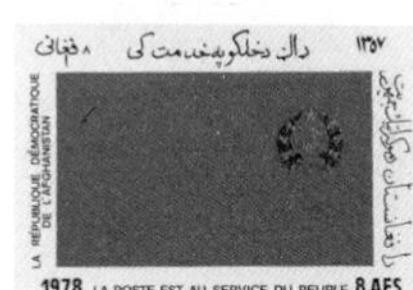
**356** Flag

**1978.** "The Mail is in the Service of the People".

| | | | | |
|---|---|---|---|---|
| 827 | **356** | 8a. red, gold and brown | 65 | 15 |
| 828 | **356** | 9a. red, gold and brown | 1·00 | 15 |

**357** Martyr

**1978.** "The People's Democratic Party Honours its Martyrs".

| | | | | |
|---|---|---|---|---|
| 829 | **357** | 18a. green | 1·00 | 40 |

**358** President Mohammed Taraki

**1978.** 14th Anniv of People's Democratic Party.

| | | | | |
|---|---|---|---|---|
| 830 | **358** | 12a. multicoloured | 75 | 25 |

**359** Emancipated Woman

**1979.** Women's Day.

| | | | | |
|---|---|---|---|---|
| 831 | **359** | 14a. blue and red | 1·20 | 50 |

**360** Farmers planting Tree

**1979.** Farmers' Day.

| | | | | |
|---|---|---|---|---|
| 832 | **360** | 1a. multicoloured | 65 | 35 |

**361** Map and Census Taking

**1979.** 1st Complete Population Census.

| | | | | |
|---|---|---|---|---|
| 833 | **361** | 3a. black, blue and red | 90 | 65 |

**362** Pres. Taraki reading "Khalq"

**1979.** 1st Publication of "Khalq" (party newspaper).

| | | | | |
|---|---|---|---|---|
| 834 | **362** | 2a. multicoloured | 65 | 15 |

**363** Pres. Taraki and Tank

**1979.** 1st Anniv of Sawr Revolution (1st issue).

| | | | | |
|---|---|---|---|---|
| 835 | **363** | 50p. multicoloured | 65 | 15 |

**364** Pres. Taraki

**1979.** 1st Anniv of Sawr Revolution (2nd issue). Multicoloured.

| | | | |
|---|---|---|---|
| 836 | 4a. Type **364** | 40 | 10 |
| 837 | 5a. Revolutionary H.Q. and Tank Monument, Kabul (47×32 mm) | 60 | 15 |
| 838 | 6a. Command room, Revolutionary H.Q. (vert) | 65 | 15 |
| 839 | 12a. House where first Khalq Party Congress was held (vert) | 80 | 25 |

**365** Carpenter and Blacksmith

**1979.** Workers' Solidarity.

| | | | | |
|---|---|---|---|---|
| 840 | **365** | 10a. multicoloured | 90 | 15 |

**366** Children on Map of Afghanistan

**1979.** International Year of the Child.

| | | | | |
|---|---|---|---|---|
| 841 | **366** | 16a. multicoloured | 1·80 | 90 |

**367** Revolutionaries and Kabul Monuments

**1979.** Independence Day.

| | | | | |
|---|---|---|---|---|
| 842 | **367** | 30a. multicoloured | 1·60 | 90 |

**368** Afghans and Flag

**1979.** Pashtunistan Day.

| | | | | |
|---|---|---|---|---|
| 843 | **368** | 9a. multicoloured | 75 | 15 |

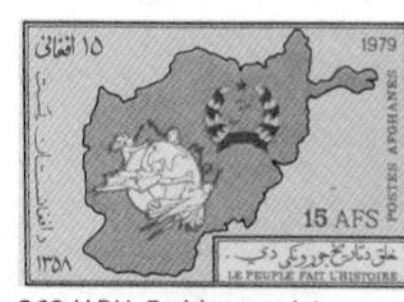
**369** U.P.U. Emblem and Arms on Map

**1979.** Stamp Day.

| | | | | |
|---|---|---|---|---|
| 844 | **369** | 15a. multicoloured | 65 | 25 |

**370** Headstone and Tomb

**1979.** Martyrs' Day.

| | | | | |
|---|---|---|---|---|
| 845 | **370** | 22a. multicoloured | 2·50 | 1·20 |

**371** Doves around Globe

**1979**

| | | | | |
|---|---|---|---|---|
| 845a | **371** | 2a. blue and red | 1·20 | 25 |

**372** Woman with Baby, Dove and Rifle

**1980.** International Women's Day.

| | | | | |
|---|---|---|---|---|
| 846 | **372** | 8a. multicoloured | 1·60 | 50 |

**373** Farmers receiving Land Grants

**1980.** Farmers' Day.

| | | | | |
|---|---|---|---|---|
| 847 | **373** | 2a. multicoloured | 2·10 | 65 |

**374** Healthy Non-smoker and Prematurely Aged Smoker

**1980.** World Health Day. Anti-smoking Campaign.
848 **374** 5a. multicoloured 1·60 65

**375** "Lenin speaking from Tribune"

**1980.** 110th Birth Anniv of Lenin.
849 **375** 12a. multicoloured 2·50 80

**376** Crowd and Clenched Fist

**1980.** 2nd Anniv of Sawr Revolution.
850 **376** 1a. multicoloured 65 15

**377** Quarry Worker and Blacksmith

**1980.** Workers' Solidarity.
851 **377** 9a. multicoloured 50 15

**378** Football

**1980.** Olympic Games, Moscow. Mult.
852 3a. Type **378** 60 15
853 6a. Wrestling 65 15
854 9a. Pigsticking 75 25
855 10a. Buzkashi 90 25

**379** Soldiers attacking Fortress

**1980.** Independence Day.
856 **379** 3a. multicoloured 65 15

**380** Pashtus with Flag

**1980.** Pashtunistan Day.
857 **380** 25a. multicoloured 1·00 40

**381** Post Office

**1980.** World U.P.U. Day.
858 **381** 20a. multicoloured 1·00 40

**382** Buzkashi

**1980**
859 **382** 50a. multicoloured 2·10 1·50
860 **382** 100a. multicoloured 4·00 1·60

**383** Arabic "H", Medina Mosque and Kaaba

**1981.** 1400th Anniv of Hegira.
861 **383** 13a.+2a. multicoloured 1·80 35

**384** Mother and Child with Dove and Globe

**1981.** International Women's Day.
862 **384** 15a. multicoloured 1·20 35

**385** Ox Plough, Tractor and Planting Trees

**1981.** Farmers' Day.
863 **385** 1a. multicoloured 1·00 25

**386** Urial

**1981.** Protected Wildlife.
864 **386** 12a. multicoloured 2·30 65

**387** Crowd and Afghan Arms

**1981.** 3rd Anniv of Sawr Revolution.
865 **387** 50p. brown 65 15

**388** Road Workers in Ravine

**1981.** Workers' Day.
866 **388** 10a. multicoloured 90 35

**389** Red Crescent enclosing Scenes of Disaster and Medical Aid

**1981.** Red Crescent Day.
867 **389** 1a.+4a. multicoloured 65 80

**390** Satellite Receiving Station

**1981.** World Telecommunications Day.
868 **390** 9a. multicoloured 65 15

**391** Map enclosing playing Children

**1981.** International Children's Day.
869 **391** 15a. multicoloured 90 40

**392** Afghans and Monument

**1981.** Independence Day.
870 **392** 4a. multicoloured 90 15

**393** Pashtus around Flag

**1981.** Pashtunistan Day.
871 **393** 2a. multicoloured 65 15

**394** Terracotta Horseman

**1981.** World Tourism Day.
872 **394** 5a. multicoloured 65 15

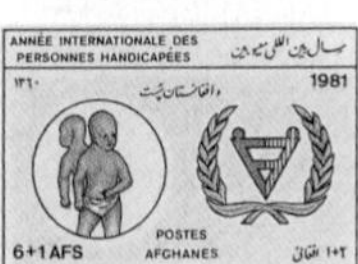

**395** Siamese Twins and I.Y.D.P. Emblem

**1981.** International Year of Disabled Persons.
873 **395** 6a.+1a. multicoloured 90 50

**396** Harvesting

**1981.** World Food Day.
874 **396** 7a. multicoloured 80 15

**397** Peace, Solidarity and Friendship Organization Emblem

**1981.** Afro-Asian Peoples' Solidarity Meeting.
875 **397** 8a. blue 75 15

**398** Heads and Clenched Fist on Globe and Emblem

**1981.** International Anti-apartheid Year.
876 **398** 4a. multicoloured 1·00 25

**399** Lion (bas-relief at Stara Zagora)

**1981.** 1300th Anniv of Bulgarian State.
877 **399** 20a. stone, purple and red 1·50 50

**400** Mother rocking Cradle

**1982.** Women's Day.
878 **400** 6a. multicoloured 60 15

**401** Farmers

**1982.** Farmers' Day.
879 **401** 4a. multicoloured 65 15

**402** Judas Tree

**1982.** Plants. Multicoloured.
880 3a. Type **402** 35 15
881 4a. Hollyhock 60 15
882 16a. Rhubarb 1·20 35

**403** Hands holding Flags and Tulip

**1982.** 4th Anniv of Sawr Revolution.

| | | | | |
|---|---|---|---|---|
| 883 | **403** | 1a. multicoloured | 1·20 | 15 |

**404** Dimitrov

**1982.** Birth Centenary of Georgi Dimitrov (Bulgarian statesman).

| | | | | |
|---|---|---|---|---|
| 884 | **404** | 30a. multicoloured | 2·30 | 80 |

**405** Blacksmith, Factory Workers, Weaver and Labourer

**1982.** Workers' Day.

| | | | | |
|---|---|---|---|---|
| 885 | **405** | 10a. multicoloured | 75 | 25 |

**406** White Storks

**1982.** Birds. Multicoloured.

| | | | | |
|---|---|---|---|---|
| 886 | | 6a. Type **406** | 1·60 | 50 |
| 887 | | 11a. Eurasian goldfinches | 2·10 | 60 |

**407** Brandt's Hedgehog

**1982.** Animals. Multicoloured.

| | | | | |
|---|---|---|---|---|
| 888 | | 3a. Type **407** | 60 | 15 |
| 889 | | 14a. Cobra | 1·50 | 25 |

**408** National Monuments

**1982.** Independence Day.

| | | | | |
|---|---|---|---|---|
| 890 | **408** | 20a. multicoloured | 1·20 | 50 |

**409** Pashtus and Flag

**1982.** Pashtunistan Day.

| | | | | |
|---|---|---|---|---|
| 891 | **409** | 32a. multicoloured | 2·50 | 75 |

**410** Tourists

**1982.** World Tourism Day.

| | | | | |
|---|---|---|---|---|
| 892 | **410** | 9a. multicoloured | 80 | 35 |

**411** Postman delivering Letter, Post Office and U.P.U. Emblem

**1982.** World U.P.U. Day.

| | | | | |
|---|---|---|---|---|
| 893 | **411** | 4a. multicoloured | 90 | 25 |

**412** Family eating Meal

**1982.** World Food Day.

| | | | | |
|---|---|---|---|---|
| 894 | **412** | 9a. multicoloured | 1·40 | 35 |

**413** U.N. Emblem illuminating Globe

**1982.** 37th Anniv of United Nations.

| | | | | |
|---|---|---|---|---|
| 895 | **413** | 15a. multicoloured | 1·00 | 40 |

**414** Earth Satellite Station

**1982.** I.T.U. Delegates' Conference, Nairobi.

| | | | | |
|---|---|---|---|---|
| 896 | **414** | 8a. multicoloured | 75 | 15 |

**415** Dr. Robert Koch

**1982.** Centenary of Discovery of Tubercle Bacillus.

| | | | | |
|---|---|---|---|---|
| 897 | **415** | 7a. black, brown & pink | 50 | 25 |

**416** Hand holding Torch, Globe and Scales

**1982.** 34th Anniv of Declaration of Human Rights.

| | | | | |
|---|---|---|---|---|
| 898 | **416** | 5a. multicoloured | 40 | 15 |

**417** Lions

**1982.** Wild Animals. Multicoloured.

| | | | | |
|---|---|---|---|---|
| 899 | | 2a. Type **417** | 40 | 15 |
| 900 | | 7a. Asiatic wild asses | 90 | 35 |
| 901 | | 12a. Sable (vert) | 2·00 | 50 |

**418** Woman releasing Dove

**1983.** International Women's Day.

| | | | | |
|---|---|---|---|---|
| 902 | **418** | 3a. multicoloured | 25 | 15 |

**419** Mir Alicher-e-Nawai (poet)

**1983.** "Mir Alicher-e-Nawai and his Times" Study Decade.

| | | | | |
|---|---|---|---|---|
| 903 | **419** | 22a. multicoloured | 90 | 35 |

**420** Distributing Land Ownership Documents

**1983.** Farmers' Day.

| | | | | |
|---|---|---|---|---|
| 904 | **420** | 10a. multicoloured | 65 | 25 |

**421** Revolution Monument

**1983.** 5th Anniv of Sawr Revolution.

| | | | | |
|---|---|---|---|---|
| 905 | **421** | 15a. multicoloured | 65 | 25 |

**422** World Map and Hands holding Cogwheel

**1983.** Labour Day.

| | | | | |
|---|---|---|---|---|
| 906 | **422** | 20a. multicoloured | 65 | 25 |

**423** Broadcasting Studio, Dish Aerial, Satellites and Television

**1983.** World Communications Year. Multicoloured.

| | | | | |
|---|---|---|---|---|
| 907 | | 4a. Type **423** | 35 | 10 |
| 908 | | 11a. Telecommunications headquarters | 60 | 15 |

**424** Hands holding Child

**1983.** International Children's Day.

| | | | | |
|---|---|---|---|---|
| 909 | **424** | 25a. multicoloured | 50 | 20 |

**425** Arms and Map of Afghanistan

**1983.** 2nd Anniv of National Fatherland Front.

| | | | | |
|---|---|---|---|---|
| 910 | **425** | 1a. multicoloured | 35 | 15 |

**426** Apollo

**1983.** Butterflies. Multicoloured.

| | | | | |
|---|---|---|---|---|
| 911 | | 9a. Type **426** | 1·00 | 75 |
| 912 | | 13a. Swallowtail | 2·30 | 1·30 |
| 913 | | 21a. Small tortoiseshell (horiz) | 3·00 | 1·60 |

**427** Racial Segregation

**1983.** Anti-apartheid Campaign.

| | | | | |
|---|---|---|---|---|
| 914 | **427** | 10a. multicoloured | 50 | 15 |

**428** National Monuments

**1983.** Independence Day.

| | | | | |
|---|---|---|---|---|
| 915 | **428** | 6a. multicoloured | 40 | 15 |

**429** Pashtus with Flag

**1983.** Pashtunistan Day.

| | | | | |
|---|---|---|---|---|
| 916 | **429** | 3a. multicoloured | 40 | 15 |

**430** Afghan riding Camel

**1983.** World Tourism Day.

| | | | | |
|---|---|---|---|---|
| 917 | **430** | 5a. multicoloured | 40 | 25 |
| 918 | - | 7a. brown and black | 60 | 25 |
| 919 | - | 12a. multicoloured | 90 | 25 |
| 920 | - | 16a. multicoloured | 1·20 | 25 |

DESIGNS—VERT: 7a. Stone carving. 16a. Carved stele. HORIZ: 12a. Three statuettes.

**431** Winter Landscape

**1983.** Multicoloured.. Multicoloured..

| | | | | |
|---|---|---|---|---|
| 921 | | 50a. Type **431** | 1·60 | 35 |
| 922 | | 100a. Woman with camel | 3·75 | 40 |

**432** "Communications"

**1983.** World Communications Year. Mult.

| | | | |
|---|---|---|---|
| 923 | 14a. Type **432** | 65 | 15 |
| 924 | 15a. Ministry of Communications, Kabul | 65 | 15 |

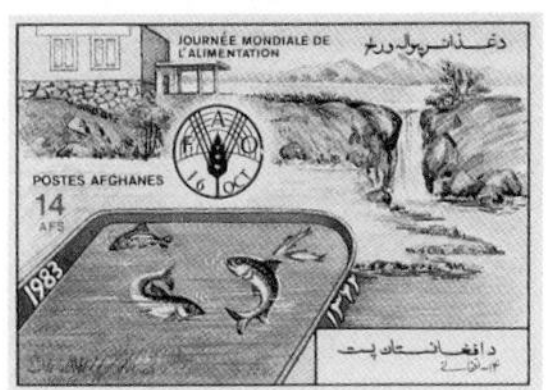

**433** Fish Breeding

**1983.** World Food Day.

| | | | | |
|---|---|---|---|---|
| 925 | **433** | 14a. multicoloured | 80 | 15 |

**434** Football

**1983.** Sports. Multicoloured.

| | | | |
|---|---|---|---|
| 926 | 1a. Type **434** | 25 | 25 |
| 927 | 18a. Boxing | 1·00 | 35 |
| 928 | 21a. Wrestling | 1·20 | 35 |

**435** Jewellery

**1983.** Handicrafts. Multicoloured.

| | | | |
|---|---|---|---|
| 929 | 2a. Type **435** | 15 | 10 |
| 930 | 8a. Polished stoneware | 35 | 15 |
| 931 | 19a. Furniture | 60 | 15 |
| 932 | 30a. Leather goods | 1·40 | 15 |

**436** Map, Sun, Scales and Torch

**1983.** 35th Anniv of Declaration of Human Rights.

| | | | | |
|---|---|---|---|---|
| 933 | **436** | 20a. multicoloured | 90 | 15 |

**437** Polytechnic Buildings and Emblem

**1983.** 20th Anniv of Kabul Polytechnic.

| | | | | |
|---|---|---|---|---|
| 934 | **437** | 30a. multicoloured | 1·20 | 25 |

**438** Ice Skating

**1984.** Winter Olympic Games, Sarajevo. Mult.

| | | | |
|---|---|---|---|
| 935 | 5a. Type **438** | 25 | 10 |
| 936 | 9a. Skiing | 35 | 10 |
| 937 | 11a. Speed skating | 50 | 10 |
| 938 | 15a. Ice hockey | 60 | 10 |
| 939 | 18a. Biathlon | 65 | 15 |
| 940 | 20a. Ski jumping | 80 | 15 |
| 941 | 22a. Bobsleigh | 1·00 | 15 |

**439** Dove, Woman and Globe

**1984.** International Women's Day.

| | | | | |
|---|---|---|---|---|
| 942 | **439** | 4a. multicoloured | 50 | 30 |

**440** Ploughing with Tractor

**1984.** Farmers' Day. Multicoloured.

| | | | |
|---|---|---|---|
| 943 | 2a. Type **440** | 15 | 10 |
| 944 | 4a. Digging irrigation channel | 15 | 10 |
| 945 | 7a. Saddling donkey by water-mill | 15 | 10 |
| 946 | 9a. Harvesting wheat | 25 | 10 |
| 947 | 15a. Building haystack | 40 | 15 |
| 948 | 18a. Showing cattle | 60 | 15 |
| 949 | 20a. Ploughing with oxen and sowing seed | 75 | 15 |

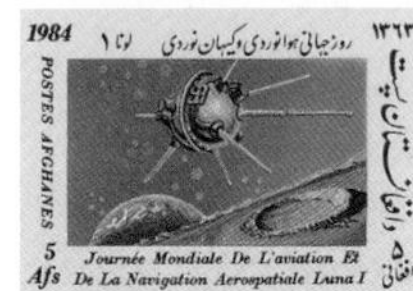

**441** "Luna I"

**1984.** World Aviation and Space Navigation Day. Multicoloured.

| | | | |
|---|---|---|---|
| 950 | 5a. Type **441** | 35 | 25 |
| 951 | 8a. "Luna II" | 40 | 25 |
| 952 | 11a. "Luna III" | 50 | 25 |
| 953 | 17a. "Apollo XI" | 65 | 25 |
| 954 | 22a. "Soyuz VI" | 80 | 35 |
| 955 | 28a. "Soyuz VII" | 80 | 35 |
| 956 | 34a. "Soyuz VI", "VII" and "VIII" | 1·00 | 40 |
| **MS**957 | 66×87 mm. 25a. Sergei Korolev (rocket designer) and rocket (29×41 mm) | 1·40 | 80 |

**442** Flags, Soldier and Workers

**1984.** 6th Anniv of Sawr Revolution.

| | | | | |
|---|---|---|---|---|
| 958 | **442** | 3a. multicoloured | 40 | 15 |

**443** Hunting Dog

**1984.** Animals. Multicoloured.

| | | | |
|---|---|---|---|
| 959 | 1a. Type **443** | 10 | 10 |
| 960 | 2a. Argali | 25 | 15 |
| 961 | 6a. Przewalski's horse (horiz) | 60 | 15 |
| 962 | 8a. Wild boar | 80 | 25 |
| 963 | 17a. Snow leopard (horiz) | 1·60 | 25 |
| 964 | 19a. Tiger (horiz) | 2·75 | 25 |
| 965 | 22a. Indian elephant | 3·00 | 35 |

**444** Postal Messenger

**1984.** 19th U.P.U. Congress, Hamburg. Mult.

| | | | |
|---|---|---|---|
| 966 | 25a. Type **444** | 90 | 15 |
| 967 | 35a. Post rider | 1·40 | 35 |
| 968 | 40a. Bird with letter | 1·80 | 35 |
| **MS**969 | 97×66 mm. 50a. black | 3·00 | 1·80 |

DESIGNS: At T **444**—35a. Post rider; 40a. Bird with letter; 25×37 mm—50a. Hamburg 1859 2s. stamp.

**445** Antonov AN-2

**1984.** 40th Anniv of Ariana Airline. Mult.

| | | | |
|---|---|---|---|
| 970 | 1a. Type **445** | 10 | 10 |
| 971 | 4a. Ilyushin Il-12 | 15 | 10 |
| 972 | 9a. Tupolev Tu-104A | 60 | 15 |
| 973 | 10a. Ilyushin Il-18 | 80 | 15 |
| 974 | 13a. Yakovlev Yak-42 | 1·10 | 15 |
| 975 | 17a. Tupolev Tu-154 | 1·40 | 15 |
| 976 | 21a. Ilyushin Il-86 | 1·60 | 15 |

**446** Ettore Bugatti (motor manufacturer) and Bugatti Type 43 Sports car, 1927

**1984.** Motor Cars. Multicoloured.

| | | | |
|---|---|---|---|
| 977 | 2a. Type **446** | 15 | 10 |
| 978 | 5a. Henry Ford and Ford Model A two-seater, 1903 | 35 | 10 |
| 979 | 8a. Rene Panhard (engineer) and Panhard Limosine, 1899 | 60 | 10 |
| 980 | 11a. Gottlieb Daimler (engineer) and Daimler DB 18 saloon, 1935 | 75 | 10 |
| 981 | 12a. Karl Benz and Benz Viktoria two-seater (inscr "Victoris"), 1893 | 1·00 | 15 |
| 982 | 15a. Armand Peugeot (motor manufacturer) and Peugeot vis-a-vis, 1892 | 1·10 | 15 |
| 983 | 22a. Louis Chevrolet (car designer) and Chevrolet Superior sedan, 1925 | 1·50 | 15 |

**447** Open Book showing Monuments and Fortress

**1984.** Independence Day.

| | | | | |
|---|---|---|---|---|
| 984 | **447** | 6a. multicoloured | 40 | 15 |

**448** Truck on Mountain Road and Pashtunistan Badge

**1984.** Pashtunistan Day.

| | | | | |
|---|---|---|---|---|
| 985 | **448** | 3a. multicoloured | 40 | 15 |

**449** Arch at Qalai Bust

**1984.** World Tourism Day. Multicoloured.

| | | | |
|---|---|---|---|
| 986 | 1a. Type **449** | 10 | 10 |
| 987 | 2a. Ornamented belt | 15 | 10 |
| 988 | 5a. Kabul monuments | 15 | 15 |
| 989 | 9a. Statuette (vert) | 25 | 15 |
| 990 | 15a. Buffalo riders in snow | 40 | 25 |
| 991 | 19a. Camel in ornate caparison | 80 | 25 |
| 992 | 21a. Buzkashi players | 1·00 | 25 |

**450** Pine Cone

**1984.** World Food Day. Multicoloured.

| | | | |
|---|---|---|---|
| 993 | 2a. Type **450** | 15 | 10 |
| 994 | 4a. Walnuts | 25 | 10 |
| 995 | 6a. Pomegranate | 35 | 10 |
| 996 | 9a. Apples | 50 | 10 |
| 997 | 13a. Cherries | 60 | 15 |
| 998 | 15a. Grapes | 75 | 15 |
| 999 | 26a. Pears | 1·20 | 15 |

**451** Globe and Emblem

**1985.** 20th Anniv (1984) of Peoples' Democratic Party.

| | | | | |
|---|---|---|---|---|
| 1000 | **451** | 25a. multicoloured | 1·20 | 40 |

**452** Cattle

**1985.** Farmers' Day. Multicoloured.

| | | | |
|---|---|---|---|
| 1001 | 1a. Type **452** | 35 | 15 |
| 1002 | 3a. Mare and foal | 35 | 15 |
| 1003 | 7a. Galloping horse | 35 | 15 |
| 1004 | 8a. Grey horse (vert) | 60 | 25 |
| 1005 | 15a. Karakul sheep and sheepskins | 90 | 25 |
| 1006 | 16a. Herder watching over cattle and sheep | 1·10 | 35 |
| 1007 | 25a. Family with pack camels | 1·50 | 40 |

**453** Map and Geologist

**1985.** Geologists' Day.

| | | | | |
|---|---|---|---|---|
| 1008 | **453** | 4a. multicoloured | 35 | 15 |

**454** Satellite

**1985.** 20th Anniv of "Intelsat" Communications Satellite. Multicoloured.

| | | | |
|---|---|---|---|
| 1009 | 6a. Type **454** | 50 | 15 |
| 1010 | 9a. "Intelsat III" | 65 | 15 |
| 1011 | 10a. Rocket launch (vert) | 90 | 15 |

**455** "Visitors for Lenin" (V. Serov)

**1985.** 115th Birth Anniv of Lenin. Multicoloured.

| | | | |
|---|---|---|---|
| 1012 | 10a. Type **455** | 65 | 25 |

1013 15a. "With Lenin" (detail, V. Serov) 80 25
1014 25a. Lenin and Red Army fighters 1·40 40
**MS**1015 90×21 mm. 50a. Lenin 2·30 1·40

**456** Revolutionaries with Flags

**1985.** 7th Anniv of Sawr Revolution.
1016 **456** 21a. multicoloured 1·00 15

**457** Olympic Stadium and Moscow Skyline

**1985.** 12th World Youth and Students' Festival, Moscow. Multicoloured.
1017 7a. Type **457** 25 10
1018 12a. Festival emblem 40 25
1019 13a. Moscow Kremlin 50 35
1020 18a. Doll 65 60

**458** Soviet Memorial, Berlin-Treptow, and Tank before Reichstag

**1985.** 40th Anniv of End of World War II. Multicoloured.
1021 6a. Type **458** 60 15
1022 9a. "Mother Homeland" war memorial, Volgograd, and fireworks over Moscow Kremlin 80 15
1023 10a. Cecilienhof Castle, Potsdam, and flags of United Kingdom, U.S.S.R. and U.S.A. 1·10 15

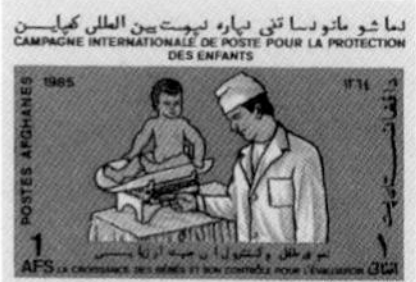


**459** Weighing Baby

**1985.** UNICEF Child Survival Campaign. Mult.
1024 1a. Type **459** 10 15
1025 2a. Vaccinating child 15 15
1026 4a. Breast-feeding baby 35 15
1027 5a. Mother and child 40 15

**460** Purple Blewit

**1985.** Fungi. Multicoloured.
1028 3a. Type **460** 15 10
1029 4a. Flaky-stemmed witches' mushroom 40 25
1030 7a. The blusher 60 35
1031 11a. Brown birch bolete 80 60
1032 12a. Common ink cap 1·10 60
1033 18a. "Hypholoma sp." 1·50 75
1034 20a. "Boletus aurantiacus" 1·60 75

**461** Emblems

**1985.** United Nations Decade for Women.
1035 **461** 10a. multicoloured 65 25

**462** Evening Primrose

**1985.** "Argentina '85" International Stamp Exhibition, Buenos Aires. Flowers. Multicoloured.
1036 2a. Type **462** 15 10
1037 4a. Cockspur coral tree 35 15
1038 8a. "Tillandsia aeranthos" 60 15
1039 13a. Periwinkle 90 25
1040 18a. Marvel-of-Peru 1·30 35
1041 25a. "Cypella herbertii" 1·80 35
1042 30a. "Clytostoma callistegioides" 2·30 35
**MS**1043 80×100 mm. 75a. "Sesbania punicea" (51×36 mm) 5·75 80

**463** Building

**1985.** Independence Day.
1044 **463** 33a. multicoloured 1·50 15

**464** Dancers in Pashtunistan Square, Kabul

**1985.** Pashtunistan Day.
1045 **464** 25a. multicoloured 1·50 15

**465** Guldara Stupa

**1985.** 10th Anniv of World Tourism Organization. Multicoloured.
1046 1a. Type **465** 15 10
1047 2a. Mirwais tomb (vert) 15 10
1048 10a. Buddha of Bamian (vert) 60 10
1049 13a. No Gumbad mosque (vert) 80 10
1050 14a. Pule Kheshti mosque 90 15
1051 15a. Arch at Qalai Bust 1·00 15
1052 20a. Ghazni minaret (vert) 1·30 15

**466** Boxing

**1985.** Sport. Multicoloured.
1053 1a. Type **466** 10 15
1054 2a. Volleyball 15 10
1055 3a. Football (vert) 50 10
1056 12a. Buzkashi 60 10
1057 14a. Weightlifting 65 15
1058 18a. Wrestling 75 15
1059 25a. Pigsticking 1·00 15

**467** Fruit Stall

**1985.** World Food Day.
1060 **467** 25a. multicoloured 90 15

**468** Flags and U.N. Building, New York

**1985.** 40th Anniv of United Nations Organization.
1061 **468** 22a. multicoloured 90 15

**469** Black-billed Magpie

**1985.** Birds. Multicoloured.
1062 2a. Type **469** 25 10
1063 4a. Green woodpecker 1·00 50
1064 8a. Common pheasants 1·10 50
1065 13a. Bluethroat, Eurasian goldfinch and hoopoe 1·60 90
1066 18a. Peregrine falcons 2·00 1·00
1067 25a. Red-legged partridge 2·75 1·50
1068 30a. Eastern white pelicans (horiz) 3·50 1·70
**MS**1069 90×20 mm. 75a. Rose-ringed parakeets (29×41 mm) 7·50 80

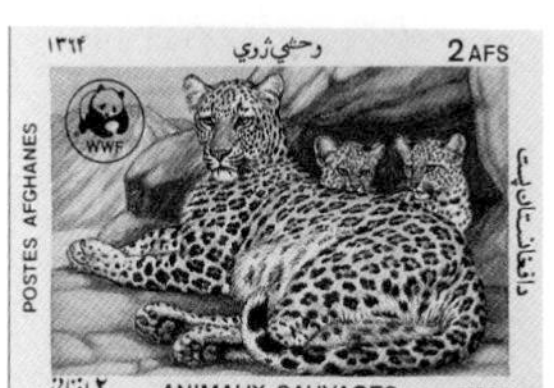


**470** Leopard and Cubs

**1985.** World Wildlife Fund. The Leopard. Mult.
1070 2a. Type **470** 40 25
1071 9a. Head of leopard 1·50 50
1072 11a. Leopard 2·50 80
1073 15a. Leopard cub 3·75 1·20

**471** Triumph 650 and Big Ben Tower

**1985.** Motorcycles. Multicoloured.
1074 2a. Type **471** 15 10
1075 4a. Motobecane and Eiffel Tower, Paris 35 10
1076 8a. Bultaco motorcycles and Don Quixote monument, Madrid 60 15
1077 13a. Honda and Mt. Fuji, Japan 90 15
1078 18a. Jawa and Old Town Hall clock, Prague 1·10 25
1079 25a. MZ motorcycle and T.V. Tower, Berlin 1·60 25
1080 30a. Motorcycle and Colosseum, Rome 2·00 25
**MS**1081 100×80 mm. 75a. Moskva Dneipr motorcycle and Red Square, Moscow 6·50 80

**472** Crowd with Flags

**1986.** 21st Anniv of Peoples' Democratic Party.
1082 **472** 2a. multicoloured 35 25

**473** Lenin writing

**1986.** 27th Soviet Communist Party Congress, Moscow.
1083 **473** 25a. multicoloured 80 40

**474** "Vostok 1"

**1986.** 25th Anniv of First Manned Space Flight. Multicoloured.
1084 3a. Type **474** 25 15
1085 7a. Russian Cosmonaut Medal (vert) 25 15
1086 9a. Launch of "Vostok 1" (vert) 40 15
1087 11a. Yuri Gagarin (first man in space) (vert) 50 15
1088 13a. Cosmonauts reading newspaper 60 25
1089 15a. Yuri Gagarin and Sergei Pavlovich Korolev (rocket designer) 60 25
1090 17a. Valentina Tereshkova (first woman in space) (vert) 75 25

**475** Footballers

**1986.** World Cup Football Championship, Mexico.
1091 **475** 3a. multicoloured 25 15
1092 - 4a. multicoloured (horiz) 35 15
1093 - 7a. multicoloured (horiz) 40 15
1094 - 11a. multicoloured 65 15
1095 - 12a. mult (horiz) 80 25
1096 - 18a. multicoloured 1·20 25
1097 - 20a. multicoloured 1·40 25
**MS**1098 120×90 mm. 75a. multicoloured (39×26 mm) 4·50 80
DESIGNS: 4a. to 75a. Various footballing scenes.

**476** Lenin

**1986.** 116th Birth Anniv of Lenin.
1099 **476** 16a. multicoloured 75 40

**477** Delegates voting

**1986.** 1st Anniv of Supreme Council Meeting of Tribal Leaders.
1100 **477** 3a. brown, red and blue 25 15

**478** Flags and Crowd

**1986.** 8th Anniv of Sawr Revolution.
1101 **478** 8a. multicoloured 40 15

**479** Worker with Cogwheel and Globe

**1986.** Labour Day.
1102 **479** 5a. multicoloured 25 15

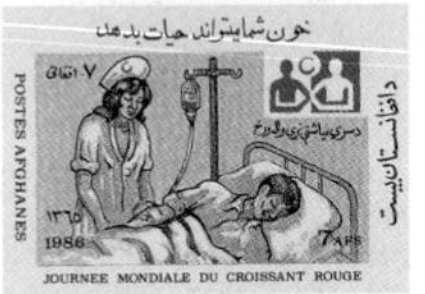
**480** Patient receiving Blood Transfusion

**1986.** International Red Cross/Crescent Day.
1103 **480** 7a. multicoloured 50 25

**481** St. Bernard

**1986.** Pedigree Dogs. Multicoloured.
1104 5a. Type **481** 25 10
1105 7a. Rough collie 40 10
1106 8a. Spaniel 50 15
1107 9a. Long-haired dachshund 60 15
1108 11a. German shepherd 65 25
1109 15a. Bulldog 90 25
1110 20a. Afghan hound 1·20 25

**482** Tiger Barb

**1986.** Fishes. Multicoloured.
1111 5a. Type **482** 25 15
1112 7a. Mbuna 40 15
1113 8a. Clown loach 50 15
1114 9a. Lisa 60 25
1115 11a. Figure-eight pufferfish 80 25
1116 15a. Six-barred distichodus 1·10 35
1117 20a. Sail-finned molly 1·40 35

**483** Mother and Children

**1986.** World Children's Day. Multicoloured.
1118 1a. Type **483** 15 15
1119 3a. Woman holding boy and emblem 15 15
1120 9a. Circle of children on map (horiz) 40 15

**484** Italian Birkenhead Locomotive

**1986.** 19th-century Railway Locomotives. Mult.
1121 4a. Type **484** 25 10
1122 5a. Norris locomotive 35 10
1123 6a. Stephenson "Patentee" type locomotive 40 15
1124 7a. Bridges Adams locomotive 50 15
1125 8a. Ansoldo locomotive 65 25
1126 9a. Locomotive "St. David" 80 25
1127 11a. Jones & Potts locomotive 90 25

**485** Cobra

**1986.** Animals. Multicoloured.
1128 3a. Type **485** 15 10
1129 4a. Lizards (vert) 25 15
1130 5a. Praying mantis 35 15
1131 8a. Beetle (vert) 50 25
1132 9a. Spider 60 35
1133 10a. Snake 65 35
1134 11a. Scorpions 80 35
Nos. 1130/2 and 1134 are wrongly inscr "Les Reptiles".

**486** Profiles on Globe

**1986.** World Youth Day.
1135 **486** 15a. multicoloured 65 25

**487** National Monuments

**1986.** Independence Day.
1136 **487** 10a. multicoloured 50 25

**488** 11th-century Ship

**1986.** "Stockholmia 86" International Stamp Exhibition. Sailing Ships. Multicoloured.
1137 4a. Type **488** 40 15
1138 5a. Roman galley 50 25
1139 6a. English royal kogge 65 25
1140 7a. Early dhow 80 25
1141 8a. Nao 1·00 25
1142 9a. Ancient Egyptian ship 1·10 25
1143 11a. Medieval galeasse 1·30 25
**MS**1144 86×64 mm. 50a. Early dhow (as 7a.) (41×29 mm) 4·00 80

**489** Tribesmen

**1986.** Pashtunistan Day.
1145 **489** 4a. multicoloured 25 15

**490** State Arms

**1986.** Supreme Council Meeting of Tribal Leaders.
1146 **490** 3a. gold, blue and black 40 25

**491** Labourer reading

**1986.** World Literacy Day.
1147 **491** 2a. multicoloured 25 15

**492** Dove and U.N. Emblem

**1986.** International Peace Year.
1148 **492** 12a. black and blue 60 25

**493** Tulips, Flame and Man with Rifle

**1986.** Afghanistan Youth Day.
1149 **493** 3a. red and black 40 25

**494** Crowd and Flags

**1987.** 9th Anniv of Sawr Revolution.
1150 **494** 3a. multicoloured 25 15

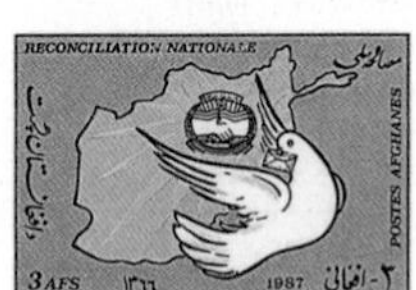
**495** Map and Dove

**1987.** National Reconciliation.
1151 **495** 3a. multicoloured 25 15

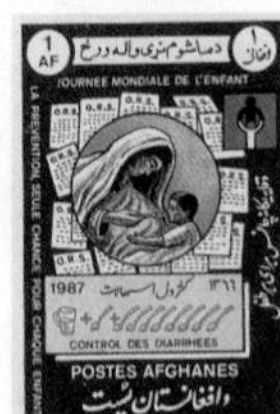
**496** Oral Rehydration

**1987.** International Children's Day. Multicoloured.
1152 1a. Type **496** 15 10
1153 5a. Weighing babies 15 10
1154 9a. Vaccinating babies 35 15

**497** Conference Delegates

**1987.** 1st Anniv of Tribal Conference.
1155 **497** 5a. multicoloured 35 25

**498** "Pieris sp."

**1987.** Butterflies and Moths. Multicoloured.
1156 7a. Type **498** 60 35
1157 9a. Brimstone and unidentified butterfly 75 35
1158 10a. Garden tiger moth (horiz) 1·00 50
1159 12a. "Parnassius sp." 1·40 50
1160 15a. Butterfly (unidentified) (horiz) 1·50 65
1161 22a. Butterfly (unidentified) (horiz) 2·10 90
1162 25a. Butterfly (unidentified) 2·50 90

**499** People on Hand

**1987.** 1st Local Government Elections.
1163 **499** 1a. multicoloured 25 15

**500** Khan Abdul Ghaffar Khan

**1987.** Pashtun and Baluch Day.
1164 **500** 4a. multicoloured 25 15

**501** "Sputnik 1"

**1987.** 30th Anniv of Launch of "Sputnik 1" (first artificial satellite). Multicoloured.
1165 10a. Type **501** 40 15
1166 15a. Rocket launch 60 15
1167 25a. "Soyuz"–"Salyut" space complex 80 15

**502** Old and Modern Post Offices

**1987.** World U.P.U. Day.
1168 **502** 22a. multicoloured 1·10 60

**503** Monument and Arch of Paghman

**1987.** Independence Day.

| | | | | |
|---|---|---|---|---|
| 1169 | **503** | 3a. multicoloured | 25 | 15 |

**504** "Communications"

**1987.** United Nations Day.

| | | | | |
|---|---|---|---|---|
| 1170 | **504** | 42a. multicoloured | 4·50 | 1·00 |

**505** Lenin

**1987.** 70th Anniv of Russian Revolution.

| | | | | |
|---|---|---|---|---|
| 1171 | **505** | 25a. multicoloured | 1·20 | 65 |

**506** Castor Oil Plant

**1987.** Plants. Multicoloured.

| | | | |
|---|---|---|---|
| 1172 | 3a. Type **506** | 15 | 15 |
| 1173 | 6a. Liquorice | 35 | 15 |
| 1174 | 9a. Camomile | 60 | 15 |
| 1175 | 14a. Thorn apple | 80 | 15 |
| 1176 | 18a. Chicory | 1·00 | 15 |

**507** Field Mice

**1987.** Mice. Multicoloured.

| | | | |
|---|---|---|---|
| 1177 | 2a. Type **507** | 40 | 15 |
| 1178 | 4a. Brown and white mice (horiz) | 50 | 15 |
| 1179 | 8a. Ginger mice (horiz) | 60 | 15 |
| 1180 | 16a. Black mice (horiz) | 1·00 | 15 |
| 1181 | 20a. Spotted and ginger mice (horiz) | 1·20 | 15 |

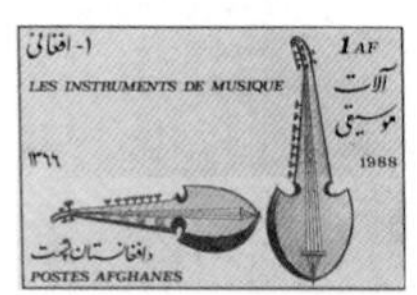


**508** Four-stringed Instrument

**1988.** Musical Instruments. Multicoloured.

| | | | |
|---|---|---|---|
| 1182 | 1a. Type **508** | 15 | 15 |
| 1183 | 3a. Drums | 15 | 15 |
| 1184 | 5a. Two-stringed instruments with two pegs | 25 | 15 |
| 1185 | 15a. Two-stringed instrument with ten pegs | 60 | 15 |
| 1186 | 18a. Two-stringed instruments with fourteen or ten pegs | 80 | 25 |
| 1187 | 25a. Four-stringed bowed instruments | 1·20 | 25 |
| 1188 | 33a. Two-stringed bowed instruments | 1·60 | 25 |

**509** Mixed Arrangement

**1988.** Flowers. Multicoloured.

| | | | |
|---|---|---|---|
| 1189 | 3a. Type **509** | 25 | 15 |
| 1190 | 5a. Tulips (horiz) | 35 | 15 |
| 1191 | 7a. Mallows | 50 | 25 |
| 1192 | 9a. Small mauve flowers | 65 | 25 |
| 1193 | 12a. Marguerites | 1·20 | 35 |
| 1194 | 15a. White flowers | 1·50 | 35 |
| 1195 | 24a. Red and blue flowers (horiz) | 2·10 | 35 |

**510** Emblems and Means of Communication

**1988.** 60th Anniv of Membership of U.P.U. and I.T.U.

| | | | | |
|---|---|---|---|---|
| 1196 | **510** | 20a. multicoloured | 80 | 50 |

**511** Tank Monument, Kabul, and Flags

**1988.** 10th Anniv of Sawr Revolution.

| | | | | |
|---|---|---|---|---|
| 1197 | **511** | 10a. multicoloured | 80 | 50 |

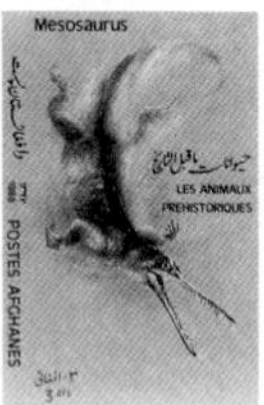


**512** Mesosaurus

**1988.** Prehistoric Animals. Multicoloured.

| | | | |
|---|---|---|---|
| 1198 | 3a. Type **512** | 15 | 10 |
| 1199 | 5a. Styracosaurus (horiz) | 25 | 10 |
| 1200 | 10a. Uintatherium (horiz) | 50 | 15 |
| 1201 | 15a. Protoceratops (horiz) | 75 | 15 |
| 1202 | 20a. Stegosaurus (horiz) | 1·00 | 25 |
| 1203 | 25a. Ceratosaurus | 1·30 | 25 |
| 1204 | 30a. Moa ("Dinornis maximus") | 1·80 | 25 |

**513** Baskets and Bowl of Fruit

**1988.** Fruit. Multicoloured.

| | | | |
|---|---|---|---|
| 1205 | 2a. Type **513** | 25 | 15 |
| 1206 | 4a. Baskets of fruit | 35 | 15 |
| 1207 | 7a. Large basket of fruit | 35 | 25 |
| 1208 | 8a. Bunch of grapes on branch (vert) | 50 | 25 |
| 1209 | 16a. Buying fruit from market stall | 80 | 35 |
| 1210 | 22a. Arranging fruit on market stall | 1·20 | 35 |
| 1211 | 25a. Stallholder weighing fruit (vert) | 1·80 | 35 |

**514** Memorial Pillar of Knowledge and Ignorance, Kabul

**1988.** Independence Day.

| | | | | |
|---|---|---|---|---|
| 1212 | **514** | 24a. multicoloured | 1·20 | 65 |

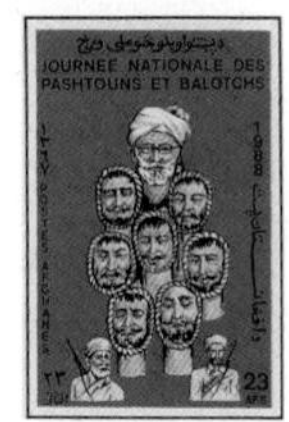


**515** Heads encircled with Rope

**1988.** Pashtunistan Day.

| | | | | |
|---|---|---|---|---|
| 1213 | **515** | 23a. multicoloured | 90 | 60 |

**516** Flags and Globe

**1988.** Afghan–Soviet Space Flight.

| | | | | |
|---|---|---|---|---|
| 1214 | **516** | 32a. multicoloured | 1·20 | 50 |

**517** Anniversary Emblem

**1988.** 125th Anniv of International Red Cross.

| | | | | |
|---|---|---|---|---|
| 1215 | **517** | 10a. multicoloured | 80 | 50 |

**518** Rocket and V. Tereshkova

**1988.** 25th Anniv of First Woman Cosmonaut Valentina Tereshkova's Space Flight. Mult.

| | | | |
|---|---|---|---|
| 1216 | 10a. Type **518** | 80 | 35 |
| 1217 | 15a. Bird, globe and rocket (vert) | 65 | 15 |
| 1218 | 25a. "Vostok 6" and globe | 1·00 | 15 |

**519** Decorated Metal Vessels

**1988.** Traditional Crafts. Multicoloured.

| | | | |
|---|---|---|---|
| 1219 | 2a. Type **519** | 10 | 10 |
| 1220 | 4a. Pottery | 15 | 10 |
| 1221 | 5a. Clothing (vert) | 25 | 15 |
| 1222 | 9a. Carpets | 35 | 15 |
| 1223 | 15a. Bags | 35 | 25 |
| 1224 | 23a. Jewellery | 90 | 25 |
| 1225 | 50a. Furniture | 1·80 | 25 |

**520** Indian Flag and Nehru

**1988.** Birth Centenary of Jawaharlal Nehru (Indian statesman).

| | | | | |
|---|---|---|---|---|
| 1226 | **520** | 40a. multicoloured | 2·10 | 80 |

**521** Emeralds

**1988.** Gemstones. Multicoloured.

| | | | |
|---|---|---|---|
| 1227 | 13a. Type **521** | 80 | 15 |
| 1228 | 37a. Lapis lazuli | 1·80 | 35 |
| 1229 | 40a. Rubies | 2·30 | 35 |

**522** Ice Skating

**1988.** Winter Olympic Games, Calgary. Mult.

| | | | |
|---|---|---|---|
| 1230 | 2a. Type **522** | 15 | 15 |
| 1231 | 5a. Slalom | 25 | 15 |
| 1232 | 9a. Two-man bobsleigh | 50 | 15 |
| 1233 | 22a. Biathlon | 90 | 15 |
| 1234 | 37a. Speed skating | 1·90 | 15 |
| **MS**1235 | 80×60 mm. 75a. Ice hockey | 4·00 | 80 |

**523** Old City

**1988.** International Campaign for Preservation of Old Sana'a, Yemen.

| | | | | |
|---|---|---|---|---|
| 1236 | **523** | 32a. multicoloured | 1·50 | 1·10 |

**524** Emblem

**1989.** 2nd Anniv of Move for Nat Reconciliation.

| | | | | |
|---|---|---|---|---|
| 1237 | **524** | 4a. multicoloured | 25 | 15 |

**525** Bishop and Game from "The Three Ages of Man" (attr. Estienne Porchier)

**1989.** Chess. Multicoloured.

| | | | |
|---|---|---|---|
| 1238 | 2a. Type **525** | 25 | 15 |
| 1239 | 3a. Faience queen and 14th century drawing of Margrave Otto IV of Brandenburg and his wife playing chess | 35 | 15 |
| 1240 | 4a. French king and game | 40 | 15 |
| 1241 | 7a. King and game | 65 | 25 |
| 1242 | 16a. Knight and game | 1·10 | 25 |
| 1243 | 24a. Arabian knight and "Great Chess" | 1·50 | 35 |
| 1244 | 45a. Bishop and teaching of game | 2·75 | 40 |

Nos. 1240/4 show illustrations from King Alfonso X's "Book of Chess, Dice and Tablings".

**526** "The Old Jew"

**1989.** Picasso Paintings. Multicoloured.

| | | | |
|---|---|---|---|
| 1245 | 4a. Type **526** | 35 | 25 |
| 1246 | 6a. "The Two Harlequins" | 40 | 25 |
| 1247 | 8a. "Portrait of Ambrouse Vollar" | 50 | 25 |
| 1248 | 22a. "Majorcan Woman" | 1·20 | 25 |
| 1249 | 35a. "Acrobat on Ball" | 2·30 | 25 |
| **MS**1250 | 70×90 mm. 75a. "Horta de Ebro Factory". Imperf | 4·00 | 80 |

**527** Euphrates Jerboa

**1989.** Animals. Multicoloured.

| | | | |
|---|---|---|---|
| 1251 | 3a. Type **527** | 35 | 25 |
| 1252 | 4a. Asiatic wild ass | 35 | 25 |
| 1253 | 14a. Lynx | 1·00 | 35 |
| 1254 | 35a. Lammergeier | 3·50 | 1·50 |
| 1255 | 44a. Markhor | 2·30 | 1·20 |
| **MS**1256 | 70×90 mm. 100a. Oxus cobra | 4·50 | 1·20 |

**528** Bomb breaking, Dove and Woman holding Wheat

**1989.** International Women's Day (1988).

| | | | | |
|---|---|---|---|---|
| 1257 | **528** | 8a. multicoloured | 40 | 15 |

**529** Cattle

**1989.** Farmers' Day. Multicoloured.

| | | | |
|---|---|---|---|
| 1258 | 1a. Type **529** | 25 | 15 |
| 1259 | 2a. Ploughing with oxen and tractors | 25 | 15 |
| 1260 | 3a. Picking cotton | 25 | 15 |

**530** Dish Aerial

**1989.** World Meteorology Day. Multicoloured.

| | | | |
|---|---|---|---|
| 1261 | 27a. Type **530** | 1·20 | 25 |
| 1262 | 32a. World Meteorological Organization emblem and state arms | 1·60 | 25 |
| 1263 | 40a. Data-collecting equipment (vert) | 2·10 | 25 |

**531** Rejoicing Crowd

**1989.** 11th Anniv of Sawr Revolution.

| | | | | |
|---|---|---|---|---|
| 1264 | **531** | 20a. multicoloured | 1·10 | 25 |

**532** Outdoor Class

**1989.** Teachers' Day.

| | | | | |
|---|---|---|---|---|
| 1265 | **532** | 42a. multicoloured | 2·10 | 35 |

**533** Eiffel Tower and Arc de Triomphe

**1989.** Bicentenary of French Revolution.

| | | | | |
|---|---|---|---|---|
| 1266 | **533** | 25a. multicoloured | 1·50 | 90 |

**534** Transmission Mast

**1989.** 10th Anniv of Asia-Pacific Telecommunity.

| | | | |
|---|---|---|---|
| 1267 | 3a. Type **534** | 15 | 15 |
| 1268 | 27a. Dish aerial | 1·10 | 25 |

**535** National Monuments

**1989.** Independence Day.

| | | | | |
|---|---|---|---|---|
| 1269 | **535** | 25a. multicoloured | 1·20 | 35 |

**536** Pashtu

**1989.** Pashtunistan Day.

| | | | | |
|---|---|---|---|---|
| 1270 | **536** | 3a. multicoloured | 35 | 25 |

**537** White Spoonbill

**1989.** Birds. Multicoloured.

| | | | |
|---|---|---|---|
| 1271 | 3a. Type **537** | 25 | 15 |
| 1272 | 5a. Purple swamphen | 50 | 25 |
| 1273 | 10a. Eurasian bittern (horiz) | 90 | 40 |
| 1274 | 15a. Eastern white pelican | 1·20 | 50 |
| 1275 | 20a. Red-crested pochard | 1·50 | 60 |
| 1276 | 25a. Mute swan | 2·10 | 65 |
| 1277 | 30a. Great cormorant (horiz) | 2·30 | 90 |

**538** Duchs Tourer, 1910

**1989.** Vintage Cars. Multicoloured.

| | | | |
|---|---|---|---|
| 1278 | 5a. Type **538** | 40 | 25 |
| 1279 | 10a. Ford Model T touring car, 1911 | 75 | 25 |
| 1280 | 20a. Renault Type AX two-seater, 1911 | 1·20 | 25 |
| 1281 | 25a. Russo-Balte tourer, 1911 | 1·50 | 35 |
| 1282 | 30a. Fiat 509 tourer, 1926 | 1·80 | 35 |

It is reported no stamps were issued by the Post Office from 1990—2001 inclusive. Any in circulation for these years are considered spurious.

Nos. 1986/8 and Types **540/2** are left for the issues of 2002, not yet received.

**543** Scales

**2002.** 55th (2003) Anniv of Universal Declaration of Human Rights

| | | | |
|---|---|---|---|
| 1989 | 4a. multicoloured | 1·70 | 1·70 |

**544** Tractor ploughing

**2003.** Farmers' Day. Multicoloured.

| | | | |
|---|---|---|---|
| 1990 | 3a. Type **544** | 15·00 | 15·00 |
| 1991 | 6a. Ploughing with oxen | 30·00 | 20·00 |

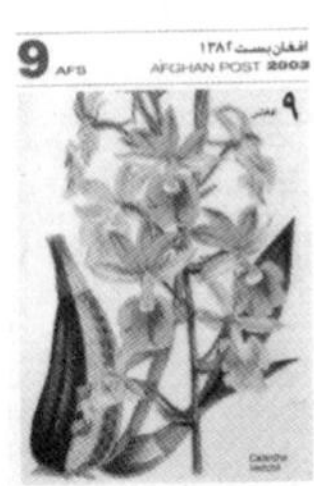
**545** *Calanthe veitchii*

**2003.** Orchids. Multicoloured.

| | | | |
|---|---|---|---|
| 1992 | 9a. Type **545** | 85 | 85 |
| 1993 | 13a. *Euanthe sanderiana* (inscr 'Eulanthe') | 1·20 | 1·20 |
| 1994 | 17a. *Ordontoglossum vuyl-stekeae* (inscr 'Ordontioda') | 1·40 | 1·40 |
| 1995 | 20a. *Dendrobium infundibulum* | 1·50 | 1·50 |
| 1996 | 30a. *Miltoniopsis roezlii* (inscr 'Miltonsiopsis') | 1·70 | 1·70 |
| 1997 | 40a. *Cattleya labiata* | 2·40 | 2·40 |
| 1998 | 100a *Vanda coerulea* | 5·25 | 5·25 |

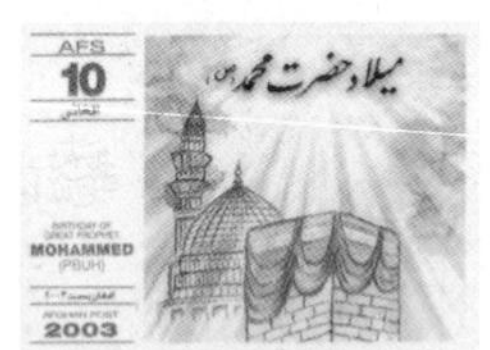
**546** Minaret, Mosque and Kaaba,

**2003.** Birthday of Prophet Mohammed.

| | | | | |
|---|---|---|---|---|
| 1999 | **546** | 10a. multicoloured | 70·00 | 30·00 |

**547** Children and 'STOP TB'

**2003.** International Tuberculosis Awareness Day. Multicoloured.

| | | | |
|---|---|---|---|
| 2000 | 1a. Type **547** | 10 | 10 |
| 2001 | 4a. Treatment (horiz) | | |
| 2002 | 9a. Infection (horiz) | 60 | 25 |

**548** Assembly

**2003.** First Anniv of Loya Jirga to elect President Hamid Karzai

| | | | | |
|---|---|---|---|---|
| 2003 | **548** | 20a. multicoloured | 1·90 | 1·90 |

**549** Map enclosing Poppy Head overlaid with Ears of Corn

**2003.** Struggle Against Narcotics Day. Multicoloured.

| | | | |
|---|---|---|---|
| 2004 | 1a Type **549** | 25 | 25 |
| 2005 | 2a Poppy head, resin and skulls (vert) | 55 | 55 |
| 2006 | 5a Tractor ploughing in poppies | 95 | 95 |
| **MS**2006a | 106×82 mmm. 10a. Poppy head, resin and skulls (different) | 1·90 | 1·90 |

**550** Rottweiler

**2003.** Dogs. Multicoloured.

| | | | |
|---|---|---|---|
| 2007 | 10a. Type **550** | 95 | 95 |
| 2008 | 20a. Cocker spaniel | 1·70 | 1·70 |
| 2009 | 30a. Doberman | 1·90 | 1·90 |
| 2010 | 40a. Afghan hound | 2·10 | 2·10 |
| 2011 | 50a. Giant schnauzer | 2·50 | 2·50 |
| 2012 | 60a. Boxer | 2·75 | 2·75 |
| **MS**2013 | 106×82 mm. 150a. Afghan hound (different) | 9·00 | 9·00 |

**551** Bird Island, South Africa

**2003.** Lighthouses. Multicoloured.

| | | | |
|---|---|---|---|
| 2014 | 10a. Type **551** | 95 | 95 |
| 2015 | 20a Cordoun, France | 1·90 | 1·90 |
| 2016 | 30a. Mahota Pagoda, China | 2·30 | 2·30 |
| 2017 | 50a Bay Canh, Vietnam | 2·75 | 2·75 |
| 2018 | 60a. Cap Roman Rock, South Africa | 3·00 | 3·00 |
| 2019 | 100a Mikomoto Shima, Japan | 4·75 | 4·75 |
| **MS**2020 | 75×106 mmm. 150a. Bell Rock, UK (inscr 'British Islands') | 9·00 | 9·00 |

**552** Monument and Arch

**2003.** Independence Day.

| | | | | |
|---|---|---|---|---|
| 2021 | **552** | 15a. multicoloured | 80·00 | 35·00 |

553 Dove Outline enclosing Students

2003. International Literacy Day.

| | | | | |
|---|---|---|---|---|
| 2022 | 553 | 2a. multicoloured | 15·00 | 15·00 |

554 Globe and Dove holding Envelope

2003. World Post Day.

| | | | | |
|---|---|---|---|---|
| 2023 | 554 | 8a. multicoloured | 45·00 | 20·00 |

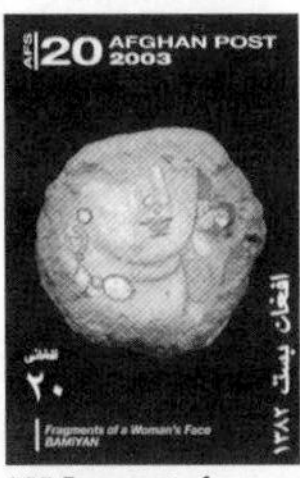
555 Fragment of Woman's Face (fresco), Bamiyan

2003. Cultural Heritage. Sheet 93×132 mm containing T 555 and similar vert designs. Multicoloured.

MS2024 20a. Type 555; 40a. Buddha's head, Gandhara; 60a. Buddha (statue), Takht-i-Bahi Monastery, Gandhara; 100a. Buddha's hand, Bamiyan 6·50 6·50

Nos. 2025/7 are vacant.

556 Quran

2003. Transmission of the Quran

| | | | | |
|---|---|---|---|---|
| 2028 | 556 | 9a. multicoloured | 3·25 | 3·25 |

557 Statue

2003. World Tourism Day. Historical Artefacts. Multicoloured.

| | | | |
|---|---|---|---|
| 2029 | 4a. Type 557 | 25·00 | 10·00 |
| 2030 | 8a. Hill fort | 45·00 | 20·00 |
| 2030a | 12a. Pot, coins and inscribed tablets | 70·00 | 30·00 |
| MS2030b | 108×82 mm. 25a. Hill fort (detail) | 1·20 | 1·20 |

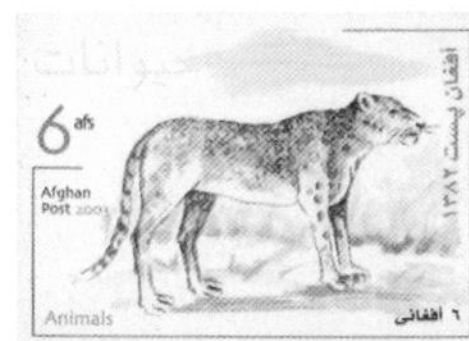
557a Leopard

2003. Animals. Multicoloured.

| | | | |
|---|---|---|---|
| 2030c | 6c. Type 557a | 10·00 | 10·00 |
| 2030d | 11a. Jackal | 65·00 | 30·00 |
| 2030e | 15a. Asiatic ibex | 80·00 | 35·00 |
| MS2030f | 107×83 mm. 40s. Leopard (different) | 6·25 | 6·25 |

558 Woman holding Book and Flame

2004. International Women's Day.

| | | | | |
|---|---|---|---|---|
| 2031 | 558 | 6a. multicoloured | 35·00 | 20·00 |

559 Woman, Pills and Blood-stained Hankerchief

2004. World TB Awareness Day. Multicoloured.

| | | | |
|---|---|---|---|
| 2032 | 1a. Type 559 | 35 | 35 |
| 2033 | 4a. Woman wearing mask and child | 50 | 50 |
| 2034 | 9a. Raising awareness | 85 | 85 |
| 2035 | 12a. TB sufferer and pills (vert) | 1·20 | 1·20 |
| 2036 | 15a. Doctor examining patient (vert) | 1·40 | 1·40 |

560 President Karzai

2004. Inauguration of President Hamid Karzai. Multicoloured.

| | | | |
|---|---|---|---|
| 2037 | 12a. Type 560 | 1·50 | 1·50 |
| MS2038 | 150×82 mm. 100a. As Type 560 (50×50 mm) | 9·25 | 9·25 |

561 Voters

2004. 1st Direct Presidential Elections.

| | | | | |
|---|---|---|---|---|
| 2039 | 561 | 15a. multicoloured | 85·00 | 40·00 |
| 2040 | - | 25a. multicoloured | 1·20 | 55·00 |

No. 2041 and Type 562 are left for Inauguration of President, Issued on 7 December 2004, not yet received.

563 Clasped Hands and Symbols of Afghanistan and China

2005. 50th Anniv of Afghanistan–China Diplomatic Relations.

| | | | | |
|---|---|---|---|---|
| 2042 | 563 | 25a. multicoloured | 1·20 | 55·00 |
| MS2042a | | 134×93 mm. Size 60×40 mm. 150a. As Type 563 | 6·50 | 6·50 |

No. MS2042 was printed on silk coated paper.

No. 2041 and Type 562 are left for Inauguration of President, Issued on 7 December 2004, not yet received.

565 Crowd

2006. 87th Anniv of Independence Day.

| | | | | |
|---|---|---|---|---|
| 2046 | 565 | 45a. multicoloured | 2·20 | 95·00 |

No. 2041 and Type 562 are left for Inauguration of President, Issued on 7 December 2004, not yet received.

566 Classroom

2006. World Literacy Day.

| | | | | |
|---|---|---|---|---|
| 2047 | 566 | 12a. multicoloured | 70·00 | 30·00 |

567 Dove enclosing Globe

2006. World Post Day. Multicoloured.

| | | | |
|---|---|---|---|
| 2048 | 15a. Type 567 | 85·00 | 40·00 |
| 2049 | 15a. As Type 567 but with inscription and colour of date changed | 85·00 | 40·00 |

567a Flags of Members

2006. 3rd Meeting of ECO Postal Authorities.

| | | | | |
|---|---|---|---|---|
| 2049a | 567a | 8a. multicoloured | 45·00 | 20·00 |

568 Lamp, Jug, Bowl and Teapot

2006. World Tourism Day. Multicoloured.

| | | | |
|---|---|---|---|
| 2050 | 15a. Type 568 | 85 | 40 |
| 2051 | 30a. Jug, coffee pot, bowl and vase | 1·50 | 60 |

No. 2052 and Type 568 are left for Elections, issued on 19 April 2007, not yet received.

No. 2053 and Type 569 are left for 800th Birth anniv of Rumi, issued on 24 May 2007, not yet received.

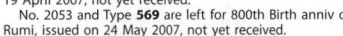

570 Dancers

2007. Aten Milli, National Dance

| | | | | |
|---|---|---|---|---|
| 2054 | 570 | 38a. multicoloured | 3·00 | 3·00 |

No. 2054 carries the imprint date '2006'.

571 Ustad Awal Mir (master singer)

2007. National Day of Fine Arts. Multicoloured.

| | | | |
|---|---|---|---|
| 2055 | 20a. Type 571 | 1·00 | 50·00 |
| 2056 | 22a. Mirmum Parwin (first female singer of Afghanistan) | 1·10 | 50·00 |

## NEWSPAPER STAMPS

N35

1928

| | | | | |
|---|---|---|---|---|
| N192 | N35 | 2p. blue | 4·00 | 4·50 |

1929

| | | | |
|---|---|---|---|
| N205A | 2p. red | 30 | 50 |

N43

1932

| | | | | |
|---|---|---|---|---|
| N215 | N43 | 2p. red | 40 | 50 |
| N216 | N43 | 2p. black | 35 | 80 |
| N217 | N43 | 2p. green | 40 | 75 |
| N219 | N43 | 2p. red | 50 | 75 |

N75 Coat-of-Arms

1939

| | | | | |
|---|---|---|---|---|
| N259 | N75 | 2p. green | 25 | 65 |
| N260 | N75 | 2p. mauve (no gum) | 15 | 1·00 |

1969. As Type N 75, but larger and with different Pushtu inscr.

| | | | |
|---|---|---|---|
| N652 | 100p. green | 25 | 25 |
| N653 | 150p. brown | 35 | 25 |

## OFFICIAL STAMPS

O27

1909

| | | | | |
|---|---|---|---|---|
| O173 | O27 | (-) red | 1·20 | 1·20 |

1939. Design 22¼×28 mm.

| | | | | |
|---|---|---|---|---|
| O281 | O86 | 15p. green | 1·10 | 80 |
| O282 | O86 | 30p. brown | 1·50 | 1·50 |
| O283 | O86 | 45p. red | 1·20 | 1·20 |
| O284 | O86 | 1a. mauve | 2·00 | 1·80 |

O86

1954. Design 24½×31 mm.

| | | | |
|---|---|---|---|
| O285b | 50p. red | 1·00 | 50 |

1965. Design 24×30½ mm.

| | | | |
|---|---|---|---|
| O287 | 50p. pink | 1·20 | 50 |

## PARCEL POST STAMPS

P27

1909

| | | | | |
|---|---|---|---|---|
| P173 | P27 | 3s. brown | 1·20 | 2·10 |

| | | | | |
|---|---|---|---|---|
| P174 | **P27** | 3s. green | 1·80 | 3·50 |
| P175 | **P27** | 1k. green | 2·10 | 3·50 |
| P176 | **P27** | 1k. red | 3·00 | 1·50 |
| P177 | **P27** | 1r. orange | 6·50 | 2·00 |
| P178 | **P27** | 1r. grey | 30·00 | |
| P179 | **P27** | 1r. brown | 3·50 | 3·50 |
| P180 | **P27** | 2r. red | 4·00 | 4·00 |
| P181 | **P27** | 2r. blue | 6·25 | 6·50 |

**P28** Old Habibia College, Kabul

**1921**

| | | | | |
|---|---|---|---|---|
| P182 | **P28** | 10p. brown | 4·00 | 5·75 |
| P183 | **P28** | 15p. brown | 5·75 | 6·50 |
| P184 | **P28** | 30p. purple | 10·50 | 6·50 |
| P185 | **P28** | 1r. blue | 12·50 | 12·50 |

**1923.** 5th Independence Day. Optd with T **28**.

| | | |
|---|---|---|
| P186 | 10p. brown | 90·00 |
| P187 | 15p. brown | £100 |
| P188 | 30p. purple | £200 |

**P35**

**P36**

**1928**

| | | | | |
|---|---|---|---|---|
| P192 | **P35** | 2a. orange | 6·50 | 5·00 |
| P193 | **P36** | 3a. green | 10·50 | 10·50 |

**1930**

| | | | | |
|---|---|---|---|---|
| P214 | **P35** | 2a. green | 7·50 | 7·50 |
| P215 | **P36** | 3a. brown | 9·00 | 10·50 |

**REGISTRATION STAMP**

**R19**

**1894.** Undated.

| | | | | |
|---|---|---|---|---|
| R155 | **R19** | 2a. black on green | 9·75 | 11·50 |

**APPENDIX**

The following stamps have either been issued in excess of postal needs or have not been available to the public in reasonable quantities at face value. Such stamps may later be given full listing if there is evidence of regular postal use. Sheets, imperforate sheetes etc, are excluded from this section.

**1961**

Agriculture Day. Fauna and Flora. 2, 2, 5, 10, 15, 25, 50, 100, 150, 175p.
Child Welfare. Sports and Games. 2, 2, 5, 10, 15, 25, 50, 100, 150, 175p.
UNICEF Surch on 1961 Child Welfare issue. 2+25, 2+25, 5+25, 10+25, 15p.+25p.
Women's Day. 50, 175p.
Independence Day. Mohamed Nadir Shah. 50, 175p.
International Exhibition, Kabul. 50, 175p.
Pashtunistan Day. 50, 175p.
National Assembly. 50, 175p.
Anti-malaria Campaign. 50, 175p.
King's 47th Birthday. 50, 175p.
Red Crescent Day. Fruits. 2, 2, 5, 10, 15, 25, 50, 100, 150, 175p.
Afghan Red Crescent Fund. 1961 Red Crescent Day issue surch 2+25, 2+25, 5+25, 10+25, 15p.+25p.
United Nations Day. 1, 2, 3, 4, 50, 75, 175p.
Teachers' Day. Flowers and Educational Scenes. 2, 2, 5, 10, 15, 25, 50, 100, 150, 175p.
UNESCO 1961 Teachers' Day issue surch 2+25, 2+25, 5+25, 10+25, 15p.+25p.

**1962**

15th Anniv (1961) of UNESCO 2, 2, 5, 10, 15, 25, 50, 75, 100p.
Ahmed Shah Baba. 50, 75, 100p.
Agriculture Day. Animals and Products. 2, 2, 5, 10, 15, 25, 50, 75, 100, 125p.
Independence Day. Marching Athletes. 25, 50, 150p.
Women's Day. Postage 25, 50p.; Air 100, 175p.
Pashtunistan Day. 25, 50, 150p.
Malaria Eradication. 2, 2, 5, 10, 15, 25, 50, 75, 100, 150, 175p.
National Assembly. 25, 50, 75, 100, 125p.
4th Asian Games, Djakarta, Indonesia. Postage 1, 2, 3, 4, 5p.; Air 25, 50, 75, 100, 150, 175p.
Children's Day. Sports and Produce. Postage 1, 2, 3, 4, 5p.; Air 75, 150, 200p.
King's 48th Birthday. 25, 50, 75, 100p.
Red Crescent Day. Fruits and Flowers. Postage 1, 2, 3, 4, 5p.; Air 25, 50, 100p.
Boy Scouts' Day. Postage 1, 2, 3, 4p.; Air 25, 50, 75, 100p.
1st Anniv of Hammarskjold's Death. Surch on 1961 UNESCO issue. 2+20, 2+20, 5+20, 10+20, 15+20, 25+20, 50+20, 75+20, 100p.+20p.
United Nations Day. Postage 1, 2, 3, 4, 5p.; Air 75, 100, 125p.
Teachers' Day. Sport and Flowers. Postage 1, 2, 3, 4, 5p.; Air 100, 150p.
World Meteorological Day. 50, 100p.

**1963**

Famous Afghans Pantheon, Kabul. 50, 75, 100p.
Agriculture Day. Sheep and Silkworms. Postage 1, 2, 3, 4, 5p.; Air 100, 150, 200p.
Freedom from Hunger. Postage 2, 3, 300p.; Air 500p.
Malaria Eradication Fund. 1962 Malaria Eradication issue surch 2+15, 2+15, 5+15, 10+15, 15+15, 25+15, 50+15, 75+15, 100+15, 150+15, 175p.+15p.
World Meteorological Day. Postage 1, 2, 3, 4, 5p.; Air 200, 300, 400, 500p.
"GANEFO" Athletic Games, Djakarta, Indonesia. Postage 2, 3, 4, 5, 10p., 9a.; Air 300, 500p.
Red Cross Centenary Postage 2, 3, 4, 5, 10p.; Air 100, 200p., 4, 6a.
Nubian Monuments Preservation. Postage 100, 200, 500p.; Air 5a., 7a.50.

**1964**

Women's Day (1963). 2, 3, 4, 5, 10p.
Afghan Boy Scouts and Girl Guides. Postage 2, 3, 4, 5, 10p.; Air 2, 2, 2a.50, 3, 4, 5, 12a.
Child Welfare Day (1963). Sports and Games. Postage 2, 3, 4, 5, 10p.; Air 200, 300p.
Afghan Red Crescent Society. Postage 100, 200p.; Air 5a., 7a.50.
Teachers' Day (1963). Flowers. Postage 2, 3, 4, 5, 10p.; Air 3a., 3a.50.
United Nations Day (1963). Postage 2, 3, 4, 5, 10p.; Air 100p., 2, 3a.
15th Anniv of Human Rights Declaration. Surch on 1964 United Nations Day issue. Postage 2+50, 3+50, 4+50, 5+50, 10p.+50p.; Air 100p.+50p., 2a.+50p., 3a.+50p.
UNICEF (dated 1963). Postage 100, 200p.; Air 5a. 7a.50.
Malaria Eradication (dated 1963). Postage 2, 3, 4, 5p., 10p. on 4p.; Air 2, 10a.

**2004**

Deer. 80a.; 115a; 100a.

**Pt. 1**

# AITUTAKI

Island in the South Pacific.

1903. 12 pence = 1 shilling; 20 shillings = 1 pound.
1967. 100 cents = 1 dollar.

## A. NEW ZEALAND DEPENDENCY

The British Government, who had exercised a protectorate over the Cook Islands group since the 1880s, handed the islands, including Aitutaki, to New Zealand administration in 1901. Cook Islands stamps were used from 1932 to 1972.

**1903.** Pictorial stamps of New Zealand surch **AITUTAKI**. and value in native language.

| | | | | |
|---|---|---|---|---|
| 1 | **23** | ½d. green | 4·75 | 6·50 |
| 2 | **42** | 1d. red | 5·00 | 5·50 |
| 4 | **26** | 2½d. blue | 14·00 | 12·00 |
| 5 | **28** | 3d. brown | 18·00 | 15·00 |
| 6 | **31** | 6d. red | 30·00 | 25·00 |
| 7 | **34** | 1s. orange | 55·00 | 85·00 |

**1911.** King Edward VII stamps of New Zealand surch **AITUTAKI**. and value in native language.

| | | | | |
|---|---|---|---|---|
| 9 | **51** | ½d. green | 1·00 | 6·50 |
| 10 | **53** | 1d. red | 3·00 | 13·00 |
| 11 | **51** | 6d. red | 50·00 | £140 |
| 12 | **51** | 1s. orange | 60·00 | £150 |

**1916.** King George V stamps of New Zealand surch **AITUTAKI**. and value in native language.

| | | | | |
|---|---|---|---|---|
| 13a | **62** | 6d. red | 7·50 | 27·00 |
| 14 | **62** | 1s. orange | 10·00 | 90·00 |

**1917.** King George V stamps of New Zealand optd **AITUTAKI**.

| | | | | |
|---|---|---|---|---|
| 19 | | ½d. green | 1·00 | 6·00 |
| 20 | **53** | 1d. red | 4·25 | 32·00 |
| 21 | **62** | 1½d. grey | 3·75 | 30·00 |
| 22 | **62** | 1½d. brown | 80 | 7·00 |
| 15a | | 2½d. blue | 1·75 | 16·00 |
| 16a | | 3d. brown | 1·50 | 27·00 |
| 17a | | 6d. red | 4·75 | 21·00 |
| 18a | | 1s. orange | 12·00 | 32·00 |

**1920.** As 1920 pictorial stamps of Cook Islands but inscr "**AITUTAKI**".

| | | | |
|---|---|---|---|
| 30 | ½d. black and green | 2·00 | 20·00 |
| 31 | 1d. black and red | 6·00 | 9·00 |
| 26 | 1½d. black and brown | 6·00 | 12·00 |
| 32 | 2½d. black and blue | 7·50 | 70·00 |
| 27 | 3d. black and blue | 2·50 | 14·00 |
| 28 | 6d. brown and grey | 5·50 | 14·00 |
| 29 | 1s. black and purple | 9·50 | 16·00 |

## B. PART OF COOK ISLANDS

On 9 August 1972 Aitutaki became a Port of Entry into the Cook Islands. Whilst remaining part of the Cook Islands, Aitutaki has a separate postal service.

**1972.** Nos. 227/8, 230, 233/4, 238, 240/1, 243 and 244 of Cook Islands optd **Aitutaki**.

| | | | | |
|---|---|---|---|---|
| 33 | **79** | ½c. multicoloured | 30 | 80 |
| 34 | - | 1c. multicoloured | 70 | 1·40 |
| 35 | - | 2½c. multicoloured | 2·25 | 7·00 |
| 36 | - | 4c. multicoloured | 70 | 85 |
| 37 | - | 5c. multicoloured | 2·50 | 7·50 |
| 38 | - | 10c. multicoloured | 2·50 | 5·50 |
| 39 | - | 20c. multicoloured | 3·75 | 1·00 |
| 40 | - | 25c. multicoloured | 70 | 1·00 |
| 41 | - | 50c. multicoloured | 2·75 | 2·75 |
| 42 | - | $1 multicoloured | 4·00 | 5·50 |

**1972.** Christmas. Nos. 406/8 of Cook Islands optd **Aitutaki**.

| | | | | |
|---|---|---|---|---|
| 43 | **130** | 1c. multicoloured | 10 | 10 |
| 44 | - | 5c. multicoloured | 15 | 15 |
| 45 | - | 10c. multicoloured | 15 | 25 |

**1972.** Royal Silver Wedding. As Nos. 413 and 415 of Cook Islands, but inscr "COOK ISLANDS Aitutaki".

| | | | | |
|---|---|---|---|---|
| 46 | **131** | 5c. black and silver | 3·50 | 2·75 |
| 47 | - | 15c. black and silver | 1·50 | 1·50 |

**1972.** No. 245 of Cook Islands optd **AITUTAKI**.

| | | | |
|---|---|---|---|
| 48 | $2 multicoloured | 50 | 75 |

**1972.** Nos. 227/8, 230, 233, 234, 238, 240, 241, 243 and 244 of Cook Islands optd **AITUTAKI** within ornamental oval.

| | | | | |
|---|---|---|---|---|
| 49 | **79** | ½c. multicoloured | 15 | 10 |
| 50 | - | 1c. multicoloured | 15 | 10 |
| 51 | - | 2½c. multicoloured | 20 | 10 |
| 52 | - | 4c. multicoloured | 25 | 15 |
| 53 | - | 5c. multicoloured | 25 | 15 |
| 54 | - | 10c. multicoloured | 35 | 25 |
| 55 | - | 20c. multicoloured | 1·25 | 50 |
| 56 | - | 25c. multicoloured | 50 | 55 |
| 57 | - | 50c. multicoloured | 75 | 90 |
| 58 | - | $1 multicoloured | 1·25 | 1·75 |

**13** "Christ Mocked" (Grunewald)

**1973.** Easter. Multicoloured.

| | | | |
|---|---|---|---|
| 59 | 1c. Type **13** | 15 | 10 |
| 60 | 1c. "St. Veronica" (Van der Weyden) | 15 | 10 |
| 61 | 1c. "The Crucified Christ with Virgin Mary, Saints and Angels" (Raphael) | 15 | 10 |
| 62 | 1c. "Resurrection" (Piero della Francesca) | 15 | 10 |
| 63 | 5c. "The Last Supper" (Master of Amiens) | 20 | 15 |
| 64 | 5c. "Condemnation" (Holbein) | 20 | 15 |
| 65 | 5c. "Christ on the Cross" (Rubens) | 20 | 15 |
| 66 | 5c. "Resurrection" (El Greco) | 20 | 15 |
| 67 | 10c. "Disrobing of Christ" (El Greco) | 25 | 15 |
| 68 | 10c. "St. Veronica" (Van Oostsanen) | 25 | 15 |
| 69 | 10c. "Christ on the Cross" (Rubens) | 25 | 15 |
| 70 | 10c. "Resurrection" (Bouts) | 25 | 15 |

**1973.** Silver Wedding Coinage. Nos. 417/23 of Cook Islands optd **AITUTAKI**.

| | | | | |
|---|---|---|---|---|
| 71 | **132** | 1c. black, red and gold | 10 | 10 |
| 72 | - | 2c. black, blue and gold | 10 | 10 |
| 73 | - | 5c. black, green and silver | 15 | 10 |
| 74 | - | 10c. black, blue and silver | 20 | 10 |
| 75 | - | 20c. black, green and silver | 30 | 15 |
| 76 | - | 50c. black, red and silver | 50 | 30 |
| 77 | - | $1 black, blue and silver | 70 | 45 |

**1973.** 10th Anniv of Treaty Banning Nuclear Testing. Nos. 236, 238, 240 and 243 of Cook Islands optd **AITUTAKI** within ornamental oval and **TENTH ANNIVERSARY CESSATION OF NUCLEAR TESTING TREATY**.

| | | | |
|---|---|---|---|
| 78 | 8c. multicoloured | 15 | 15 |
| 79 | 10c. multicoloured | 15 | 15 |
| 80 | 20c. multicoloured | 30 | 20 |
| 81 | 50c. multicoloured | 70 | 50 |

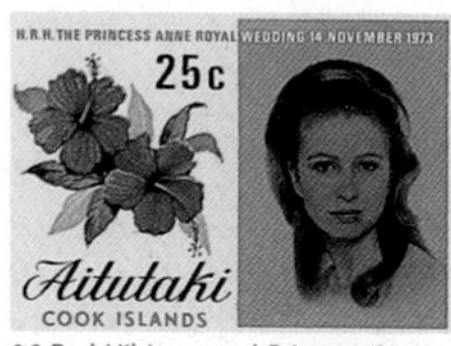


**16** Red Hibiscus and Princess Anne

**1973.** Royal Wedding. Multicoloured.

| | | | |
|---|---|---|---|
| 82 | 25c. Type **16** | 25 | 10 |
| 83 | 30c. Capt. Mark Phillips and blue hibiscus | 25 | 10 |
| **MS**84 | 114×65 mm. Nos. 82/3 | 50 | 40 |

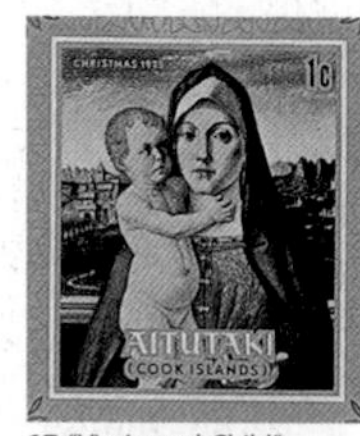


**17** "Virgin and Child" (Montagna)

**1973.** Christmas. "Virgin and Child" paintings by artists listed below. Multicoloured.

| | | | |
|---|---|---|---|
| 85 | 1c. Type **17** | 10 | 10 |
| 86 | 1c. Crivelli | 10 | 10 |
| 87 | 1c. Van Dyck | 10 | 10 |
| 88 | 1c. Perugino | 10 | 10 |
| 89 | 5c. Veronese (child at shoulder) | 25 | 10 |
| 90 | 5c. Veronese (child on lap) | 25 | 10 |
| 91 | 5c. Cima | 25 | 10 |
| 92 | 5c. Memling | 25 | 10 |
| 93 | 10c. Memling | 25 | 10 |
| 94 | 10c. Del Colle | 25 | 10 |
| 95 | 10c. Raphael | 25 | 10 |
| 96 | 10c. Lotto | 25 | 10 |

**18** Rose-branch Murex

**1974.** Sea Shells. Multicoloured.

| | | | |
|---|---|---|---|
| 97 | ½c. Type **18** | 90 | 1·00 |
| 98 | 1c. New Caledonia nautilus | 90 | 1·00 |
| 99 | 2c. Common or major harp | 90 | 1·00 |
| 100 | 3c. Striped bonnet | 90 | 1·00 |
| 101 | 4c. Mole cowrie | 90 | 1·00 |
| 102 | 5c. Pontifical mitre | 90 | 1·00 |
| 103 | 8c. Trumpet triton | 90 | 1·00 |
| 104 | 10c. Venus comb murex | 90 | 80 |
| 105 | 20c. Red-mouth olive | 1·25 | 80 |
| 106 | 25c. Ruddy frog shell | 1·25 | 80 |
| 107 | 60c. Widest pacific conch | 4·00 | 1·25 |
| 108 | $1 Maple-leaf triton or winged frog shell | 2·50 | 1·40 |
| 109 | $2 Queen Elizabeth II and Marlin-spike auger | 6·00 | 9·00 |
| 110 | $5 Queen Elizabeth II and Tiger cowrie | 29·00 | 10·00 |

The $2 and $5 are larger, 53×25 mm.

**19** Bligh and H.M.S. "Bounty"

**1974.** William Bligh's Discovery of Aitutaki. Multicoloured.

| | | | |
|---|---|---|---|
| 114 | 1c. Type **19** | 60 | 60 |
| 115 | 1c. H.M.S. "Bounty" | 60 | 60 |

| | | | |
|---|---|---|---|
| 116 | 5c. Bligh, and H.M.S. "Bounty" at Aitutaki | 1·00 | 1·00 |
| 117 | 5c. Aitutaki chart of 1856 | 1·00 | 1·00 |
| 118 | 8c. Captain Cook and H.M.S. "Resolution" | 1·40 | 1·40 |
| 119 | 8c. Map of Aitutaki and inset location map | 1·40 | 1·40 |

See also Nos. 123/8.

**20** Aitutaki Stamps of 1903, Sand Map

**1974.** Centenary of U.P.U. Multicoloured.

| | | | |
|---|---|---|---|
| 120 | 25c. Type **20** | 75 | 50 |
| 121 | 50c. Stamps of 1903 and 1920, and map | 1·00 | 75 |
| **MS**122 | 66×75 mm. Nos. 120/1 | 1·25 | 2·75 |

**1974.** Air. As Nos. 114/119 in larger size (46×26 mm), additionally inscr "AIR MAIL".

| | | | |
|---|---|---|---|
| 123 | 10c. Type **19** | 60 | 65 |
| 124 | 10c. H.M.S. "Bounty" | 60 | 65 |
| 125 | 25c. Bligh, and H.M.S. "Bounty" at Aitutaki | 70 | 75 |
| 126 | 25c. Aitutaki chart of 1856 | 70 | 75 |
| 127 | 30c. Captain Cook and H.M.S. "Resolution" | 80 | 85 |
| 128 | 30c. Map of Aitutaki and inset location map | 80 | 85 |

**21** "Virgin and Child" (Hugo van der Goes)

**1974.** Christmas. "Virgin and Child" paintings by artists named. Multicoloured.

| | | | |
|---|---|---|---|
| 129 | 1c. Type **21** | 10 | 15 |
| 130 | 5c. Bellini | 10 | 20 |
| 131 | 8c. Gerard David | 10 | 20 |
| 132 | 10c. Antonello da Messina | 10 | 15 |
| 133 | 25c. Joos van Cleve | 20 | 30 |
| 134 | 30c. Master of the Life of St. Catherine | 20 | 30 |
| **MS**135 | 127×134 mm. Nos. 129/34 | 1·40 | 1·75 |

**22** Churchill as Schoolboy

**1974.** Birth Centenary of Sir Winston Churchill. Multicoloured.

| | | | |
|---|---|---|---|
| 136 | 10c. Type **22** | 20 | 25 |
| 137 | 25c. Churchill as young man | 25 | 40 |
| 138 | 30c. Churchill with troops | 25 | 45 |
| 139 | 50c. Churchill painting | 30 | 60 |
| 140 | $1 Giving "V" sign | 40 | 75 |
| **MS**141 | 115×108 mm. Nos. 136/40 | 1·25 | 1·50 |

**1974.** Children's Christmas Fund. Nos. 129/34 surch.

| | | | | |
|---|---|---|---|---|
| 142 | 21 | 1c.+1c. multicoloured | 10 | 10 |
| 143 | - | 5c.+1c. multicoloured | 10 | 10 |
| 144 | - | 8c.+1c. multicoloured | 10 | 10 |
| 145 | - | 10c.+1c. multicoloured | 10 | 10 |
| 146 | - | 25c.+1c. multicoloured | 20 | 20 |
| 147 | - | 30c.+1c. multicoloured | 20 | 20 |

**24** Soviet and U.S. Flags

**1975.** "Apollo–Soyuz" Space Project. Mult.

| | | | |
|---|---|---|---|
| 148 | 25c. Type **24** | 30 | 20 |
| 149 | 50c. Daedalus with space capsule | 40 | 30 |
| **MS**150 | 123×61 mm. Nos. 148/9 | 1·25 | 1·10 |

**25** St. Francis

**1975.** Christmas. Multicoloured.

| | | | |
|---|---|---|---|
| 151 | 6c. Type **25** | 10 | 10 |
| 152 | 6c. Madonna and Child | 10 | 10 |
| 153 | 6c. St. John | 10 | 10 |
| 154 | 7c. King and donkey | 10 | 10 |
| 155 | 7c. Madonna, Child and King | 10 | 10 |
| 156 | 7c. Kings with gifts | 10 | 10 |
| 157 | 15c. Madonna and Child | 15 | 15 |
| 158 | 15c. St. Onufrius | 15 | 15 |
| 159 | 15c. John the Baptist | 15 | 15 |
| 160 | 20c. Shepherd and cattle | 20 | 15 |
| 161 | 20c. Madonna and Child | 20 | 15 |
| 162 | 20c. Shepherds | 20 | 15 |
| **MS**163 | 104×201 mm. Nos. 151/62 | 2·25 | 2·50 |

Stamps of the same value were printed together, se-tenant, each strip forming a composite design of a complete painting as follows: Nos. 151/3, "Madonna and Child with Saints Francis and John" (Lorenzetti); 154/6, "Adoration of the Kings" (Van der Weyden); 157/9, "Madonna and Child Enthroneth with Saints Onufrius and John the Baptist" (Montagna); 160/2, "Adoration of the Shepherds" (Reni).

**1975.** Children's Christmas Fund. Nos. 151/62 surch.

| | | | | |
|---|---|---|---|---|
| 164 | 25 | 6c.+1c. multicoloured | 10 | 10 |
| 165 | - | 6c.+1c. multicoloured | 10 | 10 |
| 166 | - | 6c.+1c. multicoloured | 10 | 10 |
| 167 | - | 7c.+1c. multicoloured | 10 | 10 |
| 168 | - | 7c.+1c. multicoloured | 10 | 10 |
| 169 | - | 7c.+1c. multicoloured | 10 | 10 |
| 170 | - | 15c.+1c. multicoloured | 15 | 15 |
| 171 | - | 15c.+1c. multicoloured | 15 | 15 |
| 172 | - | 15c.+1c. multicoloured | 15 | 15 |
| 173 | - | 20c.+1c. multicoloured | 20 | 20 |
| 174 | - | 20c.+1c. multicoloured | 20 | 20 |
| 175 | - | 20c.+1c. multicoloured | 20 | 20 |

**26** "The Descent" (detail, 15th-century Flemish School)

**1976.** Easter. Multicoloured.

| | | | |
|---|---|---|---|
| 176 | 15c. Type **26** | 15 | 10 |
| 177 | 30c. "The Descent" (detail) | 20 | 15 |
| 178 | 35c. "The Descent" (detail) | 25 | 20 |
| **MS**179 | 87×67 mm. Nos. 176/8 forming a complete picture of "The Descent" | 1·00 | 1·25 |

**27** Left Detail

**1976.** Bicentenary of American Revolution. Paintings by John Turnbull.

| | | | | |
|---|---|---|---|---|
| 180 | 27 | 30c. multicoloured | 20 | 10 |
| 181 | - | 30c. multicoloured | 20 | 10 |
| 182 | - | 30c. multicoloured | 20 | 10 |
| 183 | - | 35c. multicoloured | 20 | 15 |
| 184 | - | 35c. multicoloured | 20 | 15 |
| 185 | - | 35c. multicoloured | 20 | 15 |
| 186 | - | 50c. multicoloured | 20 | 15 |
| 187 | - | 50c. multicoloured | 20 | 15 |
| 188 | - | 50c. multicoloured | 20 | 15 |
| **MS**189 | | 132×120 mm. Nos. 180/8 | 1·75 | 1·10 |

PAINTINGS: Nos. 180/2, "The Declaration of Independence"; 183/5, "The Surrender of Lord Cornwallis at Yorktown"; 186/8, "The Resignation of General Washington".

Stamps of the same value were printed together, se-tenant, each strip forming a composite design of the whole painting.

**28** Cycling

**1976.** Olympic Games, Montreal. Multicoloured.

| | | | |
|---|---|---|---|
| 190 | 15c. Type **28** | 80 | 15 |
| 191 | 35c. Sailing | 45 | 20 |
| 192 | 60c. Hockey | 1·00 | 25 |
| 193 | 70c. Sprinting | 70 | 30 |
| **MS**194 | 107×97 mm. Nos. 190/3 | 2·50 | 1·25 |

**1976.** Royal Visit to the U.S.A. Nos. 190/3 optd **VISIT ROYAL JULY 1976**.

| | | | | |
|---|---|---|---|---|
| 195 | 28 | 15c. multicoloured | 50 | 15 |
| 196 | - | 35c. multicoloured | 45 | 25 |
| 197 | - | 60c. multicoloured | 80 | 40 |
| 198 | - | 70c. multicoloured | 70 | 45 |
| **MS**199 | | 107×97 mm. Nos. 195/8 | 2·00 | 1·25 |

**30** "The Visitation"

**1976.** Christmas.

| | | | | |
|---|---|---|---|---|
| 200 | 30 | 6c. gold and green | 10 | 10 |
| 201 | - | 6c. gold and green | 10 | 10 |
| 202 | - | 7c. gold and purple | 10 | 10 |
| 203 | - | 7c. gold and purple | 10 | 10 |
| 204 | - | 15c. gold and blue | 10 | 10 |
| 205 | - | 15c. gold and blue | 10 | 10 |
| 206 | - | 20c. gold and violet | 15 | 15 |
| 207 | - | 20c. gold and violet | 15 | 15 |
| **MS**208 | | 128×96 mm. As Nos. 200/7 but with borders on three sides | 1·00 | 1·40 |

DESIGNS: No. 201, Angel; 202, Angel; 203, Shepherds; 204, Joseph; 205, Mary and the Child; 206, Wise Man; 207, Two Wise Men.

Stamps of the same value were printed together, se-tenant, each pair forming a composite design.

**1976.** Children's Christmas Fund. Nos. 200/7 surch.

| | | | | |
|---|---|---|---|---|
| 209 | 30 | 6c.+1c. gold and green | 10 | 10 |
| 210 | - | 6c.+1c. gold and green | 10 | 10 |
| 211 | - | 7c.+1c. gold and purple | 10 | 10 |
| 212 | - | 7c.+1c. gold and purple | 10 | 10 |
| 213 | - | 15c.+1c. gold and blue | 15 | 15 |
| 214 | - | 15c.+1c. gold and blue | 15 | 15 |
| 215 | - | 20c.+1c. gold and violet | 15 | 15 |
| 216 | - | 20c.+1c. gold and violet | 15 | 15 |
| **MS**217 | | 128×96 mm. As Nos. 209/16 but with a premium of "+2c." and borders on three sides | 80 | 1·40 |

**32** Alexander Graham Bell and First Telephone

**1977.** Centenary (1976) of Telephone.

| | | | | |
|---|---|---|---|---|
| 218 | 32 | 25c. black, gold and red | 20 | 15 |
| 219 | - | 70c. black, gold and lilac | 40 | 40 |
| **MS**220 | | 116×59 mm. As Nos. 218/19 but with different colours | 70 | 1·00 |

DESIGN: 70c. Satellite and Earth station.

**33** "Christ on the Cross" (detail)

**1977.** Easter. 400th Birth Anniv of Rubens. Mult.

| | | | |
|---|---|---|---|
| 221 | 15c. Type **33** | 45 | 15 |
| 222 | 20c. "Lamentation for Christ" | 60 | 20 |
| 223 | 35c. "Christ with Straw" | 75 | 25 |
| **MS**224 | 115×57 mm. Nos. 221/3. P 13×12½ | 1·60 | 1·60 |

**34** Captain Bligh, George III and H.M.S. "Bounty"

**1977.** Silver Jubilee. Multicoloured.

| | | | |
|---|---|---|---|
| 225 | 25c. Type **34** | 35 | 35 |
| 226 | 35c. Rev. Williams, George IV and Aitutaki Church | 40 | 40 |
| 227 | 50c. Union Jack, Queen Victoria and island map | 45 | 45 |
| 228 | $1 Balcony scene, 1953 | 50 | 50 |
| **MS**229 | 130×87 mm. As Nos. 225/8 but with gold borders | 1·25 | 1·25 |

**35** The Shepherds

**1977.** Christmas. Multicoloured.

| | | | |
|---|---|---|---|
| 230 | 6c. Type **35** | 10 | 10 |
| 231 | 6c. Angel | 10 | 10 |
| 232 | 7c. Mary, Jesus and ox | 10 | 10 |
| 233 | 7c. Joseph and donkey | 10 | 10 |
| 234 | 15c. Three Kings | 10 | 10 |
| 235 | 15c. Virgin and Child | 10 | 10 |
| 236 | 20c. Joseph | 10 | 10 |
| 237 | 20c. Mary and Jesus on donkey | 10 | 10 |
| **MS**238 | 130×95 mm. Nos. 230/7 | 70 | 1·25 |

Stamps of the same value were printed together, se-tenant, forming composite designs.

**1977.** Children's Christmas Fund. Nos. 230/7 surch +1c.

| | | | |
|---|---|---|---|
| 239 | 6c.+1c. Type **35** | 10 | 10 |
| 240 | 6c.+1c. Angel | 10 | 10 |
| 241 | 7c.+1c. Mary, Jesus and ox | 10 | 10 |
| 242 | 7c.+1c. Joseph and donkey | 10 | 10 |
| 243 | 15c.+1c. Three Kings | 15 | 10 |
| 244 | 15c.+1c. Virgin and Child | 15 | 10 |
| 245 | 20c.+1c. Joseph | 15 | 10 |
| 246 | 20c.+1c. Mary and Jesus on donkey | 15 | 10 |
| **MS**247 | 130×95 mm. As Nos. 239/46 but each with premium of "+2c." | 70 | 85 |

**37** Hawaiian Goddess

**1978.** Bicentenary of Discovery of Hawaii. Mult.

| | | | |
|---|---|---|---|
| 248 | 35c. Type **37** | 35 | 25 |
| 249 | 50c. Figurehead of H.M.S. "Resolution" (horiz) | 60 | 40 |
| 250 | $1 Hawaiian temple figure | 70 | 70 |
| **MS**251 | 168×75 mm. Nos. 248/50 | 1·50 | 1·75 |

**38** "Christ on the Way to Calvary" (Martini)

**1978.** Easter. Paintings from the Louvre, Paris. Mult.

| | | | |
|---|---|---|---|
| 252 | 15c. Type **38** | 15 | 10 |
| 253 | 20c. "Pieta of Avignon" (E. Quarton) | 20 | 10 |
| 254 | 35c. "The Pilgrims at Emmaus" (Rembrandt) | 25 | 10 |
| **MS**255 | 108×83 mm. Nos. 252/4 | 75 | 75 |

**1978.** Easter. Children's Charity. Designs as Nos. 252/4, but smaller (34×26 mm) and without margins, in separate miniature sheets 75×58 mm, each with a face value of 50c. + 5c.

| | | | |
|---|---|---|---|
| **MS**256 | As Nos. 252/4 Set of 3 sheets | 1·00 | 1·00 |

**39** The Yale of Beaufort

**1978.** 25th Anniv of Coronation. Multicoloured.
257 $1 Type **39** 30 50
258 $1 Queen Elizabeth II 30 50
259 $1 Aitutaki ancestral statue 30 50
**MS**260 98×127 mm. Nos 257/9×2 75 75

Stamps from No. **MS**260 have coloured borders, the upper row in lavender and the lower in green.

**40** "Adoration of the Infant Jesus"

**1978.** Christmas. 450th Death Anniv of Durer. Multicoloured.
261 15c. Type **40** 25 15
262 17c. "The Madonna with Child" 30 15
263 30c. "The Madonna with the Iris" 45 20
264 35c. "The Madonna of the Siskin" 45 25
**MS**265 101×109 mm. As Nos. 261/4 but each with premium of "+2c." 1·10 1·00

**41** "Captain Cook" (Nathaniel Dance)

**1979.** Death Bicent of Captain Cook. Mult.
266 50c. Type **41** 1·00 80
267 75c. "H.M.S. 'Resolution' and 'Adventure' at Matavai Bay," Tahiti (W. Hodges) 1·75 95
**MS**268 94×58 mm. Nos. 266/7 2·00 2·25

**42** Girl with Flowers

**1979.** International Year of the Child. Multicoloured.
269 30c. Type **42** 20 15
270 35c. Boy playing guitar 30 20
271 65c. Children in canoe 40 30
**MS**272 104×80 mm. As Nos. 269/71, but each with a premium of "+3c." 70 1·00

**43** "Man writing a Letter" (painting by Gabriel Metsu)

**1979.** Death Centenary of Sir Rowland Hill. Multicoloured.
273 50c. Type **43** 45 45
274 50c. Sir Rowland Hill with Penny Black, 1903 ½d. and 1911 1d. stamps 45 45
275 50c. "Girl in Blue reading a Letter" (Jan Vermeer) 45 45
276 65c. "Woman writing a Letter" (Gerard Terborch) 50 50
277 65c. Sir Rowland Hill, with Penny Black, 1903 3d. and 1920 ½d. stamps 50 50
278 65c. "Lady reading a Letter" (Jan Vermeer) 50 50
**MS**279 151×85 mm. 30c.×6. As Nos. 273/8 1·75 1·75

**44** "The Burial of Christ" (left detail) (Quentin Metsys)

**1980.** Easter. Multicoloured.
280 20c. Type **44** 40 25
281 30c. "The Burial of Christ" (centre detail) 50 35
282 35c. "The Burial of Christ" (right detail) 65 45
**MS**283 93×71 mm. As Nos. 280/2, but each with premium of "+2c." 75 75

**45** Einstein as a Young Man

**1980.** 25th Death Anniv of Albert Einstein (physicist). Multicoloured.
284 12c. Type **45** 60 60
285 12c. Atom and "$E=mc^2$" equation 60 60
286 15c. Einstein in middle-age 65 65
287 15c. Cross over nuclear explosion (Test Ban Treaty, 1963) 65 65
288 20c. Einstein as an old man 75 75
289 20c. Hand preventing atomic explosion 75 75
**MS**290 113×118 mm. Nos 284/9 3·00 3·00

**46** Ancestor Figure, Aitutaki

**1980.** 3rd South Pacific Festival of Arts. Mult.
291 6c. Type **46** 10 10
292 6c. Staff god image, Rarotonga 10 10
293 6c. Trade adze, Mangaia 10 10
294 6c. Carved image of Tangaroa, Rarotonga 10 10
295 12c. Wooden image Aitutaki 10 10
296 12c. Hand club, Rarotonga 10 10
297 12c. Carved mace "god", Mangaia 10 10
298 12c. Fisherman's god, Rarotonga 10 10
299 15c. Ti'i image, Aitutaki 15 15
300 15c. Fisherman's god, Rarotonga (different) 15 15
301 15c. Carved mace "god", Cook Islands 15 15
302 15c. Carved image of Tangaroa, Rarotonga (different) 15 15
303 20c. Chief's headdress, Aitutaki 15 15
304 20c. Carved mace "god", Cook Islands (different) 15 15
305 20c. Staff god image, Rarotonga (different) 15 15
306 20c. Carved image of Tangaroa, Rarotonga (different) 15 15
**MS**307 134×194 mm. Nos. 291/306 1·60 1·75

**47** "Virgin and Child" (13th century)

**1980.** Christmas. Sculptures of "The Virgin and Child". Multicoloured.
308 15c. Type **47** 20 15
309 20c. 14th century 20 15
310 25c. 15th century 20 15
311 35c. 15th century (different) 30 20
**MS**312 82×120 mm. As Nos. 306/11 but each with premium of 2c. 70 80

**48** "Mourning Virgin"

**1981.** Easter. Details of Sculpture "Burial of Christ" by Pedro Roldan.
313 **48** 30c. gold and green 25 25
314 - 40c. gold and lilac 30 30
315 - 50c. gold and blue 30 30
**MS**316 107×60 mm. As Nos. 313/15 but each with premium of 2c. 75 85

DESIGNS: 40c. "Christ"; 50c. "Saint John".

**49** Gouldian Finch

**1981.** Birds (1st series). Multicoloured.
317 1c. Type **49** 45 30
318 1c. Common starling 45 30
319 2c. Golden whistler 50 30
320 2c. Scarlet robin 50 30
321 3c. Rufous fantail 60 30
322 3c. Peregrine falcon 60 30
323 4c. Java sparrow 70 30
324 4c. Barn owl 70 30
325 5c. Tahitian lory 70 30
326 5c. White-breasted wood swallow 70 30
327 6c. Purple swamphen 70 30
328 6c. Feral rock pigeon 70 30
329 10c. Chestnut-breasted mannikin 90 30
330 10c. Zebra dove 90 30
331 12c. Reef heron 1·00 40
332 12c. Common mynah 1·00 40
333 15c. Whimbrel (horiz) 1·25 40
334 15c. Black-browed albatross (horiz) 1·25 40
335 20c. Pacific golden plover (horiz) 1·50 55
336 20c. White tern (horiz) 1·50 55
337 25c. Pacific black duck (horiz) 1·75 70
338 25c. Brown booby (horiz) 1·75 70
339 30c. Great frigate bird (horiz) 2·00 85
340 30c. Pintail (horiz) 2·00 85
341 35c. Long-billed reed warbler 2·00 1·00
342 35c. Pomarine skua 2·00 1·00
343 40c. Buff-banded rail 2·25 1·25
344 40c. Spotted triller 2·25 1·25
345 50c. Royal albatross 2·25 1·50
346 50c. Stephen's lory 2·25 1·50
347 70c. Red-headed parrot-finch 5·50 3·00
348 70c. Orange dove 5·50 3·00
349 $1 Blue-headed flycatcher 4·50 3·75
350 $2 Red-bellied flycatcher 5·00 8·00
351 $4 Red munia 9·00 14·00
352 $5 Flat-billed kingfisher 9·00 16·00

See also Nos. 475/94.

**50** Prince Charles

**1981.** Royal Wedding. Multicoloured.
391 60c. Type **50** 30 40
392 80c. Lady Diana Spencer 40 55
393 $1.40 Prince Charles and Lady Diana (87×70 mm) 60 80

**1981.** International Year for Disabled Persons. Nos. 391/3 surch +5c.
394 60c.+5c. Type **50** 60 90
395 80c.+5c. Lady Diana Spencer 70 1·10
396 $1.40+5c. Prince Charles and Lady Diana 90 1·40

**52** Footballers

**1981.** World Cup Football Championship, Spain (1982). Football Scenes. Multicoloured.
397 12c. Ball to left of stamp 50 35
398 12c. Ball to right 50 35
399 15c. Ball to right 55 40
400 15c. Ball to left 55 40
401 20c. Ball to left 55 50
402 20c. Ball to right 55 50
403 25c. Type **52** 60 55
404 25c. "ESPANA 82" inscription 60 55
**MS**405 100×137 mm. 12c.+2c., 15c.+2c., 20c.+2c., 25c.+2c., each × 2. As Nos. 397/404 3·50 3·00

**53** "The Holy Family"

**1981.** Christmas. Etchings by Rembrandt. Each brown and gold.
406 15c. Type **53** 45 45
407 30c. "Virgin with Child" 70 70
408 40c. "Adoration of the Shepherds" (horiz) 95 95
409 50c. "The Holy Family" (horiz) 1·25 1·25
**MS**410 Designs as Nos. 406/9 in separate miniature sheets, 65×82 mm or 82×65 mm, each with a face value of 80c.+5c. Set of 4 sheets 4·00 3·00

**54** Princess of Wales

**1982.** 21st Birthday of Princess of Wales. Mult.
411 70c. Type **54** 2·00 60
412 $1 Prince and Princess of Wales 2·00 75
413 $2 Princess Diana (different) 3·25 1·50
**MS**414 82×91 mm. Nos. 411/13 6·00 2·75

**1982.** Birth of Prince William of Wales (1st issue). Nos. 391/3 optd.
415 60c. Type **50** 90 70
416 60c. Type **50** 90 70
417 80c. Lady Diana Spencer 1·10 80
418 80c. Lady Diana Spencer 1·10 80
419 $1.40 Prince Charles and Lady Diana 1·25 1·00
420 $1.40 Prince Charles and Lady Diana 1·25 1·00

OPTS: Nos. 415, 417 and 419, **21 JUNE 1982. PRINCE WILLIAM OF WALES.** Nos. 416, 418 and 420, **COMMEMORATING THE ROYAL BIRTH.**

**1982.** Birth of Prince William of Wales (2nd issue). As Nos. 411/13 but inscr "ROYAL BIRTH 21 JUNE 1982 PRINCE WILLIAM OF WALES".
421 70c. Type **54** 70 60
422 $1 Prince and Princess of Wales 80 75

423 $2 Princess Diana (different) 1·60 1·50
**MS**424 81×91 mm. Nos. 421/3 5·50 3·00

**56** "Virgin and Child" (12th-century sculpture)

**1982.** Christmas. Religious Sculptures. Multicoloured.

| | | | |
|---|---|---|---|
| 425 | 18c. Type **56** | 70 | 70 |
| 426 | 36c. "Virgin and Child" (12th-century) | 85 | 85 |
| 427 | 48c. "Virgin and Child" (13th-century) | 1·00 | 1·00 |
| 428 | 60c. "Virgin and Child" (15th-century) | 1·40 | 1·40 |
| **MS**429 | 99×115 mm. As Nos. 425/8 but each with 2c. charity premium | 2·50 | 2·75 |

**57** Aitutaki Bananas

**1983.** Commonwealth Day. Multicoloured.

| | | | |
|---|---|---|---|
| 430 | 48c. Type **57** | 75 | 50 |
| 431 | 48c. Ancient Ti'i image | 75 | 50 |
| 432 | 48c. Tourist canoeing | 75 | 50 |
| 433 | 48c. Captain William Bligh and chart | 75 | 50 |

**58** Scouts around Campfire

**1983.** 75th Anniv of Boy Scout Movement. Mult.

| | | | |
|---|---|---|---|
| 434 | 36c. Type **58** | 65 | 65 |
| 435 | 48c. Scout saluting | 75 | 75 |
| 436 | 60c. Scouts hiking | 80 | 80 |
| **MS**437 | 78×107 mm. As Nos. 434/6 but each with premium of 3c. | 1·50 | 1·75 |

**1983.** 15th World Scout Jamboree, Alberta, Canada. Nos. 434/6 optd **15TH WORLD SCOUT JAMBOREE**.

| | | | |
|---|---|---|---|
| 438 | 36c. Type **58** | 80 | 45 |
| 439 | 48c. Scout saluting | 1·00 | 55 |
| 440 | 60c. Scouts hiking | 1·25 | 75 |
| **MS**441 | 78×107 mm. As Nos. 438/40 but each with a premium of 3c. | 1·50 | 2·00 |

**60** Modern Sport Balloon

**1983.** Bicentenary of Manned Flight.

| | | | | |
|---|---|---|---|---|
| 442 | **60** | 18c. multicoloured | 55 | 30 |
| 443 | - | 36c. multicoloured | 75 | 50 |
| 444 | - | 48c. multicoloured | 90 | 60 |
| 445 | - | 60c. multicoloured | 1·00 | 80 |
| **MS**446 | | – 64×80 mm. $2.50, mult (48½×28½ mm) | 1·50 | 2·00 |

DESIGNS: 36c. to $2.50, showing different modern sports balloons.

**1983.** Various stamps surch (a) Nos. 335/48 and 352.

| | | | |
|---|---|---|---|
| 447 | 18c. on 20c. Pacific golden plover | 2·75 | 1·25 |
| 448 | 18c. on 20c. White tern | 2·75 | 1·25 |
| 449 | 36c. on 25c. Pacific black duck | 3·75 | 1·50 |
| 450 | 36c. on 25c. Brown booby | 3·75 | 1·50 |
| 451 | 36c. on 30c. Great frigate bird | 3·75 | 1·50 |
| 452 | 36c. on 30c. Pintail | 3·75 | 1·50 |
| 453 | 36c. on 35c. Long-billed reed warbler | 3·75 | 1·50 |
| 454 | 36c. on 35c. Pomarine skua | 3·75 | 1·50 |
| 455 | 48c. on 40c. Buff-banded rail | 4·25 | 1·50 |
| 456 | 48c. on 40c. Spotted triller | 4·25 | 1·50 |
| 457 | 48c. on 50c. Royal albatross | 4·25 | 1·50 |
| 458 | 48c. on 50c. Stephen's lory | 4·25 | 1·50 |
| 459 | 72c. on 70c. Red-headed parrot finch | 7·50 | 3·00 |
| 460 | 72c. on 70c. Orange dove | 7·50 | 3·00 |
| 461 | $5.60 on $5 Flat-billed kingfisher (vert) | 21·00 | 10·00 |

(b) Nos. 392/3 and 412/3.

| | | | |
|---|---|---|---|
| 462 | 96c. on 80c. Lady Diana Spencer | 3·00 | 2·50 |
| 463 | 96c. on $1 Prince and Princess of Wales | 2·75 | 2·00 |
| 464 | $1.20 on $1.40 Prince Charles and Lady Diana | 3·00 | 2·50 |
| 465 | $1.20 on $2 Princess Diana | 2·75 | 2·00 |

**63** International Mail

**1983.** World Communications Year. Multicoloured.

| | | | |
|---|---|---|---|
| 466 | 48c. Type **63** | 65 | 50 |
| 467 | 60c. Telecommunications | 95 | 70 |
| 468 | 96c. Space satellite | 1·40 | 1·00 |
| **MS**469 | 126×53 mm. Nos. 466/8 | 2·50 | 2·50 |

**64** "Madonna of the Chair"

**1983.** Christmas. 500th Birth Anniv of Raphael. Multicoloured.

| | | | |
|---|---|---|---|
| 470 | 36c. Type **64** | 75 | 40 |
| 471 | 48c. "The Alba Madonna" | 90 | 50 |
| 472 | 60c. "Conestabile Madonna" | 1·25 | 70 |
| **MS**473 | 95×116 mm. Nos. 470/2, but each with a premium of 3c. | 2·75 | 1·40 |

**1983.** Christmas. 500th Birth Anniv of Raphael. Children's Charity. Designs as Nos. 470/2 in separate miniature sheets 46×47 mm, but with different frames and a face value of 85c.+5c. Imperf.

**MS**474 As Nos. 470/2 Set of 3 sheets 3·75 2·75

**65** Gouldian Finch

**1984.** Birds (2nd series). Multicoloured.

| | | | |
|---|---|---|---|
| 475 | 2c. Type **65** | 1·75 | 1·25 |
| 476 | 3c. Common starling | 1·75 | 1·25 |
| 477 | 5c. Scarlet robin | 1·75 | 1·40 |
| 478 | 10c. Golden whistler | 2·25 | 1·40 |
| 479 | 12c. Rufous fantail | 2·25 | 1·40 |
| 480 | 18c. Peregrine falcon | 2·25 | 1·75 |
| 481 | 24c. Barn owl | 2·25 | 1·75 |
| 482 | 30c. Java sparrow | 2·25 | 1·50 |
| 483 | 36c. White-breasted wood swallow | 2·25 | 1·50 |
| 484 | 48c. Tahitian lory | 2·25 | 1·50 |
| 485 | 50c. Feral rock pigeon | 2·50 | 2·50 |
| 486 | 60c. Purple swamphen | 2·50 | 2·00 |
| 487 | 72c. Zebra dove | 3·00 | 2·50 |
| 488 | 96c. Chestnut-breasted mannikin | 3·00 | 2·50 |
| 489 | $1.20 Common mynah | 3·00 | 3·50 |
| 490 | $2.10 Reef heron | 5·00 | 3·75 |
| 491 | $3 Blue-headed flycatcher | 7·00 | 6·00 |
| 492 | $4.20 Red-bellied flycatcher | 3·50 | 6·00 |
| 493 | $5.60 Red munia | 3·50 | 9·50 |
| 494 | $9.60 Flat-billed kingfisher | 7·50 | 12·00 |

**66** Javelin throwing

**1984.** Olympic Games. Los Angeles. Multicoloured.

| | | | |
|---|---|---|---|
| 495 | 36c. Type **66** | 35 | 35 |
| 496 | 48c. Shot-putting | 40 | 45 |
| 497 | 60c. Hurdling | 45 | 55 |
| 498 | $2 Basketball | 1·75 | 1·50 |
| **MS**499 | 88×117 mm. As Nos. 495/8, but each with a charity premium of 5c. | 3·00 | 3·50 |

DESIGNS: 48c. to $2, show Memorial Coliseum and various events.

**1984.** Olympic Gold Medal Winners. Nos. 495/8 optd.

| | | | |
|---|---|---|---|
| 500 | 36c. Type **66** (optd **Javelin Throw Tessa Sanderson Great Britain**) | 35 | 35 |
| 501 | 48c. Shot-putting (optd **Shot Put Claudia Losch Germany**) | 40 | 45 |
| 502 | 60c. Hurdling (optd **Heptathlon Glynis Nunn Australia**) | 45 | 55 |
| 503 | $2 Basketball (optd **Team Basketball United States**) | 1·10 | 1·50 |

**67** Captain William Bligh and Chart

**1984.** "Ausipex" International Stamp Exhibition, Melbourne. Multicoloured.

| | | | |
|---|---|---|---|
| 504 | 60c. Type **67** | 4·00 | 3·75 |
| 505 | 96c. H.M.S. "Bounty" and map | 4·00 | 4·00 |
| 506 | $1.40 Aitutaki stamps of 1974, 1979 and 1981 with map | 4·00 | 4·25 |
| **MS**507 | 85×113 mm. As Nos. 504/6, but each with a premium of 5c. | 7·50 | 4·00 |

**1984.** Birth of Prince Henry (1st issue). No. 391 optd **15-9-84 Birth Prince Henry** and surch also.

508 $3 on 60c. Type **50** 2·00 3·25

**69** The Annunciation

**1984.** Christmas. Details from Altarpiece, St Paul's Church, Palencia, Spain. Multicoloured.

| | | | |
|---|---|---|---|
| 509 | 36c. Type **69** | 30 | 35 |
| 510 | 48c. The Nativity | 40 | 45 |
| 511 | 60c. The Epiphany | 45 | 50 |
| 512 | 96c. The Flight into Egypt | 75 | 80 |
| **MS**513 | Designs as Nos. 509/12 in separate miniature sheets, each 45×53 mm and with a face value of 90c.+7c. Imperf. Set of 4 sheets | 2·50 | 3·25 |

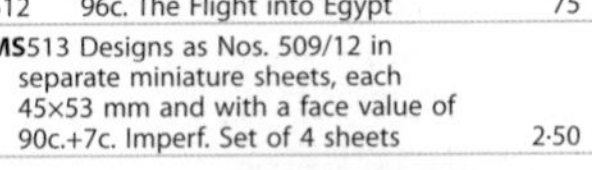

**70** Princess Diana with Prince Henry

**1984.** Birth of Prince Henry (2nd issue). Mult.

| | | | |
|---|---|---|---|
| 514 | 48c. Type **70** | 2·75 | 2·25 |
| 515 | 60c. Prince William with Prince Henry | 2·75 | 2·25 |
| 516 | $2.10 Prince and Princess of Wales with children | 3·50 | 4·50 |
| **MS**517 | 113×65 mm. As Nos. 514/16, but each with a face value of 96c.+7c. | 7·00 | 4·50 |

**71** Grey Kingbird ("Gray Kingbird")

**1985.** Birth Bicentenary of John J. Audubon (ornithologist). Designs showing original paintings. Multicoloured.

| | | | |
|---|---|---|---|
| 518 | 55c. Type **71** | 1·10 | 1·10 |
| 519 | 65c. Bohemian waxwing | 1·25 | 1·25 |
| 520 | 75c. Summer tanager | 1·40 | 1·40 |
| 521 | 95c. Common cardinal ("Cardinal") | 1·50 | 1·50 |
| 522 | $1.15 White-winged crossbill | 1·90 | 1·90 |

**72** The Queen Mother, aged Seven

**1985.** Life and Times of Queen Elizabeth the Queen Mother. Multicoloured.

| | | | |
|---|---|---|---|
| 523 | 55c. Type **72** | 45 | 50 |
| 524 | 65c. Engagement photograph, 1922 | 50 | 55 |
| 525 | 75c. With young Princess Elizabeth | 60 | 65 |
| 526 | $1.30 With baby Prince Charles | 1·00 | 1·10 |
| **MS**527 | 75×49 mm. $3 Queen Mother on her 63rd birthday | 2·25 | 2·40 |

**73** "The Calmady Children" (T. Lawrence)

**1985.** International Youth Year. Multicoloured.

| | | | |
|---|---|---|---|
| 528 | 75c. Type **73** | 3·00 | 2·75 |
| 529 | 90c. "Madame Charpentier's Children" (Renoir) | 3·00 | 3·00 |
| 530 | $1.40 "Young Girls at Piano" (Renoir) | 3·75 | 4·00 |
| **MS**531 | 103×104 mm. As Nos. 528/30, but each with a premium of 10c. | 4·75 | 3·75 |

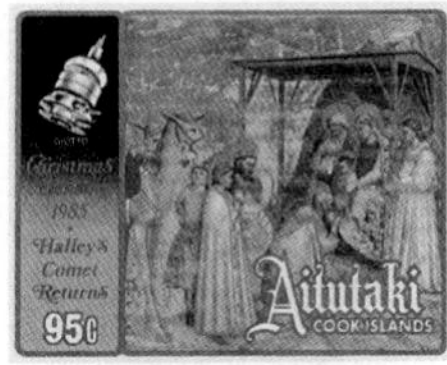

**74** "Adoration of the Magi" (Giotto) and "Giotto" Spacecraft

**1985.** Christmas. Appearance of Halley's Comet (1st issue). Multicoloured.

| | | | |
|---|---|---|---|
| 532 | 95c. Type **74** | 2·00 | 1·75 |
| 533 | 95c. As Type **74** but showing "Planet A" spacecraft | 2·00 | 1·75 |
| 534 | $1.15 Type **74** | 2·00 | 1·75 |
| 535 | $1.15 As No. 533 | 2·00 | 1·75 |
| **MS**536 | 52×55 mm. $6.40. As Type **74** but without spacecraft (30×31 mm). Imperf | 14·00 | 8·50 |

**75** Halley's Comet A.D. 684 (from "Nuremberg Chronicle")

**1986.** Appearance of Halley's Comet (2nd issue). Multicoloured.

| | | | |
|---|---|---|---|
| 537 | 90c. Type **75** | 1·25 | 90 |
| 538 | $1.25 Halley's Comet, 1066 (from Bayeux Tapestry) | 1·60 | 1·10 |
| 539 | $1.75 Halley's Comet, 1456 (from "Lucerne Chronicles") | 1·90 | 1·50 |

MS540 107×82 mm. As Nos. 537/9, but each with a face value of 95c. 5·50 2·50
MS541 65×80 mm. $4.20, "Melencolia I" (Albrecht Dürer woodcut) (61×76 mm). Imperf 6·00 3·50

76 Queen Elizabeth II on Coronation Day (from photo by Cecil Beaton)

**1986.** 60th Birthday of Queen Elizabeth II.
542 **76** 95c. multicoloured 2·00 2·25
**MS**543 58×68 mm. $4.20, As T **76**, but showing more of the portrait without oval frame 5·50 5·50

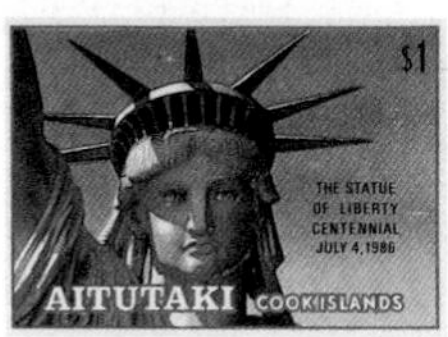

77 Head of Statue of Liberty

**1986.** Centenary of Statue of Liberty. Mult.
544 $1 Type **77** 1·25 1·25
545 $2.75 Statue of Liberty at sunset 2·75 2·75
**MS**546 91×79 mm. As Nos. 544/5, but each with a face value of $1.25 3·25 2·50

78 Prince Andrew and Miss Sarah Ferguson

**1986.** Royal Wedding.
547 **78** $2 multicoloured 2·00 2·00
**MS**548 85×70 mm. Type **78** multicoloured 6·50 8·00

**1986.** "Stampex '86" Stamp Exhibition, Adelaide. No. MS507 with "Ausipex" emblems obliterated in gold.
**MS**549 As Nos. 504/6, but each with a premium of 5c. 11·00 12·00
The "Stampex '86" exhibition emblem is overprinted on the sheet margin.

**1986.** 86th Brithday of Queen Elizabeth the Queen Mother. Nos. 523/6 in miniature sheet, 132×82 mm.
**MS**550 Nos. 523/6 11·00 10·00

79 "St. Anne with Virgin and Child"

**1986.** Christmas. Paintings by Durer. Multicoloured.
551 75c. Type **79** 1·25 1·25
552 $1.35 "Virgin and Child" 1·75 1·75
553 $1.95 "The Adoration of the Magi" 2·25 2·25
554 $2.75 "Madonna of the Rosary" 3·00 3·00
**MS**555 88×125 mm. As Nos. 551/4, but each with a face value of $1.65 13·00 14·00

**1986.** Visit of Pope John Paul II to South Pacific. Nos. 551/4 optd **NOVEMBER 21-24 1986 FIRST VISIT TO SOUTH PACIFIC** and surch also.
556 75c.+10c. Type **79** 2·75 2·50
557 $1.35+10c. "Virgin and Child" 3·25 3·00
558 $1.95+10c. "The Adoration of the Magi" 4·00 3·50
559 $2.75+10c. "Madonna of the Rosary" 5·00 5·00

**MS**560 88×125 mm. As Nos. 556/9, but each with a face value of $1.65+10c. 16·00 15·00

**1987.** Hurricane Relief Fund. Nos. 544/5, 547, 551/4 and 556/9 surch **HURRICANE RELIEF +50c**.
561 75c.+50c. Type **79** 3·25 2·75
562 75c.+10c.+50c. Type **79** 4·00 3·50
563 $1+50c. Type **77** 3·50 3·00
564 $1.35+50c. "Virgin and Child" (Durer) 3·75 3·25
565 $1.35+10c.+50c. "Virgin and Child" (Durer) 4·50 4·00
566 $1.95+50c. "The Adoration of the Magi" (Durer) 4·50 4·00
567 $1.95+10c.+50c. "The Adoration of the Magi" (Durer) 5·00 4·50
568 $2+50c. Type **78** 4·50 4·00
569 $2.75+50c. Statue of Liberty at sunset 5·00 4·50
570 $2.75+50c. "Madonna of the Rosary" (Durer) 5·00 4·50
571 $2.75+10c.+50c. "Madonna of the Rosary" (Durer) 6·50 5·50

**1987.** Royal Ruby Wedding. Nos. 391/3 surch **2.50 Royal Wedding 40th Anniv.**
572 $2.50 on 60c. Type **50** 2·00 2·50
573 $2.50 on 80c. Lady Diana Spencer 2·00 2·50
574 $2.50 on $1.40 Prince Charles and Lady Diana (87×70 mm) 2·00 2·50

83 Angels

**1987.** Christmas. Details of angels from "Virgin with Garland" by Rubens.
575 **83** 70c. multicoloured 2·00 2·00
576 - 85c. multicoloured 2·00 2·00
577 - $1.50 multicoloured 2·25 2·25
578 - $1.85 multicoloured 3·25 3·25
**MS**579 92×120 mm. As Nos. 575/8, but each with a face value of 95c. 12·00 13·00
**MS**580 96×85 mm. $6 "Virgin with Garland" (diamond, 56×56 mm) 11·00 13·00

84 Chariot Racing and Athletics

**1988.** Olympic Games, Seoul. Ancient and modern Olympic sports. Multicoloured.
581 70c. Type **84** 2·25 2·00
582 85c. Greek runners and football 2·50 2·25
583 95c. Greek wrestling and handball 2·50 2·25
584 $1.40 Greek hoplites and tennis 3·25 3·00
**MS**585 103×101 mm. As Nos. 581 and 584, but each with face value of $2 8·00 8·50

**1988.** Olympic Medal Winners, Los Angeles. Nos. 581/4 optd.
586 70c. Type **84** (optd **FLORENCE GRIFFITH JOYNER UNITED STATES 100 M AND 200 M**) 2·00 2·00
587 85c. Greek runners and football (optd **GELINDO BORDIN ITALY MARATHON**) 2·00 2·00
588 95c. Greek wrestling and handball (optd **HITOSHI SAITO JAPAN JUDO**) 2·00 2·00
589 $1.40 Greek hoplites and tennis (optd **STEFFI GRAF WEST GERMANY WOMEN'S TENNIS**) 4·50 4·00

85 "Adoration of the Shepherds" (detail)

**1988.** Christmas. Paintings by Rembrandt. Mult.
590 55c. Type **85** 2·00 1·75
591 70c. "The Holy Family" 2·25 2·00
592 85c. "Presentation in the Temple" 2·50 2·25
593 95c. "The Holy Family" (different) 2·50 2·25
594 $1.15 "Presentation in the Temple" (different) 2·75 2·50
**MS**595 85×101 mm. $4.50, As Type **85** but 52×34 mm. 5·50 6·50

86 H.M.S. "Bounty" leaving Spithead and King George III

**1989.** Bicentenary of Discovery of Aitutaki by Captain Bligh. Multicoloured.
596 55c. Type **86** 2·00 2·00
597 65c. Breadfruit plants 2·25 2·25
598 75c. Old chart showing Aitutaki and Captain Bligh 2·50 2·50
599 95c. Native outrigger and H.M.S. "Bounty" off Aitutaki 2·75 2·75
600 $1.65 Fletcher Christian confronting Bligh 3·50 3·50
**MS**601 94×72 mm. $4.20 "Mutineers casting Bligh adrift" (Robert Dodd) (60×45 mm) 8·00 9·50

87 "Apollo 11" Astronaut on Moon

**1989.** 20th Anniv of First Manned Landing on Moon. Multicoloured.
602 75c. Type **87** 2·75 2·00
603 $1.15 Conducting experiment on Moon 3·25 2·50
604 $1.80 Astronaut on Moon carrying equipment 4·00 3·50
**MS**605 105×86 mm. $6.40 Astronaut on Moon with U.S. flag (40×27 mm) 8·00 9·50

88 Virgin Mary

**1989.** Christmas. Details from "Virgin in the Glory" by Titian. Multicoloured.
606 70c. Type **88** 2·50 2·00
607 85c. Christ Child 3·00 2·50
608 95c. Angel 3·25 2·75
609 $1.25 Cherubs 3·75 3·25
**MS**610 80×100 mm. $6 "Virgin in the Glory" (45×60 mm) 8·00 9·50

89 Human Comet striking Earth

**1990.** Protection of the Environment. Mult.
611 $1.75 Type **89** 2·25 2·25
612 $1.75 Comet's tail 2·25 2·25
**MS**613 108×43 mm. Nos. 611/12 3·50 4·50
Nos. 611/12 were printed together, se-tenant, forming a composite design.

**1990.** 90th Birthday of Queen Elizabeth the Queen Mother. No. MS550 optd Ninetieth Birthday.
**MS**614 132×82 mm. Nos. 523/6 13·00 12·00

91 "Madonna of the Basket" (Correggio)

**1990.** Christmas. Religious Paintings. Mult.
615 70c. Type **91** 1·50 1·50
616 85c. "Virgin and Child" (Morando) 1·60 1·60
617 95c. "Adoration of the Child" (Tiepolo) 1·75 1·75
618 $1.75 "Mystic Marriage of St. Catherine" (Memling) 2·50 2·75
**MS**619 165×93 mm. $6 "Donne Triptych" (Memling) (horiz) 12·00 13·00

**1990.** "Birdpex '90" Stamp Exhibition, Christchurch, New Zealand. Nos. 349/50 optd Birdpex '90 and bird's head.
620 $1 Blue-headed flycatcher 4·50 4·50
621 $2 Red-bellied flycatcher 6·00 6·00

**1991.** 65th Birthday of Queen Elizabeth II. No. 352 optd **COMMEMORATING 65th BIRTHDAY OF H.M. QUEEN ELIZABETH II.**
622 $5 Flat-billed kingfisher 12·00 12·00

93 "The Holy Family" (A. Mengs)

**1991.** Christmas. Religious Paintings. Mult.
623 80c. Type **93** 1·75 1·75
624 90c. "Virgin and the Child" (Lippi) 1·75 1·75
625 $1.05 "Virgin and Child" (A. Durer) 2·00 2·00
626 $1.75 "Adoration of the Shepherds" (G. de la Tour) 2·75 3·25
**MS**627 79×103 mm. "The Holy Family" (Michelangelo) 12·00 13·00

94 Hurdling

**1992.** Olympic Games, Barcelona. Mult.
628 95c. Type **94** 1·75 1·50
629 $1.25 Weightlifting 2·00 1·75
630 $1.50 Judo 2·50 2·25
631 $1.95 Football 2·75 2·75

95 Vaka Motu Canoe

**1992.** 6th Festival of Pacific Arts, Rarotonga. Sailing Canoes. Multicoloured.
632 30c. Type **95** 65 65
633 50c. Hamatafua 80 80
634 95c. Alia Kalia Ndrua 1·50 1·50
635 $1.75 Hokule'a Hawaiian 2·25 2·75
636 $1.95 Tuamotu Pahi 2·50 3·00

**1992.** Royal Visit by Prince Edward. Nos. 632/6 optd **ROYAL VISIT**.
637 30c. Type **95** 1·25 1·25

| | | | |
|---|---|---|---|
| 638 | 50c. Hamatafua | 1·60 | 1·60 |
| 639 | 95c. Alia Kalia Ndrua | 2·50 | 2·50 |
| 640 | $1.75 Hokule'a Hawaiian | 3·50 | 3·75 |
| 641 | $1.95 Tuamotu Pahi | 3·50 | 3·75 |

96 "Virgin's Nativity" (detail) (Reni)

**1992.** Christmas. Different details from "Virgin's Nativity" by Guido Reni.

| | | | | |
|---|---|---|---|---|
| 642 | **96** | 80c. multicoloured | 1·40 | 1·40 |
| 643 | - | 90c. multicoloured | 1·60 | 1·60 |
| 644 | - | $1.05 multicoloured | 1·75 | 1·75 |
| 645 | - | $1.75 multicoloured | 2·50 | 3·00 |
| **MS**646 | | 101×86 mm. $6 multicoloured (as $1.05, but larger (36×46 mm)) | 6·50 | 8·00 |

97 The Departure from Palos

**1992.** 500th Anniv of Discovery of America by Columbus. Multicoloured.

| | | | |
|---|---|---|---|
| 647 | $1.25 Type **97** | 2·25 | 2·50 |
| 648 | $1.75 Map of voyages | 2·75 | 3·00 |
| 649 | $1.95 Columbus and crew in New World | 3·25 | 3·50 |

98 Queen Victoria and King Edward VII

**1993.** 40th Anniv of Coronation. Mult.

| | | | |
|---|---|---|---|
| 650 | $1.75 Type **98** | 3·50 | 3·00 |
| 651 | $1.75 King George V and King George VI | 3·50 | 3·00 |
| 652 | $1.75 Queen Elizabeth II in 1953 and 1986 | 3·50 | 3·00 |

99 "Madonna and Child" (Nino Pisano)

**1993.** Christmas. Religious Sculptures. Mult.

| | | | |
|---|---|---|---|
| 653 | 80c. Type **99** | 90 | 90 |
| 654 | 90c. "Virgin on Rosebush" (Luca della Robbia) | 1·00 | 1·00 |
| 655 | $1.15 "Virgin with Child and St. John" (Juan Francisco Rustici) | 1·40 | 1·40 |
| 656 | $1.95 "Virgin with Child" (Miguel Angel) | 2·25 | 2·25 |
| 657 | $3 "Madonna and Child" (Jacopo della Quercia) (32×47 mm) | 3·25 | 4·00 |

100 Ice Hockey

**1994.** Winter Olympic Games, Lillehammer. Multicoloured.

| | | | |
|---|---|---|---|
| 658 | $1.15 Type **100** | 3·50 | 3·00 |
| 659 | $1.15 Ski-jumping | 3·50 | 3·00 |
| 660 | $1.15 Cross-country skiing | 3·50 | 3·00 |

101 "Ipomoea pes–caprae"

**1994.** Flowers. Multicoloured.

| | | | |
|---|---|---|---|
| 661 | 5c. Type **101** | 10 | 10 |
| 662 | 10c. "Plumeria alba" | 10 | 10 |
| 663 | 15c. "Hibiscus rosa-sinensis" | 10 | 15 |
| 664 | 20c. "Allamanda cathartica" | 15 | 20 |
| 665 | 25c. "Delonix regia" | 20 | 25 |
| 666 | 30c. "Gardenia taitensis" | 20 | 25 |
| 667 | 50c. "Plumeria rubra" | 35 | 40 |
| 668 | 80c. "Ipomoea littoralis" | 60 | 65 |
| 669 | 85c. "Hibiscus tiliaceus" | 60 | 65 |
| 670 | 90c. "Erythrina variegata" | 65 | 70 |
| 671 | $1 "Solandra nitida" | 75 | 80 |
| 672 | $2 "Cordia subcordata" | 1·50 | 1·60 |
| 673 | $3 "Hibiscus rosa-sinensis" (different) (34×47 mm) | 2·20 | 2·30 |
| 674 | $5 As $3 (34×47 mm) | 3·75 | 4·00 |
| 675 | $8 As $3 (34×47 mm) | 5·00 | 5·25 |

Nos. 671/5 include a portrait of Queen Elizabeth II at top right.

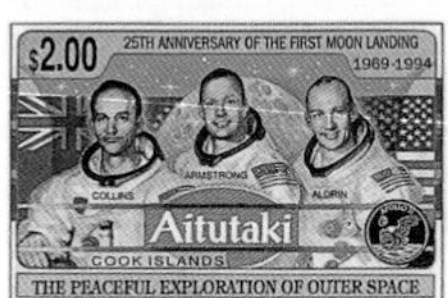

102 Cook Islands and U.S.A. Flags with Astronauts Collins, Armstrong and Aldrin

**1994.** 25th Anniv of First Manned Moon Landing. Multicoloured.

| | | | |
|---|---|---|---|
| 676 | $2 Type **102** | 7·50 | 7·50 |
| 677 | $2 "Apollo 11" re-entering atmosphere and landing in sea | 7·50 | 7·50 |

103 "The Madonna of the Basket" (Correggio)

**1994.** Christmas. Religious Paintings. Mult.

| | | | |
|---|---|---|---|
| 678 | 85c. Type **103** | 1·00 | 1·10 |
| 679 | 85c. "The Virgin and Child with Saints" (Memling) | 1·00 | 1·10 |
| 680 | 85c. "The Virgin and Child with Flowers" (Dolci) | 1·00 | 1·10 |
| 681 | 85c. "The Virgin and Child with Angels" (Bergognone) | 1·00 | 1·10 |
| 682 | 90c. "Adoration of the Kings" (Dosso) | 1·00 | 1·10 |
| 683 | 90c. "The Virgin and Child" (Bellini) | 1·00 | 1·10 |
| 684 | 90c. "The Virgin and Child" (Schiavone) | 1·00 | 1·10 |
| 685 | 90c. "Adoration of the Kings" (Dolci) | 1·00 | 1·10 |

No. 678 is inscribed "Corregio" in error.

104 Battle of Britain

**1995.** 50th Anniv of End of Second World War. Multicoloured.

| | | | |
|---|---|---|---|
| 686 | $4 Type **104** | 9·00 | 8·50 |
| 687 | $4 Battle of Midway | 9·00 | 8·50 |

105 Queen Elizabeth the Queen Mother

**1995.** 95th Birthday of Queen Elizabeth the Queen Mother.

| | | | | |
|---|---|---|---|---|
| 688 | **105** | $4 multicoloured | 7·50 | 8·00 |

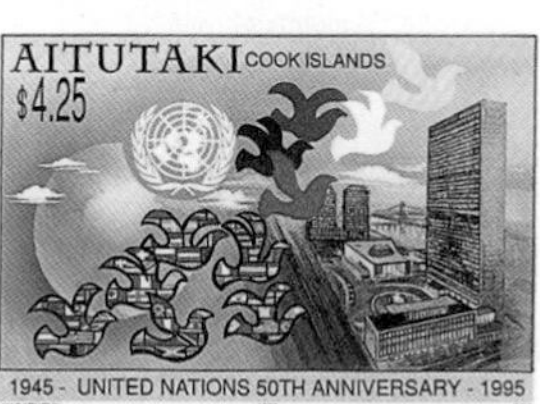

106 Globe, Doves, United Nations Emblem and Headquarters

**1995.** 50th Anniv of United Nations.

| | | | | |
|---|---|---|---|---|
| 689 | **106** | $4.25 multicoloured | 5·50 | 7·00 |

107 Green Turtle

**1995.** Year of the Sea Turtle. Multicoloured.

| | | | |
|---|---|---|---|
| 690 | 95c. Type **107** | 1·75 | 1·75 |
| 691 | $1.15 Leatherback turtle | 2·00 | 2·00 |
| 692 | $1.50 Olive Ridley turtle | 2·25 | 2·25 |
| 693 | $1.75 Loggerhead turtle | 2·50 | 2·50 |

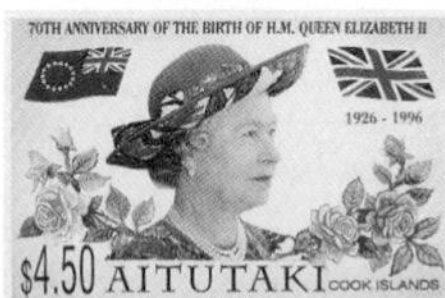

108 Queen Elizabeth II

**1996.** 70th Birthday of Queen Elizabeth II.

| | | | | |
|---|---|---|---|---|
| 694 | **108** | $4.50 multicoloured | 8·50 | 8·00 |

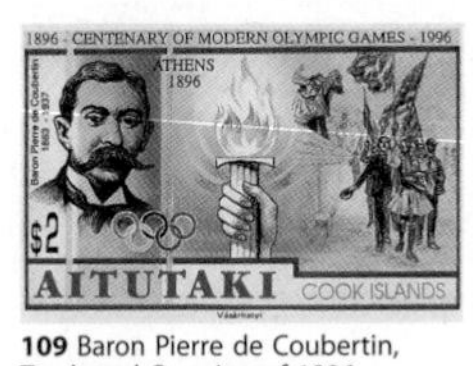

109 Baron Pierre de Coubertin, Torch and Opening of 1896 Olympic Games

**1996.** Centenary of Modern Olympic Games. Multicoloured.

| | | | |
|---|---|---|---|
| 695 | $2 Type **109** | 5·00 | 5·00 |
| 696 | $2 Athletes and American flag, 1996 | 5·00 | 5·00 |

110 Princess Elizabeth and Lieut. Philip Mountbatten with King George VI and Queen Elizabeth, 1947

**1997.** Golden Wedding of Queen Elizabeth and Prince Philip.

| | | | | |
|---|---|---|---|---|
| 697 | **110** | $2.50 multicoloured | 4·50 | 3·50 |
| **MS**698 | | 78×102 mm. **110** $6 multicoloured | 8·00 | 8·50 |

111 Diana, Princess of Wales

**1998.** Diana, Princess of Wales Commemoration.

| | | | | |
|---|---|---|---|---|
| 699 | **111** | $1 multicoloured | 1·00 | 1·00 |
| **MS**700 | | 70×100 mm. $4 Diana, Princess of Wales | 3·25 | 3·75 |

**1998.** Children's Charities. No. **MS**1427 surch **+$1 CHILDREN'S CHARITIES.**

| | | | |
|---|---|---|---|
| **MS**701 | 70×100 mm. $4 + $1 Diana, Princess of Wales | 3·75 | 4·50 |

**1999.** New Millennium. Nos. 632/6 optd KIA ORANA THIRD MILLENNIUM.

| | | | |
|---|---|---|---|
| 702 | 30c. Type **95** | 50 | 50 |
| 703 | 50c. Hamatafua | 60 | 60 |
| 704 | 95c. Alia Kalia Ndrua | 85 | 85 |
| 705 | $1.75 Hokule'a Hawaiian | 1·40 | 1·60 |
| 706 | $1.95 Tuamotu Pahi | 1·60 | 1·75 |

**2000.** Queen Elizabeth the Queen Mother's 100th Birthday. As T 277 of Cook Islands.

| | | | |
|---|---|---|---|
| 707 | $3 blue and brown | 3·25 | 3·25 |
| 708 | $3 multicoloured | 3·25 | 3·25 |
| 709 | $3 multicoloured | 3·25 | 3·25 |
| 710 | $3 green and brown | 3·25 | 3·25 |
| **MS**711 | 73×100 mm. $7.50 multicoloured | 7·00 | 8·00 |

DESIGNS: No. 707, Queen Mother in evening dress and tiara; 708, Queen Mother in evening dress standing by table; 709, Queen Mother in Garter robes; 710, King George VI and Queen Elizabeth; **MS**711 Queen Mother holding lilies.

**2000.** Olympic Games, Sydney. As T **278** of Cook Islands. Multicoloured.

| | | | |
|---|---|---|---|
| 712 | $2 Ancient Greek wrestlers | 2·00 | 2·25 |
| 713 | $2 Modern wrestlers | 2·00 | 2·25 |
| 714 | $2 Ancient Greek boxer | 2·00 | 2·25 |
| 715 | $2 Modern boxers | 2·00 | 2·25 |
| **MS**716 | 99×90 mm. $2.75 Olympic torch and Cook Island canoes | 2·25 | 2·75 |

113 Blue Lorikeets and Flowers

**2002.** Endangered Species. Blue Lorikeet. Multicoloured.

| | | | |
|---|---|---|---|
| 717 | 80c. Type **113** | 1·10 | 1·25 |
| 718 | 90c. Lorikeets and bananas | 1·10 | 1·25 |
| 719 | $1.15 Lorikeets on palm leaf | 1·40 | 1·60 |
| 720 | $1.95 Lorikeets in tree trunk | 1·90 | 2·10 |

**2003.** "United We Stand". Support for Victims of 11 September 2001 Terrorist Attacks. Design as T 282 of Cook Islands. Multicoloured.

| | | | |
|---|---|---|---|
| **MS**721 | 75×109 mm. $1.15×4 Twin Towers and flags of U.S.A. and Cook Islands | 4·75 | 5·50 |

**2005.** Pope John Paul II Commemoration. As T 285 of Cook Islands. Multicoloured.

| | | | |
|---|---|---|---|
| 722 | $1.95 Pope praying | 2·25 | 2·50 |

114 Caterpillar and Chrysalis

**2008.** Endangered Species. Blue Moon Butterfly (Hypolimna bolinas). Multicoloured.

| | | | |
|---|---|---|---|
| 723 | 80c. Type **114** | 1·40 | 1·50 |
| 724 | 90c. Female butterfly | 1·40 | 1·50 |
| 725 | $1.15 Male butterfly (wings closed) | 1·60 | 1·75 |
| 726 | $1.95 Male butterfly (wings open) | 2·10 | 2·25 |

## OFFICIAL STAMPS

**1978.** Nos. 98/105, 107/10 and 227/8 optd **O.H.M.S.** or surch also.

| | | | |
|---|---|---|---|
| O1 | 1c. multicoloured | 90 | 10 |
| O2 | 2c. multicoloured | 1·00 | 10 |
| O3 | 3c. multicoloured | 1·00 | 10 |
| O4 | 4c. multicoloured | 1·00 | 10 |
| O5 | 5c. multicoloured | 1·00 | 10 |

| | | | |
|---|---|---|---|
| O6 | 8c. multicoloured | 1·25 | 10 |
| O7 | 10c. multicoloured | 1·50 | 15 |
| O8 | 15c. on 60c. multicoloured | 2·75 | 20 |
| O9 | 18c. on 60c. multicoloured | 2·75 | 20 |
| O10 | 20c. multicoloured | 2·75 | 20 |
| O11 | 50c. multicoloured | 1·00 | 55 |
| O12 | 60c. multicoloured | 10·00 | 70 |
| O13 | $1 multicoloured (No. 108) | 10·00 | 80 |
| O14 | $2 multicoloured | 9·00 | 75 |
| O15 | $4 on $1 mult (No. 228) | 1·75 | 75 |
| O16 | $5 multicoloured | 11·00 | 1·25 |

**1985.** Nos. 351/2, 430/3, 475 and 477/94 optd **O.H.M.S.** or surch also.

| | | | |
|---|---|---|---|
| O17 | 2c. Type **65** | 1·25 | 1·50 |
| O18 | 5c. Scarlet robin | 1·50 | 1·50 |
| O19 | 10c. Golden whistler | 1·75 | 1·75 |
| O20 | 12c. Rufous fantail | 1·90 | 2·00 |
| O21 | 18c. Peregrine falcon | 3·00 | 2·25 |
| O22 | 20c. on 24 c Barn owl | 3·00 | 2·25 |
| O23 | 30c. Java sparrow | 2·25 | 1·50 |
| O24 | 40c. on 36c. White-breasted wood swallow | 2·25 | 1·50 |
| O25 | 50c. Feral rock pigeon | 2·25 | 1·50 |
| O26 | 55c. on 48c. Tahitian lory | 2·25 | 1·50 |
| O27 | 60c. Purple swamphen | 2·50 | 1·75 |
| O28 | 65c. on 72c. Zebra dove | 2·50 | 1·75 |
| O38 | 75c. on 48c. Type **57** | 1·25 | 1·40 |
| O39 | 75c. on 48c. Ancient Ti'i image | 1·25 | 1·40 |
| O40 | 75c. on 48c. Tourist canoeing | 1·25 | 1·40 |
| O41 | 75c. on 48c. Captain William Bligh and chart | 1·25 | 1·40 |
| O29 | 80c. on 96c. Chestnut-breasted mannikin | 2·50 | 1·75 |
| O30 | $1.20 Common mynah | 3·25 | 2·50 |
| O31 | $2.10 Reef heron | 4·25 | 3·75 |
| O32 | $3 Blue-headed flycatcher | 6·00 | 6·00 |
| O33 | $4.20 Red-bellied flycatcher | 7·00 | 7·00 |
| O34 | $5.60 Red munia | 8·00 | 8·00 |
| O35 | $9.60 Flat-billed kingfisher | 13·00 | 13·00 |
| O36 | $14 on $4 Red munia (35×48 mm) | 15·00 | 15·00 |
| O37 | $18 on $5 Flat-billed kingfisher (35×48 mm) | 17·00 | 17·00 |

Pt. 19

## AJMAN

One of the Trucial States in the Persian Gulf. On 18 July 1971, seven Gulf sheikhdoms, including Ajman, formed part of the State of the United Arab Emirates. The federation became effective on 1 August 1972.

1964. 100 naye paise = 1 rupee.
1967. 100 dirhams = 1 riyal.

1 Shaikh Rashid bin Humaid al Naimi and Arab Stallion

**1964.** Multicoloured. (a) Size 34½×23 mm.

| | | | |
|---|---|---|---|
| 1 | 1n.p. Type **1** | 10 | 10 |
| 2 | 2n.p. Regal angelfish | 10 | 10 |
| 3 | 3n.p. Dromedary | 10 | 10 |
| 4 | 4n.p. Yellow-banded angelfish | 10 | 10 |
| 5 | 5n.p. Tortoise | 10 | 10 |
| 6 | 10n.p. Jewel cichlid | 25 | 10 |
| 7 | 15n.p. White stork | 35 | 10 |
| 8 | 20n.p. Black-headed gulls | 35 | 10 |
| 9 | 30n.p. Lanner falcon | 60 | 25 |

(b) Size 42½×27 mm.

| | | | |
|---|---|---|---|
| 10 | 40n.p. Type **1** | 25 | 25 |
| 11 | 50n.p. Regal angelfish | 25 | 25 |
| 12 | 70n.p. Dromedary | 35 | 25 |
| 13 | 1r. Yellow-banded angelfish | 35 | 35 |
| 14 | 1r.50 Tortoise | 70 | 60 |
| 15 | 2r. Jewel cichlid | 95 | 85 |

(c) Size 53×34 mm.

| | | | |
|---|---|---|---|
| 16 | 3r. White stork | 1·60 | 1·20 |
| 17 | 5r. Black-headed gulls | 4·25 | 3·00 |
| 18 | 10r. Lanner falcon | 7·25 | 5·50 |

2 Kennedy in Football Kit

**1964.** Pres. Kennedy Commem. Perf or imperf.

| | | | | |
|---|---|---|---|---|
| 19 | 2 | 10n.p. purple and green | 10 | 10 |
| 20 | - | 15n.p. violet and turquoise | 10 | 10 |
| 21 | - | 50n.p. blue and brown | 25 | 10 |
| 22 | - | 1r. turquoise and sepia | 60 | 35 |
| 23 | - | 2r. olive and purple | 95 | 60 |
| 24 | - | 3r. brown and green | 1·40 | 95 |
| 25 | - | 5r. brown and violet | 2·40 | 2·10 |
| 26 | - | 10r. brown and blue | 4·75 | 3·50 |
| **MS**26a | | 105×140 mm. Nos. 23/6 in new colours | 24·00 | 12·00 |

DESIGNS—Various pictures of Kennedy: 15n.p. Diving; 50n.p. As naval officer; 1r. Sailing with Mrs. Kennedy; 2r. With Mrs. Eleanor Roosevelt; 3r. With wife and child; 5r. With colleagues; 10r. Full-face portrait.

3 Start of Race

**1965.** Olympic Games, Tokyo. Perf or imperf.

| | | | | |
|---|---|---|---|---|
| 27 | 3 | 5n.p. slate, brown & mauve | 10 | 10 |
| 28 | - | 10n.p. red, bronze and blue | 10 | 10 |
| 29 | 3 | 15n.p. brown, violet & green | 10 | 10 |
| 30 | - | 25n.p. black, blue and red | 25 | 10 |
| 31 | - | 50n.p. slate, purple and blue | 35 | 25 |
| 32 | - | 1r. blue, green and purple | 60 | 35 |
| 33 | - | 1r.50 purple, violet and green | 95 | 60 |
| 34 | - | 2r. blue, purple and ochre | 1·20 | 85 |
| 35 | - | 3r. violet, brown and blue | 1·80 | 1·10 |
| 36 | - | 5r. purple, green and yellow | 3·25 | 1·90 |
| **MS**36a | | 120×100 mm. Nos. 33/6 in new colours | 12·00 | 8·50 |

DESIGNS: 10n.p., 1r.50, Boxing; 25n.p., 2r. Judo; 50n.p., 5r. Gymnastics; 1, 3r. Sailing.

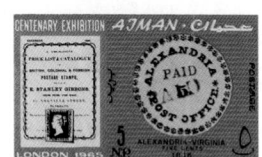

4 First Gibbons Catalogue and Alexandria (U.S.) 5c. Postmaster's Stamp

**1965.** Stanley Gibbons Catalogue Centenary Exhibition, London. Multicoloured.

| | | | |
|---|---|---|---|
| 37 | 5n.p. Type **4** | 10 | 10 |
| 38 | 10n.p. Austria (6k.) scarlet "Mercury" newspaper stamp | 10 | 10 |
| 39 | 15n.p. British Guiana "One Cent", 1856 | 10 | 10 |
| 40 | 25n.p. Canada "Twelvepence Black", 1851 | 10 | 25 |
| 41 | 50n.p. Hawaii "Missionary" 2c., 1851 | 25 | 25 |
| 42 | 1r. Mauritius "Post Office" 2d. blue, 1847 | 50 | 25 |
| 43 | 3r. Switzerland "Double Geneva" 5c.+5c., 1843 | 1·60 | 70 |
| 44 | 5r. Tuscany 3 lire, 1860 | 2·75 | 1·20 |
| **MS**44a | Two sheets, each 124×99 mm. Nos. 37, 40/1, 44 and 38/9, 42/3 | 8·50 | 8·50 |

The 5, 15 and 50n.p. and 3r. also include the First Gibbons Catalogue and the others, the Gibbons "Elizabethan" Catalogue.

**1965.** Pan Arab Games, Cairo. Perf or imperf. Nos. 29, 31 and 33/5 optd. (a) Optd **PAN ARAB GAMES CAIRO 1965**.

| | | | | |
|---|---|---|---|---|
| 45 | 3 | 15n.p. brown, violet & green | 10 | 10 |
| 46 | - | 50n.p. slate, purple and blue | 50 | 50 |
| 47 | - | 1r.50 purple, violet & green | 1·40 | 1·40 |
| 48 | - | 2r. blue, red and ochre | 2·10 | 2·10 |
| 49 | - | 3r. violet, brown and blue | 3·25 | 3·25 |

(b) Optd as Nos. 45/9 but equivalent in Arabic.

| | | | | |
|---|---|---|---|---|
| 50 | 3 | 15n.p. brown, violet & green | 10 | 10 |
| 51 | - | 50n.p. slate, purple and blue | 50 | 50 |
| 52 | - | 1r.50 purple, violet and green | 1·40 | 1·40 |
| 53 | - | 2r. blue, red and ochre | 2·10 | 2·10 |
| 54 | - | 3r. violet, brown and blue | 3·25 | 3·25 |

**1965.** Air. Designs similar to Nos. 1/9, but inscr "AIR MAIL". Mult. (a) Size 42½×25½ mm.

| | | | |
|---|---|---|---|
| 55 | 15n.p. Type **1** | 10 | 10 |
| 56 | 25n.p. Regal angelfish | 25 | 25 |
| 57 | 35n.p. Dromedary | 25 | 25 |
| 58 | 50n.p. Yellow-banded angelfish | 35 | 35 |
| 59 | 75n.p. Tortoise | 60 | 60 |
| 60 | 1r. Jewel cichlid | 85 | 85 |

(b) Size 53×34 mm.

| | | | |
|---|---|---|---|
| 61 | 2r. White stork | 1·80 | 1·80 |
| 62 | 3r. Black-headed gull | 2·40 | 2·40 |
| 63 | 5r. Lanner falcon | 4·25 | 4·25 |

**1966.** Stamp Cent Exn, Cairo. Nos. 38/9 and 41/3 optd **STAMP CENTENARY EXHIBITION CAIRO, JANUARY 1966** and pyramid motif.

| | | | |
|---|---|---|---|
| 73 | 10n.p. multicoloured | 10 | 10 |
| 74 | 15n.p. multicoloured | 25 | 25 |
| 75 | 50n.p. multicoloured | 55 | 55 |
| 76 | 1r. multicoloured | 1·00 | 1·00 |
| 77 | 3r. multicoloured | 3·00 | 3·00 |
| **MS**78 | Two sheets, each 124×99 mm. as **MS**44a | 7·75 | 4·25 |

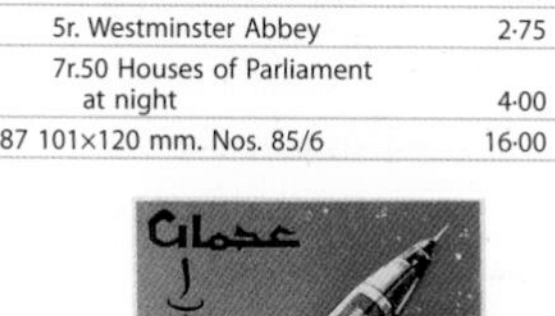

8 Sir Winston Churchill and Tower Bridge

**1966.** Churchill Commemoration. Each design includes portrait of Churchill. Multicoloured.

| | | | |
|---|---|---|---|
| 79 | 25n.p. Type **8** | 10 | 10 |
| 80 | 50n.p. Buckingham Palace | 25 | 10 |
| 81 | 75n.p. Blenheim Palace | 35 | 25 |
| 82 | 1r. British Museum | 60 | 25 |
| 83 | 2r. St. Paul's Cathedral in wartime | 1·10 | 60 |
| 84 | 3r. National Gallery and St. Martin in the Fields Church | 1·70 | 85 |
| 85 | 5r. Westminster Abbey | 2·75 | 1·40 |
| 86 | 7r.50 Houses of Parliament at night | 4·00 | 2·10 |
| **MS**87 | 101×120 mm. Nos. 85/6 | 16·00 | 8·50 |

9 Rocket

**1966.** Space Achievements. Multicoloured. (a) Postage. Size as T 9.

| | | | |
|---|---|---|---|
| 88 | 1n.p. Type **9** | 10 | 10 |
| 89 | 3n.p. Capsule | 10 | 10 |
| 90 | 5n.p. Astronaut entering capsule in space | 10 | 10 |
| 91 | 10n.p. Astronaut outside capsule in space | 10 | 10 |
| 92 | 15n.p. Astronauts and globe | 10 | 10 |
| 93 | 25n.p. Astronaut in space | 10 | 10 |
| **MS**94 | 98×88 mm. 1r. and 3r. in designs of 15n.p. and 10n.p. | 3·50 | 3·00 |

(b) Air. Size 38×38 mm.

| | | | |
|---|---|---|---|
| 95 | 50n.p. As Type **9** | 35 | 10 |
| 96 | 1r. Astronauts and globe | 60 | 25 |
| 97 | 3r. Astronaut outside capsule in space | 1·80 | 60 |
| 98 | 5r. Capsule | 3·25 | 1·10 |

**1967.** Various issues with currency names changed by overprinting in **Dh.** or **Riyals**. (a) Postage. Nos. 1/18 (1964 Definitives).

| | | | |
|---|---|---|---|
| 99 | 1d. on 1n.p. | 10 | 10 |
| 100 | 2d. on 2n.p. | 10 | 10 |
| 101 | 3d. on 3n.p. | 10 | 10 |
| 102 | 4d. on 4n.p. | 10 | 10 |
| 103 | 5d. on 5n.p. | 10 | 10 |
| 104 | 10d. on 10n.p. | 25 | 25 |
| 105 | 15d. on 15n.p. | 25 | 25 |
| 106 | 20d. on 20n.p. | 35 | 35 |
| 107 | 30d. on 30n.p. | 60 | 60 |
| 108 | 40d. on 40n.p. | 85 | 85 |
| 109 | 50d. on 50n.p. | 1·10 | 1·10 |
| 110 | 70d. on 70n.p. | 1·40 | 1·40 |
| 111 | 1r. on 1r. | 1·90 | 1·90 |
| 112 | 1r.50 on 1r.50 | 3·00 | 3·00 |
| 113 | 2r. on 2r. | 4·00 | 4·00 |
| 114 | 3r. on 3r. | 2·40 | 2·40 |
| 115 | 5r. on 5r. | 4·00 | 4·00 |
| 116 | 10r. on 10r. | 7·75 | 7·75 |

(b) Air. Nos. 55/63 (Airmails).

| | | | |
|---|---|---|---|
| 117 | 15d. on 15n.p. | 10 | 10 |
| 118 | 25d. on 25n.p. | 25 | 25 |
| 119 | 35d. on 35n.p. | 35 | 35 |
| 120 | 50d. on 50n.p. | 50 | 50 |
| 121 | 75d. on 75n.p. | 70 | 70 |
| 122 | 1r. on 1r. | 95 | 95 |
| 123 | 2r. on 2r. | 1·80 | 1·80 |
| 124 | 3r. on 3r. | 3·00 | 3·00 |
| 125 | 5r. on 5r. | 4·50 | 4·50 |

**NEW CURRENCY SURCHARGES.** Nos. 19/44 and 79/98 are known surch in new currency (dirhams and riyals), in limited quantities, but there is some doubt as to whether they were in use locally.

11 Fiat 1500 Saloon, 1962

**1967.** Transport.

| | | | | |
|---|---|---|---|---|
| 135 | 11 | 1d. brown & blk (postage) | 10 | 10 |
| 136 | - | 2d. blue and brown | 10 | 10 |
| 137 | - | 3d. mauve and black | 10 | 10 |
| 138 | - | 4d. blue and brown | 10 | 10 |
| 139 | - | 5d. green and black | 10 | 10 |
| 140 | - | 15d. blue and brown | 10 | 10 |
| 141 | - | 30d. brown and black | 25 | 10 |
| 142 | - | 50d. black and brown | 35 | 10 |
| 143 | - | 70d. violet and black | 50 | 10 |
| 144 | 11 | 1r. green and brown (air) | 60 | 25 |
| 145 | - | 2r. mauve and black | 1·20 | 50 |
| 146 | - | 3r. black and brown | 1·80 | 70 |
| 147 | - | 5r. brown and black | 3·00 | 1·20 |
| 148 | - | 10r. blue and brown | 6·00 | 2·40 |

DESIGNS: 2d., 2r. Motor coach; 3d., 3r. Motor cyclist; 4d., 5r. Boeing 707 airliner; 5d., 10r. "Brasil" (liner); 15d. "Yankee" (sail training and cruise ship); 30d. Cameleer; 50d. Arab horse; 70d. Sikorsky S-58 helicopter.

### OFFICIAL STAMPS

**1965.** Designs similar to Nos. 1/9, additionally inscr "ON STATE'S SERVICE". Multicoloured. (i) Postage. Size 43×26 mm.

| | | | |
|---|---|---|---|
| O64 | 25n.p. Type **1** | 25 | 10 |
| O65 | 40n.p. Regal angelfish | 35 | 25 |
| O66 | 50n.p. Dromedary | 50 | 35 |
| O67 | 75n.p. Yellow-banded angelfish | 60 | 50 |
| O68 | 1r. Tortoise | 95 | 60 |

(ii) Air. (a) Size 43×26 mm.

| | | | |
|---|---|---|---|
| O69 | 75n.p. Jewel cichlid | 60 | 25 |

(b) Size 53×34 mm.

| | | | |
|---|---|---|---|
| O70 | 2r. White stork | 1·90 | 70 |
| O71 | 3r. Black-headed gulls | 3·00 | 1·10 |
| O72 | 5r. Lanner falcon | 4·75 | 1·80 |

**1967.** Nos. O64/72 with currency names changed by overprinting in **Dh.** or **Riyals**.

| | | | |
|---|---|---|---|
| O126 | 25d. on 25n.p. | 25 | 25 |
| O127 | 40d. on 40n.p. | 35 | 25 |
| O128 | 50d. on 50n.p. | 50 | 25 |
| O129 | 75d. on 75n.p. (No. O67) | 60 | 50 |
| O130 | 75d. on 75n.p. (No. O69) | 95 | 60 |
| O131 | 1r. on 1r. | 70 | 85 |
| O132 | 2r. on 2r. | 3·50 | 2·10 |
| O133 | 3r. on 3r. | 7·25 | 3·00 |
| O134 | 5r. on 5r. | 13·50 | 6·25 |

For later issues see **UNITED ARAB EMIRATES**.

### APPENDIX

From June 1967 very many stamp issues were made by a succession of agencies which have been awarded contracts by the Ruler, sometimes two agencies operating at the same time. Several contradictory statements were made as to the validity of some of these issues which appeared 1967-72 and for this reason they are only listed in abbreviated form.

**1967**

50th Birth Anniv of President J. F. Kennedy. Air 10, 20, 40, 70d., 1r.50, 2, 3, 5r.
Paintings. Postage. Arab Paintings 1, 2, 3, 4, 5, 30, 70d.; Air. Asian Paintings 1, 2, 3, 5r.; Indian Painting 10r.
Tales from "The Arabian Nights". Postage 1, 2, 3, 10, 30, 50, 70d.; Air 90d., 1, 2, 3r.
World Scout Jamboree, Idaho. Postage 30, 70d., 1r.; Air 2, 3, 4r.
Olympic Games, Mexico (1968). Postage 35, 65, 75d., 1r.; Air 1r.25, 2, 3, 4r.
Winter Olympic Games, Grenoble (1968). Postage 5, 35, 60, 75d.; Air 1, 1r.25, 2, 3r.
Pres. J. F. Kennedy Memorial. Die-stamped on gold foil. Air 10r.
Paintings by Renoir and Terbrughhen. Air 35, 65d., 1, 2r.×3.

**1968**

Paintings by Velasquez. Air 1r.×2, 2r.×2.
Winter Olympic Games, Grenoble. Die-stamped on gold foil. Air 7r.
Paintings from Famous Galleries. Air 1r.×4, 2r.×6.
Costumes. Air 30d.×2, 70d.×2, 1r.×2, 2r.×2.
Olympic Games, Mexico. Postage 1r.×4; Air 2r.×4.
Satellites and Spacecraft. Air 30d.×2, 70d.×2, 1r.×2, 2r.×2, 3r.×2.
Paintings. Hunting Dogs. Air 2r.×6.
Paintings. Adam and Eve. Air 2r.×4.

Human Rights Year. Kennedy Brothers and Martin Luther King. Air 1r.×3, 2r.×3.
Kennedy Brothers Memorial. Postage 2r.; Air 5r.
Sports Champions. Inter-Milano Football Club. Postage 5, 10, 15, 20, 25d.; Air 10r.
Sports Champions. Famous Footballers. Postage 15, 20, 50, 75d., 1r.; Air 10r.
Cats. Postage 1, 2, 3d.; Air 2, 3r.
Olympic Games, Mexico. Die-stamped on gold foil. 5r.
5th Death Anniv of Pres. J. F. Kennedy. On gold foil. Air 10r.
Paintings of the Madonna. Air 30, 70d., 1, 2, 3r.
Space Exploration. Postage 5, 10, 15, 20, 25d.; Air 15r.
Olympic Games, Mexico. Gold Medals. Postage 2r.×4; Air 5r.×4.
Christmas. Air 5r.

**1969**

Sports Champions. Cyclists. Postage 1, 2, 5, 10, 15, 20d.; Air 12r.
Sports Champions. German Footballers. Postage 5, 10, 15, 20, 25d.; Air 10r.
Sports Champions. Motor-racing Drivers. Postage 1, 5, 10, 15, 25d.; Air 10r.
Motor-racing Cars. Postage 1, 5, 10, 15, 25d.; Air 10r.
Sports Champions. Boxers. Postage 5, 10, 15, 20d.; Air 10r.
Sports Champions. Baseball Players. Postage 1, 2, 5, 10, 15d.; Air 10r.
Birds. Air 1r.×11.
Roses. 1r.×6.
Wild Animals. Air 1r.×6.
Paintings. Italian Old Masters. 5, 10, 15, 20d., 10r.
Paintings. Famous Composers. Air 5, 10, 25d., 10r.
Paintings. French Artists. 1r.×4.
Paintings. Nudes. Air 2r.×4.
Three Kings Mosaic. Air 1r.×2, 3r.×2.
Kennedy Brothers. Air 2, 3, 10r.
Olympic Games, Mexico. Gold Medal Winners. Postage 1, 2d., 10r.; Air 10d., 5, 10r.
Paintings of the Madonna. Postage 10d.; Air 10r.
Space Flight of "Apollo 9". Optd on 1968 Space Exploration issue. Air 15r.
Space Flight of "Apollo 10". Optd on 1968 Space Exploration issue. Air 15r.
1st Death Anniv of Gagarin. Optd on 1968 Space Exploration issue. 5d.
2nd Death Anniv of Edward White. Optd on 1968 Space Exploration issue. 10d.
1st Death Anniv of Robert Kennedy. Optd on 1969 Kennedy Brothers issue. Air 2r.
European Football Championship. Optd on 1968 Famous Footballers issue. Air 10r.
Olympic Games, Munich (1972). Optd on 1969 Mexico Gold Medal Winners issue. Air 10d., 5, 10r.
Moon Landing of "Apollo 11". Air 1, 2, 5r.
Moon Landing of "Apollo 11". Circular designs on gold or silver foil. Air 3r.×3, 5r.×3, 10r.×14.
Paintings. Christmas. Postage 1, 2, 3, 4, 5, 15d.; Air 2, 3r.

**1970**

"Apollo" Space Flights. Postage 1, 2, 4, 5, 10d.; Air 3, 5r.
Birth Bicentenary of Napoleon Bonaparte. Die-stamped on gold foil. Air 20r.
Paintings. Easter. Postage 5, 10, 12, 30, 50, 70d.; Air 1, 2r.
Moon Landing. Die-stamped on gold foil. Air 20r.
Paintings by Michelangelo. Postage 1, 2, 4, 5, 8, 10d.; Air 3, 5r.
World Cup Football Championship, Mexico. Air 25, 50, 75d., 1, 2, 3r.
"Expo 70" World Fair, Osaka, Japan. Japanese Paintings. Postage 1, 2, 3, 4, 5, 10, 15d.; Air 1, 5r.
Birth Bicent Napoleon Bonaparte. Postage 1, 2, 4, 5, 10d.; Air 3, 5r.
Paintings. Old Masters. Postage 1, 2, 5, 6, 10d.; Air 1, 2, 3r.
Space Flight of "Apollo 13". Air 50, 75, 80d., 1, 2, 3r.
World Cup Football Championship, Mexico. Die-stamped on gold foil. Air 20r.
Olympic Games, 1960–1972. Postage 15, 30, 50, 70d.; Air 2, 5r.
"Expo 70" World Fair, Osaka, Japan. Pavilions. Postage 1, 2, 3, 4, 10, 15d.; Air 1, 3r.
Brazil's Victory in World Cup Football Championship. Optd on 1970 World Football Cup issue. Air 25, 50, 75d., 1, 2, 3r.
"Gemini" and "Apollo" Space Flights. Postage 1, 2, 3, 4, 5, 6, 8, 10, 12, 15, 20, 25, 30, 35, 40, 50d.; Air 1, 1r.50, 2, 3r.
Vintage and Veteran Cars. Postage 1, 2, 4, 5, 8, 10d.; Air 2, 3r.
Pres. D. Eisenhower Commem. Postage 30, 50, 70d.; Air 1, 2, 3r.
Paintings by Ingres. Air 25, 30, 35, 50, 70, 85d., 1, 2r.
500th Birth Anniv (1971) of Albrecht Durer. Air 25, 30, 35, 50, 70, 85d., 1, 2r.
Christmas Paintings. Air 25, 30, 35, 50, 70, 85d., 1, 2r.
Winter Olympic Games, Sapporo, Japan (1972). Die-stamped on gold foil. Air 20r.
Meeting of Eisenhower and De Gaulle, 1942. Die-stamped on gold foil. Air 20r.
General De Gaulle Commem. Air 25, 50, 75d., 1, 2, 3r.
Winter Olympic Games, Sapporo, Japan (1972). Sports. Postage 1, 2, 5, 10d.; Air 3, 5r.
J. Rindt, World Formula 1 Motor-racing Champion. Die-stamped on gold foil. Air 20r.

**1971**

"Philatokyo" Stamp Exhibition, Tokyo. Japanese Paintings. Air 25, 30, 35, 50, 70, 85d., 1, 2r.
Mars Space Project. Air 50, 75, 80d., 1, 2, 3r.
Napoleonic Military Uniforms. Postage 5, 10, 15, 20, 25, 30d.; Air 2, 3r.
Olympic Games, Munich (1972). Sports. Postage 10, 15, 25, 30, 40d.; Air 1, 2, 3r.
Paintings by Modern Artists. Air 25, 30, 35, 50, 70, 85d., 1, 2r.
Paintings by Famous Artists. Air 25, 30, 35, 50, 70, 85d., 1, 2r.
25th Anniv of United Nations. Optd on 1971 Modern Artists issue. Air 25, 30, 35, 50, 70, 85d., 1, 2r.
Olympic Games, Munich (1972). Sports. Postage 1, 2, 3, 4, 5, 6, 8, 10, 12, 15, 20, 25, 30, 35, 40, 50d.; Air 1, 1r.50, 2, 3r.
Butterflies. Air 25, 30, 35, 50, 70, 85d., 1, 2r.
Space Flight of "Apollo 14". Postage 15, 25, 50, 60, 70d.; Air 5r.
Winter Olympic Games, 1924–1968. Postage 30, 40, 50, 75d., 1r.; Air 2r.
Signs of the Zodiac. 1, 2, 5, 10, 12, 15, 25, 30, 35, 45, 50, 60d.
Famous Men. Air 65, 70, 75, 80, 85, 90d., 1, 1r.25, 1r.50, 2, 2r.50, 3r.
Death Bicent of Beethoven. 20, 30, 40, 60d., 1r.50, 2r.
Dr. Albert Schweitzer Commem. 20, 30, 40, 60d., 1r.50, 2r.
Tropical Birds. Postage 1, 2, 3, 4, 5, 10d.; Air 2, 3r.
Paintings by French Artists. Postage 1, 2, 3, 4, 5, 10d.; Air 2, 3r.
Paintings by Modern Artists. Postage 1, 2, 3, 4, 5, 10d.; Air 2, 3r.
Paintings by Degas. Postage 1, 2, 3, 4, 5, 10d.; Air 2, 3r.
Paintings by Titian. Postage 1, 2, 3, 4, 5, 10d.; Air 2, 3r.
Paintings by Renoir. Postage 1, 2, 3, 4, 5, 10d.; Air 2, 3r.
Space Flight of "Apollo 15". Postage 25, 40, 50, 60d., 1r.; Air 6r.
"Philatokyo" Stamp Exhibition, Tokyo. Stamps. Postage 10, 15, 20, 30, 35, 50, 60, 80d.; Air 1, 2r.
Tropical Birds. Postage 1, 2, 3, 5, 7, 10, 12, 15, 20, 25, 30, 40d.; Air 50, 80d., 1, 3r.
Paintings depicting Venus. Postage 1, 2, 3, 4, 5, 10d.; Air 2, 3r.
13th World Scout Jamboree, Asagiri, Japan. Scouts. Postage 1, 2, 3, 5, 7, 10, 12, 15, 20, 25, 30, 35, 40, 50, 65, 80d.; Air 1, 1r.25, 1r.50, 2r.
Lions International Clubs. Optd on 1971 Famous Paintings issue. Air 25, 30, 35, 50, 70, 85d., 1, 2r.
13th World Scout Jamboree, Asagiri, Japan. Japanese Paintings. Postage 20, 30, 40, 60, 75d.; Air 3r.
25th Anniv of UNICEF Optd on 1971 Scout Jamboree (paintings) issue. Postage 20, 30, 40, 60, 75d.; Air 3r.
Christmas 1971. (1st series. Plain frames). Portraits of Popes. Postage 1, 2, 3, 4, 5, 10d.; Air 2, 3r.
Modern Cars. Postage 10, 15, 25, 40, 50d.; Air 3r.
Olympic Games, Munich (1972). Show-jumping. Embossed on gold foil. Air 20r.
Exploration of Outer Space. Postage 15, 25, 50, 60, 70d.; Air 5r.
Royal Visit of Queen Elizabeth II to Japan. Postage 1, 2, 3, 4, 5, 10d.; Air 2, 3r.
Meeting of Pres. Nixon and Emperor Hirohito of Japan in Alaska. Design as 3r. value of 1970 Eisenhower issue but value changed and optd with commemorative inscr. Air 5r. (silver opt), 5r. (gold opt).
"Apollo" Astronants. Postage 5, 20, 35, 40, 50d.; Air 1, 2, 3r.
Discoverers of the Universe. Astronomers and Space Scientists. Postage 5, 10, 15, 20, 25, 30d.; Air 2, 5r.
"ANPHILEX 71" Stamp Exn, New York. Air 2r.50.
Christmas 1971. Portraits of Popes (2nd series. Ornamental frames). Postage 1, 2, 3, 4, 5, 10d.; Air 2, 3r.
Royal Silver Wedding of Queen Elizabeth II and Prince Philip (1972). Air 1, 2, 3r.
Space Flight of "Apollo 16". Postage 20, 30, 40, 50, 60d.; Air 3, 4r.
Fairy Tales. "Baron Munchhausen" Stories. Postage 1, 2, 4, 5, 10d.; Air 3r.
World Fair, Philadelphia (1976). Paintings. Postage 25, 50, 75d.; Air 5r.
Fairy Tales. Stories of the Brothers Grimm. Postage 1, 2, 4, 5, 10d.; Air 3r.
European Tour of Emperor Hirohito of Japan. Postage 1, 2, 4, 5, 10d.; Air 6r.
13th World Scout Jamboree, Asagiri, Japan. Postage 5, 10, 15, 20, 25d.; Air 5r.
Winter Olympic Games, Sapporo, Japan (1972). Postage 5, 10, 15, 20, 25d.; Air 5r.
Olympic Games, Munich (1972). Postage 5, 10, 15, 20, 25d.; Air 5r.
"Japanese Life". Postage 10d.×4, 20d.×4, 30d.×4, 40d.×4, 50d.×4; Air 3r.×4.
Space Flight of "Apollo 15". Postage 5, 10, 15, 20, 25, 50d.; Air 1, 2, 3, 5r.
"Soyuz 11" Disaster. Air 50d., 1r., 1r.50.
"The Future in Space". Postage 5, 10, 15, 20, 25, 50d.
2500th Anniv of Persian Empire. Postage 10, 20, 30, 40, 50d., Air 3r.
Cats. Postage 10, 15, 20, 25d.; Air 50d., 1r.
50th Anniv of Tutankhamun Tomb Discovery. Postage 1, 2, 3, 4, 5, 6, 7, 8, 9, 10, 11, 12, 13, 14, 15, 16d.; Air 1r.×4.
400th Birth Anniv of Johannes Kepler (astronomer). Postage 50d.; Air 5r.
Famous Men. Air. 1r.×5.

**1972**

150th Death Anniv of Napoleon Bonaparte (1971). Postage 10, 20, 30, 40d.; Air 1, 2, 3, 4r.
1st Death Anniv of General de Gaulle. Postage 10, 20, 30, 40d.; Air 1, 2, 3, 4r.
Wild Animals (1st series). Postage 5, 10, 15, 20, 25, 30, 35, 40d.
Tropical Fishes. Postage 5, 10, 15, 20, 25d.; Air 50, 75d., 1r.
Famous Musicians. Postage 5d.×3, 10d.×3, 15d.×3, 20d.×3, 25d.×3, 30d.×3, 35d.×3, 40d.×3.
Easter. Postage 5, 10, 15, 20, 25d.; Air 5r.
Wild Animals (2nd series). Postage 5, 10, 15, 20, 25d.; Air 5r.
"Tour de France" Cycle Race. Postage 5, 10, 15, 20, 25, 30, 35, 40, 45, 50, 55d.; Air 60, 65, 70, 75, 80, 85, 90, 95d., 1r.

Many other issues were released between 1 September 1971 and 1 August 1972, but their authenticity has been denied by the Ajman Postmaster-General. Certain issues of 1967-69 exist overprinted to commemorate other events but the Postmaster General states that these are unofficial. Ajman joined the United Arab Emirates on 1 August 1972 and the Ministry of Communications assumed responsibility for the postal services. Further stamps inscribed "Ajman" issued after that date were released without authority and had no validity.

Pt. 11

# ALAND ISLANDS

Aland is an autonomous province of Finland. From 1984 separate stamps were issued for the area although stamps of Finland could also still be used there. On 1 January 1993 Aland assumed control of its own postal service and Finnish stamps ceased to be valid there.

1984. 100 pennia = 1 markka.
2002. 100 cents = 1 euro.

**1** Fishing Boat

**1984**

| | | | | |
|---|---|---|---|---|
| 1 | **1** | 10p. mauve | 15 | 20 |
| 2 | **1** | 20p. green | 25 | 20 |
| 3 | **1** | 50p. green | 25 | 20 |
| 4 | - | 1m. green | 55 | 45 |
| 5 | **1** | 1m.10 blue | 55 | 45 |
| 6 | **1** | 1m.20 black | 55 | 55 |
| 7 | **1** | 1m.30 green | 65 | 65 |
| 8 | - | 1m.40 multicoloured | 1·20 | 80 |
| 9a | - | 1m.50 multicoloured | 1·00 | 55 |
| 10 | - | 1m.90 multicoloured | 1·00 | 95 |
| 12 | - | 3m. blue, green and black | 1·50 | 1·10 |
| 14 | - | 10m. black, chestnut & brn | 4·25 | 2·75 |
| 15 | - | 13m. multicoloured | 6·00 | 5·00 |

DESIGNS—20×29 mm: 1m.50, Midsummer pole, Storby village. 21×31 mm: 13m. Rug, 1793. 26×32 mm: 3m. Map of Aland Islands. 30×20 mm: 1m. Farjsund Bridge. 31×21 mm: 1m.40, Aland flag; 1m.90, Mariehamn Town Hall. 32×26 mm: 10m. Seal of Aland showing St. Olaf (patron saint).

**2** "Pommern" (barque) and Car Ferries, Mariehamn West Harbour

**1984.** 50th Anniv of Society of Shipowners.

| | | | | |
|---|---|---|---|---|
| 16 | **2** | 2m. multicoloured | 4·75 | 2·30 |

**3** Grove of Ashes and Hazels

**1985.** Aland Scenes. Multicoloured.

| | | | |
|---|---|---|---|
| 17 | 2m. Type **3** | 1·90 | 1·00 |
| 18 | 5m. Kokar Church and shore (horiz) | 1·90 | 1·70 |
| 19 | 8m. Windmill and farm (horiz) | 3·25 | 2·75 |

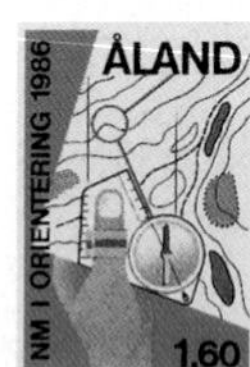

**4** Map, Compass and Measuring Instrument

**1986.** Nordic Orienteering Championships, Aland.

| | | | | |
|---|---|---|---|---|
| 20 | **4** | 1m.60 multicoloured | 3·00 | 1·70 |

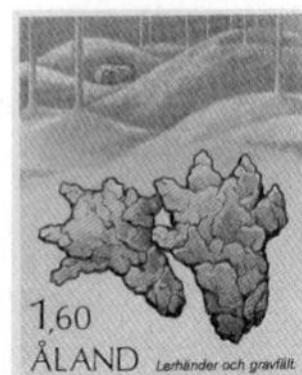

**5** Clay Hands and Burial Mounds, Skamkulla

**1986.** Archaeology. Multicoloured.

| | | | |
|---|---|---|---|
| 21 | 1m.60 Type **5** | 1·90 | 80 |
| 22 | 2m.20 Bronze staff from Finby and Apostles | 1·00 | 90 |
| 23 | 20m. Monument at ancient court site, Saltvik, and court in session (horiz) | 7·75 | 7·50 |

**6** "Onningeby" (drawing, Victor Westerholm)

**1986.** Centenary of Onnigeby Artists' Colony.

| | | | | |
|---|---|---|---|---|
| 24 | **6** | 3m.70 multicoloured | 4·00 | 2·10 |

**7** Eiders

**1987.** Birds. Multicoloured.

| | | | |
|---|---|---|---|
| 25 | 1m.70 Type **7** | 7·75 | 7·25 |
| 26 | 2m.30 Tufted ducks | 3·75 | 2·75 |
| 27 | 12m. Velvet scoters | 5·00 | 4·75 |

**8** Firemen in Horse-drawn Cart

**1987.** Centenary of Mariehamn Fire Brigade.

| | | | | |
|---|---|---|---|---|
| 28 | **8** | 7m. multicoloured | 7·00 | 7·75 |

**9** Meeting and Item 3 of Report

**1987.** 70th Anniv of Aland Municipalities Meeting, Finstrom.

| | | | | |
|---|---|---|---|---|
| 29 | **9** | 1m.70 multicoloured | 1·70 | 1·20 |

**10** Loading Mail Barrels at Eckero

**1988.** 350th Anniv of Postal Service in Aland.

| | | | | |
|---|---|---|---|---|
| 30 | **10** | 1m.80 multicoloured | 2·40 | 1·70 |

**11** Ploughing with Horses

**1988.** Centenary of Agricultural Education in Aland.

| | | | | |
|---|---|---|---|---|
| 31 | **11** | 2m.20 multicoloured | 2·10 | 2·10 |

**12** Baltic Galleass "Albanus"

**1988.** Sailing Ships. Multicoloured.

| | | | |
|---|---|---|---|
| 32 | 1m.80 Type **12** | 2·50 | 1·50 |
| 33 | 2m.40 Schooner "Ingrid" (horiz) | 3·75 | 3·25 |
| 34 | 11m. Barque "Pamir" (horiz) | 10·00 | 8·50 |

**13** St. Olaf's Church, Jomala

1988

| | | | | |
|---|---|---|---|---|
| 35 | **13** | 1m.40 multicoloured | 1·90 | 1·50 |

**14** Elder-flowered Orchid

**1989.** Orchids. Multicoloured.

| | | | |
|---|---|---|---|
| 36 | 1m.50 Type **14** | 2·50 | 1·60 |
| 37 | 2m.50 Narrow-leaved helleborine | 3·25 | 2·20 |
| 38 | 14m. Lady's slipper | 11·50 | 10·00 |

**15** Teacher and Pupils

**1989.** 350th Anniv of First Aland School, Saltvik.

| | | | | |
|---|---|---|---|---|
| 39 | **15** | 1m.90 multicoloured | 1·50 | 1·30 |

**16** St. Michael's Church, Finstrom

1989

| | | | | |
|---|---|---|---|---|
| 40 | **16** | 1m.50 multicoloured | 1·50 | 1·40 |

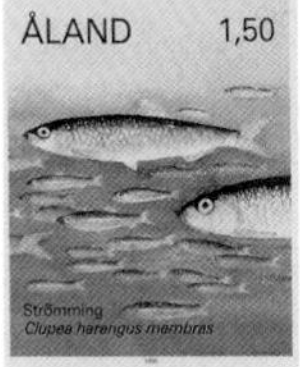
**17** Baltic Herring

**1990.** Fishes. Multicoloured.

| | | | |
|---|---|---|---|
| 41 | 1m.50 Type **17** | 1·30 | 1·00 |
| 42 | 2m. Northern pike | 1·30 | 1·00 |
| 43 | 2m.70 European flounder | 1·30 | 1·40 |

**18** St. Andrew's Church, Lumparland

1990

| | | | | |
|---|---|---|---|---|
| 44 | **18** | 1m.70 multicoloured | 1·50 | 1·30 |

**19** "St. Catherine" (fresco, St. Anna's Church, Kumlinge)

1990

| | | | | |
|---|---|---|---|---|
| 45 | **19** | 2m. multicoloured | 90 | 85 |

**20** West European Hedgehog

**1991.** Mammals. Multicoloured.

| | | | |
|---|---|---|---|
| 46 | 1m.60 Type **20** | 1·30 | 85 |
| 47 | 2m.10 Eurasian red squirrel | 1·30 | 1·00 |
| 48 | 2m.90 Roe deer | 1·50 | 1·60 |

**21** Volleyball

**1991.** Small Island Games, Mariehamn. Sheet 117×81 mm containing T **21** and similar vert designs. Multicoloured.

**MS**49 2m.10; Type **21**; 2m.10; Shooting; 2m.10; Football; 2m.10, Running 5·00 4·75

**22** Canoeing

**1991.** Nordic Countries' Postal Co-operation. Tourism. Multicoloured.

| | | | |
|---|---|---|---|
| 50 | 2m.10 Type **22** | 90 | 90 |
| 51 | 2m.90 Cycling | 1·50 | 1·50 |

**23** "League of Nations Meeting, Geneva, 1921" (print by F. Rackwitz)

**1991.** 70th Anniv of Aland Autonomy.

| | | | | |
|---|---|---|---|---|
| 52 | **23** | 16m. multicoloured | 9·00 | 7·00 |

**24** St. Mathias's Church, Vardo

1991

| | | | | |
|---|---|---|---|---|
| 53 | **24** | 1m.80 multicoloured | 1·50 | 1·00 |

**25** Von Knorring (after Karl Jansson)

**1992.** Birth Bicentenary of Rev. Frans Peter von Knorring (social reformer).

| | | | | |
|---|---|---|---|---|
| 54 | **25** | 2 klass (1m.60) mult | 1·30 | 90 |

**26** Barque "Herzogen Cecilie" and Wheat Transport Route Map

**1992.** 48th International Association of Cape Horners Congress, Mariehamn.

| | | | | |
|---|---|---|---|---|
| 55 | **26** | 1 klass (2m.10) mult | 2·00 | 1·50 |

**27** Ranno Lighthouse

**1992.** Lighthouses. Multicoloured.

| | | | |
|---|---|---|---|
| 56 | 2m.10 Type **27** | 5·75 | 2·50 |
| 57 | 2m.10 Salskar | 5·75 | 2·50 |
| 58 | 2m.10 Lagskar | 5·75 | 2·50 |
| 59 | 2m.10 Market | 5·75 | 2·50 |

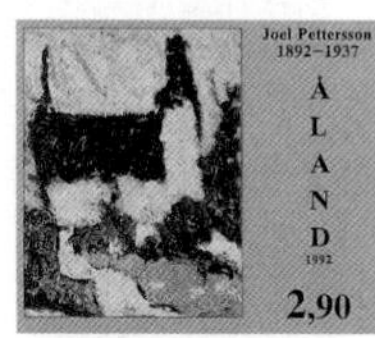
**28** "Lemland Landscape"

**1992.** Birth Cent of Joel Pettersson (painter). Mult.

| | | | |
|---|---|---|---|
| 60 | 2m.90 Type **28** | 1·30 | 1·10 |
| 61 | 16m. "Self-portrait" | 6·50 | 6·25 |

**29** Delegates processing to Church Service

**1992.** 70th Anniv of First Aland Provincial Parliament.

| | | | | |
|---|---|---|---|---|
| 62 | **29** | 3m.40 multicoloured | 1·90 | 1·50 |

**30** St. Catherine's Church, Hammarland

1992

| | | | | |
|---|---|---|---|---|
| 63 | **30** | 1m.80 multicoloured | 1·50 | 90 |

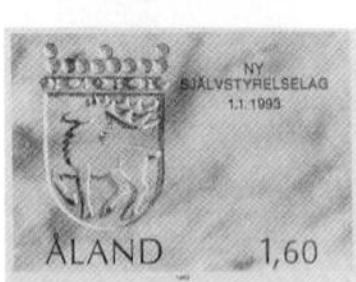
**31** Arms

**1993.** Postal Autonomy. Multicoloured.

| | | | |
|---|---|---|---|
| 64 | 1m.60 Type **31** | 1·20 | 85 |

**MS**65 129×80 mm. 1m.90 Cover with Kastelholm single-line postmark (26×35 mm); 1m.90 Mareinhamm Post Office; 1m.90 Post van leaving *Alfägeln* (ferry); 1m.90 Postal emblem (26×31 mm) 4·25 3·00

**32** Fiddler

**1993.** Nordic Countries' Postal Co-operation. Tourism. Exhibits from Jan Karlsgarden Open-air Museum.

| | | | | |
|---|---|---|---|---|
| 66 | **32** | 2m. red, pink and black | 1·00 | 85 |
| 67 | - | 2m.30 blue, black and azure | 1·00 | 1·00 |

DESIGN—HORIZ: 2m.30, Boat-house.

**33** Saltvik Woman

**1993.** Costumes. Multicoloured.

| | | | |
|---|---|---|---|
| 68 | 1m.90 Type **33** | 1·30 | 85 |
| 69 | 3m.50 Eckero and Brando women and Mariehamn couple | 1·50 | 1·50 |
| 70 | 17m. Finstrom couple | 8·25 | 7·25 |

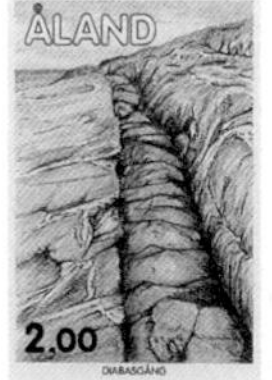
**34** Diabase Dyke, Sottunga

**1993.** Aland Geology. Multicoloured.

| | | | |
|---|---|---|---|
| 71 | 10p. Boulder field, Dano Gamlan | 25 | 20 |
| 72 | 1m.60 Drumlin (hillock), Markusbole | 75 | 75 |
| 73 | 2m. Type **34** | 90 | 70 |
| 74 | 2m.30 Pitcher of Kallskar | 90 | 75 |
| 75 | 2m.70 Pillow lava, Kumlinge | 1·20 | 90 |
| 76 | 2m.90 Red Cow (islet), Lumpurn | 1·30 | 1·30 |
| 77 | 3m.40 Erratic boulder, Torsskar, Kokar Osterbygge (horiz) | 1·40 | 1·40 |
| 78 | 6m. Folded gneiss | 2·50 | 2·30 |
| 79 | 7m. Pothole, Bano Foglo (horiz) | 2·75 | 2·50 |

**35** Mary Magdalene Church, Sottunga

1993

| | | | | |
|---|---|---|---|---|
| 80 | **35** | 1m.80 multicoloured | 1·30 | 1·20 |

**37** Glanville's Fritillary ("Melitaea cinxia")

**1994.** Butterflies. Multicoloured.

| | | | |
|---|---|---|---|
| 81 | 2m.30 Type **37** | 1·30 | 1·20 |
| 82 | 2m.30 "Quercusia querqus" | 1·30 | 1·10 |
| 83 | 2m.30 Clouded apollo ("Parnassius mnemosyne") | 1·30 | 1·20 |
| 84 | 2m.30 "Hesperia comma" | 1·30 | 1·10 |

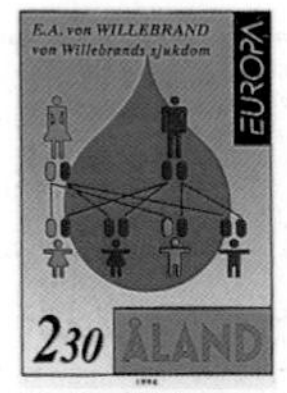
**38** Genetic Diagram

**1994.** Europa. Medical Discoveries. Multicoloured.

| | | | |
|---|---|---|---|
| 85 | 2m.30 Type **38** (discovery of Von Willebrand's disease (hereditary blood disorder)) | 2·50 | 2·00 |
| 86 | 2m.90 Molecular diagram (purification of heparin by Erik Jorpes) | 2·50 | 2·00 |

**39** Comb Ceramic and Pitted Ware Pottery

**1994.** The Stone Age.

| | | | | |
|---|---|---|---|---|
| 87 | **39** | 2m.40 brown | 1·00 | 1·20 |
| 88 | - | 2m.80 blue | 1·20 | 1·30 |
| 89 | - | 18m. green | 7·75 | 7·75 |

DESIGNS—VERT: 2m.80, Stone tools. HORIZ: 18m. Canoe and tent by river (reconstruction of Stone-age village, Langbergsoda).

**40** St. John the Baptist's Church, Sund

**1994**

| | | | | |
|---|---|---|---|---|
| 90 | **40** | 2m. multicoloured | 1·50 | 1·10 |

**42** "Skuta" (Cargo Sailing Boat)

**1995.** Cargo Sailing Ships. Multicoloured.

| | | | |
|---|---|---|---|
| 91 | 2m.30 Type **42** | 1·00 | 1·20 |
| 92 | 2m.30 "Sump" (well-boat) | 1·00 | 1·20 |
| 93 | 2m.30 "Storbat" (farm boat) | 1·00 | 1·20 |
| 94 | 2m.30 "Jakt" | 1·00 | 1·20 |

**43** National Colours and E.U. Emblem

**1995.** Admission of Aland Islands to European Union.

| | | | | |
|---|---|---|---|---|
| 95 | **43** | 2m.90 multicoloured | 1·70 | 1·30 |

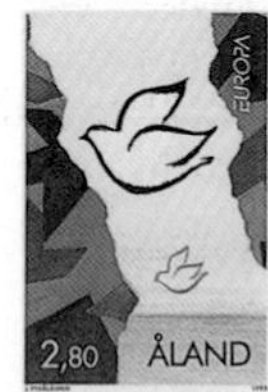

**44** Doves and Cliffs

**1995.** Europa. Peace and Freedom. Multicoloured.

| | | | |
|---|---|---|---|
| 96 | 2m.80 Type **44** | 1·30 | 1·30 |
| 97 | 2m.90 Dove, night sky and island | 1·30 | 1·40 |

**45** Golf

**1995.** Nordic Countries' Postal Co-operation. Tourism. With service indicator. Multicoloured.

| | | | |
|---|---|---|---|
| 98 | 2 klass (2m.) Type **45** | 1·30 | 1·20 |
| 99 | 1 klass (2m.30) Sport fishing | 1·50 | 1·20 |

**46** Racing Dinghies

**1995.** Optimist World Dinghy Championships, Mariehamn.

| | | | | |
|---|---|---|---|---|
| 100 | **46** | 3m.40 multicoloured | 2·00 | 1·40 |

**47** St. George's Church, Geta

**1995**

| | | | | |
|---|---|---|---|---|
| 101 | **47** | 2m. multicoloured | 1·30 | 90 |

**48** "St. Olaf" (Wooden Carving from Sund Church)

**1995.** Birth Millenary of St. Olaf.

| | | | | |
|---|---|---|---|---|
| 102 | **48** | 4m.30 multicoloured | 1·90 | 2·00 |

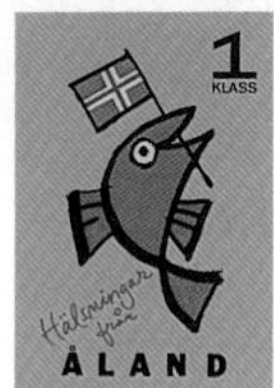

**49** Fish holding Flag in Mouth ("Greetings from Aland")

**1996.** Greetings Stamps. With service indicator. Multicoloured.

| | | | |
|---|---|---|---|
| 103 | 1 klass Type **49** | 1·50 | 1·20 |
| 104 | 1 klass Bird holding flower in beak ("Congratulations") | 1·50 | 1·20 |

**50** Landing on Branch

**1996.** Endangered Species. The Eagle Owl. Multicoloured.

| | | | |
|---|---|---|---|
| 105 | 2m.40 Type **50** | 1·00 | 1·20 |
| 106 | 2m.40 Perched on branch | 1·00 | 1·10 |
| 107 | 2m.40 Adult owl | 1·00 | 1·20 |
| 108 | 2m.40 Juvenile owl | 1·00 | 1·10 |

Nos. 105/6 form a composite design.

**51** Sally Salminen (novelist)

**1996.** Europa. Famous Women. Multicoloured.

| | | | |
|---|---|---|---|
| 109 | 2m.80 Type **51** | 1·20 | 1·10 |
| 110 | 2m.90 Fanny Sundstrom (politician) | 1·20 | 1·40 |

**52** Choir

**1996.** "Aland 96" Song and Music Festival, Mariehamn.

| | | | | |
|---|---|---|---|---|
| 111 | **52** | 2m.40 multicoloured | 1·30 | 1·10 |

**53** "Haircut"

**1996.** 150th Birth Anniv of Karl Jansson (painter).

| | | | | |
|---|---|---|---|---|
| 112 | **53** | 18m. multicoloured | 8·50 | 8·25 |

**54** "Trilobita asaphus"

**1996.** Fossils. Multicoloured.

| | | | |
|---|---|---|---|
| 113 | 40p. Type **54** | 25 | 35 |
| 114 | 9m. "Gastropoda euomophalus" | 3·50 | 3·25 |

**55** Brando Church

**1996**

| | | | | |
|---|---|---|---|---|
| 115 | **55** | 2m. multicoloured | 1·30 | 1·00 |

**56** Giant Isopod ("Saduria entomon") and Opossum Shrimp ("Mysis relicta")

**1997.** Marine Survivors from the Ice Age. Multicoloured.

| | | | |
|---|---|---|---|
| 116 | 30p. Type **56** | 25 | 25 |
| 117 | 2m.40 Four-horned sculpin ("Myotocephalus quadricornis") | 1·30 | 1·00 |
| 118 | 4m.30 Ringed seal ("Phoca hispida botrica") | 1·70 | 1·70 |

**57** Coltsfoot ("Tussilago farfara")

**1997.** Spring Flowers. Multicoloured.

| | | | |
|---|---|---|---|
| 119 | 2m.40 Type **57** | 1·00 | 1·20 |
| 120 | 2m.40 Blue anemone ("Hepatica nobilis") | 1·00 | 1·20 |
| 121 | 2m.40 Wood anemone ("Anemone nemorosa") | 1·00 | 1·20 |
| 122 | 2m.40 Yellow anemone ("Anemone ranunculoides") | 1·00 | 1·20 |

**58** Floorball

**1997.** 1st Women's Floorball World Championship, Mariehamn and Godby.

| | | | | |
|---|---|---|---|---|
| 123 | **58** | 3m.40 multicoloured | 2·00 | 1·30 |

**59** The Devil's Dance

**1997.** Europa. Tales and Legends.

| | | | | |
|---|---|---|---|---|
| 124 | **59** | 2m.90 multicoloured | 2·50 | 2·30 |

**60** Kastelholm Castle and Arms

**1997.** 600th Anniv of Kalmar Union between Sweden, Denmark and Norway.

| | | | | |
|---|---|---|---|---|
| 125 | **60** | 2m.40 multicoloured | 1·20 | 1·30 |

**61** Hologram of Schooner "Linden" and "75 Years"

**1997.** 75th Anniv of Aland Autonomy. Sheet 128×80 mm.

| | | | |
|---|---|---|---|
| **MS**126 **61** | 20m. multicoloured | 10·00 | 9·00 |

**62** "Thornbury" (freighter)

**1997.** Steam Freighters. Multicoloured.

| | | | |
|---|---|---|---|
| 127 | 2m.80 Type **62** | 1·20 | 1·20 |
| 128 | 3m.50 "Osmo" (freighter) | 1·40 | 1·30 |

**63** St George's Church, Mariehamn

**1997.** 70th Anniv of Mariehamn Church.

| | | | | |
|---|---|---|---|---|
| 129 | **63** | 1m.90 multicoloured | 1·30 | 1·00 |

**64** Man harvesting Apples

**1998.** Horticulture. Multicoloured.

| | | | |
|---|---|---|---|
| 130 | 2m. Type **64** | 75 | 85 |
| 131 | 2m.40 Woman harvesting cucumbers | 1·30 | 85 |

**65** Boy on Moped

**1998.** Youth Activities. Multicoloured.

| | | | |
|---|---|---|---|
| 132 | 2m.40 Type **65** | 1·00 | 1·20 |
| 133 | 2m.40 Laptop computer | 1·00 | 1·20 |
| 134 | 2m.40 CD disk and headphones | 1·00 | 1·20 |
| 135 | 2m.40 Step aerobics | 1·00 | 1·20 |

66 Midsummer Celebrations

1998. Europa. National Festivals.

| | | | | |
|---|---|---|---|---|
| 136 | 66 | 4m.20 multicoloured | 2·75 | 1·80 |

67 "Isabella" (car ferry)

1998. Nordic Countries' Postal Co-operation. Shipping.

| | | | | |
|---|---|---|---|---|
| 137 | 67 | 2m.40 multicoloured | 1·30 | 1·00 |

68 Waves breaking

1998. International Year of the Ocean.

| | | | | |
|---|---|---|---|---|
| 138 | 68 | 6m.30 multicoloured | 3·00 | 2·40 |

69 Players

1998. Association of Tennis Professionals Senior Tour, Mariehamn. Self-adhesive.

| | | | | |
|---|---|---|---|---|
| 139 | 69 | 2m.40 multicoloured | 1·30 | 1·00 |

70 Schooner, Compass Rose and Knots

1998. Ninth International Sea Scout Camp, Bomarsund Fortress, Aland.

| | | | | |
|---|---|---|---|---|
| 140 | 70 | 2m.80 multicoloured | 1·40 | 1·10 |

71 Seffers Homestead, Onningeby

1998. Traditional Porches. Multicoloured.

| | | | |
|---|---|---|---|
| 141 | 1m.60 Type **71** | 65 | 65 |
| 142 | 2m. Labbas homestead, Storby | 75 | 85 |
| 143 | 2m.90 Abras homestead, Bjorko | 1·20 | 1·20 |

72 Eckero Church

1998

| | | | | |
|---|---|---|---|---|
| 144 | 72 | 1m.90 multicoloured | 1·30 | 85 |

73 Sword and Dagger

1999. Bronze Age Relics. Multicoloured.

| | | | |
|---|---|---|---|
| 145 | 2m. Type **73** | 75 | 85 |
| 146 | 2m.20 "Ship" tumulus (vert) | 90 | 1·00 |

74 Wardrobe

1999. Folk Art. Decorated Furniture. Mult.

| | | | |
|---|---|---|---|
| 147 | 2m.40 Type **74** | 1·00 | 1·00 |
| 148 | 2m.40 Distaff | 1·00 | 1·00 |
| 149 | 2m.40 Chest | 1·00 | 1·00 |
| 150 | 2m.40 Spinning wheel | 1·00 | 1·00 |

75 "'Pamir' and 'Passat' (barques) off Port Victoria" (R. Castor)

1999. 50th Anniv of Rounding of Cape Horn by "Pamir" on Last Wheat-carrying Voyage.

| | | | | |
|---|---|---|---|---|
| 151 | 75 | 3m.40 multicoloured | 1·70 | 1·40 |

76 Cowslip

1999. Provincial Plant of Aland. Self-adhesive.

| | | | | |
|---|---|---|---|---|
| 152 | 76 | 2m.40 multicoloured | 1·20 | 1·00 |

77 Ido Island, Kokar

1999. Europa. Parks and Gardens.

| | | | | |
|---|---|---|---|---|
| 153 | 77 | 2m.90 multicoloured | 2·20 | 1·20 |

No. 153 is denominated both in markkas and in euros.

78 Racing Yachts

1999. Sailing.

| | | | | |
|---|---|---|---|---|
| 154 | 78 | 2m.70 multicoloured | 1·40 | 1·10 |

79 Puffed Shield Lichen ("Hypogymnia physodes")

1999. Lichens. With service indicator. Mult.

| | | | |
|---|---|---|---|
| 155 | 2 klass (2m.) Type **79** | 1·30 | 90 |
| 156 | 1 klass (2m.40) Common orange lichen ("Xanthoria parietina") | 1·50 | 1·00 |

80 Loading Avions de Transport Regional ATR72

1999. 125th Anniv of Universal Postal Union.

| | | | | |
|---|---|---|---|---|
| 157 | 80 | 2m.90 multicoloured | 1·20 | 1·30 |

81 St. Bridget's Church, Lemland

1999

| | | | | |
|---|---|---|---|---|
| 158 | 81 | 1m.90 multicoloured | 1·20 | 1·00 |

82 Runners

1999. Finnish Cross-country Championships, Mariehamn.

| | | | | |
|---|---|---|---|---|
| 159 | 82 | 3m.50 multicoloured | 1·50 | 1·30 |

**DENOMINATION**. From No. 162 to 207 Aland Islands stamps are denominated both in markkas and in euros. As no cash for the latter is in circulation, the catalogue continues to use the markka value.

83 Arctic Tern (*Sterna paradisaea*)

2000. Sea Birds. Multicoloured.

| | | | |
|---|---|---|---|
| 162 | 1m.80 Type **83** | 75 | 70 |
| 164 | 2m.20 Mew gull (*Larus canus*) (vert) | 90 | 85 |
| 166 | 2m.60 Great black-backed gull (*Larus marinus*) | 1·00 | 95 |

84 International Peace Symbol and State Flag

2000. New Millennium Sheet. 100×80 mm. Multicoloured.

**MS**171 **84** 3m.40, yellow; 3m.40, red; 3m.40, blue; 3m.40, white 8·00 5·25

85 Elk

2000. The Elk (Alces alces). Multicoloured.

| | | | |
|---|---|---|---|
| 172 | 2m.60 Type **85** | 1·00 | 1·00 |
| 173 | 2m.60 With young | 1·00 | 1·00 |
| 174 | 2m.60 Beside lake | 1·00 | 1·00 |
| 175 | 2m.60 In snow | 1·00 | 1·00 |

86 "Building Europe"

2000. Europa.

| | | | | |
|---|---|---|---|---|
| 176 | 86 | 3m. multicoloured | 2·20 | 1·60 |

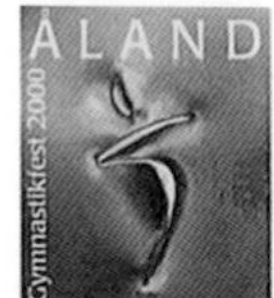
87 Gymnast

2000. Finno-Swedish Gymnastics Association Exhibition, Mariehamn. Self-adhesive.

| | | | | |
|---|---|---|---|---|
| 177 | 87 | 2m.60 multicoloured | 1·30 | 1·00 |

88 Crew and *Linden* (schooner)

2000. Visit by Cutty Sark Tall Ships' Race Competitors to Mariehamn.

| | | | | |
|---|---|---|---|---|
| 178 | 88 | 3m.40 multicoloured | 1·60 | 1·20 |

89 Lange on prow of Longship

2000. Death Millenary of Hlodver Lange the Viking.

| | | | | |
|---|---|---|---|---|
| 179 | 89 | 4m.50 multicoloured | 2·40 | 1·90 |

90 Wooden Ornamented Swiss-style House, Mariehamn

2000. 48th Death Anniv of Hilda Hongell (architect). Multicoloured.

| | | | |
|---|---|---|---|
| 180 | 3m.80 Type **90** | 1·50 | 1·30 |
| 181 | 10m. House with central front entrance, Mariehamn | 3·75 | 3·50 |

91 The Nativity

2000. 2000 Years of Christianity.

| | | | | |
|---|---|---|---|---|
| 182 | 91 | 3m. multicoloured | 1·50 | 1·20 |

92 Kokar Church

2000

| | | | | |
|---|---|---|---|---|
| 183 | 92 | 2m. multicoloured | 1·20 | 95 |

93 Steller's Eider in Flight

2001. Endangered Species. The Steller's Eider (Polysticta stelleri). Multicoloured.

| | | | |
|---|---|---|---|
| 184 | 2m.70 Type **93** | 1·00 | 1·20 |
| 185 | 2m.70 Duck and drake | 1·00 | 1·20 |
| 186 | 2m.70 Duck and drake swimming | 1·00 | 1·20 |
| 187 | 2m.70 Drake swimming | 1·00 | 1·20 |

**94** Swamp Horsetail (*Equisetum fluviatile*)

**2001.** Plants. Multicoloured.
188 1m.90 Type **94** 90 85
189 2m.80 Stiff clubmoss (*Lycopodium annotinum*) 1·20 1·20
190 3m.50 Polypody (*Polybodium vulgare*) 1·40 1·30

**95** Heart and Graffiti on Brick Wall

**2001.** St. Valentine's Day.
200 **95** 3m.20 multicoloured 1·40 1·30

**96** Fisherman and Fish

**2001.** Europa. Water Resources.
201 **96** 3m.20 multicoloured 2·10 1·90

**97** Archipelago Windmill

**2001.** Windmills. Multicoloured.
202 3m. Type **97** 1·20 1·20
203 7m. Timbered windmill (horiz) 2·75 2·50
204 20m. Nest windmill (horiz) 8·00 7·50

**98** Golden Retriever

**2001.** Puppies. Multicoloured.
205 2 klass (2m.30) Type **98** 1·20 90
206 1 klass (2m.70) Wire-haired dachshund 1·40 1·00

**99** Foglo Church

**2001**
207 **99** 2m. multicoloured 90 75

**100** Smooth Snake (*Coronella Austriaca*)

**2002.** Endangered Animals. Multicoloured.
208 5c. Type **100** 25 20
209 70c. Great crested newt (*Triturus cristatus*) 1·40 1·50

**101** Woman pushing Shopping Trolley

**2002.** Euro Currency.
210 **101** 60c. multicoloured 1·50 1·30

**102** Tidying up Christmas

**2002.** St. Canute's Day.
211 **102** €2 multicoloured 4·75 4·50

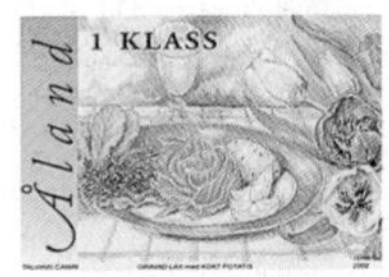

**103** Spiced Salmon and New Potatoes

**2002.** Traditional Dishes. Multicoloured.
212 1 klass (55c.) Type **103** 1·40 1·20
213 1 klass (55c.) Fried herring, mashed potatoes and beetroot 1·40 1·20
214 1 klass (55c.) Black bread and butter 1·40 1·20
215 1 klass (55c.) Aland pancake with stewed prune sauce and whipped cream 1·40 1·20

**104** Building

**2002.** Inauguration of New Post Terminal, Sviby.
216 **104** €1 multicoloured 2·50 2·20

**105** Circus Elephant and Rider

**2002.** Europa. Circus.
217 **105** 40c. multicoloured 1·50 1·20

**106** "Radar II" (sculpture, Stefan Lindfors)

**2002.** Nordic Countries' Postal Co-operation. Modern Art.
218 **106** €3 multicoloured 7·00 6·25

**107** Kayaking

**2002**
219 **107** 90c. multicoloured 2·30 2·50

**108** 8th-century Buckle, Persby, Sud

**2002.** Iron Age Jewellery found on Aland. Multicoloured.
220 2 klass. (45c.) Type **108** 1·20 1·00
221 1 klass. (55c.) 8th-century pin, Sylloda, Saltvik 1·40 1·20

**109** Saltvik Church

**2002**
222 **109** 35c. multicoloured 1·00 85

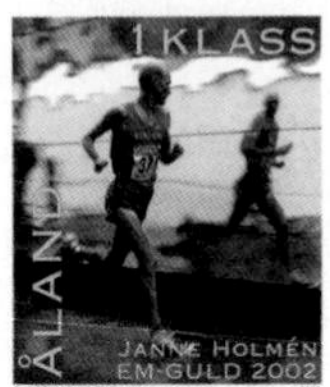

**110** Holmen

**2002.** Janne Holmen (Olympic gold medallist, men's marathon).
223 **110** 1 klass. (55c.) mult 1·40 1·20

**111** *Cantharellus cibarius*

**2003.** Fungi. Multicoloured.
224 10c. Type **111** 25 30
225 50c. *Boletus edulis* 1·30 95
226 €2.50 *Macrolepiota procera* 6·50 5·75

**112** Tovis (kitten)

**2003.** Cat Photograph Competition Winners. Multicoloured.
227 2 klass (45c.) Type **112** 1·20 1·10
228 1 klass (55c.) Randi (cat) (horiz) 1·40 1·30

**113** "Landscape in Summer" (detail) (Elin Danielson-Gambogi)

**2003.** Designs showing details of the painting. Multicoloured.
229 1 klass (55c.) Type **113** 1·40 1·30
230 1 klass (55c.) Trees and flowers 1·40 1·30
231 1 klass (55c.) Sunset over sea 1·40 1·30
232 1 klass (55c.) Shoreline and boats 1·40 1·30

**114** "Freedom of Speech and Press" (Kurt Simons)

**2003.** Europa. Poster Art.
233 **114** 45c. multicoloured 1·70 1·30

**115** "Pommern" (Arthur Victor Gregory)

**2003.** Centenary of Pommern (four mast steel barque, now museum). Self-adhesive.
234 **115** 55c. multicoloured 2·10 1·40

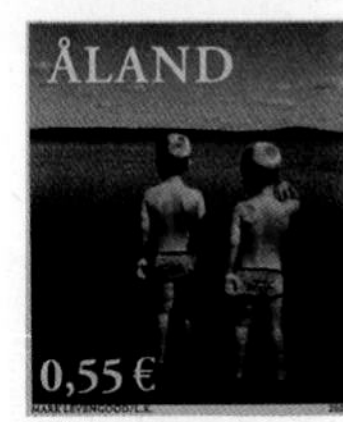

**116** Two Boys

**2003.** "My Aland". Mark Levengood.
235 **116** 55c. multicoloured 1·40 1·30

**117** Fiddle Player

**2003.** 50th Anniv of Aland Folk Music Association.
236 **117** €1.10 multicoloured 2·50 2·10

**118** Kumlinge Church

**2003**
237 **118** 40c. multicoloured 1·00 90

**119** Children dressed as St. Lucia and her Attendants

**2003.** St. Lucia Celebrations.
238 **119** 60c. multicoloured 1·50 1·20

**120** Ermine (*Mustela erminea*)

**2004.** Predators. Multicoloured.

| | | | |
|---|---|---|---|
| 239 | 20c. Type **120** | 65 | 50 |
| 240 | 60c. Fox (*Vulpes vulpes*) | 1·50 | 1·50 |
| 241 | €3 Pine marten (*Martes martes*) | 7·75 | 6·75 |

**121** Fenja and Menja (giantesses)

**2004.** Nordic Mythology. Sheet 105×70 mm.

| | | |
|---|---|---|
| **MS**250 **121** 55c. multicoloured | 1·40 | 1·30 |

Stamps of a similar theme were issued by Denmark, Faroe Islands, Finland, Greenland, Iceland, Norway and Sweden.

**122** Flag

**2004.** 50th Anniv of Aland Flag. Self-adhesive.

| | | | | |
|---|---|---|---|---|
| 251 | **122** | 1klass (60c.) multicoloured | 1·40 | 1·30 |

**123** *Cajsa* (longboat) and Passengers, 1986

**2004.** "My Aland". Mauno Koivisto (Finnish president 1982–94).

| | | | | |
|---|---|---|---|---|
| 252 | **123** | 90c. multicoloured | 2·20 | 2·00 |

**124** Yacht moored in Inlet

**2004.** Europa. Holidays.

| | | | | |
|---|---|---|---|---|
| 253 | **124** | 75c. multicoloured | 1·80 | 1·60 |

**125** Bomarsund Fortress

**2004.** 150th Anniv of Fall of Bomarsund Fortress. Sheet 170×95 mm containing T 125 and similar vert designs.

| | | |
|---|---|---|
| **MS**254 75c.×4, Type **125**; Bomarsund (different); Three soldiers; Six soldiers | 7·25 | 6·75 |

The stamps and margin of No. **MS**254 form a composite design of painting by A. Lourde-Laplace.

**126** Storklyndan, Brando

**2004.** Landscapes. Multicoloured.

| | | | |
|---|---|---|---|
| 255 | 2 klass (50c.) Type **126** | 1·00 | 1·10 |
| 256 | 1 klass (60c.) Prästgardsnaset, Findstrom | 1·70 | 1·30 |

**127** Panathenaic Stadium, Athens

**2004.** Olympic Games, Athens.

| | | | | |
|---|---|---|---|---|
| 257 | **127** | 80c. multicoloured | 1·80 | 1·70 |

**128** Father Christmas delivering Mail

**2004.** Christmas.

| | | | | |
|---|---|---|---|---|
| 258 | **128** | 45c. multicoloured | 1·20 | 1·10 |

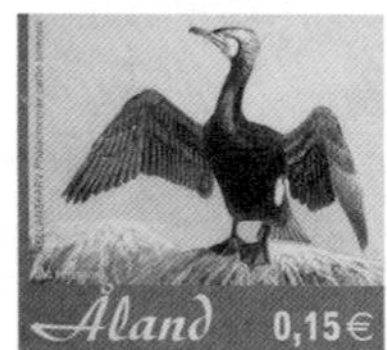


**129** Great Cormorant (*Phalacrocorax carbo sinensis*)

**2005.** Birds. Multicoloured.

| | | | |
|---|---|---|---|
| 259 | 15c. Type **129** | 50 | 45 |
| 260 | 65c. Whooper swan (*Cygnus Cygnus*) | 1·90 | 1·70 |
| 261 | €4 Grey heron (*Ardea cinerea*) | 9·50 | 8·25 |

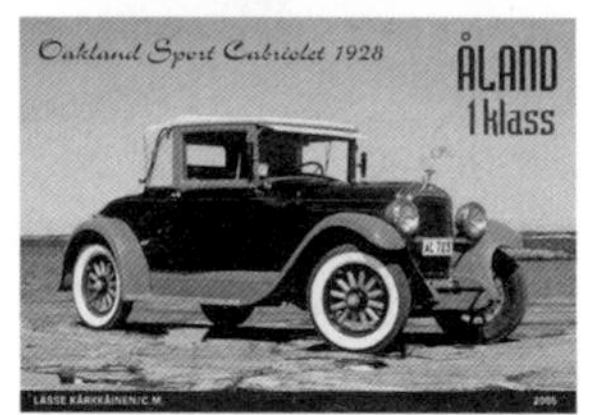


**130** Oakland Sport Chevrolet (1928) (⅔-size illustration)

**2005.** Vintage Cars. Multicoloured.

| | | | |
|---|---|---|---|
| 262 | (60c.) Type **130** | 1·70 | 1·30 |
| 263 | (60c.) Ford V8 (1939) | 1·70 | 1·30 |
| 264 | (60c.) Buick Super 4D HT (1957) | 1·70 | 1·30 |
| 265 | (60c.) Volkswagen 1200 (1964) | 1·70 | 1·30 |

**131** Family and Bonfire

**2005.** Walpurgis Night. Self-adhesive.

| | | | | |
|---|---|---|---|---|
| 266 | **131** | (50c.) multicoloured | 1·50 | 1·20 |

**132** Fish

**2005.** Europa. Gastronomy.

| | | | | |
|---|---|---|---|---|
| 267 | **132** | 90c. multicoloured | 1·90 | 1·70 |

**133** Bjorn Borg

**2005.** "My Aland". Bjorn Borg (tennis player).

| | | | | |
|---|---|---|---|---|
| 268 | **133** | 55c. multicoloured | 1·30 | 1·20 |

**134** "A Visit to Bomarsund Fortress" (Fritz von Dardel)

**2005.** 150th Anniv of Fall of Bomarsund Fortress (2004) (2nd series).

| | | | | |
|---|---|---|---|---|
| 269 | **134** | €1.30 multicoloured | 3·25 | 2·75 |

**135** *Linden* (schooner)

**2005**

| | | | | |
|---|---|---|---|---|
| 270 | **135** | 60c. multicoloured | 1·70 | 1·40 |

**136** Sando, Vardo

**2005.** Landscapes. Multicoloured.

| | | | |
|---|---|---|---|
| 271 | 70c. Type **136** | 1·90 | 1·40 |
| 272 | 80c. Grondal, Geta | 2·20 | 2·00 |

**137** Boy and Girl Brownies

**2005.** Christmas.

| | | | | |
|---|---|---|---|---|
| 273 | **137** | 45c. multicoloured | 90 | 75 |

**138** *Potosia cuprea*

**2006.** Beetles.

| | | | |
|---|---|---|---|
| 274 | 40c. Type **138** | 75 | 35 |
| 275 | 65c. *Coccinella septempunctata* | 1·30 | 85 |
| 276 | €2 *Oryctes nasicornis* | 4·50 | 3·00 |

**139** Face

**2006.** Centenary of Women's Suffrage.

| | | | | |
|---|---|---|---|---|
| 277 | **139** | 85c. multicoloured | 2·40 | 2·00 |

**140** Letesgubbe

**2006.** Nordic Mythology. Sheet 105×70 mm.

| | | |
|---|---|---|
| **MS**278 **140** 85c. multicoloured | 2·40 | 2·40 |

Stamps of a similar theme were issued by Denmark, Greenland, Faroe Islands, Finland, Iceland, Norway and Sweden.

**141** Bomarsund Fortress

**2006.** 150th Anniv of Demilitarization.

| | | | | |
|---|---|---|---|---|
| 279 | **141** | €1.50 multicoloured | 4·25 | 4·00 |

**142** Boy as King

**2006.** Europa. Integration.

| | | | | |
|---|---|---|---|---|
| 280 | **142** | €1.30 multicoloured | 3·75 | 3·50 |

**143** Girl posting Letter

**2006.** My Stamp. Self-adhesive.

| | | | | |
|---|---|---|---|---|
| 281 | **143** | 1 klass multicoloured | 1·75 | 1·50 |

**144** Sail Boat

**2006.** "My Aland". Ake Lindman (actor and filmmaker).

| | | | | |
|---|---|---|---|---|
| 282 | **144** | 75c. multicoloured | 2·10 | 2·00 |

**145** Soderby, Lemland

**2006.** Landscapes. Multicoloured.

| | | | |
|---|---|---|---|
| 283 | 55c. Type **145** | 1·50 | 1·50 |
| 284 | €1.20 Norra Essvik, Sottunga | 3·50 | 3·25 |

**146** Tribal-style Tattoo (Thomas Dahlgren)

**2006.** Tattoos. Multicoloured.

| | | | |
|---|---|---|---|
| 285 | 65c. Type **146** | 2·10 | 2·00 |
| 286 | 65c. Seaman style (Mikael Sandholm) | 2·10 | 2·00 |
| 287 | 65c. Floral (in memory of Tsunami disaster) (Linda Aberg) | 2·10 | 2·00 |

**147** Horse-drawn Sleigh

**2006.** Christmas. Inscribed "JULPOST 06".
288 **147** (50c.) multicoloured 1·40 1·40

**148** *Tripolium vulgare*

**2007.** Waterside Plants. Multicoloured.
289 80c. Type **148** 2·20 2·00
290 90c. *Lythrum salicaria* 2·60 2·50
291 €5 *Angelica archangelica* 12·50 12·00

**149** Junkers F13 flying boat

**2007.** Postal Transport. Multicoloured.
292 2klass Type **149** 1·60 1·50
293 1klass SAAB 340 2·00 1·80

**150** Skaftö, Kumlinge

**2007.** Landscape.
294 **150** 2klass multicoloured 1·60 1·50

**151** *Fillyjonks, Sea Monster and Cliffs* (painting by Tove Janson)

**2007.** Art.
295 **151** 85c. multicoloured 2·50 2·40

**152** Scout Emblem and Window

**2007.** Europa. Centenary of Scouting.
296 **152** 70c. multicoloured 2·20 2·10

**153** Bridal Crown (Titti Sundblom)

**2007.** Arts and Crafts. Multicoloured.
297 1klass Type **153** 2·20 2·00
298 1klass Flower print (Maria Korpi-Gordon and Adam Gordon) 2·20 2·00
299 1klass Ceramics (Judy Kuitunen) 2·20 2·00

**154** Two Players

**2007.** Girls' Football in Aland. Self-adhesive.
300 **154** 1klass multicoloured 2·00 1·90

**155** *Windmills* (Ture Bengtz)

**2007.** Birth Centenary of Ture Bengtz (artist and emigrant to USA). Emigration.
301 **155** 75c. multicoloured 2·10 2·00

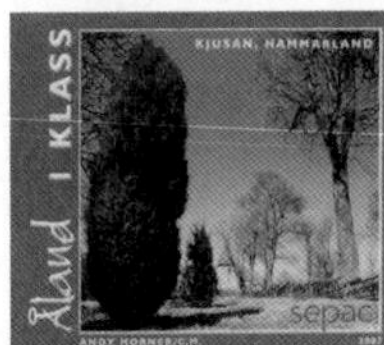


**156** Landscape, Kjusan, Hammarland

**2007.** SEPAC (small European mail services).
302 **156** 1klass multicoloured 2·00 1·90

**157** Santa Claus (poster by Haddon Sundblom)

**2007.** Christmas. Inscr 'Julpost 07'.
303 **157** (50c.) multicoloured 1·40 1·30

**158** *Perca fluviatilis*

**2008.** Fish. Paintings by Gosta Sundman. Multicoloured.
304 45c. Type **158** 1·30 1·30
305 €4.50 *Zander lucioperca* 11·50 11·50

**159** Signhild at Drottningkleven

**2008.** Nordic Mythology. Mythical Places. Sheet 105×70 mm. Inscr 'VARLDEN'.
**MS**306 **159** multicoloured 2·75 2·75

Stamps of a similar theme were issued by Denmark, Faroe Islands, Finland, Greenland, Iceland, Norway and Sweden.

The stamp and margin of No. **MS**306 form a composite design.

**MS**306 was for use on international mail and was originally on sale for 85c.

**160** Langvikshagen, Lumparland

**2008.** Landscapes. Inscr 'INRIKES'. Multicoloured.
307 (70c.) Type **160** 2·50 2·50
308 (70c.) Badhusberget, Mariehamn 2·50 2·50

Nos. 307/8 were for use on domestic mail and were originally on sale for 70c.

**161** Emblem

**2008.** Olympic Games, Beijing. Inscr 'VARLDEN'.
309 **161** (90c.) multicoloured 2·50 2·50

No. 309 was for use on international mail and was originally on sale for 90c.

**162** Letter, Ship and Sailor's Wife

**2008.** Europa. The Letter.
310 **162** €1 multicoloured 2·75 2·75

**163** Marhallan

**2008.** Lighthouses. Inscr 'EUROPA'. Multicoloured.
311 (75c.) Type **163** 2·20 2·20
312 (75c.) Gustaf Dalen 2·20 2·20
313 (75c.) Bogskar 2·20 2·20
314 (75c.) Kokarsoren 2·20 2·20

Nos. 311/14 were for use on mail within Europe and were originally on sale for 75c.

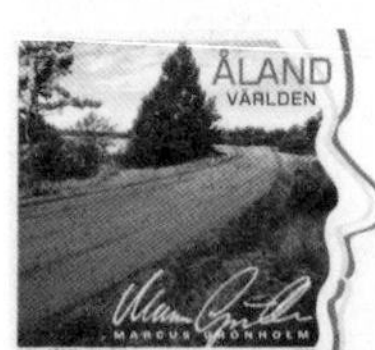


**164** Gravel Road and Profiles of Marcus Gronholm and Christoph Treier (trainer)

**2008.** My Aland. Marcus Gronholm (rally driver). Inscr 'VARLDEN'.
315 **164** (90c.) multicoloured 2·75 2·75

No. 315 was for use on international mail and was originally on sale for 90c.

**165** *Aland Peasant Bride* (Karl Emanuel Jansson)

**2008.** Art.
316 **165** €1.50 multicoloured 4·50 4·50

**166** Angel

**2008.** Christmas. Inscr 'JULPOST'.
317 **166** (55c.) multicoloured 1·50 1·50

No. 317 was on sale for 55c.

**167** Horse Rider

**2008.** My Stamp. Inscr 'EUROPA'. Self-adhesive.
318 **167** (75c.) multicoloured 2·25 2·25

No. 318 was for use on mail within Europe and was originally on sale for 75c.

**168** Boundary Post, Flojtan

**2009.** New Borders (bicentenary of Aland's integration into Russia). Inscr 'EUROPA'.
319 **168** (80c.) multicoloured 3·00 3·00

No. 319 was for use on mail within Europe and was originally on sale for 80c.

**169** Wind Turbine

**2009.** Preserve Polar Regions and Glaciers. Centenary of Electricity Supply. Sheet 120×80 mm.
**MS**320 multicoloured 7·25 7·25

**170** Ulla-Lena Lundberg

**2009.** Authors. Inscr 'EUROPA'. Multicoloured.
321 (80c.) Type **170** 3·00 3·00
322 (80c.) Anni Blomqvist 3·00 3·00
323 (80c.) Valdemar Nyman 3·00 3·00

Nos. 321/3, were issued for use on mail within Europe and were originally on sale for 80c.

**171** May Irwin and John Rice

**2009.** Centenary of Cinema in Aland.
324 **171** €1.60 multicoloured 6·00 6·00

**172** Divers and *Plus* (wreck)

**2009.** Diving. Inscr 'INRIKES'.
325 **172** (75c.) multicoloured 2·75 2·75

No. 325 was for use on mail within Aland and Finland and was originally on sale for 75c.

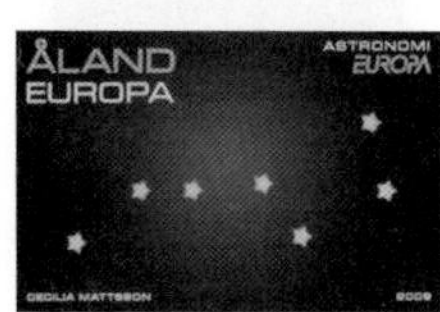

**173** The Plough (constellation)

**2009.** Europa. Astronomy. Inscr 'EUROPA'.
326 **173** (80c.) multicoloured 3·00 3·00

No. 326 was for use on mail within Europe and was originally on sale for 80c.

**174** *Viking*

**2009.** Ferries. Inscr 'INRIKES' (327)or 'EUROPA' (328). Multicoloured.
327 (75c.) Type **174** 2·50 2·50
328 (80c.) *Newbuilding* 3·25 3·25

No. 327 was for use on mail within Aland and Finland and was originally on sale for 75c.

No. 328 was for use on mail within Europe and was originally on sale for 80c.

**175** Athlete

**2009.** My Stamp. Island Games XIII, Aland. Inscr 'VARLDEN'. Self-adhesive.
329 **175** (90c.) multicoloured 3·25 3·25

No. 329 was for use on international mail and was originally on sale for 90c.

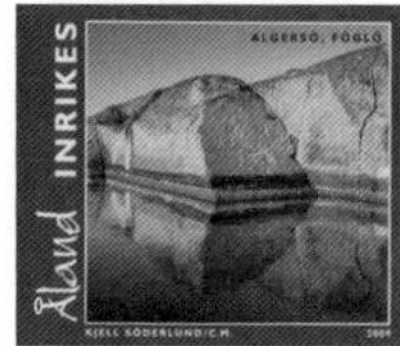

**176** Algerso, Foglo

**2009.** Landscapes. SEPAC (small european mail services) (331). Inscr 'INRIKES' (330) or 'EUROPA' (331). Multicoloured.
330 (75c.) Type **176** 2·50 2·50
331 (80c.) Orrdalsklint, Saltvik 3·25 3·25

No. 330 was for use on mail within Aland and Finland and was originally on sale for 75c.

No. 331 was for use on mail within Europe and was originally on sale for 80c.

**177** Cabin by Water

**2009.** My Aland. Martti Ahtisaari (President of Finland 1994–2000). Inscr 'VARLDEN'.
332 **177** (90c.) multicoloured 3·25 3·25

No. 332 was for use on international mail and was originally on sale for 90c.

**178** Santa's Helpers

**2009.** Christmas. Inscr 'JULPOST' (333) or 'VARLDEN' (334). Multicoloured.
333 (60c.) Type **178** 2·20 2·20
334 (90c.) Girl 3·25 3·25

No. 333 was for use on Christmas mail within Aland and Finland and was originally on sale for 60c.

No. 334 was for use on international mail and was originally on sale for 90c.

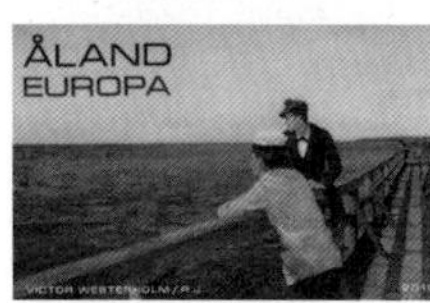

**179** *Mail Jetty at Eckero*

**2010.** 150th Birth Anniv of Victor Westerholm (artist). Inscr 'EUROPA'.
335 **179** (80c.) multicoloured 3·00 3·00

No. 335 was for use on mail within Europe and was originally on sale for 80c.

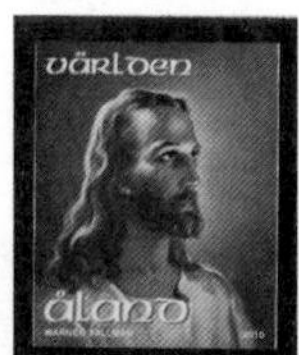

**180** *Head of Christ* (Walter Sallman)

**2010.** Religious Art. Inscr 'VARLDEN'.
336 **180** (90c.) multicoloured 3·00 3·00

No. 336 was for use on international mail and was originally on sale for 90c.

**181** Boats and Kobba Klintar (image scaled to 68% of original size)

**2010.** Life at the Coast. Kobba Klintar (heritage pilot station). Inscr 'VARLDEN'. Sheet 105×70 mm.
**MS**337 **181** multicoloured 3·00 3·00

No. 336 was for use on international mail and was originally on sale for 90c.

Stamps of a similar theme were issued by Denmark, Greenland, Faroe Islands, Finland, Iceland, Norway and Sweden.

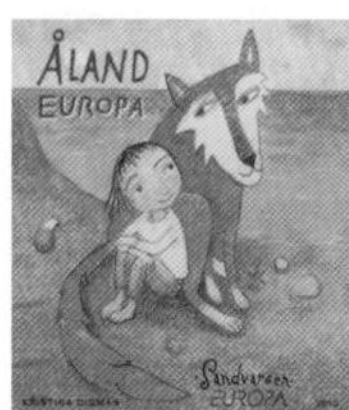

**182** Sandwolf and Zackarina (*Sandvargen* by Åsa Lind)

**2010.** Europa. Children's Books
338 **182** (85c.) multicoloured 3·25 3·25

No. 338 was for use on European mail and was originally on sale for 85c.

**183** *Skandia*

**2010.** Ferries. Multicoloured.
339 75c. Type **183** 4·25 4·25
340 €3.50 *Prinsessan* 12·00 12·00

**184** Moon Creature, c. 1960

**2010.** Plastic Toys by Plasto. Multicoloured.
341 (85c.) Type **184** 3·25 3·25
342 (85c.) Tipper lorry 3·25 3·25
343 (85c.) Ducks 3·25 3·25

No. 341/3 were for use on European mail and were originally on sale for 85c.

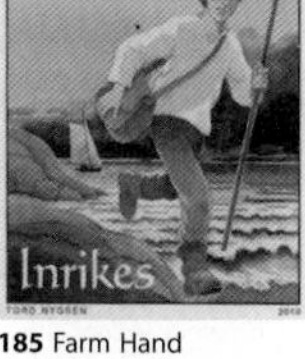

**185** Farm Hand delivering Mail

**2010.** Early Mail Delivery.
344 **185** (75c.) multicoloured 4·25 4·25

**186** Boy sailing Laser Radial

**2010.** My Stamp
345 **186** (85c.) multicoloured 3·00 3·00

No. 345 was for use on mail within Europe and was originally on sale for 85c.

**187** Stained Glass Window (detail) (Ture Bengtz), Jomala Church

**2010.** Church Interiors. Multicoloured.
346 80c. Type **187** 3·00 3·00
**MS**347 105×70 mm. €1.60 Stained glass window (horiz) 6·25 6·25

Stamps of a similar design were issued by Macau.

No. **MS**347 also contains a representation of the stamp issued by Macau.

**188** Degersand Beach, Eckerö

**2010.** Aland Scenery. Multicoloured.
348 80c. Type **188** 3·00 3·00
349 (85c.) Lillnäsberget, Sund 3·25 3·25

**189** Grannies bring Home the Christmas Tree

**2010.** Christmas
350 **189** (60c.) multicoloured 3·25 3·25

Pt. 19

# ALAOUITES

A coastal district of Syria, placed under French mandate in 1920. Became the Republic of Latakia in 1930. Incorporated with Syria in 1937.

100 centimes = 1 piastre.

**1925.** Stamps of France surch **ALAOUITES** and value in French and Arabic.

| | | | | |
|---|---|---|---|---|
| 1 | **11** | 0p.10 on 2c. purple | 2·00 | 10·50 |
| 2 | **18** | 0p.25 on 5c. orange | 2·50 | 9·00 |
| 3 | **15** | 0p.75 on 15c. green | 3·25 | 11·50 |
| 4 | **18** | 1p. on 20c. brown | 2·30 | 9·00 |
| 5 | **18** | 1p.25 on 25c. blue | 2·75 | 11·50 |
| 6 | **18** | 1p.50 on 30c. red | 9·25 | 32·00 |
| 7 | **18** | 2p. on 35c. violet | 1·00 | 9·75 |
| 8 | **13** | 2p. on 40c. red and blue | 4·00 | 12·50 |
| 9 | **13** | 2p. on 45c. green and blue | 10·00 | 32·00 |
| 10 | **13** | 3p. on 60c. violet and blue | 2·30 | 17·00 |
| 11 | **15** | 3p. on 60c. violet | 19·00 | 30·00 |
| 12 | **15** | 4p. on 85c. red | 2·00 | 8·25 |
| 13 | **13** | 5p. on 1f. red and yellow | 3·00 | 22·00 |
| 14 | **13** | 10p. on 2f. orange & grn | 5·50 | 25·00 |
| 15 | **13** | 25p. on 5f. blue and buff | 10·00 | 36·00 |

**1925.** "Pasteur" issue of France surch **ALAOUITES** and value in French and Arabic.

| | | | | |
|---|---|---|---|---|
| 16 | **30** | 0p.50 on 10c. green | 2·30 | 9·00 |
| 17 | **30** | 0p.75 on 15c. green | 1·70 | 9·25 |
| 18 | **30** | 1p.50 on 30c. red | 1·50 | 10·00 |
| 19 | **30** | 2p. on 45c. red | 2·30 | 10·50 |
| 20 | **30** | 2p.50 on 50c. blue | 3·25 | 11·50 |
| 21 | **30** | 4p. on 75c. blue | 2·50 | 13·50 |

**1925.** Air. Stamps of France optd **ALAOUITES Avion** and value in French and Arabic.

| | | | | |
|---|---|---|---|---|
| 22 | **13** | 2p. on 40c. red and blue | 6·00 | 27·00 |
| 23 | **13** | 3p. on 60c. violet and blue | 6·75 | 42·00 |
| 24 | **13** | 5p. on 1f. red and yellow | 6·00 | 24·00 |
| 25 | **13** | 10p. on 2f. orange & green | 6·00 | 28·00 |

**1925.** Pictorial stamps of Syria (1925) optd **ALAOUITES** in French and Arabic.

| | | | |
|---|---|---|---|
| 26 | 0p.10 violet | 20 | 4·25 |
| 27 | 0p.25 black | 1·10 | 7·75 |
| 28 | 0p.50 green | 1·40 | 2·00 |
| 29 | 0p.75 red | 2·10 | 6·75 |
| 30 | 1p. purple | 90 | 2·30 |
| 31 | 1p.25 green | 2·75 | 8·00 |
| 32 | 1p.50 pink | 2·00 | 5·00 |
| 33 | 2p. brown | 1·40 | 3·00 |
| 34 | 2p.50 blue | 2·40 | 7·75 |
| 35 | 3p. brown | 1·60 | 3·75 |
| 36 | 5p. violet | 1·90 | 3·25 |
| 37 | 10p. purple | 2·20 | 5·00 |
| 38 | 25p. blue | 2·75 | 13·00 |

**1925.** Air. Nos. 33 and 35/37 optd **AVION** in French and Arabic.

| | | | |
|---|---|---|---|
| 40 | 2p. brown | 2·30 | 10·50 |
| 41 | 3p. brown | 1·10 | 9·25 |
| 42 | 5p. violet | 1·20 | 7·75 |
| 43 | 10p. purple | 1·10 | 7·00 |

**1926.** Air. Air stamps of Syria with airplane overprint optd **ALAOUITES** in French and Arabic.

| | | | |
|---|---|---|---|
| 44 | 2p. brown | 2·00 | 12·00 |
| 45 | 3p. brown | 2·00 | 12·00 |
| 46 | 5p. violet | 2·00 | 12·00 |
| 47 | 10p. purple | 2·00 | 12·00 |

See also Nos. 59/60 and 63.

**1926.** Pictorial stamps of 1925 surcharged.

| | | | |
|---|---|---|---|
| 53 | 05 on 0p.10 violet | 20 | 5·00 |
| 54 | 2p. on 1p.25 green | 14·50 | 9·75 |
| 48 | 3p.50 on 0p.75 red | 90 | 5·25 |
| 49 | 4p. on 0p.25 black | 2·30 | 5·50 |
| 56 | 4p.50 on 0p.75 red | 2·50 | 7·00 |
| 50 | 6p. on 2p.50 blue | 1·40 | 6·00 |
| 57 | 7p.50 on 2p.50 blue | 2·30 | 2·50 |
| 51 | 12p. on 1p.25 green | 3·00 | 8·25 |
| 58 | 15p. on 25p. blue | 7·50 | 12·00 |
| 52 | 20p. on 1p.25 green | 3·50 | 11·00 |

**1929.** Air. (a) Pictorial stamps of Syria optd with airplane and **ALAOUITES** in French and Arabic.

| | | | |
|---|---|---|---|
| 59 | 0p.50 green | 2·30 | 9·50 |
| 60 | 1p. purple | 3·50 | 16·00 |
| 61 | 25p. blue | 20·00 | 60·00 |

(b) Nos. 54 and 58 of ALAOUITES optd with airplane.

| | | | |
|---|---|---|---|
| 62 | 2p. on 1p.25 green | 3·00 | 12·00 |
| 63 | 15p. on 25p. blue | 17·00 | 42·00 |

## POSTAGE DUE STAMPS

**1925.** Postage Due stamps of France surch **ALAOUITES** and value in French and Arabic.

| | | | | |
|---|---|---|---|---|
| D26 | **D11** | 0p.50 on 10c. brown | 1·30 | 12·50 |
| D27 | **D11** | 1p. on 20c. green | 1·10 | 12·50 |
| D28 | **D11** | 2p. on 30c. red | 1·00 | 13·00 |
| D29 | **D11** | 3p. on 50c. purple | 1·20 | 13·00 |
| D30 | **D11** | 5p. on 1f. pur on yell | 1·60 | 13·00 |

**1925.** Postage Due stamps of Syria (Nos. D192/6) optd **ALAOUITES** in French and Arabic.

| | | | |
|---|---|---|---|
| D44 | 0p.50 brown on yellow | 45 | 8·00 |
| D45 | 1p. red on red | 65 | 8·50 |
| D46 | 2p. black on blue | 90 | 9·75 |
| D47 | 3p. brown on red | 1·00 | 12·50 |
| D48 | 5p. black on green | 1·30 | 15·00 |

For later issues see **LATAKIA**.

Pt. 3

# ALBANIA

Albania, formerly part of the Turkish Empire, was declared independent on 28 November 1912, and this was recognized by Turkey in the treaty of 30 May 1913. After chaotic conditions during and after the First World War a republic was established in 1925. Three years later the country became a kingdom. From 7 April 1939 until December 1944, Albania was occupied, firstly by the Italians and then by the Germans. Following liberation a republic was set up in 1946.

1913. 40 paras = 1 piastre or grosch.
1913. 100 qint = 1 franc.
1947. 100 qint = 1 lek.

**1913.** Various types of Turkey optd with double-headed eagle and **SHQIPENIA**.

| | | | | |
|---|---|---|---|---|
| 3 | **28** | 2pa. green (No. 271) | £425 | £425 |
| 4 | **28** | 5pa. brown (No. 261) | £425 | £425 |
| 2 | **25** | 10pa. green (No. 252) | £450 | £350 |
| 5 | **28** | 10pa. green (No. 262) | £400 | £250 |
| 12 | **28** | 10pa. green (No. 289) | £900 | £850 |
| 11 | **28** | 10pa. on 20pa. red | £1300 | £1300 |
| 6 | **28** | 20pa. red (No. 263) | £375 | £250 |
| 13 | **28** | 20pa. red (No. 290) | £800 | £850 |
| 7 | **28** | 1pi. blue (No. 264) | £325 | £250 |
| 14a | **28** | 1pi. blue (No. 291) | £2000 | £1800 |
| 15 | **28** | 1pi. blk on red (No. D288) | £3250 | £2750 |
| 8 | **28** | 2pi. black (No. 265) | £550 | £475 |
| 14b | **28** | 2pi. black (No. 292) | £3500 | £3250 |
| 1 | **25** | 2½pi. brown (No. 239) | £750 | £650 |
| 9 | **28** | 5pi. purple (No. 267) | £1400 | £1200 |
| 10 | **28** | 10pi. red (No. 268) | £5000 | £4750 |

2

**1913**

| | | | | |
|---|---|---|---|---|
| 16 | **2** | 10pa. violet | 16·00 | 16·00 |
| 17 | **2** | 20pa. red and grey | 22·00 | 18·00 |
| 18 | **2** | 1g. grey | 22·00 | 21·00 |
| 19 | **2** | 2g. blue and violet | 27·00 | 21·00 |
| 20 | **2** | 5g. violet and blue | 33·00 | 27·00 |
| 21 | **2** | 10g. blue and violet | 33·00 | 27·00 |

3

**1913.** Independence Anniv.

| | | | | |
|---|---|---|---|---|
| 22 | **3** | 10pa. black and green | 5·50 | 4·25 |
| 23 | **3** | 20pa. black and red | 8·25 | 6·25 |
| 24 | **3** | 30pa. black and violet | 8·25 | 6·25 |
| 25 | **3** | 1g. black and blue | 11·00 | 9·50 |
| 26 | **3** | 2g. black | 16·00 | 10·50 |

**4** Skanderbeg (after Heinz Kautsch)

**1913**

| | | | | |
|---|---|---|---|---|
| 27 | **4** | 2q. brown and yellow | 5·50 | 2·50 |
| 28 | **4** | 5q. green and yellow | 5·50 | 2·50 |
| 29 | **4** | 10q. red | 5·50 | 2·50 |
| 30 | **4** | 25q. blue | 5·50 | 2·50 |
| 31 | **4** | 50q. mauve and red | 13·00 | 5·25 |
| 32 | **4** | 1f. brown | 30·00 | 16·00 |

**1914.** Arrival of Prince William of Wied. Optd **7 Mars 1461 RROFTE MBRETI 1914**.

| | | | |
|---|---|---|---|
| 33 | 2q. brown and yellow | 75·00 | 85·00 |
| 34 | 5q. green and yellow | 75·00 | 85·00 |
| 35 | 10q. red and rose | 75·00 | 85·00 |
| 36 | 25q. blue | 75·00 | 85·00 |
| 37 | 50q. mauve and rose | 75·00 | 85·00 |
| 38 | 1f. brown | 75·00 | 85·00 |

**1914.** Surch.

| | | | |
|---|---|---|---|
| 40 | 5pa. on 2q. brown & yellow | 3·25 | 3·25 |
| 41 | 10pa. on 5q. green & yellow | 3·25 | 3·25 |
| 42 | 20pa. on 10q. red | 5·50 | 4·25 |
| 43 | 1g. on 25q. blue | 5·50 | 4·25 |
| 44 | 2g. on 50q. mauve and red | 5·50 | 5·25 |
| 45 | 5g. on 1f. brown | 22·00 | 16·00 |

**1914.** Valona Provisional Issue. Optd **POSTE D'ALBANIE** and Turkish inscr in circle with star in centre.

| | | | |
|---|---|---|---|
| 45g | 5pa. on 2q. brown & yellow | 75·00 | 75·00 |
| 45h | 10pa. on 5q. green & yellow | £110 | £100 |
| 45i | 20pa. on 10q. red and rose | 55·00 | 50·00 |
| 45j | 1gr. on 25q. blue | 33·00 | 31·00 |
| 45k | 2gr. on 50q. mauve and red | 38·00 | 37·00 |
| 45l | 5gr. on 1f. brown | 55·00 | 50·00 |
| 45a | 2q. brown and yellow | £325 | £325 |
| 45b | 5q. green and yellow | £425 | £425 |
| 45c | 10q. red and rose | 43·00 | 42·00 |
| 45d | 25q. blue | 43·00 | 42·00 |
| 45e | 50q. mauve and red | 43·00 | 42·00 |
| 45f | 1f. brown | £800 | £800 |

11

**1917.** Inscribed "SHQIPERIE KORCE VETQEVERITARE" or "REPUBLIKA KORCE SHQIPETARE" or "QARKU-POSTES-I-KORCES".

| | | | | |
|---|---|---|---|---|
| 75 | **11** | 1c. brown and green | 3·75 | 3·25 |
| 76 | **11** | 2c. brown and green | 3·75 | 3·25 |
| 77 | **11** | 3c. grey and green | 3·75 | 3·25 |
| 78 | **11** | 5c. green and black | 5·50 | 5·25 |
| 79 | **11** | 10c. red and black | 5·50 | 5·25 |
| 72 | **11** | 25c. blue and black | 22·00 | 10·50 |
| 80 | **11** | 50c. purple and black | 9·75 | 8·25 |
| 81 | **11** | 1f. brown and black | 27·00 | 23·00 |

**1918.** No. 78 surch **QARKUI KORCES 25 CTS**.

| | | | |
|---|---|---|---|
| 81a | 25c. on 5c. green and black | £275 | £325 |

12

**1919.** Fiscal stamps used by the Austrians in Albania. Handstamped with control.

| | | | | |
|---|---|---|---|---|
| 83 | **12** | (2)q. on 2h. brown | 11·50 | 11·00 |
| 84 | **12** | 05q. on 16h. green | 11·50 | 11·00 |
| 85 | **12** | 10q. on 8h. red | 11·50 | 11·00 |
| 86 | **12** | 25q. on 64h. blue | 13·00 | 12·50 |
| 87a | **12** | 50q. on 32h. violet | 5·50 | 5·50 |
| 88 | **12** | 1f. on 1.28k. brown on blue | 14·00 | 13·50 |

Three sets may be made of this issue according to whether the handstamped control is a date, a curved comet or a comet with straight tail.

**1919.** No. 43 optd **SHKODER 1919**.

| | | | | |
|---|---|---|---|---|
| 103 | **4** | 1g. on 25q. blue | 26·00 | 17·00 |

**1919.** Fiscal stamps surch **POSTAT SHQIPTARE** and new value.

| | | | | |
|---|---|---|---|---|
| 104 | **12** | 10q. on 2h. brown | 11·00 | 7·75 |
| 111 | **12** | 10q. on 8h. red | 11·00 | 7·75 |
| 112 | **12** | 15q. on 8h. red | 11·00 | 7·75 |
| 113 | **12** | 20q. on 16h. green | 11·00 | 7·75 |
| 113b | **12** | 25q. on 32h. violet | 11·00 | 7·75 |
| 107 | **12** | 25q. on 64h. blue | 11·00 | 7·75 |
| 108 | **12** | 50q. on 32h. violet | 11·00 | 7·75 |
| 113c | **12** | 50q. on 64h. blue | 30·00 | 21·00 |
| 113d | **12** | 1f. on 96h. orange | 13·00 | 10·50 |
| 113e | **12** | 2f. on 160h. violet | 22·00 | 16·00 |

**17** Prince William I

**1920.** Optd with double-headed eagle and **SHKORDA** or surch also.

| | | | | |
|---|---|---|---|---|
| 114 | **17** | 1q. grey | 80·00 | £130 |
| 115 | **17** | 2q. on 10q. red | 12·50 | 31·00 |
| 116 | **17** | 5q. on 10q. red | 12·50 | 26·00 |
| 117 | **17** | 10q. red | 12·50 | 26·00 |
| 118 | **17** | 20q. brown | 35·00 | 50·00 |
| 119 | **17** | 25q. blue | £425 | £750 |
| 120 | **17** | 25q. on 10q. red | 12·50 | 21·00 |
| 121 | **17** | 50q. violet | 47·00 | 95·00 |
| 122 | **17** | 50q. on 10q. red | 12·50 | 42·00 |

**19** Skanderbeg

**1920.** Optd with posthorn.

| | | | | |
|---|---|---|---|---|
| 123 | **19** | 2q. orange | 9·50 | 12·50 |
| 124 | **19** | 5q. green | 17·00 | 21·00 |
| 125 | **19** | 10q. red | 28·00 | 47·00 |
| 126 | **19** | 25q. blue | 50·00 | 44·00 |
| 127 | **19** | 50q. green | 11·50 | 16·00 |
| 128 | **19** | 1f. mauve | 11·50 | 16·00 |

Stamps as Type **19** also exist optd **BESA** meaning "Loyalty".

**1922.** No. 123 surch with value in frame.

| | | | |
|---|---|---|---|
| 143 | 1q. on 2q. orange | 11·00 | 10·50 |

24

**1922.** Views.

| | | | | |
|---|---|---|---|---|
| 144 | **24** | 2q. orange (Gjinokaster) | 1·10 | 2·10 |
| 145 | **24** | 5q. green (Kanina) | 1·10 | 1·60 |
| 146 | **24** | 10q. red (Berat) | 1·10 | 1·60 |
| 147 | **24** | 25q. blue (Veziri Bridge) | 1·10 | 1·60 |
| 148 | **24** | 50q. green (Rozafat Fortress, Shkoder) | 1·10 | 1·60 |
| 149 | **24** | 1f. lilac (Korce) | 1·10 | 1·60 |
| 150 | **24** | 2f. green (Durres) | 6·50 | 8·25 |

**1924.** Opening of National Assembly. Optd **TIRANE KALLNUER** 1924 in frame with **Mbledhje Kushtetuese** above.

| | | | |
|---|---|---|---|
| 151 | 2q. orange | 27·00 | 26·00 |
| 152 | 5q. green | 27·00 | 26·00 |
| 153 | 10q. red | 20·00 | 19·00 |
| 154 | 25q. blue | 20·00 | 19·00 |
| 155 | 50q. green | 27·00 | 26·00 |

**1924.** No. 144 surch with value and bars.

| | | | |
|---|---|---|---|
| 156 | 1 on 2q. orange | 8·25 | 10·50 |

**1924.** Red Cross. (a) Surch with small red cross and premium.

| | | | |
|---|---|---|---|
| 157 | 5q.+5q. green | 27·00 | 36·00 |
| 158 | 10q.+5q. red | 27·00 | 36·00 |
| 159 | 25q.+5q. blue | 27·00 | 36·00 |
| 160 | 50q.+5q. green | 26·00 | 36·00 |

(b) Nos. 157/60 with further surch of large red cross and premium.

| | | | |
|---|---|---|---|
| 161 | 5q.+5q.+5q. green | 27·00 | 31·00 |
| 162 | 10q.+5q.+5q. red | 27·00 | 31·00 |
| 163 | 25q.+5q.+5q. blue | 27·00 | 31·00 |
| 164 | 50q.+5q.+5q. green | 27·00 | 31·00 |

**1925.** Return of Government to Capital in 1924. Optd **Triumf' i legalitetit 24 Dhetuer 1924**.

| | | | |
|---|---|---|---|
| 164a | 1 on 2q. orange (No. 156) | 8·25 | 9·50 |
| 165 | 2q. orange | 8·25 | 9·50 |
| 166 | 5q. green | 8·25 | 9·50 |
| 167 | 10q. red | 8·25 | 9·50 |
| 168 | 25q. blue | 8·25 | 9·50 |
| 169 | 50q. green | 16·00 | 18·00 |
| 170 | 1f. lilac | 16·00 | 23·00 |

**1925.** Proclamation of Republic. Optd **Republika Shqiptare 21 Kallnduer 1925**.

| | | | |
|---|---|---|---|
| 171 | 1 on 2q. orange (No. 156) | 7·00 | 10·50 |
| 172 | 2q. orange | 7·00 | 10·50 |
| 173 | 5q. green | 7·00 | 10·50 |
| 174 | 10q. red | 7·00 | 10·50 |
| 175 | 25q. blue | 7·00 | 10·50 |
| 176 | 50q. green | 7·00 | 10·50 |
| 177 | 1f. lilac | 7·00 | 10·50 |

**1925.** Optd **Republika Shqiptare**.

| | | | |
|---|---|---|---|
| 178 | 1 on 2q. orange (No. 156) | 2·20 | 2·10 |
| 179 | 2q. orange | 2·20 | 2·10 |
| 180 | 5q. green | 2·20 | 2·10 |
| 181 | 10q. red | 2·20 | 2·10 |
| 182 | 25q. blue | 2·20 | 2·10 |
| 183 | 50q. green | 2·20 | 2·10 |
| 184 | 1f. lilac | 9·75 | 5·25 |
| 185 | 2f. green | 15·00 | 5·25 |

32

**1925.** Air.

| | | | | |
|---|---|---|---|---|
| 186 | **32** | 5q. green | 4·25 | 4·25 |
| 187 | **32** | 10q. red | 4·25 | 4·25 |
| 188 | **32** | 25q. blue | 4·25 | 4·25 |
| 189 | **32** | 50q. green | 7·50 | 7·25 |
| 190 | **32** | 1f. black and violet | 13·00 | 12·50 |
| 191 | **32** | 2f. violet and olive | 22·00 | 21·00 |
| 192 | **32** | 3f. green and brown | 27·00 | 21·00 |

**33** Pres. Ahmed Zogu, later King Zog I

**34**

**1925**

| | | | | |
|---|---|---|---|---|
| 193 | **33** | 1q. yellow | 45 | 30 |
| 194 | **33** | 2q. brown | 50 | 90 |
| 195 | **33** | 5q. green | 35 | 30 |
| 196 | **33** | 10q. red | 35 | 30 |
| 197 | **33** | 15q. brown | 2·20 | 2·50 |
| 198 | **33** | 25q. blue | 55 | 30 |
| 199 | **33** | 50q. green | 2·20 | 1·90 |
| 200 | **34** | 1f. blue and red | 4·25 | 2·50 |
| 201 | **34** | 2f. orange and green | 5·50 | 2·50 |
| 202 | **34** | 3f. violet | 11·00 | 6·25 |
| 203 | **34** | 5f. black and violet | 13·00 | 9·00 |

**1927.** Air. Optd **Rep. Shqiptare**.

| | | | | |
|---|---|---|---|---|
| 204 | **32** | 5q. green | 13·00 | 12·50 |
| 205 | **32** | 10q. red | 13·00 | 12·50 |
| 206 | **32** | 25q. blue | 11·00 | 12·50 |
| 207 | **32** | 50q. green | 8·25 | 7·75 |
| 208 | **32** | 1f. black and violet | 16·00 | 12·50 |
| 209 | **32** | 2f. violet and olive | 16·00 | 12·50 |
| 210 | **32** | 3f. green and brown | 22·00 | 18·00 |

**1927.** Optd **A.Z.** and wreath.

| | | | | |
|---|---|---|---|---|
| 211 | **33** | 1q. yellow | 1·60 | 1·30 |
| 212 | **33** | 2q. brown | 85 | 50 |
| 213 | **33** | 5q. green | 3·50 | 75 |
| 214 | **33** | 10q. red | 75 | 50 |
| 215 | **33** | 15q. brown | 20·00 | 19·00 |
| 216 | **33** | 25q. blue | 1·60 | 50 |
| 217 | **33** | 50q. green | 1·60 | 50 |
| 218 | **34** | 1f. blue and red | 3·75 | 75 |
| 219 | **34** | 2f. orange and green | 3·75 | 1·00 |
| 220 | **34** | 3f. violet and brown | 6·50 | 2·10 |
| 221 | **34** | 5f. black and violet | 11·00 | 3·75 |

**1928.** Inauguration of Vlore (Valona)-Brindisi Air Service. Optd **REP. SHQYPTARE Fluturim' i I-ar Vlone-Brindisi 21.IV.1928.**

| | | | | |
|---|---|---|---|---|
| 222 | **32** | 5q. green | 13·00 | 12·50 |
| 223 | **32** | 10q. red | 13·00 | 12·50 |
| 224 | **32** | 25q. blue | 13·00 | 12·50 |
| 225 | **32** | 50q. green | 27·00 | 26·00 |
| 226 | **32** | 1f. black and violet | £140 | £140 |
| 227 | **32** | 2f. violet and olive | £140 | £140 |
| 228 | **32** | 3f. green and brown | £140 | £140 |

**1928.** Surch in figures and bars.

| | | | | |
|---|---|---|---|---|
| 229 | **33** | 1 on 10q. red (No. 214) | 1·60 | 75 |
| 230 | **33** | 5 on 25q. blue (No. 216) | 1·60 | 75 |

**39** Pres. Ahmed Zogu, later King Zog I

**40**

**1928.** National Assembly. Optd **Kujtim i Mbledhjes Kushtetuese 25.8.2.8.**

| | | | | |
|---|---|---|---|---|
| 231 | **39** | 1q. brown | 11·00 | 12·50 |
| 232 | **39** | 2q. grey | 11·00 | 12·50 |
| 233 | **39** | 5q. green | 11·00 | 16·00 |
| 234 | **39** | 10q. red | 11·00 | 16·00 |
| 235 | **39** | 15q. brown | 33·00 | 65·00 |
| 236 | **39** | 25q. blue | 13·00 | 16·00 |
| 237 | **39** | 50q. lilac | 22·00 | 21·00 |
| 238 | **40** | 1f. black and blue | 13·00 | 16·00 |

**1928.** Accession of King Zog I. Optd **Mbretnia-Shqiptare Zog I 1.IX.1928.**

| | | | | |
|---|---|---|---|---|
| 239 | **39** | 1q. brown | 27·00 | 31·00 |
| 240 | **39** | 2q. grey | 27·00 | 31·00 |
| 241 | **39** | 5q. green | 22·00 | 26·00 |
| 242 | **39** | 10q. red | 22·00 | 21·00 |
| 243 | **39** | 15q. brown | 33·00 | 37·00 |
| 244 | **39** | 25q. blue | 22·00 | 21·00 |
| 245 | **39** | 50q. lilac | 22·00 | 21·00 |
| 246 | **40** | 1f. black and blue | 27·00 | 26·00 |
| 247 | **40** | 2f. black and green | 27·00 | 26·00 |

**1928.** Optd **Mbretnia-Shqiptare** only.

| | | | | |
|---|---|---|---|---|
| 248 | **39** | 1q. brown | 1·10 | 1·60 |
| 249 | **39** | 2q. grey | 1·10 | 1·60 |
| 250 | **39** | 5q. green | 7·50 | 4·75 |
| 251 | **39** | 10q. red | 1·10 | 1·60 |
| 252 | **39** | 15q. brown | 27·00 | 31·00 |
| 253 | **39** | 25q. blue | 1·10 | 1·60 |
| 254 | **39** | 50q. lilac | 2·20 | 2·50 |
| 255 | **40** | 1f. black and blue | 4·25 | 3·25 |
| 256 | **40** | 2f. black and green | 4·25 | 5·25 |
| 257 | **40** | 3f. olive and red | 15·00 | 16·00 |
| 258 | **40** | 5f. black and violet | 16·00 | 21·00 |

**1929.** Surch **Mbr. Shqiptare** and new value.

| | | | | |
|---|---|---|---|---|
| 259 | **33** | 1 on 50q. green | 75 | 1·00 |
| 260 | **33** | 5 on 25q. blue | 75 | 1·00 |
| 261 | **33** | 15 on 10q. red | 1·30 | 1·60 |

**1929.** King Zog's 35th Birthday. Optd **RROFT-MBRETI 8.X.1929.**

| | | | | |
|---|---|---|---|---|
| 262 | | 1q. yellow | 16·00 | 26·00 |
| 263 | | 2q. brown | 16·00 | 26·00 |
| 264 | | 5q. green | 16·00 | 26·00 |
| 265 | | 10q. red | 16·00 | 26·00 |
| 266 | | 25q. blue | 16·00 | 26·00 |
| 267 | | 50q. green | 22·00 | 31·00 |
| 268 | **34** | 1f. blue and red | 30·00 | 47·00 |
| 269 | **34** | 2f. orange and green | 30·00 | 47·00 |

**1929.** Air. Optd **Mbr. Shqiptare.**

| | | | | |
|---|---|---|---|---|
| 270 | **32** | 5q. green | 11·00 | 16·00 |
| 271 | **32** | 10q. red | 11·00 | 16·00 |
| 272 | **32** | 25q. blue | 11·00 | 16·00 |
| 273 | **32** | 50q. green | £225 | £300 |
| 274 | **32** | 1f. black and violet | £425 | £500 |
| 275 | **32** | 2f. violet and olive | £500 | £550 |
| 276 | **32** | 3f. green and brown | £600 | £650 |

**49** Lake Butrinto **50** King Zog I

**1930.** 2nd Anniv of Accession of King Zog I.

| | | | | |
|---|---|---|---|---|
| 277 | **49** | 1q. grey | 55 | 30 |
| 278 | **49** | 2q. red | 55 | 30 |
| 279 | **50** | 5q. green | 55 | 30 |
| 280 | **50** | 10q. red | 55 | 50 |
| 281 | **50** | 15q. brown | 55 | 50 |
| 282 | **50** | 25q. blue | 55 | 50 |
| 283 | **49** | 50q. green | 1·10 | 75 |
| 284 | - | 1f. violet | 2·20 | 1·30 |
| 285 | - | 2f. blue | 2·75 | 1·30 |
| 286 | - | 3f. green | 8·25 | 2·10 |
| 287 | - | 5f. brown | 11·00 | 5·25 |

DESIGNS—VERT: 1, 2f. Ahmed Zog Bridge, River Mati. HORIZ: 3, 5f. Ruins of Zogu Castle.

**53** Junkers F-13 (over Tirana)

**1930.** Air. T **53** and similar view.

| | | | | |
|---|---|---|---|---|
| 288 | **53** | 5q. green | 2·20 | 2·50 |
| 289 | **53** | 15q. red | 2·20 | 2·50 |
| 290 | **53** | 20q. blue | 2·20 | 2·50 |
| 291 | **53** | 50q. olive | 5·50 | 5·25 |
| 292 | - | 1f. blue | 8·25 | 7·75 |
| 293 | - | 2f. brown | 27·00 | 26·00 |
| 294 | - | 3f. violet | 33·00 | 31·00 |

**1931.** Air. Optd **TIRANE-ROME 6 KORRIK 1931.**

| | | | | |
|---|---|---|---|---|
| 295 | **53** | 5q. green | 13·00 | 13·00 |
| 296 | **53** | 15q. red | 13·00 | 13·00 |
| 297 | **53** | 20q. blue | 13·00 | 13·00 |
| 298 | **53** | 50q. olive | 13·00 | 13·00 |
| 299 | - | 1f. blue | 75·00 | 75·00 |
| 300 | - | 2f. brown | 75·00 | 75·00 |
| 301 | - | 3f. violet | 75·00 | 75·00 |

**1934.** 10th Anniv of Revolution. Optd **1924-24 Dhetuer-1934.**

| | | | | |
|---|---|---|---|---|
| 302 | **49** | 1q. grey | 13·00 | 16·00 |
| 303 | **49** | 2q. orange | 13·00 | 16·00 |
| 304 | **50** | 5q. green | 13·00 | 16·00 |
| 305 | **50** | 10q. red | 13·00 | 16·00 |
| 306 | **50** | 15q. brown | 13·00 | 16·00 |
| 307 | **50** | 25q. blue | 16·00 | 17·00 |
| 308 | **49** | 50q. turquoise | 22·00 | 21·00 |
| 309 | - | 1f. violet (No. 284) | 22·00 | 26·00 |
| 310 | - | 2f. blue (No. 285) | 33·00 | 40·00 |
| 311 | - | 3f. green (No. 286) | 49·00 | 50·00 |

**56** Horse and Flag of Skanderbeg **57** Albania in Chains

**1937.** 25th Anniv of Independence.

| | | | | |
|---|---|---|---|---|
| 312 | **56** | 1q. violet | 55 | 50 |
| 313 | **57** | 2q. brown | 80 | 75 |
| 314 | - | 5q. green | 1·10 | 75 |
| 315 | **56** | 10q. olive | 1·10 | 1·00 |
| 316 | **57** | 15q. red | 1·60 | 1·30 |
| 317 | - | 25q. blue | 3·25 | 2·50 |
| 318 | **56** | 50q. green | 8·25 | 4·50 |
| 319 | **57** | 1f. violet | 22·00 | 7·75 |
| 320 | - | 2f. brown | 27·00 | 12·50 |

**MS**320a 140×140 mm. 20q. purple (T **56**) 33·00 £190

DESIGN: 5, 25q., 2f. As Type **57**, but eagle with opened wings (Liberated Albania).

**58** Countess Geraldine Apponyi and King Zog

**1938.** Royal Wedding.

| | | | | |
|---|---|---|---|---|
| 321 | **58** | 1q. purple | 55 | 50 |
| 322 | **58** | 2q. brown | 55 | 50 |
| 323 | **58** | 5q. green | 55 | 50 |
| 324 | **58** | 10q. olive | 2·20 | 1·00 |
| 325 | **58** | 15q. red | 2·20 | 1·00 |
| 326 | **58** | 25q. blue | 5·50 | 2·50 |
| 327 | **58** | 50q. green | 11·00 | 5·25 |
| 328 | **58** | 1f. violet | 22·00 | 10·50 |

**MS**328a 110×140 mm. 2 each 20q. purple, 30q. brown 65·00 £200

**59** National Emblems **60** King Zog

**1938.** 10th Anniv of Accession.

| | | | | |
|---|---|---|---|---|
| 329 | - | 1q. purple | 45 | 75 |
| 330 | **59** | 2q. red | 55 | 75 |
| 331 | - | 5q. green | 1·10 | 80 |
| 332 | **60** | 10q. brown | 1·10 | 1·30 |
| 333 | - | 15q. red | 2·20 | 1·60 |
| 334 | **60** | 25q. blue | 2·40 | 1·80 |
| 335 | **59** | 50q. black | 20·00 | 7·75 |
| 336 | **60** | 1f. green | 27·00 | 11·50 |

**MS**336a 110×65 mm. 15q. red (333), 20q. green (**59**), 30q. violet (**60**) 49·00 £140

DESIGN: 1, 5, 15q. As Type **60**, but Queen Geraldine's portrait.

**ITALIAN OCCUPATION**

**1939.** Optd **Mbledhja Kushtetuese 12-IV-1939 XVII.** (a) Postage.

| | | | | |
|---|---|---|---|---|
| 337 | **49** | 1q. grey | 1·60 | 1·60 |
| 338 | **49** | 2q. red | 1·60 | 1·60 |
| 339 | **50** | 5q. green | 1·10 | 1·00 |
| 340 | **50** | 10q. red | 1·10 | 1·00 |
| 341 | **50** | 15q. brown | 2·75 | 2·50 |
| 342 | **50** | 25q. blue | 3·25 | 3·25 |
| 343 | **49** | 50q. turquoise | 4·25 | 3·75 |
| 344 | - | 1f. violet (No. 284) | 6·50 | 4·75 |
| 345 | - | 2f. blue (No. 285) | 7·50 | 6·25 |
| 346 | - | 3f. green | 16·00 | 14·50 |
| 347 | - | 5f. brown | 22·00 | 25·00 |

(b) Air. Optd as Nos. 337/47 or surch also.

| | | | | |
|---|---|---|---|---|
| 348 | **53** | 5q. green | 7·50 | 6·75 |
| 349 | **53** | 15q. red | 7·00 | 7·25 |
| 350 | **53** | 20q. on 50q. olive | 12·00 | 11·50 |

**62** Gheg **64** Broken Columns, Botrint

**63** King Victor Emmanuel **65** King and Fiat G18V on Tirana–Rome Service

**1939**

| | | | | |
|---|---|---|---|---|
| 351 | **62** | 1q. blue (postage) | 1·10 | 50 |
| 352 | - | 2q. brown | 1·10 | 50 |
| 353 | - | 3q. brown | 1·10 | 50 |
| 354 | - | 5q. green | 1·60 | 20 |
| 355 | **63** | 10q. brown | 1·60 | 30 |
| 356 | **63** | 15q. red | 1·70 | 30 |
| 357 | **63** | 25q. blue | 1·70 | 1·30 |
| 358 | **63** | 30q. violet | 2·75 | 2·10 |
| 359 | - | 50q. violet | 4·25 | 1·80 |
| 360 | - | 65q. red | 12·00 | 8·25 |
| 361 | - | 1f. green | 12·00 | 5·75 |
| 362 | - | 2f. red | 27·00 | 18·00 |
| 363 | **64** | 3f. black | 46·00 | 33·00 |
| 364 | - | 5f. purple | 55·00 | 46·00 |
| 365 | **65** | 20q. brown (air) | £110 | 18·00 |

DESIGNS—SMALL: 2q. Tosk man; 3q. Gheg woman; 5, 65q. Profile of King Victor Emmanuel; 50q. Tosk woman. LARGE: 1f. Kruje Fortress; 2f. Bridge over River Kiri at Mes; 5f. Amphitheatre ruins, Berat.

**66** Sheep Farming

**1940.** Air.

| | | | | |
|---|---|---|---|---|
| 366 | **66** | 5q. green | 2·50 | 1·60 |
| 367 | - | 15q. red | 2·75 | 2·10 |
| 368 | - | 20q. blue | 5·50 | 3·25 |
| 369 | - | 50q. brown | 7·75 | 7·75 |
| 370 | - | 1f. green | 8·25 | 9·50 |
| 371 | - | 2f. black | 18·00 | 18·00 |
| 372 | - | 3f. purple | 35·00 | 31·00 |

DESIGNS: Savoia Marchetti S.M.75 airplane and—HORIZ: 20q. King of Italy and Durres harbour; 1f. Bridge over River Kiri at Mes. VERT: 15q. Aerial map; 50q. Girl and valley; 2f. Archway and wall, Durres; 3f. Women in North Eprius.

**67** King Victor Emmanuel

**1942.** 3rd Anniv of Italian Occupation.

| | | | | |
|---|---|---|---|---|
| 373 | **67** | 5q. green | 2·40 | 2·50 |
| 374 | **67** | 10q. brown | 2·40 | 2·50 |
| 375 | **67** | 15q. red | 2·40 | 2·50 |
| 376 | **67** | 25q. blue | 2·40 | 2·50 |
| 377 | **67** | 65q. brown | 7·50 | 7·75 |
| 378 | **67** | 1f. green | 7·50 | 7·75 |
| 379 | **67** | 2f. purple | 7·50 | 7·75 |

**1942.** No. 352 surch 1 QIND.

| | | | | |
|---|---|---|---|---|
| 380 | | 1q. on 2q. brown | 4·25 | 5·25 |

**69**

**1943.** Anti-tuberculosis Fund.

| | | | | |
|---|---|---|---|---|
| 381 | **69** | 5q.+5q. green | 1·80 | 2·10 |
| 382 | **69** | 10q.+10q. brown | 1·80 | 2·10 |
| 383 | **69** | 15q.+10q. red | 1·80 | 2·10 |
| 384 | **69** | 25q.+15q. blue | 2·20 | 3·25 |
| 385 | **69** | 30q.+20q. violet | 2·20 | 3·25 |
| 386 | **69** | 50q.+25q. orange | 2·20 | 3·25 |
| 387 | **69** | 65q.+30q. grey | 3·25 | 4·50 |
| 388 | **69** | 1f.+40q. brown | 5·50 | 6·25 |

**GERMAN OCCUPATION**

**1943.** Postage stamps of 1939 optd **14 Shtator 1943** or surch also.

| | | | | |
|---|---|---|---|---|
| 389 | - | 1q. on 3q. brn (No. 353) | 1·60 | 8·25 |
| 390 | - | 2q. brown (No. 352) | 1·60 | 8·25 |
| 391 | - | 3q. brown (No. 353) | 1·60 | 8·25 |
| 392 | - | 5q. green (No. 354) | 1·60 | 8·25 |
| 393 | **63** | 10q. brown | 1·60 | 8·25 |
| 394 | - | 15q. red (No. 356) | 1·60 | 8·25 |
| 395 | - | 25q. blue (No. 357) | 1·60 | 8·25 |
| 396 | - | 30q. violet (No. 358) | 1·60 | 8·25 |
| 397 | - | 50q. on 65q. brn (No. 360) | 2·20 | 12·00 |
| 398 | - | 65q. red (No. 360) | 2·20 | 12·00 |
| 399 | - | 1f. green (No. 361) | 11·00 | 24·00 |
| 400 | - | 2f. red (No. 362) | 16·00 | 80·00 |
| 401 | **64** | 3f. black | 65·00 | £200 |

**71** War Refugees

**1944.** War Refugees' Relief Fund.

| | | | | |
|---|---|---|---|---|
| 402 | **71** | 5q.+5q. green | 6·50 | 15·00 |
| 403 | **71** | 10q.+5q. brown | 6·50 | 15·00 |
| 404 | **71** | 15q.+5q. red | 6·50 | 15·00 |
| 405 | **71** | 25q.+10q. blue | 6·50 | 15·00 |
| 406 | **71** | 1f.+50q. green | 6·50 | 15·00 |
| 407 | **71** | 2f.+1f. violet | 6·50 | 15·00 |
| 408 | **71** | 3f.+1f.50 orange | 6·50 | 15·00 |

**INDEPENDENT STATE**

**1945.** Nos. 353/8 and 360/2 surch **QEVERIJA DEMOKRAT. E SHQIPERISE 22-X-1944** and value.

| | | | | |
|---|---|---|---|---|
| 409 | | 30q. on 3q. brown | 8·25 | 16·00 |
| 410 | | 40q. on 5q. green | 8·25 | 16·00 |
| 411 | | 50q. on 10q. brown | 8·25 | 16·00 |
| 412 | | 60q. on 15q. red | 8·25 | 16·00 |
| 413 | | 80q. on 25q. blue | 8·25 | 16·00 |
| 414 | | 1f. on 30q. violet | 8·25 | 16·00 |
| 415 | | 2f. on 65q. brown | 8·25 | 16·00 |
| 416 | | 3f. on 1f. green | 8·25 | 16·00 |
| 417 | | 5f. on 2f. red | 8·25 | 16·00 |

**73**

**1945.** 2nd Anniv of Formation of People's Army. Surch as T **73.**

| | | | | |
|---|---|---|---|---|
| 418 | **49** | 30q. on 1q. grey | 5·50 | 7·75 |
| 419 | **49** | 60q. on 1q. grey | 5·50 | 7·75 |
| 420 | **49** | 80q. on 1q. grey | 5·50 | 7·75 |
| 421 | **49** | 1f. on 1q. grey | 11·00 | 16·00 |
| 422 | **49** | 2f. on 2q. red | 13·00 | 18·00 |
| 423 | **49** | 3f. on 50q. green | 27·00 | 33·00 |
| 424 | - | 5f. on 2f. blue (No. 285) | 33·00 | 50·00 |

**1945.** Red Cross Fund. Surch with Red Cross, **JAVA E K.K. SHQIPTAR 4-11 MAJ 1945** and value.

| | | | | |
|---|---|---|---|---|
| 425 | **69** | 30q.+15q. on 5q.+5q. green | 11·00 | 16·00 |
| 426 | **69** | 50q.+25q. on 10q.+10q. brown | 11·00 | 16·00 |
| 427 | **69** | 1f.+50q. on 15q.+10q. red | 27·00 | 33·00 |
| 428 | **69** | 2f.+1f. on 25q.+15q. blue | 38·00 | 47·00 |

**75**

**1945**

| | | | | |
|---|---|---|---|---|
| 429 | - | 20q. green | 75 | 1·80 |
| 430 | - | 30q. orange | 1·10 | 2·50 |
| 431 | - | 40q. brown | 1·10 | 2·50 |
| 432 | - | 60q. red | 1·60 | 3·75 |
| 433 | - | 1f. red | 3·75 | 7·75 |
| 434 | **75** | 3f. blue | 27·00 | 31·00 |

DESIGNS: 20q. Latinot; 40, 60q. Bridge at Berat; 1f. Permet landscape.

**1946.** Constitutional Assembly. Optd **ASAMBLEJA KUSHTETUESE 10 KALLNUER 1946.**

| | | | | |
|---|---|---|---|---|
| 435 | | 20q. green | 1·60 | 2·10 |
| 436 | | 30q. orange | 2·20 | 2·50 |
| 437 | - | 40q. brown (No. 431) | 2·75 | 3·25 |
| 438 | - | 60q. red (No. 432) | 4·25 | 5·25 |
| 439 | - | 1f. red (No. 433) | 16·00 | 19·00 |
| 440 | - | 3f. blue (No. 434) | 27·00 | 31·00 |

## PEOPLE'S REPUBLIC

77 Globe, Dove and Olive Branch

1946. Int Women's Congress. Perf or imperf.

| | | | | |
|---|---|---|---|---|
| 441A | 77 | 20q. mauve and red | 55 | 1·60 |
| 442A | 77 | 40q. lilac and red | 1·10 | 2·10 |
| 443A | 77 | 50q. violet and red | 2·20 | 3·25 |
| 444A | 77 | 1f. blue and red | 4·25 | 6·25 |
| 445A | 77 | 2f. blue and red | 5·50 | 10·50 |

1946. Proclamation of Albanian People's Republic. Optd **REPUBLIKA POPULLORE E SHQIPERISE**.

| | | | | |
|---|---|---|---|---|
| 446 | 75 | 20q. green | 1·50 | 1·60 |
| 447 | 75 | 30q. orange | 1·70 | 2·10 |
| 448 | - | 40q. brown (No. 431) | 3·00 | 4·25 |
| 449 | - | 60q. red (No. 432) | 6·00 | 7·75 |
| 450 | - | 1f. red (No. 433) | 16·00 | 21·00 |
| 451 | - | 3f. blue (No. 434) | 27·00 | 31·00 |

1946. Albanian Red Cross Congress. Surch **KONGRESI K.K.SH. 24-25-11-46** and premium.

| | | | | |
|---|---|---|---|---|
| 452 | 75 | 20q.+10q. green | 24·00 | 37·00 |
| 453 | 75 | 30q.+15q. orange | 24·00 | 37·00 |
| 454 | - | 40q.+20q. brown | 24·00 | 37·00 |
| 455 | - | 60q.+30q. red | 24·00 | 37·00 |
| 456 | - | 1f.+50q. red | 24·00 | 37·00 |
| 457 | - | 3f.+1f.50 blue | 24·00 | 37·00 |

79 Athletes

1946. Balkan Games.

| | | | | |
|---|---|---|---|---|
| 458 | 79 | 1q. black | 16·00 | 12·50 |
| 459 | 79 | 2q. green | 16·00 | 12·50 |
| 460 | 79 | 5q. brown | 16·00 | 12·50 |
| 461 | 79 | 10q. red | 16·00 | 12·50 |
| 462 | 79 | 20q. blue | 16·00 | 12·50 |
| 463 | 79 | 40q. lilac | 16·00 | 12·50 |
| 464 | 79 | 1f. orange | 38·00 | 37·00 |

80 Qemal Stafa

1947. 5th Death Anniv of Qemal Stafa (Communist activist).

| | | | | |
|---|---|---|---|---|
| 465 | 80 | 20q. dp brown & brown | 13·00 | 16·00 |
| 466 | 80 | 28q. deep blue and blue | 13·00 | 16·00 |
| 467 | 80 | 40q. dp brown & brown | 13·00 | 16·00 |

81 Railway Construction

1947. Construction of Durres–Elbasan Railway.

| | | | | |
|---|---|---|---|---|
| 468 | 81 | 1q. black and drab | 5·50 | 1·80 |
| 469 | 81 | 4q. deep green and green | 5·50 | 1·80 |
| 470 | 81 | 10q. dp brown & brown | 5·75 | 2·10 |
| 471 | 81 | 15q. red and rose | 5·75 | 2·10 |
| 472 | 81 | 20q. black and blue | 13·00 | 2·50 |
| 473 | 81 | 28q. deep blue and blue | 18·00 | 3·25 |
| 474 | 81 | 40q. red and purple | 35·00 | 19·00 |
| 475 | 81 | 68q. dp brown & brown | 43·00 | 31·00 |

82 Partisans

83 Enver Hoxha and Vasil Shanto

1947. 4th Anniv of Formation of People's Army. Inscr "1943–1947".

| | | | | |
|---|---|---|---|---|
| 476 | 82 | 16q. brown | 9·75 | 10·50 |
| 477 | 83 | 20q. brown | 9·75 | 10·50 |
| 478 | - | 28q. blue | 9·75 | 10·50 |
| 479 | - | 40q. brown and mauve | 9·75 | 10·50 |

DESIGNS—HORIZ: 28q. Infantry column. VERT: 40q. Portrait of Vojo Kushi.

84 Ruined Conference Building

1947. 5th Anniv of Peza Conference.

| | | | | |
|---|---|---|---|---|
| 480 | 84 | 2l. purple and mauve | 7·00 | 7·75 |
| 481 | 84 | 2l.50 deep blue and blue | 7·00 | 7·75 |

85 War Invalids

1947. 1st Congress of War Invalids.

| | | | | |
|---|---|---|---|---|
| 482 | 85 | 1l. red | 16·00 | 16·00 |

86 Peasants

1947. Agrarian Reform. Inscr "REFORMA AGRARE".

| | | | | |
|---|---|---|---|---|
| 483 | 86 | 1l.50 purple | 9·75 | 10·50 |
| 484 | - | 2l. brown | 9·75 | 10·50 |
| 485 | - | 2l.50 blue | 9·75 | 10·50 |
| 486 | - | 3l. red | 9·75 | 10·50 |

DESIGNS—HORIZ: 2l. Banquet; 2l.50, Peasants rejoicing. VERT: 3l. Soldier being chaired.

87 Burning Village

1947. 3rd Anniv of Liberation. Inscr "29-XI-1944–1947".

| | | | | |
|---|---|---|---|---|
| 487 | 87 | 1l.50 red | 5·50 | 5·25 |
| 488 | - | 2l.50 purple | 5·50 | 5·25 |
| 489 | - | 5l. blue | 11·00 | 8·25 |
| 490 | - | 8l. mauve | 16·00 | 12·50 |
| 491 | - | 12l. brown | 27·00 | 21·00 |

DESIGNS: 2l.50, Riflemen; 5l. Machine-gunners; 8l. Mounted soldier; 12l. Infantry column.

1948. Nos. 429/34 surch **Lek** and value.

| | | | | |
|---|---|---|---|---|
| 492 | 75 | 0l.50 on 30q. orange | 55 | 75 |
| 493 | 75 | 1l. on 20q. green | 1·10 | 1·30 |
| 494 | - | 2l.50 on 60q. red | 2·75 | 3·75 |
| 495 | - | 3l. on 1f. red | 3·75 | 4·75 |
| 496 | - | 5l. on 3f. blue | 8·25 | 7·75 |
| 497 | - | 12l. on 40q. brown | 22·00 | 21·00 |

88 Railway Construction

1948. Construction of Durres–Tirana Railway.

| | | | | |
|---|---|---|---|---|
| 498 | 88 | 0l.50 red | 2·75 | 1·60 |
| 499 | 88 | 1l. green | 3·00 | 1·80 |
| 500 | 88 | 1l.50 red | 4·50 | 2·50 |
| 501 | 88 | 2l.50 brown | 6·50 | 3·25 |
| 502 | 88 | 5l. blue | 11·00 | 6·25 |
| 503 | 88 | 8l. orange | 18·00 | 10·50 |
| 504 | 88 | 12l. purple | 22·00 | 12·50 |
| 505 | 88 | 20l. black | 43·00 | 26·00 |

89 Parade of Infantrymen

1948. 5th Anniv of People's Army.

| | | | | |
|---|---|---|---|---|
| 506 | 89 | 2l.50 brown | 5·50 | 5·25 |
| 507 | 89 | 5l. blue | 7·50 | 7·25 |
| 508 | - | 8l. slate (Troops in action) | 14·00 | 10·50 |

90 Labourer, Globe and Flag

1949. Labour Day.

| | | | | |
|---|---|---|---|---|
| 509 | 90 | 2l.50 brown | 1·60 | 2·50 |
| 510 | 90 | 5l. blue | 3·25 | 4·25 |
| 511 | 90 | 8l. purple | 6·00 | 6·75 |

91 Soldier and Map

1949. 6th Anniv of People's Army.

| | | | | |
|---|---|---|---|---|
| 512 | 91 | 2l.50 brown | 1·60 | 2·50 |
| 513 | 91 | 5l. blue | 3·25 | 4·25 |
| 514 | 91 | 8l. orange | 6·00 | 7·75 |

92 Albanian and Kremlin Tower

1949. Albanian–Soviet Amity.

| | | | | |
|---|---|---|---|---|
| 515 | 92 | 2l.50 brown | 1·60 | 2·50 |
| 516 | 92 | 5l. blue | 3·75 | 5·25 |

93 Gen. Enver Hoxha

1949

| | | | | |
|---|---|---|---|---|
| 517 | 93 | 0l.50 purple | 35 | 10 |
| 518 | 93 | 1l. green | 40 | 10 |
| 519 | 93 | 1l.50 red | 55 | 10 |
| 520 | 93 | 2l.50 brown | 1·10 | 15 |
| 521 | 93 | 5l. blue | 2·20 | 1·00 |
| 522 | 93 | 8l. purple | 4·25 | 3·25 |
| 523 | 93 | 12l. purple | 11·50 | 5·75 |
| 524 | 93 | 20l. slate | 13·50 | 7·25 |

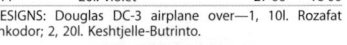

94 Soldier and Flag

1949. 5th Anniv of Liberation.

| | | | | |
|---|---|---|---|---|
| 525 | 94 | 2l.50 brown | 1·10 | 1·60 |
| 526 | - | 3l. red | 1·10 | 3·25 |
| 527 | 94 | 5l. violet | 3·25 | 4·25 |
| 528 | - | 8l. black | 6·50 | 7·75 |

DESIGN—HORIZ: 3, 8l. Street fighting.

96 Joseph Stalin

1949. Stalin's 70th Birthday.

| | | | | |
|---|---|---|---|---|
| 529 | 96 | 2l.50 brown | 1·10 | 2·10 |
| 530 | 96 | 5l. blue | 2·75 | 3·75 |
| 531 | 96 | 8l. lake | 7·00 | 9·00 |

97

1950. 75th Anniv of U.P.U.

| | | | | |
|---|---|---|---|---|
| 532 | 97 | 5l. blue | 3·00 | 6·75 |
| 533 | 97 | 8l. purple | 5·50 | 9·50 |
| 534 | 97 | 12l. black | 11·00 | 18·00 |

98 Sami Frasheri

1950. Literary Jubilee. Inscr "1950-JUBILEU I SHKRIMTAREVE TE RILINDJES".

| | | | | |
|---|---|---|---|---|
| 535 | 98 | 2l. green | 1·60 | 1·60 |
| 536 | - | 2l.50 brown | 2·20 | 2·50 |
| 537 | - | 3l. red | 4·25 | 5·25 |
| 538 | - | 5l. blue | 5·50 | 6·25 |

PORTRAITS: 2l.50, A. Zako (Cajupi); 3l. Naim Frasheri; 5l. K. Kristoforidhi.

99 Vuno-Himare

1950. Air.

| | | | | |
|---|---|---|---|---|
| 539 | 99 | 0l.50 black | 1·00 | 1·00 |
| 540 | - | 1l. purple | 1·00 | 1·00 |
| 541 | - | 2l. blue | 1·70 | 2·10 |
| 542 | 99 | 5l. green | 6·00 | 5·75 |
| 543 | - | 10l. blue | 14·00 | 10·50 |
| 544 | - | 20l. violet | 27·00 | 16·00 |

DESIGNS: Douglas DC-3 airplane over—1, 10l. Rozafat Shkodor; 2, 20l. Keshtjelle-Butrinto.

100 Stafa and Shanto

1950. Albanian Patriots.

| | | | | |
|---|---|---|---|---|
| 545 | | 2l. green | 1·40 | 1·30 |
| 546 | | 2l.50 violet | 1·60 | 1·60 |
| 547 | | 3l. red | 3·25 | 3·25 |
| 548 | | 5l. blue | 5·50 | 5·25 |
| 549 | 100 | 8l. brown | 11·00 | 10·50 |

PORTRAITS: 2l. Ahmet Haxhia, Hydajet Lezha, Naim Gjylbegu, Ndoc Mazi and Ndoc Deda; 2l.50, Asim Zeneli, Ali Demi, Kajo Karafili, Dervish Hakali and Asim Vokshi; 3l. Ataz Shehu, Baba Faja, Zoja Cure, Mustafa Matohiti and Gjok Doci; 5l. Perlat Rexhepi, Bako, Vojo Kushi, Reshit Collaku and Misto Mame.

101 Arms and Flags

1951. 5th Anniv of Republic.

| | | | | |
|---|---|---|---|---|
| 550 | 101 | 2l.50 red | 2·20 | 3·25 |

| 551 | 101 | 5l. blue | 4·25 | 6·25 |
|---|---|---|---|---|
| 552 | 101 | 8l. black | 7·00 | 9·50 |

**102** Skanderbeg

**1951.** 483rd Death Anniv of Skanderbeg (patriot).

| 553 | 102 | 2l.50 brown | 2·20 | 2·50 |
|---|---|---|---|---|
| 554 | 102 | 5l. violet | 4·25 | 5·25 |
| 555 | 102 | 8l. bistre | 7·00 | 7·75 |

**103** Gen. Enver Hoxha and Assembly

**1951.** 7th Anniv of Permet Congress.

| 556 | 103 | 2l.50 brown | 1·10 | 1·60 |
|---|---|---|---|---|
| 557 | 103 | 3l. red | 1·20 | 2·10 |
| 558 | 103 | 5l. blue | 2·75 | 3·75 |
| 559 | 103 | 8l. mauve | 5·00 | 6·25 |

**104** Child and Globe

**1951.** International Children's Day.

| 560 | 104 | 2l. green | 2·75 | 2·10 |
|---|---|---|---|---|
| 561 | - | 2l.50 brown | 3·75 | 2·50 |
| 562 | - | 3l. red | 5·00 | 3·25 |
| 563 | 104 | 5l. blue | 7·50 | 3·75 |

DESIGN—HORIZ: 2l.50, 3l. Nurse weighing baby.

**105** Enver Hoxha and Meeting-house

**1951.** 10th Anniv of Albanian Communists.

| 564 | 105 | 2l.50 brown | 65 | 1·00 |
|---|---|---|---|---|
| 565 | 105 | 3l. red | 75 | 1·40 |
| 566 | 105 | 5l. blue | 1·70 | 2·10 |
| 567 | 105 | 8l. black | 3·25 | 3·50 |

**106** Young Partisans

**1951.** 10th Anniv of Albanian Young Communists' Union. Inscr "1941–1951".

| 568 | 106 | 2l.50 brown | 1·10 | 1·60 |
|---|---|---|---|---|
| 569 | - | 5l. blue | 2·20 | 2·50 |
| 570 | - | 8l. red | 5·00 | 5·25 |

DESIGNS: Schoolgirl, railway, tractor and factories; 8l. Miniature portraits of Stafa, Spiru, Mame and Kondi.

**1952.** Air. Surch in figures.

| 571 | | 0.50l. on 2l. blue (No. 541) | £250 | £190 |
|---|---|---|---|---|
| 572 | 99 | 0.50l. on 5l. green | 49·00 | 36·00 |
| 573 | 99 | 2l.50 on 5l. green | £375 | £200 |
| 574 | - | 2l.50 on 10l. blue (No. 543) | 60·00 | 44·00 |

**108** Factory

**1953**

| 575 | 108 | 0l.50 brown | 80 | 10 |
|---|---|---|---|---|
| 576 | - | 1l. green | 1·10 | 20 |
| 577 | - | 2l.50 sepia | 1·50 | 50 |
| 578 | - | 3l. red | 1·90 | 75 |
| 579 | - | 5l. blue | 3·25 | 1·30 |
| 580 | - | 8l. olive | 3·75 | 1·60 |
| 581 | - | 12l. purple | 5·75 | 2·10 |
| 582 | - | 20l. blue | 11·00 | 4·75 |

DESIGNS—HORIZ: 1l. Canal; 2l.50, Girl and cotton mill; 3l. Girl and sugar factory; 5l. Film studio; 8l. Girl and textile machinery; 20l. Dam. VERT: 12l. Pylon and hydroelectric station.

**109** Soldiers and Flags

**1954.** 10th Anniv of Liberation.

| 583 | 109 | 0l.50 lilac | 20 | 15 |
|---|---|---|---|---|
| 584 | 109 | 1l. green | 70 | 50 |
| 585 | 109 | 2l.50 brown | 1·10 | 1·00 |
| 586 | 109 | 3l. red | 2·20 | 2·10 |
| 587 | 109 | 5l. blue | 3·25 | 3·25 |
| 588 | 109 | 8l. purple | 6·50 | 6·25 |

**110** First Albanian School

**1956.** 70th Anniv of Albanian Schools.

| 589 | 110 | 2l. purple | 55 | 50 |
|---|---|---|---|---|
| 590 | - | 2l.50 green | 90 | 1·00 |
| 591 | - | 5l. blue | 2·00 | 2·10 |
| 592 | 110 | 10l. turquoise | 6·50 | 3·75 |

DESIGN: 2l.50, 5l. Portraits of P. Sotiri, P. N. Luarasi and N. Naci.

**111**

**1957.** 15th Anniv of Albanian Workers' Party.

| 593 | 111 | 2l.50 brown | 80 | 50 |
|---|---|---|---|---|
| 594 | - | 5l. blue | 1·70 | 75 |
| 595 | - | 8l. purple | 3·00 | 3·00 |

DESIGNS: 5l. Party headquarters, Tirana; 8l. Marx and Lenin.

**112** Congress Emblem

**1957.** 4th World Trade Unions Congress, Leipzig.

| 596 | 112 | 2l.50 purple | 60 | 20 |
|---|---|---|---|---|
| 597 | 112 | 3l. red | 65 | 50 |
| 598 | 112 | 5l. blue | 75 | 75 |
| 599 | 112 | 8l. green | 2·75 | 2·40 |

**113** Lenin and Cruiser "Aurora"

**1957.** 40th Anniv of Russian Revolution.

| 600 | 113 | 2l.50 brown | 85 | 50 |
|---|---|---|---|---|
| 601 | 113 | 5l. blue | 1·60 | 1·60 |
| 602 | 113 | 8l. black | 2·10 | 1·80 |

**114** Raising the Flag

**1957.** 45th Anniv of Proclamation of Independence.

| 603 | 114 | 1l.50 purple | 80 | 30 |
|---|---|---|---|---|
| 604 | 114 | 2l.50 brown | 1·40 | 50 |
| 605 | 114 | 5l. blue | 1·80 | 1·60 |
| 606 | 114 | 8l. green | 4·25 | 2·10 |

**115** N. Veqilharxhi

**1958.** 160th Birth Anniv of Veqilharxhi (patriot).

| 607 | 115 | 2l.50 brown | 80 | 30 |
|---|---|---|---|---|
| 608 | 115 | 5l. blue | 1·60 | 50 |
| 609 | 115 | 8l. purple | 3·25 | 1·60 |

**116** L. Gurakuqi

**1958.** Removal of Ashes of Gurakuqi (patriot).

| 610 | 116 | 1l.50 green | 35 | 20 |
|---|---|---|---|---|
| 611 | 116 | 2l.50 brown | 55 | 40 |
| 612 | 116 | 5l. blue | 70 | 50 |
| 613 | 116 | 8l. sepia | 3·25 | 1·40 |

**117** Freedom Fighters

**1958.** 50th Anniv of Battle of Mashkullore.

| 614 | 117 | 2l.50 ochre | 70 | 20 |
|---|---|---|---|---|
| 615 | - | 3l. green | 70 | 20 |
| 616 | 117 | 5l. blue | 1·60 | 80 |
| 617 | - | 8l. brown | 2·75 | 1·60 |

DESIGN: 3, 8l. Tree and buildings.

**118** Soldiers in Action

**1958.** 15th Anniv of Albanian People's Army.

| 618 | 118 | 1l.50 green | 45 | 20 |
|---|---|---|---|---|
| 619 | - | 2l.50 brown | 65 | 25 |
| 620 | 118 | 8l. red | 1·60 | 1·40 |
| 621 | - | 11l. blue | 2·50 | 2·30 |

DESIGN: 2l.50, 11l. Tank-driver, sailor, infantryman and tanks.

**119** Bust of Apollo and Butrinto Amphitheatre

**1959.** Cultural Monuments Week.

| 622 | 119 | 2l.50 brown | 80 | 30 |
|---|---|---|---|---|
| 623 | 119 | 6l.50 green | 3·25 | 1·30 |
| 624 | 119 | 11l. blue | 4·25 | 2·10 |

**120** F. Joliot-Curie and Council Emblem

**1959.** 10th Anniv of World Peace Council.

| 625 | 120 | 1l.50 red | 2·20 | 50 |
|---|---|---|---|---|
| 626 | 120 | 2l.50 violet | 5·00 | 1·60 |
| 627 | 120 | 11l. blue | 11·50 | 5·25 |

**121** Basketball

**1959.** 1st National Spartacist Games.

| 628 | 121 | 1l.50 violet | 1·10 | 25 |
|---|---|---|---|---|
| 629 | - | 2l.50 green | 1·20 | 30 |
| 630 | - | 5l. red | 2·20 | 1·00 |
| 631 | - | 11l. blue | 6·50 | 3·75 |

DESIGNS: 2l.50, Football; 5l. Running; 11l. Runners with torches.

**122** Soldier

**1959.** 15th Anniv of Liberation.

| 632 | 122 | 1l.50 red | 1·20 | 25 |
|---|---|---|---|---|
| 633 | - | 2l.50 brown | 1·60 | 35 |
| 634 | - | 3l. green | 2·20 | 45 |
| 635 | - | 6l.50 red | 4·75 | 4·00 |
| **MS**635a | | 141×96 mm. Nos. 632/5 but in red. Imperf | 11·00 | 16·00 |

DESIGNS: 2l.50, Security guard. 3l. Harvester; 6l.50, Laboratory workers.

**123** Mother and Child

**1959.** 10th Anniv of Declaration of Human Rights.

| 636 | 123 | 5l. blue | 6·25 | 3·25 |
|---|---|---|---|---|
| **MS**636a | | 72×65 mm. No. 636. Imperf | 7·50 | 11·50 |

**124**

**1960.** 50th Anniv of International Women's Day.

| 637 | 124 | 2l.50 brown | 1·10 | 50 |
|---|---|---|---|---|
| 638 | 124 | 11l. red | 4·25 | 1·60 |

**125** Congress Building

**1960.** 40th Anniv of Lushnje Congress.

| 639 | 125 | 2l.50 brown | 55 | 30 |
|---|---|---|---|---|
| 640 | 125 | 7l.50 blue | 1·60 | 1·00 |

**126** A. Moisiu

**1960.** 80th Birth Anniv of Alexandre Moisiu (actor).

| 641 | 126 | 3l. brown | 70 | 50 |
|---|---|---|---|---|
| 642 | 126 | 11l. green | 2·40 | 1·00 |

**127** Lenin

**1960.** 90th Birth Anniv of Lenin.

| 643 | 127 | 4l. turquoise | 1·90 | 1·00 |
|---|---|---|---|---|
| 644 | 127 | 11l. red | 6·00 | 5·25 |

128 Vaso Pasha

1960. 80th Anniv of Albanian Alphabet Study Association.

| | | | | |
|---|---|---|---|---|
| 645 | 128 | 1l. olive | 55 | 20 |
| 646 | - | 1l.50 brown | 1·00 | 25 |
| 647 | - | 6l.50 blue | 2·10 | 85 |
| 648 | - | 11l. red | 5·50 | 2·10 |

DESIGNS: 1l.50, Jani Vreto; 6l.50, Sami Frasheri; 11l. Association statutes.

129 Frontier Guard

1960. 15th Anniv of Frontier Force.

| | | | | |
|---|---|---|---|---|
| 649 | 129 | 1l.50 red | 55 | 30 |
| 650 | 129 | 11l. blue | 3·25 | 1·50 |

130 Family with Policeman

1960. 15th Anniv of People's Police.

| | | | | |
|---|---|---|---|---|
| 651 | 130 | 1l.50 green | 55 | 25 |
| 652 | 130 | 8l.50 brown | 3·25 | 1·60 |

131 Normal School, Elbasan

1960. 50th Anniv of Normal School, Elbasan.

| | | | | |
|---|---|---|---|---|
| 653 | 131 | 5l. green | 2·75 | 1·60 |
| 654 | 131 | 6l.50 purple | 2·75 | 1·60 |

132 Soldier and Cannon

1960. 40th Anniv of Battle of Vlore.

| | | | | |
|---|---|---|---|---|
| 655 | 132 | 1l.50 brown | 75 | 50 |
| 656 | 132 | 2l.50 purple | 1·20 | 75 |
| 657 | 132 | 5l. blue | 2·75 | 1·00 |

133 Tirana Clock Tower, Kremlin and Tupolev Tu-104A Jetliner

1960. 2nd Anniv of Tirana–Moscow Jet Air Service.

| | | | | |
|---|---|---|---|---|
| 658 | 133 | 1l. brown | 1·10 | 80 |
| 659 | 133 | 7l.50 blue | 4·00 | 4·25 |
| 660 | 133 | 11l.50 grey | 6·50 | 7·25 |

134 Federation Emblem

1960. 15th Anniv of World Democratic Youth Federation.

| | | | | |
|---|---|---|---|---|
| 661 | 134 | 1l.50 blue | 65 | 30 |
| 662 | 134 | 8l.50 red | 2·20 | 1·00 |

135 Ali Kelmendi

1960. 60th Birth Anniv of Kelmendi (Communist).

| | | | | |
|---|---|---|---|---|
| 663 | 135 | 1l.50 olive | 55 | 30 |
| 664 | 135 | 11l. purple | 2·20 | 1·00 |

136 Flags of Albania and Russia, and Clasped Hands

1961. 15th Anniv of Albanian-Soviet Friendship Society.

| | | | | |
|---|---|---|---|---|
| 665 | 136 | 2l. violet | 55 | 30 |
| 666 | 136 | 8l. purple | 2·20 | 1·00 |

137 Marx and Lenin

1961. 4th Albanian Workers' Party Congress.

| | | | | |
|---|---|---|---|---|
| 667 | 137 | 2l. red | 55 | 30 |
| 668 | 137 | 8l. blue | 2·20 | 1·00 |

138 Malsi e Madhe (Shkoder) Costume

1961. Provincial Costumes.

| | | | | |
|---|---|---|---|---|
| 669 | 138 | 1l. black | 1·10 | 50 |
| 670 | - | 1l.50 purple | 1·40 | 75 |
| 671 | - | 6l.50 blue | 4·25 | 1·90 |
| 672 | - | 11l. red | 6·50 | 4·75 |

COSTUMES: 1l.50, Malsi e Madhe (Shkoder) (female); 6l.50, Lume; 11l. Mirdite.

139 European Otter

1961. Albanian Fauna.

| | | | | |
|---|---|---|---|---|
| 673 | 139 | 2l.50 blue | 4·00 | 1·00 |
| 674 | - | 6l.50 green | 8·00 | 2·40 |
| 675 | - | 11l. brown | 16·00 | 8·25 |

DESIGNS: 6l.50, Eurasian badger; 11l. Brown bear.

140 Dalmatian Pelicans

1961. Albanian Birds.

| | | | | |
|---|---|---|---|---|
| 676 | 140 | 1l.50 red on pink | 5·75 | 1·00 |
| 677 | - | 7l.50 violet on blue | 7·00 | 3·25 |
| 678 | - | 11l. brown on pink | 9·75 | 3·75 |

BIRDS: 7l.50, Grey heron; 11l. Little egret.

141 Cyclamen

1961. Albanian Flowers.

| | | | | |
|---|---|---|---|---|
| 679 | 141 | 1l.50 purple and blue | 2·20 | 50 |
| 680 | - | 8l. orange and purple | 6·00 | 2·50 |
| 681 | - | 11l. red and green | 7·50 | 3·25 |

FLOWERS: 8l. Forsythia; 11l. Lily.

142 M. G. Nikolla

1961. 50th Birth Anniv of Nikolla (poet).

| | | | | |
|---|---|---|---|---|
| 682 | 142 | 0l.50 brown | 65 | 30 |
| 683 | 142 | 8l.50 green | 2·20 | 1·60 |

143 Lenin and Marx on Flag

1961. 20th Anniv of Albanian Workers' Party.

| | | | | |
|---|---|---|---|---|
| 684 | 143 | 2l.50 red | 65 | 30 |
| 685 | 143 | 7l.50 purple | 2·00 | 1·30 |

144

1961. 20th Anniv of Albanian Young Communists' Union.

| | | | | |
|---|---|---|---|---|
| 686 | 144 | 2l.50 blue | 65 | 30 |
| 687 | 144 | 7l.50 mauve | 2·20 | 1·30 |

145 Yuri Gagarin and "Vostok 1"

1962. World's First Manned Space Flight. (a) Postage.

| | | | | |
|---|---|---|---|---|
| 688 | 145 | 0l.50 blue | 1·10 | 1·60 |
| 689 | 145 | 4l. purple | 4·25 | 4·75 |
| 690 | 145 | 11l. green | 11·00 | 11·50 |

(b) Air. Optd **POSTA AJRORE**.

| | | | |
|---|---|---|---|
| 691 | 0l.50 blue on cream | 38·00 | 50·00 |
| 692 | 4l. purple on cream | 38·00 | 50·00 |
| 693 | 11l. green on cream | 38·00 | 50·00 |

147 P. N. Luarasi

1962. 50th Death Anniv of Petro N. Luarasi (patriot).

| | | | | |
|---|---|---|---|---|
| 694 | 147 | 0l.50 blue | 55 | 30 |
| 695 | 147 | 8l.50 brown | 4·25 | 1·60 |

**IMPERF STAMPS**. Many Albanian stamps from No. 696 onwards exist imperf and/or in different colours from limited printings.

148 Campaign Emblem

1962. Malaria Eradication.

| | | | | |
|---|---|---|---|---|
| 696 | 148 | 1l.50 green | 35 | 15 |
| 697 | 148 | 2l.50 red | 55 | 30 |
| 698 | 148 | 10l. purple | 1·10 | 80 |
| 699 | 148 | 11l. blue | 1·40 | 1·00 |
| **MS**699a 90×106 mm. Nos. 696/9 | | | 38·00 | 38·00 |

149 Camomile

1962. Medicinal Plants.

| | | | | |
|---|---|---|---|---|
| 700 | 149 | 0l.50 yellow, green & blue | 55 | 30 |
| 701 | - | 8l. green, yellow and grey | 2·20 | 1·20 |
| 702 | - | 11l.50 violet, grn & ochre | 3·75 | 1·60 |

PLANTS: 8l. Silver linden; 11l.50, Sage.

150 Throwing the Javelin

1962. Olympic Games, Tokyo, 1964 (1st issue). Inscr as in T **102**.

| | | | | |
|---|---|---|---|---|
| 703 | | 0l.50 black and blue | 20 | 10 |
| 704 | | 2l.50 sepia and brown | 40 | 15 |
| 705 | | 3l. black and blue | 55 | 20 |
| 706 | 150 | 9l. purple and red | 2·20 | 1·00 |
| 707 | - | 10l. black and olive | 2·40 | 1·60 |
| **MS**707a 81×63 mm. 15l. (as 3l.) | | | 38·00 | 50·00 |

DESIGNS—VERT: 0l.50, Diving; 2l.50, Pole-vaulting; 10l. Putting the shot. HORIZ: 3l. Olympic flame.

See also Nos. 754/**MS**758a, 818/**MS**821a and 842/**MS**851a.

151 "Sputnik 1" in Orbit

1962. Cosmic Flights.

| | | | | |
|---|---|---|---|---|
| 708 | 151 | 0l.50 yellow and violet | 65 | 50 |
| 709 | - | 1l. sepia and green | 1·10 | 85 |
| 710 | - | 1l.50 yellow and red | 1·60 | 1·00 |
| 711 | - | 20l. blue and purple | 11·00 | 4·25 |
| **MS**711a 101×76 mm. 14l. (+ 6l.) brown and blue (rocket) | | | 65·00 | 80·00 |

DESIGNS: 1l. Dog "Laika" and "Sputnik 2"; 1l.50, Artificial satellite and Sun; 20l. "Lunik 3" photographing Moon.

152 Footballer and Ball in Net

1962. World Cup Football Championship, Chile.

| | | | | |
|---|---|---|---|---|
| 712 | 152 | 1l. violet and orange | 55 | 30 |
| 713 | - | 2l.50 blue and green | 1·60 | 85 |
| 714 | 152 | 6l.50 purple and brown | 2·20 | 1·00 |
| 715 | - | 15l. purple and green | 3·25 | 2·10 |
| **MS**715a 82×66 mm. 20l. brown and green (as 713 but larger) | | | 50·00 | 80·00 |

DESIGN: 2l.50, 15l. As Type **152** but globe in place of ball in net.

**153** "Europa" and Albanian Maps

**1962.** Tourist Publicity.

| No. | Type | Description | Mint | Used |
|---|---|---|---|---|
| 716 | **153** | 0l.50 red, yellow & green | 55 | 1·00 |
| 717 | - | 1l. red, purple and blue | 1·10 | 2·50 |
| 718 | - | 2l.50 red, purple and blue | 8·75 | 14·50 |
| 719 | **153** | 11l. red, yellow and grey | 16·00 | 18·00 |
| **MS**719a | | 82×63 mm. 7l. red, yellow and grey (**153**), 8l. red and grey (as 717) | 50·00 | 80·00 |

DESIGN: 1, 2l.50, Statue and map.

**154** Dardhe Woman

**1962.** Costumes of Albania's Southern Region.

| No. | Type | Description | Mint | Used |
|---|---|---|---|---|
| 720 | **154** | 0l.50 red, purple and blue | 45 | 20 |
| 721 | - | 1l. brown and buff | 55 | 40 |
| 722 | - | 2l.50 black, violet & grn | 1·60 | 1·30 |
| 723 | - | 14l. red, brown and green | 7·00 | 3·75 |

COSTUMES: 1l. Devoll man; 2l.50, Lunxheri woman; 14l. Gjirokaster man.

**155** Chamois

**1962.** Albanian Animals.

| No. | Type | Description | Mint | Used |
|---|---|---|---|---|
| 724 | **155** | 0l.50 purple and green | 55 | 40 |
| 725 | - | 1l. black and yellow | 2·20 | 1·00 |
| 726 | - | 1l.50 black and brown | 2·75 | 1·60 |
| 727 | - | 15l. brown and green | 22·00 | 5·25 |
| **MS**727a | | 72×89 mm. 20l. brown and green (as 727 but larger) | £140 | £180 |

ANIMALS—HORIZ. 1l. Lynx; 1l.50, Wild boar. VERT: 15l. Roe deer.

**156** Golden Eagle

**1962.** 50th Anniv of Independence.

| No. | Type | Description | Mint | Used |
|---|---|---|---|---|
| 728 | **156** | 1l. brown and red | 80 | 30 |
| 729 | - | 3l. black and brown | 3·75 | 1·00 |
| 730 | - | 16l. black and mauve | 7·50 | 3·75 |

DESIGNS: 3l. I. Qemali; 16l. "RPSH" and golden eagle.

**157** Revolutionaries

**1963.** 45th Anniv of October Revolution.

| No. | Type | Description | Mint | Used |
|---|---|---|---|---|
| 731 | **157** | 5l. violet and yellow | 1·30 | 75 |
| 732 | - | 10l. black and red | 3·00 | 1·90 |

DESIGN: 10l. Statue of Lenin.

**158** Henri Dunant and Globe

**1963.** Red Cross Centenary. Cross in red.

| No. | Type | Description | Mint | Used |
|---|---|---|---|---|
| 733 | **158** | 1l.50 black and red | 70 | 30 |
| 734 | **158** | 2l.50 black, red and blue | 1·10 | 50 |
| 735 | **158** | 6l. black, red and green | 2·20 | 1·00 |
| 736 | **158** | 10l. black, red and yellow | 3·75 | 2·50 |

**159** Stalin and Battle

**1963.** 20th Anniv of Battle of Stalingrad.

| No. | Type | Description | Mint | Used |
|---|---|---|---|---|
| 737 | **159** | 8l. black & grn (postage) | 11·00 | 4·25 |
| 738 | - | 7l. red and green (air) | 11·00 | 4·25 |

DESIGN: 7l. "Lenin" flag, map, tanks, etc.

**160** Nikolaev and "Vostok 3"

**1963.** 1st "Team" Manned Space Flights.

| No. | Type | Description | Mint | Used |
|---|---|---|---|---|
| 739 | **160** | 2l.50 brown and blue | 65 | 40 |
| 740 | - | 7l.50 black and blue | 1·60 | 1·00 |
| 741 | - | 20l. brown and violet | 4·25 | 3·75 |
| **MS**741a | | 88×73 mm. 25l. blue and brown (Popovich and Nikolaev) | 45·00 | 45·00 |

DESIGNS—HORIZ: 7l.50, Globe, "Vostok 3" and "Vostok 4". VERT: 20l. P. Popovic and "Vostok 4".

**161** Crawling Cockchafer

**1963.** Insects.

| No. | Type | Description | Mint | Used |
|---|---|---|---|---|
| 742 | **161** | 0l.50 brown and green | 1·30 | 50 |
| 743 | - | 1l. brown and blue | 2·20 | 1·00 |
| 744 | - | 8l. purple and red | 9·25 | 2·50 |
| 745 | - | 10l. black and yellow | 12·00 | 3·75 |

INSECTS: 1l.50, Stagbeetle; 8l. "Procerus gigas" (ground beetle); 10l. "Cicindela albanica" (tiger beetle).

**162** Policeman and Allegorical Figure

**1963.** 20th Anniv of Albanian Security Police.

| No. | Type | Description | Mint | Used |
|---|---|---|---|---|
| 746 | **162** | 2l.50 black, purple & red | 1·10 | 80 |
| 747 | **162** | 7l.50 black, lake and red | 3·75 | 2·50 |

**163** Great Crested Grebe

**1963.** Birds. Multicoloured.

| No. | Type | Description | Mint | Used |
|---|---|---|---|---|
| 748 | | 0l.50 Type **163** | 1·60 | 40 |
| 749 | | 3l. Golden eagle | 3·25 | 1·00 |
| 750 | | 6l.50 Grey partridge | 8·25 | 1·70 |
| 751 | | 11l. Western capercaillie | 11·00 | 2·50 |

**164** Official Insignia and Postmark of 1913

**1963.** 50th Anniv of First Albanian Stamps.

| No. | Type | Description | Mint | Used |
|---|---|---|---|---|
| 752 | **164** | 5l. multicoloured | 2·20 | 95 |
| 753 | - | 10l. green, black and red | 3·75 | 2·10 |

DESIGN: 10l. Albanian stamps of 1913, 1937 and 1962.

**165** Boxing

**1963.** Olympic Games, Tokyo (1964) (2nd issue).

| No. | Type | Description | Mint | Used |
|---|---|---|---|---|
| 754 | **165** | 2l. green, red and yellow | 70 | 1·00 |
| 755 | - | 3l. brown, blue & orange | 90 | 2·10 |
| 756 | - | 5l. purple, brown and blue | 1·40 | 30 |
| 757 | - | 6l. black, grey and green | 1·90 | 5·25 |
| 758 | - | 9l. blue and brown | 3·75 | 8·25 |
| **MS**758a | | 61×82 mm. 15l. mult (Torch, rings and map) | 20·00 | 27·00 |

SPORTS: 3l. Basketball; 5l. Volleyball; 6l. Cycling; 9l. Gymnastics.

**166** Gen. Enver Hoxha and Labinoti Council Building

**1963.** 20th Anniv of Albanian People's Army.

| No. | Type | Description | Mint | Used |
|---|---|---|---|---|
| 759 | **166** | 1l.50 yellow, black & red | 55 | 30 |
| 760 | - | 2l.50 bistre, brown & blue | 1·10 | 65 |
| 761 | - | 5l. black, drab & turq | 1·60 | 1·00 |
| 762 | - | 6l. blue, buff and brown | 2·20 | 1·50 |

DESIGNS: 2l.50, Soldier with weapons; 5l. Soldier attacking; 6l. Peacetime soldier.

**167** Gagarin

**1963.** Soviet Cosmonauts. Portraits in yellow and brown.

| No. | Type | Description | Mint | Used |
|---|---|---|---|---|
| 763 | **167** | 3l. violet | 1·10 | 40 |
| 764 | - | 5l. blue | 1·30 | 50 |
| 765 | - | 7l. violet and grey | 1·60 | 65 |
| 766 | - | 11l. blue and purple | 3·25 | 1·00 |
| 767 | - | 14l. blue and turquoise | 5·00 | 1·60 |
| 768 | - | 20l. blue | 7·50 | 3·75 |

COSMONAUTS: 5l. Titov; 7l. Nikolaev; 11l. Popovich; 14l. Bykovsky; 20l. Valentina Tereshkova.

**168** Volleyball (Rumania)

**1963.** European Sports Events, 1963.

| No. | Type | Description | Mint | Used |
|---|---|---|---|---|
| 769 | **168** | 2l. red, black and olive | 55 | 30 |
| 770 | - | 3l. bistre, black and red | 85 | 50 |
| 771 | - | 5l. orange, black & green | 1·10 | 85 |
| 772 | - | 7l. green, black and pink | 1·60 | 1·30 |
| 773 | - | 8l. red, black and blue | 3·75 | 1·60 |

SPORTS: 3l. Weightlifting (Sweden); 5l. Football (European Cup); 7l. Boxing (Russia); 8l. Ladies' Rowing (Russia).

**169** Celadon Swallowtail

**1963.** Butterflies and Moths.

| No. | Type | Description | Mint | Used |
|---|---|---|---|---|
| 774 | **169** | 1l. black, yellow and red | 65 | 25 |
| 775 | - | 2l. black, red and blue | 1·10 | 30 |
| 776 | - | 4l. black, yellow & purple | 2·20 | 1·00 |
| 777 | - | 5l. multicoloured | 3·25 | 95 |
| 778 | - | 8l. black, red and brown | 5·50 | 2·10 |
| 779 | - | 10l. orange, brown & blue | 7·00 | 3·25 |

DESIGNS: 2l. Jersey tiger moth; 4l. Brimstone; 5l. Death's-head hawk moth; 8l. Orange tip; 10l. Peacock.

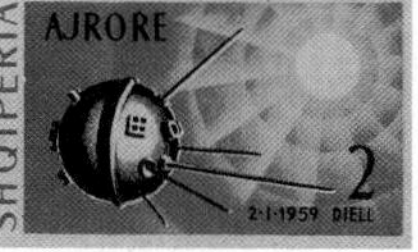


**170** Lunik 1

**1963.** Air. Cosmic Flights.

| No. | Type | Description | Mint | Used |
|---|---|---|---|---|
| 780 | **170** | 2l. olive, yellow & orange | 55 | 30 |
| 781 | - | 3l. multicoloured | 1·10 | 40 |
| 782 | - | 5l. olive, yellow & purple | 1·60 | 65 |
| 783 | - | 8l. red, yellow and violet | 2·75 | 1·20 |
| 784 | - | 12l. red, orange and blue | 5·50 | 3·75 |

DESIGNS: 3l. Lunik 2; 5l. Lunik 3; 8l. Venus 1; 12l. Mars 1.

**171** Food Processing Works

**1963.** Industrial Buildings.

| No. | Type | Description | Mint | Used |
|---|---|---|---|---|
| 785 | **171** | 2l.50 red on pink | 1·10 | 50 |
| 786 | - | 20l. green on green | 4·25 | 2·10 |
| 787 | - | 30l. purple on blue | 9·75 | 4·25 |
| 788 | - | 50l. bistre on cream | 11·00 | 5·25 |

DESIGNS—VERT: 20l. Naphtha refinery; 30l. Fruit-bottling plant. HORIZ: 50l. Copper-processing works.

**172** Shield and Banner

**1963.** 1st Army and Defence Aid Assn Congress.

| No. | Type | Description | Mint | Used |
|---|---|---|---|---|
| 789 | **172** | 2l. multicoloured | 75 | 30 |
| 790 | **172** | 8l. multicoloured | 2·20 | 1·60 |

**173** Young Men of Three Races

**1963.** 15th Anniv of Declaration of Human Rights.

| No. | Type | Description | Mint | Used |
|---|---|---|---|---|
| 791 | **173** | 3l. black and ochre | 65 | 50 |
| 792 | **173** | 5l. blue and ochre | 1·30 | 1·00 |
| 793 | **173** | 7l. violet and ochre | 2·75 | 2·10 |

**174** Bobsleighing

**1963.** Winter Olympic Games, Innsbruck. Inscr "1964".

| No. | Type | Description | Mint | Used |
|---|---|---|---|---|
| 794 | **174** | 0l.50 black and blue | 55 | 30 |
| 795 | - | 2l.50 black, red and grey | 1·00 | 50 |
| 796 | - | 6l.50 black, yellow & grey | 1·40 | 75 |
| 797 | - | 12l.50 red, black & green | 2·75 | 2·10 |
| **MS**797a | | 56×75 mm. 12l.50 black, green and blue (Ski jumper) (49×31 mm) | 35·00 | 50·00 |

DESIGNS—VERT: 2l.50, Skiing; 12l.50, Figure-skating. HORIZ: 6l.50, Ice-hockey.

**175** Lenin

**1964.** 40th Death Anniv of Lenin.

| No. | Type | Description | Mint | Used |
|---|---|---|---|---|
| 798 | **175** | 5l. olive and bistre | 1·20 | 75 |
| 799 | **175** | 10l. olive and bistre | 2·40 | 1·40 |

**176** Hurdling

**1964.** "GANEFO" Games, Djakarta (1963).

| | | | | |
|---|---|---|---|---|
| 800 | **176** | 2l.50 blue and lilac | 55 | 30 |
| 801 | - | 3l. brown and green | 1·10 | 50 |
| 802 | - | 6l.50 red and blue | 1·60 | 1·30 |
| 803 | - | 8l. ochre and blue | 2·75 | 2·10 |

SPORTS—HORIZ. 3l. Running; 6l.50, Rifle-shooting. VERT: 8l. Basketball.

**177** Common Sturgeon

**1964.** Fish. Multicoloured.

| | | | | |
|---|---|---|---|---|
| 804 | | 0l.50 Type **177** | 55 | 30 |
| 805 | | 1l. Gilthead seabream | 1·10 | 40 |
| 806 | | 1l.50 Flat-headed grey mullet | 1·60 | 50 |
| 807 | | 2l.50 Common carp | 2·20 | 1·00 |
| 808 | | 6l.50 Atlantic mackerel | 3·25 | 2·10 |
| 809 | | 10l. Lake Ochrid salmon | 5·50 | 3·25 |

**178** Eurasian Red Squirrel

**1964.** Forest Animals. Multicoloured.

| | | | | |
|---|---|---|---|---|
| 810 | | 1l. Type **178** | 55 | 25 |
| 811 | | 1l.50 Beech marten | 85 | 30 |
| 812 | | 2l. Red fox | 1·10 | 40 |
| 813 | | 2l.50 East European hedgehog | 1·60 | 50 |
| 814 | | 3l. Brown hare | 2·20 | 75 |
| 815 | | 5l. Golden jackal | 2·75 | 85 |
| 816 | | 7l. Wild cat | 4·25 | 95 |
| 817 | | 8l. Wolf | 5·50 | 1·30 |

**179** Lighting Olympic Torch

**1964.** Olympic Games, Tokyo (3rd issue). Inscr "DREJT TOKIOS".

| | | | | |
|---|---|---|---|---|
| 818 | **179** | 3l. yellow, buff and green | 55 | 75 |
| 819 | - | 5l. blue, violet and red | 75 | 1·00 |
| 820 | - | 7l. lt blue, blue & yellow | 1·10 | 1·60 |
| 821 | - | 10l. multicoloured | 1·60 | 2·50 |
| **MS**821a | | 81×91 mm. 15l. buff, blue and violet (as 820) (49×62 mm) | 30·00 | 40·00 |

DESIGNS: 5l. Torch and globes; 7l. Olympic flag and Mt. Fuji; 10l. Olympic Stadium, Tokyo.

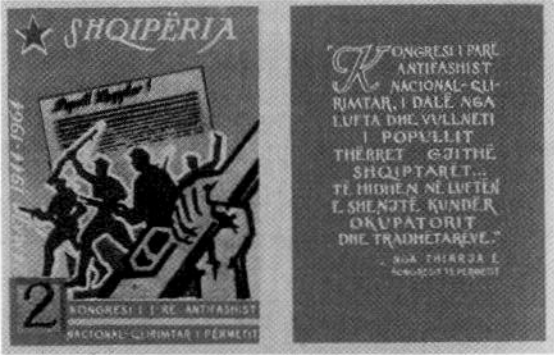

**180** Soldiers, Hand clutching Rifle, and Inscription

**1964.** 20th Anniv of Permet Congress.

| | | | | |
|---|---|---|---|---|
| 822 | **180** | 2l. sepia, red and orange | 1·60 | 1·00 |
| 823 | - | 5l. multicoloured | 3·75 | 2·10 |
| 824 | - | 8l. sepia, red and brown | 8·25 | 6·25 |

DESIGNS (each with different inscription at right): 5l. Albanian Arms; 8l. Gen. Enver Hoxha.

**181** Revolutionaries with Flag

**1964.** 40th Anniv of Revolution.

| | | | | |
|---|---|---|---|---|
| 825 | **181** | 2l.50 black and red | 55 | 30 |
| 826 | **181** | 7l.50 black and mauve | 1·60 | 1·00 |

**1964.** "Verso Tokyo" Stamp Exhibition, Rimini (Italy). Optd **Rimini 25-VI-64**.

| | | | | |
|---|---|---|---|---|
| 827 | | 10l. blue, violet, orange and black (No. 821) | 8·75 | 8·75 |

**183** Full Moon

**1964.** Moon's Phases.

| | | | | |
|---|---|---|---|---|
| 828 | **183** | 1l. yellow and violet | 55 | 20 |
| 829 | - | 5l. yellow and blue | 1·10 | 85 |
| 830 | - | 8l. yellow and blue | 1·60 | 1·00 |
| 831 | - | 11l. yellow and green | 5·50 | 2·10 |
| **MS**831a | | 67×78 mm. 15l. yellow and blue (New Moon) (34×39 mm). Imperf | 27·00 | 35·00 |

PHASES: 5l. Waxing Moon; 8l. Half-Moon; 11l. Waning Moon.

**184** Winter Wren

**1964.** Albanian Birds. Multicoloured.

| | | | | |
|---|---|---|---|---|
| 832 | | 0l.50 Type **184** | 55 | 25 |
| 833 | | 1l. Penduline tit | 1·10 | 30 |
| 834 | | 2l.50 Green woodpecker | 1·60 | 40 |
| 835 | | 3l. Common treecreeper | 2·20 | 50 |
| 836 | | 4l. Eurasian nuthatch | 2·75 | 1·00 |
| 837 | | 5l. Great tit | 3·25 | 1·30 |
| 838 | | 6l. Eurasian goldfinch | 3·75 | 1·60 |
| 839 | | 18l. Golden oriole | 8·25 | 3·75 |

**1964.** Air. Riccione "Space" Exhibition. Optd **Riccione 23-8-1964**.

| | | | | |
|---|---|---|---|---|
| 840 | **170** | 2l. olive, yellow & orange | 12·00 | 21·00 |
| 841 | - | 8l. red, yellow and violet (No. 783) | 27·00 | 31·00 |

**186** Running and Gymnastics

**1964.** Olympic Games, Tokyo.

| | | | | |
|---|---|---|---|---|
| 842 | **186** | 1l. red, blue and green | 20 | 15 |
| 843 | - | 2l. brown, blue and violet | 25 | 20 |
| 844 | - | 3l. brown, violet and olive | 35 | 20 |
| 845 | - | 4l. olive, turquoise & blue | 55 | 30 |
| 846 | - | 5l. turquoise, purple & red | 85 | 50 |
| 847 | - | 6l. ultram, lt blue & orge | 1·10 | 80 |
| 848 | - | 7l. green, orange and blue | 1·30 | 85 |
| 849 | - | 8l. grey, green and yellow | 1·40 | 95 |
| 850 | - | 9l. lt blue, yellow & purple | 1·50 | 1·00 |
| 851 | - | 10l. brown, green & turq | 1·70 | 1·60 |
| **MS**851a | | 70×96 mm. 20l. violet and bistre (Winners on Dais) (40×67 mm) | 25·00 | 30·00 |

SPORTS: 2l. Weightlifting and judo; 3l. Horse-jumping and cycling; 4l. Football and water-polo; 5l. Wrestling and boxing; 6l. Various sports and hockey; 7l. Swimming and yachting; 8l. Basketball and volleyball; 9l. Rowing and canoeing; 10l. Fencing and pistol-shooting.

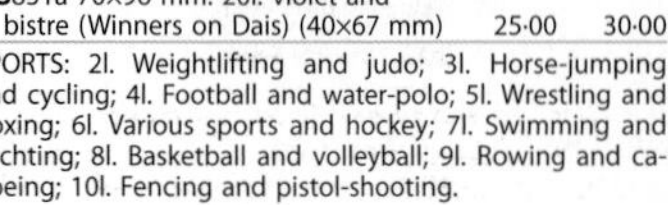

**187** Chinese Republican Emblem

**1964.** 15th Anniv of Chinese People's Republic. Inscr "I TETOR 1949 1964".

| | | | | |
|---|---|---|---|---|
| 852 | **187** | 7l. red, black and yellow | 7·75 | 3·50 |
| 853 | - | 8l. black, red and yellow | 7·75 | 4·75 |

DESIGN—HORIZ: 8l. Mao Tse-tung.

**188** Karl Marx

**1964.** Centenary of "First International".

| | | | | |
|---|---|---|---|---|
| 854 | **188** | 2l. black, red and lavender | 1·10 | 50 |
| 855 | - | 5l. slate | 2·75 | 1·60 |
| 856 | - | 8l. black, red and buff | 5·50 | 2·10 |

DESIGNS: 5l. St. Martin's Hall, London; 8l. F. Engels.

**189** J. de Rada

**1964.** 150th Birth Anniv of Jeronim de Rada (poet).

| | | | | |
|---|---|---|---|---|
| 857 | **189** | 7l. green | 1·60 | 1·00 |
| 858 | **189** | 8l. violet | 2·75 | 1·60 |

**190** Arms and Flag

**1964.** 20th Anniv of Liberation.

| | | | | |
|---|---|---|---|---|
| 859 | **190** | 1l. multicoloured | 55 | 40 |
| 860 | - | 2l. blue, red and yellow | 1·10 | 85 |
| 861 | - | 3l. brown, red and yellow | 1·60 | 1·30 |
| 862 | - | 4l. green, red and yellow | 2·20 | 1·70 |
| 863 | - | 10l. black, red and blue | 5·50 | 4·25 |

DESIGNS—HORIZ: 2l. Industrial scene; 3l. Agricultural scene. 4l. Laboratory worker. VERT: 10l. Hands holding Constitution, hammer and sickle.

**191** Mercury

**1964.** Solar System Planets. Multicoloured.

| | | | | |
|---|---|---|---|---|
| 864 | | 1l. Type **191** | 25 | 20 |
| 865 | | 2l. Venus | 55 | 30 |
| 866 | | 3l. Earth | 75 | 40 |
| 867 | | 4l. Mars | 80 | 45 |
| 868 | | 5l. Jupiter | 1·10 | 50 |
| 869 | | 6l. Saturn | 1·60 | 1·00 |
| 870 | | 7l. Uranus | 1·80 | 1·30 |
| 871 | | 8l. Neptune | 2·20 | 1·50 |
| 872 | | 9l. Pluto | 2·40 | 1·70 |
| **MS**872a | | 88×72 mm. 15l. Solar system and rocket (61×51 mm). Imperf | 35·00 | 47·00 |

**192** Chestnut

**1965.** Winter Fruits. Multicoloured.

| | | | | |
|---|---|---|---|---|
| 873 | | 1l. Type **192** | 35 | 20 |
| 874 | | 2l. Medlars | 55 | 30 |
| 875 | | 3l. Persimmon | 75 | 35 |
| 876 | | 4l. Pomegranate | 1·10 | 50 |
| 877 | | 5l. Quince | 2·20 | 75 |
| 878 | | 10l. Orange | 4·25 | 1·30 |

**193** "Industry"

**1965.** 20th Anniv of Albanian Trade Unions. Inscr "B.P.S.H. 1945–1965".

| | | | | |
|---|---|---|---|---|
| 879 | **193** | 2l. red, pink and black | 7·50 | 7·25 |
| 880 | - | 5l. black, grey and ochre | 11·50 | 11·00 |
| 881 | - | 8l. blue, lt blue & black | 14·00 | 13·50 |

DESIGNS: 5l. Set square, book and dividers ("Technocracy"); 8l. Hotel, trees and sunshade ("Tourism").

**194** Buffalo Grazing

**1965.** Water Buffaloes.

| | | | | |
|---|---|---|---|---|
| 882 | **194** | 1l. multicoloured | 1·10 | 50 |
| 883 | - | 2l. multicoloured | 2·20 | 1·00 |
| 884 | - | 3l. multicoloured | 3·25 | 1·60 |
| 885 | - | 7l. multicoloured | 7·50 | 2·10 |
| 886 | - | 12l. multicoloured | 13·00 | 2·50 |

DESIGNS: 2l. to 12l. As Type **194**, showing different views of buffalo.

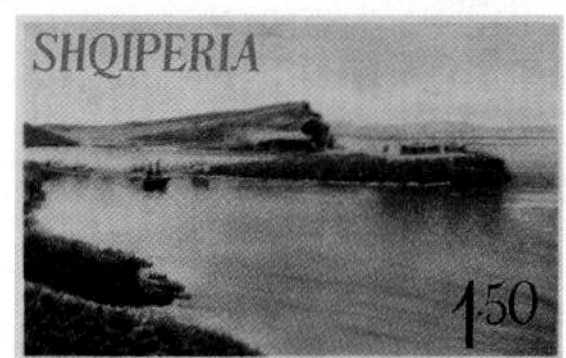

**195** Coastal View

**1965.** Albanian Scenery. Multicoloured.

| | | | | |
|---|---|---|---|---|
| 887 | | 1l.50 Type **195** | 1·60 | 50 |
| 888 | | 2l.50 Mountain forest | 3·50 | 1·00 |
| 889 | | 3l. Lugina Peak (vert) | 3·75 | 1·30 |
| 890 | | 4l. White River, Thethi (vert) | 5·00 | 1·60 |
| 891 | | 5l. Dry Mountain | 6·00 | 2·10 |
| 892 | | 9l. Lake of Flowers, Lure | 16·00 | 4·25 |

**196** Frontier Guard

**1965.** 20th Anniv of Frontier Force.

| | | | | |
|---|---|---|---|---|
| 893 | **196** | 2l.50 multicoloured | 1·60 | 1·00 |
| 894 | **196** | 12l.50 multicoloured | 9·25 | 4·25 |

**197** Rifleman

**1965.** European Shooting Championships, Bucharest.

| 895 | 197 | 1l. purple, red and violet | 35 | 20 |
|---|---|---|---|---|
| 896 | - | 2l. purple, ultram & blue | 55 | 30 |
| 897 | - | 3l. red and pink | 1·10 | 50 |
| 898 | - | 4l. multicoloured | 2·20 | 50 |
| 899 | - | 15l. multicoloured | 6·50 | 2·50 |

DESIGNS: 2, 15l. Rifle-shooting (different); 3l. "Target" map; 4l. Pistol-shooting.

**198** I.T.U. Emblem and Symbols

**1965.** Centenary of I.T.U.

| 900 | 198 | 2l.50 mauve, black & grn | 1·10 | 50 |
|---|---|---|---|---|
| 901 | 198 | 12l.50 blue, black & violet | 6·50 | 1·80 |

**199** Belyaev

**1965.** Space Flight of "Voskhod 2".

| 902 | 199 | 1l.50 brown and blue | 20 | 10 |
|---|---|---|---|---|
| 903 | - | 2l. blue, ultram & lilac | 35 | 20 |
| 904 | - | 6l.50 brown and mauve | 1·10 | 50 |
| 905 | - | 20l. yellow, black & blue | 4·25 | 2·10 |
| **MS**906 | | 71×86 mm. 20l. yellow, black and blue (as 905 but larger, 59×51 mm). Imperf | 20·00 | 31·00 |

DESIGNS: 2l. "Voskhod 2"; 6l.50, Leonov; 20l. Leonov in space.

**200** Marx and Lenin

**1965.** Postal Ministers' Congress, Peking.

| 907 | 200 | 2l.50 sepia, red & yellow | 85 | 50 |
|---|---|---|---|---|
| 908 | 200 | 7l.50 green, red & yellow | 3·50 | 2·10 |

**201** Mother and Child

**1965.** International Children's Day. Multicoloured.

| 909 | 1l. Type **201** | 25 | 15 |
|---|---|---|---|
| 910 | 2l. Children planting tree | 60 | 30 |
| 911 | 3l. Children and construction toy (horiz) | 80 | 50 |
| 912 | 4l. Child on beach | 1·10 | 85 |
| 913 | 15l. Child reading book | 4·25 | 3·25 |

**202** Wine Vessel

**1965.** Albanian Antiquities. Multicoloured.

| 914 | 1l. Type **202** | 25 | 10 |
|---|---|---|---|
| 915 | 2l. Helmet and shield | 55 | 30 |
| 916 | 3l. Mosaic of animal (horiz) | 75 | 50 |
| 917 | 4l. Statuette of man | 1·60 | 1·00 |
| 918 | 15l. Statuette of headless and limbless man | 4·00 | 2·10 |

**203** Fuchsia

**1965.** Albanian Flowers. Multicoloured.

| 919 | 1l. Type **203** | 25 | 15 |
|---|---|---|---|
| 920 | 2l. Cyclamen | 75 | 30 |
| 921 | 3l. Lilies | 1·30 | 50 |
| 922 | 3l.50 Iris | 1·60 | 75 |
| 923 | 4l. Dahlia | 1·80 | 85 |
| 924 | 4l.50 Hydrangea | 2·20 | 95 |
| 925 | 5l. Rose | 2·40 | 1·00 |
| 926 | 7l. Tulips | 3·25 | 1·30 |

**1965.** Surch.

| 927 | 5q. on 30l. (No. 787) | 85 | 85 |
|---|---|---|---|
| 928 | 15q. on 30l. (No. 787) | 1·10 | 1·00 |
| 929 | 25q. on 50l. (No. 788) | 1·60 | 1·60 |
| 930 | 80q. on 50l. (No. 788) | 3·75 | 3·75 |
| 931 | 1l.10 on 20l. (No. 786) | 5·50 | 5·25 |
| 932 | 2l. on 20l. (No. 786) | 8·75 | 8·25 |

**205** White Stork

**1965.** Migratory Birds. Multicoloured.

| 933 | 10q. Type **205** | 55 | 30 |
|---|---|---|---|
| 934 | 20q. European cuckoo | 1·10 | 50 |
| 935 | 30q. Hoopoe | 1·60 | 85 |
| 936 | 40q. European bee-eater | 2·20 | 1·00 |
| 937 | 50q. European nightjar | 2·75 | 1·30 |
| 938 | 1l.50 Common quail | 8·25 | 3·75 |

**206** "War Veterans" (after painting by B. Sejdini)

**1965.** War Veterans Conference.

| 939 | 206 | 25q. brown and black | 3·25 | 85 |
|---|---|---|---|---|
| 940 | 206 | 65q. blue and black | 8·25 | 2·10 |
| 941 | 206 | 1l.10 black | 11·00 | 4·25 |

**207** Hunter stalking Western Capercaillie

**1965.** Hunting.

| 942 | 207 | 10q. multicoloured | 55 | 20 |
|---|---|---|---|---|
| 943 | - | 20q. brown, sepia & grn | 1·10 | 20 |
| 944 | - | 30q. multicoloured | 1·60 | 30 |
| 945 | - | 40q. purple and green | 2·20 | 50 |
| 946 | - | 50q. brown, blue & black | 2·75 | 1·00 |
| 947 | - | 1l. brown, bistre & green | 5·50 | 1·60 |

DESIGNS: 20q. Shooting roe deer; 30q. Common pheasant; 40q. Shooting mallard; 50q. Dogs chasing wild boar; 1l. Hunter and brown hare.

**208** "Nerium oleander"

**1965.** Mountain Flowers. Multicoloured.

| 948 | 10q. Type **208** | 25 | 20 |
|---|---|---|---|
| 949 | 20q. "Myosotis alpestris" | 55 | 25 |
| 950 | 30q. "Dianthus glacialis" | 75 | 30 |
| 951 | 40q. "Nymphaea alba" | 1·30 | 50 |
| 952 | 50q. "Lotus corniculatus" | 1·60 | 75 |
| 953 | 1l. "Papaver rhoeas" | 4·25 | 2·10 |

**209** Tourist Hotel, Fier

**1965.** Public Buildings.

| 954 | 209 | 5q. black and blue | 10 | 10 |
|---|---|---|---|---|
| 955 | - | 10q. black and buff | 15 | 10 |
| 956 | - | 15q. black and green | 20 | 10 |
| 957 | - | 25q. black and violet | 75 | 20 |
| 958 | - | 65q. black and brown | 1·60 | 40 |
| 959 | - | 80q. black and green | 2·20 | 50 |
| 960 | - | 1l.10 black and purple | 2·75 | 75 |
| 961 | - | 1l.60 black and blue | 4·25 | 1·60 |
| 962 | - | 2l. black and pink | 5·50 | 2·10 |
| 963 | - | 3l. black and grey | 11·00 | 3·75 |

BUILDINGS: 10q. Peshkopi Hotel; 15q. Sanatorium, Tirana; 25q. "House of Rest", Pogradec; 65q. Partisans Sports Palace, Tirana; 80q. "House of Rest", Dajti Mountain; 1l.10. Palace of Culture, Tirana; 1l.60, Adriatic Hotel, Durres; 2l. Migjeni Theatre, Shkoder; 3l. "A. Moisiu" Cultural Palace, Durres.

**210** Freighter "Teuta"

**1965.** Evolution of Albanian Ships.

| 964 | 210 | 10q. green and light green | 35 | 20 |
|---|---|---|---|---|
| 965 | - | 20q. bistre and green | 45 | 20 |
| 966 | - | 30q. ultramarine and blue | 55 | 30 |
| 967 | - | 40q. violet and light violet | 75 | 50 |
| 968 | - | 50q. red and rose | 1·60 | 75 |
| 969 | - | 1l. brown and ochre | 3·75 | 1·30 |

DESIGNS: 20q. Punt; 30q. 19th-century sailing ship; 40q. 18th-century brig; 50q. Freighter "Vlora"; 1l. Illyrian galliots.

**211** Head of Brown Bear

**1965.** Brown Bears. Different Bear designs as T **211**.

| 970 | | 10q. brown and buff | 45 | 15 |
|---|---|---|---|---|
| 971 | | 20q. brown and buff | 55 | 20 |
| 972 | | 30q. brown, red and buff | 1·10 | 35 |
| 973 | | 35q. brown and buff | 1·30 | 40 |
| 974 | | 40q. brown and buff | 1·60 | 45 |
| 975 | 211 | 50q. brown and buff | 2·75 | 50 |
| 976 | - | 55q. brown and buff | 3·25 | 75 |
| 977 | - | 60q. brown, red and buff | 6·00 | 2·75 |

The 10q. to 40q. are vert.

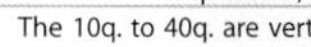

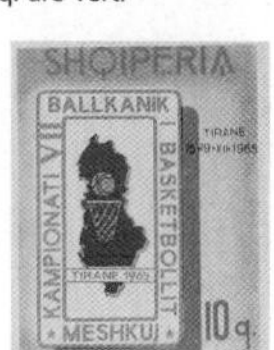

**212** Championships Emblem

**1965.** 7th Balkan Basketball Championships, Tirana. Multicoloured.

| 978 | 10q. Type **212** | 35 | 10 |
|---|---|---|---|
| 979 | 20q. Competing players | 45 | 15 |
| 980 | 30q. Clearing ball | 75 | 20 |
| 981 | 50q. Attempted goal | 1·60 | 50 |
| 982 | 1l.40 Medal and ribbon | 3·25 | 1·30 |

**213** Arms on Book

**1966.** 20th Anniv of Albanian People's Republic.

| 983 | 213 | 10q. gold, red and brown | 20 | 10 |
|---|---|---|---|---|
| 984 | - | 20q. gold, blue & ultram | 35 | 20 |
| 985 | - | 30q. gold, yellow and brown | 75 | 50 |
| 986 | - | 60q. gold, lt grn & green | 1·80 | 1·00 |
| 987 | - | 80q. gold, red and brown | 2·30 | 1·60 |

DESIGNS (Arms and): 20q. Chimney stacks; 30q. Ear of corn; 60q. Hammer, sickle and open book; 80q. Industrial plant.

**214** Cow

**1966.** Domestic Animals. Animals in natural colours; inscr in black: frame colours given.

| 988 | 214 | 10q. turquoise | 20 | 20 |
|---|---|---|---|---|
| 989 | - | 20q. green | 55 | 30 |
| 990 | - | 30q. blue | 1·30 | 40 |
| 991 | - | 35q. lavender | 1·60 | 50 |
| 992 | - | 40q. pink | 2·20 | 50 |
| 993 | - | 50q. yellow | 2·75 | 65 |
| 994 | - | 55q. blue | 3·00 | 75 |
| 995 | - | 60q. yellow | 5·50 | 1·00 |

ANIMALS—HORIZ. 20q. Pig; 30q. Sheep; 35q. Goat; 40q. Dog. VERT: 50q. Cat; 55q. Horse; 60q. Ass.

**215** Football

**1966.** World Cup Football Championships (1st series).

| 996 | 215 | 5q. orange grey & buff | 15 | 10 |
|---|---|---|---|---|
| 997 | - | 10q. multicoloured | 20 | 10 |
| 998 | - | 15q. blue, yellow & buff | 25 | 15 |
| 999 | - | 20q. multicoloured | 35 | 20 |
| 1000 | - | 25q. sepia, red and buff | 45 | 20 |
| 1001 | - | 30q. brown, green & buff | 55 | 30 |
| 1002 | - | 35q. green, blue and buff | 85 | 40 |
| 1003 | - | 40q. brown red and buff | 90 | 50 |
| 1004 | - | 50q. multicoloured | 1·10 | 75 |
| 1005 | - | 70q. multicoloured | 1·60 | 1·00 |

DESIGNS—Footballer and map showing: 10q. Montevideo (1930); 15q. Rome (1934); 20q. Paris (1938); 25q. Rio de Janeiro (1950); 30q. Berne (1954); 35q. Stockholm (1958); 40q. Santiago (1962); 50q. London (1966); 70q. World Cup and football.

See also Nos. 1035/42.

**216** A. Z. Cajupi

**1966.** Birth Centenary of Andon Cajupi (poet).

| 1006 | 216 | 40q. indigo and blue | 1·10 | 60 |
|---|---|---|---|---|
| 1007 | 216 | 1l.10 bronze and green | 3·25 | 2·10 |

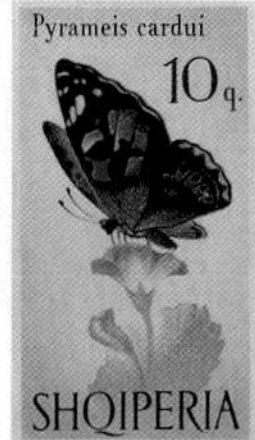

**217** Painted Lady

**1966.** Butterflies and Dragonflies. Multicoloured.

| 1008 | 10q. Type **217** | 45 | 20 |
|---|---|---|---|
| 1009 | 20q. "Calopteryx virgo" | 55 | 25 |
| 1010 | 30q. Pale clouded yellow | 75 | 30 |
| 1011 | 35q. Banded agrion | 1·10 | 35 |
| 1012 | 40q. Banded agrion (different) | 1·60 | 40 |
| 1013 | 50q. Swallowtail | 2·20 | 50 |
| 1014 | 55q. Danube clouded yellow | 2·75 | 75 |
| 1015 | 60q. Hungarian glider | 7·00 | 1·30 |

The 20, 35 and 40q. are dragonflies, remainder are butterflies.

**218** W.H.O. Building

**1966.** Inaug of W.H.O. Headquarters, Geneva.

| | | | | |
|---|---|---|---|---|
| 1016 | **218** | 25q. black and blue | 55 | 20 |
| 1017 | - | 35q. blue and orange | 1·10 | 30 |
| 1018 | - | 60q. red, blue and green | 1·60 | 75 |
| 1019 | - | 80q. blue, yellow & brn | 2·20 | 1·30 |

DESIGNS—VERT: 35q. Ambulance and patient; 60q. Nurse and mother weighing baby. HORIZ: 80q. Medical equipment.

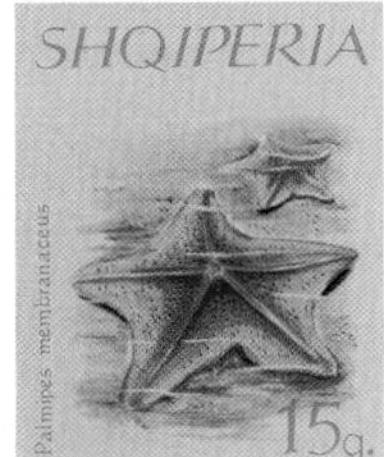

**219** Leaf Star

**1966.** "Starfish". Multicoloured.

| | | | |
|---|---|---|---|
| 1020 | 15q. Type **219** | 45 | 30 |
| 1021 | 25q. Spiny Star | 75 | 40 |
| 1022 | 35q. Brittle Star | 1·30 | 50 |
| 1023 | 45q. Sea Star | 1·60 | 65 |
| 1024 | 50q. Blood Star | 1·80 | 75 |
| 1025 | 60q. Sea Cucumber | 2·75 | 1·00 |
| 1026 | 70q. Sea Urchin | 3·25 | 2·50 |

**220** "Luna 10"

**1966.** "Luna 10". Launching.

| | | | | |
|---|---|---|---|---|
| 1027 | **220** | 20q. multicoloured | 55 | 30 |
| 1028 | - | 30q. multicoloured | 1·10 | 50 |
| 1029 | **220** | 70q. multicoloured | 2·20 | 1·00 |
| 1030 | - | 80q. multicoloured | 3·75 | 2·30 |

DESIGN: 30, 80q. Earth, Moon and trajectory of "Luna 10".

**221** Water-level Map of Albania

**1966.** International Hydrological Decade.

| | | | | |
|---|---|---|---|---|
| 1031 | **221** | 20q. black, orge & red | 55 | 30 |
| 1032 | - | 30q. multicoloured | 85 | 50 |
| 1033 | - | 70q. black and violet | 1·60 | 1·30 |
| 1034 | - | 80q. multicoloured | 2·75 | 2·10 |

DESIGNS: 30q. Water scale and fields; 70q. Turbine and electricity pylon; 80q. Hydrological decade emblem.

**222** Footballers (Uruguay, 1930)

**1966.** World Cup Football Championship (2nd series). Inscriptions and values in black.

| | | | | |
|---|---|---|---|---|
| 1035 | **222** | 10q. purple and ochre | 45 | 10 |
| 1036 | - | 20q. olive and blue | 55 | 15 |
| 1037 | - | 30q. slate and red | 75 | 20 |
| 1038 | - | 35q. red and blue | 1·00 | 25 |
| 1039 | - | 40q. brown and green | 1·10 | 30 |
| 1040 | - | 50q. green and brown | 1·30 | 50 |
| 1041 | - | 55q. green and mauve | 1·40 | 1·00 |
| 1042 | - | 60q. ochre and red | 2·75 | 1·60 |

DESIGNS—Various footballers representing World Cup winners: 20q. Italy, 1934; 30q. Italy, 1938; 35q. Uruguay, 1950; 40q. West Germany, 1954; 50q. Brazil, 1958; 55q. Brazil, 1962; 60q. Football and names of 16 finalists in 1966 Championship.

**223** Tortoise

**1966.** Reptiles. Multicoloured.

| | | | |
|---|---|---|---|
| 1043 | 10q. Type **223** | 35 | 20 |
| 1044 | 15q. Grass snake | 45 | 25 |
| 1045 | 25q. Swamp tortoise | 55 | 30 |
| 1046 | 30q. Lizard | 65 | 40 |
| 1047 | 35q. Salamander | 1·10 | 50 |
| 1048 | 45q. Green lizard | 1·30 | 60 |
| 1049 | 50q. Slow-worm | 1·40 | 75 |
| 1050 | 90q. Sand viper | 2·75 | 1·60 |

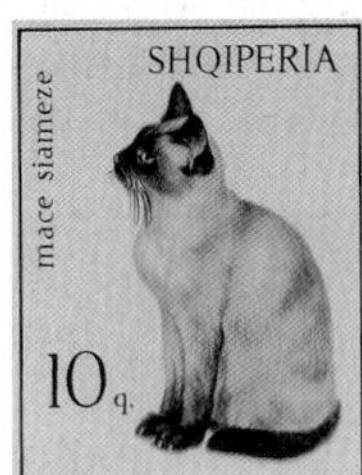

**224** Siamese Cat

**1966.** Cats. Multicoloured.

| | | | |
|---|---|---|---|
| 1051 | 10q. Type **224** | 45 | 20 |
| 1052 | 15q. Tabby | 55 | 25 |
| 1053 | 25q. Kitten | 1·10 | 30 |
| 1054 | 45q. Persian | 1·70 | 75 |
| 1055 | 60q. Persian | 2·75 | 1·00 |
| 1056 | 65q. Persian | 3·00 | 1·20 |
| 1057 | 80q. Persian | 3·75 | 1·40 |

Nos. 1053/7 are horiz.

**225** P. Budi (writer)

**1966.** 400th Birth Anniv of P. Budi.

| | | | | |
|---|---|---|---|---|
| 1058 | **225** | 25q. bronze and flesh | 1·10 | 50 |
| 1059 | **225** | 1l.75 purple and green | 3·25 | 2·50 |

**226** UNESCO Emblem

**1966.** 20th Anniv of UNESCO Multicoloured.

| | | | |
|---|---|---|---|
| 1060 | 5q. Type **226** | 35 | 15 |
| 1061 | 15q. Tulip and open book | 35 | 20 |
| 1062 | 25q. Albanian dancers | 75 | 40 |
| 1063 | 1l.55 Jug and base of column | 3·25 | 2·10 |

**227** Borzoi

**1966.** Dogs. Multicoloured.

| | | | |
|---|---|---|---|
| 1064 | 10q. Type **227** | 55 | 20 |
| 1065 | 15q. Kuvasz | 75 | 25 |
| 1066 | 25q. Setter | 1·30 | 50 |
| 1067 | 45q. Cocker spaniel | 2·00 | 1·00 |
| 1068 | 60q. Bulldog | 2·20 | 1·30 |
| 1069 | 65q. St. Bernard | 3·00 | 1·60 |
| 1070 | 80q. Dachshund | 4·25 | 2·10 |

**228** Hand holding Book

**1966.** 5th Workers Party Congress, Tirana. Multicoloured.

| | | | |
|---|---|---|---|
| 1071 | 15q. Type **228** | 35 | 15 |
| 1072 | 25q. Emblems of agriculture and industry | 60 | 15 |
| 1073 | 65q. Hammer and sickle, wheat and industrial skyline | 1·60 | 85 |
| 1074 | 95q. Hands holding banner on bayonet and implements | 2·20 | 1·30 |

**229** Ndre Mjeda (poet)

**1966.** Birth Centenary of Ndre Mjeda.

| | | | | |
|---|---|---|---|---|
| 1075 | **229** | 25q. brown and blue | 65 | 50 |
| 1076 | **229** | 1l.75 brown and green | 3·75 | 1·80 |

**230** Hammer and Sickle

**1966.** 25th Anniv of Albanian Young Communists' Union. Multicoloured.

| | | | |
|---|---|---|---|
| 1077 | 15q. Type **230** | 55 | 10 |
| 1078 | 25q. Soldier leading attack | 75 | 20 |
| 1079 | 65q. Industrial worker | 1·60 | 85 |
| 1080 | 95q. Agricultural and industrial vista | 2·20 | 1·30 |

**231** Young Communists and Banner

**1966.** 25th Anniv of Young Communists' Union. Multicoloured.

| | | | |
|---|---|---|---|
| 1081 | 5q. Manifesto (vert) | 35 | 10 |
| 1082 | 10q. Type **231** | 55 | 20 |
| 1083 | 1l.85 Partisans and banner (vert) | 3·50 | 2·30 |

**232** Golden Eagle

**1966.** Birds of Prey. Multicoloured.

| | | | |
|---|---|---|---|
| 1084 | 10q. Type **232** | 55 | 20 |
| 1085 | 15q. White-tailed sea eagle | 75 | 30 |
| 1086 | 25q. Griffon vulture | 1·10 | 50 |
| 1087 | 40q. Northern sparrow hawk | 1·30 | 65 |
| 1088 | 50q. Osprey | 1·80 | 75 |
| 1089 | 70q. Egyptian vulture | 2·75 | 1·30 |
| 1090 | 90q. Common kestrel | 3·75 | 1·60 |

**233** European Hake

**1967.** Fishes. Multicoloured.

| | | | |
|---|---|---|---|
| 1091 | 10q. Type **233** | 45 | 20 |
| 1092 | 15q. Striped red mullet | 55 | 30 |
| 1093 | 25q. Opali | 1·10 | 50 |
| 1094 | 40q. Atlantic wolffish | 1·30 | 65 |
| 1095 | 65q. Lumpsucker | 1·60 | 75 |
| 1096 | 80q. Swordfish | 2·75 | 1·30 |
| 1097 | 1l.15 Short-spined sea- scorpion | 3·25 | 1·60 |

**234** Dalmatian Pelicans

**1967.** Dalmatian Pelicans. Multicoloured.

| | | | |
|---|---|---|---|
| 1098 | 10q. Type **234** | 25 | 30 |
| 1099 | 15q. Three pelicans | 55 | 40 |
| 1100 | 25q. Pelican and chicks at nest | 1·60 | 50 |
| 1101 | 50q. Pelicans "taking off" and airborne | 3·25 | 75 |
| 1102 | 2l. Pelican "yawning" | 8·25 | 3·75 |

**235** "Camellia williamsi"

**1967.** Flowers. Multicoloured.

| | | | |
|---|---|---|---|
| 1103 | 5q. Type **235** | 20 | 10 |
| 1104 | 10q. "Chrysanthemum indicum" | 25 | 15 |
| 1105 | 15q. "Althaea rosea" | 35 | 20 |
| 1106 | 25q. "Abutilon striatum" | 1·10 | 30 |
| 1107 | 35q. "Paeonia chinensis" | 1·30 | 50 |
| 1108 | 65q. "Gladiolus gandavensis" | 2·20 | 1·00 |
| 1109 | 80q. "Freesia hybrida" | 2·75 | 1·60 |
| 1110 | 1l.15 "Dianthus caryophyllus" | 3·25 | 1·80 |

**236** Congress Emblem

**1967.** 6th Trade Unions Congress, Tirana.

| | | | | |
|---|---|---|---|---|
| 1111 | **236** | 25q. red, sepia and lilac | 1·10 | 50 |
| 1112 | **236** | 1l.75 red, green and grey | 3·25 | 2·10 |

**237** Rose

**1967.** Roses.

| | | | | |
|---|---|---|---|---|
| 1113 | **237** | 5q. multicoloured | 45 | 20 |
| 1114 | - | 10q. multicoloured | 55 | 30 |
| 1115 | - | 15q. multicoloured | 65 | 40 |
| 1116 | - | 25q. multicoloured | 75 | 50 |
| 1117 | - | 35q. multicoloured | 1·10 | 65 |
| 1118 | - | 65q. multicoloured | 1·40 | 75 |
| 1119 | - | 80q. multicoloured | 1·60 | 1·00 |
| 1120 | - | 1l.65 multicoloured | 3·25 | 1·60 |

DESIGNS: 10q. to 1l.65 Various roses as Type **237**.

**238** Borsh Coast

**1967.** Albanian Riviera. Multicoloured.

| | | | |
|---|---|---|---|
| 1121 | 15q. Butrinti (vert) | 45 | 20 |
| 1122 | 20q. Type **238** | 55 | 25 |
| 1123 | 25q. Piqeras village | 1·10 | 30 |
| 1124 | 45q. Coastal view | 1·30 | 40 |
| 1125 | 50q. Himara coast | 1·50 | 50 |
| 1126 | 65q. Fishing boat, Saranda | 2·20 | 75 |
| 1127 | 80q. Dhermi | 2·40 | 1·00 |
| 1128 | 1l. Sunset at sea (vert) | 3·25 | 1·60 |

**239** Fawn

**1967.** Roe Deer. Multicoloured.

| | | | |
|---|---|---|---|
| 1129 | 15q. Type **239** | 55 | 20 |
| 1130 | 20q. Head of buck (vert) | 55 | 30 |
| 1131 | 25q. Head of doe (vert) | 1·10 | 50 |
| 1132 | 30q. Doe and fawn | 1·10 | 50 |
| 1133 | 35q. Doe and new-born fawn | 1·60 | 75 |
| 1134 | 40q. Young buck (vert) | 1·60 | 75 |
| 1135 | 65q. Buck and doe (vert) | 3·25 | 1·00 |
| 1136 | 70q. Running deer | 4·25 | 1·60 |

**240** Costumes of Malesia e Madhe Region

**1967.** National Costumes. Multicoloured.

| | | | |
|---|---|---|---|
| 1137 | 15q. Type **240** | 45 | 15 |
| 1138 | 20q. Zadrima | 50 | 20 |
| 1139 | 25q. Kukesi | 55 | 30 |
| 1140 | 45q. Dardhe | 85 | 50 |
| 1141 | 50q. Myzeqe | 1·00 | 75 |
| 1142 | 65q. Tirana | 1·30 | 85 |
| 1143 | 80q. Dropulli | 2·20 | 1·00 |
| 1144 | 1l. Laberise | 2·30 | 1·30 |

**241** Battle Scene and Newspaper

**1967.** 25 Years of the Albanian Popular Press. Mult.

| | | | |
|---|---|---|---|
| 1145 | 25q. Type **241** | 65 | 30 |
| 1146 | 75q. Newspapers and printery | 1·70 | 75 |
| 1147 | 2l. Workers with newspaper | 4·25 | 2·10 |

**242** University, Torch and Open Book

**1967.** 10th Anniv of Tirana University.

| | | | | |
|---|---|---|---|---|
| 1148 | **242** | 25q. multicoloured | 55 | 40 |
| 1149 | **242** | 1l.75 multicoloured | 3·50 | 1·80 |

**243** Soldiers and Flag

**1967.** 25th Anniv of Albanian Democratic Front. Multicoloured.

| | | | |
|---|---|---|---|
| 1150 | 15q. Type **243** | 35 | 20 |
| 1151 | 65q. Pick, rifle and flag | 1·10 | 50 |
| 1152 | 1l.20 Torch and open book | 2·40 | 1·30 |

**244** Grey Rabbits

**1967.** Rabbit-breeding. Multicoloured.

| | | | |
|---|---|---|---|
| 1153 | 15q. Type **244** | 35 | 15 |
| 1154 | 20q. Black and white rabbit (vert) | 45 | 20 |
| 1155 | 25q. Brown hare | 65 | 30 |
| 1156 | 35q. Brown rabbits | 1·10 | 40 |
| 1157 | 40q. Common rabbits | 1·30 | 50 |
| 1158 | 50q. Grey rabbit (vert) | 2·20 | 75 |
| 1159 | 65q. Head of white rabbit (vert) | 2·40 | 85 |
| 1160 | 1l. White rabbit | 3·50 | 1·60 |

**245** "Shkoder Wedding" (detail, Kole Idromeno)

**1967.** Albanian Paintings.

| | | | | |
|---|---|---|---|---|
| 1161 | **245** | 15q. multicoloured | 55 | 20 |
| 1162 | - | 20q. multicoloured | 75 | 30 |
| 1163 | - | 25q. multicoloured | 1·10 | 40 |
| 1164 | - | 45q. multicoloured | 1·30 | 50 |
| 1165 | - | 50q. multicoloured | 1·60 | 75 |
| 1166 | - | 65q. multicoloured | 2·20 | 85 |
| 1167 | - | 80q. multicoloured | 2·40 | 1·00 |
| 1168 | - | 1l. multicoloured | 4·25 | 1·30 |

DESIGNS—VERT: 20q. "Head of the Prophet David" (detail, 16th-century fresco); 45q. Ancient mosaic head (from Durres); 50q. Detail, 16th-century icon (30×51 mm); 1l. "Our Sister" (K. Idromeno). HORIZ (51×30 mm): 25q. "Commandos of the Hakmarrja Battalion" (S. Shijaku); 65q. "Co-operative" (farm women, Z. Shoshi); 80q. "Street in Korce" (V. Mio).

**246** Lenin and Stalin

**1967.** 50th Anniv of October Revolution. Mult.

| | | | |
|---|---|---|---|
| 1169 | 15q. Type **246** | 35 | 20 |
| 1170 | 25q. Lenin with soldiers (vert) | 75 | 50 |
| 1171 | 50q. Lenin addressing meeting (vert) | 1·10 | 75 |
| 1172 | 1l.10 Revolutionaries | 2·40 | 1·00 |

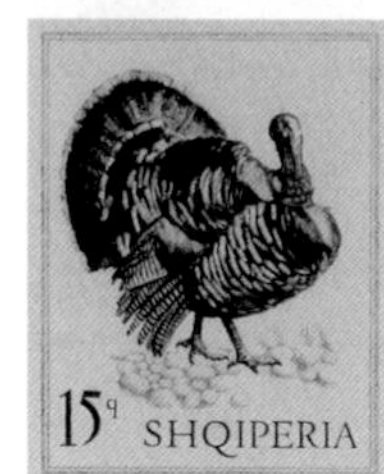

**247** Common Turkey

**1967.** Domestic Fowl. Multicoloured.

| | | | |
|---|---|---|---|
| 1173 | 15q. Type **247** | 20 | 10 |
| 1174 | 20q. Goose | 35 | 20 |
| 1175 | 25q. Hen | 55 | 30 |
| 1176 | 45q. Cockerel | 1·10 | 50 |
| 1177 | 50q. Helmeted guineafowl | 1·30 | 65 |
| 1178 | 65q. Greylag goose (horiz) | 1·60 | 75 |
| 1179 | 80q. Mallard (horiz) | 2·20 | 1·00 |
| 1180 | 1l. Chicks (horiz) | 3·25 | 1·30 |

**248** First Aid

**1967.** 6th Red Cross Congress, Tirana. Mult.

| | | | |
|---|---|---|---|
| 1181 | 15q.+5q. Type **248** | 1·10 | 65 |
| 1182 | 25q.+5q. Stretcher case | 2·20 | 1·00 |
| 1183 | 65q.+25q. Heart patient | 7·50 | 3·75 |
| 1184 | 80q.+40q. Nurse holding child | 11·00 | 5·25 |

**249** Arms of Skanderbeg

**1967.** 500th Death Anniv of Castriota Skanderbeg (patriot) (1st issue). Multicoloured.

| | | | |
|---|---|---|---|
| 1185 | 10q. Type **249** | 20 | 10 |
| 1186 | 15q. Skanderbeg | 35 | 15 |
| 1187 | 25q. Helmet and sword | 55 | 20 |
| 1188 | 30q. Kruja Castle | 65 | 30 |
| 1189 | 35q. Petrela Castle | 75 | 40 |
| 1190 | 65q. Berati Castle | 1·10 | 50 |
| 1191 | 80q. Meeting of chiefs | 2·20 | 75 |
| 1192 | 90q. Battle of Albulena | 2·30 | 1·00 |

See also Nos. 1200/7.

**250** Winter Olympic Emblem

**1967.** Winter Olympic Games, Grenoble. Mult.

| | | | |
|---|---|---|---|
| 1193 | 15q. Type **250** | 20 | 10 |
| 1194 | 25q. Ice hockey | 25 | 15 |
| 1195 | 30q. Figure skating | 35 | 20 |
| 1196 | 50q. Skiing (slalom) | 55 | 30 |
| 1197 | 80q. Skiing (downhill) | 1·10 | 50 |
| 1198 | 1l. Ski jumping | 2·40 | 1·30 |
| **MS**1199 | 58×67 mm. 2l. As Type **250** but larger. Imperf | 9·25 | 10·50 |

**251** Skanderbeg Memorial, Tirana

**1968.** 500th Death Anniv of Castriota Skanderbeg (2nd issue). Multicoloured.

| | | | |
|---|---|---|---|
| 1200 | 10q. Type **251** | 35 | 20 |
| 1201 | 15q. Skanderbeg portrait | 55 | 30 |
| 1202 | 25q. Skanderbeg portrait (different) | 1·00 | 40 |
| 1203 | 30q. Equestrian statue, Kruja (vert) | 1·10 | 45 |
| 1204 | 35q. Skanderbeg and mountains | 1·30 | 50 |
| 1205 | 65q. Bust of Skanderbeg | 2·20 | 75 |
| 1206 | 80q. Title page of biography | 3·00 | 1·60 |
| 1207 | 90q. "Skanderbeg battling with the Turks" (painting) (vert) | 3·50 | 2·10 |

**252** Alpine Dianthus

**1968.** Flowers. Multicoloured.

| | | | |
|---|---|---|---|
| 1208 | 15q. Type **252** | 20 | 10 |
| 1209 | 20q. Chinese dianthus | 25 | 15 |
| 1210 | 25q. Pink carnation | 35 | 20 |
| 1211 | 50q. Red carnation and bud | 1·10 | 30 |
| 1212 | 80q. Two red carnations | 1·60 | 50 |
| 1213 | 1l.10 Yellow carnations | 2·20 | 1·00 |

**253** Ear of Wheat and Electricity Pylon

**1968.** 5th Agricultural Co-operative Congress. Mult.

| | | | |
|---|---|---|---|
| 1214 | 25q. Type **253** | 55 | 30 |
| 1215 | 65q. Tractor (horiz) | 1·60 | 85 |
| 1216 | 1l.10 Cow | 2·20 | 1·30 |

**254** Long-horned Goat

**1968.** Goats. Multicoloured.

| | | | |
|---|---|---|---|
| 1217 | 15q. Zane female | 20 | 10 |
| 1218 | 20q. Kid | 35 | 15 |
| 1219 | 25q. Long-haired capore | 45 | 20 |
| 1220 | 30q. Black goat at rest | 55 | 25 |
| 1221 | 40q. Kids dancing | 65 | 30 |
| 1222 | 50q. Red and piebald goats | 75 | 50 |
| 1223 | 80q. Long-haired ankara | 1·60 | 65 |
| 1224 | 1l.40 Type **254** | 3·25 | 1·60 |

The 15q., 20q. and 25q. are vert.

**255** Zef Jubani

**1968.** 150th Birth Anniv of Zef Jubani (patriot).

| | | | | |
|---|---|---|---|---|
| 1225 | **255** | 25q. brown and yellow | 55 | 30 |
| 1226 | **255** | 1l.75 blue, black & vio | 2·75 | 1·60 |

**256** Doctor using Stethoscope

**1968.** 20th Anniv of W.H.O.

| | | | | |
|---|---|---|---|---|
| 1227 | **256** | 25q. red and green | 35 | 15 |
| 1228 | - | 65q. black, blue & yellow | 1·30 | 85 |
| 1229 | - | 1l.10 brown and black | 1·60 | 1·00 |

DESIGNS—HORIZ: 65q. Hospital and microscope. VERT: 1l.10, Mother feeding child.

**257** Servicewoman

**1968.** 25th Anniv of Albanian Women's Union.

| | | | | |
|---|---|---|---|---|
| 1230 | **257** | 15q. red and orange | 45 | 20 |
| 1231 | - | 25q. turquoise and green | 55 | 30 |
| 1232 | - | 60q. brown and ochre | 1·60 | 75 |
| 1233 | - | 1l. violet and light violet | 2·75 | 1·30 |

DESIGNS: 25q. Teacher; 60q. Farm-girl; 1l. Factory-worker.

**258** Karl Marx

**1968.** 150th Birth Anniv of Karl Marx. Mult.

| | | | |
|---|---|---|---|
| 1234 | 15q. Type **258** | 1·10 | 50 |
| 1235 | 25q. Marx addressing students | 1·60 | 75 |
| 1236 | 65q. "Das Kapital", "Communist Manifesto" and marchers | 2·75 | 1·60 |
| 1237 | 95q. Karl Marx | 4·25 | 3·75 |

**259** Heliopsis

**1968.** Flowers. Multicoloured.

| | | | |
|---|---|---|---|
| 1238 | 15q. Type **259** | 20 | 10 |
| 1239 | 20q. Red flax | 35 | 15 |
| 1240 | 25q. Orchid | 45 | 20 |
| 1241 | 30q. Gloxinia | 50 | 30 |
| 1242 | 40q. Orange lily | 55 | 40 |
| 1243 | 80q. Hippeastrum | 1·60 | 1·00 |
| 1244 | 1l.40 Purple magnolia | 2·75 | 1·60 |

**260** A. Frasheri and Torch

**1968.** 90th Anniv of Prizren Defence League.

| | | | | |
|---|---|---|---|---|
| 1245 | **260** | 25q. black and green | 55 | 20 |
| 1246 | - | 40q. multicoloured | 1·10 | 50 |
| 1247 | - | 85q. multicoloured | 1·60 | 1·00 |

DESIGNS: 40q. League headquarters; 85q. Frasheri's manifesto and partisans.

**261** "Shepherd" (A. Kushi)

**1968.** Paintings in Tirana Gallery. Multicoloured.

| | | | |
|---|---|---|---|
| 1248 | 15q. Type **261** | 15 | 10 |
| 1249 | 20q. "Tirana" (V. Mio) (horiz) | 20 | 10 |
| 1250 | 25q. "Highlander" (G. Madhi) | 20 | 10 |
| 1251 | 40q. "Refugees" (A. Buza) | 55 | 20 |
| 1252 | 80q. "Partisans at Shahin Matrakut" (S. Xega) | 1·10 | 30 |
| 1253 | 1l.50 "Old Man" (S. Papadhimitri) | 2·75 | 85 |
| 1254 | 1l.70 "Shkoder Gate" (S. Rrota) | 3·25 | 1·00 |
| **MS**1255 | 90×114 mm. 2l.50 "Shkoder Costume" (Z. Colombi) (51×71 mm) | 4·00 | 2·50 |

**262** Soldiers and Armoured Vehicles

**1968.** 25th Anniv of People's Army. Multicoloured.

| | | | |
|---|---|---|---|
| 1256 | 15q. Type **262** | 55 | 20 |
| 1257 | 25q. Sailor and naval craft | 65 | 25 |
| 1258 | 65q. Pilot and Ilyushin Il-28 and Mikoyan Gurevich MiG-17 aircraft (vert) | 2·20 | 1·00 |
| 1259 | 95q. Soldier and patriots | 3·25 | 1·60 |

**263** Common Squid

**1968.** Marine Fauna. Multicoloured.

| | | | |
|---|---|---|---|
| 1260 | 15q. Type **263** | 35 | 20 |
| 1261 | 20q. Common lobster | 40 | 30 |
| 1262 | 25q. Common northern whelk | 55 | 40 |
| 1263 | 50q. Edible crab | 70 | 50 |
| 1264 | 70q. Spiny lobster | 1·10 | 85 |
| 1265 | 80q. Common green crab | 1·90 | 1·00 |
| 1266 | 90q. Norwegian lobster | 2·20 | 1·60 |

**264** Relay-racing

**1968.** Olympic Games, Mexico. Multicoloured.

| | | | |
|---|---|---|---|
| 1267 | 15q. Type **264** | 15 | 10 |
| 1268 | 20q. Running | 20 | 10 |
| 1269 | 25q. Throwing the discus | 25 | 10 |
| 1270 | 30q. Horse-jumping | 35 | 20 |
| 1271 | 40q. High-jumping | 45 | 30 |
| 1272 | 50q. Hurdling | 55 | 40 |
| 1273 | 80q. Football | 1·10 | 50 |
| 1274 | 1l.40 High diving | 2·20 | 1·30 |
| **MS**1275 | 90×81 mm. 2l. Olympic Stadium (64×54 mm.) | 4·00 | 2·50 |

**265** Enver Hoxha (Party Secretary)

**1968.** Enver Hoxha's 60th Birthday.

| | | | | |
|---|---|---|---|---|
| 1276 | **265** | 25q. blue | 45 | 30 |
| 1277 | **265** | 35q. purple | 65 | 50 |
| 1278 | **265** | 80q. violet | 1·40 | 1·00 |
| 1279 | **265** | 1l.10 brown | 1·70 | 1·30 |
| **MS**1280 | | 80½×91 mm. **265** 1l.50 violet, red and gold. Imperf | £160 | £180 |

**266** Alphabet Book

**1968.** 60th Anniv of Monastir Language Congress.

| | | | | |
|---|---|---|---|---|
| 1281 | **266** | 15q. lake and green | 65 | 40 |
| 1282 | **266** | 85q. brown and green | 3·25 | 2·10 |

**267** Bohemian Waxwing

**1968.** Birds. Multicoloured.

| | | | |
|---|---|---|---|
| 1283 | 15q. Type **267** | 35 | 10 |
| 1284 | 20q. Rose-coloured starling | 55 | 20 |
| 1285 | 25q. River kingfishers | 75 | 30 |
| 1286 | 50q. Long-tailed tit | 1·10 | 50 |
| 1287 | 80q. Wallcreeper | 2·20 | 1·00 |
| 1288 | 1l.10 Bearded reedling | 3·25 | 1·60 |

**268** Mao Tse-tung

**1968.** Mao Tse-tung's 75th Birthday.

| | | | | |
|---|---|---|---|---|
| 1289 | **268** | 25q. black, red and gold | 1·10 | 50 |
| 1290 | **268** | 1l.75 black, red and gold | 7·00 | 4·75 |

**269** Adem Reka (dock foreman)

**1969.** Contemporary Heroes. Multicoloured.

| | | | |
|---|---|---|---|
| 1291 | 5q. Type **269** | 45 | 30 |
| 1292 | 10q. Pjeter Lleshi (telegraph linesman) | 55 | 40 |
| 1293 | 15q. M. Shehu and M. Kepi (fire victims) | 1·10 | 85 |
| 1294 | 25q. Shkurte Vata (railway worker) | 1·60 | 1·30 |
| 1295 | 65q. Agron Elezi (earthquake victim) | 1·90 | 1·40 |
| 1296 | 80q. Ismet Bruca (school-teacher) | 2·20 | 1·60 |
| 1297 | 1l.30 Fuat Cela (blind Co-op leader) | 3·25 | 2·10 |

**270** Meteorological Equipment

**1969.** 20th Anniv of Albanian Hydro-meteorology. Multicoloured.

| | | | |
|---|---|---|---|
| 1298 | 15q. Type **270** | 55 | 30 |
| 1299 | 25q. "Arrow" indicator | 85 | 50 |
| 1300 | 1l.60 Meteorological balloon and isobar map | 4·25 | 2·30 |

**271** "Student Revolutionaries" (P. Mele)

**1969.** Albanian Paintings since 1944. Mult.

| | | | |
|---|---|---|---|
| 1301 | 5q. Type **271** | 20 | 10 |
| 1302 | 25q. "Partisans 1914" (F. Haxhiu) (horiz) | 35 | 10 |
| 1303 | 65q. "Steel Mill" (C. Ceka) (horiz) | 55 | 20 |
| 1304 | 80q. "Reconstruction" (V. Kilica) (horiz) | 65 | 40 |
| 1305 | 1l.10 "Harvest" (N. Jonuzi) (horiz) | 1·30 | 75 |
| 1306 | 1l.15 "Seaside Terraces" (S. Kaceli) (horiz) | 1·60 | 1·30 |
| **MS**1307 | 111×91 mm. 2l. "Partisans' Meeting" (N. Zajmi). Imperf | 2·75 | 2·10 |

SIZES: The 25q., 80q., 1l.10 and 1l.15 are 50×30 mm.

**272** "Self-portrait"

**1969.** 450th Death Anniv of Leonardo da Vinci.

| | | | | |
|---|---|---|---|---|
| 1308 | **272** | 25q. agate, brown & gold | 35 | 15 |
| 1309 | - | 35q. agate, brown & gold | 65 | 20 |
| 1310 | - | 40q. agate, brown & gold | 85 | 50 |
| 1311 | - | 1l. multicoloured | 2·20 | 1·00 |
| 1312 | - | 2l. agate, brown & gold | 4·25 | 1·80 |
| **MS**1313 | | 65×95 mm. 2l. multicoloured. Imperf | 7·00 | 4·50 |

DESIGNS—VERT: 35q. "Lilies"; 1l. "Portrait of Beatrice"; 2l. "Portrait of a Lady". HORIZ: 40q. Design for "Helicopter".

**273** Congress Building

**1969.** 25th Anniv of Permet Congress. Mult.

| | | | |
|---|---|---|---|
| 1314 | 25q. Type **273** | 55 | 30 |
| 1315 | 2l.25 Two partisans | 4·25 | 3·25 |
| **MS**1316 | 95×101 mm. 1l. Albanian arms. Imperf | 50·00 | 65·00 |

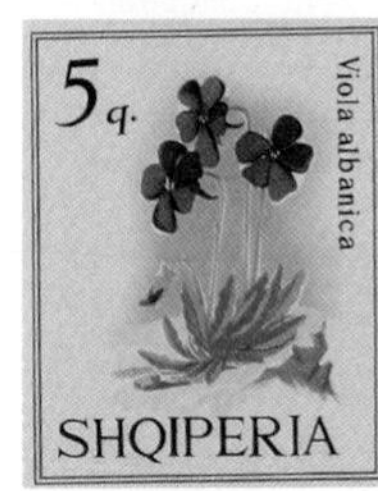

**274** "Viola albanica"

**1969.** Flowers. Viola Family. Multicoloured.

| | | | |
|---|---|---|---|
| 1317 | 5q. Type **274** | 15 | 10 |
| 1318 | 10q. "Viola hortensis" | 20 | 10 |
| 1319 | 15q. "Viola heterophylla" | 35 | 15 |
| 1320 | 20q. "Viola hortensis" (different) | 45 | 20 |
| 1321 | 25q. "Viola odorata" | 55 | 20 |
| 1322 | 80q. "Viola hortensis" (different) | 1·60 | 85 |
| 1323 | 1l.95 "Viola hortensis" (different) | 2·75 | 2·10 |

**275** Plum

**1969.** Fruit Trees. Blossom and Fruit. Mult.

| | | | |
|---|---|---|---|
| 1324 | 10q. Type **275** | 20 | 10 |
| 1325 | 15q. Lemon | 35 | 15 |
| 1326 | 25q. Pomegranate | 55 | 20 |
| 1327 | 50q. Cherry | 1·10 | 50 |
| 1328 | 80q. Apricot | 1·80 | 1·00 |
| 1329 | 1l.20 Apple | 2·75 | 1·60 |

**276** Throwing the Ball

**1969.** 16th European Basketball Championships, Naples. Multicoloured.

| | | | |
|---|---|---|---|
| 1330 | 10q. Type **276** | 35 | 10 |
| 1331 | 15q. Trying for goal | 45 | 15 |
| 1332 | 25q. Ball and net (horiz) | 55 | 20 |
| 1333 | 80q. Scoring a goal | 1·60 | 30 |
| 1334 | 2l.20 Intercepting a pass | 3·25 | 1·60 |

**277** Gymnastics

**1969.** National Spartakiad. Multicoloured.

| | | | |
|---|---|---|---|
| 1335 | 5q. Pickaxe, rifle, flag and stadium | 15 | 10 |
| 1336 | 10q. Type **277** | 20 | 10 |
| 1337 | 15q. Running | 35 | 10 |
| 1338 | 20q. Pistol-shooting | 45 | 15 |
| 1339 | 25q. Swimmer on starting block | 55 | 20 |
| 1340 | 80q. Cycling | 1·60 | 75 |
| 1341 | 95q. Football | 2·20 | 1·30 |

**278** Mao Tse-tung

**1969.** 20th Anniv of Chinese People's Republic. Multicoloured.

| | | | |
|---|---|---|---|
| 1342 | 25q. Type **278** | 1·60 | 50 |
| 1343 | 85q. Steel ladle and control room (horiz) | 5·50 | 2·10 |
| 1344 | 1l.40 Rejoicing crowd | 9·25 | 3·75 |

**279** Enver Hoxha

**1969.** 25th Anniv of 2nd National Liberation Council Meeting, Berat. Multicoloured.

| | | | |
|---|---|---|---|
| 1345 | 25q. Type **279** | 35 | 20 |
| 1346 | 80q. Star and Constitution | 85 | 50 |
| 1347 | 1l.45 Freedom-fighters | 2·20 | 1·30 |

**280** Entry of Provisional Government, Tirana

**1969.** 25th Anniv of Liberation. Multicoloured.

| | | | |
|---|---|---|---|
| 1348 | 25q. Type **280** | 45 | 20 |
| 1349 | 30q. Oil refinery | 55 | 25 |
| 1350 | 35q. Combine harvester | 75 | 30 |
| 1351 | 45q. Hydroelectric power station | 1·30 | 50 |
| 1352 | 55q. Soldier and partisans | 1·80 | 75 |
| 1353 | 1l.10 People rejoicing | 3·25 | 1·30 |

**281** Stalin

**1969.** 90th Birth Anniv of Joseph Stalin.

| | | | | |
|---|---|---|---|---|
| 1354 | **281** | 15q. lilac | 20 | 10 |
| 1355 | **281** | 25q. blue | 55 | 20 |
| 1356 | **281** | 1l. brown | 1·80 | 75 |
| 1357 | **281** | 1l.10 blue | 2·20 | 1·00 |

**282** Head of Woman

**1969.** Mosaics. (1st series). Multicoloured.

| | | | |
|---|---|---|---|
| 1358 | 15q. Type **282** | 20 | 10 |
| 1359 | 25q. Floor pattern | 35 | 20 |
| 1360 | 80q. Bird and tree | 1·10 | 50 |
| 1361 | 1l.10 Diamond floor pattern | 1·60 | 65 |
| 1362 | 1l.20 Corn in oval pattern | 2·20 | 75 |

Nos. 1359/61 are horiz.
See also Nos. 1391/6, 1564/70 and 1657/62.

**283** Manifesto and Congress Building

**1970.** 50th Anniv of Lushnje Congress.

| | | | | |
|---|---|---|---|---|
| 1363 | **283** | 25q. black, red and grey | 55 | 30 |
| 1364 | - | 1l.25 black, yell & grn | 3·25 | 2·10 |

DESIGN: 1l.25, Lushnje postmark of 1920.

**284** "25" and Workers

**1970.** 25th Anniv of Albanian Trade Unions.

| | | | | |
|---|---|---|---|---|
| 1365 | **284** | 25q. multicoloured | 55 | 30 |
| 1366 | **284** | 1l.75 multicoloured | 3·25 | 2·10 |

**285** "Lilium cernum"

**1970.** Lilies. Multicoloured.

| | | | |
|---|---|---|---|
| 1367 | 5q. Type **285** | 25 | 15 |
| 1368 | 15q. "Lilium candidum" | 35 | 20 |
| 1369 | 25q. "Lilium regale" | 55 | 30 |
| 1370 | 80q. "Lilium martagon" | 1·60 | 1·00 |
| 1371 | 1l.10 "Lilium tigrinum" | 2·20 | 1·40 |
| 1372 | 1l.15 "Lilium albanicum" | 2·75 | 1·80 |

Nos. 1370/2 are horiz.

**286** Lenin

**1970.** Birth Cent of Lenin. Each blk, silver & red.

| | | | |
|---|---|---|---|
| 1373 | 5q. Type **286** | 20 | 10 |
| 1374 | 15q. Lenin making speech | 45 | 20 |
| 1375 | 25q. As worker | 55 | 30 |
| 1376 | 95q. As revolutionary | 1·30 | 75 |
| 1377 | 1l.10 Saluting | 2·40 | 1·00 |

Nos. 1374/6 are horiz.

**287** Frontier Guard

**1970.** 25th Anniv of Frontier Force.

| | | | | |
|---|---|---|---|---|
| 1378 | **287** | 25q. multicoloured | 55 | 30 |
| 1379 | **287** | 1l.25 multicoloured | 2·75 | 1·80 |

**288** Jules Rimet Cup

**1970.** World Cup Football Championship, Mexico. Multicoloured.

| | | | |
|---|---|---|---|
| 1380 | 5q. Type **288** | 10 | 10 |
| 1381 | 10q. Aztec Stadium | 15 | 10 |
| 1382 | 15q. Three footballers | 20 | 10 |
| 1383 | 25q. Heading goal | 25 | 15 |
| 1384 | 65q. Two footballers | 55 | 20 |
| 1385 | 80q. Two footballers | 1·10 | 50 |
| 1386 | 2l. Two footballers | 2·75 | 1·40 |
| **MS**1387 | 81×74 mm. 2l. Mexican horse-man and Mt. Popocatepetil | 4·00 | 3·00 |

The design of **MS**1387 is larger, 56×45 mm.

**289** New U.P.U. Headquarters Building

**1970.** New U.P.U. Headquarters Building, Berne.

| | | | | |
|---|---|---|---|---|
| 1388 | **289** | 25q. blue, black and light blue | 35 | 15 |
| 1389 | **289** | 1l.10 pink, black & orge | 1·60 | 65 |
| 1390 | **289** | 1l.15 turq, blk & grn | 1·80 | 1·00 |

**290** Birds and Grapes

**1970.** Mosaics (2nd series). Multicoloured.

| | | | |
|---|---|---|---|
| 1391 | 5q. Type **290** | 20 | 10 |
| 1392 | 10q. Waterfowl | 35 | 10 |
| 1393 | 20q. Pheasant and tree stump | 45 | 15 |
| 1394 | 25q. Bird and leaves | 55 | 20 |
| 1395 | 65q. Fish | 1·10 | 50 |
| 1396 | 2l.25 Peacock (vert) | 3·75 | 2·10 |

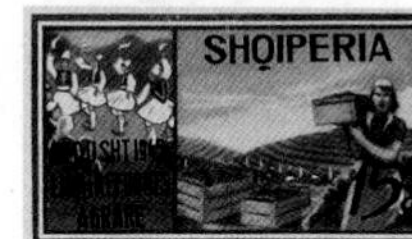

**291** Harvesters and Dancers

**1970.** 25th Anniv of Agrarian Reform.

| | | | | |
|---|---|---|---|---|
| 1397 | **291** | 15q. lilac and black | 45 | 20 |
| 1398 | - | 25q. blue and black | 55 | 30 |
| 1399 | - | 80q. brown and black | 1·60 | 50 |
| 1400 | - | 1l.30 brown and black | 2·20 | 1·00 |

DESIGNS: 25q. Ploughed fields and open-air conference; 80q. Cattle and newspapers; 1l.30, Combine-harvester and official visit.

**292** Partisans going into Battle

**1970.** 50th Anniv of Battle of Vlore.

| | | | | |
|---|---|---|---|---|
| 1401 | **292** | 15q. brown, orge & black | 35 | 20 |
| 1402 | - | 25q. brown, yell & black | 75 | 30 |
| 1403 | - | 1l.60 myrtle, grn & blk | 2·40 | 1·60 |

DESIGNS: 25q. Victory parade; 1l.60, Partisans.

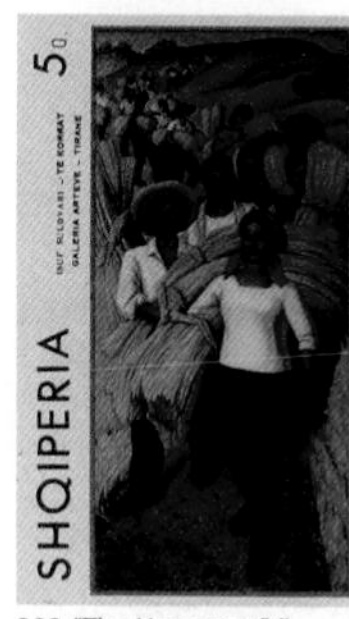

**293** "The Harvesters" (I. Sulovari)

**1970.** 25th Anniv of Liberation. Prize-winning Paintings. Multicoloured.

| | | | |
|---|---|---|---|
| 1404 | 5q. Type **293** | 10 | 10 |
| 1405 | 15q. "Return of the Partisan" (D. Trebicka) (horiz) | 20 | 10 |
| 1406 | 25q. "The Miners" (N. Zajmi) (horiz) | 25 | 15 |
| 1407 | 65q. "Instructing the Partisans" (H. Nallbani) (horiz) | 55 | 30 |
| 1408 | 95q. "Making Plans" (V. Kilica) (horiz) | 1·10 | 75 |
| 1409 | 2l. "The Machinist" (Z. Shoshi) | 3·25 | 2·10 |
| **MS**1410 | 67×96 mm. 2l. "The Guerrilla" (S. Shijaku). (54×75 mm). Imperf | 3·75 | 2·50 |

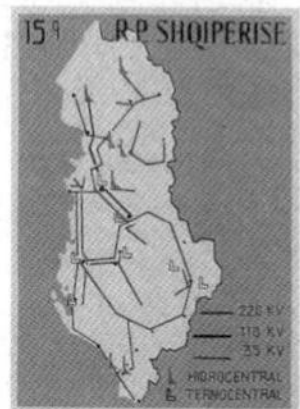

**294** Electrification Map

**1970.** Rural Electrification Completion. Mult.

| | | | |
|---|---|---|---|
| 1411 | 15q. Type **294** | 35 | 20 |
| 1412 | 25q. Lamp and graph | 55 | 30 |
| 1413 | 80q. Erecting power lines | 1·60 | 50 |
| 1414 | 1l.10 Uses of electricity | 1·80 | 1·00 |

**295** Engels

**1970.** 150th Birth Anniv of Friedrich Engels.

| | | | | |
|---|---|---|---|---|
| 1415 | **295** | 25q. blue and bistre | 55 | 20 |
| 1416 | - | 1l.10 purple and bistre | 1·60 | 75 |
| 1417 | - | 1l.15 olive and bistre | 1·80 | 85 |

DESIGNS: 1l.10, Engels as a young man; 1l.15, Engels making speech.

**295a** Tractor Factory, Tirana

**1971.** Industry. Multicoloured.

| | | | |
|---|---|---|---|
| 1417a | 10q. Type **295a** | £275 | £160 |

| | | | |
|---|---|---|---|
| 1417b | 15q. Fertiliser factory, Fier | £275 | £160 |
| 1417c | 20q. Superphosphate factory, Lac (vert) | £275 | £160 |
| 1417d | 25q. Cement factory, Elbasan | £275 | £160 |
| 1417e | 80q. Factory, Oytreki Stalin | £275 | £160 |

**296** Beethoven's Birthplace

**1970.** Birth Bicentenary of Beethoven.

| | | | | |
|---|---|---|---|---|
| 1418 | **296** | 5q. violet and gold | 20 | 10 |
| 1419 | - | 15q. purple and silver | 35 | 20 |
| 1420 | - | 25q. green and gold | 55 | 30 |
| 1421 | - | 65q. purple and silver | 1·30 | 85 |
| 1422 | - | 1l.10 blue and gold | 2·40 | 1·00 |
| 1423 | - | 1l.80 black and silver | 4·25 | 1·90 |

DESIGNS—VERT: Beethoven: 15q. In silhouette; 25q. As young man; 65q. Full-face; 1l.10, Profile. HORIZ: 1l.80, Stage performance of "Fidelio".

**297** Republican Emblem

**1971.** 25th Anniv of Republic.

| | | | | |
|---|---|---|---|---|
| 1424 | **297** | 15q. multicoloured | 35 | 20 |
| 1425 | - | 25q. multicoloured | 45 | 30 |
| 1426 | - | 80q. black, gold & green | 1·30 | 1·00 |
| 1427 | - | 1l.30 black, gold & brn | 1·80 | 1·40 |

DESIGNS: 25q. Proclamation; 80q. Enver Hoxha; 1l.30, Patriots.

**298** "Storming the Barricades"

**1971.** Centenary of Paris Commune.

| | | | | |
|---|---|---|---|---|
| 1428 | | 25q. blue and deep blue | 55 | 20 |
| 1429 | | 50q. green and grey | 75 | 40 |
| 1430 | **298** | 65q. chestnut and brown | 1·10 | 50 |
| 1431 | - | 1l.10 lilac and violet | 2·20 | 1·00 |

DESIGNS—VERT: 25q. "La Marseillaise"; 50q. Women Communards. HORIZ: 1l.10, Firing squad.

**299** "Conflict of Race"

**1971.** Racial Equality Year.

| | | | | |
|---|---|---|---|---|
| 1432 | **299** | 25q. black and brown | 35 | 20 |
| 1433 | - | 1l.10 black and red | 1·10 | 50 |
| 1434 | - | 1l.15 black and red | 1·30 | 65 |

DESIGNS—VERT: 1l.10, Heads of three races; 1l.15, Freedom fighters.

**300** Tulip

**1971.** Hybrid Tulips.

| | | | | |
|---|---|---|---|---|
| 1435 | **300** | 5q. multicoloured | 15 | 10 |
| 1436 | - | 10q. multicoloured | 20 | 10 |
| 1437 | - | 15q. multicoloured | 35 | 10 |
| 1438 | - | 20q. multicoloured | 45 | 15 |
| 1439 | - | 25q. multicoloured | 55 | 20 |
| 1440 | - | 80q. multicoloured | 1·60 | 50 |
| 1441 | - | 1l. multicoloured | 2·75 | 1·00 |
| 1442 | - | 1l.45 multicoloured | 4·25 | 2·10 |

DESIGNS: 10q. to 1l.45, Different varieties of tulips.

**301** "Postrider"

**1971.** 500th Birth Anniv of Albrecht Durer (painter and engraver).

| | | | | |
|---|---|---|---|---|
| 1443 | **301** | 10q. black and green | 20 | 10 |
| 1444 | - | 15q. black and blue | 45 | 15 |
| 1445 | - | 25q. black and blue | 55 | 20 |
| 1446 | - | 45q. black and purple | 1·10 | 50 |
| 1447 | - | 65q. multicoloured | 2·20 | 1·00 |
| 1448 | - | 2l.40 multicoloured | 6·50 | 2·10 |
| **MS**1449 | | 93×90 mm. 2l.50 multicoloured. Imperf | 5·50 | 3·75 |

DESIGNS—VERT: 15q. "Three Peasants"; 25q. "Peasant Dancers"; 45q. "The Bagpiper". HORIZ: 65q. "View of Kalchreut"; 2l.40, "View of Trient". LARGER: 2l.50, Self-portrait.

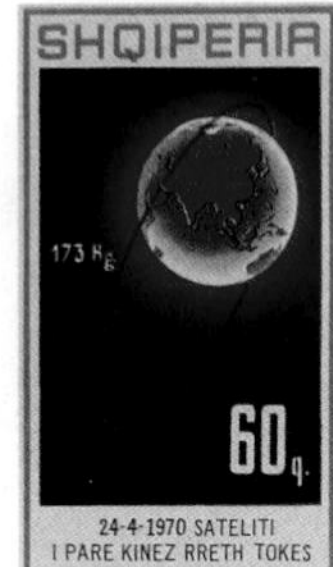


**302** Globe and Satellite (1970)

**1971.** Chinese Space Achievements. Multicoloured.

| | | | |
|---|---|---|---|
| 1450 | 60q. Type **302** | 1·10 | 50 |
| 1451 | 1l.20 Public Building, Tirana | 2·20 | 1·60 |
| 1452 | 2l.20 Globe and satellite (1971) | 4·25 | 3·25 |
| **MS**1453 | 65×112 mm. 2l.50 Globe and arrow. Imperf | 6·50 | 3·75 |

The date on No. 1451 refers to the passage of Chinese satellite over Tirana.

**303** Mao Tse-tung

**1971.** 50th Anniv of Chinese Communist Party. Multicoloured.

| | | | |
|---|---|---|---|
| 1454 | 25q. Type **303** | 85 | 50 |
| 1455 | 1l.05 Party Birthplace (horiz) | 2·20 | 1·60 |
| 1456 | 1l.20 Chinese celebrations (horiz) | 3·25 | 2·50 |

**304** Crested Tit

**1971.** Birds. Multicoloured.

| | | | |
|---|---|---|---|
| 1457 | 5q. Type **304** | 35 | 10 |
| 1458 | 10q. European serin | 45 | 15 |
| 1459 | 15q. Linnet | 65 | 15 |
| 1460 | 25q. Firecrest | 1·10 | 20 |
| 1461 | 45q. Rock thrush | 1·60 | 40 |
| 1462 | 60q. Blue tit | 2·40 | 1·00 |
| 1463 | 2l.40 Chaffinch | 9·75 | 8·25 |

**305** Running

**1971.** Olympic Games (1972). (1st issue). Mult.

| | | | |
|---|---|---|---|
| 1464 | 5q. Type **305** | 10 | 10 |
| 1465 | 10q. Hurdling | 15 | 10 |
| 1466 | 15q. Canoeing | 20 | 15 |
| 1467 | 25q. Gymnastics | 55 | 20 |
| 1468 | 80q. Fencing | 1·10 | 40 |
| 1469 | 1l.05 Football | 1·30 | 50 |
| 1470 | 3l.60 Diving | 4·50 | 1·60 |
| **MS**1471 | 70×83 mm. 2l. Runner breasting tape (47×54 mm). Imperf | 4·00 | 3·00 |

See also Nos. 1522/**MS**1530.

**306** Workers with Banner

**1971.** 6th Workers' Party Congress. Multicoloured.

| | | | |
|---|---|---|---|
| 1472 | 25q. Type **306** | 55 | 20 |
| 1473 | 1l.05 Congress hall | 1·60 | 1·40 |
| 1474 | 1l.20 "VI", flag, star and rifle (vert) | 2·20 | 1·60 |

**307** "XXX" and Red Flag

**1971.** 30th Anniv of Albanian Workers' Party. Multicoloured.

| | | | |
|---|---|---|---|
| 1475 | 15q. Workers and industry (horiz) | 20 | 10 |
| 1476 | 80q. Type **307** | 1·40 | 1·00 |
| 1477 | 1l.55 Enver Hoxha and flags (horiz) | 2·75 | 1·90 |

**308** "Young Man" (R. Kuci)

**1971.** Albanian Paintings. Multicoloured.

| | | | |
|---|---|---|---|
| 1478 | 5q. Type **308** | 10 | 10 |
| 1479 | 15q. "Building Construction" (M. Fushekati) | 15 | 10 |
| 1480 | 25q. "Partisan" (D. Jukniu) | 20 | 15 |
| 1481 | 80q. "Fighter Pilots" (S. Kristo) (horiz) | 1·10 | 20 |
| 1482 | 1l.20 "Girl Messenger" (A. Sadikaj) (horiz) | 1·40 | 85 |
| 1483 | 1l.55 "Medieval Warriors" (S. Kamberi) (horiz) | 1·60 | 1·40 |
| **MS**1484 | 89×70 mm. 2l. "Partisans in the Mountains" (I. Lulani). Imperf | 4·00 | 3·00 |

**309** Emblems and Flags

**1971.** 30th Anniv of Albanian Young Communists' Union.

| | | | | |
|---|---|---|---|---|
| 1485 | **309** | 15q. multicoloured | 20 | 10 |
| 1486 | **309** | 1l.35 multicoloured | 2·00 | 1·00 |

**310** Village Girls

**1971.** Albanian Ballet "Halili and Hajria". Mult.

| | | | |
|---|---|---|---|
| 1487 | 5q. Type **310** | 15 | 10 |
| 1488 | 10q. Parting of Halili and Hajria | 20 | 10 |
| 1489 | 15q. Hajria before Sultan Suleiman | 20 | 15 |
| 1490 | 50q. Hajria's marriage | 75 | 50 |
| 1491 | 80q. Execution of Halili | 1·30 | 75 |
| 1492 | 1l.40 Hajria killing her husband | 2·20 | 1·30 |

**311** Rifle-shooting (Biathlon)

**1972.** Winter Olympic Games, Sapporo, Japan. Multicoloured.

| | | | |
|---|---|---|---|
| 1493 | 5q. Type **311** | 10 | 10 |
| 1494 | 10q. Tobogganing | 15 | 10 |
| 1495 | 15q. Ice-hockey | 15 | 10 |
| 1496 | 20q. Bobsleighing | 20 | 10 |
| 1497 | 50q. Speed skating | 85 | 50 |
| 1498 | 1l. Slalom skiing | 1·30 | 85 |
| 1499 | 2l. Ski jumping | 2·40 | 1·90 |
| **MS**1500 | 71×91 mm. 2l.50 Figure skating. Imperf | 4·00 | 3·00 |

**312** Wild Strawberries

**1972.** Wild Fruits. Multicoloured.

| | | | |
|---|---|---|---|
| 1501 | 5q. Type **312** | 15 | 10 |
| 1502 | 10q. Blackberries | 15 | 10 |
| 1503 | 15q. Hazelnuts | 20 | 10 |
| 1504 | 20q. Walnuts | 45 | 15 |
| 1505 | 25q. Strawberry-tree fruit | 55 | 20 |
| 1506 | 30q. Dogwood berries | 75 | 50 |
| 1507 | 2l.40 Rowanberries | 4·25 | 1·60 |

**313** Human Heart

**1972.** World Health Day. Multicoloured.

| | | | |
|---|---|---|---|
| 1508 | 1l.10 Type **313** | 1·80 | 1·30 |
| 1509 | 1l.20 Treatment of cardiac patient | 2·00 | 1·40 |

**314** Congress Delegates

**1972.** 7th Albanian Trade Unions Congress. Mult.

| | | | |
|---|---|---|---|
| 1510 | 25q. Type **314** | 75 | 50 |
| 1511 | 2l.05 Congress Hall | 3·00 | 1·80 |

**315** Memorial Flame

**1972.** 30th Anniv of Martyrs' Day, and Death of Qemal Stafa.

| 1512 | **315** | 15q. multicoloured | 20 | 10 |
|---|---|---|---|---|
| 1513 | - | 25q. black, orge & grey | 55 | 20 |
| 1514 | - | 1l.90 black and ochre | 2·75 | 1·30 |

DESIGNS—VERT: 25q. "Spirit of Defiance" (statue). HORIZ: 1l.90, Qemal Stafa.

**316** "Camellia japonica Kamelie"

**1972.** Camellias.

| 1515 | **316** | 5q. multicoloured | 15 | 10 |
|---|---|---|---|---|
| 1516 | - | 10q. multicoloured | 20 | 10 |
| 1517 | - | 15q. multicoloured | 25 | 15 |
| 1518 | - | 25q. multicoloured | 55 | 20 |
| 1519 | - | 45q. multicoloured | 75 | 30 |
| 1520 | - | 50q. multicoloured | 1·30 | 50 |
| 1521 | - | 2l.50 multicoloured | 5·00 | 2·50 |

DESIGNS: Nos. 1516/21, Various camellias as Type **316**.

**317** High Jumping

**1972.** Olympic Games, Munich (2nd issue). Mult.

| 1522 | 5q. Type **317** | 10 | 10 |
|---|---|---|---|
| 1523 | 10q. Running | 15 | 10 |
| 1524 | 15q. Putting the shot | 20 | 10 |
| 1525 | 20q. Cycling | 35 | 15 |
| 1526 | 25q. Pole-vaulting | 45 | 20 |
| 1527 | 50q. Hurdling | 55 | 30 |
| 1528 | 75q. Hockey | 1·10 | 50 |
| 1529 | 2l. Swimming | 3·25 | 1·00 |
| **MS**1530 | 59×76 mm. 2l.50 High-diving (vert). Imperf | 4·00 | 3·00 |

**318** Articulated bus

**1972.** Modern Transport. Multicoloured.

| 1531 | 15q. Type **318** | 20 | 10 |
|---|---|---|---|
| 1532 | 25q. Czechoslovakian Class T699 diesel locomotive | 55 | 15 |
| 1533 | 80q. Freighter "Tirana" | 75 | 20 |
| 1534 | 1l.05 Motor-car | 1·30 | 50 |
| 1535 | 1l.20 Container truck | 2·20 | 1·00 |

**319** "Trial of Strength"

**1972.** 1st Nat Festival of Traditional Games. Mult.

| 1536 | 5q. Type **319** | 10 | 10 |
|---|---|---|---|
| 1537 | 10q. Pick-a-back ball game | 15 | 10 |
| 1538 | 15q. Leaping game | 20 | 10 |
| 1539 | 25q. Rope game | 55 | 20 |
| 1540 | 90q. Leap-frog | 1·60 | 75 |

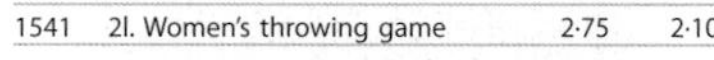

| 1541 | 2l. Women's throwing game | 2·75 | 2·10 |
|---|---|---|---|

**320** Newspaper "Mastheads"

**1972.** 30th Anniv of Press Day.

| 1542 | **320** | 15q. black and blue | 20 | 10 |
|---|---|---|---|---|
| 1543 | - | 25q. green, red & black | 35 | 15 |
| 1544 | - | 1l.90 black and mauve | 2·20 | 1·60 |

DESIGNS: 25q. Printing-press and partisan; 1l.90, Workers with newspaper.

**321** Location Map and Commemorative Plaque

**1972.** 30th Anniv of Peza Conference. Mult.

| 1545 | 15q. Type **321** | 35 | 20 |
|---|---|---|---|
| 1546 | 25q. Partisans with flag | 55 | 30 |
| 1547 | 1l.90 Conference Memorial | 3·00 | 1·90 |

**322** "Partisans Conference" (S. Capo)

**1972.** Albanian Paintings. Multicoloured.

| 1548 | 5q. Type **322** | 10 | 10 |
|---|---|---|---|
| 1549 | 10q. "Head of Woman" (I. Lulani) (vert) | 15 | 10 |
| 1550 | 15q. "Communists" (L. Shkreli) (vert) | 20 | 10 |
| 1551 | 20q. "Nendorit, 1941" (S. Shijaku) (vert) | 35 | 15 |
| 1552 | 50q. "Farm Woman" (Z. Shoshi) (vert) | 65 | 20 |
| 1553 | 1l. "Landscape" (D. Trebicka) | 1·30 | 75 |
| 1554 | 2l. "Girls with Bicycles" (V. Kilica) | 2·75 | 2·10 |
| **MS**1555 | 55×83 mm. 2l.30 "Folk Dance" (A. Buza) (vert, 40×67 mm). Imperf | 4·00 | 3·00 |

**323** Congress Emblem

**1972.** 6th Congress of Young Communists' Union.

| 1556 | **323** | 25q. gold, red and silver | 75 | 50 |
|---|---|---|---|---|
| 1557 | - | 2l.05 multicoloured | 3·00 | 1·80 |

DESIGN: 2l.05, Young worker and banner.

**324** Lenin

**1972.** 55th Anniv of Russian October Revolution. Multicoloured.

| 1558 | | 1l.10 multicoloured | 1·60 | 1·00 |
|---|---|---|---|---|
| 1559 | **324** | 1l.20 red, blk & pink | 3·25 | 1·30 |

DESIGN: 1l.10, Hammer and Sickle.

**325** Albanian Soldiers

**1972.** 60th Anniv of Independence.

| 1560 | **325** | 15q. blue, red and black | 15 | 15 |
|---|---|---|---|---|
| 1561 | - | 25q. black, red & yellow | 35 | 20 |
| 1562 | - | 65q. multicoloured | 85 | 50 |
| 1563 | - | 1l.25 black and red | 2·75 | 1·30 |

DESIGNS—VERT: 25q. Ismail Qemali; 1l.25, Albanian double-eagle emblem. HORIZ: 65q. Proclamation of Independence, 1912.

**326** Cockerel (mosaic)

**1972.** Ancient Mosaics from Apolloni and Butrint (3rd series). Multicoloured.

| 1564 | 5q. Type **326** | 10 | 10 |
|---|---|---|---|
| 1565 | 10q. Bird (vert) | 15 | 10 |
| 1566 | 15q. Partridges (vert) | 20 | 10 |
| 1567 | 25q. Warrior's leg | 45 | 30 |
| 1568 | 45q. Nude on dolphin (vert) | 55 | 40 |
| 1569 | 50q. Fish (vert) | 75 | 50 |
| 1570 | 2l.50 Warrior's head | 3·75 | 2·50 |

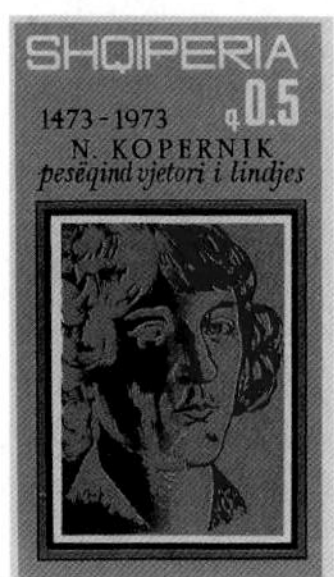

**327** Nicolas Copernicus

**1973.** 500th Birth Anniv of Copernicus. Mult.

| 1571 | 5q. Type **327** | 10 | 10 |
|---|---|---|---|
| 1572 | 10q. Copernicus and signatures | 15 | 10 |
| 1573 | 25q. Engraved portrait | 20 | 15 |
| 1574 | 80q. Copernicus at desk | 75 | 40 |
| 1575 | 1l.20 Copernicus and planets | 2·20 | 1·00 |
| 1576 | 1l.60 Planetary diagram | 3·25 | 1·60 |

**328** Policeman and Industrial Scene

**1973.** 30th Anniv of State Security Police.

| 1577 | **328** | 25q. black, blue & lt blue | 55 | 40 |
|---|---|---|---|---|
| 1578 | - | 1l.80 multicoloured | 3·00 | 1·80 |

DESIGN: 1l.80, Prisoner under escort.

**329/30** Cactus Flowers

**1973.** Cacti. As T **329/30**.

| 1579 | **329** | 10q. multicoloured | 10 | 10 |
|---|---|---|---|---|
| 1580 | **330** | 15q. multicoloured | 15 | 10 |
| 1581 | - | 20q. multicoloured | 20 | 10 |
| 1582 | - | 25q. multicoloured | 55 | 15 |
| 1583 | - | 30q. multicoloured | 4·25 | 2·50 |
| 1584 | - | 65q. multicoloured | 85 | 40 |
| 1585 | - | 80q. multicoloured | 1·10 | 50 |
| 1586 | - | 2l. multicoloured | 2·20 | 1·30 |

Nos. 1579/86 were issued together se-tenant within the sheet and in alternate formats as Types **329/30**.

**331** Common Tern

**1973.** Sea Birds. Multicoloured.

| 1587 | 5q. Type **331** | 25 | 15 |
|---|---|---|---|
| 1588 | 15q. White-winged black tern | 45 | 20 |
| 1589 | 25q. Black-headed gull | 55 | 30 |
| 1590 | 45q. Great black-headed gull | 1·10 | 75 |
| 1591 | 80q. Slender-billed gull | 2·20 | 1·60 |
| 1592 | 2l.40 Sandwich tern | 4·25 | 3·25 |

**332** Postmark of 1913, and Letters

**1973.** 60th Anniv of First Albanian Stamps. Mult.

| 1593 | 25q. Type **332** | 1·10 | 50 |
|---|---|---|---|
| 1594 | 1l.80 Postman and postmarks | 4·25 | 2·10 |

**333** Albanian Woman

**1973.** 7th Albanian Women's Congress.

| 1595 | **333** | 25q. red and pink | 55 | 30 |
|---|---|---|---|---|
| 1596 | - | 1l.80 black, orge & yell | 3·25 | 2·30 |

DESIGN: 1l.80, Albanian female workers.

**334** "Creation of the General Staff" (G. Madhi)

**1973.** 30th Anniv of Albanian People's Army. Mult.

| 1597 | 25q. Type **334** | 16·00 | 10·50 |
|---|---|---|---|
| 1598 | 40q. "August 1949" (sculpture by Sh. Haderi) (vert) | 16·00 | 10·50 |
| 1599 | 60q. "Generation after Generation" (Statue by H. Dule) (vert) | 16·00 | 10·50 |
| 1600 | 80q. "Defend Revolutionary Victories" (M. Fushekati) | 16·00 | 10·50 |

**335** "Electrification" (S. Hysa)

**1973.** Albanian Paintings. Multicoloured.

| 1601 | 5q. Type **335** | 10 | 10 |
|---|---|---|---|
| 1602 | 10q. "Textile Worker" (E. Nallbani) (vert) | 15 | 10 |
| 1603 | 15q. "Gymnastics Class" (M. Fushekati) | 15 | 10 |
| 1604 | 50q. "Aviator" (F. Stamo) (vert) | 65 | 40 |
| 1605 | 80q. "Downfall of Fascism" (A. Lakuriqi) | 75 | 50 |
| 1606 | 1l.20 "Koci Bako" (demonstrators (P. Mele)) (vert) | 1·10 | 85 |
| 1607 | 1l.30 "Peasant Girl" (Z. Shoshi) (vert) | 2·20 | 1·60 |
| **MS**1608 | 100×69 mm. 2l.05 "Battle of Tendes se Qypit" (F. Haxhiu) (88×47 mm). Imperf | 4·00 | 3·00 |

**336** "Mary Magdalene"

**1973.** 400th Birth Anniv of Caravaggio. Paintings. Multicoloured.

| | | | |
|---|---|---|---|
| 1609 | 5q. Type **336** | 10 | 10 |
| 1610 | 10q. "The Guitar Player" (horiz) | 15 | 10 |
| 1611 | 15q. Self-portrait | 20 | 10 |
| 1612 | 50q. "Boy carrying Fruit" | 65 | 40 |
| 1613 | 80q. "Basket of Fruit" (horiz) | 85 | 65 |
| 1614 | 1l.20 "Narcissus" | 1·30 | 1·00 |
| 1615 | 1l.30 "Boy peeling Apple" | 2·20 | 1·60 |
| **MS**1616 | 80×102 mm. 2l.05 "Man in Feathered Hat". Imperf | 6·00 | 5·25 |

**337** Goalkeeper with Ball

**1973.** World Cup Football Championship, Munich (1974) (1st issue). Multicoloured.

| | | | | |
|---|---|---|---|---|
| 1617 | **337** | 5q. multicoloured | 10 | 10 |
| 1618 | - | 10q. multicoloured | 15 | 10 |
| 1619 | - | 15q. multicoloured | 15 | 10 |
| 1620 | - | 20q. multicoloured | 20 | 15 |
| 1621 | - | 25q. multicoloured | 25 | 15 |
| 1622 | - | 90q. multicoloured | 1·30 | 40 |
| 1623 | - | 1l.20 multicoloured | 1·50 | 75 |
| 1624 | - | 1l.25 multicoloured | 2·20 | 1·00 |
| **MS**1625 | | 80×50 mm. 2l.05 multicoloured (Ball in net, and list of Championships). Imperf | 4·50 | 3·25 |

DESIGNS: Nos. 1618/24 are similar to Type **337**, showing goalkeepers saving goals.

See also Nos. 1663/70.

**338** Weightlifting

**1973.** World Weightlifting Championships, Havana, Cuba.

| | | | | |
|---|---|---|---|---|
| 1626 | **338** | 5q. multicoloured | 10 | 10 |
| 1627 | - | 10q. multicoloured | 15 | 10 |
| 1628 | - | 25q. multicoloured | 20 | 10 |
| 1629 | - | 90q. multicoloured | 75 | 40 |
| 1630 | - | 1l.20 mult (horiz) | 1·10 | 75 |
| 1631 | - | 1l.60 mult (horiz) | 2·20 | 1·20 |

DESIGNS: Nos. 1627/31 are similar to Type **338**, showing various lifts.

**339** Ballet Scene

**1973.** "Albanian Life and Work". Multicoloured.

| | | | |
|---|---|---|---|
| 1632 | 5q. Cement Works, Kavaje | 10 | 10 |
| 1633 | 10q. Ali Kelmendi truck factory and trucks (horiz) | 20 | 10 |
| 1634 | 15q. Type **339** | 55 | 10 |
| 1635 | 20q. Combine-harvester (horiz) | 25 | 10 |
| 1636 | 25q. "Telecommunications" | 85 | 20 |
| 1637 | 35q. Skier and hotel, Dajt (horiz) | 65 | 20 |
| 1638 | 60q. Llogora holiday village (horiz) | 1·10 | 45 |
| 1639 | 80q. Lake scene | 1·80 | 50 |
| 1640 | 1l. Textile mill (horiz) | 45 | 20 |
| 1641 | 1l.20 Furnacemen (horiz) | 1·30 | 50 |
| 1642 | 2l.40 Welder and pipeline (horiz) | 2·75 | 1·60 |
| 1643 | 3l. Skanderbeg Statue, Tirana | 4·25 | 2·50 |
| 1644 | 5l. Roman arches, Durres | 5·00 | 3·25 |

**340** Mao Tse-tung

**1973.** 80th Birth Anniv of Mao Tse-tung. Mult.

| | | | |
|---|---|---|---|
| 1645 | 85q. Type **340** | 2·75 | 1·60 |
| 1646 | 1l.20 Mao Tse-tung at parade | 3·75 | 2·50 |

**341** "Horse's Head" (Gericault)

**1974.** 150th Death Anniv of Jean-Louis Gericault (French painter).

| | | | | |
|---|---|---|---|---|
| 1647 | **341** | 10q. multicoloured | 15 | 10 |
| 1648 | - | 15q. multicoloured | 15 | 10 |
| 1649 | - | 20q. black and gold | 20 | 10 |
| 1650 | - | 25q. black, lilac and gold | 55 | 30 |
| 1651 | - | 1l.20 multicoloured | 2·20 | 75 |
| 1652 | - | 2l.20 multicoloured | 3·75 | 2·10 |
| **MS**1653 | | 90×68 mm. 2l.05 multicoloured. Imperf | 4·00 | 3·00 |

DESIGNS—VERT: 15q. "Male Model" (Gericault); 20q. "Man and Dog"; 25q. "Head of a Negro"; 1l.20, Self-portrait. HORIZ: 2l.20, "Battle of the Giants".

**342** "Lenin with Crew of the 'Aurora'" (D. Trebicka)

**1974.** 50th Death Anniv of Lenin. Multicoloured.

| | | | |
|---|---|---|---|
| 1654 | 25q. Type **342** | 55 | 30 |
| 1655 | 60q. "Lenin" (P. Mele) (vert) | 1·10 | 50 |
| 1656 | 1l.20 "Lenin" (seated) (V. Kilica) (vert) | 3·25 | 2·10 |

**343** Duck

**1974.** Ancient Mosaics from Butrint, Pogradec and Apolloni (4th series). Multicoloured.

| | | | |
|---|---|---|---|
| 1657 | 5q. Duck (different) | 10 | 10 |
| 1658 | 10q. Bird and flower | 15 | 10 |
| 1659 | 15q. Ornamental basket and grapes | 20 | 15 |
| 1660 | 25q. Type **343** | 35 | 20 |
| 1661 | 40q. Donkey and cockerel | 45 | 30 |
| 1662 | 2l.50 Dragon | 2·75 | 2·10 |

**344** Shooting at Goal

**1974.** World Cup Football Championships, Munich (2nd issue).

| | | | | |
|---|---|---|---|---|
| 1663 | **344** | 10q. multicoloured | 15 | 10 |
| 1664 | - | 15q. multicoloured | 15 | 10 |
| 1665 | - | 20q. multicoloured | 20 | 10 |
| 1666 | - | 25q. multicoloured | 35 | 15 |
| 1667 | - | 40q. multicoloured | 55 | 20 |
| 1668 | - | 80q. multicoloured | 1·10 | 50 |
| 1669 | - | 1l. multicoloured | 1·30 | 75 |
| 1670 | - | 1l.20 multicoloured | 1·80 | 1·40 |
| **MS**1671 | | 72×75 mm. 2l.05 multicoloured (Trophy and names of competing countries). Imperf | 4·00 | 3·00 |

DESIGNS: Nos. 1664/70, Players in action similar to Type **344**.

**345** Memorial and Arms

**1974.** 30th Anniv of Permet Congress. Mult.

| | | | |
|---|---|---|---|
| 1672 | 25q. Type **345** | 55 | 30 |
| 1673 | 1l.80 Enver Hoxha and text | 2·20 | 1·60 |

**346** "Solanum dulcamara"

**1974.** Useful Plants. Multicoloured.

| | | | |
|---|---|---|---|
| 1674 | 10q. Type **346** | 15 | 10 |
| 1675 | 15q. "Arbutus uva-ursi" (vert) | 15 | 10 |
| 1676 | 20q. "Convallaria majalis" (vert) | 20 | 10 |
| 1677 | 25q. "Colchicum autumnale" (vert) | 55 | 10 |
| 1678 | 40q. "Borago officinalis" | 75 | 20 |
| 1679 | 80q. "Saponaria officinalis" | 1·30 | 50 |
| 1680 | 2l.20 "Gentiana lutea" | 3·75 | 2·10 |

**347** Revolutionaries

**1974.** 50th Anniv of 1924 Revolution.

| | | | | |
|---|---|---|---|---|
| 1681 | **347** | 25q. mauve, black & red | 55 | 30 |
| 1682 | - | 1l.80 multicoloured | 2·20 | 1·60 |

DESIGN—VERT: 1l.80, Prominent revolutionaries.

**348** Redwing

**1974.** Song Birds. Multicoloured.

| | | | |
|---|---|---|---|
| 1683 | 10q. Type **348** | 20 | 10 |
| 1684 | 15q. European robin | 25 | 15 |
| 1685 | 20q. Western greenfinch | 35 | 15 |
| 1686 | 25q. Northern bullfinch (vert) | 55 | 20 |
| 1687 | 40q. Hawfinch (vert) | 85 | 25 |
| 1688 | 80q. Blackcap (vert) | 2·40 | 75 |
| 1689 | 2l.20 Nightingale (vert) | 4·25 | 2·10 |

**349** Globe and Post Office Emblem

**1974.** Centenary of Universal Postal Union. Multicoloured.

| | | | | |
|---|---|---|---|---|
| 1690 | **349** | 85q. multicoloured | 1·80 | 85 |
| 1691 | - | 1l.20 green, lilac & violet | 2·75 | 1·30 |
| **MS**1692 | | 78×78 mm. 2l.05 multicoloured. Imperf | 25·00 | 33·00 |

DESIGNS—Vert: 1l.20, U.P.U. emblem. Square: (70×70 mm.) 2l.50, Text on globe.

**350** "Widows" (Sali Shijaku)

**1974.** Albanian Paintings. Multicoloured.

| | | | |
|---|---|---|---|
| 1693 | 10q. Type **350** | 10 | 10 |
| 1694 | 15q. "Road Construction" (Danish Jukniu) (vert) | 20 | 10 |
| 1695 | 20q. "Fulfilling the Plans" (Clirim Ceka) | 25 | 10 |
| 1696 | 25q. "The Call to Action" (Spiro Kristo) (vert) | 45 | 20 |
| 1697 | 40q. "The Winter Battle" (Sabaudin Xhaferi) | 55 | 20 |
| 1698 | 80q. "Three Comrades" (Clirim Ceka) (vert) | 1·10 | 50 |
| 1699 | 1l. "Step by Step, Aid the Partisans" (Guri Madhi) | 1·60 | 1·00 |
| 1700 | 1l.20 "At the War Memorial" (Kleo Nini) | 2·20 | 1·30 |
| **MS**1701 | 87×78 mm. 2l.05 "Comrades" (Guri Madhi). Imperf | 4·00 | 3·00 |

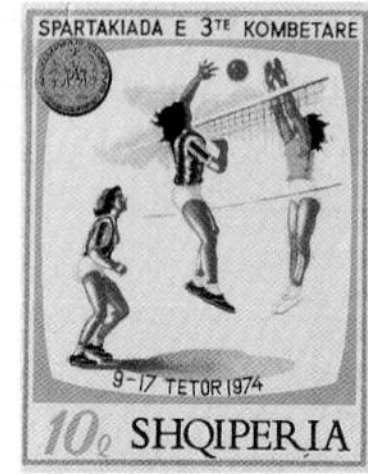


**351** Chinese Festivities

**1974.** 25th Anniv of Chinese People's Republic. Multicoloured.

| | | | | |
|---|---|---|---|---|
| 1702 | **351** | 85q. multicoloured | 3·50 | 2·10 |
| 1703 | - | 1l.20 black, red and gold | 5·50 | 3·25 |

DESIGN—VERT: 1l.20, Mao Tse-tung.

**352** Volleyball

**1974.** National Spartakiad. Multicoloured.

| | | | |
|---|---|---|---|
| 1704 | 10q. Type **352** | 10 | 10 |
| 1705 | 15q. Hurdling | 10 | 10 |
| 1706 | 20q. Hoop exercises | 15 | 10 |
| 1707 | 25q. Stadium parade | 20 | 15 |
| 1708 | 40q. Weightlifting | 55 | 20 |
| 1709 | 80q. Wrestling | 75 | 40 |
| 1710 | 1l. Rifle shooting | 1·10 | 45 |
| 1711 | 1l.20 Football | 1·60 | 50 |

**353** Berat

**1974.** 30th Anniv of 2nd Berat Liberal Council Meeting.

| | | | | |
|---|---|---|---|---|
| 1712 | **353** | 25q. red and black | 55 | 30 |
| 1713 | - | 80q. yellow, brown and black | 1·60 | 75 |
| 1714 | - | 1l. purple and black | 3·25 | 1·60 |

DESIGNS—HORIZ: 80q. "Liberation" frieze. VERT: 1l. Council members walking to meeting.

**354** Security Guards patrolling Industrial Plant

**1974.** 30th Anniv of Liberation. Multicoloured.

| | | | |
|---|---|---|---|
| 1715 | 25q. Type **354** | 15 | 10 |
| 1716 | 35q. Chemical industry | 20 | 10 |
| 1717 | 50q. Agricultural produce | 35 | 15 |
| 1718 | 80q. Cultural activities | 45 | 25 |
| 1719 | 1l. Scientific technology | 85 | 50 |
| 1720 | 1l.20 Railway construction | 1·20 | 75 |
| **MS**1721 | 81×70 mm. 2l.05 Albanians with book (60×40 mm). Imperf | 4·00 | 3·25 |

**355** Head of Artemis

**1974.** Archaeological Discoveries. Multicoloured.

| | | | | |
|---|---|---|---|---|
| 1722 | **355** | 10q. black, mauve & sil | 10 | 10 |
| 1723 | - | 15q. black, green and silver | 20 | 10 |
| 1724 | - | 20q. black, buff & silver | 35 | 20 |
| 1725 | - | 25q. black, mauve & sil | 55 | 40 |
| 1726 | - | 40q. multicoloured | 1·10 | 85 |
| 1727 | - | 80q. black, blue & silver | 1·60 | 1·30 |
| 1728 | - | 1l. black, green & silver | 2·20 | 1·60 |
| 1729 | - | 1l.20 black, sepia & sil | 3·75 | 2·10 |
| **MS**1730 | | 96×96 mm. 2l.05 multicoloured. Imperf | 4·00 | 3·25 |

DESIGNS: 15q. Statue of Zeus; 20q. Statue of Poseidon; 25q. Illyrian helmet; 40q. Greek amphora; 80q. Bust of Agrippa; 1l. Bust of Demosthenes; 1l.20, Bust of Bilia. Square: (84×84 mm.) 2l.50, Head of Artemis and Greek vase.

**356** Clasped hands

**1975.** 30th Anniv of Albanian Trade Unions. Mult.

| | | | |
|---|---|---|---|
| 1731 | 25q. Type **356** | 55 | 20 |
| 1732 | 1l.80 Workers with arms raised (horiz) | 2·20 | 1·40 |

**357** "Cichorium intybus"

**1975.** Albanian Flowers. Multicoloured.

| | | | |
|---|---|---|---|
| 1733 | 5q. Type **357** | 10 | 10 |
| 1734 | 10q. "Sempervivum montanum" | 10 | 10 |
| 1735 | 15q. "Aquilegia alpina" | 10 | 10 |
| 1736 | 20q. "Anemone hortensis" | 15 | 10 |
| 1737 | 25q. "Hibiscus trionum" | 15 | 10 |
| 1738 | 30q. "Gentiana kochiana" | 20 | 10 |
| 1739 | 35q. "Lavatera arborea" | 55 | 10 |
| 1740 | 2l.70 "Iris graminea" | 3·00 | 1·90 |

**358** Head of Jesus (detail, Doni Tondo)

**1975.** 500th Birth Anniv of Michelangelo. Mult.

| | | | | |
|---|---|---|---|---|
| 1741 | **358** | 5q. multicoloured | 10 | 10 |
| 1742 | - | 10q. brown, grey & gold | 10 | 10 |
| 1743 | - | 15q. brown, grey & gold | 15 | 10 |
| 1744 | - | 20q. sepia, grey and gold | 20 | 10 |
| 1745 | - | 25q. multicoloured | 20 | 10 |
| 1746 | - | 30q. brown, grey & gold | 20 | 10 |
| 1747 | - | 1l.20 brn, grey & gold | 1·10 | 65 |
| 1748 | - | 3l.90 multicoloured | 2·75 | 1·90 |
| **MS**1749 | | 77×86 mm. 2l.05 multicoloured. Imperf | 4·50 | 3·25 |

DESIGNS: 10q. "The Heroic Captive"; 15q. "Head of Dawn"; 20q. "Awakening Giant" (detail); 25q. "Cumaenian Sybil" (detail, Sistine chapel); 30q. "Lorenzo di Medici"; 1l.20, Head and shoulders of "David"; 3l.90, "Delphic Sybil" (detail, Sistine chapel). 70×77 mm. 2l.05, Head of Michelangelo.

**359** Horseman

**1975.** "Albanian Transport of the Past". Mult.

| | | | |
|---|---|---|---|
| 1750 | 5q. Type **359** | 10 | 10 |
| 1751 | 10q. Horse and cart | 15 | 10 |
| 1752 | 15q. Ferry | 25 | 10 |
| 1753 | 20q. Barque | 25 | 15 |
| 1754 | 25q. Horse-drawn cab | 35 | 15 |
| 1755 | 3l.35 Early car | 3·75 | 1·60 |

**360** Frontier Guard

**1975.** 30th Anniv of Frontier Force. Mult.

| | | | |
|---|---|---|---|
| 1756 | 25q. Type **360** | 55 | 30 |
| 1757 | 1l.80 Guards patrolling industrial plant | 2·20 | 1·60 |

**361** Patriot affixing Anti-fascist Placard

**1975.** 30th Anniv of "Victory over Fascism". Mult.

| | | | |
|---|---|---|---|
| 1758 | 25q. Type **361** | 35 | 20 |
| 1759 | 60q. Partisans in battle | 75 | 50 |
| 1760 | 1l.20 Patriot defeating Nazi soldier | 1·60 | 1·00 |

**362** European Wigeon

**1975.** Albanian Wildfowl. Multicoloured.

| | | | |
|---|---|---|---|
| 1761 | 5q. Type **362** | 10 | 10 |
| 1762 | 10q. Red-crested pochard | 15 | 10 |
| 1763 | 15q. White-fronted goose | 20 | 10 |
| 1764 | 20q. Pintail | 20 | 10 |
| 1765 | 25q. Red-breasted merganser | 35 | 15 |
| 1766 | 30q. Eider | 65 | 15 |
| 1767 | 35q. Whooper swans | 85 | 20 |
| 1768 | 2l.70 Common shoveler | 5·00 | 2·50 |

**363** "Shyqyri Kanapari" (Musa Qarri)

**1975.** Albanian Paintings. People's Art Exhibition, Tirana. Multicoloured.

| | | | |
|---|---|---|---|
| 1769 | 5q. Type **363** | 10 | 10 |
| 1770 | 10q. "Sea Rescue" (Agim Faja) | 10 | 10 |
| 1771 | 15q. "28 November 1912" (Petri Ceno) (horiz) | 10 | 10 |
| 1772 | 20q. "Workers' Meeting" (Sali Shijaka) | 15 | 10 |
| 1773 | 25q. "Shota Galica" (Ismail Lulani) | 15 | 10 |
| 1774 | 30q. "Victorious Fighters" (Nestor Jonuzi) | 20 | 15 |
| 1775 | 80q. "Partisan Comrades" (Vilson Halimi) | 65 | 40 |
| 1776 | 2l.25 "Republic Day Celebration" (Fatmir Haxhiu) (horiz) | 3·00 | 2·10 |
| **MS**1777 | 68×98 mm. 2l.05 "Folk dance" (Abdurahim Buza). Imperf | 3·75 | 3·25 |

**364** Farmer with Declaration of Reform

**1975.** 30th Anniv of Agrarian Reform. Mult.

| | | | |
|---|---|---|---|
| 1778 | 15q. Type **364** | 55 | 30 |
| 1779 | 2l. Agricultural scene | 2·75 | 1·80 |

**365** Dead Man's Fingers

**1975.** Marine Corals. Multicoloured.

| | | | |
|---|---|---|---|
| 1780 | 5q. Type **365** | 10 | 10 |
| 1781 | 10q. "Paramuricea chamaeleon" | 15 | 10 |
| 1782 | 20q. Red Coral | 20 | 10 |
| 1783 | 25q. Tube Coral or Sea Fan | 35 | 15 |
| 1784 | 3l.70 "Cladocora cespitosa" | 5·50 | 2·50 |

**366** Cycling

**1975.** Olympic Games, Montreal (1976). Mult.

| | | | |
|---|---|---|---|
| 1785 | 5q. Type **366** | 10 | 10 |
| 1786 | 10q. Canoeing | 10 | 10 |
| 1787 | 15q. Handball | 20 | 10 |
| 1788 | 20q. Basketball | 35 | 15 |
| 1789 | 25q. Water-polo | 45 | 15 |
| 1790 | 30q. Hockey | 55 | 20 |
| 1791 | 1l.20 Pole vaulting | 1·60 | 85 |
| 1792 | 2l.05 Fencing | 2·75 | 1·60 |
| **MS**1793 | 73×77 mm. 2l.15 Games emblem and sportsmen. Imperf | 6·50 | 6·50 |

**367** Power Lines leading to Village

**1975.** 5th Anniv of Electrification of Albanian Countryside. Multicoloured.

| | | | | |
|---|---|---|---|---|
| 1794 | **367** | 15q. multicoloured | 20 | 10 |
| 1795 | - | 25q. violet, red and lilac | 35 | 20 |
| 1796 | - | 80q. black, turq & green | 1·10 | 50 |
| 1797 | - | 85q. buff, brn & ochre | 2·20 | 1·80 |

DESIGNS: 25q. High power insulators; 80q. Dam and power station; 85q. T.V. pylons and emblems of agriculture and industry.

**368** Berat

**1975.** Air. Tourist Resorts. Multicoloured.

| | | | |
|---|---|---|---|
| 1798 | 20q. Type **368** | 35 | 20 |
| 1799 | 40q. Gjirokaster | 55 | 20 |
| 1800 | 60q. Sarande | 85 | 30 |
| 1801 | 90q. Durres | 1·60 | 50 |
| 1802 | 1l.20 Krujae | 2·20 | 1·00 |
| 1803 | 2l.40 Boga | 4·25 | 2·10 |
| 1804 | 4l.05 Tirana | 6·50 | 3·75 |

**369** Child, Rabbit and Bear planting Saplings

**1975.** Children's Tales. Multicoloured.

| | | | |
|---|---|---|---|
| 1805 | 5q. Type **369** | 10 | 10 |
| 1806 | 10q. Mrs. Fox and cub | 20 | 10 |
| 1807 | 15q. Ducks in school | 25 | 10 |
| 1808 | 20q. Bears building | 35 | 10 |
| 1809 | 25q. Animals watching television | 45 | 10 |
| 1810 | 30q. Animals with log and electric light bulbs | 50 | 10 |
| 1811 | 35q. Ants with spade and guitar | 55 | 20 |
| 1812 | 2l.70 Boy and girl with sheep and dog | 2·75 | 1·90 |

**370** Arms and Rejoicing Crowd

**1976.** 30th Anniv of Albanian People's Republic. Multicoloured.

| | | | |
|---|---|---|---|
| 1813 | 25q. Type **370** | 55 | 30 |
| 1814 | 1l.90 Folk-dancers | 3·75 | 1·60 |

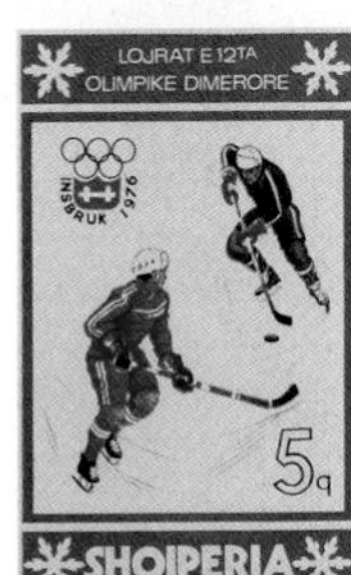


**371** Ice Hockey

**1976.** Winter Olympic Games, Innsbruck. Mult.

| | | | |
|---|---|---|---|
| 1815 | 5q. Type **371** | 10 | 10 |
| 1816 | 10q. Speed skating | 15 | 10 |
| 1817 | 15q. Rifle shooting (biathlon) | 20 | 10 |
| 1818 | 50q. Ski jumping | 35 | 15 |
| 1819 | 1l.20 Skiing (slalom) | 1·10 | 40 |
| 1820 | 2l.30 Bobsleighing | 2·00 | 1·00 |
| **MS**1821 | 66×80 mm. 2l.15 Figure skating (pairs) | 3·25 | 2·10 |

**372** "Colchicum autumnale"

**1976.** Medicinal Plants. Multicoloured.

| | | | |
|---|---|---|---|
| 1822 | 5q. Type **372** | 10 | 10 |
| 1823 | 10q. "Atropa belladonna" | 15 | 10 |
| 1824 | 15q. "Gentiana lutea" | 20 | 10 |
| 1825 | 20q. "Aesculus hippocastanum" | 20 | 10 |
| 1826 | 70q. "Polystichum filix" | 75 | 20 |
| 1827 | 80q. "Althaea officinalis" | 1·10 | 40 |
| 1828 | 2l.30 "Datura stamonium" | 2·75 | 2·10 |

**373** Wooden Bowl and Spoon

**1976.** Ethnographical Studies Conference, Tirana. Albanian Artifacts. Multicoloured.

| | | | |
|---|---|---|---|
| 1829 | 10q. Type **373** | 10 | 10 |
| 1830 | 15q. Flask (vert) | 15 | 10 |
| 1831 | 20q. Ornamental handles (vert) | 20 | 10 |
| 1832 | 25q. Pistol and dagger | 25 | 15 |
| 1833 | 80q. Hand-woven rug (vert) | 75 | 30 |
| 1834 | 1l.20 Filigree buckle and earrings | 1·10 | 50 |
| 1835 | 1l.40 Jugs with handles (vert) | 2·20 | 1·40 |

**374** "Founding the Co-operatives" (Zef Shoshi)

**1976.** Albanian Paintings. Multicoloured.

| | | | |
|---|---|---|---|
| 1836 | 5q. Type **374** | 10 | 10 |
| 1837 | 10q. "Going to Work" (Agim Zajmi) (vert) | 15 | 10 |
| 1838 | 25q. "Listening to Broadcast" (Vilson Kilica) | 20 | 10 |
| 1839 | 40q. "Female Welder" (Sabaudin Xhaferi) (vert) | 45 | 20 |
| 1840 | 50q. "Steel Workers" (Isuf Sulovari) (vert) | 85 | 30 |
| 1841 | 1l.20 "1942 Revolt" (Lec Shkreli) (vert) | 1·10 | 85 |
| 1842 | 1l.60 "Returning from Work" (Agron Dine) | 1·60 | 1·00 |
| **MS**1843 | 93×79 mm. 2l.05 "The Young Pioneer" (Andon Lakuriqi) | 3·25 | 2·10 |

**375** Demonstrators attacking Police

**1976.** 35th Anniv of Hoxha's Anti-fascist Demonstration. Multicoloured.

| | | | |
|---|---|---|---|
| 1844 | 25q. Type **375** | 55 | 20 |
| 1845 | 1l.90 Crowd with flag | 3·25 | 2·10 |

**376** Party Flag, Industry and Agriculture

**1976.** 7th Workers' Party Congress. Multicoloured.

| | | | |
|---|---|---|---|
| 1846 | 25q. Type **376** | 55 | 20 |
| 1847 | 1l.20 Hand holding Party symbols, and flag | 2·20 | 1·60 |

**377** Communist Advance

**1976.** 35th Anniv of Workers' Party. Mult.

| | | | |
|---|---|---|---|
| 1848 | 15q. Type **377** | 20 | 10 |
| 1849 | 25q. Hands holding emblems and revolutionary army | 55 | 30 |
| 1850 | 80q. "Reconstruction" | 1·10 | 50 |
| 1851 | 1l.20 "Heavy Industry and Agriculture" | 1·60 | 1·00 |
| 1852 | 1l.70 "The Arts" (ballet) | 2·20 | 1·60 |

**378** Young Communist

**1976.** 35th Anniv of Young Communists' Union. Multicoloured.

| | | | |
|---|---|---|---|
| 1853 | 80q. Type **378** | 2·10 | 1·00 |
| 1854 | 1l.25 Young Communists in action | 2·75 | 2·10 |

**379** Ballet Dancers

**1976.** Albanian Ballet "Cuca e Malexe".

| | | | | |
|---|---|---|---|---|
| 1855 | **379** | 10q. multicoloured | 10 | 30 |
| 1856 | - | 15q. multicoloured | 20 | 50 |
| 1857 | - | 20q. multicoloured | 35 | 1·00 |
| 1858 | - | 25q. multicoloured | 55 | 2·10 |
| 1859 | - | 80q. multicoloured | 1·30 | 3·25 |
| 1860 | - | 1l.20 multicoloured | 1·80 | 3·75 |
| 1861 | - | 1l.40 multicoloured | 2·20 | 4·25 |
| **MS**1862 | | 77×67 mm. 2l.05 multicoloured. Imperf | 5·00 | 5·25 |

DESIGNS: 15q. to 2l.50, Various ballet scenes.

**380** Bashtoves Castle

**1976.** Albanian Castles.

| | | | | |
|---|---|---|---|---|
| 1863 | **380** | 10q. black and blue | 10 | 10 |
| 1864 | - | 15q. black and green | 15 | 10 |
| 1865 | - | 20q. black and grey | 20 | 15 |
| 1866 | - | 25q. black and ochre | 35 | 20 |
| 1867 | - | 80q. black, pink and red | 1·10 | 50 |
| 1868 | - | 1l.20 black and blue | 1·60 | 95 |
| 1869 | - | 1l.40 black, red & pink | 1·70 | 1·00 |

DESIGNS: 15q. Gjirokaster; 20q. All Pash Tepelenes; 25q. Petreles; 80q. Berat; 1l.20, Durres; 1l.40, Krujes.

**381** Skanderbeg's Shield and Spear

**1977.** Crest and Arms of Skanderbeg's Army. Mult.

| | | | |
|---|---|---|---|
| 1870 | 15q. Type **381** | 2·20 | 50 |
| 1871 | 80q. Helmet, sword and scabbard | 7·50 | 3·75 |
| 1872 | 1l. Halberd, spear, bow and arrows | 12·00 | 9·50 |

**382** Ilya Oiqi

**1977.** Albanian Heroes. Multicoloured.

| | | | |
|---|---|---|---|
| 1873 | 5q. Type **382** | 10 | 10 |
| 1874 | 10q. Ilia Dashi | 20 | 20 |
| 1875 | 25q. Fran Ndue Ivanaj | 55 | 30 |
| 1876 | 80q. Zeliha Allmetaj | 1·60 | 50 |
| 1877 | 1l. Ylli Zaimi | 1·80 | 75 |
| 1878 | 1l.90 Isuf Plloci | 3·75 | 1·30 |

**383** Polyvinyl-chloride Plant, Vlore

**1977.** 6th Five-year Plan. Multicoloured.

| | | | |
|---|---|---|---|
| 1879 | 15q. Type **383** | 35 | 30 |
| 1880 | 25q. Naphtha plant, Ballsh | 55 | 40 |
| 1881 | 65q. Hydroelectric station, Fjerzes | 1·60 | 85 |
| 1882 | 1l. Metallurgical combinate, Elbasan | 2·40 | 1·00 |

**384** Shote Galica

**1977.** 50th Death Anniv of Shote Galica (Communist partisan).

| | | | | |
|---|---|---|---|---|
| 1883 | **384** | 80q. red and pink | 1·60 | 85 |
| 1884 | - | 1l.25 grey and blue | 2·40 | 1·50 |

DESIGN: 1l.25, Shote Galica and father.

**385** Crowd and Martyrs' Monument, Tirana

**1977.** 35th Anniv of Martyrs' Day. Multicoloured.

| | | | |
|---|---|---|---|
| 1885 | 25q. Type **385** | 55 | 30 |
| 1886 | 80q. Clenched fist and Albanian flag | 1·80 | 75 |
| 1887 | 1l.20 Bust of Qemal Stafa | 3·25 | 1·60 |

**386** Doctor calling at Village House

**1977.** "Socialist Transformation of the Villages". Multicoloured.

| | | | |
|---|---|---|---|
| 1888 | 5q. Type **386** | 10 | 10 |
| 1889 | 10q. Cowherd with cattle | 15 | 10 |
| 1890 | 20q. Harvesting | 20 | 20 |
| 1891 | 80q. Modern village | 1·60 | 75 |
| 1892 | 2l.95 Tractor and greenhouse | 6·00 | 1·60 |

**387** Workers outside Factory

**1977.** 8th Trade Unions Congress. Multicoloured.

| | | | |
|---|---|---|---|
| 1893 | 25q. Type **387** | 55 | 30 |
| 1894 | 1l.80 Three workers with flags | 3·75 | 2·10 |

**388** Advancing Soldiers

**1977.** "All the People are Soldiers". Multicoloured.

| | | | |
|---|---|---|---|
| 1895 | 15q. Type **388** | 40 | 20 |
| 1896 | 25q. Enver Hoxha and marching soldiers | 55 | 30 |
| 1897 | 80q. Soldiers and workers | 1·60 | 1·00 |
| 1898 | 1l. The Armed Forces | 2·75 | 2·10 |
| 1899 | 1l.90 Marching soldiers and workers | 4·25 | 3·75 |

**389** Two Girls with Handkerchiefs

**1977.** National Costume Dances (1st series). Mult.

| | | | |
|---|---|---|---|
| 1900 | 5q. Type **389** | 10 | 10 |
| 1901 | 10q. Two male dancers | 15 | 10 |
| 1902 | 15q. Man and woman in kerchief dance | 15 | 15 |
| 1903 | 25q. Two male dancers (different) | 20 | 15 |
| 1904 | 80q. Two women dancers with kerchiefs | 75 | 40 |
| 1905 | 1l.20 "Elbow dance" | 1·10 | 50 |
| 1906 | 1l.55 Two women with kerchiefs (different) | 1·60 | 1·00 |
| **MS**1907 | 56×74 mm. 2l.05 Sabre dance | 4·00 | 3·25 |

See also Nos. 1932/6 and 1991/5.

**390** Armed Worker with Book

**1977.** New Constitution.

| | | | | |
|---|---|---|---|---|
| 1908 | **390** | 25q. gold, red and black | 55 | 30 |
| 1909 | - | 1l.20 gold, red and black | 2·20 | 1·00 |

DESIGN: 1l.20, Industrial and agricultural symbols and hand with book.

**391** "Beni Ecen Vet"

**1977.** Albanian Films.

| No. | Type | Description | Mint | Used |
|---|---|---|---|---|
| 1910 | **391** | 10q. green and grey | 20 | 10 |
| 1911 | - | 15q. multicoloured | 35 | 10 |
| 1912 | - | 25q. green, black & grey | 55 | 30 |
| 1913 | - | 80q. multicoloured | 2·20 | 1·60 |
| 1914 | - | 1l.20 brown and grey | 3·25 | 2·50 |
| 1915 | - | 1l.60 multicoloured | 3·75 | 3·25 |

DESIGNS: 15q. "Rruge te Bardha"; 25q. "Rrugicat qe Kerkonin Diell"; 80q. "Ne Fillim te Veres"; 1l.20, "Lulekuqet Mbi Mure"; 1l.60, "Zonja nga Qyteti".

**392** Rejoicing Crowd and Independence Memorial, Tirana

**1977.** 65th Anniv of Independence. Multicoloured.

| No. | Description | Mint | Used |
|---|---|---|---|
| 1916 | 15q. Type **392** | 15 | 15 |
| 1917 | 25q. Independence leaders marching in Tirana | 55 | 30 |
| 1918 | 1l.65 Albanians dancing under national flag | 3·75 | 2·10 |

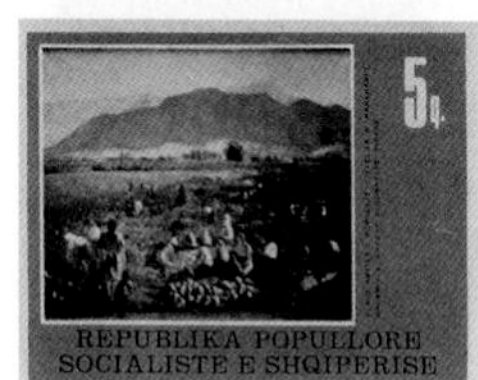

**393** "Farm Workers"

**1977.** Paintings by V. Mio. Multicoloured.

| No. | Description | Mint | Used |
|---|---|---|---|
| 1919 | 5q. Type **393** | 10 | 10 |
| 1920 | 10q. "Landscape in the Snow" | 10 | 10 |
| 1921 | 15q. "Sheep under a Walnut Tree, Springtime" | 15 | 10 |
| 1922 | 25q. "Street in Korce" | 25 | 10 |
| 1923 | 80q. "Riders in the Mountains" | 65 | 30 |
| 1924 | 1l. "Boats by the Seashore" | 1·10 | 65 |
| 1925 | 1l.75 "Tractors Ploughing" | 1·80 | 1·30 |
| **MS**1926 | 67×102 mm. 2l.05 "Self-portrait" | 4·00 | 3·25 |

**394** Pan Flute

**1978.** Folk Music Instruments.

| No. | Type | Description | Mint | Used |
|---|---|---|---|---|
| 1927 | **394** | 15q. red, black and green | 55 | 30 |
| 1928 | - | 25q. yellow, black & vio | 1·10 | 50 |
| 1929 | - | 80q. red, black and blue | 2·75 | 1·60 |
| 1930 | - | 1l.20 yellow, blk & blue | 5·50 | 3·25 |
| 1931 | - | 1l.70 lilac, black & grn | 12·00 | 7·25 |

DESIGNS: 25q. Single-string goat's head fiddle; 80q. Trumpet; 1l.20, Drum; 1l.70, Bagpipes.

**1978.** National Costume Dances (2nd series). As T **389**. Multicoloured.

| No. | Description | Mint | Used |
|---|---|---|---|
| 1932 | 5q. Girl dancers with scarves | 20 | 10 |
| 1933 | 25q. Male dancers | 35 | 20 |
| 1934 | 80q. Kneeling dancers | 85 | 50 |
| 1935 | 1l. Female dancers | 1·10 | 85 |
| 1936 | 2l.30 Male dancers with linked arms | 2·75 | 2·10 |

**395** "Tractor Drivers" (D. Trebicka)

**1978.** Paintings of the Working Class. Mult.

| No. | Description | Mint | Used |
|---|---|---|---|
| 1937 | 25q. Type **395** | 20 | 10 |
| 1938 | 80q. "Steeplejack" (S. Kristo) | 55 | 30 |
| 1939 | 85q. "A Point in the Discussion" (S. Milori) | 65 | 40 |
| 1940 | 90q. "Oil Rig Crew" (A. Cini) (vert) | 75 | 50 |
| 1941 | 1l.60 "Metal Workers" (R. Karanxha) | 1·60 | 1·00 |
| **MS**1942 | 73×99 mm. 2l.20 "The Political Discussion" (S. Sholla) | 7·50 | 4·75 |

**396** Boy and Girl

**1978.** International Children's Day. Multicoloured.

| No. | Description | Mint | Used |
|---|---|---|---|
| 1943 | 5q. Type **396** | 20 | 10 |
| 1944 | 10q. Boy and girl with pickaxe and rifle | 35 | 20 |
| 1945 | 25q. Children dancing | 75 | 50 |
| 1946 | 1l.80 Classroom scene | 4·00 | 3·25 |

**397** Woman with Pickaxe and Rifle

**1978.** 8th Women's Union Congress.

| No. | Type | Description | Mint | Used |
|---|---|---|---|---|
| 1947 | **397** | 25q. red and gold | 55 | 30 |
| 1948 | - | 1l.95 red and gold | 8·25 | 5·25 |

DESIGN: 1l.95, Peasant, Militia Guard and industrial installation.

**398** Battle of Mostar Bridge

**1978.** Centenary of the League of Prizren.

| No. | Type | Description | Mint | Used |
|---|---|---|---|---|
| 1949 | **398** | 10q. multicoloured | 20 | 10 |
| 1950 | - | 25q. multicoloured | 35 | 20 |
| 1951 | - | 80q. multicoloured | 1·60 | 1·00 |
| 1952 | - | 1l.20 blue, black & vio | 2·20 | 1·60 |
| 1953 | - | 1l.65 multicoloured | 3·25 | 2·50 |
| 1954 | - | 2l.60 lt grn, blk & grn | 5·50 | 4·75 |
| **MS**1955 | | 75×69 mm. 2l.20 multicoloured | 5·50 | 4·25 |

DESIGNS: 25q. Spirit of Skanderbeg; 80q. Albanians marching under national flag; 1l.20, Riflemen; 1l.65, Abdyl Frasheri (founder); 2l.20, League building, crossed rifles, pens and paper; 2l.60, League Headquarters, Prizren.

**399** Guerillas and Flag

**1978.** 35th Anniv of People's Army.

| No. | Description | Mint | Used |
|---|---|---|---|
| 1956 | 5q. Type **399** | 55 | 30 |
| 1957 | 25q. Men of armed forces (horiz) | 1·10 | 50 |
| 1958 | 1l.90 Men of armed forces, civil guards and Young Pioneers | 7·00 | 6·25 |

**1978.** International Fair, Riccione. No. 1832 surch **3.30L. RICCIONE 78 26.8.78.**

| No. | Description | Mint | Used |
|---|---|---|---|
| 1959 | 3l.30 on 25q. multicoloured | 17·00 | 15·00 |

**401** Man with Target Rifle

**1978.** 32nd National Shooting Championships.

| No. | Type | Description | Mint | Used |
|---|---|---|---|---|
| 1960 | **401** | 25q. black and yellow | 35 | 20 |
| 1961 | - | 80q. black and orange | 75 | 65 |
| 1962 | - | 95q. black and red | 1·10 | 85 |
| 1963 | - | 2l.40 black and red | 2·75 | 2·50 |

DESIGNS—VERT: 80q. Woman with machine carbine; 2l.40, Pistol shooting. HORIZ: 95q. Shooting from prone position.

**402** Kerchief Dance

**1978.** National Folklore Festival, Gjirokaster. Mult.

| No. | Description | Mint | Used |
|---|---|---|---|
| 1964 | 10q. Type **402** | 10 | 10 |
| 1965 | 15q. Musicians | 15 | 10 |
| 1966 | 25q. Fiddle player | 20 | 15 |
| 1967 | 80q. Singers | 55 | 30 |
| 1968 | 1l.20 Sabre dance | 1·20 | 75 |
| 1969 | 1l.90 Girl dancers | 2·40 | 1·80 |

**403** Enver Hoxha (after V. Kilica)

**1978.** Enver Hoxha's 70th Birthday.

| No. | Type | Description | Mint | Used |
|---|---|---|---|---|
| 1970 | **403** | 80q. multicoloured | 55 | 30 |
| 1971 | **403** | 1l.20 multicoloured | 1·10 | 50 |
| 1972 | **403** | 2l.40 multicoloured | 2·20 | 1·60 |
| **MS**1973 | | 68×88 mm. **403** 2l.20 multicoloured | 4·25 | 3·25 |

**404** Woman with Wheatsheaf

**1978.** Agriculture and Stock Raising. Multicoloured.

| No. | Description | Mint | Used |
|---|---|---|---|
| 1974 | 15q. Type **404** | 55 | 30 |
| 1975 | 25q. Woman with boxes of fruit | 75 | 50 |
| 1976 | 80q. Shepherd and flock | 2·75 | 2·10 |
| 1977 | 2l.60 Dairymaid and cattle | 9·75 | 7·25 |

**405** Pupils entering School

**1978**

| No. | Type | Description | Mint | Used |
|---|---|---|---|---|
| 1978 | **405** | 5q. brown, lt brn & gold | 15 | 10 |
| 1979 | - | 10q. blue, lt bl & gold | 20 | 10 |
| 1980 | - | 15q. violet, lilac and gold | 35 | 15 |
| 1981 | - | 20q. brown, drab & gold | 45 | 20 |
| 1982 | - | 25q. red, pink and gold | 55 | 30 |
| 1983 | - | 60q. green, lt grn & gold | 1·60 | 50 |
| 1984 | - | 80q. blue, lt blue & gold | 2·20 | 50 |
| 1985 | - | 1l.20 magenta, mauve and gold | 3·25 | 1·00 |
| 1986 | - | 1l.60 blue, lt blue & gold | 4·25 | 1·80 |
| 1987 | - | 2l.40 grn, lt grn & gold | 6·50 | 3·25 |
| 1988 | - | 3l. blue, lt blue & gold | 7·50 | 5·25 |

DESIGNS: 10q. Telephone, letters, telegraph wires and switchboard operators; 15q. Pouring molten iron; 20q. Dancers, musical instruments, book and artist's materials; 25q. Newspapers, radio, television and broadcasting tower; 60q. Assistant in clothes shop; 80q. Militiamen and women, tanks, ships, aircraft and radar equipment; 1l.20, Industrial complex and symbols of industry; 1l.60, Train and truck; 2l.40, Workers hoeing fields, cattle and girl holding wheat sheaf; 3l. Microscope and nurse holding up baby.

**406** Dora D'Istria

**1979.** 150th Birth Anniv of Dora D'Istria (pioneer of women's rights).

| No. | Type | Description | Mint | Used |
|---|---|---|---|---|
| 1989 | **406** | 80q. green and black | 1·60 | 1·00 |
| 1990 | - | 1l.10 grey and black | 2·75 | 2·10 |

DESIGN: 1l.10, Full-face portrait.

**1979.** National Costume Dances (3rd series). As T **389**. Multicoloured.

| No. | Description | Mint | Used |
|---|---|---|---|
| 1991 | 15q. Girl dancers with scarves | 35 | 20 |
| 1992 | 25q. Male dancers | 55 | 30 |
| 1993 | 80q. Girl dancers with scarves (different) | 2·20 | 1·00 |
| 1994 | 1l.20 Male dancers with pistols | 2·75 | 1·60 |
| 1995 | 1l.40 Female dancers with linked arms | 3·25 | 2·10 |

**407** Stone-built Galleried House

**1979.** Traditional Albanian Houses (1st series). Multicoloured.

| No. | Description | Mint | Used |
|---|---|---|---|
| 1996 | 15q. Type **407** | 20 | 10 |
| 1997 | 25q. Tower house (vert) | 35 | 15 |
| 1998 | 80q. House with wooden galleries | 1·10 | 50 |
| 1999 | 1l.20 Galleried tower house (vert) | 1·60 | 75 |
| 2000 | 1l.40 Three-storied fortified house (vert) | 2·20 | 1·30 |
| **MS**2001 | 62×75 mm. 1l.90 Fortified tower house | 8·75 | 5·25 |

See also Nos. 2116/19.

**408** Aleksander Moissi

**1979.** Birth Cententary of Aleksander Moissi (actor).

| No. | Type | Description | Mint | Used |
|---|---|---|---|---|
| 2002 | **408** | 80q. green, black & gold | 1·60 | 65 |
| 2003 | - | 1l.10 brown, blk & gold | 2·20 | 1·60 |

DESIGN: 1l.10, Aleksander Moissi (different).

**409** Vasil Shanto

**1979.** Anti-fascist Heroes (1st series). Multicoloured.

| No. | Description | Mint | Used |
|---|---|---|---|
| 2004 | 15q. Type **409** | 25 | 10 |
| 2005 | 25q. Qemal Stafa | 55 | 30 |
| 2006 | 60q. Type **409** | 2·20 | 1·00 |
| 2007 | 90q. As 25q. | 3·25 | 2·10 |

See also Nos. 2052/5, 2090/3, 2126/9, 2167/70, 2221/4, 2274/7 and 2313/5.

**410** Soldier, Crowd and Coat of Arms

**1979.** 35th Anniv of Permet Congress. Mult.

| No. | Description | Mint | Used |
|---|---|---|---|
| 2008 | 25q. Soldier, factories and wheat | 1·10 | 50 |
| 2009 | 1l.65 Type **410** | 5·00 | 2·50 |

**411** Albanian Flag

**1979.** 5th Albanian Democratic Front Congress.

| No. | Type | Description | Mint | Used |
|---|---|---|---|---|
| 2010 | **411** | 25q. multicoloured | 1·10 | 50 |
| 2011 | **411** | 1l.65 multicoloured | 5·00 | 3·25 |

**412** "Ne Stervitje" (Arben Basha)

**1979.** Paintings. Multicoloured.

2012 15q. Type **412** 10 10
2013 25q. "Shtigje Lufte" (Ismail Lulani) 20 10
2014 80q. "Agim me Fitore" (Myrteza Fushekati) 1·10 50
2015 1l.20 "Gjithe Populli ushtare" (Muhamet Deliu) 1·80 75
2016 1l.40 "Zjarret Ndezur Mbajme" (Jorgji Gjikopulli) 2·20 1·00
**MS**2017 78×103 mm. 1l.90 "Cajime Rrethime" (Fatmir Haxhiu) 4·00 3·00

**413** Athletes round Party Flag

**1979.** 35th Anniv of Liberation Spartakiad. Mult.

2018 15q. Type **413** 10 10
2019 25q. Shooting 20 10
2020 80q. Girl gymnast 1·10 50
2021 1l.10 Football 1·60 1·00
2022 1l.40 High jump 1·80 1·30

**414** Founder-president

**1979.** Centenary of Albanian Literary Society.

2023 - 25q. black, brown and gold 35 20
2024 **414** 80q. black, brown and gold 1·10 65
2025 - 1l.20 black, blue & gold 1·60 1·00
2026 - 1l.55 black, vio & gold 2·00 1·30
**MS**2027 78×66 mm. 1l.90 black, buff and gold 3·75 3·25

DESIGNS: 25q. Foundation document and seal of 1880; 1l.20, Headquarters building, 1979; 1l.55, Headquarters building, 1879; 1l.90, Four founder members, book and quill.

**415** Congress Building

**1979.** 35th Anniv of Berat Congress. Multicoloured.

2028 25q. Arms and congress document 1·40 1·00
2029 1l.65 Type **415** 4·75 3·75

**416** Workers and Industrial Complex

**1979.** 35th Anniv of Liberation. Multicoloured.

2030 25q. Type **416** 35 20
2031 80q. Wheat and hand grasping hammer and pickaxe 1·10 65
2032 1l.20 Open book, star and musical instrument 1·60 1·00
2033 1l.55 Open book, compasses and gear wheel 2·20 1·30

**417** Joseph Stalin

**1979.** Birth Centenary of Joseph Stalin.

2034 **417** 80q. blue and red 1·60 1·00
2035 - 1l.10 blue and red 2·20 1·60

DESIGN: 1l.10, Stalin and Enver Hoxha.

**418** Fireplace and Pottery, Korce

**1980.** Interiors (1st series). Multicoloured.

2036 25q. Type **418** 35 20
2037 80q. Carved bed alcove and weapons, Shkoder 75 50
2038 1l.20 Cooking hearth and carved chair, Mirdite 1·60 1·00
2039 1l.35 Turkish-style chimney, dagger and embroidered jacket, Gjirokaster 2·20 1·60

See also Nos. 2075/8.

**419** Lacework

**1980.** Handicrafts. Multicoloured.

2040 25q. Pipe and flask 35 20
2041 80q. Leather handbags 75 50
2042 1l.20 Carved eagle and embroidered rug 1·60 1·00
2043 1l.35 Type **419** 2·20 1·60

**420** Aleksander Xhuvani

**1980.** Birth Centenary of Dr. Aleksander Xhuvani.

2044 **420** 80q. blue, grey and black 2·20 1·60
2045 **420** 1l. brown, grey and black 2·75 2·10

**421** Insurrectionists

**1980.** 70th Anniv of Kosovo Insurrection.

2046 **421** 80q. black and red 2·20 1·60
2047 - 1l. black and red 3·25 2·50

DESIGN: 1l. Battle scene.

**422** "Soldiers and Workers helping Stricken Population" (D. Jukniu and L. Lulani)

**1980.** 1979 Earthquake Relief.

2048 **422** 80q. multicoloured 2·20 1·60
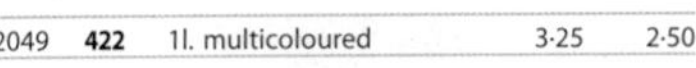
2049 **422** 1l. multicoloured 3·25 2·50

**423** Lenin

**1980.** 110th Birth Anniv of Lenin.

2050 **423** 80q. grey, red and pink 2·20 1·60
2051 **423** 1l. multicoloured 3·25 2·50

**424** Misto Mame and Ali Demi

**1980.** Anti-fascist Heroes (2nd series). Mult.

2052 25q. Type **424** 35 20
2053 80q. Sadik Staveleci, Vojo Kushi and Xhoxhi Martini 1·10 75
2054 1l.20 Bule Naipi and Persefoni Kokedhima 1·80 1·00
2055 1l.35 Ndoc Deda, Hydajet Lezha, Naim Gjylbegu, Ndoc Mazi and Ahmet Haxhia 2·20 1·60

**425** "Mirela"

**1980.** Children's Tales. Multicoloured.

2056 15q. Type **425** 10 10
2057 25q. "Shkarravina" 20 15
2058 80q. "Ariu Artist" 1·10 75
2059 2l.40 "Pika e Ujit" 4·00 3·25

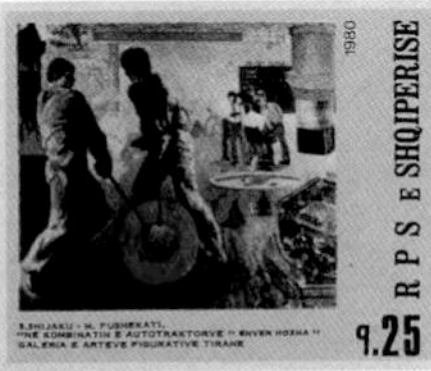

**426** "The Enver Hoxha Tractor Combine" (S. Shijaku and M. Fushekati)

**1980.** Paintings from Gallery of Figurative Arts, Tirana. Multicoloured.

2060 25q. Type **426** 35 20
2061 80q. "The Welder" (Harilla Dhima) 1·10 75
2062 1l.20 "Steel Erector (Petro Kokushta) 1·80 1·60
2063 1l.35 "Harvest Festival" (Pandeli Lena) 2·20 1·80
**MS**2064 65×82 mm. 1l.80 "Communists" (Vilson Kilica) (48×71 mm) 5·00 5·00

**427** Decorated Door (Pergamen miniature)

**1980.** Art of the Middle Ages. Each black and gold.

2065 25q. Type **427** 35 20
2066 80q. Bird (relief) 75 50
2067 1l.20 Crowned lion (relief) 1·40 1·00
2068 1l.35 Pheasant (relief) 1·60 1·30

**428** Divjaka

**1980.** National Parks. Multicoloured.

2069 80q. Type **428** 1·10 85
2070 1l.20 Lura 1·60 1·30
2071 1l.60 Thethi 2·75 2·30
**MS**2072 89×90 mm. 1l.80 Llogara (77×80 mm) 5·50 5·50

**429** Flag, Arms and rejoicing Albanians

**1981.** 35th Anniv of Albanian People's Republic. Multicoloured.

2073 80q. Type **429** 1·60 85
2074 1l. Crowd and flags outside People's Party headquarters 2·20 1·00

**1981.** Interiors (2nd series). Multicoloured.

2075 25q. As T **418** 20 15
2076 80q. Sleeping mats and spirit keg, Labara 65 50
2077 1l.20 Fireplace and covered dish mat 1·30 75
2078 1l.35 Interior and embroidered jacket, Dibres 1·80 1·40

**430** Wooden Cot

**1981.** Folk Art. Multicoloured.

2079 25q. Type **430** 35 20
2080 80q. Bucket and flask 85 75
2081 1l.20 Embroidered slippers 1·20 1·00
2082 1l.35 Jugs 1·50 1·40

**431** Footballers

**1981.** World Cup Football Championship Eliminating Rounds. Multicoloured.

2083 25q. Type **431** 1·30 60
2084 80q. Tackle 3·75 2·20
2085 1l.20 Player kicking ball 5·50 3·75
2086 1l.35 Goalkeeper saving goal 6·75 4·25

**432** Rifleman

**1981.** Cent of Battle of Shtimje. Each purple & red.

2087 80q. Type **432** 1·20 85
2088 1l. Albanian with sabre 1·50 1·00
**MS**2089 84×68 mm. 1l.80 Albanian with pistol 5·00 5·00

**1981.** Anti-fascist Heroes (3rd series). As T **424**. Multicoloured.

2090 25q. Perlat Rexhepi and Branko Kadia 35 20
2091 80q. Xheladin Beqiri and Hajdah Dushi 1·10 50
2092 1l.20 Koci Bako, Vasil Laci and Mujo Ulqinaku 1·30 1·00
2093 1l.35 Mine Peza and Zoja Cure 2·20 1·30

**433** Acrobats

**1981.** Children's Circus.

2094 - 15q. black, green & stone 15 10

2095 - 25q. black, blue and grey 20 15

2096 **433** 80q. black, mve & pink 65 50

2097 - 2l.40 black, orge & yell 2·20 2·00

DESIGNS: 15q. Monocyclists. 25q. Human pyramid; 2l.40, Acrobats spinning from marquee pole.

**434** "Rallying to the Flag, December 1911" (A. Zajmi)

**1981.** Paintings. Multicoloured.

2098 25q. "Allies" (Sh. Hysa) (horiz) 55 20

2099 80q. "Azem Galica breaking the Ring of Turks" (A. Buza) (horiz) 85 50

2100 1l.20 Type **434** 1·30 1·00

2101 1l.35 "My Flag is my Heart" (L. Cefa) 1·60 1·40

**MS**2102 81×109 mm. 1l.80 "Unite under the Flag" (N. Vasia) (55×79 mm) 5·00 5·00

**435** Weightlifting

**1981.** Albanian Participation in Inter Sports. Mult.

2103 25q. Rifle shooting 35 20

2104 80q. Type **435** 75 50

2105 1l.20 Volleyball 1·10 85

2106 1l.35 Football 1·30 1·00

**436** Flag and Hands holding Pickaxe and Rifle

**1981.** 8th Workers' Party Congress.

2107 **436** 80q. red, brown & black 85 65

2108 - 1l. red and black 1·30 1·20

DESIGN: 1l. Party flag, hammer and sickle.

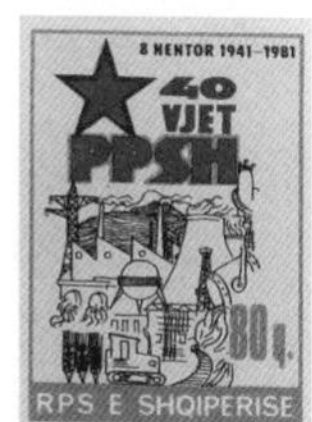


**437** Industrial and Agricultural Symbols

**1981.** 40th Anniv of Workers' Party. Mult.

2109 80q. Type **437** 55 30

2110 2l.80 Albanian flag and hand holding pickaxe and rifle 2·75 2·10

**MS**2111 79×98 mm. 1l.80 Enver Hoxha and book (50×68 mm) 5·50 5·50

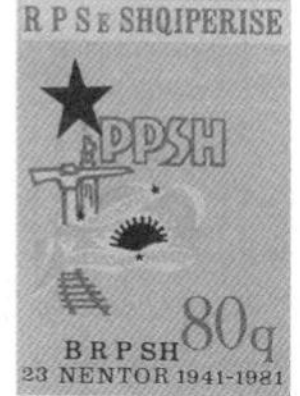


**438** Pickaxe, Rifle and Young Communists Flag

**1981.** 40th Anniv of Young Communists' Union. Multicoloured.

2112 80q. Type **438** 1·30 1·00

2113 1l. Workers' Party flag and Young Communists emblem 2·20 1·90

**439** F. S. Noli

**1981.** Birth Centenary of F. S. Noli (author).

2114 **439** 80q. green and gold 1·40 75

2115 **439** 1l.10 brown and gold 1·80 1·00

**1982.** Traditional Albanian Houses (2nd series). As T **407**, but vert. Multicoloured.

2116 25q. House in Bulqize 35 20

2117 80q. House in Kosovo 1·60 1·00

2118 1l.20 House in Bicaj 2·20 1·60

2119 1l.55 House in Mat 3·00 1·90

**440** Map, Globe and Bacillus

**1982.** Centenary of Discovery of Tubercle Bacillus.

2120 **440** 80q. multicoloured 5·50 2·10

2121 - 1l.10 brown & dp brown 7·50 3·75

DESIGN: 1l.10, Robert Koch (discoverer), microscope and bacillus.

**441** "Prizren Castle" (G. Madhi)

**1982.** Paintings of Kosovo. Multicoloured.

2122 25q. Type **441** 55 30

2123 80q. "House of the Albanian League, Prizren" (K. Buza) (horiz) 1·60 1·30

2124 1l.20 "Mountain Gorge, Rogove" (K. Buza) 2·75 1·60

2125 1l.55 "Street of the Hadhji, Zekes" (G. Madhi) 3·75 2·10

**1982.** Anti-fascist Heroes (4th series). As T **424**. Multicoloured.

2126 25q. Hibe Palikuqi and Liri Gero 55 30

2127 80q. Mihal Duri and Kojo Karafili 1·30 85

2128 1l.20 Fato Dudumi, Margarita Tutulani and Shejnaze Juka 2·00 1·40

2129 1l.55 Memo Meto and Gjok Doci 2·75 1·50

**442** Factories and Workers

**1982.** 9th Trade Unions Congress. Multicoloured.

2130 80q. Type **442** 3·75 2·20

2131 1l.10 Congress emblem 5·00 3·00

**443** Ship in Harbour

**1982.** Children's Paintings. Multicoloured.

2132 15q. Type **443** 55 20

2133 80q. Forest camp 1·10 75

2134 1l.20 House 1·60 1·30

2135 1l.65 House and garden 3·25 2·00

**444** "Village Festival" (Danish Jukniu)

**1982.** Paintings from Gallery of Figurative Arts, Tirana. Multicoloured.

2136 25q. Type **444** 35 20

2137 80q. "The Hydroelectric Station Builders" (Ali Miruku) 1·30 1·00

2138 1l.20 "Steel Workers" (Clirim Ceka) 1·60 1·30

2139 1l.55 "Oil Drillers" (Pandeli Lena) 2·75 1·60

**MS**2140 75×90 mm. 1l.90 "First Tapping of the Furnace" (Jorgji Gjikopulli) 5·50 3·75

**445** "Voice of the People" (party newspaper)

**1982.** 40th Anniv of Popular Press. Multicoloured.

2141 80q. Type **445** £120 £100

2142 1l.10 Hand duplicator producing first edition of "Voice of the People" £120 £100

**446** Heroes of Peza Monument

**1982.** 40th Anniv of Democratic Front. Mult.

2143 80q. Type **446** 8·25 4·00

2144 1l.10 Peza Conference building and marchers with flag 12·00 5·50

**447** Congress Emblem

**1982.** 8th Young Communists' Union Congress.

2145 **447** 80q. multicoloured 7·25 4·25

2146 **447** 1l.10 multicoloured 11·50 6·25

**448** Tapestry

**1982.** Handicrafts. Multicoloured.

2147 25q. Type **448** 55 30

2148 80q. Bags (vert) 1·30 75

2149 1l.20 Butter churns 1·80 1·00

2150 1l.55 Jug (vert) 2·75 1·60

**449** Freedom Fighters

**1982.** 70th Anniv of Independence.

2151 **449** 20q. deep red, red & blk 45 30

2152 - 1l.20 black, grn & red 2·20 1·30

2153 - 2l.40 brown, buff and red 4·00 2·50

**MS**2154 90×89 mm. 1l.90 multicoloured 6·50 4·25

DESIGNS: 20q. Ismail Qemali (patriot) and crowd around building; 2l.40, Six freedom fighters. (58×55 mm) 1l.90, Independence Monument, Tirana.

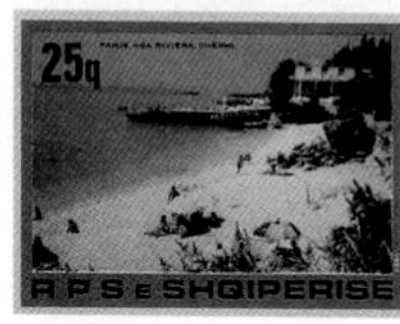


**450** Dhermi

**1982.** Coastal Views. Multicoloured.

2155 25q. Type **450** 35 20

2156 80q. Sarande 1·10 75

2157 1l.20 Ksamil 1·60 1·30

2158 1l.55 Lukove 2·40 1·60

**451** Male Dancers

**1983.** Folk Dance Assemblies Abroad. Mult.

2159 25q. Type **451** 20 10

2160 80q. Male dancers and drummer 75 50

2161 1l.20 Musicians 1·30 1·00

2162 1l.55 Group of female dancers 1·60 1·50

**452** Karl Marx

**1983.** Death Centenary of Karl Marx.

2163 **452** 80q. multicoloured 2·20 1·00

2164 **452** 1l.10 multicoloured 2·75 1·60

**453** Electricity Generation

**1983.** Energy Development.

2165 **453** 80q. blue and orange 1·40 85

2166 - 1l.10 mauve and green 1·80 1·30

DESIGN: 1l.10, Gas and oil production.

**1983.** Anti-fascist Heroes (5th series). As T **424**. Multicoloured.

2167 25q. Asim Zeneli and Nazmi Rushiti 35 20

2168 80q. Shyqyri Ishmi, Shyqyri Alimerko and Myzafer Asqeriu 1·10 50

2169 1l.20 Qybra Sokoli, Qeriba Derri and Ylbere Bilibashi 1·80 1·00

2170 1l.55 Themo Vasi and Abaz Shehu 2·75 1·60

**454** Congress Emblem

**1983.** 9th Women's Union Congress.

2171 **454** 80q. multicoloured 1·50 1·00

2172 **454** 1l.10 multicoloured 2·00 1·60

**455** Cycling

**1983.** Sport and Leisure. Multicoloured.
2173 25q. Type **455** 35 20
2174 80q. Chess 1·10 50
2175 1l.20 Gymnastics 1·80 1·00
2176 1l.55 Wrestling 2·20 1·40

**456** Soldier and Militia

**1983.** 40th Anniv of People's Army.
2177 **456** 20q. gold and red 35 20
2178 - 1l.20 gold and red 1·80 1·00
2179 - 2l.40 gold and brown 3·25 1·90
DESIGNS: 1l.20, Soldier; 2l.40 Factory guard.

**457** "Sunny Day" (Myrteza Fushekati)

**1983.** Paintings from Gallery of Figurative Arts, Tirana. Multicoloured.
2180 25q. Type **457** 35 20
2181 80q. "Morning Gossip" (Niko Progri) 1·30 75
2182 1l.20 "29th November, 1944" (Harilla Dhimo) 1·60 1·00
2183 1l.55 "Demolition" (Pandi Mele) 2·20 1·40
**MS**2184 111×74 mm. 1l.90 "Partisan Assault" (Sali Shijaku and Myrteza Fushekati) (99×59 mm) 11·00 7·50

**1983.** National Folklore Festival, Gjirokaster. As T **402**. Multicoloured.
2185 25q. Sword dance 25 15
2186 80q. Kerchief dance 1·80 1·00
2187 1l.20 Musicians 2·40 1·60
2188 1l.55 Women dancers with garlands 3·75 2·50

**458** Enver Hoxha

**1983.** 75th Birthday of Enver Hoxha.
2189 **458** 80q. multicoloured 80 65
2190 **458** 1l.20 multicoloured 1·30 1·00
2191 **458** 1l.80 multicoloured 1·80 1·40
**MS**2192 77×98 mm. 1l.90 multicoloured (as T **458** but with inscriptions differently arranged) 4·25 4·25

**459** W.C.Y. Emblem and Globe

**1983.** World Communications Year.
2193 **459** 60q. multicoloured 75 50
2194 **459** 1l.20 blue, orange & blk 2·00 1·60

**460** "Combine to Triumph" (J. Keraj)

**1983.** Skanderbeg Epoch in Art. Multicoloured.
2195 25q. Type **460** 55 20
2196 80q. "The Heroic Resistance at Krujes" (N. Bakalli) 1·60 1·00
2197 1l.20 "United we are Unconquerable by our Enemies" (N. Progri) 2·20 1·30
2198 1l.55 "Assembly at Lezhe" (B. Ahmeti) 3·25 1·80
**MS**2199 77×90 mm. 1l.90 "Victory over the Turks" (G. Madhi) 8·25 7·75

**461** Amphitheatre, Butrint (Buthrotum)

**1983.** Graeco-Roman Remains in Illyria. Mult.
2200 80q. Type **461** 2·20 1·60
2201 1l.20 Colonnade, Apoloni Cesma (Apollonium) 2·75 2·10
2202 1l.80 Vaulted gallery of amphitheatre, Dyrrah (Epidamnus) 3·25 2·50

**462** Man's Head from Apoloni

**1984.** Archaeological Discoveries (1st series). Mult.
2203 15q. Type **462** 20 15
2204 25q. Tombstone from Korce 35 20
2205 80q. Woman's head from Apoloni 1·30 85
2206 1l.10 Child's head from Tren 1·60 1·00
2207 1l.20 Man's head from Dyrrah 2·00 1·30
2208 2l.20 Bronze statuette of Eros from Dyrrah 3·25 1·60
See also Nos. 2258/61.

**463** Clock Tower, Gjirokaster

**1984.** Clock Towers.
2209 **463** 15q. purple 20 15
2210 - 25q. brown 35 20
2211 - 80q. violet 1·10 75
2212 - 1l.10 red 1·30 1·00
2213 - 1l.20 green 2·00 1·40
2214 - 2l.20 brown 3·25 2·30
DESIGNS: 25q. Kavaje; 80q. Elbasan; 1l.10, Tirana; 1l.20, Peqin; 2l.20, Kruje.

**464** Student with Microscope

**1984.** 40th Anniv of Liberation (1st issue). Mult.
2215 15q. Type **464** 20 15
2216 25q. Soldier with flag 35 20
2217 80q. Schoolchildren 1·30 85
2218 1l.10 Soldier, ships, airplanes and weapons 1·60 1·00
2219 1l.20 Workers with flag 2·00 1·30
2220 2l.20 Armed guards on patrol 3·25 1·60
See also Nos. 2255/6.

**1984.** Anti-fascist Heroes (6th series). As T **424**. Multicoloured.
2221 15q. Manush Alimani, Mustafa Matohiti and Kastriot Muco 65 20
2222 25q. Zaho Koka, Reshit Collaku and Maliq Muco 1·30 55
2223 1l.20 Lefter Talo, Tom Kola and Fuat Babani 2·40 1·40
2224 2l.20 Myslysm Shyri, Dervish Hekali and Skender Caci 4·25 2·75

**465** Enver Hoxha

**1984.** 40th Anniv of Permet Congress.
2225 **465** 80q. brown, orge & red 3·25 2·10
2226 - 1l.10 black, yell & lilac 4·00 2·50
DESIGN: 1l.10, Resistance fighter (detail of monument).

**466** Children reading Comic

**1984.** Children. Multicoloured.
2227 15q. Type **466** 55 20
2228 25q. Children with toys 1·10 50
2229 60q. Children gardening and rainbow 2·20 1·00
2230 2l.80 Children flying kite bearing Albanian arms 5·00 2·50

**467** Football in Goal

**1984.** European Football Championship Finals. Multicoloured.
2231 15q. Type **467** 1·10 30
2232 25q. Referee and football 1·60 50
2233 1l.20 Football and map of Europe 3·25 1·00
2234 2l.20 Football and pitch 3·75 2·10

**468** "Freedom is Here" (Myrteza Fushekati)

**1984.** Paintings from Gallery of Figurative Arts, Tirana. Multicoloured.
2235 15q. Type **468** 55 20
2236 25q. "Morning" (Zamir Mati) (vert) 1·10 65
2237 80q. "My Darling" (Agim Zajmi) (vert) 2·75 1·60
2238 2l.60 "For the Partisans" (Arben Basha) 4·25 2·30
**MS**2239 80×93 mm. 1l.90 "Albania" (Zamir Mati) 11·00 9·00

**469** Mulberry

**1984.** Flowers. Multicoloured.
2240 15q. Type **469** 3·25 85
2241 25q. Plantain 4·25 1·30
2242 1l.20 Hypericum 12·00 4·75
2243 2l.20 Edelweiss 24·00 9·00

**470** Sabre Dance

**1984.** "Ausipex 84" International Stamp Exhibition, Melbourne. Sheet 72×88 mm.
**MS**2244 **470** 1l.90 multicoloured 4·50 4·50

**471** Truck driving through Forest

**1984.** Forestry. Multicoloured.
2245 15q. Type **471** 1·10 65
2246 25q. Transporting logs on overhead cable 1·60 1·00
2247 1l.20 Sawmill in forest 5·50 3·25
2248 2l.20 Lumberjack sawing down trees 8·25 4·50

**472** Gjirokaster

**1984.** "Eurphila '84" Int Stamp Exn, Rome.
2249 **472** 1l.20 multicoloured 2·75 2·50

**473** Football

**1984.** 5th National Spartakiad. Multicoloured.
2250 15q. Type **473** 20 15
2251 25q. Running 55 20
2252 80q. Weightlifting 1·10 65
2253 2l.20 Pistol shooting 3·00 2·10
**MS**2254 70×90 mm. 1l.90 Opening ceremony 4·25 3·50

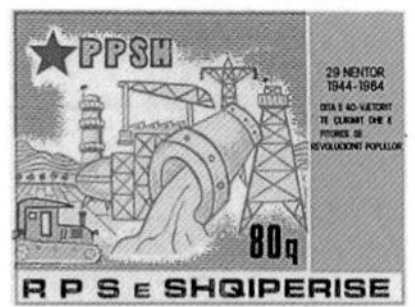

**474** Agriculture and Industry

**1984.** 40th Anniv of Liberation (2nd issue). Mult.

2255 80q. Type **474** 2·20 1·00
2256 1l.10 Soldiers and flag 2·75 1·60
**MS**2257 68×89 mm. 1l.90 Enver Hoxha making liberation speech 5·00 4·00

**1985.** Archaeological Discoveries (2nd series). As T **462**, showing Illyrian finds. Multicoloured.

2258 15q. Pot 55 20
2259 80q. Terracotta head of woman 2·20 1·00
2260 1l.20 Terracotta bust of Aphrodite 2·75 1·40
2261 1l.70 Bronze statuette of Nike 4·25 2·10

**476** Kapo (bust)

**1985.** 70th Birthday of Hysni Kapo (politician).

2262 **476** 90q. black and red 2·20 1·60
2263 **476** 1l.10 black and blue 2·75 2·10

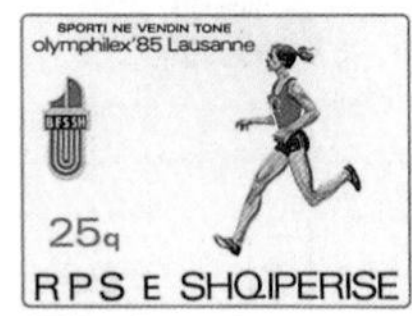

**477** Running

**1985.** "Olymphilex '85" Olympic Stamps Exhibition, Lausanne. Multicoloured.

2264 25q. Type **477** 35 20
2265 60q. Weightlifting 85 65
2266 1l.20 Football 1·60 1·30
2267 1l.50 Pistol shooting 2·75 1·60

**478** Bach

**1985.** 300th Birth Anniv of Johann Sebastian Bach (composer).

2268 **478** 80q. orange, brn & blk 22·00 13·00
2269 - 1l.20 blue, dp blue & blk 27·00 16·00

DESIGN—1l.20, Bach's birthplace, Eisenach.

**479** Hoxha

**1985.** Enver Hoxha Commemoration.

2270 **479** 80q. multicoloured 2·75 2·10
**MS**2271 67×90 mm. **479** 1l.90 multicoloured 4·25 4·25

**480** Frontier Guards

**1985.** 40th Anniv of Frontier Force. Multicoloured.

2272 25q. Type **480** 1·60 1·00
2273 80q. Frontier guard 3·75 3·25

**1985.** Anti-fascist Heroes (7th series). As T **424**. Multicoloured.

2274 25q. Mitro Xhani, Nimete Progonati and Kozma Nushi 85 50
2275 40q. Ajet Xhindoli, Mustafa Kacaci and Estref Caka 1·30 1·00
2276 60q. Celo Sinani, Llambro Andoni and Meleo Gosnishti 2·20 1·30
2277 1l.20 Thodhori Mastora, Fejzi Micoli and Hysen Cino 3·75 3·00

**481** Scarf on Rifle Barrel

**1985.** 40th Anniv of V.E. (Victory in Europe) Day. Multicoloured.

2278 25q. Type **481** 33·00 50·00
2279 80q. Crumpled swastika and hand holding rifle butt 85·00 £130

**482** "Primary School" (Thoma Malo)

**1985.** Paintings from Gallery of Figurative Arts, Tirana. Multicoloured.

2280 25q. Type **482** 35 20
2281 80q. "Heroes and Mother" (Hysen Devolli) (vert) 1·30 1·00
2282 90q. "Mother writing" (Angjelin Dodmasej) (vert) 1·60 1·30
2283 1l.20 "Women off to Work" (Ksenofen Dilo) 2·20 1·80
**MS**2284 74×88 mm. 1l.90 "Foundry Workers" (Mikel Gurashi) 5·00 3·75

**483** Scoring a Goal

**1985.** 10th World Basketball Championship, Spain.

2285 **483** 25q. blue and black 25 15
2286 - 80q. green and black 1·30 75
2287 - 1l.20 violet and black 1·80 1·30
2288 - 1l.60 red and black 2·75 2·10

DESIGNS: 80q. Player running with ball; 1l.20, Defending goal; 1l.60, Defender capturing ball.

**484** Oranges

**1985.** Fruit Trees. Multicoloured.

2289 25q. Type **484** 55 30
2290 80q. Plums 2·75 1·60
2291 1l.20 Apples 4·25 2·10
2292 1l.60 Cherries 5·50 3·25

**485** Kruja

**1985.** Architecture.

2293 **485** 25q. black and red 55 30
2294 - 80q. black, grey and brown 2·75 1·60
2295 - 1l.20 black, brown & bl 3·25 2·10
2296 - 1l.60 black, brown & red 4·25 2·50

DESIGNS: 80q. Gjirokastra; 1l.20, Berat; 1l.60, Shkoder.

**486** War Horse Dance

**1985.** National Folklore Festival. Dances.

2297 **486** 25q. brown, red & black 55 30
2298 - 80q. brown, red & black 1·60 1·00
2299 - 1l.20 brown, red & blk 2·20 1·30
2300 - 1l.60 brown, red & blk 2·75 1·80
**MS**2301 56×82 mm. 1l.90 multicoloured. Imperf 4·25 3·75

DESIGNS: 80q. Pillow dance; 1l.20, Ladies' kerchief dance; 1l.60, Men's one-legged pair dance; 1l.90, Fortress dance.

**487** State Arms

**1986.** 40th Anniv of Albanian People's Republic.

2302 **487** 25q. gold, red and black 1·60 1·00
2303 - 80q. multicoloured 3·25 2·10

DESIGN: 80q. "Comrade Hoxha announcing the News to the People" (Vilson Kilica) and arms.

**488** Dam across River Drin

**1986.** Enver Hoxha Hydroelectric Power Station. Multicoloured.

2304 25q. Type **488** 5·50 2·10
2305 80q. Control building 12·00 7·25

**489** "Gymnospermium shqipetarum"

**1986.** Flowers. Multicoloured.

2306 25q. Type **489** 2·20 1·00
2307 1l.20 "Leucojum valentinum" 8·75 4·25

**490** Maksim Gorki (writer)

**1986.** Anniversaries.

2308 **490** 25q. brown 55 30
2309 - 80q. violet 2·20 1·30
2310 - 1l.20 green 3·75 2·10
2311 - 2l.40 purple 7·50 4·75
**MS**2312 88×72 mm. 1l.90 violet, blue and yellow 5·50 4·25

DESIGNS: 25q. Type **490** (50th death anniv); 80q. Andre Ampere (physicist and mathematician, 150th death anniv); 1l.20, James Watt (inventor, 250th birth); 2l.40, Franz Liszt (composer, death cent). 88×72 mm. 1l.90, Heads of Gorki, Ampere, Watt and Liszt.

**1986.** Anti-fascist Heroes (8th series). As T **424**. Multicoloured.

2313 25q. Ramiz Aranitasi, Inajete Dumi and Laze Nuro Ferraj 2·20 1·60
2314 80q. Dine Kalenja, Kozma Naska, Met Hasa and Fahri Raalbani 5·50 2·50
2315 1l.20 Hiqmet Buzi, Bajram Tusha, Mumin Selami and Hajredin Bylyshi 8·75 5·25

**491** Trophy on Globe

**1986.** World Cup Football Championship, Mexico. Multicoloured.

2316 25q. Type **491** 55 30
2317 1l.20 Goalkeeper's hands and ball 2·75 2·10
**MS**2318 97×63 mm. 1l.90 Globe-football (40×32 mm) 4·25 3·25

**492** Car Tyre within Ship's Wheel, Diesel Train and Traffic Lights

**1986.** 40th Anniv of Transport Workers' Day.

2319 **492** 1l.20 multicoloured 14·00 7·75

**493** Naim Frasheri (poet)

**1986.** Anniversaries. Multicoloured.

2320 30q. Type **493** (140th birth anniv) 75 50
2321 60q. Ndre Mjeda (poet, 120th birth anniv) 1·30 1·00
2322 90q. Petro Nini Luarasi (jounalist, 75th death anniv) 2·20 1·60
2323 1l. Andon Zaka Cajupi (poet, 120th birth anniv) 2·75 1·90
2324 1l.20 Millosh Gjergj Nikolla (Migjeni) (revolutionary writer, 75th birth anniv) 3·25 2·30
2325 2l.60 Urani Rumbo (women's education pioneer, 50th death anniv) 8·75 4·25

**494** Congress Emblem

**1986.** 9th Workers' Party Congress, Tirana.

2326 **494** 30q. multicoloured 11·00 7·75

**495** Party Stamp and Enver Hoxha's Signature

**1986.** 45th Anniv of Workers' Party.

2327 **495** 30q. red, grey and gold 3·25 1·60
2328 - 1l.20 red, orange & gold 8·75 3·75

DESIGNS: 1l.20, Profiles of Marx, Engels, Lenin and Stalin and Tirana house where Party was founded.

**496** "Mother Albania"

**1986**

| | | | | |
|---|---|---|---|---|
| 2329 | **496** | 10q. blue | 10 | 10 |
| 2330 | **496** | 20q. red | 10 | 10 |
| 2331 | **496** | 30q. red | 10 | 10 |
| 2332 | **496** | 50q. brown | 20 | 15 |
| 2333 | **496** | 60q. green | 35 | 20 |
| 2334 | **496** | 80q. red | 55 | 30 |
| 2335 | **496** | 90q. blue | 75 | 50 |
| 2336 | **496** | 1l.20 green | 1·10 | 75 |
| 2337 | **496** | 1l.60 purple | 1·60 | 10 |
| 2338 | **496** | 2l.20 green | 2·20 | 1·60 |
| 2339 | **496** | 3l. brown | 2·75 | 2·10 |
| 2340 | **496** | 6l. yellow | 5·50 | 3·75 |

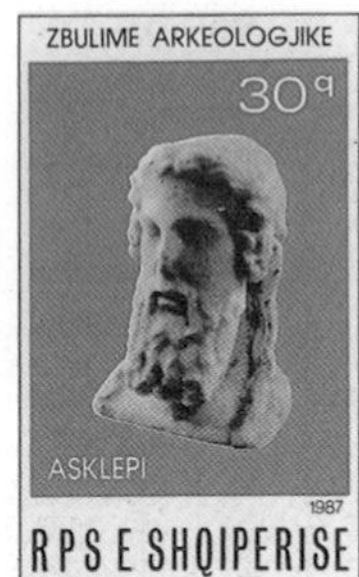

**497** Marble Head of Aesculapius

**1987.** Archaeological Discoveries (3rd series). Multicoloured.

| | | | |
|---|---|---|---|
| 2341 | 30q. Type **497** | 1·10 | 65 |
| 2342 | 80q. Terracotta figure of Aphrodite | 2·20 | 1·00 |
| 2343 | 1l. Bronze figure of Pan | 3·25 | 1·50 |
| 2344 | 1l.20 Limestone head of Jupiter | 4·25 | 2·75 |

**498** Monument and Centenary Emblem

**1987.** Centenary of First Albanian School.

| | | | | |
|---|---|---|---|---|
| 2345 | **498** | 30q. brown, lt brn & yell | 55 | 30 |
| 2346 | - | 80q. multicoloured | 1·60 | 75 |
| 2347 | - | 1l.20 multicoloured | 2·20 | 1·60 |

DESIGNS: 80q. First school building; 1l.20, Woman soldier running, girl reading book and boy doing woodwork.

**499** Victor Hugo (writer, 185th birth anniv)

**1987.** Anniversaries.

| | | | | |
|---|---|---|---|---|
| 2348 | **499** | 30q. vio, lavender & blk | 55 | 30 |
| 2349 | - | 80q. brown, lt brn & blk | 1·30 | 75 |
| 2350 | - | 90q. dp blue, blue & blk | 2·00 | 1·30 |
| 2351 | - | 1l.30 dp grn, grn & brn | 2·75 | 2·10 |

DESIGNS: 80q. Galileo Galilei (astronomer, 345th death); 90q. Charles Darwin (naturalist, 105th death); 1l.30. Miguel de Cervantes Saavedra (writer, 440th birth).

**500** "Forsythia europaea"

**1987.** Flowers. Multicoloured.

| | | | |
|---|---|---|---|
| 2352 | 30q. Type **500** | 75 | 40 |
| 2353 | 90q. "Moltkia doerfleri" | 1·40 | 1·00 |
| 2354 | 2l.10 "Wulfenia baldacii" | 3·25 | 2·75 |

**501** Congress Emblem

**1987.** 10th Trade Unions Congress, Tirana.

| | | | | |
|---|---|---|---|---|
| 2355 | **501** | 1l.20 dp red, red & gold | 5·50 | 4·25 |

**502** "The Bread of Industry" (Myrteza Fushekati)

**1987.** Paintings from Gallery of Figurative Arts, Tirana. Multicoloured.

| | | | |
|---|---|---|---|
| 2356 | 30q. Type **502** | 55 | 30 |
| 2357 | 80q. "Partisan Gift" (Skender Kokobobo) | 1·10 | 85 |
| 2358 | 1l. "Sowers" (Bujar Asllani) (horiz) | 1·60 | 1·30 |
| 2359 | 1l.20 "At the Foundry" (Clirim Ceka) (horiz) | 2·20 | 1·90 |

**503** Throwing the Hammer

**1987.** World Light Athletics Championships, Rome. Multicoloured.

| | | | |
|---|---|---|---|
| 2360 | 30q. Type **503** | 55 | 30 |
| 2361 | 90q. Running | 1·50 | 1·00 |
| 2362 | 1l.10 Putting the shot | 1·60 | 1·30 |
| **MS**2363 | 85×59 mm. 1l.90 Runner, winners' podium and banner (64×24 mm) | 4·25 | 4·25 |

**504** Themistokli Germenji (revolutionary, 70th death)

**1987.** Anniversaries.

| | | | | |
|---|---|---|---|---|
| 2364 | **504** | 30q. brown, red & black | 35 | 25 |
| 2365 | - | 80q. red, scarlet & black | 1·30 | 65 |
| 2366 | - | 90q. violet, red and black | 1·60 | 1·00 |
| 2367 | - | 1l.30 green, red & black | 2·75 | 1·90 |

DESIGNS: 80q. Bajram Curri (organizer of Albanian League, 125th birth); 90q. Aleks Stavre Drenova (poet, 40th death); 1l.30, Gjerasim Qiriazi (educational pioneer, 126th birth).

**505** Emblem

**1987.** 9th Young Communists' Union Congress, Tirana.

| | | | | |
|---|---|---|---|---|
| 2368 | **505** | 1l.20 multicoloured | 7·00 | 5·25 |

**506** National Flag

**1987.** 75th Anniv of Independence.

| | | | | |
|---|---|---|---|---|
| 2369 | **506** | 1l.20 multicoloured | 7·00 | 5·25 |

**507** Post Office Emblem

**1987.** 75th Anniv of Albanian Postal Administration. Multicoloured.

| | | | |
|---|---|---|---|
| 2370 | 90q. Type **507** | 7·50 | 5·25 |
| 2371 | 1l.20 National emblem on bronze medallion | 11·00 | 10·50 |

**508** Lord Byron (writer, bicentenary)

**1988.** Birth Anniversaries.

| | | | | |
|---|---|---|---|---|
| 2372 | **508** | 30q. black and orange | 5·50 | 4·25 |
| 2373 | - | 1l.20 black and mauve | 22·00 | 17·00 |

DESIGN: 1l.20, Eugene Delacroix (painter, 190th anniv).

**509** Oil Derrick, Tap, Houses and Wheat Ears

**1988.** 40th Anniv of W.H.O.

| | | | | |
|---|---|---|---|---|
| 2374 | **509** | 90q. multicoloured | 30·00 | 25·00 |
| 2375 | **509** | 1l.20 multicoloured | 41·00 | 33·00 |

**510** "Sideritis raeseri"

**1988.** Flowers. Multicoloured.

| | | | |
|---|---|---|---|
| 2376 | 30q. Type **510** | 11·00 | 6·25 |
| 2377 | 90q. "Lunaria telekiana" | 22·00 | 14·50 |
| 2378 | 2l.10 "Sanguisorba albanica" | 33·00 | 21·00 |

**511** Flag and Woman with Book

**1988.** 10th Women's Union Congress, Tirana.

| | | | | |
|---|---|---|---|---|
| 2379 | **511** | 90q. black, red & orange | 13·00 | 10·50 |

**512** Footballers

**1988.** 8th European Football Championship, West Germany. Multicoloured.

| | | | |
|---|---|---|---|
| 2380 | 30q. Type **512** | 2·20 | 1·90 |
| 2381 | 80q. Players jumping for ball | 3·25 | 3·00 |
| 2382 | 1l.20 Tackling | 5·50 | 5·00 |
| **MS**2383 | 78×67 mm. 1l.90 Goalkeeper saving ball. Imperf | 13·00 | 13·00 |

**513** Clasped Hands

**1988.** 110th Anniv of League of Prizren. Mult.

| | | | |
|---|---|---|---|
| 2384 | 30q. Type **513** | 45·00 | 45·00 |
| 2385 | 1l.20 League Headquarters, Prizren | 75·00 | 75·00 |

**514** Flag, Woman with Rifle and Soldier

**1988.** 45th Anniv of People's Army. Multicoloured.

| | | | |
|---|---|---|---|
| 2386 | 60q. Type **514** | 45·00 | 45·00 |
| 2387 | 90q. Army monument, partisans and Labinot house | 75·00 | 75·00 |

**515** Mihal Grameno (writer)

**1988.** Multicoloured.. Multicoloured..

| | | | |
|---|---|---|---|
| 2388 | 30q. Type **515** | 16·00 | 16·00 |
| 2389 | 90q. Bajo Topulli (revolutionary) | 27·00 | 27·00 |
| 2390 | 1l. Murat Toptani (sculptor and poet) | 33·00 | 33·00 |
| 2391 | 1l.20 Jul Variboba (poet) | 43·00 | 43·00 |

**516** Migjeni

**1988.** 50th Death Anniv of Millosh Gjergj Nikolla (Migjeni) (writer).

| | | | | |
|---|---|---|---|---|
| 2392 | **516** | 90q. silver and brown | 13·00 | 12·50 |

**517** "Dede Skurra"

**1988.** Ballads. Each black and grey.

| | | | |
|---|---|---|---|
| 2393 | 30q. Type **517** | 11·00 | 8·25 |
| 2394 | 90q. "Young Omer" | 27·00 | 23·00 |
| 2395 | 1l.20 "Gjergj Elez Alia" | 33·00 | 26·00 |

**518** Bride wearing Fezzes, Mirdita

**1988.** National Folklore Festival, Gjirokaster. Wedding Customs. Multicoloured.

| | | | |
|---|---|---|---|
| 2396 | 30q. Type **518** | 33·00 | 31·00 |
| 2397 | 1l.20 Pan Dance, Gjirokaster | £120 | 95·00 |

**519** Hoxha

**1988.** 80th Birth Anniv of Enver Hoxha. Mult.

| | | | |
|---|---|---|---|
| 2398 | 90q. Type **519** | 5·50 | 5·25 |
| 2399 | 1l.20 Enver Hoxha Museum (horiz) | 8·25 | 7·75 |

**520** Detail of Congress Document

**1988.** 80th Anniv of Monastir Language Congress. Multicoloured.

| | | | |
|---|---|---|---|
| 2400 | 60q. Type **520** | 27·00 | 23·00 |
| 2401 | 90q. Alphabet book and Congress building | 43·00 | 37·00 |

**521** Steam Locomotive and Map showing 1947 Railway line

**1989.** Railway Locomotives. Multicoloured.

| | | | |
|---|---|---|---|
| 2402 | 30q. Type **521** | 45 | 10 |
| 2403 | 90q. Polish steam locomotive and map of 1949 network | 1·30 | 50 |
| 2404 | 1l.20 Diesel locomotive and 1978 network | 1·70 | 85 |
| 2405 | 1l.80 Diesel locomotive and 1985 network | 2·50 | 1·00 |
| 2406 | 2l.40 Czechoslovakian diesel-electric locomotive and 1988 network | 5·00 | 2·10 |

**522** Entrance to Two-storey Tomb

**1989.** Archaeological Discoveries in Illyria.

| | | | | |
|---|---|---|---|---|
| 2407 | **522** | 30q. black, brown & grey | 35 | 10 |
| 2408 | - | 90q. black and green | 1·30 | 1·00 |
| 2409 | - | 2l.10 multicoloured | 2·20 | 1·90 |

DESIGNS: 90q. Buckle showing battle scene; 2l.10, Earring depicting head.

**523** Mother mourning Son

**1989.** "Kostandini and Doruntina" (folk tale). Mult.

| | | | |
|---|---|---|---|
| 2410 | 30q. Type **523** | 55 | 30 |
| 2411 | 80q. Mother weeping over tomb and son rising from dead | 1·10 | 75 |
| 2412 | 1l. Son and his sister on horseback | 1·30 | 1·00 |
| 2413 | 1l.20 Mother and daughter reunited | 1·60 | 1·30 |

**524** "Aster albanicus"

**1989.** Flowers. Multicoloured.

| | | | |
|---|---|---|---|
| 2414 | 30q. Type **524** | 35 | 10 |
| 2415 | 90q. "Orchis paparisti" | 1·30 | 1·00 |
| 2416 | 2l.10 "Orchis albanica" | 2·20 | 1·90 |

**525** Johann Strauss (composer, 90th death anniv)

**1989.** Anniversaries. Each brown and gold.

| | | | |
|---|---|---|---|
| 2417 | 30q. Type **525** | 55 | 20 |
| 2418 | 80q. Marie Curie (physicist, 55th death anniv) | 1·10 | 75 |
| 2419 | 1l. Federico Garcia Lorca (writer, 53rd death anniv) | 1·60 | 1·30 |
| 2420 | 1l.20 Albert Einstein (physicist, 110th birth anniv) | 2·20 | 1·80 |

**526** State Arms, Workers' Party Flag and Crowd

**1989.** 6th Albanian Democratic Front Congress, Tirana.

| | | | | |
|---|---|---|---|---|
| 2421 | **526** | 1l.20 multicoloured | 9·75 | 5·25 |

**527** Storming of the Bastille

**1989.** Bicentenary of French Revolution. Mult.

| | | | |
|---|---|---|---|
| 2422 | 90q. Type **527** | 75 | 50 |
| 2423 | 1l.20 Monument | 1·40 | 85 |

**528** Galley

**1989.** Ships.

| | | | | |
|---|---|---|---|---|
| 2424 | **528** | 30q. green and black | 55 | 20 |
| 2425 | - | 80q. blue and black | 1·00 | 75 |
| 2426 | - | 90q. blue and black | 1·10 | 95 |
| 2427 | - | 1l.30 lilac and black | 1·60 | 1·40 |

DESIGNS: 80q. Kogge; 90q. Schooner; 1l.30, "Tirana" (freighter).

**529** Pjeter Bogdani (writer, 300th anniv)

**1989.** Death Anniversaries. Multicoloured.

| | | | |
|---|---|---|---|
| 2428 | 30q. Type **529** | 20 | 15 |
| 2429 | 80q. Gavril Dara (writer, centenary) | 75 | 50 |
| 2430 | 90q. Thimi Mitko (writer, centenary (1990)) | 1·40 | 85 |
| 2431 | 1l.30 Kole Idromeno (painter, 50th anniv) | 2·00 | 1·00 |

**530** Engels, Marx and Marchers

**1989.** 125th Anniv of "First International". Mult.

| | | | |
|---|---|---|---|
| 2432 | 90q. Type **530** | 1·10 | 50 |
| 2433 | 1l.20 Factories, marchers and worker with pickaxe and rifle | 1·60 | 75 |

**531** Gymnastics

**1989.** 6th National Spartakiad.

| | | | | |
|---|---|---|---|---|
| 2434 | **531** | 30q. black, orange & red | 35 | 10 |
| 2435 | - | 80q. black, lt grn & grn | 75 | 50 |
| 2436 | - | 1l. black, blue & dp blue | 85 | 65 |
| 2437 | - | 1l.20 black, pur & red | 1·30 | 1·00 |

DESIGNS: 80q. Football; 1l. Cycling; 1l.20, Running.

**532** Soldier

**1989.** 45th Anniv of Liberation. Multicoloured.

| | | | |
|---|---|---|---|
| 2438 | 30q. Type **532** | 55 | 20 |
| 2439 | 80q. Date | 1·00 | 50 |
| 2440 | 1l. State arms | 1·10 | 75 |
| 2441 | 1l.20 Young couple | 1·60 | 1·30 |

**533** Chamois

**1990.** Endangered Animals. The Chamois. Mult.

| | | | |
|---|---|---|---|
| 2442 | 10q. Type **533** | 35 | 10 |
| 2443 | 30q. Mother and young | 75 | 30 |
| 2444 | 80q. Chamois keeping lookout | 2·10 | 1·00 |
| 2445 | 90q. Head of chamois | 2·20 | 1·30 |

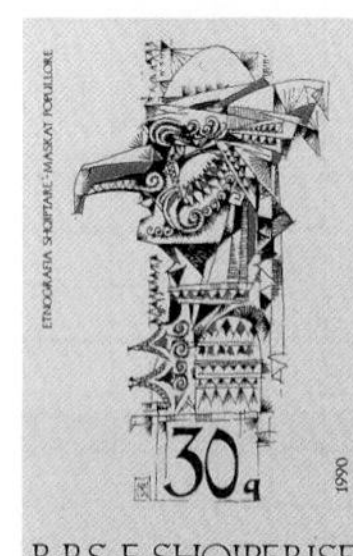


**534** Eagle Mask

**1990.** Masks. Multicoloured.

| | | | |
|---|---|---|---|
| 2446 | 30q. Type **534** | 35 | 10 |
| 2447 | 90q. Sheep | 75 | 50 |
| 2448 | 1l.20 Goat | 1·10 | 75 |
| 2449 | 1l.80 Stork | 1·60 | 1·00 |

**535** Caesar's Mushroom

**1990.** Fungi. Multicoloured.

| | | | |
|---|---|---|---|
| 2450 | 30q. Type **535** | 35 | 20 |
| 2451 | 90q. Parasol mushroom | 85 | 50 |
| 2452 | 1l.20 Cep | 1·40 | 1·20 |
| 2453 | 1l.80 "Clathrus cancelatus" | 2·00 | 1·60 |

**536** Engraving Die

**1990.** 150th Anniv of the Penny Black. Mult.

| | | | |
|---|---|---|---|
| 2454 | 90q. Type **536** | 75 | 50 |
| 2455 | 1l.20 Mounted postal messenger | 1·10 | 85 |
| 2456 | 1l.80 Mail coach passengers reading letters | 2·20 | 1·80 |

**537** Mascot and Flags

**1990.** World Cup Football Championship, Italy. Multicoloured.

| | | | |
|---|---|---|---|
| 2457 | 30q. Type **537** | 35 | 15 |
| 2458 | 90q. Mascot running | 75 | 50 |
| 2459 | 1l.20 Mascot preparing to kick ball | 1·30 | 1·00 |
| **MS**2460 | 80×62 mm. 3l.30 Mascot as goalkeeper. Imperf | 3·75 | 3·75 |

**538** Young Van Gogh and Paintings

**1990.** Death Centenary of Vincent van Gogh (painter). Multicoloured.

| No. | Description | Unused | Used |
|---|---|---|---|
| 2461 | 30q. Type **538** | 45 | 20 |
| 2462 | 90q. Van Gogh and woman in field | 85 | 50 |
| 2463 | 2l.10 Van Gogh in asylum | 2·00 | 1·60 |
| **MS**2464 | 88×73 mm. 2l.40 Van Gogh and "Wheatfield with Crows". Imperf | 3·25 | 3·25 |

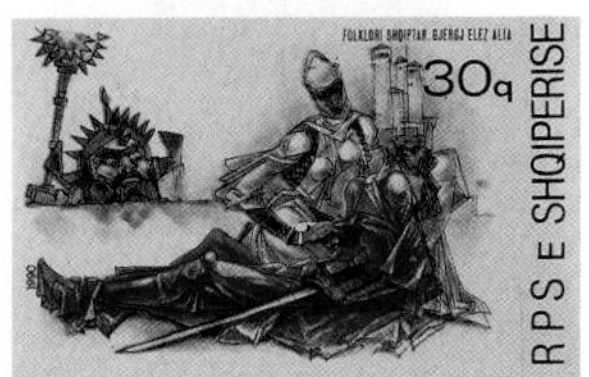

**539** Gjergj Elez Alia lying wounded

**1990.** Gjergj Elez Alia (folk hero). Multicoloured.

| No. | Description | Unused | Used |
|---|---|---|---|
| 2465 | 30q. Type **539** | 35 | 20 |
| 2466 | 90q. Alia being helped onto horse | 75 | 50 |
| 2467 | 1l.20 Alia fighting Bajloz | 1·10 | 85 |
| 2468 | 1l.80 Alia on horseback and severed head of Bajloz | 1·60 | 1·00 |

**540** Mosque

**1990.** 2400th Anniv of Berat. Multicoloured.

| No. | Description | Unused | Used |
|---|---|---|---|
| 2469 | 30q. Type **540** | 10 | 10 |
| 2470 | 90q. Triadha's Church | 60 | 40 |
| 2471 | 1l.20 River | 70 | 50 |
| 2472 | 1l.80 Onufri (artist) | 1·20 | 95 |
| 2473 | 2l.40 Nikolla | 1·40 | 1·20 |

**541** Pirroja

**1990.** Illyrian Heroes. Each black.

| No. | Description | Unused | Used |
|---|---|---|---|
| 2474 | 30q. Type **541** | 20 | 10 |
| 2475 | 90q. Teuta | 65 | 40 |
| 2476 | 1l.20 Bato | 75 | 50 |
| 2477 | 1l.80 Bardhyli | 1·10 | 85 |

**542** School and "Globe" of Books

**1990.** International Literacy Year.

| No. | Type | Description | Unused | Used |
|---|---|---|---|---|
| 2478 | **542** | 90q. multicoloured | 75 | 50 |
| 2479 | **542** | 1l.20 multicoloured | 1·10 | 85 |

**543** "Albanian Horsemen" (Eugene Delacroix)

**1990.** Albanians in Art. Multicoloured.

| No. | Description | Unused | Used |
|---|---|---|---|
| 2480 | 30q. Type **543** | 35 | 10 |
| 2481 | 1l.20 "Albanian Woman" (Camille Corot) | 1·00 | 75 |
| 2482 | 1l.80 "Skanderbeg" (anon) | 1·40 | 1·20 |

**544** Boletini

**1991.** 75th Death Anniv of Isa Boletini (revolutionary). Multicoloured.

| No. | Description | Unused | Used |
|---|---|---|---|
| 2483 | 90q. Type **544** | 65 | 40 |
| 2484 | 1l.20 Boletini and flag | 1·00 | 75 |

**545** Armorial Eagle

**1991.** 800th Anniv (1990) of Founding of Arberi State.

| No. | Type | Description | Unused | Used |
|---|---|---|---|---|
| 2485 | **545** | 90q. multicoloured | 65 | 50 |
| 2486 | **545** | 1l.20 multicoloured | 1·00 | 75 |

**546** "Woman reading"

**1991.** 150th Birth Anniv of Pierre Auguste Renoir (artist). Multicoloured.

| No. | Description | Unused | Used |
|---|---|---|---|
| 2487 | 30q. Type **546** | 55 | 10 |
| 2488 | 90q. "The Swing" | 85 | 75 |
| 2489 | 1l.20 "The Boat Club" (horiz) | 1·30 | 1·00 |
| 2490 | 1l.80 Still life (detail) (horiz) | 2·20 | 1·80 |
| **MS**2491 | 94×75 mm. 3l. "Portrait of Artist with Beard". Imperf | 4·25 | 4·25 |

**547** "Cistus albanicus"

**1991.** Flowers. Multicoloured.

| No. | Description | Unused | Used |
|---|---|---|---|
| 2492 | 30q. Type **547** | 35 | 10 |
| 2493 | 90q. "Trifolium pilczii" | 85 | 75 |
| 2494 | 1l.80 "Lilium albanicum" | 1·60 | 1·30 |

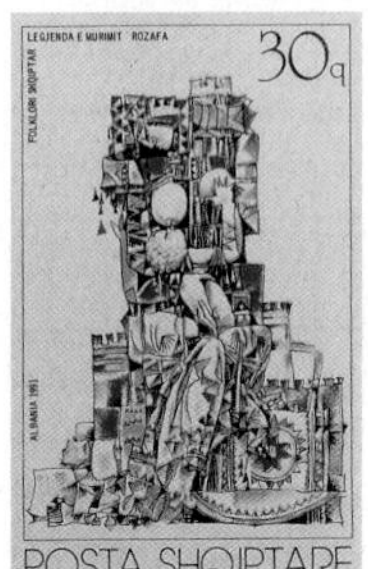

**548** Rozafa breastfeeding Child

**1991.** Imprisonment of Rozafa (folk tale). Mult.

| No. | Description | Unused | Used |
|---|---|---|---|
| 2495 | 30q. Type **548** | 20 | 10 |
| 2496 | 90q. The three brothers talking to old man | 65 | 50 |
| 2497 | 1l.20 Building of walls around Rozafa | 1·10 | 75 |
| 2498 | 1l.80 Figures symbolizing water flowing between stones | 1·50 | 1·20 |

**549** Mozart conducting

**1991.** Death Bicentenary of Wolfgang Amadeus Mozart (composer). Multicoloured.

| No. | Description | Unused | Used |
|---|---|---|---|
| 2499 | 90q. Type **549** | 75 | 50 |
| 2500 | 1l.20 Mozart and score | 1·20 | 85 |
| 2501 | 1l.80 Mozart composing | 2·10 | 1·50 |
| **MS**2502 | 88×69 mm. 3l. Mozart medallion and score. Imperf | 6·50 | 6·50 |

**550** Vitus Bering

**1992.** Explorers. Multicoloured.

| No. | Description | Unused | Used |
|---|---|---|---|
| 2503 | 30q. Type **550** | 35 | 20 |
| 2504 | 90q. Christopher Columbus and his flagship "Santa Maria" | 75 | 40 |
| 2505 | 1l.80 Ferdinand Magellan and his flagship "Vitoria" | 1·60 | 95 |

**551** Otto Lilienthal's Biplane Glider, 1896

**1992.** Aircraft.

| No. | Type | Description | Unused | Used |
|---|---|---|---|---|
| 2506 | **551** | 30q. black, red and blue | 35 | 20 |
| 2507 | - | 80q. multicoloured | 55 | 40 |
| 2508 | - | 90q. multicoloured | 75 | 65 |
| 2509 | - | 1l.20 multicoloured | 1·00 | 85 |
| 2510 | - | 1l.80 multicoloured | 1·30 | 1·20 |
| 2511 | - | 2l.40 black, grey & mve | 1·60 | 1·50 |

DESIGNS: 80q. Clement Ader's "Avion III", 1897; 90q. Wright Brothers' Type A, 1903; 1l.20, Concorde supersonic jetliner; 1l.80, Tupolev Tu-144 jetliner (wrongly inscr "114"); 2l.40, Dornier Do-31E (wrongly inscr "Dernier").

**552** Ski Jumping

**1992.** Winter Olympic Games, Albertville. Mult.

| No. | Description | Unused | Used |
|---|---|---|---|
| 2512 | 30q. Type **552** | 35 | 20 |
| 2513 | 90q. Skiing | 75 | 65 |
| 2514 | 1l.20 Ice skating (pairs) | 1·10 | 85 |
| 2515 | 1l.80 Luge | 1·60 | 1·40 |

**553** "Europe" and Doves

**1992.** Admission of Albania to European Security and Co-operation Conference at Foreign Ministers' Meeting, Berlin. Multicoloured.

| No. | Description | Unused | Used |
|---|---|---|---|
| 2516 | 90q. Type **553** | 1·20 | 1·00 |
| 2517 | 1l.20 Members' flags and map of Europe | 1·50 | 1·30 |

**554** Envelopes and Emblem

**1992.** Admission of Albania to E.P.T. Conference. Multicoloured.

| No. | Description | Unused | Used |
|---|---|---|---|
| 2518 | 90q. Type **554** | 1·30 | 1·20 |
| 2519 | 1l.20 Emblem and tape reels | 1·60 | 1·50 |

**555** Everlasting Flame

**1992.** National Martyrs' Day. Multicoloured.

| No. | Description | Unused | Used |
|---|---|---|---|
| 2520 | 90q. Type **555** | 70 | 65 |
| 2521 | 4l.10 Poppies (horiz) | 3·25 | 2·75 |

**556** Pictograms

**1992.** European Football Championship, Sweden.

| No. | Type | Description | Unused | Used |
|---|---|---|---|---|
| 2522 | **556** | 30q. light green & green | 60 | 30 |
| 2523 | - | 90q. red and blue | 1·20 | 75 |
| 2524 | - | 10l.80 ochre and brown | 7·00 | 5·25 |
| **MS**2525 | | 90×69 mm. 5l. pink, ochre and green. Imperf | 4·00 | 4·00 |

DESIGNS: 90q. to 5l., Different pictograms.

**557** Lawn Tennis

**1992.** Olympic Games, Barcelona. Multicoloured.

| No. | Description | Unused | Used |
|---|---|---|---|
| 2526 | 30q. Type **557** | 45 | 20 |
| 2527 | 90q. Baseball | 1·40 | 85 |
| 2528 | 1l.80 Table tennis | 2·75 | 1·90 |
| **MS**2529 | 89×69 mm. 5l. Torch bearer and running tracks. Imperf | 4·75 | 4·75 |

**558** Map and Doves

**1992.** European Unity.

| No. | Type | Description | Unused | Used |
|---|---|---|---|---|
| 2530 | **558** | 1l.20 multicoloured | 1·40 | 1·00 |

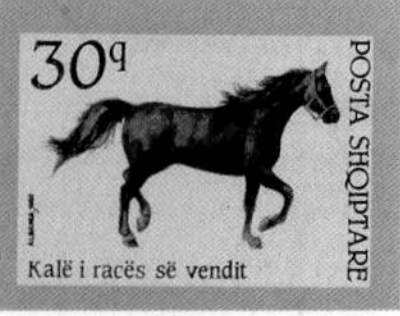

**559** Native Pony

**1992.** Horses. Multicoloured.

| No. | Description | Unused | Used |
|---|---|---|---|
| 2531 | 30q. Type **559** | 35 | 20 |
| 2532 | 90q. Hungarian nonius | 60 | 40 |
| 2533 | 1l.20 Arab (vert) | 80 | 65 |
| 2534 | 10l.60 Haflinger (vert) | 7·50 | 6·00 |

**560** Map of Americas, Columbus and Ships

**1992.** Europa. 500th Anniv of Discovery of America by Columbus. Multicoloured.

| | | | |
|---|---|---|---|
| 2535 | 60q. Type **560** | 60 | 40 |
| 2536 | 3l.20 Map of Americas and Columbus meeting Amerindians | 4·00 | 3·75 |

**MS**2537 90×70 mm. 5l. Map of America and Columbus. Imperf 85·00 85·00

**561** Mother Teresa and Child

**1992.** Mother Teresa (Agnes Gonxhe Bojaxhi) (founder of Missionaries of Charity).

| | | | | |
|---|---|---|---|---|
| 2538 | **561** | 40q. red | 10 | 10 |
| 2539 | **561** | 60q. brown | 10 | 10 |
| 2540 | **561** | 1l. violet | 10 | 10 |
| 2541 | **561** | 1l.80 grey | 15 | 10 |
| 2542 | **561** | 2l. red | 35 | 20 |
| 2543 | **561** | 2l.40 green | 45 | 30 |
| 2544 | **561** | 3l.20 blue | 60 | 50 |
| 2545 | **561** | 5l. violet | 70 | 65 |
| 2546 | **561** | 5l.60 purple | 95 | 85 |
| 2547 | **561** | 7l.20 green | 1·20 | 1·00 |
| 2548 | **561** | 10l. orange | 1·40 | 1·30 |
| 2549 | **561** | 18l. orange | 1·50 | 1·40 |
| 2550 | **561** | 20l. purple | 60 | 50 |
| 2551 | **561** | 25l. green | 2·30 | 2·10 |
| 2552 | **561** | 60l. green | 2·50 | 2·40 |

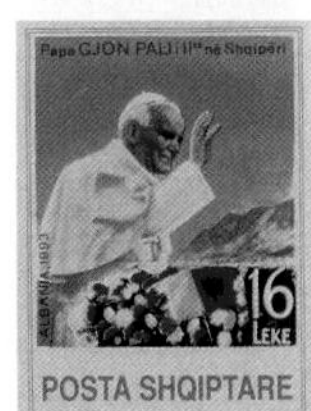

**562** Pope John Paul II

**1993.** Papal Visit.

| | | | | |
|---|---|---|---|---|
| 2555 | **562** | 16l. multicoloured | 3·00 | 2·50 |

**1993.** Nos. 2329/32 and 2335 surch **POSTA SHQIPTARE** and new value.

| | | | | |
|---|---|---|---|---|
| 2556 | **496** | 3l. on 10q. blue | 25 | 20 |
| 2557 | **496** | 6l.50 on 20q. red | 80 | 75 |
| 2558 | **496** | 13l. on 30q. red | 2·30 | 2·10 |
| 2559 | **496** | 20l. on 90q. blue | 3·50 | 3·25 |
| 2560 | **496** | 30l. on 50q. brown | 5·25 | 4·75 |

**564** Lef Nosi (first Postal Minister)

**1993.** 80th Anniv of First Albanian Stamps.

| | | | | |
|---|---|---|---|---|
| 2561 | **564** | 6l.50 brown and green | 1·20 | 1·00 |

**565** "Life Weighs Heavily on Man" (A. Zajmi)

**1993.** Europa. Contemporary Art. Multicoloured.

| | | | |
|---|---|---|---|
| 2562 | 3l. Type **565** | 1·20 | 1·00 |
| 2563 | 7l. "The Green Star" (E. Hila) (horiz) | 4·75 | 4·25 |

**MS**2564 116×121 mm. 20l. "Gjirokaster" (B. Ahmeti). Imperf 8·25 8·25

**566** Running

**1993.** Mediterranean Games, Agde and Roussillon (Languedoc), France. Multicoloured.

| | | | |
|---|---|---|---|
| 2565 | 3l. Type **566** | 25 | 20 |
| 2566 | 16l. Canoeing | 2·30 | 2·10 |
| 2567 | 21l. Cycling | 3·25 | 3·00 |

**MS**2568 117×84 mm. 20l. Map of Mediterranean. Imperf 4·00 4·00

**567** Bardhi

**1993.** 350th Death Anniv of Frang Bardhi (scholar).

| | | | | |
|---|---|---|---|---|
| 2569 | **567** | 6l.50 brown and stone | 1·40 | 1·30 |

**MS**2570 94×107 mm. 20l. brown and gold. Imperf 4·75 4·75

DESIGN: 20l. Bardhi writing at desk.

**568** Mascot and Flags around Stadium

**1994.** World Cup Football Championship, U.S.A. Multicoloured.

| | | | |
|---|---|---|---|
| 2571 | 42l. Type **568** | 1·40 | 1·30 |
| 2572 | 68l. Mascot kicking ball | 2·10 | 1·90 |

**569** Gjovalin Gjadri (construction engineer)

**1994.** Europa. Discoveries and Inventions.

| | | | | |
|---|---|---|---|---|
| 2573 | **569** | 50l. dp brn, ches & brn | 2·30 | 2·10 |
| 2574 | - | 100l. dp brn, ches & brn | 3·50 | 3·25 |

**MS**2575 60×80 mm. 150l. drab and brown. Imperf 5·75 5·75

DESIGN: 100l. Karl Ritter von Ghega (railway engineer); 150l. Sketch of traffic project.

**570** Emblem and Benz

**1995.** 150th Birth Anniv (1994) of Karl Benz (motor manufacturer). Multicoloured.

| | | | |
|---|---|---|---|
| 2576 | 5l. Type **570** | 10 | 10 |
| 2577 | 10l. Mercedes-Benz C-class saloon, 1995 Daimler motor carriage, 1886 | 25 | 20 |
| 2578 | 60l. First four-wheel Benz motor-car, 1886 | 1·40 | 1·30 |
| 2579 | 125l. Mercedes-Benz 540 K cabriolet, 1936 | 4·00 | 3·75 |

**571** Richard Wagner

**1995.** Composers. Each brown and gold.

| | | | |
|---|---|---|---|
| 2580 | 3l. Type **571** | 10 | 10 |
| 2581 | 6l.50 Edvard Grieg | 25 | 20 |
| 2582 | 11l. Charles Gounod | 35 | 30 |
| 2583 | 20l. Pyotr Tchaikovsky | 80 | 75 |

**572** Intersections

**1995.** 50th Anniv (1994) of Liberation.

| | | | | |
|---|---|---|---|---|
| 2584 | **572** | 50l. black and red | 1·70 | 1·60 |

**573** Ali Pasha

**1995.** 250th Birth Anniv (1994) of Ali Pasha of Tepelene (Pasha of Janina, 1788–1820).

| | | | | |
|---|---|---|---|---|
| 2585 | **573** | 60l. black, yellow & brn | 2·00 | 1·80 |

**MS**2586 80×60 mm. 100l. brown and orange (Administration building, Tepelene). Imperf 3·50 3·50

**574** Veskopoja, 1744 (left half)

**1995.** 250th Anniv (1994) of Veskopoja Academy. Multicoloured.

| | | | |
|---|---|---|---|
| 2587 | 42l. Type **574** | 1·20 | 1·00 |
| 2588 | 68l. Veskopoja, 1744 (right half) | 1·70 | 1·60 |

Nos. 2587/8 were issued together, se-tenant, forming a composite design.

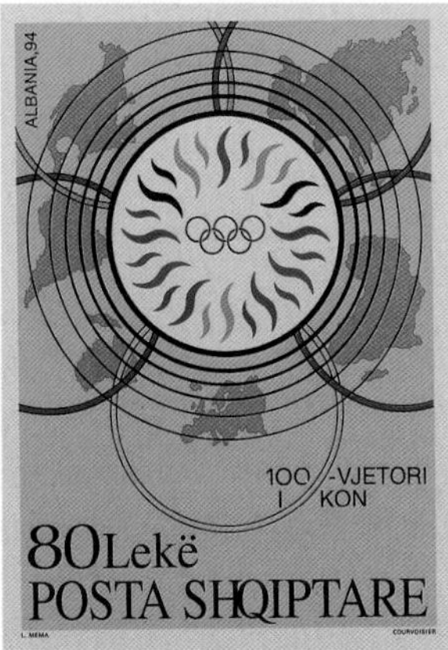

**575** Olympic Rings and Map

**1995.** Centenary of International Olympic Committee. Sheet 60×80 mm. Imperf.

**MS**2589 **575** 80l. multicoloured 2·50 2·50

**576** Palace of Europe, Strasbourg

**1995.** Admission of Albania to Council of Europe. Multicoloured.

| | | | |
|---|---|---|---|
| 2590 | 25l. Type **576** | 95 | 85 |
| 2591 | 85l. State arms and map of Europe | 3·75 | 3·25 |

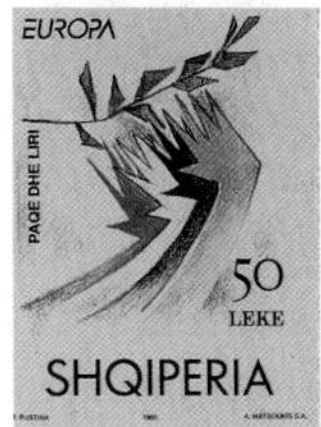

**577** Hands holding Olive Branch

**1995.** Europa. Peace and Freedom. Multicoloured.

| | | | |
|---|---|---|---|
| 2592 | 50l. Type **577** | 2·30 | 2·10 |
| 2593 | 100l. Dove flying over hands | 4·75 | 4·25 |

**MS**2594 80×60 mm. 150l. Figure stretching out hands. Imperf 7·00 7·00

**578** Mice sitting around Table and Stork with Fox

**1995.** 300th Death Anniv of Jean de La Fontaine (writer). Multicoloured.

| | | | |
|---|---|---|---|
| 2595 | 2l. Type **578** | 15 | 10 |
| 2596 | 3l. Stork with foxes around table | 25 | 10 |
| 2597 | 25l. Frogs under tree | 95 | 85 |

**MS**2598 80×60 mm. 60l. La Fontaine and animals. Imperf 2·30 2·30

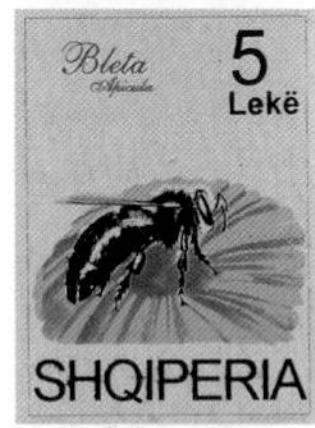

**579** Bee on Flower

**1995.** The Honey Bee. Multicoloured.

| | | | |
|---|---|---|---|
| 2599 | 5l. Type **579** | 25 | 10 |
| 2600 | 10l. Bee and honeycomb | 35 | 20 |
| 2601 | 25l. Bee on comb | 1·60 | 1·30 |

**580** Fridtjof Nansen

**1995.** Polar Explorers. Multicoloured.

| | | | |
|---|---|---|---|
| 2602 | 25l. Type **580** | 80 | 70 |
| 2603 | 25l. James Cook | 80 | 70 |
| 2604 | 25l. Roald Amundsen | 80 | 70 |
| 2605 | 25l. Robert Scott | 80 | 70 |

Nos. 2602/5 were issued together, se-tenant, forming a composite design.

**581** Flags outside U.N. Building, New York

**1995.** 50th Anniv of U.N.O. Multicoloured.

| | | | |
|---|---|---|---|
| 2606 | 2l. Type **581** | 25 | 10 |
| 2607 | 100l. Flags flying to right outside U.N. building, New York | 3·25 | 3·00 |

**582** Male Chorus

**1995.** National Folklore Festival, Berat. Mult.

2608 5l. Type **582** 35 20
2609 50l. Female participant 1·70 1·60

**583** "Poet"

**1995.** Jan Kukuzeli (11th-century poet, musician and teacher). Abstract representations of Kukuzeli. Multicoloured.

2610 18l. Type **583** 70 65
2611 20l. "Musician" 75 70
**MS**2612 80×80 mm. 100l. "Teacher". Imperf 3·50 3·50

**584** Church and Preacher, Berat Kruje

**1995.** 20th Anniv of World Tourism Organization. Multicoloured.

2613 18l. Type **584** 70 65
2614 20l. Street, Shkoder 80 75
2615 42l. Buildings, Gjirokaster 2·00 1·80

**585** Paul Eluard

**1995.** Poets' Birth Centenaries. Multicoloured.

2616 25l. Type **585** 80 75
2617 50l. Sergei Yessenin 1·60 1·50

**586** Louis, Film Reel and Projector

**1995.** Centenary of Motion Pictures. Lumiere Brothers (developers of cine camera). Mult.

2618 10l. Type **586** 25 20
2619 85l. Auguste, film reel and cinema audience 2·30 2·10

**587** Presley

**1995.** 60th Birth Anniv of Elvis Presley (entertainer). Multicoloured.

2620 3l. Type **587** 25 20
2621 60l. Presley (different) 2·10 1·90

**588** Banknotes of 1925

**1995.** 70th Anniv of Albanian National Bank. Mult.

2622 10l. Type **588** 35 20
2623 25l. Modern banknotes 95 85

**589** "5", Crumbling Star, Open Book and Peace Dove

**1995.** 5th Anniv of Democratic Movement. Mult.

2624 5l. Type **589** 25 10
2625 50l. Woman planting tree 1·90 1·70

**590** Mother Teresa

**1996.** Europa. Famous Women. Mother Teresa (founder of Missionaries of Charity).

2626 **590** 25l. multicoloured 1·20 1·00
2627 **590** 100l. multicoloured 4·00 3·75
**MS**2628 60×80 mm. 150l. Mother Teresa (different). Imperf 8·25 8·25

**591** Football, Union Flag, Map of Europe and Stadium

**1996.** European Football Championship, England. Multicoloured.

2629 25l. Type **591** 95 85
2630 100l. Map of Europe, ball and player 3·75 3·25

**592** Satellite and Radio Mast

**1996.** Inaug of Cellular Telephone Network. Mult.

2631 10l. Type **592** 35 20
2632 60l. User, truck, container ship and mobile telephone (vert) 2·00 1·80

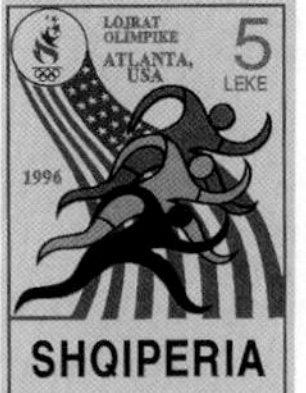

**593** Running

**1996.** Olympic Games, Atlanta, U.S.A. Mult.

2633 5l. Type **593** 25 10
2634 25l. Throwing the hammer 95 85
2635 60l. Long jumping 2·30 2·10
**MS**2636 60×80 mm. 100l. Games emblem. Imperf 3·00 3·00

**594** Linked Hands

**1996.** 75th Anniv of Albanian Red Cross.

2637 **594** 50l.+10l. mult 2·10 1·90

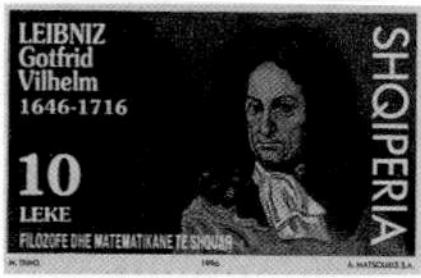

**595** Gottfried Wilhelm Leibniz (350th)

**1996.** Philosopher-mathematicians' Birth Annivs. Multicoloured.

2638 10l. Type **595** 60 40
2639 85l. Rene Descartes (400th) 3·00 2·50

**596** "The Naked Maja"

**1996.** 250th Birth Anniv of Francisco de Goya (artist). Multicoloured.

2640 10l. Type **596** 60 40
2641 60l. "Dona Isabel Cobos de Porcel" 2·10 1·90
**MS**2642 80×60 mm. 100l. "Self-portrait" (24×29 mm) 3·00 3·00

**597** Book Binding

**1996.** Christian Art Exhibition. Multicoloured.

2643 5l. Type **597** 25 10
2644 25l. Book clasp showing crucifixion 95 85
2645 85l. Book binding (different) 3·00 2·50

**598** Princess

**1996.** 50th Anniv of UNICEF Children's Paintings. Multicoloured.

2646 5l. Type **598** 25 10
2647 10l. Woman 35 20
2648 25l. Sea life 1·20 1·00
2649 50l. Harbour 1·70 1·60

**599** State Arms, Book and Fishta

**1996.** 125th Birth Anniv of Gjergj Fishta (writer and politician). Multicoloured.

2650 10l. Type **599** 35 20
2651 60l. Battle scene and Fishta 2·00 1·80

**600** Omar Khayyam and Writing Materials

**1997.** 950th Birth Anniv of Omar Khayyam (astronomer and poet). Multicoloured.

2652 20l. Type **600** 60 40
2653 50l. Omar Khayyam and symbols of astronomy 1·40 1·30

Nos. 2652/3 are inscribed "850" in error.

**601** Gutenberg

**1997.** 600th Birth Anniv of Johannes Gutenberg (printer). Multicoloured.

2654 20l. Type **601** 60 40
2655 60l. Printing press 1·70 1·60

Nos. 2654/5 were issued together, se-tenant, forming a composite design.

**602** Pelicans

**1997.** The Dalmatian Pelican. Multicoloured.

2656 10l. Type **602** 25 20
2657 80l. Pelicans on shore and in flight 2·30 2·10

Nos. 2656/7 were issued together, se-tenant, forming a composite design.

**603** Dragon

**1997.** Europa. Tales and Legends. "The Blue Pool". Multicoloured.

2658 30l. Type **603** 1·20 1·00
2659 100l. Dragon drinking from pool 4·00 3·75

**604** Konica

**1997.** 55th Death Anniv of Faik Konica (writer and politician).
2660 **604** 10l. brown and black 35 20
2661 **604** 25l. blue and black 1·00 95
**MS**2662 60×80 mm. **604** 80l. brown 3·00 3·00

**605** Male Athlete

**1997.** Mediterranean Games, Bari. Multicoloured.
2663 20l. Type **605** 60 40
2664 30l. Female athlete and rowers 1·20 1·00
**MS**2665 60×80 mm. 100l. Discus-thrower, javelin-thrower and runner. Imperf 3·00 3·00

**606** Skanderbeg

**1997**
2666 **606** 5l. red and brown 25 10
2667 **606** 10l. green and olive 35 25
2668 **606** 20l. green and deep green 65 50
2669 **606** 25l. mauve and purple 75 65
2670 **606** 30l. violet and lilac 95 80
2671 **606** 50l. grey and black 1·50 1·30
2672 **606** 60l. lt brown & brown 1·80 1·60
2673 **606** 80l. lt brown & brown 2·40 2·20
2674 **606** 100l. red and lake 3·00 2·75
2675 **606** 110l. blue and deep blue 3·25 3·00

**1997.** Mother Teresa (founder of Missionaries of Charity) Commemoration. No. 2627 optd **HOMAZH** 1910–1997.
2676 **590** 100l. multicoloured 4·00 3·50

**608** Codex Aureus (11th century)

**1997.** Codices (1st series). Multicoloured.
2677 10l. Type **608** 25 10
2678 25l. Codex Purpureus Beratinus (7th century) showing mountain and scribe 70 65
2679 60l. Codex Purpureus Beratinus showing church and scribe 1·60 1·50
See also Nos. 2712/14.

**609** Twin-headed Eagle (postal emblem)

**1997.** 85th Anniv of Albanian Postal Service.
2680 **609** 10l. multicoloured 25 10
2681 **609** 30l. multicoloured 95 85
The 30l. differs from Type **609** in minor parts of the design.

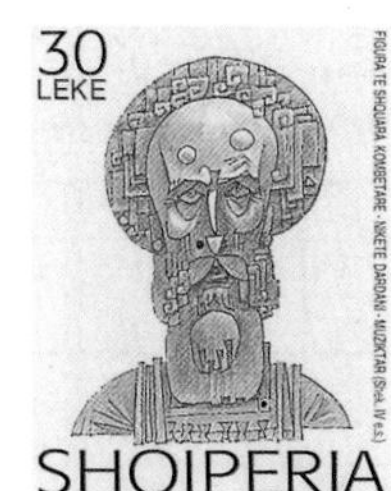

**610** Nikete of Ramesiana

**1998.** Nikete Dardani, Bishop of Ramesiana (philosopher and composer).
2682 **610** 30l. multicoloured 70 50
2683 **610** 100l. multicoloured 2·20 2·00
There are minor differences of design between the two values.

**611** Man sitting at Table

**1998.** Legend of Pogradeci Lake. Multicoloured.
2684 30l. Type **611** 70 50
2685 50l. The Three Graces 1·00 85
2686 60l. Women drawing water 1·30 1·20
2687 80l. Man of ice 1·70 1·60

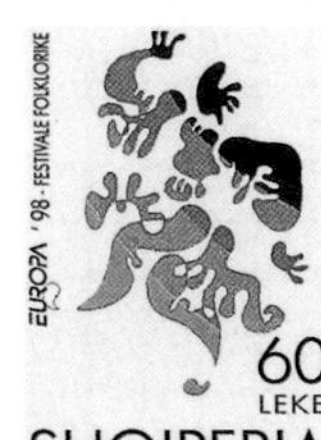

**612** Stylized Dancers

**1998.** Europa. National Festivals. Multicoloured.
2688 60l. Type **612** 2·30 2·10
2689 100l. Female dancer 3·00 2·50
**MS**2690 60×80 mm. 150l. Two dancers. Imperf 5·25 5·25

**613** Abdyl Frasheri (founder)

**1998.** 120th Anniv of League of Prizren. Mult.
2691 30l. Type **613** 70 50
2692 50l. Sulejman Vokshi and partisan 1·00 85
2693 60l. Iljaz Pashe Dibra and crossed rifles 1·30 1·20
2694 80l. Ymer Prizreni and partisans 1·70 1·60

**614** Player with Ball

**1998.** World Cup Football Championship, France. Multicoloured.
2695 60l. Type **614** 1·30 1·20
2696 100l. Player with ball (different) 2·20 2·00
**MS**2697 60×80 mm. 120l. Championship mascot. Imperf 3·00 3·00

**615** Wrestlers in National Costume

**1998.** European Junior Wrestling Championship. Multicoloured.
2698 30l. Type **615** 60 40
2699 60l. Ancient Greek wrestlers 1·30 1·20

**616** Cacej

**1998.** 90th Birth Anniv of Eqerem Cabej (linguist).
2700 **616** 60l. black and yellow 80 65
2701 **616** 80l. yellow, black & red 1·20 1·00

**617** Diana, Princess of Wales

**1998.** Diana, Princess of Wales Commemoration. Multicoloured.
2702 60l. Type **617** 1·70 1·60
2703 100l. With Mother Teresa 2·30 2·10

**618** Mother Teresa holding Child

**1998.** Mother Teresa (founder of Missionaries of Charity) Commemoration. Multicoloured.
2704 60l. Type **618** 1·40 1·30
2705 100l. Mother Teresa (vert) 2·30 2·10

**619** Detail of Painting

**1998.** 150th Birth Anniv of Paul Gauguin (artist).
Multicoloured.
2706 60l. Type **619** 1·20 1·00
2707 80l. "Women of Tahiti" 1·60 1·50
**MS**2708 60×80 mm. 120l. Face. Imperf 3·00 3·00

**620** Epitaph

**1998.** 625th Anniv of Epitaph of Gllavenica (embroidery of dead Christ). Multicoloured.
2709 30l. Type **620** 60 40
2710 80l. Close-up of upper body 1·60 1·50
**MS**2711 80×60 mm. 100l. Detail of epitaph (24×29 mm) 2·00 2·00

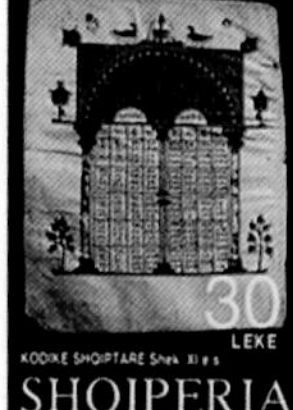

**621** Page of Codex

**1998.** Codices (2nd series). 11th-century Manuscripts. Multicoloured.
2712 30l. Type **621** 60 40
2713 50l. Front cover of manuscript 95 75
2714 80l. Page showing mosque 1·60 1·50

**1998.** "Italia '98" International Stamp Exhibition. No. **MS**2628 optd **Italia 98**.
**MS**2715 60×80 mm. 150l. mult 7·50 7·50

**623** Koliqi

**1998.** 1st Death Anniv of Cardinal Mikel Koliqi (first Albanian Cardinal). Multicoloured.
2716 30l. Type **623** 60 40
2717 100l. Koliqi (different) 2·00 1·80

**624** George Washington (first President, 1789–97)

**1999.** American Anniversaries. Multicoloured.
2718 150l. Type **624** (death bicentenary) 3·50 3·25
2719 150l. Abraham Lincoln (President 1861–65, 190th birth anniv) 3·50 3·25
2720 150l. Martin Luther King Jr. (civil rights campaigner, 70th birth anniv) 3·50 3·25

**625** Monk Seals

**1999.** The Monk Seal. Multicoloured.
2721 110l. Type **625** 2·50 2·30
2722 110l. Two seals (both facing left) 2·50 2·30
2723 150l. As No. 2722 but both facing right 3·50 3·25
2724 150l. As Type **625** but seal at back facing left and seal at front facing right 3·50 3·25
Nos. 2721/4 were issued together, se-tenant, forming a composite design.

**1999.** 50th Anniv of Council of Europe. No. 2590 surch **150 LEKE** and emblem.
2725 **576** 150l. on 25l. mult 4·00 3·50

**1999.** "iBRA '99" International Stamp Exhibition, Nuremberg, Germany. No. 2496 surch **150 LEKE** in black (new value) and multicoloured (emblem).
2726 150l. on 90q. multicoloured 3·75 3·25

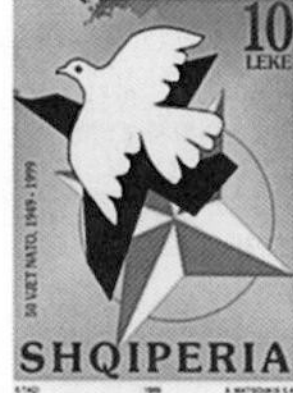

**628** Dove, Airplane and NATO Emblem

**1999.** 50th Anniv of North Atlantic Treaty Organization.
2727 **628** 10l. multicoloured 35 20
2728 **628** 100l. multicoloured 2·50 2·30
**MS**2729 69×85 mm. 250l. multicoloured 5·75 5·75

**629** Mickey Mouse

**1999.** Mickey Mouse (cartoon film character). Multicoloured.
2730 60l. Type **629** 1·40 1·30
2731 80l. Mickey writing letter 2·10 1·90
2732 110l. Mickey thinking 2·30 2·10
2733 150l. Wearing black and red jumper 3·50 3·25

**630** Thethi National Park, Shkoder

**1999.** Europa. Parks and Gardens. Multicoloured.
2734 90l. Type **630** 3·00 2·50
2735 310l. Lura National Park, Dibra 7·50 6·75
**MS**2736 80×60 mm. 350l. Divjaka National Park, Lushnje. Imperf 10·50 10·50

**631** Coin

**1999.** Illyrian Coins. Multicoloured.
2737 10l. Type **631** 25 10
2738 20l. Coins from Labeateve, Bylisi and Scutari 45 30
2739 200l. Coins of King Monuni 5·00 4·50
**MS**2740 80×60 mm. 310l. Coin of King Gent (29×49 mm) 7·50 7·50

**1999.** "Philexfrance 99" International Stamp Exhibition, Paris. No. 2512 surch with new value and Exhibition logo.
2741 **552** 150l. on 30q. mult 3·75 3·25

**633** Chaplin

**1999.** 110th Birth Anniv of Charlie Chaplin (film actor and director). Multicoloured.
2742 30l. Type **633** 70 50
2743 50l. Raising hat 1·20 1·00
2744 250l. Dancing 6·50 6·50

**635** Prisoner behind Bars

**1999.** The Nazi Holocaust.
2749 **635** 30l. multicoloured 80 70
2750 **635** 150l. black and yellow 4·00 3·75

**1999.** 125th Anniv of Universal Postal Union.
2751 **636** 20l. multicoloured 45 30
2752 **636** 60l. multicoloured 1·50 1·40

**1999.** "China 1999" International Stamp Exhibition, Peking. No. 2497 surch **150 LEKE**.
2753 150l. on 1l.20 multicoloured 3·75 3·25

**638** Javelin

**1999.** 70th Anniv of National Athletic Championships. Multicoloured.
2754 10l. Type **638** 25 10
2755 20l. Discus 45 30
2756 200l. Running 5·00 4·50

**639** Madonna and Child

**1999.** Icons by Onufri Shek (artist). Multicoloured.
2757 30l. Type **639** 90 80
2758 300l. The Resurrection 7·00 6·25

**640** Bilal Golemi (veterinary surgeon)

**1999.** Birth Anniversaries. Multicoloured.
2759 10l. Type **640** (centenary) 25 10
2760 20l. Azem Galica (revolutionary) (centenary) 45 30
2761 50l. Viktor Eftimiu (writer) (centenary) 1·30 1·20
2762 300l. Lasgush Poradeci (poet) (centenary (2000)) 7·50 6·75

**641** Carnival Mask

**1999.** Carnivals. Multicoloured.
2763 30l. Type **641** 1·10 95
2764 300l. Turkey mask 7·50 6·75

**642** Bell and Flowers

**2000.** New Millennium. The Peace Bell. Mult.
2765 40l. Type **642** 1·00 90
2766 90l. Bell and flowers (different) 2·30 2·00

**643** Woman's Costume, Librazhdi

**2000.** Regional Costumes (1st series). Mult.
2767 5l. Type **643** 10 10
2768 10l. Woman's costume, Malesia E Madhe 25 15
2769 15l. Man's costume, Malesia E Madhe 35 20
2770 20l. Man's costume, Tropoje 45 30
2771 30l. Man's costume, Dumrea 70 50
2772 35l. Man's costume, Tirana 80 65
2773 40l. Woman's costume, Tirana 95 75
2774 45l. Woman's costume, Arbereshe 1·00 85
2775 50l. Man's costume, Gjirokastra 1·20 1·00
2776 55l. Woman's costume, Lunxheri 1·30 1·20
2777 70l. Woman's costume, Cameria 1·60 1·50
2778 90l. Man's costume, Laberia 2·10 1·90

See also Nos. 2832/43, 2892/2903, 2943/54, 3053/64, 3080/91 and 3171/82.

**644** Majer

**2000.** 150th Birth Anniv of Gustav Majer (etymologist).
2779 **644** 50l. green 1·20 1·00
2780 **644** 130l. red 3·00 2·75

**645** Donald Duck

**2000.** Donald and Daisy Duck (cartoon film characters). Multicoloured.
2781 10l. Type **645** 25 10
2782 30l. Donald Duck 70 50
2783 90l. Daisy Duck 2·10 1·90
2784 250l. Donald Duck 5·75 5·25

**646** Early Racing Car

**2000.** Motor Racing. Multicoloured.
2785 30l. Type **646** 1·00 90
2786 30l. Two-man racing car 1·00 90
2787 30l. Racing car with wire nose 1·00 90
2788 30l. Racing car with solid wheels 1·00 90
2789 30l. Car No. 1 1·00 90
2790 30l. Car No. 2 1·00 90
2791 30l. White Formula 1 racing car (facing left) 1·00 90
2792 30l. Blue Formula 1 racing car 1·00 90
2793 30l. Red Formula 1 racing car 1·00 90
2794 30l. White Formula 1 racing car (front view) 1·00 90

**647** Ristoz of Mborja Church, Korca

**2000.** Birth Bimillenary of Jesus Christ. Mult.
2795 15l. Type **647** 45 30
2796 40l. St. Kolli Church, Voskopoja 1·30 1·20
2797 90l. Church of Flori and Lauri, Kosovo 3·00 2·50
**MS**2798 80×60 mm. 250l. Fountain of Shengjin (mosaic), Tirana (37×37 mm) 5·25 5·25

**648** "Building Europe"

**2000.** Europa. Multicoloured.
2799 130l. Type **648** 4·00 3·75
**MS**2800 60×80 mm. 300l. Detail of design showing boy holding star (24×29 mm) 10·50 10·50

**649** Wolf

**2000.** Animals. Multicoloured.
2801 10l. Type **649** 25 10
2802 40l. Brown bear 95 75
2803 90l. Wild boar 2·10 1·90
2804 220l. Red fox 5·00 4·50

**650** Gustav Mahler (composer) (40th death anniv)

**2000.** "WIPA 2000" International Stamp Exhibition, Vienna.
2805 **650** 130l. multicoloured 3·00 2·75

**651** Footballer saving Ball

**2000.** European Football Championship, Belgium and The Netherlands. Multicoloured.
2806 10l. Type **651** 25 10
2807 120l. Footballer heading ball 3·00 2·50
**MS**2808 80×60 mm. 260l. Footballer kicking ball. Imperf 6·25 6·25

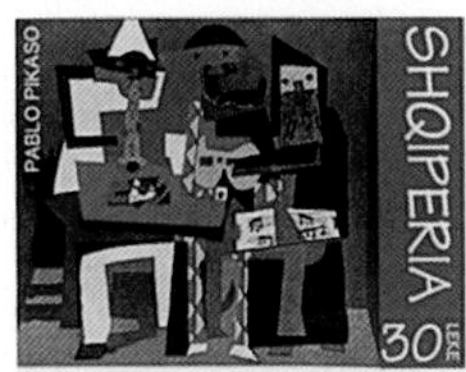

**652** Musicans

**2000.** Paintings by Picasso. Multicoloured.
2809 30l. Type **652** 70 50
2810 40l. Abstract face 1·00 85
2811 250l. Two women running along beach 5·75 5·25
**MS**2812 60×80 mm. 400l. Painting of man (24×29 mm) 9·25 9·25

**653** Basketball

**2000.** Olympic Games, Sydney. Multicoloured.
2813 10l. Type **653** 25 10
2814 40l. Football 95 75
2815 90l. Athletics 2·10 1·90
2816 250l. Cycling 5·75 5·25

**654** *LZ-1* (first Zeppelin airship) over Lake Constance, Friedrichshafen (first flight)

**2000.** Centenary of First Zeppelin Flight. Airship Development. Multicoloured.
2817 15l. Type **654** 35 20
2818 30l. Santos-Dumont airship *Ballon No. 5* and Eiffel Tower C attempted round trip from St. Cloud via Eiffel Tower, 1901 70 50
2819 300l. Beardmore airship *R-34* over New York (first double crossing of Atlantic) 6·50 5·75
**MS**2820 80×60 mm. 300l. Ferdinand von Zeppelin and airship (24×28 mm) 6·50 6·50

**655** "Self-portrait" (Picasso)

**2000.** "Espana 2000" World Stamp Exhibition, Madrid.
2821 **655** 130l. multicoloured 3·25 3·00

**656** Yellow Gentian (*Gentiana lutea*)

**2000.** Medicinal Plants. Multicoloured.
2822 50l. Type **656** 1·30 1·20
2823 70l. Cross-leaved gentian (*Gentiana cruciata*) 1·60 1·50

**657** Naim Frasheri (poet) and Landscape

**2000.** Personalities. Multicoloured.
2824 30l. Type **657** 70 50
2825 50l. Bajram Curri (revolutionary) and landscape 1·30 1·20
Nos. 2824/5 were issued together, se-tenant, forming a composite design.

**658** Mother holding Child

**2000.** 50th Anniv of United Nations High Commission for Refugees. Multicoloured.
2826 50l. Type **658** 1·40 1·30
2827 90l. Mother breastfeeding child 2·10 1·90

**659** Dede Ahmed Myftar Ahmataj

**2001.** Religious Leaders. Multicoloured.
2828 90l. Type **659** 2·30 2·10
2829 90l. Dede Sali Njazi 2·30 2·10

**2001.** "For Kosovo". Nos. 2592/3 surch **PER KOSOVEN** and new value.
2830 80l.+10l. on 50l. multicoloured 5·25 4·75
2831 130l.+20l. on 100l. multicoloured 8·75 7·75

**2001.** Regional Costumes (2nd series). As T **643**. Multicoloured.
2832 20l. Man's costume, Tropoje 60 50
2833 20l. Woman's costume, Lume 60 50
2834 20l. Woman's costume, Mirdite 60 50
2835 20l. Man's costume, Lume 60 50
2836 20l. Woman's costume, Zadrime 60 50
2837 20l. Woman's costume, Shpati 60 50
2838 20l. Man's costume, Kruje 60 50
2839 20l. Woman's costume, Macukulli 60 50
2840 20l. Woman's costume, Dardhe 60 50
2841 20l. Man's costume, Lushnje 60 50
2842 20l. Woman's costume, Dropulli 60 50
2843 20l. Woman's costume, Shmili 60 50

**661** Southern Magnolia (*Magnolia gandiflora*)

**2001.** Scented Flowers. Multicoloured.
2844 10l. Type **661** 35 20
2845 20l. Virginia rose (*Rosa virginiana*) 60 40
2846 90l. *Dianthus barbatus* 2·30 2·10
2847 140l. Lilac (*Syringa vulgaris*) 3·75 3·25

**662** Goofy in Shorts

**2001.** Goofy (cartoon film character). Multicoloured.
2848 20l. Type **662** 45 30
2849 50l. Goofy in blue hat 1·20 1·00
2850 90l. Goofy in red trousers 2·10 1·90
2851 140l. Goofy in purple waistcoat 3·25 3·00

**663** Vincenzo Bellini

**2001.** Composers' Anniversaries. Multicoloured.
2852 90l. Type **663** (birth centenary) 2·20 2·00
2853 90l. Guiseppe Verdi (death centenary) 2·20 2·00
**MS**2854 90×90 mm. 300l. Bellini and Verdi (75×38 mm) 7·00 7·00

**664** Cliffs and Stream

**2001.** Europa. Water Resources. Multicoloured.
2855 40l. Type **664** 1·20 1·00
2856 110l. Waterfall 2·30 2·10
2857 200l. Lake 4·75 4·25
**MS**2858 60×80 mm. 350l. Ripples (24×78 mm) 10·50 10·50

**665** Horse

**2001.** Domestic Animals. Multicoloured.
2859 10l. Type **665** 25 10
2860 15l. Donkey 35 20
2861 80l. Siamese cat 1·90 1·70
2862 90l. Dog 2·20 2·00
**MS**2863 80×60 mm. 300l. Head of Siamese cat (49×29 mm) 7·00 7·00

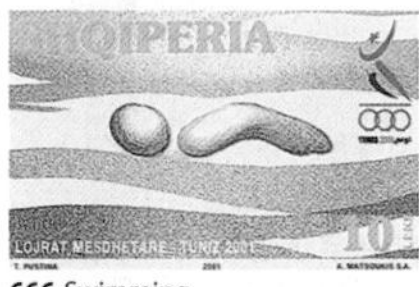

**666** Swimming

**2001.** Mediterranean Games, Tunis. Multicoloured.
2864 10l. Type **666** 35 20
2865 90l. Athletics 2·30 2·10
2866 140l. Cycling 3·75 3·25
**MS**2867 60×80 mm. 260l. Discus (29×24 mm) 6·50 6·50

**667** *Eole* (first powered take-off by Clement Ader, 1890)

**2001.** Aviation History. Multicoloured.
2868 40l. Type **667** 1·20 1·00
2869 40l. *Bleriot XI* (first powered crossing of English channel by Louis Bleriot, 1909) 1·20 1·00
2870 40l. *Spirit of St. Louis* (first solo non-stop crossing of North Atlantic from Paris to New York by Charles Lindbergh, 1927) 1·20 1·00
2871 40l. First flight to Tirana, 1925 1·20 1·00
2872 40l. Antonov AH-10 (first flight, 1956) 1·20 1·00
2873 40l. Concorde (first flight, 1969) 1·20 1·00
2874 40l. Concorde (first commercial flight, 1970) 1·20 1·00
2875 40l. Space shuttle *Colombia* (first flight, 1981) 1·20 1·00

**668** Tabakeve

**2001.** Old Bridges.
2876 **668** 10l. multicoloured 25 10
2877 - 20l. multicoloured 35 20
2878 - 40l. multicoloured 1·00 85
2879 - 90l. black 2·10 1·90
**MS**2880 80×60 mm. 2l.50 multicoloured 6·50 6·50
DESIGNS: 20l. Kamares; 40l. Golikut; 90l. Mesit. 49×22 mm—2l.50, Tabakeve.

**669** Dimitri of Arber

**2001.** Arms (1st series).
2881 20l. Type **669** 60 40
2882 45l. Balsha pricipality 1·20 1·00
2883 50l. Muzaka family 1·20 1·00
2884 90l. George Castriot (Skanderbeg) 2·30 2·10
See also Nos. 2921/4 and 2965/8.

**670** Children encircling Globe

**2001.** United Nations Year of Dialogue among Civilizations. Multicoloured, background colours given.
2885 **670** 45l. red, yellow and black 1·20 1·00
2886 **670** 50l. orange and green 1·20 1·00
2887 **670** 120l. black and red 3·00 2·50
There are minor differences in Nos. 2886/7, with each colour forming a solid block above and below the central motif.

**671** Award Ceremony (Medicins sans Frontieres, 1999 Peace Prize) and Medal

**2001.** Centenary of Nobel Prizes. Showing winners and Nobel medal. Multicoloured.
2888 10l. Type **671** 25 10
2889 20l. Wilhelm Konrad Rontgen (1901 Physics prize) 45 30
2890 90l. Ferid Murad (1998 Medicine Prize) 2·30 2·10
2891 200l. Mother Teresa (1979 Peace Prize) 4·75 4·25

**2002.** Regional Costumes (3rd series). As T **643**. Multicoloured.
2892 30l. Woman's costume, Gjakova 70 65
2893 30l. Woman's costume, Prizreni 70 65
2894 30l. Man's costume, Shkodra 70 65
2895 30l. Woman's costume, Shkodra 70 65
2896 30l. Man's costume, Berati 70 65
2897 30l. Woman's costume, Berati 70 65
2898 30l. Woman's costume, Elbasani 70 65
2899 30l. Man's costume, Elbasani 70 65
2900 30l. Woman's costume, Vlora 70 65
2901 30l. Man's costume, Vlora 70 65
2902 30l. Woman's costume, Gjirokastra 70 65
2903 30l. Woman's costume, Delvina 70 65

**672** Bambi and Thumper

**2002.** Bambi (cartoon film character). Multicoloured.

| | | | |
|---|---|---|---|
| 2904 | 20l. Type **672** | 45 | 30 |
| 2905 | 50l. Bambi alone amongst flowers | 1·20 | 1·00 |
| 2906 | 90l. Bambi and Thumper looking right | 2·00 | 1·80 |
| 2907 | 140l. Bambi with open mouth | 3·00 | 2·50 |

**673** Fireplace

**2002.** Traditional Fireplaces. T **673** and similar vert designs showing fireplaces. Multicoloured.

| | | | |
|---|---|---|---|
| **MS**2908 | 30l. Type **673**; 40l. With columns at each side; 50l. With foliage arch; 90l. With three medallions in arch | 4·75 | 4·75 |

**674** Acrobatic Jugglers

**2002.** Europa. Circus. Multicoloured.

| | | | |
|---|---|---|---|
| 2909 | 40l. Type **674** | 95 | 75 |
| 2910 | 90l. Female acrobat | 2·00 | 1·80 |
| 2911 | 220l. Tightrope performers | 5·75 | 5·25 |
| **MS**2912 | 60×80 mm. 350l. Equestrienne performer (38×38 mm) | 11·50 | 11·50 |

**675** Heading the Ball

**2002.** Football World Championship, Japan and South Korea. Multicoloured.

| | | | |
|---|---|---|---|
| 2913 | 20l. Type **675** | 45 | 30 |
| 2914 | 30l. Catching the ball | 70 | 50 |
| 2915 | 90l. Kicking the ball from horizontal position | 2·10 | 1·90 |
| 2916 | 120l. Player and ball | 2·50 | 2·30 |
| **MS**2917 | 80×60 mm. 360l. Emblem (50×30) | 8·25 | 8·25 |

**2002.** Arms (2nd series). As T **669**. Multicoloured.

| | | | |
|---|---|---|---|
| 2918 | 20l. Gropa family | 45 | 30 |
| 2919 | 45l. Skurra family | 1·00 | 85 |
| 2920 | 50l. Bua family | 1·20 | 1·00 |
| 2921 | 90l. Topia family | 2·30 | 2·10 |

**676** *Opuntia catingiola*

**2002.** Cacti. T **676** and similar triangular designs. Multicoloured.

| | | | |
|---|---|---|---|
| **MS**2922 | 50l. Type **676**; 50l. *Neoporteria pseudoreicheana*; 50l. *Lobivia shaferi* 50l. *Hylocereus undatus*; 50l. *Borzicactus madisoniorum* | 5·25 | 5·25 |

**677** Blood Group Symbols with Wings

**2002.** 50th Anniv of Blood Bank Service. Multicoloured.

| | | | |
|---|---|---|---|
| 2923 | 90l. Type **677** | 2·30 | 2·10 |
| 2924 | 90l. Blood group symbols containing figures | 2·30 | 2·10 |

**678** Naim Kryeziu (footballer)

**2002.** Sports Personalities. Multicoloured.

| | | | |
|---|---|---|---|
| 2925 | 50l. Type **678** | 1·20 | 1·00 |
| 2926 | 50l. Riza Lushta (footballer) | 1·20 | 1·00 |
| 2927 | 50l. Ymer Pampuri (weight lifter) | 1·20 | 1·00 |
| **MS**2928 | 61× 81 mm. 300l. Loro Boriçi (footballer) (vert). Imperf | 7·00 | 7·00 |

**679** Stamp, Torso and Emblem

**2002.** 50th Anniv International Federation of Stamp Dealers'Associations (IFSDA). Multicoloured.

| | | | |
|---|---|---|---|
| 2929 | 50l. Type **679** | 1·20 | 1·00 |
| 2930 | 100l. Part of stamp enlarged and emblem | 2·40 | 2·20 |

**680** Statue of Liberty

**2002.** 1st Anniv of Attacks on World Trade Centre, New York. Multicoloured.

| | | | |
|---|---|---|---|
| 2931 | 100l. Type **680** | 2·40 | 2·20 |
| 2932 | 150l. Burning towers and skyline | 3·50 | 3·25 |
| **MS**2933 | 61×81 mm. 350l. Statue of Liberty and World Trade Centre tower (vert) | 8·50 | 8·50 |

**681** Loggerhead Turtle (*Caretta caretta*)

**2002.** Fauna of Mediterranean Sea. Sheet 100×107 mm containing T **681** and similar horiz designs. Multicoloured.

| | | | |
|---|---|---|---|
| **MS**2934 | 50l. Type **681**; 50l. Common dolphin (*Delphinus delphis*); 50l. Blue shark (*Prionace glaucai*); 50l. Fin whale (*Balenoptera physalus*); 50l. Ray (*Torpedo torpedo*); 50l. Octopus (*Octopus vulgaris*) | 7·25 | 7·25 |

**682** Tefta Tashko Koço

**2002.** Personalities. The Stage. Multicoloured.

| | | | |
|---|---|---|---|
| 2935 | 50l. Type **682** (singer) | 1·20 | 1·10 |
| 2936 | 50l. Naim Frasheri (actor) | 1·20 | 1·10 |
| 2937 | 50l. Kristaq Antoniu (singer) | 1·20 | 1·10 |
| 2938 | 50l. Panajot Kanaçi (choreographer) | 1·20 | 1·10 |

**683** Flags

**2002.** 90th Anniv of Independence. Multicoloured.

| | | | |
|---|---|---|---|
| 2939 | 20l. Type **683** | 55 | 50 |
| 2940 | 90l. People and Albanian flag | 2·20 | 2·00 |

**684** Satellite Dish and Outline of Stamp

**2002.** 90th Anniv of Albanian Post and Telecommunications. Multicoloured.

| | | | |
|---|---|---|---|
| 2941 | 20l. Type **684** | 55 | 50 |
| 2942 | 90l. Airmail envelope and telegraph machine | 2·20 | 2·00 |

**2003.** Regional Costumes (4th series). As T **643**. Multicoloured.

| | | | |
|---|---|---|---|
| 2943 | 30l. Woman's costume, Kelmendi | 90 | 85 |
| 2944 | 30l. Man's costume, Zadrime | 90 | 85 |
| 2945 | 30l. Woman's costume, Zerqani | 90 | 85 |
| 2946 | 30l. Man's costume, Peshkopi | 90 | 85 |
| 2947 | 30l. Man's costume, Malesia Tiranes | 90 | 85 |
| 2948 | 30l. Woman's costume, Malesia Tiranes | 90 | 85 |
| 2949 | 30l. Woman's costume, Fushe Kruje | 90 | 85 |
| 2950 | 30l. Man's costume, Shpati | 90 | 85 |
| 2951 | 30l. Woman's costume, Myzeqe | 90 | 85 |
| 2952 | 30l. Woman's costume, Labinoti | 90 | 85 |
| 2953 | 30l. Man's costume, Korce | 90 | 85 |
| 2954 | 30l. Woman's costume, Laberi | 90 | 85 |

**685** Popeye and Bluto

**2003.** Popeye (cartoon film character). Multicoloured.

| | | | |
|---|---|---|---|
| 2955 | 40l. Type **685** | 1·20 | 1·10 |
| 2956 | 50l. Popeye running | 1·50 | 1·30 |
| 2957 | 80l. Popeye and Olive Oyl | 2·40 | 2·20 |
| 2958 | 150l. Popeye | 4·25 | 3·75 |

**686** Port Palemo Castle

**2003.** Castles. Sheet 118×98 mm. T **686** and similar horiz designs.

| | | | |
|---|---|---|---|
| **MS**2959 | 10l. grey and black; 20l. green and black; 50l. grey and black; 20l. mauve and black | 6·00 | 6·00 |

DESIGNS: 10l. Type **686**; 20l. Petrela; 50l. Kruja; 120l. Preza.

**687** Bearded Man

**2003.** Europa. Poster Art. Multicoloured.

| | | | |
|---|---|---|---|
| 2960 | 150l. Type **687** | 4·50 | 4·25 |
| 2961 | 200l. Eye, apple and piano | 6·00 | 5·50 |
| **MS**2962 | 80×61 mm. 350l. Detail of No. 2960 | 10·50 | 10·50 |

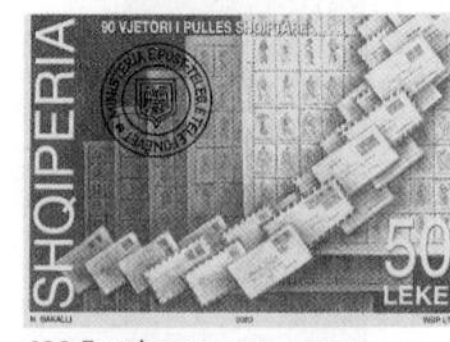


**688** Envelopes

**2003.** 90th Anniv of Albanian Post and Telecommunications (2nd series). Multicoloured.

| | | | |
|---|---|---|---|
| 2963 | 50l. Type **688** | 1·30 | 1·20 |
| 2964 | 1000l. Outline of stamps | 29·00 | 26·00 |

**2003.** Arms (3rd series). As T **669**. Multicoloured.

| | | | |
|---|---|---|---|
| 2965 | 10l. Ariantet family | 25 | 10 |
| 2966 | 20l. Jonimajt family | 65 | 60 |
| 2967 | 70l. Dukagjini family | 2·00 | 1·80 |
| 2968 | 120l. Kopili family | 3·50 | 3·00 |

**689** Pomegranate (*Punica granatum*)

**2003.** Fruit. Multicoloured. Self-adhesive.

| | | | |
|---|---|---|---|
| **MS**2969 | 50l. Type **689**; 60l. Citron (*Citrus medica*); 70l. Cantaloupe (*Cucumis melo*); 80l. Fig (*Ficus*) (inscr "Fieus") | 7·25 | 7·25 |

**690** Diocletian

**2003.** Roman Emperors. Multicoloured.

| | | | |
|---|---|---|---|
| 2970 | 70l. Type **690** | 2·00 | 1·80 |
| 2971 | 70l. Justinian | 2·00 | 1·80 |
| 2972 | 70l. Claudius II | 2·00 | 1·80 |
| 2973 | 70l. Constantine | 2·00 | 1·80 |

**691** White Stork (*Cicona cicona*)

**2003.** Birds. Sheet 100×119 mm containing T **691** and similar vert designs. Multicoloured.

| | | | |
|---|---|---|---|
| **MS**2974 | 70l. Type **691**; 70l. Golden eagle (*Aquila chrysaetos*); 70l. Eagle owl (*Bubo bubo*); 70l. Capercaillie (*Tetrao urogallus*) | 8·25 | 8·25 |

**692** Players

**2003.** 90th Anniv of Albanian Football. Each grey, black and red.

| | | | |
|---|---|---|---|
| 2975 | 80l. Type **692** | 2·20 | 2·00 |
| 2976 | 80l. Group of players | 2·20 | 2·00 |

Nos. 2975/6 were issued together, se-tenant, forming a composite design.

**693** "The Luncheon" (detail)

**2003.** 120th Death Anniv of Edouard Manet (artist). Multicoloured.

| | | | |
|---|---|---|---|
| 2977 | 40l. Type **693** | 1·10 | 95 |
| 2978 | 100l. "The Fifer" | 3·00 | 2·75 |
| **MS**2979 | 80×60 mm. 250l. Edouard Manet (horiz) | 7·00 | 7·00 |

**694** Odhise Paskall

**2003.** Albanian Sculptors. Multicoloured.

| | | | |
|---|---|---|---|
| 2980 | 50l. Type **694** | 1·30 | 1·20 |
| 2981 | 50l. Llazar Nikolla | 1·30 | 1·20 |
| 2982 | 50l. Janaq Paco | 1·30 | 1·20 |
| 2983 | 50l. Murat Toptani | 1·30 | 1·20 |

**695** Profile of Mother Teresa

**2003.** Mother Teresa (humanitarian) Commemoration. Multicoloured.

| | | | |
|---|---|---|---|
| 2984 | 40l. Type **695** | 1·30 | 1·20 |
| 2985 | 250l. Mother Teresa facing front | 6·50 | 6·00 |
| **MS**2986 | 60×60 mm. 350l. Mother Teresa (statue) (40×40 mm) | 9·25 | 9·25 |

**696** Lake, Pelicans and Pine Trees (Divjaka)

**2003.** Natural Heritage. Multicoloured.

| | | | |
|---|---|---|---|
| 2987 | 20l. Type **696** | 55 | 50 |
| 2988 | 30l. House and fir trees (Hotova forest) | 85 | 75 |
| 2989 | 200l. Snow-covered fir trees (Drenova forest) | 6·25 | 5·75 |

**697** Stylized Cyclist and Map of France

**2003.** Centenary of Tour de France Cycle Race.

| | | | | |
|---|---|---|---|---|
| 2990 | **697** | 50l. blue, red and black | 1·40 | 1·30 |
| 2991 | - | 100l. multicoloured | 2·75 | 2·50 |

DESIGN: 100l. Two cyclists.

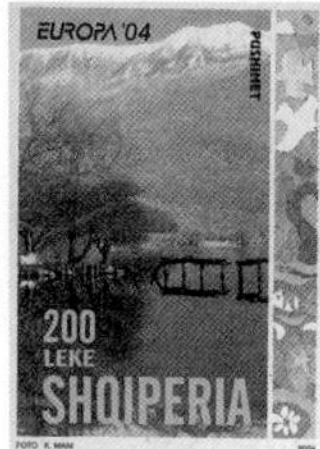


**698** Trees, Lake and Mountain, Pushimet

**2004.** Europa. Holidays. Multicoloured.

| | | | |
|---|---|---|---|
| 2992 | 200l. Type **698** | 6·00 | 5·50 |
| 2993 | 200l. Grassland, hills and mountains, Pushimet | 6·00 | 5·50 |
| **MS**2994 | 61×81 mm. 350l. Island, Pushimet | 11·00 | 11·00 |

**699** Goalkeeper

**2004.** European Football Championship 2004, Portugal. Multicoloured.

| | | | |
|---|---|---|---|
| 2995 | 20l. Type **699** | 75 | 70 |
| 2996 | 40l. Two players and goalkeeper catching ball | 1·40 | 1·30 |
| 2997 | 50l. Two players | 1·70 | 1·50 |
| 2998 | 200l. Players jumping for ball | 7·00 | 6·50 |
| **MS**2999 | 81×61 mm. 350l. Player with raised arms (38×38 mm) (circular) | 11·00 | 11·00 |

**700** Discus Thrower (statue)

**2004.** Olympic Games, Athens. Multicoloured.

| | | | |
|---|---|---|---|
| 3000 | 10l. Type **700** | 30 | 25 |
| 3001 | 200l. Face (statue) | 6·25 | 5·75 |
| **MS**3002 | 61×81 mm. 350l. Athlete carrying Olympic torch (39×55 mm) | 11·00 | 11·00 |

**701** Wilhelm von Wied

**2004.** Wilhelm von Wied (ruler, February 6th—September 5th, 1914) Commemoration. Multicoloured.

| | | | |
|---|---|---|---|
| 3003 | 40l. Type **701** | 1·30 | 1·20 |
| 3004 | 150l. Facing left | 4·75 | 4·25 |

**702** Bugs Bunny

**2004.** Bugs Bunny (cartoon character). Multicoloured.

| | | | |
|---|---|---|---|
| 3005 | 40l. Type **702** | 1·30 | 1·20 |
| 3006 | 50l. With crossed arms | 1·60 | 1·50 |
| 3007 | 80l. Wearing dinner jacket | 2·75 | 2·40 |
| 3008 | 150l. Facing left | 4·75 | 4·25 |

**703** Damaged Painting

**2004.** Mural Paintings by Nikolla Onufri, Church of Saint Mary Vllherna. Multicoloured.

| | | | |
|---|---|---|---|
| 3009 | 10l. Type **703** | 45 | 40 |
| 3010 | 20l. Mary | 75 | 70 |
| 3011 | 1000l. Saint | 34·00 | 31·00 |
| **MS**3012 | 80×65 mm. 400l. Crowned Christ | 12·50 | 12·50 |

**704** Ladybird

**2004.** Ladybird (Coccinella). Sheet 120×95 mm containing T 704 and similar horiz designs showing ladybirds. Multicoloured.

| | | | |
|---|---|---|---|
| **MS**3013 | 80l.×4, Type **704**; Six-spot; With open wings; 12-spot | 10·00 | 10·00 |

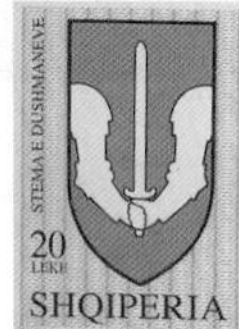


**705** Norek Luca

**2004.** Personalities. Multicoloured.

| | | | |
|---|---|---|---|
| 3014 | 50l. Type **705** (actor) (80th birth anniv) | 1·50 | 1·40 |
| 3015 | 50l. Jorgjia Truja (singer) (10th death anniv) | 1·50 | 1·40 |
| 3016 | 50l. Maria Kraja (singer) (5th death anniv) | 1·50 | 1·40 |
| 3017 | 50l. Zina Andri (actor) (80th birth anniv) | 1·50 | 1·40 |

**706** Dushmani Principality

**2004.** Arms. Multicoloured.

| | | | |
|---|---|---|---|
| 3018 | 20l. Type **706** | 80 | 75 |
| 3019 | 40l. Gjuraj family | 1·40 | 1·30 |
| 3020 | 80l. Zahariaj family | 2·75 | 2·50 |
| 3021 | 150l. Spani principality | 5·00 | 4·75 |

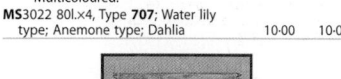

**707** Cactus-type Dahlia

**2004.** Dahlias. Sheet 164×77 mm containing T **707** and similar triangular designs showing dahlias. Multicoloured.

| | | | |
|---|---|---|---|
| **MS**3022 | 80l.×4, Type **707**; Water lily type; Anemone type; Dahlia | 10·00 | 10·00 |

**708** Madonna and Child (Anonim Shen Meria)

**2004.** 50th Anniv of National Art Gallery. Multicoloured.

| | | | |
|---|---|---|---|
| 3023 | 20l. Type **708** | 60 | 55 |
| 3024 | 20l. Saint (Mihal Anagnosti) | 60 | 55 |
| 3025 | 20l. Angel (Onufer Qiprioti) | 60 | 55 |
| 3026 | 20l. Enthroned saint holding open book (Cetiret) | 60 | 55 |
| 3027 | 20l. God and saints (Onuferi) | 60 | 55 |
| 3028 | 20l. Woman wearing scarf (Kel Kodheli) | 60 | 55 |
| 3029 | 20l. Crying woman (Vangjush Mio) | 60 | 55 |
| 3030 | 20l. Woman wearing hat (Abdurahim Buza) | 60 | 55 |
| 3031 | 20l. Semi-naked woman (Mustapha Arapi) | 60 | 55 |
| 3032 | 20l. Man with moustache (Guri Madhi) | 60 | 55 |
| 3033 | 20l. Soldier (sculpture) (Janaq Paco) | 60 | 55 |
| 3034 | 20l. Still life with grapes (Zef Kolombi) | 60 | 55 |
| 3035 | 20l. Flowers (Hasan Reci) | 60 | 55 |
| 3036 | 20l. Still life with onions (Vladimir Jani) | 60 | 55 |
| 3037 | 20l. Woman's head (sculpture) (Halim Beqiri) | 60 | 55 |
| 3038 | 20l. Men seated (Edison Gjergo) | 60 | 55 |
| 3039 | 20l. Men wearing traditional dress (Naxhi Bakalli) | 60 | 55 |
| 3040 | 20l. Family (Agron Bregu) | 60 | 55 |
| 3041 | 20l. Tree planting (Edi Hila) | 60 | 55 |
| 3042 | 20l. Holding paintbrushes (Artur Muharremi) | 60 | 55 |
| 3043 | 20l. Old man (Rembrandt) | 60 | 55 |
| 3044 | 20l. Winged horseman (Gazmend Leka) | 60 | 55 |
| 3045 | 20l. Multicoloured circle (Damien Hirst) | 60 | 55 |
| 3046 | 20l. Corpse in cave (Edvin Rama) | 60 | 55 |
| 3047 | 20l. Viking (Ibrahim Kodra) | 60 | 55 |

**709** Bunting and NATO Emblem

**2004.** 5th Anniv of NATO Peacekeeping in Kosovo. Multicoloured.

| | | | |
|---|---|---|---|
| 3048 | 100l. Type **709** | 3·00 | 2·75 |
| 3049 | 200l. Doves and United Nations flag | 6·00 | 5·50 |
| **MS**3050 | 80×60 mm. 350l. Houses flying Kosovo flag | 11·00 | 11·00 |

**710** Two Doves

**2004.** 60th Anniv of Liberation. Multicoloured.

| | | | |
|---|---|---|---|
| 3051 | 50l. Type **710** | 1·70 | 1·60 |
| 3052 | 200l. One dove | 6·25 | 5·75 |

**2004.** Regional Costumes (5th series). As T **643**. Multicoloured.

| | | | |
|---|---|---|---|
| 3053 | 30l. Back view of woman's costume, Gramshi | 90 | 85 |
| 3054 | 30l. Front view of woman's costume, Gramshi | 90 | 85 |
| 3055 | 30l. Woman's costume, Korca | 90 | 85 |
| 3056 | 30l. Man's costume, Kolonja | 90 | 85 |
| 3057 | 30l. Woman's costume, Korca (different) | 90 | 85 |
| 3058 | 30l. Woman's costume, Librazhdi | 90 | 85 |
| 3059 | 30l. Woman's costume, Permeti | 90 | 85 |
| 3060 | 30l. Woman's costume, Pogradeci | 90 | 85 |
| 3061 | 30l. Man's costume, Skrapari | 90 | 85 |
| 3062 | 30l. Woman's costume, Skrapari | 90 | 85 |
| 3063 | 30l. Woman's costume, Tepelena | 90 | 85 |
| 3064 | 30l. Woman's costume, Vlora | 90 | 85 |

**711** Emblem

**2005.** 50th Anniv of Europa Stamps. Multicoloured.

| | | | |
|---|---|---|---|
| 3065 | 200l. Type **711** | 9·00 | 8·50 |
| 3066 | 250l. Stylized figure grasping '50' | 10·50 | 10·00 |

**712** Triangular Pies

**2005.** Europa. Gastronomy. Multicoloured.

| | | | |
|---|---|---|---|
| 3068 | 200l. Type **712** | 7·00 | 6·50 |
| 3069 | 200l. Stew | 7·00 | 6·50 |

**713** Emblem

**2005.** 50th Anniv of United Nations Membership.

| | | | | |
|---|---|---|---|---|
| 3071 | **713** | 40l. multicoloured | 1·90 | 1·70 |

**714** Tom and Jerry

**2005.** Tom and Jerry (cartoon characters). Multicoloured.

| | | | |
|---|---|---|---|
| 3072 | 40l. Type **714** | 1·00 | 90 |
| 3073 | 50l. Heads of Tom and Jerry | 1·30 | 1·20 |
| 3074 | 80l. Jerry | 2·00 | 1·80 |
| 3075 | 150l. Tom | 3·50 | 3·25 |

**715** Mountain, City and Lake

**2005.** Art. Albanian Landscapes. Multicoloured.

| | | | |
|---|---|---|---|
| 3076 | 10l. Type **715** | 30 | 30 |
| 3077 | 20l. Aqueduct and castle | 65 | 60 |
| 3078 | 30l. Crowd and minaret | 95 | 90 |
| 3079 | 1000l. Lake and mountain fortress | 27·00 | 25·00 |

**2005.** Regional Costumes (6th series). As T **643**. Multicoloured.

| | | | |
|---|---|---|---|
| 3080 | 30l. Man's costume, Tirane | 1·10 | 1·00 |
| 3081 | 30l. Woman's costume, Bende Tirane | 1·10 | 1·00 |
| 3082 | 30l. Back of woman's costume, Zall Dajt | 1·10 | 1·00 |
| 3083 | 30l. Man's costume, Kavaje-Durres | 1·10 | 1·00 |
| 3084 | 30l. Woman's costume, Has | 1·10 | 1·00 |
| 3085 | 30l. Man's costume, Mat | 1·10 | 1·00 |
| 3086 | 30l. Woman's costume, Liqenas | 1·10 | 1·00 |
| 3087 | 30l. Woman's costume, Klenje | 1·10 | 1·00 |
| 3088 | 30l. Woman's costume, Maleshove | 1·10 | 1·00 |
| 3089 | 30l. Woman's costume, German | 1·10 | 1·00 |
| 3090 | 30l. Woman's costume, Kruje | 1·10 | 1·00 |
| 3091 | 30l. Man's costume, Rec | 1·10 | 1·00 |

**716** Starting Blocks

**2005.** Mediterranean Games, Almera. Multicoloured.

| | | | |
|---|---|---|---|
| 3092 | 20l. Type **716** | 85 | 70 |
| 3093 | 60l. Rings | 2·10 | 1·80 |
| 3094 | 120l. Relay baton | 4·25 | 3·50 |
| **MS**3095 | 60×80 mm. 300l. Diver (30×50 mm) | 14·50 | 14·50 |

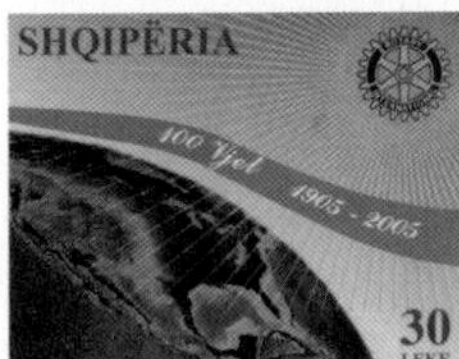

**717** Globe and Emblem

**2005.** Centenary of Rotary International. Multicoloured.

| | | | |
|---|---|---|---|
| 3096 | 30l. Type **717** | 1·00 | 90 |
| 3097 | 150l. Emblem (vert) | 5·25 | 4·50 |

**2005.** Arms (5th series). As T **706**. Multicoloured.

| | | | |
|---|---|---|---|
| 3098 | 10l. Bua | 40 | 35 |
| 3099 | 20l. Karl Topia | 1·00 | 90 |
| 3100 | 70l. Dukagjini II | 3·50 | 3·00 |
| 3101 | 120l. Engjej | 5·25 | 4·50 |

**718** Yellow-flowered Portulaca

**2005.** Portulaca. Sheet 203×60 mm containing T **718** and similar triangular designs showing portulacas. Multicoloured.

| | | | |
|---|---|---|---|
| **MS**3102 | 70l.×5, Type **718**; White flowers; Red and yellow flowers; Pale pink flowers; Double dark pink flower | 12·50 | 12·50 |

**719** Cyclists

**2005.** 80th Anniv of Cycle Race.

| | | | | |
|---|---|---|---|---|
| 3103 | **719** | 50l. multicoloured | 1·70 | 1·60 |
| 3104 | **719** | 60l. multicoloured | 2·20 | 2·00 |
| 3105 | **719** | 120l. multicoloured | 4·25 | 4·00 |

**720** Battle Scene

**2005.** 600th Birth Anniv of Gjergj Kastrioti (Skanderbeg). Sheet 240×82 mm containing T **720** and similar multicoloured designs.

| | | | |
|---|---|---|---|
| **MS**3106 | 40l. Type **720**; 50l. Chariot and fallen horse and rider; 60l. Archers, emblem and foot soldiers with spears; 70l. Shield bearer and archers; 80l. Soldier with raised sword and archers on rocks (30×30 mm) (circular); 90l. Archers firing from cliff ledge (30×30 mm) (circular) | 14·00 | 14·00 |

The stamps and margins of **MS**3106 form a composite design of battle.

**721** Roses growing through Helmet

**2005.** 60th Anniv of End of World War II. Multicoloured.

| | | | |
|---|---|---|---|
| 3107 | 50l. Type **721** | 1·70 | 1·50 |
| 3108 | 200l. Allied flags and statues | 7·25 | 6·50 |

**722** Matia Kodheli-Marubi

**2005.** National Marubi Photograph Collection. Multicoloured.

| | | | |
|---|---|---|---|
| 3109 | 10l. Type **722** | 30 | 25 |
| 3110 | 20l. Gege Marubi | 70 | 65 |
| 3111 | 70l. Pjeter Marubi (Pietro Marubbi) (photographer, artist and architect) | 2·50 | 2·30 |
| 3112 | 200l. Kel Marubi (Mikel Kodheli) | 7·25 | 6·50 |

**2006.** Various stamps, numbers given in brackets, surch **40 lek**.

| | | | |
|---|---|---|---|
| 3113 | 40l. on 30q. multicoloured (2531) | 1·40 | 1·30 |
| 3114 | 40l. on 18l. multicoloured (2549) | 1·40 | 1·30 |
| 3115 | 40l. on 2l. multicoloured (2567) | 1·40 | 1·30 |
| 3116 | 40l. on 2l. multicoloured (2595) | 1·40 | 1·30 |
| 3117 | 40l. on 3l. multicoloured (2596) | 1·40 | 1·30 |
| 3118 | 40l. on 25l. multicoloured (2597) | 1·40 | 1·30 |
| 3119 | 40l. on 2l. multicoloured (2606) | 1·40 | 1·30 |
| 3120 | 40l. on 18l. multicoloured (2610) | 1·40 | 1·30 |
| 3121 | 40l. on 18l. multicoloured (2613) | 1·40 | 1·30 |
| 3122 | 40l. on 25l. multicoloured (2620) | 1·40 | 1·30 |
| 3123 | 40l. on 25l. multicoloured (2629) | 1·40 | 1·30 |

**724** Pres. George Bush

**2007.** President George Bush's visit to Albania. Multicoloured.

| | | | |
|---|---|---|---|
| 3124 | 20l. Type **724** | 75 | 70 |
| 3125 | 40l. As Type **724** (suffused green) | 1·50 | 1·40 |
| 3126 | 80l. As Type **724** (multicoloured) | 3·00 | 2·75 |
| **MS**3127 | 97×73 mm. 200l. Statue of Liberty | 6·75 | 6·75 |

**725** Arms of Italy and Albania

**2007.** 10th Anniv of Italians in Albania.

| | | | | |
|---|---|---|---|---|
| 3128 | **725** | 40l. multicoloured | 1·80 | 1·60 |

Nos. 3129/41 and Type **726** have been left for 'Flags', issued 5 October 2007, not yet received.

Nos. 3142/52 have been left for 'Arms' (as Type **669**), issued on 15-23 October 2007, not yet received.

**727** Flags and Scouts

**2007.** Centenary of Scouting. Multicoloured.

| | | | |
|---|---|---|---|
| 3153 | 100l. Type **727** | 4·00 | 3·75 |
| 3154 | 150l. Flags and scouts (different) | 6·00 | 5·75 |
| **MS**3155 | Sheet 80×60 mm. 250l. Knot (30×25 mm) | 10·00 | 10·00 |

**728** Pink Panther

**2007.** Pink Panther (cartoon character). Mult.

| | | | |
|---|---|---|---|
| 3156 | 40l. Type **728** | 1·60 | 1·40 |
| 3157 | 50l. With Inspector Clouseau | 2·10 | 2·00 |
| 3158 | 80l. Leaning | 3·00 | 2·75 |
| 3159 | 150l. Wearing tunic | 6·50 | 6·00 |

**729** Roads (Arkida)

**2007.** Children's Drawings. Multicoloured.

| | | | |
|---|---|---|---|
| 3160 | 10l. Type **729** | 40 | 35 |
| 3161 | 40l. Boy and flowers (Amarilda Prifti) | 1·70 | 1·60 |
| 3162 | 50l. Outline of houses and viaduct (Iliaz Kasa) | 2·10 | 2·00 |
| 3163 | 80l. Buildings (K. Mezini) (horiz) | 3·50 | 3·25 |

**730** Galerio Maksimiliani

**2007.** Rulers. Multicoloured.

| | | | |
|---|---|---|---|
| 3164 | 30l. Type **730** | 1·40 | 1·20 |
| 3165 | 120l. Flavio Anastasi | 5·00 | 4·75 |

**731** Sower (fresco by David Selenica)

**2007.** Art. Multicoloured.

| | | | |
|---|---|---|---|
| 3166 | 70l. Type **731** | 3·00 | 2·75 |
| 3167 | 110l. Flowers and garlands (wall painting) (Et'hem Bey Mosque, Tirana) | 4·75 | 4·25 |

**732** Young People, Map and Stars

**2007.** Europa. Integration. Multicoloured.

| | | | |
|---|---|---|---|
| 3168 | 200l. Type **732** | 6·75 | 6·25 |
| 3169 | 200l. Young people and double-headed eagle | 6·75 | 6·25 |
| **MS**3170 | Sheet 80×60 mm. 350l. Young people and flag (30×25 mm) | 12·00 | 12·00 |

**2007.** Regional Costumes (7th series). As T **643**. Multicoloured.

| | | | |
|---|---|---|---|
| 3171 | 40l. Woman's costume (inscr 'German') | 1·30 | 1·20 |

| | | | |
|---|---|---|---|
| 3172 | 40l. Man's costume, Kubrin | 1·30 | 1·20 |
| 3173 | 40l. Woman's costume, Golloborde | 1·30 | 1·20 |
| 3174 | 40l. Man's costume, Kerrabe Malesi | 1·30 | 1·20 |
| 3175 | 40l. Woman's costume, Gur I Bardhe | 1·30 | 1·20 |
| 3176 | 40l. Woman's costume, Martanesh | 1·30 | 1·20 |
| 3177 | 40l. Woman's costume, Puke | 1·30 | 1·20 |
| 3178 | 40l. Woman's costume Serice Labinot | 1·30 | 1·20 |
| 3179 | 40l. Woman's costume Shen Gjergj | 1·30 | 1·20 |
| 3180 | 40l. Woman's costume, Tirane Qytet | 1·30 | 1·20 |
| 3181 | 40l. Man's costume, Zalle Dajt | 1·30 | 1·20 |
| 3182 | 40l. Woman's costume, Zaranike Godolesh | 1·30 | 1·20 |

Nos. 3183/94 have been left for 'Regional Costumes (8th series)' (Vert designs as T **643**), issued on 2 November 2007, not yet received.

**733** Thethi National Park (Inscr 'Parku Kombetar I Thethit')

**2007.** Tourism. Multicoloured.

| | | | |
|---|---|---|---|
| 3195 | 40l. Type **733** | 1·60 | 1·40 |
| 3196 | 50l. Luras Lake (Inscr 'Liqenet e Lures') | 2·00 | 1·80 |
| 3197 | 60l. Canine's Castle (Inscr 'Kalaja Kanines') | 2·30 | 2·10 |
| 3198 | 70l. Laguna Karavastase | 2·75 | 2·50 |

**734** Plane Tree

**2007.** Natural Heritage. Elbasan Plane Trees. Multicoloured.

| | | | |
|---|---|---|---|
| 3199 | 70l. Type **734** | 3·00 | 2·75 |
| 3200 | 90l. Hollow tree | 3·50 | 3·25 |

**735** Pope Clement II

**2007**

| | | | | |
|---|---|---|---|---|
| 3201 | **735** | 30l. multicoloured | 1·20 | 1·10 |
| 3202 | **735** | 90l. multicoloured | 4·75 | 4·25 |

**736** Leopold Senghor

**2007.** Birth Centenary (2006) of Leopold Sedar Senghor (poet and first President of Senegal 1960–80).

| | | | | |
|---|---|---|---|---|
| 3203 | **736** | 40l. multicoloured | 1·60 | 1·40 |
| 3204 | **736** | 80l. multicoloured | 3·00 | 2·75 |

**737** Team

**2007.** 60th Anniv of Albania as Balkan Football Champions.

| | | | | |
|---|---|---|---|---|
| 3205 | **737** | 10l. multicoloured | 80 | 70 |
| 3206 | **737** | 80l. multicoloured | 7·00 | 6·25 |

**738** Cannon

**2007.** World Heritage Site. Gjirokastra. Sheet 120×100 mm containing T **738** and similar vert designs. Multicoloured.

| | | |
|---|---|---|
| **MS**3207 10l. Type **738**; 20l. Flowers in a roundel; 30l. 'Kule' (building with tall basement, a first floor for use in the cold season, and a second floor for the warm season); 60l. Bridge ; 80l. Aerial view; 90l. Clock tower | 12·00 | 12·00 |

**739** Soldier wearing Gas Mask

**2007.** 10th Anniv of Albania's Participation in International Military Missions. Multicoloured.

| | | | |
|---|---|---|---|
| 3208 | 10l. Type **739** | 45 | 40 |
| 3209 | 100l. Soldiers in inflatable boat | 4·25 | 3·75 |

**740** Mother Teresa

**2007.** 10th Death Anniv of Agnes Ganzhou Bojaxhiu (Mother Teresa). Multicoloured.

| | | | | |
|---|---|---|---|---|
| 3210 | **740** | 60l. multicoloured | 3·00 | 2·75 |
| 3211 | **740** | 130l. multicoloured No. | 5·50 | 5·00 |

**MS**3212 has been left for miniature sheet, not yet received.

**741** Gaia (statue)

**2007.** Archaeology. Durres City. Multicoloured.

| | | | |
|---|---|---|---|
| 3213 | 30l. Type **741** | 1·20 | 1·10 |
| 3214 | 120l. Gaia (close up) | 4·75 | 4·25 |

No. **MS**3215 has been left for miniature sheet, not yet received.

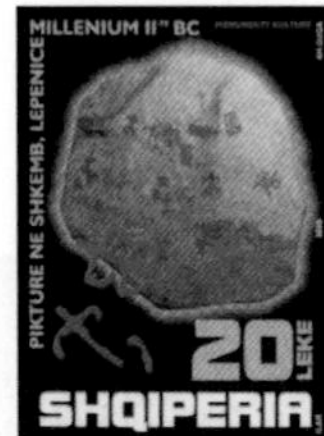

**742** Drawings

**2007.** Cultural History. Tren Cave System (first occupied during Eneolithic period c. 2500–2000 BC). Multicoloured.

| | | | |
|---|---|---|---|
| 3216 | 20l. Type **742** | 1·10 | 1·00 |
| 3217 | 100l. Drawings (different) | 4·25 | 3·75 |
| **MS**3218 | 81×61 mm. 300l. Cave (horiz) | 12·50 | 12·50 |

**743** Osman Kazazi

**2007.** Personalities (1st issue). Multicoloured.

| | | | |
|---|---|---|---|
| 3219 | 10l. Type **743** (politician) | 40 | 35 |
| 3220 | 20l. Pjeter Arbnori (politician) | 80 | 75 |
| 3221 | 60l. Llazar Sotir Gusho (Lagush Poradeci) (poet) | 2·50 | 2·40 |
| 3222 | 100l. Cesk Zadeja (composer) | 4·25 | 4·00 |

**744** Abdurrahim Buza

**2007.** Personalities (2nd issue). Multicoloured.

| | | | |
|---|---|---|---|
| 3223 | 50l. Type **744** (artist) | 2·00 | 1·90 |
| 3224 | 50l. Aleks Buda (historian) | 2·00 | 1·90 |
| 3225 | 50l. Thimi Mitko (folklorist and nationalist) | 2·00 | 1·90 |
| 3226 | 50l. Martin Camaj (writer) | 2·00 | 1·90 |

**745** Spheres as Player

**2007.** World Cup Football Championship, Germany. Multicoloured.

| | | | |
|---|---|---|---|
| 3227 | 30l. Type **745** | 1·80 | 1·70 |
| 3228 | 60l. Triangles as player | 3·00 | 2·75 |
| 3229 | 120l. Rectangles as player | 5·25 | 4·75 |
| **MS**3230 | 61×82 mm. 350l. Emblems | 13·50 | 13·50 |

The stamp and margin of **MS**3230 form a composite design.

**746** Ismail Kemal Bej Vlora (Ismail Qemali) (first head of state and government) and Arms

**2007.** 95th Anniv of Independence. Multicoloured.

| | | | |
|---|---|---|---|
| 3231 | 50l. Type **746** | 2·00 | 1·90 |
| 3232 | 110l. Ismail Qemali | 4·50 | 4·00 |

**747** Garlic

**2007.** Domestic Plants. Multicoloured.

| | | | |
|---|---|---|---|
| 3233 | 80l. Type **747** | 3·00 | 2·75 |
| 3234 | 80l. Onions | 3·00 | 2·75 |
| 3235 | 80l. Peppers | 3·00 | 2·75 |
| 3236 | 80l. Tomatoes | 3·00 | 2·75 |

**748** Blooms and Leaves

**2007.** Wulfenia baldacci. Multicoloured.

| | | | |
|---|---|---|---|
| 3237 | 70l. Type **748** | 3·00 | 2·75 |
| 3238 | 100l. Flowers on single stem | 4·25 | 4·00 |

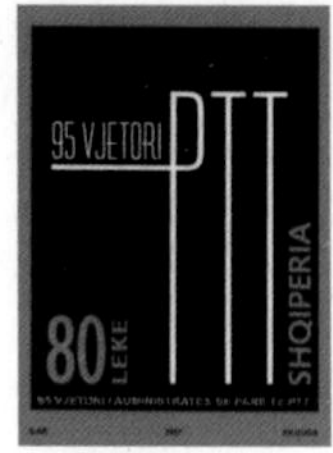

**749** Emblem

**2007.** 95th Anniv of National Post Office.

| | | | | |
|---|---|---|---|---|
| 3239 | **749** | 80l. agate and vermilion | 3·25 | 3·00 |
| 3240 | **749** | 90l. vermilion and black | 3·75 | 3·25 |

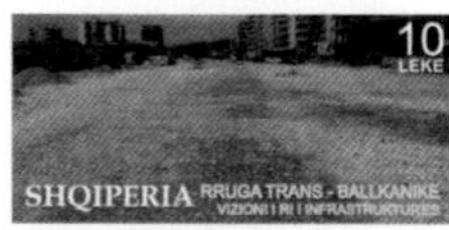

**750** New Road Surfacing

**2007.** Infrastructure Improvements. Sheet 133×107 mm containing T **750** and similar horiz designs. Multicoloured.

| | | |
|---|---|---|
| **MS**3241 10l. Type **750**; 20l. Durres port; 30l. New building, Tirana; 40l. Mother Teresa airport; 50l. Shkodra street, Hani i Hotit; 60l. Tepelene road, Gijirokastra; 70l. Fier road, Lushnje; 80l. Kalimash road, Morine | 13·50 | 13·50 |

**751** Emblem and Member Flags

**2008.** Albania in NATO. Multicoloured.

| | | | |
|---|---|---|---|
| 3242 | 40l. Type **751** | 2·00 | 1·90 |
| 3243 | 60l. Arms and emblem | 2·50 | 2·40 |

**752** Map of Switzerland

**2008.** EURO 2008–European Football Championships, Austria and Switzerland. Multicoloured.

| | | | |
|---|---|---|---|
| 3244 | 50l. Type **752** | 2·20 | 2·10 |
| 3245 | 250l. Map of Austria | 10·50 | 10·00 |
| **MS**3246 | 60×80 mm. 200l. Mascots (vert) | 9·50 | 9·50 |

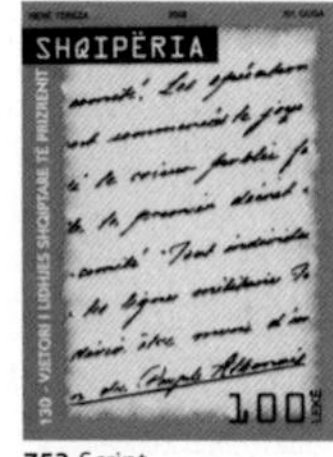

**753** Script

**2008.** 130th Anniv of Albanian League of Prizren. Multicoloured.

| | | | |
|---|---|---|---|
| 3247 | 100l. Type **753** | 4·25 | 4·00 |
| 3248 | 150l. Building | 7·00 | 6·75 |

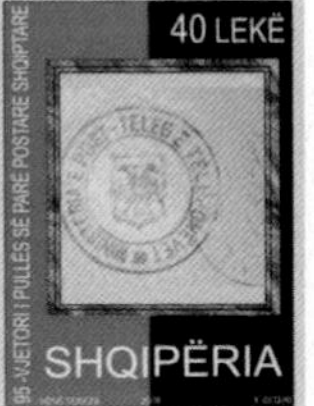

**754** Postmark

**2008.** 95th Anniv of Postal Service.

| | | | | |
|---|---|---|---|---|
| 3249 | **754** | 40l. multicoloured | 2·00 | 1·90 |

**755** John Belushi (actor)

**2008.** Personalities of Albanian Descent. Multicoloured.

| | | | |
|---|---|---|---|
| 3250 | 5l. Type **755** | 20 | 15 |
| 3251 | 10l. Gjon Mili (photographer) | 40 | 35 |
| 3252 | 20l. Koca Mi'mar Sinan Aga (Sinan) (Ottoman architect) | 80 | 75 |
| 3253 | 200l. Ibrahim Kodra (artist) | 8·75 | 8·50 |

**756** Hand holding Quill

**2008.** Europa. The Letter. Multicoloured.

| | | | |
|---|---|---|---|
| 3254 | 100l. Type **756** | 4·50 | 4·25 |
| 3255 | 150l. Hand holding quill writing Europa | 7·00 | 6·75 |
| **MS**3256 | 81×61 mm. 250l. 'Europa' (horiz) | 11·50 | 11·50 |

**757** Two Poppies

**2008.** Poppy (Papaver rhoeas). Multicoloured.

| | | | |
|---|---|---|---|
| 3257 | 50l. Type **757** | 2·20 | 2·10 |
| 3258 | 150l. Poppy | 7·00 | 6·75 |

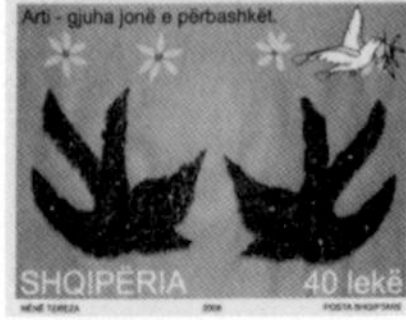

**758** Swallows

**2008.** Universal Language of Art. Multicoloured.

| | | | |
|---|---|---|---|
| 3259 | 40l. Type **758** | 2·00 | 1·90 |
| 3260 | 70l. Parachutists | 3·00 | 2·75 |

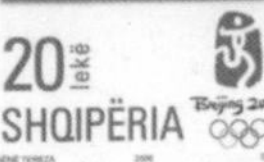

**759** Football

**2008.** Olympic Games, Beijing. Multicoloured.

| | | | |
|---|---|---|---|
| 3261 | 20l. Type **759** | 80 | 75 |
| 3262 | 30l. Water polo | 1·50 | 1·40 |
| 3263 | 40l. Athletics | 2·00 | 1·90 |
| 3264 | 50l. Cycling | 2·20 | 2·10 |

**760** Osumi Canyons

**2008.** Tourism. Multicoloured.

| | | | |
|---|---|---|---|
| 3265 | 60l. Type **760** | 2·50 | 2·40 |
| 3266 | 250l. Komani Lake | 10·50 | 10·00 |

**761** Ahmet Zogu

**2008.** 80th Anniv of Coronation of King Ahmet Zogu.

| | | | | |
|---|---|---|---|---|
| 3267 | **761** | 40l. multicoloured | 2·00 | 1·90 |
| 3268 | **761** | 100l. multicoloured | 4·50 | 4·25 |

**762** Azem Hajdari (politician)

**2008.** Personalities. Multicoloured.

| | | | |
|---|---|---|---|
| 3269 | 40l. Type **762** | 2·00 | 1·90 |
| 3270 | 200l. Adem Jashari (Kosovo nationalist) | 8·75 | 8·50 |

**763** Ymer Prizreni

**2008.** Kosovo Nationalists. Multicoloured.

| | | | |
|---|---|---|---|
| 3271 | 20l. Type **763** | 80 | 75 |
| 3272 | 30l. Isa Boletini | 1·50 | 1·40 |
| 3273 | 40l. Ibrahim Rugova | 2·00 | 1·90 |
| 3274 | 50l. Azem Galica | 2·20 | 2·10 |
| 3275 | 70l. Adem Jashari | 3·00 | 2·75 |

**764** Decius

**2008.** Roman Emperors of Illyrian Ancestry. Multicoloured.

| | | | |
|---|---|---|---|
| 3276 | 30l. Type **764** | 1·50 | 1·40 |

No. 3277 has been left for stamp not yet recieved.

**765** Harry Potter (Daniel Radcliffe) and Professor Dumbledore (Michael Gambon)

**2008.** Youth Stamps. Harry Potter (character created by J. K. Rowling). Designs showing Harry Potter and other characters. Multicoloured.

| | | | |
|---|---|---|---|
| 3278 | 20l. Type **765** | 80 | 75 |
| 3279 | 30l. With Dobby | 1·50 | 1·40 |
| 3280 | 50l. With Hermione (Emma Watson) and friends | 2·20 | 2·10 |
| 3281 | 100l. With Voldemort (Ralph Fiennes) | 4·50 | 4·25 |

**766** Congress Buildings, Monastir, Macedonia

**2008.** Centenary of Congress of Monastir (to decide on the use of Latin script for written Albanian). Multicoloured.

| | | | |
|---|---|---|---|
| 3282 | 40l. Type **766** | 2·00 | 1·90 |
| 3283 | 100l. Albanian script using Latin alphabet | 4·50 | 4·25 |

**767** Sinagogue, Saranda

**2008.** Archaeological Excavations. Multicoloured.

| | | | |
|---|---|---|---|
| 3284 | 10l. Type **767** | 80 | 75 |
| 3285 | 50l. Orikum | 2·20 | 2·10 |
| 3286 | 80l. Antigonea | 3·25 | 3·00 |

**767aa** Emblem

**2009.** 135th Anniv of Universal Postal Union

| | | | | |
|---|---|---|---|---|
| 3286a | **767aa** | 100l. multicoloured | 9·50 | 9·50 |
| 3286aa | | 200l. As Type **767aa** (vert) | 4·50 | 4·50 |

**767a** Laurel and Hardy

**2009.** Laurel and Hardy (Arthur Stanley Jefferson and Norvell Hardy) (comedians). Multicoloured.

| | | | |
|---|---|---|---|
| 3286b | 150l. Laurel and Hardy | 6·50 | 6·50 |
| 3286ba | 200l. Wearing bowler hats | 7·50 | 7·50 |
| **MS**3286c | 80×60 mm. 300l. Type **767a** | 14·00 | 14·00 |

**768** Completed Lift

**2009.** Weightlifting. Multicoloured.

| | | | |
|---|---|---|---|
| 3287 | 10l. Type **768** | 80 | 75 |
| 3288 | 60l. Jerk and lunge | 3·00 | 3·75 |
| 3289 | 120l. Squattin with barbell at shoulder hieght | 4·75 | 4·25 |
| 3290 | 150l. Squatting and grasping barbell | 7·00 | 6·75 |

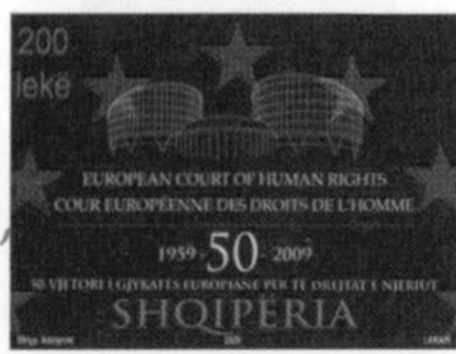

**769** Stylized Buildings

**2009.** 50th Anniv of Court of Human Rights.

| | | | | |
|---|---|---|---|---|
| 3291 | **769** | 200l. multicoloured | 9·00 | 8·50 |

**770** Flags as Map of Europe

**2009.** 60th Anniv of Council of Europe.

| | | | | |
|---|---|---|---|---|
| 3292 | **770** | 150l. multicoloured | 7·00 | 6·75 |

**771** Abidin Dino

**2009.** Painters of the Diaspora. Multicoloured.

| | | | |
|---|---|---|---|
| 3293 | 40l. Type **771** | 2·00 | 1·90 |
| 3294 | 50l. Lin Delija | 2·20 | 2·10 |
| 3295 | 60l. Lika Janko | 3·00 | 2·75 |
| 3296 | 150l. Artur Tashko | 7·00 | 6·75 |

**772** Car and Traffic Controller

**2009.** Road Traffic Control. Multicoloured.

| | | | |
|---|---|---|---|
| 3297 | 5l. Type *772* | 55 | 55 |
| 3298 | 1000l. Zebra crossing | 30·00 | 30·00 |

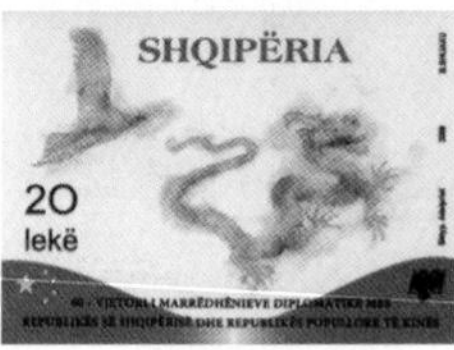

**773** Dove and Dragon

**2009.** Albania–China Diplomatic Relations.

| | | | | |
|---|---|---|---|---|
| 3299 | **773** | 20l. multicoloured | 1·50 | 1·40 |

**774** Choir

**2009.** Albanian Folk Iso–Polyphony-UNESCO Oral and Intangible Cultural Heritage of Humanity (2005). Multicoloured.

| | | | |
|---|---|---|---|
| 3300 | 40l. Type **774** | 2·00 | 2·00 |
| 3301 | 250l. Musicians | 9·00 | 9·00 |

**775** Soldier and Arms

**2009.** 65th Anniv of Liberation. Multicoloured.

| | | | |
|---|---|---|---|
| 3302 | 70l. Type **775** | 3·00 | 2·75 |
| 3303 | 200l. Arms and aircraft | 9·00 | 9·25 |

**776** Mujit Dhe e Halilit

**2009.** Albanian Folklore. Multicoloured.

| | | | |
|---|---|---|---|
| 3304 | 30l. Type **776** | 2·00 | 2·00 |

| | | | |
|---|---|---|---|
| 3305 | 200l. Couple on horseback | 9·00 | 9·00 |

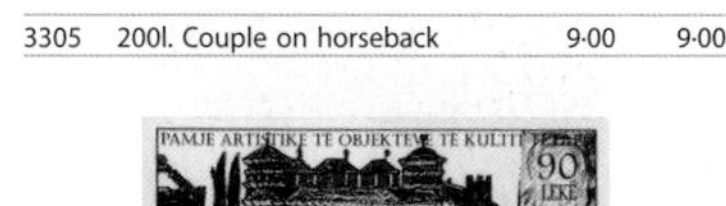

**777** Mosque, Berat (1827)

**2009.** Religious Art. Multicoloured.

| | | | |
|---|---|---|---|
| 3306 | 90l. Type **777** | 4·25 | 4·25 |
| 3307 | 100l. Fresco, Church of Mary and St. Ristozit, Mborje, Korce (1389) | 4·75 | 4·75 |
| 3308 | 120l. Frescoes, Church of St. Venerandes, Pllane-Lezhe Shek, 18th-19th century | 5·00 | 5·00 |

**778** Satellite Receiver and Planets

**2009.** Europa. Multicoloured.

| | | | |
|---|---|---|---|
| 3309 | 200l. Type **778** | 8·50 | 9·00 |
| 3310 | 200l. Landing craft and vehicles on the moon | 9·00 | 8·50 |
| **MS**3311 | 80×60 mm. Size 30×24 mm. 350l. Satellite. | 10·50 | 10·00 |

**779** Fortress of Tirana

**2009.** Archaeology. Multicoloured.

| | | | |
|---|---|---|---|
| 3312 | 30l. Type **779** | 2·50 | 2·50 |
| 3313 | 250l. Artefacts, Tumulus of Kamenica | 10·50 | 10·50 |

**780** *Rainy Beach*

**2009.** National Theatre. Multicoloured.

| | | | |
|---|---|---|---|
| 3314 | 20l. Type **780** | 2·25 | 2·25 |
| 3315 | 80l. *Pallati 176* | 3·25 | 3·25 |
| 3316 | 200l. *True Apology of Socrates* (Apologjia e vertete e Sokratit) | 8·50 | 8·50 |

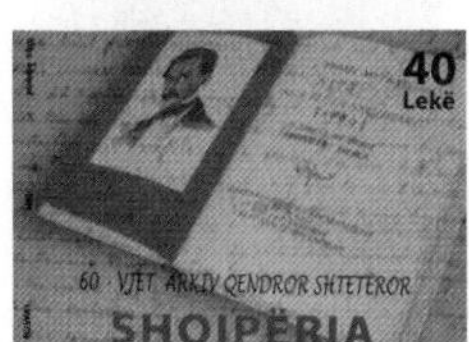


**781** Frontispiece

**2009.** 60th Anniv of State Archives. Multicoloured.

| | | | |
|---|---|---|---|
| 3317 | 40l. Type **781** | 2·00 | 2·00 |
| 3318 | 60l. Roll of parchment | 3·00 | 3·00 |

**782** Emblems

**2010.** Albania–Italy Friendship

| | | | | |
|---|---|---|---|---|
| 3319 | **782** | 40l. multicoloured | 2·00 | 2·00 |

**783** Mother Teresa

**2010.** Birth Centenary of Agnes Gonxha Bojaxhiu (Mother Teresa) (founder of Missionaries of Charity)

| | | | | |
|---|---|---|---|---|
| 3320 | **783** | 100l. multicoloured | 4·50 | 4·50 |

**784** Double-headed Eagle and European Stars

**2010.** Introduction of Visa-free Travel for Albanians in the EU

| | | | | |
|---|---|---|---|---|
| 3321 | **784** | 40l. multicoloured | 2·20 | 2·20 |

**785** Reading in Library

**2011.** 90th Anniv of State Library. Multicoloured.

| | | | |
|---|---|---|---|
| 3322 | 10l. Type **785** | 5·00 | 5·00 |
| 3323 | 1000l. Using computer in library | 45·00 | 45·00 |

Nos. 3322/3 were printed, *se-tenant*, forming a composite design

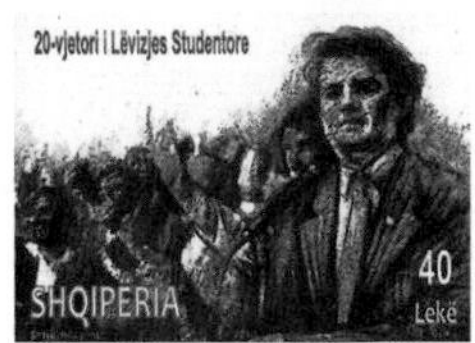


**786** Students

**2011.** 20th Anniv of Student Unrest. Multicoloured.

| | | | |
|---|---|---|---|
| 3324 | 40l. Type **786** | 2·50 | 2·50 |
| 3325 | 60l. Students protesting, rear view | 3·00 | 3·00 |
| **MS**3326 | 70×90 mm. 200l. Students making 'V' sign (vert) | 9·75 | 9·75 |

**787** Cockerel, Donkey and Sun

**2011.** Europa (2010). Multicoloured.

| | | | |
|---|---|---|---|
| 3327 | 100l. Type **787** | 4·50 | 4·50 |
| 3328 | 150l. Girl, pigeon and cat | 7·50 | 7·50 |
| **MS**3329 | 80×60 mm. 250l. Girl with pile of books (horiz) | 12·00 | 12·00 |

**EXPRESS LETTER STAMPS**
**ITALIAN OCCUPATION**

**E67** King Victor Emmanuel

**1940**

| | | | | |
|---|---|---|---|---|
| E373 | **E67** | 25q. violet | 9·75 | 10·50 |
| E374 | **E67** | 50q. red | 18·00 | 19·00 |

No. E374 is inscr "POSTAT EXPRES".

**1943.** Optd **14 Shtator 1943**.

| | | | |
|---|---|---|---|
| E402 | 25q. violet | 27·00 | 33·00 |

**POSTAGE DUE STAMPS**

**1914.** Optd TAKSE through large letter **T**.

| | | | | |
|---|---|---|---|---|
| D33 | **4** | 2q. brown and yellow | 13·00 | 5·25 |
| D34 | **4** | 5q. green and yellow | 13·00 | 5·25 |
| D35 | **4** | 10q. red and pink | 18·00 | 5·25 |
| D36 | **4** | 25q. blue | 22·00 | 5·25 |
| D37 | **4** | 50q. mauve and red | 33·00 | 17·00 |

**1914.** Nos. 40/4 optd **TAKSE**.

| | | | |
|---|---|---|---|
| D46 | 10pa. on 5q. green & yell | 6·50 | 5·25 |
| D47 | 20pa. on 10q. red and pink | 6·50 | 5·25 |
| D48 | 1g. on 25q. blue | 6·50 | 5·25 |
| D49 | 2g. on 50q. mauve and red | 6·50 | 5·25 |

**1919.** Fiscal stamps optd **TAXE**.

| | | | | |
|---|---|---|---|---|
| D89 | **12** | 4q. on 4h. pink | 16·00 | 12·50 |
| D90 | **12** | 10q. on 10k. red on grn | 16·00 | 12·50 |
| D91 | **12** | 20q. on 2k. orge on lilac | 16·00 | 12·50 |
| D92 | **12** | 50q. on 5k. brown on yell | 16·00 | 12·50 |

**D20** Fortress of Shkoder

**1920.** Optd with posthorn.

| | | | | |
|---|---|---|---|---|
| D129 | **D 20** | 4q. olive | 1·30 | 5·25 |
| D130 | **D 20** | 10q. red | 2·50 | 7·75 |
| D131 | **D 20** | 20q. brown | 2·50 | 7·75 |
| D132 | **D 20** | 50q. black | 6·50 | 21·00 |

**D22**

**1922**

| | | | | |
|---|---|---|---|---|
| D141 | **D 22** | 4q. black on red | 1·80 | 5·25 |
| D142 | **D 22** | 10q. black on red | 1·80 | 5·25 |
| D143 | **D 22** | 20q. black on red | 1·80 | 5·25 |
| D144 | **D 22** | 50q. black on red | 1·80 | 5·25 |

**1922.** Optd **Republika Shiqiptare**.

| | | | |
|---|---|---|---|
| D186 | 4q. black on red | 5·50 | 5·25 |
| D187 | 10q. black on red | 5·50 | 5·25 |
| D188 | 20q. black on red | 5·50 | 5·25 |
| D189 | 50q. black on red | 5·50 | 5·25 |

**D35**

**1925**

| | | | | |
|---|---|---|---|---|
| D204 | **D35** | 10q. blue | 2·20 | 4·25 |
| D205 | **D35** | 20q. green | 2·20 | 4·25 |
| D206 | **D35** | 30q. brown | 4·25 | 8·25 |
| D207 | **D35** | 50q. dark brown | 7·50 | 16·00 |

**D53** Arms of Albania

**1930**

| | | | | |
|---|---|---|---|---|
| D288 | **D53** | 10q. blue | 18·00 | 26·00 |
| D289 | **D53** | 20q. red | 6·50 | 16·00 |
| D290 | **D53** | 30q. violet | 6·50 | 16·00 |
| D291 | **D53** | 50q. green | 6·50 | 16·00 |

**1936.** Optd **Takse**.

| | | | | |
|---|---|---|---|---|
| D312 | **50** | 10q. red | 16·00 | 47·00 |

**D67**

**1940**

| | | | | |
|---|---|---|---|---|
| D373 | **D67** | 4q. red | 43·00 | 65·00 |
| D374 | **D67** | 10q. violet | 43·00 | 65·00 |
| D375 | **D67** | 20q. brown | 43·00 | 65·00 |
| D376 | **D67** | 30q. blue | 43·00 | 65·00 |
| D377 | **D67** | 50q. red | 43·00 | 65·00 |

Pt. 6

# ALEXANDRETTA

The territory of Alexandretta. Autonomous under French control from 1923 to September 1938.

1938. 100 centiemes = 1 piastre.

**1938.** Stamps of Syria of 1930/1 optd **Sandjak d'Alexandrette** (Nos. 1, 4, 7 and 11) or **SANDJAK D'ALEXANDRETTE** (others), Nos. 7 and 11 surch also.

| | | | |
|---|---|---|---|
| 1 | 0p.10 purple | 1·40 | 5·50 |
| 2 | 0p.20 red | 1·50 | 5·75 |
| 3 | 0p.50 violet | 1·70 | 4·50 |
| 4 | 0p.75 red | 2·40 | 5·50 |
| 5 | 1p. brown | 2·00 | 4·25 |
| 6 | 2p. violet | 2·00 | 4·75 |
| 7 | 2p.50 on 4p. orange | 3·50 | 3·50 |
| 8 | 3p. green | 3·00 | 8·25 |
| 9 | 4p. orange | 4·00 | 2·75 |
| 10 | 6p. black | 4·25 | 4·25 |
| 11 | 12p.50 on 15p. red (No. 267) | 7·50 | 8·25 |
| 12 | 25p. purple | 10·00 | 29·00 |

**1938.** Air. Stamps of Syria of 1937 (Nos. 322 etc.) optd **SANDJAK D'ALEXANDRETTE**.

| | | | |
|---|---|---|---|
| 13 | ½p. violet | 1·70 | 3·00 |
| 14 | 1p. black | 1·50 | 4·25 |
| 15 | 2p. green | 3·25 | 5·50 |
| 16 | 3p. blue | 3·75 | 9·75 |
| 17 | 5p. mauve | 9·00 | 23·00 |
| 18 | 10p. brown | 8·75 | 25·00 |
| 19 | 15p. brown | 9·25 | 28·00 |
| 20 | 25p. blue | 16·00 | 34·00 |

**1938.** 10Death of Kemal Ataturk. Nos. 4, 5, 7, 9 and 11 optd **10-11-1938** in frame.

| | | | |
|---|---|---|---|
| 27 | 0p.75 red | 43·00 | 70·00 |
| 28 | 1p. brown | 29·00 | 65·00 |
| 29 | 2p.50 on 4p. orange | 16·00 | 13·00 |
| 30 | 4p. orange | 10·00 | 17·00 |
| 31 | 12p.50 on 15p. red | 65·00 | 80·00 |

**POSTAGE DUE STAMPS**

**1938.** Postage Due stamps of Syria of 1925 optd **SANDJAK D'ALEXANDRETTE**.

| | | | | |
|---|---|---|---|---|
| D21 | **D20** | 0p.50 brown on yellow | 3·00 | 6·75 |
| D22 | **D20** | 1p. purple on pink | 2·30 | 7·25 |
| D23 | **D20** | 2p. black on blue | 3·00 | 8·00 |
| D24 | **D20** | 3p. black on red | 3·75 | 14·00 |
| D25 | **D20** | 5p. black on green | 5·75 | 11·00 |
| D26 | **D20** | 8p. black on blue | 8·25 | 11·50 |

Pt. 6

# ALEXANDRIA

Issues of the French P.O. in this Egyptian port. The French Post Offices in Egypt closed on 31 March 1931.

1899. 100 centimes = 1 franc.
1921. 10 milliemes = 1 piastre.

**1899.** Stamps of France optd **ALEXANDRIE**.

| | | | | |
|---|---|---|---|---|
| 1 | 10 | 1c. black on blue | 1·50 | 1·80 |
| 2 | 10 | 2c. brown on yellow | 2·50 | 2·50 |
| 3 | 10 | 3c. grey | 1·80 | 2·30 |
| 4 | 10 | 4c. brown on grey | 1·40 | 2·30 |
| 5 | 10 | 5c. green | 3·75 | 2·10 |
| 7 | 10 | 10c. black on lilac | 8·75 | 10·00 |
| 9 | 10 | 15c. blue | 7·25 | 5·50 |
| 10 | 10 | 20c. red on green | 9·25 | 8·50 |
| 11 | 10 | 25c. black on red | 10·50 | 90 |
| 12 | 10 | 30c. brown | 13·50 | 9·25 |
| 13 | 10 | 40c. red on yellow | 13·00 | 11·00 |
| 15 | 10 | 50c. red | 38·00 | 11·00 |
| 16 | 10 | 1f. olive | 28·00 | 12·00 |
| 17 | 10 | 2f. brown on blue | 90·00 | £100 |
| 18 | 10 | 5f. mauve on lilac | £130 | £100 |

**1902.** "Blanc", "Mouchon" and "Merson" key-types, inscr "ALEXANDRIE".

| | | | | |
|---|---|---|---|---|
| 19 | A | 1c. grey | 1·80 | 1·20 |
| 20 | A | 2c. purple | 60 | 1·90 |
| 21 | A | 3c. red | 75 | 1·60 |
| 22 | A | 4c. brown | 65 | 1·50 |
| 24 | A | 5c. green | 75 | 60 |
| 25 | B | 10c. red | 3·25 | 1·20 |
| 26 | B | 15c. red | 7·00 | 2·50 |
| 27 | B | 15c. orange | 2·50 | 2·50 |
| 28 | B | 20c. brown | 3·50 | 1·80 |
| 29 | B | 25c. blue | 2·00 | 20 |
| 30 | B | 30c. mauve | 5·00 | 3·75 |
| 31 | C | 40c. red and blue | 6·00 | 2·30 |
| 32 | C | 50c. brown and lilac | 12·00 | 90 |
| 33 | C | 1f. red and green | 22·00 | 2·30 |
| 34 | C | 2f. lilac and buff | 18·00 | 7·25 |
| 35 | C | 5f. blue and buff | 22·00 | 12·50 |

**1915.** Red Cross. Surch **5c** and Red Cross.

| | | | | |
|---|---|---|---|---|
| 36 | B | 10c. + 5c. red | 30 | 7·00 |

**1921.** Surch thus, **15 Mill.**, in one line (without bars).

| | | | | |
|---|---|---|---|---|
| 37 | A | 2m. on 5c. green | 4·00 | 9·25 |
| 38 | A | 3m. on 3c. red | 10·50 | 16·00 |
| 39 | B | 4m. on 10c. red | 3·75 | 6·50 |
| 40 | A | 5m. on 1c. grey | 13·00 | 19·00 |
| 41 | A | 5m. on 4c. brown | 10·50 | 19·00 |
| 42 | B | 6m. on 15c. orange | 2·75 | 7·75 |
| 43 | B | 8m. on 20c. brown | 5·00 | 14·00 |
| 44 | B | 10m. on 25c. blue | 3·75 | 6·50 |
| 45 | B | 12m. on 30c. mauve | 17·00 | 32·00 |
| 46 | A | 15m. on 2c. purple | 7·75 | 14·00 |
| 47 | C | 15m. on 40c. red and blue | 17·00 | 32·00 |
| 48 | C | 15m. on 50c. brown & lilac | 9·50 | 25·00 |
| 49 | C | 30m. on 1f. red and green | £140 | £140 |
| 50 | C | 60m. on 2f. lilac and buff | £160 | £160 |
| 51 | C | 150m. on 5f. blue and buff | £250 | £250 |

**1921.** Surch thus, **15 MILLIEMES**, in two lines (without bars).

| | | | | |
|---|---|---|---|---|
| 53 | A | 1m. on 1c. grey | 4·50 | 6·75 |
| 54 | A | 2m. on 5c. green | 3·50 | 5·50 |
| 55 | B | 4m. on 10c. red | 5·00 | 10·50 |
| 65 | B | 4m. on 10c. green | 3·50 | 4·50 |
| 56 | A | 5m. on 3c. orange | 6·50 | 10·00 |
| 57 | B | 6m. on 15c. orange | 3·25 | 6·00 |
| 58 | B | 8m. on 20c. brown | 3·75 | 3·75 |
| 59 | B | 10m. on 25c. blue | 1·80 | 2·75 |
| 60 | B | 10m. on 30c. mauve | 7·25 | 6·50 |
| 61 | C | 15m. on 50c. brown & lilac | 7·75 | 6·50 |
| 66 | B | 15m. on 50c. blue | 3·00 | 3·00 |
| 62 | C | 30m. on 1f. red and green | 6·00 | 3·75 |
| 63 | C | 60m. on 2f. lilac and buff | £2000 | £2000 |
| 67 | C | 60m. on 2f. red and green | 20·00 | 23·00 |
| 64 | C | 150m. on 5f. blue and buff | 21·00 | 25·00 |

**1925.** Surch in milliemes with bars over old value.

| | | | | |
|---|---|---|---|---|
| 68 | A | 1m. on 1c. grey | 20 | 4·00 |
| 69 | A | 2m. on 5c. orange | 45 | 3·00 |
| 70 | A | 2m. on 5c. green | 3·25 | 4·75 |
| 71 | B | 4m. on 10c. green | 1·00 | 5·00 |
| 72 | A | 5m. on 3c. red | 1·70 | 3·00 |
| 73 | B | 6m. on 15c. orange | 1·50 | 4·50 |
| 74 | B | 8m. on 20c. brown | 1·10 | 4·50 |
| 75 | B | 10m. on 25c. blue | 65 | 1·60 |
| 76 | B | 15m. on 50c. blue | 2·50 | 1·70 |
| 77 | C | 30m. on 1f. red and green | 1·70 | 1·00 |
| 78 | C | 60m. on 2f. red and green | 4·25 | 12·00 |
| 79 | C | 150m. on 5f. blue and buff | 6·25 | 12·50 |

**1927.** Altered key-types, inscr "Mm" below value.

| | | | | |
|---|---|---|---|---|
| 80 | A | 3m. orange | 2·75 | 6·25 |
| 81 | B | 15m. blue | 2·50 | 1·40 |
| 82 | B | 20m. mauve | 6·00 | 12·00 |
| 83 | C | 50m. red and green | 13·00 | 24·00 |
| 84 | C | 100m. blue and yellow | 16·00 | 27·00 |
| 85 | C | 250m. green and red | 20·00 | 44·00 |

**1927.** Sinking Fund. As No. 81, colour changed, surch **+ 5 Mm Caisse d'Amortissement**.

| | | | | |
|---|---|---|---|---|
| 86 | B | 15m.+5m. orange | 3·75 | 12·00 |
| 87 | B | 15m.+5m. red | 6·00 | 12·00 |
| 88 | B | 15m.+5m. brown | 11·50 | 25·00 |
| 89 | B | 15m.+5m. lilac | 15·00 | 40·00 |

### POSTAGE DUE STAMPS

**1922.** Postage Due Stamps of France surch in milliemes.

| | | | | |
|---|---|---|---|---|
| D65 | D11 | 2m. on 5c. blue | 1·80 | 10·00 |
| D66 | D11 | 4m. on 10c. brown | 3·75 | 10·00 |
| D67 | D11 | 10m. on 30c. red | 3·00 | 11·00 |
| D68 | D11 | 15m. on 50c. purple | 1·80 | 11·00 |
| D69 | D11 | 30m. on 1f. pur on yell | 2·00 | 16·00 |

D10

**1928**

| | | | | |
|---|---|---|---|---|
| D90 | D10 | 1m. grey | 1·00 | 9·00 |
| D91 | D10 | 2m. blue | 3·75 | 8·75 |
| D92 | D10 | 4m. pink | 4·00 | 9·50 |
| D93 | D10 | 5m. olive | 3·75 | 8·75 |
| D94 | D10 | 10m. red | 4·25 | 9·50 |
| D95 | D10 | 20m. purple | 5·50 | 8·75 |
| D96 | D10 | 30m. green | 10·50 | 16·00 |
| D97 | D10 | 40m. lilac | 7·25 | 16·00 |

This set was issued for use in both Alexandria and Port Said.

Pt. 6, Pt. 12

# ALGERIA

French territory in N. Africa. Stamps of France were used in Algeria from July 1958 until 3 July 1962, when the country achieved independence following a referendum.

1924. 100 centimes = 1 franc.
1964. 100 centimes = 1 dinar.

**1924.** Stamps of France optd ALGERIE.

| | | | | |
|---|---|---|---|---|
| 1 | 11 | ½c. on 1c. grey | 55 | 80 |
| 2 | 11 | 1c. grey | 60 | 2·50 |
| 3 | 11 | 2c. red | 55 | 2·75 |
| 4 | 11 | 3c. red | 70 | 2·50 |
| 5 | 11 | 4c. brown | 70 | 1·90 |
| 6 | 18 | 5c. orange | 1·40 | 70 |
| 7 | 11 | 5c. green | 70 | 15 |
| 8 | 30 | 10c. green | 1·60 | 1·40 |
| 9 | 18 | 10c. green | 40 | 50 |
| 10 | 15 | 15c. green | 1·60 | 1·40 |
| 11 | 30 | 15c. green | 70 | 2·75 |
| 12 | 18 | 15c. brown | 1·40 | 1·10 |
| 13 | 18 | 20c. brown | 1·40 | 50 |
| 14 | 18 | 25c. blue | 85 | 25 |
| 15 | 30 | 30c. red | 85 | 90 |
| 16 | 18 | 30c. blue | 70 | 15 |
| 17 | 18 | 30c. red* | 85 | 1·50 |
| 18 | 18 | 35c. violet | 1·50 | 1·70 |
| 19 | 13 | 40c. red and blue | 2·50 | 2·10 |
| 20 | 18 | 40c. olive | 1·80 | 1·90 |
| 21 | 13 | 45c. green and blue | 1·40 | 2·30 |
| 22 | 30 | 45c. red | 90 | 75 |
| 23 | 30 | 50c. blue | 1·40 | 90 |
| 24 | 15 | 60c. violet | 1·40 | 65 |
| 25 | 15 | 65c. red | 55 | 65 |
| 26 | 30 | 75c. blue | 70 | 40 |
| 27 | 15 | 80c. red | 1·20 | 75 |
| 28 | 15 | 85c. red | 1·00 | 40 |
| 29 | 13 | 1f. red and green | 2·10 | 45 |
| 30 | 18 | 1f.05 red | 1·10 | 1·50 |
| 31 | 13 | 2f. red and green | 2·30 | 3·75 |
| 32 | 13 | 3f. violet and blue | 2·50 | 3·00 |
| 33 | 13 | 5f. blue and yellow | 11·00 | 16·00 |

*No. 17 was only issued pre-cancelled and the price in the unused column is for stamps with full gum.

3 Street in the Casbah

4 Mosque of Sidi Abderahman

5 Grand Mosque

6 Bay of Algiers

**1926**

| | | | | |
|---|---|---|---|---|
| 34 | 3 | 1c. green | 30 | 1·50 |
| 35 | 3 | 2c. purple | 30 | 1·50 |
| 36 | 3 | 3c. orange | 20 | 1·50 |
| 37 | 3 | 5c. green | 45 | 15 |
| 38 | 3 | 10c. mauve | 45 | 15 |
| 39 | 4 | 15c. brown | 45 | 30 |
| 40 | 4 | 20c. green | 40 | 15 |
| 41 | 4 | 20c. red | 1·50 | 20 |
| 45 | 4 | 25c. blue | 70 | 35 |
| 46 | 4 | 30c. blue | 1·40 | 1·50 |
| 47 | 4 | 30c. green | 1·70 | 60 |
| 48 | 4 | 35c. violet | 1·70 | 5·25 |
| 49 | 4 | 40c. green | 15 | 15 |
| 50 | 5 | 45c. purple | 50 | 15 |
| 51 | 5 | 50c. blue | 50 | 15 |
| 53 | 5 | 50c. red | 1·60 | 15 |
| 54 | 5 | 60c. green | 30 | 75 |
| 55 | 5 | 65c. brown | 2·00 | 1·80 |
| 56 | 3 | 65c. blue | 2·00 | 30 |
| 57 | 5 | 75c. red | 75 | 15 |
| 58 | 5 | 75c. blue | 3·25 | 30 |
| 59 | 5 | 80c. orange | 1·20 | 2·50 |
| 60 | 5 | 90c. red | 2·50 | 2·20 |
| 61 | 6 | 1f. purple and green | 1·20 | 15 |
| 62 | 5 | 1f.05 brown | 1·10 | 2·30 |
| 63 | 5 | 1f.10 mauve | 4·50 | 7·25 |
| 64 | 6 | 1f.25 ultramarine and blue | 1·90 | 6·75 |
| 65 | 6 | 1f.50 ultramarine and blue | 3·75 | 1·50 |
| 66 | 6 | 2f. brown and green | 2·75 | 45 |
| 67 | 6 | 3f. red and mauve | 4·25 | 2·20 |
| 68 | 6 | 5f. mauve and red | 5·25 | 3·00 |
| 69 | 6 | 10f. red and brown | 75·00 | 50·00 |
| 70 | 6 | 20f. green and violet | 11·50 | 13·00 |

**1926.** Surch ½ centime.

| | | | | |
|---|---|---|---|---|
| 71 | 3 | ½c. on 1c. olive | 40 | 2·40 |

**1927.** Wounded Soldiers of Moroccan War Charity Issue. Surch with star and crescent and premium.

| | | | | |
|---|---|---|---|---|
| 72 | | 5c.+5c. green | 1·00 | 6·00 |
| 73 | | 10c.+10c. mauve | 1·20 | 6·00 |
| 74 | 4 | 15c.+15c. brown | 1·50 | 6·00 |
| 75 | 4 | 20c.+20c. red | 1·50 | 6·00 |
| 76 | 4 | 25c.+25c. green | 1·00 | 6·00 |
| 77 | 4 | 30c.+30c. blue | 2·10 | 6·00 |
| 78 | 4 | 35c.+35c. violet | 65 | 6·00 |
| 79 | 4 | 40c.+40c. olive | 1·00 | 6·00 |
| 80 | 5 | 50c.+50c. blue | 1·50 | 6·50 |
| 81 | 5 | 80c.+80c. orange | 1·30 | 6·50 |
| 82 | 6 | 1f.+1f. purple and green | 1·50 | 6·50 |
| 83 | 6 | 2f.+2f. brown and green | 32·00 | 70·00 |
| 84 | 6 | 5f.+5f. mauve and red | 70·00 | 90·00 |

**1927.** Surch in figures.

| | | | | |
|---|---|---|---|---|
| 85 | 4 | 10 on 35c. violet | 40 | 90 |
| 86 | 4 | 25 on 30c. blue | 55 | 10 |
| 87 | 4 | 30 on 25c. green | 40 | 10 |
| 88 | 5 | 65 on 60c. green | 95 | 90 |
| 89 | 5 | 90 on 80c. orange | 20 | 10 |
| 90 | 5 | 1f.10 on 1f.05 brown | 15 | 10 |
| 91 | 6 | 1f.50 on 1f.25 ultramarine and blue | 1·00 | 1·00 |

**1927.** Surch 5c.

| | | | | |
|---|---|---|---|---|
| 92 | 11 | 5c. on 4c. brown (No. 5) | 90 | 1·60 |

11 Railway Terminus, Oran

**1930.** Centenary of French Occupation.

| | | | | |
|---|---|---|---|---|
| 93 | | 5c.+5c. orange | 9·75 | 29·00 |
| 94 | - | 10c.+10c. olive | 9·75 | 22·00 |
| 95 | - | 15c.+15c. brown | 8·25 | 22·00 |
| 96 | - | 25c.+25c. grey | 8·25 | 20·00 |
| 97 | - | 30c.+30c. red | 7·00 | 28·00 |
| 98 | - | 40c.+40c. green | 5·50 | 26·00 |
| 99 | - | 50c.+50c. blue | 5·50 | 24·00 |
| 100 | - | 75c.+75c. purple | 4·75 | 24·00 |
| 101 | - | 1f.+1f. orange | 5·50 | 26·00 |
| 102 | - | 1f.50+1f.50 blue | 6·25 | 24·00 |
| 103 | - | 2f.+2f. red | 5·50 | 26·00 |
| 104 | - | 3f.+3f. green | 7·00 | 26·00 |
| 105 | - | 5f.+5f. red and green | 14·00 | 55·00 |

DESIGNS—HORIZ: 10c. Constantine; 15c. Admiralty, Algiers; 25c. Algiers; 30c. Ruins of Timgad; 40c. Ruins of Djemila. VERT: 50c. Ruins of Djemila; 75c. Tlemcen; 1f. Ghardaia; 1f.50, Tolga; 2f. Tuaregs; 3f. Native quarter, Algiers; 5f. Mosque, Algiers.

12 Bay of Algiers, after painting by Verecque

**1930.** N. African International Philatelic Exn.

| | | | | |
|---|---|---|---|---|
| 106 | 12 | 10f.+10f. brown | 34·00 | 65·00 |

15 Admiralty and Penon Lighthouse, Algiers

**1936**

| | | | | |
|---|---|---|---|---|
| 107 | A | 1c. blue | 35 | 1·50 |
| 108 | F | 2c. purple | 30 | 75 |
| 109 | B | 3c. green | 75 | 2·10 |
| 110 | C | 5c. mauve | 45 | 15 |
| 111 | 15 | 10c. green | 90 | 75 |
| 112 | D | 15c. red | 45 | 15 |
| 113 | G | 20c. green | 50 | 15 |
| 114 | E | 25c. purple | 2·20 | 60 |
| 115 | C | 30c. green | 60 | 20 |
| 116 | D | 40c. purple | 90 | 20 |
| 117 | G | 45c. blue | 1·30 | 3·75 |
| 118 | 15 | 50c. red | 3·00 | 60 |
| 119 | A | 65c. brown | 8·75 | 11·50 |
| 120 | A | 65c. red | 1·90 | 60 |
| 121 | A | 70c. brown | 75 | 90 |
| 122 | F | 75c. slate | 75 | 20 |
| 124 | B | 90c. red | 75 | 90 |
| 125 | E | 1f. brown | 75 | 20 |
| 126 | 15 | 1f.25 violet | 2·10 | 75 |
| 127 | 15 | 1f.25 red | 75 | 1·50 |
| 128 | F | 1f.50 blue | 2·75 | 90 |
| 129 | F | 1f.50 red | 3·00 | 4·50 |
| 130 | C | 1f.75 orange | 1·50 | 75 |
| 131 | B | 2f. purple | 1·00 | 15 |
| 132 | A | 2f.25 green | 19·00 | 26·00 |
| 133 | E | 2f.25 blue | 1·90 | 2·00 |
| 134 | C | 2f.50 blue | 2·20 | 3·25 |
| 135 | G | 3f. mauve | 75 | 30 |
| 136 | E | 3f.50 blue | 2·50 | 3·50 |
| 137 | 15 | 5f. slate | 1·50 | 1·60 |
| 138 | F | 10f. orange | 1·00 | 2·75 |
| 139 | D | 20f. blue | 1·90 | 3·75 |

DESIGNS—HORIZ: A, In the Sahara; B, Arc de Triomphe, Lambese; C, Ghardaia, Mzab; D, Marabouts, Touggourt; E, El Kebir Mosque, Algiers. VERT: F, Colomb Bechar-Oued; G, Cemetery, Tlemcen.

17 Exhibition Pavilion

**1937.** Paris International Exhibition.

| | | | | |
|---|---|---|---|---|
| 140 | 17 | 40c. green | 1·00 | 65 |
| 141 | 17 | 50c. red | 65 | 35 |
| 142 | 17 | 1f.50 blue | 90 | 1·00 |
| 143 | 17 | 1f.75 black | 1·90 | 1·70 |

18 Constantine in 1837

**1937.** Centenary of Capture of Constantine.

| | | | | |
|---|---|---|---|---|
| 144 | 18 | 65c. red | 1·00 | 50 |
| 145 | 18 | 1f. brown | 3·00 | 65 |
| 146 | 18 | 1f.75 blue | 30 | 75 |

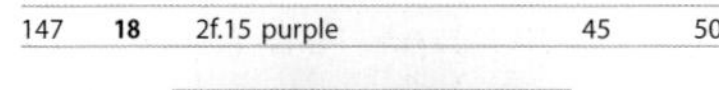

| | | | | |
|---|---|---|---|---|
| 147 | **18** | 2f.15 purple | 45 | 50 |

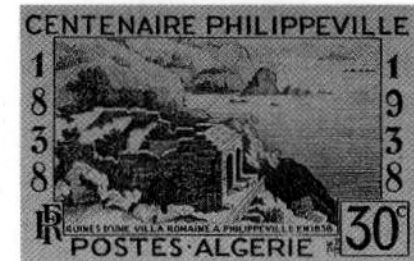

**19** Ruins of Roman Villa

**1938.** Centenary of Philippeville.

| | | | | |
|---|---|---|---|---|
| 148 | **19** | 30c. green | 1·50 | 2·50 |
| 149 | **19** | 65c. blue | 45 | 50 |
| 150 | **19** | 75c. purple | 1·80 | 2·75 |
| 151 | **19** | 3f. red | 3·75 | 4·25 |
| 152 | **19** | 5f. brown | 4·50 | 5·75 |

**1938.** 20th Anniv of Armistice Day. No. 132 surch 1918 - 11 Nov. - 1938 0.65 + 0.35.

| | | | | |
|---|---|---|---|---|
| 153 | | 65c.+35c. on 2f.25 green | 1·50 | 4·00 |

**1938.** Surch 0,25.

| | | | | |
|---|---|---|---|---|
| 154 | **15** | 25c. on 50c. red | 45 | 15 |

**22** Caillie, Lavigerie and Duveyrier

**1939.** Sahara Pioneers' Monument Fund.

| | | | | |
|---|---|---|---|---|
| 155 | **22** | 30c.+20c. green | 2·30 | 7·50 |
| 156 | **22** | 90c.+60c. red | 2·20 | 5·75 |
| 157 | **22** | 2f.25+75c. blue | 11·50 | 50·00 |
| 158 | **22** | 5f.+5f. black | 29·00 | 75·00 |

**23** "Extavia" (freighter) in Algiers Harbour

**1939.** New York World's Fair.

| | | | | |
|---|---|---|---|---|
| 159 | **23** | 20c. green | 1·50 | 3·75 |
| 160 | **23** | 40c. purple | 1·90 | 4·25 |
| 161 | **23** | 90c. brown | 2·10 | 65 |
| 162 | **23** | 1f.25 red | 6·50 | 8·25 |
| 163 | **23** | 2f.25 blue | 2·75 | 3·25 |

**1939.** Surch with new values and bars or cross.

| | | | | |
|---|---|---|---|---|
| 173 | **3** | 50c. on 65c. blue | 1·50 | 50 |
| 164 | **3** | 1f. on 90c. red | 75 | 35 |
| 173c | **B** | 90c.+60c. red (No. 124) | 90 | 35 |

**25** Algerian Soldiers

**1940.** Soldiers' Dependants' Relief Fund. Surch + and premium.

| | | | | |
|---|---|---|---|---|
| 166 | **25** | 1f.+1f. blue | 1·90 | 5·00 |
| 167 | **25** | 1f.+2f. red | 1·90 | 5·75 |
| 168 | **25** | 1f.+4f. green | 2·20 | 6·50 |
| 169 | **25** | 1f.+9f. brown | 2·50 | 8·25 |

**26** Algiers

**1941**

| | | | | |
|---|---|---|---|---|
| 170 | **26** | 30c. blue | 1·40 | 1·70 |
| 171 | **26** | 70c. brown | 1·10 | 35 |
| 172 | **26** | 1f. red | 1·10 | 35 |

**28** Marshal Petain

**1941**

| | | | | |
|---|---|---|---|---|
| 174 | **28** | 1f. blue | 60 | 1·50 |

**1941.** National Relief Fund. As No. 174, but surch +4 f and colour changed.

| | | | | |
|---|---|---|---|---|
| 175 | | 1f.+4f. black | 1·00 | 5·00 |

**1942.** National Relief Fund. Surch SECOURS NATIONAL +4f.

| | | | | |
|---|---|---|---|---|
| 176 | | 1f.+4f. blue (No. 174) | 1·20 | 6·50 |

**1942.** Various altered types. (a) As T **26**, but without "RF".

| | | | | |
|---|---|---|---|---|
| 177 | **26** | 30c. blue | 60 | 3·25 |

(b) As T **5**, but without "REPUBLIQUE FRANCAISE".

| | | | | |
|---|---|---|---|---|
| 178 | **5** | 40c. grey | 1·20 | 5·00 |
| 179 | **5** | 50c. red | 75 | 1·30 |

(c) As No. 129 but without "RF".

| | | | | |
|---|---|---|---|---|
| 180 | **F** | 1f.50 red | 1·80 | 1·10 |

**32** Arms of Oran

**1942.** Coats-of-Arms.

| | | | | |
|---|---|---|---|---|
| 190 | **A** | 10c. lilac | 1·30 | 3·50 |
| 191 | **32** | 30c. green | 1·00 | 3·75 |
| 181 | **B** | 40c. violet | 75 | 4·25 |
| 192 | **B** | 40c. lilac | 2·10 | 3·75 |
| 182 | **32** | 60c. red | 1·30 | 2·50 |
| 194 | **B** | 70c. blue | 90 | 2·30 |
| 195 | **A** | 80c. green | 1·00 | 3·75 |
| 183 | **B** | 1f.20 green | 1·30 | 3·00 |
| 184 | **A** | 1f.50 red | 45 | 50 |
| 198 | **32** | 2f. blue | 45 | 90 |
| 186 | **B** | 2f.40 red | 1·80 | 3·00 |
| 187 | **A** | 3f. blue | 45 | 65 |
| 188 | **B** | 4f. blue | 1·20 | 1·50 |
| 201 | **32** | 4f.50 purple | 90 | 15 |
| 189 | **32** | 5f. green | 1·30 | 1·70 |

ARMS: A, Algiers; B, Constantine.

**34** Marshal Petain

**1943**

| | | | | |
|---|---|---|---|---|
| 202 | **34** | 1f.50 red | 45 | 3·25 |

**35** "La Marseillaise"

**36** Allegory of Victory

**1943**

| | | | | |
|---|---|---|---|---|
| 203 | **35** | 1f.50 red | 1·00 | 3·00 |
| 204 | **36** | 1f.50 blue | 30 | 65 |

**1943.** Surch 2f.

| | | | | |
|---|---|---|---|---|
| 205 | **32** | 2f. on 5f. orange | 45 | 1·20 |

**38** Summer Palace, Algiers

**1943**

| | | | | |
|---|---|---|---|---|
| 206 | **38** | 15f. grey | 1·50 | 2·10 |
| 207 | **38** | 20f. green | 1·50 | 2·10 |
| 208 | **38** | 50f. red | 1·20 | 1·30 |
| 209 | **38** | 100f. blue | 3·00 | 3·25 |
| 210 | **38** | 200f. brown | 4·50 | 5·00 |

**39** Mother and Children

**1943.** Prisoners-of-war Relief Fund.

| | | | | |
|---|---|---|---|---|
| 211 | **39** | 50c.+4f.50 pink | 90 | 6·50 |
| 212 | **39** | 1f.50+8f.50 green | 90 | 6·50 |
| 213 | **39** | 3f.+12f. blue | 90 | 6·50 |
| 214 | **39** | 5f.+15f. brown | 90 | 6·50 |

**40** "Marianne"

**1944**

| | | | | |
|---|---|---|---|---|
| 215 | **40** | 10c. grey | 20 | 75 |
| 216 | **40** | 30c. lilac | 20 | 50 |
| 217 | **40** | 50c. red | 20 | 15 |
| 218 | **40** | 80c. green | 45 | 90 |
| 219 | **40** | 1f.20 lilac | 75 | 1·70 |
| 220 | **40** | 1f.50 blue | 20 | 15 |
| 221 | **40** | 2f.40 red | 30 | 50 |
| 222 | **40** | 3f. violet | 45 | 25 |
| 223 | **40** | 4f.50 black | 60 | 35 |

**41** Gallic Cock

**1944**

| | | | | |
|---|---|---|---|---|
| 224 | **41** | 40c. red | 45 | 3·25 |
| 225 | **41** | 1f. green | 50 | 15 |
| 226 | **41** | 2f. red | 45 | 35 |
| 227 | **41** | 2f. brown | 60 | 75 |
| 228 | **41** | 4f. blue | 1·30 | 35 |
| 229 | **41** | 10f. black | 1·50 | 2·50 |

**1944.** Surch 0f.30.

| | | | | |
|---|---|---|---|---|
| 230 | **4** | 0f.30 on 15c. brown | 60 | 1·30 |

No. 230 was only issued pre-cancelled and the price in the unused column is for stamps with full gum.

**1945.** Types of France optd ALGERIE.

| | | | | |
|---|---|---|---|---|
| 247 | **239** | 10c. black and blue | 30 | 3·75 |
| 231 | **217** | 40c. mauve | 15 | 50 |
| 232 | **217** | 50c. blue | 30 | 35 |
| 248 | - | 50c. brown, yellow and red (No. 973) | 90 | 50 |
| 233 | **218** | 60c. blue | 60 | 85 |
| 236 | **136** | 80c. green | 1·20 | 1·70 |
| 234 | **218** | 1f. red | 60 | 50 |
| 237 | **136** | 1f. blue | 90 | 50 |
| 238 | **136** | 1f.20 violet | 90 | 4·25 |
| 235 | **218** | 1f.50 lilac | 90 | 1·30 |
| 239 | **136** | 2f. brown | 30 | 15 |
| 240 | **136** | 2f.40 red | 1·00 | 2·10 |
| 242 | **219** | 2f. green | 75 | 25 |
| 241 | **136** | 3f. orange | 65 | 85 |
| 243 | **219** | 3f. red | 45 | 15 |
| 244 | **219** | 4f.50 blue | 2·10 | 50 |
| 245 | **219** | 5f. green | 35 | 25 |
| 246 | **219** | 10f. blue | 1·80 | 2·00 |

**1945.** Airmen and Dependants Fund. As No. 742 of France (bombers) optd RF ALGERIE.

| | | | | |
|---|---|---|---|---|
| 249 | **169** | 1f.50+3f.50 blue | 1·20 | 5·75 |

**1945.** Postal Employees War Victims' Fund. As No. 949 of France overprinted ALGERIE.

| | | | | |
|---|---|---|---|---|
| 250 | **223** | 4f.+6f. brown | 90 | 5·75 |

**1945.** Stamp Day. As No. 955 of France (Louis XI) optd ALGERIE.

| | | | | |
|---|---|---|---|---|
| 251 | **228** | 2f.+3f. purple | 1·20 | 5·00 |

**1946.** No. 184 surch 0f50 RF.

| | | | | |
|---|---|---|---|---|
| 252 | | 50c. on 1f.50 red | 30 | 50 |

**1946.** Type of France optd ALGERIE and surch 2F.

| | | | | |
|---|---|---|---|---|
| 253 | **136** | 2f. on 1f.50 brown | 30 | 35 |

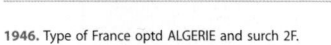

**46** Potez 56 over Algiers

**1946.** Air.

| | | | | |
|---|---|---|---|---|
| 254 | **46** | 5f. red | 1·60 | 85 |
| 255 | **46** | 10f. blue | 35 | 15 |
| 256 | **46** | 15f. green | 1·50 | 75 |
| 257a | **46** | 20f. brown | 1·50 | 35 |
| 258 | **46** | 25f. violet | 1·30 | 50 |
| 259 | **46** | 40f. black | 1·90 | 1·70 |

**1946.** Stamp Day. As No. 975 of France (De la Varane), optd ALGERIE.

| | | | | |
|---|---|---|---|---|
| 260 | **241** | 3f.+2f. red | 90 | 6·50 |

**47** Children at Spring

**1946.** Charity. Inscr as in T **47**.

| | | | | |
|---|---|---|---|---|
| 261 | **47** | 3f.+17f. green | 3·00 | 8·25 |
| 262 | **47** | 4f.+21f. red | 3·25 | 7·50 |
| 263 | **47** | 8f.+27f. purple | 4·00 | 18·00 |
| 264 | **47** | 10f.+35f. blue | 3·75 | 8·25 |

DESIGNS—VERT: 4f. Boy gazing skywards; 8f. Laurel-crowned head. HORIZ: 10f. Soldier looking at Algerian coast.

**1947.** Air. Surch -10%.

| | | | | |
|---|---|---|---|---|
| 265 | **46** | "-10%" on 5f. red | 45 | 60 |

**1947.** Stamp Day. As No. 1008 of France (Louvois), optd ALGERIE.

| | | | | |
|---|---|---|---|---|
| 266 | **253** | 4f.50+5f.50 blue | 1·20 | 7·00 |

**49** Arms of Constantine

**1947.** Various Arms.

| | | | | |
|---|---|---|---|---|
| 267 | **49** | 10c. green and red | 15 | 2·50 |
| 268 | **A** | 50c. black and orange | 15 | 35 |
| 269 | **B** | 1f. blue and yellow | 15 | 15 |
| 270 | **49** | 1f.30 black and blue | 1·50 | 4·25 |
| 271 | **A** | 1f.50 violet and yellow | 30 | 15 |
| 272 | **B** | 2f. black and green | 30 | 15 |
| 273 | **49** | 2f.50 black and red | 1·20 | 1·30 |
| 274 | **A** | 3f. red and green | 45 | 65 |
| 275 | **B** | 3f.50 green and purple | 45 | 35 |
| 276 | **49** | 4f. brown and green | 15 | 15 |
| 277 | **A** | 4f.50 blue and red | 60 | 15 |
| 278 | **A** | 5f. black and blue | 20 | 15 |
| 279 | **B** | 6f. brown and red | 45 | 15 |
| 280 | **B** | 8f. brown and blue | 30 | 15 |
| 281 | **49** | 10f. pink and brown | 60 | 25 |
| 282 | **A** | 15f. black and red | 1·80 | 15 |

ARMS: A, Algiers; B, Oran. See also Nos. 364/8 and 381/3.

**1947.** Air. 7th Anniv of Gen. de Gaulle's Call to Arms. Surch with Lorraine Cross and 18 Juin 1940 + 10 Fr.

| | | | | |
|---|---|---|---|---|
| 283 | **46** | 10f.+10f. blue | 3·25 | 8·25 |

**1947.** Resistance Movement. Type of France surch ALGERIE+10f.

| | | | | |
|---|---|---|---|---|
| 284 | **261** | 5f.+10f. grey | 1·80 | 8·25 |

**1948.** Stamp Day. Type of France (Arago) optd ALGERIE.

| | | | | |
|---|---|---|---|---|
| 285 | **267** | 6f.+4f. green | 1·50 | 8·25 |

**1948.** Air. 8th Anniv of Gen. de Gaulle's Call to Arms. Surch with Lorraine Cross and 18 JUIN 1940 + 10 Fr.

| | | | | |
|---|---|---|---|---|
| 286 | **46** | 5f.+10f. red | 3·00 | 6·50 |

**1948.** General Leclerc Memorial. Type of France surch ALGERIE + 4f.

| | | | | |
|---|---|---|---|---|
| 287 | **270** | 6f.+4f. red | 1·50 | 6·25 |

**57** Battleship "Richelieu"

**1949.** Naval Welfare Fund.

| | | | | |
|---|---|---|---|---|
| 288 | **57** | 10f.+15f. blue | 5·75 | 25·00 |
| 289 | - | 18f.+22f. red | 8·75 | 25·00 |

DESIGN: 18f. Aircraft-carrier "Arromanches".

**58** White Storks over Minaret

**1949.** Air.

| | | | | |
|---|---|---|---|---|
| 290 | **58** | 50f. green | 4·50 | 1·30 |
| 291 | - | 100f. brown | 3·00 | 85 |
| 292 | **58** | 200f. red | 8·75 | 4·25 |
| 293 | - | 500f. blue | 31·00 | 46·00 |

DESIGN—HORIZ: 100, 500f. Dewoitine D-338 trimotor air-plane over valley dwellings.

**1949.** Stamp Day. As No. 1054 of France (Choiseul) optd ALGERIE.

| | | | | |
|---|---|---|---|---|
| 294 | **278** | 15f.+5f. mauve | 95 | 6·50 |

**60** French Colonials

**1949.** 75th Anniv of U.P.U.

| | | | | |
|---|---|---|---|---|
| 295 | **60** | 5f. green | 2·40 | 5·75 |
| 296 | **60** | 15f. red | 3·00 | 5·75 |
| 297 | **60** | 25f. blue | 4·75 | 15·00 |

**61** Statue of Duke of Orleans

**1949.** Air. 25th Anniv of First Algerian Postage Stamp.

| | | | | |
|---|---|---|---|---|
| 298 | **61** | 15f.+20f. brown | 6·00 | 20·00 |

**62** Grapes

**1950**

| | | | | |
|---|---|---|---|---|
| 299 | **62** | 20f. purple, green & dp pur | 1·20 | 65 |
| 300 | - | 25f. brown, green & black | 2·40 | 1·00 |
| 301 | - | 40f. orange, green & brown | 3·00 | 2·00 |

DESIGNS: 25f. Dates; 40f. Oranges and lemons.

**1950.** Stamp Day. As No. 1091 of France (Postman), optd ALGERIE.

| | | | | |
|---|---|---|---|---|
| 302 | **292** | 12f.+3f. brown | 2·40 | 9·00 |

**63** Foreign Legionary

**1950.** Foreign Legion Welfare Fund.

| | | | | |
|---|---|---|---|---|
| 303 | **63** | 15f.+5f. green | 2·30 | 8·25 |

**64** R. P. de Foucauld and Gen. Laperrine

**1950.** 50th Anniv of French in the Sahara (25f.) and Unveiling of Monument to Abd-el-Kader (40f.).

| | | | | |
|---|---|---|---|---|
| 304 | **64** | 25f.+5f. black and green | 6·00 | 20·00 |
| 305 | - | 40f.+10f. dp brown & brn | 6·00 | 20·00 |

DESIGN: 40f. Emir Abd-el-Kader and Marshal Bugeaud.

**65** Col. C. d'Ornano

**1951.** Col. d'Ornano Monument Fund.

| | | | | |
|---|---|---|---|---|
| 306 | **65** | 15f.+5f. purple, brn blk | 1·20 | 5·75 |

**1951.** Stamp Day. As No. 1107 of France (Travelling Post Office sorting van), optd ALGERIE.

| | | | | |
|---|---|---|---|---|
| 307 | **300** | 12f.+3f. brown | 4·25 | 8·25 |

**66** Apollo of Cherchel

**1952**

| | | | | |
|---|---|---|---|---|
| 308 | **66** | 10f. sepia | 50 | 15 |
| 309 | - | 12f. brown | 60 | 25 |
| 310 | - | 15f. blue | 50 | 25 |
| 311 | - | 18f. red | 70 | 50 |
| 312 | - | 20f. green | 50 | 25 |
| 313 | **66** | 30f. blue | 85 | 50 |

STATUES: 12, 18f. Isis of Cherchel; 15, 20f. Boy and eagle.

**1952.** Stamp Day. As No. 1140 of France (Mail Coach), optd ALGERIE.

| | | | | |
|---|---|---|---|---|
| 314 | **319** | 12f.+3f. blue | 2·40 | 11·50 |

**67** Algerian War Memorial

**1952.** African Army Commemoration.

| | | | | |
|---|---|---|---|---|
| 315 | **67** | 12f. green | 95 | 2·50 |

**68** Medaille Militaire

**1952.** Military Medal Centenary.

| | | | | |
|---|---|---|---|---|
| 316 | **68** | 15f.+5f. brown, yell & grn | 2·40 | 6·50 |

**69** Fossil ("Berbericeras sekikensis")

**1952.** 19th Int Geological Convention, Algiers.

| | | | | |
|---|---|---|---|---|
| 317 | **69** | 15f. red | 3·50 | 5·75 |
| 318 | - | 30f. blue | 2·40 | 4·25 |

DESIGN: 30f. Phonolite Dyke, Hoggar.

**1952.** 10th Anniv of Battle of Bir-Hakeim. As No. 1146 of France surch ALGERIE+5 F.

| | | | | |
|---|---|---|---|---|
| 319 | **325** | 30f.+5f. blue | 2·30 | 6·50 |

**72** Bou-Nara

**1952.** Red Cross Fund.

| | | | | |
|---|---|---|---|---|
| 320 | - | 8f.+2f. red and blue | 1·20 | 5·00 |
| 321 | **72** | 12f.+3f. red | 1·80 | 8·25 |

DESIGN: 8f. El-Oued and map of Algeria.

**73** Members of Corps and Camel

**1952.** 50th Anniv of Sahara Corps.

| | | | | |
|---|---|---|---|---|
| 322 | **73** | 12f. brown | 1·80 | 3·50 |

**1953.** Stamp Day. As No. 1161 of France (Count D'Argenson), optd ALGERIE.

| | | | | |
|---|---|---|---|---|
| 323 | **334** | 12f.+3f. violet | 1·20 | 8·25 |

**74** "Victory" of Cirta

**1954.** Army Welfare Fund.

| | | | | |
|---|---|---|---|---|
| 324 | **74** | 15f.+5f. brown and sepia | 85 | 3·75 |

**75** E. Millon

**1954.** Military Health Service.

| | | | | |
|---|---|---|---|---|
| 325 | **75** | 25f. sepia and green | 95 | 65 |
| 326 | - | 40f. red and brown | 85 | 50 |
| 327 | - | 50f. indigo and blue | 1·20 | 60 |

DOCTORS—VERT: 40f. F. Maillot. HORIZ: 50f. A. Laveran.

**1954.** Stamp Day. As No. 1202 of France (Lavalette), optd ALGERIE.

| | | | | |
|---|---|---|---|---|
| 328 | **346** | 12f.+3f. red | 95 | 5·25 |

**76** French and Algerian Soldiers

**1954.** Old Soldiers' Welfare Fund.

| | | | | |
|---|---|---|---|---|
| 329 | **76** | 15f.+5f. sepia | 1·80 | 5·75 |

**77** Foreign Legionary

**1954.** Foreign Legion Welfare Fund.

| | | | | |
|---|---|---|---|---|
| 330 | **77** | 15f.+5f. green | 2·50 | 8·25 |

**78**

**1954.** 3rd International Congress of Mediterranean Citrus Fruit Culture.

| | | | | |
|---|---|---|---|---|
| 331 | **78** | 15f. blue and indigo | 1·30 | 3·00 |

**1954.** 10th Anniv of Liberation. As No. 1204 of France ("D-Day") optd ALGERIE.

| | | | | |
|---|---|---|---|---|
| 332 | **348** | 15f. red | 70 | 2·00 |

**79** Darguinah Hydroelectric Station

**1954.** Inauguration of River Agrioun Hydroelectric Installations.

| | | | | |
|---|---|---|---|---|
| 333 | **79** | 15f. purple | 1·20 | 4·00 |

**80** Courtyard of Bardo Museum

**1954**

| | | | | |
|---|---|---|---|---|
| 334 | **80** | 10f. brown & light brown | 70 | 15 |
| 335 | **80** | 12f. orange and brown (I) | 95 | 20 |
| 336 | **80** | 12f. orange and brown (II) | 60 | 50 |
| 337 | **80** | 15f. blue and light blue | 70 | 20 |
| 338 | **80** | 18f. carmine and red | 70 | 50 |
| 339 | **80** | 20f. green and light green | 90 | 1·30 |
| 340 | **80** | 25f. lilac and mauve | 95 | 30 |

12f. "POSTES" and "ALGERIE" in orange (I) or in white (II).

**1954.** 150th Anniv of Presentation of First Legion of Honour. As No. 1223 of France, optd ALGERIE.

| | | | | |
|---|---|---|---|---|
| 341 | **356** | 12f. green | 95 | 4·00 |

**81** Red Cross Nurses

**1954.** Red Cross Fund. Cross in red.

| | | | | |
|---|---|---|---|---|
| 342 | **81** | 12f.+3f. blue | 3·50 | 9·00 |
| 343 | - | 15f.+5f. violet | 4·75 | 12·00 |

DESIGN: 15f. J.H. Dunant and Djemila ruins.

**82** St. Augustine

**1954.** 1600th Birth Anniv of St. Augustine.

| | | | | |
|---|---|---|---|---|
| 344 | **82** | 15f. brown | 1·20 | 2·20 |

**83** Earthquake Victims and Ruins

**1954.** Orleansville Earthquake Relief Fund. Inscr as in T **83**.

| | | | | |
|---|---|---|---|---|
| 345 | **83** | 12f.+4f. brown | 1·40 | 6·25 |
| 346 | **83** | 15f.+5f. blue | 1·50 | 6·50 |
| 347 | - | 18f.+6f. mauve | 1·70 | 6·50 |
| 348 | - | 20f.+7f. violet | 1·80 | 7·00 |
| 349 | - | 25f.+8f. lake | 2·30 | 7·25 |
| 350 | - | 30f.+10f. turquoise | 1·70 | 8·25 |

DESIGNS—HORIZ: 18, 20f. Red Cross workers. 25, 30f. Stretcher-bearers.

**1955.** Stamp Day. As No. 1245 of France (Balloon Post), optd ALGERIE.

| | | | | |
|---|---|---|---|---|
| 351 | **364** | 12f.+3f. blue | 65 | 5·00 |

**84** Statue of Aesculapius and El Kettar Hospital

**1955.** 30th French Medical Congress.

| | | | | |
|---|---|---|---|---|
| 352 | **84** | 15f. red | 35 | 80 |

**85** Ruins of Tipasa

**1955.** Bimillenary of Tipasa.

| | | | | |
|---|---|---|---|---|
| 353 | **85** | 50f. brown | 40 | 20 |

**1955.** 50th Anniv of Rotary International. As No. 1235 of France optd ALGERIE.

354 **361** 30f. blue 45 2·30

**1955.** As Nos. 1238 and 1238b of France ("France") inscr "ALGERIE".

355 **362** 15f. red 70 20
356 **362** 20f. blue 2·10 1·50

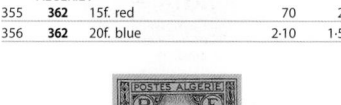

**86** Widows and Children

**1955.** War Victims' Welfare Fund.

357 **86** 15f.+5f. indigo and blue 1·40 3·25

**87** Grand Kabylie

**1955**

358 **87** 100f. indigo and blue 2·40 50

**88**

**1956.** Anti-cancer Fund.

359 **88** 15f.+5f. brown 1·60 5·50

**1956.** Stamp Day. As No. 1279 of France ("Francis of Taxis"), optd ALGERIE.

360 **383** 12f.+3f. red 95 4·50

**89** Foreign Legion Retirement Home, Sidi Bel Abbes

**1956.** Foreign Legion Welfare Fund.

361 **89** 15f.+5f. green 1·70 6·00

**90** Marshal Franchet d'Esperey (after J. Ebstein)

**1956.** Birth Cent of Marshal Franchet d'Esperey.

362 **90** 15f. indigo and blue 2·00 4·25

**91** Marshal Leclerc and Memorial

**1956.** Marshal Leclerc Commemoration.

363 **91** 15f. brown and sepia 50 4·00

**1956.** Various arms as T **49**.

364 1f. green and red 85 70
365 3f. blue and green 80 2·75
366 5f. blue and yellow 1·10 50
367 6f. green and red 1·40 3·00
368 12f. blue and red 1·60 4·50

DESIGNS: 1f. Bone; 3f. Mostaganem; 5f. Tlemcen; 6f. Algiers; 12f. Orleansville.

**92** Oran

**1956**

369 **92** 30f. purple 1·40 30
370 **92** 35f. red 1·90 5·25

**1957.** Stamp Day. As No. 1322 of France ("Felucca") optd ALGERIE.

371 **403** 12f.+3f. purple 1·80 5·00

**93** Electric Train Crossing Viaduct

**1957.** Electrification of Bone-Tebessa Railway Line.

372 **93** 40f. turquoise and green 1·80 50

**94** Fennec Fox

**1957.** Red Cross Fund. Cross in red.

373 **94** 12f.+3f. brown 3·50 15·00
374 - 15f.+5f. sepia (White storks) 3·50 15·00

**1957.** 17th Anniv of Gen. de Gaulle's Call to Arms. Surch 18 JUIN 1940 + 5F.

375 **91** 15f.+5f. red and carmine 95 5·25

**96** Beni Bahdel Barrage, Tlemcen

**1957.** Air.

376 **96** 200f. red 9·50 11·00

**97** "Horseman Crossing Ford" (after Delacroix)

**1957.** Army Welfare Fund. Inscr "OEUVRES SOCIALES DE L'ARMEE".

377 **97** 15f.+5f. red 4·75 11·00
378 - 20f.+5f. green 4·25 11·50
379 - 35f.+10f. blue 4·25 12·00

DESIGNS—HORIZ: 20f. "Lakeside View" (after Fromentin). VERT: 35f. "Arab Dancer" (after Chasseriau).

**1958.** Stamp Day. As No. 1375 of France (Rural Postal Service), optd ALGERIE.

380 **421** 15f.+5f. brown 1·60 5·00

**1958.** Arms. As T **49** but inscr "REPUBLIQUE FRANCAISE" instead of "RF" at foot.

381 2f. red and blue 60 4·00
382 6f. green and red 36·00 60·00
383 10f. purple and green 1·20 4·50

ARMS: 2f. Tizi-Ouzou; 6f. Algiers; 10f. Setif.

**99** "Strelitzia Reginae"

**1958.** Algerian Child Welfare Fund.

384 **99** 20f.+5f. orge, vio & grn 3·50 7·00

**100**

**1958.** Marshal de Lattre Foundation.

385 **100** 20f.+5f. red, grn & bl 3·50 7·00

**INDEPENDENT STATE**

**1962.** Stamps of France optd EA and with bars obliterating "REPUBLIQUE FRANCAISE".

386 **344** 10c. green 95 40
387 **463** 25c. grey and red 70 30
393 - 45c. violet, purple and sepia (No. 1463) 6·75 4·50
394 - 50c. pur & grn (No. 1464) 6·75 4·50
395 - 1f. brown, blue and myrtle (No. 1549) 4·50 1·80

**103a** Maps of Africa and Algeria

**1962.** War Orphans' Fund.

395a **103a** 1f.+9f. green, black and red £350

**1962.** As pictorial types of France but inscr "REPUBLIQUE ALGERIENNE".

396 - 5c. turquoise, grn & brn 25 10
397 **438** 10c. blue and sepia 25 10
398 - 25c. red, slate & brown 55 15
399 - 95c. blue, buff and sepia 3·50 1·10
400 - 1f. sepia and green 2·50 1·60

DESIGNS—VERT: 5c. Kerrata Gorges; 25c. Tlemcen Mosque; 95c. Oil derrick and pipeline at Hassi-Massaoud, Sahara. HORIZ: 1f. Medea.

**104** Flag, Rifle and Olive Branch

**1963.** "Return of Peace". Flag in green and red. Inscription and background colours given.

401 **104** 5c. bistre 25 10
402 **104** 10c. blue 25 10
403 **104** 25c. red 1·90 30
404 **104** 95c. violet 1·80 75
405 - 1f. green 2·20 15
406 - 2f. brown 3·75 80
407 - 5f. purple 7·00 3·00
408 - 10f. black 25·00 14·50

DESIGN: 1f. to 10f. As Type **104** but with dove and broken chain added.

**105** Campaign Emblem and Globe

**1963.** Freedom from Hunger.

409 **105** 25c. yellow, green and red 70 25

**106** Clasped Hands

**1963.** National Solidarity Fund.

410 **106** 50c.+20c. red, grn & blk 1·40 65

**107** Map and Emblems

**1963.** 1st Anniv of Independence.

411 **107** 25c. multicoloured 70 25

**108** "Arab Physicians" (13th-century MS.)

**1963.** 2nd Arab Physicians Union Congress.

412 **108** 25c. brown, green & bistre 2·10 55

**109** Branch of Orange Tree

**1963**

413 **109** 8c. orange and bronze* 10 10
414 **109** 20c. orange and green* 25 15
415 **109** 40c. orange & turq* 75 35
416 **109** 55c. orange and green* 95 55

*These stamps were only issued pre-cancelled, the unused prices being for stamps with full gum.

**110** "Constitution"

**1963.** Promulgation of Constitution.

417 **110** 25c. red, green and sepia 70 40

**111** "Freedom Fighters"

**1963.** 9th Anniv of Revolution.

418 **111** 25c. red, green and brown 70 25

**112** Centenary Emblem

**1963.** Red Cross Centenary.

419 **112** 25c. blue, red and yellow 95 55

**113** Globe and Scales of Justice

**1963.** 15th Anniv of Declaration of Human Rights.

420 **113** 25c. black and blue 70 25

**114** Labourers

**1964.** Labour Day.

421 **114** 50c. multicoloured 1·40 45

**115** Map of Africa and Flags

**1964.** 1st Anniv of Africa Day, and African Unity Charter.

422 **115** 45c. red, orange and blue 90 40

**116** Tractors

**1964**

| | | | | |
|---|---|---|---|---|
| 423 | **116** | 5c. purple | 10 | 10 |
| 424 | - | 10c. brown | 10 | 10 |
| 425 | - | 12c. green | 50 | 25 |
| 426 | - | 15c. blue | 45 | 25 |
| 427 | - | 20c. yellow | 45 | 10 |
| 428 | **116** | 25c. red | 55 | 10 |
| 429 | - | 30c. violet | 55 | 15 |
| 430 | - | 45c. lake | 70 | 25 |
| 431 | - | 50c. blue | 70 | 10 |
| 432 | - | 65c. orange | 90 | 25 |
| 433 | **116** | 85c. green | 1·40 | 25 |
| 434 | - | 95c. red | 1·80 | 25 |

DESIGNS: 10, 30, 65c. Apprentices; 12, 15, 45c. Research scientist; 20, 50, 95c. Draughtsman and bricklayer.

**117** Rameses II in War Chariot, Abu Simbel

**1964.** Nubian Monuments Preservation.

435 **117** 20c. purple, red and blue 95 40

436 - 30c. ochre, turq & red 1·20 55

DESIGN: 30c. Heads of Rameses II.

**118** Hertzian-wave Radio Transmitting Pylon

**1964.** Inauguration of Algiers–Annaba Radio-Telephone Service.

437 **118** 85c. black, blue & brown 2·10 65

**119** Fair Emblems

**1964.** Algiers Fair.

438 **119** 30c. blue, yellow and red 55 25

**120** Gas Plant

**1964.** Inaug of Natural Gas Plant at Arzew.

439 **120** 25c. blue, yellow & violet 90 50

**121** Planting Trees

**1964.** Reafforestation Campaign.

440 **121** 25c. green, red and yellow 55 25

**122** Children

**1964.** Children's Charter.

441 **122** 15c. blue, green and red 50 25

**123** Mehariste Saddle

**1965.** Saharan Handicrafts.

442 **123** 20c. multicoloured 55 25

**124** Books Aflame

**1965.** Reconstitution of Algiers University Library.

443 **124** 20c.+5c. red, blk & grn 55 40

**125** I.C.Y. Emblem

**1965.** International Co-operation Year.

444 **125** 30c. black, green and red 95 45

445 **125** 60c. black, green and blue 1·40 60

**126** I.T.U. Emblem and Symbols

**1965.** Centenary of I.T.U.

446 **126** 60c. violet, ochre & green 95 50

447 **126** 95c. brown, ochre & lake 1·40 55

**127** Musicians playing Rebbah and Lute

**1965.** Mohamed Racim's Miniatures (1st series). Multicoloured.

448 30c. Type **127** 1·80 65

449 60c. Musicians playing derbouka and tarr 2·75 1·50

450 5d. Algerian princess and sand gazelle 14·50 7·75

See also Nos. 471/3.

**128** Cattle

**1966.** Rock-paintings of Tassili-N-Ajjer (1st series).

451 **128** 1d. brown, ochre & purple 5·25 2·75

452 - 1d. multicoloured 5·25 2·75

453 - 2d. dp brown, buff & brn 11·00 4·75

454 - 3d. multicoloured 12·00 6·25

DESIGNS—VERT: No. 452, Peuhl shepherd; 454, Peuhl girls. HORIZ: No. 453, Ostriches.

See also Nos. 474/7.

**129** Pottery

**1966.** Grand Kahylie Handicrafts.

455 **129** 40c. brown, sepia and blue 55 40

456 - 50c. orange, green & bl 90 40

457 - 70c. black, red and blue 1·40 50

DESIGNS—HORIZ: 50c. Weaving. VERT: 70c. Jewellery.

**130** Meteorological Instruments

**1966.** World Meteorological Day.

458 **130** 1d. purple, green and blue 1·40 50

**131** Open Book, Cogwheel and Ear of Corn

**1966.** Literacy Campaign.

459 **131** 30c. black and ochre 50 25

460 - 60c. red, black and grey 75 40

DESIGN: 60c. Open primer, cogwheel and ear of corn.

**132** W.H.O. Building

**1966.** Inaug of W.H.O. Headquarters, Geneva.

461 **132** 30c. turq, grn & brn 45 40

462 **132** 60c. slate, blue and brown 90 40

**133** Mohammedan Scout Emblem and Banner

**1966.** 30th Anniv of Algerian Mohammedan Scouts, and 7th Arab Scout Jamboree, Jedaid (Tripoli). Multicoloured.

463 30c. Type **133** 70 40

464 1d. Jamboree emblem 1·80 65

**134** Soldiers and Battle Casualty

**1966.** Freedom Fighters' Day.

465 **134** 30c.+10c. mult 95 65

466 **134** 95c.+10c. mult 1·80 1·30

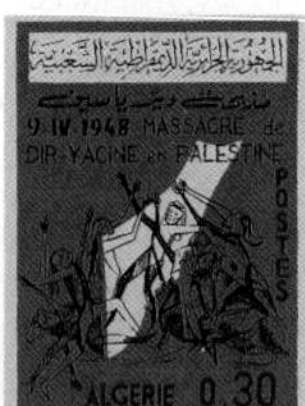

**135** Massacre Victims

**1966.** Deir Yassin Massacre (1948).

467 **135** 30c. black and red 55 25

**136** Emir Abd-el-Kader

**1966.** Return of Emir Abd-el-Kader's Remains.

468 **136** 30c. multicoloured 25 10

469 **136** 95c. multicoloured 1·10 40

See also Nos. 498/502.

**137** UNESCO Emblems

**1966.** 20th Anniv of UNESCO.

470 **137** 1d. multicoloured 1·10 40

**1966.** Mohamed Racim's Miniatures (2nd series). As T **127**. Multicoloured.

471 1d. Horseman 4·50 1·50

472 1d.50 Algerian bride 6·75 2·00

473 2d. Barbarossa 10·00 3·50

**1967.** Rock-paintings of Tassili-N-Ajjer (2nd series). As T **128**.

| | | | |
|---|---|---|---|
| 474 | 1d. violet, buff and purple | 4·50 | 1·90 |
| 475 | 2d. brown, buff and purple | 6·75 | 3·75 |
| 476 | 2d. brown, purple and buff | 7·50 | 4·00 |
| 477 | 3d. brown, buff and black | 10·50 | 5·50 |

DESIGNS: No. 474, Cow; No. 475, Antelope; No. 476, Archers; No. 477, Warrior.

**138** Bardo Museum

**1967.** "Musulman Art". Multicoloured.

| | | | |
|---|---|---|---|
| 478 | 35c. Type **138** | 45 | 25 |
| 479 | 95c. La Kalaa minaret (vert) | 95 | 45 |
| 480 | 1d.30 Sedrata ruins | 1·70 | 65 |

**139** Ghardaia

**1967.** Air.

| | | | | |
|---|---|---|---|---|
| 481 | **139** | 1d. brown, green & purple | 1·40 | 55 |
| 482 | - | 2d. brown, green and blue | 3·25 | 1·40 |
| 483 | - | 5d. brown, green and blue | 8·50 | 2·50 |

DESIGNS: 2d. Sud Aviation SE210 Caravelle over El Oued (Souf); 5d. Tipasa.

**140** View of Moretti

**1967.** International Tourist Year. Multicoloured.

| | | | |
|---|---|---|---|
| 484 | 40c. Type **140** | 70 | 40 |
| 485 | 70c. Tuareg, Tassili (vert) | 1·40 | 55 |

**141** Boy and Girl, and Red Crescent

**1967.** Algerian Red Crescent Organization.

| | | | | |
|---|---|---|---|---|
| 486 | **141** | 30c.+10c. brn, red & grn | 90 | 50 |

**142** Ostrich

**1967.** Saharan Fauna. Multicoloured.

| | | | |
|---|---|---|---|
| 487 | 5c. Shiny-tailed Lizard (horiz) | 50 | 40 |
| 488 | 20c. Type **142** | 90 | 50 |
| 489 | 40c. Sand gazelle | 1·40 | 65 |
| 490 | 70c. Fennec foxes (horiz) | 1·90 | 1·00 |

**143** Dancers with Tambourines

**1967.** National Youth Festival.

| | | | | |
|---|---|---|---|---|
| 491 | **143** | 50c. black, yellow & blue | 95 | 40 |

**144** "Athletics"

**1967.** 5th Mediterranean Games, Tunis.

| | | | | |
|---|---|---|---|---|
| 492 | **144** | 30c. black, blue and red | 70 | 40 |

**145** Skiing

**1967.** Winter Olympic Games, Grenoble (1968).

| | | | | |
|---|---|---|---|---|
| 493 | **145** | 30c. blue, green & ultram | 95 | 40 |
| 494 | - | 95c. green, violet & brown | 1·80 | 85 |

DESIGN—HORIZ (36×26 mm): 95c. Olympic rings and competitors.

**1967**

| | | | | |
|---|---|---|---|---|
| 498 | **136** | 5c. purple | 25 | 10 |
| 499 | **136** | 10c. green | 10 | 10 |
| 500 | **136** | 25c. orange | 35 | 10 |
| 501 | **136** | 30c. black | 45 | 10 |
| 502 | **136** | 30c. violet | 45 | 10 |
| 496 | **136** | 50c. red | 70 | 25 |
| 497 | **136** | 70c. blue | 90 | 25 |

The 10c. value exists in two versions, differing in the figures of value and inscription at bottom right.

**146** Scouts supporting Jamboree Emblem

**1967.** World Scout Jamboree, Idaho.

| | | | | |
|---|---|---|---|---|
| 503 | **146** | 1d. multicoloured | 2·10 | 75 |

**1967.** No. 428 surch.

| | | | | |
|---|---|---|---|---|
| 504 | **116** | 30c. on 25c. red | 70 | 25 |

**148** Kouitra

**1968.** Musical Instruments. Multicoloured.

| | | | |
|---|---|---|---|
| 505 | 30c. Type **148** | 55 | 25 |
| 506 | 40c. Lute | 90 | 40 |
| 507 | 1d.30 Rebbah | 3·00 | 1·10 |

**149** Nememcha Carpet

**1968.** Algerian Carpets. Multicoloured.

| | | | |
|---|---|---|---|
| 509 | 30c. Type **149** | 95 | 55 |
| 510 | 70c. Guergour | 1·80 | 85 |
| 511 | 95c. Djebel-Amour | 3·00 | 1·20 |
| 512 | 1d.30 Kalaa | 3·75 | 1·40 |

**150** Human Rights Emblem and Globe

**1968.** Human Rights Year.

| | | | | |
|---|---|---|---|---|
| 513 | **150** | 40c. red, yellow and blue | 75 | 40 |

**151** W.H.O. Emblem

**1968.** 20th Anniv of W.H.O.

| | | | | |
|---|---|---|---|---|
| 514 | **151** | 70c. yellow, black & blue | 90 | 40 |

**152** Emigrant

**1968.** Emigration of Algerians to Europe.

| | | | | |
|---|---|---|---|---|
| 515 | **152** | 30c. brown, slate & blue | 55 | 25 |

**153** Scouts holding Jamboree Emblem

**1968.** 8th Arab Scouts Jamboree, Algiers.

| | | | | |
|---|---|---|---|---|
| 516 | **153** | 30c. multicoloured | 70 | 25 |

**154** Torch and Athletes

**1968.** Olympic Games, Mexico. Multicoloured.

| | | | |
|---|---|---|---|
| 517 | 30c. Type **154** | 60 | 45 |
| 518 | 50c. Football | 1·10 | 65 |
| 519 | 1d. Allegory of Games (horiz) | 1·80 | 95 |

**155** Barbary Sheep

**1968.** Protected Animals. Multicoloured.

| | | | |
|---|---|---|---|
| 520 | 40c. Type **155** | 90 | 40 |
| 521 | 1d. Red deer | 2·10 | 65 |

**156** "Neptune's Chariot", Timgad

**1968.** Roman Mosaics. Multicoloured.

| | | | |
|---|---|---|---|
| 522 | 40c. "Hunting Scene" (Djemila) (vert) | 70 | 25 |
| 523 | 95c. Type **156** | 1·50 | 55 |

**157** Miner

**1968.** "Industry, Energy and Mines".

| | | | | |
|---|---|---|---|---|
| 524 | **157** | 30c. multicoloured | 50 | 25 |
| 525 | - | 30c. silver and red | 50 | 25 |
| 526 | - | 95c. red, black and silver | 1·40 | 40 |

DESIGNS: No. 525, Coiled spring ("Industry"); No. 526, Symbol of radiation ("Energy").

**158** Opuntia

**1969.** Algerian Flowers. Multicoloured.

| | | | |
|---|---|---|---|
| 527 | 25c. Type **158** | 70 | 50 |
| 528 | 40c. Dianthus | 1·10 | 65 |
| 529 | 70c. Rose | 1·80 | 75 |
| 530 | 95c. Strelitzia | 3·25 | 1·30 |

See also Nos. 621/4.

**159** Djorf Torba Dam, Oued Guir

**1969.** Saharan Public Works. Multicoloured.

| | | | |
|---|---|---|---|
| 531 | 30c. Type **159** | 70 | 25 |
| 532 | 1d.50 Route Nationale No. 51 | 2·10 | 80 |

**160** Desert Mail-coach of 1870

**1969.** Stamp Day.

| | | | | |
|---|---|---|---|---|
| 533 | **160** | 1d. sepia, brown and blue | 2·75 | 85 |

**161** The Capitol, Timgad

**1969.** Roman Ruins in Algeria. Multicoloured.

| | | | |
|---|---|---|---|
| 534 | 30c. Type **161** | 55 | 25 |
| 535 | 1d. Septimius Temple, Djemila (horiz) | 1·50 | 60 |

**162** I.L.O. Emblem

**1969.** 50th Anniv of I.L.O.

| | | | | |
|---|---|---|---|---|
| 536 | **162** | 95c. red, yellow and black | 1·30 | 45 |

**1969.** No. 425 surch.

| | | | |
|---|---|---|---|
| 537 | 20c. on 12c. green | 45 | 10 |

**164** Carved Bookcase

**1969.** Handicrafts. Multicoloured.

| | | | |
|---|---|---|---|
| 538 | 30c. Type **164** | 50 | 25 |
| 539 | 60c. Copper tray | 90 | 40 |
| 540 | 1d. Arab saddle | 1·60 | 60 |

**165** "Africa" Head

**1969.** 1st Pan-African Cultural Festival, Algiers.

| | | | | |
|---|---|---|---|---|
| 541 | **165** | 30c. multicoloured | 55 | 25 |

**166** Astronauts on Moon

**1969.** 1st Man on the Moon.

| | | | | |
|---|---|---|---|---|
| 542 | **166** | 50c. multicoloured | 1·10 | 45 |

**167** Bank Emblem

**1969.** 5th Anniv of African Development Bank.

| | | | | |
|---|---|---|---|---|
| 543 | **167** | 30c. black, yellow blue | 55 | 25 |

**168** Flood Victims

**1969.** Aid for 1969 Flood Victims.

| | | | | |
|---|---|---|---|---|
| 544 | **168** | 30c.+10c. black, flesh and blue | 75 | 45 |
| 545 | - | 95c.+25c. brown, blue and purple | 1·60 | 95 |

DESIGN: 95c. Helping hand for flood victims.

**169** "Algerian Women" (Dinet)

**1969.** Dinet's Paintings. Multicoloured.

| | | | |
|---|---|---|---|
| 546 | 1d. Type **169** | 2·10 | 85 |
| 547 | 1d.50 "The Look-outs" (Dinet) | 2·75 | 1·20 |

**170** "Mother and Child"

**1969.** "Protection of Mother and Child".

| | | | | |
|---|---|---|---|---|
| 548 | **170** | 30c. multicoloured | 70 | 40 |

**171** "Agriculture"

**1970.** Four Year Plan.

| | | | | |
|---|---|---|---|---|
| 549 | **171** | 25c. multicoloured | 30 | 25 |
| 550 | - | 30c. multicoloured | 55 | 25 |
| 551 | - | 50c. black and purple | 55 | 25 |

DESIGNS: (LARGER, 49×23 mm): 30c. "Industry and Transport"; 50c. "Industry" (abstract).

**172** Postal Deliveries by Donkey and Renault R4 Mail Van

**1970.** Stamp Day.

| | | | | |
|---|---|---|---|---|
| 552 | **172** | 30c. multicoloured | 70 | 25 |

**173** Royal Prawn

**1970.** Marine Life. Multicoloured.

| | | | |
|---|---|---|---|
| 553 | 30c. Type **173** | 70 | 25 |
| 554 | 40c. Noble pen (mollusc) | 90 | 40 |
| 555 | 75c. Neptune's basket | 1·40 | 50 |
| 556 | 1d. Red coral | 2·10 | 75 |

**174** Oranges

**1970.** "Expo 70" World Fair, Osaka, Japan. Multicoloured.

| | | | |
|---|---|---|---|
| 557 | 30c. Type **174** | 70 | 25 |
| 558 | 60c. Algerian Pavilion | 70 | 40 |
| 559 | 70c. Bunches of grapes | 1·40 | 60 |

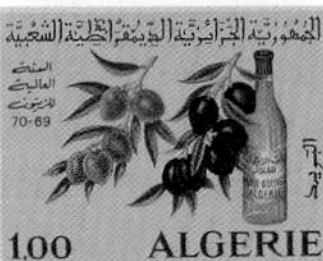


**175** Olives and Bottle of Olive-oil

**1970.** World Olive-oil Year.

| | | | | |
|---|---|---|---|---|
| 560 | **175** | 1d. multicoloured | 1·90 | 80 |

**176** New U.P.U. H.Q. Building

**1970.** Inaug of New U.P.U. Headquarters Building.

| | | | | |
|---|---|---|---|---|
| 561 | **176** | 75c. multicoloured | 1·10 | 40 |

**177** Crossed Muskets

**1970.** Algerian 18th-century Weapons. Mult.

| | | | |
|---|---|---|---|
| 562 | 40c. Type **177** | 90 | 65 |
| 563 | 75c. Sabre (vert) | 1·60 | 85 |
| 564 | 1d. Pistol | 2·30 | 1·10 |

**178** Arab League Flag, Arms and Map

**1970.** 25th Anniv of Arab League.

| | | | | |
|---|---|---|---|---|
| 565 | **178** | 30c. multicoloured | 55 | 25 |

**179** Lenin

**1970.** Birth Centenary of Lenin.

| | | | | |
|---|---|---|---|---|
| 566 | **179** | 30c. bistre and ochre | 2·75 | 40 |

**180** Exhibition Palace

**1970.** 7th International Algiers Fair.

| | | | | |
|---|---|---|---|---|
| 567 | **180** | 60c. green | 70 | 40 |

**181** I.E.Y. and Education Emblems

**1970.** International Education Year. Mult.

| | | | |
|---|---|---|---|
| 568 | 30c. Type **181** | 55 | 25 |
| 569 | 3d. Illuminated Koran (30×41 mm) | 3·50 | 1·80 |

**182** Great Mosque, Tlemcen

**1970.** Mosques.

| | | | | |
|---|---|---|---|---|
| 570 | **182** | 30c. multicoloured | 45 | 25 |
| 571 | - | 40c. brown and bistre | 55 | 25 |
| 572 | - | 1d. multicoloured | 1·00 | 40 |

DESIGNS—VERT: 40c. Ketchaoua Mosque, Algiers; 1d. Sidi-Okba Mosque.

**183** "Fine Arts"

**1970.** Algerian Fine Arts.

| | | | | |
|---|---|---|---|---|
| 573 | **183** | 1d. orange, grn & lt grn | 1·10 | 45 |

**184** G.P.O., Algiers

**1971.** Stamp Day.

| | | | | |
|---|---|---|---|---|
| 574 | **184** | 30c. multicoloured | 1·10 | 40 |

**185** Hurdling

**1971.** 6th Mediterranean Games, Izmir (Turkey).

| | | | | |
|---|---|---|---|---|
| 575 | **185** | 20c. grey and blue | 50 | 25 |
| 576 | - | 40c. grey and green | 55 | 40 |
| 577 | - | 75c. grey and brown | 1·10 | 65 |

DESIGNS—VERT: 40c. Gymnastics; 75c. Basket-ball.

**186** "Racial Equality"

**1971.** Racial Equality Year.

| | | | | |
|---|---|---|---|---|
| 578 | **186** | 60c. multicoloured | 70 | 40 |

**187** Symbols of Learning, and Students

**1971.** Inaug of Technological Institutes.

| | | | | |
|---|---|---|---|---|
| 579 | **187** | 70c. multicoloured | 90 | 30 |

**188** Red Crescent Banner

**1971.** Red Crescent Day.

| | | | | |
|---|---|---|---|---|
| 580 | **188** | 30c.+10c. red and green | 70 | 40 |

**189** Casbah, Algiers

**1971.** Air.

| | | | | |
|---|---|---|---|---|
| 581 | **189** | 2d. multicoloured | 2·50 | 1·10 |
| 582 | - | 3d. violet and black | 3·75 | 1·60 |
| 583 | - | 4d. multicoloured | 4·25 | 2·00 |

DESIGNS: 3d. Port of Oran; 4d. Rhumel Gorges.

**190** Aures Costume

**1971.** Regional Costumes (1st series). Multicoloured.

| | | | |
|---|---|---|---|
| 584 | 50c. Type **190** | 1·30 | 60 |
| 585 | 70c. Oran | 1·60 | 75 |
| 586 | 80c. Algiers | 1·90 | 95 |
| 587 | 90c. Djebel-Amour | 2·30 | 1·10 |

See also Nos. 610/13 and 659/62.

**191** UNICEF Emblem, Tree and Animals

**1971.** 25th Anniv of UNICEF.

588 **191** 60c. multicoloured 90 45

**192** Lion of St. Mark's

**1971.** UNESCO "Save Venice" Campaign. Mult.

589 80c. Type **192** 1·40 55
590 1d.15 Bridge of Sighs 2·30 95

**193** Cycling

**1972.** Olympic Games, Munich. Multicoloured.

591 25c. Type **193** 45 25
592 40c. Throwing the javelin (vert) 60 25
593 60c. Wrestling (vert) 1·10 50
594 1d. Gymnastics (vert) 1·60 55

**194** Book and Bookmark

**1972.** International Book Year.

595 **194** 1d.15 red, black and brown 90 45

**195** Algerian Postmen

**1972.** Stamp Day.

596 **195** 40c. multicoloured 70 25

**196** Jasmine

**1972.** Flowers. Multicoloured.

597 50c. Type **196** 70 40
598 60c. Violets 70 40
599 1d.15 Tuberose 2·10 65

**197** Olympic Stadium

**1972.** Inaug of Cheraga Olympic Stadium.

600 **197** 50c. green, brown & violet 70 40

**198** Festival Emblem

**1972.** 1st Festival of Arab Youth.

601 **198** 40c. brown, yellow & grn 55 25

**199** Rejoicing Algerians

**1972.** 10th Anniv of Independence.

602 **199** 1d. multicoloured 1·30 60

**1972.** Regional Costumes (2nd series). As T 190. Multicoloured.

610 50c. Hoggar 1·40 65
611 60c. Kabylie 1·80 65
612 70c. Mzab 1·90 85
613 90c. Tlemcen 2·40 1·10

**201** Child posting Letter

**1973.** Stamp Day.

614 **201** 40c. multicoloured 55 25

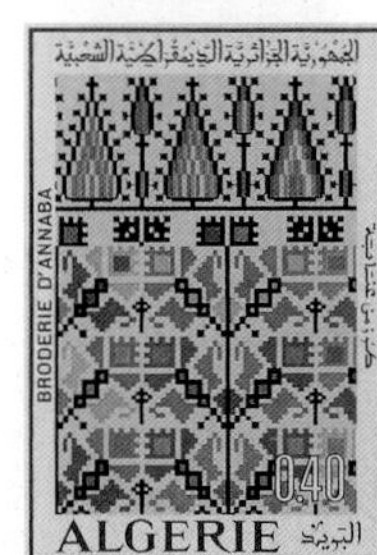

**202** Ho-Chi-Minh and Map

**1973.** "Homage to the Vietnamese People".

615 **202** 40c. multicoloured 90 40

**203** Annaba Embroidery

**1973.** Algerian Embroidery. Multicoloured.

616 40c. Type **203** 55 25
617 60c. Algiers embroidery 90 50
618 80c. Constantine embroidery 1·30 70

**204** "Food Cultivation"

**1973.** 10th Anniv of World Food Programme.

619 **204** 1d.15 multicoloured 90 40

**205** Serviceman and Flag

**1973.** National Service.

620 **205** 40c. multicoloured 55 25

**1973.** Algerian Flowers. As T 158. Multicoloured.

621 30c. Type **158** 70 25
622 40c. As No. 529 90 40
623 1d. As No. 528 1·80 65
624 1d.15 As No. 530 2·75 1·10

**206** O.A.U. Emblem

**1973.** 10th Anniv of Organization of African Unity.

625 **206** 40c. multicoloured 55 25

**207** Peasant Family

**1973.** Agrarian Revolution.

626 **207** 40c. multicoloured 70 25

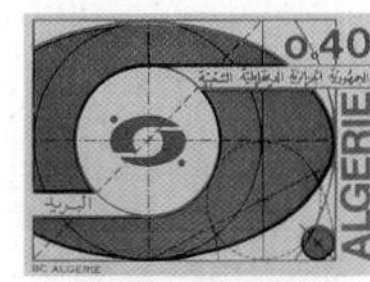

**208** Scout Badge on Map

**1973.** 24th World Scouting Congress, Nairobi, Kenya.

627 **208** 80c. mauve 75 40

**209** P.T.T. Symbol

**1973.** Inauguration of New P.T.T. Symbol.

628 **209** 40c. orange and blue 55 25

**210** Conference Emblem

**1973.** 4th Summit Conference of Non-Aligned Countries, Algiers.

629 **210** 40c. multicoloured 45 25
630 **210** 80c. multicoloured 90 40

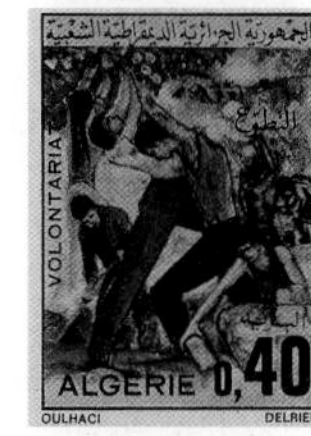

**211** "Skikda Harbour"

**1973.** Opening of Skikda Port.

631 **211** 80c. multicoloured 70 25

**212** Young Workers

**1973.** Volontariat Students' Volunteer Service.

632 **212** 40c. multicoloured 55 25

**213** Arms of Algiers

**1973.** Millenary of Algiers.

633 **213** 2d. multicoloured 3·00 1·40

**214** "Protected Infant"

**1974.** Anti-TB Campaign.

634 **214** 80c. multicoloured 90 45

**215** Industrial Scene

**1974.** Four Year Plan.

635 **215** 80c. multicoloured 90 40

**216** Arabesque Motif

**1974.** Birth Millenary of Abu-al Rayhan al-Biruni (mathematician and philosopher).

636 **216** 1d.50 multicoloured 2·50 1·40

217 Map and Arrows

**1974.** Meeting of Maghreb Committee for Co-ordination of Posts and Telecommunications, Tunis.

| | | | | |
|---|---|---|---|---|
| 637 | **217** | 40c. multicoloured | 55 | 25 |

218 Upraised Weapon and Fist

**1974.** Solidarity with South African People's Campaign.

| | | | | |
|---|---|---|---|---|
| 638 | **218** | 80c. black and red | 70 | 25 |

219 Algerian Family

**1974.** Homage to Algerian Mothers.

| | | | | |
|---|---|---|---|---|
| 639 | **219** | 85c. multicoloured | 70 | 25 |

220 Urban Scene

**1974.** Children's Drawings. Multicoloured.

| | | | |
|---|---|---|---|
| 640 | 70c. Type **220** | 75 | 35 |
| 641 | 80c. Agricultural scene | 90 | 40 |
| 642 | 90c. Tractor and sunrise | 1·10 | 65 |

Nos. 641/2 are size 49×33 mm.

**1974.** "Floralies 1974" Flower Show, Algiers. Nos. 623/4 optd FLORALIES 1974.

| | | | |
|---|---|---|---|
| 643 | 1d. multicoloured | 1·80 | 85 |
| 644 | 1d.15 multicoloured | 2·30 | 1·30 |

222 Automatic Stamp-vending Machine

**1974.** Stamp Day.

| | | | | |
|---|---|---|---|---|
| 645 | **222** | 80c. multicoloured | 80 | 35 |

223 U.P.U. Emblem on Globe

**1974.** Centenary of U.P.U.

| | | | | |
|---|---|---|---|---|
| 646 | **223** | 80c. multicoloured | 80 | 35 |

224 Revolutionaries

**1974.** 20th Anniv of Revolution. Multicoloured.

| | | | |
|---|---|---|---|
| 647 | 40c. Type **224** | 55 | 25 |
| 648 | 70c. Armed soldiers (vert) | 75 | 25 |
| 649 | 95c. Raising the flag (vert) | 90 | 40 |
| 650 | 1d. Algerians looking to Independence | 1·20 | 40 |

225 "Towards the Horizon"

**1974.** "Horizon 1980".

| | | | | |
|---|---|---|---|---|
| 651 | **225** | 95c. red, brown & black | 75 | 40 |

226 Ewer

**1974.** Algerian 17th-century Brassware. Mult.

| | | | |
|---|---|---|---|
| 652 | 50c. Type **226** | 60 | 30 |
| 653 | 60c. Coffee pot | 75 | 40 |
| 654 | 95c. Sugar basin | 1·00 | 55 |
| 655 | 1d. Bath vessel | 1·40 | 75 |

**1975.** No. 622 surch.

| | | | |
|---|---|---|---|
| 656 | 50c. on 40c. multicoloured | 2·75 | 55 |

228 Games Emblem

**1975.** 7th Mediterranean Games (1st issue).

| | | | | |
|---|---|---|---|---|
| 657 | **228** | 50c. violet, green & yellow | 50 | 25 |
| 658 | **228** | 1d. orange, violet & blue | 90 | 40 |

See also Nos. 671/5.

**1975.** Regional Costumes (3rd series). As T 190. Multicoloured.

| | | | |
|---|---|---|---|
| 659 | 1d. Algiers | 1·60 | 85 |
| 660 | 1d. The Hogger | 1·60 | 85 |
| 661 | 1d. Oran | 1·60 | 85 |
| 662 | 1d. Tlemcen | 1·60 | 85 |

229 Labour Emblems

**1975.** 10th Anniv of Arab Labour Organization.

| | | | | |
|---|---|---|---|---|
| 663 | **229** | 50c. brown | 55 | 10 |

230 Transfusion

**1975.** Blood Collection and Transfusion Service.

| | | | | |
|---|---|---|---|---|
| 664 | **230** | 50c. multicoloured | 90 | 40 |

231 El Kantara Post Office

**1975.** Stamp Day.

| | | | | |
|---|---|---|---|---|
| 665 | **231** | 50c. multicoloured | 70 | 25 |

232 Policeman and Oil Rig on Map of Algeria

**1975.** Police Day.

| | | | | |
|---|---|---|---|---|
| 666 | **232** | 50c. multicoloured | 1·10 | 40 |

233 Ground Receiving Aerial

**1975.** Satellite Telecommunications. Mult.

| | | | |
|---|---|---|---|
| 667 | 50c. Type **233** | 55 | 15 |
| 668 | 1d. Map of receiving sites | 90 | 25 |
| 669 | 1d.20 Main and subsidiary ground stations | 1·20 | 50 |

234 Revolutionary with Flag

**1975.** 20th Anniv of "Skikda" Revolution.

| | | | | |
|---|---|---|---|---|
| 670 | **234** | 1d. multicoloured | 75 | 40 |

235 Swimming

**1975.** 7th Mediterranean Games, Algiers (2nd issue). Multicoloured.

| | | | |
|---|---|---|---|
| 671 | 25c. Type **235** | 20 | 10 |
| 672 | 50c. Wrestling | 45 | 25 |
| 673 | 70c. Football (vert) | 70 | 30 |
| 674 | 1d. Athletics (vert) | 90 | 40 |
| 675 | 1d.20 Handball (vert) | 1·20 | 65 |
| **MS**676 | 136×136 mm. Nos. 671/5 | 7·75 | 6·75 |

236 "Setif-Guelma-Kherrata"

**1975.** 30th Anniv of Setif, Guelma and Kherrata Massacres (1st issue).

| | | | | |
|---|---|---|---|---|
| 677 | **236** | 5c. black and orange | 10 | 10 |
| 678 | **236** | 10c. black and green | 10 | 10 |
| 679 | **236** | 25c. black and blue | 25 | 10 |
| 680 | **236** | 30c. black and brown | 45 | 10 |
| 681 | **236** | 50c. black and green | 45 | 10 |
| 682 | **236** | 70c. black and red | 55 | 25 |
| 683 | **236** | 1d. black and red | 90 | 40 |

See also No. 698.

237 Map of the Maghreb and A.P.U. Emblem

**1975.** 10th Arab Postal Union Congress, Algiers.

| | | | | |
|---|---|---|---|---|
| 684 | **237** | 1d. multicoloured | 75 | 40 |

238 Mosaic, Palace of the Bey, Constantine

**1975.** Historic Buildings.

| | | | | |
|---|---|---|---|---|
| 685 | **238** | 1d. multicoloured | 1·10 | 40 |
| 686 | - | 2d. multicoloured | 2·20 | 95 |
| 687 | - | 2d.50 black and brown | 3·00 | 1·40 |

DESIGNS—VERT: 2d. Medersa Sidi-Boumedienne Oratory, Tlemcen. HORIZ: 2d.50, Palace of the Dey, Algiers.

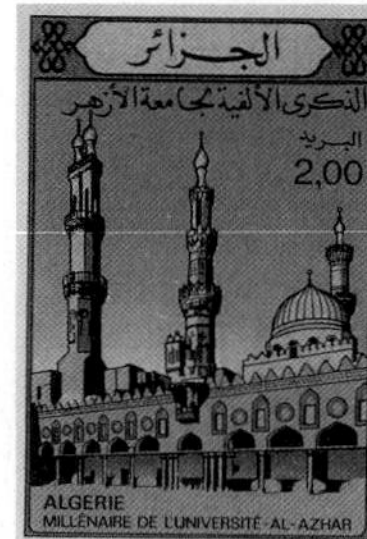


239 University Building

**1975.** Millenary of Al-Azhar University, Cairo.

| | | | | |
|---|---|---|---|---|
| 688 | **239** | 2d. multicoloured | 2·10 | 80 |

240 Red-billed Fire Finch

**1976.** Algerian Birds (1st series). Multicoloured.

| | | | |
|---|---|---|---|
| 689 | 50c. Type **240** | 1·30 | 65 |
| 690 | 1d.40 Black-headed bush shrike (horiz) | 2·50 | 1·30 |
| 691 | 2d. Blue-tit | 3·25 | 1·40 |
| 692 | 2d.50 Black-bellied sand-grouse (horiz) | 3·75 | 2·00 |

See also Nos. 722/5.

241 Early and Modern Telephones

**1976.** Telephone Centenary.

| | | | | |
|---|---|---|---|---|
| 693 | **241** | 1d.40 multicoloured | 1·10 | 55 |

**242** Map and Angolan Flag

**1976.** "Solidarity with Republic of Angola".

| 694 | **242** | 50c. multicoloured | 65 | 25 |
|---|---|---|---|---|

**243** Child on Map

**1976.** Solidarity with People of Western Sahara.

| 695 | **243** | 50c. multicoloured | 55 | 25 |
|---|---|---|---|---|

**244** Postman

**1976.** Stamp Day.

| 696 | **244** | 1d.40 multicoloured | 1·10 | 40 |
|---|---|---|---|---|

**245** People, Microscope and Slide

**1976.** Campaign Against Tuberculosis.

| 697 | **245** | 50c. multicoloured | 1·10 | 35 |
|---|---|---|---|---|

**246** "Setif-Guelma-Kherrata"

**1976.** 30th Anniv of Setif, Guelma and Kherrata Massacres (2nd issue).

| 698 | **246** | 50c. yellow and blue | 55 | 10 |
|---|---|---|---|---|

**247** Ram's Head and Landscape

**1976.** Sheep Raising.

| 699 | **247** | 50c. multicoloured | 65 | 25 |
|---|---|---|---|---|

**248** Algerians holding Torch

**1976.** National Charter.

| 700 | **248** | 50c. multicoloured | 55 | 25 |
|---|---|---|---|---|

**249** Flag and Map

**1976.** Solidarity with the Palestinian People.

| 701 | **249** | 50c. multicoloured | 70 | 25 |
|---|---|---|---|---|

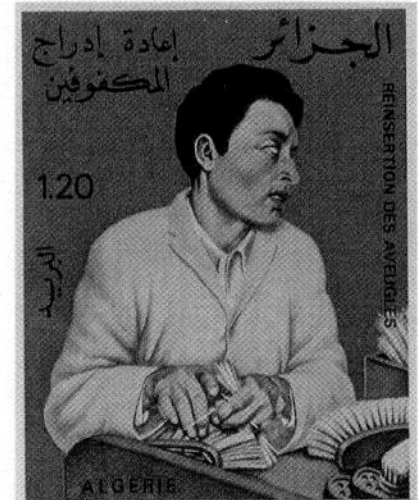

**250** Map of Africa

**1976.** 2nd Pan-African Commercial Fair, Algiers.

| 702 | **250** | 2d. multicoloured | 1·70 | 65 |
|---|---|---|---|---|

**251** Blind Man making Brushes

**1976.** Rehabilitation of the Blind. Multicoloured.

| 703 | | 1d.20 Type **251** | 1·40 | 45 |
|---|---|---|---|---|
| 704 | | 1d.40 "The Blind Man" (E. Dinet) (horiz) | 2·10 | 65 |

**252** Open Book

**1976.** The Constitution.

| 705 | **252** | 2d. multicoloured | 1·70 | 65 |
|---|---|---|---|---|

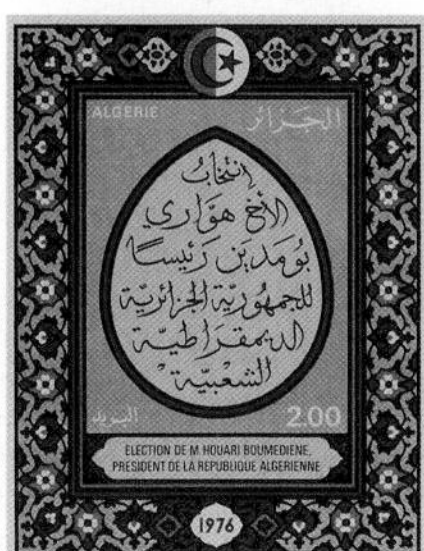

**253** Soldiers planting Seedlings

**1976.** Protection against Saharan Encroachment.

| 706 | **253** | 1d.40 multicoloured | 1·40 | 55 |
|---|---|---|---|---|

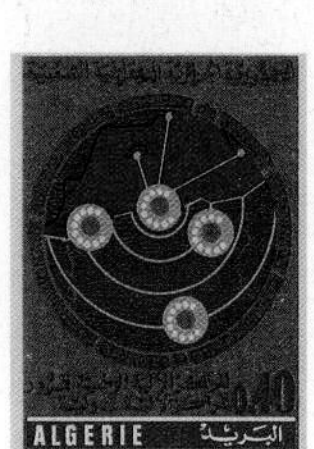

**254** Arabic Inscription

**1976.** Election of President Boumedienne.

| 707 | **254** | 2d. multicoloured | 1·70 | 65 |
|---|---|---|---|---|

**255** Map of Telephone Centres

**1977.** Inauguration of Automatic Telephone Dialling System.

| 708 | **255** | 40c. multicoloured | 50 | 25 |
|---|---|---|---|---|

**256** "Pyramid" of Heads

**1977.** 2nd General Population and Housing Census.

| 709 | **256** | 60c. on 50c. mult | 60 | 25 |
|---|---|---|---|---|

**257** Museum Building

**1977.** Sahara Museum, Ouargla.

| 710 | **257** | 60c. multicoloured | 75 | 40 |
|---|---|---|---|---|

**258** El Kantara Gorges

**1977**

| 711 | **258** | 20c. green and cream | 10 | 10 |
|---|---|---|---|---|
| 712 | **258** | 60c. mauve and cream | 25 | 10 |
| 713 | **258** | 1d. brown and cream | 60 | 25 |

**259** Assembly in Session

**1977.** National Assembly.

| 714 | **259** | 2d. multicoloured | 1·40 | 55 |
|---|---|---|---|---|

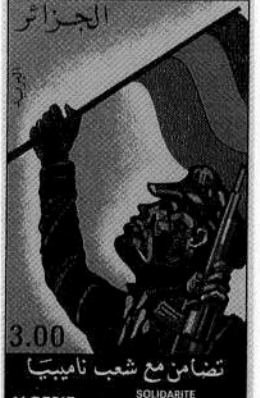

**260** Soldiers with Flag

**1977.** Solidarity with People of Zimbabwe.

| 715 | **260** | 2d. multicoloured | 1·40 | 50 |
|---|---|---|---|---|

**261** Soldier with Flag

**1977.** Solidarity with People of Namibia.

| 716 | **261** | 3d. multicoloured | 2·30 | 75 |
|---|---|---|---|---|

**262** "Winter"

**1977.** Roman Mosaics. "The Seasons". Mult.

| 717 | 1d.20 Type **262** | 1·60 | 85 |
|---|---|---|---|
| 718 | 1d.40 "Autumn" | 1·60 | 85 |
| 719 | 2d. "Summer" | 2·50 | 1·30 |
| 720 | 3d. "Spring" | 3·50 | 1·70 |
| **MS**721 | 101×145 mm. Nos. 717/20 | 13·50 | 12·00 |

**1977.** Algerian Birds (2nd series). As T 240. Multicoloured.

| 722 | 60c. Tristram's warbler | 1·20 | 70 |
|---|---|---|---|
| 723 | 1d.40 Moussier's redstart (horiz) | 2·10 | 1·10 |
| 724 | 2d. Temminck's horned lark (horiz) | 3·25 | 1·50 |
| 725 | 3d. Hoopoe | 4·00 | 2·00 |

**263** Horseman

**1977.** "The Cavaliers" (performing horsemen). Multicoloured.

| 726 | 2d. Type **263** | 2·10 | 85 |
|---|---|---|---|
| 727 | 5d. Three horsemen (horiz) | 4·75 | 1·90 |

**264** Ribbon and Games Emblem

**1977.** 3rd African Games, Algiers (1978) (1st issue). Multicoloured.

| 728 | 60c. Type **264** | 55 | 25 |
|---|---|---|---|
| 729 | 1d.40 Symbolic design and emblem | 1·50 | 50 |

See also Nos. 740/4.

**265** Tessala el Merdja

**1977.** Socialist Agricultural Villages.

| 730 | **265** | 1d.40 multicoloured | 1·00 | 40 |
|---|---|---|---|---|


**266** 12th-century Almohad Dirham

**1977.** Ancient Coins. Multicoloured.

| | | | |
|---|---|---|---|
| 731 | 60c. Type **266** | 70 | 40 |
| 732 | 1d.40 12th-century Alomhad dinar | 1·30 | 65 |
| 733 | 2d. 11th-century Almorarid dinar | 1·90 | 95 |

**267** Cherry ("Cerasus avium")

**1978.** Fruit Tree Blossom. Multicoloured.

| | | | |
|---|---|---|---|
| 734 | 60c. Type **267** | 70 | 25 |
| 735 | 1d.20 "Persica vulgaris" (peach) | 1·10 | 75 |
| 736 | 1d.30 "Amygdalus communis" (almond) | 1·10 | 75 |
| 737 | 1d.40 "Malus communis" (crab apple) | 1·60 | 80 |

**1978.** Surch.

| | | | |
|---|---|---|---|
| 738 | **236** 60c. on 50c. black & grn | 70 | 25 |

**269** Children with Traffic Signs opposing Car

**1978.** Road Safety for Children.

| | | | |
|---|---|---|---|
| 739 | **269** 60c. multicoloured | 60 | 25 |

**270** Boxing and Map of Africa

**1978.** 3rd African Games, Algiers (2nd issue). Multicoloured.

| | | | |
|---|---|---|---|
| 740 | 40c. Sports emblems and volleyball (horiz) | 25 | 10 |
| 741 | 60c. Olympic rings and table tennis symbol | 40 | 25 |
| 742 | 1d.20 Basketball symbol (horiz) | 1·00 | 40 |
| 743 | 1d.30 Hammerthrowing symbol | 1·00 | 5·00 |
| 744 | 1d.40 Type **270** | 1·30 | 60 |

**271** Patient returning to Family

**1978.** Anti-tuberculosis Campaign.

| | | | |
|---|---|---|---|
| 745 | **271** 60c. multicoloured | 60 | 25 |

**272** Ka'aba, Mecca

**1978.** Pilgrimage to Mecca.

| | | | |
|---|---|---|---|
| 746 | **272** 60c. multicoloured | 70 | 25 |

**273** Road-building

**1978.** African Unity Road.

| | | | |
|---|---|---|---|
| 747 | **273** 60c. multicoloured | 70 | 25 |

**274** Triangular Brooch

**1978.** Jewellery (1st series). Multicoloured.

| | | | |
|---|---|---|---|
| 748 | 1d.20 Type **274** | 1·20 | 55 |
| 749 | 1d.35 Circular brooch | 1·50 | 70 |
| 750 | 1d.40 Anklet | 1·80 | 80 |

See also Nos. 780/2 and 833/5.

**275** President Houari Boumedienne

**1979.** President Boumedienne Commem (1st issue).

| | | | |
|---|---|---|---|
| 751 | **275** 60c. brown, red & turq | 55 | 25 |

See also No. 753.

**276** Books and Hands holding Torch

**1979.** National Liberation Front Party Congress.

| | | | |
|---|---|---|---|
| 752 | **276** 60c. multicoloured | 55 | 25 |

**277** President Houari Boumedienne

**1979.** President Boumedienne Commem (2nd issue).

| | | | |
|---|---|---|---|
| 753 | **277** 1d.40 multicoloured | 1·40 | 50 |

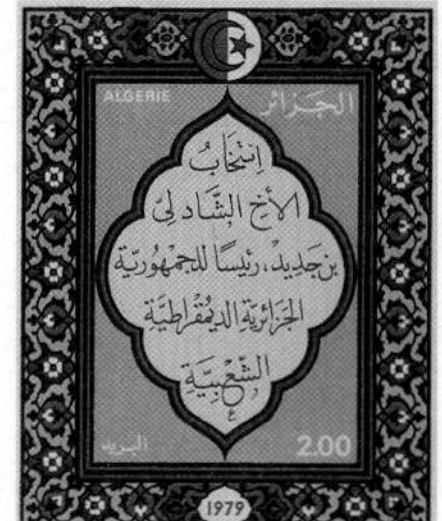

**278** Arabic Inscription

**1979.** Election of President Chadli Bendjedid.

| | | | |
|---|---|---|---|
| 754 | **278** 2d. multicoloured | 1·60 | 40 |

**279** White Storks

**1979.** Air.

| | | | |
|---|---|---|---|
| 755 | **279** 10d. blue, black and red | 6·75 | 2·50 |

**280** Ben Badis

**1979.** 90th Birth Anniv of Sheikh Abdelhamid Ben Badis (journalist and education pioneer).

| | | | |
|---|---|---|---|
| 756 | **280** 60c. multicoloured | 55 | 25 |

**281** Globe within Telephone Dial

**1979.** "Telecom 79" Exhibition. Multicoloured.

| | | | |
|---|---|---|---|
| 757 | 1d.20 Type **281** | 90 | 35 |
| 758 | 1d.40 Sound waves | 1·20 | 45 |

**282** Children dancing on Globe

**1979.** International Year of the Child. Mult.

| | | | |
|---|---|---|---|
| 759 | 60c. Picking Dates | 55 | 10 |
| 760 | 1d.40 Type **282** (vert) | 1·10 | 45 |

**283** Kabylie Nuthatch

**1979**

| | | | |
|---|---|---|---|
| 761 | **283** 1d.40 multicoloured | 2·00 | 95 |

**284** Fighting for the Revolution and Construction work

**1979.** 25th Anniv of Revolution. Multicoloured.

| | | | |
|---|---|---|---|
| 762 | 1d.40 Type **284** | 1·00 | 30 |
| 763 | 3d. Algerians with flag | 1·70 | 85 |

**285** Arabic Inscription

**1979.** 1400th Anniv of Hegira.

| | | | |
|---|---|---|---|
| 764 | **285** 3d. gold, turquoise & blue | 2·10 | 80 |

**286** Return of Dionysus (right detail)

**1980.** Dionysus Mosaic, Setif. Multicoloured.

| | | | |
|---|---|---|---|
| 765 | 1d.20 Type **286** | 1·30 | 40 |
| 766 | 1d.35 Centre detail | 1·30 | 55 |
| 767 | 1d.40 Left detail | 1·60 | 80 |

Nos. 765/7 were issued together, se-tenant, forming a composite design.

**287** Books

**1980.** Day of Knowledge.

| | | | |
|---|---|---|---|
| 768 | **287** 60c. brown, yellow & grn | 55 | 10 |

**288** Five Year Plan

**1980.** Extraordinary Congress of National Liberation Front Party.

| | | | |
|---|---|---|---|
| 769 | **288** 60c. multicoloured | 55 | 25 |

**289** Olympic Flame

**1980.** Olympic Games, Moscow. Multicoloured.

| | | | |
|---|---|---|---|
| 770 | 50c. Type **289** | 50 | 10 |
| 771 | 1d.40 Olympic sports (horiz) | 95 | 45 |

**290** Figures supporting O.P.E.C. Emblem

**1980.** 20th Anniv of Organization of Petroleum Exporting Countries.

| | | | | |
|---|---|---|---|---|
| 772 | **290** | 60c. green, blue and red | 65 | 10 |
| 773 | - | 1d.40 green and blue | 1·20 | 45 |

DESIGN: 1d.40, O.P.E.C. emblem on world map.

**291** Aures

**1980.** World Tourism Conference, Manila. Mult.

| | | | |
|---|---|---|---|
| 774 | 50c. Type **291** | 50 | 25 |
| 775 | 1d. El Oued | 90 | 25 |
| 776 | 1d.40 Tassili | 1·10 | 40 |
| 777 | 2d. Algiers | 1·90 | 65 |

**292** Ibn Sina

**1980.** Birth Millenary of Ibn Sina (Avicenna) (philosopher).

| | | | | |
|---|---|---|---|---|
| 778 | **292** | 3d. multicoloured | 2·10 | 80 |

**293** Earthquake Devastation

**1980.** El Asnam Earthquake Relief.

| | | | | |
|---|---|---|---|---|
| 779 | **293** | 3d. multicoloured | 2·10 | 55 |

**1980.** Jewellery (2nd series). As T 274. Mult.

| | | | |
|---|---|---|---|
| 780 | 60c. Necklace | 60 | 25 |
| 781 | 1d.40 Earrings and bracelet | 1·10 | 55 |
| 782 | 2d. Diadem (horiz) | 1·60 | 70 |

**294** Emblem

**1981.** Five Year Plan.

| | | | | |
|---|---|---|---|---|
| 783 | **294** | 60c. multicoloured | 40 | 10 |

**295** Basket-worker

**1981.** Traditional Arts. Multicoloured.

| | | | |
|---|---|---|---|
| 784 | 40c. Type **295** | 35 | 10 |
| 785 | 60c. Spinning | 45 | 20 |
| 786 | 1d. Copper-smith | 75 | 25 |
| 787 | 1d.40 Jeweller | 1·20 | 40 |

**296** Cedar "Cedrus atlantica"

**1981.** World Tree Day. Multicoloured.

| | | | |
|---|---|---|---|
| 788 | 60c. Type **296** | 45 | 10 |
| 789 | 1d.40 Cypress "Cupressus dupreziana" | 1·10 | 40 |

**297** Mohamed Bachir el Ibrahimi

**298** Children and Blackboard (Basic Schooling)

**1981.** Day of Knowledge.

| | | | | |
|---|---|---|---|---|
| 790 | **297** | 60c. multicoloured | 45 | 10 |
| 791 | **298** | 60c. multicoloured | 45 | 10 |

**299** Archer, Dog and Internal Organs

**1981.** 12th Int Hydatidological Congress, Algiers.

| | | | | |
|---|---|---|---|---|
| 792 | **299** | 2d. multicoloured | 1·80 | 55 |

**300** Dish Aerial and Caduceus

**1981.** World Telecommunications Day.

| | | | | |
|---|---|---|---|---|
| 793 | **300** | 1d.40 multicoloured | 1·10 | 25 |

**301** "Disabled"

**1981.** International Year of Disabled People.

| | | | | |
|---|---|---|---|---|
| 794 | **301** | 1d.20 blue, red & orange | 90 | 25 |
| 795 | - | 1d.40 multicoloured | 1·00 | 30 |

DESIGN: 1d.40, Disabled people and hand holding flower.

**302** "Papilio machaon"

**1981.** Butterflies. Multicoloured.

| | | | |
|---|---|---|---|
| 796 | 60c. Type **302** | 70 | 35 |
| 797 | 1d.20 "Rhodocera rhamni gonepteryx rhamni" | 1·20 | 50 |
| 798 | 1d.40 "Charaxes jasius" | 1·60 | 85 |
| 799 | 2d. "Papilio podalirius" | 2·10 | 90 |

**303** Mediterranean Monk Seal

**1981.** Nature Protection. Multicoloured.

| | | | |
|---|---|---|---|
| 800 | 60c. Type **303** | 80 | 40 |
| 801 | 1d.40 Barbary ape | 1·60 | 85 |

**304** Man holding Ear of Wheat

**1981.** World Food Day.

| | | | | |
|---|---|---|---|---|
| 802 | **304** | 2d. multicoloured | 1·30 | 50 |

**305** Cattle, Jabbaren

**1981.** Cave Paintings. Multicoloured.

| | | | |
|---|---|---|---|
| 803 | 60c. Mouflon, Tan Zoumaitek | 55 | 25 |
| 804 | 1d. Type **305** | 95 | 40 |
| 805 | 1d.60 Cattle, Iherir (horiz) | 1·30 | 55 |
| 806 | 2d. One-horned bull, Jabbaren (horiz) | 1·80 | 85 |

**306** Galley

**1981.** Algerian Ships of 17th and 18th Centuries. Multicoloured.

| | | | |
|---|---|---|---|
| 807 | 60c. Type **306** | 80 | 50 |
| 808 | 1d.60 Xebec | 1·80 | 1·00 |

**307** Footballers with Cup

**1982.** World Cup Football Championship, Spain. Multicoloured.

| | | | |
|---|---|---|---|
| 809 | 80c. Type **307** | 60 | 25 |
| 810 | 2d.80 Footballers and ball (horiz) | 1·90 | 75 |

**308** Microscope

**1982.** Centenary of Discovery of Tubercle Bacillus.

| | | | | |
|---|---|---|---|---|
| 811 | **308** | 80c. blue, lt blue & orge | 55 | 25 |

**309** Mirror

**1982.** Popular Traditional Arts. Multicoloured.

| | | | |
|---|---|---|---|
| 812 | 80c. Type **309** | 60 | 25 |
| 813 | 2d. Whatnot | 1·30 | 40 |
| 814 | 2d.40 Chest (48×32 mm) | 1·70 | 75 |

**310** New Mosque, Algiers

**1982.** Views of Algeria before 1830 (1st series). Size 32×22 mm.

| | | | | |
|---|---|---|---|---|
| 815 | **310** | 80c. brown | 45 | 15 |
| 816 | - | 2d.40 violet | 1·20 | 50 |
| 817 | - | 3d. green | 1·60 | 65 |

DESIGNS: 2d.40, Sidi Boumedienne Mosque, Tlemcen; 3d. Garden of Dey, Algiers.

See also Nos. 859/62, 873/5, 880/2, 999/1001, 1054/6 and 1075/86.

**311** "Callitris articulata"

**1982.** Medicinal Plants. Multicoloured.

| | | | |
|---|---|---|---|
| 818 | 50c. Type **311** | 45 | 10 |
| 819 | 80c. "Artemisia herba-alba" | 55 | 25 |
| 820 | 1d. "Ricinus communis" | 90 | 35 |
| 821 | 2d.40 "Thymus fontanesii" | 1·90 | 75 |

**312** Independence Fighter

**1982.** 20th Anniv of Independence. Mult.

| | | | |
|---|---|---|---|
| 822 | 50c. Type **312** | 40 | 15 |
| 823 | 80c. Modern soldiers | 55 | 25 |
| 824 | 2d. Algerians and symbols of prosperity | 1·40 | 55 |

**MS**825 74×82 mm. 5d. Sun rising over flames (31×39 mm) 4·25 4·00

**313** Congress House

**1982.** Soumman Congress.

| | | | | |
|---|---|---|---|---|
| 826 | **313** | 80c. multicoloured | 55 | 15 |

**314** Scout and Guide releasing Dove

**1982.** 75th Anniv of Boy Scout Movement.

| | | | | |
|---|---|---|---|---|
| 827 | **314** | 2d.80 multicoloured | 1·90 | 55 |

**315** Child

**1982.** Palestinian Children.

| | | | | |
|---|---|---|---|---|
| 828 | **315** | 1d.60 multicoloured | 95 | 30 |

**316** Waldrapp

**1982.** Nature Protection. Multicoloured.

| | | | |
|---|---|---|---|
| 829 | 50c. Type **316** | 70 | 40 |
| 830 | 80c. Houbara bustard (vert) | 95 | 65 |
| 831 | 2d. Tawny eagle | 2·20 | 1·10 |
| 832 | 2d.40 Lammergeier (vert) | 2·75 | 1·40 |

**317** Mirror

**1983.** Silver Work.

| | | | | |
|---|---|---|---|---|
| 833 | **317** | 50c. silver, black and red | 35 | 10 |
| 834 | - | 1d. multicoloured | 55 | 40 |
| 835 | - | 2d. silver, black, & purple | 1·20 | 60 |

DESIGNS—VERT. 1d. Perfume flasks. HORIZ: 2d. Belt buckle.

**318** "Abies numidica"

**1983.** World Tree Day. Multicoloured.

| | | | |
|---|---|---|---|
| 836 | 80c. Type **318** | 70 | 25 |
| 837 | 2d.80 "Acacia raddiana" | 2·10 | 75 |

**319** Mineral

**1983.** Mineral Resources.

| | | | | |
|---|---|---|---|---|
| 838 | **319** | 70c. multicoloured | 90 | 35 |
| 839 | **319** | 80c. multicoloured | 1·00 | 50 |
| 840 | **319** | 1d.20 mult (horiz) | 1·20 | 65 |
| 841 | **319** | 2d.40 mult (horiz) | 2·50 | 1·20 |

**320** Customs Officer

**1983.** 30th Anniv of Customs Co-operation Council.

| | | | | |
|---|---|---|---|---|
| 842 | **320** | 80c. multicoloured | 70 | 25 |

**321** Emir Abdelkader

**1983.** Death Centenary of Emir Abdelkader.

| | | | | |
|---|---|---|---|---|
| 843 | **321** | 4d. multicoloured | 2·30 | 95 |

**322** Fly Agaric

**1983.** Mushrooms. Multicoloured.

| | | | |
|---|---|---|---|
| 844 | 50c. Type **322** | 80 | 25 |
| 845 | 80c. Death cap | 1·10 | 65 |
| 846 | 1d.40 "Pleurotus eryngii" | 2·40 | 1·00 |
| 847 | 2d.80 "Terfezia leonis" | 3·75 | 1·70 |

**323** Ibn Khaldoun

**1983.** Ibn Khaldoun Commemoration.

| | | | | |
|---|---|---|---|---|
| 848 | **323** | 80c. multicoloured | 70 | 25 |

**324** W.C.Y. Emblem and Post Office

**1983.** World Communications Year. Mult.

| | | | |
|---|---|---|---|
| 849 | 80c. Type **324** | 55 | 25 |
| 850 | 2d.40 W.C.Y. emblem and telephone switch box | 1·50 | 65 |

**325** Goat and Tassili Mountains

**1983.** Tassili World Patrimony. Multicoloured.

| | | | |
|---|---|---|---|
| 851 | 50c. Type **325** | 40 | 10 |
| 852 | 80c. Touaregs | 55 | 25 |
| 853 | 2d.40 Rock paintings | 1·40 | 55 |
| 854 | 2d.80 Rock formation | 1·80 | 75 |

**326** Sloughi

**1983.** Sloughi. Multicoloured.

| | | | |
|---|---|---|---|
| 855 | 80c. Type **326** | 80 | 35 |
| 856 | 2d.40 Sloughi | 2·10 | 1·00 |

**327** Symbols of Economic Progress

**1983.** 5th National Liberation Front Party Congress. Multicoloured.

| | | | |
|---|---|---|---|
| 857 | 80c. Type **327** | 80 | 35 |
| **MS**858 | 75×82 mm. 5d. Party emblem (31×38 mm) | 4·25 | 4·00 |

**1984.** Views of Algeria before 1830 (2nd series). As T 310.

| | | | |
|---|---|---|---|
| 859 | 10c. blue | 10 | 10 |
| 860 | 1d. purple | 45 | 10 |
| 861 | 2d. blue | 95 | 45 |
| 862 | 4d. red | 2·10 | 65 |

DESIGNS: 10c. Oran; 1d. Sidi Abderahmane Mosque, Et Taalibi; 2d. Bejaia; 4d. Constantine.

**328** Jug

**1984.** Pottery. Multicoloured.

| | | | |
|---|---|---|---|
| 863 | 80c. Type **328** | 55 | 25 |
| 864 | 1d. Dish (horiz) | 75 | 40 |
| 865 | 2d. Lamp | 1·40 | 60 |
| 866 | 2d.40 Jug (horiz) | 1·60 | 75 |

**329** Fountain

**1984.** Fountains of Old Algiers.

| | | | | |
|---|---|---|---|---|
| 867 | **329** | 50c. multicoloured | 20 | 10 |
| 868 | - | 80c. multicoloured | 55 | 40 |
| 869 | - | 2d.40 multicoloured | 1·30 | 65 |

DESIGNS: 80c., 2d.40, Different fountains.

**330** Dove, Flames and Olympic Rings

**1984.** Olympic Games, Los Angeles.

| | | | | |
|---|---|---|---|---|
| 870 | **330** | 1d. multicoloured | 90 | 40 |

**331** Stallion

**1984.** Horses. Multicoloured.

| | | | |
|---|---|---|---|
| 871 | 80c. Type **331** | 70 | 40 |
| 872 | 2d.40 Mare | 1·90 | 1·00 |

**1984.** Views of Algeria before 1830 (3rd series). As T 310.

| | | | |
|---|---|---|---|
| 873 | 5c. purple | 10 | 10 |
| 874 | 20c. blue | 10 | 10 |
| 875 | 70c. violet | 40 | 25 |

DESIGNS: 5c. Mustapha Pacha; 20c. Bab Azzoun; 70c. Mostaganem.

**332** Lute

**1984.** Musical Instruments. Multicoloured.

| | | | |
|---|---|---|---|
| 876 | 80c. Type **332** | 55 | 25 |
| 877 | 1d. Drum | 90 | 40 |
| 878 | 2d.40 One-stringed instrument | 1·80 | 75 |
| 879 | 2d.80 Bagpipes | 2·00 | 1·00 |

**1984.** Views of Algeria before 1830 (4th series). As T 310.

| | | | |
|---|---|---|---|
| 880 | 30c. red and black | 25 | 10 |
| 881 | 40c. black | 25 | 10 |
| 882 | 50c. brown | 25 | 10 |

DESIGNS: 30c. Algiers from Admiralty; 40c. Kolea; 50c. Algiers from aqueduct.

**333** Partisans in Mountains and Flag

**1984.** 30th Anniv of Revolution. Multicoloured.

| | | | |
|---|---|---|---|
| 883 | 80c. Type **333** | 70 | 25 |
| **MS**884 | 75×82 mm. 5d. Algerian flags (31×39 mm) | 4·25 | 4·00 |

**334** Map of M'Zab Valley

**1984.** M'Zab Valley. Multicoloured.

| | | | |
|---|---|---|---|
| 885 | 80c. Type **334** | 65 | 10 |
| 886 | 2d.40 M'Zab town | 1·70 | 60 |

**335** Coffee Pot

**1985.** Ornamental Tableware.

| | | | | |
|---|---|---|---|---|
| 887 | **335** | 80c. black, silver & yellow | 55 | 25 |
| 888 | - | 2d. black, silver and green | 1·20 | 60 |
| 889 | - | 2d.40 black, silver & pink | 1·60 | 70 |

DESIGNS—HORIZ: 2d. Bowl. VERT: 2d.40, Lidded jar.

**336** Blue-finned Tuna

**1985.** Fishes. Multicoloured.

| | | | |
|---|---|---|---|
| 890 | 50c. Type **336** | 55 | 25 |
| 891 | 80c. Gilthead seabream | 95 | 40 |
| 892 | 2d.40 Dusky grouper | 2·20 | 1·10 |
| 893 | 2d.80 Smooth hound | 2·75 | 1·20 |

**337** Birds in Flight and Emblem

**1985.** National Games.

894 **337** 80c. multicoloured 65 25

**338** Stylized Trees

**1985.** Environmental Protection. Multicoloured.

895 80c. Type **338** 80 25

896 1d.40 Stylized waves 90 40

**339** Algiers Casbah

**1985**

897 **339** 20c. blue and cream 10 10

898 **339** 80c. green and cream 55 10

899 **339** 2d.40 brown and cream 1·70 10

**340** Dove within "40"

**1985.** 40th Anniv of U.N.O.

900 **340** 1d. multicoloured 90 25

**341** Figures linking arms and Emblem

**1985.** 1st National Youth Festival.

901 **341** 80c. multicoloured 70 25

**342** Figures linking arms on Globe and Dove

**1985.** International Youth Year. Multicoloured.

902 80c. Type **342** 60 25

903 1d.40 Doves making globe with laurels 90 35

**343** O.P.E.C. Emblem

**1985.** 25th Anniv of Organization of Petroleum Exporting Countries.

904 **343** 80c. multicoloured 70 25

**344** Mother and Children

**1985.** Family Planning. Multicoloured.

905 80c. Type **344** 55 25

906 1d.40 Doctor weighing baby 90 40

907 1d.70 Mother breast-feeding baby 1·10 50

**345** Chetaibi Bay

**1985.** Tourist Sites.

908 **345** 80c. blue, green & brown 45 25

909 - 2d. brown, green & blue 1·30 40

910 - 2d.40 brown, green & bl 1·60 65

DESIGNS—VERT: 2d. El Meniaa. HORIZ: 2d.40, Bou Noura.

**346** "Palm Grove"

**1985.** Paintings by N. Dinet. Multicoloured.

911 2d. Type **346** 1·50 75

912 3d. "Palm Grove" (different) 2·10 1·20

**347** Line Pattern

**1985.** Weavings. Multicoloured.

913 80c. Type **347** 70 45

914 1d.40 Diamond pattern 1·40 65

915 2d.40 Patterned horizontal stripes 2·00 1·10

916 2d.80 Vertical and horizontal stripes 2·50 1·60

**348** "Felis margarita"

**1986.** Wild Cats. Multicoloured.

917 80c. Type **348** 80 45

918 1d. Caracal 1·00 60

919 2d. Wild cat 1·90 1·10

920 2d.40 Serval (vert) 2·50 1·40

**349** Oral Vaccination

**1986.** UNESCO Child Survival Campaign. Mult.

921 80c. Type **349** 55 25

922 1d.40 Sun behind mother and baby 1·20 55

923 1d.70 Children playing 1·50 75

**350** Industrial Skyline, Clasped Hands and Emblem

**1986.** 30th Anniv of Algerian General Workers' Union.

924 **350** 2d. multicoloured 1·50 55

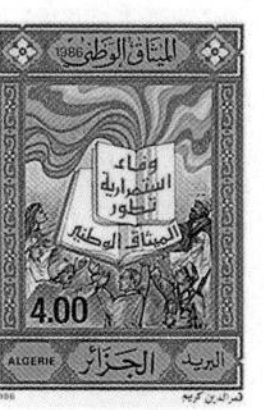

**351** Books and Crowd

**1986.** National Charter.

925 **351** 4d. multicoloured 2·75 1·20

**352** Emblem on Book and Drawing Instruments

**1986.** Disabled Persons' Day.

926 **352** 80c. multicoloured 70 30

**353** Children playing

**1986.** Anti-tuberculosis Campaign.

927 **353** 80c. multicoloured 70 35

**354** Sombrero on Football

**1986.** World Cup Football Championship, Mexico. Multicoloured.

928 2d. Type **354** 1·40 55

929 2d.40 Players and ball 1·60 70

**355** Courtyard with Fountain

**1986.** Traditional Dwellings. Multicoloured.

930 80c. Type **355** 70 30

931 2d.40 Courtyard with two beds of shrubs 1·80 1·00

932 3d. Courtyard with plants in tall pot 2·30 1·30

**356** Heart forming Drop over Patient

**1986.** Blood Donors.

933 **356** 80c. multicoloured 1·40 40

**357** Transmission Mast as Palm Tree

**1986.** Opening of Hertzian Wave Communications (Southern District).

934 **357** 60c. multicoloured 45 25

**358** Studded Gate

**1986.** Mosque Gateways. Multicoloured.

935 2d. Type **358** 1·30 55

936 2d.40 Ornate gateway 1·60 75

**359** Dove

**1986.** International Peace Year.

937 **359** 2d.40 multicoloured 1·60 55

**360** Girl dancing

**1986.** Folk Dances. Multicoloured.

938 80c. Type **360** 70 25

939 2d.40 Woman with purple dress dancing 1·70 65

940 2d.80 Veiled sword dancer 1·90 85

361 "Narcissus tazetta"

1986. Flowers. Multicoloured.

| | | | |
|---|---|---|---|
| 941 | 80c. Type **361** | 70 | 30 |
| 942 | 1d.40 "Iris unguicularis" | 1·20 | 55 |
| 943 | 2d.40 "Capparis spinosa" | 1·70 | 90 |
| 944 | 2d.80 "Gladiolus segetum" | 2·10 | 1·10 |

362 "Algerian Family"

1987. Paintings by Mohammed Issiakhem in National Museum. Multicoloured.

| | | | |
|---|---|---|---|
| 945 | 2d. Type **362** | 1·50 | 75 |
| 946 | 5d. "Man and Books" | 3·50 | 2·00 |

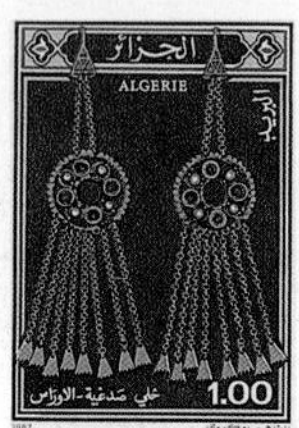
363 Earrings

1987. Jewellery from Aures. Multicoloured.

| | | | |
|---|---|---|---|
| 947 | 1d. Type **363** | 75 | 40 |
| 948 | 1d.80 Bangles | 1·20 | 60 |
| 949 | 2d.90 Brooches | 1·70 | 1·10 |
| 950 | 3d.30 Necklace (horiz) | 2·00 | 1·20 |

364 Boy and Girl

1987. Rock Carvings. Multicoloured.

| | | | |
|---|---|---|---|
| 951 | 1d. Type **364** | 90 | 55 |
| 952 | 2d.90 Goat | 2·00 | 1·30 |
| 953 | 3d.30 Animals | 2·30 | 1·40 |

365 Baby holding Syringe "Umbrella"

1987. African Vaccination Year.

| | | | | |
|---|---|---|---|---|
| 954 | **365** | 1d. multicoloured | 55 | 25 |

366 Workers and Circles

1987. Voluntary Service.

| | | | | |
|---|---|---|---|---|
| 955 | **366** | 1d. multicoloured | 55 | 30 |

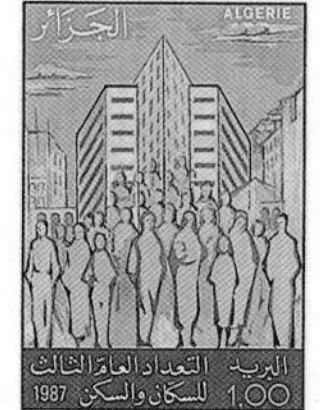
367 People and Buildings

1987. 3rd General Population Census.

| | | | | |
|---|---|---|---|---|
| 956 | **367** | 1d. multicoloured | 55 | 25 |

368 1962 War Orphans Fund Stamps and Magnifying Glass

1987. 25th Anniv of Independent Algeria Stamps.

| | | | | |
|---|---|---|---|---|
| 957 | **368** | 1d.80 multicoloured | 1·80 | 60 |

369 Hand holding Torch

1987. 25th Anniv of Independence. Multicoloured.

| | | | |
|---|---|---|---|
| 958 | 1d. Type **369** | 55 | 25 |
| **MS**959 | 75×82 mm. 5d. Sun, dove and "25" (32×39 mm) | 3·50 | 3·25 |

370 Actors in Spotlight

1987. Amateur Theatre Festival, Mostaganem. Multicoloured.

| | | | |
|---|---|---|---|
| 960 | 1d. Type **370** | 55 | 85 |
| 961 | 1d.80 Theatre | 90 | 55 |

371 Discus Thrower

1987. Mediterranean Games, Lattaquie. Mult.

| | | | |
|---|---|---|---|
| 962 | 1d. Type **371** | 55 | 30 |
| 963 | 2d.90 Tennis player (vert) | 1·50 | 70 |
| 964 | 3d.30 Footballer | 1·80 | 95 |

372 Greater Flamingo

1987. Birds. Multicoloured.

| | | | |
|---|---|---|---|
| 965 | 1d. Type **372** | 75 | 40 |
| 966 | 1d.80 Purple swamphen | 1·30 | 80 |
| 967 | 2d.50 Black-shouldered kite | 2·00 | 95 |
| 968 | 2d.90 Red kite | 1·90 | 85 |

373 Reservoir

1987. Agriculture. Multicoloured.

| | | | |
|---|---|---|---|
| 969 | 1d. Type **373** | 60 | 25 |
| 970 | 1d. Forestry (36×28 mm) | 60 | 25 |
| 971 | 1d. Foodstuffs (25×37 mm) | 60 | 25 |
| 972 | 1d. Erecting hedge against desert (25×37 mm) | 55 | 25 |

374 Map, Transmitter and Radio Waves

1987. African Telecommunications Day.

| | | | | |
|---|---|---|---|---|
| 973 | **374** | 1d. multicoloured | 70 | 25 |

375 Motorway

1987. Transport. Multicoloured.

| | | | |
|---|---|---|---|
| 974 | 2d.90 Type **375** | 1·50 | 60 |
| 975 | 3d.30 Diesel locomotive and passenger train | 2·75 | 1·20 |

376 Houari Boumedienne University, Algiers

1987. Universities. Multicoloured.

| | | | |
|---|---|---|---|
| 976 | 1d. Type **376** | 55 | 25 |
| 977 | 2d.50 Oran University | 1·30 | 45 |
| 978 | 2d.90 Constantine University | 1·50 | 60 |
| 979 | 3d.30 Emir Abdelkader University, Constantine (vert) | 1·90 | 75 |

377 Wheat, Sun and Farmer ploughing with Oxen

1988. 10th Anniv of International Agricultural Development Fund.

| | | | | |
|---|---|---|---|---|
| 980 | **377** | 1d. multicoloured | 70 | 25 |

378 Emblem as Sun above Factories

1988. Autonomy of State-owned Utilities.

| | | | | |
|---|---|---|---|---|
| 981 | **378** | 1d. multicoloured | 55 | 25 |

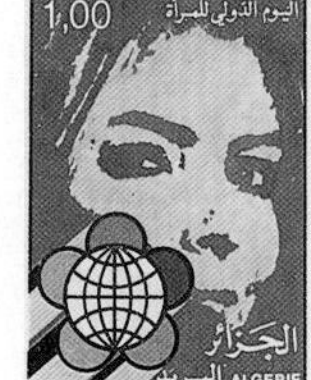
379 Woman's Face and Emblem

1988. International Women's Day.

| | | | | |
|---|---|---|---|---|
| 982 | **379** | 1d. multicoloured | 55 | 25 |

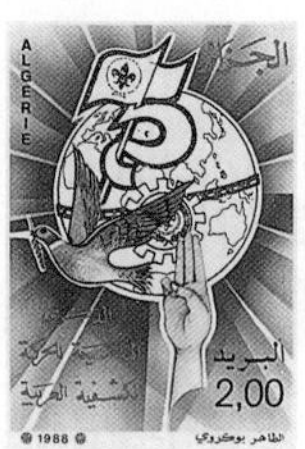
380 Globe, Flag, Wood Pigeon and Scout Salute

1988. 75th Anniv of Arab Scouting.

| | | | | |
|---|---|---|---|---|
| 983 | **380** | 2d. multicoloured | 1·10 | 45 |

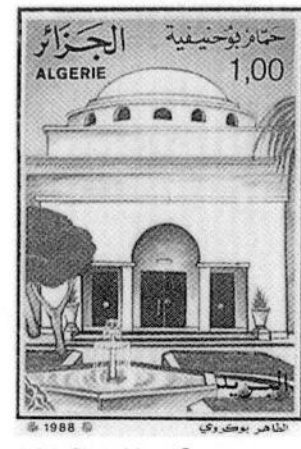
381 Bau-Hanifia

1988. Spas. Multicoloured.

| | | | |
|---|---|---|---|
| 984 | 1d. Type **381** | 55 | 25 |
| 985 | 2d.90 Chellala | 1·50 | 55 |
| 986 | 3d.30 Righa-Ain Tolba | 1·70 | 70 |

382 Running

1988. Olympic Games, Seoul.

| | | | | |
|---|---|---|---|---|
| 987 | **382** | 2d.90 multicoloured | 1·90 | 90 |

383 Pencil and Globe

1988. International Literacy Day.

| | | | | |
|---|---|---|---|---|
| 988 | **383** | 2d.90 multicoloured | 1·40 | 70 |

384 Barbary Ape

1988. Endangered Animals. Barbary Ape. Mult.

| | | | |
|---|---|---|---|
| 989 | 50c. Type **384** | 80 | 40 |
| 990 | 90c. Ape family | 1·20 | 65 |
| 991 | 1d. Ape's head and shoulders (vert) | 1·60 | 85 |
| 992 | 1d.80 Ape in tree (vert) | 2·75 | 1·50 |

385 Family Group

1988. 40th Anniv of W.H.O.

| | | | | |
|---|---|---|---|---|
| 993 | 385 | 2d.90 multicoloured | 1·30 | 60 |

386 Different Races raising Fists

1988. Anti-apartheid Campaign.

| | | | | |
|---|---|---|---|---|
| 994 | 386 | 2d.50 multicoloured | 1·20 | 50 |

387 Emblem

1988. 6th National Liberation Front Party Congress.

| | | | | |
|---|---|---|---|---|
| 995 | 387 | 1d. multicoloured | 55 | 25 |

388 Man irrigating Fields

1988. Agriculture. Multicoloured.

| | | | |
|---|---|---|---|
| 996 | 1d. Type **388** | 55 | 25 |
| 997 | 1d. Fields, cattle and man picking fruit | 55 | 25 |

389 Constantine

1989

| | | | | |
|---|---|---|---|---|
| 998 | 389 | 1d. deep green and green | 40 | 85 |

1989. Views of Algeria before 1830 (5th series). As T 310.

| | | | |
|---|---|---|---|
| 999 | 2d.50 green | 90 | 25 |
| 1000 | 2d.90 green | 1·00 | 25 |
| 1001 | 5d. brown and black | 2·10 | 40 |

DESIGNS: 2d.50, Bay; 2d.90, Harbour; 5d. View of harbour through archway.

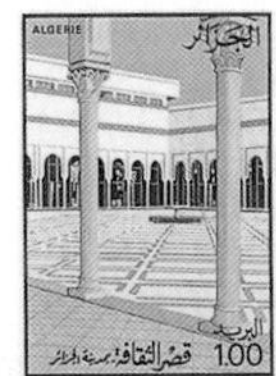
390 Courtyard

1989. National Achievements. Multicoloured.

| | | | |
|---|---|---|---|
| 1002 | 1d. Type **390** | 55 | 25 |
| 1003 | 1d. Flats (housing) | 55 | 25 |
| 1004 | 1d. Gateway, Timimoun (tourism) | 55 | 25 |
| 1005 | 1d. Dish aerial and telephones (communications) | 55 | 25 |

391 Oran Es Senia Airport

1989. Airports. Multicoloured.

| | | | |
|---|---|---|---|
| 1006 | 2d.90 Type **391** | 1·20 | 45 |
| 1007 | 3d.30 Tebessa airport | 1·40 | 60 |
| 1008 | 5d. Tamanrasset airport (vert) | 2·10 | 1·20 |

392 Irrigation

1989. Development of South. Multicoloured.

| | | | |
|---|---|---|---|
| 1009 | 1d. Type **392** | 50 | 25 |
| 1010 | 1d.80 Ouargla secondary school | 70 | 40 |
| 1011 | 2d.50 Gas complex, Hassi R'mel (vert) | 1·10 | 50 |

393 Soldiers at Various Tasks

1989. 20th Anniv of National Service.

| | | | | |
|---|---|---|---|---|
| 1012 | 393 | 2d. multicoloured | 1·30 | 65 |

394 Locusts and Crop Spraying

1989. Anti-locusts Campaign.

| | | | | |
|---|---|---|---|---|
| 1013 | 394 | 1d. multicoloured | 55 | 25 |

395 Mother and Baby

1989. International Children's Day.

| | | | | |
|---|---|---|---|---|
| 1014 | 395 | 1d.+30c. mult | 65 | 40 |

396 Moon

1989. 20th Anniv of First Manned Landing on Moon. Multicoloured.

| | | | |
|---|---|---|---|
| 1015 | 2d.90 Type **396** | 1·20 | 50 |
| 1016 | 4d. Astronaut on moon | 1·50 | 80 |

397 Globe and Emblem

1989. Centenary of Interparliamentary Union.

| | | | | |
|---|---|---|---|---|
| 1017 | 397 | 2d.90 mauve, brn & gold | 1·20 | 40 |

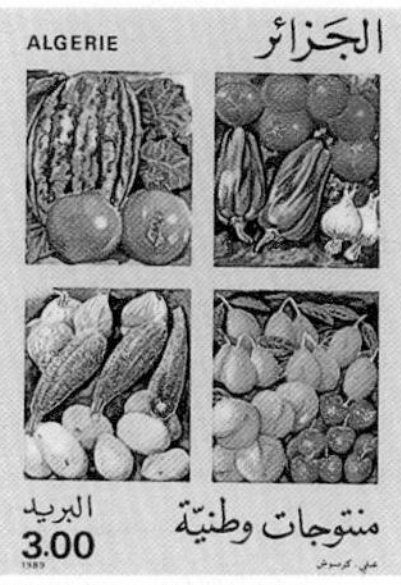
398 Fruits and Vegetables

1989. National Production.

| | | | | |
|---|---|---|---|---|
| 1018 | 398 | 2d. multicoloured | 75 | 40 |
| 1019 | - | 3d. multicoloured | 1·10 | 60 |
| 1020 | - | 5d. multicoloured | 1·90 | 1·10 |

DESIGNS: 3, 5d. Various fruits and vegetables.

399 Atlantic Bonito

1989. Fishes. Multicoloured.

| | | | |
|---|---|---|---|
| 1021 | 1d. Type **399** | 60 | 30 |
| 1022 | 1d.80 John dory | 1·10 | 45 |
| 1023 | 2d.90 Red seabream | 1·60 | 60 |
| 1024 | 3d.30 Swordfish | 1·80 | 75 |

400 "35" and Soldier with Rifle

1989. 35th Anniv of Revolution.

| | | | | |
|---|---|---|---|---|
| 1025 | 400 | 1d. multicoloured | 50 | 15 |

401 Bank Emblem, Cogwheel, Factory and Wheat

1989. 25th Anniv of African Development Bank.

| | | | | |
|---|---|---|---|---|
| 1026 | 401 | 1d. multicoloured | 45 | 25 |

402 Satan's Mushroom

1989. Fungi. Multicoloured.

| | | | |
|---|---|---|---|
| 1027 | 1d. Type **402** | 70 | 30 |
| 1028 | 1d.80 Yellow stainer | 1·20 | 45 |
| 1029 | 2d.90 Parasol mushroom | 1·90 | 75 |
| 1030 | 3d.30 Saffron milk cap | 2·20 | 95 |

403 Emblem

1990. 10th Anniv of Pan-African Postal Union.

| | | | | |
|---|---|---|---|---|
| 1031 | 403 | 1d. multicoloured | 50 | 25 |

404 Sun, Arm and Face

1990. Rational Use of Energy.

| | | | | |
|---|---|---|---|---|
| 1032 | 404 | 1d. multicoloured | 60 | 25 |

405 Emblem

1990. African Nations Cup Football Championship.

| | | | | |
|---|---|---|---|---|
| 1033 | 405 | 3d. multicoloured | 1·30 | 50 |

406 Ceramics

1990. Industries. Multicoloured.

| | | | |
|---|---|---|---|
| 1034 | 2d. Type **406** | 70 | 35 |
| 1035 | 2d.90 Car maintenance | 1·10 | 45 |
| 1036 | 3d.30 Fishing | 1·70 | 65 |

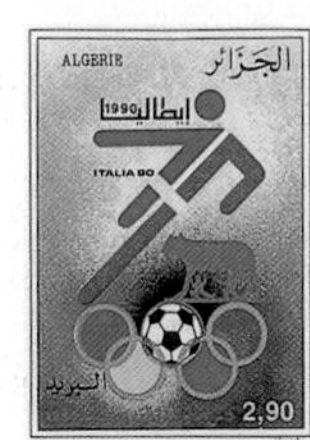
407 Pictogram and Olympic Rings

1990. World Cup Football Championship, Italy. Multicoloured.

| | | | |
|---|---|---|---|
| 1037 | 2d.90 Type **407** | 1·10 | 50 |
| 1038 | 5d. Trophy, ball and flag | 1·90 | 95 |

408 Pylons on Map

1990. Rural Electrification.

| | | | | |
|---|---|---|---|---|
| 1039 | 408 | 2d. multicoloured | 80 | 30 |

409 Young Workers

1990. Youth. Multicoloured.

| | | | |
|---|---|---|---|
| 1040 | 2d. Type **409** | 80 | 30 |
| 1041 | 3d. Youth in crowd (vert) | 1·20 | 45 |

**410** Members' Flags

**1990.** Arab Maghreb Union Summit Conference.

| | | | | |
|---|---|---|---|---|
| 1042 | **410** | 1d. multicoloured | 50 | 25 |

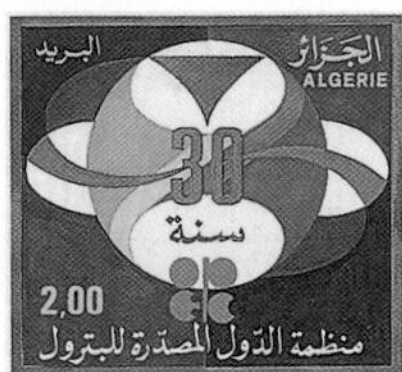

**411** Anniversary Emblem

**1990.** 30th Anniv of O.P.E.C.

| | | | | |
|---|---|---|---|---|
| 1043 | **411** | 2d. multicoloured | 80 | 30 |

**412** House and Hand holding Coin

**1990.** Savings Day.

| | | | | |
|---|---|---|---|---|
| 1044 | **412** | 1d. multicoloured | 40 | 15 |

**413** Flag, Rifle and Hands with Broken Manacles

**1990.** Namibian Independence.

| | | | | |
|---|---|---|---|---|
| 1045 | **413** | 3d. multicoloured | 1·00 | 30 |

**414** Duck

**1990.** Domestic Animals. Multicoloured.

| | | | |
|---|---|---|---|
| 1046 | 1d. Type **414** | 50 | 15 |
| 1047 | 2d. Hare (horiz) | 95 | 35 |
| 1048 | 2d.90 Common turkey | 1·30 | 55 |
| 1049 | 3d.30 Red junglefowl (horiz) | 1·60 | 75 |

**415** Dome of the Rock and Palestinians

**1990.** Palestinian "Intifada" Movement.

| | | | | |
|---|---|---|---|---|
| 1050 | **415** | 1d.+30c. mult | 60 | 40 |

**416** Crowd with Banners

**1990.** 30th Anniv of 11 December 1960 Demonstration.

| | | | | |
|---|---|---|---|---|
| 1051 | **416** | 1d. multicoloured | 30 | 10 |

**417** Families in Countryside

**1990.** Campaign against Respiratory Diseases.

| | | | | |
|---|---|---|---|---|
| 1052 | **417** | 1d. multicoloured | 30 | 10 |

**418** Sunburst, Torch and Open Book

**1991.** 2nd Anniv of Constitution.

| | | | | |
|---|---|---|---|---|
| 1053 | **418** | 1d. multicoloured | 30 | 10 |

**1991.** Views of Algeria before 1830 (6th series). As T 310.

| | | | |
|---|---|---|---|
| 1054 | 1d.50 red | 50 | 10 |
| 1055 | 4d.20 green | 1·40 | 55 |

DESIGNS: 1d.50, Kolea; 4d.20, Constantine.

**419** Bejaia

**1991.** Air. Multicoloured.

| | | | |
|---|---|---|---|
| 1056 | 10d. Type **419** | 2·75 | 1·20 |
| 1057 | 20d. Annaba | 5·50 | 2·75 |

**420** "Jasminum fruticans"

**1991.** Flowers. Multicoloured.

| | | | |
|---|---|---|---|
| 1058 | 2d. Type **420** | 70 | 30 |
| 1059 | 4d. "Dianthus crinitus" | 1·40 | 55 |
| 1060 | 5d. "Cyclamen africanum" | 1·80 | 80 |

**421** "Trip to the Country" (Mehdi Medrar)

**1991.** Children's Drawings. Multicoloured.

| | | | |
|---|---|---|---|
| 1061 | 3d. Type **421** | 90 | 25 |
| 1062 | 4d. "Children playing" (Ouidad Bounab) | 1·20 | 40 |

**422** Emblem

**1991.** 3rd Anniv of Arab Maghreb Union Summit Conference, Zeralda.

| | | | | |
|---|---|---|---|---|
| 1063 | **422** | 1d. multicoloured | 30 | 10 |

**423** Figures and Emblem

**1991.** 40th Anniv of Geneva Convention on Status of Refugees.

| | | | | |
|---|---|---|---|---|
| 1064 | **423** | 3d. multicoloured | 1·00 | 35 |

**424** Coded Letter and Target

**1991.** World Post Day (1065) and "Telecom 91" International Telecommunications Exhibition, Geneva (1066). Multicoloured.

| | | | |
|---|---|---|---|
| 1065 | 1d.50 Type **424** | 55 | 25 |
| 1066 | 4d.20 Exhibition and I.T.U. emblems (vert) | 1·20 | 45 |

**425** Spanish Festoon

**1991.** Butterflies. Multicoloured.

| | | | |
|---|---|---|---|
| 1067 | 2d. Type **425** | 60 | 30 |
| 1068 | 4d. "Melitaea didyma" | 1·00 | 45 |
| 1069 | 6d. Red admiral | 1·40 | 65 |
| 1070 | 7d. Large tortoiseshell | 1·70 | 95 |

**426** Chest Ornament

**1991.** Silver Jewellery from South Algeria. Mult.

| | | | |
|---|---|---|---|
| 1071 | 3d. Necklaces | 60 | 30 |
| 1072 | 4d. Type **426** | 80 | 45 |
| 1073 | 5d. Enamelled ornament | 90 | 65 |
| 1074 | 7d. Bangles (horiz) | 1·50 | 1·00 |

**1992.** Views of Algeria before 1830. As previous issues and new values. Size 30½×21 mm.

| | | | |
|---|---|---|---|
| 1075 | 5c. purple | 60 | 30 |
| 1076 | 10c. blue | 70 | 1·80 |
| 1077 | 20c. blue | 90 | 50 |
| 1078 | 30c. red and black | 1·30 | 35 |
| 1079 | 50c. brown | 1·30 | 35 |
| 1080 | 70c. lilac | 1·80 | 85 |
| 1081 | 80c. brown | 2·00 | 75 |
| 1082 | 1d. brown | 1·50 | 65 |
| 1083 | 2d. blue | 2·75 | 1·30 |
| 1084 | 3d. green | 3·75 | 95 |
| 1085 | 4d. red | 5·25 | 1·30 |
| 1086 | 6d.20 blue | 90 | 25 |
| 1087 | 7d.50 red | 1·20 | 25 |

DESIGNS: 5c., 6d.20, As No. 873; 10c., 7d.50, As No. 859; 20c. As No. 1000; 30c. As No. 1001; 50c. As No. 882; 70c. As No. 875; 80c. Type **310**; 1d. As No. 860; 2d. As No. 861; 3d. As No. 817; 4d. As No. 1055.

**427** Woman

**1992.** International Women's Day.

| | | | | |
|---|---|---|---|---|
| 1095 | **427** | 1d.50 multicoloured | 40 | 10 |

**428** Dorcas Gazelle

**1992.** Gazelles. Multicoloured.

| | | | |
|---|---|---|---|
| 1096 | 1d.50 Type **428** | 40 | 10 |
| 1097 | 6d.20 Edmi gazelle | 1·10 | 60 |
| 1098 | 8d.60 Addra gazelle | 1·50 | 75 |

**429** Algiers

**1992**

| | | | | |
|---|---|---|---|---|
| 1099 | **429** | 1d.50 brown & lt brown | 25 | 10 |
| 1132 | **429** | 2d. blue | 30 | 10 |
| 1147 | **429** | 3d. blue | 50 | 10 |

**430** Runners

**1992.** Olympic Games, Barcelona.

| | | | | |
|---|---|---|---|---|
| 1100 | **430** | 6d.20 multicoloured | 1·20 | 45 |

**431** Doves and Flags

**1992.** 30th Anniv of Independence.

| | | | | |
|---|---|---|---|---|
| 1101 | **431** | 5d. green, red and black | 90 | 30 |

**432** "Ajuga iva"

**1992.** Medicinal Plants. Multicoloured.

| | | | |
|---|---|---|---|
| 1102 | 1d.50 Type **432** | 25 | 10 |
| 1103 | 5d.10 Buckthorn | 90 | 40 |
| 1104 | 6d.20 Milk thistle | 1·20 | 50 |
| 1105 | 8d.60 French lavender | 1·60 | 70 |

**433** Computerized Post Office Equipment

1992. World Post Day. Modernization of Postal Service.

| | | | | |
|---|---|---|---|---|
| 1106 | 433 | 1d.50 multicoloured | 40 | 10 |

434 Boudiaf

1992. Mohammed Boudiaf (chairman of Committee of State) Commemoration.

| | | | | |
|---|---|---|---|---|
| 1107 | 434 | 2d. multicoloured | 45 | 25 |
| 1108 | 434 | 8d.60 multicoloured | 1·50 | 75 |

435 2nd-century B.C. Numidian Coin

1992. Coinage. Multicoloured.

| | | | |
|---|---|---|---|
| 1109 | 1d.50 Type **435** | 20 | 10 |
| 1110 | 2d. 14th-century Zianide dinar | 30 | 15 |
| 1111 | 5d.10 11th-century Almoravid dinar | 85 | 40 |
| 1112 | 6d.20 19th-century Emir Abd-el-Kader coin | 1·20 | 55 |

436 Short-snouted Seahorse

1992. Marine Animals. Multicoloured.

| | | | |
|---|---|---|---|
| 1113 | 1d.50 Type **436** | 35 | 10 |
| 1114 | 2d.70 Loggerhead turtle | 55 | 25 |
| 1115 | 6d.20 Mediterranean moray | 1·20 | 55 |
| 1116 | 7d.50 Lobster | 1·40 | 70 |

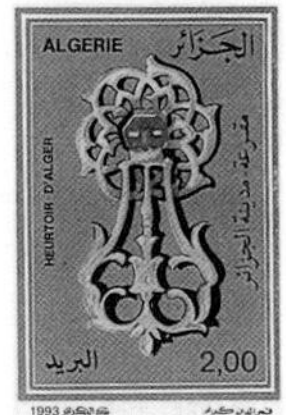

437 Algiers Door Knocker

1993. Door Knockers. Multicoloured.

| | | | |
|---|---|---|---|
| 1117 | 2d. Type **437** | 30 | 10 |
| 1118 | 5d.60 Constantine | 90 | 35 |
| 1119 | 8d.60 Tlemcen | 1·40 | 70 |

438 Medlar Blossom

1993. Fruit-tree Blossom. Multicoloured.

| | | | |
|---|---|---|---|
| 1120 | 4d.50 Type **438** | 80 | 40 |
| 1121 | 8d.60 Quince (vert) | 1·40 | 70 |
| 1122 | 11d. Apricot (vert) | 1·80 | 95 |

439 Patrol Boat, Emblem and Flag

1993. 20th Anniv of Coastguard Service.

| | | | | |
|---|---|---|---|---|
| 1123 | 439 | 2d. multicoloured | 95 | 35 |

440 Grain Storage Jar

1993. Traditional Utensils. Multicoloured.

| | | | |
|---|---|---|---|
| 1124 | 2d. Type **440** | 50 | 10 |
| 1125 | 5d.60 Grindstone | 90 | 50 |
| 1126 | 8d.60 Oil-press | 1·40 | 65 |

441 Mauretanian Royal Mausoleum, Tipaza

1993. Mausoleums. Multicoloured.

| | | | |
|---|---|---|---|
| 1127 | 8d.60 Type **441** | 1·10 | 50 |
| 1128 | 12d. Royal Mausoleum, El Khroub | 1·80 | 80 |

442 Jijelienne Coast

1993. Air.

| | | | | |
|---|---|---|---|---|
| 1129 | 442 | 50d. green, brown & blue | 5·75 | 2·00 |

443 Annaba

1993. Ports. Multicoloured.

| | | | |
|---|---|---|---|
| 1130 | 2d. Type **443** | 40 | 10 |
| 1131 | 8d.60 Arzew | 1·40 | 50 |

444 Chameleon

1993. Reptiles. Multicoloured.

| | | | |
|---|---|---|---|
| 1133 | 2d. Type **444** | 50 | 10 |
| 1134 | 8d.60 Desert monitor (horiz) | 1·60 | 85 |

445 Tipaza

1993. Tourism. Multicoloured.

| | | | |
|---|---|---|---|
| 1135 | 2d. Type **445** | 40 | 10 |
| 1136 | 8d.60 Kerzaz | 1·10 | 50 |

446 Map, Processing Plant and Uses of Hydrocarbons

1993. 30th Anniv of Sonatrach (National Society for Transformation and Commercialization of Hydrocarbons).

| | | | | |
|---|---|---|---|---|
| 1137 | 446 | 2d. multicoloured | 50 | 10 |

447 Dove, Flag and "18"

1994. National Chahid Day.

| | | | | |
|---|---|---|---|---|
| 1138 | 447 | 2d. multicoloured | 55 | 10 |

448 Crown of Statue of Liberty, Football, U.S. Flag and Trophy

1994. World Cup Football Championship, U.S.A.

| | | | | |
|---|---|---|---|---|
| 1139 | 448 | 8d.60 multicoloured | 2·75 | 85 |

449 Monkey Orchid

1994. Orchids. Multicoloured.

| | | | |
|---|---|---|---|
| 1140 | 5d.60 Type **449** | 1·20 | 65 |
| 1141 | 8d.60 "Orphrys lutea" | 1·50 | 85 |
| 1142 | 11d. Bee orchid | 2·20 | 1·30 |

450 Hoggar Script on Stone

1994. Ancient Communication. Multicoloured.

| | | | |
|---|---|---|---|
| 1143 | 3d. Type **450** | 80 | 25 |
| 1144 | 10d. Abizar stele | 1·80 | 75 |

451 Flags and Olympic Rings

1994. Cent of International Olympic Committee.

| | | | | |
|---|---|---|---|---|
| 1145 | 451 | 12d. multicoloured | 1·90 | 65 |

452 Figures and City on Globe

1994. World Population Day.

| | | | | |
|---|---|---|---|---|
| 1146 | 452 | 3d. multicoloured | 50 | 10 |

453 Sandstone

1994. Minerals. Multicoloured.

| | | | |
|---|---|---|---|
| 1148 | 3d. Type **453** | 55 | 25 |
| 1149 | 5d. Cipolin | 90 | 45 |
| 1150 | 10d. Turitella shells in chalk | 2·00 | 1·00 |

454 Brooches

1994. Saharan Silver Jewellery. Multicoloured.

| | | | |
|---|---|---|---|
| 1151 | 3d. Type **454** | 65 | 15 |
| 1152 | 5d. Belt (horiz) | 1·10 | 40 |
| 1153 | 12d. Bracelets (horiz) | 2·75 | 1·00 |

455 Soldiers

1994. 40th Anniv of Revolution.

| | | | | |
|---|---|---|---|---|
| 1154 | 455 | 3d. multicoloured | 45 | 10 |

456 Ladybirds on Leaves

1994. Insects. Multicoloured.

| | | | |
|---|---|---|---|
| 1155 | 3d. Type **456** | 50 | 15 |
| 1156 | 12d. Beetle ("Buprestidae") on plant | 1·90 | 75 |

457 Virus and Family

1994. World Anti-AIDS Campaign Day.

| | | | | |
|---|---|---|---|---|
| 1157 | 457 | 3d. black, blue & mauve | 50 | 10 |

**458** Algiers

**1994.** Regional Dances. Multicoloured.

| | | | |
|---|---|---|---|
| 1158 | 3d. Type **458** | 50 | 10 |
| 1159 | 10d. Constantine | 1·30 | 65 |
| 1160 | 12d. Alaoui | 1·40 | 75 |

**459** Southern Algeria

**1995.** 20th Anniv of World Tourism Organization.

| | | | | |
|---|---|---|---|---|
| 1161 | **459** | 3d. multicoloured | 40 | 10 |

**460** Honey Bee on Comb

**1995.** Bee-keeping. Multicoloured.

| | | | |
|---|---|---|---|
| 1162 | 3d. Type **460** | 40 | 10 |
| 1163 | 13d. Bee on flower (horiz) | 1·50 | 85 |

**461** Dahlia

**1995.** Flowers. Multicoloured.

| | | | |
|---|---|---|---|
| 1164 | 3d. Type **461** | 55 | 10 |
| 1165 | 10d. Zinnias | 1·60 | 70 |
| 1166 | 13d. Lilac | 1·80 | 85 |

**462** Circular Design

**1995.** Stucco Work from Sedrata (4th century after Hegira).

| | | | | |
|---|---|---|---|---|
| 1167 | **462** | 3d. brown | 30 | 10 |
| 1168 | - | 4d. green | 50 | 10 |
| 1169 | - | 5d. brown | 55 | 25 |

DESIGNS—4d. Circular design within square; 5d. Stylized flowers.

**463** Doves, Graves, Victims and Soldiers

**1995.** 50th Anniv of End of Second World War. Multicoloured.

| | | | |
|---|---|---|---|
| 1170 | 3d. Type **463** | 40 | 10 |
| **MS**1171 | 70×80 mm. 13d. National flag on dove (25×27 mm) | 4·50 | 3·50 |

**464** Water Pollution

**1995.** Environmental Protection. Multicoloured.

| | | | |
|---|---|---|---|
| 1172 | 3d. Type **464** | 35 | 10 |
| 1173 | 13d. Air pollution | 1·50 | 65 |

**465** Players and Anniversary Emblem

**1995.** Centenary of Volleyball.

| | | | | |
|---|---|---|---|---|
| 1174 | **465** | 3d. multicoloured | 30 | 10 |

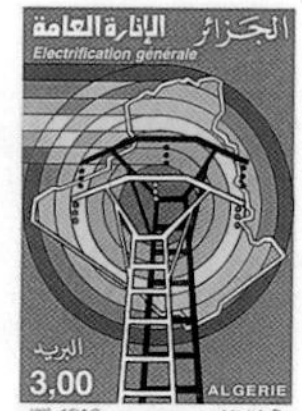

**466** Map and Pylon

**1995.** Electrification.

| | | | | |
|---|---|---|---|---|
| 1175 | **466** | 3d. multicoloured | 35 | 10 |

**467** Children and Schoolbag Contents

**1995.** National Solidarity.

| | | | | |
|---|---|---|---|---|
| 1176 | **467** | 3d.+50c. mult | 50 | 35 |

**468** Doves and Anniversary Emblem

**1995.** 50th Anniv of U.N.O.

| | | | | |
|---|---|---|---|---|
| 1177 | **468** | 13d. multicoloured | 1·40 | 75 |

**469** Pitcher from Lakhdaria

**1995.** Traditional Pottery.

| | | | | |
|---|---|---|---|---|
| 1178 | **469** | 10d. brown | 1·10 | 40 |
| 1179 | - | 20d. brown | 2·10 | 65 |
| 1180 | - | 21d. brown | 2·10 | 65 |
| 1181 | - | 30d. brown | 3·00 | 90 |

DESIGNS: 20d. Water jug (Aokas); 21d. Jar (Larbaa nath Iraten); 30d. Jar (Ouadhia).

**470** Common Shelduck

**1995.** Water Birds. Multicoloured.

| | | | |
|---|---|---|---|
| 1182 | 3d. Type **470** | 55 | 25 |
| 1183 | 5d. Common snipe | 90 | 35 |

**471** Doves flying over Javelin Thrower and Olympic Rings

**1996.** Centenary of Modern Olympic Games and Olympic Games, Atlanta.

| | | | | |
|---|---|---|---|---|
| 1184 | **471** | 20d. multicoloured | 2·20 | 1·10 |

**472** Fringed Bag

**1996.** Handicrafts. Leather Bags. Multicoloured.

| | | | |
|---|---|---|---|
| 1185 | 5d. Type **472** | 1·20 | 50 |
| 1186 | 16d. Shoulder bag with handle (vert) | 2·20 | 95 |

**473** Pasteur Institute

**1996.** Centenary (1994) of Algerian Pasteur Institute.

| | | | | |
|---|---|---|---|---|
| 1187 | **473** | 5d. multicoloured | 55 | 20 |

**474** Arabic Script and Computer

**1996.** Scientific and Technical Education Day. Multicoloured.

| | | | |
|---|---|---|---|
| 1188 | 5d. Type **474** | 55 | 25 |
| 1189 | 16d. Dove, fountain pen and symbols (vert) | 1·40 | 60 |
| 1190 | 23d. Pencil, pen, dividers and satellite over Earth on pages of open book (vert) | 2·40 | 1·10 |

**475** Iron Ore, Djebel Quenza

**1996.** Minerals. Multicoloured.

| | | | |
|---|---|---|---|
| 1191 | 10d. Type **475** | 1·20 | 50 |
| 1192 | 20d. Gold, Tirek-Amesmessa | 2·20 | 95 |

**476** "Pandoriana pandora"

**1996.** Butterflies. Multicoloured.

| | | | |
|---|---|---|---|
| 1193 | 5d. Type **476** | 65 | 25 |
| 1194 | 10d. "Coenonympha pamphilus" | 1·10 | 50 |
| 1195 | 20d. Painted lady | 2·30 | 1·10 |

| | | | |
|---|---|---|---|
| 1196 | 23d. Marbled white | 2·50 | 1·30 |

**477** Globe, Drug Addict and Drugs

**1996.** World Anti-drugs Day.

| | | | | |
|---|---|---|---|---|
| 1197 | **477** | 5d. multicoloured | 50 | 15 |

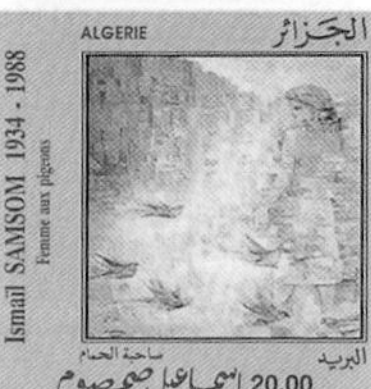

**478** "Woman with Pigeons"

**1996.** Paintings by Ismail Samsom. Multicoloured.

| | | | |
|---|---|---|---|
| 1198 | 20d. Type **478** | 1·50 | 80 |
| 1199 | 30d. "Interrogation" | 2·30 | 1·30 |

**479** Ambulance and Paramedic holding Child (Medical Aid)

**1996.** Civil Defence. Multicoloured.

| | | | |
|---|---|---|---|
| 1200 | 5d. Type **479** | 50 | 25 |
| 1201 | 23d. Globe resting in cupped hands (natural disaster prevention) (vert) | 1·80 | 85 |

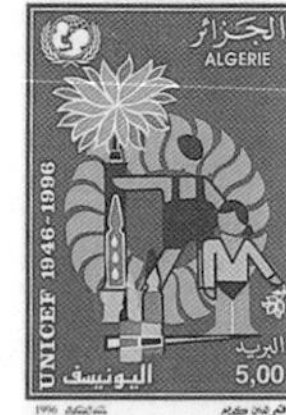

**480** Children, Syringe and Pens

**1996.** 50th Anniv of UNICEF Multicoloured.

| | | | |
|---|---|---|---|
| 1202 | 5d. Type **480** | 40 | 10 |
| 1203 | 10d. Family holding pencil, key, syringe and flower | 90 | 35 |

**481** Dar Hassan Pacha

**1996.** Algiers Courtyards. Multicoloured.

| | | | |
|---|---|---|---|
| 1204 | 5d. Type **481** | 40 | 15 |
| 1205 | 10d. Dar Kedaoudj el Amia | 75 | 40 |
| 1206 | 20d. Palais des Rais | 1·50 | 90 |
| 1207 | 30d. Villa Abdellatif | 2·40 | 1·40 |

**482** Minbar Inscription, Nedroma Mosque

**1997.** Mosque Carvings. Multicoloured.

| | | | |
|---|---|---|---|
| 1208 | 5d. Type **482** | 40 | 15 |
| 1209 | 23d. Doors, Ketchaoua Mosque, Algiers | 1·80 | 95 |

**483** Outline Map, Graph and Roofs over People

**1997.** 4th General Population and Housing Census.
1210 **483** 5d. multicoloured 40 10

**484** Soldiers controlling Crowd with Flags

**1997.** 35th Anniv of Oargla Protest.
1211 **484** 5d. multicoloured 40 10

**485** Doves above Crowd with Flags

**1997.** 35th Anniv of Victory Day.
1212 **485** 5d. multicoloured 40 10

**486** "Ficaria verna"

**1997.** Flowers. Multicoloured.
1213 5d. Type **486** 50 20
1214 16d. Honeysuckle 1·20 70
1215 23d. Common poppy 1·80 1·00

**487** "No Smoking" Sign on Map

**1997.** World No Smoking Day.
1216 **487** 5d. multicoloured 40 10

**488** Crowd and Map

**1997.** Legislative Elections.
1217 **488** 5d. multicoloured 40 10

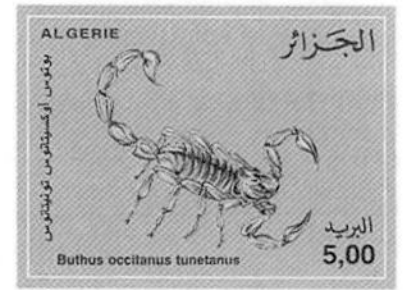

**489** "Buthus occitanus"

**1997.** Scorpions. Multicoloured.
1218 5d. Type **489** 45 15
1219 10d. "Androctonus australis" 80 45

**490** Crowd with Flags

**1997.** 35th Anniv of Independence. Multicoloured.
1220 5d. Type **490** 40 10
**MS**1221 70×80 mm. 10d. National flag behind doves and "35" between broken chain-link (25×36 mm) 1·10 85

**491** Zakaria

**1997.** 20th Death Anniv of Moufdi Zakaria (poet).
1222 **491** 5d. multicoloured 40 10

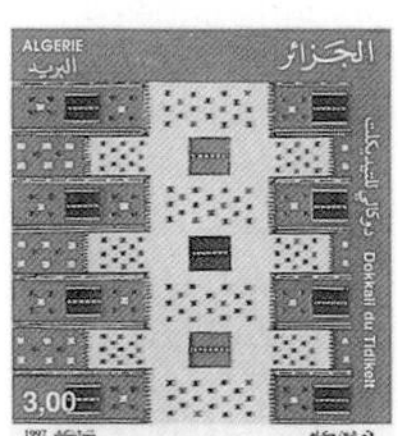

**492** Dokkali Design, Tidikelt

**1997.** Textiles. Multicoloured.
1223 3d. Type **492** 30 10
1224 5d. Tellis design, Aures 45 25
1225 10d. Bou Taleb design, M'Sila 80 40
1226 20d. Ddil design, Ait-Hichem 1·50 85

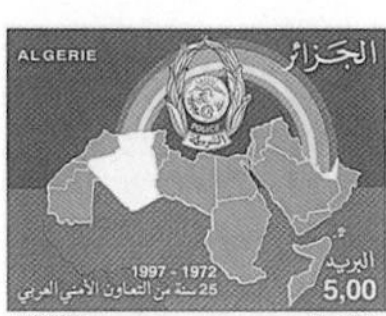

**493** Map, Emblem and Rainbow

**1997.** 25th Anniv of Pan-Arab Security Forces Organization.
1227 **493** 5d. multicoloured 40 15

**494** Packages and Express Mail Service Emblem

**1997.** World Post Day.
1228 **494** 5d. multicoloured 40 15

**495** Rising Sun on Map

**1997.** Local Elections.
1229 **495** 5d. multicoloured 40 15

**496** Tenes Lighthouse

**1997.** Lighthouses. Multicoloured.
1230 5d. Type **496** 50 25
1231 10d. Cap Caxine, Algiers (vert) 1·00 50

**497** Mail Plane and Mail Van

**1997.** 1st Anniv of Aeropostale.
1232 **497** 5d. multicoloured 50 15

**498** Variable Scallop

**1997.** Sea Shells. Multicoloured.
1233 5d. Type **498** 55 15
1234 10d. "Bolinus brandaris" 1·00 40
1235 20d. "Hinia reticulata" (vert) 1·90 80

**499** National Flag and Columned Facade

**1997.** Inauguration of Council of the Nation (upper parliamentary chamber).
1236 **499** 5d. multicoloured 40 15

**500** Flag, Ballot Box, Constitution and People

**1997.** Completion of Government Reform. Mult.
1237 5d. Type **500** (presidential election) 40 15
1238 5d. Constitution and torch (constitution referendum) 40 15
1239 5d. Ballot box and voting papers (elections to National Assembly (lower chamber of Parliament)) 40 15
1240 5d. Flag, sun and rose (local elections) 40 15
1241 5d. Flag and Parliament (elections to National Council (upper chamber)) 40 15

Nos. 1237/41 were issued together, se-tenant, forming a composite design.

**501** Exhibition Emblem

**1998.** "Expo 98" World's Fair, Lisbon. Multicoloured.
1242 5d. Type **501** 40 15
**MS**1243 80×70 mm. 24d. Mosaic of fishes (40×31 mm) Imperf 2·00 1·80

**502** Aerial Bombardment

**1998.** 40th Anniv of Bombing of Sakiet Sidi Youcef.
1244 **502** 5d. multicoloured 40 15

**503** Archives Building

**1998.** National Archives.
1245 **503** 5d. multicoloured 40 15

**504** Lalla Fadhma N'Soumeur

**1998.** International Women's Day.
1246 **504** 5d. multicoloured 35 15

**505** Players and Eiffel Tower

**1998.** World Cup Football Championship, France.
1247 **505** 24d. multicoloured 1·90 55

**506** View from Land

**1998.** Algiers Kasbah. Multicoloured.
1248 5d. Type **506** 40 30
1249 10d. Street 80 40
1250 24d. View from sea (horiz) 1·50 95

**507** Crescent and Flag

**1998.** Red Crescent.
1251 **507** 5d.+1d. red, green and black 45 25

**508** Battle Scene

**1998.** 150th Anniv of Insurrection of the Zaatcha.
1252 **508** 5d. multicoloured 40 15

**509** Parent and Child and Hand holding Rose

**1998.** International Children's Day. National Solidarity. Multicoloured.

| | | | |
|---|---|---|---|
| 1253 | 5d.+1d. Type **509** | 45 | 25 |
| 1254 | 5d.+1d. Children encircling emblem (horiz) | 45 | 25 |

**510** "Tourism and the Environment"

**1998.** Tourism. Multicoloured.

| | | | |
|---|---|---|---|
| 1255 | 5d. Type **510** | 40 | 15 |
| 1256 | 10d. Young tourists and methods of transportation (horiz) | 90 | 35 |
| 1257 | 24d. Taghit (horiz) | 1·80 | 95 |

**511** Map of North Africa and Arabia

**1998.** Arab Post Day.

| | | | | |
|---|---|---|---|---|
| 1258 | **511** | 5d. multicoloured | 90 | 10 |

**512** Interpol and Algerian Police Force Emblems

**1998.** 75th Anniv of Interpol.

| | | | | |
|---|---|---|---|---|
| 1259 | **512** | 5d. multicoloured | 40 | 10 |

**513** Provisional Government and State Flag

**1998.** 40th Anniv of Creation of Provisional Government of Algerian Republic.

| | | | | |
|---|---|---|---|---|
| 1260 | **513** | 5d. multicoloured | 40 | 15 |

**514** Arrows leading from Algeria around the World

**1998.** National Diplomacy Day.

| | | | | |
|---|---|---|---|---|
| 1261 | **514** | 5d. multicoloured | 40 | 10 |

**515** Dove and Olympic Rings

**1998.** 35th Anniv of Algerian Olympic Committee.

| | | | | |
|---|---|---|---|---|
| 1262 | **515** | 5d. multicoloured | 40 | 10 |

**516** Osprey

**1998.** Birds. Multicoloured.

| | | | |
|---|---|---|---|
| 1263 | 5d. Type **516** | 55 | 25 |
| 1264 | 10d. Audouin's gull | 1·10 | 45 |
| 1265 | 24d. Shag (vert) | 2·20 | 1·10 |
| 1266 | 30d. Common cormorant (vert) | 2·75 | 1·40 |

**517** Anniversary Emblem and Profiles

**1998.** 50th Anniv of Universal Declaration of Human Rights. Multicoloured.

| | | | |
|---|---|---|---|
| 1267 | 5d. Type **517** | 55 | 10 |
| 1268 | 24d. Anniversary emblem, dove and people | 2·00 | 90 |

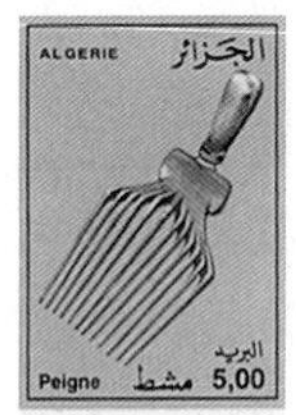
**518** Comb

**1999.** Spinning and Weaving Implements. Mult.

| | | | |
|---|---|---|---|
| 1269 | 5d. Type **518** | 50 | 25 |
| 1270 | 10d. Carding (horiz) | 90 | 40 |
| 1271 | 20d. Spindle | 1·90 | 90 |
| 1272 | 24d. Loom | 2·20 | 1·00 |

**519** Dove, Torch, Flag and Soldiers

**1999.** National Chahid Day.

| | | | | |
|---|---|---|---|---|
| 1273 | **519** | 5d. multicoloured | 40 | 15 |

**520** Pear

**1999.** Fruit Trees. Multicoloured.

| | | | |
|---|---|---|---|
| 1274 | 5d. Type **520** | 45 | 25 |
| 1275 | 10d. Plum | 80 | 45 |
| 1276 | 24d. Orange (vert) | 2·00 | 1·10 |

**521** Calligraphy

**1999.** Presidential Election.

| | | | | |
|---|---|---|---|---|
| 1277 | **521** | 5d. multicoloured | 40 | 15 |

**522** 14th-century Ceramic Mosaic, Tlemcen

**1999.** Crafts. Multicoloured.

| | | | |
|---|---|---|---|
| 1278 | 5d. Type **522** | 45 | 25 |
| 1279 | 10d. 11th-century ceramic mosaic, Kalaa des Beni Hammad | 80 | 40 |
| 1280 | 20d. Cradle (horiz) | 1·80 | 90 |
| 1281 | 24d. Table with raised rim (horiz) | 2·00 | 1·00 |

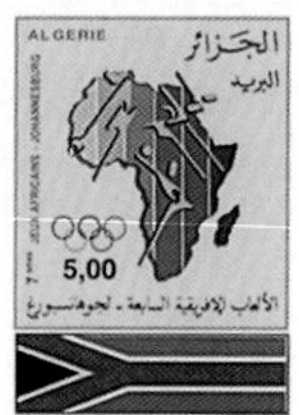
**523** Pictograms on Map of Africa and South African Flag

**1999.** 7th African Games, Johannesburg. Mult.

| | | | |
|---|---|---|---|
| 1282 | 5d. Type **523** | 45 | 25 |
| 1283 | 10d. Pictograms of athletes and South African flag (horiz) | 90 | 40 |

**524** Gneiss

**1999.** Minerals. Multicoloured.

| | | | |
|---|---|---|---|
| 1284 | 5d. Type **524** | 40 | 25 |
| 1285 | 20d. Granite | 1·60 | 90 |
| 1286 | 24d. Sericite schist | 2·00 | 1·10 |

**525** Emblem

**1999.** Organization of African Unity Summit, Algiers.

| | | | | |
|---|---|---|---|---|
| 1287 | **525** | 5d. multicoloured | 40 | 15 |

**526** Family and Map of Africa

**1999.** 40th Anniv of Organization of African Unity Convention on Refugees.

| | | | | |
|---|---|---|---|---|
| 1288 | **526** | 5d. multicoloured | 40 | 15 |

**527** Emblem and Police Officers

**1999.** Police Day.

| | | | | |
|---|---|---|---|---|
| 1289 | **527** | 5d. multicoloured | 90 | 15 |

**528** Linked Hands and "2000"

**1999.** International Year of Culture and Peace.

| | | | | |
|---|---|---|---|---|
| 1290 | **528** | 5d. multicoloured | 40 | 15 |

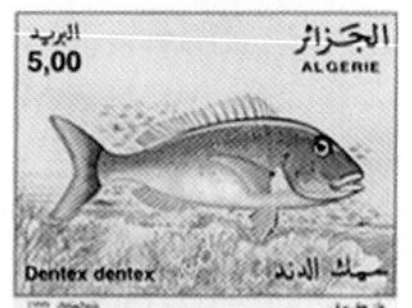
**529** Dentex Seabream

**1999.** Fishes. Multicoloured.

| | | | |
|---|---|---|---|
| 1291 | 5d. Type **529** | 55 | 25 |
| 1292 | 10d. Striped red mullet | 95 | 45 |
| 1293 | 20d. Pink dentex | 2·00 | 1·00 |
| 1294 | 24d. White seabream | 2·75 | 1·20 |

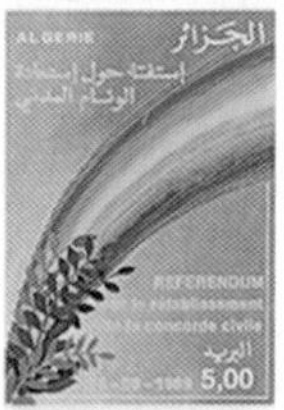
**530** Rainbow

**1999.** Referendum.

| | | | | |
|---|---|---|---|---|
| 1295 | **530** | 5d. multicoloured | 40 | 15 |

**531** Emblem and Rainbow

**1999.** 125th Anniv of Universal Postal Union. Mult.

| | | | |
|---|---|---|---|
| 1296 | 5d. Type **531** | 55 | 15 |
| 1297 | 5d. Globe, satellite and stamps | 55 | 15 |

**532** Woman's Face

**1999.** Rural Women's Day.
1298 **532** 5d. multicoloured 55 15

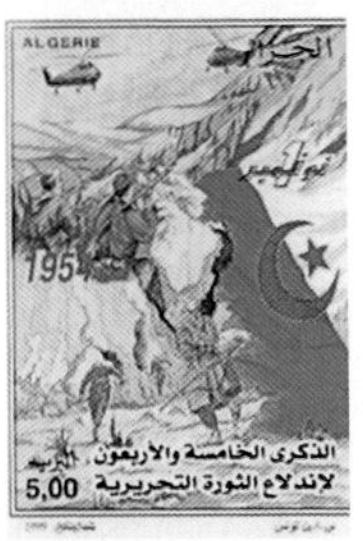
**533** Partisans and Helicopters

**1999.** 45th Anniv of Revolution. Multicoloured.
1299 5d. Type **533** 55 20
1300 5d. Partisans and fires 55 20

Nos. 1299/300 were issued together, se-tenant, forming a composite design.

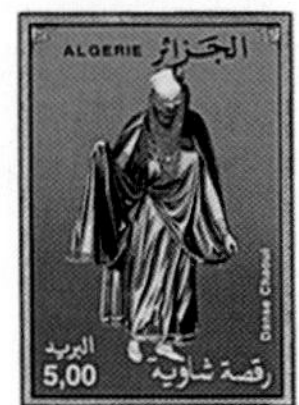
**534** Chaoui

**1999.** Folk Dances. Multicoloured.
1301 5d. Type **534** 55 25
1302 10d. Targuie 1·00 45
1303 24d. M'zab 2·00 1·10

**535** Doves

**2000.** New Millennium. Mult. Self-adhesive.
1304 5d. Type **535** (peace) 55 40
1305 5d. Plants and tree (environment) 55 40
1306 5d. Umbrella over ears of grain (food security) 55 40
1307 5d. Wind farm (new energy sources) 55 40
1308 5d. Globe and ballot box (democracy) 55 40
1309 5d. Microscope (health) 55 40
1310 5d. Cargo ship at quayside (commerce) 55 40
1311 5d. Space satellite, dish aerial, jet plane and train (communications) 55 40
1312 5d. Astronaut and lunar buggy on Moon (space) 55 40
1313 5d. Film cave paintings, mandolin and music notes (culture) 55 40
1314 5d. Outline of dove (peace) 55 40
1315 5d. Hand above flora and fauna (environment) 55 40
1316 5d. Space satellites, computer and printed circuits forming maps of Europe and Africa (communications) 55 40
1317 5d. Sun, clouds, flame and water (new energy sources) 55 40
1318 5d. Hand holding seedling (food security) 55 40
1319 5d. Staff of Aesculapius and heart (health) 55 40
1320 5d. Arrows around globe (communication) 55 40
1321 5d. Cave paintings, book, painting and violin (culture) 55 40
1322 5d. Parthenon and envelopes (democracy) 55 40
1323 5d. Space satellite, solar system, space shuttle and astronaut (space) 55 40

**536** Chaffinches

**2000.** Birds. Multicoloured.
1324 5d. Type **536** 50 35
1325 5d. Northern serin (horiz) 50 35
1326 10d. Northern bullfinch (horiz) 95 60
1327 24d. Eurasian goldfinch 2·50 1·40

**537** Emblem

**2000.** "EXPO 2000" World's Fair, Hanover.
1328 **537** 5d. multicoloured 50 30

**538** Sydney Opera House and Sports Pictograms

**2000.** Olympic Games, Sydney.
1329 **538** 24d. multicoloured 2·20 85

**539** Emblem

**2000.** Telethon 2000 (fundraising event).
1330 **539** 5d. multicoloured 50 25

**540** Crowd, Linked Hands and White Doves

**2000.** "Concorde Civile". Multicoloured.
1331 5d. Type **540** 50 15
1332 10d. Hands releasing doves (horiz) 95 40
1333 20d. Flag, doves and hands forming heart (horiz) 1·90 80
1334 24d. Doves and clasped hands above flowers 2·20 1·00

**541** Building

**2000.** National Library.
1335 **541** 5d. multicoloured 50 20

**542** Hand holding Blood Droplet

**2000.** Blood Donation Campaign.
1336 **542** 5d. multicoloured 50 25

**543** Lock

**2000.** Touareg Cultural Heritage. Multicoloured.
1337 5d. Type **543** 50 40
1338 10d. Lock (vert) 95 40

**544** Mohamed Racim (artist)

**2000.** Personalities. Multicoloured.
1339 10d. Type **544** 95 40
1340 10d. Mohammed Dib (writer) 95 40
1341 10d. Mustapha Kateb (theatre director) 95 40
1342 10d. Ali Maachi (musician) 95 40

**545** Cock-chafer

**2000.** Insects. Multicoloured.
1343 5d. Type **545** 50 30
1344 5d. Carpet beetle 50 30
1345 10d. Drugstore beetle 95 55
1346 24d. Carabus 2·50 1·20

**546** Jug

**2000.** Roman Artefacts, Tipasa. Multicoloured.
1347 5d. Type **546** 50 25
1348 10d. Vase 95 50
1349 24d. Jug 2·40 1·10

**547** *Limodorum abortivum*

**2000.** Orchids. Multicoloured.
1350 5d. Type **547** 50 25
1351 10d. *Orchis papilionacea* 95 50
1352 24d. *Orchis provincialis* 2·40 1·10

**548** Greylag Goose (*Anser anser*)

**2001.** Waterfowl. Multicoloured.
1353 5d. Type **548** 50 25
1354 5d. Avocet (*Recurvirostra avosetta*) (vert) 50 25
1355 10d. Eurasian bittern (*Botaurus stellaris*) (vert) 95 55
1356 24d. Western curlew (*Numenius arquata*) 2·50 1·10

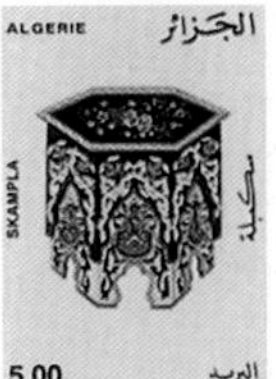
**549** Painted Table

**2001.** Traditional Crafts. Multicoloured.
1357 5d. Type **549** 50 25
1358 10d. Decorated shelf (horiz) 95 60
1359 24d. Ornate mirror 2·40 95

**550** Forest, Belezma National Park, Batna

**2001.** National Parks. Multicoloured.
1360 5d. Type **550** 50 25
1361 10d. Headland, Gouraya National Park, Bejaia (horiz) 95 45
1362 20d. Forest and mountains, Theneit el Had National Park, Tissemsilt (horiz) 1·90 80
1363 24d. El Tarf National Park 2·40 1·00

**551** St. Augustine as Child (statue)

**2001.** St. Augustine of Hippo Conference, Algiers and Annaba. Multicoloured.
1364 5d. Type **551** 50 25
1365 24d. 4th-century Christian mosaic (43×31 mm) 2·40 1·10

**552** Obverse and Reverse of Ryal Boudjou, 1830

**2001.** Coins. Multicoloured.
1366 5d. Type **552** 50 25
1367 10d. Obverse and reverse of Double Boudjou, 1826 95 45
1368 24d. Obverse and reverse of Ryal Drahem, 1771 2·40 1·00

**553** Emblem and Scouts

**2001.** National Scouts' Day.
1369 **553** 5d. multicoloured 50 30

**554** Child throwing Stones

**2001.** Intifida.
1370 **554** 5d. multicoloured 50 15

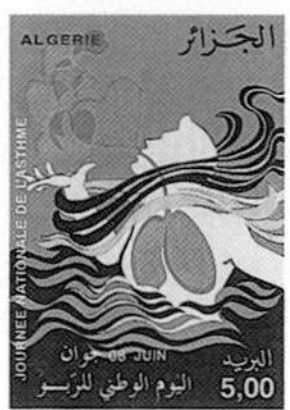
**555** Asthma Sufferer

**2001.** National Asthma Day.

| 1371 | **556** | 5d. multicoloured | 45 | 15 |
|---|---|---|---|---|

**556** Hopscotch

**2001.** Children's Games. Multicoloured.

| | | | |
|---|---|---|---|
| 1372 | 5d. Type **556** | 50 | 15 |
| 1373 | 5d. Jacks | 50 | 15 |
| 1374 | 5d. Spinning top | 50 | 15 |
| 1375 | 5d. Marbles | 50 | 15 |

**557** Runners

**2001.** 50th Anniv of Mediterranean Games. Multicoloured.

| | | | |
|---|---|---|---|
| 1376 | 5d. Type **557** | 45 | 15 |
| 1377 | 5d. Race winners and tile decoration | 45 | 15 |

**558** Emblem

**2001.** 15th World Festival of Youth and Students, Algiers.

| 1378 | **558** | 5d. multicoloured | 45 | 15 |
|---|---|---|---|---|

**559** Burning Lorry

**2001.** Freedom Fighters' Day.

| 1379 | **559** | 5d. multicoloured | 45 | 15 |
|---|---|---|---|---|

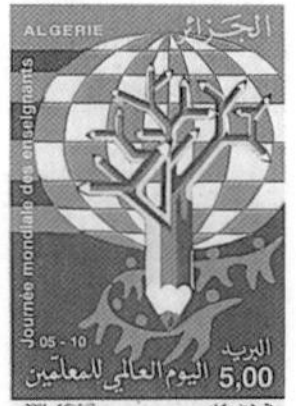
**560** Tree of Pencils

**2001.** Teacher's Day.

| 1380 | **560** | 5d. multicoloured | 45 | 15 |
|---|---|---|---|---|

**561** Children encircling Globe

**2001.** United Nations Year of Dialogue among Civilisations.

| 1381 | **561** | 5d. multicoloured | 45 | 15 |
|---|---|---|---|---|

**562** Dove and Explosion

**2001.** National Immigration Day. 40th Anniv of Demonstrations in Paris.

| 1382 | **562** | 5d. multicoloured | 45 | 20 |
|---|---|---|---|---|

**563** El Mokrani

**2001.** Resistance Fighters. Multicoloured.

| | | | |
|---|---|---|---|
| 1383 | 5d. Type **563** | 45 | 20 |
| 1384 | 5d. Cheikh Bouamama | 45 | 20 |

**564** Bab el Oued (flood damaged town)

**2001.** Flood Victims Relief Fund.

| 1385 | **564** | 5d.+5d. multicoloured | 90 | 40 |
|---|---|---|---|---|

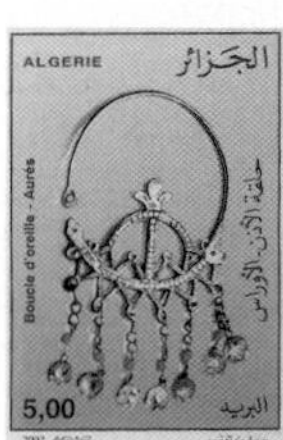
**565** Earring

**2002.** Silver Jewellery from Aures Region. Multicoloured.

| | | | |
|---|---|---|---|
| 1386 | 5d. Type **565** | 45 | 25 |
| 1387 | 5d. Fibula | 45 | 25 |
| 1388 | 24d. Pendant | 1·60 | 1·10 |

**566** Ball, Net and Goalkeeper

**2002.** World Cup Football Championship, Japan and South Korea. Multicoloured.

| | | | |
|---|---|---|---|
| 1389 | 5d. Type **566** | 45 | 25 |
| 1390 | 24d. Monk holding football (vert) | 1·80 | 1·60 |

**567** Flag, Doves and Soldiers

**2002.** 40th Anniv of Victory Day.

| 1391 | **567** | 5d. multicoloured | 45 | 30 |
|---|---|---|---|---|

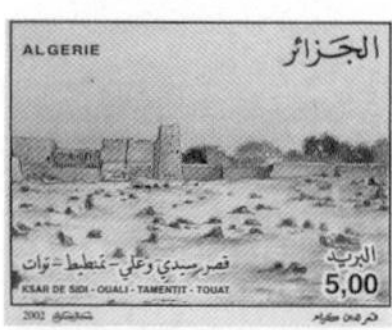
**568** Ksar Sidi Ouali Tamentit, Touat

**2002.** Fortified Castles. Multicoloured.

| | | | |
|---|---|---|---|
| 1392 | 5d. Type **568** | 45 | 30 |
| 1393 | 5d. Ksar Ighzar, Gourara | 45 | 30 |

**569** Basket, Ball and Players

**2002.** World Basketball Championship, Indianapolis, U.S.A.

| 1394 | **569** | 5d. multicoloured | 45 | 10 |
|---|---|---|---|---|

**570** Child and Table

**2002.** Children's Day. Multicoloured.

| | | | |
|---|---|---|---|
| 1395 | 5d. Type **570** | 45 | 10 |
| 1396 | 5d. Two girls | 45 | 10 |

**571** Book Illustration

**2002.** 14th Death Anniv of Mohamed Temmam (artist and musician). Multicoloured.

| | | | |
|---|---|---|---|
| 1397 | 10d. Type **571** | 90 | 40 |
| 1398 | 10d. Self-portrait | 90 | 40 |

**572** Anniversary Emblem

**2002.** 40th Anniv of Independence. Multicoloured.

| | | | |
|---|---|---|---|
| 1399 | 5d. Type **572** | 45 | 10 |
| 1400 | 24d. Flags and crowd | 1·30 | 1·00 |

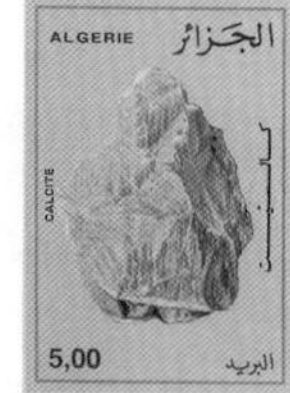
**573** Calcite

**2002.** Minerals. Multicoloured.

| | | | |
|---|---|---|---|
| 1401 | 5d. Type **573** | 30 | 10 |
| 1402 | 5d. Feldspar | 30 | 10 |
| 1403 | 5d. Galena (horiz) | 30 | 10 |
| 1404 | 5d. Conglomerate (pudding stone) (horiz) | 30 | 10 |

**574** Cherchell

**2002.** Lighthouses. Multicoloured.

| | | | |
|---|---|---|---|
| 1405 | 5d. Type **574** | 30 | 10 |
| 1406 | 10d. Cap de Fer | 60 | 40 |
| 1407 | 24d. Rachgoun island | 1·50 | 1·00 |

**575** Postal Emblem

**2002.** Re-organization of Algerian Posts.

| 1408 | **575** | 5d. multicoloured | 30 | 10 |
|---|---|---|---|---|

**576** Small Jug

**2002.** Pots. Multicoloured.

| | | | |
|---|---|---|---|
| 1409 | 5d. Type **576** | 30 | 10 |
| 1410 | 5d. Pot for cooking cous-cous | 30 | 10 |
| 1411 | 5d. Two-handled jar | 30 | 10 |
| 1412 | 5d. Oil lamp | 30 | 10 |

**577** Dove and Rainbow

**2002.** International Day of Tolerance.

| 1413 | **577** | 24d. multicoloured | 1·50 | 1·00 |
|---|---|---|---|---|

**578** *Venus verrucosa*

**2002.** Shells. Multicoloured.

| | | | |
|---|---|---|---|
| 1414 | 5d. Type **578** | 30 | 10 |
| 1415 | 5d. *Acanthocardia aculeate* | 30 | 10 |
| 1416 | 5d. *Xenophora crispa* | 30 | 10 |
| 1417 | 5d. *Epitonium commune* | 30 | 10 |

**579** *Eucalyptus globules*

2002. Medicinal Plants. Multicoloured.

| | | | |
|---|---|---|---|
| 1418 | 5d. Type **579** | 30 | 10 |
| 1419 | 10d. Mallow (*Malva sylvestris*) | 60 | 40 |
| 1420 | 24d. Laurel (*Laurus nobilis*) | 1·50 | 1·00 |

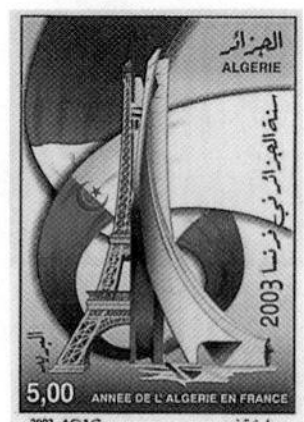

**580** Eiffel Tower, Paris and Martyr's Monument, Algiers

2003. Djazair 2003, Year of Algeria in France. Multicoloured.

| | | | |
|---|---|---|---|
| 1421 | 5d. Type **580** | 30 | 15 |
| 1422 | 24d. French and Algerian flags (horiz) | 1·50 | 1·00 |

**581** Emblem

2003. 10th Arab Games.

| | | | | |
|---|---|---|---|---|
| 1423 | **581** | 5d. multicoloured | 30 | 10 |

**582** El Maadjen, Relizane (oasis)

2003. International Year of Freshwater. Multicoloured.

| | | | |
|---|---|---|---|
| 1424 | 5d. Type **582** | 30 | 10 |
| 1425 | 10d. Traditional well, M'zab valley | 60 | 40 |
| 1426 | 24d. Kesria (irrigation), Timimoun | 1·50 | 1·00 |

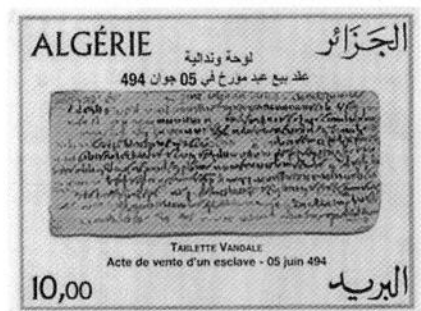

**583** Slave Sale Contract (5 June 494)

2003. Vandal Carved Tablets. Multicoloured.

| | | | |
|---|---|---|---|
| 1427 | 10d. Type **583** | 60 | 40 |
| 1428 | 24d. Mathematical chart (5 April 493) (vert) | 1·50 | 1·00 |

**584** Building Facade, Face and Books

2003. Student's Day.

| | | | | |
|---|---|---|---|---|
| 1429 | **584** | 5d. multicoloured | 30 | 10 |

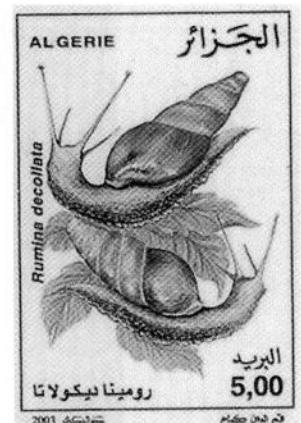

**585** *Rumina decollate*

2003. Snails. Multicoloured.

| | | | |
|---|---|---|---|
| 1430 | 5d. Type **585** | 30 | 10 |
| 1431 | 24d. *Helix aspera* | 1·50 | 1·00 |

**586** Candle, Map of Africa and Members' Flags

2003. 1st Anniv of African Union.

| | | | | |
|---|---|---|---|---|
| 1432 | **586** | 5d. multicoloured | 30 | 10 |

**587** *Ulva lactuca*

2003. Seaweeds. Multicoloured.

| | | | |
|---|---|---|---|
| 1433 | 5d. Type **587** | 30 | 10 |
| 1434 | 24d. *Gymnogongrus crenulatus* | 1·50 | 1·00 |

**588** Ploughing with Oxen

2003. Roman Mosaics. Multicoloured.

| | | | |
|---|---|---|---|
| 1435 | 5d. Type **588** | 30 | 10 |
| 1436 | 10d. Ulysses and the Sirens | 60 | 40 |
| 1437 | 24d. Hunting scene | 1·50 | 1·00 |

**589** Maouche Mohand Amokrane (founder) and Emblem

2003. 40th Anniv of Algerian Olympic Committee.

| | | | | |
|---|---|---|---|---|
| 1438 | **589** | 5d. multicoloured | 30 | 10 |

**590** Heart, Hand, Foot and Eye

2003. World Diabetes Awareness Day.

| | | | | |
|---|---|---|---|---|
| 1439 | **590** | 5d. multicoloured | 30 | 10 |

**591** Ruins

2003. Support for Earthquake Victims (21 May 2003).

| | | | | |
|---|---|---|---|---|
| 1440 | **591** | 5d.+5d. multicoloured | 60 | 40 |

**592** Doors

2003. Decorative Art. Multicoloured.

| | | | |
|---|---|---|---|
| 1441 | 5d. Type **592** | 30 | 15 |
| 1442 | 10d. Window | 60 | 40 |
| 1443 | 24d. Ceiling | 1·50 | 1·00 |

**593** Flags

2003. 45th Anniv of Algeria—China Diplomatic Relations.

| | | | | |
|---|---|---|---|---|
| 1444 | **593** | 5d. multicoloured | 30 | 10 |

**594** Hurdler

2004. Olympic Games, Athens. Multicoloured.

| | | | |
|---|---|---|---|
| 1445 | 5d. Type **594** | 30 | 10 |
| 1446 | 10d. Parthenon and hand holding Olympic torch | 60 | 40 |

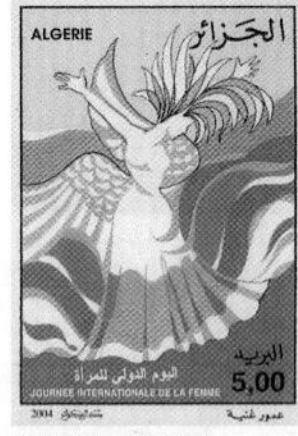

**595** Woman with Raised Arms

2004. Women's Day.

| | | | | |
|---|---|---|---|---|
| 1447 | **595** | 5d. multicoloured | 30 | 10 |

**596** Juba I

2004. Numidian Kings. Each brown, bronze and black.

| | | | |
|---|---|---|---|
| 1448 | 5d. Type **596** | 30 | 10 |
| 1449 | 5d. Juba II | 30 | 10 |
| 1450 | 5d. Micipsa | 30 | 10 |
| 1451 | 5d. Massinassa | 30 | 10 |
| 1452 | 5d. Jugurtha | 30 | 10 |

**597** Olive Tree

2004. Tree Day. Multicoloured.

| | | | |
|---|---|---|---|
| 1453 | 5d. Type **597** | 30 | 10 |
| 1454 | 10d. Date palm (vert) | 60 | 40 |

**598** Entrance to Presidential Palace

2004. Presidential Elections.

| | | | | |
|---|---|---|---|---|
| 1455 | **598** | 24d. multicoloured | 1·50 | 1·00 |

**599** Player catching Ball

2004. Centenary of FIFA (Federation Internationale de Football Association). Multicoloured.

| | | | |
|---|---|---|---|
| 1456 | 5d. Type **599** | 30 | 10 |
| 1457 | 24d. Anniversary emblem | 1·50 | 1·00 |

**600** Dromedary

2004

| | | | | |
|---|---|---|---|---|
| 1458 | **600** | 24d. multicoloured | 1·50 | 1·00 |

**601** Giving and Receiving Blood

2004. International Blood Donation Day.

| | | | | |
|---|---|---|---|---|
| 1459 | **601** | 5d. vermilion and black | 30 | 10 |

**602** Tradesmen

2004. Acquiring a Trade.

| | | | | |
|---|---|---|---|---|
| 1460 | **602** | 5d. multicoloured | 30 | 10 |

**603** Chess Pieces and Board

2004. 80th Anniv of World Chess Federation (FIDE).

| | | | | |
|---|---|---|---|---|
| 1461 | **603** | 5d. multicoloured | 30 | 10 |

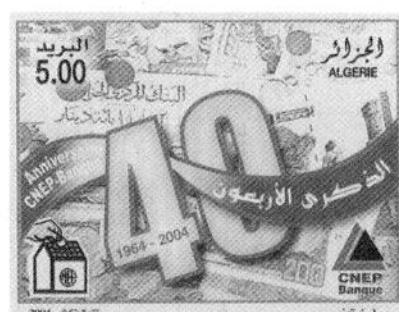


**604** Emblems and Currency

**2004.** 40th Anniv of CNEP Bank. Multicoloured.

| | | | |
|---|---|---|---|
| 1462 | 5d. Type **604** | 30 | 10 |
| 1463 | 24d. Harbour | 1·50 | 1·00 |

**605** Yellow Rose

**2004.** Roses. Multicoloured.

| | | | |
|---|---|---|---|
| 1464 | 15d. Type **605** | 1·30 | 65 |
| 1465 | 20d. Yellow rose (different) | 1·40 | 85 |
| 1466 | 30d. Orange rose | 1·80 | 1·30 |
| 1467 | 50d. Pink rose | 2·75 | 2·10 |

**606** Map and Flags

**2004.** 6th Pan African Conference, Algiers.

| | | | | |
|---|---|---|---|---|
| 1470 | **606** | 24d. multicoloured | 1·50 | 1·00 |

**607** In Tehaq Rock Formation

**2004.** Tourism. Sahara. Multicoloured.

| | | | |
|---|---|---|---|
| 1471 | 5d. Type **607** | 30 | 15 |
| 1472 | 24d. Ekanassay (vert) | 1·50 | 1·00 |

**608** TeleFood Emblem, Houses and Flowers

**2004.** World Food Day. TeleFood (UN food agency). Multicoloured.

| | | | |
|---|---|---|---|
| 1473 | 5d.+1d. Type **608** | 35 | 25 |
| 1474 | 5d.+1d. House and fruit trees | 35 | 25 |

**609** Group of Six

**2004.** 50th Anniv of Revolution. Multicoloured.

| | | | |
|---|---|---|---|
| 1475 | 15d. Type **609** | 1·30 | 65 |
| **MS**1476 70×80 mm. 30d. Emblem (30×40 mm) | | 1·80 | 1·80 |

**610** Satellite and Earth

**2004.** 2nd Anniv of Launch of D'ALSAT 1 Satellite.

| | | | | |
|---|---|---|---|---|
| 1477 | **610** | 30d. multicoloured | 1·80 | 1·30 |

**611** Rainbow and Plants

**2004.** Protection of the Environment.

| | | | | |
|---|---|---|---|---|
| 1478 | **611** | 15d. multicoloured | 1·10 | 60 |

**612** Rabah Bitat

**2004.** 4th Death Anniv of Rabah Bitat (politician).

| | | | | |
|---|---|---|---|---|
| 1479 | **612** | 15d. multicoloured | 1·10 | 60 |

**613** Wood Pigeon (*Columba palumbus*)

**2005.** Pigeons. Multicoloured.

| | | | |
|---|---|---|---|
| 1480 | 10d. Type **613** | 60 | 35 |
| 1481 | 15d. Rock dove (*Columba livia*) | 1·10 | 60 |

**614** *Echium australis*

**2005.** Flowers. Multicoloured.

| | | | |
|---|---|---|---|
| 1482 | 15d. Type **614** | 1·30 | 65 |
| 1483 | 30d. *Borago officinalis* | 1·80 | 1·30 |

**615** Eye and Hands

**2005.** National Day for the Disabled.

| | | | | |
|---|---|---|---|---|
| 1484 | **615** | 15d. multicoloured | 1·10 | 60 |

**616** Emblem

**2005.** Arab League Summit, Algeria (1485). 60th Anniv of Arab League (1486). Multicoloured.

| | | | |
|---|---|---|---|
| 1485 | 15d. Type **616** | 1·10 | 60 |
| 1486 | 30d. Emblem and "2005–1945" (vert) | 1·80 | 1·30 |

**617** Medersa D'Alger

**2005.** Medersa (seats of learning). Multicoloured.

| | | | |
|---|---|---|---|
| 1487 | 10d. Type **617** | 60 | 35 |
| 1488 | 15d. Medersa de Constantine | 1·10 | 60 |
| 1489 | 30d. Medersa de Tlemcen | 1·80 | 1·30 |

**618** Emblem

**2005.** World Intellectual Property Day.

| | | | | |
|---|---|---|---|---|
| 1490 | **618** | 15d. multicoloured | 1·10 | 60 |

**619** Workers and Hand holding Apple

**2005.** World Day for Safety and Health at Work.

| | | | | |
|---|---|---|---|---|
| 1491 | **619** | 15d. multicoloured | 1·10 | 60 |

**620** "60" and Dove

**2005.** 60th Anniv of Massacre.

| | | | | |
|---|---|---|---|---|
| 1492 | **620** | 15d. multicoloured | 1·10 | 60 |

**621** Medal and Stylized Sports

**2005.** 15th Mediterranean Games, Almeria. Multicoloured.

| | | | |
|---|---|---|---|
| 1493 | 15d. Type **621** | 1·10 | 60 |
| 1494 | 30d. Emblem (horiz) | 1·80 | 1·30 |

**622** Lakhdar Ben Khlouf

**2005.** Poets. Multicoloured.

| | | | |
|---|---|---|---|
| 1495 | 10d. Type **622** | 60 | 35 |
| 1496 | 15d. Ben M'sayeb | 1·10 | 60 |
| 1497 | 20d. Si Mohand Ou M'Hand | 1·40 | 85 |
| 1498 | 30d. Aissa El Djermouni | 1·80 | 1·30 |

**623** Children

**2005.** International Day against Drug Abuse.

| | | | | |
|---|---|---|---|---|
| 1499 | **623** | 15d. multicoloured | 1·10 | 60 |

**624** Student and Soldiers

**2005.** 50th Anniv of UGEMA (General Union of the Algerian Moslem Students).

| | | | | |
|---|---|---|---|---|
| 1500 | **624** | 15d. multicoloured | 1·10 | 60 |

**625** Cheetah

**2005.** Cheetah (inscr "Guepard"). Multicoloured.

| | | | |
|---|---|---|---|
| 1501 | 15d. Type **625** | 1·10 | 60 |
| 1502 | 30d. Standing | 1·80 | 1·30 |

**626** Emblem

**2005.** World Information Society Summit, Tunis.

| | | | | |
|---|---|---|---|---|
| 1503 | **626** | 15d. multicoloured | 1·10 | 60 |

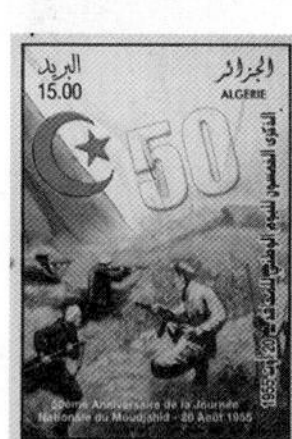


**627** "50" and Soldiers

**2005.** 50th Anniv of Uprising.

| | | | | |
|---|---|---|---|---|
| 1504 | **627** | 15d. multicoloured | 1·10 | 60 |

**628** Phare Fort

**2005.** Forts. Multicoloured.

| | | | |
|---|---|---|---|
| 1505 | 10d. Type **628** | 60 | 35 |
| 1506 | 15d. Cap Matifou | 1·10 | 60 |
| 1507 | 30d. Santa Cruz | 1·80 | 1·30 |

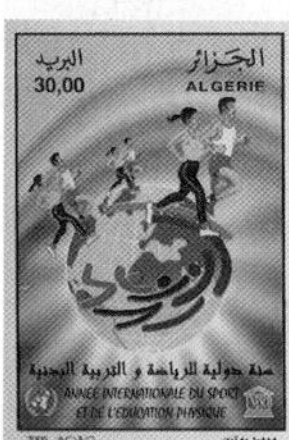


**629** Emblem and Runners

**2005.** International Year of Sports Education.

| | | | | |
|---|---|---|---|---|
| 1508 | **629** | 30d. multicoloured | 1·80 | 1·30 |

**630** Clasped Hands

**2005.** National Reconciliation.

| | | | | |
|---|---|---|---|---|
| 1509 | **630** | 15d. multicoloured | 1·10 | 60 |

**631** Flag

**2005.** Referendum.

| | | | | |
|---|---|---|---|---|
| 1510 | **631** | 15d. multicoloured | 1·10 | 60 |

**632** Flag, Emblem and Buildings

**2005.** Recovery of National Sovereignty.

| | | | | |
|---|---|---|---|---|
| 1511 | **632** | 30d. multicoloured | 1·80 | 1·30 |

**633** Saddle

**2005.** Emir Abdelkader's Possessions. Multicoloured.

| | | | |
|---|---|---|---|
| 1512 | 15d. Type **633** | 1·10 | 60 |
| 1513 | 30d. Boots | 1·80 | 1·30 |
| 1514 | 40d. Jacket (vert) | 2·40 | 1·70 |
| 1515 | 50d. Seal (vert) | 2·75 | 2·10 |

**634** Miguel de Cervantes

**2005.** Miguel de Cervantes Saavedra (writer) Commemoration.

| | | | | |
|---|---|---|---|---|
| 1516 | **634** | 30d. multicoloured | 1·80 | 1·30 |

**635** Amputee

**2005.** Anti-Personnel Mine Destruction Campaign.

| | | | | |
|---|---|---|---|---|
| 1517 | **635** | 30d. multicoloured | 1·80 | 1·30 |

**636** Emblem

**2005.** International AIDS Awareness Day.

| | | | | |
|---|---|---|---|---|
| 1518 | **636** | 30d. multicoloured | 1·80 | 1·30 |

**637** Ptolemy

**2005.** Kings. Multicoloured.

| | | | |
|---|---|---|---|
| 1519 | 15d. Type **637** | 1·10 | 60 |
| 1520 | 30d. Syphax | 1·80 | 1·30 |

**638** Building Facade

**2006.** Posts.

| | | | | |
|---|---|---|---|---|
| 1521 | **638** | 30d. multicoloured | 1·80 | 1·30 |

**639** *Ciconia ciconia*

**2006.** Waterside Birds. Multicoloured.

| | | | |
|---|---|---|---|
| 1522 | 10d. Type **639** | 60 | 35 |
| 1523 | 15d. *Ciconia nigra* | 1·10 | 60 |
| 1524 | 20d. *Platalea leucorodia* | 1·40 | 85 |
| 1525 | 30d. *Grus grus* | 1·80 | 1·30 |

**640** Skier

**2006.** Winter Olympic Games, Turin.

| | | | | |
|---|---|---|---|---|
| 1526 | **640** | 15d. multicoloured | 1·10 | 60 |

**641** Aissat Idir (founder)

**2006.** 50th Anniv of UGTA Trade Union.

| | | | | |
|---|---|---|---|---|
| 1527 | **641** | 15d. multicoloured | 1·10 | 60 |

**642** Ball and Globe

**2006.** World Cup Football Championship, Germany.

| | | | | |
|---|---|---|---|---|
| 1528 | **642** | 30d. multicoloured | 1·80 | 1·30 |

**643** Airport

**2006.** New Air Terminal, Algiers.

| | | | | |
|---|---|---|---|---|
| 1529 | **643** | 30d. multicoloured | 1·80 | 1·30 |

**645** Students

**2006.** 50th Anniv of Student's Day.

| | | | | |
|---|---|---|---|---|
| 1532 | **645** | 20d. multicoloured | 1·40 | 85 |

**646** Trees

**2006.** International Environment Day.

| | | | | |
|---|---|---|---|---|
| 1533 | **646** | 30d. multicoloured | 1·80 | 1·30 |

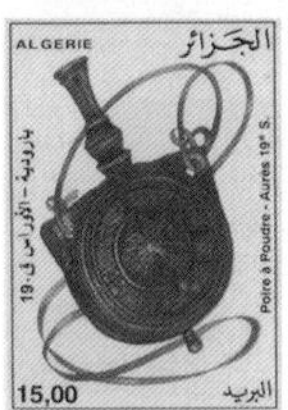
**647** Powder Holder

**2006.** Poire a Poudre (powder holders). Multicoloured.

| | | | |
|---|---|---|---|
| 1534 | 15d. Type **647** | 1·10 | 60 |
| 1535 | 20d. Powder holder (different) | 1·40 | 85 |

**648** Map

**2006.** 50th Anniv of La Soummam Congress.

| | | | | |
|---|---|---|---|---|
| 1536 | **648** | 20d. multicoloured | 1·40 | 85 |

**649** Emblem

**2006.** 16th Arab School Games.

| | | | | |
|---|---|---|---|---|
| 1537 | **649** | 30d. multicoloured | 1·80 | 1·30 |

**649a** Hand holding Pencils

**2006.** Teacher's Day

| | | | | |
|---|---|---|---|---|
| 1537a | **649a** | 20d. multicoloured | 1·40 | 85 |

**649b** Inscr "Pistachier de l'Atlas"

**2006.** Fruiting Trees. Multicoloured.

| | | | |
|---|---|---|---|
| 1537b | 20d. Type **649b** | 1·40 | 85 |
| 1537c | 30d. Inscr "Grenadier" | 1·80 | 1·30 |

**649c** Globe

**2006.** Sino-African Forum Summit, Beijing

| | | | | |
|---|---|---|---|---|
| 1537d | **649c** | 30d. multicoloured | 1·80 | 1·30 |

**650** Dunes and Oasis

**2006.** International Year of Deserts and Desertification.. Multicoloured.

| | | | | |
|---|---|---|---|---|
| 1538 | **650** | 15d. multicoloured | 1·10 | 60 |
| 1538a | | 15d. Ain Hammou-Tinerkouk-Adar | 1·10 | 60 |

**650a** Map and building

**2006.** First Anniv of Arab Transient Parliament.

| | | | | |
|---|---|---|---|---|
| 1538b | **650a** | 15d. multicoloured | 1·10 | 60 |

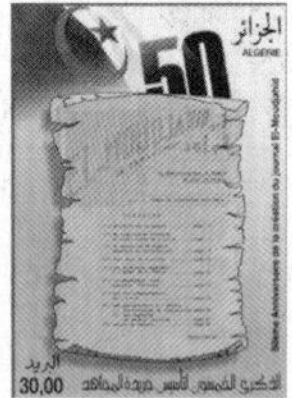
**650b** Early Edition

**2006.** 50th Anniv of El-Moudjohid (journal).

| | | | | |
|---|---|---|---|---|
| 1538c | **650b** | 30d. multicoloured | 1·80 | 1·30 |

**650c** Desalination Plant

**2006.** Desalination Plant

| | | | | |
|---|---|---|---|---|
| 1538d | **650c** | 20d. multicoloured | 1·40 | 85 |

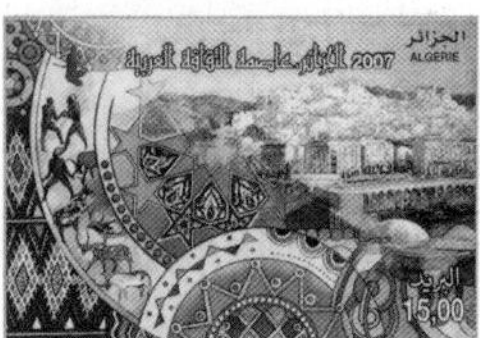
**651** Traditional Designs

**2007.** Algiers-Arab Cultural Capital-2007. Mult.

| | | | |
|---|---|---|---|
| 1539 | 15d. Type **651** | 1·10 | 60 |
| 1540 | 30d. "2007" | 1·80 | 1·30 |

**652** L'ilot d'Arzew

**2007.** Lighthouses. Multicoloured.

| | | | |
|---|---|---|---|
| 1541 | 15d. Type **652** | 1·10 | 60 |
| 1542 | 20d. Cap Sigli | 1·40 | 85 |
| 1543 | 38d. Ras-Afia | 2·20 | 1·50 |

**653** Women

**2007.** Development of Women's Employment.
1544 **653** 15d. multicoloured 1·10 60

**653a** Mohamed Ameziane Belhaddad

**2007.** Mohamed Ameziane Belhaddad Commemoration.
1545 **653a** 15d. multicoloured 1·10 60

**654** Ksar de Kenadsa

**2007.** Cultural Heritage. Multicoloured.
1546 15d. Type **654** 1·10 60
1547 15d. Ksar de Temacine (vert) 1·10 60

**655** Emblem, Map and 'JEUX AFRO-ASIATIQUES D'ALGER'

**2007.** Sport Events in Algiers. Multicoloured.
1548 15d. Type **655** 1·10 60
1549 15d. Emblem, map and 'ALL AFRICAN GAMES' (vert) 1·10 60

**656** Count Landon's Garden, Biskra

**2007.** Gardens. Multicoloured.
1550 15d. Type **656** 1·10 60
1551 20d. Ibn Badis garden, Oran 1·40 85
1552 38d. Jardin d' Essai du Hamma, Algiers 2·20 1·50

**657** Theatre de Setif

**2007.** Theatres. Multicoloured.
1553 15d. Type **657** 1·10 60
1554 15d. Theatre d'Oranen, Oran 1·10 60
1555 20d. Theatre de Annaba (*horiz*) 1·40 85
1555a 38d. Theatre d'Algers 2·20 1·50

**658** Demonstrators

**2007.** 45th Anniv of Festival of Independence and Youth. Multicoloured.
1556 15d. Type **658** 1·10 60
**MS**1557 60×77 mm. 20d. Satellite, computer and inkwell. Imperf 1·40 1·40

**659** Bottle

**2007.** Ceramics. Multicoloured.
1558 15d. Type **659** 1·10 60
1559 15d. Two handled jug 1·10 60
1560 20d. Censer 1·40 85
1561 38d. Oil lamp (horiz) 2·20 1·50

**660** Emblem

**2007.** 45th Anniv of National Police. Multicoloured.
1562 15d. Type **660** 1·10 60
1563 38d. Policeman and patrol vehicle 2·20 1·50

**661** Hyena

**2007.** Endangered Species. Multicoloured.
1564 15d. Type **661** 1·10 60
1565 38d. White-tailed red fox 2·20 1·50

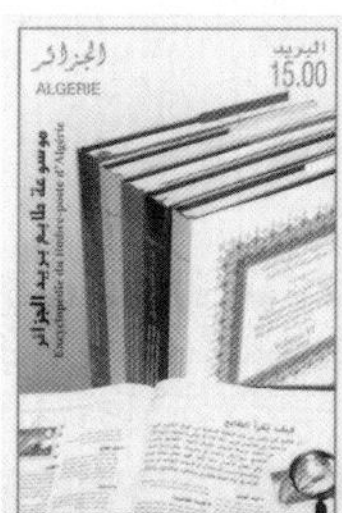


**662** Encyclopaedia of Algerian Postage Stamps

**2007**
1566 **662** 15d. multicoloured 1·10 60

**663** Ahmed Bey

**2007.** Ahmed Bey (resistance fighter) Commemoration.
1567 **663** 15d. multicoloured 1·10 60

**664** Emblem

**2007.** National Artisans' Day.
1568 **664** 15d. multicoloured 1·10 60

**665** Nile Tilapia

**2007.** Nile Tilapia (Oreochromis niloticus).
1569 **665** 15d. multicoloured 1·10 60

**666** Abd el-kader

**2007.** Birth Bicentenary of Abd al-Qadir al-Jaza'iri (Abd el-kader) (Islamic scholar, Sufi, political and military leader). Sheet 158×108 mm containing T 666 and similar vert designs.
**MS**1570 15d. Type **666**; 15d. Facing left; 38d. Wearing medals and belt 3·25 3·25

**667** Emblem

**2008.** Census.
1571 **667** 15d. multicoloured 1·10 60

**668** Doves and Emblem

**2008.** 50th Anniv of Bombing of Sakiet Sid Youcef, Tunisia.
1572 **668** 15d. multicoloured 1·10 60

A stamp of a similar design was issued by Tunisia.

**669** Ain de la Grande Rue

**2008.** Fountains. Sheet 110×90 mm containing T 669 and similar vert designs. Multicoloured.
**MS**1573 10d. Type **669**; 15d. Ain Bir Djebbah; 20d. Ain Sidi Abdellah; 38d. Ain bir Chebana 5·00 5·00

**670** Issakarassen Wetland, Tamanrasset

**2008.** Zaragoza 2008 International Water and Sustainable Development Exhibition. Sheet 110×90 mm containing T 670 and similar vert designs. Multicoloured.
**MS**1574 10d. Type **670**; 15d. Reghaia wetland; 20d. Guerbes wetland, Skikda; 38d. Emblem 2·75 2·75

**671** '50'

**2008.** 50th Anniv of National Liberation Front Football Team. Sheet 158×108 mm.
**MS**1575 multicoloured 2·30 2·30

**672** Redha Houhou

**2008.** Writers. Multicoloured (background colour given).
1576 15d. Type **672** (green) 95 50
1577 15d. Abdelhamid Benhadouga (magenta) 95 50
1578 15d. Malek Bennabi (brown) 95 50
1579 15d. Kateb Yacine (blue) 95 50

It has been reported that No. 1577 (Abdelhamid Benhadouga) has been withdrawn by Algeria Posts due to a design error.

**672a** Fencing

**2008.** Olympic Games, Beijing. Multicoloured.
1580 15d. Type **672a** 95 50
1581 15d. Wrestling 95 50

**673** Boy with Balloons

**2008.** Children and New Technologies.
1582 **673** 15d. multicoloured 95 50

**674** *Self Portrait*

**2008.** Art from National Museums. 10th Death Anniv of Baya Mahieddine (artist). Sheet 88×80 mm containing T 674 and similar horiz design. Multicoloured.
**MS**1583 15d. Type **674**; 38d. *Femme et oiseau en cage* 3·25 3·25

**675** Gare d'Alger

**2008.** Stations. Multicoloured.
1584 10d. Type **675** 60 35
1585 15d. Gare de Constantine 95 50
1586 20d. Gare d'Oran 1·25 65
1587 38d. Gare de Skikda 2·30 2·10

676 Ferhat Abbas

**2008.** Ferhat Abbas (political leader) Commemoration.

| | | | | |
|---|---|---|---|---|
| 1588 | **676** | 15d. multicoloured | 95 | 50 |

677 Script

**2008.** National Anthem.

| | | | | |
|---|---|---|---|---|
| 1589 | **677** | 15d. multicoloured | 95 | 50 |

678 Emblem

**2008.** Government Postage Stamp Printers' Association Conference.

| | | | | |
|---|---|---|---|---|
| 1590 | **678** | 15d. multicoloured | 95 | 50 |

679 Arms

**2008.** National Army.

| | | | | |
|---|---|---|---|---|
| 1591 | **679** | 15d. multicoloured | 95 | 50 |

680 Pont de Sidi M'Cid, Constantine

**2008.** Bridges. Sheet 110×88 mm containing T 680 and similar horiz designs. Multicoloured.

| | | | |
|---|---|---|---|
| **MS**1592 | 10d. Type **680**; 15d. Pont de Sidi Rached; 20d. Pont d'El Knatara; 38d. Pont de la Medersa | 5·00 | 5·00 |

681 Tebessa

**2008.** Towns. Multicoloured.

| | | | |
|---|---|---|---|
| 1593 | 10d. Type **681** | 60 | 35 |
| 1594 | 15d. Saida | 95 | 50 |
| 1595 | 20d. Miliana | 1·25 | 65 |
| 1596 | 38d. Biskra | 2·30 | 2·10 |

682 Globe and Flags

**2008.** 50th Anniv of Algeria–China Diplomatic Relations.

| | | | | |
|---|---|---|---|---|
| 1597 | **682** | 15d. multicoloured | 95 | 50 |

683 Emblem

**2008.** 60th Anniv of Anniv of Declaration of Human Rights.

| | | | | |
|---|---|---|---|---|
| 1598 | **683** | 15d. multicoloured | 95 | 50 |

684 Louis Braille and Alphabets

**2009.** Birth Bicentenary of Louis Braille (inventor of Braille writing for the blind).

| | | | | |
|---|---|---|---|---|
| 1599 | **684** | 15d. multicoloured | 95 | 50 |

685 Abderrahmene's Mausoleum, Algers

**2009.** Islamic Heritage. Mausoleums. Multicoloured.

| | | | |
|---|---|---|---|
| 1600 | 15d. Type **685** | 95 | 50 |
| 1601 | 20d. Ibrahim El Atteuf, Mausoleum (horiz) | 1·25 | 65 |

686 Figures

**2009.** National Day of Disabled Persons. Multicoloured.

| | | | |
|---|---|---|---|
| 1602 | 15d. Type **686** | 95 | 50 |
| 1603 | 20d. Emblems | 1·25 | 65 |

687 Polar Map and Hands enclosing Snowflake

**2009.** Preserve Polar Regions and Glaciers.

| | | | | |
|---|---|---|---|---|
| 1604 | **687** | 38d. multicoloured | 2·30 | 1·10 |

688 Emblem

**2009.** Presidential Elections.

| | | | | |
|---|---|---|---|---|
| 1605 | **688** | 15d. multicoloured | 95 | 50 |

689 Wooden Shoes

**2009.** Museum Exhibits. Multicoloured.

| | | | |
|---|---|---|---|
| 1606 | 15d. Type **689** | 95 | 50 |
| 1607 | 20d. Silver brooch fragment | 1·20 | 65 |
| 1608 | 30d. 19th-century waistcoat | 1·90 | 1·00 |

690 Students and University Building

**2009.** Centenary of Universite d'Alger (university).

| | | | | |
|---|---|---|---|---|
| 1609 | **690** | 15d. multicoloured | 95 | 50 |

691 Silver Fibulae

**2009.** Jewellery.

| | | | |
|---|---|---|---|
| 1610 | 1d. dull green | 10 | 10 |
| 1611 | 5d. pale brown-purple | 30 | 20 |
| 1612 | 9d. bright reddish violet | 50·00 | 30·00 |
| 1613 | 10d. olive-sepia | 60 | 35 |

DESIGNS: 1d. Type **691**; 5d. Collar with amulets; 9d. Pectoral ornament; 10d. Circular brooch.

692 Digital Code, World Map and Children on Crossing

**2009.** Protection for Children using the Internet.

| | | | | |
|---|---|---|---|---|
| 1614 | **692** | 15d. multicoloured | 95 | 50 |

693 Windsurfing

**2009.** Mediterranean Games. Multicoloured.

| | | | |
|---|---|---|---|
| 1615 | 15d. Type **693** | 95 | 50 |
| 1616 | 20d. Show jumping (horiz) | 1·20 | 65 |

694 Madaure

**2009.** Roman Sites and Monuments. Multicoloured.

| | | | |
|---|---|---|---|
| 1617 | 15d. Type **694** | 95 | 50 |
| 1618 | 20d. Khemissa | 1·20 | 65 |
| 1619 | 30d. Theatre, Guelma | 1·90 | 1·00 |

695 Symbols of Culture

**2009.** Pan African Cultural Festival, Algiers. Multicoloured.

| | | | |
|---|---|---|---|
| 1620 | 15d. Type **695** | 95 | 50 |
| 1621 | 20d. Map of Africa as design | 1·20 | 65 |

696 Symbols of Youth Development

**2009.** Algerian Youth. Multicoloured.

| | | | |
|---|---|---|---|
| 1622 | 15d. Type **696** | 95 | 50 |
| 1623 | 20d. Heart, national flag and dove | 1·20 | 65 |

697 '40'

**2009.** 40th Anniv of SONELGAZ.

| | | | | |
|---|---|---|---|---|
| 1624 | **697** | 15d. multicoloured | 95 | 50 |

698 Hand and Upturned Car

**2009.** Road Safety Campaign.

| | | | | |
|---|---|---|---|---|
| 1625 | **698** | 15d. multicoloured | 95 | 50 |

699 Bouharoun Fishing Port

**2009.** Fishing Ports. Multicoloured.

| | | | |
|---|---|---|---|
| 1626 | 15d. Type **699** | 95 | 50 |
| 1627 | 20d. Beni Saf | 1·20 | 65 |
| 1628 | 30d. Stora | 1·90 | 1·00 |

**700** Assistance

**2009.** Protection for the Elderly.

| | | | | |
|---|---|---|---|---|
| 1629 | **700** | 15d. multicoloured | 95 | 50 |

**701** Symbols of Armed Forces

**2009.** National Army.

| | | | | |
|---|---|---|---|---|
| 1630 | **701** | 15d. multicoloured | 90 | 50 |

**702** Women picking Olives

**2009.** Olive Cultivation. Multicoloured.

| | | | |
|---|---|---|---|
| 1631 | 15d. Type **702** | 95 | 50 |
| 1632 | 20d. Pressing olives (vert) | 1·20 | 65 |

**703** *La fée colombe*

**2009.** Popular Tales. Multicoloured.

| | | | |
|---|---|---|---|
| 1633 | 15d. Type **703** | 95 | 50 |
| 1634 | 15d. *La rose rouge* | 95 | 50 |
| 1635 | 15d. *Loundja la fille de l'ogre* | 95 | 50 |
| 1636 | 15d. *Badra* | 95 | 50 |

**704** *Aquila chrysaetos* (golden eagle)

**2010.** Raptors. Multicoloured.

| | | | |
|---|---|---|---|
| 1637 | 15d. Type **704** | 95 | 50 |
| 1638 | 20d. *Falco biarmicus* (Lanner falcon) (vert) | 1·20 | 65 |
| 1639 | 30d. *Falco peregrinus* (peregrine falcon) (vert) | 1·90 | 1·00 |

**705** Victim, Blast Fallout and Radiation

**2010.** Victims of Nuclear Testing.

| | | | | |
|---|---|---|---|---|
| 1640 | **705** | 15d. multicoloured | 95 | 50 |

**706** Fort de l'Empereur (Bordj Moulay Hassan), Alger

**2010.** Forts. Multicoloured.

| | | | |
|---|---|---|---|
| 1641 | 15d. Type **706** | 95 | 50 |
| 1642 | 20d. Fort Gouraya, Bejaia | 1·20 | 65 |

**707** Family and Emblem

**2010.** Expo 2010, Shanghai. Multicoloured.

| | | | |
|---|---|---|---|
| 1643 | 15d. Type **707** | 95 | 50 |
| 1644 | 38d. China pavillion | 2·30 | 1·10 |

**708** Refinery and Conference Emblem

**2010.** International Conference on Natural Liquid Gas. Multicoloured.

| | | | |
|---|---|---|---|
| 1645 | 15d. Type **708** | 95 | 50 |
| 1646 | 20d. Hill fort, coast line and conference emblem (horiz) | 1·20 | 65 |

**709** Jules Rimet Trophy and Flags

**2010.** World Cup Football Championships, South Africa. Multicoloured.

| | | | |
|---|---|---|---|
| 1647 | 15d. Type **709** | 95 | 50 |
| 1648 | 15d. Algerian player and home crowd | 95 | 50 |
| **MS**1649 | 108×88 mm. 15d. ×2 Desert fox as footballer; Player and colours | 1·90 | 1·90 |

**710** Martyrs

**2010.** 65th Anniv of May 8th Massacre

| | | | | |
|---|---|---|---|---|
| 1650 | **710** | 15d. multicoloured | 95 | 50 |

**711** Singers

**2010.** L'Ahellil du Gourara

| | | | | |
|---|---|---|---|---|
| 1651 | **711** | 15d. multicoloured | 95 | 50 |

**712** Shrine

**2010.** Martyrs Shrine

| | | | | |
|---|---|---|---|---|
| 1652 | **712** | (-) multicoloured | 95 | 50 |

**713** Hands, Dove and Map

**2010.** Year of Peace and Security in Africa

| | | | | |
|---|---|---|---|---|
| 1653 | **713** | 15d. multicoloured | 95 | 50 |

**714** Caves of Gor Beni-Add

**2010.** Caves and Grottoes. Multicoloured.

| | | | |
|---|---|---|---|
| 1654 | 15d. Type **714** | 95 | 50 |
| 1655 | 15d. Ziama Mansouriah-Jijel Grotto | 95 | 50 |

**715** Anniversary Emblem

**2010.** 50th Anniv of Organization of Petroleum Exporting Countries. Multicoloured.

| | | | |
|---|---|---|---|
| 1656 | 15d. Type **715** | 95 | 50 |
| 1657 | 38d. Emblem and oil tanker | 2·30 | 1·10 |

**716** El Hanafi-Blida Mosque

**2010.** Mosques. Multicoloured.

| | | | |
|---|---|---|---|
| 1658 | 15d. Type **716** | 95 | 50 |
| 1659 | 20d. Ali Dib-Skida | 1·20 | 65 |
| 1660 | 30d. Nedroma Gran Mosque | 1·90 | 1·00 |

**717** Dates (inscr 'Degla Beida')

**2010.** Dates. Multicoloured.

| | | | |
|---|---|---|---|
| 1661 | 15d. Type **717** | 95 | 50 |
| 1662 | 15d. Inscr 'Akerbuch' | 95 | 50 |
| 1663 | 15d. Inscr 'Deglet Noir' (vert) | 95 | 50 |
| 1664 | 15d. Inscr 'Ghars' (vert) | 95 | 50 |

**718** Ceramic Candlestick

**2010.** Traditional Crafts. Multicoloured.

| | | | |
|---|---|---|---|
| 1665 | 15d. Type **718** | 95 | 50 |
| 1666 | 20d. Quanoun (musical instrument) | 1·20 | 65 |
| 1667 | 30d. Tuareg leather chest (horiz) | 2·30 | 1·10 |

**719** Ears of Corn

**2010.** Cereal

| | | | | |
|---|---|---|---|---|
| 1668 | **719** | 1d. light green | 20 | 15 |
| 1669 | **719** | 2d. blue | 35 | 25 |

**720** Cork Oak Tree

**2011.** International Year of Forests. Multicoloured.

| | | | |
|---|---|---|---|
| 1670 | 15d. Type **720** | 95 | 50 |
| 1671 | 20d. Carob | 1·20 | 65 |
| 1672 | 30d. Soapnut | 1·00 | 1·00 |
| 1673 | 38d. Argan | 2·30 | 1·10 |

### POSTAGE DUE STAMPS

**1926.** As Postage Due stamps of France, but inscr "ALGERIE".

| | | | | |
|---|---|---|---|---|
| D34 | **D11** | 5c. blue | 70 | 6·00 |
| D35 | **D11** | 10c. brown | 60 | 1·20 |
| D36 | **D11** | 20c. olive | 1·70 | 4·75 |
| D37 | **D11** | 25c. red | 1·40 | 7·25 |
| D38 | **D11** | 30c. red | 50 | 10 |
| D39 | **D11** | 45c. green | 2·50 | 7·75 |
| D40 | **D11** | 50c. purple | 25 | 35 |
| D41 | **D11** | 60c. green | 2·50 | 6·50 |
| D42 | **D11** | 1f. red on yellow | 55 | 95 |
| D249 | **D11** | 1f.50 lilac | 2·30 | 6·00 |
| D250 | **D11** | 2f. blue | 2·75 | 5·75 |
| D43 | **D11** | 2f. mauve | 1·10 | 3·00 |
| D44 | **D11** | 3f. blue | 85 | 1·80 |
| D251 | **D11** | 5f. red | 2·50 | 6·00 |
| D252 | **D11** | 5f. green | 4·00 | 8·25 |

**1926.** As Postage Due stamps of France, but inscr "ALGERIE".

| | | | | |
|---|---|---|---|---|
| D45 | **D19** | 1c. olive | 25 | 4·75 |
| D46 | **D19** | 10c. violet | 1·20 | 2·75 |
| D47 | **D19** | 30c. bistre | 80 | 15 |
| D48 | **D19** | 60c. red | 1·30 | 15 |
| D49 | **D19** | 1f. violet | 9·00 | 1·90 |
| D50 | **D19** | 2f. blue | 13·00 | 2·75 |

**1927.** Nos. D36, D39 and D37 surch.

| | | | | |
|---|---|---|---|---|
| D92 | **D11** | 60 on 20c. olive | 1·70 | 1·10 |
| D93 | **D11** | 2f. on 45c. green | 2·75 | 5·50 |
| D94 | **D11** | 3f. on 25c. red | 1·50 | 6·50 |

**1927.** Nos. D45/8 surch.

| | | | | |
|---|---|---|---|---|
| D95 | **D19** | 10c. on 30c. bistre | 4·25 | 13·00 |
| D96 | **D19** | 1f. on 1c. olive | 2·75 | 4·50 |
| D97 | **D19** | 1f. on 60c. red | 14·00 | 75 |
| D98 | **D19** | 2f. on 10c. violet | 9·75 | 42·00 |

**1942.** As 1926 issue, but without "RF".

| | | | | |
|---|---|---|---|---|
| D181 | **D11** | 30c. red | 2·20 | 8·25 |
| D182 | **D11** | 2f. mauve | 3·00 | 7·50 |

**1944.** No. 208 surch TAXE P. C. V. DOUANE 20Fr.

| | | | | |
|---|---|---|---|---|
| D230 | **38** | 20f. on 50f. red | 3·00 | 5·25 |

**1944.** Surch T 0.50.

| | | | | |
|---|---|---|---|---|
| D231 | **4** | 50c. on 20c. green | 1·50 | 5·25 |

**1947.** Postage Due Stamps of France optd ALGERIE.

| | | | |
|---|---|---|---|
| D283 | 10c. brown (No. D985) | 45 | 5·75 |
| D284 | 30c. purple (No. D986) | 45 | 5·75 |

D53

1947

| | | | | |
|---|---|---|---|---|
| D285 | **D53** | 20c. red | 45 | 6·50 |
| D286 | **D53** | 60c. blue | 75 | 7·00 |
| D287 | **D53** | 1f. brown | 45 | 4·50 |
| D288 | **D53** | 1f.50 olive | 1·50 | 8·25 |
| D289 | **D53** | 2f. red | 35 | 3·75 |
| D290 | **D53** | 3f. violet | 60 | 4·25 |
| D291 | **D53** | 5f. blue | 60 | 1·70 |
| D292 | **D53** | 6f. black | 60 | 3·75 |
| D293 | **D53** | 10f. purple | 1·50 | 1·30 |
| D294 | **D53** | 15f. myrtle | 3·00 | 6·50 |
| D295 | **D53** | 20f. green | 1·50 | 1·30 |
| D296 | **D53** | 30f. red | 5·75 | 6·25 |
| D297 | **D53** | 50f. black | 6·50 | 10·00 |
| D298 | **D53** | 100f. blue | 28·00 | 28·00 |

**1962.** Postage Due stamps of France optd EA and with bar obliterating "REPUBLIQUE FRANCAISE".

| | | | | |
|---|---|---|---|---|
| D391 | **D457** | 5c. mauve | 20·00 | 17·00 |
| D392 | **D457** | 10c. red | 20·00 | 17·00 |
| D393 | **D457** | 20c. brown | 20·00 | 17·00 |
| D394 | **D457** | 50c. green | 40·00 | 34·00 |
| D395 | **D457** | 1f. green | 60·00 | 55·00 |

The above also exist with larger overprint applied with handstamps.

**D107** Scales of Justice

1963

| | | | | |
|---|---|---|---|---|
| D411 | **D107** | 5c. red and olive | 10 | 10 |
| D412 | **D107** | 10c. olive and red | 10 | 10 |
| D413 | **D107** | 20c. blue and black | 50 | 30 |
| D414 | **D107** | 50c. brown and green | 1·10 | 75 |
| D415 | **D107** | 1f. violet and orange | 2·20 | 1·80 |

**1968.** No. D415 surch.

| | | | |
|---|---|---|---|
| D508 | 60c. on 1f. violet and orange | 80 | 60 |

**D200** Ears of Corn

1972

| | | | | |
|---|---|---|---|---|
| D603 | **D200** | 10c. brown | 10 | 10 |
| D604 | **D200** | 20c. brown | 10 | 10 |
| D605 | **D200** | 40c. orange | 25 | 10 |
| D606 | **D200** | 50c. blue | 30 | 10 |
| D607 | **D200** | 80c. brown | 65 | 30 |
| D608 | **D200** | 1d. green | 85 | 50 |
| D609 | **D200** | 2d. blue | 1·60 | 95 |
| D610 | **D200** | 3d. violet | 50 | 25 |
| D611 | **D200** | 4d. purple | 55 | 40 |

**D644** Post Office

**2006.** Postage Due.

| | | | | |
|---|---|---|---|---|
| D1530 | **D644** | 5d. blue | 15 | 10 |
| D1531 | **D644** | 10d. green | 20 | 10 |

Pt. 7

## ALLENSTEIN

A district of E. Prussia retained by Germany as the result of a plebiscite in 1920. Stamps issued during the plebiscite period.

100 pfennig = 1 mark.

**1920.** Stamps of Germany inscr "DEUTSCHES REICH" optd **PLEBISCITE OLSZTYN ALLENSTEIN.**

| | | | | |
|---|---|---|---|---|
| 1 | **17** | 5pf. green | 55 | 1·10 |
| 2 | **17** | 10pf. red | 55 | 1·10 |
| 3 | **24** | 15pf. violet | 55 | 1·10 |
| 4 | **24** | 15pf. purple | 7·50 | 12·50 |
| 5 | **17** | 20pf. blue | 55 | 1·40 |
| 6 | **17** | 30pf. black & orge on buff | 55 | 1·40 |
| 7 | **17** | 40pf. black and red | 55 | 1·10 |
| 8 | **17** | 50pf. black & pur on buff | 55 | 1·10 |
| 9 | **17** | 75pf. black and green | 55 | 1·10 |
| 10 | **18** | 1m. red | 2·10 | 4·25 |
| 11 | **18** | 1m.25 green | 2·10 | 4·25 |
| 12 | **18** | 1m.50 brown | 1·30 | 4·25 |
| 13b | **20** | 2m.50 red | 3·25 | 12·50 |
| 14 | **21** | 3m. black | 3·25 | 4·75 |

**1920.** Stamps of Germany inscr "DEUTSCHES REICH" optd **TRAITE DE VERSAILLES** etc. in oval.

| | | | | |
|---|---|---|---|---|
| 15 | **17** | 5pf. green | 55 | 1·10 |
| 16 | **17** | 10pf. red | 55 | 1·10 |
| 17 | **24** | 15pf. violet | 55 | 1·10 |
| 18 | **24** | 15pf. purple | 27·00 | 55·00 |
| 19 | **17** | 20pf. blue | 85 | 1·70 |
| 20 | **17** | 30pf. black & orge on buff | 55 | 1·10 |
| 21 | **17** | 40pf. black and red | 55 | 1·10 |
| 22 | **17** | 50pf. black & pur on buff | 55 | 1·10 |
| 23 | **17** | 75pf. black and green | 85 | 1·70 |
| 24 | **18** | 1m. red | 2·10 | 3·25 |
| 25 | **18** | 1m.25 green | 2·10 | 3·25 |
| 26 | **18** | 1m.50 brown | 1·60 | 3·25 |
| 27 | **20** | 2m.50 red | 3·75 | 8·50 |
| 28 | **21** | 3m. black | 2·30 | 3·25 |

Pt. 6

## ALSACE AND LORRAINE

Stamps used in parts of France occupied by the German army in the war of 1870 -71, and afterwards temporarily in the annexed provinces of Alsace and Lorraine

100 pfennig = 1 mark

1

1870

| | | | | |
|---|---|---|---|---|
| 1 | **1** | 1c. green | 75·00 | £130 |
| 3 | **1** | 2c. brown | 95·00 | £170 |
| 5 | **1** | 4c. grey | 95·00 | 95·00 |
| 8 | **1** | 5c. green | 65·00 | 12·50 |
| 10 | **1** | 10c. brown | 85·00 | 18·00 |
| 14 | **1** | 20c. blue | 85·00 | 15·00 |
| 16 | **1** | 25c. brown | £140 | 95·00 |

For 1940 issues see separate lists for Alsace and Lorraine under German Occupations.

Pt. 1

## ALWAR

A state of Rajputana, N. India. Now uses Indian stamps.

12 pies = 1 anna; 16 annas = 1 rupee

**1** Native Dagger

**1877.** Roul or perf.

| | | | |
|---|---|---|---|
| 1b | ¼a. blue | 5·50 | 1·10 |
| 5 | ¼a. green | 7·00 | 2·50 |
| 2c | 1a. brown | 3·25 | 1·50 |

Pt. 6, Pt. 9

## ANDORRA

An independent state in the Pyrenees under the joint suzerainty of France and Spain.

French Post Office
1931. 100 centimes = 1 franc.
2002. 100 cents = 1 euro.

Spanish Post Office
1928. 100 centimos = 1 peseta.
2002. 100 cents = 1 euro.

### FRENCH POST OFFICES

**1931.** Stamps of France optd ANDORRE.

| | | | | |
|---|---|---|---|---|
| F1 | **11** | ½c. on 1c. grey | 1·10 | 6·50 |
| F2 | **11** | 1c. grey | 1·20 | 1·70 |
| F3 | **11** | 2c. red | 1·60 | 8·00 |
| F4 | **11** | 3c. orange | 2·10 | 4·25 |
| F5 | **11** | 5c. green | 3·25 | 8·25 |
| F6 | **11** | 10c. lilac | 5·25 | 10·00 |
| F7 | **18** | 15c. brown | 9·00 | 9·75 |
| F8 | **18** | 20c. mauve | 14·50 | 15·00 |
| F9 | **18** | 25c. brown | 12·50 | 17·00 |
| F10 | **18** | 30c. green | 12·50 | 15·00 |
| F11 | **18** | 40c. blue | 13·50 | 23·00 |
| F12 | **15** | 45c. violet | 26·00 | 31·00 |
| F13 | **15** | 50c. red | 18·00 | 20·00 |
| F14 | **15** | 65c. green | 37·00 | 41·00 |
| F15 | **15** | 75c. mauve | 42·00 | 46·00 |
| F16 | **18** | 90c. red | 55·00 | 70·00 |
| F17 | **15** | 1f. blue | 60·00 | 70·00 |
| F18 | **18** | 1f.50 blue | 65·00 | 80·00 |
| F19 | **13** | 2f. red and green | 60·00 | 90·00 |
| F20 | **13** | 3f. mauve and red | £110 | £150 |
| F21 | **13** | 5f. blue and buff | £150 | £250 |
| F22 | **13** | 10f. green and red | £325 | £450 |
| F23 | **13** | 20f. mauve and green | £425 | £500 |

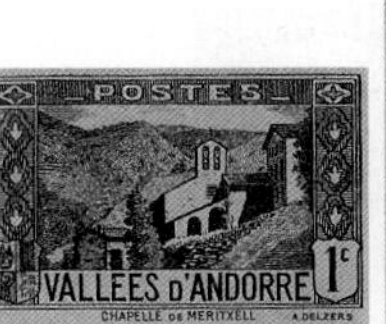
**F3** Our Lady's Chapel, Meritxell **F5** St. Michael's Church, Engolasters

1932

| | | | | |
|---|---|---|---|---|
| F24 | **F3** | 1c. slate | 75 | 2·75 |
| F25 | **F3** | 2c. violet | 1·10 | 2·30 |
| F26 | **F3** | 3c. brown | 1·20 | 2·50 |
| F27 | **F3** | 5c. green | 95 | 2·75 |
| F28 | **A** | 10c. lilac | 1·80 | 3·25 |
| F29 | **F3** | 15c. red | 2·75 | 3·50 |
| F30 | **A** | 20c. mauve | 13·50 | 17·00 |
| F31 | **F5** | 25c. brown | 5·75 | 7·50 |
| F32 | **A** | 25c. brown | 13·50 | 34·00 |
| F33 | **A** | 30c. green | 3·75 | 4·50 |
| F34 | **A** | 40c. blue | 10·50 | 9·25 |
| F35 | **A** | 40c. brown | 1·60 | 4·00 |
| F36 | **A** | 45c. red | 15·00 | 29·00 |
| F37 | **A** | 45c. green | 7·50 | 22·00 |
| F38 | **F5** | 50c. mauve | 16·00 | 17·00 |
| F39 | **A** | 50c. violet | 7·50 | 20·00 |
| F40 | **A** | 50c. green | 2·10 | 10·50 |
| F41 | **A** | 55c. violet | 32·00 | 70·00 |
| F42 | **A** | 60c. brown | 2·10 | 7·50 |
| F43 | **F5** | 65c. green | 70·00 | 75·00 |
| F44 | **A** | 65c. blue | 19·00 | 33·00 |
| F45 | **A** | 70c. red | 2·40 | 5·75 |
| F46 | **F5** | 75c. violet | 11·50 | 12·50 |
| F47 | **A** | 75c. blue | 5·25 | 17·00 |
| F48 | **A** | 80c. green | 28·00 | 70·00 |
| F49 | **B** | 80c. green | 1·70 | 6·25 |
| F50 | **B** | 90c. red | 9·50 | 9·25 |
| F51 | **B** | 90c. green | 7·50 | 15·00 |
| F52 | **B** | 1f. green | 34·00 | 23·00 |
| F53 | **B** | 1f. red | 32·00 | 34·00 |
| F54 | **B** | 1f. blue | 1·40 | 3·50 |
| F55 | **B** | 1f. 20 violet | 1·30 | 6·50 |
| F56 | **F3** | 1f. 25 mauve | 65·00 | 80·00 |
| F57 | **F3** | 1f.25 red | 8·00 | 20·00 |
| F58 | **B** | 1f.30 brown | 1·70 | 6·50 |
| F59 | **C** | 1f.50 blue | 26·00 | 37·00 |
| F60 | **B** | 1f.50 red | 1·10 | 6·50 |
| F61 | **B** | 1f.75 violet | £110 | £140 |
| F62 | **B** | 1f.75 blue | 60·00 | 75·00 |
| F63 | **B** | 2f. mauve | 10·50 | 23·00 |
| F64 | **F 3** | 2f. red | 2·10 | 8·50 |
| F65 | **F 3** | 2f. green | 1·20 | 8·50 |
| F66 | **F 3** | 2f.15 violet | 60·00 | 90·00 |
| F67 | **F 3** | 2f.25 blue | 10·50 | 30·00 |
| F68 | **F 3** | 2f.40 red | 1·40 | 6·50 |
| F69 | **F 3** | 2f.50 black | 12·50 | 36·00 |
| F70 | **F 3** | 2f.50 blue | 2·75 | 10·50 |
| F71 | **B** | 3f. brown | 25·00 | 41·00 |
| F72 | **F 3** | 3f. brown | 2·20 | 7·00 |
| F73 | **F 3** | 4f. blue | 1·60 | 6·25 |
| F74 | **F 3** | 4f.50 violet | 2·10 | 8·25 |
| F75 | **C** | 5f. brown | 1·80 | 7·00 |
| F76 | **C** | 10f. violet | 2·40 | 7·00 |
| F78 | **C** | 15f. blue | 1·60 | 4·00 |
| F79 | **C** | 20f. red | 2·10 | 3·75 |
| F81 | **A** | 50f. blue | 3·00 | 9·25 |

DESIGNS—HORIZ: A, St. Anthony's Bridge; C, Andorra la Vella. VERT: B, Valley of Sant Julia.

**1935.** No. F38 surch 20c.

| | | | | |
|---|---|---|---|---|
| F82 | **F5** | 20c. on 50c. purple | 16·00 | 29·00 |

**F9**

1936

| | | | | |
|---|---|---|---|---|
| F83 | **F9** | 1c. black | 55 | 3·25 |
| F84 | **F9** | 2c. blue | 55 | 3·25 |
| F85 | **F9** | 3c. brown | 55 | 3·25 |
| F86 | **F9** | 5c. red | 40 | 3·25 |
| F87 | **F9** | 10c. blue | 40 | 3·25 |
| F88 | **F9** | 15c. mauve | 3·25 | 5·25 |
| F89 | **F9** | 20c. green | 40 | 3·25 |
| F90 | **F9** | 30c. red | 75 | 7·00 |
| F91 | **F9** | 30c. black | 1·50 | 6·50 |
| F92 | **F9** | 35c. green | 60·00 | 90·00 |
| F93 | **F9** | 40c. brown | 1·10 | 6·25 |
| F94 | **F9** | 50c. green | 1·20 | 6·50 |
| F95 | **F9** | 60c. blue | 1·60 | 6·50 |
| F96 | **F9** | 70c. violet | 1·60 | 6·50 |

**F13** Andorra la Vella **F10**

**F14** Councillor Jaume Bonell

1944

| | | | | |
|---|---|---|---|---|
| F97 | **F10** | 10c. violet | 20 | 4·00 |
| F98 | **F10** | 30c. red | 20 | 4·00 |
| F99 | **F10** | 40c. blue | 40 | 4·00 |
| F100 | **F10** | 50c. red | 20 | 4·50 |
| F101 | **F10** | 60c. black | 40 | 4·00 |
| F102 | **F10** | 70c. mauve | 30 | 5·75 |
| F103 | **F10** | 80c. green | 20 | 5·75 |
| F104 | **F10** | 1f. blue | 1·10 | 2·40 |
| F105 | **D** | 1f. purple | 20 | 6·25 |
| F106 | **D** | 1f.20 blue | 20 | 6·25 |
| F107 | **D** | 1f.50 red | 20 | 6·25 |
| F108 | **D** | 2f. green | 20 | 4·00 |
| F109 | **E** | 2f.40 red | 20 | 4·00 |
| F110 | **E** | 2f.50 red | 4·25 | 7·00 |
| F111 | **E** | 3f. brown | 60 | 2·75 |
| F112 | **D** | 3f. red | 4·25 | 5·75 |
| F113 | **E** | 4f. blue | 55 | 6·25 |
| F114 | **E** | 4f. green | 1·10 | 7·50 |
| F115 | **D** | 4f. brown | 2·30 | 10·50 |
| F116 | **E** | 4f.50 brown | 60 | 5·75 |
| F117 | **F 13** | 4f.50 blue | 5·25 | 20·00 |
| F118 | **F 13** | 5f. blue | 55 | 6·25 |
| F119 | **F 13** | 5f. green | 1·40 | 6·50 |
| F120 | **E** | 5f. green | 3·25 | 11·50 |
| F121 | **E** | 5f. violet | 4·25 | 8·00 |
| F122 | **F 13** | 6f. red | 55 | 3·75 |
| F123 | **F 13** | 6f. purple | 55 | 5·75 |
| F124 | **E** | 6f. green | 3·25 | 7·50 |
| F125 | **F 13** | 8f. blue | 1·60 | 8·00 |
| F126 | **E** | 8f. brown | 1·10 | 3·50 |
| F127 | **F 13** | 10f. green | 40 | 5·75 |
| F128 | **F 13** | 10f. blue | 1·60 | 1·80 |
| F129 | **F 13** | 12f. red | 1·40 | 7·50 |
| F130 | **F 13** | 12f. green | 1·60 | 5·75 |
| F131 | **F 14** | 15f. purple | 65 | 6·50 |
| F132 | **F 13** | 15f. red | 85 | 3·50 |
| F133 | **F 13** | 15f. brown | 7·50 | 4·50 |
| F134 | **F 14** | 18f. blue | 3·25 | 12·00 |
| F135 | **F 13** | 18f. red | 12·50 | 26·00 |
| F136 | **F 14** | 20f. blue | 1·10 | 6·50 |
| F137 | **F 14** | 20f. violet | 3·25 | 10·00 |
| F138 | **F 14** | 25f. red | 3·75 | 10·50 |
| F139 | **F 14** | 25f. blue | 2·10 | 8·50 |
| F140 | **F 14** | 30f. blue | 21·00 | 29·00 |
| F141 | **F 14** | 40f. green | 3·25 | 9·25 |
| F142 | **F 14** | 50f. brown | 1·80 | 4·25 |

DESIGNS—HORIZ: D, Church of St. John of Caselles; E, House of the Valleys.

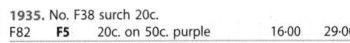

**F15** Chamois and Pyrenees

**1950.** Air.

| | | | | |
|---|---|---|---|---|
| F143 | **F15** | 100f. blue | £110 | £110 |

**F16** Les Escaldes

**1955**

| | | | | |
|---|---|---|---|---|
| F144 | **F16** | 1f. blue (postage) | 20 | 2·75 |
| F145 | **F16** | 2f. green | 55 | 2·10 |
| F146 | **F16** | 3f. red | 65 | 2·10 |
| F147 | **F16** | 5f. brown | 65 | 2·10 |
| F148 | - | 6f. green | 2·20 | 2·75 |
| F149 | - | 8f. red | 2·40 | 3·25 |
| F150 | - | 10f. violet | 4·25 | 2·75 |
| F151 | - | 12f. blue | 2·30 | 2·10 |
| F152 | - | 15f. red | 3·00 | 2·30 |
| F153 | - | 18f. blue | 2·75 | 3·75 |
| F154 | - | 20f. violet | 3·25 | 2·30 |
| F155 | - | 25f. brown | 3·50 | 4·00 |
| F156 | - | 30f. blue | 26·00 | 34·00 |
| F157 | - | 35f. blue | 13·50 | 14·50 |
| F158 | - | 40f. green | 35·00 | 55·00 |
| F159 | - | 50f. red | 4·25 | 4·50 |
| F160 | - | 65f. violet | 9·50 | 29·00 |
| F161 | - | 70f. brown | 9·25 | 22·00 |
| F162 | - | 75f. blue | 45·00 | 90·00 |
| F163 | - | 100f. green (air) | 10·50 | 15·00 |
| F164 | - | 200f. red | 21·00 | 23·00 |
| F165 | - | 500f. blue | 85·00 | 90·00 |

DESIGNS—VERT: 15f. to 25f. Gothic cross, Andorra la Vella; 100f. to 500f. East Valira River. HORIZ: 6f. to 12f. Santa Coloma Church; 30f. to 75f. Les Bons village.

**F21**

**F22** Gothic Cross, Meritxell

**1961**

| | | | | |
|---|---|---|---|---|
| F166 | **F21** | 1c. grey, blue and slate (postage) | 65 | 1·60 |
| F167 | **F21** | 2c. lt orge, blk & orge | 65 | 1·60 |
| F168 | **F21** | 5c. lt grn, blk & grn | 40 | 1·60 |
| F169 | **F21** | 10c. pink, blk & red | 45 | 45 |
| F170a | **F21** | 12c. yell, pur & grn | 2·20 | 4·50 |
| F171 | **F21** | 15c. lt bl, blk & bl | 75 | 1·60 |
| F172 | **F21** | 18c. pink, blk & mve | 1·40 | 3·25 |
| F173 | **F21** | 20c. lt yell, brn & yell | 80 | 55 |
| F174 | **F22** | 25c. blue, vio & grn | 1·10 | 1·10 |
| F175 | **F22** | 30c. pur, red & grn | 1·10 | 80 |
| F175a | **F22** | 40c. green and brown | 1·30 | 2·00 |
| F176 | **F22** | 45c. blue, ind & grn | 21·00 | 34·00 |
| F176a | **F22** | 45c. brown, bl & vio | 1·30 | 2·75 |
| F177 | **F22** | 50c. multicoloured | 2·75 | 2·75 |
| F177a | **F22** | 60c. brown & chestnut | 1·60 | 2·10 |
| F178 | **F22** | 65c. olive, bl & brn | 23·00 | 55·00 |
| F179 | **F22** | 85c. multicoloured | 23·00 | 40·00 |
| F179a | **F22** | 90c. green, bl & brn | 1·60 | 3·50 |
| F180 | **F22** | 1f. blue, brn & turq | 2·75 | 2·75 |
| F181 | - | 2f. green, red and purple (air) | 2·20 | 2·30 |
| F182 | - | 3f. purple, bl & grn | 2·40 | 2·50 |
| F183 | - | 5f. orange, pur & red | 4·00 | 4·00 |
| F184 | - | 10f. green and blue | 6·00 | 5·50 |

DESIGNS—As Type F **22**: 60c. to 1f. Engolasters Lake; 2f. to 10f. Incles Valley.

**F23** "Telstar" Satellite and part of Globe

**1962.** 1st Trans-Atlantic TV Satellite Link.

| | | | | |
|---|---|---|---|---|
| F185 | **F23** | 50c. violet and blue | 1·60 | 2·75 |

**F24** "La Sardane" (dance)

**1963.** Andorran History (1st issue).

| | | | | |
|---|---|---|---|---|
| F186 | **F24** | 20c. purple, mve & grn | 3·75 | 6·50 |
| F187 | - | 50c. red and green | 6·75 | 12·50 |
| F188 | - | 1f. green, blue & brn | 9·50 | 21·00 |

DESIGNS—LARGER (48½×27 mm): 50c. Charlemagne crossing Andorra. (48×27 mm): 1f. Foundation of Andorra by Louis le Debonnaire.

See also Nos. F190/1.

**F25** Santa Coloma Church and Grand Palais, Paris

**1964.** "PHILATEC 1964" International Stamp Exhibition, Paris.

| | | | | |
|---|---|---|---|---|
| F189 | **F25** | 25c. green, pur & brn | 1·60 | 3·25 |

**1964.** Andorran History (2nd issue). As Nos. F187/8, inscribed "1964".

| | | | | |
|---|---|---|---|---|
| F190 | | 60c. green, chestnut and brown | 11·50 | 32·00 |
| F191 | | 1f. blue, sepia and brown | 16·00 | 32·00 |

DESIGNS (48½×27 mm): 60c. "Napoleon re-establishes the Andorran Statute, 1806"; 1f. "Confirmation of the Co-government, 1288".

**F26** Virgin of Santa Coloma

**1964.** Red Cross Fund.

| | | | | |
|---|---|---|---|---|
| F192 | **F26** | 25c.+10c. red, green and blue | 21·00 | 38·00 |

**F27** "Syncom", Morse Key and Pleumeur-Bodou centre

**1965.** Centenary of I.T.U.

| | | | | |
|---|---|---|---|---|
| F193 | **F27** | 60c. violet, blue and red | 4·75 | 8·00 |

**F28** Andorra House, Paris

**1965.** Opening of Andorra House, Paris.

| | | | | |
|---|---|---|---|---|
| F194 | **F28** | 25c. brown, olive & bl | 1·10 | 2·30 |

**F29** Chair-lift

**1966.** Winter Sports.

| | | | | |
|---|---|---|---|---|
| F195 | **F29** | 25c. green, purple & bl | 1·30 | 3·25 |
| F196 | - | 40c. brown, blue & red | 2·10 | 4·00 |

DESIGN—HORIZ: 40c. Ski-lift.

**F30** Satellite "FR 1"

**1966.** Launching of Satellite "FR 1".

| | | | | |
|---|---|---|---|---|
| F197 | **F30** | 60c. blue, emer & grn | 2·10 | 4·25 |

**F31** Europa "Ship"

**1966.** Europa.

| | | | | |
|---|---|---|---|---|
| F198 | **F31** | 60c. brown | 3·50 | 6·25 |

**F32** Cogwheels

**1967.** Europa.

| | | | | |
|---|---|---|---|---|
| F199 | **F32** | 30c. indigo and blue | 4·25 | 5·75 |
| F200 | **F32** | 60c. red and purple | 5·50 | 10·50 |

**F33** "Folk Dancers" (statue)

**1967.** Centenary (1966) of New Reform.

| | | | | |
|---|---|---|---|---|
| F201 | **F33** | 30c. green, olive & slate | 1·50 | 3·50 |

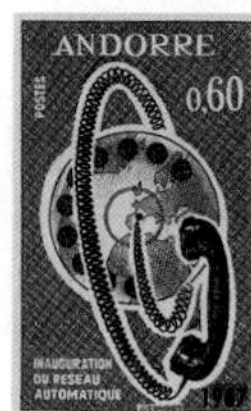

**F34** Telephone and Dial

**1967.** Inaug of Automatic Telephone Service.

| | | | | |
|---|---|---|---|---|
| F202 | **F34** | 60c. black, violet & red | 1·60 | 3·75 |

**F35** Andorran Family

**1967.** Institution of Social Security.

| | | | | |
|---|---|---|---|---|
| F203 | **F35** | 2f.30 brown & purple | 8·50 | 18·00 |

**F36** "The Temptation"

**1967.** 16th-century Frescoes in House of the Valleys (1st series).

| | | | | |
|---|---|---|---|---|
| F204 | **F36** | 25c. red and black | 1·10 | 2·75 |
| F205 | - | 30c. purple and violet | 1·20 | 3·50 |
| F206 | - | 60c. blue and indigo | 1·60 | 4·50 |

FRESCOES: 30c. "The Kiss of Judas"; 60c. "The Descent from the Cross".

See also Nos. F210/12.

**F37** Downhill Skiing

**1968.** Winter Olympic Games, Grenoble.

| | | | | |
|---|---|---|---|---|
| F207 | **F37** | 40c. purple, orge & red | 1·40 | 3·75 |

**F38** Europa "Key"

**1968.** Europa.

| | | | | |
|---|---|---|---|---|
| F208 | **F38** | 30c. blue and slate | 5·25 | 8·50 |
| F209 | **F38** | 60c. violet & brown | 8·50 | 14·00 |

**1968.** 16th-century Frescoes in House of the Valleys (2nd series). Designs as Type F 36.

| | | | | |
|---|---|---|---|---|
| F210 | | 25c. deep green and green | 95 | 3·25 |
| F211 | | 30c. purple and brown | 1·20 | 4·75 |
| F212 | | 60c. brown and red | 2·10 | 6·50 |

FRESCOES: 25c. "The Beating of Christ"; 30c. "Christ Helped by the Cyrenians"; 60c. "The Death of Christ".

**F39** High Jumping

**1968.** Olympic Games, Mexico.

| | | | | |
|---|---|---|---|---|
| F213 | **F39** | 40c. brown and blue | 2·10 | 3·75 |

**F40** Colonnade

**1969.** Europa.

| | | | | |
|---|---|---|---|---|
| F214 | **F40** | 40c. grey, blue and red | 9·50 | 11·50 |
| F215 | **F40** | 70c. red, green and blue | 13·00 | 22·00 |

**F41** Canoeing

**1969.** World Kayak-Canoeing Championships, Bourg-St. Maurice.

| | | | | |
|---|---|---|---|---|
| F216 | **F41** | 70c. dp blue, bl & grn | 2·10 | 5·25 |

**F41a** "Diamond Crystal" in Rain Drop

**1969.** European Water Charter.

| | | | | |
|---|---|---|---|---|
| F217 | **F41a** | 70c. black, blue and ultramarine | 5·25 | 9·75 |

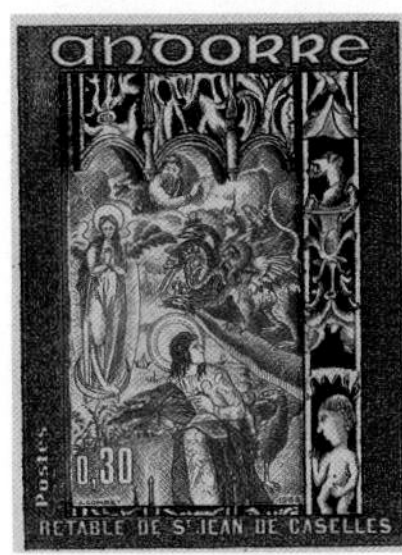


**F42** "The Apocalypse"

**1969.** Altar-screen, Church of St. John of Caselles (1st series). "The Revelation of St. John".

| | | | | |
|---|---|---|---|---|
| F218 | **F42** | 30c. red, violet & brn | 1·10 | 2·10 |
| F219 | - | 40c. bistre, brn & grey | 1·60 | 2·75 |
| F220 | - | 70c. purple, lake & red | 2·10 | 3·50 |

DESIGNS: 40c. Angel "clothed with cloud with face as the sun, and feet as pillars of fire" (Rev. 10); 70c. Christ with sword and stars, and seven candlesticks.

See also Nos. F225/7, F233/5 and F240/2.

**F43** Handball Player

**1970.** 7th World Handball Championships, France.

| | | | | |
|---|---|---|---|---|
| F221 | **F43** | 80c. blue, brn & dp bl | 2·75 | 5·25 |

**F44** "Flaming Sun"

**1970.** Europa.

| | | | | |
|---|---|---|---|---|
| F222 | **F44** | 40c. orange | 9·50 | 8·00 |
| F223 | **F44** | 80c. violet | 12·00 | 13·00 |

**F45** Putting the Shot

**1970.** 1st European Junior Athletic Championships, Paris.

| | | | | |
|---|---|---|---|---|
| F224 | **F45** | 80c. purple and blue | 2·75 | 5·50 |

**1970.** Altar-screen, Church of St. John of Caselles (2nd series). Designs as Type F 42.

| | | | |
|---|---|---|---|
| F225 | 30c. violet, brown and red | 1·50 | 2·50 |
| F226 | 40c. green and violet | 1·60 | 2·75 |
| F227 | 80c. red, blue and green | 3·25 | 4·00 |

DESIGNS: 30c. Angel with keys and padlock; 40c. Angel with pillar; 80c. St. John being boiled in cauldron of oil.

**F46** Ice Skaters

**1971.** World Ice Skating Championships, Lyon.

| | | | | |
|---|---|---|---|---|
| F228 | **F46** | 80c. violet, pur & red | 3·00 | 4·75 |

**F47** Western Capercaillie

**1971.** Nature Protection.

| | | | | |
|---|---|---|---|---|
| F229 | **F47** | 80c. multicoloured | 4·75 | 6·25 |
| F230 | - | 80c. brown, green & bl | 4·75 | 6·25 |

DESIGN: No. F230, Brown bear.

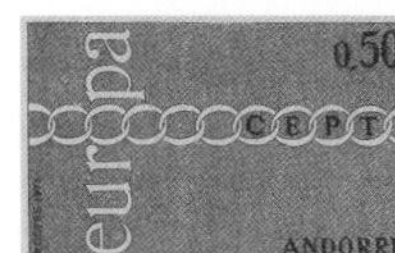


**F48** Europa Chain

**1971.** Europa.

| | | | | |
|---|---|---|---|---|
| F231 | **F48** | 50c. red | 10·50 | 12·50 |
| F232 | **F48** | 80c. green | 16·00 | 20·00 |

**1971.** Altar-screen, Church of St. John of Caselles (3rd series). As Type F 42.

| | | | |
|---|---|---|---|
| F233 | 30c. green, brown and myrtle | 1·80 | 4·50 |
| F234 | 50c. brown, orange and lake | 2·40 | 5·25 |
| F235 | 90c. blue, purple and brown | 3·75 | 7·00 |

DESIGNS: 30c. St. John in temple at Ephesus; 50c. St. John with cup of poison; 90c. St. John disputing with pagan philosophers.

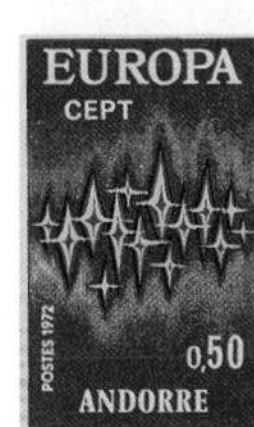


**F49** "Communications"

**1972.** Europa.

| | | | | |
|---|---|---|---|---|
| F236 | **F49** | 50c. multicoloured | 10·00 | 10·50 |
| F237 | **F49** | 90c. multicoloured | 15·00 | 18·00 |

**F50** Golden Eagle

**1972.** Nature Protection.

| | | | | |
|---|---|---|---|---|
| F238 | **F50** | 60c. olive, green & pur | 4·75 | 6·25 |

**F51** Rifle-shooting

**1972.** Olympic Games, Munich.

| | | | | |
|---|---|---|---|---|
| F239 | **F51** | 1f. purple | 3·25 | 4·50 |

**1972.** Altar-screen, Church of St. John of Caselles (4th series). As Type F 42.

| | | | |
|---|---|---|---|
| F240 | 30c. purple, grey and green | 1·40 | 2·30 |
| F241 | 50c. grey and blue | 1·70 | 2·75 |
| F242 | 90c. green and blue | 2·75 | 4·00 |

DESIGNS: 30c. St. John in discussion with bishop; 50c. St. John healing a cripple; 90c. Angel with spear.

**F52** General De Gaulle

**1972.** 5th Anniv of Gen. De Gaulle's Visit to Andorra.

| | | | | |
|---|---|---|---|---|
| F243 | **F52** | 50c. blue | 3·50 | 5·75 |
| F244 | - | 90c. red | 4·75 | 7·75 |

DESIGN: 90c. Gen. De Gaulle in Andorra la Vella, 1967.

See also Nos. F434/5.

**F53** Europa "Posthorn"

**1973.** Europa.

| | | | | |
|---|---|---|---|---|
| F245 | **F53** | 50c. multicoloured | 10·00 | 10·50 |
| F246 | **F53** | 90c. multicoloured | 10·50 | 21·00 |

**F54** "Virgin of Canolich" (wood carving)

**1973.** Andorran Art.

| | | | | |
|---|---|---|---|---|
| F247 | **F54** | 1f. lilac, blue and drab | 3·00 | 4·25 |

**F55** Lily

**1973.** Pyrenean Flowers (1st series). Multicoloured.

| | | | |
|---|---|---|---|
| F248 | 30c. Type F **55** | 1·10 | 3·25 |
| F249 | 50c. Columbine | 2·10 | 4·50 |
| F250 | 90c. Wild pinks | 1·60 | 3·50 |

See also Nos. F253/5 and F264/6.

**F56** Blue Tit ("Mesange Bleue")

**1973.** Nature Protection. Birds. Multicoloured.

| | | | |
|---|---|---|---|
| F251 | 90c. Type F **56** | 2·75 | 5·25 |
| F252 | 1f. Lesser spotted woodpecker ("Pic Epeichette") | 3·00 | 5·75 |

See also Nos. F259/60.

**1974.** Pyrenean Wild Flowers (2nd series). As Type F 55. Multicoloured.

| | | | |
|---|---|---|---|
| F253 | 45c. Iris | 55 | 4·00 |
| F254 | 65c. Tobacco Plant | 65 | 4·50 |
| F255 | 90c. Narcissus | 1·40 | 4·75 |

**F57** "The Virgin of Pal"

**1974.** Europa. Church Sculptures. Mult.

| | | | |
|---|---|---|---|
| F256 | 50c. Type F **57** | 17·00 | 11·50 |
| F257 | 90c. "The Virgin of Santa Coloma" | 23·00 | 18·00 |

**F58** Arms of Andorra

**1974.** Meeting of Co-Princes, Cahors.

| | | | | |
|---|---|---|---|---|
| F258 | **F58** | 1f. blue, violet & orge | 1·40 | 5·75 |

**1974.** Nature Protection. Birds. As Type F 56. Multicoloured.

| | | | |
|---|---|---|---|
| F259 | 60c. Citril finch ("Venturon Montagnard") | 4·25 | 7·00 |
| F260 | 80c. Northern bullfinch ("Boureuil") | 4·25 | 7·00 |

**F59** Letters crossing Globe

**1974.** Centenary of U.P.U.

| | | | | |
|---|---|---|---|---|
| F261 | **F59** | 1f.20 red, grey & brn | 2·30 | 4·25 |

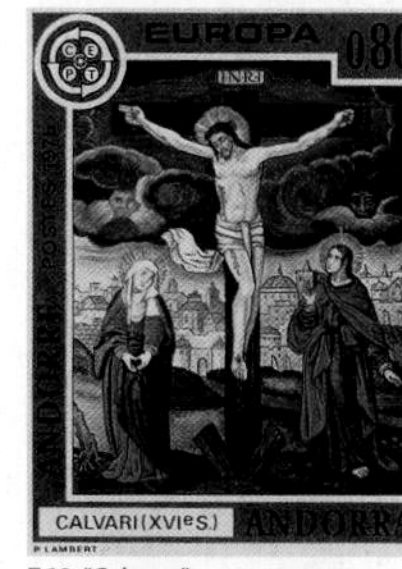


**F60** "Calvary"

**1975.** Europa. Paintings from La Cortinada Church. Multicoloured.

| | | | |
|---|---|---|---|
| F262 | 80c. Type F **60** | 8·50 | 15·00 |
| F263 | 1f.20 "Coronation of St. Martin" (horiz) | 10·50 | 23·00 |

**1975.** Pyrenean Flowers (3rd series). As Type F 55.

| | | | |
|---|---|---|---|
| F264 | 60c. multicoloured | 65 | 3·25 |
| F265 | 80c. multicoloured | 1·80 | 4·00 |
| F266 | 1f.20 yellow, red and green | 1·30 | 3·50 |

DESIGNS: 60c. Gentian; 80c. Anemone; 1f.20, Colchicum.

**F61** "Arphila" Motif

**1975.** "Arphila 75" International Stamp Exhibition, Paris.

| | | | | |
|---|---|---|---|---|
| F267 | **F61** | 2f. red, green and blue | 2·00 | 4·50 |

**F62** Pres. Pompidou (Co-prince of Andorra)

**1976.** President Pompidou of France Commem.

| | | | | |
|---|---|---|---|---|
| F268 | **F62** | 80c. black and violet | 1·10 | 3·25 |

**F63** "La Pubilla" and Emblem

**1976.** International Women's Year.

| | | | | |
|---|---|---|---|---|
| F269 | **F63** | 1f.20 black, pur & bl | 2·10 | 3·75 |

**F64** Skier

**1976.** Winter Olympic Games, Innsbruck.

| | | | | |
|---|---|---|---|---|
| F270 | **F64** | 1f.20 black, green & bl | 1·60 | 3·50 |

**F65** Telephone and Satellite

**1976.** Telephone Centenary.
F271 **F65** 1f. green, black and red 1·60 3·75

**F66** Catalan Forge

**1976.** Europa.
F272 **F66** 80c. brown, blue & grn 4·25 4·50
F273 - 1f.20 red, green & blk 5·25 5·75
DESIGN: 1f.20, Andorran folk-weaving.

**F67** Thomas Jefferson

**1976.** Bicentenary of American Revolution.
F274 **F67** 1f.20 dp grn, brn & grn 1·40 3·50

**F68** Ball-trap (clay pigeon) Shooting

**1976.** Olympic Games, Montreal.
F275 **F68** 2f. brown, violet & grn 2·10 4·00

**F69** New Chapel

**1976.** New Chapel of Our Lady, Meritxell.
F276 **F69** 1f. green, purple & brn 1·20 3·25

**F70** Apollo

**1976.** Nature Protection. Butterflies. Mult.
F277 80c. Type F **70** 3·25 6·50
F278 1f.40 Camberwell beauty 4·00 7·00

**F71** Stoat

**1977.** Nature Protection.
F279 **F71** 1f. grey, black & blue 2·40 3·75

**F72** Church of St. John of Caselles

**1977.** Europa.
F280 **F72** 1f. purple, green & bl 6·75 5·75
F281 - 1f.40 indigo, grn & bl 11·00 7·00
DESIGN: 1f.40, St. Vicens Chateau.

**F73** Book and Flowers

**1977.** 1st Anniv of Institute of Andorran Studies.
F282 **F73** 80c. brown, green & bl 1·20 2·75

**F74** St. Roma

**1977.** Reredos, St. Roma's Chapel, Les Bons.
F283 **F74** 2f. multicoloured 2·75 3·50

**F75** General Council Assembly Hall

**1977.** Andorran Institutions.
F284 **F75** 1f.10 red, blue & brn 2·75 4·00
F285 - 2f. brown and red 2·75 4·00
DESIGN—VERT. 2f. Don Guillem d'Areny Plandolit.

**F76** Eurasian Red Squirrel

**1978.** Nature Protection.
F286 **F76** 1f. brown, grn & olive 1·30 2·75

**F77** Escalls Bridge

**1978.** 700th Anniv of Parity Treaties (1st issue).
F287 **F77** 80c. green, brown & bl 85 2·75
See also No. F292.

**F78** Church at Pal

**1978.** Europa.
F288 **F78** 1f. brown, green & red 7·00 5·75
F289 - 1f.40 brown, bl & red 11·50 7·50
DESIGN: 1f.40, Charlemagne's House.

**F79** "Virgin of Sispony"

**1978.** Andorran Art.
F290 **F79** 2f. multicoloured 2·10 3·50

**F80** Tribunal Meeting

**1978.** Tribunal of Visura.
F291 **F80** 1f.20 multicoloured 1·80 2·75

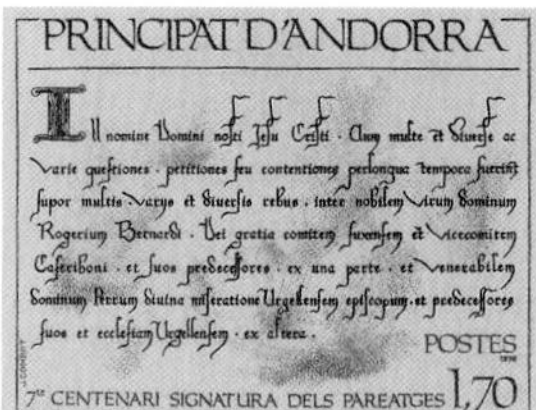

**F81** Treaty Text

**1978.** 700th Anniv of Parity Treaties (2nd issue).
F292 **F81** 1f.50 brown, grn & red 1·30 2·75

**F82** Chamois

**1978.** Nature Protection.
F293 **F82** 1f. brown, lt brn & bl 85 2·40

**F83** Rock Ptarmigans ("Perdiu Blanca")

**1979.** Nature Protection.
F294 **F83** 1f.20 multicoloured 1·70 3·25

**F84** Early 20th Century Postman and Church of St. John of Caselles

**1979.** Europa.
F295 **F84** 1f.20 black, brn & grn 3·25 4·75
F296 - 1f.70 brown, grn & mve 5·25 5·75
DESIGN: 1f.70, Old French Post Office, Andorra.

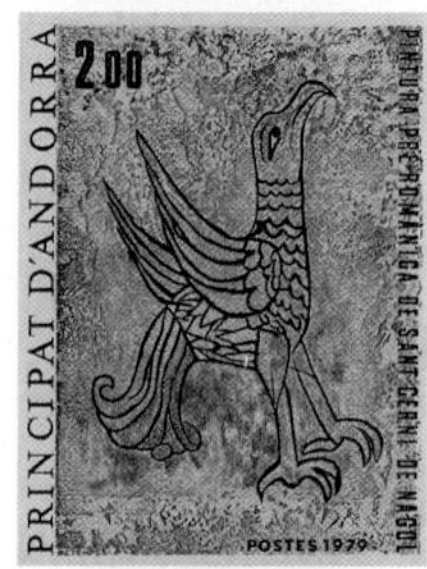

**F85** Wall painting, Church of St. Cerni, Nagol

**1979.** Pre-Romanesque Art.
F297 **F85** 2f. green, pink and brown 1·60 2·75
See also No. F309.

**F86** Boy with Sheep

**1979.** International Year of the Child.
F298 **F86** 1f.70 multicoloured 1·30 2·75

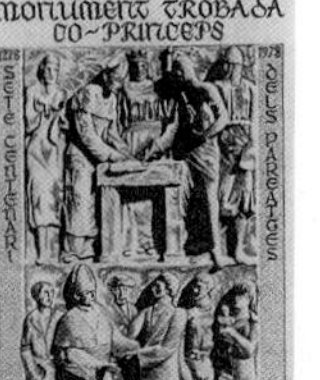

**F87** Co-princes Monument (Luigiteruggi)

**1979.** Co-princes Monument.
F299 **F87** 2f. dp green, grn & red 1·60 3·25

**F88** Judo

**1979.** World Judo Championships, Paris.
F300 **F88** 1f.30 black, dp bl & bl 1·10 2·75

**F89** Cal Pal, La Cortinada

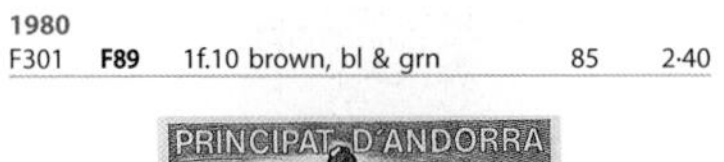

**1980**
F301 **F89** 1f.10 brown, bl & grn 85 2·40

**F90** Cross-country Skiing

**1980.** Winter Olympics, Lake Placid.
F302 **F90** 1f.80 ultram, bl & red 1·50 3·25

**F91** Charlemagne

**1980.** Europa.
F303 **F91** 1f.30 brn, chest & red 2·10 3·50
F304 - 1f.80 green and brown 2·75 4·00
DESIGN: 1f.80, Napoleon I.

**F93** Dog's-tooth Violet

**1980.** Nature Protection. Multicoloured.
F306 1f.10 Type F **93** 95 2·50
F305 1f.30 Pyrenean lily 85 2·40

**F94** Cyclists

**1980.** World Cycling Championships.
F307 **F94** 1f.20 violet, mve & brn 1·20 2·50

**F95** House of the Valleys

**1980.** 400th Anniv of Restoration of House of the Valleys (meeting place of Andorran General Council).
F308 **F95** 1f.40 brown, vio & grn 1·20 2·50

**1980.** Pre-Romanesque Art. As Type F 85. Mult.
F309 2f. Angel (wall painting, Church of St. Cerni, Nagol) (horiz) 1·70 3·25

**F97** Shepherds' Huts, Mereig

**1981.** Architecture.
F310 **F97** 1f.40 brown and blue 1·10 1·70

**F98** Bear Dance (Emcamp Carnival)

**1981.** Europa.
F311 **F98** 1f.40 black, green & bl 1·60 2·30
F312 - 2f. black, blue and red 2·10 3·50
DESIGN: 2f. El Contrapas (dance).

**F99** Bonelli's Warbler

**1981.** Nature Protection. Birds. Multicoloured.
F313 1f.20 Type F **99** 1·10 2·75
F314 1f.40 Wallcreeper 1·30 2·75

**F100** Fencing

**1981.** World Fencing Championships, Clermont-Ferrand.
F315 **F100** 2f. blue and black 1·30 2·75

**F101** Chasuble of St. Martin (miniature)

**1981.** Art.
F316 **F101** 3f. multicoloured 1·80 2·75

**F102** Fountain, Sant Julia de Loria

**1981.** International Decade of Drinking Water.
F317 **F102** 1f.60 blue and brown 1·10 2·50

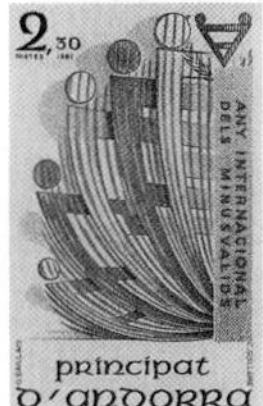


**F103** Symbolic Disabled

**1981.** International Year of Disabled Persons.
F318 **F103** 2f.30 blue, red & grn 1·50 2·75

**F104** Scroll and Badge (creation of Andorran Executive Council, 1981)

**1982.** Europa.
F319 **F104** 1f.60 blue, brn & orge 2·10 2·75
F320 - 2f.30 blue, blk & orge 2·75 3·25
DESIGN: 2f.30, Hat and cloak (creation of Land Council, 1419).

**F105** Footballer running to right

**1982.** World Cup Football Championship, Spain.
F321 **F105** 1f.60 brown and red 1·30 2·40
F322 - 2f.60 brown and red 1·90 2·75
DESIGN: 2f.60, Footballer running to left.

**F 106** 1933 1f.25 Stamp

**1982.** 1st Official Exhibition of Andorran Postage Stamps.
**MS**F323 F **106** 5f. black and red 2·75 4·00

**F107** Wall Painting, La Cortinada Church

**1982.** Romanesque Art.
F324 **F107** 3f. multicoloured 1·60 4·75

**F108** Wild Cat

**1982.** Nature Protection.
F325 **F108** 1f.80 blk, grn & grey 1·60 3·75
F326 - 2f.60 brown & green 1·40 4·00
DESIGN: 2f.60, Scots Pine.

**F109** Dr. Robert Koch

**1982.** Centenary of Discovery of Tubercle Bacillus.
F327 **F109** 2f.10 lilac 1·40 2·75

**F110** St. Thomas Aquinas

**1982.** St. Thomas Aquinas Commemoration.
F328 **F110** 2f. deep brown, brown and grey 1·30 2·75

**F111** Montgolfier and Charles Balloon over Tuileries, Paris

**1983.** Bicentenary of Manned Flight.
F329 **F111** 2f. green, red and brown 1·30 2·75

**F112** Silver Birch

**1983.** Nature Protection.
F330 **F112** 1f. red, brown and green 1·50 3·75
F331 - 1f.50 green, bl & brn 1·60 4·00
DESIGN: 1f.50, Brown trout.

**F113** Mountain Cheesery

**1983.** Europa.
F332 **F113** 1f. purple and violet 2·40 3·75
F333 - 2f.60 red, mve & pur 2·75 4·00
DESIGN: 2f.60, Catalan forge.

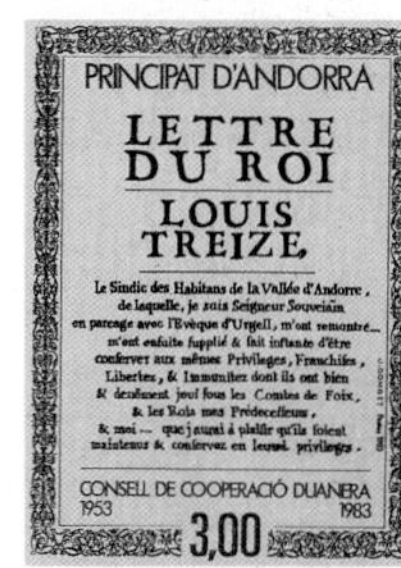


**F114** Royal Edict of Louis XIII

**1983.** 30th Anniv of Customs Co-operation Council.
F334 **F114** 3f. black and slate 2·00 5·50

**F115** Early Coat of Arms

**1983.** Inscr "POSTES".
F335 **F115** 5c. green and red 1·10 2·30
F336 **F115** 10c. dp green & green 1·10 2·30
F337 **F115** 20c. violet and mauve 1·10 2·30
F338 **F115** 30c. purple and violet 1·10 2·30
F339 **F115** 40c. blue & ultram 1·10 2·30
F340 **F115** 50c. black and red 1·10 2·30
F341 **F115** 1f. lake and red 1·10 2·30
F342 **F115** 1f.90 green 3·75 4·75
F343 **F115** 2f. red and brown 1·50 1·60
F344 **F115** 2f.10 green 1·50 2·75
F345 **F115** 2f.20 red 1·10 3·75
F346 **F115** 2f.30 red 1·40 3·75
F347 **F115** 3f. green and mauve 1·60 4·00
F348 **F115** 4f. orange and brown 3·25 6·25
F349 **F115** 5f. brown and red 2·10 5·75
F350 **F115** 10f. red and brown 4·25 6·25
F351 **F115** 15f. green & dp green 6·25 9·00
F352 **F115** 20f. blue and brown 8·00 9·25

For design as Type F **115** but inscribed "LA POSTE" see Nos. F446/9.

**F116** Wall Painting, La Cortinada Church

**1983.** Romanesque Art.
F354 **F116** 4f. multicoloured 2·10 4·00

**F117** Plandolit House

**1983**

F355 **F117** 1f.60 brown & green 1·10 1·70

**F118** Snowflakes and Olympic Torch

**1984.** Winter Olympic Games, Sarajevo.

F356 **F118** 2f.80 red, blue & grn 1·70 2·75

**F119** Pyrenees and Council of Europe Emblem

**1984.** Work Community of Pyrenees Region.

F357 **F119** 3f. blue and brown 1·80 3·25

**F120** Bridge

**1984.** Europa.

F358 **F120** 2f. green 3·75 4·00

F359 **F120** 2f.80 red 4·75 5·25

**F121** Sweet Chestnut

**1984.** Nature Protection.

F360 **F121** 1f.70 grn, brn & pur 1·30 3·75

F361 - 2f.10 green & brown 1·60 4·00

DESIGN: 2f.10, Walnut.

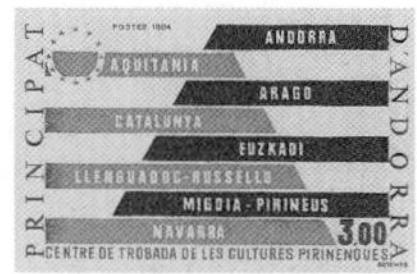

**F122** Centre Members

**1984.** Pyrenean Cultures Centre, Andorra.

F362 **F122** 3f. blue, orange & red 1·80 3·50

**F123** "St. George" (detail of fresco, Church of St. Cerni, Nagol)

**1984.** Pre-Romanesque Art.

F363 **F123** 5f. multicoloured 2·75 4·00

**F124** Sant Julia Valley

**1985**

F364 **F124** 2f. green, olive & brn 1·50 2·75

**F125** Title Page of "Le Val d'Andorre" (comic opera)

**1985.** Europa.

F365 **F125** 2f.10 green 3·75 4·00

F366 - 3f. brown & dp brown 4·75 5·25

DESIGN: 3f. Musical instruments within frame.

**F126** Teenagers holding up ball

**1985.** International Youth Year.

F367 **F126** 3f. red and brown 1·60 3·25

**F127** Mallard

**1985.** Nature Protection. Multicoloured.

F368 1f.80 Type F **127** 1·40 3·50

F369 2f.20 Eurasian goldfinch 1·70 4·00

**F128** St. Cerni and Angel (fresco, Church of St. Cerni, Nagol)

**1985.** Pre-Romanesque Art.

F370 **F128** 5f. multicoloured 2·30 4·00

**F130** 1979 Europa Stamp

**1986.** Inauguration of Postal Museum.

F381 **F130** 2f.20 brown & green 1·40 3·25

**F131** Ansalonga

**1986.** Europa.

F382 **F131** 2f.20 black and blue 4·25 4·50

F383 - 3f.20 black and green 5·25 5·50

DESIGN: 3f.20, Pyrenean chamois.

**F132** Players

**1986.** World Cup Football Championship, Mexico.

F384 **F132** 3f. grn, blk & dp grn 2·10 3·50

**F133** Angonella Lakes

**1986**

F385 **F133** 2f.20 multicoloured 1·40 2·75

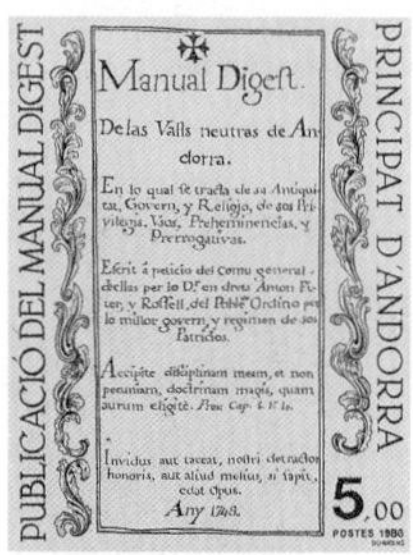

**F134** Title Page of "Manual Digest", 1748

**1986.** "Manual Digest".

F386 **F134** 5f. black, grn & brn 2·75 4·00

**F135** Dove with Twig

**1986.** International Peace Year.

F387 **F135** 1f.90 blue and indigo 1·30 2·75

**F136** St. Vincent's Chapel, Enclar

**1986**

F388 **F136** 1f.90 brn, blk & grn 1·30 2·75

**F137** Arms

**1987.** Visit of French Co-prince (French president).

F389 **F137** 2f.20 multicoloured 2·00 4·00

**F138** Meritxell Chapel

**1987.** Europa.

F390 **F138** 2f.20 purple and red 5·25 4·50

F391 - 3f.40 violet and blue 7·50 6·25

DESIGN: 3f.40, Ordino.

**F139** Ransol

**1987**

F392 **F139** 1f.90 multicoloured 1·50 3·50

**F140** Horse

**1987.** Nature Protection. Multicoloured.

F393 1f.90 Type F **140** 1·70 4·25

F394 2f.20 Isabel (moth) 2·00 4·50

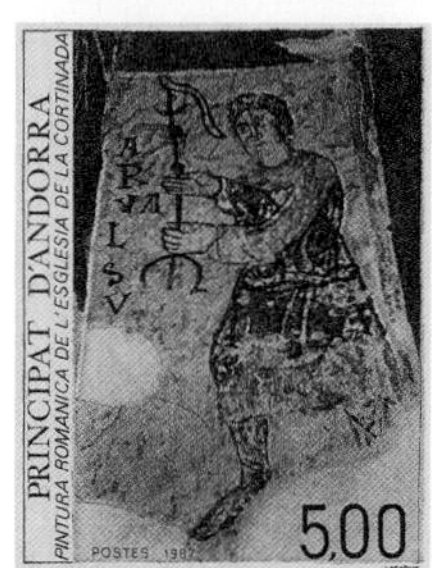

**F141** Arualsu (fresco, La Cortinada Church)

**1987.** Romanesque Art.

F395 **F141** 5f. multicoloured 3·00 4·25

**F142** Walker with Map by Signpost

**1987.** Walking.

F396 **F142** 2f. pur, grn & dp grn 1·40 2·75

**F143** Key

**1987.** La Cortinada Church Key.

F397 **F143** 3f. multicoloured 1·70 3·50

**F144** Arms

**1988**

F398 **F144** 2f.20 red 1·40 2·75

F399 **F144** 2f.30 red 1·60 4·50

F400 **F144** 2f.50 red 1·70 4·50

F401 **F144** 2f.80 red 1·80 4·25

Nos. F400/1 are inscribed "LA POSTE".

**F145** Bronze Boot and Mountains

**1988.** Archaeology.

F407 **F145** 3f. multicoloured 1·70 3·75

**F146** Players

**1988.** Rugby.
F408 **F146** 2f.20 blk, yell & grn 1·40 4·50

**F147** Enclar Aerial

**1988.** Europa. Transport and Communications. Each green, brown and blue.
F409 2f.20 Type F **147** 3·75 4·00
F410 3f.60 Hand pointing to map on screen (tourist information) 4·75 5·75

**F148** Les Escaldes Hot Spring

**1988**
F411 **F148** 2f.20 blue, brn & grn 1·40 2·75

**F149** Ansalonga Pass

**1988**
F412 **F149** 2f. blue, green & olive 1·20 2·75

**F150** Pyrenean Shepherd Dog

**1988.** Nature Protection. Multicoloured.
F413 2f. Type F **150** 1·90 4·50
F414 2f.20 Hare 2·00 4·50

**F151** Fresco, Andorra La Vella Church

**1988.** Romanesque Art.
F415 **F151** 5f. multicoloured 3·00 4·00

**F152** Birds

**1989.** Bicentenary of French Revolution.
F416 **F152** 2f.20 violet, blk & red 1·50 2·75

**F153** Pal

**1989**
F417 **F153** 2f.20 violet and blue 1·50 2·75

**F154** The Strong Horse

**1989.** Europa. Children's Games. Each brown and cream.
F418 2f.20 Type F **154** 3·25 3·50
F419 3f.60 The Handkerchief 4·25 4·75

**F155** Wounded Soldiers

**1989.** 125th Anniv of International Red Cross.
F420 **F155** 3f.60 brn, blk & red 2·10 3·50

**F156** Archaeological Find and St. Vincent's Chapel, Enclar

**1989.** Archaeology.
F421 **F156** 3f. multicoloured 1·60 3·50

**F157** Wild Boar

**1989.** Nature Protection.
F422 **F157** 2f.20 blk, grn & brn 1·60 3·50
F423 - 3f.60 black, green and deep green 2·10 4·50
DESIGN: 3f.60, Palmate newt.

**F158** Retable of St. Michael de la Mosquera, Encamp

**1989**
F424 **F158** 5f. multicoloured 3·25 5·50

**F159** La Margineda Bridge

**1990**
F425 **F159** 2f.30 blue, brn & turq 1·60 2·75

**F160** Llorts Iron Ore Mines

**1990**
F426 **F160** 3f.20 multicoloured 2·10 3·25

**F161** Exterior of Old Post Office, Andorra La Vella

**1990.** Europa. Post Office Buildings.
F427 **F161** 2f.30 red and black 4·25 5·25
F428 - 3f.20 violet and red 6·25 7·00
DESIGN: 3f.20, Interior of modern post office.

**F162** Censer, St. Roma's Chapel, Les Bons

**1990**
F429 **F162** 3f. multicoloured 2·10 3·25

**F163** Wild Roses

**1990.** Nature Protection. Multicoloured.
F430 2f.30 Type F **163** 1·60 3·25
F431 3f.20 Otter (horiz) 2·10 3·50

**F164** Tobacco-drying Sheds, Les Bons

**1990**
F432 **F164** 2f.30 yell, blk & red 1·60 2·75

**F165** Part of Mural from Santa Coloma Church

**1990**
F433 **F165** 5f. multicoloured 2·75 3·75

**1990.** Birth Centenary of Charles de Gaulle (French statesman). As Nos. F243/4 but values and inscriptions changed.
F434 **F52** 2f.30 blue 2·10 3·25
F435 **F52** 3f.20 red 2·50 3·50

**F166** Coin from St. Eulalia's Church, Encamp

**1990**
F436 **F166** 3f.20 multicoloured 2·10 3·25

**F167** Chapel of Sant Roma Dels Vilars

**1991**
F437 **F167** 2f.50 blue, blk & grn 1·60 2·75

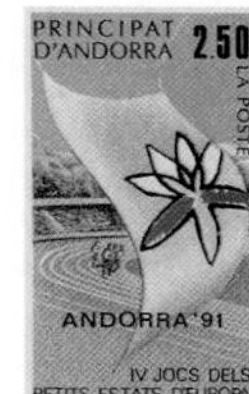


**F168** Emblem and Track

**1991.** 4th European Small States Games.
F438 **F168** 2f.50 multicoloured 1·50 2·75

**F169** Television Satellite

**1991.** Europa. Europe in Space. Multicoloured.
F439 2f.50 Type F **169** 4·25 4·50
F440 3f.50 Globe, telescope and eye (horiz) 7·50 8·00

**F170** Bottles

**1991.** Artefacts from Tomb of St. Vincent of Enclar.
F441 **F170** 3f.20 multicoloured 1·80 2·75

**F171** Sheep

**1991.** Nature Protection.
F442 **F171** 2f.50 brown, bl & blk 2·10 4·50
F443 - 3f.50 brn, mve & blk 2·20 4·75
DESIGN: 3f.50, Pyrenean cow.

**F172** Players

**1991.** World Petanque Championship, Engordany.
F444 **F172** 2f.50 blk, bistre & red 1·80 2·75

**F173** Mozart, Quartet and Organ Pipes

**1991.** Death Bicentenary of Wolfgang Amadeus Mozart (composer).
F445 **F173** 3f.40 blue, blk & turq 2·20 3·25

**1991.** As Type F 115 but inscr "LA POSTE".
F446 **F115** 2f.20 green 1·40 4·00
F447 **F115** 2f.40 green 3·00 4·50
F448 **F115** 2f.50 red 1·60 4·00
F449 **F115** 2f.70 green 2·75 4·00
F450 **F115** 2f.80 red 2·75 4·00
F451 **F115** 3f. red 2·75 4·00

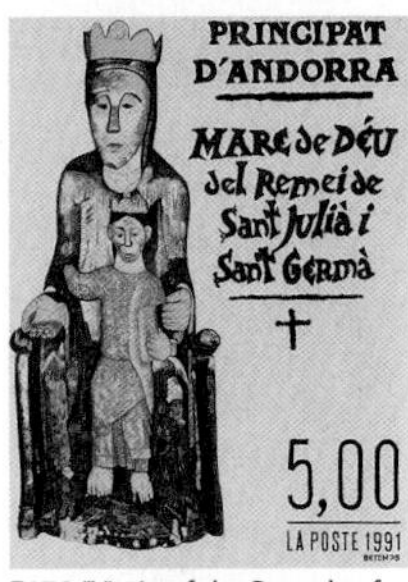


**F174** "Virgin of the Remedy of Sant Julia and Sant Germa"

**1991**
F455 **F174** 5f. multicoloured 3·25 3·75

**F175** Slalom

**1992.** Winter Olympic Games, Albertville. Mult.
F456 2f.50 Type F **175** 2·40 2·75
F457 3f.40 Figure skating 2·75 3·25

**F176** St. Andrew's Church, Arinsal

**1992**
F458 **F176** 2f.50 black and buff 1·80 2·20

**F177** Navigation Instrument and Columbus's Fleet

**1992.** Europa. 500th Anniv of Discovery of America by Columbus. Multicoloured.
F459 2f.50 Type F **177** 4·75 4·50
F460 3f.40 Fleet, Columbus and Amerindians 7·50 5·75

**F178** Canoeing

**1992.** Olympic Games, Barcelona. Multicoloured.
F461 2f.50 Type F **178** 1·90 2·30
F462 3f.40 Shooting 2·20 2·50

**F179** Globe Flowers

**1992.** Nature Protection. Multicoloured.
F463 2f.50 Type F **179** 1·70 2·40
F464 3f.40 Griffon vulture ("El Voltor") (horiz) 2·30 2·75

**F180** "Martyrdom of St. Eulalia" (altarpiece, St. Eulalia's Church, Encamp)

**1992**
F465 **F180** 4f. multicoloured 2·40 2·75

**F181** "Ordino Arcalis 91" (Mauro Staccioli)

**1992.** Modern Sculpture. Multicoloured.
F466 5f. Type F **181** 3·25 3·50
F467 5f. "Storm in a Teacup" (Dennis Oppenheim) (horiz) 3·25 3·50

**F182** Grau Roig

**1993.** Ski Resorts. Multicoloured.
F468 2f.50 Type F **182** 1·60 2·30
F469 2f.50 Ordino 1·60 2·30
F470 2f.50 Soldeu el Tarter 1·60 2·30
F471 3f.40 Pal 2·30 2·75
F472 3f.40 Arinsal 2·30 2·75

**F183** "Estructures Autogeneradores" (Jorge du Bon)

**1993.** Europa. Contemporary Art.
F473 **F183** 2f.50 dp bl, bl & vio 2·20 3·25
F474 - 3f.40 multicoloured 2·40 3·50
DESIGN—HORIZ: 3f.40, "Fisicromia per Andorra" (Carlos Cruz-Diez).

**F184** Common Blue

**1993.** Nature Protection. Butterflies. Multicoloured.
F475 2f.50 Type F **184** 2·10 3·25
F476 4f.20 "Nymphalidae" 3·00 4·00

**F185** Cyclist

**1993.** Tour de France Cycling Road Race.
F477 **F185** 2f.50 multicoloured 2·20 3·50

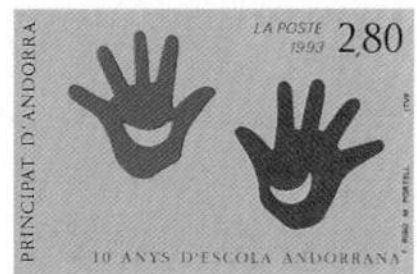


**F186** Smiling Hands

**1993.** 10th Anniv of Andorran School.
F478 **F186** 2f.80 multicoloured 2·50 3·50

**F187** "A Pagan Place" (Michael Warren)

**1993.** Modern Sculpture.
F479 **F187** 5f. black and blue 3·50 3·00
F480 - 5f. multicoloured 3·50 3·00
DESIGN: No. F480, "Pep, Lu, Canolic, Ton, Meritxell, Roma, Anna, Pau, Carles, Eugenia... and Others" (Erik Dietman).

**F188** Cross-country Skiing

**1994.** Winter Olympic Games, Lillehammer, Norway.
F481 **F188** 3f.70 multicoloured 2·20 2·50

**F189** Constitution Monument

**1994.** 1st Anniv of New Constitution.
F482 **F189** 2f.80 multicoloured 1·90 2·00
F483 - 3f.70 blk, yell & mve 2·40 3·50
DESIGN: 3f.70, Stone tablet.

**F190** AIDS Virus

**1994.** Europa. Discoveries and Inventions. Mult.
F484 2f.80 Type F **190** 2·50 2·50
F485 3f.70 Radio mast 3·00 3·00

**F191** Competitors' Flags and Football

**1994.** World Cup Football Championship, U.S.A.
F486 **F191** 3f.70 multicoloured 2·50 2·75

**F192** Horse Riding

**1994.** Tourist Activities. Multicoloured.
F487 2f.80 Type F **192** 1·90 1·90
F488 2f.80 Mountain biking 1·90 1·90
F489 2f.80 Climbing 1·90 1·90
F490 2f.80 Fishing 1·90 1·90

**F193** Scarce Swallowtail

**1994.** Nature Protection. Butterflies. Multicoloured.
F491 2f.80 Type F **193** 2·50 2·75
F492 4f.40 Small tortoiseshell 3·75 4·00

**F194** "26 10 93"

**1994.** Meeting of Co-princes.
F493 **F194** 2f.80 multicoloured 1·70 2·00

**F195** Emblem

**1995.** European Nature Conservation Year.
F494 **F195** 2f.80 multicoloured 1·90 2·10

**F196** Globe, Goal and Player

**1995.** 3rd World Cup Rugby Championship, South Africa.
F495 **F196** 2f.80 multicoloured 1·90 2·10

**F197** Dove and Olive Twig ("Peace")

**1995.** Europa. Peace and Freedom. Multicoloured.
F496 2f.80 Type F **197** 2·50 2·75
F497 3f.70 Flock of doves ("Freedom") 2·75 3·00

**F198** Emblem

**1995.** 15th Anniv of Caritas Andorrana (welfare organization).
F498 **F198** 2f.80 multicoloured 1·90 2·30

**F199** Caldea Thermal Baths, Les Escaldes-Engordany

**1995**
F499 **F199** 2f.80 multicoloured 1·90 2·30

**F200** National Auditorium, Ordino

**1995**

F500 **F200** 3f.70 black and buff 2·50 2·75

**F201** "Virgin of Meritxell"

**1995**

F501 **F201** 4f.40 multicoloured 2·75 3·00

**F202** Brimstone

**1995.** Nature Protection. Butterflies. Multicoloured.

F502 2f.80 Type F **202** 2·50 2·75

F503 3f.70 Marbled white (horiz) 3·00 3·25

**F203** National Flag over U.N. Emblem

**1995.** 50th Anniv of U.N.O. Multicoloured.

F504 2f.80 Type F **203** 2·50 2·75

F505 3f.70 Anniversary emblem over flag 2·75 3·00

**F204** National Flag and Palace of Europe, Strasbourg

**1995.** Admission of Andorra to Council of Europe.

F506 **F204** 2f.80 multicoloured 1·90 2·00

**F205** Emblem

**1996.** 4th Borrufa Trophy Skiing Competition.

F507 **F205** 2f.80 multicoloured 1·90 2·00

**F206** Basketball

**1996**

F508 **F206** 3f.70 red, blk & yell 3·00 3·75

**F207** Children

**1996.** 25th Anniv of Our Lady of Meritxell Special School.

F509 **F207** 2f.80 multicoloured 1·90 2·10

**F208** European Robin

**1996.** Nature Protection. Multicoloured.

F510 3f. Type F **208** 2·50 3·00

F511 3f.80 Great tit 3·00 3·25

**F209** Cross, St. James's Church, Engordany

**1996.** Religious Objects. Multicoloured.

F512 3f. Type F **209** 2·50 2·75

F513 3f.80 Censer, St. Eulalia's Church, Encamp (horiz) 2·75 3·00

**F210** Ermessenda de Castellbo

**1996.** Europa. Famous Women.

F514 **F210** 3f. multicoloured 2·50 2·75

**F211** Chessmen

**1996.** Chess.

F515 **F211** 4f.50 red, black & bl 2·50 2·75

**F212** Canillo

**1996.** No value expressed. Self-adhesive.

F516 **F212** (3f.) multicoloured 3·00 3·25

**F213** Cycling, Running and Throwing the Javelin

**1996.** Olympic Games, Atlanta.

F517 **F213** 3f. multicoloured 1·90 2·00

**F214** Singers

**1996.** 5th Anniv of National Youth Choir.

F518 **F214** 3f. multicoloured 1·90 2·00

**F215** Man and Boy with Animals

**1996.** Livestock Fair.

F519 **F215** 3f. yellow, red and black 1·90 2·00

**F216** St. Roma's Chapel, Les Bons

**1996.** Churches. Multicoloured.

F520 6f.70 Type F **216** 4·00 4·25

F521 6f.70 Santa Coloma 4·00 4·25

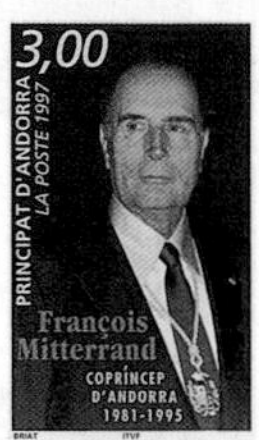


**F217** Mitterrand

**1997.** Francois Mitterrand (President of France and Co-prince of Andorra, 1981–95) Commemoration.

F522 **F217** 3f. multicoloured 1·90 2·00

**F218** Parish Emblem

**1997.** Parish of Encamp. No value expressed. Self-adhesive.

F523 **F218** (3f.) blue 1·90 2·00

**F219** Volleyball

**1997**

F524 **F219** 3f. multicoloured 1·90 2·00

**F220** The White Lady

**1997.** Europa. Tales and Legends.

F525 **F220** 3f. multicoloured 2·50 2·75

**F221** House Martin approaching Nest

**1997.** Nature Protection.

F526 **F221** 3f.80 multicoloured 1·90 2·00

**F222** Mill and Saw-mill, Cal Pal

**1997.** Tourism. Paintings by Francesc Galobardes. Multicoloured.

F527 3f. Type F **222** 2·50 2·75

F528 4f.50 Mill and farmhouse, Sole (horiz) 3·00 3·25

**F223** Monstrance, St. Iscle and St. Victoria's Church

**1997.** Religious Silver Work. Multicoloured.

F529 3f. Type F **223** 2·50 2·75

F530 15f.50 Pax, St. Peter's Church, Aixirivall 7·50 8·00

**F224** The Legend of Meritxell

**1997.** Legends. Multicoloured.

F531 3f. Type F **224** 1·90 2·10

F532 3f. The Seven-armed Cross 1·90 2·10

F533 3f.80 Wrestlers (The Fountain of Esmelicat) 3·00 3·25

3,00 EXPOSICIÓ FILATÈLICA INTERNACIONAL DEL PRINCIPAT DE MÒNACO CAPELLA DE SANT MIQUEL D'ENGOLASTERS LA POSTE 1997 PRINCIPAT D'ANDORRA

**F225** St. Michael's Chapel, Engolasters

**1997.** International Stamp Exn, Monaco.

F534 **F225** 3f. multicoloured 1·90 2·10

**F226** Harlequin juggling Candles

**1998.** Birthday Greetings Stamp.

F535 **F226** 3f. multicoloured 1·90 2·10

**F227** Super Giant Slalom

**1997.** Winter Olympic Games, Nagano, Japan.

F536 **F227** 4f.40 multicoloured 3·25 3·50

**F228** Arms of Ordino

**1998.** No value expressed. Self-adhesive.
F537 **F228** (3f.) multicoloured 1·90 2·10

**F229** Altarpiece and Vila Church

**1998**
F538 **F229** 4f.50 multicoloured 3·25 3·50

**F230** Emblem and Cogwheels

**1998.** 20th Anniv of Rotary Int in Andorra.
F539 **F230** 3f. multicoloured 1·90 2·10

**F231** Chaffinch and Berries

**1998.** Nature Protection.
F540 **F231** 3f.80 multicoloured 3·00 3·25

**F232** Players

**1998.** World Cup Football Championship, France.
F541 **F232** 3f. multicoloured 1·90 2·10

**F233** Treble Score and Stylized Orchestra

**1998.** Europa. National Festivals. Music Festival.
F542 **F233** 3f. multicoloured 1·90 2·10

**F234** River

**1998.** "Expo '98" World's Fair, Lisbon, Portugal.
F543 **F234** 5f. multicoloured 3·75 4·25

**F235** Chalice

**1998.** Chalice from the House of the Valleys.
F544 **F235** 4f.50 multicoloured 3·25 3·75

**1998.** French Victory in World Cup Football Championship. No. F541 optd FINAL FRANCA/BRASIL 3-0.
F545 **F232** 3f. multicoloured 3·75 4·25

**F237** Andorra, 1717

**1998.** Relief Maps. Multicoloured.
F546 3f. Type F **237** 1·90 2·10
F547 15f.50 Andorra, 1777 (horiz) 9·75 10·50

**F238** Museum

**1998.** Inauguration of Postal Museum.
F548 **F238** 3f. multicoloured 1·90 2·10

**F239** Front Page of First Edition

**1998.** 250th Anniv of "Manual Digest".
F549 **F239** 3f.80 multicoloured 3·00 3·25

**F240** Arms of La Massana

**1999.** No value expressed. Self-adhesive.
F550 **F240** (3f.) multicoloured 1·90 2·10

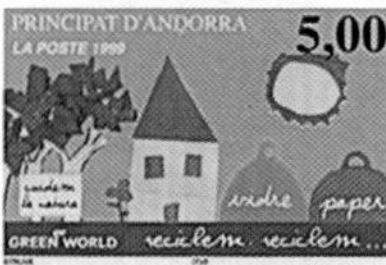
**F241** House and Recycling Bins

**1999.** "Green World". Recycling of Waste.
F551 **F241** 5f. multicoloured 3·75 4·25

**F242** Vall de Sorteny (image scaled to 63% of original size)

**1999.** Europa. Parks and Gardens.
F552 **F242** 3f. multicoloured 1·90 2·10

**F243** Council Emblem and Seat, Strasbourg

**1999.** 50th Anniv of Council of Europe.
F553 **F243** 3f.80 multicoloured 3·00 3·25

**F244** "The First Mail Coach"

**1999**
F554 **F244** 2f.70 multicoloured 1·70 1·90

**F245** Footballer and Flags

**1999.** Andorra–France Qualifying Match for European Nations Football Championship.
F555 **F245** 4f.50 multicoloured 3·50 4·00

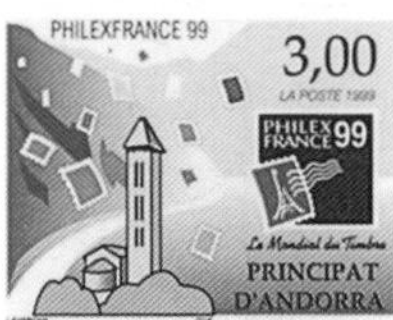
**F246** St. Michael's Church, Engolasters, and Emblem

**1999.** "Philexfrance 99" International Stamp Exhibition, Paris, France.
F556 **F246** 3f. multicoloured 1·80 2·00

**F247** Winter Scene

**1999.** Paintings of Pal by Francesc Galobardes. Multicoloured.
F557 3f. Type F **247** 1·80 2·00
F558 3f. Summer scene (horiz) 1·80 2·00

**F248** Emblem and "50"

**1999.** 50th Anniv of International Photographic Art Federation.
F559 **F248** 4f.40 multicoloured 2·75 3·00

**F249** Rull House, Sispony

**1999**
F560 **F249** 15f.50 multicoloured 7·25 8·00

**F250** Chest with Six Locks

**1999**
F561 **F250** 6f.70 multicoloured 3·25 3·50

**F251** Angels

**1999.** Christmas.
F562 **F251** 3f. multicoloured 1·80 2·00

**F252** Revellers

**2000.** New Millennium.
F563 **F252** 3f. multicoloured 1·80 2·00

**F253** Arms of La Vella

**2000.** No value expressed. Self-adhesive.
F564 **F253** (3f.) multicoloured 1·80 2·00

**F254** Snow Boarder

**2000**
F565 **F254** 4f.50 blue, brown and black 2·75 3·00

**F255** Emblem

**2000.** Montserrat Caballe International Opera Competition, Saint Julia de Loria.
F566 **F255** 3f.80 yellow and blue 2·30 2·50

**F256** *Campanula cochlearifolia*

**2000**
F567 **F256** 2f.70 multicoloured 1·80 2·00

**F257** "Building Europe"

**2000.** Europa.
F568 **F257** 3f. multicoloured 2·50 2·75

**F258** Church (Canolich Festival)

**2000.** Festivals. Multicoloured.

| | | | |
|---|---|---|---|
| F569 | 3f. Type F **258** | 1·80 | 2·00 |
| F570 | 3f. People at Our Lady's Chapel, Meritxell (Meritxell Festival) | 1·80 | 2·00 |

**F259** Sparrow

**2000**

| | | | | |
|---|---|---|---|---|
| F571 | **F259** | 4f.40 multicoloured | 2·75 | 3·00 |

**F260** Hurdling

**2000.** Olympic Games, Sydney.

| | | | | |
|---|---|---|---|---|
| F572 | **F260** | 5f. multicoloured | 3·00 | 3·50 |

**F261** Goat, Skier and Walker

**2000.** Tourism Day.

| | | | | |
|---|---|---|---|---|
| F573 | **F261** | 3f. multicoloured | 1·80 | 2·00 |

**F262** Flower, Text, Circuit Board and Emblems

**2000.** "EXPO 2000" World's Fair, Hanover.

| | | | | |
|---|---|---|---|---|
| F574 | **F262** | 3f. multicoloured | 1·80 | 2·00 |

**F263** Stone Arch and Flag

**2000.** European Community.

| | | | | |
|---|---|---|---|---|
| F575 | **F263** | 3f.80 multicoloured | 2·30 | 2·50 |

**F264** Pottery

**2000.** Prehistoric Pottery.

| | | | | |
|---|---|---|---|---|
| F576 | **F264** | 6f.70 multicoloured | 3·25 | 3·50 |

**F265** Drawing

**2000.** 25th Anniv of National Archives.

| | | | | |
|---|---|---|---|---|
| F577 | **F265** | 15f.50 multicoloured | 7·25 | 8·00 |

**F266** Arms of Saint Julia de Loria

**2001.** No value expressed. Self-adhesive.

| | | | | |
|---|---|---|---|---|
| F578 | **F266** | (3f.) multicoloured | 1·80 | 2·00 |

**F267** Ski Lift

**2001.** Canillo Aliga Club.

| | | | | |
|---|---|---|---|---|
| F579 | **F267** | 4f.50 multicoloured | 2·75 | 3·00 |

**F268** Decorative Metalwork

**2001.** Casa Cristo Museum.

| | | | | |
|---|---|---|---|---|
| F580 | **F268** | 6f.70 multicoloured | 3·25 | 3·50 |

**F269** Legend of Lake Engolasters

**2001.** Legends. Multicoloured.

| | | | |
|---|---|---|---|
| F581 | 3f. Type F **269** | 1·80 | 2·00 |
| F582 | 3f. Lords before King (foundation of Andorra) | 1·80 | 2·00 |

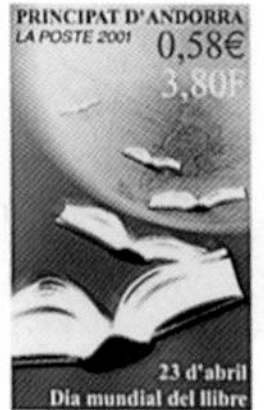


**F270** Globe and Books

**2001.** World Book Day.

| | | | | |
|---|---|---|---|---|
| F583 | **F270** | 3f.80 multicoloured | 2·30 | 2·50 |

**F271** Water Splash

**2001.** Europa. Water Resources.

| | | | | |
|---|---|---|---|---|
| F584 | **F271** | 3f. multicoloured | 2·50 | 2·75 |

**F272** Raspberry

**2001.** Multicoloured.. Multicoloured..

| | | | |
|---|---|---|---|
| F585 | 3f. Type F **272** | 2·30 | 2·50 |
| F586 | 4f.40 Jay (horiz) | 3·00 | 3·50 |

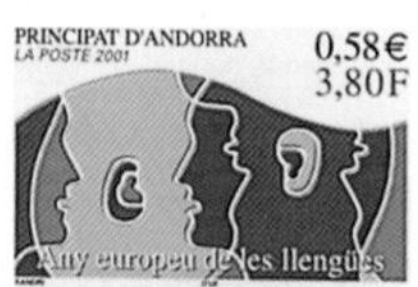


**F273** Profiles talking

**2001.** European Year of Languages.

| | | | | |
|---|---|---|---|---|
| F587 | **F273** | 3f.80 multicoloured | 2·75 | 3·25 |

**F274** Trumpeter

**2001.** Jazz Festival, Escaldes-Engordany.

| | | | | |
|---|---|---|---|---|
| F588 | **F274** | 3f. multicoloured | 2·30 | 2·50 |

**F275** Kitchen

**2001**

| | | | | |
|---|---|---|---|---|
| F589 | **F275** | 5f. multicoloured | 3·00 | 3·50 |

**F276** Chapel

**2001.** 25th Anniv of Chapel of Our Lady, Meritxell.

| | | | | |
|---|---|---|---|---|
| F590 | **F276** | 3f. multicoloured | 2·30 | 2·50 |

**F277** Hotel Pla

**2001**

| | | | | |
|---|---|---|---|---|
| F591 | **F277** | 15f.50 black, violet and green | 7·75 | 8·75 |

**F278** Cross

**2001.** Grossa Cross (boundary cross at the crossroads between Avinguda Meritxell and Carrer Bisbe Iglesias).

| | | | | |
|---|---|---|---|---|
| F592 | **F278** | 2f.70 multicoloured | 1·60 | 1·70 |

**F279** State Arms

**2002.** (a) With Face Value. Ordinary gum.

| | | | | |
|---|---|---|---|---|
| F593 | **F279** | 1c. multicoloured | 30 | 35 |
| F594 | **F279** | 2c. multicoloured | 30 | 35 |
| F595 | **F279** | 5c. multicoloured | 30 | 35 |
| F596 | **F279** | 60c. multicoloured | 1·90 | 2·10 |

(b) No value expressed.

| | | | |
|---|---|---|---|
| F598 | (46c.) multicoloured | 2·30 | 2·50 |
| F599 | (46c.) multicoloured | 2·30 | 2·50 |

(ii) Size 17×23 mm. Self-adhesive gum.

| | | | |
|---|---|---|---|
| F599a | (52c.) multicoloured | 1·70 | 1·90 |

Nos. F598/9 were sold at the rate for inland letters up to 20 grammes.

**F280** The Legend of Meritxell

**2002.** Legends. Designs as Nos. F525, F531/3 and F581/2 but with values in new currency as Type F 280. Multicoloured.

| | | | |
|---|---|---|---|
| F600 | 10c. Type F **280** | 55 | 60 |
| F601 | 20c. Wrestlers (The Fountain of Esmelicat) | 55 | 60 |
| F602 | 41c. The Piper (La joueurde cornemuse) | 1·40 | 1·60 |
| F603 | 45c. Legend of Saint Vincent Castle | 1·40 | 1·60 |
| F604 | 48c. Port Rat (horiz) | 2·10 | 2·30 |
| F604a | 48c. The Cave of Ourses | 1·40 | 1·60 |
| F604b | 49c. The Testament of Ilop | 1·40 | 1·60 |
| F604c | 50c. El tresor de la font del Manego | 1·40 | 1·60 |
| F605 | 50c. The Seven-armed Cross | 1·40 | 1·60 |
| F606 | 51c. The Devils of Aiscirivall Ches Diables d'Aixirivall | 2·10 | 2·30 |
| F606a | 75c. 'Le joueur de cornemuse' | 2·75 | 3·00 |
| F606b | 90c. Legende du pin de la "Margin eda" | 1·20 | 1·80 |
| F610 | €1 Lords before King (foundation of Andorra) | 2·75 | 3·00 |
| F611 | €2 Legend of Lake Engolasters | 5·50 | 6·25 |
| F612 | €5 The White Lady | 12·50 | 14·00 |

F281 Pedestrians on Crossing

**2002.** Schools' Road Safety Campaign.

| | | | | |
|---|---|---|---|---|
| F615 | **F281** | 69c. multicoloured | 2·50 | 2·75 |

**F282** Skier

**2002.** Winter Olympic Games, Salt Lake City, U.S.A.

| | | | | |
|---|---|---|---|---|
| F616 | **F282** | 58c. multicoloured | 1·90 | 2·10 |

**F283** Hotel Rosaleda

**2002**

| | | | | |
|---|---|---|---|---|
| F617 | **F283** | 46c. multicoloured | 1·70 | 1·80 |

**F284** Water Droplet and Clouds

**2002.** World Water Day.

| | | | | |
|---|---|---|---|---|
| F618 | **F284** | 67c. multicoloured | 2·10 | 2·30 |

**F285** Clown

**2002.** Europa. Circus.

| | | | | |
|---|---|---|---|---|
| F619 | **F285** | 46c. multicoloured | 2·50 | 2·75 |

**F286** Myrtle

**2002**

| | | | | |
|---|---|---|---|---|
| F620 | **F286** | 46c. multicoloured | 1·70 | 1·80 |

**F287** Seated Nude (Josep Viladomat)

**2002**

| | | | | |
|---|---|---|---|---|
| F621 | **F287** | €2.26 multicoloured | 6·50 | 7·00 |

**F288** Mountains from Tunnel Entrance

**2002.** Completion of the Envalira Road Tunnel between Andorra and France.

| | | | | |
|---|---|---|---|---|
| F622 | **F288** | 46c. multicoloured | 1·70 | 1·80 |

**F289** Mural (detail) (Santa Coloma Church, Andorra la Vella)

**2002**

| | | | | |
|---|---|---|---|---|
| F623 | **F289** | €1.02 multicoloured | 3·25 | 3·50 |

**F 290** Arms of Escaldes – Engordany

**2003.** Arms. No value expressed. Self-adhesive.

| | | | | |
|---|---|---|---|---|
| F624 | **F 290** | (46c.) multicoloured | 1·90 | 2·10 |

No. F624 was sold at the rate for inland letters up to 20 grammes.

**2003.** Legends. 'Legende du pinde la Margineda'. As T F 280.

| | | | |
|---|---|---|---|
| F625 | 69c. multicoloured | 1·90 | 2·10 |

**F 291** State Arms

**2003.** 10th Anniv of Constitution.

| | | | | |
|---|---|---|---|---|
| F626 | **F 291** | €2.36 multicoloured | 6·50 | 7·00 |

**F 292** Les Bons

**2003.** Architecture.

| | | | | |
|---|---|---|---|---|
| F627 | **F 292** | 67c. multicoloured | 2·50 | 2·10 |

**F 293** Hotel Mirador

**2003**

| | | | | |
|---|---|---|---|---|
| F628 | **F 293** | €1.02 multicoloured | 3·25 | 3·50 |

**F 294** Man, Dog and Sheep

**2003.** Europa. Poster Art.

| | | | | |
|---|---|---|---|---|
| F629 | **F 294** | 46c. multicoloured | 2·50 | 2·75 |

**F 295** Dancers and Fire

**2003.** Fires of St. John the Baptist Festival.

| | | | | |
|---|---|---|---|---|
| F630 | **F 295** | 50c. multicoloured | 1·90 | 2·10 |

**F 296** Cyclist and Map

**2003.** Centenary of Tour de France (cycle race).

| | | | | |
|---|---|---|---|---|
| F631 | **F 296** | 50c. multicoloured | 1·90 | 2·10 |

**F 297** Pole Vault

**2003.** World Athletics Championship, Paris.

| | | | | |
|---|---|---|---|---|
| F632 | **F 297** | 90c. multicoloured | 2·75 | 3·25 |

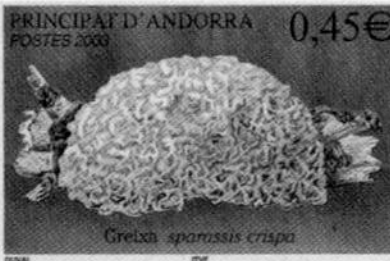
**F 298** *Greixa sparassis crispa*

**2003**

| | | | | |
|---|---|---|---|---|
| F633 | **F 298** | 45c. multicoloured | 1·30 | 1·40 |

**F 299** Red Currant

**2003**

| | | | | |
|---|---|---|---|---|
| F634 | **F 299** | 75c. multicoloured | 2·50 | 2·75 |

**F 300** Telephone, Satellite and Globe

**2003.** Centenary of First Telephone in Andorra.

| | | | | |
|---|---|---|---|---|
| F635 | **F 300** | 50c. multicoloured | 1·90 | 2·10 |

**F301** "Maternity" (Paul Gauguin)

**2003**

| | | | | |
|---|---|---|---|---|
| F636 | **F 301** | 75c. multicoloured | 2·75 | 3·00 |

**F302** St. Anthony's Market

**2004**

| | | | | |
|---|---|---|---|---|
| F637 | **F 302** | 50c. multicoloured | 1·90 | 2·10 |

**F303** Children

**2004**

| | | | | |
|---|---|---|---|---|
| F638 | **F 303** | 50c. multicoloured | 1·90 | 2·10 |

**F304** Hotel Valira

**2004**

| | | | | |
|---|---|---|---|---|
| F639 | **F 304** | €1.11 multicoloured | 3·50 | 3·75 |

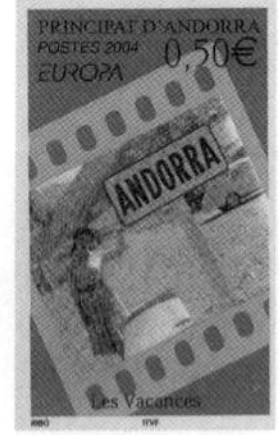
**F305** Woman and Andorra Sign

**2004.** Europa. Holidays.

| | | | | |
|---|---|---|---|---|
| F640 | **F 305** | 50c. orange, red and black | 2·10 | 2·30 |

**F306** Madriu-Perafita-Claror Valley

**2004.** UNESCO World Heritage Site.

| | | | | |
|---|---|---|---|---|
| F641 | **F 306** | 75c. multicoloured | 2·50 | 2·75 |

**F307** Poblet de Fontaneda

2004
F642 **F 307** 50c. multicoloured 1·90 2·10

**F308** Runner and Swimmer

**2004.** Olympic Games, Athens 2004.
F643 **F 308** 90c. multicoloured 3·00 3·25

**F309** "Pont de la Margineda"(sketch)

**2004.** Arts. Margineda Bridge by Joaquim Mir (Spanish artist). Multicoloured.
F644 €1 Type F **309** 3·00 3·25
F645 €2 "Pont de la Margineda" (painting) 5·75 6·25

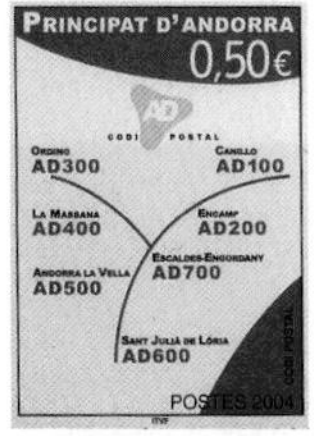
**F310** Town Names and Post Codes

**2004.** Introduction of Postal Codes.
F646 **F310** 50c. vermilion, black and lemon 1·90 2·10

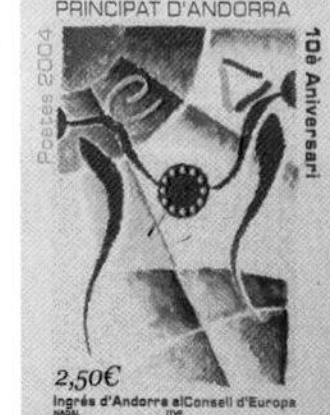
**F311** Emblem

**2004.** 10th Anniv of Entry into Council of Europe.
F647 **F311** €2.50 multicoloured 7·75 8·50

**F312** Children's Nativity

**2004.** Christmas.
F648 **F312** 50c. black, brown and bistre 1·90 2·10

**F313** Three Kings visiting Child

**2005**
F649 **F313** 50c. multicoloured 1·90 2·10

**F314** Mountains and Lake

**2005.** World Heritage Site. Madriu-Claror-Perafita Valley.
F650 **F314** 50c. multicoloured 1·90 2·10

**F 315** Tengmalm's Owl (*Aegolius funereus*)

**2005**
F651 **F315** 90c. multicoloured 2·75 3·25

**F 316** Bottle, Glass, Jug and Fruit

**2005.** Europa. Gastronomy.
F652 **F316** 55c. multicoloured 2·00 2·20

**F 317** Marksman

**2005.** Small States of Europe Games. Sheet 151×70 mm containing Type F 317 and similar vert designs. Each black and magenta.
**MS**F653 53c. Type F **317**; 55c. Runner; 82c. Swimmer; €1 Diver 9·00 9·50

**F 318** Mountain Hut, Bordes d'Ensegur

**2005**
F654 **F318** €2.50 multicoloured 8·00 8·75

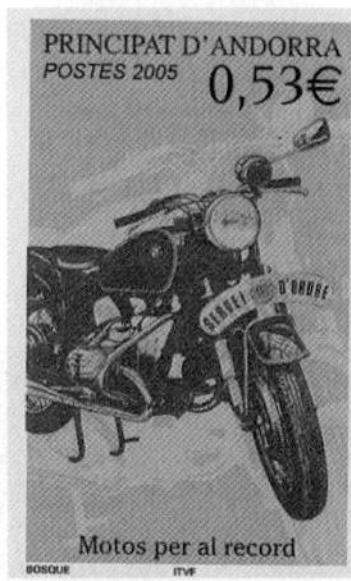
**F319** Motorcycle

**2005**
F655 **F319** 53c. sepia, brown and black 1·60 1·70

**F320** "Prats de Santa Coloma" (Joaquim Mir)

**2005.** Art.
F656 **F320** 82c. multicoloured 2·75 2·75

**F321** Hostel Calones

**2005**
F657 **F321** €1.98 multicoloured 6·25 6·50

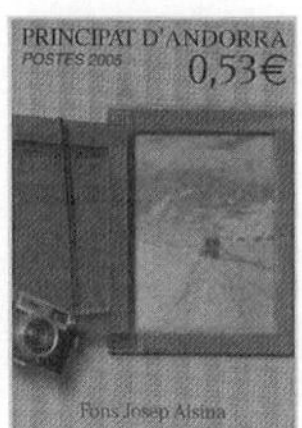
**F322** Lorry in Snow (Josep Alsina)

**2005.** Photography.
F658 **F322** 53c. multicoloured 1·70 1·80

**F323** Emblem

**2005.** Centenary of Rotary International.
F659 **F323** 55c. multicoloured 1·90 2·00

**F324** "Adoration of the Shepherds" (A. Viladomat)

**2005.** Christmas.
F660 **F324** €1.22 multicoloured 4·00 4·25

**F325** *Ursus arctos*

**2006.** Fauna. Multicoloured.
F661 53c. Type F **325** 1·70 1·80
F662 53c. *Rupicapra pyrenaica* (vert) 1·70 1·80

**F326** Alpine Skier

**2006.** Winter Olympic Games, Turin. Multicoloured.
F663 55c. Type F **326** 1·70 1·80
F664 75c. Cross country skier 2·30 2·50

**F326a** Tobacco Leaves

**2006.** Tobacco Museum, Sant Julia de Loria.
F665 **F326a** 82c. multicoloured 2·75 2·75

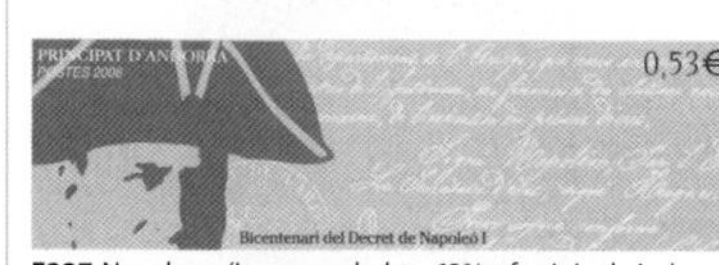
**F327** Napoleon (image scaled to 63% of original size)

**2006.** Bicentenary of Napoleon's Decree restoring Statute of Co-Principality.
F666 **F327** 53c. blue, azure and black 1·70 1·80

**F328** Coloured blocks

**2006.** Europa. Integration.
F667 **F328** 53c. multicoloured 2·00 2·10

**F329** Sorteny Valley Nature Reserve

**2006**
F668 **F329** 55c. multicoloured 1·90 2·00

**F330** Pablo Casals

**2006.** 130th Birth Anniv of Pablo Casals (cellist).
F669 **F330** 90c. multicoloured 3·00 3·25

**F331** Model T Ford

**2006**
F670 **F331** 85c. multicoloured 2·75 3·00

**F332** "Montserrat Procession" (Josep Borrell)

**2006**
F671 **F332** €1.30 multicoloured 4·25 4·50

**F333** Reredos (retable), Sant Marti de la Cortinada, Ordino

**2006**
F672 **F333** 54c. multicoloured 1·90 2·00

**F334** Marmot (*Marmota marmota*)

**2007**. Funa. Multicoloured.
F673 54c. Type F**334** 1·90 2·00
F674 60c. Eurasian red squirrel (*Sciurus vulgaris*) (horiz) 2·00 2·10

**F335** "Predel-la de Prats" (Master of Canillo)

**2007**
F675 **F335** €1.30 multicoloured 4·25 4·50

**F336** Heart enclosing Rose

**2007**. Saint George.
F676 **F336** 86c. multicoloured 3·00 3·25

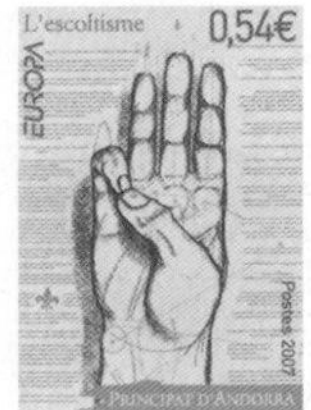


**F337** Salute

**2007**. Europa. Centenary of Scouting.
F677 **F337** 54c. multicoloured 1·90 2·00

**F338** Virgin, Meritxell

**2007**. Twinning of Meritxell and Sabart. Multicoloured.
F678 54c. Type F **338** 1·90 2·00
F679 54c. Virgin, Sabart 1·90 2·00

**F339** 'Pinette'

**2007**
F680 **F339** 60c. multicoloured 2·00 2·10

**F340** Players

**2007**. Rugby World Cup, France.
F681 **F340** 85c. multicoloured 2·75 3·00

**F341** Vall del Comapedrosa

**2007**
F682 **F341** €3.04 multicoloured 10·00 10·50

**F 341a** Prehistoric Family

**2007**. Pre-Historic Sites. El Cedre.
F683 **F 341a** 85c. multicoloured 3·00 3·25

**F 342** Cave Dwellers

**2007**. Pre-Historic Sites. La Barma de la Marginada.
F684 **F 342** 60c. multicoloured 2·00 2·10

**F343** Altarpiece, Sant Marti de la Cortinada

**2007**. Christmas.
F685 **F343** 54c. multicoloured 1·90 2·00

**F344** *Vulpes vulpes* (red fox)

**2008**. Fauna. Multicoloured.
F686 54c. Type F **344** 2·00 2·10
F687 60c. *Sus scrofa* (wild boar) (vert) 2·20 2·30

**F345** Predella's Altar of St. Michaels d'Pratts church

**2008**. Easter.
F688 **F 345** €1.33 multicoloured 5·00 5·25

**F 346** Cartercar, 1906

**2008**
F689 **F 346** 65c. multicoloured 2·75 2·75

**F 347** Symbols of Writing

**2008**. Europa. The Letter.
F690 **F 347** 55c. multicoloured 2·30 2·40

**F 348** Rowing

**2008**. Olympic Games, Beijing. Sheet 210×60 mm containing T F 348 and similar horiz designs. Multicoloured.
**MS**F691 55c.×4, Type F **348**; Running; Swimming; Judo 8·25 8·50

The stamps of **MS**F691 were not for sale separately.

**F 349** *Narcissus poeticus*

**2008**
F692 **F 349** 55c. multicoloured 2·30 2·40

**F 350** Vall d'Incles (Incles valley)

**2008**
F693 **F 350** €2.80 multicoloured 10·50 11·00

**F 351** Men

**2008**. 75th Anniv of Male Suffrage.
F694 **F 351** 55c. multicoloured 2·30 2·40

**F 352** Valley

**2008**. Sustainable Development.
F695 **F 352** 88c. multicoloured 3·75 4·00

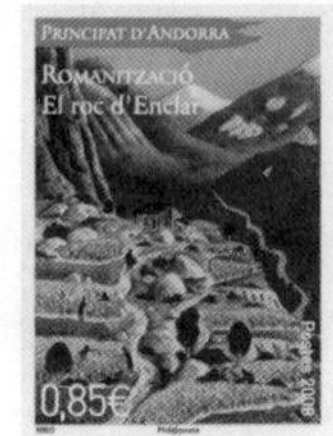


**F 353** El roc d'Enclar

**2008**
F696 **F 353** 85c. multicoloured 3·50 3·75

**F 354** St. Mark and St. Mary (alterpiece (reredos))

**2008**
F697 **F 354** 55c. multicoloured 2·75 2·75

**F 355** Louis Braille

**2009**. Birth Bicentenary of Louis Braille (inventor of Braille writing for the blind).
F698 **F 355** 88c. blue and brown 4·00 4·00

**F 356** *Equus mulus* (mule)

**2009**. Domestic Animals. Multicoloured.
F699 55c. Type F**356** 2·30 2·40
F700 65c. *Bos taurus* (cow) (horiz) 2·50 2·50

**F 357** Penguins

**2009**. Preserve Polar Regions and Glaciers. Sheet 143×120 mm containing Type F 357 and similar multicoloured design.
**MS**F701 56c. Type F **357**; 85c. Polar ice 6·25 6·50

**F 358** *Pradel la des Prats* (detail)

**2009**

| | | | | |
|---|---|---|---|---|
| F702 | **F 358** | €1.35 multicoloured | 6·00 | 6·25 |

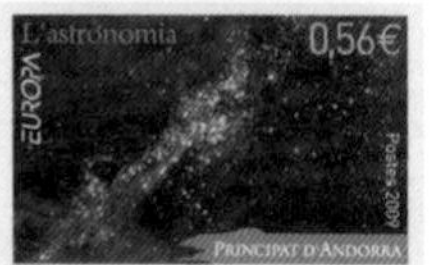


**F 359** Nebula

**2009.** Europa. Astronomy.

| | | | | |
|---|---|---|---|---|
| F703 | **F 359** | 56c. multicoloured | 2·50 | 2·50 |

**F 360** Renault Voiturette, 1898

**2009.** 1st Car manufactured by Renault.

| | | | | |
|---|---|---|---|---|
| F704 | **F 360** | 70c. multicoloured | 3·00 | 3·25 |

**F 361** *Sant Joan de Caselles* (Maurice Utrillo)

**2009.** Art.

| | | | | |
|---|---|---|---|---|
| F705 | **F 361** | 90c. multicoloured | 4·00 | 4·00 |

**F 362** Cercle dels Pessons

**2009**

| | | | | |
|---|---|---|---|---|
| F706 | **F 362** | €2.80 multicoloured | 11·50 | 12·00 |

**F 363** Cyclist

**2009.** Tour de France (cycle race).

| | | | | |
|---|---|---|---|---|
| F707 | **F 363** | 56c. multicoloured | 2·50 | 2·50 |

**F 364** Allegory

**2009.** 40th Anniv of Circle of Arts and Letters.

| | | | | |
|---|---|---|---|---|
| F708 | **F 364** | 51c. multicoloured | 2·40 | 2·40 |

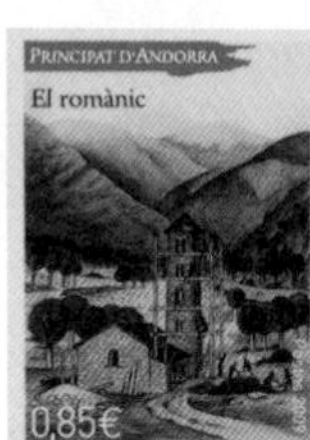


**F 365** Santa Coloma Church

**2009.** Romanesque Art in Andorra.

| | | | | |
|---|---|---|---|---|
| F709 | **F 365** | 85c. multicoloured | 3·75 | 3·75 |

**F 366** The Nativity

**2009.** Christmas.

| | | | | |
|---|---|---|---|---|
| F710 | **F 366** | 56c. multicoloured | 2·50 | 2·50 |

**F 366a** Arms

**2010.** State Arms. Background colour given. (a) With face value.

| | | | | |
|---|---|---|---|---|
| F710a | **366A** | 1c. multicoloured (pale lemon) | 20 | 25 |
| F711 | | 5c. multicoloured (cobalt) | 25 | 30 |
| F712 | | 10c. multicoloured (bright yellow-orange) | 55 | 60 |
| F713 | | 20c. multicoloured (lavender) | 55 | 60 |
| F714 | | 50c. multicoloured (olive-bistre) | 1·40 | 1·60 |

(b) No value expressed.

| | | | | |
|---|---|---|---|---|
| F715 | | (60c.) multicoloured (aqua-marine) | 2·40 | 2·50 |

Nos. F710a/F715 are as No. F **279** but with different inscriptions.

**F 367** Athlete

**2010.** Winter Olympic Games, Vancouver.

| | | | | |
|---|---|---|---|---|
| F716 | **F 367** | 85c. multicoloured | 3·75 | 3·75 |

**F 368** Casamanya Peak

**2010.** Mountains.

| | | | | |
|---|---|---|---|---|
| F717 | **F 368** | €2.80 multicoloured | 11·50 | 12·00 |

**F 369** Anniversary Emblem

**2010.** 20th Anniv of Convention on Rights of the Child. UNICEF

| | | | | |
|---|---|---|---|---|
| F718 | **F 369** | 56c. multicoloured | 2·50 | 2·50 |

No. F719 and Type F **370** are left for Le Mouton issued on 8 March 2010, not yet received.

No. F720 and Type F **371** are left for Le Vautour issued on 8 March 2010, not yet received.

No. F721 and Type F **372** are left for Ambassador to Brussles issued on 12 April 2010, not yet received.

No. F722 and Type F **373** are left for Legends issued on 26 April 2010, not yet received.

**F374** Mirror and 'Mirror, Magic Mirror, tell me which is' (from Snow White)

**2010.** Europa. Children's Books

| | | | | |
|---|---|---|---|---|
| F723 | **F 374** | 56c. silver and bright rose-red | 2·50 | 2·50 |

No. F724 and Type F **375** are left for Radio Andorra issued on 24 May 2010, not yet received. Type F **376** is vacant.

**F377** Ferrari 328 GTS

**2010.** Classic Cars

| | | | | |
|---|---|---|---|---|
| F725 | **F 377** | 70c. multicoloured | 3·00 | 3·00 |

CARME MASSANA
Natura morta
0,95€
Postes 2010
PRINCIPAT D'ANDORRA

**F378** Still Life (Carme Massana)

**2010.** Art

| | | | | |
|---|---|---|---|---|
| F726 | **F 378** | 95c. multicoloured | 3·75 | 3·75 |

**F379** The Crucifixion of Christ, Predella of the Altar of Saint-Michel De Prats Church (detail)

**2010.** Religious Art

| | | | | |
|---|---|---|---|---|
| F727 | **F 379** | €1.40 multicoloured | 2·50 | 2·50 |

See also No. F702.

## POSTAGE DUE STAMPS

**1931.** Postage Due stamps of France optd ANDORRE.

| | | | | |
|---|---|---|---|---|
| FD24 | **D11** | 5c. blue | 2·10 | 5·75 |
| FD25 | **D11** | 10c. brown | 2·10 | 4·50 |
| FD26 | **D11** | 30c. red | 1·10 | 5·25 |
| FD27 | **D11** | 50c. purple | 2·10 | 5·75 |
| FD28 | **D11** | 60c. green | 26·00 | 55·00 |
| FD29 | **D11** | 1f. brown on yellow | 2·10 | 7·00 |
| FD30 | **D11** | 2f. mauve | 17·00 | 41·00 |
| FD31 | **D11** | 3f. mauve | 4·25 | 9·75 |

**1931.** Postage Due stamps of France optd ANDORRE.

| | | | | |
|---|---|---|---|---|
| FD32 | **D43** | 1c. green | 3·25 | 5·75 |
| FD33 | **D43** | 10c. red | 6·25 | 14·00 |
| FD34 | **D43** | 60c. red | 31·00 | 48·00 |
| FD35 | **D43** | 1f. green | 95·00 | £140 |
| FD36 | **D43** | 1f.20 on 2f. blue | 90·00 | £160 |
| FD37 | **D43** | 2f. brown | £180 | £275 |
| FD38 | **D43** | 5f. on 1f. purple | 95·00 | £130 |

**FD7**

**1935**

| | | | | |
|---|---|---|---|---|
| FD82 | **FD7** | 1c. green | 4·25 | 9·25 |

**FD10**

**1937**

| | | | | |
|---|---|---|---|---|
| FD97 | **FD10** | 5c. blue | 7·50 | 16·00 |
| FD98 | **FD10** | 10c. brown | 5·25 | 30·00 |
| FD99 | **FD10** | 2f. mauve | 11·50 | 16·00 |
| FD100 | **FD10** | 5f. orange | 25·00 | 40·00 |

**FD11** Wheat Sheaves

**1943**

| | | | | |
|---|---|---|---|---|
| FD101a | **FD 11** | 10c. brown | 65 | 2·10 |
| FD102 | **FD 11** | 30c. mauve | 1·90 | 2·75 |
| FD103 | **FD 11** | 50c. green | 1·40 | 3·25 |
| FD104 | **FD 11** | 1f. blue | 2·10 | 4·75 |
| FD105 | **FD 11** | 1f.50 red | 5·75 | 14·50 |
| FD106 | **FD 11** | 2f. blue | 2·10 | 5·25 |
| FD107 | **FD 11** | 3f. red | 2·50 | 9·75 |
| FD108 | **FD 11** | 4f. violet | 5·25 | 15·00 |
| FD109 | **FD 11** | 5f. mauve | 4·25 | 14·50 |
| FD110 | **FD 11** | 10f. orange | 5·75 | 15·00 |
| FD111 | **FD 11** | 20f. brown | 8·00 | 22·00 |

**1946.** As Type FD 11, but inscr "TIMBRE-TAXE".

| | | | |
|---|---|---|---|
| FD143 | 10c. brown | 1·10 | 7·25 |
| FD144 | 1f. blue | 1·30 | 4·00 |
| FD145 | 2f. blue | 1·40 | 4·00 |
| FD146 | 3f. brown | 2·75 | 6·00 |
| FD147 | 4f. violet | 3·75 | 7·25 |
| FD148 | 5f. red | 2·10 | 5·75 |
| FD149 | 10f. orange | 3·75 | 7·50 |
| FD150 | 20f. brown | 7·50 | 13·00 |
| FD151 | 50f. green | 60·00 | 55·00 |
| FD152 | 100f. green | £110 | £160 |

**1961.** As Nos. FD143/52 but new values and colours.

| | | | |
|---|---|---|---|
| FD185 | 5c. red | 4·25 | 8·25 |
| FD186 | 10c. orange | 9·50 | 17·00 |
| FD187 | 20c. brown | 13·50 | 29·00 |
| FD188 | 50c. green | 26·00 | 47·00 |

**1964.** Designs as Nos. D1650/6 of France, but inscr "ANDORRE".

| | | | |
|---|---|---|---|
| FD192 | 5c. red, green and purple | 55 | 4·25 |
| FD193 | 10c. blue, grn & pur | 85 | 4·25 |
| FD194 | 15c. red, green and brown | 95 | 4·25 |
| FD195 | 20c. purple, green & turq | 1·10 | 4·25 |
| FD196 | 30c. blue, grn & brn | 85 | 2·50 |
| FD197 | 40c. yellow, red and green | 2·10 | 2·75 |
| FD198 | 50c. red, green and blue | 1·70 | 1·70 |

**FD129** Holly Berries

**1985.** Fruits.

| | | | | |
|---|---|---|---|---|
| FD371 | **FD129** | 10c. red and green | 1·70 | 2·75 |
| FD372 | - | 20c. brown & blue | 1·70 | 2·75 |
| FD373 | - | 30c. green and red | 1·70 | 2·75 |
| FD374 | - | 40c. brown & blk | 1·70 | 2·75 |
| FD375 | - | 50c. olive & violet | 1·70 | 2·75 |
| FD376 | - | 1f. green and blue | 1·70 | 2·75 |
| FD377 | - | 2f. red and brown | 1·80 | 3·00 |
| FD378 | - | 3f. purple & green | 2·10 | 3·50 |
| FD379 | - | 4f. olive and blue | 2·75 | 3·75 |
| FD380 | - | 5f. olive and red | 3·25 | 4·25 |

DESIGNS: 20c. Wild plum; 30c. Raspberry; 40c. Dogberry; 50c. Blackberry; 1f. Juniper; 2f. Rose hip; 3f. Elder; 4f. Bilberry; 5f. Strawberry.

## SPANISH POST OFFICES

**1928.** Stamps of Spain optd CORREOS ANDORRA.

| | | | | |
|---|---|---|---|---|
| 1B | **68** | 2c. green | 1·70 | 2·30 |
| 2B | **68** | 5c. red | 2·30 | 2·75 |
| 3B | **68** | 10c. green | 3·50 | 4·00 |
| 5B | **68** | 15c. blue | 3·50 | 4·00 |
| 6B | **68** | 20c. violet | 3·75 | 4·25 |
| 7A | **68** | 25c. red | 8·50 | 8·50 |
| 8A | **68** | 30c. brown | 29·00 | 29·00 |
| 9A | **68** | 40c. blue | 34·00 | 34·00 |
| 10A | **68** | 50c. orange | 37·00 | 37·00 |
| 11B | **69** | 1p. grey | 34·00 | 36·00 |
| 12A | **69** | 4p. red | £180 | £180 |
| 13A | **69** | 10p. brown | £250 | £250 |

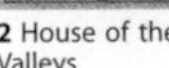

**2** House of the Valleys

**3** General Council of Andorra

**1929**

| | | | | |
|---|---|---|---|---|
| 14A | **2** | 2c. green | 2·00 | 2·30 |
| 26 | **2** | 2c. brown | 1·40 | 2·30 |
| 15A | - | 5c. purple | 3·75 | 4·00 |
| 27 | - | 5c. brown | 2·10 | 2·75 |
| 16A | - | 10c. green | 3·75 | 4·00 |
| 17A | - | 15c. blue | 5·50 | 5·75 |
| 30 | - | 15c. green | 5·75 | 7·00 |
| 18A | - | 20c. violet | 5·50 | 6·25 |
| 33 | - | 25c. red | 2·75 | 3·50 |
| 20A | **2** | 30c. brown | £150 | £160 |
| 34 | **2** | 30c. red | 2·75 | 4·00 |
| 21A | - | 40c. blue | 11·50 | 8·00 |
| 36 | **2** | 45c. red | 2·30 | 2·75 |
| 22A | - | 50c. orange | 11·50 | 7·00 |
| 38 | **2** | 60c. blue | 4·50 | 5·75 |
| 23A | **3** | 1p. slate | 23·00 | 29·00 |
| 39 | **3** | 4p. purple | 46·00 | 50·00 |
| 40 | **3** | 10p. brown | 70·00 | 75·00 |

DESIGNS: 5, 40c. Church of St. John of Caselles; 10, 20, 50c. Sant Julia de Loria; 15, 25c. Santa Coloma Church.

**7** Councillor Manuel Areny Bons

**11** Map

**1948**

| | | | | |
|---|---|---|---|---|
| 41 | **F** | 2c. olive | 1·10 | 1·70 |
| 42 | **F** | 5c. orange | 1·10 | 1·70 |
| 43 | **F** | 10c. blue | 1·10 | 1·70 |
| 44 | **7** | 20c. purple | 10·50 | 7·00 |
| 45 | **7** | 25c. orange | 7·00 | 3·50 |
| 46 | **G** | 30c. green | 23·00 | 11·50 |
| 47 | **H** | 50c. green | 34·00 | 15·00 |
| 48 | **I** | 75c. blue | 33·00 | 16·00 |
| 49 | **H** | 90c. purple | 17·00 | 11·50 |
| 50 | **I** | 1p. red | 29·00 | 15·00 |
| 51 | **G** | 1p.35 violet | 11·50 | 11·50 |
| 52 | **11** | 4p. blue | 34·00 | 29·00 |
| 53 | **11** | 10p. brown | 65·00 | 34·00 |

DESIGNS—VERT: F. Edelweiss; G. Arms; H. Market Place, Ordino; I. Shrine near Meritxell Chapel.

**12** Andorra La Vella

**1951.** Air.

| | | | | |
|---|---|---|---|---|
| 54 | **12** | 1p. brown | 40·00 | 26·00 |

**13** St. Anthony's Bridge

**1963**

| | | | | |
|---|---|---|---|---|
| 55 | **13** | 25c. brown and black | 25 | 30 |
| 56 | - | 70c. black and green | 35 | 55 |
| 57 | - | 1p. lilac and grey | 90 | 1·50 |
| 58 | - | 2p. violet and lilac | 1·10 | 1·70 |
| 59 | - | 2p.50 deep red and purple | 90 | 1·40 |
| 60 | - | 3p. slate and black | 1·10 | 1·60 |
| 61 | - | 5p. purple and brown | 3·50 | 3·75 |
| 62 | - | 6p. red and brown | 4·50 | 4·00 |

DESIGNS—VERT: 70c. Anyos meadows (wrongly inscr "AYNOS"); 1p. Canillo; 2p. Santa Coloma Church; 2p.50, Arms; 6p. Virgin of Meritxell. HORIZ: 3p. Andorra la Vella; 5p. Ordino.

**14** Daffodills

**1966.** Pyrenean Flowers.

| | | | | |
|---|---|---|---|---|
| 63 | **14** | 50c. blue and slate | 55 | 1·10 |
| 64 | - | 1p. purple and brown | 1·10 | 1·30 |
| 65 | - | 5p. blue and green | 3·25 | 3·50 |
| 66 | - | 10p. slate and violet | 1·70 | 2·75 |

DESIGNS: 1p. Carnation; 5p. Narcissus; 10p. Anemone (wrongly inscr "HELEBORUS CONI").

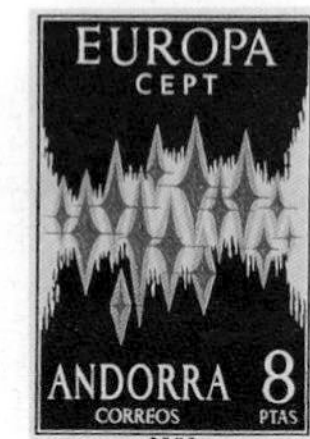

**15** "Communications"

**1972.** Europa.

| | | | | |
|---|---|---|---|---|
| 67 | **15** | 8p. multicoloured | £150 | £140 |

**16** Encamp Valley

**1972.** Tourist Views. Multicoloured.

| | | | |
|---|---|---|---|
| 68 | 1p. Type **16** | 1·00 | 1·20 |
| 69 | 1p.50 La Massana | 1·10 | 1·20 |
| 70 | 2p. Skis and snowscape, Pas de la Casa | 2·10 | 2·40 |
| 71 | 5p. Lake Pessons (horiz) | 2·30 | 2·40 |

**17** Volleyball

**1972.** Olympic Games, Munich. Multicoloured.

| | | | |
|---|---|---|---|
| 72 | 2p. Type **17** | 50 | 55 |
| 73 | 5p. Swimming (horiz) | 70 | 75 |

**18** St. Anthony's Auction

**1972.** Andorran Customs. Multicoloured.

| | | | |
|---|---|---|---|
| 74 | 1p. Type **18** | 35 | 35 |
| 75 | 1p.50 "Les Caramelles" (choir) | 35 | 35 |
| 76 | 2p. Nativity play (Christmas) | 55 | 60 |
| 77 | 5p. Giant cigar (vert) | 90 | 1·00 |
| 78 | 8p. Carved shrine, Meritxell (vert) | 1·10 | 1·20 |
| 79 | 15p. "La Marratxa" (dance) | 3·00 | 3·25 |

**19** "Peoples of Europe"

**1973.** Europa.

| | | | | |
|---|---|---|---|---|
| 80 | **19** | 2p. black, red and blue | 55 | 60 |
| 81 | - | 8p. red, brown and black | 1·70 | 1·90 |

DESIGN: 8p. Europa "Posthorn".

**20** "The Nativity"

**1973.** Christmas. Frescoes from Meritxell Chapel. Multicoloured.

| | | | |
|---|---|---|---|
| 82 | 2p. Type **20** | 55 | 60 |
| 83 | 5p. "Adoration of the Kings" | 1·70 | 1·90 |

**21** "Virgin of Ordino"

**1974.** Europa. Sculptures. Multicoloured.

| | | | |
|---|---|---|---|
| 84 | 2p. Type **21** | 2·75 | 3·00 |
| 85 | 8p. Cross | 4·00 | 4·25 |

**22** Oak Cupboard and Shelves

**1974.** Arts and Crafts. Multicoloured.

| | | | |
|---|---|---|---|
| 86 | 10p. Type **22** | 2·75 | 3·00 |
| 87 | 25p. Crown of the Virgin of the Roses | 6·25 | 6·75 |

**23** U.P.U. Monument, Berne

**1974.** Centenary of Universal Postal Union.

| | | | | |
|---|---|---|---|---|
| 88 | **23** | 15p. multicoloured | 3·50 | 3·75 |

**24** "The Nativity"

**1974.** Christmas. Carvings from Meritxell Chapel. Multicoloured.

| | | | |
|---|---|---|---|
| 89 | 2p. Type **24** | 1·10 | 1·20 |
| 90 | 5p. "Adoration of the Kings" | 3·50 | 3·75 |

**25** 19th-century Postman and Church of St. John of Caselles

**1975.** "Espana 75" Int Stamp Exhibition, Madrid.

| | | | | |
|---|---|---|---|---|
| 91 | **25** | 3p. multicoloured | 55 | 60 |

**26** "Peasant with Knife"

**1975.** Europa. 12th-century Romanesque Paintings from La Cortinada Church. Multicoloured.

| | | | |
|---|---|---|---|
| 92 | 3p. Type **26** | 2·75 | 3·00 |
| 93 | 12p. "Christ" | 5·75 | 6·25 |

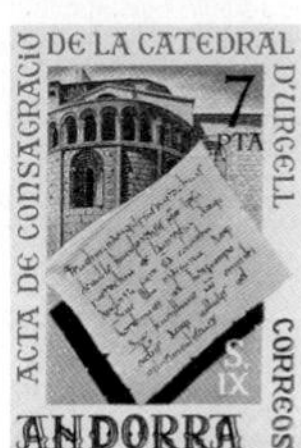

**27** Cathedral and Consecration Text

**1975.** 1100th Anniv of Consecration of Urgel Cathedral.

| | | | | |
|---|---|---|---|---|
| 94 | **27** | 7p. multicoloured | 3·50 | 3·75 |

**28** "The Nativity"

**1975.** Christmas. Paintings from La Cortinada Church. Multicoloured.

| | | | |
|---|---|---|---|
| 95 | 3p. Type **28** | 55 | 60 |
| 96 | 7p. "Adoration of The Kings" | 1·10 | 1·20 |

**29** Copper Cauldron

**1976.** Europa. Multicoloured.

| | | | |
|---|---|---|---|
| 97 | 3p. Type **29** | 70 | 75 |
| 98 | 12p. Wooden marriage chest (horiz) | 2·10 | 2·30 |

**30** Slalom Skiing

**1976.** Olympic Games, Montreal. Multicoloured.

| | | | |
|---|---|---|---|
| 99 | 7p. Type **30** | 70 | 75 |
| 100 | 15p. Canoeing (horiz) | 2·10 | 2·30 |

**31** "The Nativity"

**1976.** Christmas. Carvings from La Massana Church. Multicoloured.

| | | | |
|---|---|---|---|
| 101 | 3p. Type **31** | 40 | 45 |
| 102 | 25p. "Adoration of the Kings" | 2·50 | 2·75 |

**32** Ansalonga

**1977.** Europa. Multicoloured.

| | | | |
|---|---|---|---|
| 103 | 3p. Type **32** | 70 | 75 |
| 104 | 12p. Xuclar | 2·10 | 2·30 |

**33** Boundary Cross

**1977.** Christmas. Multicoloured.

| | | | |
|---|---|---|---|
| 105 | 5p. Type **33** | 55 | 60 |
| 106 | 12p. St. Michael's Church, Engolasters | 2·50 | 2·75 |

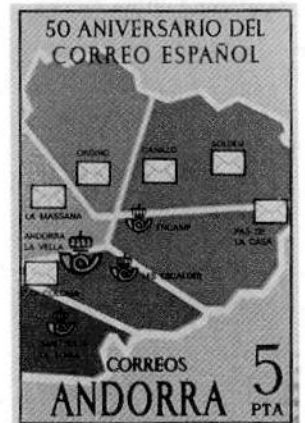

**34** Map of Andorran Post Offices

**1978.** 50th Anniv of Spanish Post Offices. Sheet 105×149 mm containing T 34 and similar vert designs. Multicoloured.

| | | | |
|---|---|---|---|
| **MS**107 | 5p. Type **34**; 10p. Postman delivering letter, 1923; 20p. Spanish Post Office, Andorra la Vella, 1928; 25p. Andorran arms | 2·75 | 3·00 |

**35** House of the Valleys

**1978.** Europa. Multicoloured.

| | | | |
|---|---|---|---|
| 108 | 5p. Type **35** | 55 | 75 |
| 109 | 12p. Church of St. John of Caselles | 1·40 | 2·30 |

**36** Crown, Mitre and Crook

**1978.** 700th Anniv of Parity Treaties.

| | | | | |
|---|---|---|---|---|
| 110 | **36** | 5p. multicoloured | 85 | 1·50 |

**37** "Holy Family"

**1978.** Christmas. Frescoes in St. Mary's Church, Encamp. Multicoloured.

| | | | |
|---|---|---|---|
| 111 | 5p. Type **37** | 40 | 45 |
| 112 | 25p. "Adoration of the Kings" | 95 | 1·10 |

**38** Young Woman's Costume

**1979.** Local Costumes. Multicoloured.

| | | | |
|---|---|---|---|
| 113 | 3p. Type **38** | 30 | 30 |
| 114 | 5p. Young man's costume | 40 | 45 |
| 115 | 12p. Newly-weds | 70 | 75 |

**39** Old Mail Bus

**1979.** Europa.

| | | | | |
|---|---|---|---|---|
| 116 | **39** | 5p. green & blue on yellow | 70 | 75 |
| 117 | - | 12p. lilac and red on yellow | 1·40 | 1·50 |

DESIGN: 12p. Pre-stamp letters.

**40** Drawing of Boy and Girl

**1979.** International Year of the Child.

| | | | | |
|---|---|---|---|---|
| 118 | **40** | 19p. blue, red and black | 1·40 | 1·50 |

**41** Agnus Dei, Santa Coloma Church

**1979.** Christmas. Multicoloured.

| | | | | |
|---|---|---|---|---|
| 119 | **41** | 8p. Santa Coloma Church | 40 | 45 |
| 120 | **41** | 25p. Type **41** | 95 | 1·10 |

**42** Pere d'Urg

**1979.** Bishops of Urgel, Co-princes of Andorra (1st series).

| | | | | |
|---|---|---|---|---|
| 121 | **42** | 1p. blue and brown | 30 | 30 |
| 122 | - | 5p. red and violet | 40 | 45 |
| 123 | - | 13p. brown and green | 85 | 90 |

DESIGNS: 5p. Joseph Caixal; 13p. Joan Benlloch.

See also Nos. 137/8, 171, 182 and 189.

**43** Antoni Fiter i Rosell

**1980.** Europa.

| | | | | |
|---|---|---|---|---|
| 124 | **43** | 8p. brown, ochre and green | 40 | 45 |
| 125 | - | 19p. black, green & dp grn | 1·70 | 1·80 |

DESIGN: 19p. Francesc Cairat i Freixes.

**44** Skiing

**1980.** Olympic Games, Moscow.

| | | | | |
|---|---|---|---|---|
| 126 | **44** | 5p. turquoise, red and blk | 30 | 30 |
| 127 | - | 8p. multicoloured | 40 | 45 |
| 128 | - | 50p. multicoloured | 1·50 | 1·70 |

DESIGNS: 8p. Boxing; 50p. Shooting.

**45** Nativity

**1980.** Christmas. Multicoloured.

| | | | |
|---|---|---|---|
| 129 | 10p. Type **45** | 40 | 45 |
| 130 | 22p. Epiphany | 95 | 1·10 |

**46** Santa Anna Dance

**1981.** Europa. Multicoloured.

| | | | |
|---|---|---|---|
| 131 | 12p. Type **46** | 70 | 75 |
| 132 | 30p. Festival of the Virgin of Canolich | 1·40 | 1·50 |

**47** Militia Members

**1981.** 50th Anniv of People's Militia.

| | | | | |
|---|---|---|---|---|
| 133 | **47** | 30p. green, grey and black | 1·40 | 1·50 |

**48** Handicapped Child learning to Write

**1981.** International Year of Disabled Persons.

| | | | | |
|---|---|---|---|---|
| 134 | **48** | 50p. multicoloured | 2·10 | 2·30 |

**49** "The Nativity"

**1981.** Christmas. Carvings from Encamp Church. Multicoloured.

| | | | |
|---|---|---|---|
| 135 | 12p. Type **49** | 70 | 75 |
| 136 | 30p. "The Adoration" | 1·40 | 1·50 |

**1981.** Bishops of Urgel, Co-princes of Andorra (2nd series). As T 42.

| | | | |
|---|---|---|---|
| 137 | 7p. purple and blue | 40 | 45 |
| 138 | 20p. brown and green | 95 | 1·10 |

DESIGNS: 7p. Salvador Casanas; 20p. Josep de Boltas.

**50** Arms of Andorra

**1982.** With "PTA" under figure of value.

| | | | | |
|---|---|---|---|---|
| 139 | **50** | 1p. mauve | 30 | 30 |
| 140 | **50** | 3p. brown | 30 | 30 |
| 141 | **50** | 7p. red | 30 | 30 |
| 142 | **50** | 12p. red | 30 | 30 |
| 143 | **50** | 15p. blue | 40 | 45 |
| 144 | **50** | 20p. green | 70 | 75 |
| 145 | **50** | 30p. red | 70 | 75 |
| 146 | **50** | 50p. green (25×31 mm) | 1·70 | 1·90 |
| 147 | **50** | 100p. blue (25×31 mm) | 3·00 | 3·50 |

See also Nos. 203/6.

**51** The New Reforms, 1866

**1982.** Europa. Multicoloured.

| | | | |
|---|---|---|---|
| 154 | 14p. Type **51** | 95 | 1·10 |
| 155 | 33p. Reform of the Institutions, 1981 | 1·80 | 2·00 |

**52** Footballers

**1982.** World Cup Football Championship, Spain. Multicoloured.

| | | | |
|---|---|---|---|
| 156 | 14p. Type **52** | 1·40 | 1·50 |
| 157 | 33p. Tackle | 2·75 | 3·00 |

**53** Arms and 1929 1p. stamp

**1982.** National Stamp Exhibition.

| | | | | |
|---|---|---|---|---|
| 158 | **53** | 14p. black and green | 1·40 | 1·50 |

**54** Spanish and French Permanent Delegations Buildings

**1982.** Anniversaries.

| | | | | |
|---|---|---|---|---|
| 159 | **54** | 9p. brown and blue | 40 | 45 |
| 160 | - | 23p. blue and brown | 70 | 75 |
| 161 | - | 33p. black and green | 1·10 | 1·20 |

DESIGNS—VERT: 9p. Type **54** (centenary of Permanent Delegations); 23p. "St. Francis feeding the Birds" (after Ciambue) (800th birth anniv of St. Francis of Assisi); 33p. Title page of "Relacio sobre la Vall de Andorra" (birth centenary of Tomas Junoy (writer)).

**55** "Virgin and Child" (statue from Andorra la Vella Parish Church)

**1982.** Christmas. Multicoloured.

| | | | |
|---|---|---|---|
| 162 | 14p. Type **55** | 70 | 75 |
| 163 | 33p. Children beating log with sticks | 2·10 | 2·30 |

**56** Building Romanesque Church

**1983.** Europa.
164 **56** 16p. green, purple & black 70 75
165 - 38p. brown, blue and black 2·10 2·30
DESIGN: 38p. 16th-century water mill.

**57** "Lactarius sanguifluus"

**1983.** Nature Protection.
166 **57** 16p. multicoloured 70 75

**58** Ballot Box on Map and Government Building

**1983.** 50th Anniv of Universal Suffrage in Andorra.
167 **58** 10p. multicoloured 70 75

**59** Mgr. Cinto Verdaguer

**1983.** Centenary of Mgr. Cinto Verdaguer's Visit.
168 **59** 50p. multicoloured 2·10 2·30

**60** Jaume Sansa Nequi

**1983.** Air. Jaume Sansa Nequi (Verger-Episcopal) Commemoration.
169 **60** 20p. deep brown & brown 70 75

**61** Wall Painting, Church of San Cerni, Nagol

**1983.** Christmas.
170 **61** 16p. multicoloured 70 75

**1983.** Bishops of Urgel, Co-princes of Andorra (3rd series). As T 42.
171 26p. brown and red 1·40 1·50
DESIGN: 26p. Joan Laguarda.

**62** Ski Jumping

**1984.** Winter Olympic Games, Sarajevo.
172 **62** 16p. multicoloured 95 1·10

**63** Exhibition and F.I.P. Emblems

**1984.** "Espana 84" Int Stamp Exhibition, Madrid.
173 **63** 26p. multicoloured 1·40 1·50

**64** Bridge

**1984.** Europa.
174 **64** 16p. brown 70 75
175 **64** 38p. blue 2·10 2·30

**65** Hurdling

**1984.** Olympic Games, Los Angeles.
176 **65** 40p. multicoloured 2·10 2·30

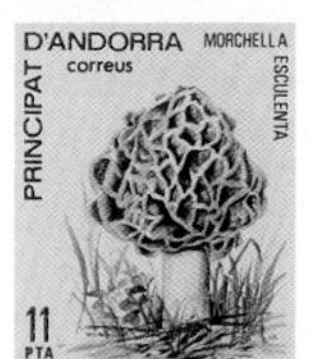

**66** Common Morel

**1984.** Nature Protection.
177 **66** 11p. multicoloured 4·25 7·50

**67** Pencil, Brush and Pen

**1984.** Pyrenean Cultures Centre, Andorra.
178 **67** 20p. multicoloured 85 90

**68** The Holy Family (wood carvings)

**1984.** Christmas.
179 **68** 17p. multicoloured 70 75

**69** Mossen Enric Marfany and Score

**1985.** Europa.
180 **69** 18p. green, purple & brown 95 1·10
181 - 45p. brown and green 1·80 2·00
DESIGN: 45p. Musician with viola (fresco detail, La Cortinada Church).

**1985.** Air. Bishops of Urgel, Co-princes of Andorra (4th series). As T 42.
182 20p. brown and ochre 70 75
DESIGN: 20p. Ramon Iglesias.

**70** Beefsteak Morel

**1985.** Nature Protection.
183 **70** 30p. multicoloured 1·40 1·50

**71** Pal

**1985**
184 **71** 17p. deep blue and blue 70 75

**72** Angels (St. Bartholomew's Chapel)

**1985.** Christmas.
185 **72** 17p. multicoloured 70 75

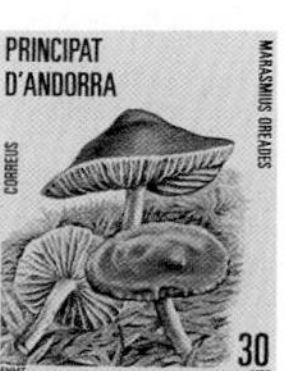

**73** Scotch Bonnet

**1986.** Nature Protection.
186 **73** 30p. multicoloured 1·40 1·50

**74** Sun, Rainbow, Lighthouse and Fish

**1986.** Europa. Each blue, red and green.
187 17p. Type **74** 1·40 1·50
188 45p. Sun and trees on rocks 2·10 2·30

**1986.** Bishops of Urgel, Co-princes of Andorra (5th series). As T 42.
189 35p. blue and brown 1·40 1·50
DESIGN: 35p. Justi Guitart.

**75** Bell of St. Roma's Chapel, Les Bons

**1986.** Christmas.
190 **75** 19p. multicoloured 70 75

**76** Arms

**1987.** Meeting of Co-princes.
191 **76** 48p. multicoloured 1·40 1·50

**77** Interior of Chapel

**1987.** Europa. Meritxell Chapel.
192 **77** 19p. brown and blue 70 75
193 - 48p. blue and brown 1·40 1·50
DESIGN: 48p. Exterior of Chapel.

**78** Emblem and House of Valleys

**1987.** Olympic Games, Barcelona (1992). Sheet 122×86 mm containing T 78 and similar horiz designs. Multicoloured.
**MS**194 20p. Type **78**; 50p. Torch carrier and St. Michael's Chapel, Fontaneda, bell tower 5·50 6·00

**79** Cep

**1987.** Nature Protection.
195 **79** 100p. multicoloured 3·50 3·75

**80** Extract from "Doctrina Pueril" by Ramon Llull

**1987.** Christmas.
196 **80** 20p. multicoloured 70 75

**81** Copper Lance Heads

**1988.** Archaeology.
197 **81** 50p. multicoloured 1·70 1·80

**82** Early 20th-century Trader and Pack Mules

**1988.** Europa. Communications. Each blue and red.
198 20p. Ancient road, Les Bons 70 75
199 45p. Type **82** 2·10 2·30

**83** Pyrenean Mountain Dog

**1988.** Nature Protection.
200 **83** 20p. multicoloured 1·40 1·50

**84** Commemorative Coin

**1988.** 700th Anniv of Second Parity Treaty.
201 **84** 20p. black, grey and brown 70 75

**85** Church of St. John of Caselles

**1988.** Christmas.
202 **85** 20p. multicoloured 70 75

**1988.** As T 50 but without "PTA" under figure of value.
203 20p. green 70 75
204 50p. green (25×31 mm) 2·10 2·30
205 100p. blue (25×31 mm) 3·75 4·25
206 500p. brown (25×31 mm) 12·50 13·50

**86** Leap-frog

**1989.** Europa. Children's Games. Multicoloured.
210 20p. Type **86** 1·40 1·50
211 45p. Girl trying to pull child from grip of other children (horiz) 2·10 2·30

**87** St. Roma's Chapel, Les Bons

**1989**
212 **87** 50p. black, green and blue 2·10 2·30

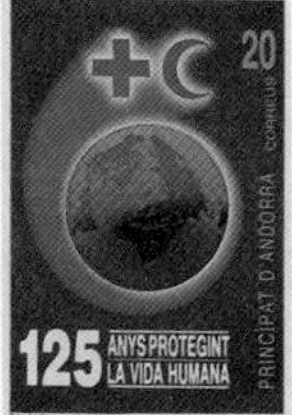

**88** Anniversary Emblem

**1989.** 125th Anniv of International Red Cross.
213 **88** 20p. multicoloured 70 75

**89** "Virgin Mary" (detail of altarpiece, Les Escaldes Church)

**1989.** Christmas.
214 **89** 20p. multicoloured 70 75

**90** Old French and Spanish Post Offices, Andorra La Vella

**1990.** Europa. Post Office Buildings. Multicoloured.
215 20p. Type **90** 70 75
216 50p. Modern Spanish post office, Andorra La Vella (vert) 2·10 2·30

**91** "Gomphidius rutilus"

**1990.** Nature Protection.
217 **91** 45p. multicoloured 2·10 2·30

**92** Plandolit House

**1990**
218 **92** 20p. brown and yellow 70 75

**93** Angel, La Massana Church

**1990.** Christmas.
219 **93** 25p. brown, stone and red 85 90

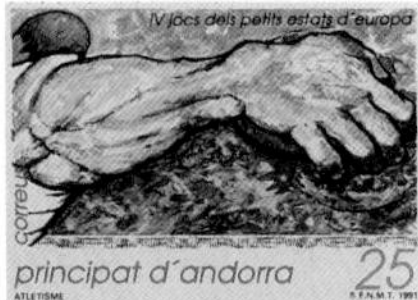

**94** Throwing the Discus

**1991.** European Small States' Games. Multicoloured.
220 25p. Type **94** 95 1·10
221 45p. High jumping and running 1·80 2·00

**95** "Olympus 1" Satellite

**1991.** Europa. Europe in Space. Multicoloured.
222 25p. Type **95** 2·10 2·30
223 55p. Close-up of "Olympus I" telecommunications satellite (horiz) 3·50 3·75

**96** Parasol Mushroom

**1991.** Nature Protection.
224 **96** 45p. multicoloured 2·10 2·30

**97** "Virgin of the Three Hands" (detail of triptych in Meritxell Chapel by Maria Assumpta Ortado i Maimo)

**1991.** Christmas.
225 **97** 25p. multicoloured 1·40 1·50

**98** Woman fetching Water from Public Tap

**1992**
226 **98** 25p. multicoloured 1·40 1·50

**99** "Santa Maria"

**1992.** Europa. 500th Anniv of Discovery of America by Columbus.
227 **99** 27p. multicoloured 2·10 2·30
228 - 45p. brown, red and orange 2·75 3·00

DESIGN—HORIZ: 45p. Engraving of King Ferdinand from map sent by Columbus to Ferdinand and Queen Isabella the Catholic.

**100** White-water Canoeing

**1992.** Olympic Games, Barcelona.
229 **100** 27p. multicoloured 1·40 1·50

**101** Benz Velo, 1894 and Sedanca de ville, 1920s

**1992.** National Motor Car Museum, Encamp.
230 **101** 27p. multicoloured 1·40 1·50

**102** "Nativity" (Fra Angelico)

**1992.** Christmas.
231 **102** 27p. multicoloured 1·40 1·50

**103** Chanterelle

**1993.** Nature Protection.
232 **103** 28p. multicoloured 1·40 1·50

**104** "Upstream" (J. A. Morrison)

**1993.** Europa. Contemporary Art. Multicoloured.
233 28p. Type **104** 1·40 1·50
234 45p. "Ritme" (Angel Calvente) (vert) 2·10 2·30

**105** Society Emblem on National Colours

**1993.** 25th Anniv of Andorran Arts and Letters Circle.
235 **105** 28p. multicoloured 1·40 1·50

**106** Illuminated "P" (Galceran de Vilanova Missal)

**1993.** Christmas.
236 **106** 28p. multicoloured 1·40 1·50

**107** National Colours

**1994.** 1st Anniv of New Constitution. Sheet 105×78 mm.
**MS**237 **107** 29p. multicoloured 2·10 2·30

**108** Sir Alexander Fleming and Penicillin

**1994.** Europa. Discoveries.
238 **108** 29p. multicoloured 1·40 1·50

239 - 55p. blue and black 2·75 3·00
DESIGN: 55p. Test tube and AIDS virus.

**109** "Hygrophorus gliocyclus"

**1994.** Nature Protection.
240 **109** 29p. multicoloured 1·40 1·50

**110** "Madonna and Child" (anon)

**1994.** Christmas.
241 **110** 29p. multicoloured 1·40 1·50

**111** Madriu Valley (south)

**1995.** European Nature Conservation Year. Mult.
242 30p. Type **111** 85 90
243 60p. Madriu Valley (north) 1·90 2·10

**112** Sun, Dove and Barbed Wire

**1995.** Europa. Peace and Freedom.
244 **112** 60p. green, orange & blk 2·10 2·30

**113** "Flight into Egypt" (altarpiece, St. Mark and St. Mary Church, Encamp)

**1995.** Christmas.
245 **113** 30p. multicoloured 1·40 1·50

**114** Palace of Europe, Strasbourg

**1995.** Admission of Andorra to Council of Europe.
246 **114** 30p. multicoloured 1·40 1·50

**115** "Ramaria aurea"

**1996.** Nature Protection. Multicoloured.
247 30p. Type **115** 1·40 1·50
248 60p. Black truffles 2·30 2·50

**116** Isabelle Sandy (writer)

**1996.** Europa. Famous Women.
249 **116** 60p. multicoloured 2·75 3·00

**117** Old Iron

**1996.** International Museums Day.
250 **117** 60p. multicoloured 2·10 2·30

**118** "The Annunciation" (altarpiece, St. Eulalia's Church, Encamp)

**1996.** Christmas.
251 **118** 30p. multicoloured 1·40 1·50

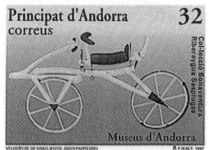

**119** Drais Velocipede, 1818

**1997.** Bicycle Museum (1st series). Multicoloured.
252 32p. Type **119** 95 1·10
253 65p. Michaux velocipede, 1861 1·90 2·10
See also Nos. 258/9 and 264/5.

**120** The Bear and The Smugglers

**1997.** Europa. Tales and Legends.
254 **120** 65p. multicoloured 2·75 3·00

**121** Dove and Cultural Symbols

**1997.** National UNESCO Commission.
255 **121** 32p. multicoloured 70 75

**122** Catalan Crib Figure

**1997.** Christmas.
256 **122** 32p. multicoloured 70 75

**123** Giant Slalom

**1998.** Winter Olympic Games, Nagano, Japan.
257 **123** 35p. multicoloured 70 75

**1998.** Bicycle Museum (2nd series). As T 119. Multicoloured.
258 35p. Kangaroo bicycle, Great Britain, 1878 95 1·10
259 70p. The Swallow, France, 1889 1·90 2·10

**124** Harlequins of Canillo

**1998.** Europa. National Festivals.
260 **124** 70p. multicoloured 2·10 2·30

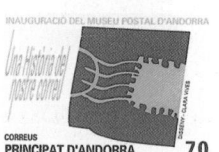

**125** Front Page of First Edition and Landscape

**1998.** 250th Anniv of "Manual Digest".
261 **125** 35p. multicoloured 70 75

**126** Emblem

**1998.** Inauguration of Postal Museum.
262 **126** 70p. violet and yellow 2·10 2·30

**127** St. Lucia Fair

**1998.** Christmas.
263 **127** 35p. multicoloured 1·40 1·50

**1999.** Bicycle Museum (3rd series). As T 119. Multicoloured.
264 35p. Salvo tricycle, 1878 (vert) 95 1·10
265 70p. Rudge tricycle, Coventry, England 1·90 2·10

**128** Mules

**1999.** Postal History.
266 **128** 35p. black and brown 1·40 1·50

**129** Palace of Human Rights, Strasbourg

**1999.** 50th Anniv of Council of Europe.
267 **129** 35p. multicoloured 1·40 1·50

**130** Vall d'Incles National Park, Canillo

**1999.** Europa. Parks and Gardens.
268 **130** 70p. multicoloured 2·10 2·30

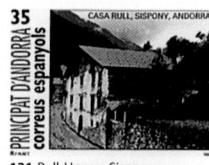

**131** Rull House, Sispony

**1999**
269 **131** 35p. multicoloured 1·40 1·50

**132** Angel (detail of altarpiece, St. Serni's Church, Canillo)

**1999.** Christmas.
270 **132** 35p. brown and light brown 1·40 1·50

**133** Santa Coloma Church

**1999.** European Heritage.
271 **133** 35p. multicoloured 1·40 1·50

**134** "Building Europe"

**2000.** Europa.
272 **134** 70p. multicoloured 2·75 3·00

**135** Angonella Lakes, Ordino

**2000**
273 **135** 35p. multicoloured 1·40 1·50

**136** Casa Lacruz

**2000.** 131st Birth Anniv of Josep Cadafalch (architect).
274 **136** 35p. multicoloured 1·40 1·50

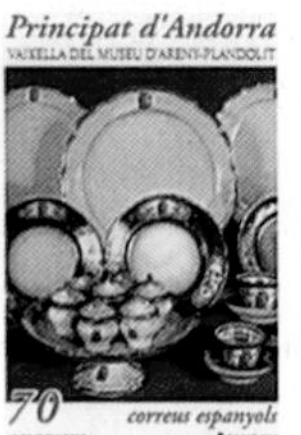


**137** Dinner Service

**2000.** D'Areny-Plandolit Museum.
275 **137** 70p. multicoloured 2·10 2·30

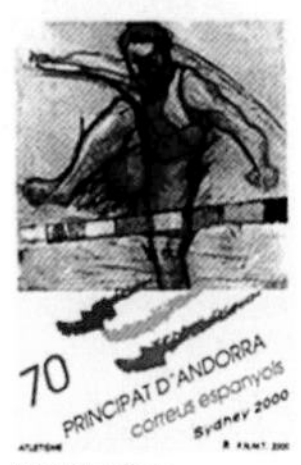


**138** Hurdling

**2000.** Olympic Games, Sydney.
276 **138** 70p. multicoloured 2·10 2·30

**139** United Nations Headquarters, Strasbourg

**2000.** 50th Anniv of United Nations Declaration of Human Rights.
277 **139** 70p. multicoloured 2·10 2·30

**140** Gradual, St. Roma, Les Bons

**2000.** 25th Anniv of the National Archives.
278 **140** 35p. multicoloured 70 75

**141** "Quadre de les Animes" (Joan Casanovas)

**2000.** Christmas.
279 **141** 35p. multicoloured 70 75

**142** Rec del Sola

**2001.** Natural Heritage.
280 **142** 40p. multicoloured 1·20 1·40

**143** Roc del Metge (thermal spring), Escaldes-Engordany

**2001.** Europa. Water Resources.
281 **143** 75p. multicoloured 2·10 2·30

**144** Casa Palau, Sant

**2001**
282 **144** 75p. multicoloured 2·10 2·30

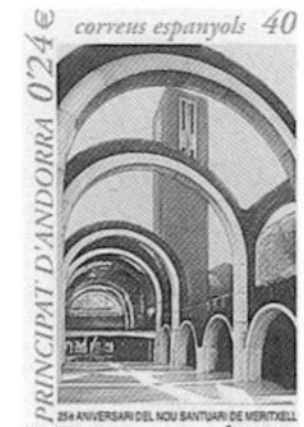


**145** Part of Sanctuary, Julia de Loria Meritxell

**2001.** 25th Anniv of Chapel of Our Lady, Meritxell.
283 **145** 40p. multicoloured 1·40 1·50

**146** Building

**2001.** 10th Anniv of National Auditorium, Ordino.
284 **146** 75p. multicoloured 2·10 2·30

**147** Angel (detail of altarpiece, Church of St. John of Caselles)

**2001.** Christmas.
285 **147** 40p. multicoloured 1·40 1·50

**148** State Arms

**2002**

| | | | | |
|---|---|---|---|---|
| 286 | **148** | 25c. orange | 70 | 75 |
| 286a | **148** | 27c. blue | 70 | 75 |
| 286b | **148** | 28c. blue | 85 | 90 |
| 286c | **148** | 29c. sepia | 85 | 90 |
| 286d | **148** | 30c. carmine | 85 | 90 |
| 287 | **148** | 50c. red | 1·40 | 1·50 |
| 288 | **148** | 52c. yellow | 1·50 | 1·70 |
| 289 | **148** | 53c. green | 1·50 | 1·70 |
| 289a | **148** | 57c. blue | 1·70 | 1·80 |
| 289b | **148** | 58c. black | 1·70 | 1·80 |
| 290 | **148** | 77c. orange | 2·20 | 2·40 |
| 291 | **148** | 78c. magenta | 2·20 | 2·40 |

**149** Alpine Accentor (*Prunella collaris*)

**2002.** Native Birds. Multicoloured.
300 25c. Type **149** 95 1·10
301 50c. Snow finch (*Montifringilla nivalis*) 1·90 2·10

**150** Emblem

**2002.** International Year of the Mountain.
302 **150** 50c. multicoloured 2·10 2·30

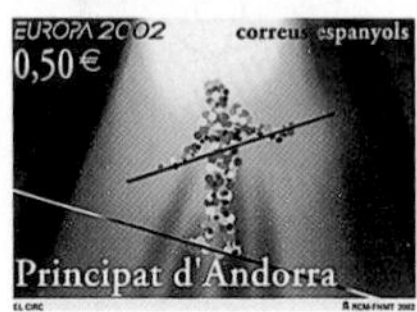


**151** Tightrope Walker

**2002.** Europa. Circus.
303 **151** 50c. multicoloured 14·00 15·00

**152** Casa Fusile, Escaldes-Engordany

**2002.** Architectural Heritage. Multicoloured.
304 €1.80 Type **152** 5·50 6·00
305 €2.10 Farga Rossell Iron Museum, La Massana 6·25 6·75

**153** Pinette Minim

**2002.** History of the Motor Car (1st series). Multicoloured.
306 25c. Type **153** 95 1·10
307 50c. Rolls Royce Silver Wraith 1·90 2·10
See also Nos. 317/18 and 324/5.

**154** Placa Benlloch, Areny-Plandolit

**2002.** Christmas.
308 **154** 25c. multicoloured 1·40 1·50

**155** Painted Medallion

**2002.** Cultural Heritage. Romanesque Murals from Santa Coloma Church, Andorra la Vella.
309 25c. Type **155** 70 75
310 50c. Part of damaged fresco showing seated figure 1·40 1·50
311 75c. Frieze 2·10 2·30

**156** Sassanat Bridge

**2003**
312 **156** 26c. multicoloured 1·40 1·50

**157** State Arms

**2003.** 10th Anniv of Constitution.
313 **157** 76c. multicoloured 2·75 3·00

**158** Man drinking, Donkey and Market Stalls

**2003.** Europa. Poster Art.
314 **158** 76c. multicoloured 2·75 3·00

**159** Northern Wheatear (*Oenanthe oenanthe*)

**2003.** Native Birds.
315 **159** 50c. multicoloured 1·40 1·50

**160** Multicoloured Stripes

**2003.** 10th Anniv of Andorras' Membership of United Nations.
316 **160** 76c. multicoloured 2·75 3·00

**161** Carter (1908)

**2003.** History of the Motor Car (2nd series). Multicoloured.
317 51c. Type **161** 1·70 1·80
318 76c. Peugeot (1928) (horiz) 2·50 2·75

**162** Roadside Cross, Andorra la Vella

**2003.** Christmas.
319 **162** 26c. multicoloured 1·40 1·50

**163** "Fira del Bestiar" (Joaquim Mir)

**2004**

320 **163** 27c. multicoloured 1·10 1·20

**164** "L'Escorxador" (Joaquim Mir)

**2004**

321 **164** 52c. multicoloured 1·90 2·10

**165** Coaches and Skiers in Snow

**2004.** Europa. Holidays.

322 **165** 77c. black 2·75 3·00

**166** Chaffinch (*Fringilla coelebs*)

**2004.** Native Birds.

323 **166** 27c. multicoloured 1·10 1·20

**167** Simca 508 C (1939)

**2004.** History of the Motor Car (3rd series).

324 €1.90 Type **167** 6·50 7·25

325 €2.19 Messerschmitt KR 1 (1955) 7·25 8·00

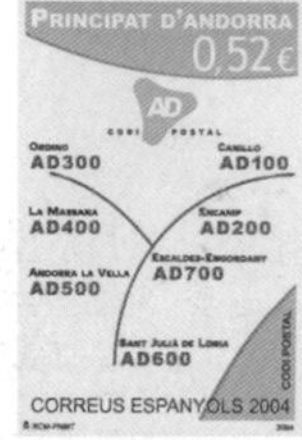


**168** Map showing Postal Districts

**2004.** Introduction of Postal Codes.

326 **168** 52c. orange, magenta and black 2·10 2·30

**169** Stars and Flag as Jigsaw Pieces

**2004.** 10th Anniv of Entry into Council of Europe.

327 **169** 52c. multicoloured 2·10 2·30

**170** Nativity

**2004.** Christmas.

328 **170** 27c. multicoloured 1·10 1·20

**171** Madriu-Perafita-Claror Valley

**2005.** UNESCO World Heritage Site.

329 **171** 28c. multicoloured 1·10 1·20

**172** "Endless" (Mark Brusse)

**2005**

330 **172** 53c. multicoloured 2·20 2·40

**174** Cyclist

**2005.** Europa. Gastronomy.

331 **173** 78c. multicoloured 3·00 3·50

**174** Cyclist

**2005.** Small States of Europe Games.

332 **174** €1.95 brown and black 5·50 6·00

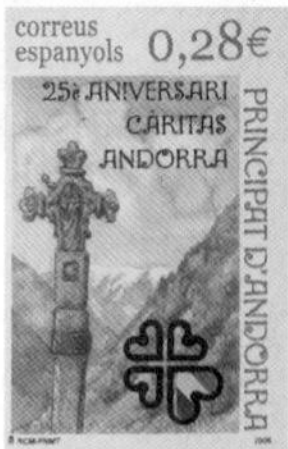


**175** Shrine

**2005.** 25th Anniv of Càritas Andorra (humanitarian organization).

333 **175** 28c. multicoloured 1·10 1·20

**176** Dipper (*Cinclus cinclus*)

**2005.** Native Birds.

334 **176** €2.21 multicoloured 6·25 6·75

**177** The Nativity (Sergei Mas)

**2005.** Christmas.

335 **177** 28c. multicoloured 1·10 1·20

**178** Skiers

**2006.** Winter Olympic Games, Turin.

336 **178** 29c. multicoloured 1·40 1·50

**179** "Ruta del Hierro" (sculpture) (Satora Sato)

**2006.** Cultural Heritage.

337 **179** 78c. multicoloured 2·50 2·75

**180** Stylized People of Many Colours and Abilities

**2006.** Europa. Integration.

338 **180** 57c. multicoloured 2·20 2·40

**181** Grey Partridge (*Perdix perdix*)

**2006.** Natural Heritage.

339 **181** €2.39 multicoloured 8·25 9·00

**182** Scrabble Letters

**2006.** Fulbright Scholarships.

340 **182** 57c. multicoloured 2·20 2·40

**183** Head Containing World Map

**2006.** 60th Anniv of UNESCO and 10th Anniv of CNAU.

341 **183** €2.33 multicoloured 8·00 8·75

**184** Nativity

**2006.** Christmas.

342 **184** 29c. multicoloured 1·20 1·20

**185** "Encamp 1994" (F. Galobardes)

**2007.** Cultural Heritage.

343 **185** 30c. multicoloured 1·20 1·20

**186** Doves and Emblem

**2007.** Europa. Centenary of Scouting.

344 **186** 58c. multicoloured 2·30 2·50

**187** 'La Familia Jordino' (sculpture by Rachid Khimoune)

**2007.** Cultural Heritage. The Iron Route (historical trail).

345 **187** €2.43 multicoloured 8·50 9·00

**188** Capercaillie (*Tetrao urogallus*)

**2007.** Natural Heritage.

346 **188** €2.49 multicoloured 8·75 9·25

**189** *Casa de la Vall* (Francesc Galobardes)

**2007.** Cultural Heritage.

347 **189** 78c. multicoloured 3·00 3·25

**190** Stylized Figures

**2007.** 25th Anniv of Andorra Red Cross.

348 **190** 30c. carmine and black 1·20 1·20

191 "Lamb kneeling before Infant Jesus" (painting by Sergi Mas)

2007. Christmas.
349 **191** 30c. multicoloured 1·20 1·20

192 *Gypaetus barbatus* (Lammergeier or bearded vulture)

2008. Natural Heritage.
350 **192** 31c. multicoloured 1·40 1·50

193 *Carro Vortiu* (sculpture by Jordi Casamajor)

2008. Cultural Heritage.
351 **193** 60c. multicoloured 2·50 2·75

194 Flag and Ballot Box

2008. 15th Anniv of Constitution.
352 **194** 31c. multicoloured 1·80 2·10

195 Envelope

2008. Europa. The Letter.
353 **195** 60c. blue and black 2·75 3·00

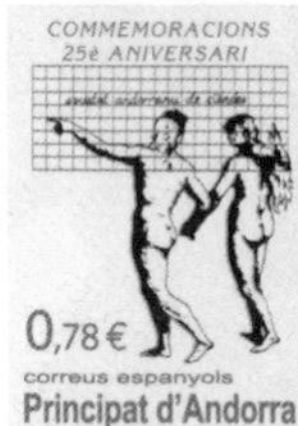
196 Adam, Eve and Graph

2008. 25th Anniv of National Science Society.
354 **196** 78c. blue and black 3·75 4·00

197 Fluvi (exhibition mascot)

2008. Zaragoza 2008 International Water and Sustainable Development Exhibition. Sheet 105×79 mm.
**MS**355 multicoloured 10·50 11·50

198 Games Emblem

2008. Olympic Games, Beijing.
356 **198** 60c. multicoloured 2·75 3·00

199 Vall del Comapedrosa

2008. Natural Heritage.
357 **199** €2.44 multicoloured 9·25 10·00

200 *Sispony* (Carme Massana)

2008. Cultural Heritage.
358 **200** 31c. multicoloured 1·60 1·80

201 Midnight Mass

2008. Christmas.
359 **201** 31c. multicoloured 1·60 1·80

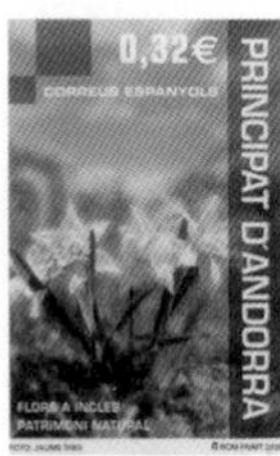
202 Narcissus

2009. Natural Heritage. Flora. Self adhesive.
360 **202** 32c. multicoloured 1·60 1·80

203 '25'

2009. 25th Anniv of Escola Andorrana.
361 **203** 62c. multicoloured 2·75 3·00

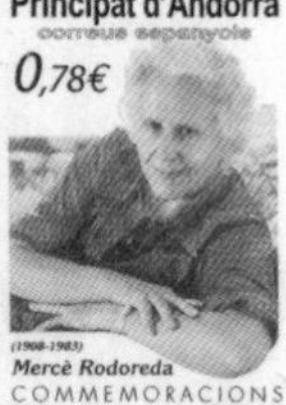
204 Merce Rodoreda

2009. Merce Rodoreda (Catalan writer) Commemoration.
362 **204** 78c. black 3·50 3·75

205 Emblem

2009. 60th Anniv of Council of Europe.
363 **205** 32c. multicoloured 1·60 1·80

206 Figures and Stars

2009. Europa. Astronomy.
364 **206** 62c. multicoloured 2·75 3·00

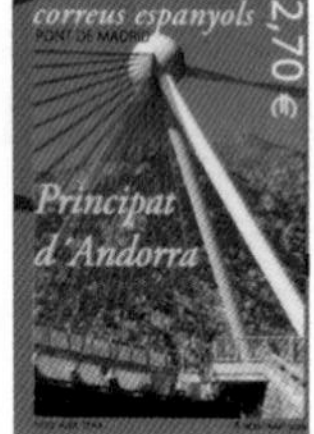
207 Bridge Strut

2009. Pont de Madrid (bridge designed by Carlos Fernandez Casado). Sheet 106×80 mm.
**MS**365 multicoloured 12·00 13·00

208 Eurasian Sparrowhawk

2009. Natural Heritage. Accipiter nisus.
366 **208** €2.47 multicoloured 9·25 10·00

209 *El Tarter* (Francesc Galobardes )

2009. Cultural Heritage. Multicoloured.
367 62c. Type **209** 2·75 3·00
368 78c. *Contrallum a Canillo* (Carme Massana) 3·50 3·75

210 Three Wise Men as Musicians (homage to National Classical Orchestra of Andorra by Sergei Mas)

2009. Christmas
369 **210** 32c. multicoloured 1·30 1·50

211 *Iris*

2010. Flora. Self-adhesive.
370 **211** 34c. multicoloured 1·70 1·90

212 Jacint Verdaguer

2010. 165th Birth Anniv of Jacint Verdaguer i Santaló (Catalan poet).
371 **212** 64c. black 2·75 3·00

213 Central Section

2010. Pont de Paris (bridge designed by Carlos Fernandez Casado).
372 **213** €2.75 multicoloured 12·00 13·00

214 Boy, Book and Fairy

2010. Europa
373 **214** 64c. multicoloured 2·75 3·00

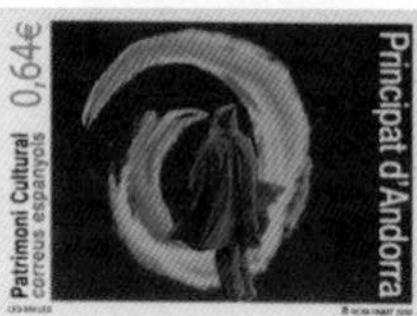
215 Circle of Flame

2010. Cultural Heritage
374 **215** 64c. multicoloured 3·25 3·50

216 Emblem and Globe

2010. World Cup Football Championships, South Africa
375 **216** 78c. multicoloured 4·00 4·25

**217** Multicoloured Ribbon

**2010.** Civic Values

| | | | | |
|---|---|---|---|---|
| 376 | **217** | €2.49 multicoloured | 11·50 | 12·00 |

**218** Mural (by Josep Oromí), Sant Joan de Sispony Church

**2010.** Christmas

| | | | | |
|---|---|---|---|---|
| 377 | **218** | 34c. multicoloured | 1·90 | 2·10 |

**EXPRESS LETTER STAMPS**

**1928.** Express Letter stamp of Spain optd CORREOS ANDORRA.

| | | | | |
|---|---|---|---|---|
| E15 | **E53** | 20c. red | 70·00 | 90·00 |

**E4** Lammergeier over Pyrenees

**1929**

| | | | | |
|---|---|---|---|---|
| E41 | **E4** | 20c. red | 8·00 | 10·50 |

**E12** Eurasian Red Squirrel (after Durer) and Arms

**1949**

| | | | | |
|---|---|---|---|---|
| E54 | **E12** | 25c. red | 7·00 | 8·00 |

Pt. 9, Pt. 12

# ANGOLA

Republic of Southern Africa. Independent of Portugal since 11 November 1975.

1870. 1000 reis = 1 milreis.
1913. 100 centavos = 1 escudo.
1932. 100 centavos = 1 angolar.
1954. 100 centavos = 1 escudo.
1977. 100 lweis = 1 kwanza.

**1870.** "Crown" key-type inscr "ANGOLA".

| | | | | |
|---|---|---|---|---|
| 7 | P | 5r. black | 1·60 | 1·10 |
| 17 | P | 10r. yellow | 16·00 | 9·25 |
| 31 | P | 10r. green | 6·00 | 3·25 |
| 9 | P | 20r. bistre | 1·70 | 1·50 |
| 26 | P | 20r. red | 14·00 | 10·50 |
| 10 | P | 25r. red | 8·25 | 6·00 |
| 27 | P | 25r. purple | 9·00 | 3·75 |
| 19b | P | 40r. blue | £180 | £130 |
| 33 | P | 40r. yellow | 8·25 | 3·75 |
| 12 | P | 50r. green | 40·00 | 11·00 |
| 30 | P | 50r. blue | 36·00 | 8·00 |
| 21a | P | 100r. lilac | 3·75 | 2·40 |
| 22 | P | 200r. orange | 3·00 | 1·50 |
| 23a | P | 300r. brown | 3·75 | 2·40 |

**1886.** "Embossed" key-type inscr "PROVINCIA DE ANGOLA".

| | | | | |
|---|---|---|---|---|
| 35 | Q | 5r. black | 9·75 | 4·50 |
| 36 | Q | 10r. green | 9·75 | 4·50 |
| 37 | Q | 20r. red | 13·00 | 9·25 |
| 39 | Q | 25r. mauve | 9·75 | 3·00 |
| 40 | Q | 40r. brown | 12·00 | 5·50 |
| 41 | Q | 50r. blue | 15·00 | 3·00 |
| 42 | Q | 100r. brown | 21·00 | 7·75 |
| 43 | Q | 200r. violet | 28·00 | 9·50 |
| 44 | Q | 300r. orange | 29·00 | 10·50 |

**1894.** "Figures" key-type inscr "ANGOLA".

| | | | | |
|---|---|---|---|---|
| 49 | R | 5r. orange | 2·30 | 1·00 |
| 62 | R | 10r. mauve | 3·25 | 2·00 |
| 63 | R | 15r. brown | 4·00 | 1·80 |
| 54 | R | 20r. lavender | 4·00 | 1·80 |
| 74 | R | 25r. green | 4·00 | 1·80 |
| 66 | R | 50r. blue | 5·00 | 2·40 |
| 67 | R | 75r. red | 8·50 | 7·25 |
| 68 | R | 80r. green | 9·75 | 5·25 |
| 69 | R | 100r. brown on buff | 9·75 | 5·25 |
| 70 | R | 150r. red on rose | 16·00 | 10·50 |
| 77 | R | 200r. blue on blue | 16·00 | 10·50 |
| 78 | R | 300r. blue on brown | 16·00 | 10·50 |

**1894.** No. N51 with circular surch **CORREIOS DE ANGOLA 25 REIS**.

| | | | | |
|---|---|---|---|---|
| 79b | V | 25r. on 2½r. brown | 46·00 | 46·00 |

**1898.** "King Carlos" key-type inscr "ANGOLA".

| | | | | |
|---|---|---|---|---|
| 80 | S | 2½r. grey | 40 | 35 |
| 81 | S | 5r. orange | 40 | 35 |
| 82 | S | 10r. green | 40 | 35 |
| 83 | S | 15r. brown | 2·30 | 1·20 |
| 142 | S | 15r. green | 1·20 | 1·10 |
| 84 | S | 20r. lilac | 50 | 40 |
| 85 | S | 25r. green | 1·20 | 50 |
| 143 | S | 25r. red | 60 | 35 |
| 86 | S | 50r. blue | 2·10 | 70 |
| 144 | S | 50r. brown | 5·75 | 1·90 |
| 145 | S | 65r. blue | 6·00 | 4·25 |
| 87 | S | 75r. red | 7·25 | 4·50 |
| 146 | S | 75r. purple | 2·30 | 1·50 |
| 88 | S | 80r. mauve | 7·25 | 2·30 |
| 89 | S | 100r. blue on blue | 1·40 | 1·00 |
| 147 | S | 115r. brown on pink | 8·00 | 5·50 |
| 148 | S | 130r. brown on yellow | 8·00 | 5·50 |
| 90 | S | 150r. brown on buff | 7·50 | 4·50 |
| 91 | S | 200r. purple on pink | 4·25 | 1·30 |
| 92 | S | 300r. blue on pink | 4·75 | 3·75 |
| 149 | S | 400r. blue on yellow | 4·25 | 2·75 |
| 93 | S | 500r. black on blue | 4·75 | 3·75 |
| 94 | S | 700r. mauve on yellow | 23·00 | 11·50 |

**1902.** "Embossed", "Figures" and "Newspaper" key-types of Angola surch.

| | | | | |
|---|---|---|---|---|
| 98 | R | 65r. on 5r. orange | 6·50 | 4·50 |
| 100 | R | 65r. on 10r. mauve | 8·00 | 4·50 |
| 102 | R | 65r. on 20r. violet | 6·50 | 4·50 |
| 104 | R | 65r. on 25r. green | 9·75 | 6·00 |
| 95 | Q | 65r. on 40r. brown | 8·00 | 4·50 |
| 96 | Q | 65r. on 300r. orange | 8·00 | 4·50 |
| 106 | Q | 115r. on 10r. green | 6·50 | 3·75 |
| 109 | R | 115r. on 80r. green | 24·00 | 6·00 |
| 111 | R | 115r. on 100r. brn on buff | 9·75 | 5·25 |
| 113 | R | 115r. on 150r. red on rose | 8·00 | 7·25 |
| 108 | Q | 115r. on 200r. violet | 6·50 | 3·75 |
| 120 | R | 130r. on 15r. brown | 4·50 | 3·75 |
| 116 | Q | 130r. on 50r. blue | 9·25 | 3·75 |
| 124 | R | 130r. on 75r. red | 4·75 | 3·25 |
| 118 | Q | 130r. on 100r. brown | 6·00 | 3·75 |
| 126 | R | 130r. on 300r. blue on brn | 13·00 | 11·00 |
| 136 | V | 400r. on 2½r. brown | 1·20 | 1·10 |
| 127 | Q | 400r. on 5r. black | 9·50 | 7·25 |
| 128 | Q | 400r. on 20r. red | 47·00 | 30·00 |
| 130 | Q | 400r. on 25r. mauve | 16·00 | 8·50 |
| 131 | R | 400r. on 50r. pale blue | 6·50 | 4·00 |
| 133 | R | 400r. on 200r. blue on blue | 6·50 | 5·50 |

**1902.** "King Carlos" key-type of Angola optd **PROVISORIO**.

| | | | | |
|---|---|---|---|---|
| 138 | S | 15r. brown | 1·60 | 1·10 |
| 139 | S | 25r. green | 1·30 | 60 |
| 140 | S | 50r. blue | 2·00 | 1·00 |
| 141 | S | 75r. red | 3·25 | 3·00 |

**1905.** No. 145 surch **50 REIS** and bar.

| | | | | |
|---|---|---|---|---|
| 150 | | 50r. on 65r. blue | 3·00 | 1·60 |

**1911.** "King Carlos" key-type optd **REPUBLICA**.

| | | | | |
|---|---|---|---|---|
| 151 | | 2½r. grey | 40 | 30 |
| 152 | | 5r. orange | 40 | 30 |
| 153 | | 10r. green | 40 | 30 |
| 154 | | 15r. green | 35 | 35 |
| 155 | | 20r. lilac | 40 | 30 |
| 156 | | 25r. red | 40 | 30 |
| 157 | | 50r. brown | 1·10 | 85 |
| 232 | | 50r. blue (No. 140) | 1·10 | 95 |
| 224 | | 75r. purple | 1·10 | 75 |
| 234 | | 75r. red (No. 141) | 1·40 | 1·10 |
| 225 | | 100r. blue on blue | 1·60 | 1·60 |
| 160 | | 115r. brown on pink | 1·60 | 95 |
| 161 | | 130r. brown on yellow | 1·60 | 95 |
| 226 | | 200r. purple on pink | 1·50 | 1·00 |
| 163 | | 400r. blue on yellow | 2·20 | 95 |
| 164 | | 500r. black on blue | 2·20 | 1·10 |
| 165 | | 700r. mauve on yellow | 2·20 | 1·40 |

**1912.** "King Manoel" key-type inscr "ANGOLA" optd **REPUBLICA**.

| | | | | |
|---|---|---|---|---|
| 166 | T | 2½r. lilac | 40 | 30 |
| 167 | T | 5r. black | 40 | 30 |
| 168 | T | 10r. green | 40 | 30 |
| 169 | T | 20r. red | 40 | 30 |
| 170 | T | 25r. brown | 40 | 30 |
| 171 | T | 50r. blue | 1·10 | 85 |
| 172 | T | 75r. brown | 1·20 | 1·10 |
| 173 | T | 100r. brown on green | 1·60 | 1·20 |
| 174 | T | 200r. green on pink | 1·60 | 1·20 |
| 175 | T | 300r. black on blue | 1·60 | 1·20 |

**1912.** "King Carlos" key-type of Angola optd **REPUBLICA** and surch.

| | | | | |
|---|---|---|---|---|
| 176 | S | 2½ on 15r. green | 2·50 | 1·60 |
| 177 | S | 5 on 15r. green | 3·00 | 1·60 |
| 178 | S | 10 on 15r. green | 1·90 | 1·60 |
| 179 | S | 25 on 75r. red (No. 141) | 36·00 | 28·00 |
| 180 | S | 25 on 75r. purple | 3·00 | 3·00 |

**1913.** Surch **REPUBLICA ANGOLA** and value in figures on "Vasco da Gama" issues of (a) Portuguese Colonies.

| | | | | |
|---|---|---|---|---|
| 181 | | ¼c. on 2½r. green | 75 | 45 |
| 182 | | ½c. on 5r. red | 75 | 45 |
| 183 | | 1c. on 10r. purple | 75 | 45 |
| 184 | | 2½c. on 25r. green | 75 | 45 |
| 185 | | 5c. on 50r. blue | 75 | 45 |
| 186 | | 7½c. on 75r. brown | 3·00 | 2·50 |
| 187 | | 10c. on 100r. brown | 1·60 | 1·10 |
| 188 | | 15c. on 150r. bistre | 95 | 80 |

(b) Macao.

| | | | | |
|---|---|---|---|---|
| 189 | | ¼c. on ½a. green | 1·10 | 95 |
| 190 | | ½c. on 1a. red | 1·10 | 95 |
| 191 | | 1c. on 2a. purple | 95 | 70 |
| 192 | | 2½c. on 4a. green | 80 | 60 |
| 193 | | 5c. on 8a. blue | 80 | 65 |
| 194 | | 7½c. on 12a. brown | 3·50 | 1·60 |
| 195 | | 10c. on 16a. brown | 1·40 | 95 |
| 196 | | 15c. on 24a. bistre | 1·25 | 95 |

(c) Timor.

| | | | | |
|---|---|---|---|---|
| 197 | | ¼c. on ½a. green | 1·10 | 95 |
| 198 | | ½c. on 1a. red | 1·10 | 95 |
| 199 | | 1c. on 2a. purple | 90 | 70 |
| 200 | | 2½c. on 4a. green | 1·90 | 60 |
| 201 | | 5c. on 8a. blue | 1·10 | 75 |
| 202 | | 7½c. on 12a. brown | 3·50 | 1·60 |
| 203 | | 10c. on 16a. brown | 1·40 | 95 |
| 204 | | 15c. on 24a. bistre | 1·30 | 95 |

**1914.** "Ceres" key-type inscr "ANGOLA".

| | | | | |
|---|---|---|---|---|
| 296 | U | ¼c. olive | 20 | 15 |
| 297 | U | ½c. black | 20 | 15 |
| 298 | U | 1c. green | 20 | 15 |
| 299 | U | 1½c. brown | 25 | 20 |
| 300 | U | 2c. red | 25 | 20 |
| 301 | U | 2c. grey | 35 | 30 |
| 281 | U | 2½c. violet | 20 | 15 |
| 303 | U | 3c. orange | 15 | 15 |
| 304 | U | 4c. red | 15 | 15 |
| 305 | U | 4½c. grey | 15 | 15 |
| 284a | U | 5c. blue | 20 | 15 |
| 307 | U | 6c. mauve | 15 | 15 |
| 308 | U | 7c. blue | 15 | 15 |
| 309 | U | 7½c. brown | 25 | 20 |
| 288 | U | 8c. grey | 20 | 20 |
| 311 | U | 10c. brown | 20 | 15 |
| 312 | U | 12c. brown | 35 | 30 |
| 313 | U | 12c. green | 35 | 30 |
| 291 | U | 15c. purple | 20 | 15 |
| 314 | U | 15c. pink | 20 | 15 |
| 315 | U | 20c. green | 85 | 70 |
| 316 | U | 24c. blue | 70 | 60 |
| 317 | U | 25c. brown | 90 | 70 |
| 217 | U | 30c. brown on green | 1·20 | 1·10 |
| 318 | U | 30c. green | 35 | 30 |
| 218 | U | 40c. brown on pink | 1·20 | 1·10 |
| 319 | U | 40c. blue | 70 | 35 |
| 219 | U | 50c. orange on pink | 4·75 | 3·50 |
| 320 | U | 50c. purple | 70 | 35 |
| 321 | U | 60c. blue | 90 | 55 |
| 322 | U | 60c. red | 43·00 | 26·00 |
| 322a | U | 80c. pink | 85 | 45 |
| 220 | U | 1e. green on blue | 3·25 | 2·20 |
| 323 | U | 1e. red | 85 | 45 |
| 325 | U | 1e. blue | 1·40 | 85 |
| 326 | U | 2e. purple | 1·20 | 60 |
| 327 | U | 5e. brown | 7·25 | 5·75 |
| 328 | U | 10e. pink | 16·00 | 13·00 |
| 329 | U | 20e. green | 55·00 | 36·00 |

**1914.** Provisional stamps of 1902 optd **REPUBLICA**.

| | | | | |
|---|---|---|---|---|
| 233 | S | 50r. on 65r. blue | 3·00 | 2·10 |
| 256 | Q | 115r. on 10r. green | 1·50 | 1·20 |
| 258 | R | 115r. on 80r. green | 1·00 | 90 |
| 261 | R | 115r. on 100r. brn on buff | 1·20 | 1·10 |
| 263 | R | 115r. on 150r. red on rose | 90 | 90 |
| 266 | Q | 115r. on 200r. violet | 1·30 | 1·10 |
| 267 | R | 130r. on 15r. brown | 1·00 | 90 |
| 246 | Q | 130r. on 50r. blue | 9·50 | 9·50 |
| 269 | R | 130r. on 75r. red | 1·80 | 1·10 |
| 273 | Q | 130r. on 100r. brown | 80 | 70 |
| 274 | R | 130r. on 300r. blue on brn | 80 | 70 |
| 254 | V | 400r. on 2½r. brown | 55 | 45 |

**1919.** Stamps of 1911, 1912 or 1914 surch.

| | | | | |
|---|---|---|---|---|
| 331 | T | ½c. on 75r. brown | 90 | 75 |
| 332 | S | ½c. on 75r. purple | 1·10 | 95 |
| 336 | T | 1c. on 50r. blue | 95 | 85 |
| 334 | S | 2½c. on 100r. brown on grn | 1·40 | 1·10 |
| 335 | S | 2½c. on 100r. blue on blue | 1·10 | 80 |
| 337 | S | 4c. on 130r. brown on yell | 1·10 | 80 |
| 339 | U | $04 on 15c. purple | 1·10 | 80 |
| 340 | U | $04 on 15c. pink | 9·00 | |
| 341 | T | $00.5 on 75r. brown | 1·10 | 90 |
| 342 | U | $00.5 on 7½c. brown | 80 | 70 |

**1925.** Nos. 136 and 133 surch **Republica 40 C**.

| | | | | |
|---|---|---|---|---|
| 343 | R | 40c. on 400r. on 200r. blue on blue | 60 | 45 |
| 345 | V | 40c. on 400r. on 2½r. brn | 55 | 55 |

**1931.** "Ceres" key-type of Angola surch.

| | | | | |
|---|---|---|---|---|
| 347 | U | 50c. on 60c. red | 1·10 | 95 |
| 348 | U | 70c. on 80c. pink | 2·20 | 1·40 |
| 349 | U | 70c. on 1e. blue | 1·80 | 1·40 |
| 350 | U | 1e.40 on 2e. purple | 1·30 | 80 |

**17** Ceres

**1932**

| | | | | |
|---|---|---|---|---|
| 351 | 17 | 1c. brown | 15 | 15 |
| 352 | 17 | 5c. sepia | 20 | 20 |
| 353 | 17 | 10c. mauve | 20 | 20 |
| 354 | 17 | 15c. black | 20 | 20 |
| 355 | 17 | 20c. grey | 20 | 20 |
| 356 | 17 | 30c. green | 20 | 20 |
| 357 | 17 | 35c. green | 4·75 | 2·50 |
| 358 | 17 | 40c. red | 30 | 15 |
| 359 | 17 | 45c. blue | 85 | 70 |
| 360 | 17 | 50c. brown | 20 | 15 |
| 361 | 17 | 60c. olive | 65 | 20 |
| 362 | 17 | 70c. brown | 65 | 20 |
| 363 | 17 | 80c. green | 40 | 15 |
| 364 | 17 | 85c. red | 2·50 | 1·20 |
| 365 | 17 | 1a. red | 60 | 20 |
| 366 | 17 | 1a.40 blue | 5·75 | 2·20 |
| 367 | 17 | 1a.75 blue | 8·00 | 3·00 |
| 368 | 17 | 2a. mauve | 2·50 | 30 |
| 369 | 17 | 5a. green | 5·75 | 95 |
| 370 | 17 | 10a. brown | 11·00 | 3·00 |
| 371 | 17 | 20a. orange | 26·00 | 3·00 |

**1934.** Surch.

| | | | | |
|---|---|---|---|---|
| 380 | | 5c. on 80c. green (A) | 65 | 30 |
| 419 | | 5c. on 80c. green (B) | 60 | 40 |
| 413 | | 10c. on 45c. blue | 1·10 | 70 |
| 381 | | 10c. on 80c. green | 85 | 45 |
| 414 | | 15c. on 45c. blue | 1·10 | 70 |
| 382 | | 15c. on 80c. green | 1·20 | 45 |
| 415 | | 20c. on 85c. red | 1·10 | 70 |
| 374 | | 30c. on 1a.40 blue | 1·90 | 1·40 |
| 416 | | 35c. on 85c. red | 1·10 | 70 |
| 417 | | 50c. on 1a.40 blue | 1·10 | 70 |
| 418 | | 60c. on 1a. red | 4·75 | 4·75 |
| 375 | | 70c. on 2a. mauve | 2·30 | 1·40 |
| 376 | | 80c. on 5a. green | 3·50 | 1·40 |

(A) surch **0,05 Cent.** in one line; (B) surch **5 CENTAVOS** in two lines.

**1935.** "Due" key-type surch CORREIOS and new value.

| | | | | |
|---|---|---|---|---|
| 377 | W | 5c. on 6c. brown | 1·20 | 85 |
| 378 | W | 30c. on 50c. grey | 1·20 | 85 |
| 379 | W | 40c. on 50c. grey | 1·20 | 85 |

**22** Vasco da Gama

**27** Airplane over Globe

**1938.** Name and value in black.

| | | | | |
|---|---|---|---|---|
| 383 | 22 | 1c. olive (postage) | 15 | 15 |
| 384 | 22 | 5c. brown | 20 | 20 |
| 385 | 22 | 10c. red | 20 | 20 |
| 386 | 22 | 15c. purple | 20 | 20 |
| 387 | 22 | 20c. grey | 20 | 20 |
| 388 | - | 30c. purple | 30 | 30 |
| 389 | - | 35c. green | 60 | 45 |
| 390 | - | 40c. brown | 20 | 15 |
| 391 | - | 50c. mauve | 30 | 15 |
| 392 | - | 60c. black | 60 | 20 |
| 393 | - | 70c. violet | 60 | 20 |
| 394 | - | 80c. orange | 60 | 20 |
| 395 | - | 1a. red | 50 | 20 |
| 396 | - | 1a.75 blue | 1·20 | 60 |
| 397 | - | 2a. red | 1·70 | 65 |
| 398 | - | 5a. olive | 7·25 | 65 |
| 399 | - | 10a. blue | 14·50 | 70 |
| 400 | - | 20a. brown | 22·00 | 1·70 |
| 401 | 27 | 10c. red (air) | 30 | 30 |
| 402 | 27 | 20c. violet | 30 | 20 |
| 403 | 27 | 50c. orange | 30 | 20 |
| 404 | 27 | 1a. blue | 30 | 20 |
| 405 | 27 | 2a. red | 60 | 20 |
| 406 | 27 | 3a. green | 55 | 35 |
| 407 | 27 | 5a. brown | 5·25 | 80 |
| 408 | 27 | 9a. red | 4·25 | 8·50 |
| 409 | 27 | 10a. mauve | 5·75 | 1·10 |

DESIGNS: 30c. to 50c. Mousinho de Albuquerque; 60c. to 1a. "Fomento" (symbolizing Progress); 1a.75, 2, 5a. Prince Henry the Navigator; 10, 20a. Afonso de Albuquerque.

**28** Portuguese Colonial Column

**1938.** President's Colonial Tour.

| | | | | |
|---|---|---|---|---|
| 410 | 28 | 80c. green | 1·70 | 1·20 |
| 411 | 28 | 1a.75 blue | 11·50 | 3·50 |
| 412 | 28 | 20a. brown | 32·00 | 17·00 |

**1945.** Nos. 394/6 surch.

| | | | | |
|---|---|---|---|---|
| 420 | | 5c. on 80c. orange | 50 | 35 |
| 421 | | 50c. on 1a. red | 50 | 35 |
| 422 | | 50c. on 1a.75 blue | 50 | 35 |

**31** Arms of Angola

**1947.** Air.

| | | | | |
|---|---|---|---|---|
| 423a | 31 | 1a. brown | 5·75 | 3·00 |
| 423b | 31 | 2a. green | 6·25 | 3·00 |
| 423c | 31 | 3a. orange | 6·25 | 3·00 |
| 423d | 31 | 3a.50 orange | 12·50 | 3·00 |
| 423e | 31 | 5a. green | 40·00 | 14·50 |
| 423f | 31 | 6a. pink | 40·00 | 9·50 |

| | | | | |
|---|---|---|---|---|
| 423g | 31 | 9a. red | £140 | £140 |
| 423h | 31 | 10a. green | 95·00 | 60·00 |
| 423i | 31 | 20a. blue | £130 | 60·00 |
| 423j | 31 | 50a. black | £200 | £140 |
| 423k | 31 | 100a. yellow | £250 | £225 |

**32** Sao Miguel Fortress, Luanda

**1948.** Tercentenary of Restoration of Angola. Inscr "Tricentenario da Restauracao de Angola 1648–1948".

| | | | | |
|---|---|---|---|---|
| 424 | 32 | 5c. violet | 15 | 10 |
| 425 | - | 10c. brown | 45 | 15 |
| 426 | - | 30c. green | 15 | 10 |
| 427 | - | 50c. purple | 15 | 10 |
| 428 | - | 1a. red | 45 | 10 |
| 429 | - | 1a.75 blue | 70 | 10 |
| 430 | - | 2a. green | 70 | 10 |
| 431 | - | 5a. black | 2·30 | 35 |
| 432 | - | 10a. mauve | 5·50 | 45 |
| 433 | - | 20a. blue | 11·50 | 2·50 |

**MS**433a 162×225 mm. Nos. 424/33 (sold at 42a.50) 60·00 60·00

DESIGNS—HORIZ: 10c. Our Lady of Nazareth Hermitage, Luanda; 1a. Surrender of Luanda; 5a. Inscribed Rocks of Yelala; 20a. Massangano Fortress. VERT (portraits): 30c. Don John IV; 50c. Salvador Correia de Sa Benevides; 1a.75, Dioga Cao; 7a. Manuel Cerveira Pereira; 10a. Paulo Dias de Novais.

**33** Our Lady of Fatima

**1948.** Honouring Our Lady of Fatima.

| | | | | |
|---|---|---|---|---|
| 434 | 33 | 50c. red | 1·80 | 1·10 |
| 435 | 33 | 3a. blue | 7·00 | 2·20 |
| 436 | 33 | 6a. orange | 22·00 | 5·50 |
| 437 | 33 | 9a. red | 60·00 | 7·00 |

**35** River Chiumbe

**36** Pedras Negras

**1949**

| | | | | |
|---|---|---|---|---|
| 438 | 35 | 20c. blue | 30 | 15 |
| 439 | 36 | 40c. brown | 30 | 10 |
| 440 | - | 50c. red | 30 | 10 |
| 441 | - | 2a.50 blue | 1·80 | 30 |
| 442 | - | 3a.50 grey | 1·80 | 1·40 |
| 443 | - | 15a. green | 14·50 | 1·40 |
| 444 | - | 50a. green | 80·00 | 5·00 |

DESIGNS—As T **35**: 50c. Luanda; 2a.50, Bandeira; 3a.50, Mocamedes; 50a. Braganza Falls. 31×26 mm: 15a. River Cubal.

**37** Aircraft and Globe

**1949.** Air.

| | | | | |
|---|---|---|---|---|
| 445 | 37 | 1a. orange | 50 | 10 |
| 446 | 37 | 2a. brown | 1·10 | 10 |
| 447 | 37 | 3a. mauve | 1·40 | 15 |
| 448 | 37 | 6a. green | 2·50 | 50 |
| 449 | 37 | 9a. purple | 3·50 | 1·20 |

**38** "Tentativa Feliz"

**1949.** Centenary of Founding of Mocamedes.

| | | | | |
|---|---|---|---|---|
| 450 | 38 | 1a. purple | 5·75 | 65 |
| 451 | 38 | 4a. green | 14·50 | 1·80 |

**39** Letter and Globe

**1949.** 75th Anniv of U.P.U.

| | | | | |
|---|---|---|---|---|
| 452 | 39 | 4a. green | 7·25 | 1·60 |

**40** Reproduction of "Crown" key-type

**1950.** Philatelic Exhibition and 80th Anniv of First Angolan Stamp.

| | | | | |
|---|---|---|---|---|
| 454 | 40 | 1a. red | 1·00 | 50 |
| 455 | 40 | 4a. black | 3·25 | 1·30 |
| 453 | 40 | 50a. green | 1·00 | 30 |

**MS**455a 120×79 mm. Nos. 453/5 (sold at 6a.50) 15·00 11·50

**41** Bells and Dove

**42** Angels holding Candelabra

**1950.** Holy Year.

| | | | | |
|---|---|---|---|---|
| 456 | 41 | 1a. violet | 70 | 15 |
| 457 | 42 | 4a. black | 3·25 | 60 |

**43** Dark Chanting Goshawk

**1951.** Birds. Multicoloured.

| | | | |
|---|---|---|---|
| 458 | 5c. Type **43** | 30 | 15 |
| 459 | 10c. Racquet-tailed roller | 30 | 15 |
| 460 | 15c. Bateleur | 45 | 15 |
| 461 | 20c. European bee eater | 45 | 30 |
| 462 | 50c. Giant kingfisher | 45 | 15 |
| 463 | 1a. Anchieta's barbet | 45 | 15 |
| 464 | 1a.50 African open-bill stork | 65 | 15 |
| 465 | 2a. Southern ground hornbill | 65 | 15 |
| 466 | 2a.50 African skimmer | 95 | 15 |
| 467 | 3a. Shikra | 65 | 15 |
| 468 | 3a.50 Senham's bustard | 95 | 15 |
| 469 | 4a. African golden oriole | 1·00 | 15 |
| 470 | 4a.50 Magpie shrike | 1·00 | 15 |
| 471 | 5a. Red-shouldered glossy starling | 3·50 | 35 |
| 472 | 6a. Sharp-tailed glossy starling | 5·00 | 95 |
| 473 | 7a. Fan-tailed whydah | 5·75 | 1·20 |
| 474 | 10a. Half-collared kingfisher | 23·00 | 1·60 |
| 475 | 12a.50 White-crowned shrike | 6·25 | 2·00 |
| 476 | 15a. White-winged starling | 5·75 | 2·00 |
| 477 | 20a. Southern yellow-billed hornbill | 55·00 | 5·00 |
| 478 | 25a. Violet starling | 20·00 | 4·25 |
| 479 | 30a. Sulphur-breasted bush shrike | 20·00 | 5·00 |
| 480 | 40a. Secretary bird | 29·00 | 7·00 |
| 481 | 50a. Peach-faced lovebird | 70·00 | 14·50 |

The 10, 15 and 20c., 2a.50, 3a., 4a.50, 12a.50 and 30a. are horiz, the remainder vert.

**44** Our Lady of Fatima

**1951.** Termination of Holy Year.

| | | | | |
|---|---|---|---|---|
| 482 | 44 | 4a. orange | 2·30 | 1·10 |

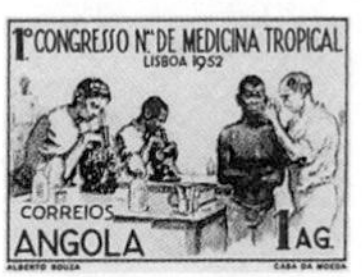

**45** Laboratory

**1952.** 1st Tropical Medicine Congress, Lisbon.

| | | | | |
|---|---|---|---|---|
| 483 | 45 | 1a. grey and blue | 80 | 30 |

**46** The Sacred Face

**1952.** Missionary Art Exhibition.

| | | | | |
|---|---|---|---|---|
| 484 | 46 | 10c. blue and flesh | 15 | 15 |
| 485 | 46 | 50c. green and stone | 65 | 15 |
| 486 | 46 | 2a. purple and flesh | 2·30 | 45 |

**47** Leopard

**1953.** Angolan Fauna. Multicoloured.

| | | | |
|---|---|---|---|
| 487 | 5c. Type **47** | 15 | 15 |
| 488 | 10c. Sable antelope (vert) | 15 | 15 |
| 489 | 20c. African elephant (vert) | 15 | 15 |
| 490 | 30c. Eland (vert) | 15 | 15 |
| 491 | 40c. Crocodile | 15 | 15 |
| 492 | 50c. Impala (vert) | 15 | 15 |
| 493 | 1a. Mountain zebra (vert) | 20 | 15 |
| 494 | 1a.50 Sitatunga (vert) | 20 | 15 |
| 495 | 2a. Black rhinoceros | 20 | 15 |
| 496 | 2a.30 Gemsbok (vert) | 20 | 15 |
| 497 | 2a.50 Lion (vert) | 30 | 15 |
| 498 | 3a. African buffalo | 35 | 15 |
| 499 | 3a.50 Springbok (vert) | 35 | 15 |
| 500 | 4a. Blue wildebeest (vert) | 12·50 | 15 |
| 501 | 5a. Hartebeest (vert) | 60 | 15 |
| 502 | 7a. Warthog (vert) | 85 | 15 |
| 503 | 10a. Waterbuck (vert) | 1·80 | 15 |
| 504 | 12a.50 Hippopotamus (vert) | 4·75 | 95 |
| 505 | 15a. Greater kudu (vert) | 5·75 | 95 |
| 506 | 20a. Giraffe (vert) | 7·25 | 60 |

**48** Stamp of 1853 and Colonial Arms

**1953.** Portuguese Stamp Centenary.

| | | | | |
|---|---|---|---|---|
| 507 | 48 | 50c. multicoloured | 45 | 35 |

**49** Father M. da Nobrega and Sao Paulo

**1954.** 4th Centenary of Sao Paulo.

| | | | | |
|---|---|---|---|---|
| 508 | 49 | 1e. black and buff | 30 | 15 |

**50** Route of President's Tour

**1954.** Presidential Visit.

| | | | | |
|---|---|---|---|---|
| 509 | 50 | 35c. multicoloured | 10 | 10 |
| 510 | 50 | 4e.50 multicoloured | 70 | 35 |

**51** Map of Angola

**1955.** Map mult. Angola territory in colour given.

| | | | | |
|---|---|---|---|---|
| 511 | 51 | 5c. white | 15 | 15 |
| 512 | 51 | 20c. salmon | 15 | 15 |
| 513 | 51 | 50c. blue | 15 | 15 |
| 514 | 51 | 1e. orange | 15 | 15 |
| 515 | 51 | 2e.30 yellow | 80 | 30 |
| 516 | 51 | 4e. blue | 1·60 | 15 |
| 517 | 51 | 10e. green | 1·40 | 15 |
| 518 | 51 | 20e. white | 2·75 | 1·20 |

**52** Col. A. de Paiva

**1956.** Birth Centenary of De Paiva.

| | | | | |
|---|---|---|---|---|
| 519 | 52 | 1e. black, blue and orange | 30 | 20 |

**53** Quela Chief

**1957.** Natives. Multicoloured.

| | | | |
|---|---|---|---|
| 520 | 5c. Type **53** | 15 | 15 |
| 521 | 10c. Andulo flute player | 15 | 15 |
| 522 | 15c. Dembos man and woman | 15 | 15 |
| 523 | 20c. Quissama dancer (male) | 15 | 15 |
| 524 | 30c. Quibala family | 15 | 15 |
| 525 | 40c. Bocolo dancer (female) | 15 | 15 |
| 526 | 50c. Quissama woman | 15 | 15 |
| 527 | 80c. Cuanhama woman | 20 | 15 |
| 528 | 1e.50 Luanda widow | 1·70 | 15 |
| 529 | 2e.50 Bocolo dancer (male) | 1·70 | 15 |
| 530 | 4e. Muquixe man | 85 | 15 |
| 531 | 10e. Cabinda chief | 1·60 | 30 |

**54** Father J. M. Antunes

**1957.** Birth Centenary of Father Antunes.

| | | | | |
|---|---|---|---|---|
| 532 | 54 | 1e. multicoloured | 60 | 30 |

**55** Exhibition Emblem, Globe and Arms

**1958.** Brussels International Exhibition.

| | | | | |
|---|---|---|---|---|
| 533 | 55 | 1e.50 multicoloured | 50 | 45 |

**56** "Securidaca longipedunculata"

**1958.** 6th Int Tropical Medicine Congress.

| | | | | |
|---|---|---|---|---|
| 534 | **56** | 2e.50 multicoloured | 1·90 | 65 |

**57** Native Doctor and Patient

**1958.** 75th Anniv of Maria Pia Hospital, Luanda.

| | | | | |
|---|---|---|---|---|
| 535 | **57** | 1e. brown, black and blue | 35 | 20 |
| 536 | - | 1e.50 multicoloured | 85 | 45 |
| 537 | - | 2e.50 multicoloured | 1·60 | 80 |

DESIGNS: 1e.50, 17th-century doctor and patient; 2e.50, Present-day doctor, orderly and patients.

**58** Welwitschia (plant)

**1959.** Centenary of Discovery of Welwitschia.

| | | | | |
|---|---|---|---|---|
| 538 | **58** | 1e.50 multicoloured | 70 | 35 |
| 539 | - | 2e.50 multicoloured | 1·10 | 45 |
| 540 | - | 5e. multicoloured | 1·80 | 45 |
| 541 | - | 10e. multicoloured | 5·50 | 1·40 |

DESIGNS: 2e.50, 5, 10e. Various types of Welwitschia ("Welwitschia mirabilis").

**59** Old Map of West Africa

**1960.** 500th Death Anniv of Prince Henry the Navigator.

| | | | | |
|---|---|---|---|---|
| 542 | **59** | 2e.50 multicoloured | 45 | 20 |

**60** "Agriculture" (distribution of seeds)

**1960.** 10th Anniv of African Technical Co-operation Commission.

| | | | | |
|---|---|---|---|---|
| 543 | **60** | 2e.50 multicoloured | 50 | 20 |

**61**

**1961.** Angolan Women. As T **61**. Portraits multicoloured; background colours given.

| | | | |
|---|---|---|---|
| 544 | 10c. green | 10 | 10 |
| 545 | 15c. blue | 10 | 10 |
| 546 | 30c. yellow | 10 | 10 |
| 547 | 40c. grey | 10 | 10 |
| 548 | 60c. brown | 10 | 10 |
| 549 | 1e.50 turquoise | 15 | 10 |
| 550 | 2e. lilac | 80 | 10 |
| 551 | 2e.50 lemon | 80 | 10 |
| 552 | 3e. pink | 3·00 | 20 |
| 553 | 4e. olive | 1·40 | 20 |
| 554 | 5e. blue | 95 | 20 |
| 555 | 7e.50 yellow | 1·30 | 65 |
| 556 | 10e. buff | 95 | 50 |
| 557 | 15e. brown | 1·40 | 65 |
| 558 | 25e. red | 2·00 | 95 |

| | | | |
|---|---|---|---|
| 559 | 50e. grey | 4·25 | 2·00 |

**62** Weightlifting

**1962.** Sports. Multicoloured.

| | | | |
|---|---|---|---|
| 560 | 50e. Flying | 15 | 15 |
| 561 | 1e. Rowing | 85 | 15 |
| 562 | 1e.50 Water polo | 60 | 20 |
| 563 | 2e.50 Throwing the hammer | 70 | 20 |
| 564 | 4e.50 High jumping | 60 | 45 |
| 565 | 15e. Type **62** | 1·40 | 1·10 |

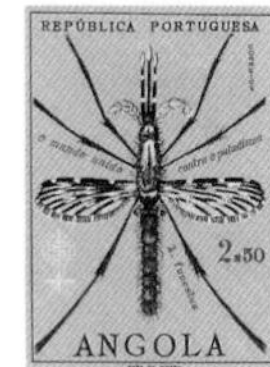


**63** "Anopheles funestus" (mosquito)

**1962.** Malaria Eradication.

| | | | | |
|---|---|---|---|---|
| 566 | **63** | 2e.50 multicoloured | 1·30 | 60 |

**64** Gen. Norton de Matos (statue)

**1962.** 50th Anniv of Nova Lisboa.

| | | | | |
|---|---|---|---|---|
| 567 | **64** | 2e.50 multicoloured | 45 | 20 |

**65** Red Locusts

**1963.** 15th Anniv of Int Locust Eradication Service.

| | | | | |
|---|---|---|---|---|
| 568 | **65** | 2e.50 multicoloured | 1·30 | 35 |

**66** Arms of St. Paul of the Assumption, Luanda

**1963.** Angolan Civic Arms (1st series). Mult.

| | | | |
|---|---|---|---|
| 569 | 5c. Type **66** | 15 | 15 |
| 570 | 10c. Massangano | 15 | 15 |
| 571 | 30c. Muxima | 15 | 15 |
| 572 | 50c. Carmona | 15 | 15 |
| 573 | 1e. Salazar | 50 | 15 |
| 574 | 1e.50 Malanje | 95 | 15 |
| 575 | 2e. Henry of Carvalho | 50 | 15 |
| 576 | 2e.50 Mocamedes | 3·00 | 45 |
| 577 | 3e. Novo Redondo | 70 | 15 |
| 578 | 3e.50 St. Salvador (Congo) | 80 | 15 |
| 579 | 5e. Luso | 70 | 20 |
| 580 | 7e.50 St. Philip (Benguela) | 95 | 80 |
| 581 | 10e. Lobito | 1·20 | 70 |
| 582 | 12e.50 Gabela | 1·30 | 1·20 |
| 583 | 15e. Sa da Bandeira | 1·30 | 1·20 |
| 584 | 17e.50 Silva Porto | 2·20 | 1·90 |
| 585 | 20e. Nova Lisboa | 2·20 | 1·60 |
| 586 | 22e.50 Cabinda | 2·20 | 1·90 |
| 587 | 30e. Serpa Pinto | 2·50 | 2·50 |

See also Nos. 589/610.

**67** Rear-Admiral A. Tomas

**1963.** Presidential Visit.

| | | | | |
|---|---|---|---|---|
| 588 | **67** | 2e.50 multicoloured | 45 | 15 |

**68** Arms of Sanza-Pombo

**1963.** Angolan Civic Arms (2nd series). Mult.

| | | | |
|---|---|---|---|
| 589 | 15c. Type **68** | 15 | 15 |
| 590 | 20c. St. Antonio do Zaire | 15 | 15 |
| 591 | 25c. Ambriz | 15 | 15 |
| 592 | 40c. Ambrizete | 15 | 15 |
| 593 | 50c. Catete | 15 | 15 |
| 594 | 70c. Quibaxe | 15 | 15 |
| 595 | 1e. Maquela do Zombo | 15 | 15 |
| 596 | 1e.20 Bembe | 15 | 15 |
| 597 | 1e.50 Caxito | 50 | 15 |
| 598 | 1e.80 Dondo | 50 | 45 |
| 599 | 2e.50 Damba | 1·90 | 15 |
| 600 | 4e. Cuimba | 45 | 15 |
| 601 | 6e.50 Negage | 45 | 30 |
| 602 | 7e. Quitexe | 65 | 45 |
| 603 | 8e. Mucaba | 65 | 50 |
| 604 | 9e. 31 de Janeiro | 95 | 80 |
| 605 | 11e. Novo Caipemba | 1·10 | 95 |
| 606 | 14e. Songo | 1·20 | 1·10 |
| 607 | 17e. Quimbele | 1·30 | 1·20 |
| 608 | 25e. Noqui | 1·60 | 1·20 |
| 609 | 35e. Santa Cruz | 2·30 | 1·90 |
| 610 | 50e. General Freire | 3·00 | 1·60 |

**69** Map of Africa, Boeing 707 and Lockheed Super Constellation Airliners

**1963.** 10th Anniv of T.A.P. Airline.

| | | | | |
|---|---|---|---|---|
| 611 | **69** | 1e. multicoloured | 85 | 30 |

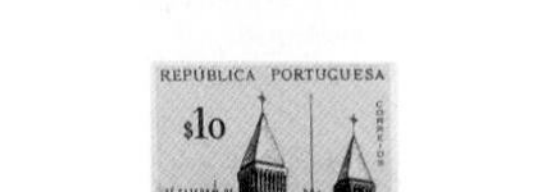

**70** Bandeira Cathedral

**1963.** Angolan Churches. Multicoloured.

| | | | |
|---|---|---|---|
| 612 | 10c. Type **70** | 10 | 10 |
| 613 | 20c. Landana | 10 | 10 |
| 614 | 30c. Luanda (Cathedral) | 10 | 10 |
| 615 | 40c. Gabela | 10 | 10 |
| 616 | 50c. St. Martin, Bay of Tigers (Chapel) | 10 | 10 |
| 617 | 1e. Melange (Cathedral) (horiz) | 15 | 15 |
| 618 | 1e.50 St. Peter, Chibia | 15 | 15 |
| 619 | 2e. Benguela (horiz) | 20 | 15 |
| 620 | 2e.50 Jesus, Luanda | 20 | 15 |
| 621 | 3e. Camabatela (horiz) | 30 | 15 |
| 622 | 3e.50 Cabinda Mission | 45 | 15 |
| 623 | 4e. Vila Folgares (horiz) | 45 | 20 |
| 624 | 4e.50 Arrabida, Lobito (horiz) | 60 | 20 |
| 625 | 5e. Cabinda | 60 | 30 |
| 626 | 7e.50 Cacuso, Malange (horiz) | 95 | 50 |
| 627 | 10e. Lubanga Mission | 1·20 | 50 |
| 628 | 12e.50 Huila Mission (horiz) | 1·40 | 80 |
| 629 | 15e. Island Cape, Luanda (horiz) | 1·60 | 85 |

**71** Dr. A. T. de Sousa

**1964.** Centenary of National Overseas Bank.

| | | | | |
|---|---|---|---|---|
| 630 | **71** | 2e.50 multicoloured | 60 | 30 |

**72** Arms and Palace of Commerce, Luanda

**1964.** Cent of Luanda Commercial Association.

| | | | | |
|---|---|---|---|---|
| 631 | **72** | 1e. multicoloured | 20 | 15 |

**73** I.T.U. Emblem and St. Gabriel

**1965.** Centenary of I.T.U.

| | | | | |
|---|---|---|---|---|
| 632 | **73** | 2e.50 multicoloured | 85 | 45 |

**74** Boeing 707 over Petroleum Refinery

**1965.** Air. Multicoloured.

| | | | |
|---|---|---|---|
| 633 | 1e.50 Type **74** | 80 | 10 |
| 634 | 2e.50 Cambabe Dam | 85 | 10 |
| 635 | 3e. Salazar Dam | 1·20 | 10 |
| 636 | 4e. Captain Trofilo Duarte Dam | 1·20 | 15 |
| 637 | 4e.50 Creveiro Lopes Dam | 85 | 15 |
| 638 | 5e. Cuango Dam | 85 | 20 |
| 639 | 6e. Quanza Bridge | 1·40 | 30 |
| 640 | 7e. Captain Trofilo Duarte Railway Bridge | 2·00 | 30 |
| 641 | 8e.50 Dr. Oliveira Salazar Bridge | 2·50 | 80 |
| 642 | 12e.50 Captain Silva Carvalho Railway Bridge | 2·50 | 1·10 |

Nos. 634/42 are horiz and each design includes a Boeing 707 airliner overhead.

**75** Fokker F.27 Friendship over Luanda Airport

**1965.** 25th Anniv of Direccao dos Transportes Aereos (Angolan airline).

| | | | | |
|---|---|---|---|---|
| 643 | **75** | 2e.50 multicoloured | 85 | 20 |

**76** Arquebusier, 1539

**1966.** Portuguese Military Uniforms. Multicoloured.

| | | | |
|---|---|---|---|
| 644 | 50c. Type **76** | 10 | 10 |
| 645 | 1e. Arquebusier, 1640 | 10 | 10 |
| 646 | 1e.50 Infantry officer, 1777 | 15 | 10 |
| 647 | 2e. Infantry standard-bearer, 1777 | 25 | 10 |
| 648 | 2e.50 Infantryman, 1777 | 25 | 10 |
| 649 | 3e. Cavalry officer, 1783 | 35 | 10 |
| 650 | 4e. Trooper, 1783 | 40 | 15 |
| 651 | 4e.50 Infantry officer, 1807 | 50 | 25 |
| 652 | 5e. Infantryman, 1807 | 60 | 25 |

653 6e. Cavalry officer, 1807 85 25

654 8e. Trooper, 1807 1·20 40

655 9e. Infantryman, 1873 1·20 60

**77** St. Paul's Hospital, Luanda, and Sarmento Rodrigues Commercial and Industrial School

**1966.** 40th Anniv of National Revolution.

656 **77** 1e. multicoloured 35 15

**78** Emblem of Brotherhood

**1966.** Centenary of Brotherhood of the Holy Spirit.

657 **78** 1e. multicoloured 25 15

**79** Mendes Barata and Cruiser "Don Carlos I"

**1967.** Centenary of Military Naval Assn. Mult.

658 1e. Type **79** 65 35

659 2e.50 Augusto de Castilho and sail/steam corvette "Mindelo" 85 35

**80** Basilica of Fatima

**1967.** 50th Anniv of Fatima Apparitions.

660 **80** 50c. multicoloured 25 15

**81** 17th-century Map and M. C. Pereira (founder)

**1967.** 350th Anniv of Benguela.

661 **81** 50c. multicoloured 25 15

**82** Town Hall, Uige-Carmona

**1967.** 50th Anniv of Uige-Carmona.

662 **82** 1e. multicoloured 15 15

**83** "The Three Orders"

**1967.** Portuguese Civil and Military Orders. Mult.

663 50c. Type **83** 15 15

664 1e. "Tower and Sword" 15 15

665 1e.50 "Avis" 15 15

666 2e. "Christ" 15 15

667 2e.50 "St. James of the Sword" 15 15

668 3e. "Empire" 25 15

669 4e. "Prince Henry" 35 35

670 5e. "Benemerencia" 40 35

671 10e. "Public Instruction" 75 85

672 20e. "Agricultural and Industrial Merit" 1·60 95

**84** Belmonte Castle

**1968.** 500th Birth Anniv of Pedro Cabral (explorer). Multicoloured.

673 50c. Our Lady of Hope (vert) 15 15

674 1e. Type **84** 25 15

675 1e.50 St. Jeronimo's hermitage (vert) 35 15

676 2e.50 Cabral's fleet (vert) 90 15

**85** Francisco Inocencio de Souza Countinho

**1969.** Bicent of Novo Redondo (Angolan city).

677 **85** 2e. multicoloured 20 10

**86** Gunboat "Loge" and Admiral Coutinho

**1969.** Birth Centenary of Admiral Gago Coutinho.

678 **86** 2e.50 multicoloured 75 25

**87** Compass

**1969.** 500th Birth Anniv of Vasco da Gama (explorer).

679 **87** 1e. multicoloured 25 15

**88** L. A. Rebello de Silva

**1969.** Cent of Overseas Administrative Reforms.

680 **88** 1e.50 multicoloured 15 15

**89** Gate of Jeronimos

**1969.** 500th Birth Anniv of King Manoel I.

681 **89** 3e. multicoloured 25 15

**90** "Angolasaurus bocagei"

**1970.** Fossils and Minerals. Multicoloured.

682 50c. Type **90** 40 15

683 1e. Ferro-meteorite 40 15

684 1e.50 Dioptase 65 40

685 2e. "Gondwanidium validium" 65 40

686 2e.50 Diamonds 65 40

687 3e. Estromatolitos 65 40

688 3e.50 Giant-toothed shark ("Procarcharodon megalodon") 1·10 65

689 4e. Dwarf lungfish ("Microceratodus angolensis") 1·10 65

690 4e.50 Muscovite (mica) 1·10 65

691 5e. Barytes 1·10 65

692 6e. "Nostoceras helicinum" 2·10 90

693 10e. "Rotula orbiculus angolensis" 2·20 1·30

**91** Marshal Carmona

**1970.** Birth Centenary of Marshal Carmona.

694 **91** 2e.50 multicoloured 35 15

**92** Cotton-picking

**1970.** Centenary of Malanje Municipality.

695 **92** 2e.50 multicoloured 40 25

**93** Mail Steamers "Infante Dom Henrique" and "Principe Perfeito" and 1870 5r. Stamp

**1970.** Stamp Centenary. Multicoloured.

696 1e.50 Type **93** (postage) 40 25

697 4e.50 Beyer-Garratt steam locomotive and 25r. stamp of 1870 2·20 2·20

698 2e.50 Fokker F.27 Friendship and Boeing 707 mail planes and 10r. stamp of 1870 (air) 1·50 65

**MS**699 150×105 mm. Nos. 696/8 (sold at 15e.) 9·50 9·50

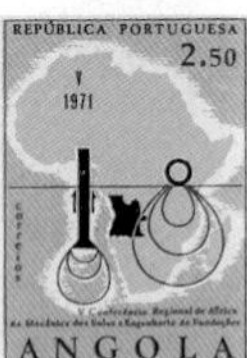


**94** Map and Emblems

**1971.** 5th Regional Soil and Foundation Engineering Conference, Luanda.

700 **94** 2e.50 multicoloured 25 15

**96** 16th-century Galleon at Mouth of Congo

**1972.** 400th Anniv of Camoens' "The Lusiads" (epic poem).

704 **96** 1e. multicoloured 50 15

**97** Sailing Yachts

**1972.** Olympic Games, Munich.

705 **97** 50c. multicoloured 50 15

**98** Fairey IIID Seaplane "Santa Cruz" near Fernando de Noronha

**1972.** 50th Anniv of 1st Flight Lisbon–Rio de Janeiro.

706 **98** 1e. multicoloured 25 15

**99** W.M.O. Emblem

**1974.** Centenary of W.M.O.

707 **99** 1e. multicoloured 35 15

**100** Dish Aerials

**1974.** Inauguration of Satellite Communications Station Network.

708 **100** 2e. multicoloured 35 25

**101** Doris Harp

**1974.** Sea Shells. Multicoloured.

709 25c. Type **101** 10 10

710 30c. West African murex 10 10

711 50c. Scaly-ridged venus 10 10

712 70c. Filose latirus 15 10

713 1e. "Cymbium cisium" 15 10

714 1e.50 West African helmet 15 10

715 2e. Rat cowrie 15 10

716 2e.50 Butterfly cone 25 10

717 3e. Bubonian conch 35 15

718 3e.50 "Tympanotonus fuscatus" 40 15

719 4e. Great ribbed cockle 40 15

720 5e. Lightning moon 50 15

721 6e. Lion's-paw scallop 60 25

722 7e. Giant tun 75 25

723 10e. Rugose donax 1·00 40

724 25e. Smith's distorsio 3·00 1·10

725 30e. "Olivancilaria acuminata" 3·00 1·30

726 35e. Giant hairy melongena 3·25 1·70

727 40e. Wavy-leaved turrid 4·50 1·80

728 50e. American sundial 5·75 2·20

**1974.** Youth Philately. No. 511 optd **1974 FILATELIA JUVENIL**.

729 **51** 5c. multicoloured 15 60

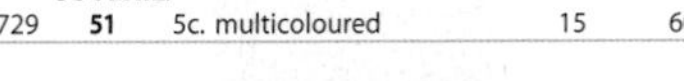

**103** Arm with Rifle and Star

**1975.** Independence.

730 **103** 1e.50 multicoloured 10 10

**104** Diquiche-ua-Puheue Mask

**1975.** Angolan Masks. Multicoloured.

| | | | | |
|---|---|---|---|---|
| 731 | | 50c. Type **104** | 10 | 10 |
| 732 | | 3e. Bui ou Congolo mask | 15 | 10 |

**105** Workers

**1976.** Workers' Day.

| | | | | |
|---|---|---|---|---|
| 733 | **105** | 1e. multicoloured | 10 | 10 |

**1976.** Stamp Day. Optd **DIA DO SELO 15 Junho 1976 REP. POPULAR DE.**

| | | | | |
|---|---|---|---|---|
| 734 | **51** | 10e. multicoloured | 1·50 | 1·25 |

**107** Pres. Agostinho Neto

**1976.** 1st Anniv of Independence.

| | | | | |
|---|---|---|---|---|
| 735 | **107** | 50c. black and grey | 10 | 10 |
| 736 | **107** | 2e. purple and grey | 10 | 10 |
| 737 | **107** | 3e. blue and grey | 10 | 10 |
| 738 | **107** | 5e. brown and buff | 15 | 10 |
| 739 | **107** | 10e. brown and drab | 25 | 10 |
| **MS**740 | | 59×75 mm. No. 739, but without President's name. Imperf | 2·00 | |

**1976.** St. Silvestre Games. Optd **S Silvestre Rep. Popular de.**

| | | | | |
|---|---|---|---|---|
| 741 | **62** | 15e. multicoloured | 55 | 35 |

**1977.** Nos. 518, 724/5 and 728 optd **REPUBLICA POPULAR DE.**

| | | | | |
|---|---|---|---|---|
| 742 | | 20e. Type **51** | 3·50 | 3·50 |
| 743 | | 25e. "Cymatium trigonum" | 60 | 15 |
| 744 | | 30e. "Olivancilaria acuminata" | 75 | 25 |
| 745 | | 50e. "Solarium granulatum" | 1·25 | 40 |

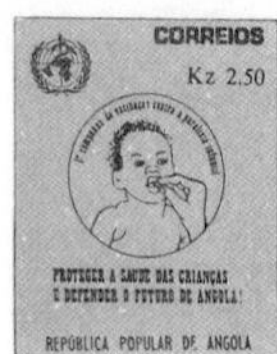


**111** Child receiving Vaccine

**1977.** Polio Vaccination Campaign.

| | | | | |
|---|---|---|---|---|
| 746 | **111** | 2k.50 blue and black | 10 | 10 |

**112** Map of Africa and Flag

**1977.** MPLA Congress.

| | | | | |
|---|---|---|---|---|
| 747 | **112** | 6k. multicoloured | 20 | 15 |

**113** Human Rights Flame

**1979.** 30th Anniv of Declaration of Human Rights.

| | | | | |
|---|---|---|---|---|
| 748 | **113** | 2k.50 yellow, red & black | 15 | 10 |

**114** Emblem

**1979.** International Anti-apartheid Year.

| | | | | |
|---|---|---|---|---|
| 749 | **114** | 1k. multicoloured | 10 | 10 |

**115** Child raising Arms to Light

**1980.** International Year of the Child (1979).

| | | | | |
|---|---|---|---|---|
| 750 | **115** | 3k.50 multicoloured | 15 | 10 |

**1980.** Nos. 697/8 optd **REPUBLICA POPULAR DE.**

| | | | | |
|---|---|---|---|---|
| 751 | | 4e.50 multicoloured (postage) | 2·75 | 1·75 |
| 752 | | 2e.50 multicoloured (air) | 15 | 10 |

**117** Pres. Agostinho Neto

**1980.** National Heroes Day. Multicoloured.

| | | | | |
|---|---|---|---|---|
| 753 | | 4k.50 Type **117** | 15 | 10 |
| 754 | | 50k. Pres. Neto with machine-gun | 1·25 | 70 |

**118** Arms and Workers

**1980.** "Popular Power".

| | | | | |
|---|---|---|---|---|
| 755 | **118** | 40k. blue and black | 1·00 | 55 |

**119** "The Liberated Angolan" (A. Vaz de Carvalho)

**1980.** 5th Anniv of Independence.

| | | | | |
|---|---|---|---|---|
| 756 | **119** | 5k.50 multicoloured | 15 | 10 |

**120** Running

**1980.** Olympic Games, Moscow.

| | | | | |
|---|---|---|---|---|
| 757 | **120** | 9k. pink and red | 20 | 10 |
| 758 | - | 12k. light blue and blue | 30 | 10 |

DESIGN: 12k. Swimming.

**121** Millet

**1980.** Angolan Produce. Multicoloured.

| | | | | |
|---|---|---|---|---|
| 759 | | 50l. Type **121** | 10 | 10 |
| 760 | | 5k. Coffee | 15 | 10 |
| 761 | | 7k.50 Sunflower | 20 | 10 |
| 762 | | 13k.50 Cotton | 30 | 15 |
| 763 | | 14k. Petroleum | 30 | 15 |
| 764 | | 16k. Diamonds | 35 | 20 |

**1981.** Nos. 708, 713/16 and 718/27 with "REPUBLICA PORTUGUESA" inscr obliterated. (a) Dish aerials.

| | | | | |
|---|---|---|---|---|
| 765 | **100** | 2e. multicoloured | 10 | 10 |

(b) Sea Shells. Multicoloured.

| | | | | |
|---|---|---|---|---|
| 766 | | 1e. "Cymbium cisium" | 10 | 10 |
| 767 | | 1e.50 West African helmet | 15 | 10 |
| 768 | | 2e. Rat cowrie | 20 | 10 |
| 769 | | 2e.50 Butterfly cone | 25 | 10 |
| 770 | | 3e.50 "Tympanotonus fuscatus" | 30 | 10 |
| 771 | | 4e. Great ribbed cockle | 35 | 15 |
| 772 | | 5e. Lightning moon | 40 | 15 |
| 773 | | 6e. Lion's-paw scallop | 45 | 20 |
| 774 | | 7e. Giant tun | 50 | 20 |
| 775 | | 10e. Rugose donax | 70 | 25 |
| 776 | | 25e. Smith's distorsio | 1·75 | 30 |
| 777 | | 30e. "Olivancilaria acuminata" | 1·90 | 65 |
| 778 | | 35e. Giant hairy melongena | 2·40 | 90 |
| 779 | | 40e. Wavy-leaved turrid | 3·00 | 1·00 |

**122** Prisoner and Protesting Crowd

**1981.** 5th Anniv of Soweto Riots in South Africa.

| | | | | |
|---|---|---|---|---|
| 780 | **122** | 4k.50 black, red & silver | 20 | 15 |

**123** Basketball and Volleyball

**1981.** 2nd Central African Games. Multicoloured.

| | | | | |
|---|---|---|---|---|
| 781 | | 50l. Cycling and Tennis | 10 | 10 |
| 782 | | 5k. Judo and Boxing | 20 | 15 |
| 783 | | 6k. Type **123** | 25 | 15 |
| 784 | | 10k. Handball and football | 40 | 20 |
| **MS**784a | | 116×129 mm. 15k. Swimming and javelin. Imperf | 80 | 85 |

**124** Statuette

**1981.** "Turipex 81".

| | | | | |
|---|---|---|---|---|
| 785 | **124** | 9k. multicoloured | 40 | 20 |

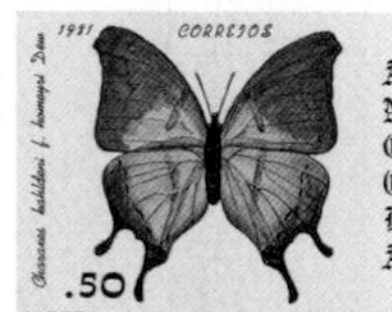


**125** "Charaxes kahldeni f. homeyri"

**1982.** Butterflies. Multicoloured.

| | | | | |
|---|---|---|---|---|
| 787 | | 50l. Type **125** | 10 | 10 |
| 788 | | 1k. "Abantis gambesiaca" | 10 | 10 |
| 789 | | 5k. "Catacroptera cloanthe" | 25 | 30 |
| 790 | | 9k. "Myrina ficedula" (vert) | 60 | 25 |
| 791 | | 10k. "Colotis danae" | 60 | 25 |
| 792 | | 15k. "Acraea acrita bella" | 80 | 30 |
| 793 | | 100k. "Precis hierta cebrese" | 5·25 | 2·40 |
| **MS**793a | | 154×104 mm. Nos. 787/93. Imperf (sold at 30k.) | 1·40 | 1·40 |

**126** "Silence of Night"

**1982.** 5th Anniv of Admission to United Nations. Multicoloured.

| | | | | |
|---|---|---|---|---|
| 794 | | 5k.50 Type **126** | 25 | 15 |
| 795 | | 7k.50 "Cotton Fields" | 35 | 15 |

**127** Worker and Building

**1982.** 20th Anniv of Angola Laboratory of Engineering. Multicoloured.

| | | | | |
|---|---|---|---|---|
| 797 | | 9k. Laboratory building (horiz) | 40 | 20 |
| 798 | | 13k. Type **127** (Research in construction materials) | 45 | 25 |
| 799 | | 100k. Geotechnical equipment | 4·00 | 2·25 |

**128** "Albizzia versicolor"

**1983.** Flowers (1st series). Multicoloured.

| | | | | |
|---|---|---|---|---|
| 800 | | 5k. "Dichrostachys glomerata" | 25 | 10 |
| 801 | | 12k. "Amblygonocarpus obtusangulus" | 45 | 20 |
| 802 | | 50k. Type **128** | 2·00 | 1·10 |

**129** Angolan Woman and Emblem

**1983.** 1st Angolan Women's Organization Congress.

| | | | | |
|---|---|---|---|---|
| 803 | **129** | 20k. multicoloured | 80 | 25 |

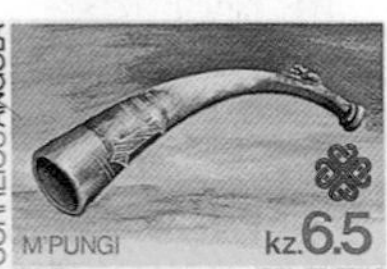


**130** M'pungi (horn)

**1983.** World Communications Year. Multicoloured.

| | | | | |
|---|---|---|---|---|
| 804 | | 6k.50 Type **130** | 25 | 20 |
| 805 | | 12k. Mondu (drum) | 50 | 45 |

**131** Spear breaking Chain around South Africa

**1983.** 30th Anniv of Organization of African Unity.
806 **131** 6k.50 multicoloured 30 25

**132** "Antestiopsis lineaticollis intricata"

**1983.** "Brasiliana 83" International Stamp Exn, Rio de Janeiro. Harmful Insects. Multicoloured.
807 4k.50 Type **132** 25 15
808 6k.50 "Stephanoderes hampei" 35 25
809 10k. "Zonocerus variegatus" 60 45

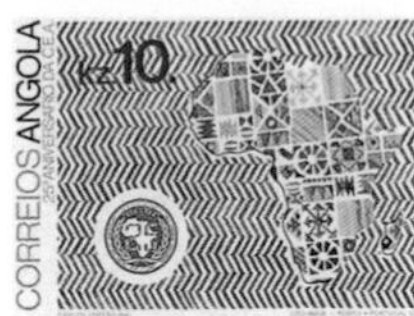

**133** Map of Africa and E.C.A. Emblem

**1983.** 25th Anniv of Economic Commission for Africa.
810 **133** 10k. multicoloured 45 40

**134** Collecting Mail

**1983.** 185th Anniv of Postal Service. Multicoloured.
811 50l. Type **134** 10 10
812 3k.50 Unloading mail from aircraft (horiz) 20 15
813 5k. Sorting mail (horiz) 35 25
814 15k. Posting letter 85 80
815 30k. Collecting mail from private box (horiz) 1·75 1·50
**MS**816 142×78 mm. Nos. 812, 813 and 815 2·20 1·90

**135** "Parasa karschi"

**1984.** Moths. Multicoloured.
817 50l. Type **135** 10 10
818 1k. "Diaphone angolensis" 10 10
819 3k.50 "Choeropais jucunda" 30 15
820 6k.50 "Hespagarista rendalli" 50 35
821 15k. "Euchromia guineensis" 95 80
822 17k.50 "Mazuca roseistriga" 1·10 95
823 20k. "Utetheisa callima" 1·40 1·25

**136** Dove

**1984.** 1st National Union of Angolan Workers Congress.
824 **136** 30k. multicoloured 1·75 1·50

**137** Flag and Agostinho Neto

**1984.** 5th National Heroes Day. Multicoloured.
825 10k.50 Type **137** 50 45
826 36k.50 Flag and Agostinho Neto (different) 1·60 1·50

**138** Southern Ground Hornbill

**1984.** Birds. Multicoloured.
827 10k.50 Type **138** 90 90
828 14k. Palm-nut vulture 1·25 1·25
829 16k. Goliath heron 1·50 1·50
830 19k.50 Eastern white pelican 1·75 1·75
831 22k. African spoonbill 2·00 2·00
832 26k. South African crowned crane 2·40 2·40

**139** Greater Kudu

**1984.** Mammals. Multicoloured.
833 1k. Type **139** 10 10
834 4k. Springbok 25 15
835 5k. Chimpanzee 30 25
836 10k. African buffalo 55 50
837 15k. Sable antelope 80 65
838 20k. Aardvark 1·25 1·10
839 25k. Spotted hyena 1·50 1·25

**140** Sao Pedro da Barra Fortress

**1985.** Monuments. Multicoloured.
840 5k. Type **140** 25 20
841 12k.50 Nova Oerias ruins 60 55
842 18k. Antiga cathedral ruins, M'Banza Kongo 80 75
843 26k. Massangano fortress 1·25 1·10
844 39k. Escravatura museum 1·75 1·60

**141** Flags on World Map

**1985.** 5th Anniv of Southern Africa Development Co-ordination Conference. Multicoloured.
845 1k. Type **141** 10 10
846 11k. Offshore drilling 1·25 50
847 57k. Conference session 2·50 2·40

**142** Flags and "XXV"

**1985.** 25th Anniv of National Union of Angolan Workers.
848 **142** 77k. multicoloured 3·50 3·25

**143** "Lonchocarpas sericeus"

**1985.** Medicinal Plants. Multicoloured.
849 1k. Type **143** 10 10
850 4k. "Gossypium sp." 20 15
851 11k. Senna 50 45
852 25k.50 "Gloriosa superba" 1·10 1·00
853 55k. "Cochlospermum angolensis" 2·50 2·40

**144** Map of Angola as Dove and Conference Emblem

**1984.** Ministerial Conference of Non-aligned Countries, Luanda.
854 **144** 35k. multicoloured 1·60 1·50

**145** Dove and U.N. Emblem

**1985.** 40th Anniv of U.N.O.
855 **145** 12k.50 multicoloured 60 55

**146** Cement Works

**1985.** 10th Anniv of Independence. Multicoloured.
856 50l. Type **146** 10 10
857 5k. Timber yard 20 15
858 7k. Quartz 30 25
859 10k. Iron works 50 45
**MS**860 210×123 mm. Nos. 856/9 1·10 95

**147** Emblem, Open Book, Soldier, Farmer and Factory

**1985.** 2nd MPLA Congress.
861 **147** 20k. multicoloured 90 85

**148** Runner on Track

**1985.** 30th Anniv of Demostenes de Almeida Clington Races. Multicoloured.
862 50l. Type **148** 10 10
863 5k. Two runners on road 20 15
864 6k.50 Three runners on road 30 25
865 10k. Two runners on track 50 45

**149** Map, Stadium and Players

**1986.** World Cup Football Championship, Mexico.
866 **149** 50l. multicoloured 10 10
867 - 3k.50 multicoloured 15 15
868 - 5k. multicoloured 30 25
869 - 7k. multicoloured 35 30
870 - 10k. multicoloured 50 45
871 - 18k. multicoloured 85 70
DESIGNS: 3k.50 to 18k. Different footballers.

**150** Crowd

**1986.** 25th Anniv of Armed Independence Movement.
872 **150** 15k. multicoloured 75 70

**151** Soviet Space Project

**1985.** 25th Anniv of First Man in Space. Mult.
873 50l. Type **151** 10 10
874 1k. "Voskhod 1" 10 10
875 5k. Cosmonaut on space walk 20 15
876 10k. Moon vehicle 50 45
877 13k. "Soyuz"–"Apollo" link-up 60 55

**152** National Flag and U.N. Emblem

**1986.** 10th Anniv of Angolan Membership of U.N.O.
878 **152** 22k. multicoloured 1·00 90

**153** People at Work

**1986.** 30th Anniv of Popular Movement for the Liberation of Angola. Multicoloured.
879 5k. Type **153** 20 15
880 5k. Emblem and people (29×36 mm) 20 15
881 5k. Soldiers fighting 20 15
Nos. 879/81 were printed together, se-tenant, forming a composite design.

**154** Lecturer and Students (Faculty of Engineering)

**1986.** 10th Anniv of Agostinho Neto University. Multicoloured.
882 50l. Type **154** 10 10
883 7k. Students and Judges (Faculty of Law) 30 25
884 10k. Students using micro-scopes and surgeons operating (Faculty of Medicine) 50 45

**155** Ouioca

**1987.** Traditional Hairstyles. Multicoloured.

| | | | |
|---|---|---|---|
| 885 | 1k. Type **155** | 10 | 10 |
| 886 | 1k.50 Luanda | 10 | 10 |
| 887 | 5k. Humbe | 20 | 15 |
| 888 | 7k. Muila | 35 | 25 |
| 889 | 20k. Muila (different) | 80 | 70 |
| 890 | 30k. Lunda, Dilolo | 1·25 | 1·00 |

**156** "Lenin in the Smolny Institute" (detail, Serov)

**1987.** 70th Anniv of Russian Revolution.

| | | | | |
|---|---|---|---|---|
| 891 | **156** | 15k. multicoloured | 60 | 25 |

**157** Pambala Beach

**1987.** Scenic Spots. Multicoloured.

| | | | |
|---|---|---|---|
| 892 | 50l. Type **157** | 10 | 10 |
| 893 | 1k.50 Quedas do Dala (waterfalls) | 10 | 10 |
| 894 | 3k.50 Black Feet Rocks, Pungo Adongo (vert) | 15 | 10 |
| 895 | 5k. Cuango River valley | 20 | 15 |
| 896 | 10k. Luanda shore (vert) | 40 | 35 |
| 897 | 20k. Serra da Leba road | 80 | 75 |

**158** Emblem

**1988.** 2nd Angolan Women's Organization Congress. Multicoloured.

| | | | |
|---|---|---|---|
| 898 | 2k. Type **158** | 10 | 10 |
| 899 | 10k. Women engaged in various pursuits | 40 | 35 |

**159** Dancers

**1988.** 10th Anniv of Vitoria Carnival. Mult.

| | | | |
|---|---|---|---|
| 900 | 5k. Type **159** | 15 | 10 |
| 901 | 10k. Revellers | 40 | 35 |

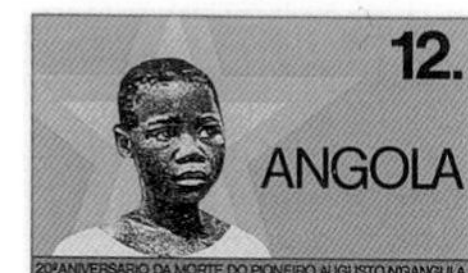

**160** Augusto N'Gangula (child revolutionary)

**1989.** Pioneers. Multicoloured.

| | | | |
|---|---|---|---|
| 902 | 12k. Type **160** (20th death anniv) | 50 | 45 |
| 903 | 15k. Pioneers (25th anniv (1988) of Agostinho Neto Pioneers Organization) | 60 | 55 |

**161** Luanda 1st August Sports Club (1979–81)

**1989.** 10th National Football League Championship. Championship Winners. Multicoloured.

| | | | |
|---|---|---|---|
| 904 | 5k. Type **161** | 15 | 15 |
| 905 | 5k. Luanda Petro Atletico (1982, 1984, 1986–88) | 15 | 15 |
| 906 | 5k. Benguela 1st May Sports Club (1983, 1985) | 15 | 15 |

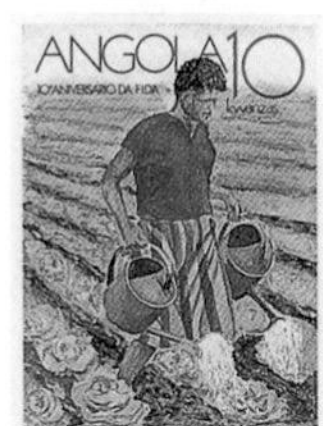

**162** Watering Cabbages

**1990.** 10th Anniv (1987) of International Fund for Agricultural Development.

| | | | | |
|---|---|---|---|---|
| 907 | **162** | 10k. multicoloured | 1·60 | 1·30 |

**163** 19th-century Middle-class Houses, Luanda

**1990.** Historical Buildings. Multicoloured.

| | | | |
|---|---|---|---|
| 908 | 1k. Type **163** | 25 | 25 |
| 909 | 2k. Cidade Alta railway station, Luanda | 50 | 30 |
| 910 | 5k. National Anthropology Museum | 60 | 40 |
| 911 | 15k. Palace of Ana Joaquina dos Santos | 1·20 | 1·20 |
| 912 | 23k. Iron Palace | 1·60 | 2·00 |
| 913 | 36k. Meteorological observatory (vert) | 2·75 | 2·50 |
| 914 | 50k. Governor's palace | 3·75 | 3·50 |

**164** "General Machado" and Route Map

**1990.** Benguela (915) and Luanda Railways. Mult.

| | | | |
|---|---|---|---|
| 915 | 5k. Type **164** | 1·00 | 1·00 |
| 916 | 12k. Beyer-Garratt steam locomotive (facing left) | 2·00 | 2·00 |
| 917 | 12k. Beyer-Garratt steam locomotive (facing right) | 2·00 | 2·00 |
| 918 | 14k. Mikado steam locomotive | 2·50 | 2·50 |
| **MS**919 | 88×69 mm. 25k. Diesel-electric locomotive (39×29 mm) | 4·25 | 4·25 |

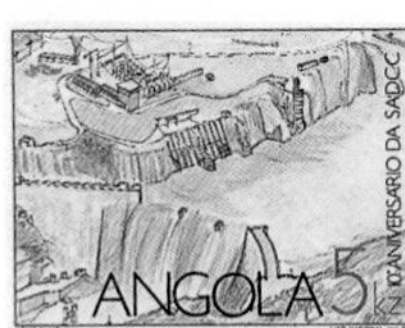

**165** Hydroelectric Production

**1990.** 10th Anniv of Southern Africa Development Co-ordinating Conference. Multicoloured.

| | | | |
|---|---|---|---|
| 920 | 5k. Type **165** | 1·00 | 80 |
| 921 | 9k. Oil industry | 2·00 | 1·75 |

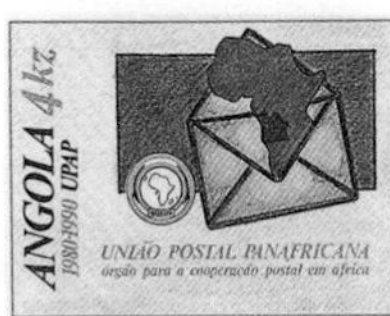

**166** Map in Envelope

**1990.** 10th Anniv of Pan-African Postal Union. Multicoloured.

| | | | |
|---|---|---|---|
| 922 | 4k. Type **166** | 90 | 70 |
| 923 | 10k. Map consisting of stamps and envelopes | 2·60 | 1·80 |

**167** "Muxima"

**1990.** "Stamp World London 90" International Stamp Exn. Paintings by Raul Indipwo. Multicoloured.

| | | | |
|---|---|---|---|
| 924 | 6k. "Three Graces" (horiz) | 1·00 | 90 |
| 925 | 9k. Type **167** | 1·80 | 1·25 |

**168** Antelope

**1990.** Protected Animals. Sable Antelope. Mult.

| | | | |
|---|---|---|---|
| 926 | 5k. Type **168** | 2·60 | 1·90 |
| 927 | 5k. Male and female | 2·60 | 1·90 |
| 928 | 5k. Female | 2·60 | 1·90 |
| 929 | 5k. Female and young | 2·60 | 1·90 |

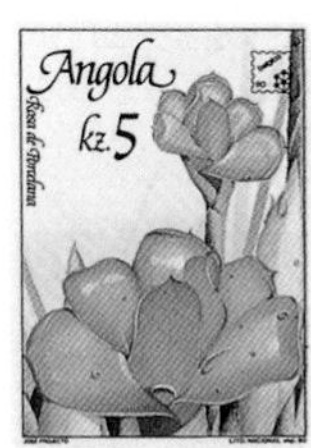

**169** Porcelain Rose

**1990.** "Belgica 90" International Stamp Exhibition, Brussels. Flowers. Multicoloured.

| | | | |
|---|---|---|---|
| 930 | 5k. Type **169** | 55 | 60 |
| 931 | 8k. Indian carnation | 90 | 80 |
| 932 | 10k. Allamanda | 1·10 | 90 |
| **MS**933 | 113×139 mm. 40k. Hibiscus and "Manneqin Pis", Brussels (49×39 mm) | 4·50 | 4·00 |

**170** Zebra Drinking

**1990.** International Literacy Year. Multicoloured.

| | | | |
|---|---|---|---|
| 934 | 5k. Type **170** | 1·10 | 80 |
| 935 | 5k. Butterfly | 1·10 | 80 |
| 936 | 5k. Horse's head | 1·10 | 80 |
| **MS**937 | 210×260 mm. 30×1k. Composite jungle-scene showing various animals and plants | 7·50 | 7·00 |

**171** Flag and People

**1990.** 10th Anniv of People's Assembly.

| | | | | |
|---|---|---|---|---|
| 938 | **171** | 10k. multicoloured | 50 | 30 |

**172** Dove, Flag and Workers

**1990.** 3rd Popular Movement for the Liberation of Angola-Labour Party Congress.

| | | | | |
|---|---|---|---|---|
| 939 | **172** | 14k. multicoloured | 80 | 50 |

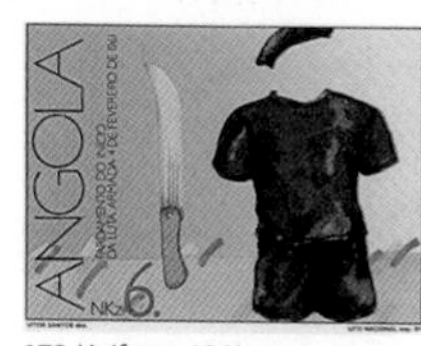

**173** Uniform, 1961

**1991.** 30th Anniv of Armed Independence Movement. Freedom Fighters' Uniforms. Mult.

| | | | |
|---|---|---|---|
| 940 | 6k. Type **173** | 1·40 | 1·00 |
| 941 | 6k. Pau N'Dulo, 1962–63 | 1·40 | 1·00 |
| 942 | 6k. Military uniform, 1968 | 1·40 | 1·00 |
| 943 | 6k. Military uniform from 1972 | 1·40 | 1·00 |

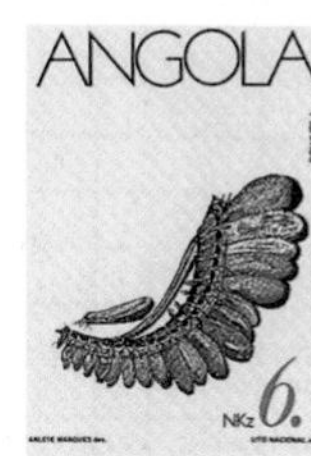

**174** Marimba

**1991.** Musical Instruments. Multicoloured.

| | | | |
|---|---|---|---|
| 944 | 6k. Type **174** | 1·20 | 85 |
| 945 | 6k. Ngoma ya Mucupela (double-ended drum) | 1·20 | 85 |
| 946 | 6k. Ngoma la Txina (floor-standing drum) | 1·20 | 85 |
| 947 | 6k. Kissange | 1·20 | 85 |

**175** Iona National Park

**1991.** African Tourism Year. Multicoloured.

| | | | |
|---|---|---|---|
| 948 | 3k. Type **175** | 50 | 40 |
| 949 | 7k. Kalandula Falls | 1·00 | 80 |
| 950 | 35k. Lobito Bay | 3·00 | 2·40 |
| 951 | 60k. "Welwitschia mirabilis" | 5·00 | 4·50 |

**176** Kabir of the Dembos

**1991.** "Espamer '91" Spain–Latin America Stamp Exhibition, Buenos Aires. Dogs. Multicoloured.

| | | | |
|---|---|---|---|
| 953 | 5k. Type **176** | 60 | 50 |
| 954 | 7k. Ombua | 90 | 70 |
| 955 | 11k. Kabir massongo | 1·50 | 1·10 |
| 956 | 12k. Kawa tchowe | 1·60 | 1·20 |

**177** Judo

**1991.** Olympic Games, Barcelona (1992) (1st issue). Multicoloured.

| | | | |
|---|---|---|---|
| 957 | 4k. Type **177** | 30 | 20 |
| 958 | 6k. Yachting | 40 | 30 |
| 959 | 10k. Marathon | 70 | 50 |
| 960 | 100k. Swimming | 6·50 | 5·25 |

**178** Mother and Child

**1991.** 13th Anniv of Angolan Red Cross. Mult.

| | | | | |
|---|---|---|---|---|
| 961 | | 20k.+5k. Type **178** | 1·40 | 1·40 |
| 962 | | 40k.+5k. Zebra and foal | 2·40 | 2·40 |

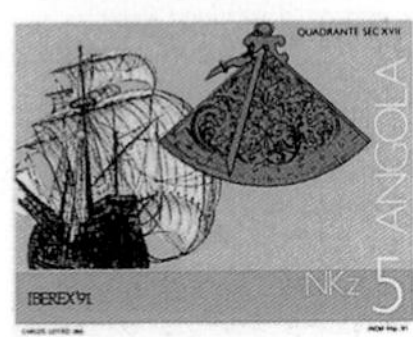

**179** Quadrant and Galleon

**1991.** "Iberex '91" Stamp Exhibition. Navigational Instruments. Multicoloured.

| | | | | |
|---|---|---|---|---|
| 963 | | 5k. Type **179** | 50 | 35 |
| 964 | | 15k. Astrolabe and caravel | 1·40 | 1·00 |
| 965 | | 20k. Cross-staff and caravel | 1·80 | 1·30 |
| 966 | | 50k. Navigation chart by Francisco Rodrigues and galleon | 4·50 | 3·25 |

**180** Common Eagle Ray

**1992.** Rays. Multicoloured.

| | | | | |
|---|---|---|---|---|
| 967 | | 40k. Type **180** | 1·20 | 50 |
| 968 | | 50k. Spotted eagle ray | 1·50 | 80 |
| 969 | | 66k. Manta ray | 2·20 | 1·20 |
| 970 | | 80k. Brown ray | 2·75 | 1·60 |
| **MS**971 | | 112×140 mm. 25k. "Atlantic manta" | 3·00 | 3·00 |

**181** Mukixi wa Mbwesu Mask

**1992.** Quioca Painted Masks (1st series).

| | | | | |
|---|---|---|---|---|
| 972 | - | 60k. orange and brown | 50 | 35 |
| 973 | - | 100k. black, verm & red | 70 | 60 |
| 974 | **181** | 150k. pink and orange | 1·00 | 95 |
| 975 | - | 250k. red and brown | 1·70 | 1·50 |

DESIGNS: 60k. Kalelwa mask; 100k. Mikixe wa Kino mask; 250k. Cikunza mask.

See also Nos. 1006/7 and 1021/4.

**182** "Ptaeroxylon obliquum"

**1992.** "Lubrapex 92" Brazilian–Portuguese Stamp Exhibition, Lisbon. Medicinal Plants. Each brown, stone and deep brown.

| | | | | |
|---|---|---|---|---|
| 976 | | 200k. Type **182** | 1·00 | 65 |
| 977 | | 300k. "Spondias mombin" | 1·50 | 1·00 |
| 978 | | 500k. "Parinari curatellifolia" | 2·50 | 1·60 |
| 979 | | 600k. "Cochlospermum angolense" | 3·00 | 1·90 |

**183** King and Missionaries

**1992.** 500th Anniv (1991) of Baptism of First Angolans. Multicoloured.

| | | | | |
|---|---|---|---|---|
| 980 | | 150k. Type **183** | 80 | 50 |
| 981 | | 420k. Ruins of M'Banza Congo Church | 2·20 | 1·40 |
| 982 | | 470k. Muxima Church | 2·40 | 1·50 |
| 983 | | 500k. Cross superimposed on children's faces | 2·60 | 1·60 |

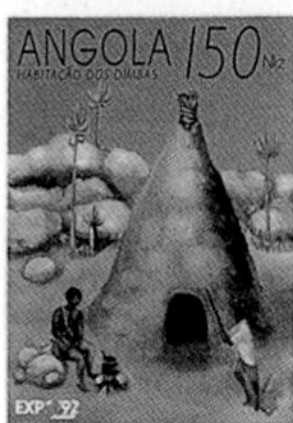

**184** Dimba House

**1992.** "Expo '92" World's Fair, Seville. Traditional Houses. Multicoloured.

| | | | | |
|---|---|---|---|---|
| 984 | | 150k. Type **184** | 4·00 | 4·00 |
| 985 | | 330k. Cokwe house | 2·20 | 1·40 |
| 986 | | 360k. Mbali house | 2·40 | 1·60 |
| 987 | | 420k. Ambwela house | 2·60 | 1·80 |
| 988 | | 500k. House of the Upper Zambezi | 3·00 | 2·50 |

**185** Lovebirds

**1992.** Nature Protection. Peach-faced Lovebirds. Multicoloured.

| | | | | |
|---|---|---|---|---|
| 989 | | 150k. Type **185** | 1·20 | 80 |
| 990 | | 200k. Birds feeding | 1·50 | 1·00 |
| 991 | | 250k. Bird in hand | 1·90 | 1·30 |
| 992 | | 300k. Bird on perch | 2·30 | 1·50 |

**186** "Crucifixion"

**1992.** Visit of Pope John Paul II. Sheet 151×90 mm containing T 186 and similar vert design plus two labels.

| | | | | |
|---|---|---|---|---|
| **MS**993 | | 340k. Type **186** 370k. "The Lost Soul" | 5·50 | 4·50 |

**187** Hurdling

**1992.** Olympic Games, Barcelona (2nd issue). Mult.

| | | | | |
|---|---|---|---|---|
| 994 | | 120k. Type **187** | 70 | 60 |
| 995 | | 180k. Cycling | 1·30 | 1·10 |
| 996 | | 240k. Roller hockey | 1·50 | 1·30 |
| 997 | | 360k. Basketball | 2·20 | 1·80 |

**188** Women with Nets

**1992.** Fishing. Multicoloured.

| | | | | |
|---|---|---|---|---|
| 998 | | 65k. Type **188** | 60 | 50 |
| 999 | | 90k. Fishermen pulling in nets | 80 | 70 |
| 1000 | | 100k. Fishermen checking traps | 90 | 80 |
| 1001 | | 120k. Fishing canoes | 1·10 | 95 |

**189** "Santa Maria"

**1992.** 500th Anniv of Discovery of America by Columbus and Genova 92 International Thematic Stamp Exhibition. Sheet 95×70 mm.

| | | | | |
|---|---|---|---|---|
| **MS**1002 | **189** | 500k. multicoloured | 7·50 | 7·00 |

**190** Crowd with Ballot Papers around Ballot Box

**1992.** 1st Free Elections. Multicoloured.

| | | | | |
|---|---|---|---|---|
| 1003 | | 120k. Type **190** | 90 | 75 |
| 1004 | | 150k. Doves, map, people and ballot box | 1·10 | 1·10 |
| 1005 | | 200k. Dove, crowd and ballot box | 1·50 | 1·20 |

**1992.** Quioca Painted Masks (2nd series). As T 181.

| | | | | |
|---|---|---|---|---|
| 1006 | | 72k. brown, black and yellow | 60 | 50 |
| 1007 | | 80k. red, black and brown | 70 | 60 |
| 1008 | | 120k. pink, black and red | 1·00 | 90 |
| 1009 | | 210k. black and yellow | 1·70 | 1·50 |

DESIGNS: 72k. Cihongo mask; 80k. Mbwasu mask; 120k. Cinhanga mask; 210k. Kalewa mask.

**191** Mail Van

**1992.** Introduction of Express Mail Service in Angola. Multicoloured.

| | | | | |
|---|---|---|---|---|
| 1010 | | 450k. Type **191** | 4·75 | 4·50 |
| 1011 | | 550k. Boeing 707 airplane | 6·75 | 5·50 |

**192** Weather Balloon

**1993.** World Meteorology Day. Meteorological Instruments. Multicoloured.

| | | | | |
|---|---|---|---|---|
| 1012 | | 250k. Type **192** | 2·75 | 1·80 |
| 1013 | | 470k. Actinometer | 3·75 | 3·00 |
| 1014 | | 500k. Rain-gauge | 4·00 | 3·25 |

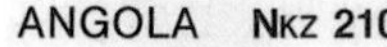

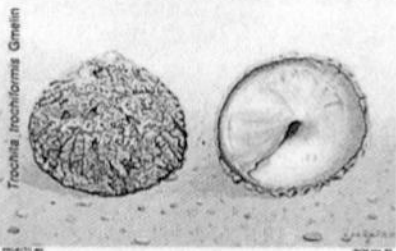
**193** Rayed Hat

**1993.** Molluscs. Multicoloured.

| | | | | |
|---|---|---|---|---|
| 1015 | | 210k. Type **193** | 75 | 60 |
| 1016 | | 330k. Bubonian conch | 1·20 | 90 |
| 1017 | | 400k. African pelican's foot | 1·50 | 1·20 |
| 1018 | | 500k. White spindle | 1·80 | 1·40 |
| **MS**1019 | | 70×90 mm. 1000k. "Pusionella nifat" | 3·50 | 3·50 |

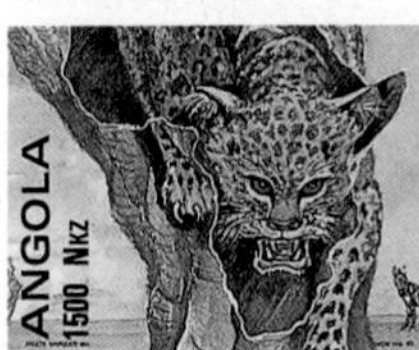

**194** Leopard

**1993.** Africa Day. Sheet 95×70 mm.

| | | | | |
|---|---|---|---|---|
| **MS**1020 | **194** | 1500k. multicoloured | 6·00 | 4·50 |

**1993.** Quioca Art (1st series). As T 181.

| | | | | |
|---|---|---|---|---|
| 1021 | | 72k. grey, red and brown | 25 | 20 |
| 1022 | | 210k. pink and brown | 60 | 55 |
| 1023 | | 420k. black, brown & orge | 1·80 | 1·50 |
| 1024 | | 600k. black, red and brown | 10 | 10 |

DESIGNS: 72k. Men with vehicles; 210k. Rider on antelope; 420k. Bird-plane; 600k. Carrying "soba".

See also Nos. 1038/41 and 1050/3.

**195** "Sansevieria cylindrica"

**1993.** Cacti and Succulents. Multicoloured.

| | | | | |
|---|---|---|---|---|
| 1025 | | 360k. Type **195** | 1·40 | 1·60 |
| 1026 | | 400k. Milk-bush | 1·80 | 1·60 |
| 1027 | | 500k. Indian fig | 2·00 | 2·30 |
| 1028 | | 600k. "Dracaena aubryana" | 2·75 | 2·40 |

**196** Atlantic Hawksbill Turtle laying Eggs and Green Turtle

**1993.** Sea Turtles. Multicoloured.

| | | | | |
|---|---|---|---|---|
| 1029 | | 180k. Type **196** | 80 | 70 |
| 1030 | | 450k. Head of Atlantic hawksbill turtle and newly hatched turtles | 2·00 | 1·70 |
| 1031 | | 550k. Leather-back turtle | 2·30 | 2·00 |
| 1032 | | 630k. Loggerhead turtles | 3·00 | 2·50 |

Nos. 1029/32 were issued together, se-tenant, forming a composite design.

**197** People Dancing

**1993.** Union of Portuguese speaking Capital Cities. Sheet 95×71 mm.

| | | | | |
|---|---|---|---|---|
| **MS**1033 | **197** | 1500k. multicoloured | 6·00 | 5·00 |

**198** Vimbundi Pipe

**1993.** Tobacco Pipes. Multicoloured.

| | | | | |
|---|---|---|---|---|
| 1034 | | 72k. Type **198** | 30 | 25 |
| 1035 | | 200k. Vimbundi pipe (different) | 9·00 | 70 |
| 1036 | | 420k. Mutopa calabash water pipe | 1·80 | 1·50 |
| 1037 | | 600k. Pexi carved-head pipe | 2·50 | 2·20 |

**1993.** Quioca Art (2nd series). As T **181**.

| | | | | |
|---|---|---|---|---|
| 1038 | | 300k. brown and orange | 95 | 80 |
| 1039 | | 600k. red and brown | 2·00 | 1·60 |
| 1040 | | 800k. black, orange and deep orange | 2·50 | 2·20 |
| 1041 | | 1000k. orange and brown | 3·25 | 2·75 |

DESIGNS: 300k. Leopard and dog; 600k. Rabbits; 800k. Birds; 1000k. Birds and cockerel.

**199** St. George's Mushroom

**1993.** Fungi. Multicoloured.

| | | | |
|---|---|---|---|
| 1042 | 300k. Type **199** | 1·20 | 95 |
| 1043 | 500k. Death cap | 2·00 | 1·50 |
| 1044 | 600k. "Amanita vaginata" | 2·20 | 1·80 |
| 1045 | 1000k. Parasol mushroom | 3·75 | 3·00 |

**200** "Cinganji" (figurine of dancer, Bie province)

**1994.** National Culture Day. "Hong Kong '94" International Stamp Exhibition. Multicoloured.

| | | | |
|---|---|---|---|
| 1046 | 500k. Type **200** | 80 | 75 |
| 1047 | 1000k. Chief's staff with carved woman's head (Bie province) | 1·60 | 1·50 |
| 1048 | 1200k. Statuette of traveller riding ox (Huambo province) | 2·00 | 1·80 |
| 1049 | 2200k. Corn pestle (Ovimbundu) | 3·50 | 3·25 |

**1994.** Quioca Art (3rd series). As T **181**.

| | | | |
|---|---|---|---|
| 1050 | 500k. multicoloured | 80 | 75 |
| 1051 | 2000k. red and brown | 1·60 | 1·50 |
| 1052 | 2500k. red and brown | 3·00 | 2·50 |
| 1053 | 3000k. carmine and red | 3·50 | 3·25 |

DESIGNS: 500k. Bird on plant; 2000k. Plant with roots; 2500k. Plant; 3000k. Fern.

**201** Orgy

**1994.** AIDS Awareness Campaign. Multicoloured.

| | | | |
|---|---|---|---|
| 1054 | 500k. Type **201** | 1·00 | 80 |
| 1055 | 1000k. Masked figure using infected syringe passing box of condoms to young couple | 2·00 | 1·70 |
| 1056 | 3000k. Victims | 5·00 | 4·50 |

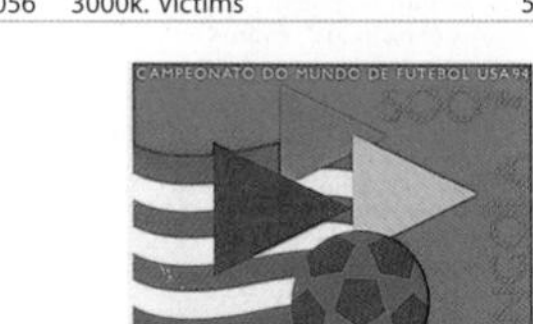


**202** Flag, Arrows and Small Ball

**1994.** World Cup Football Championship, U.S.A. Multicoloured.

| | | | |
|---|---|---|---|
| 1057 | 500k. Type **202** | 8·00 | 70 |
| 1058 | 700k. Flag, four arrows and large ball | 1·10 | 1·00 |
| 1059 | 2200k. Flag, goal net and ball | 3·50 | 3·00 |
| 1060 | 2500k. Flag, ball and boot | 4·00 | 3·50 |

**203** Brachiosaurus

**1994.** "Philakorea 1994" International and "Singpex '94" Stamp Exhibitions. Dinosaurs. Multicoloured.

| | | | |
|---|---|---|---|
| 1061 | 1000k. Type **203** | 1·00 | 50 |
| 1062 | 3000k. Spinosaurus | 1·50 | 1·00 |
| 1063 | 5000k. Ouranosaurus | 2·00 | 1·50 |
| 1064 | 10000k. Lesothosaurus | 3·50 | 3·00 |
| **MS**1065 | 102×145 mm. 19000k. Lesothosaurus and map (43×34 mm) | 4·50 | 4·50 |

**204** Brown Snake Eagle, Ostrich, Yellow-billed Stork and Pink-backed Pelican

**1994.** Tourism. Multicoloured.

| | | | |
|---|---|---|---|
| 1066 | 2000k. Type **204** | 1·00 | 80 |
| 1067 | 4000k. Animals | 1·50 | 1·30 |
| 1068 | 8000k. Women | 2·40 | 2·00 |
| 1069 | 10000k. Men | 3·00 | 2·50 |

**205** Dual-service Wall-mounted Post Box

**1994.** Post Boxes. Multicoloured.

| | | | |
|---|---|---|---|
| 1070 | 5000k. Type **205** | 70 | 65 |
| 1071 | 7500k. Wall-mounted philatelic post box | 1·30 | 1·20 |
| 1072 | 10000k. Free-standing post box | 2·60 | 2·40 |
| 1073 | 21000k. Multiple service wall-mounted post box | 3·50 | 3·00 |

**206** "Heliothis armigera" (moth)

**1994.** Cotton Pests (Insects). Multicoloured.

| | | | |
|---|---|---|---|
| 1074 | 5000k. Type **206** | 60 | 50 |
| 1075 | 6000k. "Bemisia tabasi" | 75 | 60 |
| 1076 | 10000k. "Dysdercus sp." (bug) | 1·20 | 1·00 |
| 1077 | 27000k. "Spodoptera exigua" (moth) | 3·25 | 2·50 |

**207** "100"

**1994.** Cent of International Olympic Committee.

| | | | | |
|---|---|---|---|---|
| 1078 | **207** | 27000k. red, yell & blk | 2·40 | 2·00 |

**208** Pot

**1995.** Traditional Ceramics. With service indicator. Multicoloured. (a) INLAND POSTAGE. Inscr "PORTE NACIONAL".

| | | | |
|---|---|---|---|
| 1079 | (1°) Type **208** | 8·00 | 70 |
| 1080 | (2°) Pot with figure of woman on lid | 80 | 70 |

(b) INTERNATIONAL POSTAGE. Inscr "PORTE INTERNACIONAL".

| | | | |
|---|---|---|---|
| 1081 | (1°) Pot with man's head on lid | 1·60 | 1·50 |
| 1082 | (2°) Duck-shaped pot | 1·80 | 1·70 |

**209** Making Fire

**1995.** The !Kung (Khoisan tribe). Multicoloured.

| | | | |
|---|---|---|---|
| 1083 | 10000k. Type **209** | 60 | 55 |
| 1084 | 15000k. Tipping darts with poison | 95 | 80 |
| 1085 | 20000k. Smoking | 1·30 | 1·00 |
| 1086 | 25000k. Hunting | 1·50 | 1·40 |
| 1087 | 28000k. Women and children | 1·75 | 1·50 |
| 1088 | 30000k. Painting animals on walls | 1·90 | 1·60 |

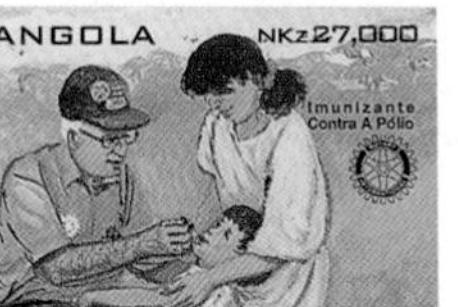


**210** Vaccinating Child against Polio

**1995.** 90th Anniv of Rotary International. Multicoloured. (a) Inscr in Portuguese.

| | | | |
|---|---|---|---|
| 1089 | 27000k. Type **210** | 2·00 | 2·00 |
| 1090 | 27000k. Examining baby | 2·00 | 2·00 |
| 1091 | 27000k. Giving child vaccination | 2·00 | 2·00 |

(b) Inscr in English.

| | | | |
|---|---|---|---|
| 1092 | 27000k. Type **210** | 2·00 | 2·00 |
| 1093 | 27000k. As No. 1090 | 2·00 | 2·00 |
| 1094 | 27000k. As No. 1091 | 2·00 | 2·00 |
| **MS**1095 | Two sheets, each 110×80 mm. 81000k. Dove flying over map. (a) Inscr in Portuguese; (b) Inscr in English Set of 2 sheets | 15·00 | 15·00 |

Nos. 1089/91 and 1092/4 respectively were issued together, se-tenant, forming composite designs.

**211** "Sputnik 1" (satellite)

**1995.** World Telecommunications Day. Mult.

| | | | |
|---|---|---|---|
| 1096 | 27000k. Type **211** | 1·70 | 1·70 |
| 1097 | 27000k. "Intelsat" satellite and space shuttle | 1·70 | 1·70 |
| **MS**1098 | 100×80 mm. Nos. 1096/7 | 3·50 | 3·50 |

**212** Doves above Baby on Daisy-covered Map

**1995.** 20th Anniv of Independence.

| | | | | |
|---|---|---|---|---|
| 1099 | **212** | 2900k. multicoloured | 1·75 | 1·75 |

**213** Child, Containers and Fork-lift Truck

**1996.** Goods Transportation. Multicoloured.

| | | | |
|---|---|---|---|
| 1100 | 200k. Type **213** | 25 | 20 |
| 1101 | 1265k. Sailing boats and "Mount Cameroon" (ferry) | 1·00 | 80 |
| 1102 | 2583k. Fork-lift trucks loading and unloading "Mount Cameroon" (ferry) | 2·00 | 1·70 |
| 1103 | 2583k. Truck | 3·00 | 1·70 |
| **MS**1104 | 106×76 mm. 1265k. Ferry | 1·50 | 1·20 |

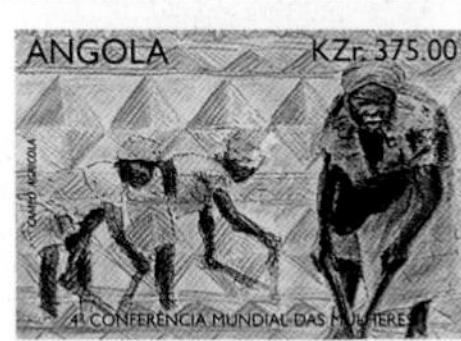


**214** Women in Agriculture

**1996.** 4th World Conference on Women, Peking (1995). Multicoloured.

| | | | |
|---|---|---|---|
| 1105 | 375k. Type **214** | 30 | 30 |
| 1106 | 1106k. Women in education | 90 | 75 |
| 1107 | 1265k. Women in business | 1·00 | 80 |
| 1108 | 2900k. Dimba servant girl (vert) | 2·30 | 1·80 |
| **MS**1109 | 106×76 mm. 1500k. Traditional education (vert) | 1·30 | 1·30 |

**215** Verdant Hawk Moth

**1996.** Flora and Fauna. Multicoloured.

| | | | |
|---|---|---|---|
| 1110 | 1500k. Type **215** | 60 | 50 |
| 1111 | 1500k. Western honey buzzard | 40 | 30 |
| 1112 | 1500k. Bateleur | 40 | 30 |
| 1113 | 1500k. Common kestrel | 40 | 30 |
| 1114 | 4400k. Water lily | 90 | 60 |
| 1115 | 4400k. Red-crested turaco | 45 | 35 |
| 1116 | 4400k. Giraffe | 40 | 35 |
| 1117 | 4400k. African elephant | 45 | 35 |
| 1118 | 5100k. Panther toad | 1·10 | 70 |
| 1119 | 5100k. Hippopotamus | 50 | 40 |
| 1120 | 5100k. Cattle egret | 50 | 40 |
| 1121 | 5100k. Lion | 50 | 40 |
| 1122 | 6000k. African hunting ("wild") dog | 1·30 | 1·10 |
| 1123 | 6000k. Helmeted turtle | 60 | 50 |
| 1124 | 6000k. African pygmy goose | 60 | 50 |
| 1125 | 6000k. Egyptian plover | 60 | 50 |
| **MS**1126 | 100×70 mm. 12000k. Spotted hyena | 2·00 | 1·60 |

Nos. 1111/13, 1115/17, 1119/21 and 1123/5 respectively were issued together, se-tenant, forming composite designs.

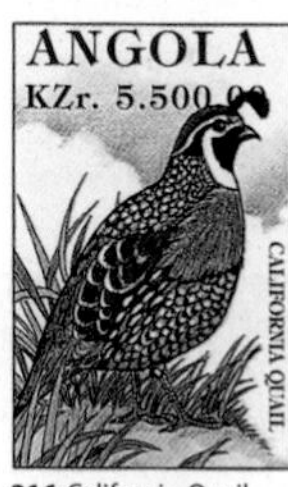


**216** California Quail

**1997.** Birds. Multicoloured.

| | | | |
|---|---|---|---|
| 1127 | 5500k. Type **216** | 50 | 35 |
| 1128 | 5500k. Prairie chicken ("Greater Prairie Chicken") | 50 | 35 |
| 1129 | 5500k. Indian blue quail ("Painted Quail") | 50 | 35 |
| 1130 | 5500k. Golden pheasant | 50 | 35 |
| 1131 | 5500k. Crested wood partridge ("Roulroul Partridge") | 50 | 35 |
| 1132 | 5500k. Ceylon spurfowl ("Ceylon Sourfowl") | 50 | 35 |
| 1133 | 5500k. Himalayan snowcock | 50 | 35 |
| 1134 | 5500k. Temminck's tragopan ("Temminicks Tragopan") | 50 | 35 |
| 1135 | 5500k. Lady Amherst's pheasant | 50 | 35 |
| 1136 | 5500k. Great curassow | 50 | 35 |
| 1137 | 5500k. Red-legged partridge | 50 | 35 |
| 1138 | 5500k. Himalayan monal pheasant ("Impeyan Pheasant") | 50 | 35 |
| 1139 | 5500k. Anna's hummingbird | 1·30 | 75 |
| 1140 | 5500k. Blue-throated hummingbird | 1·30 | 75 |
| 1141 | 5500k. Broad-tailed hummingbird | 1·30 | 75 |
| 1142 | 5500k. Costa's hummingbird | 1·30 | 75 |
| 1143 | 5500k. White-eared hummingbird | 1·30 | 75 |
| 1144 | 5500k. Calliope hummingbird | 1·30 | 75 |
| 1145 | 5500k. Violet-crowned hummingbird | 1·30 | 75 |
| 1146 | 5500k. Rufous hummingbird | 1·30 | 75 |
| 1147 | 5500k. Crimson topaz ("Crimson Topaz Hummingbird") | 1·30 | 75 |
| 1148 | 5500k. Broad-billed hummingbird | 1·30 | 75 |
| 1149 | 5500k. Frilled coquette ("Frilled Coquette Hummingbird") | 1·70 | 75 |
| 1150 | 5500k. Ruby-throated hummingbird | 1·70 | 75 |
| **MS**1151 | Two sheets, each 100×70 mm. (a) 12000k. Ring-necked pheasant; (b) 12000k. Racquet-tailed hummingbird Set of 2 sheets | 8·50 | 6·00 |

**217** Lions attacking Zebra

**1996.** African Wildlife. Multicoloured.

| | | | |
|---|---|---|---|
| 1152 | 180k. Type **217** | 80 | 55 |
| 1153 | 180k. Lions watching zebras | 80 | 55 |
| 1154 | 180k. African hunting dogs attacking gnu | 80 | 55 |
| 1155 | 180k. Pack of hunting dogs chasing herd of gnu | 80 | 55 |
| 1156 | 450k. Lions stalking isolated zebra | 80 | 55 |
| 1157 | 450k. Male lion | 80 | 55 |
| 1158 | 450k. Hunting dogs surrounding gnu | 80 | 55 |
| 1159 | 450k. Close-up of African hunting dog | 80 | 55 |
| 1160 | 550k. Cheetah | 80 | 55 |

1161 550k. Cheetah chasing springbok 80 55
1162 550k. Leopard 80 55
1163 550k. Leopard stalking oryx 80 55
1164 630k. Cheetah running beside herd of springbok 80 55
1165 630k. Cheetah overpowering springbok 80 55
1166 630k. Leopard approaching oryx 80 55
1167 630k. Leopard leaping at oryx 80 55

Nos. 1152/67 were issued together, se-tenant, in sheetlets with each horizontal strip forming a composite design of lions, cheetah, hunting dogs or leopard attacking prey.

**218** Couple with Elderly Woman

**1996.** 50th Anniv of U.N.O. Multicoloured.
1168 3500k. Type **218** 2·30 1·70
1169 3500k. Children at water pump 2·30 1·70
**MS**1170 104×74 mm. 8000k. Unloading sacks from ship 5·50 4·50

**219** "Styrbjorn" (Swedish sail warship), 1789

**1996.** Ships. Multicoloured.
1171 6000k. Type **219** 75 55
1172 6000k. U.S.S. "Constellation" (United States frigate), 1797 75 55
1173 6000k. "Taureau" (French torpedo-boat), 1865 75 55
1174 6000k. French bomb ketch 75 55
1175 6000k. "Sardegna" (Italian battleship), 1881 75 55
1176 6000k. H.M.S. "Glasgow" (frigate), 1867 75 55
1177 6000k. U.S.S. "Essex" (frigate), 1812 75 55
1178 6000k. H.M.S. "Inflexible" (battleship), 1881 75 55
1179 6000k. H.M.S. "Minotaur" (ironclad), 1863 38 55
1180 6000k. "Napoleon" (French steam ship of the line), 1854 75 55
1181 6000k. "Sophia Amalia" (Danish galleon), 1650 75 55
1182 6000k. "Massena" (French battleship), 1887 75 55
**MS**1183 Two sheets, each 105×74 mm. (a) 12000k. "Royal Prince" (English galleon), 1666 (vert); (b) 12000k. H.M.S. "Tremendous" (British ship of the line), 1806 (vert) Set of 2 sheets 5·00 4·00

**220** Mask and Drilling Platform

**1996.** 20th Anniv of Sonangol. Multicoloured.
1184 1000k. Type **220** 60 40
1185 1000k. Storage tanks and mask of woman's face 50 40
1186 2500k. Mask with beard and gas bottles 1·10 90
1187 5000k. Refuelling airplane and mask of monkey's face 2·00 1·70

**221** Slaves in Ship's Hold

**1996.** "Brapex 96" National Stamp Exhibition, Recife, Brazil. Multicoloured.
1188 20000k. Type **221** 3·00 2·50
1189 20000k. Ship capsizing 3·00 2·50
1190 30000k. Boats punting out to ship 4·75 3·50
1191 30000k. Inspection of slaves 4·75 3·50

**MS**1192 100×70 mm. 50000k. Boats (close-up of detail of No. 1190) 7·50 6·00

**222** Mission Church, Huila

**1996.** Churches. Multicoloured.
1193 5000k. Type **222** 75 65
1194 10000k. Church of Our Lady, PoPulo 1·50 1·30
1195 10000k. Church of Our Lady, Nazare 1·50 1·30
1196 25000k. St. Adriao's Church 3·75 3·25

**223** Handball

**1996.** Olympic Games, Atlanta, U.S.A. Mult.
1197 5000k. Type **223** 10 10
1198 10000k. Swimming (horiz) 15 10
1199 25000k. Athletics 2·75 2·00
1200 35000k. Shooting (horiz) 3·75 3·00
**MS**1201 76×106 mm. 65000k. Basketball (horiz) 7·00 6·50

**224** Dolphins, and Angola on Map of Africa

**1996.** 40th Anniv of Popular Movement for the Liberation of Angola (MPLA).
1202 **224** 30000k. multicoloured 4·50 4·00

The face value of No. 1202 is wrongly inscr as "300.00,00".

**225** AVE, Spain

**1997.** Trains. Multicoloured.
1203 100000k. Type **225** 1·80 1·30
1204 100000k. "Hikari", Japan 1·80 1·30
1205 100000k. "Warbonnet" diesel locomotives, U.S.A. 1·80 1·30
1206 100000k. "Deltic" diesel locomotive, Great Britain 1·80 1·30
1207 100000k. "Eurostar", France and Great Britain 1·80 1·30
1208 100000k. ETR 450, Italy 1·80 1·30
1209 140000k. Class E1300 diesel locomotive, Morocco 2·30 1·70
1210 140000k. ICE, Germany 2·30 1·70
1211 140000k. Class X2000, Sweden 2·30 1·70
1212 140000k. TGV, France 2·30 1·70
1213 250000k. Steam locomotive 3·25 3·00
1214 250000k. Garratt steam locomotive 3·25 3·00
1215 250000k. General Electric electric locomotive 3·25 3·00
**MS**1216 Two sheets. (a) 106×76 mm. 11000k. Via Rail diesel locomotive, Canada (49×37 mm); (b) 76×106 mm. 11000k. Canadian Pacific steam locomotive, Canada (37×49 mm) Set of 2 sheets 12·50 11·00

Nos. 1203/8 were issued together, se-tenant, forming a composite design.

**226** Thoroughbred

**1997.** Horses. Multicoloured.
1217 100000k. Type **226** 1·30 1·10
1218 100000k. Palomino and Appaloosa 1·30 1·10
1219 100000k. Grey and white Arabs 1·30 1·10
1220 100000k. Arab colt 1·30 1·10
1221 100000k. Thoroughbred colt 1·30 1·10
1222 100000k. Mustang (with hind quarters of another mustang) 1·30 1·10
1223 100000k. Head of mustang and hind quarters of Furioso 1·30 1·10
1224 100000k. Head and shoulders of Furioso 1·30 1·10
1225 120000k. Thoroughbred 1·70 1·30
1226 120000k. Arab and palomino 1·70 1·30
1227 120000k. Arab and Chincoteague 1·70 1·30
1228 120000k. Pintos 1·70 1·30
1229 120000k. Przewalski's Horse 1·70 1·30
1230 120000k. Thoroughbred colt 1·70 1·30
1231 120000k. Arabs 1·70 1·30
1232 120000k. New Forest pony 1·70 1·30
1233 140000k. Selle Francais 1·90 1·60
1234 140000k. Fjord 1·90 1·60
1235 140000k. Percheron 1·90 1·60
1236 140000k. Italian heavy draught horse 1·90 1·60
1237 140000k. Shagya Arab 1·90 1·60
1238 140000k. Avelignese 1·90 1·60
1239 140000k. Czechoslovakian warmblood 1·90 1·60
1240 140000k. New Forest pony 1·90 1·60
**MS**1241 Two sheets, each 100×70 mm. (a) 215000k. Thoroughbred mother and foal; (b) 220000k. Head and shoulders of thoroughbred Set of 2 sheets 8·00 6·00

Stamps of the same value were issued together, se-tenant, Nos. 1217/24 and 1225/32 respectively forming composite designs.

**227** Jules Rimet Trophy (Uruguay, 1930)

**1997.** World Cup Football Championship, France.
1242 **227** 100000k. black 1·90 1·40
1243 - 100000k. black 1·90 1·40
1244 - 100000k. multicoloured 1·90 1·40
1245 - 100000k. multicoloured 1·90 1·40
1246 - 100000k. black 1·90 1·40
1247 - 100000k. multicoloured 1·90 1·40
1248 - 100000k. black 1·90 1·40
1249 - 100000k. black 1·90 1·40
1250 - 100000k. multicoloured 1·90 1·40
1251 - 100000k. multicoloured 1·90 1·40
1252 - 100000k. black 1·90 1·40
**MS**1253 Two sheets. (a) 127×102 mm. 220000k. multicoloured (Angola team); (b) 76×102 mm. 250000k. multicoloured (Angola team, 1997) Set of 2 sheets 10·00 8·50

DESIGNS—Victory celebrations: No. 1243, Germany (1954); 1244, Brazil (1970); 1245, Maradona holding trophy (Argentina, 1986); 1246, Brazil (1994). Official team photographs: 1247, Germany (1954); 1248, Uruguay (1958); 1249, Italy (1938); 1250, Brazil (1962); 1251, Brazil (1970); 1252, Uruguay (1930).

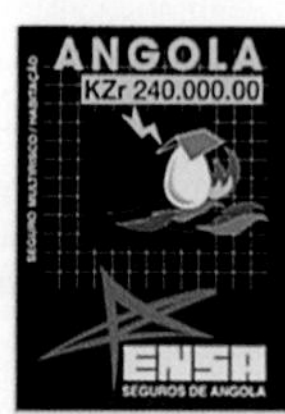

**228** House Insurance

**1998.** 20th Anniv of ENSA Insurance. Mult.
1254 240000k. Type **228** 2·10 1·80
1255 240000k. Forklift truck carrying egg (industrial risks) 2·10 1·80
1256 240000k. Egg on cross (personal accidents) 2·10 1·80
1257 240000k. Egg on waves (pleasure boating) 2·10 1·80

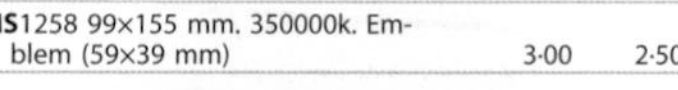
**MS**1258 99×155 mm. 350000k. Emblem (59×39 mm) 3·00 2·50

**229** Coral

**1998.** "Expo '98" World's Fair, Lisbon, Portugal. Multicoloured.
1259 100000k. Type **229** 1·70 1·30
1260 100000k. Sea urchin 1·70 1·30
1261 100000k. Seahorses 1·70 1·30
1262 100000k. Sea anemone 1·70 1·30
1263 240000k. Sea slug 4·00 3·00
1264 240000k. Finger coral 4·00 3·00

**230** Royal Assyrian ("Terinos terpander")

**1998.** Butterflies. Multicoloured.
1265 120000k. Type **230** 1·60 1·30
1266 120000k. Wanderer ("Bematistes aganice") 1·60 1·30
1267 120000k. Great orange-tip ("Hebomoia glaucippe") 1·60 1·30
1268 120000k. Alfalfa butterfly ("Colias eurytheme") 1·60 1·30
1269 120000k. Red-banded perelite ("Pereute leucodrosime") 1·60 1·30
1270 120000k. Large copper ("Lycaena dispar") 1·60 1·30
1271 120000k. Malachite ("Metamorpha stelenes") 1·60 1·30
1272 120000k. Tiger swallowtail ("Papilio glaucus") 1·60 1·30
1273 120000k. Monarch ("Danaus plexippus") 1·60 1·30
1274 120000k. Grecian shoemaker ("Catonephele numili") 1·60 1·30
1275 120000k. Silver-studded blue ("Plebejus argus") 1·60 1·30
1276 120000k. Common eggfly ("Hypolimnas bolina") 1·60 1·30
1277 120000k. Brazilian dynastor ("Dynastor napolean") (horiz) 1·60 1·30
1278 120000k. Saturn butterfly ("Zeuxidia amethystus") (horiz) 1·60 1·30
1279 120000k. Pipevine swallowtail ("Battus philenor") (horiz) 1·60 1·30
1280 120000k. Orange-barred sulphur ("Phoebis philea") (horiz) 1·60 1·30
1281 120000k. African monarch ("Danaus chrysippus") (horiz) 1·60 1·30
1282 120000k. Green-underside blue ("Glaucopsyche alexis") (horiz) 1·60 1·30
**MS**1283 Three sheets. (a) 68×98 mm. 250000k. Gold-banded forester ("Euphaedra neophron"); (b) 98×68 mm. 250000k. Hewitson's uraneis ("Uraneis ucubis") on "Armillaria straminea" (fungus); (c) 98×68 mm. 250000k. Brown hairstreak ("Thecla betulae") (horiz) Set of 3 sheets 23·00 19·00

Nos. 1265/70, 1271/6 and 1277/82 respectively were issued together, se-tenant, forming composite designs.

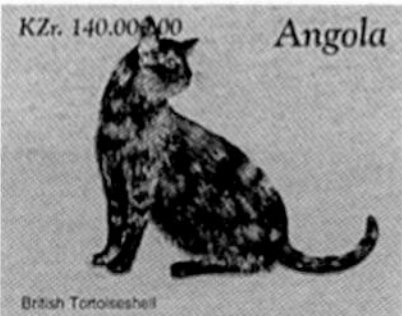

**231** British Tortoiseshell

**1998.** Cats and Dogs. Multicoloured.
1284 140000k. Type **231** 1·10 95
1285 140000k. Chinchilla 1·10 95
1286 140000k. Russian blue 1·10 95
1287 140000k. Black persian (longhair) (wrongly inscribed "Longhiar") 1·10 95
1288 140000k. British red tabby 1·10 95
1289 140000k. Birman 1·10 95
1290 140000k. West Highland white terrier 1·10 95
1291 140000k. Red setter 1·10 95
1292 140000k. Dachshund 1·10 95

| | | | |
|---|---|---|---|
| 1293 | 140000k. St. John water-dog | 1·10 | 95 |
| 1294 | 140000k. Shetland sheep-dog | 1·10 | 95 |
| 1295 | 140000k. Dalmatian | 1·10 | 95 |
| **MS**1296 | Two sheets, each 91×73 mm. (a) 500000k. Turkish van (swimming cat); (b) 500000k. Labrador retriever Set of 2 sheets | 12·00 | 11·00 |

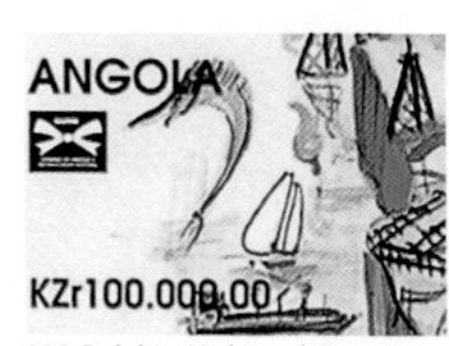

**232** Dolphin, Yacht and Container Ship

**1998.** 1st Anniv of Government of Unity and National Reconciliation. Multicoloured.

| | | | |
|---|---|---|---|
| 1297 | 100000k. Type **232** | 1·50 | 1·20 |
| 1298 | 100000k. Yacht, dolphin and container ship (different) | 1·50 | 1·20 |
| 1299 | 100000k. Yacht, container ship and railway line | 1·50 | 1·20 |
| 1300 | 100000k. Coastline and electricity pylons | 1·50 | 1·20 |
| 1301 | 200000k. Grapes, goat and railway | 3·00 | 2·40 |
| 1302 | 200000k. Village | 3·00 | 2·40 |
| 1303 | 200000k. Tractor, grapes and railway | 3·00 | 2·40 |
| 1304 | 200000k. Coal train | 3·00 | 2·40 |
| 1305 | 200000k. Railway line with branch and pylons | 3·00 | 2·40 |
| 1306 | 200000k. Elephant and tip of tree | 3·00 | 2·40 |
| 1307 | 200000k. Edge of coastline with pylon | 3·00 | 2·40 |
| 1308 | 200000k. Tree trunk and coastline | 3·00 | 2·40 |

Nos. 1297/1308 were issued together, se-tenant, forming a composite design.

**233** Ostrich, Children and Blackboard

**1998.** Decade of Education in Africa. Sheet 100×70 mm.

| | | | |
|---|---|---|---|
| **MS**1309 | **233** 400000k. mult | 5·00 | 4·00 |

**234** Lion

**1998.** Animals of the Grande Porte. Multicoloured.

| | | | |
|---|---|---|---|
| 1310 | 100000k. Type **234** | 1·50 | 1·20 |
| 1311 | 100000k. Hippopotamus ("Hippopotamus amphibius") | 1·50 | 1·20 |
| 1312 | 100000k. African elephant ("Loxodonta africana") | 1·50 | 1·20 |
| 1313 | 100000k. Giraffe ("Giraffa campelopardalis") | 1·50 | 1·20 |
| 1314 | 220000k. African buffalo ("Synceros caffer") | 3·00 | 2·40 |
| 1315 | 220000k. Gorilla ("Gorilla gorilla") | 3·00 | 2·40 |
| 1316 | 220000k. White rhinoceros ("Ceratotherium simum") | 3·00 | 2·40 |
| 1317 | 220000k. Gemsbok ("Oryx gazella") | 3·00 | 2·40 |

There are errors in the Latin inscriptions.

**235** Man kicking Football

**1998.** Eradication of Polio in Angola. Sheet 100×70 mm.

| | | | |
|---|---|---|---|
| **MS**1318 | **235** 500000k. mult | 6·00 | 5·00 |

**236** Diana, Princess of Wales

**1998.** Diana, Princess of Wales Commemoration. Multicoloured.

| | | | |
|---|---|---|---|
| 1319 | 100000k. Type **236** | 1·40 | 1·20 |
| 1320 | 100000k. Wearing white balldress | 1·40 | 1·20 |
| 1321 | 100000k. Holding handbag | 1·40 | 1·20 |
| 1322 | 100000k. Wearing black evening dress | 1·40 | 1·20 |
| 1323 | 100000k. Holding bouquet (white jacket) | 1·40 | 1·20 |
| 1324 | 100000k. Wearing pearl necklace (looking down) | 1·40 | 1·20 |
| 1325 | 100000k. Wearing pearl necklace (head raised) | 1·40 | 1·20 |
| 1326 | 100000k. Speaking, wearing green velvet jacket | 1·40 | 1·20 |
| 1327 | 100000k. Wearing sunglasses | 1·40 | 1·20 |
| 1328 | 100000k. Wearing black jacket and white blouse | 1·40 | 1·20 |
| 1329 | 100000k. Wearing green blouse | 1·40 | 1·20 |
| 1330 | 100000k. Holding flowers (black jacket) | 1·40 | 1·20 |
| 1331 | 150000k. With young girl amputee | 2·20 | 1·80 |
| 1332 | 150000k. With two amputees | 2·20 | 1·80 |
| 1333 | 150000k. Walking through minefield | 2·20 | 1·80 |
| **MS**1334 | 76×106 mm. 400000k. In mine protective clothing | 6·50 | 5·50 |

**237** "Pagurites sp."

**1998.** International Year of the Ocean. Mult.

| | | | |
|---|---|---|---|
| 1335 | 100000k. Type **237** | 45 | 35 |
| 1336 | 100000k. "Callinectes marginatus" (crab) | 90 | 80 |
| 1337 | 100000k. "Thais forbesi" | 90 | 90 |
| 1338 | 100000k. "Ostrea tulipa" | 90 | 80 |
| 1339 | 100000k. "Balanus amphitrite" | 90 | 80 |
| 1340 | 100000k. "Uca tangeri" | 90 | 80 |
| 1341 | 170000k. "Littorina angulifera" | 1·60 | 1·40 |
| 1342 | 170000k. Great hairy melongena ("Semifusus morio") | 1·60 | 1·40 |
| 1343 | 170000k. "Thais coronata" | 1·60 | 1·40 |
| 1344 | 170000k. "Cerithium atratum" on red branch | 1·60 | 1·40 |
| 1345 | 170000k. "Ostrea tulipa" (different) | 1·60 | 1·40 |
| 1346 | 170000k. "Cerithium atratum" on green branch | 1·60 | 1·40 |
| **MS**1347 | Two sheets, each 85×110 mm. (a) 300000k. "Goniopsis" (crab) (horiz); (b) 300000k. Shell Set of 2 sheets | 6·00 | 5·50 |

**238** Mangos

**1998.** "Portugal 98" International Stamp Exhibition, Lisbon. Fruit and Vegetables. Multicoloured.

| | | | |
|---|---|---|---|
| 1348 | 100000k. Type **238** | 1·40 | 1·10 |
| 1349 | 100000k. Guava | 1·40 | 1·10 |
| 1350 | 120000k. Chillies | 1·60 | 1·30 |
| 1351 | 120000k. Sweet corn | 1·60 | 1·30 |
| 1352 | 140000k. Sliced bananas | 1·90 | 1·50 |
| 1353 | 140000k. Avocadoes | 1·90 | 1·50 |

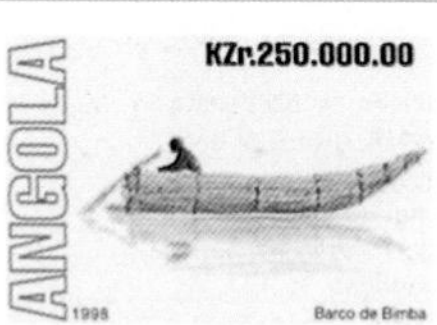

**239** Bimba Canoe

**1998.** Canoes. Multicoloured.

| | | | |
|---|---|---|---|
| 1354 | 250000k. Type **239** | 2·75 | 2·50 |
| 1355 | 250000k. Sailing canoe, Ndongo | 2·75 | 2·50 |
| 1356 | 250000k. Building canoes in Ndongo | 2·75 | 2·50 |

**240** "Titanic"

**1998.** The "Titanic" (liner that sank on maiden voyage, 1912). Sheet 200×160 mm containing T **240** and similar designs. Multicoloured.

| | | | |
|---|---|---|---|
| **MS**1357 | 350000k. Type **240**; 350000k. Stern of "Titanic"; 350000k. "Titanic" under full steam (75×30 mm); 350000k. Bow of "Titanic" (37×60 mm) | 11·00 | 10·00 |

**241** Ultralight Plane

**1998.** Aircraft. Multicoloured.

| | | | |
|---|---|---|---|
| 1358 | 150000k. Type **241** | 1·00 | 80 |
| 1359 | 150000k. Gyroplane | 1·00 | 80 |
| 1360 | 150000k. Business jet | 1·00 | 80 |
| 1361 | 150000k. Convertible plane | 1·00 | 80 |
| 1362 | 150000k. Chuterplane | 1·00 | 80 |
| 1363 | 150000k. Twin-rotor craft | 1·00 | 80 |
| 1364 | 150000k. Skycrane | 1·00 | 80 |
| 1365 | 150000k. British Aerospace/Aerospatiale Concorde Supersonic airliner | 1·00 | 80 |
| 1366 | 150000k. Flying boat | 1·00 | 80 |
| 1367 | 200000k. Boeing 737-100 | 1·80 | 1·40 |
| 1368 | 200000k. Ilyushin Il-62M | 1·80 | 1·40 |
| 1369 | 250000k. Pedal-powered plane | 1·20 | 90 |
| 1370 | 250000k. Sail plane | 1·20 | 90 |
| 1371 | 250000k. Aerobatic plane | 1·20 | 90 |
| 1372 | 250000k. Hang-gliding | 1·20 | 90 |
| 1373 | 250000k. Balloon | 1·20 | 90 |
| 1374 | 250000k. Glidercraft | 1·20 | 90 |
| 1375 | 250000k. Model airplane | 1·20 | 90 |
| 1376 | 250000k. Air racing | 1·20 | 90 |
| 1377 | 250000k. Solar-celled plane | 1·20 | 90 |
| **MS**1378 | Four sheets. (a) 110×85 mm. 1000000k. Boeing 777 (84×28 mm); (b) 85×110 mm. 1000000k. Space shuttle Columbia (28×84 mm); (c) 100×70 mm. 1000000k. Boeing 737-200 (84×28 mm); (d) 100×70 mm. 1000000k. Boeing 747-300 (84×28 mm) Set of 4 sheets | 18·00 | 15·00 |

Nos. 1358/66 and 1369/77 respectively were issued together, se-tenant, forming composite designs.

**242** Parasaurolophus

**1998.** Prehistoric Animals. Multicoloured.

| | | | |
|---|---|---|---|
| 1379 | 120000k. Type **242** | 90 | 80 |
| 1380 | 120000k. Elaphosaurus | 90 | 80 |
| 1381 | 120000k. Iguanodon | 90 | 80 |
| 1382 | 120000k. Maiasaura | 90 | 80 |
| 1383 | 120000k. Brontosaurus | 90 | 80 |
| 1384 | 120000k. Plateosaurus | 90 | 80 |
| 1385 | 120000k. Brachiosaurus | 90 | 80 |
| 1386 | 120000k. Anatosaurus | 90 | 80 |
| 1387 | 120000k. Tyrannosaurus rex | 90 | 80 |
| 1388 | 120000k. Carnotaurus | 90 | 80 |
| 1389 | 120000k. Corythosaurus | 90 | 80 |
| 1390 | 120000k. Stegosaurus | 90 | 80 |
| 1391 | 120000k. Iguanodon (different) | 90 | 80 |
| 1392 | 120000k. Hadrosaurus (horiz) | 90 | 80 |
| 1393 | 120000k. Ouranosaurus (horiz) | 90 | 80 |
| 1394 | 120000k. Hypsilophodon (horiz) | 90 | 80 |
| 1395 | 120000k. Brachiosaurus (horiz) | 90 | 80 |
| 1396 | 120000k. Shunosaurus (horiz) | 90 | 80 |
| 1397 | 120000k. Amargasaurus (horiz) | 90 | 80 |
| 1398 | 120000k. Tuojiangosaurus (horiz) | 90 | 80 |
| 1399 | 120000k. Monoclonius | 90 | 80 |
| 1400 | 120000k. Struthiosaurus (horiz) | 90 | 80 |
| **MS**1401 | Two sheets, each 85×110 mm. (a) 550000k. Tyrannosaurus (different); (b) 550000k. Triceratops Set of 2 sheets | 48·00 | 48·00 |

**243** Head

**1999.** Endangered Species. The Lesser Flamingo (Phoenicopterus minor). Multicoloured.

| | | | |
|---|---|---|---|
| 1402 | 300000k. Type **243** | 1·60 | 1·30 |
| 1403 | 300000k. Flamingo with wings outstretched | 1·60 | 1·30 |
| 1404 | 300000k. Flamingo facing left | 1·60 | 1·30 |
| 1405 | 300000k. Front view of flamingo | 1·40 | 1·30 |

**244** Hyacinth Macaw (*Anodorhynchus hyacinthinus*)

**1999.** Animals and Birds. Multicoloured.

| | | | |
|---|---|---|---|
| 1406 | 300000k. Type **244** | 1·60 | 1·30 |
| 1407 | 300000k. Penguin (*Sphenisciformes*) (vert) | 1·60 | 1·30 |
| 1408 | 300000k. Przewalski's horse (*Equus caballus przewalski*) (wrongly inscr "Equis") | 1·60 | 1·30 |
| 1409 | 300000k. American bald eagle (*Haliaetus leucocephalus*) (vert) | 1·60 | 1·30 |
| 1410 | 300000k. Spectacled bear (*Tremarctos ornatus*) | 1·50 | 1·20 |
| 1411 | 300000k. Jay (*Aphelocoma*) | 1·50 | 1·20 |
| 1412 | 300000k. Bare-legged scops owl (*Otus insularis*) | 1·50 | 1·20 |
| 1413 | 300000k. Whale-headed stork (*Balaeniceps rex*) | 1·50 | 1·20 |
| 1414 | 300000k. Atlantic ridley turtle (*Lepidochelys kempii*) | 1·50 | 1·20 |
| 1415 | 300000k. Canadian river otter (*Lutra canadensis*) | 1·50 | 1·20 |
| 1416 | 300000k. Swift fox (*Vulpes velox hebes*) | 1·50 | 1·20 |
| 1417 | 300000k. Deer (*Odocoileus*) | 1·50 | 1·20 |
| 1418 | 300000k. Orang-utan (*Pongo pygmaeus*) | 1·50 | 1·20 |
| 1419 | 300000k. Golden lion tamarin (*Leontopithecus rosalia rosalia*) (inscr "Leontopitecus") | 1·50 | 1·20 |
| 1420 | 300000k. Tiger (*Panthera tigris altaica*) | 1·50 | 1·20 |
| 1421 | 300000k. Polecat (wrongly inscr "Tragelaphus eurycerus") | 1·50 | 1·20 |
| **MS**1422 | Two sheets, each 110×85 mm. (a) 1000000k. Brown bear (*Ursus arctos horribilis*); (b) 1000000k. Giant panda (*Ailuropoda melanoleuca*) | 10·00 | 9·00 |

**245** Satellite circling Earth

**1999.** International Telecommunications Day.

| | | | | |
|---|---|---|---|---|
| 1423 | **245** | 500000k. multicoloured | 2·30 | 2·00 |

**246** Waterfall, Andulo, Bie

**1999.** Waterfalls. Multicoloured.

| | | | |
|---|---|---|---|
| 1424 | 500000k. Type **246** | 2·30 | 2·00 |
| 1425 | 500000k. Chiumbo, Lunda | 2·30 | 2·00 |
| 1426 | 500000k. Ruacana, Cunene | 2·30 | 2·00 |
| 1427 | 500000k. Coemba, Moxico | 2·30 | 2·00 |

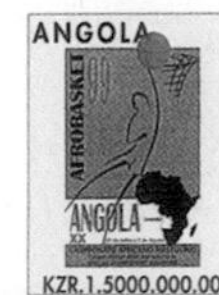

**247** Emblem

**1999.** "Afrobasket '99" (Men's African Basketball Championship). Multicoloured.

1428 15000000k. Type **247** 1·30 1·30
1429 15000000k. Ball teetering on the edge of net, and players' hands 1·60 1·30
1430 15000000k. Hand scooping ball from edge of net 1·60 1·30
1431 15000000k. Flower holding ball 1·60 1·30
**MS**1432 95×83 mm. 25000000k. Enlarged detail from No. 1441 (39×29 mm) 7·25 2·20

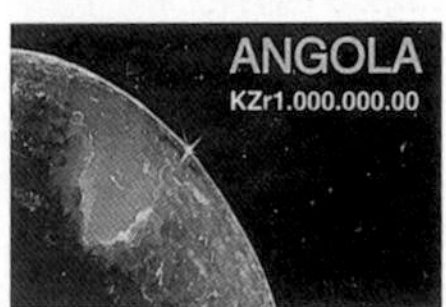

**248** African Continent

**1999.** South African Development Community (S.A.D.C.).
1433 **248** 1000000k. multicoloured 2·00 1·80

**249** Duke and Duchess of York, 1923

**1999.** 100th Birthday of Queen Elizabeth, the Queen Mother. Multicoloured.

1434 **249** 200000k. black and gold 1·50 90
1435 - 200000k. mult 1·50 90
1436 - 200000k. mult 1·50 90
1437 - 200000k. mult 1·50 90
**MS**1438 154×157 mm. 500000k. Queen Mother in academic robes (37×50 mm) 3·00 2·50

DESIGNS: No. 1435, Portrait of Queen Mother wearing Star of the Garter; 1436, Queen Mother wearing fur stole; 1437, Queen Mother wearing blue hat.

**250** Ekuikui II

**1999.** Rulers. Multicoloured.

1439 500000k. Type **250** 2·20 1·90
1440 500000k. Mvemba Nzinga 2·20 1·90
1441 500000k. Mwata Yamvu Nawej II 2·20 1·90
1442 500000k. Njinga Mbande 2·20 1·90
**MS**1443 104×76 mm. 1000000k. Mandume Ndemufayo 5·00 4·50

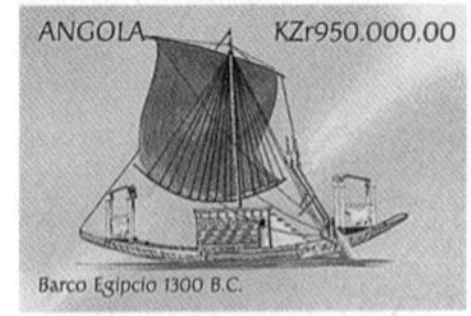

**251** 13th-century B.C. Pharaonic Barque

**1999.** Ships. Multicoloured.

1444 950000k. Type **251** 1·10 80
1445 950000k. Flemish carrack, 1480 1·10 80
1446 950000k. H.M.S. *Beagle* (Darwin), 1830 1·10 80
1447 950000k. *North Star* (paddle-steamer), 1852 1·10 80
1448 950000k. *Fram* (schooner, Amundsen and Nansen), 1892 1·10 80
1449 950000k. *Unyo Maru* (sail/steam freighter), 1909 (inscr "Unyon") 1·10 80
1450 950000k. *Juan Sebastian de Elcano* (cadet schooner), 1927 1·10 80
1451 950000k. *Tovarishch*, (three-masted cadet barque), 1933 1·10 80
1452 950000k. *Bucentaur* (Venetian state galley), 1728 1·10 80
1453 950000k. *Clermont* (first commercial paddle-steamer), 1807 1·10 80
1454 950000k. *Savannah* (paddle-steamer), 1819 1·10 80
1455 950000k. *Dromedary* (steam tug), 1844 1·10 80
1456 950000k. *Iberia* (steam freighter), 1881 1·10 80
1457 950000k. *Gluckauf* (tanker), 1886 1·10 80
1458 950000k. *Cidade de Paris* (ocean steamer), 1888 1·10 80
1459 950000k. *Mauretania* (liner), 1906 1·10 80
1460 950000k. *La Gloire* (first armoured-hull ship), 1859 1·10 80
1461 950000k. *L'Ocean*, (French battery ship), 1868 1·10 80
1462 950000k. *Dandolo* (Italian cruiser), 1876 (inscr "Dandalo") and stern of H.M.S. *Dreadnought* 1·10 80
1463 950000k. H.M.S. *Dreadnought* (battleship), 1906 1·10 80
1464 950000k. *Bismarck* (battleship), 1939 and stern of U.S.S. *Cleveland* 1·10 80
1465 950000k. U.S.S. *Cleveland* (cruiser), 1946 1·10 80
1466 950000k. U.S.S. *Boston* (first guided-missile cruiser), 1942 and stern of U.S.S. *Long Beach* 1·10 80
1467 950000k. U.S.S. *Long Beach* (first nuclear-powered cruiser), 1959 1·10 80
**MS**1468 Four sheets, each 75×70 mm. (a) 5000000k. 18th-century junk; (b) 5000000k. *Madre de Dios* (carrack) (wrongly inscr "Deus"), 1609; (c) 5000000k. Catamaran, 1861; (d) 5000000k. *Natchez* (Mississippi paddle-steamer), 1870 22·00 16·00

Nos. 1474/5, 1476/7 and 1478/9 respectively were issued together, se-tenant, forming a composite design.

**252** Fly Agaric (*Amanita muscaria*)

**1999.** Fungi. Multicoloured.

1469 1000000k. Type **252** (wrongly inscr "Aminita") 1·00 75
1470 1000000k. Bronze boletus (*Boletus* ) 1·00 75
1471 1000000k. Lawyer's wig (*Coprinus comatus*) 1·00 75
1472 1000000k. The blusher (*Amanita rubescens*) (inscr "Aminita") 1·00 75
1473 1000000k. Slimy-branded cort (*Cortinarius collinitus*) 1·00 75
1474 1000000k. Devil's boletus (*Boletus satanas*) 1·00 75
1475 1000000k. Parasol mushroom (*Lepiota procera*) 1·00 75
1476 1000000k. Trumpet agaric (*Clitocybe geotropa*) 1·00 75
1477 1000000k. *Morchella crassipes* 1·00 75
1478 1000000k. *Boletus rufescens* 1·00 75
1479 1000000k. Death cap (*Amanita phalloides*) 1·00 75
1480 1000000k. *Collybia iocephala* 1·00 75
1481 1000000k. *Tricholoma aurantium* 1·00 75
1482 1000000k. *Cortinarius violaceus* 1·00 75
1483 1000000k. *Mycena polygramma* 1·00 75
1484 1000000k. *Psalliota augusta* 1·00 75
1485 1000000k. *Russula nigricans* 1·00 75
1486 1000000k. Granulated boletus (*Boletus granulatus*) 1·00 75
1487 1000000k. *Mycena strobilinoides* 1·00 75
1488 1000000k. Caesar's mushroom (*Amanita caesarea*) 1·00 75
1489 1000000k. Fly agaric (*Amanita muscaria*) (different) 1·00 75
1490 1000000k. *Boletus crocipodius* 1·00 75
1491 1000000k. Cracked green russula (*Russula virescens*) 1·00 75
1492 1000000k. Saffron milk cap (*Lactarius deliciosus*) 1·00 75
1493 1250000k. Caesar's mushroom (*Amanita caesarea*) (different) 1·50 1·40
1495 1250000k. Red cracked boletus (*Boletus chrysenteron*) (wrongly inscr "chyrsenteron") 1·50 1·40
1496 1250000k. Butter mushroom (*Boletus luteus*) 1·50 1·40
1497 1250000k. Lawyer's wig (*Coprinus comatus*) (different) 1·50 1·40
1498 1250000k. Witch's hat (*Hygrocybe conica*) 1·50 1·40
1499 1250000k. *Psalliota xanthoderma* 1·50 1·40
**MS**1500 Two sheets, each 75×105 mm. (a) 5000000k. *Mycena lilacifolia*; (b) 5000000k. *Psalliota haemorrhoidaria* 11·00 8·00

**253** Mercury and Venus

**1999.** 30th Anniv of First Manned Moon Landing. Multicoloured.

1501 3500000k. Type **253** 1·10 75
1502 3500000k. Jupiter 1·10 75
1503 3500000k. Neptune and Pluto 1·10 75
1504 3500000k. Earth and Mars 1·10 75
1505 3500000k. Saturn 1·10 75
1506 3500000k. Uranus 1·10 75
1507 3500000k. Explorer 17 satellite, 1963 1·10 75
1508 3500000k. Intelsat 4A satellite, 1975 1·10 75
1509 3500000k. GOES-D (Geostationary Operational Environmental Satellite), 1980 1·10 75
1510 3500000k. Intelsat 2 satellite, 1966 1·10 75
1511 3500000k. Navstar 2 (Navigation System with Timing And Ranging), 1978 1·10 75
1512 3500000k. S.M.S. (Solar Maximum Mission) satellite, 1980 1·10 75
1513 3500000k. Earth and astronaut walking in space 1·10 75
1514 3500000k. Mariner 8 spacecraft 1·10 75
1515 3500000k. Viking 10 spacecraft 1·10 75
1516 3500000k. Ginga satellite 1·10 75
1517 3500000k. Soyuz 19 spacecraft (inscr "satelite") 1·10 75
1518 3500000k. Voyager spacecraft 1·10 75
1519 3500000k. Hubble space telescope (vert) 1·10 75
1520 3500000k. Launch of space shuttle *Atlantis* (vert) 1·10 75
1521 3500000k. Uhuru satellite (vert) 1·10 75
1522 3500000k. Mir space station (vert) 1·10 75
1523 3500000k. Gemini 7 spacecraft (vert) 1·10 75
1524 3500000k. Venera 7 spacecraft (vert) 1·10 75
**MS**1525 Five sheets (a) 95×85 mm. 6000000k. Astronaut from Apollo 17 walking on moon (vert); (b) 95×85 mm. 6000000k. Astronaut driving moon buggy (vert); (c) 85×110 mm. 12000000k. Launch of commercial satellite SBS 4 (vert); (d) 85×110 mm. Neil Armstrong (astronaut) (vert); (e) 110×85 mm. 12000000k. Earth and *Columbia* spacecraft 18·00 15·00

No. 1523 is inscribed "GEMNI" in error.

**254** 'Night Attack by 47 Ronin'

**1999.** 150th Death Anniv of Katushika Hokusai (artist). Multicoloured.

1526 3500000k. Type **254** 1·10 75
1527 3500000k. "Usigafuchi no Kudan" 1·10 75
1528 3500000k. Sketch of seated man 1·10 75
1529 3500000k. Sketch of animals and birds 1·10 75
1530 3500000k. "Autumn Pheasant" 1·10 75
1531 3500000k. Rural landscape 1·10 75
1532 3500000k. "Survey of the region" 1·10 75
1533 3500000k. Kabuki theatre 1·10 75
1534 3500000k. Sketch of hen 1·10 75
1535 3500000k. Sketch of wheelwright 1·10 75
1536 3500000k. "Excursion to Enoshima" 1·10 75
1537 3500000k. Sumida River landscape 1·10 75
**MS**1538 Two sheets, each 100×70 mm. (a) 12000000k. Japanese calligraphy between woman and child (vert); (b) 12000000k. Woman dressing hair (vert) 8·00 6·50

**255** SNCF Class 242 Steam Locomotive

**2000.** "PHILEX FRANCE 99" International Stamp Exhibition, Paris. Locomotives. Two sheets, each 111×80 mm containing T **255** and similar horiz design. Multicoloured.

**MS**1539 (a) 12k. Type **255** (b) 12k. Prototype Linear Propulsion Hover Train 13·50 12·00

**257** Zebra

**2000.** Fauna. Multicoloured.

1540 1k.50 Type **256** 1·00 90
1541 2k. Short-tailed fruit bat 1·30 1·20
1542 3k. California condor 1·90 1·80
1543 5k.50 Lion 3·50 3·25
**MS**1544 Eight sheets:—140×179 mm. (a) 3k.50×6, Florida white-tailed deer; Turkey; Beaver; Bullfrog; Manatee; Greenback cutthroat trout; (b) 3k.50×6, White-faced sapajou; Toucan; Eyelash viper; Tree frog; Golden lion tamarin; Harpy eagle:—140×179 mm. (vert) (c) 3k.50×6, Mountain gorilla; Black rhino; Cape buffalo; Jackson chameleon; Cape cobra; Meerkats; (d) 3k.50×6, Kangaroo; Koala; Rainbow bee-eater; Red-eyed tree frog; Townsville blue-eye; Snake-necked tortoise:—107×77 mm. (vert) (e) 12k. Three-toed sloth; (f) 12k. Cheetah; (g) 12k. Orang-utan:—70×100 mm. (vert) 12k. Ring-tailed lemur 40·00 34·00

**256** Harpy Eagle

**2000.** Birds. Multicoloured.

1545 1k.50 Type **257** 1·40 1·10
1546 2k. Andean condor 1·50 1·40
1547 3k. Lappet-faced vulture (vert) 2·30 2·00
1547a 5k.50 Vulture 4·25 4·00
**MS**1548 Eight sheets 128×127 mm. (a) 3k.50×6, American kestrel (*Falco sparverius*) (inscr "sperterius"); Spectacled owl (*Pulsatrix perspicillata*); White-tailed kite (*Eleanus leucurus*) (inscr "Elemus"); Boobook owl (*Ninox novaeseelandiae*) (inscr "novaseseelandiar"); *Polemaetus bellicosus* (inscr "Polmactus"); Caracara (*Polyborus plancus*); (b) 3k.50×6, Northern goshawk (*Accipiter gentiles*) (inscr "Acolpiler genttlis"); Hawk owl (*Surnia ulula*) (wrongly inscr "Surnis"); Peregrine falcon (*Falco prregrinus*); Eastern screech owl (*Otus asio*); African fish eagle (*Haliaeetus vocifer*) (inscr "Haliaectus"); Laughing falcon (*Herpetotheres cachinnans*) (inscr "Herpetothers"):—85×127 mm. (c) 6k.50×3, Verreaux's eagle; Bonelli's eagle; African fish eagle:—127×85 mm. (d) 6k.50×3, Bald eagle (vert); Tawny eagle (vert); Eagle (vert); (e) 85×110 mm. 12k. Lanner falcon (vert); (f) 110×85 mm. 12k. King vultures; (g) 85×111 mm. 15k. Secretary bird (*Sagittarius serpentarius*); (h) 15k. Golden eagle (*Aquila chrysaetos*) (inscr "chrysectos") 40·00 40·00

**258** Zebra (*Equs zebra*)

**2000.** Animals and Birds. Multicoloured.

1549 1k.50 Type **258** 1·00 80
1550 1k.50 Golden palm weaver (*Ploceus xanthops*) 1·00 80
1551 1k.50 Hunting dog (*Lycaon pictus*) 1·00 80
1552 1k.50 Cheetah (*Acinonyx jubatus*) 1·30 1·00
1553 1k.50 Gemsbok (*Oryx gazelle*) 1·00 80
1554 1k.50 Cape fox (*Vulpes chama*) (inscr "Otocyon megalotis") 1·00 80
1555 1k.50 Giraffe (*Giraffa camelopardalis*) 1·00 80
1556 1k.50 Golden jackal (*Canis aureus*) (inscr "adustus") 1·00 80
1557 1k.50 Potto (*Perodicticus potto*) 1·00 80
1558 1k.50 Lion (*Panthera leo*) 1·00 80
1559 1k.50 Lilac-breasted roller (*Coracias caudate*) (inscr "Coracus") 1·30 1·00
1560 1k.50 Bat-eared fox (*Otocyon megalotis*) 1·00 80
1561 2k. Ostrich (*Struthio camelus*) 1·50 1·20
1562 2k. African wild cat (*Felis lybica*) 1·50 1·20
1563 2k. Impala (*Aepyceros melampus*) 1·50 1·20
1564 2k. Savanna monkey (*Cercopithecus aethiops*) 1·50 1·20
1565 2k. Black rhino (*Diceros bicornis*) 1·50 1·20
1566 2k. Baboon (*Papio*) 1·50 1·20
1567 2k. Caracal (*Felis caracal*) 1·50 1·20
1568 2k. Secretary bird (*Sagittarius serpentarius*) 1·75 1·50
1569 2k. Warthog (*Phacochoerus aethiopicus*) 1·50 1·20
1570 2k. Afro-Australian fur seal (*Arctocephalus pusillus*) 1·50 1·20
1571 2k. Malachite kingfisher (*Alcedo cristata*) 2·00 1·75
1572 2k. Hippopotamus (*Hippopotamus amphibious*) 1·50 1·20
**MS**1573 Two sheets. (a) 85×110 mm.12k. Savanna monkey (vert); (b) 110×85 mm. 12k. Elephant (*Loxodonta Africana*) (vert) 13·00 13·00

**259** Flowers and Birds (Lai-Ji)

**2000.** Millennium (1st issue). Cultural Events of the 16th-century. Multicoloured.

1574 2k.50 Type **259** 2·75 1·50
1575 2k.50 "Last Judgement", Orvieto Cathedral (Luca Signorelli) 2·75 1·50
1576 2k.50 "Enchanted Garden" (Hieronymus Bosch) 2·75 1·50
1577 2k.50 Machiavelli (author of O Principe (beginning of modern politics)) 2·75 1·50
1578 2k.50 Illustration from Utopia (Sir Thomas More) 2·75 1·50
1579 2k.50 Martin Luther (church reform) 2·75 1·50
1580 2k.50 Charles I of Spain (holy Roman Emperor (unification of Europe)) 2·75 1·50
1581 2k.50 "School of Athens" (Rafael) 2·75 1·50
1582 2k.50 Juan Sebastion Elcano (first circumnavigation of the world) 3·25 1·50
1583 2k.50 Henry VIII (separation from Catholic church) 3·25 1·50
1584 2k.50 Spanish conquering Aztecs and Incas (exploration of Americas) 2·75 1·50
1585 2k.50 Plasencia Cathedral (beginning of Romanesque architecture) 2·75 1·50
1586 2k.50 Potatoes (first introduction into Europe) 3·25 1·50
1587 2k.50 Astrolabe (Copernicus' theory of the universe) 3·25 1·50
1588 2k.50 Priest and courtiers (Portuguese-Japanese trade) 2·75 1·50
1589 2k.50 "Self Portrait" (Albrecht Durer (death, 1528)) (60×40 mm) 2·75 1·50
1590 2k.50 Woman, hourglass, inkwell and cross (declaration of rights of indigenous Americans by Queen Isabel of Castille) 2·75 1·50

**260** Henry II of Germany

**2000.** Millennium (2nd issue). Monarchs and Popes. Multicoloured.

**MS**1591 Twelve sheets:—165×198 mm. (a) 3k.×4, Type **260**; Marina Mniszech, Queen Consort of Tsar Lzhedmitry (false Dmitri); Tsar Ivan IV; Tsar Ivan III; (b) 3k.×4, Charles II of England; Lady Jane Grey; Leopold III of Belgium; Louis XV of France; (c) 3k.×6, James I of England; James II of England; James VI of Scotland; Brian Boru, King of Ireland; William I of Prussia (inscr "William I of Germany"); Edward VI of England; (d) 3k.×6, Pope Nicholas II; Pope Pascal II; Pope Sergius IV; Pope Victor II; Pope Victor III; Pope Urban III; Pope Innocent II; (e) 3k.×6, Pope John XIII; Pope Agapetus II; Pope John XVIII; Pope Lucius II; (f) 3k.×6, Pope Celestine II; Pope Clement II; Pope Clement III; Pope Gelasius II; Pope Benedict VII; Pope Gregory V:—109×129 mm. (g) 12k. William IV of England; (h) 12k. Tsar Fyodor I; (i) 12k. Tsar Lzhedmitry; (j) 12k. Pope Gregory VII; (k) 12k. Pope Leo XIII; (l) 12k. Pope Leo IX 60·00 60·00

**261** Damaged Building, Kuito

**2000.** Buildings and People. Multicoloured.

1592 3k. Type **261** 1·90 1·90
1593 3k. People and Kunje–Kuito road 1·90 1·90
1594 4k. Post Office building 2·50 2·50
1595 4k. Police headquarters 2·50 2·50
1596 5k. Damaged apartments 3·25 3·25
1597 5k. Independence Plaza 3·25 3·25
1598 6k. Children 3·75 3·75
1599 6k. Man carrying sack 3·75 3·75

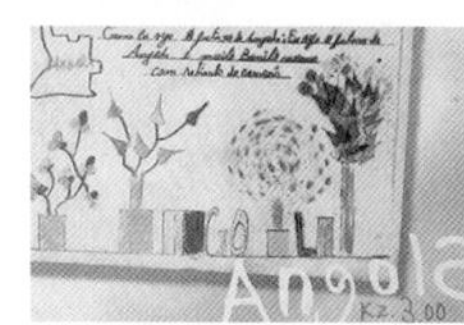

**262** Trees

**2000.** Children's Paintings. Multicoloured.

1600 3k. Type **262** 1·50 1·50
1601 4k. Wall 1·90 1·90
1602 5k. Rural scene 2·40 2·40

**263** Directorate of Communications, Telephones and Telegraphs, Luanda

**2000.** Postal Buildings. Multicoloured.

1603 5k. Type **263** 2·30 2·00
1604 5k. ETP building, Mbanza Congo 2·30 2·00
1605 5k. CTT building, Namibe 2·30 2·00
1606 8k. ECP building, Luanda 3·75 3·50
1607 8k. ETP building, Lobito 3·75 3·50
1608 8k. ECP building, Luanda (different) 3·75 3·50

**264** Tank, Rifle and Dove

**2001.** 25th Anniv of Independence. Sheet 140×47 mm containing T **264** and similar horiz design. Multicoloured.

**MS**1609 12k. Type **264**; 12k. Dove, mattock and tractor 6·00 6·00

**265** Radio Studio

**2001.** 25th Anniv of Public Radio (**MS**1613a, **MS**1613c) and Television (others). Four sheets containing T **265** and similar multicoloured designs.

**MS**1610 (a) 154×80 mm. 9k.50, Type **265**; 9k.50, Reporter in war zone; 9k.50 Carrying stretcher from burning aeroplane. (b) 154×80 mm. 9k.50, Television studio; 9k.50, Cameraman filming tank; 9k.50, Women and children crossing water. (c) 99×60 mm. 12k. Reporter in war zone (detail) (42×28 mm). (d) 99×60 mm. 12k. Cameraman filming tank (detail) (28×42 mm) (vert) 30·00 30·00

**266** Hands holding Book

**2001.** Africa Day. Multicoloured.

1611 10k. Type **266** 2·75 2·30
1612 10k. Hands and xylophone 2·75 2·30
**MS**1613 130×90 mm. 30k. Map of Africa 8·00 8·00

**267** *Nicolaia speciosa*

**2001.** Flowers. Belgica 2001 International Stamp Exhibition. Multicoloured.

1614 8k. Type **267** 2·75 2·50
1615 9k. *Allamanda cathartica* (inscr "cathartca") 3·00 2·75
1616 10k. *Welwitschia mirabilis* 3·50 3·00
1617 10k. *Tagetes patula* 3·50 3·00
**MS**1618 130×90 mm. 30k. No. 1616 10·50 10·00

**268** Man wearing Dark Glasses

**2001.** Total Eclipse of the Sun, 21 June 2001. Sheet 130×90 mm.

**MS**1619 30k. multicoloured 7·50 7·50

**269** West African Lungfish (*Protopterus annectens*)

**2001.** Freshwater Fish. Multicoloured.

1620 11k. Type **269** 2·00 1·50
1621 17k. *Protopterus amphibious* 3·00 2·40
1622 18k. *Tilapia ruweti* 3·25 2·50
**MS**1623 130×90 mm. 36k. Red-breasted tilapia (*Tilapia rendalli*) 6·50 6·50

**270** Ovambo Efundula, Cunene

**2001.** Traditional Dances. Multicoloured.

1624 11k. Type **270** 1·50 1·30
1625 11k. Massembo, Luanda 1·60 1·30
1626 17k. Macolo Batuque, Uige 2·50 2·00
1627 18k. Mukixi, Lunda Tchokwe 2·60 2·20
1628 18k. Humbi Puberdade, Namibe 2·60 2·20
**MS**1629 130×90 mm. 36k. Carnival Juvenil, Luanda 5·50 5·50

**271** Hand-woven Hat, Banda

**2001.** Woven Crafts. Sheet 130×90 mm containing T **271** and similar horiz design. Multicoloured.

**MS**1630 17k. Type **271**; 18k. Hat with extensions, Kijinga 5·25 5·25

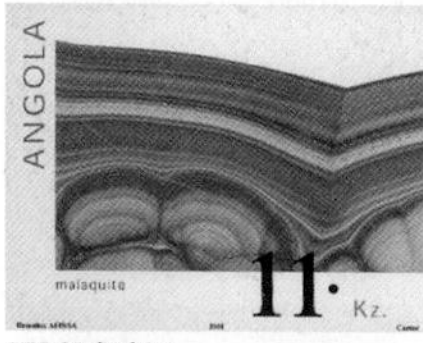

**272** Malachite

**2001.** Minerals. Multicoloured.

1631 11k. Type **272** 2·00 1·80
1632 11k. Hematite 2·00 1·80
1633 18k. Diamond 3·25 2·75
1634 18k. Psilomelane 3·25 2·75

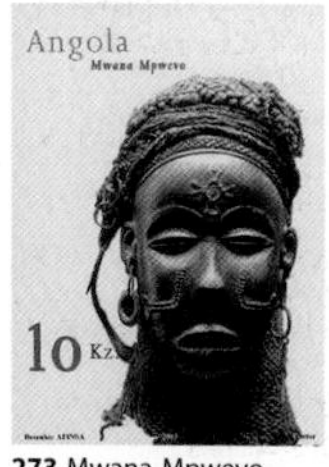

**273** Mwana Mpwevo

**2002.** Masks. Multicoloured.

1635 10k. Type **273** (Ngangela animistic ritual) 1·40 1·30
1636 11k. Mukixi (Cokwe circumcision ritual) 1·80 1·40
1637 11k. Mbunda (comic) 1·80 1·40
1638 17k. Mwana Pwo (Cokwe circumcision ritual) 2·50 2·10
1639 18k. Likisi-Cinganji (supernatural incarnation) 2·75 2·20
**MS**1640 90×80 mm. 36k. Ndemba (Bakongo circumcision ritual) 6·00 5·00

**274** Players and Football

**2002.** Football World Cup Championship, Japan and South Korea. Multicoloured.

1641 35k. Type **274** 4·50 3·00
1642 37k. Players and ball (different) 4·75 3·25
**MS**1643 55×120 mm. Nos. 1641/2 8·50 6·50

**275** Figure with Target on Chest

**2002.** Socialist International Congress. Multicoloured.

1644 10k. Type **275** (abolition of the death penalty) 1·20 80
1645 10k. Woman (end to violence against women) 1·20 80
1646 10k. Faces (combating poverty) 1·20 80
1647 10k. Map and dollar sign (eliminate foreign debt) 1·20 80
1648 10k. Map ("Africa in Peril" combating poverty) 1·20 80
**MS**1649 40×30 mm. Nos. 1644/7 6·50 6·00

**276** National Map, Rainbow and Dove

**2002.** Peace and Reconciliation Commission.
1650 **276** 35k. multicoloured 2·00 1·60

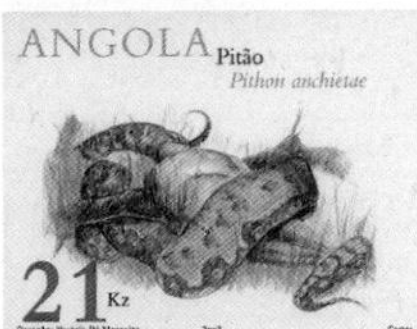

**277** Python (*Python anchietae*) (inscr "pithon")

**2002.** Reptiles. Multicoloured.
1651 21k. Type **277** 1·50 1·10
1652 35k. *Lacerta* (lizard) 2·50 1·90
1653 37k. *Naja Nigricollis* (spitting cobra) 2·60 2·00
1654 40k. *Crocodylus niloticus* 2·75 2·20

**278** Lighthouse, Barra do Dande

**2002.** Lighthouses and Buoys. Multicoloured.
1655 45k. Type **278** 3·50 2·50
1656 45k. Snake Head lighthouse, Soyo 3·50 2·50
1657 45k. Tafe lighthouse, Cabinda Bay 3·50 2·50
1658 45k. Moita Seca lighthouse, South Margin Bay 3·50 2·50
1659 45k. Red buoy no. 9, Luanda Bay 3·50 2·50
1660 45k. Green buoy no. 1, Luanda Bay 3·50 2·50

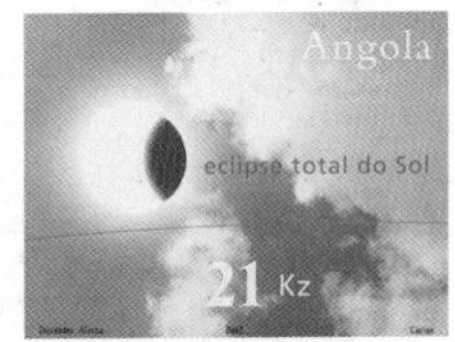

**279** Partial Eclipse (one third)

**2002.** Total Eclipse of the Sun (21 June 2001). Sheet 155×80 mm containing T **279** and similar horiz designs showing stages of eclipse. Multicoloured.
**MS**1661 21k. Type **279**; 35k. Two thirds; 37k. Total eclipse 6·00 6·00

**280** Antonio Manuel (17th-century Congolese ambassador to Pope Paul V) and Lion

**2002.** Angola—Italy Friendship. Multicoloured.
1662 35k. Type **280** 2·20 1·80
1663 45k. Antonio Manuel and papal plaque 3·00 2·20
**MS**1664 120×72 mm. Nos. 1662/3 4·00 4·00

**281** Omolingui (Ovimbundo water pot)

**2002.** Pottery. Multicoloured.
1665 27k. Type **281** 2·00 1·20
1666 45k. Mulondo (Luvale drinking jar) 3·00 2·00
1667 47k. Ombya Yo Tuma (Ovimbundo food pot) 3·25 2·20
**MS**1668 120×72 mm. 51k. Sanga (Bakongo drinking vessel) 4·00 3·00

**282** Trees, Satellite Dish and UN Emblem

**2003.** 3rd United Nations Science, Technology and Development Meeting.
1669 **282** 50k. multicoloured 2·75 2·20

**283** Stylized Bi-plane

**2003.** Centenary of Powered Flight.
1670 **283** 25k. multicoloured 2·75 2·75

**284** Antonio Jacinto

**2003.** Writers. Multicoloured.
1671 27k. Type **284** 1·50 1·20
1672 45k. Antonio Agostinho Neto 2·20 1·70
**MS**1673 121×90 mm. 27k. Antonio Jacinto wearing cap; 45k. Agostinho Neto as younger man 3·75 3·75

**285** Two Antelope

**2003.** Sable Antelope (Hippotragus niger). Multicoloured.
1674 27k. Type **285** 1·50 1·20
1675 45k. Two antelope with straight horns 2·20 1·70
1676 47k. One antelope with curved horns 2·50 2·00

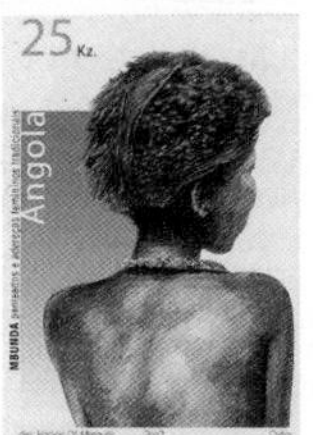

**286** Mbunda Woman

**2003.** Traditional Women's Hairstyles. Sheet 130×120 mm containing T **286** and similar vert designs.
**MS**1677 25k.×6, Type **286**; Soyo; Huila; Humbi; Cabinda; Quipungu 8·00 8·00

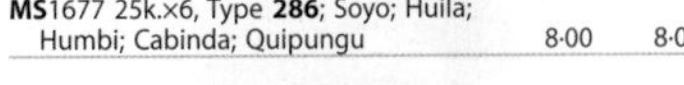

**287** Musicians (detail, "Ascensao") (Jorge Afonso)

**2003.** Christmas. Multicoloured.
1678 27k. Type **287** 1·50 1·20
1679 27k. "Adoraçao dos Pastores" (Andre Reinoso) 1·50 1·20
1680 45k. Holy Family (detail, "Adoraçao dos Pastores") (Josefa de Obidos) 2·20 1·70
1681 45k. Cherubs (detail, "Adoraçao dos Pastores") (Josefa de Obidos) 2·20 1·70
**MS**1682 110×92 mm. Nos. 1678/81 7·50 7·50

**288** Bryde's Whale (*Balaenoptera edeni*)

**2003.** Marine Mammals. Multicoloured.
1683 27k. Type **288** 2·50 2·20
1684 45k. Heaviside's dolphin (*Cephalorhynchus heavisidii*) 4·50 3·50
**MS**1685 120×84 mm. 27k. Type **288**; 47k. Pilot whale (Globicephala melaena) (inscr "Giobiocephaia") 7·00 6·00

**289** Tawny Eagle (*Aquila rapax*)

**2003.** Eagles. Multicoloured.
1686 20k. Type **289** 2·00 1·70
1687 20k. Martial eagle (*Hieraaetus bellicosus*) (inscr "Polemaetus") 2·00 1·70
1688 25k. African fish eagle (*Haliaeetus vocifer*) 2·50 2·20
1689 25k. Bateleur (*Terathopius ecaudatus*) 2·50 2·20
**MS**1690 120×80 mm. 45k. Verreaux's eagle (*Aquila verreauxi*) 5·50 5·00

**290** Chess Pieces

**2003.** Chess. Multicoloured.
1691 45k. Type **290** 3·50 3·00
1692 45k. Board and pieces 3·50 3·00

**291** Pope John Paul II

**2003.** 25th Anniv of the Pontificate of Pope John Paul II. Multicoloured.
1693 27k. Type **291** 2·20 1·70
1694 27k. Pope John Paul II with raised hand 2·20 1·70

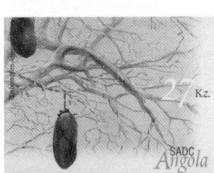

**292** *Adansonia digitata*

**2004.** Southern African Development Community. Plants. Multicoloured.
1695 27k. Type **292** 1·80 1·30
1695a 27k. *Psidium guayava* 1·80 1·30
1696 45k. *Carica papaya* 3·00 2·20
1697 45k. *Cymbopogon citrates* 3·00 2·20
**MS**1698 129×105 mm. Nos. 1695/7 8·00 6·00

**293** Basketball

**2004.** Olympic Games, Athens. Multicoloured.
1699 27k. Type **293** 1·50 1·10
1700 27k. Handball 1·50 1·10
1701 45k. Running 2·50 1·80
1702 45k. Volleyball 2·50 1·80

**294** Humpback Whales (*Megaptera novaeangliae*)

**2004.** Sea Mammals. Multicoloured.
1703 27k. Type **294** 1·50 1·10
1704 27k. Heaviside's dolphin (*Cephalorhynchus heavisidii*) 1·50 1·10
1705 45k. Bottlenose dolphin (*Tursiops truncates*) 2·50 1·80
**MS**1706 135×80 mm. 99k. *Megaptera novaeangliae* (different) 5·50 5·00

Nos. 1703/5 were issued together, se-tenant, forming a composite design.

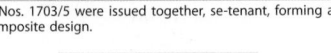

**295** Saddle Tanker (Benguela)

**2004.** Trains. Multicoloured.
1707 27k. Type **295** 1·50 1·10
1708 27k. Diesel locomotive (Mocamedes) 1·50 1·10
1709 27k. Locomotive CFB 225 (Benguela) 1·50 1·10

**296** Fireman and Campaign Emblem

**2004.** Fire Emergency Phone Number Publicity Campaign. Multicoloured.
1710 27k. Type **296** 1·50 1·10
1711 27k. Fire appliance 1·50 1·10
1712 45k. Fire appliance facing right 2·50 1·80
**MS**1713 130×80 mm. Nos. 1710/12 5·00 5·50

**297** Globe and Footballers

**2004.** Centenary of FIFA (Federation Internationale de Football Association).
1714 **297** 45k. multicoloured 2·00 1·60

**298** Three Kings

**2004.** Christmas. Multicoloured.
1715 27k. Type **298** 1·20 95
1716 45k. Nativity 2·00 1·60

Nos. 1715/16 were issued together, se-tenant, forming a composite design.

**299** Family of Monkeys

**2004.** Colobus Monkey (Colobus angolensis). Multicoloured.
1717 27k. Type **299** 1·20 1·20
1718 27k. Mother and baby 1·20 1·20
1719 27k. Male 1·20 1·20
1720 27k. Facing left 1·20 1·20

300 Woman and City Skyline

**2005.** 50th Anniv of Rotary of Luanda. Multicoloured.

| | | | |
|---|---|---|---|
| 1721 | 45k. Type **300** | 2·00 | 1·60 |
| 1722 | 51k. Woman and countryside | 2·75 | 2·00 |
| **MS**1723 | 120×80 mm. Nos. 1721/2 | 5·50 | 5·00 |

Nos. 1724/7 and Type **301** are left for Basketry, issued on 6 September 2005, not yet received.

Nos. 1728/9 and Type **302** are left for 30th Anniv of Independence, issued on 8 November 2005, not yet received.

Nos. 1730/1and Type **303** are left for World Summit on the Information Society (WSIS), issued on 8 November 2005, not yet received.

Nos. 1732/5 and Type **304** are left for Ministerial Conference of African Oil Producers , issued on 24 April 2006, not yet received.

Nos. 1736/7 and Type **305** are left for World Cup, issued on 30 August 2006, not yet received.

**306** Dogs

**2006.** Tenth Anniv of Countries of Portuguese Language Community. Lubrapex International Stamp Exhibition, Rio de Janeiro, Brazil. Multicoloured.

| | | | |
|---|---|---|---|
| 1738 | 27k. Type **306** | 35 | 15 |
| 1739 | 45k. Grey parrots | 65 | 25 |
| 1740 | 45k. Helmeted guinea fowl | 65 | 25 |

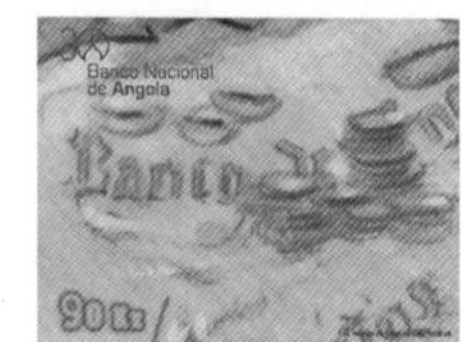
**307** Currency

**2006.** 30th Anniv of National Bank. Multicoloured.

| | | | |
|---|---|---|---|
| **MS**1745 | 200×136 mm. 90k. Type **307** | 1·90 | 1·90 |

No. 1746 and Type **308** are left for Paralympic Committee, issued on 29 December 2006, not yet received.

No. 1747 and Type **309** are left for Five Years of Peace, issued on 20 April 2007, not yet received.

Nos. 1748/9 and Type **310** are left for Venice Biennial, issued on 20 April 2007, not yet received.

No. 1750 and Type **311** are left for Africa Day, issued on 25 May 2007, not yet received.

Nos. 1751/5 and Type **312** are left for Centenary of Scouting, issued on 1 June 2007, not yet received.

No. 1756 and Type **313** are left for 27th Anniv of SADC , issued on 17 August 2007, not yet received.

No. 1757 and Type **314** are left for Olympic Games, Beijing, issued on 20 September 2007, not yet received.

**315** Malange

**2007.** World Post Day. Multicoloured.

| | | | |
|---|---|---|---|
| **MS**1758 | 45k.×2, Type **315**; Huambo | 1·10 | 1·10 |

**316** *Caretta caretta*

**2007.** Marine Turtles. Multicoloured.

| | | | |
|---|---|---|---|
| **MS**1759 | 126×104 mm. 27k. Type **316**; 27k. *Chelonia mydas* ; 45k. *Eretmochelys imbricata* ; 45k. *Lepidochelys olivacea* | 45 | 45 |
| **MS**1760 | 142×108 mm. 130k. *Dermochelys coriacea* (37×39 mm) | 1·30 | 1·30 |

**317** Meat and Dumplings

**2008.** Angolan Gastronomy. Multicoloured.

| | | | |
|---|---|---|---|
| 1761 | 37k. Type **317** | 40 | 14 |
| 1762 | 40k. Greens and dumplings | 40 | 15 |
| 1763 | 59k. Stew with greens (Calulu) | 1·10 | 35 |
| **MS**1764 | 160×90 mm. 153k. Chicken stew (Muamba) | 1·90 | 1·90 |

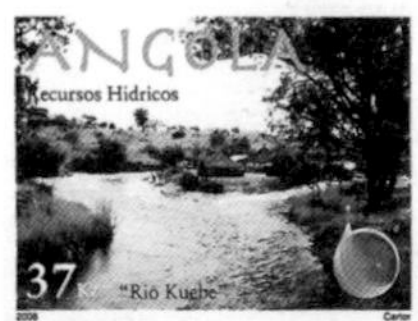

**318** Rio Kuebe

**2008.** Rivers. Multicoloured.

| | | | |
|---|---|---|---|
| 1765 | 37k. Type **318** | 40 | 15 |
| 1766 | 37k. Rapidos do Kuanza (Rapids of Kwanza) | 40 | 15 |
| 1767 | 40k. Rio Kuanza | 55 | 20 |
| 1768 | 40k. Foz do Rio Mbridge (Mbridge rivermouth) | 55 | 20 |
| **MS**1769 | 160×90 mm. 153k. Recursos Hidricos (waterfall (water resources)) | 1·90 | 1·10 |

**319** Landmine Clearance

**2008.** Tenth Anniv of Lwini Social Solidarity Fund (to help landmine victims). Multicoloured.

| | | | |
|---|---|---|---|
| **MS**1770 | 37k. Type **319**; 40k. Information literature (horiz); 40k. Princess Diana and Ana Paula dos Santos (foundation president) (horiz); 59k. Children in wheelchairs (horiz); 59k. Landmine victims making baskets (horiz) | 2·75 | 2·75 |

**320** Water Jug

**2008.** Water Jugs. Multicoloured.

| | | | |
|---|---|---|---|
| 1771 | 37k. Type **320** | 40 | 15 |
| 1772 | 37k. Incised jug with several handles | 40 | 15 |
| 1773 | 40k. Green jug with spout, handle and lid | 55 | 20 |
| 1774 | 40k. White jug with figure as lid | 55 | 20 |

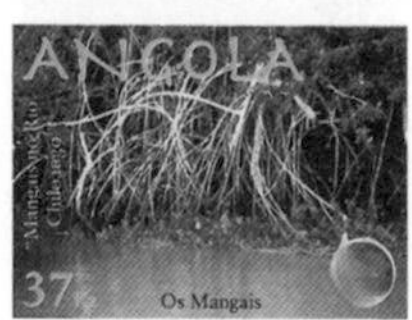

**321** Mangroves

**2008.** Mangroves on Rio Chiloango. Multicoloured.

| | | | |
|---|---|---|---|
| 1775 | 37k. Mangroves | 60 | 25 |
| 1776 | 37k. River bordered by mangroves | 60 | 25 |
| 1777 | 59k. Type **321** | 85 | 35 |

**322** Coffee Berries

**2009.** Angolan Coffee, Amboim. Multicoloured.

| | | | |
|---|---|---|---|
| 1778 | 37k. Type **322** | 40 | 15 |
| 1779 | 45k. Branches of coffee plant | 55 | 30 |
| 1780 | 45k. Woman picking coffee (horiz) | 55 | 30 |

**323** Antonio Agostinho Neto

**2009.** Antonio Agostinho Neto (first president of Angola) Commemoration.

| | | | |
|---|---|---|---|
| 1781 | 40k. black and scarlet-vermilion | 45 | 30 |
| 1782 | 50k. multicoloured | 45 | 35 |
| **MS**1783 | 160×90 mm. 150k. multicoloured | 1·20 | 1·20 |

DESIGNS: 40k. Type **323**; 50k. Wearing uniform; 150k. With school children.

**324** Pope Benedict XVI

**2009.** Visit of Pope Benedict XVI to Angola

| | | | |
|---|---|---|---|
| **MS**1784 **324** | 150×60mm. 100k. multicoloured | 2·75 | 2·75 |

**325** Cabinda Stadium

**2010.** COCAN 2010, African Cup of Nations Football Competition. Multicoloured.

| | | | |
|---|---|---|---|
| 1785 | 40k. Type **325** | 40 | 15 |
| 1786 | 40k. Benguela | 40 | 15 |
| 1787 | 50k. Huila | 45 | 20 |
| 1788 | 50k. Luanda | 45 | 20 |

## APPENDIX

**1995**

90th Anniv of Rotary International (on gold foil). 81000k.

## CHARITY TAX STAMPS

Used on certain days of the year as an additional tax on internal letters. If one was not used in addition to normal postage, postage due stamps were used to collect the deficiency and the fine.

**1925.** Marquis de Pombal Commemorative stamps of Portugal but inscr "ANGOLA".

| | | | | |
|---|---|---|---|---|
| C343 | **C73** | 15c. violet | 90 | 85 |
| C344 | - | 15c. violet | 90 | 85 |
| C345 | **C75** | 15c. violet | 90 | 85 |

**C15**

**1929**

| | | | | |
|---|---|---|---|---|
| C347 | **C15** | 50c. blue | 4·50 | 1·50 |

**C29**

**1939.** No gum.

| | | | | |
|---|---|---|---|---|
| C413 | **C29** | 50c. green | 2·40 | 20 |
| C414 | **C29** | 1a. red | 3·50 | 1·60 |

**C52** Old Man

**1955.** Heads in brown.

| | | | | |
|---|---|---|---|---|
| C646 | **C52** | 50c. orange | 15 | 10 |
| C647 | - | 1e. red (Boy) | 15 | 10 |
| C648 | - | 1e.50 green (Girl) | 15 | 10 |
| C522 | - | 2e.50 blue (Old woman) | 60 | 35 |

**1957.** Surch.

| | | | | |
|---|---|---|---|---|
| C535 | **C52** | 10c. on 50c. orange | 20 | 15 |
| C534 | **C52** | 30c. on 50c. orange | 25 | 25 |

**C58** Mother and Child

**1959**

| | | | | |
|---|---|---|---|---|
| C538 | **C58** | 10c. black and orange | 20 | 15 |
| C539 | - | 30c. black and slate | 20 | 15 |

DESIGN: 30c. Boy and girl.

**C65** Yellow, White and Black Men

**1962.** Provincial Settlement Committee.

| | | | | |
|---|---|---|---|---|
| C568 | **C65** | 50c. multicoloured | 25 | 15 |
| C569 | **C65** | 1e. multicoloured | 40 | 15 |

**C75** "Full Employment"

**1965.** Provincial Settlement Committee.

| | | | | |
|---|---|---|---|---|
| C644 | **C75** | 1e. multicoloured | 20 | 15 |
| C645 | **C75** | 2e. multicoloured | 25 | 15 |
| C643 | **C75** | 50e. multicoloured | 20 | 15 |

**C95** Planting Tree

**1972.** Provincial Settlement Committee.

| | | | | |
|---|---|---|---|---|
| C701 | **C95** | 50c. red and brown | 15 | 15 |
| C702 | - | 1e. black and green | 15 | 15 |
| C703 | - | 2e. black and brown | 15 | 15 |

DESIGNS: 1e. Agricultural workers; 2e. Corncobs and flowers.

## NEWSPAPER STAMP

**1893.** "Newspaper" key-type inscr "ANGOLA".

| | | | | |
|---|---|---|---|---|
| N51 | **V** | 2½r. brown | 2·30 | 1·10 |

## POSTAGE DUE STAMPS

**1904.** "Due" key-type inscr "ANGOLA".

| | | | | |
|---|---|---|---|---|
| D150 | **W** | 5r. green | 30 | 30 |
| D151 | **W** | 10r. grey | 30 | 30 |
| D152 | **W** | 20r. brown | 65 | 35 |
| D153 | **W** | 30r. orange | 65 | 35 |
| D154 | **W** | 50r. brown | 85 | 55 |
| D155 | **W** | 60r. brown | 7·50 | 4·00 |
| D156 | **W** | 100r. mauve | 3·25 | 2·10 |
| D157 | **W** | 130r. blue | 3·25 | 2·10 |
| D158 | **W** | 200r. red | 9·25 | 5·00 |
| D159 | **W** | 500r. lilac | 7·75 | 4·25 |

See also Nos. D343/52.

**1911.** Nos. D150/9 optd **REPUBLICA**.

| | | | |
|---|---|---|---|
| D166 | 5r. green | 25 | 20 |
| D167 | 10r. grey | 25 | 20 |
| D168 | 20r. brown | 25 | 20 |
| D169 | 30r. orange | 40 | 20 |
| D170 | 50r. brown | 40 | 20 |
| D171 | 60r. brown | 1·10 | 70 |

| | | | |
|---|---|---|---|
| D172 | 100r. mauve | 1·10 | 70 |
| D173 | 130r. blue | 1·30 | 85 |
| D174 | 200r. red | 1·50 | 85 |
| D175 | 500r. lilac | 1·70 | 1·50 |

**1921.** Values in new currency.

| | | | |
|---|---|---|---|
| D343 | ½c. green | 25 | 20 |
| D344 | 1c. grey | 25 | 20 |
| D345 | 2c. brown | 25 | 20 |
| D346 | 3c. orange | 25 | 20 |
| D347 | 5c. brown | 25 | 20 |
| D348 | 6c. brown | 25 | 20 |
| D349 | 10c. mauve | 35 | 30 |
| D350 | 13c. blue | 70 | 65 |
| D351 | 20c. red | 70 | 65 |
| D352 | 50c. grey | 70 | 65 |

**1925.** Marquis de Pombal stamps of Angola, as Nos. C343/5, optd **MULTA**.

| | | | | |
|---|---|---|---|---|
| D353 | **C73** | 30c. violet | 90 | 85 |
| D354 | - | 30c. violet | 90 | 85 |
| D355 | **C 75** | 30c. violet | 90 | 85 |

**1949.** Surch **PORTEADO** and value.

| | | | | |
|---|---|---|---|---|
| D438 | **17** | 10c. on 20c. grey | 25 | 20 |
| D439 | **17** | 20c. on 30c. green | 45 | 40 |
| D440 | **17** | 30c. on 50c. brown | 70 | 60 |
| D441 | **17** | 40c. on 1a. red | 1·00 | 95 |
| D442 | **17** | 50c. on 2a. mauve | 1·50 | 1·40 |
| D443 | **17** | 1a. on 5a. green | 1·70 | 1·60 |

**D45**

**1952.** Numerals in red, name in black.

| | | | | |
|---|---|---|---|---|
| D483 | **D45** | 10c. brown and olive | 20 | 15 |
| D484 | **D45** | 30c. green and blue | 20 | 15 |
| D485 | **D45** | 50c. brown & lt brn | 20 | 15 |
| D486 | **D45** | 1a. blue, green & orge | 40 | 40 |
| D487 | **D45** | 2a. brown and red | 55 | 50 |
| D488 | **D45** | 5a. brown and blue | 55 | 50 |

Pt. 9

## ANGRA

A district of the Azores, which used the stamps of the Azores except from 1892 to 1905.

1000 reis = 1 milreis.

**1892.** As T **4** of Funchal, inscr "ANGRA".

| | | | |
|---|---|---|---|
| 16 | 5r. yellow | 4·25 | 2·50 |
| 5 | 10r. mauve | 4·75 | 2·50 |
| 6 | 15r. brown | 5·50 | 3·75 |
| 7 | 20r. violet | 5·50 | 3·75 |
| 8 | 25r. green | 7·50 | 1·70 |
| 9 | 50r. blue | 11·00 | 5·75 |
| 10 | 75r. red | 13·00 | 7·50 |
| 11 | 80r. green | 15·00 | 14·00 |
| 24 | 100r. brown on yellow | 55·00 | 20·00 |
| 13 | 150r. red on rose | 75·00 | 60·00 |
| 14 | 200r. blue on blue | 75·00 | 60·00 |
| 15 | 300r. blue on brown | 75·00 | 60·00 |

**1897.** "King Carlos" key-type inscr "ANGRA".

| | | | | |
|---|---|---|---|---|
| 28 | **S** | 2½r. grey | 1·00 | 65 |
| 29 | **S** | 5r. red | 1·00 | 65 |
| 30 | **S** | 10r. green | 1·00 | 65 |
| 31 | **S** | 15r. brown | 13·00 | 8·50 |
| 43 | **S** | 15r. green | 1·30 | 80 |
| 32 | **S** | 20r. lilac | 2·50 | 1·90 |
| 33 | **S** | 25r. green | 4·25 | 1·70 |
| 44 | **S** | 25r. red | 90 | 80 |
| 34 | **S** | 50r. blue | 7·75 | 2·40 |
| 46 | **S** | 65r. blue | 1·80 | 80 |
| 35 | **S** | 75r. red | 4·75 | 2·30 |
| 47 | **S** | 75r. brown on yellow | 19·00 | 15·00 |
| 36 | **S** | 80r. mauve | 2·10 | 1·70 |
| 37 | **S** | 100r. blue on blue | 3·75 | 2·40 |
| 48 | **S** | 115r. red on pink | 3·75 | 2·75 |
| 49 | **S** | 130r. brown on cream | 3·75 | 2·75 |
| 38 | **S** | 150r. brown on yellow | 3·75 | 2·40 |
| 50 | **S** | 180r. grey on pink | 4·75 | 4·25 |
| 39 | **S** | 200r. purple on pink | 7·75 | 6·75 |
| 40 | **S** | 300r. blue on pink | 11·50 | 8·75 |
| 41 | **S** | 500r. black on blue | 24·00 | 19·00 |

Pt. 1

## ANGUILLA

St. Christopher, Nevis and Anguilla were granted Associated Statehood on 27 February 1967, but following a referendum Anguilla declared her independence and the St. Christopher authorities withdrew. On 7 July 1969, the Anguilla post office was officially recognised by the Government of St. Christopher, Nevis and Anguilla and normal postal communications via St. Christopher were resumed.

By the Anguilla Act of 27 July 1971, the island was restored to direct British control.

100 cents = 1 West Indian dollar.

**1967.** Nos. 129/44 of St. Kitts-Nevis optd **Independent Anguilla** and bar.

| | | | | |
|---|---|---|---|---|
| 1 | - | ½c. sepia and blue | 55·00 | 26·00 |
| 2 | **33** | 1c. multicoloured | 65·00 | 11·00 |
| 3 | - | 2c. multicoloured | 60·00 | 2·25 |
| 4 | - | 3c. multicoloured | 65·00 | 5·50 |
| 5 | - | 4c. multicoloured | 65·00 | 6·50 |
| 6 | - | 5c. multicoloured | £250 | 27·00 |
| 7 | - | 6c. multicoloured | £110 | 16·00 |
| 8 | - | 10c. multicoloured | 65·00 | 9·00 |
| 9 | - | 15c. multicoloured | £120 | 15·00 |
| 10 | - | 20c. multicoloured | £250 | 20·00 |
| 11 | - | 25c. multicoloured | £200 | 35·00 |
| 12 | - | 50c. multicoloured | £3750 | £700 |
| 13 | - | 60c. multicoloured | £4500 | £1400 |
| 14 | - | $1 yellow and blue | £3250 | £600 |
| 15 | - | $2.50 multicoloured | £2500 | £400 |
| 16 | - | $5 multicoloured | £2750 | £425 |

Owing to the limited stocks available for overprinting, the sale of the stamps was personally controlled by the Postmaster and no orders from the trade were accepted.

**2** Mahogany Tree, The Quarter

**1967**

| | | | | |
|---|---|---|---|---|
| 17 | **2** | 1c. green, brown and orange | 10 | 1·00 |
| 18 | - | 2c. turquoise and black | 10 | 2·75 |
| 19 | - | 3c. black and green | 10 | 10 |
| 20 | - | 4c. blue and black | 10 | 10 |
| 21 | - | 5c. multicoloured | 10 | 10 |
| 22 | - | 6c. red and black | 10 | 10 |
| 23 | - | 10c. multicoloured | 15 | 10 |
| 24 | - | 15c. multicoloured | 2·50 | 20 |
| 25 | - | 20c. multicoloured | 1·25 | 2·50 |
| 26 | - | 25c. multicoloured | 60 | 20 |
| 27 | - | 40c. green, blue and black | 1·00 | 25 |
| 28 | - | 60c. multicoloured | 4·50 | 4·75 |
| 29 | - | $1 multicoloured | 1·75 | 3·25 |
| 30 | - | $2.50 multicoloured | 2·00 | 7·00 |
| 31 | - | $5 multicoloured | 3·00 | 4·25 |

DESIGNS: 2c. Sombrero Lighthouse; 3c. St. Mary's Church; 4c. Valley Police Station; 5c. Old Plantation House, Mt. Fortune; 6c. Valley Post Office; 10c. Methodist Church, West End; 15c. Wall Blake Airport; 20c. Beech A90 King Air aircraft over Sandy Ground; 25c. Island harbour; 40c. Map of Anguilla; 60c. Hermit crab and starfish; $1, Hibiscus; $2.50, Local scene; $5, Spiny lobster.

**17** Yachts in Lagoon

**1968.** Anguillan Ships. Multicoloured.

| | | | |
|---|---|---|---|
| 32 | 10c. Type **17** | 35 | 10 |
| 33 | 15c. Boat on beach | 40 | 10 |
| 34 | 25c. Schooner "Warspite" | 55 | 15 |
| 35 | 40c. Schooner "Atlantic Star" | 65 | 20 |

**18** Purple-throated Carib

**1968.** Anguillan Birds. Multicoloured.

| | | | |
|---|---|---|---|
| 36 | 10c. Type **18** | 65 | 15 |
| 37 | 15c. Bananaquit | 80 | 20 |
| 38 | 25c. Black-necked stilt (horiz) | 85 | 20 |
| 39 | 40c. Royal tern (horiz) | 90 | 30 |

**19** Guides' Badge and Anniversary Years

**1968.** 35th Anniv of Anguillan Girl Guides. Mult.

| | | | |
|---|---|---|---|
| 40 | 10c. Type **19** | 10 | 10 |
| 41 | 15c. Badge and silhouettes of guides (vert) | 15 | 10 |
| 42 | 25c. Guides' badge and Headquarters | 20 | 15 |
| 43 | 40c. Association and proficiency badges (vert) | 25 | 15 |

**20** The Three Kings

**1968.** Christmas.

| | | | | |
|---|---|---|---|---|
| 44 | **20** | 1c. black and red | 10 | 10 |
| 45 | - | 10c. black and blue | 10 | 10 |
| 46 | - | 15c. black and brown | 15 | 10 |
| 47 | - | 40c. black and blue | 15 | 10 |
| 48 | - | 50c. black and green | 20 | 15 |

DESIGNS—VERT: 10c. The Wise Men; 15c. Holy Family and manger. HORIZ: 40c. The Shepherds; 50c. Holy Family and donkey.

**21** Bagging Salt

**1969.** Anguillan Salt Industry. Multicoloured.

| | | | |
|---|---|---|---|
| 49 | 10c. Type **21** | 25 | 10 |
| 50 | 15c. Packing salt | 30 | 10 |
| 51 | 40c. Salt pond | 35 | 10 |
| 52 | 50c. Loading salt | 35 | 10 |

**1969.** Expiration of Interim Agreement on Status of Anguilla. Nos. 17/22, 23, 24 and 26/7 optd **INDEPENDENCE JANUARY 1969.**

| | | | |
|---|---|---|---|
| 52a | 1c. green, brown and orange | 10 | 40 |
| 52b | 2c. green and black | 10 | 40 |
| 52c | 3c. black and green | 10 | 40 |
| 52d | 4c. blue and black | 10 | 40 |
| 52e | 5c. multicoloured | 10 | 20 |
| 52f | 6c. red and black | 10 | 20 |
| 52g | 10c. multicoloured | 10 | 30 |
| 52h | 15c. multicoloured | 90 | 30 |
| 52i | 25c. multicoloured | 80 | 30 |
| 52j | 40c. green, blue and black | 1·00 | 40 |

The remaining values of the 1967 series, nos. 17/31, also come with this overprint but these are outside the scope of this catalogue.

**22** "The Crucifixion" (Studio of Massys)

**1969.** Easter Commemoration. Multicoloured.

| | | | |
|---|---|---|---|
| 53 | 25c. Type **22** | 25 | 15 |
| 54 | 40c. "The Last Supper" (ascribed to Roberti) | 35 | 15 |

**23** Amaryllis

**1969.** Flowers of the Caribbean. Multicoloured.

| | | | |
|---|---|---|---|
| 55 | 10c. Type **23** | 15 | 20 |
| 56 | 15c. Bougainvillea | 15 | 25 |
| 57 | 40c. Hibiscus | 20 | 50 |
| 58 | 50c. "Cattleya" orchid | 1·00 | 1·60 |

**24** Superb Gaza, Channelled Turban, Chestnut Turban and Carved Star Shell

**1969.** Sea Shells. Multicoloured.

| | | | |
|---|---|---|---|
| 59 | 10c. Type **24** | 20 | 20 |
| 60 | 15c. American thorny oysters | 20 | 20 |
| 61 | 40c. Scotch, royal and smooth scotch bonnets | 30 | 30 |
| 62 | 50c. Atlantic trumpet triton | 40 | 30 |

**1969.** Christmas. Nos. 17 and 25/8 optd with different seasonal emblems.

| | | | |
|---|---|---|---|
| 63 | 1c. green, brown and orange | 10 | 10 |
| 64 | 20c. multicoloured | 20 | 10 |
| 65 | 25c. multicoloured | 20 | 10 |
| 66 | 40c. green, blue and black | 25 | 15 |
| 67 | 60c. multicoloured | 40 | 20 |

**30** Spotted Goatfish

**1969.** Fishes. Multicoloured.

| | | | |
|---|---|---|---|
| 68 | 10c. Type **30** | 45 | 15 |
| 69 | 15c. Blue-striped grunt | 60 | 15 |
| 70 | 40c. Nassau grouper | 75 | 20 |
| 71 | 50c. Banded butterflyfish | 80 | 20 |

**31** "Morning Glory"

**1970.** Flowers. Multicoloured.

| | | | |
|---|---|---|---|
| 72 | 10c. Type **31** | 25 | 10 |
| 73 | 15c. Blue petrea | 35 | 10 |
| 74 | 40c. Hibiscus | 50 | 20 |
| 75 | 50c. "Flame Tree" | 60 | 25 |

**32** "The Crucifixion" (Masaccio)

**1970.** Easter. Multicoloured.

| | | | |
|---|---|---|---|
| 76 | 10c. "The Ascent to Calvary" (Tiepolo) (horiz) | 15 | 10 |
| 77 | 20c. Type **32** | 20 | 10 |
| 78 | 40c. "Deposition" (Rosso Fiorentino) | 25 | 15 |
| 79 | 60c. "The Ascent to Calvary" (Murillo) (horiz) | 25 | 15 |

**33** Scout Badge and Map

**1970.** 40th Anniv of Scouting in Anguilla. Multicoloured.

| | | | |
|---|---|---|---|
| 80 | 10c. Type **33** | 15 | 15 |
| 81 | 15c. Scout camp, and cubs practising first aid | 20 | 20 |

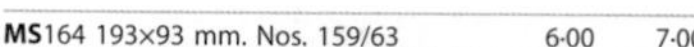

| No. | Description | Unused | Used |
|---|---|---|---|
| 82 | 40c. Monkey bridge | 25 | 30 |
| 83 | 50c. Scout H.Q. building and Lord Baden-Powell | 35 | 30 |

**34** Boatbuilding

**1970.** Multicoloured.. Multicoloured..

| No. | Description | Unused | Used |
|---|---|---|---|
| 84 | 1c. Type **34** | 30 | 40 |
| 85 | 2c. Road construction | 30 | 40 |
| 86 | 3c. Quay, Blowing Point | 30 | 20 |
| 87 | 4c. Broadcaster, Radio Anguilla | 30 | 50 |
| 88 | 5c. Cottage Hospital extension | 40 | 50 |
| 89 | 6c. Valley Secondary School | 30 | 50 |
| 90 | 10c. Hotel extension | 30 | 30 |
| 91 | 15c. Sandy Ground | 30 | 30 |
| 92 | 20c. Supermarket and cinema | 70 | 30 |
| 93 | 25c. Bananas and mangoes | 35 | 1·00 |
| 94 | 40c. Wall Blake Airport | 4·00 | 3·25 |
| 95 | 60c. Sandy Ground jetty | 65 | 3·50 |
| 96 | $1 Administration buildings | 1·25 | 1·40 |
| 97 | $2.50 Livestock | 1·50 | 4·00 |
| 98 | $5 Sandy Hill Bay | 3·25 | 3·75 |

**35** "The Adoration of the Shepherds" (Reni)

**1970.** Christmas. Multicoloured.

| No. | Description | Unused | Used |
|---|---|---|---|
| 99 | 1c. Type **35** | 10 | 10 |
| 100 | 20c. "The Virgin and Child" (Gozzoli) | 30 | 20 |
| 101 | 25c. "Mystic Nativity" (detail, Botticelli) | 30 | 20 |
| 102 | 40c. "The Santa Margherita Madonna" (detail, Mazzola) | 40 | 25 |
| 103 | 50c. "The Adoration of the Magi" (detail, Tiepolo) | 40 | 25 |

**36** "Ecce Homo" (detail, Correggio)

**1971.** Easter. Paintings. Multicoloured.

| No. | Description | Unused | Used |
|---|---|---|---|
| 104 | 10c. Type **36** | 25 | 10 |
| 105 | 15c. "Christ appearing to St Peter" (detail, Carracci) | 25 | 10 |
| 106 | 40c. "Angels weeping over the Dead Christ" (detail, Guercino) (horiz) | 30 | 10 |
| 107 | 50c. "The Supper at Emmaus" (detail, Caravaggio) (horiz) | 30 | 15 |

**37** "Hypolimnas misippus"

**1971.** Butterflies. Multicoloured.

| No. | Description | Unused | Used |
|---|---|---|---|
| 108 | 10c. Type **37** | 1·60 | 70 |
| 109 | 15c. "Junonia evarete" | 1·60 | 80 |
| 110 | 40c. "Agraulis vanillae" | 2·00 | 1·25 |
| 111 | 50c. "Danaus plexippus" | 2·00 | 1·50 |

**38** "Magnanime" and "Aimable" in Battle

**1971.** Sea-battles of the West Indies. Multicoloured.

| No. | Description | Unused | Used |
|---|---|---|---|
| 112 | 10c. Type **38** | 1·10 | 1·40 |
| 113 | 15c. H.M.S. "Duke", "Glorieux" and H.M.S. "Agamemnon" | 1·25 | 1·60 |
| 114 | 25c. H.M.S. "Formidable" and H.M.S. "Namur" against "Ville de Paris" | 1·50 | 1·75 |
| 115 | 40c. H.M.S. "Canada" | 1·60 | 1·90 |
| 116 | 50c. H.M.S. "St. Albans" and wreck of "Hector" | 1·75 | 2·00 |

Nos. 112/116 were issued together, se-tenant, forming a composite design.

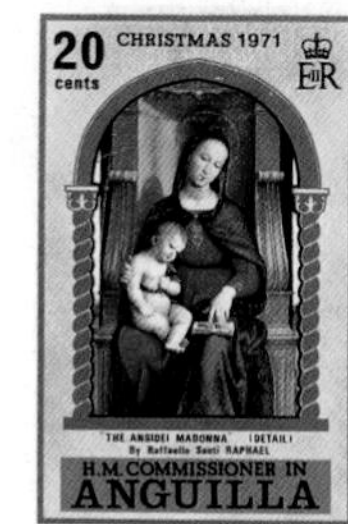


**39** "The Ansidei Madonna" (detail, Raphael)

**1971.** Christmas. Multicoloured.

| No. | Description | Unused | Used |
|---|---|---|---|
| 117 | 20c. Type **39** | 25 | 30 |
| 118 | 25c. "Mystic Nativity" (detail, Botticelli) | 25 | 30 |
| 119 | 40c. "Adoration of the Shepherds" (detail, ascr to Murillo) | 30 | 40 |
| 120 | 50c. "The Madonna of the Iris" (detail, ascr to Durer) | 35 | 70 |

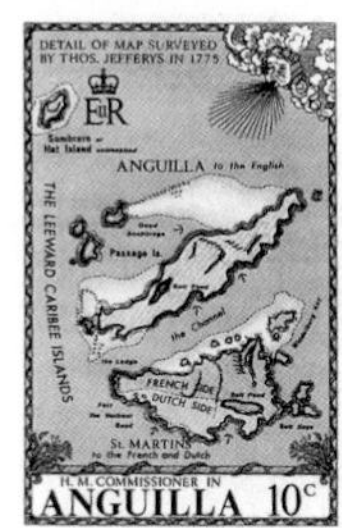


**40** Map of Anguilla and St. Martin by Thomas Jefferys, 1775

**1972.** Caribbean Maps depicting Anguilla. Multicoloured.

| No. | Description | Unused | Used |
|---|---|---|---|
| 121 | 10c. Type **40** | 25 | 10 |
| 122 | 15c. Samuel Fahlberg's Map, 1814 | 35 | 15 |
| 123 | 40c. Thomas Jefferys' Map, 1775 (horiz) | 50 | 25 |
| 124 | 50c. Captain E. Barnett's Map, 1847 (horiz) | 60 | 25 |

**41** "Jesus Buffeted"

**1972.** Easter. Multicoloured.

| No. | Description | Unused | Used |
|---|---|---|---|
| 125 | 10c. Type **41** | 25 | 25 |
| 126 | 15c. "The Way of Sorrows" | 30 | 30 |
| 127 | 25c. "The Crucifixion" | 30 | 30 |
| 128 | 40c. "Descent from the Cross" | 35 | 35 |
| 129 | 50c. "The Burial" | 40 | 40 |

**42** Loblolly Tree

**1972.** Multicoloured.. Multicoloured..

| No. | Description | Unused | Used |
|---|---|---|---|
| 130 | 1c. Spear fishing | 10 | 40 |
| 131 | 2c. Type **42** | 10 | 40 |
| 132 | 3c. Sandy Ground | 10 | 40 |
| 133 | 4c. Ferry at Blowing Point | 1·75 | 20 |
| 134 | 5c. Agriculture | 15 | 1·00 |
| 135 | 6c. St. Mary's Church | 25 | 20 |
| 136 | 10c. St. Gerard's Church | 25 | 40 |
| 137 | 15c. Cottage hospital extension | 25 | 30 |
| 138 | 20c. Public library | 30 | 35 |
| 139 | 25c. Sunset at Blowing Point | 40 | 2·00 |
| 140 | 40c. Boat building | 5·00 | 1·50 |
| 141 | 60c. Hibiscus | 4·00 | 4·00 |
| 142 | $1 Magnificent frigate bird ("Man-o'-War") | 10·00 | 8·00 |
| 143 | $2.50 Frangipani | 5·00 | 10·00 |
| 144 | $5 Brown pelican | 16·00 | 17·00 |
| 144a | $10 Green-back turtle | 15·00 | 18·00 |

**1972.** Royal Silver Wedding. As T **52** of Ascension, but with Schooner and Common dolphin in background.

| No. | Description | Unused | Used |
|---|---|---|---|
| 145 | 25c. green | 50 | 75 |
| 146 | 40c. brown | 50 | 75 |

**44** Flight into Egypt

**1972.** Christmas. Multicoloured.

| No. | Description | Unused | Used |
|---|---|---|---|
| 147 | 1c. Type **44** | 10 | 10 |
| 148 | 20c. Star of Bethlehem | 20 | 20 |
| 149 | 25c. Holy Family | 20 | 20 |
| 150 | 40c. Arrival of the Magi | 20 | 25 |
| 151 | 50c. Adoration of the Magi | 25 | 25 |

**45** "The Betrayal of Christ"

**1973.** Easter. Multicoloured.

| No. | Description | Unused | Used |
|---|---|---|---|
| 152 | 1c. Type **45** | 10 | 10 |
| 153 | 10c. "The Man of Sorrows" | 10 | 10 |
| 154 | 20c. "Christ bearing the Cross" | 10 | 15 |
| 155 | 25c. "The Crucifixion" | 15 | 15 |
| 156 | 40c. "The Descent from the Cross" | 15 | 15 |
| 157 | 50c. "The Resurrection" | 15 | 20 |
| **MS**158 | 140×141 mm. Nos. 152/7. Bottom panel in gold and mauve | 70 | 80 |

**46** "Santa Maria"

**1973.** Columbus Discovers the West Indies. Multicoloured.

| No. | Description | Unused | Used |
|---|---|---|---|
| 159 | 1c. Type **46** | 10 | 10 |
| 160 | 20c. Early map | 1·50 | 1·25 |
| 161 | 40c. Map of voyages | 1·60 | 1·40 |
| 162 | 70c. Sighting land | 1·90 | 1·75 |
| 163 | $1.20 Landing of Columbus | 2·50 | 2·25 |
| **MS**164 | 193×93 mm. Nos. 159/63 | 6·00 | 7·00 |

**47** Princess Anne and Captain Mark Phillips

**1973.** Royal Wedding. Multicoloured. Background colours given.

| No. | Type | Description | Unused | Used |
|---|---|---|---|---|
| 165 | **47** | 60c. green | 20 | 15 |
| 166 | **47** | $1.20 mauve | 30 | 15 |

**48** "The Adoration of the Shepherds" (Reni)

**1973.** Christmas. Multicoloured.

| No. | Description | Unused | Used |
|---|---|---|---|
| 167 | 1c. Type **48** | 10 | 10 |
| 168 | 10c. "The Madonna and Child with Saints Jerome and Dominic" (Filippino Lippi) | 10 | 10 |
| 169 | 20c. "The Nativity" (Master of Brunswick) | 15 | 15 |
| 170 | 25c. "Madonna of the Meadow" (Bellini) | 15 | 15 |
| 171 | 40c. "Virgin and Child" (Cima) | 20 | 20 |
| 172 | 50c. "Adoration of the Kings" (Geertgen) | 20 | 20 |
| **MS**173 | 148×149 mm. Nos. 167/72 | 80 | 1·60 |

**49** "The Crucifixion" (Raphael)

**1974.** Easter.

| No. | Type | Description | Unused | Used |
|---|---|---|---|---|
| 174 | **49** | 1c. multicoloured | 10 | 10 |
| 175 | - | 15c. multicoloured | 10 | 10 |
| 176 | - | 20c. multicoloured | 15 | 15 |
| 177 | - | 25c. multicoloured | 15 | 15 |
| 178 | - | 40c. multicoloured | 15 | 15 |
| 179 | - | $1 multicoloured | 20 | 25 |
| **MS**180 | | 123×141 mm. Nos. 174/9 | 1·00 | 1·25 |

DESIGNS: 15c. to $1, Details of Raphael's "Crucifixion".

**50** Churchill Making "Victory" Sign

**1974.** Birth Centenary of Sir Winston Churchill. Multicoloured.

| No. | Description | Unused | Used |
|---|---|---|---|
| 181 | 1c. Type **50** | 10 | 10 |
| 182 | 20c. Churchill with Roosevelt | 20 | 20 |
| 183 | 25c. Wartime broadcast | 20 | 20 |
| 184 | 40c. Birthplace, Blenheim Palace | 30 | 30 |
| 185 | 60c. Churchill's statue | 30 | 35 |
| 186 | $1.20 Country residence, Chartwell | 45 | 55 |
| **MS**187 | 195×96 mm. Nos. 181/6 | 1·40 | 2·50 |

**51** U.P.U. Emblem

**1974.** Centenary of U.P.U.

| | | | | |
|---|---|---|---|---|
| 188 | **51** | 1c. black and blue | 10 | 10 |
| 189 | **51** | 20c. black and orange | 15 | 15 |
| 190 | **51** | 25c. black and yellow | 15 | 15 |
| 191 | **51** | 40c. black and mauve | 20 | 25 |
| 192 | **51** | 60c. black and green | 30 | 40 |
| 193 | **51** | $1.20 black and blue | 50 | 60 |
| **MS**194 | | 195×96 mm. Nos. 188/93 | 1·25 | 2·25 |

**52** Anguillan pointing to Star

**1974.** Christmas. Multicoloured.

| | | | |
|---|---|---|---|
| 195 | 1c. Type **52** | 10 | 10 |
| 196 | 20c. Child in Manger | 10 | 20 |
| 197 | 25c. King's offering | 10 | 20 |
| 198 | 40c. Star over map of Anguilla | 15 | 20 |
| 199 | 60c. Family looking at star | 15 | 20 |
| 200 | $1.20 Angels of Peace | 20 | 30 |
| **MS**201 | 177×85 mm. Nos. 195/200 | 1·00 | 2·00 |

**53** "Mary, John and Mary Magdalene" (Matthias Grunewald)

**1975.** Easter. Details from Isenheim Altarpiece, Colmar Museum. Multicoloured.

| | | | |
|---|---|---|---|
| 202 | 1c. Type **53** | 10 | 10 |
| 203 | 10c. "The Crucifixion" | 15 | 15 |
| 204 | 15c. "St. John the Baptist" | 15 | 15 |
| 205 | 20c. "St. Sebastian and Angels" | 15 | 20 |
| 206 | $1 "The Entombment" (horiz) | 20 | 35 |
| 207 | $1.50 "St. Anthony the Hermit" | 25 | 45 |
| **MS**208 | 134×127 mm. Nos. 202/7 (imperf) | 1·00 | 2·00 |

**54** Statue of Liberty

**1975.** Bicentenary of American Revolution. Mult.

| | | | |
|---|---|---|---|
| 209 | 1c. Type **54** | 10 | 10 |
| 210 | 10c. The Capitol | 20 | 10 |
| 211 | 15c. "Congress voting for Independence" (Pine and Savage) | 30 | 15 |
| 212 | 20c. Washington and map | 30 | 15 |
| 213 | $1 Boston Tea Party | 45 | 40 |
| 214 | $1.50 Bicentenary logo | 50 | 60 |
| **MS**215 | 198×97 mm. Nos. 209/14 | 1·25 | 2·50 |

**55** "Madonna, Child and the Infant John the Baptist" (Raphael)

**1975.** Christmas. "Madonna and Child" paintings by artists named. Multicoloured.

| | | | |
|---|---|---|---|
| 216 | 1c. Type **55** | 10 | 10 |
| 217 | 10c. Cima | 15 | 15 |
| 218 | 15c. Dolci | 20 | 15 |
| 219 | 20c. Durer | 20 | 20 |
| 220 | $1 Bellini | 35 | 25 |
| 221 | $1.50 Botticelli | 45 | 35 |
| **MS**222 | 130×145 mm. Nos. 216/21 | 2·00 | 2·25 |

**1976.** New Constitution. Nos. 130 etc optd **NEW CONSTITUTION 1976** or surch also.

| | | | |
|---|---|---|---|
| 223 | 1c. Spear fishing | 30 | 40 |
| 224 | 2c. on 1c. Spear fishing | 30 | 40 |
| 225 | 2c. Type **42** | 7·50 | 1·75 |
| 226 | 3c. on 40c. Boat building | 75 | 70 |
| 227 | 4c. Ferry at Blowing Point | 1·00 | 1·00 |
| 228 | 5c. on 40c. Boat building | 30 | 50 |
| 229 | 6c. St. Mary's Church | 30 | 50 |
| 230 | 10c. on 20c. Public library | 30 | 50 |
| 231 | 10c. St. Gerard's Church | 7·50 | 4·75 |
| 232 | 15c. Cottage Hospital extension | 30 | 1·25 |
| 233 | 20c. Public library | 30 | 50 |
| 234 | 25c. Sunset at Blowing Point | 30 | 50 |
| 235 | 40c. Boat building | 1·00 | 70 |
| 236 | 60c. Hibiscus | 70 | 70 |
| 237 | $1 Magnificent frigate bird | 6·50 | 2·25 |
| 238 | $2.50 Frangipani | 2·25 | 2·25 |
| 239 | $5 Brown pelican | 8·00 | 8·50 |
| 240 | $10 Green-back turtle | 3·00 | 6·00 |

**57** Almond

**1976.** Flowering Trees. Multicoloured.

| | | | |
|---|---|---|---|
| 241 | 1c. Type **57** | 10 | 10 |
| 242 | 10c. Autograph | 20 | 20 |
| 243 | 15c. Calabash | 20 | 20 |
| 244 | 20c. Cordia | 20 | 20 |
| 245 | $1 Papaya | 30 | 45 |
| 246 | $1.50 Flamboyant | 35 | 55 |
| **MS**247 | 194×99 mm. Nos. 241/6 | 1·50 | 2·00 |

**58** The Three Marys

**1976.** Easter. Showing portions of the Altar Frontal Tapestry, Rheinau. Multicoloured.

| | | | |
|---|---|---|---|
| 248 | 1c. Type **58** | 10 | 10 |
| 249 | 10c. The Crucifixion | 10 | 10 |
| 250 | 15c. Two Soldiers | 15 | 15 |
| 251 | 20c. The Annunciation | 15 | 15 |
| 252 | $1 The complete tapestry (horiz) | 65 | 65 |
| 253 | $1.50 The Risen Christ | 80 | 80 |
| **MS**254 | 138×130 mm. Nos. 248/53 (imperf) | 1·75 | 2·10 |

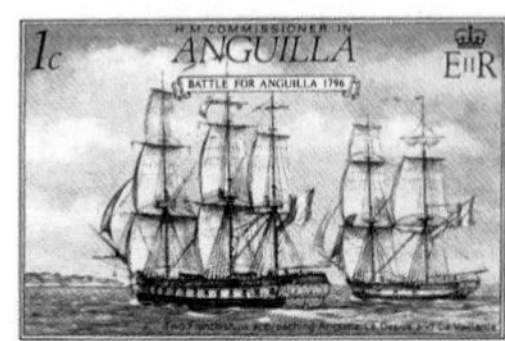


**59** French Ships approaching Anguilla

**1976.** Bicentenary of Battle of Anguilla. Mult.

| | | | |
|---|---|---|---|
| 255 | 1c. Type **59** | 10 | 10 |
| 256 | 3c. "Margaret" (sloop) leaving Anguilla | 1·25 | 35 |
| 257 | 15c. Capture of "Le Desius" | 1·50 | 55 |
| 258 | 25c. "La Vaillante" forced aground | 1·50 | 80 |
| 259 | $1 H.M.S. "Lapwing" | 2·00 | 1·25 |
| 260 | $1.50 "Le Desius" burning | 2·25 | 1·75 |
| **MS**261 | 205×103 mm. Nos. 255/60 | 7·50 | 6·00 |

**60** "Christmas Carnival" (A. Richardson)

**1976.** Christmas. Children's Paintings. Mult.

| | | | |
|---|---|---|---|
| 262 | 1c. Type **60** | 10 | 10 |
| 263 | 3c. "Dreams of Christmas Gifts" (J. Connor) | 10 | 10 |
| 264 | 15c. "Carolling" (P. Richardson) | 15 | 15 |
| 265 | 25c. "Candle-light Procession" (A. Mussington) | 20 | 20 |
| 266 | $1 "Going to Church" (B. Franklin) | 30 | 30 |
| 267 | $1.50 "Coming Home for Christmas" (E. Gumbs) | 40 | 40 |
| **MS**268 | 232×147 mm. Nos. 262/7 | 1·50 | 1·75 |

**61** Prince Charles and H.M.S. "Minerva" (frigate)

**1977.** Silver Jubilee. Multicoloured.

| | | | |
|---|---|---|---|
| 269 | 25c. Type **61** | 15 | 10 |
| 270 | 40c. Prince Philip landing by launch at Road Bay, 1964 | 15 | 10 |
| 271 | $1.20 Coronation scene | 20 | 20 |
| 272 | $2.50 Coronation regalia and map of Anguilla | 25 | 30 |
| **MS**273 | 145×96 mm. Nos. 269/72 | 65 | 90 |

**62** Yellow-crowned Night Heron

**1977.** Multicoloured.. Multicoloured..

| | | | |
|---|---|---|---|
| 274 | 1c. Type **62** | 30 | 1·25 |
| 275 | 2c. Great barracuda | 30 | 2·50 |
| 276 | 3c. Queen or pink conch | 2·00 | 3·25 |
| 277 | 4c. Spanish bayonet (flower) | 40 | 70 |
| 278 | 5c. Honeycomb trunkfish | 1·50 | 30 |
| 279 | 6c. Cable and Wireless building | 30 | 30 |
| 280 | 10c. American kestrel ("American Sparrow Hawk") | 5·00 | 3·00 |
| 281 | 15c. Ground orchid | 2·75 | 1·75 |
| 282 | 20c. Stop-light parrotfish | 3·25 | 75 |
| 283 | 22c. Lobster fishing boat | 50 | 60 |
| 284 | 35c. Boat race | 1·40 | 70 |
| 285 | 50c. Sea bean | 90 | 50 |
| 286 | $1 Sandy Island | 60 | 50 |
| 287 | $2.50 Manchineel | 1·00 | 1·00 |
| 288 | $5 Ground lizard | 2·00 | 1·75 |
| 289 | $10 Red-billed tropic bird | 9·00 | 4·25 |

**63** "The Crucifixion" (Massys)

**1977.** Easter. Paintings by Castagno ($1.50) or Ugolino (others). Multicoloured.

| | | | |
|---|---|---|---|
| 291 | 1c. Type **63** | 10 | 10 |
| 292 | 3c. "The Betrayal" | 10 | 10 |
| 293 | 22c. "The Way to Calvary" | 20 | 20 |
| 294 | 30c. "The Deposition" | 25 | 25 |
| 295 | $1 "The Resurrection" | 50 | 50 |
| 296 | $1.50 "The Crucifixion" | 65 | 65 |
| **MS**297 | 192×126 mm. Nos. 291/6 | 1·60 | 1·75 |

**1977.** Royal Visit. Nos. 269/72 optd **ROYAL VISIT TO WEST INDIES.**

| | | | |
|---|---|---|---|
| 298 | 25c. Type **61** | 10 | 10 |
| 299 | 40c. Prince Philip landing at Road Bay, 1964 | 10 | 15 |
| 300 | $1.20 Coronation scene | 20 | 25 |
| 301 | $1.50 Coronation regalia and map of Anguilla | 25 | 35 |
| **MS**302 | 145×96 mm. Nos. 298/301 | 80 | 60 |

**65** "Le Chapeau de Paille"

**1977.** 400th Birth Anniv of Rubens. Multicoloured.

| | | | |
|---|---|---|---|
| 303 | 25c. Type **65** | 15 | 15 |
| 304 | 40c. "Helene Fourment and her Two Children" | 20 | 25 |
| 305 | $1.20 "Rubens and his Wife" | 60 | 65 |
| 306 | $2.50 "Marchesa Brigida Spinola-Doria" | 75 | 95 |
| **MS**307 | 90×145 mm. Nos. 303/6 | 2·00 | 2·10 |

**1977.** Christmas. Nos. 262/7 with old date blocked out and additionally inscr "1977", some also surch.

| | | | |
|---|---|---|---|
| 308 | 1c. Type **60** | 10 | 10 |
| 309 | 5c. on 3c. "Dreams of Christmas Gifts" | 10 | 10 |
| 310 | 12c. on 15c. "Carolling" | 15 | 15 |
| 311 | 18c. on 25c. "Candle-light Procession" | 20 | 20 |
| 312 | $1 "Going to Church" | 45 | 45 |
| 313 | $2.50 on $1.50 "Coming Home for Christmas" | 90 | 90 |
| **MS**314 | 232×147 mm. Nos. 308/13 | 2·50 | 2·50 |

**1978.** Easter. Nos. 303/6 optd **EASTER 1978.**

| | | | |
|---|---|---|---|
| 315 | 25c. Type **65** | 15 | 20 |
| 316 | 40c. "Helene Fourment with her Two Children" | 15 | 20 |
| 317 | $1.20 "Rubens and his Wife" | 35 | 40 |
| 318 | $2.50 "Marchesa Brigida Spinola-Doria" | 45 | 60 |
| **MS**319 | 93×145 mm. Nos. 315/18 | 1·25 | 1·50 |

**68** Coronation Coach at Admiralty Arch

**1978.** 25th Anniv of Coronation. Multicoloured.

| | | | |
|---|---|---|---|
| 320 | 22c. Buckingham Palace | 10 | 10 |
| 321 | 50c. Type **68** | 10 | 10 |
| 322 | $1.50 Balcony scene | 15 | 15 |
| 323 | $2.50 Royal coat of arms | 25 | 25 |
| **MS**324 | 138×92 mm. Nos. 320/3 | 60 | 60 |

**1978.** Anniversaries. Nos. 283/4 and 287 optd **VALLEY SECONDARY SCHOOL 1953–1978** and Nos. 285/6 and 288 optd **ROAD METHODIST CHURCH 1878–1978,** or surch also.

| | | | |
|---|---|---|---|
| 325 | 22c. Lobster fishing boat | 20 | 15 |
| 326 | 35c. Boat race | 30 | 20 |
| 327 | 50c. Sea bean | 30 | 30 |
| 328 | $1 Sandy Island | 35 | 40 |
| 329 | $1.20 on $5 Ground lizard | 40 | 45 |
| 330 | $1.50 on $2.50 Manchineel | 45 | 55 |

**71** Mother and Child

**1978.** Christmas. Children's Paintings. Mult.

| | | | |
|---|---|---|---|
| 331 | 5c. Type **71** | 10 | 10 |
| 332 | 12c. Christmas masquerade | 15 | 10 |
| 333 | 18c. Christmas dinner | 15 | 10 |
| 334 | 22c. Serenading | 15 | 10 |
| 335 | $1 Child in manger | 45 | 20 |
| 336 | $2.50 Family going to church | 90 | 40 |
| **MS**337 | 191×101 mm. Nos. 331/6 | 1·60 | 1·75 |

**1979.** International Year of the Child. As Nos. 331/6, but additionally inscr "1979 INTERNATIONAL YEAR OF THE CHILD" and emblem. Borders in different colours.

| | | | |
|---|---|---|---|
| 338 | 5c. Type **71** | 10 | 10 |
| 339 | 12c. Christmas masquerade | 10 | 10 |
| 340 | 18c. Christmas dinner | 10 | 10 |
| 341 | 22c. Serenading | 10 | 10 |
| 342 | $1 Child in manger | 30 | 30 |
| 343 | $2.50 Family going to church | 50 | 50 |
| **MS**344 | 205×112 mm. Nos. 338/43 | 2·25 | 2·50 |

**1979.** Nos. 274/7 and 279/80 surch.

| | | | |
|---|---|---|---|
| 345 | 12c. on 2c. Great barracuda | 50 | 50 |
| 346 | 14c. on 4c. Spanish bayonet | 40 | 50 |
| 347 | 18c. on 3c. Queen conch | 80 | 55 |
| 348 | 25c. on 6c. Cable and Wireless building | 55 | 50 |
| 349 | 38c. on 10c. American kestrel | 2·50 | 70 |
| 350 | 40c. on 1c. Type **62** | 2·50 | 70 |

**73** Valley Methodist Church

**1979.** Easter. Church Interiors. Multicoloured.

| | | | |
|---|---|---|---|
| 351 | 5c. Type **73** | 10 | 10 |
| 352 | 12c. St. Mary's Anglican Church, The Valley | 10 | 10 |
| 353 | 18c. St. Gerard's Roman Catholic Church, The Valley | 15 | 15 |
| 354 | 22c. Road Methodist Church | 15 | 15 |
| 355 | $1.50 St. Augustine's Anglican Church, East End | 60 | 60 |
| 356 | $2.50 West End Methodist Church | 75 | 75 |
| **MS**357 | 190×105 mm. Nos. 351/6 | 1·75 | 2·25 |

**74** Cape of Good Hope 1d. "Woodblock" of 1881

**1979.** Death Centenary of Sir Rowland Hill. Multicoloured.

| | | | |
|---|---|---|---|
| 358 | 1c. Type **74** | 10 | 10 |
| 359 | 1c. U.S.A. "inverted Jenny" of 1918 | 10 | 10 |
| 360 | 22c. Penny Black ("V.R." Official) | 15 | 15 |
| 361 | 35c. Germany 2m, "Graf Zeppelin" of 1928 | 20 | 20 |
| 362 | $1.50 U.S.A. $5 "Columbus" of 1893 | 40 | 60 |
| 363 | $2.50 Great Britain £5 orange of 1882 | 60 | 95 |
| **MS**364 | 187×123 mm. Nos. 358/63 | 1·25 | 2·40 |

**75** Wright "Flyer I" (1st powered Flight, 1903)

**1979.** History of Powered Flight. Multicoloured.

| | | | |
|---|---|---|---|
| 365 | 5c. Type **75** | 20 | 10 |
| 366 | 12c. Louis Bleriot at Dover after Channel crossing, 1909 | 25 | 10 |
| 367 | 18c. Vickers FB-27 Vimy (1st non-stop crossing of Atlantic, 1919) | 30 | 15 |
| 368 | 22c. Ryan NYP Special "Spirit of St Louis" (1st solo Atlantic flight by Charles Lindbergh, 1927) | 30 | 20 |
| 369 | $1.50 Airship LZ 127 "Graf Zeppelin", 1928 | 65 | 60 |
| 370 | $2.50 Concorde, 1979 | 3·25 | 90 |
| **MS**371 | 200×113 mm. Nos. 365/70 | 3·50 | 3·25 |

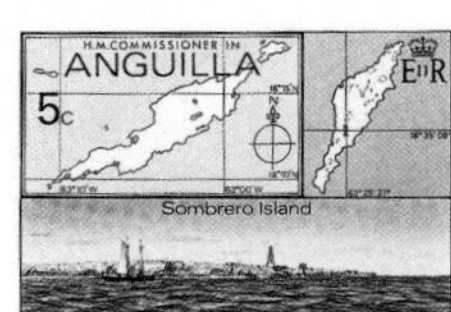


**76** Sombrero Island

**1979.** Outer Islands. Multicoloured.

| | | | |
|---|---|---|---|
| 372 | 5c. Type **76** | 15 | 10 |
| 373 | 12c. Anguillita Island | 15 | 10 |
| 374 | 18c. Sandy Island | 15 | 15 |
| 375 | 25c. Prickly Pear Cays | 15 | 15 |
| 376 | $1 Dog Island | 40 | 40 |
| 377 | $2.50 Scrub Island | 60 | 70 |
| **MS**378 | 180×91 mm. Nos. 372/7 | 2·75 | 2·25 |

**77** Red Poinsettia

**1979.** Christmas. Multicoloured.

| | | | |
|---|---|---|---|
| 379 | 22c. Type **77** | 15 | 20 |
| 380 | 35c. Kalanchoe | 20 | 30 |
| 381 | $1.50 Cream poinsettia | 40 | 50 |
| 382 | $2.50 White poinsettia | 60 | 70 |
| **MS**383 | 146×164 mm. Nos. 379/82 | 1·75 | 2·25 |

**78** Exhibition Scene

**1979.** "London 1980" International Stamp Exhibition (1st issue). Multicoloured.

| | | | |
|---|---|---|---|
| 384 | 35c. Type **78** | 15 | 20 |
| 385 | 50c. Earls Court Exhibition Centre | 15 | 25 |
| 386 | $1.50 Penny Black and Two-penny Blue stamps | 25 | 60 |
| 387 | $2.50 Exhibition Logo | 45 | 95 |
| **MS**388 | 150×94 mm. Nos. 384/7 | 1·40 | 2·00 |

See also Nos. 407/9.

**79** Games Site

**1980.** Winter Olympic Games, Lake Placid, U.S.A. Multicoloured.

| | | | |
|---|---|---|---|
| 389 | 5c. Type **79** | 10 | 10 |
| 390 | 18c. Ice hockey | 20 | 10 |
| 391 | 35c. Ice skating | 20 | 20 |
| 392 | 50c. Bobsleighing | 20 | 20 |
| 393 | $1 Skiing | 20 | 35 |
| 394 | $2.50 Luge-tobogganing | 40 | 80 |
| **MS**395 | 136×128 mm. Nos. 389/94 | 1·00 | 2·00 |

**80** Salt ready for "Reaping"

**1980.** Salt Industry. Multicoloured.

| | | | |
|---|---|---|---|
| 396 | 5c. Type **80** | 10 | 10 |
| 397 | 12c. Tallying salt | 10 | 10 |
| 398 | 18c. Unloading salt flats | 15 | 15 |
| 399 | 22c. Salt storage heap | 15 | 15 |
| 400 | $1 Salt for bagging and grinding | 30 | 40 |
| 401 | $2.50 Loading salt for export | 50 | 70 |
| **MS**402 | 180×92 mm. Nos. 396/401 | 1·10 | 1·75 |

**1980.** Anniversaries. Nos. 280, 282 and 287/8 optd **50th Anniversary Scouting 1980** (10c., $2.50) or **75th Anniversary Rotary 1980** (others).

| | | | |
|---|---|---|---|
| 403 | 10c. American kestrel | 1·75 | 15 |
| 404 | 20c. Stop-light parrotfish | 1·00 | 20 |
| 405 | $2.50 Manchineel | 1·75 | 1·25 |
| 406 | $5 Ground lizard | 2·50 | 1·90 |

**83** Palace of Westminster and Great Britain 1970 9d. "Philympia" Commemoration

**1980.** "London 1980" International Stamp Exhibition (2nd issue). Multicoloured.

| | | | |
|---|---|---|---|
| 407 | 50c. Type **83** | 55 | 75 |
| 408 | $1.50 City Hall, Toronto and "Capex 1978" stamp of Canada | 85 | 1·25 |
| 409 | $2.50 Statue of Liberty and 1976 "Interphil" stamp of U.S.A. | 1·10 | 1·40 |
| **MS**410 | 157×130 mm. Nos. 407/9 | 2·25 | 3·00 |

**84** Queen Elizabeth the Queen Mother

**1980.** 80th Birthday of The Queen Mother.

| | | | | |
|---|---|---|---|---|
| 411 | **84** | 35c. multicoloured | 70 | 40 |
| 412 | **84** | 50c. multicoloured | 85 | 50 |
| 413 | **84** | $1.50 multicoloured | 1·50 | 1·50 |
| 414 | **84** | $3 multicoloured | 2·25 | 2·50 |
| **MS**415 | | 160×110 mm. Nos. 411/14 | 5·50 | 4·75 |

**85** Brown Pelicans ("Pelican")

**1980.** Christmas. Birds. Multicoloured.

| | | | |
|---|---|---|---|
| 416 | 5c. Type **85** | 30 | 10 |
| 417 | 22c. Great blue heron ("Great Grey Heron") | 75 | 20 |
| 418 | $1.50 Barn swallow ("Swallow") | 1·75 | 60 |
| 419 | $3 Ruby-throated hummingbird ("Hummingbird") | 2·25 | 1·40 |
| **MS**420 | 126×160 mm. Nos. 416/19 | 10·00 | 7·50 |

**1980.** Separation from St. Kitts. Nos. 274, 277, 280/9, 334 and 418/19 optd **SEPARATION 1980** or surch also.

| | | | |
|---|---|---|---|
| 421 | 1c. Type **62** | 20 | 80 |
| 422b | 2c. on 4c. Spanish bayonet | 20 | 80 |
| 423 | 5c. on 15c. Ground orchid | 1·50 | 80 |
| 424 | 5c. on $1.50 Barn swallow | 1·50 | 80 |
| 425 | 5c. on $3 Ruby-throated hummingbird | 1·50 | 80 |
| 426 | 10c. American kestrel | 1·75 | 80 |
| 427 | 12c. on $1 Sandy Island | 20 | 80 |
| 428 | 14c. on $2.50 Manchineel | 20 | 80 |
| 429 | 15c. Ground orchid | 1·50 | 80 |
| 430 | 18c. on $5 Ground lizard | 25 | 80 |
| 431 | 20c. Stop-light parrotfish | 25 | 80 |
| 432 | 22c. Lobster fishing boat | 25 | 80 |
| 433 | 25c. on 15c. Ground orchid | 1·50 | 85 |
| 434 | 35c. Boat race | 30 | 85 |
| 435 | 38c. on 22c. Serenading | 30 | 85 |
| 436 | 40c. on 1c. Type **62** | 30 | 85 |
| 437 | 50c. Sea bean | 35 | 95 |
| 438 | $1 Sandy Island | 50 | 1·25 |
| 439 | $2.50 Manchineel | 1·25 | 3·00 |
| 440 | $5 Ground lizard | 2·25 | 4·00 |
| 441 | $10 Red-billed tropic bird | 5·00 | 6·00 |
| 442 | $10 on 6c. Cable and Wireless Building | 5·00 | 6·00 |

**87** First Petition for Separation, 1825

**1980.** Separation from St. Kitts. Multicoloured.

| | | | |
|---|---|---|---|
| 443 | 18c. Type **87** | 10 | 10 |
| 444 | 22c. Referendum ballot paper, 1967 | 15 | 10 |
| 445 | 35c. Airport blockade, 1967 | 30 | 15 |
| 446 | 50c. Anguillan flag | 60 | 20 |
| 447 | $1 Separation celebration, 1980 | 40 | 35 |
| **MS**448 | 178×92 mm. Nos. 443/7 | 1·40 | 1·25 |

**88** "Nelson's Dockyard" (R. Granger Barrett)

**1981.** 175th Death Anniv of Lord Nelson. Mult.

| | | | |
|---|---|---|---|
| 449 | 22c. Type **88** | 2·50 | 50 |
| 450 | 35c. "Ships in which Nelson Served" (Nicholas Pocock) | 2·50 | 70 |
| 451 | 50c. "H.M.S. Victory" (Monamy Swaine) | 3·00 | 1·50 |
| 452 | $3 "Battle of Trafalgar" (Clarkson Stanfield) | 3·75 | 6·50 |
| **MS**453 | 82×63 mm. $5 "Horatio Nelson" (L. F. Abbott) and coat of arms | 3·00 | 3·25 |

**89** Minnie Mouse being chased by Bees

**1981.** Easter. Walt Disney Cartoon Characters. Multicoloured.

| | | | |
|---|---|---|---|
| 454 | 1c. Type **89** | 10 | 10 |
| 455 | 2c. Pluto laughing at Mickey Mouse | 10 | 10 |
| 456 | 3c. Minnie Mouse tying ribbon round Pluto's neck | 10 | 10 |
| 457 | 5c. Minnie Mouse confronted by love-struck bird who fancies her bonnet | 10 | 10 |
| 458 | 7c. Dewey and Huey admiring themselves in mirror | 10 | 10 |
| 459 | 9c. Horace Horsecollar and Clarabelle Cow out for a stroll | 10 | 10 |
| 460 | 10c. Daisy Duck with hat full of Easter eggs | 10 | 10 |
| 461 | $2 Goofy unwrapping Easter hat | 1·40 | 1·40 |
| 462 | $3 Donald Duck in his Easter finery | 1·60 | 1·60 |
| **MS**463 | 134×108 mm. $5 Chip and Dale making off with hat | 3·50 | 3·50 |

**90** Prince Charles, Lady Diana Spencer and St. Paul's Cathedral

**1981.** Royal Wedding. Multicoloured.

| | | | |
|---|---|---|---|
| 464 | 50c. Type **90** | 15 | 20 |
| 465 | $2.50 Althorp | 30 | 50 |
| 466 | $3 Windsor Castle | 35 | 60 |
| **MS**467 | 90×72 mm. Buckingham Palace | 1·25 | 1·50 |

**91** Children playing in Tree

**1981.** 35th Anniv of UNICEF Multicoloured.

| | | | |
|---|---|---|---|
| 470 | 5c. Type **91** | 20 | 30 |
| 471 | 10c. Children playing by pool | 20 | 30 |
| 472 | 15c. Children playing musical instruments | 20 | 30 |
| 473 | $3 Children playing with pets | 2·50 | 3·00 |
| **MS**474 | 78×106 mm. Children playing football (vert) | 3·50 | 5·00 |

**1981.** Christmas. Designs as T **89** showing scenes from Walt Disney's cartoon film "The Night before Christmas".

| | | | |
|---|---|---|---|
| 475 | 1c. multicoloured | 10 | 10 |
| 476 | 2c. multicoloured | 10 | 10 |
| 477 | 3c. multicoloured | 10 | 10 |
| 478 | 5c. multicoloured | 15 | 10 |
| 479 | 7c. multicoloured | 15 | 10 |
| 480 | 10c. multicoloured | 15 | 10 |
| 481 | 12c. multicoloured | 15 | 10 |
| 482 | $2 multicoloured | 3·75 | 1·25 |

| | | | |
|---|---|---|---|
| 483 | $3 multicoloured | 3·75 | 1·60 |
| **MS**484 | 130×105 mm. $5 multicoloured | 5·50 | 3·50 |

**92** Red Grouper

**1982.** Multicoloured.. Multicoloured..

| | | | |
|---|---|---|---|
| 485 | 1c. Type **92** | 15 | 1·00 |
| 486 | 5c. Ferry service, Blowing Point | 30 | 1·00 |
| 487 | 10c. Island dinghies | 20 | 60 |
| 488 | 15c. Majorettes | 20 | 60 |
| 489 | 20c. Launching boat, Sandy Hill | 40 | 60 |
| 490 | 25c. Corals | 1·50 | 60 |
| 491 | 30c. Little Bay cliffs | 30 | 75 |
| 492 | 35c. Fountain Cave interior | 1·50 | 80 |
| 493 | 40c. Sunset over Sandy Island | 30 | 75 |
| 494 | 45c. Landing at Sombrero | 50 | 80 |
| 495 | 60c. Seine fishing | 3·25 | 3·25 |
| 496 | 75c. Boat race at sunset, Sandy Ground | 1·00 | 2·00 |
| 497 | $1 Bagging lobster at Island Harbour | 2·25 | 2·00 |
| 498 | $5 Brown pelicans | 16·00 | 13·00 |
| 499 | $7.50 Hibiscus | 11·00 | 15·00 |
| 500 | $10 Queen triggerfish | 16·00 | 15·00 |

**1982.** No. 494 surch **50c.**

| | | | |
|---|---|---|---|
| 501 | 50c. on 45c. Landing at Sombrero | 50 | 35 |

**94** Anthurium and "Heliconius charithonia"

**1982.** Easter. Flowers and Butterflies. Multicoloured.

| | | | |
|---|---|---|---|
| 502 | 10c. Type **94** | 1·10 | 15 |
| 503 | 35c. Bird of paradise and "Junonia evarete" | 2·00 | 40 |
| 504 | 75c. Allamanda and "Danaus plexippus" | 2·25 | 70 |
| 505 | $3 Orchid tree and "Biblis hyperia" | 3·50 | 2·25 |
| **MS**506 | 65×79 mm. $5 Amaryllis and "Dryas julia" | 2·75 | 3·50 |

**95** Lady Diana Spencer in 1961

**1982.** 21st Birthday of Princess of Wales. Mult.

| | | | |
|---|---|---|---|
| 507 | 10c. Type **95** | 50 | 20 |
| 508 | 30c. Lady Diana Spencer in 1968 | 1·75 | 25 |
| 509 | 40c. Lady Diana in 1970 | 50 | 30 |
| 510 | 60c. Lady Diana in 1974 | 55 | 35 |
| 511 | $2 Lady Diana in 1981 | 80 | 1·10 |
| 512 | $3 Lady Diana in 1981 (different) | 5·50 | 1·40 |
| **MS**513 | 72×90 mm. $5 Princess of Wales | 7·50 | 3·00 |
| **MS**514 | 125×125 mm. As Nos. 507/12, but with buff borders | 8·50 | 6·50 |

**96** Pitching Tent

**1982.** 75th Anniv of Boy Scout Movement. Multicoloured.

| | | | |
|---|---|---|---|
| 515 | 10c. Type **96** | 45 | 20 |
| 516 | 35c. Scout band | 85 | 50 |
| 517 | 75c. Yachting | 1·25 | 90 |
| 518 | $3 On parade | 3·00 | 2·75 |
| **MS**519 | 90×72 mm. $5 Cooking | 4·50 | 4·00 |

**1982.** World Cup Football Championship, Spain. Horiz designs as T **89** showing scenes from Walt Disney's cartoon film "Bedknobs and Broomsticks".

| | | | |
|---|---|---|---|
| 520 | 1c. multicoloured | 10 | 10 |
| 521 | 3c. multicoloured | 10 | 10 |
| 522 | 4c. multicoloured | 10 | 10 |
| 523 | 5c. multicoloured | 10 | 10 |
| 524 | 7c. multicoloured | 10 | 10 |
| 525 | 9c. multicoloured | 10 | 10 |
| 526 | 10c. multicoloured | 10 | 10 |
| 527 | $2.50 multicoloured | 2·25 | 1·75 |
| 528 | $3 multicoloured | 2·25 | 2·00 |
| **MS**529 | 126×101 mm. $5 multicoloured | 9·00 | 8·50 |

**1982.** Commonwealth Games, Brisbane. Nos. 487, 495/6 and 498 optd **COMMONWEALTH GAMES 1982.**

| | | | |
|---|---|---|---|
| 530 | 10c. Island dinghies | 15 | 25 |
| 531 | 60c. Seine fishing | 45 | 60 |
| 532 | 75c. Boat race at sunset, Sandy Ground | 60 | 80 |
| 533 | $5 Brown pelicans | 3·25 | 3·75 |

**1982.** Birth Cent of A. A. Milne (author). As T **89**.

| | | | |
|---|---|---|---|
| 534 | 1c. multicoloured | 25 | 20 |
| 535 | 2c. multicoloured | 25 | 20 |
| 536 | 3c. multicoloured | 25 | 20 |
| 537 | 5c. multicoloured | 35 | 20 |
| 538 | 7c. multicoloured | 35 | 25 |
| 539 | 10c. multicoloured | 50 | 15 |
| 540 | 12c. multicoloured | 60 | 20 |
| 541 | 20c. multicoloured | 90 | 25 |
| 542 | $5 multicoloured | 9·00 | 9·50 |
| **MS**543 | 120×93 mm. $5 multicoloured | 7·50 | 9·00 |

DESIGNS—HORIZ: 1c. to $5 Scenes from various "Winnie the Pooh" stories.

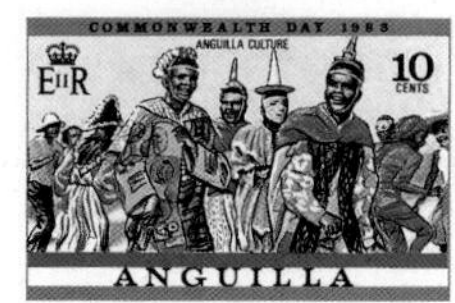


**98** Culture

**1983.** Commonwealth Day. Multicoloured.

| | | | |
|---|---|---|---|
| 544 | 10c. Type **98** | 10 | 15 |
| 545 | 35c. Anguilla and British flags | 30 | 30 |
| 546 | 75c. Economic co-operation | 60 | 1·00 |
| 547 | $2.50 Salt industry (salt pond) | 3·75 | 4·50 |
| **MS**548 | 76×61 mm. World map showing positions of Commonwealth countries | 2·50 | 2·50 |

**99** "I am the Lord Thy God"

**1983.** Easter. The Ten Commandments. Mult.

| | | | |
|---|---|---|---|
| 549 | 1c. Type **99** | 10 | 10 |
| 550 | 2c. "Thou shalt not make any graven image" | 10 | 10 |
| 551 | 3c. "Thou shalt not take My Name in vain" | 10 | 10 |
| 552 | 10c. "Remember the Sabbath Day" | 25 | 10 |
| 553 | 35c. "Honour thy father and mother" | 65 | 20 |
| 554 | 60c. "Thou shalt not kill" | 1·00 | 40 |
| 555 | 75c. "Thou shalt not commit adultery" | 1·25 | 50 |
| 556 | $2 "Thou shalt not steal" | 2·75 | 1·50 |
| 557 | $2.50 "Thou shalt not bear false witness" | 3·00 | 1·50 |
| 558 | $5 "Thou shalt not covet" | 4·25 | 2·75 |
| **MS**559 | 126×102 mm. $5 "Moses receiving the Tablets" (16th-century woodcut) | 2·75 | 3·00 |

**100** Leatherback Turtle

**1983.** Endangered Species. Turtles. Multicoloured.

| | | | |
|---|---|---|---|
| 560 | 10c. Type **100** | 3·50 | 80 |
| 561 | 35c. Hawksbill turtle | 6·50 | 1·25 |
| 562 | 75c. Green turtle | 7·50 | 3·50 |
| 563 | $1 Loggerhead turtle | 8·50 | 7·50 |
| **MS**564 | 93×72 mm. $5 Leatherback turtle (different) | 22·00 | 4·00 |

**101** Montgolfier Hot Air Balloon, 1783

**1983.** Bicentenary of Manned Flight. Multicoloured.

| | | | |
|---|---|---|---|
| 565 | 10c. Type **101** | 50 | 50 |
| 566 | 60c. Blanchard and Jefferies crossing English Channel by balloon, 1785 | 1·25 | 85 |
| 567 | $1 Henri Giffard's steam-powered dirigible airship, 1852 | 1·75 | 1·50 |
| 568 | $2.50 Otto Lillienthal and biplane glider, 1890–96 | 2·50 | 3·00 |
| **MS**569 | 72×90 mm. $5 Wilbur Wright flying round Statue of Liberty, 1909 | 2·75 | 3·50 |

**102** Boys' Brigade Band and Flag

**1983.** Centenary of Boys' Brigade. Multicoloured.

| | | | |
|---|---|---|---|
| 570 | 10c. Type **102** | 50 | 15 |
| 571 | $5 Brigade members marching | 3·50 | 2·75 |
| **MS**572 | 96×115 mm. Nos. 570/1 | 3·25 | 4·50 |

**1983.** 150th Anniv of Abolition of Slavery (1st issue). Nos. 487, 493 and 497/8 optd **150TH ANNIVERSARY ABOLITION OF SLAVERY ACT.**

| | | | |
|---|---|---|---|
| 573 | 10c. Island dinghies | 20 | 10 |
| 574 | 40c. Sunset over Sandy Island | 30 | 25 |
| 575 | $1 Bagging lobster at Island Harbour | 70 | 50 |
| 576 | $5 Brown pelicans | 8·50 | 2·75 |

See also Nos. 616/23.

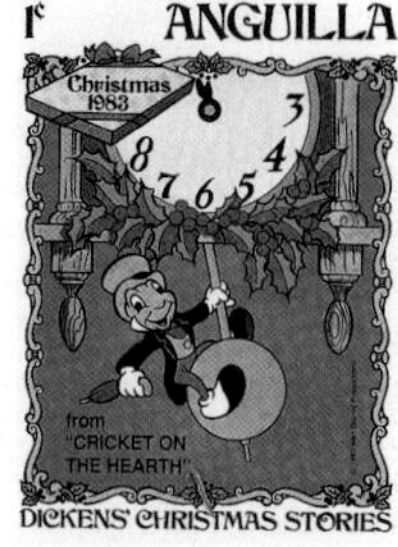


**104** Jiminy on Clock ("Cricket on the Hearth")

**1983.** Christmas. Walt Disney Cartoon Characters. Multicoloured.

| | | | |
|---|---|---|---|
| 577 | 1c. Type **104** | 10 | 10 |
| 578 | 2c. Jiminy with fiddle ("Cricket on the Hearth") | 10 | 10 |
| 579 | 3c. Jiminy among toys ("Cricket on the Hearth") | 10 | 10 |
| 580 | 4c. Mickey as Bob Cratchit ("A Christmas Carol") | 10 | 10 |
| 581 | 5c. Donald Duck as Scrooge ("A Christmas Carol") | 10 | 10 |
| 582 | 6c. Mini and Goofy in "The Chimes" | 10 | 10 |
| 583 | 10c. Goofy sees an imp appearing from bells ("The Chimes") | 10 | 10 |
| 584 | $2 Donald Duck as Mr. Pickwick ("The Pickwick Papers") | 3·25 | 2·75 |
| 585 | $3 Disney characters as Pickwickians ("The Pickwick Papers") | 3·75 | 2·25 |
| **MS**586 | 130×104 mm. Donald Duck as Mr. Pickwick with gifts ("The Pickwick Papers") | 10·00 | 11·00 |

**105** 100 Metres Race

**1984.** Olympic Games, Los Angeles. Multicoloured. (A) Inscr "1984 Los Angeles".

| | | | |
|---|---|---|---|
| 587A | 1c. Type **105** | 10 | 10 |
| 588A | 2c. Long jumping | 10 | 10 |
| 589A | 3c. Shot-putting | 10 | 10 |
| 590A | 4c. High jumping | 10 | 10 |
| 591A | 5c. 400 metres race | 10 | 10 |
| 592A | 6c. Hurdling | 10 | 10 |
| 593A | 10c. Discus-throwing | 10 | 10 |
| 594A | $1 Pole-vaulting | 3·25 | 1·25 |
| 595A | $4 Javelin-throwing | 6·00 | 3·50 |
| **MS**596A | 117×93 mm. $5 1500 metres race | 7·50 | 4·50 |

(B) Inscr "1984 Olympics Los Angeles" and Olympic emblem.

| | | | |
|---|---|---|---|
| 587B | 1c. Type **105** | 10 | 10 |
| 588B | 2c. Long jumping | 10 | 10 |
| 589B | 3c. Shot-putting | 10 | 10 |
| 590B | 4c. High jumping | 10 | 10 |
| 591B | 5c. 400 metres race | 10 | 10 |
| 592B | 6c. Hurdling | 10 | 10 |
| 593B | 10c. Discus-throwing | 10 | 10 |
| 594B | $1 Pole-vaulting | 3·75 | 3·00 |
| 595B | $4 Javelin-throwing | 7·50 | 8·50 |
| **MS**596B | 117×93 mm. $5 1500 metres race | 7·50 | 4·50 |

**106** "Justice"

**1984.** Easter. Multicoloured.

| | | | |
|---|---|---|---|
| 597 | 10c. Type **106** | 15 | 10 |
| 598 | 25c. "Poetry" | 20 | 20 |
| 599 | 35c. "Philosophy" | 30 | 30 |
| 600 | 40c. "Theology" | 30 | 30 |
| 601 | $1 "Abraham and Paul" | 85 | 95 |
| 602 | $2 "Moses and Matthew" | 1·60 | 2·25 |
| 603 | $3 "John and David" | 2·25 | 3·00 |
| 604 | $4 "Peter and Adam" | 2·50 | 3·00 |
| **MS**605 | 83×110 mm. $5 "Astronomy" | 3·50 | 3·00 |

Nos. 597/605 show details from "La Stanza della Segnatura" by Raphael.

**1984.** Nos. 485, 491, 498/500 surch.

| | | | |
|---|---|---|---|
| 606 | 25c. on $7.50 Hibiscus | 65 | 35 |
| 607 | 35c. on 30c. Little Bay cliffs | 50 | 40 |
| 608 | 60c. on 1c. Type **92** | 55 | 45 |
| 609 | $2.50 on $5 Brown pelicans | 3·00 | 1·50 |
| 610 | $2.50 on $10 Queen triggerfish | 1·75 | 1·50 |

**108** 1913 1d. Kangaroo Stamp

**1984.** "Ausipex 84" International Stamp Exhibition. Multicoloured.

| | | | |
|---|---|---|---|
| 611 | 10c. Type **108** | 40 | 30 |
| 612 | 75c. 1914 6d. Laughing Kookaburra | 1·25 | 1·25 |
| 613 | $1 1932 2d. Sydney Harbour Bridge | 1·75 | 1·75 |
| 614 | $2.50 1938 10s. King George VI | 2·25 | 3·75 |
| **MS**615 | 95×86 mm. $5 £1 Bass and £2 Admiral King | 5·00 | 7·00 |

**109** Thomas Fowell Buxton

**1984.** 150th Anniv of Abolition of Slavery (2nd issue). Multicoloured.

| | | | |
|---|---|---|---|
| 616 | 10c. Type **109** | 10 | 10 |
| 617 | 25c. Abraham Lincoln | 25 | 25 |
| 618 | 35c. Henri Christophe | 35 | 35 |
| 619 | 60c. Thomas Clarkson | 50 | 50 |
| 620 | 75c. William Wilberforce | 60 | 60 |
| 621 | $1 Olaudah Equiano | 70 | 70 |
| 622 | $2.50 General Charles Gordon | 1·60 | 1·60 |
| 623 | $5 Granville Sharp | 3·00 | 3·00 |
| **MS**624 | 150×121 mm. Nos. 616/23 | 7·50 | 10·00 |

**1984.** Universal Postal Union Congress, Hamburg. Nos. 486/7 and 498 optd **U.P.U. CONGRESS HAMBURG 1984** or surch also (No 626).

| | | | |
|---|---|---|---|
| 625 | 5c. Ferry service, Blowing Point | 30 | 10 |
| 626 | 20c. on 10c. Island dinghies | 30 | 15 |
| 627 | $5 Brown pelicans | 5·50 | 3·50 |

**1984.** Birth of Prince Henry. Nos. 507/12 optd **PRINCE HENRY BIRTH 15.9.84.**

| | | | |
|---|---|---|---|
| 628 | 10c. Type **95** | 20 | 10 |
| 629 | 30c. Lady Diana Spencer in 1968 | 40 | 25 |
| 630 | 40c. Lady Diana in 1970 | 20 | 30 |
| 631 | 60c. Lady Diana in 1974 | 30 | 45 |
| 632 | $2 Lady Diana in 1981 | 75 | 1·25 |
| 633 | $3 Lady Diana in 1981 (different) | 1·25 | 1·75 |
| **MS**634 | 72×90 mm. $5 Princess of Wales | 2·00 | 3·00 |
| **MS**635 | 125×125 mm. As Nos. 628/33, but with buff borders | 2·50 | 4·00 |

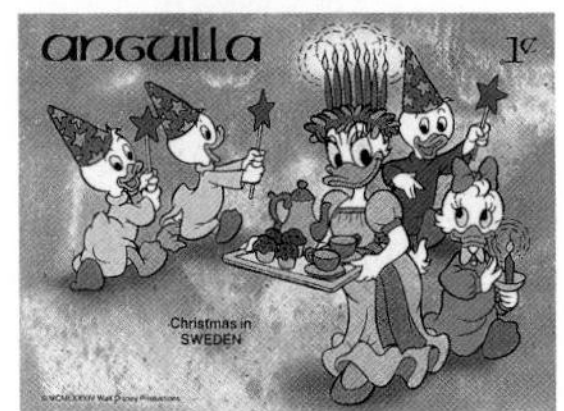

**112** Christmas in Sweden

**1984.** Christmas. Walt Disney Cartoon Characters. National Scenes. Multicoloured.

| | | | |
|---|---|---|---|
| 636 | 1c. Type **112** | 10 | 10 |
| 637 | 2c. Italy | 10 | 10 |
| 638 | 3c. Holland | 10 | 10 |
| 639 | 4c. Mexico | 10 | 10 |
| 640 | 5c. Spain | 10 | 10 |
| 641 | 10c. Disneyland, U.S.A. | 10 | 10 |
| 642 | $1 Japan | 3·00 | 2·00 |
| 643 | $2 Anguilla | 4·00 | 4·75 |
| 644 | $4 Germany | 6·50 | 8·00 |
| **MS**645 | 126×102 mm. $5 England | 7·00 | 5·00 |

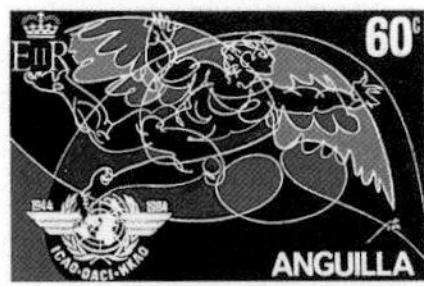

**113** Icarus in Flight

**1984.** 40th Anniv of International Civil Aviation Authority. Multicoloured.

| | | | |
|---|---|---|---|
| 646 | 60c. Type **113** | 60 | 75 |
| 647 | 75c. "Solar Princess" (abstract) | 80 | 90 |
| 648 | $2.50 I.C.A.O. emblem (vert) | 2·25 | 3·00 |
| **MS**649 | 65×49 mm. $5 Map of air routes serving Anguilla | 3·00 | 4·50 |

**114** Barn Swallow

**1985.** Birth Bicentenary of John J. Audubon (ornithologist). Multicoloured.

| | | | |
|---|---|---|---|
| 650 | 10c. Type **114** | 80 | 65 |
| 651 | 60c. American wood stork ("Woodstork") | 1·50 | 1·25 |
| 652 | 75c. Roseate tern | 1·50 | 1·25 |
| 653 | $5 Osprey | 4·50 | 6·00 |
| **MS**654 | Two sheets, each 73×103 mm. $4 Western tanager (horiz); (b) $4 Solitary vireo (horiz) Set of 2 sheets | 8·50 | 5·00 |

**115** The Queen Mother visiting King's College Hospital, London

**1985.** Life and Times of Queen Elizabeth the Queen Mother. Multicoloured.

| | | | |
|---|---|---|---|
| 655 | 10c. Type **115** | 10 | 10 |
| 656 | $2 The Queen Mother inspecting Royal Marine Volunteer Cadets, Deal | 80 | 1·25 |
| 657 | $3 The Queen Mother outside Clarence House | 1·10 | 1·50 |
| **MS**658 | 56×85 mm. $5 At Ascot, 1979 | 1·75 | 2·50 |

**116** White-tailed Tropic Bird

**1985.** Birds. Multicoloured.

| | | | |
|---|---|---|---|
| 659 | 5c. Brown pelican | 1·75 | 1·75 |
| 660 | 10c. Mourning dove ("Turtle Dove") | 1·75 | 1·75 |
| 661 | 15c. Magnificent frigate bird (inscr "Man-o-War") | 1·75 | 1·75 |
| 662 | 20c. Antillean crested hummingbird | 1·75 | 1·75 |
| 663 | 25c. Type **116** | 1·75 | 1·75 |
| 664 | 30c. Caribbean elaenia | 1·75 | 1·75 |
| 665 | 35c. Black-whiskered vireo | 7·50 | 5·00 |
| 665a | 35c. Lesser Antillean bullfinch | 3·00 | 1·75 |
| 666 | 40c. Yellow-crowned night heron | 1·75 | 1·75 |
| 667 | 45c. Pearly-eyed thrasher | 1·75 | 1·75 |
| 668 | 50c. Laughing gull | 1·75 | 1·75 |
| 669 | 65c. Brown booby | 1·75 | 1·75 |
| 670 | 80c. Grey kingbird | 2·25 | 3·00 |
| 671 | $1 Audubon's shearwater | 2·25 | 3·00 |
| 672 | $1.35 Roseate tern | 1·75 | 3·00 |
| 673 | $2.50 Bananaquit | 5·50 | 8·00 |
| 674 | $5 Belted kingfisher | 4·25 | 8·00 |
| 675 | $10 Green-backed heron ("Green Heron") | 7·00 | 10·00 |

**1985.** 75th Anniv of Girl Guide Movement. Nos. 486, 491, 496 and 498 optd **GIRL GUIDES 75TH ANNIVERSARY 1910–1985** and anniversary emblem.

| | | | |
|---|---|---|---|
| 676 | 5c. Ferry service, Blowing Point | 30 | 30 |
| 677 | 30c. Little Bay cliffs | 40 | 35 |
| 678 | 75c. Boat race at sunset, Sandy Ground | 60 | 85 |
| 679 | $5 Brown pelicans | 9·00 | 8·50 |

**118** Goofy as Huckleberry Finn Fishing

**1985.** 150th Birth Anniv of Mark Twain (author). Walt Disney cartoon characters in scenes from "Huckleberry Finn". Multicoloured.

| | | | |
|---|---|---|---|
| 680 | 10c. Type **118** | 70 | 20 |
| 681 | 60c. Pete as Pap surprising Huck | 2·25 | 85 |
| 682 | $1 "Multiplication tables" | 2·75 | 1·25 |
| 683 | $3 The Duke reciting Shakespeare | 4·00 | 4·00 |
| **MS**684 | 127×102 mm. $5 "In school but out" | 8·50 | 8·00 |

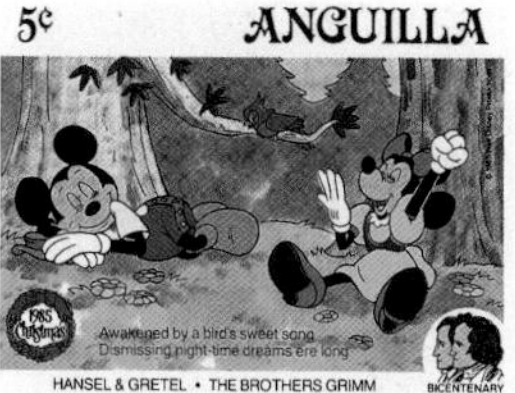

**119** Hansel and Gretel (Mickey and Minnie Mouse) awakening in Forest

**1985.** Birth Bicentenaries of Grimm Brothers (folklorists). Designs showing Walt Disney cartoon characters in scenes from "Hansel and Gretel". Multicoloured.

| | | | |
|---|---|---|---|
| 685 | 5c. Type **119** | 55 | 55 |
| 686 | 50c. Hansel and Gretel find the gingerbread house | 1·50 | 60 |
| 687 | 90c. Hansel and Gretel meeting the Witch | 2·00 | 1·00 |
| 688 | $4 Hansel and Gretel captured by the Witch | 3·50 | 5·00 |
| **MS**689 | 128×101 mm. $5 Hansel and Gretel riding on swan | 8·00 | 9·00 |

**120** Statue of Liberty and "Danmark" (Denmark)

**1985.** Centenary of the Statue of Liberty (1986). The Statue of Liberty and Cadet ships.

| | | | |
|---|---|---|---|
| 690 | 10c. Type **120** | 1·00 | 85 |
| 691 | 20c. "Eagle" (U.S.A.) | 1·25 | 90 |
| 692 | 60c. "Amerigo Vespucci" (Italy) | 1·60 | 1·50 |
| 693 | 75c. "Sir Winston Churchill" (Great Britain) | 1·60 | 1·50 |
| 694 | $2 "Nippon Maru" (Japan) | 1·75 | 4·00 |
| 695 | $2.50 "Gorch Fock" (West Germany) | 1·75 | 4·00 |
| **MS**696 | 96×69 mm. $5 Statue of Liberty (vert) | 7·00 | 4·50 |

**1985.** 80th Anniv of Rotary (10, 35c.) and International Youth Year (others). Nos. 487, 491 and 497 optd or surch **80TH ANNIVERSARY ROTARY 1985** and emblem (10, 35c.) or **INTERNATIONAL YOUTH YEAR** and emblem ($1, $5).

| | | | |
|---|---|---|---|
| 697 | 10c. Island dinghies | 25 | 15 |
| 698 | 35c. on 30c. Little Bay cliffs | 55 | 30 |
| 699 | $1 Bagging lobster at Island Harbour | 1·25 | 80 |
| 700 | $5 on 30c. Little Bay cliffs | 4·00 | 4·50 |

**123** Johannes Hevelius (astronomer) and Mayan Temple Observatory

**1986.** Appearance of Halley's Comet. Multicoloured.

| | | | |
|---|---|---|---|
| 701 | 5c. Type **123** | 55 | 55 |
| 702 | 10c. "Viking Lander" space vehicle on Mars, 1976 | 55 | 55 |
| 703 | 60c. Comet in 1664 (from "Theatri Cosmicum", 1668) | 1·50 | 85 |
| 704 | $4 Comet over Mississippi riverboat, 1835 (150th birth anniv of Mark Twain) | 4·50 | 5·00 |
| **MS**705 | 101×70 mm. $5 Halley's Comet over Anguilla | 4·50 | 6·00 |

**124** "The Crucifixion"

**1986.** Easter.

| | | | | |
|---|---|---|---|---|
| 706 | **124** | 10c. multicoloured | 20 | 20 |
| 707 | - | 25c. multicoloured | 35 | 35 |
| 708 | - | 45c. multicoloured | 65 | 65 |
| 709 | - | $4 multicoloured | 3·25 | 3·75 |
| **MS**710 | - | 93×75 mm. $5 multicoloured (horiz) | 5·50 | 7·50 |

DESIGNS: 25c. to $5 Different stained glass windows from Chartres Cathedral.

**125** Princess Elizabeth inspecting Guards, 1946

**1986.** 60th Birthday of Queen Elizabeth II.

| | | | | |
|---|---|---|---|---|
| 711 | **125** | 20c. black and yellow | 40 | 20 |
| 712 | - | $2 multicoloured | 1·75 | 1·50 |
| 713 | - | $3 multicoloured | 1·75 | 1·75 |
| **MS**714 | - | 120×85 mm. $5 black and brown | 2·75 | 3·75 |

DESIGNS: $2 Queen at Garter Ceremony; $3 At Trooping the Colour; $5 Duke and Duchess of York with baby Princess Elizabeth, 1926.

**1986.** "Ameripex" International Stamp Exhibition, Chicago. Nos. 659, 667, 671, 673 and 675 optd **AMERIPEX 1986.**

| | | | |
|---|---|---|---|
| 715 | 5c. Brown pelican | 60 | 75 |
| 716 | 45c. Pearly-eyed thrasher | 1·25 | 45 |
| 717 | $1 Audubon's shearwater | 2·00 | 1·10 |
| 718 | $2.50 Bananaquit | 2·75 | 3·00 |
| 719 | $10 Green-backed heron | 6·50 | 8·50 |

**127** Prince Andrew and Miss Sarah Ferguson

**1986.** Royal Wedding. Multicoloured.

| | | | |
|---|---|---|---|
| 720 | 10c. Type **127** | 50 | 15 |
| 721 | 35c. Prince Andrew | 85 | 35 |
| 722 | $2 Miss Sarah Ferguson | 2·25 | 1·50 |
| 723 | $3 Prince Andrew and Miss Sarah Ferguson (diffferent) | 2·50 | 2·00 |
| **MS**724 | 119×90 mm. $6 Westminster Abbey | 5·50 | 6·50 |

**1986.** International Peace Year. Nos. 616/23 optd **INTERNATIONAL YEAR OF PEACE.**

| | | | |
|---|---|---|---|
| 725 | 10c. Type **109** | 90 | 60 |
| 726 | 25c. Abraham Lincoln | 1·25 | 50 |
| 727 | 35c. Henri Christophe | 1·40 | 55 |
| 728 | 60c. Thomas Clarkson | 2·00 | 80 |
| 729 | 75c. William Wilberforce | 2·00 | 1·00 |
| 730 | $1 Olaudah Equiano | 2·00 | 1·25 |
| 731 | $2.50 General Gordon | 3·50 | 4·75 |
| 732 | $5 Granville Sharp | 4·25 | 7·00 |
| **MS**733 | 150×121 mm. Nos. 725/32 | 15·00 | 17·00 |

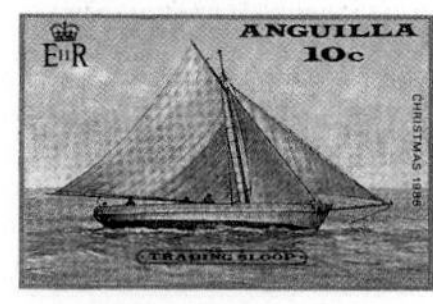

**129** Trading Sloop

**1986.** Christmas. Ships. Multicoloured.

| | | | |
|---|---|---|---|
| 734 | 10c. Type **129** | 1·75 | 60 |
| 735 | 45c. "Lady Rodney" (cargo liner) | 3·25 | 1·10 |
| 736 | 80c. "West Derby" (19th-century sailing ship) | 4·25 | 2·50 |
| 737 | $3 "Warspite" (local sloop) | 8·50 | 10·00 |
| **MS**738 | 130×100 mm. $4 Boat-race day (vert) | 17·00 | 19·00 |

**130** Christopher Columbus with Astrolabe

**1986.** 500th Anniv (1992) of Discovery of America by Columbus (1st issue). Multicoloured.

| | | | |
|---|---|---|---|
| 739 | 5c. Type **130** | 60 | 60 |
| 740 | 10c. Columbus on board ship | 1·00 | 60 |

| | | | |
|---|---|---|---|
| 741 | 35c. "Santa Maria" | 2·10 | 1·10 |
| 742 | 80c. King Ferdinand and Queen Isabella of Spain (horiz) | 1·50 | 1·75 |
| 743 | $4 Caribbean Indians smoking tobacco (horiz) | 3·25 | 5·00 |
| MS744 | Two sheets, each 96×66 mm. (a) $5 Caribbean manatee (horiz). (b) $5 Dragon tree Set of 2 sheets | 15·00 | 17·00 |

See also Nos. 902/6.

**131** "Danaus plexippus"

**1987.** Easter. Butterflies. Multicoloured.

| | | | |
|---|---|---|---|
| 745 | 10c. Type **131** | 1·50 | 70 |
| 746 | 80c. "Anartia jatrophae" | 4·00 | 2·75 |
| 747 | $1 "Heliconius charithonia" | 4·25 | 2·75 |
| 748 | $2 "Junonia evarete" | 7·00 | 8·50 |
| MS749 | 90×69 mm. $6 "Dryas julia" | 11·00 | 13·00 |

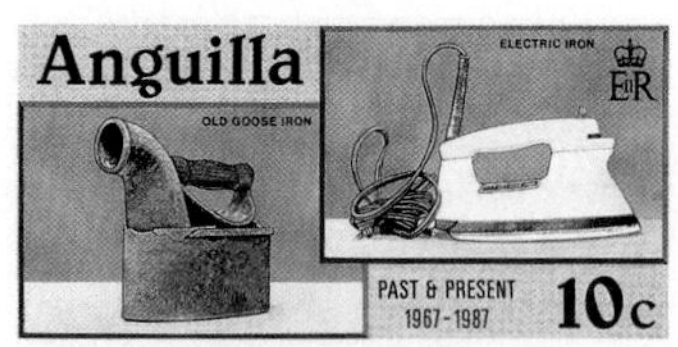


**132** Old Goose Iron and Modern Electric Iron

**1987.** 20th Anniv of Separation from St. Kitts-Nevis. Multicoloured.

| | | | |
|---|---|---|---|
| 750 | 10c. Type **132** | 70 | 40 |
| 751 | 35c. Old East End School and Albena Lake-Hodge Comprehensive College | 75 | 45 |
| 752 | 45c. Past and present markets | 85 | 50 |
| 753 | 80c. Previous sailing ferry and new motor ferry, Blowing Point | 2·50 | 1·25 |
| 754 | $1 Original mobile post office and new telephone exchange | 2·50 | 1·40 |
| 755 | $2 Open-air meeting, Burrowes Park and House of Assembly in session | 2·75 | 3·25 |
| MS756 | 159×127 mm. Nos. 750/5 | 12·00 | 15·00 |

**1987.** "Capex '87" International Stamp Exhibition, Toronto. Nos. 665a, 667, 670 and 675 optd **CAPEX'87.**

| | | | |
|---|---|---|---|
| 757 | 35c. Lesser Antillean bullfinch | 2·25 | 80 |
| 758 | 45c. Pearly-eyed thrasher | 2·25 | 80 |
| 759 | 80c. Grey kingbird | 3·25 | 1·25 |
| 760 | $10 Green-backed heron | 11·00 | 13·00 |

**1987.** 20th Anniv of Independence. Nos. 659, 661/4 and 665a/75 optd **20 YEARS OF PROGRESS 1967–1987,** No. 762 surch also.

| | | | |
|---|---|---|---|
| 761 | 5c. Brown pelican | 2·75 | 2·75 |
| 762 | 10c. on 15c. Magnificent frigate bird | 2·75 | 2·75 |
| 763 | 15c. Magnificent frigate bird | 3·00 | 3·00 |
| 764 | 20c. Antillean crested hummingbird | 3·00 | 3·00 |
| 765 | 25c. Type **116** | 3·00 | 3·00 |
| 766 | 30c. Caribbean elaenia | 3·00 | 3·00 |
| 767 | 35c. Lesser Antillean bullfinch | 3·00 | 3·00 |
| 768 | 40c. Yellow-crowned night heron | 3·00 | 3·00 |
| 769 | 45c. Pearly-eyed thrasher | 3·00 | 3·00 |
| 770 | 50c. Laughing gull | 3·00 | 3·00 |
| 771 | 65c. Brown booby | 3·25 | 3·25 |
| 772 | 80c. Grey kingbird | 3·25 | 3·25 |
| 773 | $1 Audubon's shearwater | 3·25 | 3·25 |
| 774 | $1.35 Roseate tern | 3·75 | 4·00 |
| 775 | $2.50 Bananaquit | 4·50 | 6·00 |
| 776 | $5 Belted kingfisher | 6·00 | 8·50 |
| 777 | $10 Green-backed heron | 8·00 | 11·00 |

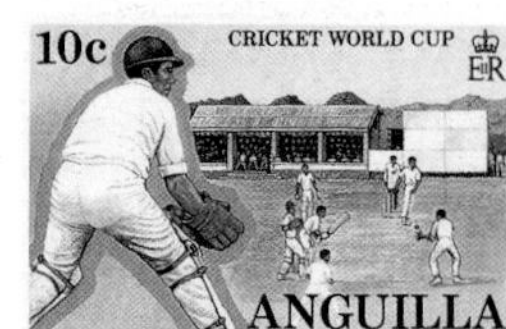


**135** Wicket Keeper and Game in Progress

**1987.** Cricket World Cup. Multicoloured.

| | | | |
|---|---|---|---|
| 778 | 10c. Type **135** | 2·25 | 80 |
| 779 | 35c. Batsman and local Anguilla team | 2·25 | 70 |
| 780 | 45c. Batsman and game in progress | 2·75 | 75 |
| 781 | $2.50 Bowler and game in progress | 5·00 | 8·50 |
| MS782 | 100×75 mm. $6 Batsman and game in progress (different) | 15·00 | 16·00 |

**136** West Indian Top Shell

**1987.** Christmas. Sea Shells and Crabs. Mult.

| | | | |
|---|---|---|---|
| 783 | 10c. Type **136** | 1·50 | 55 |
| 784 | 35c. Ghost crab | 2·25 | 60 |
| 785 | 50c. Spiny Caribbean vase | 3·00 | 1·40 |
| 786 | $2 Great land crab | 6·00 | 8·00 |
| MS787 | 101×75 mm. $6 Queen or pink conch | 12·00 | 13·00 |

**1987.** Royal Ruby Wedding. Nos. 665a, 671/2 and 675 optd **40TH WEDDING ANNIVERSARY H.M. QUEEN ELIZABETH II H.R.H. THE DUKE OF EDINBURGH.**

| | | | |
|---|---|---|---|
| 788 | 35c. Lesser Antillean bullfinch | 1·50 | 55 |
| 789 | $1 Audubon's shearwater | 2·25 | 80 |
| 790 | $1.35 Roseate tern | 2·50 | 90 |
| 791 | $10 Green-backed heron | 6·50 | 8·50 |

**138** "Crinum erubescens"

**1988.** Easter. Lilies. Multicoloured.

| | | | |
|---|---|---|---|
| 792 | 30c. Type **138** | 60 | 25 |
| 793 | 45c. Spider lily | 70 | 25 |
| 794 | $1 "Crinum macowanii" | 1·75 | 85 |
| 795 | $2.50 Day lily | 2·00 | 3·00 |
| MS796 | 100×75 mm. $6 Easter lily | 2·75 | 4·50 |

**139** Relay Racing

**1988.** Olympic Games, Seoul. Multicoloured.

| | | | |
|---|---|---|---|
| 797 | 35c. Type **139** | 45 | 30 |
| 798 | 45c. Windsurfing | 55 | 45 |
| 799 | 50c. Tennis | 1·50 | 1·10 |
| 800 | 80c. Basketball | 6·50 | 2·75 |
| MS801 | 104×78 mm. $6 Athletics | 3·00 | 4·50 |

**140** Common Sea Fan

**1988.** Christmas. Marine Life. Multicoloured.

| | | | |
|---|---|---|---|
| 802 | 35c. Type **140** | 1·00 | 30 |
| 803 | 80c. Coral crab | 1·75 | 70 |
| 804 | $1 Grooved brain coral | 2·00 | 1·00 |
| 805 | $1.60 Queen triggerfish | 2·75 | 3·25 |
| MS806 | 103×78 mm. $6 West Indian spiny lobster | 3·00 | 4·50 |

**1988.** Visit of Princess Alexandra. Nos. 665a, 670/1 and 673 optd **H.R.H. PRINCESS ALEXANDRA'S VISIT NOVEMBER 1988.**

| | | | |
|---|---|---|---|
| 807 | 35c. Lesser Antillean bullfinch | 2·50 | 70 |
| 808 | 80c. Grey kingbird | 3·25 | 1·40 |
| 809 | $1 Audubon's shearwater | 3·25 | 1·60 |
| 810 | $2.50 Bananaquit | 5·00 | 5·50 |

**142** Wood Slave

**1989.** Lizards. Multicoloured.

| | | | |
|---|---|---|---|
| 811 | 45c. Type **142** | 1·75 | 50 |
| 812 | 80c. Slippery back | 2·50 | 85 |
| 813 | $2.50 "Iguana delicatissima" | 4·50 | 4·75 |
| MS814 | 101×75 mm. $6 Tree lizard | 14·00 | 4·75 |

**143** "Christ Crowned with Thorns" (detail) (Bosch)

**1989.** Easter. Religious Paintings. Multicoloured.

| | | | |
|---|---|---|---|
| 815 | 35c. Type **143** | 80 | 25 |
| 816 | 80c. "Christ bearing the Cross" (detail) (Gerard David) | 1·25 | 75 |
| 817 | $1 "The Deposition" (detail) (Gerard David) | 1·40 | 80 |
| 818 | $1.60 "Pieta" (detail) (Rogier van der Weyden) | 2·00 | 2·75 |
| MS819 | 103×77 mm. $6 "Crucified Christ with the Virgin Mary and Saints" (detail) (Raphael) | 2·75 | 4·25 |

**144** University Arms

**1989.** 40th Anniv of University of the West Indies.

| | | | | |
|---|---|---|---|---|
| 820 | **144** | $5 multicoloured | 3·75 | 4·25 |

**1989.** 20th Anniv of First Manned Landing on Moon. Nos. 670/2 and 674 optd **20TH ANNIVERSARY MOON LANDING.**

| | | | |
|---|---|---|---|
| 821 | 80c. Grey kingbird | 2·75 | 90 |
| 822 | $1 Audubon's shearwater | 2·75 | 1·00 |
| 823 | $1.35 Roseate tern | 3·00 | 1·75 |
| 824 | $5 Belted kingfisher | 7·50 | 10·00 |

**146** Lone Star (house), 1930

**1989.** Christmas. Historic Houses. Multicoloured.

| | | | |
|---|---|---|---|
| 825 | 5c. Type **146** | 50 | 1·00 |
| 826 | 35c. Whitehouse, 1906 | 1·00 | 45 |
| 827 | 45c. Hodges House | 1·10 | 50 |
| 828 | 80c. Warden's Place | 1·75 | 1·75 |
| MS829 | 102×77 mm. $6 Wallblake House, 1787 | 3·75 | 6·00 |

**147** Bigeye ("Blear Eye")

**1990.** Fish. Multicoloured.

| | | | |
|---|---|---|---|
| 830B | 5c. Type **147** | 60 | 75 |
| 831B | 10c. Long-spined squirrelfish ("Redman") | 60 | 75 |
| 832A | 15c. Stop-light parrotfish ("Speckletail") | 60 | 60 |
| 833A | 25c. Blue-striped grunt | 70 | 80 |
| 834A | 30c. Yellow jack | 70 | 80 |
| 835B | 35c. Red hind | 75 | 75 |
| 836A | 40c. Spotted goatfish | 90 | 80 |
| 837A | 45c. Queen triggerfish ("Old wife") | 90 | 60 |
| 838A | 50c. Coney ("Butter fish") | 90 | 80 |
| 839A | 65c. Smooth trunkfish ("Shell fish") | 1·00 | 80 |
| 840A | 80c. Yellow-tailed snapper | 1·25 | 90 |
| 841A | $1 Banded butterflyfish ("Katy") | 1·25 | 1·00 |
| 842A | $1.35 Nassau grouper | 1·50 | 1·50 |
| 843A | $2.50 Blue tang ("Doctor fish") | 2·25 | 3·50 |
| 844A | $5 Queen angelfish | 3·00 | 5·00 |
| 845A | $10 Great barracuda | 4·75 | 8·00 |

**148** The Last Supper

**1990.** Easter. Multicoloured.

| | | | |
|---|---|---|---|
| 846 | 35c. Type **148** | 1·25 | 40 |
| 847 | 45c. The Trial | 1·25 | 40 |
| 848 | $1.35 The Crucifixion | 3·00 | 2·25 |
| 849 | $2.50 The Empty Tomb | 3·50 | 5·00 |
| MS850 | 114×84 mm. $6 The Resurrection | 11·00 | 13·00 |

**149** G.B. 1840 Penny Black

**1990.** "Stamp World London 90" International Stamp Exhibition. Multicoloured.

| | | | |
|---|---|---|---|
| 851 | 25c. Type **149** | 1·25 | 35 |
| 852 | 50c. G.B. 1840 Twopenny Blue | 1·75 | 50 |
| 853 | $1.50 Cape of Good Hope 1861 1d. "woodblock" (horiz) | 3·00 | 3·25 |
| 854 | $2.50 G.B. 1882 £5 (horiz) | 3·50 | 4·25 |
| MS855 | 86×71 mm. $6 Penny Black and Twopence Blue (horiz) | 12·00 | 15·00 |

**1990.** Anniversaries and Events. Nos. 841/4 optd.

| | | | |
|---|---|---|---|
| 856 | $1 Banded butterflyfish (optd **EXPO '90**) | 1·50 | 1·00 |
| 857 | $1.35 Nassau grouper (optd **1990 INTERNATIONAL LITERACY YEAR**) | 1·60 | 1·25 |
| 858 | $2.50 Blue tang (optd **WORLD CUP FOOTBALL CHAMPIONSHIPS 1990**) | 6·00 | 6·00 |
| 859 | $5 Queen angelfish (optd **90TH BIRTHDAY H.M. THE QUEEN MOTHER**) | 11·00 | 11·00 |

**151** Mermaid Flag

**1990.** Island Flags. Multicoloured.

| | | | |
|---|---|---|---|
| 860 | 50c. Type **151** | 1·75 | 60 |
| 861 | 80c. New Anguilla official flag | 2·25 | 1·00 |
| 862 | $1 Three Dolphins flag | 2·50 | 1·10 |
| 863 | $5 Governor's official flag | 7·00 | 9·00 |

**152** Laughing Gulls

**1990.** Christmas. Sea Birds. Multicoloured.

| | | | |
|---|---|---|---|
| 864 | 10c. Type **152** | 60 | 50 |
| 865 | 35c. Brown booby | 1·00 | 50 |
| 866 | $1.50 Bridled tern | 2·00 | 2·00 |

| | | | |
|---|---|---|---|
| 867 | $3.50 Brown pelican | 3·25 | 4·75 |
| **MS**868 | 101×76 mm. $6 Least tern | 8·50 | 11·00 |

**1991.** Easter. Nos. 846/9 optd **1991**.

| | | | |
|---|---|---|---|
| 869 | 35c. Type **148** | 1·50 | 60 |
| 870 | 45c. The Trial | 1·60 | 60 |
| 871 | $1.35 The Crucifixion | 3·00 | 2·00 |
| 872 | $2.50 The Empty Tomb | 4·25 | 7·50 |
| **MS**873 | 114×84 mm. $6 The Resurrection | 12·00 | 14·00 |

**154** Angel

**1991.** Christmas.

| | | | | |
|---|---|---|---|---|
| 874 | **154** | 5c. violet, brown & black | 1·00 | 1·00 |
| 875 | - | 35c. multicoloured | 2·50 | 55 |
| 876 | - | 80c. multicoloured | 2·50 | 2·25 |
| 877 | - | $1 multicoloured | 3·50 | 2·25 |
| **MS**878 | – | 131×97 mm. $5 multicoloured | 11·00 | 13·00 |

DESIGNS—VERT: 35c. Father Christmas. HORIZ: 80c. Church and house; $1 Palm trees at night; $5 Anguilla village.

**155** Angels with Palm Branches outside St. Gerard's Church

**1992.** Easter. Multicoloured.

| | | | |
|---|---|---|---|
| 879 | 30c. Type **155** | 1·25 | 45 |
| 880 | 45c. Angels singing outside Methodist Church | 1·50 | 45 |
| 881 | 80c. Village (horiz) | 2·50 | 90 |
| 882 | $1 Congregation going to St. Mary's Church | 2·50 | 1·00 |
| 883 | $5 Dinghy regatta (horiz) | 6·50 | 9·50 |

**1992.** No. 834 surch **$1.60**.

| | | | |
|---|---|---|---|
| 884 | $1.60 on 30c. Yellow jack | 2·75 | 2·25 |

**157** Anguillan Flags

**1992.** 25th Anniv of Separation from St. Kitts-Nevis. Multicoloured.

| | | | |
|---|---|---|---|
| 885 | 80c. Type **157** | 2·75 | 1·50 |
| 886 | $1 Present official seal | 2·75 | 1·50 |
| 887 | $1.60 Anguillan flags at airport | 4·00 | 3·75 |
| 888 | $2 Royal Commissioner's official seal | 4·00 | 4·50 |
| **MS**889 | 116×117 mm. $10 "Independent Anguilla" overprinted stamps of 1967 (85×85 mm) | 14·00 | 15·00 |

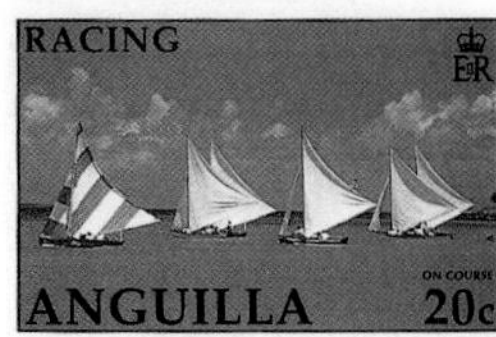


**158** Dinghy Race

**1992.** Sailing Dinghy Racing.

| | | | | |
|---|---|---|---|---|
| 890 | **158** | 20c. multicoloured | 1·75 | 75 |
| 891 | - | 35c. multicoloured | 2·25 | 65 |
| 892 | - | 45c. multicoloured | 2·50 | 65 |
| 893 | - | 80c. multicoloured | 3·25 | 4·50 |
| 894 | - | 80c. black and blue | 3·25 | 4·50 |
| 895 | - | $1 multicoloured | 3·25 | 2·75 |
| **MS**896 | – | 129×30 mm. $6 multicoloured | 9·00 | 11·00 |

DESIGNS—VERT: 35c. Stylized poster; 80c. (No. 893) "Blue Bird" in race; 80c. (No. 894) Construction drawings of "Blue Bird" by Douglas Pyle; $1 Stylized poster (different). HORIZ: 45c. Dinghies on beach. (97×32 mm)—$6 Composite designs as 20 and 45c. values.

**159** Mucka Jumbie on Stilts

**1992.** Christmas. Local Traditions. Mult.

| | | | |
|---|---|---|---|
| 897 | 20c. Type **159** | 1·00 | 40 |
| 898 | 70c. Masqueraders | 2·00 | 60 |
| 899 | $1.05 Baking in old style oven | 2·25 | 1·25 |
| 900 | $2.40 Collecting presents from Christmas tree | 4·00 | 6·00 |
| **MS**901 | 128×101 mm. $5 As No. 900 | 3·75 | 6·00 |

**160** Columbus landing in New World

**1992.** 500th Anniv of Discovery of America by Columbus (2nd issue).

| | | | | |
|---|---|---|---|---|
| 902 | **160** | 80c. multicoloured | 3·00 | 1·25 |
| 903 | - | $1 black and brown | 3·00 | 1·25 |
| 904 | - | $2 multicoloured | 4·00 | 4·50 |
| 905 | - | $3 multicoloured | 4·50 | 6·50 |
| **MS**906 | – | 78×54 mm. $6 multicoloured | 11·00 | 12·00 |

DESIGNS—VERT: $1 Christopher Columbus; $6 Columbus and map of West Indies. HORIZ: $2 Fleet of Columbus; $3 "Pinta".

**161** "Kite Flying" (Kyle Brooks)

**1993.** Easter. Children's Paintings. Mult.

| | | | |
|---|---|---|---|
| 907 | 20c. Type **161** | 2·00 | 75 |
| 908 | 45c. "Clifftop Village Service" (Kara Connor) | 2·50 | 70 |
| 909 | 80c. "Morning Devotion on Sombrero" (Junior Carty) | 3·25 | 1·40 |
| 910 | $1.50 "Hill Top Church Service" (Leana Harris) | 4·50 | 7·00 |
| **MS**911 | 90×110 mm. $5 "Good Friday Kites" (Marvin Hazel and Kyle Brooks) (39×53 mm) | 5·50 | 7·50 |

**162** Salt Picking

**1993.** Traditional Industries. Mult.

| | | | |
|---|---|---|---|
| 912 | 20c. Type **162** | 3·50 | 1·25 |
| 913 | 80c. Tobacco growing | 2·75 | 1·25 |
| 914 | $1 Cotton picking | 2·75 | 1·25 |
| 915 | $2 Harvesting sugar cane | 4·75 | 7·00 |
| **MS**916 | 111×85 mm. $6 Fishing | 12·00 | 14·00 |

**163** Lord Great Chamberlain presenting Spurs of Charity to Queen

**1993.** 40th Anniv of Coronation. Mult.

| | | | |
|---|---|---|---|
| 917 | 80c. Type **163** | 2·25 | 80 |
| 918 | $1 The Benediction | 2·50 | 90 |
| 919 | $2 Queen Elizabeth II in Coronation robes | 3·25 | 3·50 |
| 920 | $3 St. Edward's Crown | 3·75 | 4·50 |
| **MS**921 | 114×95 mm. $6 The Queen and Prince Philip in Coronation coach | 13·00 | 14·00 |

**164** Carnival Pan Player

**1993.** Anguilla Carnival. Multicoloured.

| | | | |
|---|---|---|---|
| 922 | 20c. Type **164** | 80 | 40 |
| 923 | 45c. Revellers dressed as pirates | 90 | 50 |
| 924 | 80c. Revellers dressed as stars | 1·25 | 40 |
| 925 | $1 Mas dancing | 2·25 | 80 |
| 926 | $2 Masked couple | 3·50 | 4·50 |
| 927 | $3 Revellers dressed as commandos | 4·25 | 6·00 |
| **MS**928 | 123×94 mm. $5 Revellers in fantasy costumes | 12·00 | 14·00 |

**165** Mucka Jumbies Carnival Characters

**1993.** Christmas. Multicoloured.

| | | | |
|---|---|---|---|
| 929 | 20c. Type **165** | 1·25 | 80 |
| 930 | 35c. Local carol singers | 1·60 | 70 |
| 931 | 45c. Christmas home baking | 1·75 | 70 |
| 932 | $3 Decorating Christmas tree | 5·50 | 7·50 |
| **MS**933 | 123×118 mm. $4 Mucka Jumbies and carol singers (58½×47 mm) | 3·50 | 5·00 |

**166** Travelling Branch Post Van at Sandy Ground

**1994.** Delivering the Mail. Multicoloured.

| | | | |
|---|---|---|---|
| 934 | 20c. Type **166** | 2·00 | 80 |
| 935 | 45c. "Betsy R" (mail schooner) at The Forest (vert) | 2·50 | 80 |
| 936 | 80c. Mail van at old Post Office | 3·00 | 1·60 |
| 937 | $1 Jeep on beach, Island Harbour (vert) | 3·00 | 1·60 |
| 938 | $4 New Post Office | 4·75 | 8·00 |

**167** Princess Alexandra, 1988

**1994.** Royal Visitors. Multicoloured.

| | | | |
|---|---|---|---|
| 939 | 45c. Type **167** | 1·75 | 75 |
| 940 | 50c. Princess Alice, 1960 | 1·75 | 75 |
| 941 | 80c. Prince Philip, 1993 | 2·50 | 1·50 |
| 942 | $1 Prince Charles, 1973 | 2·75 | 1·50 |
| 943 | $2 Queen Elizabeth II, 1994 | 3·50 | 5·00 |
| **MS**944 | 162×90 mm. Nos. 939/43 | 12·00 | 13·00 |

**168** "The Crucifixion"

**1994.** Easter. Stained-glass Windows. Multicoloured.

| | | | |
|---|---|---|---|
| 945 | 20c. Type **168** | 1·00 | 50 |
| 946 | 45c. "The Empty Tomb" | 1·40 | 45 |
| 947 | 80c. "The Resurrection" | 2·00 | 90 |
| 948 | $3 "Risen Christ with Disciples" | 4·50 | 7·50 |

**169** Cameroun Player and Pontiac Silverdome, Detroit

**1994.** World Cup Football Championship, U.S.A. Multicoloured.

| | | | |
|---|---|---|---|
| 949 | 20c. Type **169** | 85 | 50 |
| 950 | 70c. Argentine player and Foxboro Stadium, Boston | 1·50 | 70 |
| 951 | $1.80 Italian player and RFK Memorial Stadium, Washington | 2·50 | 3·00 |
| 952 | $2.40 German player and Soldier Field, Chicago | 3·50 | 4·00 |
| **MS**953 | 112×85 mm. $6 American and Colombian players | 11·00 | 12·00 |

**170** "The Nativity" (Gustave Dore)

**1994.** Christmas. Religious Paintings. Mult.

| | | | |
|---|---|---|---|
| 954 | 20c. Type **170** | 1·00 | 80 |
| 955 | 30c. "The Wise Men guided by the Star" (Dore) | 1·25 | 80 |
| 956 | 35c. "The Annunciation" (Dore) | 1·25 | 80 |
| 957 | 45c. "Adoration of the Shepherds" (detail) (Poussin) | 1·40 | 80 |
| 958 | $2.40 "The Flight into Egypt" (Dore) | 4·50 | 6·00 |

**171** Pair of Zenaida Doves

**1995.** Easter. Zenaida Doves. Multicoloured.

| | | | |
|---|---|---|---|
| 959 | 20c. Type **171** | 50 | 40 |
| 960 | 45c. Dove on branch | 75 | 50 |
| 961 | 50c. Guarding nest | 80 | 55 |
| 962 | $5 With chicks | 5·50 | 7·00 |

**172** Trygve Lie (first Secretary-General) and General Assembly

**1995.** 50th Anniv of United Nations. Multicoloured.

| | | | |
|---|---|---|---|
| 963 | 20c. Type **172** | 30 | 30 |
| 964 | 80c. Flag and building showing "50" | 60 | 65 |

| | | | |
|---|---|---|---|
| 965 | $1 Dag Hammarskjold and U Thant (former Secretary-Generals) and U.N. Charter | 70 | 75 |
| 966 | $5 U.N. Building (vert) | 4·00 | 7·00 |

**173** Anniversary Emblem and Map of Anguilla

**1995.** 25th Anniv of Caribbean Development Bank. Multicoloured.

| | | | |
|---|---|---|---|
| 967 | 45c. Type **173** | 1·50 | 1·75 |
| 968 | $5 Bank building and launches | 3·00 | 4·25 |

**174** Blue Whale

**1995.** Endangered Species. Whales. Multicoloured.

| | | | |
|---|---|---|---|
| 969 | 20c. Type **174** | 2·50 | 85 |
| 970 | 45c. Right whale (vert) | 2·75 | 75 |
| 971 | $1 Sperm whale | 3·25 | 1·75 |
| 972 | $5 Humpback whale | 8·50 | 9·00 |

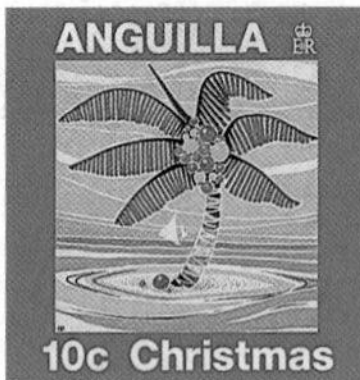


**175** Palm Tree

**1995.** Christmas. Multicoloured.

| | | | |
|---|---|---|---|
| 973 | 10c. Type **175** | 90 | 90 |
| 974 | 25c. Balloons and fishes | 1·25 | 60 |
| 975 | 45c. Shells | 1·50 | 60 |
| 976 | $5 Fishes in shape of Christmas tree | 9·00 | 10·00 |

**176** Deep Water Gorgonia

**1996.** Corals. Multicoloured.

| | | | |
|---|---|---|---|
| 977 | 20c. Type **176** | 1·75 | 80 |
| 978 | 80c. Common sea fan | 2·75 | 1·00 |
| 979 | $5 Venus sea fern | 8·00 | 10·00 |

**177** Running

**1996.** Olympic Games, Atlanta. Multicoloured.

| | | | |
|---|---|---|---|
| 980 | 20c. Type **177** | 1·00 | 60 |
| 981 | 80c. Javelin throwing and wheelchair basketball | 3·00 | 1·25 |
| 982 | $1 High jumping and hurdles | 1·50 | 1·25 |
| 983 | $3.50 Olympic rings and torch with Greek and American flags | 5·50 | 5·50 |

**178** Siege of Sandy Hill Fort

**1996.** Bicentenary of the Battle for Anguilla. Multicoloured.

| | | | |
|---|---|---|---|
| 984 | 60c. Type **178** | 1·25 | 1·00 |
| 985 | 75c. French troops destroying church (horiz) | 1·25 | 1·00 |
| 986 | $1.50 Naval battle (horiz) | 2·75 | 2·50 |
| 987 | $4 French troops landing at Rendezvous Bay | 4·00 | 5·50 |

**179** Gooseberry

**1997.** Fruit. Multicoloured.

| | | | |
|---|---|---|---|
| 988 | 10c. Type **179** | 50 | 60 |
| 989 | 20c. West Indian cherry | 60 | 30 |
| 990 | 40c. Tamarind | 75 | 30 |
| 991 | 50c. Pomme-surette | 80 | 40 |
| 992 | 60c. Sea almond | 90 | 55 |
| 993 | 75c. Sea grape | 1·00 | 85 |
| 994 | 80c. Banana | 1·10 | 85 |
| 995 | $1 Genip | 1·25 | 1·00 |
| 996 | $1.10 Coco plum | 1·40 | 1·60 |
| 997 | $1.25 Pope | 1·75 | 2·00 |
| 998 | $1.50 Pawpaw | 1·75 | 2·00 |
| 999 | $2 Sugar apple | 2·25 | 3·00 |
| 1000 | $3 Soursop | 3·00 | 3·75 |
| 1001 | $4 Pomegranate | 3·50 | 4·25 |
| 1002 | $5 Cashew | 4·00 | 5·00 |
| 1003 | $10 Mango | 7·00 | 8·00 |

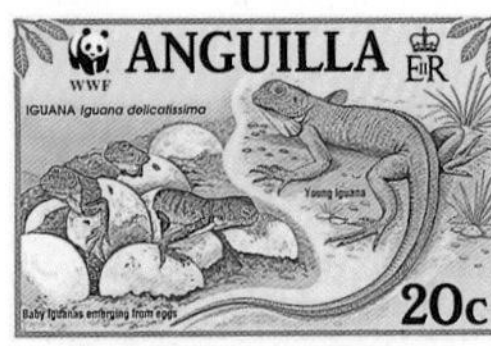


**180** West Indian Iguanas hatching

**1997.** Endangered Species. West Indian Iguanas. Multicoloured.

| | | | |
|---|---|---|---|
| 1004 | 20c. Type **180** | 1·75 | 1·50 |
| 1005 | 50c. On rock | 2·00 | 1·60 |
| 1006 | 75c. On branch | 2·25 | 2·00 |
| 1007 | $3 Head of West Indian iguana | 3·25 | 4·00 |

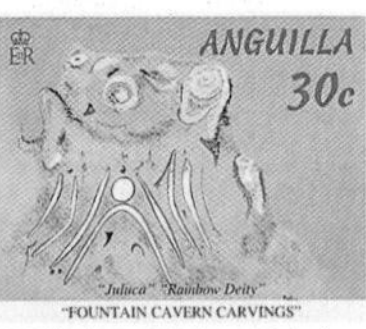


**181** "Juluca, Rainbow Deity"

**1997.** Ancient Stone Carvings from Fountain Cavern. Multicoloured.

| | | | |
|---|---|---|---|
| 1008 | 30c. Type **181** | 55 | 35 |
| 1009 | $1.25 "Lizard with front legs extended" | 1·10 | 1·00 |
| 1010 | $2.25 "Chief" | 1·75 | 2·50 |
| 1011 | $2.75 "Jocahu, the Creator" | 2·25 | 3·00 |

**182** Diana, Princess of Wales

**1998.** Diana, Princess of Wales Commemoration. Multicoloured.

| | | | |
|---|---|---|---|
| 1012 | 15c. Type **182** | 2·00 | 1·25 |
| 1013 | $1 Wearing yellow blouse | 2·75 | 1·60 |
| 1014 | $1.90 Wearing tiara | 3·00 | 3·00 |
| 1015 | $2.25 Wearing blue short-sleeved Red Cross blouse | 3·25 | 3·25 |

**183** "Treasure Island" (Valarie Alix)

**1998.** International Arts Festival. Multicoloured.

| | | | |
|---|---|---|---|
| 1016 | 15c. Type **183** | 60 | 60 |
| 1017 | 30c. "Posing in the Light" (Melsadis Fleming) (vert) | 60 | 40 |
| 1018 | $1 "Pescadores de Anguilla" (Juan Garcia) (vert) | 90 | 80 |
| 1019 | $1.50 "Fresh Catch" (Verna Hart) | 1·25 | 1·75 |
| 1020 | $1.90 "The Bell Tower of St. Mary's" (Ricky Racardo Edwards) (vert) | 1·50 | 2·25 |

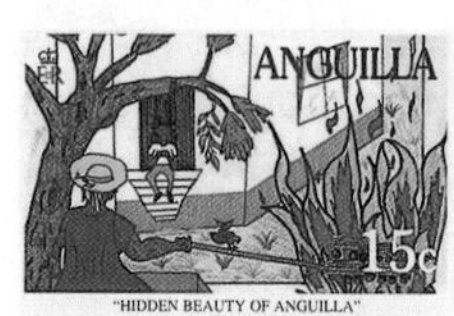


**184** Roasting Corn-cobs on Fire

**1998.** Christmas. "Hidden Beauty of Anguilla". Children's Paintings. Multicoloured.

| | | | |
|---|---|---|---|
| 1021 | 15c. Type **184** | 35 | 30 |
| 1022 | $1 Fresh fruit and market stallholder | 80 | 50 |
| 1023 | $1.50 Underwater scene | 1·00 | 1·25 |
| 1024 | $3 Cacti and view of sea | 1·60 | 2·50 |

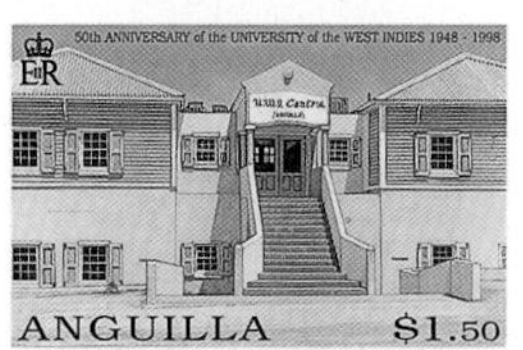


**185** University of West Indies Centre, Anguilla

**1998.** 50th Anniv of University of West Indies. Multicoloured.

| | | | |
|---|---|---|---|
| 1025 | $1.50 Type **185** | 80 | 90 |
| 1026 | $1.90 Man with torch and University arms | 1·10 | 1·50 |

**186** Sopwith Camel and Bristol F2B Fighters

**1998.** 80th Anniv of Royal Air Force. Multicoloured.

| | | | |
|---|---|---|---|
| 1027 | 30c. Type **186** | 1·00 | 50 |
| 1028 | $1 Supermarine Spitfire Mk II and Hawker Hurricane Mk I | 2·00 | 90 |
| 1029 | $1.50 Avro Lancaster | 2·25 | 2·25 |
| 1030 | $1.90 Panavia Tornado F3 and Harrier GR7 | 2·75 | 3·00 |

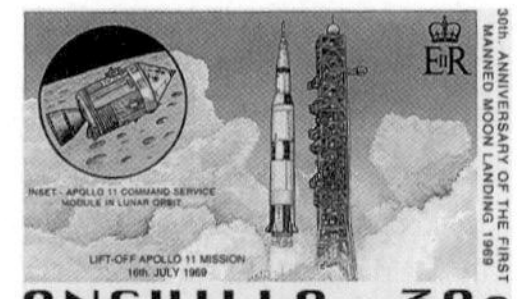


**187** Saturn 5 Rocket and "Apollo 11" Command Module

**1999.** 30th Anniv of First Manned Landing on Moon. Multicoloured.

| | | | |
|---|---|---|---|
| 1031 | 30c. Type **187** | 55 | 35 |
| 1032 | $1 Astronaut Edwin Aldrin, Lunar Module "Eagle" and first footprint on Moon | 1·00 | 70 |
| 1033 | $1.50 Lunar Module leaving Moon's surface | 1·00 | 1·00 |
| 1034 | $1.90 Recovery of Command Module | 1·40 | 2·00 |

**188** Albena Lake Hodge

**1999.** Anguillan Heroes and Heroines (1st series). Each black, green and cream.

| | | | |
|---|---|---|---|
| 1035 | 30c. Type **188** | 40 | 30 |
| 1036 | $1 Collins O. Hodge | 80 | 65 |
| 1037 | $1.50 Edwin Wallace Rey | 1·00 | 1·25 |
| 1038 | $1.90 Walter G. Hodge | 1·25 | 2·00 |

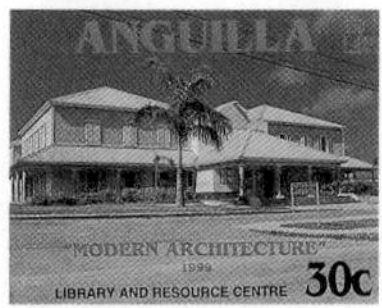


**189** Library and Resource Centre

**1999.** Modern Architecture. Multicoloured.

| | | | |
|---|---|---|---|
| 1039 | 30c. Type **189** | 45 | 35 |
| 1040 | 65c. Parliamentary building and Court House | 65 | 60 |
| 1041 | $1 Caribbean Commercial Bank | 1·00 | 80 |
| 1042 | $1.50 Police Headquarters | 2·25 | 2·00 |
| 1043 | $1.90 Post Office | 1·75 | 2·50 |

**190** Beach Barbeque and Fireworks

**1999.** Christmas and New Millennium. Mult.

| | | | |
|---|---|---|---|
| 1044 | 30c. Type **190** | 55 | 30 |
| 1045 | $1 Musicians around globe | 1·25 | 55 |
| 1046 | $1.50 Family at Christmas dinner | 1·75 | 1·75 |
| 1047 | $1.90 Celebrations around decorated shrub | 2·00 | 2·50 |

**191** Shoal Bay (East)

**2000.** Beaches. Multicoloured.

| | | | |
|---|---|---|---|
| 1048 | 15c. Type **191** | 30 | 40 |
| 1049 | 30c. Maundys Bay | 35 | 30 |
| 1050 | $1 Rendezvous Bay | 75 | 50 |
| 1051 | $1.50 Meads Bay | 1·00 | 1·25 |
| 1052 | $1.90 Little Bay | 1·25 | 1·75 |
| 1053 | $2 Sandy Ground | 1·25 | 1·75 |
| **MS**1054 | 144×144 mm. Nos. 1048/53 | 4·25 | 4·75 |

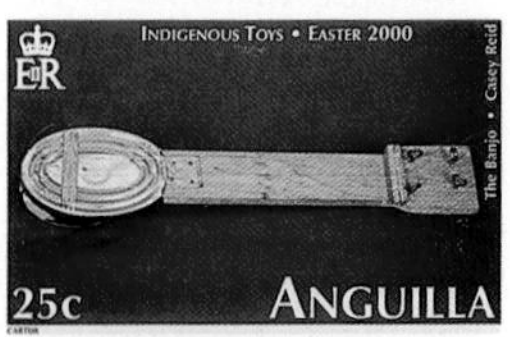


**192** Toy Banjo (Casey Reid)

**2000.** Easter. Indigenous Toys. Multicoloured.

| | | | |
|---|---|---|---|
| 1055 | 25c. Type **192** | 40 | 30 |
| 1056 | 30c. Spinning top (Johniela Harrigan) | 40 | 30 |
| 1057 | $1.50 Catapult (Akeem Rogers) | 1·10 | 1·10 |
| 1058 | $1.90 Roller (Melisa Mussington) | 1·40 | 1·75 |
| 1059 | $2.50 Killy Ban (trap) (Casey Reid) | 1·75 | 2·25 |
| **MS**1060 | 145×185 mm. 75c. Rag Doll (Jahia Esposito) (vert); $1 Kite (Javed Maynard) (vert); $1.25, Cricket ball (Jevon Lake) (vert); $4 Pond boat (Corvel Flemming) (vert) | 4·75 | 5·50 |

**193** Lanville Harrigan

**2000.** West Indies Cricket Tour and 100th Test Match at Lord's. Multicoloured.

| | | | |
|---|---|---|---|
| 1061 | $2 Type **193** | 2·00 | 2·00 |
| 1062 | $4 Cardigan Connor | 3·00 | 4·00 |
| **MS**1063 | 119×102 mm. $6 Lord's Cricket Ground (horiz) | 9·00 | 9·00 |

**2000.** "The Stamp Show 2000" International Stamp Exhibition, London. Beaches. As No. **MS**1054, but with exhibition logo on bottom margin. Mult.

| | | | |
|---|---|---|---|
| **MS**1064 | 144×144 mm. Nos. 1048/53 | 4·75 | 6·00 |

**194** Prince William and Royal Family after Trooping the Colour

**2000.** 18th Birthday of Prince William. Mult.

| | | | |
|---|---|---|---|
| 1065 | 30c. Type **194** | 1·50 | 50 |
| 1066 | $1 Prince and Princess of Wales with sons | 2·25 | 85 |
| 1067 | $1.90 With Prince Charles and Prince Harry | 2·75 | 2·75 |
| 1068 | $2.25 Skiing with father and brother | 3·25 | 3·25 |
| **MS**1069 | 125×95 mm. $8 Prince William as pupil at Eton | 7·00 | 8·00 |

**195** Queen Elizabeth the Queen Mother and Prince William

**2000.** 100th Birthday of Queen Elizabeth the Queen Mother. Showing different portraits. Multicoloured.

| | | | |
|---|---|---|---|
| 1070 | 30c. Type **195** | 65 | 40 |
| 1071 | $1.50 Island scene | 1·50 | 1·00 |
| 1072 | $1.90 Clarence House | 1·75 | 1·60 |
| 1073 | $5 Castle of Mey | 3·25 | 4·00 |

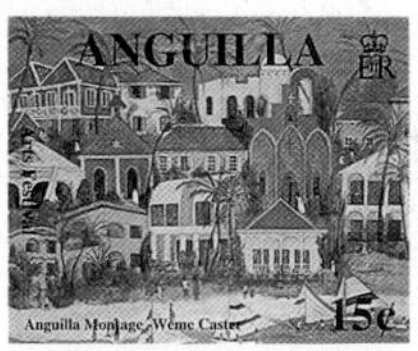

**196** "Anguilla Montage" (Weme Caster)

**2000.** International Arts Festival. Multicoloured.

| | | | |
|---|---|---|---|
| 1074 | 15c. Type **196** | 30 | 40 |
| 1075 | 30c. "Serenity" (Damien Carty) | 35 | 35 |
| 1076 | 65c. "Inter Island Cargo" (Paula Walden) | 55 | 45 |
| 1077 | $1.50 "Rainbow City where Spirits find Form" (Fiona Percy) | 1·25 | 1·50 |
| 1078 | $1.90 "Sailing Silver Seas" (Valerie Carpenter) | 1·40 | 2·00 |
| **MS**1079 | 75×100 mm. $7 "Historic Anguilla" (Melsadis Fleming) (42×28 mm) | 4·75 | 6·00 |

**197** Dried Flower Arrangement

**2000.** Christmas. Flower and Garden Show.

| | | | | |
|---|---|---|---|---|
| 1080 | **197** | 15c. multicoloured | 25 | 25 |
| 1081 | - | 25c. multicoloured | 30 | 25 |
| 1082 | - | 30c. multicoloured | 30 | 25 |
| 1083 | - | $1 multicoloured | 75 | 60 |
| 1084 | - | $1.50 multicoloured | 1·25 | 1·50 |
| 1085 | - | $1.90 multicoloured | 1·50 | 2·25 |

DESIGNS: 25c. to $1.90, Different floral arrangements.

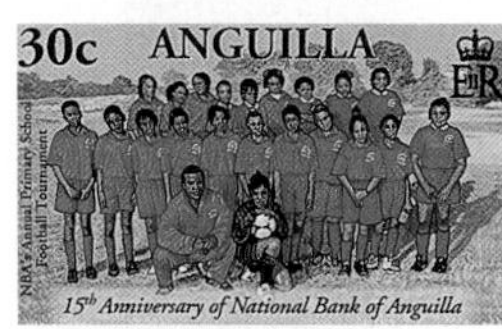

**198** Winning Primary School Football Team (Bank Sponsorship)

**2000.** 15th Anniv of National Bank of Anguilla. Multicoloured.

| | | | |
|---|---|---|---|
| 1086 | 30c. Type **198** | 30 | 25 |
| 1087 | $1 *De-Chan* (yacht) (Bank sponsorship) (vert) | 70 | 60 |
| 1088 | $1.50 Bank crest (vert) | 1·25 | 1·50 |
| 1089 | $1.90 New Bank Headquarters | 1·50 | 2·00 |

**199** Ebenezer Methodist Church in 19th Century

**2000.** 170th Anniv of Ebenezer Methodist Church.

| | | | | |
|---|---|---|---|---|
| 1090 | **199** | 30c. brown and black | 30 | 20 |
| 1091 | - | $1.90 multicoloured | 1·50 | 2·00 |

DESIGN: $1.90, Church in 2000.

**200** Soroptomist Day Care Centre

**2001.** United Nations Women's Human Rights Campaign. Multicoloured.

| | | | |
|---|---|---|---|
| 1092 | 25c. Type **200** | 30 | 30 |
| 1093 | 30c. Britannia Idalia Gumbs (Anguillan politician) (vert) | 30 | 30 |
| 1094 | $2.25 "Caribbean Woman II" (Leisel Renee Jobity) (vert) | 1·60 | 2·25 |

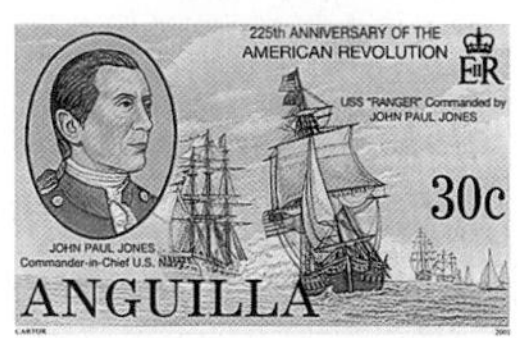

**201** John Paul Jones and U.S.S. *Ranger* (frigate)

**2001.** 225th Anniv of American War of Independence. Multicoloured.

| | | | |
|---|---|---|---|
| 1095 | 30c. Type **201** | 1·25 | 60 |
| 1096 | $1 George Washington and Battle of Yorktown | 1·50 | 1·00 |
| 1097 | $1.50 Thomas Jefferson and submission of Declaration of Independence to Congress | 2·00 | 2·50 |
| 1098 | $1.90 John Adams and the signing of the Treaty of Paris | 2·00 | 2·50 |

**202** Bahama Pintail

**2001.** Anguillian Birds. Multicoloured.

| | | | |
|---|---|---|---|
| 1099 | 30c. Type **202** | 75 | 50 |
| 1100 | $1 Black-faced grassquit (vert) | 1·00 | 80 |
| 1101 | $1.50 Common noddy | 1·60 | 1·60 |
| 1102 | $2 Black-necked stilt (vert) | 2·00 | 2·25 |
| 1103 | $3 Kentish plover ("Snowy Plover") | 2·50 | 2·75 |
| **MS**1104 | 124×88 mm. 25c. Snowy egret; 65c. Red-billed tropic bird; $1.35, Greater yellowlegs; $2.25, Sooty tern | 6·00 | 6·00 |

**203** "Children encircling Globe" (Urska Golob)

**2001.** U.N. Year of Dialogue among Civilisations.

| | | | | |
|---|---|---|---|---|
| 1105 | **203** | $1.90 multicoloured | 1·60 | 2·25 |

**204** Triangle

**2001.** Christmas. Indigenous Musical Instruments. Multicoloured.

| | | | |
|---|---|---|---|
| 1106 | 15c. Type **204** | 25 | 30 |
| 1107 | 25c. Maracas | 35 | 35 |
| 1108 | 30c. Guiro (vert) | 35 | 35 |
| 1109 | $1.50 Marimba | 1·25 | 1·25 |
| 1110 | $1.90 Tambu (hand drum) (vert) | 1·50 | 1·75 |
| 1111 | $2.50 Bass pan | 2·00 | 2·50 |
| **MS**1112 | 110×176 mm. 75c. Banjo (vert); $1 Quatro (vert); $1.25, Ukelele (vert); $3 Cello (vert) | 5·00 | 6·00 |

**205** Sombrero Lighthouse, 1962

**2002.** Commissioning of New Sombrero Lighthouse. Multicoloured.

| | | | |
|---|---|---|---|
| 1113 | 30c. Type **205** | 75 | 55 |
| 1114 | $1.50 Old and new lighthouses (horiz) | 1·75 | 1·75 |
| 1115 | $1.90 New, fully-automated lighthouse, 2001 | 2·00 | 2·25 |

**206** Artist, Entertainer and Sportsmen

**2002.** 20th Anniv of Social Security Board. Multicoloured (except 30c.).

| | | | |
|---|---|---|---|
| 1116 | 30c. Type **206** (ultramarine and blue) | 40 | 30 |
| 1117 | 75c. Anguillans of all ages | 70 | 65 |
| 1118 | $2.50 Anguillan workers (horiz) | 2·25 | 2·75 |

**207** H.M.S. *Antrim* (destroyer), 1967

**2002.** Ships of the Royal Navy. Multicoloured.

| | | | |
|---|---|---|---|
| 1119 | 30c. Type **207** | 60 | 45 |
| 1120 | 50c. H.M.S. *Formidable* (aircraft carrier), 1939 | 80 | 60 |
| 1121 | $1.50 H.M.S. *Dreadnought* (battleship), 1906 | 1·25 | 1·50 |
| 1122 | $2 H.M.S. *Warrior* (ironclad), 1860 | 1·75 | 2·00 |
| **MS**1123 | 102×77 mm. H.M.S. *Ark Royal* (aircraft carrier), 1981 (vert) | 6·50 | 7·00 |

**208** Princess Elizabeth with Prince Charles

**2002.** Golden Jubilee. Multicoloured.

| | | | |
|---|---|---|---|
| 1124 | 30c. Type **208** | 40 | 30 |
| 1125 | $1.50 Queen Elizabeth wearing white coat | 1·10 | 1·10 |
| 1126 | $1.90 Queen Elizabeth in evening dress | 1·75 | 1·75 |
| 1127 | $5 Wearing yellow hat and coat | 4·25 | 4·50 |
| **MS**1128 | 106×75 mm. $8 Queen Elizabeth sitting at desk | 8·50 | 9·50 |

**209** Valley Health Centre

**2002.** Centenary of Pan American Health Organization. Multicoloured.

| | | | |
|---|---|---|---|
| 1129 | 30c. Type **209** | 45 | 25 |
| 1130 | $1.50 Centenary of PAHO logo | 1·25 | 1·60 |

**210** *Finance* (sloop)

**2003.** Past Sailing Vessels of Anguilla. Multicoloured.

| | | | |
|---|---|---|---|
| 1131 | 15c. Type **210** | 40 | 40 |
| 1132 | 30c. *Tiny Gull* | 50 | 30 |
| 1133 | 65c. *Lady Laurel* (schooner) | 70 | 40 |
| 1134 | 75c. *Spitfire* (gaff rigged sloop) | 70 | 40 |
| 1135 | $1 *Liberator* (schooner) | 90 | 50 |
| 1136 | $1.35 *Excelsior* (schooner) | 1·00 | 70 |
| 1137 | $1.50 *Rose Millicent* | 1·25 | 1·00 |
| 1138 | $1.90 *Betsy R.* (sloop) | 1·40 | 1·10 |
| 1139 | $2 *Sunbeam R.* (sloop) | 1·50 | 1·40 |
| 1140 | $2.25 *New London* | 1·75 | 1·90 |
| 1141 | $3 *Ismay* (schooner) | 2·25 | 2·50 |
| 1142 | $10 *Warspite* (schooner) | 7·00 | 7·50 |

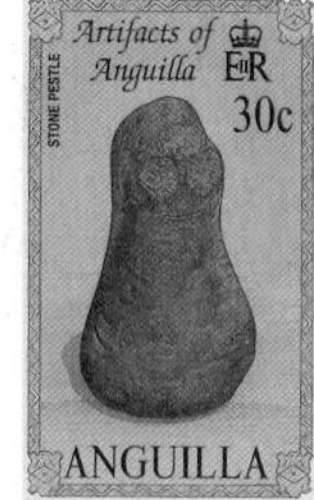

**211** Stone Pestle

**2003.** Artifacts of Anguilla. Multicoloured.

| | | | |
|---|---|---|---|
| 1143 | 30c. Type **211** | 50 | 25 |
| 1144 | $1 Frog worked shell ornament | 1·00 | 60 |
| 1145 | $1.50 Pottery | 1·25 | 1·10 |
| 1146 | $1.90 Mask worked shell ornament | 1·50 | 1·75 |

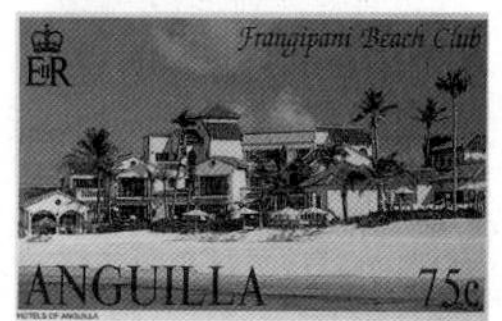

**212** Frangipani Beach Club

**2003.** Hotels of Anguilla. Multicoloured.

| | | | |
|---|---|---|---|
| 1147 | 75c. Type **212** | 70 | 45 |
| 1148 | $1 Pimms, Cap Juluca | 85 | 55 |
| 1149 | $1.35 Cocoloba Beach Resort | 1·00 | 80 |
| 1150 | $1.50 Malliouhana Hotel | 1·25 | 1·10 |
| 1151 | $1.90 Carimar Beach Club | 1·40 | 1·40 |
| 1152 | $3 Covecastles | 2·00 | 2·50 |

**213** "Eudice's Garden" (Eunice Summer)

**2004.** International Arts Festival. Multicoloured.

| | | | |
|---|---|---|---|
| 1153 | 15c. Type **213** | 40 | 30 |
| 1154 | 30c. "Hammocks" (Lisa Davenport) | 50 | 30 |
| 1155 | $1 "Conched Out" (Richard Shaffett) | 90 | 70 |
| 1156 | $1.50 "Islands Rhythms"(Carol Garvin) | 1·10 | 1·10 |
| 1157 | $1.90 "Party at the Beach"(Jean-Pierre Ballagny) | 1·40 | 1·40 |
| 1158 | $3 "Shoal Bay before Luis"(Jacqueline Mariethoz) | 2·00 | 2·50 |

**214** Athlete (400 Metres)

**2004.** Olympic Games, Athens. Multicoloured.

| | | | |
|---|---|---|---|
| 1159 | 30c. Type **214** | 50 | 30 |
| 1160 | $1 Laser dinghies (sailing) | 90 | 60 |
| 1161 | $1.50 Gymnastics (rings) | 1·10 | 1·10 |
| 1162 | $1.90 The Acropolis, Athens, Pierre de Coubertin (founder of modern Olympics) and Dimetrios Vikelas (first IOC President) (horiz) | 1·40 | 1·75 |

**215** Goat

**2004.** Goats of Anguilla. Multicoloured.

| | | | |
|---|---|---|---|
| 1163 | 30c. Type **215** | 50 | 30 |
| 1164 | 50c. Black and white goat | 60 | 35 |
| 1165 | $1 Black and tan goat (vert) | 90 | 60 |
| 1166 | $1.50 Chestnut goat | 1·10 | 1·10 |
| 1167 | $1.90 Chestnut and white goat (vert) | 1·40 | 1·50 |
| 1168 | $2.25 Two kids | 1·75 | 2·00 |

**216** Cordless Telephone

**2004.** Development of the Telephone. Multicoloured.

| | | | |
|---|---|---|---|
| 1169 | 30c. Type **216** | 30 | 20 |
| 1170 | $1 Touch tone telephone | 90 | 70 |
| 1171 | $1.50 Cellular phone | 1·25 | 1·40 |
| 1172 | $1.90 Circular dial telephone (horiz) | 1·60 | 1·75 |
| 1173 | $3.80 Magneto telephone | 3·25 | 3·50 |

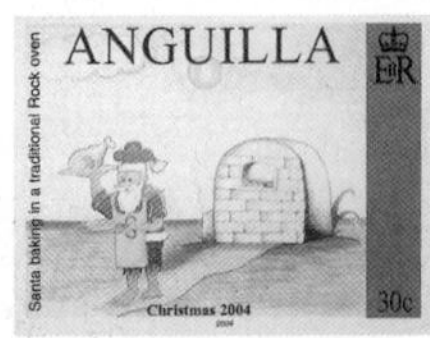

**217** Santa baking in Traditional Rock Oven

**2004.** Christmas. Multicoloured.

| | | | |
|---|---|---|---|
| 1174 | 30c. Type **217** | 30 | 20 |
| 1175 | $1.50 Santa climbing coconut tree | 1·25 | 1·40 |
| 1176 | $1.90 Santa's string band | 1·40 | 1·60 |
| 1177 | $3.80 Santa delivering gifts by donkey | 2·75 | 3·00 |
| **MS**1178 | 107×76 mm. $8 Santa delivering gifts by boat | 6·00 | 7·00 |

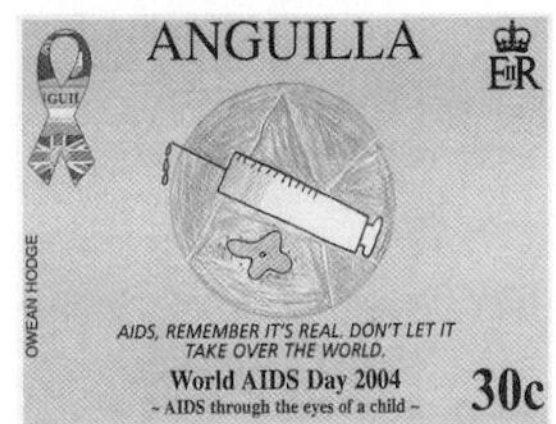

**218** "AIDS, Remember it's Real. Don't let it take over the World" (Owean Hodge)

**2005.** World AIDS Day 2004—"AIDS through the Eyes of a Child". Children's paintings. Multicoloured.

| | | | |
|---|---|---|---|
| 1179 | 30c. Type **218** | 30 | 20 |
| 1180 | $1.50 "Arm Yourself against AIDS" (Lydia Fleming) | 1·25 | 1·40 |
| 1181 | $1.90 "AIDS is Your Concern" (Nina Rodriguez) | 1·40 | 1·60 |
| **MS**1182 | 144×144 mm. 15c. Classroom (Kenswick Richardson); 75c. Dancer, Schoolgirl, Teacher, Smoker (Toniquewah Ruan); $1 Girls and Tree (Elizabeth Anne Orchard); $2 "Even I can get AIDS" (Tricia Watty-Beard) | 3·00 | 3·25 |

**219** Arms of Anguilla and Rotary Emblem

**2005.** Centenary of Rotary International and 25th Anniv of Anguilla Rotary Club. Multicoloured.

| | | | |
|---|---|---|---|
| 1183 | 30c. Type **219** | 30 | 20 |
| 1184 | $1 Brown pelican and palm tree (District 7020) | 80 | 70 |
| 1185 | $1.50 Paul Harris (founder) | 1·25 | 1·40 |
| 1186 | $1.90 Children on slide (School Playground Project) | 1·40 | 1·60 |

**220** Grey Dog

**2005.** Dogs of Anguilla. Multicoloured.

| | | | |
|---|---|---|---|
| 1187 | 30c. Type **220** | 30 | 20 |
| 1188 | $1.50 Black and tan dog with puppy (vert) | 1·25 | 1·40 |
| 1189 | $1.90 Black and tan dog (vert) | 1·40 | 1·60 |
| 1190 | $2.25 Tan dog | 1·70 | 1·80 |

**221** Air Anguilla Cessna 402

**2006.** Early Airlines. Multicoloured.

| | | | |
|---|---|---|---|
| 1191 | 30c. Type **221** | 40 | 30 |
| 1192 | 40c. LIAT DHC Dash 8 | 45 | 30 |
| 1193 | 60c. Winair Foxtrot DHC Twin Otter | 70 | 40 |
| 1194 | $1 Anguilla Airways Piper Aztec | 1·00 | 70 |
| 1195 | $1.50 St. Thomas Air Transport Piper Aztec | 1·40 | 1·60 |
| 1196 | $1.90 Carib Air Service Piper Aztec | 1·90 | 2·10 |

**222** *Appias drusillia*

**2006.** Butterflies. Multicoloured.

| | | | |
|---|---|---|---|
| 1197 | 30c. Type **222** | 40 | 30 |
| 1198 | $1.50 *Danaus plexippus megalippe* | 1·25 | 1·40 |
| 1199 | $1.90 *Phoebis sennae* | 1·70 | 1·80 |
| 1200 | $2.75 *Papilio demoleus* | 2·40 | 2·50 |
| **MS**1201 | 126×88 mm. 40c. *Aphrissa statira*; 60c. *Eurema elathea*; $1 *Danaus plexippusmegalippe*; $3 *Agraulis vanillae* | 4·75 | 5·00 |

**223** Soroptimist International Logo

**2007.** 25th Anniv (2006) of Anguilla Soroptimist Club. Multicoloured.

| | | | |
|---|---|---|---|
| 1202 | $1.90 Type **223** | 1·70 | 1·80 |
| 1203 | $2.75 Alecia Ballin | 2·75 | 2·50 |

**224** St. Bruno (Carthusian founder)

**2007.** Bronze Devotional Medallions. Designs showing medallions from Spanish ship El Buen Consejo, sunk in 1772 off Anguilla coast. Multicoloured.

| | | | |
|---|---|---|---|
| 1204 | 30c. Type **224** | 25 | 30 |
| 1205 | $1.50 Our Lady of Sorrows | 1·25 | 1·40 |
| 1206 | $1.90 Five Wounds of Jesus | 1·50 | 1·60 |
| 1207 | $2.75 Virgin and Child | 2·25 | 2·40 |

**225** Hyacinth Carty

**2008.** 40th Anniv of the Revolution (independence from St. Kitts-Nevis). Multicoloured.

| | | | |
|---|---|---|---|
| 1208 | 30c. Type **225** | 25 | 30 |
| 1209 | $1 Edward Duncan | 75 | 80 |
| 1210 | $1.50 Connell Harrigan | 1·25 | 1·40 |
| 1211 | $1.90 Reverend Leonard Carty | 1·50 | 1·60 |
| 1212 | $2.25 Jeremiah Gumbs | 1·75 | 1·90 |
| 1213 | $3.75 Atlin Harrigan | 3·00 | 3·25 |

**226** White-painted House with Gabled Roof and Lean-to

**2008.** Historical Architecture. Local Houses of the 1930s–1960s. Multicoloured.

| | | | |
|---|---|---|---|
| 1214 | 30c. Type **226** | 15 | 25 |
| 1215 | $1 House with gabled roof and lean-to at back | 45 | 50 |
| 1216 | $1.25 House with double hipped roof and flight of steps | 55 | 65 |
| 1217 | $1.50 House on seashore with hipped roof | 90 | 95 |
| 1218 | $1.90 House with double gabled roof | 1·10 | 1·25 |
| 1219 | $2.40 House with double hipped roof and verandah | 1·25 | 1·40 |
| 1220 | $2.75 House with hipped roof and verandah | 1·75 | 1·90 |
| 1221 | $3.75 House with gabled roof and flight of steps | 2·00 | 2·10 |

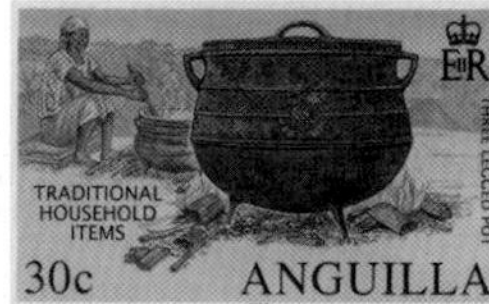

**227** Three Legged Pot

**2009.** Traditional Household Items. Multicoloured.

| | | | |
|---|---|---|---|
| 1222 | 30c Type **227** | 10 | 15 |
| 1223 | $1 Mortar and pestle | 45 | 50 |
| 1224 | $1.50 Gas and coal irons | 90 | 95 |
| 1225 | $1.90 Oil and gas lamps | 1·10 | 1·25 |
| 1226 | $2 Coal pots | 1·40 | 1·50 |
| 1227 | $2.25 Enamel and aluminium utensils (wrongly inscr 'USTENSILS') | 1·60 | 1·75 |

**228** *Tabebuia heterophylla*

**2009.** Wild Flowers. Multicoloured.

| | | | |
|---|---|---|---|
| 1228 | 30c Type **228** | 45 | 50 |
| 1229 | $1 *Argemone mexicana* | 80 | 90 |
| 1230 | $1.50 *Catharanthus roseus* | 1·00 | 1·10 |
| 1231 | $1.90 *Datura stramonium* | 1·25 | 1·40 |
| 1232 | $2 *Centrosema virginianum* | 1·50 | 1·60 |
| 1233 | $2.25 *Tetramicra canaliculata* | 1·50 | 1·60 |

Pt. 6

## ANJOUAN

One of the Comoro Is. between Madagascar and the East coast of Africa. Used stamps of Madagascar from 1914 and became part of the Comoro Islands in 1950.

100 centimes = 1 franc.

**1892.** "Tablet" key-type inscr "SULTANAT D'ANJOUAN".

| | | | | |
|---|---|---|---|---|
| 1 | D | 1c. black on blue | 1·40 | 2·00 |
| 2 | D | 2c. brown on buff | 2·10 | 2·30 |
| 3 | D | 4c. brown on grey | 3·25 | 3·75 |
| 4 | D | 5c. green on green | 5·50 | 7·75 |
| 5 | D | 10c. black on lilac | 7·75 | 7·25 |
| 14 | D | 10c. red | 25·00 | 33·00 |
| 6 | D | 15c. blue | 11·00 | 11·50 |
| 15 | D | 15c. grey | 13·00 | 21·00 |
| 7 | D | 20c. red on green | 12·00 | 15·00 |
| 8 | D | 25c. black on pink | 12·00 | 15·00 |
| 16 | D | 25c. blue | 16·00 | 28·00 |
| 9 | D | 30c. brown on grey | 27·00 | 30·00 |
| 17 | D | 35c. black on yellow | 8·25 | 9·25 |
| 10 | D | 40c. red on yellow | 32·00 | 27·00 |
| 18 | D | 45c. black on green | £100 | £120 |
| 11 | D | 50c. red on pink | 36·00 | 48·00 |
| 19 | D | 50c. brown on blue | 22·00 | 40·00 |
| 12 | D | 75c. brown on orange | 33·00 | 55·00 |
| 13 | D | 1f. green | 70·00 | 90·00 |

**1912.** Surch in figures.

| | | | |
|---|---|---|---|
| 20A | 05 on 2c. brown on buff | 2·75 | 5·50 |
| 21A | 05 on 4c. brown on grey | 1·40 | 3·00 |
| 22A | 05 on 15c. blue | 1·40 | 3·00 |
| 23A | 05 on 20c. red on green | 2·30 | 7·00 |
| 24A | 05 on 25c. black on pink | 1·60 | 3·50 |
| 25A | 05 on 30c. brown on grey | 2·50 | 3·00 |
| 26A | 10 on 40c. red on yellow | 1·50 | 1·80 |
| 27A | 10 on 45c. black on green | 1·40 | 1·70 |
| 28A | 10 on 50c. red on pink | 2·40 | 10·50 |
| 29A | 10 on 75c. brown on orange | 3·00 | 9·00 |
| 30A | 10 on 1f. green | 4·25 | 8·25 |

Pt. 6

## ANNAM AND TONGKING

Later part of Indo-China and now included in Vietnam

100 centimes = 1 franc.

**1888.** Stamps of French Colonies, "Commerce" type, surch **A & T** and value in figures.

| | | | | |
|---|---|---|---|---|
| 1 | J | 1 on 2c. brown on yellow | 65·00 | 55·00 |
| 2 | J | 1 on 4c. lilac on grey | 55·00 | 37·00 |
| 3 | J | 5 on 10c. black on lilac | 50·00 | 50·00 |

Pt. 1

# ANTIGUA

One of the Leeward Is., Br. W. Indies. Used general issues for Leeward Islands, concurrently with Antiguan stamps until 1 July 1956. Ministerial Government introduced on 1 January 1960. Achieved Associated Statehood on 3 March 1967 and Independence within the Commonwealth on 1 November 1981. Nos. 718/21 and 733 onwards are inscribed "Antigua and Barbuda".

1862. 12 pence = 1 shilling; 20 shillings = 1 pound.
1951. 100 cents = 1 West Indian dollar.

1

**1862**

| | | | | |
|---|---|---|---|---|
| 5 | 1 | 1d. mauve | £130 | 70·00 |
| 25 | 1 | 1d. red | 2·25 | 3·75 |
| 29 | 1 | 6d. green | 60·00 | £120 |

3

**1879**

| | | | | |
|---|---|---|---|---|
| 21 | 3 | ½d. green | 3·25 | 16·00 |
| 22 | 3 | 2½d. brown | £190 | 55·00 |
| 27 | 3 | 2½d. blue | 7·00 | 14·00 |
| 23 | 3 | 4d. blue | £275 | 15·00 |
| 28 | 3 | 4d. brown | 2·25 | 3·00 |
| 30 | 3 | 1s. mauve | £160 | £140 |

4

**1903**

| | | | | |
|---|---|---|---|---|
| 31 | 4 | ½d. black and green | 3·75 | 6·50 |
| 41 | 4 | ½d. green | 4·50 | 4·75 |
| 32 | 4 | 1d. black and red | 9·50 | 1·25 |
| 43 | 4 | 1d. red | 9·50 | 2·25 |
| 45 | 4 | 2d. purple and brown | 4·75 | 32·00 |
| 34 | 4 | 2½d. black and blue | 12·00 | 19·00 |
| 46 | 4 | 2½d. blue | 20·00 | 16·00 |
| 47 | 4 | 3d. green and brown | 6·50 | 19·00 |
| 48 | 4 | 6d. purple and black | 7·50 | 40·00 |
| 49 | 4 | 1s. blue and purple | 22·00 | 70·00 |
| 50 | 4 | 2s. green and violet | £110 | £130 |
| 39 | 4 | 2s.6d. black and purple | 26·00 | 65·00 |
| 40 | 5 | 5s. green and violet | £100 | £150 |

5

**1913.** Head of King George V.

| | | | | |
|---|---|---|---|---|
| 51 | 5 | 5s. green and violet | 90·00 | £150 |

**1916.** Optd **WAR STAMP**.

| | | | | |
|---|---|---|---|---|
| 53 | 4 | ½d. green | 1·50 | 2·50 |
| 54 | 4 | 1½d. orange | 1·00 | 1·25 |

8

**1921**

| | | | | |
|---|---|---|---|---|
| 62 | 8 | ½d. green | 3·00 | 50 |
| 63 | 8 | 1d. red | 4·25 | 50 |
| 64 | 8 | 1d. violet | 6·00 | 1·50 |
| 67 | 8 | 1½d. orange | 5·50 | 7·00 |
| 68 | 8 | 1½d. red | 9·00 | 1·75 |
| 69 | 8 | 1½d. brown | 3·00 | 60 |
| 70 | 8 | 2d. grey | 4·00 | 75 |
| 72 | 8 | 2½d. yellow | 2·50 | 17·00 |
| 73 | 8 | 2½d. blue | 11·00 | 5·50 |
| 74 | 8 | 3d. purple on yellow | 10·00 | 8·50 |
| 56 | 8 | 4d. black and red on yellow | 2·25 | 5·50 |
| 75 | 8 | 6d. purple | 6·50 | 5·50 |
| 57 | 8 | 1s. black on green | 4·25 | 9·00 |
| 58 | 8 | 2s. purple and blue on blue | 13·00 | 27·00 |
| 78 | 8 | 2s.6d. black and red on blue | 45·00 | 32·00 |
| 79 | 8 | 3s. green and violet | 50·00 | £100 |
| 80 | 8 | 4s. black and red | 50·00 | 75·00 |
| 60 | 8 | 5s. green and red on yellow | 8·50 | 50·00 |
| 61 | 8 | £1 purple and black on red | £250 | £350 |

**9** Old Dockyard, English Harbour

**10** Government House, St. John's

**1932.** Tercentenary. Designs with medallion portrait of King George V.

| | | | | |
|---|---|---|---|---|
| 81 | 9 | ½d. green | 4·50 | 7·50 |
| 82 | - | 1d. red | 5·50 | 7·50 |
| 83 | - | 1½d. brown | 3·75 | 4·75 |
| 84 | 10 | 2d. grey | 7·00 | 25·00 |
| 85 | 10 | 2½d. blue | 7·00 | 8·50 |
| 86 | 10 | 3d. orange | 7·00 | 12·00 |
| 87 | - | 6d. violet | 15·00 | 12·00 |
| 88 | - | 1s. olive | 20·00 | 32·00 |
| 89 | - | 2s.6d. purple | 55·00 | 75·00 |
| 90 | - | 5s. black and brown | £110 | £140 |

DESIGNS—HORIZ: 6d. to 2s.6d. Nelson's "Victory"; 5s. Sir Thomas Warner's "Conception".

**13** Windsor Castle

**1935.** Silver Jubilee.

| | | | | |
|---|---|---|---|---|
| 91 | 13 | 1d. blue and red | 3·00 | 4·00 |
| 92 | 13 | 1½d. blue and grey | 2·75 | 1·50 |
| 93 | 13 | 2½d. brown and blue | 7·00 | 1·60 |
| 94 | 13 | 1s. grey and purple | 8·50 | 17·00 |

**1937.** Coronation. As T **2** of Aden.

| | | | |
|---|---|---|---|
| 95 | 1d. red | 70 | 2·75 |
| 96 | 1½d. brown | 60 | 2·50 |
| 97 | 2½d. blue | 2·25 | 3·00 |

**15** English Harbour

**16** Nelson's Dockyard

**1938**

| | | | | |
|---|---|---|---|---|
| 98 | 15 | ½d. green | 40 | 1·25 |
| 99 | 16 | 1d. red | 3·25 | 2·50 |
| 100a | 16 | 1½d. brown | 2·75 | 3·50 |
| 101 | 15 | 2d. grey | 1·00 | 1·00 |
| 102 | 16 | 2½d. blue | 1·00 | 80 |
| 103 | - | 3d. orange | 1·00 | 1·00 |
| 104 | - | 6d. violet | 4·00 | 1·25 |
| 105 | - | 1s. black and brown | 6·00 | 2·00 |
| 106a | - | 2s.6d. purple | 32·00 | 18·00 |
| 107 | - | 5s. olive | 14·00 | 11·00 |
| 108 | 16 | 10s. mauve | 18·00 | 32·00 |
| 109 | - | £1 green | 38·00 | 60·00 |

DESIGNS—HORIZ: 3d., 2s.6d., £1, Fort James. VERT: 6d., 1s., 5s. St. John's Harbour.

**1946.** Victory. As T **9** of Aden.

| | | | |
|---|---|---|---|
| 110 | 1½d. brown | 30 | 10 |
| 111 | 3d. orange | 30 | 50 |

**1949.** Silver Wedding. As T **10/11** of Aden.

| | | | |
|---|---|---|---|
| 112 | 2½d. blue | 50 | 2·75 |
| 113 | 5s. green | 14·00 | 12·00 |

**20** Hermes, Globe and Forms of Transport

**21** Hemispheres, Jet-powered Vickers Viking Airliner and Steamer

**22** Hermes and Globe

**23** U.P.U. Monument

**1949.** 75th Anniv of U.P.U.

| | | | | |
|---|---|---|---|---|
| 114 | 20 | 2½d. blue | 40 | 75 |
| 115 | 21 | 3d. orange | 2·00 | 3·00 |
| 116 | 22 | 6d. purple | 45 | 2·75 |
| 117 | 23 | 1s. brown | 45 | 1·25 |

**24** Arms of University

**25** Princess Alice

**1951.** Inauguration of B.W.I. University College.

| | | | | |
|---|---|---|---|---|
| 118 | 24 | 3c. black and brown | 55 | 1·75 |
| 119 | 25 | 12c. black and violet | 1·00 | 2·00 |

**1953.** Coronation. As T **13** of Aden.

| | | | |
|---|---|---|---|
| 120 | 2c. black and green | 30 | 75 |

**27** Martello Tower

**1953.** Designs as 1938 issues but with portrait of Queen Elizabeth II as in T **27**.

| | | | | |
|---|---|---|---|---|
| 120a | - | ½c. brown | 40 | 30 |
| 121 | 15 | 1c. grey | 30 | 1·50 |
| 122 | 16 | 2c. green | 30 | 10 |
| 123 | 16 | 3c. black and yellow | 40 | 20 |
| 153 | 15 | 4c. red | 30 | 1·75 |
| 154 | 16 | 5c. black and lilac | 20 | 10 |
| 155 | - | 6c. yellow | 60 | 30 |
| 156 | 27 | 8c. blue | 30 | 20 |
| 157 | - | 12c. violet | 75 | 20 |
| 129 | - | 24c. black and brown | 4·00 | 15 |
| 130 | 27 | 48c. purple and blue | 9·50 | 2·75 |
| 131 | - | 60c. purple | 7·50 | 80 |
| 132a | - | $1.20 olive | 3·50 | 1·00 |
| 133 | 16 | $2.40 purple | 16·00 | 12·00 |
| 134 | - | $4.80 slate | 21·00 | 26·00 |

DESIGNS—HORIZ: ½, 6, 60c., $4.80, Fort James. VERT: 12, 24c., $1.20, St John's Harbour.

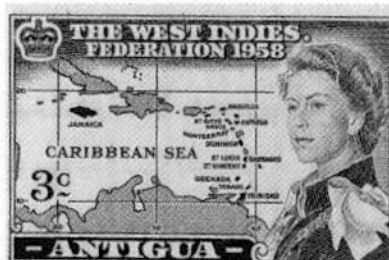

**28** Federation Map

**1958.** Inaug of British Caribbean Federation.

| | | | | |
|---|---|---|---|---|
| 135 | 28 | 3c. green | 1·25 | 30 |
| 136 | 28 | 6c. blue | 1·40 | 2·75 |
| 137 | 28 | 12c. red | 1·60 | 75 |

**1960.** New Constitution. Nos. 123 and 157 optd **COMMEMORATION ANTIGUA CONSTITUTION**.

| | | | | |
|---|---|---|---|---|
| 138 | 16 | 3c. black and yellow | 15 | 15 |
| 139 | - | 12c. violet | 15 | 15 |

**30** Nelson's Dockyard and Admiral Nelson

**1961.** Restoration of Nelson's Dockyard.

| | | | | |
|---|---|---|---|---|
| 140 | 30 | 20c. purple and brown | 1·40 | 1·60 |
| 141 | 30 | 30c. green and blue | 1·40 | 2·00 |

**31** Stamp of 1862 and R.M.S.P. "Solent I" at English Harbour

**1962.** Stamp Centenary.

| | | | | |
|---|---|---|---|---|
| 142 | 31 | 3c. purple and green | 90 | 10 |
| 143 | 31 | 10c. blue and green | 1·00 | 10 |
| 144 | 31 | 12c. sepia and green | 1·10 | 10 |
| 145 | 31 | 50c. brown and green | 1·50 | 2·25 |

**1963.** Freedom from Hunger. As T **28** of Aden.

| | | | |
|---|---|---|---|
| 146 | 12c. green | 15 | 15 |

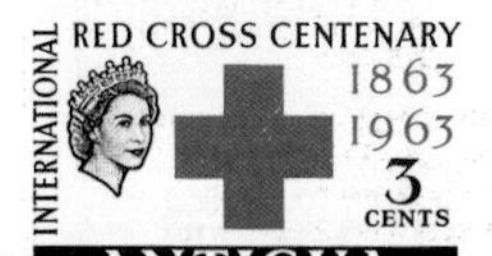

**33** Red Cross Emblem

**1963.** Centenary of Red Cross.

| | | | | |
|---|---|---|---|---|
| 147 | 33 | 3c. red and black | 30 | 75 |
| 148 | 33 | 12c. red and blue | 45 | 1·25 |

**34** Shakespeare and Memorial Theatre, Stratford-upon-Avon

**1964.** 400th Birth Anniv of Shakespeare.

| | | | | |
|---|---|---|---|---|
| 164 | 34 | 12c. brown | 30 | 10 |

**1965.** No. 157 surch **15c.**

| | | | |
|---|---|---|---|
| 165 | 15c. on 12c. violet | 10 | 10 |

**36** I.T.U. Emblem

**1965.** Centenary of I.T.U.

| | | | | |
|---|---|---|---|---|
| 166 | 36 | 2c. blue and red | 25 | 15 |
| 167 | 36 | 50c. yellow and blue | 75 | 1·25 |

**37** I.C.Y. Emblem

**1965.** International Co-operation Year.

| | | | | |
|---|---|---|---|---|
| 168 | 37 | 4c. purple and turquoise | 20 | 10 |
| 169 | 37 | 15c. green and lavender | 30 | 20 |

**38** Sir Winston Churchill, and St. Paul's Cathedral in Wartime

**1966.** Churchill Commemoration. Designs in black, red and gold with background in colours given.

| | | | | |
|---|---|---|---|---|
| 170 | **38** | ½c. blue | 10 | 1·75 |
| 171 | **38** | 4c. green | 65 | 10 |
| 172 | **38** | 25c. brown | 1·50 | 45 |
| 173 | **38** | 35c. violet | 1·50 | 55 |

**39** Queen Elizabeth II and Duke of Edinburgh

**1966.** Royal Visit.

| | | | | |
|---|---|---|---|---|
| 174 | **39** | 6c. black and blue | 1·50 | 1·10 |
| 175 | **39** | 15c. black and mauve | 1·50 | 1·40 |

**40** Footballer's Legs, Ball and Jules Rimet Cup

**1966.** World Cup Football Championship.

| | | | | |
|---|---|---|---|---|
| 176 | **40** | 6c. multicoloured | 20 | 75 |
| 177 | **40** | 35c. multicoloured | 60 | 25 |

**41** W.H.O. Building

**1966.** Inaug of W.H.O. Headquarters, Geneva.

| | | | | |
|---|---|---|---|---|
| 178 | **41** | 2c. black, green and blue | 20 | 25 |
| 179 | **41** | 15c. black, purple & brn | 1·25 | 25 |

**42** Nelson's Dockyard

**1966**

| | | | | |
|---|---|---|---|---|
| 180 | **42** | ½c. green and blue | 10 | 1·25 |
| 181 | - | 1c. purple and mauve | 10 | 30 |
| 182 | - | 2c. blue and orange | 10 | 20 |
| 183a | - | 3c. red and black | 15 | 15 |
| 184a | - | 4c. violet and brown | 15 | 30 |
| 185 | - | 5c. blue and green | 10 | 10 |
| 186 | - | 6c. orange and purple | 1·50 | 30 |
| 187 | - | 10c. green and red | 15 | 10 |
| 188a | - | 15c. brown and blue | 55 | 10 |
| 189 | - | 25c. blue and brown | 35 | 20 |
| 190a | - | 35c. mauve and brown | 60 | 1·00 |
| 191a | - | 50c. green and black | 70 | 2·25 |
| 192 | - | 75c. blue and ultra-marine | 4·00 | 2·50 |
| 193b | - | $1 mauve and green | 1·25 | 5·00 |
| 194a | - | $2.50 black and mauve | 1·50 | 8·00 |
| 195 | - | $5 green and violet | 10·00 | 6·50 |

DESIGNS: 1c. Old Post Office, St John's; 2c. Health Centre; 3c. Teachers' Training College; 4c. Martello Tower, Barbuda; 5c. Ruins of Officers' Quarters, Shirley Heights; 6c. Government House, Barbuda; 10c. Princess Margaret School; 15c. Air terminal building; 25c. General Post Office; 35c. Clarence House; 50c. Government House, St. John's; 75c. Administration building; $1 Court-house, St. John's; $2.50, Magistrates' Court; $5 St. John's Cathedral.

**54** "Education"

**55** "Science"

**56** "Culture"

**1966.** 20th Anniv of UNESCO.

| | | | | |
|---|---|---|---|---|
| 196 | **54** | 4c. violet, yellow & orange | 20 | 10 |
| 197 | **55** | 25c. yellow, violet and olive | 45 | 10 |
| 198 | **56** | $1 black, purple and orange | 90 | 2·25 |

**57** State Flag and Maps

**1967.** Statehood. Multicoloured.

| | | | | |
|---|---|---|---|---|
| 199 | | 4c. Type **57** | 10 | 10 |
| 200 | | 15c. State Flag | 10 | 20 |
| 201 | | 25c. Premier's Office and State Flag | 10 | 25 |
| 202 | | 35c. As 15c. | 15 | 25 |

**60** Gilbert Memorial Church

**1967.** Attainment of Autonomy by the Methodist Church.

| | | | | |
|---|---|---|---|---|
| 203 | **60** | 4c. black and red | 10 | 10 |
| 204 | - | 25c. black and green | 15 | 15 |
| 205 | - | 35c. black and blue | 15 | 15 |

DESIGNS: 25c. Nathaniel Gilbert's House; 35c. Caribbean and Central American map.

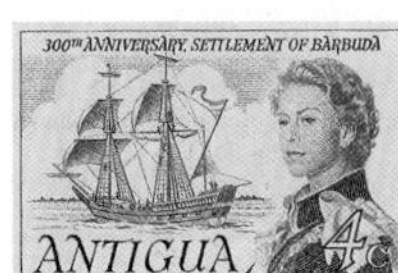

**63** Coat of Arms

**1967.** 300th Anniv of Treaty of Breda and Grant of New Arms.

| | | | | |
|---|---|---|---|---|
| 206 | **63** | 15c. multicoloured | 15 | 10 |
| 207 | **63** | 35c. multicoloured | 15 | 10 |

**64** "Susan Constant" (settlers' ship)

**1967.** 300th Anniv of Barbuda Settlement.

| | | | | |
|---|---|---|---|---|
| 208 | **64** | 4c. blue | 45 | 10 |
| 209 | - | 6c. purple | 45 | 1·25 |
| 210 | **64** | 25c. green | 50 | 20 |
| 211 | - | 35c. black | 55 | 25 |

DESIGN: 6, 35c. Blaeu's Map of 1665.

**66** Tracking Station

**1968.** N.A.S.A. Apollo Project. Inauguration of Dow Hill Tracking Station.

| | | | | |
|---|---|---|---|---|
| 212 | **66** | 4c. blue, yellow and black | 10 | 10 |
| 213 | - | 15c. blue, yellow and black | 20 | 10 |
| 214 | - | 25c. blue, yellow and black | 20 | 10 |
| 215 | - | 50c. blue, yellow and black | 30 | 40 |

DESIGNS: 15c. Antenna and spacecraft taking off; 25c. Spacecraft approaching Moon; 50c. Re-entry of space capsule.

**70** Limbo-dancing

**1968.** Tourism. Multicoloured.

| | | | | |
|---|---|---|---|---|
| 216 | | ½c. Type **70** | 10 | 50 |
| 217 | | 15c. Water-skier and bathers | 30 | 10 |
| 218 | | 25c. Yachts and beach | 30 | 10 |
| 219 | | 35c. Underwater swimming | 30 | 10 |
| 220 | | 50c. Type **70** | 35 | 1·25 |

**74** Old Harbour in 1768

**1968.** Opening of St. John's Deep Water Harbour.

| | | | | |
|---|---|---|---|---|
| 221 | **74** | 2c. blue and red | 10 | 40 |
| 222 | - | 15c. green and sepia | 35 | 10 |
| 223 | - | 25c. yellow and blue | 40 | 10 |
| 224 | - | 35c. salmon and emerald | 50 | 10 |
| 225 | **74** | $1 black | 90 | 2·00 |

DESIGNS: 15c. Old harbour in 1829; 25c. Freighter and chart of new harbour; 35c. New harbour.

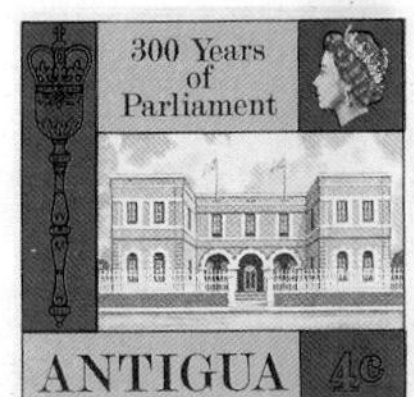

**78** Parliament Buildings

**1969.** Tercentenary of Parliament. Multicoloured.

| | | | | |
|---|---|---|---|---|
| 226 | | 4c. Type **78** | 10 | 10 |
| 227 | | 15c. Antigua Mace and bearer | 20 | 10 |
| 228 | | 25c. House of Representative's Room | 20 | 10 |
| 229 | | 50c. Coat of arms and Seal of Antigua | 30 | 1·60 |

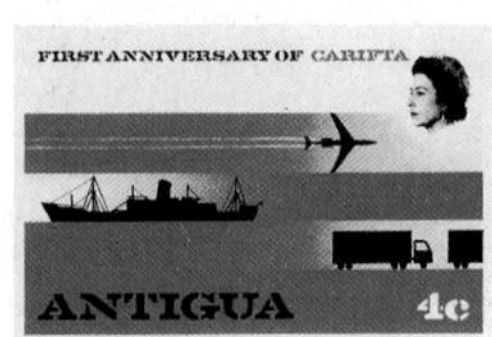

**82** Freight Transport

**1969.** 1st Anniv of Caribbean Free Trade Area.

| | | | | |
|---|---|---|---|---|
| 230 | **82** | 4c. black and purple | 10 | 10 |
| 231 | **82** | 15c. black and blue | 20 | 30 |
| 232 | - | 25c. brown, black & ochre | 25 | 30 |
| 233 | - | 35c. chocolate, blk & brn | 25 | 30 |

DESIGN—VERT: 25, 35c. Crate of cargo.

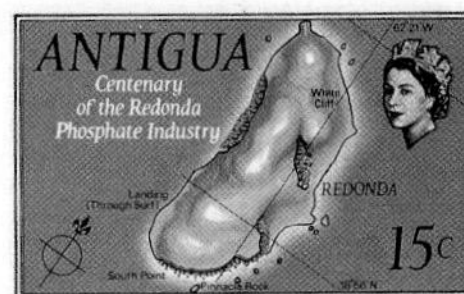

**84** Island of Redonda (Chart)

**1969.** Centenary of Redonda Phosphate Industry. Multicoloured.

| | | | | |
|---|---|---|---|---|
| 249 | | 15c. Type **84** | 20 | 10 |
| 250 | | 25c. View of Redonda from the sea | 20 | 10 |
| 251 | | 50c. Type **84** | 45 | 75 |

**86** "The Adoration of the Magi" (Marcillat)

**1969.** Christmas. Stained Glass Windows. Mult.

| | | | | |
|---|---|---|---|---|
| 252 | | 6c. Type **86** | 10 | 10 |
| 253 | | 10c. "The Nativity" (unknown German artist, 15th century) | 10 | 10 |
| 254 | | 35c. Type **86** | 25 | 10 |
| 255 | | 50c. As 10c. | 50 | 40 |

**1970.** Surch **20c** and bars.

| | | | | |
|---|---|---|---|---|
| 256 | | 20c. on 25c. (No. 189) | 10 | 10 |

**89** Coat of Arms

**1970.** Coil Stamps.

| | | | | |
|---|---|---|---|---|
| 257A | **89** | 5c. blue | 10 | 40 |
| 258A | **89** | 10c. green | 10 | 35 |
| 259A | **89** | 25c. red | 20 | 35 |

**90** Sikorsky S-38 Flying Boat

**1970.** 40th Anniv of Antiguan Air Services. Multicoloured.

| | | | | |
|---|---|---|---|---|
| 260 | | 5c. Type **90** | 50 | 10 |
| 261 | | 20c. Dornier Do-X flying boat | 80 | 10 |
| 262 | | 35c. Hawker Siddeley H.S.748 | 1·00 | 10 |
| 263 | | 50c. Douglas C-124C Globe-master II | 1·00 | 1·50 |
| 264 | | 75c. Vickers Super VC-10 | 1·25 | 2·00 |

**91** Dickens and Scene from "Nicholas Nickleby"

**1970.** Death Centenary of Charles Dickens.

| | | | | |
|---|---|---|---|---|
| 265 | **91** | 5c. bistre, sepia and black | 10 | 10 |
| 266 | - | 20c. turq, sepia & blk | 20 | 10 |
| 267 | - | 35c. blue, sepia and black | 30 | 10 |
| 268 | - | $1 red, sepia and black | 75 | 80 |

DESIGNS: All stamps show Dickens and scene from: 20c. "Pickwick Papers"; 35c. "Oliver Twist"; $1 "David Copperfield".

**92** Carib Indian and War Canoe

**1970.** Multicoloured.. Multicoloured..

| No. | Description | Mint | Used |
|---|---|---|---|
| 323 | ½c. Type **92** | 20 | 50 |
| 270 | 1c. Columbus and "Nina" | 30 | 1·50 |
| 271 | 2c. Sir Thomas Warner's emblem and "Concepcion" | 40 | 3·25 |
| 325 | 3c. Viscount Hood and H.M.S. "Barfleur" | 35 | 1·25 |
| 273 | 4c. Sir George Rodney and H.M.S. "Formidable" | 40 | 3·00 |
| 274 | 5c. Nelson and H.M.S. "Boreas" | 50 | 40 |
| 275 | 6c. William IV and H.M.S. "Pegasus" | 1·75 | 4·00 |
| 276 | 10c. "Blackbeard" and pirate ketch | 80 | 20 |
| 277 | 15c. Collingwood and H.M.S. "Pelican" | 9·00 | 1·00 |
| 278 | 20c. Nelson and H.M.S. "Victory" | 1·25 | 40 |
| 279 | 25c. "Solent I" (paddle-steamer) | 1·25 | 40 |
| 280 | 35c. George V (when Prince George) and H.M.S. "Canada" (screw corvette) | 2·00 | 80 |
| 281 | 50c. H.M.S. "Renown" (battle cruiser) | 4·00 | 6·00 |
| 331 | 75c. "Federal Maple" (freighter) | 7·50 | 3·00 |
| 332 | $1 "Sol Quest" (yacht) and class emblem | 3·00 | 1·75 |
| 333 | $2.50 H.M.S. "London" (destroyer) | 2·75 | 6·50 |
| 285 | $5 "Pathfinder" (tug) | 2·50 | 6·00 |

**93** "The Small Passion" (detail) (Durer)

**1970.** Christmas.

| No. | Type | Description | Mint | Used |
|---|---|---|---|---|
| 286 | **93** | 3c. black and blue | 10 | 10 |
| 287 | - | 10c. purple and pink | 10 | 10 |
| 288 | **93** | 35c. black and red | 30 | 10 |
| 289 | - | 50c. black and lilac | 45 | 50 |

DESIGN: 10, 50c. "Adoration of the Magi" (detail)(Durer).

**94** 4th King's Own Regiment, 1759

**1970.** Military Uniforms (1st series). Mult.

| No. | Description | Mint | Used |
|---|---|---|---|
| 290 | ½c. Type **94** | 10 | 10 |
| 291 | 10c. 4th West India Regiment, 1804 | 50 | 10 |
| 292 | 20c. 60th Regiment, The Royal American, 1809 | 75 | 10 |
| 293 | 35c. 93rd Regiment, Sutherland Highlanders, 1826–34 | 1·00 | 10 |
| 294 | 75c. 3rd West India Regiment, 1851 | 1·75 | 2·00 |
| **MS**295 | 128×164 mm. Nos. 290/4 | 5·50 | 11·00 |

See also Nos. 303/8, 313/18, 353/8 and 380/5.

**95** Market Woman casting Vote

**1971.** 20th Anniv of Adult Suffrage.

| No. | Type | Description | Mint | Used |
|---|---|---|---|---|
| 296 | **95** | 5c. brown | 10 | 10 |
| 297 | - | 20c. olive | 10 | 10 |
| 298 | - | 35c. purple | 10 | 10 |
| 299 | - | 50c. blue | 15 | 30 |

DESIGNS: People voting: 20c. Executive; 35c. Housewife; 50c. Artisan.

**96** "The Last Supper"

**1971.** Easter. Works by Durer.

| No. | Type | Description | Mint | Used |
|---|---|---|---|---|
| 300 | **96** | 5c. black grey and red | 10 | 10 |
| 301 | - | 35c. black, grey and violet | 10 | 10 |
| 302 | - | 75c. black, grey and gold | 20 | 30 |

DESIGNS: 35c. "The Crucifixion"; 75c. "The Resurrection".

**1971.** Military Uniforms (2nd series). As T **94**. Multicoloured.

| No. | Description | Mint | Used |
|---|---|---|---|
| 303 | ½c. Private, 12th Regiment, The Suffolk (1704) | 10 | 10 |
| 304 | 10c. Grenadier, 38th Regiment, South Staffordshire (1751) | 35 | 10 |
| 305 | 20c. Light Company, 5th Regiment, Royal Northumberland Fusiliers (1778) | 50 | 10 |
| 306 | 35c. Private, 48th Regiment, The Northamptonshire (1793) | 60 | 10 |
| 307 | 75c. Private, 15th Regiment, East Yorks (1805) | 1·00 | 3·00 |
| **MS**308 | 127×144 mm. Nos. 303/7 | 4·50 | 6·50 |

**97** "Madonna and Child" (detail, Veronese)

**1971.** Christmas. Multicoloured.

| No. | Description | Mint | Used |
|---|---|---|---|
| 309 | 3c. Type **97** | 10 | 10 |
| 310 | 5c. "Adoration of the Shepherds" (detail, Veronese) | 10 | 10 |
| 311 | 35c. Type **97** | 25 | 10 |
| 312 | 50c. As 5c. | 40 | 30 |

**1972.** Military Uniforms (3rd series). As T **94**. Multicoloured.

| No. | Description | Mint | Used |
|---|---|---|---|
| 313 | ½c. Battalion Company Officer, 25th Foot, 1815 | 10 | 10 |
| 314 | 10c. Sergeant, 14th Foot, 1837 | 85 | 10 |
| 315 | 20c. Private, 67th Foot, 1853 | 1·60 | 15 |
| 316 | 35c. Officer, Royal Artillery, 1854 | 1·90 | 20 |
| 317 | 75c. Private, 29th Foot, 1870 | 2·25 | 4·00 |
| **MS**318 | 125×141 mm. Nos. 313/17 | 7·00 | 8·50 |

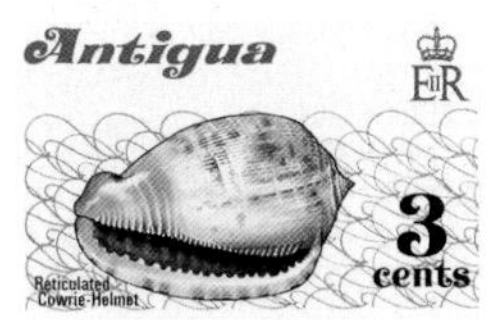


**98** Reticulated Cowrie Helmet

**1972.** Shells. Multicoloured.

| No. | Description | Mint | Used |
|---|---|---|---|
| 319 | 3c. Type **98** | 50 | 10 |
| 320 | 5c. Measled cowrie | 50 | 10 |
| 321 | 35c. West Indian fighting conch | 1·40 | 15 |
| 322 | 50c. Hawk-wing conch | 1·60 | 3·00 |

**99** St. John's Cathedral, Side View

**1972.** Christmas and 125th Anniv of St. John's Cathedral. Multicoloured.

| No. | Description | Mint | Used |
|---|---|---|---|
| 335 | 35c. Type **99** | 20 | 10 |
| 336 | 50c. Cathedral interior | 25 | 25 |
| 337 | 75c. St. John's Cathedral | 30 | 60 |
| **MS**338 | 165×102 mm. Nos. 335/7 | 65 | 1·00 |

**1972.** Royal Silver Wedding. As T **52** of Ascension, but with floral background.

| No. | Description | Mint | Used |
|---|---|---|---|
| 339 | 20c. blue | 15 | 15 |
| 340 | 35c. blue | 15 | 15 |

**101** Batsman and Map

**1972.** 50th Anniv of Rising Sun Cricket Club. Multicoloured.

| No. | Description | Mint | Used |
|---|---|---|---|
| 341 | 5c. Type **101** | 55 | 15 |
| 342 | 35c. Batsman and wicket-keeper | 65 | 10 |
| 343 | $1 Club badge | 1·00 | 2·25 |
| **MS**344 | 88×130 mm. Nos. 341/3 | 3·25 | 7·50 |

**102** Yacht and Map

**1972.** Inauguration of Antigua and Barbuda Tourist Office in New York. Multicoloured.

| No. | Description | Mint | Used |
|---|---|---|---|
| 345 | 35c. Type **102** | 15 | 10 |
| 346 | 50c. Yachts | 20 | 15 |
| 347 | 75c. St. John's G.P.O. | 25 | 25 |
| 348 | $1 Statue of Liberty | 25 | 25 |
| **MS**349 | 100×94 mm. Nos. 346, 348 | 75 | 1·25 |

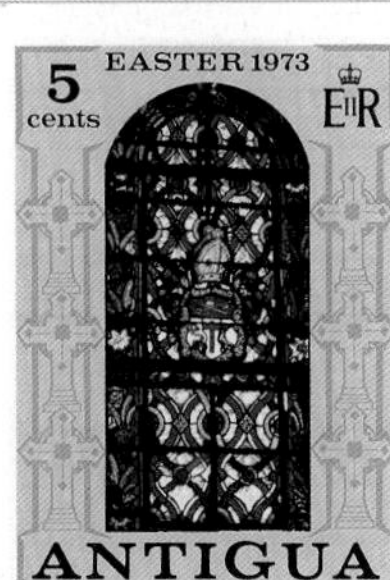


**103** "Episcopal Coat of Arms"

**1973.** Easter. Multicoloured.

| No. | Type | Description | Mint | Used |
|---|---|---|---|---|
| 350 | **103** | 5c. Type **103** | 10 | 10 |
| 351 | - | 35c. "The Crucifixion" | 15 | 10 |
| 352 | - | 75c. "Arms of 1st Bishop of Antigua" | 25 | 30 |

Nos. 350/2 show different stained-glass windows from St. John's Cathedral.

**1973.** Military Uniforms (4th series). As T **94**. Multicoloured.

| No. | Description | Mint | Used |
|---|---|---|---|
| 353 | ½c. Private, Zachariah Tiffin's Regiment of Foot, 1701 | 10 | 10 |
| 354 | 10c. Private, 63rd Regiment of Foot, 1759 | 40 | 10 |
| 355 | 20c. Light Company Officer, 35th Regiment of Foot, 1828 | 50 | 15 |
| 356 | 35c. Private, 2nd West India Regiment, 1853 | 65 | 15 |
| 357 | 75c. Sergeant, 49th Regiment, 1858 | 1·00 | 1·25 |
| **MS**358 | 127×145 mm. Nos. 353/7 | 3·75 | 3·25 |

**104** Butterfly Costumes

**1973.** Carnival. Multicoloured.

| No. | Description | Mint | Used |
|---|---|---|---|
| 359 | 5c. Type **104** | 10 | 10 |
| 360 | 20c. Carnival street scene | 15 | 10 |
| 361 | 35c. Carnival troupe | 20 | 10 |
| 362 | 75c. Carnival Queen | 30 | 30 |
| **MS**363 | 134×95 mm. Nos. 359/62 | 65 | 1·00 |

**105** "Virgin of the Milk Porridge" (Gerard David)

**1973.** Christmas. Multicoloured.

| No. | Description | Mint | Used |
|---|---|---|---|
| 364 | 3c. Type **105** | 10 | 10 |
| 365 | 5c. "Adoration of the Magi" (Stomer) | 10 | 10 |
| 366 | 20c. "The Granducal Madonna" (Raphael) | 15 | 10 |
| 367 | 35c. "Nativity with God the Father and Holy Ghost" (Battista) | 20 | 10 |
| 368 | $1 "Madonna and Child" (Murillo) | 40 | 60 |
| **MS**369 | 130×128 mm. Nos. 364/8 | 1·10 | 1·75 |

**106** Princess Anne and Captain Mark Phillips

**1973.** Royal Wedding.

| No. | Type | Description | Mint | Used |
|---|---|---|---|---|
| 370 | **106** | 35c. multicoloured | 10 | 10 |
| 371 | - | $2 multicoloured | 25 | 25 |
| **MS**372 | | 78×100 mm. Nos. 370/1 | 50 | 40 |

The $2 is as Type **106** but has a different border.

**1973.** Nos. 370/1 optd **HONEYMOON VISIT DECEMBER 16TH 1973**.

| No. | Type | Description | Mint | Used |
|---|---|---|---|---|
| 373 | **106** | 35c. multicoloured | 15 | 10 |
| 374 | - | $2 multicoloured | 30 | 30 |
| **MS**375 | | 78×100 mm. Nos. 373/4 | 55 | 55 |

**108** Coat of Arms of Antigua and University

**1974.** 25th Anniv of University of West Indies. Multicoloured.

| No. | Description | Mint | Used |
|---|---|---|---|
| 376 | 5c. Type **108** | 15 | 10 |
| 377 | 20c. Extra-mural art | 20 | 10 |
| 378 | 35c. Antigua campus | 20 | 10 |
| 379 | 75c. Antigua chancellor | 25 | 35 |

**1974.** Military Uniforms (5th series). As T **94**. Multicoloured.

| No. | Description | Mint | Used |
|---|---|---|---|
| 380 | ½c. Officer, 59th Foot, 1797 | 10 | 10 |
| 381 | 10c. Gunner, Royal Artillery, 1800 | 35 | 10 |
| 382 | 20c. Private, 1st West India Regiment, 1830 | 50 | 10 |
| 383 | 35c. Officer, 92nd Foot, 1843 | 60 | 10 |
| 384 | 75c. Private, 23rd Foot, 1846 | 75 | 2·25 |
| **MS**385 | 125×145 mm. Nos. 380/4 | 2·25 | 2·50 |

**109** English Postman, Mailcoach and Westland Dragonfly Helicopter

**1974.** Centenary of U.P.U. Multicoloured.

| No. | Description | Mint | Used |
|---|---|---|---|
| 386 | ½c. Type **109** | 10 | 10 |
| 387 | 1c. Bellman, mail steamer "Orinoco" and satellite | 10 | 10 |
| 388 | 2c. Train guard, post-bus and hydrofoil | 10 | 10 |
| 389 | 5c. Swiss messenger, Wells Fargo coach and Concorde | 60 | 30 |
| 390 | 20c. Postilion, Japanese postmen and carrier pigeon | 35 | 10 |
| 391 | 35c. Antiguan postman, Sikorsky S-88 flying boat and tracking station | 45 | 15 |
| 392 | $1 Medieval courier, American express train and Boeing 747-100 | 1·75 | 2·00 |
| **MS**393 | 141×161 mm. Nos. 386/92 | 3·50 | 2·50 |

On the ½c. English is spelt "Enlish" and on the 2c. Postal is spelt "Fostal".

**110** Traditional Player

**1974.** Antiguan Steel Bands.

394 **110** 5c. dp red, red and black 10 10
395 - 20c. brown, lt brn & blk 10 10
396 - 35c. lt green, green & blk 10 10
397 - 75c. blue, dp blue & blk 20 1·10
**MS**398 115×108 mm. Nos. 394/7 35 1·25

DESIGNS—HORIZ: 20c. Traditional band; 35c. Modern band. VERT: 75c. Modern player.

**111** Footballers

**1974.** World Cup Football Championships.

399 **111** 5c. multicoloured 10 10
400 - 35c. multicoloured 15 10
401 - 75c. multicoloured 30 30
402 - $1 multicoloured 35 40
**MS**403 135×130 mm. Nos. 399/402 85 90

Nos. 400/2 show various footballing designs similar to Type **111**.

**1974.** Earthquake Relief Fund. Nos. 400/2 and 397 optd or surch **EARTHQUAKE RELIEF**.

404 35c. multicoloured 20 10
405 75c. multicoloured 30 25
406 $1 multicoloured 40 30
407 $5 on 75c. deep blue, blue and black 1·25 2·00

**113** Churchill as Schoolboy and School College Building, Harrow

**1974.** Birth Centenary of Sir Winston Churchill. Multicoloured.

408 5c. Type **113** 15 10
409 35c. Churchill and St. Paul's Cathedral 20 10
410 75c. Coat of arms and catafalque 30 65
411 $1 Churchill, "reward" notice and South African escape route 45 1·00
**MS**412 107×82 mm. Nos. 408/11 1·00 1·50

**114** "Madonna of the Trees" (Bellini)

**1974.** Christmas. "Madonna and Child" paintings by named artists. Multicoloured.

413 ½c. Type **114** 10 10
414 1c. Raphael 10 10
415 2c. Van der Weyden 10 10
416 3c. Giorgione 10 10
417 5c. Mantegna 10 10
418 20c. Vivarini 20 10
419 35c. Montagna 30 10
420 75c. Lorenzo Costa 55 1·10
**MS**421 139×126 mm. Nos. 413/20 95 1·40

**1975.** Nos. 390/2 and 331 surch.

422 50c. on 20c. multicoloured 1·25 2·00
423 $2.50 on 35c. multicoloured 2·00 5·50
424 $5 on $1 multicoloured 6·50 7·00
425 $10 on 75c. multicoloured 2·00 7·50

**116** Carib War Canoe, English Harbour, 1300

**1975.** Nelson's Dockyard. Multicoloured.

427 5c. Type **116** 20 10
428 15c. Ship of the line, English Harbour, 1770 80 15
429 35c. H.M.S "Boreas" at anchor, and Lord Nelson, 1787 1·25 15
430 50c. Yachts during "Sailing Week", 1974 1·25 1·50
431 $1 Yacht Anchorage, Old Dockyard, 1970 1·50 2·25
**MS**432 130×134 mm. As Nos. 427/31, but in larger format, 43×28 mm 3·25 2·00

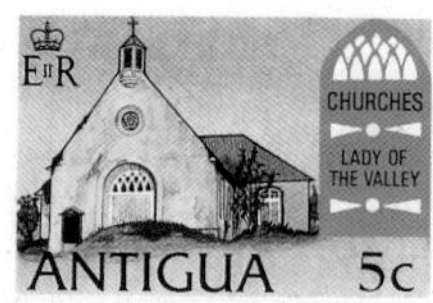

**117** Lady of the Valley Church

**1975.** Antiguan Churches. Multicoloured.

433 5c. Type **117** 10 10
434 20c. Gilbert Memorial 10 10
435 35c. Grace Hill Moravian 15 10
436 50c. St. Phillips 20 20
437 $1 Ebenezer Methodist 35 50
**MS**438 91×101 mm. Nos. 435/7 65 1·25

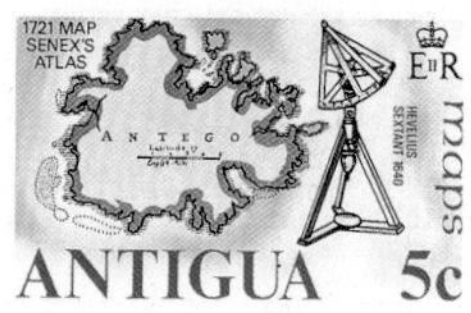

**118** Map of 1721 and Sextant of 1640

**1975.** Maps of Antigua. Multicoloured.

439 5c. Type **118** 30 15
440 20c. Map of 1775 and galleon 55 15
441 35c. Maps of 1775 and 1955 70 15
442 $1 1973 maps of Antigua and English Harbour 1·40 2·25
**MS**443 130×89 mm. Nos. 439/42 3·00 3·25

**119** Scout Bugler

**1975.** World Scout Jamboree, Norway. Mult.

444 15c. Type **119** 25 15
445 20c. Scouts in camp 30 15
446 35c. "Lord Baden-Powell" (D. Jagger) 50 20
447 $2 Scout dancers from Dahomey 1·50 2·25
**MS**448 145×107 mm. Nos. 444/7 3·25 3·50

**120** "Eurema elathea"

**1975.** Butterflies. Multicoloured.

449 ½c. Type **120** 10 30
450 1c. "Danaus plexippus" 10 30
451 2c. "Phoebis philea" 10 30
452 5c. "Hypolimnas misippus" 20 10
453 20c. "Eurema proterpia" 75 40
454 35c. "Battus polydamas" 1·40 50
455 $2 "Cynthia cardui" 4·00 9·00
**MS**456 147×94 mm. Nos. 452/5 6·00 11·00

No. 452 is incorrectly captioned "Marpesia petreus thetys".

**121** "Madonna and Child" (Correggio)

**1975.** Christmas. "Madonna and Child" paintings by artists named. Multicoloured.

457 ½c. Type **121** 10 10
458 1c. El Greco 10 10
459 2c. Durer 10 10
460 3c. Antonello 10 10
461 5c. Bellini 10 10
462 10c. Durer (different) 10 10
463 35c. Bellini (different) 40 10
464 $2 Durer (different again) 1·00 1·00
**MS**465 138×119 mm. Nos. 461/4 1·50 1·60

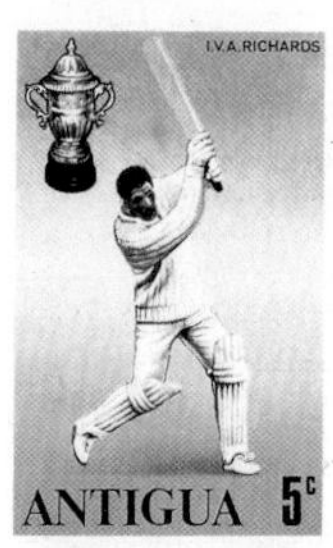

**122** Vivian Richards

**1975.** World Cricket Cup Winners. Multicoloured.

466 5c. Type **122** 1·25 20
467 35c. Andy Roberts 2·25 60
468 $2 West Indies team (horiz) 4·25 8·00

**123** Antillean Crested Hummingbird

**1976.** Multicoloured.. Multicoloured..

469A ½c. Type **123** 40 50
470A 1c. Imperial amazon ("Imperial Parrot") 1·40 50
471A 2c. Zenaida dove 1·40 50
472A 3c. Loggerhead kingbird 1·40 60
473A 4c. Red-necked pigeon 1·40 2·00
474A 5c. Rufous-throated solitaire 2·00 10
475A 6c. Orchid tree 30 2·00
476A 10c. Bougainvillea 30 10
477A 15c. Geiger tree 35 10
478A 20c. Flamboyant 35 35
479A 25c. Hibiscus 40 15
480A 35c. Flame of the wood 40 40
481A 50c. Cannon at Fort James 55 60
482A 75c. Premier's Office 60 2·00
483A $1 Potworks Dam 75 1·00
484A $2.50 Diamond irrigation scheme (44×28 mm) 1·00 5·00
485B $5 Government House (44×28 mm) 1·50 7·50
486A $10 Coolidge International Airport (44×28 mm) 3·50 8·00

**124** Privates, Clark's Illinois Regiment

**1976.** Bicentenary of American Revolution. Mult.

487 ½c. Type **124** 10 10
488 1c. Rifleman, Pennsylvania Militia 10 10
489 2c. Powder horn 10 10
490 5c. Water bottle 10 10
491 35c. American flags 50 10
492 $1 "Montgomery" (American brig) 1·00 40
493 $5 "Ranger" (privateer sloop) 1·75 2·25
**MS**494 71×84 mm. $2.50, Congress flag 1·00 1·40

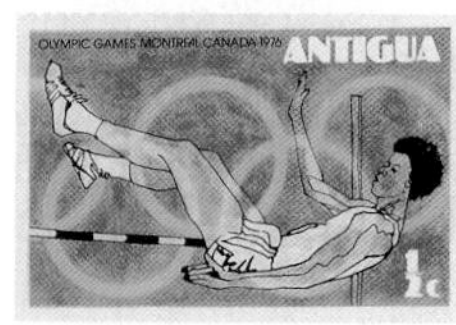

**125** High Jump

**1976.** Olympic Games, Montreal.

495 **125** ½c. brown, yellow & black 10 10
496 - 1c. violet, blue and black 10 10
497 - 2c. green and black 10 10
498 - 15c. blue and black 15 10
499 - 30c. brown, yell & blk 20 15
500 - $1 orange, red and black 40 40
501 - $2 red and black 60 80
**MS**502 88×138 mm. Nos. 498/501 1·75 1·25

DESIGNS: 1c. Boxing; 2c. Pole vault; 15c. Swimming; 30c. Running; $1 Cycling; $2 Shot put.

**126** Water Skiing

**1976.** Water Sports. Multicoloured.

503 ½c. Type **126** 10 10
504 1c. Sailing 10 10
505 2c. Snorkeling 10 10
506 20c. Deep sea fishing 50 10
507 50c. Scuba diving 75 35
508 $2 Swimming 1·25 1·25
**MS**509 89×114 mm. Nos. 506/8 1·75 1·75

**127** French Angelfish

**1976.** Fishes. Multicoloured.

510 15c. Type **127** 40 15
511 30c. Yellow-finned grouper 55 30
512 50c. Yellow-tailed snapper 70 50
513 90c. Shy hamlet 90 1·50

**128** The Annunciation

**1976.** Christmas. Multicoloured.

514 8c. Type **128** 10 10
515 10c. The Holy Family 10 10
516 15c. The Magi 10 10
517 50c. The Shepherds 20 25
518 $1 Epiphany scene 30 50

**129** Mercury and U.P.U. Emblem

**1976.** Special Events, 1976. Multicoloured.

519 ½c. Type **129** 10 10
520 1c. Alfred Nobel 10 10
521 10c. Space satellite 30 10
522 50c. Viv Richards and Andy Roberts 3·50 1·75
523 $1 Bell and telephones 1·00 2·00
524 $2 Yacht "Freelance" 2·25 4·50
**MS**525 127×101 mm. Nos. 521/4 7·50 13·00

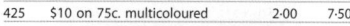

**130** Royal Family

**1977.** Silver Jubilee. Multicoloured. (a) Perf.

| | | | |
|---|---|---|---|
| 526 | 10c. Type **130** | 10 | 10 |
| 527 | 30c. Royal Visit, 1966 | 10 | 10 |
| 528 | 50c. The Queen enthroned | 15 | 15 |
| 529 | 90c. The Queen after Coronation | 15 | 25 |
| 530 | $2.50 Queen and Prince Charles | 30 | 55 |
| **MS**531 | 116×78 mm. $5 Queen and Prince Philip | 65 | 85 |

(b) Roulximperf. Self-adhesive.

| | | | |
|---|---|---|---|
| 532 | 50c. As 90c. | 35 | 75 |
| 533 | $5 The Queen and Prince Philip | 2·00 | 3·75 |

Nos. 532/3 come from booklets.

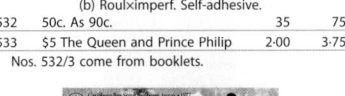

**131** Making Camp

**1977.** Caribbean Scout Jamboree, Jamaica. Mult.

| | | | |
|---|---|---|---|
| 534 | ½c. Type **131** | 10 | 10 |
| 535 | 1c. Hiking | 10 | 10 |
| 536 | 2c. Rock-climbing | 10 | 10 |
| 537 | 10c. Cutting logs | 15 | 10 |
| 538 | 30c. Map and sign reading | 40 | 10 |
| 539 | 50c. First aid | 65 | 25 |
| 540 | $2 Rafting | 1·25 | 2·50 |
| **MS**541 | 127×114 mm. Nos. 538/40 | 3·00 | 4·00 |

**132** Carnival Costume

**1977.** 21st Anniv of Carnival. Multicoloured.

| | | | |
|---|---|---|---|
| 542 | 10c. Type **132** | 10 | 10 |
| 543 | 30c. Carnival Queen | 25 | 10 |
| 544 | 50c. Butterfly costume | 30 | 15 |
| 545 | 90c. Queen of the band | 40 | 25 |
| 546 | $1 Calypso King and Queen | 40 | 30 |
| **MS**547 | 140×120 mm. Nos. 542/6 | 1·10 | 1·60 |

**1977.** Royal Visit. Nos. 526/30 optd **ROYAL VISIT 28TH OCTOBER 1977.**

| | | | |
|---|---|---|---|
| 548 | 10c. Type **130** | 10 | 10 |
| 549 | 30c. Royal Visit, 1966 | 15 | 10 |
| 550 | 50c. The Queen enthroned | 20 | 10 |
| 551 | 90c. The Queen after Coronation | 30 | 20 |
| 552 | $2.50 Queen and Prince Charles | 50 | 35 |
| **MS**553 | 116×178 mm. $5 Queen and Prince Philip | 1·00 | 1·00 |

**134** "Virgin and Child Enthroned" (Tura)

**1977.** Christmas. Paintings by artists listed. Mult.

| | | | |
|---|---|---|---|
| 554 | ½c. Type **134** | 10 | 20 |
| 555 | 1c. Crivelli | 10 | 20 |
| 556 | 2c. Lotto | 10 | 20 |
| 557 | 8c. Pontormo | 15 | 10 |
| 558 | 10c. Tura (different) | 15 | 10 |
| 559 | 25c. Lotto (different) | 30 | 10 |
| 560 | $2 Crivelli (different) | 85 | 1·00 |

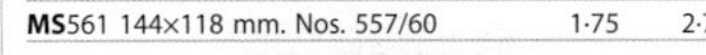

| | | | |
|---|---|---|---|
| **MS**561 | 144×118 mm. Nos. 557/60 | 1·75 | 2·75 |

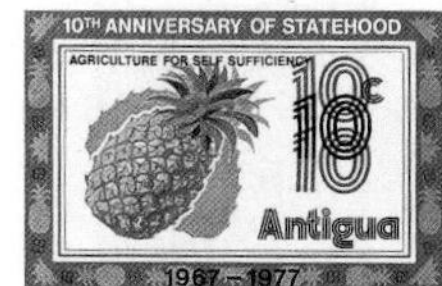

**135** Pineapple

**1977.** 10th Anniv of Statehood. Multicoloured.

| | | | |
|---|---|---|---|
| 562 | 10c. Type **135** | 10 | 10 |
| 563 | 15c. State flag | 60 | 20 |
| 564 | 50c. Police band | 2·50 | 80 |
| 565 | 90c. Premier V. C. Bird | 55 | 80 |
| 566 | $2 State Coat of Arms | 90 | 2·00 |
| **MS**567 | 129×99 mm. Nos. 563/6 | 3·50 | 3·00 |

**136** Wright Glider III, 1902

**1978.** 75th Anniv of Powered Flight. Mult.

| | | | |
|---|---|---|---|
| 568 | ½c. Type **136** | 10 | 10 |
| 569 | 1c. Wright Flyer I, 1903 | 10 | 10 |
| 570 | 2c. Launch system and engine | 10 | 10 |
| 571 | 10c. Orville Wright (vert) | 30 | 10 |
| 572 | 50c. Wright Flyer III, 1905 | 60 | 15 |
| 573 | 90c. Wilbur Wright (vert) | 80 | 30 |
| 574 | $2 Wright Type B, 1910 | 1·00 | 80 |
| **MS**575 | 90×75 mm. $2.50, Wright Flyer I on launch system | 1·25 | 2·75 |

**137** Sunfish Regatta

**1978.** Sailing Week. Multicoloured.

| | | | |
|---|---|---|---|
| 576 | 10c. Type **137** | 20 | 10 |
| 577 | 50c. Fishing and work boat race | 35 | 20 |
| 578 | 90c. Curtain Bluff race | 60 | 35 |
| 579 | $2 Power boat rally | 1·10 | 1·25 |
| **MS**580 | 110×77 mm. $2.50, Guadeloupe–Antigua race | 1·50 | 1·75 |

**138** Queen Elizabeth and Prince Philip

**1978.** 25th Anniv of Coronation. Mult. (a) Perf.

| | | | |
|---|---|---|---|
| 581 | 10c. Type **138** | 10 | 10 |
| 582 | 30c. Crowning | 10 | 10 |
| 583 | 50c. Coronation procession | 15 | 10 |
| 584 | 90c. Queen seated in St. Edward's Chair | 20 | 15 |
| 585 | $2.50 Queen wearing Imperial State Crown | 40 | 40 |
| **MS**586 | 114×104 mm. $5 Queen and Prince Philip | 80 | 80 |

(b) Roulximperf. Self-adhesive. Horiz designs as Type **138**.

| | | | |
|---|---|---|---|
| 587 | 25c. Glass Coach | 15 | 30 |
| 588 | 50c. Irish State Coach | 25 | 50 |
| 589 | $5 Coronation Coach | 1·75 | 3·00 |

Nos. 587/9 come from booklets.

**140** Player running with Ball

**1978.** World Cup Football Championship, Argentina. Multicoloured.

| | | | |
|---|---|---|---|
| 590 | 10c. Type **140** | 15 | 10 |
| 591 | 15c. Players in front of goal | 15 | 10 |
| 592 | $3 Referee and player | 2·00 | 1·75 |
| **MS**593 | 126×88 mm. 25c. Player crouching with ball; 30c. Players heading ball; 50c. Players running with ball; $2 Goalkeeper diving. All horiz | 3·25 | 2·50 |

**141** Petrea

**1978.** Flowers. Multicoloured.

| | | | |
|---|---|---|---|
| 594 | 25c. Type **141** | 25 | 10 |
| 595 | 50c. Sunflower | 35 | 20 |
| 596 | 90c. Frangipani | 60 | 30 |
| 597 | $2 Passion flower | 1·25 | 2·00 |
| **MS**598 | 118×85 mm. $2.50, Hibiscus | 1·40 | 1·60 |

**142** "St. Ildefonso receiving the Chasuble from the Virgin" (Rubens)

**1978.** Christmas. Multicoloured.

| | | | |
|---|---|---|---|
| 599 | 8c. Type **142** | 10 | 10 |
| 600 | 25c. "The Flight of St. Barbara" (Rubens) | 20 | 10 |
| 601 | $2 "Madonna and Child, with St. Joseph, John the Baptist and Donor" | 65 | 55 |
| **MS**602 | 170×113 mm. $4 "The Annunciation" (Rubens) | 1·25 | 1·50 |

The painting shown on No. 601 is incorrectly attributed to Rubens on the stamp. The artist was Sebastiano del Piombo.

**143** 1d. Stamp of 1863

**1979.** Death Centenary of Sir Rowland Hill. Mult.

| | | | |
|---|---|---|---|
| 603 | 25c. Type **143** | 10 | 10 |
| 604 | 50c. 1840 Penny Black | 20 | 15 |
| 605 | $1 Mail coach and woman posting letter, c. 1840 | 30 | 20 |
| 606 | $2 Modern transport | 1·10 | 60 |
| **MS**607 | 108×82 mm. $2.50, Sir Rowland Hill | 80 | 90 |

**144** "The Deposition from the Cross" (painting)

**1979.** Easter. Works by Durer.

| | | | | |
|---|---|---|---|---|
| 608 | **144** | 10c. multicoloured | 10 | 10 |
| 609 | - | 50c. multicoloured | 35 | 20 |
| 610 | - | $4 black, mauve and yellow | 1·00 | 90 |
| **MS**611 | – | 114×99 mm. $2.50, multicoloured | 80 | 80 |

DESIGNS: 50c., $2.50, "Christ on the Cross–The Passion" (wood engravings) (both different); $4 "Man of Sorrows with Hands Raised" (wood engraving).

**145** Toy Yacht and Child's Hand

**1979.** International Year of the Child. Mult.

| | | | |
|---|---|---|---|
| 612 | 25c. Type **145** | 10 | 10 |
| 613 | 50c. Rocket | 25 | 15 |
| 614 | 90c. Car | 40 | 25 |
| 615 | $2 Toy train | 1·00 | 90 |
| **MS**616 | 80×112 mm. $5 Aeroplane | 1·10 | 1·10 |

Nos. 612/16 also show the hands of children of different races.

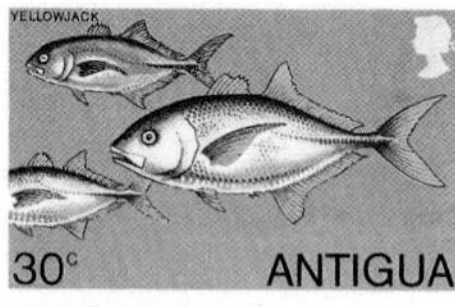

**146** Yellow Jack

**1979.** Fishes. Multicoloured.

| | | | |
|---|---|---|---|
| 617 | 30c. Type **146** | 35 | 15 |
| 618 | 50c. Blue-finned tuna | 40 | 25 |
| 619 | 90c. Sailfish | 60 | 40 |
| 620 | $3 Wahoo | 1·75 | 1·75 |
| **MS**621 | 122×75 mm. $2.50, Great barracuda | 1·50 | 1·40 |

**147** Cook's Birthplace, Marton

**1979.** Death Bicentenary of Captain Cook. Mult.

| | | | |
|---|---|---|---|
| 622 | 25c. Type **147** | 65 | 25 |
| 623 | 50c. H.M.S. "Endeavour" | 1·25 | 60 |
| 624 | 90c. Marine chronometer | 75 | 80 |
| 625 | $3 Landing at Botany Bay | 1·75 | 3·00 |
| **MS**626 | 110×85 mm. $2.50, H.M.S. "Resolution" | 2·25 | 1·50 |

**148** The Holy Family

**1979.** Christmas. Multicoloured.

| | | | |
|---|---|---|---|
| 627 | 8c. Type **148** | 10 | 10 |
| 628 | 25c. Virgin and Child on ass | 15 | 10 |
| 629 | 50c. Shepherd and star | 25 | 35 |
| 630 | $4 Wise Men with gifts | 85 | 2·50 |
| **MS**631 | 113×94 mm. $3 Angel with trumpet | 1·00 | 1·50 |

**149** Javelin Throwing

**1980.** Olympic Games, Moscow. Multicoloured.

| | | | |
|---|---|---|---|
| 632 | 10c. Type **149** | 20 | 10 |
| 633 | 25c. Running | 20 | 10 |
| 634 | $1 Pole vault | 50 | 50 |
| 635 | $2 Hurdles | 70 | 1·75 |
| **MS**636 | 127×96 mm. $3 Boxing (horiz) | 80 | 90 |

**150** Mickey Mouse and Airplane

**1980.** International Year of the Child. Walt Disney Cartoon Characters. Multicoloured.

| | | | |
|---|---|---|---|
| 637 | ½c. Type **150** | 10 | 10 |
| 638 | 1c. Donald Duck driving car (vert) | 10 | 10 |
| 639 | 2c. Goofy driving taxi | 10 | 10 |
| 640 | 3c. Mickey and Minnie Mouse on motorcycle | 10 | 10 |
| 641 | 4c. Huey, Dewey and Louie on a bicycle for three | 10 | 10 |
| 642 | 5c. Grandma Duck and truck of roosters | 10 | 10 |
| 643 | 10c. Mickey Mouse in jeep (vert) | 10 | 10 |
| 644 | $1 Chip and Dale in yacht | 2·00 | 2·00 |
| 645 | $4 Donald Duck riding toy train (vert) | 4·00 | 6·50 |
| **MS**646 | 101×127 mm. $2.50, Goofy flying biplane | 4·50 | 3·25 |

**1980.** "London 1980" International Stamp Exhibition. Nos. 603/6 optd **LONDON 1980**.

| | | | |
|---|---|---|---|
| 647 | 25c. Type **143** | 25 | 15 |
| 648 | 50c. Penny Black | 35 | 35 |
| 649 | $1 Stage-coach and woman posting letter, c. 1840 | 60 | 70 |
| 650 | $2 Modern mail transport | 3·25 | 3·00 |

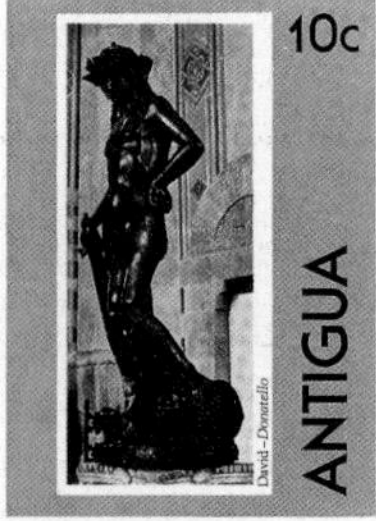

**152** "David" (statue, Donatello)

**1980.** Famous Works of Art. Multicoloured.

| | | | |
|---|---|---|---|
| 651 | 10c. Type **152** | 10 | 10 |
| 652 | 30c. "The Birth of Venus" (painting, Botticelli) (horiz) | 30 | 15 |
| 653 | 50c. "Reclining Couple" (sarcophagus), Cerveteri (horiz) | 40 | 40 |
| 654 | 90c. "The Garden of Earthly Delights" (painting by Bosch) (horiz) | 55 | 65 |
| 655 | $1 "Portinari Altarpiece" (painting, van der Goes) (horiz) | 65 | 75 |
| 656 | $4 "Eleanora of Toledo and her Son, Giovanni de'Medici" (painting, Bronzino) | 1·75 | 3·00 |
| **MS**657 | 99×124 mm. $5 "The Holy Family" (painting, Rembrandt) | 2·50 | 1·75 |

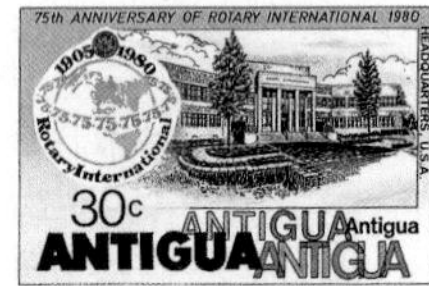

**153** Anniversary Emblem and Headquarters, U.S.A.

**1980.** 75th Anniv of Rotary International. Mult.

| | | | |
|---|---|---|---|
| 658 | 30c. Type **153** | 30 | 30 |
| 659 | 50c. Rotary anniversary emblem and Antigua Rotary Club banner | 40 | 50 |
| 660 | 90c. Map of Antigua and Rotary emblem | 60 | 70 |
| 661 | $3 Paul P. Harris (founder) and Rotary emblem | 2·00 | 3·50 |
| **MS**662 | 102×78 mm. $5 Antiguan flags and Rotary emblems | 1·25 | 2·00 |

**154** Queen Elizabeth the Queen Mother

**1980.** 80th Birthday of The Queen Mother.

| | | | |
|---|---|---|---|
| 663 | **154** 10c. multicoloured | 40 | 10 |
| 664 | **154** $2.50 multicoloured | 1·50 | 1·75 |
| **MS**665 | 68×90 mm. As T **154**. $3 multicoloured | 1·75 | 2·25 |

**155** Ringed Kingfisher

**1980.** Birds. Multicoloured.

| | | | |
|---|---|---|---|
| 666 | 10c. Type **155** | 70 | 30 |
| 667 | 30c. Plain pigeon | 1·00 | 50 |
| 668 | $1 Green-throated carib | 1·50 | 2·00 |
| 669 | $2 Black-necked stilt | 2·00 | 4·00 |
| **MS**670 | 73×73 mm. $2.50, Roseate tern | 7·00 | 4·50 |

**1980.** Christmas. Walt Disney's "Sleeping Beauty". As T **150**. Multicoloured.

| | | | |
|---|---|---|---|
| 671 | ½c. The Bad Fairy with her raven | 10 | 10 |
| 672 | 1c. The good fairies | 10 | 10 |
| 673 | 2c. Aurora | 10 | 10 |
| 674 | 4c. Aurora pricks her finger | 10 | 10 |
| 675 | 8c. The prince | 10 | 10 |
| 676 | 10c. The prince fights the dragon | 15 | 10 |
| 677 | 25c. The prince awakens Aurora with a kiss | 20 | 20 |
| 678 | $2 The prince and Aurora's betrothal | 2·25 | 2·25 |
| 679 | $2.50 The prince and princess | 2·50 | 2·50 |
| **MS**680 | 126×101 mm. $4 multicoloured (vert) | 5·00 | 3·25 |

**156** Diesel Locomotive No. 15

**1981.** Sugar Cane Railway Locomotives. Mult.

| | | | |
|---|---|---|---|
| 681 | 25c. Type **156** | 15 | 15 |
| 682 | 50c. Narrow-gauge steam locomotive | 30 | 30 |
| 683 | 90c. Diesel locomotives Nos. 1 and 10 | 55 | 60 |
| 684 | $3 Steam locomotive hauling sugar cane | 2·00 | 2·25 |
| **MS**685 | 82×111 mm. $2.50, Antiguan sugar factory, railway yard and sheds | 1·75 | 1·75 |

**1981.** Independence. Nos. 475/6 and 478/86 optd **"INDEPENDENCE 1981"**.

| | | | |
|---|---|---|---|
| 686B | 6c. Orchid tree | 10 | 30 |
| 687B | 10c. Bougainvillea | 10 | 10 |
| 688B | 20c. Flamboyant | 10 | 10 |
| 689B | 25c. Hibiscus | 15 | 15 |
| 690B | 35c. Flame of the wood | 20 | 20 |
| 691B | 50c. Cannon at Fort James | 35 | 35 |
| 692B | 75c. Premier's Office | 40 | 60 |
| 693B | $1 Potworks Dam | 55 | 70 |
| 694B | $2.50 Irrigation scheme, Diamond Estate | 75 | 1·75 |
| 695B | $5 Government House | 1·40 | 3·00 |
| 696B | $10 Coolidge International Airport | 3·25 | 5·50 |

**158** "Pipes of Pan"

**1981.** Birth Centenary of Picasso. Multicoloured.

| | | | |
|---|---|---|---|
| 697 | 10c. Type **158** | 10 | 10 |
| 698 | 50c. "Seated Harlequin" | 30 | 30 |
| 699 | 90c. "Paulo as Harlequin" | 55 | 55 |
| 700 | $4 "Mother and Child" | 2·00 | 2·00 |
| **MS**701 | 115×140 mm. $5 "Three Musicians" (detail) | 1·75 | 2·75 |

**159** Prince Charles and Lady Diana Spencer

**1981.** Royal Wedding (1st issue). Multicoloured.

| | | | |
|---|---|---|---|
| 702 | 25c. Type **159** | 10 | 10 |
| 703 | 50c. Glamis Castle | 10 | 10 |
| 704 | $4 Prince Charles skiing | 80 | 80 |
| **MS**705 | 96×82 mm. $5 Glass coach | 80 | 80 |

**160** Prince of Wales at Investiture, 1969

**1981.** Royal Wedding (2nd issue). Multicoloured. Roul×imperf. Self-adhesive.

| | | | |
|---|---|---|---|
| 706 | 25c. Type **160** | 15 | 25 |
| 707 | 25c. Prince Charles as baby, 1948 | 15 | 25 |
| 708 | $1 Prince Charles at R.A.F. College, Cranwell, 1971 | 25 | 50 |
| 709 | $1 Prince Charles attending Hill House School, 1956 | 25 | 50 |
| 710 | $2 Prince Charles and Lady Diana Spencer | 50 | 75 |
| 711 | $2 Prince Charles at Trinity College, 1967 | 50 | 75 |
| 712 | $5 Prince Charles and Lady Diana (different) | 1·00 | 1·50 |

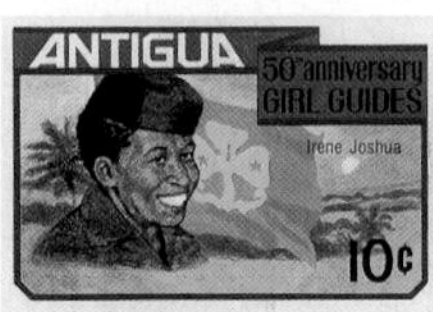

**161** Irene Joshua (founder)

**1981.** 50th Anniv of Antigua Girl Guide Movement. Multicoloured.

| | | | |
|---|---|---|---|
| 713 | 10c. Type **161** | 15 | 10 |
| 714 | 50c. Campfire sing-song | 45 | 35 |
| 715 | 90c. Sailing | 75 | 65 |
| 716 | $2.50 Animal tending | 1·75 | 2·00 |
| **MS**717 | 110×85 mm. $5 Raising the flag | 4·50 | 3·00 |

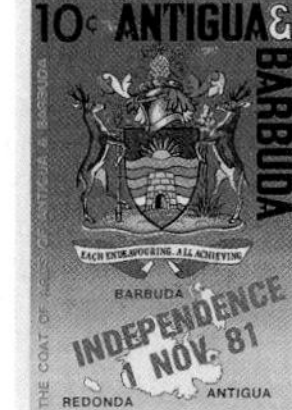

**162** Antigua and Barbuda Coat of Arms

**1981.** Independence. Multicoloured.

| | | | |
|---|---|---|---|
| 718 | 10c. Type **162** | 25 | 10 |
| 719 | 50c. Pineapple, with Antigua and Barbuda flag and map | 2·00 | 60 |
| 720 | 90c. Prime Minister Vere Bird | 55 | 55 |
| 721 | $2.50 St. John's Cathedral (38×25 mm) | 1·50 | 3·50 |
| **MS**722 | 105×79 mm. $5 Map of Antigua and Barbuda (42×42 mm) | 4·50 | 2·75 |

**163** "Holy Night" (Jacques Stella)

**1981.** Christmas. Paintings. Multicoloured.

| | | | |
|---|---|---|---|
| 723 | 8c. Type **163** | 15 | 10 |
| 724 | 30c. "Mary with Child" (Julius Schnorr von Carolfeld) | 40 | 15 |
| 725 | $1 "Virgin and Child" (Alonso Cano) | 75 | 90 |
| 726 | $3 "Virgin and Child" (Lorenzo di Credi) | 1·10 | 3·75 |
| **MS**727 | 77×111 mm. $5 "Holy Family" (Pieter von Avon) | 2·50 | 4·50 |

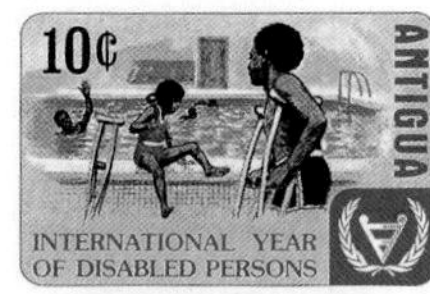

**164** Swimming

**1981.** International Year of Disabled People. Sports for the Disabled. Multicoloured.

| | | | |
|---|---|---|---|
| 728 | 10c. Type **164** | 10 | 10 |
| 729 | 50c. Discus-throwing | 20 | 30 |
| 730 | 90c. Archery | 40 | 55 |
| 731 | $2 Baseball | 1·00 | 1·40 |
| **MS**732 | 108×84 mm. $4 Basketball | 5·00 | 2·75 |

**165** Scene from Football Match

**1982.** World Cup Football Championship, Spain.

| | | | |
|---|---|---|---|
| 733 | **165** 10c. multicoloured | 30 | 10 |
| 734 | - 50c. multicoloured | 60 | 35 |
| 735 | - 90c. multicoloured | 1·10 | 70 |
| 736 | - $4 multicoloured | 3·50 | 3·50 |
| **MS**737 | – 75×92 mm. $5 multicoloured | 8·50 | 10·00 |

DESIGNS: 50c. to $5, Scenes from various matches.

**166** Airbus Industrie A300

**1982.** Coolidge International Airport. Mult.

| | | | |
|---|---|---|---|
| 738 | 10c. Type **166** | 10 | 10 |
| 739 | 50c. Hawker-Siddeley H.S.748 | 30 | 30 |
| 740 | 90c. De Havilland D.H.C.6 Twin Otter | 60 | 60 |
| 741 | $2.50 Britten Norman Islander | 1·75 | 1·75 |

| | | | |
|---|---|---|---|
| **MS**742 | 99×73 mm. $5 Boeing 747-100 (horiz) | 2·75 | 4·00 |

**167** Cordia

**1982.** Death Centenary of Charles Darwin. Fauna and Flora. Multicoloured.

| | | | |
|---|---|---|---|
| 743 | 10c. Type **167** | 30 | 10 |
| 744 | 50c. Small Indian mongoose (horiz) | 60 | 40 |
| 745 | 90c. Corallita | 1·00 | 75 |
| 746 | $2 Mexican bulldog bat (horiz) | 2·50 | 3·25 |
| **MS**747 | 107×85 mm. $5 Carribbean monk seal | 7·50 | 8·00 |

**168** Queen's House, Greenwich

**1982.** 21st Birthday of Princess of Wales. Mult.

| | | | |
|---|---|---|---|
| 748 | 90c. Type **168** | 45 | 45 |
| 749 | $1 Prince and Princess of Wales | 65 | 50 |
| 750 | $4 Princess Diana | 3·00 | 2·00 |
| **MS**751 | 102×75 mm. $5 Type **169** | 3·75 | 2·50 |

**170** Boy Scouts decorating Streets for Independence Parade

**1982.** 75th Anniv of Boy Scout Movement. Multicoloured.

| | | | |
|---|---|---|---|
| 752 | 10c. Type **170** | 25 | 10 |
| 753 | 50c. Boy Scout giving helping hand during street parade | 60 | 40 |
| 754 | 90c. Boy Scouts attending H.R.H. Princess Margaret at Independence Ceremony | 1·00 | 75 |
| 755 | $2.20 Cub Scout giving directions to tourists | 1·90 | 2·75 |
| **MS**756 | 102×72 mm. $5 Lord Baden-Powell | 5·50 | 5·50 |

**1982.** Birth of Prince William of Wales. Nos. 748/50 optd **ROYAL BABY 21.6.82.**

| | | | |
|---|---|---|---|
| 757 | 90c. Type **168** | 45 | 45 |
| 758 | $1 Prince and Princess of Wales | 50 | 50 |
| 759 | $4 Princess Diana | 2·00 | 1·50 |
| **MS**760 | 102×75 mm. $5 Type **169** | 2·40 | 2·50 |

**172** Roosevelt in 1940

**1982.** Birth Centenary of Franklin D. Roosevelt. (Nos. 761, 763 and 765/6) and 250th Birth Anniv of George Washington (others). Multicoloured.

| | | | |
|---|---|---|---|
| 761 | 10c. Type **172** | 20 | 10 |
| 762 | 25c. Washington as blacksmith | 45 | 15 |
| 763 | 45c. Churchill, Roosevelt and Stalin at Yalta Conference | 1·75 | 40 |
| 764 | 60c. Washington crossing the Delaware (vert) | 1·00 | 40 |
| 765 | $1 "Roosevelt Special" train (vert) | 1·75 | 90 |
| 766 | $3 Portrait of Roosevelt (vert) | 1·40 | 2·40 |
| **MS**767 | 92×87 mm. $4 Roosevelt and Wife | 2·00 | 1·75 |
| **MS**768 | 92×87 mm. $4 Portrait of Washington (vert) | 2·00 | 1·75 |

No. **MS**768 also exists imperf.

**173** "Annunciation"

**1982.** Christmas. Religious Paintings by Raphael. Multicoloured.

| | | | |
|---|---|---|---|
| 769 | 10c. Type **173** | 10 | 10 |
| 770 | 30c. "Adoration of the Magi" | 15 | 15 |
| 771 | $1 "Presentation at the Temple" | 50 | 50 |
| 772 | $4 "Coronation of the Virgin" | 2·10 | 2·25 |
| **MS**773 | 95×124 mm. $5 "Marriage of the Virgin" | 2·75 | 2·50 |

**174** Tritons and Dolphins

**1983.** 500th Birth Anniv of Raphael. Details from "Galatea" Fresco. Multicoloured.

| | | | |
|---|---|---|---|
| 774 | 45c. Type **174** | 20 | 25 |
| 775 | 50c. Sea nymph carried off by Triton | 25 | 30 |
| 776 | 60c. Winged angel steering dolphins (horiz) | 30 | 35 |
| 777 | $4 Cupids shooting arrows (horiz) | 1·60 | 2·00 |
| **MS**778 | 101×125 mm. $5 Galatea pulled along by dolphins | 1·50 | 2·25 |

**175** Pineapple Produce

**1983.** Commonwealth Day. Multicoloured.

| | | | |
|---|---|---|---|
| 779 | 25c. Type **175** | 15 | 15 |
| 780 | 45c. Carnival | 20 | 25 |
| 781 | 60c. Tourism | 30 | 35 |
| 782 | $3 Airport | 1·00 | 1·50 |

**176** T.V. Satellite Coverage of Royal Wedding

**1983.** World Communications Year. Multicoloured.

| | | | |
|---|---|---|---|
| 783 | 15c. Type **176** | 40 | 20 |
| 784 | 50c. Police communications | 2·25 | 1·50 |
| 785 | 60c. House-to-train telephone call | 2·25 | 1·50 |
| 786 | $3 Satellite earth station with planets Jupiter and Saturn | 4·75 | 5·00 |
| **MS**787 | 100×90 mm. $5 "Comsat" satellite over West Indies | 2·00 | 3·75 |

**177** Bottle-nosed Dolphin

**1983.** Whales. Multicoloured.

| | | | |
|---|---|---|---|
| 788 | 15c. Type **177** | 85 | 20 |
| 789 | 50c. Fin whale | 1·75 | 1·25 |
| 790 | 60c. Bowhead whale | 2·00 | 1·25 |
| 791 | $3 Spectacled porpoise | 3·75 | 4·25 |
| **MS**792 | 122×101 mm. $5 Narwhal | 8·50 | 6·00 |

**178** Cashew Nut

**1983.** Fruits and Flowers. Multicoloured.

| | | | |
|---|---|---|---|
| 793 | 1c. Type **178** | 15 | 1·00 |
| 794 | 2c. Passion fruit | 15 | 1·00 |
| 795 | 3c. Mango | 15 | 1·00 |
| 796 | 5c. Grapefruit | 20 | 75 |
| 797a | 10c. Pawpaw | 30 | 20 |
| 798 | 15c. Breadfruit | 75 | 20 |
| 799 | 20c. Coconut | 50 | 20 |
| 800a | 25c. Oleander | 75 | 20 |
| 801 | 30c. Banana | 60 | 40 |
| 802a | 40c. Pineapple | 75 | 30 |
| 803a | 45c. Cordia | 85 | 40 |
| 804 | 50c. Cassia | 90 | 60 |
| 805 | 60c. Poui | 1·50 | 1·00 |
| 806a | $1 Frangipani | 2·00 | 1·50 |
| 807a | $2 Flamboyant | 3·50 | 4·50 |
| 808 | $2.50 Lemon | 3·75 | 6·50 |
| 809 | $5 Linum vitae | 5·00 | 13·00 |
| 810 | $10 National flag and coat of arms | 8·00 | 17·00 |

**179** Dornier Do-X Flying Boat

**1983.** Bicentenary of Manned Flight. Mult.

| | | | |
|---|---|---|---|
| 811 | 30c. Type **179** | 1·00 | 30 |
| 812 | 50c. Supermarine S.6B seaplane | 1·25 | 60 |
| 813 | 60c. Curtiss F-9C Sparrowhawk biplane and airship U.S.S. "Akron" | 1·40 | 85 |
| 814 | $4 Hot-air balloon "Pro Juventute" | 3·25 | 5·00 |
| **MS**815 | 80×105 mm. $5 Airship LZ-127 "Graf Zeppelin" | 1·75 | 2·25 |

**180** "Sibyls and Angels" (detail) (Raphael)

**1983.** Christmas. 500th Birth Anniv of Raphael.

| | | | | |
|---|---|---|---|---|
| 816 | **180** | 10c. multicoloured | 30 | 20 |
| 817 | - | 30c. multicoloured | 65 | 35 |
| 818 | - | $1 multicoloured | 1·50 | 1·25 |
| 819 | - | $4 multicoloured | 3·00 | 5·00 |
| **MS**820 | – | 101×103 mm. $5 multicoloured | 1·50 | 2·25 |

DESIGNS—HORIZ: 10c. to $4, Different details from "Sibyls and Angels". VERT: $5 "The Vision of Ezekiel".

**181** John Wesley (founder)

**1983.** Bicentenary of Methodist Church (1984). Multicoloured.

| | | | |
|---|---|---|---|
| 821 | 15c. Type **181** | 25 | 15 |
| 822 | 50c. Nathaniel Gilbert (founder in Antigua) | 70 | 50 |
| 823 | 60c. St. John Methodist Church steeple | 75 | 65 |
| 824 | $3 Ebenezer Methodist Church, St. John's | 2·00 | 4·00 |

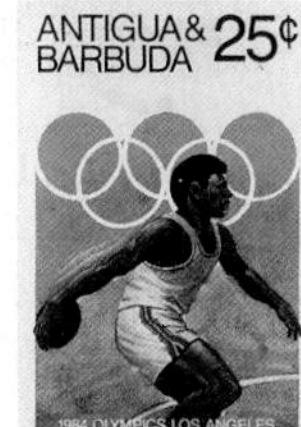


**182** Discus

**1984.** Olympic Games, Los Angeles. Multicoloured.

| | | | |
|---|---|---|---|
| 825 | 25c. Type **182** | 20 | 15 |
| 826 | 50c. Gymnastics | 35 | 30 |
| 827 | 90c. Hurdling | 65 | 70 |
| 828 | $3 Cycling | 2·50 | 3·75 |
| **MS**829 | 82×67 mm. $5 Volleyball | 2·75 | 3·00 |

**183** "Booker Vanguard" (freighter)

**1984.** Ships. Multicoloured.

| | | | |
|---|---|---|---|
| 830 | 45c. Type **183** | 1·00 | 55 |
| 831 | 50c. S.S. "Canberra" (liner) | 1·25 | 80 |
| 832 | 60c. Yachts | 1·50 | 1·00 |
| 833 | $4 "Fairwind" (cargo liner) | 3·00 | 7·00 |
| **MS**834 | 107×80 mm. $5 18th-century British man-of-war (vert) | 1·75 | 3·50 |

**184** Chenille

**1984.** Universal Postal Union Congress, Hamburg. Multicoloured.

| | | | |
|---|---|---|---|
| 835 | 15c. Type **184** | 40 | 15 |
| 836 | 50c. Shell flower | 80 | 70 |
| 837 | 60c. Anthurium | 85 | 1·10 |
| 838 | $3 Angels trumpet | 2·75 | 6·50 |
| **MS**839 | 100×75 mm. $5 Crown of Thorns | 1·50 | 3·25 |

**1984.** Various stamps surch. (a) Nos. 702/4.

| | | | |
|---|---|---|---|
| 840 | $2 on 25c. Type **159** | 2·50 | 2·50 |
| 841 | $2 on 50c. Glamis Castle | 2·50 | 2·50 |
| 842 | $2 on $4 Prince Charles skiing | 2·50 | 2·50 |
| **MS**843 | 96×82 mm. $2 on $5 Glass coach | 4·00 | 4·00 |

(b) Nos. 748/50.

| | | | |
|---|---|---|---|
| 844 | $2 on 90c. Type **168** | 2·00 | 2·00 |
| 845 | $2 on $1 Prince and Princess of Wales | 2·00 | 2·00 |
| 846 | $2 on $4 Princess Diana | 2·00 | 2·00 |
| **MS**847 | 102×75 mm. Type **169** | 4·00 | 4·00 |

(c) Nos. 757/9.

| | | | |
|---|---|---|---|
| 848 | $2 on 90c. Type **168** | 2·00 | 2·00 |
| 849 | $2 on $1 Prince and Princess of Wales | 2·00 | 2·00 |
| 850 | $2 on $4 Princess Diana | 2·00 | 2·00 |
| **MS**851 | 102×75 mm. $2 on $5 Type **169** | 4·00 | 4·00 |

(d) Nos. 779/82.

| | | | |
|---|---|---|---|
| 852 | $2 on 25c. Type **175** | 2·75 | 1·25 |
| 853 | $2 on 45c. Carnival | 2·75 | 1·25 |
| 854 | $2 on 60c. Tourism | 2·75 | 1·25 |
| 855 | $2 on $3 Airport | 2·75 | 1·25 |

**187** Abraham Lincoln

**1984.** Presidents of the United States of America. Multicoloured.

| | | | |
|---|---|---|---|
| 856 | 10c. Type **187** | 15 | 10 |
| 857 | 20c. Harry S. Truman | 20 | 15 |

| | | | |
|---|---|---|---|
| 858 | 30c. Dwight D. Eisenhower | 30 | 25 |
| 859 | 40c. Ronald W. Reagan | 50 | 30 |
| 860 | 90c. Gettysburg Address, 1863 | 90 | 75 |
| 861 | $1.10 Formation of N.A.T.O.,1949 | 1·25 | 1·25 |
| 862 | $1.50 Eisenhower during the war | 1·60 | 1·75 |
| 863 | $2 Reagan and Caribbean Basin Initiative | 1·75 | 2·00 |

**188** View of Moravian Mission

**1984.** 150th Anniv of Abolition of Slavery. Multicoloured.

| | | | |
|---|---|---|---|
| 864 | 40c. Type **188** | 90 | 50 |
| 865 | 50c. Antigua Courthouse, 1823 | 1·00 | 65 |
| 866 | 60c. Planting sugar-cane, Monks Hill | 1·10 | 75 |
| 867 | $3 Boiling house, Delaps' estate | 4·25 | 6·00 |
| **MS**868 | 95×70 mm. $5 Loading sugar, Willoughby Bay | 6·50 | 4·75 |

**189** Rufous-sided Towhee

**1984.** Songbirds. Multicoloured.

| | | | |
|---|---|---|---|
| 869 | 40c. Type **189** | 1·25 | 85 |
| 870 | 50c. Parula warbler | 1·40 | 1·10 |
| 871 | 60c. House wren | 1·50 | 1·50 |
| 872 | $2 Ruby-crowned kinglet | 2·00 | 3·75 |
| 873 | $3 Common flicker ("Yellow-shafted Flicker") | 2·75 | 5·00 |
| **MS**874 | 76×76 mm. $5 Yellow-breasted chat | 2·50 | 6·00 |

**190** Grass-skiing

**1984.** "Ausipex" International Stamp Exhibition, Melbourne, Australian Sports. Multicoloured.

| | | | |
|---|---|---|---|
| 875 | $1 Type **190** | 1·25 | 1·50 |
| 876 | $5 Australian football | 3·75 | 5·50 |
| **MS**877 | 108×78 mm. $5 Boomerang-throwing | 2·50 | 4·00 |

**191** "The Virgin and Infant with Angels and Cherubs"

**1984.** 450th Death Anniv of Correggio (painter). Multicoloured.

| | | | |
|---|---|---|---|
| 878 | 25c. Type **191** | 40 | 20 |
| 879 | 60c. "The Four Saints" | 80 | 50 |
| 880 | 90c. "St. Catherine" | 1·10 | 90 |
| 881 | $3 "The Campori Madonna" | 2·25 | 4·25 |
| **MS**882 | 90×60 mm. $5 "St. John the Baptist" | 2·00 | 2·75 |

**192** "The Blue Dancers"

**1984.** 150th Birth Anniv of Edgar Degas (painter). Multicoloured.

| | | | |
|---|---|---|---|
| 883 | 15c. Type **192** | 35 | 15 |
| 884 | 50c. "The Pink Dancers" | 80 | 60 |
| 885 | 70c. "Two Dancers" | 1·10 | 85 |
| 886 | $4 "Dancers at the Bar" | 2·50 | 4·75 |
| **MS**887 | 90×60 mm. "The Folk dancers" (40×27 mm) | 2·00 | 2·75 |

**193** Sir Winston Churchill

**1984.** Famous People. Multicoloured.

| | | | |
|---|---|---|---|
| 888 | 60c. Type **193** | 1·10 | 1·50 |
| 889 | 60c. Mahatma Gandhi | 1·10 | 1·50 |
| 890 | 60c. John F. Kennedy | 1·10 | 1·50 |
| 891 | 60c. Mao Tse-tung | 1·10 | 1·50 |
| 892 | $1 Churchill with General De Gaulle, Paris, 1944 (horiz) | 1·25 | 1·75 |
| 893 | $1 Gandhi leaving London by train, 1931 (horiz) | 1·25 | 1·75 |
| 894 | $1 Kennedy with Chancellor Adenauer and Mayor Brandt, Berlin, 1963 (horiz) | 1·25 | 1·75 |
| 895 | $1 Mao Tse-tung with Lin Piao, Peking, 1969 (horiz) | 1·25 | 1·75 |
| **MS**896 | 114×80 mm. $5 Flags of Great Britain, India, the United States and China | 9·00 | 4·50 |

**194** Donald Duck fishing

**1984.** Christmas. 50th Birthday of Donald Duck. Walt Disney Cartoon Characters. Multicoloured.

| | | | |
|---|---|---|---|
| 897 | 1c. Type **194** | 10 | 10 |
| 898 | 2c. Donald Duck lying on beach | 10 | 10 |
| 899 | 3c. Donald Duck and nephews with fishing rods and fishes | 10 | 10 |
| 900 | 4c. Donald Duck and nephews in boat | 10 | 10 |
| 901 | 5c. Wearing diving masks | 10 | 10 |
| 902 | 10c. In deckchairs reading books | 10 | 10 |
| 903 | $1 With toy shark's fin | 2·25 | 1·25 |
| 904 | $2 In sailing boat | 2·50 | 3·00 |
| 905 | $5 Attempting to propel boat | 5·50 | 6·00 |
| **MS**906 | Two sheets, each 125×100 mm. (a) $5 Nephews with crayon and paintbrushes (horiz). (b) $5 Donald Duck in deckchair Set of 2 sheets | 9·00 | 13·00 |

**195** Torch from Statue in Madison Square Park, 1885

**1985.** Centenary (1986) of Statue of Liberty (1st issue). Multicoloured.

| | | | |
|---|---|---|---|
| 907 | 25c. Type **195** | 30 | 20 |
| 908 | 30c. Statue of Liberty and scaffolding ("Restoration and Renewal") (vert) | 30 | 20 |
| 909 | 50c. Frederic Bartholdi (sculptor) supervising construction, 1876 | 40 | 40 |
| 910 | 90c. Close-up of statue | 60 | 75 |
| 911 | $1 Statue and cadet ship ("Operation Sail", 1976) (vert) | 1·60 | 1·40 |
| 912 | $3 Dedication ceremony, 1886 | 1·75 | 3·00 |
| **MS**913 | 110×80 mm. $5 Port of New York | 3·75 | 3·75 |

See also Nos. 1110/19.

**196** Arawak Pot Sherd and Indians making Clay Utensils

**1985.** Native American Artefacts. Multicoloured.

| | | | |
|---|---|---|---|
| 914 | 15c. Type **196** | 15 | 10 |
| 915 | 50c. Arawak body design and Arawak Indians tattooing | 30 | 40 |
| 916 | 60c. Head of the god "Yocahu" and Indians harvesting manioc | 40 | 50 |
| 917 | $3 Carib war club and Carib Indians going into battle | 1·25 | 2·50 |
| **MS**918 | 97×68 mm. $5 Taino Indians worshipping stone idol | 1·50 | 2·50 |

**197** Triumph 2hp "Jap", 1903

**1985.** Centenary of the Motorcycle. Multicoloured.

| | | | |
|---|---|---|---|
| 919 | 10c. Type **197** | 65 | 15 |
| 920 | 30c. "Indian Arrow", 1949 | 1·10 | 40 |
| 921 | 60c. BMW "R100RS", 1976 | 1·60 | 1·25 |
| 922 | $4 Harley-Davidson "Model II", 1916 | 5·50 | 9·00 |
| **MS**923 | 90×93 mm. $5 Laverda "Jota", 1975 | 5·50 | 7·00 |

**198** Slavonian Grebe ("Horned Grebe")

**1985.** Birth Bicentenary of John J. Audubon (ornithologist) (1st issue). Multicoloured. Designs showing original paintings.

| | | | |
|---|---|---|---|
| 924 | 90c. Type **198** | 1·75 | 1·25 |
| 925 | $1 British storm petrel ("Least Petrel") | 2·00 | 1·25 |
| 926 | $1.50 Great blue heron | 2·50 | 3·25 |
| 927 | $3 Double-crested cormorant | 3·75 | 6·00 |
| **MS**928 | 103×72 mm. $5 White-tailed tropic bird (vert) | 7·00 | 6·00 |

See also Nos. 990/4.

**199** "Anaea cyanea"

**1985.** Butterflies. Multicoloured.

| | | | |
|---|---|---|---|
| 929 | 25c. Type **199** | 1·00 | 30 |
| 930 | 60c. "Leodonta dysoni" | 2·25 | 1·25 |
| 931 | 90c. "Junea doraete" | 2·75 | 1·50 |
| 932 | $4 "Prepona pylene" | 7·50 | 10·50 |
| **MS**933 | 132×105 mm. $5 "Caerois gerdtrudtus" | 4·50 | 6·50 |

**200** Cessna 172D Skyhawk

**1985.** 40th Anniv of International Civil Aviation Organization. Multicoloured.

| | | | |
|---|---|---|---|
| 934 | 30c. Type **200** | 1·25 | 30 |
| 935 | 90c. Fokker D.VII | 2·75 | 1·25 |
| 936 | $1.50 SPAD VII | 3·75 | 3·25 |
| 937 | $3 Boeing 747-100 | 5·50 | 7·50 |
| **MS**938 | 97×83 mm. $5 De Havilland D.H.C.6 twin otter | 4·50 | 6·50 |

**201** Maimonides

**1985.** 850th Birth Anniv of Maimonides (physician, philosopher and scholar).

| | | | |
|---|---|---|---|
| 939 | **201** $2 green | 4·00 | 3·25 |
| **MS**940 | 70×84 mm. Type **201** $5 brown | 7·00 | 4·50 |

**202** Young Farmers with Produce

**1985.** International Youth Year. Multicoloured.

| | | | |
|---|---|---|---|
| 941 | 25c. Type **202** | 25 | 20 |
| 942 | 50c. Hotel management trainees | 40 | 50 |
| 943 | 60c. Girls with goat and boys with football ("Environment") | 1·00 | 70 |
| 944 | $3 Windsurfing ("Leisure") | 2·75 | 5·50 |
| **MS**945 | 102×72 mm. $5 Young people with Antiguan flags | 2·75 | 3·25 |

**203** The Queen Mother attending Church

**1985.** Life and Times of Queen Elizabeth the Queen Mother. Multicoloured.

| | | | |
|---|---|---|---|
| 946 | $1 Type **203** | 45 | 60 |
| 947 | $1.50 Watching children playing in London garden | 60 | 85 |
| 948 | $2.50 The Queen Mother in 1979 | 90 | 1·40 |
| **MS**949 | 56×85 mm. $5 With Prince Edward at Royal Wedding, 1981 | 5·50 | 3·00 |

Stamps as Nos. 946/8, but with face values of 90c., $1 and $3 exist from additional sheetlets with changed background colours.

**204** Magnificent Frigate Bird

**1985.** Marine Life. Multicoloured.

| | | | |
|---|---|---|---|
| 950 | 15c. Type **204** | 1·00 | 30 |
| 951 | 45c. Brain coral | 2·00 | 95 |
| 952 | 60c. Cushion star | 2·25 | 1·75 |
| 953 | $3 Spotted moray | 7·00 | 9·00 |
| **MS**954 | 110×80 mm. $5 Elkhorn coral | 9·00 | 7·00 |

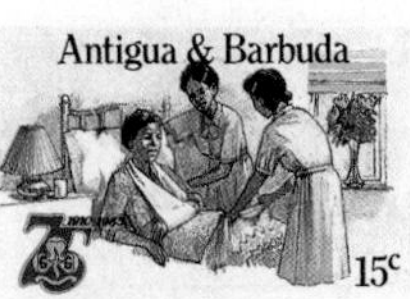


**205** Girl Guides Nursing

**1985.** 75th Anniv of Girl Guide Movement. Multicoloured.

| | | | |
|---|---|---|---|
| 955 | 15c. Type **205** | 75 | 20 |
| 956 | 45c. Open-air Girl Guide meeting | 1·40 | 60 |
| 957 | 60c. Lord and Lady Baden-Powell | 1·75 | 90 |
| 958 | $3 Girl Guides gathering flowers | 4·25 | 4·50 |

| | | | |
|---|---|---|---|
| MS959 | 67×96 mm. $5 Barn swallow (Nature study) | 6·50 | 8·50 |

**206** Bass Trombone

**1985.** 300th Birth Anniv of Johann Sebastian Bach (composer).

| | | | | |
|---|---|---|---|---|
| 960 | **206** | 25c. multicoloured | 1·40 | 55 |
| 961 | - | 50c. multicoloured | 1·75 | 1·10 |
| 962 | - | $1 multicoloured | 3·25 | 1·75 |
| 963 | - | $3 multicoloured | 6·00 | 7·00 |
| MS964 | – | 104×73 mm. $5 black and grey | 4·50 | 4·75 |

DESIGNS:50c. English horn; $1 Violino piccolo; $3 Bass rackett; $5 Johann Sebastian Bach.

**207** Flags of Great Britain and Antigua

**1985.** Royal Visit. Multicoloured.

| | | | |
|---|---|---|---|
| 965 | 60c. Type **207** | 1·00 | 65 |
| 966 | $1 Queen Elizabeth II (vert) | 1·50 | 1·25 |
| 967 | $4 Royal Yacht "Britannia" | 3·25 | 7·00 |
| MS968 | 110×83 mm. $5 Map of Antigua | 3·00 | 3·25 |

**1985.** 150th Birth Anniv of Mark Twain (author). As T **118** of Anguilla showing Walt Disney cartoon characters in scenes from "Roughing It". Multicoloured.

| | | | |
|---|---|---|---|
| 969 | 25c. Donald Duck and Mickey Mouse meeting Indians | 1·00 | 20 |
| 970 | 50c. Mickey Mouse, Donald Duck and Goofy canoeing | 1·50 | 55 |
| 971 | $1.10 Goofy as Pony Express rider | 2·50 | 2·25 |
| 972 | $1.50 Donald Duck and Goofy hunting buffalo | 3·00 | 3·75 |
| 973 | $2 Mickey Mouse and silver mine | 3·50 | 4·50 |
| MS974 | 127×101 mm. $5 Mickey Mouse driving stagecoach | 8·00 | 7·50 |

**1985.** Birth Bicentenaries of Grimm Brothers (folklorists). As T **119** of Anguilla showing Walt Disney cartoon characters in scenes from "Spindle, Shuttle and Needle". Multicoloured.

| | | | |
|---|---|---|---|
| 975 | 30c. The Prince (Mickey Mouse) searches for a bride | 1·25 | 40 |
| 976 | 60c. The Prince finds the Orphan Girl (Minnie Mouse) | 1·75 | 80 |
| 977 | 70c. The Spindle finds the Prince | 2·00 | 1·40 |
| 978 | $1 The Needle tidies the Girl's house | 2·50 | 1·75 |
| 979 | $3 The Prince proposes | 4·75 | 7·50 |
| MS980 | 125×101 mm. $5 The Orphan Girl and spinning wheel on Prince's horse | 8·00 | 7·50 |

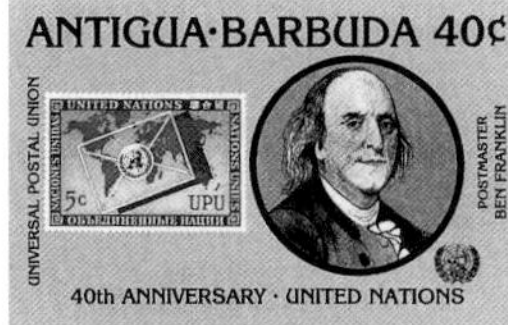

**208** Benjamin Franklin and U.N. (New York) 1953 U.P.U. 5c. Stamp

**1985.** 40th Anniv of United Nations Organization. Multicoloured.

| | | | |
|---|---|---|---|
| 981 | 40c. Type **208** | 1·00 | 70 |
| 982 | $1 George Washington Carver (agricultural chemist) and 1982 Nature Conservation 28c. stamp | 2·00 | 2·00 |
| 983 | $3 Charles Lindbergh (aviator) and 1978 I.C.A.O. 25c. stamp | 4·75 | 7·50 |
| MS984 | 101×77 mm. $5 Marc Chagall (artist) (vert) | 6·50 | 4·75 |

Nos. 981/4 each include a United Nations (New York) stamp design.

**209** "Madonna and Child" (De Landi)

**1985.** Christmas. Religious Paintings. Mult.

| | | | |
|---|---|---|---|
| 985 | 10c. Type **209** | 30 | 15 |
| 986 | 25c. "Madonna and Child" (Berlinghiero) | 55 | 25 |
| 987 | 60c. "The Nativity" (Fra Angelico) | 70 | 60 |
| 988 | $4 "Presentation in the Temple" (Giovanni di Paolo) | 1·75 | 4·25 |
| MS989 | 113×81 mm. $5 "The Nativity" (Antoniazzo Romano) | 3·00 | 3·75 |

**1986.** Birth Bicentenary of John J. Audubon (ornithologist) (2nd issue). As T **198** showing original paintings. Multicoloured.

| | | | |
|---|---|---|---|
| 990 | 60c. Mallard | 2·25 | 1·50 |
| 991 | 90c. North American black duck ("Dusky Duck") | 2·75 | 2·00 |
| 992 | $1.50 Pintail ("Common Pintail") | 3·50 | 4·50 |
| 993 | $3 American wigeon ("Wigeon") | 4·75 | 6·50 |
| MS994 | 102×73 mm. Eider ("Common Eider") | 7·00 | 5·50 |

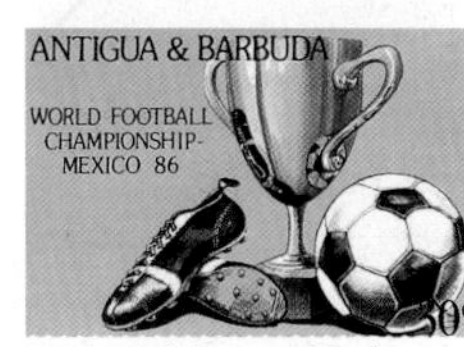

**210** Football, Boots and Trophy

**1986.** World Cup Football Championship, Mexico. Multicoloured.

| | | | |
|---|---|---|---|
| 995 | 30c. Type **210** | 1·50 | 40 |
| 996 | 60c. Goalkeeper (vert) | 2·00 | 85 |
| 997 | $1 Referee blowing whistle (vert) | 2·50 | 1·75 |
| 998 | $4 Ball in net | 6·50 | 9·00 |
| MS999 | 87×76 mm. $5 Two players competing for ball | 8·50 | 7·50 |

**1986.** Appearance of Halley's Comet (1st issue). As T **123** of Anguilla. Multicoloured.

| | | | |
|---|---|---|---|
| 1000 | 5c. Edmond Halley and Old Greenwich Observatory | 30 | 20 |
| 1001 | 10c. Messerschmitt Me 163B Komet (fighter aircraft), 1944 | 30 | 15 |
| 1002 | 60c. Montezuma (Aztec emperor) and Comet in 1517 (from "Historias de las Indias de Neuva Espana") | 1·50 | 70 |
| 1003 | $4 Pocahontas saving Capt. John Smith and Comet in 1607 | 4·50 | 5·50 |
| MS1004 | 101×70 mm. $5 Halley's Comet over English Harbour, Antigua | 3·50 | 3·75 |

See also Nos. 1047/51.

**1986.** 60th Birthday of Queen Elizabeth II. As T **125** of Anguilla.

| | | | |
|---|---|---|---|
| 1005 | 60c. black and yellow | 30 | 35 |
| 1006 | $1 multicoloured | 50 | 55 |
| 1007 | $4 multicoloured | 1·40 | 1·90 |
| MS1008 | 120×85 mm. $5 black and brown | 2·00 | 3·00 |

DESIGNS: 60c. Wedding photograph, 1947; $1 Queen at Trooping the Colour; $4 In Scotland; $5 Queen Mary and Princess Elizabeth, 1927.

**211** Tug

**1986.** Local Boats. Multicoloured.

| | | | |
|---|---|---|---|
| 1009 | 30c. Type **211** | 25 | 20 |
| 1010 | 60c. Game fishing boat | 45 | 35 |
| 1011 | $1 Yacht | 75 | 60 |
| 1012 | $4 Lugger with auxiliary sail | 2·50 | 3·25 |
| MS1013 | 108×78 mm. $5 Boats under construction | 3·00 | 4·00 |

**212** "Hiawatha" express

**1986.** "Ameripex '86" International Stamp Exhibition, Chicago. Famous American Trains. Multicoloured.

| | | | |
|---|---|---|---|
| 1014 | 25c. Type **212** | 1·25 | 50 |
| 1015 | 50c. "Grand Canyon" express | 1·50 | 80 |
| 1016 | $1 "Powhattan Arrow" express | 1·75 | 1·75 |
| 1017 | $3 "Empire State" express | 3·00 | 6·00 |
| MS1018 | 116×87 mm. $5 Southern Pacific "Daylight" express | 6·00 | 11·00 |

**213** Prince Andrew and Miss Sarah Ferguson

**1986.** Royal Wedding. Multicoloured.

| | | | |
|---|---|---|---|
| 1019 | 45c. Type **213** | 70 | 35 |
| 1020 | 60c. Prince Andrew | 80 | 45 |
| 1021 | $4 Prince Andrew with Prince Philip | 2·75 | 3·50 |
| MS1022 | 88×88 mm. $5 Prince Andrew and Miss Sarah Ferguson (different) | 5·00 | 4·50 |

**214** Fly-specked Cerith

**1986.** Sea Shells. Multicoloured.

| | | | |
|---|---|---|---|
| 1023 | 15c. Type **214** | 75 | 50 |
| 1024 | 45c. Smooth Scotch bonnet | 1·75 | 1·25 |
| 1025 | 60c. West Indian crown conch | 2·00 | 2·00 |
| 1026 | $3 Ciboney murex | 6·50 | 10·00 |
| MS1027 | 109×75 mm. $5 Colourful Atlantic moon (horiz) | 7·50 | 8·50 |

**215** Water Lily

**1986.** Flowers. Multicoloured.

| | | | |
|---|---|---|---|
| 1028 | 10c. Type **215** | 20 | 15 |
| 1029 | 15c. Queen of the night | 20 | 15 |
| 1030 | 50c. Cup of gold | 55 | 55 |
| 1031 | 60c. Beach morning glory | 70 | 70 |
| 1032 | 70c. Golden trumpet | 80 | 80 |
| 1033 | $1 Air plant | 90 | 1·10 |
| 1034 | $4 Purple wreath | 1·75 | 3·00 |
| 1035 | $4 Zephyr lily | 2·00 | 3·75 |
| MS1036 | Two sheets, each 102×72 mm. (a) $4 Dozakie. (b) $5 Four o'clock flower Set of 2 sheets | 5·00 | 7·50 |

**1986.** World Cup Football Championship Winners, Mexico. Nos. 995/8 optd **WINNERS Argentina 3 W.Germany 2.**

| | | | |
|---|---|---|---|
| 1037 | 30c. Type **210** | 1·25 | 40 |
| 1038 | 60c. Goalkeeper (vert) | 1·75 | 75 |
| 1039 | $1 Referee blowing whistle (vert) | 2·25 | 1·10 |
| 1040 | $4 Ball in net | 5·50 | 4·50 |
| MS1041 | 87×76 mm. $5 Two players competing for ball | 5·50 | 4·00 |

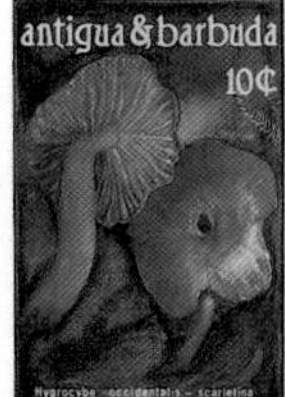

**217** "Hygrocybe occidentalis var. scarletina"

**1986.** Mushrooms. Multicoloured.

| | | | |
|---|---|---|---|
| 1042 | 10c. Type **217** | 30 | 25 |
| 1043 | 50c. "Trogia buccinalis" | 70 | 55 |
| 1044 | $1 "Collybia subpruinosa" | 1·25 | 1·25 |
| 1045 | $4 "Leucocoprinus brebissonii" | 3·00 | 4·50 |
| MS1046 | 102×82 mm. $5 "Pyrrhoglossum pyrrhum" | 13·00 | 11·00 |

**(218)**

**1986.** Appearance of Halley's Comet (2nd issue). Nos. 1000/3 optd with T **218**.

| | | | |
|---|---|---|---|
| 1047 | 5c. Edmond Halley and Old Greenwich Observatory | 20 | 10 |
| 1048 | 10c. Messerschmitt Me 163B Komet (fighter aircraft), 1944 | 50 | 10 |
| 1049 | 60c. Montezuma (Aztec emperor) and Comet in 1517 (from "Historias de las Indias de Neuva Espana") | 1·25 | 65 |
| 1050 | $4 Pocahontas saving Capt. John Smith and Comet in 1607 | 4·50 | 4·00 |
| MS1051 | 101×70 mm. $5 Halley's Comet over English Harbour, Antigua | 6·00 | 6·50 |

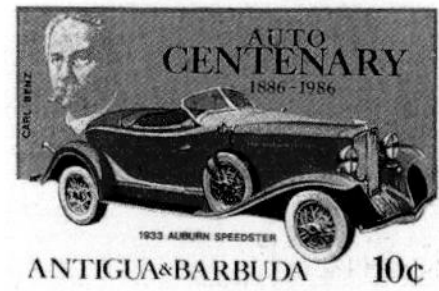

**219** Auburn "Speedster" (1933)

**1986.** Centenary of First Benz Motor Car. Mult.

| | | | |
|---|---|---|---|
| 1052 | 10c. Type **219** | 15 | 10 |
| 1053 | 15c. Mercury "Sable" (1986) | 20 | 10 |
| 1054 | 50c. Cadillac (1959) | 55 | 30 |
| 1055 | 60c. Studebaker (1950) | 70 | 45 |
| 1056 | 70c. Lagonda "V-12" (1939) | 80 | 55 |
| 1057 | $1 Adler "Standard" (1930) | 1·10 | 75 |
| 1058 | $3 DKW (1956) | 2·50 | 2·50 |
| 1059 | $4 Mercedes "500K" (1936) | 3·00 | 3·00 |
| MS1060 | Two sheets, each 99×70 mm. (a) $5 Daimler (1896). (b) $5 Mercedes "Knight" (1921) Set of 2 sheets | 9·00 | 6·50 |

**220** Young Mickey Mouse playing Santa Claus

**1986.** Christmas. Designs showing Walt Disney cartoon characters as babies. Multicoloured.

| | | | |
|---|---|---|---|
| 1061 | 25c. Type **220** | 60 | 35 |
| 1062 | 30c. Mickey and Minnie Mouse building snowman | 70 | 40 |
| 1063 | 40c. Aunt Matilda and Goofy baking | 75 | 45 |
| 1064 | 60c. Goofy and Pluto | 1·00 | 85 |
| 1065 | 70c. Pluto, Donald and Daisy Duck carol singing | 1·10 | 1·00 |
| 1066 | $1.50 Donald Duck, Mickey Mouse and Pluto stringing popcorn | 1·75 | 2·50 |
| 1067 | $3 Grandma Duck and Minnie Mouse | 3·00 | 4·50 |
| 1068 | $4 Donald Duck and Pete | 3·25 | 4·50 |
| MS1069 | Two sheets, each 127×102 mm. (a) $5 Goofy, Donald Duck and Minnie Mouse playing with reindeer. (b) $5 Mickey Mouse, Donald and Daisy Duck playing with toys Set of 2 sheets | 13·00 | 14·00 |

**221** Arms of Antigua

| 1986 | | | |
|---|---|---|---|
| 1070 **221** | 10c. blue | 50 | 50 |
| 1071 - | 25c. red | 75 | 75 |

DESIGN: 25c. Flag of Antigua.

**222** "Canada I" (1981)

**1987.** America's Cup Yachting Championship. Multicoloured.

| | | | |
|---|---|---|---|
| 1072 | 30c. Type **222** | 45 | 20 |
| 1073 | 60c. "Gretel II" (1970) | 60 | 50 |
| 1074 | $1 "Sceptre" (1958) | 85 | 1·00 |
| 1075 | $3 "Vigilant" (1893) | 2·25 | 3·00 |
| **MS**1076 | 113×84 mm. $5 "Australia II" defeating "Liberty" (1983) (horiz) | 4·00 | 5·00 |

**223** Bridled Burrfish

**1987.** Marine Life. Multicoloured.

| | | | |
|---|---|---|---|
| 1077 | 15c. Type **223** | 2·50 | 50 |
| 1078 | 30c. Common noddy ("Brown Noddy") | 4·50 | 60 |
| 1079 | 40c. Nassau grouper | 3·00 | 70 |
| 1080 | 50c. Laughing gull | 5·50 | 1·50 |
| 1081 | 60c. French angelfish | 3·50 | 1·50 |
| 1082 | $1 Porkfish | 3·50 | 1·75 |
| 1083 | $2 Royal tern | 7·50 | 6·00 |
| 1084 | $3 Sooty tern | 7·50 | 8·00 |
| **MS**1085 | Two sheets, each 120×94 mm. (a) $5 Banded butterflyfish. (b) $5 Brown booby Set of 2 sheets | 17·00 | 14·00 |

Nos. 1078, 1080 and 1083/5 are without the World Wildlife Fund logo shown on Type **223**.

**224** Handball

**1987.** Olympic Games, Seoul (1988) (1st issue). Multicoloured.

| | | | |
|---|---|---|---|
| 1086 | 10c. Type **224** | 60 | 10 |
| 1087 | 60c. Fencing | 85 | 35 |
| 1088 | $1 Gymnastics | 1·25 | 80 |
| 1089 | $3 Football | 2·50 | 4·00 |
| **MS**1090 | 100×72 mm. $5 Boxing gloves | 3·50 | 4·25 |

See also Nos. 1222/6.

**225** "The Profile"

**1987.** Birth Centenary of Marc Chagall (artist). Multicoloured.

| | | | |
|---|---|---|---|
| 1091 | 10c. Type **225** | 30 | 15 |
| 1092 | 30c. "Portrait of the Artist's Sister" | 45 | 30 |
| 1093 | 40c. "Bride with Fan" | 50 | 40 |
| 1094 | 60c. "David in Profile" | 55 | 45 |
| 1095 | 90c. "Fiancee with Bouquet" | 75 | 60 |
| 1096 | $1 "Self Portrait with Brushes" | 75 | 65 |
| 1097 | $3 "The Walk" | 1·75 | 2·25 |
| 1098 | $4 "Three Candles" | 2·00 | 2·50 |
| **MS**1099 | Two sheets, each 110×95 mm. (a) $5 "Fall of Icarus" (104×89 mm). (b) $5 "Myth of Orpheus" (104×89 mm). Imperf Set of 2 sheets | 6·50 | 6·00 |

**226** "Spirit of Australia" (fastest powerboat), 1978

**1987.** Milestones of Transportation. Multicoloured.

| | | | |
|---|---|---|---|
| 1100 | 10c. Type **226** | 80 | 40 |
| 1101 | 15c. Werner von Siemens's electric locomotive, 1879 | 1·50 | 50 |
| 1102 | 30c. U.S.S. "Triton" (first submerged circum-navigation), 1960 | 1·25 | 50 |
| 1103 | 50c. Trevithick's steam carriage (first passenger-carrying vehicle), 1801 | 1·75 | 60 |
| 1104 | 60c. U.S.S. "New Jersey" (battleship), 1942 | 1·75 | 85 |
| 1105 | 70c. Draisaine bicycle, 1818 | 2·00 | 1·00 |
| 1106 | 90c. "United States" (liner) (holder of Blue Riband), 1952 | 1·75 | 1·00 |
| 1107 | $1.50 Cierva C.4 (first autogyro), 1923 | 1·75 | 2·75 |
| 1108 | $2 Curtiss NC-4 flying boat (first transatlantic flight), 1919 | 2·00 | 3·00 |
| 1109 | $3 "Queen Elizabeth 2" (liner), 1969 | 3·50 | 4·50 |

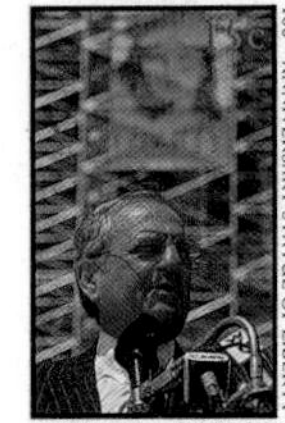


**227** Lee Iacocca at Unveiling of Restored Statue

**1987.** Centenary of Statue of Liberty (1986) (2nd issue). Multicoloured.

| | | | |
|---|---|---|---|
| 1110 | 15c. Type **227** | 15 | 15 |
| 1111 | 30c. Statue at sunset (side view) | 20 | 20 |
| 1112 | 45c. Aerial view of head | 30 | 30 |
| 1113 | 50c. Lee Iacocca and torch | 35 | 35 |
| 1114 | 60c. Workmen inside head of Statue (horiz) | 35 | 35 |
| 1115 | 90c. Restoration work (horiz) | 50 | 50 |
| 1116 | $1 Head of Statue | 55 | 55 |
| 1117 | $2 Statue at sunset (front view) | 1·00 | 1·50 |
| 1118 | $3 Inspecting restoration work (horiz) | 1·25 | 2·00 |
| 1119 | $5 Statue at night | 2·00 | 3·50 |

**228** Grace Kelly

**1987.** Entertainers. Multicoloured.

| | | | |
|---|---|---|---|
| 1120 | 15c. Type **228** | 90 | 40 |
| 1121 | 30c. Marilyn Monroe | 2·75 | 80 |
| 1122 | 45c. Orson Welles | 90 | 60 |
| 1123 | 50c. Judy Garland | 90 | 65 |
| 1124 | 60c. John Lennon | 4·25 | 1·25 |
| 1125 | $1 Rock Hudson | 1·40 | 1·10 |
| 1126 | $2 John Wayne | 2·50 | 2·00 |
| 1127 | $3 Elvis Presley | 10·00 | 4·50 |

**229** Scouts around Camp Fire and Red Kangaroo

**1987.** 16th World Scout Jamboree, Australia. Mult.

| | | | |
|---|---|---|---|
| 1128 | 10c. Type **229** | 65 | 20 |
| 1129 | 60c. Scouts canoeing and blue-winged kookaburra | 1·25 | 80 |
| 1130 | $1 Scouts on assault course and ring-tailed rock wallaby | 1·00 | 85 |
| 1131 | $3 Field kitchen and koala | 1·50 | 4·25 |
| **MS**1132 | 103×78 mm. $5 Flags of Antigua, Australia and Scout Movement | 3·25 | 3·50 |

**230** Whistling Frog

**1987.** "Capex '87" International Stamp Exhibition, Toronto. Reptiles and Amphibians. Mult.

| | | | |
|---|---|---|---|
| 1133 | 30c. Type **230** | 55 | 20 |
| 1134 | 60c. Croaking lizard | 75 | 40 |
| 1135 | $1 Antiguan anole | 1·00 | 70 |
| 1136 | $3 Red-footed tortoise | 2·00 | 3·00 |
| **MS**1137 | 106×76 mm. $5 Ground lizard | 2·25 | 2·75 |

**1987.** 10th Death Anniv of Elvis Presley (entertainer). No. 1127 optd **10th ANNIVERSARY 16th AUGUST 1987**.

| | | | |
|---|---|---|---|
| 1138 | $3 Elvis Presley | 8·00 | 4·75 |

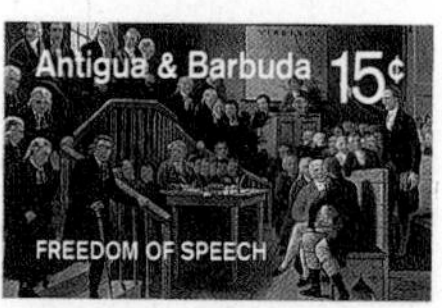


**232** House of Burgesses, Virginia ("Freedom of Speech")

**1987.** Bicentenary of U.S. Constitution. Mult.

| | | | |
|---|---|---|---|
| 1139 | 15c. Type **232** | 10 | 10 |
| 1140 | 45c. State Seal, Connecticut | 20 | 25 |
| 1141 | 60c. State Seal, Delaware | 25 | 35 |
| 1142 | $4 Governor Morris (Pennsylvania delegate) (vert) | 1·75 | 2·25 |
| **MS**1143 | 105×75 mm. $5 Roger Sherman (Connecticut delegate) (vert) | 2·00 | 2·75 |

**233** "Madonna and Child" (Bernardo Daddi)

**1987.** Christmas. Religious Paintings. Mult.

| | | | |
|---|---|---|---|
| 1144 | 45c. Type **233** | 50 | 15 |
| 1145 | 60c. St. Joseph (detail, "The Nativity" (Sano di Pietro)) | 65 | 30 |
| 1146 | $1 Virgin Mary (detail, "The Nativity" (Sano di Pietro)) | 85 | 55 |
| 1147 | $4 "Music-making Angel" (Melozzo da Forli) | 2·25 | 3·50 |
| **MS**1148 | 99×70 mm. $5 "The Flight into Egypt" (Sano di Pietro) | 2·25 | 2·75 |

**234** Wedding Photograph, 1947

**1988.** Royal Ruby Wedding.

| | | | |
|---|---|---|---|
| 1149 **234** | 25c. brown, black and blue | 30 | 15 |
| 1150 - | 60c. multicoloured | 60 | 40 |
| 1151 - | $2 brown, black and green | 1·10 | 1·10 |
| 1152 - | $3 multicoloured | 1·50 | 1·60 |
| **MS**1153 | 107×77 mm. $5 multicoloured | 2·50 | 2·75 |

DESIGNS: 60c. Queen Elizabeth II; $2 Princess Elizabeth and Prince Philip with Prince Charles at his christening, 1948; $3 Queen Elizabeth (from photo by Tim Graham), 1980; $5 Royal family, 1952.

**235** Great Blue Heron

**1988.** Birds of Antigua. Multicoloured.

| | | | |
|---|---|---|---|
| 1154 | 10c. Type **235** | 45 | 40 |
| 1155 | 15c. Ringed kingfisher (horiz) | 50 | 40 |
| 1156 | 50c. Bananaquit (horiz) | 90 | 50 |
| 1157 | 60c. American purple gallinule ("Purple Gallinule") (horiz) | 90 | 50 |
| 1158 | 70c. Blue-hooded euphonia (horiz) | 1·00 | 55 |
| 1159 | $1 Brown-throated conure ("Caribbean Parakeet") | 1·25 | 75 |
| 1160 | $3 Troupial (horiz) | 2·50 | 3·50 |
| 1161 | $4 Purple-throated carib ("Hummingbird") (horiz) | 2·50 | 3·50 |
| **MS**1162 | Two sheets, each 115×86 mm. (a) $5 Greater flamingo. (b) $5 Brown pelican Set of 2 sheets | 4·50 | 5·50 |

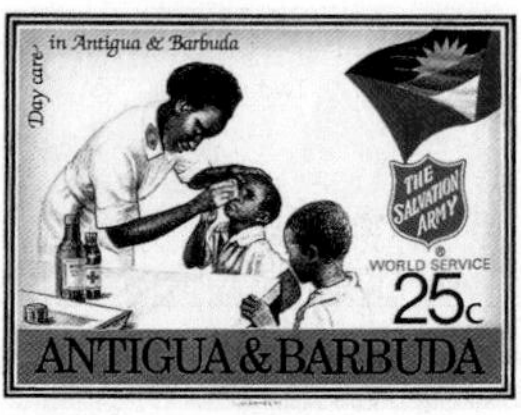


**236** First Aid at Daycare Centre, Antigua

**1988.** Salvation Army's Community Service. Multicoloured.

| | | | |
|---|---|---|---|
| 1163 | 25c. Type **236** | 80 | 65 |
| 1164 | 30c. Giving penicillin injection, Indonesia | 80 | 65 |
| 1165 | 40c. Children at daycare centre, Bolivia | 90 | 75 |
| 1166 | 45c. Rehabilitation of the handicapped, India | 90 | 75 |
| 1167 | 50c. Training blind man, Kenya | 1·00 | 1·25 |
| 1168 | 60c. Weighing baby, Ghana | 1·00 | 1·25 |
| 1169 | $1 Training typist, Zambia | 1·40 | 1·75 |
| 1170 | $2 Emergency food kitchen, Sri Lanka | 2·00 | 3·50 |
| **MS**1171 | 152×83 mm. $5 General Eva Burrows | 3·75 | 4·50 |

**237** Columbus's Second Fleet, 1493

**1988.** 500th Anniv (1992) of Discovery of America by Columbus (1st issue). Multicoloured.

| | | | |
|---|---|---|---|
| 1172 | 10c. Type **237** | 80 | 40 |
| 1173 | 30c. Painos. Indian village and fleet | 80 | 45 |
| 1174 | 45c. "Santa Mariagalante" (flagship) and Painos. village | 1·00 | 45 |
| 1175 | 60c. Painos Indians offering Columbus fruit and vegetables | 80 | 50 |
| 1176 | 90c. Painos Indian and Columbus with scarlet macaw | 2·00 | 1·00 |
| 1177 | $1 Columbus landing on island | 1·50 | 1·00 |
| 1178 | $3 Spanish soldier and fleet | 2·25 | 3·00 |
| 1179 | $4 Fleet under sail | 2·50 | 3·00 |
| **MS**1180 | Two sheets, each 110×80 mm. (a) $5 Queen Isabella's cross. (b) $5 Gold coin of Ferdinand and Isabella Set of 2 sheets | 6·50 | 7·00 |

See also Nos. 1267/71, 1360/8, 1503/11, 1654/60 and 1670/1.

**238** "Bust of Christ"

**1988.** Easter. 500th Birth Anniv of Titian (artist). Multicoloured.

1181 30c. Type **238** 40 20
1182 40c. "Scourging of Christ" 45 25
1183 45c. "Madonna in Glory with Saints" 45 25
1184 50c. "The Averoldi Polyptych" (detail) 45 35
1185 $1 "Christ Crowned with Thorns" 70 55
1186 $2 "Christ Mocked" 1·10 1·25
1187 $3 "Christ and Simon of Cyrene" 1·50 1·75
1188 $4 "Crucifixion with Virgin and Saints" 1·75 2·25
**MS**1189 Two sheets, each 110×95 mm. (a) $5 "Ecce Homo" (detail). (b) $5 "Noli me Tangere" (detail) Set of 2 sheets 7·00 8·50

**239** Two Yachts rounding Buoy

**1988.** Sailing Week. Multicoloured.

1190 30c. Type **239** 35 20
1191 60c. Three yachts 50 40
1192 $1 British yacht under way 60 55
1193 $3 Three yachts (different) 1·10 2·50
**MS**1194 103×92 mm. $5 Two yachts 1·75 3·25

**240** Mickey Mouse and Diver with Porpoise

**1988.** Disney EPCOT Centre, Orlando, Florida. Designs showing cartoon characters and exhibits. Multicoloured.

1195 1c. Type **240** 10 10
1196 2c. Goofy and Mickey Mouse with futuristic car (vert) 10 10
1197 3c. Mickey Mouse and Goofy as Atlas (vert) 10 10
1198 4c. Mickey Mouse and "Edaphosaurus" (prehistoric reptile) 10 10
1199 5c. Mickey Mouse at Journey into Imagination exhibit 15 10
1200 10c. Mickey Mouse collecting vegetables (vert) 20 10
1201 25c. Type **240** 55 25
1202 30c. As 2c. 55 25
1203 40c. As 3c. 60 30
1204 60c. As 4c. 85 50
1205 70c. As 5c. 95 60
1206 $1.50 As 10c. 2·00 2·00
1207 $3 Goofy and Mickey Mouse with robot (vert) 2·50 2·75
1208 $4 Mickey Mouse and Clarabelle at Horizons exhibit 2·50 2·75
**MS**1209 Two sheets, each 125×99 mm. (a) $5 Mickey Mouse and monorail (vert). (b) $5 Mickey Mouse flying over EPCOT Centre Set of 2 sheets 7·00 6·50

**1988.** Stamp Exhibitions. Nos. 1083/4 optd.

1210 $2 Royal tern (optd **Praga '88**, Prague) 5·50 2·75
1211 $3 Sooty tern (optd **INDEPENDENCE 40**, Israel) 5·50 3·50
**MS**1212 Two sheets, each 120×94 mm. (a) $5 Banded butterflyfish (optd **"OLYM-PHILEX '88"**, Seoul). (b) $5 brown booby (optd **"FINLANDIA 88"**, Helsinki). Set of 2 sheets 17·00 10·00

**242** Jacaranda

**1988.** Flowering Trees. Multicoloured.

1213 10c. Type **242** 30 20
1214 30c. Cordia 40 20
1215 50c. Orchid tree 60 40
1216 90c. Flamboyant 70 50
1217 $1 African tulip tree 75 55
1218 $2 Potato tree 1·40 1·60
1219 $3 Crepe myrtle 1·60 2·00
1220 $4 Pitch apple 1·75 2·75
**MS**1221 Two sheets, each 106×76 mm. (a) $5 Cassia. (b) $5 Chinaberry Set of 2 sheets 5·00 6·00

**243** Gymnastics

**1988.** Olympic Games, Seoul (2nd issue). Mult.

1222 40c. Type **243** 30 25
1223 60c. Weightlifting 40 30
1224 $1 Water polo (horiz) 80 50
1225 $3 Boxing (horiz) 1·50 2·25
**MS**1226 114×80 mm. $5 Runner with Olympic torch 2·00 3·00

**244** "Danaus plexippus"

**1988.** Caribbean Butterflies. Multicoloured.

1227 1c. Type **244** 60 1·00
1228 2c. "Greta diaphanus" 70 1·00
1229 3c. "Calisto archebates" 70 1·00
1230 5c. "Hamadryas feronia" 85 1·00
1231 10c. "Mestra dorcas" 1·00 30
1232 15c. "Hypolimnas misippus" 1·50 30
1233 20c. "Dione juno" 1·60 30
1234 25c. "Heliconius charithonia" 1·60 30
1235 30c. "Eurema pyro" 1·60 30
1236 40c. "Papilio androgeus" 1·60 30
1237 45c. "Anteos maerula" 1·60 30
1238 50c. "Aphrissa orbis" 1·75 45
1239 60c. "Astraptes xagua" 2·00 60
1240 $1 "Heliopetes arsalte" 2·25 1·00
1241 $2 "Polites baracoa" 3·25 3·75
1242 $2.50 "Phocides pigmalion" 4·00 5·00
1243 $5 "Prepona amphitoe" 5·50 7·50
1244 $10 "Oarisma nanus" 7·50 11·00
1244a $20 "Parides lycimenes" 15·00 20·00

**245** President Kennedy and Family

**1988.** 25th Death Anniv of John F. Kennedy (American statesman). Multicoloured.

1245 1c. Type **245** 10 10
1246 2c. Kennedy commanding "PT109" 10 10
1247 3c. Funeral cortege 10 10
1248 4c. In motorcade, Mexico City 10 10
1249 30c. As 1c. 35 15
1250 60c. As 4c. 1·00 40
1251 $1 As 3c. 1·10 75
1252 $4 As 2c. 3·00 3·50
**MS**1253 105×75 mm. $5 Kennedy taking presidential oath of office 2·50 3·25

**246** Minnie Mouse carol singing

**1988.** Christmas. "Mickey's Christmas Chorale". Design showing Walt Disney cartoon characters. Multicoloured.

1254 10c. Type **246** 40 30
1255 25c. Pluto 55 45
1256 30c. Mickey Mouse playing ukelele 55 45
1257 70c. Donald Duck and nephew 90 80
1258 $1 Mordie and Ferdie carol singing 90 1·00
1259 $1 Goofy carol singing 90 1·00
1260 $1 Chip n'Dale sliding off roof 90 1·00
1261 $1 Two of Donald Duck's nephews at window 90 1·00
1262 $1 As 10c. 90 1·00
1263 $1 As 25c. 90 1·00
1264 $1 As 30c. 90 1·00
1265 $1 As 70c. 90 1·00
**MS**1266 Two sheets, each 127×102 mm. (a) $7 Donald Duck playing trumpet and Mickey and Minnie Mouse in carriage. (b) $7 Mickey Mouse and friends singing carols on roller skates (horiz) Set of 2 sheets 8·50 8·50

Nos. 1258/65 were printed together, se-tenant, forming a composite design.

**247** Arawak Warriors

**1989.** 500th Anniv of Discovery of America by Columbus (1992) (2nd issue). Pre-Columbian Arawak Society. Multicoloured.

1267 $1.50 Type **247** 1·10 1·40
1268 $1.50 Whip dancers 1·10 1·40
1269 $1.50 Whip dancers and chief with pineapple 1·10 1·40
1270 $1.50 Family and camp fire 1·10 1·40
**MS**1271 71×84 mm. $6 Arawak chief 2·75 3·00

Nos. 1267/70 were printed together, se-tenant, forming a composite design.

**248** De Havilland Comet 4 Airliner

**1989.** 50th Anniv of First Jet Flight. Mult.

1272 10c. Type **248** 90 45
1273 30c. Messerschmitt Me 262 fighter 1·50 45
1274 40c. Boeing 707 airliner 1·50 45
1275 60c. Canadair CL-13 Sabre (inscr "F-86") fighter 1·90 55
1276 $1 Lockheed F-104 Starfighters 2·25 1·10
1277 $2 McDonnell Douglas DC-10 airliner 3·00 3·00
1278 $3 Boeing 747-300/400 airliner 3·25 4·50
1279 $4 McDonnell Douglas F-4 Phantom II fighter 3·25 4·50
**MS**1280 Two sheets, each 114×83 mm. (a) $7 Grumman F-14A Tomcat fighter. (b) $7 Concorde airliner Set of 2 sheets 9·50 12·00

**249** "Festivale"

**1989.** Caribbean Cruise Ships. Multicoloured.

1281 25c. Type **249** 1·75 50
1282 45c. "Southward" 2·00 50
1283 50c. "Sagafjord" 2·00 50
1284 60c. "Daphne" 2·00 60
1285 75c. "Cunard Countess" 2·25 1·00
1286 90c. "Song of America" 2·50 1·10
1287 $3 "Island Princess" 4·00 5·50
1288 $4 "Galileo" 4·00 5·50
**MS**1289 (a) 113×87 mm. $6 "Norway". (b) 111×82 mm. $6 "Oceanic" Set of 2 sheets 7·00 11·00

**250** "Fish swimming by Duck half-submerged in Stream"

**1989.** Japanese Art. Paintings by Hiroshige. Mult.

1290 25c. Type **250** 1·00 50
1291 45c. "Crane and Wave" 1·25 50
1292 50c. "Sparrows and Morning Glories" 1·40 50
1293 60c. "Crested Blackbird and Flowering Cherry" 1·50 60
1294 $1 "Great Knot sitting among Water Grass" 1·75 80
1295 $2 "Goose on a Bank of Water" 2·50 2·50
1296 $3 "Black Paradise Flycatcher and Blossoms" 3·00 3·00
1297 $4 "Sleepy Owl perched on a Pine Branch" 3·00 3·00
**MS**1298 Two sheets, each 102×75 mm. (a) $5 "Bullfinch flying near a Clematis Branch". (b) $5 "Titmouse on a Cherry Branch" Set of 2 sheets 9·00 9·50

**251** Mickey and Minnie Mouse in Helicopter over River Seine

**1989.** "Philexfrance 89" International Stamp Exhibition, Paris. Walt Disney cartoon characters in Paris. Multicoloured.

1299 1c. Type **251** 10 10
1300 2c. Goofy and Mickey Mouse passing Arc de Triomphe 10 10
1301 3c. Mickey Mouse painting picture of Notre Dame 10 10
1302 4c. Mickey and Minnie Mouse with Pluto leaving Metro station 10 10
1303 5c. Minnie Mouse as model in fashion show 10 10
1304 10c. Daisy Duck, Minnie Mouse and Clarabelle as Folies Bergere dancers 10 10
1305 $5 Mickey and Minnie Mouse shopping in street market 7·00 7·00
1306 $6 Mickey and Minnie Mouse, Jose Carioca and Donald Duck at pavement cafe 7·00 7·00
**MS**1307 Two sheets, each 127×101 mm. (a) $5 Mickey and Minnie Mouse in hot air balloon. (b) $5 Mickey Mouse at Pompidou Centre cafe (vert) Set of 2 sheets 11·00 13·00

**252** Goalkeeper

**1989.** World Cup Football Championship, Italy (1990). Multicoloured.

1308 15c. Type **252** 85 30
1309 25c. Goalkeeper moving towards ball 90 30
1310 $1 Goalkeeper reaching for ball 2·00 1·25
1311 $4 Goalkeeper saving goal 3·50 5·00
**MS**1312 Two sheets, each 75×105 mm. (a) $5 Three players competing for ball (horiz). (b) $5 Ball and player' legs (horiz) Set of 2 sheets 8·00 10·00

**253** "Mycena pura"

**1989.** Fungi. Multicoloured.

1313 10c. Type **253** 75 50

| | | | |
|---|---|---|---|
| 1314 | 25c. "Psathyrella tuberculata" (vert) | 1·10 | 40 |
| 1315 | 50c. "Psilocybe cubensis" | 1·50 | 60 |
| 1316 | 60c. "Leptonia caeruleocapitata" (vert) | 1·50 | 70 |
| 1317 | 75c. "Xeromphalina tenuipes" (vert) | 1·75 | 1·10 |
| 1318 | $1 "Chlorophyllum molybdites" (vert) | 1·75 | 1·25 |
| 1319 | $3 "Marasmius haematocephalus" | 2·75 | 3·75 |
| 1320 | $4 "Cantharellus cinnabarinus" | 2·75 | 3·75 |
| **MS**1321 | Two sheets, each 88×62 mm. (a) $6 "Leucopaxillus gracillimus" (vert). (b) $6 "Volvariella volvacea" Set of 2 sheets | 13·00 | 15·00 |

**254** Desmarest's Hutia

**1989.** Local Fauna. Multicoloured.

| | | | |
|---|---|---|---|
| 1322 | 25c. Type **254** | 80 | 50 |
| 1323 | 45c. Caribbean monk seal | 2·50 | 1·00 |
| 1324 | 80c. Mustache bat (vert) | 1·50 | 1·00 |
| 1325 | $4 American manatee (vert) | 3·50 | 5·50 |
| **MS**1326 | 113×87 mm. $5 West Indian giant rice rat | 7·00 | 9·00 |

**255** Goofy and Old Printing Press

**1989.** "American Philately". Walt Disney cartoon characters with stamps and the logo of the American Philatelic Society. Multicoloured.

| | | | |
|---|---|---|---|
| 1327 | 1c. Type **255** | 10 | 10 |
| 1328 | 2c. Donald Duck cancelling first day cover for Mickey Mouse | 10 | 10 |
| 1329 | 3c. Donald Duck's nephews reading recruiting poster for Pony Express riders | 10 | 10 |
| 1330 | 4c. Morty and Ferdie as early radio broadcasters | 10 | 10 |
| 1331 | 5c. Donald Duck and water buffalo watching television | 10 | 10 |
| 1332 | 10c. Donald Duck with stamp album | 10 | 10 |
| 1333 | $4 Daisy Duck with computer system | 4·75 | 6·00 |
| 1334 | $6 Donald's nephews with stereo radio, trumpet and guitar | 6·00 | 7·00 |
| **MS**1335 | Two sheets, each 127×102 mm. (a) $5 Donald's nephews donating stamps to charity. (b) $5 Minnie Mouse flying mailplane upside down (horiz) Set of 2 sheets | 11·00 | 13·00 |

**256** Mickey Mouse and Donald Duck with Camden and Amboy Locomotive "John Bull", 1831

**1989.** "World Stamp Expo '89" International Stamp Exhibition, Washington. Walt Disney cartoon characters and locomotives. Mult.

| | | | |
|---|---|---|---|
| 1336 | 25c. Type **256** | 90 | 50 |
| 1337 | 45c. Mickey Mouse and friends with "Atlantic", 1832 | 1·10 | 50 |
| 1338 | 50c. Mickey Mouse and Goofy with "William Crooks", 1861 | 1·10 | 50 |
| 1339 | 60c. Mickey Mouse and Goofy with "Minnetonka", 1869 | 1·10 | 65 |
| 1340 | $1 Chip n'Dale with "Thatcher Perkins", 1863 | 1·40 | 75 |
| 1341 | $2 Mickey and Minnie Mouse with "Pioneer", 1848 | 2·25 | 2·25 |
| 1342 | $3 Mickey Mouse and Donald Duck with cog railway locomotive "Peppersass", 1869 | 3·00 | 4·00 |
| 1343 | $4 Mickey Mouse with Huey, Dewey and Louie aboard N.Y. World's Fair "Gimbels Flyer", 1939 | 3·25 | 4·00 |
| **MS**1344 | Two sheets, each 127×101 mm. (a) $6 Mickey Mouse and locomotive "Thomas Jefferson", 1835 (vert). (b) $6 Mickey Mouse and friends at Central Pacific "Golden Spike" ceremony, 1869 Set of 2 sheets | 7·50 | 9·00 |

**258** Launch of "Apollo II"

**1989.** 20th Anniv of First Manned Landing on Moon. Multicoloured.

| | | | |
|---|---|---|---|
| 1346 | 10c. Type **258** | 50 | 30 |
| 1347 | 45c. Aldrin on Moon | 1·25 | 30 |
| 1348 | $1 Module "Eagle" over Moon (horiz) | 1·75 | 1·10 |
| 1349 | $4 Recovery of "Apollo II" crew after splashdown (horiz) | 2·75 | 5·00 |
| **MS**1350 | 107×77 mm. $5 Astronaut Neil Armstrong | 4·50 | 5·50 |

**259** "The Small Cowper Madonna" (Raphael)

**1989.** Christmas. Paintings by Raphael and Giotto. Multicoloured.

| | | | |
|---|---|---|---|
| 1351 | 10c. Type **259** | 30 | 15 |
| 1352 | 25c. "Madonna of the Goldfinch" (Raphael) | 45 | 20 |
| 1353 | 30c. "The Alba Madonna" (Raphael) | 45 | 20 |
| 1354 | 50c. Saint (detail, "Bologna Altarpiece") (Giotto) | 65 | 30 |
| 1355 | 60c. Angel (detail, "Bologna Altarpiece") (Giotto) | 70 | 35 |
| 1356 | 70c. Angel slaying serpent (detail, "Bologna Altarpiece") (Giotto) | 80 | 40 |
| 1357 | $4 Evangelist (detail, "Bologna Altarpiece") (Giotto) | 3·00 | 4·50 |
| 1358 | $5 "Madonna of Foligno" (detail) (Raphael) | 3·00 | 4·50 |
| **MS**1359 | Two sheets, each 71×96 mm. (a) $5 "The Marriage of the Virgin" (detail) (Raphael). (b) $5 Madonna and Child (detail, "Bologna Altarpiece") (Giotto) Set of 2 sheets | 9·00 | 12·00 |

**260** Star-eyed Hermit Crab

**1990.** 500th Anniv (1992) of Discovery of America by Columbus (3rd issue). New World Natural History–Marine Life. Multicoloured.

| | | | |
|---|---|---|---|
| 1360 | 10c. Type **260** | 45 | 20 |
| 1361 | 20c. Spiny lobster | 65 | 25 |
| 1362 | 25c. Magnificent banded fanworm | 65 | 25 |
| 1363 | 45c. Cannonball jellyfish | 80 | 40 |
| 1364 | 60c. Red-spiny sea star | 1·00 | 60 |
| 1365 | $2 Peppermint shrimp | 2·00 | 2·50 |
| 1366 | $3 Coral crab | 2·25 | 3·75 |
| 1367 | $4 Branching fire coral | 2·25 | 3·75 |
| **MS**1368 | Two sheets, each 100×69 mm. (a) $5 Common sea fan. (b) $5 Portuguese man-of-war Set of 2 sheets | 8·00 | 9·00 |

**261** "Vanilla mexicana"

**1990.** "Expo '90" International Garden and Greenery Exhibition, Osaka. Orchids. Multicoloured.

| | | | |
|---|---|---|---|
| 1369 | 15c. Type **261** | 75 | 50 |
| 1370 | 45c. "Epidendrum ibaguense" | 1·10 | 50 |
| 1371 | 50c. "Epidendrum secundum" | 1·25 | 55 |
| 1372 | 60c. "Maxillaria conferta" | 1·40 | 55 |
| 1373 | $1 "Oncidium altissimum" | 1·50 | 1·00 |
| 1374 | $2 "Spiranthes lanceolata" | 2·00 | 2·50 |
| 1375 | $3 "Tonopsis utricularioides" | 2·25 | 3·50 |
| 1376 | $5 "Epidendrum nocturnum" | 3·25 | 4·50 |
| **MS**1377 | Two sheets, each 102×70 mm. (a) $6 "Octomeria graminifolia". (b) $6 "Rodriguezia lanceolata" Set of 2 sheets | 6·50 | 8·00 |

**262** Queen Victoria and Queen Elizabeth II

**1990.** 150th Anniv of the Penny Black.

| | | | | |
|---|---|---|---|---|
| 1378 | **262** | 45c. green | 1·00 | 40 |
| 1379 | - | 60c. mauve | 1·25 | 65 |
| 1380 | - | $5 blue | 3·75 | 5·50 |
| **MS**1381 | | 102×80 mm. Type **262** $6 purple | 5·00 | 6·50 |

DESIGNS: 60c., $5 As Type **262**, but with different backgrounds.

**263** "Britannia" (mail paddle-steamer), 1840

**1990.** "Stamp World London '90" International Stamp Exhibition.

| | | | | |
|---|---|---|---|---|
| 1382 | **263** | 50c. green and red | 1·00 | 35 |
| 1383 | - | 75c. brown and red | 1·50 | 90 |
| 1384 | - | $4 blue and red | 4·00 | 5·50 |
| **MS**1385 | – | 104×81 mm. $6 brown and red | 3·75 | 6·00 |

DESIGNS: 75c. Travelling Post Office sorting van, 1892; $4 Short S.23 Empire "C" Class flying boat "Centaurus", 1938; $6 Post Office underground railway, London, 1927.

**264** Flamefish

**1990.** Reef Fishes. Multicoloured.

| | | | |
|---|---|---|---|
| 1386 | 10c. Type **264** | 65 | 55 |
| 1387 | 15c. Coney | 80 | 55 |
| 1388 | 50c. Long-spined squirrelfish | 1·25 | 60 |
| 1389 | 60c. Sergeant major | 1·25 | 60 |
| 1390 | $1 Yellow-tailed snapper | 1·50 | 85 |
| 1391 | $2 Rock beauty | 2·25 | 2·75 |
| 1392 | $3 Spanish hogfish | 2·75 | 3·75 |
| 1393 | $4 Striped parrotfish | 2·75 | 3·75 |
| **MS**1394 | Two sheets, each 90×70 mm. (a) $5 Black-barred soldierfish. (b) $4 Four-eyed butterflyfish Set of 2 sheets | 10·00 | 11·00 |

**265** "Voyager 2" passing Saturn

**1990.** Achievement in Space. Multicoloured.

| | | | |
|---|---|---|---|
| 1395 | 45c. Type **265** | 1·00 | 85 |
| 1396 | 45c. "Pioneer 11" photographing Saturn | 1·10 | 85 |
| 1397 | 45c. Astronaut in transporter | 1·10 | 85 |
| 1398 | 45c. Space shuttle "Columbia" | 1·10 | 85 |
| 1399 | 45c. "Apollo 10" command module on parachutes | 1·10 | 85 |
| 1400 | 45c. "Skylab" space station | 1·10 | 85 |
| 1401 | 45c. Astronaut Edward White in space | 1·10 | 85 |
| 1402 | 45c. "Apollo" spacecraft on joint mission | 1·10 | 85 |
| 1403 | 45c. "Soyuz" spacecraft on joint mission | 1·10 | 85 |
| 1404 | 45c. "Mariner 1" passing Venus | 1·10 | 85 |
| 1405 | 45c. "Gemini 4" capsule | 1·10 | 85 |
| 1406 | 45c. "Sputnik 1" | 1·10 | 85 |
| 1407 | 45c. Hubble space telescope | 1·10 | 85 |
| 1408 | 45c. North American X-15 rocket plane | 1·10 | 85 |
| 1409 | 45c. Bell XS-1 airplane | 1·10 | 85 |
| 1410 | 45c. "Apollo 17" astronaut and lunar rock formation | 1·10 | 85 |
| 1411 | 45c. Lunar Rover | 1·10 | 85 |
| 1412 | 45c. "Apollo 14" lunar module | 1·10 | 85 |
| 1413 | 45c. Astronaut Buzz Aldrin on Moon | 1·10 | 85 |
| 1414 | 45c. Soviet "Lunokhod" lunar vehicle | 1·10 | 85 |

**266** Queen Mother in Evening Dress

**1990.** 90th Birthday of Queen Elizabeth the Queen Mother.

| | | | | |
|---|---|---|---|---|
| 1415 | **266** | 15c. multicoloured | 55 | 20 |
| 1416 | - | 35c. multicoloured | 75 | 25 |
| 1417 | - | 75c. multicoloured | 1·00 | 85 |
| 1418 | - | $3 multicoloured | 2·50 | 3·50 |
| **MS**1419 | – | 67×98 mm. mult | 4·00 | 4·50 |

DESIGNS: Nos. 1416/19, Recent photographs of the Queen Mother.

**267** Mickey Mouse as Animator

**1990.** Mickey Mouse in Hollywood. Walt Disney cartoon characters. Multicoloured.

| | | | |
|---|---|---|---|
| 1420 | 25c. Type **267** | 60 | 25 |
| 1421 | 45c. Minnie Mouse learning lines while being dressed | 80 | 25 |
| 1422 | 50c. Mickey Mouse with clapper board | 90 | 30 |
| 1423 | 60c. Daisy Duck making-up Mickey Mouse | 1·00 | 35 |
| 1424 | $1 Clarabelle Cow as Cleopatra | 1·25 | 70 |
| 1425 | $2 Mickey Mouse directing Goofy and Donald Duck | 1·75 | 2·25 |
| 1426 | $3 Mickey Mouse directing Goofy as birdman | 2·25 | 3·50 |
| 1427 | $4 Donald Duck and Mickey Mouse editing film | 2·25 | 3·50 |
| **MS**1428 | Two sheets, each 132×95 mm. (a) $5 Minnie Mouse, Daisy Duck and Clarabelle as musical stars. (b) $5 Mickey Mouse on set as director Set of 2 sheets. | 7·00 | 9·00 |

**268** Men's 20 Kilometres Walk

**1990.** Olympic Games, Barcelona (1992) (1st issue). Multicoloured.

| | | | |
|---|---|---|---|
| 1429 | 50c. Type **268** | 75 | 40 |
| 1430 | 75c. Triple jump | 1·00 | 75 |
| 1431 | $1 Men's 10,000 metres | 1·25 | 85 |

1432 $5 Javelin 3·50 6·00

**MS**1433 100×70 mm. $6 Athlete lighting Olympic flame at Los Angeles Olympics 5·50 7·00

See also Nos. 1553/61 and 1609/17.

**269** Huey and Dewey asleep ("Christmas Stories")

**1990.** International Literacy Year. Walt Disney cartoon characters illustrating works by Charles Dickens. Multicoloured.

1434 15c. Type **269** 65 35
1435 45c. Donald Duck as Poor Jo looking at grave ("Bleak House") 1·00 45
1436 50c. Dewey as Oliver asking for more ("Oliver Twist") 1·10 50
1437 60c. Daisy Duck as The Marchioness ("Old Curiosity Shop") 1·25 55
1438 $1 Little Nell giving nosegay to her grandfather ("Little Nell") 1·40 85
1439 $2 Scrooge McDuck as Mr. Pickwick ("Pickwick Papers") 2·00 2·50
1440 $3 Minnie Mouse as Florence and Mickey Mouse as Paul ("Dombey and Son") 2·25 3·50
1441 $5 Minnie Mouse as Jenny Wren ("Our Mutual Friend") 2·75 4·50

**MS**1442 Two sheets, each 126×102 mm. (a) $6 Artful Dodger picking pocket ("Oliver Twist"). (b) $6 Unexpected arrivals at Mr. Peggoty's ("David Copperfield") Set of 2 sheets 10·00 12·00

**1990.** World Cup Football Championship Winners, Italy. Nos. 1308/11 optd **Winners West Germany 1 Argentina 0**.

1443 15c. Type **252** 75 40
1444 25c. Goalkeeper moving towards ball 75 40
1445 $1 Goalkeeper reaching for ball 1·75 1·60
1446 $4 Goalkeeper saving goal 3·75 5·50

**MS**1447 Two sheets, each 75×105 mm. (a) $5 Three players competing for ball (horiz). (b) $5 Ball and players' legs (horiz) Set of 2 sheets 9·50 11·00

**271** Pearly-eyed Thrasher

**1990.** Birds. Multicoloured.

1448 10c. Type **271** 45 30
1449 25c. Purple-throated carib 45 35
1450 50c. Common yellowthroat 50 40
1451 60c. American kestrel 1·00 70
1452 $1 Yellow-bellied sapsucker 1·00 80
1453 $2 American purple gallinule ("Purple Gallinule") 2·00 2·25
1454 $3 Yellow-crowned night heron 2·10 3·00
1455 $4 Blue-hooded euphonia 2·10 3·00

**MS**1456 Two sheets, each 76×60 mm. (a) $6 Brown pelican. (b) $6 Magnificent frigate bird Set of 2 sheets 14·00 16·00

**272** "Madonna and Child with Saints" (detail, Sebastiano del Piombo)

**1990.** Christmas. Paintings by Renaissance Masters. Multicoloured.

1457 25c. Type **272** 80 30
1458 30c. "Virgin and Child with Angels" (detail, Grunewald) (vert) 90 30
1459 40c. "The Holy Family and a Shepherd" (detail, Titian) 1·00 30
1460 60c. "Virgin and Child" (detail, Lippi) (vert) 1·40 40
1461 $1 "Jesus, St. John and Two Angels" (Rubens) 1·75 70
1462 $2 "Adoration of the Shepherds" (detail, Vincenzo Catena) 2·50 2·75
1463 $4 "Adoration of the Magi" (detail, Giorgione) 4·00 5·50
1464 $5 "Virgin and Child adored by Warrior" (detail, Vincenzo Catena) 4·00 5·50

**MS**1465 Two sheets, each 71×101 mm. (a) $6 "Allegory of the Blessings of Jacob" (detail, Rubens) (vert). (b) $6 "Adoration of the Magi" (detail, Fra Angelico) (vert) Set of 2 sheets 6·50 7·50

**273** "Rape of the Daughters of Leucippus" (detail)

**1991.** 350th Death Anniv of Rubens. Mult.

1466 25c. Type **273** 1·00 40
1467 45c. "Bacchanal" (detail) 1·50 45
1468 50c. "Rape of the Sabine Women" (detail) 1·50 50
1469 60c. "Battle of the Amazons" (detail) 1·60 65
1470 $1 "Rape of the Sabine Women" (different detail) 2·00 1·00
1471 $2 "Bacchanal" (different detail) 2·50 2·50
1472 $3 "Rape of the Sabine Women" (different detail) 3·50 4·25
1473 $4 "Bacchanal" (different detail) 3·50 5·00

**MS**1474 Two sheets, each 101×71 mm. (a) $6 "Rape of Hippoda-meia" (detail). (b) $6 "Battle of the Amazons" (different detail) Set of 2 sheets 8·50 10·00

**274** U.S. Troops cross into Germany, 1944

**1991.** 50th Anniv of Second World War. Mult.

1475 10c. Type **274** 1·10 65
1476 15c. Axis surrender in North Africa, 1943 1·25 50
1477 25c. U.S. tanks invade Kwajalein, 1944 1·25 50
1478 45c. Roosevelt and Churchill meet at Casablanca, 1943 2·50 70
1479 50c. Marshal Badoglio, Prime Minister of Italian anti-fascist government, 1943 1·50 70
1480 $1 Lord Mountbatten, Supreme Allied Commander South-east Asia, 1943 3·00 1·50
1481 $2 Greek victory at Koritza, 1940 2·25 2·75
1482 $4 Anglo-Soviet mutual assistance pact, 1941 3·25 4·25
1483 $5 Operation Torch landings, 1942 3·25 4·25

**MS**1484 Two sheets, each 108×80 mm. (a) $6 Japanese attack on Pearl Harbor, 1941. (b) $6 U.S.A.A.F. daylight raid on Schweinfurt, 1943 Set of 2 sheets 9·00 11·00

**275** Locomotive "Prince Regent", Middleton Colliery, 1812

**1991.** Cog Railways. Multicoloured.

1485 25c. Type **275** 1·25 55
1486 30c. Snowdon Mountain Railway 1·25 55
1487 40c. First railcar at Hell Gate, Manitou Pike's Peak Railway, U.S.A 1·40 65
1488 60c. P.N.K.A. rack railway, Java 1·60 70
1489 $1 Green Mountain Railway, Maine, 1883 2·00 1·00
1490 $2 Rack locomotive "Pike's Peak", 1891 3·00 3·00
1491 $4 Vitznau–Rigi Railway, Switzerland, and Mt. Rigi hotel local post stamp 3·75 4·75
1492 $5 Leopoldina Railway, Brazil 3·75 4·75

**MS**1493 Two sheets, each 100×70 mm. (a) $6 Electric towing locomotives, Panama Canal. (b) $6 Gornergracht Railway, Switzerland (vert) Set of 2 sheets 12·00 13·00

**276** "Heliconius charithonia"

**1991.** Butterflies. Multicoloured.

1494 10c. Type **276** 65 50
1495 35c. "Marpesia petreus" 1·10 50
1496 50c. "Anartia amathea" 1·25 60
1497 75c. "Siproeta stelenes" 1·50 1·00
1498 $1 "Battus polydamas" 1·75 1·10
1499 $2 "Historis odius" 2·25 2·75
1500 $4 "Hypolimnas misippus" 3·25 4·25
1501 $5 "Hamadryas feronia" 3·25 4·25

**MS**1502 Two sheets. (a) 73×100 mm. $6 "Vanessa cardui" caterpillar (vert) (b) 100×73 mm. $6 "Danaus plexippus" caterpillar (vert) Set of 2 sheets 14·00 16·00

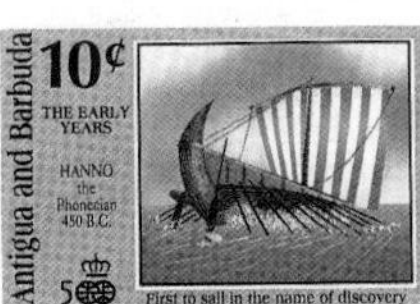


**277** Hanno the Phoenician, 450 B.C.

**1991.** 500th Anniv of Discovery of America by Columbus (1992) (4th issue). History of Exploration.

1503 **277** 10c. multicoloured 70 40
1504 - 15c. multicoloured 80 40
1505 - 45c. multicoloured 1·25 50
1506 - 60c. multicoloured 1·40 60
1507 - $1 multicoloured 1·75 85
1508 - $2 multicoloured 2·25 2·75
1509 - $4 multicoloured 3·00 4·00
1510 - $5 multicoloured 3·00 4·00

**MS**1511 – Two sheets, each 106×76 mm. (a) $6 black and red. (b) $6 black and red Set of 2 sheets 7·00 9·00

DESIGNS—HORIZ: 15c. Pytheas the Greek, 325 B.C.; 45c. Erik the Red discovering Greenland, 985 A.D.; 60c. Leif Eriksson reaching Vinland, 1000 A.D.; $1 Scylax the Greek in the Indian Ocean, 518 A.D.; $2 Marco Polo sailing to the Orient, 1259 A.D.; $4 Ship of Queen Hatshepsut of Egypt, 1493 B.C.; $5 St. Brendan's coracle, 500 A.D. VERT: $6 (No. **MS**1511a) Engraving of Columbus as Admiral; $6 (No. **MS**1511b) Engraving of Columbus bare-headed.

**278** "Camille Roulin" (Van Gogh)

**1991.** Death Centenary (1990) of Vincent van Gogh (artist). Multicoloured.

1512 5c. Type **278** 70 85
1513 10c. "Armand Roulin" 70 60
1514 15c. "Young Peasant Woman with Straw Hat sitting in the Wheat" 85 50
1515 25c. "Adeline Ravoux" 1·00 50
1516 30c. "The Schoolboy" 1·00 50
1517 40c. "Doctor Gachet" 1·10 50
1518 50c. "Portrait of a Man" 1·25 50
1519 75c. "Two Children" 1·75 80
1520 $2 "The Postman Joseph Roulin" 2·75 2·75
1521 $3 "The Seated Zouave" 3·75 4·00
1522 $4 "L'Arlesienne" 4·00 4·50
1523 $5 "Self-Portrait, November/December 1888" 4·00 4·50

**MS**1524 Three sheets, each 102×76 mm. (a) $5 "Farmhouse in Provence" (horiz). (b) $5 "Flowering Garden" (horiz). (c) $6 "The Bridge at Trinquetaille" (horiz) Imperf Set of 3 sheets 16·00 18·00

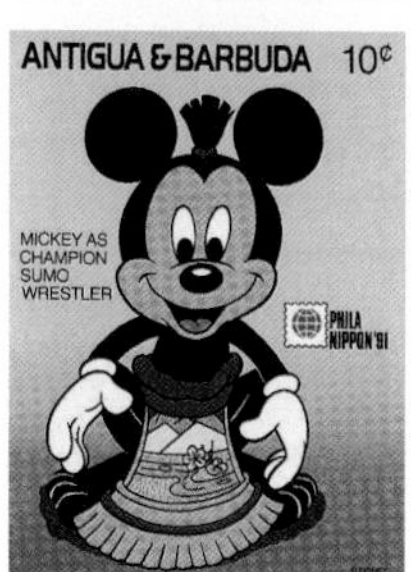


**279** Mickey Mouse as Champion Sumo Wrestler

**1991.** "Philanippon '91" International Stamp Exhibition, Tokyo. Walt Disney cartoon characters participating in martial arts. Multicoloured.

1525 10c. Type **279** 80 20
1526 15c. Goofy using the tonfa (horiz) 90 25
1527 45c. Donald Duck as a Ninja (horiz) 1·60 50
1528 60c. Mickey armed for Kung fu 2·00 65
1529 $1 Goofy with Kendo sword 2·50 1·25
1530 $2 Mickey and Donald demonstrating Aikido (horiz) 3·00 3·00
1531 $4 Mickey and Donald in Judo bout (horiz) 4·00 5·00
1532 $5 Mickey performing Yabusame (mounted archery) 4·00 5·00

**MS**1533 Two sheets, each 127×102 mm. (a) $6 Mickey delivering Karate kick (horiz). (b) $6 Mickey demonstrating Tamashiwara Set of 2 sheets 10·00 12·00

**280** Queen Elizabeth and Prince Philip in 1976

**1991.** 65th Birthday of Queen Elizabeth II. Multicoloured.

1534 15c. Type **280** 30 10
1535 20c. The Queen and Prince Philip in Portugal, 1985 30 10
1536 $2 Queen Elizabeth II 1·50 1·50
1537 $4 The Queen and Prince Philip at Ascot, 1986 2·75 3·25

**MS**1538 68×90 mm. $4 The Queen at National Theatre, 1986, and Prince Philip 3·25 4·00

**1991.** 10th Wedding Anniv of Prince and Princess of Wales. As T **280**. Multicoloured.

1539 10c. Prince and Princess of Wales at party, 1986 40 10
1540 40c. Separate portraits of Prince, Princess and sons 80 25
1541 $1 Prince Henry and Prince William 1·10 70
1542 $5 Princess Diana in Australia and Prince Charles in Hungary 4·25 4·50

**MS**1543 68×90 mm. $4 Prince Charles in Hackney and Princess and sons in Majorca, 1987 5·00 5·50

**281** Daisy Duck teeing-off

**1991.** Golf. Walt Disney cartoon characters. Mult.

1544 10c. Type **281** 70 50
1545 15c. Goofy playing ball from under trees 75 50
1546 45c. Mickey Mouse playing deflected shot 1·25 50
1547 60c. Mickey hacking divot out of fairway 1·50 65
1548 $1 Donald Duck playing ball out of pond 1·75 1·10
1549 $2 Minnie Mouse hitting ball over pond 2·50 2·75
1550 $4 Donald in a bunker 3·25 4·00
1551 $5 Goofy trying snooker shot into hole 3·25 4·00

| | | | |
|---|---|---|---|
| **MS**1552 | Two sheets, each 127×102 mm. (a) $6 Grandma Duck in senior tournament. (b) $6 Mickey and Minnie Mouse on course (horiz) Set of 2 sheets | 10·00 | 12·00 |

**282** Moose receiving Gold Medal

**1991.** 50th Anniv of Archie Comics, and Olympic Games, Barcelona (1992) (2nd issue). Multicoloured.

| | | | |
|---|---|---|---|
| 1553 | 10c. Type **282** | 55 | 40 |
| 1554 | 25c. Archie playing polo on a motorcycle (horiz) | 85 | 40 |
| 1555 | 40c. Archie and Betty at fencing class | 1·10 | 45 |
| 1556 | 60c. Archie joining girls' volleyball team | 1·40 | 65 |
| 1557 | $1 Archie with tennis ball in his mouth | 1·75 | 1·10 |
| 1558 | $2 Archie running marathon | 2·50 | 3·00 |
| 1559 | $4 Archie judging women's gymnastics (horiz) | 3·75 | 4·50 |
| 1560 | $5 Archie watching the cheerleaders | 3·75 | 4·50 |
| **MS**1561 | Two sheets, each 128×102 mm. (a) $6 Archie heading football. (b) $6 Archie catching baseball (horiz) Set of 2 sheets | 11·00 | 13·00 |

**283** Presidents De Gaulle and Kennedy, 1961

**1991.** Birth Centenary of Charles de Gaulle (French statesman). Multicoloured.

| | | | |
|---|---|---|---|
| 1562 | 10c. Type **283** | 80 | 50 |
| 1563 | 15c. General De Gaulle with President Roosevelt, 1945 (vert) | 80 | 50 |
| 1564 | 45c. President De Gaulle with Chancellor Adenauer, 1962 (vert) | 1·25 | 50 |
| 1565 | 60c. De Gaulle at Arc de Triomphe, Liberation of Paris, 1944 (vert) | 1·50 | 65 |
| 1566 | $1 General De Gaulle crossing the Rhine, 1945 | 1·75 | 1·25 |
| 1567 | $2 General De Gaulle in Algiers, 1944 | 2·50 | 3·00 |
| 1568 | $4 Presidents De Gaulle and Eisenhower, 1960 | 3·25 | 4·50 |
| 1569 | $5 De Gaulle returning from Germany, 1968 (vert) | 3·25 | 4·50 |
| **MS**1570 | Two sheets. (a) 76×106 mm. $6 De Gaulle with crowd. (b) 106×76 mm. $6 De Gaulle and Churchill at Casablanca, 1943 Set of 2 sheets | 14·00 | 13·00 |

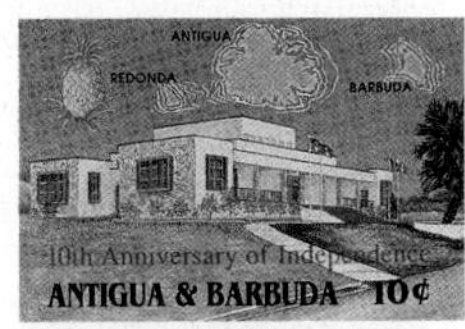


**284** Parliament Building and Map

**1991.** 10th Anniv of Independence.

| | | | |
|---|---|---|---|
| 1571 | **284** 10c. multicoloured | 75 | 50 |
| **MS**1572 | 87×97 mm. $6 Old Post Office, St. Johns, and stamps of 1862 and 1981 (50×37 mm) | 6·00 | 7·50 |

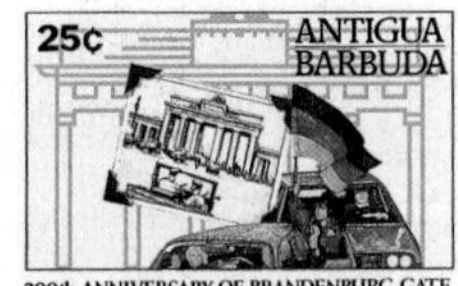


**285** Germans celebrating Reunification

**1991.** Anniversaries and Events. Multicoloured.

| | | | |
|---|---|---|---|
| 1573 | 25c. Type **285** | 30 | 30 |
| 1574 | 75c. Cubs erecting tent | 70 | 50 |
| 1575 | $1.50 "Don Giovanni" and Mozart | 5·00 | 3·00 |
| 1576 | $2 Chariot driver and Gate at night | 1·10 | 2·00 |
| 1577 | $2 Lord Baden-Powell and members of 3rd Antigua Methodist cub pack (vert) | 3·00 | 2·75 |
| 1578 | $2 Lilienthal's signature and glider "Flugzeug Nr. 5" | 3·25 | 2·75 |
| 1579 | $2.50 Driver in Class P36 steam locomotive (vert) | 6·00 | 4·00 |
| 1580 | $3 Statues from podium | 1·75 | 3·25 |
| 1581 | $3.50 Cubs and camp fire | 2·50 | 3·25 |
| 1582 | $4 St. Peter's Cathedral, Salzburg | 9·00 | 7·50 |
| **MS**1583 | Two sheets. (a) 100×72 mm. $4 Detail of chariot and helmet; (b) 89×117 mm. $5 Antiguan flag and Jamboree emblem (vert) Set of 2 sheets | 8·00 | 11·00 |

ANNIVERSARIES AND EVENTS: Nos. 1573, 1576, 1580, **MS**1583a, Bicentenary of Brandenburg Gate, Germany; 1574, 1577, 1581, **MS**1583b, 17th World Scout Jamboree, Korea; 1575, 1582, Death bicentenary of Mozart (composer); 1578, Centenary of Otto Lilienthal's gliding experiments; 1579, Centenary of Trans-Siberian Railway.

**286** "Nimitz" Class Carrier and "Ticonderoga" Class Cruiser

**1991.** 50th Anniv of Japanese Attack on Pearl Harbor. Multicoloured.

| | | | |
|---|---|---|---|
| 1585 | $1 Type **286** | 2·25 | 1·75 |
| 1586 | $1 Tourist launch | 2·25 | 1·75 |
| 1587 | $1 U.S.S. "Arizona" memorial | 2·25 | 1·75 |
| 1588 | $1 Wreaths on water and aircraft | 2·25 | 1·75 |
| 1589 | $1 White tern | 2·25 | 1·75 |
| 1590 | $1 Mitsubishi A6M Zero-Sen fighters over Pearl City | 2·25 | 1·75 |
| 1591 | $1 Mitsubishi A6M Zero-Sen fighters attacking | 2·25 | 1·75 |
| 1592 | $1 Battleship Row in flames | 2·25 | 1·75 |
| 1593 | $1 U.S.S. "Nevada" (battleship) underway | 2·25 | 1·75 |
| 1594 | $1 Mitsubishi A6M Zero-Sen fighters returning to carriers | 2·25 | 1·75 |

**287** "The Annunciation"

**1991.** Christmas. Religious Paintings by Fra Angelico. Multicoloured.

| | | | |
|---|---|---|---|
| 1595 | 10c. Type **287** | 40 | 30 |
| 1596 | 30c. "Nativity" | 65 | 30 |
| 1597 | 40c. "Adoration of the Magi" | 75 | 30 |
| 1598 | 60c. "Presentation in the Temple" | 1·00 | 45 |
| 1599 | $1 "Circumcision" | 1·25 | 65 |
| 1600 | $3 "Flight into Egypt" | 2·50 | 3·50 |
| 1601 | $4 "Massacre of the Innocents" | 2·50 | 4·00 |
| 1602 | $5 "Christ teaching in the Temple" | 2·50 | 4·00 |
| **MS**1603 | Two sheets, each 102×127 mm. (a) $6 "Adoration of the Magi" (Cook Tondo). (b) $6 "Adoration of the Magi" (different) Set of 2 sheets | 13·00 | 14·00 |

**288** Queen Elizabeth II and Bird Sanctuary

**1992.** 40th Anniv of Queen Elizabeth II's Accession. Multicoloured.

| | | | |
|---|---|---|---|
| 1604 | 10c. Type **288** | 1·25 | 40 |
| 1605 | 30c. Nelson's Dockyard | 1·50 | 40 |
| 1606 | $1 Ruins on Shirley Heights | 1·50 | 70 |
| 1607 | $5 Beach and palm trees | 3·00 | 4·25 |
| **MS**1608 | Two sheets, each 75×98 mm. (a) $6 Beach. (b) $6 Hillside foliage Set of 2 sheets | 8·50 | 9·00 |

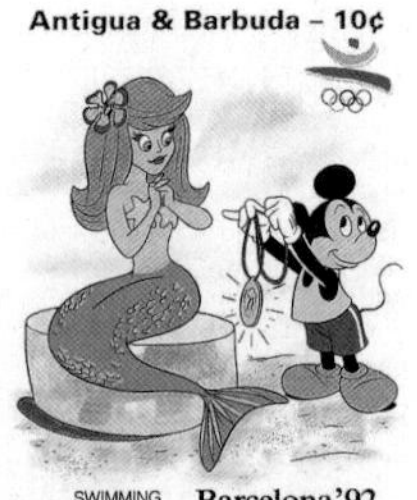


**289** Mickey Mouse awarding Swimming Gold Medal to Mermaid

**1992.** Olympic Games, Barcelona (3rd issue). Walt Disney cartoon characters. Multicoloured.

| | | | |
|---|---|---|---|
| 1609 | 10c. Type **289** | 70 | 30 |
| 1610 | 15c. Huey, Dewey and Louie with kayak | 80 | 30 |
| 1611 | 30c. Donald Duck and Uncle Scrooge in yacht | 1·00 | 35 |
| 1612 | 50c. Donald and horse playing water polo | 1·40 | 50 |
| 1613 | $1 Big Pete weightlifting | 2·00 | 85 |
| 1614 | $2 Donald and Goofy fencing | 3·00 | 3·00 |
| 1615 | $4 Mickey and Donald playing volleyball | 4·00 | 4·50 |
| 1616 | $5 Goofy vaulting | 4·00 | 4·50 |
| **MS**1617 | Four sheets, each 123×98 mm. (a) $6 Mickey playing football. (b) $6 Mickey playing basketball (horiz). (c) $6 Minnie Mouse on uneven parallel bars (horiz). (d) $6 Mickey, Goofy and Donald judging gymnastics (horiz) Set of 4 sheets | 14·00 | 15·00 |

**290** Pteranodon

**1992.** Prehistoric Animals. Mult.

| | | | |
|---|---|---|---|
| 1618 | 10c. Type **290** | 65 | 40 |
| 1619 | 15c. Brachiosaurus | 65 | 40 |
| 1620 | 30c. Tyrannosaurus Rex | 85 | 40 |
| 1621 | 50c. Parasaurolophus | 1·00 | 50 |
| 1622 | $1 Deinonychus (horiz) | 1·50 | 1·00 |
| 1623 | $2 Triceratops (horiz) | 2·00 | 2·00 |
| 1624 | $4 Protoceratops hatching (horiz) | 2·25 | 2·75 |
| 1625 | $5 Stegosaurus (horiz) | 2·25 | 2·75 |
| **MS**1626 | Two sheets, each 100×70 mm. (a) $6 Apatosaurus (horiz). (b) $6 Allosaurus (horiz) Set of 2 sheets | 8·50 | 9·50 |

**291** "Supper at Emmaus" (Caravaggio)

**1992.** Easter. Religious Paintings. Multicoloured.

| | | | |
|---|---|---|---|
| 1627 | 10c. Type **291** | 60 | 25 |
| 1628 | 15c. "The Vision of St. Peter" (Zurbaran) | 75 | 25 |
| 1629 | 30c. "Christ driving the Money-changers from the Temple" (Tiepolo) | 1·00 | 40 |
| 1630 | 40c. "Martyrdom of St. Bartholomew" (detail) (Ribera) | 1·25 | 50 |
| 1631 | $1 "Christ driving the Money-changers from the Temple" (detail) (Tiepolo) | 2·00 | 1·00 |
| 1632 | $2 "Crucifixion" (detail) (Altdorfer) | 3·00 | 3·00 |
| 1633 | $4 "The Deposition" (detail) (Fra Angelico) | 4·00 | 5·00 |
| 1634 | $5 "The Deposition" (different detail) (Fra Angelico) | 4·00 | 5·00 |
| **MS**1635 | Two sheets. (a) 102×71 mm. $6 "The Last Supper" (detail, Masip). (b) 71×102 mm. $6 "Crucifixion" (detail, Altdorfer) (vert) Set of 2 sheets | 9·50 | 12·00 |

**292** "The Miracle at the Well" (Alonso Cano)

**1992.** "Granada '92" International Stamp Exhibition, Spain. Spanish Paintings. Multicoloured.

| | | | |
|---|---|---|---|
| 1636 | 10c. Type **292** | 50 | 30 |
| 1637 | 15c. "The Poet Luis de Goingora y Argote" (Velazquez) | 65 | 30 |
| 1638 | 30c. "The Painter Francisco Goya" (Vincente Lopez Portana) | 85 | 40 |
| 1639 | 40c. "Maria de las Nieves Michaela Fourdinier" (Luis Paret y Alcazar) | 95 | 50 |
| 1640 | $1 "Carlos III eating before his Court" (Alcazar) (horiz) | 1·75 | 1·25 |
| 1641 | $2 "Rain Shower in Granada" (Antonio Munoz Degrain) (horiz) | 2·50 | 2·75 |
| 1642 | $4 "Sarah Bernhardt" (Santiago Rusinol i Prats) | 3·50 | 4·00 |
| 1643 | $5 "The Hermitage Garden" (Joaquim Mir Trinxet) | 3·50 | 4·00 |
| **MS**1644 | Two sheets, each 120×95 mm. (a) $6 "The Ascent of Monsieur Boucle's Montgolfier Balloon in the Gardens of Aranjuez" (Antonio Carnicero) (112×87 mm). (b) $6 "Olympus: Battle with the Giants" (Francisco Bayeu y Subías) (112×87 mm). Imperf Set of 2 sheets | 14·00 | 15·00 |

**293** "Amanita caesarea"

**1992.** Fungi. Multicoloured.

| | | | |
|---|---|---|---|
| 1645 | 10c. Type **293** | 70 | 40 |
| 1646 | 15c. "Collybia fusipes" | 85 | 40 |
| 1647 | 30c. "Boletus aereus" | 1·25 | 40 |
| 1648 | 40c. "Laccaria amethystina" | 1·25 | 50 |
| 1649 | $1 "Russula virescens" | 2·00 | 1·25 |
| 1650 | $2 "Tricholoma equestre" ("Tricholoma auratum") | 2·75 | 2·75 |
| 1651 | $4 "Calocybe gambosa" | 3·50 | 4·00 |
| 1652 | $5 "Lentinus tigrinus" ("Panus tigrinus") | 3·50 | 4·00 |
| **MS**1653 | Two sheets, each 100×70 mm. (a) $6 "Clavariadelphus truncatus". (b) $6 "Auricularia auricula-judae" Set of 2 sheets | 12·00 | 13·00 |

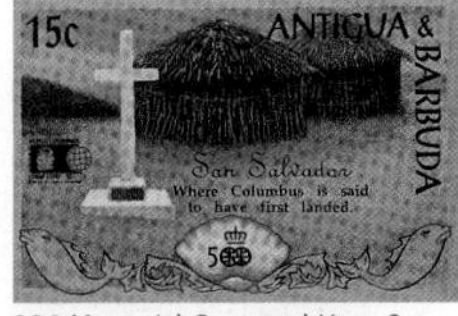


**294** Memorial Cross and Huts, San Salvador

**1992.** 500th Anniv of Discovery of America by Columbus (5th issue). World Columbian Stamp "Expo '92", Chicago. Multicoloured.

| | | | |
|---|---|---|---|
| 1654 | 15c. Type **294** | 30 | 20 |
| 1655 | 30c. Martin Pinzon with telescope | 45 | 25 |
| 1656 | 40c. Christopher Columbus | 65 | 35 |
| 1657 | $1 "Pinta" | 2·50 | 1·25 |
| 1658 | $2 "Nina" | 2·75 | 2·75 |
| 1659 | $4 "Santa Maria" | 3·50 | 5·50 |
| **MS**1660 | Two sheets, each 108×76 mm. (a) $6 Ship and map of West Indies. (b) $6 Sea monster Set of 2 sheets | 8·50 | 11·00 |

**295** Antillean Crested Hummingbird and Wild Plantain

**1992**. "Genova '92" International Thematic Stamp Exhibition. Hummingbirds and Plants. Multicoloured.

1661 10c. Type **295** 35 50
1662 25c. Green mango and parrot's plantain 50 40
1663 45c. Purple-throated carib and lobster claws 70 45
1664 60c. Antillean mango and coral plant 80 55
1665 $1 Vervain hummingbird and cardinal's guard 1·10 85
1666 $2 Rufous-breasted hermit and heliconia 1·75 2·00
1667 $4 Blue-headed hummingbird and red ginger 3·00 3·50
1668 $5 Green-throated carib and ornamental banana 3·00 3·50
**MS**1669 Two sheets, each 100×70 mm. (a) $6 Bee hummingbird and jungle flame. (b) $6 Western streamertail and bignonia Set of 2 sheets 10·00 12·00

**296** Columbus meeting Amerindians

**1992**. 500th Anniv of Discovery of America by Columbus (6th issue). Organization of East Caribbean States. Multicoloured.

1670 $1 Type **296** 85 65
1671 $2 Ships approaching island 1·40 1·60

**297** Ts'ai Lun and Paper

**1992**. Inventors and Inventions. Mult.

1672 10c. Type **297** 25 25
1673 25c. Igor Sikorsky and "Bolshoi Baltiskii" (first four-engined airplane) 1·50 40
1674 30c. Alexander Graham Bell and early telephone 55 45
1675 40c. Johannes Gutenberg and early printing press 55 45
1676 60c. James Watt and stationary steam engine 3·50 1·25
1677 $1 Anton van Leeuwenhoek and early microscope 1·75 1·40
1678 $4 Louis Braille and hands reading braille 4·50 5·00
1679 $5 Galileo and telescope 4·50 5·00
**MS**1680 Two sheets, each 100×73 mm. (a) $6 Edison and Latimer's phonograph. (b) $6 "Clermont" (first commercial paddle-steamer) Set of 2 sheets 9·50 12·00

**298** Elvis looking Pensive

**1992**. 15th Death Anniv of Elvis Presley. Mult.

1681 $1 Type **298** 1·75 1·10
1682 $1 Wearing black and yellow striped shirt 1·75 1·10
1683 $1 Singing into microphone 1·75 1·10
1684 $1 Wearing wide-brimmed hat 1·75 1·10
1685 $1 With microphone in right hand 1·75 1·10
1686 $1 In Army uniform 1·75 1·10
1687 $1 Wearing pink shirt 1·75 1·10
1688 $1 In yellow shirt 1·75 1·10
1689 $1 In jacket and bow tie 1·75 1·10

**299** Madison Square Gardens

**1992**. Postage Stamp Mega Event, New York. Sheet 100×70 mm.

**MS**1690 $6 multicoloured 4·25 5·50

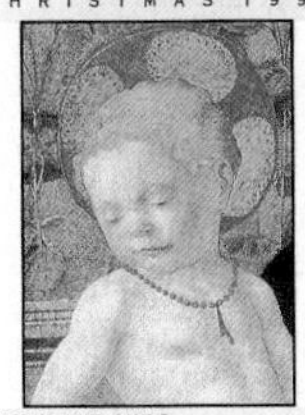


**300** "Virgin and Child with Angels" (detail) (School of Piero della Francesca)

**1992**. Christmas. Details of the Holy Child from various paintings. Multicoloured.

1691 10c. Type **300** 60 30
1692 25c. "Madonna degli Alberelli" (Giovanni Bellini) 90 30
1693 30c. "Madonna and Child with St. Anthony Abbot and St. Sigismund" (Neroccio) 95 30
1694 40c. "Madonna and the Grand Duke" (Raphael) 1·00 30
1695 60c. "The Nativity" (Georges de la Tour) 1·50 60
1696 $1 "Holy Family" (Jacob Jordaens) 1·75 1·00
1697 $4 "Madonna and Child Enthroned" (Magaritone) 3·75 4·75
1698 $5 "Madonna and Child on a Curved Throne" (Byzantine school) 3·75 4·75
**MS**1699 Two sheets, each 76×102 mm. (a) $6 "Madonna and Child" (Domenco Ghirlando). (b) $6 "The Holy Family" (Pontormo) Set of 2 sheets 9·50 12·00

**301** Russian Cosmonauts

**1992**. Anniversaries and Events. Mult.

1700 10c. Type **301** 70 60
1701 40c. "Graf Zeppelin" (airship), 1929 1·50 65
1702 45c. Bishop Daniel Davis 50 40
1703 75c. Konrad Adenauer making speech 65 65
1704 $1 Bus Mosbacher and "Weatherly" (yacht) 1·25 1·25
1705 $1.50 Rain forest 1·40 1·50
1706 $2 Tiger 6·00 4·00
1707 $2 National flag, plant and emblem (horiz) 4·50 3·00
1708 $2 Members of Community Players company (horiz) 2·00 3·00
1709 $2.25 Women carrying pots 2·00 3·00
1710 $3 Lions Club emblem 2·25 3·25
1711 $4 Chinese rocket on launch tower 4·00 4·50
1712 $4 West German and N.A.T.O. flags 4·50 4·75
1713 $6 Hugo Eckener (airship pioneer) 4·50 5·50
**MS**1714 Four sheets, each 100×71 mm. (a) $6 Projected European space station. (b) $6 Airship LZ-129 "Hindenburg", 1936. (c) $6 Brandenburg Gate on German flag. (d) $6 "Danaus plexippus" (butterfly) Set of 4 sheets 21·00 22·00

ANNIVERSARIES AND EVENTS: Nos. 1700, 1711, **MS**1714a, International Space Year; 1701, 1713, **MS**1714b, 75th death anniv of Count Ferdinand von Zeppelin; 1702, 150th anniv of Anglican Diocese of North-eastern Caribbean and Aruba; 1703, 1712, **MS**1714c, 25th death anniv of Konrad Adenauer (German statesman); 1704, Americas Cup yachting championship; 1705/6, **MS**1714d, Earth Summit '92, Rio; 1707, 50th anniv of Inter-American Institute for Agricultural Co-operation; 1708, 40th anniv of Cultural Development; 1709, United Nations World Health Organization Projects; 1710, 75th anniv of International Association of Lions Clubs.

**302** Boy Hiker resting

**1993**. Hummel Figurines. Multicoloured.

1715 15c. Type **302** 35 15
1716 30c. Girl sitting on fence 55 25
1717 40c. Boy hunter 65 35
1718 50c. Boy with umbrella 75 45
1719 $1 Hikers at signpost 1·25 75
1720 $2 Boy hiker with pack and stick 1·75 2·25
1721 $4 Girl with young child and goat 2·75 3·50
1722 $5 Boy whistling 2·75 3·50
**MS**1723 Two sheets, each 97×122 mm. (a) $1.50×4, As Nos. 1715/18. (b) $1.50×4, As Nos. 1719/22 Set of 2 sheets 13·00 14·00

**303** Goofy playing Golf

**1993**. Opening of Euro-Disney Resort, Paris. Multicoloured.

1724 10c. Type **303** 80 30
1725 25c. Chip and Dale at Davy Crockett's campground 1·00 30
1726 30c. Donald Duck at the Cheyenne Hotel 1·00 35
1727 40c. Goofy at the Santa Fe Hotel 1·10 35
1728 $1 Mickey and Minnie Mouse at the New York Hotel 2·25 1·25
1729 $2 Mickey, Minnie and Goofy in car 2·75 2·75
1730 $4 Goofy at Pirates of the Caribbean 4·00 5·00
1731 $5 Donald at Adventureland 4·00 5·00
**MS**1732 Four sheets, each 127×102 mm. (a) $6 Mickey in bellboy outfit. (b) $6 Mickey on star (vert). (c) $6 Mickey on opening poster (vert). (d) $6 Mickey and balloons on opening poster (vert) Set of 2 sheets 16·00 18·00

**304** Cardinal's Guard

**1993**. Flowers. Multicoloured.

1733 15c. Type **304** 1·00 40
1734 25c. Giant granadilla 1·10 40
1735 30c. Spider flower 1·10 40
1736 40c. Gold vine 1·25 40
1737 $1 Frangipani 2·00 1·25
1738 $2 Bougainvillea 2·75 2·75
1739 $4 Yellow oleander 3·75 4·50
1740 $5 Spicy jatropha 3·75 4·50
**MS**1741 Two sheets, each 100×70 mm. (a) $6 Birdlime tree. (b) Fairy lily Set of 2 sheets 9·00 12·00

**305** "The Destiny of Marie de' Medici" (upper detail)

**1993**. Bicentenary of the Louvre, Paris. Paintings by Peter Paul Rubens. Multicoloured.

1742 $1 Type **305** 95 85
1743 $1 "The Birth of Marie de' Medici" 95 85
1744 $1 "The Education of Marie de' Medici" 95 85
1745 $1 "The Destiny of Marie de' Medici" (lower detail) 95 85
1746 $1 "Henry VI receiving the Portrait of Marie" 95 85
1747 $1 "The Meeting of the King and Marie at Lyons" 95 85
1748 $1 "The Marriage by Proxy" 95 85
1749 $1 "The Birth of Louis XIII" 95 85
1750 $1 "The Capture of Juliers" 95 85
1751 $1 "The Exchange of the Princesses" 95 85
1752 $1 "The Regency" 95 85
1753 $1 "The Majority of Louis XIII" 95 85
1754 $1 "The Flight from Blois" 95 85
1755 $1 "The Treaty of Angouleme" 95 85
1756 $1 "The Peace of Angers" 95 85
1757 $1 "The Reconciliation of Louis and Marie de' Medici" 95 85
**MS**1758 70×100 mm. $6 "Helene Fourment with a Coach" (52×85 mm) 5·50 7·00

Nos. 1742/57 depict details from "The Story of Marie de' Medici".

**306** St. Lucia Amazon ("St. Lucia Parrot")

**1993**. Endangered Species. Multicoloured.

1759 $1 Type **306** 90 90
1760 $1 Cahow 90 90
1761 $1 Swallow-tailed kite 90 90
1762 $1 Everglade kite ("Everglades Kite") 90 90
1763 $1 Imperial amazon ("Imperial Parrot") 90 90
1764 $1 Humpback whale 90 90
1765 $1 Plain pigeon ("Puerto Rican Plain Pigeon") 90 90
1766 $1 St. Vincent amazon ("St. Vincent Parrot") 90 90
1767 $1 Puerto Rican amazon ("Puerto Rican Parrot") 90 90
1768 $1 Leatherback turtle 90 90
1769 $1 American crocodile 90 90
1770 $1 Hawksbill turtle 90 90
**MS**1771 Two sheets, each 100×70 mm. (a) $6 As No. 1764. (b) West Indian manatee Set of 2 sheets 8·00 10·00

Nos. 1759/70 were printed together, se-tenant, with the background forming a composite design.

**307** Queen Elizabeth II at Coronation (photograph by Cecil Beaton)

**1993**. 40th Anniv of Coronation (1st issue).

1772 **307** 30c. multicoloured 60 60
1773 - 40c. multicoloured 70 70
1774 - $2 blue and black 1·75 2·00
1775 - $4 multicoloured 2·25 2·50
**MS**1776 70×100 mm. $6 multicoloured 5·00 6·00

DESIGNS: 40c. Queen Elizabeth the Queen Mother's Crown, 1937; $2 Procession of heralds; $4 Queen Elizabeth II and Prince Edward. (28½×42½ mm)—$6 "Queen Elizabeth II" (detail) (Dennis Fildes).

**308** Princess Margaret and Antony Armstrong-Jones

**1993.** 40th Anniv of Coronation (2nd issue).

| | | | |
|---|---|---|---|
| 1777-1808 | $1×32 either grey and black or multicoloured | 26·00 | 28·00 |

DESIGNS: Various views as Type **308** from each decade of the reign.

**309** Edward Stanley Gibbons and Catalogue of 1865

**1993.** Famous Professional Philatelists (1st series).

| | | | | |
|---|---|---|---|---|
| 1809 | **309** | $1.50 brown, black & grn | 1·25 | 1·25 |
| 1810 | - | $1.50 multicoloured | 1·25 | 1·25 |
| 1811 | - | $1.50 multicoloured | 1·25 | 1·25 |
| 1812 | - | $1.50 multicoloured | 1·25 | 1·25 |
| 1813 | - | $1.50 multicoloured | 1·25 | 1·25 |
| 1814 | - | $1.50 multicoloured | 1·25 | 1·25 |
| **MS**1815 | | 98×69 mm. $3 black; $3 black | 5·50 | 6·50 |

DESIGNS: No. 1810, Theodore Champion and France 1849 1f. stamp; 1811, J. Walter Scott and U.S.A. 1918 24c. "Inverted Jenny" error; 1812, Hugo Michel and Bavaria 1849 1k. stamp; 1813, Alberto and Giulio Bolaffi with Sardinia 1851 5c. stamp; 1814, Richard Borek and Brunswick 1865 1gr. stamp; **MS**1815, Front pages of "Mekeel's Weekly Stamp News" in 1891 (misdated 1890) and 1993.

See also No. 1957.

**310** Paul Gascoigne

**1993.** World Cup Football Championship, U.S.A. (1st issue). English Players. Multicoloured.

| | | | |
|---|---|---|---|
| 1816 | $2 Type **310** | 1·50 | 1·40 |
| 1817 | $2 David Platt | 1·50 | 1·40 |
| 1818 | $2 Martin Peters | 1·50 | 1·40 |
| 1819 | $2 John Barnes | 1·50 | 1·40 |
| 1820 | $2 Gary Lineker | 1·50 | 1·40 |
| 1821 | $2 Geoff Hurst | 1·50 | 1·40 |
| 1822 | $2 Bobby Charlton | 1·50 | 1·40 |
| 1823 | $2 Bryan Robson | 1·50 | 1·40 |
| 1824 | $2 Bobby Moore | 1·50 | 1·40 |
| 1825 | $2 Nobby Stiles | 1·50 | 1·40 |
| 1826 | $2 Gordon Banks | 1·50 | 1·40 |
| 1827 | $2 Peter Shilton | 1·50 | 1·40 |
| **MS**1828 | Two sheets, each 135×109 mm. (a) $6 Bobby Moore holding World Cup. (b) $6 Gary Lineker and Bobby Robson Set of 2 sheets | 9·00 | 11·00 |

See also Nos. 2039/45.

**311** Grand Inspector W. Heath

**1993.** Anniversaries and Events. Multicoloured.

| | | | |
|---|---|---|---|
| 1829 | 10c. Type **311** | 2·00 | 1·00 |
| 1830 | 15c. Rodnina and Oulanov (U.S.S.R.) (pairs figure skating) (horiz) | 1·25 | 50 |
| 1831 | 30c. Present Masonic Hall, St. John's (horiz) | 2·25 | 1·00 |
| 1832 | 30c. Willy Brandt with Helmut Schmidt and George Leber (horiz) | 70 | 40 |
| 1833 | 30c. "Cat and Bird" (Picasso) (horiz) | 70 | 40 |
| 1834 | 40c. Previous Masonic Hall, St. John's (horiz) | 2·25 | 1·00 |
| 1835 | 40c. "Fish on a Newspaper" (Picasso) (horiz) | 70 | 50 |
| 1836 | 40c. Early astronomical equipment | 70 | 50 |
| 1837 | 40c. Prince Naruhito and engagement photographs (horiz) | 70 | 50 |
| 1838 | 60c. Grand Inspector J. Jeffery | 3·00 | 1·25 |
| 1839 | $1 "Woman combing her Hair" (W. Slewinski) (horiz) | 1·25 | 1·25 |
| 1840 | $3 Masako Owada and engagement photographs (horiz) | 2·50 | 3·00 |
| 1841 | $3 "Artist's Wife with Cat" (Konrad Kryzanowski) (horiz) | 2·50 | 3·00 |
| 1842 | $4 Willy Brandt and protest march (horiz) | 3·00 | 3·50 |
| 1843 | $4 Galaxy | 3·00 | 3·50 |
| 1844 | $5 Alberto Tomba (Italy) (giant slalom) (horiz) | 3·00 | 3·50 |
| 1845 | $5 "Dying Bull" (Picasso) (horiz) | 3·00 | 3·50 |
| 1846 | $5 Pres. Clinton and family (horiz) | 3·00 | 3·50 |
| **MS**1847 | Seven sheets. (a) 106×75 mm. $5 Copernicus. (b) 106×75 mm. $6 Womens' 1500 metre speed skating medallists (horiz). (c) 106×75 mm. $6 Willy Brandt at Warsaw Ghetto Memorial (horiz). (d) 106×75 mm. $6 "Woman with a Dog" (detail) (Picasso) (horiz). (e) 106×75 mm. $6 Masako Owada. (f) 70×100 mm. $6 "General Confusion" (S. I. Witkiewicz). (g) 106×75 mm. $6 Pres. Clinton taking the Oath (42½×57 mm) Set of 7 sheets | 25·00 | 28·00 |

ANNIVERSARIES AND EVENTS: Nos. 1829, 1831, 1834, 1838, 150th anniv of St. John's Masonic Lodge No. 492; 1830, 1844, **MS**1847b, Winter Olympic Games '94, Lillehammer; 1832, 1842, **MS**1847c, 80th birth anniv of Willy Brandt (German politician); 1833, 1835, 1845, **MS**1847d, 20th death anniv of Picasso (artist); 1836, 1843, **MS**1847a, 450th death anniv of Copernicus (astronomer); 1837, 1840, **MS**1847e, Marriage of Crown Prince Naruhito of Japan; 1839, 1841, **MS**1847f, "Polska '93" International Stamp Exhibition, Poznan; 1846, **MS**1847g, Inauguration of U.S. President William Clinton.

**312** Hugo Eckener and Dr. W. Beckers with Airship "Graf Zeppelin" over Lake George, New York

**1993.** Aviation Anniversaries. Multicoloured.

| | | | |
|---|---|---|---|
| 1848 | 30c. Type **312** | 1·00 | 70 |
| 1849 | 40c. Chicago World's Fair from "Graf Zeppelin" | 1·00 | 1·00 |
| 1850 | 40c. Gloster Whittle E.28/39, 1941 | 1·00 | 1·00 |
| 1851 | 40c. George Washington writing balloon mail letter (vert) | 1·00 | 1·00 |
| 1852 | $4 Pres. Wilson and Curtiss JN-4 Jenny | 3·75 | 4·50 |
| 1853 | $5 Airship "Hindenburg" over Ebbets Field baseball stadium, 1937 | 3·75 | 4·50 |
| 1854 | $5 Gloster Meteor in dogfight | 3·75 | 4·50 |
| **MS**1855 | Three sheets. (a) 86×105 mm. $6 Hugo Eckener (vert). (b) 105×86 mm. $6 Consolidated PBY-5 Catalina flying boat (57×42½ mm). (c) 105×86 mm. $6 Alexander Hamilton, Washington and John Jay watching Blanchard's balloon, 1793 (horiz) Set of 3 sheets | 16·00 | 18·00 |

ANNIVERSARIES: Nos. 1848/9, 1853, **MS**1855a, 125th birth anniv of Hugo Eckener (airship commander); 1850, 1854, **MS**1855b, 75th anniv of Royal Air Force; 1851/2, **MS**1855c, Bicentenary of first airmail flight.

**313** Lincoln Continental

**1993.** Centenaries of Henry Ford's First Petrol Engine (Nos. 1856, 1858), and Karl Benz's First Four-wheeled Car (others). Multicoloured.

| | | | |
|---|---|---|---|
| 1856 | 30c. Type **313** | 1·00 | 75 |
| 1857 | 40c. Mercedes racing car, 1914 | 1·00 | 75 |
| 1858 | $4 Ford "GT40", 1966 | 4·00 | 4·50 |
| 1859 | $5 Mercedes Benz "gull-wing" coupe, 1954 | 4·00 | 4·50 |
| **MS**1860 | Two sheets. (a) 114×87 mm. $6 Ford's Mustang emblem. (b) 87×114 mm. $6 Germany 1936 12pf. Benz and U.S.A. 1968 12c. Ford stamps Set of 2 sheets | 9·00 | 12·00 |

**314** "The Musical Farmer", 1932

**1993.** Mickey Mouse Film Posters. Mult.

| | | | |
|---|---|---|---|
| 1861 | 10c. Type **314** | 75 | 30 |
| 1862 | 15c. "Little Whirlwind", 1941 | 85 | 35 |
| 1863 | 30c. "Pluto's Dream House", 1940 | 1·00 | 40 |
| 1864 | 40c. "Gulliver Mickey", 1934 | 1·00 | 40 |
| 1865 | 50c. "Alpine Climbers", 1936 | 1·00 | 50 |
| 1866 | $1 "Mr. Mouse Takes a Trip", 1940 | 1·50 | 1·00 |
| 1867 | $2 "The Nifty Nineties", 1941 | 2·25 | 2·50 |
| 1868 | $4 "Mickey Down Under", 1948 | 3·25 | 4·50 |
| 1869 | $5 "The Pointer", 1939 | 3·25 | 4·50 |
| **MS**1870 | Two sheets, each 125×105 mm. (a) $6 "The Simple Things", 1953. (b) $6 "The Prince and the Pauper", 1990 Set of 2 sheets | 11·00 | 14·00 |

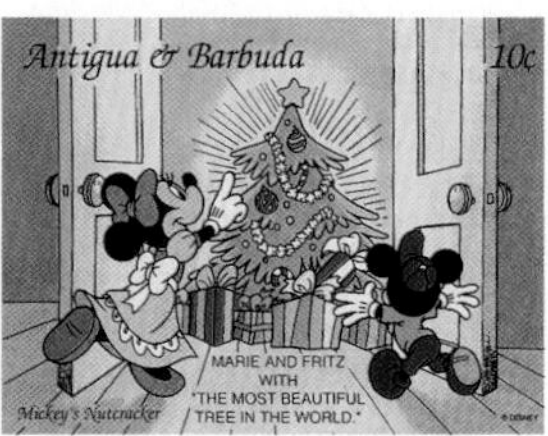


**315** Marie and Fritz with Christmas Tree

**1993.** Christmas. Mickey's Nutcracker. Walt Disney cartoon characters in scenes from "The Nutcracker". Multicoloured.

| | | | |
|---|---|---|---|
| 1871 | 10c. Type **315** | 75 | 40 |
| 1872 | 15c. Marie receives Nutcracker from Godfather Drosselmeir | 80 | 40 |
| 1873 | 20c. Fritz breaks Nutcracker | 80 | 40 |
| 1874 | 30c. Nutcracker with sword | 90 | 40 |
| 1875 | 40c. Nutcracker and Marie in the snow | 95 | 40 |
| 1876 | 50c. Marie and the Prince meet Sugar Plum Fairy | 1·00 | 60 |
| 1877 | 60c. Marie and Prince in Crystal Hall | 1·00 | 60 |
| 1878 | $3 Huey, Dewey and Louie as Cossack dancers | 3·25 | 4·00 |
| 1879 | $6 Mother Ginger and her puppets | 4·50 | 6·50 |
| **MS**1880 | Two sheets, each 127×102 mm. (a) $6 Marie and Prince in sleigh. (b) $6 The Prince in sword fight (vert) Set of 2 sheets | 9·00 | 12·00 |

**316** "Hannah and Samuel" (Rembrandt)

**1993.** Famous Paintings by Rembrandt and Matisse. Multicoloured.

| | | | |
|---|---|---|---|
| 1881 | 15c. Type **316** | 40 | 30 |
| 1882 | 15c. "Guitarist" (Matisse) | 40 | 30 |
| 1883 | 30c. "The Jewish Bride" (Rembrandt) | 55 | 30 |
| 1884 | 40c. "Jacob wrestling with the Angel" (Rembrandt) | 60 | 30 |
| 1885 | 60c. "Interior with a Goldfish Bowl" (Matisse) | 80 | 50 |
| 1886 | $1 "Mlle Yvonne Landsberg" (Matisse) | 1·25 | 80 |
| 1887 | $4 "The Toboggan" (Matisse) | 3·00 | 4·25 |
| 1888 | $5 "Moses with the Tablets of the Law" (Rembrandt) | 3·00 | 4·25 |
| **MS**1889 | Two sheets. (a) 124×99 mm. $6 "The Blinding of Samson by the Philistines" (detail) (Rembrandt). (b) 99×124 mm. $6 "The Three Sisters" (detail) (Matisse) Set of 2 sheets | 9·50 | 12·00 |

**317** Hong Kong 1981 $1 Golden Threadfin Bream Stamp and Sampans, Shau Kei Wan

**1994.** "Hong Kong '94" International Stamp Exhibition (1st issue). Multicoloured.

| | | | |
|---|---|---|---|
| 1890 | 40c. Type **317** | 80 | 80 |
| 1891 | 40c. Antigua 1990 $2 Rock beauty stamp and sampans, Shau Kei Wan | 80 | 80 |

Nos. 1890/1 were printed together, se-tenant, forming a composite design.

See also Nos. 1892/7 and 1898/1905.

**318** Terracotta Warriors

**1994.** "Hong Kong '94" International Stamp Exhibition (2nd issue). Qin Dynasty Terracotta Figures. Multicoloured.

| | | | |
|---|---|---|---|
| 1892 | 40c. Type **318** | 75 | 60 |
| 1893 | 40c. Cavalryman and horse | 75 | 60 |
| 1894 | 40c. Warriors in armour | 75 | 60 |
| 1895 | 40c. Painted bronze chariot and team | 75 | 60 |
| 1896 | 40c. Pekingese dog | 75 | 60 |
| 1897 | 40c. Warriors with horses | 75 | 60 |

**319** Mickey Mouse in Junk

**1994.** "Hong Kong '94" International Stamp Exhibition (3rd issue). Walt Disney cartoon characters. Multicoloured.

| | | | |
|---|---|---|---|
| 1898 | 10c. Type **319** | 70 | 30 |
| 1899 | 15c. Minnie Mouse as mandarin | 75 | 35 |
| 1900 | 30c. Donald and Daisy Duck on houseboat | 90 | 45 |
| 1901 | 50c. Mickey holding bird in cage | 1·10 | 60 |
| 1902 | $1 Pluto and ornamental dog | 1·75 | 1·00 |
| 1903 | $2 Minnie and Daisy celebrating Bun Festival | 2·50 | 2·50 |
| 1904 | $4 Goofy making noodles | 3·50 | 4·50 |
| 1905 | $5 Goofy pulling Mickey in rickshaw | 3·50 | 4·50 |
| **MS**1906 | Two sheets, each 133×109 mm. (a) $5 Mickey and Donald on harbour ferry (horiz). (b) $5 Mickey in traditional dragon dance (horiz) Set of 2 sheets | 7·00 | 9·00 |

**320** Sumatran Rhinoceros lying down

**1994.** Centenary (1992) of Sierra Club (environmental protection society). Endangered Species. Multicoloured.

| | | | |
|---|---|---|---|
| 1907 | $1.50 Type **320** | 1·25 | 1·25 |
| 1908 | $1.50 Sumatran rhinoceros feeding | 1·25 | 1·25 |
| 1909 | $1.50 Ring-tailed lemur on ground | 1·25 | 1·25 |

| | | | |
|---|---|---|---|
| 1910 | $1.50 Ring-tailed lemur on branch | 1·25 | 1·25 |
| 1911 | $1.50 Red-fronted brown lemur on branch | 1·25 | 1·25 |
| 1912 | $1.50 Head of red-fronted brown lemur | 1·25 | 1·25 |
| 1913 | $1.50 Head of red-fronted brown lemur in front of trunk | 1·25 | 1·25 |
| 1914 | $1.50 Sierra Club Centennial emblem | 80 | 80 |
| 1915 | $1.50 Head of Bactrian camel | 1·25 | 1·25 |
| 1916 | $1.50 Bactrian camel | 1·25 | 1·25 |
| 1917 | $1.50 African elephant drinking | 1·25 | 1·25 |
| 1918 | $1.50 Head of African elephant | 1·25 | 1·25 |
| 1919 | $1.50 Leopard sitting upright | 1·25 | 1·25 |
| 1920 | $1.50 Leopard in grass (em-blem at right) | 1·25 | 1·25 |
| 1921 | $1.50 Leopard in grass (em-blem at left) | 1·25 | 1·25 |
| **MS**1922 | Four sheets. (a) 100×70 mm. $1.50, Sumatran rhinoceros (horiz). (b) 70×100 mm. $1.50, Ring-tailed lemur (horiz). (c) 70×100 mm. $1.50, Bactrian camel (horiz). (d) 100×70 mm. $1.50, African elephant (horiz) Set of 4 sheets | 6·00 | 8·00 |

**321** West Highland White Terrier

**1994.** Dogs of the World. Chinese New Year ("Year of the Dog"). Multicoloured.

| | | | |
|---|---|---|---|
| 1923 | 50c. Type **321** | 75 | 65 |
| 1924 | 50c. Beagle | 75 | 65 |
| 1925 | 50c. Scottish terrier | 75 | 65 |
| 1926 | 50c. Pekingese | 75 | 65 |
| 1927 | 50c. Dachshund | 75 | 65 |
| 1928 | 50c. Yorkshire terrier | 75 | 65 |
| 1929 | 50c. Pomeranian | 75 | 65 |
| 1930 | 50c. Poodle | 75 | 65 |
| 1931 | 50c. Shetland sheepdog | 75 | 65 |
| 1932 | 50c. Pug | 75 | 65 |
| 1933 | 50c. Shih Tzu | 75 | 65 |
| 1934 | 50c. Chihuahua | 75 | 65 |
| 1935 | 75c. Mastiff | 75 | 65 |
| 1936 | 75c. Border collie | 75 | 65 |
| 1937 | 75c. Samoyed | 75 | 65 |
| 1938 | 75c. Airedale terrier | 75 | 65 |
| 1939 | 75c. English setter | 75 | 65 |
| 1940 | 75c. Rough collie | 75 | 65 |
| 1941 | 75c. Newfoundland | 75 | 65 |
| 1942 | 75c. Weimarana | 75 | 65 |
| 1943 | 75c. English springer spaniel | 75 | 65 |
| 1944 | 75c. Dalmatian | 75 | 65 |
| 1945 | 75c. Boxer | 75 | 65 |
| 1946 | 75c. Old English sheepdog | 75 | 65 |
| **MS**1947 | Two sheets, each 93×58 mm. (a) $6 Welsh corgi. (b) $6 Labrador retriever Set of 2 sheets | 9·00 | 12·00 |

**322** "Spiranthes lanceolata"

**1994.** Orchids. Multicoloured.

| | | | |
|---|---|---|---|
| 1948 | 10c. Type **322** | 70 | 60 |
| 1949 | 20c. "Ionopsis utricularioides" | 1·00 | 50 |
| 1950 | 30c. "Tetramicra canaliculata" | 1·25 | 50 |
| 1951 | 50c. "Oncidium picturatum" | 1·50 | 65 |
| 1952 | $1 "Epidendrum difforme" | 2·00 | 1·25 |
| 1953 | $2 "Epidendrum ciliare" | 3·00 | 2·75 |
| 1954 | $4 "Epidendrum ibaguense" | 4·00 | 4·25 |
| 1955 | $5 "Epidendrum nocturnum" | 4·00 | 4·25 |
| **MS**1956 | Two sheets, each 100×73 mm. (a) $6 "Rodriguezia lanceolata". (b) $6 "Encyclia cochleata" Set of 2 sheets | 9·00 | 12·00 |

**323** Hermann E. Sieger, Germany 1931 1m. Zeppelin Stamp and Airship LZ-127 "Graf Zeppelin"

**1994.** Famous Professional Philatelists (2nd series).

| | | | | |
|---|---|---|---|---|
| 1957 | **323** | $1.50 multicoloured | 2·75 | 2·50 |

**324** "Danaus plexippus"

**1994.** Butterflies. Multicoloured.

| | | | |
|---|---|---|---|
| 1958 | 10c. Type **324** | 85 | 75 |
| 1959 | 15c. "Appias drusilla" | 1·00 | 45 |
| 1960 | 30c. "Eurema lisa" | 1·25 | 55 |
| 1961 | 40c. "Anaea troglodyta" | 1·25 | 60 |
| 1962 | $1 "Urbanus proteus" | 2·00 | 1·25 |
| 1963 | $2 "Junonia evarete" | 2·75 | 2·75 |
| 1964 | $4 "Battus polydamas" | 3·50 | 4·50 |
| 1965 | $5 "Heliconius charitonia" | 3·50 | 4·50 |
| **MS**1966 | Two sheets, each 102×72 mm. (a) $6 "Phoebis sennae". (b) $6 "Hemiargus hanno" Set of 2 sheets | 9·00 | 12·00 |

No. 1959 is inscribed "Appisa drusilla" and No. 1965 "Heliconius charitonius", both in error.

**325** Bottlenose Dolphin

**1994.** Marine Life. Multicoloured.

| | | | |
|---|---|---|---|
| 1967 | 50c. Type **325** | 75 | 75 |
| 1968 | 50c. Killer whale | 75 | 75 |
| 1969 | 50c. Spinner dolphin | 75 | 75 |
| 1970 | 50c. Oceanic sunfish | 75 | 75 |
| 1971 | 50c. Caribbean reef shark and short fin pilot whale | 75 | 75 |
| 1972 | 50c. Copper-banded but-terflyfish | 75 | 75 |
| 1973 | 50c. Mosaic moray | 75 | 75 |
| 1974 | 50c. Clown triggerfish | 75 | 75 |
| 1975 | 50c. Red lobster | 75 | 75 |
| **MS**1976 | Two sheets, each 106×76 mm. (a) $6 Seahorse. (b) $6 Swordfish ("Blue Marlin") (horiz) Set of 2 sheets | 11·00 | 12·00 |

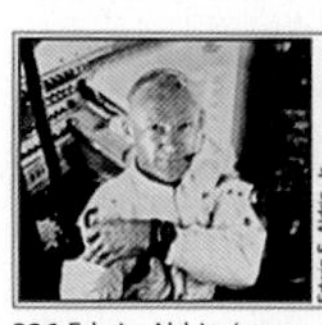


**326** Edwin Aldrin (astronaut)

**1994.** 25th Anniv of First Manned Moon Landing. Multicoloured.

| | | | |
|---|---|---|---|
| 1977 | $1.50 Type **326** | 1·75 | 1·50 |
| 1978 | $1.50 First lunar footprint | 1·75 | 1·50 |
| 1979 | $1.50 Neil Armstrong (as-tronaut) | 1·75 | 1·50 |
| 1980 | $1.50 Aldrin stepping onto Moon | 1·75 | 1·50 |
| 1981 | $1.50 Aldrin and equipment | 1·75 | 1·50 |
| 1982 | $1.50 Aldrin and U.S.A. flag | 1·75 | 1·50 |
| 1983 | $1.50 Aldrin at Tranquility Base | 1·75 | 1·50 |
| 1984 | $1.50 Moon plaque | 1·75 | 1·50 |
| 1985 | $1.50 "Eagle" leaving Moon | 1·75 | 1·50 |
| 1986 | $1.50 Command module in lunar orbit | 1·75 | 1·50 |
| 1987 | $1.50 First day cover of U.S.A. 1969 10c. First Man on Moon stamp | 1·75 | 1·50 |
| 1988 | $1.50 Pres. Nixon and astronauts | 1·75 | 1·50 |
| **MS**1989 | 72×102 mm. $6 Armstrong and Aldrin with postal official | 4·00 | 5·00 |

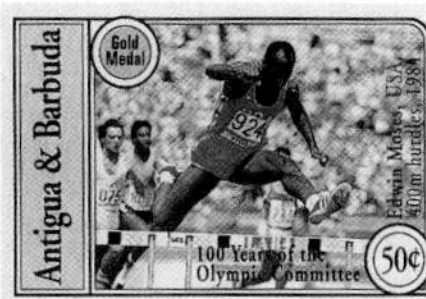


**327** Edwin Moses (U.S.A.) (400 m hurdles, 1984)

**1994.** Centenary of International Olympic Committee. Gold Medal Winners. Multicoloured.

| | | | |
|---|---|---|---|
| 1990 | 50c. Type **327** | 40 | 30 |
| 1991 | $1.50 Steffi Graf (Germany) (tennis, 1988) | 1·75 | 1·75 |
| **MS**1992 | 79×110 mm. $6 Johann Olav Koss (Norway) (500, 1500 and 10,000 metre speed skating), 1994 | 5·00 | 5·50 |

**328** Antiguan Family

**1994.** International Year of the Family.

| | | | | |
|---|---|---|---|---|
| 1993 | **328** | 90c. multicoloured | 1·00 | 1·00 |

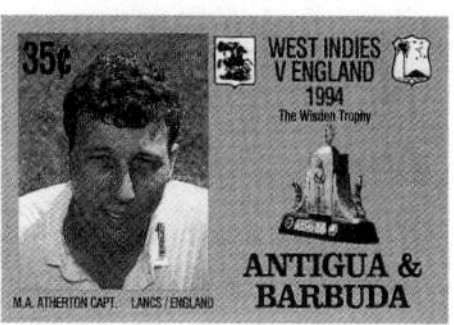


**329** Mike Atherton (England) and Wisden Trophy

**1994.** Centenary (1995) of First English Cricket Tour to the West Indies. Multicoloured.

| | | | |
|---|---|---|---|
| 1994 | 35c. Type **329** | 1·00 | 65 |
| 1995 | 75c. Viv Richards (West Indies) (vert) | 1·75 | 1·25 |
| 1996 | $1.20 Richie Richardson (West Indies) and Wisden Trophy | 2·25 | 2·50 |
| **MS**1997 | 80×100 mm. $3 English team, 1895 (black and brown) | 2·50 | 3·00 |

**330** Entrance Bridge, Songgwangsa Temple

**1994.** "Philakorea '94" International Stamp Exhibition, Seoul. Multicoloured.

| | | | |
|---|---|---|---|
| 1998 | 40c. Type **330** | 50 | 40 |
| 1999 | 75c. Long-necked bottle | 70 | 75 |
| 2000 | 75c. Punch'ong ware jar with floral decoration | 70 | 75 |
| 2001 | 75c. Punch'ong ware jar with blue dragon pattern | 70 | 75 |
| 2002 | 75c. Ewer in shape of bamboo shoot | 70 | 75 |
| 2003 | 75c. Punch'ong ware green jar | 70 | 75 |
| 2004 | 75c. Pear-shaped bottle | 70 | 75 |
| 2005 | 75c. Porcelain jar with brown dragon pattern | 70 | 75 |
| 2006 | 75c. Porcelain jar with floral pattern | 70 | 75 |
| 2007 | 90c. Song-op Folk Village, Cheju | 70 | 75 |
| 2008 | $3 Port Sogwipo | 1·75 | 2·25 |
| **MS**2009 | 104×71 mm. $4 Ox herder playing flute (vert) | 3·25 | 4·00 |

**331** Short S.25 Sunderland (flying boat)

**1994.** 50th Anniv of D-Day. Multicoloured.

| | | | |
|---|---|---|---|
| 2010 | 40c. Type **331** | 1·00 | 40 |
| 2011 | $2 Lockheed P-38 Lightning fighters attacking train | 2·75 | 2·75 |
| 2012 | $3 Martin B-26 Marauder bombers | 3·25 | 3·75 |
| **MS**2013 | 108×78 mm. $6 Hawker Typhoon fighter bomber | 6·00 | 6·50 |

**332** Travis Tritt

**1994.** Stars of Country and Western Music. Multicoloured.

| | | | |
|---|---|---|---|
| 2014 | 75c. Type **332** | 70 | 70 |
| 2015 | 75c. Dwight Yoakam | 70 | 70 |
| 2016 | 75c. Billy Ray Cyrus | 70 | 70 |
| 2017 | 75c. Alan Jackson | 70 | 70 |
| 2018 | 75c. Garth Brooks | 70 | 70 |
| 2019 | 75c. Vince Gill | 70 | 70 |
| 2020 | 75c. Clint Black | 70 | 70 |
| 2021 | 75c. Eddie Rabbit | 70 | 70 |
| 2022 | 75c. Patsy Cline | 70 | 70 |
| 2023 | 75c. Tanya Tucker | 70 | 70 |
| 2024 | 75c. Dolly Parton | 70 | 70 |
| 2025 | 75c. Anne Murray | 70 | 70 |
| 2026 | 75c. Tammy Wynette | 70 | 70 |
| 2027 | 75c. Loretta Lynn | 70 | 70 |
| 2028 | 75c. Reba McEntire | 70 | 70 |
| 2029 | 75c. Skeeter Davis | 70 | 70 |
| 2030 | 75c. Hank Snow | 70 | 70 |
| 2031 | 75c. Gene Autry | 70 | 70 |
| 2032 | 75c. Jimmie Rodgers | 70 | 70 |
| 2033 | 75c. Ernest Tubb | 70 | 70 |
| 2034 | 75c. Eddy Arnold | 70 | 70 |
| 2035 | 75c. Willie Nelson | 70 | 70 |
| 2036 | 75c. Johnny Cash | 70 | 70 |
| 2037 | 75c. George Jones | 70 | 70 |
| **MS**2038 | Three sheets. (a) 100×70 mm. $6 Hank Williams Jr. (b) 100×70 mm. $6 Hank Williams Sr. (c) 70×100 mm. $6 Kitty Wells (horiz) Set of 3 sheets | 14·00 | 14·00 |

**333** Hugo Sanchez (Mexico)

**1994.** World Cup Football Championship, U.S.A. (2nd issue). Multicoloured.

| | | | |
|---|---|---|---|
| 2039 | 15c. Type **333** | 75 | 30 |
| 2040 | 35c. Jurgen Klinsmann (Germany) | 1·25 | 45 |
| 2041 | 65c. Antiguan player | 1·50 | 55 |
| 2042 | $1.20 Cobi Jones (U.S.A.) | 2·00 | 1·75 |
| 2043 | $4 Roberto Baggio (Italy) | 3·25 | 4·00 |
| 2044 | $5 Bwalya Kalusha (Zambia) | 3·25 | 4·00 |
| **MS**2045 | Two sheets. (a) 72×105 mm. $6 Maldive Islands player (vert). (b) 107×78 mm. $6 World Cup trophy (vert) Set of 2 sheets | 8·00 | 9·00 |

No. 2040 is inscribed "Klinsman" in error.

**334** Sir Shridath Ramphal

**1994.** 1st Recipients of Order of the Caribbean Community. Multicoloured.

| | | | |
|---|---|---|---|
| 2046 | 65c. Type **334** | 50 | 40 |
| 2047 | 90c. William Demas | 65 | 60 |
| 2048 | $1.20 Derek Walcott | 2·00 | 1·50 |

**335** Pair of Magnificent Frigate Birds

**1994.** Birds. Multicoloured.

| | | | |
|---|---|---|---|
| 2049 | 10c. Type **335** | 55 | 45 |
| 2050 | 15c. Bridled quail dove | 65 | 40 |
| 2051 | 30c. Magnificent frigate bird chick hatching | 85 | 70 |
| 2052 | 40c. Purple-throated carib (vert) | 85 | 70 |
| 2053 | $1 Male magnificent frigate bird in courtship display (vert) | 1·10 | 1·25 |
| 2054 | $1 Broad-winged hawk (vert) | 1·10 | 1·25 |

| No. | Description | Unused | Used |
|---|---|---|---|
| 2055 | $3 Young magnificent frigate bird | 2·25 | 3·25 |
| 2056 | $4 Yellow warbler | 2·25 | 3·25 |
| **MS**2057 | Two sheets. (a) 70×100 mm. $6 Female magnificent frigate bird (vert). (b) 100×70 mm. $6 Black-billed whistling duck ducklings Set of 2 sheets | 8·00 | 9·00 |

Nos. 2049, 2051, 2053 and 2055 also show the W.W.F. Panda emblem.

**336** "The Virgin and Child by the Fireside" (Robert Campin)

**1994.** Christmas. Religious Paintings. Multicoloured.

| No. | Description | Unused | Used |
|---|---|---|---|
| 2058 | 15c. Type **336** | 80 | 30 |
| 2059 | 35c. "The Reading Madonna" (Giorgione) | 1·10 | 30 |
| 2060 | 40c. "Madonna and Child" (Giovanni Bellini) | 1·25 | 30 |
| 2061 | 45c. "The Litta Madonna" (Da Vinci) | 1·25 | 30 |
| 2062 | 65c. "The Virgin and Child under the Apple Tree" (Lucas Cranach the Elder) | 1·60 | 55 |
| 2063 | 75c. "Madonna and Child" (Master of the Female Half-lengths) | 1·75 | 70 |
| 2064 | $1.20 "An Allegory of the Church" (Alessandro Allori) | 2·25 | 2·00 |
| 2065 | $5 "Madonna and Child wreathed with Flowers" (Jacob Jordaens) | 3·75 | 5·50 |
| **MS**2066 | Two sheets. (a) 123×88 mm. $6 "Madonna and Child with Commissioners" (detail) (Palma Vecchio) (b) 88×123 mm. $6 "The Virgin Enthroned with Child" (detail) (Bohemian master) Set of 2 sheets | 7·50 | 9·00 |

**337** Magnificent Frigate Bird

**1995.** Birds. Multicoloured.

| No. | Description | Unused | Used |
|---|---|---|---|
| 2067 | 15c. Type **337** | 30 | 10 |
| 2068 | 25c. Blue-hooded euphonia | 40 | 15 |
| 2069 | 35c. Eastern meadowlark ("Meadowlark") | 45 | 20 |
| 2070 | 40c. Red-billed tropic bird | 45 | 20 |
| 2071 | 45c. Greater flamingo | 45 | 25 |
| 2072 | 60c. Yellow-faced grassquit | 50 | 30 |
| 2073 | 65c. Yellow-billed cuckoo | 50 | 30 |
| 2074 | 70c. Purple-throated carib | 55 | 35 |
| 2075 | 75c. Bananaquit | 55 | 35 |
| 2076 | 90c. Painted bunting | 65 | 40 |
| 2077 | $1.20 Red-legged honeycreeper | 90 | 55 |
| 2078 | $2 Northern jacana ("Jacana") | 1·50 | 1·00 |
| 2079 | $5 Greater Antillean bullfinch | 3·25 | 3·00 |
| 2080 | $10 Caribbean elaenia | 6·00 | 6·50 |
| 2081 | $20 Brown trembler ("Trembler") | 10·00 | 11·00 |

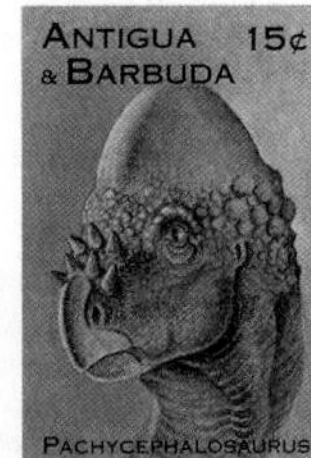


**338** Head of Pachycephalosaurus

**1995.** Prehistoric Animals. Multicoloured.

| No. | Description | Unused | Used |
|---|---|---|---|
| 2082 | 15c. Type **338** | 60 | 60 |
| 2083 | 20c. Head of afrovenator | 60 | 60 |
| 2084 | 65c. Centrosaurus | 80 | 80 |
| 2085 | 75c. Kronosaurus (horiz) | 80 | 80 |
| 2086 | 75c. Ichthyosaurus (horiz) | 80 | 80 |
| 2087 | 75c. Plesiosaurus (horiz) | 80 | 80 |
| 2088 | 75c. Archelon (horiz) | 80 | 80 |
| 2089 | 75c. Pair of tyrannosaurus (horiz) | 80 | 80 |
| 2090 | 75c. Tyrannosaurus (horiz) | 80 | 80 |
| 2091 | 75c. Parasaurolophus (horiz) | 80 | 80 |
| 2092 | 75c. Pair of parasaurolophus (horiz) | 80 | 80 |
| 2093 | 75c. Oviraptor (horiz) | 80 | 80 |
| 2094 | 75c. Protoceratops with eggs (horiz) | 80 | 80 |
| 2095 | 75c. Pteranodon and protoceratops (horiz) | 80 | 80 |
| 2096 | 75c. Pair of protoceratops (horiz) | 80 | 80 |
| 2097 | 90c. Pentaceratops drinking | 1·00 | 1·00 |
| 2098 | $1.20 Head of tarbosaurus | 1·25 | 1·25 |
| 2099 | $5 Head of styracosaurus | 3·25 | 4·00 |
| **MS**2100 | Two sheets, each 101×70 mm. (a) $6 Head of Corythosaurus (horiz). (b) $6 Head of Carnotaurus (horiz) Set of 2 sheets | 9·50 | 12·00 |

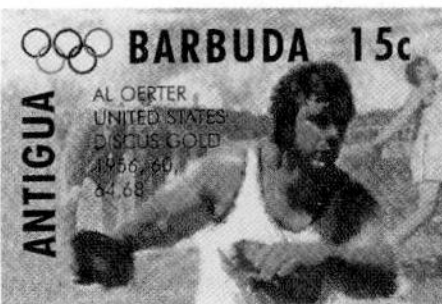


**339** Al Oerter (U.S.A.) (discus – 1956, 1960, 1964, 1968)

**1995.** Olympic Games, Atlanta (1996). Previous Gold Medal Winners (1st issue). Multicoloured.

| No. | Description | Unused | Used |
|---|---|---|---|
| 2101 | 15c. Type **339** | 60 | 30 |
| 2102 | 20c. Greg Louganis (U.S.A.) (diving – 1984, 1988) | 60 | 30 |
| 2103 | 65c. Naim Suleymanoglu (Turkey) (weightlifting – 1988) | 75 | 50 |
| 2104 | 90c. Louise Ritter (U.S.A.) (high jump – 1988) | 1·00 | 70 |
| 2105 | $1.20 Nadia Comaneci (Rumania) (gymnastics –1976) | 2·00 | 1·40 |
| 2106 | $5 Olga Bondarenko (Russia) (10,000 metres – 1988) | 3·25 | 5·00 |
| **MS**2107 | Two sheets, each 106×76 mm. (a) $6 United States crew (eight-oared shell — 1964). (b) $6 Lutz Hessilch (Germany) (cycling — 1988) (vert) Set of 2 sheets | 11·00 | 12·00 |

No. 2106 is inscribed "BOLDARENKO" in error.

See also Nos. 2302/23.

**340** Map of Berlin showing Russian Advance

**1995.** 50th Anniv of End of Second World War in Europe. Multicoloured.

| No. | Description | Unused | Used |
|---|---|---|---|
| 2108 | $1.20 Type **340** | 1·40 | 1·25 |
| 2109 | $1.20 Russian tank and infantry | 1·40 | 1·25 |
| 2110 | $1.20 Street fighting in Berlin | 1·40 | 1·25 |
| 2111 | $1.20 German tank exploding | 1·40 | 1·25 |
| 2112 | $1.20 Russian air raid | 1·40 | 1·25 |
| 2113 | $1.20 German troops surrendering | 1·40 | 1·25 |
| 2114 | $1.20 Hoisting the Soviet flag on the Reichstag | 1·40 | 1·25 |
| 2115 | $1.20 Captured German standards | 1·40 | 1·25 |
| **MS**2116 | 104×74 mm. $6 Gen. Konev (vert) | 4·50 | 5·50 |

See also Nos. 2132/8.

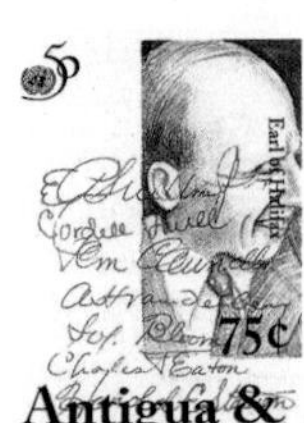


**341** Signatures and Earl of Halifax

**1995.** 50th Anniv of United Nations. Multicoloured.

| No. | Description | Unused | Used |
|---|---|---|---|
| 2117 | 75c. Type **341** | 70 | 1·00 |
| 2118 | 90c. Virginia Gildersleeve | 70 | 1·00 |
| 2119 | $1.20 Harold Stassen | 70 | 1·00 |
| **MS**2120 | 100×70 mm. $6 Pres. Franklin D. Roosevelt | 3·50 | 4·25 |

Nos. 2117/19 were printed together, se-tenant, forming a composite design.

**342** Woman buying Produce from Market

**1995.** 50th Anniv of F.A.O. Multicoloured.

| No. | Description | Unused | Used |
|---|---|---|---|
| 2121 | 75c. Type **342** | 70 | 1·00 |
| 2122 | 90c. Women shopping | 70 | 1·00 |
| 2123 | $1.20 Women talking | 70 | 1·00 |
| **MS**2124 | 100×70 mm. $6 Tractor | 3·00 | 3·75 |

Nos. 2121/3 were printed together, se-tenant, forming a composite design.

**343** Beach and Rotary Emblem

**1995.** 90th Anniv of Rotary International.

| No. | Description | Unused | Used |
|---|---|---|---|
| 2125 | **343** $5 multicoloured | 3·50 | 4·00 |
| **MS**2126 | 74×104 mm. $6 National flag and emblem | 3·50 | 4·00 |

**344** Queen Elizabeth the Queen Mother

**1995.** 95th Birthday of Queen Elizabeth the Queen Mother.

| No. | Description | Unused | Used |
|---|---|---|---|
| 2127 | - $1.50 brown, light brown and black | 1·50 | 1·50 |
| 2128 | **344** $1.50 multicoloured | 1·50 | 1·50 |
| 2129 | - $1.50 multicoloured | 1·50 | 1·50 |
| 2130 | - $1.50 multicoloured | 1·50 | 1·50 |
| **MS**2131 | 100×127 mm. $6 multicoloured | 5·50 | 5·50 |

DESIGNS: No. 2127, Queen Elizabeth the Queen Mother (pastel drawing); 2129, At desk (oil painting); 2130, Wearing green dress; **MS**2131, Wearing blue dress.

**1995.** 50th Anniv of End of Second World War in the Pacific. As T **340**. Multicoloured.

| No. | Description | Unused | Used |
|---|---|---|---|
| 2132 | $1.20 Gen. Chang Kai-Shek and Chinese guerrillas | 1·10 | 1·25 |
| 2133 | $1.20 Gen. Douglas MacArthur and beach landing | 1·10 | 1·25 |
| 2134 | $1.20 Gen. Claire Chennault and U.S. fighter aircraft | 1·10 | 1·25 |
| 2135 | $1.20 Brig. Orde Wingate and supply drop | 1·10 | 1·25 |
| 2136 | $1.20 Gen. Joseph Stilwell and U.S. supply plane | 1·10 | 1·25 |
| 2137 | $1.20 Field-Marshal Bill Slim and loading cow into plane | 1·10 | 1·25 |
| **MS**2138 | 108×76 mm. $3 Admiral Nimitz and aircraft carrier | 2·75 | 3·50 |

**345** Family ("Caring")

**1995.** Tourism. Sheet 95×72 mm, containing T **345** and similar horiz designs. Multicoloured.

| No. | Description | Unused | Used |
|---|---|---|---|
| **MS**2139 | $2 Type **345**; $2 Market trader ("Marketing"); $2 Workers and housewife ("Working"); $2 Leisure pursuits ("Enjoying Life") | 5·50 | 7·00 |

**346** Purple-throated Carib

**1995.** Birds. Multicoloured.

| No. | Description | Unused | Used |
|---|---|---|---|
| 2140 | 75c. Type **346** | 1·00 | 85 |
| 2141 | 75c. Antillean crested hummingbird | 1·00 | 85 |
| 2142 | 75c. Bananaquit | 1·00 | 85 |
| 2143 | 75c. Mangrove cuckoo | 1·00 | 85 |
| 2144 | 75c. Troupial | 1·00 | 85 |
| 2145 | 75c. Green-throated carib | 1·00 | 85 |
| 2146 | 75c. Yellow warbler | 1·00 | 85 |
| 2147 | 75c. Antillean euphonia ("Blue-hooded Euphonia") | 1·00 | 85 |
| 2148 | 75c. Scaly-breasted thrasher | 1·00 | 85 |
| 2149 | 75c. Burrowing owl | 1·00 | 85 |
| 2150 | 75c. Carib grackle | 1·00 | 85 |
| 2151 | 75c. Adelaide's warbler | 1·00 | 85 |
| 2152 | 75c. Ring-necked duck | 1·00 | 85 |
| 2153 | 75c. Ruddy duck | 1·00 | 85 |
| 2154 | 75c. Green-winged teal | 1·00 | 85 |
| 2155 | 75c. Wood duck | 1·00 | 85 |
| 2156 | 75c. Hooded merganser | 1·00 | 85 |
| 2157 | 75c. Lesser scaup | 1·00 | 85 |
| 2158 | 75c. Black-billed whistling duck ("West Indian Tree Duck") | 1·00 | 85 |
| 2159 | 75c. Fulvous whistling duck | 1·00 | 85 |
| 2160 | 75c. Bahama pintail | 1·00 | 85 |
| 2161 | 75c. Northern shoveler | 1·00 | 85 |
| 2162 | 75c. Masked duck | 1·00 | 85 |
| 2163 | 75c. American wigeon | 1·00 | 85 |
| **MS**2164 | Two sheets, each 104×74 mm. (a) $6 American purple gallinule. (b) $6 Heads of Blue-winged teal Set of 2 sheets | 13·00 | 13·00 |

Nos. 2140/51 and 2152/63 respectively were printed together, se-tenant, forming composite designs.

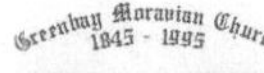

ANTIGUA
BARBUDA 20c

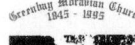

**347** Original Church, 1845

**1995.** 150th Anniv of Greenbay Moravian Church. Multicoloured.

| No. | Description | Unused | Used |
|---|---|---|---|
| 2165 | 20c. Type **347** | 70 | 30 |
| 2166 | 60c. Church in 1967 | 1·00 | 40 |
| 2167 | 75c. Present church | 1·25 | 50 |
| 2168 | 90c. Revd. John Buckley (first minister of African descent) | 1·40 | 60 |
| 2169 | $1.20 Bishop John Ephraim Knight (longest-serving minister) | 1·75 | 1·75 |
| 2170 | $2 As 75c. | 2·75 | 3·50 |
| **MS**2171 | 110×81 mm. $6 Front of present church | 4·50 | 6·00 |

**348** Mining Bees

**1995.** Bees. Multicoloured.

| No. | Description | Unused | Used |
|---|---|---|---|
| 2172 | 90c. Type **348** | 1·00 | 70 |
| 2173 | $1.20 Solitary bee | 1·40 | 90 |
| 2174 | $1.65 Leaf-cutter bee | 2·00 | 2·00 |
| 2175 | $1.75 Honey bees | 2·00 | 2·00 |
| **MS**2176 | 110×80 mm. $6 Solitary mining bee | 4·00 | 5·00 |

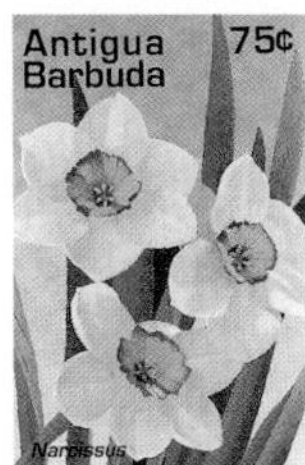


**349** Narcissus

**1995.** Flowers. Multicoloured.

| | | | |
|---|---|---|---|
| 2177 | 75c. Type **349** | 80 | 80 |
| 2178 | 75c. Camellia | 80 | 80 |
| 2179 | 75c. Iris | 80 | 80 |
| 2180 | 75c. Tulip | 80 | 80 |
| 2181 | 75c. Poppy | 80 | 80 |
| 2182 | 75c. Peony | 80 | 80 |
| 2183 | 75c. Magnolia | 80 | 80 |
| 2184 | 75c. Oriental lily | 80 | 80 |
| 2185 | 75c. Rose | 80 | 80 |
| 2186 | 75c. Pansy | 80 | 80 |
| 2187 | 75c. Hydrangea | 80 | 80 |
| 2188 | 75c. Azaleas | 80 | 80 |
| **MS**2189 | 80×100 mm. $6 Calla lily | 4·00 | 5·00 |

No. 2186 is inscribed "Pansie" in error.

**350** Somali

**1995.** Cats. Multicoloured.

| | | | |
|---|---|---|---|
| 2190 | 45c. Type **350** | 75 | 60 |
| 2191 | 45c. Persian and butterflies | 75 | 60 |
| 2192 | 45c. Devon rex | 75 | 60 |
| 2193 | 45c. Turkish angora | 75 | 60 |
| 2194 | 45c. Himalayan | 75 | 60 |
| 2195 | 45c. Maine coon | 75 | 60 |
| 2196 | 45c. Ginger non-pedigree | 75 | 60 |
| 2197 | 45c. American wirehair | 75 | 60 |
| 2198 | 45c. British shorthair | 75 | 60 |
| 2199 | 45c. American curl | 75 | 60 |
| 2200 | 45c. Black non-pedigree and butterfly | 75 | 60 |
| 2201 | 45c. Birman | 75 | 60 |
| **MS**2202 | 104×74 mm. $6 Siberian kitten (vert) | 7·50 | 7·50 |

Nos. 2190/2201 were printed together, se-tenant, forming a composite design.

**351** The Explorer Tent

**1995.** 18th World Scout Jamboree, Netherlands. Tents. Multicoloured.

| | | | |
|---|---|---|---|
| 2203 | $1.20 Type **351** | 1·60 | 1·60 |
| 2204 | $1.20 Camper tent | 1·60 | 1·60 |
| 2205 | $1.20 Wall tent | 1·60 | 1·60 |
| 2206 | $1.20 Trail tarp | 1·60 | 1·60 |
| 2207 | $1.20 Miner's tent | 1·60 | 1·60 |
| 2208 | $1.20 Voyager tent | 1·60 | 1·60 |
| **MS**2209 | Two sheets, each 76×106 mm. (a) $6 Scout and camp fire. (b) $6 Scout with back pack (vert) Set of 2 sheets | 8·50 | 10·00 |

**352** Trans-Gabon Diesel-electric Train

**1995.** Trains of the World. Multicoloured.

| | | | |
|---|---|---|---|
| 2210 | 35c. Type **352** | 1·00 | 65 |
| 2211 | 65c. Canadian Pacific diesel-electric locomotive | 1·50 | 90 |
| 2212 | 75c. Santa Fe Railway diesel-electric locomotive, U.S.A. | 1·60 | 1·00 |
| 2213 | 90c. High Speed Train, Great Britain | 1·60 | 1·00 |
| 2214 | $1.20 TGV express train, France | 1·60 | 1·60 |
| 2215 | $1.20 Diesel-electric locomotive, Australia | 1·60 | 1·60 |
| 2216 | $1.20 Pendolino "ETR 450" electric train, Italy | 1·60 | 1·60 |
| 2217 | $1.20 Diesel-electric locomotive, Thailand | 1·60 | 1·60 |
| 2218 | $1.20 Pennsylvania Railroad Type K4 steam locomotive, U.S.A. | 1·60 | 1·60 |
| 2219 | $1.20 Beyer-Garratt steam locomotive, East African Railways | 1·60 | 1·60 |
| 2220 | $1.20 Natal Government steam locomotive | 1·60 | 1·60 |
| 2221 | $1.20 Rail gun, American Civil War | 1·60 | 1·60 |
| 2222 | $1.20 Locomotive "Lion" (red livery), Great Britain | 1·60 | 1·60 |
| 2223 | $1.20 William Hedley's "Puffing Billy" (green livery), Great Britain | 1·60 | 1·60 |
| 2224 | $6 Amtrak high speed diesel locomotive, U.S.A. | 3·75 | 4·50 |
| **MS**2225 | Two sheets, each 110×80 mm. (a) $6 Locomotive "Iron Rooster", China (vert). (b) $6 "Indian-Pacific" diesel-electric locomotive, Australia (vert) Set of 2 sheets | 13·00 | 13·00 |

**353** Dag Hammarskjold (1961 Peace)

**1995.** Cent of Nobel Prize Trust Fund. Mult.

| | | | |
|---|---|---|---|
| 2226 | $1 Type **353** | 1·10 | 1·10 |
| 2227 | $1 Georg Wittig (1979 Chemistry) | 1·10 | 1·10 |
| 2228 | $1 Wilhelm Ostwald (1909 Chemistry) | 1·10 | 1·10 |
| 2229 | $1 Robert Koch (1905 Medicine) | 1·10 | 1·10 |
| 2230 | $1 Karl Ziegler (1963 Chemistry) | 1·10 | 1·10 |
| 2231 | $1 Alexander Fleming (1945 Medicine) | 1·10 | 1·10 |
| 2232 | $1 Hermann Staudinger (1953 Chemistry) | 1·10 | 1·10 |
| 2233 | $1 Manfred Eigen (1967 Chemistry) | 1·10 | 1·10 |
| 2234 | $1 Arno Penzias (1978 Physics) | 1·10 | 1·10 |
| 2235 | $1 Shmuel Agnon (1966 Literature) | 1·10 | 1·10 |
| 2236 | $1 Rudyard Kipling (1907 Literature) | 1·10 | 1·10 |
| 2237 | $1 Aleksandr Solzhenitsyn (1970 Literature) | 1·10 | 1·10 |
| 2238 | $1 Jack Steinberger (1988 Physics) | 1·10 | 1·10 |
| 2239 | $1 Andrei Sakharov (1975 Peace) | 1·10 | 1·10 |
| 2240 | $1 Otto Stern (1943 Physics) | 1·10 | 1·10 |
| 2241 | $1 John Steinbeck (1962 Literature) | 1·10 | 1·10 |
| 2242 | $1 Nadine Gordimer (1991 Literature) | 1·10 | 1·10 |
| 2243 | $1 William Faulkner (1949 Literature) | 1·10 | 1·10 |
| **MS**2244 | Two sheets, each 100×70 mm. (a) $6 Elie Wiesel (1986 Peace) (vert). (b) $6 The Dalai Lama (1989 Peace) (vert) Set of 2 sheets | 8·00 | 9·50 |

**354** Elvis Presley

**1995.** 60th Birth Anniv of Elvis Presley. Mult.

| | | | |
|---|---|---|---|
| 2245 | $1 Type **354** | 1·25 | 95 |
| 2246 | $1 Holding microphone in right hand | 1·25 | 95 |
| 2247 | $1 In blue shirt and with neck of guitar | 1·25 | 95 |
| 2248 | $1 Wearing blue shirt and smiling | 1·25 | 95 |
| 2249 | $1 On wedding day | 1·25 | 95 |
| 2250 | $1 In army uniform | 1·25 | 95 |
| 2251 | $1 Wearing red shirt | 1·25 | 95 |
| 2252 | $1 Wearing white shirt | 1·25 | 95 |
| 2253 | $1 In white shirt with microphone | 1·25 | 95 |
| **MS**2254 | 101×71 mm. $6 "Ghost" image of Elvis amongst the stars | 7·00 | 5·50 |

**355** John Lennon and Signature

**1995.** 15th Death Anniv of John Lennon (entertainer). Multicoloured.

| | | | |
|---|---|---|---|
| 2255 | 45c. Type **355** | 50 | 40 |
| 2256 | 50c. In beard and spectacles | 50 | 50 |
| 2257 | 65c. Wearing sunglasses | 55 | 55 |
| 2258 | 75c. In cap with heart badge | 65 | 65 |
| **MS**2259 | 103×73 mm. $6 As 75c. | 5·50 | 6·50 |

**1995.** Hurricane Relief. Nos. 2203/8 optd **"Hurricane Relief"**.

| | | | |
|---|---|---|---|
| 2260 | $1.20 Type **351** | 1·25 | 1·25 |
| 2261 | $1.20 Camper tent | 1·25 | 1·25 |
| 2262 | $1.20 Wall tent | 1·25 | 1·25 |
| 2263 | $1.20 Trail tarp | 1·25 | 1·25 |
| 2264 | $1.20 Miner's tent | 1·25 | 1·25 |
| 2265 | $1.20 Voyager tent | 1·25 | 1·25 |
| **MS**2266 | Two sheets, each 76×106 mm. (a) $6 Scout and camp fire. (b) $6 Scout with back pack (vert) Set of 2 sheets | 12·00 | 15·00 |

**357** "Rest on the Flight into Egypt" (Paolo Veronese)

**1995.** Christmas. Religious Paintings. Multicoloured.

| | | | |
|---|---|---|---|
| 2267 | 15c. Type **357** | 30 | 30 |
| 2268 | 35c. "Madonna and Child" (Van Dyck) | 40 | 40 |
| 2269 | 65c. "Sacred Conversation Piece" (Veronese) | 60 | 50 |
| 2270 | 75c. "Vision of St. Anthony" (Van Dyck) | 70 | 60 |
| 2271 | 90c. "Virgin and Child" (Van Eyck) | 80 | 65 |
| 2272 | $6 "The Immaculate Conception" (Giovanni Tiepolo) | 3·00 | 4·25 |
| **MS**2273 | Two sheets. (a) 101×127 mm. $5 "Christ appearing to his Mother" (detail) (Van der Weyden). (b) 127×101 mm. $6 "The Infant Jesus and Young St. John" (Murillo) Set of 2 sheets | 7·50 | 9·00 |

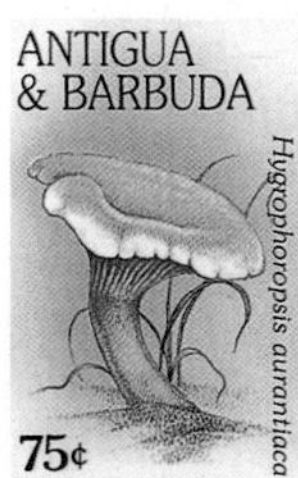


**358** "Hygrophoropsis aurantiaca"

**1996.** Fungi. Multicoloured.

| | | | |
|---|---|---|---|
| 2274 | 75c. Type **358** | 60 | 70 |
| 2275 | 75c. "Hygrophorus bakerensis" | 60 | 70 |
| 2276 | 75c. "Hygrophorus conicus" | 60 | 70 |
| 2277 | 75c. "Hygrophorus miniatus" ("Hygrocybe miniata") | 60 | 70 |
| 2278 | 75c. "Suillus brevipes" | 60 | 70 |
| 2279 | 75c. "Suillus luteus" | 60 | 70 |
| 2280 | 75c. "Suillus granulatus" | 60 | 70 |
| 2281 | 75c. "Suillus caerulescens" | 60 | 70 |
| **MS**2282 | Two sheets, each 105×75 mm. (a) $6 "Conocybe filaris". (b) $6 "Hygrocybe flavescens" Set of 2 sheets | 7·00 | 8·00 |

**359** H.M.S. "Resolution" (Cook)

**1996.** Sailing Ships. Multicoloured.

| | | | |
|---|---|---|---|
| 2283 | 15c. Type **359** | 70 | 40 |
| 2284 | 25c. "Mayflower" (Pilgrim Fathers) | 70 | 40 |
| 2285 | 45c. "Santa Maria" (Columbus) | 1·00 | 40 |
| 2286 | 75c. "Aemilia" (Dutch galleon) | 1·00 | 90 |
| 2287 | 75c. "Sovereign of the Seas" (English galleon) | 1·00 | 90 |
| 2288 | 90c. H.M.S. "Victory" (Nelson) | 1·25 | 90 |
| 2289 | $1.20 As No. 2286 | 1·50 | 1·60 |
| 2290 | $1.20 As No. 2287 | 1·50 | 1·60 |
| 2291 | $1.20 "Royal Louis" (French galleon) | 1·50 | 1·60 |
| 2292 | $1.20 H.M.S. "Royal George" (ship of the line) | 1·50 | 1·60 |
| 2293 | $1.20 "Le Protecteur" (French frigate) | 1·50 | 1·60 |
| 2294 | $1.20 As No. 2288 | 1·50 | 1·60 |
| 2295 | $1.50 As No. 2285 | 1·50 | 1·60 |
| 2296 | $1.50 "Vitoria" (Magellan) | 1·60 | 1·75 |
| 2297 | $1.50 "Golden Hind" (Drake) | 1·60 | 1·75 |
| 2298 | $1.50 As No. 2284 | 1·60 | 1·75 |
| 2299 | $1.50 "Griffin" (La Salle) | 1·60 | 1·75 |
| 2300 | $1.50 Type **359** | 1·60 | 1·75 |
| **MS**2301 | Two sheets. (a) 102×72 mm. $6 U.S.S. "Constitution" (frigate). (b) 98×67 mm. $6 "Grande" "Hermine" (Cartier) Set of 2 sheets | 7·50 | 9·00 |

**360** Florence Griffith Joyner (U.S.A.) (Gold – track, 1988)

**1996.** Olympic Games, Atlanta. Previous Medal Winners (2nd issue). Multicoloured.

| | | | |
|---|---|---|---|
| 2302 | 65c. Type **360** | 60 | 60 |
| 2303 | 75c. Olympic Stadium, Seoul (1988) (horiz) | 65 | 65 |
| 2304 | 90c. Allison Jolly and Lynne Jewell (U.S.A.) (Gold – yachting, 1988) (horiz) | 70 | 70 |
| 2305 | 90c. Wolfgang Nordwig (Germany) (Gold – pole vaulting, 1972) | 70 | 75 |
| 2306 | 90c. Shirley Strong (Great Britain) (Silver – 100 metres hurdles, 1984) | 70 | 75 |
| 2307 | 90c. Sergei Bubka (Russia) (Gold – pole vault, 1988) | 70 | 75 |
| 2308 | 90c. Filbert Bayi (Tanzania) (Silver – 3000 metres steeplechase, 1980) | 70 | 75 |
| 2309 | 90c. Victor Saneyev (Russia) (Gold – triple jump, 1968, 1972, 1976) | 70 | 75 |
| 2310 | 90c. Silke Renk (Germany) (Gold – javelin, 1992) | 70 | 75 |
| 2311 | 90c. Daley Thompson (Great Britain) (Gold – decathlon, 1980, 1984) | 70 | 75 |
| 2312 | 90c. Robert Richards (U.S.A.) (Gold – pole vault, 1952, 1956) | 70 | 75 |
| 2313 | 90c. Parry O'Brien (U.S.A.) (Gold – shot put, 1952, 1956) | 70 | 75 |
| 2314 | 90c. Ingrid Kramer (Germany) (Gold – women's platform diving, 1960) | 70 | 75 |
| 2315 | 90c. Kelly McCormick (U.S.A.) (Silver – women's springboard diving, 1984) | 70 | 75 |
| 2316 | 90c. Gary Tobian (U.S.A.) (Gold – men's springboard diving, 1960) | 70 | 75 |
| 2317 | 90c. Greg Louganis (U.S.A.) (Gold – men's diving, 1984 and 1988) | 70 | 75 |
| 2318 | 90c. Michelle Mitchell (U.S.A.) (Silver – women's platform diving, 1984 and 1988) | 70 | 75 |
| 2319 | 90c. Zhou Jihong (China) (Gold – women's platform diving, 1984) | 70 | 75 |
| 2320 | 90c. Wendy Wyland (U.S.A.) (Bronze – women's platform diving, 1984) | 70 | 75 |
| 2321 | 90c. Xu Yanmei (China) (Gold – women's platform diving, 1988) | 70 | 75 |

| | | | |
|---|---|---|---|
| 2322 | 90c. Fu Mingxia (China) (Gold – women's platform diving, 1992) | 70 | 75 |
| 2323 | $1.20 2000 metre tandem cycle race (horiz) | 1·00 | 1·00 |
| **MS**2324 | Two sheets, each 106×76 mm. (a) $5 Bill Toomey (U.S.A.) (Gold—Decathlon, 1968) (horiz). (b) $6 Mark Lenzi (U.S.A.) (Gold—Men's springboard diving, 1992) Set of 2 sheets | 7·00 | 8·00 |

Nos. 2305/13 and 2314/22 respectively were printed together, se-tenant, with the background forming a composite design.

**361** Black Skimmer

**1996.** Sea Birds. Multicoloured.

| | | | |
|---|---|---|---|
| 2325 | 75c. Type **361** | 70 | 75 |
| 2326 | 75c. Black-capped petrel | 70 | 75 |
| 2327 | 75c. Sooty tern | 70 | 75 |
| 2328 | 75c. Royal tern | 70 | 75 |
| 2329 | 75c. Pomarine skua ("Pomarine Jaegger") | 70 | 75 |
| 2330 | 75c. White-tailed tropic bird | 70 | 75 |
| 2331 | 75c. Northern gannet | 70 | 75 |
| 2332 | 75c. Laughing gull | 70 | 75 |
| **MS**2333 | Two sheets, each 105×75 mm. (a) $5 Magnificent frigate bird ("Great Frigate Bird"). (b) $6 Brown pelican Set of 2 sheets | 7·50 | 9·00 |

**362** Mickey and Goofy on Elephant ("Around the World in Eighty Days")

**1996.** Novels of Jules Verne. Walt Disney cartoon characters in scenes from the books. Multicoloured.

| | | | |
|---|---|---|---|
| 2334 | 1c. Type **362** | 15 | 25 |
| 2335 | 2c. Mickey, Donald and Goofy entering cave ("A Journey to the Centre of the Earth") | 20 | 25 |
| 2336 | 5c. Mickey and Minnie driving postcart ("Michel Strogoff") | 30 | 25 |
| 2337 | 10c. Mickey, Donald and Goofy in space rocket ("From the Earth to the Moon") | 40 | 20 |
| 2338 | 15c. Mickey and Goofy in balloon ("Five Weeks in a Balloon") | 40 | 20 |
| 2339 | 20c. Mickey and Goofy in China ("Around the World in Eighty Days") | 40 | 20 |
| 2340 | $1 Mickey, Goofy and Pluto on island ("The Mysterious Island") | 2·00 | 85 |
| 2341 | $2 Mickey, Pluto, Goofy and Donald on Moon ("From the Earth to the Moon") | 2·50 | 2·50 |
| 2342 | $3 Mickey being lifted by bird ("Captain Grant's Children") | 3·00 | 3·25 |
| 2343 | $5 Mickey with seal and squid ("Twenty Thousand Leagues Under the Sea") | 4·25 | 5·00 |
| **MS**2344 | Two sheets, each 124×99 mm. (a) $6 Mickey on "Nautilus" ("Twenty Thousand Leagues Under the Sea"). (b) $6 Mickey and Donald on raft ("A Journey to the Centre of the Earth") Set of 2 sheets | 11·00 | 11·00 |

**363** Bruce Lee

**1996.** "CHINA '96" 9th Asian International Stamp Exhibition, Peking. Bruce Lee (actor). Multicoloured.

| | | | |
|---|---|---|---|
| 2345 | 75c. Type **363** | 70 | 70 |
| 2346 | 75c. Bruce Lee in white shirt and red tie | 70 | 70 |
| 2347 | 75c. In plaid jacket and tie | 70 | 70 |
| 2348 | 75c. In mask and uniform | 70 | 70 |
| 2349 | 75c. Bare-chested | 70 | 70 |
| 2350 | 75c. In mandarin jacket | 70 | 70 |
| 2351 | 75c. In brown jumper | 70 | 70 |
| 2352 | 75c. In fawn shirt | 70 | 70 |
| 2353 | 75c. Shouting | 70 | 70 |
| **MS**2354 | 76×106 mm. $5 Bruce Lee | 3·75 | 4·00 |

**364** Queen Elizabeth II

**1996.** 70th Birthday of Queen Elizabeth II. Multicoloured.

| | | | |
|---|---|---|---|
| 2355 | $2 Type **364** | 1·25 | 1·50 |
| 2356 | $2 With bouquet | 1·25 | 1·50 |
| 2357 | $2 In Garter robes | 1·25 | 1·50 |
| **MS**2358 | 96×111 mm. $6 Wearing white dress | 5·50 | 6·00 |

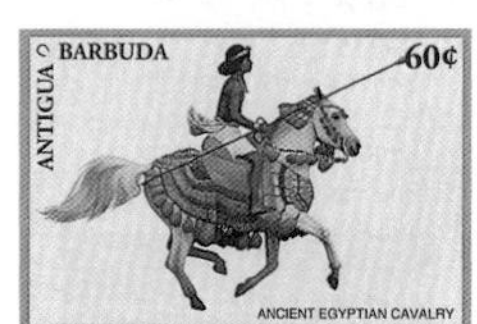


**365** Ancient Egyptian Cavalryman

**1996.** Cavalry through the Ages. Multicoloured.

| | | | |
|---|---|---|---|
| 2359 | 60c. Type **365** | 50 | 55 |
| 2360 | 60c. 13th-century English knight | 50 | 55 |
| 2361 | 60c. 16th-century Spanish lancer | 50 | 55 |
| 2362 | 60c. 18th-century Chinese cavalryman | 50 | 55 |
| **MS**2363 | 100×70 mm. $6 19th-century French cuirassier | 3·25 | 3·75 |

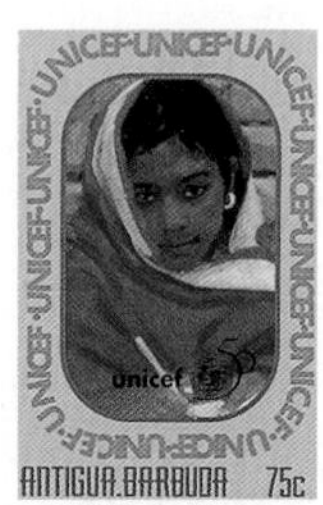


**366** Girl in Red Sari

**1996.** 50th Anniv of UNICEF Multicoloured.

| | | | |
|---|---|---|---|
| 2364 | 75c. Type **366** | 60 | 60 |
| 2365 | 90c. South American mother and child | 70 | 70 |
| 2366 | $1.20 Nurse with child | 90 | 1·00 |
| **MS**2367 | 114×74 mm. $6 Chinese child | 3·25 | 3·75 |

**367** Tomb of Zachariah and "Verbascum sinuatum"

**1996.** 3000th Anniv of Jerusalem. Multicoloured.

| | | | |
|---|---|---|---|
| 2368 | 75c. Type **367** | 65 | 65 |
| 2369 | 90c. Pool of Siloam and "Hyacinthus orientalis" | 75 | 75 |
| 2370 | $1.20 Hurva Synagogue and "Ranunculus asiaticus" | 1·10 | 1·10 |
| **MS**2371 | 66×80 mm. $6 Model of Herrod's Temple and "Cerics siliquastrum" | 5·50 | 5·50 |

**368** Kate Smith

**1996.** Cent of Radio. Entertainers. Mult.

| | | | |
|---|---|---|---|
| 2372 | 65c. Type **368** | 50 | 50 |
| 2373 | 75c. Dinah Shore | 60 | 60 |
| 2374 | 90c. Rudy Vallee | 70 | 70 |
| 2375 | $1.20 Bing Crosby | 90 | 1·00 |
| **MS**2376 | 72×104 mm. $6 Jo Stafford (28×42 mm) | 3·25 | 3·75 |

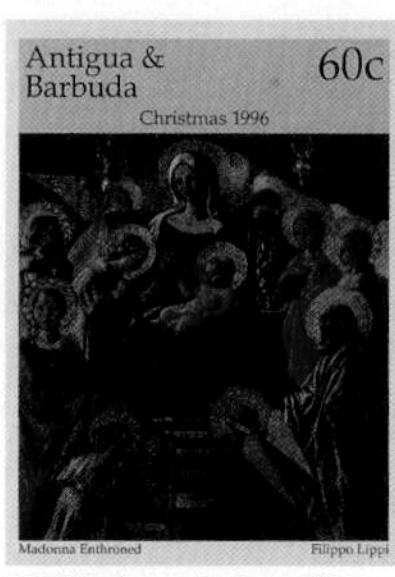


**369** "Madonna Enthroned"

**1996.** Christmas. Religious Paintings by Filippo Lippi. Multicoloured.

| | | | |
|---|---|---|---|
| 2377 | 60c. Type **369** | 70 | 40 |
| 2378 | 90c. "Adoration of the Child and Saints" | 80 | 55 |
| 2379 | $1 "The Annunciation" | 95 | 70 |
| 2380 | $1.20 "Birth of the Virgin" | 1·10 | 1·10 |
| 2381 | $1.60 "Adoration of the Child" | 1·50 | 1·75 |
| 2382 | $1.75 "Madonna and Child" | 1·75 | 2·00 |
| **MS**2383 | Two sheets, each 76×106 mm. (a) $6 "Madonna and Child" (different). (b) $6 "The Circumcision" Set of 2 sheets | 10·00 | 11·00 |

**370** Robert Preston ("The Music Man")

**1997.** Broadway Musical Stars. Multicoloured.

| | | | |
|---|---|---|---|
| 2384 | $1 Type **370** | 90 | 90 |
| 2385 | $1 Michael Crawford ("Phantom of the Opera") | 90 | 90 |
| 2386 | $1 Zero Mostel ("Fiddler on the Roof") | 90 | 90 |
| 2387 | $1 Patti Lupone ("Evita") | 90 | 90 |
| 2388 | $1 Raul Julia ("Threepenny Opera") | 90 | 90 |
| 2389 | $1 Mary Martin ("South Pacific") | 90 | 90 |
| 2390 | $1 Carol Channing ("Hello Dolly") | 90 | 90 |
| 2391 | $1 Yul Brynner ("The King and I") | 90 | 90 |
| 2392 | $1 Julie Andrews ("My Fair Lady") | 90 | 90 |
| **MS**2393 | 106×76 mm. $6 Mickey Rooney ("Sugar Babies") | 4·00 | 5·00 |

**371** Goofy and Wilbur

**1997.** Walt Disney Cartoon Characters. Mult.

| | | | |
|---|---|---|---|
| 2394 | 1c. Type **371** | 10 | 10 |
| 2395 | 2c. Donald and Goofy in boxing ring | 10 | 10 |
| 2396 | 5c. Donald, Panchito and Jose Carioca | 10 | 10 |
| 2397 | 10c. Mickey and Goofy playing chess | 20 | 15 |
| 2398 | 15c. Chip and Dale with acorns | 20 | 15 |
| 2399 | 20c. Pluto and Mickey | 20 | 15 |
| 2400 | $1 Daisy and Minnie eating ice-cream | 90 | 75 |
| 2401 | $2 Daisy and Minnie at dressing table | 1·50 | 1·75 |
| 2402 | $3 Gus Goose and Donald | 2·00 | 2·50 |
| **MS**2403 | Two sheets. (a) 102×127 mm. $6 Goofy. (b) 127×102 mm. Donald Duck playing guitar (vert) Set of 2 sheets | 8·00 | 8·50 |

**372** Charlie Chaplin as Young Man

**1997.** 20th Death Anniv of Charlie Chaplin (film star). Multicoloured.

| | | | |
|---|---|---|---|
| 2404 | $1 Type **372** | 70 | 70 |
| 2405 | $1 Pulling face | 70 | 70 |
| 2406 | $1 Looking over shoulder | 70 | 70 |
| 2407 | $1 In cap | 70 | 70 |
| 2408 | $1 In front of star | 70 | 70 |
| 2409 | $1 In "The Great Dictator" | 70 | 70 |
| 2410 | $1 With movie camera and megaphone | 70 | 70 |
| 2411 | $1 Standing in front of camera lens | 70 | 70 |
| 2412 | $1 Putting on make-up | 70 | 70 |
| **MS**2413 | 76×106 mm. $6 Charlie Chaplin | 4·00 | 4·25 |

Nos. 2404/12 were printed together, se-tenant, with the backgrounds forming a composite design.

**373** "Charaxes porthos"

**1997.** Butterflies. Multicoloured.

| | | | |
|---|---|---|---|
| 2414 | 90c. Type **373** | 65 | 50 |
| 2415 | $1.10 "Charaxes protoclea protoclea" | 70 | 80 |
| 2416 | $1.10 "Byblia ilithyia" | 70 | 80 |
| 2417 | $1.10 Black-headed tchagra (bird) | 70 | 80 |
| 2418 | $1.10 "Charaxes nobilis" | 70 | 80 |
| 2419 | $1.10 "Pseudacraea boisduvali trimeni" | 70 | 80 |
| 2420 | $1.10 "Charaxes smaragdalis" | 70 | 80 |
| 2421 | $1.10 "Charaxes lasti" | 70 | 80 |
| 2422 | $1.10 "Pseudacrea poggei" | 70 | 80 |
| 2423 | $1.10 "Graphium colonna" | 70 | 80 |
| 2424 | $1.10 Carmine bee eater (bird) | 70 | 80 |
| 2425 | $1.10 "Pseudacraea eurytus" | 70 | 80 |
| 2426 | $1.10 "Hypolimnas monteironis" | 70 | 80 |
| 2427 | $1.10 "Charaxes anticlea" | 70 | 80 |
| 2428 | $1.10 "Graphium leonidas" | 70 | 80 |
| 2429 | $1.10 "Graphium illyris" | 70 | 80 |
| 2430 | $1.10 "Nephronia argia" | 70 | 80 |
| 2431 | $1.10 "Graphium policenes" | 70 | 80 |
| 2432 | $1.10 "Papilio dardanus" | 70 | 80 |
| 2433 | $1.20 "Aethiopana honorius" | 70 | 80 |
| 2434 | $1.60 "Charaxes hadrianus" | 1·00 | 1·10 |
| 2435 | $1.75 "Precis westermanni" | 1·25 | 1·40 |
| **MS**2436 | Three sheets, each 106×76 mm. (a) $6 "Charaxes lactitinctus" (horiz). (b) $6 "Eupheadra neophron". (c) $6 "Euxanthe tiberius" (horiz) Set of 3 sheets | 11·00 | 13·00 |

Nos. 2415/23 and 2424/32 respectively were printed together, se-tenant, with the backgrounds forming a composite design.

No. 2430 is inscribed "Nepheronia argia" in error.

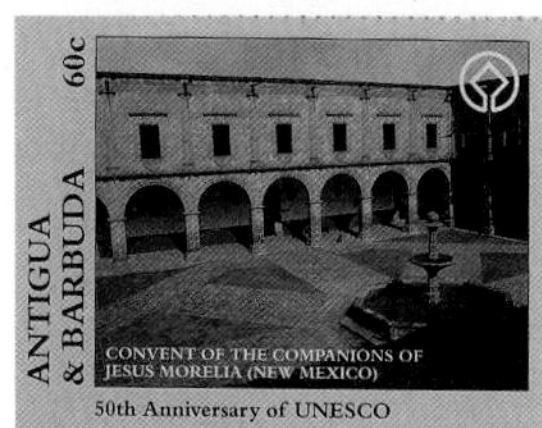


**374** Convent of The Companions of Jesus, Morelia, Mexico

**1997.** 50th Anniv of UNESCO Multicoloured.

| | | | |
|---|---|---|---|
| 2437 | 60c. Type **374** | 60 | 35 |
| 2438 | 90c. Fortress at San Lorenzo, Panama (vert) | 70 | 50 |
| 2439 | $1 Canaima National Park, Venezuela (vert) | 80 | 55 |
| 2440 | $1.10 Aerial view of church with tower, Guanajuato, Mexico (vert) | 80 | 90 |
| 2441 | $1.10 Church facade, Guanajuato, Mexico (vert) | 80 | 90 |
| 2442 | $1.10 Aerial view of churches with domes, Guanajuato, Mexico (vert) | 80 | 90 |
| 2443 | $1.10 Jesuit Missions of the Chiquitos, Bolivia (vert) | 80 | 90 |
| 2444 | $1.10 Huascaran National Park, Peru (vert) | 80 | 90 |
| 2445 | $1.10 Jesuit Missions of La Santisima, Paraguay (vert) | 80 | 90 |
| 2446 | $1.10 Cartagena, Colombia (vert) | 80 | 90 |
| 2447 | $1.10 Fortification, Havana, Cuba (vert) | 80 | 90 |
| 2448 | $1.20 As No. 2444 (vert) | 85 | 90 |
| 2449 | $1.60 Church of San Fransisco, Guatemala (vert) | 1·25 | 1·40 |
| 2450 | $1.65 Tikal National Park, Guatemala | 1·50 | 1·60 |
| 2451 | $1.65 Rio Platano Reserve, Honduras | 1·50 | 1·60 |
| 2452 | $1.65 Ruins of Copan, Honduras | 1·50 | 1·60 |
| 2453 | $1.65 Antigua ruins, Guatemala | 1·50 | 1·60 |
| 2454 | $1.65 Teotihuacan, Mexico | 1·50 | 1·60 |
| 2455 | $1.75 Santo Domingo, Dominican Republic (vert) | 1·60 | 1·75 |
| **MS**2456 | Two sheets, each 127×102 mm. (a) $6 Tikal National Park, Guatemala. (b) $6 Teotihuacan pyramid, Mexico Set of 2 sheets | 9·00 | 9·50 |

No. 2446 is inscribed "Columbia" in error.

**375** Red Bishop

**1997.** Endangered Species. Multicoloured.

| | | | |
|---|---|---|---|
| 2457 | $1.20 Type **375** | 1·25 | 1·25 |
| 2458 | $1.20 Yellow baboon | 1·25 | 1·25 |
| 2459 | $1.20 Superb starling | 1·25 | 1·25 |
| 2460 | $1.20 Ratel | 1·25 | 1·25 |
| 2461 | $1.20 Hunting dog | 1·25 | 1·25 |
| 2462 | $1.20 Serval | 1·25 | 1·25 |
| 2463 | $1.65 Okapi | 1·40 | 1·40 |
| 2464 | $1.65 Giant forest squirrel | 1·40 | 1·40 |
| 2465 | $1.65 Lesser masked weaver | 1·40 | 1·40 |
| 2466 | $1.65 Small-spotted genet | 1·40 | 1·40 |
| 2467 | $1.65 Yellow-billed stork | 1·40 | 1·40 |
| 2468 | $1.65 Red-headed agama | 1·40 | 1·40 |
| **MS**2469 | Three sheets, each 106×76 mm. (a) $6 South African crowned crane. (b) $6 Bat-eared fox. (c) $6 Malachite kingfisher Set of 3 sheets | 14·00 | 15·00 |

Nos. 2457/62 and 2463/8 respectively were printed together, se-tenant, with the backgrounds forming composite designs.

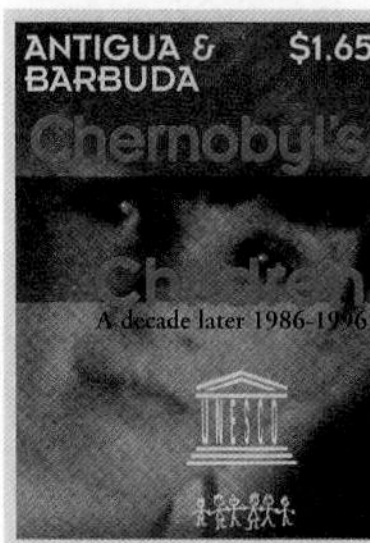


**376** Child's Face and UNESCO Emblem

**1997.** 10th Anniv of Chernobyl Nuclear Disaster. Multicoloured.

| | | | |
|---|---|---|---|
| 2470 | $1.65 Type **376** | 1·25 | 1·40 |
| 2471 | $2 As Type **376**, but inscr "CHABAD'S CHILDREN OF CHERNOBYL" at foot | 1·50 | 1·60 |

**377** Paul Harris and James Grant

**1997.** 50th Death Anniv of Paul Harris (founder of Rotary International).

| | | | |
|---|---|---|---|
| 2472 | $1.75 Type **377** | 1·25 | 1·50 |
| **MS**2473 | 78×107 mm. $6 Group study exchange, New Zealand | 3·50 | 4·00 |

**378** Queen Elizabeth II

**1997.** Golden Wedding of Queen Elizabeth and Prince Philip. Multicoloured.

| | | | |
|---|---|---|---|
| 2474 | $1 Type **378** | 1·00 | 1·00 |
| 2475 | $1 Royal coat of arms | 1·00 | 1·00 |
| 2476 | $1 Queen Elizabeth and Prince Philip at reception | 1·00 | 1·00 |
| 2477 | $1 Queen Elizabeth and Prince Philip in landau | 1·00 | 1·00 |
| 2478 | $1 Balmoral | 1·00 | 1·00 |
| 2479 | $1 Prince Philip | 1·00 | 1·00 |
| **MS**2480 | 100×71 mm. $6 Queen Elizabeth with Prince Philip in naval uniform | 4·00 | 4·50 |

**379** Kaiser Wilhelm I and Heinrich von Stephan

**1997.** "Pacific '97" International Stamp Exhibition, San Francisco. Death Centenary of Heinrich von Stephan (founder of the U.P.U.).

| | | | | |
|---|---|---|---|---|
| 2481 | **379** | $1.75 blue | 1·10 | 1·40 |
| 2482 | - | $1.75 brown | 1·10 | 1·40 |
| 2483 | - | $1.75 mauve | 1·10 | 1·40 |
| **MS**2484 | | 82×119 mm. $6 violet | 3·75 | 4·50 |

DESIGNS: No. 2482, Von Stephan and Mercury; 2483, Carrier pigeon and loft; **MS**2484, Von Stephan and 15th-century Basle messenger.

No. 2483 is inscribed "PIDGEON" in error.

**380** The Two Ugly Sisters and their Mother

**1997.** 175th Anniv of Brothers Grimm's Third Collection of Fairy Tales. Cinderella. Multicoloured.

| | | | |
|---|---|---|---|
| 2485 | $1.75 Type **380** | 1·40 | 1·50 |
| 2486 | $1.75 Cinderella and her Fairy Godmother | 1·40 | 1·50 |
| 2487 | $1.75 Cinderella and the Prince | 1·40 | 1·50 |
| **MS**2488 | 124×96 mm. $6 Cinderella trying on slipper | 4·00 | 4·50 |

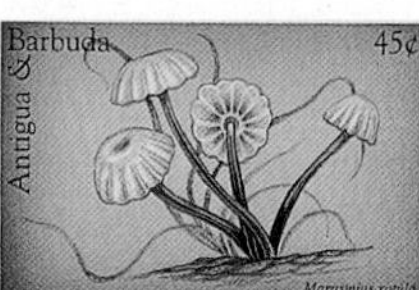


**381** "Marasmius rotula"

**1997.** Fungi. Multicoloured.

| | | | |
|---|---|---|---|
| 2489 | 45c. Type **381** | 50 | 30 |
| 2490 | 65c. "Cantharellus cibarius" | 60 | 40 |
| 2491 | 70c. "Lepiota cristata" | 60 | 40 |
| 2492 | 90c. "Auricularia mesenteric" | 70 | 50 |
| 2493 | $1 "Pholiota alnicola" | 75 | 55 |
| 2494 | $1.65 "Leccinum aurantiacum" | 1·10 | 1·25 |
| 2495 | $1.75 "Entoloma serrulatum" | 1·25 | 1·40 |
| 2496 | $1.75 "Panaeolus sphinctrinus" | 1·25 | 1·40 |
| 2497 | $1.75 "Volvariella bombycina" | 1·25 | 1·40 |
| 2498 | $1.75 "Conocybe percincta" | 1·25 | 1·40 |
| 2499 | $1.75 "Pluteus cervinus" | 1·25 | 1·40 |
| 2500 | $1.75 "Russula foetens" | 1·25 | 1·40 |
| **MS**2501 | Two sheets, each 106×76 mm. (a) $6 "Amanita cothurnata". (b) $6 "Panellus serotinus" Set of 2 sheets | 7·50 | 8·50 |

**382** "Odontoglossum cervantesii"

**1997.** Orchids of the World. Multicoloured.

| | | | |
|---|---|---|---|
| 2502 | 45c. Type **382** | 50 | 30 |
| 2503 | 65c. "Phalaenopsis" Medford Star | 60 | 40 |
| 2504 | 75c. "Vanda Motes" Resplendent | 65 | 45 |
| 2505 | 90c. "Odontonia" Debutante | 70 | 50 |
| 2506 | $1 "Iwanagaara" Apple Blossom | 75 | 55 |
| 2507 | $1.65 "Cattleya" Sophia Martin | 1·10 | 1·25 |
| 2508 | $1.65 Dogface Butterfly | 1·10 | 1·25 |
| 2509 | $1.65 "Laeliocattleya" Mini Purple | 1·10 | 1·25 |
| 2510 | $1.65 "Cymbidium" Showgirl | 1·10 | 1·25 |
| 2511 | $1.65 "Brassolaeliocattleya" Dorothy Bertsch | 1·10 | 1·25 |
| 2512 | $1.65 "Disa Blackii" | 1·10 | 1·25 |
| 2513 | $1.65 "Paphiopedilum leeanum" | 1·10 | 1·25 |
| 2514 | $1.65 "Paphiopedilum macranthum" | 1·10 | 1·25 |
| 2515 | $1.65 "Brassocattleya" Angel Lace | 1·10 | 1·25 |
| 2516 | $1.65 "Saphrolae liocattleya" Precious Stones | 1·10 | 1·25 |
| 2517 | $1.65 Orange Theope Butterfly | 1·10 | 1·25 |
| 2518 | $1.65 "Promenaea xanthina" | 1·10 | 1·25 |
| 2519 | $1.65 "Lycasle macrobulbon" | 1·10 | 1·25 |
| 2520 | $1.65 "Amestella philippinensis" | 1·10 | 1·25 |
| 2521 | $1.65 "Masdevallia" Machu Picchu | 1·10 | 1·25 |
| 2522 | $1.65 "Phalaenopsis" Zuma Urchin | 1·10 | 1·25 |
| 2523 | $2 "Dendrobium victoria-reginae" | 1·40 | 1·60 |
| **MS**2524 | Two sheets, each 76×106 mm. (a) "Mitonia" Seine. (b) "Pouphiopedilum gratrixanum" Set of 2 sheets | 7·50 | 8·50 |

Nos. 2507/14 and 2515/22 respectively were printed together, se-tenant, with the backgrounds forming composite designs.

**383** Maradona holding World Cup Trophy, 1986

**1997.** World Cup Football Championship, France (1998).

| | | | | |
|---|---|---|---|---|
| 2525 | **383** | 60c. multicoloured | 50 | 35 |
| 2526 | - | 75c. brown | 60 | 45 |
| 2527 | - | 90c. multicoloured | 70 | 50 |
| 2528 | - | $1 brown | 75 | 75 |
| 2529 | - | $1 brown | 75 | 75 |
| 2530 | - | $1 brown | 75 | 75 |
| 2531 | - | $1 black | 75 | 75 |
| 2532 | - | $1 brown | 75 | 75 |
| 2533 | - | $1 brown | 75 | 75 |
| 2534 | - | $1 brown | 75 | 75 |
| 2535 | - | $1 brown | 75 | 75 |
| 2536 | - | $1.20 multicoloured | 75 | 75 |
| 2537 | - | $1.65 multicoloured | 1·10 | 1·25 |
| 2538 | - | $1.75 multicoloured | 1·10 | 1·40 |
| **MS**2539 | | Two sheets, each 102×127 mm. (a) $6 multicoloured. (b) $6 mult Set of 2 sheets | 7·50 | 8·50 |

DESIGNS—HORIZ: No. 2526, Fritzwalter, West Germany, 1954; 2527, Zoff, Italy, 1982; 2536, Moore, England, 1966; 2537, Alberto, Brazil, 1970; 2538, Matthaus, West Germany, 1990; **MS**2539 (b) West German players celebrating, 1990. VERT: No. 2528, Ademir, Brazil, 1950; 2529, Eusebio, Portugal, 1966; 2530, Fontaine, France, 1958; 2531, Schillaci, Italy, 1990; 2532, Leonidas, Brazil, 1938; 2533, Stabile, Argentina, 1930; 2534, Nejedly, Czechoslovakia, 1934; 2535, Muller, West Germany, 1970; **MS**2539 (a) Bebeto, Brazil.

**384** Scottish Fold Kitten

**1997.** Cats and Dogs. Multicoloured.

| | | | |
|---|---|---|---|
| 2540 | $1.65 Type **384** | 1·40 | 1·25 |
| 2541 | $1.65 Japanese bobtail | 1·40 | 1·25 |
| 2542 | $1.65 Tabby manx | 1·40 | 1·25 |
| 2543 | $1.65 Bicolor American shorthair | 1·40 | 1·25 |
| 2544 | $1.65 Sorrel Abyssinian | 1·40 | 1·25 |
| 2545 | $1.65 Himalayan blue point | 1·40 | 1·25 |
| 2546 | $1.65 Dachshund | 1·40 | 1·25 |
| 2547 | $1.65 Staffordshire terrier | 1·40 | 1·25 |
| 2548 | $1.65 Shar-pei | 1·40 | 1·25 |
| 2549 | $1.65 Beagle | 1·40 | 1·25 |
| 2550 | $1.65 Norfolk terrier | 1·40 | 1·25 |
| 2551 | $1.65 Golden retriever | 1·40 | 1·25 |
| **MS**2552 | Two sheets, each 107×77 mm. (a) $6 Red tabby (vert). (b) $6 Siberian husky (vert) Set of 2 sheets | 7·50 | 8·50 |

**385** Original Drawing by Trevithick, 1803

**1997.** Railway Locomotives of the World. Multicoloured.

| | | | |
|---|---|---|---|
| 2553 | $1.65 Type **385** | 1·40 | 1·25 |
| 2554 | $1.65 William Hedley's "Puffing Billy", (1813–14) | 1·40 | 1·25 |
| 2555 | $1.65 Crampton locomotive of French Nord Railway, 1858 | 1·40 | 1·25 |
| 2556 | $1.65 Lawrence Machine Shop locomotive, U.S.A., 1860 | 1·40 | 1·25 |
| 2557 | $1.65 Natchez and Hamburg Railway steam locomotive "Mississippi", U.S.A., 1834 | 1·40 | 1·25 |
| 2558 | $1.65 Bury "Coppernob" locomotive, Furness Railway, 1846 | 1·40 | 1·25 |
| 2559 | $1.65 David Joy's "Jenny Lind", 1847 | 1·40 | 1·25 |
| 2560 | $1.65 Schenectady Atlantic locomotive, U.S.A., 1899 | 1·40 | 1·25 |
| 2561 | $1.65 Kitsons Class 1800 tank locomotive, Japan, 1881 | 1·40 | 1·25 |
| 2562 | $1.65 Pennsylvania Railroad express frieght | 1·40 | 1·25 |
| 2563 | $1.65 Karl Golsdorf's 4 cylinder locomotive, Austria | 1·40 | 1·25 |
| 2564 | $1.65 Series "E" locomotive, Russia, 1930 | 1·40 | 1·25 |
| **MS**2565 | Two sheets, each 72×100 mm. (a) $6 George Stephenson "Patentee" type locomotive, 1843. (b) $6 Brunel's trestle bridge over River Lynher, Cornwall Set of 2 sheets | 7·50 | 8·50 |

No. 2554 is dated "1860" in error.

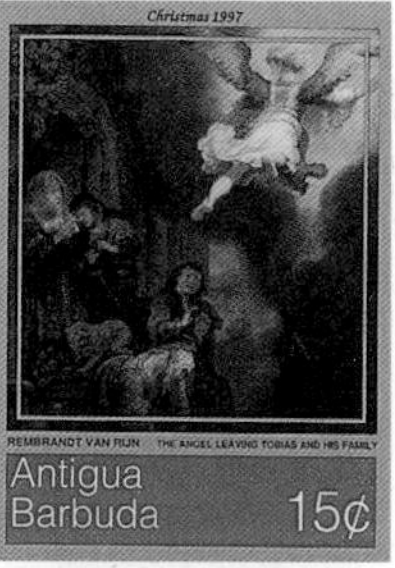


**386** "The Angel leaving Tobias and his Family" (Rembrandt)

**1997.** Christmas. Religious Paintings. Multicoloured.

| | | | |
|---|---|---|---|
| 2566 | 15c. Type **386** | 20 | 15 |
| 2567 | 25c. "The Resurrection" (Martin Knoller) | 30 | 20 |
| 2568 | 60c. "Astronomy" (Raphael) | 50 | 40 |
| 2569 | 75c. "Music-making Angel" (Melozzo da Forli) | 60 | 55 |
| 2570 | 90c. "Amor" (Parmigianino) | 70 | 60 |
| 2571 | $1.20 "Madonna and Child with Saints" (Rosso Fiorentino) | 80 | 85 |
| **MS**2572 | Two sheets, each 105×96 mm. (a) $6 "The Wedding of Tobias" (Gianantonio and Francesco Guardi) (horiz). (b) $6 "The Portinari Altarpiece" (Hugo van der Goes) (horiz) Set of 2 sheets | 7·50 | 8·50 |

**387** Diana, Princess of Wales

**1998.** Diana, Princess of Wales Commemoration. Multicoloured (except Nos. 2574 and 2581/2).

| | | | |
|---|---|---|---|
| 2573 | $1.65 Type **387** | 1·10 | 1·10 |
| 2574 | $1.65 Wearing hoop earrings (red and black) | 1·10 | 1·10 |
| 2575 | $1.65 Carrying bouquet | 1·10 | 1·10 |
| 2576 | $1.65 Wearing floral hat | 1·10 | 1·10 |
| 2577 | $1.65 With Prince Harry | 1·10 | 1·10 |
| 2578 | $1.65 Wearing white jacket | 1·10 | 1·10 |
| 2579 | $1.65 In kitchen | 1·10 | 1·10 |
| 2580 | $1.65 Wearing black and white dress | 1·10 | 1·10 |
| 2581 | $1.65 Wearing hat (brown and black) | 1·10 | 1·10 |
| 2582 | $1.65 Wearing floral print dress (brown and black) | 1·10 | 1·10 |
| 2583 | $1.65 Dancing with John Travolta | 1·10 | 1·10 |
| 2584 | $1.65 Wearing white hat and jacket | 1·10 | 1·10 |
| **MS**2585 | Two sheets, each 70×100 mm. (a) $6 Wearing red jumper. (b) $6 Wearing black dress for papal audience (brown and black) Set of 2 sheets | 7·50 | 8·00 |

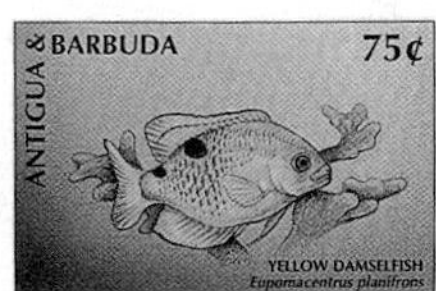


**388** Yellow Damselfish

**1998.** Fishes. Multicoloured.

| | | | |
|---|---|---|---|
| 2586 | 75c. Type **388** | 55 | 40 |
| 2587 | 90c. Barred hamlet | 65 | 50 |
| 2588 | $1 Yellow-tailed damselfish ("Jewelfish") | 70 | 55 |
| 2589 | $1.20 Blue-headed wrasse | 75 | 60 |
| 2590 | $1.50 Queen angelfish | 85 | 85 |
| 2591 | $1.65 Jackknife-fish | 90 | 95 |
| 2592 | $1.65 Spot-finned hogfish | 90 | 95 |
| 2593 | $1.65 Sergeant major | 90 | 95 |
| 2594 | $1.65 Neon goby | 90 | 95 |
| 2595 | $1.65 Jawfish | 90 | 95 |
| 2596 | $1.65 Flamefish | 90 | 95 |
| 2597 | $1.65 Rock beauty | 90 | 95 |
| 2598 | $1.65 Yellow-tailed snapper | 90 | 95 |
| 2599 | $1.65 Creole wrasse | 90 | 95 |
| 2600 | $1.65 Slender filefish | 90 | 95 |
| 2601 | $1.65 Long-spined squirrelfish | 90 | 95 |
| 2602 | $1.65 Royal gramma ("Fairy Basslet") | 90 | 95 |
| 2603 | $1.75 Queen triggerfish | 1·00 | 1·10 |
| **MS**2604 | Two sheets, each 80×110 mm. (a) $6 Porkfish. (b) $6 Black-capped basslet Set of 2 sheets | 7·50 | 8·50 |

Nos. 2591/6 and 2597/2602 respectively were printed together, se-tenant, with the backgrounds forming composite designs.

**389** First Church and Manse, 1822–40

**1998.** 175th Anniv of Cedar Hall Moravian Church. Multicoloured.

| | | | |
|---|---|---|---|
| 2605 | 20c. Type **389** | 20 | 20 |
| 2606 | 45c. Cedar Hall School, 1840 | 35 | 30 |
| 2607 | 75c. Hugh A. King, minister 1945–53 | 55 | 45 |
| 2608 | 90c. Present Church building | 65 | 50 |
| 2609 | $1.20 Water tank, 1822 | 75 | 65 |
| 2610 | $2 Former Manse, demolished 1978 | 1·25 | 1·50 |
| **MS**2611 | 100×70 mm. $6 Present church building (different) (50×37 mm.) | 3·25 | 4·00 |

**390** Europa Point Lighthouse, Gibraltar

**1998.** Lighthouses of the World. Multicoloured.

| | | | |
|---|---|---|---|
| 2612 | 45c. Type **390** | 50 | 40 |
| 2613 | 65c. Tierra del Fuego, Argentina (horiz) | 60 | 40 |
| 2614 | 75c. Point Loma, California, U.S.A. (horiz) | 70 | 45 |
| 2615 | 90c. Groenpoint, Cape Town, South Africa | 80 | 45 |
| 2616 | $1 Youghal, Cork, Ireland | 85 | 55 |
| 2617 | $1.20 Launceston, Tasmania, Australia | 90 | 75 |
| 2618 | $1.65 Point Abino, Ontario, Canada (horiz) | 1·25 | 1·50 |
| 2619 | $1.75 Great Inagua, Bahamas | 1·40 | 1·75 |
| **MS**2620 | 99×70 mm. $6 Cap Hatteras, North Carolina, U.S.A. | 5·00 | 5·50 |

No. 2613 is inscribed "Terra Del Fuego" in error.

**391** Pooh and Tigger (January)

**1998.** Through the Year with Winnie the Pooh. Multicoloured.

| | | | |
|---|---|---|---|
| 2621 | $1 Type **391** | 85 | 85 |
| 2622 | $1 Pooh and Piglet indoors (February) | 85 | 85 |
| 2623 | $1 Piglet hang-gliding with scarf (March) | 85 | 85 |
| 2624 | $1 Tigger, Pooh and Piglet on pond (April) | 85 | 85 |
| 2625 | $1 Kanga and Roo with posy of flowers (May) | 85 | 85 |
| 2626 | $1 Pooh on balloon and Owl (June) | 85 | 85 |
| 2627 | $1 Pooh, Eeyore, Tigger and Piglet gazing at stars (July) | 85 | 85 |
| 2628 | $1 Pooh and Piglet by stream (August) | 85 | 85 |
| 2629 | $1 Christopher Robin going to school (September) | 85 | 85 |
| 2630 | $1 Eeyore in fallen leaves (October) | 85 | 85 |
| 2631 | $1 Pooh and Rabbit gathering pumpkins (November) | 85 | 85 |
| 2632 | $1 Pooh and Piglet skiing (December) | 85 | 85 |
| **MS**2633 | Four sheets, each 126×101 mm. (a) $6 Pooh, Rabbit and Piglet with blanket (Spring). (b) $6 Pooh by pond (Summer). (c) $6 Pooh sweeping fallen leaves (Autumn). (d) $6 Pooh and Eeyore on ice (Winter) Set of 4 sheets | 16·00 | 16·00 |

**392** Miss Nellie Robinson (founder)

**1998.** Centenary of Thomas Oliver Robinson Memorial School.

| | | | | |
|---|---|---|---|---|
| 2634 | **392** | 20c. green and black | 20 | 15 |
| 2635 | - | 45c. multicoloured | 40 | 25 |
| 2636 | - | 65c. green and black | 55 | 45 |
| 2637 | - | 75c. multicoloured | 60 | 55 |
| 2638 | - | 90c. multicoloured | 70 | 60 |
| 2639 | - | $1.20 brown, green and black | 90 | 1·10 |
| **MS**2640 | | 106×76 mm. $6 brown | 3·25 | 3·75 |

DESIGNS—HORIZ: 45c. School photo, 1985; 65c. Former school building, 1930–49; 75c. Children with Mrs. Natalie Hurst (present headmistress); $1.20, Present school building, 1950. VERT: 90c. Miss Ina Loving (former teacher); $6 Miss Nellie Robinson (different).

**393** Spotted Eagle Ray

**1998.** International Year of the Ocean. Multicoloured.

| | | | |
|---|---|---|---|
| 2641-2665 | 40c.×25 Type **393**; Manta ray; Hawksbill turtle; Jellyfish; Queen angelfish; Octopus; Emperor angelfish; Regal angelfish; Porkfish; Racoon butterflyfish; Atlantic barracuda; Sea horse; Nautilus; Trumpetfish; White tip shark; Sunken Spanish galleon; Black-tip shark; Long-nosed butterflyfish; Green moray eel; Captain Nemo; Treasure chest; Hammerhead shark; Divers; Lionfish; Clownfish | | |
| 2666-2677 | 75c.×12 Maroon-tailed conure; Cocoi heron; Common tern; Rainbow lory ("Rainbow Lorikeet"); Saddleback butterflyfish; Goatfish and cat shark; Blue shark and stingray; Majestic snapper; Nassau grouper; Black-cap gramma and blue tang; Stingrays; Stingrays and giant starfish | | |
| **MS**2678 | Two sheets. (a) 68×98 mm. $6 Humpback whale. (b) 98×68 mm. $6 Fiddler ray Set of 2 sheets | 7·00 | 7·50 |

Nos. 2641/65 and 2666/77 respectively were printed together, se-tenant, with the backgrounds forming composite designs.

**394** "Savannah" (paddle-steamer)

**1998.** Ships of the World. Multicoloured.

| | | | |
|---|---|---|---|
| 2679 | $1.75 Type **394** | 1·25 | 1·40 |
| 2680 | $1.75 Viking longship | 1·25 | 1·40 |
| 2681 | $1.75 Greek galley | 1·25 | 1·40 |
| 2682 | $1.75 Sailing clipper | 1·25 | 1·40 |
| 2683 | $1.75 Dhow | 1·25 | 1·40 |
| 2684 | $1.75 Fishing catboat | 1·25 | 1·40 |
| **MS**2685 | Three sheets, each 100×70 mm. (a) $6 13th-century English warship (41×22 mm). (b) $6 Sailing dory (22×41 mm). (c) $6 Baltimore clipper (41×22 mm) Set of 3 sheets | 11·00 | 12·00 |

**395** Flags of Antigua and CARICOM

**1998.** 25th Anniv of Caribbean Community.

| | | | | |
|---|---|---|---|---|
| 2686 | **395** | $1 multicoloured | 1·25 | 1·25 |

**396** Ford, 1896

**1998.** Classic Cars. Multicoloured.

| | | | |
|---|---|---|---|
| 2687 | $1.65 Type **396** | 1·00 | 1·10 |
| 2688 | $1.65 Ford A, 1903 | 1·00 | 1·10 |
| 2689 | $1.65 Ford T, 1928 | 1·00 | 1·10 |
| 2690 | $1.65 Ford T, 1922 | 1·00 | 1·10 |
| 2691 | $1.65 Ford Blackhawk, 1929 | 1·00 | 1·10 |
| 2692 | $1.65 Ford Sedan, 1934 | 1·00 | 1·10 |
| 2693 | $1.65 Torpedo, 1911 | 1·00 | 1·10 |
| 2694 | $1.65 Mercedes 22, 1913 | 1·00 | 1·10 |
| 2695 | $1.65 Rover, 1920 | 1·00 | 1·10 |
| 2696 | $1.65 Mercedes-Benz, 1956 | 1·00 | 1·10 |
| 2697 | $1.65 Packard V-12, 1934 | 1·00 | 1·10 |
| 2698 | $1.65 Opel, 1924 | 1·00 | 1·10 |
| **MS**2699 | Two sheets, each 70×100 mm. (a) $6 Ford, 1908 (60×40 mm). (b) $6 Ford, 1929 (60×40 mm) Set of 2 sheets | 7·50 | 8·00 |

**397** Lockheed-Boeing General Dynamics Yf-22

**1998.** Modern Aircraft. Multicoloured.

| | | | |
|---|---|---|---|
| 2700 | $1.65 Type **397** | 1·10 | 1·25 |
| 2701 | $1.65 Dassault-Breguet Rafale BO 1 | 1·10 | 1·25 |
| 2702 | $1.65 MiG 29 | 1·10 | 1·25 |
| 2703 | $1.65 Dassault-Breguet Mirage 2000D | 1·10 | 1·25 |
| 2704 | $1.65 Rockwell B-1B "Lancer" | 1·10 | 1·25 |
| 2705 | $1.65 McDonnell-Douglas C-17A | 1·10 | 1·25 |
| 2706 | $1.65 Space Shuttle | 1·10 | 1·25 |
| 2707 | $1.65 SAAB "Grippen" | 1·10 | 1·25 |
| 2708 | $1.65 Eurofighter EF-2000 | 1·10 | 1·25 |
| 2709 | $1.65 Sukhoi SU 27 | 1·10 | 1·25 |
| 2710 | $1.65 Northrop B-2 | 1·10 | 1·25 |
| 2711 | $1.65 Lockheed F-117 "Nighthawk" | 1·10 | 1·25 |
| **MS**2712 | Two sheets, each 110×85 mm. (a) $6 F18 Hornet. (b) $6 Sukhoi SU 35 Set of 2 sheets | 7·50 | 8·00 |

No. **MS**2712b is inscribed "Sukhi" in error.

**398** Karl Benz (internal-combustion engine)

**1998.** Millennium Series. Famous People of the Twentieth Century. Inventors. Multicoloured.

| | | | |
|---|---|---|---|
| 2713 | $1 Type **398** | 80 | 80 |
| 2714 | $1 Early Benz car and Mercedes-Benz racing car (53×38 mm) | 80 | 80 |
| 2715 | $1 Atom bomb mushroom cloud (53×38 mm) | 80 | 80 |
| 2716 | $1 Albert Einstein (theory of relativity) | 80 | 80 |
| 2717 | $1 Leopold Godowsky Jr. and Leopold Damrosch Mannes (Kodachrome film) | 80 | 80 |
| 2718 | $1 Camera and transparencies (53×38 mm) | 80 | 80 |
| 2719 | $1 Heinkel He 178 (first turbo jet plane) (53×38 mm) | 80 | 80 |
| 2720 | $1 Dr. Hans Pabst von Ohain (jet turbine engine) | 80 | 80 |
| 2721 | $1 Rudolf Diesel (diesel engine) | 80 | 80 |
| 2722 | $1 Early Diesel engine and forms of transport (53×38 mm) | 80 | 80 |
| 2723 | $1 Zeppelin airship (53×38 mm) | 80 | 80 |
| 2724 | $1 Count Ferdinand von Zeppelin (airship pioneer) | 80 | 80 |
| 2725 | $1 Wilhelm Conrad Rontgen (X-rays) | 80 | 80 |
| 2726 | $1 X-ray of hand (53×38 mm) | 80 | 80 |
| 2727 | $1 Launch of Saturn rocket (53×38 mm) | 80 | 80 |
| 2728 | $1 Wernher von Braun (rocket research) | 80 | 80 |
| **MS**2729 | Two sheets, each 106×76 mm. (a) $6 Hans Geiger (Geiger counter). (b) $6 William Shockley (research into semi-conductors) Set of 2 sheets | 7·50 | 8·00 |

No. 2713 is inscribed "CARL BENZ" in error.

**399** Stylized Americas

**1998.** 50th Anniv of Organization of American States.

| | | | | |
|---|---|---|---|---|
| 2730 | **399** | $1 multicoloured | 70 | 70 |

**400** "Figures on the Seashore"

**1998.** 25th Death Anniv of Pablo Picasso (painter). Multicoloured.
2731 $1.20 Type **400** 75 70
2732 $1.65 "Three Figures under a Tree" (vert) 85 90
2733 $1.75 "Two Women running on the Beach" 95 1·10
**MS**2734 126×102 mm. $6 "Bullfight" 3·25 3·50

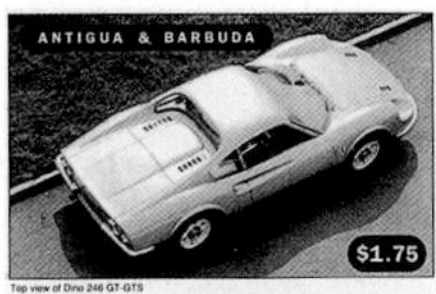

**401** Dino 246 GT-GTS

**1998.** Birth Centenary of Enzo Ferrari (car manufacturer). Multicoloured.
2735 $1.75 Type **401** 2·25 2·25
2736 $1.75 Front view of Dino 246 GT-GTS 2·25 2·25
2737 $1.75 365 GT4 BB 2·25 2·25
**MS**2738 104×72 mm. $6 Dino 246 GT-GTS (91×34 mm) 6·00 6·00

**402** Scout Handshake

**1998.** 19th World Scout Jamboree, Chile. Multicoloured.
2739 90c. Type **402** 60 55
2740 $1 Scouts hiking 75 70
2741 $1.20 Scout salute 90 1·10
**MS**2742 68×98 mm. $6 Lord Baden-Powell 3·25 3·50

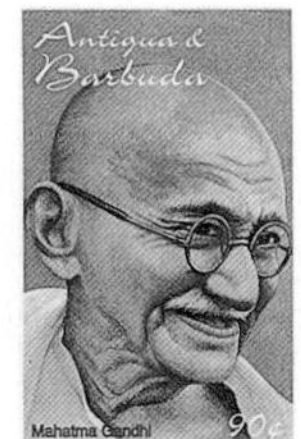

**403** Mahatma Gandhi

**1998.** 50th Death Anniv of Mahatma Gandhi. Multicoloured.
2743 90c. Type **403** 75 60
2744 $1 Gandhi seated 90 75
2745 $1.20 As young man 1·25 1·10
2746 $1.65 At primary school in Rajkot, aged 7 1·75 1·90
**MS**2747 100×70 mm. $6 Gandhi with staff 3·75 4·00

**404** McDonnell Douglas Phantom F-GR1

**1998.** 80th Anniv of Royal Air Force. Multicoloured.
2748 $1.75 Type **404** 1·25 1·40
2749 $1.75 Two Sepecat Jaguar GR1As 1·25 1·40
2750 $1.75 Panavia Tornado F3 1·25 1·40
2751 $1.75 McDonnell Douglas Phantom F-GR2 1·25 1·40
**MS**2752 Two sheets, each 90×68 mm. (a) $6 Golden eagle (bird) and Bristol F2B Fighter. (b) $6 Hawker Hurricane and EF-2000 Eurofighter Set of 2 sheets 8·00 8·50

**405** Diana, Princess of Wales

**1998.** 1st Death Anniv of Diana, Princess of Wales.
2753 **405** $1.20 multicoloured 1·00 1·00

**406** Brown Pelican

**1998.** Sea Birds of the World. Multicoloured.
2754 15c. Type **406** 30 20
2755 25c. Dunlin 40 20
2756 45c. Atlantic puffin 50 25
2757 75c. King eider 65 70
2758 75c. Inca tern 65 70
2759 75c. Little auk ("Dovekie") 65 70
2760 75c. Ross's gull 65 70
2761 75c. Common noddy ("Brown Noddy") 65 70
2762 75c. Marbled murrelet 65 70
2763 75c. Northern gannet 65 70
2764 75c. Razorbill 65 70
2765 75c. Long-tailed skua ("Long-tailed Jaegar") 65 70
2766 75c. Black guillemot 65 70
2767 75c. Whimbrel 65 70
2768 75c. American oystercatcher ("Oystercatcher") 30 35
2769 90c. Pied cormorant 65 70
**MS**2770 Two sheets, each 100×70 mm. (a) $6 Black skimmer. (b) $6 Wandering albatross Set of 2 sheets 7·50 8·00

Nos. 2757/68 were printed together, se-tenant, with the backgrounds forming a composite design.

No. 2760 is inscribed "ROSS' BULL" in error.

**407** Border Collie

**1998.** Christmas. Dogs. Multicoloured.
2771 15c. Type **407** 30 20
2772 25c. Dalmatian 40 20
2773 65c. Weimaraner 55 40
2774 75c. Scottish terrier 60 40
2775 90c. Long-haired dachshund 70 50
2776 $1.20 Golden retriever 90 90
2777 $2 Pekingese 1·60 1·90
**MS**2778 Two sheets, each 75×66 mm. (a) $6 Dalmatian. (b) $6 Jack Russell terrier Set of 2 sheets 7·50 8·00

**408** Mickey Mouse Sailing

**1999.** 70th Birthday of Mickey Mouse. Walt Disney characters participating in water sports. Multicoloured.
2779 $1 Type **408** 80 80
2780 $1 Mickey and Goofy sailing 80 80
2781 $1 Goofy windsurfing 80 80
2782 $1 Mickey sailing and seagull 80 80
2783 $1 Goofy sailing 80 80
2784 $1 Mickey windsurfing 80 80
2785 $1 Goofy running with surfboard 80 80
2786 $1 Mickey surfing 80 80
2787 $1 Donald Duck holding surfboard 80 80
2788 $1 Donald on surfboard (face value at right) 80 80
2789 $1 Minnie Mouse surfing in green shorts 80 80
2790 $1 Goofy surfing 80 80
2791 $1 Goofy in purple shorts waterskiing 80 80
2792 $1 Mickey waterskiing 80 80
2793 $1 Goofy waterskiing with Mickey 80 80
2794 $1 Donald on surfboard (face value at left) 80 80
2795 $1 Goofy in yellow shorts waterskiing 80 80
2796 $1 Minnie in pink shorts surfing 80 80
**MS**2797 Four sheets, each 127×102 mm. (a) $6 Goofy (horiz). (b) $6 Donald Duck. (c) $6 Minnie Mouse. (d) $6 Mickey Mouse Set of 4 sheets 14·00 15·00

**409** Hell's Gate Steel Orchestra, 1996

**1999.** 50th Anniv of Hell's Gate Steel Orchestra. Multicoloured.
2798 20c. Type **409** 20 15
2799 60c. Orchestra members, New York, 1992 40 35
2800 75c. Orchestra members with steel drums, 1950 50 45
2801 90c. Eustace Henry, 1964 60 50
2802 $1.20 Alston Henry playing double tenor 85 1·10
**MS**2803 Two sheets. (a) 100×70 mm. $4 Orchestra members, 1950 (vert). (b) 70×100 mm. $4 Eustace Henry, 1964 (vert) Set of 2 sheets 5·50 6·00

**410** Tulips

**1999.** Flowers. Multicoloured.
2804 60c. Type **410** 40 30
2805 75c. Fuschia 50 35
2806 90c. Morning glory (horiz) 60 60
2807 90c. Geranium (horiz) 60 60
2808 90c. Blue hibiscus (horiz) 60 60
2809 90c. Marigolds (horiz) 60 60
2810 90c. Sunflower (horiz) 60 60
2811 90c. Impatiens (horiz) 60 60
2812 90c. Petunia (horiz) 60 60
2813 90c. Pansy (horiz) 60 60
2814 90c. Saucer magnolia (horiz) 60 60
2815 $1 Primrose (horiz) 70 70
2816 $1 Bleeding heart (horiz) 70 70
2817 $1 Pink dogwood (horiz) 70 70
2818 $1 Peony (horiz) 70 70
2819 $1 Rose (horiz) 70 70
2820 $1 Hellebores (horiz) 70 70
2821 $1 Lily (horiz) 70 70
2822 $1 Violet (horiz) 70 70
2823 $1 Cherry blossom (horiz) 70 70
2824 $1.20 Calla lily 75 75
2825 $1.65 Sweet pea 90 1·10
**MS**2826 Two sheets. (a) 76×100 mm. $6 Sangria lily. (b) 106×76 mm. $6 Zinnias Set of 2 sheets 7·50 8·00

Nos. 2806/14 and 2815/23 respectively were each printed together, se-tenant, forming composite designs.

**411** Elle Macpherson

**1999.** "Australia '99" International Stamp Exhibition, Melbourne (1st issue). Elle Macpherson (model). Multicoloured.
2827 $1.20 Type **411** 75 80
2828 $1.20 Lying on couch 75 80
2829 $1.20 In swimsuit 75 80
2830 $1.20 Looking over shoulder 75 80
2831 $1.20 Wearing cream shirt 75 80
2832 $1.20 Wearing stetson 75 80
2833 $1.20 Wearing black T-shirt 75 80
2834 $1.20 Holding tree branch 75 80

See also Nos. 2875/92.

**412** "Luna 2" Moon Probe

**1999.** Satellites and Spacecraft. Multicoloured.
2835 $1.65 Type **412** 1·10 1·10
2836 $1.65 "Mariner 2" space probe 1·10 1·10
2837 $1.65 "Giotto" space probe 1·10 1·10
2838 $1.65 Rosat satellite 1·10 1·10
2839 $1.65 International Ultraviolet Explorer 1·10 1·10
2840 $1.65 "Ulysses" space probe 1·10 1·10
2841 $1.65 "Mariner 10" space probe 1·10 1·10
2842 $1.65 "Luna 9" Moon probe 1·10 1·10
2843 $1.65 Advanced X-ray Astrophysics Facility 1·10 1·10
2844 $1.65 "Magellan" space probe 1·10 1·10
2845 $1.65 "Pioneer – Venus 2" space probe 1·10 1·10
2846 $1.65 Infra-red Astronomy Satellite 1·10 1·10
**MS**2847 Two sheets, each 106×76 mm. (a) $6 "Salyut 1" space station (horiz). (b) $6 "MIR" space station (horiz) Set of 2 sheets 7·50 8·00

Nos. 2835/40 and 2841/46 repectively were each printed together, se-tenant, with the backgrounds forming composite designs.

**413** John Glenn entering "Mercury" Capsule, 1962

**1999.** John Glenn's Return to Space. Multicoloured.
2848 $1.75 Type **413** 1·25 1·25
2849 $1.75 Glenn in "Mercury" mission spacesuit 1·25 1·25
2850 $1.75 Fitting helmet for "Mercury" mission 1·25 1·25
2851 $1.75 Outside pressure chamber 1·25 1·25

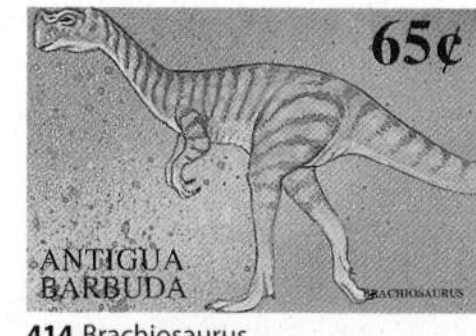

**414** Brachiosaurus

**1999.** Prehistoric Animals. Multicoloured.
2852 65c. Type **414** 65 40
2853 75c. Oviraptor (vert) 70 40
2854 $1 Homotherium 80 45
2855 $1.20 Macrauchenia (vert) 90 60
2856 $1.65 Struthiomimus 1·00 1·00
2857 $1.65 Corythosaurus 1·00 1·00
2858 $1.65 Dsungaripterus 1·00 1·00
2859 $1.65 Compsognathus 1·00 1·00
2860 $1.65 Prosaurolophus 1·00 1·00
2861 $1.65 Montanoceratops 1·00 1·00
2862 $1.65 Stegosaurus 1·00 1·00
2863 $1.65 Deinonychus 1·00 1·00
2864 $1.65 Ouranosaurus 1·00 1·00
2865 $1.65 Leptictidium 1·00 1·00
2866 $1.65 Ictitherium 1·00 1·00
2867 $1.65 Plesictis 1·00 1·00
2868 $1.65 Hemicyon 1·00 1·00
2869 $1.65 Diacodexis 1·00 1·00
2870 $1.65 Stylinodon 1·00 1·00
2871 $1.65 Kanuites 1·00 1·00
2872 $1.65 Chriacus 1·00 1·00
2873 $1.65 Argyrolagus 1·00 1·00
**MS**2874 Two sheets, each 110×85 mm. (a) $6 Eurhinodelphis. (b) $6 Pteranodon Set of 2 sheets 7·50 8·00

Nos. 2856/64 and 2865/73 respectively were each printed together, se-tenant, with the backgrounds forming composite designs.

**415** Two White Kittens

**1999.** "Australia '99" International Stamp Exhibition, Melbourne (2nd issue). Cats. Mult.

| | | | |
|---|---|---|---|
| 2875 | 35c. Type **415** | 30 | 20 |
| 2876 | 45c. Kitten with string | 40 | 25 |
| 2877 | 60c. Two kittens under blanket | 50 | 35 |
| 2878 | 75c. Two kittens in basket | 60 | 45 |
| 2879 | 90c. Kitten with ball | 70 | 50 |
| 2880 | $1 White kitten | 80 | 60 |
| 2881 | $1.65 Two kittens playing | 1·00 | 1·00 |
| 2882 | $1.65 Black and white kitten | 1·00 | 1·00 |
| 2883 | $1.65 Black kitten and sleeping cream kitten | 1·00 | 1·00 |
| 2884 | $1.65 White kitten with green string | 1·00 | 1·00 |
| 2885 | $1.65 Two sleeping kittens | 1·00 | 1·00 |
| 2886 | $1.65 White kitten with black tip to tail | 1·00 | 1·00 |
| 2887 | $1.65 Kitten with red string | 1·00 | 1·00 |
| 2888 | $1.65 Two long-haired kittens | 1·00 | 1·00 |
| 2889 | $1.65 Ginger kitten | 1·00 | 1·00 |
| 2890 | $1.65 Kitten playing with mouse | 1·00 | 1·00 |
| 2891 | $1.65 Kitten asleep on blue cushion | 1·00 | 1·00 |
| 2892 | $1.65 Tabby kitten | 1·00 | 1·00 |

**MS**2893 Two sheets, each 70×100 mm. (a) $6 Cat carrying kitten in mouth. (b) $6 Kitten in tree Set of 2 sheets 7·50 8·00

**416** Early Leipzig–Dresden Railway Carriage and Caroline Islands 1901 Yacht Type 5m. Stamp

**1999.** "iBRA '99" International Stamp Exhibition, Nuremberg. Multicoloured.

| | | | |
|---|---|---|---|
| 2894 | $1 Type **416** | 70 | 60 |
| 2895 | $1.20 Golsdorf steam locomotive and Caroline Islands 1901 Yacht type 1m. | 80 | 70 |
| 2896 | $1.65 Early Leipzig–Dresden Railway carriage and Caroline Islands 1899 20pf. optd on Germany | 1·00 | 1·10 |
| 2897 | $1.90 Golsdorf steam locomotive and Caroline Islands 1901 Yacht type 5pf. and 20pf. | 1·40 | 1·75 |

**MS**2898 165×110 mm. $6 Registration label for Ponape, Caroline Islands 3·25 3·50

**417** "People on Balcony of Sazaido" (Hokusai)

**1999.** 150th Death Anniv of Katsushika Hokusai (Japanese artist). Multicoloured.

| | | | |
|---|---|---|---|
| 2899 | $1.65 Type **417** | 1·00 | 1·00 |
| 2900 | $1.65 "Nakahara in Sagami Province" | 1·00 | 1·00 |
| 2901 | $1.65 "Defensive Positions" (two wrestlers) | 1·00 | 1·00 |
| 2902 | $1.65 "Defensive Positions" (three wrestlers) | 1·00 | 1·00 |
| 2903 | $1.65 "Mount Fuji in Clear Weather" | 1·00 | 1·00 |
| 2904 | $1.65 "Nihonbashi in Edo" | 1·00 | 1·00 |
| 2905 | $1.65 "Asakusa Honganji" | 1·00 | 1·00 |
| 2906 | $1.65 "Dawn at Isawa in Kai Province" | 1·00 | 1·00 |
| 2907 | $1.65 "Samurai with Bow and Arrow" (with arrows on ground) | 1·00 | 1·00 |
| 2908 | $1.65 "Samurai with Bow and Arrow" (trees in background) | 1·00 | 1·00 |
| 2909 | $1.65 "Kajikazawa in Kai Province" | 1·00 | 1·00 |
| 2910 | $1.65 "A Great Wave" | 1·00 | 1·00 |

**MS**2911 Two sheets, each 100×71 mm. (a) $6 "A Netsuke Workshop" (vert). (b) $6 "Gotenyama at Shinagawa on Tokaido Highway" (vert) Set of 2 sheets 7·50 8·00

No. 2903 is inscribed "MOUNT FUGI" in error.

**418** Sophie Rhys-Jones

**1999.** Royal Wedding. Multicoloured.

| | | | |
|---|---|---|---|
| 2912 | $3 Type **418** | 1·75 | 2·00 |
| 2913 | $3 Sophie and Prince Edward | 1·75 | 2·00 |
| 2914 | $3 Prince Edward | 1·75 | 2·00 |

**MS**2915 108×78 mm. $6 Prince Edward with Sophie Rhys-Jones and Windsor Castle (horiz) 3·25 3·50

**419** Three Children

**1999.** 10th Anniv of United Nations Rights of the Child Convention. Multicoloured.

| | | | |
|---|---|---|---|
| 2916 | $3 Type **419** | 1·75 | 2·00 |
| 2917 | $3 Adult hand holding child's hand | 1·75 | 2·00 |
| 2918 | $3 Dove and U.N. Headquarters | 1·75 | 2·00 |

**MS**2919 112×70 mm. $6 Dove 3·25 3·50

Nos. 2916/18 were printed together, se-tenant, forming a composite design.

**420** Crampton Type Railway Locomotive, 1855–69

**1999.** "PhilexFrance '99" International Stamp Exhibition, Paris. Railway Locomotives. Two sheets, each 106×81 mm, containing T **420** and similar design. Multicoloured.

**MS**2920 (a) $6 Type **420**. (b) $6 Compound type No. 232-U1 steam locomotive, 1949 Set of 2 sheets 7·50 8·00

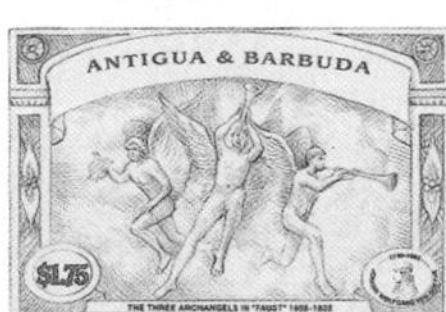

**421** Three Archangels from "Faust"

**1999.** 250th Birth Anniv of Johann von Goethe (German writer).

| | | | | |
|---|---|---|---|---|
| 2921 | **421** | $1.75 purple, mauve and black | 1·10 | 1·25 |
| 2922 | - | $1.75 blue, violet and black | 1·10 | 1·25 |
| 2923 | - | $1.75 green and black | 1·10 | 1·25 |

**MS**2924 – 79×101 mm. $6 black and brown 3·25 3·50

DESIGNS: No. 2922, Von Goethe and Von Schiller; 2923, Faust reclining with spirits; **MS**2924 Wolfgang von Goethe.

**422** "Missa Ferdie" (fishing launch)

**1999.** Local Ships and Boats. Multicoloured.

| | | | |
|---|---|---|---|
| 2925 | 25c. Type **422** | 25 | 20 |
| 2926 | 45c. Yachts in 32nd Annual Antigua International Sailing Week | 40 | 25 |
| 2927 | 60c. "Jolly Roger" (tourist ship) | 50 | 40 |
| 2928 | 90c. "Freewinds" (cruise liner) (10th anniv of first visit) | 70 | 60 |
| 2929 | $1.20 "Monarch of the Seas" (cruise liner) | 95 | 1·10 |

**MS**2930 98×62 mm. $4 "Freewinds" (11th anniv of maiden voyage) (50×37 mm) 2·75 3·00

**423** Fiery Jewel

**1999.** Butterflies. Multicoloured.

| | | | |
|---|---|---|---|
| 2931 | 65c. Type **423** | 60 | 40 |
| 2932 | 75c. Hewitson's blue hairstreak | 70 | 45 |
| 2933 | $1 California dog face (horiz) | 80 | 80 |
| 2934 | $1 Small copper (horiz) | 80 | 80 |
| 2935 | $1 Zebra swallowtail (horiz) | 80 | 80 |
| 2936 | $1 White "M" hairstreak (horiz) | 80 | 80 |
| 2937 | $1 Old world swallowtail (horiz) | 80 | 80 |
| 2938 | $1 Buckeye (horiz) | 80 | 80 |
| 2939 | $1 Apollo (horiz) | 80 | 80 |
| 2940 | $1 Sonoran blue (horiz) | 80 | 80 |
| 2941 | $1 Purple emperor (horiz) | 80 | 80 |
| 2942 | $1.20 Scarce bamboo page (horiz) | 90 | 90 |
| 2943 | $1.65 Paris peacock (horiz) | 1·25 | 1·40 |

**MS**2944 Two sheets. (a) 85×110 mm. $6 Monarch. (b) 110×85 mm. $6 Cairns birdwing (horiz) Set of 2 sheets 7·50 5·00

Nos. 2933/41 were printed together, se-tenant, forming a composite design.

**424** "Madonna and Child in Wreath of Flowers" (Rubens)

**1999.** Christmas. Religious Paintings.

| | | | | |
|---|---|---|---|---|
| 2945 | **424** | 15c. multicoloured | 20 | 10 |
| 2946 | - | 25c. black, stone & yellow | 25 | 15 |
| 2947 | - | 45c. multicoloured | 40 | 25 |
| 2948 | - | 60c. multicoloured | 50 | 30 |
| 2949 | - | $2 multicoloured | 1·50 | 1·60 |
| 2950 | - | $4 black, stone & yell | 2·75 | 3·25 |

**MS**2951 – 76×106 mm. $6 multicoloured 3·50 3·75

DESIGNS: 25c. "Shroud of Christ held by Two Angels" (Durer); 45c. "Madonna and Child enthroned between Two Saints" (Raphael); 60c. "Holy Family with Lamb" (Raphael); $2 "The Transfiguration" (Raphael); $4 "Three Putti holding Coat of Arms (Durer); $6 "Coronation of St. Catharine" (Rubens).

**425** Katharine Hepburn (actress)

**2000.** Senior Celebrities of the 20th Century. Mult.

| | | | |
|---|---|---|---|
| 2952 | 90c. Type **425** | 55 | 55 |
| 2953 | 90c. Martha Graham (dancer) | 55 | 55 |
| 2954 | 90c. Eubie Blake (jazz pianist) | 55 | 55 |
| 2955 | 90c. Agatha Christie (novelist) | 55 | 55 |
| 2956 | 90c. Eudora Welty (American novelist) | 55 | 55 |
| 2957 | 90c. Helen Hayes (actress) | 55 | 55 |
| 2958 | 90c. Vladimir Horowitz (concert pianist) | 55 | 55 |
| 2959 | 90c. Katharine Graham (newspaper publisher) | 55 | 55 |
| 2960 | 90c. Pablo Casals (cellist) | 55 | 55 |
| 2961 | 90c. Pete Seeger (folk singer) | 55 | 55 |
| 2962 | 90c. Andres Segovia (guitarist) | 55 | 55 |
| 2963 | 90c. Frank Lloyd Wright (architect) | 55 | 55 |

**426** Sir Cliff Richard

**2000.** 60th Birthday of Sir Cliff Richard (entertainer).

| | | | | |
|---|---|---|---|---|
| 2964 | **426** | $1.65 multicoloured | 1·00 | 1·00 |

**427** Charlie Chaplin

**2000.** Charlie Chaplin (actor and director) Commemoration. Showing film scenes. Mult.

| | | | |
|---|---|---|---|
| 2965 | $1.65 Standing in street (*Modern Times*) | 90 | 90 |
| 2966 | $1.65 Hugging man (*The Gold Rush*) | 90 | 90 |
| 2967 | $1.65 Type **427** | 90 | 90 |
| 2968 | $1.65 Wielding tools (*Modern Times*) | 90 | 90 |
| 2969 | $1.65 With hands on hips (*The Gold Rush*) | 90 | 90 |
| 2970 | $1.65 Wearing cape (*The Gold Rush*) | 90 | 90 |

**428** Streamertail

**2000.** "The Stamp Show 2000" International Stamp Exhibition, London. Birds of the Caribbean. Mult.

| | | | |
|---|---|---|---|
| 2971 | 75c. Type **428** | 50 | 35 |
| 2972 | 90c. Yellow-bellied sapsucker | 60 | 40 |
| 2973 | $1.20 Rufous-tailed jacamar | 75 | 75 |
| 2974 | $1.20 Scarlet macaw | 75 | 75 |
| 2975 | $1.20 Yellow-crowned amazon ("Yellow-fronted Amazon") | 75 | 75 |
| 2976 | $1.20 Golden conure ("Queen-of-Bavaria") | 75 | 75 |
| 2977 | $1.20 Nanday conure | 75 | 75 |
| 2978 | $1.20 Jamaican tody | 75 | 75 |
| 2979 | $1.20 Smooth-billed ani | 75 | 75 |
| 2980 | $1.20 Puerto Rican woodpecker | 75 | 75 |
| 2981 | $1.20 Ruby-throated hummingbird | 75 | 75 |
| 2982 | $1.20 Common ground dove | 75 | 75 |
| 2983 | $1.20 American wood ibis ("Wood Stork") | 75 | 75 |
| 2984 | $1.20 Saffron finch | 75 | 75 |
| 2985 | $1.20 Green-backed heron | 75 | 75 |
| 2986 | $1.20 Lovely cotinga | 75 | 75 |
| 2987 | $1.20 St. Vincent amazon ("St. Vincent Parrot") | 75 | 75 |
| 2988 | $1.20 Cuban grassquit | 75 | 75 |
| 2989 | $1.20 Red-winged blackbird | 75 | 75 |
| 2990 | $2 Spectacled owl | 1·40 | 1·50 |

**MS**2991 Two sheets, each 80×106 mm. (a) $6 Vermillion flycatcher (50×37 mm). (b) $6 Red-capped manakin (37×50 mm) Set of 2 sheets 7·00 7·50

Nos. 2974/81 and 2982/9 were each printed together, se-tenant, with the backgrounds forming composite designs.

No. 2981 is inscribed "Arhilochus colubria" in error.

**429** "Arthur Goodwin"

**2000.** 400th Birth Anniv of Sir Anthony Van Dyck (Flemish painter). Multicoloured.

| No. | Description | Unused | Used |
|---|---|---|---|
| 2992 | $1.20 Type **429** | 75 | 75 |
| 2993 | $1.20 "Sir Thomas Wharton" | 75 | 75 |
| 2994 | $1.20 "Mary Villiers, Daughter of Duke of Buckingham" | 75 | 75 |
| 2995 | $1.20 "Christina Bruce, Countess of Devonshire" | 75 | 75 |
| 2996 | $1.20 "James Hamilton, Duke of Hamilton" | 75 | 75 |
| 2997 | $1.20 "Henry Danvers, Earl of Danby" | 75 | 75 |
| 2998 | $1.20 "Marie de Raet, Wife of Philippe le Roy" | 75 | 75 |
| 2999 | $1.20 "Jacomo de Cachiopin" | 75 | 75 |
| 3000 | $1.20 "Princess Henrietta of Lorraine attended by a Page" | 75 | 75 |
| 3001 | $1.20 "Portrait of a Man" | 75 | 75 |
| 3002 | $1.20 "Portrait of a Woman" | 75 | 75 |
| 3003 | $1.20 "Philippe le Roy, Seigneur de Ravels" | 75 | 75 |
| 3004 | $1.20 "Charles I in State Robes" | 75 | 75 |
| 3005 | $1.20 "Queen Henrietta Maria" (in white dress) | 75 | 75 |
| 3006 | $1.20 "Queen Henrietta Maria with Sir Jeffrey Hudson" | 75 | 75 |
| 3007 | $1.20 "Charles I in Armour" | 75 | 75 |
| 3008 | $1.20 "Queen Henrietta Maria in Profile facing right" | 75 | 75 |
| 3009 | $1.20 "Queen Henrietta Maria" (in black dress) | 75 | 75 |
| **MS**3010 | Six sheets. (a) 102×128 mm. $5 "Charles I on Horseback". (b) 102×128 mm. $5 "Charles I Hunting". (c) 128×102 mm. $5 "Charles I with Queen Henrietta Maria". (d) 128×102 mm. $5 "Charles I" (from Three Aspects portrait). (e) 102×128 mm. $6 "William, Lord Russell". (f) 102×128 mm. $6 "Two Sons of Duke of Lennox" Set of 6 sheets | 17·00 | 19·00 |

No. 2994 is inscribed "Mary Villers", 3002 "Portrait of a Women", 3005 "Henrieta Maria" and **MS**3010f "Duke of Lenox", all in error.

**430** *Eupolea miniszeki*

**2000.** Butterflies. Multicoloured.

| No. | Description | Unused | Used |
|---|---|---|---|
| 3011 | $1.65 Type **430** | 90 | 90 |
| 3012 | $1.65 *Heliconius doris* | 90 | 90 |
| 3013 | $1.65 *Evenus coronata* | 90 | 90 |
| 3014 | $1.65 *Papilio anchisiades* | 90 | 90 |
| 3015 | $1.65 *Syrmatia dorilas* | 90 | 90 |
| 3016 | $1.65 *Morpho patroclus* | 90 | 90 |
| 3017 | $1.65 *Mesosemia loruhama* | 90 | 90 |
| 3018 | $1.65 *Bia actorion* | 90 | 90 |
| 3019 | $1.65 *Anteos clorinde* | 90 | 90 |
| 3020 | $1.65 *Menander menande* | 90 | 90 |
| 3021 | $1.65 *Catasticta manco* | 90 | 90 |
| 3022 | $1.65 *Urania leilus* | 90 | 90 |
| 3023 | $1.65 *Theope eudocia* (vert) | 90 | 90 |
| 3024 | $1.65 *Uranus sloanus* (vert) | 90 | 90 |
| 3025 | $1.65 *Helicopis cupido* (vert) | 90 | 90 |
| 3026 | $1.65 *Papilio velovis* (vert) | 90 | 90 |
| 3027 | $1.65 *Graphium androcles* (vert) | 90 | 90 |
| 3028 | $1.65 *Mesene phareus* (vert) | 90 | 90 |
| **MS**3029 | Three sheets. (a) 110×85 mm. $6 *Graphium encelades*. (b) 110×85 mm. $6 *Graphium milon*. (c) 85×110 mm. $6 *Hemlargus isola* (vert) Set of 3 sheets | 9·50 | 10·00 |

Nos. 3011/16, 3017/22 and 3023/8 were each printed together, se-tenant, with the backgrounds forming composite designs.

**431** Boxer

**2000.** Cats and Dogs. Multicoloured.

| No. | Description | Unused | Used |
|---|---|---|---|
| 3030 | 90c. Type **431** | 60 | 40 |
| 3031 | $1 Alaskan malamute | 70 | 45 |
| 3032 | $1.65 Bearded collie | 90 | 90 |
| 3033 | $1.65 Cardigan Welsh corgi | 90 | 90 |
| 3034 | $1.65 Saluki (red) | 90 | 90 |
| 3035 | $1.65 Basset hound | 90 | 90 |
| 3036 | $1.65 White standard poodle | 90 | 90 |
| 3037 | $1.65 Boston terrier | 90 | 90 |
| 3038 | $1.65 Long-haired blue and white cat (horiz) | 90 | 90 |
| 3039 | $1.65 Snow shoe (horiz) | 90 | 90 |
| 3040 | $1.65 Persian (horiz) | 90 | 90 |
| 3041 | $1.65 Chocolate lynx point (horiz) | 90 | 90 |
| 3042 | $1.65 Brown and white sphynx (horiz) | 90 | 90 |
| 3043 | $1.65 White tortoiseshell (horiz) | 90 | 90 |
| 3044 | $2 Wirehaired pointer | 1·10 | 1·10 |
| 3045 | $4 Saluki (black) | 2·00 | 2·25 |
| **MS**3046 | Two sheets. (a) 106×71 mm. $6 Cavalier King Charles spaniel. (b) 111×81 mm. $6 Lavender tortie Set of 2 sheets | 7·50 | 8·00 |

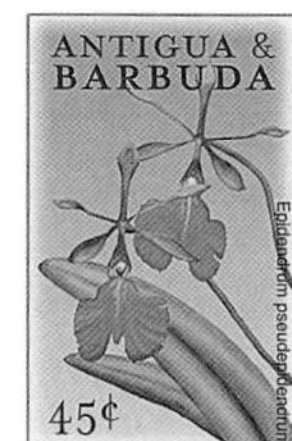

**432** *Epidendrum pseudepidendrum*

**2000.** Flowers of the Caribbean. Multicoloured.

| No. | Description | Unused | Used |
|---|---|---|---|
| 3047 | 45c. Type **432** | 35 | 25 |
| 3048 | 65c. *Odontoglossum cervantesii* | 50 | 30 |
| 3049 | 75c. *Cattleya dowiana* | 60 | 35 |
| 3050 | 90c. *Beloperone guttata* | 70 | 40 |
| 3051 | $1 *Colliandra haematocephala* | 75 | 50 |
| 3052 | $1.20 *Brassavola nodosa* | 85 | 65 |
| 3053 | $1.65 *Pseudocalymna alliaceum* | 1·00 | 1·00 |
| 3054 | $1.65 *Datura candida* | 1·00 | 1·00 |
| 3055 | $1.65 *Ipomoea tuberosa* | 1·00 | 1·00 |
| 3056 | $1.65 *Allamanda cathartica* | 1·00 | 1·00 |
| 3057 | $1.65 *Aspasia epidendroides* | 1·00 | 1·00 |
| 3058 | $1.65 *Maxillaria cucullata* | 1·00 | 1·00 |
| 3059 | $1.65 *Anthurium andreanum* | 1·00 | 1·00 |
| 3060 | $1.65 *Doxantha unguiscati* | 1·00 | 1·00 |
| 3061 | $1.65 *Hibiscus rosa-sinensis* | 1·00 | 1·00 |
| 3062 | $1.65 *Canna indica* | 1·00 | 1·00 |
| 3063 | $1.65 *Heliconius umilis* | 1·00 | 1·00 |
| 3064 | $1.65 *Strelitzia reginae* | 1·00 | 1·00 |
| 3065 | $1.65 *Masdevallia coccinea* | 1·00 | 1·00 |
| 3066 | $1.65 *Paphinia cristata* | 1·00 | 1·00 |
| 3067 | $1.65 *Vanilla planifolia* | 1·00 | 1·00 |
| 3068 | $1.65 *Cattleya forbesii* | 1·00 | 1·00 |
| 3069 | $1.65 *Lycaste skinneri* | 1·00 | 1·00 |
| 3070 | $1.65 *Cattleya percivaliana* | 1·00 | 1·00 |
| **MS**3071 | Three sheets, each 74×103 mm. (a) $6 *Cattleya leopoldiie*. (b) $6 *Strelitzia reginae*. (c) $6 *Rossioglossum grande* Set of 3 sheets | 9·50 | 10·00 |

No. 3061 is inscribed "rosa-senensis" and **MS**3071b "regenae", both in error.

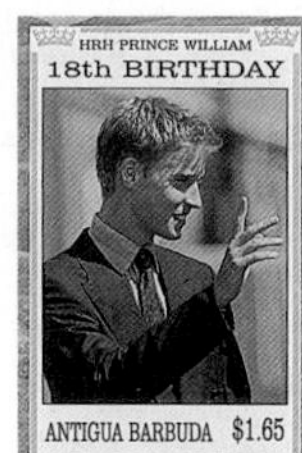

**433** Prince William

**2000.** 18th Birthday of Prince William. Multicoloured.

| No. | Description | Unused | Used |
|---|---|---|---|
| 3072 | $1.65 Prince William waving | 1·00 | 1·00 |
| 3073 | $1.65 Wearing Eton school uniform | 1·00 | 1·00 |
| 3074 | $1.65 Wearing grey suit | 1·00 | 1·00 |
| 3075 | $1.65 Type **433** | 1·00 | 1·00 |
| **MS**3076 | 100×80 mm. $6 Princess Diana with Princes William and Harry (37×50 mm) | 3·50 | 3·75 |

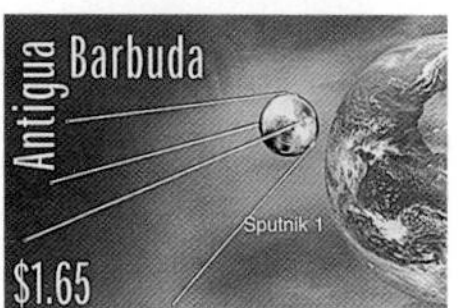

**434** "Sputnik I"

**2000.** "EXPO 2000" World Stamp Exhibition, Anaheim, U.S.A. Space Satellites. Multicoloured.

| No. | Description | Unused | Used |
|---|---|---|---|
| 3077 | $1.65 Type **434** | 1·00 | 1·00 |
| 3078 | $1.65 "Explorer I" | 1·00 | 1·00 |
| 3079 | $1.65 "Mars Express" | 1·00 | 1·00 |
| 3080 | $1.65 "Lunik I Solnik" | 1·00 | 1·00 |
| 3081 | $1.65 "Ranger 7" | 1·00 | 1·00 |
| 3082 | $1.65 "Mariner 4" | 1·00 | 1·00 |
| 3083 | $1.65 "Mariner 10" | 1·00 | 1·00 |
| 3084 | $1.65 "Soho" | 1·00 | 1·00 |
| 3085 | $1.65 "Mariner 2" | 1·00 | 1·00 |
| 3086 | $1.65 "Giotto" | 1·00 | 1·00 |
| 3087 | $1.65 "Exosat" | 1·00 | 1·00 |
| 3088 | $1.65 "Pioneer Venus" | 1·00 | 1·00 |
| **MS**3089 | Two sheets, each 106×76 mm. (a) $6 "Vostok I". (b) $6 Hubble Space Telescope Set of 2 sheets | 7·50 | 8·00 |

Nos. 3077/82 and 3083/8 were each printed together, se-tenant, with the backgrounds forming composite designs.

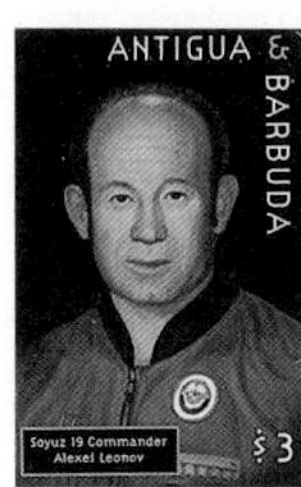

**435** Alexei Leonov (Commander of "Soyuz 19")

**2000.** 25th Anniv of "Apollo–Soyuz" Joint Project. Multicoloured.

| No. | Description | Unused | Used |
|---|---|---|---|
| 3090 | $3 Type **435** | 1·75 | 2·00 |
| 3091 | $3 "Soyuz 19" | 1·75 | 2·00 |
| 3092 | $3 Valeri Kubasov ("Soyuz 19" engineer) | 1·75 | 2·00 |
| **MS**3093 | 71×88 mm. $6 Alexei Leonov and Thomas Stafford (Commander of "Apollo 18") | 3·25 | 3·50 |

**436** Anna Karina in *Une Femme est Une Femme*, 1961

**2000.** 50th Anniv of Berlin Film Festival. Designs showing actors, directors and film scenes. Mult.

| No. | Description | Unused | Used |
|---|---|---|---|
| 3094 | $1.65 Type **436** | 1·00 | 1·00 |
| 3095 | $1.65 *Carmen Jones*, 1955 | 1·00 | 1·00 |
| 3096 | $1.65 *Die Ratten*, 1955 | 1·00 | 1·00 |
| 3097 | $1.65 *Die Vier im Jeep*, 1951 | 1·00 | 1·00 |
| 3098 | $1.65 Sidney Poitier in *Lilies of the Field*, 1963 | 1·00 | 1·00 |
| 3099 | $1.65 *Invitation to the Dance*, 1956 | 1·00 | 1·00 |
| **MS**3100 | 97×103 mm. $6 Kate Winslet in *Sense and Sensibility*, 1996 | 3·25 | 3·50 |

No. 3096 is inscribed "GOLDER BERLIN BEAR" and **MS**3100 shows the award date "1966" in error.

**437** George Stephenson and *Locomotion No. 1*, 1825

**2000.** 175th Anniv of Stockton and Darlington Line (first public railway). Multicoloured.

| No. | Description | Unused | Used |
|---|---|---|---|
| 3101 | $3 Type **437** | 2·00 | 2·25 |
| 3102 | $3 Camden and Amboy Railroad locomotive *John Bull*, 1831 | 2·00 | 2·25 |

**438** Statue of Johann Sebastian Bach

**2000.** 250th Death Anniv of Johann Sebastian Bach (German composer). Sheet 77×88 mm.

| No. | Description | Unused | Used |
|---|---|---|---|
| **MS**3103 | $6 multicoloured | 3·50 | 3·75 |

**439** Albert Einstein

**2000.** Election of Albert Einstein (mathematical physicist) as Time Magazine "Man of the Century". Sheet 117×91 mm.

| No. | Description | Unused | Used |
|---|---|---|---|
| **MS**3104 | $6 multicoloured | 3·25 | 3·50 |

**440** LZ-1 Airship, 1900

**2000.** Centenary of First Zeppelin Flight.

| No. | Type | Description | Unused | Used |
|---|---|---|---|---|
| 3105 | **440** | $3 brown, black and blue | 1·75 | 2·00 |
| 3106 | - | $3 brown, black and blue | 1·75 | 2·00 |
| 3107 | - | $3 multicoloured | 1·75 | 2·00 |
| **MS**3108 | – | 93×66 mm. $6 multicoloured | 3·25 | 3·50 |

DESIGNS: No. 3106, LZ-2, 1906; 3107, LZ-3, 1906. (50×37 mm)—No. **MS**3108, LZ-7 *Deutschland*, 1910.

Nos. 3105/7 were printed together, se-tenant, with the backgrounds forming a composite design.

**441** Marcus Latimer Hurley (cycling), St. Louis (1904)

**2000.** Olympic Games, Sydney. Multicoloured.

| No. | Description | Unused | Used |
|---|---|---|---|
| 3109 | $2 Type **441** | 1·40 | 1·40 |
| 3110 | $2 Diving | 1·40 | 1·40 |
| 3111 | $2 Flaminio Stadium, Rome (1960) and Italian flag | 1·40 | 1·40 |
| 3112 | $2 Ancient Greek javelin thrower | 1·40 | 1·40 |

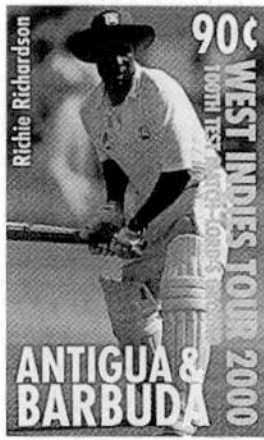

**442** Richie Richardson

**2000.** West Indies Cricket Tour and 100th Test Match at Lord's. Multicoloured.

| No. | Description | Unused | Used |
|---|---|---|---|
| 3113 | 90c. Type **442** | 75 | 40 |
| 3114 | $5 Viv Richards | 3·25 | 3·50 |
| **MS**3115 | 121×104 mm. $6 Lord's Cricket Ground (horiz) | 3·50 | 3·75 |

No. 3114 is inscribed "Viv Richard" in error.

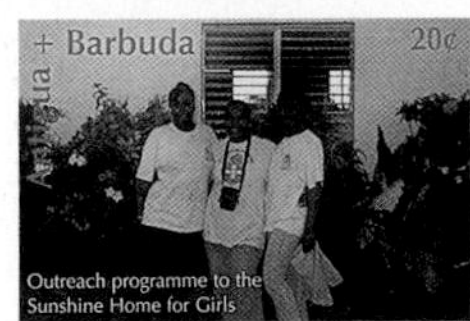

**443** Outreach Programme at Sunshine Home for Girls

**2000.** Girls Brigade. Multicoloured.

| | | | |
|---|---|---|---|
| 3116 | 20c. Type **443** | 20 | 15 |
| 3117 | 60c. Ullida Rawlins Gill (International Vice President) (vert) | 40 | 30 |
| 3118 | 75c. Officers and girls | 50 | 35 |
| 3119 | 90c. Girl with flag (vert) | 70 | 50 |
| 3120 | $1.20 Members of 8th Antigua Company with flag (vert) | 95 | 1·10 |
| **MS**3121 | 102×124 mm. $5 Girl Brigade badge (vert) | 3·00 | 3·25 |

**444** Lady Elizabeth Bowes-Lyon as Young Girl

**2000.** "Queen Elizabeth the Queen Mother's Century".

| | | | | |
|---|---|---|---|---|
| 3122 | **444** | $2 multicoloured | 1·40 | 1·40 |
| 3123 | - | $2 black and gold | 1·40 | 1·40 |
| 3124 | - | $2 black and gold | 1·40 | 1·40 |
| 3125 | - | $2 multicoloured | 1·40 | 1·40 |
| **MS**3126 | - | 153×157 mm. $6 multicoloured | 3·50 | 3·75 |

DESIGNS: No. 3123, Queen Elizabeth in 1940; 3124, Queen Mother with Princess Anne, 1951; 3125, Queen Mother in Canada, 1989; **MS**3126, Queen Mother inspecting guard of honour.

No. **MS**3126 also shows the Royal Arms embossed in gold.

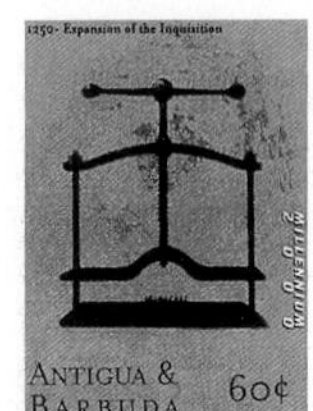

**445** Thumbscrew (Expansion of Inquisition, 1250)

**2000.** New Millennium. People and Events of Thirteenth Century (1250–1300). Multicoloured (except No. 3127).

| | | | |
|---|---|---|---|
| 3127 | 60c. Type **445** (black and red) | 40 | 40 |
| 3128 | 60c. Chartres Cathedral (completed, 1260) | 40 | 40 |
| 3129 | 60c. Donor's sculpture, Naumberg (completed, 1260) | 40 | 40 |
| 3130 | 60c. Delegates (Simon de Montfort's Parliament, 1261) | 40 | 40 |
| 3131 | 60c. "Maesta" (Cimabue) (painted 1270) | 40 | 40 |
| 3132 | 60c. Marco Polo (departure from Venice, 1271) | 40 | 40 |
| 3133 | 60c. "Divine Wind" (Kamikaze wind saves Japan from invasion, 1274) | 40 | 40 |
| 3134 | 60c. St. Thomas Aquinas (died 1274) | 40 | 40 |
| 3135 | 60c. Arezzo Cathedral (completed 1277) | 40 | 40 |
| 3136 | 60c. Margrethe ("The Maid of Norway") (crowned Queen of Scotland, 1286) | 40 | 40 |
| 3137 | 60c. Jewish refugees (Expulsion of Jews from England, 1290) | 40 | 40 |
| 3138 | 60c. Muslim horseman (capture of Acre, 1291) | 40 | 40 |
| 3139 | 60c. Moshe de Leon (compiles *The Zohar*, 1291) | 40 | 40 |
| 3140 | 60c. Knights in combat (German Civil War, 1292–98) | 40 | 40 |
| 3141 | 60c. Kublai Khan (died 1294) | 40 | 40 |
| 3142 | 60c. Dante (writes *La Vita Nuova*, 1295) (59×39 mm) | 40 | 40 |
| 3143 | 60c. "Autumn Colours on Quiao and Hua Mountains" (Zhan Mengfu) (painted 1296) | 40 | 40 |

**446** "Admonishing the Court Ladies" (after Ku K'ai-Chih)

**2000.** New Millennium. Two Thousand Years of Chinese Paintings. Multicoloured.

| | | | |
|---|---|---|---|
| 3144 | 25c. Type **446** | 20 | 20 |
| 3145 | 25c. Ink on silk drawing from Zhan Jadashan | 20 | 20 |
| 3146 | 25c. Ink and colour on silk drawing from Mawangdui Tomb | 20 | 20 |
| 3147 | 25c. "Scholars collating Texts" (attr Yang Zihua) | 20 | 20 |
| 3148 | 25c. "Spring Outing" (attr Zhan Ziqian) | 20 | 20 |
| 3149 | 25c. "Portrait of the Emperors" (attr Yen Liben) | 20 | 20 |
| 3150 | 25c. "Sailing Boats and Riverside Mansion" (attr Li Sixun) | 20 | 20 |
| 3151 | 25c. "Two Horses and Groom" (Han Kan) | 20 | 20 |
| 3152 | 25c. "King's Portrait" (attr Wu Daozi) | 20 | 20 |
| 3153 | 25c. "Court Ladies wearing Flowered Headdresses" (attr Zhou Fang) | 20 | 20 |
| 3154 | 25c. "Distant Mountain Forest" (mountain) (Juran) | 20 | 20 |
| 3155 | 25c. "Mount Kuanglu" (Jiang Hao) | 20 | 20 |
| 3156 | 25c. "Pheasant and Small Birds" (Huang Jucai) | 20 | 20 |
| 3157 | 25c. "Deer among Red Maples" (anon) | 20 | 20 |
| 3158 | 25c. "Distant Mountain Forest" (river and fields) (Juran) | 20 | 20 |
| 3159 | 25c. "Literary Gathering" (Han Huang) (57×39 mm) | 20 | 20 |
| 3160 | 25c. "Birds and Insects" (Huang Quan) | 20 | 20 |

No. 3148 is inscribed "SPRINTING", No. 3150 "MASION" and No. 3153 "HEADRESSES", all in error.

**447** King Donald III of Scotland

**2000.** Monarchs of the Millennium.

| | | | | |
|---|---|---|---|---|
| 3161 | **447** | $1.65 black, stone and brown | 1·00 | 1·00 |
| 3162 | - | $1.65 black, stone and brown | 1·00 | 1·00 |
| 3163 | - | $1.65 black, stone and brown | 1·00 | 1·00 |
| 3164 | - | $1.65 black, stone and brown | 1·00 | 1·00 |
| 3165 | - | $1.65 black, stone and brown | 1·00 | 1·00 |
| 3166 | - | $1.65 black, stone and brown | 1·00 | 1·00 |
| 3167 | - | $1.65 multicoloured | 1·00 | 1·00 |
| 3168 | - | $1.65 multicoloured | 1·00 | 1·00 |
| 3169 | - | $1.65 multicoloured | 1·00 | 1·00 |
| 3170 | - | $1.65 multicoloured | 1·00 | 1·00 |
| 3171 | - | $1.65 multicoloured | 1·00 | 1·00 |
| 3172 | - | $1.65 multicoloured | 1·00 | 1·00 |
| **MS**3173 | - | Two sheets, each 115×135 mm. (a) $6 mult. (b) $6 mult Set of 2 sheets | 7·50 | 8·00 |

DESIGNS: No. 3162, King Duncan I of Scotland; 3163, King Duncan II of Scotland; 3164, King Macbeth of Scotland; 3165, King Malcolm III of Scotland; 3166, King Edgar of Scotland; 3167, King Charles I of England and Scotland; 3168, King Charles II of England and Scotland; 3169, Prince Charles Edward Stuart ("The Young Pretender"); 3170, King James II of England and VII of Scotland; 3171, King James II of Scotland; 3172, King James III of Scotland; **MS**3173a, King Robert I of Scotland; **MS**3173b, Queen Anne of Great Britain.

No. 3169 is inscribed "George III 1760–1820 Great Britain" in error.

**2000.** Popes of the Millennium. As T **447**. Each black, yellow and green.

| | | | |
|---|---|---|---|
| 3174 | $1.65 Alexander VI (bareheaded) | 1·00 | 1·00 |
| 3175 | $1.65 Benedict XIII | 1·00 | 1·00 |
| 3176 | $1.65 Boniface IX | 1·00 | 1·00 |
| 3177 | $1.65 Alexander VI (wearing cap) | 1·00 | 1·00 |
| 3178 | $1.65 Clement VIII | 1·00 | 1·00 |
| 3179 | $1.65 Clement VI | 1·00 | 1·00 |
| 3180 | $1.65 John Paul II | 1·00 | 1·00 |
| 3181 | $1.65 Benedict XV | 1·00 | 1·00 |
| 3182 | $1.65 John XXIII | 1·00 | 1·00 |
| 3183 | $1.65 Pius XI | 1·00 | 1·00 |
| 3184 | $1.65 Pius XII | 1·00 | 1·00 |
| 3185 | $1.65 Paul VI | 1·00 | 1·00 |
| **MS**3186 | Two sheets, each 115×135 mm. (a) $6 Pius II (black, yellow and black). (b) $6 Pius VII (black, yellow and black) Set of 2 sheets | 7·50 | 8·00 |

No. 3181 is inscribed "BENIDICT XV" in error.

**448** Agouti

**2000.** Fauna of the Rain Forest. Multicoloured.

| | | | |
|---|---|---|---|
| 3187 | 75c. Type **448** | 60 | 35 |
| 3188 | 90c. Capybara | 70 | 40 |
| 3189 | $1.20 Basilisk lizard | 80 | 55 |
| 3190 | $1.65 Green violetear ("Green Violet-Ear Hummingbird") | 1·00 | 1·00 |
| 3191 | $1.65 Harpy eagle | 1·00 | 1·00 |
| 3192 | $1.65 Three-toed sloth | 1·00 | 1·00 |
| 3193 | $1.65 White uakari monkey | 1·00 | 1·00 |
| 3194 | $1.65 Anteater | 1·00 | 1·00 |
| 3195 | $1.65 Coati | 1·00 | 1·00 |
| 3196 | $1.75 Red-eyed tree frog | 1·00 | 1·00 |
| 3197 | $1.75 Black spider monkey | 1·00 | 1·00 |
| 3198 | $1.75 Emerald toucanet | 1·00 | 1·00 |
| 3199 | $1.75 Kinkajou | 1·00 | 1·00 |
| 3200 | $1.75 Spectacled bear | 1·00 | 1·00 |
| 3201 | $1.75 Tapir | 1·00 | 1·00 |
| 3202 | $2 Heliconid butterfly | 1·25 | 1·25 |
| **MS**3203 | Two sheets. (a) 90×65 mm. $6 Keel-billed toucan (horiz). (b) 65×90 mm. $6 Scarlet macaw Set of 2 sheets | 7·50 | 8·00 |

Nos. 3190/5 and 3196/201 were printed together, se-tenant, forming composite designs.

**449** "Sea Cliff" Submarine

**2000.** Submarines. Multicoloured.

| | | | |
|---|---|---|---|
| 3204 | 65c. Type **449** | 40 | 30 |
| 3205 | 75c. "Beaver Mark IV" | 50 | 35 |
| 3206 | 90c. "Reef Ranger" | 60 | 40 |
| 3207 | $1 "Cubmarine" | 70 | 45 |
| 3208 | $1.20 "Alvin" | 80 | 55 |
| 3209 | $2 H.M.S. *Revenge* | 1·25 | 1·40 |
| 3210 | $2 *Walrus*, Netherlands | 1·25 | 1·40 |
| 3211 | $2 U.S.S. *Los Angeles* | 1·25 | 1·40 |
| 3212 | $2 *Daphne*, France | 1·25 | 1·40 |
| 3213 | $2 U.S.S. *Ohio* | 1·25 | 1·40 |
| 3214 | $2 U.S.S. *Skipjack* | 1·25 | 1·40 |
| 3215 | $3 "Argus", Russia | 1·60 | 1·75 |
| **MS**3216 | Two sheets, each 107×84 mm. (a) $6 "Trieste". (b) $6 Type 209 U-boat, Germany Set of 2 sheets | 7·50 | 8·00 |

Nos. 3209/14 were printed together, se-tenant, with the backgrounds forming a composite design.

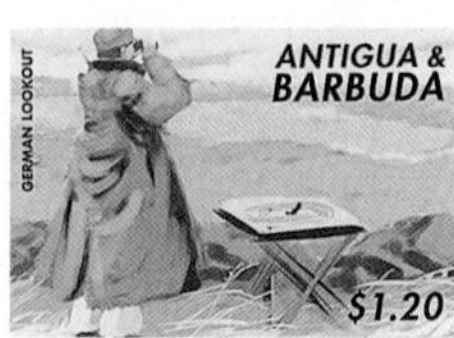

**450** German Lookout

**2000.** 60th Anniv of Battle of Britain. Multicoloured (except No. 3222).

| | | | |
|---|---|---|---|
| 3217 | $1.20 Type **450** | 1·00 | 1·00 |
| 3218 | $1.20 Children's evacuation train | 1·00 | 1·00 |
| 3219 | $1.20 Evacuating hospital patients | 1·00 | 1·00 |
| 3220 | $1.20 Hawker Hurricane (fighter) | 1·00 | 1·00 |
| 3221 | $1.20 Rescue team | 1·00 | 1·00 |
| 3222 | $1.20 Churchill cartoon (black) | 1·00 | 1·00 |
| 3223 | $1.20 King George VI and Queen Elizabeth inspecting bomb damage | 1·00 | 1·00 |
| 3224 | $1.20 Barrage balloon above Tower Bridge | 1·00 | 1·00 |
| 3225 | $1.20 Bristol Blenheim (bomber) | 1·00 | 1·00 |
| 3226 | $1.20 Prime Minister Winston Churchill | 1·00 | 1·00 |
| 3227 | $1.20 Bristol Blenheim and barrage balloons | 1·00 | 1·00 |
| 3228 | $1.20 Heinkel (fighter) | 1·00 | 1·00 |
| 3229 | $1.20 Supermarine Spitfire (fighter) | 1·00 | 1·00 |
| 3230 | $1.20 German rescue launch | 1·00 | 1·00 |
| 3231 | $1.20 Messerschmitt 109 (fighter) | 1·00 | 1·00 |
| 3232 | $1.20 R.A.F. rescue launch | 1·00 | 1·00 |
| **MS**3233 | Two sheets, each 90×60 mm. (a) $6 Junkers 87B (dive bomber). (b) $6 Supermarine Spitfires at dusk Set of 2 sheets | 10·00 | 11·00 |

No. **MS**3233a is inscribed "JUNKERS 878" in error.

**451** "The Defence of Cadiz" (Zurbaran)

**2000.** "Espana 2000" International Stamp Exhibition, Madrid. Paintings from the Prado Museum. Mult.

| | | | |
|---|---|---|---|
| 3234 | $1.65 Type **451** | 90 | 90 |
| 3235 | $1.65 "The Defence of Cadiz" (General and galleys) | 90 | 90 |
| 3236 | $1.65 "The Defence of Cadiz" (officers) | 90 | 90 |
| 3237 | $1.65 "Vulcan's Forge" (Vulcan) (Velazquez) | 90 | 90 |
| 3238 | $1.65 "Vulcan's Forge" (working metal) | 90 | 90 |
| 3239 | $1.65 "Vulcan's Forge" (workers with hammers) | 90 | 90 |
| 3240 | $1.65 "Family Portrait" (three men) (Adriaen Key) | 90 | 90 |
| 3241 | $1.65 "Family Portrait" (one man) | 90 | 90 |
| 3242 | $1.65 "Family Portrait" (three women) | 90 | 90 |
| 3243 | $1.65 "The Devotion of Rudolf I" (horseman with lantern) (Rubens and Jan Wildens) | 90 | 90 |
| 3244 | $1.65 "The Devotion of Rudolf I" (priest on horseback) | 90 | 90 |
| 3245 | $1.65 "The Devotion of Rudolf I" (huntsman) | 90 | 90 |
| 3246 | $1.65 "The Concert" (lute player) (Vincente Gonzalez) | 90 | 90 |
| 3247 | $1.65 "The Concert" (lady with fan) | 90 | 90 |
| 3248 | $1.65 "The Concert" (two gentlemen) | 90 | 90 |
| 3249 | $1.65 "The Adoration of the Magi" (Wise Man) (Juan Maino) | 90 | 90 |
| 3250 | $1.65 "The Adoration of the Magi" (two Wise Men) | 90 | 90 |
| 3251 | $1.65 "The Adoration of the Magi" (Holy Family) | 90 | 90 |
| **MS**3252 | Three sheets. (a) 115×90 mm. $6 "The Deliverance of St. Peter" (Jose de Ribera) (horiz). (b) 110×90 mm. $6 "The Fan Seller" (Jose del Castillo). (c) 110×90 mm. $6 "Family in a Garden" (Jan van Kessel the Younger) Set of 3 sheets | 9·50 | 10·00 |

Nos. 3246/8 are inscribed "Gonzlez" with No. 3248 additionally inscribed "Francisco Rizi", all in error.

**452** Two Angels

**2000.** Christmas and Holy Year. Multicoloured.

| | | | |
|---|---|---|---|
| 3253 | 25c. Type **452** | 20 | 15 |
| 3254 | 45c. Heads of two angels looking down | 35 | 25 |
| 3255 | 90c. Heads of two angels, one looking up | 60 | 40 |
| 3256 | $1.75 Type **452** | 1·10 | 1·25 |

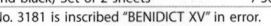

3257 $1.75 As 45c. 1·10 1·25
3258 $1.75 As 90c. 1·10 1·25
3259 $1.75 As $5 1·10 1·25
3260 $5 Two angels with drapery 3·00 3·50
**MS**3261 110×120 mm. $6 Holy Child 3·25 3·50

**453** "Dr. Ephraim Bueno" (Rembrandt)

**2000.** Bicentenary of Rijksmuseum, Amsterdam. Dutch Paintings. Multicoloured.

3262 $1 Type **453** 60 60
3263 $1 "Woman writing a Letter" (Frans van Meris de Oude) 60 60
3264 $1 "Mary Magdalen" (Jan van Scorel) 60 60
3265 $1 "Anna Coddle" (Maerten van Heemskerck) 60 60
3266 $1 "Cleopatra's Banquet" (Gerard Lairesse) 60 60
3267 $1 "Titus in Friar's Habit" (Rembrandt) 60 60
3268 $1.20 "Saskia" (Rembrandt) 70 70
3269 $1.20 "In the Month of July" (Paul Joseph Constantin Gabriel) 70 70
3270 $1.20 "Maria Trip" (Rembrandt) 70 70
3271 $1.20 "Still Life with Flowers" (Jan van Huysum) 70 70
3272 $1.20 "Haesje van Cleyburgh" (Rembrandt) 70 70
3273 $1.20 "Girl in a White Kimono" (George Hendrick Breitner) 70 70
3274 $1.65 "Man and Woman at a Spinning Wheel" (Pieter Pietersz) 90 90
3275 $1.65 "Self-portrait" (Rembrandt) 90 90
3276 $1.65 "Jeremiah lamenting the Destruction of Jerusalem" (Rembrandt) 90 90
3277 $1.65 "The Jewish Bride" (Rembrandt) 90 90
3278 $1.65 "Anna accused by Tobit of stealing a Kid" (Rembrandt) 90 90
3279 $1.65 "The Prophetess Anna" (Rembrandt) 90 90
**MS**3280 Three sheets, each 118×88 mm. (a) $6 "Doubting Thomas" (Hendrick ter Brugghen). (b) $6 "Still Life with Cheeses" (Floris van Dijck); (c) $6 "Isaac Blessing Jacob" (Govert Flinck) Set of 3 sheets 9·50 10·00

**454** "Starmie No. 121"

**2001.** Characters from "Pokemon" (children's cartoon series). Multicoloured.

3281 $1.75 Type **454** 1·10 1·10
3282 $1.75 "Misty" 1·10 1·10
3283 $1.75 "Brock" 1·10 1·10
3284 $1.75 "Geodude No. 74" 1·10 1·10
3285 $1.75 "Krabby No. 98" 1·10 1·10
3286 $1.75 "Ash" 1·10 1·10
**MS**3287 74×114 mm. $6 "Charizard No. 6" 3·25 3·50

**455** Blue-toothed Entoloma

**2001.** "Hong Kong 2001" Stamp Exhibition. Tropical Fungi. Multicoloured.

3288 25c. Type **455** 30 20
3289 90c. Common morel 60 40
3290 $1 Red cage fungus 75 45
3291 $1.65 Copper trumpet 90 90
3292 $1.65 Field mushroom ("Meadow Mushroom") 90 90
3293 $1.65 Green gill ("Green-gilled Parasol") 90 90
3294 $1.65 The panther 90 90
3295 $1.65 Death cap 90 90
3296 $1.65 Royal boletus ("King Bolete") 90 90
3297 $1.65 Lilac fairy helmet ("Lilac Bonnet") 90 90
3298 $1.65 Silky volvar 90 90
3299 $1.65 Agrocybe mushroom ("Poplar Field Cap") 90 90
3300 $1.65 Saint George's mushroom 90 90
3301 $1.65 Red-stemmed tough shank 90 90
3302 $1.65 Fly agaric 90 90
3303 $1.75 Common fawn agaric ("Fawn Shield-Cap") 1·00 1·00
**MS**3304 Two sheets, each 70×90 mm. (a) $6 Yellow parasol. (b) $6 Mutagen milk cap Set of 2 sheets 7·50 8·00

Nos. 3291/6 and 3297/302 were each printed together, se-tenant, with the backgrounds forming composite designs.

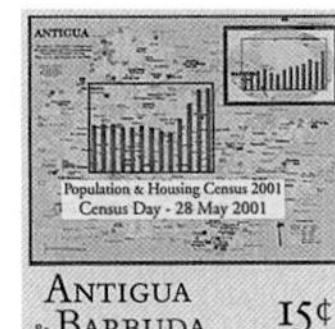

**456** Map and Graphs

**2001.** Population and Housing Census.

3305 **456** 15c. multicoloured 15 10
3306 - 25c. multicoloured 20 15
3307 - 65c. multicoloured 55 50
3308 - 90c. multicoloured 70 70
**MS**3309 – 55×50 mm. $6 multicoloured (Map and census logo) 3·50 3·75

DESIGNS: 25c. to 90c. Map and different form of graph.

**457** "Yuna (Bath-house Women)" (detail)

**2001.** "PHILANIPPON 2001" International Stamp Exhibition, Tokyo. Traditional Japanese Paintings. Multicoloured.

3310 45c. Type **457** 30 25
3311 60c. "Yuna (Bath-house Women)" (different detail) 40 30
3312 65c. "Yuna (Bath-house Women)" (different detail) 40 30
3313 75c. "The Hikone Screen" (detail) 50 35
3314 $1 "The Hikone Screen" (different detail) 60 45
3315 $1.20 "The Hikone Screen" (different detail) 70 55
3316 $1.65 Galleon and Dutch merchants with horse 90 90
3317 $1.65 Galleon and merchants with tiger 90 90
3318 $1.65 Merchants unpacking goods 90 90
3319 $1.65 Merchants with parasol and horse 90 90
3320 $1.65 Women packing food 90 90
3321 $1.65 Picnic under the cherry tree 90 90
3322 $1.65 Palanquins and resting bearers 90 90
3323 $1.65 Women dancing 90 90
3324 $1.65 Three samurai 90 90
3325 $1.65 One samurai 90 90
**MS**3326 Three sheets, each 80×110 mm. (a) $6 "Harunobu Suzuki" (Shiba Kokani) (38×50 mm). (b) $6 "Daruma" (Tsujo Kako) (38×50 mm). (c) $6 "Visiting a Shrine on a Rainy Night" (Harunobu Suziki) (38×50 mm) Set of 3 sheets 9·50 10·00

Nos. 3316/19 ("The Namban Screen" by Kano Nizen) and Nos. 3320/5 ("Merry-making under the Cherry Blossoms" by Kano Naganobu) were each printed together, se-tenant, with both sheetlets forming the entire painting.

**458** Lucille Ball leaning on Mantelpiece

**2001.** Scenes from I Love Lucy (American T.V. comedy series). Eight sheets each containing multicoloured design as T **458**.

**MS**3327 (a) 118×92 mm. $6 Type **458**. (b) 98×120 mm. $6 Desi Arnaz laughing. (c) 93×130 mm. $6 William Frawley at table. (d) 114×145 mm. $6 Lucille Ball with William Frawley. (e) 114×145 mm. $6 Lucille Ball in blue dress. (f) 119×111 mm. $6 Lucille Ball sitting at table. (g) 128×100 mm. $6 Lucille Ball as scarecrow. (h) 93×125 mm. $6 William Frawley shouting at Desi Arnaz (horiz) Set of 8 sheets 22·00 24·00

**462** Young Queen Victoria in Blue Dress

**459** *Hintleya burtii*

**2001.** Caribbean Orchids. Multicoloured.

3328 45c. Type **459** 40 25
3329 75c. *Neomoovea irrovata* 50 35
3330 90c. *Comparettia speciosa* 60 40
3331 $1 *Cypredepium crapeanum* 70 45
3332 $1.20 *Trichoceuos muralis* (vert) 75 75
3333 $1.20 *Dracula rampira* (vert) 75 75
3334 $1.20 *Psychopsis papilio* (vert) 75 75
3335 $1.20 *Lycaste clenningiana* (vert) 75 75
3336 $1.20 *Telipogon nevuosus* (vert) 75 75
3337 $1.20 *Masclecallia ayahbacana* (vert) 75 75
3338 $1.65 *Cattleya dowiana* (vert) 90 90
3339 $1.65 *Dendiobium cruentum* (vert) 90 90
3340 $1.65 *Bulbophyllum lobb* (vert) 90 90
3341 $1.65 *Chysis laevis* (vert) 90 90
3342 $1.65 *Ancistrochilus rothschildicanus* (vert) 90 90
3343 $1.65 *Angraecum sororium* (vert) 90 90
3344 $1.65 *Rhyncholaelia glanca* (vert) 90 90
3345 $1.65 *Oncidium barbatum* (vert) 90 90
3346 $1.65 *Phaius tankervillege* (vert) 90 90
3347 $1.65 *Ghies brechtiana* (vert) 90 90
3348 $1.65 *Angraecum leonis* (vert) 90 90
3349 $1.65 *Cycnoches loddigesti* (vert) 90 90
**MS**3350 Two sheets. (a) 68×104 mm. $6 *Symphalossum sanquinem* (vert). (b) 104×68 mm. $6 *Trichopilia fragrans* (vert) Set of 2 sheets 7·50 8·00

**460** Yellowtail Damselfish

**2001.** Tropical Marine Life. Multicoloured.

3351 25c. Type **460** 20 15
3352 45c. Indigo hamlet 30 25
3353 65c. Great white shark 45 30
3354 90c. Bottle-nose dolphin 60 50
3355 90c. Palette surgeonfish 60 50
3356 $1 Octopus 65 50
3357 $1.20 Common dolphin 70 70
3358 $1.20 Franklin's gull 70 70
3359 $1.20 Rock beauty 70 70
3360 $1.20 Bicoloured angelfish 70 70
3361 $1.20 Beaugregory 70 70
3362 $1.20 Banded butterflyfish 70 70
3363 $1.20 Common tern 70 70
3364 $1.20 Flying fish 70 70
3365 $1.20 Queen angelfish 70 70
3366 $1.20 Blue-striped grunt 70 70
3367 $1.20 Porkfish 70 70
3368 $1.20 Blue tang 70 70
3369 $1.65 Red-footed booby 90 90
3370 $1.65 Bottle-nose dolphin 90 90
3371 $1.65 Hawksbill turtle 90 90
3372 $1.65 Monk seal 90 90
3373 $1.65 Great white shark (inscr "Bull Shark") 90 90
3374 $1.65 Lemon shark 90 90
3375 $1.65 Dugong 90 90
3376 $1.65 White-tailed tropicbird 90 90
3377 $1.65 Bull shark 90 90
3378 $1.65 Manta ray 90 90
3379 $1.65 Green turtle 90 90
3380 $1.65 Spanish grunt 90 90
**MS**3381 Four sheets. (a) 68×98 mm. $5 Sailfish. (b) 68×98 mm. $5 Brown pelican and beaugregory (vert). (c) 98×68 mm. $6 Queen triggerfish. (d) 96×68 mm. $6 Hawksbill turtle Set of 4 sheets 12·00 13·00

Nos. 3357/62, 3363/8, 3369/74 and 3375/80 were each printed together, se-tenant, the backgrounds forming composite designs.

**461** *Freewinds* (liner) and Police Band, Antigua

**2001.** Work of Freewinds (Church of Scientology flagship) in Caribbean. Multicoloured.

3382 30c. Type **461** 40 30
3383 45c. At anchor off St. Barthelemy 45 30
3384 75c. At sunset 70 60
3385 90c. Off Bonaire 90 90
3386 $1.50 *Freewinds* anchored off Bequia 1·25 1·40
**MS**3387 Two sheets, each 85×60 mm. (a) $4 *Freewinds* alongside quay, Curacao. (b) $4 Decorated with lights Set of 2 sheets 5·50 6·00

**2001.** Death Centenary of Queen Victoria. Multicoloured.

3388 $2 Type **462** 1·40 1·40
3389 $2 Queen Victoria wearing red head-dress 1·40 1·40
3390 $2 Queen Victoria with jewelled hair ornament 1·40 1·40
3391 $2 Queen Victoria, after Chalon, in brooch 1·40 1·40
**MS**3392 70×82 mm. $5 Queen Victoria in old age 3·00 3·50

**463** "Water Lilies"

**2001.** 75th Death Anniv of Claude-Oscar Monet (French painter). Multicoloured.

3393 $2 Type **463** 1·25 1·40
3394 $2 "Rose Portals, Giverny" 1·25 1·40
3395 $2 "Water Lily Pond, Harmony in Green" 1·25 1·40
3396 $2 "Artist's Garden, Irises" 1·25 1·40
**MS**3397 136×111 mm. $5 "Jerusalem Artichoke Flowers" (vert) 3·00 3·25

No. 3396 is inscribed "Artists's" in error.

**464** Duchess of York with Baby Princess Elizabeth (1926)

**2001.** 75th Birthday of Queen Elizabeth II. Multicoloured.

| | | | |
|---|---|---|---|
| 3398 | $1 Type **464** | 75 | 75 |
| 3399 | $1 Queen in Coronation robes (1953) | 75 | 75 |
| 3400 | $1 Young Princess Elizabeth (1938) | 75 | 75 |
| 3401 | $1 Queen Elizabeth in Garter robes (1956) | 75 | 75 |
| 3402 | $1 Princess Elizabeth with pony (1939) | 75 | 75 |
| 3403 | $1 Queen Elizabeth in red dress and pearls (1985) | 75 | 75 |
| **MS**3404 | 90×72 mm. $6 Princess Elizabeth and Queen Elizabeth (1940) | 3·50 | 3·75 |

**465** Verdi in Top Hat

**2001.** Death Centenary of Giuseppe Verdi (Italian composer). Multicoloured.

| | | | |
|---|---|---|---|
| 3405 | $2 Type **465** | 1·75 | 1·75 |
| 3406 | $2 Don Carlos and part of opera score | 1·75 | 1·75 |
| 3407 | $2 Conductor and score for *Aida* | 1·75 | 1·75 |
| 3408 | $2 Musicians and score for *Rigoletto* | 1·75 | 1·75 |
| **MS**3409 | 77×117 mm. $5 Verdi in evening dress | 4·50 | 4·75 |

Nos. 3405/8 were printed together, se-tenant, the backgrounds forming a composite design.

**466** "Georges-Henri Manuel"

**2001.** Death Centenary of Henri de Toulouse-Lautrec (French painter). Multicoloured.

| | | | |
|---|---|---|---|
| 3410 | $2 Type **466** | 1·25 | 1·40 |
| 3411 | $2 "Louis Pascal" | 1·25 | 1·40 |
| 3412 | $2 "Romain Coolus" | 1·25 | 1·40 |
| 3413 | $2 "Monsieur Fourcade" | 1·25 | 1·40 |
| **MS**3414 | 67×84 mm. $5 "Dancing at the Moulin de la Galette" | 3·00 | 3·25 |

No 3412 is inscribed "ROMAN" in error.

**467** Marlene Dietrich smoking

**2001.** Birth Centenary of Marlene Dietrich (actress and singer).

| | | | | |
|---|---|---|---|---|
| 3415 | **467** | $2 black, purple and red | 1·25 | 1·40 |
| 3416 | - | $2 black, purple and red | 1·25 | 1·40 |
| 3417 | - | $2 multicoloured | 1·25 | 1·40 |
| 3418 | - | $2 black, purple and red | 1·25 | 1·40 |

DESIGNS: No. 3416, Marlene Dietrich, in evening gown, sitting on settee; 3417, In black dress; 3418, Sitting on piano.

**468** Collared Peccary

**2001.** Vanishing Fauna of the Caribbean. Multicoloured.

| | | | |
|---|---|---|---|
| 3419 | 25c. Type **468** | 30 | 20 |
| 3420 | 30c. Baird's tapir | 30 | 20 |
| 3421 | 45c. Agouti | 40 | 25 |
| 3422 | 75c. Bananaquit | 50 | 35 |
| 3423 | 90c. Six-banded armadillo | 60 | 40 |
| 3424 | $1 Roseate spoonbill | 75 | 45 |
| 3425 | $1.80 Mouse opossum | 1·25 | 1·40 |
| 3426 | $1.80 Magnificent black frigate bird | 1·25 | 1·40 |
| 3427 | $1.80 Northern jacana | 1·25 | 1·40 |
| 3428 | $1.80 Painted bunting | 1·25 | 1·40 |
| 3429 | $1.80 Haitian solenodon | 1·25 | 1·40 |
| 3430 | $1.80 St. Lucia iguana | 1·25 | 1·40 |
| 3431 | $2.50 West Indian iguana | 1·60 | 1·75 |
| 3432 | $2.50 Scarlet macaw | 1·60 | 1·75 |
| 3433 | $2.50 Cotton-topped tamarin | 1·60 | 1·75 |
| 3434 | $2.50 Kinkajou | 1·60 | 1·75 |
| **MS**3435 | Two sheets. (a) 117×85 mm. $6 Ocelot (vert). (b) 162×116 mm. $6 King vulture (vert) Set of 2 sheets | 7·50 | 8·00 |

**469** Sara Crewe (*The Little Princess*) reading a Letter

**2001.** Shirley Temple Films. Multicoloured. Showing film scenes. (a) *The Little Princess*. Multicoloured.

| | | | |
|---|---|---|---|
| 3436 | $1.50 Type **469** | 90 | 90 |
| 3437 | $1.50 Sara in pink dressing gown | 90 | 90 |
| 3438 | $1.50 Sara cuddling doll | 90 | 90 |
| 3439 | $1.50 Sara as Princess on throne | 90 | 90 |
| 3440 | $1.50 Sara talking to man in frock coat | 90 | 90 |
| 3441 | $1.50 Sara blowing out candles | 90 | 90 |
| 3442 | $1.80 Sara with Father (horiz) | 1·00 | 1·00 |
| 3443 | $1.80 Sara scrubbing floor (horiz) | 1·00 | 1·00 |
| 3444 | $1.80 Sara and friend with Headmistress (horiz) | 1·00 | 1·00 |
| 3445 | $1.80 Sara with Queen Victoria (horiz) | 1·00 | 1·00 |
| **MS**3446 | 106×76 mm. $6 Sara with wounded Father | 3·25 | 3·50 |

(b) *Baby, Take a Bow*.

| | | | |
|---|---|---|---|
| 3447 | $1.65 Shirley in dancing class (horiz) | 90 | 90 |
| 3448 | $1.65 Shirley cuddling Father (horiz) | 90 | 90 |
| 3449 | $1.65 Shirley at bedtime with parents (horiz) | 90 | 90 |
| 3450 | $1.65 Shirley in yellow dress with Father (horiz) | 90 | 90 |
| 3451 | $1.65 Shirley and Father at Christmas party (horiz) | 90 | 90 |
| 3452 | $1.65 Shirley and gangster looking in cradle (horiz) | 90 | 90 |
| 3453 | $1.65 Shirley in spotted dress | 90 | 90 |
| 3454 | $1.65 Shirley on steps with gangster | 90 | 90 |
| 3455 | $1.65 Shirley with gangster holding gun | 90 | 90 |
| 3456 | $1.65 Shirley with Mother | 90 | 90 |
| **MS**3457 | 106×76 mm. $6 Shirley in spotted dress | 3·25 | 3·50 |

**470** Rudolph Valentino in *Blood and Sand*, 1922

**2001.** 75th Death Anniv of Rudolph Valentino (Italian film actor).

| | | | | |
|---|---|---|---|---|
| 3458 | **470** | $1 brown and black | 70 | 70 |
| 3459 | - | $1 lilac and black | 70 | 70 |
| 3460 | - | $1 brown and black | 70 | 70 |
| 3461 | - | $1 brown and black | 70 | 70 |
| 3462 | - | $1 red and black | 70 | 70 |
| 3463 | - | $1 lilac and black | 70 | 70 |
| 3464 | - | $1 multicoloured | 70 | 70 |
| 3465 | - | $1 multicoloured | 70 | 70 |
| 3466 | - | $1 multicoloured | 70 | 70 |
| 3467 | - | $1 multicoloured | 70 | 70 |
| 3468 | - | $1 multicoloured | 70 | 70 |
| 3469 | - | $1 multicoloured | 70 | 70 |
| **MS**3470 | | Two sheets. (a) 90×125 mm. $6 multicoloured. (b) 68×95 mm. $6 multicoloured Set of 2 sheets | 7·50 | 8·00 |

DESIGNS: No. 3459, In *Eyes of Youth* with Clara Kimbal Young, 1919; 3460, In *All Night Long* with Carmel Meyers, 1918; 3461, Valentino in 1926; 3462, In *Camille* with Alla Nazimova, 1921; 3463, In *Cobra* with Nita Naldi, 1925; 3464, In *The Son of the Sheik* with Vilma Banky, 1926; 3465, In *The Young Rajah*, 1922; 3466, In *The Eagle* with Vilma Banky, 1925; 3467, In *The Sheik* with Agnes Ayres, 1921; 3468, In *A Sainted Devil*, 1924; 3469, In *Monsieur Beaucaire*, 1924; **MS**3470, (a) Valentino with Natacha Rambova. (b) In *The Four Horseman of the Apocalypse*, 1921.

Nos. 3464 and 3466 are inscribed "BLANKY" and No. 3467 "AYERS", all in error.

**471** Queen Elizabeth

**2001.** Golden Jubilee (1st issue).

| | | | | |
|---|---|---|---|---|
| 3471 | **471** | $1 multicoloured | 1·00 | 1·00 |

No. 3471 was printed in sheetlets of 8, containing two vertical rows of four, separated by a large illustrated central gutter. Both the stamp and the illustration on the central gutter are made up of a collage of miniature flower photographs.

See also Nos. 3535/8.

**472** Melvin Calvin, 1961

**2001.** Centenary of Nobel Prizes. Chemistry Winners. Multicoloured.

| | | | |
|---|---|---|---|
| 3472 | $1.50 Type **472** | 90 | 90 |
| 3473 | $1.50 Linus Pauling, 1954 | 90 | 90 |
| 3474 | $1.50 Vincent du Vigneaud, 1955 | 90 | 90 |
| 3475 | $1.50 Richard Synge, 1952 | 90 | 90 |
| 3476 | $1.50 Archer Martin, 1952 | 90 | 90 |
| 3477 | $1.50 Alfred Werner, 1913 | 90 | 90 |
| 3478 | $1.50 Robert Curl Jr., 1996 | 90 | 90 |
| 3479 | $1.50 Alan Heeger, 2000 | 90 | 90 |
| 3480 | $1.50 Michael Smith, 1993 | 90 | 90 |
| 3481 | $1.50 Sidney Altman, 1989 | 90 | 90 |
| 3482 | $1.50 Elias Corey, 1990 | 90 | 90 |
| 3483 | $1.50 William Giauque, 1949 | 90 | 90 |
| **MS**3484 | Three sheets, each 107×75 mm. (a) $6 Ernest Rutherford, 1908. (b) $6 Ernst Fischer, 1973. (c) $6 American volunteers, International Red Cross (Peace Prize, 1944) Set of 3 sheets | 9·50 | 10·00 |

**473** "Madonna and Child with Angels" (Filippo Lippi)

**2001.** Christmas. Italian Religious Paintings. Multicoloured.

| | | | |
|---|---|---|---|
| 3485 | 25c. Type **473** | 20 | 15 |
| 3486 | 45c. "Madonna of Corneto Tarquinia" (Lippi) | 35 | 25 |
| 3487 | 50c. "Madonna and Child" (Domenico Ghirlandaio) | 35 | 25 |
| 3488 | 75c. "Madonna and Child" (Lippi) | 60 | 35 |
| 3489 | $4 "Madonna Delceppo" (Lippi) | 2·50 | 3·00 |
| **MS**3490 | 106×136 mm. $6 "Madonna enthroned with Angels and Saints" (Lippi) | 3·25 | 3·50 |

**474** Final between Uruguay and Brazil, Brazil 1950

**2001.** World Cup Football Championship, Japan and Korea (2002). Multicoloured.

| | | | |
|---|---|---|---|
| 3491 | $1.50 Type **474** | 90 | 90 |
| 3492 | $1.50 Ferenc Puskas (Hungary), Switzerland 1954 | 90 | 90 |
| 3493 | $1.50 Raymond Kopa (France), Sweden 1958 | 90 | 90 |
| 3494 | $1.50 Mauro (Brazil), Chile 1962 | 90 | 90 |
| 3495 | $1.50 Gordon Banks (England), England 1966 | 90 | 90 |
| 3496 | $1.50 Pele (Brazil), Mexico 1970 | 90 | 90 |
| 3497 | $1.50 Daniel Passarella (Argentina), Argentina 1978 | 90 | 90 |
| 3498 | $1.50 Karl-Heinz Rummenigge (Germany), Spain 1982 | 90 | 90 |
| 3499 | $1.50 World Cup Trophy, Mexico 1986 | 90 | 90 |
| 3500 | $1.50 Diego Maradona (Argentina), Italy 1990 | 90 | 90 |
| 3501 | $1.50 Roger Milla (Cameroun), U.S.A. 1994 | 90 | 90 |
| 3502 | $1.50 Zinedine Zidane (France), France 1998 | 90 | 90 |
| **MS**3503 | Two sheets, each 88×75 mm. (a) $6 Detail of Jules Rimet Trophy, Uruguay, 1930. (b) $6 Detail of World Cup Trophy, Japan/Korea, 2002 Set of 2 sheets | 7·50 | 8·00 |

No. 3500 is inscribed "Deigo" in error.

**475** Battle of Nashville, 1864

**2002.** American Civil War. Multicoloured.

| | | | |
|---|---|---|---|
| 3504 | 45c. Type **475** | 55 | 55 |
| 3505 | 45c. Capture of Atlanta, 1864 | 55 | 55 |
| 3506 | 45c. Battle of Spotsylvania, 1864 | 55 | 55 |
| 3507 | 45c. Battle of The Wilderness, 1864 | 55 | 55 |
| 3508 | 45c. Battle of Chickamauga Creek, 1863 | 55 | 55 |
| 3509 | 45c. Battle of Gettysburg, 1863 | 55 | 55 |
| 3510 | 45c. Lee and Jackson at Chancellorsville, 1863 | 55 | 55 |
| 3511 | 45c. Battle of Fredericksburg, 1862 | 55 | 55 |
| 3512 | 45c. Battle of Antietam, 1862 | 55 | 55 |
| 3513 | 45c. Second Battle of Bull Run, 1862 | 55 | 55 |
| 3514 | 45c. Battle of Five Forks, 1865 | 55 | 55 |
| 3515 | 45c. Seven Days' Battles, 1862 | 55 | 55 |
| 3516 | 45c. First Battle of Bull Run, 1861 | 55 | 55 |
| 3517 | 45c. Battle of Shiloh, 1862 | 55 | 55 |
| 3518 | 45c. Battle of Seven Pines, 1862 | 55 | 55 |
| 3519 | 45c. Bombardment of Fort Sumter, 1861 | 55 | 55 |
| 3520 | 45c. Battle of Chattanooga, 1863 | 55 | 55 |

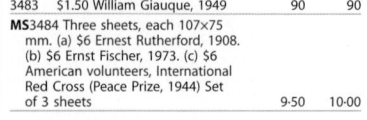

3521 45c. Grant and Lee at Appomattox, 1865 55 55
3522 50c. General Ulysses S. Grant (vert) 55 55
3523 50c. President Abraham Lincoln (vert) 55 55
3524 50c. President Jefferson Davis (vert) 55 55
3525 50c. General Robert E. Lee (vert) 55 55
3526 50c. General George Custer (vert) 55 55
3527 50c. Admiral Andrew Hull Foote (vert) 55 55
3528 50c. General "Stonewall" Jackson (vert) 55 55
3529 50c. General Jeb Stuart (vert) 55 55
3530 50c. General George Meade (vert) 55 55
3531 50c. General Philip Sheridan (vert) 55 55
3532 50c. General James Longstreet (vert) 55 55
3533 50c. General John Mosby (vert) 55 55
**MS**3534 Two sheets, each 105×76 mm. (a) $6 Confederate ironclad *Merrimack* attacking *Cumberland* (Federal sloop) (51×38 mm). (b) $6 *Monitor* (Federal ironclad) Set of 2 sheets 9·50 10·00

**476** Queen Elizabeth presenting Rosettes

**2002.** Golden Jubilee (2nd issue). Multicoloured.
3535 $2 Type **476** 1·75 1·75
3536 $2 Queen Elizabeth at garden party 1·75 1·75
3537 $2 Queen Elizabeth in evening dress 1·75 1·75
3538 $2 Queen Elizabeth in cream coat 1·75 1·75
**MS**3539 76×108 mm. $6 Princesses Elizabeth and Margaret as bridesmaids 3·50 3·75

**477** U.S. Flag as Statue of Liberty and Antigua & Barbuda Flag

**2002.** "United We Stand". Support for Victims of 11 September 2001 Terrorist Attacks.
3540 **477** $2 multicoloured 1·25 1·40

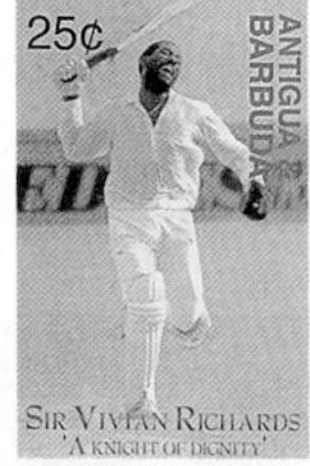

**478** Sir Vivian Richards waving Bat

**2002.** 50th Birthday of Sir Vivian Richards (West Indian cricketer). Multicoloured.
3541 25c. Type **478** 70 30
3542 30c. Sir Vivian Richards receiving presentation from Antigua Cricket Association 80 35
3543 50c. Sir Vivian Richards wearing sash 90 45
3544 75c. Sir Vivian Richards batting 1·10 70
3545 $1.50 Sir Vivian Richards and Lady Richards 1·75 1·75
3546 $1.80 Sir Vivian Richards with enlarged action photograph of himself 2·00 2·25
**MS**3547 Two sheets, each 68×95 mm. (a) $6 Sir Vivian Richards with guard of honour. (b) $6 Sir Vivian Richards in Indian traditional dress Set of 2 sheets 10·00 10·50

**479** Thick-billed Parrot

**2002.** Flora and Fauna. Multicoloured.
3548 50c. Type **479** 40 30
3549 75c. Lesser long-nosed bat 50 35
3550 90c. Quetzal 60 60
3551 90c. Two-toed sloth 60 60
3552 90c. Lovely cotinga 60 60
3553 90c. *Pseudolycaena marsyas* (butterfly) 60 60
3554 90c. Magenta-throated woodstar 60 60
3555 90c. *Automeris rubrescens* (moth) 60 60
3556 90c. *Bufo periglenes* (toad) 60 60
3557 90c. Collared peccary 60 60
3558 90c. Tamandua anteater 60 60
3559 $1 St. Lucia parrot 70 70
3560 $1 Cuban kite 70 70
3561 $1 West Indian whistling-duck 70 70
3562 $1 *Eurema amelia* (butterfly) 70 70
3563 $1 Scarlet ibis 70 70
3564 $1 Black-capped petrel 70 70
3565 $1 *Cnemidophorus vanzoi* (lizard) 70 70
3566 $1 Cuban solenodon 70 70
3567 $1 *Papilio thersites* (butterfly) 70 70
3568 $1.50 Montserrat oriole 95 95
3569 $1.80 *Leptotes perkinsae* (butterfly) 1·25 1·40
**MS**3570 Two sheets, each 110×85 mm. (a) $6 Olive Ridley turtle. (b) $6 Margay Set of 2 sheets 7·50 8·00

Nos. 3550/8 and 3559/67 were each printed together, se-tenant, with the backgrounds forming composite designs.

**480** Community Players wearing Straw Hats

**2002.** 50th Anniv of Community Players. Multicoloured. Showing scenes from various productions.
3571 20c. Type **480** 25 20
3572 25c. Men in suits with women in long dresses 25 20
3573 30c. In *Pirates of Penzance* 25 20
3574 75c. Female choir 50 35
3575 90c. In Mexican dress 60 40
3576 $1.50 Members at a reception 95 1·10
3577 $1.80 Production in the open air 1·25 1·40
**MS**3578 Two sheets, each 76×84 mm. (a) $4 Mrs. Edie Hill-Thibou (former President) (vert). (b) $4 Miss Yvonne Maginley (Acting President and Director of Music) (vert) Set of 2 sheets 5·50 6·00

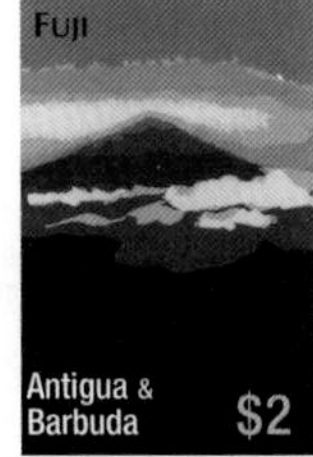

**481** Mount Fuji, Japan

**2002.** International Year of Mountains. Mult.
3579 $2 Type **481** 1·25 1·40
3580 $2 Machu Picchu, Peru 1·25 1·40
3581 $2 The Matterhorn, Switzerland 1·25 1·40

**482** Cross-country Skiing

**2002.** Winter Olympic Games, Salt Lake City. Multicoloured.
3582 $2 Type **482** 1·25 1·40
3583 $2 Pairs figure skating 1·25 1·40
**MS**3584 84×114 mm. Nos. 3582/3 2·25 2·50

**483** Amerigo Vespucci wearing Skullcap

**2002.** 500th Anniv of Amerigo Vespucci's Third Voyage. Multicoloured.
3585 $2.50 Type **483** 1·60 1·75
3586 $2.50 Vespucci as an old man 1·60 1·75
3587 $2.50 16th-century map 1·60 1·75
**MS**3588 49×68 mm. $5 Vespucci holding dividers (vert) 3·00 3·25

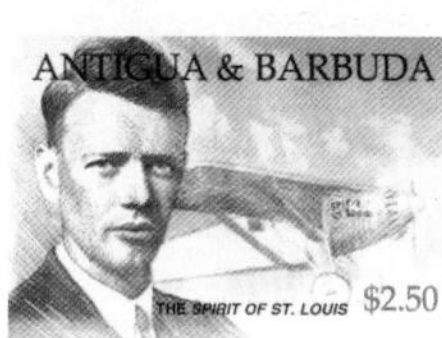

**484** *Spirit of St. Louis* and Charles Lindbergh (pilot)

**2002.** 75th Anniv of First Solo Transatlantic Flight. Multicoloured.
3589 $2.50 Type **484** 1·60 1·75
3590 $2.50 *Spirit of St. Louis* at Le Bourget, Paris, 1927 1·60 1·75
3591 $2.50 Charles Lindbergh in New York ticker-tape parade, 1927 1·60 1·75
**MS**3592 80×110 mm. $6 Charles Lindbergh wearing flying helmet 3·25 3·50

**485** Princess Diana

**2002.** 5th Death Anniv of Diana, Princess of Wales. Multicoloured.
3593 $1.80 Type **485** 1·10 1·25
3594 $1.80 Princess Diana in tiara (looking left) 1·10 1·25
3595 $1.80 Wearing hat 1·10 1·25
3596 $1.80 Princess Diana wearing pearl drop earrings and black dress 1·10 1·25
3597 $1.80 Wearing tiara (facing front) 1·10 1·25
3598 $1.80 Princess Diana wearing pearl drop earrings 1·10 1·25
**MS**3599 91×106 mm. $6 Princess Diana 3·25 3·50

**486** Kennedy Brothers

**2002.** Presidents John F. Kennedy and Ronald Reagan Commemoration. Multicoloured.
3600 $1.50 Type **486** 90 90
3601 $1.50 John Kennedy with Danny Kaye (American entertainer) 90 90
3602 $1.50 Delivering Cuban Blockade speech, 1962 90 90
3603 $1.50 With Jacqueline Kennedy 90 90
3604 $1.50 Meeting Bill Clinton (future president) 90 90
3605 $1.50 Family at John Kennedy's funeral 90 90
3606 $1.50 President and Mrs. Reagan with Pope John Paul II, 1982 90 90
3607 $1.50 As George Gipp in *Knute Rockne - All American*, 1940 90 90
3608 $1.50 With General Matthew Ridgeway, Bitburg Military Cemetery, Germany, 1985 90 90
3609 $1.50 With George H. Bush and Secretary Mikhail Gorbachev of U.S.S.R., 1988 90 90

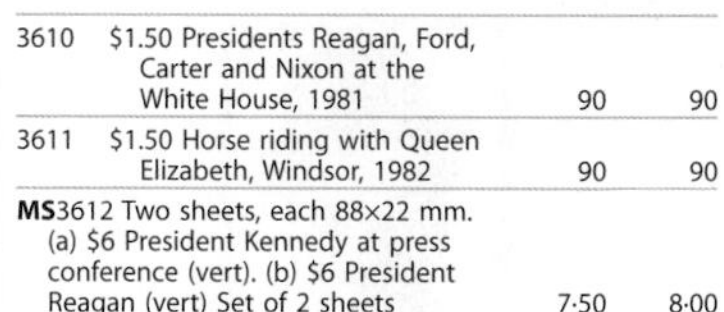
3610 $1.50 Presidents Reagan, Ford, Carter and Nixon at the White House, 1981 90 90
3611 $1.50 Horse riding with Queen Elizabeth, Windsor, 1982 90 90
**MS**3612 Two sheets, each 88×22 mm. (a) $6 President Kennedy at press conference (vert). (b) $6 President Reagan (vert) Set of 2 sheets 7·50 8·00

**487** Red-billed Tropicbird

**2002.** Endangered Species of Antigua. Multicoloured.
3613 $1.50 Type **487** 90 90
3614 $1.50 Brown pelican 90 90
3615 $1.50 Magnificent frigate bird 90 90
3616 $1.50 Ground lizard 90 90
3617 $1.50 West Indian whistling duck 90 90
3618 $1.50 Antiguan racer snake 90 90
3619 $1.50 Spiny lobster 90 90
3620 $1.50 Hawksbill turtle 90 90
3621 $1.50 Queen conch 90 90

**488** Elvis Presley

**2002.** 25th Death Anniv of Elvis Presley (American entertainer).
3622 **488** $1 multicoloured 1·40 1·25

**489** Cheerleader Teddy

**2002.** Centenary of the Teddy Bear. Girl Teddies. Multicoloured.
3623 $2 Type **489** 1·25 1·40
3624 $2 Figure skater 1·25 1·40
3625 $2 Ballet dancer 1·25 1·40
3626 $2 Aerobics instructor 1·25 1·40

**490** "Croconaw No. 159"

**2002.** Pokemon (children's cartoon series). Mult.
3627 $1.50 Type **490** 90 90
3628 $1.50 "Mantine No. 226" 90 90
3629 $1.50 "Feraligatr No. 160" 90 90
3630 $1.50 "Qwilfish No. 211" 90 90
3631 $1.50 "Remoraid No. 223" 90 90
3632 $1.50 "Quagsire No. 195" 90 90
**MS**3633 80×106 mm. $6 "Chinchou No. 170" 3·25 3·50

**491** Charlie Chaplin

**2002.** 25th Death Anniv of Charlie Chaplin (British actor). Each black, grey and light grey.

| | | | |
|---|---|---|---|
| 3634 | $1.80 Type **491** | 1·25 | 1·40 |
| 3635 | $1.80 Wearing waistcoat and spotted bow-tie | 1·25 | 1·40 |
| 3636 | $1.80 In top hat | 1·25 | 1·40 |
| 3637 | $1.80 Wearing coat and bowler hat | 1·25 | 1·40 |
| 3638 | $1.80 Charlie Chaplin in old age | 1·25 | 1·40 |
| 3639 | $1.80 With finger on chin | 1·25 | 1·40 |
| **MS**3640 | 90×105 mm. $6 Charlie Chaplin as The Tramp | 3·50 | 3·75 |

**492** Bob Hope

**2002.** Bob Hope (American entertainer) Commemoration. Designs showing him entertaining American troops. Multicoloured.

| | | | |
|---|---|---|---|
| 3641 | $1.50 Type **492** | 1·10 | 1·25 |
| 3642 | $1.50 Wearing bush hat,Vietnam, 1972 | 1·10 | 1·25 |
| 3643 | $1.50 On board U.S.S. *John F. Kennedy* (aircraft carrier) | 1·10 | 1·25 |
| 3644 | $1.50 With hawk badge on sleeve, Berlin, 1948 | 1·10 | 1·25 |
| 3645 | $1.50 Wearing desert fatigues | 1·10 | 1·25 |
| 3646 | $1.50 In white cap and stars on collar | 1·10 | 1·25 |

**493** Lee Strasberg

**2002.** 20th Death Anniv of Lee Strasberg (pioneer of "Method Acting").

| | | | | |
|---|---|---|---|---|
| 3647 | **493** | $1 black and stone | 75 | 75 |

**494** Marlene Dietrich

**2002.** 10th Death Anniv of Marlene Dietrich (actress and singer). Each black and grey.

| | | | |
|---|---|---|---|
| 3648 | $1.50 Type **494** | 90 | 90 |
| 3649 | $1.50 Wearing top hat | 90 | 90 |
| 3650 | $1.50 In chiffon dress | 90 | 90 |
| 3651 | $1.50 Resting chin on left hand | 90 | 90 |
| 3652 | $1.50 In cloche hat | 90 | 90 |
| 3653 | $1.50 Wearing black evening gloves | 90 | 90 |
| **MS**3654 | 83×108 mm. $6 Marlene Dietrich wearing chiffon scarf | 3·25 | 3·50 |

**495** Ferrari 801, 1957

**2002.** Ferrari Racing Cars. Multicoloured.

| | | | |
|---|---|---|---|
| 3655 | 20c. Type **495** | 20 | 20 |
| 3656 | 25c. Ferrari 256, 1959 | 25 | 20 |
| 3657 | 30c. Ferrari 246 P, 1960 | 25 | 20 |
| 3658 | 90c. Ferrari 246, 1966 | 60 | 50 |
| 3659 | $1 Ferrari 312 B2, 1971 | 70 | 55 |
| 3660 | $1.50 Ferrari 312, 1969 | 90 | 90 |
| 3661 | $2 Ferrari F310 B, 1997 | 1·25 | 1·40 |
| 3662 | $4 Ferrari F2002, 2002 | 2·25 | 2·50 |

**496** Antigua & Barbuda Flag

**2002.** 21st Anniv of Independence. Multicoloured.

| | | | |
|---|---|---|---|
| 3663 | 25c. Type **496** | 35 | 25 |
| 3664 | 30c. Antigua & Barbuda coat of arms (vert) | 35 | 25 |
| 3665 | $1.50 Mount St. John's Hospital under construction | 1·25 | 1·25 |
| 3666 | $1.80 Parliament Building, St. John's | 1·40 | 1·60 |
| **MS**3667 | Two sheets, each 77×81 mm. (a) $6 Sir Vere Bird (Prime Minister, 1967–94) (38×51 mm). (b) $6 Lester Bird (Prime Minister since 1994) (38×51 mm) Set of 2 sheets | 7·50 | 8·00 |

**497** Juan Valeron (Spain)

**2002.** World Cup Football Championship, Japan and Korea. Multicoloured.

| | | | |
|---|---|---|---|
| 3668 | $1.65 Type **497** | 90 | 90 |
| 3669 | $1.65 Iker Casillas (Spain) | 90 | 90 |
| 3670 | $1.65 Fernando Hierro (Spain) | 90 | 90 |
| 3671 | $1.65 Gary Kelly (Ireland) | 90 | 90 |
| 3672 | $1.65 Damien Duff (Ireland) | 90 | 90 |
| 3673 | $1.65 Matt Holland (Ireland) | 90 | 90 |
| 3674 | $1.65 Pyo Lee (South Korea) | 90 | 90 |
| 3675 | $1.65 Ji Sung Park (South Korea) | 90 | 90 |
| 3676 | $1.65 Jung Hwan Ahn (South Korea) | 90 | 90 |
| 3677 | $1.65 Filippo Inzaghi (Italy) | 90 | 90 |
| 3678 | $1.65 Paolo Maldini (Italy) | 90 | 90 |
| 3679 | $1.65 Dammiano Tommasi (Italy) | 90 | 90 |
| **MS**3680 | Four sheets, each 82×82 mm. (a) $3 Jose Camacho (Spanish coach); $3 Raul Gonzales Blanco (Spain). (b) $3 Robbie Keane (Ireland); $3 Mick McCarthy (Irish coach). (c) $3 Guus Hiddink (South Korean coach); $3 Chul Sang Yoo (South Korea). (d) $3 Francesco Totti (Italy); $3 Giovanni Trapattoni (Italian coach) Set of 4 sheets | 12·00 | 13·00 |

No. **MS**3680a is inscribed "Carlos Gamarra" in error.

**498** "Coronation of the Virgin" (Domenico Ghirlandaio)

**2002.** Christmas. Religious Paintings. Multicoloured.

| | | | |
|---|---|---|---|
| 3681 | 25c. Type **498** | 20 | 15 |
| 3682 | 45c. "Adoration of the Magi" (detail) (D. Ghirlandaio) | 30 | 25 |
| 3683 | 75c. "Annunciation" (Simone Martini) (vert) | 50 | 35 |
| 3684 | 90c. "Adoration of the Magi" (different detail) (D. Ghirlandaio) | 60 | 40 |
| 3685 | $5 "Madonna and Child" (Giovanni Bellini) | 3·00 | 3·50 |
| **MS**3686 | 76×110 mm. $6 "Madonnna and Child" (S. Martini) | 3·25 | 3·50 |

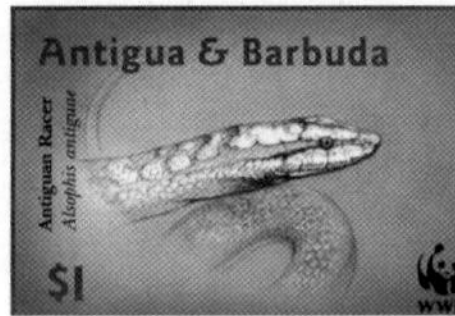


**499** Antiguan Racer Snake Head

**2002.** Endangered Species. Antiguan Racer Snake. Multicoloured.

| | | | |
|---|---|---|---|
| 3687 | $1 Type **499** | 70 | 70 |
| 3688 | $1 Coiled Antiguan racer snake with tail at right | 70 | 70 |
| 3689 | $1 Antiguan racer snake with pebbles and leaves | 70 | 70 |
| 3690 | $1 Coiled Antiguan racer snake with tail at left | 70 | 70 |

**500** Magnificent Frigate Bird

**2002.** Fauna and Flora. Multicoloured.

| | | | |
|---|---|---|---|
| 3691 | $1.50 Type **500** | 90 | 90 |
| 3692 | $1.50 Sooty tern | 90 | 90 |
| 3693 | $1.50 Bananaquit | 90 | 90 |
| 3694 | $1.50 Yellow-crowned night heron | 90 | 90 |
| 3695 | $1.50 Greater flamingo | 90 | 90 |
| 3696 | $1.50 Belted kingfisher | 90 | 90 |
| 3697 | $1.50 Killer whale | 90 | 90 |
| 3698 | $1.50 Sperm whale | 90 | 90 |
| 3699 | $1.50 Minke whale | 90 | 90 |
| 3700 | $1.50 Blainville's beaked whale | 90 | 90 |
| 3701 | $1.50 Blue whale | 90 | 90 |
| 3702 | $1.50 Cuvier's beaked whale | 90 | 90 |
| 3703 | $1.80 *Epidendrum fragans* | 1·10 | 1·10 |
| 3704 | $1.80 *Dombeya wallichii* | 1·10 | 1·10 |
| 3705 | $1.80 *Abebuia serratifolia* | 1·10 | 1·10 |
| 3706 | $1.80 *Cryptostegia grandiflora* | 1·10 | 1·10 |
| 3707 | $1.80 *Hylocereus undatus* | 1·10 | 1·10 |
| 3708 | $1.80 *Rodriguezia lanceolata* | 1·10 | 1·10 |
| 3709 | $1.80 *Diphthera festiva* | 1·10 | 1·10 |
| 3710 | $1.80 *Hypocrita dejanira* | 1·10 | 1·10 |
| 3711 | $1.80 *Eupseudosoma involutum* | 1·10 | 1·10 |
| 3712 | $1.80 *Composia credula* | 1·10 | 1·10 |
| 3713 | $1.80 *Citherania magnifica* | 1·10 | 1·10 |
| 3714 | $1.80 *Divana diva* | 1·10 | 1·10 |
| **MS**3715 | Four sheets, each 75×45 mm. (a) $5 Snowy egret. (b) $5 *Rothschildia orizaba* (moth). (c) $6 Humpback whale. (d) $6 *Ionopsis utricularioides* (flower) Set of 4 sheets | 12·00 | 13·00 |

Nos. 3691/6 (birds), 3697/702 (whales), 3703/8 (moths) and 3709/14 (flowers) were each printed together, se-tenant, with the backgrounds forming composite designs.

**501** Dr. Margaret O'garro

**2002.** Centenary of Pan American Health Organization. Health Professionals. Multicoloured.

| | | | |
|---|---|---|---|
| 3716 | $1.50 Type **501** | 90 | 90 |
| 3717 | $1.50 Ineta Wallace (nurse) | 90 | 90 |
| 3718 | $1.50 Vincent Edwards (public health official) | 90 | 90 |

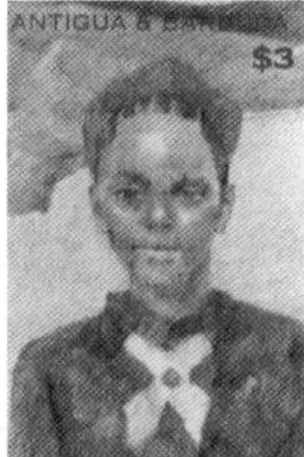


**502** Antiguan Brownie

**2002.** 20th World Scout Jamboree, Thailand. Each lilac and brown (Nos. 3719/21) or multicoloured (others).

| | | | |
|---|---|---|---|
| 3719 | $3 Type **502** | 1·75 | 1·90 |
| 3720 | $3 Brownie with badge on cap | 1·75 | 1·90 |
| 3721 | $3 Brownie without badge on cap | 1·75 | 1·90 |
| 3722 | $3 Robert Baden-Powell on horseback, 1896 (horiz) | 1·75 | 1·90 |
| 3723 | $3 Ernest Thompson Seton (founder, Boy Scouts of America), 1910, and American scout badge (horiz) | 1·75 | 1·90 |
| 3724 | $3 First black scout troop, Virginia, 1928 (horiz) | 1·75 | 1·90 |
| **MS**3725 | Two sheets. (a) 80×113 mm. $6 Ernest Thompson Seton. (b) 110×83 mm. $6 Scout salute Set of 2 sheets | 7·50 | 8·00 |

Nos. 3719/21 were printed together, se-tenant, forming a composite design.

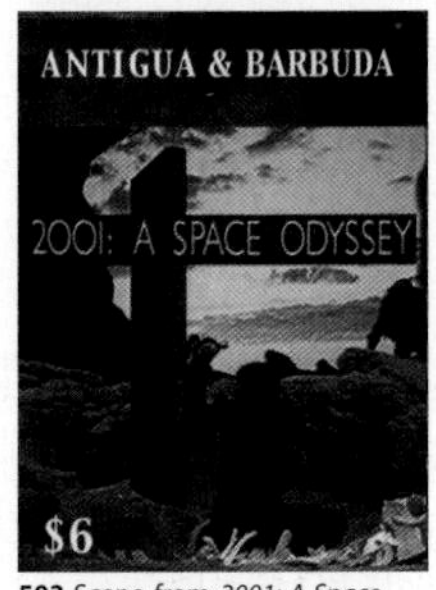


**503** Scene from *2001: A Space Odyssey* (Arthur C. Clarke)

**2002.** Famous Science Fiction Authors. Three sheets, each 150×108 mm, containg vert designs as T **503**. Multicoloured.

| | | | |
|---|---|---|---|
| **MS**3726 | Three sheets. (a) $6 Type **503**. (b) $6 Scene from *The Monuments of Mars* (Richard C. Hoagland). (c) $6 Nostradamus with globe Set of 3 sheets | 9·50 | 10·00 |

**504** "Goat and Kids" (Liu Jiyou)

**2003.** Chinese New Year ("Year of the Goat").

| | | | | |
|---|---|---|---|---|
| 3727 | **504** | $1.80 multicoloured | 1·10 | 1·10 |

**505** "Lucretia"

**2003.** 450th Death Anniv of Lucas Cranach the Elder (artist). Multicoloured.

| | | | |
|---|---|---|---|
| 3728 | 75c. Type **505** | 50 | 35 |
| 3729 | 90c. "Venus and Cupid" (detail) | 60 | 40 |
| 3730 | $1 "Judith with Head of Holofernes" (c. 1530) | 70 | 60 |
| 3731 | $1.50 "Portrait of a Young Lady" (detail) | 90 | 1·00 |

| | | |
|---|---|---|
| **MS**3732 152×188 mm. $2 "Portrait of the Wife of a Jurist"; $2 "Portrait of a Jurist"; $2 "Johannes Cuspinian"; $2 "Portrait of Anna Cuspinian" | 3·50 | 3·75 |
| **MS**3733 120×100 mm. $6 "Judith with Head of Holofernes" (c. 1532) | 3·50 | 3·75 |

**506** "A High Class Maid training in a Samurai Household"

**2003.** Japanese Art of Taiso Yoshitoshi. Multicoloured.

| | | |
|---|---|---|
| 3734 25c. Type **506** | 25 | 15 |
| 3735 50c. "A Castle-Toppler known as a Keisei" | 40 | 25 |
| 3736 $1 "Stylish Young Geisha battling a Snowstorm on her Way to Work" | 70 | 55 |
| 3737 $5 "A Lady in Distress being treated with Moxa" | 3·00 | 3·50 |
| **MS**3738 178×140 mm. $2 "A Lady of the Imperial Court wearing Four Layers of Robes"; $2 "Young Mother adoring her Infant Son"; $2 "Lady-in-Waiting looking amused over a Veranda in the Household of a Great Lord"; $2 "A High Ranking Courtesan known as an "Oiran", waiting for a Private Assignation" | 5·00 | 5·50 |
| **MS**3739 135×67 mm. $6 "A Girl teasing her Cat" | 3·25 | 3·50 |

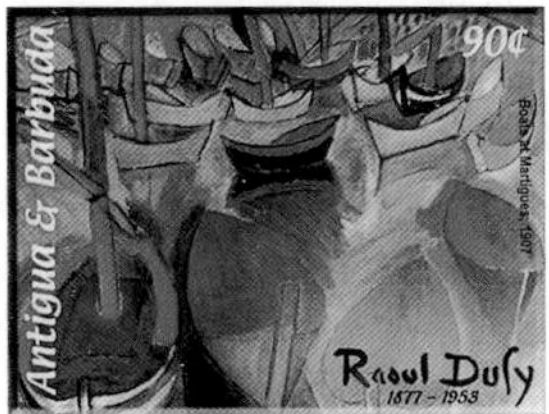


**507** "Boats at Martigues"

**2003.** 50th Death Anniv of Raoul Dufy (artist). Multicoloured.

| | | |
|---|---|---|
| 3740 90c. Type **507** | 60 | 40 |
| 3741 $1 "Harvesting" | 70 | 45 |
| 3742 $1.80 "Sailboats in the Port of Le Havre" | 1·10 | 1·10 |
| 3743 $5 "The Big Bather" (vert) | 3·00 | 3·50 |
| **MS**3744 173×124 mm. $2 "The Beach and the Pier at Trouville"; $2 "Port with Sailing Ships"; $2 "Black Cargo"; $2 "Nice, The Bay of Anges" | 5·00 | 5·50 |
| **MS**3745 Two sheets, each 95×76 mm. (a) $6 "Vence". (b) $6 "The Interior with an Open Window". Both Imperf | 7·50 | 8·00 |

**508** Queen Elizabeth II at Trooping the Colour

**2003.** 50th Anniv of Coronation. Multicoloured.

| | | |
|---|---|---|
| **MS**3746 155×93 mm. $3 Type **508**; $3 Queen wearing fawn beret with single feather; $3 Queen wearing feathered hat | 5·50 | 6·00 |
| **MS**3747 105×75 mm. $6 Princess Elizabeth | 3·50 | 3·75 |

**509** Prince William

**2003.** 21st Birthday of Prince William of Wales. Multicoloured.

| | | |
|---|---|---|
| **MS**3748 147×77 mm. $3 Type **509**; $3 Prince william wearing polo helmet; $3 Wearing blue T-shirt | 5·50 | 3·75 |
| **MS**3749 67×97 mm. $6 As teenager holding bouquet | 3·50 | 3·75 |

**510** Tamarind Tree, Parham

**2003.** Centenary of Salvation Army in Antigua. Multicoloured.

| | | |
|---|---|---|
| 3750 30c. Type **510** | 40 | 25 |
| 3751 90c. Salvation Army pre-school | 80 | 45 |
| 3752 $1 Meals on wheels (horiz) | 95 | 65 |
| 3753 $1.50 St. John Citadel band (horiz) | 1·40 | 1·40 |
| 3754 $1.80 Salvation Army Citadel (horiz) | 1·75 | 2·00 |
| **MS**3755 146×78 mm. $6 As Type **510** but without badge and centenary inscription | 4·25 | 4·50 |

**511** First Anglican Scout Troop, 1931

**2003.** 90th Anniv of Antigua and Barbuda Scouts Association. Multicoloured (except No. 3756).

| | | |
|---|---|---|
| 3756 30c. Type **511** (black and brown) | 25 | 20 |
| 3757 $1 National Scout Camp, 2002 | 70 | 55 |
| 3758 $1.50 Woodbadge Training course, 2000 (horiz) | 90 | 90 |
| 3759 $1.80 Visitors to National Camp, 1986 (horiz) | 1·10 | 1·10 |
| **MS**3760 136×96 mm. 90c. Edris George; 90c. Theodore George; 90c. Edris James (all Deputy Commissioners) | 1·60 | 1·75 |
| **MS**3761 74×101 mm. $6 Scout leader demonstrating semaphore | 3·25 | 3·50 |

**512** Cesar Garin (1903)

**2003.** Centenary of Tour de France Cycle Race. Past winners. Multicoloured.

| | | |
|---|---|---|
| **MS**3762 160×100 mm. $2 Type **512**; $2 Caricature of Henri Cornet (1904); $2 Louis Trousselier (1905); $2 Rene Pottier (1906) | 7·00 | 7·00 |
| **MS**3763 160×100 mm. $2 Lucien Petit-Breton (1907); $2 Lucien Petit-Breton (1908); $2 Francois Faber (1909); $2 Octave Lapize (1910) | 7·00 | 7·00 |
| **MS**3764 160×100 mm. $2 Gustave Garrigou (1911); $2 Odile Defraye (1912); $2 Phillipe Thys (1913); $2 Phillipe Thys (1914) | 7·00 | 7·00 |
| **MS**3765 Three sheets, each 100×70 mm. (a) $6 Henri Desgranges (editor of *L'Auto*). (b) $6 Pierre Giffard (editor of *Le Velo*). (c) $6 Le Compte de Dion (sponsor) Set of 3 sheets | 12·00 | 13·00 |

**513** Frigate Bird and Emblem

**2003.** 30th Anniv of CARICOM.

| | | |
|---|---|---|
| 3766 **513** $1 multicoloured | 1·00 | 80 |

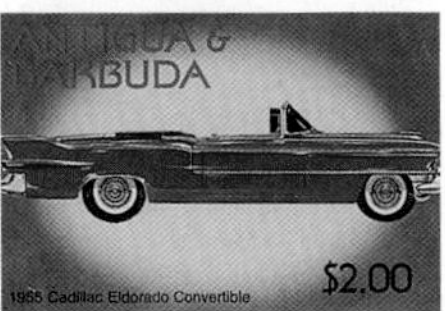


**514** Cadillac Eldorado Convertible (1955)

**2003.** Centenary of General Motors Cadillac. Multicoloured.

| | | |
|---|---|---|
| **MS**3767 110×150 mm. $2 Type **514**; $2 Cadillac Series 60 (1937); $2 Cadillac Eldorado (1959); $2 Cadillac Eldorado (2002) | 5·00 | 5·50 |
| **MS**3768 102×76 mm. $6 Cadillac Eldorado (1953) | 3·25 | 3·50 |

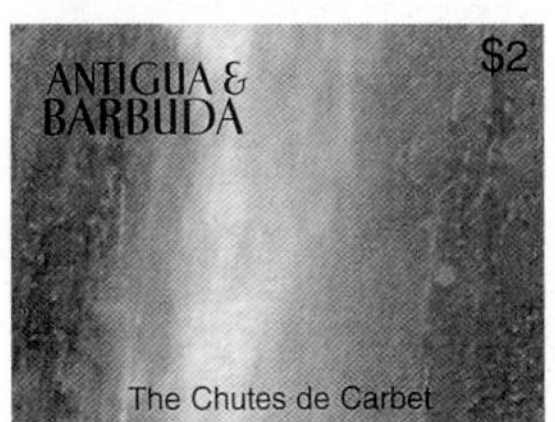


**515** Chutes de Carbet Waterfall, Guadeloupe

**2003.** International Year of Freshwater. Multicoloured.

| | | |
|---|---|---|
| **MS**3769 94×180 mm. $2 Type **515**; $2 Foot of Chutes de Carbet waterfall; $2 Rapids at foot of Chutes de Carbet waterfall | 3·25 | 3·50 |
| **MS**3770 96×67 mm. $6 Waterfall, Ocho Rios, Jamaica (vert) | 3·25 | 3·50 |

**516** Corvette Convertible (1954)

**2003.** 50th Anniv of General Motors Chevrolet Corvette. Multicoloured.

| | | |
|---|---|---|
| **MS**3771 110×151 mm. $2 Type **516**; $2 Corvette Sting Ray (1964); $2 Corvette Sting Ray Convertible (1964); $2 Corvette Convertible (1998) | 5·00 | 5·50 |
| **MS**3772 102×74 mm. $6 Corvette Convertible (1956) | 3·25 | 3·50 |

**517** *Flyer I* (first manned powered flight), 1903

**2003.** Centenary of Powered Flight. Multicoloured.

| | | |
|---|---|---|
| **MS**3773 176×106 mm. $2 Type **517**; $2 Paul Cornu's helicopter on first helicopter flight, 1907; $2 E.B. Ely's biplane making first landing on ship, 1911; $2 Curtiss A-1 (first seaplane), 1911 | 5·00 | 5·50 |
| **MS**3774 176×106 mm. $2 Bell X-5 research aircraft with variable wings, 1951; $2 Convair XFY-1 vertical take-off and landing; $2 North American X-15 rocket aircraft, 1959; $2 Alexei Leonov on first spacewalk, 1965 | 5·00 | 5·50 |
| **MS**3775 176×106 mm. $2 Concorde, 1969; $2 Martin X-24 Lifting Body Vehicle Pre-Space Shuttle, 1969; $2 Apollo-Soyuz, 1975; $2 Viking Robot Mars Expedition, 1976 | 3·25 | 3·50 |
| **MS**3776 Three sheets, each 106×76 mm. (a) $6 Boeing Model 200 Monomail with retractable landing gear, 1930. (b) $6 Bell XS-1 rocket plane breaking sound barrier, 1947. (c) $6 Grumman X-29 with forward swept wings, 1984 | 3·25 | 3·50 |

**2003.** As Nos. 2067/81, with country name overprint smaller and bird inscriptions in English only.

| | | |
|---|---|---|
| 3777 $5 Greater Antillean bullfinch | 2·00 | 2·10 |
| 3778 $10 Caribbean elaenia | 4·25 | 4·50 |

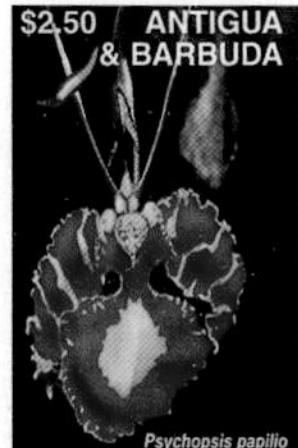


**518** *Psychopsis papilio*

**2003.** Orchids. Multicoloured.

| | | |
|---|---|---|
| **MS**3779 96×138 mm. $2.50 Type **518**; $2.50 *Amesiella philippinensis*; $2.50 *Maclellanara* "Pagan Dove Song"; $2.50 *Phalaenopsis* "Little Hal" | 5·50 | 6·00 |
| **MS**3780 205×124 mm. $2.50 *Daeliocattleya* "Amber Glow"; $2.50 *Hygrochilus parishii*; $2.50 *Dendrobium crystallinum*; $2.50 *Disa* hybrid (all horiz) | 5·50 | 6·00 |
| **MS**3781 98×68 mm. $5 *Cattleya deckeri* (horiz) | 3·25 | 3·50 |

**519** Bull Shark

**2003.** Sharks. Multicoloured.

| | | |
|---|---|---|
| **MS**3782 128×128 mm. $2 Type **519**; $2 Grey reef shark; $2 Black tip shark; $2 Leopard shark | 5·00 | 5·50 |
| **MS**3783 88×88 mm. $5 Great white shark | 3·25 | 3·50 |

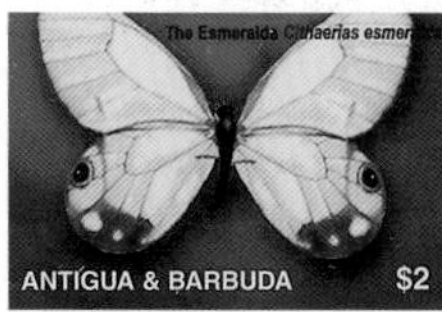


**520** Esmeralda

**2003.** Butterflies. Multicoloured.

| | | |
|---|---|---|
| **MS**3784 105×86 mm. $2 Type **520**; $2 Tiger pierid; $2 Blue night butterfly; $2 *Charaxes nobilis* | 5·00 | 5·50 |
| **MS**3785 205×132 mm. $2.50 Orange-barred sulphur; $2.50 Scarce bamboo page; $2.50 *Charaxes latona*; $2.50 Hewitson's blue hairstreak | 6·00 | 6·50 |
| **MS**3786 98×68 mm. $5 *Diaethia merdionalis* | 3·25 | 3·50 |

**521** Apes

**2003.** Centenary of Circus Clowns. Multicoloured.

| | | |
|---|---|---|
| **MS**3787 119×195 mm. $1.80 Type **521**; $1.80 Mo Lite; $1.80 Gigi; $1.80 "Buttons" M. C. Bride | 4·25 | 4·50 |
| **MS**3788 145×218 mm. $1.80 Chun Group; $1.80 Casselly Sisters (acrobats); $1.80 Oliver Groszer; $1.80 Keith Nelson (sword swallower) | 4·25 | 4·50 |

No. **MS**3787 is cut in the shape of a clown on a bicycle and No. **MS**3788 in the shape of a circus elephant.

**522** "Madonna and Child" (detail) (Bartolommeo Vivarini)

**2003.** Christmas. Multicoloured.

| | | |
|---|---|---|
| 3789 25c. Type **522** | 20 | 10 |
| 3790 30c. "Holy Family" (detail) (Pompeo Girolano Batoni) | 25 | 15 |

3791 45c. "Madonna and Child" (detail) (Benozzo Gozzoli) 35 25
3792 50c. "Madonna and Child" (detail) (Benozzo Gozzoli), Calci Parish Church 35 25
3793 75c. "Madonna and Child giving Blessings" (Benozzo Gozzoli) 50 35
3794 90c. "Madonna and Child" (detail) (Master of the Female Half-Figures) 60 40
3795 $2.50 "The Benois Madonna" (detail) (da Vinci) 1·50 1·75
**MS**3796 70×110 mm. $6 "The Virgin and Child with Angels" (Rosso Fiorentino) 3·25 3·50

**523** Blue and Yellow Macaw ("Blue and Gold Macaw")

**2003.** Birds. Multicoloured.
**MS**3797 96×137 mm. $2.50 Type **523**; $2.50 Green-winged macaw; $2.50 Rainbow lory ("Green-naped Lorikeet"); $2.50 Lesser sulphur-crested cockatoo 5·50 6·00
**MS**3798 205×133 mm. $2.50 Chestnut-fronted macaw ("Severe Macaw"); $2.50 Blue-headed parrot; $2.50 Budgerigar; $2.50 Sun conure (all horiz) 5·50 6·00
**MS**3799 98×68 mm. $5 Waldrapp ("Bald Ibis") (horiz) 3·25 3·50

**524** Diana Monkey

**2004.** Chinese New Year ("Year of the Monkey"). Multicoloured.
**MS**3800 152×95 mm. $1.50 Type **524**; $1.50 Mandrill; $1.50 Lar gibbon; $1.50 Red howler monkey 3·25 3·50

**525** Mountain Landscape

**2004.** Hong Kong 2004 International Stamp Exhibition. Paintings by Ren Xiong. Multicoloured.
**MS**3801 131×138 mm. $1.50 Type **525**; $1.50 "Myriad Bamboo in Misty Rain"; $1.50 Winter landscape; $1.50 House and tree 3·25 3·50
**MS**3802 170×137 mm. $1.50 "Myriad Sceptres worshipping Heaven"; $1.50 Misty mountain landscape; $1.50 Myriad cherry trees; $1.50 Mountain landscape with two streams; $1.50 "Myriad Valleys with competing Streams"; $1.50 Myriad lights 5·00 5·50
**MS**3803 74×153 mm. $2.50 Bird singing from flowering cherry branch; $2.50 Bird in maple tree 3·00 3·25

Nos. **MS**3801/2 show paintings from *The Ten Myriads* album and No. **MS**3803 paintings from *Album after the Poems of Yao Xie*.

**526** Binky skating

**2004.** Arthur the Aardvark by Marc Brown (children's books and TV programme). T **526** and similar vert designs. Multicoloured.
**MS**3804 150×183 mm. $1.50 Type **526**; $150 Buster skating; $1.50 Francine skating; $1.50 D.W.; $1.50 Sue Ellen; $1.50 Muffy skating 5·00 5·50
**MS**3805 150×183 mm. $1.80 Binky in baseball game; $1.80 Muffy with bat; $1.80 Francine running; $1.80 Buster catching ball 4·00 4·50
**MS**3806 150×183 mm. $2.50 Arthur hitting ball; $2.50 Sue Ellen with bat; $2.50 Binky holding bat; $2.50 Arthur with bat raised 4·00 4·50

No. **MS**3804 shows Arthur characters skating and **MS**3805/6 show them playing baseball.

**527** "Freedom of Speech"

**2004.** 25th Death Anniv of Norman Rockwell (artist) (2003). T **527** and similar vert designs. Multicoloured.
**MS**3807 135×145 mm. $2 Type **527**; $2 "Freedom to Worship"; $2 "Freedom from Want"; $2 "Freedom from Fear" 5·00 5·50
**MS**3808 62×82 mm. $6 "Do Unto Others as you would have them Do Unto You". Imperf 5·00 5·50

No. **MS**3807 shows a series of posters and **MS**3808 a painting for Saturday Evening Post cover, 1961.

**528** "Woman with a Flower"

**2004.** 30th Death Anniv of Pablo Picasso (artist). T **528** and similar vert designs. Multicoloured.
**MS**3809 177×127 mm. $2 Type **528**; $2 "Marie-Therese Seated"; $2 The Red Armchair (Marie-Therese) Seated"; $2 "The Dream (Marie-Therese) Seated" 5·00 5·50
**MS**3810 58×69 mm. $5 "Bust of a Girl (Marie-Therese)". Imperf 3·25 3·50

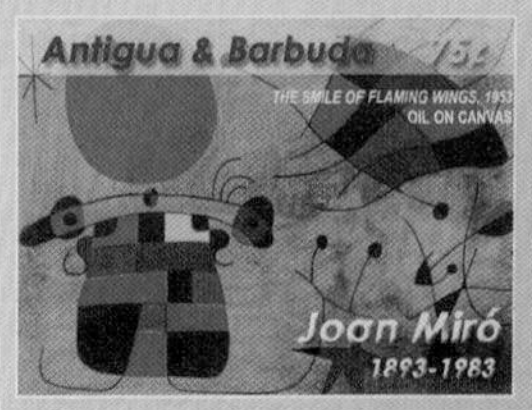

**529** "The Smile of Flaming Wings, 1953"

**2004.** 20th Death Anniv of Joan Miro (artist). Multicoloured.
3811 75c. Type **529** 50 35
3812 90c. "The Bird's Song in the Dew of the Moon, 1955" 60 40
3813 $1 "Dancer II, 1957" (vert) 70 45
3814 $4 "Painting, 1954" (vert) 2·50 3·00
**MS**3815 Sheet 181×152 mm containing four different $2 designs, each entitled "Painting Based on a Collage, 1933" 4·75 5·50
**MS**3816 Two sheets. (a) 102×83 mm. $5 "Bather, 1932". (b) 83×102 mm. $6 "Flame in Space and Nude Woman, 1932." Both imperf. Set of 2 sheets 6·25 6·75

**530** "Vaite Goupil"

**2004.** Death Centenary of Paul Gauguin (2003) (artist). Multicoloured.
3817 25c. Type **530** 25 20
3818 30c. "Autoportrait. Pres du Golgotha" 25 20
3819 75c. "Le Moulin David A Pont-Aven" (horiz) 60 40
3820 $2.50 "Moisson en Bretagne" 1·75 1·90
**MS**3821 77×62 mm. $4 "Cavaliers sur la Plage". Imperf 2·50 2·75

**531** Felipe de Borbon and Letizia Ortiz

**2004.** Marriage of Crown Prince Felipe de Borbon and Letizia Ortiz. Multicoloured.
3822 30c. Type **531** 25 15
3823 50c. Felipe de Borbon and Letizia Ortiz in gardens 35 25
3824 75c. Letizia Ortiz 50 30
3825 90c. Felipe de Borbon 60 40
3826 $1 Felipe de Borbon and Letizia Ortiz wearing dark coats 70 55
3827 $5 Felipe de Borbon and Letizia Ortiz at social function 3·00 3·25
**MS**3828 190×174 mm. $1.80 Family photo; $1.80 Felipe de Borbon swearing allegiance to the Flag; $1.80 Felipe de Borbon with father and grandfather; $1.80 With King Juan Carlos I and Queen Sofia (horiz); $1.80 As No. 3824; $1.80 As No. 3825 6·00 6·50
**MS**3829 Six sheets, each 138×123 mm. (a) $5 Family photo. (b) $5 Felipe de Borbon with father and grandfather. (c) $5 Felipe de Borbon and Letizia Ortiz laughing. (d) $6 With King Juan Carlos I and Queen Sofia (horiz). (e) $6 Felipe de Borbon swearing allegiance to the Flag. (f) $6 Letizia Ortiz reading news Set of 6 sheets 17·00 18·00

**532** Dove carrying Olive Branch

**2004.** United Nations International Year of Peace. Sheet 146×86 mm containing T **532** and similar horiz designs. Multicoloured.
**MS**3830 $3 Type **532**; $3 Dove with olive branch and globe; $3 Dove with olive branch and United Nations emblem 5·50 6·00

**533** King Class 4-6-0

**2004.** Bicentenary of Steam Locomotives. Six sheets containing T **533** and similar multicoloured designs.
**MS**3831 Three sheets. (a) 147×175 mm. $1 Type **533**; $1 Argentinian 11B Class 2-8-0; $1 Baldwin Mikado; $1 Track signal; $1 Signal block instrument; $1 Forders Sidings signal box; $1 Signal on line; $1 Signal in snow; $1 Interior of signal box; $1 Two light signals. (b) 147×176 mm. $1 Class 2-4-0T, Douglas–Port Erin line; $1 Class 4-8-2S, South African; $1 Class 2-8-2, China; $1 St. Pancras Station; $1 Ulverston Station; $1 Bolton Station; $1 Liverpool Street Station; $1 Cannon Street Station; $1 Malvern Station. (c) 146×177 mm. $1 Evening Star (horiz); $1 Indian Railways XC Pacific (horiz); $1 German Kreigslokomotive (horiz); $1 Bullied Light Pacific and Corfe Castle (horiz); $1 Copper cap chimney (horiz); $1 Tallylyn Railway (horiz); $1 Preservation volunteers (horiz); $1 Class Y7 0-4-0T (horiz); $1 Asmara Locoshed and Breda 0-4-0, Eritrea (horiz) Set of 3 sheets 14·00 15·00
**MS**3832 Three sheets, each 97×67 mm. (a) $5 Settle–Carlisle line (horiz). (b) $6 Lake Egridir (horiz). (c) $6 Douro Valley railway (horiz) Set of 3 sheets 9·00 9·50

**534** Pope John Paul II and Mother Teresa

**2004.** 25th Anniv of the Pontificate of Pope John Paul II. Sheet 162×152 mm containing T **534** and similar horiz designs. Multicoloured.
**MS**3833 $1.80 Type **534**; $1.80 At the Wailing Wall; $1.80 With Pres. George W. Bush; $1.80 Waving with left hand; $1.80 Waving with right hand 7·50 7·50

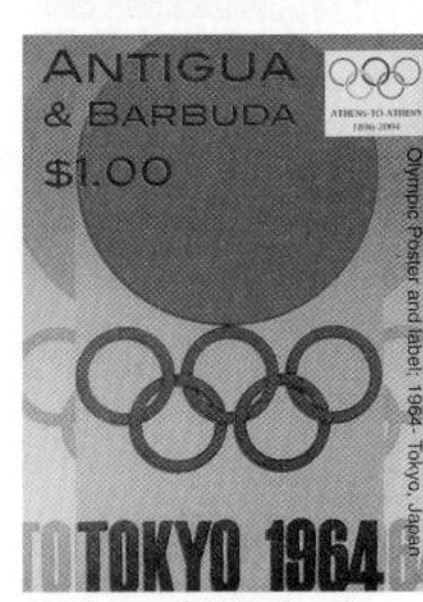

**535** Poster of 1964 Olympic Games, Tokyo

**2004.** Olympic Games, Athens. Multicoloured.
3834 $1 Type **535** 70 50
3835 $1.65 Commemorative medal of 1964 Olympic Games, Tokyo 1·00 1·00
3836 $1.80 Fencing (horiz) 1·10 1·25
3837 $2 Pankration (wrestling, Greek art) (horiz) 1·25 1·40

**536** Milan Galic (Yugoslav player)

**2004.** European Football Championship 2004, Portugal. Commemoration of First European Football Championship (1960). T **536** and similar multicoloured designs.
**MS**3838 147×86 mm. $2 Type **536**; $2 Slava Metreveli (USSR player); $2 Igor Netto (USSR player); $2 Parc des Princes stadium 4·75 5·50
**MS**3839 98×85 mm. $6 USSR football team, 1960 (50×37 *mm*) 3·25 3·50

**537** Derrick Tysoe (Durham Light Infantry)

**2004.** 60th Anniv of D-Day Landings.
3840 **537** 30c. multicoloured 25 20
3841 - 45c. multicoloured 30 20
3842 - $1.50 multicoloured 95 95
3843 - $3 multicoloured 1·75 1·90
**MS**3844 Two sheets, each 177×107 mm. (a) $2 purple, mauve and black; $2 multicoloured; $2 purple; $2 lilac and black. (b) $2 deep blue and black; $2 blue and black; $2 slate and black; $2 slate violet and black Set of 2 sheets 9·00 9·50
**MS**3845 Two sheets, each 100×69 mm. (a) $6 purple and black. (b) $6 brown and black Set of 2 sheets 7·50 8·00

DESIGNS: No. 3840 Type **537**; No. 3841 Lt. Gen. Walter Bedell Smith; 3842 Les Perry, 1st Battalion, Suffolk Regiment; 3843 Major Gen. Percy Hobart; **MS**3844 (a) $2 Tiger II tank; $2 Kurt Meyer and tactics; $2 Canadian infantry; $2 British infantry; (b) $2 Hamilcar and Tetrarch tank; $2 Horsa Glider and soldiers; $2 Beachheads; $2 Soldiers and civilians; **MS**3845 (a) $6 Mulberry Harbour; (b) $6 Sherman tank.

**538** Queen Juliana

**2004.** Queen Juliana of the Netherlands. Sheet, 170×180 mm, containing T **538** and similar horiz designs. Multicoloured.
**MS**3846 $2 Type **538**; $2 With Prince Bernhard; $2 With Princess Beatrix; $2 With Princess Irene; $2 With Princess Margriet; $2 With Princess Christina 7·50 8·00

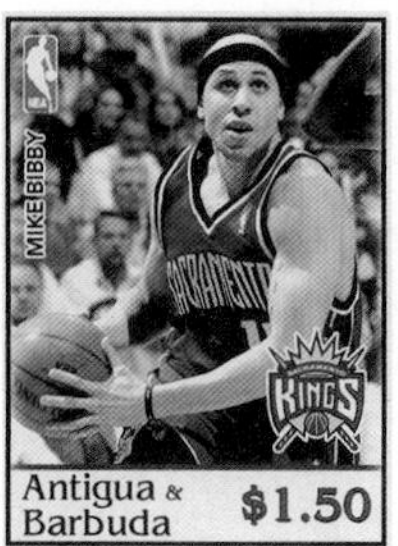

**539** Mike Bibby

**2004.** National Basketball Association, China. Sheet, 204×140 mm, containing T **539** and similar vert designs. Multicoloured.
**MS**3847 Type **539**; $1.50 Jim Jackson; $1.50 Tracy McGrady; $1.50 Chris Webber; $1.50 Peja Stojakovic; $1.50 Yao Ming 7·00 7·00

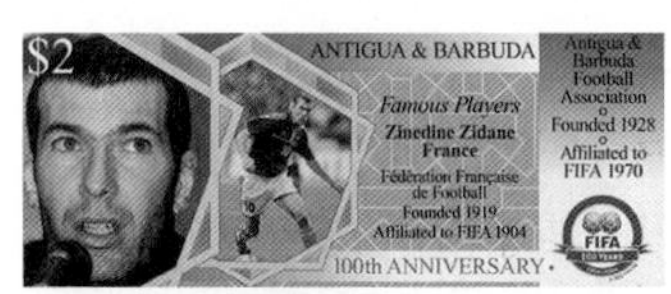

**540** Zinedine Zidane (France)

**2004.** Centenary of FIFA (Federation Internationale de Football Association). T **540** and similar horiz designs. Multicoloured.
**MS**3848 193×97 mm. $2 Type **540**; $2 Roberto Baggio (Italy); $2 Franz Beckenbaur (Germany); $2 Ossie Ardiles (Argentina) 3·50 3·75
**MS**3849 108×87 mm. $6 Jimmy Greaves (England) 3·50 3·75

**541** George Herman "Babe" Ruth

**2004.** Centenary of Baseball World Series. Sheet 127×118 mm containing T **541** and similar vert designs showing portraits of George Herman Ruth Jr ("Babe Ruth"). Multicoloured.
**MS**3850 $1.80 Type **541**; $1.80 Wearing crown; $1.80 Wearing striped cap; $1.80 Holding baseball bat over shoulder 3·50 3·75

**542** John Denver

**2004.** John Denver Commemoration. Sheet 117×107 mm containing T **542** and similar vert designs. Multicoloured.
**MS**3851 $1.50 Type **542**; $1.50 John Denver (wearing pale waistcoat); $1.50 Wearing dark waistcoat; $1.50 Facing left 3·25 3·50

**543** "If you had wider shoulders..."

**2004.** "The Family Circus" (cartoon). T **543** and similar vert designs. Multicoloured.
**MS**3852 115×176 mm. $2 Type **543**; $2 "Billy attacked me too hard!" (red border); $2 "Who tee-peed the mummies?"; $2 "Looking out there makes me realize its indeed the little things that count" 4·25 4·50
**MS**3853 115×176 mm. $2 "Billy attacked me too hard!" (purple border); $2 "His ears came from where his eyes are"; $2 "Tennessee!"; $2 "One candy, or one bowl?" 4·25 4·50
**MS**3854 176×115 mm. $2 "Someday I might travel to another planet, but I'm not sure why"; $2 "Adam and Eve were lucky. They didn't have any history to learn"; $2 "My backpack is too full. Will somebody help me to stand up?"; $2 "I tripped because one foot tried to hug the other foot" 4·25 4·50
**MS**3855 176×115 mm. $2 "If you don't put enough stamps on it the mailman will only take it part way"; $2 "Gee, Grandma, you have a lot of thoughts on your wall"; $2 "Shall I play for you, pa-rum-pa-rum-pummm..."; $2 "You have to do that when you're married" 4·25 4·50
**MS**3856 192×105 mm. $2 Billy; $2 Jeffy; $2 PJ; $2 Dolly 4·25 4·50

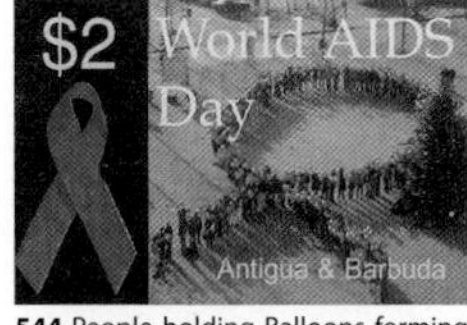

**544** People holding Balloons forming AIDS Ribbon

**2004.** World AIDS Day.
3857 **544** $2 multicoloured 1·25 1·40

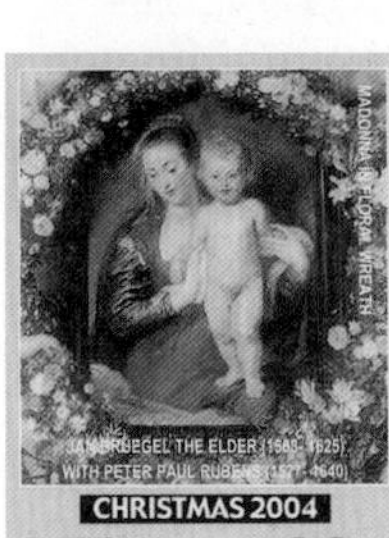

**545** "Madonna in Floral Wreath" (Bruegel the Elder with Rubens)

**546** Santa on Skis

**2004.** Christmas. Multicoloured. (a) As T **545**.
3858 20c. Type **545** 20 15
3859 25c. "Madonna and Child" (detail) (Mabuse (Jan Gossaert)) 20 25
3860 $1 "Floral Wreath with Virgin and Child" (detail) (Daniel Seghers) 70 45
3861 $1.80 "Madonna and Child" (detail) (Andrea Mantegna) 1·10 1·25
**MS**3862 70×100 mm. $6 "Madonna in a Floral Wreath" (Daniel Seghers) 3·25 3·50

(b) As T **546**.
3863 30c. Type **546** 25 15
3864 45c. Santa ornament with arms raised 30 25
3865 50c. Santa on chimney 35 25

**547** American Pit (inscr "Pitt") Bull Terrier

**2005.** Cats and Dogs. Multicoloured.
3866 30c. Type **547** 30 20
3867 75c. Golden Persian 50 40
3868 90c. Maltese (dog) 60 45
3869 $1 Calico shorthair (cat) 70 60
3870 $1.50 Siamese 90 90
3871 $1.50 Rottweiler 90 90
3872 $3 Tabby Persian 1·75 2·00
3873 $3 Australian terrier 1·75 2·00
**MS**3874 Two sheets, each 100×70 mm. (a) $5 Turkish cat. (b) $5 German shepherd dog (horiz) 6·00 6·50

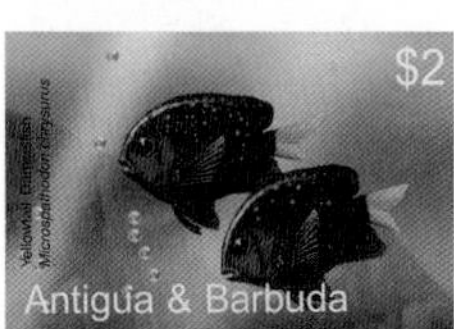

**548** Yellowtail Damselfish

**2005.** Tropical Sea Life. Multicoloured.
**MS**3875 143×84 mm. $2 Type **548**; $2 French angelfish; $2 Horseshoe crab; $2 Emerald mithrax crab 4·75 5·00
**MS**3876 100×70 mm. $6 Spanish hogfish 3·25 3·50

The stamps within **MS**3875 form a composite design of a coral reef.

**549** Figure-of-eight Butterfly

**2005.** Insects. Multicoloured.
**MS**3877 143×83 mm. $2 Type **549**; $2 Honey bee; $2 Migratory grasshopper; $2 Hercules beetle 4·75 5·00
**MS**3878 100×70 mm. $5 Cramer's mesene butterfly (vert) 3·00 3·25

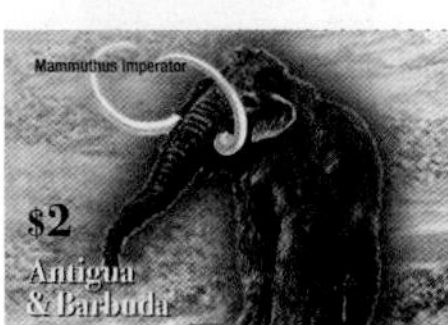

**550** Mammuthus imperator

**2005.** Prehistoric Animals. Multicoloured.
**MS**3879 Three sheets, each 140×110 mm. (a) $2 Type **550**; $2 Brontops; $2 Hyracotherium; $2 Propalaeotherium. (b) $2.50 Ceratosaurs; $2.50 Coelurosaurs; $2.50 Ornitholestes; $2.50 Baryonyx. (c) $3 Plateosaurus; $3 Yangchuanosaurus; $3 Ceolophysis; $3 Lystrosaurus 15·00 16·00
**MS**3880 Three sheets, each 98×70 mm. (a) $4 Triceratops. (b) $5 Stegosaurus. (c) $6 Coelodonta 6·00 6·25

The stamps within Nos. **MS**3879a/c each form composite background designs.

**551** Uruguay Team, 1930

**2005.** 75th Anniv of First World Cup Football Championship, Uruguay. Multicoloured.
3881 $2.50 Type **551** 1·50 1·60
3882 $2.50 Hector Castro scoring goal against Argentina, World Cup final, 1930 1·50 1·60
3883 $2.50 Estadio Centenario 1·50 1·60
3884 $2.50 Hector Castro 1·50 1·60
**MS**3885 111×86 mm. $6 Players after victory of Uruguay, 1930 3·25 3·50

**552** Bust of Von Schiller (C. L. Richter), Central Park, New York

**2005.** Death Bicentenary of Friedrich von Schiller (poet and dramatist). Multicoloured.
3886 $3 Type **552** 1·75 2·00
3887 $3 Modern performance of *Kabale und Liebe* 1·75 2·00
3888 $3 Von Schiller's birthplace, Marbach, Germany 1·75 2·00
**MS**3889 66×95 mm. $6 Von Schiller and statue, Lincoln Park, Chicago 3·25 3·50

**553** *Misterio en la Isla de los Monstruos*, 1961

**2005.** Death Centenary of Jules Verne (writer). Posters from films of Jules Verne's novels. Multicoloured.
3890 $2 Type **553** 1·25 1·40
3891 $2 *Journey to the Centre of the Earth*, 1961 1·25 1·40
3892 $2 *From the Earth to the Moon*, 1956 1·25 1·40
3893 $2 *Los Diablos del Mar*, 1961 1·25 1·40
**MS**3894 103×97 mm. $5 Michael Strogoff (56×41 mm) 3·00 3·25

**554** British attempting to Board Spanish Ship *Santisima Trinidad*

**2005.** Bicentenary of the Battle of Trafalgar. Multicoloured.
3895 90c. Type **554** 1·00 70
3896 $1 Sailors clinging to wreckage and HMS *Royal Sovereign*, *Santa Ana*, HMS *Mars*, *Fouguex* and HMS *Temeraire* 1·25 90
3897 $1.50 HMS *Britannia* firing on crippled French *Bucentaure* 1·50 1·50
3898 $1.80 French *Redoubtable* and HMS *Victory* 1·75 2·00

| | | | |
|---|---|---|---|
| **MS**3899 | 90×122 mm. $6 Crew of HMS *Victory* firing during battle | 4·75 | 5·00 |

**555** Ronald Reagan

**2005.** Ronald Reagan (US President 1981–9) Commemoration.

| | | | |
|---|---|---|---|
| 3900 | **555** $1.50 multicoloured | 90 | 90 |

**556** Defeated German Soldiers, Red Square, 9 May 1945

**2005.** 60th Anniv of Victory in Europe Day. Multicoloured.

| | | | |
|---|---|---|---|
| 3901 | $1.50 Type **556** | 90 | 90 |
| 3902 | $1.50 General Montgomery | 90 | 90 |
| 3903 | $1.50 Marshal Zhukov | 90 | 90 |
| 3904 | $1.50 General Bradley | 90 | 90 |

**557** Churchill, Roosevelt and Stalin at Yalta Summit, 1945

**2005.** 60th Anniv of Victory in Japan Day. Multicoloured.

| | | | |
|---|---|---|---|
| 3905 | $2 Type **557** | 1·25 | 1·25 |
| 3906 | $2 US troops raising flag on Mt. Suribachi | 1·25 | 1·25 |
| 3907 | $2 Gen. McArthur signing Japanese surrender documents | 1·25 | 1·25 |
| 3908 | $2 Surrendering Japanese officials, 2 September 1945 | 1·25 | 1·25 |

**558** "Mother Hen and her Brood" (Wang Ning)

**2005.** Chinese New Year ("Year of the Rooster"). Multicoloured.

| | | | |
|---|---|---|---|
| 3909 | $1 Type **558** | 70 | 75 |
| **MS**3910 | 75×105 mm. $4 "Mother Hen and her Brood" (Wang Ning) | 2·50 | 2·75 |

**559** Dwight Howard, Orlando Magic

**2005.** US National Basketball Association Players. Multicoloured.

| | | | |
|---|---|---|---|
| 3911 | 75c. Type **559** | 70 | 55 |
| 3912 | 75c. Lucious Harris, Cleveland Cavaliers | 70 | 55 |
| 3913 | 75c. Emeka Okafor, Charlotte Bobcats | 70 | 55 |
| 3914 | 75c. Antonio McDyess, Detroit Pistons | 70 | 55 |
| 3915 | 75c. Ray Allen, Seattle Supersonics | 70 | 55 |

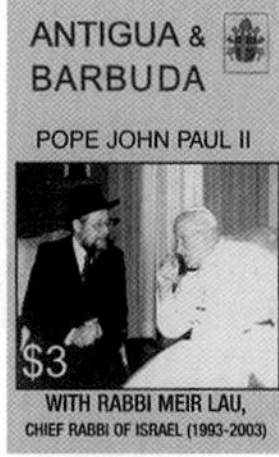

**560** Pope John Paul II with Rabbi Meir Lau (Chief Rabbi of Israel, 1993–2003)

**2005.** Pope John Paul II Commemoration.

| | | | |
|---|---|---|---|
| 3916 | **560** $3 multicoloured | 2·75 | 2·75 |

**561** Italy 1979 World Rotary Congress Stamp

**2005.** Centenary of Rotary International. Multicoloured.

| | | | |
|---|---|---|---|
| 3917 | $3 Type **561** | 1·75 | 1·90 |
| 3918 | $3 Paul Harris medallion and "Sow the Seeds of Love" | 1·75 | 1·90 |
| 3919 | $3 Paul Harris (founder), Tokyo, 1935 | 1·75 | 1·90 |
| **MS**3920 | 100×70 mm. $6 Young African children (horiz) | 3·25 | 3·50 |

**562** Albert Einstein

**2005.** 50th Death Anniv of Albert Einstein (physicist). Multicoloured.

| | | | |
|---|---|---|---|
| 3921 | $3 Type **562** | 1·75 | 1·90 |
| 3922 | $3 On bicycle | 1·75 | 1·90 |
| 3923 | $3 Albert Einstein (grey background) | 1·75 | 1·90 |

**563** Hans Christian Andersen

**2005.** Birth Bicentenary of Hans Christian Andersen (writer). Multicoloured.

| | | | |
|---|---|---|---|
| 3924 | $3 Type **563** | 1·75 | 1·90 |
| 3925 | $3 Statue in Central Park, New York | 1·75 | 1·90 |
| 3926 | $3 Tombstone | 1·75 | 1·90 |
| **MS**3927 | 100×70 mm. $6 Hans Christian Andersen seated in chair | 3·25 | 3·50 |

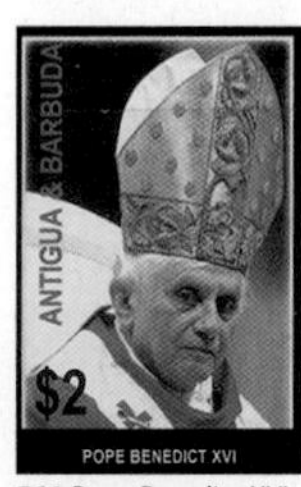

**564** Pope Benedict XVI

**2005.** Election of Pope Benedict XVI.

| | | | |
|---|---|---|---|
| 3928 | **564** $2 multicoloured | 1·75 | 1·75 |

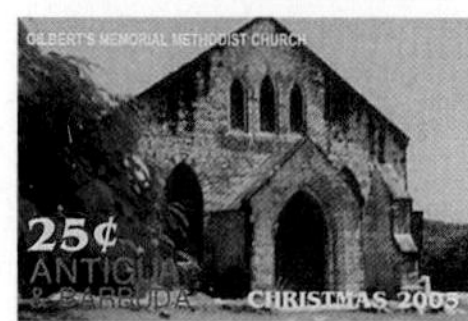

**565** Gilbert's Memorial Methodist Church

**2005.** Christmas. Churches. Multicoloured.

| | | | |
|---|---|---|---|
| 3929 | 25c. Type **565** | 25 | 15 |
| 3930 | 30c. The People's Church, Barbuda | 30 | 20 |
| 3931 | 30c. Tyrell's Roman Catholic Church | 30 | 20 |
| 3932 | 45c. St. Barnabas Anglican Church | 35 | 20 |
| 3933 | 50c. St. Peter's Anglican Church | 40 | 30 |
| 3934 | 75c. Spring Gardens Moravian Church | 50 | 40 |
| 3935 | 75c. St. Steven's Anglican Church | 50 | 40 |
| 3936 | 90c. Pilgrim Holiness Church (vert) | 60 | 45 |
| 3937 | 90c. Holy Family Catholic Cathedral | 60 | 45 |
| 3938 | $1 Ebenezer Methodist Church | 70 | 75 |
| **MS**3939 | Two sheets, each 100×70 mm. (a) $5 St. John's Cathedral. (b) $5 Service at Spring Gardens Moravian Church (vert) | 6·00 | 6·50 |

**566** The Joiners Loft, Nelson's Dockyard

**2005.** National Parks of Antigua. Multicoloured.

| | | | |
|---|---|---|---|
| 3940 | 20c. Type **566** | 15 | 20 |
| 3941 | 20c. Pay Office, Nelson's Dockyard (vert) | 15 | 20 |
| 3942 | 30c. Bakery, Nelson's Dockyard | 30 | 20 |
| 3943 | 30c. Admirals House Museum, Nelson's Dockyard | 30 | 20 |
| 3944 | 75c. Devil's Bridge National Park | 50 | 40 |
| 3945 | 75c. View from Shirley Heights Lookout, Nelson's Dockyard National Park | 50 | 40 |
| 3946 | 90c. Green Castle Hill National Park | 60 | 45 |
| 3947 | 90c. Fort Berkeley, Nelson's Dockyard National Park | 60 | 45 |
| 3948 | $1.50 Pigeon Point Beach, Nelson's Dockyard National Park | 90 | 90 |
| 3949 | $1.50 Half Moon Bay National Park | 90 | 90 |
| 3950 | $1.80 Cannon at Fort Berkeley | 1·10 | 1·25 |
| **MS**3951 | Two sheets. (a) 96×67 mm. $5 Frigate birds nesting at Codrington Lagoon National Park, Barbuda. (b) 65×96 mm. $5 Cannon and Admirals House Museum, Nelson's Dockyard (vert) | 6·00 | 6·50 |

**567** Yellowstone National Park

**2006.** National Parks of the USA. Multicoloured.

| | | | |
|---|---|---|---|
| 3952 | $1.50 Type **567** | 90 | 90 |
| 3953 | $1.50 Olympic National Park | 90 | 90 |
| 3954 | $1.50 Glacier National Park | 90 | 90 |
| 3955 | $1.50 Grand Canyon National Park | 90 | 90 |
| 3956 | $1.50 Yosemite National Park | 90 | 90 |
| 3957 | $1.50 Great Smoky Mountains National Park | 90 | 90 |
| **MS**3958 | 95×70 mm. $6 Mount Rainier National Park (42×28 mm) | 3·25 | 3·50 |

**568** Bishop John Ephraim Knight

**2006.** 250th Anniv of Moravian Church in Antigua. Moravian Church Antigua Conference. Multicoloured.

| | | | |
|---|---|---|---|
| 3959 | 30c. Type **568** | 25 | 15 |
| 3960 | $1 John Andrew Buckley (minister 1856–79) | 70 | 55 |
| 3961 | $1.50 Old Spring Gardens Moravian Church, 1854–1963 (horiz) | 90 | 90 |
| **MS**3962 | Three sheets, each 95×60 mm. (a) $5 Westerby Memorial, St. John's. (b) $5 Sandbox Tree (site of beginnings of Antigua Moravian Church). (c) $5 Spring Gardens Teachers College, 1854–1958 (horiz) | 5·50 | 6·00 |

**569** Princess Elizabeth

**2006.** 80th Birthday of Queen Elizabeth II. Multicoloured.

| | | | |
|---|---|---|---|
| 3963 | $2 Type **569** | 1·10 | 1·10 |
| 3964 | $2 Princess Elizabeth wearing cream dress and pearl necklace | 1·10 | 1·10 |
| 3965 | $2 Princess Elizabeth wearing white blouse | 1·10 | 1·10 |
| 3966 | $2 Queen Elizabeth II wearing diadem and red dress | 1·10 | 1·10 |
| **MS**3967 | 120×120 mm. $6 Queen Elizabeth II wearing diadem and drop earrings | 3·00 | 3·25 |

**570** Marilyn Monroe

**2006.** 80th Birth Anniv of Marilyn Monroe (actress).

| | | | |
|---|---|---|---|
| 3968 | **570** $3 multicoloured | 1·75 | 1·75 |

**571** Austria 2s.20 Ice Hockey Stamp

**2006.** Winter Olympic Games, Turin. Showing Austrian stamps issued for 1964 Olympic Games, Innsbruck (Nos. 3964/6) or poster (No. 3967). Multicoloured.

| | | | |
|---|---|---|---|
| 3969 | 75c. Type **571** | 50 | 40 |
| 3970 | 75c. Poster for Winter Olympic Games, Sapporo, 1972 (vert) | 50 | 40 |
| 3971 | 90c. Japan 1972 Winter Olympics 20y. skiing stamp (vert) | 60 | 40 |
| 3972 | 90c. (1s.80) Figure skating stamp | 60 | 40 |
| 3973 | $2 4s. Bobsleighing stamp | 1·25 | 1·25 |
| 3974 | $3 Poster for Winter Olympic Games, Innsbruck, 1964 (vert) | 1·75 | 1·75 |

**572** Benjamin Franklin

**2006.** Washington 2006 International Stamp Exhibition. Showing Benjamin Franklin. Multicoloured.

**MS**3975 Two sheets, each 140×152 mm. (a) $3×4 Type **572**,Wearing red in oval portrait in gold frame (84×93 mm) (imperf); USA 1847 5c. stamp; Close-up portrait. (b) $3×3 Round portraits in gold frames: Wearing red; Sitting at desk; In close-up 11·00 12·00

**573** Mozart's Viola

**2006.** 250th Birth Anniv of Wolfgang Amadeus Mozart (composer). Multicoloured.

3976 $3 Type **573** 1·75 1·75
3977 $3 Mozart aged eleven 1·75 1·75
3978 $3 Young Mozart 1·75 1·75
3979 $3 Mozart in Verona, 1770 1·75 1·75

**574** Elvis Presley in "Charro!"

**2006.** 50th Anniv of Elvis Presley's Film Debut. Sheet 190×127 mm containing T **574** and similar vert designs showing film posters. Multicoloured.

3980 $3 Type **574** 1·75 1·75
3981 $3 "Follow That Dream" 1·75 1·75
3982 $3 "G I Blues" 1·75 1·75
3983 $3 "Blue Hawaii" 1·75 1·75

**575** Leaders after Garbage Collection Race, 2002

**2006.** 75th Anniv of Antigua and Barbuda Girl Guides. Multicoloured.

3984 25c. Type **575** 20 10
3985 30c. Girl guides colour party (horiz) 25 15
3986 45c. Uniformed and non-uniformed members 30 20
3987 50c. Girl guides marching band (horiz) 30 25
3988 $1 Leeward Islands leaders training camp, 1946 (horiz) 70 55

**MS**3989 Three sheets, each 100×70 mm. (a) $5 Enrolment ceremony, 2006 (horiz). (b) $5 Girl guides gathering at Fort James, 1935 (horiz). (c) $5 Lisa Simon, Assistant Commissioner 8·25 8·50

**576** HS-748 Hawker Siddely Avro

**2006.** 50th Anniv of LIAT (Leeward Islands Air Transport) Airline. Multicoloured.

3990 30c. Type **576** 25 15
3991 50c. BN2 Islanders on ground 30 20
3992 50c. BN2 Norman Islander 30 20
3993 50c. Beechcraft Twin Bonanza (vert) 30 20
3994 $1.50 BAC111-orange and HS748-pink/lilac on ground 90 90
3995 $2.50 Present brand DH8-300 50 seater De Havilland on ground 1·60 1·40

**MS**3996 70×100 mm. $5 Sir Frank Delisle (founder) and first Beechcraft Twin Bonanza N9614R (vert) 2·75 3·00

**577** Magnificent Frigate Bird

**2006.** 25th Anniv of Independence. Multicoloured.

3997 25c. Type **577** 20 10
3998 25c. Fallow deer hinds 20 10
3999 25c. Fallow deer stag on beach 20 10
4000 25c. Magnificent frigate birds in flight and on nest 20 10
4001 30c. Pineapple 25 15
4002 $1 National flag 70 55
4003 $1.50 Coat of Arms 90 90

**MS**4004 100×70 mm. $5 New Parliament building (38×49 mm) 2·75 3·00

**578** JSC Shuttle Mission Simulator (SMS)

**2006.** Space Anniversaries. Multicoloured. (a) 25th Anniv of First Flight of Space Shuttle "Columbia".

4005 $2 Type **578** 1·25 1·25
4006 $2 STS-1 prime crew during classroom session 1·25 1·25
4007 $2 STS-1 "Columbia" on launch pad 1·25 1·25
4008 $2 STS-1 "Columbia" blast-off 1·25 1·25
4009 $2 Pre-touchdown landing of "Columbia" at Edwards AFB, California 1·25 1·25
4010 $2 Space shuttle "Columbia" landing at Edwards Air Force Base 1·25 1·25

(b) 40th Anniv of "Luna 9" Moon Landing.

4011 $3 Molniya 8K78M rocket on launch vehicle 1·75 1·75
4012 $3 "Luna 9" flight apparatus 1·75 1·75
4013 $3 Image of Moon's surface transmitted by "Luna 9" 1·75 1·75
4014 $3 "Luna 9" capsule 1·75 1·75

(c) 30th Anniv (2005) of "Apollo-Soyuz" Test Project.

4015 $3 "Apollo" crew boarding transfer van 1·75 1·75
4016 $3 Handshake after "Apollo-Soyuz" linkup 1·75 1·75
4017 $3 Display of ASTP commemorative plaque 1·75 1·75
4018 $3 Recovery of ASTP Apollo command module 1·75 1·75

**MS**4019 Three sheets, each 100×70 mm. (a) $6 Calipso satellite. (b) $6 SS *Atlantis* docking on Space Station "MIR". (c) $6 Artist's concept of a NASA spaceship to orbit the Moon 9·00 9·75

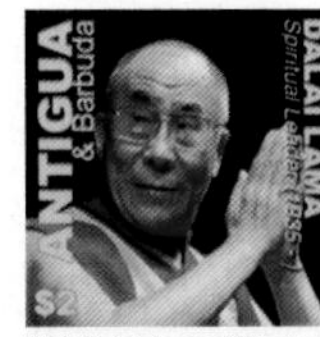


**579** Dalai Lama (Tibetan leader)

**2006.** Civil Rights. Multicoloured.

4020 $2 Type **579** 1·25 1·25
4021 $2 Abraham Lincoln (slavery abolitionist) 1·25 1·25
4022 $2 Susan Anthony (women's suffragist) 1·25 1·25
4023 $2 Harriet Tubman (slave liberator) 1·25 1·25
4024 $2 Mahatma Gandhi (Indian leader) 1·25 1·25
4025 $2 Nelson Mandela (anti-apartheid leader) 1·25 1·25
4026 $2 Rosa Parks (civil rights activist) 1·25 1·25

**MS**4027 70×100 mm. $5 Martin Luther King (civil rights leader) 2·75 3·00

**580** "Landscape with the Baptism of the Eunuch" (detail)

**2006.** 400th Birth Anniv of Rembrandt Harmenszoon van Rijn (artist). Multicoloured.

4028 50c. Type **580** 30 20
4029 75c. "Landscape with a Coach" (detail) 50 40
4030 $1 "River Landscape with Ruins" (detail) 70 55
4031 $2 "Landscape with a Castle" (detail) 1·25 1·25
4032 $2 "Samson Posing the Riddle to the Wedding Guests" (detail, Samson's bride) 1·25 1·25
4033 $2 "Samson Posing the Riddle to the Wedding Guests" (detail, two men) 1·25 1·25
4034 $2 "Samson Posing the Riddle to the Wedding Guests" (detail, two guests listening) 1·25 1·25
4035 $2 "Samson Posing the Riddle to the Wedding Guests" (detail, woman) 1·25 1·25
4036 $2 "The Holy Family (detail, man sitting at table) 1·25 1·25
4037 $2 "The Good Samaritan arriving at the Inn" (detail) 1·25 1·25
4038 $2 "Rebecca Taking Leave of her Family" (detail) 1·25 1·25
4039 $2 "The Holy Family" (detail, man sitting) 1·25 1·25

**MS**4040 Two sheets, each 70×100 mm. (a) $5 "Self-Portrait". (b) $5 "Rembrandt's Mother". Both imperf 5·50 6·00

**581** Bauble

**2006.** Christmas. Multicoloured.

4041 30c. Type **581** 25 15
4042 90c. Gold star 65 50
4043 $1 Red bell 70 55
4044 $1.50 Miniature tree 90 75

**MS**4045 100×150 mm. $2×4 As Nos. 4041/4 5·00 4·50

**MS**4046 100×70 mm. $6 Santa on beach with wrapped presents 3·00 2·75

Nos. 4041/5 show Christmas tree decorations.

Stamps from **MS**4045 are in similar designs to Nos. 4041/4 but have the country inscription at top and no coloured panel at the foot of the stamp.

The background of **MS**4045 forms a composite design showing a decorated Christmas tree.

**582** Betty Boop

**2006.** Betty Boop. Multicoloured.

4047 $1.50 Type **582** 90 75
4048 $1.50 Leaning forward 90 75
4049 $1.50 Holding mirror 90 75
4050 $1.50 Holding microphone 90 75
4051 $1.50 Seated, looking over shoulder 90 75
4052 $1.50 Wearing red heart garter 90 75

**MS**4053 70×100 mm. $3 "BETTY BOOP"; $3 With yellow fur stole 3·00 2·75

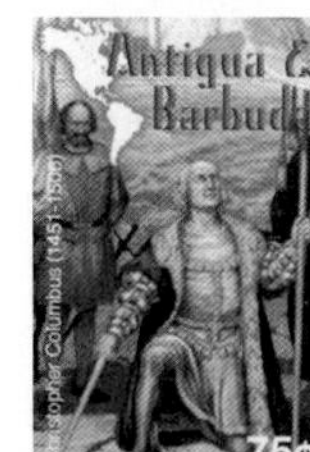


**583** Columbus landing in New World

**2007.** 500th Death Anniv of Christopher Columbus. Multicoloured.

4054 75c. Type **583** 50 40
4055 90c. Christopher Columbus 60 45
4056 $2 Columbus (portrait in oval frame) 1·25 1·25
4057 $3 Columbus (in profile) 1·75 1·75

**MS**4058 100×70 mm. $6 *Nina, Pinta* and *Santa Maria* 3·00 3·25

**584** National Flags forming Knot

**2007.** Centenary of World Scout Movement. Multicoloured.

4059 $4 Type **584** 2·25 2·25

**MS**4060 110×80 mm. $6 National flags forming knot 3·00 3·25

**585** Ensign Kennedy

**2007.** 90th Birth Anniv of John F. Kennedy (American President 1960–3). Multicoloured.

4061 $3 Type **585** 1·75 1·75
4062 $3 Kennedy and crew members 1·75 1·75
4063 $3 Kennedy at the USS *PT-109* 1·75 1·75
4064 $3 Kennedy in the South Pacific 1·75 1·75
4065 $3 Campaigning on crutches 1·75 1·75
4066 $3 "The New Congressman" 1·75 1·75
4067 $3 John F. Fitzgerald, Joseph Kennedy and John F. Kennedy 1·75 1·75
4068 $3 "Celebrating Victory" 1·75 1·75

Nos. 4061/4 (showing John Kennedy in the Navy, 1941–5) and 4065/8 (showing his election to the House of Representatives, 1947–53).

**586** *Alamanda*

**587** *Callicore maimuna* (figure-of-eight butterfly)

**2007.** Flowers. Multicoloured.

4069 75c. Type **586** 50 40
4070 90c. *Bidens sulphurea* 60 45
4071 $1 *Alstroemeria caryophyllacea* 70 55
4072 $2 *Canna limbata* (horiz) 1·25 1·25
4073 $2 *Gazania rigens* (horiz) 1·25 1·25
4074 $2 *Gloriosa rothschildiana* (horiz) 1·25 1·25
4075 $2 *Hibiscus sinensis* (horiz) 1·25 1·25
4076 $4 *Bougainvillea* 2·25 2·25

**MS**4077 100×70 mm. $6 *Caesalpinia pulcherrima* 3·00 3·25

**2007.** Butterflies of the Caribbean. Multicoloured.

4078 75c. Type **587** 50 40
4079 90c. *Dismorphia amphione* (tiger pierid) 60 45

4080 $1 *Eryphanis polyxena* (purple mort bleu) 70 55

4081 $4 *Colobura dirce* (mosaic butterfly) 2·25 2·25

**MS**4082 130×108 mm. $2×4 *Actinote pellenea* (small lacewing); *Anteos clorinde* (clorinde); *Morpho peleides* (common morpho); *Anartia jatrophae* (white peacock) 4·50 4·50

**MS**4083 70×99 mm. $5 *Catonephele numilia* (Grecian shoemaker) 2·75 2·75

The stamps and margins of No. **MS**4082 form a composite design of palm tree foliage.

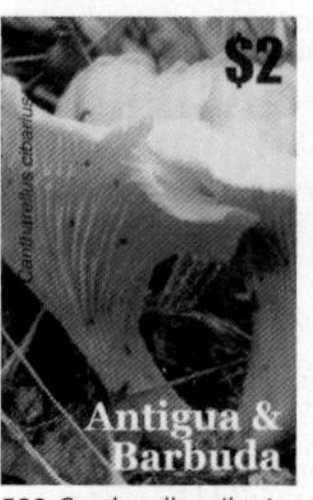

**588** *Cantharellus cibarius* **590** Kenneth Benjamin

**589** *Oncidium flexuosum*

**2007.** Mushrooms of the Caribbean. Multicoloured.

**MS**4084 131×108 mm. $2×4 Type **588**; *Auricularia auricula-judae*; *Mycena acicula*; *Peziza vesiculosa* 4·50 4·50

**MS**4085 100×70 mm. $6 *Pleurotus djamor* 3·00 3·25

The stamps and margins of No. **MS**4084 form a composite design.

**2007.** Orchids. Multicoloured.

4086 $3 Type **589** 1·75 1·75

4087 $3 *Paphiopedilum Pinocchio* 1·75 1·75

4088 $3 *Cattleyopsis lindenii* 1·75 1·75

4089 $3 *Cattleyopsis cubensis* 1·75 1·75

**MS**4090 100×70 mm. $6 *Osmoglossum pulchellum* (*vert*) 3·00 3·25

**2007.** World Cup Cricket, West Indies. Famous West Indian Cricketers. Multicoloured.

4091 25c. Type **590** 15 10

4092 30c. Anderson Roberts 20 15

4093 90c. Ridley Jacobs 60 45

4094 $1 Curtly Ambrose 70 55

4095 $1.50 Richard (Richie) Richardson 90 75

**MS**4096 117×90 mm. $5 Sir Vivian Richards 2·75 3·00

**591** Princess Elizabeth and Duke of Edinburgh

**2007.** Diamond Wedding of Queen Elizabeth II and Duke of Edinburgh. Multicoloured.

4097 $1.50 Type **591** 90 75

4098 $1.50 Wedding shoes 90 75

**MS**4099 101×70 mm. $6 On wedding day with family (*vert*) 3·00 3·25

**592** Camellias and Butterfly

**2007.** 50th Death Anniv of Qi Baishi (artist). Paintings on Fans. Multicoloured.

4100 $1.50 Type **592** 90 75

4101 $1.50 Two shrimps and arrowhead leaves 90 75

4102 $1.50 Gourd and ladybug 90 75

4103 $1.50 Bird 90 75

4104 $1.50 Landscape 90 75

4105 $1.50 Five shrimps 90 75

**MS**4106 (a) 102×72 mm. $3 Chrysanthemums; $3 Maple leaves (both vert). (b) 72×102 mm. $6 Wisteria (*vert*) 7·00 7·50

**593** Ferrari 365 GTS4, 1969

**2007.** Ferrari Classic Cars. Multicoloured.

4107 $1.40 Type **593** 85 70

4108 $1.40 Superamerica, 2005 85 70

4109 $1.40 F1 90, 1990 85 70

4110 $1.40 400 Automatic, 1976 85 70

4111 $1.40 250 GT Coupe, 1954 85 70

4112 $1.40 156 F2, 1960 85 70

4113 $1.40 312 P, 1972 85 70

4114 $1.40 D 50, 1956 85 70

**594** Concorde 01 rolled out, Filton, 20 Sept 1971

**2007.** Concorde. Multicoloured.

4115 $1.50 Type **594** 90 75

4116 $1.50 Concorde 01 (G-AXDN) in flight (green border) 90 75

4117 $1.50 As Type **594** (violet border) 90 75

4118 $1.50 As No. 4116 (magenta) 90 75

4119 $1.50 As Type **594** (green border) 90 75

4120 $1.50 As No. 4116 (violet border) 90 75

4121 $1.50 Concorde and London Eye (green inscr) 90 75

4122 $1.50 Concorde and Sydney Opera House (black inscr) 90 75

4123 $1.50 As No. 4121 (magenta inscr) 90 75

4124 $1.50 As No. 4122 (orange inscr) 90 75

4125 $1.50 As No. 4121 (black inscr) 90 75

4126 $1.50 As No. 4122 (blue inscr) 90 75

Nos. 4115/20 show Concorde 01, the first pre-production aircraft.

Nos. 4121/6 commemorate the London to Sydney flight record set on 13 February 1985. The colours given for Nos. 4121/6 are those of the country inscription 'ANTIGUA & BARBUDA'.

**595** NH-90 Helicopter

**2007.** Centenary of the Helicopter. Multicoloured.

4127 $1.50 Type **595** 90 75

4128 $1.50 BO 105 helicopter carrying pipes 90 75

4129 $1.50 NH-90 helicopter on ground 90 75

4130 $1.50 AS-61 helicopter 6-15 over sea 90 75

4131 $1.50 BO 105 helicopter and lighthouse 90 75

4132 $1.50 AS-61 helicopter 6-26 90 75

**MS**4133 100×71 mm. $6 Bell UH-1 Iroquois 'Huey' troop carrier (*vert*) 3·00 3·25

**596** Pope Benedict XVI

**2007.** 80th Birthday of Pope Benedict XVI.

4134 **596** $1.40 multicoloured 85 70

**597** Elvis Presley

**2007.** 30th Death Anniv of Elvis Presley. Multicoloured.

4135 $1.50 Type **597** 90 75

4136 $1.50 Wearing striped shirt, seen in profile 90 75

4137 $1.50 Holding guitar, wearing jacket and bow tie 90 75

4138 $1.50 Wearing striped shirt, smiling 90 75

4139 $1.50 Wearing red shirt 90 75

4140 $1.50 Holding guitar, seen in half-profile 90 75

**598** Diana, Princess of Wales

**2007.** 10th Death Anniv of Diana, Princess of Wales. Multicoloured.

4141 $2 Type **598** 1·25 1·25

4142 $2 Wearing pale mauve and drop earrings 1·25 1·25

4143 $2 Wearing purple jacket with black edging on collar 1·25 1·25

4144 $2 Wearing brownish grey and white dress and hat 1·25 1·25

**MS**4145 70×100 mm. $6 Wearing headscarf 3·00 2·75

**599** *Strelitzia parvifolia* (bird of paradise)

**2007.** Plants and Trees. Multicoloured.

4146 15c. Type **599** 15 10

4147 20c. *Thespesia populnea* (seaside mahoe) 20 15

4148 30c. *Hibiscus rosa sinensis* 25 15

4149 50c. *Agave karatto* 30 20

4150 70c. *Barringtonia asiatica* 45 35

4151 75c. *Cocos nucifera* (coconut) 50 40

4152 90c. *Prosopis chilensis* (mesquite) (*horiz*) 60 45

4153 $1 *Tamarindus indica* 70 55

4154 $1.50 *Capparis cynophallophora* (black willow) (*horiz*) 90 75

4155 $1.80 Baobab (*horiz*) 1·10 1·10

4156 $2 *Petrea volubilis* 1·25 1·25

4157 $2.50 *Opuntia cochenillifera* (cactus) (*horiz*) 1·50 1·50

4158 $5 *Hymenaea courbaril* (locust fruit) (*horiz*) 2·75 3·00

4159 $10 *Caesalpinia ciliata* (Barbuda black warri) 5·25 5·50

4160 $20 *Ricinus communis* (castor oil plant) 10·00 10·50

**600** John W. Ashe, Antigua & Barbuda

**2007.** Holocaust Remembrance. Multicoloured.

4161 $1.40 Type **600** 85 70

4162 $1.40 Alfred Capelle, Marshall Islands 85 70

4163 $1.40 Masao Nakayama, Micronesia 85 70

4164 $1.40 Gilles Noghes, Monaco 85 70

4165 $1.40 Baatar Choisuren, Mongolia 85 70

4166 $1.40 Filipe Chiduma, Mozambique 85 70

4167 $1.40 Marlene Moses, Nauru 85 70

4168 $1.40 Franciscus Majoor, Netherlands 85 70

**601** Antigua and Barbuda on Bauble

**2007.** Christmas. Multicoloured.

4169 30c. Type **601** 25 15

4170 90c. Decorated palm tree and parade dancers on beach 65 50

4171 $1 Cake decorations 70 55

4172 $1.50 Parade costume 90 75

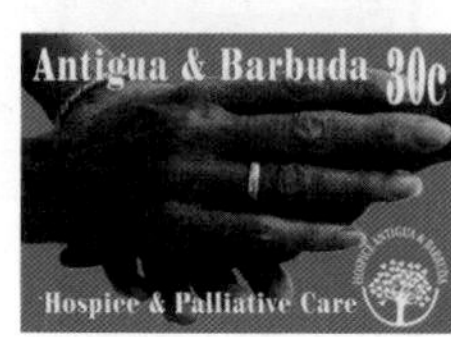


**602** Hands

**2007.** World Hospice and Palliative Care Day. Multicoloured.

4173 30c. Type **602** 25 15

4174 30c. Clock 25 15

**603** King Court (Prince Klaas), 1691–1736

**2008.** National Heroes. Multicoloured.

4175 90c. Type **603** 65 50

4176 90c. Dame Georgiana E. (Nellie) Robinson, 1880–1972 65 50

4177 $1 Sir Vivian Richards 75 60

4178 $1.50 Sir V. C. Bird Snr, 1909–99 1·25 1·00

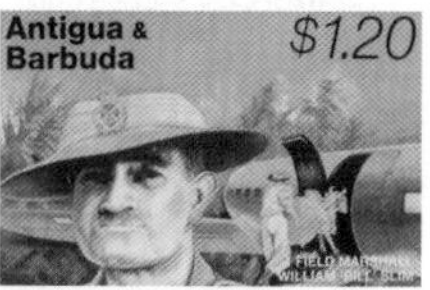


**603a** Field Marshal William 'Bill' Slim

**2008.** Field Marshal William 'Bill' Slim Commemoration.

4178a **603a** $1.20 multicoloured 1·25 1·10

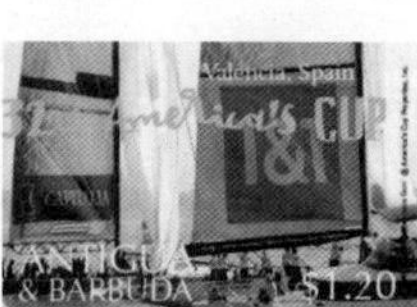


**604** Americas Cup Yachts

**2008.** 32nd Americas Cup Yachting Championship, Valencia, Spain. Multicoloured.

4179 $1.20 Type **604** 90 75

4180 $1.80 Two yachts, yellow-hulled *Lladro* at right 1·40 1·40

4181 $3 Two yachts 2·25 1·50

4182 $5 Five yachts 3·75 4·00

**605** Pierre de Coubertin (founder of modern Olympics), 1896

**2008.** Olympic Games, Beijing. Multicoloured.

| | | | |
|---|---|---|---|
| 4183 | $1.40 Type **605** | 1·10 | 1·10 |
| 4184 | $1.40 Poster for first modern Olympic Games, Athens, 1896 | 1·10 | 1·10 |
| 4185 | $1.40 Spiridon Louis of Greece, marathon gold medallist, 1896 | 1·10 | 1·10 |
| 4186 | $1.40 Paul Masson of France, cycling gold medallist, 1896 | 1·10 | 1·10 |

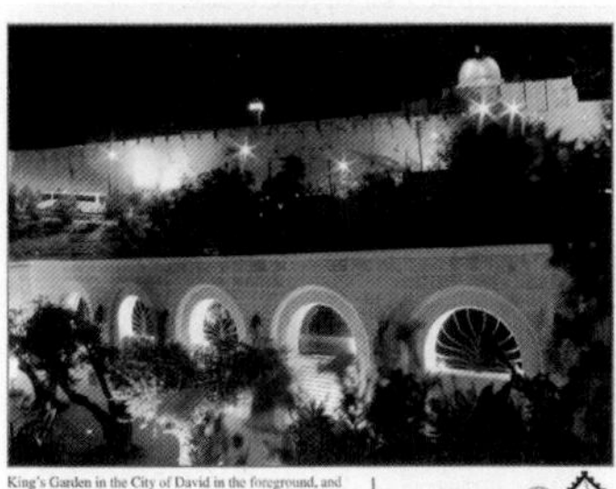

ANTIGUA &
BARBUDA $6
WORLD STAMP CHAMPIONSHIP ISRAEL 2008
May 14 - 21


**606** King's Garden, Walls of Old City and Al-Aqsa Mosque, Jerusalem (image scaled to 44% of original size)

**2008.** Israel 2008 World Stamp Championship. Sheet 110×100 mm.

**MS**4187 multicoloured 4·50 4·75

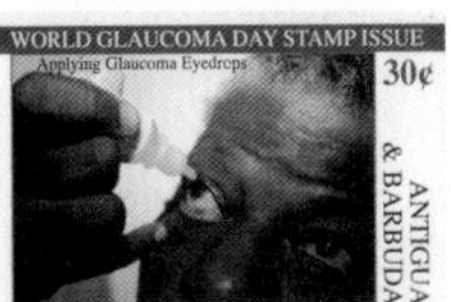


**607** Applying Eye Drops

**2008.** World Glaucoma Day. Multicoloured.

| | | | |
|---|---|---|---|
| 4188 | 30c. Type **607** | 25 | 15 |
| 4189 | 50c. Normal and glaucomatous optic nerves | 40 | 25 |
| 4190 | $1 Using braille typewriter | 75 | 60 |

**608** Pope Benedict XVI

**2008.** 1st Visit of Pope Benedict XVI to the United States

4191 **608** $2 multicoloured 1·50 1·25

**609** Elvis Presley

**2008.** 50th Anniv of Elvis Presley's Induction into the US Army. Sheet 160×130 mm containing T **609** and similar vert designs. Multicoloured.

**MS**4192 Type **609**; In light grey uniform; In dark grey uniform; In light grey uniform with cap 6·00 5·75

The stamps within **MS**4192 share a composite background design.

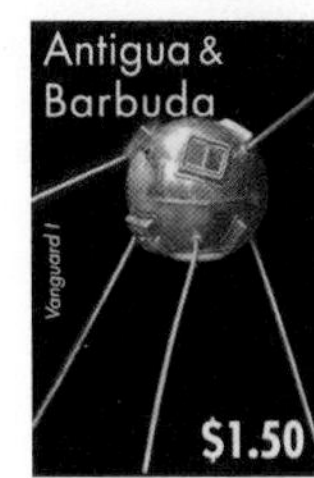


**610** *Vanguard I*, 1958

**2008.** 50 Years of Space Exploration and Satellites. Multicoloured.

| | | | |
|---|---|---|---|
| 4193 | $1.50 Type **610** | 1·25 | 1·00 |
| 4194 | $1.50 *Vanguard I* (green and white background) | 1·25 | 1·00 |
| 4195 | $1.50 *Vanguard I* (sphere and base) | 1·25 | 1·00 |
| 4196 | $1.50 *Explorer III*, 1958 | 1·25 | 1·00 |
| 4197 | $1.50 *Explorer III* orbiting Earth | 1·25 | 1·00 |
| 4198 | $1.50 Van Allen radiation belt (discovered by Explorer programme) | 1·25 | 1·00 |
| 4199 | $2 *Vanguard I* and Moon | 1·50 | 1·25 |
| 4200 | $2 *Vanguard I* orbiting Earth at sunrise | 1·50 | 1·25 |
| 4201 | $2 *Explorer III* (deep brown-red and light green background) | 1·50 | 1·25 |
| 4202 | $2 *Explorer III* | 1·50 | 1·25 |

**MS**4203 Two sheets, each 100×70 mm. (a) $6 *Vanguard I* above Earth (horiz). (b) $6 *Explorer III* and Earth (horiz) 9·00 8·75

**611** Capt Kirk and Mr. Spock

**2008.** Star Trek. Multicoloured.

| | | | |
|---|---|---|---|
| 4204 | $1.50 Type **611** | 1·25 | 1·10 |
| 4205 | $1.50 Mr. Spock, Capt. Kirk, Dr. Leonard McCoy and Lt. Cmdr Scott | 1·25 | 1·10 |
| 4206 | $1.50 Mr. Spock and Lt. Uhura | 1·25 | 1·10 |
| 4207 | $1.50 Enterprise crew in alien city | 1·25 | 1·10 |
| 4208 | $1.50 Lt. Uhura (Nichelle Nichols) on bridge of Enterprise | 1·25 | 1·00 |
| 4209 | $1.50 Lt. Cmdr Scott (James Doohan) | 1·25 | 1·00 |
| 4210 | $2 Dr. Leonard McCoy (DeForest Kelley) (50×37 mm) | 1·50 | 1·25 |
| 4211 | $2 Mr. Spock (Leonard Nimoy) (50×37 mm) | 1·50 | 1·25 |
| 4212 | $2 Captain Kirk (William Shatner) (50×37 mm) | 1·50 | 1·25 |
| 4213 | $2 Hikaru Sulu (George Takei) (50×37 mm) | 1·50 | 1·25 |

**612** Muhammad Ali

**2008.** Muhammad Ali (world heavyweight boxing champion, 1964, 1974–8). Multicoloured.

| | | | |
|---|---|---|---|
| 4214-4219 | $1.50×6 Type **612** and similar designs showing Muhammad Ali speaking | 7·00 | 6·75 |
| 4220-4223 | $2×4 Hitting punchbag; Wearing white robe, speaking; With white robe over back of shoulders; Wearing helmet (all 37×50 mm) | 6·00 | 6·75 |

**613** John F. Kennedy (in profile)

**2008.** John F. Kennedy (US President 1960–3) Commemoration. Sheet 100×130 mm containing T **613** and similar vert designs showing President Kennedy. Multicoloured.

**MS**4224 Type **613**; Facing straight ahead; Head turned to left; With hand raised to chin 6·00 5·75

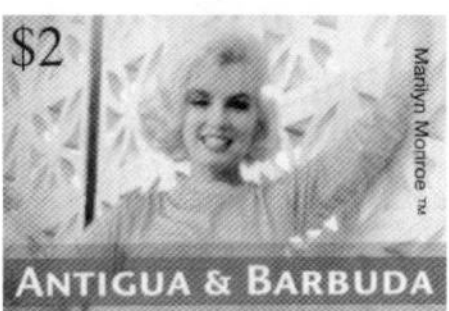


**614** Marilyn Monroe

**2008.** Marilyn Monroe Commemoration. Sheet 100×140 mm containing T **614** and similar horiz designs. Multicoloured.

**MS**4225 Type **614**; Head turned to left; Wearing deep orange; Wearing mauve sweater 6·00 7·75

**615** Holy Family

**2009.** Christmas. Designs showing stained glass windows. Multicoloured.

| | | | |
|---|---|---|---|
| 4226 | 30c. Type **615** | 25 | 15 |
| 4227 | 90c. Baby Jesus in manger | 60 | 50 |
| 4228 | $1 Mary and infant Jesus with hands held together in prayer (vert) | 75 | 60 |
| 4229 | $1.50 Mary and infant Jesus standing on her lap (vert) | 1·25 | 1·00 |

**616** Baseball

**2009.** Olympic Games, Beijing (2008). Sports of the Summer Games. Sheet 130×94 mm containing T **616** and similar vert designs. Multicoloured.

**MS**4230 Type **616**; Beach volleyball; Gymnastics; Judo 4·25 4·00

**617** First Inaugural Address of Pres. Lincoln, 4 March 1861

**2009.** Birth Bicentenary of Abraham Lincoln (US President 1861–5). Sheet 130×100 mm containing T **617** and similar horiz designs. Multicoloured.

**MS**4231 Type **617**; Abraham Lincoln; Crowd at his second inaugural address, 4 March 1865; Crowd and Abraham Lincoln 6·00 5·75

The stamps and margins of No. **MS**4231 form composite designs.

**618** Pres. Barack Obama (in profile)

**2009.** Inauguration of President Barack Obama. Multicoloured.

**MS**4232 130×100 mm. $2.75 Type **618**×4 3·00 2·75

**MS**4232a 100×70 mm. $10 Pres. Obama (in front of US flag) (37×50 mm) 7·50 7·00

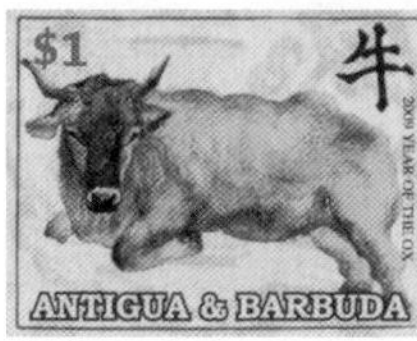


**619** Ox

**2009.** Chinese New Year. Year of the Ox. Sheet 190×78 mm.

**MS**4233 $1 Type **619**×4 multicoloured 4·00 3·75

**620** Xian

**2009.** China 2009 World Stamp Exhibition, Luoyang (1st issue). Sites and Scenes of China. Multicoloured.

**MS**4234 100×145 mm. $1.40×4 Type **620**; Harbinn; Chongqing; Tianjin 1·40 1·40

**621** Emperor Quin Shi Huang

**2009.** China 2009 World Stamp Exhibition, Luoyang (2nd issue). First Emperor Quin Shi Huang (221–210BC) and his Terracotta Army. Multicoloured.

**MS**4235 120×150 mm. $1.40×4 Type **621**; Horses; Warriors; Excavation with army in columns 1·40 1·40

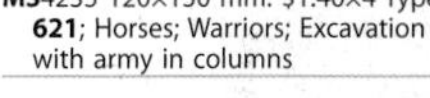

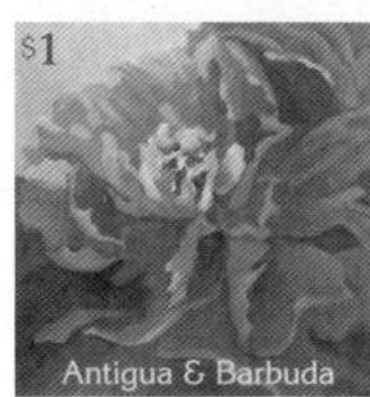


**622** Peony

**2009.** China 2009 World Stamp Exhibition, Luoyang (3rd issue). Peonies. Multicoloured.

4236 $1 Type **622** 95 90

**MS**4237 100×70 mm. $5 Black and dull pink peony design (triangular 35×30 mm) 4·75 4·75

**623** Elvis Presley

**2009.** Elvis Presley Commemoration. Multicoloured.

**MS**4238 185×125 mm. $1.50×6 Type **623**; Wearing jacket and tie (orange background); Standing with hands on hips; Wearing pale orange jacket with white stripe; Playing guitar, wearing lei; Wearing jacket and tie (sky background) 3·25 3·25

**624**

**2009.** National Stamp Day.

4239 **624** $4 multicoloured 3·75 3·50

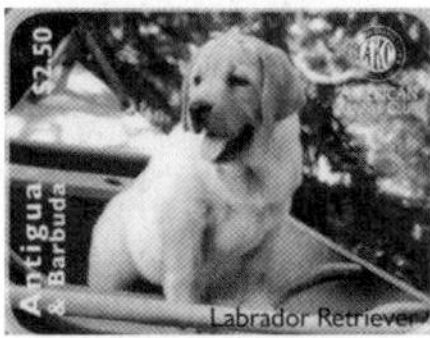


**625** Labrador Retriever

**2009.** 125th Anniv of the American Kennel Club. Two sheets, each 100×120 mm, containing T **625** and similar horiz designs showing Labrador Retriever puppies (**MS**4240) or Dachshunds (**MS**4241). Multicoloured.

**MS**4240 Type **625**; Two golden labrador puppies; Black and golden labrador puppies carrying stick; Golden labrador puppy in tub 9·75 9·75

**MS**4241 Black and tan dachshund pawing case; Tan dachshund in green wooden crate; Two dachshund puppies in wooden trug; Wire-haired dachshund 9·75 9·75

**626** Michael Jackson

**2009.** Michael Jackson Commemoration. Multicoloured.

**MS**4242 158×112 mm. $2.50×4 Type **626**; Wearing black with gold crossbelts and waistband; Wearing orange-red with black diagonal band; Wearing silver jacket with eagle design 9·75 9·75

**MS**4243 130×100 mm. $2.50×4 Wearing plain white shirt; Wearing white jacket with black armbands 9·75 9·75

**MS**4244 150×110 mm. $6 Wearing white T-shrit and white shirt (38×51 mm) 4·75 4·75

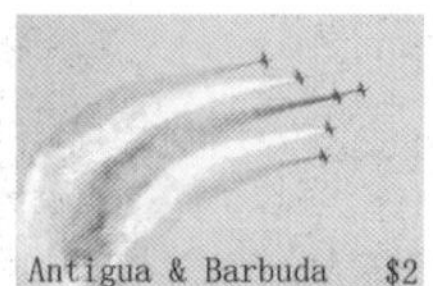


**627** Flypast of Fighter Jets

**2009.** Centenary of Chinese Aviation and Aeropex 2009 Exhibition, Beijing. T **627** and similar horiz designs. Multicoloured.

**MS**4245 145×95 mm. $2×4 Type **627**; Jet fighters flying to right; Jet fighters flying to left; Jet fighters flying in fan formation 3·75 3·75

**MS**4246 120×80 mm. $6 J–7GB fighter jet (50×38 mm) 3·75 3·75

**628** Pres. Barack Obama

**2009.** Meeting of US President Barack Obama and Pope Benedict XVI, Vatican, 10 July 2009. Multicoloured.

**MS**4247 150×100 mm. $2.75×3 Type **628**; Pope Benedict XVI; Michelle Obama 2·75 2·75

**MS**4248 110×90 mm. $6 Pope Benedict XVI and Pres. Barack Obama (horiz) 3·75 3·75

**629** Apollo 11 Emblem

**2009.** 40th Anniv of First Manned Moon Landing and International Year of Astronomy. Multicoloured.

**MS**4249 151×100 mm. $2.50×4 Type **629**; Lunar Module *Eagle*; Passive Seismic Experiment Package; Apollo 11 2·40 2·40

**MS**4250 101×71 mm. $6 Apollo 11 orbiting Moon 3·75 3·75

**630** Poster for *King Creole*, 1958

**2009.** Elvis Presley in Film *King Creole*. Multicoloured.

**MS**4251 125×90 mm. $6 Type **630** 3·75 3·75

**MS**4252 90×125 mm. $6 Elvis Presley playing guitar 3·75 3·75

**MS**4253 90×125 mm. $6 Elvis Presley with arms raised (horiz) 3·75 3·75

**MS**4254 125×90 mm. $6 Elvis Presley playing guitar (horiz) 3·75 3·75

**631** Candles and Wreath

**2009.** Christmas. Showing Christmas lights. Multicoloured.

4255 90c. Type **631** 90 85

4256 $1 Gold, red and green lights 95 90

4257 $1.80 Three bells and tree branches 1·75 1·60

4258 $3 Nativity 2·75 2·50

**632** Pair of Caribbean Coot

**2009.** Endangered Species. Caribbean Coot (*Fulica caribaea*). Multicoloured.

4259 $2.65 Type **632** 2·50 2·50

4260 $2.65 Pair landing 2·50 2·50

4261 $2.65 Pair with chick 2·50 2·50

4262 $2.65 Adult feeding chick 2·50 2·50

**MS**4263 112×165 mm. Nos. 4259/62, each ×2 20·00 20·00

**633** Sir Vere Cornwall Bird

**2009.** Birth Centenary of Rt. Honourable Dr. Sir Vere Cornwall Bird Sr. (first Chief Minister, Premier and Prime Minister of Antigua). Multicoloured.

4264 30c. Type **633** 30 25

4265 75c. Sir V. C. Bird (Antigua flag in background) 75 70

4266 90c. Wearing red jacket and hat 90 85

4267 $1.50 Sir V. C. Bird (black and white photo) 1·40 1·25

**MS**4268 160×110 mm. $2.50×4 As Nos. 4265/7 9·75 9·75

**MS**4269 100×70 mm. $6 Sir V. C. Bird (Antigua flag and outline map in background) 5·75 5·75

**634** Glossy Ibis (*Plegadis falcinellus*)

**2009.** Birds of Antigua and Barbuda. Multicoloured.

4270 $1.20 Type **634** 1·25 1·10

4271 $1.80 Green-winged teal (*Anas carolinensis*) 1·75 1·60

4272 $3 California clapper rail (*Rallus longirostris obsoletus*) 2·75 2·50

4273 $5 Cattle egret (*Bubulcus ibis*) (vert) 4·75 4·50

**MS**4274 90×90 mm. $2.50×4 Green heron (*Butorides virescens*); Common ground dove (*Columbina passerina*); White-tailed hawk (*Buteo albicaudatus*); Black-faced grassquit (*Tiaris bicolor*) 6·50 6·50

**MS**4275 70×100 mm. $3×2 Bananaquit (*Coereba flaveola*); Osprey (*Pandion haliaetus*) 5·75 5·75

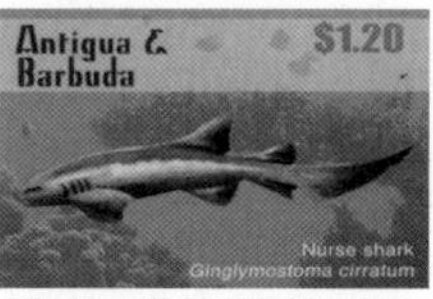


**634a** Nurse Shark (*Ginglymostoma cirratum*)

**2010.** Sharks of the Caribbean. Multicoloured.

4275*a* $1.20 Type **634a** 1·25 1·10

4275*b* $1.80 Caribbean reef shark (*Carcharhinus perezi*) 1·75 1·60

4275*c* $3 Tiger Shark (*Galeocerdo cuvier*) 2·25 2·00

4275*d* $5 Whale shark (*Rhincodon typus*) 3·50 3·25

**MS**4275*e* $2.75x4 170×100 mm. $2.75×4 Caribbean sharpnose shark (*Rhizoprionodon porosus*); Blacktip shark (*Carcharhinus limbatus*); Oceanic whitetip shark (*Carcharhinus longimanus*); Bull shark (*Carcharhinus leucas* 5·50 5·25

The stamps and margins of **MS**4275e form a composite design.

**634b** Rat

**2010.** Chinese Lunar Calendar.. Multicoloured.

**MS**4275*f* 60c.x12 Type **634b**; Ox; Tiger; Rabbit; Dragon; Snake; Horse; Ram; Monkey; Rooster; Dog; Pig 3·50 3·25

**634c** Bronze Tiger, Western Han Dynasty, China

**2010.** Chinese New Year. Year of the Tiger.. Multicoloured.

**MS**4275*g* $5 Type **634c**; $5 Bronze tiger, Shang Dynasty, China 4·75 4·50

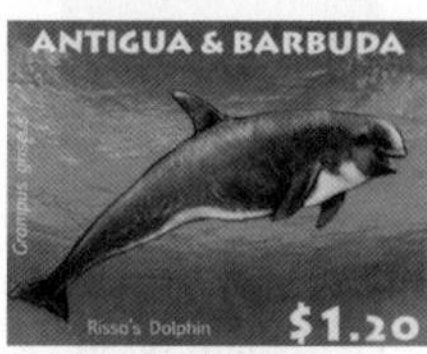


**635** Risso's Dolphin (*Grampus griseus*)

**2010.** Whales and Dolphins of the Caribbean. Multicoloured.

4276 $1.20 Type **635** 1·25 1·10

4277 $1.80 Common dolphin (*Delphinus delphis*) 1·75 1·60

4278 $3 Humpback whale (*Megaptera novaeangliae*) 2·25 2·00

4279 $5 Sperm whale (*Physeter macrocephalus*) 3·75 3·50

**MS**4280 100×140 mm. $2×6 Short-snout dolphin (*Lagenodelphis hosei*); Spotted dolphin (*Stenella frontalis*); Cuvier's beaked whale (*Ziphius cavirostris*); Shortfin pilot whale (*Globicephala macrorhynchus*); Gulf Stream beaked whale (*Mesoplodon europaeus*); Rough-toothed dolphin (*Stenobredanensis*) 9·00 8·75

**636** Diana, Princess of Wales

**2010.** Diana, Princess of Wales Commemoration. Sheet 130×90 mm containing T **636** and similar vert designs. Multicoloured.

**MS**4281 Type **636**; Wearing pink; Wearing pale mauve; Wearing pale green 6·00 5·75

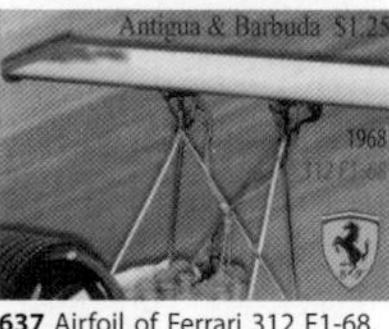


**637** Airfoil of Ferrari 312 F1-68, 1968

**2010.** Ferrari Cars. Multicoloured.

4282 $1.25 Type **637** 75 70

4283 $1.25 Ferrari 312 F1-68, 1968 75 70

4284 $1.25 Engine of Ferrari 246 P F1, 1960 75 70

4285 $1.25 Ferrari 246 P F1, 1960 (car no. 34) 75 75

4286 $1.25 Interior of Ferrari 365 P Speciale, 1966 75 70

4287 $1.25 Ferrari 365 P Speciale, 1966 75 70

4288 $1.25 Engine of Ferrari 158 F1, 1964 75 70

4289 $1.25 Ferrari 158 F1, 1964 (car no. 20) 75 70

**638** Common Buckeye (Junonia coenia)

**2010.** Butterflies of the Caribbean. Multicoloured.

4290 $1.20 Type **638** 1·25 1·10

4291 $1.80 Red postman (*Heliconius erato*) 1·75 1·60

4292 $3 Red admiral (*Vanessa atalanta*) 2·25 2·10

4293 $5 Zebra longwing (*Heliconius charithonia*) 3·50 3·25

**MS**4294 140×100 mm. $2×6 Orange sulphur (inscr 'sulfur') (*Colias eurytheme*); Blue morpho (*Morpho peleides*); Queen butterfly (*Danaus gilippus*); Zebra swallowtail (*Eurytides marcellus*); Malachite (*Siproata stelenes*); Gatekeeper butterfly (*Pyronia tithonus*) 6·00 5·75

The stamps and margins of **MS**4294 form a composite background design of a flowering plant.

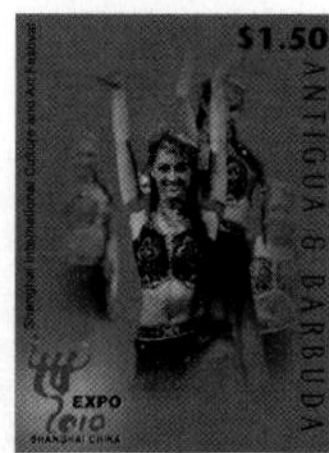


**639** Dancers, Shanghai International Culture and Art Festival

**2010.** Expo 2010, Shanghai, China. Multicoloured.

**MS**4295 $1.50×4 Type **639**; China National Grand Theatre, Beijing; Green rice terrace, Guangxi Province, China; Dance performance, Beijing (yellow background) 3·25 3·00

**640** Mother Teresa with Princess Diana, New York

**2010.** Birth Centenary of Mother Teresa. Multicoloured.

**MS**4296 $2.50×4 Type **640**; Receiving Order of Merit from Queen Elizabeth II, India; Receiving Medal of Freedom from Pres. Reagan; With Pope John Paul II, Calcutta, India 5·25 5·00

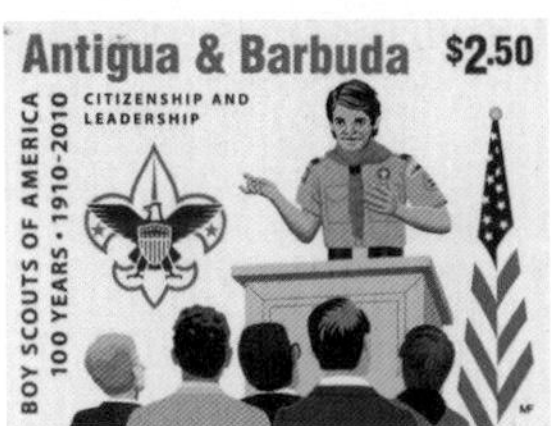

**641** Scout giving Lecture ('Citizenship and Leadership')

**2010.** Centenary of Boy Scouts of America. Multicoloured.

**MS**4297 $2.50 Type **641**×2; $2.50 Two scouts in kayak ('Aquatic sport adventures')×2 5·25 5·00

**MS**4298 $2.50 Statue of Liberty giving Scout salute×2; $2.50 Two scouts ('Navigation with map and compass')×2

**642** Elvis Presley

**2010.** 75th Birth Anniv of Elvis Presley. Multicoloured.

**MS**4299 $2.75×4 Type **642**; Facing forward, singing; Facing left, guitar strap over face; Three images of Elvis Presley 5·25 5·00

**MS**4300 $2.75×4 Wearing white with pattern; Wearing open neck shirt; Two images of Elvis Presley; Wearing white jacket with dark piping 5·25 5·00

The stamps and margins of **MS**4299 form a composite design spelling out 'ELV75'.

**643** Pres. Obama holding Nobel Peace Prize

**2010.** Pres. Barack Obama's Nobel Peace Prize (2009). Multicoloured.

**MS**4301 $2.75×4 Type **643**; Speaking (side view) ; Speaking from podium; Holding Nobel Peace Prize, smiling 5·50 5·25

**644** Princess Diana on Visit to Hindu Mission, UK

**2010.** Princess Diana Commemoration. Multicoloured.

**MS**4302 $2.75×4 Type **644**; Visit to Pakistan; Visit to Dubai; Visit to Japan 5·50 5·25

**MS**4303 $2.75×4 Wearing tiara with pearls and pearl drop earrings; Wearing tiara and sapphire and diamond earrings; Wearing tiara and pearl drop earrings; Wearing tiara and white jacket with stand-up collar 5·00 5·25

**645** Rainbows

**2010.** Centenary of Girlguiding. Multicoloured.

**MS**4304 150×100 mm. $2.75×4 Type **645**; Brownies in kayaks; Three guides; Three Senior Section guides hiking 5·50 5·25

**MS**4305 70×100 mm. $6 Guides 4·25 4·00

**646** Abraham Lincoln

**2010.** Birth Bicentenary (2009) of Abraham Lincoln (US President 1861–5). Multicoloured.

**MS**4306 $2.75×4 Type **646**; With beard, facing forward; With beard, looking to left; Profile, facing left 5·50 5·25

**MS**4307 $2.75×4 Type **646**; With beard, facing forward; With beard, looking to left; Profile, facing left 5·50 5·25

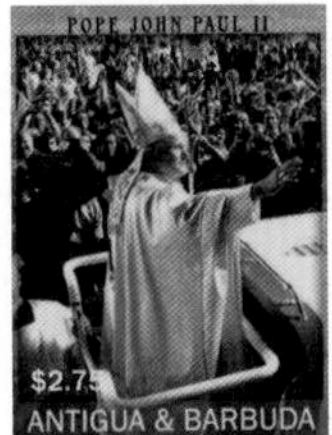

**647** Pope John Paul II

**2010.** Pope John Paul II Commemoration. Multicoloured.

**MS**4308 $2.75 Type **647**×4 1·50 1·25

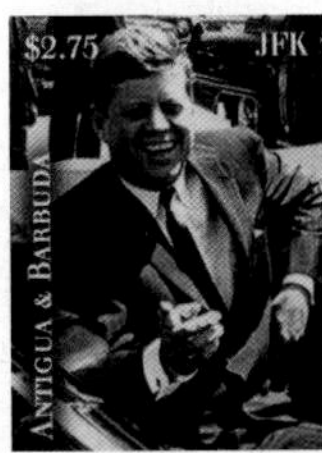

**648** Pres. John F. Kennedy

**2010.** 50th Anniv of Election of Pres. John F. Kennedy. Multicoloured.

**MS**4309 $2.75×4 Type **648**; Pres. John F. Kennedy; Seated in chair (bookcase in background); Speaking 5·50 5·25

**649** Three Stooges

**2010.** The Three Stooges. Multicoloured.

**MS**4310 $2.50×4 Type **649**; The Three Stooges as decorators, Curly holding cloth to Moe's neck; The Three Stooges as doctors and patient, Larry holding scissors to Curly's nose; Larry and Moe with Curly's head in guillotine 7·00 7·00

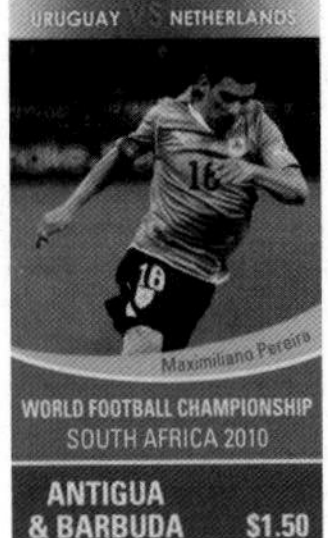

**650** Maximiliano Pereira (Uruguay)

**2010.** World Cup Football Championship, South Africa. Multicoloured.

**MS**4311 130×150 mm. $1.50×6 Type **650**; John Heitinga (Netherlands); Edinson Cavani (Uruguay); Mark Van Bommel (Netherlands); Martin Caceres (Uruguay); Giovanni van Bronckhorst (Netherlands) 8·00 7·75

**MS**4312 85×90 mm. $3.50 Oscar Tabarez (Uruguay coach); $3.50 Uruguay flag on football 5·50 5·25

**MS**4313 85×90 mm. $3.50 Bert van Marwijk (Dutch coach); $3.50 Dutch flag on football 5·50 5·25

**651** California Spangled Cat

**2010.** Cats of the World. Multicoloured.

**MS**4314 150×100 mm. $2.50×6 Type **651**; Siamese; British shorthair; Norwegian forest; Egyptian mau; American curl longhair 3·75 3·75

**MS**4315 100×70 mm. $6 Manx cat 3·75 3·75

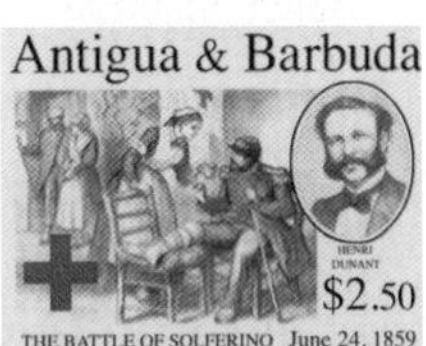

**652** Henri Dunant and Nurses with Wounded Soldiers

**2010.** Death Centenary of Henri Dunant (instigator of Red Cross). Multicoloured.

**MS**4316 150×100 mm. $2.50×4 Type **652**; Wounded laying on battlefield; Cavalry; Cavalry and soldiers 2·40 2·40

**MS**4317 70×100 mm. $6 Battle of Solferino 3·75 3·75

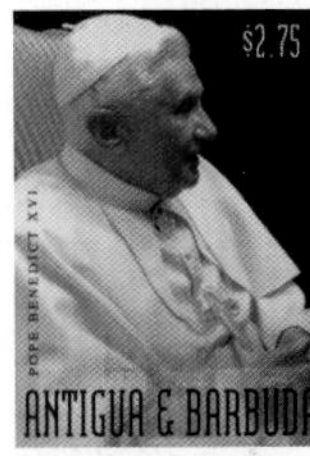

**653** Pope Benedict XVI

**2010.** Fifth Anniv of Papacy of Pope Benedict XVI. Multicoloured.

**MS**4318 142×153 mm. $2.75 Type **653**×4 9·75 9·75

**MS**4319 171×113 mm. $2.75 Pope Benedict XVI (facing left)×4 9·75 9·75

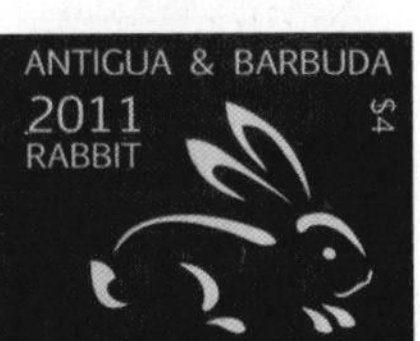

**654** Rabbit

**2011.** Chinese New Year. Year of the Rabbit

**MS**4320 $4 Type **654**; $4 Chinese rabbit symbol 6·00 6·00

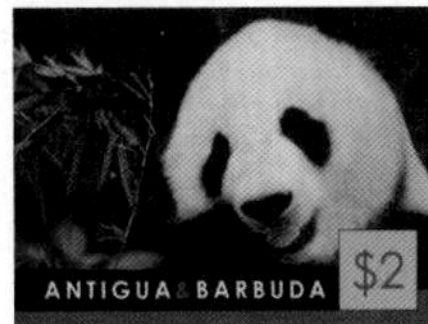

**655** Giant Panda

**2011.** Beijing 2010 International Stamp and Coin Exposition. Giant Panda. Multicoloured.

**MS**4321 170×95 mm. $2×4 Type **655**; Close-up of face; Panda with bamboo plant; Panda eating leaves (side view) 2·40 2·40

**MS**4322 62×90 mm. $5 Giant panda (facing right) 3·25 3·25

**656** *Casini Madonna* (Masaccio)

**2011.** Christmas. Multicoloured.

| | | | |
|---|---|---|---|
| 4323 | 30c. Type **656** | 30 | 25 |
| 4324 | 75c. *Madonna of the Stars* (Tintoretto) | 70 | 65 |
| 4325 | 90c. Wall mosaic showing magi from Basilica of Sant Apollinan, Nuovo, Italy | 90 | 85 |
| 4326 | $1.50 *The Annunciation* (Fra Angelico) | 1·40 | 1·25 |

Pt. 20

## ANTIOQUIA

One of the states of the Granadine Confederation. A department of Colombia from 1886, now uses Colombian stamps.

100 centavos = 1 peso.

1

**1868.** Various arms designs. Imperf.

| | | | | |
|---|---|---|---|---|
| 1 | 1 | 2½c. blue | £1200 | £700 |
| 2 | - | 5c. green | £900 | £500 |
| 3 | - | 10c. lilac | £2750 | £900 |
| 4 | - | 1p. red | £700 | £450 |

5

6

**1869.** Various frames. Imperf.

| | | | | |
|---|---|---|---|---|
| 5 | **5** | 2½c. blue | 5·00 | 4·25 |
| 6 | **5** | 5c. green | 7·75 | 7·00 |
| 8 | **5** | 10c. mauve | 10·00 | 5·00 |
| 9 | **5** | 20c. brown | 10·00 | 5·00 |
| 10 | **6** | 1p. red | 20·00 | 17·00 |

7

**1873.** Arms designs inscr "E.S." (or "Eo. So." or "Estado Soberano") "de Antioquia". Imperf.

| | | | | |
|---|---|---|---|---|
| 11 | 7 | 1c. green | 7·25 | 5·25 |
| 12 | - | 5c. green | 12·00 | 8·50 |
| 13 | - | 10c. mauve | 35·00 | 28·00 |
| 14 | - | 20c. brown | 12·00 | 10·00 |
| 15 | - | 50c. blue | 2·75 | 2·10 |
| 16 | - | 1p. red | 5·00 | 3·75 |
| 17 | - | 2p. black on yellow | 12·00 | 10·50 |
| 18 | - | 5p. black on red | 90·00 | 75·00 |

The 5p. is larger (25½×31½ mm).

15

**1875.** Imperf.

| | | | | |
|---|---|---|---|---|
| 20 | **15** | 1c. black on green | 2·40 | 3·25 |
| 21 | **15** | 1c. black | 1·80 | 3·25 |
| 43 | **15** | 1c. mauve | 3·50 | 5·25 |
| 52 | **15** | 1c. green | 3·50 | 5·25 |
| 22 | - | 2½c. blue (Arms) | 3·50 | 2·75 |
| 23 | - | 5c. green ("Liberty") | 22·00 | 19·00 |
| 25 | - | 10c. mauve (J. Berrio) | 35·00 | 28·00 |

20

21 Liberty

23 Liberty

**1879.** Imperf.

| | | | | |
|---|---|---|---|---|
| 30 | **20** | 2½c. blue | 3·75 | 3·50 |
| 38 | **20** | 2½c. green | 3·50 | 2·75 |
| 45 | **20** | 2½c. black on buff | 10·00 | 8·50 |
| 39 | **21** | 5c. green | 6·00 | 5·00 |
| 40 | **21** | 5c. violet | 13·00 | 10·00 |
| 32 | - | 10c. violet (Arms) | £1400 | £900 |
| 36 | **23** | 10c. violet | £275 | 85·00 |
| 41 | **23** | 10c. red | 3·50 | 2·75 |
| 42 | **21** | 20c. brown | 6·00 | 5·00 |

25 Liberty

**1883.** Various frames. Head of Liberty to left. Imperf.

| | | | | |
|---|---|---|---|---|
| 47 | **25** | 5c. yellow | 7·75 | 5·75 |
| 48 | **25** | 5c. green | £225 | £100 |
| 53 | **25** | 5c. brown | 7·25 | 4·50 |
| 49 | **25** | 10c. green | 7·75 | 7·00 |
| 50 | **25** | 10c. mauve | 17·00 | 10·00 |
| 55 | **25** | 10c. blue | 7·75 | 5·75 |
| 51 | **25** | 20c. blue | 7·25 | 5·75 |

28

**1886.** Imperf.

| | | | | |
|---|---|---|---|---|
| 57 | **28** | 1c. green on pink | 90 | 75 |
| 65 | **28** | 1c. red on lilac | 65 | 55 |
| 58 | **28** | 2½c. black on orange | 90 | 75 |
| 66 | **28** | 2½c. mauve on pink | 65 | 75 |
| 59 | **28** | 5c. blue on buff | 5·00 | 4·25 |
| 67 | **28** | 5c. red on green | 5·00 | 2·30 |
| 68 | **28** | 5c. lake on buff | 90 | 85 |
| 60 | **28** | 10c. red on buff | 1·00 | 1·20 |
| 69 | **28** | 10c. brown on green | 1·00 | 1·20 |
| 61 | **28** | 20c. purple on buff | 2·40 | 2·10 |
| 62 | **28** | 50c. yellow on buff | 4·50 | 3·75 |
| 63 | **28** | 1p. yellow on green | 7·25 | 5·75 |
| 64 | **28** | 2p. green on lilac | 7·25 | 5·75 |

31

**1888.** Various sizes and frames. Inscr "MEDELLIN". Imperf.

| | | | | |
|---|---|---|---|---|
| 70 | **31** | 2½c. black on yellow | 22·00 | 19·00 |
| 71 | **31** | 2½c. red on white | 11·00 | 9·00 |
| 72 | **31** | 5c. black on yellow | 12·00 | 10·00 |
| 73 | **31** | 5c. red on orange | 7·25 | 5·75 |

34

**1889.** Arms in various frames.

| | | | | |
|---|---|---|---|---|
| 74 | **34** | 1c. black on red | 35 | 30 |
| 75 | **34** | 2½c. black on blue | 35 | 30 |
| 76 | **34** | 5c. black on yellow | 45 | 45 |
| 77 | **34** | 10c. black on green | 45 | 45 |
| 95 | **34** | 10c. brown | 35 | 30 |
| 78 | **34** | 20c. blue | 2·00 | 1·90 |
| 79 | **34** | 50c. brown | 3·75 | 3·75 |
| 80 | **34** | 50c. green | 2·75 | 2·75 |
| 81 | **34** | 1p. red | 2·75 | 2·75 |
| 82 | **34** | 2p. black on mauve | 20·00 | 19·00 |
| 83 | **34** | 5p. black on red | 29·00 | 28·00 |

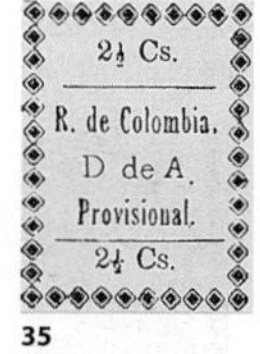
35

**1890.** Perf.

| | | | | |
|---|---|---|---|---|
| 84 | **35** | 2½c. black on buff | 2·75 | 2·75 |
| 85 | **35** | 5c. black on yellow | 2·75 | 2·75 |
| 86 | **35** | 10c. black on buff | 9·25 | 9·00 |
| 87 | **35** | 10c. black on red | 12·00 | 11·50 |
| 88 | **35** | 20c. black on yellow | 12·00 | 11·50 |

36

**1892**

| | | | | |
|---|---|---|---|---|
| 89 | **36** | 1c. brown on buff | 55 | 55 |
| 90 | **36** | 1c. blue | 35 | 30 |
| 91 | **36** | 2½c. violet on lilac | 55 | 55 |
| 92 | **36** | 2½c. green | 55 | 55 |
| 93 | **36** | 5c. black | 1·50 | 75 |
| 94 | **36** | 5c. red | 35 | 30 |

37

**1896**

| | | | | |
|---|---|---|---|---|
| 96 | **37** | 2c. grey | 35 | 30 |
| 107 | **37** | 2c. red | 35 | 55 |
| 97 | **37** | 2½c. brown | 35 | 30 |
| 108 | **37** | 2½c. blue | 35 | 30 |
| 98 | **37** | 3c. red | 35 | 30 |
| 109 | **37** | 3c. olive | 35 | 30 |
| 99 | **37** | 5c. green | 35 | 30 |
| 110 | **37** | 5c. yellow | 45 | 45 |
| 100 | **37** | 10c. lilac | 75 | 75 |
| 111 | **37** | 10c. brown | 75 | 75 |
| 101 | **37** | 20c. brown | 2·00 | 1·90 |
| 112 | **37** | 20c. blue | 2·00 | 1·90 |
| 102 | **37** | 50c. sepia | 2·00 | 1·90 |
| 113 | **37** | 50c. red | 1·80 | 1·70 |
| 103 | **37** | 1p. black and blue | 24·00 | 23·00 |
| 114 | **37** | 1p. black and red | 24·00 | 23·00 |
| 104 | **37** | 2p. black and orange | 75·00 | 75·00 |
| 115 | **37** | 2p. black and green | 75·00 | 75·00 |
| 105 | **37** | 5p. black and mauve | £130 | £130 |

39 Gen. Cordoba

**1899**

| | | | | |
|---|---|---|---|---|
| 118 | **39** | ½c. blue | 20 | 20 |
| 119 | **39** | 1c. blue | 20 | 20 |
| 120 | **39** | 2c. black | 20 | 20 |
| 121 | **39** | 3c. red | 20 | 20 |
| 122 | **39** | 4c. brown | 20 | 20 |
| 123 | **39** | 5c. green | 20 | 20 |
| 124 | **39** | 10c. red | 20 | 20 |
| 125 | **39** | 20c. violet | 20 | 20 |
| 126 | **39** | 50c. yellow | 20 | 20 |
| 127 | **39** | 1p. green | 20 | 20 |
| 128 | **39** | 2p. green | 20 | 20 |

43

**1901.** Various frames.

| | | | | |
|---|---|---|---|---|
| 132 | **43** | 1c. red | 35 | 30 |
| 133 | **43** | 1c. brown | 90 | 85 |
| 134 | **43** | 1c. blue | 90 | 85 |

Nos. 132 and 134 also exist with "CENTAVO" inside the rectangle below figure "1".

46

47

48 Girardot

**1902**

| | | | | |
|---|---|---|---|---|
| 138 | **46** | 1c. red | 35 | 30 |
| 139 | **46** | 1c. blue | 35 | 30 |
| 140 | **46** | 2c. blue | 35 | 30 |
| 141 | **46** | 2c. violet | 35 | 30 |
| 142 | **46** | 3c. green | 35 | 30 |
| 143 | **46** | 4c. purple | 35 | 30 |
| 144 | **47** | 5c. red | 35 | 30 |
| 145 | **47** | 10c. mauve | 35 | 30 |
| 147 | **47** | 20c. green | 35 | 30 |
| 148 | **47** | 30c. red | 35 | 30 |
| 149 | **48** | 40c. blue | 35 | 30 |
| 150 | **48** | 50c. brown on yellow | 35 | 30 |
| 152 | - | 1p. black and violet | 1·10 | 1·10 |
| 153 | - | 2p. black and red | 1·10 | 1·10 |
| 154 | - | 5p. black and blue | 2·00 | 1·90 |

DESIGN: 1p. to 5p. Dr. J. Felix de Restrepo.
No. 145 also exists with smaller head.

54

55

56 Zea

**1903**

| | | | | |
|---|---|---|---|---|
| 159 | **54** | 4c. brown | 35 | 30 |
| 160 | **54** | 5c. blue | 35 | 30 |
| 161 | **55** | 10c. yellow | 35 | 30 |
| 162 | **55** | 20c. lilac | 35 | 30 |
| 163 | **55** | 30c. brown | 90 | 85 |
| 164 | **55** | 40c. green | 90 | 85 |
| 165 | **55** | 50c. red | 35 | 30 |
| 166 | **56** | 1p. green | 90 | 85 |
| 167 | **56** | 2p. mauve (Rovira) | 90 | 85 |
| 168 | **56** | 3p. blue (La Pola) | 90 | 85 |
| 169 | **56** | 4p. red (Restrepo) | 1·50 | 1·50 |
| 170 | **56** | 5p. brown (Madrid) | 4·50 | 2·10 |
| 171 | **56** | 10p. red (Corral) | 9·25 | 5·25 |

### ACKNOWLEDGEMENT OF RECEIPT STAMPS

AR53

**1902**

| | | | | |
|---|---|---|---|---|
| AR157 | **AR53** | 5c. black on red | 1·40 | 1·40 |
| AR158 | **AR53** | 5c. green | 45 | 45 |

### REGISTRATION STAMPS

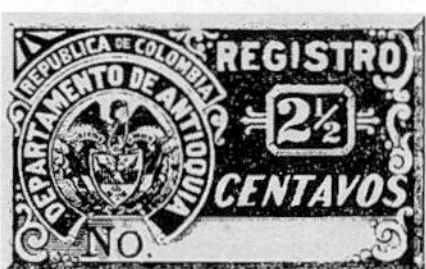
R38

**1896**

| | | | | |
|---|---|---|---|---|
| R106 | **R38** | 2½c. pink | 1·80 | 1·80 |
| R117 | **R38** | 2½c. blue | 1·80 | 1·70 |

**R41** Gen. Cordoba

**R42**

**1899**

| | | | | |
|---|---|---|---|---|
| R130 | **R41** | 2½c. blue | 35 | 30 |
| R131 | **R42** | 10c. red | 35 | 30 |

R52

**1902**

| | | | | |
|---|---|---|---|---|
| R156 | **R52** | 10c. violet on green | 45 | 45 |

### TOO LATE STAMPS

**L40** Gen. Cordoba

**1899**

| | | | | |
|---|---|---|---|---|
| L129 | **L40** | 2½c. green | 35 | 30 |

**1901.** As T 43, but inscr "RETARDO" at sides.

| | | | |
|---|---|---|---|
| L137a | 2½c. purple | 1·10 | 1·10 |

L51

**1902**

| | | | | |
|---|---|---|---|---|
| L155 | **L51** | 2½c. lilac | 35 | 30 |

Pt. 8

## ARBE

During the period of D'Annunzio's Italian Regency of Carnaro (Fiume), separate issues were made forArbe (now Rab).

100 centesimi = 1lira

**1920.** No. 148, etc of Fiume optd **ARBE**.

| | | | |
|---|---|---|---|
| 1B | 5c. green | 10·50 | 10·50 |
| 2B | 10c. red | 21·00 | 21·00 |
| 3B | 20c. brown | 55·00 | 32·00 |
| 4B | 25c. blue | 32·00 | 32·00 |
| 5 | 50c. on 20c. brown | 55·00 | 32·00 |
| 6 | 55c. on 5c. green | 55·00 | 32·00 |

### EXPRESS LETTER STAMPS

**1920.** Nos. E163/4 of Fiume optd **ARBE**.

| | | | |
|---|---|---|---|
| E7 | 30c. on 20c. brown | £190 | £110 |
| E8 | 50c. on 5c. green | £130 | £110 |

Pt. 20

# ARGENTINE REPUBLIC

A republic in the S.E. of S. America formerly part of the Spanish Empire.

1858. 100 centavos = 1 peso.
1985. 100 centavos = 1 austral.
1992. 100 centavos = 1 peso.

1 Argentine Confederation

**1858.** Imperf.

| 1 | 1 | 5c. red | 1·00 | 25·00 |
|---|---|---|---|---|
| 2 | 1 | 10c. green | 1·50 | 55·00 |
| 3 | 1 | 15c. blue | 14·00 | £160 |

3 Argentine Confederation

**1862.** Imperf.

| 10 | 3 | 5c. red | 16·00 | 18·00 |
|---|---|---|---|---|
| 8 | 3 | 10c. green | £150 | 60·00 |
| 9 | 3 | 15c. blue | £300 | £190 |

5 Rivadavia 6 Rivadavia

**1864.** Imperf.

| 14 | 6 | 10c. green | £2250 | £1300 |
|---|---|---|---|---|
| 15 | 5 | 15c. blue | £7500 | £4500 |
| 24 | 5 | 5c. red | £190 | 80·00 |

**1864.** Perf.

| 16 |  | 5c. red | 26·00 | 10·50 |
|---|---|---|---|---|
| 17 | 6 | 10c. green | 70·00 | 24·00 |
| 18 | 5 | 15c. blue | £200 | 80·00 |

9 Rivadavia 10 Gen. Belgrano 11 Gen. San Martin

**1867.** Perf.

| 28 | 9 | 5c. red | 12·50 | 1·00 |
|---|---|---|---|---|
| 29 | 10 | 10c. green | 41·00 | 8·75 |
| 30a | 11 | 15c. blue | 85·00 | 16·00 |

12 Balcarce

**1873.** Portraits. Perf.

| 31 | 12 | 1c. violet | 6·25 | 2·00 |
|---|---|---|---|---|
| 32 | - | 4c. brown (Moreno) | 5·00 | 45 |
| 33 | - | 30c. orange (Alvear) | £100 | 19·00 |
| 34 | - | 60c. black (Posadas) | £100 | 4·50 |
| 35 | - | 90c. blue (Saavedra) | 26·00 | 2·75 |

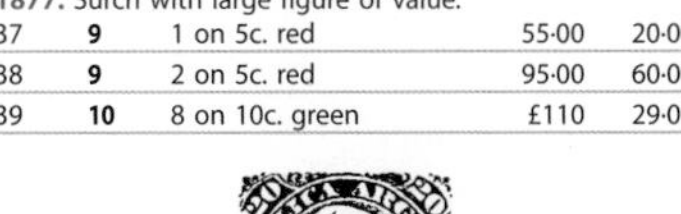

**1877.** Surch with large figure of value.

| 37 | 9 | 1 on 5c. red | 55·00 | 20·00 |
|---|---|---|---|---|
| 38 | 9 | 2 on 5c. red | 95·00 | 60·00 |
| 39 | 10 | 8 on 10c. green | £110 | 29·00 |

22 Sarsfield

**1876.** Roul.

| 36 | 9 | 5c. red | £180 | 75·00 |
|---|---|---|---|---|
| 40 | 9 | 8c. lake | 21·00 | 35 |
| 41 | 10 | 16c. green | 10·00 | 1·20 |
| 42 | 22 | 20c. blue | 12·50 | 2·75 |
| 43 | 11 | 24c. blue | 21·00 | 2·75 |

24 Lopez

**1877.** Perf.

| 46 | 24 | 2c. green | 4·50 | 85 |
|---|---|---|---|---|
| 44 | 9 | 8c. lake | 4·25 | 50 |
| 45 | 11 | 24c. blue | 24·00 | 1·80 |
| 47 | - | 25c. lake (Alvear) | 22·00 | 6·00 |

**1882.** Surch 1/2 (PROVISORIO).

| 51 | 9 | ½ on 5c. red | 1·40 | 1·40 |
|---|---|---|---|---|

29

**1882**

| 52 | 29 | ½c. brown | 1·60 | 1·00 |
|---|---|---|---|---|
| 55 | 29 | 1c. red | 3·50 | 1·00 |
| 54 | 29 | 12c. blue | 50·00 | 8·75 |

**1884.** Surch 1884 and value in figures or words.

| 90 | 9 | ½c. on 5c. red | 2·75 | 2·20 |
|---|---|---|---|---|
| 92 | 11 | ½c. on 15c. blue | 11·00 | 8·00 |
| 94 | 11 | 1c. on 15c. blue | 11·00 | 8·75 |
| 100 | 9 | 4c. on 5c. red | 7·00 | 4·50 |

33

**1884**

| 101 | 33 | ½c. brown | 1·30 | 50 |
|---|---|---|---|---|
| 102 | 33 | 1c. red | 6·25 | 50 |
| 103 | 33 | 12c. blue | 30·00 | 1·20 |

34 Urquiza 45 Mitre

**1888.** Portrait types, inscr "CORREOS ARGENTINOS".

| 108 | 34 | ½c. blue | 1·00 | 50 |
|---|---|---|---|---|
| 110 | - | 2c. green (Lopez) | 12·00 | 7·25 |
| 111 | - | 3c. green (Celman) | 2·10 | 75 |
| 113 | - | 5c. red (Rivadavia) | 15·00 | 1·30 |
| 114 | - | 6c. red (Sarmiento) | 31·00 | 18·00 |
| 115 | - | 10c. brown (Avellaneda) | 18·00 | 1·00 |
| 116 | - | 15c. orange (San Martin) | 21·00 | 1·60 |
| 117a | - | 20c. green (Roca) | 14·50 | 1·20 |
| 118 | - | 25c. violet (Belgrano) | 21·00 | 2·50 |
| 119 | - | 30c. brown (Dorrego) | 26·00 | 3·00 |
| 120a | - | 40c. grey (Moreno) | 31·00 | 3·50 |
| 121 | 45 | 50c. blue | £120 | 7·75 |

51 Rivadavia 60 Paz

**1888.** Portrait types, inscr "CORREOS Y TELEGRAFOS" except No. 126.

| 137 | 60 | ¼c. green | 50 | 30 |
|---|---|---|---|---|
| 122 | - | ½c. blue (Urquiza) | 50 | 30 |
| 123 | - | 1c. brown (Sarsfield) | 1·00 | 50 |
| 125 | - | 2c. violet (Derqui) | 1·00 | 50 |
| 126 | - | 3c. green (Celman) | 3·00 | 80 |
| 127 | 51 | 5c. red | 3·00 | 50 |
| 129 | - | 6c. blue (Sarmiento) | 2·10 | 55 |
| 130 | - | 10c. brown (Avellaneda) | 3·00 | 50 |
| 131 | - | 12c. blue (Alberti) | 6·25 | 2·00 |
| 132 | - | 40c. grey (Moreno) | 6·25 | 1·00 |
| 133 | - | 50c. orange (Mitre) | 6·25 | 1·00 |
| 134 | - | 60c. black (Posadas) | 15·00 | 3·00 |

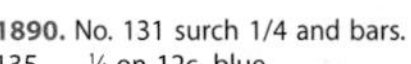

**1890.** No. 131 surch 1/4 and bars.

| 135 |  | ¼ on 12c. blue | 35 | 35 |
|---|---|---|---|---|

52 Rivadavia

**1890**

| 128a | 52 | 5c. red | 1·80 | 20 |
|---|---|---|---|---|

63 La Madrid

**1891.** Portraits.

| 139 | - | 1p. blue (San Martin) | 55·00 | 9·75 |
|---|---|---|---|---|
| 140 | 63 | 5p. blue | £275 | 50·00 |
| 141 | - | 20p. green (G. Brown) | £425 | £130 |

61 Rivadavia

**1891**

| 138 | 61 | 8c. red | 1·30 | 50 |
|---|---|---|---|---|

65 Rivadavia 66 Belgrano 67 San Martin

**1892**

| 142 | 65 | ½c. blue | 30 | 15 |
|---|---|---|---|---|
| 143 | 65 | 1c. brown | 50 | 15 |
| 144 | 65 | 2c. green | 60 | 20 |
| 145 | 65 | 3c. orange | 1·20 | 20 |
| 146 | 65 | 5c. red | 1·20 | 20 |
| 147 | 66 | 10c. red | 9·50 | 35 |
| 148 | 66 | 12c. blue | 7·25 | 35 |
| 149 | 66 | 16c. slate | 12·00 | 45 |
| 150 | 66 | 24c. sepia | 12·00 | 45 |
| 257 | 66 | 30c. orange | 32·00 | 2·00 |
| 151 | 66 | 50c. green | 18·00 | 45 |
| 188 | 66 | 80c. lilac | 8·50 | 45 |
| 152a | 67 | 1p. red | 8·75 | 65 |
| 190 | 67 | 1p.20 black | 8·50 | 1·70 |
| 153 | 67 | 2p. green | 18·00 | 1·80 |
| 154 | 67 | 5p. blue | 24·00 | 1·80 |

70 Fleet of Columbus

**1892.** 4th Centenary of Discovery of America by Columbus.

| 219 | 70 | 2c. blue | 7·75 | 3·25 |
|---|---|---|---|---|
| 220 | 70 | 5c. blue | 8·25 | 4·00 |

71 "Liberty" and Shield

**1899**

| 221 | 71 | ½c. brown | 30 | 20 |
|---|---|---|---|---|
| 222 | 71 | 1c. green | 1·30 | 40 |
| 223 | 71 | 2c. grey | 40 | 20 |
| 224 | 71 | 3c. orange | 40 | 35 |
| 225 | 71 | 4c. yellow | 65 | 40 |
| 226 | 71 | 5c. red | 40 | 20 |
| 227 | 71 | 6c. black | 40 | 40 |
| 228 | 71 | 10c. green | 1·00 | 25 |
| 229a | 71 | 12c. blue | 65 | 40 |
| 230 | 71 | 12c. green | 65 | 40 |
| 231 | 71 | 15c. blue | 1·40 | 40 |
| 232 | 71 | 16c. orange | 5·50 | 4·00 |
| 233 | 71 | 20c. red | 1·10 | 20 |
| 234 | 71 | 24c. purple | 2·75 | 70 |
| 235 | 71 | 30c. red | 5·00 | 40 |
| 237 | 71 | 50c. blue | 2·75 | 35 |
| 238 | 71 | 1p. black and blue | 8·50 | 70 |
| 239 | 71 | 5p. black and orange | 32·00 | 6·00 |
| 240 | 71 | 10p. black and green | 42·00 | 10·00 |
| 241 | 71 | 20p. black and red | £110 | 20·00 |

The peso values are larger (19×32 mm).

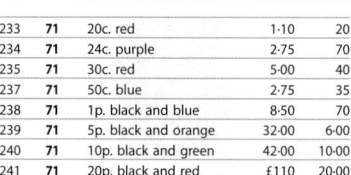

73 Port Rosario

**1902.** Completion of Port Rosario Docks.

| 290 | 73 | 5c. blue | 4·00 | 1·70 |
|---|---|---|---|---|

74 Gen. San Martin

**1908**

| 291B | 74 | ½c. violet | 35 | 20 |
|---|---|---|---|---|
| 292B | 74 | 1c. brown | 35 | 20 |
| 293B | 74 | 2c. brown | 40 | 20 |
| 294B | 74 | 3c. green | 40 | 25 |
| 295B | 74 | 4c. mauve | 85 | 25 |
| 296B | 74 | 5c. red | 40 | 20 |
| 297B | 74 | 6c. green | 60 | 40 |
| 298B | 74 | 10c. green | 1·30 | 20 |
| 299A | 74 | 12c. brown | 40 | 40 |
| 300B | 74 | 12c. blue | 1·30 | 20 |
| 301A | 74 | 15c. green | 4·25 | 1·20 |
| 302B | 74 | 20c. blue | 85 | 20 |
| 303B | 74 | 24c. red | 2·50 | 40 |
| 304B | 74 | 30c. red | 4·25 | 40 |
| 305B | 74 | 50c. black | 4·25 | 35 |
| 306A | 74 | 1p. red and blue | 12·50 | 1·70 |

The 1p. is larger (21½×27 mm) with portrait at upper left.

76 Pyramid of May 78 Azcuenaga and Alberti

80 Saavedra

**1910.** Cent of Deposition of the Spanish Viceroy.

| 366 | 76 | ½c. blue and grey | 50 | 30 |
|---|---|---|---|---|
| 367 | - | 1c. black and green | 50 | 30 |
| 368 | - | 2c. black and green | 50 | 30 |
| 369 | 78 | 3c. green | 1·00 | 40 |
| 370 | - | 4c. green and blue | 1·00 | 40 |
| 371 | 80 | 5c. red | 75 | 30 |
| 372 | - | 10c. black and brown | 1·10 | 50 |
| 373 | - | 12c. blue | 1·10 | 50 |
| 374 | - | 20c. black and brown | 3·00 | 70 |
| 375 | - | 24c. blue and brown | 2·75 | 1·20 |
| 376 | - | 30c. black and lilac | 2·75 | 1·00 |
| 377 | - | 50c. black and red | 6·25 | 1·20 |
| 378 | - | 1p. blue | 9·50 | 3·00 |
| 379 | - | 5p. purple and orange | 75·00 | 36·00 |
| 380 | - | 10p. black and orange | £100 | 60·00 |
| 381 | - | 20p. black and blue | £160 | £100 |

DESIGNS—VERT: 50c. Crowds on 25 May 1810; 10p. Centenary Monument; 20p. San Martin. HORIZ: 1c. Pena and Vieytes; 2c. Meeting at Pena's house; 4c. Fort of the Viceroys, Buenos Aires; 10c. Distribution of cockades; 12c. Congress Building; 20c. Castelli and Matheu; 24c. First National Council; 30c. Belgrano and Larrea; 1p. Moreno and Paso; 5p. "Oath of the Junta".

90 Sarmiento

1911. Birth Centenary of Pres. Sarmiento.

| 382 | 90 | 5c. black and brown | 85 | 40 |
|---|---|---|---|---|

91 Ploughman

1911

| 383 | 91 | 5c. red | 40 | 15 |
|---|---|---|---|---|
| 384 | 91 | 12c. blue | 5·25 | 45 |

92 Ploughman 94

1911

| 395 | 92 | ½c. violet | 45 | 45 |
|---|---|---|---|---|
| 396 | 92 | 1c. brown | 45 | 45 |
| 397 | 92 | 2c. brown | 65 | 45 |
| 398 | 92 | 3c. green | 65 | 65 |
| 399a | 92 | 4c. purple | 75 | 75 |
| 400 | 92 | 5c. red | 55 | 45 |
| 401 | 92 | 10c. green | 2·20 | 45 |
| 402 | 92 | 12c. blue | 75 | 45 |
| 403 | 92 | 20c. blue | 4·00 | 65 |
| 404 | 92 | 24c. brown | 8·25 | 2·75 |
| 405 | 92 | 30c. red | 9·25 | 1·40 |
| 406 | 92 | 50c. black | 13·00 | 1·30 |
| 408 | 94 | 1p. red and blue | 13·00 | 1·40 |
| 409 | 94 | 5p. green and grey | 24·00 | 8·00 |
| 410 | 94 | 10p. blue and violet | £100 | 20·00 |
| 411 | 94 | 20p. red and blue | £225 | £100 |

95 Dr. F. N. Laprida 96 Declaration of Independence

97 San Martin

1916. Centenary of Independence.

| 417 | 95 | ½c. violet | 75 | 45 |
|---|---|---|---|---|
| 418 | 95 | 1c. brown | 75 | 55 |
| 419 | 95 | 2c. brown | 75 | 45 |
| 420 | 95 | 3c. green | 75 | 75 |
| 421 | 95 | 4c. purple | 75 | 75 |
| 422 | 96 | 5c. red | 75 | 9·50 |
| 423 | 96 | 10c. green | 2·10 | 45 |
| 424 | 97 | 12c. blue | 75 | 45 |
| 425 | 97 | 20c. blue | 75 | 75 |
| 426 | 97 | 24c. red | 3·25 | 1·60 |
| 427 | 97 | 30c. red | 3·25 | 95 |
| 428 | 97 | 50c. black | 5·00 | 95 |
| 429 | 97 | 1p. red and blue | 13·00 | 7·00 |
| 430 | 97 | 5p. green and grey | £130 | 80·00 |
| 431 | 97 | 10p. blue and violet | £200 | £160 |
| 432 | 97 | 20p. red and grey | £170 | £130 |

98 San Martin

1917

| 450A | 98 | ½c. violet | 45 | 20 |
|---|---|---|---|---|
| 451A | 98 | 1c. buff | 45 | 20 |
| 452A | 98 | 2c. brown | 45 | 20 |
| 453A | 98 | 3c. green | 65 | 20 |
| 454A | 98 | 4c. purple | 65 | 20 |
| 455B | 98 | 5c. red | 45 | 20 |
| 439A | 98 | 10c. green | 45 | 45 |
| 457B | - | 12c. blue | 1·70 | 20 |
| 458B | - | 20c. blue | 1·70 | 20 |
| 459B | - | 24c. red | 3·25 | 20 |
| 460B | - | 30c. red | 4·00 | 45 |
| 461B | - | 50c. black | 8·25 | 65 |
| 445B | - | 1p. red and blue | 8·25 | 75 |
| 446B | - | 5p. green and grey | 21·00 | 3·75 |
| 447B | - | 10p. blue and violet | 65·00 | 16·00 |
| 448B | - | 20p. red and grey | £130 | 75·00 |

The 12c. to 20p. values are larger (21×27 mm).

100 Dr. Juan Pujol

1918. Birth Centenary of Juan Pujol, 1st P.M.G. of Argentina.

| 449 | 100 | 5c. grey and bistre | 1·00 | 45 |
|---|---|---|---|---|

102 Mausoleum of Belgrano 103 Creation of Argentine Flag

1920. Death Centenary of Gen. Manuel Belgrano.

| 478 | 102 | 2c. red | 70 | 15 |
|---|---|---|---|---|
| 479 | 103 | 5c. blue and red | 70 | 15 |
| 480 | - | 12c. blue and green | 1·40 | 60 |

DESIGN—VERT: 12c. Gen. Belgrano.

106 General Urquiza

1920. Gen. Urquiza's Victory at Cepada.

| 488 | 106 | 5c. blue | 55 | 30 |
|---|---|---|---|---|

107 General Mitre

1921. Birth Centenary of Gen. Mitre.

| 490 | 107 | 2c. brown | 55 | 30 |
|---|---|---|---|---|
| 491 | 107 | 5c. blue | 55 | 30 |

108

1921. 1st Pan-American Postal Congress.

| 492 | 108 | 3c. lilac | 75 | 45 |
|---|---|---|---|---|
| 493 | 108 | 5c. blue | 1·90 | 10 |
| 494 | 108 | 10c. brown | 2·20 | 45 |
| 495 | 108 | 12c. red | 2·75 | 95 |

1921. As T 108, but smaller. Inscr "BUENOS AIRES AGOSTO DE 1921".

| 496A | 5c. red | 40 | 25 |
|---|---|---|---|

1921. As No. 496, but inscr "REPUBLICA ARGENTINA" at foot.

| 511A | 5c. red | 3·00 | 25 |
|---|---|---|---|

112

1923. With or without stop below "c".

| 529 | 112 | ½c. purple | 35 | 15 |
|---|---|---|---|---|
| 530 | 112 | 1c. brown | 35 | 15 |
| 531 | 112 | 2c. brown | 35 | 15 |
| 516A | 112 | 3c. green | 35 | 25 |
| 517A | 112 | 4c. red | 35 | 25 |
| 534 | 112 | 5c. red | 35 | 15 |
| 535 | 112 | 10c. green | 35 | 20 |
| 536 | 112 | 12c. blue | 40 | 20 |
| 537 | 112 | 20c. blue | 65 | 20 |
| 538 | 112 | 24c. brown | 1·80 | 80 |
| 539 | 112 | 25c. violet | 85 | 20 |
| 540 | 112 | 30c. red | 1·80 | 20 |
| 541 | 112 | 50c. black | 4·25 | 20 |
| 542 | - | 1p. red and blue | 7·00 | 35 |
| 543 | - | 5p. green and lilac | 21·00 | 4·00 |
| 544 | - | 10p. blue and red | 65·00 | 10·00 |
| 545 | - | 20p. lake and slate | 85·00 | 30·00 |

The peso values are larger (21×27 mm).

114 B. Rivadavia

1926. Rivadavia Centenary.

| 546 | 114 | 5c. red | 55 | 30 |
|---|---|---|---|---|

115 Rivadavia 116 San Martin

117 G.P.O., 1926 118 G.P.O., 1826

1926. Postal Centenary.

| 547 | 115 | 3c. green | 35 | 20 |
|---|---|---|---|---|
| 548 | 116 | 5c. red | 35 | 20 |
| 549 | 117 | 12c. blue | 1·10 | 30 |
| 550 | 118 | 25c. brown | 2·75 | 85 |

120 Biplane and Globe 122

1928. Air.

| 558 | 120 | 5c. red | 1·80 | 75 |
|---|---|---|---|---|
| 559 | 120 | 10c. blue | 2·75 | 1·10 |
| 560 | - | 15c. brown | 2·75 | 1·10 |
| 561 | 120 | 18c. violet | 5·00 | 3·75 |
| 562 | - | 20c. blue | 3·25 | 1·10 |
| 563 | - | 24c. blue | 5·50 | 3·75 |
| 564 | 122 | 25c. violet | 5·50 | 1·70 |
| 565 | 122 | 30c. red | 6·50 | 1·30 |
| 566 | - | 35c. red | 5·50 | 1·20 |
| 567a | 120 | 36c. brown | 3·00 | 1·50 |
| 568 | - | 50c. black | 5·50 | 75 |
| 569 | - | 54c. brown | 5·50 | 2·30 |
| 570 | - | 72c. green | 6·50 | 2·30 |
| 571 | 122 | 90c. purple | 12·00 | 2·30 |
| 572 | 122 | 1p. red and blue | 14·50 | 1·10 |
| 573 | 122 | 1p.08 blue and red | 22·00 | 5·75 |
| 574 | - | 1p.26 green and violet | 29·00 | 10·50 |
| 575 | - | 1p.80 red and blue | 29·00 | 10·50 |
| 576 | - | 3p.60 blue and grey | 55·00 | 23·00 |

DESIGNS—VERT: 15, 20, 24, 54, 72c. Yellow-headed Caracara over sea. HORIZ: 35, 50c., 1p.26, 1p.80, 3p.60, Andean Condor on mountain top.

124 Arms of Argentina and Brazil

1928. Centenary of Peace with Brazil.

| 577 | 124 | 5c. red | 1·90 | 65 |
|---|---|---|---|---|
| 578 | 124 | 12c. blue | 3·25 | 85 |

125 Torch illuminating New World

1929. "Day of the Race" issue.

| 579 | 125 | 2c. brown | 2·75 | 55 |
|---|---|---|---|---|
| 580 | - | 5c. red | 2·75 | 45 |
| 581 | - | 12c. blue | 8·25 | 1·30 |

DESIGNS: 5c. Symbolical figures, Spain and Argentina; 12c. American offering laurels to Columbus.

(128)

1930. Air. "Zeppelin" Europe–Pan-America Flight. Optd with T 128.

| 587 | - | 20c. blue (No. 562) | 14·50 | 8·50 |
|---|---|---|---|---|
| 588 | - | 50c. black (No. 568) | 19·00 | 13·00 |
| 589 | 122 | 90c. purple | 13·00 | 8·50 |
| 584 | 122 | 1p. red and blue | 29·00 | 14·00 |
| 585 | - | 1p.80 (No. 575) | 85·00 | 37·00 |
| 586 | - | 3p.60 (No. 576) | £225 | £110 |

129 Soldier and Civilian Insurgents 130 The Victorious March, 6 September 30

1930. Revolution of 6 September 1930.

| 592 | 129 | ½c. violet | 55 | 30 |
|---|---|---|---|---|
| 611 | 130 | ½c. mauve | 45 | 30 |
| 593 | 129 | 1c. green | 55 | 35 |
| 612 | 130 | 1c. black | 1·30 | 1·10 |
| 594 | 130 | 2c. lilac | 65 | 30 |
| 595 | 129 | 3c. green | 55 | 45 |
| 613 | 130 | 3c. green | 90 | 65 |
| 596 | 129 | 4c. violet | 55 | 45 |
| 614 | 130 | 4c. lake | 55 | 45 |
| 597 | 129 | 5c. red | 45 | 30 |
| 615 | 130 | 5c. red | 45 | 30 |
| 598 | 129 | 10c. black | 1·10 | 55 |
| 616 | 130 | 10c. green | 1·90 | 65 |
| 599 | 130 | 12c. blue | 90 | 45 |
| 600 | 130 | 20c. buff | 90 | 35 |
| 601 | 130 | 24c. brown | 3·50 | 2·30 |
| 602 | 130 | 25c. green | 4·25 | 2·30 |
| 603 | 130 | 30c. violet | 6·50 | 3·50 |
| 604 | 130 | 50c. black | 9·25 | 4·50 |
| 605 | 130 | 1p. red and blue | 19·00 | 14·00 |
| 606 | 130 | 2p. orange and black | 33·00 | 16·00 |
| 607 | 130 | 5p. black and green | £100 | 49·00 |
| 608 | 130 | 10p. blue and lake | £130 | 60·00 |
| 609 | 130 | 20p. blue and green | £350 | £130 |
| 610 | 130 | 50p. violet and green | £1000 | £750 |

1931. 1st Anniv of 1930 Revolution. Optd 6 Septembre 1930 - 1931.

| 617 | 112 | 3c. green (postage) | 45 | 45 |
|---|---|---|---|---|
| 618 | 112 | 10c. green | 90 | 85 |
| 624 | 129 | 18c. violet (air) | 2·75 | 1·60 |
| 619 | 112 | 30c. red | 5·00 | 4·50 |
| 620 | 112 | 50c. black | 5·00 | 4·50 |
| 625 | - | 72c. green (No. 570) | 22·00 | 14·00 |
| 626 | 122 | 90c. purple | 22·00 | 14·00 |
| 621 | 112 | 1p. red and blue | 6·00 | 4·50 |
| 627 | - | 1p.80 red & bl (No. 575) | 44·00 | 34·00 |
| 623 | 130 | 2p. orange and black | 19·00 | 13·00 |
| 628 | - | 3p.60 bl & grey (No. 576) | 85·00 | 60·00 |
| 622 | 112 | 5p. green and lilac | £100 | 28·00 |

1932. Zeppelin Air stamps. Optd GRAF ZEPPELIN 1932.

| 629 | 120 | 5c. red | 3·25 | 2·10 |
|---|---|---|---|---|
| 630 | 120 | 18c. violet | 14·00 | 9·50 |
| 631 | 122 | 90c. purple | 50·00 | 28·00 |

134 Refrigerating Plant

**1932.** 6th International Refrigerating Congress.

| | | | | |
|---|---|---|---|---|
| 632 | **134** | 3c. green | 1·30 | 65 |
| 633 | **134** | 10c. red | 2·75 | 55 |
| 634 | **134** | 12c. blue | 7·75 | 1·90 |

**135** Port La Plata

**1933.** 50th Anniv of La Plata City.

| | | | | |
|---|---|---|---|---|
| 635 | **135** | 3c. brown and green | 55 | 35 |
| 636 | - | 10c. purple and orange | 65 | 30 |
| 637 | - | 15c. blue | 5·00 | 2·30 |
| 638 | - | 20c. brown and lilac | 2·20 | 1·40 |
| 639 | - | 30c. red and green | 21·00 | 8·00 |

DESIGNS: 10c. President J. A. Roca; 15c. Municipal buildings; 20c. La Plata Cathedral; 30c. Dr. D. Rocha.

**139** Christ of the Andes

**1934.** 32nd Int Eucharistic Congress, Buenos Aires.

| | | | | |
|---|---|---|---|---|
| 640 | **139** | 10c. red | 1·10 | 30 |
| 641 | - | 15c. blue | 2·20 | 65 |

DESIGN—HORIZ: 15c. Buenos Aires Cathedral.

**141** "Liberty" with Arms of Brazil and Argentina

**1935.** Visit of President Vargas of Brazil. Inscr "MAYO DE 1935".

| | | | | |
|---|---|---|---|---|
| 642 | **141** | 10c. red | 1·10 | 30 |
| 643 | - | 15c. blue | 2·20 | 65 |

DESIGN: 15c. Clasped hands and flags.

**143** D. F. Sarmiento

**1935.** Portraits.

| | | | | |
|---|---|---|---|---|
| 644 | | ½c. purple (Belgrano) | 30 | 20 |
| 645 | | 1c. brown (Type **143**) | 30 | 20 |
| 646 | | 2c. brown (Urquiza) | 35 | 20 |
| 647 | | 3c. green (San Martin) | 35 | 20 |
| 648 | | 4c. grey (G. Brown) | 35 | 20 |
| 653b | | 5c. brown (Moreno) | 70 | 20 |
| 650 | | 6c. green (Alberdi) | 40 | 20 |
| 653d | | 10c. red (Rivadavia) | 2·10 | 20 |
| 651 | | 12c. purple (Mitre) | 45 | 30 |
| 708 | | 15c. grey (Martin Guemes) | 55 | 35 |
| 652 | | 20c. blue (Juan Martin Guemes) | 90 | 20 |
| 653 | | 20c. blue (Martin Guemes) | 55 | 20 |

See also Nos. 671 etc.

**1935.** Philatelic Exhibition, Buenos Aires (Ex. Fl. B.A.). Sheet 83×100 mm.

| | | |
|---|---|---|
| **MS**654 **112** 10c. green ×4 (sold at 1p.) | 95·00 | 45·00 |

**146** Prize Bull

**151** With Boundary Lines

**1936.** Production and Industry.

| | | | | |
|---|---|---|---|---|
| 676 | **146** | 15c. blue | 55 | 30 |
| 677a | **146** | 20c. blue (19½×26 mm) | 35 | 20 |
| 755 | **146** | 20c. blue (22×33 mm) | 2·75 | 10 |
| 656 | - | 25c. red and pink | 45 | 20 |
| 757 | - | 30c. brown and yellow | 1·20 | 10 |
| 658 | - | 40c. purple and mauve | 55 | 20 |
| 659 | - | 50c. red and salmon | 45 | 20 |
| 660 | **151** | 1p. blue and brown | 24·00 | 1·20 |
| 760 | - | 1p. blue and brown | 5·00 | 10 |
| 661 | - | 2p. blue and purple | 1·30 | 20 |
| 662 | - | 5p. green and blue | 6·50 | 45 |
| 763 | - | 10p. black and purple | 22·00 | 2·00 |
| 764 | - | 20p. brown and blue | 19·00 | 2·00 |

DESIGNS—VERT: 25c. Ploughman; 50c. Oil well; 1p. (No. 760) as Type **151** but without country boundaries; 5p. Iguazu Falls; 10p. Grapes; 20p. Cotton plant. HORIZ: 30c. Patagonian ram; 40c. Sugar cane and factory; 2p. Fruit products.

**157**

**1936.** Pan-American Peace Conference.

| | | | | |
|---|---|---|---|---|
| 665 | **157** | 10c. red | 90 | 25 |

**158** Pres. Sarmiento

**1938.** President's 50th Death Anniv.

| | | | | |
|---|---|---|---|---|
| 666 | **158** | 3c. green | 65 | 55 |
| 667 | **158** | 5c. red | 65 | 55 |
| 668 | **158** | 15c. blue | 1·30 | 65 |
| 669 | **158** | 50c. orange | 4·25 | 1·40 |

**159** "Presidente Sarmiento"

**1939.** Last Voyage of Cadet Ship "Presidente Sarmiento".

| | | | | |
|---|---|---|---|---|
| 670 | **159** | 5c. green | 55 | 30 |

**1939.** Portraits as T **143**.

| | | | | |
|---|---|---|---|---|
| 671 | | 2½c. black | 30 | 20 |
| 672 | | 3c. grey (San Martin) | 40 | 20 |
| 672a | | 3c. grey (Moreno) | 40 | 20 |
| 673 | | 4c. green | 35 | 20 |
| 894 | | 5c. brown (16½×22½ mm) | 25 | 10 |
| 674 | | 8c. orange | 35 | 20 |
| 678 | | 10c. purple | 30 | 20 |
| 675 | | 12c. red | 30 | 20 |
| 895 | | 20c. lilac (21×27 mm) | 90 | 20 |
| 895b | | 20c. lilac (19½×25½ mm) | 90 | 20 |

PORTRAITS: 2½c. L. Braille; 4c. G. Brown; 5c. Jose Hernandez; 8c. N. Avellaneda; 10c. B. Rivadavia; 12c. B. Mitre; 20c. G. Brown.

**160** Allegory of the Post

**1939.** 11th U.P.U. Congress, Buenos Aires.

| | | | | |
|---|---|---|---|---|
| 679 | **160** | 5c. red | 90 | 20 |
| 680 | - | 15c. grey | 90 | 45 |
| 681 | - | 20c. blue | 90 | 20 |
| 682 | - | 25c. green | 1·30 | 45 |
| 683 | - | 50c. brown | 2·20 | 85 |
| 684 | - | 1p. purple | 5·50 | 2·10 |
| 685 | - | 2p. mauve | 24·00 | 13·00 |
| 686 | - | 5p. violet | 55·00 | 27·00 |

DESIGNS—VERT: 20c. Seal of Argentina; 1p. Symbols of postal communications; 2p. Argentina, "Land of Promise" from a pioneer painting. HORIZ: 15c. G.P.O.; 25c. Iguazu Falls; 50c. Mt. Bonete; 5p. Lake Frias.

**1939.** International Philatelic Exhibition, Buenos Aires. Two sheets se-tenant horiz or vert, each comprising Nos. 679, 681/3 arranged differently.

| | | |
|---|---|---|
| **MS**686a Two sheets, 190×95 mm or 95×190 mm | 17·00 | 16·00 |

**165** Working-class Family and New Home

**1939.** 1st Pan-American Housing Congress.

| | | | | |
|---|---|---|---|---|
| 687 | **165** | 5c. green | 45 | 20 |

**167** North and South America

**1940.** 50th Anniv of Pan-American Union.

| | | | | |
|---|---|---|---|---|
| 688 | **167** | 15c. blue | 55 | 20 |

**168** Corrientes Type **5**

**1940.** Centenary of First Adhesive Postage Stamps and Philatelic Exhibition, Cordoba. Sheet 111×111 mm containing early Argentine issues as T 168.

| | | |
|---|---|---|
| **MS**688a 5c. blue (Type **168**); 5c. blue (Cordoba T **3**); 5c. red (Type **1**); 5c. red (Type **3**); 10c. blue (Buenos Aires T **1**) | 13·00 | 10·50 |

**169** Airplane and Envelope

**1940.** Air.

| | | | | |
|---|---|---|---|---|
| 689 | **169** | 30c. orange | 8·75 | 45 |
| 690 | - | 50c. brown | 13·00 | 45 |
| 691 | **169** | 1p. red | 3·25 | 10 |
| 692 | - | 1p.25 green | 90 | 10 |
| 693 | **169** | 2p.50 blue | 2·75 | 50 |

DESIGNS—VERT: 50c. "Mercury"; 1p.25, Douglas DC-2 in clouds.

**172** Gen. French, Col. Beruti and Rosette of the "Legion de Patricios"

**1941.** 131st Anniv of Rising against Spain.

| | | | | |
|---|---|---|---|---|
| 694 | **172** | 5c. blue | 45 | 20 |

**173** Marco M. de Avellaneda

**1941.** Death Centenary of Avellaneda (patriot).

| | | | | |
|---|---|---|---|---|
| 695 | **173** | 5c. blue | 45 | 20 |

**174** Statue of Gen. J. A. Roca

**1941.** Dedication of Statue of Gen. Roca.

| | | | | |
|---|---|---|---|---|
| 696 | **174** | 5c. green | 45 | 20 |

**175** Pellegrini (founder) and National Bank

**1941.** 50th Anniv of National Bank.

| | | | | |
|---|---|---|---|---|
| 697 | **175** | 5c. lake | 45 | 20 |

**176** Gen. Juan Lavalle

**1941.** Death Centenary of Gen. Lavalle.

| | | | | |
|---|---|---|---|---|
| 698 | **176** | 5c. blue | 45 | 20 |

**177** New P.O. Savings Bank

**1942.** Inauguration of P.O. Savings Bank.

| | | | | |
|---|---|---|---|---|
| 699 | **177** | 1c. green | 35 | 20 |

**178** Jose Manuel Estrada

**1942.** Birth Centenary of Estrada (patriot).

| | | | | |
|---|---|---|---|---|
| 700 | **178** | 5c. purple | 45 | 20 |

**180** G.P.O., Buenos Aires

**1942.** Postage and Express Stamps.

| | | | | |
|---|---|---|---|---|
| 717 | **180** | 35c. blue | 4·75 | 20 |
| 746 | **180** | 35c. blue | 1·90 | 30 |

No. 717 is inscr "PALACIO CENTRAL DE CORREOS Y TELEGRAFOS" and No. 746 "PALACIO CENTRAL DE CORREOS Y TELECOMUNICACIONES".

**181** Proposed Columbus Lighthouse

**1942.** 450th Anniv of Discovery of America by Columbus.

| | | | | |
|---|---|---|---|---|
| 721b | **181** | 15c. blue | 6·50 | 65 |

**182** Dr. Paz (founder of "La Prensa")

**1942.** Birth Centenary of Dr. Jose C. Paz.

| | | | | |
|---|---|---|---|---|
| 722 | **182** | 5c. blue | 45 | 15 |

**183** Flag of Argentina and Books

**1943.** 1st National Book Fair.

| | | | | |
|---|---|---|---|---|
| 723 | **183** | 5c. blue | 45 | 15 |

**184** Arms of Argentina

**1943.** Revolution of 4 June 1943.

| | | | | |
|---|---|---|---|---|
| 724 | **184** | 5c. red | 35 | 15 |
| 725 | **184** | 15c. green | 1·00 | 20 |
| 726 | **184** | 20c. blue (larger) | 1·50 | 20 |

**185** National Independence House

**1943.** Restoration of Tucuman Museum.

| | | | | |
|---|---|---|---|---|
| 727b | **185** | 5c. green | 45 | 15 |

**186** Head of Liberty, Money-box and Laurels

**1943.** 1st Savings Bank Conference.

| | | | | |
|---|---|---|---|---|
| 728 | **186** | 5c. brown | 35 | 10 |

**187** Buenos Aires in 1800

**1944.** Export Day.

| | | | | |
|---|---|---|---|---|
| 729 | **187** | 5c. black | 35 | 10 |

**188** Postal Union of the Americas and Spain

**189** Alexander Graham Bell

**1944.** Postmen's Benefit Fund. Inscr "PRO-CARTERO".

| | | | | |
|---|---|---|---|---|
| 730 | - | 3c.+2c. black and violet | 80 | 65 |
| 731 | **188** | 5c.+5c. black and red | 1·10 | 30 |
| 732 | **189** | 10c.+5c. black and orge | 2·20 | 75 |
| 733 | - | 25c.+15c. black and brn | 2·75 | 1·30 |
| 734 | - | 1p.+50c. black and green | 13·00 | 10·50 |

DESIGNS: 3c. Samuel Morse; 25c. Rowland Hill; 1p. Columbus landing in America.

**191** Liner, Warship and Yacht

**1944.** Naval Week.

| | | | | |
|---|---|---|---|---|
| 735 | **191** | 5c. blue | 35 | 10 |

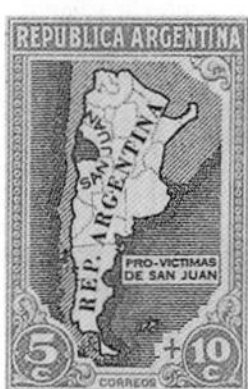

**192** Argentina

**1944.** San Juan Earthquake Relief Fund.

| | | | | |
|---|---|---|---|---|
| 736 | **192** | 5c.+10c. black & olive | 1·40 | 65 |
| 737 | **192** | 5c.+50c. black and red | 5·50 | 2·30 |
| 738 | **192** | 5c.+1p. black & orange | 17·00 | 10·50 |
| 739 | **192** | 5c.+20p. black & blue | 40·00 | 21·00 |

**193** Arms of Argentina

**1944.** 1st Anniv of Revolution of 4 June 1943.

| | | | | |
|---|---|---|---|---|
| 740 | **193** | 5c. blue | 45 | 15 |

**193a** National Flag

**1944.** National Anthem and Aid for La Rioja and Catamarca Provinces. Two sheets 75×110 mm each containing T 193a.

| | | |
|---|---|---|
| **MS**740a 5c.+1p. blue and plum | 22·00 | 7·00 |
| **MS**740b 5c.+50p. blue and indigo | £650 | £650 |

**194** Archangel Gabriel

**195** Cross of Palermo

**1944.** 4th National Eucharistic Congress.

| | | | | |
|---|---|---|---|---|
| 741 | **194** | 3c. green | 50 | 20 |
| 742 | **195** | 5c. red | 50 | 20 |

**196** Allegory of Savings

**1944.** 20th Anniv of Universal Savings Day.

| | | | | |
|---|---|---|---|---|
| 743 | **196** | 5c. black | 35 | 15 |

**197** Reservists

**1944.** Reservists' Day.

| | | | | |
|---|---|---|---|---|
| 744 | **197** | 5c. blue | 35 | 15 |

**198** Bernardino Rivadavia

**199** Rivadavia's Mausoleum

**1945.** Rivadavia's Death Centenary.

| | | | | |
|---|---|---|---|---|
| 770 | **198** | 3c. green | 45 | 15 |
| 771 | - | 5c. red | 45 | 15 |
| 772 | **199** | 20c. blue | 55 | 20 |

DESIGN—As Type **198**: 5c. Rivadavia and Scales of Justice.

**200** San Martin

**1945**

| | | | | |
|---|---|---|---|---|
| 773 | **200** | 5c. red | 35 | 15 |

**201** Monument to Andes Army, Mendoza

**1946.** "Homage to the Unknown Soldier of Independence".

| | | | | |
|---|---|---|---|---|
| 776 | **201** | 5c. purple | 45 | 15 |

**202** Pres. Roosevelt

**1946.** 1st Death Anniv of Pres. Franklin Roosevelt.

| | | | | |
|---|---|---|---|---|
| 777 | **202** | 5c. grey | 35 | 15 |

**203** "Affirmation"

**1946.** Installation of Pres. Juan Peron.

| | | | | |
|---|---|---|---|---|
| 778 | **203** | 5c. blue | 35 | 15 |

**204** Airplane over Iguazu Falls

**1946.** Air.

| | | | | |
|---|---|---|---|---|
| 779 | **204** | 15c. red | 45 | 15 |
| 780 | - | 25c. green | 45 | 15 |

DESIGN: 25c. Airplane over Andes.

**205** "Flight"

**1946.** Aviation Week.

| | | | | |
|---|---|---|---|---|
| 781 | **205** | 15c. green on green | 90 | 30 |
| 782 | - | 60c. purple on buff | 90 | 30 |

DESIGN: 60c. Hand upholding globe.

**207** "Argentina and Populace"

**1946.** 1st Anniv of Peron's Defeat of Counter-revolution.

| | | | | |
|---|---|---|---|---|
| 783 | **207** | 5c. mauve | 65 | 45 |
| 784 | **207** | 10c. green | 90 | 55 |
| 785 | **207** | 15c. blue | 1·10 | 85 |
| 786 | **207** | 50c. brown | 90 | 65 |
| 787 | **207** | 1p. red | 2·10 | 1·70 |

**208** Money-box and Map

**1946.** Annual Savings Day.

| | | | | |
|---|---|---|---|---|
| 788 | **208** | 30c. red | 90 | 30 |

**209** Industry

**1946.** Industrial Exhibition.

| | | | | |
|---|---|---|---|---|
| 789 | **209** | 5c. purple | 55 | 15 |

**210** Argentine–Brazil International Bridge

**1947.** Opening of Bridge between Argentina and Brazil.

| | | | | |
|---|---|---|---|---|
| 790 | **210** | 5c. green | 45 | 15 |

**211** South Pole

**1947.** 43rd Anniv of 1st Argentine Antarctic Mail.

| | | | | |
|---|---|---|---|---|
| 791 | **211** | 5c. violet | 65 | 20 |
| 792 | **211** | 20c. red | 1·40 | 20 |

**212** "Justice"

**1947.** 1st Anniv of Col. Juan Peron's Presidency.

| | | | | |
|---|---|---|---|---|
| 793 | **212** | 5c. purple and buff | 45 | 15 |

**213** Icarus Falling

**1947.** "Week of the Wing".

| | | | | |
|---|---|---|---|---|
| 794 | **213** | 15c. purple | 45 | 15 |

**214** "Presidente Sarmiento"

**1947.** 50th Anniv of Launching of Cadet Ship "Presidente Sarmiento".

| | | | | |
|---|---|---|---|---|
| 795 | **214** | 5c. blue | 45 | 15 |

**215** Cervantes and "Don Quixote"

**1947.** 400th Birth Anniv of Cervantes.

| | | | | |
|---|---|---|---|---|
| 796 | **215** | 5c. green | 45 | 15 |

**216** Gen. San Martin and Urn

**1947.** Arrival from Spain of Ashes of Gen. San Martin's Parents.

| | | | | |
|---|---|---|---|---|
| 797 | **216** | 5c. green | 45 | 15 |

**217** Young Crusaders

**1947.** Educational Crusade for Universal Peace.

| | | | | |
|---|---|---|---|---|
| 798 | **217** | 5c. green | 45 | 15 |
| 799 | **217** | 20c. brown | 55 | 15 |

**218** Statue of Araucarian Indian

**1948.** American Indian Day.

| | | | | |
|---|---|---|---|---|
| 801 | **218** | 25c. brown | 45 | 15 |

**219** Phrygian Cap and Sprig of Wheat

**1948.** 5th Anniv of Anti-isolationist Revolution of 4 June 1943.

| | | | | |
|---|---|---|---|---|
| 802 | **219** | 5c. blue | 35 | 15 |

**220** "Stop"

**1948.** Safety First Campaign.

| | | | | |
|---|---|---|---|---|
| 803 | **220** | 5c. yellow and brown | 40 | 15 |

**221** Posthorn and Oak Leaves

**1948.** Bicent of Postal Service in Rio de la Plata.

| | | | | |
|---|---|---|---|---|
| 804 | **221** | 5c. mauve | 40 | 15 |

**222** Argentine Farmers

**1948.** Agriculture Day.

| | | | | |
|---|---|---|---|---|
| 805 | **222** | 10c. brown | 35 | 15 |

**223** "Liberty and Plenty"

**1948.** Re-election of President Peron.

| | | | | |
|---|---|---|---|---|
| 806 | **223** | 25c. red | 55 | 20 |

**225** Statue of Atlas

**226** Map, Globe and Compasses

**1948.** Air. 4th Meeting of Pan-American Cartographers.

| | | | | |
|---|---|---|---|---|
| 807 | **225** | 45c. brown | 65 | 20 |
| 808 | **226** | 70c. green | 1·30 | 55 |

**226a** Buenos Aires

**1948.** Bicentenary of Postal Service in Rio de la Plata (2nd issue). Two sheets containing designs as T 226a.

**MS**808a 144×101 mm. (horiz designs). 15c. green (Mail coach, 1865); 45c. brown (Type **226a**); 55c. brown (First train, 1857); 85c. ultramarine (Sailing ship, 1767) 8·75 3·75

**MS**808b 102×144 mm (vert designs). 85c. brown (Domingo de Basavilibaso); 1p.50 green (Postrider, 1748); 1p.20 indigo (Sailing ship, 1798); 1p.90 purple (Courier in the Andes, 1772) Price for 2 sheets 60·00 13·00

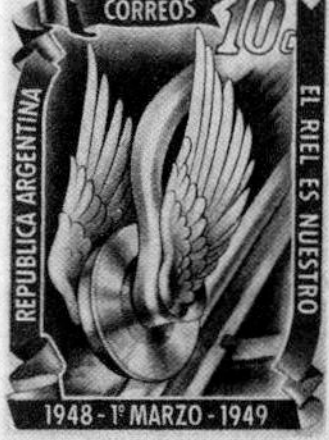


**227** Winged Railway Wheel

**1949.** 1st Anniv of Nationalization of Argentine Railways.

| | | | | |
|---|---|---|---|---|
| 809 | **227** | 10c. blue | 55 | 20 |

**228** Head of Liberty

**1949.** Constitution Day.

| | | | | |
|---|---|---|---|---|
| 810 | **228** | 1p. purple and red | 70 | 30 |

**229** Trophy and Target

**1949.** Air. International Shooting Championship.

| | | | | |
|---|---|---|---|---|
| 811 | **229** | 75c. brown | 1·20 | 30 |

**230** "Intercommunication"

**1949.** 75th Anniv of U.P.U.

| | | | | |
|---|---|---|---|---|
| 812 | **230** | 25c. green and olive | 35 | 15 |

**231** San Martin

**232** San Martin at Boulogne

**1950.** San Martin's Death Cent. Dated "1850 1950".

| | | | | |
|---|---|---|---|---|
| 813 | - | 10c. purple and blue | 20 | 10 |
| 814 | **231** | 20c. brown and red | 20 | 10 |
| 815 | **232** | 25c. brown | 35 | 10 |
| 816 | - | 50c. blue and green | 75 | 30 |
| 817 | - | 75c. green and brown | 75 | 30 |
| 818 | - | 1p. green | 2·00 | 30 |
| 819 | - | 2p. purple | 1·10 | 55 |

**MS**819a 120×150 mm. Nos. 813/14 and 816/17. Imperf 3·75 2·75

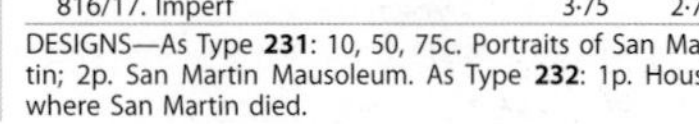

DESIGNS—As Type **231**: 10, 50, 75c. Portraits of San Martin; 2p. San Martin Mausoleum. As Type **232**: 1p. House where San Martin died.

**233** Stamp Designer

**1950.** Int Philatelic Exhibition, Buenos Aires.

| | | | | |
|---|---|---|---|---|
| 820 | **233** | 10c.+10c. violet (postage) | 20 | 15 |
| 821 | - | 45c.+45c. blue (air) | 35 | 30 |
| 822 | - | 70c.+70c. brown | 55 | 50 |
| 823 | - | 1p.+1p. red | 2·20 | 1·60 |
| 824 | - | 2p.50+2p.50 olive | 12·00 | 8·00 |
| 825 | - | 5p.+5p. green | 19·00 | 13·00 |

**MS**825a 120×150 mm. Nos. 820/2. Imperf 8·75 8·00

DESIGNS: 45c. Engraver; 70c. Proofing; 1p. Printer; 2p.50, Woman reading letter; 5p. San Martin.

**234** S. America and Antarctic

**1951**

| | | | | |
|---|---|---|---|---|
| 826 | **234** | 1p. blue and brown | 1·00 | 20 |

**235** Douglas DC-3 and Andean Condor

**1951.** Air. 10th Anniv of State Airlines.

| | | | | |
|---|---|---|---|---|
| 827 | **235** | 20c. olive | 70 | 20 |

**236** Pegasus and Steam Locomotive

**1951.** Five-year Plan.

| | | | | |
|---|---|---|---|---|
| 828 | **236** | 5c. brown (postage) | 1·20 | 20 |
| 829 | - | 25c. green | 2·40 | 35 |
| 830 | - | 40c. purple | 3·25 | 35 |
| 831 | - | 20c. blue (air) | 95 | 20 |

DESIGNS—HORIZ: 25c. "President Peron" (liner) and common dolphin. VERT: 20c. Douglas DC-4 and Andean condor; 40c. Head of Mercury and telephone.

**237** Woman Voter and "Argentina"

**1951.** Women's Suffrage in Argentina.

| | | | | |
|---|---|---|---|---|
| 832 | **237** | 10c. purple | 55 | 15 |

238 "Piety"

1951. Air. Eva Peron Foundation Fund.

| | | | | |
|---|---|---|---|---|
| 833 | 238 | 2p.45+7p.55 olive | 34·00 | 20·00 |

239 Eva Peron 240 Eva Peron

1952. (a) Size 20×26 mm.

| | | | | |
|---|---|---|---|---|
| 834 | 239 | 1c. brown | 35 | 15 |
| 835 | 239 | 5c. grey | 35 | 15 |
| 836 | 239 | 10c. red | 35 | 15 |
| 837 | 239 | 20c. red | 35 | 15 |
| 838 | 239 | 25c. green | 35 | 15 |
| 839 | 239 | 40c. purple | 35 | 15 |
| 841 | 239 | 45c. blue | 70 | 20 |
| 840 | 239 | 50c. bistre | 70 | 20 |

(b) Size 22×33 mm. Without inscr "EVA PERON".

| | | | | |
|---|---|---|---|---|
| 842 | 240 | 1p. brown | 70 | 20 |
| 843 | 240 | 1p.50 green | 3·50 | 20 |
| 844 | 240 | 2p. red | 70 | 20 |
| 845 | 240 | 3p. blue | 2·10 | 20 |

(c) Size 22×33 mm. Inscr "EVA PERON".

| | | | | |
|---|---|---|---|---|
| 846 | | 1p. brown | 55 | 20 |
| 847 | | 1p.50 green | 2·10 | 20 |
| 848 | | 2p. red | 2·10 | 20 |
| 849 | | 3p. blue | 5·25 | 75 |

(d) Size 30½×40 mm. Inscr "EVA PERON".

| | | | | |
|---|---|---|---|---|
| 850 | | 5p. brown | 5·25 | 1·00 |
| 851 | 239 | 10p. red | 12·50 | 2·20 |
| 852 | 240 | 20p. green | 21·00 | 5·25 |
| 853 | 239 | 50p. blue | 37·00 | 13·00 |

241 Indian Funeral Urn

1953. 4th Centenary of Santiago del Estero.

| | | | | |
|---|---|---|---|---|
| 854 | 241 | 50c. green | 35 | 10 |

242 Rescue Ship "Uruguay"

1953. 50th Anniv of Rescue of the "Antarctic".

| | | | | |
|---|---|---|---|---|
| 855 | 242 | 50c. blue | 1·90 | 65 |

243 Planting Flag in S. Orkneys

1954. 50th Anniv of Argentine P.O. in South Orkneys.

| | | | | |
|---|---|---|---|---|
| 856 | 243 | 1p.45 blue | 1·70 | 45 |

244 "Telegraphs"

1954. International Telecommunications Conference. Symbolical designs inscr as in T 244.

| | | | | |
|---|---|---|---|---|
| 857 | 244 | 1p.50 purple | 70 | 20 |
| 858 | - | 3p. blue | 2·10 | 35 |
| 859 | - | 5p. red | 2·75 | 65 |

DESIGNS—VERT: 3p. "Radio". HORIZ: 5p. "Television".

245 Pediment, Buenos Aires Stock Exchange

1954. Centenary of Argentine Stock Exchange.

| | | | | |
|---|---|---|---|---|
| 860 | 245 | 1p. green | 70 | 10 |

246 Eva Peron

1954. 2nd Death Anniv of Eva Peron.

| | | | | |
|---|---|---|---|---|
| 861 | 246 | 3p. red | 3·00 | 55 |

247 San Martin 249 Wheat

250 Mt. Fitz Roy

1954

| | | | | |
|---|---|---|---|---|
| 862 | 247 | 20c. red | 25 | 10 |
| 863 | 247 | 40c. red | 35 | 10 |
| 868 | - | 50c. blue (33×22 mm) | 35 | 10 |
| 869 | - | 50c. blue (32×21 mm) | 75 | 20 |
| 870 | 249 | 80c. brown | 35 | 10 |
| 871 | - | 1p. brown | 45 | 10 |
| 872 | - | 1p.50 blue | 35 | 10 |
| 873 | - | 2p. red | 55 | 20 |
| 874 | - | 3p. purple | 55 | 20 |
| 875a | - | 5p. green | 10·50 | 25 |
| 876 | - | 10p. green and grey | 11·00 | 25 |
| 877 | 250 | 20p. violet | 16·00 | 70 |
| 1018 | - | 22p. blue | 2·40 | 25 |
| 878 | - | 50p. indigo and blue (30½×40½ mm) | 13·50 | 1·40 |
| 1023 | - | 50p. blue (29½×40 mm) | 12·00 | 70 |
| 1287 | - | 50p. blue (22½×32½ mm) | 1·80 | 25 |

DESIGNS—As Type **249**: HORIZ: 50c. Port of Buenos Aires; 1p. Cattle; 2p. Eva Peron Foundation; 3p. El Nihuil Dam. As Type **250**: VERT: 1p.50, 22p. Industrial Plant; 5p. Iguazu Falls; 50p. San Martin. HORIZ: 10p. Humahuaca Ravine.

For 43p. in the design of the 1p.50 and 22p. see No. 1021.

For 65c. in same design see No. 1313.

248 "Prosperity"

1954. Centenary of Argentine Corn Exchange.

| | | | | |
|---|---|---|---|---|
| 867 | 248 | 1p.50 grey | 1·00 | 25 |

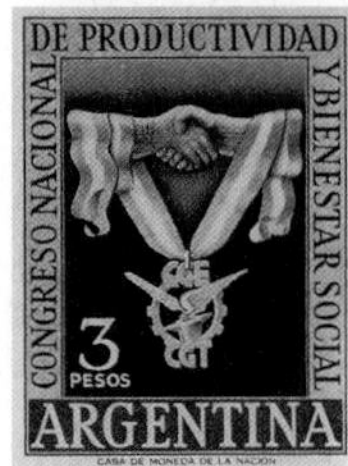

251 Clasped Hands and Congress Emblem

1955. Productivity and Social Welfare Congress.

| | | | | |
|---|---|---|---|---|
| 879 | 251 | 3p. brown | 1·70 | 35 |

252 Father and Son with Model Airplane

1955. 25th Anniv of Commercial Air Services.

| | | | | |
|---|---|---|---|---|
| 880 | 252 | 1p.50 grey | 1·40 | 25 |

253 "Liberation"

1955. Anti-Peronist Revolution of 16 Sept. 1955.

| | | | | |
|---|---|---|---|---|
| 881 | 253 | 1p.50 olive | 1·00 | 25 |

254 Forces Emblem

1955. Armed Forces Commemoration.

| | | | | |
|---|---|---|---|---|
| 882 | 254 | 3p. blue | 70 | 20 |

255 Gen. Urquiza (after J. M. Blanes)

1956. 104th Anniv of Battle of Caseros.

| | | | | |
|---|---|---|---|---|
| 883 | 255 | 1p.50 green | 1·10 | 35 |

256 Detail from "Antiope" (Correggio)

1956. Infantile Paralysis Relief Fund.

| | | | | |
|---|---|---|---|---|
| 884 | 256 | 20c.+30c. grey | 45 | 30 |

257 Coin and Die

1956. 75th Anniv of National Mint.

| | | | | |
|---|---|---|---|---|
| 885 | 257 | 2p. brown and sepia | 45 | 25 |

258 Corrientes Stamp of 1856 259 Dr. J. G. Pujol

1956. Centenary of 1st Argentine Stamps.

| | | | | |
|---|---|---|---|---|
| 886 | 258 | 40c. blue and green | 35 | 10 |
| 887 | 258 | 2p.40 mauve and brown | 45 | 20 |
| 888 | 259 | 4p.40 blue | 1·00 | 35 |

The 40c. shows a 1r. stamp of 1856.

260 Cotton, Chaco

1956. New Provinces.

| | | | | |
|---|---|---|---|---|
| 889 | - | 50c. blue | 80 | 20 |
| 890 | 260 | 1p. lake | 90 | 20 |
| 891 | - | 1p.50 green | 1·00 | 20 |

DESIGNS—HORIZ: 50c. Lumbering, La Pampa. VERT: 1p.50, Mate tea plant, Misiones.

261 "Liberty"

1956. 1st Anniv of Revolution.

| | | | | |
|---|---|---|---|---|
| 892 | 261 | 2p.40 mauve | 1·10 | 35 |

262 Detail from "Virgin of the Rocks" (Leonardo)

1956. Air. Infantile Paralysis Victims, Gratitude for Help.

| | | | | |
|---|---|---|---|---|
| 893 | 262 | 1p. purple | 1·10 | 35 |

**1956.** Argentine Stamp Centenary (2nd issue) and Corrientes Stamp Centenary Exhibition. Nos. 886/7 but in litho and colours changed and No. 888 in sheet.

| | | | |
|---|---|---|---|
| **MS**893a | 147×169 mm. 40c. indigo and green; 2p.40 claret and purple; 4p.40 blue | 7·50 | 7·25 |

**264** Esteban Echeverria (writer)

**265** F. Ameghino (anthropologist)

**266** Roque Saenz Pena (statesman)

**1956**

| | | | | |
|---|---|---|---|---|
| 896 | **264** | 2p. purple | 35 | 20 |
| 897 | **265** | 2p.40 brown | 45 | 20 |
| 898 | **266** | 4p.40 green | 70 | 30 |

**267** Franklin

**1956.** 250th Birth Anniv of Benjamin Franklin.

| | | | | |
|---|---|---|---|---|
| 899 | **267** | 40c. blue | 45 | 20 |

**268** "Hercules" (sail frigate)

**269** Admiral G. Brown

**1957.** Death Cent of Admiral Guillermo Brown.

| | | | | |
|---|---|---|---|---|
| 900 | **268** | 40c. blue (postage) | 25 | 10 |
| 901 | - | 2p.40 green | 55 | 10 |
| 902 | - | 60c. grey (air) | 35 | 10 |
| 903 | - | 1p. mauve | 25 | 10 |
| 904 | **269** | 2p. brown | 35 | 10 |

DESIGNS—HORIZ: 60c. "Zefiro" and "Nancy" (sail warships) at Battle of Montevideo; 1p. L. Rosales and T. Espora. VERT: 2p.40, Admiral Brown in later years.

**270** Church of Santo Domingo

**1957.** 150th Anniv of Defence of Buenos Aires.

| | | | | |
|---|---|---|---|---|
| 905 | **270** | 40c. green | 35 | 10 |

**271** Map of the Americas and Badge of Buenos Aires

**1957.** Air. Inter-American Economic Conference.

| | | | | |
|---|---|---|---|---|
| 906 | **271** | 2p. purple | 55 | 15 |

**272** "La Portena", 1857

**1957.** Centenary of Argentine Railways.

| | | | | |
|---|---|---|---|---|
| 907 | **272** | 40c. sepia (postage) | 1·40 | 35 |
| 908 | - | 60c. grey (air) | 1·40 | 35 |

DESIGN: 60c. Diesel locomotive.

**273** Globe, Flag and Compass Rose

**1957.** Air. Int Tourist Congress, Buenos Aires.

| | | | | |
|---|---|---|---|---|
| 909 | **273** | 1p. brown | 35 | 25 |
| 910 | - | 2p. turquoise | 35 | 25 |

DESIGN: 2p. Symbolic key of tourism.

**274** Head of Liberty

**1957.** Reform Convention.

| | | | | |
|---|---|---|---|---|
| 911 | **274** | 40c. red | 45 | 15 |

**275**

**1957.** Air. International Correspondence Week.

| | | | | |
|---|---|---|---|---|
| 912 | **275** | 1p. blue | 70 | 30 |

**276** "Wealth in Oil"

**1957.** 50th Anniv of Argentine Oil Industry.

| | | | | |
|---|---|---|---|---|
| 913 | **276** | 40c. blue | 1·00 | 35 |

**277** La Plata Museum

**1958.** 75th Anniv of Founding of La Plata.

| | | | | |
|---|---|---|---|---|
| 914 | **277** | 40c. black | 35 | 15 |

**278** Health Emblem and Flower

**1958.** Air. Child Welfare.

| | | | | |
|---|---|---|---|---|
| 915 | **278** | 1p.+50c. red | 45 | 45 |

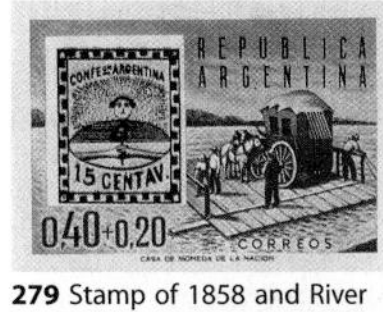

**279** Stamp of 1858 and River Ferry

**280** Stamp of 1858

**1958.** Centenary of Argentine Confederation Stamps and Philatelic Exhibition, Buenos Aires.

| | | | | |
|---|---|---|---|---|
| 916 | **279** | 40c.+20c. purple and green (postage) | 85 | 60 |
| 917 | - | 2p.40+1p.20 blue and black | 90 | 65 |
| 918 | - | 4p.40+2p.20 pur & bl | 95 | 70 |
| 919 | **280** | 1p.+50c. blue and olive (air) | 90 | 85 |
| 920 | **280** | 2p.+1p. violet and red | 1·10 | 95 |
| 921 | **280** | 3p.+1p.50 brown & grn | 1·10 | 1·00 |
| 922 | **280** | 5p.+2p.50 red and olive | 1·40 | 1·30 |
| 923 | **280** | 10p.+5p. sepia & olive | 2·30 | 1·80 |

DESIGNS—HORIZ: 2p.40, Magnifier, stamp album and stamp of 1858; 4p.40, P.O. building of 1858.

**281** Steam Locomotive and Arms of Argentina and Bolivia

**1958.** Argentine–Bolivian Friendship. (a) Inauguration of Yacuiba–Santa Cruz Railway.

| | | | | |
|---|---|---|---|---|
| 924 | **281** | 40c. red and slate | 90 | 30 |

**282** Douglas DC-6 over Map of Argentine-Bolivian Frontier

(b) Exchange of Presidential Visits.

| | | | | |
|---|---|---|---|---|
| 925 | **282** | 1p. brown | 90 | 30 |

**283** "Liberty and Flag"

**1958.** Transfer of Presidential Mandate. Head of "Liberty" in grey; inscr black; flag yellow and blue; background colours given.

| | | | | |
|---|---|---|---|---|
| 926 | **283** | 40c. buff | 15 | 10 |
| 927 | **283** | 1p. salmon | 35 | 10 |
| 928 | **283** | 2p. green | 70 | 35 |

**284** Farman H.F.20 Biplane

**1958.** 50th Anniv of Argentine Aero Club.

| | | | | |
|---|---|---|---|---|
| 929 | **284** | 2p. brown | 35 | 20 |

**285** National Flag Monument, Rosario

**1958.** 1st Anniv of Inauguration of National Flag Monument.

| | | | | |
|---|---|---|---|---|
| 930 | **285** | 40c. grey and blue | 35 | 20 |

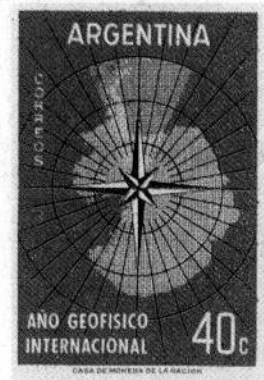


**286** Map of Antarctica

**1958.** International Geophysical Year.

| | | | | |
|---|---|---|---|---|
| 931 | **286** | 40c. black and red | 1·10 | 35 |

**287** Confederation Stamp and "The Santa Fe Mail" (after J. L. Palliere)

**1958.** Cent of Argentine Confederation Stamps.

| | | | | |
|---|---|---|---|---|
| 932 | - | 40c. grn & blue (postage) | 35 | 25 |
| 933 | - | 80c. blue & yellow (air) | 45 | 25 |
| 934 | **287** | 1p. blue and orange | 40 | 25 |

DESIGNS: 40c. First local Cordoba 5c. stamp of 1858 and mail coach; 80c. Buenos Aires Type **1** of 1858 and "View of Buenos Aires" (after Deroy).

**288** Aerial view of Flooded Town

**1958.** Flood Disaster Relief Fund. Inscr as in T 288.

| | | | | |
|---|---|---|---|---|
| 935 | **288** | 40c.+20c. brn (postage) | 35 | 25 |
| 936 | - | 1p.+50c. plum (air) | 35 | 25 |
| 937 | - | 5p.+2p.50 blue | 1·20 | 1·10 |

DESIGNS—HORIZ: 1p. Different aerial view of flooded town; 5p. Truck in flood water and garage.

**289** Child receiving Blood

**1958.** Leukaemia Relief Campaign.

| | | | | |
|---|---|---|---|---|
| 938 | **289** | 1p.+50c. red and black | 1·30 | 35 |

**290** U.N. Emblem and "Dying Captive" (after Michelangelo)

**1959.** 10th Anniv of Declaration of Human Rights.

| | | | | |
|---|---|---|---|---|
| 939 | **290** | 40c. grey and brown | 35 | 20 |

**291** Hawker Siddeley Comet 4

**1959.** Air. Inauguration of Comet Jet Airliners by Argentine National Airlines.

| | | | | |
|---|---|---|---|---|
| 940 | **291** | 5p. black and green | 50 | 10 |

**292** Orchids and Globe

**1959.** 1st Int Horticultural Exn, Buenos Aires.

| | | | | |
|---|---|---|---|---|
| 941 | **292** | 1p. purple | 35 | 20 |

**293** Pope Pius XII

**1959.** Pope Pius XII Commemoration.

| | | | | |
|---|---|---|---|---|
| 942 | **293** | 1p. black and yellow | 50 | 20 |

**294** William Harvey

**1959.** 21st International Physiological Science Congress. Medical Scientists.

| | | | | |
|---|---|---|---|---|
| 943 | **294** | 50c. green | 25 | 10 |
| 944 | - | 1p. red | 30 | 10 |
| 945 | - | 1p.50 brown | 35 | 10 |

PORTRAITS: 1p. Claude Bernard; 1p.50, Ivan P. Pavlov.

**295** Creole Horse

**296** Tierra del Fuego

**1959**

| | | | | |
|---|---|---|---|---|
| 946 | | 10c. green | 60 | 20 |
| 947 | | 20c. purple | 60 | 20 |
| 948 | | 50c. ochre | 60 | 20 |
| 950 | **295** | 1p. red | 60 | 20 |
| 1016 | - | 1p. brown | 25 | 10 |
| 1027 | - | 1p. brown | 25 | 10 |
| 1035 | - | 2p. red | 50 | 10 |
| 951 | - | 3p. blue | 50 | 20 |
| 1036 | - | 4p. red | 1·50 | 25 |
| 952 | **296** | 5p. brown | 75 | 30 |
| 1037 | - | 8p. red | 75 | 15 |
| 1038 | - | 10p. red | 1·00 | 20 |
| 1286 | - | 10p. brown | 75 | 25 |
| 1017 | - | 12p. purple | 1·50 | 25 |
| 954 | - | 20p. green | 4·25 | 25 |
| 1039 | - | 20p. red | 50 | 10 |
| 1019 | - | 23p. green | 7·25 | 25 |
| 1020 | - | 25p. lilac | 2·20 | 25 |
| 1021 | - | 43p. lake | 10·50 | 25 |
| 1022 | - | 45p. brown | 6·00 | 25 |
| 1025 | - | 100p. blue | 11·00 | 25 |
| 1026 | - | 300p. violet | 5·50 | 25 |
| 1032 | - | 500p. green | 2·20 | 25 |
| 1290 | - | 1000p. blue | 5·25 | 85 |

DESIGNS—As Type **295**—HORIZ: 10c. Spectacled caiman; 20c. Llama; 50c. Puma. VERT: 2, 4, 8, 10p. (No 1038), 20p. (No. 1039) San Martin. As Type **296**—HORIZ: 3p. Zapata Hill, Catamarca; 300p. Mar del Plata (40×29½ mm). VERT: 1p. (No. 1016) Sunflowers; 1p. (No. 1027) Sunflower (22×32 mm); 10p. (No. 1286) Inca Bridge, Mendoza; 12, 23, 25p. Red quebracho tree; 20p. (No. 954) Lake Nahuel Huapi; 43, 45p. Industrial plant (30×39½ mm); 100p. Ski-jumper; 500p. Red deer (stag); 1,000p. Leaping salmon.

For these designs with face values in revalued currency, see Nos. 1300 etc.

**298** Runner

**1959.** 3rd Pan-American Games, Chicago. Designs embody torch emblem. Centres and torch in black.

| | | | | |
|---|---|---|---|---|
| 955 | **298** | 20c.+10c. green (postage) | 25 | 10 |
| 956 | - | 50c.+20c. yellow | 35 | 20 |
| 957 | - | 1p.+50c. purple | 50 | 25 |
| 958 | - | 2p.+1p. blue (air) | 60 | 25 |
| 959 | - | 3p.+1p.50 olive | 85 | 70 |

DESIGNS—VERT: 50c. Basketball; 1p. Boxing. HORIZ: 2p. Rowing; 3p. High-diving.

**299**

**1959.** Red Cross Hygiene Campaign.

| | | | | |
|---|---|---|---|---|
| 960 | **299** | 1p. red, blue and black | 35 | 15 |

**300** Child with Toys

**1959.** Mothers' Day.

| | | | | |
|---|---|---|---|---|
| 961 | **300** | 1p. red and black | 35 | 15 |

**301** Buenos Aires 1p. stamp of 1859

**1959.** Stamp Day.

| | | | | |
|---|---|---|---|---|
| 962 | **301** | 1p. blue and grey | 35 | 15 |

**302** B. Mitre and J. J. de Urquiza

**1959.** Centenary of Pact of San Jose de Flores.

| | | | | |
|---|---|---|---|---|
| 963 | **302** | 1p. plum | 35 | 15 |

**303** Andean Condor

**1960.** Child Welfare. Birds.

| | | | | |
|---|---|---|---|---|
| 964 | **303** | 20c.+10c. blue (postage) | 1·50 | 25 |
| 965 | - | 50c.+20c. violet | 1·80 | 25 |
| 966 | - | 1p.+50c. brown | 1·50 | 25 |
| 967 | - | 2p.+1p. mauve (air) | 1·50 | 35 |
| 968 | - | 3p.+1p.50 green | 1·50 | 70 |

BIRDS: 50c. Fork-tailed flycatcher; 1p. Magellanic wood-pecker; 2p. Red-winged tinamou; 3p. Greater rhea.

**304** "Uprooted Tree"

**1960.** World Refugee Year.

| | | | | |
|---|---|---|---|---|
| 969 | **304** | 1p. red and brown | 50 | 25 |
| 970 | **304** | 4p.20 purple and green | 50 | 25 |

**MS**971 113×85 mm. No. 969/70 with premium added for aid to refugees 1p.50c. and 4p.20+2p.10. Imperf 2·10 1·90

**305** Abraham Lincoln

**1960.** 150th Birth Anniv of Abraham Lincoln.

| | | | | |
|---|---|---|---|---|
| 972 | **305** | 5p. blue | 60 | 25 |

**306** Saavedra and Chapter Hall, Buenos Aires

**1960.** 150th Anniv of May Revolution.

| | | | | |
|---|---|---|---|---|
| 973 | **306** | 1p. purple (postage) | 25 | 10 |
| 974 | - | 2p. green | 25 | 10 |
| 975 | - | 4p.20 green and grey | 35 | 20 |
| 976 | - | 10p.70 blue and slate | 60 | 25 |
| 977 | - | 1p.80 brown (air) | 25 | 10 |
| 978 | - | 5p. purple and brown | 50 | 20 |

**MS**979 Two sheets each 104×156 mm. Nos. 973/4, 977 in red-brown. Nos. 975/6, 978 in green 5·25 5·00

DESIGNS—Chapter Hall and: 1p.80, Moreno; 2p. Paso; 4p.20, Alberti and Azcuenaga; 5p. Belgrano and Castelli; 10p.70, Larrea and Matheu.

**307** Dr. L. Drago

**1960.** Birth Centenary of Drago.

| | | | | |
|---|---|---|---|---|
| 980 | **307** | 4p.20 brown | 35 | 20 |

**308** "Five Provinces"

**1960.** Air. New Argentine Provinces.

| | | | | |
|---|---|---|---|---|
| 981 | **308** | 1p.80 blue and red | 35 | 20 |

**309** "Market Place 1810" (Buenos Aires)

**1960.** Air. Inter-American Philatelic Exhibition, Buenos Aires ("EFIMAYO") and 150th Anniv of Revolution. Inscr "EFIMAYO 1960".

| | | | | |
|---|---|---|---|---|
| 982 | **309** | 2p.+1p. lake | 25 | 10 |
| 983 | - | 6p.+3p. grey | 50 | 20 |
| 984 | - | 10p.70+5p.30 blue | 85 | 45 |
| 985 | - | 20p.+10p. turquoise | 1·50 | 1·20 |

DESIGNS: 6p. "The Water Carrier"; 10p.70, "The Landing Place"; 20p. "The Fort".

**310** J. B. Alberdi

**1960.** 150th Birth Anniv of J. B. Alberdi (statesman).

| | | | | |
|---|---|---|---|---|
| 986 | **310** | 1p. green | 35 | 20 |

**311** Seibo (Argentine National Flower)

**1960.** Air. Chilean Earthquake Relief Fund. Inscr "AYUDA CHILE".

| | | | | |
|---|---|---|---|---|
| 987 | **311** | 6p.+3p. red | 50 | 25 |
| 988 | - | 10p.70+5p.30 red | 75 | 45 |

DESIGN: 10p.70, Copihue (Chilean national flower).

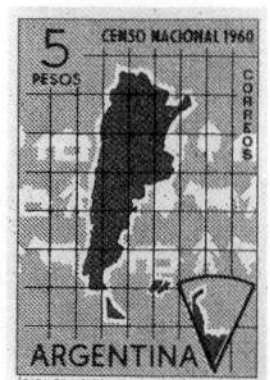

**312** Map of Argentina

**1960.** Census.

| | | | | |
|---|---|---|---|---|
| 989 | **312** | 5p. lilac | 1·20 | 35 |

**313** Galleon

**1960.** 8th Spanish-American P.U. Congress.

| | | | | |
|---|---|---|---|---|
| 990 | **313** | 1p. green (postage) | 35 | 10 |
| 991 | **313** | 5p. brown | 85 | 25 |
| 992 | **313** | 1p.80 purple (air) | 35 | 10 |
| 993 | **313** | 10p.70 turquoise | 1·10 | 35 |

**1960.** Air. U.N. Day. Nos. 982/5 optd DIA DE LAS NACIONES UNIDAS 24 DE OCTUBRE.

| | | | | |
|---|---|---|---|---|
| 994 | **309** | 2p.+1p. red | 25 | 10 |
| 995 | - | 6p.+3p. black | 50 | 35 |
| 996 | - | 10p.70+5p.30 blue | 75 | 60 |
| 997 | - | 20p.+10p. turquoise | 1·30 | 1·10 |

**315** Blessed Virgin of Lujan

**1960.** 1st Inter-American Marian Congress.

| | | | | |
|---|---|---|---|---|
| 998 | **315** | 1p. blue | 1·00 | 25 |

**316** Jacaranda

**1960.** International Thematic Stamp Exhibition ("TEMEX"). Inscr "TEMEX-61".

| | | | | |
|---|---|---|---|---|
| 999 | **316** | 50c.+50c. blue | 10 | 10 |
| 1000 | - | 1p.+1p. turquoise | 20 | 10 |
| 1001 | - | 3p.+3p. brown | 60 | 25 |
| 1002 | - | 5p.+5p. brown | 85 | 60 |

FLOWERS: 1p. Passion flowers; 3p. Hibiscus; 5p. Black lapacho.

**317** Argentine Scout Badge

**1961.** International Scout (Patrol) Camp.
1003 **317** 1p. red and black 50 20

**318** "Shipment of Cereals" (after B. Q. Martin)

**1961.** Export Campaign.
1004 **318** 1p. brown 50 20

**319** Emperor Penguin and Chick

**1961.** Child Welfare. Inscr "PRO-INFANCIA".
1005 - 4p.20+2p.10 brown (postage) 1·70 95
1006 **319** 1p.80+90c. black (air) 85 60
DESIGN: 4p.20, Blue-eyed cormorant.

**320** "America"

**1961.** 150th Anniv of Battle of San Nicolas.
1007 **320** 2p. black 50 20

**321** Dr. M. Moreno

**1961.** 150th Death Anniv of Dr. M. Moreno.
1008 **321** 2p. blue 35 15

**322** Emperor Trajan

**1961.** Visit of President of Italy.
1009 **322** 2p. green 35 15

**1961.** Americas Day. Nos. 999/1002 optd 14 DE ABRIL DE LAS AMERICAS.
1010 **316** 50c.+50c. blue 25 10
1011 - 1p.+1p. turquoise 25 10
1012 - 3p.+3p. brown 35 25
1013 - 5p.+5p. brown 75 45

**324** Tagore

**1961.** Birth Centenary of Rabindranath Tagore (Indian poet).
1014 **324** 2p. violet on green 1·10 25

**325** San Martin Monument, Madrid

**1961.** Inaug of Spanish San Martin Monument.
1015 **325** 1p. black 35 20

**331a** Gen. Belgrano (after monument by Rocha, Buenos Aires)

**1961.** Gen. Manuel Belgrano Commemoration.
1034 **331a** 2p. blue 1·00 25

**333** Antarctic Scene

**1961.** 10th Anniv of San Martin Antarctic Base.
1044 **333** 2p. black 1·00 25

**334** Conquistador and Sword

**1961.** 4th Centenary of Jujuy City.
1045 **334** 2p. red and black 35 20

**335** Sarmiento Statue (Rodin)

**1961.** 150th Birth Anniv of Sarmiento.
1046 **335** 2p. violet 35 20

**336** Cordoba Cathedral

**1961.** "Argentina 62" International Philatelic Exn.
1047 **336** 2p.+2p. purple (postage) 35 25
1048 - 3p.+3p. green 50 35
1049 - 10p.+10p. blue 1·10 95
**MS**1050 86×86 mm. Nos. 1047/9 each indigo. Imperf 3·75 2·50

**343** 15c. Stamp of 1862

1059 **343** 6p.50+6p.50 blue and turquoise (air) 1·00 85
DESIGNS—HORIZ: 10p. Buenos Aires Cathedral. VERT: 3p. As Type **343** but showing 10c. value and different inscr.

**337**

**1961.** World Town-planning Day.
1052 **337** 2p. blue and yellow 35 20

**338** "The Flight into Egypt" (after Ana Maria Moncalvo)

**1961.** Child Welfare.
1053 **338** 2p.+1p. brown & lilac 25 10
1054 **338** 10p.+5p. purple & mve 75 20

**339** Belgrano Statue (C. Belleuse)

**1962.** 150th Anniv of National Flag.
1055 **339** 2p. blue 35 20

**340** Mounted Grenadier

**1962.** 150th Anniv of Gen. San Martin's Mounted Grenadiers.
1056 **340** 2p. red 1·00 25

**341** Mosquito and Emblem

**1962.** Malaria Eradication.
1057 **341** 2p. black and red 60 20

**342** Lujan Basilica

**1962.** 75th Anniv of Coronation of the Holy Virgin of Lujan.
1058 **342** 2p. black and brown 35 10

**344** Juan Jufre (founder)

**1962.** 400th Anniv of San Juan.
1060 **344** 2p. blue 35 20

**345** UNESCO Emblem

**1962.** Air. 15th Anniv of UNESCO.
1061 **345** 13p. brown and ochre 60 35

**346** "Flight"

**1962.** 50th Anniv of Argentine Air Force.
1062 **346** 2p. blue, black & purple 35 20

**347** Juan Vucetich (fingerprints pioneer)

**1962.** Vucetich Commem.
1063 **347** 2p. green 35 15

**348** 19th-century Mail Coach

**1962.** Air. Postman's Day.
1064 **348** 5p.60 black and drab 1·00 25

**1962.** Air. Surch AEREO and value.
1065 **296** 5p.60 on 5p. brown 35 25
1066 **296** 18p. on 5p. brn on grn 1·50 35

**350** U.P.A.E. Emblem

**1962.** Air. 50th Anniv of Postal Union of Latin America.
1067 **350** 5p.60 blue 50 15

**351** Pres. Sarmiento

**1962**
1073 **351** 2p. green 1·00 25
1069 - 4p. red 75 25
1071 - 6p. brown 50 10
1075 - 6p. red 2·40 25
1072 - 90p. bistre 4·00 45
PORTRAITS: 4, 6p. Jose Hernandez; 90p. G. Brown.

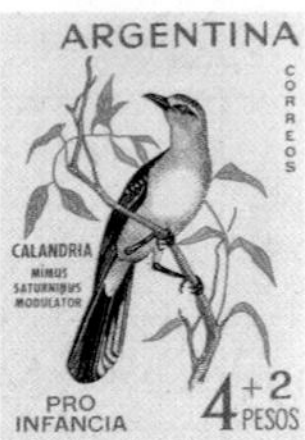


**352** Chalk-browed Mockingbird

**1962.** Child Welfare.

| | | | | |
|---|---|---|---|---|
| 1076 | **352** | 4p.+2p. sepia, turquoise and brown | 2·00 | 1·10 |
| 1077 | - | 12p.+6p. brown, yellow and slate | 3·00 | 1·50 |

DESIGN—VERT: 12p. Rufous-collared sparrow.

See also Nos. 1101/2, 1124/5, 1165/6, 1191/2, 1214/15, 1264/5, 1293/4, 1394/5, 1415/16 and 1441/2.

**353** Skylark 3 Glider

**1963.** Air. 9th World Gliding Championships, Junin.

| | | | | |
|---|---|---|---|---|
| 1078 | **353** | 5p.60 black and blue | 25 | 10 |
| 1079 | - | 11p. black, red and blue | 60 | 35 |

DESIGN: 11p. Super Albatross glider.

**354** "20 de Febrero" Monument, Salta

**1963.** 150th Anniv of Battle of Salta.

| | | | | |
|---|---|---|---|---|
| 1080 | **354** | 2p. green | 1·00 | 25 |

**355** Cogwheels

**1963.** 75th Anniv of Argentine Industrial Union.

| | | | | |
|---|---|---|---|---|
| 1081 | **355** | 4p. red and grey | 1·00 | 25 |

**356** National College

**1963.** Centenary of National College, Buenos Aires.

| | | | | |
|---|---|---|---|---|
| 1082 | **356** | 4p. black and buff | 1·10 | 35 |

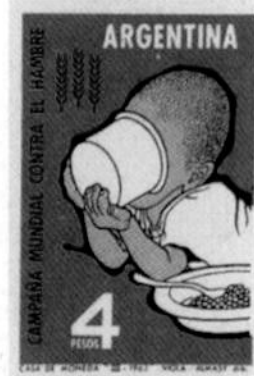


**357** Child drinking Milk

**1963.** Freedom from Hunger.

| | | | | |
|---|---|---|---|---|
| 1083 | **357** | 4p. ochre, black and red | 35 | 20 |

**358** "Flight"

**1963.** Air. (a) As T 358.

| | | | | |
|---|---|---|---|---|
| 1084 | **358** | 5p.60 green, mve & pur | 35 | 20 |
| 1085 | **358** | 7p. black & yellow (I) | 85 | 25 |
| 1086 | **358** | 7p. black & yellow (II) | 7·25 | 1·40 |
| 1087 | **358** | 11p. purple, green & blk | 35 | 20 |
| 1088 | **358** | 18p. blue, red and mauve | 1·50 | 35 |
| 1089 | **358** | 21p. grey, red and brown | 2·40 | 45 |

Two types of 7p. I, "ARGENTINA" reads down, and II, "ARGENTINA" reads up as in Type **358**.

(b) As T 358 but inscr "REPUBLICA ARGENTINA" reading down.

| | | | |
|---|---|---|---|
| 1147 | 12p. lake and brown | 2·30 | 35 |
| 1148 | 15p. blue and red | 1·60 | 35 |
| 1291 | 26p. ochre | 25 | 10 |
| 1150 | 27p.50 green and black | 2·50 | 60 |
| 1151 | 30p.50 brown and blue | 3·25 | 95 |
| 1292 | 40p. lilac | 4·00 | 25 |
| 1153 | 68p. green | 5·75 | 70 |
| 1154 | 78p. blue | 2·40 | 95 |

See also Nos. 1374/80 in revalued currency.

**359** Football

**1963.** 4th Pan-American Games, Sao Paulo.

| | | | | |
|---|---|---|---|---|
| 1090 | **359** | 4p.+2p. green, black and pink (postage) | 35 | 20 |
| 1091 | - | 12p.+6p. purple, black and salmon | 75 | 60 |
| 1092 | - | 11p.+5p. red, black and green (air) | 85 | 70 |

DESIGNS: 11p. Cycling; 12p. Show-jumping.

**360** Frigate "La Argentina" (after Bouchard)

**1963.** Navy Day.

| | | | | |
|---|---|---|---|---|
| 1093 | **360** | 4p. blue | 1·10 | 35 |

**361** Assembly House and Seal

**1963.** 150th Anniv of 1813 Assembly.

| | | | | |
|---|---|---|---|---|
| 1094 | **361** | 4p. black and blue | 1·00 | 25 |

**362** Battle Scene

**1963.** 150th Anniv of Battle of San Lorenzo.

| | | | | |
|---|---|---|---|---|
| 1095 | **362** | 4p. black & green on grn | 1·00 | 25 |

**363** Queen Nefertari (bas-relief)

**1963.** UNESCO Campaign for Preservation of Nubian Monuments.

| | | | | |
|---|---|---|---|---|
| 1096 | **363** | 4p. black, green & buff | 1·00 | 25 |

**364** Government House

**1963.** Presidential Installation.

| | | | | |
|---|---|---|---|---|
| 1097 | **364** | 5p. brown and pink | 1·00 | 25 |

**365** "Science"

**1963.** 10th Latin-American Neurosurgery Congress.

| | | | | |
|---|---|---|---|---|
| 1098 | **365** | 4p. blue, black & brown | 1·10 | 35 |

**366** Blackboards

**1963.** "Alliance for Progress".

| | | | | |
|---|---|---|---|---|
| 1099 | **366** | 5p. red, black and blue | 35 | 20 |

**367** F. de las Carreras (President of Supreme Court)

**1963.** Centenary of Judicial Power.

| | | | | |
|---|---|---|---|---|
| 1100 | **367** | 5p. green | 35 | 20 |

**1963.** Child Welfare. As T 352. Mult.

| | | | |
|---|---|---|---|
| 1101 | 4p.+2p. Vermilion flycatcher (postage) | 1·80 | 60 |
| 1102 | 11p.+5p. Great kiskadee (air) | 2·40 | 95 |

**368** Kemal Ataturk

**1963.** 25th Death Anniv of Kemal Ataturk.

| | | | | |
|---|---|---|---|---|
| 1103 | **368** | 12p. grey | 75 | 25 |

**369** "Payador" (after Castagnino)

**1964.** 4th National Folklore Festival.

| | | | | |
|---|---|---|---|---|
| 1104 | **369** | 4p. black, blue & ultram | 1·00 | 25 |

**370** Map of Antarctic Islands

**1964.** Antarctic Claims Issue.

| | | | | |
|---|---|---|---|---|
| 1105 | **370** | 2p. bl & ochre (postage) | 2·50 | 35 |
| 1106 | - | 4p. bistre and blue | 3·75 | 45 |
| 1107 | - | 18p. bl & bistre (air) | 3·75 | 85 |

DESIGNS—VERT: (30×39½ mm): 4p. Map of Argentina and Antarctica. HORIZ: (as Type **291**): 18p. Map of "Islas Malvinas" (Falkland Islands).

**371** Jorge Newbery in Airplane

**1964.** 50th Death Anniv of Jorge Newbery (aviator).

| | | | | |
|---|---|---|---|---|
| 1108 | **371** | 4p. green | 1·10 | 35 |

**372** Pres. Kennedy

**1964.** President Kennedy Memorial Issue.

| | | | | |
|---|---|---|---|---|
| 1109 | **372** | 4p. blue and mauve | 75 | 25 |

**373** Father Brochero

**1964.** 50th Death Anniv of Father J. G. Brochero.

| | | | | |
|---|---|---|---|---|
| 1110 | **373** | 4p. brown | 1·10 | 35 |

**374** U.P.U. Monument, Berne

**1964.** Air. 15th U.P.U. Congress, Vienna.

| | | | | |
|---|---|---|---|---|
| 1111 | **374** | 18p. purple and red | 90 | 35 |

**375** Soldier of the Patricios Regiment

**1964.** Army Day.

| | | | | |
|---|---|---|---|---|
| 1112 | **375** | 4p. multicoloured | 1·30 | 25 |

See also Nos. 1135, 1170, 1201, 1223, 1246, 1343, 1363, 1399, 1450, 1515, 1564, 1641 and 1678.

**376** Pope John XXIII

**1964.** Pope John Commemoration.

| | | | | |
|---|---|---|---|---|
| 1113 | **376** | 4p. black and orange | 40 | 20 |

**377** Olympic Stadium

**1964.** Olympic Games, Tokyo.

| | | | | |
|---|---|---|---|---|
| 1114 | **377** | 4p.+2p. brown, yellow and red (postage) | 40 | 20 |
| 1115 | - | 12p.+6p. black & green | 75 | 35 |
| 1116 | - | 11p.+5p. blk & bl (air) | 1·50 | 70 |

DESIGNS—VERT: 11p. Sailing; 12p. Fencing.

**378** University Arms

**1964.** 350th Anniv of Cordoba University.

| | | | | |
|---|---|---|---|---|
| 1117 | **378** | 4p. yellow, blue & black | 40 | 10 |

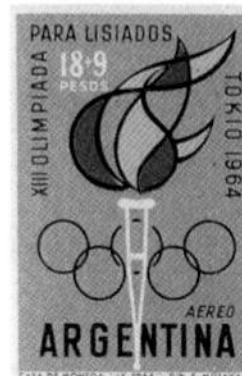


**379** Olympic Flame and Crutch

**1964.** Air. Invalids Olympic Games, Tokyo.

| | | | | |
|---|---|---|---|---|
| 1118 | **379** | 18p.+9p. multicoloured | 1·00 | 85 |

**380** "The Discovery of America" (Florentine woodcut)

**1964.** Air. "Columbus Day" (or "Day of the Race").

| | | | | |
|---|---|---|---|---|
| 1119 | **380** | 13p. black and drab | 1·40 | 45 |

**381** Pigeons and U.N. Headquarters

**1964.** United Nations Day.

| | | | | |
|---|---|---|---|---|
| 1120 | **381** | 4p. ultramarine and blue | 65 | 20 |

**382** J. V. Gonzalez (medallion)

**1964.** Birth Centenary of J. V. Gonzalez.

| | | | | |
|---|---|---|---|---|
| 1121 | **382** | 4p. red | 1·00 | 25 |

**383** Gen. J. Roca

**1964.** 50th Death Anniv of General Julio Roca.

| | | | | |
|---|---|---|---|---|
| 1122 | **383** | 4p. blue | 40 | 10 |

**384** "Market-place, Montserrat Square" (after C. Morel)

**1964.** "Argentine Painters".

| | | | | |
|---|---|---|---|---|
| 1123 | **384** | 4p. sepia | 50 | 35 |

**1964.** Child Welfare. As T 352. Multicoloured.

| | | | | |
|---|---|---|---|---|
| 1124 | | 4p.+2p. Red-crested cardinal (postage) | 1·60 | 45 |
| 1125 | | 18p.+9p. Chilean swallow (air) | 3·25 | 1·20 |

**385** Icebreaker "General San Martin" and Bearded Penguin

**1965.** "National Territory of Tierra del Fuego, Antarctic and South Atlantic Isles".

| | | | | |
|---|---|---|---|---|
| 1126 | - | 2p. purple (postage) | 75 | 20 |
| 1127 | **385** | 4p. blue | 1·90 | 35 |
| 1128 | - | 11p. red (air) | 90 | 25 |

DESIGNS: 2p. General Belgrano Base (inscr "BASE DE EJERCITO" etc); 11p. Teniente Matienzo Joint Antarctic Base (inscr "BASE CONJUNTA" etc).

**1965.** Air. 1st Rio Plata Philatelists' Day. Optd PRIMERAS JORNADAS FILATELICAS RIOPLATENSES.

| | | | | |
|---|---|---|---|---|
| 1129 | **358** | 7p. black & yellow (II) | 40 | 20 |

**387** Young Saver

**1965.** 50th Anniv of National Postal Savings Bank.

| | | | | |
|---|---|---|---|---|
| 1130 | **387** | 4p. black and red | 35 | 10 |

**388** I.T.U. Emblem

**1965.** Air. Centenary of I.T.U.

| | | | | |
|---|---|---|---|---|
| 1131 | **388** | 18p. multicoloured | 65 | 25 |

**389** I.Q.S.Y. Emblem

**1965.** Int Quiet Sun Year and Space Research.

| | | | | |
|---|---|---|---|---|
| 1132 | **389** | 4p. black, orange and blue (postage) | 1·00 | 35 |
| 1133 | - | 18p. red (air) | 1·10 | 45 |
| 1134 | - | 50p. blue | 1·60 | 95 |

DESIGNS—VERT: 18p. Rocket launching. HORIZ: 50p. Earth, trajectories and space phenomena (both inscr "INVESTIGACIONES ESPACIALES").

**391** Ricardo Guiraldes

**1965.** Army Day (29 May).

| | | | | |
|---|---|---|---|---|
| 1135 | **390** | 8p. multicoloured | 90 | 35 |

See also Nos. 1170, 1201, 1223, 1246, 1343, 1363, 1399, 1450, 1515, 1564 and 1641.

**391** Ricardo Guiraldes

**1965.** Argentine Writers (1st series). Each brown.

| | | | |
|---|---|---|---|
| 1136 | 8p. Type **391** | 65 | 25 |
| 1137 | 8p. E. Larreta | 65 | 25 |
| 1138 | 8p. L. Lugones | 65 | 25 |
| 1139 | 8p. R. J. Payro | 65 | 25 |
| 1140 | 8p. R. Rojas | 65 | 25 |

See also Nos 1174/8.

**392** H. Yrigoyen (statesman)

**1965.** Hipolito Yrigoyen Commemoration.

| | | | | |
|---|---|---|---|---|
| 1141 | **392** | 8p. black and red | 40 | 20 |

**393** "Children looking through a Window"

**1965.** International Mental Health Seminar.

| | | | | |
|---|---|---|---|---|
| 1142 | **393** | 8p. black and brown | 1·00 | 45 |

**394** Ancient Map and Funeral Urn

**1965.** 400th Anniv of San Miguel de Tucuman.

| | | | | |
|---|---|---|---|---|
| 1143 | **394** | 8p. multicoloured | 50 | 25 |

**395** Mgr. Dr. J. Cagliero

**1965.** Cagliero Commemoration.

| | | | | |
|---|---|---|---|---|
| 1144 | **395** | 8p. violet | 40 | 10 |

**396** Dante (statue in Church of the Holy Cross, Florence)

**1965.** 700th Birth Anniv of Dante.

| | | | | |
|---|---|---|---|---|
| 1145 | **396** | 8p. blue | 1·00 | 25 |

**397** Sail Merchantman "Mimosa"

**1965.** Centenary of Welsh Colonisation of Chubut and Foundation of Rawson.

| | | | | |
|---|---|---|---|---|
| 1146 | **397** | 8p. black and red | 50 | 20 |

**398** Police Emblem on Map of Buenos Aires

**1965.** Federal Police Day.

| | | | | |
|---|---|---|---|---|
| 1155 | **398** | 8p. red | 50 | 35 |

**399** Schoolchildren

**1965.** 81st Anniv of Law 1420 (Public Education).

| | | | | |
|---|---|---|---|---|
| 1156 | **399** | 8p. black and green | 50 | 20 |

**400** St. Francis's Church, Catamarca

**1965.** Brother Mamerto Esquiu Commemoration.

| | | | | |
|---|---|---|---|---|
| 1157 | **400** | 8p. brown and yellow | 40 | 10 |

**401** R. Dario (Nicaraguan poet)

**1965.** 50th Death Anniv of Ruben Dario.

| | | | | |
|---|---|---|---|---|
| 1158 | **401** | 15p. violet on grey | 40 | 20 |

**402** "The Orange-seller" (detail)

**1966.** Prilidiano Pueyrredon's Paintings. Designs show details from the original works, each green.

| | | | |
|---|---|---|---|
| 1159 | 8p. Type **402** | 1·10 | 60 |
| 1160 | 8p. "A Halt at the Village Grocer's Shop" | 1·10 | 60 |
| 1161 | 8p. "San Fernando Landscape" | 1·10 | 60 |
| 1162 | 8p. "Bathing Horses on the Banks of the River Plate" | 1·10 | 60 |

**403** Rocket "Centaur" and Antarctic Map

**1966.** Air. Rocket Launches in Antarctica.

| | | | | |
|---|---|---|---|---|
| 1163 | **403** | 27p.50 red, black & blue | 1·50 | 1·20 |

**404** Dr. Sun Yat-sen

**1966.** Birth Centenary of Dr. Sun Yat-sen.
1164 **404** 8p. brown 1·10 25

**1966.** Child Welfare. As T 352, inscr "R. ARGENTINA". Multicoloured.
1165 8p.+4p. Southern lapwing (postage) 2·00 85
1166 27p.50+12p.50 Rufous hornero (air) 1·60 1·20

**405** "Rivadavia" 5c. stamp of 1864

**1966.** 2nd Rio Plata Philatelists Days and Exhibition. Miniature sheet containing designs as T 405.
**MS**1167 141×100 mm. 4p. red and grey (T **405**); 5p. green and grey (10c. stamp); 8p. blue and grey (15c. stamp) 1·60 1·50

**406** "Human Races"

**1966.** Inaug of W.H.O. Headquarters, Geneva.
1168 **406** 8p. black and brown 50 20

**407** Magellan Gull

**1966.** Air. 50th Anniv of Naval Aviation School, Puerto Militar.
1169 **407** 12p. multicoloured 75 35

**1966.** Army Day (29 May). As T 390.
1170 8p. multicoloured 1·00 25
DESIGN: 8p. Militiaman of Guemes's "Infernals".

**408** Arms of Argentina

**1966.** Air. "Argentina '66" Philatelic Exhibition, Buenos Aires.
1171 **408** 10p.+10p. multicoloured 2·75 1·90

**409**

**1966.** 150th Anniv of Independence. Sheet of 25 (5×5) comprising different 10p. designs–national, federal and provincial arms and maps, as T 409. Inscr "1816–1966". Multicoloured.
**MS**1172 Sheet of 25 stamps 65·00 60·00

**410** "Charity" Emblem

**1966.** Argentine Charities.
1173 **410** 10p. blue, black & green 40 10

**1966.** Argentine Writers (2nd series). Portraits as T 391. Each green.
1174 10p. H. Ascasubi 65 25
1175 10p. Estanislao del Campo 65 25
1176 10p. M. Cane 65 25
1177 10p. Lucio V. Lopez 65 25
1178 10p. R. Obligado 65 25

**411** Anchor

**1966.** 25th Anniv of Argentine Mercantile Marine.
1179 **411** 4p. multicoloured 40 20

**412** L. Agote

**1966.** Argentine Scientists. Each violet.
1180 10p. Type **412** 65 25
1181 10p. J. B. Ambrosetti 65 25
1182 10p. M. I. Lillo 65 25
1183 10p. F. P. Moreno 65 25
1184 10p. F. J. Muniz 65 25

**413** Map and Flags of the American States

**1966.** 7th American Armies Conf, Buenos Aires.
1185 **413** 10p. multicoloured 40 10

**414** Bank Facade

**1966.** 75th Anniv of Argentine National Bank.
1186 **414** 10p. green 40 10

**415** La Salle Statue and College

**1966.** 75th Anniv of La Salle College, Buenos Aires.
1187 **415** 10p. black and brown 40 10

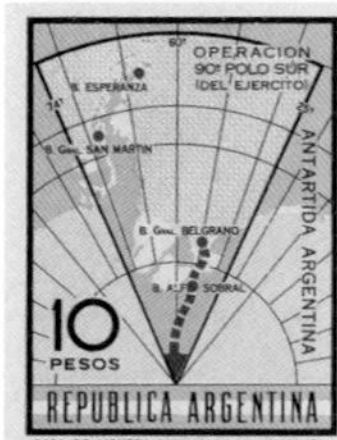

**416** Antarctic Map with Expedition Route

**1966.** Argentine South Pole Expedition, 1965–66.
1188 **416** 10p. multicoloured 1·30 25

**417** Gen. J. M. de Pueyrredon

**1966.** Gen. J. M. de Pueyrredon Commemoration.
1189 **417** 10p. red 50 20

**418** Gen. J. G. de Las Heras

**1966.** Gen. Juan G. de Las Heras Commemoration.
1190 **418** 10p. black 40 10

**1967.** Child Welfare. As T 352, inscr "R. ARGENTINA". Multicoloured.
1191 10p.+5p. Scarlet-headed blackbird (horiz) (postage) 2·30 1·10
1192 15p.+7p. Blue and yellow tanager (air) 2·75 1·70

**419** Ancient Pot

**1967.** 20th Anniv of UNESCO.
1193 **419** 10p. multicoloured 50 20

**420** "The Meal" (after F. Fader)

**1967.** Fernando Fader (painter).
1194 **420** 10p. brown 50 20

**421** Juana Azurduy de Padilla

**1967.** Famous Argentine Women. Each sepia.
1195 6p. Type **421** 65 25
1196 6p. J. M. Gorriti 65 25
1197 6p. C. Grierson 65 25
1198 6p. J. P. Manson 65 25
1199 6p. A. Storni 65 25

**422** Schooner "Invencible"

**1967.** Navy Day.
1200 **422** 20p. multicoloured 1·80 45

**1967.** Army Day (29 May). As T 390.
1201 20p. multicoloured 1·10 25
DESIGN: 20p. Soldier of the Arribenos Regiment.

**423** M. Belgrano (6p.) and J. G. de Artigas (22p.)

**1967.** 3rd Rio Plata Philatelists Days and Exhibition. Sheet 63×55 mm comprising designs as T 423.
**MS**1202 6p. and 22p. each brown and grey 75 70

**424** Suitcase and Dove

**1967.** International Tourist Year.
1203 **424** 20p. multicoloured 50 20

**425** PADELAI Emblem and Sun

**1967.** 75th Anniv of PADELAI (Argentine Children's Welfare Association).
1204 **425** 20p. multicoloured 40 10

**426** Teodoro Fels's Bleriot XI

**1967.** Air. 50th Anniv of 1st Argentine–Uruguay Airmail Flight.
1205 **426** 26p. brown, olive & blue 40 10

**427** Ferreyra's Oxwagon and Skyscrapers

**1967.** Centenary of Villa Maria.
1206 **427** 20p. multicoloured 40 10

**428** "General San Martin" (from statue by M. P. Nunez de Ibarra)

**1967.** 150th Anniv of Battle of Chacabuco.

| | | | | |
|---|---|---|---|---|
| 1207 | **428** | 20p. brown and yellow | 90 | 25 |
| 1208 | - | 40p. blue | 1·40 | 45 |

DESIGN—(48×31 mm)—HORIZ: 40p. "Battle of Chacabuco" (from painting by P. Subercaseaux).

**429** Interior of Museum

**1967.** 10th Anniv of Government House Museum.

| | | | | |
|---|---|---|---|---|
| 1209 | **429** | 20p. blue | 40 | 20 |

**430** Pedro Zanni and "Provincia de Buenos Aires"

**1967.** Aeronautics Week.

| | | | | |
|---|---|---|---|---|
| 1210 | **430** | 20p. multicoloured | 50 | 20 |

**431** Cadet Ship "General Brown" (from painting by E. Biggeri)

**1967.** "Temex 67" Stamp Exhibition and 95th Anniv of Naval Military School.

| | | | | |
|---|---|---|---|---|
| 1211 | **431** | 20p. multicoloured | 1·90 | 60 |

**432** Ovidio Lagos and Front Page of "La Capital" (newspaper)

**1967.** Centenary of "La Capital".

| | | | | |
|---|---|---|---|---|
| 1212 | **432** | 20p. brown | 40 | 10 |

**433** St. Barbara (from altar-painting, Segovia, Spain)

**1967.** Artillery Day (4 Dec).

| | | | | |
|---|---|---|---|---|
| 1213 | **433** | 20p. red | 50 | 15 |

**1967.** Child Welfare. Bird designs as T 352. Multicoloured.

| | | | |
|---|---|---|---|
| 1214 | 20p.+10p. Amazon kingfisher (postage) | 2·00 | 60 |
| 1215 | 26p.+13p. Toco toucan (air) | 2·50 | 85 |

**434** "Sivori's Wife"

**1968.** 50th Death Anniv of Eduardo Sivori (painter).

| | | | | |
|---|---|---|---|---|
| 1216 | **434** | 20p. green | 50 | 20 |

**435** "Almirante Brown" Scientific Station

**1968.** "Antarctic Territories".

| | | | | |
|---|---|---|---|---|
| 1217 | - | 6p. multicoloured | 90 | 20 |
| 1218 | **435** | 20p. multicoloured | 1·30 | 25 |
| 1219 | - | 40p. multicoloured | 2·10 | 85 |

DESIGNS—VERT (22½×32 mm): 6p. Map of Antarctic radio-postal stations. HORIZ (as Type **435**): 40p. Aircraft over South Pole ("Trans-Polar Round Flight").

**436** Man in Wheelchair

**1968.** Rehabilitation Day for the Handicapped.

| | | | | |
|---|---|---|---|---|
| 1220 | **436** | 20p. black and green | 40 | 25 |

**437** "St. Gabriel" (detail from "The Annunciation" by Leonardo da Vinci)

**1968.** St. Gabriel (patron saint of army communications).

| | | | | |
|---|---|---|---|---|
| 1221 | **437** | 20p. mauve | 40 | 25 |

**438** Children and W.H.O. Emblem

**1968.** 20th Anniv of W.H.O.

| | | | | |
|---|---|---|---|---|
| 1222 | **438** | 20p. blue and red | 40 | 25 |

**1968.** Army Day (29 May). As T 390.

| | | | |
|---|---|---|---|
| 1223 | 20p. multicoloured | 1·30 | 25 |

DESIGN: 20p. Iriarte's artilleryman.

**439** Full-rigged Cadet Ship "Libertad" (E. Biggeri)

**1968.** Navy Day.

| | | | | |
|---|---|---|---|---|
| 1224 | **439** | 20p. multicoloured | 2·10 | 35 |

**440** G. Rawson and Hospital

**1968.** Centenary of Guillermo Rawson Hospital.

| | | | | |
|---|---|---|---|---|
| 1225 | **440** | 6p. bistre | 50 | 25 |

**441** Vito Dumas and "Legh II"

**1968.** Air. Vito Dumas' World Voyage in Yacht "Legh II".

| | | | | |
|---|---|---|---|---|
| 1226 | **441** | 68p. multicoloured | 1·00 | 60 |

**442** Children using Zebra crossing

**1968.** Road Safety.

| | | | | |
|---|---|---|---|---|
| 1227 | **442** | 20p. multicoloured | 1·00 | 35 |

**443** "O'Higgins greeting San Martin" (P. Subercaseaux)

**1968.** 150th Anniv of Battle of the Maipu.

| | | | | |
|---|---|---|---|---|
| 1228 | **443** | 40p. blue | 1·10 | 45 |

**444** Dr. O. Magnasco (lawyer)

**1968.** Magnasco Commemoration.

| | | | | |
|---|---|---|---|---|
| 1229 | **444** | 20p. brown | 65 | 30 |

**445** "The Sea" (E. Gomez)

**446** "Grandmother's Birthday" (P. Lynch)

**1968.** Children's Stamp Design Competition.

| | | | | |
|---|---|---|---|---|
| 1230 | **445** | 20p. multicoloured | 50 | 20 |
| 1231 | **446** | 20p. multicoloured | 50 | 20 |

**447** Mar del Plata at Night

**1968.** 4th Plenary Assembly of Int Telegraph and Telephone Consultative Committee, Mar del Plata.

| | | | | |
|---|---|---|---|---|
| 1232 | **447** | 20p. black, yellow and blue (postage) | 40 | 20 |
| 1233 | - | 40p. black, mauve and blue (air) | 75 | 20 |
| 1234 | - | 68p. multicoloured | 1·10 | 45 |

DESIGNS (as Type **447**): 40p. South America in Assembly hemisphere. (Larger, 40×30 mm): 68p. Assembly emblem.

**448** Mounted Gendarme

**1968.** National Gendarmerie.

| | | | | |
|---|---|---|---|---|
| 1235 | **448** | 20p. multicoloured | 50 | 20 |

**449** Coastguard Cutter "Lynch"

**1968.** National Maritime Prefecture (Coastguard).

| | | | | |
|---|---|---|---|---|
| 1236 | **449** | 20p. black, grey and blue | 50 | 20 |

**450** A. de Anchorena and "Pampero"

**1968.** Aeronautics Week.

| | | | | |
|---|---|---|---|---|
| 1237 | **450** | 20p. multicoloured | 50 | 20 |

**451** St. Martin of Tours (A. Guido)

**1968.** St. Martin of Tours (patron saint of Buenos Aires).

| | | | | |
|---|---|---|---|---|
| 1238 | **451** | 20p. brown and lilac | 40 | 20 |

**452** Bank Emblem

**1968.** Municipal Bank of Buenos Aires.

| | | | | |
|---|---|---|---|---|
| 1239 | **452** | 20p. black, green & yell | 40 | 20 |

**453** Anniversary and A.L.P.I. Emblems

**1968.** 25th Anniv of "Fight Against Polio Association" (A.L.P.I.).

| | | | | |
|---|---|---|---|---|
| 1240 | **453** | 20p. green and red | 40 | 20 |

**454** "My Grandmother's Birthday" (Patricia Lynch)

**1968.** 1st "Solidarity" Philatelic Exn, Buenos Aires.

| | | | | |
|---|---|---|---|---|
| 1241 | **454** | 40p.+20p. multicoloured | 90 | 60 |

**455** "The Potter Woman" (Ramon Gomez Cornet)

**1968.** Cent of Whitcomb Gallery, Buenos Aires.

| | | | | |
|---|---|---|---|---|
| 1242 | **455** | 20p. red | 90 | 60 |

**456** Emblem of State Coalfields

**1968.** Coal and Steel Industries. Multicoloured.

| | | | |
|---|---|---|---|
| 1243 | 20p. Type **456** | 50 | 20 |
| 1244 | 20p. Ladle and emblem of Military Steel-manufacturing Agency ("FM") | 50 | 20 |

**457** Illustration from Schmidl's book "Journey to the River Plate and Paraguay"

**1969.** Ulrich Schmidl Commemoration.

| | | | | |
|---|---|---|---|---|
| 1245 | **457** | 20p. yellow, red & black | 90 | 60 |

**1969.** Army Day (29 May). As T 390.

| | | | |
|---|---|---|---|
| 1246 | 20p. Sapper, Buenos Aires Army, 1856 | 1·50 | 25 |

**459** Sail Frigate "Hercules"

**1969.** Navy Day.

| | | | | |
|---|---|---|---|---|
| 1247 | **459** | 20p. multicoloured | 2·75 | 45 |

**460** "Freedom and Equality" (from poster by S. Zagorski)

**1969.** Human Rights Year.

| | | | | |
|---|---|---|---|---|
| 1254 | **460** | 20p. black and yellow | 40 | 20 |

**461** I.L.O. Emblem within Honeycomb

**1969.** 50th Anniv of I.L.O.

| | | | | |
|---|---|---|---|---|
| 1255 | **461** | 20p. multicoloured | 40 | 20 |

**462** P. N. Arata (biologist)

**1969.** Argentine Scientists.

| | | | | |
|---|---|---|---|---|
| 1256 | **462** | 6p. brown on yellow | 75 | 30 |
| 1257 | - | 6p. brown on yellow | 75 | 30 |
| 1258 | - | 6p. brown on yellow | 75 | 30 |
| 1259 | - | 6p. brown on yellow | 75 | 30 |
| 1260 | - | 6p. brown on yellow | 75 | 30 |

PORTRAITS: No. 1257, M. Fernandez (zoologist); 1258, A. P. Gallardo (biologist); 1259, C. M. Hicken (botanist); 1260, E. L. Holmberg (botanist).

**463** Dish Aerial and Satellite

**1969.** Satellite Communications.

| | | | | |
|---|---|---|---|---|
| 1261 | **463** | 20p. blk & yell (postage) | 50 | 20 |
| 1262 | - | 40p. blue (air) | 1·10 | 35 |

DESIGN—HORIZ: 40p. Earth station and dish aerial.

**464** Nieuport 28 and Route Map

**1969.** 50th Anniv of 1st Argentine Airmail Service.

| | | | | |
|---|---|---|---|---|
| 1263 | **464** | 20p. multicoloured | 50 | 20 |

**1969.** Child Welfare. As T 352, inscr "R. ARGENTINA". Multicoloured.

| | | | |
|---|---|---|---|
| 1264 | 20p.+10p. White-faced whistling duck (postage) | 2·50 | 70 |
| 1265 | 26p.+13p. Lineated woodpecker (air) | 2·75 | 85 |

**465** College Entrance

**1969.** Centenary of Argentine Military College.

| | | | | |
|---|---|---|---|---|
| 1266 | **465** | 20p. multicoloured | 50 | 20 |

**466** General Pacheco (from painting by R. Guidice)

**1969.** Death Centenary of General Angel Pacheco.

| | | | | |
|---|---|---|---|---|
| 1267 | **466** | 20p. green | 40 | 20 |

**467** Bartolome Mitre and Logotypes of "La Nacion"

**1969.** Centenary of Newspapers "La Nacion" and "La Prensa".

| | | | | |
|---|---|---|---|---|
| 1268 | **467** | 20p. black, emer & grn | 1·10 | 45 |
| 1269 | - | 20p. black orange & yell | 1·10 | 45 |

DESIGN: No. 1269 "The Lantern" (masthead) and logotypes of "La Prensa".

**468** J. Aguirre

**1969.** Argentine Musicians.

| | | | | |
|---|---|---|---|---|
| 1270 | **468** | 6p. green and blue | 1·10 | 45 |
| 1271 | - | 6p. green and blue | 1·10 | 45 |
| 1272 | - | 6p. green and blue | 1·10 | 45 |
| 1273 | - | 6p. green and blue | 1·10 | 45 |
| 1274 | - | 6p. green and blue | 1·10 | 45 |

MUSICIANS: No. 1271, F. Boero; 1272, C. Gaito; 1273, C. L. Buchardo; 1274, A. Williams.

**469** Hydro-electric Project on Rivers Limay and Neuquen

**1969.** National Development Projects. Mult.

| | | | |
|---|---|---|---|
| 1275 | 6p. Type **469** (postage) | 90 | 25 |
| 1276 | 20p. Parana–Santa Fe river tunnel | 1·80 | 35 |
| 1277 | 26p. Atomic power plant, Atucha (air) | 2·50 | 1·30 |

**470** Lieut. B. Matienzo and Nieuport 28 Biplane

**1969.** Aeronautics Week.

| | | | | |
|---|---|---|---|---|
| 1278 | **470** | 20p. multicoloured | 90 | 20 |

**471** Capital "L" and Lions Emblem

**1969.** 50th Anniv of Lions International.

| | | | | |
|---|---|---|---|---|
| 1279 | **471** | 20p. olive, orge & green | 1·10 | 25 |

**472** "Madonna and Child" (after R. Soldi)

**1969.** Christmas.

| | | | | |
|---|---|---|---|---|
| 1280 | **472** | 20p. multicoloured | 1·10 | 35 |

**1970.** Child Welfare. As T 352, but differently arranged and inscr "REPUBLICA ARGENTINA". Multicoloured.

| | | | |
|---|---|---|---|
| 1293 | 20c.+10c. Slender-tailed wood-star (postage) | 2·00 | 70 |
| 1294 | 40c.+20c. Chilean flamingo (air) | 2·50 | 85 |

See also Nos. 1394/5, 1415/16 and 1441/2.

**474** "General Belgrano" (lithograph by Gericault)

**1970.** Birth Bicent of General Manuel Belgrano.

| | | | | |
|---|---|---|---|---|
| 1295 | **474** | 20c. brown | 65 | 20 |
| 1296 | - | 50c. black, flesh & blue | 1·30 | 35 |

DESIGN—HORIZ (56×15 mm): 50c. "Monument to the Flag" (bas-relief by Jose Fioravanti).

**475** Early Fire Engine

**1970.** Air. Centenary of Buenos Aires Fire Brigade.

| | | | | |
|---|---|---|---|---|
| 1297 | **475** | 40c. multicoloured | 2·30 | 45 |

**476** Naval Schooner "Juliet", 1814

**1970.** Navy Day.

| | | | | |
|---|---|---|---|---|
| 1298 | **476** | 20c. multicoloured | 2·00 | 60 |

**477** San Jose Palace

**1970.** President Justo de Urquiza Commemoration.

| | | | | |
|---|---|---|---|---|
| 1299 | **477** | 20c. multicoloured | 40 | 20 |

**478** General Belgrano

**1970.** Revalued currency. Previous designs with values in centavos and pesos as T **478**. Inscr "REPUBLICA ARGENTINA" or "ARGENTINA".

| | | | | |
|---|---|---|---|---|
| 1300 | | 1c. green (No. 1016) | 25 | 10 |
| 1301 | - | 3c. red (No. 951) | 25 | 10 |
| 1302 | **296** | 5c. blue | 25 | 10 |
| 1303 | **478** | 6c. blue | 40 | 15 |
| 1304 | **478** | 8c. green | 25 | 10 |
| 1305 | - | 10c. brown (No. 1286)* | 50 | 15 |
| 1306 | - | 10c. red (No. 1286) | 2·40 | 45 |
| 1307 | - | 10c. brown (No. 1286)* | 65 | 25 |
| 1308 | **478** | 10c. brown | 25 | 10 |
| 1309 | - | 25c. brown | 65 | 15 |
| 1310 | **478** | 30c. purple | 50 | 20 |
| 1311 | - | 50c. red | 1·50 | 30 |
| 1312 | **478** | 60c. yellow | 50 | 25 |
| 1313 | - | 65c. brown (No. 878) | 1·50 | 25 |
| 1314 | - | 70c. blue | 25 | 15 |
| 1315 | - | 90c. green (No. 878) | 4·50 | 30 |
| 1316a | - | 1p. brown (as No. 1027, but 23×29 mm) | 4·50 | 25 |
| 1317 | - | 1p.15 blue (No. 1072) | 1·50 | 25 |
| 1318 | - | 1p.20 orange (No. 878) | 1·60 | 30 |
| 1319 | - | 1p.20 red | 50 | 20 |
| 1320 | - | 1p.80 brn (as No. 1072) | 50 | 20 |
| 1321 | **478** | 1p.80 blue | 50 | 25 |
| 1322 | - | 2p. brown | 50 | 15 |
| 1323 | - | 2p.70 bl (as No. 878) | 50 | 25 |
| 1323a | **478** | 3p. grey | 50 | 20 |
| 1392 | - | 4p.50 green (as No. 1288) (G. Brown) | 1·10 | 20 |
| 1325 | - | 5p. green (as No. 1032) | 1·90 | 35 |
| 1326 | - | 6p. red | 50 | 20 |
| 1327 | - | 6p. green | 50 | 20 |

| | | | | |
|---|---|---|---|---|
| 1328 | - | 7p.50 grn (as No. 878) | 1·60 | 30 |
| 1329 | - | 10p. blue (as No. 1033) | 2·50 | 25 |
| 1329a | - | 12p. green | 65 | 20 |
| 1329b | - | 12p. red | 65 | 20 |
| 1330 | - | 13p.50 red (as No. 1072) | 1·60 | 60 |
| 1331 | - | 13p.50 red (as No. 1072 but larger, 16×24 mm) | 75 | 25 |
| 1332 | - | 15p. red | 50 | 15 |
| 1333 | - | 15p. blue | 50 | 15 |
| 1334 | - | 20p. red | 50 | 20 |
| 1335 | - | 22p.50 blue (as No. 878) (22×32½ mm) | 1·30 | 25 |
| 1393 | - | 22p.50 blue (as No. 878) (26×39 mm) | 2·20 | 70 |
| 1336 | - | 30p. red | 65 | 20 |
| 1337 | **478** | 40p. green | 1·80 | 25 |
| 1338 | - | 40p. red | 50 | 15 |
| 1339 | **478** | 60p. blue | 2·50 | 30 |
| 1340 | - | 70p. blue | 2·50 | 45 |
| 1340a | **478** | 90p. green | 1·30 | 30 |
| 1340b | - | 100p. red | 1·30 | 30 |
| 1340c | - | 110p. red | 65 | 25 |
| 1340d | - | 120p. red | 50 | 30 |
| 1340e | - | 130p. red | 90 | 35 |

DESIGNS—VERT (as Type **478**): 25, 50, 70c., 1p.20, 2, 6, 12, 15p. (No. 1332), 20, 30, 40p. (No. 1338), 100, 110, 120, 130p. General Jose de San Martin; 15p. (No. 1333), 70p. Guillermo Brown.

*No. 1307 differs from Nos. 1305/6 in being without imprint. It also has "CORREOS" at top right.

**482** Wireless Set of 1920 and Radio "Waves"

**1970.** 50th Anniv of Argentine Radio Broadcasting.

| | | | | |
|---|---|---|---|---|
| 1341 | **482** | 20c. multicoloured | 75 | 45 |

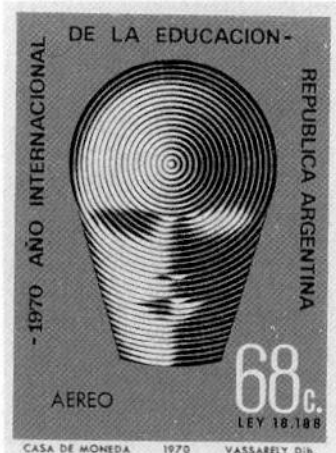


**483** Emblem of Education Year

**1970.** Air. International Education Year.

| | | | | |
|---|---|---|---|---|
| 1342 | **483** | 68c. black and blue | 65 | 30 |

**1970.** Military Uniforms. As T 390. Multicoloured.

| | | | |
|---|---|---|---|
| 1343 | 20c. Military courier, 1879 | 1·50 | 25 |

**484** "Liberation Fleet leaving Valparaiso" (A. Abel)

**1970.** 150th Anniv of Peruvian Liberation.

| | | | | |
|---|---|---|---|---|
| 1344 | **484** | 26c. multicoloured | 1·90 | 60 |

**485** "United Nations"

**1970.** 25th Anniv of U.N.

| | | | | |
|---|---|---|---|---|
| 1345 | **485** | 20c. multicoloured | 40 | 20 |

**486** Cordoba Cathedral

**1970.** 400th Anniv of Tucuman Diocese.

| | | | | |
|---|---|---|---|---|
| 1346 | **486** | 50c. blk & grey (postage) | 1·40 | 35 |
| 1347 | - | 40c. multicoloured (air) | 1·50 | 60 |

DESIGN—HORIZ: 40c. Chapel, Sumampa.

**487** Planetarium

**1970.** Air. Buenos Aires Planetarium.

| | | | | |
|---|---|---|---|---|
| 1348 | **487** | 40c. multicoloured | 1·10 | 35 |

**488** "Liberty" and Mint Building

**1970.** 25th Anniv of State Mint Building, Buenos Aires.

| | | | | |
|---|---|---|---|---|
| 1349 | **488** | 20c. black, green & gold | 40 | 10 |

**489** "The Manger" (H. G. Gutierrez) (image scaled to 63% of original size)

**1970.** Christmas.

| | | | | |
|---|---|---|---|---|
| 1350 | **489** | 20c. multicoloured | 90 | 60 |

**490** Jorge Newbery and Morane Saulnier Type L Airplane

**1970.** Air. Aeronautics Week.

| | | | | |
|---|---|---|---|---|
| 1351 | **490** | 26c. multicoloured | 65 | 25 |

**491** St. John Bosco and College Building

**1970.** Salesian Mission in Patagonia.

| | | | | |
|---|---|---|---|---|
| 1352 | **491** | 20c. black and green | 40 | 20 |

**492** "Planting the Flag"

**1971.** 5th Anniv of Argentine Expedition to the South Pole.

| | | | | |
|---|---|---|---|---|
| 1353 | **492** | 20c. multicoloured | 2·30 | 35 |

**493** Dorado (image scaled to 64% of original size)

**1971.** Child Welfare. Fishes. Multicoloured.

| | | | |
|---|---|---|---|
| 1354 | 20c.+10c. Type **493** (postage) | 2·00 | 70 |
| 1355 | 40c.+20c. River Plate pejerry (air) | 1·80 | 60 |

**494** Einstein and Scanners

**1971.** Electronics in Postal Development.

| | | | | |
|---|---|---|---|---|
| 1356 | **494** | 25c. multicoloured | 75 | 45 |

**495** E. I. Alippi

**1971.** Argentine Actors and Actresses. Each black and brown.

| | | | |
|---|---|---|---|
| 1357 | 15c. Type **495** | 50 | 15 |
| 1358 | 15c. J. A. Casaberta | 50 | 15 |
| 1359 | 15c. R. Casaux | 50 | 15 |
| 1360 | 15c. Angelina Pagano | 50 | 15 |
| 1361 | 15c. F. Parravicini | 50 | 15 |

**496** Federation Emblem

**1971.** Inter-American Regional Meeting of International Roads Federation.

| | | | | |
|---|---|---|---|---|
| 1362 | **496** | 25c. black and blue | 50 | 20 |

**1971.** Army Day. As T 390.

| | | | |
|---|---|---|---|
| 1363 | 25c. multicoloured | 2·10 | 25 |

DESIGN: 25c. Artilleryman of 1826.

**1971.** Navy Day. As T 476.

| | | | |
|---|---|---|---|
| 1364 | 25c. multicoloured | 2·30 | 25 |

DESIGN: Sloop "Carmen".

**498** "General Guemes" (L. Gigli)

**1971.** 150th Death Anniv of General M. de Guemes. Multicoloured.

| | | | |
|---|---|---|---|
| 1365 | 25c. Type **498** | 90 | 25 |
| 1366 | 25c. "Death of Guemes" (A. Alice) (84×29 mm) | 90 | 25 |

**499** Order of the Peruvian Sun

**1971.** 150th Anniv of Peruvian Independence.

| | | | | |
|---|---|---|---|---|
| 1367 | **499** | 31c. yellow, black & red | 1·10 | 25 |

**500** Stylized Tulip

**1971.** 3rd Int and 8th Nat Horticultural Exhibition.

| | | | | |
|---|---|---|---|---|
| 1368 | **500** | 25c. multicoloured | 65 | 20 |

**501** Dr. A. Saenz (founder) (after Jose Gut)

**1971.** 150th Anniv of Buenos Aires University.

| | | | | |
|---|---|---|---|---|
| 1369 | **501** | 25c. multicoloured | 50 | 20 |

**502** Arsenal Emblem

**1971.** 30th Anniv of Fabricaciones Militares (Arsenals).

| | | | | |
|---|---|---|---|---|
| 1370 | **502** | 25c. multicoloured | 50 | 20 |

**503** Road Transport

**1971.** Nationalized Industries.

| | | | | |
|---|---|---|---|---|
| 1371 | **503** | 25c. mult (postage) | 90 | 15 |
| 1372 | - | 65c. multicoloured | 2·30 | 45 |
| 1373 | - | 31c. yell, blk & red (air) | 1·00 | 35 |

DESIGNS: 31c. Refinery and formula ("Petrochemicals"); 65c. Tree and paper roll ("Paper and Cellulose").

**1971.** Air. Revalued currency. Face values in centavos.

| | | | | |
|---|---|---|---|---|
| 1374 | **358** | 45c. brown | 4·50 | 60 |
| 1375 | **358** | 68c. red | 65 | 25 |
| 1376a | **358** | 70c. blue | 3·25 | 25 |
| 1377 | **358** | 90c. green | 3·25 | 25 |
| 1378 | **358** | 1p.70 blue | 1·00 | 25 |
| 1379 | **358** | 1p.95 green | 1·00 | 25 |
| 1380 | **358** | 2p.65 purple | 1·00 | 25 |

**504** Constellation and Telescope

**1971.** Centenary of Cordoba Observatory.

| | | | | |
|---|---|---|---|---|
| 1381 | **504** | 25c. multicoloured | 1·10 | 25 |

**505** Capt. D. L. Candelaria and Morane Saulnier Type P Airplane

**1971.** 25th Aeronautics and Space Week.

| | | | | |
|---|---|---|---|---|
| 1382 | **505** | 25c. multicoloured | 65 | 20 |

**506** "Stamps" (Mariette Lydis)

**1971.** 2nd Charity Stamp Exhibition.
1383 **506** 1p.+50c. multicoloured 75 45

**507** "Christ in Majesty" (tapestry by Butler)

**1971.** Christmas.
1384 **507** 25c. multicoloured 40 20

**1972.** Child Welfare. As T 352, but differently arranged and inscr "REPUBLICA ARGENTINA".
1394 25c.+10c. Saffron finch (vert) 1·90 45
1395 65c.+30c. Rufous-bellied thrush (horiz) 2·50 60

**508** "Maternity" (J. Castagnino)

**1972.** 25th Anniv of UNICEF.
1396 **508** 25c. black and brown 40 15

**509** Treaty Emblem, "Libertad" (liner) and Almirante Brown Base

**1972.** 10th Anniv of Antarctic Treaty.
1397 **509** 25c. multicoloured 1·10 45

**510** Postman's Mail Pouch

**1972.** Bicentenary of 1st Buenos Aires Postman.
1398 **510** 25c. multicoloured 35 10

**1972.** Army Day. As T 390. Multicoloured.
1399 25c. Sergeant of Negro and Mulatto Battalion (1806–7) 1·10 45

**1972.** Navy Day. As T 476. Multicoloured.
1400 25c. Brigantine "Santisima Trinidad" 1·60 50

**512** Sonic Balloon

**1972.** National Meteorological Service.
1401 **512** 25c. multicoloured 50 15

**513** Oil Pump

**1972.** 50th Anniv of State Oilfields (Y.P.F.).
1402 **513** 45c. black, blue & gold 1·40 25

**514** Forest Centre

**1972.** 7th World Forestry Congress, Buenos Aires.
1403 **514** 25c. black, blue & lt bl 1·10 35

**515** Arms and Cadet Ship "Presidente Sarmiento"

**1972.** Centenary of Naval School.
1404 **515** 25c. multicoloured 1·30 25

**516** Baron A. de Marchi, Balloon and Voisin "Boxkite"

**1972.** Aeronautics Week.
1405 **516** 25c. multicoloured 75 40

**517** Bartolome Mitre

**1972.** 150th Birth Anniv of General Bartolome Mitre.
1406 **517** 25c. blue 70 40

**518** Heart and Flower

**1972.** World Health Day.
1407 **518** 90c. blk, violet & blue 90 45

**519** "Martin Fierro" (J. C. Castignino)

**1972.** Int Book Year and Cent of "Martin Fierro" (poem by Jose Hernandez). Multicoloured.
1408 50c. Type **519** 50 15
1409 90c. "Spirit of the Gaucho" (V. Forte) 1·00 45

**520** Iguazu Falls

**1972.** American Tourist Year.
1410 **520** 45c. multicoloured 50 20

**521** "Wise Man on Horseback" (18th-century wood-carving)

**1972.** Christmas.
1411 **521** 50c. multicoloured 75 25

**522** Cockerel Emblem

**1973.** 150th Anniv of Federal Police Force.
1412 **522** 50c. multicoloured 50 20

**523** Bank Emblem and First Coin

**1973.** 150th Anniv of Provincial Bank of Buenos Aires.
1413 **523** 50c. multicoloured 40 15

**524** Douglas DC-3 Aircraft and Polar Map

**1973.** 10th Anniv of 1st Argentine Flight to South Pole.
1414 **524** 50c. multicoloured 2·50 95

**1973.** Child Welfare. As T 473, but differently arranged and inscr "R. ARGENTINA". Mult.
1415 50c.+25c. Crested screamer (vert) 2·00 95
1416 90c.+45c. Saffron-cowled blackbird (horiz) 2·50 1·50

**525** Presidential Chair

**1973.** Presidential Inauguration.
1417 **525** 50c. multicoloured 40 10

**526** San Martin and Bolivar

**1973.** San Martin's Farewell to People of Peru. Multicoloured.
1418 50c. Type **526** 50 20
1419 50c. "San Martin" (after Gil de Castro) (vert) 50 20

**527** "Eva Peron – Eternally with her People"

**1973.** Eva Peron Commemoration.
1420 **527** 70c. multicoloured 40 15

**528** "House of Viceroy Sobremonte" (H. de Virgilio)

**1973.** 4th Centenary of Cordoba.
1421 **528** 50c. multicoloured 45 15

**529** "Woman" (L. Spilimbergo)

**1973.** Philatelists' Day. Argentine Paintings. Mult.
1422 15c.+15c. "Nature Study" (A. Guttero) (horiz) 50 10
1423 70c. Type **529** 1·30 25
1424 90c.+90c. "Nude" (M. C. Victorica) (horiz) 1·60 1·10

See also Nos. 1434/6 and 1440.

**530** "La Argentina" (sail frigate)

**1973.** Navy Day.
1425 **530** 70c. multicoloured 1·30 25

**531** Early and Modern Telephones

**1973.** 25th Anniv of National Telecommunications Enterprise (E.N.T.E.L.).

| | | | | |
|---|---|---|---|---|
| 1426 | **531** | 70c. multicoloured | 65 | 15 |

**532** Quill Pen of Flags

**1973.** 12th International Latin Notaries Congress.

| | | | | |
|---|---|---|---|---|
| 1427 | **532** | 70c. multicoloured | 40 | 15 |

**533** Lujan Basilica

**1973**

| | | | | |
|---|---|---|---|---|
| 1428 | **533** | 18c. brown and yellow | 25 | 10 |
| 1429 | **533** | 50c. purple and black | 25 | 10 |
| 1429a | **533** | 50c. blue and brown | 25 | 10 |
| 1430 | **533** | 50c. purple | 25 | 10 |

**1973.** Transfer of Presidency of General Juan Peron. No. 1318 optd TRANSMISION DEL MANDO PRESIDENCIAL 12 OCTUBRE 1973.

| | | | |
|---|---|---|---|
| 1431 | 1p.20 orange | 1·40 | 25 |

**535** "Virgin and Child" (stained-glass window)

**1973.** Christmas. Multicoloured.

| | | | |
|---|---|---|---|
| 1432 | 70c. Type **535** | 65 | 25 |
| 1433 | 1p.20 "The Manger" (B. Venier) | 1·10 | 45 |

**1974.** Argentine Paintings. As T 529. Mult.

| | | | |
|---|---|---|---|
| 1434 | 50c. "Houses" (E. Daneri) (horiz) | 65 | 20 |
| 1435 | 70c. "The Lama" (J. B. Planas) | 70 | 25 |
| 1436 | 90c. "Homage to the Blue Grotto" (E. Pettoruti) (horiz) | 75 | 35 |

**536** View of Mar del Plata

**1974.** Centenary of Mar del Plata.

| | | | | |
|---|---|---|---|---|
| 1437 | **536** | 70c. multicoloured | 50 | 20 |

**537** "Fray Justo Santa Maria de Oro" (anon.)

**1974.** Birth Bicentenary of Fray Justo Santa Maria de Oro.

| | | | | |
|---|---|---|---|---|
| 1438 | **537** | 70c. multicoloured | 40 | 10 |

**538** Weather Contrasts

**1974.** Cent of World Meteorological Organization.

| | | | | |
|---|---|---|---|---|
| 1439 | **538** | 1p.20 multicoloured | 1·00 | 35 |

**1974.** "Prenfil 74" Philatelic Press Exhibition, Buenos Aires. As No. 1435.

| | | | |
|---|---|---|---|
| 1440 | 70c.+30c. multicoloured | 75 | 30 |

**1974.** Child Welfare. As T 352 but differently arranged and inscr "REPUBLICA ARGENTINA". Multicoloured.

| | | | |
|---|---|---|---|
| 1441 | 70c.+30c. Double-collared seedeater | 2·00 | 60 |
| 1442 | 1p.20+60c. Hooded siskin | 2·50 | 85 |

**539** B. Roldan

**1974.** Birth Centenary of Belisario Roldan (writer).

| | | | | |
|---|---|---|---|---|
| 1443 | **539** | 70c. brown and blue | 35 | 15 |

**540** O.E.A. Member Countries

**1974.** 25th Anniv of Organization of American States' Charter.

| | | | | |
|---|---|---|---|---|
| 1444 | **540** | 1p.38 multicoloured | 40 | 15 |

**541** Posthorn Emblem

**1974.** Creation of State Posts and Telecommunications Enterprise (E.N.C.O.T.E.L.).

| | | | | |
|---|---|---|---|---|
| 1445 | **541** | 1p.20 blue, black & gold | 75 | 15 |

**542** Flags of Member Countries

**1974.** 6th Meeting of River Plate Countries' Foreign Ministers.

| | | | | |
|---|---|---|---|---|
| 1446 | **542** | 1p.38 multicoloured | 40 | 20 |

**543** El Chocon Hydro-electric Complex

**1974.** Nationalized Industries. Multicoloured.

| | | | |
|---|---|---|---|
| 1447 | 70c. Type **543** | 65 | 15 |
| 1448 | 1p.20 Blast furnace, Somisa steel mills | 1·00 | 45 |
| 1449 | 4p.50 General Belgrano Bridge (61×25 mm) | 3·25 | 70 |

**1974.** Army Day. As T 390. Multicoloured.

| | | | |
|---|---|---|---|
| 1450 | 1p.20 Mounted Grenadier | 1·00 | 20 |

See also Nos. 1515 and 1564.

**544** A. Mascias and Bleriot XI

**1974.** Air Force Day.

| | | | | |
|---|---|---|---|---|
| 1451 | **544** | 1p.20 multicoloured | 1·00 | 20 |

**545** Brigantine "Belgrano"

**1974.** 150th Anniv of San Martin's Departure into Exile.

| | | | | |
|---|---|---|---|---|
| 1452 | **545** | 1p.20 multicoloured | 1·80 | 45 |

**546** San Francisco Convent, Santa Fe

**1974.** 400th Anniv of Santa Fe.

| | | | | |
|---|---|---|---|---|
| 1453 | **546** | 1p.20 multicoloured | 65 | 15 |

**547** Symbolic Posthorn

**1974.** Centenary of U.P.U.

| | | | | |
|---|---|---|---|---|
| 1454 | **547** | 2p.65 multicoloured | 1·40 | 35 |

**548** Mariano Necochea

**1974.** 150th Anniv of Battles of Junin and Ayacucho. Sheet 143×134 mm comprising T 548 and similar vert designs. Multicoloured.

| | | | |
|---|---|---|---|
| **MS**1455 | (a) 1p. Type **548**; (b) 1p.20 San Martin; (c) 1p.70 Manuel Isidoro Suarez; (d) 1p.90 Juan Pascual Pringles; (e) 2p.70 Latin American flags; (f) 4p.50 Jose Felix Bogado | 5·25 | 5·00 |

**549** Congress Building, Buenos Aires

**1974**

| | | | | |
|---|---|---|---|---|
| 1456 | **549** | 30p. purple and yellow | 3·25 | 25 |

**550** Boy examining Stamp

**1974.** International Year of Youth Philately.

| | | | | |
|---|---|---|---|---|
| 1457 | **550** | 1p.70 black and yellow | 65 | 15 |

**551** "Christmas in Peace" (V. Campanella)

**1974.** Christmas. Multicoloured.

| | | | |
|---|---|---|---|
| 1458 | 1p.20 Type **551** | 1·10 | 25 |
| 1459 | 2p.65 "St. Anne and the Virgin Mary" | 1·30 | 45 |

**552** "Space Monsters" (R. Forner)

**1975.** Contemporary Argentine Paintings. Mult.

| | | | |
|---|---|---|---|
| 1460 | 2p.70 Type **552** | 1·50 | 35 |
| 1461 | 4p.50 "Sleep" (E. Centurion) | 2·75 | 60 |

**553** Cathedral and Weaver, Catamarca (image scaled to 58% of original size)

**1975.** Tourist Views (1st series). Multicoloured.

| | | | |
|---|---|---|---|
| 1462 | 1p.20 Type **553** | 40 | 20 |
| 1463 | 1p.20 Street scene and carved pulpit, Jujuy | 40 | 20 |
| 1464 | 1p.20 Monastery and tree- felling, Salta | 40 | 20 |
| 1465 | 1p.20 Dam and vase, Santiago del Estero | 40 | 20 |
| 1466 | 1p.20 Colombres Museum and farm cart, Tucuman | 40 | 20 |

See also Nos. 1491/3.

**554** "We're Vaccinated Now" (M. L. Alonso)

**1975.** Children's Vaccination Campaign.

| | | | | |
|---|---|---|---|---|
| 1467 | **554** | 2p. multicoloured | 75 | 20 |

**555** "Don Quixote" (Zuloaga)

**1975.** Air. "Espana 75" International Stamp Exhibition, Madrid.

| | | | | |
|---|---|---|---|---|
| 1468 | **555** | 2p.75 black, yell & red | 1·00 | 40 |

**556** Hugo S. Acuna and South Orkneys Base

**1975.** Antarctic Pioneers. Multicoloured.

| | | | |
|---|---|---|---|
| 1469 | 2p. Type **556** | 50 | 15 |
| 1470 | 2p. Francisco P. Moreno and Quetrihue Peninsula | 50 | 15 |
| 1471 | 2p. Capt. Carlos M. Moyano and Cerra Torre, Santa Cruz | 50 | 15 |
| 1472 | 2p. Lt. Col. Luis Piedra Buena and naval cutter "Luisito" in the Antarctic | 50 | 15 |
| 1473 | 2p. Ensign Jose M. Sobral and "Snow Hill" House | 50 | 15 |

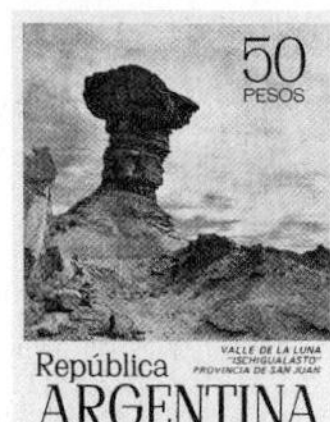


**557** Valley of the Moon, San Juan Province

**1975**

| | | | | |
|---|---|---|---|---|
| 1474 | **557** | 50p. multicoloured | 4·00 | 45 |
| 1474a | **557** | 300p. multicoloured | 4·50 | 45 |
| 1474b | - | 500p. multicoloured | 8·75 | 1·20 |
| 1474c | - | 1000p. multicoloured | 7·00 | 1·40 |

DESIGNS—HORIZ: 500p. Admiral Brown Antarctic Station; 1000p. San Francisco Church, Salta.

**1975.** Air. Surch.

| | | | | |
|---|---|---|---|---|
| 1475 | **358** | 9p.20 on 5p.60 green, mauve and purple | 1·50 | 35 |
| 1476 | **358** | 19p.70 on 5p.60 green, mauve and purple | 2·10 | 70 |
| 1477 | **358** | 100p. on 5p.60 green, mauve and purple | 9·50 | 3·75 |

**559** Eduardo Bradley and Balloon

**1975.** Air Force Day.

| | | | | |
|---|---|---|---|---|
| 1478 | **559** | 6p. multicoloured | 75 | 25 |

**560** Sail Frigate "25 de Mayo"

**1975.** Navy Day.

| | | | | |
|---|---|---|---|---|
| 1479 | **560** | 6p. multicoloured | 1·50 | 35 |

**561** "Oath of the 33 Orientales on the Beach of La Agraciada" (J. Blanes)

**1975.** 150th Anniv of Uruguayan Independence.

| | | | | |
|---|---|---|---|---|
| 1480 | **561** | 6p. multicoloured | 1·30 | 35 |

**1975.** Air. Surch. REVALORIZADO and value.

| | | | | |
|---|---|---|---|---|
| 1481 | **358** | 9p.20 on 5p.60 green, mauve and purple | 1·10 | 45 |
| 1482 | **358** | 19p.70 on 5p.60 green, mauve and purple | 2·00 | 95 |

**563** Flame Emblem

**1975.** 30th Anniv of Pres. Peron's Seizure of Power.

| | | | | |
|---|---|---|---|---|
| 1483 | **563** | 6p. multicoloured | 65 | 25 |

**1975.** Surch REVALORIZADO and value.

| | | | | |
|---|---|---|---|---|
| 1484 | **533** | 5p. on 18c. brown & yell | 75 | 15 |

**565** Bridge and Flags of Argentina and Uruguay

**1975.** "International Bridge" between Colon (Argentina) and Paysandu (Uruguay).

| | | | | |
|---|---|---|---|---|
| 1485 | **565** | 6p. multicoloured | 75 | 20 |

**566** Posthorn Emblem

**1975.** Introduction of Postal Codes.

| | | | | |
|---|---|---|---|---|
| 1486 | **566** | 10p. on 20c. yellow, black and green | 90 | 20 |

**1975.** Nos. 951 and 1288 surch REVALORIZADO and value.

| | | | |
|---|---|---|---|
| 1487 | 6c. on 3p. blue | 40 | 10 |
| 1488 | 30c. on 90p. bistre | 40 | 10 |

**568** "The Nativity" (stained-glass window)

**1975.** Christmas.

| | | | | |
|---|---|---|---|---|
| 1489 | **568** | 6p. multicoloured | 75 | 20 |

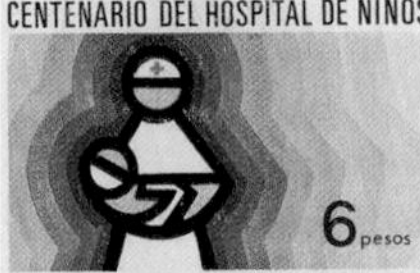


**569** Stylized Nurse and Child

**1975.** Centenary of Children's Hospital.

| | | | | |
|---|---|---|---|---|
| 1490 | **569** | 6p. multicoloured | 1·30 | 35 |

**1975.** Tourist Views (2nd series). As T 553. Mult.

| | | | |
|---|---|---|---|
| 1491 | 6p. Mounted patrol and oil rig, Chubut | 90 | 25 |
| 1492 | 6p. Glacier and sheep-shearing, Santa Cruz | 90 | 25 |
| 1493 | 6p. Lake Lapataia, Tierra del Fuego, and Antarctic scene | 90 | 25 |

**570** "Numeral"

**1976**

| | | | | |
|---|---|---|---|---|
| 1494 | **570** | 12c. grey and black | 40 | 15 |
| 1495 | **570** | 50c. slate and green | 40 | 15 |
| 1496 | **570** | 1p. red and black | 40 | 15 |
| 1497 | **570** | 4p. blue and black | 40 | 15 |
| 1498 | **570** | 5p. yellow and black | 50 | 15 |
| 1499 | **570** | 6p. brown and black | 50 | 15 |
| 1500 | **570** | 10p. grey and violet | 90 | 20 |
| 1501 | **570** | 27p. green and black | 65 | 20 |
| 1502 | **570** | 30p. blue and black | 3·25 | 25 |
| 1503 | **570** | 45p. yellow and black | 1·80 | 25 |
| 1504 | **570** | 50p. green and black | 1·80 | 25 |
| 1505 | **570** | 100p. green and red | 1·80 | 25 |

**571** Airliner in Flight

**1976.** 25th Anniv of "Aerolineas Argentinas".

| | | | | |
|---|---|---|---|---|
| 1513 | **571** | 30p. multicoloured | 2·00 | 25 |

**572** Sail Frigate "Heroina" and Map of Malvinas

**1976.** Argentine Claims to Falkland Islands (Malvinas).

| | | | | |
|---|---|---|---|---|
| 1514 | **572** | 6p. multicoloured | 5·75 | 60 |

**1976.** Army Day. As T 390. Multicoloured.

| | | | |
|---|---|---|---|
| 1515 | 12p. Infantryman of Conde's 7th Regiment | 75 | 20 |

**573** Louis Braille

**1976.** Louis Braille (inventor of characters for the Blind) Commemoration.

| | | | | |
|---|---|---|---|---|
| 1516 | **573** | 19p.70 blue | 50 | 15 |

**574** Plush-crested Jay

**1976.** Argentine Philately. Multicoloured.

| | | | |
|---|---|---|---|
| 1517 | 7p.+3p.50 Type **574** | 1·40 | 80 |
| 1518 | 13p.+6p.50 Yellow-collared macaw | 1·50 | 80 |
| 1519 | 20p.+10p. "Begonia micranthera" | 1·70 | 85 |
| 1520 | 40p.+20p. "Echinopsis shaferi" (teasel) | 2·10 | 1·00 |

**575** Schooner "Rio de la Plata"

**1976.** Navy Day.

| | | | | |
|---|---|---|---|---|
| 1521 | **575** | 12p. multicoloured | 95 | 25 |

**576** Dr. Bernardo Houssay (Medicine)

**1976.** Argentine Nobel Prize Winners.

| | | | | |
|---|---|---|---|---|
| 1522 | **576** | 10p. black, orge & grey | 50 | 15 |
| 1523 | - | 15p. black, yell & grey | 50 | 15 |
| 1524 | - | 20p. black, brn & grey | 65 | 25 |

DESIGNS: 15p. Dr. Luis Leloir (chemistry); 20p. Dr. Carlos Lamas (peace).

**577** Bridge and Ship

**1976.** "International Bridge" between Unzue (Argentina) and Fray Bentos (Uruguay).

| | | | | |
|---|---|---|---|---|
| 1525 | **577** | 12p. multicoloured | 1·30 | 25 |

**578** Cooling Tower and Pipelines

**1976.** General Mosconi Petrochemical Project.

| | | | | |
|---|---|---|---|---|
| 1526 | **578** | 28p. multicoloured | 75 | 20 |

**579** Teodoro Fels and Bleriot XI

**1976.** Air Force Day.

| | | | | |
|---|---|---|---|---|
| 1527 | **579** | 15p. multicoloured | 65 | 15 |

**580** "Nativity" (E. Chiapetto)

**1976.** Christmas.

| | | | | |
|---|---|---|---|---|
| 1528 | **580** | 20p. multicoloured | 1·10 | 45 |

**581** Dr. D. Velez Sarsfield (statesman)

**1977.** Death Cent (1975) of Dr. D. V. Sarsfield.

| | | | | |
|---|---|---|---|---|
| 1529 | **581** | 50p. brown and red | 1·30 | 45 |

**582** Conference Emblem

**1977.** United Nations Water Conference.

| | | | | |
|---|---|---|---|---|
| 1530 | **582** | 70p. multicoloured | 1·10 | 35 |

**583** "The Visit" (Horacio Butler)

**1977.** Plastic Arts. Multicoloured.

| | | | |
|---|---|---|---|
| 1531 | 50p. Type **583** | 1·00 | 25 |
| 1532 | 70p. "Consecration" (M. P. Caride) (vert) | 1·40 | 45 |

**584** World Cup Emblem

**1977.** World Cup Football Championship, Argentina. Multicoloured.

| | | | |
|---|---|---|---|
| 1533 | 30p. Type **584** | 75 | 25 |
| 1534 | 70p. Stadium and flags (vert) | 1·40 | 35 |

**585** City of La Plata Museum

**1977**

| | | | | |
|---|---|---|---|---|
| 1535 | **585** | 5p. black and brown | 40 | 10 |
| 1536 | - | 10p. black and blue | 25 | 10 |
| 1538 | - | 20p. black and yellow | 40 | 10 |
| 1539 | - | 40p. black and blue | 50 | 10 |
| 1540 | - | 50p. black and yellow | 65 | 20 |
| 1541 | - | 50p. black and brown | 65 | 15 |
| 1542 | - | 100p. black and pink | 50 | 10 |
| 1543 | - | 100p. black and orange | 65 | 15 |
| 1544 | - | 100p. black and green | 50 | 10 |
| 1545 | - | 200p. black and blue | 75 | 25 |
| 1546 | - | 280p. black and lilac | 11·50 | 1·30 |
| 1547b | - | 300p. black and yellow | 1·20 | 25 |
| 1548 | - | 480p. black and yellow | 1·80 | 35 |
| 1549b | - | 500p. black and green | 2·20 | 25 |
| 1550 | - | 520p. black and orange | 2·40 | 35 |
| 1551 | - | 800p. black and purple | 2·75 | 35 |
| 1552a | - | 1000p. black and gold | 3·75 | 35 |
| 1553 | - | 1000p. black and yellow | 3·25 | 45 |
| 1554 | - | 2000p. multicoloured | 2·75 | 45 |

DESIGNS—HORIZ: 10p. House of Independence, Tucuman; 20p. Type **585**; 50p. (No. 1541), Cabildo, Buenos Aires; 100p. (Nos. 1542/3), Columbus Theatre, Buenos Aires; 280p., 300p. Rio Grande Museum Chapel, Tierra del Fuego; 480p., 520p., 800p. San Ignacio Mission Church ruins; 500p. Candonga Chapel; 1000p. General Post Office, Buenos Aires (No. 1552 39×29 mm, No. 1553 32×21 mm); 2000p. Civic Centre, Bariloche. VERT: 40p. Cabildo, Salta; 50p. (No. 1540), Cabildo, Buenos Aires; 200p. Monument to the Flag, Rosario.

**586** Morse Key and Satellite

**1977.** "Argentine Philately". Multicoloured.

| | | | |
|---|---|---|---|
| 1560 | 10p.+5p. Type **586** | 55 | 30 |
| 1561 | 20p.+10p. Old and modern mail vans | 65 | 65 |
| 1562 | 60p.+30p. Old and modern ships | 1·30 | 1·00 |
| 1563 | 70p.+35p. SPAD XIII and Boeing 707 aircraft | 1·60 | 1·00 |

**1977.** Army Day. As T 390. Multicoloured.

| | | | |
|---|---|---|---|
| 1564 | 30p. Trooper of 16th Lancers | 1·50 | 35 |

**587** Schooner "Sarandi"

**1977.** Navy Day.

| | | | | |
|---|---|---|---|---|
| 1565 | **587** | 30p. multicoloured | 1·50 | 35 |

**1977.** 150th Anniv of Uruguay Post Office. As No. 1325 but colour changed. Surch 100 PESOS 150 ANIV. DEL CORREO NACIONAL DEL URUGUAY.

| | | | |
|---|---|---|---|
| 1566 | 100p. on 5p. brown | 2·50 | 1·10 |

**1977.** "Argentina '77" Exhibition. As No. 1474c, but inscr "EXPOSICION ARGENTINA '77".

| | | | |
|---|---|---|---|
| 1567 | 160p.+80p. multicoloured | 4·50 | 3·00 |

**589** Admiral Guillermo Brown

**1977.** Birth Bicent of Admiral Guillermo Brown.

| | | | | |
|---|---|---|---|---|
| 1568 | **589** | 30p. multicoloured | 65 | 20 |

**590** Civic Centre, Santa Rosa (La Pampa)

**1977.** Provinces of the Argentine. Multicoloured.

| | | | |
|---|---|---|---|
| 1569 | 30p. Type **590** | 65 | 25 |
| 1570 | 30p. Sierra de la Ventana (Buenos Aires) | 65 | 25 |
| 1571 | 30p. Skiers at Chapelco, San Martin de los Andes (Neuquen) | 65 | 25 |
| 1572 | 30p. Lake Fonck (Rio Negro) | 65 | 25 |

**591** Savoia S.16 ter Flying Boat over Rio de la Plata

**1977.** Air Force and 1926 Buenos Aires–New York Flight Commemoration.

| | | | | |
|---|---|---|---|---|
| 1573 | **591** | 40p. multicoloured | 50 | 20 |

**592** Jet Fighter Outline

**1977.** 50th Anniv of Military Aviation Factory.

| | | | | |
|---|---|---|---|---|
| 1574 | **592** | 30p. blue, pale blue and black | 40 | 10 |

**593** "The Adoration of the Kings" (stained-glass window, Holy Sacrament Basilica, Buenos Aires)

**1977.** Christmas.

| | | | | |
|---|---|---|---|---|
| 1575 | **593** | 100p. multicoloured | 1·60 | 25 |

**1978.** World Cup Football Championship, Argentina. Sheet 102×133 mm containing No. 1567×4 optd Argentina 78 and logo.

| | | | |
|---|---|---|---|
| **MS**1576 | 160p.+80p. multicoloured | 33·00 | 31·00 |

**595** World Cup Emblem

**1978.** World Cup Football Championship, Argentina.

| | | | | |
|---|---|---|---|---|
| 1577 | **595** | 200p. green and blue | 1·50 | 45 |

**596** Rosario

**1978.** World Cup Football Championship (3rd issue). Match Sites. Multicoloured.

| | | | |
|---|---|---|---|
| 1578 | 50p. Type **596** | 50 | 20 |
| 1579 | 100p. Cordoba | 50 | 20 |
| 1580 | 150p. Mendoza | 90 | 25 |
| 1581 | 200p. Mar del Plata | 90 | 25 |
| 1582 | 300p. Buenos Aires | 1·60 | 45 |

**597** Children and Institute Emblem

**1978.** 50th Anniv of Inter-American Children's Institute.

| | | | | |
|---|---|---|---|---|
| 1583 | **597** | 100p. multicoloured | 65 | 30 |

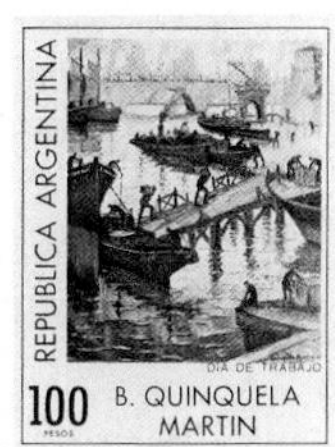

**598** "The Working Day" (B. Quinquela Martin)

**1978.** Argentine Art. Multicoloured.

| | | | |
|---|---|---|---|
| 1584 | 100p. Type **598** | 90 | 25 |
| 1585 | 100p. "Bust of an Unknown Woman" (Orlando Pierri) | 90 | 25 |

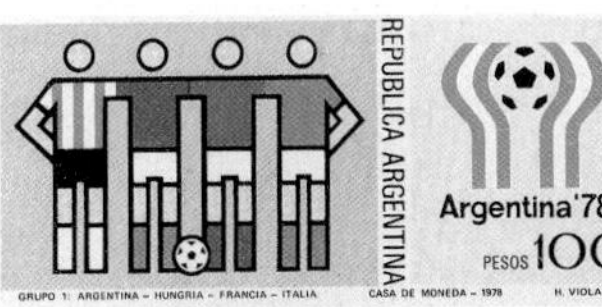

**599** Players from Argentina, Hungary, France and Italy (Group One)

**1978.** World Cup Football Championship, Argentina. Multicoloured.

| | | | |
|---|---|---|---|
| 1586 | 100p. Type **599** | 50 | 20 |
| 1587 | 200p. Group Two players | 1·30 | 25 |
| 1588 | 300p. Group Three players | 1·80 | 35 |
| 1589 | 400p. Group Four players | 2·40 | 45 |
| **MS**1590 | 89×60 mm. 700p. black and flesh | 5·00 | 4·75 |

DESIGN: (39×26 mm) 700p. River Plate Stadium.

**600** Hooded Siskin

**1978.** Inter-American Philatelic Exhibition. Mult.

| | | | |
|---|---|---|---|
| 1591 | 50p.+50p. Type **600** | 2·10 | 1·50 |
| 1592 | 100p.+100p. Double-collared seedeater | 2·30 | 1·50 |
| 1593 | 150p.+150p. Saffron-cowled blackbird | 3·25 | 2·20 |
| 1594 | 200p.+200p. Vermilion flycatcher | 3·50 | 2·50 |
| 1595 | 500p.+500p. Great kiskadee | 7·50 | 6·00 |

**601** Young Tree with Support

**1978.** Technical Co-operation among Developing Countries Conference, Buenos Aires.

| | | | | |
|---|---|---|---|---|
| 1596 | **601** | 100p. multicoloured | 65 | 20 |

**602** River Plate Stadium

**1978.** Argentina's Victory in World Cup Football Championship. Sheet 88×60 mm.

| | | | | |
|---|---|---|---|---|
| **MS**1597 | **602** | 1000p. black, stone and red | 6·25 | 6·00 |

**603** Bank Emblems of 1878 and 1978

**1978.** Centenary of Bank of Buenos Aires.

| | | | | |
|---|---|---|---|---|
| 1598 | **603** | 100p. multicoloured | 65 | 20 |

**604** General Manuel Savio and Steel Production

**1978.** 30th Death Anniv of General Manuel Savio (director of military manufacturing).

| | | | | |
|---|---|---|---|---|
| 1599 | **604** | 100p. multicoloured | 65 | 20 |

**605** San Martin

**1978.** Birth Bicentenary of Gen. San Martin.

| | | | | |
|---|---|---|---|---|
| 1600 | **605** | 2000p. green | 7·50 | 45 |
| 1600a | **605** | 10000p. blue | 11·50 | 60 |

**606** Numeral

**1978**

| | | | | |
|---|---|---|---|---|
| 1601 | **606** | 150p. blue and light blue | 65 | 25 |
| 1602 | **606** | 180p. blue and light blue | 65 | 25 |
| 1603 | **606** | 200p. blue and light blue | 60 | 25 |

**607** Chessboard, Pawn and Queen

**1978.** 23rd Chess Olympiad, Buenos Aires.
1604 **607** 200p. multicoloured 6·25 95

**608** Argentine Flag supporting Globe

**1978.** 12th Int Cancer Congress, Buenos Aires.
1605 **608** 200p. multicoloured 1·40 25

**609** "Correct Franking"

**1978.** Postal Publicity.

| No. | Type | Description | Mint | Used |
|---|---|---|---|---|
| 1606 | **609** | 20p. blue | 25 | 10 |
| 1607 | - | 30p. green | 40 | 15 |
| 1608 | - | 50p. red | 65 | 15 |

DESIGN—VERT: 30p. "Collect postage stamps". HORIZ: 50p. "Indicate the correct post code".

**610** Push-pull Tug

**1978.** 20th Anniv of Argentine River Fleet. Mult.

| No. | Description | Mint | Used |
|---|---|---|---|
| 1609 | 100p. Type **610** | 50 | 20 |
| 1610 | 200p. Tug "Legador" | 90 | 25 |
| 1611 | 300p. Tug "Rio Parana Mini" | 1·30 | 35 |
| 1612 | 400p. River passenger ship "Ciudad de Parana" | 1·80 | 35 |

**611** Bahia Blanca and Arms

**1978.** 150th Anniv of Bahia Blanca.
1613 **611** 200p. multicoloured 90 35

**612** "To Spain" (Arturo Dresco)

**1978.** Visit of King and Queen of Spain.
1614 **612** 300p. multicoloured 5·00 60

**613** Stained-glass Window, San Isidro Cathedral, Buenos Aires

**1978.** Christmas.
1615 **613** 200p. multicoloured 1·10 25

**614** "Chacabuco Slope" (Pedro Subercaseaux)

**1978.** Birth Bicent of General Jose de San Martin.

| No. | Description | Mint | Used |
|---|---|---|---|
| 1616 | 500p. Type **614** | 3·25 | 45 |
| 1617 | 1000p. "The Embrace of Maipo" (Pedro Subercaseaux) (vert) | 6·25 | 60 |

**615** San Martin Stamp of 1877 and U.P.U. Emblem

**1979.** Cent of Argentine Membership of U.P.U.
1618 **615** 200p. blue, black & brn 90 20

**616** Mariano Moreno (revolutionary)

**1979.** Celebrities.

| No. | Type | Description | Mint | Used |
|---|---|---|---|---|
| 1619 | **616** | 200p. yellow, blk & red | 90 | 20 |
| 1620 | - | 200p. blue, blk & dp bl | 90 | 20 |

DESIGNS: No. 1620, Adolfo Alsina (statesman).

**617** "Still Life" (Ernesto de la Carcova)

**1979.** Argentine Paintings. Multicoloured.

| No. | Description | Mint | Used |
|---|---|---|---|
| 1621 | 200p. Type **617** | 75 | 25 |
| 1622 | 300p. "The Washer-woman" (F. Brughetti) | 1·50 | 45 |

**618** Balcarce Antenna and Radio Waves

**1979.** 3rd Inter-American Telecommunications Conference.
1623 **618** 200p. multicoloured 1·00 35

**619** Rosette

**1979**

| No. | Type | Description | Mint | Used |
|---|---|---|---|---|
| 1624 | **619** | 240p. blue and brown | 65 | 25 |
| 1625 | **619** | 260p. blue and black | 65 | 25 |
| 1626 | **619** | 290p. blue and brown | 75 | 25 |
| 1627 | **619** | 310p. blue and purple | 75 | 25 |
| 1628 | **619** | 350p. blue and red | 1·00 | 25 |
| 1629 | **619** | 450p. blue and ultram | 90 | 25 |
| 1630 | **619** | 600p. blue and green | 90 | 25 |
| 1631 | **619** | 700p. blue and black | 1·10 | 25 |
| 1632 | **619** | 800p. blue and orange | 75 | 25 |
| 1632a | **619** | 1100p. blue and grey | 1·60 | 25 |
| 1632b | **619** | 1500p. blue and black | 90 | 2·40 |
| 1632c | **619** | 1700p. blue and green | 90 | 25 |

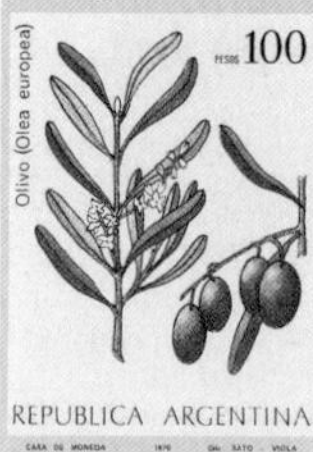


**620** Olives

**1979.** Agricultural Products. Multicoloured.

| No. | Description | Mint | Used |
|---|---|---|---|
| 1633 | 100p. Type **620** | 75 | 45 |
| 1634 | 200p. Tea | 1·00 | 60 |
| 1635 | 300p. Sorghum | 1·90 | 70 |
| 1636 | 400p. Flax | 2·10 | 95 |

**621** "75" and Symbol

**1979.** 75th Anniv of Argentine Automobile Club.
1637 **621** 200p. multicoloured 65 30

**622** Laurel Leaves and Army Emblem

**1979.** Naming of Village Subteniente Berdina, Tucuman.
1638 **622** 200p. multicoloured 70 30

**623** Wheat Exchange and Emblem

**1979.** 125th Anniv of Wheat Exchange, Buenos Aires.
1639 **623** 200p. blue, gold & black 65 30

**624** "Uruguay" (sail/steam gunboat)

**1979.** Navy Day.
1640 **624** 250p. multicoloured 1·50 60

**1979.** Army Day. As T 390. Multicoloured.
1641 200p. Trooper of Mounted Chasseurs, 1817 1·80 45

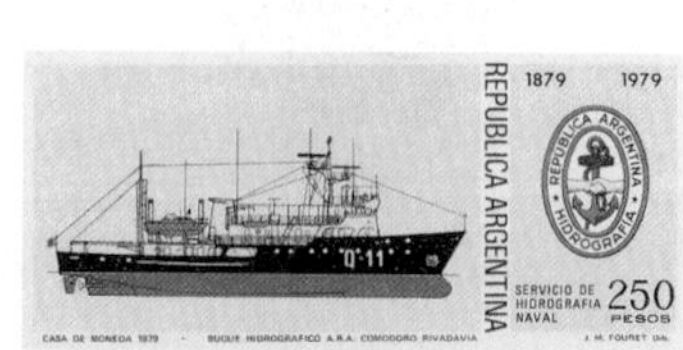


**625** "Comodoro Rivadavia" (hydrographic survey ship)

**1979.** Naval Hydrographic Service.
1642 **625** 250p. multicoloured 1·50 60

**626** Tree and Man Symbol

**1979.** Ecology Day.
1643 **626** 250p. multicoloured 1·00 35

**627** SPAD XIII and Vicente Almandos

**1979.** Air Force Day.
1644 **627** 250p. multicoloured 1·30 35

**628** "Military Occupation of Rio Negro by Gen. Julio A. Roca's Expedition" (detail, J. M. Blanes)

**1979.** Centenary of Conquest of the Desert.
1645 **628** 250p. multicoloured 1·30 35

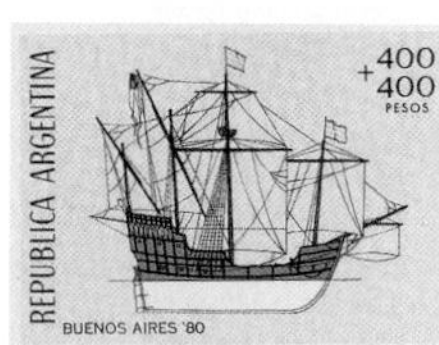


**629** Caravel "Magdalena"

**1979.** "Buenos Aires '80" International Stamp Exhibition. Multicoloured.

| No. | Description | Mint | Used |
|---|---|---|---|
| 1646 | 400p.+400p. Type **629** | 6·25 | 3·75 |
| 1647 | 500p.+500p. Three-masted sailing ship | 7·50 | 4·25 |
| 1648 | 600p.+600p. Corvette "Descubierta" | 10·50 | 8·75 |
| 1649 | 1500p.+1500p. Yacht "Fortuna" | 25·00 | 13·00 |

**630** Rowland Hill

**1979.** Death Centenary of Sir Rowland Hill.
1650 **630** 300p. black, grey & red 1·00 35

**631** Francisco de Viedma y Narvaez Monument (A. Funes and J. Agosta)

**1979.** Bicentenary of Founding of Viedma and Carmen de Patagones Towns.
1651 **631** 300p. multicoloured 1·50 35

**632** Pope Paul VI

**1979.** Election of Pope John Paul I.

| | | | | |
|---|---|---|---|---|
| 1652 | **632** | 500p. black | 1·80 | 45 |
| 1653 | - | 500p. black | 1·80 | 45 |

DESIGN: No. 1653, Pope John Paul I.

**633** Molinas Church

**1979.** Churches. Multicoloured.

| | | | | |
|---|---|---|---|---|
| 1654 | | 100p.+50p. Purmamarca Church | 50 | 20 |
| 1655 | | 200p.+100p. Type **633** | 75 | 25 |
| 1656 | | 300p.+150p. Animana Church | 1·10 | 45 |
| 1657 | | 400p.+200p. San Jose de Lules Church | 1·60 | 70 |

**1979.** 75th Anniv of Rosario Philatelic Society. No. 1545 optd 75 ANIV. SOCIEDAD FILATELICA DE ROSARIO.

| | | | | |
|---|---|---|---|---|
| 1658 | | 200p. blue and black | 1·10 | 35 |

**635** Children's Faces, and Sun on Map of Argentina

**1979.** Resettlement Policy.

| | | | | |
|---|---|---|---|---|
| 1659 | **635** | 300p. yellow, black & bl | 1·30 | 45 |

**636** Stained-glass Window, Salta Cathedral

**1979.** Christmas.

| | | | | |
|---|---|---|---|---|
| 1660 | **636** | 300p. multicoloured | 1·10 | 35 |

**637** Institute Emblem

**1979.** Centenary of Military Geographical Institute.

| | | | | |
|---|---|---|---|---|
| 1661 | **637** | 300p. multicoloured | 1·30 | 45 |

**638** General Mosconi and Oil Rig

**1979.** Birth Centenary of General Enrique Mosconi.

| | | | | |
|---|---|---|---|---|
| 1662 | **638** | 1000p. blue and black | 2·75 | 85 |

**639** Buenos Aires 3p. Stamp of 1858

**1979.** Prenfil 80 International Exhibition of Philatelic Literature and Journalism, Buenos Aires. Four sheets 89×60 mm containing designs as T 639.

**MS**1663 (a) 250p.+250p. black, stone and vermilion; (b) 750p.+750p. flesh and black; (c) 1000p.+1000p. multicoloured; (d) 2000p.+2000p. black, green and vermilion 32·00 30·00

DESIGNS—VERT: 750p. Rowland Hill; 2000p. International Year of the Child emblem. HORIZ: 1000p. Argentine 5c. Columbus stamp of 1892.

**640** Rotary Emblem and Globe

**1979.** 75th Anniv of Rotary International.

| | | | | |
|---|---|---|---|---|
| 1664 | **640** | 300p. multicoloured | 3·25 | 60 |

**641** Girl with Ruddy Ground Doves

**1979.** International Year of the Child.

| | | | | |
|---|---|---|---|---|
| 1665 | **641** | 500p. brown, blue & blk | 1·40 | 60 |
| 1666 | - | 1000p. multicoloured | 2·75 | 70 |

DESIGN: 1000p. "Family".

**642** Guillermo Brown

**1980**

| | | | | |
|---|---|---|---|---|
| 1667 | **642** | 5000p. black | 9·50 | 35 |
| 1668 | **642** | 30000p. black and blue | 5·75 | 1·10 |

**643** I.T.U. Emblem and Microphone

**1980.** Regional Administrative Conference on Broadcasting, Buenos Aires.

| | | | | |
|---|---|---|---|---|
| 1669 | **643** | 500p. blue, gold & ultram | 2·50 | 35 |

**644** Organization of American States Emblem

**1980.** Day of the Americas.

| | | | | |
|---|---|---|---|---|
| 1670 | **644** | 500p. multicoloured | 1·00 | 30 |

**645** Angel

**1980.** Centenary of Argentinian Red Cross.

| | | | | |
|---|---|---|---|---|
| 1671 | **645** | 500p. multicoloured | 1·00 | 30 |

**646** Salto Grande Hydro-electric Complex

**1980.** National Development Projects. Mult.

| | | | | |
|---|---|---|---|---|
| 1672 | | 300p. Type **646** | 90 | 35 |
| 1673 | | 300p. Zarate-Brazo Largo bridge | 90 | 35 |
| 1674 | | 300p. Dish aerials, Balcarce | 90 | 35 |

**647** Hipolito Bouchard and Sail Frigate "La Argentina"

**1980.** Navy Day.

| | | | | |
|---|---|---|---|---|
| 1675 | **647** | 500p. multicoloured | 1·30 | 45 |

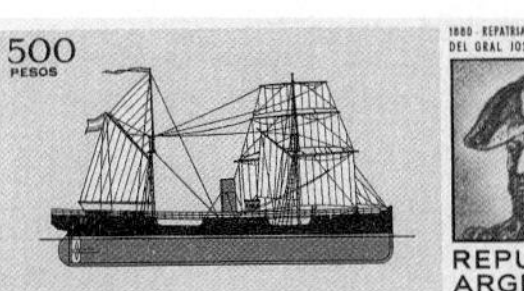


**648** "Villarino" and Woodcut of San Martin Theodore by Gericault

**1980.** Centenary of Return of General Jose de San Martin's Remains.

| | | | | |
|---|---|---|---|---|
| 1676 | **648** | 500p. multicoloured | 1·30 | 45 |

**649** "Gazeta de Buenos-Ayres" and Signature of Dr. Mariano Moreno (first editor)

**1980.** Journalists' Day.

| | | | | |
|---|---|---|---|---|
| 1677 | **649** | 500p. multicoloured | 1·00 | 25 |

**650** Part of Mural

**1980.** 400th Anniv of Buenos Aires. Sheet 249×103 mm containing T 650 and similar vert designs forming a composite design depicting the ceramic mural by Rodolfo Franco in Cathedral Underground Station.

**MS**1678 500p.×14 multicoloured 23·00 21·00

**651** Soldier feeding Dove

**1980.** Army Day.

| | | | | |
|---|---|---|---|---|
| 1679 | **651** | 500p. green, blk & gold | 1·50 | 45 |

**652** Lt. Gen. Aramburu

**1980.** 10th Death Anniv of Lt. Gen. Pedro Eugenio Aramburu.

| | | | | |
|---|---|---|---|---|
| 1680 | **652** | 500p. yellow and black | 1·00 | 35 |

**653** Gen. Juan Gregorio de Las Heras

**1980.** National Heroes.

| | | | | |
|---|---|---|---|---|
| 1681 | **653** | 500p. stone and black | 1·00 | 35 |
| 1682 | - | 500p. yellow, blk & pur | 1·00 | 35 |
| 1683 | - | 500p. mauve and black | 1·00 | 35 |

DESIGNS: No. 1682, Bernardino Rivadavia; 1683, Brigadier-General Jose Matias Zapiola.

**654** University of La Plata

**1980.** 75th Anniv of La Plata University.

| | | | | |
|---|---|---|---|---|
| 1684 | **654** | 500p. multicoloured | 1·00 | 30 |

**655** Major Francisco de Arteaga and Avro 504K

**1980.** Air Force Day.

| | | | | |
|---|---|---|---|---|
| 1685 | **655** | 500p. multicoloured | 1·10 | 30 |

**656** Flag and "Pencil" Figure

**1980.** National Census.

| | | | | |
|---|---|---|---|---|
| 1686 | **656** | 500p. black and blue | 2·00 | 30 |

**657** King Penguin

**1980.** 75th Anniv of Argentine Presence in South Orkneys and 150th Anniv of Political and Military Command for the Malvinas. Two sheets each 151×174 mm containing T 657 and similar vert designs. Multicoloured.

**MS**1687 Two sheets (a) 150p.×12 Centre two stamps depict South Orkneys Naval Station; (b) 500p.×12 Centre two stamps depict "Puerto Soledad 1829" by Luisa Vernet 44·00 41·00

**658** Congress Emblem

**1980.** National Marian Congress, Mendoza.
1688 **658** 700p. multicoloured 1·50 35

**659** Heart pierced by Cigarette

**1980.** Anti-smoking Campaign.
1689 **659** 700p. multicoloured 1·60 35

**660** Part of Mural

**1980.** Buenos Aires 80 International Stamp Exhibition. Sheet 251×105 mm containing T 660 and similar vert designs forming a composite design depicting the ceramic mural by Alfredo Guido in the 9th July Underground Station.
**MS**1690 500p.×14 multicoloured 20·00 19·00

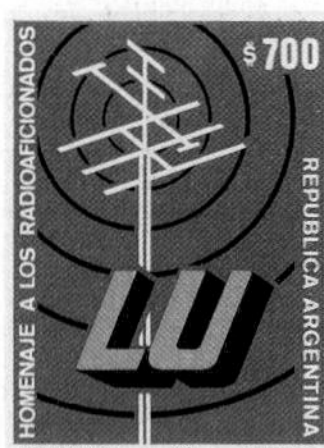


**661** Radio Antenna and Call Sign

**1980.** Radio Amateurs.
1691 **661** 700p. blue, black & green 1·40 35

**662** Academy Emblem

**1980.** 50th Anniv of Technical Military Academy.
1692 **662** 700p. multicoloured 1·40 35

**663** Commemorative Medallion

**1980.** Christmas. 150th Anniv of Appearance of Holy Virgin to St. Catherine Laboure.
1693 **663** 700p. multicoloured 1·40 35

**664** Plan of Lujan Cathedral and Outline of Virgin

**1980.** Christmas. 350th Anniv of Appearance of Holy Virgin at Lujan.
1694 **664** 700p. green and brown 1·40 35

**665** Simon Bolivar

**1980.** 150th Death Anniv of Simon Bolivar.
1695 **665** 700p. multicoloured 1·40 35

**666** Football and Flags of Competing Nations

**1981.** Gold Cup Football Competition, Montevideo.
1696 **666** 1000p. multicoloured 2·00 35

**667** "Lujan Landscape" (Marcos Tiglio)

**1981.** Paintings. Multicoloured.
1697 1000p. Type **667** 1·60 60
1698 1000p. "Effect of Light on Lines" (Miguel Angel Vidal) 1·60 60

**668** Congress Emblem

**1981.** International Congress on Medicine and Sciences applied to Sport.
1699 **668** 1000p. blue, brown & blk 1·40 35

**669** Esperanza Army Base, Antarctica

**1981.** 20th Anniv of Antarctic Treaty. Mult.
1700 1000p. Type **669** 2·50 70
1701 2000p. Map of Vicecomodoro Marambio Island and De Havilland Twin Otter airplane (59½×25 mm) 4·50 95
1702 2000p. Icebreaker "Almirante Irizar" 4·50 95

**670** Military Club

**1981.** Centenary of Military Club. Multicoloured.
1703 1000p. Type **670** 1·30 35
1704 2000p. Blunderbusses 1·50 45

**671** "Minuet" (Carlos E. Pellegrini)

**1981.** "Espamer '81" International Stamp Exhibition, Buenos Aires (1st issue).
1705 **671** 500p.+250p. purple, gold and brown 1·40 70
1706 - 700p.+350p. green, gold and brown 2·00 1·20
1707 - 800p.+400p. brown, gold and deep brown 2·10 1·50
1708 - 1000p.+500p. mult 2·75 2·10

DESIGNS: 700p. "La Media Cana" (Carlos Morel); 800p. "Cielito" (Carlos E. Pellegrini); 1000p. "El Gato" (Juan Leon Palliere).

See also Nos. 1719 and 1720/1.

**672** Juan A. Alvarez de Arenales

**1981.** Celebrities' Anniversaries.
1709 **672** 1000p. black, yell & brn 1·30 35
1710 - 1000p. blk, pink & lilac 1·30 35
1711 - 1000p. black, pale green and green 1·30 35

DESIGNS: No. 1709, Type **672** (patriot, 150th death anniv); 1710, Felix G. Frias (writer and politician, death centenary); 1711, Jose E. Uriburu (statesman, 150th birth centenary).

**1981.** 50th Anniv of Bahia Blanca Philatelic and Numismatic Society. No. 1553 optd 50 ANIV DE LA ASOCIACION FILATELICA Y NUMISMATICA DE BAHIA BLANCA.
1712 1000p. black and yellow 3·25 60

**674** World Map divided into Time Zones and Sun

**1981.** Centenary of Naval Observatory.
1713 **674** 1000p. multicoloured 1·90 45

**675** "St. Cayetano" (detail, stained-glass window, San Cayetano Basilica)

**1981.** 500th Death Anniv of St. Cayetano (founder of Teatino Order).
1714 **675** 1000p. multicoloured 1·30 35

**676** Pablo Castaibert and Bleriot XI

**1981.** Air Force Day.
1715 **676** 1000p. multicoloured 2·10 45

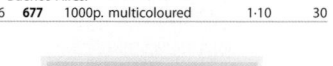

**677** First Argentine Blast Furnace, Sierra de Palpala

**1981.** 22nd Latin American Steel-makers Congress, Buenos Aires.
1716 **677** 1000p. multicoloured 1·10 30

**678** Emblem of National Directorate for Special Education

**1981.** International Year of Disabled People.
1717 **678** 1000p. multicoloured 1·30 30

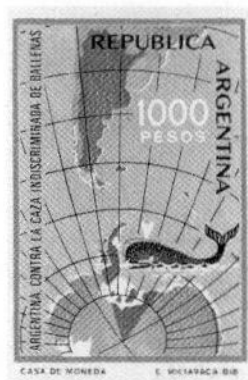


**679** Sperm Whale and Map of Argentina and Antarctica

**1981.** Campaign against Indiscriminate Whaling.
1718 **679** 1000p. multicoloured 9·25 60

**680** "Espamer 81" Emblem and 15th-century Caravel

**1981.** "Espamer 81" International Stamp Exhibition, Buenos Aires (2nd issue).
1719 **680** 1300p. pink, brn & blk 1·60 60

**681** "San Martin at the Battle of Bailen" (equestrian statuette)

**1981.** "Espamer 81" International Stamp Exhibition, Buenos Aires (3rd issue).
1720 **681** 1000p. multicoloured 65 30
1721 **681** 1500p. multicoloured 90 35

**682** Argentine Army Emblem

**1981.** Argentine Army. 175th Anniv of Infantry Regiment No. 1 "Patricios". Multicoloured.
1722 1500p. Type **682** 75 35
1723 1500p. "Patricios" badge 75 35

**1981.** Philatelic Services Course, Postal Union of the Americas and Spain Technical Training School, Buenos Aires. Optd CURSO SUPERIOR DE ORGANIZACION DE SERVICIOS FILATELICOS-UPAE-BUENOS AIRES-1981.

| | | | | |
|---|---|---|---|---|
| 1724 | **680** | 1300p. pink, brn & blk | 2·50 | 45 |

**684** Football

**1981.** Espamer 81 International Stamp Exhibition, Buenos Aires (4th issue). Sheet 137×130 mm containing T 684 and similar vert designs. Multicoloured.

| | | | |
|---|---|---|---|
| **MS**1725 2000p. Type **684**; 3000p. Tackle; 5000p. Dribbling; 15000p. Goalkeeper | | 12·50 | 12·00 |

**685** "Patacon" (one peso piece)

**1981.** Centenary of First Argentine Coins.

| | | | | |
|---|---|---|---|---|
| 1726 | **685** | 2000p. silver, blk & pur | 90 | 25 |
| 1727 | - | 3000p. gold, black & bl | 1·10 | 35 |

DESIGN: 3000p. Argentine oro (five pesos piece).

**686** Stained-glass Window, Church of Our Lady of Mercy, Tucuman

**1981.** Christmas.

| | | | | |
|---|---|---|---|---|
| 1728 | **686** | 1500p. multicoloured | 3·75 | 85 |

**687** "Drive Carefully"

**1981.** Road Safety. Multicoloured.

| | | | |
|---|---|---|---|
| 1729 | 1000p. "Observe traffic lights" | 2·50 | 60 |
| 1730 | 2000p. Type **687** | 1·30 | 70 |
| 1731 | 3000p. Zebra Crossing ("Cross at the white lines") (horiz) | 1·90 | 75 |
| 1732 | 4000p. Headlights ("Don't dazzle") (horiz) | 2·10 | 85 |

**688** Francisco Luis Bernardez

**1982.** Authors. Multicoloured.

| | | | | |
|---|---|---|---|---|
| 1733 | | 1000p. Type **688** | 2·50 | 60 |
| 1734 | | 2000p. Lucio V. Mansilla | 1·30 | 65 |
| 1735 | | 3000p. Conrado Nale Roxlo | 1·90 | 85 |
| 1736 | | 4000p. Victoria Ocampo | 2·50 | 95 |

**689** Emblem

**1982.** 22nd American Air Force Commanders Conference, Buenos Aires.

| | | | | |
|---|---|---|---|---|
| 1737 | **689** | 2000p. multicoloured | 2·00 | 45 |

**690** Dr. Robert Koch

**1982.** 25th World Tuberculosis Conf, Buenos Aires.

| | | | | |
|---|---|---|---|---|
| 1738 | **690** | 2000p. brown, red & blk | 1·90 | 45 |

**691** Pre-Columbian Artwork and Signature of Hernando de Lerma (founder)

**1982.** 400th Anniv of Salta City.

| | | | | |
|---|---|---|---|---|
| 1739 | **691** | 2000p. green, blk & gold | 2·50 | 45 |
| **MS**1740 89×60 mm. **691** 5000p. green, black and gold (39×26 mm) | | | 5·00 | 4·75 |

**1982.** Argentine Invasion of the Falkland Islands. Optd LAS MALVINAS SON ARGENTINAS.

| | | | | |
|---|---|---|---|---|
| 1741 | **619** | 1700p. blue and green | 1·00 | 35 |

**693** "Poseidon with Trophies of War" (sculpture) and Naval Centre Arms

**1982.** Centenary of Naval Centre.

| | | | | |
|---|---|---|---|---|
| 1742 | **693** | 2000p. multicoloured | 1·30 | 45 |

**694** "Chorisia speciosa"

**1982.** Flowers. Multicoloured.

| | | | |
|---|---|---|---|
| 1743 | 200p. "Zinnia peruviana" | 50 | 15 |
| 1744 | 300p. "Ipomoea purpurea" | 50 | 15 |
| 1745 | 400p. "Tillandsia aeranthos" | 50 | 15 |
| 1746 | 500p. Type **694** | 50 | 15 |
| 1747 | 800p. "Oncidium bifolium" | 50 | 15 |
| 1748 | 1000p. "Erythrina crista-galli" | 50 | 15 |
| 1749 | 2000p. "Jacaranda mimosifolia" | 55 | 15 |
| 1750 | 3000p. "Bauhinia candicans" | 1·00 | 35 |
| 1751 | 5000p. "Tecoma stans" | 1·00 | 35 |
| 1752 | 10000p. "Tabebuia ipe" | 1·80 | 35 |
| 1753 | 20000p. "Passiflora coerulea" | 1·90 | 35 |
| 1754 | 30000p. "Aristolochia littoralis" | 2·75 | 60 |
| 1755 | 50000p. "Oxalis enneaphylla" | 5·25 | 85 |

**695** Juan C. Sanchez

**1982.** 10th Death Anniv of Lt. Gen. Juan C. Sanchez.

| | | | | |
|---|---|---|---|---|
| 1761 | **695** | 5000p. multicoloured | 1·50 | 35 |

**696** Don Luis Verne (first Commander)

**1982.** 153rd Anniv of Political and Military Command for the Malvinas.

| | | | | |
|---|---|---|---|---|
| 1762 | **696** | 5000p. black and brown | 2·50 | 85 |
| 1763 | - | 5000p. light bl, blk & bl | 1·90 | 60 |

DESIGN (82×28 mm): No. 1763, Map of the South Atlantic Islands.

**697** Pope John Paul II

**1982.** Papal Visit.

| | | | | |
|---|---|---|---|---|
| 1764 | **697** | 5000p. multicoloured | 3·25 | 85 |

**698** San Martin

**1982**

| | | | | |
|---|---|---|---|---|
| 1765 | **698** | 50000p. brown and red | 12·00 | 1·40 |

**699** "The Organ Player" (detail, Aldo Severi)

**1982.** Paintings. Multicoloured.

| | | | |
|---|---|---|---|
| 1766 | 2000p. Type **699** | 1·30 | 40 |
| 1767 | 3000p. "Flowers" (Santiago Cogorno) | 1·40 | 45 |

**700** "Gen. de Sombras" (Sylvia Sieburger)

**1982.** "Argentine Philately". Tapestries. Mult.

| | | | |
|---|---|---|---|
| 1768 | 1000p.+500p. Type **700** | 75 | 60 |
| 1769 | 2000p.+1000p. "Inter-pretation of a Rectangle" (Silke Haupt) | 90 | 70 |
| 1770 | 3000p.+1500p. "Canal" (detail, Beatriz Bongliani) (horiz) | 1·00 | 85 |
| 1771 | 4000p.+2000p. "Pueblito de Tilcara" (Tana Sachs) (horiz) | 1·10 | 95 |

**701** Petrol Pump and Sugar Cane

**1982.** Alconafta (petrol-alcohol mixture) Campaign.

| | | | | |
|---|---|---|---|---|
| 1772 | **701** | 2000p. multicoloured | 1·40 | 35 |

**1982.** 50th Anniv of Tucuman Philatelic Society. No. 1751 optd 50 ANIVERSARIO SOCIEDAD FILATELICA DE TUCUMAN.

| | | | |
|---|---|---|---|
| 1773 | 5000p. multicoloured | 3·75 | 1·40 |

**703** Belt Buckle with Argentine Scout Emblem

**1982.** 75th Anniv of Boy Scout Movement.

| | | | | |
|---|---|---|---|---|
| 1774 | **703** | 5000p. multicoloured | 3·50 | 60 |

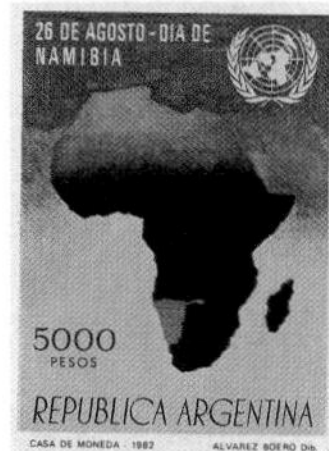


**704** Map of Africa showing Namibia

**1982.** Namibia Day.

| | | | | |
|---|---|---|---|---|
| 1775 | **704** | 5000p. multicoloured | 1·50 | 35 |

**705** Rio Tercero Nuclear Power Station

**1982.** Atomic Energy. Multicoloured.

| | | | |
|---|---|---|---|
| 1776 | 2000p. Type **705** | 65 | 15 |
| 1777 | 2000p. Control room of Rio Tercero power station | 65 | 15 |

**706** Our Lady of Itati, Corrientes

**1982.** Churches and Cathedrals of the North-east Provinces.

| | | | | |
|---|---|---|---|---|
| 1778 | **706** | 2000p. green and black | 90 | 55 |
| 1779 | - | 3000p. grey and purple | 1·00 | 60 |
| 1780 | - | 5000p. blue and purple | 1·60 | 65 |
| 1781 | - | 10000p. brown and black | 2·50 | 85 |

DESIGNS—VERT: 3000p. Resistencia Cathedral, Chaco. HORIZ: 5000p. Formosa Cathedral; 10000p. Ruins of San Ignacio, Misiones.

707 "Sidereal Tension" (M. A. Agatiello)

**1982.** Art. Multicoloured.

| | | | |
|---|---|---|---|
| 1782 | 2000p. Type **707** | 1·40 | 60 |
| 1783 | 3000p. "Sugerencia II" (E. MacEntyre) | 1·50 | 65 |
| 1784 | 5000p. "Storm" (Carlos Silva) | 2·10 | 70 |

708 Games Emblem and Santa Fe Bridge

**1982.** 2nd "Southern Cross" Games, Rosario and Santa Fe.

| | | | | |
|---|---|---|---|---|
| 1785 | **708** | 2000p. blue and black | 90 | 35 |

709 Volleyball

**1982.** 10th Men's Volleyball World Championship.

| | | | | |
|---|---|---|---|---|
| 1786 | **709** | 2000p. multicoloured | 50 | 25 |
| 1787 | **709** | 5000p. multicoloured | 1·00 | 35 |

710 Road Signs

**1982.** 50th Anniv of National Roads Administration.

| | | | | |
|---|---|---|---|---|
| 1788 | **710** | 5000p. multicoloured | 1·00 | 30 |

711 Monument to the Army of the Andes

**1982.** Centenary of "Los Andes" Newspaper.

| | | | | |
|---|---|---|---|---|
| 1789 | **711** | 5000p. multicoloured | 90 | 25 |

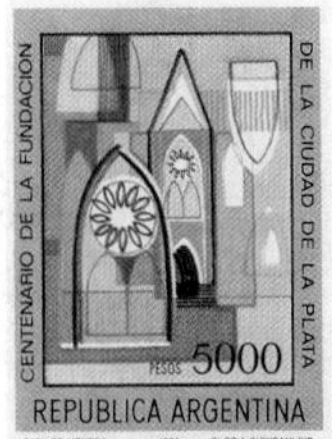
712 La Plata Cathedral

**1982.** Centenary of La Plata. Multicoloured.

| | | | |
|---|---|---|---|
| 1790 | 5000p. Type **712** | 1·40 | 35 |
| 1791 | 5000p. Municipal Palace | 1·40 | 35 |

**MS**1792 120×115 mm. 2500p.×6 (a) Cathedral; (b) Allegorical head (top); (c) Observatory; (d) Municipal Palace; (e) Allegorical head (bottom); (f) Natural Sciences Museum 4·00 3·75

713 First Oil Rig

**1982.** 75th Anniv of Discovery of Oil in Comodoro Rivadavia.

| | | | | |
|---|---|---|---|---|
| 1793 | **713** | 5000p. multicoloured | 1·90 | 35 |

714 Dr. Carlos Pellegrini (founder) (after J. Sorolla y Bastida)

**1982.** Cent of Buenos Aires Jockey Club. Mult.

| | | | |
|---|---|---|---|
| 1794 | 5000p. Jockey Club emblem | 1·50 | 35 |
| 1795 | 5000p. Type **714** | 1·50 | 35 |

715 Cross of St. Damian, Assisi

**1982.** 800th Birth Anniv of St. Francis of Assisi.

| | | | | |
|---|---|---|---|---|
| 1796 | **715** | 5000p. multicoloured | 2·10 | 35 |

716 "St. Vincent de Paul" (stained-glass window, Our Lady of the Miraculous Medal, Buenos Aires)

**1982.** Christmas.

| | | | | |
|---|---|---|---|---|
| 1797 | **716** | 3000p. multicoloured | 3·25 | 60 |

717 Pedro B. Palacios

**1982.** Authors. Each red and green.

| | | | |
|---|---|---|---|
| 1798 | 1000p. Type **717** | 40 | 10 |
| 1799 | 2000p. Leopoldo Marechal | 50 | 15 |
| 1800 | 3000p. Delfina Bunge de Galvez | 65 | 20 |
| 1801 | 4000p. Manuel Galvez | 75 | 25 |
| 1802 | 5000p. Evaristo Carriego | 90 | 30 |

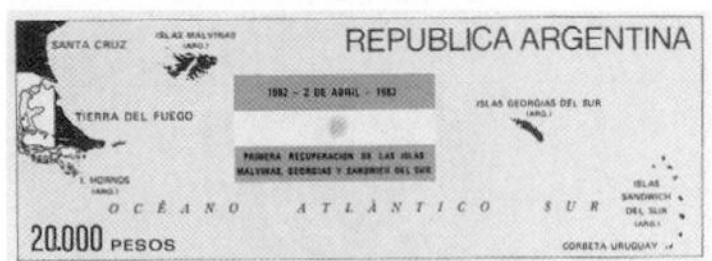
718 Argentine Flag and Map of South Atlantic Islands (image scaled to 58% of original size)

**1983.** 1st Anniv of Argentine Invasion of Falkland Islands.

| | | | | |
|---|---|---|---|---|
| 1803 | **718** | 20000p. multicoloured | 2·50 | 85 |

719 Sitram (automatic message transmission service) Emblem

**1983.** Information Technology. Multicoloured.

| | | | |
|---|---|---|---|
| 1804 | 5000p. Type **719** | 2·00 | 95 |
| 1805 | 5000p. Red Arpac (data communications system) emblem | 2·00 | 95 |

720 Naval League Emblem

**1983.** Navy Day. 50th Anniv of Naval League.

| | | | | |
|---|---|---|---|---|
| 1806 | **720** | 5000p. multicoloured | 1·00 | 35 |

721 Allegorical Figure (Victor Rebuffo)

**1983.** 25th Anniv of National Arts Fund.

| | | | | |
|---|---|---|---|---|
| 1807 | **721** | 5000p. multicoloured | 75 | 25 |

722 Golden Saloon

**1983.** 75th Anniv of Columbus Theatre, Buenos Aires. Multicoloured.

| | | | |
|---|---|---|---|
| 1808 | 5000p. Type **722** | 1·10 | 60 |
| 1809 | 10000p. Stage curtain | 1·60 | 70 |

723 Marbles

**1983.** Argentine Philately. Children's Games (1st series). Multicoloured.

| | | | |
|---|---|---|---|
| 1810 | 20c.+10c. Type **723** | 50 | 30 |
| 1811 | 30c.+15c. Skipping | 65 | 35 |
| 1812 | 50c.+25c. Hopscotch | 1·40 | 45 |
| 1813 | 1p.+50c. Boy with kite | 1·80 | 70 |
| 1814 | 2p.+1p. Boy with spinning top | 2·50 | 95 |

See also Nos. 1870/4.

724 Maned Wolf

**1983.** Protected Animals (1st series). Mult.

| | | | |
|---|---|---|---|
| 1815 | 1p. Type **724** | 1·60 | 35 |
| 1816 | 1p.50 Pampas deer | 2·40 | 45 |
| 1817 | 2p. Giant anteater | 2·50 | 60 |
| 1818 | 2p.50 Jaguar | 3·00 | 70 |

See also Nos 1883/87.

**1983.** Flowers. As T 694 but inscr in new currency. Multicoloured.

| | | | |
|---|---|---|---|
| 1819 | 5c. Type **694** | 75 | 20 |
| 1820 | 10c. "Erythrina crista-galli" | 25 | 10 |
| 1821 | 20c. "Jacaranda mimosifolia" | 25 | 10 |
| 1822 | 30c. "Bauhinia candicans" | 65 | 20 |
| 1823 | 40c. "Eichhornia crassipes" | 40 | 10 |
| 1824 | 50c. "Tecoma stans" | 25 | 10 |
| 1825 | 1p. "Tabebuia ipe" | 50 | 10 |
| 1826 | 1p.80 "Mutisia retusa" | 40 | 10 |
| 1827 | 2p. "Passiflora coerulea" | 50 | 10 |
| 1828 | 3p. "Aristolochia littoralis" | 65 | 10 |
| 1829 | 5p. "Oxalis enneaphylla" | 90 | 15 |
| 1830 | 10p. "Alstroemeria aurantiaca" | 1·50 | 25 |
| 1831 | 20p. "Ipomoea purpurea" | 65 | 10 |
| 1832 | 30p. "Embothrium coccineum" | 3·25 | 25 |
| 1833 | 50p. "Tillandsia aeranthos" | 90 | 25 |
| 1834 | 100p. "Oncidium bifolium" | 2·50 | 25 |
| 1835 | 300p. "Cassia carnaval" | 2·75 | 70 |

725 "Founding of City of Catamarca" (detail, Luis Varela Lezana)

**1983.** 300th Anniv of San Fernando del Valle de Catamarca.

| | | | | |
|---|---|---|---|---|
| 1836 | **725** | 1p. multicoloured | 65 | 30 |

726 Brother Mamerto Esquiu

**1983.** Death Centenary of Brother Mamerto Esquiu, Bishop of Cordoba.

| | | | | |
|---|---|---|---|---|
| 1837 | **726** | 1p. black, red and grey | 65 | 30 |

727 Bolivar (painting by Herrera Toro after engraving by C. Turner)

**1983.** Birth Bicentenary of Simon Bolivar.

| | | | | |
|---|---|---|---|---|
| 1838 | **727** | 1p. multicoloured | 65 | 30 |
| 1839 | - | 2p. red and black | 1·00 | 45 |

DESIGN: 2p. Bolivar (engraving by Kepper).

728 San Martin

1983

| | | | | |
|---|---|---|---|---|
| 1840 | 728 | 10p. green and black | 4·50 | 60 |
| 1841 | - | 20p. blue and black | 4·00 | 2·40 |
| 1842 | 728 | 50p. brown and blue | 3·50 | 2·50 |
| 1843 | - | 200p. black and blue | 3·25 | 1·80 |
| 1844 | - | 500p. blue and brown | 3·50 | 85 |

DESIGNS: 20, 500p. Guillermo Brown; 200p. Manuel Belgrano.

729 Gen. Toribio de Luzuriaga

**1983.** Birth Bicentenary (1982) of Gen. Toribio de Luzuriaga.

| | | | | |
|---|---|---|---|---|
| 1845 | 729 | 1p. multicoloured | 90 | 35 |

730 Grand Bourg House, Buenos Aires

**1983.** 50th Anniv of Sanmartinian National Institute.

| | | | | |
|---|---|---|---|---|
| 1846 | 730 | 2p. brown and black | 1·00 | 35 |

731 Dove and Rotary Emblem

**1983.** Rotary International South American Regional Conference, Buenos Aires.

| | | | | |
|---|---|---|---|---|
| 1847 | 731 | 1p. multicoloured | 1·00 | 35 |

732 Running Track and Games Emblem

**1983.** 9th Pan-American Games, Venezuela.

| | | | | |
|---|---|---|---|---|
| 1848 | 732 | 1p. red, green & black | 75 | 25 |
| 1849 | - | 2p. multicoloured | 1·00 | 35 |

DESIGN: 2p. Games emblem.

733 W.C.Y. Emblem

**1983.** World Communications Year (1st issue).

| | | | | |
|---|---|---|---|---|
| 1850 | 733 | 2p. multicoloured | 1·00 | 35 |

See also Nos. 1853/6 and 1857.

734 "The Squash Peddler" (Antonio Berni)

**1983.** Argentine Paintings. Multicoloured.

| | | | |
|---|---|---|---|
| 1851 | 1p. Type **734** | 75 | 25 |
| 1852 | 2p. "Figure in Yellow" (Luis Seoane) | 1·00 | 35 |

735 Ox-drawn Wagon

**1983.** World Communications Year (2nd issue). Mail Transport. Multicoloured.

| | | | |
|---|---|---|---|
| 1853 | 1p. Type **735** | 90 | 45 |
| 1854 | 2p. Horse-drawn mail cart | 1·00 | 60 |
| 1855 | 4p. Locomotive "La Portena" | 1·50 | 65 |
| 1856 | 5p. Tram | 1·60 | 70 |

736 "Central Post Office, Buenos Aires" (Lola Frexas)

**1983.** World Communications Year (3rd issue).

| | | | | |
|---|---|---|---|---|
| 1857 | 736 | 2p. multicoloured | 65 | 30 |

737 Rockhopper Penguin

**1983.** Fauna and Pioneers of Southern Argentina. Multicoloured.

| | | | |
|---|---|---|---|
| 1858a | 2p. Type **737** | 65 | 35 |
| 1858b | 2p. Wandering albatross | 65 | 35 |
| 1858c | 2p. Black-browed albatross | 65 | 35 |
| 1858d | 2p. Macaroni penguin | 65 | 35 |
| 1858e | 2p. Luis Piedra Buena (after Juan R. Mezzadra) | 65 | 35 |
| 1858f | 2p. Carlos Maria Moyano (after Mezzadra) | 65 | 35 |
| 1858g | 2p. Luis Py (after Mezzadra) | 65 | 35 |
| 1858h | 2p. Augusto Lasserre (after Horacio Alvarez Boero) | 65 | 35 |
| 1858i | 2p. Light-mantled sooty albatross | 65 | 35 |
| 1858j | 2p. Leopard seal | 65 | 35 |
| 1858k | 2p. Crabeater seal | 65 | 35 |
| 1858l | 2p. Weddell seal | 65 | 35 |

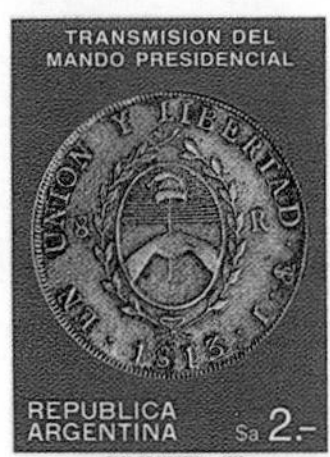

738 Coin of 1813

**1983.** Transfer of Presidency.

| | | | | |
|---|---|---|---|---|
| 1859 | 738 | 2p. silver, black and blue | 1·00 | 20 |

739 "Christmas Manger" (tapestry by Silke)

**1983.** Christmas. Multicoloured.

| | | | |
|---|---|---|---|
| 1860 | 2p. Type **739** | 95 | 20 |
| 1861 | 3p. Stained-glass window, San Carlos de Bariloche Church | 1·50 | 45 |

740 Printing Cylinder and Newspaper

**1984.** Centenary of "El Dia" Newspaper.

| | | | | |
|---|---|---|---|---|
| 1862 | 740 | 4p. multicoloured | 75 | 20 |

741 Compass Rose

**1984.** "Espana 84" (Madrid) and "Argentina 85" (Buenos Aires) International Stamp Exhibitions (1st issue). Multicoloured.

| | | | |
|---|---|---|---|
| 1863 | 5p.+2p.50 Type **741** | 1·30 | 45 |
| 1864 | 5p.+2p.50 Arms of Spain and Argentine Republic | 1·30 | 45 |
| 1865 | 5p.+2p.50 Arms of Christopher Columbus | 1·30 | 45 |
| 1866 | 5p.+2p.50 "Nina" | 1·30 | 45 |
| 1867 | 5p.+2p.50 "Pinta" | 1·30 | 45 |
| 1868 | 5p.+2p.50 "Santa Maria" | 1·30 | 45 |

See also Nos. 1906/10, 1917/18 and 1920/4.

742 College

**1984.** Centenary of Alejandro Carbo Teacher Training College, Cordoba.

| | | | | |
|---|---|---|---|---|
| 1869 | 742 | 10p. multicoloured | 75 | 30 |

**1984.** Argentine Philately. Children's Games (2nd series). As T 723. Multicoloured.

| | | | |
|---|---|---|---|
| 1870 | 2p.+1p. Blind man's buff | 65 | 35 |
| 1871 | 3p.+1p.50 Girls throwing hoop | 70 | 40 |
| 1872 | 4p.+2p. Leap frog | 75 | 55 |
| 1873 | 5p.+2p.50 Boy rolling hoop | 90 | 60 |
| 1874 | 6p.+3p. Ball and stick | 1·10 | 85 |

743 Rowing and Basketball

**1984.** Olympic Games, Los Angeles. Mult.

| | | | |
|---|---|---|---|
| 1875 | 5p. Type **743** | 50 | 35 |
| 1876 | 5p. Weightlifting and discus | 50 | 35 |
| 1877 | 10p. Cycling and swimming | 90 | 45 |
| 1878 | 10p. Pole vault and fencing | 90 | 45 |

744 Wheat

**1984.** Food Supplies. Multicoloured.

| | | | |
|---|---|---|---|
| 1879 | 10p. Type **744** (18th F.A.O. Latin American Regional Conference, Buenos Aires) | 1·00 | 45 |
| 1880 | 10p. Sunflowers (World Food Day) | 1·00 | 45 |
| 1881 | 10p. Maize (3rd National Maize Congress, Pergamino) | 1·00 | 45 |

745 Stock Exchange

**1984.** Centenary of Rosario Stock Exchange.

| | | | | |
|---|---|---|---|---|
| 1882 | 745 | 10p. multicoloured | 90 | 45 |

**1984.** Protected Animals (2nd series). As T 724. Multicoloured.

| | | | |
|---|---|---|---|
| 1883 | 20p. Brazilian merganser | 1·60 | 45 |
| 1884 | 20p. Black-fronted piping guan | 1·60 | 45 |
| 1885 | 20p. Hooded grebes | 1·60 | 45 |
| 1886 | 20p. Vicunas | 1·60 | 45 |
| 1887 | 20p. Chilean guemal | 1·60 | 45 |

746 Festival Emblem

**1984.** 1st Latin American Theatre Festival, Cordoba.

| | | | | |
|---|---|---|---|---|
| 1888 | 746 | 20p. multicoloured | 65 | 35 |

747 "Apostles' Communion" (detail, Fra Angelico)

**1984.** 50th Anniv of Buenos Aires International Eucharist Congress.

| | | | | |
|---|---|---|---|---|
| 1889 | 747 | 20p. multicoloured | 75 | 45 |

748 Antonio Oneto and Railway Station (Puerto Deseado)

**1984.** City Centenaries. Multicoloured.

| | | | |
|---|---|---|---|
| 1890 | 20p. Type **748** | 1·30 | 45 |
| 1891 | 20p. 19th-century view and sail/steam corvette "Parana" (Ushuaia) | 1·30 | 45 |

749 Glacier

**1984.** World Heritage Site. Los Glaciares National Park. Multicoloured.

| | | | |
|---|---|---|---|
| 1892 | 20p. Glacier (different) | 1·10 | 35 |
| 1893 | 30p. Type **749** | 1·90 | 45 |

**1984.** 50th Anniv of Buenos Aires Philatelic Centre. No. 1830 optd 1934–50°ANIVERSARIO-1984 CENTRO FILATELICO BUENOS-AIRES.

| | | | |
|---|---|---|---|
| 1894 | 10p. multicoloured | 75 | 55 |

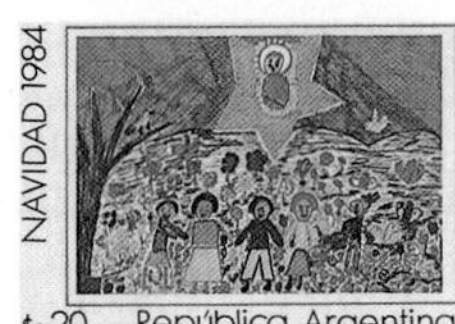

**751** "Jesus and the Star" (Diego Aguero)

**1984.** Christmas. Multicoloured.

| | | | |
|---|---|---|---|
| 1895 | 20p. Type **751** | 1·00 | 40 |
| 1896 | 30p. "The Three Kings" (Leandro Ruiz) | 1·30 | 45 |
| 1897 | 50p. "The Holy Family" (Maria Castillo) (vert) | 1·40 | 55 |

**752** "Sheds (La Boca)" (Marcos Borio)

**1984.** Argentine Paintings. Multicoloured.

| | | | |
|---|---|---|---|
| 1898 | 20p. Type **752** | 90 | 40 |
| 1899 | 20p. "View of the Zoo" (Fermin Eguia) (horiz) | 90 | 40 |
| 1900 | 20p. "Floodlit Congress Building" (Francisco Travieso) | 90 | 40 |

**753** Angel J. Carranza (historian, 150th)

**1985.** Birth Anniversaries.

| | | | | |
|---|---|---|---|---|
| 1901 | **753** | 10p. deep blue & blue | 75 | 35 |
| 1902 | - | 20p. deep brown & brn | 90 | 45 |
| 1903 | - | 30p. deep blue & blue | 1·00 | 60 |
| 1904 | - | 40p. black and green | 1·60 | 65 |

DESIGNS: 20p. Estanislao del Campo (poet, 150th); 30p. Jose Hernandez (journalist, 150th); 40p. Vicente Lopez y Planes (President of Argentine Confederation 1827–28, birth bicent).

**754** Guemes and "Infernal" (soldier)

**1985.** Birth Bicentenary of General Martin Miguel de Guemes (Independence hero).

| | | | | |
|---|---|---|---|---|
| 1905 | **754** | 30p. multicoloured | 50 | 30 |

**755** Teodoro Fels's Bleriot XI Gnome

**1985.** "Argentina '85" International Stamp Exhibition. Buenos Aires (2nd issue). First Airmail Flights. Multicoloured.

| | | | |
|---|---|---|---|
| 1906 | 20p. Type **755** (Buenos Aires–Montevideo, 1917) | 40 | 20 |
| 1907 | 40p. Junkers F-13L (Cordoba–Villa Dolores, 1925) | 65 | 35 |
| 1908 | 60p. Saint-Exupery's Latecoere 25 (first Bahia Blanca-Comodoro Rivadavia, 1929) | 1·00 | 40 |
| 1909 | 80p. "Graf Zeppelin" airship (Argentina-Germany, 1934) | 1·30 | 60 |
| 1910 | 100p. Consolidated PBY-5A Catalina amphibian (to Argentine Antarctic, 1952) | 1·80 | 70 |

**756** Central Bank

**1985.** 50th Anniv of Central Bank, Buenos Aires.

| | | | | |
|---|---|---|---|---|
| 1911 | **756** | 80p. multicoloured | 1·10 | 35 |

**757** Jose A. Ferreyra and "Munequitas Portenas"

**1985.** Argentine Film Directors. Multicoloured.

| | | | |
|---|---|---|---|
| 1912 | 100p. Type **757** | 1·30 | 60 |
| 1913 | 100p. Leopoldo Torre Nilsson and "Martin Fierro" | 1·30 | 60 |

**758** "Carlos Gardel" (Hermenegildo Sabat)

**1985.** 50th Death Anniv of Carlos Gardel (entertainer). Multicoloured.

| | | | |
|---|---|---|---|
| 1914 | 200p. Type **758** | 2·50 | 70 |
| 1915 | 200p. "Carlos Gardel" (Carlos Alonso) | 2·50 | 70 |
| 1916 | 200p. "Carlos Gardel" (Aldo Severi and Martiniano Arce) | 2·50 | 70 |

**759** "The Arrival" (Pedro Figari)

**1985.** "Argentina '85" International Stamp Exhibition (3rd issue). Multicoloured.

| | | | |
|---|---|---|---|
| 1917 | 20c. Type **759** | 1·50 | 60 |
| 1918 | 30c. "Mail Coach Square" (detail, Cesareo B. de Quiros) | 1·80 | 65 |
| **MS**1919 | 146×74 mm. 20c. (29×39 mm), 30c. (39×29 mm) Details of "Halt in the Country" (Prilidiano Pueyrredon) | 6·25 | 6·00 |

**760** Cover of 1917 Teodoro Fels Flight

**1985.** "Argentina '85" International Stamp Exhibition (4th issue). Multicoloured.

| | | | |
|---|---|---|---|
| 1920 | 10c. Type **760** | 75 | 35 |
| 1921 | 10c. Cover of 1925 Cordoba–Villa Dolores flight | 75 | 35 |
| 1922 | 10c. Cover of 1929 Saint-Exupery flight | 75 | 35 |
| 1923 | 10c. Cover of 1934 "Graf Zeppelin" flight | 75 | 35 |
| 1924 | 10c. Cover of 1952 Antarctic flight | 75 | 35 |

**1985.** Flowers. As T **694** but with currency expressed as "A". Multicoloured.

| | | | |
|---|---|---|---|
| 1930 | ½c. "Oxalis enneaphylla" | 90 | 15 |
| 1931 | 1c. "Alstroemeria aurantiaca" | 50 | 10 |
| 1932 | 2c. "Ipomoea purpurea" | 50 | 10 |
| 1933 | 3c. "Embothrium coccineum" | 50 | 10 |
| 1934a | 5c. "Tillandsia aeranthos" | 50 | 10 |
| 1927 | 8½c. "Erythrina crista-galli" | 50 | 10 |
| 1935a | 10c. "Oncidium bifolium" | 90 | 15 |
| 1936a | 20c. "Chorisia speciosa" | 65 | 35 |
| 1937 | 30c. "Cassia carnaval" | 1·50 | 60 |
| 1938 | 50c. "Zinnia peruviana" | 1·90 | 45 |
| 1941 | 1a. "Begonia micranthera var. Hieronymi" | 2·50 | 45 |
| 1941a | 2a. "Bauhinia candicans" | 1·00 | 30 |
| 1942 | 5a. "Gymnocalyciun bruchii" | 6·25 | 4·25 |
| 1942a | 10a. "Eichhornia crassipes" | 50 | 30 |
| 1942b | 20a. "Mutisia retusa" | 15 | 10 |
| 1942c | 50a. Passion flower | 50 | 30 |
| 1943 | 100a. "Alstroemeria aurantiaca" | 65 | 20 |
| 1943a | 300a. "Ipomoea purpurea" | 2·00 | 95 |
| 1943b | 500a. "Embothrium coccineum" | 3·25 | 1·50 |
| 1943c | 1000a. "Aristolochia littoralis" | 1·00 | 60 |
| 1943d | 5000a. "Erythrina crista-galli" | 4·75 | 65 |
| 1943e | 10000a. "Jacaranda mimosifolia" | 7·50 | 4·75 |

No. 1927 is 15×23 mm, the remainder 22×32 mm.

**761** "Woman with Bird" (Juan del Prete)

**1985.** Argentine Paintings. Multicoloured.

| | | | |
|---|---|---|---|
| 1944 | 20c. Type **761** | 1·50 | 60 |
| 1945 | 30c. "Illuminated Fruits" (Fortunato Lacamera) | 1·80 | 70 |

**762** Musical Bow

**1985.** Traditional Musical Instruments. Mult.

| | | | |
|---|---|---|---|
| 1946 | 20c. Type **762** | 1·00 | 40 |
| 1947 | 20c. Long flute with drum accompaniment | 1·00 | 40 |
| 1948 | 20c. Frame drum | 1·00 | 40 |
| 1949 | 20c. Pan's flute | 1·00 | 40 |
| 1950 | 20c. Jew's harp | 1·00 | 40 |

**763** Juan Bautista Alberdi (writer)

**1985.** Anniversaries.

| | | | |
|---|---|---|---|
| 1951 | 10c. Type **763** (death centenary (1984)) | 40 | 20 |
| 1952 | 20c. Nicolas Avellaneda (President 1874–80, death centenary) | 75 | 35 |
| 1953 | 30c. Brother Luis Beltran (Independence hero, birth bicentenary (1984)) | 1·10 | 60 |
| 1954 | 40c. Ricardo Levene (historian) (birth centenary) | 2·00 | 70 |

**764** Roller Skaters

**1985.** International Youth Year.

| | | | | |
|---|---|---|---|---|
| 1955 | **764** | 20c. black and blue | 1·00 | 40 |
| 1956 | - | 30c. multicoloured | 1·10 | 45 |
| **MS**1957 | | 146×74 mm. 1a. multicoloured. Imperf | 6·25 | 6·00 |

DESIGNS: 30c. "Disappointment". 137×66 mm "Halt in the Country" (Prilidiano Pueyrredon).

**765** "Rothschildia jacobaeae"

**1985.** Argentine Philately. Butterflies.

| | | | |
|---|---|---|---|
| 1958 | 5c.+2c. Type **765** | 1·40 | 45 |
| 1959 | 10c.+5c. "Heliconius erato phyllis" | 1·50 | 60 |
| 1960 | 20c.+10c. "Precis evarete hilaris" | 2·10 | 1·10 |
| 1961 | 25c.+13c. "Cyanopepla pretiosa" | 3·25 | 1·80 |
| 1962 | 40c.+20c. "Papilio androgeus" | 4·25 | 2·50 |

**766** Forclaz Windmill (Entre Rios)

**1985.** Tourism. Argentine Provinces. Mult.

| | | | |
|---|---|---|---|
| 1963 | 10c. Type **766** | 75 | 20 |
| 1964 | 10c. Sierra de la Ventana (Buenos Aires) | 75 | 20 |
| 1965 | 10c. Potrero de los Funes artificial lake (San Luis) | 75 | 20 |
| 1966 | 10c. Church belfry (North-west Argentina) | 75 | 20 |
| 1967 | 10c. Magellanic penguins, Punta Tombo (Chubut) | 75 | 20 |
| 1968 | 10c. Sea of Mirrors (Cordoba) | 75 | 20 |

**767** Hand holding White Stick

**1985.** National Campaign for the Prevention of Blindness.

| | | | | |
|---|---|---|---|---|
| 1969 | **767** | 10c. multicoloured | 65 | 20 |

**768** "Birth of Our Lord" (Carlos Cortes)

**1985.** Christmas. Multicoloured.

| | | | |
|---|---|---|---|
| 1970 | 10c. Type **768** | 65 | 25 |
| 1971 | 20c. "Christmas" (Hector Viola) | 1·40 | 70 |

**769** Rio Gallegos Cathedral

**1985.** Centenary of Rio Gallegos.

| | | | | |
|---|---|---|---|---|
| 1972 | **769** | 10c. multicoloured | 2·50 | 60 |

**770** Grape Harvesting

**1986.** 50th Anniv of Grape Harvest Nat Festival.
1973 **770** 10c. multicoloured 75 15

**771** House of Valentin Alsina (Italian Period)

**1986.** Buenos Aires Architecture, 1880–1930. Mult.
1974 20c. Type **771** 1·00 45
1975 20c. 1441 Calle Cerrito (French period) 1·00 45
1976 20c. Customs House (Academic period) (horiz) 1·00 45
1977 20c. House, Avenido de Mayo (Art Nouveau) 1·00 45
1978 20c. Isaac Fernandez Blanco Museum (National Restoration period) (horiz) 1·00 45

**772** Jubany Base

**1986.** Argentine Antarctic Research. Mult.
1979 10c. Type **772** 1·50 1·00
1980 10c. Kerguelen fur seal 1·50 1·00
1981 10c. Southern sealion 1·50 1·00
1982 10c. General Belgrano Base 1·50 1·00
1983 10c. Pintado petrel 1·50 1·00
1984 10c. Black-browed albatross 1·50 1·00
1985 10c. King penguin 1·50 1·00
1986 10c. Giant petrel 1·50 1·00
1987 10c. Hugo Alberto Acuna (explorer) 1·50 1·00
1988 10c. Magellanic penguin 1·50 1·00
1989 10c. Magellan snipe 1·50 1·00
1990 10c. Capt. Augustin Servando del Castillo (explorer) 1·50 1·00

**773** "Foundation of Nereid" (detail, Lola Mora)

**1986.** Sculpture. Multicoloured.
1991 20c. Type **773** 1·40 45
1992 30c. "Work Song" (detail, Rogelio Yrurtia) 1·50 55

**774** Dr. Alicia Moreau de Justo (suffragist, d. 1986)

**1986.** Anniversaries.
1993 **774** 10c. black, yellow & brn 75 35
1994 - 10c. black, turq & blue 75 35
1995 - 30c. black, red & mauve 2·30 1·10
DESIGNS: No. 1994, Dr. Emilio Ravignani (historian, birth centenary); 1995, Indira Gandhi (Prime Minister of India, 1st death anniv).

**775** Dr. Francisco Narciso Laprida

**1986.** Birth Bicentenaries of Independence Heroes. Each brown, yellow and black.
1996 20c. Type **775** 90 45
1997 20c. Brig. Gen. Estanislao Lopez 90 45
1998 20c. Gen. Francisco Ramirez 90 45

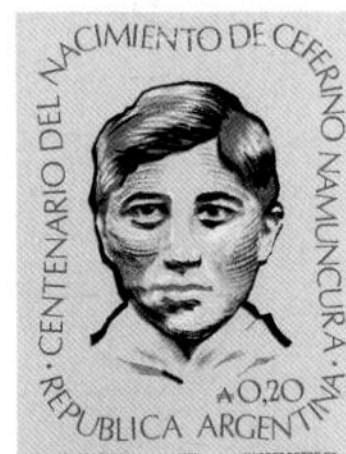

**776** Namuncura

**1986.** Birth Centenary of Ceferino Namuncura (first Indian seminary student).
1999 **776** 20c. multicoloured 1·00 60

**777** Drawing by Nazarena Pastor

**1986.** Argentine Philately. Children's Drawings. Multicoloured.
2000 5c.+2c. Type **777** 40 20
2001 10c.+5c. Girl and boy holding flowers and balloon (Tatiana Valleistein) (horiz) 65 30
2002 20c.+10c. Boy and girl (Juan Manel Flores) 1·00 95
2003 25c.+13c. Town and waterfront (Marcelo E. Pezzuto) (horiz) 1·40 1·20
2004 40c.+20c. Village (Esteban Diehl) (horiz) 2·00 1·80

**1986.** No. 1825 surch A0,10.
2005 10c. on 1p. "Tabebuia ipe" 1·90 85

**779** Argentine Team (value top left)

**1986.** Argentina, World Cup Football Championship (Mexico) Winners. Multicoloured.
2006 75c. Type **779** 2·10 1·80
2007 75c. Argentine team (value top right) 2·10 1·80
2008 75c. Argentine team (value bottom left) 2·10 1·80
2009 75c. Argentine team (value bottom right) 2·10 1·80
2010 75c. Player shooting for goal 2·10 1·80
2011 75c. Player tackling and goal-keeper on ground 2·10 1·80
2012 75c. Player number 11 2·10 1·80
2013 75c. Player number 7 2·10 1·80
2014 75c. Crowd and Argentina player 2·10 1·80
2015 75c. West German player 2·10 1·80
2016 75c. Goalkeeper on ground 2·10 1·80
2017 75c. Footballers' legs 2·10 1·80
2018 75c. Hand holding World Cup trophy 2·10 1·80
2019 75c. Raised arm and crowded stadium 2·10 1·80
2020 75c. People with flags and cameras 2·10 1·80
2021 75c. Player's body and crowd 2·10 1·80

Nos. 2006/13 were printed together se-tenant in a sheetlet of eight stamps arranged in two blocks, each block forming a composite design. Nos. 2014/21 were similarly arranged in a second sheetlet.

**780** Municipal Building

**1986.** Centenary of San Francisco City.
2022 **780** 20c. multicoloured 90 55

**781** Old Railway Station

**1986.** Centenary of Trelew City.
2023 **781** 20c. multicoloured 90 55

**782** Emblem and Colours

**1986.** Mutualism Day.
2024 **782** 20c. multicoloured 90 55

**783** "Primitive Retable" (Aniko Szabo)

**1986.** Christmas. Multicoloured.
2025 20c. Type **783** 1·60 60
2026 30c. "Everybody's Tree" (Franca Delacqua) 1·90 70

**784** St. Rosa of Lima

**1986.** 400th Birth Anniv of St. Rosa de Lima.
2027 **784** 50c. multicoloured 2·50 1·20

**785** Municipal Building

**1986.** Anniversaries. Multicoloured.
2028 20c. Type **785** (bicentenary of Rio Cuarto city) 1·50 45
2029 20c. Palace of Justice, Cordoba (50th anniv) 1·50 45

**786** Marine Biology

**1987.** 25th Anniv of Antarctic Treaty. Mult.
2030 20c. Type **786** 1·50 60
2031 30c. Study of native birds 2·10 70
**MS**2032 159×89 mm. As Nos. 2030/1 but each 39×49 mm 9·50 8·75

**787** Emblem

**1987.** Centenary of National Mortgage Bank.
2033 **787** 20c. yellow, brown & blk 1·30 70

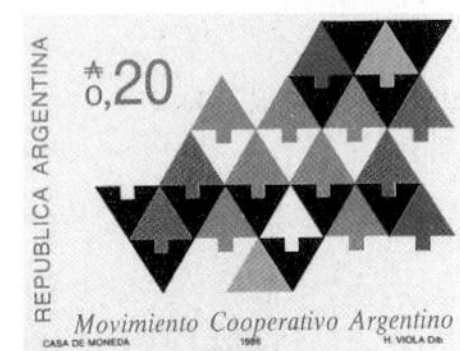

**788** Stylized Pine Trees

**1987.** Argentine Co-operative Movement.
2034 **788** 20c. multicoloured 1·30 70

**789** Pope

**1987.** 2nd Visit of Pope John Paul II.
2035 **789** 20c. blue and red 65 35
2036 - 80c. brown and green 2·50 1·20
**MS**2037 160×90 mm. 1a. multicoloured (34×45 mm) 4·50 4·25
DESIGNS: 80c. Pope in robes with Crucifix; 1a. Pope and children.

**790** Flag forming "PAZ" (peace)

**1987.** International Peace Year.
2038 **790** 20c. blue, dp blue & blk 1·10 35
2039 - 30c. multicoloured 1·20 45
DESIGN: 30c. "Pigeon" (sculpture, Victor Kaniuka).

**791** "Polo Players" (Alejandro Moy)

**1987.** World Polo Championships, Palermo.
2040 **791** 20c. multicoloured 1·50 35

**792** "Supplicant" (Museum of Natural Sciences, La Plata)

**1987.** 14th International Museums Council General Conference, Buenos Aires. Multicoloured.

| | | | |
|---|---|---|---|
| 2041 | 25c. Conference emblem | 75 | 35 |
| 2042 | 25c. Shield of Potosi (National History Museum, Buenos Aires) | 75 | 35 |
| 2043 | 25c. Statue of St. Bartholomew (Enrique Larreta Spanish Art Museum, Buenos Aires) | 75 | 35 |
| 2044 | 25c. Cudgel with animal design (Patagonia Museum, San Carlos de Bariloche) | 75 | 35 |
| 2045 | 25c. Type **792** | 75 | 35 |
| 2046 | 25c. Grate from Argentine Confederation House (Entre Rios Historical Museum, Parana) | 75 | 35 |
| 2047 | 25c. Statue of St. Joseph (Northern Historical Museum, Salta) | 75 | 35 |
| 2048 | 25c. Funeral urn (Provincial Archaeological Museum, Santiago del Estero) | 75 | 35 |

**793** Pillar Box

**1987.** No value expressed. (a) Inscr "C" and "TARIFA INTERNA/HASTA 10 GRAMOS".

| | | | |
|---|---|---|---|
| 2049 **793** | (18c.) red, black & yell | 1·60 | 45 |

(b) Inscr "C" and "TARIFA INTERNA/DE 11 A 20 GRAMOS".

| | | | |
|---|---|---|---|
| 2050 | (33c.) black, yell & grn | 1·90 | 60 |

**794** Spotted Metynis ("Metynnis maculatus")

**1987.** Argentine Philately. River Fishes. Mult.

| | | | |
|---|---|---|---|
| 2051 | 10c.+5c. Type **794** | 45 | 15 |
| 2052 | 10c.+5c. Black-finned pearlfish ("Cynolebias nigripinnis") | 45 | 15 |
| 2053 | 10c.+5c. Solar's leporinus ("Leporinus solarii") | 45 | 15 |
| 2054 | 10c.+5c. Red-flanked bloodfin ("Aphyocharax rathbuni") | 45 | 15 |
| 2055 | 10c.+5c. Bronze catfish ("Corydoras aeneus") | 45 | 15 |
| 2056 | 10c.+5c. Giant hatchetfish ("Thoracocharax securis") | 45 | 15 |
| 2057 | 10c.+5c. Black-striped pearlfish ("Cynolebias melanotaenia") | 45 | 15 |
| 2058 | 10c.+5c. Chanchito cichlid ("Cichlasoma facetum") | 45 | 15 |
| 2059 | 20c.+10c. Silver tetra ("Tetragonopterus argente") | 80 | 30 |
| 2060 | 20c.+10c. Buenos Aires tetra ("Hemigrammus caudovittatus") | 80 | 30 |
| 2061 | 20c.+10c. Two-spotted astyanax ("Astyanax bimaculatus") | 80 | 30 |
| 2062 | 20c.+10c. Black widow tetra ("Gymnocorymbus ternetzi") | 80 | 30 |
| 2063 | 20c.+10c. Trahira ("Hoplias malabaricus") | 80 | 30 |
| 2064 | 20c.+10c. Blue-finned tetra ("Aphyocharax rubripinnis") | 80 | 30 |
| 2065 | 20c.+10c. Agassiz's dwarf cichlid ("Apistogramma agassizi") | 80 | 30 |
| 2066 | 20c.+10c. Fanning pyrrhulina ("Pyrrhulina rachoviana") | 80 | 30 |

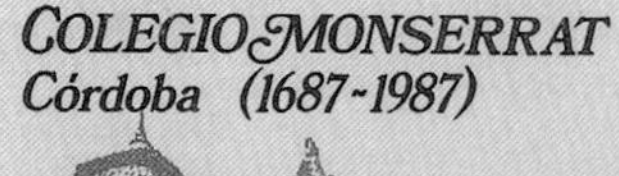

**795** College Facade and Arms (image scaled to 63% of original size)

**1987.** 300th Anniv of Montserrat College, Cordoba and Montserrat/87 National Stamp Exhibition. Sheet 75×110 mm. Imperf.

| | | | |
|---|---|---|---|
| **MS**2067 **795** | 1a. multicoloured | 2·50 | 2·40 |

**796** Jorge Luis Borges (writer)

**1987.** Anniversaries. Multicoloured.

| | | | |
|---|---|---|---|
| 2068 | 20c. Type **796** (1st death anniv) | 65 | 15 |
| 2069 | 30c. Armando Discepolo, (dramatist and theatre director, birth cent) | 75 | 25 |
| 2070 | 50c. Dr Carlos Alberto Pueyrredon (historian, birth centenary) | 90 | 40 |

**797** Drawing by Leonardo da Vinci

**1987.** "The Post, a Medium for Communication and Prevention of Addictions".

| | | | |
|---|---|---|---|
| 2071 **797** | 30c. multicoloured | 1·90 | 45 |

**798** "The Sower" (Julio Vanzo)

**1987.** 75th Anniv of Argentine Farmers' Union.

| | | | |
|---|---|---|---|
| 2072 **798** | 30c. multicoloured | 1·30 | 45 |

**799** Basketball

**1987.** 10th Pan-American Games, Indianapolis. Multicoloured.

| | | | |
|---|---|---|---|
| 2073 | 20c. Type **799** | 75 | 35 |
| 2074 | 30c. Rowing | 90 | 40 |
| 2075 | 50c. Dinghies | 1·00 | 45 |

**800** Col. Maj. Ignacio Alvarez Thomas

**1987.** Anniversaries. Multicoloured.

| | | | |
|---|---|---|---|
| 2076 | 25c. Type **800** (birth bicent) | 90 | 35 |
| 2077 | 25c. Col. Manuel Dorrego (birth bicentenary) | 90 | 35 |
| 2078 | 50c. 18th-century Spanish map of Falkland Islands (death bicentenary of Jacinto de Altolaguirre, governor of Islands) (horiz) | 1·80 | 60 |
| 2079 | 50c. "Signing the Accord" (Rafael del Villar) (50th anniv of House of Accord Museum, San Nicolas) (horiz) | 1·80 | 60 |

**801** Children as Nurse and Mother

**1987.** UNICEF Child Vaccination Campaign.

| | | | |
|---|---|---|---|
| 2080 **801** | 30c. multicoloured | 90 | 30 |

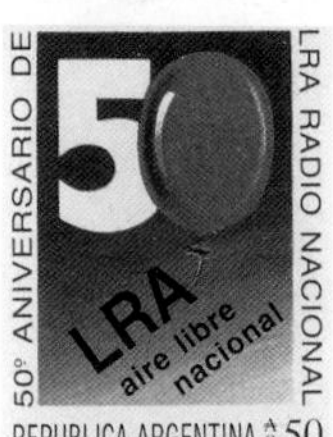


**802** Balloon

**1987.** Anniversaries. Multicoloured.

| | | | |
|---|---|---|---|
| 2081 | 50c. Type **802** (50th anniv of LRA National Radio) | 1·30 | 70 |
| 2082 | 50c. Celendonio Galvan Moreno (first editor) (50th anniv of "Postas Argentinas" magazine) | 1·30 | 70 |
| 2083 | 1a. Dr. Jose Marco del Pont (founder) (centenary of Argentine Philatelic Society) | 2·50 | 95 |

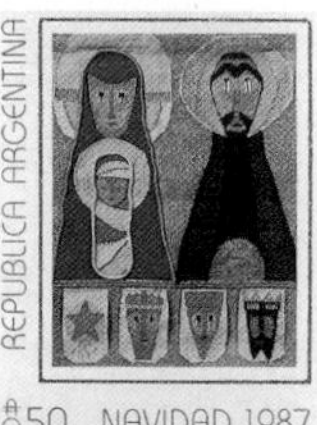


**803** "Nativity" (tapestry, Alisia Frega)

**1987.** Christmas. Multicoloured.

| | | | |
|---|---|---|---|
| 2084 | 50c. Type **803** | 1·00 | 35 |
| 2085 | 1a. Doves and flowers (tapestry, Silvina Trigos) | 2·10 | 95 |

**804** Crested Oropendola, Baritu National Park

**1987.** National Parks (1st series). Multicoloured.

| | | | |
|---|---|---|---|
| 2086 | 50c. Type **804** | 2·30 | 60 |
| 2087 | 50c. Otter, Nahuel Huapi National Park | 2·30 | 60 |
| 2088 | 50c. Night monkey, Rio Pilcomayo National Park | 2·30 | 60 |
| 2089 | 50c. Kelp goose, Tierra del Fuego National Park | 2·30 | 60 |
| 2090 | 50c. Alligator, Iguazu National Park | 2·30 | 60 |

See also Nos. 2150/4, 2222/6 and 2295/9.

**805** "Caminito" (Jose Canella)

**1988.** Historical and Tourist Sites. Multicoloured.

| | | | |
|---|---|---|---|
| 2090a | 3a. "Purmamarca" (Nestor Martin) (33×22 mm) | 1·10 | 45 |
| 2091 | 5a. Type **805** | 4·00 | 2·00 |
| 2092 | 10a. "Old Almacen" (Jose Canella) (A) | 8·25 | 4·25 |
| 2092a | 10a. "Old Almacen" (Jose Canella) (B) | 2·10 | 95 |
| 2095 | 20a. "Ushuaia" (Nestor Martin) (vert) | 7·50 | 3·00 |
| 2099 | 50a. Type **805** | 2·10 | 95 |

10a. A. Inscr "Viejo Almacen". B. Inscr "El Viejo Almacen".

**806** "Minstrel singing in a Grocer's Shop" (Carlos Morel)

**1988.** Argentine Paintings. Multicoloured.

| | | | |
|---|---|---|---|
| 2105 | 1a. Type **806** | 1·50 | 60 |
| 2106 | 1a. "Curuzu" (detail, Candido Lopez) | 1·50 | 60 |

**807** Hand arranging Coloured Cubes

**1988.** Argentine–Brazil Economic Co-operation.

| | | | |
|---|---|---|---|
| 2107 **807** | 1a. multicoloured | 1·00 | 45 |

**808** St. Anne's Chapel, Corrientes

**1988.** 400th Annivs of Corrientes and Alta Gracia. Multicoloured.

| | | | |
|---|---|---|---|
| 2108 | 1a. Type **808** | 1·50 | 60 |
| 2109 | 1a. Alta Gracia church | 1·50 | 60 |

**809** Men Stacking Sacks

**1988.** Labour Day. Details of mural "Cereals" (Nueve de Julio station, Buenos Aires underground railway). Multicoloured.

| | | | |
|---|---|---|---|
| 2110 | 50c. Type **809** | 90 | 75 |
| 2111 | 50c. Sacks | 90 | 75 |
| 2112 | 50c. Men unloading truck | 90 | 75 |
| 2113 | 50c. Horse and cart | 90 | 75 |

Nos. 2110/13 were printed together, se-tenant, forming a composite design.

**810** Steam Locomotive "Yatay" and Tender, 1888 (image scaled to 54% of original size)

**1988.** "Prenfil '88" Philatelic Literature Exhibition, Buenos Aires (1st issue). Railways. Multicoloured.

| | | | |
|---|---|---|---|
| 2114 | 1a.+50c. Type **810** | 1·30 | 85 |
| 2115 | 1a.+50c. Electric passenger coach, 1914 | 1·30 | 85 |
| 2116 | 1a.+50c. Type B-15 loco-motive and tender, 1942 | 1·30 | 85 |

2117 1a.+50c. Type GT-22 diesel locomotive, 1988 1·30 85

See also Nos. 2134/7.

**811** Running

**1988.** Olympic Games, Seoul. Multicoloured.

2118 1a. Type **811** 65 35
2119 2a. Football 1·60 45
2120 3a. Hockey 2·30 95
2121 4a. Tennis 2·75 1·20

**812** Bank Facade

**1988.** Centenary of Bank of Mendoza.

2122 **812** 2a. multicoloured 1·30 55

**813** Arms of Guemes and National Guard Emblem

**1988.** 50th Anniv of National Guard.

2123 **813** 2a. multicoloured 1·30 55

**814** "St. Cayetano (patron saint of workers)" (C. Quaglia)

**1988.** Philatelic Anniversaries and Events. Mult.

2124 2a. Type **814** (50th anniv of Liniers (Buenos Aires) Philatelic Circle) 1·40 70
2125 3a. "Our Lady of Carmen (patron saint of Cuyo)" (window, Carlos Quaglia) (50th anniv of West Argentina Philatelic Society) 1·50 85
**MS**2126 145×73 mm. 5a. "Love" (mural, Antonio Berni) (Li-men 88 national stamp exhibition, Buenos Aires) (39×29 mm) 4·50 4·25

**815** Sarmiento (after Mario Chierico) and Cathedral of the North School

**1988.** Death Centenary of Domingo Faustino Sarmiento (President, 1868–74).

2127 **815** 3a. multicoloured 2·10 85

**816** "San Isidro" (Enrique Castro)

**1988.** Horse Paintings. Multicoloured.

2128 2a.+1a. Type **816** 1·90 95
2129 2a.+1a. "Waiting" (Gustavo Solari) 1·90 95
2130 2a.+1a. "Beside the Pond" (F. Romero Carranza) 1·90 95
2131 2a.+1a. "Mare and Colt" (Enrique Castro) 1·90 95
2132 2a.+1a. "Under the Tail" (Enrique Castro) 1·90 95

**1988.** 21st International Urological Society Congress. No. 2091 optd XXI CONGRESO DE LA SOCIEDAD INTERNACIONAL DE UROLOGIA SIU 88.

2133 **805** 5a. multicoloured 7·50 2·40

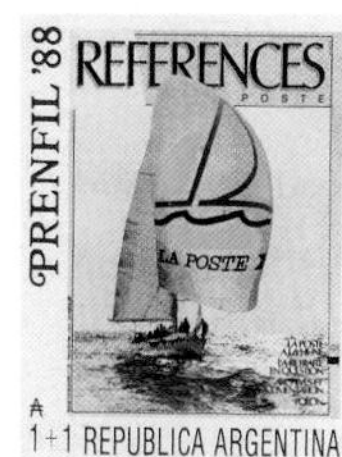

**818** Cover of "References de la Poste"

**1988.** "Prenfil '88" Philatelic Literature Exhibition, Buenos Aires (2nd issue). Designs showing magazine covers. Multicoloured.

2134 1a.+1a. Type **818** 75 35
2135 1a.+1a. "Cronaca Filatelica" 75 35
2136 1a.+1a. "Co Fi" 75 35
2137 2a.+2a. "Postas Argentinas" 95 60

**819** "Immaculate Conception"

**1988.** Arbrafax 88 Argentinian–Brazilian Stamp Exhibition, Buenos Aires. Sheet 156×80 mm containing T 819 and similar horiz design. Multicoloured.

**MS**2138 2a.+2a. "Candle Delivery at San Ignacio" (Leonie Matthis); 3a.+3a. Type **819** 5·00 4·75

**820** Underground Train

**1988.** 75th Anniv of Buenos Aires Underground Railway.

2139 **820** 5a. multicoloured 2·10 95

**821** "Virgin of Tenderness"

**1988.** Christmas. Virgins in Ucrania Cathedral, Buenos Aires. Multicoloured.

2140 5a. Type **821** 1·90 70
2141 5a. "Virgin of Protection" 1·90 70

**822** Ushuaia and St. John

**1989.** Death Centenary (1988) of St. John Bosco (founder of Salesian Brothers).

2142 **822** 5a. multicoloured 1·30 35

**823** "Rincon de los Areneros" (Justo Lynch)

**1989.** Paintings. Multicoloured.

2143 5a. Type **823** 2·75 45
2144 5a. "Blancos" (Fernando Fader) 2·75 45

**824** "Crowning with Thorns" and Church of Our Lady of Carmen, Tandil

**1989.** Holy Week. Multicoloured.

2145 2a. Type **824** 50 25
2146 2a. "Jesus of Nazareth" and Buenos Aires Cathedral 50 25
2147 3a. "Our Lady of Sorrows" and Humahuaca Church, Jujuy 65 30
2148 3a. "Jesus Meets His Mother" (statue) and La Quebrada Church, San Luis 65 30

**825** Shattering Drinking Glass

**1989.** Anti-alcoholism Campaign.

2149 **825** 5a. multicoloured 1·30 45

**1989.** National Parks (2nd series). As T 804. Mult.

2150 5a. Crested gallito ("Gallito Capeton"), Lihue Calel National Park 1·30 45
2151 5a. Lizard, El Palmar National Park 1·30 45
2152 5a. Tapirs, Calilegua National Park 1·30 45
2153 5a. Howler monkey, Chaco National Park 1·30 45
2154 5a. Magellanic woodpecker ("Carpintero Negro Patagonico"), Los Glaciares National Park 1·30 45

**826** Emblem

**1989.** Cent of Argentine Membership of I.T.U.

2155 **826** 10a. multicoloured 2·75 60

**827** Class 1A Glider Entries

**1989.** World Model Airplane Championships, La Cruz-Embals-Cordoba. Multicoloured.

2156 5a. Type **827** 1·00 35
2157 5a. Class 1B rubber-powered entries 1·00 35

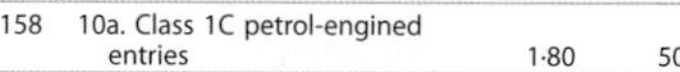

2158 10a. Class 1C petrol-engined entries 1·80 50

**828** Otuno ("Diplomystes viedmensis")

**1989.** Argentine Philately. Fishes. Multicoloured.

2159 10a.+5a. Type **828** 1·00 60
2160 10a.+5a. Striped galaxiid ("Haplochiton taeniatus") 1·00 60
2161 10a.+5a. Creole perch ("Jenyns percichthys tucha") 1·00 60
2162 10a.+5a. River Plate galaxiid ("Galaxias platei") 1·00 60
2163 10a.+5a. Brown trout ("Salmo fario") 1·00 60

**829** "All Men are Born Free and Equal"

**1989.** Bicentenary of French Revolution.

2164 **829** 10a. red, blue and black 1·00 45
2165 - 15a. black, red and blue 1·10 50
**MS**2166 146×74 mm. 25a. multicoloured 2·10 2·00

DESIGNS: 15a. "Marianne" (Gandon) and French flag; 25a. "Liberty guiding the People" (detail, E. Delacroix).

**830** "Weser" (steamer)

**1989.** Immigration. Multicoloured.

2167 150a. Type **830** 2·75 85
2168 200a. Immigrants' hostel 3·25 1·10
**MS**2169 155×80 mm. As Nos. 2167/8 but each 35×25 mm 5·00 4·75

**831** "Republic" (bronze bust)

**1989.** Transference of Presidency. Unissued stamp surch as in T 831.

2170 **831** 300a. on 50a. mult 2·75 85

**832** Arms of Columbus and Title Page of "Book of Privileges"

**1989.** "Espamer '90" Spain–Latin America Stamp Exhibition. Chronicles of Discovery. Each yellow, black and red.

2171 100a.+50a. Type **832** 75 70
2172 150a.+50a. Illustration from "New Chronicle and Good Government" (Guaman Poma de Ayala) 1·00 95
2173 200a.+100a. Illustration from "Discovery and Conquest of Peru" (Pedro de Cieza de Leon) 1·50 1·40

2174 250a.+100a. Illustration from "A Journey to the River Plate" (Ulrico Schmidl) 1·80 1·70

**833** Fr. Guillermo Furlong and Title Page of "Los Jesuitas"

**1989.** Birth Anniversaries.

2175 **833** 150a. black, light green and green (centenary) 90 55
2176 - 150a. black, buff and brown (centenary) 90 55
2177 - 200a. black, light blue and blue (bicentenary) 1·00 60

DESIGNS: No. 2176, Dr. Gregorio Alvarez (physician) and title page of "Canto A Chos Mala"; 2177, Brigadier Gen. Enrique Martinez and "Battle of Maipu" (detail of lithograph, Theodore Gericault).

**834** Wooden Mask from Atajo

**1989.** America. Pre-Columbian Artefacts. Mult.

2178 200a. Type **834** 1·60 60
2179 300a. Urn from Punta de Balastro 2·10 65

**835** "Policewoman with Children" (Diego Molinari)

**1989.** Federal Police Week. Winning entries in a schools' painting competition.

2180 100a. Type **835** 95 35
2181 100a. "Traffic policeman" (Carlos Alberto Sarago) 95 35
2182 150a. "Adults and child by traffic lights" (Roxana Andrea Osuna) 1·30 60
2183 150a. "Policeman and child stopping traffic at crossing" (Pablo Javier Quaglia) 1·30 60

**836** "Dream of Christmas" (Maria Carballido)

**1989.** Christmas. Multicoloured.

2184 200a. Type **836** 1·10 35
2185 200a. "Cradle Song for Baby Jesus" (Gato Frias) 1·10 35
2186 300a. "Christ of the Hills" (statue, Chipo Cespedes) (vert) 1·30 45

**837** "Battle of Vuelta de Obligado" (Ulde Todo)

**1989**

2187 **837** 300a. multicoloured 2·10 45

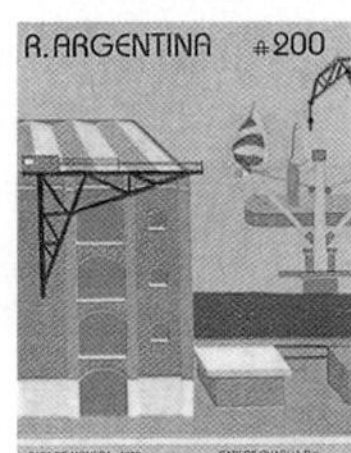


**838** Port Building

**1990.** Cent of Buenos Aires Port. Multicoloured.

2188 200a. Type **838** 2·50 1·00
2189 200a. Crane and bows of container and sailing ships 2·50 1·00
2190 200a. Truck on quay and ships in dock 2·50 1·00
2191 200a. Van and building 2·50 1·00

Nos. 2188/91 were printed together, se-tenant, forming a composite design.

**839** Aconcagua Peak and Los Horcones Lagoon

**1990.** Aconcagua International Fair. Mult.

2192 500a. Type **839** 1·80 75
2193 500a. Aconcagua Peak and Los Horcones Lagoon (right-hand detail) 1·80 75

Nos. 2192/3 were printed together, se-tenant, forming a composite design.

**840** "75" and Girl with Savings Box

**1990.** 75th Anniv of National Savings and Insurance Fund.

2194 **840** 1000a. multicoloured 1·00 45

**841** Footballer in Striped Shirt

**1990.** World Cup Football Championship, Italy. Multicoloured.

2195 2500a. Type **841** 2·20 1·00
2196 2500a. Upper body of footballer in blue shirt 2·20 1·00
2197 2500a. Ball and footballers' legs 2·20 1·00
2198 2500a. Lower body of footballer 2·20 1·00

Nos. 2195/8 were printed together, se-tenant, forming a composite design.

**842** Flowers

**1990.** Anti-drugs Campaign.

2199 **842** 2000a. multicoloured 1·90 85

**843** School Emblem and Pellegrini

**1990.** Centenary of Carlos Pellegrini Commercial High School.

2200 **843** 2000a. multicoloured 1·90 85

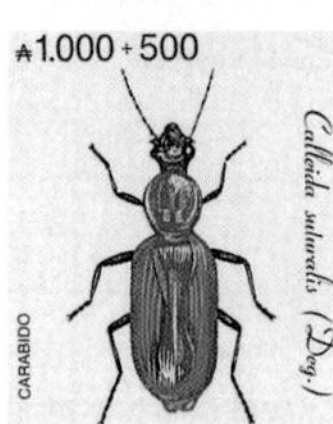


**844** "Calleida suturalis"

**1990.** Argentine Philately. Insects. Multicoloured.

2201 1000a.+500a. Type **844** 1·80 1·20
2202 1000a.+500a. "Adalia bipunctata" 1·80 1·20
2203 1000a.+500a. "Hippodamia convergens" 1·80 1·20
2204 1000a.+500a. "Nabis punctipennis" 1·80 1·20
2205 1000a.+500a. "Podisus nigrispinus" 1·80 1·20

**845** Letters and Globe

**1990.** International Literacy Year.

2206 **845** 2000a. multicoloured 1·50 85

**846** Marcos Zar and Savoia S-16 Flying Boat

**1990.** Air. Aerofildae 90 National Air Mail Exhibition, Buenos Aires. Sheet 158×78 mm containing T 846 and similar horiz design. Multicoloured.

**MS**2207 2000a.+ 2000a. Type **846**; 3000a.+3000a. Capt. Antonio Parodi and biplane 12·50 12·00

**847** Players

**1990.** World Basketball Championship. Mult.

2208 2000a. Type **847** 3·25 2·10
**MS**2209 5000a. Detail of No. 2208 (29×39 mm) 8·25 7·00

**848** Junkers Ju 52/3m

**1990.** Air. 50th Anniv of LADE (airline). Mult.

2210 2500a. Type **848** 2·10 1·10
2211 2500a. Grumman SA-16 Albatross flying boat 2·10 1·10
2212 2500a. Fokker Friendship 2·10 1·10
2213 2500a. Fokker Fellowship 2·10 1·10

**849** Arms of West Indies Maritime Post

**1990.** 14th Postal Union of the Americas and Spain Congress, Buenos Aires.

2214 **849** 3000a. brown & black 2·50 1·00
2215 - 3000a. multicoloured 2·50 1·00
2216 - 3000a. multicoloured 2·50 1·00
2217 - 3000a. multicoloured 2·50 1·00

DESIGNS: No. 2215, Sailing packet and despatch boat; 2216, "Rio Carcarana" (cargo liner); 2217, Boeing 707 airplane and mail van.

**850** "Descubierta"

**1990.** Espamer 91 Spain–Latin America Stamp Exhibition, Buenos Aires. Sheet 109×114 mm containing T 850 and similar vert designs. Multicoloured.

**MS**2218 2000a.+1000a.×4: Type **850**; Alejandro Malaspina (explorer) and "Atrevide"; Amerindians; Artist drawing Amerindians 12·50 12·00

**851** "Hamelia erecta" and Iguazu Falls

**1990.** America. Natural World. Multicoloured.

2219 3000a. Type **851** 2·50 1·00
2220 3000a. Sea cow, Puerto Deseado 2·50 1·00

**852** U.P.U. Emblem on "Stamp"

**1990.** World Post Day.

2221 **852** 3000a. multicoloured 2·30 85

**1990.** National Parks (3rd series). As T 804. Mult.

2222 3000a. Anteater, El Rey National Park 2·40 95
2223 3000a. Black-necked swans ("Cisne de Cuello Negro"), Laguna Blanca National Park 2·40 95
2224 3000a. Black-chested buzzard eagle ("Aguila Mora"), Lanin National Park 2·40 95
2225 3000a. Armadillo, Perito Moreno National Park 2·40 95
2226 3000a. Pudu, Puelo National Park 2·40 95

**853** Hands (after Michelangelo) and Army Emblem

**1990.** Cent of Salvation Army in Argentina (2227) and Nat University of the Littoral (2228). Mult.

2227 3000a. Type **853** 2·30 1·10
2228 3000a. University building and emblem 2·30 1·10

**854** Archangel Gabriel

**1990.** Christmas. Stained-glass windows by Carlos Quaglia from Church of Immaculate Conception, Villaguay. Multicoloured.

| | | | |
|---|---|---|---|
| 2229 | 3000a. Dove's wing and hand | 2·10 | 1·10 |
| 2230 | 3000a. Dove and Mary | 2·10 | 1·10 |
| 2231 | 3000a. Type **854** | 2·10 | 1·10 |
| 2232 | 3000a. Lower half of Mary and open book | 2·10 | 1·10 |
| 2233 | 3000a. Joseph | 2·10 | 1·10 |
| 2234 | 3000a. Star, shepherds and head of Mary | 2·10 | 1·10 |
| 2235 | 3000a. Manger | 2·10 | 1·10 |
| 2236 | 3000a. Baby Jesus in Mary's arms | 2·10 | 1·10 |
| 2237 | 3000a. Joseph with two doves and Mary | 2·10 | 1·10 |
| 2238 | 3000a. Simeon | 2·10 | 1·10 |
| 2239 | 3000a. Lower halves of Joseph and Mary | 2·10 | 1·10 |
| 2240 | 3000a. Lower half of Simeon and altar | 2·10 | 1·10 |

Nos. 2229/32, 2233/6 and 2237/40 were printed together in se-tenant sheetlets of four stamps, each sheetlet forming a composite design of stained glass windows entitled "Incarnation of Son of God", "The Birth of Christ" and "Presentation of Jesus in the Temple".

**855** Putting the Shot

**1990.** Espamer 91 Spain–Latin America Stamp Exhibition, Buenos Aires (2nd issue) and Olympic Games, Barcelona (1992). Sheet 103×125 mm containing T 855 and similar vert designs. Multicoloured.

| | | | |
|---|---|---|---|
| **MS**2241 | 2000a.+2000a.×4: Type **855**; High jumping; Hurdling; Pole vaulting | 19·00 | 18·00 |

**856** "Landscape" (Pio Collivadino)

**1991.** Paintings. Multicoloured.

| | | | |
|---|---|---|---|
| 2242 | 4000a. Type **856** | 1·80 | 1·00 |
| 2243 | 4000a. "Weeping Willows" (Atilio Malinverno) (horiz) | 1·80 | 1·00 |

**857** Juan Manuel Fangio

**1991.** Espamer 91 Spain–Latin America Stamp Exhibition, Buenos Aires (3rd issue). Racing Drivers. Sheet 104×125 mm containing T 857 and similar vert designs. Multicoloured.

| | | | |
|---|---|---|---|
| **MS**2244 | 2500a.+2500a.×4: Type **857**; Juan Manuel Bordeau; Carlos Alberto Reutemann; Oscar and Juan Galvez | 9·50 | 9·25 |

**858** Rosas

**1991.** Return of Remains of Brig. Gen. Juan Manuel de Rosas.

| | | | | |
|---|---|---|---|---|
| 2245 | **858** | 4000a. multicoloured | 1·80 | 1·00 |

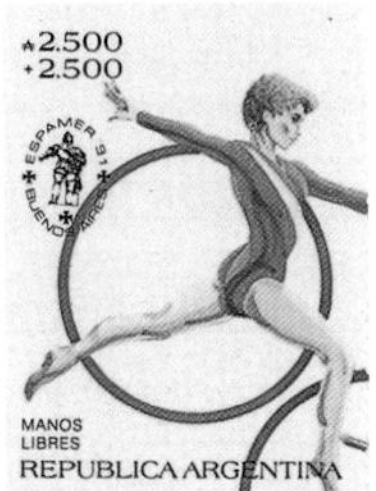

**859** Freestyle Gymnastics

**1991.** Espamer 91 Spain–Latin America Stamp Exhibition, Buenos Aires (4th issue) and Olympic Games, Barcelona (1992) (2nd issue). Gymnastics. Sheet 103×125 mm containing T 859 and similar vert designs. Multicoloured.

| | | | |
|---|---|---|---|
| **MS**2246 | 2500a.+2500a.×4: Type **859**; Asymmetric bars; Beam; Hoop exercise | 9·50 | 9·25 |

**860** "Hernan, the Pirate" (Jose Salinas)

**1991.** Comic Strips. Each black and blue.

| | | | |
|---|---|---|---|
| 2247 | 4000a. Type **860** | 1·80 | 1·00 |
| 2248 | 4000a. "Don Fulgencio" (Lino Palacio) | 1·80 | 1·00 |
| 2249 | 4000a. "Tablas Medicas de Salerno" (Oscar Conti) | 1·80 | 1·00 |
| 2250 | 4000a. "Buenos Aires en Camiseta" (Alejandro del Prado) | 1·80 | 1·00 |
| 2251 | 4000a. "Girls!" (Jose Divito) | 1·80 | 1·00 |
| 2252 | 4000a. "Langostino" (Eduardo Ferro) | 1·80 | 1·00 |
| 2253 | 4000a. "Mafalda" (Joaquin Lavado) | 1·80 | 1·00 |
| 2254 | 4000a. "Mort Cinder" (Alberto Breccia) | 1·80 | 1·00 |

**861** "Flags" (Maria Augustina Ferreyra)

**1991.** 700th Anniv of Swiss Confederation.

| | | | | |
|---|---|---|---|---|
| 2255 | **861** | 4000a. multicoloured | 1·80 | 85 |

**862** Divine Child Mayor

**1991.** 400th Anniv of La Rioja City.

| | | | | |
|---|---|---|---|---|
| 2256 | **862** | 4000a. multicoloured | 1·80 | 85 |

**863** Eduardo Bradley, Angel Zuloaga and Balloon "Eduardo Newbery"

**1991.** 75th Anniv of Crossing of Andes by Balloon.

| | | | | |
|---|---|---|---|---|
| 2257 | **863** | 4000a. multicoloured | 1·80 | 85 |

**864** "Vitoria" (Magellan's galleon)

**1991.** America. Voyages of Discovery. Mult.

| | | | |
|---|---|---|---|
| 2258 | 4000a. Type **864** | 2·50 | 1·00 |
| 2259 | 4000a. Juan Diaz de Solis's fleet | 2·50 | 1·00 |

**865** "Virgin of the Valley, Catamarca" (top half)

**1991.** Christmas. Stained-glass Windows from Church of Our Lady of Lourdes, Santos Lugares, Buenos Aires. Multicoloured.

| | | | |
|---|---|---|---|
| 2260 | 4000a. Type **865** | 2·10 | 1·00 |
| 2261 | 4000a. "Virgin of the Valley" (bottom half) | 2·10 | 1·00 |
| 2262 | 4000a. Church and "Virgin of the Rosary of the Miracle, Cordoba" (top half) | 2·10 | 1·00 |
| 2263 | 4000a. "Virgin of the Rosary of the Miracle" (bottom half) | 2·10 | 1·00 |

Nos. 2260/3 were issued together, se-tenant, Nos. 2260/1 and 2262/3 forming composite designs.

**866** Enrique Pestalozzi (editor) and Masthead

**1991.** Centenaries. Multicoloured.

| | | | |
|---|---|---|---|
| 2264 | 4000a. Type **866** ("Argentinisches Tageblatt" (1989)) | 1·80 | 85 |
| 2265 | 4000a. Leandro Alem (founder) and flags (Radical Civic Union) | 1·80 | 85 |
| 2266 | 4000a. Marksman (Argentine Shooting Federation) | 1·80 | 85 |
| 2267 | 4000a. Dr. Nicasio Etchepareborda (first professor) and emblem (Buenos Aires Faculty of Odontology) | 1·80 | 85 |
| 2268 | 4000a. Dalmiro Huergo and emblem (Graduate School of Economics) | 1·80 | 85 |

**867** Gen. Juan Lavalle and Medal

**1991.** Anniversaries. Multicoloured.

| | | | |
|---|---|---|---|
| 2269 | 4000a. Type **867** (150th death anniv) | 1·80 | 85 |
| 2270 | 4000a. Gen. Jose Maria Paz and Battle of Ituzaingo medal (birth bicentenary) | 1·80 | 85 |
| 2271 | 4000a. Dr. Marco Avellaneda and opening words of "Ode to the 25th May" (politician and writer, 150th death anniv) | 1·80 | 85 |
| 2272 | 4000a. William Henry Hudson and title page of "Far Away and Long Ago" (writer, 150th birth anniv) | 1·80 | 85 |

**868** "Castor" (rocket)

**1991.** "Iberoprenfil '92" Iberia–Latin America Philatelic Literature Exhibition, Buenos Aires (1st issue). Multicoloured.

| | | | |
|---|---|---|---|
| 2273 | 4000a.+4000a. Type **868** | 4·00 | 1·60 |
| 2274 | 4000a.+4000a. "Lusat-1" satellite | 4·00 | 1·60 |

See also Nos. 2313/14 and 2325/8.

**869** Guiana Crested Eagle ("Morphnu guianensis")

**1991.** Birds. Multicoloured.

| | | | |
|---|---|---|---|
| 2275 | 4000a. Type **869** | 2·50 | 1·10 |
| 2276 | 4000a. Green-winged macaw ("Ara chloroptera") | 2·50 | 1·10 |
| 2277 | 4000a. Lesser rhea ("Pterocnemia pennata") | 2·50 | 1·10 |

**870** Gaucho with Woman

**1992.** Abrafex 92 Argentinian–Brazilian Stamp Exhibition, Porto Algere, Brazil. Sheet 103×126 mm containing T 870 and similar vert designs. Multicoloured.

| | | | |
|---|---|---|---|
| **MS**2278 | 38c. Type **870**; 38c. Gaucho with horse; 38c. Gaucho in grocer's shop; 38c. Ranch owner | 8·25 | 8·00 |

**871** Golden Tops

**1992.** Fungi.

| | | | |
|---|---|---|---|
| 2279 | 10c. Type **871** | 75 | 25 |
| 2280 | 25c. Common ink cap | 1·30 | 35 |
| 2281 | 38c. Type **871** | 1·30 | 45 |
| 2282 | 48c. As 25c. | 1·50 | 55 |
| 2283 | 50c. Granulated boletus | 2·50 | 70 |
| 2284 | 51c. Common morel | 1·60 | 60 |
| 2285 | 61c. Fly agaric | 2·00 | 65 |
| 2286 | 68c. Lawyer's wig | 3·25 | 80 |
| 2289 | 1p. As 61c. | 5·00 | 1·10 |

2290 1p.25 As 50c. 5·00 1·10
2293 2p. As 51c. 9·50 2·75
For redrawn, smaller, designs see Nos. 2365/77.

**1992.** National Parks (4th series). As T 804. Multicoloured.
2295 38c. Chucao tapaculo ("Chucao"), Los Alerces National Park 1·50 85
2296 38c. Opossum, Los Arrayanes National Park 1·50 85
2297 38c. Giant armadillo, Formosa Nature Reserve 1·50 85
2298 38c. Cavy, Petrified Forests Natural Monument 1·50 85
2299 38c. James's flamingo ("Parina chica"), Laguna de los Pozuelos Natural Monument 1·50 85

**872** Soldier and Truck

**1992.** National Heroes Commem. Multicoloured.
2300 38c. Type **872** 1·30 70
2301 38c. "General Belgrano" (cruiser) 1·30 70
2302 38c. FMA Pucara fighter 1·30 70

**873** "Carnotaurus sastrei"

**1992.** Dinosaurs. Multicoloured.
2303 38c.+38c. Type **873** 2·75 1·80
2304 38c.+38c. "Amargasaurus cazaui" 2·75 1·80

**874** "Tileforo Areco"

**1992.** Birth Centenary (1991) of Florencio Molina Campios (painter). Multicoloured.
2305 38c. Type **874** 1·50 85
2306 38c. "In the Shade" (horiz) 1·50 85

**875** Deer

**1992.** Conference on Environment and Development, Rio de Janeiro. Sheet 85×82 mm containing T 875 and similar square designs. Multicoloured.
**MS**2307 38c. Type **875**; 38c. Birds; 38c. Butterflies; 38c. Whale 12·00 12·00

**876** General Lucio N. Mansilla and "San Martin" (frigate)

**1992.** Birth Anniversaries. Multicoloured.
2308 38c. Type **876** (bicentenary) 1·50 85
2309 38c. Jose Manuel Estrada (historian, 150th) 1·50 85
2310 38c. General Jose I. Garmendia (150th) 1·50 85

**877** Hearts as Flowers

**1992.** Anti-drugs Campaign.
2311 **877** 38c. multicoloured 1·90 95

**878** Steam Pump Fire Engine and Calaza

**1992.** 140th Birth Anniv of Col. Jose Calaza (founder of fire service).
2312 **878** 38c. multicoloured 1·60 90

**879** "The Party"

**1992.** "Iberoprenfil '92" Iberia–Latin America Philatelic Literature Exhibition, Buenos Aires (2nd issue). Paintings by Raul Soldi. Multicoloured.
2313 76c.+76c. Type **879** 6·25 4·75
2314 76c.+76c. "Church of St. Anne of Glew" 6·25 4·75

**880** Columbus, European Symbols and "Santa Maria"

**1992.** America. 500th Anniv of Discovery of America by Columbus. Multicoloured.
2315 38c. Type **880** 2·50 1·20
2316 38c. American symbols and Columbus 2·50 1·20

**1992.** 50th Anniv of Neuquen and Rio Negro Philatelic Centre. Unissued stamp as T 871 optd 50ºANIVERSARIO CENTRO FILATELICO DE NEUQUEN Y RIO NEGRO. Multicoloured.
2317 1p.77 Verdigris agaric 7·50 4·75

**882** "God Pays You"

**1992.** Argentine Films. Advertising posters. Mult.
2318 38c. Type **882** 1·80 85
2319 38c. "The Turbid Waters" 1·80 85
2320 38c. "Un Guapo del 900" 1·80 85
2321 38c. "The Truce" 1·80 85
2322 38c. "The Official Version" 1·80 85

**883** Flags of Paraguay and Argentina as Stamps

**1992.** "Parafil '92" Paraguay–Argentina Stamp Exhibition, Buenos Aires.
2323 **883** 76c.+76c. mult 6·00 4·50

**884** Angel and Baby Jesus

**1992.** Christmas.
2324 **884** 38c. multicoloured 1·80 85

**885** Punta Mogotes Lighthouse

**1992.** "Iberoprenfil '92" Iberia–Latin America Philatelic Literature Exhibition, Buenos Aires (3rd issue). Lighthouses. Multicoloured.
2325 38c. Type **885** 1·80 85
2326 38c. Rio Negro 1·80 85
2327 38c. San Antonio 1·80 85
2328 38c. Cabo Blanco 1·80 85

**886** Campaign Emblem

**1992.** Anti-AIDS Campaign.
2329 **886** 10c. black, red and blue 3·25 60
2330 - 26c. multicoloured 5·75 1·00
DESIGN: 26c. AIDS cloud over house of life.

**887** "Sac-B" Research Satellite

**1992.** International Space Year.
2331 **887** 38c. multicoloured 2·00 95

**888** "The Lord of the Miracle" (Matriz Church, Salta)

**1992.** 400th Anniv of Arrival of the "Lord of the Miracle" in America. Sheet 72×112 mm.
**MS**2332 **888** 76c. multicoloured 7·00 4·75

**889** Footballers and Emblem

**1993.** Centenary of Argentine Football Assn.
2333 **889** 38c. multicoloured 1·80 85

**890** Arquebusier and Arms of Francisco de Arganaras (founder)

**1993.** 400th Anniv of Jujuy.
2334 **890** 38c. multicoloured 1·80 85

**891** Government Tower, Poznan

**1993.** International Stamp Exhibitions. Sheet 84×119 mm containing T 891 and similar square designs. Multicoloured.
**MS**2335 38c. Type **891** (Polska 93); 48c."Christ the Redeemer" (Statue), Rio de Janeiro (Brasiliana 93); 76c. Palace dome, Bangkok (Bangkok 1993) 6·50 6·50

**892** Order of San Martin

**1993.** Anniversaries. Multicoloured.
2336 38c. Type **892** (50th anniv) 1·80 85
2337 38c. Entrance to and emblem of National History Academy (centenary) 1·80 85

**893** Flag-bearer and Arms of Gendarmerie

**1993.** National Heroes Commemoration. Mult.
2338 38c. Type **893** 1·80 85
2339 38c. "Rio Iguazu" (coastguard corvette) 1·80 85

**894** Luis Candelaria and Morane Saulnier Type P Monoplane

**1993.** 75th Anniv of First Flight over the Andes.
2340 **894** 38c. multicoloured 1·90 95

**895** Snowy Egret ("Egretta thula")

**1993.** Paintings of Birds by Axel Amuchastegui. Multicoloured.
2341 38c.+38c. Type **895** 2·75 2·10
2342 38c.+38c. Scarlet-headed blackbird ("Amblyramphus holosericeus") 2·75 2·10
2343 38c.+38c. Red-crested cardinal ("Paroaria coronata") 2·75 2·10
2344 38c.+38c. Amazon kingfisher ("Chloroceryle amazona") 2·75 2·10

**896** "Coming Home" (Adriana Zaefferer)

**1993.** Paintings. Multicoloured.
2345 38c. Type **896** 1·80 85
2346 38c. "The Old House" (Norberto Russo) 1·80 85

**897** Pato

**1993.** 40th Anniv of Declaration of Pato as National Sport.
2347 **897** 1p. multicoloured 3·75 2·20

**898** Segurola's Pacara ("Enterolobium contortisiliquum")

**1993.** Old Trees in Buenos Aires. Multicoloured.
2348 75c. Type **898** (Puan and Baldomero Fernandez Moreno Streets) 2·50 1·40
2349 75c. Pueyrredon's carob tree ("Prosopis alba") (Pueyrredon Square) 2·50 1·40
2350 1p.50 Alvear's coral tree ("Erythrina falcata") (Lavalle Square) 5·25 2·50
2351 1p.50 Avellaneda's magnolia ("Magnolia grandiflora") (Adolfo Berro Avenue) 5·25 2·50

**899** Southern Right Whale

**1993.** America. Endangered Animals. Mult.
2352 50c. Type **899** 2·00 1·10
2353 75c. Commerson's dolphin 3·00 1·80

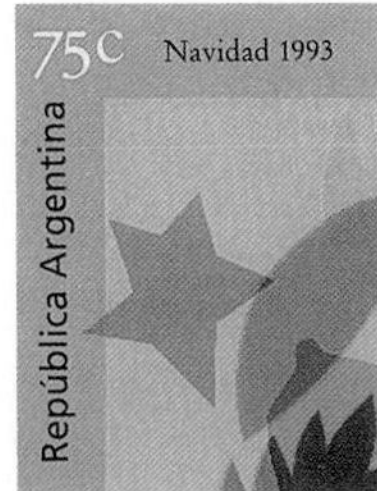

**900** Star, Leaf and Bell (Christmas)

**1993.** Christmas and New Year. Festive Symbols. Multicoloured.
2354 75c. Type **900** 3·00 1·80
2355 75c. Leaf, sun and moon (New Year) 3·00 1·80
2356 75c. Leaf and fir tree (Christmas) 3·00 1·80
2357 75c. Fish and moon (New Year) 3·00 1·80

Nos. 2354/7 were issued together, se-tenant, forming a composite design.

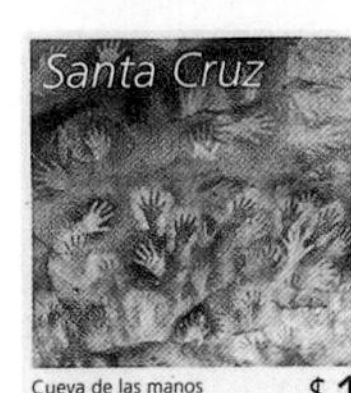

**901** Cave Painting

**1993.** Cave of Hands, Santa Cruz.
2358 **901** 1p. multicoloured 3·75 2·20

**902** Emblem

**1994.** New Argentine Post Emblem.
2359 **902** 75c. multicoloured 5·00 1·70

**903** Brazil Player

**1994.** World Cup Football Championship, U.S.A. (1st issue). Multicoloured.
2360 25c. German player 1·00 60
2361 50c. Type **903** 1·90 1·20
2362 75c. Argentine player 2·50 1·80
2363 1p. Italian player 3·75 2·40
**MS**2364 151×99 mm. 1p.50 As No. 2362 but 39×49 mm 5·75 5·25

See also Nos. 2380/3.

**904** Golden Tops

**1994.** Fungi. Multicoloured.
2365 10c. Type **904** 50 25
2366 25c. Common ink cap 75 45
2369 50c. Granulated boletus 1·50 95
2374 1p. Fly agaric 3·25 1·90
2377 2p. Common morel 6·25 3·75

**905** Argentine Player with Ball (Matias Taylor)

**1994.** World Cup Football Championship, U.S.A. (2nd issue). Winning entries in children's competition. Multicoloured.
2380 75c. Type **905** 2·75 1·20
2381 75c. Tackle (Torcuato Santiago Gonzalez Agote) 2·75 1·20
2382 75c. Players (Julian Lisenberg) (horiz) 2·75 1·20
2383 75c. Match scene (Maria Paula Palma) (horiz) 2·75 1·20

**906** Black-throated Finch

**1994.** Animals of the Falkland Islands (Islas Malvinas). Multicoloured.
2384 25c. Type **906** 1·00 60
2385 50c. Gentoo penguins 1·50 85
2386 75c. Falkland Islands flightless steamer ducks 2·50 1·20
2387 1p. Southern elephant-seal 3·25 2·10

**907** Town Arms

**1994.** Anniversaries. Multicoloured.
2388 75c. Type **907** (400th anniv of San Luis) 2·75 1·20
2389 75c. Arms (3rd anniv of provincial status of Tierra del Fuego, Antarctica and South Atlantic Islands) 3·75 1·80

**908** Ladislao Jose Biro

**1994.** Inventors. Multicoloured.
2390 75c. Type **908** (ball-point pen) 2·75 1·20
2391 75c. Raul Pateras de Pescara (helicopter) 2·75 1·20
2392 75c. Quirino Cristiani (animated films) 2·75 1·20
2393 75c. Enrique Finochietto (surgical instruments) 2·75 1·20

**909** Star, Purple Bauble and Bell

**1994.** UNICEF Children's Fund in Argentina. Multicoloured.
2394 50c. Type **909** 1·90 85
2395 75c. Bell, red bauble and star 2·75 1·20

**910** Children holding Globe (Ivana Mirna de Caro)

**1994.** "Care of the Planet". Children's Painting Competition. Multicoloured.
2396 25c. Type **910** 90 40
2397 25c. Girl polishing sunbeam and boy tending tree (Elena Tsouprik) 90 40
2398 50c. Children of all races around globe (Estefania Navarro) (horiz) 1·90 85
2399 50c. Globe as house (Maria Belen Gidoni) (horiz) 1·90 85

**911** Star and Angel (The Annunciation)

**1994.** Christmas. Multicoloured.
2400 50c. Type **911** 1·90 85
2401 75c. Madonna and Child (Nativity) 2·75 1·20

**912** Running

**1995.** 12th Pan-American Games, Mar del Plata. Multicoloured.
2402 75c. Type **912** 2·75 1·20
2403 75c. Cycling 2·75 1·20
2404 75c. Diving 2·75 1·20
2405 1p.25 Football (vert) 3·75 1·80
2406 1p.25 Gymnastics (vert) 3·75 1·80

**913** Postal Emblem

**1995.** Self-adhesive.
2407 **913** 25c. yellow, blue & black 10·00 95
2408 **913** 75c. yellow, blue & black 3·50 1·70

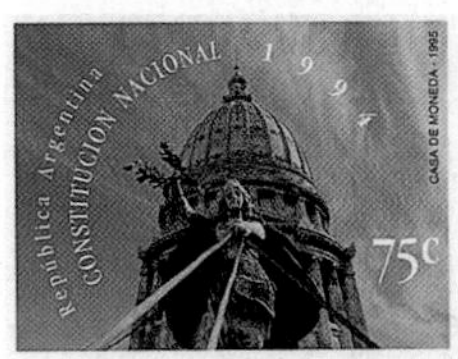

**914** National Congress Building and "The Republic Triumphant" (statue, detail)

**1995.** New Constitution, August 1994.
2409 **914** 75c. multicoloured 2·75 1·80

**915** Letters and Disk (image scaled to 75% of original size)

**1995.** 21st International Book Fair.
2410 **915** 75c. multicoloured 2·75 1·80

**916** Bay-winged Cowbird

**1995.** Birds. Multicoloured.

| | | | |
|---|---|---|---|
| 2412 | 5p. Hooded siskin | 16·00 | 12·00 |
| 2413 | 9p.40 Type **916** | 27·00 | 21·00 |
| 2414 | 10p. Rufous-collared sparrow | 29·00 | 23·00 |

**917** Clouds seen through Atrium

**1995.** Centenary of Argentine Engineers' Centre, Buenos Aires.

| | | | | |
|---|---|---|---|---|
| 2420 | **917** | 75c. multicoloured | 2·75 | 1·70 |

**918** Antoine de Saint-Exupery (pilot and writer)

**1995.** Aerofila 96 Latin American Airmail Exhibition. Sheet 130×90 mm containing T 918 and similar multicoloured design.

| | | | |
|---|---|---|---|
| **MS**2421 | 25c.+25c. Type **918**; 75c.+75c. Illustration from "The Little Prince" | 12·50 | 12·00 |

**919** "Bahia Aguirre" (supply ship)

**1995.** Argentine Antarctic. Sheet 171×91 mm containing T 919 and similar horiz design. Multicoloured.

| | | | |
|---|---|---|---|
| **MS**2422 | 75c.+25c. Type **919**; 1p.25+75c. Lockheed C-130 Hercules transport plane | 14·00 | 14·00 |

**920** Jose Marti

**1995.** Revolutionaries' Anniversaries. Mult.

| | | | |
|---|---|---|---|
| 2423 | 1p. Type **920** (death cent) | 3·75 | 2·40 |
| 2424 | 1p. Antonio de Sucre (birth bicentenary) | 3·75 | 2·40 |

**921** Greater Rhea

**1995.** Birds. Multicoloured.

| | | | |
|---|---|---|---|
| 2425 | 5c. Type **921** | 15 | 10 |
| 2425a | 10c. Giant wood rail ("ipecae") | 65 | 25 |
| 2426 | 25c. King penguin | 90 | 40 |
| 2427 | 50c. Toco toucan | 1·90 | 80 |
| 2428 | 75c. Andean condor | 2·75 | 1·60 |
| 2429 | 1p. Barn owl | 5·00 | 2·40 |
| 2430 | 2p. Olivaceous cormorant | 8·75 | 4·75 |
| 2431 | 2p.75 Southern lapwing | 10·50 | 6·25 |
| 2432 | 3p.25 Southern lapwing | 15·00 | 7·75 |

**1995.** Animals. As T 921. Multicoloured.

| | | | |
|---|---|---|---|
| 2436 | 25c. Alligator | 90 | 55 |
| 2437 | 50c. Red fox | 1·90 | 1·20 |
| 2438 | 75c. Anteater | 2·75 | 1·70 |
| 2439 | 75c. Vicuna | 2·75 | 1·70 |
| 2440 | 75c. Sperm whale | 2·75 | 1·70 |

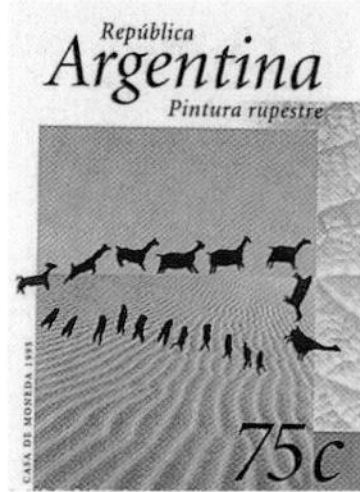


**922** Cave Painting (Patagonia)

**1995.** Archaeology. Multicoloured.

| | | | |
|---|---|---|---|
| 2441 | 75c. Type **922** | 2·75 | 1·70 |
| 2442 | 75c. Stone mask (Tafi culture, Tucuman) | 2·75 | 1·70 |
| 2443 | 75c. Anthropomorphic vase (Catamarca) | 2·75 | 1·70 |
| 2444 | 75c. Woven cloth (North Patagonia) | 2·75 | 1·70 |

**923** Peron

**1995.** Birth Centenary of Juan Peron (President, 1946–55 and 1973–74).

| | | | | |
|---|---|---|---|---|
| 2445 | **923** | 75c. blue and bistre | 2·75 | 1·70 |

**924** Postal Emblem on Sunflower

**1995**

| | | | | |
|---|---|---|---|---|
| 2446 | **924** | 75c. multicoloured | 8·75 | 2·40 |

**925** "50" Emblem

**1995.** Anniversaries. Sheet 110×80 mm containing T 925 and similar horiz designs. Multicoloured.

| | | | |
|---|---|---|---|
| **MS**2447 | 75c. Type **925** (50th anniv of United Nations Organization); 75c. "50" and emblem (50th anniv of International Civil Aviation Organization); 75c. "50" and emblem (50th anniv of Food and Agriculture Organization); 75c. "75" and emblem (75th anniv of International Labour Organization) | 12·00 | 12·00 |

**926** Christmas Tree

**1995.** Christmas. Multicoloured.

| | | | |
|---|---|---|---|
| 2448 | 75c. Type **926** | 2·75 | 1·70 |
| 2449 | 75c. "1996" | 2·75 | 1·70 |
| 2450 | 75c. Glasses of champagne | 2·75 | 1·70 |
| 2451 | 75c. Present | 2·75 | 1·70 |
| 2452 | 75c. Type **926** | 2·75 | 1·70 |

**927** "Les 400 Coups" (dir. Francois Truffaut)

**1995.** Centenary of Motion Pictures. Each black, grey and orange.

| | | | |
|---|---|---|---|
| 2453 | 75c. "Battleship Potemkin" (dir. Sergei Eisenstein) | 2·75 | 1·70 |
| 2454 | 75c. "Casablanca" (dir. Michael Curtiz) | 2·75 | 1·70 |
| 2455 | 75c. "Bicycle Thieves" (dir. Vittorio de Sica) | 2·75 | 1·70 |
| 2456 | 75c. Charlie Chaplin in "Limelight" | 2·75 | 1·70 |
| 2457 | 75c. Type **927** | 2·75 | 1·70 |
| 2458 | 75c. "Chronicle of an Only Child" (dir. Leonardo Favio) | 2·75 | 1·70 |

**928** Horse-drawn Mail Coach

**1995.** America (1994). Postal Transport. Mult.

| | | | |
|---|---|---|---|
| 2459 | 75c. Type **928** | 2·75 | 1·70 |
| 2460 | 75c. Early postal van | 2·75 | 1·70 |

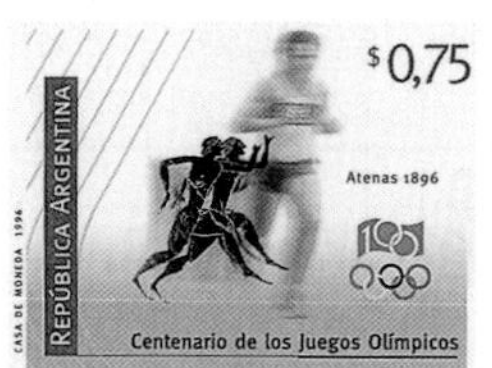


**929** Dirigible Airship

**1995.** The Sky. Multicoloured.

| | | | |
|---|---|---|---|
| 2461 | 25c. Type **929** | 1·00 | 65 |
| 2462 | 25c. Kite | 1·00 | 65 |
| 2463 | 25c. Hot-air balloon | 1·00 | 65 |
| 2464 | 50c. Balloons | 2·00 | 1·30 |
| 2465 | 50c. Paper airplane | 2·00 | 1·30 |
| 2466 | 75c. Airplane | 2·75 | 1·70 |
| 2467 | 75c. Helicopter | 2·75 | 1·70 |
| 2468 | 75c. Parachute | 2·75 | 1·70 |

**930** Ancient Greek and Modern Runners

**1996.** Multicoloured. (a) Centenary of Modern Olympic Games. Horiz designs.

| | | | |
|---|---|---|---|
| 2471 | 75c. Type **930** | 2·75 | 1·70 |
| 2472 | 1p. "The Discus Thrower" (ancient Greek statue, Miron) and modern thrower | 4·00 | 2·50 |

(b) Olympic Games. Vert designs.

| | | | |
|---|---|---|---|
| 2473 | 75c. Torch bearer (Buenos Aires, 2004) | 2·75 | 1·70 |
| 2474 | 1p. Rowing (Atlanta, 1996) | 4·00 | 2·50 |

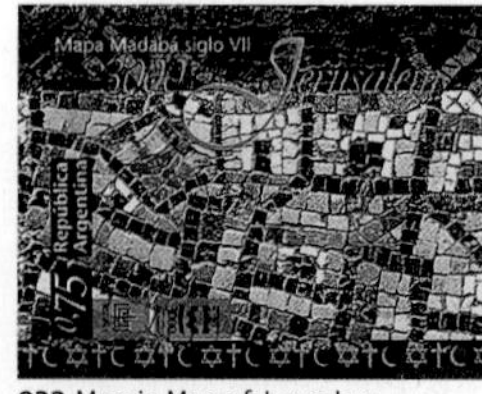


**931** Francisco Muniz (founder of Academy of Medicine and Public Hygiene Council)

**1996.** Physicians' Anniversaries. Multicoloured.

| | | | |
|---|---|---|---|
| 2475 | 50c. Type **931** (birth bicentenary (1995)) | 2·00 | 1·30 |
| 2476 | 50c. Ricardo Gutierrez (founder of Children's Hospital and co-founder of periodical "La Patria Argentina", death centenary) | 2·00 | 1·30 |
| 2477 | 50c. Ignacio Pirovano (death centenary (1995)) | 2·00 | 1·30 |
| 2478 | 50c. Esteban Maradona (birth centenary (1995) and first death anniv) | 2·00 | 1·30 |

**932** Mosaic Map of Jerusalem (left-hand detail)

**1996.** 3000th Anniv of Jerusalem. Multicoloured.

| | | | |
|---|---|---|---|
| 2479 | 75c. Type **932** | 2·75 | 1·70 |
| 2480 | 75c. Map (right-hand detail) | 2·75 | 1·70 |

Nos. 2479/80 were issued together, se-tenant, forming a composite design.

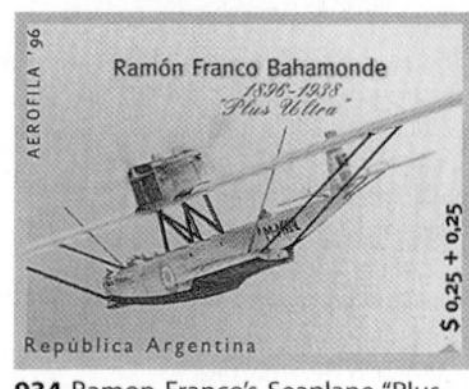


**933** Capybaras

**1996.** America. Endangered Species. Mult.

| | | | |
|---|---|---|---|
| 2481 | 75c. Type **933** | 2·75 | 1·70 |
| 2482 | 75c. Guanacos | 2·75 | 1·70 |

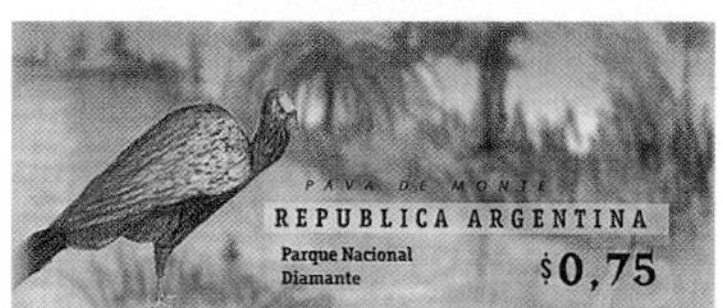


**934** Ramon Franco's Seaplane "Plus Ultra"

**1996.** "Aerofila '96" Latin American Airmail Exhibition. Aircraft. Multicoloured.

| | | | |
|---|---|---|---|
| 2483 | 25c.+25c. Type **934** | 2·00 | 1·30 |
| 2484 | 25c.+25c. Alberto Santos-Dumont's biplane "14 bis" | 2·00 | 1·30 |
| 2485 | 50c.+50c. Charles Lindbergh's "Spirit of St. Louis" | 4·00 | 2·50 |
| 2486 | 50c.+50c. Eduardo Olivero's biplane "Buenos Aires" | 4·00 | 2·50 |

**1996.** As Nos. 2407/8. Self-adhesive. Imperf.

| | | | | |
|---|---|---|---|---|
| 2486a | **913** | 25c. yellow and blue | 2·40 | 1·50 |
| 2486b | **913** | 75c. yellow and blue | 4·50 | 2·75 |

**935** Dusky-legged Guan, Diamante National Park (image scaled to 75% of original size)

**1996.** National Parks. Multicoloured.

| | | | |
|---|---|---|---|
| 2487 | 75c. Type **935** | 2·75 | 1·70 |
| 2488 | 75c. Mountain viscacha, El Leoncito Nature Reserve | 2·75 | 1·70 |
| 2489 | 75c. Marsh deer, Otamendi Nature Reserve | 2·75 | 1·70 |
| 2490 | 75c. Red-spectacled amazon, San Antonio Nature Reserve | 2·75 | 1·70 |

**936** Dragon

**1996.** Murals from Buenos Aires Underground Railway. Multicoloured.

| | | | |
|---|---|---|---|
| 2491 | 1p.+50c. Type **936** | 5·25 | 2·75 |
| 2492 | 1p.50+1p. Bird | 8·75 | 4·75 |

**937** "San Antonio" (tank landing ship)

**1996.** Cent of Port Belgrano Naval Base. Mult.

| | | | |
|---|---|---|---|
| 2493 | 25c. Type **937** | 1·30 | 80 |
| 2494 | 50c. "Rosales" (corvette) | 2·00 | 1·30 |
| 2495 | 75c. "Hercules" (destroyer) | 2·75 | 1·70 |
| 2496 | 1p. "25 de Mayo" (aircraft carrier) | 3·75 | 2·40 |

**938** Decorative Panel

**1996.** Carousel. Multicoloured.

| | | | |
|---|---|---|---|
| 2497 | 25c. Type **938** | 1·00 | 65 |
| 2498 | 25c. Child on horse | 1·00 | 65 |
| 2499 | 25c. Carousel | 1·00 | 65 |
| 2500 | 50c. Fairground horses | 2·00 | 1·30 |
| 2501 | 50c. Child in airplane | 2·00 | 1·30 |
| 2502 | 50c. Pig | 2·00 | 1·30 |
| 2503 | 75c. Child in car | 2·75 | 1·70 |

**939** Head Post Office, Buenos Aires

**1996.** Size 24½×34½ mm. Self-adhesive. Imperf.

| | | | | |
|---|---|---|---|---|
| 2504 | **939** | 75c. multicoloured | 3·75 | 2·00 |

See also Nos. 2537/8.

**940** "Adoration of the Wise Men" (Gladys Rinaldi)

**1996.** Christmas. Tapestries. Multicoloured.

| | | | |
|---|---|---|---|
| 2505 | 75c. Type **940** | 2·75 | 1·70 |
| 2506 | 1p. Abstract (Norma Bonet de Maekawa) (horiz) | 4·00 | 2·50 |

**941** Melchior Base

**1996.** Argentinian Presence in Antarctic. Mult.

| | | | |
|---|---|---|---|
| 2507 | 75c. Type **941** | 2·75 | 1·70 |
| 2508 | 1p.25 "Irizar" (ice-breaker) | 5·00 | 3·25 |

**942** "Vahine no te Miti" (Gauguin)

**1996.** Cent of National Gallery of Fine Arts. Mult.

| | | | |
|---|---|---|---|
| 2509 | 75c. Type **942** | 2·50 | 1·60 |
| 2510 | 1p. "The Nymph surprised" (Edouard Manet) | 3·25 | 2·00 |
| 2511 | 1p. "Figure of Woman" (Amedeo Modigliani) | 3·25 | 2·00 |
| 2512 | 1p.25 "Woman lying down" (Pablo Picasso) (horiz) | 3·75 | 2·40 |

**943** Granite Mining, Cordoba

**1997.** Mining Industry. Multicoloured.

| | | | |
|---|---|---|---|
| 2513 | 75c. Type **943** | 2·75 | 1·70 |
| 2514 | 1p.25 Borax mining, Salta | 5·00 | 3·25 |

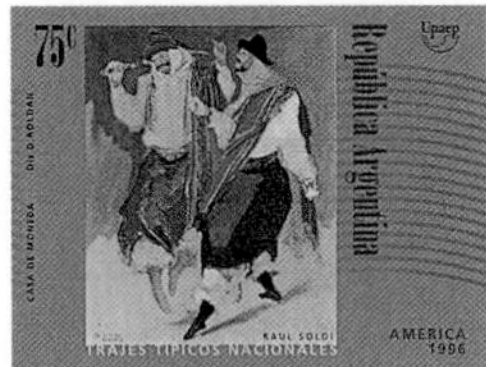


**944** "They amuse Themselves in Dancing" (Raul Soldi)

**1997.** America (1996). National Costume.

| | | | | |
|---|---|---|---|---|
| 2515 | **944** | 75c. multicoloured | 2·75 | 1·70 |

**945** Arms, Sabre and Shako

**1997.** Centenary of Repatriation of General San Martin's Sabre.

| | | | | |
|---|---|---|---|---|
| 2516 | **945** | 75c. multicoloured | 2·75 | 1·70 |

**946** Match Scene

**1997.** 29th World Rugby Youth Championship, Argentina.

| | | | | |
|---|---|---|---|---|
| 2517 | **946** | 75c. multicoloured | 2·75 | 1·70 |

**947** "Fortuna" (yacht)

**1997.** 50th Anniv of Buenos Aires to Rio de Janeiro Regatta.

| | | | | |
|---|---|---|---|---|
| 2518 | **947** | 75c. multicoloured | 2·75 | 1·70 |

**948** Ceres Design, France (1849–52)

**1997.** "Mevifil '97" First Int Exn of Philatelic Audio-visual and Computer Systems. Mult.

| | | | |
|---|---|---|---|
| 2519 | 50c.+50c. Type **948** | 4·50 | 2·75 |
| 2520 | 50c.+50c. Queen Isabella II design, Spain (1851) | 4·50 | 2·75 |
| 2521 | 50c.+50c. Rivadavia design, Argentine Republic (1864) | 4·50 | 2·75 |
| 2522 | 50c.+50c. Paddle-steamer design, Buenos Aires (1858) | 4·50 | 2·75 |

Nos. 2519/22 were issued together, se-tenant, with the centre of the block forming the composite design of an eye.

**949** Museum

**1997.** Centenary of National History Museum, Buenos Aires.

| | | | | |
|---|---|---|---|---|
| 2523 | **949** | 75c. multicoloured | 2·75 | 1·70 |

**950** Seal and Oak Leaf

**1997.** Centenary of La Plata National University.

| | | | | |
|---|---|---|---|---|
| 2524 | **950** | 75c. multicoloured | 2·75 | 1·70 |

**951** Carcano (after Dolores Capdevila)

**1997.** 50th Death Anniv (1996) of Ramon Carcano (postal reformer).

| | | | | |
|---|---|---|---|---|
| 2525 | **951** | 75c. multicoloured | 2·75 | 1·70 |

**952** Cabo Virgenes Lighthouse

**1997.** Lighthouses. Multicoloured.

| | | | |
|---|---|---|---|
| 2526 | 75c. Type **952** | 2·75 | 1·70 |
| 2527 | 75c. Isla Pinguino | 2·75 | 1·70 |
| 2528 | 75c. San Juan de Salvamento | 2·75 | 1·70 |
| 2529 | 75c. Punta Delgada | 2·75 | 1·70 |

**953** Condor and Olympic Rings

**1997.** Inclusion of Buenos Aires in Final Selection Round for 2004 Olympic Games.

| | | | | |
|---|---|---|---|---|
| 2530 | **953** | 75c. multicoloured | 2·75 | 1·70 |

**954** Lacroze Company Suburban Service, 1912

**1997.** Centenary of First Electric Tramway in Buenos Aires. Illustrations from "History of the Tram" by Marcelo Mayorga. Multicoloured.

| | | | |
|---|---|---|---|
| 2531 | 75c. Type **954** | 2·75 | 1·70 |
| 2532 | 75c. Lacroze Company urban service, 1907 | 2·75 | 1·70 |
| 2533 | 75c. Anglo Argentina Company tramcar, 1930 | 2·75 | 1·70 |
| 2534 | 75c. City of Buenos Aires Transport Corporation tramcar, 1942 | 2·75 | 1·70 |
| 2535 | 75c. Fabricaciones Militares tramcar, 1956 | 2·75 | 1·70 |
| 2536 | 75c. Electricos de Sur Company tramcar, 1908 | 2·75 | 1·70 |

Nos. 2531/6 were issued together, se-tenant, showing a composite design of a tram in a city street.

**1997.** As No. 2504 but size 23×35 mm. Self-adhesive. Imperf.

| | | | | |
|---|---|---|---|---|
| 2537 | **939** | 25c. multicoloured | 1·00 | 65 |
| 2538 | **939** | 75c. multicoloured | 2·75 | 1·70 |

**955** Monument (by Mauricio Molina)

**1997.** Inauguration of Monument to Joaquin Gonzalez (politician) at La Rioja.

| | | | | |
|---|---|---|---|---|
| 2539 | **955** | 75c. multicoloured | 2·75 | 1·70 |

**956** Alberto Ginastera (after Carlos Nine)

**1997.** Composers. Multicoloured.

| | | | |
|---|---|---|---|
| 2540 | 75c. Type **956** | 2·75 | 1·70 |
| 2541 | 75c. Astor Piazzolla (after Carlos Alonso) | 2·75 | 1·70 |
| 2542 | 75c. Anibal Troilo (after Hermenegildo Sabat) | 2·75 | 1·70 |
| 2543 | 75c. Atahualpa Yupanqui (after Luis Scafati) | 2·75 | 1·70 |

**957** "Tren a las Nubes", Salta

**1997.** Trains. Multicoloured.

| | | | |
|---|---|---|---|
| 2544 | 50c.+50c. Type **957** | 4·50 | 2·75 |
| 2545 | 50c.+50c. Preserved steam locomotive, Buenos Aires | 4·50 | 2·75 |
| 2546 | 50c.+50c. Patagonian express "La Trochita" Rio Negro–Chubut | 4·50 | 2·75 |
| 2547 | 50c.+50c. Austral Fueguino Railway locomotive No. 2, Tierra del Fuego | 4·50 | 2·75 |

**958** Eva Peron (after Raul Manteola)

**1997.** 50th Anniv of Women's Suffrage.

| | | | | |
|---|---|---|---|---|
| 2548 | **958** | 75c. pink and grey | 2·75 | 1·70 |

**959** Jorge Luis Borges and Maze

**1997.** Writers. Multicoloured.

| | | | |
|---|---|---|---|
| 2549 | 1p. Type **959** | 3·75 | 2·40 |
| 2550 | 1p. Julio Cortazar and hop-scotch grid | 3·75 | 2·40 |

**1997.** 70th Anniv of Air Mail in Argentina. No. MS2421 optd 1927 1997 ANIVERSARIO AEROPOSTA ARGENTINA in margin.

| | | | |
|---|---|---|---|
| **MS**2551 | 25c.+25c. multicoloured; 75c.+75c. multicoloured | 12·00 | 7·50 |

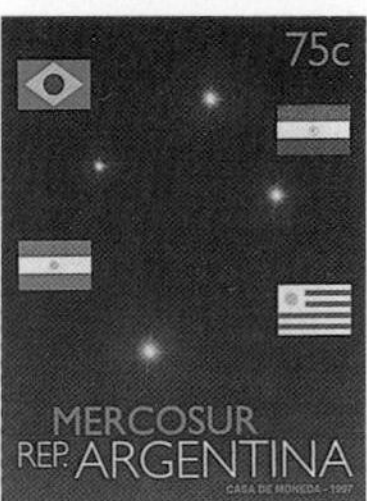


**961** Members' Flags and Southern Cross

**1997.** Mercosur (South American Common Market).

2552 **961** 75c. multicoloured 3·25 2·00

**962** "Presidente Sarmiento" (Hugo Leban)

**1997.** Centenary of Launch of "Presidente Sarmiento" (cadet ship). Multicoloured.

2553 75c. Type **962** 3·25 2·00

**MS**2554 150×100 mm. 75c. "Presidente Sarmiento" at sea; 75c. Figurehead (vert) 8·75 5·50

**963** Guevara

**1997.** 30th Death Anniv of Ernesto "Che" Guevara (revolutionary).

2555 **963** 75c. brown, red & black 3·75 2·00

**964** Vicuna (Julian Chiapparo)

**1997.** "Draw an Ecostamp" Children's Competition Winners. Multicoloured.

2556 50c. Type **964** 2·10 1·30

2557 50c. Vicuna (Leandro Lopez Portal) 2·10 1·30

2558 75c. Seal (Andres Lloren) (horiz) 3·00 1·90

2559 75c. Ashy-headed goose (Jose Saccone) (horiz) 3·00 1·90

**965** "Nativity" (Mary Jose)

**1997.** Christmas. Tapestries of the Nativity. Designs by artists named. Mult. (a) Size 45×34 mm.

2560 75c. Type **965** 3·00 2·00

(b) Size 44×27 mm. Self-adhesive. Imperf.

2561 25c. Elena Aguilar 95 65

2562 25c. Silvia Pettachi 95 65

2563 50c. Ana Escobar 2·00 1·30

2564 50c. Alejandra Martinez 2·00 1·30

2565 75c. As No. 2560 but with inscriptions differently arranged 3·00 2·00

2566 75c. Nidia Martinez 3·00 2·00

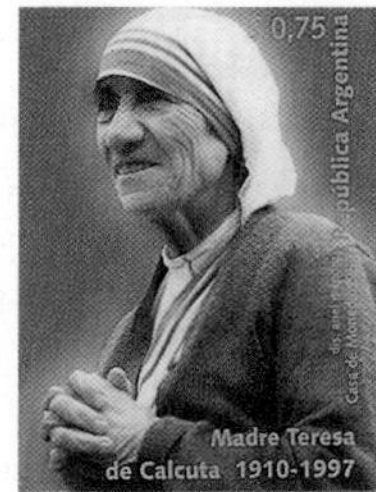


**966** Mother Teresa

**1997.** Mother Teresa (founder of the Missionaries of Charity) Commemoration.

2567 **966** 75c. multicoloured 3·00 2·00

**967** Houssay

**1998.** 50th Anniv (1997) of Award to Bernardo Houssay of Nobel Prize for Medicine and Physiology.

2568 **967** 75c. multicoloured 3·00 2·00

**968** Mountaineers

**1998.** Cent of First Ascent of Mt. Aconcagua.

2569 **968** 1p.25 multicoloured 5·25 3·50

**969** San Martin de los Andes and Lake Lacar

**1998.** Centenary of San Martin de los Andes.

2570 **969** 75c. multicoloured 3·00 2·00

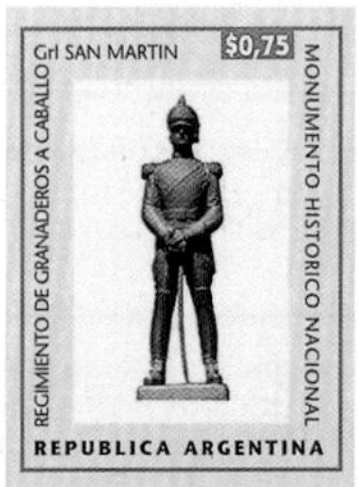


**970** Grenadier Monument (Juan Carlos Ferraro)

**1998.** Declaration as National Historical Monument of Palermo Barracks of General San Martin Horse Grenadiers. Multicoloured.

2571 75c. Type **970** 3·00 2·00

2572 75c. Sevres urn with portrait of San Martin 3·00 2·00

2573 75c. Regiment coat of arms 3·00 2·00

2574 75c. Main facade of barracks 3·00 2·00

**971** Globe and Baby

**1998.** Protection of Ozone Layer.

2575 **971** 75c. multicoloured 3·00 2·00

**972** Postman, 1920

**1998.** America. The Postman. Multicoloured.

2576 75c. Type **972** 3·00 2·00

2577 75c. Postman, 1998 3·00 2·00

**973** "El Reino del Reves"

**1998.** Stories by Maria Elena Walsh. Illustrations by Eduardo and Ricardo Fuhrmann. Multicoloured. Self-adhesive.

2578 75c. Type **973** 3·00 2·00

2579 75c. "Zoo Loco" 3·00 2·00

2580 75c. "Dailan Kifki" 3·00 2·00

2581 75c. "Manuelita" 3·00 2·00

**974** St Peter's, Fiambala, Catamarca

**1998.** Historic Chapels. Multicoloured.

2582 75c. Type **974** 3·00 2·00

2583 75c. Huacalera, Jujuy 3·00 2·00

2584 75c. St. Dominic's, La Rioja 3·00 2·00

2585 75c. Tumbaya, Jujuy 3·00 2·00

**975** Raised Hands

**1998.** White Helmets (volunteer humanitarian workers).

2586 **975** 1p. multicoloured 4·25 2·75

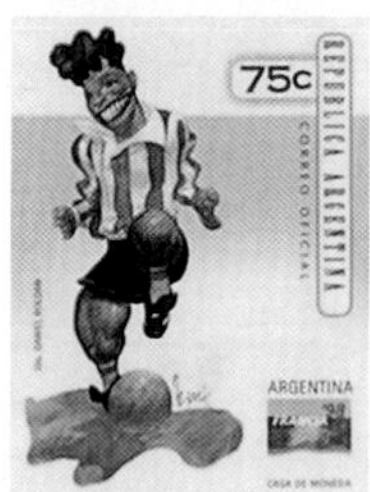


**976** Argentine Player

**1998.** World Cup Football Championship, France. Multicoloured.

2587 75c. Type **976** 3·00 2·00

2588 75c. Croatian player 3·00 2·00

2589 75c. Jamaican player 3·00 2·00

2590 75c. Japanese player 3·00 2·00

**977** Typewriter, Camera, Pen, Computer and Satellite

**1998.** Journalism Day.

2591 **977** 75c. multicoloured 3·00 2·00

**978** Corrientes 1860 3c. Stamps and Postal Emblem

**1998.** 250th Anniv of Establishment of Regular Postal Service in Rio de la Plata (Spanish dominion in South America). Multicoloured.

2592 75c. Type **978** 3·00 2·00

2593 75c. Buenos Aires Post Office and pillar box 3·00 2·00

**979** Jesuit Ruins, San Ignacio Mini

**1998.** Mercosur Missions.

2594 **979** 75c. multicoloured 3·00 2·00

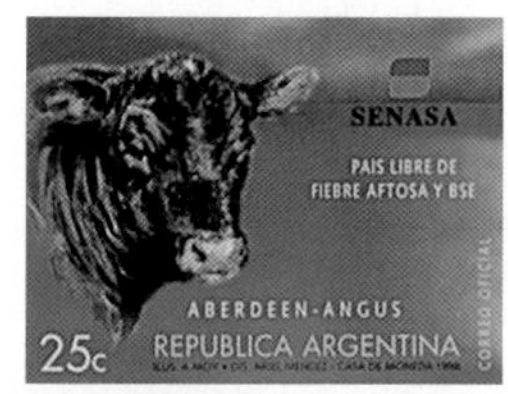


**980** Aberdeen Angus

**1998.** Cattle. Multicoloured.

2595 25c. Type **980** 1·20 80

2596 25c. Brahman 1·20 80

2597 50c. Hereford 2·10 1·40

2598 50c. Criolla 2·10 1·40

2599 75c. Holando-Argentina 3·00 2·00

2600 75c. Shorthorn 3·00 2·00

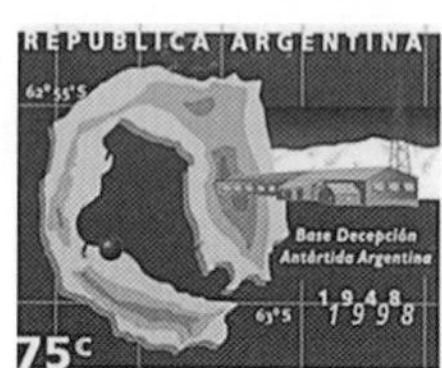


**981** Map and Base

**1998.** 50th Anniv of Decepcion Antarctic Base.

2601 **981** 75c. multicoloured 3·25 2·00

**982** Anniversary Emblem

**1998.** 50th Anniv of State of Israel.

2602 **982** 75c. multicoloured 3·25 2·00

**983** Bridge in Japanese Garden, Buenos Aires

**1998.** Cent of Argentina–Japan Friendship Treaty.

2603 **983** 75c. multicoloured 3·25 2·00

**984** Facade and clock

**1998.** 70th Anniv of Head Post Office, Buenos Aires. Multicoloured.

| | | | |
|---|---|---|---|
| 2604 | 75c. Type **984** | 3·25 | 2·00 |
| 2605 | 75c. Capital and bench | 3·25 | 2·00 |

**985** Patoruzu (Quinterno)

**1998.** Comic Strip Characters. Multicoloured.

| | | | |
|---|---|---|---|
| 2606 | 75c. Type **985** | 3·25 | 2·00 |
| 2607 | 75c. Matias (Sendra) | 3·25 | 2·00 |
| 2608 | 75c. Clemente (Caloi) | 3·25 | 2·00 |
| 2609 | 75c. El Eternauta (Oesterheld Solano Lopez) | 3·25 | 2·00 |
| 2610 | 75c. Loco Chavez (Trillo Altuna) | 3·25 | 2·00 |
| 2611 | 75c. Inodoro Pereyra (Fontanarrosa) | 3·25 | 2·00 |
| 2612 | 75c. Tia Vicenta (Landru) | 3·25 | 2·00 |
| 2613 | 75c. Gaturro (Nik) | 3·25 | 2·00 |

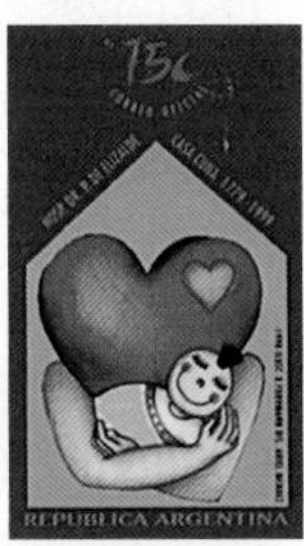

**986** Heart with Arms holding Baby

**1998.** 220th Anniv of Dr. Pedro de Elizalde Children's Hospital.

| | | | | |
|---|---|---|---|---|
| 2614 | **986** | 75c. multicoloured | 3·25 | 2·00 |

**987** Post Banner and Pennant, 1785, and Arms of Maritime Post

**1998.** "Espamer '98" Iberian–Latin American Stamp Exhibition, Buenos Aires. Mult. Self-adhesive.

| | | | |
|---|---|---|---|
| 2615 | 25c. Type **987** | 1·10 | 70 |
| 2616 | 75c. Mail brigantine | 3·25 | 2·00 |
| 2617 | 75c.+75c. Mail brigantine (different) | 6·50 | 4·25 |
| 2618 | 1p.25+1p.25 Mail brig | 10·50 | 7·00 |

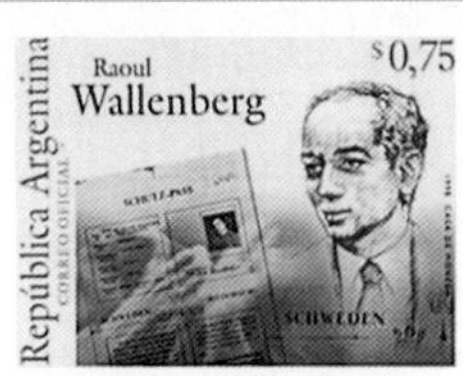

**988** Passport and Wallenberg

**1998.** Raoul Wallenberg (Swedish diplomat in Hungary who helped Jews escape, 1944–45) Commemoration.

| | | | | |
|---|---|---|---|---|
| 2619 | **988** | 75c. multicoloured | 3·00 | 2·00 |

**989** Aguada Culture Bird

**1998.** 50th Anniv of Organization of American States.

| | | | | |
|---|---|---|---|---|
| 2620 | **989** | 75c. multicoloured | 3·00 | 2·00 |

**990** Eoraptor

**1998.** Prehistoric Animals. Multicoloured.

| | | | |
|---|---|---|---|
| 2621 | 75c. Type **990** | 3·50 | 2·40 |
| 2622 | 75c. Gasparinisaura | 3·50 | 2·40 |
| 2623 | 75c. Giganotosaurus | 3·50 | 2·40 |
| 2624 | 75c. Patagosaurus | 3·50 | 2·40 |

Nos. 2621/4 were issued together, se-tenant, forming a composite design.

**991** Child as Angel, Stars and Score

**1998.** Christmas.

| | | | | |
|---|---|---|---|---|
| 2625 | **991** | 75c. multicoloured | 3·00 | 2·00 |

**992** Juan Figueroa (founder) and First Issue

**1998.** Centenary of "El Liberal" (newspaper).

| | | | | |
|---|---|---|---|---|
| 2626 | **992** | 75c. multicoloured | 3·00 | 2·00 |

**993** Postman

**1998.** Postmen. Size 25×35 mm. Multicoloured. Self-adhesive.

| | | | |
|---|---|---|---|
| 2627 | 25c. Type **993** | 95 | 65 |
| 2628 | 75c. Modern postman | 3·00 | 2·00 |

For 75c. in reduced size see No. 2640.

**1998.** Birds. As T 921. Multicoloured. Self-adhesive.

| | | | |
|---|---|---|---|
| 2629 | 60c. Red-tailed comet | 2·10 | 1·40 |

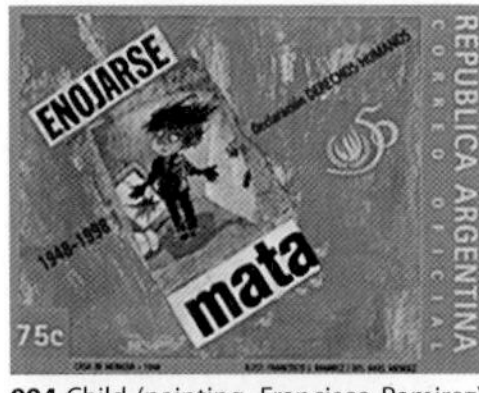

**994** Child (painting, Francisco Ramirez)

**1998.** 50th Anniv of Universal Declaration of Human Rights.

| | | | | |
|---|---|---|---|---|
| 2635 | **994** | 75c. multicoloured | 3·00 | 2·00 |

**995** Enrique Julio (founder) and Newspaper Offices

**1998.** Cent of "La Nueva Provincia" (newspaper).

| | | | | |
|---|---|---|---|---|
| 2636 | **995** | 75c. multicoloured | 3·00 | 2·00 |

**996** "Haggadah" of Pessah (exhibit) and Carving on Cathedral

**1998.** Permanent Exhibition commemorating Holocaust Victims, Buenos Aires Cathedral.

| | | | | |
|---|---|---|---|---|
| 2637 | **996** | 75c. multicoloured | 3·00 | 2·00 |

**1999.** Postmen. Size 21×27 mm. Mult. Self-adhesive.

| | | | |
|---|---|---|---|
| 2638 | 25c. Type **993** | 85 | 55 |
| 2639 | 50c. Postman, 1950 | 1·50 | 1·00 |
| 2640 | 75c. As No. 2628 | 2·40 | 1·60 |

**997** Oil-smeared Magellanic Penguin

**1999.** International Year of the Ocean. Mult.

| | | | |
|---|---|---|---|
| 2641 | 50c. Type **997** | 1·70 | 1·10 |
| 2642 | 75c. Dolphins (horiz) | 2·50 | 1·70 |

**998** Buildings and Draughtsman's Instruments

**1999.** National Arts Fund.

| | | | | |
|---|---|---|---|---|
| 2643 | **998** | 75c. multicoloured | 2·40 | 1·60 |

**999** Computer and Book

**1999.** 25th Book Fair, Buenos Aires. Multicoloured.

| | | | |
|---|---|---|---|
| 2644 | 75c. Type **999** | 2·75 | 1·80 |
| 2645 | 75c. Obelisk, compact disk case and readers | 2·75 | 1·80 |

Nos. 2644/5 were issued together, se-tenant, forming a composite design.

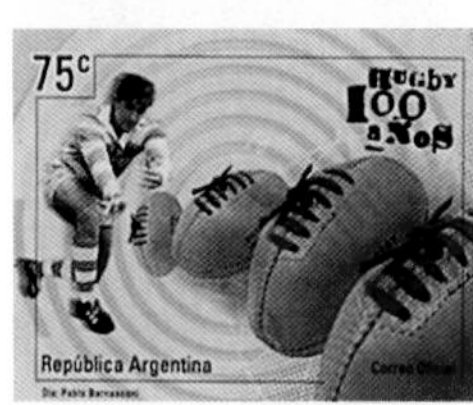

**1000** Rugby Balls and Player

**1999.** Centenary of Argentine Rugby Union. Multicoloured.

| | | | |
|---|---|---|---|
| 2646 | 75c. Type **1000** | 2·75 | 1·80 |
| **MS**2647 | 120×90 mm. 1p.50 19th-century and modern players | 5·00 | 4·00 |

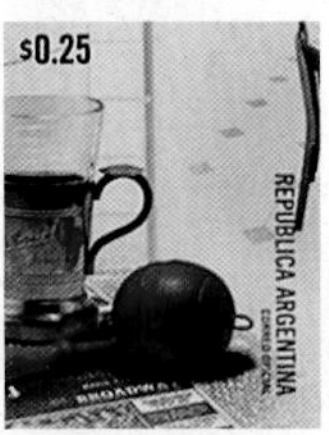

**1001** Glass, La Giralda

**1999.** Cafes. Multicoloured. Self-adhesive.

| | | | |
|---|---|---|---|
| 2648 | 25c. Type **1001** | 85 | 55 |
| 2649 | 75c. Two glasses, Cafe Homero Manzi | 2·50 | 1·70 |

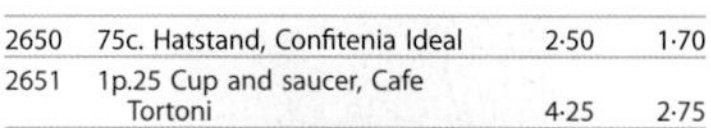

| | | | |
|---|---|---|---|
| 2650 | 75c. Hatstand, Confitenia Ideal | 2·50 | 1·70 |
| 2651 | 1p.25 Cup and saucer, Cafe Tortoni | 4·25 | 2·75 |

**1002** Pierre de Coubertin, 1924 Olympic Gold Medal and Olympic Rings

**1999.** 75th Anniv of Argentine Olympic Committee.

| | | | | |
|---|---|---|---|---|
| 2652 | **1002** | 75c. multicoloured | 2·50 | 1·70 |

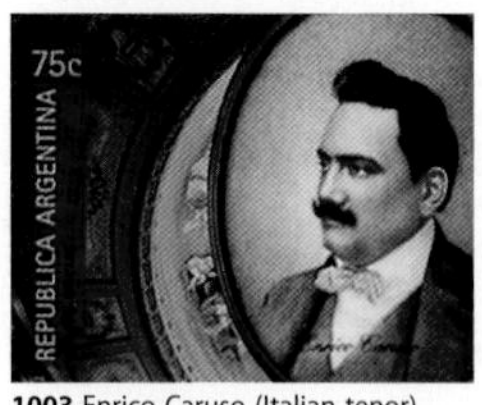

**1003** Enrico Caruso (Italian tenor)

**1999.** Opera. Multicoloured.

| | | | |
|---|---|---|---|
| 2653 | 75c. Type **1003** (125th birth anniv and centenary of American debut) | 2·50 | 1·60 |
| 2654 | 75c. Singer and musical instruments | 2·50 | 1·60 |
| 2655 | 75c. Buenos Aires Opera House | 2·50 | 1·60 |
| 2656 | 75c. Scene from "El Matrero" (Felipe Boero) | 2·50 | 1·60 |

**1004** Rosario Vera Penaloza (educationist)

**1999.** America (1998). Famous Women. Mult.

| | | | |
|---|---|---|---|
| 2659 | 75c. Type **1004** | 2·50 | 1·70 |
| 2660 | 75c. Julieta Lanteri (women's rights campaigner) | 2·50 | 1·70 |

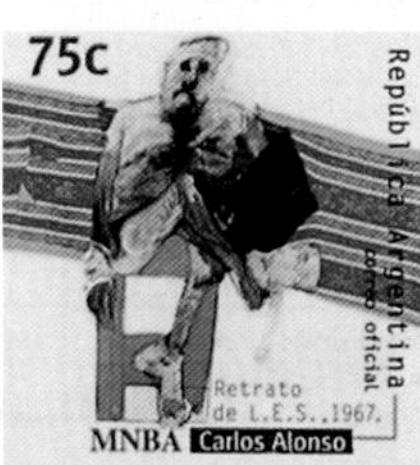

**1005** "Portrait of L. E. S." (Carlos Alonso)

**1999.** Paintings. Two sheets each 150×100 mm containing multicoloured designs as T 1005.

| | | | |
|---|---|---|---|
| **MS**2661 | Two sheets. (a) 75c. "Anarchy of Year 20" (Luis Felipe Noe) (78×39 mm); 75c. Type **1005**. (b) 75c. "Typical Orchestra" (Antonio Berni) (69×49 mm); 75c. Unititled (Aida Carballo) (39×49 mm) | 10·00 | 10·00 |

**1006** Local Road Network

**1999.** Bulk Mailing Stamps. Mult. Self-adhesive.

| | | | |
|---|---|---|---|
| 2662 | 35c. Type **1006** | 1·20 | 80 |
| 2663 | 40c. Town plan | 1·30 | 85 |
| 2664 | 50c. Regional map | 1·70 | 1·10 |

**1007** Carrier Pigeon

**1999**

| | | | | |
|---|---|---|---|---|
| 2665 | **1007** | 75c. multicoloured | 2·75 | 1·90 |

**1008** Boxer

**1999.** Dogs. Multicoloured.

| | | | |
|---|---|---|---|
| 2666 | 25c. Type **1008** | 70 | 45 |
| 2667 | 25c. Old English sheepdog | 70 | 45 |
| 2668 | 50c. Welsh collie | 1·30 | 85 |
| 2669 | 50c. St. Bernard | 1·30 | 85 |
| 2670 | 75c. German shepherd | 2·10 | 1·40 |
| 2671 | 75c. Siberian husky | 2·10 | 1·40 |

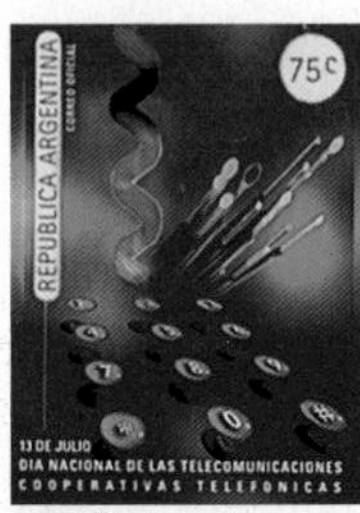

**1009** Telephone Keypad

**1999.** National Telecommunications Day.

| | | | | |
|---|---|---|---|---|
| 2672 | **1009** | 75c. multicoloured | 2·50 | 1·70 |

**1010** College Gates

**1999.** 150th Anniv of Justo Jose de Urquiza College, Concepcion del Uruguay.

| | | | | |
|---|---|---|---|---|
| 2673 | **1010** | 75c. multicoloured | 2·50 | 1·70 |

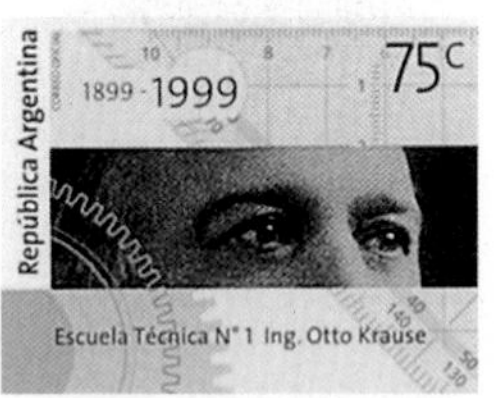

**1011** Krause (engineer) and Industrial Instruments

**1999.** Centenary of Technical School No. 1 Otto Krause.

| | | | | |
|---|---|---|---|---|
| 2674 | **1011** | 75c. multicoloured | 2·50 | 1·70 |

**1012** Nativity

**1999.** Bethlehem 2000.

| | | | | |
|---|---|---|---|---|
| 2675 | **1012** | 75c. blue, gold and red | 3·50 | 2·00 |

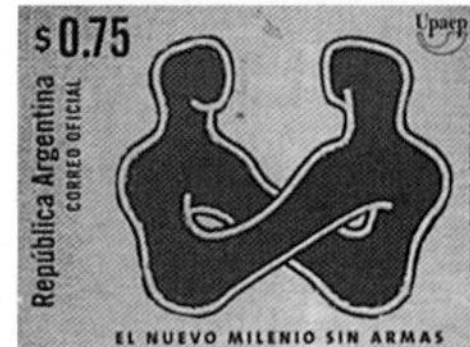

**1013** Brotherhood among Men

**1999.** America. A New Millennium without Arms. Multicoloured.

| | | | |
|---|---|---|---|
| 2676 | 75c. Type **1013** | 2·50 | 1·70 |
| 2677 | 75c. Liberty Tree (vert) | 2·50 | 1·70 |

**1014** Coypu ("Myocastor coypus"), Mburucuya National Park

**1999.** National Parks. Multicoloured.

| | | | |
|---|---|---|---|
| 2678 | 50c. Type **1014** | 1·70 | 1·00 |
| 2679 | 50c. Andean condor, Quebrada de los Condoritos National Park | 1·70 | 1·00 |
| 2680 | 50c. Vicuna, San Guillermo National Park | 1·70 | 1·00 |
| 2681 | 75c. Puma, Sierra de las Quijadas National Park | 2·50 | 1·70 |
| 2682 | 75c. Argentine grey fox ("Dusicyon griseus"), Talampaya National Park | 2·50 | 1·70 |

**1015** Map of the Americas, Road Network and Wickerwork

**1999.** 40th Anniv of Inter-American Development Bank.

| | | | | |
|---|---|---|---|---|
| 2683 | **1015** | 75c. multicoloured | 2·50 | 1·70 |

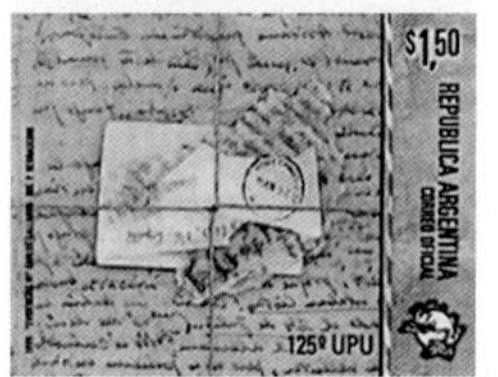

**1016** "Evidencias VI" (Carlos Gallardo)

**1999.** 125th Anniv of Universal Postal Union.

| | | | | |
|---|---|---|---|---|
| 2684 | **1016** | 1p.50 multicoloured | 5·00 | 3·25 |

**1017** "Fournier" and Map

**1999.** 50th Anniv of Sinking of the "Fournier" (minesweeper) in Antarctica.

| | | | | |
|---|---|---|---|---|
| 2685 | **1017** | 75c. multicoloured | 2·50 | 1·70 |

**1018** "Nothofagus pumillio"

**1999.** Trees (1st series). Multicoloured.

| | | | |
|---|---|---|---|
| 2686 | 75c. Type **1018** | 2·50 | 1·70 |
| 2687 | 75c. "Prosopis caldenia" | 2·50 | 1·70 |
| 2688 | 75c. "Schinopsis balansae" | 2·50 | 1·70 |
| 2689 | 75c. "Cordia trichotoma" | 2·50 | 1·70 |

Nos. 2686/9 were issued together, se-tenant, forming a composite design.

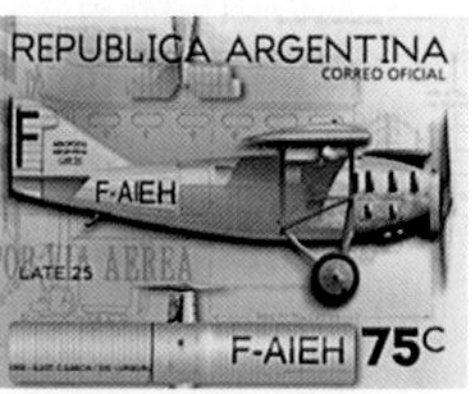

**1019** Latecoere 25 Mailplane

**1999.** 50th Anniv of World Record for Consecutive Parachute Jumps. Multicoloured.

| | | | |
|---|---|---|---|
| 2690 | 75c. Type **1019** | 2·50 | 1·70 |
| 2691 | 75c. Parachutists | 2·50 | 1·70 |

**1020** Accordionist "The Tango"

**1999.** The New Millennium. Three sheets each 150×100 mm containing multicoloured designs as T 1020.

| | | | |
|---|---|---|---|
| **MS**2692 | Three sheets. (a) 50, 75c. "The Tango"; (b) 50, 75c. Jorge Luis Borges (writer); (c) 50, (horiz), 75c. Football | 12·00 | 12·00 |

**1021** Boca Juniors Club Supporters

**1999.** Football. Multicoloured. (a) Size 42×33 mm.

| | | | |
|---|---|---|---|
| 2693 | 75c. Type **1021** | 2·50 | 1·70 |
| 2694 | 75c. River Plate Club supporters | 2·50 | 1·70 |

(b) Size 37×34 mm (1p.50) or 37×27 mm (others) (i) Boca Juniors.

| | | | |
|---|---|---|---|
| 2695 | 25c. Two players and ball | 85 | 55 |
| 2696 | 50c. Club badge | 1·50 | 1·00 |
| 2697 | 50c. Players hugging | 1·50 | 1·00 |
| 2698 | 75c. Supporters and balloons | 2·40 | 1·60 |
| 2699 | 75c. Club banner | 2·40 | 1·60 |
| 2700 | 75c. Players | 2·40 | 1·60 |
| 2701 | 1p.50 Player making high kick | 4·75 | 3·25 |

(ii) River Plate.

| | | | |
|---|---|---|---|
| 2702 | 25c. Stadium | 85 | 55 |
| 2703 | 50c. Players arriving on pitch | 1·50 | 1·00 |
| 2704 | 50c. Supporters waving flags | 1·50 | 1·00 |
| 2705 | 75c. Club badge | 2·40 | 1·60 |
| 2706 | 75c. Trophy | 2·40 | 1·60 |
| 2707 | 75c. Supporters with banner | 2·40 | 1·60 |
| 2708 | 1p.50 Player preparing to kick ball | 4·75 | 3·25 |

Nos. 2695/708 are self-adhesive.

**1022** Planisphere of Central South America (Pierre Descelliers, 1546)

**1999.** Maps. Multicoloured.

| | | | |
|---|---|---|---|
| 2709 | 25c.+25c. Type **1022** | 1·50 | 1·00 |
| 2710 | 50c.+50c. 17th-century map of estuary of the River Plate (Claes Voogt) | 3·00 | 2·00 |
| 2711 | 50c.+50c. Buenos Aires (Military Geographical Institute, 1910) | 3·00 | 2·00 |
| 2712 | 75c.+75c. Mouth of Riachuelo river and Buenos Aires harbour (satellite picture, 1999) | 4·75 | 3·25 |

**1023** Valdivielso and St. Peter's Cathedral, Rome

**1999.** Canonization of Hector Valdivielso Saez (Brother of the Christian Schools).

| | | | | |
|---|---|---|---|---|
| 2713 | **1023** | 75c. multicoloured | 2·50 | 1·70 |

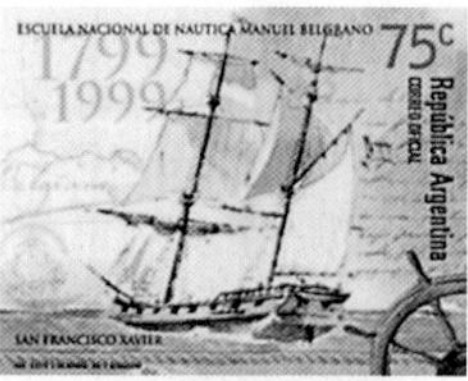

**1024** "San Francisco Xavier" (brig)

**1999.** Bicentenary of Manuel Belgrano Naval Academy.

| | | | | |
|---|---|---|---|---|
| 2714 | **1024** | 75c. multicoloured | 2·50 | 1·70 |

**1025** "Uruguay"

**1999.** 125th Anniv of Launch of "Uruguay" (sail/steam corvette). Sheet 150×100 mm.

| | | | | |
|---|---|---|---|---|
| **MS**2715 | **1025** | 1p.50 multicoloured | 4·75 | 4·75 |

**1026** Holy Family

**1999.** Christmas. Multicoloured.

| | | | |
|---|---|---|---|
| 2716 | 25c. Wise Man (29×29 mm) | 85 | 55 |
| 2717 | 25c. Bell (29×29 mm) | 85 | 55 |
| 2718 | 50c. Two kings and camels (39×29 mm) | 1·70 | 1·10 |
| 2719 | 50c. Holly leaf (39×29 mm) | 1·70 | 1·10 |
| 2720 | 75c. Angel with star (39×30 mm) | 2·50 | 1·70 |
| 2721 | 75c. Star (29×30 mm) | 2·50 | 1·70 |
| 2722 | 75c. Nativity (39×29 mm) | 2·50 | 1·70 |
| 2723 | 75c. Tree decorations (29×29 mm) | 2·50 | 1·70 |
| 2724 | 75c. Type **1026** | 2·50 | 1·70 |

**1027** Grape on Vine

**2000.** Wine Making. Multicoloured.

| | | | |
|---|---|---|---|
| 2725 | 25c. Type **1027** | 85 | 55 |
| 2726 | 25c. Glass and bottle of wine | 85 | 55 |
| 2727 | 50c. Wine bottles | 1·70 | 1·10 |
| 2728 | 50c. Cork screw and cork | 1·70 | 1·10 |

**1028** Mathematical Symbol and "2000"

**2000.** International Mathematics Year.

| | | | | |
|---|---|---|---|---|
| 2729 | **1028** | 75c. multicoloured | 2·50 | 1·70 |

**1029** White-fronted Dove

**2000.** Doves and Pigeon. Mult. Self-adhesive.

| | | | |
|---|---|---|---|
| 2730 | 75c. Type **1029** | 2·75 | 2·00 |
| 2731 | 75c. Picazuro pigeon (*Columba picazuro*) | 2·75 | 2·00 |
| 2732 | 75c. Picui dove (*Columbina picni*) | 2·75 | 2·00 |
| 2733 | 75c. Eared dove (*Fenaida auriculata*) | 2·75 | 2·00 |

**1030** *Venda coerulea*

**2000.** Bangkok 2000 International Stamp Exhibition. Plants. Sheet 100×76 mm containing T 1030 and similar horiz design. Multicoloured.

| | | | |
|---|---|---|---|
| **MS**2734 | 25c. Type **1030**; 75c. Coral tree | 3·50 | 3·50 |

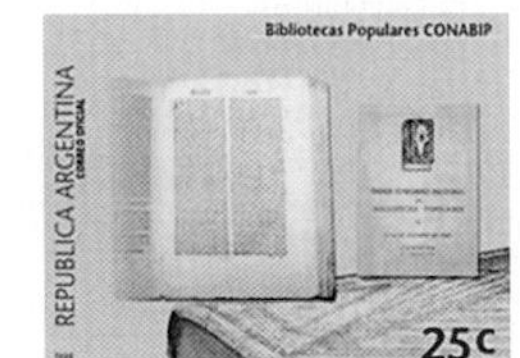

**1031** Open Book (CONABIP Library)

**2000.** Libraries. Multicoloured.

| | | | |
|---|---|---|---|
| 2735 | 25c. Type **1031** | 90 | 65 |
| 2736 | 50c. Building facade (Jujuy library) | 1·80 | 1·30 |
| 2737 | 75c. Hands and braille book (Argentine Library for the Blind) | 2·75 | 2·00 |
| 2738 | $1 Open book and building (National Library) | 3·50 | 2·75 |

No. 2737 has an inscription in braille across the stamp.

**1032** Caravel, Compass Rose and Letter

**2000.** 500th Anniv of the Discovery of Brazil. Multicoloured.

| | | | |
|---|---|---|---|
| 2739 | 25c. Type **1032** | 90 | 65 |
| 2740 | 75c. Pedro Alvares Cabral (discoverer) and map of South America | 2·75 | 2·00 |

**1033** Lieutenant General Luis Maria Campos (founder)

**2000.** Centenary of the Higher Military Academy.

| | | | | |
|---|---|---|---|---|
| 2741 | **1033** | 75c. multicoloured | 2·75 | 2·00 |

**1034** Penny Black and *La Portena* (steam locomotive), 1857

**2000.** The Stamp Show 2000 International Stamp Exhibition, London. Sheet 99×76 mm containing T 1034 and similar horiz design. Multicoloured.

| | | | |
|---|---|---|---|
| **MS**2742 | 25c. Type **1034**; 75c. Two 1862 15c. stamps and modern pillar box | 3·50 | 3·50 |

**1035** Convention Emblem

**2000.** 91st Rotary International Convention, Buenos Aires.

| | | | | |
|---|---|---|---|---|
| 2743 | **1035** | 75c. multicoloured | 2·75 | 2·10 |

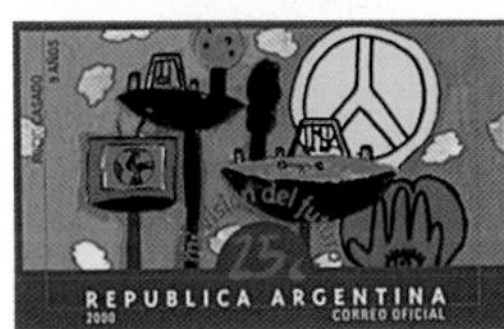

**1036** Futuristic Houses and Emblems (Rocio Casado)

**2000.** "Stampin' the Future". Winning Entries in Children's International Painting Competition. Mult.

| | | | |
|---|---|---|---|
| 2744 | 25c. Type **1036** | 1·00 | 75 |
| 2745 | 50c. Sea and clouds (Carolina Cacerez) (vert) | 1·90 | 1·40 |
| 2746 | 75c. Flower (Valeria A. Pizarro) | 3·00 | 2·30 |
| 2747 | $1 Flying cars (Cristina Ayala Castro) (vert) | 3·75 | 2·75 |

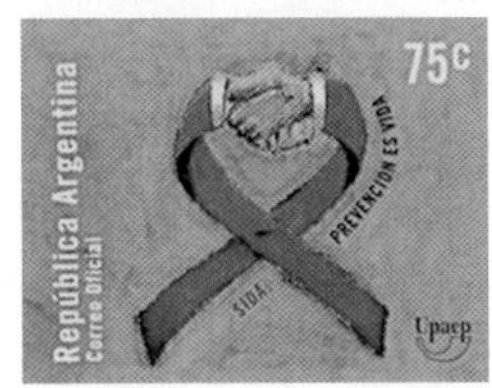

**1037** Ribbon

**2000.** America. AIDS Awareness. Multicoloured.

| | | | |
|---|---|---|---|
| 2748 | 75c. Type **1037** | 3·00 | 2·30 |
| 2749 | 75c. Arms circling faces | 3·00 | 2·30 |

**1038** Potez 25 Biplane

**2000.** Birth Centenary of Antoine de Saint-Exupery (novelist and pilot). Multicoloured.

| | | | |
|---|---|---|---|
| 2750 | 25c. Type **1038** | 1·00 | 75 |
| 2751 | 50c. Late 28 | 2·00 | 1·50 |

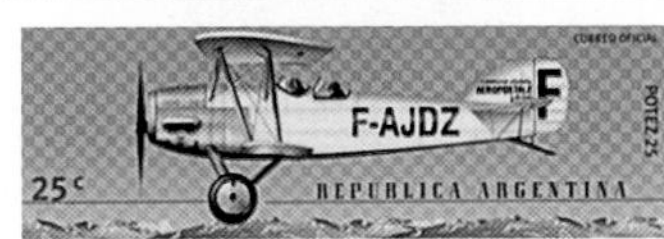

**1039** Potez 25 Biplane

**2000.** "Aerofila 2000" Mercosur Air Philately Exhibition, Buenos Aires. Multicoloured.

| | | | |
|---|---|---|---|
| 2752 | 25c. As Type **1039** | 1·00 | 75 |
| 2753 | 25c. Antoine de Saint-Exupery (novelist and pilot) (29×29 mm) | 1·00 | 75 |
| 2754 | 50c. Late 28 | 2·00 | 1·50 |
| 2755 | 50c. Henri Guillaumet, Almonacid and Jean Mermoz (aviation pioneers) (29×29 mm) | 2·00 | 1·50 |
| 2756 | 50c. Map of South America and tail of Late 25 (39×39 mm) | 2·00 | 1·50 |
| 2757 | $1 Late 25 and cover (39×29 mm) | 4·00 | 3·00 |

**1040** Illia

**2000.** Birth Centenary of Arturo U. Illia (President, 1963–66).

| | | | | |
|---|---|---|---|---|
| 2758 | **1040** | 75c. multicoloured | 3·00 | 2·30 |

**1041** San Martin

**2000.** 150th Death Anniv of General Jose de San Martin.

| | | | | |
|---|---|---|---|---|
| 2759 | **1041** | 75c. multicoloured | 3·00 | 2·30 |

**1042** Siku Pipes

**2000.** Argentine Culture. Multicoloured.

| | | | |
|---|---|---|---|
| 2760 | 10c. Ceremonial axe | 30 | 25 |
| 2761 | 25c. Type **1042** | 90 | 60 |
| 2762 | 50c. Andean loom | 1·80 | 1·20 |
| 2763 | 60c. Pampeana poncho | 2·30 | 1·50 |
| 2764 | 75c. Funeral mask | 2·75 | 1·80 |
| 2765 | $1 Basket | 3·50 | 2·40 |
| 2766 | $2 Kultun ritual drum | 7·25 | 4·75 |
| 2767 | $3.25 Ceremonial tiger mask | 11·50 | 7·50 |
| 2768 | $5 Funeral urn | 18·00 | 12·00 |
| 2770 | $9.40 Suri ceremonial costume | 34·00 | 23·00 |

**1043** Sarsfield, Signature and Cordoba Province Arms

**2000.** Birth Bicentenary of Dalmacio Velez Sarsfield (lawyer).

| | | | | |
|---|---|---|---|---|
| 2775 | **1043** | 75c. multicoloured | 3·25 | 2·40 |

**1044** Windsurfing

**2000.** Olympic Games, Sydney. Multicoloured.

| | | | |
|---|---|---|---|
| 2776 | 75c. Type **1044** | 3·25 | 2·40 |
| 2777 | 75c. Hockey | 3·25 | 2·40 |
| 2778 | 75c. Volleyball | 3·25 | 2·40 |
| 2779 | 75c. High jump and pole vault | 3·25 | 2·40 |

**1045** Argentine Petiso

**2000.** "Espana 2000" International Stamp Exhibition, Madrid. Horses. Multicoloured.

| | | | |
|---|---|---|---|
| 2780 | 25c. Type **1045** | 1·00 | 75 |
| 2781 | 25c. Carriage horse | 1·00 | 75 |
| 2782 | 50c. Peruvian horse | 2·00 | 1·50 |
| 2783 | 50c. Criolla | 2·00 | 1·50 |
| 2784 | 75c. Saddle horse | 3·25 | 2·40 |
| 2785 | 75c. Polo horse | 3·25 | 2·40 |
| **MS**2786 | 100×75 mm. 25c. Stagecoach (39×29 mm); 75c. Horse's head (39×29 mm) | 4·25 | 4·25 |

**1046** Man on Bicycle and Las Nereidas Fountain (image scaled to 73% of original size)

**2000.** Transportation. Multicoloured.

| | | | |
|---|---|---|---|
| 2787 | 25c.+25c. Type **1046** | 2·00 | 1·50 |
| 2788 | 50c.+50c. *Graf Zeppelin* over Buenos Aires | 4·25 | 3·25 |
| 2789 | 50c.+50c. *Ganz* (diesel locomotive) | 4·25 | 3·25 |
| 2790 | 75c.+75c. Tram | 6·25 | 4·75 |

**1047** Nuclear Reactor

**2000.** 50th Anniv of National Commission for Atomic Energy.

| | | | | |
|---|---|---|---|---|
| 2791 | **1047** | 75c. multicoloured | 3·25 | 2·40 |

**1048** "Filete" (left-hand detail)

**2000.** Fileteado (painting genre) (Nos. 2792/3) and Tango (dance) (Nos. 2794/5). Multicoloured.

| | | | |
|---|---|---|---|
| 2792 | 75c. Type **1048** | 3·25 | 2·40 |
| 2793 | 75c. "Filete" (right-hand detail) (Brunetti brothers) | 3·25 | 2·40 |
| 2794 | 75c. Tango orchestra | 3·25 | 2·40 |
| 2795 | 75c. Couple dancing | 3·25 | 2·40 |

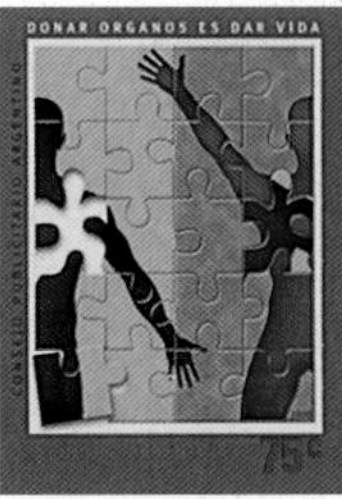

**1049** Human Bodies on Jigsaw

**2000.** 40th Anniv of Organ Donation Publicity Campaign.

| | | | | |
|---|---|---|---|---|
| 2796 | **1049** | 75c. multicoloured | 3·25 | 2·40 |

**1050** "Birth of Jesus" (stained glass window, Sanctuary of Our Lady of the Rosary, New Pompeii)

**2000.** Christmas.

| | | | | |
|---|---|---|---|---|
| 2797 | **1050** | 75c. multicoloured | 3·25 | 2·40 |

**1051** *Commelina erecta*

**2000.** Medicinal Plants. Multicoloured.

| | | | |
|---|---|---|---|
| 2798 | 75c. Type **1051** | 3·25 | 2·40 |
| 2799 | 75c. *Senna corymbosa* | 3·25 | 2·40 |
| 2800 | 75c. *Mirabilis jalapa* | 3·25 | 2·40 |
| 2801 | 75c. *Eugenia uniflora* | 3·25 | 2·40 |

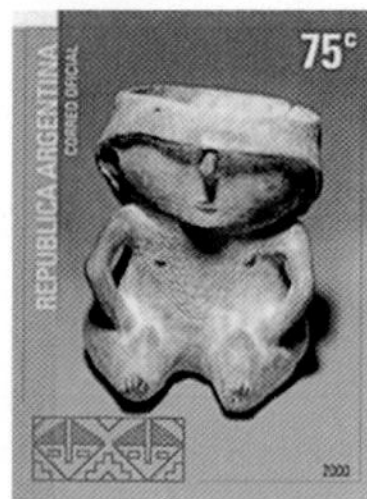

**1052** Human-shaped Vessel, Cienaga

**2000.** Traditional Crafts. Multicoloured.

| | | | |
|---|---|---|---|
| 2802 | 75c. Type **1052** | 3·25 | 2·40 |
| 2803 | 75c. Painted human-shaped vase, Vaquerias | 3·25 | 2·40 |
| 2804 | 75c. Animal-shaped vessel, Condorhuasi | 3·25 | 2·40 |
| 2805 | 75c. Human-shaped vase, Candelaria | 3·25 | 2·40 |

**1053** "U. P." Unidad Postal

**2001.** Postal Agents' Stamps. Multicoloured, background colours given. Self-adhesive gum.

| | | | | |
|---|---|---|---|---|
| 2806 | **1053** | 10c. turquoise | 25 | 20 |
| 2807 | **1053** | 25c. green | 70 | 55 |
| 2808 | **1053** | 60c. yellow | 1·60 | 1·20 |
| 2809 | **1053** | 75c. red | 2·20 | 1·70 |
| 2810 | **1053** | $1 blue | 3·00 | 2·20 |
| 2811 | **1053** | $3 red | 9·00 | 6·75 |
| 2812 | **1053** | $3.25 yellow | 9·75 | 7·25 |
| 2813 | **1053** | $5.50 mauve | 16·00 | 12·00 |

Nos. 2806/13 were issued for use by Postal Agents as opposed to branches of the Argentine Post Office.

**1054** *Megatherium americanum* ("Megaterio")

**2001.** Cainozoic Mammals. Multicoloured.

| | | | |
|---|---|---|---|
| 2820 | 75c. Type **1054** | 3·25 | 2·40 |
| 2821 | 75c. *Doedicurus clavcaudatus* ("Gliptodonte") | 3·25 | 2·40 |
| 2822 | 75c. *Macrauchenia patachonica* ("Macrauqueria") | 3·25 | 2·40 |
| 2823 | 75c. *Toxodon platensis* ("Toxodonte") | 3·25 | 2·40 |

**1055** Map, South Polar Skua and San Martin Base

**2001.** 50th Anniv of San Martín and Brown Antarctic Bases. Multicoloured.

| | | | |
|---|---|---|---|
| 2824 | 75c. Type **1055** | 3·25 | 2·40 |
| 2825 | 75c. Blue-eyed cormorant, map and Brown Base | 3·25 | 2·40 |

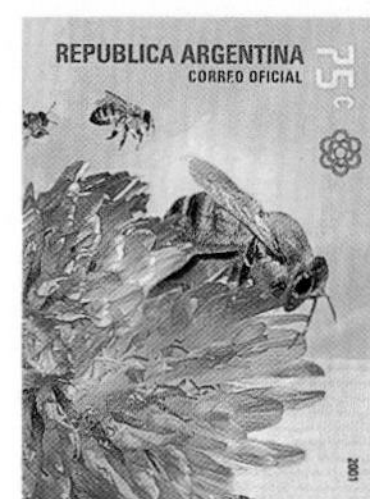

**1056** Bees on Clover Flower

**2001.** Apiculture. Multicoloured.

| | | | |
|---|---|---|---|
| 2826 | 75c. Type **1056** | 3·25 | 2·40 |
| 2827 | 75c. Bees on honeycomb | 3·25 | 2·40 |
| 2828 | 75c. Bees and bee-keeper attending hives | 3·25 | 2·40 |
| 2829 | 75c. Jar of honey and swizzle | 3·25 | 2·40 |

Nos. 2826/9 were issued together, se-tenant, forming a composite design.

**1057** Scientist with Fossilized Bones

**2001.** 50th Anniv of Argentine Antarctic Institute. Sheet 150×99 mm containing T 1057 and similar horiz design. Multicoloured.

| | | | |
|---|---|---|---|
| **MS**2830 | 75c. Type **1057**; 75c. Scientist and surveying equipment | 6·25 | 6·25 |

**1058** Dornier Do-j Wal Flying Boat *Plus Ultra* and Route Map

**2001.** 75th Anniv of Major Ramon Franco's Flight from Spain to Argentina.

| | | | | |
|---|---|---|---|---|
| 2831 | **1058** | 75c. multicoloured | 3·25 | 2·40 |

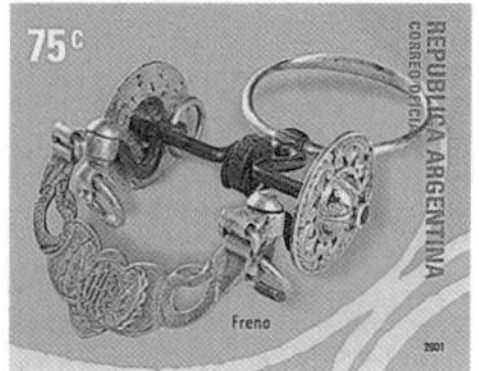

**1059** Horse's Bridle Fittings

**2001.** Silver Work. Each blue, silver and black.

| | | | |
|---|---|---|---|
| 2832 | 75c. Type **1059** | 3·25 | 2·40 |
| 2833 | 75c. Stirrups | 3·25 | 2·40 |
| 2834 | 75c. Spurs | 3·25 | 2·40 |
| 2835 | 75c. Rastra (gaucho belt decoration) | 3·25 | 2·40 |

**1060** "Washerwoman by the Banks of Belgrano" (detail, Prilidiano Pueyrredon)

**2001.** Belgica 2001 International Stamp Exhibition, Brussels. 500th Anniv of European Postal Service. Sheet 99×75 mm containing T 1060 and similar horiz design. Multicoloured.

| | | | |
|---|---|---|---|
| **MS**2836 | 25c. Type **1060**; 75c. "Hay Harvest" (detail, Pieter Bruegel, the Elder) | 4·50 | 4·50 |

**1061** Goalkeeper catching Ball

**2001.** Under 20's World Youth Football Championship, Argentine Republic. Multicoloured.

| | | | |
|---|---|---|---|
| 2837 | 75c. Type **1061** | 3·25 | 2·40 |
| 2838 | 75c. Player kicking ball | 3·25 | 2·40 |

**1062** People and Buildings

**2001.** National Census.

| | | | | |
|---|---|---|---|---|
| 2839 | **1062** | 75c. multicoloured | 3·25 | 2·40 |

**1063** SAC-C Satellite, Seagulls and Sunflowers

**2001.** Environmental Protection. Satellite Tracking Project.

| | | | | |
|---|---|---|---|---|
| 2840 | **1063** | 75c. multicoloured | 3·25 | 2·40 |

**1064** Puma

**2001.** Wild Cats. Multicoloured.

| | | | |
|---|---|---|---|
| 2841 | 25c. Type **1064** | 1·00 | 75 |
| 2842 | 25c. Jaguar | 1·00 | 75 |
| 2843 | 50c. Jaguarundi | 2·00 | 1·50 |
| 2844 | 50c. Ocelot | 2·00 | 1·50 |
| 2845 | 75c. Geoffroy's Cat | 3·25 | 2·40 |
| 2846 | 75c. Kodkod | 3·25 | 2·40 |

**1065** "Bandoneon Recital" (painting, Aldo Severi)

**2001**

| | | | | |
|---|---|---|---|---|
| 2847 | **1065** | 75c. multicoloured | 3·25 | 2·40 |

**1066** Couple dancing the Tango

**2001.** PHILA NIPPON 01 International Stamp Exhibition, Tokyo. Sheet 100×75 mm containing T 1066 and similar horiz design. Multicoloured.

| | | | |
|---|---|---|---|
| **MS**2848 | 75c. Type **1066**; 75c. Kabuki performer | 6·25 | 6·25 |

**1067** Discepolo

**2001.** Birth Centenary of Enriques Santos Discepolo (actor and lyric writer).

| | | | | |
|---|---|---|---|---|
| 2849 | **1067** | 75c. multicoloured | 3·50 | 2·50 |

**1068** Courtyard, Caroya Estancia, Angel and Chapel, Estancia Santa Catalina

**2001.** UNESCO World Heritage Sites. Mult.

| | | | |
|---|---|---|---|
| 2850 | 75c. Type **1068** | 3·50 | 2·50 |
| 2851 | 75c. Emblem and chapel, Estancia La Candelaria, dome of Estancia Alta Gracia and belfry, Estancia Jesus Maria | 3·50 | 2·50 |

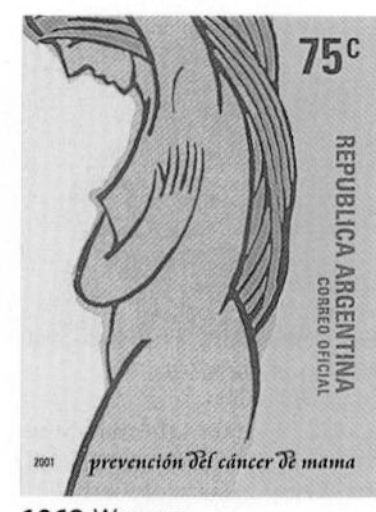

**1069** Woman

**2001.** Breast Cancer Awareness.

| | | | | |
|---|---|---|---|---|
| 2852 | **1069** | 75c. multicoloured | 3·50 | 2·50 |

**1070** Burmeister's Porpoise (image scaled to 73% of original size)

**2001.** Marine Mammals. Multicoloured.

| | | | |
|---|---|---|---|
| 2853 | 25c.+25c. Type **1070** | 2·30 | 2·10 |
| 2854 | 50c.+50c. La Plata River dolphin | 4·75 | 4·25 |
| 2855 | 50c.+50c. Minke whale | 4·75 | 4·25 |
| 2856 | 75c.+75c. Humpback whale | 7·25 | 6·50 |

**1071** Alfa Romeo 159 Alfetta, Spain, 1951

**2001.** Formula 1 Racing Cars driven by Juan Manuel Fangio. Multicoloured.

| | | | |
|---|---|---|---|
| 2857 | 75c. Type **1071** | 3·25 | 2·40 |
| 2858 | 75c. Mercedes Benz W 196, France, 1954 | 3·25 | 2·40 |
| 2859 | 75c. Lancia-Ferrari D50, Monaco, 1956 | 3·25 | 2·40 |
| 2860 | 75c. Maserati 250 F, Germany, 1957 | 3·25 | 2·40 |

**1072** Palo Santo Tree (*Bulnesia sarmientoi*)

**2001.** Mercosur (South American Common Market).

| | | | | |
|---|---|---|---|---|
| 2861 | **1072** | 75c. multicoloured | 3·25 | 2·40 |

**1073** Justo Jose de Urquiza

**2001.** Birth Anniversaries. Multicoloured.

| | | | |
|---|---|---|---|
| 2862 | 75c. Type **1073** (politician) (bicentenary) | 3·25 | 2·40 |
| 2863 | 75c. Roque Saenz Pena (President 1910—14) (150th anniv) | 3·25 | 2·40 |

**1074** 18th-century Mail Courier

**2001.** HAFNIA 01 International Stamp Exhibition, Copenhagen. Sheet 100×75 mm containing T 1074 and similar horiz design. Multicoloured.

| | | | |
|---|---|---|---|
| **MS**2864 | 25c. Type **1074**; 75c. 17th-century mail courier | 5·00 | 5·00 |

**1075** "La Pobladora" Carriage (Enrique Udaondo Graphic Museum Complex)

**2001.** Museums. Multicoloured.

| | | | |
|---|---|---|---|
| 2865 | 75c. Type **1075** | 3·25 | 2·40 |
| 2866 | 75c. Ebony and silver crucifix (Brigadier General Juan Martin de Pueyrredon Museum) (vert) | 3·25 | 2·40 |
| 2867 | 75c. Funerary urn (Emilio and Duncan Wagner Museum of Anthropological and Natural Sciences) (vert) | 3·25 | 2·40 |
| 2868 | 75c. Skeleton of Carnotaurus sastrei (Argentine Natural Science Museum) | 3·25 | 2·40 |

**1076** "The Power of the Most High will Overshadow You" (Martin La Spina)

**2001.** Christmas.

| | | | |
|---|---|---|---|
| 2869 | **1076** 75c. multicoloured | 3·25 | 2·40 |

**1077** Carola Lorenzini and Focke Wulf 44-J

**2001.** Aviation. Multicoloured.

| | | | |
|---|---|---|---|
| 2870 | 75c. Type **1077** | 3·25 | 2·40 |
| 2871 | 75c. Jean Mermoz and Arc-en-Ciel | 3·25 | 2·40 |

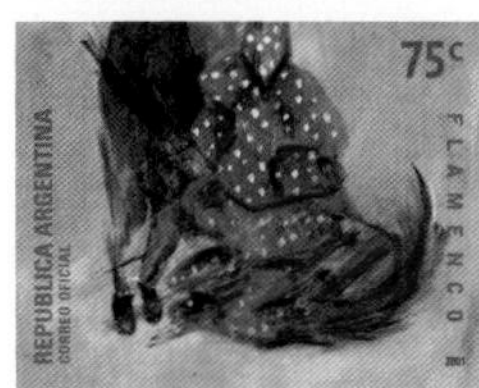


**1078** Dancers (Flamenco)

**2001.** Dances. Multicoloured.

| | | | |
|---|---|---|---|
| 2872 | 75c. Type **1078** | 3·25 | 2·40 |
| 2873 | 75c. Dancers (purple skirt) (Vals) | 3·25 | 2·40 |
| 2874 | 75c. Dancers (orange skirt) (Zamba) | 3·25 | 2·40 |
| 2875 | 75c. Dancers (Tango) | 3·25 | 2·40 |

**1079** Scene from "Apollon Musagete" (Igor Stravinsky)

**2001.** National Day of the Dancer.

| | | | |
|---|---|---|---|
| 2876 | **1079** 75c. multicoloured | 3·25 | 2·40 |

**1080** Television Set, Camera and Microphone

**2001.** 50th Anniv of Television in Argentina. Multicoloured.

| | | | |
|---|---|---|---|
| 2877 | 75c. Type **1080** | 3·25 | 2·40 |
| 2878 | 75c. Television set and video tapes | 3·25 | 2·40 |
| 2879 | 75c. Satellite dish and astronaut | 3·25 | 2·40 |
| 2880 | 75c. Colour television cables and remote control | 3·25 | 2·40 |

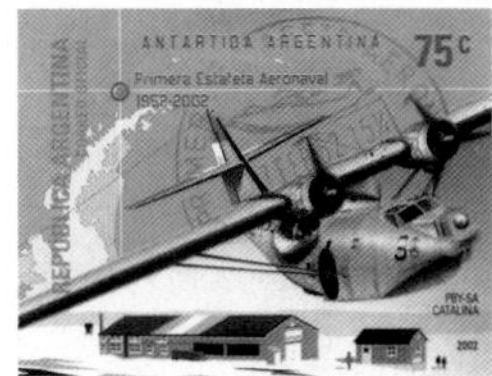


**1081** Consolidated PBY-5A Catalina (amphibian) and Cancellation

**2002.** 50th Anniv of Argentine Antarctic Programme. Multicoloured.

| | | | |
|---|---|---|---|
| 2881 | 75c. Type **1081** (first air and sea courier service) | 3·25 | 2·40 |
| 2882 | 75c. *Chiriguano* (minesweeper) and buildings (foundation of Esparanza Base) | 3·25 | 2·40 |

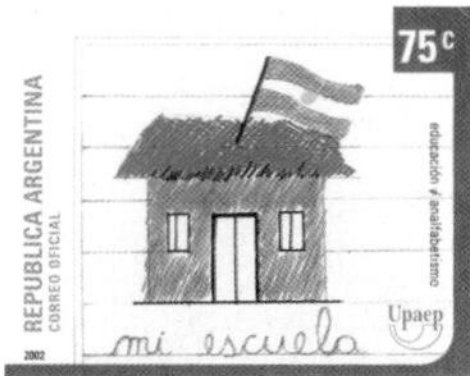


**1082** House and Flag

**2002.** America. Education and Literacy Campaign. Multicoloured.

| | | | |
|---|---|---|---|
| 2883 | 75c. Type **1082** | 3·25 | 2·40 |
| 2884 | 75c. Children playing hopscotch | 3·25 | 2·40 |

**1083** Two-banded Plover (*Charadrius falklandicus*)

**2002.** Birds. Multicoloured.

| | | | |
|---|---|---|---|
| 2885 | 50c. Type **1083** | 1·80 | 1·30 |
| 2886 | 50c. Dolphin gull (*Larus scoresbii*) | 1·80 | 1·30 |
| 2887 | 75c. Ruddy-headed goose (*Chloephaga rubidiceps*) (vert) | 2·75 | 2·00 |
| 2888 | 75c. King penguin (*Aptenodytes patagonicus*) (vert) | 2·75 | 2·00 |

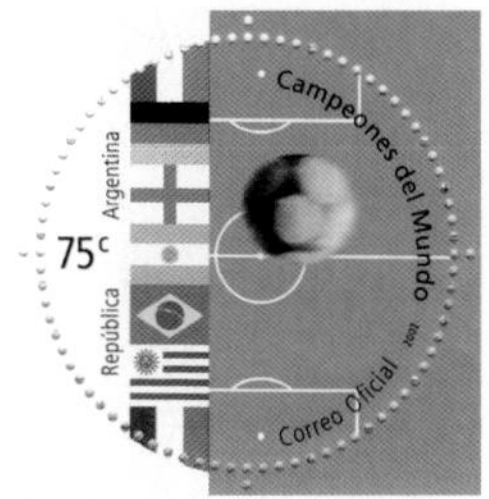


**1084** Flags of Championship Winners and Football

**2002.** 20th-century World Cup Football Champions. Multicoloured.

| | | | |
|---|---|---|---|
| 2889 | 75c. Type **1084** | 2·75 | 2·00 |
| 2890 | 75c. Argentine footballer | 2·75 | 2·00 |

**1085** Parana River and Emblem

**2002.** Anniversaries. Multicoloured.

| | | | |
|---|---|---|---|
| 2891 | 25c. Type **1085** (150th anniv of Rosario City) | 90 | 65 |
| 2892 | 25c. National flag and monument | 90 | 65 |
| 2893 | 50c. Mount Fitzroy (150th birth anniv of Francisco Pascasio Moreno (Perito) (explorer and founder of Argentine Scouts movement)) | 1·80 | 1·30 |
| 2894 | 50c. Dr. Moreno | 1·80 | 1·30 |
| 2895 | 75c. Flower and view of city (centenary of foundation San Carlos de Bariloche) | 2·75 | 2·00 |
| 2896 | 75c. Capilla San Eduardo (St. Edward's chapel) and city plan | 2·75 | 2·00 |

**1086** Fruit, Mother, Boy, Bread and Health Centre

**2002.** Centenary of Pan-American Health Organization.

| | | | |
|---|---|---|---|
| 2897 | **1086** 75c. multicoloured | 2·75 | 2·00 |

**1087** Cosme Mariano Argerich, 1758–1820

**2002.** Doctors. Multicoloured.

| | | | |
|---|---|---|---|
| 2898 | 50c. Type **1087** | 1·80 | 1·30 |
| 2899 | 50c. Jose Maria Ramos Mejia, 1849–1914 | 1·80 | 1·30 |
| 2900 | 50c. Salvador Mazza, 1886–1946 | 1·80 | 1·30 |
| 2901 | 50c. Carlos Arturo Gianononio, 1926–1995 | 1·80 | 1·30 |

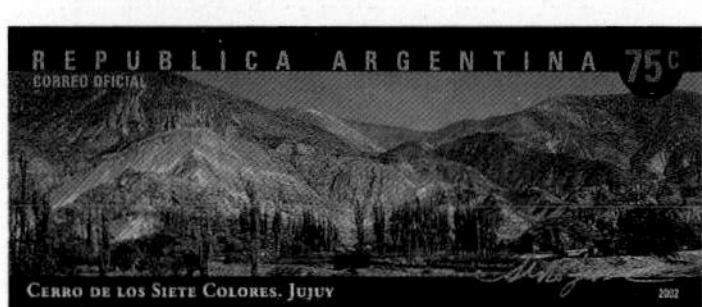


**1088** Hill of Seven Colours, Jujuy (image scaled to 74% of original size)

**2002.** Landscapes. Multicoloured.

| | | | |
|---|---|---|---|
| 2902 | 75c. Type **1088** | 2·75 | 2·00 |
| 2903 | 75c. Iguazu waterfall, Misiones | 2·75 | 2·00 |
| 2904 | 75c. Talampaya National Park | 2·75 | 2·00 |
| 2905 | 75c. Agoncagua mountain, Mendoza | 2·75 | 2·00 |
| 2906 | 75c. Rosedal Park, Buenos Aires | 2·75 | 2·00 |
| 2907 | 75c. San Jorge lighthouse, Chubut | 2·75 | 2·00 |
| 2908 | 75c. Perito Moreno glacier, Santa Cruz | 2·75 | 2·00 |
| 2909 | 75c. Lapataia Bay, Tierra del Fuego | 2·75 | 2·00 |

See also Nos. 2980/7 and 3022/9.

**1089** Pampas Deer (*Ozotoceros bezoarticus*)

**2002.** Endangered Species. Multicoloured.

| | | | |
|---|---|---|---|
| 2910 | $1 Type **1089** | 3·25 | 2·20 |
| 2911 | $1 Vicuna (*Vicugna vicugna*) | 3·25 | 2·20 |
| 2912 | $1 Southern pudu (*Pudu pudu*) | 3·25 | 2·20 |
| 2913 | $1 Chaco peccary (*Catgonus wagneri*) | 3·25 | 2·20 |

**1090** Eva Peron

**2002.** 50th Death Anniv of Eva Peron. Multicoloured.

| | | | |
|---|---|---|---|
| 2914 | 75c. Type **1090** | 2·75 | 2·00 |
| 2915 | 75c. In cameo | 2·75 | 2·00 |
| 2916 | 75c. At microphone | 2·75 | 2·00 |
| 2917 | 75c. In profile wearing earrings | 2·75 | 2·00 |

**1091** Argentine Footballer

**2002.** Philakorea 2002 International Stamp Exhibition. Sheet 100×75 mm containing T 1091 and similar horiz design. Multicoloured.

| | | | |
|---|---|---|---|
| **MS**2918 | $1.50 Type **1091**; $1.50 Korean footballer | 6·75 | 6·75 |

**1092** Boa Constrictor (*Boa lampalagua*) (image scaled to 73% of original size)

**2002.** Reptiles. Multicoloured.

| | | | |
|---|---|---|---|
| 2919 | 25c.+25c. Type **1092** | 1·10 | 80 |
| 2920 | 50c.+50c. Caiman (*Caiman yacare*) | 2·30 | 1·60 |
| 2921 | 50c.+50c. Argentine black and white tegu (*Tupinambis merianae*) | 2·30 | 1·60 |
| 2922 | 75c.+75c. Red-footed tortoise (*Chelonoidis carbonaria*) | 3·50 | 2·40 |

**1093** Whale's Head

**2002.** Mercosur (South American Common Market). Multicoloured.

| | | | |
|---|---|---|---|
| 2923 | 75c. Type **1093** | 1·30 | 85 |
| 2924 | 75c. Whale's tail | 1·30 | 85 |

**1094** *Edessa meditabunda*

**2002.** Insects. Multicoloured.

2925 25c. Type **1094** 65 45
2926 50c. *Elaeochlora viridis* 1·30 85
2927 75c. *Chrysodina aurata* 1·90 1·30
2928 75c. *Steirastoma breve* 2·50 1·70

**1095** Players, Ball and Net

**2002.** World Men's Volleyball Championships. Multicoloured.

2929 75c. Type **1095** 1·90 1·30
2930 75c. Two players ball and net 1·90 1·30
2931 75c. Hands, net, ball and head 1·90 1·30
2932 75c. Players congratulating one another 1·90 1·30

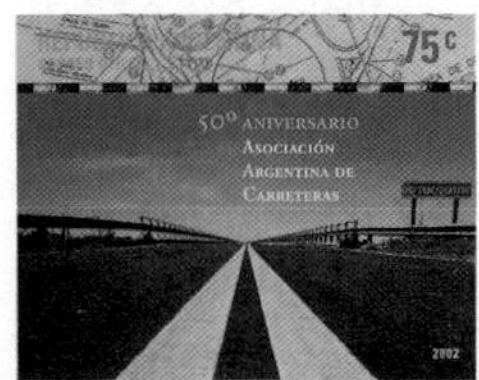

**1096** Roadway

**2002.** 50th Anniv of Argentine Highways Department.

2933 **1096** 75c. multicoloured 1·90 1·30

**1097** Roberto Arlt

**2002.** Death Anniversaries. Multicoloured.

2934 75c. Type **1097** (writer, 60th) 1·90 1·30
2935 75c. Luis Sandrini (actor and director, 22nd) 1·90 1·30
2936 75c. Nini Marshall (actor, 6th) 1·90 1·30
2937 75c. Beatriz Guido (writer, 14th) 1·90 1·30

**1101** Andres Chazarreta (composer)

**2002.** Folklorists. Multicoloured.

2945 75c. Type **1101** 1·90 1·30
2946 75c. Gustavo "Cuchi" Leguizamon (songwriter) 1·90 1·30
2947 75c. Carlos Vega (guitarist) 1·90 1·30
2948 75c. Armando Tejada Gomez (poet and songwriter) 1·90 1·30

**1098** Immigrant Hotel, Mother and Child

**2002.** Immigration. Multicoloured.

2938 75c. Type **1098** 1·90 1·30
2939 75c. Two men and ship 1·90 1·30
2940 75c. Two men and immigrant hotel 1·90 1·30
2941 75c. Horse-drawn farm implement and family 1·90 1·30

Nos. 2938/41 were issued in horizontal se-tenant strips of four stamps within the sheet, each pair (2938/9 and 2940/1) forming a composite design.

**1099** Envelope, Horse-drawn Coach and Head

**2002.** 50th Anniv of Argentine Federation of Philatelic Entities (FAEF). Multicoloured.

2942 75c. Type **1099** 1·90 1·30
2943 75c. Flag, figure, ship and arms 1·90 1·30

**1100** Joseph leading Donkey carrying Mary and Jesus

**2002.** Christmas.

2944 **1100** 75c. multicoloured 1·90 1·30

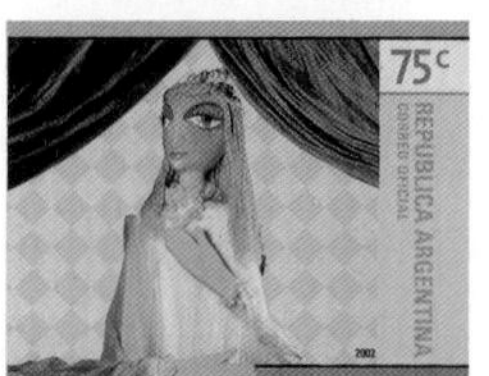

**1102** Girl (rod puppet)

**2002.** Puppets. Multicoloured.

2949 75c. Type **1102** 1·90 1·30
2950 75c. Fish and king (marionettes) 1·90 1·30
2951 75c. Man (marote puppet) 1·90 1·30
2952 75c. Figures (shadow puppets) 1·90 1·30

**1103** Cabbage containing Hands

**2003.** "Pro Huerta" (communal gardens initiative). Multicoloured.

2953 75c. Type **1103** 1·90 1·30
2954 75c. Street map as corn cob (vert) 1·90 1·30

**1104** Woven Bag and Band

**2003.** Mercosur (South American Common Market). Multicoloured.

2955 75c. Type **1104** (Pilaga and Toba people, Formosa province) 1·90 1·30
2956 75c. Basketwork sieve (Mbya people, Misiones province) and wooden servers (Wichi people, Salta province) 1·90 1·30

**1105** Squirrel Cuckoo (*Piaya cayana*) (Colonia Benitez reserve) (image scaled to 73% of original size)

**2003.** National Parks. Multicoloured.

2957 50c. Type **1105** 1·30 85
2958 50c. Grey brocket (*Mazama gouzoupira*) (Copo park) 1·30 85
2959 50c. Guanaco (*Lama guanicoe*) (Los Cardones) 1·30 85
2960 75c. Magellanic penguin (*Speniscus magellanicus*) (Monte Leon) 1·90 1·30
2961 75c. *Tinamotis pentlandii* (Campo de los Alisos) 1·90 1·30

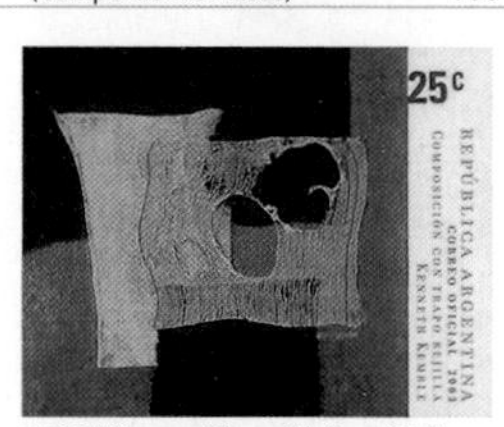

**1106** "Composition with Rag Grid" (Kenneth Kemble)

**2003.** Art. Multicoloured.

2962 25c. Type **1106** 65 45
2963 25c. "Painting" (Roberto Aizenberg) (vert) 65 45
2964 50c. "Screen" (Romulo Maccio) (vert) 1·30 85
2965 75c. "La Gioconda" (Guillemo Roux) 1·90 1·30
2966 75c. "To Flee" (Antonio Segui) 1·90 1·30
2967 $1 "San P." (Xul Solar) (vert) 2·50 1·70

**1107** Hockey Player

**2003.** Sport. Multicoloured.

2968 75c. Type **1107** (Women's Hockey World Champions, 2002) 1·90 1·30
2969 75c. Footballer (World Blind Football Champions, 2002) 1·90 1·30

No. 2969 was embossed with the face value in Braille.

**1108** Mago Fafa (Broccoli)

**2003.** Cartoons. Sheet 156×120 mm containing T 1108 and similar vert designs. Multicoloured.

**MS**2970 25c. Type **1108**; 25c. Astronauta (Crist); 50c. Hijitus (Garcia Ferre); 50c. Savarese (Mandrafina and Robin Wood); 75c. Sonoman (Oswal); 75c. El Tipito (Daniel Paz and Rudy); 75c. La Vaca Aurora (Mirco); 75c. Diogenes y el Linyera (Tabare) 7·50 7·50

**1109** 19th-century Soup Tureen

**2003.** Silver Work. Multicoloured.

2971 75c. Type **1109** 1·90 1·30
2972 75c. Kettle, *mate de campana* and drinking tube 1·90 1·30
2973 75c. Chocolate pot and jug 1·90 1·30
2974 75c. 19th-century sugar bowl 1·90 1·30

Nos. 2971/4 were issued together, se-tenant, forming a composite design.

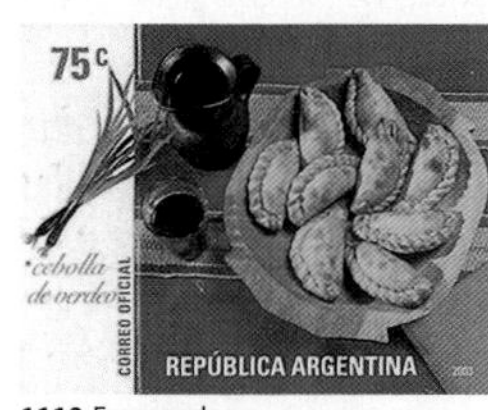

**1110** Empanadas

**2003.** Traditional Foods. Multicoloured.

2975 75c. Type **1110** (turnovers) 1·90 1·30
2976 75c. Locro (corn and bean stew) 1·90 1·30
2977 75c. Parillada (mixed grill) 1·90 1·30
2978 75c. Pastilitos (miniature pastries) 1·90 1·30

**1111** El Elastico (elastic)

**2003.** Children's Games. Sheet 108×88 mm containing T 1111 and similar horiz designs. Multicoloured.

**MS**2979 50c.×4 Type **1111**; La escondida (hide and seek); La mancha (tag); Martin pescador (Martin the fisherman) 4·50 4·50

**2003.** Landscapes. As T 1088. Multicoloured.

2980 75c. Mbigua marsh, Formosa 1·90 1·30
2981 75c. Dead Man's salt flat, Catamarca 1·90 1·30
2982 75c. Quilmes ruins, Tucuman 1·90 1·30
2983 75c. Ibera marshland, Corrientes 1·90 1·30
2984 75c. Moon Valley, Ischigualasto park, San Juan 1·90 1·30
2985 75c. Mar del Plata city, Buenos Aires 1·90 1·30
2986 75c. Caleu Caleu, La Pampa 1·90 1·30
2987 75c. Lanin National Park, Neuqueen 1·90 1·30

**1112** Velocipede (1855) (image scaled to 67% of original size)

**2003.** Evolution of the Bicycle. Multicoloured.

2988 25c.+25c. Type **1112** 1·10 80
2989 50c.+50c. Penny farthing (1867) 2·30 1·60
2990 50c.+50c. Touring bicycle 2·30 1·60
2991 75c.+75c. Racing bicycle 3·50 2·40

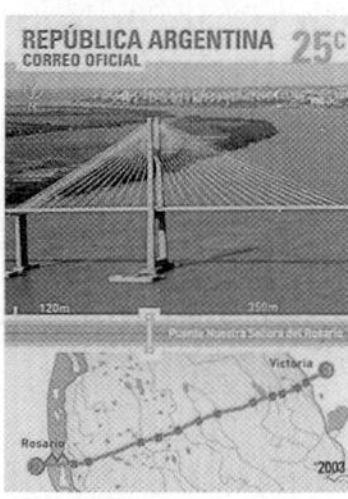

**1113** Bridge

**2003.** Inauguration of Nuestra Senora de Rosario Bridge over Parana River. Multicoloured.

2992 25c. Type **1113** 65 45
2993 75c. Ship and bridge 1·90 1·30

Nos. 2992/3 were issued together, se-tenant, forming a composite design of the bridge.

**1114** Provincial Emblem

**2003.** Rio Negro Province.

| | | | | |
|---|---|---|---|---|
| 2994 | **1114** | 75c. multicoloured | 1·90 | 1·30 |

**1115** Dr. Vicente Fidel Lopez

**2003.** Anniversaries. Multicoloured.

| | | | |
|---|---|---|---|
| 2995 | 75c. Type **1115** (politician) (death centenary) | 1·90 | 1·30 |
| 2996 | 75c. General San Martin Regiment (centenary of modern regiment) | 1·90 | 1·30 |
| 2997 | 75c. Script and Bautista Alberdi (constitutional pioneer) (150th anniv of constitution) | 1·90 | 1·30 |
| 2998 | 75c. Presidential palace and symbols of office | 1·90 | 1·30 |

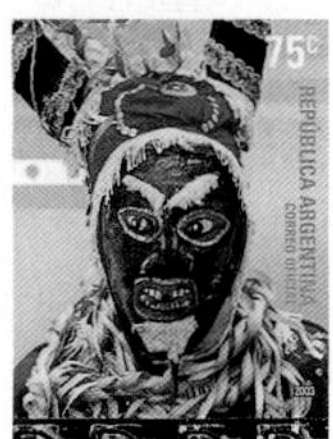


**1116** Demon Mask

**2003.** Bangkok 2003 International Stamp Exhibition. Sheet 150×100 mm containing T 1116 and similar vert design. Multicoloured.

| | | | |
|---|---|---|---|
| **MS**2999 | 75c.×2 Type **1116** (Quebrada de Humahuaca carnival, Argentine); Spirit mask (Phi Ta Khon festival, Thailand) | 3·50 | 3·50 |

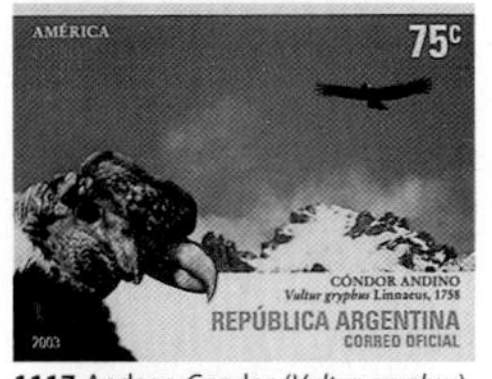


**1117** Andean Condor (*Vultur gryphus*)

**2003.** America. Flora and Fauna. Multicoloured.

| | | | |
|---|---|---|---|
| 3000 | 75c. Type **1117** | 1·90 | 1·30 |
| 3001 | 75c. *Nothofagus pumilio* (tree), forest and mountains | 1·90 | 1·30 |

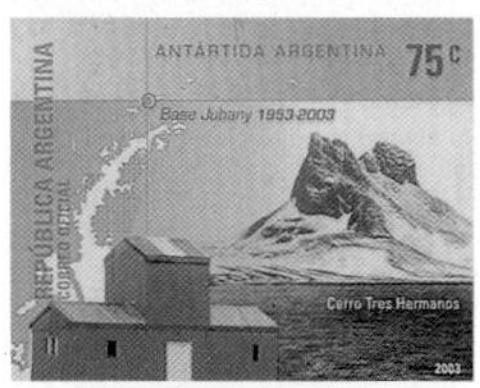


**1118** Map, Laboratory and Tres Hermanos Mountain

**2003.** 50th Anniv of Jubany Antarctic Base.

| | | | | |
|---|---|---|---|---|
| 3002 | **1118** | 75c. multicoloured | 1·90 | 1·30 |

**1119** Cattle

**2003.** National Products. Multicoloured.

| | | | |
|---|---|---|---|
| 3003 | 75c. Type **1119** (livestock) | 1·90 | 1·30 |
| 3004 | 75c. Soya beans (agriculture) | 1·90 | 1·30 |
| 3005 | 75c. Telecobalt therapy machines (nuclear medicine) | 1·90 | 1·30 |
| 3006 | 75c. Drums and bars (aluminium production) | 1·90 | 1·30 |

**1120** Corvette *Uruguay*

**2003.** Centenary of Rescue of Swedish Scientists by Argentine Corvette Uruguay. Multicoloured.

| | | | |
|---|---|---|---|
| 3007 | 75c. Type **1120** | 1·90 | 1·30 |
| **MS**3008 | 150×99 mm. 75c.×2 Swedish ship (40×30 mm); Captain Julian Irizar and *Uruguay* (40×30 mm) | 3·50 | 3·50 |

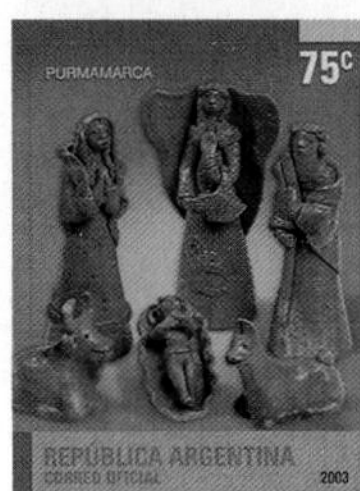


**1121** The Nativity (clay figures)

**2003.** Christmas. Multicoloured.

| | | | |
|---|---|---|---|
| 3009 | 75c. Type **1121** | 1·90 | 1·30 |
| 3010 | 75c. "Guacho Birth" (wooden carving) (Eloy Lopez) | 1·90 | 1·30 |

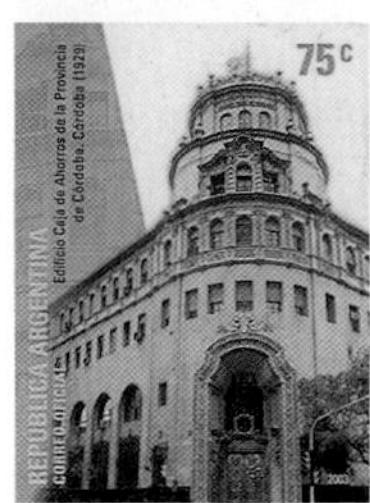


**1122** Savings Bank Building, Cordoba

**2003.** 20th-Century Architecture. Multicoloured.

| | | | |
|---|---|---|---|
| 3011 | 75c. Type **1122** | 1·90 | 1·30 |
| 3012 | 75c. Bank, San Miguel de Tucuman | 1·90 | 1·30 |
| 3013 | 75c. Minetti Palace, Rosario | 1·90 | 1·30 |
| 3014 | 75c. Barolo Palace, Buenos Aires | 1·90 | 1·30 |

**1123** Helicopter over Orcados Base

**2004.** Centenary of Orcados Base and Orcados del Sud Post Office, Antarctica. Multicoloured.

| | | | |
|---|---|---|---|
| 3015 | 75c. Type **1123** | 1·90 | 1·30 |
| **MS**3016 | 150×100 mm. 75c.×2, 5 cent 1904 stamp and "Orcados del Sud" 1904 postmark; Orcados meteorological observatory, 1904 | 3·50 | 3·50 |

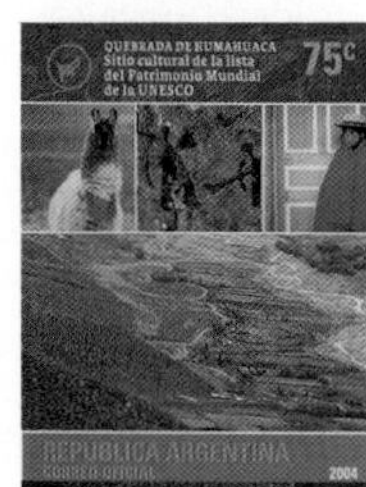


**1124** Llama, Cave Painting, Painted Door and Rio Grande Valley

**2004.** UNESCO World Heritage Site. Quebrada de Humahuaca. Multicoloured.

| | | | |
|---|---|---|---|
| 3017 | 75c. Type **1124** | 1·90 | 1·30 |
| 3018 | 75c. Church, festival procession and valley | 1·90 | 1·30 |

Nos. 3017/18 were issued together, se-tenant, forming a composite design.

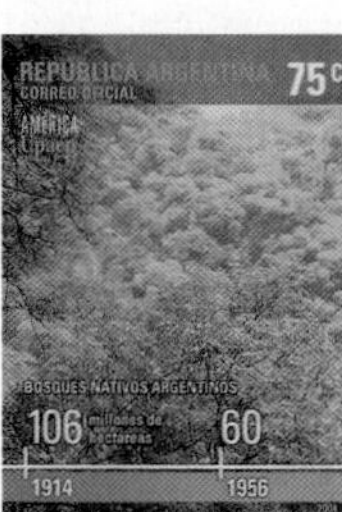


**1125** Green Forest

**2004.** America. Endangered Species. Destruction of the Rainforest. Multicoloured.

| | | | |
|---|---|---|---|
| 3019 | 75c. Type **1125** | 1·90 | 1·30 |
| 3020 | 75c. Dying forest | 1·90 | 1·30 |

Nos. 3019/20 were issued together, se-tenant, forming a composite design.

The centre of No. 3020 has been removed to simulate burning.

**1126** Masthead of First Edition and Modern Copy

**2004.** Centenary of "La Voz del Interior" Newspaper.

| | | | | |
|---|---|---|---|---|
| 3021 | **1126** | 75c. multicoloured | 1·90 | 1·30 |

**2004.** Landscapes. As T 1088. Multicoloured.

| | | | |
|---|---|---|---|
| 3022 | 75c. Drying peppers, Molinas, Salta | 1·90 | 1·30 |
| 3023 | 75c. Man leading donkey, Pampa del Indio Park, Chaco | 1·90 | 1·30 |
| 3024 | 75c. Dam on Rio Dulce river, Rio Hondo, Santiago del Estero | 1·90 | 1·30 |
| 3025 | 75c. Bridge over Setubal lagoon, Santa Fe de la Vera Cruz | 1·90 | 1·30 |
| 3026 | 75c. San Roque lake, Cordoba | 1·90 | 1·30 |
| 3027 | 75c. Palm Grove National Park, Entre Rios | 1·90 | 1·30 |
| 3028 | 75c. Potero de los Funes, San Luis | 1·90 | 1·30 |
| 3029 | 75c. Tronador mountain, Rio Negro | 1·90 | 1·30 |

**1127** Street Football

**2004.** Centenary of FIFA (Federation Internationale de Football Association). Paintings by Ruben Ramonda. Multicoloured.

| | | | |
|---|---|---|---|
| 3030 | 75c. Type **1127** | 1·90 | 1·30 |
| 3031 | 75c. The Tunnel | 1·90 | 1·30 |

**1128** "Back from Fishing" (Joaquin Sorolla y Bastida)

**2004.** Espana 2004 International Stamp Exhibition, Valencia. Sheet 150×100 mm containing T 1128 and similar multicoloured design.

| | | | |
|---|---|---|---|
| **MS**3032 | 75c. Type **1128**; 75c. "At Rest in the Pampa" (Angel Della Valle) (vert) | 3·50 | 3·50 |

**1129** Compass in Case

**2004.** 125th Anniv of Naval Hydro-Graphic Service. Multicoloured.

| | | | |
|---|---|---|---|
| 3033 | 75c. Type **1129** | 1·90 | 1·30 |
| 3034 | 75c. Sextant | 1·90 | 1·30 |
| 3035 | 75c. Cabo Virgenes lighthouse | 1·90 | 1·30 |
| 3036 | 75c. *Puerto Deseado* (hydrographic ship) | 1·90 | 1·30 |

**1130** Performing Dogs

**2004.** Circus. Sheet 109×88 mm containing T 1130 and similar horiz designs. Multicoloured.

| | | | |
|---|---|---|---|
| **MS**3037 | 50c. Type **1130**; 50c. Trapeze artiste; 50c. Clown riding unicycle; 50c. Equestrienne | 4·00 | 4·00 |

The stamps of No. **MS**3037 form a composite design of a circus ring.

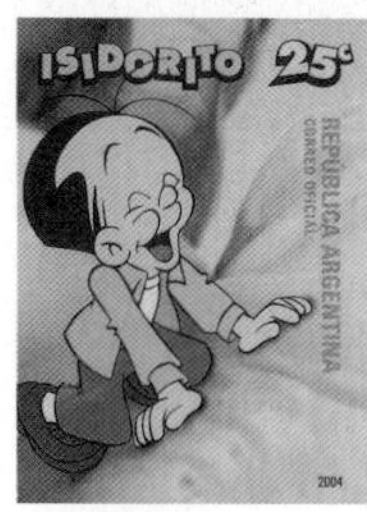


**1131** Isidorito

**2004.** Patorutzito (character from graphic magazine by Dante Quinterno). Designs showing characters. Multicoloured.

| | | | |
|---|---|---|---|
| 3038 | 75c. Patoruzito (20×60 mm) | 1·90 | 1·30 |
| 3039 | 75c. Pamperito (20×60 mm) | 1·90 | 1·30 |
| 3040 | 75c. Isidorito (30×29 mm) | 1·90 | 1·30 |
| 3041 | 75c. Malen | 1·90 | 1·30 |
| 3042 | 75c. Upita | 1·90 | 1·30 |
| 3043 | 75c. Chacha | 1·90 | 1·30 |
| **MS**3044 | 167×118 mm. 25c. Type **1131**; 25c. Upita (different); 50c. Patoruzito; 50c. Malen (different); 75c. Pamperito; 75c. Chacha plus 2 stamp size labels | 7·00 | 7·00 |

The stamps and labels contained in **MS**3044 form a composite design.

**1132** Woman and Guide Dog

**2004.** Working Dogs. Multicoloured.

| | | | |
|---|---|---|---|
| 3045 | 75c. Type **1132** | 1·90 | 1·30 |
| 3046 | 75c. Rescue dog (horiz) | 1·90 | 1·30 |

**1133** *Patagonotothen ramsay*

**2004.** Endangered Species. Fish. Multicoloured.

| | | | |
|---|---|---|---|
| 3047 | 75c. Type **1133** | 1·90 | 1·30 |
| 3048 | 75c. *Bathyraja griseocauda* | 1·90 | 1·30 |
| 3049 | 75c. *Salilota australis* | 1·90 | 1·30 |
| 3050 | 75c. *Dissostichus eleginoides* | 1·90 | 1·30 |

**1134** Cycling

**2004.** Olympic Games, Athens 2004. Multicoloured.

| | | | |
|---|---|---|---|
| 3051 | 75c. Type **1134** | 1·90 | 1·30 |
| 3052 | 75c. Judo | 1·90 | 1·30 |
| 3053 | 75c. Swimming | 1·90 | 1·30 |
| 3054 | 75c. Tennis | 1·90 | 1·30 |

**1135** *Villarino (image scaled to 73% of original size)*

**2004.** Naval Carriers. Multicoloured.

| | | | |
|---|---|---|---|
| 3055 | 25c.+25c. Type **1135** | 90 | 70 |
| 3056 | 50c.+50c. *Pampa* | 1·80 | 1·30 |
| 3057 | 50c.+50c. *Bahia Thetis* | 1·80 | 1·30 |
| 3058 | 75c.+75c. *Cabo de Hornis* | 2·50 | 2·20 |

Nos. 3055/8 were issued together, se-tenant, forming a composite design.

**1136** Queen Palm Fruit (*Syagrus romanzoffiana*)

**2004.** Singapore 2004 International Stamp Exhibition. Fruit. Sheet 150×100 mm containing T 1136 and similar vert designs.
**MS**3059 75c.×2, Type **1136**; Mango 2·50 1·70

**1137** El Pehuen

**2004.** Legends and Traditions. Multicoloured.
3060 75c. Type **1137** (legend of araucaria tree) 1·60 1·10
3061 75c. La Yacumama (Diaguita water goddess) 1·60 1·10
3062 75c. La Pachamama (earth goddess) 1·60 1·10
3063 75c. La Difunta Correa (legend of mother who died of thirst) 1·60 1·10

**1138** Early Students and Microscope

**2004.** Centenaries. Multicoloured.
3064 75c. Type **1138** (Agronomy and Veterinary Science Institute) 1·60 1·10
3065 75c. Jose san Martin (statue) and road and rail bridges over Nequen river (Neuqin city) 1·60 1·10
3066 75c. Monument and cover of "La Coleccionista" (Rosario Philatelic Association) 1·60 1·10

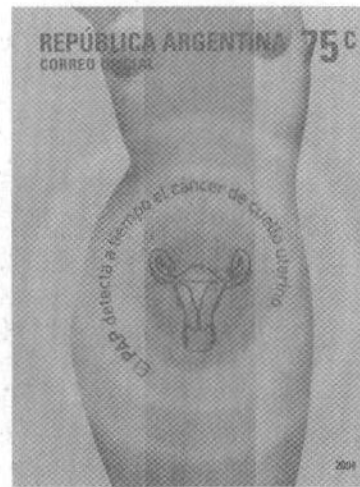

**1139** Woman's Torso and Campaign Emblem

**2004.** Cervical Cancer Awareness Campaign.
3067 **1139** 75c. multicoloured 1·60 1·10

**1140** Hourglass containing Clear Water

**2004.** Mercosur. Water Conservation Campaign. Multicoloured.
3068 75c. Type **1140** 1·60 1·10
3069 75c. Hourglass containing contaminated water 1·60 1·10

**1141** Mary

**2004.** Christmas. Multicoloured.
3070 75c. Type **1141** 1·60 1·10
3071 75c. The Nativity 1·60 1·10

**1142** Reverse

**2004.** 1813 One Ounce Gold Coin. Multicoloured.
3072 75c. Type **1142** 1·60 1·10
3073 75c. Obverse 1·60 1·10

Nos. 3072/3 were issued together, se-tenant, forming a composite design.

**1143** "Spanish Grammar for Americans" and Andres Bello (author)

**2004.** 3rd International Spanish Language Congress.
3074 **1143** 75c. multicoloured 1·60 1·10

**1144** Exchange Building

**2004.** 150th Anniv of Buenos Aires Commodities Exchange.
3075 **1144** 75c. multicoloured 1·60 1·10

**1145** "Aloysia citriodora"

**2004.** Aromatic Plants. Multicoloured.
3076 75c. Type **1145** 1·60 1·10
3077 75c. "Minthostachys mollis" 1·60 1·10
3078 75c. "Tagetes minuta" 1·60 1·10
3079 75c. "Lippia turbinate" 1·60 1·10

**1146** Emblem and Scout

**2005.** 12th Pan American Scout Jamboree, Mendoza.
3080 **1146** 75c. multicoloured 1·60 1·10

**1147** Ram Klong Yao Dance (Thailand)

**2005.** 50th Anniv of Thailand—Argentina Diplomatic Relations. Multicoloured.
3081 75c. Type **1147** 1·60 1·10
3082 75c. Tango (Argentina) 1·60 1·10

**1148** "Woman in Red Sweater"

**2005.** Birth Centenary of Alberto Berni (artist). Details from painting. Multicoloured.
3083 75c. Type **1148** 1·60 1·10
**MS**3084 150×99 mm. 75c.×2 Face (detail); Baby and men wearing hats (detail) (horiz) 3·25 3·25

The stamps and margin of No. **MS**3084 form a composite design of "Manifestation".

**1149** Rotary International Emblem, Children and Vaccine

**2005.** Centenary of Rotary International (charitable organization). Eradication of Polio Campaign.
3085 **1149** 75c. multicoloured 1·60 1·10

**1150** Silvina Ocampo

**2005.** Mercosaur. Writers. Multicoloured.
3086 75c. Type **1150** (1903–1993) 1·60 1·10
3087 75c. Ezequiel Martinez Estrada (1895–1964) 1·60 1·10

**1151** Sedan Graciela

**2005.** National Motor Industry. Multicoloured.
3088 75c. Type **1151** 1·60 1·10
3089 75c. Justicalista sport 1·60 1·10
3090 75c. Rastrojero diesel 1·60 1·10
3091 75c. Siam di Tella 1500 1·60 1·10
3092 75c. Torino 380W 1·60 1·10

**1152** Jose Antonio Balseiro (founder) and Nuclear Reactor

**2005.** 50th Anniv of Balseiro Institute. International Year of Physics. Multicoloured.
3093 75c. Type **1152** 1·60 1·10
3094 75c. Albert Einstein and frontispiece of *Theory of Special Relativity* 1·60 1·10

**1153** Pope John Paul II

**2005.** Pope John Paul II Commemoration. Multicoloured.
3095 75c. Type **1153** 1·60 1·10
**MS**3096 150×99 mm. 75c.×2, (each 40×50 mm) Wearing mitre and carrying pastoral staff; Saying farewell 3·25 3·25

**1154** Workers at Machines and Demonstrators

**2005.** Anniversaries. Multicoloured.
3097 75c. Type **1154** (75th anniv of Workers Confederation) 1·60 1·10
3098 75c. Mar del Plata and *La Capital* (centenary of *La Capital* newspaper) 1·60 1·10
3099 75c. Alfredo Palacios (centenary of Sunday blue law) 1·60 1·10

**1155** Cesar Milstein

**2005.** Cesar Milstein (Nobel Prize for Medicine, 1984) Commemoration.
3100 **1155** 75c. multicoloured 1·60 1·10

**1156** Orestes Liberti (1st Commander) and Horse-drawn Fire Engine

**2005.** Volunteer Fire Fighters. Multicoloured.
3101 75c. Type **1156** 1·60 1·10
3102 75c. Fighting fire and modern engine 1·60 1·10

**1157** Early and Modern Red Cross Workers

**2005.** 125th Anniv of Argentine Red Cross Society.
3103 **1157** 75c. multicoloured 1·60 1·10

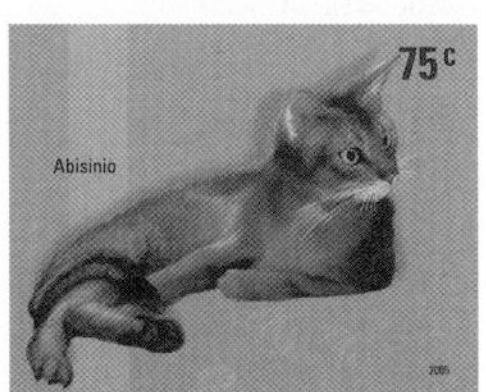

**1158** Abyssinian

**2005.** Cats. Sheet 117×166 mm containing T 1158 and similar horiz designs. Multicoloured.
**MS**3104 25c. Birman; 25c. Siamese; 50c. Oriental shorthair; 50c. Persian; 75c. Type **1158**; 75c. European shorthair 5·00 5·00

**1159** Juan Filloy

**2005.** 5th Death Anniv of Juan Filloy (writer).
3105 **1159** 75c. multicoloured 1·60 1·10

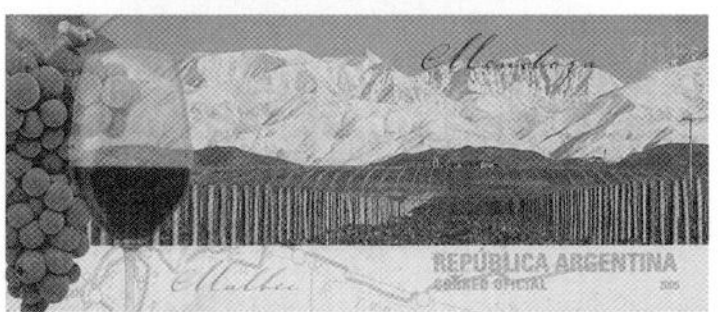

**1160** Malbec (image scaled to 73% of original size)

**2005.** Tourism. Wine. Multicoloured.
3106 75c. Type **1160** (Mendoza, Tupungato Valley) 1·60 1·10
3107 75c. Merlot (Rio Negro, Alto Valle de Rio Negro) 1·60 1·10
3108 75c. Syrah (San Juan - Zonda Valley) 1·60 1·10
3109 75c. Torrontes (Salta - Cafayate, Calchaquies Valleys) 1·60 1·10
See also Nos. 3202/4.

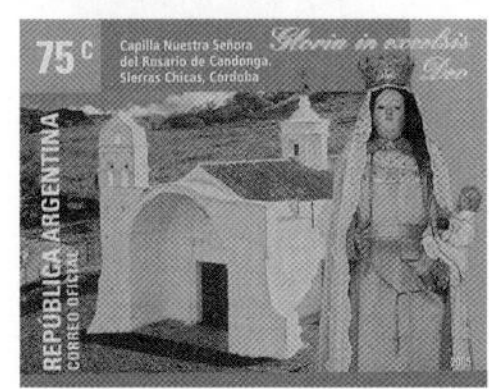

**1161** Our Lady of the Rosary Candonga Chapel, Sierras Chicas, Cordoba

**2005.** Places of Worship. Multicoloured.
3110 75c. Type **1161** 1·60 1·10
3111 75c. Al Ahmad Mosque, Buenos Aires 1·60 1·10
3112 75c. Israelite Congregation of Argentine Temple, Buenos Aires 1·60 1·10
3113 75c. Vision of the Middle Buddhist Temple, Buenos Aires 1·60 1·10

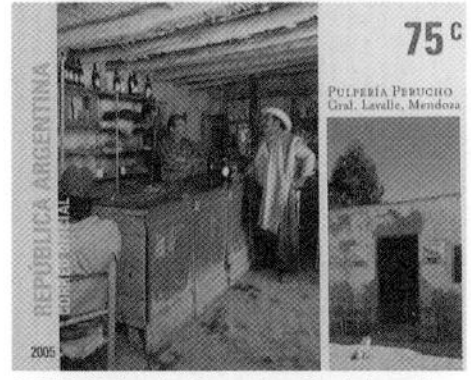

**1162** Pulperia Perucho, Gral, Lavalle, Mendoza

**2005.** Stores (Pulperias). Multicoloured.
3114 75c. Type **1162** 1·60 1·10
3115 75c. El Torito, Baradero, Buenos Aires 1·60 1·10
3116 75c. Impini, Larroque, Entre Rios 1·60 1·10
3117 75c. Pulperia de Cacho di Catarina 1·60 1·10

**1163** *Rio De la Plata* (merchant vessel) (image scaled to 67% of original size)

**2005.** Ships. Multicoloured.
3118 25c.+25c. Type **1163** 95 60
3119 50c.+50c. *Libertad* (passenger ship) 1·80 1·00
3120 50c.+50c. *Camopo Duran* (tanker) 1·80 1·00
3121 75c.+75c. *Isla Soledad* (container ship) 2·50 2·20
Nos. 3118/21 were issued together, se-tenant, forming a composite design.

**1164** Julio Bocca (dancer)

**2005.** Colon Theatre. Multicoloured.
3122 75c. Type **1164** 1·60 1·10
3123 75c. Theatre orchestra, opera singers and choir 1·60 1·10

**1165** Ice Flow

**2005.** 1st Anniv of Antarctic Treaty Secretariat, Buenos Aires (3124). General Hernan Pujato's Expeditions to Antarctica (MS3125). Mult.
3124 75c. Type **1165** 1·60 1·10
**MS**3125 150×100 mm. 75c.×2, Divers and boat; General Pujato and team members 3·25 3·25

**1166** Virgin and Child (detail)

**2005.** Christmas. Showing parts of the painting "Retablo" by Elena Strorni. Multicoloured.
3126 75c. Type **1166** 1·60 1·10
**MS**3127 150×100 mm. 75c.×4, The Annunciation (40×40 mm); The Nativity (40×40 mm); Three Wise Men (40×40 mm); Presenting Jesus in the temple (40×40 mm) 6·25 6·25

**1167** Solar Panel and Light Bulb

**2005.** Alternative Energy. Multicoloured.
3128 75c. Type **1167** 1·60 1·10
3129 $4 Wind generators 6·25 4·75

**1168** Mar de Plata Port and Summit Emblem

**2005.** 4th Americas' Summit.
3130 **1168** 75c. multicoloured 1·60 1·10

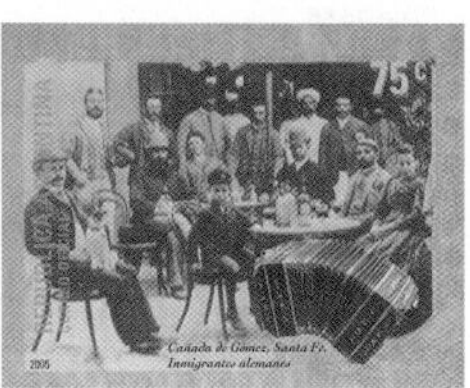

**1169** German Immigrants, Canada de Gomez, Santa Fe

**2005.** Immigration. Multicoloured.
3131 75c. Type **1169** 1·60 1·10
3132 75c. Slovakian women and children, Immigrant Hotel, Buenos Aires 1·60 1·10
3133 75c. Welsh immigrants, Chubut Central Railway, Trelew 1·60 1·10
3134 75c. Jewish colony, Moises Ville, Santa Fe 1·60 1·10

**1170** Luis Angel Firpo

**2005.** Sport. Boxers. Multicoloured.
3135 75c. Type **1170** 1·60 1·10
3136 75c. Nicolino Locche 1·60 1·10

**1171** Man (film, "Ivan & Eva")

**2005.** Design. Multicoloured.
3137 75c. Type **1171** 1·60 1·10
3138 75c. Dress (Nadine Zlotogora) (clothes and textile) (vert) 1·60 1·10
3139 75c. Aluminium chair (Ricardo Blanco) (industrial design) (vert) 1·60 1·10
3140 75c. CD case (Claudia Smith) (graphic design) 1·60 1·10

**1172** Bartolme Mitre

**2006.** Death Centenary of Bartolme Mitre (journalist and president 1862–8).
3141 **1172** 75c. multicoloured 1·60 1·10

**1173** Snow-covered City

**2006.** Centenary of Esquel.
3142 **1173** 75c. multicoloured 1·60 1·10

**2006.** Tourism. Wine. As T 1160. Multicoloured.
3143 50c. Vineyard, Alto Valle del Rio Negro (Merlot wine) (Rio Negro) (70×30 mm) 1·10 75
3144 75c. Wine barrels (Salta) 1·60 1·10
3145 1p. Grape harvest (San Juan) 2·20 1·50
3146 1p.25 Vineyard, Valle del Tupungato (Malbec wine) (Mendoza) (70×30 mm) 2·40 1·60
3147 2p.75 Wine tasting (Mendoza) 2·50 1·70
3148 3p. Vineyard, Valle del Zonda (Syrah wine) (San Juan) (70×30 mm) 2·75 1·90
3149 3p.25 Vineyard, Cafayate, Valles Calchaquies (Torrentes wine) (Salta) (70×30 mm) 3·00 2·00
3150 3p.50 Wine vats (Rio Negro) 3·25 2·20

**1175** Ramon Carrillo

**2006.** Birth Centenary of Ramon Carrillo (health care specialist).
3151 **1175** 75c. multicoloured 1·60 95

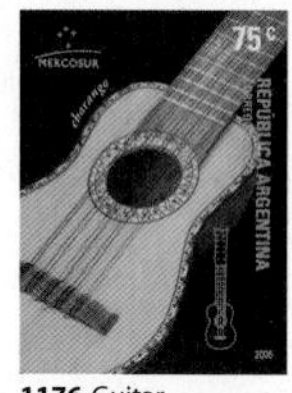

**1176** Guitar

**2006.** Mercosur. Musical Instruments. Mult.
3152 75c. Type **1176** 1·60 95
3153 $3.50 Drum 5·00 3·50

**1177** 1 de Mayo Lighthouse

**2006.** Lighthouses. Multicoloured.
3154 75c. Type **1177** 1·60 90
3155 75c. Ano Nuevo 1·60 90
3156 75c. El Rincon 1·60 90
3157 75c. Recalada a Bahia Blanca 1·60 90

**1178** Escuela de Mecanica de la Armada (concentration camp) (1976)

**2006.** "From Horror to Hope". 30th Anniv of Military Dictatorship. Sheet 151×99 mm containing T 1178 and similar vert design. Multicoloured.
**MS**3158 75c.×2, Type **1178**; Escuela de Mecanica de la Armada (memorial museum) (2006) 3·25 3·25

**1179** Crown

**2006.** 18th-century Religious Silverware. Multicoloured.
3159 75c. Type **1179** 1·60 95
3160 75c. Candelabra 1·60 95
3161 75c. Chalice 1·60 95
3162 75c. Viaticum 1·60 95

**1180** Toyota Corolla WRC (Luis Perez Companc—Rally Nacional A8 category)

**2006.** National Motor Racing Champions. Multicoloured.

3163 75c. Type **1180** 1·60 95
3164 75c. Ford Falcon (Juan Manuel Silva—Turismo Carretera category) 1·60 95
3165 75c. Ford Focus (Gabriel Ponce de Leon—Turismo Competición 2000 category) 1·60 95
3166 75c. Ford Escort (Patricio di Palma—Class 3 Nacional category) 1·60 95

**1181** Springer Spaniel

**2006.** Dogs. Sheet 117×166 mm containing T 1181 and similar horiz designs. Multicoloured.

**MS**3167 25c. Type **1181**; 25c. Yorkshire terrier; 50c. Argentine dogo (Argentinian mastiff); 50c. Miniature schnauzer; 75c. Poodle; 75c. Chow 6·50 2·75

No. **MS**3167 also contains two illustrated stamp size labels forming a composite design.

**1182** Argentine Player

**2006.** World Cup Football Championship, Germany. Multicoloured.

1p. Serbia and Montenegro 1·90 1·90
3168 1p. Type **1182** 1·90 1·90
3170 1p. Ivory Coast 1·90 1·90
3171 1p. Netherlands 1·90 1·90
3172 4p. Football in net 5·75 4·25
**MS**3173 149x100 mm. 1p.50 As No. 3168 (detail) 2·75 2·75

**1183** Knotted Cigarette (image scaled to 49% of original size)

**2006.** World Health Organization No Tobacco Day.

3174 **1183** 75c. multicoloured 1·60 95

**1184** Lizard Outline and Dead Tree

**2006.** International Year of Deserts and Desertification. Multicoloured.

3175 75c. Type **1184** 1·60 95
3176 75c. *Lilotaemus* (lizard) and *Calycera crassifolia* 1·60 95

**1185** Mauricio Borensztein (Tato Bores) (actor)

**2006.** Personalities. Multicoloured.

3177 75c. Type **1185** 1·60 95
3178 75c. Rodolfo Walsh (journalist) 1·60 95

**1186** Alpine Skiing

**2006.** Winter Sports. Multicoloured.

3179 75c. Type **1186** 1·60 95
3180 75c. Snowboarding 1·60 95
3181 75c. Cross-country skiing 1·60 95
3182 75c. Biathlon 1·60 95

**1187** Musician

**2006.** Tango. Multicoloured.

3183 75c. Type **1187** 1·60 95
3184 $4 Dancers 1·60 95

Stamps of a similar design were issued by France.

**1188** Patoruzito riding Pamperito

**2006.** Patoruzito (character from graphic magazine by Dante Quinterno). Opening of "Patoruzito—La Gran Adventura" (film).

3185 **1188** 75c. multicoloured 1·60 95

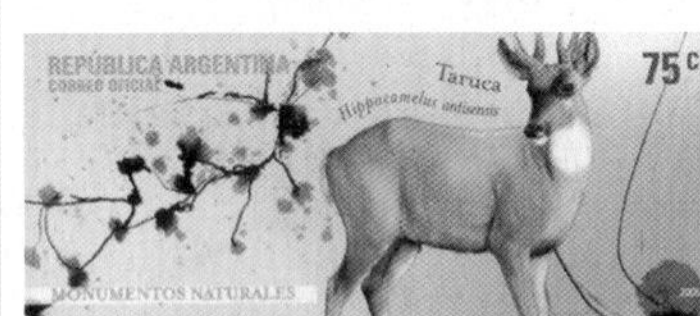


**1189** Taruca (*Hippocamelus antisensis*) (image scaled to 74% of original size)

**2006.** Natural Monuments. Multicoloured.

3186 75c. Type **1189** 1·60 95
3187 75c. Southern right whale (*Eubaluena australis*) 1·60 95
3188 75c. Huemul (*Hippocamelus bisculus*) 1·60 95
3189 75c. Jaguar (*Panthera onca*) 1·60 95

**1190** House as Money Box and Plug connected to Sun (Florencia Tovi)

**2006.** America. Energy Conservation. Winning Designs in Children's Drawing Competition. Multicoloured.

3190 75c. Type **1190** 1·60 95
3191 75c. Window, table and standard lamp (Camila Suarez) 1·60 95

**1191** "The Re-conquest of Buenos Aires" (Charles Fouqueray)

**2006.** Bicentenary of British Invasion and Defeat. Sheet 99×75 mm.

**MS**3192 **1191** 1p.50 multicoloured 2·75 2·75

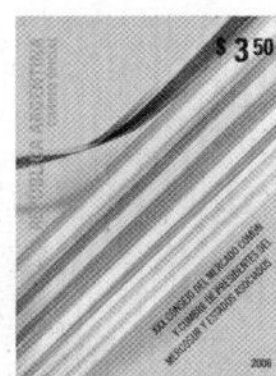


**1192** Flags as Ribbons

**2006.** 30th Council of the Common Market. Mercosur and Associate States' Presidents' Summit.

3193 **1192** 3p.50 multicoloured 1·60 95

**1193** Ciudad de Buenos Aires (image scaled to 49% of original size)

**2006.** River Transport. Multicoloured.

3194 25c.+25c. Type **1193** 1·60 95
3195 50c.+50c. Lambare 1·60 95
3196 50c.+50c. Madrid 1·60 95
3197 75c.+75c. Rawson 1·60 95

**1194** "150 Anos"

**2006.** 150th Anniv of First Argentine Stamp. Multicoloured.

3198 75c. Type **1194** 1·60 95
**MS**3199 151×99 mm. $1.50 As Type **3** (1856 1 real stamp) (40×40 mm) 2·75 2·75

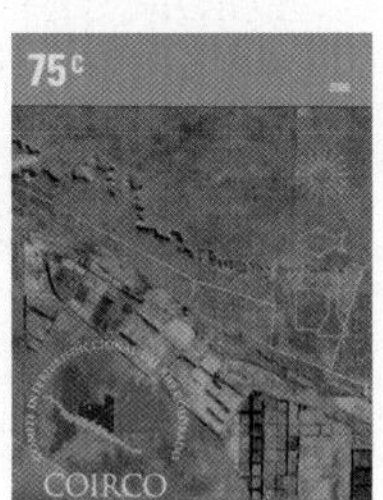


**1195** Colorado River Basin

**2006.** 30th Anniv of Comite Interjurisdiccional de Rio Colorado (COIRCO) (inter-jurisdictional committee on the Colorado river).

3200 **1195** 75c. multicoloured 1·60 95

**1196** Legion de Patricios Rifleman (1806–9)

**2006.** Bicentenary of Infantry Corps "Patricios".

3201 **1196** 75c. multicoloured 1·60 95

**2006.** Tourism. Wine. As T 1160. Multicoloured.

3202 75c. Syrah (Catamarcaungato Valley) 1·60 95
3203 75c. Torrontes Riojano (La Rioja) 1·60 95
3204 75c. Pinot noir (Neuquen) 1·60 95

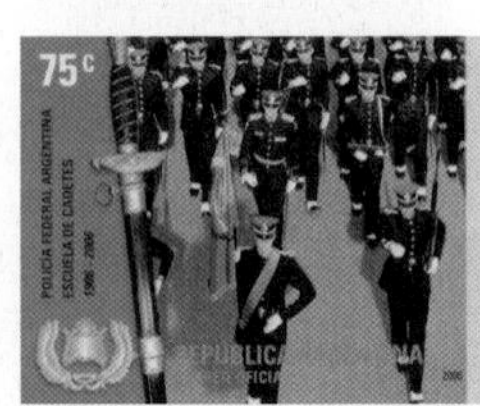


**1197** Cadets

**2006.** Centenary of Ramon L. Falcon Cadet School.

3205 **1197** 75c. multicoloured 1·60 95

**1198** Puente San Roque Gonzalez de Santa Cruz, between Argentina and Paraguay (image scaled to 73% of original size)

**2006.** International Bridges in Argentina. Multicoloured.

3206 75c. Type **1198** 1·60 95
3207 75c. Puente Presidente Tancredo Neves, between Argentina and Brazil 1·60 95

**1199** "Madona y Paloma"

**2006.** Christmas. Paintings by Alfredo Guttero. Multicoloured.

3208 75c. Type **1199** 1·60 95
3209 75c. "Anunciacion" (horiz) 1·60 95

**1200** Research Activities

**2006.** National Institute of Farming Technology.

3210 **1200** 75c. multicoloured 1·60 95

**1201** Norberto Napolitano (Pappo)

**2006.** 40th Anniv of Argentinean Rock Music. Multicoloured.

3211 75c. Type **1201** 1·60 95
3212 75c. Luca George (Luca) Prodan 1·60 95
3213 75c. Miguel Angel Peralta (Miguel Abuelo) 1·60 95
3214 75c. Jose Alberto Iglesias (Tanguito) 1·60 95

**1202** Valentin Sayhueque

**2006.** Caciques (tribal chiefs). Multicoloured.

3215 75c. Type **1202** (Huilliche people) 1·60 95
3216 75c. Casimiro Bigua (Tehuelche people) 1·60 95

**1203** *Hercules* (detail from painting *Combate de Marin Garcia* by Emilio Biggeri)

**2007.** 150th Death Anniv of Admiral William Brown.

| | | | | |
|---|---|---|---|---|
| 3217 | **1203** | 75c. multicoloured | 1·60 | 95 |

**1204** Grapes (Neuquen)

**2007.** Tourism. Wine. Multicoloured.

| | | | |
|---|---|---|---|
| 3218 | 75c. Type **1204** | 1·60 | 95 |
| 3219 | 75c. Grapes (Catamarca) | 1·60 | 95 |
| 3220 | 75c. Grapes (La Rioja) | 1·60 | 95 |
| 3221 | 3p.25 Bottle (Neuquen) | 3·75 | 2·40 |
| 3222 | 3p.25 Bottle (Catamarca) | 3·75 | 2·40 |
| 3223 | 3p.25 Bottle (La Rioja) | 3·75 | 2·40 |

**1205** 1982 18 pesos Stamp and Ofincina Radiopostal Islas Malvinas Postmark

**2007.** 25th Anniv of South Atlantic Conflict. Multicoloured.

| | | | |
|---|---|---|---|
| 3224 | 75c. Type **1205** | 1·60 | 95 |
| 3225 | 75c. IAI Dagger Fighter aircraft | 1·60 | 95 |
| 3226 | 75c. Battle Cruiser *General Belgrano* | 1·60 | 95 |
| 3227 | 75c. Decorated veteran | 1·60 | 95 |
| 3228 | 75c. Decoration awarded to all veterans (*vert*) | 1·60 | 95 |

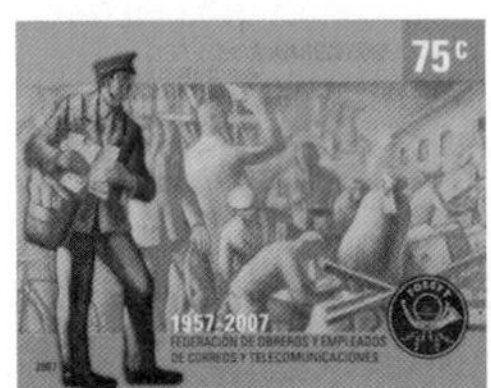
**1206** Postal Workers (detail from painting by Jose Murcia)

**2007.** 50th Anniv of Postal and Telecommunications Workers Federation (FOECYT).

| | | | | |
|---|---|---|---|---|
| 3229 | **1206** | 75c. multicoloured | 1·60 | 95 |

**1207** *Phalacrocorax atriceps* (Imperial or blue-eyed cormorant)

**2007.** Argentina in Antarctica. Multicoloured.

| | | | |
|---|---|---|---|
| 3230 | 75c. Type **1207** | 1·60 | 95 |
| 3231 | 75c. *Leptonychotes weddellii* (Weddell seal) | 1·60 | 95 |
| 3232 | 75c. *Sterna vittata* (Antarctic tern) | 1·60 | 95 |
| 3233 | 75c. *Sterna vittata* (Antarctic tern) | 1·60 | 95 |
| 3234 | 75c. *Pysoscelis adeliae* (Adelie penguin ) | 1·60 | 95 |
| 3235 | 75c. *Chionis alba* (snowy or yellow-billed sheathbill) | 1·60 | 95 |
| 3236 | 75c. *Pygoscelis papua* (gentoo penguins) | 1·60 | 95 |
| 3237 | 75c. *Pygoscelis papua* (gentoo penguins) | 1·60 | 95 |
| 3238 | 4p. *Almirante Irízar* (ice breaker) | 5·00 | 3·50 |

Nos. 3232/3 and 3236/7 were issued together, se-tenant, forming a composite design.

**1208** Latin American Art Museum, Buenos Aires

**2007.** Architecture. Multicoloured.

| | | | |
|---|---|---|---|
| 3239 | 75c. Type **1208** | 1·60 | 95 |
| 3240 | 3p.25. High Mountain Archaeological Museum, Salta | 4·50 | 3·00 |

**1209** Rocking Horse

**2007.** Toys. Multicoloured.

| | | | |
|---|---|---|---|
| 3241 | 75c. Type **1209** | 1·60 | 95 |
| 3242 | 75c. Tea set | 1·60 | 95 |
| 3243 | 75c. Train set | 1·60 | 95 |
| 3244 | 75c. Soldiers | 1·60 | 95 |

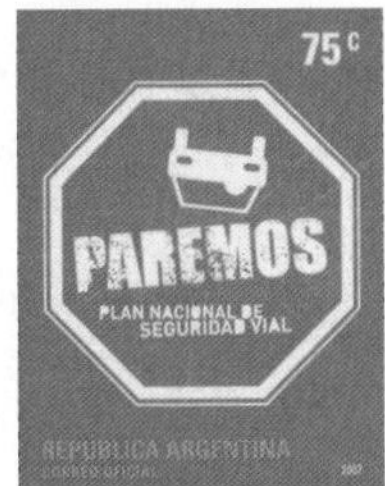
**1210** Emblem

**2007.** National Road Safety Campaign.

| | | | | |
|---|---|---|---|---|
| 3245 | **1210** | 75c. red and silver | 1·60 | 95 |

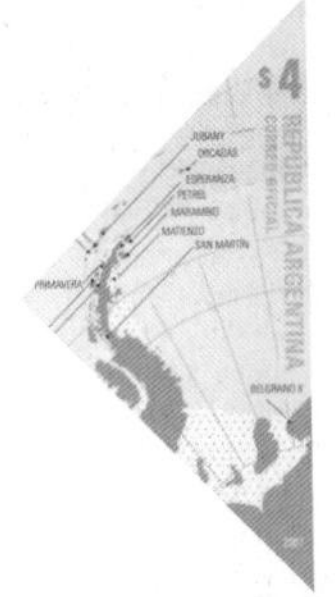
**1211** Argentine Bases

**2007.** International Polar Year. Sheet 150×98 mm.

| | | | |
|---|---|---|---|
| **MS**3246 | 4p. multicoloured | 5·00 | 3·50 |

**1212** *Combate de Santo Domingo* (Eleodora Marenco)

**2007.** Bicentenary of Defence of Buenos Aires.

| | | | | |
|---|---|---|---|---|
| 3247 | **1212** | 75c. multicoloured | 1·60 | 95 |

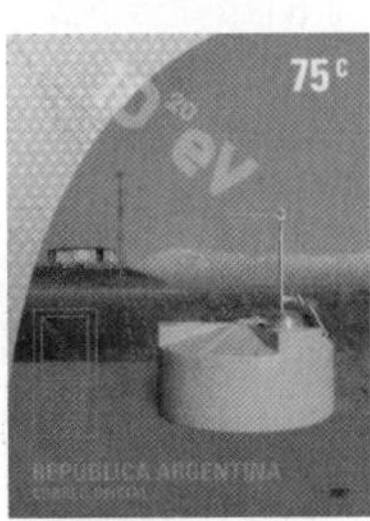
**1213** Radiation and Fluorescence Detectors

**2007.** Pierre Auger Observatory.

| | | | | |
|---|---|---|---|---|
| 3248 | **1213** | 75c. multicoloured | 1·60 | 95 |

**1214** St. Jose de Calasanz and Pupils (stained glass window, San Jose de Calasanz Church, Buenos Aires)

**2007.** 450th Birth Anniv of Jose de Calasanz (founder of first free school in modern Europe).

| | | | | |
|---|---|---|---|---|
| 3249 | **1214** | 1p. multicoloured | 1·90 | 1·20 |

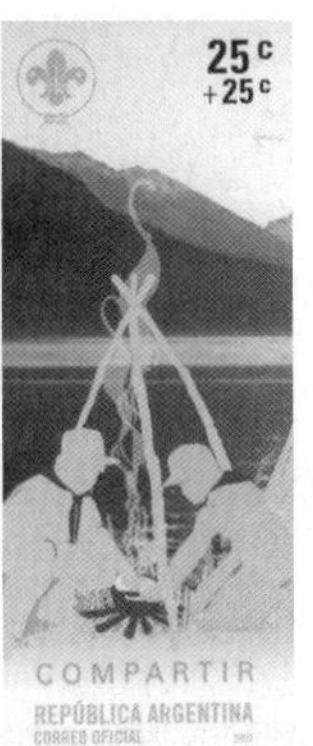
**1215** Campfire

**2007.** Centenary of Scouting. Multicoloured.

| | | | |
|---|---|---|---|
| 3250 | 25c.+25c. Type **1215** | 90 | 60 |
| 3251 | 50c.+50c. Tent and scout saluting | 1·80 | 1·20 |
| 3252 | 75c.+75c. Scout wearing pack | 2·20 | 1·50 |
| 3253 | 1p.+1p. Scouts pulling guy rope | 2·50 | 1·70 |

Nos. 3250/3 were issued together, se-tenant, forming a composite design.

**1216** *El Chaco* (meteorite)

**2007.** Meteorites of Campo Del Cielo. Sheet 148×99 mm.

| | | | |
|---|---|---|---|
| **MS**3254 | 6p. multicoloured | 6·25 | 6·00 |

**1217** *Homero Manzi* (Hermenegildo Sabat)

**2007.** Birth Centenary of Homero Nicolas Manzione Prestera (Homero Manzi) (lyricist).

| | | | | |
|---|---|---|---|---|
| 3255 | **1217** | 1p. multicoloured | 1·60 | 95 |

**1218** Road leading to S. C. de Bariloche (Rio Negro)

**2007.** Tourism. National Route 40. Sheet 496×99 mm containing T 1218 and similar horiz designs. Multicoloured.

| | | | |
|---|---|---|---|
| **MS**3256 | 50c. Type **1218**; 50c. Abra El Acay (40×30 mm); 1p. Road to Perito Moreno (Santa Cruz) (70×30 mm); 1p. *La Trochita* locomotive (Chubut) (40×30 mm); 1p. Lanin volcano (Neuquen) (40×30 mm), 1p. Rio Grande (Mendoza) (50×30 mm); 1p. Goats, San Jose Jachal (San Juan) (40×30 mm); 1p. Cuesta de Miranda (La Rioja) (50×30 mm); 1p. Capel Nuestra Senora del Transito (Catamarca); 1p. Ruins of Quilmes (Tucuman); 1p. Road leading to Oratorio (Jujuy) (40×30 mm) | 10·00 | 9·50 |

**1219** Houses with Blocked and Free-flowing Chimneys (Julieta Saavedra Barrgan)

**2007.** Carbon Monoxide Inhalation Prevention Campaign. Winning Designs in Children's Drawing Competition. Multicoloured.

| | | | |
|---|---|---|---|
| 3257 | 1p. Type **1219** | 1·80 | 1·20 |
| 3258 | 1p. Dirty and clean flames (Efrain Osvaldo Rost) (vert) | 1·80 | 1·20 |
| 3259 | 1p. Engineer and gas cooker (Camila Micaela Alvarez Petrone) (vert) | 1·80 | 1·20 |
| 3260 | 1p. Smoking fire (Leandro Ventancour) | 1·80 | 1·20 |

**1220** Accordion

**2007.** 150th Anniv of Argentine–Germany Bilateral Relations. Sheet 150×100 mm.

| | | | |
|---|---|---|---|
| **MS**3261 | 4p. multicoloured | 5·25 | 5·25 |

**1221** Emblem

**2007.** Centenary of Club Atletico San Lorenzo de Almagro.

| | | | | |
|---|---|---|---|---|
| 3262 | **1221** | 1p. multicoloured | 1·80 | 1·20 |

**1222** Ceferino Namuncura

**2007.** Beatification of Ceferino Namuncura.

| | | | | |
|---|---|---|---|---|
| 3263 | **1222** | 1p. multicoloured | 1·80 | 1·20 |

**1223** *Corrientes esquina Uruguay* (Horacio Cuppola)

**2007.** Contemporary Art. Multicoloured.

| | | | |
|---|---|---|---|
| 3264 | 1p. Type **1223** | 1·80 | 1·20 |
| 3265 | 1p. *Dialogo* (Liliana Porter) (vert) | 1·80 | 1·20 |
| 3266 | 1p. *0611* (detail) (Pablo Siqier) | 1·80 | 1·20 |

| | | | | |
|---|---|---|---|---|
| 3267 | | 1p. *Imaginando el estupor* (detail) (Marta Minujin) (vert) | 1·80 | 1·20 |

**1224** Three Wise Men

**2007.** Christmas. Showing detail from The Birth (stained glass window)). Multicoloured.

| | | | | |
|---|---|---|---|---|
| 3268 | | 25c. Type **1224** | 1·80 | 1·20 |
| 3269 | | 1p. Holy Family | 1·80 | 1·20 |

**1225** Early Drilling Site

**2007.** Centenary of Oil and Gas Discovery in Argentina.

| | | | | |
|---|---|---|---|---|
| 3270 | **1225** | 1p. multicoloured | 1·80 | 1·20 |

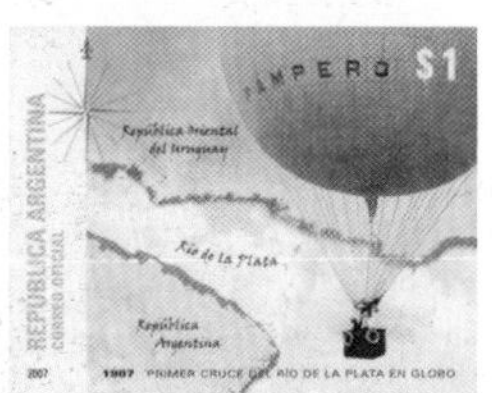


**1226** *Pampero* (balloon) and River Plate

**2007.** Centenary of Aaron de Anchorena and Jorge Newbery's Balloon Flight across the River Plate.

| | | | | |
|---|---|---|---|---|
| 3271 | **1226** | 1p. multicoloured | 1·80 | 1·20 |

**1227** Ceremonial Staff

**2007.** Presidential Inauguration. 24th Anniv of Democracy.

| | | | | |
|---|---|---|---|---|
| 3272 | **1227** | 1p. multicoloured | 1·80 | 1·20 |

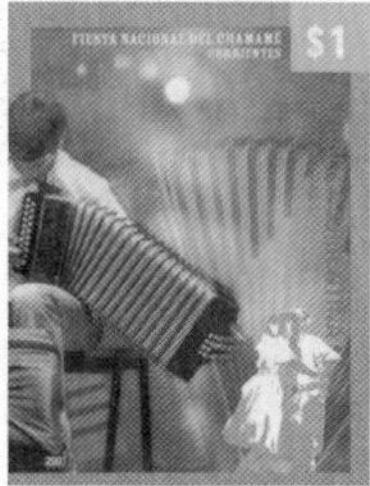


**1228** Accordionist and Dancers

**2007.** Festivals. Multicoloured.

| | | | | |
|---|---|---|---|---|
| 3273 | | 1p. Type **1228** (National Chamame (dance) festival) | 1·80 | 1·20 |
| 3274 | | 1p. Ponchos and dancers (National and International Poncho festival) | 1·80 | 1·20 |
| 3275 | | 1p. Horseman, fireworks, guitar and dancers (National and International Dressage and Folklore festival) | 1·80 | 1·20 |
| 3276 | | 1p. Snow Queen and skier (National Snow festival) | 1·80 | 1·20 |

## BULK MAIL STAMPS

**BP999** Post Office Building, Buenos Aires

**1999.** Bulk Mail. Self-adhesive. Imperf.

| | | | | |
|---|---|---|---|---|
| BP2644 | **BP999** | $7 black and blue | 21·00 | 14·00 |
| BP2645 | **BP999** | $11 black and red | 33·00 | 22·00 |
| BP2646 | **BP999** | $16 black and yellow | 50·00 | 35·00 |
| BP2647 | **BP999** | $23 black and green | 70·00 | 47·00 |

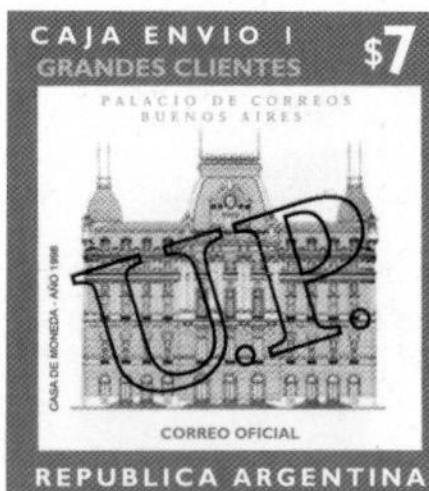


**BP1069**

**2001.** Bulk Mail. Additionally overprinted UP. Imperf.

| | | | | |
|---|---|---|---|---|
| BP2853 | **BP1069** | $7 black and blue | 19·00 | 17·00 |
| BP2854 | **BP1069** | $11 black and red | 29·00 | 26·00 |

## EXPRESS SERVICE MAIL

**E999** Express Service Emblem

**1999.** Self-adhesive.

| | | | | |
|---|---|---|---|---|
| E2644 | **E999** | 8p.75 blue and silver | 30·00 | 20·00 |
| E2645 | - | 17p.50 blue and gold | 65·00 | 43·00 |

DESIGN: 24-hour service emblem.

No. E2644 was for express service mail and No. E2645 for use on 24-hour express service mail.

## OFFICIAL STAMPS

**1884.** Optd OFICIAL.

| | | | | |
|---|---|---|---|---|
| O66 | **33** | ½c. brown | 15·00 | 12·00 |
| O69 | **33** | 1c. red | 60 | 40 |
| O70 | **24** | 2c. green | 60 | 40 |
| O71 | - | 4c. brown (No. 32) | 60 | 40 |
| O72 | **9** | 8c. red | 60 | 55 |
| O73 | **10** | 10c. green | 50·00 | 30·00 |
| O76 | **33** | 12c. blue | 1·00 | 80 |
| O77 | **10** | 16c. green | 2·00 | 1·20 |
| O78 | **22** | 20c. blue | 10·00 | 8·25 |
| O79 | **11** | 24c. blue (roul) | 12·50 | 8·50 |
| O80 | **11** | 24c. blue (perf) | 1·20 | 90 |
| O81 | - | 25c. red (No. 47) | 20·00 | 15·00 |
| O82 | - | 30c. orange (No. 33) | 42·00 | 24·00 |
| O83 | - | 60c. black (No. 34) | 25·00 | 15·00 |
| O84 | - | 90c. blue (No. 35) | 25·00 | 19·00 |

**O73**

**1901**

| | | | | |
|---|---|---|---|---|
| O275 | **O73** | 1c. grey | 20 | 15 |
| O276 | **O73** | 2c. brown | 20 | 15 |
| O277 | **O73** | 5c. red | 20 | 15 |
| O278 | **O73** | 10c. green | 40 | 15 |
| O279 | **O73** | 30c. blue | 2·75 | 80 |
| O280 | **O73** | 50c. orange | 1·80 | 70 |

**1938.** (a) Optd SERVICIO OFICIAL in two lines.

| | | | | |
|---|---|---|---|---|
| O668 | **143** | 1c. brown (No. 645) | 45 | 20 |
| O669 | - | 2c. brown (No. 646) | 45 | 20 |
| O670 | - | 3c. green (No. 647) | 1·20 | 20 |
| O679 | - | 3c. grey (No. 672) | 45 | 20 |
| O771 | - | 3c. grey (No. 672a) | 3·50 | 1·40 |
| O671 | - | 5c. brown (No. 653b) | 45 | 20 |
| O782 | **200** | 5c. red (No. 773) | 10 | 10 |
| O667 | - | 10c. red (No. 653d) | 55 | 20 |
| O773 | - | 10c. purple (No. 678) | 55 | 20 |
| O681 | **146** | 15c. blue (No. 676) | 55 | 20 |
| O683 | **146** | 20c. blue (19½x26 mm) | 1·40 | 45 |
| O774 | - | 15c. grey (No. 708) | 65 | 20 |
| O872 | **247** | 20c. red | 45 | 10 |
| O813 | - | 25c. (No. 673) | 65 | 20 |
| O674 | - | 40c. (No. 658) | 1·80 | 45 |
| O675 | - | 50c. (No. 659) | 45 | 20 |
| O676 | **152** | 1p. (No. 760) | 55 | 45 |
| O827 | **234** | 1p. (No. 826) | 90 | 20 |
| O778 | - | 2p. (No. 661) | 55 | 20 |
| O779 | - | 5p. (No. 662) | 55 | 20 |
| O780 | - | 10p. (No. 763) | 65 | 45 |
| O781 | - | 20p. (No. 764) | 1·80 | 1·40 |

(b) Optd SERVICIO OFICIAL in one line.

| | | | | |
|---|---|---|---|---|
| O897 | | 20c. lilac (No. 895) | 45 | 20 |

**1953.** Eva Peron stamps optd SERVICIO OFICIAL.

| | | | | |
|---|---|---|---|---|
| O854 | **239** | 5c. grey | 45 | 15 |
| O855 | **239** | 10c. red | 45 | 15 |
| O856 | **239** | 20c. red | 45 | 15 |
| O857 | **239** | 25c. green | 45 | 15 |
| O858 | **239** | 40c. purple | 45 | 15 |
| O859 | **239** | 45c. blue | 55 | 45 |
| O860 | **239** | 50c. bistre | 45 | 15 |
| O862 | **240** | 1p. brown (No. 846) | 55 | 20 |
| O863 | **240** | 1p.50 green (No. 847) | 55 | 20 |
| O864 | **240** | 2p. red (No. 848) | 55 | 20 |
| O865 | **240** | 3p. blue (No. 849) | 70 | 45 |
| O866 | **240** | 5p. brown | 1·40 | 65 |
| O867 | **239** | 10p. red | 7·50 | 6·00 |
| O868 | **240** | 20p. green | 65·00 | 35·00 |

**1955.** Stamps of 1954 optd SERVICIO OFICIAL in one line.

| | | | | |
|---|---|---|---|---|
| O869 | **247** | 20c. red | 45 | 10 |
| O870 | **247** | 40c. red | 45 | 10 |
| O880 | - | 1p. brown (No. 871) | 45 | 20 |
| O882 | - | 3p. purple (No. 874) | 55 | 20 |
| O883 | - | 5p. green (No. 875) | 55 | 20 |
| O884 | - | 10p. green and grey (No. 876) | 65 | 20 |
| O886 | **250** | 20p. violet | 1·50 | 70 |

**1955.** Various stamps optd. (a) Optd S. OFICIAL.

| | | | | |
|---|---|---|---|---|
| O896 | - | 5c. brown (No. 894) | 45 | 20 |
| O955 | - | 10c. green (No. 946) | 50 | 20 |
| O956 | - | 20c. purple (No. 947) | 60 | 20 |
| O879 | - | 50c. blue (No. 868) | 45 | 20 |
| O957 | - | 50c. ochre (No. 948) | 50 | 20 |
| O1034 | - | 1p. brn (No. 1016) | 60 | 35 |
| O899 | **264** | 2p. purple | 45 | 20 |
| O1050 | - | 2p. red (No. 1035) | 50 | 10 |
| O959 | - | 3p. blue (No. 951) | 50 | 20 |
| O1051 | - | 4p. red (No. 1036) | 75 | 10 |
| O961 | **296** | 5p. brown | 60 | 20 |
| O1052 | - | 8p. red (No. 1037) | 50 | 10 |
| O962 | - | 10p. brown (No. 1286) | 60 | 20 |
| O1036 | - | 12p. dull purple (No. 1028) | 1·10 | 25 |
| O1053 | - | 10p. red (No. 1038) | 60 | 10 |
| O964 | - | 20p. green (No. 954) | 60 | 20 |
| O1055 | - | 20p. red (No. 1039) | 55 | 25 |
| O1037 | - | 22p. blue (No. 1018) | 1·30 | 45 |
| O1038 | - | 23p. green (No. 1019) | 1·60 | 60 |
| O1039 | - | 25p. lilac (No. 1020) | 1·30 | 60 |
| O1040 | - | 43p. lake (No. 1021) | 3·00 | 1·30 |
| O1041 | - | 45p. brn (No. 1022) | 3·00 | 1·30 |
| O1042 | - | 50p. blue (No. 1023) | 5·00 | 1·50 |
| O1043 | - | 50p. blue (No. 1287) | 6·75 | 1·50 |
| O1045 | - | 100p. blue (No. 1289) | 3·25 | 1·30 |
| O1046 | - | 300p. violet (No. 1026) | 9·75 | 4·75 |

(b) Optd SERVICIO OFICIAL.

| | | | | |
|---|---|---|---|---|
| O900 | **265** | 2p.40 brown | 45 | 20 |
| O958 | - | 3p. blue (No. 951) | 50 | 20 |
| O901 | **266** | 4p.40 green | 45 | 20 |
| O960 | **296** | 5p. brown | 60 | 20 |
| O887 | | 50p. ind & bl (No. 878) | 3·00 | 1·30 |
| O1049 | - | 500p. grn (No. 1032) | 16·00 | 7·75 |

For lists of stamps optd **M.A.**, **M.G.**, **M.H.**, **M.I.**, **M.J.I.**, **M.M.**, **M.O.P.** or **M.R.C.** for use in ministerial offices see the Stanley Gibbons Catalogue Part 20 (South America).

**1963.** Nos. 1068, etc., optd S. OFICIAL.

| | | | | |
|---|---|---|---|---|
| O1076 | **351** | 2p. green | 60 | 10 |
| O1080 | - | 4p. red (No. 1069) | 75 | 15 |
| O1081 | - | 6p. red (No. 1070) | 85 | 45 |
| O1078 | - | 90p. bistre (No. 1288) | 8·00 | 3·75 |

## RECORDED MESSAGE STAMPS

**RM166** Winged Messenger

**1939.** Various symbolic designs inscr "CORREOS FONOPOSTAL".

| | | | | |
|---|---|---|---|---|
| RM688 | **RM166** | 1p.18 blue | 19·00 | 10·50 |
| RM689 | - | 1p.32 blue | 19·00 | 10·50 |
| RM690 | - | 1p.50 brown | 65·00 | 45·00 |

DESIGNS—VERT: 1p.32, Head of Liberty and National Arms. HORIZ: 1p.50, Record and winged letter.

## TELEGRAPH STAMPS USED FOR POSTAGE

**PT34**

**PT35** (Sun closer to "NACIONAL")

**1887**

| | | | | |
|---|---|---|---|---|
| PT104 | **PT34** | 10c. red | 1·10 | 15 |
| PT105 | **PT35** | 10c. red | 1·10 | 15 |
| PT106 | **PT34** | 40c. blue | 1·20 | 15 |
| PT107 | **PT35** | 40c. blue | 1·20 | 15 |

Pt. 10

# ARMENIA

Formerly part of Transcaucasian Russia. Temporarily independent after the Russian revolution of 1917. From 12 March 1922, Armenia, Azerbaijan and Georgia formed the Transcaucasian Federation. Issues for the federation were superseded by those of the Soviet Union in 1924.

With the dissolution of the Soviet Union in 1991 Armenia once again became independent.

NOTE. Only one price is given for Nos. 3/245, which applies to unused or cancelled to order. Postally used copies are worth more.

All the overprints and surcharges were handstamped and consequently were applied upright or inverted indiscriminately, some occurring only inverted.

1919. 100 kopeks = 1 rouble.
1994. 100 luna = 1 dram.

### NATIONAL REPUBLIC

28 May 1918 to 2 December 1920 and 18 February to 2 April 1921.

**1919.** Arms type of Russia and unissued Postal Savings Bank stamp (No. 6) surch. Imperf or perf. (a) Surch thus k. 60 k with or without stops.

| No. | Type | Description | Price |
|---|---|---|---|
| 3 | 22 | 60k. on 1k. orange | 65 |
| 6 | - | 60k. on 1k. red on buff | 12·00 |

(b) Surch in figures only.

| No. | Type | Description | Price |
|---|---|---|---|
| 7 | 22 | 60k. on 1k. orange | 30·00 |
| 8 | 22 | 120k. on 1k. orange | 30·00 |

(6)

**1919.** Stamps of Russia optd as T 6 in various sizes, with or without frame. Imperf or perf. (a) Arms types.

| No. | Type | Description | Price |
|---|---|---|---|
| 53B | 22 | 1k. orange | 12·50 |
| 54B | 22 | 2k. green | 3·00 |
| 55B | 22 | 3k. red | 2·40 |
| 11B | 23 | 4k. red | 80 |
| 12B | 22 | 5k. red | 1·30 |
| 13B | 23 | 10k. blue | 90 |
| 14B | 22 | 10k. on 7k. blue | 1·20 |
| 15B | 10 | 15k. blue and purple | 1·50 |
| 16B | 14 | 20k. red and blue | 1·60 |
| 17B | 10 | 25k. mauve and green | 2·00 |
| 45B | 10 | 35k. green and purple | 2·20 |
| 19B | 14 | 50k. green and purple | 1·00 |
| 30aB | 22 | 60k. on 1k. orange (No. 3) | 2·50 |
| 31B | 10 | 70k. orange and brown | 1·00 |
| 32B | 15 | 1r. orange and brown | 2·20 |
| 33B | 11 | 3r.50 green and brown | 3·50 |
| 23B | 20 | 5r. green and blue | 5·00 |
| 24B | 11 | 7r. pink and green | 9·00 |
| 62B | 11 | 7r. yellow and black | 40·00 |
| 52B | 20 | 10r. grey, red and yellow | 11·00 |

(b) Romanov type.

| No. | Type | Description | Price |
|---|---|---|---|
| 63B | 20 | 4k. red (No. 129) | 2·00 |

(c) Unissued Postal Savings Bank stamp.

| No. | Type | Description | Price |
|---|---|---|---|
| 64A | | 1k. red on buff | 6·50 |

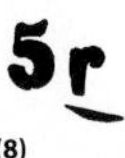
(8)

**1920.** Stamps of Russia surch as T 8 in various types and sizes. Imperf or perf. (a) Arms types.

| No. | Type | Description | Price |
|---|---|---|---|
| 65B | 22 | 1r. on 1k. orange | 3·25 |
| 94B | 22 | 1r. on 60k. on 1k. orange (No. 3) | 4·50 |
| 66B | 22 | 3r. on 3k. red | 2·10 |
| 67B | 22 | 3r. on 4k. red | 7·25 |
| 97B | 22 | 5r. on 2k. green | 2·50 |
| 69B | 23 | 5r. on 4k. red | 1·30 |
| 70B | 22 | 5r. on 5k. red | 1·80 |
| 71B | 22 | 5r. on 7k. blue | 1·20 |
| 72B | 23 | 5r. on 10k. blue | 1·60 |
| 73B | 22 | 5r. on 10 on 7k. blue | 2·10 |
| 74B | 10 | 5r. on 14k. red and blue | 2·30 |
| 75B | 10 | 5r. on 15k. blue and purple | 2·10 |
| 76aB | 10 | 5r. on 20 on 14k. red and blue | 8·50 |
| 76B | 14 | 5r. on 20k. red and blue | 2·10 |
| 77B | 10 | 5r. on 25k. mauve and green | 8·50 |
| 111B | 22 | 5r. on 3r. on 5k. red | 11·00 |
| 78B | 10 | 10r. on 25k. mauve and green | 2·00 |
| 79B | 10 | 10r. on 35k. green and purple | 1·50 |
| 80B | 14 | 10r. on 50k. green and purple | 4·00 |
| 80aB | 9 | 25r. on 1k. orange | 40·00 |
| 80bB | 9 | 25r. on 3k. red | 40·00 |
| 80cB | 9 | 25r. on 5k. purple | 40·00 |
| 80dB | 22 | 25r. on 10 on 7k. blue | 40·00 |
| 80eB | 10 | 25r. on 15k. blue and purple | 40·00 |
| 81B | 14 | 25r. on 20k. red and blue | 4·50 |
| 82B | 10 | 25r. on 25k. mauve and green | 3·75 |
| 83B | 10 | 25r. on 35k. green and purple | 2·75 |
| 84B | 14 | 25r. on 50k. green and purple | 3·50 |
| 85B | 10 | 25r. on 70k. orange and brown | 5·00 |
| 104aB | 9 | 50r. on 1k. orange | 45·00 |
| 104bB | 9 | 50r. on 3k. red | 48·00 |
| 85bB | 10 | 50r. on 4k. red | 45·00 |
| 104cB | 14 | 50r. on 5k. purple | 48·00 |
| 85cB | 10 | 50r. on 15k. blue and purple | 45·00 |
| 85dB | 14 | 50r. on 20k. red and blue | 45·00 |
| 85eB | 10 | 50r. on 35k. green & purple | 45·00 |
| 85fB | 14 | 50r. on 50k. green & purple | 25·00 |
| 105B | 10 | 50r. on 70k. orange and brown | 6·25 |
| 106B | 15 | 50r. on 1r. orange and brown | 6·50 |
| 107B | 15 | 100r. on 1r. orange and brown | 6·00 |
| 108B | 11 | 100r. on 3r.50 green and brown | 18·00 |
| 88B | 20 | 100r. on 5r. green and blue | 15·00 |
| 89B | 11 | 100r. on 7r. yellow and black | 19·00 |
| 90B | 11 | 100r. on 7r. pink and green | 10·00 |
| 93B | 20 | 100r. on 10r. grey, red and yellow | 15·00 |

(b) Romanov issue of 1913.

| No. | Type | Description | Price |
|---|---|---|---|
| 112 | 20 | 1r. on 1k. orange | 10·50 |
| 113 | 20 | 3r. on 3k. red | 13·00 |
| 114 | 20 | 5r. on 4k. red | 5·50 |
| 115 | 20 | 5r. on 10 on 7k. brown | 3·25 |
| 116 | 20 | 5r. on 14k. green | 39·00 |
| 117 | 20 | 5r. on 20 on 14k. green | 5·25 |
| 118 | 20 | 25r. on 4k. red | 6·50 |
| 118a | 20 | 100r. on 1k. orange | 65·00 |
| 119 | 20 | 100r. on 2k. green | 65·00 |
| 120 | 20 | 100r. on 3r. violet | 65·00 |

(c) War Charity issues of 1914 and 1915.

| No. | Type | Description | Price |
|---|---|---|---|
| 121 | 15 | 25r. on 1k. green and red on yellow | 39·00 |
| 122 | 15 | 25r. on 3k. green and red on rose | 39·00 |
| 123 | 15 | 50r. on 7k. green and brown on buff | 48·00 |
| 124 | 15 | 50r. on 10k. brown and blue | 48·00 |
| 125 | 15 | 100r. on 1k. green and red on yellow | 48·00 |
| 126 | 15 | 100r. on 1k. grey and brown | 48·00 |
| 127 | 15 | 100r. on 3k. green and red on rose | 48·00 |
| 128 | 15 | 100r. on 7k. green and brown on buff | 48·00 |
| 129 | 15 | 100r. on 10k. brown and blue | 48·00 |

**1920.** Arms types of Russia optd as T 6 in various sizes with or without frame, and surch as T 8 or with value only in various types and sizes. Imperf or perf.

| No. | Type | Description | Price |
|---|---|---|---|
| 155B | 22 | 1r. on 60k. on 1k. orange (No. 3) | 1·30 |
| 156A | 22 | 3r. on 3k. red | 2·50 |
| 157A | 22 | 5r. on 2k. green | 1·10 |
| 141A | 23 | 5r. on 4k. red | 4·50 |
| 158A | 22 | 5r. on 5k. red | 4·25 |
| 142A | 23 | 5r. on 10k. blue | 4·50 |
| 143A | 22 | 5r. on 10 on 7k. blue | 4·50 |
| 144A | 10 | 5r. on 15k. blue & pur | 2·40 |
| 145A | 14 | 5r. on 20k. red and blue | 2·40 |
| 132B | 10 | 10r. on 15k. blue & pur | 12·00 |
| 145aB | 14 | 10r. on 20k. red & blue | 1·20 |
| 146A | 10 | 10r. on 25k. mauve and green | 2·40 |
| 147B | 10 | 10r. on 35k. green and purple | 1·20 |
| 148A | 14 | 10r. on 50k. green and purple | 3·00 |
| 159A | 10 | 10r. on 70k. orange and brown | 14·00 |
| 163A | 22 | 10r. on 5r. on 5k. red | 30·00 |
| 164A | 10 | 10r. on 5r. on 25k. mauve and green | 32·00 |
| 165A | 10 | 10r. on 5r. on 35k. green and purple | 11·00 |
| 138A | 10 | 25r. on 70k. orange and brown | 8·00 |
| 161B | 15 | 50r. on 1r. orange and brown | 2·75 |
| 135B | 11 | 100r. on 3r.50 green and brown | 3·00 |
| 151A | 20 | 100r. on 5r. green & bl | 8·00 |
| 136A | 11 | 100r. on 7r. pink and green | 9·00 |
| 154aA | 20 | 100r. on 10r. grey, red and yellow | 12·00 |
| 166A | 20 | 100r. on 25r. on 5r. green and blue | 30·00 |

**1920.** Stamps of Russia optd as T 6 in various sizes, with or without frame and surch 10. Perf. (a) Arms types.

| No. | Type | Description | Price |
|---|---|---|---|
| 168 | 14 | 10 on 20k. red and blue | 30·00 |
| 169 | 10 | 10 on 25k. mauve and green | 30·00 |
| 170 | 10 | 10 on 35k. green and purple | 20·00 |
| 171 | 14 | 10 on 50k. green and purple | 24·00 |

(b) Romanov type.

| No. | Type | Description | Price |
|---|---|---|---|
| 172 | | 10 on 4k. red (No. 129) | 48·00 |

**1920.** Stamps of Russia optd with monogram as in T 8 in various types and sizes and surch 10. Imperf or perf. (a) Arms types.

| No. | Type | Description | Price |
|---|---|---|---|
| 173 | 23 | 10 on 4k. red | 48·00 |
| 174 | 22 | 10 on 5k. red | 48·00 |
| 175 | 10 | 10 on 15k. blue & purple | 48·00 |
| 176 | 14 | 10 on 20k. red and blue | 45·00 |
| 176a | 10 | 10 on 20 on 14k. red and blue | 24·00 |
| 177 | 10 | 10 on 25k. mauve & green | 24·00 |
| 178 | 10 | 10 on 35k. green & purple | 24·00 |
| 179 | 14 | 10 on 50k. green & purple | 24·00 |

(b) Romanov type.

| No. | Type | Description | Price |
|---|---|---|---|
| 181 | | 10 on 4k. red (No. 129) | 60·00 |

### SOVIET REPUBLIC

Stamps in Types **11**, **12** and a similar horizontal type showing a woman spinning were printed in Paris to the order of the Armenian National Government, but were not issued in Armenia as the Bolshevists had assumed control. (Price 10p. each).

**11**

**12** Mt. Ararat

(13)

**1921.** Arms types of Russia surch with T 13. Perf.

| No. | Type | Description | Price |
|---|---|---|---|
| 182 | 15 | 5000r. on 1r. orange and brown | 6·50 |
| 183 | 11 | 5000r. on 3r.50 grn & brn | 6·50 |
| 184 | 20 | 5000r. on 5r. green & blue | 6·50 |
| 185 | 11 | 5000r. on 7r. pink and green | 6·50 |
| 186 | 20 | 5000r. on 10r. grey, red & yellow | 6·50 |

### TRANSCAUCASIAN FEDERATION ISSUES FOR ARMENIA

**14** Common Crane

**16** Village Scene

**1922.** Unissued stamps surch in gold kopeks. Imperf.

| No. | Type | Description | Price |
|---|---|---|---|
| 187 | 14 | 1 on 250r. red | 9·75 |
| 188 | 14 | 1 on 250r. slate | 13·00 |
| 189 | 16 | 2 on 500r. red | 5·25 |
| 190 | 16 | 3 on 500r. slate | 5·25 |
| 191 | - | 4 on 1000r. red | 5·25 |
| 192 | - | 4 on 1000r. slate | 9·75 |
| 193 | - | 5 on 2000r. slate | 30·00 |
| 194 | - | 10 on 2000r. red | 30·00 |
| 195 | - | 15 on 5000r. red | 23·00 |
| 196 | - | 20 on 5000r. slate | 5·25 |

DESIGNS (sizes in mm): 1000r. Woman at well (17×26); 2000r. Erivan railway station (35×24½); 5000r. Horseman and Mt. Ararat (39½×24½).

**17** Soviet Emblems

**18** Wall Sculpture at Ani

**19** Mt. Aragatz

**1922.** Unissued stamps as T 17/19 surch in gold kopeks in figures. Imperf or perf.

| No. | Type | Description | Price |
|---|---|---|---|
| 210 | 17 | 1 on 1r. green | 9·75 |
| 198 | 18 | 2 on 2r. slate | 15·00 |
| 212 | - | 3 on 3r. red | 18·00 |
| 213 | - | 4 on 25r. green | 3·75 |
| 201 | - | 5 on 50r. red | 5·00 |
| 215 | - | 10 on 100r. orange | 13·00 |
| 203 | - | 15 on 250r. blue | 2·20 |
| 204a | 19 | 20 on 500r. purple | 3·00 |
| 205 | - | 35 on 20,000r. red | 24·00 |
| 206a | - | 50 on 25,000r. green | 48·00 |
| 209 | - | 50 on 25,000r. blue | 6·50 |

DESIGNS (sizes in mm): 3r. (29×22) and 250r. (21×35) Soviet emblems; 25r. (30×22½); 100r. (34½×23) and 20,000r. (43×27) Mythological sculptures, Ani. 50r. (25½×37). Armenian soldier; 25,000r. (45½×27½) Mt. Ararat.

The above and other values were not officially issued without the surcharges.

**1923.** As T 19, etc., surch in gold kopeks in figures. Imperf or perf.

| No. | Type | Description | Price |
|---|---|---|---|
| 219 | - | 1 on 250r. blue | 6·50 |
| 217 | 19 | 2 on 500r. purple | 6·50 |
| 218 | - | 3 on 20000r. lake | 13·00 |

**26** Mt. Ararat and Soviet Emblems

**28** Ploughing

**1923.** Unissued stamps in various designs as T 26/28 surch in Transcaucasian roubles in figures. Perf.

| No. | Type | Description | Price |
|---|---|---|---|
| 227 | 26 | 10,000r. on 50r. green and red | 1·80 |
| 228 | - | 15,000r. on 300r. blue and buff | 1·80 |
| 229 | - | 25,000r. on 400r. blue and pink | 1·80 |
| 240B | - | 30,000r. on 500r. violet and lilac | 2·00 |
| 231 | - | 50,000r. on 1000r. blue | 1·80 |
| 232 | - | 75,000r. on 3000r. black and green | 2·00 |
| 233 | - | 100,000r. on 2000r. black and grey | 2·40 |
| 243 | - | 200,000r. on 4000r. black and brn | 1·20 |
| 235 | - | 300,000r. on 5000r. black and red | 3·25 |
| 245 | 28 | 500,000r. on 10,000r. black and red | 1·50 |

DESIGNS (sizes in mm): 300r. (26×35) Star over Mt. Ararat; 400r. (26×34½) Soviet emblems; 500r. (26×34½) Crane (bird); 1000r. (19×25) Peasant in punt; 2000r. (26×31) Human-headed bird from old bas-relief; 3000r. (26½×36) Sower; 4000r. (26×31½) Star and dragon; 5000r. (26×32) Blacksmith.

### INDEPENDENT REPUBLIC

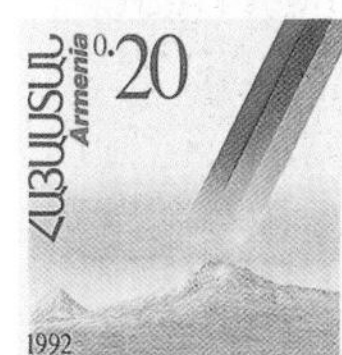
**31** Mount Ararat and National Colours

**1992.** Independence Day.

| No. | Type | Description | Unused | Used |
|---|---|---|---|---|
| 246 | 31 | 20k. multicoloured | 15 | 15 |
| 247 | 31 | 2r. multicoloured | 70 | 70 |
| 248 | 31 | 5r. multicoloured | 1·70 | 1·70 |
| **MS**249 | | 80×80 mm. 7r. multicoloured (Mt. Ararat and eagle) | 43·00 | 43·00 |

**32** Dish Aerial and World Map

**1992.** Inauguration of International Direct-dial Telephone System.

| | | | | |
|---|---|---|---|---|
| 250 | **32** | 50k. multicoloured | 3·00 | 3·00 |

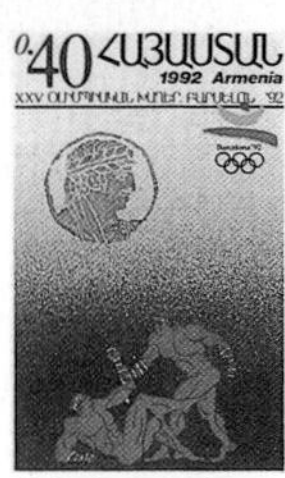

**33** Ancient Greek Wrestling

**1992.** Olympic Games, Barcelona. Multicoloured.

| | | | |
|---|---|---|---|
| 251 | 40k. Type **33** | 10 | 35 |
| 252 | 3r.60 Boxing | 40 | 40 |
| 253 | 5r. Weightlifting | 60 | 60 |
| 254 | 12r. Gymnastics (ring exercises) | 1·40 | 1·40 |

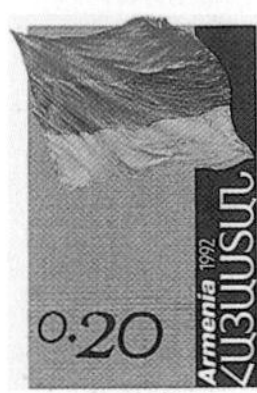

**34** National Flag

**1992**

| | | | | |
|---|---|---|---|---|
| 255 | **34** | 20k. multicoloured (postage) | 10 | 10 |
| 256 | - | 1r. black | 15 | 15 |
| 257 | - | 3r. brown | 45 | 45 |
| 258 | - | 3r. brown | 30 | 30 |
| 259 | - | 5r. black | 60 | 60 |
| 260 | - | 20r. grey | 65 | 65 |
| 261 | - | 2r. blue (air) | 30 | 30 |

DESIGNS: 1r. Goddess Waroubini statuette from Orgov radio-optical telescope; 2r. Zvartnots Airport, Yerevan; 3r. (No. 257) Goddess Anahit; 3r. (No. 258) Runic inscription Karmir-Blour; 5r. U.P.U. Monument, Berne, Switzerland; 20r. Silver cup from Karashamb.

See also Nos. 275/82.

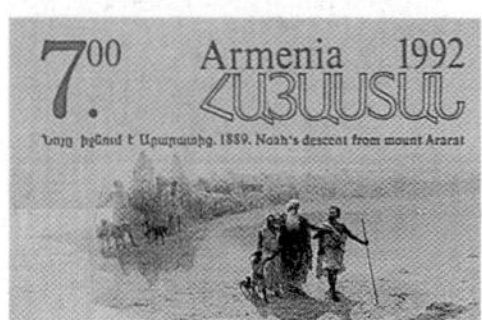

**35** "Noah's Descent from Mt. Ararat"

**1993.** 175th Birth Anniv of Hovhannes Aivazovsky (painter). Sheet 95×63 mm.

| | | | |
|---|---|---|---|
| **MS**262 | **35** 7r. multicoloured | 2·10 | 2·10 |

**36** Engraved 10th- century Tombstone, Makenis

**1993.** Armenian Cultural History. Multicoloured.

| | | | |
|---|---|---|---|
| 263 | 40k. Type **36** | 10 | 10 |
| 264 | 80k. Illuminated page from Gospel of 1295 | 20 | 20 |
| 265 | 3r.60 13th-century bas-relief, Gandzasar | 75 | 75 |
| 266 | 5r. "Glorious Mother of God" (18th-century painting, H. Hovnatanian) | 1·30 | 1·30 |
| **MS**267 | 93x73mm. 12r. "David of Sassoun", 1922 (painting, H. Kojoian) | 6·25 | 5·75 |

**37** Garni Canyon

**1993.** Landscapes. Multicoloured.

| | | | |
|---|---|---|---|
| 268 | 40k. Type **37** | 10 | 10 |
| 269 | 80k. Shaki Falls, Zangezur | 10 | 10 |
| 270 | 3r.60 River Arpa gorge, Vike | 35 | 35 |
| 271 | 5r. Lake Sevan (horiz) | 50 | 50 |
| 272 | 12r. Mount Ararat (horiz) | 1·20 | 1·20 |

**38** Temple of Garni

**1993.** "YEREVAN '93" International Stamp Exn.

| | | | | |
|---|---|---|---|---|
| 273 | **38** | 10r. red, black and brown | 10 | 10 |
| **MS**274 | | 133×111 mm. No. 273×6 plus two labels | 4·50 | 4·25 |

**1994.** As T 34 but new currency.

| | | | |
|---|---|---|---|
| 275 | 10l. agate and brown | 10 | 10 |
| 277 | 50l. deep brown and brown | 60 | 60 |
| 280 | 10d. brown and grey | 60 | 60 |
| 282 | 25d. gold and red | 1·50 | 1·50 |

DESIGNS: 10l. Shivini, Sun God (Karmir-Blour); 50l. Tayshaba, God of the Elements (Karmir-Blour); 10d. Khaldi, Supreme God (Karmir-Blour); 25d. National arms.

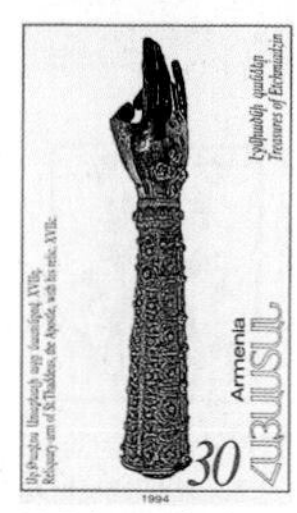

**39** Reliquary for Arm of St. Thaddeus (17th century)

**1994.** Treasures of Etchmiadzin (seat of Armenian church). Multicoloured.

| | | | |
|---|---|---|---|
| 286 | 3d. Descent from the Cross (9th-century wooden panel) | 10 | 10 |
| 287 | 5d. Gilded silver reliquary of Holy Cross of Khotakerats (1300) | 10 | 10 |
| 288 | 12d. Cross with St. Karapet's right hand (14th century) | 1·00 | 1·00 |
| 289 | 30d. Type **39** | 50 | 50 |
| 290 | 50d. Gilded silver chrism vessel (1815) | 1·40 | 1·40 |

**40** (40) **40** (41)

**1994.** Stamp Exhibitions, Yerevan. (a) "Armenia '94" National Exn. No. 273 surch with T 40.

| | | | |
|---|---|---|---|
| 291 | 40d. on 10r. red, blk & brn | 3·75 | 3·75 |

(b) "Armenia–Argentina" Exhibition. No. 273 surch with T 41.

| | | | |
|---|---|---|---|
| 292 | 40d. on 10r. red, blk & brn | 3·75 | 3·75 |

**42** Cancelled Stamps of 1919

**1994.** 75th Anniv of First Stamp Issue.

| | | | | |
|---|---|---|---|---|
| 293 | **42** | 16d. multicoloured | 30 | 30 |

**43** Stadium and Arms of National Committee

**1994.** Olympic Committees. Multicoloured.

| | | | |
|---|---|---|---|
| 294 | 30d. Type **43** | 45 | 45 |
| 295 | 40d. Olympic rings (centenary of Int Olympic Committee) | 65 | 65 |

**44** Haroutune Shmavonian

**1994.** Bicentenary of "Azdarar" (first Armenian periodical).

| | | | | |
|---|---|---|---|---|
| 296 | **44** | 30d. brown and green | 40 | 40 |

**45** Ervand Otian

**1994.** 125th Birth Anniversaries.

| | | | | |
|---|---|---|---|---|
| 297 | **45** | 50d. drab and brown | 30 | 30 |
| 298 | - | 50d. brown | 30 | 30 |

DESIGN—HORIZ: 50d. Levon Shant.

**46** "Cross" (from Gospel)

**1995.** 1700th Anniv (2001) of Christianity in Armenia (1st issue). Works of art. Multicoloured.

| | | | |
|---|---|---|---|
| 299 | 60d. Type **46** | 55 | 55 |
| 300 | 70d. "St. Bartholomew and St. Thaddeus the Apostles" (Hovnatan Hovnatanian) (45×39 mm) | 55 | 55 |
| 301 | 70d. "Kings Abhar and Trdat" (Mkrtoum Hovnatanian) (45×39 mm) | 55 | 55 |
| 302 | 80d. "St. Gregory the Illuminator" | 70 | 70 |
| 303 | 90d. "The Baptism of Armenian People" (H. Aivazovsky) | 85 | 85 |
| **MS**304 | 97×71 mm. 400d. black and ochre ("Echmiadzin Monastery" (detail of engraving by Jacob Peeters)) | 2·75 | 2·75 |

See also Nos. **MS**331, 362/**MS**367, 382/**MS**387 and **MS**401.

**47** Vazgen I

**1995.** 1st Death Anniv of Vazgen I (Patriarch of Armenian Orthodox Church).

| | | | | |
|---|---|---|---|---|
| 305 | **47** | 150d. black and grey | 70 | 70 |

**48** Black-polished Pottery

**1995.** Museum Artefacts (1st series). Multicoloured.

| | | | |
|---|---|---|---|
| 306 | 30d. Type **48** | 25 | 25 |
| 307 | 60d. Silver horn | 50 | 50 |
| 308 | 130d. Gohar carpet | 1·20 | 1·20 |

See also Nos. 332/4.

**49** Red Kite and Oak

**1995.** Birds and Trees. Multicoloured.

| | | | |
|---|---|---|---|
| 309 | 40d. Type **49** | 40 | 55 |
| 310 | 60d. Golden eagle and juniper | 50 | 60 |

**50** Workers building "Honeycomb" Map

**1995.** Hyastan All-Armenian Fund.

| | | | | |
|---|---|---|---|---|
| 311 | **50** | 90d. multicoloured | 65 | 65 |

**51** Rainbows around U.N. Emblem

**1995.** 50th Anniv of U.N.O.

| | | | | |
|---|---|---|---|---|
| 312 | **51** | 90d. multicoloured | 65 | 65 |

**52** Commander P. Kitsook (408th Rifle Division)

**1995.** 50th Anniv of End of Second World War. (a) Size 40×23 mm. Each black, orange and blue.

| | | | |
|---|---|---|---|
| 313 | 60d. Type **52** | 40 | 40 |
| 314 | 60d. Commanders S. Chernikov, N. Tavartkeladze and V. Penkovsky (76th Mountain Rifle Red-banner (51st Guard) Division) | 40 | 40 |
| 315 | 60d. Commanders S. Zakian, H. Babayan and I. Lyudnikov (390th Rifle Division) | 40 | 40 |
| 316 | 60d. Commanders A. Vasilian, M. Dobrovolsky, Y. Grechany and G. Sorokin (409th Rifle Division) | 40 | 40 |
| 317 | 60d. Commanders A. Sargissian and N. Safarian (89th Taman Triple Order Bearer Rifle Division) | 40 | 40 |

(b) Size 23×35 mm. Each blue, orange and brown.

| | | | |
|---|---|---|---|
| 318 | 60d. Marshal Hovhannes Baghramian | 60 | 60 |
| 319 | 60d. Admiral Hovhannes Issakov | 60 | 60 |

| | | | | |
|---|---|---|---|---|
| 320 | | 60d. General Marshal Hamazasp Babajanian | 60 | 60 |
| 321 | | 60d. Marshal Sergey Khoudyakov | 60 | 60 |
| **MS**322 | | 120×90 mm. 300d. "Return of the Hero" (Mariam Aslamazian) | 2·50 | 2·50 |

**53** Ghevond Alishan (historian and geographer)

**1995.** Writers' Anniversaries.

| | | | | |
|---|---|---|---|---|
| 323 | **53** | 90d. green and black | 55 | 55 |
| 324 | - | 90d. sepia, brown & yellow | 55 | 55 |
| 325 | - | 90d. blue and red | 60 | 60 |

DESIGNS: No. 323, Type **53** (175th birth); 324, Grigor Artsruni (journalist, 150th birth); 325, Franz Werfel (50th death).

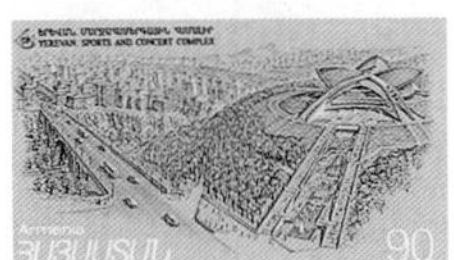

**54** Sports and Concert Complex

**1995.** Yerevan.

| | | | | |
|---|---|---|---|---|
| 326 | | 60d. black and orange | 30 | 30 |
| 327 | | 80d. black and pink | 40 | 40 |
| 328 | **54** | 90d. black and buff | 45 | 45 |
| 329 | - | 100d. black and buff | 60 | 60 |
| 330 | - | 120d. black and pink | 80 | 80 |
| **MS**331 | | 90×65 mm. 400d. multicoloured | 2·40 | 2·40 |

DESIGNS—As T **54**: 60d. Brandy distillery and wine cellars; 80d. Abovian Street; 400d. Panoramic view of Yerevan. 60×23 mm: 100d. Baghramian Avenue; 120d. Republic Square.

No. **MS**331 also commemorates the 1700th anniv (2001) of Christianity in Armenia.

**1995.** Museum Artefacts (2nd series). As T 48. Mult.

| | | | |
|---|---|---|---|
| 332 | 40d. Four-wheeled carriages (horiz) | 25 | 25 |
| 333 | 60d. Bronze model of solar system | 45 | 45 |
| 334 | 90d. Tombstone from Loriberd | 65 | 65 |

**55** Katsian and Spectators watching Flight

**1995.** Air. 86th Anniv of Artiom Katsian's 1909 World Record for Range and Altitude.

| | | | | |
|---|---|---|---|---|
| 335 | **55** | 90d. ochre, brown and blue | 60 | 60 |

[illegible]փnus 40

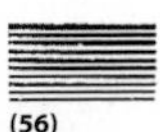

**(56)**

**1996.** No. 275 surch as T 56.

| | | | |
|---|---|---|---|
| 336 | 40d. on 10l. agate and brown | 95 | 95 |
| 337 | 100d. on 10l. agate and brown | 2·30 | 2·30 |
| 338 | 150d. on 10l. agate and brown | 3·50 | 3·50 |
| 339 | 200d. on 10l. agate and brown | 5·00 | 5·00 |

**57** Griboedov

**1996.** Birth Bicentenary of Aleksandr Griboedov (historian).

| | | | | |
|---|---|---|---|---|
| 340 | **57** | 90d. stone, brown and red | 65 | 65 |

**58** Hayrik Khrimian (patriarch of Armenian Orthodox Church, 175th birth anniv (1995))

**1996.** Anniversaries.

| | | | | |
|---|---|---|---|---|
| 341 | **58** | 90d. blue & brn (postage) | 55 | 55 |
| 342 | - | 90d. multicoloured | 55 | 55 |
| 343 | - | 90d. grey, blue & red (air) | 55 | 55 |

DESIGNS—HORIZ: No. 342, Lazar Serebryakov (Admiral of the Fleet, and 19th-century Russian warships, birth bicentenary (1995)). VERT: No. 343, Nelson Stepanian (Second World War pilot, 50th death anniv (1994)).

**59** Opening Frame from First Armenian Film

**1996.** Centenary of Motion Pictures.

| | | | | |
|---|---|---|---|---|
| 344 | **59** | 60d. black, grey and blue | 40 | 40 |

**60** Angel and Red Cross

**1996.** 75th Anniv of Armenian Red Cross Society.

| | | | | |
|---|---|---|---|---|
| 345 | **60** | 60d. multicoloured | 40 | 40 |

**61** Wild Goats

**1996.** Mammals. Multicoloured.

| | | | |
|---|---|---|---|
| 346 | 40d. Type **61** | 60 | 20 |
| 347 | 60d. Leopards | 55 | 65 |

**62** Nansen and "Fram"

**1996.** Centenary of Return of Fridtjof Nansen's Arctic Expedition.

| | | | | |
|---|---|---|---|---|
| 348 | **62** | 90d. multicoloured | 70 | 70 |

**63** Cycling

**1996.** Olympic Games, Atlanta. Multicoloured.

| | | | |
|---|---|---|---|
| 349 | 40d. Type **63** | 25 | 25 |
| 350 | 60d. Triple jumping | 40 | 40 |
| 351 | 90d. Wrestling | 70 | 70 |

Nos. 349/51 were issued together, se-tenant, the backgrounds forming a composite design showing ancient Greek athletes.

**64** Torch Bearer

**1996.** Centenary of Modern Olympic Games.

| | | | | |
|---|---|---|---|---|
| 352 | **64** | 60d. multicoloured | 35 | 35 |

**65** Genrikh Kasparian (first prize winner, "Chess in USSR" competition, 1939)

**1996.** 32nd Chess Olympiad, Yerevan. Designs showing positions from previous games. Mult.

| | | | |
|---|---|---|---|
| 353 | 40d. Type **65** | 35 | 35 |
| 354 | 40d. Tigran Petrosian v. Mikhail Botvinnik (World Championship, Moscow, 1963) | 35 | 35 |
| 355 | 40d. Gary Kasparov v. Anatoly Karpov (World Championship, Leningrad, 1986) | 35 | 35 |
| 356 | 40d. Olympiad emblem | 35 | 35 |

**66** Tigran Petrosian (World chess champion, 1963–69) and Tigran Petrosian Chess House, Yerevan

**1996**

| | | | | |
|---|---|---|---|---|
| 357 | **66** | 90d. multicoloured | 65 | 65 |

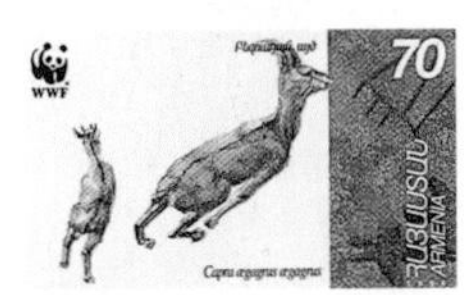

**67** Goats

**1996.** The Wild Goat. Multicoloured.

| | | | |
|---|---|---|---|
| 358 | 70d. Type **67** | 35 | 35 |
| 359 | 100d. Lone female | 45 | 45 |
| 360 | 130d. Lone male | 60 | 60 |
| 361 | 350d. Heads of male and female | 1·70 | 1·70 |

**68** Church of the Holy Mother, Samarkand, Uzbekistan

**1997.** 1700th Anniv (2001) of Christianity in Armenia (2nd issue). Armenian Apostolic Overseas Churches. Multicoloured.

| | | | |
|---|---|---|---|
| 362 | 100d. Type **68** | 50 | 50 |
| 363 | 100d. Church of the Holy Mother, Kishinev, Moldova | 50 | 50 |
| 364 | 100d. St. Hripsime's Church, Yalta, Ukraine | 50 | 50 |
| 365 | 100d. St. Catherine's Church, St. Petersburg, Russia | 50 | 50 |
| 366 | 100d. Church, Lvov, Ukraine | 50 | 50 |
| **MS**367 | 92×66 mm. 500d. St. George of Echmiadzin's Church, Tbilisi, Georgia | 2·50 | 2·50 |

**69** Man operating Printing Press

**1997.** 225th Anniv of First Printing Press in Armenia.

| | | | | |
|---|---|---|---|---|
| 368 | **69** | 70d. multicoloured | 85 | 85 |

**70** Jivani and Mount Ararat

**1997.** 150th Birth Anniv of Jivani (folk singer).

| | | | | |
|---|---|---|---|---|
| 369 | **70** | 90d. multicoloured | 45 | 45 |

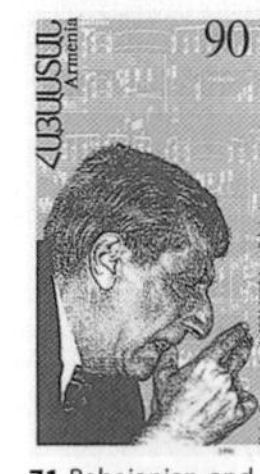

**71** Babajanian and Score of "Heroic Ballad"

**1997.** 75th Birth Anniv (1996) of Arno Babajanian (composer and pianist).

| | | | | |
|---|---|---|---|---|
| 370 | **71** | 90d. black, lilac & purple | 45 | 45 |

**72** Countryside (Gevorg Bashinjaghian)

**1997.** Exhibits in National Gallery of Armenia (1st series). Multicoloured.

| | | | |
|---|---|---|---|
| 371 | 150d. Type **72** | 75 | 75 |
| 372 | 150d. "One of My Dreams" (Eghishe Tadevossian) | 75 | 75 |
| 373 | 150d. "Portrait of Natalia Tehumian" (Hakob Hovnatanian) (vert) | 75 | 75 |
| 374 | 150d. "Salome" (Vardges Sureniants) (vert) | 75 | 75 |

See also Nos. 390/2 and 512/13.

**73** Mamulian

**1997.** Birth Centenary of Rouben Mamulian (film director).

| | | | | |
|---|---|---|---|---|
| 375 | **73** | 150d. multicoloured | 80 | 80 |

**74** St. Basil's Cathedral, Moscow

**1997.** "Moscow 97" Int Stamp Exhibition.

| | | | | |
|---|---|---|---|---|
| 376 | **74** | 170d. multicoloured | 85 | 85 |

**75** Hayk and Bel

**1997.** Europa. Tales and Legends. Multicoloured.

| | | | |
|---|---|---|---|
| 377 | 170d. Type **75** | 2·00 | 2·00 |

378 250d. The Song of Vahagn 2·50 2·50

**76** Charents

**1997.** Birth Centenary of Eghishe Charents (poet).
379 **76** 150d. brown and red 75 75

**77** "Iris lycotis"

**1997.** Irises. Multicoloured.
380 40d. Type **77** 15 15
381 170d. "Iris elegantissima" 75 75

**78** St. Gregory the Illuminator Cathedral, Anthelias, Libya

**1997.** 1700th Anniv (2001) of Christianity in Armenia (3rd issue). Armenian Overseas Educational Centres. Multicoloured.
382 100d. Type **78** 50 50
383 100d. St. Khach Armenian Church, Nakhijevan, Rostov-on-Don 50 50
384 100d. St. James's Monastery, Jerusalem (horiz) 50 50
385 100d. Nercissian School, Tblisi, Georgia (60×21 mm) 50 50
386 100d. San Lazzaro Mekhitarian Congregation, Venice (horiz) 50 50
**MS**387 90×45 mm. 500d. Lazarian Seminary, Moscow (horiz) 2·40 2·40

**79** Baby Jesus, Angel and Mary

**1997.** Christmas.
388 **79** 40d. multicoloured 30 30

**80** Eagle and Demonstrator with Flag

**1998.** 10th Anniv of Karabakh Movement.
389 **80** 250d. multicoloured 1·60 1·60

**1998.** Exhibits in National Gallery of Armenia (2nd series). As T 72. Multicoloured.
390 150d. "Family. Generations" (Yervand Kochar) (vert) 75 75
391 150d. "Tartar Women's Dance" (Alexander Bazhbeouk-Melikian) 75 75
392 150d. "Spring in Our Yard" (Haroutiun Kalents) (vert) 75 75

**81** Diana, Princess of Wales

**1998.** Diana, Princess of Wales Commemoration.
393 **81** 250d. multicoloured 90 90

**82** Eiffel Tower, Ball and Pitch

**1998.** World Cup Football Championship, France.
394 **82** 250d. multicoloured 1·20 1·20

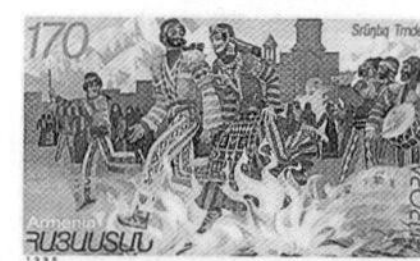
**83** Couple leaping through Flames (Trndez)

**1998.** Europa. National Festivals. Multicoloured.
395 170d. Type **83** 1·30 1·30
396 250d. Girls in traditional costume (Ascension) 2·20 2·20

**84** Southern Swallowtail

**1998.** Insects. Multicoloured.
397 170d. Type **84** 85 85
398 250d. "Rethera komarovi" (moth) 1·20 1·20

**85** Ayrarat Couple

**1998.** Traditional Costumes (1st series). Mult.
399 170d. Type **85** 85 85
400 250d. Vaspurakan family 1·20 1·20
See also Nos. 408/9, 492/3, 591/2 and 620/1.

**86** St. Forty Children's Church, Milan

**1998.** 1700th Anniv (2001) of Christianity in Armenia (4th issue). Sheet 143×71 mm. Multicoloured.
**MS**401 100d. Type **86**; 100d. St. Sargis's Church, London; 100d. St. Vardan's Cathedral, New York; 100d. St. Hovhannes's Cathedral, Paris; 100d. St. Gregory the Illuminator's Cathedral, Buenos Aires 2·50 2·50

**87** Fissure in Earth's Surface

**1998.** 10th Anniv of Armenian Earthquake.
402 **87** 250d. black, red and lilac 1·20 1·20

**88** Pyrite

**1998.** Minerals. Multicoloured.
403 170d. Type **88** 90 90
404 250d. Agate 1·30 1·30

**89** Briusov

**1998.** 125th Birth Anniv of Valery Briusov (Russian translator of Armenian works).
405 **89** 90d. multicoloured 45 45

**90** Parajanov

**1999.** 75th Birth Anniv of Sergei Parajanov (film director and artist). Sheet 74 ×65 mm.
**MS**406 **90** 500d. multicoloured 2·75 2·75
**MS**407 As No. **MS**406 but with emblem in margin of "iBRA" International Stamp Exhibition, Nuremberg, Germany 3·00 3·00

**1999.** Traditional Costumes (2nd series). As T 85.
408 170d. Mother and child from Karin 90 90
409 250d. Zangezour couple 1·30 1·30

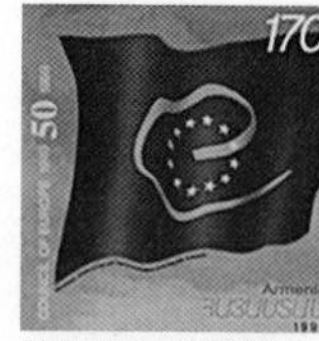
**91** Khosrov Reserve

**1999.** Europa. Parks and Gardens. Multicoloured.
410 170d. Type **91** 85 85
411 250d. Dilijan Reserve 1·00 1·00

**92** Anniversary Emblem on Flag

**1999.** 50th Anniv of Council of Europe.
412 **92** 170d. multicoloured 1·80 1·80

**93** Medieval Kogge and Map

**1999.** Ships of the Armenian Kingdom of Cilicia (11–14th centuries). Multicoloured.
413 170d. Type **93** 85 85
414 250d. Medieval single-masted sailing ships 1·30 1·30
415 250d. As No. 414 but with emblem of "Philexfrance 99" International Stamp Exhibition, Paris, France, in lower right corner 1·30 1·30

**94** Armenian Gampr

**1999.** Domestic Pets. Multicoloured.
416 170d. Type **94** 85 85
417 250d. Turkish van cat 1·30 1·30
418 250d. As No. 417 but with emblem of "China 1999" International Stamp Exhibition, Peking, China, in lower right corner 1·40 1·40

**95** Obverse and Reverse of Medal

**1999.** 1st Pan-Armenian Games, Yerevan. Sheet 58×40 mm.
**MS**419 **95** 250d. multicoloured 2·20 2·20

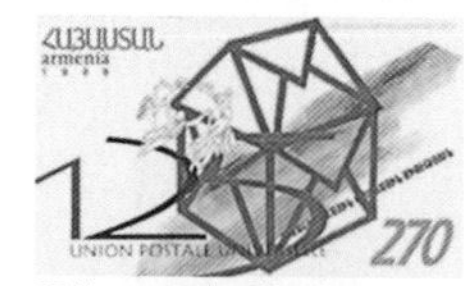
**96** St. Gregory the Illuminator's Church, Cairo

**1999.** 1700th Anniv (2001) of Christianity in Armenia (5th issue). Sheet 121×65 mm containing T 96 and similar horiz designs. Multicoloured.
**MS**420 70d. Type **96**; 70d. St. Gregory the Illuminator's Church, Singapore; 70d. St. Khach's Church, Suchava; 70d. St. Saviour's Church, Worcester; 70d. Church of the Holy Mother, Madras 1·90 1·90

**97** House made of Envelopes

**1999.** 125th Anniv of Universal Postal Union.
421 **97** 270d. multicoloured 1·60 1·60

**98** Karen Demirchyan (Speaker of the National Assembly)

**2000.** Commemoration of Victims of Attack on National Assembly. Multicoloured.
422 250d. Type **98** 1·40 1·40
423 250d. Vazgen Sargsyan (Prime Minister) 1·40 1·40
**MS**424 60×40 mm. 540d. Demirchyan Sargsyan, Yuri Bakshyan, Ruben Mirochyan, Henrik Abrahamyan, Armenak Armenakyan, Leonard Petrossyan and Mikael Kotanyan 3·00 3·00

**99** Sevan Trout

**2000.** Fishes. Multicoloured.
425 50d. Type **99** 35 35
426 270d. Sevan barbel 1·50 1·50

**100** The Liar Hunter

**2000.** National Fairy Tales. Multicoloured.
427 70d. Type **100** 40 40
428 130d. The King and the Peddler 70 70

**101** "Building Europe"

**2000.** Europa.

| | | | | |
|---|---|---|---|---|
| 429 | **101** | 40d. multicoloured | 35 | 35 |
| 430 | **101** | 500d. multicoloured | 4·25 | 4·25 |

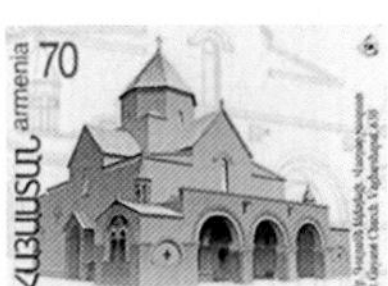

**102** St. Gayane Church, Vagharshapat

**2000.** 1700th Anniv (2001) of Christianity in Armenia (6th issue). Sheet 121×65 mm containing T 102 and similar horiz designs. Multicoloured.

**MS**431 70d. Type **102**; 70d. Etchmiadzin Cathedral, Vagharshapat; 70d. Church of the Holy Mother, Khor Virap; 70d. St. Shoghakat Church, Vagharshapat; 70d. St. Hrip'sime Church, Vagharshapat 2·75 2·75

**103** Basketball

**2000.** Olympic Games, Sydney. Multicoloured.

| | | | | |
|---|---|---|---|---|
| 432 | | 10d. Type **103** | 10 | 10 |
| 433 | | 30d. Tennis | 25 | 25 |
| 434 | | 500d. Weightlifting | 4·25 | 4·25 |

**104** Quartz

**2000.** Minerals. Multicoloured.

| | | | | |
|---|---|---|---|---|
| 435 | | 170d. Type **104** | 1·30 | 1·30 |
| 436 | | 250d. Molybdenite | 1·90 | 1·90 |

**105** Shnorhali

**2000.** 900th Birth Anniv of Nerses Shnorhali (writer and musician).

| | | | | |
|---|---|---|---|---|
| 437 | **105** | 270d. multicoloured | 1·60 | 1·60 |

**106** Adoration of the Magi

**2000.** Christmas.

| | | | | |
|---|---|---|---|---|
| 438 | **106** | 170d. multicoloured | 1·00 | 1·00 |

**107** Issahakian

**2000.** 125th Birth Anniv of Avetik Issahakian (poet).

| | | | | |
|---|---|---|---|---|
| 439 | **107** | 130d. multicoloured | 60 | 60 |

**108** Dhol

**2000.** Musical Instruments. Multicoloured.

| | | | | |
|---|---|---|---|---|
| 440 | | 170d. Type **108** | 95 | 95 |
| 441 | | 250d. Duduk (wind instrument) | 1·30 | 1·30 |

**109** Viktor Hambartsoumian (astrophysicist)

**2000.** New Millennium. Famous Armenians. Mult.

| | | | | |
|---|---|---|---|---|
| 442 | | 110d. Type **109** | 65 | 65 |
| 443 | | 110d. Abraham Alikhanov (physicist) | 65 | 65 |
| 444 | | 110d. Andranik Iossifan (electrical engineer) | 65 | 65 |
| 445 | | 110d. Sargis Saltikov (metallurgist) | 65 | 65 |
| 446 | | 110d. Samval Kochariants (electrical engineer) | 65 | 65 |
| 447 | | 110d. Artem Mikoyan (aircraft designer) | 65 | 65 |
| 448 | | 110d. Norayr Sisisakian (biochemist) | 65 | 65 |
| 449 | | 110d. Ivan Knunyants (chemist) | 65 | 65 |
| 450 | | 110d. Nikoghayos Yenikolopian (physical chemist) | 65 | 65 |
| 451 | | 110d. Nikoghayos Adonts (historian) | 65 | 65 |
| 452 | | 110d. Manouk Abeghian (folklore scholar) | 65 | 65 |
| 453 | | 110d. Hovhannes Toumanian (poet) | 65 | 65 |
| 454 | | 110d. Hrachya Ajarian (linguist) | 65 | 65 |
| 455 | | 110d. Gevorg Emin (poet) | 65 | 65 |
| 456 | | 110d. Yervand Lalayan (anthropologist) | 65 | 65 |
| 457 | | 110d. Daniel Varoujan (poet) | 65 | 65 |
| 458 | | 110d. Paruyr Sevak (poet) | 65 | 65 |
| 459 | | 110d. William Saroyan (dramatist and novelist) | 65 | 65 |
| 460 | | 110d. Hamo Beknazarian (film director) | 65 | 65 |
| 461 | | 110d. Alexandre Tamanian (architect) | 65 | 65 |
| 462 | | 110d. Vahram Papazian (actor) | 65 | 65 |
| 463 | | 110d. Vasil Tahirov (viticulturist) | 65 | 65 |
| 464 | | 110d. Leonid Yengibarian (mime artist) | 65 | 65 |
| 465 | | 110d. Haykanoush Danielian (singer) | 65 | 65 |
| 466 | | 110d. Sergo Hambartsoumian (weight lifter) | 65 | 65 |
| 467 | | 110d. Hrant Shahinian (gymnast) | 65 | 65 |
| 468 | | 110d. Toros Toramanian (architect) | 65 | 65 |
| 469 | | 110d. Komitas (composer) | 65 | 65 |
| 470 | | 110d. Aram Khachatourian (composer) | 65 | 65 |
| 471 | | 110d. Martiros Sarian (artist) | 65 | 65 |
| 472 | | 110d. Avet Terterian (composer) | 65 | 65 |
| 473 | | 110d. Alexandre Spendiarian (composer) | 65 | 65 |
| 474 | | 110d. Arshile Gorky (artist) | 65 | 65 |
| 475 | | 110d. Minas Avetissian (artist) | 65 | 65 |
| 476 | | 110d. (Levon Orbeli physiologist) | 65 | 65 |
| 477 | | 110d. Hripsimeh Simonian (ceramics artist) | 65 | 65 |

**110** Soldiers

**2001.** 1550th Anniv of Battle of Avarayr. Sheet 90×65 mm containing T 110 and similar vert design. Multicoloured.

**MS**478 170d. Type **110**; 270d. Vardan Mamikonian 3·00 3·00

**111** Narekatsi and Text

**2001.** Millenary of A Record of Lamentations by Grigor Narekatsi.

| | | | | |
|---|---|---|---|---|
| 479 | **111** | 25d. multicoloured | 55 | 55 |

**112** Lake Sevan

**2001.** Europa. Water Resources. Multicoloured.

| | | | | |
|---|---|---|---|---|
| 480 | | 50d. Type **112** | 25 | 25 |
| 481 | | 500d. Spandarian Reservoir | 2·75 | 2·75 |

**113** Emblem

**2001.** Armenian Membership of Council of Europe.

| | | | | |
|---|---|---|---|---|
| 482 | **113** | 240d. multicoloured | 1·10 | 1·10 |

**114** Trophy

**2001.** 2nd Pan-Armenian Games. Sheet 58×40 mm.

**MS**483 **114** 300d. multicoloured 2·20 2·20

**115** Persian Squirrel

**2001.** Endangered Species. Persian Squirrel (*Sciurus persicus*). Multicoloured.

| | | | | |
|---|---|---|---|---|
| 484 | **113** | 40d. Type **115** | 40 | 40 |
| 485 | **113** | 50d. Adult sitting on branch with young in tree hole | 50 | 50 |
| 486 | **113** | 80d. Head of squirrel | 85 | 85 |
| 487 | **113** | 120d. On ground | 1·30 | 1·30 |

**116** Cathedral Facade

**2001.** 1700th Anniv of Christianity in Armenia (7th issue). St. Gregory the Illuminator Cathedral, Yerevan. Multicoloured.

| | | | | |
|---|---|---|---|---|
| 488 | | 50d. Type **116** | 35 | 35 |
| 489 | | 205d. Interior elevation of Cathedral (44×30 mm) | 1·40 | 1·40 |
| 490 | | 240d. Exterior elevation of Cathedral (44×30 mm) | 1·70 | 1·70 |


**117** Lazarian and Institute

**2001.** Death Bicentenary of Hovhannes Lazarian (founder of Institute of Oriental Languages, Moscow).

| | | | | |
|---|---|---|---|---|
| 491 | **117** | 300d. multicoloured | 1·70 | 1·70 |

A stamp in a similar design was issued by Russia.

**2001.** Traditional Costumes (3rd series). As T 85. Multicoloured.

| | | | | |
|---|---|---|---|---|
| 492 | | 50d. Javakhch couple | 40 | 40 |
| 493 | | 250d. Artzakh couple | 1·70 | 1·70 |

**118** Emblem

**2001.** 6th World Wushu Championships, Yerevan.

| | | | | |
|---|---|---|---|---|
| 494 | **118** | 180d. black | 1·00 | 1·00 |

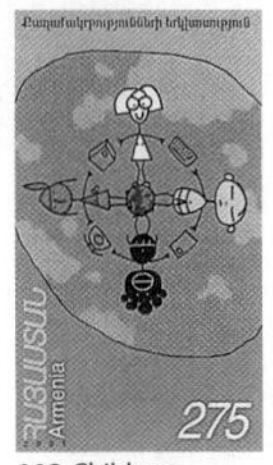

**119** Children encircling Globe

**2001.** United Nations Year of Dialogue among Civilizations.

| | | | | |
|---|---|---|---|---|
| 495 | **119** | 275d. multicoloured | 1·60 | 1·60 |

**120** Emblem

**2001.** 10th Anniv of Commonwealth of Independent States.

| | | | | |
|---|---|---|---|---|
| 496 | **120** | 205d. multicoloured | 1·20 | 1·20 |

**121** Profiles

**2001.** European Year of Languages.

| | | | | |
|---|---|---|---|---|
| 497 | **121** | 350d. multicoloured | 2·30 | 2·30 |

**122** Flag

**2001.** 10th Anniv of Independence.

| | | | | |
|---|---|---|---|---|
| 498 | **122** | 300d. multicoloured | 1·70 | 1·70 |

**123** Cart

**2001.** Transport. Multicoloured.

| | | | | |
|---|---|---|---|---|
| 499 | | 180d. Type **123** | 1·30 | 1·30 |
| 500 | | 205d. Phaeton | 1·40 | 1·40 |

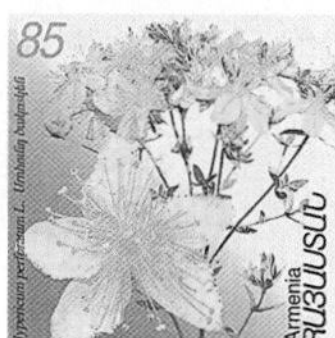


**124** *Hypericum perforatum*

**2001.** Medicinal Plants. Multicoloured.

| | | | |
|---|---|---|---|
| 501 | 85d. Type **124** | 60 | 60 |
| 502 | 205d. *Thymus serpyllum* | 1·50 | 1·50 |

**125** Eagle

**2002**

| | | | | |
|---|---|---|---|---|
| 503 | **125** | 10d. brown | 10 | 10 |
| 504 | **125** | 25d. green | 20 | 20 |
| 506 | **125** | 50d. blue | 35 | 35 |
| 507 | **125** | 70d. rose | 20 | 20 |
| 508 | **125** | 300d. blue | 1·50 | 1·50 |
| 509 | **125** | 500d. brown | 1·90 | 1·90 |

**126** Calendar Belt (2000 B.C.) and Copper Works

**2002.** Traditional Production. Multicoloured.

| | | | |
|---|---|---|---|
| 510 | 120d. Type **126** | 75 | 75 |
| 511 | 350d. Beer vessels (7th century B.C.) and modern brewing equipment | 2·10 | 2·10 |

**2002.** Exhibits in National Gallery of Armenia (3rd series). Vert designs as T 72.

| | | | |
|---|---|---|---|
| 512 | 200d. black, grey and green | 1·00 | 1·00 |
| 513 | 200d. black, grey and red | 1·00 | 1·00 |

DESIGNS: No. 512, "Lily" (Edgar Chahine); 513, "Salome" (sculpture, Hakob Gurjian).

**127** Football and Maps of Japan and South Korea

**2002.** World Cup Football Championships, Japan and South Korea.

| | | | | |
|---|---|---|---|---|
| 514 | **127** | 350d. multicoloured | 1·90 | 1·90 |

**128** Pushman and "The Silent Order" (detail, painting)

**2002.** 125th Birth Anniv of Hovsep Pushman (artist). Sheet 75×65 mm.

| | | | |
|---|---|---|---|
| **MS**515 | 650d. multicoloured | 3·50 | 3·50 |

**129** Technical Drawings, Tevossian and Factory

**2002.** Birth Centenary of Hovhannes Tevossian (metallurgical engineer).

| | | | | |
|---|---|---|---|---|
| 516 | **129** | 350d. multicoloured | 1·90 | 1·90 |

**130** Birds, Playing Cards, Ribbons and Magician's Hat

**2002.** Europa. Circus. Multicoloured.

| | | | |
|---|---|---|---|
| 517 | 70d. Type **130** | 40 | 40 |
| 518 | 500d. Clown juggling | 2·10 | 2·10 |

**131** Aivazian

**2002.** Birth Centenary of Artemy Aivazian (composer).

| | | | | |
|---|---|---|---|---|
| 519 | **131** | 600d. multicoloured | 3·25 | 3·25 |

**132** Ani Cathedral

**2002.** Sheet 90×60 mm.

| | | | |
|---|---|---|---|
| **MS**520 | **132** 550d. multicoloured | 2·75 | 2·75 |

**133** Kaputjugh Mountain

**2002.** International Year of Mountains.

| | | | | |
|---|---|---|---|---|
| 521 | **133** | 350d. multicoloured | 2·10 | 2·10 |

**134** Armenian Lizard (*Lacerta armeniaca*)

**2002.** Reptiles. Multicoloured.

| | | | |
|---|---|---|---|
| 522 | 170d. Type **134** | 1·10 | 1·10 |
| 523 | 220d. Radde's viper (*Vipera raddei*) | 1·40 | 1·40 |

**135** Woman and Dove

**2002.** United Nations Development Fund for Women.

| | | | | |
|---|---|---|---|---|
| 524 | **135** | 220d. multicoloured | 1·60 | 1·60 |

**136** Steam Locomotive

**2002.** Centenary of Alexandrapol–Yerevan Railway.

| | | | | |
|---|---|---|---|---|
| 525 | **136** | 350d. multicoloured | 2·50 | 2·50 |

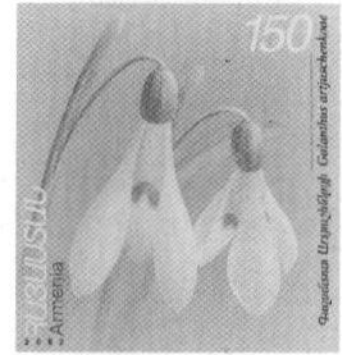


**137** *Galanthus artjuschenkoae*

**2002.** Flowers. Multicoloured.

| | | | |
|---|---|---|---|
| 526 | 150d. Type **137** | 1·00 | 1·00 |
| 527 | 200d. *Merendera mirzoevae* | 1·50 | 1·50 |

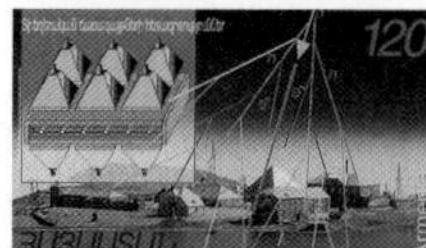


**138** Research Station, Yerevan Physics Institute

**2002.** Space Research. Multicoloured.

| | | | |
|---|---|---|---|
| 528 | 120d. Type **138** | 85 | 85 |

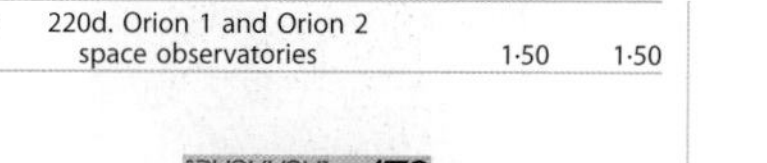

| | | | |
|---|---|---|---|
| 529 | 220d. Orion 1 and Orion 2 space observatories | 1·50 | 1·50 |

**139** "Handle with Care" (Artak Baghdassaryan)

**2003.** Europa. Poster Art. Multicoloured.

| | | | |
|---|---|---|---|
| 530 | 170d. Type **139** | 1·30 | 1·30 |
| 531 | 250d. "Armenia our Home" (Kearen Kojoyan) | 1·70 | 1·70 |

**140** Aram Khachatourian

**2003.** Birth Centenary of Aram Khachatourian (composer).

| | | | | |
|---|---|---|---|---|
| 532 | **140** | 350d. multicoloured | 1·90 | 1·90 |

**141** Armenian Gull (*Larus Armenicus*)

**2003.** World Environment Day. Rehabilitation of Lake Gilli.

| | | | | |
|---|---|---|---|---|
| 533 | **141** | 220d. multicoloured | 1·30 | 1·30 |

**142** Viaduct and Emblem

**2003.** 10th Anniv of TRACEA (transport corridor Europe–Caucasus–Asia) Programme. Sheet 74×55 mm.

| | | | |
|---|---|---|---|
| **MS**534 | **142** 480d. multicoloured | 2·75 | 2·75 |

**143** Horse-drawn Cart, Map of Route and First Postal Seal

**2003.** 175th Anniv of First Armenian Postal Dispatch.

| | | | | |
|---|---|---|---|---|
| 535 | **143** | 70d. multicoloured | 40 | 40 |

**144** Siamanto and Script

**2003.** 125th Birth Anniv of Siamanto (Atom Yarchanyan) (writer).

| | | | | |
|---|---|---|---|---|
| 536 | **144** | 350d. multicoloured | 1·90 | 1·90 |

**145** Coins and Currency Notes

**2003.** 10th Anniv of Armenian Currency.

| | | | | |
|---|---|---|---|---|
| 537 | **145** | 170d. multicoloured | 95 | 95 |

**146** Vahan Tekeyan

**2003.** 125th Birth Anniv of Vahan Tekeyan (writer).

| | | | | |
|---|---|---|---|---|
| 538 | **146** | 200d. multicoloured | 1·10 | 1·10 |

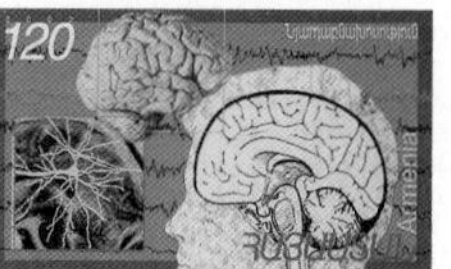


**147** Profile showing Brain

**2003.** Neurophysiology.

| | | | | |
|---|---|---|---|---|
| 539 | **147** | 120d. multicoloured | 65 | 65 |

**148** Sports and Culture Complex, Yerevan

**2003.** 3rd Armenian Games. Sheet 58×40 mm.

| | | | |
|---|---|---|---|
| **MS**540 | **148** 350d. multicoloured | 2·00 | 2·00 |

**149** "The Baptism" (6–7th century), Gospel of Ejmiatsin

**2003.** Armenian Miniatures. Sheet 65×74 mm.

| | | | |
|---|---|---|---|
| **MS**541 | **149** 550d. multicoloured | 3·25 | 3·25 |

**150** "Still Life" (Alexander Shevchenko)

**2004.** Art. Multicoloured.

| | | | |
|---|---|---|---|
| 542 | 200d. Type **150** | 1·20 | 1·20 |
| 543 | 220d. "In a Restaurant" (Konstantin Roudakon) | 1·30 | 1·30 |

**151** "100" and Football

**2004.** Centenary of FIFA (Federation Internationale de Football Association).

| | | | | |
|---|---|---|---|---|
| 544 | **151** | 350d. multicoloured | 1·70 | 1·70 |

**152** White Voskehat Grapes

**2004.** Grapes. Multicoloured.

| | | | |
|---|---|---|---|
| 545 | 170d. Type **152** | 1·00 | 1·00 |
| 546 | 220d. Black Areni grapes | 1·20 | 1·20 |

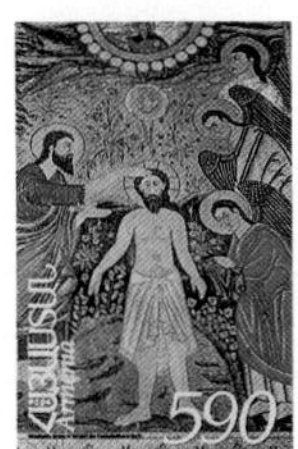


**153** 17th-century Frescos, Vifliem Church

**2004.** 400th Anniv of New Julfa (Armenian settlement in Iran). Sheet 55×56 mm.

| | | | |
|---|---|---|---|
| **MS**547 | 590d. multicoloured | 3·00 | 3·00 |

**154** *The Cat and the Dog*, 1937

**2004.** Animated Films. Multicoloured.

| | | | |
|---|---|---|---|
| 548 | 70d. Type **154** | 40 | 40 |
| 549 | 120d. *Foxbook*, 1975 | 70 | 70 |

**155** Aramayis Yerznkian

**2004.** 125th Birth Anniv of Aramayis Yerznkian (politician).

| | | | | |
|---|---|---|---|---|
| 550 | **155** | 220d. multicoloured | 1·10 | 1·10 |

**156** Karabakh Horse

**2005**

| | | | | |
|---|---|---|---|---|
| 551 | **156** | 350d. multicoloured | 1·80 | 1·80 |

**157** Hand and Olympic Rings

**2005.** Olympic Games, Athens (2004). Multicoloured.

| | | | |
|---|---|---|---|
| 552 | 70d. Type **157** | 40 | 40 |
| 553 | 170d. Hand as runner | 1·00 | 1·00 |
| 554 | 350d. Hand as pistol | 2·10 | 2·10 |

**158** Hands enclosing Seedling

**2005.** International Day against Desertification.

| | | | | |
|---|---|---|---|---|
| 555 | **158** | 360d. multicoloured | 1·90 | 1·90 |

**159** Laboratory Vessel and Chemical Formula

**2005.** Chemistry.

| | | | | |
|---|---|---|---|---|
| 556 | **159** | 220d. multicoloured | 1·10 | 1·10 |

**160** Michael Nalbandian and Script

**2005.** 175th Birth Anniv of Michael Nalbandian (writer).

| | | | | |
|---|---|---|---|---|
| 557 | **160** | 220d. multicoloured | 1·10 | 1·10 |

**161** Mouratsan and Forest

**2005.** 150th Birth Anniv of Grigor Ter-Hovhanissian (Mouratsan) (writer).

| | | | | |
|---|---|---|---|---|
| 558 | **161** | 350d. multicoloured | 1·80 | 1·80 |

**162** Tigran petrossian

**2005.** 75th Birth Anniv of Tigran Petrossian (chess player).

| | | | | |
|---|---|---|---|---|
| 559 | **162** | 220d. multicoloured | 1·10 | 1·10 |

**163** Man sitting on Flower

**2005.** Europa. Holidays (2004). Multicoloured.

| | | | |
|---|---|---|---|
| 560 | 70d. Type **163** | 25 | 25 |
| 561 | 350d. Footprint in sand | 1·70 | 1·70 |

**164** Goshavank Church

**2005.** Goshavank Monastery (12th–13th century). Sheet 84×84 mm.

| | | | |
|---|---|---|---|
| **MS**562 | 480d. multicoloured | 2·40 | 2·40 |

**165** Armen Tigranian, Musical Scores and Landscape

**2005.** 125th Birth Anniv of Armen Tigranian (composer and musician).

| | | | | |
|---|---|---|---|---|
| 563 | **165** | 220d. multicoloured | 1·10 | 1·10 |

**166** Xachkar (cross)

**2005.** 90th Anniv of Armenian Genocide.

| | | | | |
|---|---|---|---|---|
| 564 | **166** | 350d. multicoloured | 1·90 | 1·90 |

**167** Mother Armenia (statue)

**2005.** 60th Anniv of End of World War II.

| | | | | |
|---|---|---|---|---|
| 565 | **167** | 350d. multicoloured | 1·90 | 1·90 |

**168** Anushavan Arzumanian

**2005.** Birth Centenary of Anushavan Arzumanian (economist).

| | | | | |
|---|---|---|---|---|
| 566 | **168** | 220d. multicoloured | 1·10 | 1·10 |

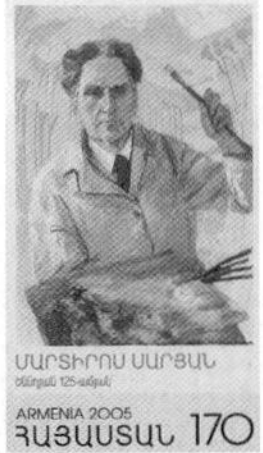


**169** "Self Portrait"

**2005.** 125th Birth Anniv of Martiros Sarian (artist). Multicoloured.

| | | | |
|---|---|---|---|
| 567 | 170d. Type **169** | 80 | 80 |
| 568 | 200d. "Mount Aragats" | 90 | 90 |

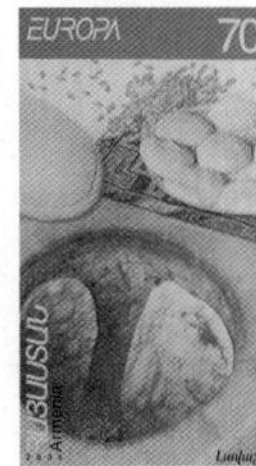


**170** Lavash Bread

**2005.** Europa. Gastronomy. Multicoloured.

| | | | |
|---|---|---|---|
| 569 | 70d. Type **170** | 25 | 25 |
| 570 | 350d. Harisa porridge | 1·90 | 1·90 |

**171** Fragment of 16th-century Khachkar

**2005.** Mother's Day.

| | | | | |
|---|---|---|---|---|
| 571 | **171** | 350d. multicoloured | 1·90 | 1·90 |

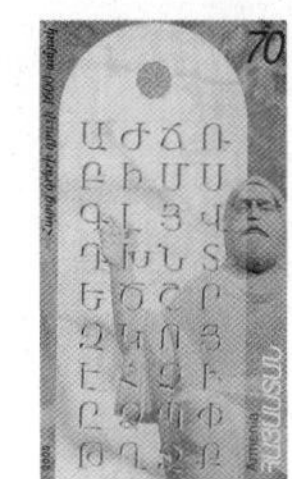


**172** Alphabet and Mesrob Mashots (inventor) (statue)

**2005.** 1600th Anniv of Armenian Alphabet.

| | | | | |
|---|---|---|---|---|
| 572 | **172** | 70d. multicoloured | 25 | 25 |

**173** Vardan Ajemian (actor and theatre director)

**2005.** Anniversaries. Multicoloured.

| | | | |
|---|---|---|---|
| 573 | 70d. Type **173** (birth centenary) | 25 | 25 |
| 574 | 170d. Anania Shirakatsi (scientist) (1400th birth anniv) | 80 | 80 |

**174** Carpet (Artzakh) (19th-century)

**2005.** Carpets. Multicoloured.

| | | | |
|---|---|---|---|
| 575 | 60d. Type **174** | 15 | 15 |
| 576 | 350d. Carpet (Zangezour) (1904) | 1·90 | 1·90 |
| **MS**577 | 92×65 mm. 480d. Carpet (Artzakh) (18th-century) (28×42 mm) | 2·50 | 2·50 |

**175** Mher Mkrtchian (actor)

**2005.** Anniversaries. Multicoloured.

| | | | |
|---|---|---|---|
| 578 | 120d. Type **175** (75th birth anniv) | 45 | 45 |
| 579 | 350d. Artem Mikoyan (aircraft designer) (birth centenary) | 1·90 | 1·90 |

**176** Armenian and Russian Flags and Arms

**2006.** Year of Armenia in Russia.

| | | | | |
|---|---|---|---|---|
| 580 | **176** | 350d. multicoloured | 1·90 | 1·90 |

A stamp of the same design was issued by Russia.

**177** Alexandre Melik-Pashaev (conductor)

**2006.** Birth Centenaries. Multicoloured.

| | | | |
|---|---|---|---|
| 581 | 70d. Type **177** | 25 | 25 |
| 582 | 170d. Vakhtang Ananian (writer) | 80 | 80 |

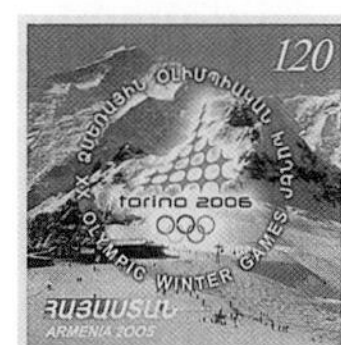
**178** Emblem

**2006.** Winter Olympic Games, Turin. Multicoloured.

| | | | |
|---|---|---|---|
| 583 | 120d. Type **178** | 45 | 45 |
| 584 | 170d. Map of Italy on skis | 80 | 80 |

**179** Cathedral Facade

**2006.** St. Mary's Cathedral of Russian Orthodox.

| | | | | |
|---|---|---|---|---|
| 585 | **179** | 170d. multicoloured | 80 | 80 |

**180** Raphael Patakanian

**2006.** 175th Birth Anniv of Raphael Patkanian (writer).

| | | | | |
|---|---|---|---|---|
| 586 | **180** | 220d. multicoloured | 1·10 | 1·10 |

**181** "P" and Emblem

**2006.** 50th Anniv of Europa Stamps. Multicoloured.

| | | | |
|---|---|---|---|
| 587 | 70d. Type **181** | 20 | 20 |
| 588 | 70d. "T" and emblem | 20 | 20 |
| 589 | 70d. "C" and emblem | 20 | 20 |
| 590 | 70d. "E" and emblem | 20 | 20 |

**2006.** Traditional Costumes (4th series). As T 85.

| | | | |
|---|---|---|---|
| 591 | 170d. Sassoun family | 60 | 60 |
| 592 | 200d. Shatakhk couple | 65 | 65 |

**182** *Porphyrophora hamelii*

**2006.** Insects. Multicoloured.

| | | | |
|---|---|---|---|
| 593 | 170d. Type **182** | 60 | 60 |
| 594 | 220d. *Procerus fallettianus* | 70 | 70 |

**183** Spiridon Melikian

**2006.** 125th (2005) Birth Anniv of Spiridon Melikian (composer).

| | | | | |
|---|---|---|---|---|
| 595 | **183** | 350d. multicoloured | 90 | 90 |

**184** "Adoration of the Magi" (1391), Gospel of Vostan

**2006.** Armenian Miniatures (2nd series). Sheet 75×65 mm.

| | | | |
|---|---|---|---|
| **MS**596 | **184** 480d. multicoloured | 1·40 | 1·40 |

**185** "15"

**2006.** 15th Anniv of Republic of Armenia. Sheet 70×70 mm.

| | | | |
|---|---|---|---|
| **MS**597 | **185** 480d. multicoloured | 1·80 | 1·80 |

**186** Dove

**2006.** Peace.

| | | | | |
|---|---|---|---|---|
| 598 | **186** | 50d. multicoloured | 1·00 | 1·00 |

**187** "To Jerusalem" (1211), Gospel of Haghpat

**2006.** Armenian Miniatures (3rd series). Sheet 65×76 mm.

| | | | |
|---|---|---|---|
| **MS**599 | **187** 220d. multicoloured | 2·75 | 2·75 |

**188** Watch Mechanism

**2006.** Europa. Integration. Multicoloured.

| | | | |
|---|---|---|---|
| 600 | 200d. Type **188** | 2·75 | 2·75 |
| 601 | 350d. Golden key and rusty keys | 4·50 | 4·50 |

**189** Ball, Trophy, Flags and Emblem

**2006.** World Cup Football Championship, Germany.

| | | | | |
|---|---|---|---|---|
| 602 | **189** | 350d. multicoloured | 4·50 | 4·50 |

**190** Boghos Nubar

**2006.** Centenary of General Benevolent Union. Sheet 110×77 mm containing T 190 and similar vert designs. Multicoloured.

| | | | |
|---|---|---|---|
| **MS**603 | 120d.×3, Type **190** (benefactor); Minutes of first meeting; Alex Manoogian (benefactor) | 4·50 | 4·50 |

**191** Sergey Merkurov and "Naked" (sculpture)

**2006.** 125th Birth Anniv of Sergey Merkurov (artist and sculptor).

| | | | | |
|---|---|---|---|---|
| 604 | **191** | 230d. multicoloured | 2·75 | 2·75 |

**192** *Testudo horsfieldii*

**2007.** Endangered Species. Testudo horsfieldii. Multicoloured.

| | | | |
|---|---|---|---|
| 605 | 70d. Type **192** | 95 | 95 |
| 606 | 70d. Facing left | 95 | 95 |
| 607 | 70d. Facing right | 95 | 95 |
| 608 | 70d. Amongst leaves | 95 | 95 |

**193** Trophy

**2007.** Armenia—37th World Chess Olympiad Champions. Multicoloured.

| | | | |
|---|---|---|---|
| 609 | 170d. Type **193** | 2·20 | 2·20 |
| 610 | 220d. Medal | 2·75 | 2·75 |
| 611 | 280d. Chess pieces | 2·75 | 2·75 |
| 612 | 350d. Queen | 4·50 | 4·50 |

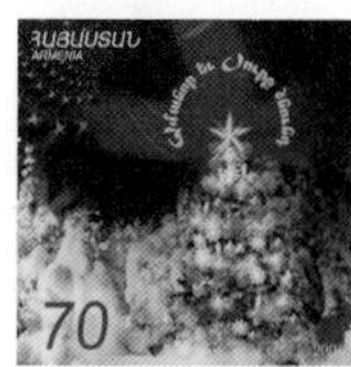
**194** Decorated Tree

**2007.** Christmas and New Year.

| | | | | |
|---|---|---|---|---|
| 613 | **194** | 70d. multicoloured | 95 | 95 |

**195** Clown and Circus Building

**2007.** 50th Anniv of National Circus Collective.

| | | | | |
|---|---|---|---|---|
| 614 | **195** | 70d. multicoloured | 95 | 95 |

**196** Stepan Shahumian Monument

**2007.** Armenian Settlements. Stepanavan. Multicoloured.

| | | | |
|---|---|---|---|
| 615 | 110d. Type **196** | 1·40 | 1·40 |
| 616 | 120d. Memorial fountain | 1·50 | 1·50 |
| 617 | 170d. Rock of Lori Bridge | 2·25 | 2·25 |
| 618 | 200d. Bear Rock | 2·50 | 2·50 |

**197** Sculpture

**2007.** 50th Anniv of Yerevan Mathematical Machines Scientific Research Institute.

| | | | | |
|---|---|---|---|---|
| 619 | **197** | 120d. multicoloured | 1·50 | 1·50 |

**2007.** Traditional Costumes (5th series). As T 85.

| | | | |
|---|---|---|---|
| 620 | 170d. Taron couple | 2·25 | 2·25 |
| 621 | 230d. Shirak couple | 2·75 | 2·75 |

**198** Voski

**2007.** Apricot (Armeniaca vulgaris). Multicoloured.

| | | | |
|---|---|---|---|
| 622 | 230d. Type **198** | 2·25 | 2·25 |
| 623 | 230d. Yerevani | 2·25 | 2·25 |
| 624 | 230d. Ghevondi | 2·25 | 2·25 |
| 625 | 230d. Karmir Nakhijevanik | 2·25 | 2·25 |
| 626 | 230d. Deghin Nakhijevanik | 2·25 | 2·25 |
| 627 | 230d. Khosroveni karmir | 2·25 | 2·25 |
| 628 | 230d. Deghnanush vaghahas | 2·25 | 2·25 |
| 629 | 230d. Vaghahas vardaguyn | 2·25 | 2·25 |
| 630 | 230d. Karmreni | 2·25 | 2·25 |
| 631 | 230d. Sateni deghin | 2·25 | 2·25 |

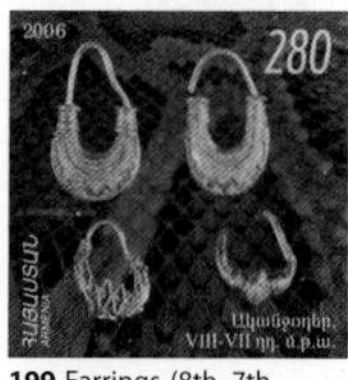
**199** Earrings (8th–7th century BC)

**2007.** Jewellery. Multicoloured.

| | | | |
|---|---|---|---|
| 632 | 280d. Type **199** | 2·75 | 2·75 |
| 633 | 280d. Pendant (3rd century BC) | 2·75 | 2·75 |
| 634 | 280d. Earrings with pendants (10th–11th century) | 2·75 | 2·75 |
| 635 | 280d. Gospel with encrusted cover (1484) | 2·75 | 2·75 |
| 636 | 280d. Chalice (1623) | 2·75 | 2·75 |
| 637 | 280d. Mitre (1765) | 2·75 | 2·75 |
| 638 | 280d. Dove-shaped vessel (1797) | 2·75 | 2·75 |
| 639 | 280d. Knar-diadem (19th century) | 2·75 | 2·75 |
| 640 | 280d. Bracelet (early 20th century) | 2·75 | 2·75 |
| 641 | 280d. Incensory (19th century) | 2·75 | 2·75 |

**200** "Pallas Athena or Armoured Figure"

**2007.** 400th Birth Anniv (2006) of Rembrandt Harmenszoon van Rijn (artist). Multicoloured.

| | | | |
|---|---|---|---|
| 642 | 70d. Type **200** | 95 | 95 |
| 643 | 350d. "Portrait of an Old Man" | 4·50 | 4·50 |
| **MS**644 | 128×89 mm. 70d. "Self Portrait with Saskia"; 170d. "Juno"; 280d. "Woman with Fan"; 350d. "Portrait of Jan Six" | 10·00 | 10·00 |

**201** Mozart as a Young Man (detail)

**2007.** 250th Birth Anniv (2006) of Wolfgang Amadeus Mozart (composer and musician). Multicoloured.

645 70d. Type **201** 95 95
646 350d. Mozart facing left (vert) 4·50 4·50
**MS**647 128×89 mm. 70d. Mozart and score (42×28 mm); 170d. Mozart and script (42×28 mm); 280d. Mozart and stringed instrument (42×28 mm); 350d. Mozart as young man (28×42 mm) 10·00 10·00

**202** Artashes Shahinian

**2007.** Birth Centenary of Artashes Shahinian (scientist).

648 **202** 230d. multicoloured 1·90 1·90

**203** Blue Mosque

**2007**

649 **203** 350d. multicoloured 4·50 4·50

**204** 'L'Ange au Sourire' (the angel with a smile), Rheims Cathedral

**2007.** Year of Armenia in France. Multicoloured.

650 70d. Type **204** 1·00 1·00
651 350d. The Nativity (15th-century miniature) 4·50 4·50

**205** Apricot

**2007**

652 **205** 350d. multicoloured 4·25 4·25

**206** Tirgran the Great

**2007**

653 **206** 50d. multicoloured 80 80
654 **206** 60d. multicoloured 90 90
655 **206** 70d. multicoloured 1·00 1·00
656 **206** 120d. multicoloured 1·80 1·80

**207** Hands

**2007.** Centenary of Scouting.

657 **207** 350d. multicoloured 4·50 4·50

**208** Gusan Sheram

**2007.** 150th Birth Anniv of Talyan Grigor Karapet (Gusan Sheram) (composer and singer).

658 **208** 280d. multicoloured 3·75 3·75

**209** Margar Sedrakyan

**2007.** Birth Centenary of Margar Sedrakyan (Cognac maker).

659 **209** 170d. multicoloured 2·30 2·30

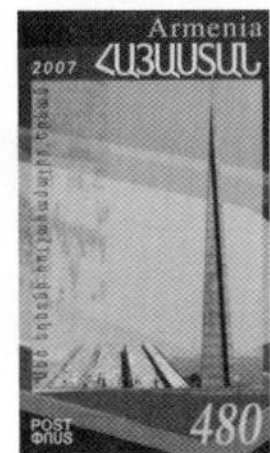
**210** Memorial

**2007.** 40th Anniv of Genocide Museum. Sheet 74×65 mm.

**MS**660 480d. multicoloured 6·00 6·00

**211** *Sparrows* (Yeva Karapetyan)

**2007.** Children's Drawings.

661 **211** 35d. multicoloured 1·00 1·00

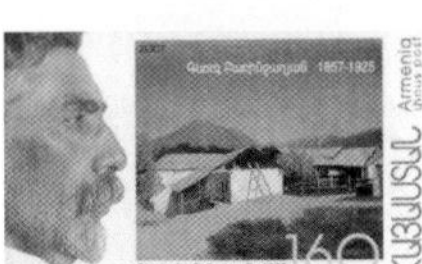
**212** Gevorg Bashinjaghyan and *Gyughakan Tesaran*

**2007.** 150th Birth Anniv of Gevorg Bashinjaghyan (artist). Multicoloured.

662 160d. Type **212** 2·30 2·30
663 220d. *Aragats* 3·00 3·00

**213** Jean Garzou in his Studio

**2007.** Birth Centenary of Garnik Zulumyan (Jean Garzou) (artist). Multicoloured.

664 180d. Type **213** 2·50 2·50
665 220d. *Portrait of Seda (vert)* 2·75 2·75

**214** Hands holding Trophy

**2007.** Pan Armenian Games, Yerevan. Sheet 40×58 mm.

**MS**666 360d. multicoloured 4·75 4·75

**215** Norayr Sisakyan

**2007.** Birth Centenary of Norayr Sisakyan (biochemist).

667 **215** 120d. multicoloured 1·60 1·60

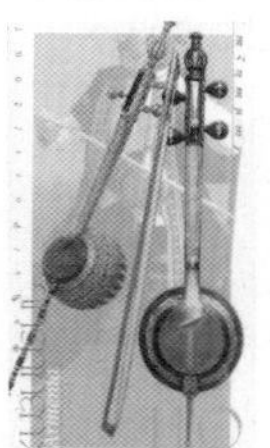
**216** Kamancha

**2007.** Traditional Instruments.

668 **216** 110d. multicoloured 1·60 1·60

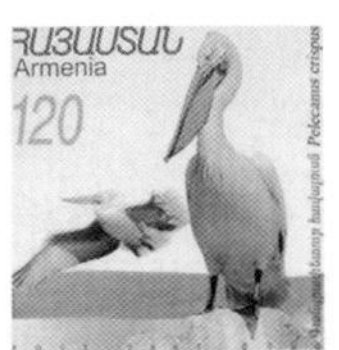
**217** *Pelecanus crispus* (Dalmatian pelican)

**2007.** Endangered Species. Multicoloured.

669 120d. Type **217** 1·50 1·50
670 200d. *Aegypius monachus* (Eurasian black vulture) 2·75 2·75

**218** Matenadaran

**2007.** Matenadaran Manuscript and Book Depository.

671 **218** 200d. multicoloured 2·50 2·50

**219** Bagrat Nalbandyan

**2007.** Bagrat Nalbandyan (communications commissar) Commemoration.

672 **219** 230d. multicoloured 3·00 3·00

**220** Nemrut Baghdasaryan

**2007.** Birth Centenary of Nemrut Baghdasaryan (photojournalist).

673 **220** 200d. multicoloured 2·50 2·50

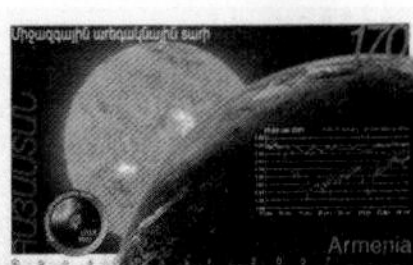
**221** Sun and Earth

**2007.** International Year of Solar Physics. 50th Anniv of Geophysics.

674 **221** 170d. multicoloured 2·30 2·30

**222** *Aphrodite* (Greek)

**2007.** Statues. Multicoloured.

675 70d. Type **222** 1·00 1·00
676 350d. *Anahit* (Armenian) 4·50 4·50

Stamps of the same design were issued by Greece.

**223** Family (Eduard Ghazaryan)

**2008.** International Children's Day.

677 **223** 70d. multicoloured 1·50 1·50

No. 677 includes the se-tenant premium-carrying tab shown in Type **223**, the premium for the benefit of children's charities.

**224** Chinese Dragon

**2008.** Olympic Games, Beijing.

678 **224** 350d. multicoloured 5·00 5·00

**225** Carving

**2008.** Woodcraft.

679 **225** 120d. multicoloured 7·75 7·75

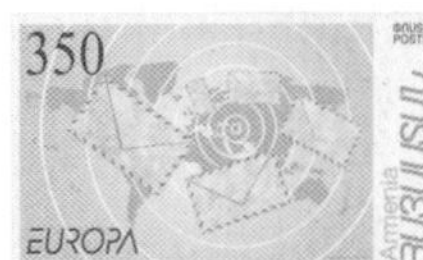
**226** Envelopes and Map

**2008.** Europa. The Letter.

680 **226** 350d. multicoloured 5·00 5·00

**227** Alexander Shirvanzade

**2008.** 150th Birth Anniv of Alexander Shirvanzade (writer).

681 **227** 280d. multicoloured 4·00 4·00

**2008.** Tirgran the Great.

682 **206** 10d. multicoloured 30 30
683 **206** 20d. multicoloured 55 55
684 **206** 50d. multicoloured 1·30 1·30
685 **206** 1100d. multicoloured 13·75 13·75

See also Nos. 653/6.

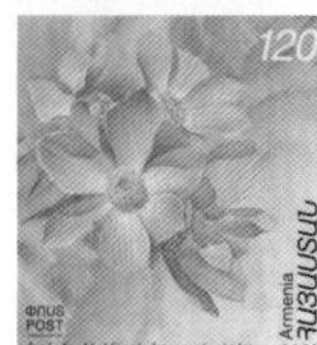

**228** *Anemone fasciculata*

**2008.** Flowers. Multicoloured.

| | | | | |
|---|---|---|---|---|
| 686 | | 120d. Type **228** | 2·75 | 2·75 |
| 687 | | 280d. *Scabiosa caucasica* | 4·00 | 4·00 |

**229** Building Facade

**2008.** 75th Anniv of Polytechnic Institute.

| | | | | |
|---|---|---|---|---|
| 688 | **229** | 220d. multicoloured | 3·75 | 3·75 |

**230** William Saroyan

**2008.** Birth Centenary of William Saroyan (dramatist and writer).

| | | | | |
|---|---|---|---|---|
| 689 | **230** | 350d. multicoloured | 5·75 | 5·75 |

**231** Viktor Ambartsumyan

**2008.** Birth Centenary of Viktor Amazaspovich Ambartsumyan (scientist).

| | | | | |
|---|---|---|---|---|
| 690 | **231** | 120d. multicoloured | 2·00 | 2·00 |

**232** Peyo Yavorov (Bulgarian poet and revolutionary)

**2008.** Nationalist Liberation Movements of Bulgaria and Armenia. Multicoloured.

| | | | | |
|---|---|---|---|---|
| 691 | | 70d. Type **232** | 1·00 | 1·00 |
| 692 | | 350d. Andranik Ozanyan (Armenian general in Balkan Wars of Independence) | 4·75 | 4·75 |

**2009.** Tirgran the Great. Size 19×23 mm.

| | | | | |
|---|---|---|---|---|
| 693 | **206** | 10d. multicoloured (dull yellow-green) | 15 | 15 |
| 694 | **206** | 25d. multicoloured (orange-yellow) | 25 | 25 |
| 695 | **206** | 50d. multicoloured (bright magenta) | 55 | 55 |
| 696 | **206** | 70d. multicoloured (olive-sepia) | 75 | 75 |
| 697 | **206** | 120d. multicoloured (reddish violet) | 1·30 | 1·30 |
| 698 | **206** | 220d. multicoloured (deep blue) | 2·75 | 2·75 |
| 699 | **206** | 280d. multicoloured (deep dull violet blue) | 3·75 | 3·75 |
| 700 | **206** | 350d. multicoloured (bright crimson) | 4·25 | 2·25 |

See also Nos. 653/6 and 682/5.

**233** Dancer holding Sword

**2009.** Dances. Multicoloured.

| | | | | |
|---|---|---|---|---|
| 701 | | 70d. Type **233** | 1·20 | 1·20 |
| 702 | | 350d. Couple | 3·75 | 3·75 |

**234** Ruins

**2009.** Tushpa-Van–Ancient Capital of Armenia.

| | | | | |
|---|---|---|---|---|
| 703 | **234** | 220d. multicoloured | 2·50 | 2·50 |

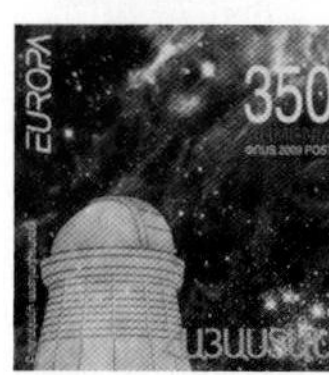

**235** Observatory

**2009.** Europa. Astronomy.

| | | | | |
|---|---|---|---|---|
| 704 | **235** | 350d. multicoloured | 4·75 | 4·75 |

**236** Armenian Chess Team

**2009.** Armenia Gold Medalists at Chess Olympiad 2008, Dresden, Germany. Multicoloured.

| | | | | |
|---|---|---|---|---|
| 705 | | 70d. Type **236** | 2·50 | 2·50 |
| 706 | | 280d. Chess pieces | 11·00 | 11·00 |

**237** Stylized Buildings

**2009.** 50th Anniv of European Court of Human Rights.

| | | | | |
|---|---|---|---|---|
| 707 | **237** | 70d. multicoloured | 95 | 95 |

**238** '60' and Emblem

**2009.** 60th Anniv of Council of Europe

| | | | | |
|---|---|---|---|---|
| 708 | **238** | 280d. multicoloured | 3·50 | 3·50 |

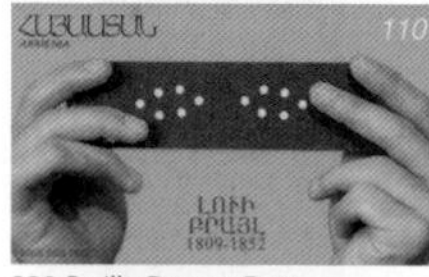

**239** Braille Dots as Eyes

**2009.** Birth Bicentenary of Louis Braille (inventor of Braille writing for the blind).

| | | | | |
|---|---|---|---|---|
| 709 | **239** | 110d. multicoloured | 1·40 | 1·40 |

**240** Daniel Varuzhan

**2009.** 125th Birth Anniv of Daniel Varuzhan (writer).

| | | | | |
|---|---|---|---|---|
| 710 | **240** | 230d. multicoloured | 2·75 | 2·75 |

**241** Monument

**2009.** 50th Anniv of Monument to Davit of Sasun (epic hero). Sheet 69×90 mm.

| | | | | |
|---|---|---|---|---|
| **MS**711 | | multicoloured | 4·50 | 4·50 |

**242** Hrant Shahinyan, Helsinki–1952

**2009.** Olympic Champions. Sheet 119×59 mm containing T 242 and square designs. Multicoloured.

| | | | | |
|---|---|---|---|---|
| **MS**712 | | 70d. Type **242**; 120d. Igor Novikov, Melbourne–1956, Tokyo–1964;160d. Albert Azaryan, Melbourne–1956, Rome–1960 | 4·50 | 4·50 |

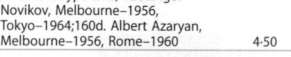

**243** Khachatur Abovyan

**2009.** Birth Bicentenary of Khachatur Abovyan (educator, poet and advocate of modernization).

| | | | | |
|---|---|---|---|---|
| 713 | **243** | 170d. multicoloured | 2·00 | 2·00 |

**244** *Panna Paskevich* (Georgi Yakulov)

**2009.** Art from National Gallery. Multicoloured.

| | | | | |
|---|---|---|---|---|
| 714 | | 200d. Type **244** | 2·50 | 2·50 |
| 715 | | 200d. *Autumn. A Corner in Yerevan* (Sedrak Arakelyan) | 2·50 | 2·50 |

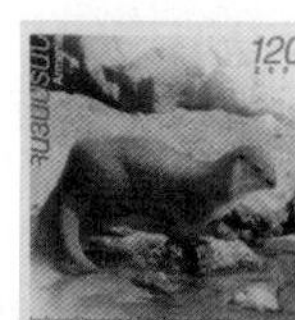

**245** *Lutra lutra meridionalis* (European otter)

**2009.** Fauna. Multicoloured.

| | | | | |
|---|---|---|---|---|
| 716 | | 120d. Type **245** | 2·10 | 2·10 |
| 717 | | 160d. *Ursus arctos syriacus* (Syrian brown bear) | 2·75 | 2·75 |

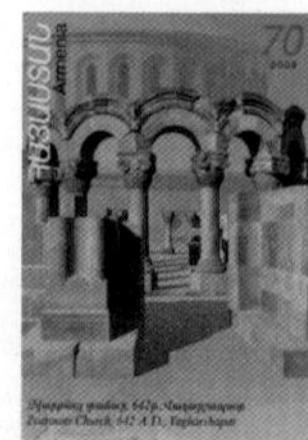

**246** Zvartnots Church, 642 AD,

**2009.** Churches in Vagharshapat. Sheet 145×69 mm containing T 246 and similar vert designs. Multicoloured.

| | | | | |
|---|---|---|---|---|
| **MS**718 | | 70d.×4, Type **246**; St. Hripsime church, 618 AD; Mother See of Holy Etchmiadzin, 301–303 AD; St. Gayane church, 630 AD | 3·50 | 3·50 |

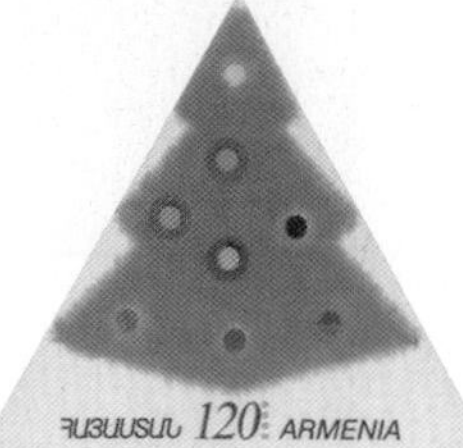

**247** Decorated Tree

**2009.** New Year.

| | | | | |
|---|---|---|---|---|
| 719 | **247** | 120d. multicoloured | 1·60 | 1·60 |

The tree shown on No. 719 was printed with a flocked surface and simulated baubles.

**248** Virgin and Child

**2009.** Christmas. Multicoloured.

| | | | | |
|---|---|---|---|---|
| 720 | | 280d. Type **248** | 3·50 | 3·50 |
| **MS**721 | | 80×105 mm. Size 60×30 mm. 650d. As Type **248** but design enlarged | 8·00 | 8·00 |

**2010.** Tirgran the Great

(a) Ordinary gum

| | | | | |
|---|---|---|---|---|
| 722 | **206** | 10d. magenta | 40 | 40 |
| 723 | | 25d. ultramarine | 60 | 60 |
| 724 | | 50d. yellow-ochre | 75 | 75 |
| 725 | | 70d. bright vermilion | 1·00 | 1·00 |
| 726 | | 100d. purple-brown | 1·50 | 1·50 |
| 727 | | 120d. claret | 1·80 | 1·80 |
| 728 | | 200d. pale greenish grey | 2·50 | 2·50 |
| 729 | | 220d. bright reddish violet | 2·75 | 2·75 |
| 730 | | 280d. scarlet | 3·75 | 3·75 |
| 731 | | 650d. apple green | 4·50 | 4·50 |

(b) Self-adhesive

| | | | | |
|---|---|---|---|---|
| 732 | **206** | 10d. magenta | 40 | 40 |
| 733 | | 25d. ultramarine | 60 | 60 |
| 734 | | 50d. yellow-ochre | 75 | 75 |
| 735 | | 70d. bright vermilion | 1·00 | 1·00 |
| 736 | | 100d. purple-brown | 1·50 | 1·50 |
| 737 | | 120d. claret | 1·80 | 1·80 |
| 738 | | 200d. pale greenish grey | 2·50 | 2·50 |
| 739 | | 220d. bright reddish violet | 2·75 | 2·75 |
| 740 | | 280d. scarlet | 3·75 | 3·75 |
| 741 | | 650d. apple green | 4·50 | 4·50 |

**249** Henrik Kasparyan and Chessboard

**2010.** Birth Centenary of Henrik Kasparyan

| | | | | |
|---|---|---|---|---|
| 742 | **249** | 870d. multicoloured | 9·50 | 9·50 |

**250** Victory Monument

**2010.** 65th Anniv of End of World War II

| | | | | |
|---|---|---|---|---|
| 743 | **250** | 350d. multicoloured | 4·75 | 4·75 |

251 Memorial Complex

**2010.** Russian Officer Cemetery. Multicoloured.

| No. | Type | Description | Mint | Used |
|---|---|---|---|---|
| 744 | | 350d. Type **251** | 5·00 | 5·00 |
| **MS**745 | | 102×77 mm. 650d. As Type **251** | 5·00 | 8·00 |

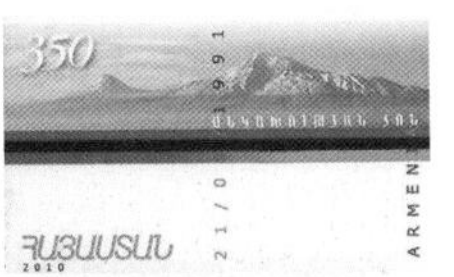
**252** Mount Ararat

**2010.** Independence Day

| No. | Type | Description | Mint | Used |
|---|---|---|---|---|
| 746 | | 350d. Type **252** | 4·50 | 4·50 |
| 747 | | 650d. National flag (30×30 mm) | 8·50 | 8·50 |

**253** Armenian Pavillion (image scaled to 68% of original size)

**2010.** Expo 2010, Shanghai. Multicoloured.

| No. | Type | Description | Mint | Used |
|---|---|---|---|---|
| 748 | | 280d Type **253** | 3·75 | 3·75 |

No. 749 is left for stamp known, but not yet received

**254** Medieval Women

**2010.** Europa

| No. | Type | Description | Mint | Used |
|---|---|---|---|---|
| 750 | **254** | 350d. multicoloured | 4·50 | 4·50 |

**255** Vladimir Yengibaryan (Melbourne, 1956)

**2010.** Olympic Champions. Multicoloured.

| No. | Type | Description | Mint | Used |
|---|---|---|---|---|
| **MS**751 | | 160d.×3, Type **255**; Faina Melnik (Munich, 1972); Yuri Vardanyan (Moscow, 1980) | 6·50 | 6·50 |

**256** Cross Country Skier

**2010.** Winter Olympic Games, Vancouver. Multicoloured.

| No. | Type | Description | Mint | Used |
|---|---|---|---|---|
| **MS**752 | | 350d. Type **256**; 500d. Alpine houses and cross country skier; 600d. Alpine skier | 19·00 | 19·00 |

**257** Games Emblem and Pictograms

**2010.** Olympic Youth Games, Singapore

| No. | Type | Description | Mint | Used |
|---|---|---|---|---|
| 753 | **257** | 870d. multicoloured | 11·50 | 11·50 |

**258** Ball and Globe

**2010.** Football World Cup Championships, South Africa

| No. | Type | Description | Mint | Used |
|---|---|---|---|---|
| 754 | **258** | 1100d. multicoloured | 14·50 | 14·50 |

Pt. 4

# ARUBA

An island in the Caribbean, formerly part of Netherlands Antilles. In 1986 became an autonomous country within the Kingdom of the Netherlands.

100 cents = 1 gulden.

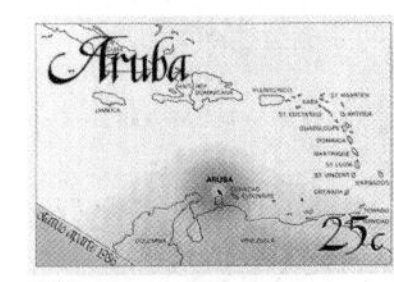

**1** Map

**1986.** New Constitution.

| No. | Type | Description | Mint | Used |
|---|---|---|---|---|
| 1 | **1** | 25c. yellow, blue and black | 1·70 | 55 |
| 2 | - | 45c. multicoloured | 2·00 | 1·10 |
| 3 | - | 55c. black, grey and red | 2·50 | 1·50 |
| 4 | - | 100c. multicoloured | 3·25 | 2·50 |

DESIGNS—VERT: 45c. Aruban arms; 55c. National anthem. HORIZ: 100c. Aruban flag.

**2** House

**1986**

| No. | Type | Description | Mint | Used |
|---|---|---|---|---|
| 5 | **2** | 5c. black and yellow | 55 | 10 |
| 6 | - | 15c. black and blue | 1·20 | 55 |
| 7 | - | 20c. black and grey | 90 | 35 |
| 8 | - | 25c. black and violet | 1·70 | 55 |
| 9 | - | 30c. black and red | 1·70 | 90 |
| 10 | - | 35c. black and bistre | 1·70 | 90 |
| 12 | - | 45c. black and blue | 2·00 | 1·20 |
| 14 | - | 55c. black and grey | 1·70 | 90 |
| 15 | - | 60c. black and blue | 1·90 | 1·10 |
| 16 | - | 65c. black and blue | 1·80 | 1·50 |
| 18 | - | 75c. black and brown | 2·00 | 1·50 |
| 20 | - | 85c. black and orange | 2·00 | 1·10 |
| 21 | - | 90c. black and green | 2·20 | 1·50 |
| 22 | - | 100c. black and brown | 2·20 | 1·50 |
| 23 | - | 150c. black and green | 3·75 | 2·20 |
| 24 | - | 250c. black and green | 5·25 | 4·50 |

DESIGNS: 15c. Clock tower; 20c. Container crane; 25c. Lighthouse; 30c. Snake; 35c. Burrowing owl; 45c. Carib-bean vase (shell); 55c. Frog; 60c. Water-skier; 65c. Fisherman casting net; 75c. Hurdy-gurdy; 85c. Pot; 90, 250c. Different cacti; 100c. Maize; 150c. Watapana Tree.

**3** People and Two Ropes

**1986.** "Solidarity". Multicoloured.

| No. | Type | Description | Mint | Used |
|---|---|---|---|---|
| 25 | | 30c.+10c. Type **3** | 2·00 | 1·10 |
| 26 | | 35c.+15c. People and three ropes | 2·00 | 1·10 |
| 27 | | 60c.+25c. People and one rope | 2·75 | 1·70 |

**4** Dove between Scenes of Peace and War

**1986.** International Peace Year. Multicoloured.

| No. | Type | Description | Mint | Used |
|---|---|---|---|---|
| 28 | | 60c. Type **4** | 5·00 | 1·70 |
| 29 | | 100c. Doves flying over broken barbed wire | 10·00 | 3·25 |

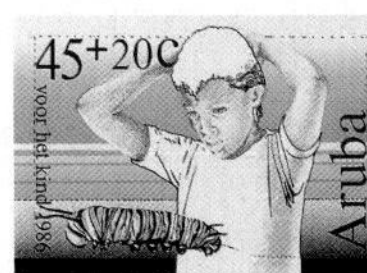

**5** Boy and Caterpillar

**1986.** Child Welfare. Multicoloured.

| No. | Type | Description | Mint | Used |
|---|---|---|---|---|
| 30 | | 45c.+20c. Type **5** | 2·75 | 1·10 |
| 31 | | 70c.+25c. Boy and shell | 3·25 | 1·70 |
| 32 | | 100c.+40c. Girl and butterfly | 4·00 | 2·50 |

**6** Engagement Picture

**1987.** Golden Wedding of Princess Juliana and Prince Bernhard.

| No. | Type | Description | Mint | Used |
|---|---|---|---|---|
| 33 | **6** | 135c. orange, black and gold | 4·50 | 2·50 |

**7** Queen Beatrix and Prince Claus

**1987.** Royal Visit. Multicoloured.

| No. | Type | Description | Mint | Used |
|---|---|---|---|---|
| 34 | | 55c. Type **7** | 2·20 | 1·10 |
| 35 | | 60c. Prince Willem-Alexander | 2·20 | 1·10 |

**8** Woman looking at Beach

**1987.** Tourism. Multicoloured.

| No. | Type | Description | Mint | Used |
|---|---|---|---|---|
| 36 | | 60c. Type **8** | 2·20 | 1·50 |
| 37 | | 100c. Woman looking at desert landscape | 3·25 | 2·00 |

**9** Child with Book on Beach

**1987.** Child Welfare. Multicoloured.

| No. | Type | Description | Mint | Used |
|---|---|---|---|---|
| 38 | | 25c.+10c. Type **9** | 1·70 | 90 |
| 39 | | 45c.+20c. Children drawing Christmas tree | 2·20 | 1·10 |
| 40 | | 70c.+30c. Child gazing at Nativity crib | 3·25 | 1·70 |

**10** Plantation

**1988.** "Aloe vera". Multicoloured.

| No. | Type | Description | Mint | Used |
|---|---|---|---|---|
| 41 | | 45c. Type **10** | 2·00 | 1·10 |
| 42 | | 60c. Stem and leaves of plant | 2·20 | 1·50 |
| 43 | | 100c. Harvesting aloes | 2·75 | 1·70 |

**11** 25c. Coin

**1988.** Coins. Multicoloured.

| No. | Type | Description | Mint | Used |
|---|---|---|---|---|
| 44 | | 25c. Type **11** | 1·50 | 55 |
| 45 | | 55c. Square 50c. coin | 2·00 | 1·10 |
| 46 | | 65c. 5c. and 10c. coins | 2·20 | 1·50 |
| 47 | | 150c. 1 gulden coin | 4·00 | 2·50 |

**12** Bananaquits, Country Scene and "Love"

**1988.** Greetings Stamps. Multicoloured.

| No. | Type | Description | Mint | Used |
|---|---|---|---|---|
| 48 | | 70c. Type **12** | 2·00 | 1·10 |
| 49 | | 135c. West Indian crown conch, West Indian chank (shells), seaside scene and "Love" | 2·75 | 2·00 |

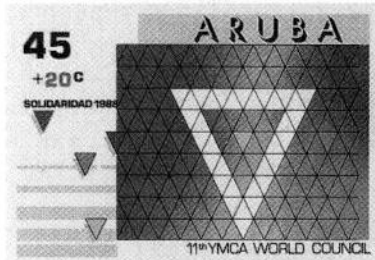

**13** White Triangle on Shaded Background

**1988.** "Solidarity". 11th Y.M.C.A. World Council. Multicoloured.

| No. | Type | Description | Mint | Used |
|---|---|---|---|---|
| 50 | | 45c.+20c. Type **13** | 2·20 | 1·10 |
| 51 | | 60c.+25c. Interlocking triangles | 2·20 | 1·70 |
| 52 | | 100c.+50c. Shaded triangle on white background | 2·75 | 2·20 |

**14** Torch

**1988.** Olympic Games, Seoul. Multicoloured.

| No. | Type | Description | Mint | Used |
|---|---|---|---|---|
| 53 | | 35c. Type **14** | 1·70 | 90 |
| 54 | | 100c. Games and Olympic emblems | 2·75 | 1·70 |

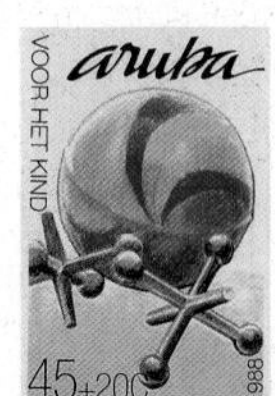

**15** Jacks

**1988.** Child Welfare. Toys. Multicoloured.

| No. | Type | Description | Mint | Used |
|---|---|---|---|---|
| 55 | | 45c.+20c. Type **15** | 2·20 | 1·10 |
| 56 | | 70c.+30c. Spinning top | 2·20 | 1·70 |
| 57 | | 100c.+50c. Kite | 2·75 | 2·20 |

**16** Children

**1989.** Carnival. Multicoloured.

| No. | Type | Description | Mint | Used |
|---|---|---|---|---|
| 58 | | 45c. Type **16** | 2·20 | 1·10 |
| 59 | | 60c. Girl in costume | 2·20 | 1·10 |
| 60 | | 100c. Lights | 2·75 | 1·70 |

**17** Maripampun

**1989.** Maripampun. Multicoloured.

| No. | Type | Description | Mint | Used |
|---|---|---|---|---|
| 61 | | 35c. Type **17** | 1·70 | 85 |
| 62 | | 55c. Seed pods | 1·70 | 1·10 |
| 63 | | 200c. Pod distributing seeds | 4·50 | 3·25 |

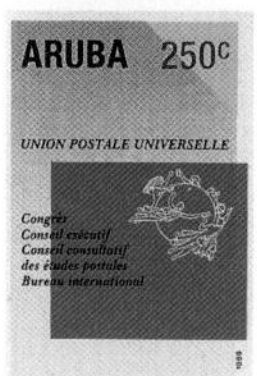

**18** Emblem

**1989.** Universal Postal Union.

| | | | | |
|---|---|---|---|---|
| 64 | **18** | 250c. multicoloured | 6·75 | 4·25 |

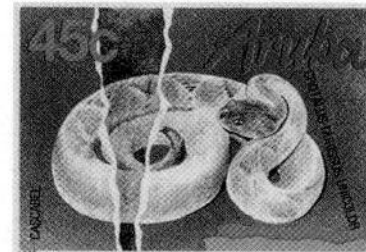
**19** Snake

**1989.** South American Rattlesnake.

| | | | | |
|---|---|---|---|---|
| 65 | **19** | 45c. multicoloured | 1·70 | 90 |
| 66 | - | 55c. multicoloured | 2·00 | 1·10 |
| 67 | - | 60c. multicoloured | 2·00 | 1·10 |

DESIGNS: 55, 60c. Snake (different).

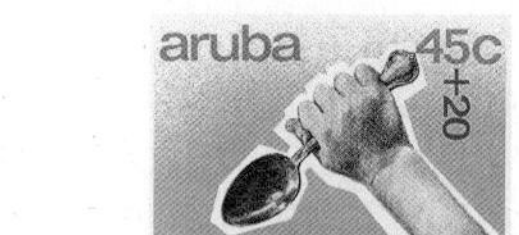

**20** Spoon in Child's Hand

**1989.** Child Welfare. Multicoloured.

| | | | |
|---|---|---|---|
| 68 | 45c +20c. Type **20** | 2·00 | 1·10 |
| 69 | 60c.+30c. Child playing football | 2·20 | 1·20 |
| 70 | 100c.+50c. Child's hand in adult's hand (vert) | 3·25 | 2·20 |

**21** Violin, Tambour and Cuatro Players

**1989.** New Year. Dande Musicians. Multicoloured.

| | | | |
|---|---|---|---|
| 71 | 25c. Type **21** | 1·10 | 55 |
| 72 | 70c. Guitar and cuatro players and singer with hat | 1·60 | 1·10 |
| 73 | 150c. Cuatro, accordion and wiri players | 3·00 | 2·20 |

**22** Tractor and Natural Vegetation

**1990.** Environmental Protection. Multicoloured.

| | | | |
|---|---|---|---|
| 74 | 45c. Type **22** | 1·50 | 1·10 |
| 75 | 55c. Face and wildlife (vert) | 1·70 | 1·10 |
| 76 | 100c. Marine life | 2·75 | 2·00 |

**23** Giant Caribbean Anemone and Pederson's Cleaning Shrimp

**1990.** Marine Life. Multicoloured.

| | | | |
|---|---|---|---|
| 77 | 60c. Type **23** | 1·70 | 1·10 |
| 78 | 70c. Queen angelfish and red coral | 2·20 | 1·70 |
| 79 | 100c. Banded coral shrimp, fire sponge and yellow boring sponge | 3·25 | 2·50 |

**24** Ball

**1990.** World Cup Football Championship, Italy. Multicoloured.

| | | | |
|---|---|---|---|
| 80 | 35c. Type **24** | 1·50 | 90 |
| 81 | 200c. Mascot | 4·50 | 3·25 |

**25** Emblem of Committee of Tanki Leendert Association Youth Centre

**1990.** "Solidarity". Multicoloured.

| | | | |
|---|---|---|---|
| 82 | 55c.+25c. Type **25** | 2·20 | 1·80 |
| 83 | 100c.+50c. Emblem of Foundation for Promotion of Responsible Parenthood | 4·00 | 3·00 |

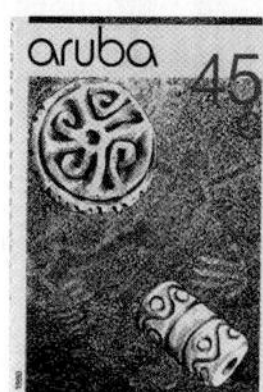

**26** Clay Painting Stamps

**1990.** Archaeology. Multicoloured.

| | | | |
|---|---|---|---|
| 84 | 45c. Type **26** | 1·50 | 1·10 |
| 85 | 60c. Stone figure | 1·70 | 1·10 |
| 86 | 100c. Dabajuroid-style jar | 2·75 | 1·70 |

**27** Sailboards and Fishes

**1990.** Child Welfare. Multicoloured.

| | | | |
|---|---|---|---|
| 87 | 45c.+20c. Type **27** | 1·70 | 1·10 |
| 88 | 60c.+30c. Parakeets and coconut trees | 2·20 | 1·70 |
| 89 | 100c.+50c. Kites and lizard | 3·25 | 2·75 |

**28** Mountain and Shoreline

**1991.** Landscapes. Multicoloured.

| | | | |
|---|---|---|---|
| 90 | 55c. Type **28** | 1·40 | 1·10 |
| 91 | 65c. Cacti and Haystack mountain | 1·70 | 1·50 |
| 92 | 100c. House, mountain and ocean, Jaburibari | 2·50 | 2·20 |

**29** Woman holding Herbs ("Carer")

**1991.** Women and Work. Multicoloured.

| | | | |
|---|---|---|---|
| 93 | 35c. Type **29** | 1·10 | 55 |
| 94 | 70c. Women and kitchen ("Housewife") | 1·70 | 1·50 |
| 95 | 100c. Women and telephone ("Woman in the World") | 2·20 | 2·00 |

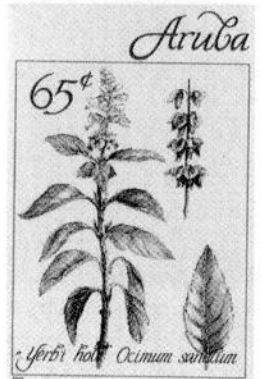

**30** "Ocimum sanctum"

**1991.** Medicinal Plants. Multicoloured.

| | | | |
|---|---|---|---|
| 96 | 65c. Type **30** | 1·70 | 1·10 |
| 97 | 75c. "Jatropha gossypifolia" | 2·00 | 1·50 |
| 98 | 95c. "Croton flavens" | 2·20 | 1·70 |

**31** Fishing Net, Float and Needle

**1991.** Traditional Crafts.

| | | | | |
|---|---|---|---|---|
| 99 | **31** | 35c. black, ultram & blue | 1·10 | 90 |
| 100 | - | 250c. black, lilac & purple | 5·00 | 4·25 |

DESIGNS: 250c. Hat, straw and hat-block.

**32** Child's Hand taking Book from Shelf

**1991.** Child Welfare. Multicoloured.

| | | | |
|---|---|---|---|
| 101 | 45c.+25c. Type **32** | 1·70 | 1·50 |
| 102 | 60c.+35c. Child's finger pointing to letter "B" | 2·20 | 1·70 |
| 103 | 100c.+50c. Child reading | 3·25 | 2·50 |

**33** Toucan saying "Welcome"

**1991.** Tourism. Multicoloured.

| | | | |
|---|---|---|---|
| 104 | 35c. Type **33** | 1·10 | 1·10 |
| 105 | 70c. Aruban youth welcoming tourist | 1·70 | 1·10 |
| 106 | 100c. Windmill and Bubali swamp | 2·75 | 2·20 |

**34** Government Decree of 1892 establishing first Aruban Post Office

**1992.** Centenary of Postal Service (1st issue). Mult.

| | | | |
|---|---|---|---|
| 107 | 60c. Type **34** | 1·40 | 1·10 |
| 108 | 75c. Lt.-Governor's building (mail service office, 1892–1908) (horiz) | 1·70 | 1·10 |
| 109 | 80c. Present Oranjestad P.O. (horiz) | 2·20 | 1·70 |

See also Nos. 117/19.

**35** Equality of Sexes

**1992.** Equality. Multicoloured.

| | | | |
|---|---|---|---|
| 110 | 100c. Type **35** | 2·20 | 1·70 |
| 111 | 100c. People of different races (equality of nations) | 2·20 | 1·70 |

**36** Aruban Flag, Guide Emblem and Girl Guides

**1992.** "Solidarity". Multicoloured.

| | | | |
|---|---|---|---|
| 112 | 55c.+30c. Type **36** | 2·20 | 1·70 |
| 113 | 100c.+50c. Open hand with Cancer Fund emblem | 3·25 | 2·50 |

**37** Columbus, Map and Clouds

**1992.** 500th Anniv of Discovery of America by Columbus. Multicoloured.

| | | | |
|---|---|---|---|
| 114 | 30c. Type **37** | 1·70 | 55 |
| 115 | 40c. Caravel (from navigation chart, 1525) | 1·70 | 90 |
| 116 | 50c. Indians, queen conch shell and 1540 map | 1·70 | 1·10 |

**38** "I Love Post" (Jelissa Boekhoudt)

**1992.** Child Welfare. Centenary of Postal Service (2nd issue). Children's Drawings. Multicoloured.

| | | | |
|---|---|---|---|
| 117 | 50c.+30c. Type **38** | 2·00 | 1·50 |
| 118 | 70c.+35c. Airplane dropping letters (Marianne Fingal) | 2·20 | 1·70 |
| 119 | 100c.+50c. Pigeon carrying letter in beak (Minorenti Jacobs) (vert) | 3·25 | 2·50 |

**39** Seroe Colorado Bridge

**1992.** Natural Bridges. Multicoloured.

| | | | |
|---|---|---|---|
| 120 | 70c. Type **39** | 1·60 | 1·10 |
| 121 | 80c. Natural Bridge | 2·00 | 1·70 |

**41** Rocks at Ayo

**1993.** Rock Formations. Multicoloured.

| | | | |
|---|---|---|---|
| 123 | 50c. Type **41** | 1·10 | 1·10 |
| 124 | 60c. Casibari | 1·50 | 1·10 |
| 125 | 100c. Ayo (different) | 2·20 | 2·00 |

**42** Traditional Instruments

**1993.** Cock's Burial (part of St. John's Feast celebrations). Multicoloured.

| | | | |
|---|---|---|---|
| 126 | 40c. Type **42** | 1·10 | 1·10 |
| 127 | 70c. "Cock's Burial" (painting, Leo Kuiperi) | 1·50 | 1·10 |
| 128 | 80c. Verses of song, yellow flag, and calabashes | 1·70 | 1·70 |

**43** Sailfish dinghy

**1993.** Sports. Multicoloured.

| | | | |
|---|---|---|---|
| 129 | 50c. Type **43** | 1·10 | 1·10 |

| | | | |
|---|---|---|---|
| 130 | 65c. Land sailing | 1·50 | 1·10 |
| 131 | 75c. Sailboard | 1·70 | 1·50 |

**44** Young Iguana

**1993.** The Iguana. Multicoloured.

| | | | |
|---|---|---|---|
| 132 | 35c. Type **44** | 1·50 | 90 |
| 133 | 60c. Young adult | 1·70 | 1·50 |
| 134 | 100c. Adult (vert) | 2·20 | 2·20 |

**45** Aruban House, Landscape and Cacti

**1993.** Child Welfare. Multicoloured.

| | | | |
|---|---|---|---|
| 135 | 50c.+30c. Type **45** | 1·60 | 1·50 |
| 136 | 75c.+40c. Face, bridge and sea (vert) | 2·20 | 2·20 |
| 137 | 100c.+50c. Bridge, buildings and landscape | 3·00 | 2·75 |

**46** Owls

**1994.** The Burrowing Owl. Multicoloured.

| | | | |
|---|---|---|---|
| 138 | 5c. Type **46** | 1·80 | 40 |
| 139 | 10c. Pair with young | 1·80 | 90 |
| 140 | 35c. Owl with locust in claw (vert) | 2·10 | 1·10 |
| 141 | 40c. Owl (vert) | 2·10 | 1·70 |

**47** Athlete

**1994.** Centenary of Int Olympic Committee. Mult.

| | | | |
|---|---|---|---|
| 142 | 50c. Type **47** | 1·30 | 1·10 |
| 143 | 90c. Baron Pierre de Coubertin (founder) | 2·00 | 1·70 |

**48** Family in House

**1994.** "Solidarity". Int Year of The Family. Mult.

| | | | |
|---|---|---|---|
| 144 | 50c.+35c. Type **48** | 1·70 | 1·60 |
| 145 | 100c.+50c. Family outside house | 3·00 | 3·00 |

**49** Flags of U.S.A. and Aruba, Ball and Players

**1994.** World Cup Football Championship, U.S.A. Multicoloured.

| | | | |
|---|---|---|---|
| 146 | 65c. Type **49** | 1·70 | 1·50 |
| 147 | 150c. Mascot | 3·25 | 2·75 |

**50** West Indian Cherry

**1994.** Wild Fruits. Multicoloured.

| | | | |
|---|---|---|---|
| 148 | 40c. Type **50** | 1·10 | 1·10 |
| 149 | 70c. Geiger tree | 1·70 | 1·10 |
| 150 | 85c. "Pithecellobium unguis-cati" | 2·00 | 1·70 |
| 151 | 150c. Sea grape | 3·75 | 2·75 |

**51** Children with Umbrella sitting on Anchor (shelter and security)

**1994.** Child Welfare. Influence of the Family. Mult.

| | | | |
|---|---|---|---|
| 152 | 50c.+30c. Type **51** | 2·00 | 1·70 |
| 153 | 80c.+35c. Children in smiling sun (warmth of nurturing home) | 2·50 | 2·20 |
| 154 | 100c.+50c. Child flying on owl (wisdom guiding the child) | 2·75 | 2·75 |

**52** Government Building, 1888

**1995.** Historic Buildings. Multicoloured.

| | | | |
|---|---|---|---|
| 155 | 35c. Type **52** | 90 | 75 |
| 156 | 60c. Ecury Residence, 1929 (vert) | 1·50 | 1·10 |
| 157 | 100c. Protestant Church, 1846 (vert) | 2·20 | 2·00 |

**53** Dove, Emblem and Flags

**1995.** 50th Anniv of U.N.O. Multicoloured.

| | | | |
|---|---|---|---|
| 158 | 30c. Type **53** | 1·50 | 90 |
| 159 | 200c. Emblem, flags, globe and doves | 4·00 | 3·75 |

**54** Casanova II and Rosettes

**1995.** Interpaso Horses. Multicoloured.

| | | | |
|---|---|---|---|
| 160 | 25c. Type **54** | 90 | 50 |
| 161 | 75c. Horse performing Paso Fino | 1·70 | 1·50 |
| 162 | 80c. Horse performing Figure 8 (vert) | 1·70 | 1·70 |
| 163 | 90c. Girl on horseback (vert) | 2·00 | 1·70 |

**55** Cowpea

**1995.** Vegetables. Multicoloured.

| | | | |
|---|---|---|---|
| 164 | 25c. Type **55** | 85 | 50 |
| 165 | 50c. Apple cucumber | 1·40 | 1·10 |
| 166 | 70c. Okra | 1·60 | 1·40 |
| 167 | 85c. Pumpkin | 1·80 | 1·70 |

**56** Hawksbill Turtle

**1995.** Turtles. Multicoloured.

| | | | |
|---|---|---|---|
| 168 | 15c. Type **56** | 1·70 | 40 |
| 169 | 50c. Green turtle | 2·10 | 90 |
| 170 | 95c. Loggerhead turtle | 2·30 | 1·70 |
| 171 | 100c. Leatherback turtle | 2·75 | 1·70 |

**57** Children holding Balloons outside House (Christina Trejo)

**1995.** Child Welfare. Children's Drawings. Mult.

| | | | |
|---|---|---|---|
| 172 | 50c.+25c. Type **57** | 1·70 | 1·40 |
| 173 | 70c.+35c. Children at seaside (Julysses Tromp) | 2·20 | 2·00 |
| 174 | 100c.+50c. Children and adults gardening (Ronald Tromp) | 3·25 | 2·75 |

**58** Henry Eman

**1996.** 10th Anniv of Internal Autonomy. Politicians. Multicoloured.

| | | | |
|---|---|---|---|
| 175 | 100c. Type **58** | 2·00 | 1·70 |
| 176 | 100c. Juancho Irausquin | 2·00 | 1·70 |
| 177 | 100c. Shon Eman | 2·00 | 1·70 |
| 178 | 100c. Betico Croes | 2·00 | 1·70 |

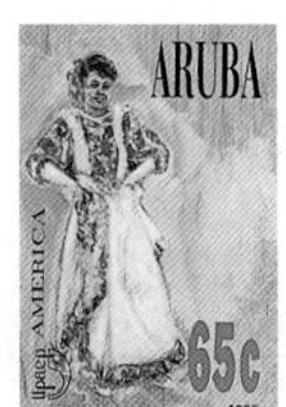

**59** Woman

**1996.** America. Traditional Costumes. Mult.

| | | | |
|---|---|---|---|
| 179 | 65c. Type **59** | 2·20 | 1·10 |
| 180 | 70c. Man | 2·20 | 1·10 |
| 181 | 100c. Couple dancing (horiz) | 2·75 | 1·70 |

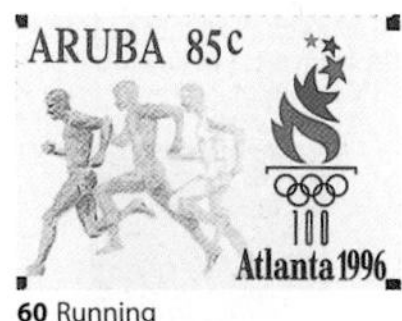

**60** Running

**1996.** Olympic Games, Atlanta. Multicoloured.

| | | | |
|---|---|---|---|
| 182 | 85c. Type **60** | 2·20 | 1·50 |
| 183 | 130c. Cycling | 2·75 | 2·50 |

**61** Mathematical Instruments, "G" and Rising Sun

**1996.** "Solidarity". 75th Anniv of Freemasons' Lodge El Sol Naciente. Multicoloured.

| | | | |
|---|---|---|---|
| 184 | 60c.+30c. Type **61** | 2·50 | 1·50 |
| 185 | 100c.+50c. Globes on top of columns and doorway | 3·25 | 2·50 |

**62** Livia Ecury (teacher and nurse)

**1996.** Anniversaries. Multicoloured.

| | | | |
|---|---|---|---|
| 186 | 60c. Type **62** (5th death) | 1·50 | 1·50 |
| 187 | 60c. Laura Wernet-Paskel (teacher and politician, 85th birth) | 1·50 | 1·50 |
| 188 | 60c. Lolita Euson (poet, 2nd death) | 1·50 | 1·50 |

**63** Rabbits at Bus-stop

**1996.** Child Welfare. Comic Strips. Multicoloured.

| | | | |
|---|---|---|---|
| 189 | 50c.+25c. Type **63** | 1·90 | 1·50 |
| 190 | 70c.+35c. Mother accompanying young owl to school | 2·30 | 2·00 |
| 191 | 100c.+50c. Boy flying kite with friend | 2·75 | 2·50 |

**64** Children at the Seaside and Words on Signpost

**1997.** "Year of Papiamento" (Creole language). Multicoloured.

| | | | |
|---|---|---|---|
| 192 | 50c. Type **64** | 1·10 | 1·10 |
| 193 | 140c. Sunrise over ocean | 2·75 | 2·75 |

**65** Postman on Bicycle, 1936–57

**1997.** America. The Postman. Multicoloured.

| | | | |
|---|---|---|---|
| 194 | 60c. Type **65** | 2·75 | 1·70 |
| 195 | 70c. Postman delivering package by jeep, 1957–88 | 2·75 | 1·70 |
| 196 | 80c. Postman delivering letter from motor scooter, 1995 | 2·75 | 1·70 |

**66** Decorated Cunucu House

**1997.** Aruban Architecture. Multicoloured.

| | | | |
|---|---|---|---|
| 197 | 30c. Type **66** | 90 | 60 |
| 198 | 65c. Bannistered steps | 1·70 | 1·50 |
| 199 | 100c. Arends Building (vert) | 2·20 | 2·00 |

**67** Merlin and Lighthouse

**1997.** "Pacific 97" International Stamp Exhibition, San Francisco. Multicoloured.

| | | | |
|---|---|---|---|
| 200 | 90c. Type **67** | 2·75 | 2·20 |
| 201 | 90c. Windswept trees and dolphin | 2·75 | 2·20 |
| 202 | 90c. Iguana on rock and cacti | 2·75 | 2·20 |
| 203 | 90c. Three types of fishes and one dolphin | 2·75 | 2·20 |
| 204 | 90c. Two dolphins and fishes | 2·75 | 2·20 |

| | | | |
|---|---|---|---|
| 205 | 90c. Burrowing owl on shore, turtle and lionfish | 2·75 | 2·20 |
| 206 | 90c. Stingray, rock beauty, angelfishes, squirrelfish and coral reef | 2·75 | 2·20 |
| 207 | 90c. Diver and stern of shipwreck | 2·75 | 2·20 |
| 208 | 90c. Shipwreck, reef and fishes | 2·75 | 2·20 |

Nos. 200/8 were issued together, se-tenant, forming a composite design.

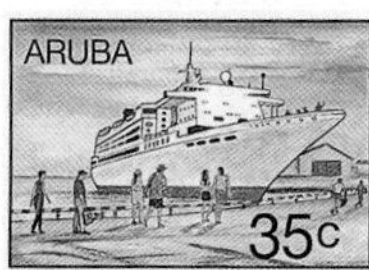

**68** Passengers approaching Cruise Liner

**1997.** Cruise Tourism. Multicoloured.

| | | | |
|---|---|---|---|
| 209 | 35c. Type **68** | 1·10 | 90 |
| 210 | 50c. Passengers disembarking | 1·50 | 1·10 |
| 211 | 150c. Cruise liner at sea and launch at shore | 3·00 | 2·75 |

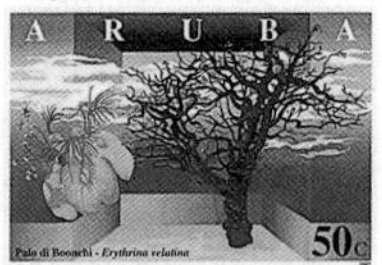

**69** Coral Tree

**1997.** Trees. Multicoloured.

| | | | |
|---|---|---|---|
| 212 | 50c. Type **69** | 1·50 | 1·10 |
| 213 | 60c. "Cordia dentata" | 1·70 | 1·50 |
| 214 | 70c. "Tabebuia billbergii" | 2·00 | 1·50 |
| 215 | 130c. Lignum vitae | 2·75 | 2·20 |

**70** Girl among Aloes

**1997.** Child Welfare. Child and Nature. Mult.

| | | | |
|---|---|---|---|
| 216 | 50c.+25c. Type **70** | 1·70 | 1·40 |
| 217 | 70c.+35c. Boy and butterfly (vert) | 2·50 | 2·20 |
| 218 | 100c.+50c. Girl swimming underwater by coral reef | 2·50 | 2·75 |

**71** Fort Zoutman

**1998.** Bicentenary of Fort Zoutman.

| | | | | |
|---|---|---|---|---|
| 219 | **71** | 30c. multicoloured | 1·10 | 90 |
| 220 | **71** | 250c. multicoloured | 4·75 | 4·25 |

Each design consists of alternating strips in brown tones or black and white. When the 250c. is laid on top of the 30c., the brown strips form a composite design of the fort in its early years and the black and white strips a composite design of the fort after 1929, when various alterations were made.

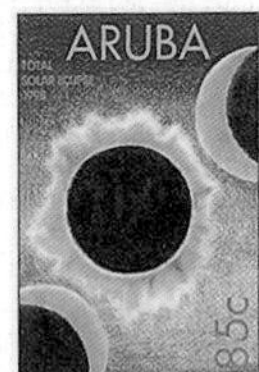

**72** Stages of Eclipse

**1998.** Total Solar Eclipse. Multicoloured.

| | | | |
|---|---|---|---|
| 221 | 85c. Type **72** | 2·20 | 1·50 |
| 222 | 100c. Globe showing path of eclipse and map of Aruba plotting duration of total darkness | 2·50 | 1·70 |

**73** Globe, Emblem and Wheelchair balanced on Map of Aruba

**1998.** "Solidarity" Anniversaries. Multicoloured.

| | | | |
|---|---|---|---|
| 223 | 60c.+30c. Type **73** (50th anniv of Lions Club of Aruba) | 2·20 | 1·60 |
| 224 | 100c.+50c. Boy reading, emblem and grandmother in rocking chair (60th anniv of Rotary Club of Aruba) | 3·25 | 2·50 |

**74** Tropical Mockingbird

**1998.** Birds. Multicoloured.

| | | | |
|---|---|---|---|
| 225 | 50c. Type **74** | 1·90 | 1·10 |
| 226 | 60c. American kestrel (vert) | 2·20 | 1·50 |
| 227 | 70c. Troupial (vert) | 2·20 | 1·50 |
| 228 | 150c. Bananaquit | 3·75 | 3·25 |

**75** Villagers processing Corn

**1998.** World Stamp Day.

| | | | | |
|---|---|---|---|---|
| 229 | **75** | 225c. multicoloured | 6·25 | 5·00 |

**76** Ribbon Dance

**1998.** Child Welfare. Multicoloured.

| | | | |
|---|---|---|---|
| 230 | 50c.+25c. Type **76** | 1·60 | 1·50 |
| 231 | 80c.+40c. Boy playing cuarta (four-string guitar) | 2·50 | 2·50 |
| 232 | 100c. + 50c. Basketball | 3·25 | 2·75 |

**77** Two Donkeys

**1999.** The Donkey. Multicoloured.

| | | | |
|---|---|---|---|
| 233 | 40c. Type **77** | 1·60 | 90 |
| 234 | 65c. Two adults and foal | 1·80 | 1·50 |
| 235 | 100c. Adult and foal | 2·75 | 2·20 |

**78** "Opuntia wentiana"

**1999.** Cacti. Multicoloured.

| | | | |
|---|---|---|---|
| 236 | 50c. Type **78** | 1·50 | 1·00 |
| 237 | 60c. "Lemaireocereus griseus" | 1·70 | 1·20 |
| 238 | 70c. "Cephalocereus lanuginosus" ("Cadushi di carona") | 1·70 | 1·50 |
| 239 | 75c. "Cephalocereus lanuginosus" ("Cadushi") | 2·00 | 1·70 |

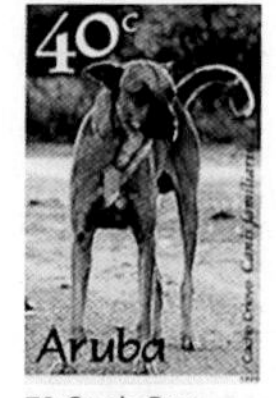

**79** Creole Dog

**1999.** Creole Dogs ("Canis familiaris"). Mult.

| | | | |
|---|---|---|---|
| 240 | 40c. Type **79** | 1·70 | 1·10 |
| 241 | 60c. White dog standing on rock | 2·00 | 1·50 |
| 242 | 80c. Dog sitting by sea | 2·20 | 1·70 |
| 243 | 165c. Black and tan dog sitting on rock | 3·75 | 3·25 |

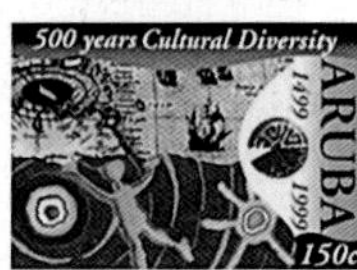

**80** Indian Cave Drawings and Antique Map

**1999.** 500 Years of Cultural Diversity. Mult.

| | | | |
|---|---|---|---|
| 244 | 150c. Type **80** | 2·75 | 2·50 |
| 245 | 175c. Indian cave drawings and carnival headdress | 3·25 | 3·00 |
| **MS**246 | 90×60 mm. Nos. 244/5 | 6·75 | 5·50 |

**81** Public Library and Children

**1999.** 50th Anniv of Public Library Service. Mult.

| | | | |
|---|---|---|---|
| 247 | 70c. Type **81** | 1·60 | 1·70 |
| 248 | 100c. Library, Santa Cruz | 2·30 | 2·00 |

**82** Boy with Fisherman

**1999.** Child Welfare. Multicoloured.

| | | | |
|---|---|---|---|
| 249 | 60c.+30c. Type **82** | 1·70 | 1·50 |
| 250 | 80c.+40c. Man reading to children | 2·50 | 2·20 |
| 251 | 100c.+50c. Woman with child (vert) | 3·25 | 2·75 |

**83** Three Wise Men

**1999.** Christmas. Multicoloured. Self-adhesive.

| | | | |
|---|---|---|---|
| 252 | 40c. Type **83** | 1·80 | 1·10 |
| 253 | 70c. Shepherds | 2·20 | 1·50 |
| 254 | 100c. Holy Family | 2·75 | 2·00 |

**84** *Norops lineatus*

**2000.** Reptiles. Multicoloured.

| | | | |
|---|---|---|---|
| 255 | 40c. Type **84** | 7·75 | 80 |
| 256 | 60c. Greeen iguana (vert) | 1·60 | 1·50 |
| 257 | 75c. Annulated snake (vert) | 1·80 | 1·50 |
| 258 | 150c. Racerunner | 3·75 | 2·50 |

**85** Flags

**2000.** America. A.I.D.S. Awareness. Multicoloured.

| | | | |
|---|---|---|---|
| 259 | 75c. Type **85** | 2·00 | 2·00 |
| 260 | 175c. Ribbon on globe (vert) | 3·75 | 3·75 |

**86** Bank Facade

**2000.** Anniversaries. Multicoloured.

| | | | |
|---|---|---|---|
| 261 | 150c. Type **86** (75th anniv of Aruba Bank) | 3·25 | 2·50 |
| 262 | 165c. Chapel (250th anniv of Alto Vista Chapel) | 3·25 | 2·75 |

**87** West Indian Top Shell

**2000.** Aspects of Aruba. Multicoloured.

| | | | |
|---|---|---|---|
| 263 | 15c. Type **87** | 50 | 40 |
| 264 | 25c. Guadirikiri cave | 85 | 50 |
| 265 | 35c. Mud-house (vert) | 1·00 | 80 |
| 267 | 55c. Cacti | 1·50 | 1·10 |
| 269 | 85c. Hooiberg | 2·00 | 1·70 |
| 271 | 100c. Gold smelter, Balashi (vert) | 2·50 | 2·00 |
| 272 | 250c. Rock crystal | 5·00 | 4·50 |
| 275 | 500c. Conchi | 9·50 | 8·25 |

**88** Children at Beach Playground

**2000.** "Solidarity". Multicoloured.

| | | | |
|---|---|---|---|
| 280 | 75c.+35c. Type **88** | 2·10 | 1·80 |
| 281 | 100c.+50c. Children building sandcastles | 3·50 | 2·75 |

**89** "Solar Energy" (Nikki Johanna Teresia Willems)

**2000.** Child Welfare. "Stampin' the Future". Winning Entries in Children's International Painting Competition. Multicoloured.

| | | | |
|---|---|---|---|
| 282 | 60c.+30c. Type **89** | 2·10 | 1·70 |
| 283 | 80c.+40c. "Environmental Protection" (Samantha Jeanne Tromp) | 2·30 | 2·00 |
| 284 | 100c.+50c. "Future Vehicles" (Jennifer Huntington) | 3·25 | 2·75 |

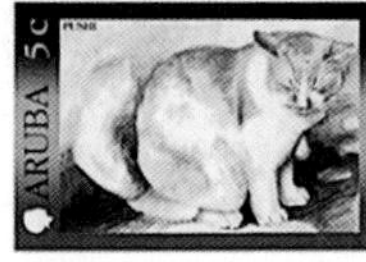

**90** Cat

**2001.** Domestic Animals. Multicoloured.

| | | | |
|---|---|---|---|
| 285 | 5c. Type **90** | 65 | 35 |
| 286 | 30c. Tortoise | 1·70 | 1·10 |
| 287 | 50c. Rabbit | 1·70 | 1·10 |
| 288 | 200c. Brown-throated conure | 4·50 | 4·00 |

**91** Shaman preparing for Sun Ceremony

**2001.** 40 Years of Mascaruba (amateur theatre group). Depicting scenes from Macuarima, History or Legend? (musical play). Mult.

| | | | |
|---|---|---|---|
| 289 | 60c. Type **91** | 1·60 | 1·10 |
| 290 | 150c. Love scene between Guadarikiri and Blanco | 3·00 | 2·75 |

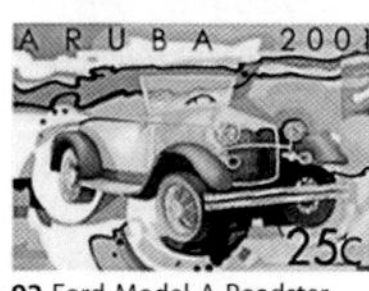

**92** Ford Model A Roadster, 1930

**2001.** Motor Cars. Multicoloured.

| | | | |
|---|---|---|---|
| 291 | 25c. Type **92** | 1·80 | 1·10 |
| 292 | 40c. Citroen Comerciale saloon, 1933 | 1·80 | 1·10 |
| 293 | 70c. Plymouth Pick-up, 1948 | 2·00 | 1·70 |
| 294 | 75c. Edsel corsair convertable, 1959 | 2·10 | 1·70 |

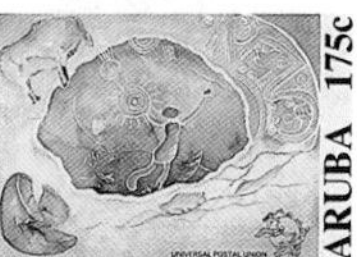

**93** Rock Drawings

**2001.** Universal Postal Union. United Nations Year of Dialogue among Civilizations.

| | | | | |
|---|---|---|---|---|
| 295 | **93** | 175c. multicoloured | 4·00 | 3·25 |

**94** Pedestrians using Crossing

**2001.** Child Welfare. International Year of Volunteers. Multicoloured.

| | | | |
|---|---|---|---|
| 296 | 40c. + 20c. Type **94** | 1·60 | 1·10 |
| 297 | 60c. + 30c. Boys walking dogs | 2·10 | 1·70 |
| 298 | 100c. + 50c. Children putting litter in bin | 3·25 | 2·75 |

**95** Dakota Airport, 1950

**2002.** Queen Beatrix Airport. Multicoloured.

| | | | |
|---|---|---|---|
| 299 | 30c. Type **95** | 1·00 | 55 |
| 300 | 75c. Queen Beatrix Airport, 1972 | 1·90 | 1·50 |
| 301 | 175c. Queen Beatrix Airport, 2000 | 3·75 | 3·25 |

Dakota Airport was re-named Princess Beatrix Airport in 1955 and Queen Beatrix Airport in 1972.

**96** Prince Willem-Alexander and Princess Maxima

**2002.** Wedding of Crown Prince Willem-Alexander to Maxima Zorreguieta. Multicoloured.

| | | | |
|---|---|---|---|
| 302 | 60c. Type **96** | 1·50 | 1·10 |
| 303 | 300c. Prince Willem-Alexander and Princess Máxima facing right | 5·50 | 5·50 |

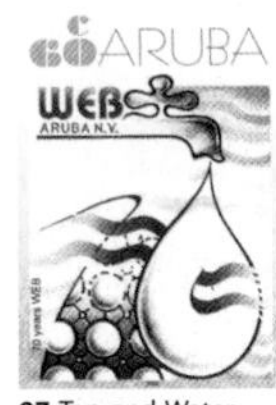

**97** Tap and Water Droplet

**2002.** 70th Anniv of Water Company (W. E. B.). Multicoloured.

| | | | |
|---|---|---|---|
| 304 | 60c. Type **97** | 1·20 | 1·10 |
| 305 | 85c. Water pipes (horiz) | 1·70 | 1·60 |
| 306 | 165c. Water meter and meter reader | 3·25 | 3·25 |

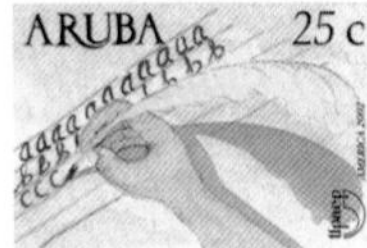

**98** Hand holding Quill Pen

**2002.** America. Literacy Campaign. Multicoloured.

| | | | |
|---|---|---|---|
| 307 | 25c. Type **98** | 1·10 | 90 |
| 308 | 100c. Alphabet on wall and boy on step-ladder | 2·20 | 1·90 |

**99** *U-156* Submarine firing on Lago Oil Refinery

**2002.** Second World War. Multicoloured.

| | | | |
|---|---|---|---|
| 309 | 60c. Type **99** | 2·20 | 1·10 |
| 310 | 75c. *Pedernales* (oil-tanker) in flames | 2·20 | 1·40 |
| 311 | 150c. "Boy" Ecury (resistance fighter) (statue) (vert) | 3·25 | 2·75 |

**100** Boy, Iguana and Goat

**2002.** Child Welfare. Animals. Multicoloured.

| | | | |
|---|---|---|---|
| 312 | 40c.+20c. Type **100** | 1·20 | 1·10 |
| 313 | 60c.+30c. Girl, turtle and crab (horiz) | 2·50 | 1·70 |
| 314 | 100c.+50c. Pelicans, boy and parakeet | 3·00 | 2·75 |

**101** House at Fontein

**2003.** Mud Houses. Multicoloured.

| | | | |
|---|---|---|---|
| 315 | 40c. Type **101** | 90 | 80 |
| 316 | 60c. House at Ari Kok | 1·20 | 1·10 |
| 317 | 75c. House at Fontein | 1·60 | 1·50 |

**102** The Trupialen Boys Choir

**2003.** 50th Anniv of "De Trupialen" (boys' organization). Multicoloured.

| | | | |
|---|---|---|---|
| 318 | 30c. Type **102** | 65 | 55 |
| 319 | 50c. Puppet theatre posters | 1·10 | 1·00 |
| 320 | 100c. Organization emblems | 2·20 | 1·90 |

**103** *Schomburgkia humboldtii*

**2003.** Orchids. Multicoloured.

| | | | |
|---|---|---|---|
| 321 | 75c. Type **103** | 1·80 | 1·70 |
| 322 | 500c. *Brassavola nodosa* | 11·00 | 9·00 |

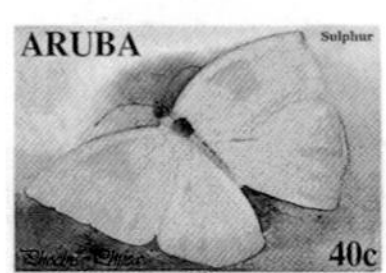

**104** Orange-barred Sulphur Butterfly

**2003.** Butterflies. Multicoloured.

| | | | |
|---|---|---|---|
| 323 | 40c. Type **104** | 1·30 | 1·10 |
| 324 | 75c. Monarch | 1·90 | 1·60 |
| 325 | 85c. Hairstreak | 2·20 | 1·80 |
| 326 | 175c. Gulf fritillary | 3·75 | 3·25 |

**105** Hawksbill Turtle (*Eretmochelys imbricate*)

**2003.** Endangered Species. Turtles. Multicoloured.

| | | | |
|---|---|---|---|
| 327 | 25c. Type **105** | 1·20 | 1·00 |
| 328 | 60c. Leatherback turtle (*Dermochelys coricea*) (horiz) | 1·40 | 1·20 |
| 329 | 75c. Green turtle (*Chelonia mydas*) | 1·80 | 1·50 |
| 330 | 150c. Loggerhead turtle (*Caretta caretta*) (horiz) | 3·50 | 3·00 |

**106** Baseball

**2003.** Child Welfare. Children and Sport.

| | | | |
|---|---|---|---|
| 331 | 40c.+20c. Type **106** | 1·20 | 1·00 |
| 332 | 60c.+30c. Volleyball | 1·80 | 1·50 |
| 333 | 100c.+50c. Football | 3·50 | 3·00 |

**107** Masks and Headdresses

**2004.** 50th Anniv of Carnival. Multicoloured.

| | | | |
|---|---|---|---|
| 334 | 60c. Type **107** | 95 | 80 |
| 335 | 75c. Woman's face (vert) | 1·40 | 1·20 |
| 336 | 150c. Heads wearing carnival headdresses | 3·00 | 2·50 |

**108** Sandwich Tern (*Sterna sandvicensis*)

**2004.** Birds. Multicoloured.

| | | | |
|---|---|---|---|
| 337 | 70c. Type **108** | 1·40 | 1·20 |
| 338 | 75c. Brown pelican (*Pelecanus occidentalis*) | 1·60 | 1·30 |
| 339 | 80c. Frigate bird (*Fregata magnificens*) | 1·70 | 1·40 |
| 340 | 90c. Laughing gull (*Larus atricilla*) | 1·80 | 1·50 |

**109** Parrotfish

**2004.** Fish. Multicoloured.

| | | | |
|---|---|---|---|
| 341 | 40c. Type **109** | 1·10 | 90 |
| 342 | 60c. Queen angelfish | 1·30 | 1·10 |
| 343 | 75c. Squirrelfish | 1·60 | 1·30 |
| 344 | 100c. Small-mouthed grunt | 1·90 | 1·60 |

**110** Children holding Maracas

**2004.** Child Welfare. Musical Instruments. Multicoloured.

| | | | |
|---|---|---|---|
| 345 | 60c.+30c. Type **110** | 1·80 | 1·50 |
| 346 | 85c.+40c. Three children and steel drum | 2·40 | 2·10 |
| 347 | 100c.+50c. Boy playing wiri and girl holding tambourine | 3·00 | 2·50 |

**111** Presents and Decorated Tree

**2004.** Christmas and New Year. Multicoloured.

| | | | |
|---|---|---|---|
| 348 | 50c. Type **111** | 95 | 80 |
| 349 | 85c. Parcels, carol singers and candle | 1·70 | 1·40 |
| 350 | 125c. Fireworks | 2·40 | 2·10 |

**112** Interconnecting Islands (Aruba, Curacao, Bonaire, Saba, St. Maarten and St. Eustatius)

**2004.** 50th Anniv of Charter of the Kingdom (statute establishing partial autonomy). Multicoloured.

| | | | |
|---|---|---|---|
| 351 | 160c. Type **112** | 2·30 | 2·00 |
| 352 | 165c. Kingdom Statute monument | 2·40 | 2·10 |

**113** Sun and Flower

**2004.** Greetings Stamps. Multicoloured.

| | | | |
|---|---|---|---|
| 353 | 60c. Type **113** ("Thank you") | 1·10 | 90 |
| 354 | 75c. Two rabbits ("Love") | 1·20 | 1·00 |
| 355 | 135c. Fish ("Get well soon") | 1·90 | 1·60 |
| 356 | 215c. Balloons ("Congratulations") | 3·50 | 3·00 |

**114** Race Car and Spectators

**2005.** Drag Racing. Multicoloured.

| | | | |
|---|---|---|---|
| 357 | 60c. Type **114** | 1·20 | 1·00 |
| 358 | 85c. Parachute opening at race end | 1·80 | 1·50 |
| 359 | 185c. Race start | 3·00 | 2·50 |

**115** Queen Beatrix and Prince Claus

**2005.** 25th Anniv of Coronation of Queen Beatrix. Sheet 144×75 mm containing T 115 and similar vert designs. Multicoloured.

| | | | |
|---|---|---|---|
| **MS**360 | 30c. Type **115**; 60c. Seated; 75c. With Nelson Mandela; 105c.Wearing glasses; 215c. Wearing hat | 7·75 | 7·75 |

**116** Sunset

**2005.** Tourism. Sunsets. Multicoloured.

| | | | |
|---|---|---|---|
| 361 | 60c. Type **116** | 95 | 80 |
| 362 | 100c. Palm tree | 1·60 | 1·30 |
| 363 | 205c. Pelicans | 3·25 | 2·75 |

**117** American Kestrel (*Falco sparverius*)

**2005.** Birds. Multicoloured.

| | | | |
|---|---|---|---|
| 364 | 60c. Type **117** | 1·20 | 1·00 |
| 365 | 75c. Burrowing owl (*Athene cunicularia*) | 1·60 | 1·30 |
| 366 | 135c. Osprey (*Pandion haliaetus*) | 2·30 | 2·00 |
| 367 | 200c. Common caracara (*Polyborus plancus*) | 3·50 | 3·00 |
| **MS**368 | 110×70 mm. Nos. 364/7 | 7·75 | 7·75 |

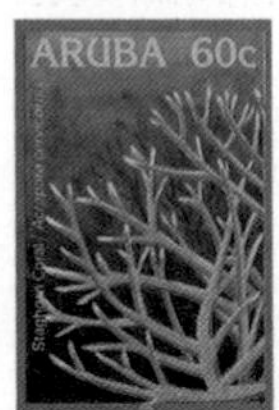

**118** *Acropora cervicornis*

**2005.** Corals. Multicoloured.

| | | | |
|---|---|---|---|
| 369 | 60c. Type **118** | 1·10 | 95 |
| 370 | 75c. *Millepora complanata* | 1·40 | 1·20 |
| 371 | 100c. *Iciligorgia schrammi* | 1·80 | 1·50 |
| 372 | 215c. *Diploria strigosa* | 3·75 | 3·25 |

**119** Girl and Stamps

**2005.** Child Welfare. Philately. Multicoloured.

| | | | |
|---|---|---|---|
| 373 | 75c. Type **119** | 1·50 | 1·30 |
| 374 | 85c. Boy holding magnifier and album | 1·60 | 1·40 |
| 375 | 125c. Boy putting stamps in album | 2·30 | 2·00 |

**120** "House of Savaneta" (Jean George Pandellis)

**2006.** Art. Multicoloured.

| | | | |
|---|---|---|---|
| 376 | 60c. Type **120** | 1·20 | 1·00 |
| 377 | 75c. "Haf di Rei" (Mateo Hayde) | 1·50 | 1·30 |
| 378 | 185c. "Landscape" (Julie Oduber) | 3·50 | 3·00 |

**121** Emblem

**2006.** 50th Anniv of YMCA. Multicoloured.

| | | | |
|---|---|---|---|
| 379 | 75c. Type **121** | 1·50 | 1·30 |
| 380 | 205c. Children at play (horiz) | 3·75 | 3·25 |

**122** Tree and Log Bridge

**2006.** Washington 2006 International Stamp Exhibition. Sheet 98×88 mm containing T 122 and similar multicoloured design.

| | | | |
|---|---|---|---|
| **MS**381 | 500c.×2, Type **122**; Cacti and boats (vert) | 13·50 | 13·50 |

The stamps and margins of **MS**381 form a composite design.

**123** Goalkeeper

**2006.** World Cup Football Championship, Germany. Multicoloured.

| | | | |
|---|---|---|---|
| 382 | 75c. Type **123** | 1·40 | 1·20 |
| 383 | 215c. Hands holding globe as football | 3·75 | 3·25 |

**124** Surf Boards, Boats, Windsurfers and Kitesurfer

**2006.** 20th Anniv of Hi-Winds Windsurfing Competition. Multicoloured.

| | | | |
|---|---|---|---|
| 384 | 60c. Type **124** | 1·00 | 85 |
| 385 | 100c. Leaping kitesurfer | 1·60 | 1·30 |
| 386 | 125c. Windsurfers | 2·00 | 1·70 |

**125** Fire Hazards

**2006.** Fire Prevention. Multicoloured.

| | | | |
|---|---|---|---|
| 387 | 60c. Type **125** | 1·00 | 85 |
| 388 | 100c. Firefighters | 1·60 | 1·30 |
| 389 | 205c. Fire appliances | 3·25 | 2·75 |

**126** House and Goat

**2006.** Arikok National Park. Multicoloured.

| | | | |
|---|---|---|---|
| 390 | 75c. Type **126** | 1·30 | 1·10 |
| 391 | 100c. Cacti, valley and eagle (vert) | 1·60 | 1·30 |
| 392 | 200c. Cacti and owl | 3·25 | 2·75 |

**127** Dancers and Boar

**2007.** New Year. Year of the Pig. Sheet 78×62 mm containing T 127 and similar multicoloured design.

| | | | |
|---|---|---|---|
| **MS**393 | 205c. Type **127**; 215c. Dragon (*vert*) | 6·50 | 6·50 |

The stamp and margin of **MS393** form a composite design.

**128** Luciana Maria Koolman and Original Building

**2007.** 50th Anniv of Casa Cuna Children's Home Foundation. Multicoloured.

| | | | |
|---|---|---|---|
| 394 | 50c. Type **128** | 85 | 70 |
| 395 | 125c. Children enclosed in hands | 2·00 | 1·70 |
| 396 | 150c. New building | 2·40 | 2·10 |

**129** Museum of Antiquities

**2007.** Museums. Multicoloured.

| | | | |
|---|---|---|---|
| 397 | 70c. Type **129** | 1·10 | 95 |
| 398 | 85c. Numismatic museum | 1·30 | 1·10 |
| 399 | 100c. Archaeological museum | 1·50 | 1·30 |
| 400 | 135c. Historical museum | 2·10 | 1·80 |

**130** Pipeline of *Pedernalis* (wrecked oil tanker)

**2007.** Wrecks and Reefs. Sheet 87×70 mm containing T 130 and similar horiz designs. Multicoloured.

| | | | |
|---|---|---|---|
| **MS**401 | 200c. Type **130**; 300c. Convair 400 aircraft wreck; 500c. Sea turtle and *Jane* (wrecked freighter); 500c. *Antilla* (wrecked freighter) and fish | 17·00 | 17·00 |

The stamps and margins of **MS**401 form a composite design.

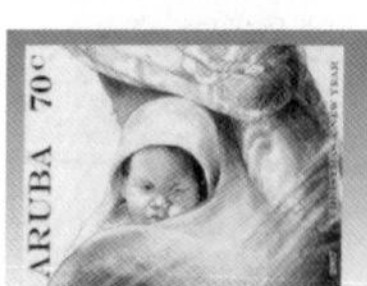

**131** Mother and Child

**2007.** Christmas. Multicoloured.

| | | | |
|---|---|---|---|
| 402 | 70c. Type **131** | 1·20 | 1·10 |
| 403 | 100c. Girl with presents | 1·70 | 1·50 |
| 404 | 150c. Child with balloon | 2·50 | 2·30 |

**132** Beached Catamarans

**2007.** Catamaran Regatta. Multicoloured.

| | | | |
|---|---|---|---|
| 405 | 40c. Type **132** | 70 | 60 |
| 406 | 80c. Two catamarans and buoy | 1·40 | 1·20 |
| 407 | 125c. Tacking | 2·10 | 1·90 |

| | | | |
|---|---|---|---|
| 408 | 130c. Racing | 2·20 | 2·00 |

**133** As Small Child

**2008.** 70th Birth Anniv of Queen Beatrix. Multicoloured.

| | | | |
|---|---|---|---|
| 409 | 75c. Type **133** | 1·30 | 1·10 |
| 410 | 125c. With Prince Claus and new born Prince Willem Alexander | 2·10 | 1·90 |
| 411 | 250c. Wearing regalia on day of accession | 4·25 | 3·75 |
| 412 | 300c. With Crown Prince Willem Alexander and his family | 5·00 | 4·50 |

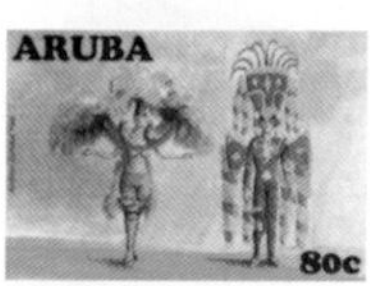

**134** Carnival

**2008.** Cultural Heritage. Multicoloured.

| | | | |
|---|---|---|---|
| 413 | 80c. Type **134** | 1·40 | 1·20 |
| 414 | 130c. Street entertainers | 2·20 | 2·00 |
| 415 | 250c. Musicians, dancers, cockerel and campfire | 3·50 | 3·00 |
| 416 | 300c. Musicians and house-holders | 4·75 | 4·25 |

**135** Athletics

**2008.** Olympic Games, Beijing. Multicoloured.

| | | | |
|---|---|---|---|
| 417 | 50c. Type **135** | 85 | 75 |
| 418 | 75c. Synchronised swimming | 1·30 | 1·10 |
| 419 | 100c. Gymnastics (vert) | 1·70 | 1·50 |
| 420 | 175c. Judo | 2·10 | 1·90 |

**136** Burrowing Owl

**2008.** Aruban Cultural Year. Burrowing Owl Athene cunicularia arubensis . Multicoloured.

| | | | |
|---|---|---|---|
| 421 | 100c. Type **136** | 1·80 | 1·60 |
| 422 | 150c. Two owls (horiz ) | 2·75 | 2·40 |
| 423 | 350c. Head | 6·25 | 5·75 |

**137** FRX Super Glide Big Boy

**2008.** Harley Davidson Motorcycles. Multicoloured.

| | | | |
|---|---|---|---|
| 424 | 175c. Type **137** | 3·25 | 3·00 |
| 425 | 225c. Knucklehead | 4·00 | 3·50 |
| 426 | 305c. Roadking | 5·25 | 4·75 |

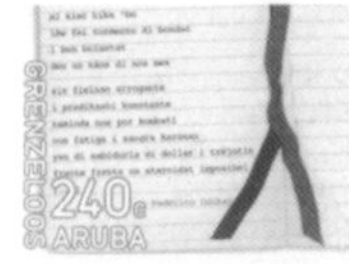

**138** Script (poem by Frederico Oduber)

**2008.** Netherlands and Beyond. Sheet 145×75 mm containing T 138 and similar multicoloured designs.

| | | | |
|---|---|---|---|
| **MS**427 | 240c. Type **138**; 240c. *Wata-pana* (first magazine in Papiamento (local language)) (vert); 240c. Henry Habibe and poem (vert) | 14·50 | 14·50 |

No. **MS**427 also includes a Netherlands Antilles 5c. stamp (Houses (architecture)) and a Netherlands 92c. stamp (chillies and cheese (food)).

The 'foreign' stamps could only be used in their country of origin.

**139** *Calatropis procea*

**2008.** Flowers. Multicoloured.

| | | | |
|---|---|---|---|
| 428 | 100c. Type **139** | 1·80 | 1·60 |
| 429 | 185c. *Thespesia populnea* | 3·50 | 3·00 |
| 430 | 200c. *Cryptostegia grandiflora* | 3·50 | 3·25 |
| 431 | 215c. *Passiflora foetida* | 3·75 | 3·50 |

**140** *Self Portrait*

**2008.** International Culture. Drawings by Rembrandt. Multicoloured.

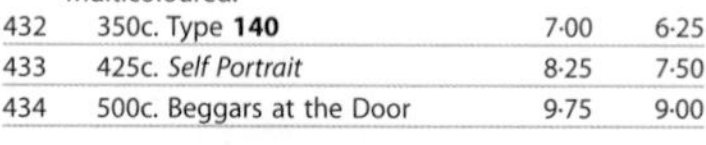

| | | | |
|---|---|---|---|
| 432 | 350c. Type **140** | 7·00 | 6·25 |
| 433 | 425c. *Self Portrait* | 8·25 | 7·50 |
| 434 | 500c. Beggars at the Door | 9·75 | 9·00 |

**141** Donkeys transporting Water

**2008.** Aruba in the Old Days. Each brown and ochre.

| | | | |
|---|---|---|---|
| 435 | 100c. Type **141** | 2·00 | 1·80 |
| 436 | 200c. Two roomed clay house | 4·00 | 3·50 |
| 437 | 215c. Harvesting *Aloe vera* | 4·25 | 3·75 |

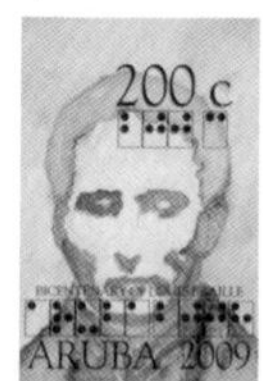

**142** Louis Braille

**2009.** Birth Bicentenary of Louis Braille (inventor of Braille writing for the blind). Multicoloured.

| | | | |
|---|---|---|---|
| 438 | 200c. Type **142** | 4·00 | 3·50 |
| 439 | 215c. Hand holding white stick | 4·25 | 3·75 |

**143** Carnival Queen

**2009.** 55th Anniv of Aruba Carnival. Sheet 115×95 mm containing T 143 and similar horiz designs. Multicoloured.

| | | | |
|---|---|---|---|
| **MS**440 | 75c. Type **143**; 100c. Float with clown; 175c. Float with champagne bottle, large '55' bottom left; 225c. Dancers | 11·00 | 11·50 |

**143a** Kapel Alto Vista

**2009.** Architecture

| | | | | |
|---|---|---|---|---|
| 440a | **143a** | 5c. multicoloured | 10 | 10 |
| 440b | | 10c. multicoloured | 15 | 10 |
| 440c | | 25c. multicoloured | 40 | 25 |
| 440d | | 50c. multicoloured | 85 | 65 |
| 440e | | 85c. multicoloured | 1·20 | 1·00 |
| 440f | | 90c. multicoloured | 1·50 | 1·30 |
| 440g | | 100c. multicoloured | 1·70 | 1·50 |
| 440h | | 125c. multicoloured | 2·40 | 1·90 |
| 440i | | 130c. multicoloured | 2·50 | 1·90 |
| 440j | | 135c. multicoloured | 2·60 | 2·20 |
| 440k | | 140c. multicoloured | 2·60 | 2·20 |

| | | | |
|---|---|---|---|
| 440l | 200c. multicoloured | 3·50 | 2·75 |
| 440m | 215c. multicoloured | 3·75 | 3·25 |
| 440n | 220c. multicoloured | 4·00 | 3·50 |

**144** Tunnel of Love (Baranca Suna) Cave

**2009.** Caves. Multicoloured.

| | | | |
|---|---|---|---|
| 441 | 175c. Type **144** | 3·50 | 3·25 |
| 442 | 200c. Fountain (Fontein) | 4·00 | 3·50 |
| 443 | 225c. Guardirikiri (Quadirikiri Grot) | 4·25 | 4·00 |

**145** Ozone Layer

**2009.** Global Warming Awareness Campaign. Sheet 82×64 mm containing T 145 and similar horiz designs. Multicoloured.

**MS**444 200c. Type **145**; 250c. Melting ice caps; 250c. Pollution; 300c. Alternative energy sources 17·00 17·00

**146** California Lighthouse

**2009.** Architecture. Sheet 86×86 mm containing T 146 and similar multicoloured designs.

**MS**445 175c. Type **146**; 250c. Plaza Daniel Leo, Oranjestad (horiz); 275c. Henriquez Building (horiz); 325c. Main Building, Ecury Complex 18·00 18·00

**147** Girl Reading

**2009.** 60th Anniv of National Library. Each black and new blue.

| | | | |
|---|---|---|---|
| 446 | 185c. Type **147** | 3·50 | 3·25 |
| 447 | 300c. Woman reading | 6·00 | 5·25 |

**148** *Stenella frontalis* (Atlantic spotted dolphin)

**2009.** Dophins. Multicoloured.

| | | | |
|---|---|---|---|
| 448 | 125c. Type **148** | 1·90 | 1·50 |
| 449 | 200c. *Steno bredanensis* (rough-toothed dolphin) | 4·00 | 3·50 |
| 450 | 300c. Two Atlantic spotted dolphins facing right | 6·00 | 5·25 |
| 451 | 325c. Several rough-toothed dolphins | 6·50 | 5·75 |

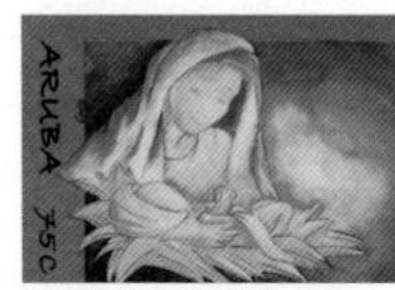

**149** Virgin and Child

**2009.** Christmas. Multicoloured.

| | | | |
|---|---|---|---|
| 452 | 75c. Type **149** | 1·30 | 1·10 |
| 453 | 120c. Angel | 1·90 | 1·70 |
| 454 | 125c. Hands holding globe, '2009' and 'Peace' | 2·10 | 1·90 |
| 455 | 210c. Shepherds and star | 4·50 | 3·50 |

**150** Palm Tree, Wall and Fish (paper)

**2010.** Recycle. Multicoloured.

| | | | |
|---|---|---|---|
| 456 | 90c. Type **150** | 1·80 | 1·60 |
| 457 | 180c. House and cow (card-board and pasta) | 3·50 | 3·25 |
| 458 | 325c. Fish and boat (paper, bottle tops and lolly sticks) | 6·50 | 5·75 |

**151** Seaplane

**2010.** Historic Aircraft. Multicoloured.

| | | | |
|---|---|---|---|
| 459 | 250c. Type **151** | 4·50 | 4·25 |
| 460 | 500c. Curtiss NC-4 | 8·75 | 8·50 |

**152** Two Junior Scouts

**2010.** Scouting. Multicoloured.

| | | | |
|---|---|---|---|
| 461 | 85c. Type **152** | 60 | 55 |
| 462 | 95c. Two scouts and campfire | 75 | 70 |
| 463 | 135c. Scout emerging from tent | 1·50 | 1·40 |
| 464 | 180c. Four scouts map reading | 2·00 | 1·90 |

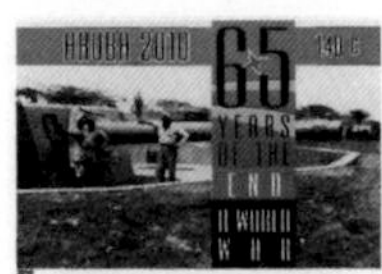

**153** Soldiers in Gun Placement

**2010.** 65th Anniv of End of World War II. Multicoloured.

| | | | |
|---|---|---|---|
| 465 | 140c. Type **153** | 1·60 | 1·50 |
| 466 | 200c. Soldiers and missile | 2·50 | 2·40 |
| 467 | 275c. Guns on foundering ship | 3·00 | 2·75 |

**154** Blue and Gold Macaw

**2010.** Parrots. Multicoloured.

| | | | |
|---|---|---|---|
| 468 | 85c. Type **154** | 70 | 55 |
| 469 | 90c. Green Amazonian | 90 | 65 |
| 470 | 180c. Scarlet macaw | 2·00 | 1·70 |

**155** Self-Portrait

**2010.** Art. Multicoloured.

| | | | |
|---|---|---|---|
| 471 | 200c. Type **155** | 1·30 | 1·00 |
| 472 | 250c. Vase with Fifteen Sunflowers | 1·90 | 1·50 |
| 473 | 305c. The Starry Night | 3·00 | 2·50 |
| 474 | 500c. *Wheat Field Under Threatening Skies* (detail) | 5·25 | 4·75 |

**156** Essoville Rum Shop

**2010.** Rum Shops. Multicoloured.

| | | | |
|---|---|---|---|
| 475 | 100c. Type **156** | 2·50 | 2·20 |
| 476 | 200c. Aruba Rum Shop | 4·50 | 4·25 |
| 477 | 255c. Caribbean Store | 5·50 | 5·25 |

**157** *Caesalpinia pulcherrima*

**2010.** Flowers. Multicoloured.

| | | | |
|---|---|---|---|
| 478 | 200c. Type **157** | 3·25 | 2·75 |
| 479 | 200c. *Dipladenia sanderi* | 3·25 | 2·75 |
| 480 | 200c. *Dipladenia sanderi* | 3·25 | 2·75 |
| 481 | 200c. *Adenium obesum* | 3·25 | 2·75 |
| 482 | 200c. *Bougainvillea* | 3·25 | 2·75 |
| 483 | 200c. *Ixora* | 3·25 | 2·75 |
| 484 | 200c. *Eichhornia crassipes* | 3·25 | 2·75 |
| 485 | 200c. *Passiflora caerulea* | 3·25 | 2·75 |
| 486 | 200c. *Allamanda cathartica* | 3·25 | 2·75 |
| 487 | 200c. *Nerium oleander* | | |

**158** Beth Israel Synagogue

**2010.** Places of Worship. Multicoloured.

| | | | |
|---|---|---|---|
| 488 | 85c. Type **158** | 1·50 | 1·20 |
| 489 | 90c. Protestant Church | 1·90 | 1·50 |
| 490 | 135c. St. Fransiscus Catholic Church | 3·00 | 2·50 |
| 491 | 240c. Interior, St. Fransiscus Church | 5·50 | 2·00 |

**159** *Falco sparverius* (American kestrel)

**2010.** Birds. Multicoloured.

| | | | |
|---|---|---|---|
| 492 | 200c. Type **159** | 4·25 | 3·75 |
| 493 | 200c. *Icterus icterus* (troupial) | 4·25 | 3·75 |
| 494 | 200c. *Mimus gilvus* (tropical mockingbird) | 4·25 | 3·75 |
| 495 | 200c. *Egretta alba* (great white egret) | 4·25 | 3·75 |
| 496 | 200c. *Aratinga pertinax* (brown-throated parakeet) | 4·75 | 3·75 |
| 497 | 200c. *Pelicanus occidentalis* (eastern brown pelican) | 4·25 | 3·75 |
| 498 | 200c. *Athena cunicularia* (burrowing owl) | 4·25 | 3·75 |
| 499 | 200c. *Coereba flaveola* (bananaquit) | 4·25 | 3·75 |
| 500 | 200c. *Polyborus plancus* (caracara) | 4·25 | 3·75 |
| 501 | 200c. *Colibri thalassinus* (green violet-ear) | 4·25 | 3·75 |

**160** Caribbean Reef Octopus

**2010.** Caribbean Reef Octopus (*Octopus briareus*). Multicoloured.

| | | | |
|---|---|---|---|
| 502 | 100c. Type **160** | 2·10 | 1·90 |
| 503 | 175c. With tenacles extended downwards | 4·25 | 3·75 |
| 504 | 255c. With tenacles extended upwards | 5·00 | 4·50 |
| 505 | 300c. Coiled on sea bed | 6·00 | 5·50 |

**161** *Heliconius hecale*

**2010.** Butterflies. Multicoloured.

| | | | |
|---|---|---|---|
| 506 | 200c. Type **161** | 4·00 | 3·50 |
| 507 | 200c. *Morpho peleides* (inscr 'Morpho paleides') | 4·00 | 3·50 |
| 508 | 200c. *Danaus plexippus* | 4·00 | 3·50 |
| 509 | 200c. *Anartia jatrophae* | 5·00 | 3·50 |
| 511 | 200c. *Phoebis sennae* | 4·00 | 3·50 |
| 511 | 200c. *Heliconius charithorius* (inscr 'Heliconius charithorius') | 4·00 | 3·50 |
| 512 | 200c. *Siproeta stelenes* | 4·00 | 3·50 |
| 513 | 200c. *Caligo memmon* | 4·00 | 3·50 |
| 514 | 200c. *Heliconius melpomene* | 4·00 | 3·50 |
| 515 | 200c *Agraulis vanilla* | 4·00 | 3·50 |

**EXPRESS MAIL SERVICE**

**E40** Globe, Planets and Aruban Arms

**1993**

| | | | | |
|---|---|---|---|---|
| E122 | **E40** | 200c. multicoloured | 4·50 | 3·25 |

Pt. 1

# ASCENSION

An island in South Atlantic. A dependency of St. Helena.

1922. 12 pence = 1 shilling; 20 shillings = 1 pound.
1971. 100 pence = 1 pound.

**1922.** Stamps of St. Helena of 1912 optd ASCENSION.

| | | | |
|---|---|---|---|
| 1 | ½d. black and green | 6·00 | 24·00 |
| 2 | 1d. green | 6·00 | 23·00 |
| 3 | 1½d. red | 17·00 | 48·00 |
| 4 | 2d. black and slate | 17·00 | 13·00 |
| 5 | 3d. blue | 13·00 | 24·00 |
| 6 | 8d. black and purple | 27·00 | 50·00 |
| 9 | 1s. black on green | 28·00 | 48·00 |
| 7 | 2s. black and blue on blue | £110 | £130 |
| 8 | 3s. black and violet | £140 | £160 |

**2** Badge of St. Helena

**1924**

| | | | | |
|---|---|---|---|---|
| 10 | 2 | ½d. black | 5·00 | 18·00 |
| 11 | 2 | 1d. black and green | 6·00 | 13·00 |
| 12 | 2 | 1½d. red | 10·00 | 38·00 |
| 13 | 2 | 2d. black and grey | 18·00 | 12·00 |
| 14 | 2 | 3d. blue | 8·00 | 18·00 |
| 15 | 2 | 4d. black on yellow | 50·00 | 90·00 |
| 15d | 2 | 5d. purple and green | 16·00 | 26·00 |
| 16 | 2 | 6d. black and purple | 60·00 | £110 |
| 17 | 2 | 8d. black and violet | 16·00 | 45·00 |
| 18 | 2 | 1s. black and brown | 21·00 | 55·00 |
| 19 | 2 | 2s. black and blue on blue | 75·00 | 95·00 |
| 20 | 2 | 3s. black on blue | 95·00 | £100 |

**3** Georgetown

**4** Ascension Island

**1934.** Medallion portrait of King George V (except 1s.).

| No. | Type | Description | Unused | Used |
|---|---|---|---|---|
| 21 | **3** | ½d. black and violet | 90 | 80 |
| 22 | **4** | 1d. black and green | 1·75 | 1·50 |
| 23 | - | 1½d. black and red | 1·75 | 2·25 |
| 24 | **4** | 2d. black and orange | 1·75 | 2·50 |
| 25 | - | 3d. black and blue | 2·00 | 1·50 |
| 26 | - | 5d. black and blue | 2·25 | 3·25 |
| 27 | **4** | 8d. black and brown | 4·25 | 4·75 |
| 28 | - | 1s. black and red | 18·00 | 10·00 |
| 29 | **4** | 2s.6d. black and purple | 45·00 | 48·00 |
| 30 | - | 5s. black and brown | 50·00 | 60·00 |

DESIGNS—HORIZ: 1½d. The Pier; 3d. Long Beach; 5d. Three Sisters; 1s. Sooty tern ("Wideawake Fair"); 5s. Green mountain.

**1935.** Silver Jubilee. As T **13** of Antigua.

| No. | Description | Unused | Used |
|---|---|---|---|
| 31 | 1½d. blue and red | 3·50 | 12·00 |
| 32 | 2d. blue and grey | 11·00 | 32·00 |
| 33 | 5d. green and blue | 23·00 | 32·00 |
| 34 | 1s. grey and purple | 23·00 | 40·00 |

**1937.** Coronation. As T 2 of Aden.

| No. | Description | Unused | Used |
|---|---|---|---|
| 35 | 1d. green | 50 | 1·40 |
| 36 | 2d. orange | 1·00 | 60 |
| 37 | 3d. blue | 1·00 | 50 |

**10** Green Mountain

**1938**

| No. | Type | Description | Unused | Used |
|---|---|---|---|---|
| 38 | **A** | ½d. black and violet | 5·50 | 2·75 |
| 38b | **A** | ½d. black and violet | 1·40 | 3·00 |
| 39 | **B** | 1d. black and green | 45·00 | 12·00 |
| 39b | **B** | 1d. black and orange | 45 | 60 |
| 39d | **C** | 1d. black and green | 60 | 1·50 |
| 40b | **10** | 1½d. black and red | 1·00 | 80 |
| 40d | **10** | 1½d. black and pink | 1·50 | 1·00 |
| 41a | **B** | 2d. black and orange | 80 | 40 |
| 41c | **B** | 2d. black and red | 1·25 | 1·75 |
| 42 | **D** | 3d. black and blue | £100 | 29·00 |
| 42b | **D** | 3d. black and grey | 70 | 80 |
| 42d | **B** | 4d. black and blue | 5·00 | 3·00 |
| 43 | **C** | 6d. black and blue | 10·00 | 2·25 |
| 44a | **A** | 1s. black and brown | 4·75 | 2·00 |
| 45 | **10** | 2s.6d. black and red | 42·00 | 9·50 |
| 46a | **D** | 5s. black and brown | 38·00 | 38·00 |
| 47a | **C** | 10s. black and purple | 48·00 | 60·00 |

DESIGNS: A, Georgetown; B, Green Mountain; C, Three Sisters; D, Long Beach.

**1946.** Victory. As T 9 of Aden.

| No. | Description | Unused | Used |
|---|---|---|---|
| 48 | 2d. orange | 40 | 1·00 |
| 49 | 4d. blue | 40 | 60 |

**1948.** Silver Wedding. As T 10/11 of Aden.

| No. | Description | Unused | Used |
|---|---|---|---|
| 50 | 3d. black | 50 | 30 |
| 51 | 10s. mauve | 55·00 | 50·00 |

**1949.** U.P.U. As T 20/23 of Antigua.

| No. | Description | Unused | Used |
|---|---|---|---|
| 52 | 3d. red | 1·00 | 2·00 |
| 53 | 4d. blue | 4·00 | 1·50 |
| 54 | 6d. olive | 2·00 | 3·50 |
| 55 | 1s. black | 2·00 | 1·50 |

**1953.** Coronation. As T 13 of Aden.

| No. | Description | Unused | Used |
|---|---|---|---|
| 56 | 3d. black and grey | 1·00 | 1·75 |

**15** Water Catchment

**1956**

| No. | Type | Description | Unused | Used |
|---|---|---|---|---|
| 57 | **15** | ½d. black and brown | 10 | 50 |
| 58 | - | 1d. black and mauve | 3·75 | 2·25 |
| 59 | - | 1½d. black and orange | 1·00 | 1·00 |
| 60 | - | 2d. black and red | 4·75 | 2·75 |
| 61 | - | 2½d. black and brown | 2·00 | 2·75 |
| 62 | - | 3d. black and blue | 4·75 | 1·25 |
| 63 | - | 4d. black and turquoise | 1·25 | 2·00 |
| 64 | - | 6d. black and blue | 1·50 | 2·50 |
| 65 | - | 7d. black and olive | 3·25 | 1·50 |
| 66 | - | 1s. black and red | 1·00 | 1·25 |
| 67 | - | 2s.6d. black and purple | 28·00 | 8·00 |
| 68 | - | 5s. black and green | 38·00 | 18·00 |
| 69 | - | 10s. black and purple | 48·00 | 40·00 |

DESIGNS: 1d. Map of Ascension; 1½d. Georgetown; 2d. Map showing Atlantic cables; 2½d. Mountain road; 3d. White-tailed tropic bird ("Boatswain Bird"); 4d. Yellow-finned tuna; 6d. Rollers on seashore; 7d. Turtles; 1s. Land crab; 2s.6d. Sooty tern ("Wideawake"); 5s. Perfect Crater; 10s. View of Ascension from north-west.

**28** Brown Booby

**1963.** Birds. Multicoloured.

| No. | Description | Unused | Used |
|---|---|---|---|
| 70 | 1d. Type **28** | 1·50 | 30 |
| 71 | 1½d. White-capped noddy ("Black Noddy") | 2·00 | 1·00 |
| 72 | 2d. White tern ("Fairy Tern") | 1·25 | 30 |
| 73 | 3d. Red-billed tropic bird | 1·75 | 30 |
| 74 | 4½d. Common noddy ("Brown Noddy") | 1·75 | 30 |
| 75 | 6d. Sooty tern ("Wideawake Tern") | 1·25 | 30 |
| 76 | 7d. Ascension frigate bird ("Frigate bird") | 1·25 | 30 |
| 77 | 10d. Blue-faced booby ("White Booby") | 1·25 | 50 |
| 78 | 1s. White-tailed tropic bird ("Yellow-billed Tropicbird") | 1·25 | 30 |
| 79 | 1s.6d. Red-billed tropic bird | 4·50 | 1·75 |
| 80 | 2s.6d. Madeiran storm petrel | 8·50 | 11·00 |
| 81 | 5s. Red-footed booby (brown phase) | 10·00 | 11·00 |
| 82 | 10s. Ascension frigate birds ("Frigate birds") | 13·00 | 13·00 |
| 83 | £1 Red-footed booby (white phase) | 20·00 | 15·00 |

**1963.** Freedom from Hunger. As T **28** of Aden.

| No. | Description | Unused | Used |
|---|---|---|---|
| 84 | 1s.6d. red | 75 | 40 |

**1963.** Centenary of Red Cross. As T **33** of Antigua.

| No. | Description | Unused | Used |
|---|---|---|---|
| 85 | 3d. red and black | 1·50 | 1·25 |
| 86 | 1s.6d. red and blue | 2·50 | 2·25 |

**1965.** Centenary of I.T.U. As T **36** of Antigua.

| No. | Description | Unused | Used |
|---|---|---|---|
| 87 | 3d. mauve and violet | 50 | 65 |
| 88 | 6d. turquoise and brown | 75 | 65 |

**1965.** I.C.Y. As T **37** of Antigua.

| No. | Description | Unused | Used |
|---|---|---|---|
| 89 | 1d. purple and turquoise | 40 | 60 |
| 90 | 6d. green and lavender | 60 | 90 |

**1966.** Churchill Commemoration. As T **38** of Antigua.

| No. | Description | Unused | Used |
|---|---|---|---|
| 91 | 1d. blue | 50 | 75 |
| 92 | 3d. green | 2·00 | 1·25 |
| 93 | 6d. brown | 2·25 | 1·50 |
| 94 | 1s.6d. violet | 3·00 | 2·00 |

**1966.** World Cup Football Championship. As T **40** of Antigua.

| No. | Description | Unused | Used |
|---|---|---|---|
| 95 | 3d. multicoloured | 1·50 | 60 |
| 96 | 6d. multicoloured | 1·50 | 80 |

**1966.** Inauguration of W.H.O. Headquarters, Geneva. As T **41** of Antigua.

| No. | Description | Unused | Used |
|---|---|---|---|
| 97 | 3d. black, green and blue | 1·75 | 1·00 |
| 98 | 1s.6d. black, purple and ochre | 4·75 | 2·00 |

**36** Satellite Station

**1966.** Opening of Apollo Communication Satellite Earth Station.

| No. | Type | Description | Unused | Used |
|---|---|---|---|---|
| 99 | **36** | 4d. black and violet | 10 | 10 |
| 100 | **36** | 8d. black and green | 15 | 15 |
| 101 | **36** | 1s.3d. black and brown | 15 | 20 |
| 102 | **36** | 2s.6d. black and blue | 15 | 20 |

**37** B.B.C. Emblem

**1966.** Opening of B.B.C. Relay Station.

| No. | Type | Description | Unused | Used |
|---|---|---|---|---|
| 103 | **37** | 1d. gold and blue | 10 | 10 |
| 104 | **37** | 3d. gold and green | 15 | 15 |
| 105 | **37** | 6d. gold and violet | 15 | 15 |
| 106 | **37** | 1s.6d. gold and red | 15 | 15 |

**1967.** 20th Anniv of UNESCO As T **54/56** of Antigua.

| No. | Description | Unused | Used |
|---|---|---|---|
| 107 | 3d. multicoloured | 2·00 | 1·50 |
| 108 | 6d. yellow, violet and olive | 2·75 | 2·00 |
| 109 | 1s.6d. black, purple and orange | 4·50 | 2·50 |

**44** Human Rights Emblem and Chain Links

**1968.** Human Rights Year.

| No. | Type | Description | Unused | Used |
|---|---|---|---|---|
| 110 | **44** | 6d. orange, red and black | 15 | 15 |
| 111 | **44** | 1s.6d. blue, red and black | 20 | 25 |
| 112 | **44** | 2s.6d. green, red and black | 20 | 30 |

**45** Black Durgon ("Ascension Black-Fish")

**1968.** Fishes (1st series).

| No. | Type | Description | Unused | Used |
|---|---|---|---|---|
| 113 | **45** | 4d. black, grey and blue | 30 | 40 |
| 114 | - | 8d. multicoloured | 35 | 70 |
| 115 | - | 1s.9d. multicoloured | 40 | 80 |
| 116 | - | 2s.3d. multicoloured | 40 | 85 |

DESIGNS: 8d. Scribbled filefish ("Leather-jacket"); 1s.9d. Yellow-finned tuna; 2s.3d. Short-finned mako.

See also Nos. 117/20 and 126/9.

**1969.** Fishes (2nd series). As T **45**. Multicoloured.

| No. | Description | Unused | Used |
|---|---|---|---|
| 117 | 4d. Sailfish | 75 | 90 |
| 118 | 6d. White seabream ("Old wife") | 1·00 | 1·25 |
| 119 | 1s.6d. Yellowtail | 1·25 | 2·50 |
| 120 | 2s.11d. Rock hind ("Jack") | 1·50 | 3·00 |

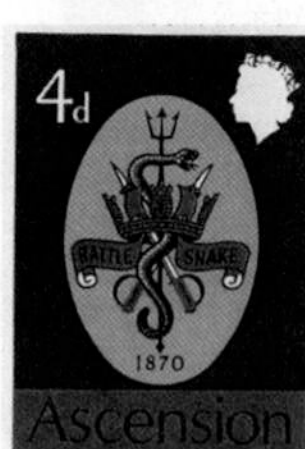

**46** H.M.S. *Rattlesnake*

**1969.** Royal Navy Crests (1st series).

| No. | Type | Description | Unused | Used |
|---|---|---|---|---|
| 121 | **46** | 4d. multicoloured | 60 | 30 |
| 122 | - | 9d. multicoloured | 75 | 35 |
| 123 | - | 1s.9d. blue and gold | 1·10 | 45 |
| 124 | - | 2s.3d. multicoloured | 1·25 | 55 |
| **MS**125 | | 165×105 mm. Nos. 121/4 | 6·50 | 13·00 |

DESIGNS: 9d. H.M.S. "Weston"; 1s.9d. H.M.S. "Undaunted"; 2s.3d. H.M.S. "Eagle".

See also Nos. 130/3, 149/52, 154/7 and 166/9.

**1970.** Fishes (3rd series). As T **45**. Multicoloured.

| No. | Description | Unused | Used |
|---|---|---|---|
| 126 | 4d. Wahoo | 4·50 | 2·75 |
| 127w | 9d. Ascension jack ("Coalfish") | 3·00 | 1·25 |
| 128 | 1s.9d. Pompouno dolphin | 5·50 | 3·50 |
| 129w | 2s.3d. Squirrelfish ("Soldier") | 3·00 | 1·50 |

**1970.** Royal Navy Crests (2nd series). As T **46**. Multicoloured.

| No. | Description | Unused | Used |
|---|---|---|---|
| 130 | 4d. H.M.S. "Penelope" | 1·00 | 1·00 |
| 131 | 9d. H.M.S. "Carlisle" | 1·25 | 1·50 |
| 132 | 1s.6d. H.M.S. "Amphion" | 1·75 | 2·00 |
| 133 | 2s.6d. H.M.S. "Magpie" | 1·75 | 2·00 |
| **MS**134 | 159×96 mm. Nos. 130/3 | 11·00 | 15·00 |

**50** Early Chinese Rocket

**1971.** Decimal Currency. Evolution of Space Travel. Multicoloured.

| No. | Description | Unused | Used |
|---|---|---|---|
| 135 | ½p. Type **50** | 15 | 20 |
| 136 | 1p. Medieval Arab astronomers | 20 | 20 |
| 137 | 1½p. Tycho Brahe's observatory, quadrant and supernova (horiz) | 30 | 30 |
| 138 | 2p. Galileo, Moon and telescope (horiz) | 40 | 30 |
| 139 | 2½p. Isaac Newton, instruments and apple (horiz) | 1·75 | 1·00 |
| 140 | 3½p. Harrison's chronometer and H.M.S. "Deptford" (frigate), 1735 (horiz) | 2·50 | 1·50 |
| 141 | 4½p. Space rocket taking off | 1·25 | 1·00 |
| 142 | 5p. World's largest telescope, Palomar (horiz) | 1·00 | 1·00 |
| 143 | 7½p. World's largest radio telescope, Jodrell Bank (horiz) | 4·00 | 1·75 |
| 144 | 10p. "Mariner VII" and Mars (horiz) | 3·50 | 1·75 |
| 145 | 12½p. "Sputnik II" and Space dog, Laika (horiz) | 5·00 | 2·00 |
| 146 | 25p. Walking in Space | 6·00 | 2·25 |
| 147 | 50p. "Apollo XI" crew on Moon (horiz) | 5·00 | 2·75 |
| 148 | £1 Future Space Research station (horiz) | 5·00 | 4·50 |

**1971.** Royal Navy Crests (3rd series). As T **46**. Mult.

| No. | Description | Unused | Used |
|---|---|---|---|
| 149 | 2p. H.M.S. "Phoenix" | 1·00 | 30 |
| 150 | 4p. H.M.S. "Milford" | 1·00 | 55 |
| 151 | 9p. H.M.S. "Pelican" | 1·25 | 80 |
| 152 | 15p. H.M.S. "Oberon" | 1·25 | 1·00 |
| **MS**153 | 151×104 mm. Nos. 149/52 | 4·00 | 15·00 |

**1972.** Royal Navy Crests (4th series). As T **46**. Mult.

| No. | Description | Unused | Used |
|---|---|---|---|
| 154 | 1½p. H.M.S. "Lowestoft" | 50 | 50 |
| 155 | 3p. H.M.S. "Auckland" | 55 | 75 |
| 156 | 6p. H.M.S. "Nigeria" | 60 | 1·25 |
| 157 | 17½p. H.M.S. "Bermuda" | 90 | 2·50 |
| **MS**158 | 157×93 mm. Nos. 154/7 | 2·25 | 7·50 |

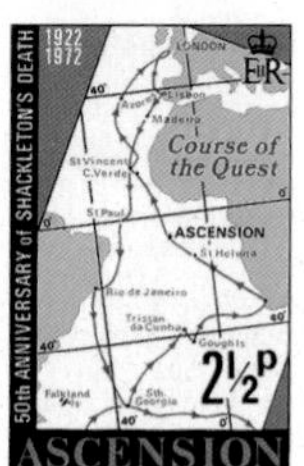

**51** Course of the "Quest"

**1972.** 50th Anniv of Shackleton's Death. Mult.

| No. | Description | Unused | Used |
|---|---|---|---|
| 159 | 2½p. Type **51** | 30 | 60 |
| 160 | 4p. Shackleton and "Quest" (horiz) | 35 | 60 |
| 161 | 7½p. Shackleton's cabin and "Quest" (horiz) | 35 | 65 |
| 162 | 11p. Shackleton statue and memorial | 40 | 80 |
| **MS**163 | 139×114 mm. Nos. 159/62 | 1·25 | 6·00 |

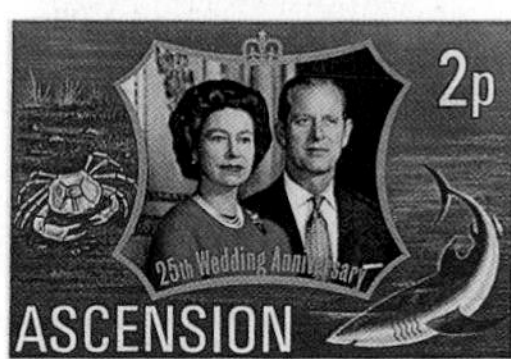

**52** Land Crab and Short-finned Mako

**1972.** Royal Silver Wedding. Multicoloured.

| No. | Type | Description | Unused | Used |
|---|---|---|---|---|
| 164 | **52** | 2p. violet | 15 | 10 |
| 165 | **52** | 16p. red | 35 | 30 |

**1973.** Royal Naval Crests (5th series). As T **46**. Multicoloured.

| No. | Description | Unused | Used |
|---|---|---|---|
| 166 | 2p. H.M.S. "Birmingham" | 2·00 | 1·50 |
| 167 | 4p. H.M.S. "Cardiff" | 2·25 | 1·50 |
| 168 | 9p. H.M.S. "Penzance" | 3·00 | 1·75 |
| 169 | 13p. H.M.S. "Rochester" | 3·25 | 1·75 |
| **MS**170 | 109×152 mm. Nos. 166/9 | 28·00 | 10·00 |

**53** Green Turtle

**1973.** Turtles. Multicoloured.

| No. | Description | Unused | Used |
|---|---|---|---|
| 171 | 4p. Type **53** | 2·75 | 1·75 |
| 172 | 9p. Loggerhead turtle | 3·00 | 2·00 |
| 173 | 12p. Hawksbill turtle | 3·25 | 2·25 |

**54** Sergeant, R.M. Light Infantry, 1900

**1973.** 50th Anniv of Departure of Royal Marines from Ascension. Multicoloured.

| | | | |
|---|---|---|---|
| 174 | 2p. Type **54** | 1·50 | 1·50 |
| 175 | 6p. R.M. Private, 1816 | 2·25 | 1·50 |
| 176 | 12p. R.M. Light Infantry Officer, 1880 | 2·50 | 2·25 |
| 177 | 20p. R.M. Artillery Colour Sergeant, 1910 | 3·00 | 2·50 |

**1973.** Royal Wedding. As T **47** of Anguilla. Multicoloured. Background colours given.

| | | | |
|---|---|---|---|
| 178 | 2p. brown | 15 | 10 |
| 179 | 18p. green | 20 | 20 |

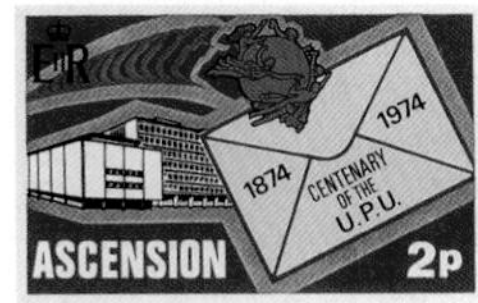

**55** Letter and H.Q., Berne

**1974.** Centenary of Universal Postal Union. Mult.

| | | | |
|---|---|---|---|
| 180 | 2p. Type **55** | 20 | 30 |
| 181 | 9p. Hermes and U.P.U. monument | 30 | 45 |

**56** Churchill as a Boy, and Birthplace, Blenheim Palace

**1974.** Birth Centenary of Sir Winston Churchill. Multicoloured.

| | | | |
|---|---|---|---|
| 182 | 5p. Type **56** | 20 | 35 |
| 183 | 25p. Churchill as statesman, and U.N. Building | 30 | 75 |
| **MS**184 | 93×87 mm. Nos. 182/3 | 1·00 | 2·50 |

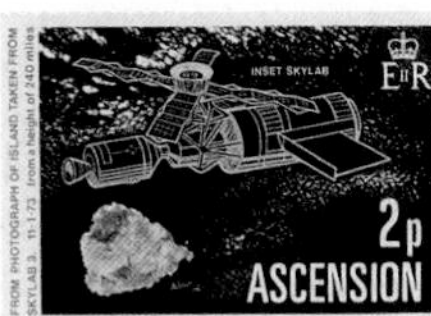

**57** "Skylab 3" and Photograph of Ascension

**1975.** Space Satellites. Multicoloured.

| | | | |
|---|---|---|---|
| 185 | 2p. Type **57** | 20 | 30 |
| 186 | 18p. "Skylab 4" Command module and photograph | 30 | 40 |

**58** U.S.A.F. Lockheed C-141A Starlifter

**1975.** Wideawake Airfield. Multicoloured.

| | | | |
|---|---|---|---|
| 187 | 2p. Type **58** | 80 | 65 |
| 188 | 5p. R.A.F. Lockheed C-130 Hercules | 80 | 85 |
| 189 | 9p. Vickers Super VC-10 | 80 | 1·40 |
| 190 | 24p. U.S.A.F. Lockheed C-5A Galaxy | 1·25 | 2·50 |
| **MS**191 | 144×99 mm. Nos. 187/90 | 14·00 | 22·00 |

**1975.** "Apollo-Soyuz" Space Link. Nos. 141 and 145/6 optd APOLLO-SOYUZ LINK 1975.

| | | | |
|---|---|---|---|
| 192 | 4½p. multicoloured | 15 | 20 |
| 193 | 12½p. multicoloured | 15 | 25 |
| 194 | 25p. multicoloured | 25 | 40 |

**60** Arrival of Royal Navy, 1815

**1975.** 160th Anniv of Occupation. Multicoloured.

| | | | |
|---|---|---|---|
| 195 | 2p. Type **60** | 25 | 25 |
| 196 | 5p. Water supply, Dampiers Drip | 25 | 40 |
| 197 | 9p. First landing, 1815 | 25 | 60 |
| 198 | 15p. The garden on Green Mountain | 35 | 85 |

**61** Yellow Canaries ("Canary")

**1976.** Multicoloured.. Multicoloured..

| | | | |
|---|---|---|---|
| 199 | 1p. Type **61** | 40 | 1·50 |
| 200 | 2p. White tern ("Fairy Tern") (vert) | 50 | 1·50 |
| 201 | 3p. Common waxbill ("Waxbill") | 50 | 1·50 |
| 202 | 4p. White-capped noddy ("Black Noddy") (vert) | 50 | 1·50 |
| 203 | 5p. Common noddy ("Brown Noddy") | 70 | 1·50 |
| 204 | 6p. Common mynah | 70 | 1·50 |
| 205 | 7p. Madeiran storm petrel (vert) | 70 | 1·50 |
| 206 | 8p. Sooty tern | 70 | 1·50 |
| 207 | 9p. Blue-faced booby ("White Booby") (vert) | 70 | 1·50 |
| 208 | 10p. Red-footed booby | 70 | 1·50 |
| 209 | 15p. Red-necked spurfowl ("Red-throated Francolin") (vert) | 85 | 1·50 |
| 210 | 18p. Brown booby (vert) | 85 | 1·50 |
| 211 | 25p. Red-billed tropic bird ("Red-billed Bo'sun Bird") | 90 | 1·50 |
| 212 | 50p. White-tailed tropic bird ("Yellow-billed Tropic Bird") | 1·00 | 1·75 |
| 213 | £1 Ascension frigate-bird (vert) | 1·00 | 2·25 |
| 214 | £2 Boatswain Bird Island Sanctuary (50×38 mm) | 2·00 | 5·00 |

**63** G.B. Penny Red with Ascension Postmark

**1976.** Festival of Stamps, London.

| | | | | |
|---|---|---|---|---|
| 215 | **63** | 5p. red, black and brown | 15 | 15 |
| 216 | - | 9p. green, black and brown | 15 | 20 |
| 217 | - | 25p. multicoloured | 25 | 45 |
| **MS**218 | | 133×121 mm. No. 217 with St. Helena No. 318 and Tristan da Cunha No. 206 | 1·75 | 2·00 |

DESIGNS—VERT: 9p. ½d. stamp of 1922. HORIZ: 25p. "Southampton Castle" (liner).

**64** U.S. Base, Ascension

**1976.** Bicentenary of American Revolution. Multicoloured.

| | | | |
|---|---|---|---|
| 219 | 8p. Type **64** | 30 | 40 |
| 220 | 9p. NASA Station at Devils Ashpit | 30 | 45 |
| 221 | 25p. "Viking" landing on Mars | 50 | 80 |

**65** Visit of Prince Philip, 1957

**1977.** Silver Jubilee. Multicoloured.

| | | | |
|---|---|---|---|
| 222 | 8p. Type **65** | 15 | 15 |
| 223 | 12p. Coronation Coach leaving Buckingham Palace (horiz) | 20 | 20 |
| 224 | 25p. Coronation Coach (horiz) | 35 | 40 |

**66** Tunnel carrying Water Pipe

**1977.** Water Supplies. Multicoloured.

| | | | |
|---|---|---|---|
| 225 | 3p. Type **66** | 15 | 15 |
| 226 | 5p. Breakneck Valley wells | 20 | 20 |
| 227 | 12p. Break tank (horiz) | 30 | 35 |
| 228 | 25p. Water catchment (horiz) | 45 | 65 |

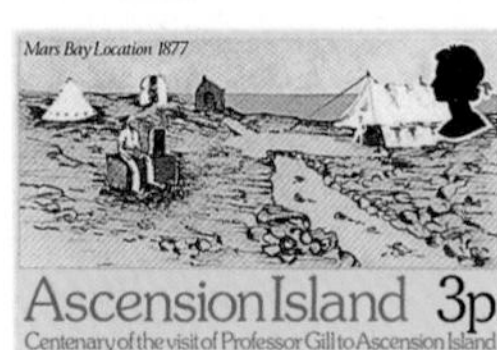

**67** Mars Bay Location, 1877

**1977.** Centenary of Visit of Professor Gill (astronomer). Multicoloured.

| | | | |
|---|---|---|---|
| 229 | 3p. Type **67** | 15 | 20 |
| 230 | 8p. Instrument sites, Mars Bay | 15 | 25 |
| 231 | 12p. Sir David and Lady Gill | 20 | 40 |
| 232 | 25p. Maps of Ascension | 60 | 70 |

**68** Lion of England

**1978.** 25th Anniv of Coronation.

| | | | | |
|---|---|---|---|---|
| 233 | **68** | 25p. yellow, brown and silver | 35 | 50 |
| 234 | - | 25p. multicoloured | 35 | 50 |
| 235 | - | 25p. yellow, brown and silver | 35 | 50 |

DESIGNS: No 234, Queen Elizabeth II; No 235, Green turtle.

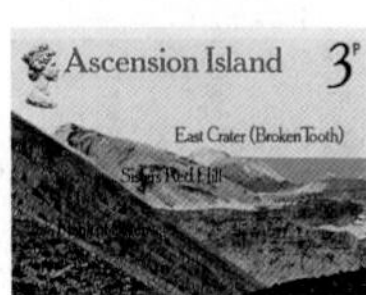

**70** Flank of Sisters, Sisters' Red Hill and East Crater

**1978.** Ascension Island Volcanic Rock Formations. Multicoloured.

| | | | |
|---|---|---|---|
| 236 | 3p. Type **70** | 15 | 20 |
| 237 | 5p. Holland's Crater (Hollow Tooth) | 20 | 30 |
| 238 | 12p. Street Crater, Lower Valley Crater and Bear's Back | 25 | 40 |
| 239 | 15p. Butt Crater, Weather Post and Green Mountain | 30 | 45 |
| 240 | 25p. Flank of Sisters, Thistle Hill and Two Boats Village | 35 | 50 |
| **MS**241 | 185×100 mm. Nos. 236/40, each × 2 | 2·00 | 5·00 |

Nos. 236/40 were issued as a se-tenant strip within the sheet, forming a composite design.

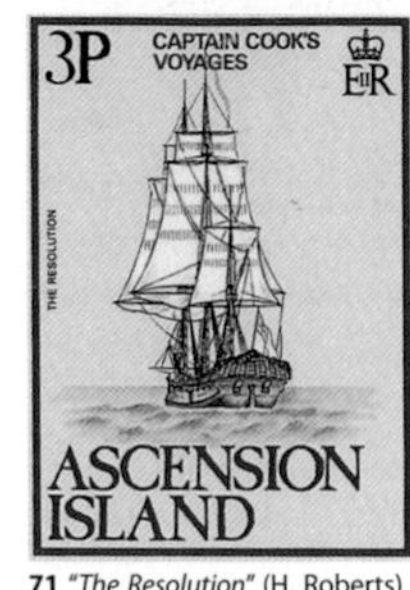

**71** *"The Resolution"* (H. Roberts)

**1979.** Bicentenary of Captain Cook's Voyages, 1768–79. Multicoloured.

| | | | |
|---|---|---|---|
| 242 | 3p. Type **71** | 30 | 25 |
| 243 | 8p. Cook's chronometer | 25 | 40 |
| 244 | 12p. Green turtle | 30 | 50 |
| 245 | 25p. Flaxman/Wedgwood medallion of Cook | 30 | 70 |

**72** St. Mary's Church, Georgetown

**1979.** Ascension Day. Multicoloured.

| | | | |
|---|---|---|---|
| 246 | 8p. Type **72** | 10 | 20 |
| 247 | 12p. Map of Ascension | 15 | 30 |
| 248 | 50p. "The Ascension" (painting by Rembrandt) | 30 | 90 |

**73** Landing Cable, Comfortless Cove

**1979.** 80th Anniv of Eastern Telegraph Company's Arrival on Ascension.

| | | | | |
|---|---|---|---|---|
| 249 | **73** | 3p. black and red | 10 | 10 |
| 250 | - | 8p. black and green | 15 | 15 |
| 251 | - | 12p. black and yellow | 20 | 20 |
| 252 | - | 15p. black and violet | 20 | 25 |
| 253 | - | 25p. black and brown | 25 | 35 |

DESIGNS—HORIZ: 8p. C.S. "Anglia"; 15p. C.S. "Seine"; 25p. Cable and Wireless earth station. VERT: 12p. Map of Atlantic cable network.

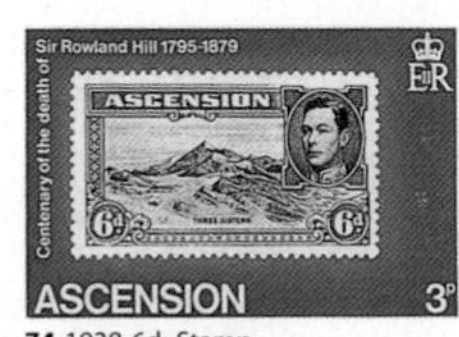

**74** 1938 6d. Stamp

**1979.** Death Centenary of Sir Rowland Hill.

| | | | | |
|---|---|---|---|---|
| 254 | **74** | 3p. black and blue | 10 | 10 |
| 255 | - | 8p. black, green and pale green | 15 | 20 |
| 256 | - | 12p. black, blue and pale blue | 15 | 25 |
| 257 | - | 50p. black and red | 40 | 90 |

DESIGNS—HORIZ: 8p. 1956 5s. definitive. VERT: 12p. 1924 3s. stamp; 50p. Sir Rowland Hill.

**75** *Anogramma ascensionis*

**1980.** Ferns and Grasses. Multicoloured.

| | | | |
|---|---|---|---|
| 258 | 3p. Type **75** | 10 | 15 |
| 259 | 6p. "Xiphopteris ascensionense" | 10 | 20 |
| 260 | 8p. "Sporobolus caespitosus" | 10 | 20 |
| 261 | 12p. "Dryopteris durus" (vert) | 15 | 30 |
| 262 | 18p. "Dryopteris ascensionis" (vert) | 15 | 40 |
| 263 | 24p. "Marattia purpurascens" (vert) | 20 | 55 |

**76** 17th-Century Bottle Post

**1980.** "London 1980" International Stamp Exhibition. Multicoloured.

| | | | |
|---|---|---|---|
| 264 | 8p. Type **76** | 15 | 20 |
| 265 | 12p. 19th-century chance calling ship | 20 | 25 |
| 266 | 15p. "Garth Castle" (regular mail service from 1863) | 20 | 30 |
| 267 | 50p. "St. Helena" (mail services, 1980) | 60 | 90 |
| **MS**268 | 102×154 mm. Nos. 264/7 | 1·00 | 2·40 |

**77** H.M. Queen Elizabeth the Queen Mother

**1980.** 80th Birthday of The Queen Mother.

| | | | | |
|---|---|---|---|---|
| 269 | **77** | 15p. multicoloured | 40 | 40 |

**78** Lubbock's Yellowtail

**1980.** Fish. Multicoloured.

| | | | |
|---|---|---|---|
| 270 | 3p. Type **78** | 20 | 25 |
| 271 | 10p. Resplendent angelfish | 20 | 25 |
| 272 | 25p. Bicoloured butterflyfish | 30 | 55 |
| 273 | 40p. Marmalade razorfish | 40 | 75 |

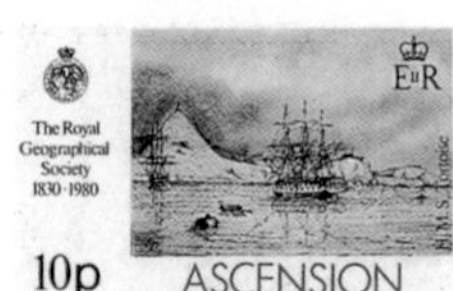


**79** H.M.S. *Tortoise*

**1980.** 150th Anniv of Royal Geographical Society. Multicoloured.

| | | | |
|---|---|---|---|
| 274 | 10p. Type **79** | 20 | 40 |
| 275 | 15p. "Wideawake Fair" | 25 | 45 |
| 276 | 60p. Mid-Atlantic Ridge (38×48 mm) | 65 | 1·25 |

**80** Green Mountain Farm, 1881

**1981.** Green Mountain Farm. Multicoloured.

| | | | |
|---|---|---|---|
| 277 | 12p. Type **80** | 15 | 35 |
| 278 | 15p. Two Boats, 1881 | 15 | 40 |
| 279 | 20p. Green Mountain and Two Boats, 1981 | 20 | 50 |
| 280 | 30p. Green Mountain Farm, 1981 | 30 | 70 |

**81** Cable and Wireless Earth Station

**1981.** "Space Shuttle" Mission and Opening of 2nd Earth Station.

| | | | | |
|---|---|---|---|---|
| 281 | **81** | 15p. black, blue and pale blue | 30 | 35 |

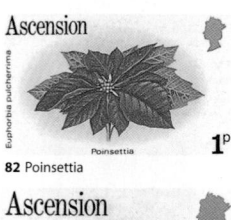

**82** Poinsettia

**83** Solanum

**1981.** Flowers. Multicoloured.

| | | | |
|---|---|---|---|
| 282A | 1p. Type **82** | 70 | 1·25 |
| 283B | 2p. Clustered wax flower | 50 | 1·25 |
| 284B | 3p. Kolanchoe (vert) | 50 | 1·25 |
| 285A | 4p. Yellow pops | 80 | 1·25 |
| 286A | 5p. Camels foot creeper | 80 | 1·25 |
| 287A | 8p. White oleander | 80 | 1·25 |
| 288B | 10p. Ascension lily (vert) | 45 | 75 |
| 289A | 12p. Coral plant (vert) | 1·50 | 1·10 |
| 290B | 15p. Yellow allamanda | 50 | 75 |
| 291B | 20p. Ascension euphorbia | 1·00 | 75 |
| 292A | 30p. Flame of the forest (vert) | 1·25 | 1·25 |
| 293A | 40p. Bougainvillea "King Leopold" | 1·25 | 3·00 |
| 294A | 50p. Type **83** | 1·75 | 3·25 |
| 295B | £1 Ladies petticoat | 2·00 | 3·00 |
| 296A | £2 Red hibiscus | 3·50 | 6·00 |

Nos. 294/6 are as Type **83**.

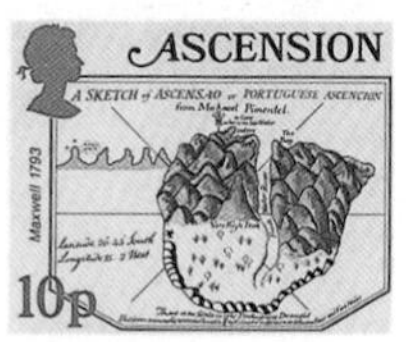


**84** Map by Maxwell, 1793

**1981.** Early Maps of Ascension.

| | | | | |
|---|---|---|---|---|
| 297 | **84** | 10p. black, gold and blue | 20 | 35 |
| 298 | - | 12p. black, gold and green | 20 | 35 |
| 299 | - | 15p. black, gold and stone | 20 | 35 |
| 300 | - | 40p. black, gold and yellow | 50 | 70 |
| **MS**301 | | 79×64 mm. 5p. × 4 multi-coloured | 60 | 75 |

DESIGNS: 12p. Maxwell, 1793 (different); 15p. Ekeberg and Chapman, 1811; 40p. Campbell, 1819; miniature sheet, Linschoten, 1599.

Stamps from **MS**301 form a composite design.

**85** Wedding Bouquet from Ascension

**1981.** Royal Wedding. Multicoloured.

| | | | |
|---|---|---|---|
| 302 | 10p. Type **85** | 15 | 15 |
| 303 | 15p. Prince Charles in Fleet Air Arm flying kit | 30 | 30 |
| 304 | 50p. Prince Charles and Lady Diana Spencer | 65 | 90 |

**87** "Interest"

**1981.** 25th Anniv of Duke of Edinburgh Award Scheme. Multicoloured.

| | | | |
|---|---|---|---|
| 305 | 5p. Type **87** | 15 | 15 |
| 306 | 10p. "Physical activities" | 15 | 15 |
| 307 | 15p. "Service" | 20 | 20 |
| 308 | 40p. Duke of Edinburgh | 45 | 45 |

**88** Scout crossing Rope Bridge

**1982.** 75th Anniv of Boy Scout Movement.

| | | | | |
|---|---|---|---|---|
| 309 | **88** | 10p. black, blue and light blue | 15 | 35 |
| 310 | - | 15p. black, brown and yellow | 15 | 50 |
| 311 | - | 25p. black, mve & lt mve | 20 | 60 |
| 312 | - | 40p. black, red and orange | 30 | 85 |
| **MS**313 | | 121×121 mm. 10, 15, 25, 40p. As Nos. 309/12 (each diamond 40×40 mm) | 1·00 | 2·50 |

DESIGNS: 15p. 1st Ascension Scout Group flag; 25p. Scouts learning to use radio; 40p. Lord Baden-Powell.

**89** Charles Darwin

**1982.** 150th Anniv of Charles Darwin's Voyage. Multicoloured.

| | | | |
|---|---|---|---|
| 314 | 10p. Type **89** | 20 | 40 |
| 315 | 12p. Darwin's pistols | 20 | 50 |
| 316 | 15p. Rock crab | 25 | 55 |
| 317 | 40p. H.M.S. "Beagle" | 60 | 95 |

**90** Fairey Swordfish Torpedo Bomber

**1982.** 40th Anniv of Wideawake Airfield. Multicoloured.

| | | | |
|---|---|---|---|
| 318 | 5p. Type **90** | 75 | 35 |
| 319 | 10p. North American B-25C Mitchell | 1·00 | 40 |
| 320 | 15p. Boeing EC-135N Aria | 1·25 | 55 |
| 321 | 50p. Lockheed C-130 Hercules | 1·75 | 1·10 |

**91** Ascension Coat of Arms

**1982.** 21st Birthday of Princess of Wales. Mult.

| | | | |
|---|---|---|---|
| 322 | 12p. Type **91** | 20 | 20 |
| 323 | 15p. Lady Diana Spencer in Music Room, Buckingham Palace | 20 | 20 |
| 324 | 25p. Bride and Earl Spencer leaving Clarence House | 30 | 30 |
| 325 | 50p. Formal portrait | 65 | 65 |

**1982.** Commonwealth Games, Brisbane. Nos. 290/1 optd 1st PARTICIPATION COMMON-WEALTH GAMES 1982.

| | | | |
|---|---|---|---|
| 326 | 15p. Yellow allamanda | 30 | 40 |
| 327 | 20p. Ascension euphorbia | 40 | 45 |

**94** Bush House, London

**1982.** Christmas. 50th Anniv of B.B.C. External Broadcasting. Multicoloured.

| | | | |
|---|---|---|---|
| 328 | 5p. Type **94** | 15 | 20 |
| 329 | 10p. Atlantic relay station | 20 | 30 |
| 330 | 25p. Lord Reith, first Director-General | 30 | 60 |
| 331 | 40p. King George V making his first Christmas broadcast, 1932 | 45 | 75 |

**95** *Marasmius thwaitesii* ("*Marasmius echinosphaerus*")

**1983.** Fungi. Multicoloured.

| | | | |
|---|---|---|---|
| 332 | 7p. Type **95** | 25 | 30 |
| 333 | 12p. "Chlorophyllum molybdites" | 35 | 45 |
| 334 | 15p. "Leucocoprinus cepaestripes" | 40 | 50 |
| 335 | 20p. "Lycoperdon marginatum" | 45 | 65 |
| 336 | 50p. "Marasmiellus distantifolius" | 55 | 1·25 |

**96** Aerial View of Georgetown

**1983.** Island Views (1st series). Multicoloured.

| | | | |
|---|---|---|---|
| 337 | 12p. Type **96** | 15 | 25 |
| 338 | 15p. Green Mountain farm | 15 | 25 |
| 339 | 20p. Boatswain Bird Island | 20 | 40 |
| 340 | 60p. Telemetry Hill by night | 40 | 80 |

See also Nos. 367/70.

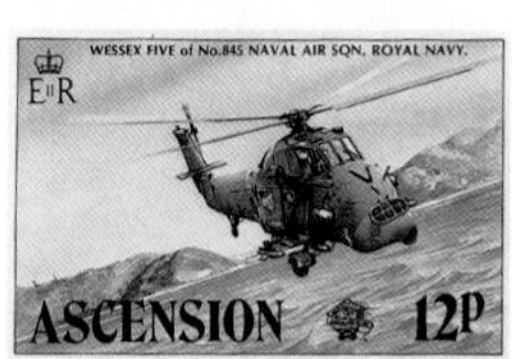


**97** Westland Wessex 5 Helicopter of No. 845 Naval Air Squadron

**1983.** Bicentenary of Manned Flight. British Military Aircraft. Multicoloured.

| | | | |
|---|---|---|---|
| 341 | 12p. Type **97** | 40 | 65 |
| 342 | 15p. Avro Vulcan B.2 of No. 44 Squadron | 40 | 75 |
| 343 | 20p. Hawker Siddeley Nimrod M.R.2P of No. 20 Squadron | 40 | 85 |
| 344 | 60p. Handey Page Victor K2 of No. 55 Squadron | 60 | 2·00 |

**98** Iguanid

**1983.** Introduced Species. Multicoloured.

| | | | |
|---|---|---|---|
| 345 | 12p. Type **98** | 25 | 30 |
| 346 | 15p. Common rabbit | 30 | 35 |
| 347 | 20p. Cat | 40 | 45 |
| 348 | 60p. Donkey | 75 | 1·40 |

**99** Speckled Tellin (*Tellina listeri*)

**1983.** Sea Shells. Multicoloured.

| | | | |
|---|---|---|---|
| 349 | 7p. Type **99** | 15 | 20 |
| 350 | 12p. Lion's paw scallop | 15 | 30 |
| 351 | 15p. Lurid cowrie | 20 | 35 |
| 352 | 20p. Ascension nerite | 20 | 45 |
| 353 | 50p. Miniature melo | 40 | 1·10 |

**100** 1922 1½d. Stamp

**1984.** 150th Anniv of St. Helena as a British Colony. Multicoloured.

| | | | |
|---|---|---|---|
| 354 | 12p. Type **100** | 20 | 45 |
| 355 | 15p. 1922 2d. stamp | 20 | 50 |
| 356 | 20p. 1922 8d. stamp | 20 | 55 |
| 357 | 60p. 1922 1s. stamp | 50 | 1·40 |

**101** Prince Andrew

**1984.** Visit of Prince Andrew. Sheet 124×90 mm.

| | | | |
|---|---|---|---|
| **MS**358 | 12p. Type **101**; 70p. Prince Andrew in naval uniform | 1·00 | 1·60 |

**102** Naval Semaphore

**1984.** 250th Anniv of "Lloyd's List" (newspaper). Multicoloured.

| | | | |
|---|---|---|---|
| 359 | 12p. Type **102** | 50 | 30 |
| 360 | 15p. "Southampton Castle" (liner) | 50 | 35 |
| 361 | 20p. Pier head | 55 | 45 |
| 362 | 70p. "Dane" (screw steamer) | 1·25 | 1·50 |

**103** Penny Coin and Yellow-finned Tuna

**1984.** New Coinage. Multicoloured.

| | | | |
|---|---|---|---|
| 363 | 12p. Type **103** | 35 | 35 |
| 364 | 15p. Twopenny coin and donkey | 40 | 40 |
| 365 | 20p. Fifty pence coin and green turtle | 45 | 50 |
| 366 | 70p. Pound coin and sooty tern | 80 | 1·75 |

**1984.** Island Views (2nd series). As T **96**. Mult.

| | | | |
|---|---|---|---|
| 367 | 12p. The Devil's Riding-school | 20 | 30 |
| 368 | 15p. St. Mary's Church | 25 | 35 |
| 369 | 20p. Two Boats Village | 25 | 45 |
| 370 | 70p. Ascension from the sea | 80 | 1·50 |

**104** Bermuda Cypress

**1985.** Trees. Multicoloured.

| | | | |
|---|---|---|---|
| 371 | 7p. Type **104** | 20 | 20 |
| 372 | 12p. Norfolk Island pine | 25 | 30 |
| 373 | 15p. Screwpine | 25 | 35 |
| 374 | 20p. Eucalyptus | 25 | 45 |
| 375 | 65p. Spore tree | 70 | 1·40 |

**105** The Queen Mother with Prince Andrew at Silver Jubilee Service

**1985.** Life and Times of Queen Elizabeth the Queen Mother. Multicoloured.

| | | | |
|---|---|---|---|
| 376 | 12p. With the Duke of York at Balmoral, 1924 | 25 | 35 |
| 377 | 15p. Type **105** | 25 | 40 |
| 378 | 20p. The Queen Mother at Ascot | 30 | 55 |
| 379 | 70p. With Prince Henry at his christening (from photo by Lord Snowdon) | 80 | 1·75 |
| **MS**380 | 91×73 mm. 75p. Visiting the "Queen Elizabeth 2" at Southampton, 1968 | 1·10 | 1·60 |

**106** 32 Pdr. Smooth Bore Muzzle-loader, *c* 1820, and Royal Marine Artillery Hat Plate, *c* 1816

**1985.** Guns on Ascension Island. Multicoloured.

| | | | |
|---|---|---|---|
| 381 | 12p. Type **106** | 40 | 90 |
| 382 | 15p. 7 inch rifled muzzle-loader, c. 1866, and Royal Cypher on barrel | 40 | 1·00 |
| 383 | 20p. 7 pdr rifled muzzle-loader, c. 1877, and Royal Artillery Badge | 40 | 1·25 |
| 384 | 70p. 5.5 inch gun, 1941, and crest from H.M.S. "Hood" | 80 | 3·00 |

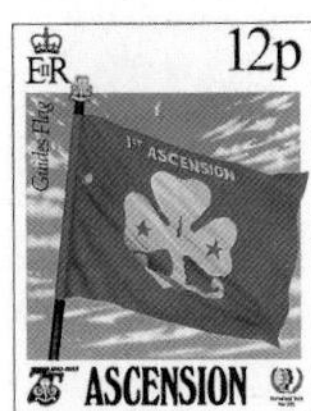


**107** Guide Flag

**1985.** 75th Anniv of Girl Guide Movement and International Youth Year. Multicoloured.

| | | | |
|---|---|---|---|
| 385 | 12p. Type **107** | 30 | 70 |
| 386 | 15p. Practising first aid | 30 | 80 |
| 387 | 20p. Camping | 30 | 90 |
| 388 | 70p. Lady Baden-Powell | 80 | 2·50 |

**108** *Clerodendrum fragrans*

**1985.** Wild Flowers. Multicoloured.

| | | | |
|---|---|---|---|
| 389 | 12p. Type **108** | 30 | 75 |
| 390 | 15p. Shell ginger | 30 | 90 |
| 391 | 20p. Cape daisy | 35 | 90 |
| 392 | 70p. Ginger lily | 70 | 2·50 |

**109** Newton's Reflector Telescope

**1986.** Appearance of Halley's Comet. Mult.

| | | | |
|---|---|---|---|
| 393 | 12p. Type **109** | 40 | 1·10 |
| 394 | 15p. Edmond Halley and Old Greenwich Observatory | 40 | 1·25 |
| 395 | 20p. Short's Gregorian telescope and comet, 1759 | 40 | 1·25 |
| 396 | 70p. Ascension satellite tracking station and ICE spacecraft | 1·10 | 3·50 |

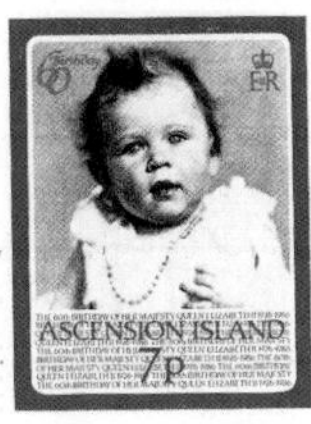


**110** Princess Elizabeth in 1926

**1986.** 60th Birthday of Queen Elizabeth II. Mult.

| | | | |
|---|---|---|---|
| 397 | 7p. Type **110** | 15 | 25 |
| 398 | 15p. Queen making Christmas broadcast, 1952 | 15 | 40 |
| 399 | 20p. At Garter ceremony, Windsor Castle, 1983 | 20 | 50 |
| 400 | 35p. In Auckland, New Zealand, 1981 | 30 | 80 |
| 401 | £1 At Crown Agents' Head Office, London, 1983 | 75 | 2·25 |

**111** 1975 Space Satellites 2p. Stamp

**1986.** "Ameripex '86" International Stamp Exhibition, Chicago. Designs showing previous Ascension stamps. Multicoloured.

| | | | |
|---|---|---|---|
| 402 | 12p. Type **111** | 25 | 60 |
| 403 | 15p. 1980 "London 1980" International Stamp Exhibition 50p. | 20 | 70 |
| 404 | 20p. 1976 Bicentenary of American Revolution 8p. | 25 | 90 |
| 405 | 70p. 1982 40th anniv of Wideawake Airfield 10p. | 70 | 2·00 |
| **MS**406 | 60×75 mm. 75p. Statue of Liberty | 1·50 | 2·75 |

**112** Prince Andrew and Miss Sarah Ferguson

**1986.** Royal Wedding. Multicoloured.

| | | | |
|---|---|---|---|
| 407 | 15p. Type **112** | 25 | 50 |
| 408 | 35p. Prince Andrew aboard H.M.S. "Brazen" | 50 | 1·00 |

**113** H.M.S. *Ganymede* (*c* 1811)

**1986.** Ships of the Royal Navy. Multicoloured.

| | | | |
|---|---|---|---|
| 409 | 1p. Type **113** | 55 | 1·50 |
| 410 | 2p. H.M.S. "Kangaroo" (c.1811) | 60 | 1·50 |
| 411 | 4p. H.M.S. "Trinculo" (c.1811) | 60 | 1·50 |
| 412 | 5p. H.M.S. "Daring" (c.1811) | 60 | 1·50 |
| 413 | 9p. H.M.S. "Thais" (c.1811) | 70 | 1·50 |
| 414 | 10p. H.M.S. "Pheasant" (1819) | 70 | 1·50 |
| 415 | 15p. H.M.S. "Myrmidon" (1819) | 80 | 1·75 |
| 416 | 18p. H.M.S. "Atholl" (1825) | 90 | 1·75 |
| 417 | 20p. H.M.S. "Medina" (1830) | 90 | 1·75 |
| 418 | 25p. H.M.S. "Saracen" (1840) | 1·00 | 2·00 |
| 419 | 30p. H.M.S. "Hydra" (c.1845) | 1·00 | 2·00 |
| 420 | 50p. H.M.S. "Sealark" (1849) | 1·00 | 2·50 |
| 421 | 70p. H.M.S. "Rattlesnake" (1868) | 1·00 | 3·00 |
| 422 | £1 H.M.S. "Penelope" (1889) | 1·25 | 3·75 |
| 423 | £2 H.M.S. "Monarch" (1897) | 2·50 | 6·50 |

**114** Cape Gooseberry

**1987.** Edible Bush Fruits. Multicoloured.

| | | | |
|---|---|---|---|
| 424 | 12p. Type **114** | 65 | 90 |
| 425 | 15p. Prickly pear | 65 | 1·00 |
| 426 | 20p. Guava | 70 | 1·10 |
| 427 | 70p. Loquat | 1·10 | 2·75 |

**115** Ignition of Rocket Motors

**1987.** 25th Anniv of First American Manned Earth Orbit. Multicoloured.

| | | | |
|---|---|---|---|
| 428 | 15p. Type **115** | 55 | 75 |
| 429 | 18p. Lift-off | 60 | 80 |
| 430 | 25p. Re-entry | 75 | 95 |
| 431 | £1 Splashdown | 2·50 | 3·25 |
| **MS**432 | 92×78 mm. 70p. "Friendship 7" capsule | 1·75 | 2·00 |

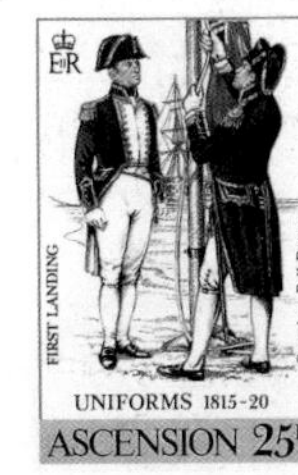


**116** Captains in Full Dress raising Red Ensign

**1987.** 19th-century Uniforms (1st series). Royal Navy, 1815–20. Multicoloured.

| | | | |
|---|---|---|---|
| 433 | 25p. Type **116** | 50 | 60 |
| 434 | 25p. Surgeon and seamen | 50 | 60 |
| 435 | 25p. Seaman with water-carrying donkey | 50 | 60 |
| 436 | 25p. Midshipman and gun | 50 | 60 |
| 437 | 25p. Commander in undress uniform surveying | 50 | 60 |

See also Nos. 478/82.

**117** *Cynthia cardui*

**1987.** Insects (1st series). Multicoloured.

| | | | |
|---|---|---|---|
| 438 | 15p. Type **117** | 55 | 65 |
| 439 | 18p. "Danaus chrysippus" | 60 | 75 |
| 440 | 25p. "Hypolimnas misippus" | 75 | 85 |
| 441 | £1 "Lampides boeticus" | 1·50 | 2·50 |

See also Nos. 452/5 and 483/6.

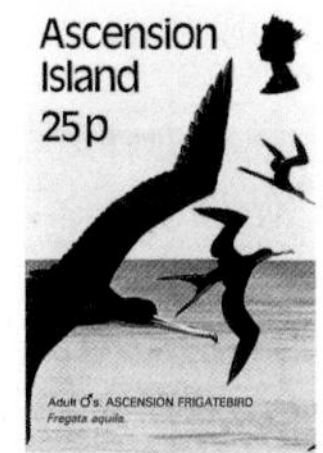


**118** Male Ascension Frigate Birds

**1987.** Sea Birds (1st series). Multicoloured.

| | | | |
|---|---|---|---|
| 442 | 25p. Type **118** | 1·60 | 2·00 |
| 443 | 25p. Juvenile Ascension frigate bird, brown booby and blue-faced boobies | 1·60 | 2·00 |
| 444 | 25p. Male Ascension frigate bird and blue-faced boobies | 1·60 | 2·00 |
| 445 | 25p. Female Ascension frigate bird | 1·60 | 2·00 |

| | | | |
|---|---|---|---|
| 446 | 25p. Adult male feeding juvenile Ascension frigate bird | 1·60 | 2·00 |

Nos. 442/6 were printed together, se-tenant, forming a composite design.
See also Nos. 469/73.

**1987.** Royal Ruby Wedding. Nos. 397/401 optd 40TH WEDDING ANNIVERSARY.

| | | | |
|---|---|---|---|
| 447 | 7p. Type **110** | 15 | 15 |
| 448 | 15p. Queen making Christmas broadcast, 1952 | 20 | 20 |
| 449 | 20p. At Garter ceremony, Windsor Castle, 1983 | 25 | 25 |
| 450 | 35p. In Auckland, New Zealand, 1981 | 40 | 45 |
| 451 | £1 At Crown Agents' Head Office, London, 1983 | 1·00 | 1·10 |

**1988.** Insects (2nd series). As T **117**. Multicoloured.

| | | | |
|---|---|---|---|
| 452 | 15p. "Gryllus bimaculatus" (field cricket) | 30 | 30 |
| 453 | 18p. "Ruspolia differeus" (bush cricket) | 35 | 35 |
| 454 | 25p. "Chilomenus lunata" (ladybird) | 40 | 40 |
| 455 | £1 "Diachrysia orichalcea" (moth) | 1·50 | 1·50 |

**120** Bate's Memorial, St. Mary's Church

**1988.** 150th Death Anniv of Captain William Bate (garrison commander, 1828–38). Multicoloured.

| | | | |
|---|---|---|---|
| 456 | 9p. Type **120** | 25 | 25 |
| 457 | 15p. Commodore's Cottage | 30 | 30 |
| 458 | 18p. North East Cottage | 35 | 35 |
| 459 | 25p. Map of Ascension | 45 | 45 |
| 460 | 70p. Captain Bate and marines | 1·00 | 1·00 |

**121** H.M.S. *Resolution* (ship of the line), 1667

**1988.** Bicentenary of Australian Settlement. Ships of the Royal Navy. Multicoloured.

| | | | |
|---|---|---|---|
| 461 | 9p. Type **121** | 1·25 | 45 |
| 462 | 18p. H.M.S. "Resolution" (Captain Cook), 1772 | 1·75 | 70 |
| 463 | 25p. H.M.S. "Resolution" (battleship), 1892 | 1·75 | 85 |
| 464 | 65p. H.M.S. "Resolution" (battleship), 1916 | 2·50 | 1·50 |

**1988.** "Sydpex '88" National Stamp Exhibition, Sydney. Nos. 461/4 optd SYDPEX 88 30.7.88 - 7.8.88.

| | | | |
|---|---|---|---|
| 465 | 9p. Type **121** | 50 | 40 |
| 466 | 18p. H.M.S. "Resolution" (Captain Cook), 1772 | 75 | 60 |
| 467 | 25p. H.M.S. "Resolution" (battleship), 1892 | 85 | 70 |
| 468 | 65p. H.M.S. "Resolution" (battleship), 1916 | 1·60 | 1·40 |

**1988.** Sea Birds (2nd series). Sooty Tern. As T **118**. Multicoloured.

| | | | |
|---|---|---|---|
| 469 | 25p. Pair displaying | 1·60 | 1·25 |
| 470 | 25p. Turning egg | 1·60 | 1·25 |
| 471 | 25p. Incubating egg | 1·60 | 1·25 |
| 472 | 25p. Feeding chick | 1·60 | 1·25 |
| 473 | 25p. Immature sooty tern | 1·60 | 1·25 |

Nos. 469/73 were printed together, se-tenant, forming a composite design of a nesting colony.

**123** Lloyd's Coffee House, London, 1688

**1988.** 300th Anniv of Lloyd's of London. Mult.

| | | | |
|---|---|---|---|
| 474 | 8p. Type **123** | 25 | 25 |
| 475 | 18p. "Alert IV" (cable ship) (horiz) | 65 | 65 |
| 476 | 25p. Satellite recovery in space (horiz) | 80 | 80 |
| 477 | 65p. "Good Hope Castle" (cargo liner) on fire off Ascension, 1973 | 1·75 | 1·75 |

**1988.** 19th-century Uniforms (2nd series). Royal Marines 1821–34. As T **116**. Multicoloured.

| | | | |
|---|---|---|---|
| 478 | 25p. Marines landing on Ascension, 1821 | 1·10 | 1·60 |
| 479 | 25p. Officer and Marine at semaphore station, 1829 | 1·10 | 1·60 |
| 480 | 25p. Sergeant and Marine at Octagonal Tank, 1831 | 1·10 | 1·60 |
| 481 | 25p. Officers at water pipe tunnel, 1833 | 1·10 | 1·60 |
| 482 | 25p. Officer supervising construction of barracks, 1834 | 1·10 | 1·60 |

**1989.** Insects (3rd series). As T **117**. Mult.

| | | | |
|---|---|---|---|
| 483 | 15p. "Trichoptilus wahlbergi" (moth) | 75 | 50 |
| 484 | 18p. "Lucilia sericata" (fly) | 80 | 55 |
| 485 | 25p. "Alceis ornatus" (weevil) | 1·10 | 70 |
| 486 | £1 "Polistes fuscatus" (wasp) | 3·00 | 2·40 |

**124** Two Land Crabs

**1989.** Ascension Land Crabs. Multicoloured.

| | | | |
|---|---|---|---|
| 487 | 15p. Type **124** | 40 | 45 |
| 488 | 18p. Crab with claws raised | 45 | 50 |
| 489 | 25p. Crab on rock | 60 | 70 |
| 490 | £1 Crab in surf | 2·00 | 2·50 |
| **MS**491 | 98×101 mm. Nos. 487/90 | 3·00 | 3·75 |

**125** 1949 75th Anniversary of U.P.U. 1s. Stamp

**1989.** "Philexfrance '89" International Stamp Exhibition, Paris, and "World Stamp Expo '89", Washington (1st issue). Sheet 104×86 mm.

| | | | |
|---|---|---|---|
| **MS**492 | 75p. multicoloured | 3·00 | 3·75 |

See also Nos. 498/503.

**126** "Apollo 7" Tracking Station, Ascension

**1989.** 20th Anniv of First Manned Landing on Moon. Multicoloured.

| | | | |
|---|---|---|---|
| 493 | 15p. Type **126** | 65 | 45 |
| 494 | 18p. Launch of "Apollo 7" (30×30 mm) | 70 | 50 |
| 495 | 25p. "Apollo 7" emblem (30×30 mm) | 90 | 70 |
| 496 | 70p. "Apollo 7" jettisoning expended Saturn rocket | 1·75 | 1·75 |
| **MS**497 | 101×83 mm. £1 Diagram of "Apollo 11" mission | 2·00 | 2·10 |

**127** *Queen Elizabeth 2* (liner) and U.S.S. *John F. Kennedy* (aircraft carrier) in New York Harbour

**1989.** "Philexfrance 89" International Stamp Exhibition, Paris, and "World Stamp Expo '89", Washington (1st issue). Designs showing Statue of Liberty and Centenary celebrations. Multicoloured.

| | | | |
|---|---|---|---|
| 498 | 15p. Type **127** | 50 | 50 |
| 499 | 15p. Cleaning statue | 50 | 50 |
| 500 | 15p. Statue of Liberty | 50 | 50 |
| 501 | 15p. Crown of statue | 50 | 50 |
| 502 | 15p. Warships and New York skyline | 50 | 50 |
| 503 | 15p. "Jean de Vienne" (French destroyer) and skyscrapers | 50 | 50 |

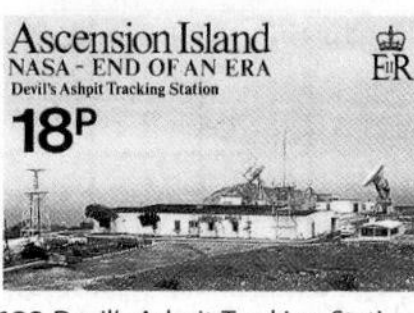

**128** Devil's Ashpit Tracking Station

**1989.** Closure of Devil's Ashpit Tracking Station, Ascension. Multicoloured.

| | | | |
|---|---|---|---|
| 504 | 18p. Type **128** | 80 | 50 |
| 505 | 25p. Launch of shuttle "Atlantis" | 80 | 55 |

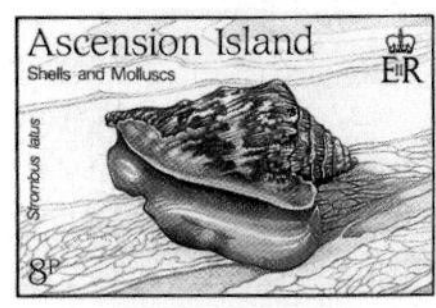

**129** Bubonian Conch (*Strombus latus*)

**1989.** Sea Shells. Multicoloured.

| | | | |
|---|---|---|---|
| 506 | 8p. Type **129** | 40 | 30 |
| 507 | 18p. Giant tun | 70 | 50 |
| 508 | 25p. Doris loup | 90 | 65 |
| 509 | £1 Atlantic trumpet triton | 2·75 | 2·50 |

**130** Donkeys

**1989.** Ascension Wildlife. Multicoloured.

| | | | |
|---|---|---|---|
| 510 | 18p. Type **130** | 1·00 | 1·25 |
| 511 | 25p. Green turtle | 1·00 | 1·25 |

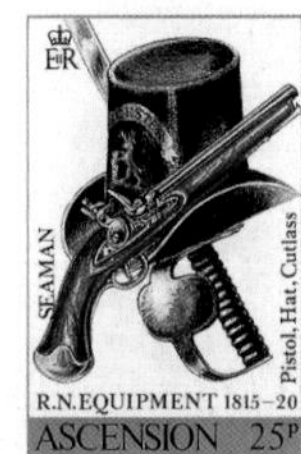

**131** Seaman's Pistol, Hat and Cutlass

**1990.** Royal Navy Equipment, 1815–20. Mult.

| | | | |
|---|---|---|---|
| 512 | 25p. Type **131** | 70 | 70 |
| 513 | 25p. Midshipman's belt plate, button, sword and hat | 70 | 70 |
| 514 | 25p. Surgeon's hat, sword and instrument chest | 70 | 70 |
| 515 | 25p. Captain's hat, telescope and sword | 70 | 70 |
| 516 | 25p. Admiral's epaulette, megaphone, hat and pocket | 70 | 70 |

See also Nos. 541/5.

**132** Pair of Ascension Frigate Birds with Young

**1990.** Endangered Species. Ascension Frigate Bird. Multicoloured.

| | | | |
|---|---|---|---|
| 517 | 9p. Type **132** | 1·50 | 1·00 |
| 518 | 10p. Fledgeling | 1·50 | 1·00 |
| 519 | 11p. Adult male in flight | 1·50 | 1·00 |
| 520 | 15p. Female and immature birds in flight | 1·75 | 1·25 |

**133** Penny Black and Twopence Blue

**1990.** "Stamp World London 90" International Stamp Exhibition. Multicoloured.

| | | | |
|---|---|---|---|
| 521 | 9p. Type **133** | 50 | 40 |
| 522 | 18p. Ascension postmarks used on G.B. stamps | 70 | 60 |
| 523 | 25p. Unloading mail at Wideawake Airfield | 95 | 85 |
| 524 | £1 Mail van and Main Post Office | 2·25 | 2·75 |

**134** "Queen Elizabeth, 1940" (Sir Gerald Kelly)

**1990.** 90th Birthday of Queen Elizabeth the Queen Mother.

| | | | | |
|---|---|---|---|---|
| 525 | **134** | 25p. multicoloured | 75 | 75 |
| 526 | - | £1 black and lilac | 2·25 | 2·25 |

DESIGN—29×37 mm: £1 King George VI and Queen Elizabeth with Bren-gun carrier.

**136** "Madonna and Child" (sculpture, Dino Felici)

**1990.** Christmas. Works of Art. Multicoloured.

| | | | |
|---|---|---|---|
| 527 | 8p. Type **136** | 70 | 70 |
| 528 | 18p. "Madonna and Child" (anon) | 1·25 | 1·25 |
| 529 | 25p. "Madonna and Child with St. John" (Johann Gebhard) | 1·75 | 1·75 |
| 530 | 65p. "Madonna and Child" (Giacomo Gritti) | 3·00 | 4·00 |

**137** *Garth Castle* (mail steamer), 1910

**1990.** Maiden Voyage of "St. Helena II". Mult.

| | | | |
|---|---|---|---|
| 531 | 9p. Type **137** | 90 | 90 |
| 532 | 18p. "St. Helena I" during Falkland Islands campaign, 1982 | 1·25 | 1·25 |
| 533 | 25p. Launch of "St. Helena II" | 1·75 | 1·75 |
| 534 | 70p. Duke of York launching "St. Helena II" | 3·00 | 4·25 |
| **MS**535 | 100×100 mm. £1 "St. Helena II" and outline map of Ascension | 3·50 | 5·00 |

**1991.** 175th Anniv of Occupation. Nos. 418, 420 and 422 optd **BRITISH FOR 175 YEARS**.

| | | | |
|---|---|---|---|
| 536 | 25p. H.M.S. "Saracen" (1840) | 2·00 | 2·50 |

| | | | |
|---|---|---|---|
| 537 | 50p. H.M.S. "Sealark" (1849) | 2·50 | 3·50 |
| 538 | £1 H.M.S. "Penelope" (1889) | 3·75 | 5·00 |

**139** Queen Elizabeth II at Trooping the Colour

**1991.** 65th Birthday of Queen Elizabeth II and 70th Birthday of Prince Philip. Multicoloured.

| | | | |
|---|---|---|---|
| 539 | 25p. Type **139** | 1·25 | 1·60 |
| 540 | 25p. Prince Philip in naval uniform | 1·25 | 1·60 |

**1991.** Royal Marines Equipment, 1821–1844. As T **131**. Multicoloured.

| | | | |
|---|---|---|---|
| 541 | 25p. Officer's shako, epaulettes, belt plate and button | 1·10 | 1·60 |
| 542 | 25p. Officer's cap, sword, epaulettes and belt plate | 1·10 | 1·60 |
| 543 | 25p. Drum major's shako and staff | 1·10 | 1·60 |
| 544 | 25p. Sergeant's shako, chevrons, belt plate and canteen | 1·10 | 1·60 |
| 545 | 25p. Drummer's shako and side-drum | 1·10 | 1·60 |

**140** B.B.C. World Service Relay Station

**1991.** 25th Anniv of B.B.C. Atlantic Relay Station. Multicoloured.

| | | | |
|---|---|---|---|
| 546 | 15p. Type **140** | 90 | 1·10 |
| 547 | 18p. Transmitters at English Bay | 1·00 | 1·25 |
| 548 | 25p. Satellite receiving station (vert) | 1·25 | 1·40 |
| 549 | 70p. Antenna support tower (vert) | 2·50 | 4·00 |

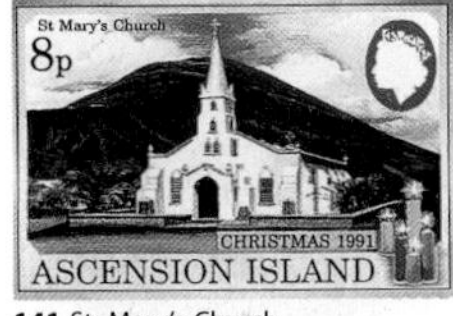

**141** St. Mary's Church

**1991.** Christmas. Ascension Churches. Mult.

| | | | |
|---|---|---|---|
| 550 | 8p. Type **141** | 55 | 55 |
| 551 | 18p. Interior of St. Mary's Church | 1·00 | 1·00 |
| 552 | 25p. Our Lady of Ascension Grotto | 1·25 | 1·25 |
| 553 | 65p. Interior of Our Lady of Ascension Grotto | 2·75 | 5·00 |

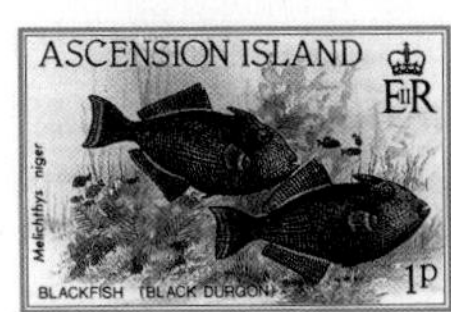

**142** Black Durgon ("Blackfish")

**1991.** Fish. Multicoloured.

| | | | |
|---|---|---|---|
| 554 | 1p. Type **142** | 1·25 | 60 |
| 555 | 2p. Sergeant major ("Five finger") | 1·25 | 60 |
| 556 | 4p. Resplendent angelfish | 1·50 | 70 |
| 557 | 5p. Derbio ("Silver fish") | 1·50 | 70 |
| 558 | 9p. Spotted scorpionfish ("Gurnard") | 1·75 | 80 |
| 559 | 10p. St. Helena parrotfish ("Blue dad") | 1·75 | 80 |
| 560 | 15p. St. Helena butterflyfish ("Cunning fish") | 2·25 | 1·00 |
| 561 | 18p. Rock hind ("Grouper") | 2·25 | 1·00 |
| 562 | 20p. Spotted moray | 2·25 | 1·25 |
| 563 | 25p. Squirrelfish ("Hardback soldierfish") | 2·25 | 1·25 |
| 564 | 30p. Blue marlin | 2·25 | 1·40 |
| 565 | 50p. Wahoo | 3·00 | 2·00 |
| 566 | 70p. Yellow-finned tuna | 3·00 | 2·75 |
| 567 | £1 Blue shark | 3·25 | 3·50 |
| 568 | £2.50 Bottlenose dolphin | 7·00 | 7·00 |

**143** Holland's Crater

**1992.** 40th Anniv of Queen Elizabeth II's Accession. Multicoloured.

| | | | |
|---|---|---|---|
| 569 | 9p. Type **143** | 30 | 30 |
| 570 | 15p. Green Mountain | 50 | 50 |
| 571 | 18p. Boatswain Bird Island | 60 | 60 |
| 572 | 25p. Three portraits of Queen Elizabeth | 80 | 80 |
| 573 | 70p. Queen Elizabeth II | 2·00 | 2·00 |

The portraits shown on the 25p. are repeated from the three lower values of the set.

**144** Compass Rose and *Eye of the Wind* (cadet brig)

**1992.** 500th Anniv of Discovery of America by Columbus and Re-enactment Voyages. Mult.

| | | | |
|---|---|---|---|
| 574 | 9p. Type **144** | 1·25 | 80 |
| 575 | 18p. Map of re-enactment voyages and "Soren Larsen" (cadet brigantine) | 1·75 | 1·25 |
| 576 | 25p. "Santa Maria", "Pinta" and "Nina" | 2·25 | 1·50 |
| 577 | 70p. Columbus and "Santa Maria" | 3·75 | 3·50 |

**145** Control Tower, Wideawake Airfield

**1992.** 50th Anniv of Wideawake Airfield. Multicoloured.

| | | | |
|---|---|---|---|
| 578 | 15p. Type **145** | 65 | 65 |
| 579 | 18p. Nose hangar | 70 | 70 |
| 580 | 25p. Site preparation by U.S. Army engineers | 90 | 90 |
| 581 | 70p. Laying fuel pipeline | 2·25 | 2·25 |

**146** Hawker Siddeley Nimrod

**1992.** 10th Anniv of Liberation of Falkland Islands. Aircraft. Multicoloured.

| | | | |
|---|---|---|---|
| 582 | 15p. Type **146** | 1·50 | 1·75 |
| 583 | 18p. Vickers VC-10 landing at Ascension | 1·50 | 1·75 |
| 584 | 25p. Westland Wessex HU Mk 5 helicopter lifting supplies | 2·00 | 1·75 |
| 585 | 65p. Avro Vulcan B.2 over Ascension | 3·25 | 4·75 |
| **MS**586 | 116×116 mm. 15p.+3p. Type **146**; 18p.+4p. As No. 583; 25p.+5p. As No. 584; 65p.+13p. As No. 585 | 4·00 | 6·00 |

The premiums on No. **MS**586 were for the S.S.A.F.A.

**147** "Christmas in Great Britain and Ascension"

**1992.** Christmas. Children's Paintings. Mult.

| | | | |
|---|---|---|---|
| 587 | 8p. Type **147** | 80 | 1·00 |
| 588 | 18p. "Santa Claus riding turtle" | 1·25 | 1·50 |
| 589 | 25p. "Nativity" | 1·50 | 1·75 |
| 590 | 65p. "Nativity with rabbit" | 2·75 | 5·00 |

**148** Male Canary Singing

**1993.** Yellow Canary. Multicoloured.

| | | | |
|---|---|---|---|
| 591 | 15p. Type **148** | 75 | 80 |
| 592 | 18p. Adult male and female | 85 | 90 |
| 593 | 25p. Young birds calling for food | 95 | 1·10 |
| 594 | 70p. Adults and young birds on the wing | 2·50 | 4·00 |

**149** Sopwith Snipe

**1993.** 75th Anniv of Royal Air Force. Multicoloured.

| | | | |
|---|---|---|---|
| 595 | 20p. Type **149** | 2·00 | 1·75 |
| 596 | 25p. Supermarine Southampton | 2·00 | 1·75 |
| 597 | 30p. Avro Type 652 Anson | 2·00 | 1·90 |
| 598 | 70p. Vickers-Armstrong Wellington | 3·25 | 4·50 |
| **MS**599 | 110×77 mm. 25p. Westland Lysander; 25p. Armstrong-Whitworth Meteor ("Gloster Meteor"); 25p. De Havilland D.H.106 Comet; 25p. Hawker Siddeley H.S.801 Nimrod | 3·00 | 4·00 |

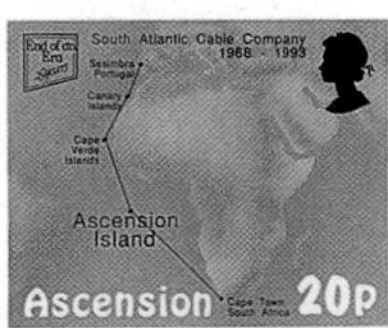

**150** Map of South Atlantic Cable

**1993.** 25th Anniv of South Atlantic Cable Company. Multicoloured.

| | | | |
|---|---|---|---|
| 600 | 20p. Type **150** | 80 | 90 |
| 601 | 25p. "Sir Eric Sharpe" laying cable | 90 | 1·00 |
| 602 | 30p. Map of Ascension | 1·00 | 1·25 |
| 603 | 70p. "Sir Eric Sharpe" (cable ship) off Ascension | 2·25 | 2·75 |

**151** Lanatana Camara

**1993.** Local Flowers. Multicoloured.

| | | | |
|---|---|---|---|
| 604 | 20p. Type **151** | 1·50 | 1·00 |
| 605 | 25p. Moonflower | 1·60 | 1·10 |
| 606 | 30p. Hibiscus | 1·60 | 1·25 |
| 607 | 70p. Frangipani | 3·00 | 3·25 |

**152** Posting Christmas Card to Ascension

**1993.** Christmas. Multicoloured.

| | | | |
|---|---|---|---|
| 608 | 12p. Type **152** | 45 | 45 |
| 609 | 20p. Loading mail onto R.A.F. Lockheed TriStar at Brize Norton | 95 | 70 |
| 610 | 25p. TriStar over South Atlantic | 1·25 | 90 |
| 611 | 30p. Unloading mail at Wideawake Airfield | 1·40 | 1·10 |
| 612 | 65p. Receiving card and Georgetown Post Office | 1·60 | 3·25 |
| **MS**613 | 161×76 mm. Nos. 608/12 | 10·00 | 10·00 |

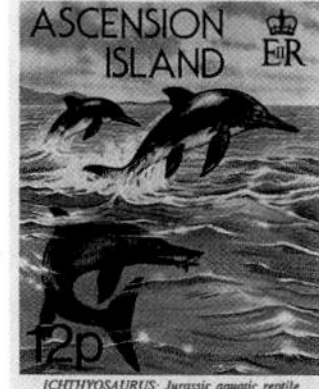

**153** Ichthyosaurus

**1994.** Prehistoric Aquatic Reptiles. Mult.

| | | | |
|---|---|---|---|
| 614 | 12p. Type **153** | 70 | 1·10 |
| 615 | 20p. Metriorhynchus | 85 | 1·25 |
| 616 | 25p. Mosasaurus | 90 | 1·40 |
| 617 | 30p. Elasmosaurus | 90 | 1·50 |
| 618 | 65p. Plesiosaurus | 1·75 | 2·75 |

**1994.** "Hong Kong '94" International Stamp Exhibition. Nos. 614/18 optd **HONG KONG '94** and emblem.

| | | | |
|---|---|---|---|
| 619 | 12p. Type **153** | 1·00 | 1·50 |
| 620 | 20p. Metriorhynchus | 1·25 | 1·60 |
| 621 | 25p. Mosasaurus | 1·25 | 1·90 |
| 622 | 30p. Elasmosaurus | 1·40 | 2·00 |
| 623 | 65p. Plesiosaurus | 2·50 | 4·00 |

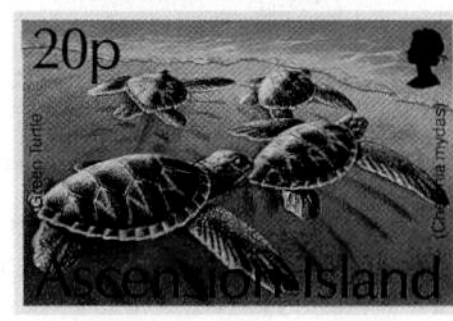

**155** Young Green Turtles heading towards Sea

**1994.** Green Turtles. Multicoloured.

| | | | |
|---|---|---|---|
| 624 | 20p. Type **155** | 2·25 | 2·25 |
| 625 | 25p. Turtle digging nest | 2·25 | 2·25 |
| 626 | 30p. Turtle leaving sea | 2·25 | 2·25 |
| 627 | 65p. Turtle swimming | 3·75 | 6·00 |
| **MS**628 | 116×90 mm. 30p. Turtle leaving sea (different); 30p. Turtle digging nest (different); 30p. Young turtles heading towards sea (different); 30p. Young turtle leaving nest | 12·00 | 12·00 |

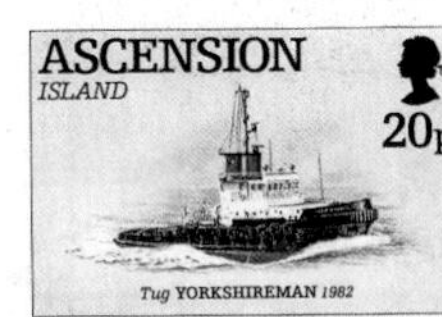

**156** *Yorkshireman* (tug)

**1994.** Civilian Ships used in Liberation of Falkland Islands, 1982. Multicoloured.

| | | | |
|---|---|---|---|
| 629 | 20p. Type **156** | 2·75 | 2·25 |
| 630 | 25p. "St. Helena I" (minesweeper support ship) | 2·75 | 2·25 |
| 631 | 30p. "British Esk" (tanker) | 2·75 | 2·50 |
| 632 | 65p. "Uganda" (hospital ship) | 5·00 | 6·00 |

**157** Sooty Tern Chick

**1994.** Sooty Tern. Multicoloured.

| | | | |
|---|---|---|---|
| 633 | 20p. Type **157** | 90 | 1·50 |
| 634 | 25p. Juvenile bird | 95 | 1·50 |
| 635 | 30p. Brooding adult | 1·10 | 1·60 |
| 636 | 65p. Adult male performing courting display | 1·75 | 2·75 |
| **MS**637 | 77×58 mm. £1 Flock of sooty terns | 3·50 | 5·50 |

**158** Donkey Mare with Foal

**1994.** Christmas. Donkeys. Multicoloured.

| | | | |
|---|---|---|---|
| 638 | 12p. Type **158** | 1·60 | 1·40 |
| 639 | 20p. Juvenile | 1·90 | 1·75 |
| 640 | 25p. Foal | 1·90 | 1·75 |
| 641 | 30p. Adult and cattle egrets | 1·90 | 1·90 |
| 642 | 65p. Adult | 3·75 | 5·00 |

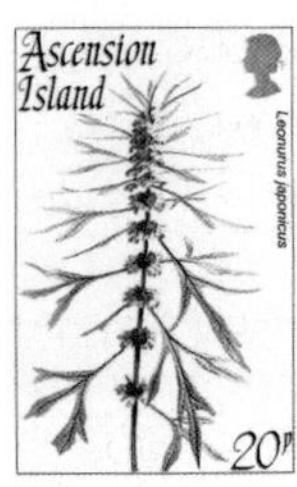


**159** *Leonurus japonicus*

**1995.** Flowers. Multicoloured.

| | | | |
|---|---|---|---|
| 643 | 20p. Type **159** | 2·75 | 2·25 |
| 644 | 25p. "Catharanthus roseus" (horiz) | 2·75 | 2·25 |
| 645 | 30p. "Mirabilis jalapa" | 3·00 | 2·50 |
| 646 | 65p. "Asclepias curassavica" (horiz) | 3·75 | 5·50 |

**160** Two Boats and Green Mountain

**1995.** Late 19th-century Scenes. Each in cinnamon and brown.

| | | | |
|---|---|---|---|
| 647 | 12p. Type **160** | 50 | 80 |
| 648 | 20p. Island Stewards' Store | 70 | 90 |
| 649 | 25p. Navy headquarters and barracks | 90 | 1·10 |
| 650 | 30p. Police office | 1·75 | 1·75 |
| 651 | 65p. Pierhead | 2·00 | 3·50 |

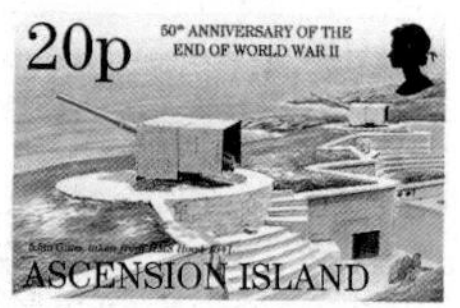


**161** 5.5-inch Coastal Battery

**1995.** 50th Anniv of End of Second World War. Multicoloured.

| | | | |
|---|---|---|---|
| 652 | 20p. Type **161** | 1·75 | 2·00 |
| 653 | 25p. Fairey Swordfish aircraft | 2·00 | 2·00 |
| 654 | 30p. H.M.S. "Dorsetshire" (cruiser) | 2·25 | 3·25 |
| 655 | 65p. H.M.S. "Devonshire" (cruiser) | 3·75 | 4·50 |
| **MS**656 | 75×85 mm. £1 Reverse of 1939–45 War Medal (vert) | 2·50 | 3·25 |

**162** Male and Female *Lampides boeticus*

**1995.** Butterflies. Multicoloured.

| | | | |
|---|---|---|---|
| 657 | 20p. Type **162** | 1·50 | 1·50 |
| 658 | 25p. "Vanessa cardui" | 1·75 | 1·75 |
| 659 | 30p. Male "Hypolimnas misippus" | 1·75 | 1·75 |
| 660 | 65p. "Danaus chrysippus" | 2·75 | 3·50 |
| **MS**661 | 114×85 mm. £1 "Vanessa atalanta" | 5·50 | 6·00 |

No. **MS**661 includes the "Singapore '95" International Stamp Exhibition logo on the sheet margin.

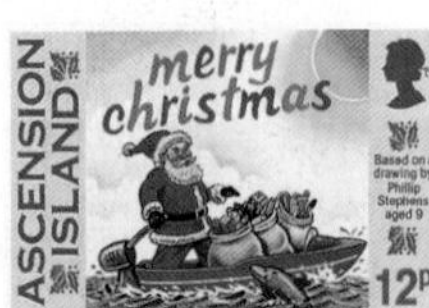


**163** "Santa Claus on Boat" (Phillip Stephens)

**1995.** Christmas. Children's Drawings. Mult.

| | | | |
|---|---|---|---|
| 662 | 12p. Type **163** | 1·75 | 1·25 |
| 663 | 20p. "Santa sitting on Wall" (Kelly Lemon) | 2·00 | 1·75 |
| 664 | 25p. "Santa in Chimney" (Mario Anthony) | 2·00 | 1·75 |
| 665 | 30p. "Santa riding Dolphin" (Verena Benjamin) | 2·00 | 1·75 |
| 666 | 65p. "Santa in Sleigh over Ascension" (Tom Butler) | 3·50 | 5·00 |

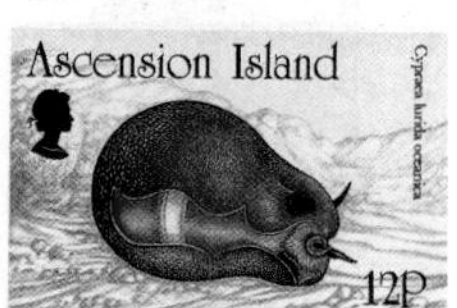


**164** *Cypraea lurida oceanica*

**1996.** Molluscs. Multicoloured.

| | | | |
|---|---|---|---|
| 667 | 12p. Type **164** | 2·75 | 3·00 |
| 668 | 25p. "Cypraea spurca sanctaehelenae" | 3·00 | 3·25 |
| 669 | 30p. "Harpa doris" | 3·00 | 3·25 |
| 670 | 65p. "Umbraculum umbraculum" | 3·75 | 4·00 |

Nos. 667/70 were printed together, se-tenant, forming a composite design.

**165** Queen Elizabeth II and St. Mary's Church

**1996.** 70th Birthday of Queen Elizabeth II. Mult.

| | | | |
|---|---|---|---|
| 671 | 20p. Type **165** | 55 | 60 |
| 672 | 25p. The Residency | 60 | 60 |
| 673 | 30p. The Roman Catholic Grotto | 70 | 75 |
| 674 | 65p. The Exiles' Club | 1·75 | 2·00 |

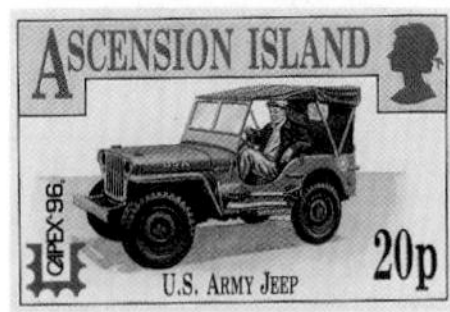


**166** American Army Jeep

**1996.** "CAPEX '96" International Stamp Exhibition, Toronto. Island Transport. Multicoloured.

| | | | |
|---|---|---|---|
| 675 | 20p. Type **166** | 1·50 | 1·50 |
| 676 | 25p. Citroen 7.5hp two-seater car, 1924 | 1·60 | 1·60 |
| 677 | 30p. Austin ten tourer car, 1930 | 1·60 | 1·60 |
| 678 | 65p. Series 1 Land Rover | 2·75 | 3·25 |

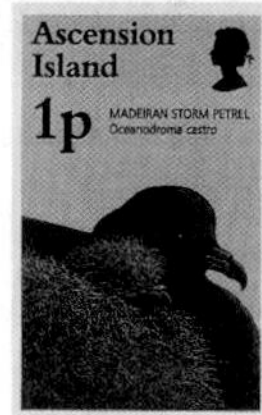


**167** Madeiran Storm Petrel

**1996.** Birds and their Young. Multicoloured.

| | | | |
|---|---|---|---|
| 679 | 1p. Type **167** | 75 | 1·00 |
| 680 | 2p. Red-billed tropic bird | 75 | 1·00 |
| 681 | 4p. Common mynah | 75 | 1·00 |
| 682 | 5p. House sparrow | 75 | 1·00 |
| 683 | 7p. Common waxbill | 1·00 | 1·25 |
| 684 | 10p. White tern | 1·25 | 1·25 |
| 685 | 12p. Red-necked spurfowl | 1·50 | 1·25 |
| 686 | 15p. Common noddy ("Brown Noddy") | 1·50 | 1·50 |
| 687 | 20p. Yellow canary | 1·75 | 1·50 |
| 688 | 25p. White-capped noddy ("Black Noddy") | 1·75 | 1·50 |
| 689 | 30p. Red-footed booby | 1·75 | 1·50 |
| 690 | 40p. White-tailed tropic bird ("Yellow-billed Tropicbird") | 2·00 | 2·00 |
| 691 | 65p. Brown booby | 2·75 | 3·00 |
| 692 | £1 Blue-faced booby ("Masked Booby") | 3·25 | 3·50 |
| 693 | £2 Sooty tern | 5·00 | 6·00 |
| 694 | £3 Ascension frigate bird | 7·00 | 8·00 |

See also Nos. 726/7.

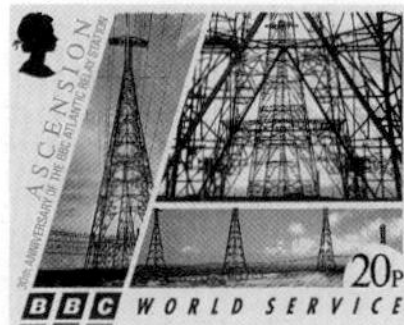


**168** Pylons

**1996.** 30th Anniv of B.B.C. Atlantic Relay Station. Multicoloured.

| | | | |
|---|---|---|---|
| 695 | 20p. Type **168** | 75 | 75 |
| 696 | 25p. Pylons (different) | 80 | 80 |
| 697 | 30p. Pylons and station buildings | 90 | 90 |
| 698 | 65p. Dish aerial, pylon and beach | 1·90 | 1·90 |

**169** Santa Claus on Dish Aerial

**1996.** Christmas. Santa Claus. Multicoloured.

| | | | |
|---|---|---|---|
| 699 | 12p. Type **169** | 50 | 50 |
| 700 | 20p. Playing golf | 75 | 75 |
| 701 | 25p. In deck chair | 75 | 75 |
| 702 | 30p. On top of aircraft | 85 | 85 |
| 703 | 65p. On funnel of "St. Helena II" (mail ship) | 1·90 | 2·25 |

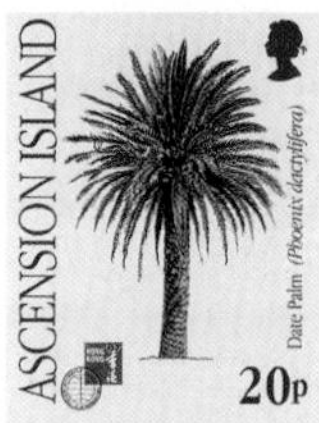


**170** Date Palm

**1997.** "Hong Kong '97" International Stamp Exhibition. Trees. Multicoloured.

| | | | |
|---|---|---|---|
| 704 | 20p. Type **170** | 75 | 75 |
| 705 | 25p. Mauritius hemp | 85 | 85 |
| 706 | 30p. Norfolk Island pine | 95 | 95 |
| 707 | 65p. Dwarf palm | 2·00 | 2·50 |

**1997.** "HONG KONG '97" International Stamp Exhibition. Sheet 130×90 mm containing design as No. 691. Multicoloured.

| | | | |
|---|---|---|---|
| **MS**708 | 65p. Brown booby | 1·50 | 1·75 |

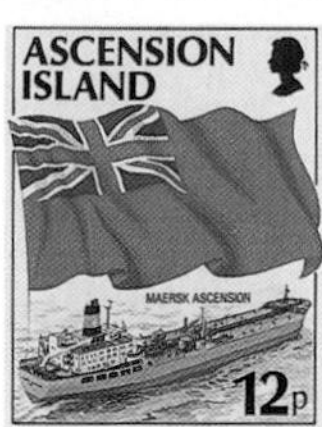


**171** Red Ensign and *Maersk Ascension* (tanker)

**1997.** Flags. Multicoloured.

| | | | |
|---|---|---|---|
| 709 | 12p. Type **171** | 1·00 | 80 |
| 710 | 25p. R.A.F. flag and Tristar airliner | 1·40 | 1·10 |
| 711 | 30p. N.A.S.A. emblem and Space Shuttle "Atlantis" landing | 1·40 | 1·25 |
| 712 | 65p. White Ensign and H.M.S. "Northumberland" (frigate) | 2·75 | 2·75 |

**172** *Solanum sodomaeum*

**1997.** Wild Herbs. Multicoloured.

| | | | |
|---|---|---|---|
| 713 | 30p. Type **172** | 1·40 | 1·60 |
| 714 | 30p. "Ageratum conyzoides" | 1·40 | 1·60 |
| 715 | 30p. "Leonurus sibiricus" | 1·40 | 1·60 |
| 716 | 30p. "Cerastium vulgatum" | 1·40 | 1·60 |
| 717 | 30p. "Commelina diffusa" | 1·40 | 1·60 |

Nos. 713/17 were printed together, se-tenant, with the backgrounds forming a composite design.

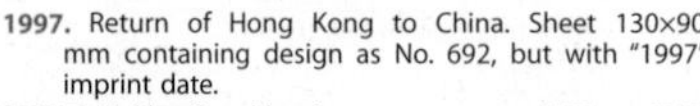

**1997.** Return of Hong Kong to China. Sheet 130×90 mm containing design as No. 692, but with "1997" imprint date.

| | | | |
|---|---|---|---|
| **MS**718 | £1 Blue-faced booby | 1·50 | 2·10 |

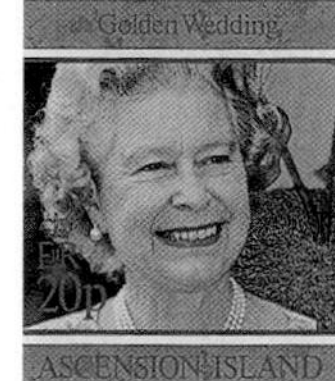


**173** Queen Elizabeth II

**1997.** Golden Wedding of Queen Elizabeth and Prince Philip. Multicoloured.

| | | | |
|---|---|---|---|
| 719 | 20p. Type **173** | 1·50 | 2·00 |
| 720 | 20p. Prince Philip on horseback | 1·50 | 2·00 |
| 721 | 25p. Queen Elizabeth with polo pony | 1·50 | 2·00 |
| 722 | 25p. Prince Philip in Montserrat | 1·50 | 2·00 |
| 723 | 30p. Queen Elizabeth and Prince Philip | 1·50 | 2·00 |
| 724 | 30p. Prince William and Prince Harry on horseback | 1·50 | 2·00 |
| **MS**725 | 110×70 mm. $1.50, Queen Elizabeth and Prince Philip in landau (horiz) | 3·50 | 3·50 |

Nos. 719/20, 721/2 and 723/4 respectively were printed together, se-tenant, with the backgrounds forming composite designs.

**1997.** Birds and their Young. As Nos. 683 and 687, but smaller, size 20×24 mm. Multicoloured.

| | | | |
|---|---|---|---|
| 726 | 15p. Common waxbill | 2·00 | 2·25 |
| 727 | 35p. Yellow canary | 2·00 | 2·25 |

**174** Black Marlin

**1997.** Gamefish. Multicoloured.

| | | | |
|---|---|---|---|
| 728 | 12p. Type **174** | 75 | 75 |
| 729 | 20p. Atlantic sailfish | 1·00 | 1·00 |
| 730 | 25p. Swordfish | 1·10 | 1·10 |
| 731 | 30p. Wahoo | 1·25 | 1·25 |
| 732 | £1 Yellowfin tuna | 3·00 | 4·00 |

**175** Interior of St. Mary's Church

**1997.** Christmas. Multicoloured.

| | | | |
|---|---|---|---|
| 733 | 15p. Type **175** | 1·00 | 1·00 |
| 734 | 35p. Falklands memorial window showing Virgin and child | 1·60 | 1·60 |
| 735 | 40p. Falklands memorial window showing Archangel | 1·75 | 1·90 |
| 736 | 50p. Pair of stained glass windows | 2·00 | 2·25 |

**176** *Cactoblastis cactorum* (caterpillar and moth)

**1998.** Biological Control using Insects. Mult.

| | | | |
|---|---|---|---|
| 737 | 15p. Type **176** | 2·00 | 1·75 |
| 738 | 35p. "Teleonemia scrupulosa" (lace-bug) | 2·50 | 2·25 |
| 739 | 40p. "Neltumius arizonensis" (beetle) | 2·50 | 2·75 |
| 740 | 50p. "Algarobius prosopis" (beetle) | 2·75 | 3·25 |

**177** Diana, Princess of Wales, 1985

**1998.** Diana, Princess of Wales Commemoration. Sheet 145×70 mm, containing T 177 and similar vert designs. Multicoloured.

| | | | |
|---|---|---|---|
| **MS**741 | 35p. Type **177**; 35p. Wearing yellow blouse, 1992; 35p. Wearing grey jacket, 1984; 35p. Carrying bouquets (sold at £1.40 + 20p. charity premium) | 2·25 | 3·75 |

**178** Fairey Fawn

**1998.** 80th Anniv of Royal Air Force. Mult.

| | | | |
|---|---|---|---|
| 742 | 15p. Type **178** | 1·50 | 1·25 |
| 743 | 35p. Vickers Vernon | 2·25 | 2·25 |
| 744 | 40p. Supermarine Spitfire F.22 | 2·25 | 2·50 |
| 745 | 50p. Bristol Britannia C.2 | 2·50 | 3·00 |
| **MS**746 | 110×77 mm. 50p. Blackburn Kangaroo; 50p. S.E.5a; 50p. Curtiss Kittyhawk III; 50p. Boeing Fortress II | 4·75 | 4·75 |

**179** Barn Swallow

**1998.** Migratory Birds. Multicoloured.

| | | | |
|---|---|---|---|
| 747 | 15p. Type **179** | 1·25 | 1·25 |
| 748 | 25p. House martin | 1·50 | 1·50 |
| 749 | 35p. Cattle egret | 1·75 | 1·75 |
| 750 | 40p. Eurasian swift ("Swift") | 1·90 | 1·90 |
| 751 | 50p. Allen's gallinule | 2·00 | 2·00 |

**180** Cricket

**1998.** Sporting Activities. Multicoloured.

| | | | |
|---|---|---|---|
| 752 | 15p. Type **180** | 2·75 | 1·75 |
| 753 | 35p. Golf | 3·50 | 2·25 |
| 754 | 40p. Football | 2·00 | 2·50 |
| 755 | 50p. Shooting | 2·00 | 2·50 |

**181** Children in Nativity Play

**1998.** Christmas. Multicoloured.

| | | | |
|---|---|---|---|
| 756 | 15p. Type **181** | 1·25 | 1·25 |
| 757 | 35p. Santa Claus arriving on Ascension | 1·75 | 1·75 |
| 758 | 40p. Santa Claus on carnival float | 1·75 | 1·75 |
| 759 | 50p. Carol singers | 1·75 | 1·75 |

**182** Curtiss C-46 Commando

**1999.** Aircraft. Multicoloured.

| | | | |
|---|---|---|---|
| 760 | 15p. Type **182** | 1·75 | 1·75 |
| 761 | 35p. Douglas C-47 Dakota | 2·25 | 2·25 |
| 762 | 40p. Douglas C-54 Skymaster | 2·25 | 2·25 |
| 763 | 50p. Consolidated Liberator Mk. V | 2·25 | 2·50 |
| **MS**764 | 120×85 mm. $1.50, Consolidated Liberator LB-30 | 11·00 | 11·00 |

No. **MS**764 also commemorates the 125th birth anniv of Sir Winston Churchill.

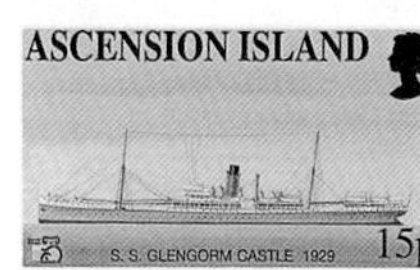

**183** *Glengorm Castle* (mail ship), 1929

**1999.** "Australia '99" World Stamp Exhibition, Melbourne. Ships. Multicoloured.

| | | | |
|---|---|---|---|
| 765 | 15p. Type **183** | 1·75 | 1·75 |
| 766 | 35p. "Gloucester Castle" (mail ship), 1930 | 2·25 | 2·25 |
| 767 | 40p. "Durham Castle" (mail ship), 1930 | 2·25 | 2·25 |
| 768 | 50p. "Garth Castle" (mail ship), 1930 | 2·25 | 2·50 |
| **MS**769 | 121×82 mm. £1 H.M.S. "Endeavour" (Cook) | 3·00 | 4·00 |

**184** Pair of White Terns ("Fairy Terns")

**1999.** Endangered Species. White Tern ("Fairy Tern"). Multicoloured.

| | | | |
|---|---|---|---|
| 770 | 10p. Type **184** | 45 | 55 |
| 771 | 10p. On branch | 45 | 55 |
| 772 | 10p. Adult and fledgeling | 45 | 55 |
| 773 | 10p. In flight | 45 | 55 |

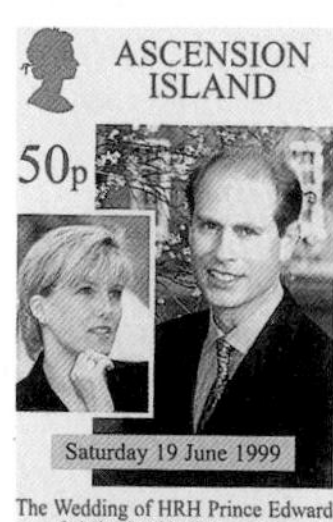

**185** Prince Edward and Miss Sophie Rhys-Jones

**1999.** Royal Wedding. Multicoloured.

| | | | |
|---|---|---|---|
| 774 | 50p. Type **185** | 1·25 | 1·50 |
| 775 | £1 Engagement photograph | 2·25 | 2·75 |

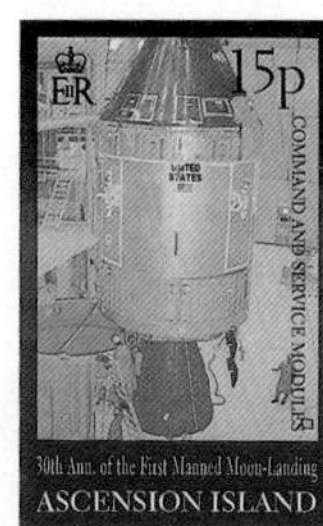

**186** Command and Service Modules

**1999.** 30th Anniv of First Manned Landing on Moon. Multicoloured.

| | | | |
|---|---|---|---|
| 776 | 15p. Type **186** | 75 | 1·10 |
| 777 | 35p. Moon from "Apollo 11" | 1·25 | 1·60 |
| 778 | 40p. Devil's Ashpit Tracking Station and command module | 1·25 | 1·60 |
| 779 | 50p. Lunar module leaving Moon | 1·25 | 1·60 |
| **MS**780 | 90×80 mm. $1.50, Earth as seen from Moon (circular, 40 mm diam) | 3·75 | 5·00 |

**187** King George VI, Queen Elizabeth and Prime Minister Winston Churchill, 1940

**1999.** "Queen Elizabeth the Queen Mother's Century". Multicoloured.

| | | | |
|---|---|---|---|
| 781 | 15p. Type **187** | 1·25 | 1·25 |
| 782 | 35p. With Prince Charles at Coronation, 1953 | 1·75 | 1·75 |
| 783 | 40p. On her 88th Birthday, 1988 | 1·75 | 1·75 |
| 784 | 50p. With Guards' drummers, 1988 | 1·75 | 1·75 |
| **MS**785 | 145×70 mm. £1.50, Lady Elizabeth Bowes-Lyon, and "Titanic" (liner) (black) | 3·75 | 5·00 |

**188** Babies with Toys

**1999.** Christmas. Multicoloured.

| | | | |
|---|---|---|---|
| 786 | 15p. Type **188** | 1·50 | 1·50 |
| 787 | 35p. Children dressed as clowns | 2·00 | 2·00 |
| 788 | 40p. Getting ready for bed | 2·00 | 2·00 |
| 789 | 50p. Children dressed as pirates | 2·00 | 2·00 |

**189** *Anglia* (cable ship), 1900

**1999.** Centenary of Cable & Wireless Communications plc on Ascension.

| | | | | |
|---|---|---|---|---|
| 790 | **189** | 15p. black, brown and bistre | 1·75 | 1·75 |
| 791 | - | 35p. black, brown and bistre | 2·25 | 2·25 |
| 792 | - | 40p. multicoloured | 2·25 | 2·25 |
| 793 | - | 50p. black, brown and bistre | 2·50 | 2·50 |
| **MS**794 | - | 105×90 mm. £1.50, multicoloured | 3·75 | 4·00 |

DESIGNS: 35p. "Cambria" (cable ship), 1910; 40p. Cable network map; 50p. "Colonia" (cable ship), 1910; £1.50, "Seine" (cable ship), 1899.

**190** Baby Turtles

**2000.** Turtle Project on Ascension. Multicoloured.

| | | | |
|---|---|---|---|
| 795 | 15p. Type **190** | 1·25 | 1·25 |
| 796 | 35p. Turtle on beach | 1·75 | 1·75 |
| 797 | 40p. Turtle with tracking device | 1·75 | 1·75 |
| 798 | 50p. Turtle heading for sea | 1·75 | 1·75 |
| **MS**799 | 197×132 mm. 25p. Head of turtle; 25p. Type **190**; 25p. Turtle on beach; 25p. Turtle entering sea (each 40×26 mm) | 5·00 | 5·50 |

**2000.** "The Stamp Show 2000" International Stamp Exhibition, London. As No. **MS**799, but with "The Stamp Show 2000" added to the bottom right corner of the margin.

| | | | |
|---|---|---|---|
| **MS**800 | 197×132 mm. 25p. Head of turtle; 25p. Type **190**; 25p. Turtle on beach; 25p. Turtle entering sea (each 40×26 mm) | 2·75 | 3·25 |

**191** Prince William as Toddler, 1983

**2000.** 18th Birthday of Prince William. Mult.

| | | | |
|---|---|---|---|
| 801 | 15p. Type **191** | 1·00 | 1·00 |
| 802 | 35p. Prince William in 1994 | 1·50 | 1·50 |
| 803 | 40p. Skiing at Klosters, Switzerland (horiz) | 1·50 | 1·50 |
| 804 | 50p. Prince William in 1997 (horiz) | 1·50 | 1·50 |
| **MS**805 | 175×95 mm. 10p. As baby with toy mouse (horiz) and Nos. 801/4 | 7·00 | 7·00 |

**192** Royal Marine and Early Fort, 1815

**2000.** Forts. Multicoloured.

| | | | |
|---|---|---|---|
| 806 | 15p. Type **192** | 1·75 | 1·75 |
| 807 | 35p. Army officer and Fort Thornton, 1817 | 2·50 | 2·50 |
| 808 | 40p. Soldier and Fort Hayes, 1860 | 2·50 | 2·50 |
| 809 | 50p. Naval lieutenant and Fort Bedford, 1940 | 2·75 | 2·75 |

**193** Ships and Dockside Crane ("I saw Three Ships")

**2000.** Christmas. Carols. Multicoloured.

| | | | |
|---|---|---|---|
| 810 | 15p. Type **193** | 1·50 | 1·20 |
| 811 | 25p. Choir and musicians on beach ("Silent Night") | 1·75 | 1·25 |
| 812 | 40p. Donkeys and church ("Away in a Manger") | 2·50 | 2·00 |
| 813 | 90p. Carol singers outside church ("Hark the Herald Angels Sing") | 4·50 | 7·00 |

**194** Green Turtle

**2001.** "Hong Kong 2001" Stamp Exhibition. Sheet 150×90 mm, containing T 194. Multicoloured.

| | | | |
|---|---|---|---|
| **MS**814 | 25p. Type **194**; 40p. Loggerhead turtle | 3·75 | 4·50 |

**195** Captain William Dampier

**2001.** Centenary of Wreck of the Roebuck. Mult.

| | | | |
|---|---|---|---|
| 815 | 15p. Type **195** | 2·25 | 2·25 |
| 816 | 35p. Construction drawing (horiz) | 2·75 | 2·75 |
| 817 | 40p. Cave dwelling at Dampier's Drip (horiz) | 2·75 | 2·75 |
| 818 | 50p. Map of Ascension | 3·50 | 3·50 |

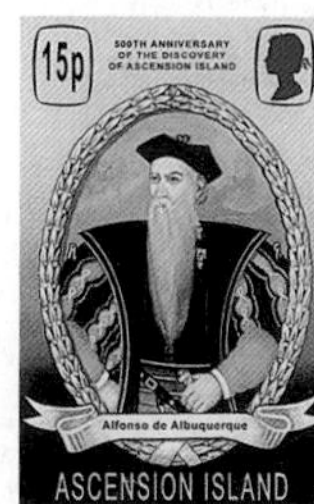

**196** Alfonso de Albuquerque

**2001.** 500th Anniv of the Discovery of Ascension Island. Multicoloured.

| | | | |
|---|---|---|---|
| 819 | 15p. Type **196** | 2·25 | 2·25 |
| 820 | 35p. Portuguese caravel | 3·25 | 3·25 |
| 821 | 40p. Cantino map | 3·50 | 3·50 |
| 822 | 50p. Rear Admiral Sir George Cockburn | 3·50 | 3·50 |

**197** Great Britain 1d. Stamp used on Ascension, 1855

**2001.** Death Centenary of Queen Victoria. Mult.

| | | | |
|---|---|---|---|
| 823 | 15p. Type **197** | 1·25 | 1·25 |
| 824 | 25p. Navy church parade, 1901 (horiz) | 1·50 | 1·50 |
| 825 | 35p. H.M.S. *Phoebe* (cruiser) (horiz) | 2·00 | 2·00 |
| 826 | 40p. The Red Lion, 1863 (horiz) | 2·00 | 2·00 |
| 827 | 50p. "Queen Victoria" | 2·00 | 2·00 |
| 828 | 65p. Sir Joseph Hooker (botanist) | 2·00 | 2·75 |
| **MS**829 | 105×80 mm. £1.50, Queen Victoria's coffin on the steps of St. George's Chapel, Windsor (horiz) | 5·50 | 6·50 |

**198** Islander Hostel

**2001.** "BELGICA 2001" International Stamp Exhibition, Brussels. Tourism. Multicoloured.

| | | | |
|---|---|---|---|
| 830 | 35p. Type **198** | 2·50 | 3·00 |
| 831 | 35p. The Residency | 2·50 | 3·00 |
| 832 | 40p. The Red Lion | 2·50 | 3·00 |
| 833 | 40p. Turtle Ponds | 2·50 | 3·00 |

**199** Female Ascension Frigate Bird

**2001.** Birdlife World Bird Festival (1st series). Ascension Frigate Birds. Multicoloured.

| | | | |
|---|---|---|---|
| 834 | 15p. Type **199** | 1·25 | 1·25 |
| 835 | 35p. Fledgeling | 1·75 | 1·75 |
| 836 | 40p. Male bird in flight (horiz) | 1·75 | 1·75 |
| 837 | 50p. Male bird with pouch inflated (horiz) | 1·75 | 1·75 |
| **MS**838 | 175×80 mm. 10p. Male and female birds on rock (horiz) and Nos. 834/7 | 6·50 | 7·50 |

See also Nos. 889/94 and 921/**MS**926.

**200** Princess Elizabeth and Dog

**2002.** Golden Jubilee.

| | | | |
|---|---|---|---|
| 839 | **200** 15p. agate, mauve and gold | 1·50 | 1·50 |
| 840 | - 35p. multicoloured | 2·00 | 2·00 |
| 841 | - 40p. multicoloured | 2·00 | 2·00 |
| 842 | - 50p. multicoloured | 2·00 | 2·00 |
| **MS**843 | - 162×95 mm. Nos. 839/42 and 60p. multicoloured | 7·50 | 8·50 |

DESIGNS—HORIZ: 35p. Queen Elizabeth wearing tiara, 1978; 40p. Princess Elizabeth, 1946; 50p. Queen Elizabeth visiting Henley-on-Thames, 1998. VERT: (38×51 mm)—50p. Queen Elizabeth after Annigoni.

**201** Royal Marines landing at English Bay

**2002.** 20th Anniv of Liberation of the Falkland Islands. Multicoloured.

| | | | |
|---|---|---|---|
| 844 | 15p. Type **201** | 1·25 | 1·25 |
| 845 | 35p. Weapons testing | 1·60 | 1·60 |
| 846 | 40p. H.M.S. *Hermes* (aircraft carrier) | 1·60 | 1·60 |
| 847 | 50p. R.A.F. Vulcan at Wideawake Airfield | 1·60 | 1·60 |

**202** Duchess of York at Harrow Hospital, 1931

**2002.** Queen Elizabeth the Queen Mother Commemoration.

| | | | |
|---|---|---|---|
| 848 | **202** 35p. black, gold and purple | 1·40 | 1·40 |
| 849 | - 40p. multicoloured | 1·40 | 1·40 |
| **MS**850 | - 145×70 mm. 50p. brown and gold; £1 multicoloured | 6·50 | 7·50 |

DESIGNS: 40p. Queen Mother on her birthday, 1997; 50p. Duchess of York, 1925; £1 Queen Mother, Scrabster, 1992.

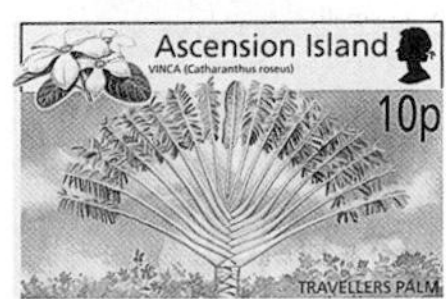


**203** Travellers Palm and Vinca

**2002.** Island Views. Multicoloured.

| | | | |
|---|---|---|---|
| 851 | 10p. Type **203** | 75 | 1·00 |
| 852 | 15p. Broken Tooth (volcanic crater) and Mexican poppy | 1·00 | 75 |
| 853 | 20p. St. Mary's Church and Ascension lily | 1·00 | 75 |
| 854 | 25p. Boatswain Bird Island and goatweed | 1·40 | 1·25 |
| 855 | 30p. Cannon and Mauritius hemp | 1·40 | 1·40 |
| 856 | 35p. The Guest House and frangipani | 1·50 | 1·25 |
| 857 | 40p. Wideawake tern and Ascension spurge | 2·00 | 2·00 |
| 858 | 50p. The Pier Head and lovechaste | 2·00 | 2·25 |
| 859 | 65p. Sisters' Peak and yellowboy | 2·25 | 2·75 |
| 860 | 90p. Two Boats School and Persian lilac | 3·00 | 3·25 |
| 861 | £2 Green turtle and wild currant | 6·00 | 7·00 |
| 862 | £5 Wideawake Airfield and coral tree | 13·00 | 14·00 |

**204** "Ecce Ancilla Dominii" (Dante Rossetti)

**2002.** Christmas. Religious Paintings. Mult.

| | | | |
|---|---|---|---|
| 863 | 15p. Type **204** | 70 | 70 |
| 864 | 25p. "The Holy Family and Shepherd" (Titian) (horiz) | 95 | 95 |
| 865 | 35p. "Christ carrying the Cross" (A. Bergognone) | 1·25 | 1·25 |
| 866 | 75p. Sketch for "The Ascension" (Benjamin West) | 2·50 | 2·50 |

**205** Ariane 4 Rocket on Gantry

**2003.** Ariane Downrange Station. Multicoloured.

| | | | |
|---|---|---|---|
| 867 | 35p. Type **205** | 1·40 | 1·40 |
| 868 | 40p. Map of Ariane Downrange stations (horiz) | 1·50 | 1·50 |
| 869 | 65p. Automated Transfer Vehicle (ATV) in Space (horiz) | 2·50 | 2·50 |
| 870 | 90p. Launch of Ariane 5 | 3·75 | 4·25 |
| **MS**871 | 170×88 mm. Nos. 867/70 | 8·25 | 8·25 |

**206** Coronation Coach in Procession

**2003.** 50th Anniv of Coronation. Multicoloured.

| | | | |
|---|---|---|---|
| 872 | 40p. Type **206** | 1·50 | 1·00 |
| 873 | £1 Newly crowned Queen with bishops and peers | 3·25 | 3·75 |
| **MS**874 | 95×115 mm. As Nos. 872/3 | 4·75 | 4·75 |

Nos. 872/3 have red frame; stamps from **MS**874 have no frame and country name in mauve panel.

**207** Queen Elizabeth II

**2003**

| | | | |
|---|---|---|---|
| 875 | **207** £3 black, green and myrtle | 6·50 | 7·00 |

**208** Prince William at Tidworth Polo Club and on Skiing Holiday, 2002

**2003.** 21st Birthday of Prince William of Wales. Multicoloured.

| | | | |
|---|---|---|---|
| 876 | 75p. Type **208** | 2·75 | 2·75 |
| 877 | 75p. On Raleigh International Expedition, 2000 and at Queen Mother's 101st Birthday, 2001 | 2·75 | 2·75 |

**209** Bleriot XI

**2003.** Centenary of Powered Flight. Multicoloured.

| | | | |
|---|---|---|---|
| 878 | 15p. Type **209** | 85 | 85 |
| 879 | 20p. Vickers VC-10 | 90 | 90 |
| 880 | 35p. BAe Harrier FRS Mk1 | 1·60 | 1·60 |
| 881 | 40p. Westland Sea King HAS Mk. 4 helicopter | 1·75 | 1·75 |
| 882 | 50p. Rockwell Space Shuttle | 1·75 | 1·75 |
| 883 | 90p. General Dynamics F-16 Fighting Falcon | 3·25 | 3·50 |
| **MS**884 | 115×65 mm. £1.50 Fairey Swordfish Mk II. | 6·50 | 7·00 |

**210** Casting Vote into Ballot Box

**2003.** Christmas. First Anniv of Democracy on Ascension. Multicoloured.

| | | | |
|---|---|---|---|
| 885 | 15p. Type **210** | 75 | 55 |
| 886 | 25p. Island Council session | 90 | 65 |
| 887 | 40p. Students ("HIGHER EDUCATION") | 1·40 | 1·10 |
| 888 | £1 Government Headquarters | 2·75 | 3·50 |

**211** Adult with Fledgling

**2004.** Birdlife International (2nd series). Masked Booby. Multicoloured.

| | | | |
|---|---|---|---|
| 889 | 15p. Type **211** | 85 | 75 |
| 890 | 35p. Pair (vert) | 1·40 | 1·00 |
| 891 | 40p. In flight (vert) | 1·40 | 1·25 |
| 892 | 50p. Adult calling | 1·50 | 1·50 |
| 893 | 90p. Masked booby | 3·00 | 3·50 |
| **MS**894 | 175×80 mm. Nos. 889/93 | 7·00 | 7·50 |

**212** *Bougainvillea glabra* (orange)

**2004.** Bicentenary of the Royal Horticultural Society. Multicoloured.

| | | | |
|---|---|---|---|
| 895 | 15p. Type **212** | 75 | 75 |
| 896 | 35p. *Bougainvillea glabra* (pink) | 1·40 | 1·00 |
| 897 | 40p. *Bougainvillea glabra* (white) | 1·50 | 1·10 |
| 898 | 90p. *Bougainvillea spectabilis* (red) | 2·75 | 3·50 |
| **MS**899 | 105×80 mm. £1.50 *Pteris adscensionis* | 6·00 | 6·50 |

**213** Blue Marlin

**2004.** Sport Fishing (1st series). Multicoloured.

| | | | |
|---|---|---|---|
| 900 | 15p. Type **213** | 75 | 75 |
| 901 | 35p. Swordfish | 1·40 | 1·00 |
| 902 | 40p. Sailfish | 1·50 | 1·10 |
| 903 | 90p. White marlin | 2·75 | 3·50 |
| **MS**904 | 61×51 mm. £1.50 Blue marlin | 5·00 | 6·00 |

See also Nos. 927/**MS**931.

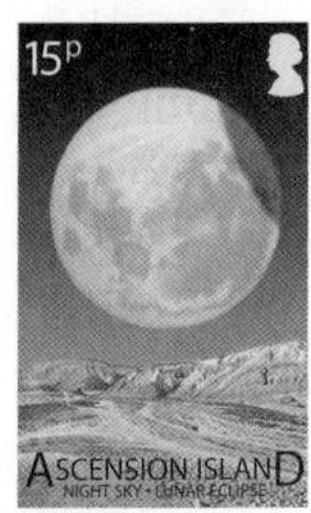


**214** Moon over Hummock Point

**2004.** Lunar Eclipse. Multicoloured.

| | | | |
|---|---|---|---|
| 905 | 15p. Type **214** | 75 | 75 |
| 906 | 25p. Yellow moon over Sisters Peak (North side) | 1·25 | 1·00 |
| 907 | 35p. Orange moon over Daly's Craggs | 1·50 | 1·00 |
| 908 | £1.25 Red moon and birds over Mars Bay | 3·75 | 4·50 |
| **MS**909 | 130×55 mm. £1.25 As No. 908 | 4·00 | 5·00 |

**215** MV *Ascension*

**2004.** Merchant Ships. Multicoloured.

| | | | |
|---|---|---|---|
| 910 | 15p. Type **215** | 1·25 | 1·00 |
| 911 | 35p. *St. Helena* (mail ship) | 2·00 | 1·25 |
| 912 | 40p. *Caronia* (mail ship) | 2·00 | 1·50 |
| 913 | £1.25 MV *Maersk Gannet* | 6·00 | 7·50 |

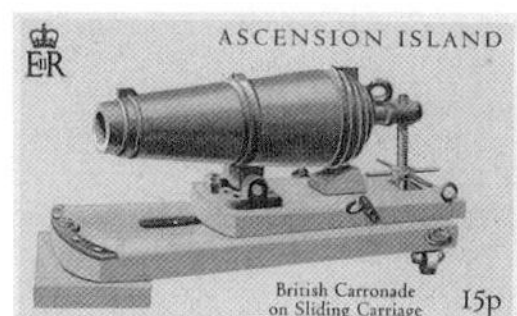

**216** British Carronade on Sliding Carriage

**2005.** Bicentenary of Battle of Trafalgar (1st issue). Multicoloured.

| No. | Description | Unused | Used |
|---|---|---|---|
| 914 | 15p. Type **216** | 75 | 65 |
| 915 | 25p. Royal Marine drummer boy, 1805 (vert) | 1·25 | 90 |
| 916 | 35p. HMS *Britannia* (vert) | 1·40 | 1·25 |
| 917 | 40p. Admiral Nelson | 1·50 | 1·50 |
| 918 | 50p. HMS *Neptune* and *Santissima Trinidad* | 1·60 | 1·60 |
| 919 | 90p. HMS *Victory* | 2·75 | 4·00 |
| **MS**920 | 120×80 mm. £1 Lord Nelson (vert); £1 *Neptune* (vert) | 6·50 | 7·50 |

No. 919 contains traces of powdered wood from HMS *Victory*.

See also Nos. 937/9.

**217** White Tern ("Fairy Tern")

**2005.** Birdlife International (3rd series). "The Sea Birds Return". Multicoloured.

| No. | Description | Unused | Used |
|---|---|---|---|
| 921 | 15p. Type **217** | 55 | 55 |
| 922 | 35p. White-tailed tropic bird | 1·10 | 1·10 |
| 923 | 40p. Brown booby | 1·25 | 1·40 |
| 924 | 50p. Common noddy ("Brown Noddy") | 1·40 | 1·40 |
| 925 | £1.25 Red-billed tropic bird | 3·25 | 4·25 |
| **MS**926 | 170×80 mm. Nos. 921/5 | 8·00 | 8·50 |

**218** Yellowfin Tuna

**2005.** Sport Fishing (2nd series). Tuna. Mult.

| No. | Description | Unused | Used |
|---|---|---|---|
| 927 | 35p. Type **218** | 1·25 | 1·25 |
| 928 | 40p. Skipjack tuna | 1·40 | 1·40 |
| 929 | 50p. Albacore tuna | 1·50 | 1·50 |
| 930 | £1.25 Bigeye tuna | 3·50 | 4·00 |
| **MS**931 | 61×51 mm. £1.50 Yellowfin tuna hunting herrings | 4·50 | 5·50 |

**219** Pope John Paul II

**2005.** Pope John Paul II Commemoration.

| No. | Type | Description | Unused | Used |
|---|---|---|---|---|
| 932 | **219** | 40p. multicoloured | 1·75 | 1·75 |

**220** *The Little Fir Tree*

**2005.** Christmas. Birth Bicentenary of Hans Christian Andersen (writer). Multicoloured.

| No. | Description | Unused | Used |
|---|---|---|---|
| 933 | 15p. Type **220** | 1·00 | 1·00 |
| 934 | 25p. *The Mail-Coach Passengers* | 1·25 | 1·25 |
| 935 | 35p. *The Little Match Girl* | 1·50 | 1·50 |
| 936 | £1.25 *The Snow Man* | 4·00 | 5·00 |

**221** HMS *Victory*

**2005.** Bicentenary of the Battle of Trafalgar (2nd issue). Multicoloured.

| No. | Description | Unused | Used |
|---|---|---|---|
| 937 | 40p. Type **221** | 1·50 | 1·40 |
| 938 | 65p. Ships engaged in battle (horiz) | 2·50 | 3·00 |
| 939 | 90p. "Admiral Lord Nelson" | 3·50 | 4·00 |

**222** Black Jack

**2006.** Sport Fishing (3rd series). Jacks. Multicoloured.

| No. | Description | Unused | Used |
|---|---|---|---|
| 940 | 20p. Type **222** | 1·00 | 1·00 |
| 941 | 35p. Almaco jack | 1·60 | 1·40 |
| 942 | 50p. Horse-eye jack | 2·00 | 2·00 |
| 943 | £1 Rainbow runner | 3·50 | 4·25 |
| **MS**944 | 61×50 mm. £1.50 Longfin crevalle jack | 4·50 | 5·50 |

**223** Princess Elizabeth

**2006.** 80th Birthday of Queen Elizabeth II. Multicoloured.

| No. | Description | Unused | Used |
|---|---|---|---|
| 945 | 20p. Type **223** | 80 | 80 |
| 946 | 40p. Queen Elizabeth II, c. 1952 | 1·00 | 1·25 |
| 947 | 50p. Queen Elizabeth II | 1·75 | 1·90 |
| 948 | £1.30 Wearing Garter robes | 4·25 | 8·00 |
| **MS**949 | 144×75 mm. £1 Queen, c. 1952; £1 Queen in 1960s | 6·00 | 7·00 |

**224** HMS *Beagle* (175th anniv of Darwin's voyage)

**2006.** Exploration and Innovation. Anniversaries. Multicoloured.

| No. | Description | Unused | Used |
|---|---|---|---|
| 950 | 20p. Type **224** | 1·25 | 1·25 |
| 951 | 20p. Charles Darwin (originator of theory of evolution) | 1·25 | 1·25 |
| 952 | 35p. *Great Britain* (steam/sail) | 2·00 | 2·00 |
| 953 | 35p. Isambard Kingdom Brunel (engineer, birth bicentenary) | 2·00 | 2·00 |
| 954 | 40p. *Nina* (Columbus) | 2·25 | 2·25 |
| 955 | 40p. Christopher Columbus (discoverer of New World, 500th death anniv) | 2·25 | 2·25 |
| 956 | 50p. World map with lines of magnetic variation | 2·25 | 2·25 |
| 957 | 50p. Edmund Halley (astronomer, 350th birth anniv) and Halley's comet | 2·25 | 2·25 |

Nos. 950/1, 952/3, 954/5 and 956/7 were each printed together, se-tenant, forming a composite background design.

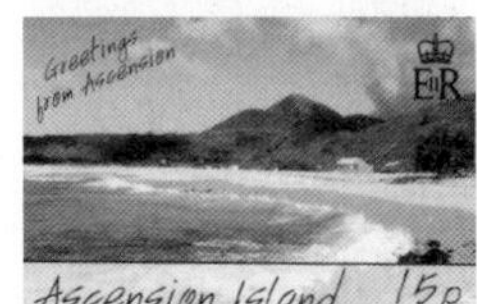

**225** Long Beach ("Greetings from Ascension")

**2006.** Christmas. Views of Ascension Island. Multicoloured.

| No. | Description | Unused | Used |
|---|---|---|---|
| 958 | 15p. Type **225** | 85 | 85 |
| 959 | 25p. Coastal rocks at sunset ("Merry Christmas") | 1·25 | 1·25 |
| 960 | 35p. Dewpond ("Seasons Greetings") | 1·60 | 1·25 |
| 961 | £1.25 Coast and Boatswain Bird Island ("Happy New Year") | 4·25 | 5·00 |

**226** Resplendent Angelfish

**2007.** Endangered Species. Resplendent Angelfish (Centropyge resplendens). Multicoloured.

| No. | Description | Unused | Used |
|---|---|---|---|
| 962 | 35p. Type **226** | 1·40 | 1·10 |
| 963 | 40p. Shoal of resplendent angelfish | 1·60 | 1·60 |
| 964 | 50p. Three angelfish near red coral and rocks | 1·60 | 1·60 |
| 965 | £1.25 Large male angelfish and three smaller females | 4·00 | 4·50 |

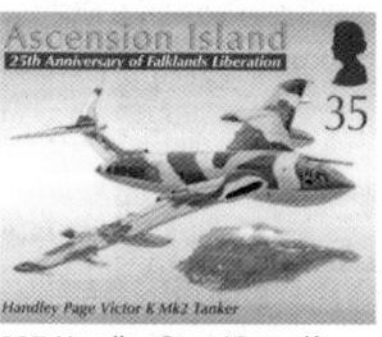

**227** Handley Page Victor K Mk2 Tanker

**2007.** 25th Anniv of the Liberation of the Falkland Islands. Multicoloured.

| No. | Description | Unused | Used |
|---|---|---|---|
| 966 | 35p. Type **227** | 1·50 | 1·10 |
| 967 | 40p. HMS *Dumbarton Castle* (offshore patrol vessel) and Chinook helicopter | 1·90 | 1·90 |
| 968 | 50p. HMS *Fearless* with helicopter and landing craft | 1·90 | 1·90 |
| 969 | £1.25 Vulcan XM607 taking off | 4·50 | 5·00 |
| **MS**970 | Two sheets, each 183×89 mm. (a) As Type **227**; 40p. Vickers VC10 Transport; 50p. Nimrod MR2 Maritime Reconnaissance; As No. 969. (b) 35p. RFA *Tidespring* refuelling HMS *Antrim*; As No. 967; As No. 968; £1.25 *Atlantic Conveyor* and Harrier fighter | 9·00 | 10·00 |

Stamps from the two miniature sheets **MS**970a/b do not have white borders.

The 50p. stamp from **MS**970(a) has an incorrect spelling "Reconaissance".

**228** Ascension Scouts forming Fleur-de-Lis Emblem

**2007.** Centenary of Scouting. Multicoloured.

| No. | Description | Unused | Used |
|---|---|---|---|
| 971 | 35p. Type **228** | 1·40 | 1·10 |
| 972 | 40p. Scouts rescuing stranded turtle | 1·60 | 1·60 |
| 973 | 50p. Ascension Scout Troop sitting on gun from HMS *Hood* | 1·60 | 1·60 |
| 974 | £1.25 Scouts on top of their Land Rover near Butt Crater | 4·00 | 5·00 |

**229** Mother Teresa and Princess Diana, Rome, 1992

**2007.** 10th Death Anniv of Diana, Princess of Wales.

| No. | Type | Description | Unused | Used |
|---|---|---|---|---|
| 975 | **229** | 50p. multicoloured | 1·60 | 1·60 |

**230** Engagement Photograph, July 1947

**2007.** Diamond Wedding of Queen Elizabeth II and Duke of Edinburgh. Multicoloured.

| No. | Description | Unused | Used |
|---|---|---|---|
| 976 | 35p. Type **230** | 2·00 | 2·50 |
| 977 | 90p. Wedding programme | 4·00 | 4·50 |
| 978 | £1.25 Queen and Duke of Edinburgh at St. Paul's Cathedral for 80th birthday Thanksgiving Service | 4·25 | 4·75 |

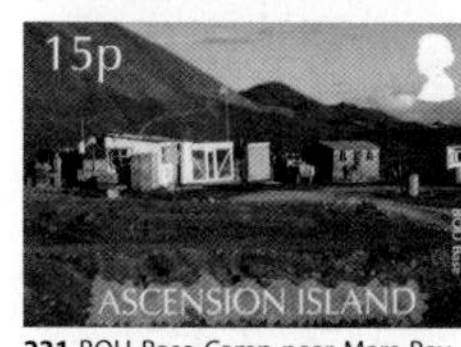

**231** BOU Base Camp near Mars Bay

**2007.** 50th Anniv of the British Ornithologists' Union Centenary Expedition (1957–9). Multicoloured.

| No. | Description | Unused | Used |
|---|---|---|---|
| 979 | 15p. Type **231** | 1·00 | 1·25 |
| 980 | 15p. Peter Mundy's drawing of extinct flightless rail, 1656 | 1·00 | 1·25 |
| 981 | 25p. Team member recording sooty tern ('Wideawake') | 1·25 | 1·50 |
| 982 | 25p. Sooty terns ('Wideawake') | 1·25 | 1·50 |
| 983 | 40p. BOU outpost, Boatswain-bird Island | 4·50 | 5·00 |
| 984 | 40p. Masked booby | 2·25 | 2·50 |
| 985 | 50p. Team members with expedition dinghy *Overdraft* | 2·25 | 2·50 |
| 986 | 50p. Red-footed booby | 2·25 | 2·50 |

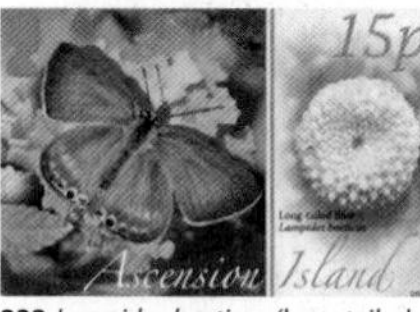

**232** *Lampides boeticus* (long-tailed blue butterfly)

**2008.** Fauna and their Eggs. Multicoloured.

| No. | Description | Unused | Used |
|---|---|---|---|
| 987 | 15p. Type **232** | 45 | 50 |
| 988 | 20p. *Cheilomenes lunata* (ladybird) | 60 | 65 |
| 989 | 25p. *Panulirus echinatus* (spiny lobster) | 75 | 80 |
| 990 | 30p. *Schistocerca gregaria* (desert locust) | 90 | 85 |
| 991 | 35p. *Chelonia mydas* (green turtle) | 1·10 | 1·20 |
| 992 | 40p. *Gecarcinus lagostoma* (landcrab) | 1·20 | 1·30 |
| 993 | 50p. *Sula sula* (red-footed booby) | 1·50 | 1·60 |
| 994 | 65p. *Hemdactylus mercatorius* (coconut-palm gecko) | 1·90 | 2·00 |
| 995 | 90p. *Estrilda astrild* (common waxbill) | 2·75 | 3·00 |
| 996 | £1 *Stegastes lubbocki* (yellowtail damselfish) | 3·00 | 3·25 |
| 997 | £2.50 *Oceanodroma castro* (Madeiran storm-petrel) | 7·50 | 7·75 |
| 998 | £5 *Francolinus afer* (red-necked francolin) | 15·00 | 15·00 |

**233** Bluntnose Sixgill Shark

**2008.** Sharks. Multicoloured.

| No. | Description | Unused | Used |
|---|---|---|---|
| 999 | 35p. Type **233** | 1·75 | 2·25 |
| 1000 | 40p. Scalloped hammerhead | 1·75 | 2·25 |
| 1001 | 50p. Shortfin mako | 1·75 | 2·25 |
| 1002 | £1.25 Whale shark | 3·75 | 2·25 |
| **MS**1003 | 70×45 mm. £1.50 Bigeye thresher | 5·00 | 5·50 |

**234** Bell X-1E NACA X-Plane, 1958

**2008.** 50th Anniv of NASA. Multicoloured.

| | | | |
|---|---|---|---|
| 1004 | 35p. Type **234** | 1·10 | 1·20 |
| 1005 | 35p. Apollo 11 Moon Walk, 1969 | 1·10 | 1·20 |
| 1006 | 40p. Apollo 17 Lunar Roving Vehicle, 1972 | 1·10 | 1·20 |
| 1007 | 50p. STS1 Space Shuttle *Columbia*, 1981 | 1·50 | 1·60 |
| 1008 | 65p. The Hubble Space Telescope, 1990 | 1·90 | 1·80 |
| 1009 | 90p. International Space Station, 2006 | 2·75 | 3·00 |

**235** Sopwith 7F.1 Snipe

**2008.** 90th Anniv of the Royal Air Force. Multicoloured.

| | | | |
|---|---|---|---|
| 1010 | 15p. Type **235** | 1·10 | 90 |
| 1011 | 35p. Vickers Wellington Mk 1C | 1·90 | 1·75 |
| 1012 | 40p. Supermarine Spitfire Mk IX | 2·00 | 2·00 |
| 1013 | 50p. Gloster Meteor F.IV | 2·00 | 2·00 |
| 1014 | 65p. BAe Hawk | 2·50 | 2·75 |
| 1015 | 90p. Typhoon F2 (Eurofighter) | 3·25 | 3·50 |

**236** Valerius Cordus (1515–44) and *Cordia sebestena*

**2008.** Botanists and Plants named after them. Multicoloured.

| | | | |
|---|---|---|---|
| 1016 | 35p. Type **236** | 1·50 | 1·25 |
| 1017 | 40p. Nehemiah Grew (1641–1712) and *Grewia occidentalis* | 1·75 | 1·75 |
| 1018 | 50p. Charles Plumier (1646–1704) and *Plumeria rubra* | 1·75 | 1·75 |
| 1019 | £2 Carl Peter Thunberg (1743–1828) and *Thunbergia grandiflora* | 6·50 | 7·00 |

**237** Father Christmas

**2008.** Christmas. Designs showing illustrations of Father Christmas from Father Christmas and Father Christmas Goes on Holiday by Raymond Briggs superimposed over Ascension Island scenes. Multicoloured.

| | | | |
|---|---|---|---|
| 1020 | 15p. Type **237** | 70 | 70 |
| 1021 | 25p. Father Christmas in reindeer-drawn sleigh above surf of western coast | 1·00 | 1·00 |
| 1022 | 50p. Father Christmas lying on inflatable | 1·75 | 1·75 |
| 1023 | £2 Father Christmas and his laden sleigh above Green Mountain and Two Boats Village | 6·50 | 7·00 |

**238** King Henry III (1216–72) and the Tower of London

**2008.** Britain's Longest Reigning Monarchs. Multicoloured.

| | | | |
|---|---|---|---|
| 1024 | 35p. Type **238** | 1·90 | 1·60 |
| 1025 | 40p. King James VI (1567–1625) and Stirling Castle | 2·00 | 2·00 |
| 1026 | 50p. King George III (1760–1820) and Windsor Castle | 2·25 | 2·25 |
| 1027 | 65p. Queen Victoria (1837–1901) and Osborne House | 2·50 | 2·75 |
| 1028 | £1.25 Queen Elizabeth II (from 1952) and Buckingham Palace | 4·75 | 5·50 |

**239** Bottlenose Dolphin (*Tursiops truncatus*)

**2009.** Whales and Dolphins. Multicoloured.

| | | | |
|---|---|---|---|
| 1029 | 35p. Type **239** | 1·10 | 1·20 |
| 1030 | 40p. Pantropical spotted dolphin (*Stenella attenuata*) | 1·20 | 1·30 |
| 1031 | 50p. Sperm whale (*Physeter macrocephalus*) and squid (prey) | 1·50 | 1·60 |
| 1032 | £1.25 Gervais' beaked whale (*Mesoplodon europeus*) | 3·75 | 4·00 |
| **MS**1033 | 111×65 mm. £2 Humpback whale (*Megaptera novaeangliae*) | 6·00 | 6·25 |

**240** Flt. SLt. Rex Warneford

**2009.** Centenary of Naval Aviation. Victoria Cross of the Fleet Air Arm. Multicoloured.

| | | | |
|---|---|---|---|
| 1034 | 35p. Type **240** | 1·75 | 1·75 |
| 1035 | 35p. Moraine-Saulnier L destroys Zeppelin LZ37, Belgium, 6/7 June 1915 | 1·75 | 1·75 |
| 1036 | 35p. Sqn. Cdr. Richard Bell Davies | 1·75 | 1·75 |
| 1037 | 35p. Nieuport 10 takes off pursued by enemy soldiers, Bulgaria, 19 November 1915 | 1·75 | 1·75 |
| 1038 | 40p. Lt. Cdr. (A) Eugene Esmonde | 1·75 | 1·75 |
| 1039 | 40p. Fairey Swordfish aircraft attacking German heavy cruisers, 12 February 1942 | 1·75 | 1·75 |
| 1040 | 50p. Lt. Robert Hampton Gray | 1·75 | 1·75 |
| 1041 | 50p. Corsair bombing Japanese warship | 1·75 | 1·75 |

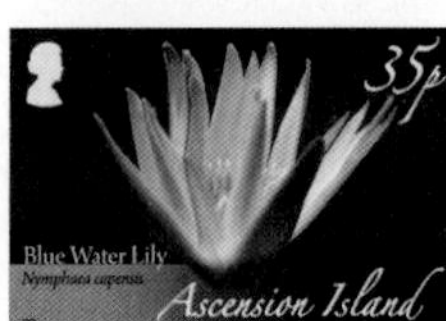

**241** Blue Water Lily (*Nymphaea capensis*)

**2009.** Introduced Plant Species. Multicoloured.

| | | | |
|---|---|---|---|
| 1042 | 35p. Type **241** | 1·10 | 1·20 |
| 1043 | 35p. Raspberry (*Rubus rosifolius*) | 1·10 | 1·20 |
| 1044 | 40p. Prickly pear (*Optunia vulgaris*) | 1·20 | 1·30 |
| 1045 | 50p. Ascension lily (*Hippeastrum reginae*) | 1·50 | 1·60 |
| 1046 | 65p. Yellowboy (*Tecoma stans*) | 1·90 | 2·00 |
| 1047 | 90p. Portraits of young and old Joseph Dalton Hooker (botanist) | 2·75 | 3·00 |

**242** Dr. Archie Carr with Early Turtle Tracking Equipment

**2009.** Turtle Research and Conservation and Birth Centenary of Dr. Archie Carr (sea turtle biologist). T 242 and similar horiz designs, each showing either head of turtle at left (Nos. 1048, 1050, 1052, 1054) or outline map of Ascension Island at right (others). Multicoloured.

| | | | |
|---|---|---|---|
| 1048 | 15p. Type **242** | 80 | 1·00 |
| 1049 | 15p. Dr. Archie Carr attaching tracking floats to turtle | 80 | 2·00 |
| 1050 | 35p. Female laying eggs | 1·40 | 1·60 |
| 1051 | 35p. Turtle hatchlings | 1·40 | 1·60 |
| 1052 | 40p. Beach raking to remove turtle tracks after counting | 1·40 | 1·75 |
| 1053 | 40p. Population monitoring | 1·40 | 1·75 |
| 1054 | 65p. Rescuer with turtle | 2·00 | 2·50 |
| 1055 | 65p. Two rescuers with turtle | 2·00 | 2·50 |

Nos. 1048/9, 1050/1, 1052/3 and 1054/5 were each printed together, se-tenant, each pair forming a composite design.

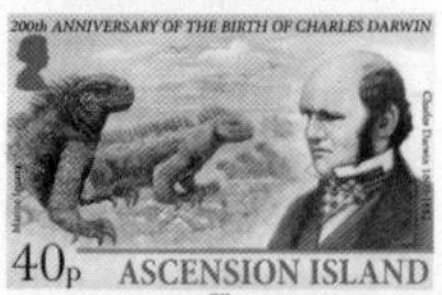

**243** Charles Darwin and Woodpecker Finch

**2009.** Birth Bicentenary of Charles Darwin (naturalist and evolutionary theorist). Each showing a different portrait. Multicoloured.

| | | | |
|---|---|---|---|
| 1056 | 35p. Type **243** | 1·75 | 1·50 |
| 1057 | 40p. Charles Darwin (in profile) and marine iguanas | 1·75 | 1·75 |
| 1058 | 50p. Charles Darwin and Galapagos tortoise | 1·75 | 1·75 |
| 1059 | £2 Charles Darwin as old man, Galapagos penguins and *Beagle* | 6·50 | 7·00 |

**244** Juvenile White-tailed Tropic Bird

**2009.** White-tailed Tropic Bird (Phaethon lepturus). Multicoloured.

| | | | |
|---|---|---|---|
| 1060 | 35p. Type **244** | 1·75 | 2·00 |
| 1061 | 40p. Adult feeding juvenile | 1·75 | 2·00 |
| 1062 | 50p. Juvenile in flight | 1·75 | 2·00 |
| 1063 | £1.25 Adult in flight | 3·50 | 4·00 |

**245** Hardback Soldier Fish (*Holocentrus adscensionis*)

**2010.** Reef Fish. Multicoloured.

| | | | |
|---|---|---|---|
| 1064 | 35p. Type **245** | 1·60 | 1·60 |
| 1065 | 40p. Grouper (*Epinephelus adscensionis*) | 1·75 | 1·75 |
| 1066 | 50p. Five fingers (*Abudefduf saxatilis*) | 1·75 | 1·75 |
| 1067 | £1.25 Rock bullseye (*Heteropriacanthus cruentatus*) | 3·50 | 4·00 |
| **MS**1068 | 84×59 mm. £2 Softback soldier fish (*Myripristis jacobus*) | 6·50 | 7·00 |

**246** Guides

**2010.** Centenary of Girl Guiding. Multicoloured.

| | | | |
|---|---|---|---|
| 1069 | 40p. Type **246** | 1·60 | 1·60 |
| 1070 | 50p. Guides and large fish catch | 1·75 | 1·75 |
| 1071 | 90p. Guide leaders and 'Celebrating 100 Years of Guiding' celebration cake | 3·00 | 3·25 |
| 1072 | £1.25 Guide abseiling | 3·75 | 4·00 |
| **MS**1073 | 160×80 mm. £1×3 Olave, Lady Baden-Powell (Chief Guide 1918–77); Agnes Baden-Powell (founder); Lord Baden-Powell (founder of Scout Movement) (all vert) | 9·00 | 9·00 |

**247** Supermarine Spitfire R6803, 65 Squadron

**2010.** London 2010 Festival of Stamps. 70th Anniv of the Battle of Britain. Multicoloured.

| | | | |
|---|---|---|---|
| 1074 | 50p. Type **247** | 1·75 | 2·00 |
| 1075 | 50p. Hawker Hurricane V7383, 615 Squadron | 1·75 | 2·00 |
| 1076 | 50p. Supermarine Spitfire X4036, 234 Squadron | 1·75 | 2·00 |
| 1077 | 50p. Hawker Hurricane R4175, 303 Squadron | 1·75 | 2·00 |
| 1078 | 50p. Supermarine Spitfire R6885, 41 Squadron | 1·75 | 2·00 |
| 1079 | 50p. Hawker Hurricane V6684, 303 Squadron | 1·75 | 2·00 |
| 1080 | 50p. Supermarine Spitfire K9998, 603 Squadron | 1·75 | 2·00 |
| 1081 | 50p. Hawker Hurricane R4118, 605 Squadron | 1·75 | 2·00 |

Nos. 1080/1 were printed together, se-tenant, forming composite background design.

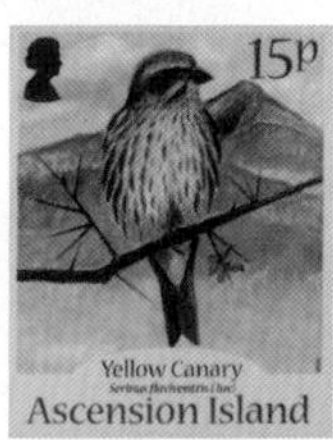

**248** Juvenile Yellow Canary

**2010.** Yellow Canary (*Serinus flaviventris*). Multicoloured.

| | | | |
|---|---|---|---|
| 1082 | 15p. Type **248** | 70 | 70 |
| 1083 | 35p. Adult male (perched) | 1·25 | 1·25 |
| 1084 | 60p. Adult female | 2·00 | 2·00 |
| 1085 | 90p. Adult male (on ground) | 2·75 | 2·75 |

**249** Christmas Lunch

**2010.** Christmas on Ascension Island. Multicoloured.

| | | | |
|---|---|---|---|
| 1086 | 15p. Type **249** | 45 | 50 |
| 1087 | 40p. Santa riding in decorated pick-up truck in Christmas parade | 1·10 | 1·20 |
| 1088 | 50p. Three children at Christingle service | 1·50 | 1·60 |
| 1089 | £1.25 Children's nativity play | 3·50 | 3·75 |

**250** HMS Erebus and Terror approaching Ascension

**2011.** Parsley Fern (*Anogramma ascensionis*). Multicoloured.

| | | | |
|---|---|---|---|
| 1090 | 15p. Type **250** | 15 | 15 |
| 1091 | 25p. Parsley fern | 80 | 80 |
| 1092 | 35p. Parsley fern in situ | 1·10 | 1·10 |
| 1093 | 40p. Parsley fern seedlings | 1·25 | 1·25 |
| 1094 | £1 Parsley fern cultivation, Kew Gardens | 3·00 | 3·00 |

**251** Queen Elizabeth II, Westminster Abbey, 12 April 2001

**2011.** Queen Elizabeth II and Prince Philip 'A Lifetime of Service'. Multicoloured.

| | | | |
|---|---|---|---|
| 1095 | 15p. Type **251** | 45 | 45 |
| 1096 | 25p. Queen Elizabeth and Prince Philip, 1953 | 80 | 80 |
| 1097 | 35p. Queen Elizabeth and Prince Philip, Buckingham Palace, 1999 | 1·10 | 1·10 |
| 1098 | 40p. Queen Elizabeth and Prince Philip, The Mall, London, 24 February 2009 | 1·25 | 1·25 |
| 1099 | 60p. Queen Elizabeth and Prince Philip in Balmoral Castle grounds, September 1960 | 1·75 | 1·75 |
| 1100 | £1.25 Duke of Edinburgh, Westminster Abbey, 12 April 2001 | 3·75 | 3·75 |
| **MS**1101 | 174×163 mm. Nos. 1095/100 and three stamp-size labels | 9·00 | 9·00 |

| | | |
|---|---|---|
| **MS**1102 110×70 mm. £2 Queen Elizabeth II and Prince Philip, Westminster Abbey, 1977 | 6·00 | 6·00 |

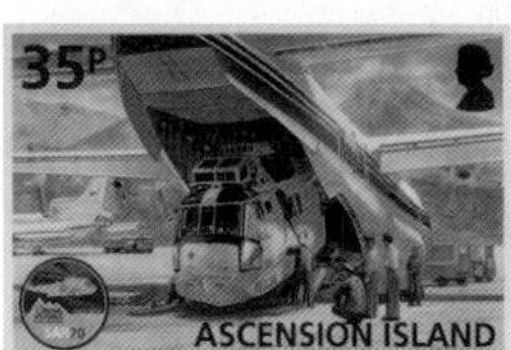

**252** Unloading Sea King Helicopter from Hold of Short Belfast Aircraft, 8 May 1982

**2011.** 70th Anniv of RAF Search and Rescue. Multicoloured.

| | | | |
|---|---|---|---|
| 1103 | 35p. Type **252** | 1·10 | 1·25 |
| 1104 | 40p. Westland Sea King HAR3 helicopter XZ593 over Ascension Island | 1·25 | 1·40 |
| 1105 | 90p. Sea King helicopter XZ593 delivering stores to HMS *Dumbarton Castle* (Castle Class patrol ship), 1982 | 2·75 | 3·00 |
| 1106 | £1 Sea King helicopter XZ593 airlifting casualty from nuclear submarine HMS *Spartan*, 1982 | 3·00 | 3·25 |
| **MS**1107 | 64×94 mm. £2.50 Sea King helicopter XZ593 | 7·50 | 7·50 |

**POSTAGE DUE STAMPS**

**D1** Outline Map of Ascension

**1986**

| | | | | |
|---|---|---|---|---|
| D1 | **D1** | 1p. deep brown and brown | 15 | 30 |
| D2 | **D1** | 2p. brown and orange | 15 | 30 |
| D3 | **D1** | 5p. brown and orange | 15 | 30 |
| D4 | **D1** | 7p. black and violet | 20 | 40 |
| D5 | **D1** | 10p. black and blue | 25 | 45 |
| D6 | **D1** | 25p. black and green | 65 | 1·10 |

Pt. 1

# AUSTRALIA

An island continent to the S.E. of Asia. A Commonwealth consisting of the states of New S. Wales, Queensland, S. Australia, Tasmania, Victoria and W. Australia.

1913. 12 pence = 1 shilling; 20 shillings = 1 pound.
1966. 100 cents = 1 dollar.

**1** Eastern Grey Kangaroo

**1913**

| | | | | |
|---|---|---|---|---|
| 1 | 1 | ½d. green | 8·00 | 4·50 |
| 2 | 1 | 1d. red | 13·00 | 1·00 |
| 35 | 1 | 2d. grey | 42·00 | 7·50 |
| 36 | 1 | 2½d. blue | 23·00 | 10·00 |
| 37 | 1 | 3d. olive | 35·00 | 4·75 |
| 6 | 1 | 4d. orange | 80·00 | 24·00 |
| 8 | 1 | 5d. brown | 70·00 | 35·00 |
| 38 | 1 | 6d. blue | 75·00 | 7·50 |
| 73 | 1 | 6d. brown | 25·00 | 1·75 |
| 133 | 1 | 9d. violet | 32·00 | 2·25 |
| 40 | 1 | 1s. green | 45·00 | 5·00 |
| 41 | 1 | 2s. brown | £200 | 13·00 |
| 134 | 1 | 2s. purple | 7·00 | 1·00 |
| 135 | 1 | 5s. grey and yellow | £150 | 17·00 |
| 136 | 1 | 10s. grey and pink | £400 | £140 |
| 15 | 1 | £1 brown and blue | £2000 | £2000 |
| 137 | 1 | £1 grey | £600 | £275 |
| 138 | 1 | £2 black and pink | £3500 | £550 |

**3**

**1913**

| | | | | |
|---|---|---|---|---|
| 20 | **3** | ½d. green | 3·75 | 1·00 |
| 94 | **3** | ½d. orange | 2·25 | 1·40 |
| 17 | **3** | 1d. red | 2·75 | 4·75 |
| 57 | **3** | 1d. violet | 5·00 | 1·50 |
| 125 | **3** | 1d. green | 1·75 | 20 |
| 59a | **3** | 1½d. brown | 6·50 | 60 |
| 61 | **3** | 1½d. green | 4·00 | 80 |
| 77 | **3** | 1½d. red | 2·25 | 40 |
| 62 | **3** | 2d. orange | 12·00 | 1·00 |
| 98 | **3** | 2d. brown | 10·00 | 9·50 |
| 127 | **3** | 2d. red | 1·75 | 10 |
| 128 | **3** | 3d. blue | 18·00 | 1·25 |
| 22 | **3** | 4d. orange | 30·00 | 2·50 |
| 64 | **3** | 4d. violet | 14·00 | 15·00 |
| 65 | **3** | 4d. blue | 48·00 | 8·50 |
| 129 | **3** | 4d. olive | 18·00 | 1·25 |
| 92 | **3** | 4½d. violet | 18·00 | 3·75 |
| 130 | **3** | 5d. brown | 15·00 | 20 |
| 131 | **3** | 1s.4d. blue | 50·00 | 3·50 |

**4** Laughing Kookaburra

**1913**

| | | | | |
|---|---|---|---|---|
| 19 | **4** | 6d. purple | 75·00 | 55·00 |

**8** Parliament House, Canberra

**1927.** Opening of Parliament House.

| | | | | |
|---|---|---|---|---|
| 105 | **8** | 1½d. lake | 50 | 50 |

**1928.** National Stamp Exhibition, Melbourne.

| | | | | |
|---|---|---|---|---|
| 106 | **4** | 3d. blue | 4·25 | 6·50 |
| **MS**106a | | 65×70 mm. No. 106×4 | £110 | £200 |

**9** De Havilland Hercules and Pastoral Scene

**1929.** Air.

| | | | | |
|---|---|---|---|---|
| 115 | **9** | 3d. green | 8·00 | 4·25 |

**10** Black Swan

**1929.** Centenary of Western Australia.

| | | | | |
|---|---|---|---|---|
| 116 | **10** | 1½d. red | 1·25 | 1·60 |

**11** "Capt. Chas Sturt" (J. H. Crossland)

**1930.** Centenary of Sturt's Exploration of River Murray.

| | | | | |
|---|---|---|---|---|
| 117 | **11** | 1½d. red | 1·25 | 1·00 |
| 118 | **11** | 3d. blue | 6·00 | 8·50 |

**1930.** Surch in words.

| | | | | |
|---|---|---|---|---|
| 119 | **3** | 2d. on 1½d. red | 1·50 | 1·00 |
| 120 | **3** | 5d. on 4½d. violet | 9·50 | 13·00 |

**13** The "Southern Cross" above Hemispheres

**1931.** Kingsford Smith's Flights.

| | | | | |
|---|---|---|---|---|
| 121 | **13** | 2d. red (postage) | 1·00 | 1·00 |
| 122 | **13** | 3d. blue | 6·50 | 5·50 |
| 123 | **13** | 6d. violet (air) | 5·50 | 16·00 |

**1931.** Air. As T **13** but inscr "AIR MAIL SERVICE".

| | | | |
|---|---|---|---|
| 139 | 6d. brown | 17·00 | 16·00 |

**1931.** Air. No. 139 optd O S.

| | | | |
|---|---|---|---|
| 139a | 6d. brown | 30·00 | 55·00 |

**17** Superb Lyrebird

**1932**

| | | | | |
|---|---|---|---|---|
| 140 | **17** | 1s. green | 38·00 | 2·75 |

**18** Sydney Harbour Bridge

**1932.** Opening of Sydney Harbour Bridge.

| | | | | |
|---|---|---|---|---|
| 144 | **18** | 2d. red | 4·00 | 1·40 |
| 142 | **18** | 3d. blue | 7·00 | 8·50 |
| 143 | **18** | 5s. green | £425 | £200 |

**19** Laughing Kookaburra

**1932**

| | | | | |
|---|---|---|---|---|
| 146 | **19** | 6d. brown | 16·00 | 55 |

**20** Melbourne and River Yarra

**1934.** Centenary of Victoria.

| | | | | |
|---|---|---|---|---|
| 147 | **20** | 2d. red | 2·50 | 1·75 |
| 148 | **20** | 3d. blue | 4·00 | 5·50 |
| 149 | **20** | 1s. black | 55·00 | 20·00 |

**21** Merino Ram

**1934.** Death Centenary of Capt. John Macarthur (founder of Australian sheep-farming).

| | | | | |
|---|---|---|---|---|
| 150 | **21** | 2d. red | 8·00 | 1·50 |
| 151 | **21** | 3d. blue | 13·00 | 17·00 |
| 152 | **21** | 9d. purple | 28·00 | 48·00 |

**22** Hermes

**1934**

| | | | | |
|---|---|---|---|---|
| 153b | **22** | 1s.6d. purple | 2·00 | 1·40 |

**23** Cenotaph, Whitehall

**1935.** 20th. Anniv of Gallipoli Landing.

| | | | | |
|---|---|---|---|---|
| 154 | **23** | 2d. red | 2·00 | 30 |
| 155 | **23** | 1s. black | 50·00 | 45·00 |

**24** King George V on "Anzac"

**1935.** Silver Jubilee.

| | | | | |
|---|---|---|---|---|
| 156 | **24** | 2d. red | 2·50 | 30 |
| 157 | **24** | 3d. blue | 8·00 | 11·00 |
| 158 | **24** | 2s. violet | 35·00 | 55·00 |

**25** Amphitrite and Telephone Cable

**1936.** Opening of Submarine Telephone Cable to Tasmania.

| | | | | |
|---|---|---|---|---|
| 159 | **25** | 2d. red | 1·75 | 50 |
| 160 | **25** | 3d. blue | 4·00 | 2·75 |

**26** Site of Adelaide, 1836; Old Gum Tree, Glenelg; King William Street, Adelaide

**1936.** Centenary of South Australia.

| | | | | |
|---|---|---|---|---|
| 161 | **26** | 2d. red | 2·25 | 40 |
| 162 | **26** | 3d. blue | 8·50 | 3·50 |
| 163 | **26** | 1s. green | 14·00 | 9·00 |

**27** Wallaroo

**28** Queen Elizabeth

**29** King George VI

**30** King George VI

**31** King George VI

**33** Merino Ram

**38** Queen Elizabeth

**40** King George VI and Queen Elizabeth

**1937**

| | | | | |
|---|---|---|---|---|
| 228 | **27** | ½d. orange | 20 | 10 |
| 165 | **28** | 1d. green | 1·00 | 50 |
| 180 | - | 1d. green | 6·50 | 60 |
| 181 | - | 1d. purple | 1·50 | 50 |
| 182 | **29** | 1½d. purple | 4·75 | 13·00 |
| 183 | **29** | 1½d. green | 1·25 | 1·75 |
| 167 | **30** | 2d. red | 1·00 | 50 |
| 184 | - | 2d. red | 4·75 | 20 |
| 185 | **30** | 2d. purple | 50 | 2·00 |
| 186 | **31** | 3d. blue | 45·00 | 3·75 |
| 187 | **31** | 3d. brown | 40 | 10 |
| 188 | - | 4d. green | 1·00 | 10 |
| 189 | **33** | 5d. purple | 50 | 2·25 |
| 190a | - | 6d. brown | 1·75 | 10 |
| 191 | - | 9d. brown | 1·00 | 30 |
| 192 | - | 1s. green | 1·75 | 10 |
| 175 | **31** | 1s.4d. mauve | 2·50 | 2·50 |
| 176a | **38** | 5s. purple | 4·00 | 2·75 |
| 177 | - | 10s. purple | 48·00 | 17·00 |
| 178 | **40** | £1 slate | 65·00 | 35·00 |

DESIGNS—As Type **28**: 4d. Koala; 6d. Kookaburra; 1s. Lyrebird. As Type **33**: 9d. Platypus. As Type **38**: 10s. King George VI.

Nos. 180 and 184 are as Types **28** and **30** but with completely shaded background.

**41** Governor Phillip at Sydney Cove (J. Alcott)

**1937.** 150th Anniv of New South Wales.

| | | | | |
|---|---|---|---|---|
| 193 | **41** | 2d. red | 3·00 | 30 |
| 194 | **41** | 3d. blue | 6·50 | 2·25 |
| 195 | **41** | 9d. purple | 22·00 | 12·00 |

**42** A.I.F. and Nurse

**1940.** Australian Imperial Forces.

| | | | | |
|---|---|---|---|---|
| 196 | **42** | 1d. green | 2·25 | 2·75 |
| 197 | **42** | 2d. red | 2·00 | 1·50 |
| 198 | **42** | 3d. blue | 15·00 | 10·00 |
| 199 | **42** | 6d. purple | 29·00 | 26·00 |

**1941.** Surch with figures and bars.

| | | | | |
|---|---|---|---|---|
| 200 | **30** | 2½d. on 2d. red | 1·00 | 70 |
| 201 | **31** | 3½d. on 3d. blue | 2·00 | 2·25 |
| 202 | **33** | 5½d. on 5d. purple | 4·00 | 5·50 |

**46a** Queen Elizabeth **47** King George VI **48** King George VI

**49** King George VI **50** Emu

**1942**

| | | | | |
|---|---|---|---|---|
| 203 | **46a** | 1d. purple | 1·75 | 10 |
| 204 | **46a** | 1½d. green | 2·25 | 10 |
| 205 | **47** | 2d. purple | 1·75 | 2·00 |
| 206 | **48** | 2½d. red | 40 | 10 |
| 207 | **49** | 3½d. blue | 2·25 | 60 |
| 208 | **50** | 5½d. grey | 1·00 | 20 |

**52** Duke and Duchess of Gloucester

**1945.** Royal Visit.

| | | | | |
|---|---|---|---|---|
| 209 | **52** | 2½d. red | 20 | 10 |
| 210 | **52** | 3½d. blue | 40 | 1·25 |
| 211 | **52** | 5½d. grey | 50 | 1·25 |

**53** Star and Wreath

**1946.** Victory. Inscr "PEACE 1945".

| | | | | |
|---|---|---|---|---|
| 213 | **53** | 2½d. red | 20 | 10 |
| 214 | - | 3½d. blue | 55 | 1·75 |
| 215 | - | 5½d. green | 60 | 1·00 |

DESIGNS—HORIZ: 3½d. Flag and dove. VERT: 5½d. Angel.

**56** Sir Thomas Mitchell and Queensland

**1946.** Centenary of Mitchell's Central Queensland Exploration.

| | | | | |
|---|---|---|---|---|
| 216 | **56** | 2½d. red | 25 | 10 |
| 217 | **56** | 3½d. blue | 75 | 1·50 |
| 218 | **56** | 1s. green | 75 | 65 |

**57** Lt. John Shortland, R.N. **58** Steel Foundry

**1947.** 150th Anniv of City of Newcastle.

| | | | | |
|---|---|---|---|---|
| 219 | **57** | 2½d. lake | 20 | 10 |
| 220 | **58** | 3½d. blue | 60 | 1·50 |
| 221 | - | 5½d. green | 60 | 75 |

DESIGNS—As Type **58**: HORIZ: 5½d. Coal carrier cranes.

**60** Queen Elizabeth II when Princess

**1947.** Wedding of Princess Elizabeth.

| | | | | |
|---|---|---|---|---|
| 222a | **60** | 1d. purple | 10 | 10 |

**61** Hereford Bull **61a** Hermes and Globe

**62** Aboriginal Art **62a** Commonwealth Coat of Arms

**1948**

| | | | | |
|---|---|---|---|---|
| 223 | **61** | 1s.3d. brown | 2·00 | 1·10 |
| 223a | **61a** | 1s.6d. brown | 1·00 | 10 |
| 224 | **62** | 2s. brown | 1·50 | 10 |
| 224a | **62a** | 5s. red | 3·50 | 20 |
| 224b | **62a** | 10s. purple | 18·00 | 85 |
| 224c | **62a** | £1 blue | 40·00 | 4·00 |
| 224d | **62a** | £2 green | 85·00 | 15·00 |

**63** William J. Farrer

**1948.** W. J. Farrer (wheat research) Commem.

| | | | | |
|---|---|---|---|---|
| 225 | **63** | 2½d. red | 40 | 10 |

**64** Ferdinand von Mueller

**1948.** Sir Ferdinand von Mueller (botanist) Commemoration.

| | | | | |
|---|---|---|---|---|
| 226 | **64** | 2½d. red | 30 | 10 |

**65** Boy Scout

**1948.** Pan-Pacific Scout Jamboree, Wonga Park.

| | | | | |
|---|---|---|---|---|
| 227 | **65** | 2½d. lake | 30 | 10 |

For 3½d. value dates "1952–53", see No. 254.

**66** "Henry Lawson" (Sir Lionel Lindsay)

**1949.** Henry Lawson (poet) Commemoration.

| | | | | |
|---|---|---|---|---|
| 231 | **66** | 2½d. purple | 40 | 10 |

**67** Mounted Postman and Convair CV 240 Aircraft

**1949.** 75th Anniv of U.P.U.

| | | | | |
|---|---|---|---|---|
| 232 | **67** | 3½d. blue | 50 | 60 |

**68** John, Lord Forrest of Bunbury

**1949.** John, Lord Forrest (explorer and politician) Commemoration.

| | | | | |
|---|---|---|---|---|
| 233 | **68** | 2½d. red | 55 | 10 |

**69** Queen Elizabeth **70** King George VI **81** King George VI

**80** King George VI **71** Aborigine **82** King George VI

**1950**

| | | | | |
|---|---|---|---|---|
| 236 | **69** | 1½d. green | 40 | 40 |
| 237 | **69** | 2d. green | 15 | 10 |
| 234 | **70** | 2½d. red | 10 | 10 |
| 237c | **70** | 2½d. brown | 15 | 35 |
| 235 | **70** | 3d. red | 15 | 25 |
| 237d | **70** | 3d. green | 15 | 10 |
| 247 | **81** | 3½d. purple | 10 | 10 |
| 248 | **81** | 4½d. red | 15 | 1·25 |
| 249 | **81** | 6½d. brown | 20 | 1·25 |
| 250 | **81** | 6½d. green | 20 | 45 |
| 251 | **80** | 7½d. blue | 15 | 80 |
| 238 | **71** | 8½d. brown | 20 | 1·00 |
| 252 | **82** | 1s.0½d. blue | 85 | 60 |
| 253 | **71** | 2s.6d. brown (21×25½ mm) | 1·75 | 1·00 |

**72** Reproduction of First Stamp of N.S.W. **73** Reproduction of First Stamp of Victoria

**1950.** Centenary of Australian States Stamps.

| | | | | |
|---|---|---|---|---|
| 239 | **72** | 2½d. purple | 50 | 10 |
| 240 | **73** | 2½d. purple | 50 | 10 |

**75** Sir Henry Parkes **77** Federal Parliament House, Canberra

**1951.** 50th Anniv of Commonwealth. Inscr as in T 75 and 77.

| | | | | |
|---|---|---|---|---|
| 241 | **75** | 3d. lake | 1·40 | 10 |
| 242 | - | 3d. lake | 1·40 | 10 |
| 243 | - | 5½d. blue | 45 | 2·25 |
| 244 | **77** | 1s.6d. brown | 1·00 | 50 |

DESIGNS—As Type **70**: No. 242, Sir Edmund Barton. As Type **77**: No. 243, Opening first Federal Parliament.

**78** E. H. Hargraves **79** C. J. Latrobe

**1951.** Centenaries. Discovery of Gold in Australia and of Responsible Government in Victoria.

| | | | | |
|---|---|---|---|---|
| 245 | **78** | 3d. purple | 1·00 | 10 |
| 246 | **79** | 3d. purple | 1·00 | 10 |

**1952.** Pan-Pacific Scout Jamboree, Greystanes. As T 65 but dated "1952–53".

| | | | | |
|---|---|---|---|---|
| 254 | **65** | 3½d. lake | 20 | 10 |

**83** Butter

**1953.** Food Production. Inscr "PRODUCE FOOD!".

| | | | | |
|---|---|---|---|---|
| 255 | **83** | 3d. green | 30 | 10 |
| 256 | - | 3d. green (Wheat) | 30 | 10 |
| 257 | - | 3d. green (Beef) | 30 | 10 |
| 258 | **83** | 3½d. red | 30 | 10 |
| 259 | - | 3½d. red (Wheat) | 30 | 10 |
| 260 | - | 3½d. red (Beef) | 30 | 10 |

**86** Queen Elizabeth II

**1953**

| | | | | |
|---|---|---|---|---|
| 261 | **86** | 1d. purple | 15 | 15 |
| 261a | **86** | 2½d. blue | 20 | 15 |
| 262 | **86** | 3d. green | 20 | 10 |
| 263 | **86** | 3½d. red | 20 | 10 |
| 263a | **86** | 6½d. orange | 2·50 | 50 |

**87** Queen Elizabeth II

**1953.** Coronation.

| | | | | |
|---|---|---|---|---|
| 264 | **87** | 3½d. red | 40 | 10 |
| 265 | **87** | 7½d. violet | 75 | 1·40 |
| 266 | **87** | 2s. green | 2·50 | 1·40 |

**88** Young Farmers and Calf

**1953.** 25th Anniv of Australian Young Farmers' Clubs.

| | | | | |
|---|---|---|---|---|
| 267 | **88** | 3½d. brown and green | 10 | 10 |

**89** Lt.-Gov. D. Collins **90** Lt.-Gov. W. Paterson

**91** Sullivan Cove, Hobart, 1804

**1953.** 150th Anniv of Settlement in Tasmania.

| | | | | |
|---|---|---|---|---|
| 268 | **89** | 3½d. purple | 35 | 10 |
| 269 | **90** | 3½d. purple | 35 | 10 |
| 270 | **91** | 2s. green | 1·25 | 2·75 |

**92** Stamp of 1853

**1953.** 1st Centenary of Tasmania Postage Stamps.

| | | | | |
|---|---|---|---|---|
| 271 | **92** | 3d. red | 10 | 40 |

**93** Queen Elizabeth II and Duke of Edinburgh **94** Queen Elizabeth II

**1954.** Royal Visit.

| | | | | |
|---|---|---|---|---|
| 272 | **93** | 3½d. red | 20 | 10 |
| 273 | **94** | 7½d. purple | 30 | 1·25 |
| 274 | **93** | 2s. green | 60 | 65 |

**95** "Telegraphic Communications"

**1954.** Centenary of Telegraph.

| | | | | |
|---|---|---|---|---|
| 275 | **95** | 3½d. brown | 10 | 10 |

**96** Red Cross and Globe

**1954.** 40th Anniv of Australian Red Cross Society.

| | | | | |
|---|---|---|---|---|
| 276 | **96** | 3½d. blue and red | 10 | 10 |

**97** Mute Swan

**1954.** Centenary of Western Australian Stamps.

| | | | | |
|---|---|---|---|---|
| 277 | **97** | 3½d. black | 20 | 10 |

**98** Locomotives of 1854 and 1954

**1954.** Centenary of Australian Railways.

| | | | | |
|---|---|---|---|---|
| 278 | **98** | 3½d. purple | 30 | 10 |

**99** Territory Badge

**1954.** Australian Antarctic Research.

| | | | | |
|---|---|---|---|---|
| 279 | **99** | 3½d. black | 15 | 10 |

**100** Olympic Games Symbol

**1954.** Olympic Games Propaganda.

| | | | | |
|---|---|---|---|---|
| 280 | **100** | 2s. blue | 1·50 | 1·00 |
| 280a | **100** | 2s. green | 1·75 | 2·50 |

**101** Rotary Symbol, Globe and Flags

**1955.** 50th Anniv of Rotary International.

| | | | | |
|---|---|---|---|---|
| 281 | **101** | 3½d. red | 10 | 10 |

**103** American Memorial, Canberra

**1955.** Australian–American Friendship.

| | | | | |
|---|---|---|---|---|
| 283 | **103** | 3½d. blue | 10 | 10 |

**101a** Queen Elizabeth II **102** Queen Elizabeth II

**1955**

| | | | | |
|---|---|---|---|---|
| 282a | **101a** | 4d. lake | 20 | 10 |
| 282b | **101a** | 7½d. violet | 60 | 1·50 |
| 282c | **101a** | 10d. blue | 60 | 1·25 |
| 282 | **102** | 1s.0½d. blue | 1·25 | 1·25 |
| 282d | **102** | 1s.7d. brown | 1·25 | 45 |

**104** Cobb & Co. Coach (from etching by Sir Lionel Lindsay)

**1955.** Mail-coach Pioneers Commemoration.

| | | | | |
|---|---|---|---|---|
| 284 | **104** | 3½d. sepia | 25 | 10 |
| 285 | **104** | 2s. brown | 1·00 | 1·40 |

**105** Y.M.C.A. Emblem and Map of the World

**1955.** World Centenary of Y.M.C.A.

| | | | | |
|---|---|---|---|---|
| 286 | **105** | 3½d. green and red | 10 | 10 |

**106** Florence Nightingale and Young Nurse

**1955.** Nursing Profession Commemoration.

| | | | | |
|---|---|---|---|---|
| 287 | **106** | 3½d. lilac | 10 | 10 |

**107** Queen Victoria

**1955.** Centenary of South Australian Postage Stamps.

| | | | | |
|---|---|---|---|---|
| 288 | **107** | 3½d. green | 10 | 10 |

**108** Badges of N.S.W., Victoria and Tasmania

**1956.** Centenary of Responsible Government in N.S.W., Victoria and Tasmania.

| | | | | |
|---|---|---|---|---|
| 289 | **108** | 3½d. lake | 10 | 10 |

**109** Arms of Melbourne **110** Olympic Torch and Symbol

**111** Collins Street, Melbourne

**1956.** Olympic Games, Melbourne.

| | | | | |
|---|---|---|---|---|
| 290 | **109** | 4d. red | 25 | 10 |
| 291 | **110** | 7½d. blue | 60 | 1·40 |
| 292 | **111** | 1s. multicoloured | 70 | 30 |
| 293 | - | 2s. multicoloured | 1·00 | 1·40 |

DESIGN—As Type **111**: 2s. Melbourne across River Yarra.

**115** South Australia Coat of Arms

**1957.** Centenary of Responsible Government in South Australia.

| | | | | |
|---|---|---|---|---|
| 296 | **115** | 4d. brown | 10 | 10 |

**116** Map of Australia and Caduceus

**1957.** Royal Flying Doctor Service of Australia.

| | | | | |
|---|---|---|---|---|
| 297 | **116** | 7d. blue | 15 | 10 |

**117** "The Spirit of Christmas" (after Sir Joshua Reynolds)

**1957.** Christmas.

| | | | | |
|---|---|---|---|---|
| 298 | **117** | 3½d. red | 10 | 20 |
| 299 | **117** | 4d. purple | 10 | 10 |

**118** Lockheed Super Constellation Airliner

**1958.** Inaug of Australian "Round-the-World" Air Service.

| | | | | |
|---|---|---|---|---|
| 301 | **118** | 2s. blue | 1·00 | 1·00 |

**119** Hall of Memory, Sailor and Airman

**1958**

| | | | | |
|---|---|---|---|---|
| 302 | **119** | 5½d. lake | 40 | 30 |
| 303 | - | 5½d. lake | 40 | 30 |

No. 303 shows a soldier and servicewoman instead of the sailor and airman.

**120** Sir Charles Kingsford Smith and the "Southern Cross"

**1958.** 30th Anniv of 1st Air Crossing of the Tasman Sea.

| | | | | |
|---|---|---|---|---|
| 304 | **120** | 8d. blue | 60 | 1·00 |

**121** Silver Mine, Broken Hill

**1958.** 75th Anniv of Founding of Broken Hill.

| | | | | |
|---|---|---|---|---|
| 305 | **121** | 4d. brown | 30 | 10 |

**122** The Nativity

**1958.** Christmas Issue.

| | | | | |
|---|---|---|---|---|
| 306 | **122** | 3½d. red | 20 | 30 |
| 307 | **122** | 4d. violet | 20 | 10 |

**124** Queen Elizabeth II **126** Queen Elizabeth II **127** Queen Elizabeth II

**128** Queen Elizabeth II **129** Queen Elizabeth II

**1959**

| | | | | |
|---|---|---|---|---|
| 308 | - | 1d. purple | 10 | 10 |
| 309 | **124** | 2d. brown | 50 | 20 |
| 311 | **126** | 3d. turquoise | 15 | 10 |
| 312 | **127** | 3½d. green | 15 | 15 |
| 313 | **128** | 4d. red | 1·75 | 10 |

| | | | | |
|---|---|---|---|---|
| 314 | 129 | 5d. blue | 1·25 | 10 |

No. 308 shows a head and shoulders portrait as in Type **128** and is vert.

**131** Numbat **137** Christmas Bells

**142** Aboriginal Stockman

**1959**

| | | | | |
|---|---|---|---|---|
| 316 | 131 | 6d. brown | 1·50 | 10 |
| 317 | - | 8d. brown | 75 | 10 |
| 318 | - | 9d. sepia | 1·75 | 55 |
| 319 | - | 11d. blue | 1·00 | 15 |
| 320 | - | 1s. green | 1·75 | 40 |
| 321 | - | 1s.2d. purple | 1·00 | 15 |
| 322 | 137 | 1s.6d. red on yellow | 1·50 | 1·00 |
| 323 | - | 2s. blue | 70 | 10 |
| 324 | - | 2s.3d. green on yellow | 1·00 | 10 |
| 324a | - | 2s.3d. green | 2·50 | 75 |
| 325 | - | 2s.5d. brown on yellow | 3·50 | 75 |
| 326 | - | 3s. red | 1·25 | 20 |
| 327 | 142 | 5s. brown | 12·00 | 2·75 |

DESIGNS—As Type **131**: VERT: 8d. Tiger Cat; 9d. Eastern grey kangaroo; 11d. Common rabbit bandicoot; 1s. Platypus. HORIZ: 1s.2d. Thylacine. As Type **137**: 2s. Flannel flower; 2s.3d. Wattle; 2s.5d. Banksia (plant); 3s. Waratah.

**143** Postmaster Isaac Nichols boarding the Brig "Experiment"

**1959.** 150th Anniv of Australian P.O.

| | | | | |
|---|---|---|---|---|
| 331 | 143 | 4d. slate | 15 | 10 |

**144** Parliament House, Brisbane, and Arms of Queensland

**1959.** Centenary of Queensland Self-Government.

| | | | | |
|---|---|---|---|---|
| 332 | 144 | 4d. lilac and green | 10 | 10 |

**145** "The Approach of the Magi"

**1959.** Christmas.

| | | | | |
|---|---|---|---|---|
| 333 | 145 | 5d. violet | 10 | 10 |

**146** Girl Guide and Lord Baden-Powell

**1960.** 50th Anniv of Girl Guide Movement.

| | | | | |
|---|---|---|---|---|
| 334 | 146 | 5d. blue | 30 | 15 |

**147** "The Overlanders" (after Sir Daryl Lindsay)

**1960.** Centenary of Northern Territory Exploration.

| | | | | |
|---|---|---|---|---|
| 335 | 147 | 5d. mauve | 50 | 15 |

**148** "Archer" and Melbourne Cup

**1960.** 100th Melbourne Cup Race Commemoration.

| | | | | |
|---|---|---|---|---|
| 336 | 148 | 5d. sepia | 20 | 10 |

**149** Queen Victoria

**1960.** Centenary of Queensland Stamps.

| | | | | |
|---|---|---|---|---|
| 337 | 149 | 5d. green | 25 | 10 |

**150** Open Bible and Candle

**1960.** Christmas Issue.

| | | | | |
|---|---|---|---|---|
| 338 | 150 | 5d. lake | 10 | 10 |

**151** Colombo Plan Bureau Emblem

**1961.** Colombo Plan.

| | | | | |
|---|---|---|---|---|
| 339 | 151 | 1s. brown | 10 | 10 |

**152** Melba (after bust by Sir Bertram Mackennal)

**1961.** Birth Centenary of Dame Nellie Melba (singer).

| | | | | |
|---|---|---|---|---|
| 340 | 152 | 5d. blue | 30 | 15 |

**153** Open Prayer Book and Text

**1961.** Christmas Issue.

| | | | | |
|---|---|---|---|---|
| 341 | 153 | 5d. brown | 10 | 10 |

**154** J. M. Stuart

**1962.** Centenary of Stuart's South to North Crossing of Australia.

| | | | | |
|---|---|---|---|---|
| 342 | 154 | 5d. red | 40 | 10 |

**155** Flynn's Grave and Nursing Sister

**1962.** 50th Anniv of Australian Inland Mission.

| | | | | |
|---|---|---|---|---|
| 343 | 155 | 5d. multicoloured | 30 | 15 |

**156** "Woman"

**1962.** "Associated Country Women of the World" Conference, Melbourne.

| | | | | |
|---|---|---|---|---|
| 344 | 156 | 5d. green | 10 | 10 |

**157** "Madonna and Child"

**1962.** Christmas.

| | | | | |
|---|---|---|---|---|
| 345 | 157 | 5d. violet | 15 | 10 |

**158** Perth and Kangaroo Paw (plant)

**1962.** British Empire and Commonwealth Games, Perth. Multicoloured.

| | | | |
|---|---|---|---|
| 346 | 5d. Type **158** | 50 | 10 |
| 347 | 2s.3d. Arms of Perth and running track | 2·00 | 2·75 |

**160** Queen Elizabeth II

**1963.** Royal Visit.

| | | | | |
|---|---|---|---|---|
| 348 | 160 | 5d. green | 35 | 10 |
| 349 | - | 2s.3d. lake | 1·50 | 3·00 |

DESIGN: 2s.3d. Queen Elizabeth II and Duke of Edinburgh.

**162** Arms of Canberra and W. B. Griffin (architect)

**1963.** 50th Anniv of Canberra.

| | | | | |
|---|---|---|---|---|
| 350 | 162 | 5d. green | 15 | 10 |

**163** Centenary Emblem

**1963.** Centenary of Red Cross.

| | | | | |
|---|---|---|---|---|
| 351 | 163 | 5d. red, grey and blue | 60 | 10 |

**164** Blaxland, Lawson and Wentworth on Mount York

**1963.** 150th Anniv of First Crossing of Blue Mountains.

| | | | | |
|---|---|---|---|---|
| 352 | 164 | 5d. blue | 15 | 10 |

**165** "Export"

**1963.** Export Campaign.

| | | | | |
|---|---|---|---|---|
| 353 | 165 | 5d. red | 10 | 10 |

**1963.** As T 160 but smaller 17½×21½ mm "5D" at top right replacing "ROYAL VISIT 1963" and oak leaves omitted.

| | | | |
|---|---|---|---|
| 354 | 5d. green | 1·00 | 10 |
| 354c | 5d. red | 55 | 10 |

**167** Tasman and "Heemskerk"

**1963.** Navigators.

| | | | | |
|---|---|---|---|---|
| 355 | 167 | 4s. blue | 3·00 | 55 |
| 356 | - | 5s. brown | 3·75 | 1·75 |
| 357 | - | 7s.6d. olive | 19·00 | 16·00 |
| 358 | - | 10s. purple | 25·00 | 5·00 |
| 359 | - | £1 violet | 35·00 | 16·00 |
| 360 | - | £2 sepia | 55·00 | 75·00 |

DESIGNS—As Type **167**: 7s.6d. Captain Cook; 10s. Flinders and "Investigator". 20½×5½ mm: 5s. Dampier and "Roebuck"; £1 Bass and "Tom Thumb" (whale boat); £2 Admiral King and "Mermaid" (survey cutter).

**173** "Peace on Earth..."

**1963.** Christmas.

| | | | | |
|---|---|---|---|---|
| 361 | 173 | 5d. blue | 10 | 10 |

**174** "Commonwealth Cable"

**1963.** Opening of COMPAC (Trans-Pacific Telephone Cable).

| | | | | |
|---|---|---|---|---|
| 362 | 174 | 2s.3d. multicoloured | 1·50 | 2·75 |

**176** Black-backed Magpie

**1964.** Birds.

| | | | | |
|---|---|---|---|---|
| 363 | - | 6d. multicoloured | 1·00 | 25 |
| 364 | 176 | 9d. black, grey and green | 1·00 | 2·75 |
| 365 | - | 1s.6d. multicoloured | 75 | 1·40 |
| 366 | - | 2s. yellow, black and pink | 1·40 | 50 |
| 367 | - | 2s.5d. multicoloured | 1·75 | 3·50 |
| 368 | - | 2s.6d. multicoloured | 2·50 | 3·75 |
| 369 | - | 3s. multicoloured | 2·50 | 1·75 |

BIRDS—HORIZ: 6d. Yellow-tailed thornbill; 2s.6d. Scarlet robin. VERT: 1s.6d. Galah (cockatoo); 2s. Golden whistler (Thickhead); 2s.5d. Blue wren; 3s. Straw-necked ibis.

**182** Bleriot XI Aircraft (type flown by M. Guillaux, 1914)

**1964.** 50th Anniv of 1st Australian Airmail Flight.

| | | | | |
|---|---|---|---|---|
| 370 | 182 | 5d. green | 30 | 10 |
| 371 | 182 | 2s.3d. red | 1·50 | 2·75 |

**183** Child looking at Nativity Scene

**1964.** Christmas.

| | | | | |
|---|---|---|---|---|
| 372 | 183 | 5d. red, blue, buff and black | 10 | 10 |

**184** "Simpson and his Donkey"

**1965.** 50th Anniv of Gallipoli Landing.

| | | | | |
|---|---|---|---|---|
| 373 | **184** | 5d. brown | 50 | 10 |
| 374 | **184** | 8d. blue | 75 | 2·50 |
| 375 | **184** | 2s.3d. purple | 1·50 | 2·50 |

**185** "Telecommunications"

**1965.** Centenary of I.T.U.

| | | | | |
|---|---|---|---|---|
| 376 | **185** | 5d. black, brown and blue | 60 | 10 |

**186** Sir Winston Churchill

**1965.** Churchill Commemoration.

| | | | | |
|---|---|---|---|---|
| 377 | **186** | 5d. multicoloured | 30 | 10 |

**187** General Monash

**1965.** Birth Centenary of General Sir John Monash (engineer and soldier).

| | | | | |
|---|---|---|---|---|
| 378 | **187** | 5d. multicoloured | 15 | 10 |

**188** Hargrave and "Multiplane" Seaplane (1902)

**1965.** 50th Death Anniv of Lawrence Hargrave (aviation pioneer).

| | | | | |
|---|---|---|---|---|
| 379 | **188** | 5d. multicoloured | 25 | 10 |

**189** I.C.Y. Emblem

**1965.** International Co-operation Year.

| | | | | |
|---|---|---|---|---|
| 380 | **189** | 2s.3d. green and blue | 65 | 1·50 |

**190** "Nativity Scene"

**1965.** Christmas.

| | | | | |
|---|---|---|---|---|
| 381 | **190** | 5d. multicoloured | 15 | 10 |

**191** Queen Elizabeth II **192** Blue-faced Honeyeater

**1966.** Decimal currency. As earlier issues but with values in cents and dollars as in T 191/2. Also some new designs.

| | | | | |
|---|---|---|---|---|
| 382 | **191** | 1c. brown | 25 | 10 |
| 383 | **191** | 2c. green | 70 | 10 |
| 384 | **191** | 3c. green | 70 | 10 |
| 404 | **191** | 3c. black, pink and green | 45 | 1·25 |
| 385 | **191** | 4c. red | 20 | 10 |
| 405 | **191** | 4c. black, brown and red | 35 | 60 |
| 386 | - | 5c. multicoloured (as 363) | 25 | 10 |
| 386c | **191** | 5c. blue | 70 | 10 |
| 405a | **191** | 5c. black, brown and blue | 40 | 10 |
| 387 | **192** | 6c. multicoloured | 1·25 | 1·00 |
| 387a | **191** | 6c. orange | 1·00 | 10 |
| 388 | - | 7c. multicoloured | 60 | 10 |
| 388a | **191** | 7c. purple | 1·25 | 10 |
| 389 | - | 8c. multicoloured | 60 | 1·00 |
| 390 | - | 9c. multicoloured | 60 | 20 |
| 391 | - | 10c. multicoloured | 60 | 10 |
| 392 | - | 13c. multicoloured | 1·50 | 25 |
| 393 | - | 15c. multicoloured (as 365) | 1·25 | 1·75 |
| 394 | - | 20c. yellow, black and pink (as 366) | 1·50 | 15 |
| 395 | - | 24c. multicoloured | 65 | 1·25 |
| 396 | - | 25c. multicoloured (as 368) | 1·50 | 30 |
| 397 | - | 30c. multicoloured (as 369) | 4·50 | 1·25 |
| 398 | **167** | 40c. blue | 3·00 | 10 |
| 399 | - | 50c. brown (as 356) | 3·00 | 10 |
| 400 | - | 75c. olive (as 357) | 1·00 | 1·00 |
| 401 | - | $1 purple (as 358) | 1·50 | 20 |
| 402 | - | $2 violet (as 359) | 6·00 | 1·00 |
| 403 | - | $4 brown (as 360) | 6·00 | 6·50 |

DESIGNS—VERT: 7c. White-tailed Dascyllus ("Humbug fish"); 8c. Copper-banded butterflyfish ("Coral fish"); 9c. Hermit crab; 10c. Orange clownfish ("Anemone fish"); 13c. Red-necked avocet. HORIZ: 24c. Azure kingfisher.

**200** "Saving Life"

**1966.** 75th Anniv of Royal Life Saving Society.

| | | | | |
|---|---|---|---|---|
| 406 | **200** | 4c. black, lt bl & bl | 15 | 10 |

**201** "Adoration of the Shepherds"

**1966.** Christmas.

| | | | | |
|---|---|---|---|---|
| 407 | **201** | 4c. black and olive | 10 | 10 |

**202** "Eendracht"

**1966.** 350th Anniv of Dirk Hartog's Landing in Australia.

| | | | | |
|---|---|---|---|---|
| 408 | **202** | 4c. multicoloured | 10 | 10 |

**203** Open Bible

**1967.** 150th Anniv of British and Foreign Bible Society in Australia.

| | | | | |
|---|---|---|---|---|
| 409 | **203** | 4c. multicoloured | 10 | 10 |

**204** Ancient Keys and Modern Lock

**1967.** 150th Anniv of Australian Banking.

| | | | | |
|---|---|---|---|---|
| 410 | **204** | 4c. black, blue and green | 10 | 10 |

**205** Lions Badge and 50 Stars

**1967.** 50th Anniv of Lions International.

| | | | | |
|---|---|---|---|---|
| 411 | **205** | 4c. black, gold and blue | 10 | 10 |

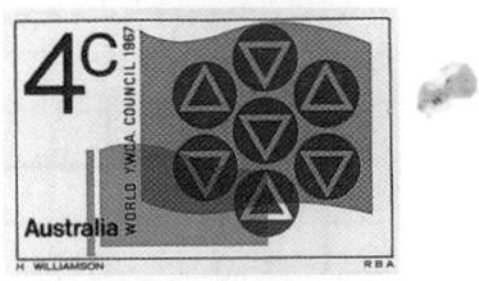


**206** Y.W.C.A. Emblem

**1967.** World Y.W.C.A. Council Meeting, Monash University, Melbourne.

| | | | | |
|---|---|---|---|---|
| 412 | **206** | 4c. multicoloured | 10 | 10 |

**207** Anatomical Figures

**1967.** 5th World Gynaecology and Obstetrics Congress, Sydney.

| | | | | |
|---|---|---|---|---|
| 413 | **207** | 4c. black, blue and violet | 10 | 10 |

**1967.** No. 385 surch.

| | | | | |
|---|---|---|---|---|
| 414 | **191** | 5c. on 4c. red | 25 | 10 |

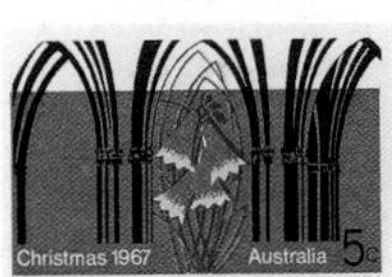


**209** Christmas Bells and Gothic Arches

**1967.** Christmas. Multicoloured.

| | | | |
|---|---|---|---|
| 415 | 5c. Type **209** | 20 | 10 |
| 416 | 25c. Religious symbols (vert) | 1·00 | 1·90 |

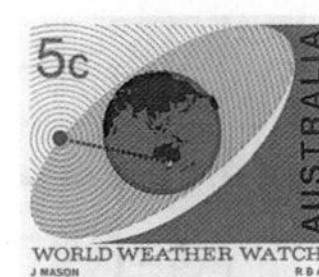


**211** Satellite in Orbit

**1968.** World Weather Watch. Multicoloured.

| | | | |
|---|---|---|---|
| 417 | 5c. Type **211** | 30 | 10 |
| 418 | 20c. World weather map | 1·10 | 2·75 |

**213** Radar Antenna

**1968.** World Telecommunications via Intelsat II.

| | | | | |
|---|---|---|---|---|
| 419 | **213** | 25c. blue, black and green | 1·00 | 2·00 |

**214** Kangaroo Paw (Western Australia)

**1968.** State Floral Emblems. Multicoloured.

| | | | |
|---|---|---|---|
| 420 | 6c. Type **214** | 45 | 1·25 |
| 421 | 13c. Pink Heath (Victoria) | 50 | 70 |
| 422 | 15c. Tasmanian Blue Gum (Tasmania) | 50 | 40 |
| 423 | 20c. Sturt's Desert Pea (South Australia) | 1·00 | 75 |
| 424 | 25c. Cooktown Orchid (Queensland) | 1·10 | 75 |
| 425 | 30c. Waratah (New South Wales) | 50 | 10 |

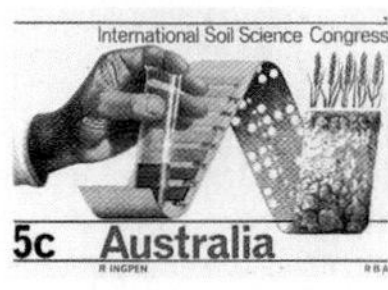


**220** Soil Sample Analysis

**1968.** International Soil Science Congress and World Medical Association Assembly. Mult.

| | | | |
|---|---|---|---|
| 426 | 5c. Type **220** | 10 | 10 |
| 427 | 5c. Rubber-gloved hands, syringe and head of Hippocrates | 10 | 10 |

**222** Athlete carrying Torch and Sunstone Symbol

**1968.** Olympic Games, Mexico City. Mult.

| | | | |
|---|---|---|---|
| 428 | 5c. Type **222** | 30 | 10 |
| 429 | 25c. Sunstone symbol and Mexican flag | 40 | 1·50 |

**224** Houses and Dollar Signs

**1968.** Building and Savings Societies Congress.

| | | | | |
|---|---|---|---|---|
| 430 | **224** | 5c. multicoloured | 10 | 40 |

**225** Church Window and View of Bethlehem

**1968.** Christmas.

| | | | | |
|---|---|---|---|---|
| 431 | **225** | 5c. multicoloured | 10 | 10 |

**226** Edgeworth David (geologist)

**1968.** Famous Australians (1st series).

| | | | | |
|---|---|---|---|---|
| 432 | **226** | 5c. green on myrtle | 25 | 20 |
| 433 | - | 5c. black on blue | 25 | 20 |
| 434 | - | 5c. brown on buff | 25 | 20 |
| 435 | - | 5c. violet on lilac | 25 | 20 |

DESIGNS: No. 433, A. B. Paterson (poet); No. 434, Albert Namatjira (artist); No. 435, Caroline Chrisholm (social worker).

Nos. 432/5 were only issued in booklets and exist with one or two sides imperf.

See also Nos. 446/9, 479/82, 505/8, 537/40, 590/5, 602/7 and 637/40.

**230** Macquarie Lighthouse

**1968.** 150th Anniv of Macquarie Lighthouse.

| | | | | |
|---|---|---|---|---|
| 436 | **230** | 5c. black and yellow | 30 | 70 |

**231** Pioneers and Modern Building, Darwin

**1969.** Centenary of Northern Territory Settlement.

| | | | | |
|---|---|---|---|---|
| 437 | **231** | 5c. brown, olive and ochre | 10 | 10 |

**232** Melbourne Harbour

**1969.** 6th Biennial Conference of International Association of Ports and Harbours, Melbourne.

| | | | | |
|---|---|---|---|---|
| 438 | **232** | 5c. multicoloured | 20 | 10 |

**233** Concentric Circles (symbolizing Management, Labour and Government)

**1969.** 50th Anniv of I.L.O.

| | | | | |
|---|---|---|---|---|
| 439 | **233** | 5c. multicoloured | 15 | 10 |

**234** Sugar Cane

**1969.** Primary Industries. Multicoloured.

| | | | |
|---|---|---|---|
| 440 | 7c. Type **234** | 50 | 1·50 |
| 441 | 15c. Timber | 75 | 2·50 |
| 442 | 20c. Wheat | 30 | 60 |
| 443 | 25c. Wool | 50 | 1·50 |

**238** "The Nativity" (stained glass window)

**1969.** Christmas. Multicoloured.

| | | | |
|---|---|---|---|
| 444 | 5c. Type **238** | 20 | 10 |
| 445 | 25c. "Tree of Life", Christ in crib and Christmas Star (abstract) | 1·00 | 2·00 |

**240** Edmund Barton

**1969.** Famous Australians (2nd series). Prime Ministers.

| | | | | |
|---|---|---|---|---|
| 446 | **240** | 5c. black on green | 40 | 20 |
| 447 | - | 5c. black on green | 40 | 20 |
| 448 | - | 5c. black on green | 40 | 20 |
| 449 | - | 5c. black on green | 40 | 20 |

DESIGNS: No. 447, Alfred Deakin; 448, J. C. Watson; 449, G. H. Reid.

Nos. 446/9 were only issued in booklets and only exist with one or two adjacent sides imperf.

**244** Capt. Ross Smith's Vickers Vimy, 1919

**1969.** 50th Anniv of 1st England–Australia Flight.

| | | | | |
|---|---|---|---|---|
| 450 | **244** | 5c. multicoloured | 15 | 10 |
| 451 | - | 5c. red, black and green | 15 | 10 |
| 452 | - | 5c. multicoloured | 15 | 10 |

DESIGNS: No. 451, Lt. H. Fysh and Lt. P. McGinness on 1919 survey with Ford Model T runabout; 452, Capt. Wrigley and Sgt. Murphy in Royal Aircraft Factory B.E.2E taking off to meet the Smiths.

**247** Symbolic Track and Diesel Locomotive

**1970.** Sydney–Perth Standard Gauge Railway Link.

| | | | | |
|---|---|---|---|---|
| 453 | **247** | 5c. multicoloured | 15 | 10 |

**248** Australian Pavilion, Osaka

**1970.** World Fair, Osaka.

| | | | | |
|---|---|---|---|---|
| 454 | **248** | 5c. multicoloured | 15 | 10 |
| 455 | - | 20c. red and black | 35 | 65 |

DESIGN: 20c., "Southern Cross" and "from the Country of the south with warm feelings" (message).

**251** Australian Flag

**1970.** Royal Visit.

| | | | | |
|---|---|---|---|---|
| 456 | | 5c. black and ochre | 35 | 15 |
| 457 | **251** | 30c. multicoloured | 1·10 | 2·50 |

DESIGN: 5c. Queen Elizabeth II and Duke of Edinburgh.

**252** Lucerne Plant, Bull and Sun

**1970.** 11th International Grasslands Congress, Queensland.

| | | | | |
|---|---|---|---|---|
| 458 | **252** | 5c. multicoloured | 10 | 80 |

**253** Captain Cook and H.M.S. "Endeavour"

**1970.** Bicentenary of Captain Cook's Discovery of Australia's East Coast. Multicoloured.

| | | | |
|---|---|---|---|
| 459 | 5c. Type **253** | 35 | 10 |
| 460 | 5c. Sextant and H.M.S. "Endeavour" | 35 | 10 |
| 461 | 5c. Landing at Botany Bay | 35 | 10 |
| 462 | 5c. Charting and exploring | 35 | 10 |
| 463 | 5c. Claiming possession | 35 | 10 |
| 464 | 30c. Captain Cook, H.M.S. "Endeavour", sextant, aborigines and kangaroo (63×30 mm) | 1·25 | 2·50 |
| **MS**465 | 157×129 mm. Nos. 459/64. Imperf | 7·50 | 9·00 |

Nos. 459/63 were issued together, se-tenant, forming a composite design.

**259** Sturt's Desert Rose

**1970.** Coil Stamps. Multicoloured.

| | | | |
|---|---|---|---|
| 465a | 2c. Type **259** | 40 | 20 |
| 466 | 4c. Type **259** | 85 | 2·00 |
| 467 | 5c. Golden wattle | 20 | 10 |
| 468 | 6c. Type **259** | 1·25 | 1·00 |
| 468b | 7c. Sturt's desert pea | 40 | 70 |
| 468d | 10c. As 7c. | 60 | 1·50 |

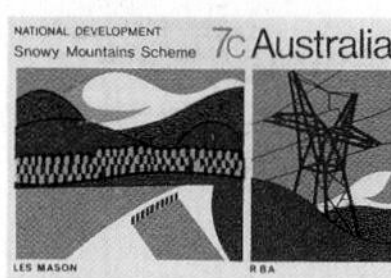


**264** Snowy Mountains Scheme

**1970.** National Development (1st series). Mult.

| | | | |
|---|---|---|---|
| 469 | 7c. Type **264** | 20 | 80 |
| 470 | 8c. Ord River scheme | 10 | 15 |
| 471 | 9c. Bauxite to aluminium | 15 | 15 |
| 472 | 10c. Oil and natural gas | 30 | 10 |

See also Nos. 541/4.

**265** Rising Flames

**1970.** 16th Commonwealth Parliamentary Association Conference, Canberra.

| | | | | |
|---|---|---|---|---|
| 473 | **265** | 6c. multicoloured | 10 | 10 |

**266** Milk Analysis and Dairy Herd

**1970.** 18th International Dairy Congress, Sydney.

| | | | | |
|---|---|---|---|---|
| 474 | **266** | 6c. multicoloured | 10 | 10 |

**267** "The Nativity"

**1970.** Christmas.

| | | | | |
|---|---|---|---|---|
| 475 | **267** | 6c. multicoloured | 10 | 10 |

**268** U.N. "Plant" and Dove of Peace

**1970.** 25th Anniv of United Nations.

| | | | | |
|---|---|---|---|---|
| 476 | **268** | 6c. multicoloured | 15 | 10 |

**269** Boeing 707 and Avro 504

**1970.** 50th Anniv of QANTAS Airline.

| | | | | |
|---|---|---|---|---|
| 477 | **269** | 6c. multicoloured | 30 | 10 |
| 478 | - | 30c. multicoloured | 70 | 1·50 |

DESIGN: 30c. Avro 504 and Boeing 707.

**1970.** Famous Australians (3rd series). As T 226.

| | | | |
|---|---|---|---|
| 479 | 6c. blue | 35 | 20 |
| 480 | 6c. black on brown | 35 | 20 |
| 481 | 6c. purple on pink | 35 | 20 |
| 482 | 6c. red on pink | 35 | 20 |

DESIGNS: No. 479, The Duigan brothers (pioneer aviators); 480, Lachlan Macquarie (Governor of New South Wales); 481, Adam Lindsay Gordon (poet); 482, E. J. Eyre (explorer).

**271** "Theatre"

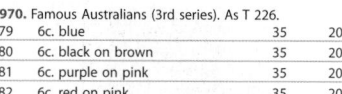

**1971.** "Australia–Asia". 28th International Congress of Orientalists, Canberra. Multicoloured.

| | | | |
|---|---|---|---|
| 483 | 7c. Type **271** | 45 | 60 |
| 484 | 15c. "Music" | 85 | 1·00 |
| 485 | 20c. "Sea Craft" | 65 | 90 |

**272** The Southern Cross

**1971.** Centenary of Australian Natives' Association.

| | | | | |
|---|---|---|---|---|
| 486 | **272** | 6c. black, red and blue | 10 | 10 |

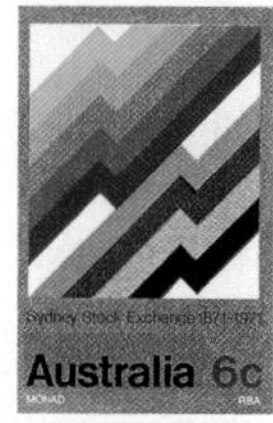


**273** Market "Graph"

**1971.** Centenary of Sydney Stock Exchange.

| | | | | |
|---|---|---|---|---|
| 487 | **273** | 6c. multicoloured | 10 | 10 |

**274** Rotary Emblem

**1971.** 50th Anniv of Rotary International in Australia.

| | | | | |
|---|---|---|---|---|
| 488 | **274** | 6c. multicoloured | 15 | 10 |

**275** Dassault Mirage Jets and De Havilland D.H.9A Biplane

**1971.** 50th Anniv of R.A.A.F.

| | | | | |
|---|---|---|---|---|
| 489 | **275** | 6c. multicoloured | 70 | 10 |

**276** Draught-horse, Cat and Dog

**1971.** Animals. Multicoloured.

| | | | |
|---|---|---|---|
| 490 | 6c. Type **276** | 20 | 10 |
| 491 | 12c. Vet and lamb ("Animal Science") | 45 | 20 |
| 492 | 18c. Red Kangaroo ("Fauna Conservation") | 1·25 | 35 |
| 493 | 24c. Guide-dog ("Animals Aid to Man") | 1·00 | 1·50 |

The 6c. commemorates the Centenary of the Australian R.S.P.C.A.

**277** Bark Painting

**1971.** Aboriginal Art. Multicoloured.

| 494 | 20c. Type **277** | 20 | 20 |
|---|---|---|---|
| 495 | 25c. Body decoration | 20 | 55 |
| 496 | 30c. Cave painting (vert) | 65 | 20 |
| 497 | 35c. Grave posts (vert) | 30 | 15 |

**278** The Three Kings and the Star

**1971.** Christmas. Colours of star and colour of "AUSTRALIA" given.

| 498 | **278** | 7c. blue, mauve and brown | 50 | 15 |
|---|---|---|---|---|
| 499 | **278** | 7c. mauve, brown and white | 50 | 15 |
| 500 | **278** | 7c. mauve, white and black | 2·75 | 80 |
| 501 | **278** | 7c. black, green and black | 50 | 15 |
| 502 | **278** | 7c. lilac, green and mauve | 50 | 15 |
| 503 | **278** | 7c. black, brown and white | 50 | 15 |
| 504 | **278** | 7c. blue, mauve and green | 14·00 | 2·25 |

**1972.** Famous Australians. (4th series). As T 240. Prime Ministers.

| 505 | 7c. blue | 30 | 20 |
|---|---|---|---|
| 506 | 7c. blue | 30 | 20 |
| 507 | 7c. red | 30 | 20 |
| 508 | 7c. red | 30 | 20 |

DESIGNS: No. 505, Andrew Fisher; 506, W. M. Hughes; 507, Joseph Cook; 508, S. M. Bruce.

**280** Cameo Brooch

**1972.** 50th Anniv of Country Women's Association.

| 509 | **280** | 7c. multicoloured | 20 | 10 |
|---|---|---|---|---|

**281** Fruit

**1972.** Primary Industries. Multicoloured.

| 510 | 20c. Type **281** | 1·00 | 2·50 |
|---|---|---|---|
| 511 | 25c. Rice | 1·00 | 4·00 |
| 512 | 30c. Fish | 1·00 | 1·00 |
| 513 | 35c. Beef | 2·25 | 75 |

**282** Worker in Wheelchair

**1972.** Rehabilitation of the Disabled.

| 514 | **282** | 12c. brown and green | 10 | 10 |
|---|---|---|---|---|
| 515 | - | 18c. green and orange | 1·00 | 35 |
| 516 | - | 24c. blue and brown | 15 | 10 |

DESIGNS—HORIZ: 18c. Patient and teacher. VERT: 24c. Boy playing with ball.

**283** Telegraph Line

**1972.** Centenary of Overland Telegraph Line.

| 517 | **283** | 7c. multicoloured | 15 | 15 |
|---|---|---|---|---|

**284** Athletics

**1972.** Olympic Games, Munich. Multicoloured.

| 518 | 7c. Type **284** | 25 | 25 |
|---|---|---|---|
| 519 | 7c. Rowing | 25 | 25 |
| 520 | 7c. Swimming | 25 | 25 |
| 521 | 35c. Equestrian | 1·25 | 3·50 |

**285** Numerals and Computer Circuit

**1972.** 10th Int Congress of Accountants, Sydney.

| 522 | **285** | 7c. multicoloured | 15 | 15 |
|---|---|---|---|---|

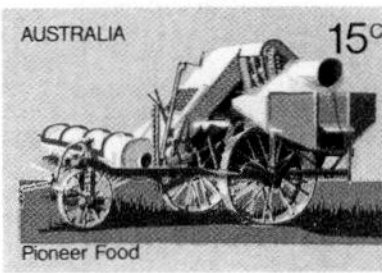

**286** Australian-built Harvester

**1972.** Pioneer Life. Multicoloured.

| 523 | 5c. Pioneer family (vert) | 10 | 10 |
|---|---|---|---|
| 524 | 10c. Water-pump (vert) | 20 | 10 |
| 525 | 15c. Type **286** | 15 | 10 |
| 526 | 40c. House | 15 | 30 |
| 527 | 50c. Stage-coach | 35 | 20 |
| 528 | 60c. Morse key (vert) | 30 | 80 |
| 529 | 80c. "Gem" (paddle-steamer) | 30 | 80 |

**287** Jesus with Children

**1972.** Christmas. Multicoloured.

| 530 | 7c. Type **287** | 30 | 10 |
|---|---|---|---|
| 531 | 35c. Dove and spectrum motif (vert) | 2·75 | 5·00 |

**288** "Length"

**1973.** Metric Conversion. Multicoloured.

| 532 | 7c. Type **288** | 45 | 60 |
|---|---|---|---|
| 533 | 7c. "Volume" | 45 | 60 |
| 534 | 7c. "Mass" | 45 | 60 |
| 535 | 7c. "Temperature" (horiz) | 45 | 60 |

**289** Caduceus and Laurel Wreath

**1973.** 25th Anniv of World Health Organization.

| 536 | **289** | 7c. multicoloured | 30 | 15 |
|---|---|---|---|---|

**1973.** Famous Australians (5th series). As T 226.

| 537 | 7c. brown and black | 35 | 45 |
|---|---|---|---|
| 538 | 7c. lilac and black | 35 | 45 |
| 539 | 7c. brown and black | 35 | 45 |
| 540 | 7c. lilac and black | 35 | 45 |

PORTRAITS: No. 537, William Wentworth (statesman and explorer); 538, Isaac Issacs (1st Australian-born Governor-General); 539, Mary Gilmore (writer); 540, Marcus Clarke (author).

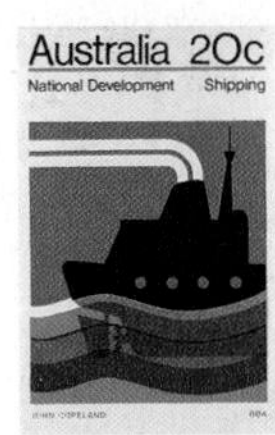

**291** Shipping

**1973.** National Development (2nd series). Mult.

| 541 | 20c. Type **291** | 1·50 | 2·75 |
|---|---|---|---|
| 542 | 25c. Iron ore and steel | 1·50 | 2·75 |
| 543 | 30c. Beef roads | 1·50 | 2·75 |
| 544 | 35c. Mapping | 2·25 | 2·75 |

**292** Banded Coral Shrimp

**1973.** Marine Life and Gemstones. Multicoloured.

| 545 | 1c. Type **292** | 10 | 10 |
|---|---|---|---|
| 546 | 2c. Fiddler crab | 10 | 10 |
| 547 | 3c. Coral crab | 10 | 10 |
| 548 | 4c. Mauve stinger | 15 | 55 |
| 549 | 6c. Chrysoprase (vert) | 25 | 60 |
| 550 | 7c. Agate (vert) | 20 | 10 |
| 551 | 8c. Opal (vert) | 35 | 10 |
| 552 | 9c. Rhodonite (vert) | 50 | 15 |
| 552a | 10c. Star sapphire (vert) | 75 | 10 |

**293** Children at Play

**1973.** 50th Anniv of Legacy (welfare organization).

| 553 | **293** | 7c. brown, red and green | 30 | 10 |
|---|---|---|---|---|

**294** John baptizing Jesus

**1973.** Christmas. Multicoloured.

| 554 | 7c. Type **294** | 35 | 10 |
|---|---|---|---|
| 555 | 30c. The Good Shepherd | 1·75 | 2·25 |

**295** Sydney Opera House

**1973.** Architecture.

| 556 | **295** | 7c. blue and pale blue | 30 | 15 |
|---|---|---|---|---|
| 557 | - | 10c. ochre and brown | 80 | 70 |
| 558 | - | 40c. grey, brown and black | 1·25 | 2·50 |
| 559 | - | 50c. multicoloured | 1·25 | 2·75 |

DESIGNS—HORIZ: 10c. Buchanan's Hotel, Townsville; 40c. Como House, Melbourne. VERT: 50c. St. James's Church, Sydney.

**296** Wireless Receiver and Speaker

**1973.** 50th Anniv of Regular Radio Broadcasting.

| 560 | **296** | 7c. blue, red and black | 15 | 10 |
|---|---|---|---|---|

**297** Common Wombat

**1974.** Animals. Multicoloured.

| 561 | 20c. Type **297** | 25 | 10 |
|---|---|---|---|
| 562 | 25c. Short-nosed echidna (inscr "Spiny Anteater") | 60 | 60 |
| 563 | 30c. Brush-tailed possum | 75 | 15 |
| 564 | 75c. Pygmy (inscr "Feather-tailed") glider | 80 | 1·00 |

**298** "Sergeant of Light Horse" (G. Lambert)

**1974.** Australian Paintings. Multicoloured.

| 565 | $1 Type **298** | 1·00 | 10 |
|---|---|---|---|
| 566 | $2 "Red Gums of the Far North" (H. Heysen) (horiz) | 1·25 | 25 |
| 566b | $4 "Shearing the Rams" (Tom Roberts) (horiz) | 2·00 | 2·25 |
| 567 | $5 "McMahon's Point" (Sir Arthur Streeton) | 3·25 | 2·25 |
| 567a | $10 "Coming South" (Tom Roberts) | 4·50 | 3·50 |

**299** Supreme Court Judge

**1974.** 150th Anniv of Australia's Third Charter of Justice.

| 568 | **299** | 7c. multicoloured | 20 | 10 |
|---|---|---|---|---|

**300** Rugby Football

**1974.** Non-Olympic Sports. Multicoloured.

| 569 | 7c. Type **300** | 40 | 50 |
|---|---|---|---|
| 570 | 7c. Bowls | 40 | 50 |
| 571 | 7c. Australian football (vert) | 40 | 50 |
| 572 | 7c. Cricket (vert) | 40 | 50 |
| 573 | 7c. Golf (vert) | 40 | 50 |
| 574 | 7c. Surfing (vert) | 40 | 50 |
| 575 | 7c. Tennis (vert) | 40 | 50 |

**301** "Transport of Mails"

**1974.** Centenary of U.P.U. Multicoloured.

| 576 | 7c. Type **301** | 40 | 20 |
|---|---|---|---|
| 577 | 30c. Three-part version of T **301** (vert) | 85 | 1·90 |

**302** Letter "A" and W. C. Wentworth (co-founder)

**1974.** 150th Anniv of First Independent Newspaper, "The Australian".

| | | | | |
|---|---|---|---|---|
| 578 | **302** | 7c. black and brown | 50 | 40 |

**1974.** No. 551 surch.

| | | | |
|---|---|---|---|
| 579 | 9c. on 8c. multicoloured | 15 | 15 |

**304** "The Adoration of the Magi"

**1974.** Christmas. Woodcuts by Durer.

| | | | | |
|---|---|---|---|---|
| 580 | **304** | 10c. black on cream | 25 | 10 |
| 581 | - | 35c. black on cream | 80 | 1·00 |

DESIGN: 35c. "The Flight into Egypt".

**305** "Pre-school Education"

**1974.** Education in Australia. Multicoloured.

| | | | |
|---|---|---|---|
| 582 | 5c. Type **305** | 25 | 40 |
| 583 | 11c. "Correspondence Schools" | 25 | 60 |
| 584 | 15c. "Science Education" | 40 | 40 |
| 585 | 60c. "Advanced Education" (vert) | 50 | 2·00 |

**306** "Road Safety"

**1975.** Environment Dangers. Multicoloured.

| | | | |
|---|---|---|---|
| 586 | 10c. Type **306** | 50 | 50 |
| 587 | 10c. "Pollution" (horiz) | 50 | 50 |
| 588 | 10c. "Bush Fires" (horiz) | 50 | 50 |

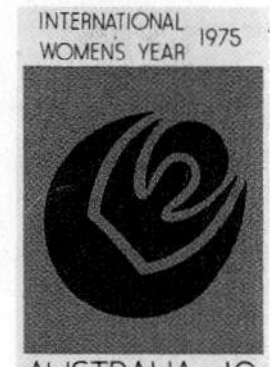

**307** Australian Women's Year Emblem

**1975.** International Women's Year.

| | | | | |
|---|---|---|---|---|
| 589 | **307** | 10c. blue, green and violet | 20 | 15 |

**308** J. H. Scullin

**1975.** Famous Australians (6th series). Prime Ministers. Multicoloured.

| | | | |
|---|---|---|---|
| 590 | 10c. Type **308** | 25 | 35 |
| 591 | 10c. J. A. Lyons | 25 | 35 |
| 592 | 10c. Earle Page | 25 | 35 |
| 593 | 10c. Arthur Fadden | 25 | 35 |
| 594 | 10c. John Curtin | 25 | 35 |

| | | | |
|---|---|---|---|
| 595 | 10c. J. B. Chifley | 25 | 35 |

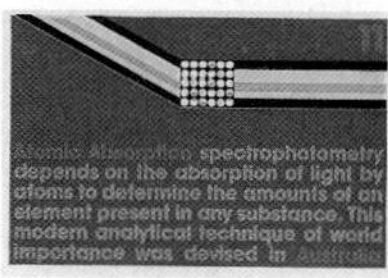

**309** Atomic Absorption Spectrophotometry

**1975.** Scientific Development. Multicoloured.

| | | | |
|---|---|---|---|
| 596 | 11c. Type **309** | 70 | 75 |
| 597 | 24c. Radio astronomy | 1·25 | 2·00 |
| 598 | 33c. Immunology | 1·25 | 2·00 |
| 599 | 48c. Oceanography | 1·50 | 2·75 |

**310** Logo of Australian Postal Commission

**1975.** Inauguration of Australian Postal and Telecommunications Commissions.

| | | | | |
|---|---|---|---|---|
| 600 | **310** | 10c. black, red and grey | 25 | 10 |
| 601 | - | 10c. black, orange and grey | 25 | 10 |

DESIGN: No. 601, Logo of Australian Tele-communications Commission.

**311** Edith Cowan

**1975.** Famous Australians (7th series). Australian Women. Multicoloured.

| | | | |
|---|---|---|---|
| 602 | 10c. Type **311** | 55 | 70 |
| 603 | 10c. Louisa Lawson | 55 | 70 |
| 604 | 10c. "Henry Richardson" (pen name of Ethel Richardson) | 55 | 70 |
| 605 | 10c. Catherine Spence | 55 | 70 |
| 606a | 10c. Constance Stone | 55 | 70 |
| 607 | 10c. Truganini | 55 | 70 |

**312** "Helichrysum thomsonii"

**1975.** Wild Flowers. Multicoloured.

| | | | |
|---|---|---|---|
| 608 | 18c. Type **312** | 25 | 10 |
| 609 | 45c. "Callistemon teretifolius" (horiz) | 50 | 10 |

**313** "Tambaran" House and Sydney Opera House

**1975.** Independence of Papua New Guinea. Mult.

| | | | |
|---|---|---|---|
| 610 | 18c. Type **313** | 20 | 10 |
| 611 | 25c. "Freedom" (bird in flight) (horiz) | 50 | 1·50 |

**314** Epiphany Scene

**1975.** Christmas.

| | | | | |
|---|---|---|---|---|
| 612 | **314** | 15c. multicoloured | 40 | 10 |
| 613 | - | 45c. violet, blue and silver | 1·00 | 3·00 |

DESIGN—HORIZ: 45c. "Shining Star".

**315** Australian Coat of Arms

**1976.** 75th Anniv of Nationhood.

| | | | | |
|---|---|---|---|---|
| 614 | **315** | 18c. multicoloured | 40 | 20 |

**316** Telephone-user, c. 1878

**1976.** Centenary of Telephone.

| | | | | |
|---|---|---|---|---|
| 615 | **316** | 18c. multicoloured | 20 | 15 |

**317** John Oxley

**1976.** 19th Century Explorers. Multicoloured.

| | | | |
|---|---|---|---|
| 616 | 18c. Type **317** | 35 | 50 |
| 617 | 18c. Hume and Hovell | 35 | 50 |
| 618 | 18c. John Forrest | 35 | 50 |
| 619 | 18c. Ernest Giles | 35 | 50 |
| 620 | 18c. William Gosse | 35 | 50 |
| 621 | 18c. Peter Warburton | 35 | 50 |

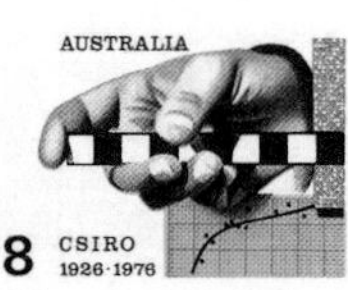

**318** Measuring Stick, Graph and Computer Tape

**1976.** 50th Anniv of Commonwealth Scientific and Industrial Research Organization.

| | | | | |
|---|---|---|---|---|
| 622 | **318** | 18c. multicoloured | 20 | 15 |

**319** Football

**1976.** Olympic Games, Montreal. Multicoloured.

| | | | |
|---|---|---|---|
| 623 | 18c. Type **319** | 20 | 20 |
| 624 | 18c. Gymnastics (vert) | 20 | 20 |
| 625 | 25c. Diving (vert) | 35 | 80 |
| 626 | 40c. Cycling | 1·25 | 1·25 |

**320** Richmond Bridge, Tasmania

**1976.** Australian Scenes. Multicoloured.

| | | | |
|---|---|---|---|
| 627 | 5c. Type **320** | 20 | 10 |
| 628 | 25c. Broken Bay, N.S.W | 65 | 10 |
| 629 | 35c. Wittenoom Gorge, W.A | 45 | 20 |
| 630 | 50c. Mt. Buffalo, Victoria (vert) | 90 | 20 |
| 631 | 70c. Barrier Reef | 1·25 | 1·25 |
| 632 | 85c. Ayers Rock, N.T | 1·50 | 2·25 |

**321** Blamire Young (designer of first Australian stamp)

**1976.** National Stamp Week.

| | | | | |
|---|---|---|---|---|
| 633 | **321** | 18c. multicoloured | 15 | 15 |
| **MS**634 | | 101×112 mm. Nos. 633×4 | 75 | 1·50 |

**322** "Virgin and Child" (detail, Simone Contarini)

**1976.** Christmas.

| | | | | |
|---|---|---|---|---|
| 635 | **322** | 15c. mauve and blue | 20 | 10 |
| 636 | - | 45c. multicoloured | 50 | 90 |

DESIGN: 45c. Toy koala bear and decorations.

**323** John Gould

**1976.** Famous Australians. (8th series). Scientists. Multicoloured.

| | | | |
|---|---|---|---|
| 637 | 18c. Type **323** | 35 | 50 |
| 638 | 18c. Thomas Laby | 35 | 50 |
| 639 | 18c. Sir Baldwin Spencer | 35 | 50 |
| 640 | 18c. Griffith Taylor | 35 | 50 |

**324** "Music"

**1977.** Performing Arts. Multicoloured.

| | | | |
|---|---|---|---|
| 641 | 20c. Type **324** | 15 | 25 |
| 642 | 30c. Drama | 20 | 35 |
| 643 | 40c. Dance | 25 | 40 |
| 644 | 60c. Opera | 1·50 | 1·75 |

**325** Queen Elizabeth II

**1977.** Silver Jubilee. Multicoloured.

| | | | |
|---|---|---|---|
| 645 | 18c. Type **325** | 30 | 10 |
| 646 | 45c. The Queen and Duke of Edinburgh | 70 | 90 |

**326** Fielder and Wicket Keeper

**1977.** Centenary of Australia–England Test Cricket.

| | | | |
|---|---|---|---|
| 647 | 18c. Type **326** | 40 | 65 |
| 648 | 18c. Umpire and batsman | 40 | 65 |
| 649 | 18c. Fielders | 40 | 65 |
| 650 | 18c. Batsman and umpire | 40 | 65 |
| 651 | 18c. Bowler and fielder | 40 | 65 |
| 652 | 45c. Batsman facing bowler | 50 | 1·25 |

**327** Parliament House

**1977.** 50th Anniv of Opening of Parliament House, Canberra.

| | | | | |
|---|---|---|---|---|
| 653 | **327** | 18c. multicoloured | 15 | 10 |

**328** Trade Union Workers

**1977.** 50th Anniv of Australian Council of Trade Unions.
654 **328** 18c. multicoloured 15 10

**329** Surfing Santa

**1977.** Christmas. Multicoloured.
655 15c. Type **329** 25 10
656 45c. Madonna and Child 75 1·25

**330** National Flag

**1978.** Australia Day.
657 **330** 18c. multicoloured 20 15

**331** Harry Hawker and Sopwith Atlantic

**1978.** Early Australian Aviators. Multicoloured.
658 18c. Type **331** 30 50
659 18c. Bert Hinkler and Avro Type 581 Avian 30 50
660 18c. Sir Charles Kingsford Smith and "Southern Cross" 30 50
661 18c. Charles Ulm and "Southern Cross" 30 50
**MS**662 100×112 mm. Nos. 658/61×2. Imperf 75 1·75

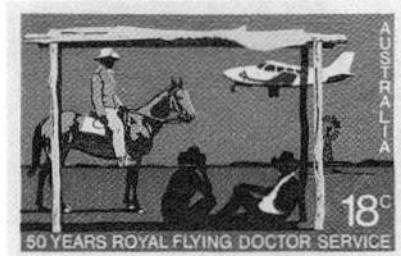

**332** Piper PA-31 Navajo landing at Station Airstrip

**1978.** 50th Anniv of Royal Flying Doctor Service.
663 **332** 18c. multicoloured 20 15

**333** Illawarra Flame Tree

**1978.** Trees. Multicoloured.
664 18c. Type **333** 20 15
665 25c. Ghost gum 35 1·40
666 40c. Grass tree 45 2·00
667 45c. Cootamundra wattle 45 70

**334** Sturt's Desert Rose and Map

**1978.** Establishment of State Government for the Northern Territory.
668 **334** 18c. multicoloured 20 15

**335** Hooded Plover

**1978.** Birds (1st series). Multicoloured.
669 1c. Spotted-sided ("Zebra") finch 10 20
670 2c. Crimson finch 10 20
671 5c. Type **335** 50 10
672 15c. Forest kingfisher (vert) 20 20
673 20c. Australian dabchick ("Little Grebe") 70 10
674 20c. Yellow robin ("Eastern Yellow Robin") 75 10
675 22c. White-tailed kingfisher (22×29 mm) 30 10
676 25c. Masked ("Spur-wing") plover 1·00 1·25
677 30c. Pied oystercatcher 1·00 25
678 40c. Variegated ("Lovely") wren (vert) 30 45
679 50c. Flame robin (vert) 1·00 1·00
680 55c. Comb-crested jacana ("Lotus-Bird") 1·40 60
See also Nos. 734/40.

**336** 1928 3d. National Stamp Exhibition Commemorative

**1978.** 50th Anniv of National Stamp Week, and National Stamp Exhibition.
694 **336** 20c. multicoloured 15 15
**MS**695 78×113 mm. No. 694×4 75 1·50

**337** "The Madonna and the Child" (after van Eyck)

**1978.** Christmas. Multicoloured.
696 15c. Type **337** 30 10
697 25c. "The Virgin and Child" (Marmion) 45 65
698 55c. "The Holy Family" (del Vaga) 70 1·00

**338** "Tulloch"

**1978.** Horse-racing. Multicoloured.
699 20c. Type **338** 30 10
700 35c. "Bernborough" (vert) 45 85
701 50c. "Phar Lap" (vert) 60 1·25
702 55c. "Peter Pan" 60 1·10

**339** Raising the Flag, Sydney Cove, 26 January 1788

**1979.** Australia Day.
703 **339** 20c. multicoloured 15 15

**340** "Canberra" (paddle-steamer)

**1979.** Ferries and Murray River Steamers. Mult.
704 20c. Type **340** 20 10
705 35c. "Lady Denman" 40 70
706 50c. "Murray River Queen" (paddle-steamer) 50 1·40
707 55c. "Curl Curl" (hydrofoil) 55 1·25

**341** Port Campbell, Victoria

**1979.** National Parks. Multicoloured.
708 20c. Type **341** 30 40
709 20c. Uluru, Northern Territory 30 40
710 20c. Royal, New South Wales 30 40
711 20c. Flinders Ranges, South Australia 30 40
712 20c. Nambung, Western Australia 30 40
713 20c. Girraween, Queensland (vert) 30 40
714 20c. Mount Field, Tasmania (vert) 30 40

**342** "Double Fairlie" Type Locomotive, Western Australia

**1979.** Steam Railways. Multicoloured.
715 20c. Type **342** 30 10
716 35c. Locomotive, Puffing Billy Line, Victoria 60 70
717 50c. Locomotive, Pichi Richi Line, South Australia 70 1·50
718 55c. Locomotive, Zig Zag Railway, New South Wales 80 1·40

**343** Symbolic Swan

**1979.** 150th Anniv of Western Australia.
719 **343** 20c. multicoloured 15 15

**344** Children playing on Slide

**1979.** International Year of the Child.
720 **344** 20c. multicoloured 15 10

**345** Letters and Parcels

**1979.** Christmas. Multicoloured.
721 15c. "Christ's Nativity" (Eastern European icon) 15 10
722 25c. Type **345** 15 65
723 55c. "Madonna and Child" (Buglioni) 25 80

**346** Fly-fishing

**1979.** Fishing.
724 **346** 20c. multicoloured 15 10
725 - 35c. blue and violet 25 70
726 - 50c. multicoloured 35 90
727 - 55c. multicoloured 35 85
DESIGNS: 35c. Spinning; 50c. Deep sea game-fishing; 55c. Surf-fishing.

**347** Matthew Flinders

**1980.** Australia Day.
728 **347** 20c. multicoloured 20 10

**348** Dingo

**1980.** Dogs. Multicoloured.
729 20c. Type **348** 40 10
730 25c. Border collie 40 50
731 35c. Australian terrier 45 70
732 50c. Australian cattle dog 80 2·00
733 55c. Australian kelpie 80 1·40

**1980.** Birds (2nd series). As T 335. Multicoloured.
734 10c. Golden-shouldered parrot (vert) 50 10
734b 18c. Spotted catbird (vert) 50 1·75
735 28c. Australian bee eater ("Rainbow Bird") (vert) 50 20
736 35c. Regent bower bird (vert) 50 10
737 45c. Masked wood swallow 50 10
738 60c. Australian king parrot ("King Parrot") (vert) 50 15
739 80c. Rainbow pitta 1·00 75
740 $1 Black-backed magpie ("Western Magpie") (vert) 1·00 10

**349** Queen Elizabeth II

**1980.** Birthday of Queen Elizabeth II.
741 **349** 22c. multicoloured 30 20

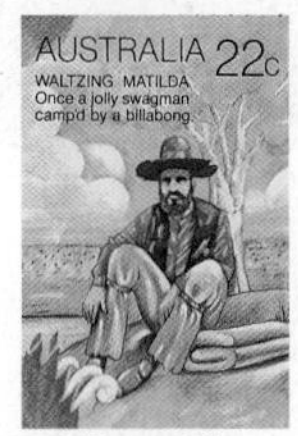

**350** "Once a jolly Swagman camp'd by a Billabong"

**1980.** Folklore. "Waltzing Matilda". Multicoloured.
742 22c. Type **350** 25 40
743 22c. "And he sang as he shoved that jumbuck in his tuckerbag" 25 40
744 22c. "Up rode the squatter mounted on his thorough-bred" 25 40
745 22c. "Down came the troopers one, two, three" 25 40
746 22c. "And his ghost may be heard as you pass by that billabong" 25 40

**351** High Court Building, Canberra

**1980.** Opening of High Court Building.

| | | | | |
|---|---|---|---|---|
| 747 | **351** | 22c. multicoloured | 20 | 20 |

**352** Salvation Army

**1980.** Community Welfare. Multicoloured.

| | | | |
|---|---|---|---|
| 748 | 22c. Type **352** | 30 | 30 |
| 749 | 22c. St. Vincent de Paul Society (vert) | 30 | 30 |
| 750 | 22c. Meals on Wheels (vert) | 30 | 30 |
| 751 | 22c. "Life. Be in it" | 30 | 30 |

**353** Postbox, c. 1900

**1980.** National Stamp Week. Multicoloured.

| | | | |
|---|---|---|---|
| 752 | 22c. Type **353** | 25 | 40 |
| 753 | 22c. Postman, facing left | 25 | 40 |
| 754 | 22c. Ford Model T mail van | 25 | 40 |
| 755 | 22c. Postman, facing right | 25 | 40 |
| 756 | 22c. Postman and postbox | 25 | 40 |
| **MS**757 | 95×100 mm. Nos. 752, 754 and 756 | 1·10 | 1·60 |

**354** "Holy Family" (painting, Prospero Fontana)

**1980.** Christmas. Multicoloured.

| | | | |
|---|---|---|---|
| 758 | 15c. "The Virgin Enthroned" (Justin O'Brien) (detail) | 15 | 10 |
| 759 | 28c. Type **354** | 25 | 40 |
| 760 | 60c. "Madonna and Child" (sculpture by School of M. Zuern) | 50 | 1·10 |

**355** Commonwealth Aircraft Factory Wackett, 1941

**1980.** Australian Aircraft. Multicoloured.

| | | | |
|---|---|---|---|
| 761 | 22c. Type **355** | 30 | 10 |
| 762 | 40c. Commonwealth Aircraft Factory Winjeel, 1955 | 50 | 75 |
| 763 | 45c. Commonwealth Aircraft Factory Boomerang, 1944 | 50 | 85 |
| 764 | 60c. Government Aircraft Factory Nomad, 1975 | 65 | 1·40 |

**356** Flag in shape of Australia

**1981.** Australia Day.

| | | | | |
|---|---|---|---|---|
| 765 | **356** | 22c. multicoloured | 20 | 20 |

**357** Caricature of Darby Munro (jockey)

**1981.** Sporting Personalities. Caricatures. Mult.

| | | | |
|---|---|---|---|
| 766 | 22c. Type **357** | 20 | 10 |
| 767 | 35c. Victor Trumper (cricket) | 40 | 60 |
| 768 | 55c. Sir Norman Brookes (tennis) | 40 | 1·00 |
| 769 | 60c. Walter Lindrum (billiards) | 40 | 1·25 |

**358** 1931 Kingsford Smith's Flights 6d. Commemorative

**1981.** 50th Anniversary of Official Australia–U.K. Airmail Service.

| | | | | |
|---|---|---|---|---|
| 770 | **358** | 22c. lilac, red and blue | 15 | 10 |
| 771 | - | 60c. lilac, red and blue | 40 | 90 |

DESIGN—HORIZ: 60c. As T **358**, but format changed.

**359** Apex Emblem and Map of Australia

**1981.** 50th Anniv of Apex (young men's service club).

| | | | | |
|---|---|---|---|---|
| 772 | **359** | 22c. multicoloured | 20 | 20 |

**360** Queen's Personal Standard for Australia

**1981.** Birthday of Queen Elizabeth II.

| | | | | |
|---|---|---|---|---|
| 773 | **360** | 22c. multicoloured | 20 | 20 |

**361** "Licence Inspected"

**1981.** Gold Rush Era. Sketches by S. T. Gill. Mult.

| | | | |
|---|---|---|---|
| 774 | 22c. Type **361** | 20 | 25 |
| 775 | 22c. "Puddling" | 20 | 25 |
| 776 | 22c. "Quality of washing stuff" | 20 | 25 |
| 777 | 22c. "On route to deposit gold" | 20 | 25 |

**362** "On the Wallaby Track" (Fred McCubbin)

**1981.** Paintings. Multicoloured.

| | | | |
|---|---|---|---|
| 778 | $2 Type **362** | 1·00 | 30 |
| 779 | $5 "A Holiday at Mentone, 1888" (Charles Conder) | 3·00 | 1·00 |

**363** Thylacine

**363a** Blue Mountain Tree Frog

**363b** "Papilio ulysses" (butterfly)

**1981.** Wildlife. Multicoloured.

| | | | |
|---|---|---|---|
| 781 | 1c. Lace monitor | 10 | 20 |
| 782 | 3c. Corroboree frog | 10 | 10 |
| 783 | 4c. Regent skipper (butterfly) (vert) | 55 | 80 |
| 784 | 5c. Queensland hairy-nosed wombat (vert) | 10 | 10 |
| 785 | 10c. Cairns birdwing (butterfly) (vert) | 60 | 10 |
| 786 | 15c. Eastern snake-necked tortoise | 1·00 | 1·00 |
| 787 | 20c. MacLeay's swallowtail (butterfly) (vert) | 80 | 35 |
| 788 | 24c. Type **363** | 45 | 10 |
| 789 | 25c. Common rabbit-bandicoot (inscr "Greater Bilby") (vert) | 40 | 1·00 |
| 790a | 27c. Type **363a** | 1·00 | 45 |
| 791 | 27c. Type **363b** | 1·00 | 30 |
| 792 | 30c. Bridle nail-tailed wallaby (vert) | 90 | 20 |
| 792a | 30c. Chlorinda hairstreak (butterfly) (vert) | 1·00 | 20 |
| 793 | 35c. Blue tiger (butterfly) (vert) | 1·00 | 30 |
| 794 | 40c. Smooth knob-tailed gecko | 45 | 30 |
| 795 | 45c. Big greasy (butterfly) (vert) | 1·00 | 30 |
| 796 | 50c. Leadbeater's possum | 50 | 10 |
| 797 | 55c. Stick-nest rat (vert) | 50 | 30 |
| 798 | 60c. Wood white (butterfly) (vert) | 1·10 | 30 |
| 799 | 65c. Yellow-faced whip snake | 1·75 | 1·50 |
| 800 | 70c. Crucifix toad | 65 | 1·75 |
| 801 | 75c. Eastern water dragon | 1·25 | 90 |
| 802 | 80c. Amaryllis azure (butterfly) (vert) | 1·40 | 2·00 |
| 803 | 85c. Centralian blue-tongued lizard | 1·10 | 1·25 |
| 804 | 90c. Freshwater crocodile | 1·60 | 1·25 |
| 805 | 95c. Thorny devil | 1·60 | 2·00 |
| 806 | $1 Sword-grass brown (butterfly) (vert) | 1·40 | 30 |

**364** Prince Charles and Lady Diana Spencer

**1981.** Royal Wedding.

| | | | | |
|---|---|---|---|---|
| 821 | **364** | 24c. multicoloured | 20 | 10 |
| 822 | **364** | 60c. multicoloured | 55 | 1·00 |

**365** "Cortinarius cinnabarinus"

**1981.** Australian Fungi. Multicoloured.

| | | | |
|---|---|---|---|
| 823 | 24c. Type **365** | 30 | 10 |
| 824 | 35c. "Coprinus comatus" | 50 | 1·10 |
| 825 | 55c. "Armillaria luteobubalina" | 65 | 1·25 |
| 826 | 60c. "Cortinarius austro-venetus" | 75 | 1·40 |

**366** Disabled People playing Basketball

**1981.** International Year for Disabled Persons.

| | | | | |
|---|---|---|---|---|
| 827 | **366** | 24c. multicoloured | 20 | 20 |

**367** "Christmas Bush for His Adorning"

**1981.** Christmas. Scenes and Verses from Carols by W. James and J. Wheeler. Multicoloured.

| | | | |
|---|---|---|---|
| 828 | 18c. Type **367** | 20 | 10 |
| 829 | 30c. "The Silver Stars are in the Sky" | 25 | 25 |
| 830 | 60c. "Noeltime" | 40 | 90 |

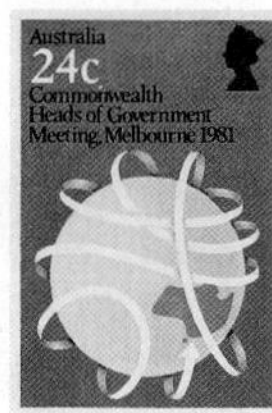

**368** Globe depicting Australia

**1981.** Commonwealth Heads of Government Meeting, Melbourne.

| | | | | |
|---|---|---|---|---|
| 831 | **368** | 24c. black, blue and gold | 15 | 10 |
| 832 | **368** | 60c. black, blue and silver | 45 | 75 |

**369** "Ragamuffin" ocean racing yacht

**1981.** Yachts. Multicoloured.

| | | | |
|---|---|---|---|
| 833 | 24c. Type **369** | 25 | 10 |
| 834 | 35c. "Sharpie" | 40 | 55 |
| 835 | 55c. "12 Metre" | 55 | 1·50 |
| 836 | 60c. "Sabot" | 80 | 1·50 |

**370** Aborigine, Governor Phillip (founder of N.S.W., 1788) and Post World War II Migrant

**1982.** Australia Day. "Three Great Waves of Migration".

| | | | | |
|---|---|---|---|---|
| 837 | **370** | 24c. multicoloured | 35 | 25 |

**371** Humpback Whale

**1982.** Whales. Multicoloured.

| | | | |
|---|---|---|---|
| 838 | 24c. Sperm whale | 30 | 10 |
| 839 | 35c. Black (inscr "Southern") right whale (vert) | 40 | 60 |
| 840 | 55c. Blue whale (vert) | 60 | 1·50 |
| 841 | 60c. Type **371** | 70 | 1·50 |

**372** Queen Elizabeth II

**1982.** Birthday of Queen Elizabeth II.

| | | | | |
|---|---|---|---|---|
| 842 | **372** | 27c. multicoloured | 35 | 15 |

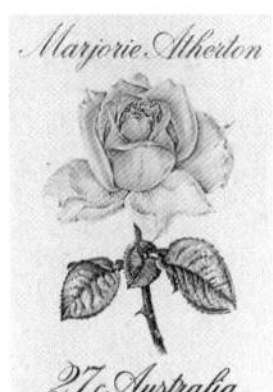


**373** "Marjorie Atherton"

**1982.** Roses. Multicoloured.

| | | | |
|---|---|---|---|
| 843 | 27c. Type **373** | 25 | 15 |
| 844 | 40c. "Imp" | 30 | 60 |
| 845 | 65c. "Minnie Watson" | 50 | 2·00 |
| 846 | 75c. "Satellite" | 50 | 1·25 |

**374** Radio Announcer and 1930-style Microphone

**1982.** 50th Anniv of ABC (Australian Broadcasting Commission). Multicoloured.

| | | | |
|---|---|---|---|
| 847 | 27c. Type **374** | 30 | 65 |
| 848 | 27c. ABC logo | 30 | 65 |

**375** Forbes Post Office

**1982.** Historic Australian Post Offices. Mult.

| | | | |
|---|---|---|---|
| 849 | 27c. Type **375** | 30 | 40 |
| 850 | 27c. Flemington Post Office | 30 | 40 |
| 851 | 27c. Rockhampton Post Office | 30 | 40 |
| 852 | 27c. Kingston S. E. Post Office (horiz) | 30 | 40 |
| 853 | 27c. York Post Office (horiz) | 30 | 40 |
| 854 | 27c. Launceston Post Office | 30 | 40 |
| 855 | 27c. Old Post and Telegraph Station, Alice Springs (horiz) | 30 | 40 |

**376** Early Australian Christmas Card

**1982.** Christmas. Multicoloured.

| | | | |
|---|---|---|---|
| 856 | 21c. Bushman's Hotel with Cobb's coach arriving (horiz) | 25 | 10 |
| 857 | 35c. Type **376** | 40 | 60 |
| 858 | 75c. Little girl offering Christmas pudding to swagman | 60 | 1·60 |

**377** Boxing

**1982.** Commonwealth Games, Brisbane.

| | | | | |
|---|---|---|---|---|
| 859 | **377** | 27c. stone, yellow and red | 25 | 25 |
| 860 | - | 27c. yellow, stone and green | 25 | 25 |
| 861 | - | 27c. stone, yellow and brown | 25 | 25 |
| 862 | - | 75c. multicoloured | 60 | 1·25 |
| **MS**863 | | 130×95 mm. Nos. 859/61 | 1·25 | 1·75 |

DESIGNS: No. 860, Archery; No. 861, Weight-lifting; No. 862, Pole-vaulting.

**378** Sydney Harbour Bridge 5s. Stamp of 1932

**1982.** National Stamp Week.

| | | | | |
|---|---|---|---|---|
| 864 | **378** | 27c. multicoloured | 35 | 30 |

**379** "Yirawala" Bark Painting

**1982.** Opening of Australian National Gallery.

| | | | | |
|---|---|---|---|---|
| 865 | **379** | 27c. multicoloured | 30 | 25 |

**380** Mimi Spirits Dancing

**1982.** Aboriginal Culture. Music and Dance.

| | | | | |
|---|---|---|---|---|
| 866 | **380** | 27c. multicoloured | 20 | 10 |
| 867 | - | 40c. multicoloured | 30 | 60 |
| 868 | - | 65c. multicoloured | 45 | 1·00 |
| 869 | - | 75c. multicoloured | 50 | 1·00 |

DESIGN: 40c. to 75c. Aboriginal bark paintings of Mimi Spirits.

**381** "Eucalyptus calophylla" "Rosea"

**1982.** Eucalyptus Flowers. Multicoloured.

| | | | |
|---|---|---|---|
| 870 | 1c. Type **381** | 10 | 30 |
| 871 | 2c. "Eucalyptus casia" | 10 | 30 |
| 872 | 3c. "Eucalyptus ficifolia" | 1·25 | 2·25 |
| 873 | 10c. "Eucalyptus globulus" | 1·25 | 2·25 |
| 874 | 27c. "Eucalyptus forrestiana" | 30 | 40 |

**382** Shand Mason Steam Fire Engine, 1891

**1983.** Historic Fire Engines. Multicoloured.

| | | | |
|---|---|---|---|
| 875 | 27c. Type **382** | 35 | 10 |
| 876 | 40c. Hotchkiss fire engine, 1914 | 45 | 75 |
| 877 | 65c. Ahrens-Fox fire engine, 1929 | 70 | 1·60 |
| 878 | 75c. Merryweather manual fire appliance, 1851 | 70 | 1·40 |

**383** H.M.S. "Sirius"

**1983.** Australia Day. Multicoloured.

| | | | |
|---|---|---|---|
| 879 | 27c. Type **383** | 40 | 75 |
| 880 | 27c. H.M.S. "Supply" | 40 | 75 |

**384** Stylized Kangaroo and Kiwi

**1983.** Closer Economic Relationship Agreement with New Zealand.

| | | | | |
|---|---|---|---|---|
| 881 | **384** | 27c. multicoloured | 30 | 30 |

**385** Equality and Dignity

**1983.** Commonwealth Day. Multicoloured.

| | | | |
|---|---|---|---|
| 882 | 27c. Type **385** | 20 | 25 |
| 883 | 27c. Liberty and Freedom | 20 | 25 |
| 884 | 27c. Social Justice and Co-operation | 20 | 25 |
| 885 | 75c. Peace and Harmony | 50 | 1·50 |

**386** R.Y. "Britannia" passing Sydney Opera House

**1983.** Birthday of Queen Elizabeth II.

| | | | | |
|---|---|---|---|---|
| 886 | **386** | 27c. multicoloured | 50 | 30 |

**387** "Postal and Telecommunications Services"

**1983.** World Communications Year.

| | | | | |
|---|---|---|---|---|
| 887 | **387** | 27c. multicoloured | 30 | 30 |

**388** Badge of the Order of St. John

**1983.** Centenary of St. John Ambulance in Australia.

| | | | | |
|---|---|---|---|---|
| 888 | **388** | 27c. black and blue | 35 | 30 |

**389** Jaycee Members and Badge

**1983.** 50th Anniv of Australian Jaycees.

| | | | | |
|---|---|---|---|---|
| 889 | **389** | 27c. multicoloured | 30 | 30 |

**390** "The Bloke"

**1983.** Folklore. "The Sentimental Bloke" (humorous poem by C. J. Dennis). Multicoloured.

| | | | |
|---|---|---|---|
| 890 | 27c. Type **390** | 30 | 50 |
| 891 | 27c. "Doreen—The Intro" | 30 | 50 |
| 892 | 27c. "The Stror' at Coot" | 30 | 50 |
| 893 | 27c. "Hitched" | 30 | 50 |
| 894 | 27c. "The Mooch o' Life" | 30 | 50 |

**391** Nativity Scene

**1983.** Christmas. Children's Paintings. Mult.

| | | | |
|---|---|---|---|
| 895 | 24c. Type **391** | 20 | 10 |
| 896 | 35c. Kookaburra | 35 | 45 |
| 897 | 85c. Father Christmas in sleigh over beach | 90 | 1·40 |

**392** Sir Paul Edmund de Strzelecki

**1983.** Explorers of Australia. Multicoloured.

| | | | |
|---|---|---|---|
| 898 | 30c. Type **392** | 25 | 40 |
| 899 | 30c. Ludwig Leichhardt | 25 | 40 |
| 900 | 30c. William John Wills and Robert O'Hara Burke | 25 | 40 |
| 901 | 30c. Alexander Forrest | 25 | 40 |

**393** Cook Family Cottage, Melbourne

**1984.** Australia Day.

| | | | | |
|---|---|---|---|---|
| 902 | **393** | 30c. black and stone | 30 | 35 |

**394** Charles Ulm, "Faith in Australia" and Trans-Tasman Cover

**1984.** 50th Anniv of First Official Airmail Flights, New Zealand–Australia and Australia–Papua New Guinea. Multicoloured.

| | | | |
|---|---|---|---|
| 903 | 45c. Type **394** | 75 | 1·25 |
| 904 | 45c. As Type **394** but showing flown cover to Papua New Guinea | 75 | 1·25 |

**395** Thomson "Steamer", 1898

**1984.** Veteran and Vintage Cars. Multicoloured.

| | | | |
|---|---|---|---|
| 905 | 30c. Type **395** | 50 | 70 |
| 906 | 30c. Tarrant two seater, 1906 | 50 | 70 |
| 907 | 30c. Gordon & Co "Australian Six" two seater, 1919 | 50 | 70 |
| 908 | 30c. Summit tourer, 1923 | 50 | 70 |
| 909 | 30c. Chic two seater, 1924 | 50 | 70 |

**396** Queen Elizabeth II

**1984.** Birthday of Queen Elizabeth II.

| | | | | |
|---|---|---|---|---|
| 910 | **396** | 30c. multicoloured | 30 | 35 |

**397** "Cutty Sark"

**1984.** Clipper Ships. Multicoloured.

| | | | |
|---|---|---|---|
| 911 | 30c. Type **397** | 35 | 25 |
| 912 | 45c. "Orient" (horiz) | 50 | 80 |
| 913 | 75c. "Sobraon" (horiz) | 70 | 1·75 |
| 914 | 85c. "Thermopylae" | 70 | 1·50 |

**398** Freestyle

**1984.** Skiing. Multicoloured.

| | | | |
|---|---|---|---|
| 915 | 30c. Type **398** | 30 | 45 |
| 916 | 30c. Downhill racer | 30 | 45 |
| 917 | 30c. Slalom (horiz) | 30 | 45 |
| 918 | 30c. Nordic (horiz) | 30 | 45 |

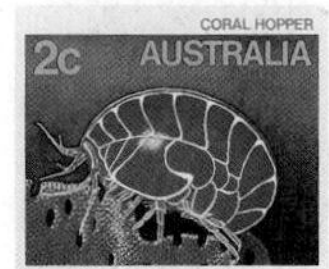

**399** Coral Hopper

**1984.** Marine Life. Multicoloured.

| | | | |
|---|---|---|---|
| 919 | 2c. Type **399** | 10 | 30 |
| 920 | 3c. Jimble | 40 | 30 |
| 921 | 5c. Tasselled frogfish ("Anglerfish") | 15 | 10 |
| 922 | 10c. Rough stonefish | 1·00 | 50 |
| 923 | 20c. Red handfish | 65 | 40 |
| 924 | 25c. Orange-lipped cowrie | 45 | 40 |
| 925 | 30c. Choat's wrasse | 45 | 40 |
| 926 | 33c. Leafy seadragon | 65 | 10 |
| 927 | 40c. Red velvetfish | 85 | 1·75 |
| 928 | 45c. Textile or cloth of gold cone | 1·50 | 50 |
| 929 | 50c. Clown surgeonfish | 80 | 50 |
| 930 | 55c. Bennet's nudibranch | 80 | 50 |
| 931 | 60c. Zebra lionfish | 1·50 | 70 |
| 932 | 65c. Banded stingray | 1·50 | 2·25 |
| 933 | 70c. Southern blue-ringed octopus | 1·50 | 1·75 |
| 934 | 80c. Pineconefish ("Pineapple fish") | 1·25 | 1·75 |
| 935 | 85c. Royal angelfish | 90 | 70 |
| 936 | 90c. Crab-eyed goby | 1·60 | 75 |
| 937 | $1 Crown of thorns starfish | 1·50 | 80 |

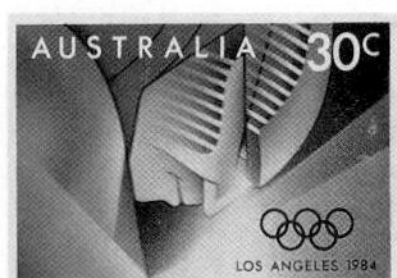

**400** Before the Event

**1984.** Olympic Games, Los Angeles. Multicoloured.

| | | | |
|---|---|---|---|
| 941 | 30c. Type **400** | 25 | 40 |
| 942 | 30c. During the event | 25 | 40 |
| 943 | 30c. After the event (vert) | 25 | 40 |

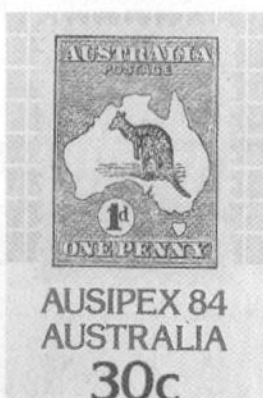

**401** Australian 1913 1d. Kangaroo Stamp

**1984.** "Ausipex '84" International Stamp Exhibition, Melbourne.

| | | | |
|---|---|---|---|
| 944 | **401** 30c. multicoloured | 35 | 30 |
| **MS**945 | 126×175 mm. 30c. × 7, Victoria 1850 3d. "Half Length"; New South Wales 1850 1d. "Sydney View"; Tasmania 1853 1d.; South Australia 1855 1d.; Western Australia 1854 1d. "Black Swan"; Queensland 1860 6d.; Type **401** | 3·50 | 4·50 |

**402** "Angel" (stained-glass window, St. Francis's Church, Melbourne)

**1984.** Christmas. Stained-glass Windows. Mult.

| | | | |
|---|---|---|---|
| 946 | 24c. "Angel and Child" (Holy Trinity Church, Sydney) | 15 | 10 |
| 947 | 30c. "Veiled Virgin and Child" (St. Mary's Catholic Church, Geelong) | 20 | 10 |
| 948 | 40c. Type **402** | 30 | 75 |
| 949 | 50c. "Three Kings" (St. Mary's Cathedral, Sydney) | 40 | 90 |
| 950 | 85c. "Madonna and Child" (St. Bartholomew's Church, Norwood) | 50 | 1·60 |

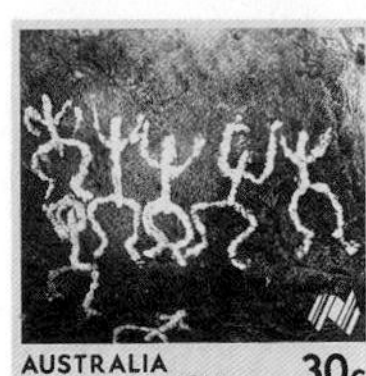

**403** "Stick Figures" (Cobar Region)

**1984.** Bicentenary (1988) of Australian Settlement (1st issue). The First Australians. Multicoloured.

| | | | |
|---|---|---|---|
| 951 | 30c. Type **403** | 20 | 45 |
| 952 | 30c. "Bunjil" (large figure), Grampians | 20 | 45 |
| 953 | 30c. "Quikans" (tall figures), Cape York | 20 | 45 |
| 954 | 30c. "Wandjina Spirit and Baby Snakes" (Gibb River) | 20 | 45 |
| 955 | 30c. "Rock Python" (Gibb River) | 20 | 45 |
| 956 | 30c. "Silver Barramundi" (fish) (Kakadu National Park) | 20 | 45 |
| 957 | 30c. Bicentenary emblem | 20 | 45 |
| 958 | 85c. "Rock Possum" (Kakadu National Park) | 50 | 1·40 |

See also Nos. 972/5, 993/6, 1002/7, 1019/22, 1059/63, 1064/6, 1077/81, 1090/2, 1110, 1137/41, 1145/8 and 1149.

**404** Yellow-tufted Honeyeater

**1984.** 150th Anniv of Victoria.

| | | | |
|---|---|---|---|
| 959 | 30c. Type **404** | 40 | 65 |
| 960 | 30c. Leadbeater's possum | 40 | 65 |

**405** "Musgrave Ranges" (Sidney Nolan)

**1985.** Australia Day. Birth Bicentenary of Dorothea Mackellar (author of poem "My Country"). Multicoloured.

| | | | |
|---|---|---|---|
| 961 | 30c. Type **405** | 50 | 80 |
| 962 | 30c. "The Walls of China" (Russell Drysdale) | 50 | 80 |

**406** Young People of Different Races and Sun

**1985.** International Youth Year.

| | | | |
|---|---|---|---|
| 963 | **406** 30c. multicoloured | 40 | 30 |

**407** Royal Victorian Volunteer Artillery

**1985.** 19th-Century Australian Military Uniforms. Multicoloured.

| | | | |
|---|---|---|---|
| 964 | 33c. Type **407** | 50 | 70 |
| 965 | 33c. Western Australian Pinjarrah Cavalry | 50 | 70 |
| 966 | 33c. New South Wales Lancers | 50 | 70 |
| 967 | 33c. New South Wales Contingent to the Sudan | 50 | 70 |
| 968 | 33c. Victorian Mounted Rifles | 50 | 70 |

**408** District Nurse of early 1900s

**1985.** Centenary of District Nursing Services.

| | | | |
|---|---|---|---|
| 969 | **408** 33c. multicoloured | 45 | 35 |

**409** Sulphur-crested Cockatoos

**1985.** Multicoloured, background colour given.

| | | | |
|---|---|---|---|
| 970 | **409** 1c. flesh | 1·75 | 2·75 |
| 971 | **409** 33c. turquoise | 45 | 55 |

**410** Abel Tasman and Journal Entry

**1985.** Bicentenary (1988) of Australian Settlement (2nd issue). Navigators. Multicoloured.

| | | | |
|---|---|---|---|
| 972 | 33c. Type **410** | 45 | 35 |
| 973 | 33c. Dirk Hartog's "Eendracht" (detail, Aert Anthonisz) | 45 | 35 |
| 974 | 33c. "William Dampier" (detail, T. Murray) | 45 | 35 |
| 975 | 90c. Globe and hand with extract from Dampier's journal | 1·00 | 2·50 |
| **MS**976 | 150×115 mm. As Nos. 972/5, but with cream-coloured margins | 3·25 | 4·50 |

**411** Sovereign's Badge of Order of Australia

**1985.** Queen Elizabeth II's Birthday.

| | | | |
|---|---|---|---|
| 977 | **411** 33c. multicoloured | 40 | 30 |

**412** Tree, and Soil running through Hourglass ("Soil")

**1985.** Conservation. Multicoloured.

| | | | |
|---|---|---|---|
| 978 | 33c. Type **412** | 25 | 20 |
| 979 | 50c. Washing on line and smog ("air") | 50 | 85 |
| 980 | 80c. Tap and flower ("water") | 65 | 1·50 |
| 981 | 90c. Chain encircling flames ("energy") | 80 | 2·00 |

**413** "Elves and Fairies" (Annie Rentoul and Ida Rentoul Outhwaite)

**1985.** Classic Australian Children's Books. Mult.

| | | | |
|---|---|---|---|
| 982 | 33c. Type **413** | 40 | 75 |
| 983 | 33c. "The Magic Pudding" (Norman Lindsay) | 40 | 75 |
| 984 | 33c. "Ginger Meggs" (James Charles Bancks) | 40 | 75 |
| 985 | 33c. "Blinky Bill" (Dorothy Wall) | 40 | 75 |
| 986 | 33c. "Snugglepot and Cuddlepie" (May Gibbs) | 40 | 75 |

**414** Dish Aerials

**1985.** Electronic Mail Service.

| | | | |
|---|---|---|---|
| 987 | **414** 33c. multicoloured | 35 | 30 |

**415** Angel in Sailing Ship

**1985.** Christmas. Multicoloured.

| | | | |
|---|---|---|---|
| 988 | 27c. Angel with holly wings | 25 | 10 |
| 989 | 33c. Angel with bells | 30 | 10 |
| 990 | 45c. Type **415** | 40 | 35 |
| 991 | 55c. Angel with star | 50 | 70 |
| 992 | 90c. Angel with Christmas tree bauble | 75 | 1·75 |

**416** Astrolabe ("Batavia", 1629)

**1985.** Bicentenary (1988) of Australian Settlement (3rd issue). Relics from Early Shipwrecks. Multicoloured.

993 33c. Type **416** 35 15
994 50c. German beardman jug ("Vergulde Draeck", 1656) 60 1·00
995 90c. Wooden bobbins ("Batavia", 1629) and encrusted scissors ("Zeewijk", 1727) 1·00 3·25
996 $1 Silver and brass buckle ("Zeewijk", 1727) 1·00 2·25

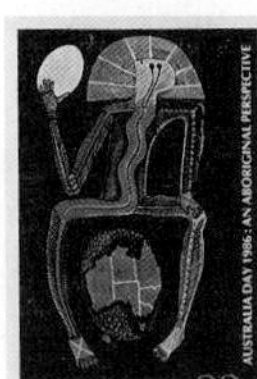

**417** Aboriginal Wandjina Spirit, Map of Australia and Egg

**1986.** Australia Day.

997 **417** 33c. multicoloured 40 30

**418** AUSSAT Satellite, Moon and Earth's Surface

**1986.** AUSSAT National Communications Satellite System. Multicoloured.

998 33c. Type **418** 40 15
999 80c. AUSSAT satellite in orbit 1·00 2·25

**419** H.M.S. "Buffalo"

**1986.** 150th Anniv of South Australia. Mult.

1000 33c. Type **419** 70 1·25
1001 33c. "City Sign" sculpture (Otto Hajek), Adelaide 70 1·25

Nos. 1000/1 were printed together se-tenant, the background of each horiz pair showing an extract from the colony's Letters Patent of 1836.

**420** "Banksia serrata"

**1986.** Bicentenary (1988) of Australian Settlement (4th issue). Cook's Voyage to New Holland. Multicoloured.

1002 33c. Type **420** 50 35
1003 33c. "Hibiscus meraukensis" 50 35
1004 50c. "Dillenia alata" 70 1·10
1005 80c. "Correa reflexa" 1·50 2·75
1006 90c. "Joseph Banks" (botanist) (Reynolds) and Banks with Dr. Solander 2·00 2·75
1007 90c. "Sydney Parkinson" (self-portrait) and Parkinson drawing 2·00 2·75

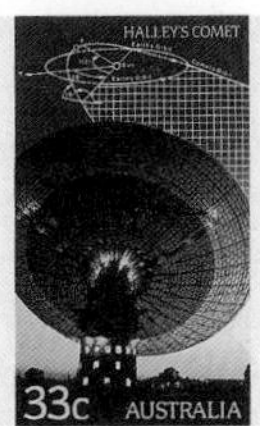

**421** Radio Telescope, Parkes, and Diagram of Comet's Orbit

**1986.** Appearance of Halley's Comet.

1008 **421** 33c. multicoloured 50 35

**422** Queen Elizabeth II

**1986.** 60th Birthday of Queen Elizabeth.

1009 **422** 33c. multicoloured 55 35

**423** Brumbies (wild horses)

**1986.** Australian Horses. Multicoloured.

1010 33c. Type **423** 60 15
1011 80c. Mustering 1·50 2·25
1012 90c. Show-jumping 1·50 2·50
1013 $1 Child on pony 1·75 2·25

**424** "The Old Shearer stands"

**1986.** Folklore. Scenes and Verses from the Folksong "Click go the Shears". Multicoloured.

1014 33c. Type **424** 45 80
1015 33c. "The ringer looks around" 45 80
1016 33c. "The boss of the board" 45 80
1017 33c. "The tar-boy is there" 45 80
1018 33c. "Shearing is all over" 45 80

Nos. 1014/18 were printed together, se-tenant, forming a composite design.

**425** "King George III" (A. Ramsay) and Convicts

**1986.** Bicentenary (1988) of Australian Settlement (5th issue). Convict Settlement in New South Wales. Multicoloured.

1019 33c. Type **425** 60 65
1020 33c. "Lord Sydney" (Gilbert Stuart) and convicts 60 65
1021 33c. "Captain Arthur Phillip" (F. Wheatley) and ship 60 65
1022 $1 "Captain John Hunter" (W. B. Bennett) and aborigines 1·75 5·50

**426** Red Kangaroo

**1986.** Australian Wildlife (1st series). Mult.

1023 36c. Type **426** 70 95
1024 36c. Emu 70 95
1025 36c. Koala 70 95
1026 36c. Laughing kookaburra ("Kookaburra") 70 95
1027 36c. Platypus 70 95

See also Nos. 1072/6.

**427** Royal Bluebell

**1986.** Alpine Wildflowers. Multicoloured.

1028 3c. Type **427** 50 75
1029 5c. Alpine marsh marigold 2·00 3·25
1030 25c. Mount Buffalo sunray 2·00 3·25
1031 36c. Silver snow daisy 45 30

**428** Pink Enamel Orchid

**1986.** Native Orchids. Multicoloured.

1032 36c. Type **428** 75 20
1033 55c. "Dendrobium nindii" 1·50 1·25
1034 90c. Duck orchid 2·25 4·00
1035 $1 Queen of Sheba orchid 2·25 2·75

**429** "Australia II" crossing Finishing Line

**1986.** Australian Victory in America's Cup, 1983. Multicoloured.

1036 36c. Type **429** 75 75
1037 36c. Boxing kangaroo flag of winning syndicate 75 75
1038 36c. America's Cup trophy 75 75

**430** Dove with Olive Branch and Sun

**1986.** International Peace Year.

1039 **430** 36c. multicoloured 65 40

**431** Mary and Joseph

**1986.** Christmas. Scenes from children's nativity play. Multicoloured.

1040 30c. Type **431** 40 30
1041 36c. Three Wise Men leaving gifts 50 45
1042 60c. Angels (horiz) 90 1·75

**MS**1043 147×70 mm. 30c. Three angels and shepherd (horiz); 30c. Kneeling shepherds (horiz); 30c. Mary, Joseph and three angels; 30c. Innkeeper and two angels; 30c. Three Wise Men (horiz) 3·50 4·00

**432** Australian Flag on Printed Circuit Board

**1987.** Australia Day. Multicoloured.

1044 36c. Type **432** 55 75
1045 36c. "Australian Made" Campaign logos 55 75

**433** Aerial View of Yacht

**1987.** America's Cup Yachting Championship. Multicoloured.

1046 36c. Type **433** 30 20
1047 55c. Two yachts tacking 60 1·00
1048 90c. Two yachts beating 80 2·50
1049 $1 Two yachts under full sail 90 1·50

**434** Grapes and Melons

**1987.** Australian Fruit. Multicoloured.

1050 36c. Type **434** 30 20
1051 65c. Tropical and sub-tropical fruits 80 1·50
1052 90c. Citrus fruit, apples and pears 1·25 2·50
1053 $1 Stone and berry fruits 1·25 1·60

**435** Livestock

**1987.** Agricultural Shows. Multicoloured.

1054 36c. Type **435** 60 20
1055 65c. Produce 1·00 1·75
1056 90c. Sideshows 1·25 3·00
1057 $1 Competitions 1·50 2·40

**436** Queen Elizabeth in Australia, 1986

**1987.** Queen Elizabeth II's Birthday.

1058 **436** 36c. multicoloured 55 60

**437** Convicts on Quay

**1987.** Bicentenary (1988) of Australian Settlement (6th issue). Departure of the First Fleet. Multicoloured.

1059 36c. Type **437** 80 1·10
1060 36c. Royal Marines officer and wife 80 1·10
1061 36c. Sailors loading supplies 80 1·10

| | | | |
|---|---|---|---|
| 1062 | 36c. Officers being ferried to ships | 80 | 1·10 |
| 1063 | 36c. Fleet in English Channel | 80 | 1·10 |

See also Nos. 1064/6, 1077/81 and 1090/2.

**1987.** Bicentenary (1988) of Australian Settlement (7th issue). First Fleet at Tenerife. As T 437. Multicoloured.

| | | | |
|---|---|---|---|
| 1064 | 36c. Ferrying supplies, Santa Cruz | 70 | 1·00 |
| 1065 | 36c. Canary Islands fishermen and departing fleet | 70 | 1·00 |
| 1066 | $1 Fleet arriving at Tenerife | 1·75 | 2·25 |

Nos. 1064/5 were printed together, se-tenant, forming a composite design.

**438** "At the Station"

**1987.** Folklore. Scenes and Verses from Poem "The Man from Snowy River". Multicoloured.

| | | | |
|---|---|---|---|
| 1067 | 36c. Type **438** | 80 | 1·10 |
| 1068 | 36c. "Mountain bred" | 80 | 1·10 |
| 1069 | 36c. "That terrible descent" | 80 | 1·10 |
| 1070 | 36c. "At their heels" | 80 | 1·10 |
| 1071 | 36c. "Brought them back" | 80 | 1·10 |

Nos. 1067/71 were printed together, se-tenant, forming a composite background design of mountain scenery.

**1987.** Australian Wildlife (2nd series). As T 426. Multicoloured.

| | | | |
|---|---|---|---|
| 1072 | 37c. Common brushtail possum | 55 | 85 |
| 1073 | 37c. Sulphur-crested cockatoo ("Cockatoo") | 55 | 85 |
| 1074 | 37c. Common wombat | 55 | 85 |
| 1075 | 37c. Crimson rosella ("Rosella") | 55 | 85 |
| 1076 | 37c. Echidna | 55 | 85 |

**1987.** Bicentenary (1988) of Australian Settlement (8th issue). First Fleet at Rio de Janeiro. As T 437. Multicoloured.

| | | | |
|---|---|---|---|
| 1077 | 37c. Sperm whale and fleet | 80 | 1·10 |
| 1078 | 37c. Brazilian coast | 80 | 1·10 |
| 1079 | 37c. British officers in market | 80 | 1·10 |
| 1080 | 37c. Religious procession | 80 | 1·10 |
| 1081 | 37c. Fleet leaving Rio | 80 | 1·10 |

Nos. 1077/81 were printed together, se-tenant, forming a composite design.

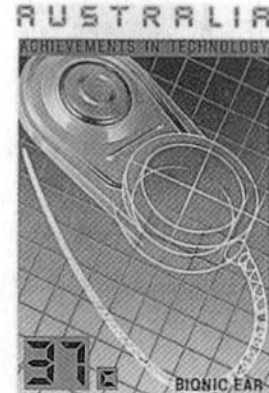


**439** Bionic Ear

**1987.** Australian Achievements in Technology. Mult.

| | | | |
|---|---|---|---|
| 1082 | 37c. Type **439** | 30 | 15 |
| 1083 | 53c. Microchips | 55 | 45 |
| 1084 | 63c. Robotics | 60 | 70 |
| 1085 | 68c. Ceramics | 65 | 75 |

**440** Catching Crayfish

**1987.** "Aussie Kids". Multicoloured.

| | | | |
|---|---|---|---|
| 1086 | 37c. Type **440** | 40 | 15 |
| 1087 | 55c. Playing cat's cradle | 60 | 75 |
| 1088 | 90c. Young football supporters | 1·00 | 2·50 |
| 1089 | $1 Children with kangaroo | 1·00 | 1·50 |

**1987.** Bicentenary (1988) of Australian Settlement (9th issue). First Fleet at Cape of Good Hope. As T 437. Multicoloured.

| | | | |
|---|---|---|---|
| 1090 | 37c. Marine checking list of livestock | 65 | 1·00 |
| 1091 | 37c. Loading livestock | 65 | 1·00 |
| 1092 | $1 First Fleet at Cape Town | 1·50 | 2·50 |

Nos. 1090/1 were printed together, se-tenant, forming a composite design.

**441** Detail of Spearthrower, Western Australia

**1987.** Aboriginal Crafts. Multicoloured.

| | | | |
|---|---|---|---|
| 1093 | 3c. Type **441** | 1·10 | 1·50 |
| 1094 | 15c. Shield pattern, New South Wales | 5·50 | 7·50 |
| 1095 | 37c. Basket weave, Queensland | 1·10 | 1·50 |
| 1096 | 37c. Bowl design, Central Australia | 90 | 1·25 |
| 1097 | 37c. Belt pattern, Northern Territory | 1·10 | 1·50 |

**442** Grandmother and Granddaughters with Candles

**1987.** Christmas. Designs showing carol singing by candlelight. Multicoloured.

| | | | |
|---|---|---|---|
| 1098 | 30c. Type **442** | 50 | 65 |
| 1099 | 30c. Father and daughters | 50 | 65 |
| 1100 | 30c. Four children | 50 | 65 |
| 1101 | 30c. Family | 50 | 65 |
| 1102 | 30c. Six teenagers | 50 | 65 |
| 1103 | 37c. Choir (horiz) | 50 | 65 |
| 1104 | 63c. Father and two children (horiz) | 85 | 1·25 |

**1988.** Bicentenary of Australian Settlement (10th issue). Arrival of First Fleet. As T 437. Mult.

| | | | |
|---|---|---|---|
| 1105 | 37c. Aborigines watching arrival of Fleet, Botany Bay | 65 | 95 |
| 1106 | 37c. Aborigine family and anchored ships | 65 | 95 |
| 1107 | 37c. Fleet arriving at Sydney Cove | 65 | 95 |
| 1108 | 37c. Ship's boat | 65 | 95 |
| 1109 | 37c. Raising the flag, Sydney Cove, 26 January 1788 | 65 | 95 |

Nos. 1105/9 were printed together, se-tenant, forming a composite design.

**443** Koala with Stockman's Hat and Eagle dressed as Uncle Sam

**1988.** Bicentenary of Australian Settlement (11th issue). Joint issue with U.S.A.

| | | | | |
|---|---|---|---|---|
| 1110 | **443** | 37c. multicoloured | 60 | 35 |

**444** "Religion" (A. Horner)

**1988.** "Living Together". Designs showing cartoons. Multicoloured (except 30c.).

| | | | |
|---|---|---|---|
| 1111 | 1c. Type **444** | 50 | 70 |
| 1112 | 2c. "Industry" (P. Nicholson) | 50 | 60 |
| 1113 | 3c. "Local Government" (A. Collette) | 50 | 60 |
| 1114 | 4c. "Trade Unions" (Liz Honey) | 10 | 20 |
| 1115 | 5c. "Parliament" (Bronwyn Halls) | 50 | 50 |
| 1116 | 10c. "Transport" (Meg Williams) | 30 | 50 |
| 1117 | 15c. "Sport" (G. Cook) | 1·75 | 60 |
| 1118 | 20c. "Commerce" (M. Atcherson) | 70 | 1·00 |
| 1119 | 25c. "Housing" (C. Smith) | 45 | 40 |
| 1120 | 30c. "Welfare" (R. Tandberg) (black and lilac) | 55 | 1·25 |
| 1121 | 37c. "Postal Services" (P. Viska) | 50 | 50 |
| 1121b | 39c. "Tourism" (J. Spooner) | 60 | 50 |
| 1122 | 40c. "Recreation" (R. Harvey) | 70 | 70 |
| 1123 | 45c. "Health" (Jenny Coopes) | 70 | 1·25 |
| 1124 | 50c. "Mining" (G. Haddon) | 70 | 50 |
| 1125 | 53c. "Primary Industry" (S. Leahy) | 1·75 | 2·00 |
| 1126 | 55c. "Education" (Victoria Roberts) | 1·50 | 2·00 |
| 1127 | 60c. "Armed Forces" (B. Green) | 1·50 | 70 |
| 1128 | 63c. "Police" (J. Russell) | 2·50 | 1·40 |
| 1129 | 65c. "Telecommunications" (B. Petty) | 1·50 | 2·50 |
| 1130 | 68c. "The Media" (A. Langoulant) | 2·25 | 3·25 |
| 1131 | 70c. "Science and Technology" (J. Hook) | 1·75 | 1·75 |
| 1132 | 75c. "Visual Arts" (G. Dazeley) | 1·00 | 1·00 |
| 1133 | 80c. "Performing Arts" (A. Stitt) | 1·25 | 1·00 |
| 1134 | 90c. "Banking" (S. Billington) | 1·50 | 1·50 |
| 1135 | 95c. "Law" (C. Aslanis) | 1·00 | 2·00 |
| 1136 | $1 "Rescue and Emergency" (M. Leunig) | 1·10 | 1·00 |

**445** "Government House, Sydney, 1790" (George Raper)

**1988.** Bicentenary of Australian Settlement (12th issue). "The Early Years, 1788–1809". Mult.

| | | | |
|---|---|---|---|
| 1137 | 37c. Type **445** | 65 | 1·00 |
| 1138 | 37c. "Government Farm, Parramatta, 1791" ("The Port Jackson Painter") | 65 | 1·00 |
| 1139 | 37c. "Parramatta Road, 1796" (attr Thomas Watling) | 65 | 1·00 |
| 1140 | 37c. "View of Sydney Cove, c. 1800" (detail) (Edward Dayes) | 65 | 1·00 |
| 1141 | 37c. "Sydney Hospital, 1803", (detail) (George William Evans) | 65 | 1·00 |

Nos. 1137/41 were printed together, se-tenant, forming a composite background design from the painting "View of Sydney from the East Side of the Cove, c. 1808" by John Eyre.

**446** Queen Elizabeth II (from photo by Tim Graham)

**1988.** Queen Elizabeth II's Birthday.

| | | | | |
|---|---|---|---|---|
| 1142 | **446** | 37c. multicoloured | 50 | 40 |

**447** Expo '88 Logo

**1988.** "Expo '88" World Fair, Brisbane.

| | | | | |
|---|---|---|---|---|
| 1143 | **447** | 37c. multicoloured | 50 | 40 |

**448** New Parliament House

**1988.** Opening of New Parliament House, Canberra.

| | | | | |
|---|---|---|---|---|
| 1144 | **448** | 37c. multicoloured | 50 | 40 |

**449** Early Settler and Sailing Clipper

**1988.** Bicentenary of Australian Settlement (13th issue). Multicoloured.

| | | | |
|---|---|---|---|
| 1145 | 37c. Type **449** | 75 | 1·00 |
| 1146 | 37c. Queen Elizabeth II with British and Australian Parliament Buildings | 75 | 1·00 |
| 1147 | $1 W. G. Grace (cricketer) and tennis racquet | 1·50 | 2·25 |
| 1148 | $1 Shakespeare, John Lennon (entertainer) and Sydney Opera House | 1·50 | 2·25 |

Stamps in similar designs were also issued by Great Britain.

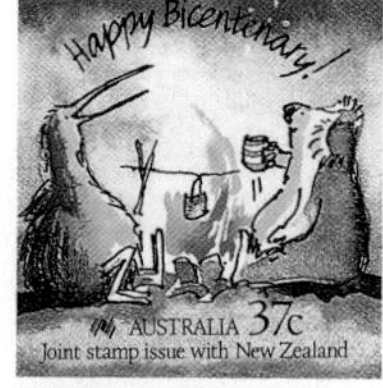


**450** Kiwi and Koala at Campfire

**1988.** Bicentenary of Australian Settlement (14th issue).

| | | | | |
|---|---|---|---|---|
| 1149 | **450** | 37c. multicoloured | 65 | 40 |

A stamp in a similar design was also issued by New Zealand.

**451** "Bush Potato Country" (Turkey Tolsen Tjupurrula and David Corby Tjapaltjarri)

**1988.** Art of the Desert. Aboriginal Paintings from Central Australia. Multicoloured.

| | | | |
|---|---|---|---|
| 1150 | 37c. Type **451** | 25 | 30 |
| 1151 | 55c. "Courtship Rejected" (Limpi Puntungka Tjapangati) | 45 | 70 |
| 1152 | 90c. "Medicine Story" (artist unknown) | 65 | 2·40 |
| 1153 | $1 "Ancestor Dreaming" (Tim Leura Tjapaltjarri) | 65 | 1·50 |

**452** Basketball

**1988.** Olympic Games, Seoul. Multicoloured.

| | | | |
|---|---|---|---|
| 1154 | 37c. Type **452** | 50 | 40 |
| 1155 | 65c. Athlete crossing finish line | 60 | 1·75 |
| 1156 | $1 Gymnast with hoop | 85 | 1·75 |

**453** Rod and Mace

**1988.** 34th Commonwealth Parliamentary Conference, Canberra.

| | | | | |
|---|---|---|---|---|
| 1157 | **453** | 37c. multicoloured | 50 | 60 |

**454** Necklace by Peter Tully

**1988.** Australian Crafts. Multicoloured.

| | | | |
|---|---|---|---|
| 1158 | 2c. Type **454** | 4·00 | 6·00 |
| 1159 | 5c. Vase by Colin Levy | 4·00 | 6·00 |
| 1160 | 39c. Teapot by Frank Bauer | 50 | 35 |

**455** Pinnacles Desert

**1988.** Panorama of Australia. Multicoloured.
1161 39c. Type **455** 70 40
1162 55c. Flooded landscape, Arnhem Land 1·00 1·00
1163 65c. Twelve Apostles, Victoria 1·50 2·50
1164 70c. Mountain Ash wood 1·50 2·50

**456** "The Nativity" (Danielle Hush)

**1988.** Christmas. Multicoloured.
1165 32c. Type **456** 35 10
1166 39c. "Koala as Father Christmas" (Kylie Courtney) 35 10
1167 63c. "Christmas Cockatoo" (Benjamin Stevenson) 70 1·40

**457** Sir Henry Parkes

**1989.** Australia Day. Centenary of Federation Speech by Sir Henry Parkes (N.S.W. Prime Minister).
1168 **457** 39c. multicoloured 45 40

**458** Bowls

**1989.** Sports. Multicoloured.
1169 1c. Type **458** 10 50
1170 2c. Tenpin-bowling 10 20
1171 3c. Australian football 1·00 1·00
1172 5c. Kayaking and canoeing 15 10
1174 10c. Sailboarding 15 15
1176 20c. Tennis 20 25
1179 39c. Fishing 45 40
1180 41c. Cycling 40 35
1181 43c. Skateboarding 50 40
1184 55c. Kite-flying 50 45
1186 65c. Rock-climbing 80 70
1187 70c. Cricket 1·90 80
1188 75c. Netball 70 1·50
1189 80c. Squash 1·00 65
1190 85c. Diving 1·75 80
1191 90c. Soccer 1·75 2·00
1192 $1 Fun-run 1·00 50
1193 $1.10 Golf 3·50 1·00
1194 $1.20 Hang-gliding 4·50 1·10

**459** Merino

**1989.** Sheep in Australia. Multicoloured.
1195 39c. Type **459** 70 50
1196 39c. Poll Dorset 70 50
1197 85c. Polwarth 1·75 3·50
1198 $1 Corriedale 1·75 2·00

**460** Adelaide Botanic Garden

**1989.** Botanic Gardens. Multicoloured.
1199 $2 Noroo, New South Wales 1·50 30
1200 $5 Mawarra, Victoria 4·25 60
1201 $10 Type **460** 7·50 1·00
1201a $20 "A View of the Artist's House and Garden in Mills Plains, Van Diemen's Land" (John Glover) 19·00 8·00

**461** "Queen Elizabeth II" (sculpture, John Dowie)

**1989.** Queen Elizabeth II's Birthday.
1202 **461** 39c. multicoloured 55 50

**462** Arrival of Immigrant Ship, 1830s

**1989.** Colonial Development (1st issue). Pastoral Era 1810–1850. Multicoloured.
1203 39c. Type **462** 45 60
1204 39c. Pioneer cottage and wool dray 45 60
1205 39c. Squatter's homestead 45 60
1206 39c. Shepherd with flock (from Joseph Lycett's "Views of Australia") 45 60
1207 39c. Explorer in desert (after watercolour by Edward Frome) 45 60

See also Nos. 1254/8 and 1264/8.

**463** Gladys Moncrieff and Roy Rene

**1989.** Australian Stage and Screen Personalities. Multicoloured.
1208 39c. Type **463** 40 40
1209 85c. Charles Chauvel and Chips Rafferty 80 2·00
1210 $1 Nellie Stewart and J. C. Williamson 80 1·25
1211 $1.10 Lottie Lyell and Raymond Longford 80 1·50

**464** "Impression" (Tom Roberts)

**1989.** Australian Impressionist Paintings. Mult.
1212 41c. Type **464** 45 50
1213 41c. "Impression for Golden Summer" (Sir Arthur Streeton) 45 50
1214 41c. "All on a Summer's Day" (Charles Conder) (vert) 45 50
1215 41c. "Petit Dejeuner" (Frederick McCubbin) 45 50

**465** Freeways

**1989.** The Urban Environment.
1216 **465** 41c. black, purple and green 80 1·40
1217 - 41c. black, purple and mauve 80 1·25
1218 - 41c. black, purple and blue 80 1·40

DESIGNS: No. 1217, City buildings, Melbourne; No. 1218, Commuter train at platform.

**466** Hikers outside Youth Hostel

**1989.** 50th Anniv of Australian Youth Hostels.
1219 **466** 41c. multicoloured 55 50

**467** Horse Tram, Adelaide, 1878

**1989.** Historic Trams. Multicoloured.
1220 41c. Type **467** 70 75
1221 41c. Steam tram, Sydney, 1884 70 75
1222 41c. Cable tram, Melbourne, 1886 70 75
1223 41c. Double-deck electric tram, Hobart, 1893 70 75
1224 41c. Combination electric tram, Brisbane, 1901 70 75

**468** "Annunciation" (15th-century Book of Hours)

**1989.** Christmas. Illuminated Manuscripts. Mult.
1225 36c. Type **468** 30 10
1226 41c. "Annunciation to the Shepherds" (Wharncliffe Book of Hours, c. 1475) 35 10
1227 80c. "Adoration of the Magi" (15th-century Parisian Book of Hours) 1·00 1·75

**469** Radio Waves and Globe

**1989.** 50th Anniv of Radio Australia.
1228 **469** 41c. multicoloured 55 50

**470** Golden Wattle

**1990.** Australia Day.
1229 **470** 41c. multicoloured 55 50

**471** Australian Wildflowers

**1990.** Greetings Stamps.
1230 **471** 41c. multicoloured 65 65
1231 **471** 43c. multicoloured 50 50

**472** Dr. Constance Stone (first Australian woman doctor), Modern Doctor and Nurses

**1990.** Centenary of Women in Medical Practice.
1232 **472** 41c. multicoloured 50 45

**473** Greater Glider

**1990.** Animals of the High Country. Multicoloured.
1233 41c. Type **473** 60 45
1234 65c. Tiger cat ("Spotted-tailed Quoll") 90 1·90
1235 70c. Mountain pygmy-possum 95 1·90
1236 80c. Brush-tailed rock-wallaby 1·10 1·90

**474** "Stop Smoking"

**1990.** Community Health. Multicoloured.
1237 41c. Type **474** 55 55
1238 41c. "Drinking and driving don't mix" 55 55
1239 41c. "No junk food, please" 55 55
1240 41c. "Guess who's just had a check up?" 55 55

**475** Soldiers from Two World Wars

**1990.** "The Anzac Tradition". Multicoloured.
1241 41c. Type **475** 70 40
1242 41c. Fighter pilots and munitions worker 70 40
1243 65c. Veterans and Anzac Day parade 1·10 1·25
1244 $1 Casualty evacuation, Vietnam, and disabled veteran 1·60 1·40
1245 $1.10 Letters from home and returning troopships 1·75 1·50

**476** Queen at Australian Ballet Gala Performance, London, 1988

**1990.** Queen Elizabeth II's Birthday.

| No. | Type | Description | | |
|---|---|---|---|---|
| 1246 | **476** | 41c. multicoloured | 1·00 | 50 |

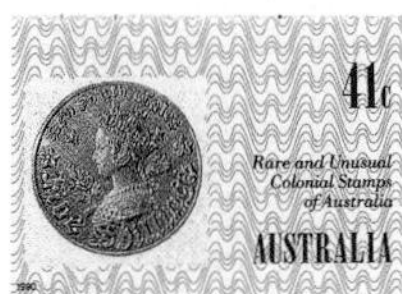

**477** New South Wales 1861 5s. Stamp

**1990.** 150th Anniv of the Penny Black. Designs showing stamps. Multicoloured.

| No. | Description | | |
|---|---|---|---|
| 1247 | 41c. Type **477** | 70 | 90 |
| 1248 | 41c. South Australia 1855 unissued 1s. | 70 | 90 |
| 1249 | 41c. Tasmania 1853 4d. | 70 | 90 |
| 1250 | 41c. Victoria 1867 5s. | 70 | 90 |
| 1251 | 41c. Queensland 1897 unissued 6d. | 70 | 90 |
| 1252 | 41c. Western Australia 1855 4d. with inverted frame | 70 | 90 |
| **MS**1253 | 122×85 mm. Nos. 1247/52 | 3·75 | 4·75 |

**478** Gold Miners on Way to Diggings

**1990.** Colonial Development (2nd issue). Gold Fever. Multicoloured.

| No. | Description | | |
|---|---|---|---|
| 1254 | 41c. Type **478** | 85 | 1·00 |
| 1255 | 41c. Mining camp | 85 | 1·00 |
| 1256 | 41c. Panning and washing for gold | 85 | 1·00 |
| 1257 | 41c. Gold Commissioner's tent | 85 | 1·00 |
| 1258 | 41c. Moving gold under escort | 85 | 1·00 |

**479** Glaciology Research

**1990.** Australian–Soviet Scientific Co-operation in Antarctica. Multicoloured.

| No. | Description | | |
|---|---|---|---|
| 1261 | 41c. Type **479** | 65 | 40 |
| 1262 | $1.10 Krill (marine biology research) | 1·60 | 1·75 |
| **MS**1263 | 85×65 mm. Nos. 1261/2 | 2·25 | 2·25 |

Stamps in similar designs were also issued by Russia.

**480** Auctioning Building Plots

**1990.** Colonial Development (3rd issue). Boomtime. Multicoloured.

| No. | Description | | |
|---|---|---|---|
| 1264 | 41c. Type **480** | 55 | 55 |
| 1265 | 41c. Colonial mansion | 55 | 55 |
| 1266 | 41c. Stock exchange | 55 | 55 |
| 1267 | 41c. Fashionable society | 55 | 55 |
| 1268 | 41c. Factories | 55 | 55 |

**481** "Salmon Gums" (Robert Juniper)

**1990.** "Heidelberg and Heritage" Art Exhibition. Multicoloured.

| No. | Description | | |
|---|---|---|---|
| 1269 | 28c. Type **481** | 2·50 | 3·50 |
| 1270 | 43c. "The Blue Dress" (Brian Dunlop) | 40 | 45 |

**482** "Adelaide Town Hall" (Edmund Gouldsmith)

**1990.** 150th Anniv of Local Government.

| No. | Type | Description | | |
|---|---|---|---|---|
| 1271 | **482** | 43c. multicoloured | 75 | 50 |

**483** Laughing Kookaburras and Gifts

**1990.** Christmas. Multicoloured.

| No. | Description | | |
|---|---|---|---|
| 1272 | 38c. Type **483** | 50 | 25 |
| 1273 | 43c. Baby Jesus with koalas and wallaby (vert) | 50 | 25 |
| 1274 | 80c. Possum on Christmas tree | 1·50 | 3·50 |

**484** National Flag

**1991.** Australia Day. 90th Anniv of Australian Flag.

| No. | Type | Description | | |
|---|---|---|---|---|
| 1275 | **484** | 43c. blue, red and grey | 55 | 25 |
| 1276 | - | 90c. multicoloured | 1·25 | 1·25 |
| 1277 | - | $1 multicoloured | 1·25 | 1·40 |
| 1278 | - | $1.20 red, blue and grey | 1·60 | 1·75 |

DESIGNS: 90c. Royal Australian Navy ensign; $1 Royal Australian Air Force standard; $1.20, Australian merchant marine ensign.

**485** Black-necked Stork

**1991.** Waterbirds. Multicoloured.

| No. | Description | | |
|---|---|---|---|
| 1279 | 43c. Type **485** | 80 | 50 |
| 1280 | 43c. Black swan (horiz) | 80 | 50 |
| 1281 | 85c. Cereopsis goose ("Cape Barren") | 2·25 | 3·00 |
| 1282 | $1 Chestnut-breasted teal ("Chestnut Teal") (horiz) | 2·25 | 2·50 |

**486** Recruitment Poster (Women's Services)

**1991.** Anzac Day. 50th Anniversaries.

| No. | Type | Description | | |
|---|---|---|---|---|
| 1283 | **486** | 43c. multicoloured | 60 | 40 |
| 1284 | - | 43c. black, green & brn | 60 | 40 |
| 1285 | - | $1.20 multicoloured | 2·25 | 2·00 |

DESIGNS: 43c. (No. 1284) Patrol (Defence of Tobruk); $1.20, "V-P Day Canberra" (Harold Abbot) (Australian War Memorial).

**487** Queen Elizabeth at Royal Albert Hall, London

**1991.** Queen Elizabeth II's Birthday.

| No. | Type | Description | | |
|---|---|---|---|---|
| 1286 | **487** | multicoloured | 1·00 | 50 |

**488** "Tectocoris diophthalmus" (bug)

**1991.** Insects. Multicoloured.

| No. | Description | | |
|---|---|---|---|
| 1287 | 43c. Type **488** | 75 | 45 |
| 1288 | 43c. "Cizara ardeniae" (hawk moth) | 75 | 45 |
| 1289 | 80c. "Petasida ephippigera" (grasshopper) | 2·25 | 2·00 |
| 1290 | $1 "Castiarina producta" (beetle) | 2·25 | 1·50 |

**489** "Bondi" (Max Dupain)

**1991.** 150 Years of Photography in Australia.

| No. | Type | Description | | |
|---|---|---|---|---|
| 1291 | **489** | 43c. black, brown and blue | 80 | 65 |
| 1292 | - | 43c. black, green & brn | 80 | 65 |
| 1293 | - | 70c. black, green & brn | 1·50 | 1·10 |
| 1294 | - | $1.20 black, brn & grn | 2·00 | 1·50 |

DESIGNS: No. 1292, "Gears for the Mining Industry, Vickers Ruwolt, Melbourne" (Wolfgang Sievers): 1293, "The Wheel of Youth" (Harold Cazneaux): 1294, "Teacup Ballet" (Olive Cotton).

**490** Singing Group

**1991.** Australian Radio Broadcasting. Designs showing listeners and scenes from radio programmes. Multicoloured.

| No. | Description | | |
|---|---|---|---|
| 1295 | 43c. Type **490** | 70 | 45 |
| 1296 | 43c. "Blue Hills" serial | 70 | 45 |
| 1297 | 85c. "The Quiz Kids" | 1·40 | 1·50 |
| 1298 | $1 "Argonauts' Club" children's programme | 1·60 | 1·40 |

**491** Puppy

**1991.** Domestic Pets. Multicoloured.

| No. | Description | | |
|---|---|---|---|
| 1299 | 43c. Type **491** | 70 | 45 |
| 1300 | 43c. Kitten | 70 | 45 |
| 1301 | 70c. Pony | 1·40 | 2·50 |
| 1302 | $1 Sulphur-crested cockatoo | 1·90 | 1·50 |

**492** George Vancouver (1791) and Edward Eyre (1841)

**1991.** Exploration of Western Australia.

| No. | Type | Description | | |
|---|---|---|---|---|
| 1303 | **492** | $1.05 multicoloured | 1·25 | 1·10 |
| **MS**1304 | | 100×65 mm. No. 1303 | 1·25 | 1·40 |

**493** "Seven Little Australians" (Ethel Turner)

**1991.** Australian Writers of the 1890s. Multicoloured.

| No. | Description | | |
|---|---|---|---|
| 1305 | 43c. Type **493** | 50 | 45 |
| 1306 | 75c. "On Our Selection" (Steele Rudd) | 80 | 1·00 |
| 1307 | $1 "Clancy of the Overflow" (poem, A. B. Paterson) (vert) | 1·10 | 1·00 |
| 1308 | $1.20 "The Drover's Wife" (short story, Henry Lawson) (vert) | 1·25 | 1·60 |

**494** Shepherd

**1991.** Christmas. Multicoloured.

| No. | Description | | |
|---|---|---|---|
| 1309 | 38c. Type **494** | 40 | 15 |
| 1310 | 43c. Infant Jesus | 45 | 15 |
| 1311 | 90c. Wise Man | 1·50 | 1·75 |

**495** Parma Wallaby

**1992.** Threatened Species. Multicoloured. Ordinary or self-adhesive gum.

| No. | Description | | |
|---|---|---|---|
| 1312 | 45c. Type **495** | 80 | 90 |
| 1313 | 45c. Ghost bat | 80 | 90 |
| 1314 | 45c. Long-tailed dunnart | 80 | 90 |
| 1315 | 45c. Little pygmy-possum | 80 | 90 |
| 1316 | 45c. Dusky hopping-mouse | 80 | 90 |
| 1317 | 45c. Squirrel glider | 80 | 90 |

**496** Basket of Wild Flowers

**1992.** Greetings Stamp.

| No. | Type | Description | | |
|---|---|---|---|---|
| 1318 | **496** | 45c. multicoloured | 50 | 50 |

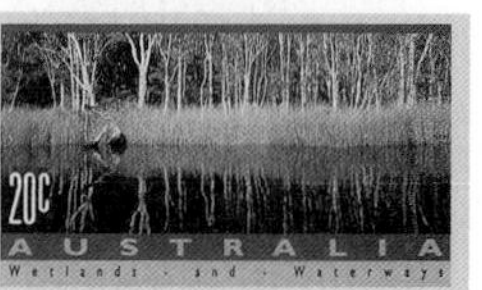

**497** Noosa River, Queensland

**1992.** Wetlands and Waterways. Multicoloured.

| No. | Description | | |
|---|---|---|---|
| 1319 | 20c. Type **497** | 1·75 | 2·50 |
| 1320 | 45c. Lake Eildon, Victoria | 40 | 45 |

**498** "Young Endeavour" (brigantine)

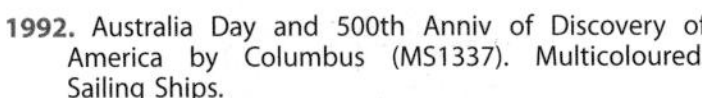

**1992.** Australia Day and 500th Anniv of Discovery of America by Columbus (MS1337). Multicoloured. Sailing Ships.

| | | | |
|---|---|---|---|
| 1333 | 45c. Type **498** | 80 | 50 |
| 1334 | 45c. "Britannia" (yacht) (vert) | 80 | 50 |
| 1335 | $1.05 "Akarana" (cutter) (vert) | 1·75 | 2·75 |
| 1336 | $1.20 "John Louis" (pearling lugger) | 2·00 | 2·00 |
| **MS**1337 | 147×64 mm. Nos. 1333/6 | 4·75 | 5·25 |

**499** Bombing of Darwin

**1992.** 50th Anniv of Second World War Battles. Multicoloured.

| | | | |
|---|---|---|---|
| 1338 | 45c. Type **499** | 80 | 45 |
| 1339 | 75c. Anti-aircraft gun and fighters, Milne Bay | 1·50 | 1·60 |
| 1340 | 75c. Infantry on Kokoda Trail | 1·50 | 1·60 |
| 1341 | $1.05 H.M.A.S. "Australia" (cruiser) and U.S.S. "Yorktown" (aircraft carrier), Coral Sea | 1·75 | 2·00 |
| 1342 | $1.20 Australians advancing, El Alamein | 2·00 | 1·75 |

**500** "Helix Nebula"

**1992.** International Space Year. Multicoloured.

| | | | |
|---|---|---|---|
| 1343 | 45c. Type **500** | 85 | 45 |
| 1344 | $1.05 "The Pleiades" | 2·00 | 1·25 |
| 1345 | $1.20 "Spiral Galaxy, NGC 2997" | 2·25 | 1·50 |
| **MS**1346 | 133×70 mm. Nos. 1343/5 | 4·50 | 4·50 |

**501** Hunter Valley, New South Wales

**1992.** Vineyard Regions. Multicoloured.

| | | | |
|---|---|---|---|
| 1347 | 45c. Type **501** | 80 | 1·00 |
| 1348 | 45c. North-east Victoria | 80 | 1·00 |
| 1349 | 45c. Barossa Valley, South Australia | 80 | 1·00 |
| 1350 | 45c. Coonawarra, South Australia | 80 | 1·00 |
| 1351 | 45c. Margaret River, Western Australia | 80 | 1·00 |

**502** 3½d. Stamp of 1953

**1992.** Queen Elizabeth II's Birthday.

| | | | | |
|---|---|---|---|---|
| 1352 | **502** | 45c. multicoloured | 1·00 | 60 |

**503** Salt Action

**1992.** Land Conservation. Multicoloured.

| | | | |
|---|---|---|---|
| 1353 | 45c. Type **503** | 85 | 1·10 |
| 1354 | 45c. Farm planning | 85 | 1·10 |
| 1355 | 45c. Erosion control | 85 | 1·10 |
| 1356 | 45c. Tree planting | 85 | 1·10 |
| 1357 | 45c. Dune care | 85 | 1·10 |

**504** Cycling

**1992.** Olympic Games and Paralympic Games (No. 1359), Barcelona. Multicoloured.

| | | | |
|---|---|---|---|
| 1358 | 45c. Type **504** | 60 | 25 |
| 1359 | $1.20 High jumping | 1·50 | 1·75 |
| 1360 | $1.20 Weightlifting | 1·50 | 1·75 |

**505** Echidna

**1992.** Australian Wildlife (1st series). Multicoloured.

| | | | |
|---|---|---|---|
| 1361 | 30c. Saltwater crocodile | 25 | 20 |
| 1362 | 35c. Type **505** | 65 | 30 |
| 1363 | 40c. Platypus | 2·00 | 70 |
| 1364 | 50c. Koala | 60 | 35 |
| 1365 | 60c. Common bushtail possum | 1·50 | 1·50 |
| 1366 | 70c. Laughing kookaburra ("Kookaburra") | 2·25 | 1·00 |
| 1367 | 85c. Australian pelican ("Pelican") | 75 | 70 |
| 1368a | 90c. Eastern grey kangaroo | 2·25 | 2·50 |
| 1369 | 95c. Common wombat | 1·00 | 2·50 |
| 1370a | $1.20 Major Mitchell's cockatoo ("Pink Cockatoo") | 2·00 | 1·10 |
| 1371 | $1.35 Emu | 1·75 | 2·50 |

See also Nos. 1459/64.

**506** Sydney Harbour Tunnel (value at left)

**1992.** Opening of Sydney Harbour Tunnel. Mult.

| | | | |
|---|---|---|---|
| 1375b | 45c. Type **506** | 1·90 | 1·90 |
| 1376b | 45c. Sydney Harbour Tunnel (value at right) | 1·90 | 1·90 |

Nos. 1375/6 were printed together, se-tenant, forming a composite design.

**507** Warden's Courthouse, Coolgardie

**1992.** Centenary of Discovery of Gold at Coolgardie and Kalgoorlie. Multicoloured.

| | | | |
|---|---|---|---|
| 1377 | 45c. Type **507** | 80 | 50 |
| 1378 | 45c. Post Office, Kalgoorlie | 80 | 50 |
| 1379 | $1.05 York Hotel, Kalgoorlie | 1·75 | 2·50 |
| 1380 | $1.20 Town Hall, Kalgoorlie | 2·25 | 2·50 |

**508** Bowler of 1892

**1992.** Centenary of Sheffield Shield Cricket Tournament. Multicoloured.

| | | | |
|---|---|---|---|
| 1381 | 45c. Type **508** | 1·00 | 50 |
| 1382 | $1.20 Batsman and wicket-keeper | 2·00 | 3·00 |

**509** Children's Nativity Play

**1992.** Christmas. Multicoloured.

| | | | |
|---|---|---|---|
| 1383 | 40c. Type **509** | 40 | 15 |
| 1384 | 45c. Child waking on Christmas Day | 60 | 15 |
| 1385 | $1 Children carol singing | 2·00 | 1·75 |

**510** "Ghost Gum, Central Australia" (Namatjira)

**1993.** Australia Day. Paintings by Albert Namatjira. Multicoloured.

| | | | |
|---|---|---|---|
| 1386 | 45c. Type **510** | 90 | 1·40 |
| 1387 | 45c. "Across the Plain to Mount Giles" | 90 | 1·40 |

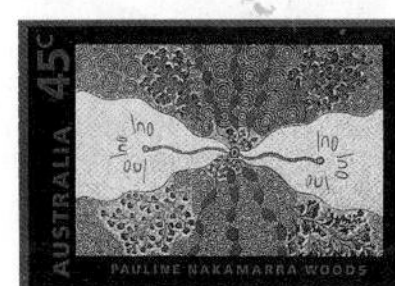


**511** "Wild Onion Dreaming" (Pauline Nakamarra Woods)

**1993.** "Dreamings". Paintings by Aboriginal Artists. Multicoloured.

| | | | |
|---|---|---|---|
| 1388 | 45c. Type **511** | 60 | 30 |
| 1389 | 75c. "Yam Plants" (Jack Wunuwun) (vert) | 1·10 | 1·10 |
| 1390 | 85c. "Goose Egg Hunt" (George Milpurrurru) (vert) | 1·25 | 1·60 |
| 1391 | $1 "Kalumpiwarra-Ngulalintji" (Rover Thomas) | 1·40 | 1·40 |

**512** Uluru (Ayers Rock) National Park

**1993.** World Heritage Sites (1st series). Multicoloured.

| | | | |
|---|---|---|---|
| 1392 | 45c. Type **512** | 60 | 30 |
| 1393 | 85c. Rain forest, Fraser Island | 1·50 | 1·75 |
| 1394 | 95c. Beach, Shark Bay | 1·50 | 1·75 |
| 1395 | $2 Waterfall, Kakadu | 2·75 | 2·50 |

See also Nos. 1582/5.

**513** Queen Elizabeth II on Royal Visit, 1992

**1993.** Queen Elizabeth II's Birthday.

| | | | | |
|---|---|---|---|---|
| 1396 | **513** | 45c. multicoloured | 1·00 | 65 |

**514** H.M.A.S. "Sydney" (cruiser, launched 1934) in Action

**1993.** Second World War Naval Vessels. Mult.

| | | | |
|---|---|---|---|
| 1397 | 45c. Type **514** | 80 | 45 |
| 1398 | 85c. H.M.A.S. "Bathurst" (minesweeper) | 2·00 | 1·75 |
| 1399 | $1.05 H.M.A.S. "Arunta" (destroyer) | 2·25 | 2·75 |
| 1400 | $1.20 "Centaur" (hospital ship) and tug | 2·25 | 2·75 |

**515** "Work in the Home"

**1993.** Working Life in the 1890s. Mult.

| | | | |
|---|---|---|---|
| 1401 | 45c. Type **515** | 55 | 50 |
| 1402 | 45c. "Work in the Cities" | 55 | 50 |
| 1403 | $1 "Work in the Country" | 1·10 | 1·25 |
| 1404 | $1.20 Trade Union banner | 1·50 | 2·00 |

**516** "Centenary Special", Tasmania, 1971

**1993.** Australian Trains. Multicoloured.

| | | | |
|---|---|---|---|
| 1405 | 45c. Type **516** | 65 | 95 |
| 1406 | 45c. "Spirit of Progress", Victoria | 65 | 95 |
| 1407 | 45c. "Western Endeavour", Western Australia, 1970 | 65 | 95 |
| 1408 | 45c. "Silver City Comet", New South Wales | 65 | 95 |
| 1409 | 45c. Cairns–Kuranda tourist train, Queensland | 65 | 95 |
| 1410 | 45c. "The Ghan", Northern Territory | 65 | 95 |

Nos. 1405/10 also come self-adhesive.

**517** "Black Cockatoo Feather" (Fiona Foley)

**1993.** International Year of Indigenous Peoples. Aboriginal Art. Multicoloured.

| | | | |
|---|---|---|---|
| 1417 | 45c. Type **517** | 35 | 30 |
| 1418 | 75c. "Ngarrgooroon Country" (Hector Jandany) (horiz) | 60 | 1·50 |
| 1419 | $1 "Ngak Ngak" (Ginger Riley Munduwalawala) (horiz) | 75 | 1·60 |
| 1420 | $1.05 "Untitled" (Robert Cole) | 90 | 2·50 |

**518** Conference Emblem

**1993.** Inter-Parliamentary Union Conference and 50th Anniv of Women in Federal Parliament. Multicoloured.

| | | | |
|---|---|---|---|
| 1421 | 45c. Type **518** | 75 | 1·50 |
| 1422 | 45c. Dame Enid Lyons and Senator Dorothy Tangney | 75 | 1·50 |

**519** Ornithocheirus

**1993.** Prehistoric Animals. Multicoloured.

| | | | |
|---|---|---|---|
| 1423 | 45c. Type **519** | 60 | 50 |
| 1424 | 45c. Leaellynasaura (25×30 mm) | 60 | 50 |
| 1425 | 45c. Timimus (26×33 mm) | 60 | 50 |
| 1426 | 45c. Allosaurus (26×33 mm) | 60 | 50 |
| 1427 | 75c. Muttaburrasaurus (30×50 mm) | 1·00 | 90 |
| 1428 | $1.05 Minmi (50×30 mm) | 1·50 | 1·50 |
| **MS**1429 | 166×73 mm. Nos. 1423/8 | 4·50 | 6·50 |

Nos. 1423/4 also come self-adhesive.

**520** "Goodwill"

**1993.** Christmas. Multicoloured.

| | | | |
|---|---|---|---|
| 1432 | 40c. Type **520** | 40 | 10 |
| 1433 | 45c. "Joy" | 55 | 10 |
| 1434 | $1 "Peace" | 1·50 | 1·60 |

**521** "Shoalhaven River Bank—Dawn" (Arthur Boyd)

**1994.** Australia Day. Landscape Paintings. Mult.

| | | | |
|---|---|---|---|
| 1435 | 45c. Type **521** | 40 | 20 |
| 1436 | 85c. "Wimmera" (Sir Sidney Nolan) | 80 | 90 |
| 1437 | $1.05 "Lagoon, Wimmera" (Nolan) | 90 | 1·25 |
| 1438 | $2 "White Cockatoos with Flame Trees" (Boyd) (vert) | 1·60 | 2·10 |

**522** Teaching Lifesaving Techniques

**1994.** Centenary of Organized Life Saving in Australia. Multicoloured.

| | | | |
|---|---|---|---|
| 1439 | 45c. Type **522** | 45 | 30 |
| 1440 | 45c. Lifeguard on watch | 45 | 30 |
| 1441 | 95c. Lifeguard team | 90 | 1·10 |
| 1442 | $1.20 Lifeguards on surf boards | 1·25 | 1·50 |

Nos. 1439/40 also come self-adhesive.

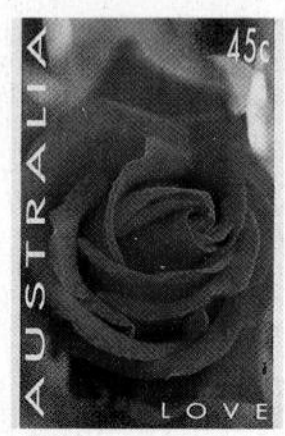


**523** Rose

**1994.** Greetings Stamps. Flower photographs by Lariane Fonseca. Multicoloured.

| | | | |
|---|---|---|---|
| 1445 | 45c. Type **523** | 40 | 45 |
| 1446 | 45c. Tulips | 40 | 45 |
| 1447 | 45c. Poppies | 40 | 45 |

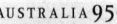

**524** Bridge and National Flags

**1994.** Opening of Friendship Bridge between Thailand and Laos.

| | | | | |
|---|---|---|---|---|
| 1448 | **524** | 95c. multicoloured | 1·25 | 1·40 |

**525** "Queen Elizabeth II" (Sir William Dargie)

**1994.** Queen Elizabeth II's Birthday.

| | | | | |
|---|---|---|---|---|
| 1449 | **525** | 45c. multicoloured | 1·00 | 70 |

**526** "Family in Field" (Bobbie-Lea Blackmore)

**1994.** International Year of the Family. Children's Paintings. Multicoloured.

| | | | |
|---|---|---|---|
| 1450 | 45c. Type **526** | 55 | 20 |
| 1451 | 75c. "Family on Beach" (Kathryn Teoh) | 75 | 1·00 |
| 1452 | $1 "Family around Fire" (Maree McCarthy) | 1·00 | 1·25 |

**1994.** Australian Wildlife (2nd series). As T 505. Multicoloured. Ordinary or self-adhesive gum.

| | | | |
|---|---|---|---|
| 1459 | 45c. Kangaroo | 60 | 85 |
| 1460 | 45c. Female kangaroo with young | 60 | 85 |
| 1461 | 45c. Two kangaroos | 60 | 85 |
| 1462 | 45c. Family of koalas on branch | 60 | 85 |
| 1463 | 45c. Koala on ground | 60 | 85 |
| 1464 | 45c. Koala asleep in tree | 60 | 85 |

**527** Suffragettes

**1994.** Centenary of Women's Emancipation in South Australia.

| | | | | |
|---|---|---|---|---|
| 1465 | **527** | 45c. multicoloured | 60 | 60 |

**528** Bunyip from Aboriginal Legend

**1994.** The Bunyip (mythological monster). Mult.

| | | | |
|---|---|---|---|
| 1466 | 45c. Type **528** | 55 | 70 |
| 1467 | 45c. Nature spirit bunyip | 55 | 70 |
| 1468 | 90c. "The Bunyip of Berkeley's Creek" (book illustration) | 1·00 | 2·00 |
| 1469 | $1.35 Bunyip as natural history | 1·40 | 2·50 |

**529** "Robert Menzies" (Sir Ivor Hele)

**1994.** Wartime Prime Ministers. Multicoloured.

| | | | |
|---|---|---|---|
| 1470 | 45c. Type **529** | 1·25 | 1·50 |
| 1471 | 45c. "Arthur Fadden" (William Dargie) | 1·25 | 1·50 |
| 1472 | 45c. "John Curtin" (Anthony Dattilo-Rubbo) | 1·25 | 1·50 |
| 1473 | 45c. "Francis Forde" (Joshua Smith) | 1·25 | 1·50 |
| 1474 | 45c. "Joseph Chifley" (A. D. Colquhoun) | 1·25 | 1·50 |

**530** Lawrence Hargrave and Box Kites

**1994.** Aviation Pioneers.

| | | | | |
|---|---|---|---|---|
| 1475 | **530** | 45c. brown, green and cinnamon | 90 | 50 |
| 1476 | - | 45c. brown, red and lilac | 90 | 50 |
| 1477 | - | $1.35 brown, violet and blue | 2·75 | 3·75 |
| 1478 | - | $1.80 brown, deep green and green | 3·00 | 3·75 |

DESIGNS: No. 1476, Ross and Keith Smith with Vickers Vimy (first England–Australia flight); 1477, Ivor McIntyre, Stanley Goble and Fairey IIID seaplane (first aerial circumnavigation of Australia); 1478, Freda Thompson and De Havilland Moth Major "Christopher Robin" (first Australian woman to fly solo from England to Australia).

**531** Scarlet Macaw

**1994.** Australian Zoos. Endangered Species. Mult.

| | | | |
|---|---|---|---|
| 1479 | 45c. Type **531** | 80 | 55 |
| 1480 | 45c. Cheetah (25×30 mm) | 80 | 55 |
| 1481 | 45c. Orang-utan (26×37 mm) | 80 | 55 |
| 1482 | 45c. Fijian crested iguana (26×37 mm) | 80 | 55 |
| 1483 | $1 Asian elephants (49×28 mm) | 2·75 | 1·60 |
| **MS**1484 | 166×73 mm. Nos. 1479/83 | 4·50 | 4·50 |

Nos. 1479/80 also come self-adhesive.

**532** "Madonna and Child" (detail)

**1994.** Christmas. "The Adoration of the Magi" by Giovanni Toscani. Multicoloured.

| | | | |
|---|---|---|---|
| 1487 | 40c. Type **532** | 40 | 15 |
| 1488 | 45c. "Wise Man and Horse" (detail) (horiz) | 60 | 15 |
| 1489 | $1 "Wise Man and St. Joseph" (detail) (horiz) | 1·50 | 1·00 |
| 1490 | $1.80 Complete painting (49×29 mm) | 2·25 | 2·75 |

**533** Yachts outside Sydney Harbour

**1994.** 50th Sydney to Hobart Yacht Race. Mult.

| | | | |
|---|---|---|---|
| 1491 | 45c. Type **533** | 1·00 | 80 |
| 1492 | 45c. Yachts passing Tasmania coastline | 1·00 | 80 |

Nos. 1491/92 also come self-adhesive.

**534** Symbolic Kangaroo

**1994.** Self-adhesive. Automatic Cash Machine Stamps.

| | | | | |
|---|---|---|---|---|
| 1495 | **534** | 45c. gold, emerald and green | 55 | 80 |
| 1496 | **534** | 45c. gold, green and blue | 55 | 80 |
| 1497 | **534** | 45c. gold, green and lilac | 55 | 80 |
| 1498 | **534** | 45c. gold, emerald and green | 55 | 80 |
| 1499 | **534** | 45c. gold, emerald and green | 55 | 80 |
| 1500 | **534** | 45c. gold, green and pink | 55 | 80 |
| 1501 | **534** | 45c. gold, green and red | 55 | 80 |
| 1502 | **534** | 45c. gold, green and brown | 55 | 80 |

**535** "Back Verandah" (Russell Drysdale)

**1995.** Australia Day. Paintings. Multicoloured.

| | | | |
|---|---|---|---|
| 1503 | 45c. Type **535** | 60 | 45 |
| 1504 | 45c. "Skull Springs Country" (Guy Grey-Smith) | 60 | 45 |
| 1505 | $1.05 "Outcamp" (Robert Juniper) | 1·60 | 1·50 |
| 1506 | $1.20 "Kite Flying" (Ian Fairweather) | 1·75 | 1·50 |

**536** Red Heart and Rose

**1995.** St. Valentine's Day. Multicoloured.

| | | | |
|---|---|---|---|
| 1507 | 45c. Type **536** | 55 | 55 |
| 1508 | 45c. Gold and red heart with rose | 55 | 55 |
| 1509 | 45c. Gold heart and roses | 85 | 1·25 |

**537** "Endeavour" Replica at Sea

**1995.** Completion of "Endeavour" Replica. Mult.

| | | | |
|---|---|---|---|
| 1510 | 45c. Type **537** | 1·50 | 1·75 |
| 1511 | 45c. "Captain Cook's Endeavour" (detail) (Oswald Brett) | 1·50 | 1·75 |
| 1512 | 20c. Type **537** (44×26 mm) | 1·00 | 1·75 |

**538** Coalport Plate and Bracket Clock, Old Government House, Parramatta

**1995.** 50th Anniv of Australian National Trusts.

| | | | | |
|---|---|---|---|---|
| 1514 | **538** | 45c. blue and brown | 45 | 45 |
| 1515 | - | 45c. green and brown | 45 | 45 |
| 1516 | - | $1 red and blue | 1·00 | 95 |
| 1517 | - | $2 green and blue | 1·90 | 1·90 |

DESIGNS: No. 1515, Steiner doll and Italian-style chair, Ayers House, Adelaide; 1516, "Advance Australia" teapot and parian-ware statuette, Victoria; 1517, Silver bowl and china urn, Old Observatory, Perth.

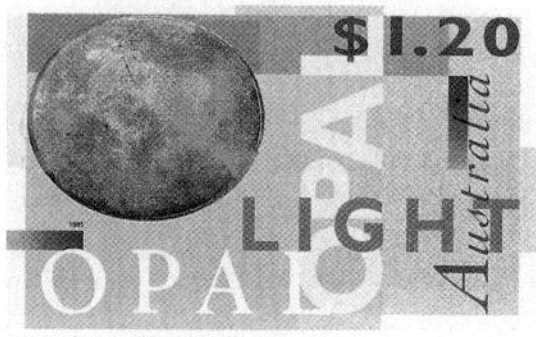


**539** Light Opal (hologram)

**1995.** Opals. Multicoloured.

| | | | |
|---|---|---|---|
| 1518 | $1.20 Type **539** | 3·50 | 1·25 |
| 1519 | $2.50 Black opal (hologram) | 4·50 | 3·75 |

**540** Queen Elizabeth II at Gala Concert, 1992

**1995.** Queen Elizabeth II's Birthday.

| | | | | |
|---|---|---|---|---|
| 1520 | **540** | 45c. multicoloured | 75 | 75 |

**541** Sir Edward Dunlop and P.O.W. Association Badge

**1995.** Australian Second World War Heroes (1st series). Mult. Ordinary or self-adhesive gum.

| | | | |
|---|---|---|---|
| 1521 | 45c. Type **541** | 60 | 60 |
| 1522 | 45c. Mrs. Jessie Vasey and War Widows' Guild badge | 60 | 60 |
| 1523 | 45c. Sgt. Tom Derrick and Victoria Cross | 60 | 60 |
| 1524 | 45c. Flt. Sgt. Rawdon Middleton and Victoria Cross | 60 | 60 |

See also Nos. 1545/8.

**542** Children and Globe of Flags

**1995.** 50th Anniv of United Nations.

| | | | | |
|---|---|---|---|---|
| 1529 | **542** | 45c. multicoloured | 75 | 75 |

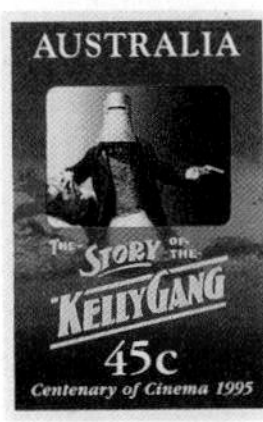


**543** "The Story of the Kelly Gang"

**1995.** Centenary of Cinema. Scenes from Films. Multicoloured. (a) Size 23×35 mm.

| | | | |
|---|---|---|---|
| 1530 | 45c. Type **543** | 1·40 | 1·50 |
| 1531 | 45c. "On Our Selection" | 1·40 | 1·50 |
| 1532 | 45c. "Jedda" | 1·40 | 1·50 |
| 1533 | 45c. "Picnic at Hanging Rock" | 1·40 | 1·50 |
| 1534 | 45c. "Strictly Ballroom" | 1·40 | 1·50 |

(b) Self-adhesive. Size 19×30½ mm.

| | | | |
|---|---|---|---|
| 1535 | 45c. Type **543** | 1·10 | 1·50 |
| 1536 | 45c. "On Our Selection" | 1·10 | 1·50 |
| 1537 | 45c. "Jedda" | 1·10 | 1·50 |
| 1538 | 45c. "Picnic at Hanging Rock" | 1·10 | 1·50 |
| 1539 | 45c. "Strictly Ballroom" | 1·10 | 1·50 |

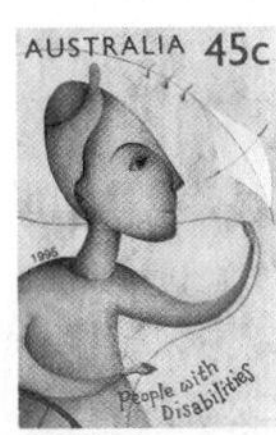


**544** Man in Wheelchair flying Kite

**1995.** People with Disabilities. Multicoloured.

| | | | |
|---|---|---|---|
| 1540 | 45c. Type **544** | 1·25 | 1·40 |
| 1541 | 45c. Blind woman playing violin | 1·25 | 1·40 |

**1995.** 50th Anniv of Peace in the Pacific. Designs as 1946 Victory Commemoration (Nos. 213/15) redrawn with new face values.

| | | | | |
|---|---|---|---|---|
| 1542 | **53** | 45c. red | 1·00 | 70 |
| 1543 | - | 45c. green | 1·00 | 70 |
| 1544 | - | $1.50 blue | 2·25 | 2·75 |

DESIGNS—VERT: No. 1543, Angel. HORIZ: No. 1544, Flag and dove.

**1995.** Australian Second World War Heroes (2nd series). As T 541. Multicoloured.

| | | | |
|---|---|---|---|
| 1545 | 45c. Sister Ellen Savage and George Medal | 1·50 | 1·75 |
| 1546 | 45c. Chief Petty Officer Percy Collins and Distinguished Service Medal and Bar | 1·50 | 1·75 |
| 1547 | 45c. Lt-Comm. Leon Goldsworthy and George Cross | 1·50 | 1·75 |
| 1548 | 45c. Warrant Officer Len Waters and R.A.A.F. wings | 1·50 | 1·75 |

**545** Koala with Cub

**1995.** Australia–China Joint Issue. Endangered Species. Multicoloured.

| | | | |
|---|---|---|---|
| 1549 | 45c. Type **545** | 70 | 1·00 |
| 1550 | 45c. Giant panda with cubs | 70 | 1·00 |
| **MS**1551 | Two sheets, each 106×70 mm. (a) No. 1549. (b) No. 1550 Set of 2 sheets | 2·00 | 2·25 |

**546** Father Joseph Slattery, Thomas Lyle and Walter Filmer (Radiology)

**1995.** Medical Scientists. Multicoloured.

| | | | |
|---|---|---|---|
| 1552 | 45c. Type **546** | 1·25 | 1·25 |
| 1553 | 45c. Dame Jean Macnamara and Sir Macfarlane Burnet (viruses) | 1·25 | 1·25 |
| 1554 | 45c. Fred Hollows (ophthalmology) (vert) | 1·25 | 60 |
| 1555 | $2.50 Sir Howard Florey (antibiotics) (vert) | 5·50 | 6·00 |

**547** Flatback Turtle

**1995.** Marine Life. Multicoloured. Ordinary or self-adhesive gum.

| | | | |
|---|---|---|---|
| 1556 | 45c. Type **547** | 55 | 55 |
| 1557 | 45c. Flame angelfish and nudibranch | 55 | 55 |
| 1558 | 45c. Potato grouper ("Potato cod") and hump-headed wrasse ("Maori wrasse") | 55 | 55 |
| 1559 | 45c. Giant trevally | 55 | 55 |
| 1560 | 45c. Black marlin | 55 | 55 |
| 1561 | 45c. Mako and tiger sharks | 55 | 55 |
| **MS**1562 | 166×73 mm. Nos. 1556/61 | 3·50 | 3·00 |

**548** "Madonna and Child"

**1995.** Christmas. Stained-glass Windows from Our Lady Help of Christians Church, Melbourne. Multicoloured.

| | | | |
|---|---|---|---|
| 1569 | 40c. Type **548** | 80 | 15 |
| 1570 | 45c. "Angel carrying the Gloria banner" | 80 | 15 |
| 1571 | $1 "Rejoicing Angels" | 3·00 | 3·25 |

No. 1569 also comes self-adhesive.

**549** "West Australian Banksia" (Margaret Preston)

**1996.** Australia Day. Paintings. Multicoloured.

| | | | |
|---|---|---|---|
| 1573 | 45c. Type **549** | 1·00 | 30 |
| 1574 | 85c. "The Babe is Wise" (Lina Bryans) | 2·00 | 2·25 |
| 1575 | $1 "The Bridge in Curve" (Grace Cossington Smith) (horiz) | 2·25 | 2·00 |
| 1576 | $1.20 "Beach Umbrellas" (Vida Lahey) (horiz) | 2·50 | 3·25 |

**550** Gold Heart and Rose

**1996.** St. Valentine's Day.

| | | | | |
|---|---|---|---|---|
| 1577 | **550** | 45c. multicoloured | 1·00 | 1·00 |

**551** Bristol Type 156 Beaufighter and Curtiss P-40E Kittyhawk I

**1996.** Military Aviation. Multicoloured.

| | | | |
|---|---|---|---|
| 1578 | 45c. Type **551** | 2·00 | 2·00 |
| 1579 | 45c. Hawker Sea Fury and Fairey Firefly | 2·00 | 2·00 |
| 1580 | 45c. Bell Kiowa helicopters | 2·00 | 2·00 |
| 1581 | 45c. Government Aircraft Factory Hornets | 2·00 | 2·00 |

**552** Tasmanian Wilderness

**1996.** World Heritage Sites (2nd series). Mult.

| | | | |
|---|---|---|---|
| 1582 | 45c. Type **552** | 90 | 7·25 |
| 1583 | 75c. Willandra Lakes | 2·25 | 2·50 |
| 1584 | 95c. Naracoorte Fossil Cave | 2·50 | 3·50 |
| 1585 | $1 Lord Howe Island | 2·50 | 2·25 |

**553** Australian Spotted Cuscus

**1996.** Australia–Indonesia Joint Issue. Mult.

| | | | |
|---|---|---|---|
| 1586 | 45c. Type **553** | 1·25 | 1·75 |
| 1587 | 45c. Indonesian bear cuscus | 1·25 | 1·75 |
| **MS**1588 | 106×70 mm. Nos. 1586/7 | 2·50 | 3·50 |

**554** Head of Queen Elizabeth II

**1996.** Queen Elizabeth II's Birthday.

| | | | | |
|---|---|---|---|---|
| 1589 | **554** | 45c. multicoloured | 1·25 | 1·00 |

**555** North Melbourne Players

**1996.** Centenary of Australian Football League. Players from different teams. Multicoloured. Ordinary or self-adhesive gum.

| | | | |
|---|---|---|---|
| 1606 | 45c. Type **555** | 50 | 90 |
| 1607 | 45c. Brisbane (red and yellow shirt) | 50 | 90 |
| 1608 | 45c. Sydney (red and white shirt) | 50 | 90 |
| 1609 | 45c. Carlton (black shirt with white emblem) | 50 | 90 |
| 1610 | 45c. Adelaide (black, red and yellow shirt) | 50 | 90 |
| 1611 | 45c. Fitzroy (yellow, red and blue shirt) | 50 | 90 |
| 1612 | 45c. Richmond (black shirt with yellow diagonal stripe) | 50 | 90 |
| 1613 | 45c. St. Kilda (red, white and black shirt) | 50 | 90 |
| 1614 | 45c. Melbourne (black shirt with red top) | 50 | 90 |
| 1615 | 45c. Collingwood (black and white vertical striped shirt) | 50 | 90 |
| 1616 | 45c. Fremantle (green, red, white and blue shirt) | 50 | 90 |
| 1617 | 45c. Footscray (blue, white and red shirt) | 50 | 90 |
| 1618 | 45c. West Coast (deep blue shirt with yellow stripes) | 50 | 90 |
| 1619 | 45c. Essendon (black shirt with red stripe) | 50 | 90 |
| 1620 | 45c. Geelong (black and white horizontal striped shirt) | 50 | 90 |
| 1621 | 45c. Hawthorn (black and yellow vertical striped shirt) | 50 | 90 |

**556** Leadbeater's Possum

**1996.** Fauna and Flora (1st series). Central Highlands Forest, Victoria. Multicoloured.

| | | | |
|---|---|---|---|
| 1622 | 5c. Type **556** | 30 | 10 |
| 1623 | 10c. Powerful owl | 1·50 | 20 |
| 1624 | $2 Blackwood wattle | 1·40 | 1·50 |
| 1625 | $5 Soft tree fern and mountain ash (30×50 mm) | 7·50 | 3·75 |

See also Nos. 1679/90, 1854/66, 2130/33, 2200/3, 2272/6 and 2377/80.

**1996.** "China '96" 9th Asian International Stamp Exhibition, Peking. Sheet 120×65 mm, containing Nos. 1453b, 1454b and 1455b. Multicoloured.

| | | | |
|---|---|---|---|
| **MS**1626 | 45c. Kangaroo; 45c. Female kangaroo with young; 45c. Two kangaroos | 2·00 | 2·25 |

**557** Edwin Flack (800 and 1500 metres gold medal winner, 1896)

**1996.** Centennial Olympic Games and 10th Paralympic Games, Atlanta. Multicoloured.

| | | | |
|---|---|---|---|
| 1627 | 45c. Type **557** | 80 | 80 |
| 1628 | 45c. Fanny Durack (100 metres freestyle swimming gold medal winner, 1912) | 80 | 80 |
| 1629 | $1.05 Wheelchair athletes | 2·00 | 2·00 |

**558** "Animalia" (Graeme Base)

**1996.** 50th Anniv of Children's Book Council Awards. Designs taken from book covers. Ordinary or self-adhesive gum. Multicoloured.

| | | | |
|---|---|---|---|
| 1630 | 45c. Type **558** | 60 | 60 |
| 1631 | 45c. "Greetings from Sandy Beach" (Bob Graham) | 60 | 60 |
| 1632 | 45c. "Who Sank the Boat?" (Pamela Allen) | 60 | 60 |
| 1633 | 45c. "John Brown, Rose and the Midnight Cat" (Jenny Wagner, illustrated by Ron Brooks) | 60 | 60 |

**559** American Bald Eagle, Kangaroo and Olympic Flame

**1996.** Passing of Olympic Flag to Sydney.

| | | | | |
|---|---|---|---|---|
| 1638 | **559** | 45c. multicoloured | 55 | 50 |

**560** Margaret Windeyer

**1996.** Centenary of the National Council of Women.

| | | | | |
|---|---|---|---|---|
| 1639 | **560** | 45c. purple and yellow | 50 | 50 |
| 1640 | - | $1 blue and yellow | 1·25 | 2·00 |

DESIGN: $1 Rose Scott.

**561** Pearl

**1996.** Pearls and Diamonds. Multicoloured.

| | | | |
|---|---|---|---|
| 1641 | 45c. Type **561** | 60 | 50 |
| 1642 | $1.20 Diamond | 1·40 | 1·50 |

The pearl on the 45c. is shown as an exelgram (holographic printing on ultra thin plastic film) and the diamond on the $1.20 as a hologram, each embossed on to the stamp.

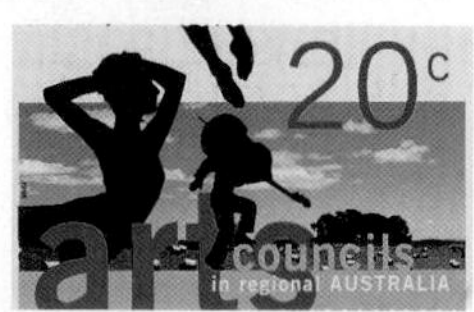


**562** Silhouettes of Female Dancer and Musician on Rural Landscape

**1996.** 50th Anniv of Arts Councils. Multicoloured.

| | | | |
|---|---|---|---|
| 1643 | 20c. Type **562** | 1·40 | 2·25 |
| 1644 | 45c. Silhouettes of musician and male dancer on landscape | 35 | 45 |

**563** Ginger Cats

**1996.** Australian Pets. Multicoloured.

| | | | |
|---|---|---|---|
| 1645 | 45c. Type **563** | 75 | 75 |
| 1646 | 45c. Blue heeler dogs | 75 | 75 |
| 1647 | 45c. Sulphur-crested cockatoo (30×25 mm) | 75 | 75 |
| 1648 | 45c. Duck with ducklings (25×30 mm) | 75 | 75 |
| 1649 | 45c. Dog and cat (25×30 mm) | 75 | 75 |
| 1650 | 45c. Ponies (30×50 mm) | 75 | 75 |
| **MS**1651 | 166×73 mm. Nos. 1645/50 | 4·00 | 4·00 |

Nos. 1645/6 also come self-adhesive.

**564** Ferdinand von Mueller

**1996.** Australia–Germany Joint Issue. Death Centenary of Ferdinand von Mueller (botanist).

| | | | | |
|---|---|---|---|---|
| 1654 | **564** | $1.20 multicoloured | 1·25 | 2·00 |

**565** Willem de Vlamingh

**1996.** 300th Anniv of the Visit of Willem de Vlamingh to Western Australia.

| | | | | |
|---|---|---|---|---|
| 1655 | **565** | 45c. multicoloured | 1·00 | 1·50 |

**566** Madonna and Child

**1996.** Christmas. Multicoloured.

| | | | |
|---|---|---|---|
| 1656 | 40c. Type **566** | 55 | 15 |
| 1657 | 45c. Wise man with gift | 55 | 15 |
| 1658 | $1 Shepherd boy with lamb | 1·25 | 1·50 |

No. 1656 also comes self-adhesive.

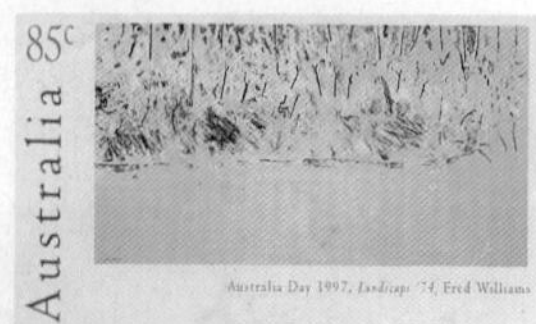


**567** "Landscape '74" (Fred Williams)

**1997.** Australia Day. Contemporary Paintings. Multicoloured.

| | | | |
|---|---|---|---|
| 1660 | 85c. Type **567** | 1·10 | 1·10 |
| 1661 | 90c. "The Balcony 2" (Brett Whiteley) | 1·10 | 1·10 |
| 1662 | $1.20 "Fire Haze at Gerringong" (Lloyd Rees) | 1·40 | 1·40 |

**568** Sir Donald Bradman

**1997.** Australian Legends (1st series). Sir Donald Bradman (cricketer). Multicoloured.

| | | | |
|---|---|---|---|
| 1663 | 45c. Type **568** | 55 | 55 |
| 1664 | 45c. Bradman playing stroke | 55 | 55 |

See also Nos. 1731/42, 1838/9, 1947/50, 2069/70, 2165/9, 2264/7, 2348/9, 2473/8, 2577/81 and 2741/58.

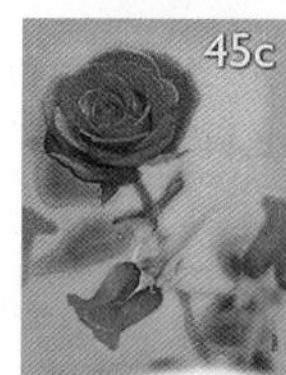


**569** Red Roses

**1997.** St. Valentine's Day. Ordinary or self-adhesive gum.

| | | | | |
|---|---|---|---|---|
| 1665 | **569** | 45c. multicoloured | 50 | 50 |

**570** Ford Coupe Utility, 1934

**1997.** Classic Cars. Multicoloured. Ordinary or self-adhesive gum.

| | | | |
|---|---|---|---|
| 1667 | 45c. Type **570** | 60 | 75 |
| 1668 | 45c. Holden 48-215 (FX) sedan, 1948 | 60 | 75 |
| 1669 | 45c. Austin Lancer sedan, 1958 | 60 | 75 |
| 1670 | 45c. Chrysler Valiant "R" Series sedan, 1962 | 60 | 75 |

**571** May Wirth and Horse

**1997.** 150th Anniv of the Circus in Australia. Multicoloured.

| | | | |
|---|---|---|---|
| 1675 | 45c. Type **571** | 55 | 75 |
| 1676 | 45c. Con Colleano on tightrope | 55 | 75 |
| 1677 | 45c. Clowns | 55 | 75 |
| 1678 | 45c. Acrobats | 55 | 75 |

**1997.** Fauna and Flora (2nd series). Kakadu Wetlands, Northern Territory. As T 556. Mult.

| | | | |
|---|---|---|---|
| 1679 | 20c. Saltwater crocodile | 15 | 20 |
| 1680 | 25c. Northern dwarf tree frog | 20 | 25 |
| 1681 | 45c. Comb-crested jacana ("Jacana") | 75 | 75 |
| 1682 | 45c. Mangrove kingfisher ("Little Kingfisher") | 75 | 75 |
| 1683 | 45c. Brolga | 75 | 75 |
| 1684 | 45c. Black-necked stork ("Jabiru") | 75 | 75 |
| 1685 | $1 "Cressida cressida" (butterfly) | 70 | 75 |
| 1686 | $10 Kakadu Wetlands (50×30 mm) | 7·00 | 5·00 |
| **MS**1686a | 106×70 mm. No. 1686 | 9·00 | 11·00 |

Nos. 1681/84 also come self-adhesive.

**572** Royal Wedding 1d. Stamp of 1947

**1997.** Queen Elizabeth II's Birthday.

| | | | | |
|---|---|---|---|---|
| 1691 | **572** | 45c. purple | 60 | 60 |

**573** Hand holding Globe and Lion's Emblem

**1997.** 50th Anniv of First Australian Lions Club.

| | | | | |
|---|---|---|---|---|
| 1692 | **573** | 45c. blue, brown and purple | 50 | 50 |

**574** Doll holding Teddy Bear (Kaye Wiggs)

**1997.** Dolls and Teddy Bears. Multicoloured.

| | | | |
|---|---|---|---|
| 1693 | 45c. Type **574** | 45 | 50 |
| 1694 | 45c. Teddy bear standing (Jennifer Laing) | 45 | 50 |
| 1695 | 45c. Doll wearing white dress with teddy bear (Susie McMahon) | 45 | 50 |
| 1696 | 45c. Doll in brown dress and bonnet (Lynda Jacobson) | 45 | 50 |
| 1697 | 45c. Teddy bear sitting (Helen Williams) | 45 | 50 |

**575** Police Rescue Helicopter

**1997.** Emergency Services. Multicoloured.

| | | | |
|---|---|---|---|
| 1698 | 45c. Type **575** | 1·40 | 1·00 |
| 1699 | 45c. Emergency Service volunteers carrying victim | 1·40 | 1·00 |
| 1700 | $1.05 Fire service at fire | 2·50 | 2·25 |
| 1701 | $1.20 Loading casualty into ambulance | 2·75 | 2·00 |

**576** George Peppin Jnr (breeder) and Merino Sheep

**1997.** Bicentenary of Arrival of Merino Sheep in Australia. Multicoloured.

| | | | |
|---|---|---|---|
| 1702 | 45c. Type **576** | 70 | 1·00 |
| 1703 | 45c. Pepe chair, cloth and wool logo | 70 | 1·00 |

**577** Dumbi the Owl

**1997.** "The Dreaming". Cartoons from Aboriginal Stories. Multicoloured.

| | | | |
|---|---|---|---|
| 1704 | 45c. Type **577** | 65 | 30 |
| 1705 | $1 The Two Willy-Willies | 1·25 | 1·10 |
| 1706 | $1.20 How Brolga became a Bird | 1·25 | 2·00 |
| 1707 | $1.80 Tuggan-Tuggan | 1·75 | 3·75 |

**578** "Rhoetosaurus brownei"

**1997.** Prehistoric Animals. Multicoloured.

| | | | |
|---|---|---|---|
| 1708 | 45c. Type **578** | 45 | 60 |
| 1709 | 45c. "Mcnamaraspis kaprios" | 45 | 60 |
| 1710 | 45c. "Ninjemys oweni" | 45 | 60 |
| 1711 | 45c. "Paracylotosaurus davidi" | 45 | 60 |
| 1712 | 45c. "Woolungasaurus glendowerensis" | 45 | 60 |

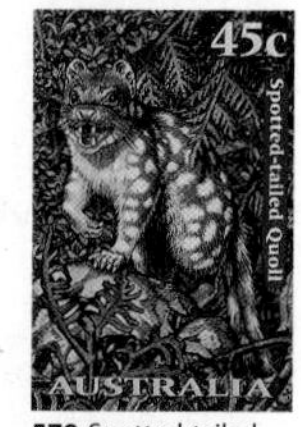


**579** Spotted-tailed Quoll

**1997.** Nocturnal Animals. Multicoloured.

| | | | |
|---|---|---|---|
| 1713 | 45c. Type **579** | 70 | 90 |
| 1714 | 45c. Barking owl | 70 | 90 |
| 1715 | 45c. Platypus (30×25 mm) | 70 | 90 |
| 1716 | 45c. Brown antechinus (30×25 mm) | 70 | 90 |
| 1717 | 45c. Dingo (30×25 mm) | 70 | 90 |
| 1718 | 45c. Yellow-bellied glider (50×30 mm) | 70 | 90 |
| **MS**1719 | 166×78 mm. Nos. 1713/18 | 4·75 | 4·75 |

Nos. 1713/14 also come self-adhesive.

**580** Woman

**1997.** Breast Cancer Awareness Campaign.

| | | | | |
|---|---|---|---|---|
| 1722 | **580** | 45c. multicoloured | 1·25 | 60 |

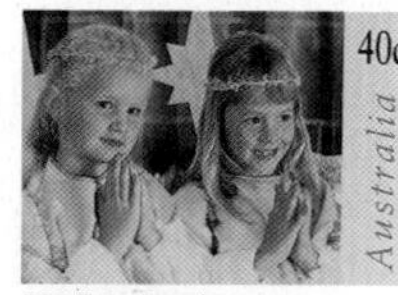


**581** Two Angels

**1997.** Christmas. Children's Nativity Play. Mult.

| | | | |
|---|---|---|---|
| 1723 | 40c. Type **581** | 50 | 15 |
| 1724 | 45c. Mary | 55 | 15 |
| 1725 | $1 Three Kings | 1·25 | 1·50 |

No. 1723 also comes self-adhesive.

**582** "Flying Cloud" (clipper) (J. Scott)

**1998.** Ship Paintings. Multicoloured.

| | | | |
|---|---|---|---|
| 1727 | 45c. Type **582** | 60 | 30 |
| 1728 | 85c. "Marco Polo" (full-rigged ship) (T. Robertson) | 1·00 | 1·00 |
| 1729 | $1 "Chusan I" (steamship) (C. Gregory) | 1·25 | 1·10 |
| 1730 | $1.20 "Heather Belle" (clipper) | 1·50 | 1·75 |

**583** Betty Cuthbert (1956)

**1998.** Australian Legends (2nd series). Olympic Gold Medal Winners. Multicoloured. Ordinary or self-adhesive gum.

| | | | |
|---|---|---|---|
| 1731 | 45c. Type **583** | 45 | 65 |
| 1732 | 45c. Betty Cuthbert running | 45 | 65 |
| 1733 | 45c. Herb Elliott (1960) | 45 | 65 |
| 1734 | 45c. Herb Elliott running | 45 | 65 |
| 1735 | 45c. Dawn Fraser (1956, 1960 and 1964) | 45 | 65 |
| 1736 | 45c. Dawn Fraser swimming | 45 | 65 |
| 1737 | 45c. Marjorie Jackson (1952) | 45 | 65 |
| 1738 | 45c. Marjorie Jackson running | 45 | 65 |
| 1739 | 45c. Murray Rose (1956) | 45 | 65 |
| 1740 | 45c. Murray Rose swimming | 45 | 65 |
| 1741 | 45c. Shirley Strickland (1952 and 1956) | 45 | 65 |
| 1742 | 45c. Shirley Strickland hurdling | 45 | 65 |

**584** "Champagne" Rose

**1998.** Greeting Stamp. Ordinary or self-adhesive gum.
1755 **584** 45c. multicoloured 55 50

**585** Queen Elizabeth II

**1998.** Queen Elizabeth II's Birthday.
1757 **585** 45c. multicoloured 60 50

**586** Sea Hawk (helicopter) landing on Frigate

**1998.** 50th Anniv of Royal Australian Navy Fleet Air Arm.
1758 **586** 45c. multicoloured 75 50

**587** Sheep Shearer and Sheep

**1998.** Farming. Multicoloured. Ordinary or self-adhesive gum.
1759 45c. Type **587** 45 50
1760 45c. Barley and silo 45 50
1761 45c. Farmers herding beef cattle 45 50
1762 45c. Sugar cane harvesting 45 50
1763 45c. Two dairy cows 45 50

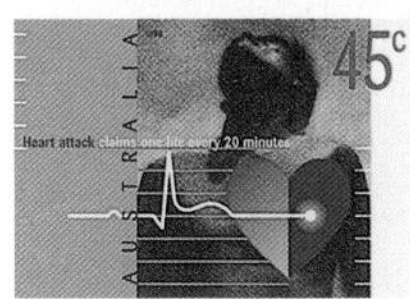

**588** Cardiograph Trace and Heart

**1998.** Heart Disease Awareness.
1769 **588** 45c. multicoloured 65 50

**589** Johnny OKeefe ("The Wild One", 1958)

**1998.** Australian Rock and Roll. Multicoloured. Ordinary or self-adhesive gum.
1770 45c. Type **589** 45 50
1771 45c. Col Joye ("Oh Yeah Uh Huh", 1959) 45 50
1772 45c. Little Pattie ("He's My Blonde Headed Stompie Wompie Real Gone Surfer Boy", 1963) 45 50
1773 45c. Normie Rowe ("Shakin all Over", 1965) 45 50
1774 45c. Easybeats ("She's so Fine", 1965) 45 50
1775 45c. Russell Morris ("The Real Thing", 1969) 45 50
1776 45c. Masters Apprentices ("Turn Up Your Radio", 1970) 45 50
1777 45c. Daddy Cool ("Eagle Rock", 1971) 45 50
1778 45c. Billy Thorpe and the Aztecs ("Most People I know think I'm Crazy", 1972) 45 50
1779 45c. Skyhooks ("Horror Movie", 1974) 45 50
1780 45c. AC/DC ("It's a Long Way to the Top", 1975) 45 50

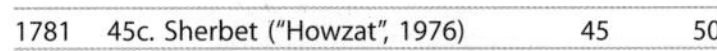
1781 45c. Sherbet ("Howzat", 1976) 45 50

**590** Yellow-tufted Honeyeater ("Helmeted Honeyeater")

**1998.** Endangered Species. Multicoloured.
1794 5c. Type **590** 45 45
1795 5c. Orange-bellied parrot 45 45
1796 45c. Red-tailed cockatoo ("Red-tailed Black-Cockatoo") 80 80
1797 45c. Gouldian finch 80 80

**591** French Horn and Cello Players

**1998.** Youth Arts, Australia. Multicoloured.
1798 45c. Type **591** 50 50
1799 45c. Dancers 50 50

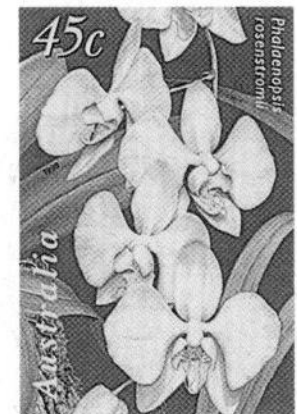

**592** "Phalaenopsis rosenstromii"

**1998.** Australia–Singapore Joint Issue. Orchids.
1800 45c. Type **592** 55 40
1801 85c. "Arundina graminifolia" 1·00 1·00
1802 $1 "Grammatophyllum speciosum" 1·40 1·25
1803 $1.20 "Dendrobium phalaenopsis" 1·50 1·60
**MS**1804 138×72 mm. Nos. 1800/3 4·00 3·75

**593** Flying Angel with Teapot (cartoon by Michael Leunig)

**1998.** "The Teapot of Truth" (cartoons by Michael Leunig). Multicoloured.
1805 45c. Type **593** 75 80
1806 45c. Two birds in heart-shaped tree 75 80
1807 45c. Pouring tea 75 80
1808 $1 Mother and child (29×24 mm) 1·40 1·75
1809 $1.20 Cat with smiling face (29×24 mm) 1·40 1·75

**594** Red Lacewing

**1998.** Butterflies. Multicoloured. Ordinary or self-adhesive gum.
1815 45c. Type **594** 75 85
1816 45c. Dull oakblue 75 85
1817 45c. Meadow argus 75 85
1818 45c. Ulysses butterfly 75 85
1819 45c. Common red-eye 75 85

**595** Flinders' Telescope and Map of Tasmania

**1998.** Bicentenary of the Circumnavigation of Tasmania by George Bass and Matthew Flinders. Multicoloured.
1820 45c. Type **595** 75 65
1821 45c. Sextant and letter from Bass 75 65

**596** Weedy Seadragon

**1998.** International Year of the Ocean. Multicoloured.
1822 45c. Type **596** 65 65
1823 45c. Bottlenose dolphin 65 65
1824 45c. Fiery squid (24×29 mm) 65 65
1825 45c. Manta ray (29×24 mm) 65 65
1826 45c. White pointer shark (29×49 mm) 65 65
1827 45c. Southern right whale (49×29 mm) 65 65
**MS**1828 166×73 mm. Nos. 1822/7 2·75 2·75

Nos. 1822/3 also come self-adhesive.

**597** Rose of Freedom

**1998.** 50th Anniv of Universal Declaration of Human Rights.
1831 **597** 45c. multicoloured 50 50

**598** Three Kings

**1998.** Christmas. Multicoloured.
1832 40c. Type **598** 40 15
1833 45c. Nativity scene 40 15
1834 $1 Mary and Joseph 1·10 1·10

No. 1832 also comes self-adhesive.

**599** Australian Coat of Arms

**1999.** 50th Anniv of Australian Citizenship. Ordinary or self-adhesive gum.
1837 **599** 45c. multicoloured 40 40

**600** Arthur Boyd

**1999.** Australian Legends (3rd series). Arthur Boyd (painter). Multicoloured. Ordinary or self-adhesive gum.
1838 45c. Type **600** 50 50
1839 45c. "Nebuchadnezzer on fire falling over Waterfall" (Arthur Boyd) 50 50

**601** Red Roses

**1999.** Greetings Stamp. Romance. Ordinary or self-adhesive gum.
1843 **601** 45c. multicoloured 40 40

**602** Elderly Man and Grandmother with Boy

**1999.** International Year of Older Persons. Mult.
1844 45c. Type **602** 50 50
1845 45c. Elderly woman and grandfather with boy 50 50

**603** "Polly Woodside" (barque)

**1999.** Sailing Ships. Multicoloured.
1846 45c. Type **603** 60 35
1847 85c. "Alma Doepel" (topsail schooner) 1·00 1·10
1848 $1 "Enterprize" replica (topsail schooner) 1·25 1·10
1849 $1.05 "Lady Nelson" replica (topsail schooner) 1·40 1·90

**1999.** Australia—Ireland Joint Issue. "Polly Woodside" (barque). Sheet 137×72 mm. Mult.
**MS**1850 45c. Type **603**; 30p. Type **374** of Ireland (No. **MS**1850 was sold at $1.25 in Australia) 1·25 1·40

**1999.** Australia—Canada. Joint Issue. "Marco Polo" (emigrant ship). Sheet 160×95 mm. Mult.
**MS**1851 85c. As No. 1728; 46c. Type **701** of Canada (No. **MS**1851 was sold at $1.30 in Australia) 1·25 1·40

**1999.** "Australia '99" International Stamp Exhibition, Melbourne. Two sheets, each 142×76 mm, containing designs as Nos. 398/403 and all with face value of 45c.
**MS**1852 (a) 45c. ultramarine (Type **167**); 45c. grey (Captain Cook); 45c. brown (Flinders). (b) 45c. red (Type **168**); 45c. brown (Bass); 45c. purple (King) Set of 2 sheets 2·50 2·75

**604** Olympic Torch and 1956 7½d. Stamp

**1999.** Olympic Torch Commemoration.
1853 **604** $1.20 multicoloured 1·10 1·10

**605** "Correa reflexa" (native fuchsia)

**1999.** Fauna and Flora (3rd series). Coastal Environment. Multicoloured.
1854 45c. Type **605** 50 50
1855 45c. "Hibbertia scandens" (guinea flower) 50 50
1856 45c. "Ipomoea pre-caprae" (beach morning glory) 50 50
1857 45c. "Wahlenbergia stricta" (Australian bluebells) 50 50
1858 70c. Humpback whales and zebra volute shell (29×24 mm) 60 70
1859 90c. Brahminy kite and checkerboard helmet shell (29×24 mm) 65 70

1860 90c. Fraser Island and chambered nautilus (29×24 mm) 65 70

1861 $1.05 Loggerhead turtle and melon shell (29×24 mm) 75 80

1862 $1.20 White-bellied sea eagle and Campbell's stromb shell (29×24 mm) 85 90

Nos. 1859/60 were printed together, se-tenant, forming a composite design.

Nos. 1854/7 also come self-adhesive.

**606** Queen Elizabeth II with The Queen Mother

**1999.** Queen Elizabeth II's Birthday.

1870 **606** 45c. multicoloured 70 50

**607** "Here's Humphrey"

**1999.** Children's Television Programmes. Multicoloured. Ordinary or self-adhesive gum.

1871 45c. Type **607** 45 45

1872 45c. "Bananas in Pyjamas" 45 45

1873 45c. "Mr. Squiggle" 45 45

1874 45c. "Play School" (teddy bears) 45 45

1875 45c. "Play School" (clock, toy dog and doll) 45 45

**608** Obverse and Reverse of 1899 Sovereign

**1999.** Centenary of the Perth Mint.

1881 **608** $2 gold, blue and green 2·00 1·75

**609** Lineout against New Zealand

**1999.** Centenary of Australian Test Rugby. Mult.

1882 45c. Type **609** 50 40

1883 45c. Kicking the ball against England 50 40

1884 $1 Try against South Africa (horiz) 1·00 85

1885 $1.20 Passing the ball against Wales (horiz) 1·10 1·25

Nos. 1882/3 also come self-adhesive.

**610** Drilling at Burn's Creek and Rock Bolting in Tumut 2 Power Station Hall

**1999.** 50th Anniv of Snowy Mountain Scheme (hydro-electric project). Multicoloured. Ordinary or self-adhesive gum.

1888 45c. Type **610** 65 65

1889 45c. English class for migrant workers, Cooma 65 65

1890 45c. Tumut 2 Tailwater Tunnel and Eucumbene Dam 65 65

1891 45c. German carpenters and Island Bend Dam 65 65

**611** Calligraphy Pen and Letter

**1999.** Greetings Stamps. Multicoloured.

1896 45c. Type **611** 65 65

1897 45c. Wedding rings 65 65

1898 45c. Birthday cake 65 65

1899 45c. Christmas decoration 65 65

1900 45c. Teddy bear 65 65

1901 $1 Koala 1·25 1·25

See also No. 1921.

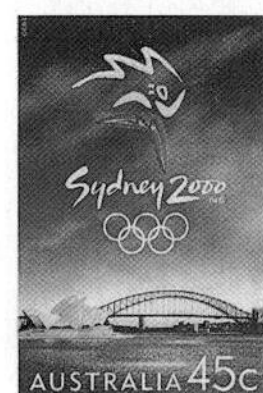


**612** Sydney Olympic Emblem

**1999.** Olympic Games, Sydney (2000) (1st issue).

1902 **612** 45c. multicoloured 1·25 60

See also Nos. 2015/24.

**613** Australia Post Symbol, 1975

**1999.** "Sydney Design '99" International Congress and Exhibition. Multicoloured.

1903 45c. Type **613** 45 30

1904 90c. Embryo chair, 1988 80 80

1905 $1.35 Possum skin textile, c.1985 1·25 1·25

1906 $1.50 Storey Hall, R.M.I.T. University, 1995 1·25 1·50

**614** Magnificent Tree Frog

**1999.** National Stamp Collecting Month, Small Pond Life. Multicoloured. Ordinary or self-adhesive gum.

1907 45c. Type **614** 55 55

1908 45c. Sacred kingfisher 55 55

1909 45c. Roth's tree frog (29×24 mm) 55 55

1910 45c. Dragonfly (29×24 mm) 55 55

1911 50c. Javelin frog (24×29 mm) 65 65

1912 50c. Northern dwarf tree frog (24×29 mm) 65 65

**MS**1913 166×73 mm. Nos. 1907/12 3·00 3·25

**615** Madonna and Child

**1999.** Christmas. Multicoloured.

1918 40c. Type **615** 50 30

1919 $1 Tree of Life (horiz) 1·00 1·00

No. 1918 also comes self-adhesive.

**616** Fireworks and Hologram

**1999.** Millennium Greetings stamp.

1921 **616** 45c. multicoloured 50 50

**617** Rachel Thomson (college administrator)

**2000.** New Millennium. "Face of Australia". Mult.

1922 45c. Nicholle and Meghan Triandis (twin babies) 40 60

1923 45c. David Willis (cattleman) 40 60

1924 45c. Natasha Bramley (scuba diver) 40 60

1925 45c. Cyril Watson (Aborigine boy) 40 60

1926 45c. Mollie Dowdall (wearing red hat) (vineyard worker) 40 60

1927 45c. Robin Dicks (flying instructor) 40 60

1928 45c. Mary Simons (retired nurse) 40 60

1929 45c. Peta and Samantha Nieuwerth (mother and baby) 40 60

1930 45c. John Matthews (doctor) 40 60

1931 45c. Edith Dizon-Fitzimmons (wearing drop earrings) (music teacher) 40 60

1932 45c. Philippa Weir (wearing brown hat) (teacher) 40 60

1933 45c. John Thurgar (in bush hat and jacket) (farmer) 40 60

1934 45c. Miguel Alzona (with face painted) (schoolboy) 40 60

1935 45c. Type **617** 40 60

1936 45c. Necip Akarsu (wearing blue shirt) (postmaster) 40 60

1937 45c. Justin Allan (R.A.N. sailor) 40 60

1938 45c. Wadad Dennaoui (wearing checked shirt) (student) 40 60

1939 45c. Jack Laity (market gardener) 40 60

1940 45c. Kelsey Stubbin (wearing cricket cap) (schoolboy) 40 60

1941 45c. Gianna Rossi (resting chin on hand) (church worker) 40 60

1942 45c. Paris Hansch (toddler) 40 60

1943 45c. Donald George Whatham (in blue shirt and tie) (retired teacher) 40 60

1944 45c. Stacey Coull (wearing pendant) 40 60

1945 45c. Alex Payne (wearing cycle helmet) (schoolgirl) 40 60

1946 45c. John Lodge (Salvation Army member) 40 60

**618** Walter Parker

**2000.** Australian Legends (4th series). "The Last Anzacs". Multicoloured. Ordinary of sels-adhesive gum.

1951 45c. Type **618** 35 40

1952 45c. Roy Longmore 35 40

1953 45c. Alec Campbell 35 40

1954 45c. 1914–15 Star (medal) 35 40

**619** Scenes from "Cloudstreet" (play) (Perth Festival)

**2000.** Arts Festivals. Multicoloured.

1955 45c. Type **619** 55 55

1956 45c. Belgian dancers from Rosas Company (Adelaide Festival) 55 55

1957 45c. "Guardian Angel" (sculpture) and dancer (Sydney Festival) 55 55

1958 45c. Musician and Balinese dancer (Melbourne Festival) 55 55

1959 45c. Members of Vusa Dance Company of South Africa (Brisbane Festival) 55 55

**620** Coast Banksia, False Sarsaparilla and Swamp Bloodwood (plants)

**2000.** Gardens. Multicoloured. Ordinary or self-adhesive gum.

1965 45c. Type **620** 35 40

1966 45c. Eastern spinebill on swamp bottlebrush in foreground 35 40

1967 45c. Border of cannas 35 40

1968 45c. Roses, lake and ornamental bridge 35 40

1969 45c. Hibiscus with bandstand in background 35 40

**621** Queen Elizabeth II in 1996

**2000.** Queen Elizabeth II's Birthday.

1970 **621** 45c. multicoloured 65 50

**622** Medals and Korean Landscape

**2000.** 50th Anniv of Korean War.

1971 **622** 45c. multicoloured 50 50

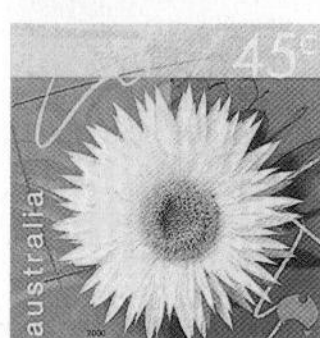


**623** Daisy

**2000.** Nature and Nation. Greeting stamps. Mult.

1972 45c. Type **623** 45 50

1973 45c. Australia on globe 45 50

1974 45c. Red kangaroo and flag 45 50

1975 45c. Sand, sea and sky 45 50

1976 45c. Rainforest 45 50

**624** Taking the Vote, New South Wales

**2000.** Centenary of Commonwealth of Australia Constitution Act. Multicoloured.

1977 45c. Type **624** 45 40

1978 45c. Voters waiting for results, Geraldton, Western Australia 45 40

1979 $1.50 Queen Victoria (29×49 mm) 1·40 1·40

1980 $1.50 Women dancing ("The Fair New Nation") (29×49 mm) 1·40 1·40

**MS**1981 155×189 mm. Nos. 1977/80 3·25 3·25

**625** Sydney Opera House, New South Wales

**2000.** International Stamps. Views of Australia (1st series). Multicoloured.

| | | | |
|---|---|---|---|
| 1982 | 50c. Type **625** | 90 | 20 |
| 1983 | $1 Nandroya Falls, Queensland | 1·60 | 30 |
| 1984 | $1.50 Sydney Harbour Bridge, New South Wales | 2·00 | 75 |
| 1985 | $2 Cradle Mountain, Tasmania | 2·25 | 75 |
| 1986 | $3 The Pinnacles, Western Australia | 2·50 | 1·25 |
| 1987 | $4.50 Flinders Ranges, South Australia (51×24 mm) | 3·75 | 2·25 |
| 1988 | $5 Twelve Apostles, Victoria (51×24 mm) | 4·00 | 2·25 |
| 1989 | $10 Devils Marbles, Northern Territory (51×24 mm) | 8·25 | 4·50 |

Nos. 1982/9 were intended for international postage which, under changes in Australian tax laws from 1 July 2000, remained exempt from General Sales Tax.

From 1 February 2001 only international stamps were valid on overseas mail and from that date could not be used on items posted to Australian addresses.

See also Nos. 2151/5 and 2195/9.

**626** Tennis Player in Wheelchair

**2000.** Paralympic Games, Sydney (1st issue). Multicoloured. Ordinary or self-adhesive gum.

| | | | |
|---|---|---|---|
| 1990 | 45c. Type **626** | 50 | 50 |
| 1991 | 45c. Amputee sprinting | 50 | 50 |
| 1992 | 49c. Basketball player in wheelchair | 50 | 50 |
| 1993 | 49c. Blind cyclist | 50 | 50 |
| 1994 | 49c. Amputee putting the shot | 50 | 50 |

See also Nos. 2053/4.

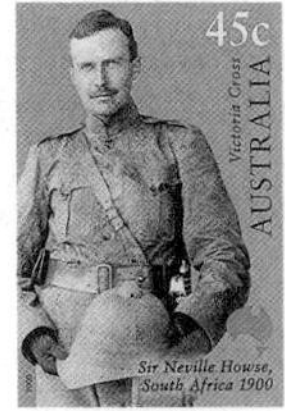


**627** Sir Neville Howse (first Australian recipient of Victoria Cross, 1900)

**2000.** Cent of Australia's First Victoria Cross Award.

| | | | | |
|---|---|---|---|---|
| 2000 | **627** | 45c. multicoloured | 70 | 50 |
| 2001 | - | 45c. brown, gold and black | 70 | 50 |
| 2002 | - | 45c. multicoloured | 70 | 50 |
| 2003 | - | 45c. multicoloured | 70 | 50 |
| 2004 | - | 45c. brown, gold and black | 70 | 50 |

DESIGNS: No. 2001, Sir Roden Cutler, 1941; 2002, Victoria Cross; 2003, Private Edward Kenna, 1945; 2004, Warrant Officer Keith Payne, 1969.

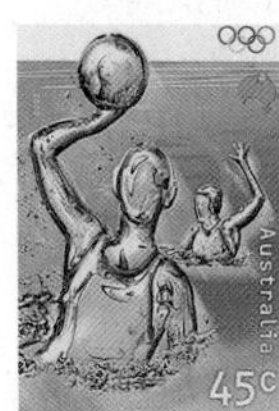


**628** Water Polo

**2000.** Olympic Games, Sydney (2nd issue). Multicoloured. Ordinary or self-adhesive gum. Competitors highlighted in varnish.

| | | | |
|---|---|---|---|
| 2005 | 45c. Type **628** | 40 | 50 |
| 2006 | 45c. Hockey | 40 | 50 |
| 2007 | 45c. Swimming | 40 | 50 |
| 2008 | 45c. Basketball | 40 | 50 |
| 2009 | 45c. Cycling (triathlon) | 40 | 50 |
| 2010 | 45c. Horse riding | 40 | 50 |
| 2011 | 45c. Tennis | 40 | 50 |
| 2012 | 45c. Gymnastics | 40 | 50 |
| 2013 | 45c. Running | 40 | 50 |
| 2014 | 45c. Rowing | 40 | 50 |

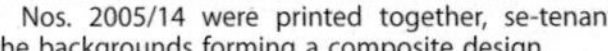

Nos. 2005/14 were printed together, se-tenant, with the backgrounds forming a composite design.

**629** Olympic Flag, Flame and Parthenon

**2000.** Transfer of Olympic Flag from Sydney to Athens. Joint issue with Greece. Multicoloured.

| | | | |
|---|---|---|---|
| 2025 | 45c. Type **629** | 50 | 40 |
| 2026 | $1.50 Olympic Flag, Flame and Sydney Opera House | 1·50 | 1·50 |

Stamps in similar designs were issued by Greece.

**630** Ian Thorpe (Men's 400m Freestyle Swimming)

**2000.** Australian Gold Medal Winners at Sydney Olympic Games. Multicoloured.

| | | | |
|---|---|---|---|
| 2027A | 45c. Type **630** | 40 | 45 |
| 2028A | 45c. Australian team (Men's 4×100 m Freestyle Swimming Relay) | 40 | 45 |
| 2029A | 45c. Michael Diamond (Men's Trap Shooting) | 40 | 45 |
| 2030A | 45c. Australian team (Three Day Equestrian Event) | 40 | 45 |
| 2031A | 45c. Susie O'Neill (Women's 200 m Freestyle Swimming) | 40 | 45 |
| 2032A | 45c. Australian team (Men's 4×200 m Freestyle Swimming Relay) | 40 | 45 |
| 2033A | 45c. Simon Fairweather (Men's Individual Archery) | 40 | 45 |
| 2034A | 45c. Australian team (Men's Madison Cycling) | 40 | 45 |
| 2035A | 45c. Grant Hackett (Men's 1500 m Freestyle Swimming) | 40 | 45 |
| 2036A | 45c. Australian team (Women's Water Polo) | 40 | 45 |
| 2037A | 45c. Australian team (Women's Beach Volleyball) | 40 | 45 |
| 2038A | 45c. Cathy Freeman (Women's 400 m Athletics) | 40 | 45 |
| 2039A | 45c. Lauren Burns (Women's under 49 kg Taekwondo) | 40 | 45 |
| 2040A | 45c. Australian team (Women's Hockey) | 40 | 45 |
| 2041A | 45c. Australian crew (Women's 470 Dinghy Sailing) | 40 | 45 |
| 2042A | 45c. Australian crew (Men's 470 Dinghy Sailing) | 40 | 45 |

**631** Martian Terrain

**2000.** Stamp Collecting Month. Exploration of Mars. Multicoloured. (a) Ordinary gum.

| | | | |
|---|---|---|---|
| 2043 | 45c. Type **631** | 45 | 45 |
| 2044 | 45c. Astronaut using thruster | 45 | 45 |
| 2045 | 45c. Spacecraft (50×30 mm) | 45 | 45 |
| 2046 | 45c. Flight crew (30×25 mm) | 45 | 45 |
| 2047 | 45c. Launch site (30×50 mm) | 45 | 45 |
| 2048 | 45c. Robots on kelp rod (25×30 mm) | 45 | 45 |
| **MS**2049 | 166×73 mm. Nos. 2043/8 | 2·50 | 2·50 |

(b) Self-adhesive. Designs 21×32 mm.

| | | | |
|---|---|---|---|
| 2050 | 45c. Type **631** | 45 | 45 |
| 2051 | 45c. Astronaut using thruster | 45 | 45 |

**632** Cathy Freeman with Olympic Torch and Ring of Flames

**2000.** Opening Ceremony, Olympic Games, Sydney.

| | | | | |
|---|---|---|---|---|
| 2052 | **632** | 45c. multicoloured | 1·00 | 50 |

**633** Blind Athlete carrying Olympic Torch

**2000.** Paralympic Games, Sydney (2nd issue). Multicoloured.

| | | | |
|---|---|---|---|
| 2053 | 45c. Type **633** | 55 | 50 |
| 2054 | 45c. Paralympic Games logo | 55 | 50 |

**634** Siobhan Paton (swimmer)

**2000.** Siobhan Paton, Paralympian of the Year.

| | | | | |
|---|---|---|---|---|
| 2055 | **634** | 45c. multicoloured | 1·00 | 60 |

**635** "Sleep in Heavenly Peace"

**2000.** Christmas. "Silent Night" (carol). Multicoloured. (a) Ordinary gum.

| | | | |
|---|---|---|---|
| 2056 | 40c. Type **635** | 50 | 25 |
| 2057 | 45c. "All is Calm, All is Bright" | 50 | 25 |
| **MS**2058 | 165×75 mm. Nos. 2056/7 | 1·00 | 1·00 |

(b) Self-adhesive.

| | | | |
|---|---|---|---|
| 2059 | 40c. Type **635** | 45 | 35 |

(c) International Mail. As T 625 inscr "Season's Greetings".

| | | | |
|---|---|---|---|
| 2060 | 80c. Byron Bay, New South Wales | 70 | 85 |

**2001.** International Mail. No. 1901 optd International POST.

| | | | |
|---|---|---|---|
| 2061 | $1 Koala | 2·00 | 1·25 |

**637** Parade passing Federation Arch, Sydney

**2001.** Centenary of Federation. Multicoloured. (a) Ordinary gum.

| | | | |
|---|---|---|---|
| 2062 | 49c. Type **637** | 65 | 55 |
| 2063 | 49c. Edmund Barton (first Federal Prime Minister) | 65 | 55 |
| 2064 | $2 "Australia For Ever" (song sheet) and celebration picnic (50×30 mm) | 2·40 | 2·10 |
| 2065 | $2 State Banquet, Sydney (30×50 mm) | 2·40 | 2·10 |
| **MS**2066 | 166×73 mm. Nos. 2062/5 | 4·75 | 5·00 |

(b) Self-adhesive.

| | | | |
|---|---|---|---|
| 2067 | 49c. Type **637** | 60 | 60 |
| 2068 | 49c. Edmund Barton (first Federal Prime Minister) | 60 | 60 |

**638** Slim Dusty with Guitar in 1940s

**2001.** Australian Legends (5th series). Slim Dusty (country music singer). Multicoloured. Ordinary or self-adhesive gum.

| | | | |
|---|---|---|---|
| 2069 | 45c. Type **638** | 50 | 50 |
| 2070 | 45c. Slim Dusty wearing "Sundowner" hat | 50 | 50 |

**639** Light Horse Parade, 1940, and Command Post, New Guinea, 1943

**2001.** Centenary of Australian Army. Multicoloured.

| | | | |
|---|---|---|---|
| 2073 | 45c. Type **639** | 1·00 | 65 |
| 2074 | 45c. Soldier carrying Rwandan child and officers on the Commando Selection Course | 1·00 | 65 |

**640** Entry Canopy, Skylights and Site Plan

**2001.** Opening of the National Museum, Canberra. Multicoloured.

| | | | |
|---|---|---|---|
| 2075 | 49c. Type **640** | 50 | 50 |
| 2076 | 49c. Skylights and "Pangk" (wallaby sculpture) | 50 | 50 |

**2001.** Sir Donald Bradman (cricketer) Commemoration. Nos. 1663/4 additionally inscribed "1908–2001" in red. Multicoloured.

| | | | |
|---|---|---|---|
| 2077 | 45c. Type **568** | 50 | 50 |
| 2078 | 45c. Bradman playing stroke | 50 | 50 |

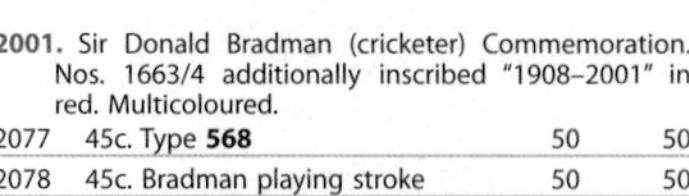

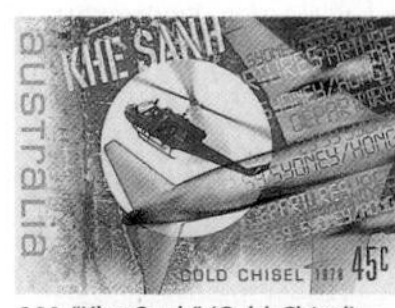


**641** "Khe Sanh" (Cold Chisel), 1978

**2001.** Australian Rock and Pop Music. Multicoloured. Ordinary or self-adhesive gum.

| | | | |
|---|---|---|---|
| 2089 | 45c. Type **641** | 45 | 60 |
| 2090 | 45c. "Down Under" (Men at Work), 1981 | 45 | 60 |
| 2091 | 45c. "Power and the Passion" (Midnight Oil), 1983 | 45 | 60 |
| 2092 | 45c. "Original Sin" (INXS), 1984 | 45 | 60 |
| 2093 | 45c. "You're the Voice" (John Farnham), 1986 | 45 | 60 |
| 2094 | 45c. "Don't Dream it's Over" (Crowded House), 1986 | 45 | 60 |
| 2095 | 45c. "Treaty" (Yothu Yindi), 1991 | 45 | 60 |
| 2096 | 45c. "Tomorrow" (Silverchair), 1994 | 45 | 60 |
| 2097 | 45c. "Confide in Me" (Kylie Minogue), 1994 | 45 | 60 |
| 2098 | 45c. "Truly, Madly, Deeply" (Savage Garden), 1997 | 45 | 60 |

**642** Queen Elizabeth II holding Bouquet

**2001.** Queen Elizabeth II's Birthday.

| | | | | |
|---|---|---|---|---|
| 2099 | **642** | 45c. multicoloured | 1·50 | 65 |

**643** Party Balloons

**2001.** "Colour My Day". Greetings Stamps. (a) Domestic Mail.

| | | | |
|---|---|---|---|
| 2100 | 45c. Type **643** | 30 | 35 |
| 2101 | 45c. Smiling Flower | 30 | 35 |
| 2102 | 45c. Hologram and party streamers | 30 | 35 |

(b) International Mail.

| | | | |
|---|---|---|---|
| 2103 | $1 Kangaroo and joey | 1·00 | 80 |
| 2104 | $1.50 The Bayulu Banner | 1·40 | 1·75 |

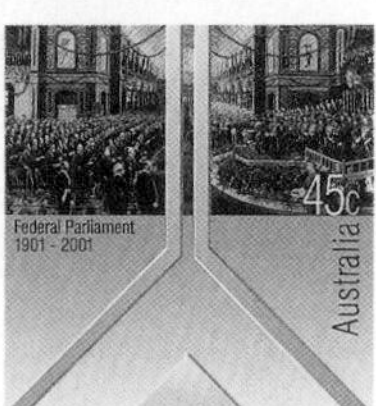


**644** "Opening of the First Federal Parliament" (Charles Nuttall)

**2001.** Centenary of Federal Parliament. Paintings. Multicoloured.

2105 45c. Type **644** 50 40
2106 $2.45 "Prince George opening the First Parliament of the Commonwealth of Australia" (Tom Roberts) 2·25 2·50
**MS**2107 Two sheets, each 166×75 mm. (a) No. 2105. (b) No. 2106 Set of 2 sheets 2·75 3·00

**645** Telecommunications Tower

**2001.** Outback Services. Multicoloured. Ordinary or self-adhesive gum.

2108 45c. Type **645** 90 75
2109 45c. Road train 90 75
2110 45c. School of the Air pupil 90 75
2111 45c. Outback family and mail box 90 75
2112 45c. Royal Flying Doctor Service aircraft and ambulance 90 75

**646** Dragon Boat and Hong Kong Convention and Exhibition Centre

**2001.** Joint Issue with Hong Kong. Dragon Boat Racing. Multicoloured. (a) Domestic Mail.

2118 45c. Type **646** 50 45

(b) International Mail.

2119 $1 Dragon boat and Sydney Opera House 1·00 1·00
**MS**2120 115×70 mm. Nos. 2118/19 1·40 1·40

**2001.** International Stamps. Views of Australia (2nd series). As T 625. Multicoloured.

2121 50c. The Three Sisters, Blue Mountains, New South Wales 1·00 40
2122 $1 The Murrumbidgee River, Australian Capital Territory 1·50 40
2123 $1.50 Four Mile Beach, Port Douglas, Queensland 2·25 1·00
2124 $20 Uluru Rock at dusk, Northern Territory (52×24 mm) 21·00 16·00

**647** Variegated Wren ("Variegated Fairy-Wren")

**2001.** Fauna and Flora (4th series). Desert Birds. Multicoloured. Ordinary or self-adhesive gum.

2130 45c. Type **647** 50 50
2131 45c. Painted finch ("Painted Firetail") 50 50
2132 45c. Crimson chat 50 50
2133 45c. Budgerigar 50 50

**648** Daniel Solander (Swedish botanist) and Mango Tree

**2001.** Australia–Sweden Joint Issue. Daniel Solander's Voyage with Captain Cook. Multicoloured. (a) Domestic Mail.

2134 45c. Type **648** 75 50

(b) International Mail.

2135 $1.50 H.M.S. *Endeavour* on reef and Kapok tree 2·25 2·50

**649** Christmas Tree

**2001.** Christmas (1st issue). Multicoloured. (a) Domestic Mail.

2136 40c. Type **649** 40 35

(b) International Mail.

2137 80c. Star 1·00 1·00

See also Nos. 2157/8.

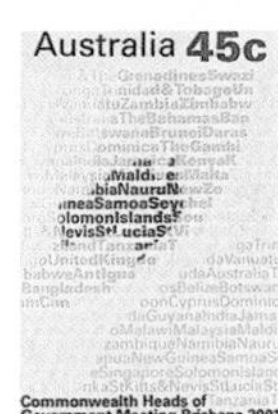


**650** Australia on Globe

**2001.** Commonwealth Heads of Government Meeting (No. 2138) and Commonwealth Parliamentary Conference (No. 2139). Mult.

2138 45c. Type **650** 50 50
2139 45c. Southern Cross 50 50

**651** Wedge-tailed Eagle

**2001.** Centenary of Birds of Australia. Birds of Prey. Multicoloured.

2140 49c. Type **651** 75 75
2141 49c. Australian kestrel ("Nankeen Kestrel") 75 75
2142 98c. Red goshawk (vert) 1·50 2·00
2143 98c. Spotted harrier (vert) 1·50 2·00

**652** Cockatoos dancing to Animal Band

**2001.** National Stamp Collecting Month. "Wild Babies" (cartoons). Multicoloured. Ordinary or self-adhesive gum.

2144 45c. Type **652** 55 45
2145 45c. Kevin Koala with birthday cake 55 45
2146 45c. Ring-tailed possums eating 55 45
2147 45c. Bilbies at foot of tree 55 45
2148 45c. James Wombat on rope ladder 55 45
2149 45c. Wallaby, echidna and platypus on rope ladder 55 45
**MS**2150 Two sheets, each 175×75 mm. (a) Nos. 2144/6. (b) 2147/9. Ordinary gum 2·50 2·50

**653** "Adoration of the Magi"

**2001.** Christmas (2nd issue). Miniatures from "Wharncliffe Hours Manuscript". Multicoloured.

2157 40c. Type **653** 1·10 30
2158 45c. "Flight into Egypt" 1·10 35

No. 2157 also comes self-adhesive.

**654** Sir Gustav Nossal (immunologist)

**2002.** Australian Legends. (6th series). Medical Scientists. Ordinary or self-adhesive gum. Multicoloured.

2165 45c. Type **654** 40 55
2166 45c. Nancy Millis (microbiologist) 40 55
2167 45c. Peter Doherty (immunologist) 40 55
2168 45c. Fiona Stanley (epidemiologist) 40 55
2169 45c. Donald Metcalf (haematologist) 40 55

**655** Queen Elizabeth in 1953

**2002.** Golden Jubilee. Multicoloured.

2170 45c. Type **655** 50 35
2171 $2.45 Queen Elizabeth in Italy, 2000 2·25 3·50
**MS**2172 160×77 mm. Nos. 2170/1 3·00 3·50

**656** Steven Bradbury (Men's 1000m Short Track Speed Skating)

**2002.** Australian Gold Medal Winners at Salt Lake City Winter Olympic Games. Multicoloured.

2173 45c. Type **656** 95 60
2174 45c. Alisa Camplin (Women's Aerials Freestyle Skiing) 95 60

**657** Austin 7 and Bugatti Type 40, Australian Grand Prix, Phillip Island, 1928

**2002.** Centenary of Motor Racing in Australia and New Zealand. Ordinary or self-adhesive gum. Multicoloured.

2175 45c. Type **657** 80 85
2176 45c. Jaguar Mark II, Australian Touring Car Championship, Mallala, 1963 80 85
2177 45c. Repco-Brabham, Tasman Series, Sandown, 1966 80 85
2178 45c. Holden Torana and Ford Falcon, Hardie-Ferodo 500, Bathurst, 1972 80 85
2179 45c. William's Ford, Australian Grand Prix, Calder, 1980 80 85
2180 45c. Benetton-Renault, Australian Grand Prix, Albert Park, 2001 80 85

**658** Macquarie Lighthouse

**2002.** Lighthouses. Multicoloured.

2187 45c. Type **658** 75 35
2188 49c. Cape Naturaliste 90 80
2189 49c. Troubridge Island 90 80
2190 $1.50 Cape Bruny 2·25 2·25

Nos. 2188/9 also come self-adhesive.

**659** Nicolas Baudin, Kangaroo, *Geographe* (ship) and Map

**2002.** Australia—France Joint Issue. Bicentenary of Flinders—Baudin Meeting at Encounter Bay. Multicoloured. (a) Domestic Mail.

2193 45c. Type **659** 50 40

(b) International Mail.

2194 $1.50 Matthew Flinders, Port Lincoln Parrot, *Investigator* (ship) and Map 1·75 1·75

**2002.** International Stamps. Views of Australia (3rd series). As T 625. Multicoloured.

2195 50c. Walker Flat, River Murray, South Australia 65 40
2196 $1 Mt. Roland, Tasmania 1·25 60
2197 $1.50 Cape Leveque, Western Australia 1·60 1·25

Nos. 2195/6 also come self-adhesive.

**660** Desert Star Flower

**2002.** Fauna and Flora (5th series). Great Sandy Desert. Multicoloured.

2200 50c. Type **660** 40 35
2201 $1 Bilby 80 65
2202 $1.50 Thorny Devil 1·20 1·60
2203 $2 Great Sandy Desert landscape (50×30 mm) 1·60 1·90

No. 2200 also comes self-adhesive.

**661** "Ghost Gum, Mt Sonder" (Albert Namatjira)

**2002.** Birth Centenary of Albert Namatjira (artist). Multicoloured. Nos. 2204/7, ordinary or self-adhesive gum.

**MS**2208 133×70 mm. Nos. 2204/7 1·75 1·75
2209 45c. Type **661** 40 55
2210 45c. "Mt Hermannsburg" 40 55
2211 45c. "Glen Helen Country" 40 55
2212 45c. "Simpsons Gap" 40 55

**662** *Nelumbo nucifera*

**2002.** Australia–Thailand Joint Issue. 50th Anniv of Diplomatic Relations. Water Lilies. Multicoloured. (a) Domestic Mail.

2213 45c. Type **662** 60 35

(b) International Mail.

2214 $1 *Nymphaea immutabilis* 1·40 75
**MS**2215 107×70 mm. Nos. 2214/15 1·75 1·75

**663** Star, Presents and Baubles

**2002.** International Greetings. Multicoloured.

2216 90c. Type **663** 85 80
2217 $1.10 Koala 1·00 95
2218 $1.65 "Puja" (painting by Ngarralja Tommy May) 1·50 1·40

**2002.** International Stamps. Views of Australia (4th series). As T 625. Multicoloured.

2219 $1.10 Coonawarra, South Australia 1·60 70
2220 $1.65 Gariwerd (Grampians), Victoria 2·25 1·40
2221 $2.20 National Library, Canberra 2·50 2·25
2222 $3.30 Cape York, Queensland 3·75 3·75

**664** Lilly-pilly

**2002.** "Bush Tucker". Edible Plants from the Outback. Multicoloured. Ordinary or self-adhesive gum.

| | | | |
|---|---|---|---|
| 2228 | 49c. Type **664** | 55 | 55 |
| 2229 | 49c. Honey Grevillea | 55 | 55 |
| 2230 | 49c. Quandong | 55 | 55 |
| 2231 | 49c. Acacia seeds | 55 | 55 |
| 2232 | 49c. Murnong | 55 | 55 |

**665** Bunyip

**2002.** Stamp Collecting Month. The Magic Rainforest, (book by John Marsden). Multicoloured. Nos. 2233/8, ordinary or self-adhesive gum.

| | | | |
|---|---|---|---|
| 2233 | 45c. Type **665** | 50 | 50 |
| 2234 | 45c. Fairy on branch | 50 | 50 |
| 2235 | 45c. Gnome with sword | 50 | 50 |
| 2236 | 45c. Goblin with stock whip | 50 | 50 |
| 2237 | 45c. Wizard | 50 | 50 |
| 2238 | 45c. Sprite | 50 | 50 |
| **MS**2239 | 170×90 mm. Nos. 2234/9 | 3·00 | 3·00 |

**666** "Wakeful"

**2002.** Champion Racehorses. Multicoloured.

| | | | |
|---|---|---|---|
| 2246 | 45c. Type **666** | 1·10 | 1·10 |
| 2247 | 45c. "Rising Fast" | 1·10 | 1·10 |
| 2248 | 45c. "Manikato" | 1·10 | 1·10 |
| 2249 | 45c. "Might and Power" | 1·10 | 1·10 |
| 2250 | 45c. "Sunline" | 1·10 | 1·10 |

**667** Nativity

**2002.** Christmas. Multicoloured.

| | | | |
|---|---|---|---|
| 2251 | 40c. Type **667** | 75 | 35 |
| 2252 | 45c. The Three Wise Men | 75 | 35 |

No. 2251 also comes self-adhesive.

**668** Two Daisies

**2003.** Greetings Stamps. Some adapted from previous issues. Multicoloured.

| | | | |
|---|---|---|---|
| 2254 | 50c. Type **668** | 40 | 45 |
| 2255 | 50c. Wedding rings and yellow roses | 40 | 45 |
| 2256 | 50c. Hearts and pink roses | 40 | 45 |
| 2257 | 50c. Birthday cake and present | 40 | 45 |
| 2258 | 50c. Seated teddy bear | 40 | 45 |
| 2259 | 50c. Balloons | 40 | 45 |
| 2260 | 50c. Red kangaroo and flag | 40 | 45 |
| 2261 | 50c. Australia on globe | 40 | 45 |
| 2262 | 50c. Sports car | 40 | 45 |
| 2263 | $1 Wedding rings and pink rose | 80 | 85 |

**669** Margaret Court with Wimbledon Trophy

**2003.** Australian Legends (7th series). Tennis Players. Ordinary or self-adhesive gum. Multicoloured.

| | | | |
|---|---|---|---|
| 2264 | 50c. Type **669** | 65 | 50 |
| 2265 | 50c. Margaret Court in action | 65 | 50 |
| 2266 | 50c. Rod Laver with Wimbledon Trophy | 65 | 50 |
| 2267 | 50c. Rod Laver in action | 65 | 50 |

**670** Blue Orchid

**2003.** Fauna and Flora (6th series). Rainforest, Daintree National Park. Multicoloured. Ordinary or self-adhesive gum.

| | | | |
|---|---|---|---|
| 2272 | 50c. Orange-thighed tree frog | 70 | 60 |
| 2273 | 50c. Green-spotted triangle (butterfly) | 70 | 60 |
| 2274 | 50c. Striped possum | 70 | 60 |
| 2275 | 50c. Yellow-bellied sunbird | 70 | 60 |
| 2276 | $1.45 Type **670** | 1·50 | 1·25 |

**671** Snapper and Fishing from Beach

**2003.** Angling in Australia. Multicoloured.

| | | | |
|---|---|---|---|
| 2282 | 50c. Type **671** | 60 | 60 |
| 2283 | 50c. Murray cod and flooded wood | 60 | 60 |
| 2284 | 50c. Brown trout and fly-fishing | 60 | 60 |
| 2285 | 50c. Yellow-finned tuna and sea-fishing from launch | 60 | 60 |
| 2286 | 50c. Barramundi and anglers in mangrove swamp | 60 | 60 |

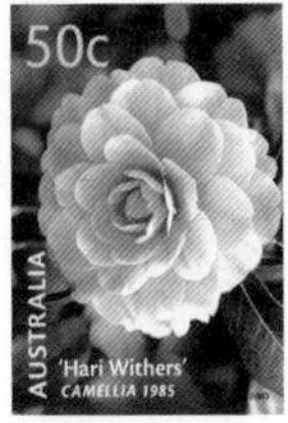


**672** "Hari Withers" Camellia

**2003.** Australian Horticulture. Multicoloured. (a) Size 25×36 mm. Ordinary gum.

| | | | |
|---|---|---|---|
| 2287 | 50c. Type **672** | 55 | 50 |
| 2288 | 50c. "Victoria Gold" rose | 55 | 50 |
| 2289 | 50c. "Superb" grevillea | 55 | 50 |
| 2290 | 50c. "Bush Tango" kangaroo paw | 55 | 50 |
| 2291 | 50c. "Midnight" rhododendron | 55 | 50 |

(b) Size 21×33 mm. Self-adhesive.

| | | | |
|---|---|---|---|
| 2292 | 50c. Type **672** | 50 | 60 |
| 2293 | 50c. "Victoria Gold" rose | 50 | 60 |
| 2294 | 50c. "Superb" grevillea | 50 | 60 |
| 2295 | 50c. "Bush Tango" kangaroo paw | 50 | 60 |
| 2296 | 50c. "Midnight" rhododendron | 50 | 60 |

**673** "Ned Kelly" (Sir Sidney Nolan)

**2003.** Australian Paintings (1st series). Multicoloured.

| | | | |
|---|---|---|---|
| 2297 | $1 Type **673** | 1·25 | 1·40 |
| 2298 | $1 "Family Home, Suburban Exterior" (Howard Arkley) | 1·25 | 1·40 |
| 2299 | $1.45 "Cord Long Drawn, Expectant" (Robert Jacks) | 1·75 | 1·90 |
| 2300 | $2.45 "Girl" (Joy Hester) | 2·50 | 3·25 |

**674** Queen Elizabeth II, 1953 (photograph by Cecil Beaton)

**2003.** 50th Anniv of Coronation. Multicoloured.

| | | | |
|---|---|---|---|
| 2301 | 50c. Type **674** | 75 | 45 |
| 2302 | $2.45 St. Edward's Crown | 2·50 | 3·50 |
| **MS**2303 | 105×70 mm. Nos. 2301/2 | 3·25 | 4·00 |

No. 2301 also comes self-adhesive.

**675** Untitled Painting by Ningura Napurrula

**2003.** International Stamps. Art of Papunya Tula Movement. Showing untitled paintings by Aboriginal artists. Multicoloured.

| | | | |
|---|---|---|---|
| 2305 | $1.10 Type **675** | 1·50 | 70 |
| 2306 | $1.65 Naata Nungurrayi | 2·25 | 1·40 |
| 2307 | $2.20 Graham Tjupurrula (55×24 mm) | 2·50 | 2·00 |
| 2308 | $3.30 Dini Campbell Tjampitjinpa (55×24 mm) | 3·75 | 3·50 |

**676** Kangaroo Chromosomes

**2003.** 50th Anniv of Discovery of DNA. Multicoloured.

| | | | |
|---|---|---|---|
| 2309 | 50c. Type **676** | 80 | 80 |
| 2310 | 50c. DNA double helix | 80 | 80 |

**677** *Oscar W* (paddle-steamer)

**2003.** 150th Anniv of Murray River Shipping. Multicoloured. Ordinary or self-adhesive gum.

| | | | |
|---|---|---|---|
| 2311 | 50c. Type **677** | 65 | 55 |
| 2312 | 50c. *Marion* (paddle-steamer) | 65 | 55 |
| 2313 | 50c. *Ruby* (paddle-steamer) | 65 | 55 |
| 2314 | 50c. *Pyap* (cruise vessel) | 65 | 55 |
| 2315 | 50c. *Adelaide* (paddle-steamer) | 65 | 55 |

**678** Christmas Tree

**2003.** Greetings Stamps. Peace and Goodwill. Design, adapted from Christmas 2001 (1st issue) (Nos. 2136/7). Multicoloured. (a) Domestic Mail.

| | | | |
|---|---|---|---|
| 2321 | 50c. Type **678** | 40 | 45 |

(b) International Mail.

| | | | |
|---|---|---|---|
| 2322 | 90c. Star | 75 | 80 |

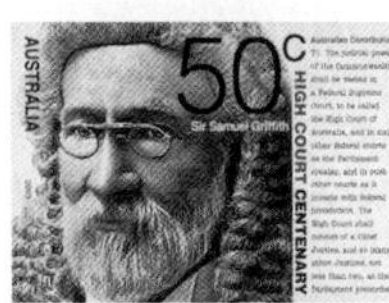


**679** Sir Samuel Griffith (first Chief Justice)

**2003.** Centenary of High Court of Australia.

| | | | | |
|---|---|---|---|---|
| 2323 | **679** | 50c. purple, black and red | 55 | 45 |
| 2324 | - | $1.45 vermilion, red and black | 1·50 | 1·50 |
| **MS**2325 | | 105×70 mm. Nos. 2323/4 | 2·50 | 2·25 |

DESIGN: $1.45, "JUSTICE".

**680** Ulysses Butterfly

**2003.** Stamp Collecting Month. Bugs and Butterflies. Multicoloured. Ordinary or self-adhesive gum.

| | | | |
|---|---|---|---|
| 2326 | 50c. Type **680** | 50 | 45 |
| 2327 | 50c. Leichhardt's grasshopper | 50 | 45 |
| 2328 | 50c. Vedalia ladybird | 50 | 45 |
| 2329 | 50c. Green mantid and captured damselfly | 50 | 45 |
| 2330 | 50c. Emperor gum moth caterpillar | 50 | 45 |
| 2331 | 50c. Fiddler beetle | 50 | 45 |
| **MS**2332 | 170×85 mm. Nos. 2326/31 | 3·00 | 3·00 |

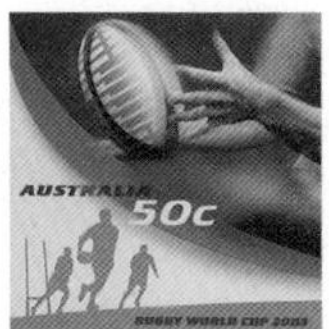


**681** Hands passing Ball and Players

**2003.** Rugby World Cup Championship, Australia. Multicoloured. (a) Domestic Mail.

| | | | |
|---|---|---|---|
| 2339 | 50c. Type **681** | 55 | 45 |

(b) International Mail.

| | | | |
|---|---|---|---|
| 2340 | $1.10 Trophy (Webb Ellis Cup) and Telstra Stadium | 1·10 | 1·00 |
| 2341 | $1.65 Hand grasping ball and player taking shot at goal | 1·50 | 2·00 |
| **MS**2342 | 115×70 mm. Nos. 2339/41 | 2·75 | 3·00 |

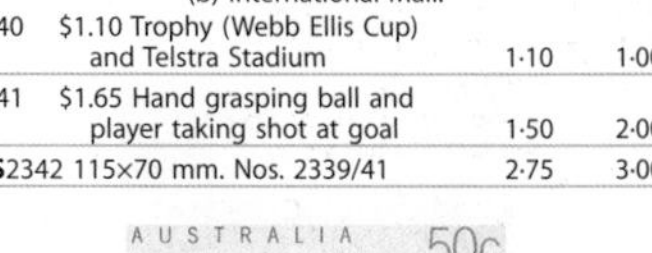

**682** "Active with ASTHMA" and Silhouettes of Sportspeople

**2003.** National Asthma Week Campaign.

| | | | | |
|---|---|---|---|---|
| 2343 | **682** | 50c. multicoloured | 1·00 | 45 |

**683** Mary, Baby Jesus and Angels

**2003.** Christmas. Multicoloured.

| | | | |
|---|---|---|---|
| 2344 | 45c. Type **683** | 45 | 15 |
| 2345 | 50c. Three Wise Men | 45 | 15 |
| 2346 | 90c. Angel appearing to shepherds | 80 | 90 |

No. 2344 also comes self-adhesive.

**684** Joan Sutherland as *Lucia di Lammermoor*, 1980

**2004.** Australian Legends (8th series). Dame Joan Sutherland (opera singer). Multicoloured. Ordinary or self-adhesive gum.

| | | | |
|---|---|---|---|
| 2350 | 50c. Type **684** | 80 | 80 |
| 2351 | 50c. Joan Sutherland | 80 | 80 |

**685** Aboriginal shell necklace and bracelet

**2004.** Bicentenary of Settlement of Hobart, Tasmania. Multicoloured.

| | | | |
|---|---|---|---|
| 2352 | 50c. Type **685** | 85 | 70 |
| 2353 | 50c. Cheshunt House, Deloraine | 85 | 70 |
| 2354 | $1 "Mount Wellington and Hobart Town from Kangaroo Point" (John Glover) | 1·75 | 1·75 |

| | | | |
|---|---|---|---|
| 2355 | $1 Mountains, south west Tasmania | 1·75 | 1·75 |
| **MS**2356 | 135×72 mm. Nos. 2352/5 | 4·25 | 4·25 |

**686** Ross Bridge, Tasmania, 1836

**2004.** Landmark Bridges. Multicoloured. Ordinary or self-adhesive gum.

| | | | |
|---|---|---|---|
| 2357 | 50c. Type **686** | 90 | 70 |
| 2358 | 50c. Lockyer Creek Bridge, Queensland, 1911 | 90 | 70 |
| 2359 | 50c. Sydney Harbour Bridge, 1932 | 90 | 70 |
| 2360 | 50c. Birkenhead Bridge, Adelaide, 1940 | 90 | 70 |
| 2361 | 50c. Bolte Bridge, Melbourne, 1999 | 90 | 70 |

**687** Stylized "Southern Cross"

**2004.** Greetings Stamp.

| | | | | |
|---|---|---|---|---|
| 2367 | **687** | 50c. multicoloured | 70 | 55 |

**688** Solar Systems CS500 Dish ("solar")

**2004.** Renewable Energy. Multicoloured. Ordinary or self-adhesive gum.

| | | | |
|---|---|---|---|
| 2368 | 50c. Type **688** | 85 | 85 |
| 2369 | 50c. Wind turbines ("wind") | 85 | 85 |
| 2370 | 50c. Snowy Mountains Hydro-electric Scheme ("hydro") | 85 | 85 |
| 2371 | 50c. Sugar cane field, bagasse (waste plant fibre) and sugar mill ("biomass") | 85 | 85 |

**689** Queen Elizabeth II (from photo by Dorothy Wilding)

**2004.** 50th Anniv of Royal Tour to Australia.

| | | | | |
|---|---|---|---|---|
| 2376 | **689** | 50c. purple, black and grey | 1·25 | 55 |

**690** Red Lacewing

**2004.** Fauna and Flora (7th series). Rainforest Butterflies. Multicoloured.

| | | | |
|---|---|---|---|
| 2377 | 5c. Type **690** | 15 | 15 |
| 2378 | 10c. Blue-banded eggfly | 15 | 15 |
| 2379 | 75c. Cruiser | 1·00 | 50 |
| 2380 | $2 Ulysses and red lacewing butterflies and Daintree Rain-forest (50×30 mm) | 3·00 | 2·50 |

**691** Cockatoos and Aircraft

**2004.** Australian Innovations. Multicoloured. Ordinary or self-adhesive gum.

| | | | |
|---|---|---|---|
| 2381 | 50c. Type **691** (black box flight recorder, 1961) | 1·00 | 90 |
| 2382 | 50c. Pregnant woman (ultra-sound imaging equipment, 1976) | 1·00 | 90 |
| 2383 | 50c. Driver's hands on wheel (Racecam TV sport coverage, 1979) | 1·00 | 90 |
| 2384 | 50c. Kangaroo with joey and car (baby safety capsule, 1984) | 1·00 | 90 |
| 2385 | 50c. Portion of banknote and tree (polymer banknotes, 1988) | 1·00 | 90 |

**692** Shaw Savill Lines *Dominion Monarch*

**2004.** "Bon Voyage". Ocean Liners. Advertising posters. Multicoloured.

| | | | |
|---|---|---|---|
| 2391 | 50c. Type **692** | 90 | 45 |
| 2392 | $1 Union Steam Ship Co. *Awatea* | 1·50 | 85 |
| 2393 | $1.45 Orient Line *Ormonde* & *Orsova* | 2·00 | 2·00 |
| 2394 | $2 Aberdeen & Commonwealth Line liner passing under bridge | 2·75 | 2·75 |

No. 2395 also comes self-adhesive.

**693** Eureka Flag (Southern Cross)

**2004.** 150th Anniv of Eureka Stockade. Multicoloured.

| | | | |
|---|---|---|---|
| 2396 | 50c. Type **693** | 60 | 45 |
| 2397 | $2.45 Peter Lalor (gold diggers leader) and detail from "Swearing allegiance to the Southern Cross 1854" (Alphonse Doudiet) | 2·75 | 3·00 |
| **MS**2398 | 106×69 mm. Nos. 2396/7 | 3·25 | 3·25 |

**694** Koala

**2004.** "Impressions". Australian Wildlife and Heritage. Multicoloured.

| | | | |
|---|---|---|---|
| 2399 | $1 Type **694** | 1·50 | 1·50 |
| 2400 | $1 Little penguin | 1·50 | 1·50 |
| 2401 | $1.45 Clown anemonefish (horiz) | 1·75 | 1·75 |
| 2402 | $2.45 Gold Coast (horiz) | 2·75 | 3·25 |

**695** Swimming

**2004.** Olympic Games, Athens, Greece. Multicoloured.

| | | | |
|---|---|---|---|
| 2403 | 50c. Type **695** | 60 | 45 |
| 2404 | $1.65 Sprinting | 1·90 | 1·90 |
| 2405 | $1.65 Cycling | 2·75 | 1·90 |

**696** Ian Thorpe (Men's 400m Freestyle Swimming)

**2004.** Australian Gold Medal Winners at Olympic Games, Athens. Multicoloured.

| | | | |
|---|---|---|---|
| 2406 | 50c. Type **696** | 80 | 70 |
| 2407 | 50c. Women's 4×100m relay team | 80 | 70 |
| 2408 | 50c. Sara Carrigan (Road Race Cycling) | 80 | 70 |
| 2409 | 50c. Petria Thomas (Women's 100m Butterfly Swimming) | 80 | 70 |
| 2410 | 50c. Suzanne Balogh (Women's Trap Shooting) | 80 | 70 |
| 2411 | 50c. Ian Thorpe (Men's 200m Freestyle Swimming) | 80 | 70 |
| 2412 | 50c. Jodie Henry (Women's 100m Freestyle Swimming) | 80 | 70 |
| 2413 | 50c. Anna Meares (Women's 500m Time Trial Cycling) | 80 | 70 |
| 2414 | 50c. James Tomkins and Drew Ginn (Men's Pair Rowing) | 80 | 70 |
| 2415 | 50c. Grant Hacket (Men's 1500m Freestyle Swimming) | 80 | 70 |
| 2416 | 50c. Women's 4×100m Medley Relay Swimming Team | 80 | 70 |
| 2417 | 50c. Chantelle Newberry (Women's 10m Platform Diving) | 80 | 70 |
| 2418 | 50c. Men's 4000m pursuit cycling team | 80 | 70 |
| 2419 | 50c. Ryan Bayley (Men's Individual Sprint Cycling) | 80 | 70 |
| 2420 | 50c. Graeme Brown and Stuart O'Grady (Men's Madison Cycling) | 80 | 70 |
| 2421 | 50c. Ryan Bayley (Men's Keirin Cycling) | 80 | 70 |
| 2422 | 50c. Men's hockey team | 80 | 70 |

**697** Entrance Beach, Broome, Western Australia

**2004.** International Stamps. Coastlines. Multicoloured.

| | | | |
|---|---|---|---|
| 2423 | $1.20 Type **697** | 2·00 | 50 |
| 2424 | $1.80 Mt. William National Park, Tasmania | 2·50 | 90 |
| 2425 | $2.40 Potato Point, Bodalla, New South Wales | 3·25 | 1·50 |
| 2426 | $3.60 Point Gibbon, Eyre Peninsula, South Australia | 4·50 | 2·75 |

**698** Sheet of Early Australian Stamp (No. 16) (image scaled to 47% of original size)

**2004.** Treasures from the Archives (1st series). Ordinary or self-adhesive gum.

| | | | | |
|---|---|---|---|---|
| 2427 | **698** | $5 multicoloured | 6·50 | 7·50 |

See also No. 2555.

**699** Stephenson 2-4-0 (Melbourne–Sandridge, 1854)

**2004.** 150th Anniv of Australian Railways. Multicoloured. Ordinary or self-adhesive gum.

| | | | |
|---|---|---|---|
| 2429 | 50c. Type **699** | 1·00 | 1·10 |
| 2430 | 50c. Locomotive No. 1 (Sydney–Parramatta, 1855) | 1·00 | 1·10 |
| 2431 | 50c. B12 Class locomotive (Helidon–Toowoomba, 1867) | 1·00 | 1·10 |
| 2432 | 50c. G Class train (Kalgoorlie–Port Augusta, 1917) | 1·00 | 1·10 |
| 2433 | 50c. *The Ghan* (Alice Springs–Darwin, 2004) | 1·00 | 1·10 |

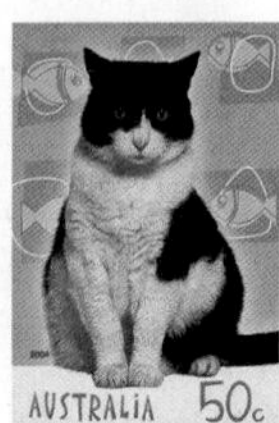

**700** "Ezzie" (black and white cat)

**2004.** Stamp Collecting Months. Cats and Dogs. Multicoloured. (a) Ordinary gum.

| | | | |
|---|---|---|---|
| 2439 | 50c. Type **700** | 90 | 90 |
| 2440 | 50c. "Tinkerbell" (ginger and white kitten) | 90 | 90 |
| 2441 | 50c. "Max" (Labrador puppy) | 90 | 90 |
| 2442 | 50c. "Bridie" and "Lily" (West Highland terriers) | 90 | 90 |
| 2443 | $1 "Edward" (Jack Russell terrier) | 2·00 | 1·50 |
| **MS**2444 | 170×85 mm. Nos. 2439/43 | 5·00 | 4·50 |

(b) Self-adhesive.

| | | | |
|---|---|---|---|
| 2445 | 50c. "Max" (Labrador puppy) | 70 | 80 |
| 2446 | 50c. Type **700** | 70 | 80 |
| 2447 | 50c. "Bridie" and "Lily" (West Highland Terriers) | 70 | 80 |
| 2448 | 50c. "Tinkerbell" (ginger and white kitten) | 70 | 80 |
| 2449 | $1 "Edward" (Jack Russell terrier) | 1·50 | 1·60 |

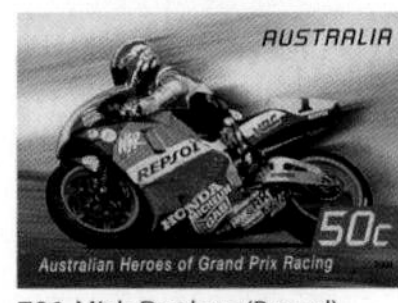

**701** Mick Doohan (Repsol)

**2004.** Formula 1 Motorcycle Racing. Multicoloured. Ordinary or self-adhesive gum.

| | | | |
|---|---|---|---|
| 2455 | 50c. Type **701** | 80 | 90 |
| 2456 | 50c. Wayne Gardner (Racing Honda) | 80 | 90 |
| 2457 | 50c. Troy Bayliss (Ducati) | 80 | 90 |
| 2458 | 50c. Daryl Beattie (Team Suzuki) | 80 | 90 |
| 2459 | 50c. Garry McCoy (Red Bull) | 80 | 90 |

**702** Mary and Jesus

**2004.** Christmas. Multicoloured. (a) Domestic mail.

| | | | |
|---|---|---|---|
| 2460 | 45c. Type **702** | 40 | 15 |
| 2461 | 50c. The Angel and the shepherds | 45 | 15 |

(b) International mail.

| | | | |
|---|---|---|---|
| 2462 | $1 The Three Wise Men (horiz) | 80 | 80 |

(c) Self-adhesive.

| | | | |
|---|---|---|---|
| 2464 | $1 The Three Wise Men (horiz) | 80 | 1·10 |

**703** Tennis Player and Match, Warehousemen's Cricket Ground, Melbourne, c. 1905

**2005.** Centenary of Australian Open Tennis Championships. Multicoloured.

| | | | |
|---|---|---|---|
| 2465 | 50c. Type **703** | 1·50 | 50 |
| 2466 | $1.80 Woman player and match, Melbourne Park, c. 2005 | 3·00 | 2·75 |

**704** Prue Acton

**2005.** Australian Legends (9th series). Fashion Designers. Multicoloured. Ordinary or self-adhesive gum.

| | | | |
|---|---|---|---|
| 2473 | 50c. Type **704** | 80 | 90 |
| 2474 | 50c. Jenny Bannister | 80 | 90 |
| 2475 | 50c. Collette Dinnigan | 80 | 90 |
| 2476 | 50c. Akira Isogawa | 80 | 90 |
| 2477 | 50c. Joe Saba | 80 | 90 |
| 2478 | 50c. Carla Zampatti | 80 | 90 |

**705** Princess Parrot

**2005.** Australian Parrots. Multicoloured. Ordinary or self-adhesive gum.

| | | | |
|---|---|---|---|
| 2484 | 50c. Type **705** | 1·10 | 1·10 |
| 2485 | 50c. Rainbow lorikeet | 1·10 | 1·10 |
| 2486 | 50c. Green rosella | 1·10 | 1·10 |
| 2487 | 50c. Red-capped parrot | 1·10 | 1·10 |
| 2488 | 50c. Purple-crowned lorikeet | 1·10 | 1·10 |

**706** Sir Donald Bradman's Cap

**2005.** Sporting Treasures. Multicoloured.

| | | | |
|---|---|---|---|
| 2489 | 50c. Type **706** | 1·00 | 85 |
| 2490 | 50c. Lionel Rose's boxing gloves | 1·00 | 85 |
| 2491 | $1 Marjorie Jackson's running spikes | 1·50 | 1·50 |
| 2492 | $1 Phar Lap's racing silks | 1·50 | 1·50 |

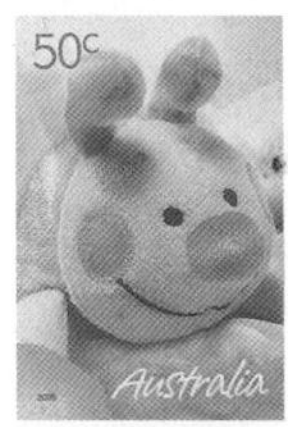


**707** Bumble Bee Toy

**2005.** Greetings Stamps (1st series). "Marking the Occasion". Multicoloured.

| | | | |
|---|---|---|---|
| 2493 | 50c. Type **707** | 1·00 | 1·10 |
| 2494 | 50c. Red roses | 1·00 | 1·10 |
| 2495 | 50c. Wrapped presents | 1·00 | 1·10 |
| 2496 | 50c. Kangaroos at sunset | 1·00 | 1·10 |
| 2497 | 50c. Bouquet of white flowers | 1·00 | 1·10 |
| 2498 | $1 Hand holding bouquet of cream roses | 1·75 | 1·25 |
| 2499 | $1.10 Koala | 1·75 | 1·50 |
| 2500 | $1.20 Shell on sandy beach | 2·00 | 2·25 |
| 2501 | $1.80 Sydney Opera House | 3·50 | 3·50 |

Nos. 2493/8 are for domestic use and 2499/51 are for international use.

See also Nos. 2556/7.

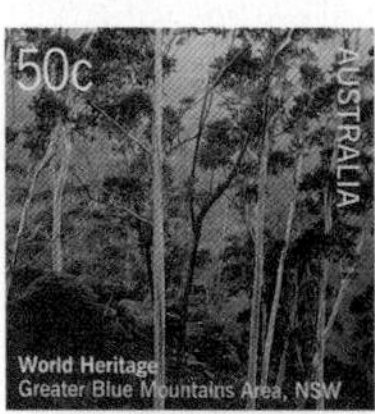


**708** Greater Blue Mountains Area, New South Wales

**2005.** World Heritage Sites. Multicoloured.

| | | | |
|---|---|---|---|
| 2502 | 50c. Type **708** | 1·00 | 85 |
| 2503 | 50c. Blenheim Palace, England | 1·00 | 85 |
| 2504 | 50c. Wet Tropics, Queensland | 1·00 | 85 |
| 2505 | 50c. Stonehenge, England | 1·00 | 85 |
| 2506 | $1 Purnululu National Park, West Australia | 1·75 | 1·50 |
| 2507 | $1 Heart of Neolithic Orkney, Scotland | 1·75 | 1·50 |
| 2508 | $1.80 Uluru-Kata Tjuta National Park, Northern Territories | 2·50 | 2·75 |
| 2509 | $1.80 Hadrian's Wall, England | 2·50 | 2·75 |

Nos. 2502/7 are for domestic use and 2508/9 are for international use.

Stamps in similar designs were also issued by Great Britain.

**709** Tribrachidium

**2005.** Creatures of the Slime (Ediacaran fossils). Multicoloured.

| | | | |
|---|---|---|---|
| 2510 | 50c. Type **709** | 1·00 | 85 |
| 2511 | 50c. Dickinsonia | 1·00 | 85 |
| 2512 | 50c. Spriggina | 1·00 | 85 |
| 2513 | 50c. Kimberella | 1·00 | 85 |
| 2514 | 50c. Inaria | 1·00 | 85 |
| 2515 | $1 Charniodiscus 1.501 | 1·75 | 1·50 |
| **MS**2516 | 170×210 mm. Nos. 2510/15 | 5·50 | 5·50 |

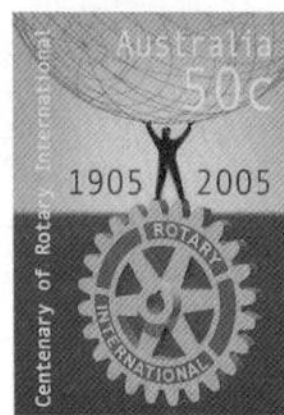


**710** Rotary Emblem and Man supporting Globe

**2005.** Centenary of Rotary International. Ordinary or self-adhesive gum.

| | | | | |
|---|---|---|---|---|
| 2517 | **710** | 50c. multicoloured | 1·25 | 85 |

**711** Obverse of Coin showing Head of Queen Victoria

**2005.** 150th Anniv of First Australian Coin. Design showing one sovereign coin and Sydney Mint building. Multicoloured.

| | | | |
|---|---|---|---|
| 2519 | 50c. Type **711** | 1·25 | 85 |
| 2520 | $2.45 Reverse of coin showing olive wreath | 4·00 | 3·25 |
| **MS**2521 | 105×69 mm. As Nos. 2519/20 but coins in gold foil | 4·75 | 4·25 |

**712** Queen at Opening Ceremony for Commonwealth Heads of Government Meeting, Queensland, 2002

**2005.** Queen's Birthday.

| | | | | |
|---|---|---|---|---|
| 2522 | **712** | 50c. multicoloured | 1·25 | 60 |

**713** Superb Lyrebird

**2005.** International Stamps. Bush Wildlife. Multicoloured.

| | | | |
|---|---|---|---|
| 2523 | $1 Type **713** | 1·50 | 60 |
| 2524 | $1.10 Laughing kookaburra | 1·50 | 65 |
| 2525 | $1.20 Koala | 1·60 | 80 |
| 2526 | $1.80 Red kangaroo | 2·50 | 1·50 |

Nos. 2524/6 also come self-adhesive.

**714** Sturt's Desert Pea

**2005.** Australian Wildflowers (1st series). Multicoloured. Ordinary or self-adhesive gum.

| | | | |
|---|---|---|---|
| 2530 | 50c. Type **714** | 85 | 85 |
| 2531 | 50c. Coarse-leaved mallee | 85 | 85 |
| 2532 | 50c. Common fringe lily | 85 | 85 |
| 2533 | 50c. Swamp daisy | 85 | 85 |

See also Nos. 2590/**MS**2594 and 2759/62.

**715** Vineyard

**2005.** Australian Wine. Multicoloured.

| | | | |
|---|---|---|---|
| 2538 | 50c. Type **715** | 90 | 85 |
| 2539 | 50c. Ripening grapes | 90 | 85 |
| 2540 | $1 Harvesting grapes | 1·75 | 1·50 |
| 2541 | $1 Casks of wine | 1·75 | 1·50 |
| 2542 | $1.45 Glasses of red and white wine and cheese | 2·50 | 2·50 |

Nos. 2538/9 also come self-adhesive.

**716** Snowgum

**2005.** Native Trees. Multicoloured. Ordinary or self-adhesive gum.

| | | | |
|---|---|---|---|
| 2550 | 50c. Type **716** | 80 | 90 |
| 2551 | 50c. Wollemi pine | 80 | 90 |
| 2552 | 50c. Boab | 80 | 90 |
| 2553 | 50c. Karri | 80 | 90 |
| 2554 | 50c. Moreton Bay fig | 80 | 90 |

**717** 1888 20s. New South Wales Stamps (image scaled to 47% of original size)

**2005.** Treasures from the Archives (2nd issue).

| | | | | |
|---|---|---|---|---|
| 2555 | **717** | $5 multicoloured | 9·00 | 9·50 |

**718** Christmas Tree with Lights

**2005.** Greetings Stamps. "Marking the Occasion" (2nd series). Multicoloured.

| | | | |
|---|---|---|---|
| 2556 | 45c. Type **718** | 85 | 85 |
| 2557 | 50c. Map of Australia with stars | 85 | 85 |

**719** Chloe the Chicken

**2005.** Stamp Collecting Month. "Down on the Farm". Multicoloured.

| | | | |
|---|---|---|---|
| **MS**2564 | 170×85 mm. Nos. 2558/63 | 5·00 | 5·50 |
| 2565 | 50c. Type **719** | 70 | 80 |
| 2566 | 50c. Lucy the Lamb | 70 | 80 |
| 2567 | 50c. Gilbert the Goat | 70 | 80 |
| 2568 | 50c. Ralph the Piglet | 70 | 80 |
| 2569 | 50c. Abigail the Cow | 70 | 80 |
| 2570 | $1 Harry the Horse | 1·50 | 1·75 |

Nos. 2558/2563 also come self-adhesive.

**720** Madonna and Child

**2005.** Christmas. Multicoloured. Ordinary or self-adhesive gum. (i) Domestic mail.

| | | | |
|---|---|---|---|
| 2571 | 45c. Type **720** | 75 | 15 |

(ii) International Mail.

| | | | |
|---|---|---|---|
| 2572 | $1 Adoring angel (horiz) | 1·50 | 85 |

**721** Emblem

**2006.** Commonwealth Games, Melbourne (1st issue). Ordinary or self-adhesive gum.

| | | | | |
|---|---|---|---|---|
| 2575 | **721** | 50c. multicoloured | 60 | 45 |

See also Nos. 2596/2600 and **MS**2607/**MS**2623.

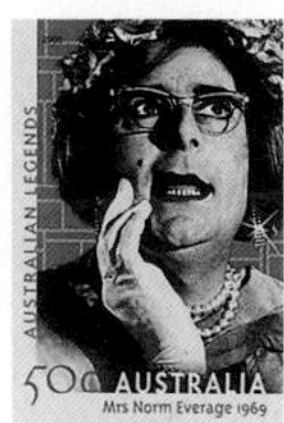


**722** Mrs. Norm Everage, 1969

**2006.** Australian Legends (10th series). Barry Humphries (satirist and actor). Multicoloured. Ordinary or self-adhesive gum.

| | | | |
|---|---|---|---|
| 2582 | 50c. Type **722** | 85 | 1·00 |
| 2583 | 50c. As Mrs. Edna Everage, 1973 | 85 | 1·00 |
| 2584 | 50c. As Dame Edna Everage, 1982 | 85 | 1·00 |
| 2585 | 50c. As Dame Edna Everage, 2004 | 85 | 1·00 |
| 2586 | 50c. Barry Humphries | 85 | 1·00 |

**723** Red Rose

**2006.** Greetings Stamp. Roses. Ordinary or self-adhesive gum.

| | | | | |
|---|---|---|---|---|
| 2587 | **723** | 50c. multicoloured | 1·00 | 45 |

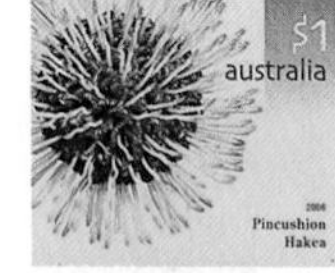


**724** *Pincushion Hakea*

**2006.** Australian Wildflowers (2nd series). Multicoloured.

| | | | |
|---|---|---|---|
| 2590 | $1 Type **724** | 1·60 | 50 |
| 2591 | $2 Donkey orchid | 3·25 | 1·25 |
| 2592 | $5 Mangles kangaroo paw (49×29 mm) | 6·50 | 4·50 |
| 2593 | $10 Waratah (49×29 mm) | 12·00 | 9·00 |
| **MS**2594 | 105×70 mm. $10 As No. 2593 (49×29 mm) | 11·00 | 12·00 |

**725** Dale Begg-Smith

**2006.** Dale-Begg Smith's Gold Medal for Men's Moguls Skiing at Winter Olympic Games, Turin.

| | | | | |
|---|---|---|---|---|
| 2595 | **725** | 50c. multicoloured | 1·00 | 75 |

**726** Athlete at Start

**2006.** Commonwealth Games, Melbourne (2nd issue). Multicoloured. (a) Ordinary gum. (i) Domestic Mail.

| | | | |
|---|---|---|---|
| 2596 | 50c. Type **726** | 50 | 45 |

(ii) International Post.

| | | | |
|---|---|---|---|
| 2597 | $1.25 Cyclist | 2·25 | 2·00 |
| 2598 | $1.85 Netball | 2·75 | 3·25 |
| **MS**2599 | 142×75 mm. Nos. 2596/8 | 5·50 | 5·50 |

(b) Self-adhesive.

| | | | |
|---|---|---|---|
| 2600 | 50c. Type **726** | 75 | 80 |

**727** Platypus

**2006.** International Post. Native Wildlife. Multicoloured.

| | | | |
|---|---|---|---|
| 2601 | 5c. Type **727** | 10 | 10 |
| 2602 | 25c. Short-beaked echidna | 30 | 25 |
| 2603 | $1.25 Common wombat | 2·00 | 1·10 |
| 2604 | $1.85 Tasmanian devil | 2·75 | 1·60 |
| 2605 | $2.50 Greater bilby | 3·75 | 2·00 |
| 2606 | $3.70 Dingo | 5·50 | 3·25 |

**728** Tram with Feathered "Wings" (Opening Ceremony)

**2006.** Commonwealth Games (3rd issue). Seventeen sheets each 180×200 mm containing horiz designs as T 728 showing opening/closing ceremonies (Nos. MS2607, MS2622) or Australian gold medal winners (others). Multicoloured.

| | | |
|---|---|---|
| **MS**2607 50c.×5 No. 1 Opening Ceremony | 2·75 | 3·25 |
| **MS**2608 50c.×5 No. 2 | 2·75 | 3·25 |
| **MS**2609 50c.×10 No. 3 | 5·00 | 6·00 |
| **MS**2610 50c.×5 No. 4 | 2·75 | 3·25 |
| **MS**2611 50c.×10 No. 5 | 5·00 | 6·00 |
| **MS**2612 50c.×5 No. 6 | 2·75 | 3·25 |
| **MS**2613 50c.×5 No. 7 | 2·75 | 3·25 |
| **MS**2614 50c.×10 No. 8 | 5·00 | 6·00 |
| **MS**2615 50c.×5 No. 9 | 2·75 | 3·25 |
| **MS**2616 50c.×10 No. 10 | 5·00 | 6·00 |
| **MS**2617 50c.×5 No. 11 | 2·75 | 3·25 |
| **MS**2618 50c.×10 No. 12 | 5·00 | 6·00 |
| **MS**2619 50c.×10 No. 13 | 5·00 | 6·00 |
| **MS**2620 50c.×10 No. 14 | 5·00 | 6·00 |
| **MS**2621 50c.×5 No. 15 | 2·75 | 3·25 |
| **MS**2622 50c.×5 No. 16 Closing Ceremony | 2·75 | 3·25 |
| **MS**2623 50c.×10 No. 17 Most memorable moment Kerryn McCann's Marathon victory | 5·00 | 6·00 |

Nos. **MS**2607/23 are numbered from 1 to 17 at the foot of the sheet.

**729** "Queen Elizabeth II in Garter Robes" (Pietro Annigoni)

**2006.** 80th Birthday of Queen Elizabeth II. Multicoloured. (a) Ordinary gum.

| | | | |
|---|---|---|---|
| 2624 | 50c. Type **729** | 1·00 | 45 |
| 2625 | $2.45 Queen Elizabeth II (photo by Cecil Beaton) | 4·00 | 4·00 |
| **MS**2626 | 105×70 mm. Nos. 2624/5 | 5·00 | 4·25 |

No. **MS**2626 also commemorates the 50th anniversary of the portrait by Annigoni.

(b) Self-adhesive.

| | | | |
|---|---|---|---|
| 2627 | 50c. Type **729** | 75 | 1·00 |

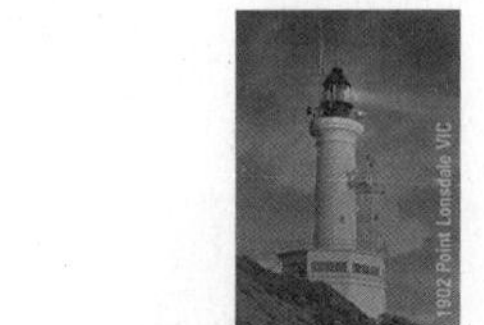

**730** Point Lonsdale, Victoria, 1902

**2006.** Lighthouses of the 20th Century. Ordinary or self-adhesive gum. Multicoloured.

| | | | |
|---|---|---|---|
| 2628 | 50c. Type **730** | 1·00 | 1·00 |
| 2629 | 50c. Cape Don, Northern Territory, 1916 | 1·00 | 1·00 |
| 2630 | 50c. Wollongong Head, New South Wales, 1937 | 1·00 | 1·00 |
| 2631 | 50c. Casuarina Point, West Australia, 1971 | 1·00 | 1·00 |
| 2632 | 50c. Point Cartwright, Queensland, 1979 | 1·00 | 1·00 |

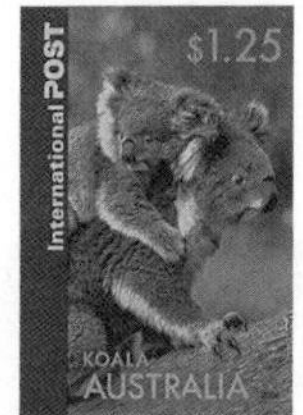

**731** Koala with Cub

**2006.** International Stamps. "Greetings from Australia". Ordinary or self-adhesive gum. Multicoloured.

| | | | |
|---|---|---|---|
| 2638 | $1.25 Type **731** | 1·60 | 1·25 |
| 2639 | $1.85 Royal Exhibition Building, Melbourne | 2·40 | 2·75 |

**732** Boy heading Ball ("PLAY")

**2006.** World Cup Football Championship, Germany. Soccer in Australia. Ordinary gum. Multicoloured. (i) Domestic Mail.

| | | | |
|---|---|---|---|
| 2642 | 50c. Type **732** | 70 | 80 |
| 2643 | 50c. Player kicking ball ("GOAL") | 70 | 80 |

(ii) International Post.

| | | | |
|---|---|---|---|
| 2644 | $1.25 Goalkeeper ("SAVE") | 1·75 | 1·50 |
| 2645 | $1.85 Player with ball ("SHOT") | 2·40 | 2·75 |
| **MS**2646 | Circular 170×170 mm. Nos. 2642/5 | 4·75 | 4·75 |

(b) Self-adhesive.

| | | | |
|---|---|---|---|
| 2647 | 50c. Type **732** | 75 | 90 |
| 2648 | 50c. As No. 2643 | 75 | 90 |

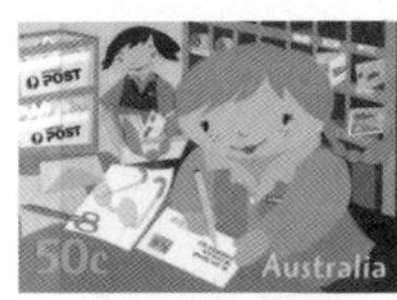

**733** Kate sorting Mail

**2006.** "Postie Kate". Ordinary or self-adhesive gum. Multicoloured.

| | | | |
|---|---|---|---|
| 2649 | 50c. Type **733** | 80 | 80 |
| 2650 | 50c. On motorcycle, giving letter to woman | 80 | 80 |
| 2651 | 50c. With van, delivering parcel | 80 | 80 |
| 2652 | 50c. Riding motorcycle. passing mailbox | 80 | 80 |
| 2653 | 50c. With mail satchel on shoulder | 80 | 80 |

**734** Blue Whale

**2006.** Endangered Species. Whales. Multicoloured. (a) Ordinary gum. (i) Domestic Mail.

| | | | |
|---|---|---|---|
| 2659 | 50c. Type **734** | 75 | 60 |
| 2660 | 50c. Humpback whale | 75 | 60 |

(ii) International Post.

| | | | |
|---|---|---|---|
| 2661 | $1.25 Fin whale | 1·75 | 1·25 |
| 2662 | $1.85 Southern bottlenose whale | 2·75 | 2·75 |
| **MS**2663 | 69×66 mm. Nos. 2659/62 | 5·50 | 5·00 |

(b) Self-adhesive. (i) Domestic Mail.

| | | | |
|---|---|---|---|
| 2664 | 50c. Type **734** | 75 | 90 |
| 2665 | 50c. As No. 2660 | 75 | 90 |

(ii) International Post.

| | | | |
|---|---|---|---|
| 2666 | $1.25 As No. 2661 | 1·60 | 2·00 |
| 2667 | $1.85 As No. 2662 | 2·40 | 2·75 |

**2006.** Le Salon du Timbre Stamp Exhibition, Paris. No. MS2646 inscr "LE SALON DU TIMBRE & DE L'ECRIT 17 AU 25 JUIN 2006 PARC FLORAL DE PARIS www.salondutimbre.fr" on sheet margin.

| | | | |
|---|---|---|---|
| **MS**2668 | Circular 170×170 mm. Nos. 2642/5 | 4·25 | 4·75 |

**735** Surfing

**2006.** Extreme Sports. Multicoloured.

| | | | |
|---|---|---|---|
| 2669 | 50c. Type **735** | 90 | 50 |
| 2670 | $1 Snowboarding | 1·75 | 1·25 |
| 2671 | $1.45 Skateboarding | 2·00 | 2·25 |
| 2672 | $2 Freestyle motoX | 3·50 | 3·50 |

**736** Ford TT Truck, 1917

**2006.** Driving through the Years. Multicoloured. (a) Ordinary or self-adhesive gum.

| | | | |
|---|---|---|---|
| 2678 | 50c. Type **736** | 70 | 80 |
| 2679 | 50c. Holden FE, 1956 | 70 | 80 |
| 2680 | 50c. Morris 850 (Mini Minor), 1961 | 70 | 80 |
| 2681 | 50c. Holden Sandman HX panel van, 1976 | 70 | 80 |
| 2682 | 50c. Toyota LandCruiser FJ60, 1985 | 70 | 80 |

**737** "Sunbury Rock Festival" (1972)

**2006.** Rock Posters (1st series). Multicoloured. (a) Ordinary or self-adhesive gum.

| | | | |
|---|---|---|---|
| 2683 | 50c. Type **737** | 90 | 90 |
| 2684 | 50c. "Magic Dirt" (2002) | 90 | 90 |
| 2685 | 50c. "Masters Apprentices" (1969) | 90 | 90 |
| 2686 | 50c. "Goanna's Spirit of Place" (1983) | 90 | 90 |
| 2687 | 50c. "Angels/Sports/Paul Kelly" (c. 1979) | 90 | 90 |
| 2688 | 50c. "Midnight Oil" (c. 1979) | 90 | 90 |
| 2689 | 50c. "Big Day Out" (2003) | 90 | 90 |
| 2690 | 50c. "Apollo Bay Music Festival" (1999) | 90 | 90 |
| 2691 | 50c. "Rolling Stones Australian Tour" (1973) | 90 | 90 |
| 2692 | 50c. "Mental as Anything" (1990) | 90 | 90 |

See also Nos. 2808/11.

**738** White Shark

**2006.** Stamp Collecting Month. Dangerous Australians. Multicoloured. (a) Ordinary gum.

| | | | |
|---|---|---|---|
| 2703 | 50c. Type **738** | 1·00 | 1·00 |
| 2704 | 50c. Eastern brown snake | 1·00 | 1·00 |
| 2705 | 50c. Box jellyfish | 1·00 | 1·00 |
| 2706 | 50c. Saltwater crocodile | 1·00 | 1·00 |
| 2707 | 50c. Blue-ringed octopus | 1·00 | 1·00 |
| 2708 | $1 Yellow-bellied sea snake | 1·50 | 1·25 |
| **MS**2709 | 130×90 mm. Nos. 2703/8 | 5·00 | 5·00 |

(b) Self-adhesive.

| | | | |
|---|---|---|---|
| 2710 | 50c. Type **738** | 90 | 90 |
| 2711 | 50c. As No. 2704 | 90 | 90 |
| 2712 | 50c. As No. 2705 | 90 | 90 |
| 2713 | 50c. As No. 2706 | 90 | 90 |
| 2714 | 50c. As No. 2707 | 90 | 90 |
| 2715 | $1 As No. 2708 | 1·40 | 1·40 |

**739** "In Melbourne Tonight"

**2006.** 50th Anniv of Television in Australia. Multicoloured. (a) Ordinary or self-adhesive gum.

| | | | |
|---|---|---|---|
| 2716 | 50c. Type **739** | 70 | 70 |
| 2717 | 50c. "Homicide" | 70 | 70 |
| 2718 | 50c. "Dateline" | 70 | 70 |
| 2719 | 50c. "Neighbours" | 70 | 70 |
| 2720 | 50c. "Kath and Kim" | 70 | 70 |

**2006.** China 2006 Stamp and Coin Expo. Two sheets, each 110×80 mm containing No. 2638, design on sheet margin given.

| | | |
|---|---|---|
| **MS**2726 **731** (a) $1.25 multicoloured (Great Wall of China). (b) $1.25 multicoloured (Sydney Opera House) | 3·75 | 3·75 |

**740** 2s. Melbourne across River Yarra Stamp

**2006.** 50th Anniv of Olympic Games, Melbourne. Showing Australia 1956 Olympic Games stamps and contemporary photographs of Melbourne. Multicoloured.

| | | | |
|---|---|---|---|
| 2727 | 50c. Type **740** | 1·25 | 1·00 |
| 2728 | 50c. River Yarra, Melbourne | 1·25 | 1·00 |
| 2729 | $1 1s. Collins Street stamp | 1·75 | 1·50 |
| 2730 | $1 Collins Street, Melbourne | 1·75 | 1·50 |

**741** Virgin Mary and Baby Jesus

**2006.** Christmas. Multicoloured. (a) Ordinary gum. (i) Domestic mail.

| | | | |
|---|---|---|---|
| 2731 | 45c. Type **741** | 80 | 30 |
| 2732 | 50c. Magi with gift | 80 | 35 |

(ii) International Mail.

| | | | |
|---|---|---|---|
| 2733 | $1.05 Young shepherd with lamb | 1·40 | 1·10 |

(b) Self-adhesive. Smaller design 22×33 mm. (i) Domestic mail.

| | | | |
|---|---|---|---|
| 2734 | 45c. Type **741** | 70 | 60 |

(ii) International Mail.

| | | | |
|---|---|---|---|
| 2735 | $1.05 As No. 2733 | 1·25 | 1·50 |

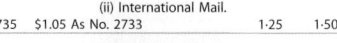

**742** Victorious Australian Cricketers

**2007.** "Australia wins the Ashes". Multicoloured. (a) Ordinary gum. (i) Domestic Mail.

| | | | |
|---|---|---|---|
| 2736 | 50c. Type **742** | 1·25 | 1·00 |

(ii) International Post.

| | | | |
|---|---|---|---|
| 2737 | $1.85 Australian team with Ashes Urn | 3·25 | 3·50 |
| **MS**2738 | 160×80 mm. Nos. 2736/7 | 4·50 | 4·50 |

(b) Self-adhesive. (i) Domestic Mail.

| | | | |
|---|---|---|---|
| 2739 | 50c. As No. 2736 | 1·00 | 1·00 |

(ii) International Post.

| | | | |
|---|---|---|---|
| 2740 | $1.85 As No. 2737 | 3·00 | 4·00 |

**743** Scobie Breasley (jockey), 1936

**2007.** Australian Legends (11th series). Legends of Australian Horse Racing. Multicoloured. (a) Ordinary gum.

| | | | |
|---|---|---|---|
| 2741 | 50c. Type **743** | 75 | 85 |
| 2742 | 50c. Scobie Breasley on "Santa Claus" after winning English Derby | 75 | 85 |
| 2743 | 50c. Bart Cummings (trainer) holding binoculars, 1966 | 75 | 85 |
| 2744 | 50c. Bart Cummings holding Melbourne Cup | 75 | 85 |
| 2745 | 50c. Roy Higgins (jockey), 1965 | 75 | 85 |
| 2746 | 50c. Roy Higgins riding "Light Fingers" to win Melbourne Cup, 1965 | 75 | 85 |
| 2747 | 50c. Bob Ingham (breeder), c. 1972 | 75 | 85 |

| | | | |
|---|---|---|---|
| 2748 | 50c. Bob Ingham leading "Lonhro", 2004 | 75 | 85 |
| 2749 | 50c. George Moore (jockey), 1957 | 75 | 85 |
| 2750 | 50c. George Moore riding "Tulloch", 1960 | 75 | 85 |
| 2751 | 50c. John Tapp (race commentator), 1972 | 75 | 85 |
| 2752 | 50c. John Tapp at microphone, 1998 | 75 | 85 |

(b) Self-adhesive.

| | | | |
|---|---|---|---|
| 2753 | 50c. Type **743** | 70 | 80 |
| 2754 | 50c. As No. 2743 | 70 | 80 |
| 2755 | 50c. As No. 2746 | 70 | 80 |
| 2756 | 50c. As No. 2748 | 70 | 80 |
| 2757 | 50c. As No. 2749 | 70 | 80 |
| 2758 | 50c. As No. 2751 | 70 | 80 |

**744** Tasmanian Christmas Bell

**2007.** Australian Wildflowers (3rd series). Multicoloured. Ordinary or self-adhesive gum.

| | | | |
|---|---|---|---|
| 2759 | 50c. Type **744** | 90 | 90 |
| 2760 | 50c. Green spider flower | 90 | 90 |
| 2761 | 50c. Sturt's desert rose | 90 | 90 |
| 2762 | 50c. *Phebalium whitei* | 90 | 90 |

**745** Swimmer

**2007.** 12th FINA (Federation Internationale de Natation) World Championships, Melbourne. Ordinary or self-adhesive gum.

| | | | | |
|---|---|---|---|---|
| 2767 | **745** | 50c. multicoloured | 70 | 70 |

**746** Maria Island, Tasmania

**2007.** International Post. Island Jewels. Multicoloured. (a) Ordinary gum.

| | | | |
|---|---|---|---|
| 2769 | 10c. Type **746** | 15 | 10 |
| 2770 | 30c. Rottnest Island, West Australia | 45 | 40 |
| 2771 | $1.30 Green Island, Queensland | 2·00 | 2·10 |
| 2772 | $1.95 Fraser Island, Queensland | 2·50 | 2·25 |
| 2773 | $2.60 Kangaroo Island, South Australia | 3·25 | 3·00 |
| 2774 | $3.85 Lord Howe Island, New South Wales | 3·75 | 3·50 |

(b) Self-adhesive gum.

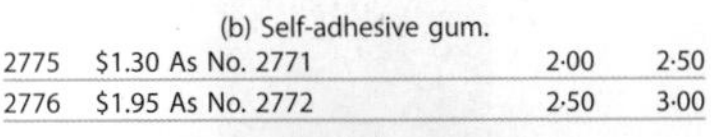

| | | | |
|---|---|---|---|
| 2775 | $1.30 As No. 2771 | 2·00 | 2·50 |
| 2776 | $1.95 As No. 2772 | 2·50 | 3·00 |

**747** Female Lifeguard with Reel

**2007.** Year of the Surf Lifesaver. Multicoloured. (a) Ordinary gum.

| | | | |
|---|---|---|---|
| 2777 | 50c. Type **747** | 70 | 70 |
| 2778 | 50c. Male lifeguards | 70 | 70 |
| 2779 | $1 Surf boat | 2·50 | 2·25 |
| 2780 | $2 "Nippers" (life saving club's children's programme) | 3·50 | 4·00 |

(b) Self-adhesive gum.

| | | | |
|---|---|---|---|
| 2781 | 50c. As No. 2778 | 70 | 1·00 |
| 2782 | 50c. Type **747** | 70 | 1·00 |
| **MS**2783 | 160×90 mm. $2.45 Inflatable rescue boat ×2 | 6·50 | 6·75 |

**748** Aries

**2007.** Signs of the Zodiac. Multicoloured. Ordinary or self-adhesive gum.

| | | | |
|---|---|---|---|
| 2784 | 50c. Type **748** | 70 | 80 |
| 2785 | 50c. Taurus | 70 | 80 |
| 2786 | 50c. Gemini | 70 | 80 |
| 2787 | 50c. Cancer | 70 | 80 |
| 2788 | 50c. Leo | 70 | 80 |
| 2789 | 50c. Virgo | 70 | 80 |
| 2790 | 50c. Libra | 70 | 80 |
| 2791 | 50c. Scorpio | 70 | 80 |
| 2792 | 50c. Sagittarius | 70 | 80 |
| 2793 | 50c. Capricorn | 70 | 80 |
| 2794 | 50c. Aquarius | 70 | 80 |
| 2795 | 50c. Pisces | 70 | 80 |

**749** "At the Beach" (Percy Trompf)

**2007.** Poster Art (2nd series). Nostalgic Tourism. Showing 1930s tourism posters. Multicoloured.

| | | | |
|---|---|---|---|
| 2808 | 50c. Type **749** | 70 | 70 |
| 2809 | $1 "Fishing" (John Vickery) | 1·40 | 1·25 |
| 2810 | $2 "Riding in the Country" (James Northfield) | 3·00 | 3·50 |
| 2811 | $2.45 "Winter Sport" (James Northfield) | 3·75 | 4·50 |

**750** Queen Elizabeth II in Australia, March 2006

**2007.** Queen's Birthday.

| | | | | |
|---|---|---|---|---|
| 2812 | **750** | 50c. multicoloured | 1·00 | 1·00 |

**751** *Admella* (steamship), 1859

**2007.** Historic Shipwrecks. Multicoloured.

| | | | |
|---|---|---|---|
| 2813 | 50c. Type **751** | 80 | 70 |
| 2814 | $1 *Loch Ard* (clipper), 1878 | 1·50 | 1·25 |
| 2815 | $2 *Dunbar* (clipper), 1857 | 3·00 | 4·00 |

**752** Yellow-footed Rock-wallaby

**2007.** International Post. "Country to Coast". Multicoloured.

| | | | |
|---|---|---|---|
| 2816 | $1.30 Type **752** | 2·00 | 1·75 |
| 2817 | $1.95 Sydney Harbour Bridge | 3·25 | 2·75 |

**753** "The Burning Bicycle"

**2007.** Circus: Under the Big Top. Multicoloured. Ordinary or self-adhesive gum.

| | | | |
|---|---|---|---|
| 2818 | 50c. Type **753** | 80 | 80 |
| 2819 | 50c. "The Inside-out Man" | 80 | 80 |
| 2820 | 50c. "The Dental Trapeze" | 80 | 80 |
| 2821 | 50c. "The Banana Lady" | 80 | 80 |
| 2822 | 50c. "The Human Cannonball" | 80 | 80 |

**754** Big Golden Guitar, Tamworth, New South Wales

**2007.** Big Things

| | | | |
|---|---|---|---|
| 2828 | 50c. Type **754** | 80 | 85 |
| 2829 | 50c. Big lobster, Kingston SE, South Australia | 80 | 85 |
| 2830 | 50c. Big banana, Coffs Harbour, New South Wales | 80 | 85 |
| 2831 | 50c. Big Merino ram, Goulburn, New South Wales | 80 | 85 |
| 2832 | 50c. Big pineapple, Nambour, Queensland | 80 | 85 |

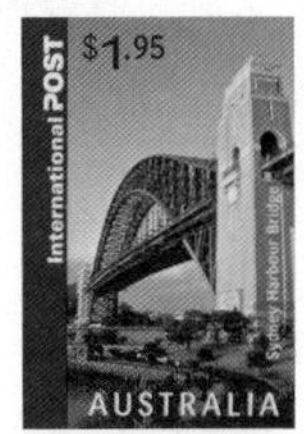


**755** Sydney Harbour Bridge

**2007.** International Post. 75th Anniv of Sydney Harbour Bridge. Sheet 130×90 mm.

| | | | |
|---|---|---|---|
| **MS**2838 | (a) $1.95×2 multicoloured. (b) $1.95×2 multicoloured (emblem and '15 JUNE 2007 SYDNEY NSW 2000' inscr in gold on sheet margin) Set of 2 sheets | 11·00 | 11·00 |

**756** Grey-headed flying-fox

**2007.** Threatened Wildlife. Multicoloured. (i) Domestic mail.

| | | | |
|---|---|---|---|
| 2839 | 50c. Type **756** | 90 | 90 |
| 2840 | 50c. Mountain Pygmy-possum | 90 | 90 |

(ii) International Post.

| | | | |
|---|---|---|---|
| 2841 | $1.25 Flatback turtle | 2·25 | 2·25 |
| 2842 | $1.30 Wandering albatross | 2·25 | 2·25 |

**757** Former ICI House, Melbourne, 1973

**2007.** Landmarks: Modernist Australian Architecture. Multicoloured.

| | | | |
|---|---|---|---|
| 2843 | 50c. Type **757** | 90 | 90 |
| 2844 | 50c. Academy of Science, Canberra, 1958 | 90 | 90 |
| 2845 | $1 Council House, Perth, 1962 | 1·60 | 1·25 |
| 2846 | $2.45 Sydney Opera House, 1973 | 4·00 | 4·50 |

| | | | |
|---|---|---|---|
| **MS**2847 | 90×90 mm. Nos. 2843/6 | 6·75 | 6·75 |

**758** Delicatessen, Dairy Produce Hall, Queen Victoria Market, Melbourne

**2007.** Market Feast. Multicoloured. Ordinary or self-adhesive gum.

| | | | |
|---|---|---|---|
| 2848 | 50c. Type **758** | 80 | 90 |
| 2849 | 50c. Banana seller, Rusty's Market, Cairns | 80 | 90 |
| 2850 | 50c. Sydney Fish Market | 80 | 90 |
| 2851 | 50c. Vegetable stall, Adelaide Central Market | 80 | 90 |
| 2852 | 50c. Potato seller, Hume Murray Farmers Market, Albury Wodonga | 80 | 90 |

**2007.** BANGKOK 2007

| | | | |
|---|---|---|---|
| **MS**2857b | 130×90 mm. **755** $1.95×2 multicoloured | 6·50 | 5·75 |

**759** APEC Logo and Half Globe

**2007.** Asia-Pacific Economic Cooperation Forum, Australia. Ordinary or self-adhesive gum.

| | | | | |
|---|---|---|---|---|
| 2858 | **759** | 50c. multicoloured | 70 | 70 |

**760** SAS Soldiers, Helicopter and Parachutist

**2007.** 50th Anniv of the Special Air Service.

| | | | | |
|---|---|---|---|---|
| 2860 | **760** | 50c. multicoloured | 1·00 | 80 |

**761** Brisbane Botanic Gardens, Mt. Coot-tha

**2007.** Australian Botanic Gardens. Multicoloured. Ordinary or self-adhesive gum.

| | | | |
|---|---|---|---|
| 2861 | 50c. Type **761** | 80 | 80 |
| 2862 | 50c. Kings Park and Botanic Garden, Perth | 80 | 80 |
| 2863 | 50c. Royal Botanic Gardens and Domain, Sydney | 80 | 80 |
| 2864 | 50c. Royal Botanic Gardens, Melbourne | 80 | 80 |
| 2865 | 50c. Botanic Gardens of Adelaide | 80 | 80 |

**2007.** Collectors International Fair, Prague. No. MS2838 inscr 'SBERATEL SAMMLER COLLECTOR' and emblem on sheet margin.

| | | | |
|---|---|---|---|
| **MS**2871 | 130×90 mm. **755** $1.95×2 multicoloured | 5·75 | 5·75 |

**762** Sputnik (first satellite), 1957

**2007.** Stamp Collecting Month. Blast Off! 50 Years in Space. Multicoloured.

| | | | |
|---|---|---|---|
| 2872 | 50c. Type **762** | 70 | 70 |
| 2873 | 50c. Cosmonaut Alexei Leonov on first space walk, 1965 | 70 | 70 |
| 2874 | 50c. Neil Armstrong walking on Moon, 1969 | 70 | 70 |
| 2875 | 50c. *Voyager* space probe, 1977 | 70 | 70 |
| 2876 | 50c. International Space Station, 1998 | 70 | 70 |

2877 $1 Hubble Space Telescope and galaxy, 1990 1·25 1·25
**MS**2878 160×90 mm. Nos. 2872/7 and as No. 2877 but 51×37 mm 6·25 6·50
Nos. 2872/6 also come self-adhesive.

**763** Family Picnic outside Caravan, 1950s

**2007.** Caravanning through the Years. Multicoloured. Ordinary or self-adhesive gum.
2884 50c. Type **763** 70 80
2885 50c. Family with kangaroos outside caravan, 1960s 70 80
2886 50c. Family outside caravan, 1970s 70 80
2887 50c. Woman and girl outside caravan, 1980s 70 80
2888 50c. Elderly couple sitting outside caravan, c. 2007 70 80

**764** Surfing Santa Stamp Design by Roger Roberts, 1977

**2007.** Christmas. 50 Years of Christmas Stamps. Multicoloured designs showing Christmas stamp designs from previous years redrawn without the face values. (a) Ordinary gum. (i) Domestic Mail.
2894 45c. Type **764** 80 20
2895 45c. Bush Nativity (Baby Jesus with koalas and wallaby) by Marg Towt, 1990 80 1·00
2896 45c. Madonna and Child 80 1·00
2897 50c. The Spirit of Christmas 80 70

(ii) International Post.
2898 $1.10 Madonna and Child from stained-glass window, 1984 1·50 1·50

(b) Self-adhesive. (i) Domestic Mail.
2899 45c. As Type **764** 65 60
2900 45c. As No. 2895 65 65
2901 45c. As No. 2896 65 65
2902 50c. As No. 2897 70 85

(ii) International Post.
2903 $1.10 As No. 2898 1·50 1·75
**MS**2904 156×100 mm. As No. 2899 and Nos. 2900/3 4·75 4·75

**765** Red Rose

**2008.** Greetings stamp. 'Love Blooms'. Ordinary or self-adhesive gum.
2905 **765** 50c. multicoloured 80 70

**766** Dame Elisabeth Murdoch

**2008.** Australian Legends (12th series). Philanthropists. Multicoloured. Ordinary or self-dhesive gum.
2907 50c. Type **766** 1·00 1·00
2908 50c. Victor Smorgon and Loti Smorgon 1·00 1·00
2909 50c. Lady (Mary) Fairfax 1·00 1·00
2910 50c. Frank Lowy 1·00 1·00

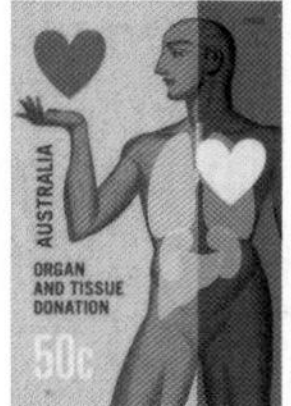

**767** Human Body showing Organs

**2008.** Organ and Tissue Donation. Ordinary or self-adhesive gum.
2915 **767** 50c. multicoloured 75 75

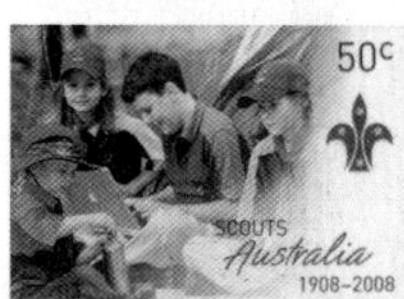

**768** Scout Camp

**2008.** Centenary of Scouting in Australia. T 768 and similar horiz designs. Multicoloured. (a) Ordinary gum. (i) Domestic Mail.
2917 50c. Type **768** 75 75

(ii) International Post.
2918 $1.35 Scouts in circle 1·90 2·00
2919 $2 Lord Baden-Powell (founder) 2·75 3·75

(b) Self-adhesive. (i) Domestic Mail.
2920 50c. As Type **768** 75 1·00

(ii) International Post.
2921 $1.35 As No. 2918 3·50 4·25
2922 $2 As No. 2919 4·75 6·00

**769** Hanging Rock, Grose River Gorge, New South Wales

**2008.** International Post. 'Gorgeous Australia'. Multicoloured. (a) Ordinary gum.
2923 $1.35 Type **769** 1·90 1·90
2924 $2 Walpa Gorge, Northern Territory 3·00 2·75
2925 $2.70 Katherine Gorge, Northern Territory (horiz) 4·00 4·00
2926 $4 Geikie Gorge, West Australia (horiz) 6·50 6·50

(b) Self-adhesive
2927 $1.35 As Type 769 3·50 4·25
2928 $2 As No. 2924 4·75 6·00

**770** Pope Benedict XVI

**2008.** World Youth Day, Sydney. Multicoloured. (a) Ordinary gum (i) Domestic Mail.
2929 50c. Type **770** 1·00 75

(ii) International Post
2930 $1.35 Pope holding crosier 2·50 2·50
2931 $2 Pope giving blessing 3·00 3·25

(b) Self-adhesive. (ii) International Post
2932 $1.35 As No. 2930 2·25 2·50
2933 $2 As No. 2931 3·75 4·50

**2008.** Canberra Stamp Show. Sheet 130×90 mm containing No. 2919×2. Multicoloured.
**MS**2934 $2×2 Lord Baden-Powell 5·50 5·50

**771** Bulldogs

**2008.** Centenary of Rugby League. Multicoloured. (a) Ordinary gum.
2935 50c. Type **771** 80 90
2936 50c. Titans 80 90
2937 50c. Sharks 80 90
2938 50c. Knights 80 90
2939 50c. Cowboys 80 90
2940 50c. Broncos 80 90
2941 50c. Sea Eagles 80 90
2942 50c. Storm 80 90
2943 50c. Roosters 80 90
2944 50c. Raiders 80 90
2945 50c. Rabbitohs 80 90
2946 50c. Panthers 80 90
2947 50c. Dragons 80 90
2948 50c. Eels 80 90
2949 50c. Wests Tigers 80 90
2950 50c. Warriors 80 90

(b) Self-adhesive.
2951 50c. As No. 2942 75 90
2952 50c. As No. 2937 75 90
2953 50c. As No. 2943 75 90
2954 50c. As Type **771** 75 90
2955 50c. As No. 2938 75 90
2956 50c. As No. 2939 75 90
2957 50c. As No. 2945 75 90
2958 50c. As No. 2944 75 90
2959 50c. As No. 2948 75 90
2960 50c. As No. 2949 75 90
2961 50c. As No. 2947 75 90
2962 50c. As No. 2941 75 90
2963 50c. As No. 2940 75 90
2964 50c. As No. 2936 75 90
2965 50c. As No. 2946 75 90
2966 50c. As No. 2950 75 90

**772** Face Shovel in Mine

**2008.** Heavy Haulers. Multicoloured. (a) Ordinary or self-adhesive gum.
2967 50c. Type **772** 1·00 1·00
2968 50c. 200 tonne mine haul truck 1·00 1·00
2969 50c. Road train 1·00 1·00
2970 50c. Ore train, West Australia 1·00 1·00
2971 50c. MS *Berge Stahl* (world?s largest bulk carrier) 1·00 1·00

**773** Veterans marching

**2008.** 'Lest We Forget': ANZAC Day. Multicoloured. (a) Ordinary gum.
2977 50c. Type **773** 85 85
2978 50c. Laying wreaths at war memorial 85 85
2979 50c. Playing the *Last Post* 85 85
2980 50c. War veteran and young boy 85 85
2981 50c. Young Australians at Gallipoli 85 85
**MS**2982 160×90 mm. Nos. 2977/81 3·75 3·75

(b) Self-adhesive.
2983 50c. As Type **773** 90 1·00
2984 50c. As No. 2978 90 1·00
2985 50c. As No. 2979 90 1·00
2986 50c. As No. 2980 90 1·00
2987 50c. As No. 2981 90 1·00

**774** Queen Elizabeth II at Official Dinner, Parliament House, Canberra, 2006

**2008.** Queen's Birthday. Multicoloured. (i) Domestic Mail.
2988 50c. Type**774** 1·00 75

(ii) International Post.
2989 $2 Sovereign's badge, Order of Australia 3·00 3·50
**MS**2990 106×70 mm. Nos. 2988/9 4·00 4·25

**775** Balloons over Sydney, New South Wales

**2008.** 'Up Up and Away'. 150th Anniv of First Hot Air Balloon Flight in Australia. Multicoloured. Ordinary or self adhesive gum.
2991 50c. Type **775** 1·10 1·10
2992 50c. Orange and white balloons over Mt. Feathertop, Victoria 1·10 1·10
2993 50c. Multicoloured balloons over the Western MacDonnell Ranges, Northern Territories 1·10 1·10
2994 50c. Balloons over Canberra, Australian Central Territory 1·10 1·10

**2008.** WSC Israel 2008 World Stamp Championship, Tel-Aviv. Sheet 130×90 mm containing No. 2979×4. Multicoloured.
**MS**2999 50c.× 4 Playing *The Last Post* 3·50 3·50

**776** German Shepherd Dog

**2008.** Working Dogs. Multicoloured. Ordinary or self-adhesive gum.
3005 50c. Type **776** 85 1·10
3006 50c. Australian cattle dog 85 1·10
3007 50c. Beagle 85 1·10
3008 50c. Border collie 85 1·10
3009 50c. Labrador 85 1·10

**777** Chinese Dragon

**2008.** Olympic Games, Beijing. Ordinary or self-adhesive gum.
3010 **777** 50c. multicoloured 1·00 1·00

**778** Watering Can and Rubber Duck ('SAVE WATER')

**2008.** Living Green
3012 50c. Type **778** 80 80
3013 50c. Hand holding bin ('REDUCE WASTE') 80 80
3014 50c. Bus with legs ('TRAVEL SMART') 80 80
3015 50c. Crescent moon with light switch ('SAVE ENERGY') 80 80

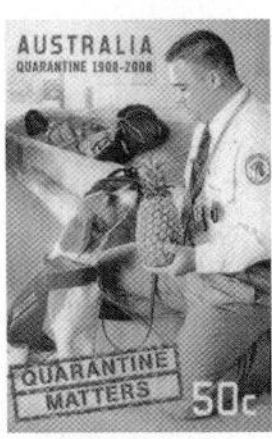

**779** Quarantine Detector Dog and Handler

**2008.** Centenary of the Quarantine Act. Ordinary or self-adhesive gum.

3020 **779** 50c. multicoloured 1·00 1·00

**780** Pilgrims with Flags at Barangaroo for Opening Mass

**2008.** World Youth Day (2nd issue). Multicoloured.

3022 50c. Type **780** 1·40 1·40
3023 50c. Pope Benedict XVI at Barangaroo 1·40 1·40
3024 50c. Re-enactment of Stations of the Cross 1·40 1·40
3025 50c. Start of Pilgrimage Walk at Sydney Harbour Bridge 1·40 1·40
3026 50c. Pope Benedict XVI at Final Mass, Southern Cross Precinct 1·40 1·40

**781** Football Game, Melbourne, 1866

**2008.** 150th Anniv of Australian Football.

3027 **781** 50c. multicoloured 1·00 1·00

**782** Basketball

**2008.** Olympic Games, Beijing. Multicoloured.

3028 50c. Type **782** 1·00 50
3029 $1.30 Cycling 2·25 2·50
3030 $1.35 Gymnastics 2·25 2·50

Nos. 3029/3030 also come self-adesive.

**783** Bristol Tourer

**2008.** Aviation. Multicoloured. (a) Ordinary gum. (i) Domestic mail

3033 50c. Type **783** 1·10 1·10
3034 50c. Short S.30 Empire flying boat 1·10 1·10
3035 50c. Lockheed Super Constellation 1·10 1·10

(ii) International Post.

3036 $2 Airbus A320 4·25 4·25

(b) Self-adhesive.

3037 $2 As No. 3036 3·25 3·75

**784** Stephanie Rice (swimming: women's 400m individual medley)

**2008.** Ausralian Gold Medal Winners at Olympic Games, Beijing. Multicoloured.

3038A 50c. Type **784** 1·00 1·00
3039A 50c. Lisbeth Trickett (swimming: women's 100m butterfly) 1·00 1·00
3040A 50c. Leisel Jones (swimming: women's 100m breaststroke) 1·00 1·00
3041A 50c. Stephanie Rice (swimming: women's 200m individual medley) 1·00 1·00
3042A 50c. Women's 4×200m freestyle relay swimming team 1·00 1·00
3043A 50c. Drew Ginn and Duncan Free (rowing: men's pair) 1·00 1·00
3044A 50c. David Crawshay and Scott Brennan (rowing: men's double sculls) 1·00 1·00
3045A 50c. Women's 4×100m medley relay swimming team 1·00 1·00
3046A 50c. Emma Snowsill (women's triathlon) 1·00 1·00
3047A 50c. Malcolm Page and Nathan Wilmott (sailing: men's 470) 1·00 1·00
3048A 50c. Tessa Parkinson and Elise Rechichi (sailing: women's 470) 1·00 1·00
3049A 50c. Ken Wallace (canoe/kayak: men's K-1 500m) 1·00 1·00
3050A 50c. Steven Hooker (athletics: men's pole vault) 1·00 1·00
3051A 50c. Matthew Mitcham (diving: men's 10m platform) 1·00 1·00

**2008.** SunStamp 2008 National Stamp Exhibition, Brisbane. Sheet 130×90 mm containing Nos. 2998 and 3036, each ×2. Multicoloured.

**MS**3052 50c.×2 Multicoloured balloons over the Western MacDonnell Ranges, Northern Territories; $2×2 Airbus A320 8·00 8·00

**785** Luna Park, Melbourne

**2008.** Tourist Precincts. Multicoloured.

3053 55c. Type **785** 80 80
3054 55c. South Bank, Brisbane 80 80
3055 55c. The Rocks, Sydney 80 80
3056 55c. Fisherman's Wharf, Fremantle 80 80
3057 $1.10 Foreshore, Cairns 1·50 1·40
3058 $1.65 Salamanca Place, Hobart 2·40 2·25
3059 $2.75 Glenelg, Adelaide (50×30 mm) 4·00 4·25

Nos. 3053/3056 also come self-adhesive.

**786** Russell Falls, Tasmania

**2008.** International Post. Waterfalls of Australia. Multicoloured.

3064 $1.40 Type **786** 2·00 1·25
3065 $2.05 Jim Jim Falls, Northern Territory 3·00 3·00
3066 $2.80 Spa Pool, Hamersley Gorge, Western Australia 4·00 4·00
3067 $4.10 Mackenzie Falls, Victoria 6·00 6·00

Nos. 3064/3065 also come self-adhesive.

**787** Silver Rings

**2008.** Greetings Stamps. 'For Every Occasion'. Multicoloured.

3070 55c. Type **787** 80 80
3071 55c. Gold rings 80 80
3072 55c. Baby's feet 80 80
3073 55c. Gold heart and pink roses 80 80
3074 55c. Balloons 80 80
3075 55c. Bird flying over beach 80 80
3076 55c. Outline map of Australia as sun and stylised landscape 80 80
3077 55c. Sparklers 80 80
3078 55c. Australia and Antarctica on globe (30×30 mm) 80 80
3079 $1.10 Embroidery from wedding dress and pale pink roses 1·60 1·60

**788** Genyornis

**2008.** Stamp Collecting Month. Megafauna of Australia. Multicoloured.

3080 55c. Type **788** 80 80
3081 55c. Diprotodon 80 80
3082 55c. Thylacoleo 80 80
3083 55c. Thylacine 80 80
3084 $1.10 Megalania (52×37 mm) 1·50 1·50
3085 $1.10 Procoptodon (52×37 mm) 1·50 1·50
**MS**3086 170×90 mm. Nos. 3080/5 6·00 6·00

Nos. 3080/3083 also come self-adhesive.

**2008.** Beijing Expo. No. MS3086 optd with emblem and BEIJING 24-27 OCTOBER 2008.

**MS**3091 170×90 mm. Nos. 3080/5 7·00 7·00

**789** Matthew Cowdrey

**2008.** Paralympian of the Year.

3092 **789** 55c. multicoloured 1·00 80

**790** Baubles

**2008.** Christmas. Multicoloured. (a) Ordinary gum. (i) Domestic Mail

3093 50c. Type **790** 75 75
3094 50c. Virgin Mary and baby Jesus 75 75
3095 55c. Angel 75 75

(ii) International Post.

3096 $1.20 Wise man carrying gift 1·75 1·75

(b) Self-adhesive. (i) Domestic Mail.

3097 50c. As Type **790** 85 85
3098 50c. As Type **790** but gold foil star on bottom left bauble 85 85
3099 50c. As No. 3094 85 85

(ii) International Post.

3100 $1.20 As No. 3096 1·75 2·00

**791** *The Adventures of Priscilla, Queen of the Desert*

**2008.** Favourite Australian Films. Multicoloured. Self-adhesive.

3106 55c. Type **791** 85 95
3107 55c. *The Castle* 85 95
3108 55c. *Muriel's Wedding* 85 95
3109 55c. *Lantana* 85 95
3110 55c. *Gallipoli* 85 95

Nos. 3106/3110 also came with ordinary gum.

**2008.** Discovery of the HMAS Sydney. Sheet 130×90 mm containing Nos. 2977/8, each ×2. Multicoloured.

**MS**3111 50c.×2 Type **773**; 50c.×2 Laying wreaths at war memorial 3·00 3·00

**2008.** 90th Anniv of the End of World War I. Sheet 160×90 mm containing Nos. 2978/9, each ×2. Multicoloured.

**MS**3112 50c.×2 Laying wreaths at war memorial; 50c.×2 Playing the *Last Post* 3·00 3·00

**792** Nicole Kidman

**2009.** Australian Legends (13th series). 'Legends of the Screen'. Multicoloured.

3113 55c. Type **792** 1·00 1·00
3114 55c. Russell Crowe 1·00 1·00
3115 55c. Geoffrey Rush 1·00 1·00
3116 55c. Cate Blanchett 1·00 1·00
3117 55c. Russell Crowe in *Gladiator*, 2000 1·00 1·00
3118 55c. Nicole Kidman in *Moulin Rouge!*, 2001 1·00 1·00
3119 55c. Cate Blanchett in *Elizabeth: The Golden Age*, 2007 1·00 1·00
3120 55c. Geoffrey Rush in *Shine*, 1996 1·00 1·00

Nos. 3113/3120 also come self-adhesive.

**793** Red Roses

**2009.** Greetings Stamps. 'With Love'. Azure (3131, 3134, 3136) or multicoloured (others). (a) Ordinary gum.

3129 55c. Type **793** 95 95
3130 55c. Heart flowers 95 95
3131 55c. Fiigree heart 95 95

(a) Ordinary gum.

3132 55c. Type **793** 95 95
3133 55c. As No. 3130 but with white border 95 95
3134 55c. As No. 3131 but with white border 95 95
3135 55c. As No. 3130 but with red foil applied to hearts and white border 95 95
3136 55c. As No. 3131 but with flocking applied to filigree heart and white border 95 95

**794** Esky (coolbox) and Wine Cask

**2009.** Inventive Australia. Designs showing Australian inventions. Multicoloured. (a) Ordinary gum.

3137 55c. Type **794** 95 95
3138 55c. Girl swinging on Hills hoist (rotary clothes line) 95 95
3139 55c. Girl wearing Speedo swimsuit and boy and girl wearing zinc cream 95 95
3140 55c. Ute and B&D Roll-a-Door (garage door) 95 95
3141 55c. Victa rotary lawnmower 95 95
**MS**3142 170×84 mm. Nos. 3137/41 4·25 4·25

(b) Self-adhesive.

3143 55c. As Type **794** 95 95
3144 55c. As No. 3138 95 95
3145 55c. As No. 3139 95 95
3146 55c. As No. 3140 95 95
3147 55c. As No. 3141 95 95

**2009.** Greetings Stamps. 'For Every Occasion' (2nd series). As Nos. 3071/2, 3074, 3077 and 3079. Multicoloured. Self-adhesive.

| No. | Description | | |
|---|---|---|---|
| 3148 | 55c. Gold rings ( 3071) | 95 | 95 |
| 3149 | 55c. Baby's feet (3072) | 95 | 95 |
| 3150 | 55c. Balloons (3074) | 95 | 95 |
| 3151 | 55c. Sparklers (3077) | 95 | 95 |
| 3152 | $1.10 Embroidery from wedding dress and pale pink roses ( 3079) | 2·50 | 2·50 |

Nos. 3149/51 differ from Nos. 3072, 3074 and 3077 by having white borders.

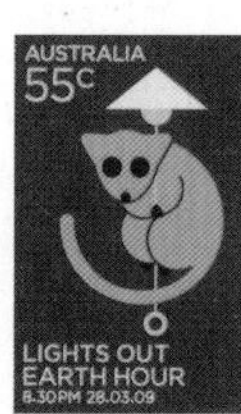


**795** Possum ('LIGHTS OUT')

**2009.** Earth Hour. Multicoloured. (a) Ordinary gum. (i) Domestic Mail

| No. | Description | | |
|---|---|---|---|
| 3153 | 55c. Type **795** | 1·00 | 1·00 |
| 3154 | 55c. Owl ('SWITCH OFF') | 1·00 | 1·00 |
| | (ii) International Post | | |
| 3155 | $2.05 Orang-utan ('SAVE ENERGY') | 3·50 | 3·50 |
| | (b) Self-adhesive. | | |
| 3156 | 55c. As Type **795** | 90 | 90 |
| 3157 | 55c. As No. 3154 | 90 | 90 |

**796** Isaac Nicholls, First Postmaster of New South Wales, boarding Ship to Collect Incoming Mail, 1809

**2009.** Bicentenary of Postal Services in Australia (1st issue). Multicoloured. Ordinary or self-adhesive gum.

| No. | Description | | |
|---|---|---|---|
| 3158 | 55c. Type **796** | 1·00 | 1·00 |
| 3159 | 55c. Menzies Creek Post Office, Victoria, 1900s ('Early post office') | 1·00 | 1·00 |
| 3160 | 55c. Early posting box | 1·00 | 1·00 |
| 3161 | 55c. Australian soldiers reading letters, France, 1918 ('News from home') | 1·00 | 1·00 |
| 3162 | 55c. First Quantas air mail service, Brisbane–Charleville, 1929 ('Early air mail') | 1·00 | 1·00 |
| 3163 | 55c. Home delivery | 1·00 | 1·00 |
| 3164 | 55c. Family reading letter ('Post-war immigration') | 1·00 | 1·00 |
| 3165 | 55c. Retail PostShop | 1·00 | 1·00 |
| 3166 | 55c. Express Post | 1·00 | 1·00 |
| 3167 | 55c. Australia Post lorry ('Part of every day') | 1·00 | 1·00 |

**797** *Mamu* (Nura Rupert), 2002

**2009.** Indigenous Culture. Designs showing aboriginal paintings. Multicoloured. (a) Ordinary gum. (i) Domestic Mail

| No. | Description | | |
|---|---|---|---|
| 3178 | 55c. Type **797** | 1·00 | 1·00 |
| 3179 | 55c. *All the Jila* (Jan Billycan), 2006 | 1·00 | 1·00 |
| 3180 | 55c. *Mina Mina* (Judy Napangardi Watson), 2004 | 1·00 | 1·00 |
| | (ii) International Post | | |
| 3181 | $1.40 Untitled (from the Mission series) (Elaine Russell), 2006 | 2·75 | 2·75 |
| 3182 | $2.05 *Natjula* (Tjuruparu Watson), 2003 | 3·25 | 3·25 |
| | (b) Self-adhesive. | | |
| 3183 | $1.40 As No. 3181 | 2·25 | 2·50 |
| 3184 | $2.05 As No. 3182 | 3·25 | 3·25 |

**798** Queen Elizabeth II riding Side Saddle at Trooping the Colour

**2009.** Queen's Birthday. Multicoloured.

| No. | Description | | |
|---|---|---|---|
| 3185 | 55c. Type **798** | 80 | 80 |
| 3186 | $2.05 Queen Elizabeth and Prince Philip riding in carriage at Trooping the Colour | 3·25 | 3·25 |
| **MS**3187 | 106×70 mm. Nos. 3185/6 | 4·00 | 4·00 |

**2009.** 23rd Asian International Stamp Exhibition, Hong Kong. Sheet 130×90 mm containing Nos. 3053/6. Multicoloured.

| No. | Description | | |
|---|---|---|---|
| **MS**3188 | 55c. Type **785**; 55c. South Bank, Brisbane; 55c. The Rocks, Sydney; 55c. Fisherman's Wharf, Fremantle | 3·50 | 3·50 |

**799** Anna Pavlova (ballerina) and Pavlova (meringue, whipped cream and fruit)

**2009.** 'Not Just Desserts'. Multicoloured.

| No. | Description | | |
|---|---|---|---|
| 3189 | 55c. Type **799** | 1·10 | 1·10 |
| 3190 | 55c. Dame Nellie Melba (opera singer) and peach melba | 1·10 | 1·10 |
| 3191 | 55c. Second Baron Lamington (Governor of Queensland, 1896–1901), Lady Lamington and lamingtons (sponge cake squares with chocolate and coconut) | 1·10 | 1·10 |
| 3192 | 55c. ANZAC soldiers of 1915 and Anzac biscuits | 1·10 | 1·10 |

Nos. 3189/3192 also come self-adhesive.

**800** Indian Ocean ('Spotted') Bottlenose Dolphin

**2009.** Endangered Species. Dolphins of the Australian Coastline. Multicoloured. (a) Ordinary gum. (i) Domestic Mail.

| No. | Description | | |
|---|---|---|---|
| 3197 | 55c. Type **800** | 90 | 90 |
| | (ii) International Post. | | |
| 3198 | $1.35 Hourglass dolphin | 2·10 | 2·10 |
| 3199 | $1.40 Southern right whale dolphin | 2·10 | 2·10 |
| 3200 | $2.05 Dusky dolphin | 3·25 | 3·25 |
| **MS**3201 | 136×70 mm. Nos. 3197/200 | 8·25 | 8·25 |
| | (b) Self-adhesive. | | |
| 3202 | $1.35 As No. 3198 | 2·25 | 2·25 |
| 3203 | $1.40 As No. 3199 | 2·25 | 2·25 |
| 3204 | $2.05 As No. 3200 | 3·75 | 3·75 |

**801** Queensland Parliament House, Brisbane, Windmill and Outback Red Sands

**2009.** 150th Anniv of Queensland. Multicoloured.

| No. | Description | | |
|---|---|---|---|
| 3205 | 55c. Type **801** | 90 | 90 |
| 3206 | $2.75 Great Barrier Reef, red-eyed tree frog, rainforest and beach | 4·50 | 4·50 |
| **MS**3207 | 106×70 mm. Nos. 3205/6 | 5·25 | 5·25 |

**802** 1913 £2 Kangaroo and Map Stamp

**2009.** Bicentenary of Postal Services in Australia (2nd issue). Australia's Favourite Stamps. Multicoloured.

| No. | Description | | |
|---|---|---|---|
| 3208 | 55c. Type **802** | 95 | 95 |
| 3209 | 55c. 1932 5s. Sydney Harbour Bridge stamp | 95 | 95 |
| 3210 | 55c. 1946 Victory Commemoration 2½d. 'Peace' stamp | 95 | 95 |
| 3211 | 55c. 1950 8½d. Aborigine stamp | 95 | 95 |
| 3212 | 55c. 1914 6d. Kookaburra stamp | 95 | 95 |

Nos. 3208/3212 also come self-adhesive.

**803** Koala (*Phascolarctos cinereus*)

**2009.** International Post. Australian Bush Babies. Multicoloured.

| No. | Description | | |
|---|---|---|---|
| 3218 | $1.45 Type **803** | 2·50 | 1·75 |
| 3219 | $2.10 Eastern grey kangaroo (*Macropus giganteus*) | 3·00 | 3·50 |
| 3220 | $2.90 Brushtail possum (*Trichosurus vulpecula*) (horiz) | 5·50 | 5·50 |
| 3221 | $4.20 Common wombat (*Vombatus ursinus*) | 7·00 | 7·00 |

Nos. 3218/3219 also come self-adhesive.

**804** Fitzroy Gardens, Melbourne

**2009.** Australian Parks and Gardens. Multicoloured.

| No. | Description | | |
|---|---|---|---|
| 3224 | 55c. Type **804** | 95 | 95 |
| 3225 | 55c. Roma Street Parkland, Brisbane | 95 | 95 |
| 3226 | 55c. St. David's Park, Hobart | 95 | 95 |
| 3227 | 55c. Commonwealth Park, Canberra | 95 | 95 |
| 3228 | 55c. Hyde Park, Sydney | 95 | 95 |

Nos. 3224/3228 also come self-adhesive.

**2009.** Melbourne Stampshow 2009 National Stamp Exhibition. Sheet 140×95 mm. Sheet containing Nos. 3192, 3208, 3212 and 3224.

| No. | Description | | |
|---|---|---|---|
| **MS**3234 | 55c.×4 ANZAC soldiers of 1915 and Anzac biscuits; Type **802**; 1914 6d. Kookaburra stamp; Type **804** | 3·50 | 3·50 |

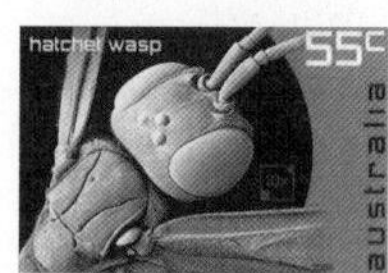


**805** Hatchet Wasp

**2009.** Micro Monsters. Multicoloured.

| No. | Description | | |
|---|---|---|---|
| 3235 | 55c. Type **805** | 1·10 | 1·10 |
| 3236 | 55c. Praying mantis | 1·10 | 1·10 |
| 3237 | 55c. Ground beetle | 1·10 | 1·10 |
| 3238 | 55c. Jumping spider | 1·10 | 1·10 |
| 3239 | 55c. Ant | 1·10 | 1·10 |
| 3240 | $1.10 Weevil | 2·10 | 2·10 |
| **MS**3241 | 160×85 mm. As Nos. 3235/40 | 6·75 | 6·75 |

Nos. 3235/3239 also come self-adhesive.

**806** Bridled Nailtail Wallaby (Australia)

**2009.** Species at Risk. Multicoloured.

| No. | Description | | |
|---|---|---|---|
| 3247 | 55c. Type **806** | 1·10 | 1·10 |
| 3248 | 55c. Norfolk Island green parrot (Norfolk Island) | 1·10 | 1·10 |
| 3249 | 55c. Subantarctic fur seal (Australian Antarctic Territory) | 1·10 | 1·10 |
| 3250 | 55c. Christmas Island blue-tailed skink) (Christmas Island) | 1·10 | 1·10 |
| 3251 | 55c. Green turtle (Cocos (Keeling) Islands) | 1·10 | 1·10 |
| **MS**3252 | 150×85 mm. As Nos. 3247/51 | 5·00 | 5·00 |

Nos. 3247/3251 also come self-adhesive.

**807** Water Tank, Fleurieu Peninsula, South Australia

**2009.** Corrugated Landscapes. Multicoloured.

| No. | Description | | |
|---|---|---|---|
| 3258 | 55c. Type **807** | 95 | 95 |
| 3259 | 55c. Traditional home, Broken Hill, New South Wales | 95 | 95 |
| 3260 | 55c. Nissen hut converted into shearing shed, Bushy Park Cattle Station, Queensland | 95 | 95 |
| 3261 | 55c. Magney House, Bingie Bingie Point, New South Wales | 95 | 95 |

Nos. 3258/3261 also come self-adhesive.

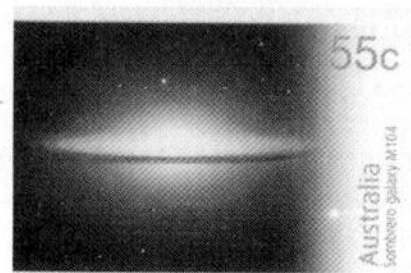


**808** Sombrero Galaxy M104

**2009.** International Year of Astronomy. Stargazing: The Southern Skies. Multicoloured. (i) Domestic Mail.

| No. | Description | | |
|---|---|---|---|
| 3266 | 55c. Type **808** | 1·25 | 1·00 |
| | (ii) International Post. | | |
| 3267 | $1.45 Reflection nebula M78 | 2·75 | 2·75 |
| 3268 | $2.10 Spiral galaxy M83 | 3·75 | 4·00 |
| **MS**3269 | 141×75 mm. Nos. 3266/8 | 7·00 | 7·00 |

**809** Green Catbird (*Ailuroedus crassirostris*)

**2009.** Australian Songbirds. Multicoloured.

| No. | Description | | |
|---|---|---|---|
| 3270 | 55c. Type **809** | 1·10 | 60 |
| 3271 | $1.10 Noisy scrub-bird (*Atrichornis clamosus*) | 2·25 | 1·90 |
| 3272 | $1.65 Mangrove golden whistler (*Pachycephala melanura*) (male) | 3·25 | 3·25 |
| 3273 | $2.75 Pair of scarlet honeyeaters (*Myzomela sanguinolenta*) | 5·00 | 6·00 |

No. 3270 also comes self-adhesive.

**810** Cyclops Pedal Car

**2009.** Classic Toys. Multicoloured.

| No. | Description | | |
|---|---|---|---|
| 3275 | 55c. Type **810** | 1·10 | 1·10 |
| 3276 | 55c. Test Match board game | 1·10 | 1·10 |
| 3277 | 55c. Barbie doll | 1·10 | 1·10 |
| 3278 | 55c. Malvern Star Dragstar bicycle | 1·10 | 1·10 |
| 3279 | 55c. Cabbage Patch Kids doll | 1·10 | 1·10 |

Nos. 3275/3279 also come self-adhesive.

**811** Australian Rules Football

**2009.** Stamp Collecting Month. 'Let's Get active!'. Multicoloured.

| | | | |
|---|---|---|---|
| 3285 | 55c. Type **811** | 1·10 | 1·10 |
| 3286 | 55c. Basketball | 1·10 | 1·10 |
| 3287 | 55c. Soccer | 1·10 | 1·10 |
| 3288 | 55c. Netball | 1·10 | 1·10 |
| 3289 | 55c. Cricket | 1·10 | 1·10 |
| 3290 | 55c. Tennis | 1·10 | 1·10 |
| **MS**3291 | 160×89 mm. Nos. 3285/90 | 6·00 | 6·00 |

Nos. 3285/3290 come self-adhesive.

**812** Patrica Crabb

**2009.** Bicentenary of Postal Services in Australia (3rd issue). 'Our People Your Post'. Multicoloured.

| | | | |
|---|---|---|---|
| 3298 | 55c. Type **812** | 1·10 | 1·10 |
| 3299 | 55c. Shirley Freeman (behind counter, wearing red blouse) | 1·10 | 1·10 |
| 3300 | 55c. Vinko Romank (carrying box of Express Post) | 1·10 | 1·10 |
| 3301 | 55c. Valda Knott (in front of shelving) | 1·10 | 1·10 |
| 3302 | 55c. Gordon Morgan (in front of Australia Post motorcycles) | 1·10 | 1·10 |
| 3303 | 55c. Vongpradith Phongsavan (wearing striped shirt and fluorescent tabard) | 1·10 | 1·10 |
| 3304 | 55c. Norma Thomas and Australia Post contractor's van | 1·10 | 1·10 |
| 3305 | 55c. John Marsh (wearing pale blue shirt) | 1·10 | 1·10 |
| 3306 | 55c. Anne Brun (behind counter) | 1·10 | 1·10 |
| 3307 | 55c. Russell Price (wearing blue jacket with Australia Post emblem) | 1·10 | 1·10 |

**813** Virgin Mary and Infant Jesus

**2009.** Christmas (1st issue). Multicoloured. (a) Ordinary gum. (i) Domestic mail.

| | | | |
|---|---|---|---|
| 3308 | 50c. Type **813** | 95 | 95 |

(ii) International Post.

| | | | |
|---|---|---|---|
| 3309 | $1.25 The Magi | 2·40 | 2·40 |
| **MS**3310 | 106×70 mm. Nos. 3308/9 | 3·25 | 3·25 |

(b) Self-adhesive. (i) Domestic mail.

| | | | |
|---|---|---|---|
| 3311 | 50c. As Type **813** | 1·00 | 1·00 |

(ii) International Post.

| | | | |
|---|---|---|---|
| 3312 | $1.25 As No. 3309 | 2·25 | 2·25 |

**814** Candles enclosed in Star

**2009.** Christmas (2nd issue). Multicoloured. (a) Ordinary gum.

| | | | |
|---|---|---|---|
| 3313 | 50c. Type **814** | 95 | 95 |
| 3314 | 50c. Decorated Christmas tree | 95 | 95 |
| 3315 | 50c. Wrapped gifts enclosed in Santa hat | 95 | 95 |
| 3316 | 50c. Baubles enclosed in bell | 95 | 95 |
| 3317 | 50c. Candy canes enclosed in stocking | 95 | 95 |

(b) Self-adhesive.

| | | | |
|---|---|---|---|
| 3318 | 50c. As Type **814** | 95 | 95 |
| 3319 | 50c. As No. 3314 | 95 | 95 |
| 3320 | 50c. As No. 3315 | 95 | 95 |
| 3321 | 50c. As No. 3316 | 95 | 95 |
| 3322 | 50c. As No. 3317 | 95 | 95 |

(c) Self-adhesive.

| | | | |
|---|---|---|---|
| 3323 | 50c. As Type **814** but gold foil star outline | 1·00 | 1·00 |
| 3324 | 50c. As No. 3314 but gold foil Christmas tree outline | 1·00 | 1·00 |
| 3325 | 50c. As No. 3315 but gold foil Santa hat outline | 1·00 | 1·00 |
| 3326 | 50c. As No. 3316 but gold foil bell outline | 1·00 | 1·00 |
| 3327 | 50c. As No. 3317 but gold foil stocking outline | 1·00 | 1·00 |

**815** Peter Carey

**2010.** Australian Legends (14th series). 'Legends of the Written Word'. Multicoloured. (a) Ordinary gum.

| | | | |
|---|---|---|---|
| 3328 | 55c. Type **815** | 1·10 | 1·10 |
| 3329 | 55c. Peter Carey (black/white photo) | 1·10 | 1·10 |
| 3330 | 55c. David Malouf (black/white photo) | 1·10 | 1·10 |
| 3331 | 55c. David Malouf | 1·10 | 1·10 |
| 3332 | 55c. Colleen McCullough | 1·10 | 1·10 |
| 3333 | 55c. Colleen McCullough (black/white photo) | 1·10 | 1·10 |
| 3334 | 55c. Bryce Courtenay (black/white photo) | 1·10 | 1·10 |
| 3335 | 55c. Bryce Courtenay | 1·10 | 1·10 |
| 3336 | 55c. Thomas Keneally | 1·10 | 1·10 |
| 3337 | 55c. Thomas Keneally (black/white photo) | 1·10 | 1·10 |
| 3338 | 55c. Tim Winton (black/white photo) | 1·10 | 1·10 |
| 3339 | 55c. Tim Winton | 1·10 | 1·10 |

(b) Self-adhesive.

| | | | |
|---|---|---|---|
| 3340 | 55c. As Type **815** | 1·00 | 1·00 |
| 3341 | 55c. As No. 3331 | 1·00 | 1·00 |
| 3342 | 55c. As No. 3332 | 1·00 | 1·00 |
| 3343 | 55c. As No. 3335 | 1·00 | 1·00 |
| 3344 | 55c. As No. 3336 | 1·00 | 1·00 |
| 3345 | 55c. As No. 3339 | 1·00 | 1·00 |

**816** Governor Macquarie and North View of Sydney

**2010.** Bicentenary of Arrival of Governor Lachlan Macquarie in New South Wales. Multicoloured.

| | | | |
|---|---|---|---|
| 3346 | 55c. Type **816** | 1·25 | 1·25 |
| 3347 | 55c. Port Jackson and Sydney Town | 1·25 | 1·25 |
| 3348 | 55c. Parramatta Female Penitentiary, 1818 | 1·25 | 1·25 |
| 3349 | 55c. Government Stables, Sydney, 1817 | 1·25 | 1·25 |

**817** Coat of Arms on Reverse of Florin

**2010.** Centenary of First Australian Commonwealth Coins. Multicoloured.

| | | | |
|---|---|---|---|
| 3350 | 55c. Type **817** | 1·10 | 60 |
| 3351 | $2.75 King Edward VII on Obverse of Florin | 5·50 | 6·60 |
| **MS**3352 | 106×70 mm. As Nos. 3350/1 | 6·50 | 6·50 |

**818** Torah Bright (snowboard – halfpipe)

**2010.** Australian Gold Medallists at Olympic Winter Games, Vancouver. Multicoloured.

| | | | |
|---|---|---|---|
| 3353 | 55c. Type **818** | 1·10 | 1·10 |
| 3354 | 55c. Lydia Lassila (freestyle skiing - aerials) | | |

**819** Colin Defries flying modified Wright Model A *The Stella*, Victoria Park Racecourse, Sydney, 9 December 1909

**2010.** Centenary of Powered Flight. Multicoloured. (a) Ordinary gum. (i) Domestic Mail.

| | | | |
|---|---|---|---|
| 3355 | 55c. Type **819** (first powered flight in Australia) | 1·10 | 60 |

(ii) International Post.

| | | | |
|---|---|---|---|
| 3356 | $1.45 John Duigan's flight, Mia Mia, Victoria, 7 October 1910 (first flight by Australian in Australian plane) | 2·75 | 2·75 |
| 3357 | $2.10 Harry Houdini flying Voisin aircraft, Diggers Rest, Victoria, 18 March 1910 | 3·75 | 4·25 |

(b) Self-adhesive.

| | | | |
|---|---|---|---|
| 3358 | $1.45 As No. 3356 | 2·75 | 2·75 |
| 3359 | $2.10 As No. 3357 | 3·75 | 4·25 |

**2010.** Canberra Stampshow 2010. Sheet 140×95 mm containing Nos. 3346, 3351, and 3355/6.

| | | | |
|---|---|---|---|
| **MS**3360 | 55c. Type **816**; 55c. Type **819**; $1.45 John Duigan's flight, Mia Mia, Victoria, 7 October 1910 (first flight by Australian in Australian plane); $2.75 King Edward VII on obverse of florin coin | 9·00 | 9·00 |

**820** Prize Bull

**2010.** 'Come to the Show'. Multicoloured.

| | | | |
|---|---|---|---|
| 3361 | 55c. Type **820** | 1·00 | 1·00 |
| 3362 | 55c. Cake decorating | 1·00 | 1·00 |
| 3363 | 55c. Winning show horse | 1·00 | 1·00 |
| 3364 | 55c. Wood chopping | 1·00 | 1·00 |
| 3365 | 55c. Prizewinning dog | 1·00 | 1·00 |
| **MS**3366 | 170×85 mm. Nos. 3361/5 | 4·75 | 4·75 |

Nos. 3361/3365 also come self-adhesive.

**821** Queen Elizabeth II leaving St. Andrew's Cathedral, Sydney, 2006

**2010.** Queen's Birthday. Ordinary or self-adhesive gum.

| | | | | |
|---|---|---|---|---|
| 3372 | **821** | 55c. multicoloured | 1·00 | 60 |

**822** Australian Soldiers on Kokoda Trail, 1942

**2010.** Kokoda. Multicoloured. (a) Ordinary gum. (i) Domestic mail.

| | | | |
|---|---|---|---|
| 3374 | 55c. Type **822** | 1·10 | 1·10 |
| 3375 | 55c. Papua New Guineans helping wounded soldiers along trail, 1942 | 1·10 | 1·10 |
| 3376 | 55c. Kokoda veterans | 1·10 | 1·10 |
| 3377 | 55c. Trekker, guide and memorial | 1·10 | 1·10 |

(ii) International Post.

| | | | |
|---|---|---|---|
| 3378 | $1.45 Veterans at Kokoda Isurava Memorial | 2·75 | 2·75 |
| **MS**3379 | 160×90 mm. Nos. 3374/8 | 6·25 | 6·25 |

(b) Self-adhesive.

| | | | |
|---|---|---|---|
| 3380 | 55c. As Type **822** | 1·10 | 1·10 |
| 3381 | 55c. As No. 3375 | 1·10 | 1·10 |
| 3382 | 55c. As No. 3376 | 1·10 | 1·10 |
| 3383 | 55c. As No. 3377 | 1·10 | 1·10 |

Stamps in similar designs were issued by Papua New Guinea.

**823** The Ghan'

**2010.** Great Australian Railway Journeys. Multicoloured.

(a) Ordinary paper. (i) Domestic Mail.

| | | | |
|---|---|---|---|
| 3384 | Type **823** | 1·10 | 1·10 |
| 3385 | 55c. West Coast Wilderness Railway, Tasmania | 1·10 | 1·10 |
| 3386 | 55c. 'The Indian Pacific' | 1·10 | 1·10 |

(ii) International Post. Size 50×30 mm.

| | | | |
|---|---|---|---|
| 3387 | $2.10 Kuranda Scenic Railway, Queensland | 3·75 | 3·75 |
| **MS**3388 | 140×90 mm. No. 3387 | 7·00 | 7·00 |

(b) Self-adhesive. Phosphor over parts of design. (i) Domestic Mail.

| | | | |
|---|---|---|---|
| 3389 | 55c. As Type **823** | 1·10 | 1·10 |
| 3390 | 55c. As No. 3385 | 1·10 | 1·10 |
| 3391 | 55c. As No. 3386 | 1·10 | 1·10 |

(ii) International Post. Size 50×30 mm.

| | | | |
|---|---|---|---|
| 3392 | $2.10 As No. 3387 | 3·75 | 75 |

**824** Queen Victoria

**2010.** Colonial Heritage: Empire (1st issue)

| | | | | |
|---|---|---|---|---|
| 3393 | **824** | $5 multicoloured | 9·50 | 9·50 |
| **MS**3394 | | 140×90 mm. No. 3393 | 9·50 | 9·50 |

**2010.** London 2010 Festival of Stamps. Multicoloured.

| | | | |
|---|---|---|---|
| **MS**3395 | 140×90 mm. Type **819**×2; No. 3356×2 | 4·00 | 4·00 |
| **MS**3396 | 140×90 mm. Type **821**; Type **774**; Type **798**; Type **729** | 9·50 | 9·50 |
| **MS**3397 | 140×90 mm. No. 3387 | 7·50 | 7·50 |
| **MS**3398 | 140×90 mm. No. 3393 | 4·00 | 4·00 |

**825** Peng Peng (Australian kookaburra mascot)

**2010.** Expo 2010, Shanghai, China. Multicoloured.

| | | | |
|---|---|---|---|
| 3399 | 55c. Type **825** | 1·10 | 1·10 |
| 3400 | 55c. Australian pavilion | 1·10 | 1·00 |

**826** Purnululu National Park, Western Australia

**2010.** Australian UNESCO World Heritage Sites. Multicoloured.

(a) Ordinary gum.

| | | | |
|---|---|---|---|
| 3401 | 55c. Type **826** | 1·10 | 1·10 |
| 3402 | 55c. Kakadu National Park, Northern Territory | 1·10 | 1·10 |
| 3403 | $1.10 Mount Warning, Gondwana Rainforests | 2·25 | 2·25 |
| 3404 | $1.10 Tasmanian Wilderness | 2·25 | 2·25 |

(b) Self-adhesive. Partial phosphor frame (at left and foot).

| | | | |
|---|---|---|---|
| 3405 | 55c. As No. 3402 | 1·10 | 1·10 |
| 3406 | 55c. As Type **826** | 1·10 | 1·10 |

**827** Coral Rabbitfish

**2010.** Fish of the Reef. Multicoloured.

(a) Ordinary gum

| | | | |
|---|---|---|---|
| 3407 | 5c. Type **827** | 15 | 15 |
| 3408 | 60c. Clown triggerfish | 1·10 | 1·10 |
| 3409 | 60c. Spotted sweetlips | 1·10 | 1·10 |
| 3410 | 60c. Golden damselfish | 1·10 | 1·10 |
| 3411 | 50c. Regal angelfish | 1·10 | 1·10 |
| 3412 | $1.20 Saddle butterflyfish | 2·50 | 2·50 |
| 3413 | $1.80 Chevron butterflyfish | 2·75 | 2·75 |
| 3414 | $3 Orangefin anemonefish (50×30 mm) | 5·50 | 5·50 |

(b) Self-adhesive

| | | | |
|---|---|---|---|
| 3415 | 5c. As Type **827** | 15 | 15 |
| 3416 | 60c. As No. 3408 | 1·10 | 1·10 |
| 3417 | 60c. As No. 3409 | 1·10 | 1·10 |
| 3418 | 60c. As No. 3410 | 1·10 | 1·10 |
| 3419 | 60c. As No. 3411 | 1·10 | 1·10 |

Nos. 3420/5 are left vacant for possible additions to this series of definitive stamps.

**828** Bay of Fires, Tasmania

**2010.** International Stamps. Australian Beaches. Multicoloured.

(a) Ordinary gum

| | | | |
|---|---|---|---|
| 3426 | $1.50 Type **828** | 3·25 | 3·25 |
| 3427 | $2.20 Cape Tribulation, Queensland | 4·25 | 4·25 |
| 3428 | $4.30 Hellfire Bay, Western Australia (50×30 mm) | 7·50 | 7·50 |

(b) Self-adhesive

| | | | |
|---|---|---|---|
| 3429 | $1.50 As Type **828** | 3·25 | 3·25 |
| 3430 | $2.20 As No. 3427 | 4·25 | 4·25 |

**829** 'Piper'

**2010.** Adopted and Adored. Dogs. Multicoloured.

(a) Ordinary paper

| | | | |
|---|---|---|---|
| 3431 | 60c. Type **829** | 1·20 | 1·20 |
| 3432 | 60c. Jessie | 1·20 | 1·20 |
| 3433 | 60c. Buckley | 1·20 | 1·20 |
| 3434 | 60c. Daisy | 1·20 | 1·20 |
| 3435 | 60c. Tigger | 1·20 | 1·20 |

(b) Self-adhesive

| | | | |
|---|---|---|---|
| 3436 | 60c. As Type **829** | 1·20 | 1·20 |
| 3437 | 60c. As No. 3432 | 1·20 | 1·20 |
| 3438 | 60c. As No. 3433 | 1·20 | 1·20 |
| 3439 | 60c. As No. 3434 | 1·20 | 1·20 |
| 3440 | 60c. As No. 3435 | 1·20 | 1·20 |

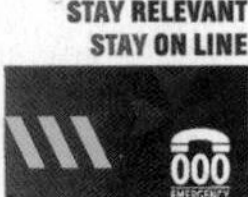


**830** 'STAY FOCUSED STAY RELEVANT STAY ON LINE'

**2010.** Emergency Services. Multicoloured.

(a) Ordinary gum

| | | | |
|---|---|---|---|
| 3441 | 60c. Type **830** | 1·20 | 1·20 |
| 3442 | 60c. Police helicopter | 1·20 | 1·20 |
| 3443 | 60c. Fire emblem | 1·20 | 1·20 |
| 3444 | 60c. Ambulance service emblem | 1·20 | 1·20 |

(b) Self-adhesive

| | | | |
|---|---|---|---|
| 3445 | 60c. As Type **830** | 1·20 | 1·20 |
| 3446 | 60c. As No. 3442 | 1·20 | 1·20 |
| 3447 | 60c. As No. 3443 | 1·20 | 1·20 |
| 3448 | 60c. As No. 3444 | 1·20 | 1·20 |

**831** Gold and White Design

**2010.** Greetings Stamps. 'For Special Occasions'. Multicoloured.

(a) Ordinary gum

| | | | |
|---|---|---|---|
| 3449 | 60c. Type **831** | 1·10 | 1·10 |
| 3450 | 60c. Pink tulips | 1·10 | 1·10 |
| 3451 | 60c. Cream roses | 1·10 | 1·10 |
| 3452 | 60c. Glasses of champagne | 1·10 | 1·10 |
| 3453 | 60c. Three balloons | 1·10 | 1·10 |
| 3454 | 60c. Teddy bear holding daisy | 1·10 | 1·10 |
| 3455 | 60c. Wattle flowers | 1·10 | 1·10 |
| 3456 | 60c. Southern Cross (deep blue background) (30×30 mm) | 1·10 | 1·10 |
| 3457 | 60c. Southern Cross (orange and pink background) (30×30 mm) | 1·10 | 1·10 |
| 3458 | $1.20 Wedding and engagement rings | 2·50 | 2·50 |

(b) Self-adhesive

| | | | |
|---|---|---|---|
| 3459 | 60c. As No. 3450 | 1·10 | 1·10 |
| 3460 | 60c. As No. 3451 | 1·10 | 1·10 |
| 3461 | 60c. As No. 3453 | 1·10 | 1·10 |
| 3462 | 60c. As No. 3454 | 1·10 | 1·10 |
| 3463 | 60c. As No. 3455 | 1·10 | 1·10 |
| 3464 | $1.20 As No. 3458 | 2·50 | 2·50 |

**832** Construction Worker, Doctor and Teacher

**2010.** Centenary of Australian Taxation Office

| | | | | |
|---|---|---|---|---|
| 3465 | **832** | 60c. multicoloured | 1·10 | 1·10 |

**833**

**2010.** 150th Anniv of Departure of Burke and Wills Expedition. Multicoloured.

(a) Ordinary gum

| | | | |
|---|---|---|---|
| 3466 | 60c. Type **833** | 1·20 | 1·20 |
| 3467 | 60c. Expedition leaving Melbourne, August 1860 | 1·20 | 1·20 |
| 3468 | $1.20 Return of Burke, Wills and John King from Gulf of Carpentaria to Cooper's Creek, April 1861 | 2·50 | 2·50 |
| 3469 | $1.20 Burke, Wills and King on journey to Mount Hopeless | 2·50 | 2·50 |

(b) Self-adhesive

| | | | |
|---|---|---|---|
| 3470 | 60c. As No. 3467 | 1·20 | 1·20 |
| 3471 | 60c. As Type **833** | 1·20 | 1·20 |

**2010.** Bangkok 2010 25th Asian International Stamp Exhibition. Multicoloured.

| | | | |
|---|---|---|---|
| **MS**3472 | 5c. Coral Rabbitfish×2; 60c. Oriental sweetlips; 60c. Clown triggerfish | 2·40 | 2·40 |

**2010.** Stampex '10 National Stamp Exhibition, Adelaide. Multicoloured.

| | | | |
|---|---|---|---|
| **MS**3473 | 60c. Type **833**; $2.05 Jade iceberg | 5·25 | 5·25 |

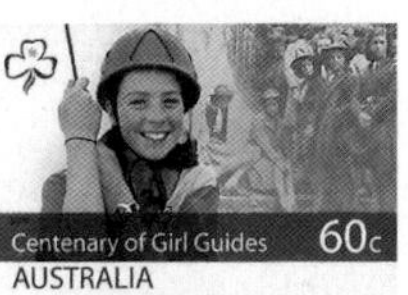


**834**

**2010.** Centenary of Girl Guides Australia. Multicoloured.

(a) Ordinary gum. (i) Domestic Mail

| | | | |
|---|---|---|---|
| 3474 | 60c. Type **834** | 1·50 | 1·50 |

(ii) International Mail

| | | | |
|---|---|---|---|
| 3475 | $1.50 Two guides making guide sign | 2·75 | 2·75 |
| 3476 | $2.20 Olave Baden-Powell (founder) | 4·50 | 4·50 |

(b) Self-adhesive. (i) Domestic Mail

| | | | |
|---|---|---|---|
| 3477 | 60c. As Type **834** | 1·50 | 1·50 |

(ii) International Post

| | | | |
|---|---|---|---|
| 3478 | $1.50 As No. 3475 | 2·75 | 4·50 |
| 3479 | $2.20 As No. 3476 | 4·50 | 4·50 |

**835**

**2010.** National Service Memorial, Canberra

(a) Ordinary gum

| | | | | |
|---|---|---|---|---|
| 3480 | **835** | 60c. multicoloured | 1·30 | 1·30 |

(b) Self-adhesive. Irregular partial phosphor frame.

| | | | | |
|---|---|---|---|---|
| 3481 | **835** | 60c. multicoloured | 1·30 | 1·30 |

**836** Children on Beach, 1950s

**2010.** 'Long Weekend'. Multicoloured.

(a) Ordinary gum

| | | | |
|---|---|---|---|
| 3482 | 60c. Type **836** | 1·30 | 1·30 |
| 3483 | 60c. Family camping, 1960s | 1·30 | 1·30 |
| 3484 | 60c. Surfers on beach, 1970s | 1·30 | 1·30 |
| 3485 | 60c. Family on shore and houseboat on Lake Eildon, Victoria, 1980s | 1·30 | 1·30 |
| 3486 | 60c. Children playing in snow, 1990s | 1·30 | 1·30 |

(b) Self-adhesive. Phosphor over parts of design

| | | | |
|---|---|---|---|
| 3487 | 60c. As Type **836** | 1·30 | 1·30 |
| 3488 | 60c. As No. 3483 | 1·30 | 1·30 |
| 3489 | 60c. As No. 3484 | 1·30 | 1·30 |
| 3490 | 60c. As No. 3485 | 1·30 | 1·30 |
| 3491 | 60c. As No. 3486 | 1·30 | 1·30 |

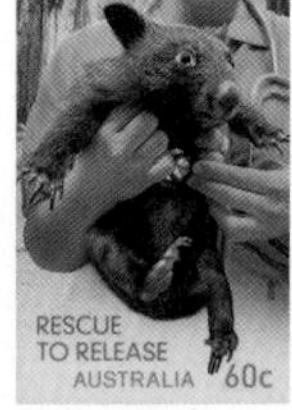


**837** Common Wombat

**2010.** Wildlife Caring: Rescue to Release. Multicoloured.

(a) Ordinary gum

| | | | |
|---|---|---|---|
| 3492 | 60c. Type **837** | 1·20 | 1·20 |
| 3493 | 60c. Eastern grey kangaroo | 1·20 | 1·20 |
| 3494 | 60c. Koala | 1·20 | 1·20 |
| 3495 | 60c. Grey-headed flying fox | 1·20 | 1·20 |
| 3496 | 60c. Southern boobook owl | 1·20 | 1·20 |
| 3497 | $1.20 Ringtail possum | 3·00 | 3·00 |
| **MS**3498 | 170×85 mm. Nos. 3492/7 | 8·50 | 8·50 |

(b) Self-adhesive

| | | | |
|---|---|---|---|
| 3499 | 60c. As Type **837** | 1·20 | 1·20 |
| 3500 | 60c. As No. 3493 | 1·20 | 1·20 |
| 3501 | 60c. As No. 3494 | 1·20 | 1·20 |
| 3502 | 60c. As No. 3495 | 1·20 | 1·20 |
| 3503 | 60c. As No. 3496 | 1·20 | 1·20 |

**838** Mary MacKillop

**2010.** Canonisation of Mary MacKillop (Mother Mary of the Cross, founder of Sisters of St. Joseph of the Sacred Heart)

| | | | | |
|---|---|---|---|---|
| 3504 | **838** | 60c. multicoloured | 1·20 | 1·20 |

**839** Red-backed Kingfisher (*Todiramphus pyrrhopygius*)

**2010.** Australian Kingfishers. Multicoloured.

(a) Ordinary gum

| | | | |
|---|---|---|---|
| 3505 | 60c. Type **839** | 1·50 | 1·50 |
| 3506 | $1.20 Sacred kingfisher (*Todiramphus sanctus*) | 1·70 | 1·70 |
| 3507 | $1.80 Blue-winged kookaburra (*Dacelo leachii*) | 3·00 | 3·00 |
| 3508 | $3 Yellow-billed kingfisher (*Syma torotoro*) | 5·75 | 5·75 |

(b) Self-adhesive

| | | | |
|---|---|---|---|
| 3509 | 60c. As Type **839** | 1·20 | 1·20 |

**840** Melbourne Cup, 2010

**2010.** 150th Anniv of Melbourne Cup Horse Race. Multicoloured.

(a) Ordinary gum

| | | | |
|---|---|---|---|
| 3510 | 60c. Type **840** | 1·20 | 1·20 |

3511 60c. Carbine, 1890 (horiz) 1·20 1·20
3512 60c. Phar Lap, 1930 (horiz) 1·20 1·20
3513 60c. Saintly, 1996 (horiz) 1·20 1·20
**MS**3514 160×85 mm. Nos. 3510/13 5·00 5·00

(b) Self-adhesive

3515 60c. As No. 3511 1·20 1·20
3516 60c. As No. 3512 1·20 1·20
3517 60c. As No. 3513 1·20 1·20

**841** Young Girl writing Letter

**2010.** Christmas (1st issue). Dear Santa. Multicoloured.

(a) Ordinary gum

3518 55c. Type **841** 1·20 1·20
3519 55c. Santa reading letter 1·20 1·20

(b) Self-adhesive

3520 55c. As No. 3519 1·20 1·20
3521 55c. As Type **841** 1·20 1·20
3522 55c. As Type **841** but foil 'AUSTRALIA' and varnish on letter and stocking 1·20 1·20
3523 55c. As No. 3519 but foil 'AUSTRALIA' and varnish on Santa's beard, cuffs and boots 1·20 1·20

**842** Madonna and Child

**2010.** Christmas (2nd issue). Multicoloured.

(a) Ordinary gum

(i) Domestic mail

3524 55c. Type **842** 1·20 1·20

(ii) International Post

3525 $1.30 Angel and shepherds 2·50 2·50

(b) Self-adhesive

(i) Domestic mail

3526 55c. As Type **842** 1·20 1·20

(ii) International Post

3527 $1.30 As No. 3525 2·50 2·50

**843** 'LOVE' and Red Roses

**2010.** Greetings Stamps. Multicoloured.

(a) Ordinary gum

3528 60c. Type **843** 1·20 1·20
3529 60c. Pattern of hearts, flowers and vine leaves 1·20 1·20

(b) Self-adhesive

3530 60c. As Type **843** 1·20 1·20
3531 60c. As No. 3529 1·20 1·20
3532 60c. As No. 3452 1·20 1·20

**844** Eva Cox (feminist)

**2011.** Australian Legends (15th series). Multicoloured.

(a) Ordinary gum

3533 60c. Type **844** 1·20 1·20
3534 60c. Germaine Greer (feminist author) 1·20 1·20
3535 60c. Elizabeth Evatt (former chief judge) 1·20 1·20
3536 60c. Anne Summers (writer and co-founder of first women's refuge) 1·20 1·20

(b) Self-adhesive

3537 60c. As Type **844** 1·20 1·20
3538 60c. As No. 3534 1·20 1·20
3539 60c. As No. 3535 1·20 1·20
3540 60c. As No. 3536

Nos. 3541/50, T **845** are left for Premier's Flood Relief Appeal sheetlet, issued 27 January 2011, not yet received.

**846** Women's Eyes

**2011.** Centenary of International Women's Day
3551 **846** 60c. multicoloured 1·30 1·30

**847** F-111 ('Pig')

**2011.** Royal Australian Air Force (RAAF) Aviation. Multicoloured.

(a) Ordinary gum

3552 60c. Type **847** 1·30 1·30
3553 60c. F/A -18F 1·30 1·30
3554 $1.20 Wedgetail 3·25 3·25
3555 $3 C-17 Globemaster III 5·75 5·75
**MS**3556 135×72 mm. Nos. 3552/5 11·50 11·50

(b) Self-adhesive

3557 60c. As Type **847** 1·30 1·30
3558 60c. As No. 3553 1·30 1·30

Nos. 3552/3 were printed together, *se-tenant*, as horizontal pairs, each pair forming a composite background design. The stamps and margins of **MS**3556 form a composite design.

**848** Gerbera

**2011.** Floral Festivals Australia. Multicoloured.

(a) Ordinary paper

3559 60c. Type **848** (Melbourne International Flower and Garden Show) 1·30 1·30
3560 60c. Jacaranda (Jacaranda Festival, Grafton) 1·30 1·30
3561 60c. Australian everlasting (Kings Park Festival, Perth) 1·30 1·30
3562 60c. Violet (Toowoomba Carnival of Flowers) 1·30 1·30
3563 60c. Tulip (Floriade, Canberra) 1·30 1·30

(b) Self-adhesive

3564 60c. As Type **848** 1·30 1·30
3565 60c. As No. 3560 1·30 1·30
3566 60c. As No. 3561 1·30 1·30
3567 60c. As No. 3562 1·30 1·30
3568 60c. As No. 3563 1·30 1·30

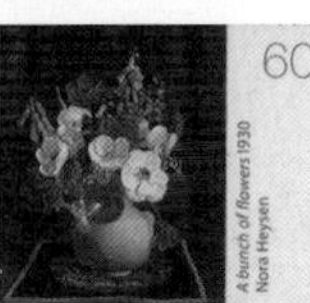


**849** *A Bunch of Flowers* (Nora Heysen), 1930

**2011.** The Gallery Series. National Gallery of Victoria: Flowers (1st series). Multicoloured.

(a) Ordinary gum

3569 60c. Type **849** 1·30 1·30
3570 60c. *Camellias* (Arnold Shore), 1937 1·30 1·30
3571 60c. *Fruit and Flowers* (Vida Lahey), c. 1924 1·30 1·30
3572 60c. *Still Life, Zinnias* (Roy de Maistre), 1925–30 1·30 1·30
3573 60c. *A Cottage Bunch* (Hans Heysen), 1930 1·30 1·30

(b) Self-adhesive

3574 60c. As Type **849** 1·30 1·30
3575 60c. As No. 3570 1·30 1·30
3576 60c. As No. 3571 1·30 1·30
3577 60c. As No. 3572 1·30 1·30
3578 60c. As No. 3573 1·30 1·30

**850** Salt Pan ('The Dry')

**2011.** Lake Eyre. Multicoloured.

(a) Ordinary gum. (i) Domestic mail

3579 60c. Type **850** 1·30 1·30

(ii) Internatonal Post

3580 $1.55 Green land with pools of water ('New Growth') 3·00 3·00
3581 $2.25 Australian pelican flying over breeding colony on island ('Bird Life') 3·75 3·75
3582 $3.10 Lake Eyre ('In Flood') 6·75 6·75

(b) Self-adhesive

3583 $1.55 As No. 3580 2·10 2·10
3584 $2.25 As No. 3581 3·00 3·00

**851** Queen Elizabeth II, 1984 (Brian Dunlop)

**2011.** 85th Birthday of Queen Elizabeth II. Multicoloured.

(i) Domestic Mail

3585 60c. Type **851** 1·30 1·30

(ii) International Post

3586 $2.25 Queen Elizabeth II, 2005 (Rolf Harris) 4·75 4·75
**MS**3587 106×70 mm. Nos. 3585/6 6·25 6·25

**852** Prince William and Miss Catherine Middleton

**2011.** Royal Wedding. Multicoloured.

(a) Ordinary gum. (i) Domestic mail

3588 60c. Type **852** 1·30 1·30

(ii) International Post

3589 $2.25 As Type **852** but white background 5·00 5·00
**MS**3590 106×70 mm. Nos. 3588/9 6·25 6·25

(b) Self-adhesive

3591 60c. As Type **852** 1·30 1·30

**845** Rescuer carrying Baby

**2011.** Premier's Flood Relief Appeal. Multicoloured.

3541 60c. Type **845** 1·30 1·30
3542 60c. House surrounded by floodwater 1·30 1·30
3543 60c. Rescuing cat from flooded house 1·30 1·30
3544 60c. Wallaby on debris in floodwater 1·30 1·30
3545 60c. Aerial view of flooded houses and street 1·30 1·30

Each sheetlet was sold at $8, a $2 premium over face value. This premium went to the Premier's Flood Relief Appeal.

Nos. 3546/50 are vacant.

### OFFICIAL STAMPS

**1931.** Optd O.S. (a) Kangaroo issue.

O133 **1** 6d. brown 28·00 20·00

(b) King George V issue.

O128 **3** ½d. orange 6·00 1·50
O129 **3** 1d. green 3·25 45
O130 **3** 2d. red 16·00 55
O131 **3** 3d. blue 7·50 4·50
O126 **3** 4d. olive 19·00 3·00
O132 **3** 5d. brown 40·00 27·00

(c) Various issues.

O123 **13** 2d. red 65·00 23·00
O134 **18** 2d. red 6·00 2·00
O124 **13** 3d. blue £250 27·00
O135 **18** 3d. blue 14·00 5·00
O136 **17** 1s. green 45·00 27·00

### POSTAGE DUE STAMPS

**D1**

**1902.** White space below value at foot.

D1 **D1** ½d. green 3·25 4·75
D2 **D1** 1d. green 20·00 9·50
D3 **D1** 2d. green 50·00 11·00
D4 **D1** 3d. green 42·00 25·00
D5 **D1** 4d. green 42·00 12·00
D6 **D1** 6d. green 60·00 9·50
D7 **D1** 8d. green 95·00 80·00
D8 **D1** 5s. green £200 70·00

**D3**

**1902.** White space filled in.

D22 **D3** ½d. green 15·00 11·00
D23 **D3** 1d. green 15·00 4·25
D24 **D3** 2d. green 38·00 3·00
D25 **D3** 3d. green 70·00 16·00
D26 **D3** 4d. green 60·00 16·00
D17 **D3** 5d. green 60·00 13·00
D28 **D3** 6d. green 65·00 10·00
D29 **D3** 8d. green £130 55·00
D18 **D3** 10d. green 85·00 17·00
D19 **D3** 1s. green 65·00 14·00
D20 **D3** 2s. green £120 18·00
D33 **D3** 5s. green £325 22·00
D43 **D3** 10s. green £1800 £1800
D44 **D3** 20s. green £4000 £2250

**1908.** As Type D 3, but stroke after figure of value, thus "5/-".

D58 1s. green 90·00 11·00
D60 2s. green £1000 £14000
D59 5s. green £250 48·00
D61 10s. green £2500 £22000
D62 20s. green £6500 £45000

**D7**

**1909**

D132 **D7** ½d. red and green 4·00 3·50
D133 **D7** 1d. red and green 2·50 3·00
D93 **D7** 1½d. red and green 1·50 9·00
D121 **D7** 2d. red and green 6·00 1·25
D134 **D7** 3d. red and green 1·75 3·00
D109 **D7** 4d. red and green 8·50 3·75
D124 **D7** 5d. red and green 16·00 7·00
D137 **D7** 6d. red and green 2·50 2·00
D126 **D7** 7d. red and green 2·25 1·50
D127 **D7** 8d. red and green 3·25 15·00
D139 **D7** 10d. red and green 3·25 1·75
D128 **D7** 1s. red and green 17·00 1·75

| | | | | |
|---|---|---|---|---|
| D70 | **D7** | 2s. red and green | 70·00 | 8·50 |
| D71 | **D7** | 5s. red and green | 90·00 | 11·00 |
| D72 | **D7** | 10s. red and green | £250 | £150 |
| D73 | **D7** | £1 red and green | £500 | £300 |

**D10**

**1953**

| | | | | |
|---|---|---|---|---|
| D140 | **D10** | 1s. red and green | 5·50 | 2·25 |
| D130 | **D10** | 2s. red and green | 14·00 | 7·00 |
| D131a | **D10** | 5s. red and green | 12·00 | 1·00 |

Pt. 1

## AUSTRALIAN ANTARCTIC TERRITORY

By an Order in Council of 7 February 1933, the territory S. of latitude 60°S. between 160th and 145th meridians of East longitude (excepting Adelie Land) was placed under Australian administration. Until 1957 stamps of Australia were used from the base.

1957. 12 pence = 1 shilling; 20 shillings = 1 pound.
1966. 100 cents = 1 dollar.

**1** 1954 Expedition at Vestfold Hills and Map

**1957**

| | | | | |
|---|---|---|---|---|
| 1 | **1** | 2s. blue | 1·00 | 50 |

**2** Members of Shackleton Expedition at S. Magnetic Pole, 1909

**3** Weazel and Team

**1959**

| | | | | |
|---|---|---|---|---|
| 2 | **2** | 5d. on 4d. black and sepia | 60 | 15 |
| 3 | **3** | 8d. on 7d. black and blue | 1·75 | 2·25 |
| 4 | - | 1s. myrtle | 2·25 | 2·00 |
| 5 | - | 2s.3d. green | 7·00 | 3·00 |

DESIGNS—VERT (as Type **3**): 1s. Dog-team and iceberg; 2s.3d. Map of Antarctica and emperor penguins.

**6**

**1961**

| | | | | |
|---|---|---|---|---|
| 6 | **6** | 5d. blue | 1·00 | 20 |

**7** Sir Douglas Mawson (Expedition leader)

**1961.** 50th Anniv of 1911–14 Australian Antarctic Expedition.

| | | | | |
|---|---|---|---|---|
| 7 | **7** | 5d. myrtle | 35 | 20 |

**8** Aurora and Camera Dome

**1966.** Multicoloured.. Multicoloured..

| | | | |
|---|---|---|---|
| 8 | 1c. Type **8** | 70 | 30 |
| 9 | 2c. Emperor penguins | 3·00 | 80 |
| 10 | 4c. Ship and iceberg | 1·00 | 90 |
| 11 | 5c. Banding southern elephant-seals | 2·25 | 1·75 |
| 12 | 7c. Measuring snow strata | 80 | 80 |
| 13 | 10c. Wind gauges | 1·00 | 1·10 |
| 14 | 15c. Weather balloon | 5·00 | 2·00 |
| 15 | 20c. Bell Trooper helicopter (horiz) | 9·00 | 2·50 |
| 16 | 25c. Radio operator (horiz) | 1·75 | 2·25 |
| 17 | 50c. Ice-compression tests (horiz) | 2·50 | 4·00 |
| 18 | $1 Parahelion ("mock sun") (horiz) | 19·00 | 12·00 |

**11** Sastrugi (Snow Ridges)

**1971.** 10th Anniv of Antarctic Treaty.

| | | | | |
|---|---|---|---|---|
| 19 | **11** | 6c. blue and black | 75 | 1·00 |
| 20 | - | 30c. multicoloured | 2·75 | 6·00 |

DESIGN: 30c. Pancake ice.

**12** Capt. Cook, Sextant and Compass

**1972.** Bicentenary of Cook's Circumnavigation of Antarctica. Multicoloured.

| | | | |
|---|---|---|---|
| 21 | 7c. Type **12** | 1·00 | 75 |
| 22 | 35c. Chart and H.M.S. "Resolution" | 3·00 | 1·25 |

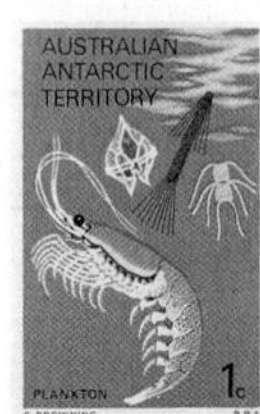

**13** Plankton

**1973.** Multicoloured.. Multicoloured..

| | | | |
|---|---|---|---|
| 23 | 1c. Type **13** | 30 | 20 |
| 24 | 5c. Mawson's De Havilland Gipsy Moth, 1931 | 55 | 1·00 |
| 25 | 7c. Adelie penguin | 1·50 | 1·00 |
| 26 | 8c. De Havilland Fox Moth, 1934–37 | 60 | 1·25 |
| 27 | 9c. Leopard seal (horiz) | 40 | 1·25 |
| 28 | 10c. Killer whale (horiz) | 2·25 | 2·00 |
| 29 | 20c. Wandering albatross ("Albatross") (horiz) | 1·50 | 1·00 |
| 30 | 25c. Wilkins's Lockheed Vega "San Francisco", 1928 (horiz) | 55 | 1·00 |
| 31 | 30c. Ellsworth's Northrop Gamma "Polar Star", 1935 | 55 | 1·00 |
| 32 | 35c. Christensen's Avro Type 581 Avian, 1934 (horiz) | 55 | 1·00 |
| 33 | 50c. Byrd's Ford Trimotor "Floyd Bennett", 1929 | 55 | 1·25 |
| 34 | $1 Sperm whale | 75 | 1·40 |

**14** Admiral Byrd (expedition leader), Ford Trimotor "Floyd Bennett" and Map of South Pole

**1979.** 50th Anniv of First Flight over South Pole. Multicoloured.

| | | | |
|---|---|---|---|
| 35 | 20c. Type **14** | 25 | 60 |
| 36 | 55c. Admiral Byrd, aircraft and Antarctic terrain | 50 | 1·25 |

**15** "Thala Dan" (supply ship)

**1979.** Ships. Multicoloured.

| | | | |
|---|---|---|---|
| 37 | 1c. "Aurora" (horiz) | 15 | 10 |
| 38 | 2c. "Penola" (Rymill's ship) | 40 | 10 |
| 39 | 5c. Type **15** | 30 | 40 |
| 40 | 10c. H.M.S. "Challenger" (survey ship) (horiz) | 50 | 1·50 |
| 41 | 15c. "Morning" (bow view) (whaling ship) (horiz) | 2·00 | 3·00 |
| 42 | 15c. "Nimrod" (stern view) (Shackleton's ship) (horiz) | 1·40 | 2·00 |
| 43 | 20c. "Discovery II" (supply ship) (horiz) | 1·50 | 1·50 |
| 44 | 22c. "Terra Nova" (Scott's ship) | 1·00 | 1·25 |
| 45 | 25c. "Endurance" (Shackleton's ship) | 60 | 1·00 |
| 46 | 30c. "Fram" (Amundsen's ship) (horiz) | 60 | 1·75 |
| 47 | 35c. "Nella Dan" (supply ship) (horiz) | 80 | 1·75 |
| 48 | 40c. "Kista Dan" (supply ship) | 1·25 | 2·25 |
| 49 | 45c. "L'Astrolabe" (D'Urville's ship) (horiz) | 70 | 1·50 |
| 50 | 50c. "Norvegia" (supply ship) (horiz) | 70 | 70 |
| 51 | 55c. "Discovery" (Scott's ship) | 1·00 | 2·00 |
| 52 | $1 H.M.S. "Resolution" (Cook's ship) | 1·75 | 2·50 |

No. 41 is incorrectly inscr "S.Y. Nimrod".

**16** Sir Douglas Mawson in Antarctic Terrain

**1982.** Birth Centenary of Sir Douglas Mawson (Antarctic explorer). Multicoloured.

| | | | |
|---|---|---|---|
| 53 | 27c. Type **16** | 25 | 25 |
| 54 | 75c. Sir Douglas Mawson and map of Australian Antarctic Territory | 75 | 1·50 |

**17** Light-mantled Sooty Albatross

**1983.** Regional Wildlife. Multicoloured.

| | | | |
|---|---|---|---|
| 55 | 27c. Type **17** | 60 | 90 |
| 56 | 27c. King cormorant ("Macquarie Island shag") | 60 | 90 |
| 57 | 27c. Southern elephant seal | 60 | 90 |
| 58 | 27c. Royal penguin | 60 | 90 |
| 59 | 27c. Dove prion ("Antarctic prion") | 60 | 90 |

**18** Antarctic Scientist

**1983.** 12th Antarctic Treaty Consultative Meeting. Canberra.

| | | | | |
|---|---|---|---|---|
| 60 | **18** | 27c. multicoloured | 55 | 1·00 |

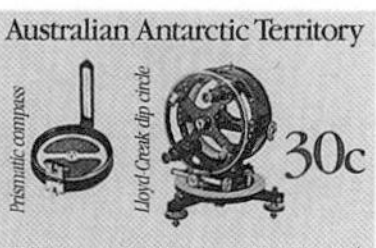

**19** Prismatic Compass and Lloyd-Creak Dip Circle

**1984.** 75th Anniv of Magnetic Pole Expedition. Multicoloured.

| | | | |
|---|---|---|---|
| 61 | 30c. Type **19** | 30 | 30 |
| 62 | 85c. Aneroid barometer and theodolite | 70 | 1·25 |

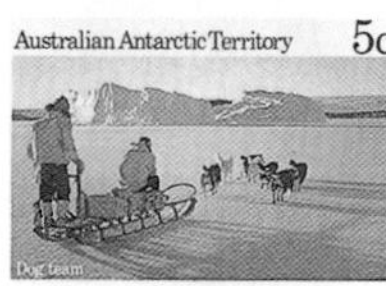

**20** Dog Team pulling Sledge

**1984.** Antarctic Scenes. Multicoloured.

| | | | |
|---|---|---|---|
| 63 | 2c. Summer afternoon, Mawson Station | 20 | 1·00 |
| 64 | 5c. Type **20** | 20 | 30 |
| 65 | 10c. Late summer evening, MacRobertson Land | 20 | 40 |
| 66 | 15c. Prince Charles Mountains | 20 | 1·00 |
| 67 | 20c. Summer morning, Wilkesland | 20 | 1·50 |
| 68 | 25c. Sea-ice and iceberg | 60 | 1·50 |
| 69 | 30c. Mount Coates | 25 | 50 |
| 70 | 33c. "Iceberg Alley", Mawson | 25 | 1·00 |
| 71 | 36c. Early winter evening, Casey Station | 50 | 50 |
| 72 | 45c. Brash ice (vert) | 70 | 2·00 |
| 73 | 60c. Midwinter shadows, Casey Station | 50 | 65 |
| 74 | 75c. Coastline | 2·25 | 3·00 |
| 75 | 85c. Landing strip | 2·50 | 3·00 |
| 76 | 90c. Pancake ice (vert) | 75 | 80 |
| 77 | $1 Emperor penguins | 3·00 | 1·50 |

**21** Prince Charles Mountains near Mawson Station

**1986.** 25th Anniv of Antarctic Treaty.

| | | | | |
|---|---|---|---|---|
| 78 | **21** | 36c. multicoloured | 1·25 | 1·10 |

**22** Hourglass Dolphins and "Nella Dan"

**1988.** Environment, Conservation and Technology. Multicoloured.

| | | | |
|---|---|---|---|
| 79 | 37c. Type **22** | 1·10 | 1·40 |
| 80 | 37c. Emperor penguins and Davis Station | 1·10 | 1·40 |
| 81 | 37c. Crabeater seal and Hughes 500D helicopters | 1·10 | 1·40 |
| 82 | 37c. Adelie penguins and tracked vehicle | 1·10 | 1·40 |
| 83 | 37c. Grey-headed albatross and photographer | 1·10 | 1·40 |

**23** "Antarctica"

**1989.** Antarctic Landscape Paintings by Sir Sidney Nolan. Multicoloured.

| | | | |
|---|---|---|---|
| 84 | 39c. Type **23** | 1·50 | 1·75 |
| 85 | 39c. "Iceberg Alley" | 1·50 | 1·75 |
| 86 | 60c. "Glacial Flow" | 2·50 | 2·75 |
| 87 | 80c. "Frozen Sea" | 3·00 | 3·25 |

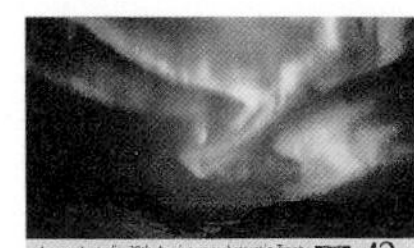

**24** "Aurora Australis"

**1991.** 30th Anniv of Antarctic Treaty (43c.) and Maiden Voyage of "Aurora Australis" (research ship) ($1.20). Multicoloured.

| | | | |
|---|---|---|---|
| 88 | 43c. Type **24** | 75 | 60 |
| 89 | $1.20 "Aurora Australis" off Heard Island | 2·75 | 4·25 |

**25** Adelie Penguin and Chick

**1992.** Antarctic Wildlife. Multicoloured.

| | | | |
|---|---|---|---|
| 90 | 45c. Type **25** | 75 | 50 |
| 91 | 75c. Elephant seal with pup | 1·25 | 90 |
| 92 | 85c. Hall's giant petrel ("Northern giant petrel") on nest with fledgeling | 1·40 | 1·00 |
| 93 | 95c. Weddell seal and pup | 1·50 | 1·00 |
| 94 | $1 Royal penguin | 1·60 | 1·00 |
| 95 | $1.20 Emperor penguins with chicks (vert) | 1·75 | 1·40 |
| 96 | $1.40 Fur seal | 1·75 | 1·75 |
| 97 | $1.50 King penguin (vert) | 1·75 | 2·25 |

**26** Head of Husky

**1994.** Departure of Huskies from Antarctica. Multicoloured.

| | | | |
|---|---|---|---|
| 104 | 45c. Type **26** | 1·75 | 75 |
| 105 | 75c. Dogs pulling sledge (horiz) | 2·00 | 2·00 |
| 106 | 85c. Husky in harness | 2·25 | 2·25 |
| 107 | $1.05 Dogs on leads (horiz) | 2·50 | 2·50 |

**27** Humpback Whale with Calf

**1995.** Whales and Dolphins. Multicoloured.

| | | | |
|---|---|---|---|
| 108 | 45c. Type **27** | 1·75 | 80 |
| 109 | 45c. Pair of hourglass dolphins (vert) | 1·75 | 1·75 |
| 110 | 45c. Pair of minke whales (vert) | 1·75 | 1·75 |
| 111 | $1 Killer whale | 3·00 | 3·00 |
| **MS**112 | 146×64 mm. Nos. 108/11 | 8·00 | 8·00 |

Nos. 109/10 were printed together, se-tenant, forming a composite design.

**28** "Rafting Sea Ice" (Christian Clare Robertson)

**1996.** Paintings by Christian Clare Robertson. Multicoloured.

| | | | |
|---|---|---|---|
| 113 | 45c. Type **28** | 90 | 1·25 |
| 114 | 45c. "Shadow on the Plateau" | 90 | 1·25 |
| 115 | $1 "Ice Cave" | 1·90 | 2·00 |
| 116 | $1.20 "Twelve Lake" | 2·25 | 2·50 |

**29** Apple Huts

**1997.** 50th Anniv of Australian National Antarctic Research Expeditions (A.N.A.R.E.). Multicoloured.

| | | | |
|---|---|---|---|
| 117 | 45c. Type **29** | 1·00 | 1·10 |
| 118 | 45c. Tuning a radio receiver | 1·00 | 1·10 |
| 119 | 95c. Summer surveying | 1·60 | 2·00 |
| 120 | $1.05 Scientists in cage above sea ice | 1·75 | 2·00 |
| 121 | $1.20 Scientists and tents | 1·90 | 2·25 |

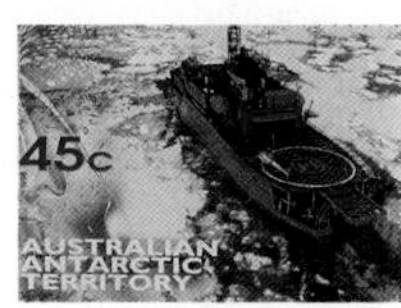

**30** "Aurora Australis" (research ship)

**1998.** Antarctic Transport. Multicoloured.

| | | | |
|---|---|---|---|
| 122 | 45c. Type **30** | 2·25 | 2·25 |
| 123 | 45c. "Skidoo" | 2·25 | 2·25 |
| 124 | $1 Helicopter lifting quad motorcycle (vert) | 4·25 | 3·25 |
| 125 | $2 Hagglunds tractor and trailer (vert) | 4·75 | 6·00 |

**31** Sir Douglas Mawson (expedition leader, 1911–14) and "Aurora" (research ship)

**1999.** Restoration of Mawson's Huts, Cape Denison. Each including a background drawing of a hut. Multicoloured.

| | | | |
|---|---|---|---|
| 126 | 45c. Type **31** | 2·00 | 2·00 |
| 127 | 45c. Huts in blizzard | 2·00 | 2·00 |
| 128 | 90c. Husky team | 3·25 | 3·25 |
| 129 | $1.35 Conservation in progress | 3·25 | 3·25 |

**32** Emperor Penguins

**2000.** Penguins. Multicoloured.

| | | | |
|---|---|---|---|
| 130 | 45c. Type **32** | 2·75 | 2·75 |
| 131 | 45c. Adelie penguins | 2·75 | 2·75 |

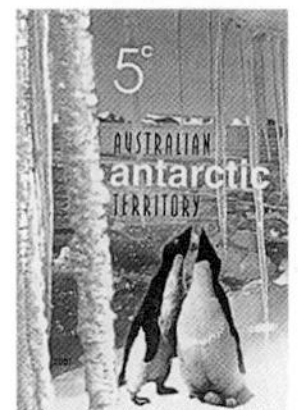

**33** Adelie Penguins with Egg

**2001.** Centenary of Australian Antarctic Exploration. Multicoloured.

| | | | |
|---|---|---|---|
| 132 | 5c. Type **33** | 75 | 80 |
| 133 | 5c. Louis Bernacchi (physicist) | 75 | 80 |
| 134 | 5c. *Nimrod* (Shackleton) | 75 | 80 |
| 135 | 5c. Mackay, Edgeworth David and Mawson at South Magnetic Pole, 1909 | 75 | 80 |
| 136 | 5c. Taylor and Debenham (geologists) | 75 | 80 |
| 137 | 10c. Early radio set | 75 | 80 |
| 138 | 10c. Lockheed-Vega aircraft and husky team | 75 | 80 |
| 139 | 10c. Sir Douglas Mawson | 75 | 80 |
| 140 | 10c. Members of BANZARE Expedition, 1929–31 | 75 | 80 |
| 141 | 10c. Hoisting Union Jack | 75 | 80 |
| 142 | 25c. Hoisting Australian flag, 1948 | 80 | 85 |
| 143 | 25c. Hagglund vehicle and helicopter | 80 | 85 |
| 144 | 25c. *Aurora australis* over Casey | 80 | 85 |
| 145 | 25c. Scientist with weather balloon | 80 | 85 |
| 146 | 25c. Modern Antarctic clothing and "apple" hut | 80 | 85 |
| 147 | 45c. *Nella Dan* (supply ship) and emperor penguins | 85 | 90 |
| 148 | 45c. Male and female scientists taking ice sample | 85 | 90 |
| 149 | 45c. Scientist using satellite phone | 85 | 90 |
| 150 | 45c. Weddell seal and tourists | 85 | 90 |
| 151 | 45c. Satellite photograph of Antarctica | 85 | 90 |

Nos. 132/51 were printed together, se-tenant, with the backgrounds forming a composite design.

Each stamp carries an inscription on the reverse, printed over the gum.

**34** Female Leopard Seal and Pup

**2001.** Endangered Species. Leopard Seal. Mult.

| | | | |
|---|---|---|---|
| 152 | 45c. Type **34** | 1·75 | 1·75 |
| 153 | 45c. Male seal on ice floe chasing adelie penguins | 1·75 | 1·75 |
| 154 | 45c. Female seal and pup swimming underwater | 1·75 | 1·75 |
| 155 | 45c. Adult seal chasing adelie penguins underwater | 1·75 | 1·75 |

**35** Light Detection and Ranging Equipment, Davis Base

**2002.** Antarctic Research. Multicoloured.

| | | | |
|---|---|---|---|
| 156 | 45c. Type **35** | 2·00 | 2·00 |
| 157 | 45c. Magnified diatom and coastline, Casey Base | 2·00 | 2·00 |
| 158 | 45c. Wandering albatross, Macquarie Base | 2·00 | 2·00 |
| 159 | 45c. Adelie penguin, Mawson Base | 2·00 | 2·00 |

**36** *Kista Dan* in Heavy Seas

**2003.** Antarctic Supply Ships. Multicoloured.

| | | | |
|---|---|---|---|
| 160 | 50c. Type **36** | 2·25 | 2·25 |
| 161 | 50c. *Magga Dan* entering pack ice | 2·25 | 2·25 |
| 162 | $1 *Thala Dan* and iceberg (vert) | 3·25 | 2·25 |
| 163 | $1.45 *Nella Dan* unloading in Antarctic (vert) | 4·00 | 4·50 |

**37** Naming Ceremony, 1954

**2004.** 50th Anniv of Mawson Station. Multicoloured.

| | | | |
|---|---|---|---|
| 164 | 50c. Type **37** | 2·00 | 2·00 |
| 165 | 50c. Mawson Station, 2004 | 2·00 | 2·00 |
| 166 | $1 Accomodation "caravan", 1950s | 2·75 | 2·25 |
| 167 | $1.45 Emperor penguin rookery | 3·50 | 4·00 |

**38** Hughes 500 Helicopter

**2005.** Aviation in the Australian Antarctic Territory. Multicoloured.

| | | | |
|---|---|---|---|
| 168 | 50c. Type **38** | 1·75 | 1·75 |
| 169 | 50c. De Haviland DHC-2 Beaver | 1·75 | 1·75 |
| 170 | $1 Pilatus PC06 Porter | 2·75 | 2·25 |
| 171 | $1.45 Douglas DC-3/Dakota C-47 | 3·25 | 3·75 |

**39** Mackerel Icefish

**2006.** Fish of the Australian Antarctic Territory. Multicoloured.

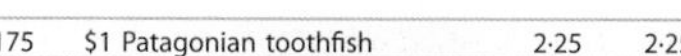

| | | | |
|---|---|---|---|
| 172 | 50c. Type **39** | 1·75 | 1·75 |
| 173 | 50c. Lanternfish | 1·75 | 1·75 |
| 174 | $1 Eaton's skate | 2·25 | 2·25 |
| 175 | $1 Patagonian toothfish | 2·25 | 2·25 |

**40** Royal Penguins

**2007.** Endangered Species. Royal Penguins (*Eudyptes schlegeli*). Multicoloured.

| | | | |
|---|---|---|---|
| 176 | 50c. Type **40** | 1·75 | 1·75 |
| 177 | 50c. Penguin with egg | 1·75 | 1·75 |
| 178 | $1 Two penguins sparring | 2·25 | 2·25 |
| 179 | $1 Pair snuggling together | 2·25 | 2·25 |

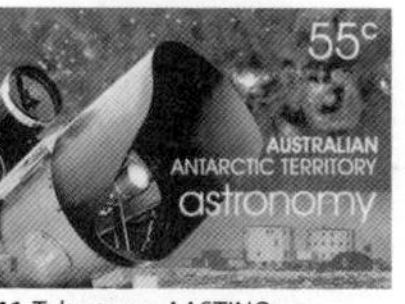

**41** Telescope, AASTINO Observatory, Stars and Gas Cloud (Astronomy from the Polar Plateaus)

**2008.** International Polar Year 2007–08. Multicoloured.

| | | | |
|---|---|---|---|
| 180 | 55c. Type **41** | 1·50 | 1·50 |
| 181 | 55c. Scientists drilling through sea ice (Sea Ice Physics and Ecosystem Experiment) | 1·50 | 1·50 |
| 182 | $1.10 Pteropod, pelagic snail *Limacina helicina* and emperor penguin (marine biology) | 2·00 | 2·00 |
| 183 | $1.10 CTD (conductivity-temperature-depth) probe and ocean (Climate of Antarctica and the Southern Ocean project) | 2·00 | 2·00 |
| **MS**184 | 160×90 mm. Nos. 180/3 | 6·50 | 6·50 |

**42** Unloading *Nimrod*

**2009.** Centenary of the First Expedition to the South Magnetic Pole. Each black, grey and blue.

| | | | |
|---|---|---|---|
| 185 | 55c. Type **42** | 1·00 | 1·00 |
| 186 | 55c. Arroll-Johnston car towing provisions on sledge | 1·00 | 1·00 |
| 187 | $1.10 Northern Party camp | 1·75 | 1·75 |
| 188 | $1.10 Alistair Mackay, Douglas Mawson and Edgeworth David raising Union Jack at South Magnetic Pole | 1·75 | 1·75 |
| **MS**189 | 170×85 mm. Nos. 185/8 | 5·50 | 5·50 |

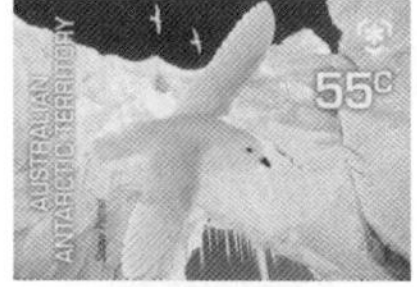

**43** Snow Petrel

**2009.** Preserve the Polar Regions and Glaciers. Multicoloured. (i) Domestic Mail

| | | | |
|---|---|---|---|
| 190 | 55c. Type **43** | 1·00 | 1·00 |
| 191 | $2.05 Jade iceberg | 4·00 | 4·00 |
| **MS**192 | 120x80mm. Nos. 190/1 | 5·00 | 5·00 |

**44** Pleurophyllum hookeri

**2010.** Macquarie Island. Multicoloured.

| | | | |
|---|---|---|---|
| 193 | 60c. Type **44** | 1·60 | 1·60 |
| 194 | 60c. Southern elephant seal | 1·60 | 1·60 |
| 195 | $1.20 Mawson Point Stacks | 2·10 | 2·10 |
| 196 | $1.20 Caroline Cove | 2·10 | 2·10 |
| **MS**197 | 159×85 mm. Nos. 193/6 | 7·25 | 7·25 |

Pt. 2

# AUSTRIA

A state of central Europe, part of the Austro-Hungarian Monarchy and Empire until 1918. At the end of the First World War the Empire was dismembered and German-spealing Austria became a Republic.

Austria was absorbed into the German Reich in 1938 and remained part of Germany until 1945. Following occupation of the four Allied Powers the Austrian Republic was re-establihed on 14 May 1945.

1850. 60 kreuzer = 1 gulden.
1858. 100 kreuzer = 1 gulden.
1899. 100 heller = 1 krone.
1925. 100 groschen = 1 schilling.
1938. 100 pfennig = 1 German reichsmark.
1945. 100 groschen = 1 schilling.
2002. 100 cents = 1 euro.

**1** Arms of Austria

**1850.** Imperf.

| | | | | |
|---|---|---|---|---|
| 6a | **1** | 1k. yellow | £1800 | £110 |
| 7 | **1** | 2k. black | £2250 | £100 |
| 8a | **1** | 3k. red | £600 | 4·75 |
| 9 | **1** | 6k. brown | £1300 | 8·50 |
| 10 | **1** | 9k. blue | £1300 | 3·75 |

For stamps in Type **1** with values in "CENTES", see Lombardy and Venetia.

**4**

**5**

**1858**

| | | | | |
|---|---|---|---|---|
| 22a | **5** | 2k. yellow | £1500 | 70·00 |
| 23 | **4** | 3k. black | £2250 | £375 |
| 24 | **4** | 3k. green | £1900 | £225 |
| 25a | **5** | 5k. red | £500 | 2·75 |
| 26a | **5** | 10k. brown | £1200 | 4·25 |
| 27a | **5** | 15k. blue | £1100 | 2·75 |

For stamps in Types **4** and **5** with values in "SOLDI", see Lombardy and Venetia.

The portraits on Austrian stamps to 1906 are of the Emperor Francis Joseph I.

**10**

**1860**

| | | | | |
|---|---|---|---|---|
| 33 | **10** | 2k. yellow | £550 | 43·00 |
| 34 | **10** | 3k. green | £475 | 38·00 |
| 35 | **10** | 5k. red | £350 | 1·10 |
| 36 | **10** | 10k. brown | £450 | 2·75 |
| 37 | **10** | 15k. blue | £600 | 1·90 |

**12** Arms of Austria

**1863**

| | | | | |
|---|---|---|---|---|
| 45 | **12** | 2k. yellow | £250 | 17·00 |
| 46 | **12** | 3k. green | £250 | 17·00 |
| 47 | **12** | 5k. red | 70·00 | 55 |
| 48 | **12** | 10k. blue | £300 | 4·25 |
| 49 | **12** | 15k. brown | £300 | 2·40 |

**A H14**

**A H16**

**1867**

| | | | | |
|---|---|---|---|---|
| 59 | **AH14** | 2k. yellow | 19·00 | 1·10 |
| 60 | **AH14** | 3k. green | 95·00 | 1·10 |
| 62 | **AH14** | 5k. red | 3·00 | 20 |
| 63 | **AH14** | 10k. blue | £225 | 1·10 |
| 64 | **AH14** | 15k. brown | 21·00 | 17·00 |
| AH56a | **AH14** | 25k. grey | 65·00 | 24·00 |
| 66 | **AH16** | 50k. brown | 19·00 | £250 |

**20**

**1883**

| | | | | |
|---|---|---|---|---|
| 70c | **20** | 2k. brown | 8·25 | 45 |
| 71c | **20** | 3k. green | 8·25 | 30 |
| 72c | **20** | 5k. red | £150 | 20 |
| 73c | **20** | 10k. blue | 21·00 | 45 |
| 74c | **20** | 20k. grey | £200 | 4·25 |
| 75a | **20** | 50k. mauve | £475 | £160 |

**23**

**24**

**1890**

| | | | | |
|---|---|---|---|---|
| 79 | **23** | 1k. grey | 2·10 | 55 |
| 80 | **23** | 2k. brown | 50 | 20 |
| 81 | **23** | 3k. green | 60 | 20 |
| 82 | **23** | 5k. red | 60 | 20 |
| 83 | **23** | 10k. blue | 1·50 | 20 |
| 84 | **23** | 12k. purple | 3·50 | 55 |
| 85 | **23** | 15k. purple | 3·50 | 55 |
| 86 | **23** | 20k. green | 55·00 | 3·25 |
| 87 | **23** | 24k. blue | 3·00 | 1·90 |
| 88 | **23** | 30k. brown | 3·00 | 1·30 |
| 89 | **23** | 50k. mauve | 8·25 | 15·00 |
| 90 | **24** | 1g. blue | 6·25 | 4·25 |
| 105 | **24** | 1g. lilac | £100 | 6·50 |
| 91 | **24** | 2g. red | 10·50 | 38·00 |
| 106 | **24** | 2g. green | 41·00 | 65·00 |

**25**

**1891.** Figures in black.

| | | | | |
|---|---|---|---|---|
| 92 | **25** | 20k. green | 5·25 | 20 |
| 93 | **25** | 24k. blue | 7·25 | 1·30 |
| 94 | **25** | 30k. brown | 5·25 | 20 |
| 95 | **25** | 50k. mauve | 6·25 | 55 |

**27**

**28**

**29**

**30**

**1899.** Corner numerals in black on heller values.

| | | | | |
|---|---|---|---|---|
| 107 | **27** | 1h. mauve | 1·00 | 20 |
| 108 | **27** | 2h. grey | 4·25 | 85 |
| 140 | **27** | 3h. brown | 1·00 | 20 |
| 141b | **27** | 5h. green | 1·00 | 20 |
| 142b | **27** | 6h. orange | 1·00 | 20 |
| 143b | **28** | 10h. red | 1·00 | 20 |
| 144b | **28** | 20h. brown | 1·00 | 20 |
| 145b | **28** | 25h. blue | 1·00 | 20 |
| 146b | **28** | 30h. mauve | 2·10 | 1·10 |
| 147b | **29** | 35h. green | 1·50 | 30 |
| 148b | **29** | 40h. green | 2·10 | 5·25 |
| 149b | **29** | 50h. blue | 5·25 | 13·00 |
| 150b | **29** | 60h. brown | 2·10 | 1·10 |
| 119a | **30** | 1k. red | 11·50 | 20 |
| 120 | **30** | 2k. lilac | £150 | 65 |
| 121 | **30** | 4k. green | 26·00 | 32·00 |

**33**

**35**

**1904.** Types as before, but with corners containing figures altered as T 33 and 35. Figures in black on white on 10h. to 30h. only.

| | | | | |
|---|---|---|---|---|
| 169 | **33** | 1h. purple | 20 | 65 |
| 170 | **33** | 2h. black | 20 | 45 |
| 171 | **33** | 3h. brown | 40 | 10 |
| 173 | **33** | 6h. orange | 60 | 10 |
| 160 | **28** | 10h. red | 5·25 | 20 |
| 161 | **28** | 20h. brown | 47·00 | 1·60 |
| 162 | **28** | 25h. blue | 45·00 | 1·30 |
| 163 | **28** | 30h. mauve | 70·00 | 2·75 |
| 178 | **35** | 35h. green | 5·25 | 55 |
| 179 | **35** | 40h. purple | 5·25 | 1·40 |
| 180 | **35** | 50h. blue | 5·25 | 4·75 |
| 181 | **35** | 60h. brown | 5·25 | 1·30 |
| 168 | **35** | 72h. red | 6·25 | 2·10 |

**1906.** Figures on plain white ground and stamps printed in one colour.

| | | | | |
|---|---|---|---|---|
| 183 | **28** | 5h. yellow-green | 40 | 10 |
| 184 | **28** | 10h. red | 50 | 20 |
| 185 | **28** | 12h. violet | 1·50 | 1·10 |
| 186 | **28** | 20h. brown | 5·00 | 30 |
| 187 | **28** | 25h. blue | 5·00 | 75 |
| 188 | **28** | 30h. red | 12·50 | 55 |

**37** Francis Joseph I

**38** Francis Joseph I

**41** Schonbrunn

**42** Francis Joseph I

**1908.** 60th Anniv of Emperor's Accession.

| | | | | |
|---|---|---|---|---|
| 189A | - | 1h. black | 40 | 20 |
| 190A | - | 2h. violet | 40 | 20 |
| 191B | - | 3h. purple | 30 | 10 |
| 192B | **37** | 5h. green | 20 | 10 |
| 193A | - | 6h. brown | 95 | 1·10 |
| 194B | **37** | 10h. red | 20 | 10 |
| 195A | - | 12h. red | 2·10 | 1·60 |
| 196B | - | 20h. brown | 2·75 | 50 |
| 197B | **37** | 25h. blue | 2·50 | 45 |
| 198B | - | 30h. green | 6·25 | 65 |
| 199A | - | 35h. grey | 6·00 | 40 |
| 200 | **38** | 50h. green | 2·00 | 55 |
| 201 | - | 60h. red | 40 | 20 |
| 202 | **38** | 72h. brown | 5·00 | 55 |
| 203 | - | 1k. violet | 21·00 | 55 |
| 204 | **41** | 2k. green and red | 36·00 | 1·10 |
| 205 | - | 5k. purple and brown | 65·00 | 8·50 |
| 206 | **42** | 10k. brown, blue & ochre | £300 | £110 |

DESIGNS—As Type **37**: 1h. Charles VI; 2h. Maria Theresa; 3h. Joseph II; 6h. Leopold II; 12h. Francis I; 20h. Ferdinand; 30h. Francis Joseph I in 1848; 35h. Same in 1878. As Type **38**: 60h. Francis Joseph I on horseback; 1k. Same in ceremonial robes. As Type **41**: 5k. Hofburg.

**45**

**1910.** 80th Birthday of Francis Joseph I. As issue of 1908 but with dates added as T 45.

| | | | | |
|---|---|---|---|---|
| 223 | | 1h. black | 6·25 | 10·50 |
| 224 | | 2h. violet | 8·25 | 21·00 |
| 225 | | 3h. purple | 7·25 | 18·00 |
| 226 | | 5h. green | 20 | 45 |
| 227 | | 6h. brown | 4·25 | 16·00 |
| 228 | | 10h. red | 20 | 45 |
| 229 | | 12h. red | 5·25 | 18·00 |
| 230 | | 20h. brown | 13·50 | 20·00 |
| 231 | | 25h. blue | 3·75 | 4·25 |
| 232 | | 30h. green | 5·25 | 16·00 |
| 233 | | 35h. grey | 5·25 | 17·00 |
| 234 | | 50h. green | 7·25 | 20·00 |
| 235 | | 60h. red | 7·25 | 20·00 |
| 236 | | 1k. violet | 5·75 | 9·50 |
| 237 | | 2k. green and red | £200 | £325 |
| 238 | | 5k. purple and brown | £150 | £300 |
| 239 | | 10k. brown, blue and ochre | £275 | £475 |

**47**

**1914.** War Charity Funds.

| | | | | |
|---|---|---|---|---|
| 240 | **47** | 5h.+(2h.) green | 30 | 45 |
| 241 | **47** | 10h.+(2h.) red | 40 | 75 |

**48** Cavalry

**1915.** War Charity Funds.

| | | | | |
|---|---|---|---|---|
| 242 | - | 3h.+1h. brown | 10 | 55 |
| 243 | **48** | 5h.+2h. green | 10 | 10 |
| 244 | - | 10h.+2h. red | 10 | 10 |
| 245 | - | 20h.+3h. green | 60 | 3·25 |
| 246 | - | 35h.+3h. blue | 3·00 | 7·50 |

DESIGNS: 3h. Infantry; 10h. Artillery; 20h. Battleship "Viribus Unitas" (Navy); 35h. Lohner Pfeilflieger B-1 biplane (Air Force).

**49** Imperial Austrian Crown

**50** Francis Joseph I

**51** Arms of Austria

**52**

**1916**

| | | | | |
|---|---|---|---|---|
| 247 | **49** | 3h. violet | 10 | 10 |
| 248 | **49** | 5h. green | 10 | 10 |
| 249 | **49** | 6h. orange | 40 | 1·60 |
| 250 | **49** | 10h. red | 10 | 10 |
| 251 | **49** | 12h. blue | 40 | 2·75 |
| 252 | **50** | 15h. red | 60 | 20 |
| 253 | **50** | 20h. brown | 3·75 | 40 |
| 254 | **50** | 25h. blue | 8·25 | 75 |
| 255 | **50** | 30h. slate | 7·50 | 1·30 |
| 256 | **51** | 40h. olive | 20 | 10 |
| 257 | **51** | 50h. green | 20 | 10 |
| 258 | **51** | 60h. blue | 20 | 10 |
| 259 | **51** | 80h. brown | 20 | 10 |
| 260 | **51** | 90h. purple | 20 | 10 |
| 261 | **51** | 1k. red on yellow | 40 | 15 |
| 262aa | **52** | 2k. blue | 10 | 20 |
| 263aa | **52** | 3k. red | 30 | 1·10 |
| 264a | **52** | 4k. green | 4·25 | 1·60 |
| 265aa | **52** | 10k. violet | 10·50 | 43·00 |

On Nos. 254/5 the portrait is full face. The 1k. has floral sprays each side of the coat-of-arms.

**60** Charles I

**1917**

| | | | | |
|---|---|---|---|---|
| 290 | **60** | 15h. red | 20 | 30 |
| 291a | **60** | 20h. green | 20 | 30 |
| 292 | **60** | 25h. blue | 1·00 | 30 |
| 293 | **60** | 30h. violet | 1·00 | 30 |

**1918.** Air. Optd FLUGPOST or surch also.

| | | | | |
|---|---|---|---|---|
| 296A | **52** | 1k.50 on 2k. mauve | 2·10 | 9·75 |
| 297B | **52** | 2k.50 on 3k. brown | 10·50 | 32·00 |
| 298A | **52** | 4k. grey | 7·25 | 23·00 |

**1918.** Optd Deutschosterreich.

| | | | | |
|---|---|---|---|---|
| 299 | **49** | 3h. violet | 10 | 10 |
| 300 | **49** | 5h. green | 10 | 10 |
| 301 | **49** | 6h. orange | 30 | 2·75 |
| 302 | **49** | 10h. red | 10 | 10 |
| 303 | **49** | 12h. blue | 30 | 2·75 |
| 304 | **60** | 15h. red | 30 | 1·60 |
| 305 | **60** | 20h. green | 10 | 10 |
| 306 | **60** | 25h. blue | 10 | 30 |
| 307 | **60** | 30h. violet | 10 | 10 |
| 308 | **51** | 40h. olive | 10 | 10 |
| 309 | **51** | 50h. green | 60 | 2·10 |
| 310 | **51** | 60h. blue | 55 | 2·00 |
| 311 | **51** | 80h. brown | 20 | 20 |
| 312 | **51** | 90h. red | 20 | 65 |
| 313 | **51** | 1k. red on yellow | 20 | 30 |
| 314 | **52** | 2k. blue | 10 | 10 |
| 315 | **52** | 3k. red | 40 | 1·10 |
| 316 | **52** | 4k. green | 2·10 | 4·25 |
| 317 | **52** | 10k. violet | 10·50 | 27·00 |

**64** Posthorn **65** Republican Arms **66** "New Republic"

**1919.** Imperf or perf.

| | | | | |
|---|---|---|---|---|
| 336 | **64** | 3h. grey | 10 | 10 |
| 337 | **65** | 5h. green | 10 | 10 |
| 338 | **65** | 5h. grey | 10 | 10 |
| 339 | **64** | 6h. orange | 10 | 65 |
| 340 | **65** | 10h. red | 10 | 10 |
| 342 | **64** | 12h. blue | 10 | 1·30 |
| 343a | **64** | 15h. brown | 10 | 10 |
| 344 | **66** | 20h. green | 10 | 10 |
| 346 | **65** | 25h. blue | 10 | 10 |
| 347 | **64** | 25h. violet | 10 | 10 |
| 348 | **66** | 30h. brown | 10 | 10 |
| 349 | **66** | 40h. violet | 10 | 10 |
| 350 | **66** | 40h. red | 10 | 10 |
| 351 | **65** | 45h. green | 20 | 1·10 |
| 352 | **66** | 50h. blue | 10 | 10 |
| 353 | **64** | 60h. green | 10 | 10 |
| 354 | **65** | 1k. red on yellow | 10 | 10 |
| 355 | **65** | 1k. blue | 40 | 1·10 |

**67** Parliament Building

**1919**

| | | | | |
|---|---|---|---|---|
| 356 | **67** | 2k. black and red | 30 | 1·10 |
| 357 | **67** | 2½k. bistre | 20 | 55 |
| 358 | **67** | 3k. brown and blue | 10 | 10 |
| 359 | **67** | 4k. black and red | 10 | 10 |
| 360 | **67** | 5k. black | 10 | 30 |
| 361 | **67** | 7½k. purple | 30 | 55 |
| 362 | **67** | 10k. brown and green | 25 | 55 |
| 363 | **67** | 20k. brown and violet | 10 | 55 |
| 364 | **67** | 50k. violet on yellow | 70 | 1·60 |

**71** Republican Arms

**1920**

| | | | | |
|---|---|---|---|---|
| 402 | **71** | 80h. red | 10 | 20 |
| 403 | **71** | 1k. brown | 10 | 20 |
| 404 | **71** | 1½k. green | 30 | 20 |
| 405 | **71** | 2k. blue | 10 | 20 |
| 406 | **71** | 3k. black and green | 10 | 30 |
| 407 | **71** | 4k. claret and red | 10 | 20 |
| 408 | **71** | 5k. red and lilac | 10 | 20 |
| 409 | **71** | 7½k. brown and orange | 10 | 30 |
| 410 | **71** | 10k. blue and violet | 10 | 20 |

The frames of the 3 to 10k. differ.

**1920.** Issues for Carinthian Plebiscite. Optd Karnten Abstimmung (T 65/7 in new colours). (a) Perf.

| | | | | |
|---|---|---|---|---|
| 411 | **65** | 5h. (+10h.) grey on yell | 70 | 2·10 |
| 412 | **65** | 10h. (+20h.) red on pink | 70 | 1·60 |
| 413 | **64** | 15h. (+30h.) brn on yell | 30 | 1·10 |
| 414 | **66** | 20h. (+40h.) green on bl | 30 | 85 |
| 415 | **64** | 25h. (+50h.) pur on pink | 30 | 90 |
| 416 | **66** | 30h. (+60h.) brn on buff | 1·80 | 3·75 |
| 417 | **66** | 40h. (+80h.) red on yell | 30 | 1·10 |
| 418 | **66** | 50h. (+100h.) indigo on blue | 30 | 85 |
| 419 | **64** | 60h. (+120h.) green on bl | 1·80 | 3·75 |
| 420 | **71** | 80h. (+160h.) red | 45 | 95 |
| 421 | **71** | 1k. (+2k.) brown | 45 | 1·10 |
| 422 | **71** | 2k. (+4k.) blue | 45 | 1·10 |

(b) Imperf.

| | | | | |
|---|---|---|---|---|
| 423 | **67** | 2½k. (+5k.) brown | 50 | 1·40 |
| 424 | **67** | 3k. (+6k.) green & blue | 60 | 1·70 |
| 425 | **67** | 4k. (+8k.) violet & red | 85 | 2·00 |
| 426 | **67** | 5k. (+10k.) blue | 75 | 1·70 |
| 427 | **67** | 7½k. (+15k.) green | 75 | 1·70 |
| 428 | **67** | 10k. (+20k.) red & green | 85 | 1·90 |
| 429 | **67** | 20k. (+40k.) brn & lilac | 95 | 2·40 |

The plebiscite was to decide whether Carinthia should be part of Austria or Yugoslavia, and the premium was for a fund to promote a vote in favour of remaining in Austria. The result was a vote for Austria.

**1921.** Flood Relief Fund. Optd Hochwasser 1920 (colours changed).

| | | | | |
|---|---|---|---|---|
| 430 | **65** | 5h. (+10h.) grey on yell | 30 | 1·10 |
| 431 | **65** | 10h. (+20h.) brown | 30 | 1·10 |
| 432 | **64** | 15h. (+30h.) grey | 30 | 1·10 |
| 433 | **66** | 20h. (+40h.) green on yell | 30 | 1·10 |
| 434 | **64** | 25h. (+50h.) blue on yell | 30 | 1·10 |
| 435 | **66** | 30h. (+60h.) purple on bl | 65 | 2·10 |
| 436 | **66** | 40h. (+80h.) brn on red | 75 | 2·75 |
| 437 | **66** | 50h. (+100h.) green on bl | 1·70 | 4·75 |
| 438 | **64** | 60h. (+120h.) pur on yell | 50 | 2·10 |
| 439 | **71** | 80h. (+160h.) blue | 50 | 2·10 |
| 440 | **71** | 1k. (+2k.) orange on blue | 45 | 2·10 |
| 441 | **71** | 1½k. (+3k.) green on yell | 25 | 1·10 |
| 442 | **71** | 2k. (+4k.) brown | 25 | 1·10 |
| 443 | **67** | 2½k. (+5k.) blue | 30 | 1·10 |
| 444 | **67** | 3k. (+6k.) red & green | 30 | 1·10 |
| 445 | **67** | 4k. (+8k.) brown & lilac | 1·00 | 3·75 |
| 446 | **67** | 5k. (+10k.) green | 30 | 2·10 |
| 447 | **67** | 7½k. (+15k.) red | 30 | 2·10 |
| 448 | **67** | 10k. (+20k.) green & blue | 30 | 2·10 |
| 449 | **67** | 20k. (+40k.) pur & red | 60 | 3·25 |

**80** Pincers and Hammer **81** Ear of Corn

**1922**

| | | | | |
|---|---|---|---|---|
| 461 | **81** | ½k. brown | 10 | 85 |
| 462 | **80** | 1k. brown | 10 | 10 |
| 463 | **80** | 2k. blue | 10 | 10 |
| 464 | **81** | 2½k. brown | 10 | 10 |
| 465 | **80** | 4k. purple | 10 | 1·40 |
| 466 | **80** | 5k. green | 10 | 10 |
| 467 | **81** | 7½k. violet | 10 | 10 |
| 468 | **80** | 10k. red | 10 | 10 |
| 469 | **81** | 12½k. green | 10 | 10 |
| 470 | **81** | 15k. turquoise | 10 | 10 |
| 471 | **81** | 20k. blue | 10 | 10 |
| 472 | **81** | 25k. red | 10 | 10 |
| 473 | **80** | 30k. grey | 10 | 10 |
| 474 | **80** | 45k. red | 10 | 10 |
| 475 | **80** | 50k. brown | 10 | 10 |
| 476 | **80** | 60k. green | 10 | 10 |
| 477 | **80** | 75k. blue | 10 | 10 |
| 478 | **80** | 80k. yellow | 10 | 10 |
| 479 | **81** | 100k. grey | 10 | 10 |
| 480 | **81** | 120k. brown | 10 | 10 |
| 481 | **81** | 150k. orange | 10 | 10 |
| 482 | **81** | 160k. green | 10 | 10 |
| 483 | **81** | 180k. red | 10 | 10 |
| 484 | **81** | 200k. pink | 10 | 10 |
| 485 | **81** | 240k. violet | 10 | 10 |
| 486 | **81** | 300k. blue | 10 | 10 |
| 487 | **81** | 400k. green | 1·50 | 55 |
| 488 | **81** | 500k. yellow | 10 | 10 |
| 489 | **81** | 600k. slate | 10 | 10 |
| 490 | **81** | 700k. brown | 2·50 | 20 |
| 491 | **81** | 800k. violet | 1·00 | 2·75 |
| 492 | **80** | 1000k. mauve | 1·30 | 20 |
| 493 | **80** | 1200k. red | 85 | 65 |
| 494 | **80** | 1500k. orange | 85 | 20 |
| 495 | **80** | 1600k. slate | 4·25 | 4·25 |
| 496 | **80** | 2000k. blue | 5·25 | 3·75 |
| 497 | **80** | 3000k. blue | 15·00 | 2·75 |
| 498 | **80** | 4000k. blue on blue | 7·75 | 3·75 |

**82**

**1922**

| | | | | |
|---|---|---|---|---|
| 499 | **82** | 20k. sepia | 10 | 20 |
| 500 | **82** | 25k. blue | 10 | 20 |
| 501 | **82** | 50k. red | 10 | 20 |
| 502 | **82** | 100k. green | 10 | 20 |
| 503 | **82** | 200k. purple | 10 | 20 |
| 504 | **82** | 500k. orange | 40 | 2·10 |
| 505 | **82** | 1000k. violet on yellow | 10 | 20 |
| 506 | **82** | 2000k. green on yellow | 10 | 20 |
| 507 | **82** | 3000k. red | 13·00 | 1·10 |
| 508 | **82** | 5000k. black | 2·40 | 2·10 |
| 509 | **82** | 10,000k. brown | 5·75 | 7·50 |

**85** Mozart

**1922.** Musicians' Fund.

| | | | | |
|---|---|---|---|---|
| 519b | - | 2½k. brown | 9·25 | 13·00 |
| 520 | **85** | 5k. blue | 1·50 | 2·75 |
| 521 | - | 7½k. black | 2·50 | 4·25 |
| 522 | - | 10k. purple | 3·00 | 5·25 |
| 523 | - | 25k. green | 5·75 | 10·50 |
| 524 | - | 50k. red | 3·00 | 5·25 |
| 525 | - | 100k. green | 9·25 | 21·00 |

COMPOSERS: 2½k. Haydn; 7½k. Beethoven; 10k. Schubert; 25k. Bruckner; 50k. J. Strauss; 100k. Wolf.

**87** Hawk **88** W. Kress

**1922.** Air.

| | | | | |
|---|---|---|---|---|
| 546 | **87** | 300k. red | 40 | 2·40 |
| 547 | **87** | 400k. green | 6·25 | 21·00 |
| 548 | **87** | 600k. olive | 40 | 2·10 |
| 549 | **87** | 900k. red | 40 | 2·10 |
| 550 | **88** | 1200k. purple | 40 | 2·10 |
| 551 | **88** | 2400k. slate | 40 | 2·10 |
| 552 | **88** | 3000k. brown | 4·25 | 13·00 |
| 553 | **88** | 4800k. blue | 4·25 | 13·00 |

**89** Bregenz

**1923.** Artists' Charity Fund.

| | | | | |
|---|---|---|---|---|
| 554 | **89** | 100k. green | 5·25 | 10·50 |
| 555 | - | 120k. blue | 5·25 | 10·50 |
| 556 | - | 160k. purple | 5·25 | 10·50 |
| 557 | - | 180k. purple | 5·25 | 10·50 |
| 558 | - | 200k. red | 5·25 | 10·50 |
| 559 | - | 240k. brown | 5·25 | 10·50 |
| 560 | - | 400k. brown | 5·25 | 10·50 |
| 561 | - | 600k. green | 6·25 | 10·50 |
| 562 | - | 1000k. black | 9·25 | 17·00 |

DESIGNS: 120k. Salzburg; 160k. Eisenstadt; 180k. Klagenfurt; 200k. Innsbruck; 240k. Linz; 400k. Graz; 600k. Melk; 1000k. Vienna.

**90** "Art the Comforter"

**1924.** Artists' Charity Fund.

| | | | | |
|---|---|---|---|---|
| 563 | **90** | 100k.+300k. green | 5·25 | 13·00 |
| 564 | - | 300k.+900k. brown | 5·25 | 13·00 |
| 565 | - | 500k.+1500k. purple | 5·25 | 14·00 |
| 566 | - | 600k.+1800k. turquoise | 10·50 | 25·00 |
| 567 | - | 1000k.+3000k. brown | 15·00 | 31·00 |

DESIGNS: 300k. "Agriculture and Handicraft"; 500k. "Mother Love"; 600k. "Charity"; 1000k. "Fruitfulness".

**91** **92** Plains **93** Minorite Church, Vienna

**1925**

| | | | | |
|---|---|---|---|---|
| 568 | **91** | 1g. grey | 25 | 20 |
| 569 | **91** | 2g. red | 50 | 20 |
| 570 | **91** | 3g. red | 50 | 20 |
| 571 | **91** | 4g. blue | 1·50 | 20 |
| 572 | **91** | 5g. brown | 2·10 | 20 |
| 573 | **91** | 6g. blue | 1·50 | 20 |
| 574 | **91** | 7g. brown | 2·10 | 20 |
| 575 | **91** | 8g. green | 5·25 | 20 |
| 576 | **92** | 10g. brown | 1·00 | 20 |
| 577 | **92** | 15g. red | 1·00 | 20 |
| 578 | **92** | 16g. blue | 1·00 | 20 |
| 579 | **92** | 18g. green | 1·50 | 1·10 |
| 580 | - | 20g. violet | 1·00 | 20 |
| 581 | - | 24g. red | 1·20 | 55 |
| 582 | - | 30g. brown | 1·50 | 20 |
| 583 | - | 40g. blue | 1·90 | 20 |
| 584 | - | 45g. brown | 2·10 | 20 |
| 585 | - | 50g. grey | 2·10 | 30 |
| 586 | - | 80g. blue | 4·75 | 6·00 |
| 587 | **93** | 1s. green | 23·00 | 2·10 |
| 588 | - | 2s. red | 8·75 | 14·00 |

DESIGN—As T **92**—20g. to 80g. Golden eagle on mountains.

**96** Pilot and Hansa Brandenburg C-1 **97** de Havilland D.H.34 and Common Crane

**1925.** Air.

| | | | | |
|---|---|---|---|---|
| 616 | **96** | 2g. brown | 50 | 1·30 |
| 617 | **96** | 5g. red | 30 | 45 |
| 618 | **96** | 6g. blue | 1·00 | 2·10 |
| 619 | **96** | 8g. green | 1·00 | 2·40 |
| 620 | **97** | 10g. red | 1·30 | 3·75 |
| 621 | **96** | 10g. orange | 1·30 | 2·75 |
| 622 | **97** | 15g. red | 1·00 | 2·10 |
| 623 | **96** | 15g. mauve | 50 | 1·10 |
| 624 | **96** | 20g. brown | 14·00 | 16·00 |
| 625 | **96** | 25g. violet | 6·25 | 12·00 |
| 626 | **97** | 30g. purple | 1·20 | 3·75 |
| 627 | **96** | 30g. bistre | 10·50 | 13·00 |
| 628 | **97** | 50g. grey | 1·20 | 3·75 |
| 629 | **96** | 50g. blue | 18·00 | 19·00 |
| 630 | **96** | 80g. green | 3·00 | 5·25 |
| 631 | **97** | 1s. blue | 10·50 | 14·00 |
| 632 | **97** | 2s. green | 2·10 | 5·25 |
| 633 | **97** | 3s. brown | 65·00 | 85·00 |
| 634 | **97** | 5s. blue | 18·00 | 38·00 |
| 635 | **97** | 10s. brown on grey (25×32 mm) | 10·50 | 32·00 |

**98** Siegfried and Dragon

**1926.** Child Welfare. Scenes from the Nibelung Legend.

| | | | | |
|---|---|---|---|---|
| 636 | **98** | 3g.+2g. brown | 1·20 | 1·20 |
| 637 | - | 8g.+2g. blue | 20 | 55 |
| 638 | - | 15g.+5g. red | 40 | 55 |
| 639 | - | 20g.+5g. green | 60 | 1·10 |
| 640 | - | 24g.+6g. violet | 60 | 1·10 |
| 641 | - | 40g.+10g. brown | 4·25 | 7·00 |

DESIGNS: 8g. Gunther's voyage; 15g. Kriemhild and Brunhild; 20g. Hagen and the Rhine maidens; 24g. Rudiger and the Nibelungs; 40g. Dietrich's fight with Hagen.

**99** Dr. Michael Hainisch

**1928.** 10th Anniv of Republic and War Orphans and Invalid Children's Fund.

| | | | | |
|---|---|---|---|---|
| 642 | **99** | 10g. (+10g.) brown | 6·25 | 16·00 |
| 643 | **99** | 15g. (+15g.) red | 6·25 | 16·00 |
| 644 | **99** | 30g. (+30g.) black | 6·25 | 16·00 |
| 645 | **99** | 40g. (+40g.) blue | 6·25 | 16·00 |

**100** Gussing

**101** National Library, Vienna

**1929.** Views. Size 25½×21½ mm.

| | | | | |
|---|---|---|---|---|
| 646 | **100** | 10g. orange | 1·00 | 10 |
| 647 | **100** | 10g. brown | 1·00 | 10 |
| 648 | - | 15g. purple | 1·00 | 1·80 |
| 649 | - | 16g. black | 20 | 10 |
| 650 | - | 18g. green | 50 | 65 |
| 651 | - | 20g. black | 50 | 10 |
| 653 | - | 24g. purple | 7·25 | 75 |
| 654 | - | 30g. violet | 8·25 | 10 |
| 655 | - | 40g. blue | 10·50 | 30 |
| 656 | - | 50g. violet | 39·00 | 30 |
| 657 | - | 60g. green | 31·00 | 55 |
| 658 | **101** | 1s. brown | 8·25 | 55 |
| 659 | - | 2s. green | 19·00 | 17·00 |

VIEWS—As T **100**: 15g. Hochosterwitz; 16, 20g. Durnstein; 18g. Traunsee; 24g. Salzburg; 30g. Seewiesen; 40g. Innsbruck; 50g. Worthersee; 60g. Hohenems. As T **101**: 2s. St. Stephen's Cathedral, Vienna.

See also Nos. 678/91.

**102** Pres. Wilhelm Miklas

**1930.** Anti-tuberculosis Fund.

| | | | | |
|---|---|---|---|---|
| 660 | **102** | 10g. (+10g.) brown | 10·50 | 30·00 |
| 661 | **102** | 20g. (+20g.) red | 10·50 | 30·00 |
| 662 | **102** | 30g. (+30g.) purple | 10·50 | 30·00 |
| 663 | **102** | 40g. (+40g.) blue | 10·50 | 30·00 |
| 664 | **102** | 50g. (+50g.) green | 10·50 | 30·00 |
| 665 | **102** | 1s. (+1s.) brown | 10·50 | 30·00 |

**1930.** Rotarian Congress. Optd with Rotary Int emblem and CONVENTION WIEN 1931.

| | | | | |
|---|---|---|---|---|
| 666 | **100** | 10g. (+10g.) brown | 50·00 | 85·00 |
| 667 | - | 20g. (+20g.) grey (No. 651) | 50·00 | 85·00 |
| 668 | - | 30g. (+30g.) vio (No. 654) | 50·00 | 85·00 |
| 669 | - | 40g. (+40g.) bl (No. 655) | 50·00 | 85·00 |
| 670 | - | 50g. (+50g.) vio (No. 656) | 50·00 | 85·00 |
| 671 | **101** | 1s. (+1s.) brown | 50·00 | 85·00 |

**104** Johann Nestroy

**1931.** Austrian Writers and Youth Unemployment Fund.

| | | | | |
|---|---|---|---|---|
| 672 | - | 10g. (+10g.) purple | 21·00 | 45·00 |
| 673 | - | 20g. (+20g.) grey | 21·00 | 45·00 |
| 674 | **104** | 30g. (+30g.) red | 21·00 | 45·00 |
| 675 | - | 40g. (+40g.) blue | 21·00 | 45·00 |
| 676 | - | 50g. (+50g.) green | 21·00 | 45·00 |
| 677 | - | 1s. (+1s.) brown | 21·00 | 45·00 |

DESIGNS: 10g. F. Raimund; 20g. E. Grillparzer; 40g. A Stifter; 50g. L. Anzengruber; 1s. P. Rosegger.

**105**

**1932.** Designs as No. 646 etc, but size reduced to 20½×16 mm as T 105.

| | | | | |
|---|---|---|---|---|
| 678 | **105** | 10g. brown | 1·00 | 20 |
| 679 | - | 12g. green | 2·10 | 20 |
| 680 | - | 18g. green | 2·10 | 3·50 |
| 681 | - | 20g. black | 1·00 | 20 |
| 682 | - | 24g. red | 6·75 | 20 |
| 683 | - | 24g. violet | 4·25 | 20 |
| 684 | - | 30g. violet | 23·00 | 20 |
| 685 | - | 30g. red | 8·25 | 30 |
| 686 | - | 40g. blue | 27·00 | 2·10 |
| 687 | - | 40g. violet | 10·50 | 55 |
| 688 | - | 50g. violet | 31·00 | 55 |
| 689 | - | 50g. blue | 10·50 | 55 |
| 690 | - | 60g. green | 70·00 | 5·25 |
| 691 | - | 64g. green | 23·00 | 55 |

DESIGNS (new values): 12g. Traunsee; 64g. Hohenems.

**106** Dr. Ignaz Seipel

**1932.** Death of Dr. Seipel (Chancellor), and Ex-servicemen's Fund.

| | | | | |
|---|---|---|---|---|
| 692 | **106** | 50g. (+50g.) blue | 19·00 | 38·00 |

**107** Hans Makart

**1932.** Austrian Painters.

| | | | | |
|---|---|---|---|---|
| 693 | - | 12g. (+12g.) green | 31·00 | 65·00 |
| 694 | - | 24g. (+24g.) purple | 31·00 | 65·00 |
| 695 | - | 30g. (+30g.) red | 31·00 | 65·00 |
| 696 | **107** | 40g. (+40g.) grey | 31·00 | 65·00 |
| 697 | - | 64g. (+64g.) brown | 31·00 | 65·00 |
| 698 | - | 1s. (+1s.) red | 31·00 | 65·00 |

DESIGNS: 12g. F. G. Waldmuller; 24g. Von Schwind; 30g. Alt; 64g. Klimt; 1s. A. Egger-Lienz.

**108** The Climb

**1933.** International Ski Championship Fund.

| | | | | |
|---|---|---|---|---|
| 699 | **108** | 12g. (+12g.) green | 10·50 | 27·00 |
| 700 | - | 24g. (+24g.) violet | £140 | £190 |
| 701 | - | 30g. (+30g.) red | 21·00 | 38·00 |
| 702 | - | 50g. (+50g.) blue | £140 | £190 |

DESIGNS: 24g. Start; 30g. Race; 50g. Ski jump.

**109** "The Honeymoon" (M. von Schwind)

**1933.** International Philatelic Exn, Vienna (WIPA).

| | | | | |
|---|---|---|---|---|
| 703 | **109** | 50g. (+50g.) blue | £200 | £350 |
| **MS**705 | | 127×105 mm. As No. 703 (+1s.60 admission) in block of four | £3500 | £5000 |

**111** John Sobieski

**1933.** 250th Anniv of Relief of Vienna and Pan-German Catholic Congress.

| | | | | |
|---|---|---|---|---|
| 706 | - | 12g. (+12g.) green | 33·00 | 55·00 |
| 707 | - | 24g. (+24g.) violet | 31·00 | 48·00 |
| 708 | - | 30g. (+30g.) red | 31·00 | 48·00 |
| 709 | **111** | 40g. (+40g.) grey | 44·00 | 85·00 |
| 710 | - | 50g. (+50g.) blue | 31·00 | 48·00 |
| 711 | - | 64g. (+64g.) brown | 36·00 | 75·00 |

DESIGNS—VERT: 12g. Vienna in 1683; 24g. Marco d'Aviano; 30g. Count von Starhemberg; 50g. Charles of Lorraine; 64g. Burgomaster Liebenberg.

**1933.** Winter Relief Fund. Surch with premium and Winterhilfe (5g.) or WINTERHILFE (others).

| | | | | |
|---|---|---|---|---|
| 712 | **91** | 5g.+2g. green | 20 | 75 |
| 713 | - | 12g.+3g. blue (as 679) | 30 | 1·10 |
| 714 | - | 24g.+6g. brn (as 682) | 20 | 75 |
| 715 | **101** | 1s.+50g. red | 41·00 | 95·00 |

**114**

**115**

**1934**

| | | | | |
|---|---|---|---|---|
| 716 | **114** | 1g. violet | 10 | 10 |
| 717 | **114** | 3g. red | 10 | 10 |
| 718 | - | 4g. green | 10 | 10 |
| 719 | - | 5g. purple | 10 | 10 |
| 721 | - | 6g. blue | 20 | 10 |
| 722 | - | 8g. green | 10 | 10 |
| 723 | - | 12g. brown | 10 | 10 |
| 724 | - | 20g. brown | 20 | 10 |
| 725 | - | 24g. turquoise | 10 | 10 |
| 726 | - | 25g. violet | 20 | 25 |
| 727 | - | 30g. red | 20 | 10 |
| 728 | - | 35g. red | 40 | 50 |
| 729 | **115** | 40g. grey | 50 | 30 |
| 730 | **115** | 45g. brown | 45 | 20 |
| 731 | - | 60g. blue | 70 | 55 |
| 732 | - | 64g. brown | 1·00 | 20 |
| 733 | - | 1s. purple | 1·50 | 85 |
| 735 | - | 2s. green | 4·75 | 8·50 |
| 736 | - | 3s. orange | 18·00 | 32·00 |
| 737 | - | 5s. black | 41·00 | 70·00 |

DESIGNS (Austrian costumes of the districts named)—As Type **114**: 1, 3g. Burgenland; 4, 5g. Carinthia; 6, 8g. Lower Austria; 12, 20g. Upper Austria; 24, 25g. Salzburg; 30, 35g. Styria (Steiermark). As Type **115**: 40, 45g. Tyrol; 60, 64g. Vorarlberg; 1s. Vienna; 2s. Army officer and soldiers. 30×31 mm: 3s. Harvesters; 5s. Builders.

**117** Chancellor Dollfuss

**1934.** Dollfuss Mourning Stamp.

| | | | | |
|---|---|---|---|---|
| 738 | **117** | 24g. black | 60 | 1·10 |

See also No. 762.

**118** Anton Pilgram

**1934.** Welfare Funds. Austrian Architects.

| | | | | |
|---|---|---|---|---|
| 739 | **118** | 12g. (+12g.) black | 14·50 | 32·00 |
| 740 | - | 24g. (+24g.) violet | 14·50 | 32·00 |
| 741 | - | 30g. (+30g.) red | 14·50 | 32·00 |
| 742 | - | 40g. (+40g.) brown | 14·50 | 32·00 |
| 743 | - | 60g. (+60g.) blue | 14·50 | 32·00 |
| 744 | - | 64g. (+64g.) green | 14·50 | 32·00 |

DESIGNS: 24g. Fischer von Erlach; 30g. J. Prandtauer; 40g. A. von Siccardsburg and E. van der Null; 60g. H. von Ferstel; 64g. Otto Wagner.

**119** "Mother and Child" (J. Danhauser)

**1935.** Mothers Day.

| | | | | |
|---|---|---|---|---|
| 745 | **119** | 24g. blue | 70 | 55 |

**1935.** 1st Anniv of Assassination of Dr. Dollfuss.

| | | | | |
|---|---|---|---|---|
| 762 | **117** | 24g. blue | 1·50 | 1·40 |

**121** Maria Worth Castle, Carinthia

**122** Zugspitze Aerial Railway

**1935.** Air. Designs showing Junkers airplane (except 10s.) and landscape.

| | | | | |
|---|---|---|---|---|
| 763 | - | 5g. purple | 30 | 85 |
| 764 | **121** | 10g. orange | 10 | 55 |
| 765 | - | 15g. green | 1·00 | 2·75 |
| 766 | - | 20g. blue | 10 | 55 |
| 767 | - | 25g. purple | 10 | 55 |
| 768 | - | 30g. red | 10 | 55 |
| 769 | - | 40g. green | 10 | 55 |
| 770 | - | 50g. blue | 20 | 95 |
| 771 | - | 60g. sepia | 40 | 1·40 |
| 772 | - | 80g. brown | 50 | 1·80 |
| 773 | - | 1s. red | 40 | 1·60 |
| 774 | - | 2s. green | 3·00 | 8·50 |
| 775 | - | 3s. brown | 9·25 | 32·00 |
| 776 | **122** | 5s. green | 5·25 | 23·00 |
| 777 | - | 10s. blue | 85·00 | £170 |

DESIGNS—As T **121**: 5g. Gussing Castle; 15g. Durnstein; 20g. Hallstatt; 25g. Salzburg; 30g. Dachstein Mts.; 40g. Wettersee; 50g. Stuben am Arlberg; 60g. St. Stephen's Cathedral, Vienna; 80g. Minorite Church, Vienna. As T **122**: 1s. River Danube; 2s. Tauern railway viaduct; 3s. Grossglockner mountain roadway; 10s. Glider and yachts on the Attersee.

**1935.** Winter Relief Fund. As Nos. 719, 723, 725 and 733, but colours changed, surch Winterhilfe (778/80) or WINTERHILFE (781) and premium.

| | | | | |
|---|---|---|---|---|
| 778 | | 5g.+2g. green | 70 | 1·60 |
| 779 | | 12g.+3g. blue | 1·20 | 2·10 |
| 780 | | 24g.+6g. brown | 70 | 1·60 |
| 781 | | 1s.+50g. red | 41·00 | 90·00 |

**123** Prince Eugene of Savoy (born 1663, not 1667 as given)

**1935.** Welfare Funds. Austrian Heroes.

| | | | | |
|---|---|---|---|---|
| 782 | **123** | 12g. (+12g.) brown | 15·00 | 32·00 |
| 783 | - | 24g. (+24g.) green | 15·00 | 32·00 |
| 784 | - | 30g. (+30g.) purple | 15·00 | 32·00 |
| 785 | - | 40g. (+40g.) blue | 15·00 | 32·00 |
| 786 | - | 60g. (+60g.) blue | 15·00 | 32·00 |
| 787 | - | 64g. (+64g.) violet | 15·00 | 32·00 |

PORTRAITS: 24g. Baron von Laudon; 30g. Archduke Charles; 40g. Field-Marshal Radetzky; 60g. Vice-Admiral von Tegetthoff; 64g. Field-Marshal Conrad von Hotzendorff.

**124** Slalom Course Skier

**1936.** International Ski Championship Fund. Inscr "WETTKAMPFE 1936".

| | | | | |
|---|---|---|---|---|
| 788 | **124** | 12g. (+12g.) green | 3·00 | 6·50 |
| 789 | - | 24g. (+24g.) violet | 5·25 | 8·50 |
| 790 | - | 35g. (+35g.) red | 31·00 | 75·00 |
| 791 | - | 60g. (+60g.) blue | 31·00 | 75·00 |

DESIGNS: 24g. Skier on mountain slope; 35g. Woman slalom course skier; 60g. View of Maria Theresienstrasse, Innsbruck.

**125** Madonna and Child

**1936.** Mothers' Day.

| | | | | |
|---|---|---|---|---|
| 792 | **125** | 24g. blue | 40 | 1·30 |

**126** Chancellor Dollfuss

**1936.** 2nd Anniv of Assassination of Dr. Dollfuss.

| | | | | |
|---|---|---|---|---|
| 793 | **126** | 10s. blue | £950 | £1500 |

**127** "St. Martin sharing Cloak"

**1936.** Winter Relief Fund. Inscr "WINTERHILFE 1936/37".

| | | | | |
|---|---|---|---|---|
| 794 | **127** | 5g.+2g. green | 35 | 1·10 |
| 795 | - | 12g.+3g. violet | 35 | 1·10 |
| 796 | - | 24g.+6g. blue | 35 | 1·10 |
| 797 | - | 1s.+1s. red | 9·25 | 25·00 |

DESIGNS: 12g. "Healing the sick"; 24g. "St. Elizabeth feeding the hungry"; 1s. "Warming the poor".

**128** J. Ressel

**1936.** Welfare Funds. Austrian Inventors.

| | | | | |
|---|---|---|---|---|
| 798 | **128** | 12g. (+12g.) brown | 3·50 | 10·00 |
| 799 | - | 24g. (+24g.) violet | 3·50 | 10·00 |
| 800 | - | 30g. (+30g.) red | 3·50 | 10·00 |
| 801 | - | 40g. (+40g.) black | 3·50 | 10·00 |
| 802 | - | 60g. (+60g.) blue | 3·50 | 10·00 |
| 803 | - | 64g. (+64g.) green | 3·50 | 10·00 |

PORTRAITS: 24g. Karl Ritter von Ghega; 30g. J. Werndl; 40g. Carl Freih. Auer von Welsbach; 60g. R. von Lieben; 64g. V. Kaplan.

**129** Mother and Child

**1937.** Mothers' Day.

| | | | | |
|---|---|---|---|---|
| 804 | **129** | 24g. red | 30 | 55 |

**130** "Maria Anna"

**1937.** Centenary of Regular Danube Services of Danube Steam Navigation Co. Paddle-steamers.

| | | | | |
|---|---|---|---|---|
| 805 | **130** | 12g. red | 85 | 1·10 |
| 806 | - | 24g. blue | 85 | 1·10 |
| 807 | - | 64g. green | 85 | 2·10 |

DESIGNS: 24g. "Helios"; 64g. "Oesterreich".

**131** "Child Welfare"

**1937.** Winter Relief Fund. Inscr "WINTERHILFE 1937 1938".

| | | | | |
|---|---|---|---|---|
| 808 | **131** | 5g.+2g. green | 20 | 65 |
| 809 | - | 12g.+3g. brown | 20 | 65 |
| 810 | - | 24g.+6g. blue | 20 | 65 |
| 811 | - | 1s.+1s. red | 4·75 | 18·00 |

DESIGNS: 12g. "Feeding the Children"; 24g. "Protecting the Aged"; 1s. "Nursing the Sick".

**132** Steam Locomotive "Austria", 1837

**1937.** Railway Centenary.

| | | | | |
|---|---|---|---|---|
| 812 | **132** | 12g. brown | 20 | 40 |
| 813 | - | 25g. violet | 85 | 1·60 |
| 814 | - | 35g. red | 2·50 | 3·75 |

DESIGNS: 25g. Steam locomotive, 1936; 35g. Electric locomotive.

**133** Dr. G. Van Swieten

**1937.** Welfare Funds. Austrian Doctors.

| | | | | |
|---|---|---|---|---|
| 815 | **133** | 5g. (+5g.) brown | 2·75 | 7·50 |
| 816 | - | 8g. (+8g.) red | 2·75 | 7·50 |
| 817 | - | 12g. (+12g.) brown | 2·75 | 7·50 |
| 818 | - | 20g. (+20g.) green | 2·75 | 7·50 |
| 819 | - | 24g. (+24g.) violet | 2·75 | 7·50 |
| 820 | - | 30g. (+30g.) red | 2·75 | 7·50 |
| 821 | - | 40g. (+40g.) olive | 2·75 | 7·50 |
| 822 | - | 60g. (+60g.) blue | 2·75 | 7·50 |
| 823 | - | 64g. (+64g.) purple | 2·75 | 7·50 |

DESIGNS: 8g. L. A. von Auenbrugg; 12g. K. von Rokitansky; 20g. J. Skoda; 25g. F. von Hebra; 30g. F. von Arlt; 40g. J. Hyrtl; 60g. T. Billroth; 64g. T. Meynert.

**134** Nosegay and Signs of the Zodiac

**1937.** Christmas Greetings.

| | | | | |
|---|---|---|---|---|
| 824 | | 12g. green | 10 | 30 |
| 825 | **134** | 24g. red | 10 | 30 |

**ALLIED OCCUPATION.** Nos. 826/905 were issued in the Russian Zone of occupation and Nos. 906/22 were a joint issue for use in the British, French and American zones.

**1945.** Hitler portrait stamps of Germany optd. (a) Optd Osterreich only.

| | | | | |
|---|---|---|---|---|
| 826 | **173** | 5pf. green | 30 | 1·40 |
| 827 | **173** | 8pf. red | 40 | 1·10 |

(b) Optd Osterreich and bar.

| | | | | |
|---|---|---|---|---|
| 828 | | 6pf. violet | 60 | 1·60 |
| 829 | | 12pf. red | 60 | 1·60 |

**(137)**

**1945.** 1941 and 1944 Hitler stamps of Germany optd as T 137.

| | | | | |
|---|---|---|---|---|
| 830 | **137** | 1pf. grey | 6·25 | 13·00 |
| 831 | **137** | 3pf. brown | 3·25 | 11·00 |
| 832 | **137** | 4pf. grey | 17·00 | 38·00 |
| 833 | **137** | 5pf. green | 4·25 | 11·00 |
| 834 | **137** | 6pf. violet | 1·60 | 2·20 |
| 835 | **137** | 8pf. red | 1·30 | 3·25 |
| 836 | **137** | 10pf. brown | 4·25 | 11·00 |
| 837 | **137** | 12pf. red | 60 | 1·10 |
| 838 | **137** | 15pf. red | 1·60 | 5·50 |
| 839 | **137** | 16pf. green | 40·00 | 85·00 |
| 840 | **137** | 20pf. blue | 4·25 | 8·50 |
| 841 | **137** | 24pf. brown | 37·00 | 85·00 |
| 842 | **173** | 25pf. blue | 5·25 | 11·00 |
| 843 | **173** | 30pf. green | 5·25 | 11·00 |
| 844 | **173** | 40pf. mauve | 5·75 | 11·50 |
| 845 | **225** | 42pf. green | 8·25 | 19·00 |
| 846 | **173** | 50pf. green | 6·75 | 13·00 |
| 847 | **173** | 60pf. brown | 7·25 | 16·00 |
| 848 | **173** | 80pf. blue | 6·25 | 15·00 |
| 853 | **182** | 1rm. green | 34·00 | 70·00 |
| 850 | **182** | 2rm. violet | 29·00 | 60·00 |
| 855 | **182** | 3rm. red | 60·00 | £130 |
| 856 | **182** | 5rm. blue | £425 | £900 |

**1945.** Stamps of Germany surch OSTERREICH and new value.

| | | | | |
|---|---|---|---|---|
| 857 | **186** | 5pf. on 12+88pf. green | 85 | 2·75 |
| 858 | - | 6pf. on 6+14pf. brown and blue (No. 811) | 10·50 | 24·00 |
| 859 | **220** | 8pf. on 42+108pf. brn | 1·40 | 4·75 |
| 860 | - | 12pf. on 3+7pf. blue (No. 810) | 85 | 2·75 |

**(140)**

**1945.** 1941 and 1944 Hitler stamps of Germany optd as T 140.

| | | | | |
|---|---|---|---|---|
| 862 | **173** | 5pf. green | 1·60 | 5·50 |
| 863 | **173** | 6pf. violet | 1·00 | 4·25 |
| 864 | **173** | 8pf. red | 85 | 4·50 |
| 865 | **173** | 12pf. red | 1·00 | 5·50 |
| 866 | **173** | 30pf. green | 10·50 | 27·00 |
| 867a | **225** | 42pf. green | 23·00 | 44·00 |

**141** New National Arms

**142** New National Arms

**1945**

| | | | | |
|---|---|---|---|---|
| 868 | **141** | 3pf. brown | 20 | 20 |
| 869 | **141** | 4pf. blue | 20 | 45 |
| 870 | **141** | 5pf. green | 20 | 25 |
| 871 | **141** | 6pf. purple | 20 | 25 |
| 872 | **141** | 8pf. orange | 20 | 25 |
| 873 | **141** | 10pf. brown | 20 | 25 |
| 874 | **141** | 12pf. red | 20 | 25 |
| 875 | **141** | 15pf. orange | 20 | 30 |
| 876 | **141** | 16pf. green | 25 | 65 |
| 877 | **141** | 20pf. blue | 20 | 30 |
| 878 | **141** | 24pf. orange | 20 | 45 |
| 879 | **141** | 25pf. blue | 20 | 35 |
| 880 | **141** | 30pf. green | 20 | 25 |
| 881 | **141** | 38pf. blue | 20 | 35 |
| 882 | **141** | 40pf. purple | 20 | 40 |
| 883 | **141** | 42pf. grey | 30 | 45 |
| 884 | **141** | 50pf. green | 20 | 55 |
| 885 | **141** | 60pf. red | 20 | 55 |
| 886 | **141** | 80pf. violet | 20 | 45 |
| 887 | **142** | 1rm. green | 40 | 1·10 |
| 888 | **142** | 2rm. violet | 45 | 1·20 |
| 889 | **142** | 3rm. purple | 50 | 1·70 |
| 890 | **142** | 5rm. brown | 70 | 2·30 |

Nos. 877/86 are 24×28 mm.

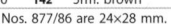

**144** Allegorical of the Home Land

**1945.** Austrian Welfare Charities.

| | | | | |
|---|---|---|---|---|
| 905 | **144** | 1s.+10s. green | 1·80 | 3·50 |

**145** Posthorn

**1945**

| | | | | |
|---|---|---|---|---|
| 906 | **145** | 1g. blue | 20 | 85 |
| 907 | **145** | 3g. orange | 20 | 30 |
| 908 | **145** | 4g. brown | 20 | 30 |
| 909 | **145** | 5g. green | 20 | 25 |
| 910 | **145** | 6g. purple | 20 | 25 |
| 911 | **145** | 8g. red | 20 | 25 |
| 912 | **145** | 10g. grey | 20 | 25 |
| 913 | **145** | 12g. brown | 20 | 25 |
| 914 | **145** | 15g. red | 20 | 30 |
| 915 | **145** | 20g. brown | 20 | 30 |
| 916 | **145** | 25g. blue | 20 | 30 |
| 917 | **145** | 30g. mauve | 20 | 30 |
| 918 | **145** | 40g. blue | 20 | 30 |
| 919 | **145** | 60g. olive | 20 | 45 |
| 920 | **145** | 1s. violet | 40 | 85 |
| 921 | **145** | 2s. yellow | 50 | 1·70 |
| 922 | **145** | 5s. blue | 55 | 1·80 |

**146** Salzburg **148** Durnstein

**1945.** Views as T 146/8.

| | | | | |
|---|---|---|---|---|
| 923 | - | 3g. blue | 20 | 20 |
| 924 | - | 4g. red | 20 | 20 |
| 925 | - | 5g. red | 20 | 20 |
| 926 | **146** | 6g. green | 20 | 20 |
| 927 | - | 8g. brown | 20 | 20 |
| 928 | - | 8g. purple | 20 | 20 |
| 929 | - | 8g. green | 20 | 20 |
| 930 | - | 10g. green | 20 | 20 |
| 931 | - | 10g. purple | 20 | 20 |
| 932 | - | 12g. brown | 20 | 20 |
| 933 | - | 15g. blue | 20 | 20 |
| 934 | - | 16g. brown | 20 | 20 |
| 935 | - | 20g. blue | 20 | 20 |
| 936 | - | 24g. green | 20 | 20 |
| 937 | - | 25g. grey | 20 | 20 |
| 938 | - | 30g. red | 20 | 20 |
| 939 | - | 30g. blue | 50 | 55 |
| 940 | - | 35g. red | 20 | 20 |
| 941 | - | 38g. green | 20 | 20 |
| 942 | - | 40g. grey | 20 | 20 |
| 943 | - | 42g. red | 20 | 20 |
| 944 | - | 45g. blue | 30 | 55 |
| 945 | - | 50g. blue | 20 | 20 |
| 946 | - | 50g. purple | 85 | 85 |
| 947 | - | 60g. blue | 30 | 30 |
| 948 | - | 60g. violet | 3·00 | 3·75 |
| 949 | - | 70g. blue | 35 | 55 |
| 950 | - | 80g. brown | 40 | 75 |
| 951 | - | 90g. green | 1·70 | 3·25 |
| 952A | **148** | 1s. brown | 1·00 | 1·60 |
| 953A | - | 2s. grey | 3·50 | 5·50 |
| 954A | - | 3s. green | 1·20 | 2·75 |
| 955A | - | 5s. red | 2·10 | 3·75 |

DESIGNS—As Type **146**: 3g. Lermoos; 4g. Iron-ore mine, Erzberg; 5g. Leopoldsberg, Vienna; 8g. (927), Prater Woods, Vienna; 8g. (928/9), Town Hall Park, Vienna; 10g. (930/1), Hochosterwitz; 12g. Schafberg; 15g. Forchtenstein; 16g. Gesauseeingang. 23½×29 mm: 20g. Gebhartsberg; 24g. Holdrichsmuhle, near Modling; 25g. Vent im Otztal; 30g. (938/9), Neusiedler Lake; 35g. Belvedere Palace, Vienna; 38g. Langbath Lake; 40g. Mariazell; 42g. Traunstein; 45g. Burg Hartenstein; 50g. (945/6), Silvretta Peaks, Vorarlberg; 60g. (947/8), Semmering; 70g. Badgastein; 80g. Kaisergebirge; 90g. Wayside shrine near Tragoss. As T **148**: 2s. St. Christof; 3s. Heiligenblut; 5s. Schonbrunn Palace, Vienna.

See also Nos. 1072/86a.

**1946.** 1st Anniv of U.N.O. No. 938 surch 26. JUNI 1945+20 g 26. JUNI 1946 and globe.

| | | | | |
|---|---|---|---|---|
| 971 | | 30g.+20g. red | 3·00 | 6·50 |

**151** Dr. Karl Renner

**1946.** 1st Anniv of Establishment of Renner Government.

| | | | | |
|---|---|---|---|---|
| 972 | **151** | 1s.+1s. green | 6·25 | 11·00 |
| 973 | **151** | 2s.+2s. violet | 6·25 | 11·00 |
| 974 | **151** | 3s.+3s. purple | 6·25 | 11·00 |
| 975 | **151** | 5s.+5s. brown | 6·25 | 11·00 |
| **MS**976 | | Four sheets, each 180×155 mm, each with block of 8 of one value (972/5) and Arms in centre. Imperf Set 4 sheets | £2500 | £17000 |

**152** Dagger and Map

**1946.** "Anti-Fascist" Exhibition.

| | | | | |
|---|---|---|---|---|
| 977 | **152** | 5g.+3g. sepia | 60 | 1·30 |
| 978 | - | 6g.+4g. green | 40 | 95 |
| 979 | - | 8g.+6g. orange | 40 | 95 |
| 980 | - | 12g.+12g. blue | 40 | 95 |
| 981 | - | 30g.+30g. violet | 40 | 1·10 |
| 982 | - | 42g.+42g. brown | 60 | 1·10 |
| 983 | - | 1s.+1s. red | 50 | 1·60 |
| 984 | - | 2s.+2s. red | 1·20 | 2·75 |

DESIGNS: 6g. Broom sweeping Nazi and Fascist emblems; 8g. St. Stephen's Cathedral in flames; 12g. Hand and barbed wire; 30g. Hand strangling snake; 42g. Hammer and broken column; 1s. Hand and Austrian flag; 2s. Eagle and smoking Nazi emblem.

(153)

**1946.** Congress of Society for Promotion of Cultural and Economic Relations with the Soviet Union. No. 932 optd with T 153.

| | | | | |
|---|---|---|---|---|
| 985 | | 12g. brown | 20 | 55 |

**154** Mare and Foal

**1946.** Austria Prize Race Fund.

| | | | | |
|---|---|---|---|---|
| 986 | **154** | 16g.+16g. red | 2·50 | 5·50 |
| 987 | - | 24g.+24g. violet | 2·10 | 4·25 |
| 988 | - | 60g.+60g. green | 2·10 | 4·25 |
| 989 | - | 1s.+1s. blue | 2·10 | 4·25 |
| 990 | - | 2s.+2s. brown | 7·25 | 11·00 |

DESIGNS: 24g. Two horses' heads; 60g. Racehorse clearing hurdle; 1s. Three racehorses; 2s. Three horses' heads.

**155** Ruprecht's Church, Vienna

**1946.** 950th Anniv of First recorded use of name "Osterreich".

| | | | | |
|---|---|---|---|---|
| 991 | **155** | 30g.+70g. red | 50 | 1·10 |

**156** Statue of Duke Rudolf

**1946.** St. Stephen's Cathedral Reconstruction Fund. Architectural and Sculptural designs.

| | | | | |
|---|---|---|---|---|
| 992 | **156** | 3g.+12g. brown | 20 | 1·10 |
| 993 | - | 5g.+20g. purple | 20 | 1·10 |
| 994 | - | 6g.+24g. blue | 20 | 1·10 |
| 995 | - | 8g.+32g. green | 20 | 1·10 |
| 996 | - | 10g.+40g. blue | 20 | 1·10 |
| 997 | - | 12g.+48g. violet | 50 | 2·20 |
| 998 | - | 30g.+1s.20 red | 1·80 | 2·20 |
| 999 | - | 50g.+1s.80 blue | 2·30 | 6·50 |
| 1000 | - | 1s.+5s. purple | 3·00 | 8·50 |
| 1001 | - | 2s.+10s. brown | 6·25 | 11·00 |

DESIGNS: 5g. Tomb of Frederick III; 6g. Pulpit; 8g. Statue of St. Stephen; 10g. Statue of Madonna and Child; 12g. Altar; 30g. Organ; 50g. Anton Pilgram; 1s. N.E. Tower; 2s. S.W. Spire.

**157** Franz Grillparzer (dramatic poet)

**1947.** Famous Austrians.

| | | | | |
|---|---|---|---|---|
| 1002 | | 12g. green | 30 | 55 |
| 1003 | **157** | 18g. purple | 30 | 30 |
| 1004 | - | 20g. green | 50 | 30 |
| 1005 | - | 40g. brown | 10·50 | 6·00 |
| 1006 | - | 40g. green | 10·50 | 11·00 |
| 1007 | - | 60g. lake | 50 | 45 |

PORTRAITS: 12g. Franz Schubert (composer); 20g. Carl Michael Ziehrer (composer); 40g. (No. 1005), Adalbert Stifter (poet); 40g. (No. 1006), Anton Bruckner (composer); 60g. Friedrich Amerling (painter).

**158** Harvesting

**1947.** Vienna Fair Fund.

| | | | | |
|---|---|---|---|---|
| 1009 | **158** | 3g.+2g. brown | 50 | 1·10 |
| 1010 | - | 8g.+2g. green | 50 | 1·10 |
| 1011 | - | 10g.+5g. slate | 50 | 1·10 |
| 1012 | - | 12g.+8g. violet | 50 | 1·10 |
| 1013 | - | 18g.+12g. olive | 50 | 1·10 |
| 1014 | - | 30g.+10g. purple | 50 | 1·10 |
| 1015 | - | 35g.+15g. red | 50 | 1·60 |
| 1016 | - | 60g.+20g. blue | 50 | 1·70 |

DESIGNS: 8g. Logging; 10g. Factory; 12g. Pithead; 18g. Oil wells; 30g. Textile machinery; 35g. Foundry; 60g. Electric cables.

**159** Airplane over Hinterstoder

**1947.** Air.

| | | | | |
|---|---|---|---|---|
| 1017 | | 50g. brown | 50 | 1·10 |
| 1018 | | 1s. purple | 50 | 1·10 |
| 1019 | | 2s. green | 50 | 2·20 |
| 1020 | **159** | 3s. brown | 3·50 | 7·50 |
| 1021 | - | 4s. green | 2·50 | 7·50 |
| 1022 | - | 5s. blue | 2·50 | 7·50 |
| 1023 | - | 10s. blue | 1·30 | 13·00 |

DESIGNS—Airplane over: 50g. Windmill at St. Andra; 1s. Heidentor; 2s. Gmund; 4s. Pragraten; 5s. Torsaule; 10s. St. Charles's Church, Vienna.

**160** Beaker (15th century)

**1947.** National Art Exhibition Fund.

| | | | | |
|---|---|---|---|---|
| 1024 | **160** | 3g.+2g. brown | 50 | 85 |
| 1025 | - | 8g.+2g. green | 50 | 85 |
| 1026 | - | 10g.+5g. red | 50 | 85 |
| 1027 | - | 12g.+8g. violet | 50 | 85 |
| 1028 | - | 18g.+12g. brown | 50 | 85 |
| 1029 | - | 20g.+10g. violet | 50 | 1·10 |
| 1030 | - | 30g.+10g. green | 50 | 1·10 |
| 1031 | - | 35g.+15g. red | 50 | 1·10 |
| 1032 | - | 48g.+12g. purple | 1·60 | 1·40 |
| 1033 | - | 60g.+20g. blue | 1·60 | 1·40 |

DESIGNS: 8g. Statue of "Providence" (Donner); 10g. Benedictine Monastery, Melk; 12g. "Wife of Dr. Brante of Vienna"; 18g. "Children in a Window" (Waldmuller); 20g. Belvedere Palace Gateway; 30g. Figure of "Egeria" on fountain at Schonbrunn; 35g. National Library, Vienna; 48g. "Copper Printer's (Ernst Rohm) Workshop" (Ferdinand Schmutzer); 60g. "Girl in Straw Hat" (Amerling).

**161** Racehorse

**1947.** Vienna Prize Race Fund.

| | | | | |
|---|---|---|---|---|
| 1034 | **161** | 60+20g. blue on pink | 30 | 1·40 |

**163** Prisoner-of-war

**1947.** Prisoners-of-war Relief Fund.

| | | | | |
|---|---|---|---|---|
| 1063 | **163** | 8g.+2g. green | 30 | 85 |
| 1064 | - | 12g.+8g. brown | 30 | 85 |
| 1065 | - | 18g.+12g. black | 30 | 85 |
| 1066 | - | 35g.+15g. purple | 30 | 85 |
| 1067 | - | 60g.+20g. blue | 30 | 85 |
| 1068 | - | 1s.+40g. brown | 30 | 1·60 |

DESIGNS: 12g. Letter from home; 18g. Gruesome camp visitor; 35g. Soldier and family reunited; 60g. Industry beckons returned soldier; 1s. Soldier sowing.

**1947.** Nos. 934 and 941 surch.

| | | | | |
|---|---|---|---|---|
| 1069 | | 75g. on 38g. green | 50 | 1·60 |
| 1070 | | 1s.40 on 16g. brown | 30 | 55 |

**165** Globe and Tape Machine

**1947.** Telegraph Centenary.

| | | | | |
|---|---|---|---|---|
| 1071 | **165** | 40g. violet | 40 | 65 |

**1947.** Currency Revaluation. (a) As T 146.

| | | | | |
|---|---|---|---|---|
| 1072 | | 3g. red (Lermoos) | 40 | 20 |
| 1073 | | 5g. red (Leopoldsberg) | 40 | 20 |
| 1074 | | 10g. red (Hochosterwitz) | 40 | 20 |
| 1075 | | 15g. red (Forchtenstein) | 2·50 | 2·40 |
| | | (b) As T 146 but larger (23½x29 mm). | | |
| 1076 | | 20g. red (Gebhartsberg) | 50 | 20 |
| 1077 | | 30g. red (Neusiedler Lake) | 60 | 30 |
| 1078 | | 40g. red (Mariazell) | 1·00 | 20 |
| 1079 | | 50g. red (Silvretta Peaks) | 1·00 | 20 |
| 1080 | | 60g. red (Semmering) | 12·50 | 2·75 |
| 1081 | | 70g. red (Badgastein) | 5·25 | 20 |
| 1082 | | 80g. red (Kaisergebirge) | 5·25 | 55 |
| 1083 | | 90g. red (Wayside shrine, Tragoss) | 6·25 | 1·40 |
| | | (c) As T 148. | | |
| 1084 | | 1s. violet (Durnstein) | 1·30 | 30 |
| 1085 | | 2s. violet (St. Christof) | 1·60 | 55 |
| 1086 | | 3s. violet (Heiligenblut) | 31·00 | 2·20 |
| 1086a | | 5s. violet (Schonbrunn) | 31·00 | 2·75 |

Nos. 1072/86a in new currency replaced previous issue at rate of 3s. (old) = 1s. (new).

**166** Sacred Olympic Flame

**1948.** Fund for Entries to 5th Winter Olympic Games, St. Moritz.

| | | | | |
|---|---|---|---|---|
| 1087 | **166** | 1s.+50g. blue | 50 | 85 |

**167** Laabenbach Viaduct, Neulenbach

**1948.** Reconstruction Fund.

| | | | | |
|---|---|---|---|---|
| 1088 | **167** | 10g.+5g. grey | 20 | 30 |
| 1089 | - | 20g.+10g. violet | 20 | 30 |
| 1090 | - | 30g.+10g. green | 50 | 65 |
| 1091 | - | 40g.+20g. green | 20 | 30 |
| 1092 | - | 45g.+20g. blue | 20 | 30 |
| 1093 | - | 60g.+30g. red | 20 | 30 |
| 1094 | - | 75g.+35g. purple | 30 | 45 |
| 1095 | - | 80g.+40g. purple | 30 | 45 |
| 1096 | - | 1s.+50g. blue | 30 | 45 |
| 1097 | - | 1s.40+70g. lake | 60 | 75 |

DESIGNS (showing reconstruction): 20g. Vermunt Lake Dam; 30g. Danube Port, Vienna; 40g. Erzberg open-cast mine; 45g. Southern Railway Station, Vienna; 60g. Flats; 75g. Vienna Gas Works; 80g. Oil refinery; 1s. Mountain roadway; 1s.40, Parliament Building.

**169** Violets

**1948.** Anti-tuberculosis Fund.

| | | | | |
|---|---|---|---|---|
| 1098 | **169** | 10g.+5g. violet, mauve and green | 35 | 35 |
| 1099 | - | 20g.+10g. green, light green and yellow | 35 | 35 |
| 1100 | - | 30g.+10g. brown, yellow and green | 4·50 | 4·50 |
| 1101 | - | 40g.+20g. green, yellow and orange | 85 | 85 |
| 1102 | - | 45g.+20g. purple, mauve and yellow | 30 | 30 |
| 1103 | - | 60g.+30g. red, mauve and green | 30 | 30 |
| 1104 | - | 75g.+35g. green, pink and yellow | 30 | 30 |
| 1105 | - | 80g.+40g. blue, pink and green | 40 | 40 |
| 1106 | - | 1s.+50g. blue, ultramarine and green | 40 | 40 |
| 1107 | - | 1s.40+70g. green, blue and yellow | 2·75 | 2·75 |

FLOWERS: 20g. Anemone; 30g. Crocus; 40g. Primrose; 45g. Pasque flower; 60g. Rhododendron; 75g. Wild rose; 80g. Cyclamen; 1s. Gentian; 1s.40, Edelweiss.

**170** Vorarlberg Montafon

**1948.** Provincial Costumes.

| | | | | |
|---|---|---|---|---|
| 1108 | | 3g. grey | 85 | 1·10 |
| 1109 | | 5g. green | 30 | 20 |
| 1110 | | 10g. blue | 30 | 20 |
| 1111 | | 15g. brown | 50 | 20 |
| 1112 | **170** | 20g. green | 30 | 20 |
| 1113 | - | 25g. brown | 30 | 20 |
| 1114 | - | 30g. red | 3·50 | 20 |
| 1115 | - | 30g. violet | 1·00 | 20 |
| 1116 | - | 40g. violet | 4·25 | 20 |
| 1117 | - | 40g. green | 85 | 20 |
| 1118 | - | 45g. blue | 4·25 | 75 |
| 1119 | - | 50g. brown | 1·20 | 20 |
| 1120 | - | 60g. red | 85 | 20 |
| 1121 | - | 70g. green | 85 | 20 |
| 1122 | - | 75g. blue | 7·25 | 75 |
| 1123 | - | 80g. rose | 1·00 | 20 |
| 1124 | - | 90g. purple | 55·00 | 55 |
| 1125 | - | 1s. blue | 16·00 | 20 |
| 1126 | - | 1s. red | £130 | 20 |
| 1127 | - | 1s. green | 70 | 20 |
| 1128 | - | 1s.20 violet | 1·00 | 20 |
| 1129 | - | 1s.40 brown | 3·00 | 30 |
| 1130 | - | 1s.45 red | 2·50 | 20 |
| 1131 | - | 1s.50 blue | 2·10 | 20 |
| 1132 | - | 1s.60 red | 85 | 20 |
| 1133 | - | 1s.70 blue | 4·25 | 1·30 |
| 1134 | - | 2s. green | 1·60 | 20 |
| 1135 | - | 2s.20 slate | 8·25 | 30 |
| 1136 | - | 2s.40 blue | 2·10 | 25 |
| 1137 | - | 2s.50 brown | 5·75 | 2·20 |
| 1138 | - | 2s.70 brown | 1·00 | 1·40 |
| 1139 | - | 3s. lake | 2·25 | 20 |
| 1140 | - | 3s.50 green | 34·00 | 30 |
| 1141 | - | 4s.50 purple | 1·00 | 1·30 |
| 1142 | - | 5s. purple | 1·60 | 20 |
| 1143 | - | 7s. olive | 6·25 | 2·20 |
| 1144 | - | 10s. grey | 50·00 | 7·50 |

DESIGNS—As T **170**: 3g. "Tirol Inntal"; 5g. "Salzburg Pinzgau"; 10, 75g. "Steiermark Salzkammergut" (different designs); 15g. "Burgenland Lutzmannsburg"; 25g., 1s.60, "Wien 1850" (two different designs); 30g. (2) "Salzburg Pongau"; 40g. (2) "Wien 1840"; 45g. "Karnten Lesachtal"; 50g. "Vorarlberg Bregenzerwald"; 60g. "Karnten Lavanttal"; 70g. "Niederosterreich Wachau"; 80g. "Steiermark Ennstal"; 90g. "Steiermark Mittelsteier"; 1s. (3) "Tirol Pustertal"; 1s.20, "Niederosterreich Wienerwald"; 1s.40, "Oberosterreich Innviertel"; 1s.45, "Wilter bei Innsbruck"; 1s.50, "Wien 1853"; 1s.70, "Ost Tirol Kals"; 2s. "Oberosterreich"; 2s.20, "Ischl 1820"; 2s.40, "Kitzbuhel"; 2s.50, "Obersteiermark 1850"; 2s.70, "Kleines Walsertal"; 3s. "Burgenland"; 3s.50, "Niederosterreich 1850"; 4s.50, "Gailtal"; 5s. "Zillertal"; 7s. "Steiermark Sulmtal". 25×35 mm: 10s. "Wien 1850".

**172** Kunstlerhaus

**173** Hans Makart

**1948.** 80th Anniv of Creative Artists' Association.

| | | | | |
|---|---|---|---|---|
| 1145 | **172** | 20g.+10g. green | 10·50 | 8·50 |
| 1146 | **173** | 30g.+15g. brown | 3·50 | 4·25 |
| 1147 | - | 40g.+20g. blue | 3·50 | 4·25 |
| 1148 | - | 50g.+25g. violet | 6·25 | 7·50 |
| 1149 | - | 60g.+30g. red | 7·25 | 6·50 |
| 1150 | - | 1s.+50g. blue | 7·25 | 8·50 |
| 1151 | - | 1s.40+70g. brown | 21·00 | 26·00 |

PORTRAITS: 40g. K. Kundmann; 50g. A. von Siccardsburg; 60g. H. Canon; 1s. W. Unger; 1s.40, Friedr. Schmidt.

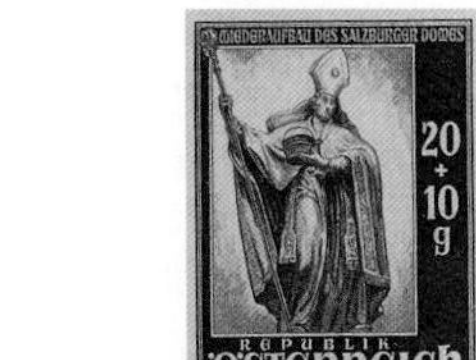

**174** St. Rupert

**1948.** Salzburg Cathedral Reconstruction Fund.

| | | | | |
|---|---|---|---|---|
| 1152 | **174** | 20g.+10g. green | 10·50 | 11·00 |
| 1153 | - | 30g.+15g. brown | 3·00 | 4·25 |
| 1154 | - | 40g.+20g. green | 3·50 | 4·25 |
| 1155 | - | 50g.+25g. brown | 1·00 | 1·10 |
| 1156 | - | 60g.+30g. red | 1·00 | 1·10 |
| 1157 | - | 80g.+40g. purple | 1·00 | 1·10 |
| 1158 | - | 1s.+50g. blue | 1·00 | 1·60 |
| 1159 | - | 1s.40+70g. green | 3·00 | 4·25 |

DESIGNS: 30, 40, 50, 80g. Views of Salzburg Cathedral; 60g. St. Peter's; 1s. Cathedral and Fortress; 1s.40, Madonna.

**175** Pres. Renner

**1948.** 30th Anniv of Republic.

| | | | | |
|---|---|---|---|---|
| 1160 | **175** | 1s. blue | 3·00 | 2·75 |

See also Nos. 1224 and 1333.

**176** F. Gruber and J. Mohr

**1948.** 130th Anniv of Composition of Carol "Silent Night, Holy Night".

| | | | | |
|---|---|---|---|---|
| 1161 | **176** | 60g. brown | 8·50 | 8·50 |

**177** Boy and Hare

**1949.** Child Welfare Fund.

| | | | | |
|---|---|---|---|---|
| 1162 | **177** | 40g.+10g. purple | 22·00 | 24·00 |
| 1163 | - | 60g.+20g. red | 22·00 | 24·00 |
| 1164 | - | 1s.+25g. blue | 22·00 | 24·00 |
| 1165 | - | 1s.40+35g. green | 25·00 | 27·00 |

DESIGNS: 60g. Two girls and apples in boot; 1s. Boy and birthday cake; 1s.40, Girl praying before candle.

**178** Boy and Dove

**1949.** U.N. Int. Children's Emergency Fund.

| | | | | |
|---|---|---|---|---|
| 1166 | **178** | 1s. blue | 16·00 | 4·25 |

**179** Johann Strauss

**1949.** 50th Death Anniv of Johann Strauss the Younger (composer).

| | | | | |
|---|---|---|---|---|
| 1167 | **179** | 1s. blue | 4·25 | 3·00 |

See also Nos. 1174, 1207 and 1229.

**180** Esperanto Star

**1949.** Esperanto Congress, Vienna.

| | | | | |
|---|---|---|---|---|
| 1168 | **180** | 20g. green | 1·40 | 1·40 |

**181** St. Gebhard

**1949.** Birth Millenary of St. Gebhard (Bishop of Vorarlberg).

| | | | | |
|---|---|---|---|---|
| 1169 | **181** | 30g. violet | 2·50 | 2·50 |

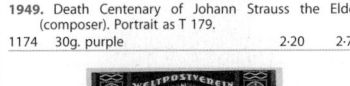

**182** Seal of Duke Friedrich II, 1230

**1949.** Prisoners-of-war Relief Fund. Arms.

| | | | | |
|---|---|---|---|---|
| 1170 | **182** | 40g.+10g. yell & brn | 14·00 | 13·00 |
| 1171 | - | 60g.+15g. pink & pur | 12·00 | 11·00 |
| 1172 | - | 1s.+25g. red & blue | 12·00 | 11·00 |
| 1173 | - | 1s.60+40g. pink and green | 16·00 | 16·00 |

ARMS: 60g. Princes of Austria, 1450; 1s. Austria, 1600; 1s.60, Austria, 1945.

**1949.** Death Centenary of Johann Strauss the Elder (composer). Portrait as T 179.

| | | | | |
|---|---|---|---|---|
| 1174 | | 30g. purple | 2·20 | 2·75 |

**183** Allegory of U.P.U.

**1949.** 75th Anniv of U.P.U.

| | | | | |
|---|---|---|---|---|
| 1175 | **183** | 40g. green | 5·50 | 5·50 |
| 1176 | - | 60g. red | 6·50 | 5·50 |
| 1177 | - | 1s. blue | 11·00 | 9·75 |

DESIGNS: 60g. Children holding "75"; 1s. Woman's head.

**185** Magnifying Glass and Covers

**1949.** Stamp Day.

| | | | | |
|---|---|---|---|---|
| 1206 | **185** | 60g.+15g. brown | 4·25 | 3·75 |

**1949.** 50th Death Anniv of Karl Millocker (composer). Portrait as T 179.

| | | | | |
|---|---|---|---|---|
| 1207 | | 1s. blue | 22·00 | 17·00 |

**186** M. M. Daffinger

**1950.** 160th Birth Anniv of Moritz Michael Daffinger (painter).

| | | | | |
|---|---|---|---|---|
| 1208 | **186** | 60g. brown | 11·00 | 8·50 |

**187** A. Hofer

**1950.** 140th Death Anniv of Andreas Hofer (patriot).

| | | | | |
|---|---|---|---|---|
| 1209 | **187** | 60g. violet | 17·00 | 13·00 |

See also Nos. 1211, 1223, 1232, 1234, 1243, 1253, 1288 and 1386.

**188** Stamp of 1850

**1950.** Austrian Stamp Centenary.

| | | | | |
|---|---|---|---|---|
| 1210 | **188** | 1s. black on yellow | 2·75 | 2·20 |

**1950.** Death Centenary of Josef Madersperger (sewing machine inventor). Portrait as T 187.

| | | | | |
|---|---|---|---|---|
| 1211 | | 60g. violet | 9·75 | 5·50 |

**189** Arms of Austria and Carinthia

**1950.** 30th Anniv of Carinthian Plebiscite.

| | | | | |
|---|---|---|---|---|
| 1212 | **189** | 60g.+15g. grn & brn | 43·00 | 38·00 |
| 1213 | - | 1s.+25g. red & orange | 55·00 | 43·00 |
| 1214 | - | 1s.70+40g. blue and turquoise | 55·00 | 49·00 |

DESIGNS: 1s. Carinthian waving Austrian flag; 1s.70, Hand and ballot box.

**190** Rooks

**1950.** Air.

| | | | | |
|---|---|---|---|---|
| 1215 | **190** | 60g. violet | 6·50 | 5·50 |
| 1216 | - | 1s. violet (Barn swallows) | 32·00 | 30·00 |
| 1217 | - | 2s. blue (Black-headed gulls) | 22·00 | 11·00 |
| 1218 | - | 3s. turquoise (Great cormorants) | £190 | £160 |
| 1219 | - | 5s. brown (Common buzzard) | £190 | £160 |
| 1220 | - | 10s. purple (Grey heron) | 85·00 | 75·00 |
| 1221 | - | 20s. sepia (Golden eagle) | 16·00 | 4·25 |

**191** Philatelist

**1950.** Stamp Day.

| | | | | |
|---|---|---|---|---|
| 1222 | **191** | 60g.+15g. green | 13·00 | 11·00 |

**1950.** Birth Centenary of Alexander Girardi (actor). Portrait as T 187.

| | | | | |
|---|---|---|---|---|
| 1223 | | 30g. blue | 2·40 | 1·90 |

**192** Dr. Renner

**1951.** Death of Pres. Karl Renner.

| | | | | |
|---|---|---|---|---|
| 1224 | **192** | 1s. black on lemon | 1·90 | 85 |

**193** Miner

**1951.** Reconstruction Fund.

| | | | | |
|---|---|---|---|---|
| 1225 | **193** | 40g.+10g. purple | 22·00 | 24·00 |
| 1226 | - | 60g.+15g. green | 22·00 | 24·00 |
| 1227 | - | 1s.+25g. brown | 22·00 | 24·00 |
| 1228 | - | 1s.70+40g. blue | 22·00 | 24·00 |

DESIGNS: 60g. Bricklayer; 1s. Bridge-builder; 1s.70, Telegraph engineer.

**1951.** 150th Birth Anniv of Joseph Lanner (composer). Portrait as T 179.

| | | | | |
|---|---|---|---|---|
| 1229 | | 60g. green | 7·00 | 3·75 |

**194** Martin Johann Schmidt

**1951.** 150th Death Anniv of Schmidt (painter).

| | | | | |
|---|---|---|---|---|
| 1230 | **194** | 1s. red | 10·00 | 4·75 |

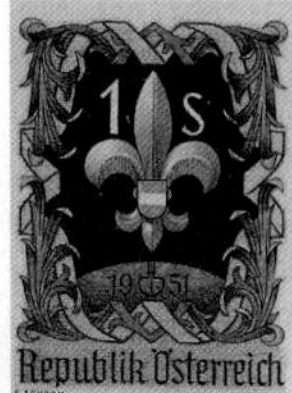

**195** Scout Badge

**1951.** Boy Scout Jamboree.

| | | | | |
|---|---|---|---|---|
| 1231 | **195** | 1s. red, yellow & green | 7·00 | 6·50 |

**1951.** 10th Death Anniv of Wilhelm Kienzl (composer). Portrait as T 187.

| | | | | |
|---|---|---|---|---|
| 1232 | | 1s.50 blue | 4·75 | 3·25 |

**196** Laurel Branch and Olympic Emblem

**1952.** 6th Winter Olympic Games, Oslo.
1233 **196** 2s.40+60g. green 32·00 30·00

**1952.** 150th Birth Anniv of Karl Ritter von Ghega (railway engineer). Portrait as T 187.
1234 1s. green 11·00 3·25

**197** Schrammel

**1952.** Birth Cent of Josef Schrammel (composer).
1235 **197** 1s.50 blue 11·00 3·25
See also No. 1239.

**198** Cupid and Letter

**1952.** Stamp Day.
1236 **198** 1s.50+35g. purple 32·00 31·00

**199** Breakfast Pavilion

**1952.** Bicentenary of Schonbrunn Menagerie.
1237 **199** 1s.50 green 9·75 3·25

**200**

**1952.** Int Union of Socialist Youth Camp, Vienna.
1238 **200** 1s.50 blue 11·00 2·20

**1952.** 150th Birth Anniv of Nikolaus Lenau (writer). Portrait as T 197.
1239 1s. green 11·00 3·25

**202**

**1952.** International Children's Correspondence.
1240 **202** 2s.40 blue 18·00 4·25

**203** "Christus Pantocrator" (sculpture)

**1952.** Austrian Catholics' Day.
1241 **203** 1s.+25g. olive 16·00 15·00

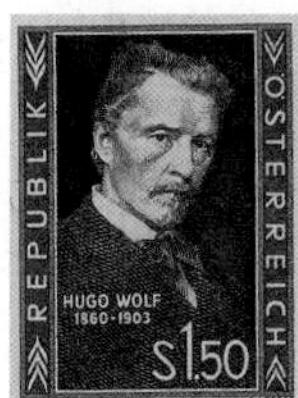

**204** Hugo Wolf

**1953.** 50th Death Anniv of Wolf (composer).
1242 **204** 1s.50 blue 12·00 3·25

**1953.** President Korner's 80th Birthday. As T 187 but portrait of Korner.
1243 1s.50 blue 12·00 3·25
For 1s.50 black, see No. 1288.

**1953.** 60th Anniv of Austrian Trade Union Movement. As No. 955 (colour changed) surch GEWERKSCHAFTS BEWEGUNG 60 JAHRE 1s+25g.
1244 1s.+25g. on 5s. blue 4·75 4·25

**206** Linz National Theatre

**1953.** 150th Anniv of Linz National Theatre.
1245 **206** 1s.50 turquoise 27·00 4·25

**207** Meeting-house, Steyr

**1953.** Vienna Evangelical School Rebuilding Fund.
1246 **207** 70g.+15g. purple 45 45
1247 - 1s.+25g. blue 45 45
1248 - 1s.50+40g. brown 1·10 1·10
1249 - 2s.40+60g. green 4·75 4·75
1250 - 3s.+75g. lilac 12·00 12·00
DESIGNS: 1s. J. Kepler (astronomer); 1s.50, Lutheran Bible, 1534; 2s.40, T. von Hansen (architect); 3s. School after reconstruction.

**208** Child and Christmas Tree

**1953.** Christmas.
1251 **208** 1s. green 1·80 1·10
See also No. 1266.

**209**

**1953.** Stamp Day.
1252 **209** 1s.+25g. brown 12·00 11·00

**1954.** 150th Birth Anniv of M. Von Schwind (painter). As T 187 but portrait of Von Schwind.
1253 1s.50 lilac 23·00 4·25

**210** Baron K. von Rokitansky

**1954.** 150th Birth Anniv of Von Rokitansky (anatomist).
1254 **210** 1s.50 violet 26·00 4·25
See also No. 1264.

**1954.** Avalanche Fund. As No. 953 (colour changed) surch LAWINENOPFER 1954 1s+20g.
1255 1s.+20g. blue 55 55

**212** Surgeon with Microscope

**1954.** Health Service Fund.
1256 - 30g.+10g. violet 1·60 1·60
1257 **212** 70g.+15g. brown 55 55
1258 - 1s.+25g. blue 55 55
1259 - 1s.45+35g. green 85 1·10
1260 - 1s.50+35g. red 7·75 11·00
1261 - 2s.40+60g. purple 9·25 12·00
DESIGNS: 30g. Boy patient and sun-ray lamp; 1s. Mother and children; 1s.45, Operating theatre; 1s.50, Baby on scales; 2s.40, Red Cross nurse and ambulance.

**213** Esperanto Star

**1954.** 50th Anniv of Esperanto in Austria.
1262 **213** 1s. green and brown 7·50 75

**214** J. M. Rottmayr von Rosenbrunn

**1954.** Birth Tercentenary of Rottmayr von Rosenbrunn (painter).
1263 **214** 1s. green 19·00 4·75

**1954.** 25th Death Anniv of Dr. Auer von Welsbach (inventor). Portrait as T 210.
1264 1s.50 blue 55·00 4·25

**216** Great Organ, Church of St. Florian

**1954.** 2nd International Congress of Catholic Church Music, Vienna.
1265 **216** 1s. brown 3·50 65

**1954.** Christmas. As No. 1251, but colour changed.
1266 **208** 1s. blue 6·00 1·10

**217** 18th-century River Boat

**1954.** Stamp Day.
1267 **217** 1s.+25g. green 11·00 9·75

**218** Arms of Austria and Newspapers

**1954.** 150th Anniv of State Printing Works and 250th Anniv of "Wiener-Zeitung" (newspaper).
1268 **218** 1s. black and red 4·25 85

**219** "Freedom"

**1955.** 10th Anniv of Re-establishment of Austrian Republic.
1269 - 70g. purple 3·25 55
1270 - 1s. blue 8·50 55
1271 **219** 1s.45 red 14·00 7·00
1272 - 1s.50 brown 36·00 60
1273 - 2s.40 green 14·00 9·75
DESIGNS: 70g. Parliament Buildings; 1s. Western Railway terminus, Vienna; 1s.50, Modern houses; 2s.40, Limberg Dam.

**1955.** Austrian State Treaty. As No. 888, but colour changed, optd STAATSVERTRAG 1955.
1274 **142** 2s. grey 4·25 1·10

**221** "Strength through Unity"

**1955.** 4th World Trade Unions Congress, Vienna.
1275 **221** 1s. blue 4·25 3·75

**222** "Return to Work"

**1955.** Returned Prisoners-of-war Relief Fund.
1276 **222** 1s.+25g. brown 3·75 3·25

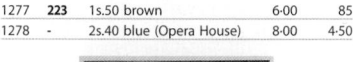

**223** Burgtheater, Vienna

**1955.** Re-opening of Burgtheater and State Opera House, Vienna.
1277 **223** 1s.50 brown 6·00 85
1278 - 2s.40 blue (Opera House) 8·00 4·50

**224** Globe and Flags

**1955.** 10th Anniv of U.N.O.
1279 **224** 2s.40 green 24·00 5·50

**225** Stamp Collector

**1955.** Stamp Day.
1280 **225** 1s.+25g. brown 6·50 6·00

226 Mozart

**1956.** Birth Bicentenary of Mozart (composer).
1281 **226** 2s.40 blue 9·75 2·75

227

**1956.** Admission of Austria into U.N.
1282 **227** 2s.40 brown 19·00 3·75

228

**1956.** 5th World Power Conference, Vienna.
1283 **228** 2s.40 blue 17·00 4·25

229 Vienna and Five New Towns

**1956.** 23rd International Town Planning Congress.
1284 **229** 1s.45 red, black & green 5·50 1·70

230 J. B. Fischer von Erlach

**1956.** Birth Tercentenary of Fischer von Erlach (architect).
1285 **230** 1s.50 brown 1·80 1·80

231 "Stamp Day"

**1956.** Stamp Day.
1286 **231** 1s.+25g. red 5·50 5·50

**1956.** Hungarian Relief Fund. As No. 1173, but colours changed, surch 1956 1.50 +50 UNGARNHILFE.
1287 1s.50+50g. on 1s.60+40g. red and grey 1·10 1·10

**1957.** Death of Pres. Korner. As No. 1243, but colour changed.
1288 1s.50 black 3·25 2·75

233 J. Wagner von Jauregg

**1957.** Birth Centenary of Wagner von Jauregg (psychiatrist).
1289 **233** 2s.40 brown 6·50 4·25

234 Anton Wildgans

**1957.** 25th Death Anniv of Anton Wildgans (poet).
1290 **234** 1s. blue 85 75

235 Daimber (1907), Graf and Stift (1957) Post Buses

**1957.** 50th Anniv of Postal Coach Service.
1291 **235** 1s. black on yellow 85 75

237 Mt. Gasherbrum II

**1957.** Austrian Himalaya–Karakorum Expedition, 1956.
1293 **237** 1s.50 blue 75 75

236 Mariazell Basilica

**1957.** Buildings. (a) Size 20½×24½ mm.

| | | | | |
|---|---|---|---|---|
| 1295 | - | 20g. purple | 55 | 20 |
| 1296 | - | 30g. green | 65 | 20 |
| 1297 | - | 40g. red | 45 | 20 |
| 1298 | - | 50g. grey | 45 | 20 |
| 1299 | - | 60g. brown | 45 | 20 |
| 1300 | - | 70g. blue | 90 | 20 |
| 1301 | - | 80g. brown | 70 | 20 |
| 1302 | **236** | 1s. brown | 1·90 | 30 |
| 1303 | - | 1s. brown | 1·20 | 20 |
| 1304 | - | 1s.20 purple | 1·30 | 45 |
| 1305 | - | 1s.30 green | 30 | 20 |
| 1306 | - | 1s.40 blue | 1·10 | 30 |
| 1307 | - | 1s.50 red | 1·30 | 20 |
| 1308 | - | 1s.80 blue | 1·40 | 20 |
| 1309 | - | 2s. blue | 6·50 | 30 |
| 1310 | - | 2s. blue | 2·20 | 60 |
| 1311 | - | 2s.20 green | 1·40 | 20 |
| 1312 | - | 2s.50 violet | 3·00 | 1·10 |
| 1313 | - | 3s. blue | 1·60 | 20 |
| 1314 | - | 3s.40 green | 2·30 | 1·10 |
| 1315 | - | 3s.50 mauve | 2·40 | 65 |
| 1316 | - | 4s. violet | 2·50 | 55 |
| 1317 | - | 4s.50 green | 3·25 | 85 |
| 1318 | - | 5s.50 green | 2·40 | 1·20 |
| 1319 | - | 6s. violet | 2·50 | 50 |
| 1320 | - | 6s.40 blue | 4·00 | 1·10 |
| 1321 | - | 8s. purple | 5·50 | 1·10 |

(b) Larger.

| | | | |
|---|---|---|---|
| 1322 | 10s. green | 5·50 | 55 |
| 1323 | 20s. purple | 6·50 | 1·70 |

(c) Smaller, size 17½×21 mm.

| | | | | |
|---|---|---|---|---|
| 1324 | - | 50g. grey | 45 | 30 |
| 1325 | **236** | 1s. brown | 45 | 30 |
| 1326 | - | 1s.50 purple | 55 | 30 |

DESIGNS: 20g. Old Courtyard, Morbisch; 30g. Vienna Town Hall; 40g. Porcia Castle, Spittal; 50g. Heiligenstadt flats; 60g. Lederer Tower, Wels; 70g. Archbishop's Palace, Salzburg; 80g. Old farmhouse, Pinzgau; 1s. (1303) Millstatt; 1s.20, Corn Measurer's House, Bruck-on-the-Mur; 1s.30, Schattenburg Castle; 1s.40, Klagenfurt Town Hall; 1s.50, "Rabenhof" Flats, Erdberg, Vienna; 1s.80, Mint Tower, Hall-in-Tyrol; 2s. (1309) Christkindl Church; 2s. (1310) Dragon Fountain, Klagenfurt; 2s.20, Beethoven's House, Heiligenstadt, Vienna; 2s.50, Danube Bridge, Linz; 3s. "Swiss Portal", Imperial Palace, Vienna; 3s.40, Stein Gate, Krems-on-the-Danube; 3s.50, Esterhazy Palace, Eisenstadt; 4s. Vienna Gate, Hainburg; 4s.50, Schwechat Airport; 5s.50, Chur Gate, Feldkirch; 6s. Graz Town Hall; 6s.40, "Golden Roof", Innsbruck; 8s. Steyr Town Hall. 22×28½ mm: 10s. Heidenreichstein Castle. 28½×37½ mm: 20s. Melk Abbey.

238 Post Office, Linz

**1957.** Stamp Day.
1327 **238** 1s.+25g. green 4·75 4·25

239 Badgastein

**1958.** International Alpine Ski Championships, Badgastein.
1328 **239** 1s.50 blue 65 55

240 Vickers Viscount 800 OE-LAB

**1958.** Austrian Airlines Inaugural Flight, Vienna–London.
1329 **240** 4s. red 1·60 85

241 Mother and Child

**1958.** Mothers' Day.
1330 **241** 1s.50 blue 65 55

242 Walther von der Vogelweide (after 12th-century manuscript)

**1958.** 3rd Austrian Choir Festival, Vienna.
1331 **242** 1s.50 multicoloured 65 55

243 Dr. O. Redlich

**1958.** Birth Cent of Dr. Oswald Redlich (historian).
1332 **243** 2s.40 blue 95 65

**1958.** 40th Anniv of Republic. As T 175 but inscr "40 JAHRE".
1333 **175** 1s.50 green 1·10 95

244 Post Office, Kitzbuhel

**1958.** Stamp Day.
1334 **244** 2s.40+60g. blue 1·60 1·40

245 "E" building on Map of Europe

**1959.** Europa.
1335 **245** 2s.40 green 3·75 75

246 Monopoly Emblem and Cigars

**1959.** 175th Anniv of Austrian Tobacco Monopoly.
1336 **246** 2s.40 brown 95 55

247 Archduke Johann

**1959.** Death Cent of Archduke Johann of Austria.
1337 **247** 1s.50 green 65 45

248 Western Capercaillie

**1959.** International Hunting Congress, Vienna.

| | | | | |
|---|---|---|---|---|
| 1338 | **248** | 1s. purple | 55 | 30 |
| 1339 | - | 1s.50 blue (Roebuck) | 85 | 20 |
| 1340 | - | 2s.40 grn (Wild boar) | 1·40 | 1·50 |
| 1341 | - | 3s.50 brown (Red deer family) | 95 | 65 |

249 Haydn

**1959.** 150th Death Anniv of Haydn.
1342 **249** 1s.50 purple 85 55

250 Tyrolean Eagle

**1959.** 150th Anniv of Tyrolese Rising.

| | | | | |
|---|---|---|---|---|
| 1343 | **250** | 1s.50 red | 65 | 40 |

**251** Microwave Transmitting Aerial, Zugspitze

**1959.** Inaug of Austrian Microwave Network.

| | | | | |
|---|---|---|---|---|
| 1344 | **251** | 2s.40 blue | 85 | 55 |

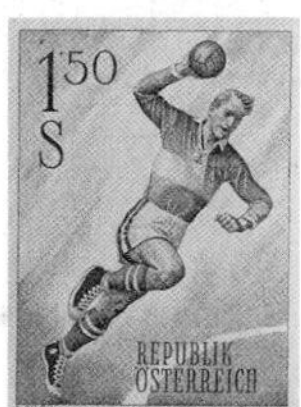

**252** Handball Player

**1959.** Sports.

| | | | | |
|---|---|---|---|---|
| 1345 | - | 1s. violet | 65 | 30 |
| 1346 | **252** | 1s.50 green | 95 | 65 |
| 1347 | - | 1s.80 red | 65 | 55 |
| 1348 | - | 2s. purple | 55 | 45 |
| 1349 | - | 2s.20 blue | 65 | 55 |

DESIGNS: 1s. Runner; 1s.80, Gymnast; 2s. Hurdling; 2s.20, Hammer thrower.

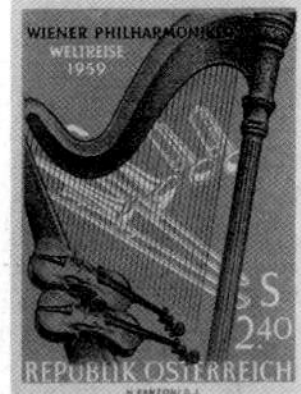

**253** Orchestral Instruments

**1959.** Vienna Philharmonic Orchestra's World Tour.

| | | | | |
|---|---|---|---|---|
| 1350 | **253** | 2s.40 black and blue | 85 | 60 |

**254** Roman Coach

**1959.** Stamp Day.

| | | | | |
|---|---|---|---|---|
| 1351 | **254** | 2s.40+60g. blk & mve | 1·30 | 1·20 |

**255** Refugees

**1960.** World Refugee Year.

| | | | | |
|---|---|---|---|---|
| 1352 | **255** | 3s. turquoise | 95 | 70 |

**256** Pres. Adolf Scharf

**1960.** President's 70th Birthday.

| | | | | |
|---|---|---|---|---|
| 1353 | **256** | 1s.50 green | 95 | 50 |

**257** Youth Hostellers

**1960.** Youth Hostels Movement.

| | | | | |
|---|---|---|---|---|
| 1354 | **257** | 1s. red | 55 | 50 |

**258** Dr. Eiselsberg

**1960.** Birth Cent of Dr. Anton Eiselsberg (surgeon).

| | | | | |
|---|---|---|---|---|
| 1355 | **258** | 1s.50 sepia and cream | 1·10 | 50 |

**259** Gustav Mahler

**1960.** Birth Centenary of Gustav Mahler (composer).

| | | | | |
|---|---|---|---|---|
| 1356 | **259** | 1s.50 brown | 1·10 | 50 |

**260** Jakob Prandtauer

**1960.** 300th Birth Anniv of Jakob Prandtauer (architect).

| | | | | |
|---|---|---|---|---|
| 1357 | **260** | 1s.50 brown | 1·10 | 50 |

**261** Grossglockner Highway

**1960.** 25th Anniv of Grossglockner Alpine Highway.

| | | | | |
|---|---|---|---|---|
| 1358 | **261** | 1s.80 blue | 2·20 | 90 |

**262** Ionic Capital

**1960.** Europa.

| | | | | |
|---|---|---|---|---|
| 1359 | **262** | 3s. black | 2·75 | 2·30 |

**263** Griffen, Carinthia

**1960.** 40th Anniv of Carinthian Plebiscite.

| | | | | |
|---|---|---|---|---|
| 1360 | **263** | 1s.50 green | 85 | 50 |

**264** Examining Proof of Engraved Stamp

**1960.** Stamp Day.

| | | | | |
|---|---|---|---|---|
| 1361 | **264** | 3s.+70g. brown | 2·20 | 2·00 |

**265** "Freedom"

**1961.** Austrian Freedom Martyrs' Commem.

| | | | | |
|---|---|---|---|---|
| 1362 | **265** | 1s.50 red | 95 | 60 |

**266** Hansa Brandenburg C-1

**1961.** "LUPOSTA" Exhibition, Vienna, and 1st Austrian Airmail Service Commemoration.

| | | | | |
|---|---|---|---|---|
| 1363 | **266** | 5s. blue | 1·60 | 1·50 |

**267** Transport and Multi-unit Electric Train

**1961.** European Transport Ministers' Meeting.

| | | | | |
|---|---|---|---|---|
| 1364 | **267** | 3s. olive and red | 1·10 | 1·00 |

**268** "Mower in the Alps" (Detail, A. Egger-Lienz)

**1961.** Centenary of Kunstlerhaus, Vienna. Inscr as in T 268.

| | | | | |
|---|---|---|---|---|
| 1365 | **268** | 1s. purple and brown | 55 | 30 |
| 1366 | - | 1s.50 lilac and brown | 55 | 30 |
| 1367 | - | 3s. green and brown | 1·60 | 1·20 |
| 1368 | - | 5s. violet and brown | 1·60 | 1·20 |

PAINTINGS: 1s.50, "The Kiss" (after A. von Pettenkofen). 3s. "Portrait of a Girl" (after A. Romako). 5s. "The Triumph of Ariadne" (detail of Ariadne, after Hans Makart).

**269** Observatory on Sonnblick Mountain

**1961.** 75th Anniv of Sonnblick Meteorological Observatory.

| | | | | |
|---|---|---|---|---|
| 1369 | **269** | 1s.80 blue | 85 | 60 |

**270** Lavanttaler Colliery

**1961.** 15th Anniv of Nationalized Industries. Inscr "JAHRE VERSTAATLICHTE UNTERNEHMUNGEN".

| | | | | |
|---|---|---|---|---|
| 1370 | **270** | 1s. black | 30 | 25 |
| 1371 | - | 1s.50 green | 30 | 25 |
| 1372 | - | 1s.80 red | 95 | 90 |
| 1373 | - | 3s. mauve | 1·30 | 1·20 |
| 1374 | - | 5s. blue | 1·60 | 1·40 |

DESIGNS: 1s.50, Turbine; 1s.80, Industrial plant; 3s. Steelworks, Linz; 5s. Oil refinery, Schwechat.

**271** Mercury

**1961.** World Bank Congress, Vienna.

| | | | | |
|---|---|---|---|---|
| 1375 | **271** | 3s. black | 95 | 90 |

**272** Arms of Burgenland

**1961.** 40th Anniv of Burgenland.

| | | | | |
|---|---|---|---|---|
| 1376 | **272** | 1s.50 red, yellow & sepia | 65 | 60 |

**273** Liszt

**1961.** 150th Birth Anniv of Franz Liszt (composer).

| | | | | |
|---|---|---|---|---|
| 1377 | **273** | 3s. brown | 85 | 60 |

**274** Rust Post Office

**1961.** Stamp Day.

| | | | | |
|---|---|---|---|---|
| 1378 | **274** | 3s.+70g. green | 2·00 | 2·00 |

**275** Court of Accounts

**1961.** Bicentenary of Court of Accounts.

| | | | | |
|---|---|---|---|---|
| 1379 | **275** | 1s. sepia | 55 | 50 |

**276** Glockner-Kaprun Power Station

**1962.** 15th Anniv of Electric Power Nationalization. Inscr as in T 276.

| | | | | |
|---|---|---|---|---|
| 1380 | **276** | 1s. blue | 20 | 25 |
| 1381 | - | 1s.50 purple | 45 | 40 |
| 1382 | - | 1s.80 green | 1·20 | 1·10 |
| 1383 | - | 3s. brown | 85 | 80 |
| 1384 | - | 4s. red | 95 | 90 |
| 1385 | - | 6s.40 black | 2·75 | 2·50 |

DESIGNS: 1s.50, Ybbs-Persenbeug (Danube); 1s.80, Luner See; 3s. Grossraming (Enns River); 4s. Bisamberg Transformer Station; 6s.40, St. Andra Power Stations.

**1962.** Death Cent of Johann Nestroy (playwright). Portrait as T 187.

| | | | | |
|---|---|---|---|---|
| 1386 | | 1s. violet | 65 | 60 |

**277** F. Gauermann

**1962.** Death Cent of Friedrich Gauermann (painter).

| | | | | |
|---|---|---|---|---|
| 1387 | **277** | 1s.50 blue | 65 | 60 |

**278** Scout Badge and Handclasp

**1962.** 50th Anniv of Austrian Scout Movement.

| | | | | |
|---|---|---|---|---|
| 1388 | **278** | 1s.50 green | 85 | 80 |

**279** Forest and Lake

**1962.** "The Austrian Forest".

| | | | | |
|---|---|---|---|---|
| 1389 | **279** | 1s. grey | 75 | 70 |
| 1390 | - | 1s.50 brown | 85 | 80 |
| 1391 | - | 3s. myrtle | 2·75 | 2·50 |

DESIGNS: 1s.50, Deciduous forest; 3s. Fir and larch forest.

**280** Electric Locomotive and Steam Locomotive "Austria" (1837)

**1962.** 125th Anniv of Austrian Railways.

| | | | | |
|---|---|---|---|---|
| 1392 | **280** | 3s. black and buff | 2·20 | 1·50 |

**281** Engraving Die

**1962.** Stamp Day.

| | | | | |
|---|---|---|---|---|
| 1393 | **281** | 3s.+70g. violet | 2·75 | 2·50 |

**282** Postal Officials of 1863

**1963.** Centenary of Paris Postal Conference.

| | | | | |
|---|---|---|---|---|
| 1394 | **282** | 3s. sepia and yellow | 1·30 | 90 |

**283** Hermann Bahr

**1963.** Birth Centenary of Hermann Bahr (writer).

| | | | | |
|---|---|---|---|---|
| 1395 | **283** | 1s.50 sepia and blue | 85 | 40 |

**284** St. Florian (statue)

**1963.** Cent of Austrian Voluntary Fire Brigade.

| | | | | |
|---|---|---|---|---|
| 1396 | **284** | 1s.50 black and pink | 85 | 50 |

**285** Flag and Emblem

**1963.** 5th Austrian Trade Unions Federation Congress.

| | | | | |
|---|---|---|---|---|
| 1397 | **285** | 1s.50 red, sepia & grey | 65 | 40 |

**286** Crests of Tyrol and Austria

**1963.** 600th Anniv of Tyrol as an Austrian Province.

| | | | | |
|---|---|---|---|---|
| 1398 | **286** | 1s.50 multicoloured | 65 | 40 |

**287** Prince Eugene of Savoy

**1963.** Birth Tercent of Prince Eugene of Savoy.

| | | | | |
|---|---|---|---|---|
| 1399 | **287** | 1s.50 violet | 65 | 40 |

**288** Centenary Emblem

**1963.** Centenary of Red Cross.

| | | | | |
|---|---|---|---|---|
| 1400 | **288** | 3s. silver, red and black | 95 | 80 |

**289** Skiing (slalom)

**1963.** Winter Olympic Games, Innsbruck, 1964. Centres black; inscr gold; background colours given.

| | | | | |
|---|---|---|---|---|
| 1401 | **289** | 1s. grey | 30 | 20 |
| 1402 | - | 1s.20 blue | 45 | 30 |
| 1403 | - | 1s.50 grey | 55 | 40 |
| 1404 | - | 1s.80 purple | 65 | 60 |
| 1405 | - | 2s.20 green | 1·10 | 1·00 |
| 1406 | - | 3s. slate | 75 | 60 |
| 1407 | - | 4s. blue | 1·30 | 1·20 |

DESIGNS: 1s.20, Skiing (biathlon); 1s.50, Ski jumping; 1s.80, Figure skating; 2s.20, Ice hockey; 3s. Tobogganing; 4s. Bobsleighing.

**290** Vienna "101" P.O. and Railway Shed

**1963.** Stamp Day.

| | | | | |
|---|---|---|---|---|
| 1408 | **290** | 3s.+70g. black & drab | 1·10 | 1·00 |

**291** "The Holy Family" (Josef Stammel)

**1963.** Christmas.

| | | | | |
|---|---|---|---|---|
| 1409 | **291** | 2s. green | 65 | 40 |

**292** Nasturtium

**1964.** Int Horticultural Exn, Vienna. Mult.

| | | | | |
|---|---|---|---|---|
| 1410 | | 1s. Type **292** | 30 | 20 |
| 1411 | | 1s.50 Peony | 40 | 25 |
| 1412 | | 1s.80 Clematis | 45 | 40 |
| 1413 | | 2s.20 Dahlia | 95 | 90 |
| 1414 | | 3s. Convolvulus | 1·10 | 1·00 |
| 1415 | | 4s. Mallow | 1·60 | 1·50 |

**293** Gothic Statue and Stained-glass Window

**1964.** Romanesque Art Exhibition, Vienna.

| | | | | |
|---|---|---|---|---|
| 1416 | **293** | 1s.50 blue and black | 65 | 60 |

**294** Pallas Athene and Interior of Assembly Hall, Parliament Building

**1964.** 2nd Parliamentary and Scientific Conference, Vienna.

| | | | | |
|---|---|---|---|---|
| 1417 | **294** | 1s.80 black and green | 55 | 50 |

**295** "The Kiss" (Gustav Klimt)

**1964.** Re-opening of "Viennese Secession" Exn Hall.

| | | | | |
|---|---|---|---|---|
| 1418 | **295** | 3s. multicoloured | 95 | 90 |

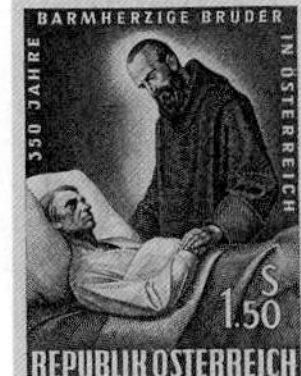


**296** "Comforting the Sick"

**1964.** 350th Anniv of Order of Brothers of Mercy in Austria.

| | | | | |
|---|---|---|---|---|
| 1419 | **296** | 1s.50 blue | 75 | 70 |

**297** "Bringing News of the Victory at Kunersdorf" (Bellotto)

**1964.** 15th U.P.U. Congress, Vienna. Paintings.

| | | | | |
|---|---|---|---|---|
| 1420 | **297** | 1s. purple | 20 | 15 |
| 1421 | - | 1s.20 brown | 45 | 30 |
| 1422 | - | 1s.50 blue | 30 | 25 |
| 1423 | - | 1s.80 violet | 65 | 60 |
| 1424 | - | 2s.20 black | 85 | 80 |
| 1425 | - | 3s. purple | 55 | 50 |
| 1426 | - | 4s. green | 1·10 | 1·00 |
| 1427 | - | 6s.40 purple | 3·50 | 3·25 |

PAINTINGS: 1s.20, "Changing Horses" (Hormann); 1s.50, "The Wedding Trip" (Schwind); 1s.80, "Postboys returning Home" (Raffalt); 2s.20, "The Vienna Mail Coach" (Klein); 3s. "Changing Horses" (Gauermann); 4s. "Postal Tracked-vehicle in Mountain Village" (Pilch); 6s.40, "Saalbach Post Office and Post-bus" (Pilch).

**298** Vienna, from the Hochhaus (N.)

**1964.** "WIPA" Stamp Exhibition, Vienna (1965) (1st issue). Multicoloured.

| | | | |
|---|---|---|---|
| 1428 | 1s.50+30g. Type **298** | 65 | 65 |
| 1429 | 1s.50+30g. N.E. | 65 | 65 |
| 1430 | 1s.50+30g. E. | 65 | 65 |
| 1431 | 1s.50+30g. S.E. | 65 | 65 |
| 1432 | 1s.50+30g. S. | 65 | 65 |
| 1433 | 1s.50+30g. S.W. | 65 | 65 |
| 1434 | 1s.50+30g. W. | 65 | 65 |
| 1435 | 1s.50+30g. N.W. | 65 | 65 |

The designs show a panoramic view of Vienna, looking to different points of compass (indicated on stamps). The inscription reads "Vienna welcomes you to WIPA 1965".

See also Nos. 1447/52.

**299** "Workers"

**1964.** Centenary of Austrian Workers' Movement.

| | | | | |
|---|---|---|---|---|
| 1436 | **299** | 1s. black | 55 | 45 |

**300** Europa "Flower"

**1964.** Europa.

| | | | | |
|---|---|---|---|---|
| 1437 | **300** | 3s. blue | 2·40 | 85 |

**301** Radio Receiver Dial

**1964.** 40th Anniv of Austrian Broadcasting Service.
1438 **301** 1s. sepia and red 55 45

**302** Old Printing Press

**1964.** 6th International Graphical Federation Congress, Vienna.
1439 **302** 1s.50 black and drab 55 45

**303** Post-bus Station, St. Gilgen

**1964.** Stamp Day.
1440 **303** 3s.+70g. multicoloured 1·60 1·30

**304** Dr. Adolf Scharf

**1965.** Pres. Scharf Commemoration.
1441 **304** 1s.50 blue and black 85 45

**305** "Reconstruction"

**1965.** "20 Years of Reconstruction".
1442 **305** 1s.80 lake 65 50

**306** University Seal, 1365

**1965.** 600th Anniv of Vienna University.
1443 **306** 3s. red and gold 95 80

**307** "St. George" (after engraving by Altdorfer)

**1965.** Danubian Art.
1444 **307** 1s.80 blue 65 50

**308** I.T.U. Emblem, Morse Key and T.V. Aerial

**1965.** Centenary of I.T.U.
1445 **308** 3s. violet 95 50

**309** F. Raimund

**1965.** 175th Birth Anniv of Ferdinand Raimund (actor and playwright).
1446 **309** 3s. purple 85 45

**310** Egyptian Hieroglyphs on Papyrus

**1965.** "WIPA" Stamp Exhibition, Vienna (2nd issue). "Development of the Letter".
1447 **310** 1s.50+40g. black and pink 55 45
1448 - 1s.80+50g. black and yellow 65 50
1449 - 2s.20+60g. black and lilac 1·20 95
1450 - 3s.+80g. black & yell 95 80
1451 - 4s.+1s. black & blue 1·50 1·20
1452 - 5s.+1s.20 black & grn 2·20 1·70
DESIGNS: 1s.80, Cuneiform writing; 2s.20, Latin; 3c. Ancient letter and seal; 4s.19th-century letter; 5s. Typewriter.

**311** Gymnasts with Wands

**1965.** 4th Gymnaestrada, Vienna.
1453 **311** 1s.50 black and blue 55 25
1454 - 3s. black and brown 85 45
DESIGNS: 3s. Girls exercising with tambourines.

**312** Dr. I. Semmelweis

**1965.** Death Cent of Ignaz Semmelweis (physician).
1455 **312** 1s.50 lilac 55 25

**313** F. G. Waldmuller (self-portrait)

**1965.** Death Cent of F. G. Waldmuller (painter).
1456 **313** 3s. black 95 50

**314** Red Cross and Gauze

**1965.** Red Cross Conference, Vienna.
1457 **314** 3s. red and black 95 45

**315** Flag and Crowned Eagle

**1965.** 50th Anniv of Austrian Towns Union.
1458 **315** 1s.50 multicoloured 85 50

**316** Austrian Flag, U. N. Emblem and Headquarters

**1965.** 10th Anniv of Austria's Membership of U.N.O.
1459 **316** 3s. sepia, red and blue 95 50

**317** University Building

**1965.** 150th Anniv of University of Technology, Vienna.
1460 **317** 1s.50 violet 65 35

**318** Bertha von Suttner

**1965.** 60th Anniv of Nobel Peace Prize Award to Bertha von Suttner (writer).
1461 **318** 1s.50 black 65 35

**319** Postman delivering Mail

**1965.** Stamp Day.
1462 **319** 3s.+70g. green 1·60 1·30

**320** Postal Code Map

**1966.** Introduction of Postal Code System.
1463 **320** 1s.50 black, red & yell 65 35

**321** P.T.T. Headquarters

**1966.** Centenary of Austrian Posts and Telegraphs Administration.
1464 **321** 1s.50 black on cream 65 35

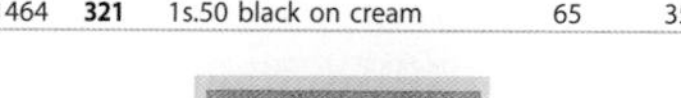

**322** M. Ebner-Eschenbach

**1966.** 50th Death Anniv of Maria Ebner-Eschenbach (writer).
1465 **322** 3s. purple 95 45

**323** Big Wheel

**1966.** Bicentenary of Vienna Prater.
1466 **323** 1s.50 green 65 25

**324** Josef Hoffmann

**1966.** 10th Death Anniv of Josef Hoffmann (architect).
1467 **324** 3s. brown 95 50

**325** Bank Emblem

**1966.** 150th Anniv of Austrian National Bank.
1468 **325** 3s. brown, grn & drab 95 50

**326** Arms of Wiener Neustadt

**1966.** "Wiener Neustadt 1440–93" Art Exhibition.
1469 **326** 1s.50 multicoloured 65 35

**327** Puppy

**1966.** 120th Anniv of Vienna Animal Protection Society.
1470 **327** 1s.80 black and yellow 65 50

**328** Columbine

**1966.** Alpine Flora. Multicoloured.

| | | | |
|---|---|---|---|
| 1471 | 1s.50 Type **328** | 50 | 25 |
| 1472 | 1s.80 Turk's cap | 55 | 25 |
| 1473 | 2s.20 Wulfenia | 65 | 40 |
| 1474 | 3s. Globe flower | 75 | 45 |
| 1475 | 4s. Orange lily | 85 | 60 |
| 1476 | 5s. Alpine anemone | 1·90 | 85 |

**329** Fair Building

**1966.** Wels International Fair.

| | | | | |
|---|---|---|---|---|
| 1477 | **329** | 3s. blue | 95 | 45 |

**330** Peter Anich

**1966.** Death Bicent of Peter Anich (cartographer).

| | | | | |
|---|---|---|---|---|
| 1478 | **330** | 1s.80 black | 65 | 35 |

**331** "Suffering"

**1966.** 15th International Occupational Health Congress, Vienna.

| | | | | |
|---|---|---|---|---|
| 1479 | **331** | 3s. black and red | 95 | 50 |

**332** "Eunuchus" by Terence (engraving, Johann Gruninger)

**1966.** Austrian National Library, Vienna. Mult.

| | | | |
|---|---|---|---|
| 1480 | 1s.50 Type **332** (Theatre collection) | 45 | 20 |
| 1481 | 1s.80 Detail of title page of Willem Blaeu's atlas (Cartography collection) | 50 | 25 |
| 1482 | 2s.20 "Herrengasse, Vienna" (Anton Stutzinger (Pictures and portraits collection)) | 55 | 35 |
| 1483 | 3s. Illustration from Rene of Anjou's "Livre du Cuer d'Amours Espris" (Manuscripts collection) | 1·10 | 50 |

**333** Young Girl

**1966.** Austrian "Save the Children" Fund.

| | | | | |
|---|---|---|---|---|
| 1484 | **333** | 3s. black and blue | 85 | 45 |

**334** Strawberries

**1966.** Fruits. Multicoloured.

| | | | |
|---|---|---|---|
| 1485 | 50g. Type **334** | 55 | 25 |
| 1486 | 1s. Grapes | 55 | 20 |
| 1487 | 1s.50 Apple | 55 | 25 |
| 1488 | 1s.80 Blackberries | 85 | 70 |
| 1489 | 2s.20 Apricots | 85 | 70 |
| 1490 | 3s. Cherries | 95 | 80 |

**335** 16th-century Postman

**1966.** Stamp Day.

| | | | | |
|---|---|---|---|---|
| 1491 | **335** | 3s.+70g. multicoloured | 1·10 | 85 |

**336** Arms of Linz University

**1966.** Inauguration of Linz University.

| | | | | |
|---|---|---|---|---|
| 1492 | **336** | 3s. multicoloured | 95 | 50 |

**337** Skater of 1867

**1967.** Centenary of Vienna Skating Assn.

| | | | | |
|---|---|---|---|---|
| 1493 | **337** | 3s. indigo and blue | 95 | 50 |

**338** Dancer with Violin

**1967.** Centenary of "Blue Danube" Waltz.

| | | | | |
|---|---|---|---|---|
| 1494 | **338** | 3s. purple | 95 | 45 |

**339** Dr. Schonherr

**1967.** Birth Cent of Dr. Karl Schonherr (poet).

| | | | | |
|---|---|---|---|---|
| 1495 | **339** | 3s. brown | 95 | 50 |

**340** Ice Hockey Goalkeeper

**1967.** World Ice Hockey Championships, Vienna.

| | | | | |
|---|---|---|---|---|
| 1496 | **340** | 3s. blue and green | 95 | 80 |

**341** Violin and Organ

**1967.** 125th Anniv of Vienna Philharmonic Orchestra.

| | | | | |
|---|---|---|---|---|
| 1497 | **341** | 3s.50 blue | 95 | 45 |

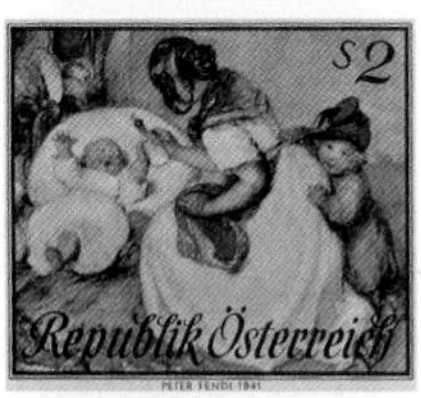


**342** "Mother and Children" (aquarelle, Peter Fendi)

**1967.** Mother's Day.

| | | | | |
|---|---|---|---|---|
| 1498 | **342** | 2s. multicoloured | 65 | 50 |

**343** "Madonna" (Gothic wood-carving)

**1967.** "Gothic Art in Austria" Exhibition, Krems.

| | | | | |
|---|---|---|---|---|
| 1499 | **343** | 3s. green | 95 | 35 |

**344** Jewelled Cross

**1967.** "Salzburg Treasures" Exhibition, Salzburg Cathedral.

| | | | | |
|---|---|---|---|---|
| 1500 | **344** | 3s.50 multicoloured | 95 | 50 |

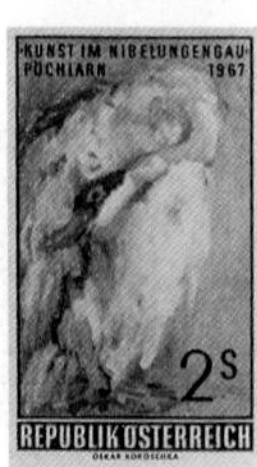


**345** "The White Swan" (from Kokoschkas tapestry "Cupid and Psyche")

**1967.** "Art of the Nibelungen District" Exhibition, Pochlarn.

| | | | | |
|---|---|---|---|---|
| 1501 | **345** | 2s. multicoloured | 65 | 35 |

**346** Vienna

**1967.** 10th European Talks, Vienna.

| | | | | |
|---|---|---|---|---|
| 1502 | **346** | 3s. black and red | 85 | 45 |

**347** Champion Bull

**1967.** Centenary of Ried Fair.

| | | | | |
|---|---|---|---|---|
| 1503 | **347** | 2s. purple | 65 | 35 |

**348** Colorado Potato Beetle

**1967.** 6th Int Plant Protection Congress, Vienna.

| | | | | |
|---|---|---|---|---|
| 1504 | **348** | 3s. multicoloured | 95 | 50 |

**349** Locomotive No. 671

**1967.** Centenary of Brenner Railway.

| | | | | |
|---|---|---|---|---|
| 1505 | **349** | 3s.50 green and brown | 95 | 50 |

**350** "Christ" (fresco detail)

**1967.** Lambach Frescoes.

| | | | | |
|---|---|---|---|---|
| 1506 | **350** | 2s. multicoloured | 65 | 45 |

**351** Prater Hall, Vienna

**1967.** International Trade Fairs Congress, Vienna.

| | | | | |
|---|---|---|---|---|
| 1507 | **351** | 2s. purple and cream | 85 | 45 |

**352** Rector's Medallion and Chain

**1967.** 275th Anniv of Fine Arts Academy, Vienna.

| | | | | |
|---|---|---|---|---|
| 1508 | **352** | 2s. brown, yellow & blue | 85 | 45 |

**353** Bible on Rock (from commemorative coin of 1717)

**1967.** 450th Anniv of the Reformation.

| | | | | |
|---|---|---|---|---|
| 1509 | **353** | 3s.50 blue | 85 | 45 |

**354** Forest Trees

**1967.** 100 Years of Austrian University Forestry Studies.

| 1510 | **354** | 3s.50 green | 1·30 | 70 |
|---|---|---|---|---|

**355** Memorial, Vienna

**1967.** 150th Anniv of Land Registry.

| 1511 | **355** | 2s. green | 55 | 25 |
|---|---|---|---|---|

**356** "St. Leopold" (stained-glass window, Heiligenkreuz Monastery)

**1967.** Margrave Leopold the Holy.

| 1512 | **356** | 1s.80 multicoloured | 55 | 25 |
|---|---|---|---|---|

**357** "Music and Art"

**1967.** 150th Anniv of Academy of Music and Dramatic Art, Vienna.

| 1513 | **357** | 3s.50 black and violet | 95 | 50 |
|---|---|---|---|---|

**358** St. Mary's Altar, Nonnberg Convent, Salzburg

**1967.** Christmas.

| 1514 | **358** | 2s. green | 65 | 35 |
|---|---|---|---|---|

**359** "The Letter- carrier" (from playing-card)

**1967.** Stamp Day.

| 1515 | **359** | 3s.50+80g. mult | 1·60 | 85 |
|---|---|---|---|---|

**360** Ski Jump, Stadium and Mountains

**1968.** Winter University Games, Innsbruck.

| 1516 | **360** | 2s. blue | 65 | 35 |
|---|---|---|---|---|

**361** C. Sitte

**1968.** 125th Birth Anniv of Camillo Sitte (architect).

| 1517 | **361** | 2s. brown | 55 | 45 |
|---|---|---|---|---|

**362** Mother and Child

**1968.** Mothers' Day.

| 1518 | **362** | 2s. olive | 55 | 45 |
|---|---|---|---|---|

**363** "Veterinary Medicine"

**1968.** Bicentenary of Vienna Veterinary College.

| 1519 | **363** | 3s.50 gold, pur & drab | 85 | 70 |
|---|---|---|---|---|

**364** Bride with Lace Veil

**1968.** Centenary of Vorarlberg Lace.

| 1520 | **364** | 3s.50 blue | 85 | 70 |
|---|---|---|---|---|

**365** Etrich Limousine

**1968.** "IFA Wien 1968" Airmail Stamp Exhibition, Vienna.

| 1521 | **365** | 2s. brown | 55 | 45 |
|---|---|---|---|---|
| 1522 | - | 3s.50 green | 95 | 80 |
| 1523 | - | 5s. blue | 1·70 | 1·40 |

DESIGNS: 3s.50, Sud Aviation SE 210 Caravelle; 5s. Douglas DC-8 A-8021.

**367** Landsteiner

**1968.** Birth Centenary of Dr. Karl Landsteiner (physician and pathologist).

| 1525 | **367** | 3s.50 blue | 95 | 50 |
|---|---|---|---|---|

**368** P. Rosegger

**1968.** 50th Death Anniv of Peter Rosegger (writer).

| 1526 | **368** | 2s. green | 65 | 35 |
|---|---|---|---|---|

**369** A. Kauffmann (self-portrait)

**1968.** Exhibition of Angelica Kauffmann's Paintings, Bregenz.

| 1527 | **369** | 2s. violet | 65 | 45 |
|---|---|---|---|---|

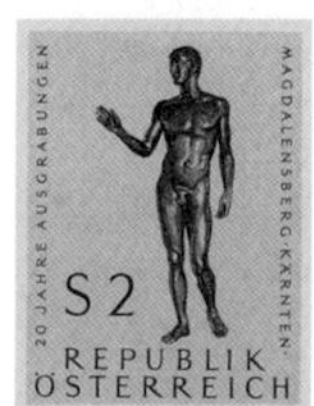


**370** Statue of Young Man (Helenenberg site)

**1968.** Magdalensberg Excavations, Carinthia.

| 1528 | **370** | 2s. black and green | 55 | 35 |
|---|---|---|---|---|

**371** "The Bishop" (Romanesque carving)

**1968.** 750th Anniv of Graz-Seckau Diocese.

| 1529 | **371** | 2s. grey | 55 | 35 |
|---|---|---|---|---|

**372** K. Moser

**1968.** 50th Death Anniv of Koloman Moser (graphic artist).

| 1530 | **372** | 2s. brown and red | 55 | 35 |
|---|---|---|---|---|

**373** Human Rights Emblem

**1968.** Human Rights Year.

| 1531 | **373** | 1s.50 red, green & grey | 95 | 50 |
|---|---|---|---|---|

**374** Arms and Provincial Shields

**1968.** 50th Anniv of Republic. Multicoloured.

| 1532 | 2s. Type **374** | 55 | 35 |
|---|---|---|---|
| 1533 | 2s. Karl Renner (first President of Second Republic) | 55 | 35 |
| 1534 | 2s. First Article of Constitution | 55 | 35 |

**375** Crib, Oberndorf, Salzburg

**1968.** 150th Anniv of "Silent Night, Holy Night" (carol).

| 1535 | **375** | 2s. green | 65 | 35 |
|---|---|---|---|---|

**376** Mercury

**1968.** Stamp Day.

| 1536 | **376** | 3s.50+80g. green | 1·10 | 1·10 |
|---|---|---|---|---|

**377** Fresco (Troger), Melk Monastery

**1968.** Baroque Frescoes. Designs showing frescoes in locations given. Multicoloured.

| 1537 | 2s. Type **377** | 65 | 60 |
|---|---|---|---|
| 1538 | 2s. Altenburg Monastery | 65 | 60 |
| 1539 | 2s. Rohrenbach-Greillenstein | 65 | 60 |
| 1540 | 2s. Ebenfurth Castle | 65 | 60 |
| 1541 | 2s. Halbthurn Castle | 65 | 60 |
| 1542 | 2s. Maria Treu Church, Vienna | 65 | 60 |

Nos. 1537/9 are the work of Anton Troger and Nos. 1540/2 that of Franz Maulbertsch.

378 "Madonna and Child"

1969. 500th Anniv of Vienna Diocese. Statues in St. Stephen's Cathedral, Vienna.

| | | | | |
|---|---|---|---|---|
| 1543 | 378 | 2s. blue | 65 | 60 |
| 1544 | - | 2s. grey | 65 | 60 |
| 1545 | - | 2s. green | 65 | 60 |
| 1546 | - | 2s. purple | 65 | 60 |
| 1547 | - | 2s. black | 65 | 60 |
| 1548 | - | 2s. brown | 65 | 60 |

DESIGNS: No. 1544, "St. Christopher"; No. 1545, "St. George"; No. 1546, "St. Paul"; No. 1547, "St. Sebastian"; No. 1548, "St. Stephen".

379 Parliament Building, Vienna

1969. Interparliamentary Union Meeting, Vienna.

| | | | | |
|---|---|---|---|---|
| 1549 | 379 | 2s. green | 55 | 35 |

380 Colonnade

1969. Europa.

| | | | | |
|---|---|---|---|---|
| 1550 | 380 | 2s. multicoloured | 1·60 | 45 |

381 "Council Members"

1969. 20th Anniv of Council of Europe.

| | | | | |
|---|---|---|---|---|
| 1551 | 381 | 3s.50 multicoloured | 95 | 60 |

382 Soldiers

1969. Austrian Armed Forces.

| | | | | |
|---|---|---|---|---|
| 1552 | 382 | 2s. brown and red | 65 | 35 |

383 "Don Giovanni"

1969. Centenary of State Opera, Vienna. Sheet 182×212 mm. T 383 and similar scenes.

| | | |
|---|---|---|
| MS1553 2s.×8 each brown, red and gold | 6·50 | 6·50 |

DESIGNS—Scenes from Opera and Ballet: "Don Giovanni" (Mozart), "The Magic Flute" (Mozart), "Fidelio" (Beethoven), "Lohengrin" (Wagner), "Don Carlos" (Verdi), "Carmen" (Bizet), "Der Rosenkavlier" (R. Strauss) and "Swan Lake" (Tchaikovsky).

384 Maximilian's Armour

1969. "Maximilian I" Exhibition, Innsbruck.

| | | | | |
|---|---|---|---|---|
| 1554 | 384 | 2s. black | 65 | 35 |

385 Viennese "Privilege" Seal

1969. 19th International Union of Local Authorities Congress, Vienna.

| | | | | |
|---|---|---|---|---|
| 1555 | 385 | 2s. red, brown & ochre | 65 | 35 |

386 Young Girl

1969. 20th Anniv of "SOS" Children's Villages Movement.

| | | | | |
|---|---|---|---|---|
| 1556 | 386 | 2s. brown and green | 65 | 35 |

387 Hands clasping Spanner

1969. 50th Anniv of Int Labour Organization.

| | | | | |
|---|---|---|---|---|
| 1557 | 387 | 2s. green | 65 | 35 |

388 Austrian "Flag" encircling Globe

1969. "Austrians Living Abroad" Year.

| | | | | |
|---|---|---|---|---|
| 1558 | 388 | 3s.50 red and green | 95 | 50 |

389 "El Cid killing a Bull" (Goya)

1969. Bicentenary of Albertina Art Collection, Vienna. Multicoloured.

| | | | |
|---|---|---|---|
| 1559 | 2s. Type 389 | 55 | 55 |
| 1560 | 2s. "Young Hare" (Durer) | 55 | 55 |
| 1561 | 2s. "Madonna with Pomegranate" (Raphael) | 55 | 55 |
| 1562 | 2s. "The Painter and the Amateur" (Bruegel) | 55 | 55 |
| 1563 | 2s. "Rubens's Son, Nicholas" (Rubens) | 55 | 55 |
| 1564 | 2s. "Self-portrait" (Rembrandt) | 55 | 55 |
| 1565 | 2s. "Madame de Pompadour" (detail, Guerin) | 55 | 55 |
| 1566 | 2s. "The Artist's Wife" (Schiele) | 55 | 55 |

390 Pres. Jonas

1969. Pres. Franz Jonas's 70th Birthday.

| | | | | |
|---|---|---|---|---|
| 1567 | 390 | 2s. blue and grey | 55 | 45 |

391 Posthorn and Lightning over Globe

1969. 50th Anniv of Post and Telegraph Employees Union.

| | | | | |
|---|---|---|---|---|
| 1568 | 391 | 2s. multicoloured | 55 | 45 |

392 Savings Bank (c. 1450)

1969. 150th Anniv of Austrian Savings Bank.

| | | | | |
|---|---|---|---|---|
| 1569 | 392 | 2s. green and silver | 55 | 45 |

393 "The Madonna" (Egger-Lienz)

1969. Christmas.

| | | | | |
|---|---|---|---|---|
| 1570 | 393 | 2s. purple and yellow | 55 | 45 |

394 Unken, Salzburg, Post-house Sign (after F. Zeller)

1969. Stamp Day.

| | | | | |
|---|---|---|---|---|
| 1571 | 394 | 3s.50+80g. black, red and stone | 95 | 85 |

395 J. Schoffel

1970. 60th Death Anniv of Josef Schoffel ("Saviour of the Vienna Woods").

| | | | | |
|---|---|---|---|---|
| 1572 | 395 | 2s. purple | 45 | 35 |

396 St. Clement Hofbauer

1970. 150th Death Anniv of St. Clement Hofbauer (theologian).

| | | | | |
|---|---|---|---|---|
| 1573 | 396 | 2s. brown and green | 45 | 35 |

397 Chancellor Leopold Figl

1970. 25th Anniv of Austrian Republic.

| | | | | |
|---|---|---|---|---|
| 1574 | 397 | 2s. olive | 65 | 35 |
| 1575 | - | 2s. brown | 65 | 35 |

DESIGN: No. 1575, Belvedere Castle.

398 Krimml Waterfalls

1970. Nature Conservation Year.

| | | | | |
|---|---|---|---|---|
| 1576 | 398 | 2s. green | 1·10 | 70 |

399 Oldest University Seal

1970. 300th Anniv of Leopold Franz University, Innsbruck.

| | | | | |
|---|---|---|---|---|
| 1577 | 399 | 2s. black and red | 55 | 45 |

400 "Musikverein" Organ

1970. Centenary of "Musikverein" Building.

| | | | | |
|---|---|---|---|---|
| 1578 | 400 | 2s. purple and gold | 55 | 45 |

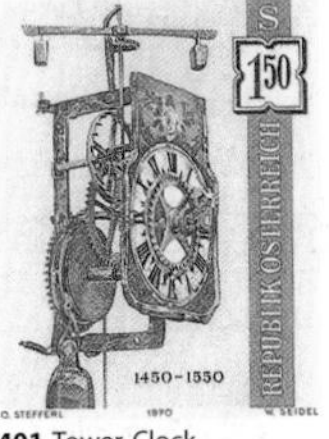
401 Tower Clock, 1450–1550

1970. Antique Clocks.

| | | | | |
|---|---|---|---|---|
| 1579 | 401 | 1s.50 brown and cream | 55 | 45 |
| 1580 | - | 1s.50 green & lt green | 55 | 45 |
| 1581 | - | 2s. blue and pale blue | 65 | 50 |
| 1582 | - | 2s. red and purple | 65 | 50 |
| 1583 | - | 3s.50 brown and buff | 1·10 | 85 |
| 1584 | - | 3s.50 purple and lilac | 1·10 | 85 |

DESIGNS: No. 1580, Empire "lyre" clock, 1790–1815; No. 1581, Pendant ball clock, 1600–50; No. 1582, Pocket-watch and signet, 1800–30; No. 1583, Bracket clock, 1720–60; No. 1584, "Biedermeier" pendulum clock and musical-box, 1820–50.

**402** "The Beggar Student" (Millocker)

**1970.** Famous Operettas.

| | | | | |
|---|---|---|---|---|
| 1585 | **402** | 1s.50 turquoise & green | 55 | 45 |
| 1586 | - | 1s.50 blue and yellow | 55 | 45 |
| 1587 | - | 2s. purple and pink | 65 | 50 |
| 1588 | - | 2s. brown and green | 65 | 50 |
| 1589 | - | 3s.50 blue and light blue | 1·10 | 85 |
| 1590 | - | 3s.50 blue and buff | 1·10 | 85 |

OPERETTAS: No. 1586, "Die Fledermaus" (Johann Strauss the younger); 1587, "A Waltz Dream" (O. Straus); 1588, "The Birdseller" (C. Zeller); 1589, "The Merry Widow" (F. Lehar); 1590, "Two Hearts in Waltz-time" (R. Stoiz).

**403** Scene from "The Gipsy Baron" (J. Strauss)

**1970.** 25th Anniv of Bregenz Festival.

| | | | | |
|---|---|---|---|---|
| 1591 | **403** | 3s.50 blue, buff & ult | 95 | 50 |

**404** Festival Emblem

**1970.** 50th Anniv of Salzburg Festival.

| | | | | |
|---|---|---|---|---|
| 1592 | **404** | 3s.50 multicoloured | 95 | 50 |

**405** T. Koschat

**1970.** 125th Birth Anniv of Thomas Koschat (composer and poet).

| | | | | |
|---|---|---|---|---|
| 1593 | **405** | 2s. brown | 55 | 45 |

**406** "Head of St. John", from sculpture "Mount of Olives", Ried Church (attributed to T. Schwanthaler)

**1970.** 13th World Veterans Federation General Assembly.

| | | | | |
|---|---|---|---|---|
| 1594 | **406** | 3s.50 sepia | 95 | 50 |

**407** Climbers and Mountains

**1970.** "Walking and Mountaineering".

| | | | | |
|---|---|---|---|---|
| 1595 | **407** | 2s. blue and mauve | 55 | 35 |

**408** A. Cossmann

**1970.** Birth Cent of Alfred Cossmann (engraver).

| | | | | |
|---|---|---|---|---|
| 1596 | **408** | 2s. brown | 55 | 35 |

**409** Arms of Carinthia

**1970.** 50th Anniv of Carinthian Plebiscite.

| | | | | |
|---|---|---|---|---|
| 1597 | **409** | 2s. multicoloured | 55 | 35 |

**410** U.N. Emblem

**1970.** 25th Anniv of United Nations.

| | | | | |
|---|---|---|---|---|
| 1598 | **410** | 3s.50 blue and black | 95 | 50 |

**411** "Adoration of the Shepherds" (carving, Garsten Monastery)

**1970.** Christmas.

| | | | | |
|---|---|---|---|---|
| 1599 | **411** | 2s. blue | 45 | 35 |

**412** Saddle, Harness and Posthorn

**1970.** Stamp Day.

| | | | | |
|---|---|---|---|---|
| 1600 | **412** | 3s.50+80g. black, yellow and grey | 1·10 | 1·10 |

**413** Pres. K. Renner

**1970.** Birth Centenary of Pres. Renner.

| | | | | |
|---|---|---|---|---|
| 1601 | **413** | 2s. purple | 55 | 35 |

**414** Beethoven (after painting by Waldmuller)

**1970.** Birth Bicentenary of Beethoven.

| | | | | |
|---|---|---|---|---|
| 1602 | **414** | 3s.50 black and stone | 95 | 60 |

**415** E. Handel-Mazzetti

**1971.** Birth Centenary of Enrica Handel-Mazzetti (novelist).

| | | | | |
|---|---|---|---|---|
| 1603 | **415** | 2s. brown | 45 | 25 |

**416** "Safety for Children"

**1971.** Road Safety.

| | | | | |
|---|---|---|---|---|
| 1604 | **416** | 2s. multicoloured | 65 | 35 |

**417** Florentine Bowl, c. 1580

**1971.** Austrian Art Treasures (1st series). Sculpture and Applied Art.

| | | | | |
|---|---|---|---|---|
| 1605 | **417** | 1s.50 green and grey | 55 | 45 |
| 1606 | - | 2s. purple and grey | 85 | 70 |
| 1607 | - | 3s.50 yellow, brn & grey | 1·30 | 1·00 |

DESIGNS: 2s. Ivory equestrian statuette of Joseph I, 1693 (Matthias Steinle); 3s.50, Salt-cellar, c. 1570 (Cellini).

See also Nos. 1609/11, 1632/4 and 1651/3.

**418** Shield of Trade Association

**1971.** 23rd International Chamber of Commerce Congress, Vienna.

| | | | | |
|---|---|---|---|---|
| 1608 | **418** | 3s.50 multicoloured | 85 | 50 |

**419** "Jacopo de Strada" (Titian)

**1971.** Austrian Art Treasures (2nd series).

| | | | | |
|---|---|---|---|---|
| 1609 | **419** | 1s.50 purple | 55 | 45 |
| 1610 | - | 2s. black | 85 | 70 |
| 1611 | - | 3s.50 brown | 1·30 | 1·00 |

PAINTINGS: 2s. "The Village Feast" (Brueghel); 3s.50, "Young Venetian Woman" (Durer).

**420** Notary's Seal

**1971.** Austrian Notarial Statute Cent Congress.

| | | | | |
|---|---|---|---|---|
| 1612 | **420** | 3s.50 purple and brown | 85 | 45 |

**421** "St. Matthew" (altar sculpture)

**1971.** "Krems Millennium of Art" Exhibition.

| | | | | |
|---|---|---|---|---|
| 1613 | **421** | 2s. brown and purple | 45 | 25 |

**422** Dr. A. Neilreich

**1971.** Death Cent of Dr. August Neilreich (botanist).

| | | | | |
|---|---|---|---|---|
| 1614 | **422** | 2s. brown | 45 | 25 |

**423** Singer with Lyre

**1971.** International Choir Festival, Vienna.

| | | | | |
|---|---|---|---|---|
| 1615 | **423** | 4s. blue, gold & lt blue | 95 | 80 |

**424** Arms of Kitzbuhel

**1971.** 700th Anniv of Kitzbuhel.

| | | | | |
|---|---|---|---|---|
| 1616 | **424** | 2s.50 multicoloured | 55 | 45 |

**425** Stock Exchange Building

**1971.** Bicentenary of Vienna Stock Exchange.

| | | | | |
|---|---|---|---|---|
| 1617 | **425** | 4s. brown | 85 | 50 |

**426** Old and New Fair Halls

**1971.** "50 Years of Vienna International Fairs".

| | | | | |
|---|---|---|---|---|
| 1618 | **426** | 2s.50 purple | 55 | 45 |

**427** O.G.B. Emblem

**1971.** 25th Anniv of Austrian Trade Unions Federation.

| | | | | |
|---|---|---|---|---|
| 1619 | **427** | 2s. multicoloured | 45 | 35 |

428 Arms and Insignia

**1971.** 50th Anniv of Burgenland Province.

| | | | | |
|---|---|---|---|---|
| 1620 | **428** | 4s. multicoloured | 45 | 35 |

429 "Marcus" Veteran Car

**1971.** 75th Anniv of Austrian Automobile, Motor Cycle and Touring Club.

| | | | | |
|---|---|---|---|---|
| 1621 | **429** | 4s. black and green | 85 | 60 |

430 Europa Bridge, Brenner Highway

**1971.** Inauguration of Brenner Highway.

| | | | | |
|---|---|---|---|---|
| 1622 | **430** | 4s. blue | 85 | 60 |

431 Iron-ore Workings, Erzberg

**1971.** 25 Years of Nationalized Industries.

| | | | | |
|---|---|---|---|---|
| 1623 | **431** | 1s.50 brown | 55 | 45 |
| 1624 | - | 2s. blue | 55 | 45 |
| 1625 | - | 4s. green | 1·10 | 85 |

DESIGNS: 2s. Nitrogen Works, Linz; 4s. Iron and Steel works, Linz.

432 Electric Train on the Semmering Line

**1971.** Railway Anniversaries.

| | | | | |
|---|---|---|---|---|
| 1626 | **432** | 2s. purple | 55 | 45 |

433 E. Tschermak-Seysenegg

**1971.** Birth Centenary of Dr. E. Tshermak-Seysenegg (biologist).

| | | | | |
|---|---|---|---|---|
| 1627 | **433** | 2s. purple and grey | 45 | 35 |

434 Angling

**1971.** Sports.

| | | | | |
|---|---|---|---|---|
| 1628 | **434** | 2s. brown | 45 | 35 |

435 "The Infant Jesus as Saviour" (from miniature by Durer)

**1971.** Christmas.

| | | | | |
|---|---|---|---|---|
| 1629 | **435** | 2s. multicoloured | 55 | 45 |

436 "50 Years"

**1971.** 50th Anniv of Austrian Philatelic Clubs Association.

| | | | | |
|---|---|---|---|---|
| 1630 | **436** | 4s.+1s.50 pur & gold | 1·30 | 1·00 |

437 Franz Grillparzer (from miniature by Daffinger)

**1972.** Death Centenary of Grillparzer (dramatist).

| | | | | |
|---|---|---|---|---|
| 1631 | **437** | 2s. black, brown & stone | 65 | 35 |

438 Roman Fountain, Friesach

**1972.** Austrian Art Treasures (3rd series). Fountains.

| | | | | |
|---|---|---|---|---|
| 1632 | **438** | 1s.50 purple | 55 | 45 |
| 1633 | - | 2s. brown | 85 | 70 |
| 1634 | - | 2s.50 green | 1·30 | 1·00 |

DESIGNS: 2s. Lead Fountain, Heiligenkreuz Abbey; 2s.50. Leopold Fountain, Innsbruck.

439 Hofburg Palace

**1972.** 4th European Postal Ministers' Conf, Vienna.

| | | | | |
|---|---|---|---|---|
| 1635 | **439** | 4s. violet | 95 | 80 |

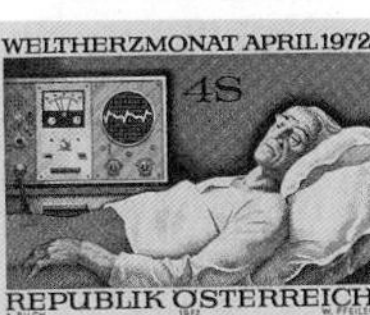
440 Heart Patient

**1972.** World Heart Month.

| | | | | |
|---|---|---|---|---|
| 1636 | **440** | 4s. brown | 95 | 80 |

441 "Woman's Head" (sculpture, Gurk Cathedral)

**1972.** 900th Anniv of Gurk Diocese.

| | | | | |
|---|---|---|---|---|
| 1637 | **441** | 2s. purple and gold | 65 | 50 |

442 Vienna Town Hall and Congress Emblem

**1972.** 9th International Public and Co-operative Economy Congress, Vienna.

| | | | | |
|---|---|---|---|---|
| 1638 | **442** | 4s. black, red and yellow | 1·10 | 70 |

443 Lienz–Pelos Pylon Line

**1972.** 25th Anniv of Electric Power Nationalization.

| | | | | |
|---|---|---|---|---|
| 1639 | **443** | 70g. violet and grey | 45 | 35 |
| 1640 | - | 2s.50 brown and grey | 65 | 50 |
| 1641 | - | 4s. blue and grey | 1·10 | 85 |

DESIGNS: 2s.50, Vienna-Semmering Power Station; 4s. Zemm Dam and lake.

444 Runner with Torch

**1972.** Passage of the Olympic Torch through Austria.

| | | | | |
|---|---|---|---|---|
| 1642 | **444** | 2s. brown and red | 55 | 45 |

445 "Hermes" (C. Laib)

**1972.** "Late Gothic Art" Exhibition, Salzburg.

| | | | | |
|---|---|---|---|---|
| 1643 | **445** | 2s. purple | 55 | 45 |

446 Pears

**1972.** Amateur Gardeners' Congress, Vienna.

| | | | | |
|---|---|---|---|---|
| 1644 | **446** | 2s.50 multicoloured | 75 | 60 |

447 "Spanish Walk"

**1972.** 400th Anniv of the Spanish Riding School, Vienna. Sheet 136×181 mm containing T 447 and similar square designs each in purple, red and gold.

**MS**1645 2s. Type **447**; 2s. "Piaffe"; 2s.50 "Levade"; 2s.50 "On the long rein"; 4s. "Capriole"; 4s. "Courbette" 5·50 5·50

448 University Arms

**1972.** Cent of University of Agriculture, Vienna.

| | | | | |
|---|---|---|---|---|
| 1646 | **448** | 2s. multicoloured | 55 | 45 |

449 Old University Buildings (after F. Danreiter)

**1972.** 350th Anniv of Paris Lodron University, Salzburg.

| | | | | |
|---|---|---|---|---|
| 1647 | **449** | 4s. brown | 95 | 80 |

450 C. M. Ziehrer

**1972.** 50th Death Anniv of Carl M. Ziehrer (composer and conductor).

| | | | | |
|---|---|---|---|---|
| 1648 | **450** | 2s. red | 55 | 45 |

451 "Virgin and Child", Inzersdorf Church

**1972.** Christmas.

| | | | | |
|---|---|---|---|---|
| 1649 | **451** | 2s. purple and green | 65 | 50 |

452 18th-century Viennese Postman

**1972.** Stamp Day.

| | | | | |
|---|---|---|---|---|
| 1650 | **452** | 4s.+1s. green | 1·30 | 1·00 |

453 State Sledge of Maria Theresa

**1972.** Austrian Art Treasures (4th series). Carriages from the Imperial Coach House.

| | | | | |
|---|---|---|---|---|
| 1651 | **453** | 1s.50 brown and bistre | 55 | 45 |
| 1652 | - | 2s. green and bistre | 85 | 70 |
| 1653 | - | 2s.50 purple and bistre | 1·30 | 1·00 |

DESIGNS: 2s. Coronation landau; 2s.50, Hapsburg State Coach.

454 Telephone Network

**1972.** Completion of Austrian Telephone System Automation.
1654 **454** 2s. black and yellow 55 45

**455** "Drug Addict"

**1973.** Campaign against Drug Abuse.
1655 **455** 2s. multicoloured 75 45

**456** A. Petzold

**1973.** 50th Death Anniv of Alfons Petzold (writer).
1656 **456** 2s. purple 55 45

**457** Korner

**1973.** Birth Centenary of Pres. Theodor Korner (President, 1951–57).
1657 **457** 2s. purple and grey 55 45

**458** McDonell DC-9 OE-LDA

**1973.** Austrian Aviation Anniversaries.
1658 **458** 2s. blue and red 55 45

**459** Otto Loewi

**1973.** Birth Cent of Otto Loewi (pharmacologist).
1659 **459** 4s. violet 95 70

**460** "Succour"

**1973.** 25th Anniv of National Federation of Austrian Social Insurance Institutes.
1660 **460** 2s. blue 55 45

**461** Telephone Dial within Posthorn

**1973.** Europa.
1661 **461** 2s.50 black, yell & orge 2·20 70

**462** Fair Emblem

**1973.** 25th Dornbirn Fair.
1662 **462** 2s. multicoloured 65 35

**463** Military Pentathlon

**1973.** 25th Anniv of International Military Sports Council and 23rd Military Pentathlon Championships, Wiener Neustadt.
1663 **463** 4s. green 1·00 55

**464** Leo Slezak

**1973.** Birth Centenary of Leo Slezak (operatic tenor).
1664 **464** 4s. brown 1·00 55

**465** Main Entrance, Hofburg Palace

**1973.** 39th International Statistical Institute's Congress, Vienna.
1665 **465** 2s. brown, red and grey 55 30

**466** "Admiral Tegetthof Icebound" (J. Payer)

**1973.** Centenary of Discovery of Franz Josef Land.
1666 **466** 2s.50 green 80 45

**467** I.U.L.C.S. Arms

**1973.** 13th International Union of Leather Chemists' Societies Congress, Vienna.
1667 **467** 4s. multicoloured 1·00 65

**468** "Academy of Sciences, Vienna" (B. Bellotto)

**1973.** Cent of Int Meteorological Organization.
1668 **468** 2s.50 violet 80 45

**469** Max Reinhardt

**1973.** Birth Centenary of Max Reinhardt (theatrical director).
1669 **469** 2s. purple 55 45

**470** F. Hanusch

**1973.** 50th Death Anniv of Ferdinand Hanusch (politician).
1670 **470** 2s. purple 55 30

**471** Light Harness Racing

**1973.** Centenary of Vienna Trotting Assn.
1671 **471** 2s. green 65 55

**472** Radio Operator

**1973.** 50th Anniv of International Criminal Police Organization (Interpol).
1672 **472** 4s. violet 90 65

**473** Petzval Camera Lens

**1973.** "Europhot" (professional photographers) Congress, Vienna.
1673 **473** 2s.50 multicoloured 90 55

**474** Aqueduct, Hollen Valley

**1973.** Centenary of Vienna's 1st Mountain-spring Aqueduct.
1674 **474** 2s. brown, red & blue 55 30

**475** Almsee

**1973.** Views. (a) Size 23×29 mm.

| | | | | |
|---|---|---|---|---|
| 1674a | - | 20g. blue and light blue | 90 | 45 |
| 1675 | - | 50g. green & lt green | 45 | 25 |
| 1676 | - | 1s. sepia and brown | 45 | 25 |
| 1677 | - | 1s.50 purple and pink | 65 | 30 |
| 1678 | - | 2s. indigo and blue | 80 | 30 |
| 1679 | - | 2s.50 deep lilac & lilac | 90 | 30 |
| 1680 | - | 3s. ultramarine & blue | 1·10 | 30 |
| 1680a | - | 3s.50 brown & orange | 1·10 | 45 |
| 1681 | **475** | 4s. violet and lilac | 1·10 | 30 |
| 1681a | - | 4s.20 black and grey | 1·70 | 95 |
| 1682 | - | 4s.50 dp green & green | 1·50 | 45 |
| 1683 | - | 5s. violet and lilac | 1·50 | 45 |
| 1683a | - | 5s.50 blue and violet | 2·50 | 1·90 |
| 1683b | - | 5s.60 olive and green | 3·25 | 2·75 |
| 1684 | - | 6s. lilac and pink | 2·10 | 30 |
| 1684a | - | 6s.50 blue & turquoise | 2·00 | 45 |
| 1685 | - | 7s. deep green & green | 2·75 | 45 |
| 1685a | - | 7s.50 purple & mauve | 3·25 | 45 |
| 1686 | - | 8s. brown and pink | 2·75 | 65 |
| 1686a | - | 9s. red and pink | 3·25 | 65 |
| 1687 | - | 10s. myrtle and green | 3·25 | 45 |
| 1688 | - | 11s. red and orange | 4·00 | 45 |
| 1688a | - | 12s. sepia and brown | 4·00 | 95 |
| 1688b | - | 14s. myrtle and green | 5·00 | 95 |
| 1688c | - | 16s. brown and orange | 5·50 | 95 |
| 1688d | - | 20s. green and bistre | 6·75 | 95 |

(b) Size 28×37 mm.
1689 50s. violet and grey 20·00 2·40

(c) Size 17×20 mm.
1690 3s. ultramarine and blue 80 65

DESIGNS: 20g. Friedstadt Keep, Muhlviertel; 50g. Zillertal; 1s. Kahlenbergerdorf, Vienna; 1s.50, Bludenz; 2s. Old bridge, Finstermunz; 2s.50, Murau, Styria; 3s. Bischofsmutze and Alpine farm; 3s.50, Osterkirche, Oberwart; 4s.20, Hirschegg, Kleinwalsertal; 4s.50, Windmill, Retz; 5s. Ruins of Aggstein Castle; 5s.50, Peace Chapel, Stoderzinken; 5s.60, Riezlern, Kleinwalsertal; 6s. Lindauer Hut, Ratikon Massif; 6s.50, Villach, Carinthia; 7s. Falkenstein Castle; 7s.50, Hohensalzburg Fortress; 8s. Votive column, Reiteregg, Styria; 9s. Asten valley; 10s. Neusiedlersee; 11s. Enns; 12s. Kufstein Fortress; 14s. Weiszsee, Salzburg; 16s. Bad Tatzmannsdorf open-air museum; 20s. Myra Falls, Muggendorf; 50s. Hofburg, Vienna.

**476** "The Nativity" (stained-glass window, St. Erhard Church, Bretenau)

**1973.** Christmas.
1691 **476** 2s. multicoloured 55 30

**477** "Archangel Gabriel" (carving by Lorenz Luchsperger)

**1973.** Stamp Day.
1692 **477** 4s.+1s. purple 1·20 1·20

**478** Dr. Fritz Pregl

**1973.** 50th Anniv of Award of Nobel Prize for Chemistry to Fritz Pregl.
1693 **478** 4s. blue 1·00 65

**479** Telex Machine and Globe

**1974.** 50th Anniv of Radio Austria.
1694 **479** 2s.50 blue & ultramarine 80 45

**480** Hugo Hofmannsthal

**1974.** Birth Cent of Hugo Hofmannsthal (writer).
1695 **480** 4s. blue 1·00 65

**481** Anton Bruckner (composer)

**1974.** Inaug of Bruckner Memorial Centre, Linz.
1696 **481** 4s. brown 1·10 65

**482** Vegetables

**1974.** 2nd Int Horticultural Show, Vienna. Mult.
1697 2s. Type **482** 55 45
1698 2s.50 Fruit 90 75
1699 4s. Flowers 1·10 95

**483** Head from Ancient Seal

**1974.** 750th Anniv of Judenburg.
1700 **483** 2s. multicoloured 65 40

**484** Karl Kraus

**1974.** Birth Centenary of Karl Kraus (poet).
1701 **484** 4s. red 1·00 65

**485** "St. Michael" (wood-carving, Thomas Schwanthaler)

**1974.** "Sculptures by the Schwanthaler Family" Exhibition, Reichersberg.
1702 **485** 2s.50 green 90 45

**486** "King Arthur" (statue, Innsbruck)

**1974.** Europa.
1703 **486** 2s.50 blue and brown 2·20 95

**487** Early De Dion-Bouton Motor-tricycle

**1974.** 75th Anniv of Austrian Association of Motoring, Motor Cycling and Cycling.
1704 **487** 2s. brown and grey 55 45

**488** Mask of Satyr's Head

**1974.** "Renaissance in Austria" Exhibition, Schallaburg Castle.
1705 **488** 2s. black, brown & gold 55 45

**489** I.R.U. Emblem

**1974.** 14th International Road Haulage Union Congress, Innsbruck.
1706 **489** 4s. black and orange 1·10 65

**490** F. A. Maulbertsch

**1974.** 205th Birth Anniv of Franz Maulbertsch (painter).
1707 **490** 2s. brown 65 30

**491** Gendarmes of 1849 and 1974

**1974.** 125th Anniv of Austrian Gendarmerie.
1708 **491** 2s. multicoloured 65 30

**492** Fencing

**1974.** Sports.
1709 **492** 2s.50 black and orange 80 45

**493** Transport Emblems

**1974.** European Transport Ministers' Conference, Vienna.
1710 **493** 4s. multicoloured 1·00 65

**494** "St. Virgilius" (wood-carving)

**1974.** 1200 Years of Christianity in Salzburg.
1711 **494** 2s. blue 65 30

**495** Pres. F. Jonas

**1974.** Pres. Franz Jonas Commemoration.
1712 **495** 2s. black 65 30

**496** F. Stelzhamer

**1974.** Death Cent of Franz Stelzhamer (poet).
1713 **496** 2s. blue 65 30

**497** Diving

**1974.** 13th European Swimming, Diving and Water-polo Championships.
1714 **497** 4s. brown and blue 1·10 65

**498** F. R. von Hebra (founder of German scientific dermatology)

**1974.** 30th Meeting of German-speaking Dermatologists Association, Graz.
1715 **498** 4s. brown 1·00 65

**499** A. Schonberg

**1974.** Birth Cent of Arnold Schonberg (composer).
1716 **499** 2s.50 purple 90 45

**500** Broadcasting Studios, Salzburg

**1974.** 50th Anniv of Austrian Broadcasting.
1717 **500** 2s. multicoloured 65 30

**501** E. Eysler

**1974.** 25th Death Anniv of Edmund Eysler (composer).
1718 **501** 2s. green 55 45

**502** 19th-century Postman and Mail Transport

**1974.** Centenary of U.P.U.
1719 **502** 2s. brown and mauve 65 55
1720 - 4s. blue and grey 1·00 85
DESIGN: 4s. Modern postman and mail transport.

**503** Sports Emblem

**1974.** 25th Anniv of Football Pools in Austria.
1721 **503** 70g. red, black and green 55 30

**504** Steel Gauntlet grasping Rose

**1974.** Nature Protection.
1722 **504** 2s. multicoloured 90 55

**505** C. D. von Dittersdorf

**1974.** 175th Death Anniv of Carl Ditters von Dittersdorf (composer).
1723 **505** 2s. green 65 30

**506** Mail Coach and P.O., 1905

**1974.** Stamp Day.
1724 **506** 4s.+2s. blue 1·50 95

**507** "Virgin Mary and Child" (wood-carving)

**1974.** Christmas.
1725 **507** 2s. brown and gold 55 40

**508** F. Schmidt

**1974.** Birth Centenary of Franz Schmidt (composer).
1726 **508** 4s. black and stone 1·00 65

**509** "St. Christopher and Child" (altarpiece)

**1975.** European Architectural Heritage Year and 125th Anniv of Austrian Commission for Preservation of Monuments.
1727 **509** 2s.50 brown and grey 80 40

**510** Slalom

**1975.** Winter Olympics, Innsbruck (1976) (1st issue). Multicoloured.
1728 1s.+50g. Type **510** 35 30
1729 1s.50+70g. Ice hockey 45 40
1730 2s.+90g. Ski-jumping 65 55
1731 4s.+1s.90 Bobsleighing 1·30 1·10
See also Nos. 1747/50.

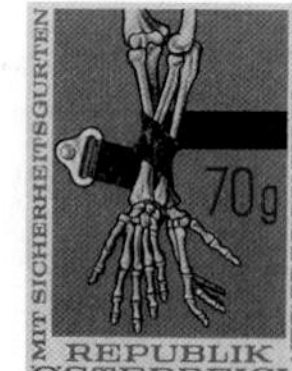

**511** Seat-belt around Skeletal Limbs

**1975.** Car Safety-belts Campaign.
1732 **511** 70g. multicoloured 45 40

**512** Stained-glass Window, Vienna Town Hall

**1975.** 11th European Communities' Day.
1733 **512** 2s.50 multicoloured 65 45

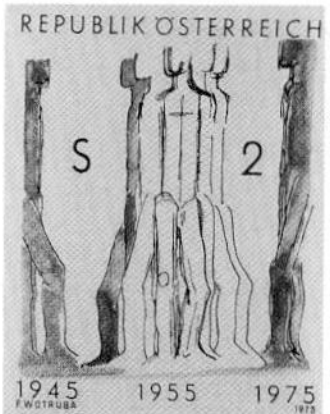

**513** "The Buffer State"

**1975.** 30th Anniv of Foundation of Austrian Second Republic.
1734 **513** 2s. black and brown 55 30

**514** Forest Scene

**1975.** 50th Anniv of Foundation of Austrian Forests Administration.
1735 **514** 2s. green 80 40

**515** "The High Priest" (M. Pacher)

**1975.** Europa.
1736 **515** 2s.50 multicoloured 2·20 45

**516** Gosaukamm Cable-way

**1975.** 4th International Ropeways Congress, Vienna.
1737 **516** 2s. blue and red 65 30

**517** J. Misson

**1975.** Death Centenary of Josef Misson (poet).
1738 **517** 2s. brown and red 55 30

**518** "Setting Sun"

**1975.** Nat Pensioners' Assn Meeting, Vienna.
1739 **518** 1s.50 multicoloured 55 30

**519** F. Porsche

**1975.** Birth Centenary of Prof. Ferdinand Porsche (motor engineer).
1740 **519** 1s.50 purple & green 55 30

**520** L. Fall

**1975.** 50th Death Anniv of Leo Fall (composer).
1741 **520** 2s. violet 55 30

**521** Judo "Shoulder Throw"

**1975.** World Judo Championships, Vienna.
1742 **521** 2s.50 multicoloured 80 45

**522** Heinrich Angeli

**1975.** 50th Death Anniv of Heinrich Angeli (court painter).
1743 **522** 2s. purple 65 30

**523** J. Strauss

**1975.** 150th Birth Anniv of Johann Strauss the Younger (composer).
1744 **523** 4s. brown and ochre 1·10 65

**524** "The Cellist"

**1975.** 75th Anniv of Vienna Symphony Orchestra.
1745 **524** 2s.50 blue and silver 65 40

**525** "One's Own House"

**1975.** 50th Anniv of Austrian Building Societies.
1746 **525** 2s. multicoloured 55 30

**1975.** Winter Olympic Games, Innsbruck (1976) (2nd issue). As T 510. Multicoloured.
1747 70g.+30g. Figure-skating (pairs) 45 40
1748 2s.+1s. Cross-country skiing 55 45
1749 2s.50+1s. Tobogganing 90 75
1750 4s.+2s. Rifle-shooting (biathlon) 1·30 1·10

**526** Scene on Folding Fan

**1975.** Bicentenary of Salzburg State Theatre.
1751 **526** 1s.50 multicoloured 55 30

**527** Austrian Stamps of 1850, 1922 and 1945

**1975.** Stamp Day. 125th Anniv of Austrian Postage Stamps.
1752 **527** 4s.+2s. multicoloured 1·30 1·10

**528** "Virgin and Child" (Schottenaltar, Vienna)

**1975.** Christmas.
1753 **528** 2s. lilac and gold 65 40

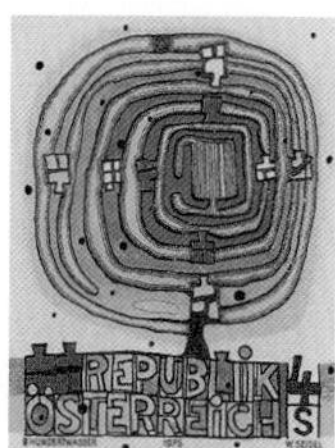

**529** "Spiralbaum" (F. Hundertwasser)

**1975.** Modern Austrian Art.
1754 **529** 4s. multicoloured 1·70 1·20

**530** Old Theatre Building

**1976.** Bicentenary of the Burgtheatre, Vienna. Sheet 130×60 mm containing T 530 and similar horiz design.
**MS**1755 3s. blue (Type **530**); 3s. brown (Interior of the modern theatre) 2·00 2·00

**531** Dr. R. Barany

**1976.** Birth Centenary of Dr. Robert Barany (Nobel prizewinner for Medicine, 1915).
1756 **531** 3s. brown and blue 1·00 45

**532** Ammonite Fossil

**1976.** Cent Exn, Vienna Natural History Museum.
1757 **532** 3s. multicoloured 1·00 45

**533** 9th-century Coronation Throne

**1976.** Millenary of Carinthia.

| | | | | |
|---|---|---|---|---|
| 1758 | **533** | 3s. black and yellow | 1·00 | 45 |

**534** Stained-glass Window, Klosterneuburg

**1976.** Babenberg Exhibition, Lilienfeld.

| | | | | |
|---|---|---|---|---|
| 1759 | **534** | 3s. multicoloured | 1·00 | 45 |

**535** "The Siege of Linz" (contemporary engraving)

**1976.** 350th Anniv of the Peasants' War in Upper Austria.

| | | | | |
|---|---|---|---|---|
| 1760 | **535** | 4s. black and green | 1·00 | 55 |

**536** Bowler delivering Ball

**1976.** 11th World Skittles Championships, Vienna.

| | | | | |
|---|---|---|---|---|
| 1761 | **536** | 4s. black and orange | 1·00 | 55 |

**537** "St. Wolfgang" (altar painting by Michael Pacher)

**1976.** International Art Exhibition, St. Wolfgang.

| | | | | |
|---|---|---|---|---|
| 1762 | **537** | 6s. purple | 1·70 | 95 |

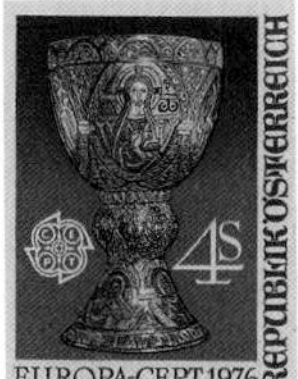

**538** Tassilo Cup, Kremsmunster

**1976.** Europa.

| | | | | |
|---|---|---|---|---|
| 1763 | **538** | 4s. multicoloured | 2·75 | 95 |

**539** Fair Emblem

**1976.** 25th Austrian Timber Fair, Klagenfurt.

| | | | | |
|---|---|---|---|---|
| 1764 | **539** | 3s. multicoloured | 1·00 | 45 |

**540** Constantin Economo

**1976.** Birth Centenary of Constantin Economo (brain specialist).

| | | | | |
|---|---|---|---|---|
| 1765 | **540** | 3s. brown | 1·00 | 45 |

**541** Bohemian Court Chancellery, Vienna

**1976.** Centenary of Administrative Court.

| | | | | |
|---|---|---|---|---|
| 1766 | **541** | 6s. brown | 1·70 | 95 |

**542** Arms of Lower Austria

**1976.** Millenary of Austria. Sheet 135×180 mm containing T 542 and similar vert designs showing provincial arms.

| | | | |
|---|---|---|---|
| **MS**1767 | 2s.×9 multicoloured | 5·00 | 5·00 |

DESIGNS: Arms of Lower Austria, Upper Austria, Styria, Carinthia, Vorarlberg, Salzberg, Burgenland and Vienna.

**543** Cancer the Crab

**1976.** Fight against Cancer.

| | | | | |
|---|---|---|---|---|
| 1768 | **543** | 2s.50 multicoloured | 80 | 45 |

**544** U.N. Emblem and Bridge

**1976.** 10th Anniv of U.N. Industrial Development Organization.

| | | | | |
|---|---|---|---|---|
| 1769 | **544** | 3s. blue and gold | 1·00 | 55 |

**545** Punched Tapes and Map of Europe

**1976.** 30th Anniv of Austrian Press Agency.

| | | | | |
|---|---|---|---|---|
| 1770 | **545** | 1s.50 multicoloured | 45 | 30 |

**546** V. Kaplan

**1976.** Birth Centenary of Viktor Kaplan (inventor of turbine).

| | | | | |
|---|---|---|---|---|
| 1771 | **546** | 2s.50 multicoloured | 65 | 55 |

**547** "The Birth of Christ" (Konrad von Friesach)

**1976.** Christmas.

| | | | | |
|---|---|---|---|---|
| 1772 | **547** | 3s. multicoloured | 90 | 45 |

**548** Postilion's Hat and Posthorn

**1976.** Stamp Day.

| | | | | |
|---|---|---|---|---|
| 1773 | **548** | 6s.+2s. black & lilac | 1·80 | 1·50 |

**549** R. M. Rilke

**1976.** 50th Death Anniv of Rainer Maria Rilke (poet).

| | | | | |
|---|---|---|---|---|
| 1774 | **549** | 3s. violet | 90 | 45 |

**550** "Augustin the Piper" (Arik Brauer)

**1976.** Austrian Modern Art.

| | | | | |
|---|---|---|---|---|
| 1775 | **550** | 6s. multicoloured | 1·70 | 95 |

**551** City Synagogue

**1976.** 150th Anniv of Vienna City Synagogue.

| | | | | |
|---|---|---|---|---|
| 1776 | **551** | 1s.50 multicoloured | 45 | 30 |

**552** N. J. von Jacquin

**1977.** 250th Birth Anniv of Nikolaus Joseph Freiherrn von Jacquin (botanist).

| | | | | |
|---|---|---|---|---|
| 1777 | **552** | 4s. brown | 1·00 | 65 |

**553** Oswald von Wolkenstein

**1977.** 600th Birth Anniv of Oswald von Wolkenstein (poet).

| | | | | |
|---|---|---|---|---|
| 1778 | **553** | 3s. multicoloured | 90 | 45 |

**554** Handball

**1977.** World Indoor Handball Championships, Group B, Austria.

| | | | | |
|---|---|---|---|---|
| 1779 | **554** | 1s.50 multicoloured | 45 | 30 |

**555** A. Kubin

**1977.** Birth Centenary of Alfred Kubin (writer and illustrator).

| | | | | |
|---|---|---|---|---|
| 1780 | **555** | 6s. blue | 1·70 | 95 |

**556** Cathedral Spire

**1977.** 25th Anniv of Re-opening of St. Stephen's Cathedral, Vienna.

| | | | | |
|---|---|---|---|---|
| 1781 | **556** | 2s.50 brown | 90 | 75 |
| 1782 | - | 3s. blue | 1·00 | 85 |
| 1783 | - | 4s. purple | 1·50 | 1·20 |

DESIGNS: 3s. West front; 4s. Interior.

**557** F. Herzmanovsky-Orlando

**1977.** Birth Centenary of Fritz Herzmanovsky-Orlando (writer).

| | | | | |
|---|---|---|---|---|
| 1784 | **557** | 6s. green and gold | 1·70 | 95 |

**558** I.A.E.A. Emblem

**1977.** 20th Anniv of Int Atomic Energy Agency.

| | | | | |
|---|---|---|---|---|
| 1785 | **558** | 3s. lt blue, gold & blue | 90 | 45 |

**559** Arms of Schwanenstadt

**1977.** 350th Anniv of Schwanenstadt.

| | | | | |
|---|---|---|---|---|
| 1786 | **559** | 3s. multicoloured | 90 | 45 |

**560** Attersee

**1977.** Europa.

| | | | | |
|---|---|---|---|---|
| 1787 | **560** | 6s. green | 4·00 | 1·40 |

**561** Globe (Vincenzo Coronelli)

**1977.** 5th International Symposium and 25th Anniv of Coronelli World Federation of Globe Friends.
1788 **561** 3s. black and stone 90 45

**562** Canoeist

**1977.** World "White Water" Canoe Championships.
1789 **562** 4s. multicoloured 1·00 55

**563** "The Samaritan" (Francesco Bassano)

**1977.** 50th Anniv of Austrian Workers' Samaritan Federation.
1790 **563** 1s.50 multicoloured 55 30

**564** Papermakers' Arms

**1977.** 17th Conference of European Committee of Pulp and Paper Technology.
1791 **564** 3s. multicoloured 90 45

**565** "Freedom"

**1977.** Martyrs for Austrian Freedom.
1792 **565** 2s.50 blue and red 80 45

**566** Steam Locomotive, "Austria", 1837

**1977.** 140th Anniv of Austrian Railways. Mult.
1793 1s.50 Type **566** 65 55
1794 2s.50 Type 214 steam locomotive, 1928 1·00 85
1795 3s. Type 1044 electric locomotive, 1974 1·70 1·40

**567** "Madonna and Child" (wood carving, Mariastein Pilgrimage Church)

**1977.** Christmas.
1796 **567** 3s. multicoloured 90 45

**568** "Danube Maiden" (Wolfgang Hutter)

**1977.** Austrian Modern Art.
1797 **568** 6s. multicoloured 1·70 95

**569** Emanuel Herrmann (inventor of postcard)

**1977.** Stamp Day.
1798 **569** 6s.+2s. brown and cinnamon 2·00 1·40

**570** Egon Friedell

**1978.** Birth Centenary of Egon Friedell (writer).
1799 **570** 3s. black and blue 90 45

**571** Underground Train

**1978.** Opening of Vienna Underground Railway.
1800 **571** 3s. multicoloured 1·10 55

**572** Rifleman and Skier

**1978.** Biathlon World Championships, Hochfilzen.
1801 **572** 4s. multicoloured 1·10 65

**573** Aztec Feather Shield

**1978.** 30th Anniv of Museum of Ethnology, Vienna.
1802 **573** 3s. multicoloured 1·00 45

**574** Leopold Kunschak

**1978.** 25th Death Anniv of Leopold Kunschak (politician).
1803 **574** 3s. blue 1·00 45

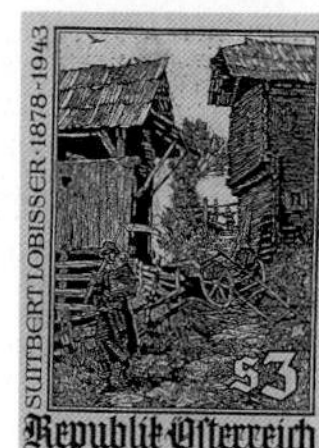

**575** "Mountain Peasants"

**1978.** Birth Centenary of Suitbert Lobisser (wood engraver).
1804 **575** 3s. brown and stone 1·00 45

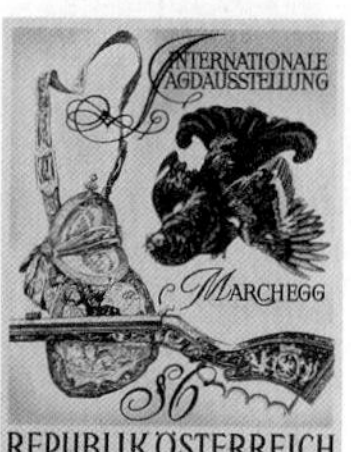

**576** Black Grouse, Hunting Satchel and Fowling Piece

**1978.** International Hunting Exn, Marchegg.
1805 **576** 6s. blue, brown & turq 1·70 95

**577** Map of Europe and Austrian Parliament Building

**1978.** 3rd Interparliamentary European Security Conference, Vienna.
1806 **577** 4s. multicoloured 1·00 65

**578** Riegersburg Castle, Styria

**1978.** Europa.
1807 **578** 6s. purple 4·00 95

**579** "Admont Pieta" (Salzburg Circle Master)

**1978.** "Gothic Art in Styria" Exhibition.
1808 **579** 2s.50 black and ochre 65 55

**580** Ort Castle

**1978.** 700th Anniv of Gmunden Town Charter.
1809 **580** 3s. multicoloured 1·10 45

**581** Face surrounded by Fruit and Flowers

**1978.** 25th Anniv of Austrian Association for Social Tourism.
1810 **581** 6s. multicoloured 1·70 95

**582** Franz Lehar and Villa at Bad Ischl

**1978.** International Lehar Congress.
1811 **582** 6s. blue 1·70 95

**583** Tools and Globe

**1978.** 15th Congress of International Federation of Building and Wood Workers.
1812 **583** 1s.50 black, yellow & red 55 45

**584** Knights Jousting

**1978.** 700th Anniv of Battle of Durnkrut and Jedenspeigen.
1813 **584** 3s. multicoloured 1·10 65

**585** Bridge over River Drau

**1978.** 1100th Anniv of Villach.
1814 **585** 3s. multicoloured 1·10 65

**586** City Seal, 1440

**1978.** 850th Anniv of Graz.
1815 **586** 4s. brown, green & grey 1·30 75

**587** Angler

**1978.** 25th Sport Fishing Championships, Vienna.
1816 **587** 4s. multicoloured 1·30 75

**588** Distorted Pattern

**1978.** Handicapped People.
1817 **588** 6s. black and brown 1·70 95

**589** Concrete Chain

**1978.** 9th International Concrete and Prefabrication Industry Congress, Vienna.
1818 **589** 2s.50 multicoloured 65 55

**590** "Grace" (Albin Egger-Lienz)

**1978.** European Family Congress.
1819 **590** 6s. multicoloured 1·70 95

**591** Lise Meitner

**1978.** Birth Centenary of Lise Meitner (physicist).
1820 **591** 6s. violet 1·70 95

**592** Victor Adler (bust, Anton Hamek)

**1978.** 60th Death Anniv of Victor Adler (statesman).
1821 **592** 3s. black and red 1·10 45

**593** Franz Schubert (after Josef Kriehuber)

**1978.** 150th Death Anniv of Franz Schubert (composer).
1822 **593** 6s. brown 2·00 95

**594** "Madonna and Child" (Martino Altomonte, Wilhering Collegiate Church)

**1978.** Christmas.
1823 **594** 3s. multicoloured 1·00 45

**595** Postbus, 1913

**1978.** Stamp Day.
1824 **595** 10s.+5s. multicoloured 3·00 2·50

**596** "Archduke Johann Hut, Grossglockner" (E. T. Compton)

**1978.** Centenary of Austrian Alpine Club.
1825 **596** 1s.50 violet and gold 55 45

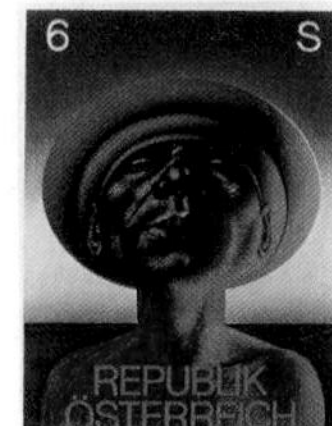


**597** "Adam" (Rudolf Hausner)

**1978.** Austrian Modern Art.
1826 **597** 6s. multicoloured 1·70 95

**598** Bound Hands

**1978.** 30th Anniv of Declaration of Human Rights.
1827 **598** 6s. purple 1·70 95

**599** "CCIR"

**1979.** 50th Anniv of International Radio Consultative Committee.
1828 **599** 6s. multicoloured 1·50 75

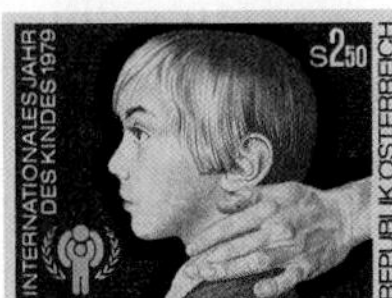


**600** Adult protecting Child

**1979.** International Year of the Child.
1829 **600** 2s.50 multicoloured 65 55

**601** Air Rifle, Pistol and Target

**1979.** Centenary of Austrian Shooting Club, and European Air Rifle and Air Pistol Shooting Championships.
1830 **601** 6s. multicoloured 1·70 75

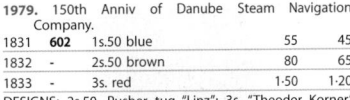

**602** "Franz I" (paddle-steamer)

**1979.** 150th Anniv of Danube Steam Navigation Company.
1831 **602** 1s.50 blue 55 45
1832 - 2s.50 brown 80 65
1833 - 3s. red 1·50 1·20

DESIGNS: 2s.50, Pusher tug "Linz"; 3s. "Theodor Korner" (passenger vessel).

**603** Skater

**1979.** World Ice Skating and Dancing Championships. Vienna.
1834 **603** 4s. multicoloured 1·10 75

**604** Fashion Drawing by Theo Zache, 1900

**1979.** 50th Viennese Int Ladies' Fashion Week.
1835 **604** 2s.50 multicoloured 65 55

**605** Wiener Neustadt Cathedral

**1979.** 700th Anniv of Wiener Neustadt Cathedral.
1836 **605** 4s. blue and grey 1·10 65

**606** Relief from Emperor Joseph II Monument, Vienna

**1979.** Bicentenary of Education for the Deaf.
1837 **606** 2s.50 green, black & gold 80 45

**607** Population Graph

**1979.** 150th Anniv of Austrian Central Statistical Office.
1838 **607** 2s.50 multicoloured 90 45

**608** Laurenz Koschier (postal reformer)

**1979.** Europa.
1839 **608** 6s. brown and ochre 3·75 95

**609** Section through Diesel Engine

**1979.** 13th Congress of International Combustion Engine Council.
1840 **609** 4s. multicoloured 1·10 65

**610** Town Arms of Ried, Braunau and Scharding

**1979.** Bicentenary of Innviertel District.
1841 **610** 3s. multicoloured 1·10 45

**611** Water Pollution

**1979.** Prevention of Water Pollution.
1842 **611** 2s.50 green and grey 90 45

**612** Arms of Rottenmann

**1979.** 700th Anniv of Rottenmann.
1843 **612** 3s. multicoloured 1·70 45

**613** Jodok Fink

**1979.** 50th Death Anniv of Jodok Fink (politician).
1844 **613** 3s. brown 1·10 45

**614** Arms of Wels and Returned Soldiers League Badge

**1979.** 5th European Meeting of Returned Soldiers.
1845 **614** 4s. green and black 1·10 65

**615** Flower

**1979.** U.N. Conference on Science and Technology for Development, Vienna.
1846 **615** 4s. blue 1·10 65

**616** Vienna International Centre

**1979.** Opening of U.N.O. Vienna Int Centre.
1847 **616** 6s. slate 1·70 95

**617** Eye and Blood Vessels of Diabetic

**1979.** 10th World Congress of International Diabetes Federation, Vienna.
1848 **617** 2s.50 multicoloured 80 45

**618** Stanzer Valley seen from Arlberg Road Tunnel

**1979.** 16th World Road Congress, Vienna.
1849 **618** 4s. multicoloured 1·10 65

**619** Steam-driven Printing Press

**1979.** 175th Anniv of State Printing Works.
1850 **619** 3s. black and stone 90 55

**620** Richard Zsigmondy

**1979.** 50th Death Anniv of Dr. Richard Zsigmondy (Nobel Prize winner for Chemistry).
1851 **620** 6s. brown 1·70 95

**621** Bregenz Festival and Congress Hall

**1979.** Bregenz Festival and Congress Hall.
1852 **621** 2s.50 lilac 90 45

**622** Burning Match

**1979.** "Save Energy".
1853 **622** 2s.50 multicoloured 90 45

**623** Lions Emblem

**1979.** 25th European Lions Forum, Vienna.
1854 **623** 4s. yellow, gold and lilac 1·10 65

**624** Wilhelm Exner (founder)

**1979.** Centenary of Industrial Museum and Technical School, Vienna.
1855 **624** 2s.50 dp purple & purple 80 45

**625** "The Suffering Christ" (Hans Fronius)

**1979.** Austrian Modern Art.
1856 **625** 4s. black and stone 1·10 75

**626** Series 52 Goods Locomotive

**1979.** Centenary of Raab (Gyor)–Odenburg (Sopron)-Ebenfurt Railway.
1857 **626** 2s.50 multicoloured 1·10 75

**627** August Musger

**1979.** 50th Death Anniv of August Musger (pioneer of slow-motion photography).
1858 **627** 2s.50 black and grey 80 45

**628** "Nativity" (detail of icon by Moses Subotic, St. Barbara Church, Vienna)

**1979.** Christmas.
1859 **628** 4s. multicoloured 1·10 65

**629** Neue Hofburg, Vienna

**1979.** "WIPA 1981" International Stamp Exhibition, Vienna (1st issue). Inscr "1. Phase".
1860 **629** 16s.+8s. multicoloured 4·75 4·50

See also No. 1890.

**630** Arms of Baden

**1980.** 500th Anniv of Baden.
1861 **630** 4s. multicoloured 1·10 65

**631** Loading Exports

**1980.** Austrian Exports.
1862 **631** 4s. blue, red and black 1·10 65

**632** Rheumatic Hand holding Stick

**1980.** Fight against Rheumatism.
1863 **632** 2s.50 red and blue 80 45

**633** Emblems of 1880 and 1980

**1980.** Centenary of Austrian Red Cross.
1864 **633** 2s.50 multicoloured 80 45

**634** Kirchschlager

**1980.** Pres. Rudolf Kirchschlager's 65th Birthday.
1865 **634** 4s. brown and red 1·10 65

**635** Robert Hamerling

**1980.** 150th Birth Anniv of Robert Hamerling (writer).
1866 **635** 2s.50 green 80 45

**636** Town Seal

**1980.** 750th Anniv of Hallein.
1867 **636** 4s. black and red 1·10 65

**637** "Maria Theresa as a Young Woman" (Andreas Moller)

**1980.** Death Bicentenary of Empress Maria Theresa.
1868 **637** 2s.50 purple 1·10 95
1869 - 4s. blue 1·50 1·20
1870 - 6s. brown 2·50 2·10

DESIGNS: 4s. "Maria Theresa with St. Stephen's Crown" (Martin van Meytens); 6s. "Maria Theresa as Widow" (Joseph Ducreux).

**638** Flags of Treaty Signatories

**1980.** 25th Anniv of Austrian State Treaty.
1871 **638** 4s. multicoloured 1·10 65

**639** St. Benedict (statue, Meinrad Guggenbichler)

**1980.** Congress of Austrian Benedictine Orders, Mariazell.
1872 **639** 2s.50 green 80 45

**640** "Hygieia" (Gustav Klimt)

**1980.** 175th Anniv of Hygiene Education.
1873 **640** 4s. multicoloured 1·10 65

**641** Dish Aerial, Aflenz

**1980.** Inauguration of Aflenz Satellite Communications Earth Station.
1874 **641** 6s. multicoloured 1·70 95

**642** Steyr (copperplate engraving, 1693)

**1980.** Millenary of Steyr.
1875 **642** 4s. brown, black & gold 1·10 65

**643** Oil Driller

**1980.** 50th Anniv of Oil Production in Austria.
1876 **643** 2s.50 multicoloured 80 45

**644** Town Seal of 1267

**1980.** 800th Anniv of Innsbruck.
1877 **644** 2s.50 yellow, blk & red 80 45

**645** Ducal Crown

**1980.** 800th Anniv of Elevation of Styria to Dukedom.
1878 **645** 4s. multicoloured 1·10 65

**646** Leo Ascher

**1980.** Birth Cent of Leo Ascher (composer).
1879 **646** 3s. violet 80 45

**647** "Abraham" (illustration from "Viennese Genesis")

**1980.** 10th Congress of International Organization for Study of the Old Testament.
1880 **647** 4s. multicoloured 1·10 65

**648** Robert Stolz

**1980.** Europa and Birth Centenary of Robert Stolz (composer).
1881 **648** 6s. red 3·25 95

**649** Falkenstein Railway Bridge

**1980.** 11th International Association of Bridge and Structural Engineering Congress, Vienna.
1882 **649** 4s. multicoloured 1·10 65

**650** "Moon Figure" (Karl Brandstatter)

**1980.** Austrian Modern Art.
1883 **650** 4s. multicoloured 1·10 65

**651** Customs Officer

**1980.** 150th Anniv of Customs Service.
1884 **651** 2s.50 brown and red 80 45

**652** Masthead of 1810

**1980.** 350th Anniv of "Linzer Zeitung" (Linz newspaper).
1885 **652** 2s.50 black, red & gold 80 45

**653** Frontispiece of Waidhofen Municipal Book

**1980.** 750th Anniv of Waidhofen.
1886 **653** 2s.50 multicoloured 80 45

**654** Heads

**1980.** 25th Anniv of Federal Army.
1887 **654** 2s.50 green and red 80 45

**655** Alfred Wegener

**1980.** Birth Centenary of Alfred Wegener (explorer and geophysicist).
1888 **655** 4s. blue 1·10 65

**656** Robert Musil

**1980.** Birth Centenary of Robert Musil (writer).
1889 **656** 4s. brown 1·10 65

**1980.** "WIPA 1981" International Stamp Exhibition, Vienna (2nd issue). Inscr "2. Phase".
1890 **629** 16s.+8s. mult 4·75 4·50

**657** "Adoration of the Kings" (stained-glass window, Viktring Collegiate Church)

**1980.** Christmas.
1891 **657** 4s. multicoloured 1·10 65

**658** Ribbon in National Colours

**1981.** 25th Anniv of General Social Insurance Act.
1892 **658** 2s.50 red, green & black 55 45

**1981.** WIPA. 1981 International Stamp Exhibtion, Vienna (3rd issue). Sheet 90×71 mm. containing horiz designs as T 629 but in finished state.
**MS**1893 16s. + 8s. multicoloured 5·50 5·50

**659** Unissued Design for 1926 Child Welfare Stamps

**1981.** Birth Centenary of Wilhelm Dachauer (artist).
1894 **659** 3s. brown 80 45

**660** Disabled Person operating Machine Tool

**1981.** 3rd European Regional Conference of Rehabilitation International.
1895 **660** 6s. brown, blue and red 1·30 85

**661** Sigmund Freud

**1981.** 125th Birth Anniv of Sigmund Freud (psychoanalyst).
1896 **661** 3s. purple 80 45

**662** Long-distance Heating System

**1981.** 20th International Union of Long-distance Heat Distributors Congress, Vienna.
1897 **662** 4s. multicoloured 1·10 65

**663** "Azzo and his Vassals" (cover of Monastery's "bearskin" Manuscript)

**1981.** Kuenring Exhibition, Zwettl Monastery.
1898 **663** 3s. multicoloured 80 45

**664** Maypole

**1981.** Europa.
1899 **664** 6s. multicoloured 4·50 1·40

**665** Early Telephone

**1981.** Centenary of Austrian Telephone System.
1900 **665** 4s. multicoloured 1·10 65

**666** "The Frog King"

**1981.** Art Education in Schools.
1901 **666** 3s. multicoloured 80 45

**667** Research Centre

**1981.** 25th Anniv of Seibersdorf Research Centre.
1902 **667** 4s. blue, dp blue & orge 1·10 65

**668** Town Hall and Seal

**1981.** 850th Anniv of St. Veit-on-Glan.
1903 **668** 4s. yellow, brown & red 1·10 65

**669** Johann Florian Heller (chemist)

**1981.** 11th Int Clinical Chemistry Congress, Vienna.
1904 **669** 6s. brown 1·30 95

**670** Boltzmann

**1981.** 75th Death Anniv of Ludwig Boltzmann (physicist).
1905 **670** 3s. green 80 45

**671** Otto Bauer

**1981.** Birth Centenary of Otto Bauer (writer and politician).
1906 **671** 4s. multicoloured 1·10 65

**672** Chemical Balance

**1981.** International Pharmaceutical Federation Congress, Vienna.
1907 **672** 6s. black, brown and red 1·20 75

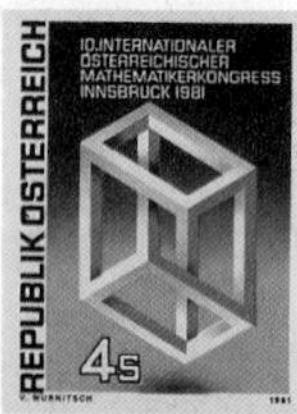

**673** Impossible Construction (M. C. Escher)

**1981.** 10th International Austrian Mathematicians' Congress, Innsbruck.
1908 **673** 4s. lt blue, blue & dp blue 1·10 65

**674** "Coronation of Virgin Mary" (detail)

**1981.** 500th Anniv of Michael Pacher's Altarpiece at St. Wolfgang, Abersee.
1909 **674** 3s. blue 80 45

**675** Compass Rose

**1981.** 75th Anniv of Graz S.E. Exhibition.
1910 **675** 4s. multicoloured 1·10 65

**676** "Holy Trinity" (illuminated MS, 12th century)

**1981.** 16th International Congress of Byzantine Scholars, Vienna.
1911 **676** 6s. multicoloured 1·20 75

**677** Josef II

**1981.** Bicentenary of Toleration Act (giving freedom of worship to Protestants).
1912 **677** 4s. black, blue & bistre 1·10 65

**678** Hans Kelsen

**1981.** Bicentenary of Hans Kelsen (law lecturer and contributor to shaping of Austrian Constitution).
1913 **678** 3s. red 80 45

**679** Full and Empty Bowls and F.A.O. Emblem

**1981.** World Food Day.
1914 **679** 6s. multicoloured 1·20 75

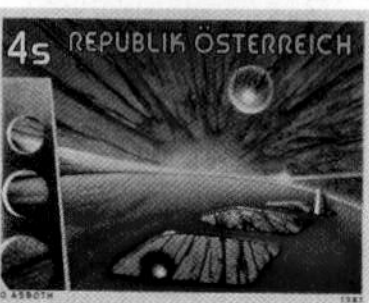

**680** "Between the Times" (Oscar Asboth)

**1981.** Austrian Modern Art.
1915 **680** 4s. multicoloured 1·10 65

**681** Workers and Emblem

**1981.** 7th International Catholic Employees' Meeting, Vienna-Lainz.
1916 **681** 3s. multicoloured 80 45

**682** Hammer-Purgstall

**1981.** 125th Death Anniv of Josef Hammer-Purgstall (orientalist).
1917 **682** 3s. multicoloured 80 45

**683** Julius Raab

**1981.** 90th Birth Anniv of Julius Raab (politician).
1918 **683** 6s. purple 1·10 95

**684** Stefan Zweig

**1981.** Birth Centenary of Stefan Zweig (writer).
1919 **684** 4s. lilac 90 75

**685** Christmas Crib, Burgenland

**1981.** Christmas.
1920 **685** 4s. multicoloured 90 75

**686** Arms of St. Nikola

**1981.** 800th Anniv of St. Nikola-on-Danube.
1921 **686** 4s. multicoloured 90 75

**687** Volkswagen Transporter Ambulance

**1981.** Cent of Vienna's Emergency Medical Service.
1922 **687** 3s. multicoloured 80 45

**688** Skier

**1982.** Alpine Skiing World Championship, Schladming-Haus.
1923 **688** 4s. multicoloured 80 45

**689** Dorotheum Building

**1982.** 275th Anniv of Dorotheum Auction, Pawn and Banking Society.
1924 **689** 4s. multicoloured 80 45

**690** Lifesaving

**1982.** 25th Anniv of Austrian Water Lifesaving Service.
1925 **690** 5s. blue, red & light blue 1·00 85

**691** St. Severin

**1982.** "St. Severin and the End of the Roman Period" Exhibition, Enns.
1926 **691** 3s. multicoloured 80 45

**692** Sebastian Kneipp (pioneer of holistic medicine)

**1982.** International Kneipp Congress, Vienna.
1927 **692** 4s. multicoloured 80 65

**693** Printers' Coat-of-arms

**1982.** 500th Anniv of Printing in Austria.
1928 **693** 4s. multicoloured 80 65

**694** Urine Analysis from "Canon Medicinae" by Avicenna

**1982.** 5th European Union for Urology Congress, Vienna.
1929 **694** 6s. multicoloured 1·10 95

**695** St. Francis preaching to Animals (miniature)

**1982.** "Franciscan Art and Culture in the Middle Ages" Exhibition, Krems-Stein.
1930 **695** 3s. multicoloured 80 45

**696** Haydn and Birthplace, Rohrau

**1982.** "Joseph Haydn and His Time" Exhibition, Eisenstadt.
1931 **696** 3s. green 1·10 95

**697** Globe within Milk Churn

**1982.** World Dairying Day.
1932 **697** 7s. multicoloured 1·70 95

**698** Town Arms (1804 flag)

**1982.** 800th Anniv of Gfohl.
1933 **698** 4s. multicoloured 80 65

**699** Tennis Player

**1982.** 80th Anniv of Austrian Lawn Tennis Assn.
1934 **699** 3s. multicoloured 80 45

**700** Main Square, Langenlois

**1982.** 900th Anniv of Langenlois.
1935 **700** 4s. multicoloured 90 45

**701** Town Arms

**1982.** 800th Anniv of Weiz.
1936 **701** 4s. multicoloured 1·70 75

**702** Linz–Freistadt–Budweis Horse-drawn Railway

**1982.** Europa.
1937 **702** 6s. brown 5·00 1·00

**703** Ignaz Seipel

**1982.** 50th Death Anniv of Ignaz Seipel (Federal Chancellor).
1938 **703** 3s. purple 80 50

**704** Postbus

**1982.** 75th Anniv of Post-bus Service.
1939 **704** 4s. multicoloured 90 80

**705** Rocket Launch

**1982.** Second U.N. Conference on the Exploration and Peaceful Uses of Outer Space, Vienna.
1940 **705** 4s. multicoloured 1·10 1·00

**706** Globe (Federal Office for Standardization and Surveying, Vienna)

**1982.** Geodesists' Day.
1941 **706** 3s. multicoloured 80 50

**707** Great Bustard ("Grosstrappe")

**1982.** Endangered Animals. Multicoloured.
1942 3s. Type **707** 80 70
1943 4s. Eurasian beaver 1·00 90
1944 6s. Western capercaillie ("Auerhahn") 1·60 1·40

**708** Institute Building, Laxenburg

**1982.** 10th Anniv of International Institute for Applied Systems Analysis.
1945 **708** 3s. black and brown 65 60

**709** St. Apollonia (patron saint of dentists)

**1982.** 70th International Dentists Federation Congress, Vienna.
1946 **709** 4s. multicoloured 90 80

**710** Emmerich Kalman

**1982.** Birth Cent of Emmerich Kalman (composer).
1947 **710** 3s. blue 80 50

**711** Max Mell

**1982.** Birth Centenary of Max Mell (writer).
1948 **711** 3s. multicoloured 80 50

**712** Christmas Crib, Damuls Church

**1982.** Christmas.
1949 **712** 4s. multicoloured 90 80

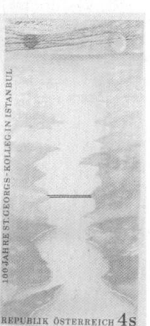

**713** Aerial View of Bosphorus

**1982.** Centenary of St. George's Austrian College, Istanbul.
1950 **713** 4s. multicoloured 90 80

**714** "Mainz-Weber" Mailbox, 1870

**1982.** Stamp Day.
1951 **714** 6s.+3s. multicoloured 2·20 2·00

**715** "Muse of the Republic" (Ernst Fuchs)

**1982.** Austrian Modern Art.
1952 **715** 4s. red and violet 1·10 1·00

**716** Bank, Vienna

**1983.** Centenary of Postal Savings Bank.
1953 **716** 4s. yellow, black and blue 90 80

**717** Hildegard Burjan

**1983.** Birth Centenary of Hildegard Burjan (founder of Caritas Socialis (religious sisterhood)).
1954 **717** 4s. red 90 80

**718** Linked Arms

**1983.** World Communications Year.
1955 **718** 7s. multicoloured 1·50 1·00

**719** Young Girl

**1983.** 75th Anniv of Children's Friends Organization.
1956 **719** 4s. black, blue and red 90 80

**720** Josef Matthias Hauer

**1983.** Birth Centenary of Josef Matthias Hauer (composer).
1957 **720** 3s. purple 65 60

**721** Douglas DC-9-80 Super Eighty

**1983.** 25th Anniv of Austrian Airlines.
1958 **721** 6s. multicoloured 1·30 1·20

**722** Hands protecting Workers

**1983.** Cent of Government Work Inspection Law.
1959 **722** 4s. grn, dp grn & brn 90 80

**723** Wels (engraving, Matthaeus Merian)

**1983.** "Millenary of Upper Austria" Exn, Wels.
1960 **723** 3s. multicoloured 65 60

**724** Human Figure, Heart and Electrocardiogram

**1983.** 7th World Symposium on Pacemakers.
1961 **724** 4s. red, mauve and blue 90 80

**725** Monastery Arms

**1983.** 900th Anniv of Gottweig Monastery.
1962 **725** 3s. multicoloured 65 60

**726** Weitra

**1983.** 800th Anniv of Weitra.
1963 **726** 4s. black, red and gold 90 80

**727** Cap, Stick, Ribbon and Emblems

**1983.** 50th Anniv of MKV and CCV Catholic Students' Organizations.
1964 **727** 4s. multicoloured 90 80

**728** Glopper Castle and Town Arms

**1983.** 650th Anniv of Hohenems Town Charter.
1965 **728** 4s. multicoloured 90 80

**729** Hess

**1983.** Europa. Birth Centenary of Viktor Franz Hess (physicist and Nobel Prize winner).
1966 **729** 6s. green 5·00 1·00

**730** Vienna City Hall

**1983.** 25th Anniv of Vienna City Hall.
1967 **730** 4s. multicoloured 90 80

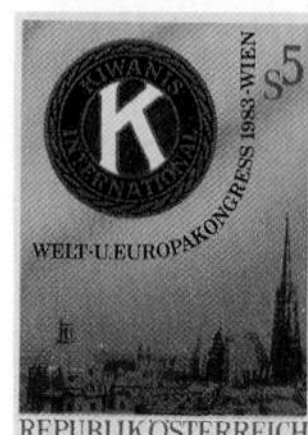


**731** Kiwanis Emblem and View of Vienna

**1983.** Kiwanis International, World and European Conference, Vienna.
1968 **731** 5s. multicoloured 1·10 1·00

**732** Congress Emblem

**1983.** 7th World Psychiatry Congress, Vienna.
1969 **732** 4s. multicoloured 90 60

**733** Hasenauer and Natural History Museum, Vienna

**1983.** 150th Birth Anniv of Carl Freiherr von Hasenauer (architect).
1970 **733** 3s. brown 90 50

**734** Institute for Promotion of Trade and Industry, Linz

**1983.** 27th International Professional Competition for Young Skilled Workers, Linz.
1971 **734** 4s. multicoloured 1·10 70

**735** Symbols of Penicillin V Efficacy and Cancer

**1983.** 13th Int Chemotherapy Congress, Vienna.
1972 **735** 5s. red and green 1·10 80

**736** Pope John Paul II

**1983.** Papal Visit.
1973 **736** 6s. black, red and gold 1·70 1·00

**737** "Relief of Vienna, 1683" (Franz Geffels)

**1983.** 300th Anniv of Relief of Vienna. Sheet 90×70 mm.
**MS**1974 **737** 6s. multicoloured 2·20 2·00

**738** Spectrum around Cross

**1983.** Austrian Catholics' Day.
1975 **738** 3s. multicoloured 80 50

**739** Vienna Town Hall

**1983.** Centenary of Vienna Town Hall.
1976 **739** 4s. multicoloured 1·10 60

**740** Karl von Terzaghi

**1983.** Birth Centenary of Karl von Terzaghi (soil mechanics and foundations engineer).
1977 **740** 3s. blue 90 50

**741** Initials of Federation

**1983.** 10th Austrian Trade Unions Federation Congress.
1978 **741** 3s. red and black 80 50

**742** "Evening Sun in Burgenland" (Gottfried Kumpf)

**1983.** Austrian Modern Art.
1979 **742** 4s. multicoloured 1·10 80

**743** Tram No. 5, 1883

**1983.** Centenary of Modling–Hinterbruhl Electric Railway.
1980 **743** 3s. multicoloured 1·10 50

**744** Boy looking at Stamped Envelope

**1983.** Stamp Day.
1981 **744** 6s.+3s. multicoloured 2·00 1·60

**745** Francisco Carolinum Museum, Linz

**1983.** 150th Anniv of Upper Austrian Provincial Museum.
1982 **745** 4s. multicoloured 1·10 70

**746** Crib by Johann Giner the Elder, Kitzbuhel Church

**1983.** Christmas.
1983 **746** 4s. multicoloured 90 80

**747** Parliament Building

**1983.** Centenary of Parliament Building, Vienna.
1984 **747** 4s. blue 1·10 70

**748** "St. Nicholas" (Maria Freund)

**1983.** Youth Stamp.
1985 **748** 3s. multicoloured 80 50

**749** Wolfgang Pauli

**1983.** 25th Death Anniv of Wolfgang Pauli (Nobel Prize winner for Physics).
1986 **749** 6s. brown 1·30 1·00

**750** Gregor Mendel

**1984.** Death Cent of Gregor Mendel (geneticist).

| | | | | |
|---|---|---|---|---|
| 1987 | **750** | 4s. ochre and brown | 90 | 80 |

**751** Hanak at Work

**1984.** 50th Death Anniv of Anton Hanak (sculptor).

| | | | | |
|---|---|---|---|---|
| 1988 | **751** | 3s. brown and black | 80 | 50 |

**752** Disabled Skier

**1984.** 3rd World Winter Games for the Disabled, Innsbruck.

| | | | | |
|---|---|---|---|---|
| 1989 | **752** | 4s.+2s. multicoloured | 1·30 | 1·20 |

**753** Memorial, Wollersdorf

**1984.** 50th Anniv of 1934 Insurrections.

| | | | | |
|---|---|---|---|---|
| 1990 | **753** | 4s.50 red and black | 90 | 60 |

**754** Founders' Stone

**1984.** 900th Anniv of Reichersberg Monastery.

| | | | | |
|---|---|---|---|---|
| 1991 | **754** | 3s.50 stone, brown & bl | 80 | 50 |

**755** Geras Monastery

**1984.** Monasteries and Abbeys.

| | | | | |
|---|---|---|---|---|
| 1992 | - | 50g. yellow, black & grey | 20 | 20 |
| 1993 | - | 1s. yellow, black & mve | 45 | 20 |
| 1994 | - | 1s.50 yellow, red & blue | 45 | 25 |
| 1995 | - | 2s. yellow, green & black | 80 | 30 |
| 1996 | **755** | 3s.50 yellow, sep & brn | 1·30 | 40 |
| 1997 | - | 4s. yellow, purple & red | 1·30 | 30 |
| 1998 | - | 4s.50 yellow, lilac & blue | 1·50 | 50 |
| 1999 | - | 5s. yellow, purple & orge | 1·50 | 50 |
| 2000 | - | 5s.50 yell, dp vio & vio | 1·80 | 50 |
| 2001 | - | 6s. yellow, green & emer | 1·80 | 30 |
| 2002 | - | 7s. yellow, green & blue | 2·75 | 40 |
| 2003 | - | 7s.50 yell, dp brn & brn | 2·50 | 50 |
| 2004 | - | 8s. yellow, blue and red | 2·50 | 50 |
| 2005 | - | 10s. yellow, red & grey | 3·00 | 50 |
| 2006 | - | 11s. yellow, black & brn | 3·25 | 80 |
| 2007 | - | 12s. yellow, brn & orge | 5·00 | 1·20 |
| 2008 | - | 17s. yellow, ultram & bl | 5·50 | 1·30 |
| 2009 | - | 20s. yellow, brown & red | 6·75 | 1·50 |

DESIGNS: 50g. Vorau Monastery; 1s. Wettingen Abbey, Mehrerau; 1s.50, Monastery of Teutonic Order, Vienna; 2s. Michaelbeuern Benedictine Monastery, Salzburg; 4s. Stams Monastery; 4s.50, Schlagl Monastery; 5s. St. Paul's Monastery, Lavanttal; 5s.50, St. Gerold's Priory, Vorarlberg; 6s. Rein Monastery; 7s. Loretto Monastery; 7s.50, Dominican Monastery, Vienna; 8s. Cistercian Monastery, Zwettl; 10s. Premonstratensian Monastery, Wilten; 11s. Trappist Monastery, Engelszell; 12s. Monastery of the Hospitallers, Eisenstadt; 17s. St. Peter's Abbey, Salzburg; 20s. Wernberg Convent, Carinthia.

**756** Cigar Band showing Tobacco Plant

**1984.** Bicentenary of Tobacco Monopoly.

| | | | | |
|---|---|---|---|---|
| 2012 | **756** | 4s.50 multicoloured | 90 | 60 |

**757** Kostendorf

**1984.** 1200th Anniv of Kostendorf.

| | | | | |
|---|---|---|---|---|
| 2013 | **757** | 4s.50 multicoloured | 90 | 60 |

**758** Wheel Bearing

**1984.** 20th International Federation of Automobile Engineers' Associations World Congress, Vienna.

| | | | | |
|---|---|---|---|---|
| 2014 | **758** | 5s. multicoloured | 1·10 | 80 |

**759** Bridge

**1984.** Europa. 25th Anniv of E.P.T. Conference.

| | | | | |
|---|---|---|---|---|
| 2015 | **759** | 6s. blue and ultramarine | 4·50 | 1·00 |

**760** Archduke Johann (after Schnorr von Carolsfeld)

**1984.** 125th Death Anniv of Archduke Johann.

| | | | | |
|---|---|---|---|---|
| 2016 | **760** | 4s.50 multicoloured | 90 | 60 |

**761** Aragonite

**1984.** "Ore and Iron in the Green Mark" Exhibition, Eisenerz.

| | | | | |
|---|---|---|---|---|
| 2017 | **761** | 3s.50 multicoloured | 65 | 50 |

**762** Binding of "Das Buch vom Kaiser", by Max Herzig

**1984.** Lower Austrian "Era of Emperor Franz Joseph: From Revolution to Grunderzeit" Exhibition, Grafenegg Castle.

| | | | | |
|---|---|---|---|---|
| 2018 | **762** | 3s.50 red and gold | 90 | 50 |

**763** Upper City Tower and Arms

**1984.** 850th Anniv of Vocklabruch.

| | | | | |
|---|---|---|---|---|
| 2019 | **763** | 4s.50 multicoloured | 1·10 | 80 |

**764** Dionysus (Virunum mosaic)

**1984.** Centenary of Carinthia Provincial Museum, Klagenfurt.

| | | | | |
|---|---|---|---|---|
| 2020 | **764** | 3s.50 stone, brn & grey | 80 | 50 |

**765** "Meeting of Austrian Army with South Tyrolean Reserves" (detail, Schnorr von Carolsfeld)

**1984.** "Jubilee of Tyrol Province" Exhibition.

| | | | | |
|---|---|---|---|---|
| 2021 | **765** | 3s.50 multicoloured | 80 | 50 |

**766** Ralph Benatzky

**1984.** Birth Cent of Ralph Benatzky (composer).

| | | | | |
|---|---|---|---|---|
| 2022 | **766** | 4s. brown | 90 | 60 |

**767** Flood Control Barriers

**1984.** Centenary of Flood Control Systems.

| | | | | |
|---|---|---|---|---|
| 2023 | **767** | 4s.50 green | 1·10 | 70 |

**768** Christian von Ehrenfels

**1984.** 125th Death Anniv of Christian von Ehrenfels (philosopher).

| | | | | |
|---|---|---|---|---|
| 2024 | **768** | 3s.50 multicoloured | 80 | 50 |

**769** Models of European Monuments

**1984.** 25th Anniv of Minimundus (model world), Worthersee.

| | | | | |
|---|---|---|---|---|
| 2025 | **769** | 4s. yellow and black | 90 | 80 |

**770** Blockheide Eibenstein National Park

**1984.** Natural Beauty Spots.

| | | | | |
|---|---|---|---|---|
| 2026 | **770** | 4s. pink and olive | 90 | 80 |

**771** Electric Train on Schanatobel Bridge (Arlberg Railway Centenary)

**1984.** Railway Anniversaries.

| | | | | |
|---|---|---|---|---|
| 2027 | **771** | 3s.50 brown, gold & red | 1·10 | 1·00 |
| 2028 | - | 4s.50 blue, silver and red | 1·30 | 1·20 |

DESIGN: 4s.50, Electric train on Falkenstein Bridge (75th anniv of Tauern Railway).

**772** Johann Georg Stuwer's Flight in Montgolfier Balloon

**1984.** Bicentenary of First Manned Balloon Flight in Austria.

| | | | | |
|---|---|---|---|---|
| 2029 | **772** | 6s. multicoloured | 1·50 | 90 |

**773** Lake Neusiedl

**1984.** Natural Beauty Spots.

| | | | | |
|---|---|---|---|---|
| 2030 | **773** | 4s. purple and blue | 90 | 80 |

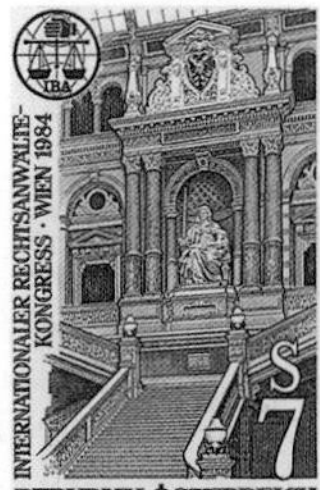

**774** Palace of Justice, Vienna

**1984.** 20th Int Bar Assn Congress, Vienna.

| | | | | |
|---|---|---|---|---|
| 2031 | **774** | 7s. multicoloured | 1·50 | 1·30 |

**775** "Joseph Hyrtl" (window, Innsbruck Anatomy Institute)

**1984.** 7th European Anatomists' Congress, Innsbruck.
2032 **775** 6s. multicoloured 1·30 80

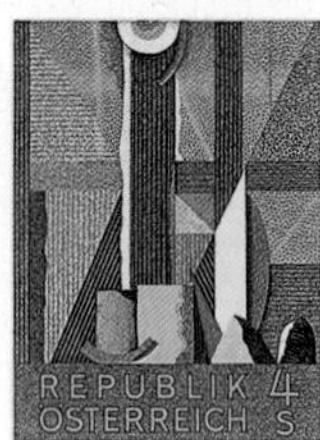


**776** "Window" (Karl Korab)

**1984.** Austrian Modern Art.
2033 **776** 4s. multicoloured 1·10 80

**777** Clock of Imms (astrolabe)

**1984.** 600th Birth Anniv of Johannes von Gmunden (astronomer and mathematician).
2034 **777** 3s.50 multicoloured 80 50

**778** Quill

**1984.** 125th Anniv of Concordia Press Club.
2035 **778** 4s.50 black, gold & red 90 60

**779** Fanny Elssler

**1984.** Death Centenary of Fanny Elssler (dancer).
2036 **779** 4s. multicoloured 1·00 60

**780** "Holy Family" (detail, Aggsbach Old High Altar)

**1984.** Christmas.
2037 **780** 4s.50 multicoloured 1·00 90

**781** Detail from Burial Chamber Wall of Seschemnofer III

**1984.** Stamp Day.
2038 **781** 6s.+3s. multicoloured 2·00 1·60

**782** Coat of Arms

**1985.** 400th Anniv of Graz University.
2039 **782** 3s.50 multicoloured 80 70

**783** Dr. Lorenz Bohler

**1985.** Birth Centenary of Prof. Dr. Lorenz Bohler (surgeon).
2040 **783** 4s.50 purple 90 60

**784** Ski Jumping, Skiing and Emblem

**1985.** World Nordic Skiing Championship, Seefeld.
2041 **784** 4s. multicoloured 1·00 90

**785** Linz Cathedral

**1985.** Bicentenary of Linz Diocese.
2042 **785** 4s.50 multicoloured 90 60

**786** Alban Berg

**1985.** Birth Centenary of Alban Berg (composer).
2043 **786** 6s. blue 1·30 1·00

**787** Institute Emblem

**1985.** 25th Anniv of Institute for Vocational Advancement.
2044 **787** 4s.50 multicoloured 90 60

**788** Stylized "B" and Clouds

**1985.** 2000th Anniv of Bregenz.
2045 **788** 4s. black, ultram & blue 80 50

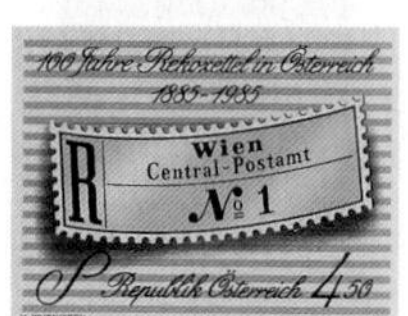


**789** 1885 Registration Label

**1985.** Centenary of Registration Labels in Austria.
2046 **789** 4s.50 black, yell & grey 90 60

**790** Josef Stefan

**1985.** 150th Birth Anniv of Josef Stefan (physicist).
2047 **790** 6s. brown, stone and red 1·30 90

**791** St. Leopold (Margrave and patron saint)

**1985.** Lower Austrian Provincial Exhibition, Klosterneuburg Monastery.
2048 **791** 3s.50 multicoloured 80 50

**792** "The Story-teller"

**1985.** 150th Birth Anniv of Franz Defregger (artist).
2049 **792** 3s.50 multicoloured 80 70

**793** Barbed Wire, Broken Tree and New Shoot

**1985.** 40th Anniv of Liberation.
2050 **793** 4s.50 multicoloured 90 60

**794** Johann Joseph Fux (composer)

**1985.** Europa. Music Year.
2051 **794** 6s. brown and grey 4·25 1·00

**795** Flags and Caduceus

**1985.** 25th Anniv of European Free Trade Association.
2052 **795** 4s. multicoloured 1·00 70

**796** Town and Arms

**1985.** Millenary of Boheimkirchen.
2053 **796** 4s.50 multicoloured 1·00 70

**797** Bishop's Gate, St. Polten

**1985.** Bicentenary of St. Polten Diocese.
2054 **797** 4s.50 multicoloured 1·00 70

**798** Johannes von Nepomuk Church, Innsbruck

**1985.** Gumpp Family (architects) Exn, Innsbruck.
2055 **798** 3s.50 multicoloured 80 60

**799** Garsten (copperplate, George Matthaus Fischer)

**1985.** Millenary of Garsten.
2056 **799** 4s.50 multicoloured 1·10 80

**800** U.N. Emblem and Austrian Arms

**1985.** 40th Anniv of U.N.O. and 30th Anniv of Austrian Membership.
2057 **800** 4s. multicoloured 1·00 70

**801** Association Headquarters, Vienna

**1985.** 13th International Suicide Prevention Association Congress, Vienna.
2058 **801** 5s. brown, lt yell & yell 1·10 80

**802** Woodland

**1985.** Forestry Year. Sheet 90×70 mm.
**MS**2059 **802** 6s. multicoloured 2·20 2·20

**803** Operetta Emblem and Spa Building

**1985.** 25th Bad Ischl Operetta Week.
2060 **803** 3s.50 multicoloured 1·00 70

**804** Fireman and Emblem

**1985.** 8th International Fire Brigades Competition, Vocklabruck.
2061 **804** 4s.50 black, green & red 1·30 80

**805** Grossglockner Mountain Road

**1985.** 50th Anniv of Grossglockner Mountain Road.
2062 **805** 4s. multicoloured 1·00 70

**806** Chessboard as Globe

**1985.** World Chess Association Congress, Graz.
2063 **806** 4s. multicoloured 90 80

**807** "Founding of Konigstetten" (August Stephan)

**1985.** Millenary of Konigstetten.
2064 **807** 4s.50 multicoloured 1·00 70

**808** Webern Church and Arms of Hofkirchen and Taufkircher

**1985.** 1200th Anniversaries of Hofkirchen, Weibern and Taufkirchen.
2065 **808** 4s.50 multicoloured 1·00 70

**809** Dr. Adam Politzer

**1985.** 150th Birth Anniv of Dr. Adam Politzer (otologist).
2066 **809** 3s.50 violet 90 60

**810** Emblem and View of Vienna

**1985.** International Association of Forwarding Agents World Congress, Vienna.
2067 **810** 6s. multicoloured 1·30 90

**811** "Clowns Riding High Bicycles" (Paul Flora)

**1985.** Austrian Modern Art.
2068 **811** 4s. multicoloured 1·10 1·00

**812** St. Martin, Patron Saint of Burgenland

**1985.** 25th Anniv of Eisenstadt Diocese.
2069 **812** 4s.50 black, bistre & red 1·10 80

**813** Roman Mounted Courier

**1985.** 50th Anniv of Stamp Day.
2070 **813** 6s.+3s. multicoloured 2·00 1·80

**814** Hanns Horbiger

**1985.** 125th Birth Anniv of Hanns Horbiger (design engineer).
2071 **814** 3s.50 purple and gold 90 80

**815** "Adoration of the Christ Child" (marble relief)

**1985.** Christmas.
2072 **815** 4s.50 multicoloured 80 50

**816** Aqueduct

**1985.** 75th Anniv of Second Vienna Waterline.
2073 **816** 3s.50 black, red & blue 80 50

**818** Chateau de la Muette (headquarters)

**1985.** 25th Anniv of Organization of Economic Co-operation and Development.
2080 **818** 4s. black, gold & mauve 95 85

**819** Johann Bohm

**1986.** Birth Centenary of Johann Bohm (founder of Austrian Trade Unions Federation).
2081 **819** 4s.50 black and red 1·00 70

**820** Dove and Globe

**1986.** International Peace Year.
2082 **820** 6s. multicoloured 1·30 85

**821** Push-button Dialling

**1986.** Introduction of Digital Preselection Telephone System.
2083 **821** 5s. multicoloured 1·00 60

**822** Albrechtsberger and Organ

**1986.** 250th Birth Anniv of Johann Georg Albrechtsberger (composer).
2084 **822** 3s.50 multicoloured 80 70

**823** Main Square and Arms

**1986.** 850th Anniv of Korneuburg.
2085 **823** 5s. multicoloured 1·20 70

**824** Kokoschka (self-portrait)

**1986.** Birth Centenary of Oskar Kokoschka (artist).
2086 **824** 4s. black and pink 1·00 60

**825** Council Flag

**1986.** 30th Anniv of Membership of Council of Europe.
2087 **825** 6s. black, red and blue 1·30 85

**826** Holzmeister and Salzburg Festival Hall

**1986.** Birth Centenary of Professor Clemens Holzmeister (architect).
2088 **826** 4s. grey, brown & lt brn 80 70

**827** Road, Roll of Material, and Congress Emblem

**1986.** 3rd International Geotextile Congress, Vienna.
2089 **827** 5s. multicoloured 1·00 60

**828** Schlosshof Palace (after Bernardo Bellotto) and Prince Eugene

**1986.** "Prince Eugene and the Baroque Era" Exhibition, Schlosshof and Niederweiden.
2090 **828** 4s. multicoloured 95 70

**829** St. Florian Monastery

**1986.** Upper Austrian "World of Baroque" Exhibition, St. Florian Monastery.
2091 **829** 4s. multicoloured 1·00 70

**830** Herberstein Castle and Styrian Arms

**1986.** "Styria – Bridge and Bulwark" Exhibition, Herberstein Castle, near Stubenberg.
2092 **830** 4s. multicoloured 1·00 70

**831** Large Pasque Flower

**1986.** Europa.
2093 **831** 6s. multicoloured 3·50 1·00

**832** Wagner and Scene from Opera "Lohengrin"

**1986.** International Richard Wagner (composer) Congress, Vienna.
2094 **832** 4s. multicoloured 95 85

**833** Antimonite Crystal

**1986.** Burgenland "Mineral and Fossils" Exhibition, Oberpullendorf.
2095 **833** 4s. multicoloured 95 85

**834** Martinswall, Zirl

**1986.** Natural Beauty Spots.
2096 **834** 5s. brown and blue 1·20 85

**835** Waidhofen

**1986.** 800th Anniv of Waidhofen on Ybbs.
2097 **835** 4s. multicoloured 1·20 85

**836** Tschauko Falls, Ferlach

**1986.** Natural Beauty Spots.
2098 **836** 5s. green and brown 1·20 85

**837** 19th-century Steam and Modern Articulated Trams

**1986.** Cent of Salzburg Local Transport System.
2099 **837** 4s. multicoloured 1·20 1·00

**838** Enns and Seals of Signatories

**1986.** 800th Anniv of Georgenberg Treaty (between Duke Leopold V of Austria and Duke Otakar IV of Styria).
2100 **838** 5s. multicoloured 1·20 85

**839** Tandler

**1986.** 50th Death Anniv of Julius Tandler (social reformer).
2101 **839** 4s. multicoloured 95 85

**840** "Observatory, 1886" (A. Heilmann)

**1986.** Centenary of Sonnblick Observatory.
2102 **840** 4s. black, blue and gold 95 85

**841** Man collecting Mandragora (from "Codex Tacuinum Sanitatis")

**1986.** 7th European Anaesthesia Congress, Vienna.
2103 **841** 5s. multicoloured 1·20 85

**842** Fire Assistant

**1986.** 300th Anniv of Vienna Fire Brigade.
2104 **842** 4s. multicoloured 1·70 1·00

**843** Stoessl

**1986.** 50th Death Anniv of Otto Stoessl (writer).
2105 **843** 4s. multicoloured 95 85

**844** Viennese Hunting Tapestry (detail)

**1986.** 5th International Oriental Carpets and Tapestry Conference, Vienna and Budapest.
2106 **844** 5s. multicoloured 1·20 85

**845** Minister in Pulpit

**1986.** 125th Anniv of Protestants Act and 25th Anniv of Protestants Law.
2107 **845** 5s. black and violet 1·20 85

**846** "Decomposition" (Walter Schmogner)

**1986.** Austrian Modern Art.
2108 **846** 4s. multicoloured 1·20 85

**847** Liszt, Birthplace and Score

**1986.** 175th Birth Anniv of Franz Liszt (composer).
2109 **847** 5s. green and brown 1·20 85

**848** Aerial View of Vienna (image scaled to 60% of original size)

**1986.** European Security and Co-operation Conference Review Meeting, Vienna. Sheet 90×70 mm.
**MS**2110 **848** 6s. multicoloured 1·70 1·60

**849** Strettweg Religious Carriage

**1986.** 175th Anniv of Styrian Joanneum Museum.
2111 **849** 4s. multicoloured 95 85

**850** "Nuremberg Letter Messenger" (16th century woodcut)

**1986.** Stamp Day.
2112 **850** 6s.+3s. multicoloured 2·20 1·70

**851** "Adoration of the Shepherds" (woodcut, Johann Georg Schwanthaler)

**1986.** Christmas.
2113 **851** 5s. brown and gold 1·20 85

**852** Headquarters

**1986.** 40th Anniv of Federal Chamber of Trade and Industry.
2114 **852** 5s. multicoloured 1·20 85

**853** Foundry Worker

**1986.** Austrian World of Work (1st series).
2115 **853** 4s. multicoloured 95 85

See also Nos. 2144, 2178, 2211, 2277, 2386, 2414, 2428, 2486, 2520, 2572 and 2605.

**854** "The Educated Eye"

**1987.** Centenary of Adult Education in Vienna.
2116 **854** 5s. multicoloured 1·20 85

**855** "Large Blue Madonna" (Anton Faistauer)

**1987.** Painters' Birth Centenaries. Multicoloured.
2117 4s. Type **855** 95 85
2118 6s. "Self-portrait" (Albert Paris Gutersloh) 1·40 1·20

**856** Hundertwasser House, Vienna

**1987.** Europa and "Europalia 1987 Austria" Festival, Belgium.
2119 **856** 6s. multicoloured 6·50 2·10

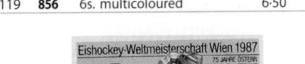

**857** Ice Hockey Players

**1987.** World Ice Hockey Championships, Vienna, and 75th Anniv of Austrian Ice Hockey Association.
2120 **857** 5s. multicoloured 1·50 1·00

**858** Austria Centre

**1987.** Inaug of Austria Conference Centre, Vienna.
2121 **858** 5s. multicoloured 1·50 1·00

**859** Salzburg

**1987.** 700th Anniv of Salzburg Town Charter.
2122 **859** 5s. multicoloured 1·50 1·00

**860** Machine Shop, 1920

**1987.** Upper Austrian "Work–Men–Machines, the Route to Industrialized Society" Exhibition, Steyr.
2123 **860** 4s. black and red 1·20 70

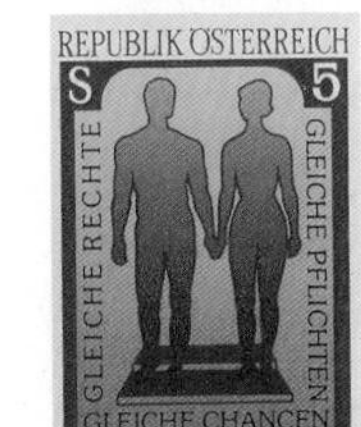

**861** Man and Woman

**1987.** Equal Rights for Men and Women.
2124 **861** 5s. multicoloured 1·20 85

**862** "Adele Bloch-Bauer I" (detail, Gustav Klimt)

**1987.** Lower Austrian "Era of Emperor Franz Joseph: Splendour and Misery" Exhibition, Grafenegg Castle.
2125 **862** 4s. multicoloured 1·20 70

**863** Archbishop and Salzburg

**1987.** 400th Anniv of Election of Prince Wolf Dietrich von Raitenau as Archbishop of Salzburg.
2126 **863** 4s. multicoloured 95 85

**864** Schnitzler

**1987.** 125th Birth Anniv of Arthur Schnitzler (dramatist).
2127 **864** 6s. multicoloured 1·30 95

**865** Lace and Arms

**1987.** 1100th Anniv of Lustenau.
2128 **865** 5s. multicoloured 1·20 85

**866** Anniversary Emblem (William Slattery)

**1987.** 150th Anniv of Austrian Railways. Sheet 90×70 mm.
**MS**2129 **866** 6s. silver, red and black 2·30 2·10

**867** Dachstein Giant Ice Cave

**1987.** Natural Beauty Spots.
2130 **867** 5s. green and black 1·20 85

**868** Engraver at Work

**1987.** 8th European Association of Engravers and Flexographers International Congress, Vienna.
2131 **868** 5s. brown, pink and grey 1·20 60

**869** Dr. Karl Josef Bayer (chemist)

**1987.** 8th International Light Metal Meeting, Leoben and Vienna.
2132 **869** 5s. multicoloured 1·20 60

**870** Passenger Ferry

**1987.** Centenary of 1st Achensee Steam Service.
2133 **870** 4s. multicoloured 1·20 1·00

**871** Office Building, Vienna

**1987.** 10th Anniv of Office of Ombudsmen.
2134 **871** 5s. black, yellow and red 1·20 85

**872** Schrodinger

**1987.** Birth Cent of Erwin Schrodinger (physicist).
2135 **872** 5s. brown, cream and bistre 1·20 85

**873** Freistadt Town Square

**1987.** 125th Anniv of Freistadt Exhibitions.
2136 **873** 5s. multicoloured 1·20 60

**874** Arbing Church

**1987.** 850th Anniv of Arbing.
2137 **874** 5s. multicoloured 1·20 60

**875** Gauertal and Montafon Valleys, Voralberg

**1987.** Natural Beauty Spots.
2138 **875** 5s. brown and yellow 1·20 85

**876** Cyclist

**1987.** World Cycling Championship, Vienna and Villach.
2139 **876** 5s. multicoloured 1·20 1·00

**877** Emblem

**1987.** World Congress of International Institute of Savings Banks, Vienna.
2140 **877** 5s. multicoloured 1·20 85

**878** Hofhaymer at Organ

**1987.** 450th Death Anniv of Paul Hofhaymer (composer and organist).
2141 **878** 4s. blue, black and gold 95 85

**879** Haydn and Salzburg

**1987.** 250th Birth Anniv of Michael Haydn (composer).
2142 **879** 4s. lilac 95 85

**880** Lammergeier ("Bartgeier")

**1987.** 25th Anniv of Alpine Zoo, Innsbruck.
2143 **880** 4s. multicoloured 95 85

**881** Woman using Word Processor

**1987.** Austrian World of Work (2nd series).
2144 **881** 4s. multicoloured 1·00 70

**882** "Tree Goddesses" (Arnulf Neuwirth)

**1987.** Austrian Modern Art.
2145 **882** 5s. multicoloured 1·20 85

**883** Lottery Wheel

**1987.** Bicentenary of Gambling Monopoly.
2146 **883** 5s. multicoloured 1·20 85

**884** Helmer

**1987.** Birth Centenary of Oskar Helmer (politician).
2147 **884** 4s. multicoloured 95 85

**885** Gluck

**1987.** Death Bicentenary of Christoph Willibald Gluck (composer).
2148 **885** 5s. brown and ochre 1·20 85

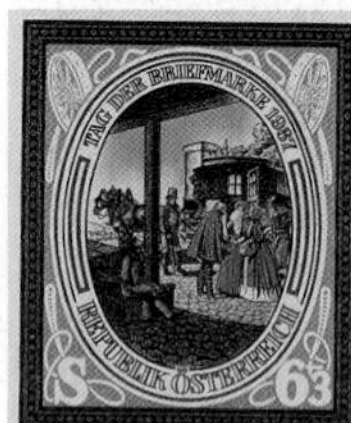


**886** Stagecoach and Passengers (lithograph, Carl Schuster)

**1987.** Stamp Day.
2149 **886** 6s.+3s. multicoloured 2·20 1·80

**887** Josef Mohr and Franz Xaver Gruber (composers of "Silent Night")

**1987.** Christmas.
2150 **887** 5s. multicoloured 1·70 1·00

**888** Bosco and Boys

**1988.** International Educational Congress of St. John Bosco's Salesian Brothers, Vienna.
2151 **888** 5s. purple and orange 1·20 85

**889** Cross-country Sledging

**1988.** 4th World Winter Games for the Disabled, Innsbruck.
2152 **889** 5s.+2s.50 multicoloured 2·00 1·30

**890** Mach

**1988.** 150th Birth Anniv of Ernst Mach (physicist and philosopher).
2153 **890** 6s. multicoloured 1·40 95

**891** "Village with Bridge"

**1988.** 25th Death Anniv of Franz von Zulow (artist).
2154 **891** 4s. multicoloured 1·20 85

**892** "The Confiscation" (Ferdinand Georg Waldmuller)

**1988.** "Patriotism and Protest: Viennese Biedermeier and Revolution" Exhibition, Vienna.
2155 **892** 4s. multicoloured 1·20 85

**893** Barbed Wire, Flag and Crosses

**1988.** 50th Anniv of Annexation of Austria by Germany.
2156 **893** 5s. green, brown and red 1·40 90

**894** Steam Locomotive "Aigen", Muhlkreis Railway, 1887

**1988.** Railway Centenaries. Multicoloured.
2157 4s. Type **894** 1·20 1·00
2158 5s. Modern electric tram and Josefsplatz stop (Viennese Local Railways Stock Corporation) 1·50 1·30

**895** European Bee Eater

**1988.** 25th Anniv of World Wildlife Fund, Austria.
2159 **895** 5s. multicoloured 1·40 1·00

**896** Decanter and Beaker

**1988.** Styrian "Glass and Coal" Exn, Barnbach.
2160 **896** 4s. multicoloured 95 85

**897** Late Gothic Silver Censer

**1988.** Lower Austrian "Art and Monastic Life at the Birth of Austria" Exhibition, Seitenstetten Benedictine Monastery.
2161 **897** 4s. multicoloured 95 85

**898** Taking Casualty to Volkswagen Transporter Ambulance and Red Cross

**1988.** 125th Anniv of Red Cross.
2162 **898** 12s. black, red and green 2·50 1·90

**899** Dish Aerials, Aflenz

**1988.** Europa. Telecommunications.
2163 **899** 6s. multicoloured 4·75 1·60

**900** Mattsee Monastery

**1988.** Salzburg "Bajuvars from Severin to Tassilo" Exhibition, Mattsee Monastery.
2164 **900** 4s. multicoloured 95 85

**901** Weinberg Castle

**1988.** Upper Austrian "Muhlviertel: Nature, Culture, Life" Exhibition, Weinberg Castle, near Kefermarkt.
2165 **901** 4s. multicoloured 95 85

**902** Horvath

**1988.** 50th Death Anniv of Odon von Horvath (writer).
2166 **902** 6s. black and bistre 1·40 95

**903** Stockerau Town Hall

**1988.** 25th Anniv of Stockerau Festival.
2167 **903** 5s. multicoloured 1·20 85

**904** Motorway

**1988.** Completion of Tauern Motorway.
2168 **904** 4s. multicoloured 95 85

**905** Brixlegg

**1988.** 1200th Anniv of Brixlegg.
2169 **905** 5s. multicoloured 1·20 85

**906** Klagenfurt (after Matthaus Merian)

**1988.** 400th Anniv of Regular Postal Services in Carinthia.
2170 **906** 5s. multicoloured 1·20 85

**907** Parish Church and Dean's House

**1988.** 1200th Anniv of Brixen im Thale, Tyrol.
2171 **907** 5s. multicoloured 1·20 85

**908** Krimml Waterfalls, Upper Tauern National Park

**1988.** Natural Beauty Spots.
2172 **908** 5s. black and blue 1·20 85

**909** Town Arms

**1988.** 1100th Anniv of Feldkirchen, Carinthia.
2173 **909** 5s. multicoloured 1·20 85

**910** Feldbach

**1988.** 800th Anniv of Feldbach.
2174 **910** 5s. multicoloured 1·20 85

**911** Ansfelden

**1988.** 1200th Anniv of Ansfelden.
2175 **911** 5s. multicoloured 1·20 85

**912** Hologram of Export Emblem

**1988.** Federal Economic Chamber Export Congress.
2176 **912** 8s. multicoloured 3·00 2·30

**913** Concert Hall

**1988.** 75th Anniv of Vienna Concert Hall.
2177 **913** 5s. multicoloured 1·20 85

**914** Laboratory Assistant

**1988.** Austrian World of Work (3rd series).
2178 **914** 4s. multicoloured 1·00 70

**915** "Guards" (Giselbert Hoke)

**1988.** Austrian Modern Art.
2179 **915** 5s. multicoloured 1·20 85

**916** Schonbauer

**1988.** Birth Centenary of Dr. Leopold Schonbauer (neurosurgeon and politician).
2180 **916** 4s. multicoloured 1·00 70

**917** Carnation

**1988.** Cent of Austrian Social Democratic Party.
2181 **917** 4s. multicoloured 95 85

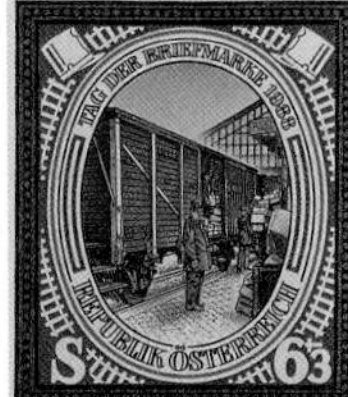

**918** Loading Railway Mail Van at Pardubitz Station, 1914

**1988.** Stamp Day.
2182 **918** 6s.+3s. multicoloured 2·30 1·70

**919** "Nativity" (St. Barbara's Church, Vienna)

**1988.** Christmas.
2183 **919** 5s. multicoloured 1·20 85

**920** "Madonna" (Lucas Cranach)

**1989.** 25th Anniv of Diocese of Innsbruck.
2184 **920** 4s. multicoloured 95 60

**921** Margrave Leopold II leading Abbot Sigibold and Monks to Melk (detail of fresco, Paul Troger)

**1989.** 900th Anniv of Melk Benedictine Monastery.
2185 **921** 5s. multicoloured 1·20 85

**922** Marianne Hainisch

**1989.** 150th Birth Anniv of Marianne Hainisch (women's rights activist).
2186 **922** 6s. multicoloured 1·40 1·00

**923** Glider and Paraskier

**1989.** World Gliding Championships, Wiener Neustadt, and World Paraskiing Championships, Damuls.
2187 **923** 6s. multicoloured 1·40 1·00

**924** "The Painting"

**1989.** 50th Death Anniv of Rudolf Jettmar (painter).
2188 **924** 5s. multicoloured 1·20 85

**925** "Bruck an der Leitha" (17th-century engraving, Georg Vischer)

**1989.** 750th Anniv of Bruck an der Leitha.
2189 **925** 5s. multicoloured 1·20 85

**926** Wittgenstein

**1989.** Birth Centenary of Ludwig Wittgenstein (philosopher).
2190 **926** 5s. multicoloured 1·20 70

**927** Holy Trinity Church, Stadl-Paura

**1989.** 250th Death Anniv of Johann Michael Prunner (architect).
2191 **927** 5s. multicoloured 1·20 70

**928** Suess (after Josef Kriehuber) and Map

**1989.** 75th Death Anniv of Eduard Suess (geologist and politician).
2192 **928** 6s. multicoloured 1·30 85

**929** "Judenburg" (17th-century engraving, Georg Vischer)

**1989.** Upper Styrian "People, Coins, Markets" Exhibition, Judenburg.
2193 **929** 4s. multicoloured 1·00 70

**930** Steam Engine (Vinzenz Prick)

**1989.** Lower Austrian "Magic of Industry" Exhibition, Pottenstein.
2194 **930** 4s. blue and gold 1·00 70

**931** Radstadt

**1989.** 700th Anniv of Radstadt.
2195 **931** 5s. multicoloured 1·20 85

**932** Wooden Salt Barge from Viechtau

**1989.** Europa. Children's Toys.
2196 **932** 6s. multicoloured 4·00 1·00

**933** "St. Adalbero and Family before Madonna and Child" (Monastery Itinerary Book)

**1989.** Upper Austrian "Graphic Art" Exhibition and 900th Anniv of Lambach Monastery Church.
2197 **933** 4s. multicoloured 1·00 70

**934** "Gisela" (paddle-steamer)

**1989.** 150th Anniv of Passenger Shipping on Traunsee.
2198 **934** 5s. multicoloured 1·70 1·00

**935** Hansa Brandenburg C-1 Mail Biplane at Vienna, 1918

**1989.** Stamp Day.
2199 **935** 6s.+3s. multicoloured 2·00 1·70

**936** St. Andra (after Matthaus Merian)

**1989.** 650th Anniv of St. Andra.
2200 **936** 5s. multicoloured 1·20 85

**937** Strauss

**1989.** 125th Birth Anniv of Richard Strauss (composer).
2201 **937** 6s. red, brown and gold 1·40 1·00

**938** Locomotive

**1989.** Centenary of Achensee Steam Rack Railway.
2202 **938** 5s. multicoloured 1·50 85

**939** Parliament Building, Vienna

**1989.** Centenary of Interparliamentary Union.
2203 **939** 6s. multicoloured 1·40 95

**940** Anniversary Emblem

**1989.** Centenary of National Insurance in Austria.
2204 **940** 5s. multicoloured 1·20 70

**941** U.N. Building, Vienna

**1989.** 10th Anniv of U.N. Vienna Centre.
2205 **941** 8s. multicoloured 2·00 1·00

**942** Lusthaus Water, Prater Woods, Vienna

**1989.** Natural Beauty Spots.
2206 **942** 5s. black and buff 1·20 1·00

**943** Wildalpen and Hammerworks

**1989.** 850th Anniv of Wildalpen.
2207 **943** 5s. multicoloured 1·20 85

**944** Emblem

**1989.** 33rd Congress of European Organization for Quality Control, Vienna.
2208 **944** 6s. multicoloured 1·40 95

**945** Palace of Justice, Vienna

**1989.** 14th Congress of Int Assn of Criminal Law.
2209 **945** 6s. multicoloured 1·30 90

**946** "Tree of Life" (Ernst Steiner)

**1989.** Austrian Modern Art.
2210 **946** 5s. multicoloured 1·40 95

**947** Bricklayer

**1989.** Austrian World of Work (4th series).
2211 **947** 5s. multicoloured 1·40 95

**948** Ludwig Anzengruber (150th birth anniv)

**1989.** Writers' Anniversaries. Multicoloured.
2212 4s. Type **948** 1·20 85
2213 4s. Georg Trakl (75th death anniv) 1·20 85

**949** Fried

**1989.** 125th Birth Anniv of Alfred Fried (Peace Movement worker).
2214 **949** 6s. multicoloured 1·50 1·00

**950** "Adoration of the Shepherds" (detail, Johann Carl von Reslfeld)

**1989.** Christmas.
2215 **950** 5s. multicoloured 1·20 85

**951** "Courier" (Albrecht Durer)

**1990.** 500th Anniv of Regular European Postal Services.
2216 **951** 5s. chocolate, cinnamon and brown 1·30 85

**952** Streif Downhill and Ganslern Slalom Runs

**1990.** 50th Hahnenkamm Ski Championships, Kitzbuhel.
2217 **952** 5s. multicoloured 1·20 85

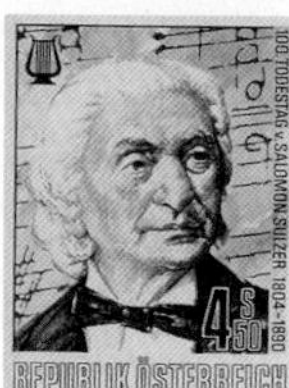

**953** Sulzer

**1990.** Death Centenary of Salomon Sulzer (creator of modern Synagogue songs).
2218 **953** 4s.50 multicoloured 1·00 60

**954** Emich

**1990.** 50th Death Anniv of Friedrich Emich (microchemist).
2219 **954** 6s. purple and green 1·20 85

**955** Emperor Friedrich III (miniature by Ulrich Schreier)

**1990.** 500th Anniv of Linz as Capital of Upper Austria.
2220 **955** 5s. multicoloured 1·20 85

**956** University Seals

**1990.** 625th Anniv of Vienna University and 175th Anniv of Vienna University of Technology.
2221 **956** 5s. red, gold and lilac 1·20 85

**957** South Styrian Vineyards

**1990.** Natural Beauty Spots.
2222 **957** 5s. black and yellow 1·20 85

**958** Parish Church

**1990.** 1200th Anniv of Anthering.
2223 **958** 7s. multicoloured 1·90 95

**959** 1897 May Day Emblem

**1990.** Centenary of Labour Day.
2224 **959** 4s.50 multicoloured 1·00 95

**960** "Our Dear Housewife of Seckau" (relief)

**1990.** 850th Anniv of Seckau Abbey.
2225 **960** 4s.50 blue 1·00 70

**961** Ebene Reichenau Post Office

**1990.** Europa. Post Office Buildings.
2226 **961** 7s. multicoloured 5·25 1·20

**962** Thematic Stamp Motifs

**1990.** Stamp Day.
2227 **962** 7s.+3s. multicoloured 2·30 1·90

**963** Makart (self-portrait)

**1990.** 150th Birth Anniv of Hans Makart (painter).
2228 **963** 4s.50 multicoloured 1·20 1·00

**964** Schiele (self-portrait)

**1990.** Birth Centenary of Egon Schiele (painter).
2229 **964** 5s. multicoloured 1·20 1·00

**965** Raimund

**1990.** Birth Bicentenary of Ferdinand Raimund (actor and playwright).
2230 **965** 4s.50 multicoloured 1·20 1·00

**966** "The Hundred Guilden Note" (Rembrandt)

**1990.** 2nd Int Christus Medicus Congress, Bad Ischl.
2231 **966** 7s. multicoloured 1·90 95

**967** Hardegg

**1990.** 700th Anniv of Hardegg's Elevation to Status of Town.
2232 **967** 4s.50 multicoloured 1·20 85

**968** Oberdrauburg (copperplate engraving, Freiherr von Valvasor)

**1990.** 750th Anniv of Oberdrauburg.
2233 **968** 5s. multicoloured 1·30 60

**969** Church and Town Hall

**1990.** 850th Anniv of Gumpoldskirchen.
2234 **969** 5s. multicoloured 1·30 60

**970** Zdarsky skiing

**1990.** 50th Death Anniv of Mathias Zdarsky (developer of alpine skiing).
2235 **970** 5s. multicoloured 1·30 60

**971** "Telegraph", 1880, and "Anton Chekhov", 1978

**1990.** 150th Anniv of Modern (metal) Shipbuilding in Austria.
2236 **971** 9s. multicoloured 2·10 1·20

**972** Perkonig

**1990.** Birth Centenary of Josef Friedrich Perkonig (writer).
2237 **972** 5s. sepia, brown & gold 1·20 85

**973** "Man of Rainbows" (Robert Zeppel-Sperl)

**1990.** Austrian Modern Art.
2238 **973** 5s. multicoloured 1·20 85

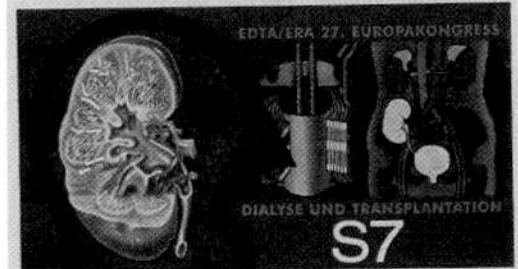
**974** Kidney, Dialysis Machine and Anatomical Diagram

**1990.** 27th European Dialysis and Transplantation Federation Congress, Vienna.
2239 **974** 7s. multicoloured 1·90 95

**975** Werfel

**1990.** Birth Centenary of Franz Werfel (writer).
2240 **975** 5s. multicoloured 1·20 85

**976** U.N. and Austrian Flags

**1990.** 30th Anniv of Austrian Participation in U.N. Peace-keeping Forces.
2241 **976** 7s. multicoloured 1·90 95

**977** Arms of Provinces

**1990.** 45th Anniv of First Provinces Conference (established Second Republic as Federal State).
2242 **977** 5s. multicoloured 1·20 60

**978** University Seal

**1990.** 150th Anniv of Mining University, Leoben.
2243 **978** 4s.50 black, red & green 1·00 60

**979** Vogelsang

**1990.** Death Centenary of Karl von Vogelsang (Christian social reformer).
2244 **979** 4s.50 multicoloured 1·00 60

**980** Metal Workers

**1990.** Centenary of Metal, Mining and Energy Trade Union.
2245 **980** 5s. multicoloured 1·20 60

**981** Player

**1990.** 3rd World Ice Curling Championships, Vienna.
2246 **981** 7s. multicoloured 1·90 95

**982** Greenhouse

**1990.** Re-opening of Schonbrunn Greenhouse.
2247 **982** 5s. multicoloured 1·20 60

**983** "Birth of Christ"

**1990.** Christmas. Detail of Altarpiece by Master Nikolaus of Verdun, Klosterneuburg Monastery.
2248 **983** 5s. multicoloured 1·20 60

**984** Grillparzer

**1991.** Birth Bicent of Franz Grillparzer (dramatist).
2249 **984** 4s.50 multicoloured 1·20 60

**985** Skier

**1991.** World Alpine Skiing Championships, Saalbach-Hinterglemm.
2250 **985** 5s. multicoloured 1·20 85

**986** Kreisky

**1991.** 80th Birth Anniv of Bruno Kreisky (Chancellor, 1970–82).
2251 **986** 5s. multicoloured 1·20 85

**987** Schmidt and Vienna Town Hall

**1991.** Death Centenary of Friedrich von Schmidt (architect).
2252 **987** 7s. multicoloured 1·90 1·20

**988** Fountain, Vienna

**1991.** Anniversaries. Multicoloured.
2253 4s.50 Type **988** (250th death anniv of Georg Raphael Donner (sculptor)) 1·00 95
2254 5s. "Kitzbuhel in Winter" (birth centenary of Alfons Walde (artist and architect)) 1·20 1·00
2255 7s. Vienna Stock Exchange (death centenary of Theophil von Hansen (architect)) 1·70 1·60
See also No. 2269.

**989** M. von Ebner-Eschenbach

**1991.** 75th Death Anniv of Marie von Ebner-Eschenbach (writer).
2256 **989** 4s.50 purple 1·20 85

**990** Mozart

**1991.** Death Bicentenary of Wolfgang Amadeus Mozart (composer). Sheet 115×69 mm containing T 990 and similar vert design, each purple, mauve and gold.
**MS**2257 5s. Type **990**; 5s. "The Magic Flute" (statue, Vienna) 3·50 3·00

**991** Obir Stalactite Caverns, Eisenkappel

**1991.** Natural Beauty Spots.
2258 **991** 5s. multicoloured 1·30 90

**992** Spittal an der Drau (after Matthaus Merian)

**1991.** 800th Anniv of Spittal an der Drau.
2259 **992** 4s.50 multicoloured 1·30 90

**993** "ERS-1" European Remote Sensing Satellite

**1991.** Europa. Europe in Space.
2260 **993** 7s. multicoloured 6·00 1·30

**994** "Garden Party" (Anthoni Bays)

**1991.** Vorarlberg "Clothing and People" Exhibition, Hohenems.
2261 **994** 5s. multicoloured 1·30 90

**995** Grein

**1991.** 500th Anniv of Grein Town Charter.
2262 **995** 4s.50 multicoloured 1·30 90

**996** Bedding Plants forming Arms

**1991.** 1200th Anniv of Tulln.
2263 **996** 5s. multicoloured 1·30 90

**997** Military History Museum

**1991.** Vienna Museum Centenaries. Multicoloured.
2264 5s. Type **997** 1·30 1·10
2265 7s. Museum of Art History 1·60 1·50

**998** "B" and "P"

**1991.** Stamp Day.
2266 **998** 7s.+3s. brown, sepia and black 2·30 2·00

This is the first of a series of ten annual stamps, each of which will illustrate two letters. The complete series will spell out the words "Briefmarke" and "Philatelie".

**999** Tunnel Entrance

**1991.** Opening of Karawanken Road Tunnel between Carinthia and Slovenia.
2267 **999** 7s. multicoloured 1·60 1·20

**1000** Town Hall

**1991.** 5th Anniv of St. Polten as Capital of Lower Austria.
2268 **1000** 5s. multicoloured 1·40 90

**1991.** 150th Birth Anniv of Otto Wagner (architect). As T 988. Multicoloured.
2269 4s.50 Karlsplatz Station, Vienna City Railway 1·30 1·10

**1001** Rowing

**1991.** Junior World Canoeing Championships and World Rowing Championships, Vienna.
2270 **1001** 5s. multicoloured 1·30 90

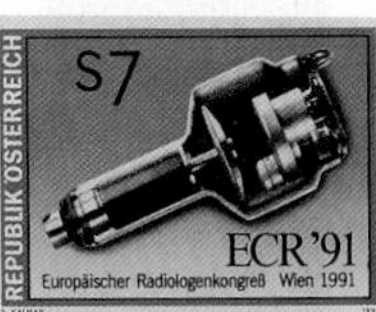


**1002** X-ray Tube

**1991.** European Radiology Congress, Vienna.
2271 **1002** 7s. multicoloured 1·60 1·10

**1003** Paracelsus

**1991.** 450th Death Anniv of Theophrastus Bombastus von Hohenheim (Paracelsus) (physician and scientist).
2272 **1003** 4s. black, red & brown 1·30 90

**1004** "Mir" Space Station

**1991.** "Austro Mir 91" Soviet–Austrian Space Flight.
2273 **1004** 9s. multicoloured 2·10 1·50

**1005** Almabtrieb (driving cattle from mountain pastures) (Zell, Tyrol)

**1991.** Folk Customs and Art (1st series). Mult.
2274 4s.50 Type **1005** 1·00 90
2275 5s. Vintage Crown (Neustift, Vienna) 1·10 1·00
2276 7s. Harvest monstrance (Nestelbach, Styria) 1·60 1·50

See also Nos. 2305/7, 2349/51, 2363/5, 2393/5, 2418, 2432/3, 2450, 2482, 2491, 2500/1, 2508, 2524, 2546, 2547, 2550, 2552, 2569, 2581, 2587, 2595, 2718, 2776 and 2815.

**1006** Weaver

**1991.** Austrian World of Work (5th series).
2277 **1006** 4s.50 multicoloured 1·10 80

**1007** "The General" (Rudolf Pointner)

**1991.** Austrian Modern Art.
2278 **1007** 5s. multicoloured 1·30 90

**1008** Raab

**1991.** Birth Centenary of Julius Raab (Chancellor, 1953–61).
2279 **1008** 4s.50 brown & chestnut 1·30 90

**1009** "Birth of Christ" (detail of fresco, Baumgartenberg Church)

**1991.** Christmas.
2280 **1009** 5s. multicoloured 1·30 1·10

**1010** Clerks

**1992.** Centenary of Trade Union of Clerks in Private Enterprise.
2281 **1010** 5s.50 multicoloured 1·40 1·00

**1011** Emblems of Games and Olympic Rings

**1992.** Winter Olympic Games, Albertville, and Summer Games, Barcelona.
2282 **1011** 7s. multicoloured 2·00 1·10

**1012** Competitor

**1992.** 8th World Toboggan Championships on Natural Runs, Bad Goisern.
2283 **1012** 5s. multicoloured 1·30 90

**1013** Hollow Stone, Klostertal

**1992.** Natural Beauty Spots.
2284 **1013** 5s. multicoloured 1·30 90

**1014** Saiko

**1992.** Birth Centenary of George Saiko (writer).
2285 **1014** 5s.50 brown 1·40 1·00

**1015** "Athlete with Ball" (Christian Attersee)

**1992.** Centenary of Workers' Sport Movement.
2286 **1015** 5s.50 multicoloured 1·40 1·00

**1016** Franz Joseph Muller (chemist and mineralogist)

**1992.** Scientific Anniversaries. Multicoloured.
2287 5s. Type **1016** (250th birth anniv) 1·30 1·10
2288 5s.50 Paul Kitaibel (botanist, 175th death anniv) 1·40 1·20
2289 6s. Christian Doppler (physicist) (150th anniv of observation of Doppler Effect) 1·50 1·30
2290 7s. Richard Kuhn (chemist, 25th death anniv) 1·60 1·50

**1017** Angels playing Instruments

**1992.** 150th Anniv of Vienna Philharmonic Orchestra. Sheet 90×70 mm.
**MS**2291 **1017** 5s.50 black, brown and gold 2·30 2·00

**1018** First and Present Emblems

**1992.** Centenary of Railway Workers' Trade Union.
2292 **1018** 5s.50 red and black 1·30 80

**1019** Hanrieder

**1992.** 150th Birth Anniv of Norbert Hanrieder (writer).
2293 **1019** 5s.50 lilac & brown 1·40 90

**1020** Scenes from "The Birdseller" (Zeller) and "The Beggar Student" (Millocker)

**1992.** 150th Birth Anniversaries of Carl Zeller and Karl Millocker (composers).
2294 **1020** 6s. multicoloured 1·50 1·10

**1021** Foundry and Process

**1992.** Ironworks Day. 40th Anniv of First LD-Process Steel Works, Linz.
2295 **1021** 5s. multicoloured 1·30 90

**1022** Woodcut of the Americas by Sebastian Munster (from "Geographia Universalis" by Claudius Ptolomaus)

**1992.** Europa. 500th Anniv of Discovery of America by Columbus.
2296 **1022** 7s. multicoloured 6·00 1·70

**1023** Dredger

**1992.** Centenary of Treaty for International Regulation of the Rhine.
2297 **1023** 7s. multicoloured 2·00 1·30

**1024** Rieger

**1992.** Centenary of Adoption of Pseudonym Reimmichl by Sebastian Rieger (writer).
2298 **1024** 5s. brown 1·30 90

**1025** Flags and Alps

**1992.** Alpine Protection Convention.
2299 **1025** 5s.50 multicoloured 1·40 1·00

**1026** Dr. Anna Dengel

**1992.** Birth Centenary of Dr. Anna Dengel (founder of Medical Missionary Sisters).
2300 **1026** 5s.50 multicoloured 1·50 90

**1027** "R" and "H"

**1992.** Stamp Day.
2301 **1027** 7s.+3s. multicoloured 2·30 2·00

See note below No. 2266.

**1028** Town Hall

**1992.** 750th Anniv of First Documentation of Lienz as a Town.
2302 **1028** 5s. multicoloured 1·30 90

**1029** "Billroth in Lecture Room" (A. F. Seligmann)

**1992.** Austrian Surgery Society International Congress, Eisenstadt.
2303 **1029** 6s. multicoloured 1·40 1·00

**1030** Waldheim

**1992.** Presidency of Dr. Kurt Waldheim.
2304 **1030** 5s.50 black, red & grey 1·30 90

**1992.** Folk Customs and Art (2nd series). As T 1005. Multicoloured.
2305 5s. Target with figure of Zieler, Lower Austria, 1732 1·30 1·10
2306 5s.50 Chest, Carinthia 1·50 1·30
2307 7s. Votive tablet from Venser Chapel, Vorarlberg 1·60 1·50

**1031** Bridge over Canal

**1992.** Completion of Marchfeld Canal System.
2308 **1031** 5s. multicoloured 1·30 90

**1032** "The Purification of Sea Water" (Peter Pongratz)

**1992.** Austrian Modern Art.
2309 **1032** 5s.50 multicoloured 1·50 1·10

**1033** Gateway, Hofburg Palace (venue)

**1992.** 5th Int Ombudsmen's Conference, Vienna.
2310 **1033** 5s.50 multicoloured 1·30 90

**1034** Academy Seal

**1992.** 300th Anniv of Academy of Fine Arts, Vienna.
2311 **1034** 5s. blue and red 1·30 90

**1035** "The Annunciation"

**1992.** Death Bicentenary of Veit Koniger (sculptor).
2312 **1035** 5s. multicoloured 1·30 1·10

**1036** "Birth of Christ" (Johann Georg Schmidt)

**1992.** Christmas.
2313 **1036** 5s.50 multicoloured 1·40 90

**1037** Earth and Satellite

**1992.** Birth Centenary of Hermann Potocnik (alias Noordung) (space travel pioneer).
2314 **1037** 10s. multicoloured 2·30 1·70

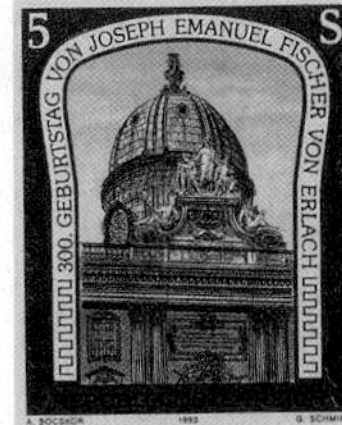

**1038** Dome of Michael Wing, Hofburg Palace, Vienna

**1993.** Architects' Anniversaries. Multicoloured.
2315 5s. Type **1038** (Joseph Emanuel Fischer von Erlach, 300th birth) 1·10 1·00
2316 5s.50 Kinsky Palace, Vienna (Johann Lukas von Hildebrandt, 325th birth) 1·20 1·10
2317 7s. State Opera House, Vienna (Eduard van der Null and August Siccard von Siccardsburg, 125th death annivs) 1·80 1·70

**1039** Emergency Vehicle's Flashing Lantern

**1993.** 25th Anniv of Radio-controlled Emergency Medical Service.
2318 **1039** 5s. multicoloured 1·20 90

**1040** Wilder Kaiser Massif, Tyrol

**1993.** Natural Beauty Spots.
2319 **1040** 6s. multicoloured 1·40 1·00

**1041** Mitterhofer Typewriter

**1993.** Death Centenary of Peter Mitterhofer (typewriter pioneer).

| | | | | |
|---|---|---|---|---|
| 2320 | **1041** | 17s. multicoloured | 4·25 | 2·75 |

**1042** "Strada del Sole" (record sleeve)

**1993.** "Austro Pop" (1st series). Rainhard Fendrich (singer).

| | | | | |
|---|---|---|---|---|
| 2321 | **1042** | 5s.50 multicoloured | 1·40 | 1·10 |

See also Nos. 2356 and 2368.

**1043** Games Emblem

**1993.** Winter Special Olympics, Salzburg and Schladming.

| | | | | |
|---|---|---|---|---|
| 2322 | **1043** | 6s.+3s. multicoloured | 3·50 | 2·00 |

**1044** Sealsfield

**1993.** Birth Bicent of Charles Sealsfield (novelist).

| | | | | |
|---|---|---|---|---|
| 2323 | **1044** | 10s. red, blue and gold | 3·50 | 1·50 |

**1045** Girl realizing her Rights

**1993.** Ratification of U.N. Convention on Children's Rights.

| | | | | |
|---|---|---|---|---|
| 2324 | **1045** | 7s. multicoloured | 1·80 | 1·10 |

**1046** "Death" (detail of sculpture, Josef Stammel), Admont Monastery, Styria

**1993.** Monasteries and Abbeys.

| | | | | |
|---|---|---|---|---|
| 2325 | - | 1s. brown, black & grn | 35 | 35 |
| 2326 | **1046** | 5s.50 black, yell & grn | 2·40 | 55 |
| 2327 | - | 6s. black, mauve & yell | 1·40 | 35 |
| 2328 | - | 7s. brown, black & grey | 2·40 | 1·50 |
| 2329 | - | 7s.50 brown, bl & blk | 2·40 | 55 |
| 2330 | - | 8s. orange, black & bl | 3·00 | 90 |
| 2331 | - | 10s. black, blue & orge | 3·25 | 1·30 |
| 2332 | - | 20s. black, blue & yell | 7·25 | 1·10 |
| 2333 | - | 26s. orange, black & bis | 7·75 | 1·10 |
| 2334 | - | 30s. red, yellow & black | 10·50 | 1·80 |

DESIGNS: 1s. The Annunciation (detail of crosier of Abbess), St. Gabriel Benedictine Abbey, Bertholdstein; 6s. St. Benedict of Nursia (glass painting), Mariastern Abbey, Gwiggen; 7s. Marble lion, Franciscan Monastery, Salzburg; 7s.50, Virgin Mary (detail of cupola painting by Paul Troger), Altenburg Monastery; 8s. Early Gothic doorway, Wilhering Monastery; 10s. "The Healing of St. Peregrinus" (altarpiece), Maria Luggau Monastery; 20s. Hartmann Crosier, St. Georgenberg Abbey, Fiecht; 26s. "Master Dolorosa" (sculpture), Franciscan Monastery, Schwaz; 30s. Madonna and Child, Monastery of the Scottish Order, Vienna.

**1047** "Flying Harlequin" (Paul Flora)

**1993.** Europa. Contemporary Art.

| | | | | |
|---|---|---|---|---|
| 2345 | **1047** | 7s. multicoloured | 4·50 | 1·10 |

**1048** Silhouette, Script and Signature

**1993.** 150th Birth Anniv of Peter Rosegger (writer and newspaper publisher).

| | | | | |
|---|---|---|---|---|
| 2346 | **1048** | 5s.50 black and green | 1·20 | 1·10 |

**1049** "Hohentwiel" (lake steamer) and Flags

**1993.** Lake Constance European Region.

| | | | | |
|---|---|---|---|---|
| 2347 | **1049** | 6s. multicoloured | 1·80 | 1·10 |

**1050** Knights in Battle and "I"s

**1993.** Stamp Day.

| | | | | |
|---|---|---|---|---|
| 2348 | **1050** | 7s.+3s. gold, black and blue | 2·20 | 2·00 |

See note below No. 2266.

**1005** Almabtrieb (driving cattle from mountain pastures) (Zell, Tyrol)

**1993.** Folk Customs and Art (3rd series). As T 1005. Multicoloured.

| | | | |
|---|---|---|---|
| 2349 | 5s. Corpus Christi Day procession, Hallstatt, Upper Austria | 1·10 | 1·00 |
| 2350 | 5s.50 Drawing the block (log), Burgenland | 1·20 | 1·10 |
| 2351 | 7s. Aperschnalzen (whipping the snow away), Salzburg | 1·60 | 1·50 |

**1051** Human Rights Emblem melting Bars

**1993.** U.N. World Conf on Human Rights, Vienna.

| | | | | |
|---|---|---|---|---|
| 2352 | **1051** | 10s. multicoloured | 2·20 | 1·50 |

**1052** Jagerstatter

**1993.** 50th Death Anniv of Franz Jagerstatter (conscientious objector).

| | | | | |
|---|---|---|---|---|
| 2353 | **1052** | 5s.50 multicoloured | 1·20 | 1·10 |

**1053** Train approaching Wolfgangsee

**1993.** Centenary of Schafberg Cog Railway.

| | | | | |
|---|---|---|---|---|
| 2354 | **1053** | 6s. multicoloured | 1·60 | 1·10 |

**1054** "Self-portrait with Doll"

**1993.** Birth Centenary of Rudolf Wacker (artist).

| | | | | |
|---|---|---|---|---|
| 2355 | **1054** | 6s. multicoloured | 1·20 | 1·10 |

**1993.** "Austro Pop" (2nd series). Ludwig Hirsch (singer and actor). As T 1042. Multicoloured.

| | | | |
|---|---|---|---|
| 2356 | 5s.50 "Die Omama" (record sleeve) | 1·40 | 1·10 |

**1055** "Concert in Dornbacher Park" (Balthasar Wigand)

**1993.** 150th Anniv of Vienna Male Choral Society.

| | | | | |
|---|---|---|---|---|
| 2357 | **1055** | 5s. multicoloured | 1·20 | 90 |

**1056** "Easter" (Max Weiler)

**1993.** Austrian Modern Art.

| | | | | |
|---|---|---|---|---|
| 2358 | **1056** | 5s.50 multicoloured | 1·20 | 90 |

**1057** "99 Heads" (detail, Friedensreich Hundertwasser)

**1993.** Council of Europe Heads of State Conference, Vienna.

| | | | | |
|---|---|---|---|---|
| 2359 | **1057** | 7s. multicoloured | 3·00 | 2·00 |

**1058** Statue of Athene, Parliament Building

**1993.** 75th Anniv of Austrian Republic.

| | | | | |
|---|---|---|---|---|
| 2360 | **1058** | 5s. multicoloured | 1·20 | 90 |

**1059** Workers

**1993.** Cent of 1st Austrian Trade Unions Congress.

| | | | | |
|---|---|---|---|---|
| 2361 | **1059** | 5s.50 multicoloured | 1·20 | 90 |

**1060** "Birth of Christ" (Krainburg Altar, Styria)

**1993.** Christmas.

| | | | | |
|---|---|---|---|---|
| 2362 | **1060** | 5s.50 multicoloured | 1·20 | 90 |

**1994.** Folk Customs and Art (4th series). As T 1005. Multicoloured.

| | | | |
|---|---|---|---|
| 2363 | 5s.50 Rocking cradle, Vorarlberg | 1·20 | 1·10 |
| 2364 | 6s. Carved sleigh, Styria | 1·40 | 1·30 |
| 2365 | 7s. Godparent's bowl and lid, Upper Austria | 1·60 | 1·50 |

**1061** Winter Sports

**1994.** Winter Olympic Games, Lillehammer, Norway.

| | | | | |
|---|---|---|---|---|
| 2366 | **1061** | 7s. multicoloured | 1·40 | 1·30 |

**1062** Early Production of Coins

**1994.** 800th Anniv of Vienna Mint.

| | | | | |
|---|---|---|---|---|
| 2367 | **1062** | 6s. multicoloured | 1·20 | 1·10 |

**1994.** "Austro Pop" (3rd series). Falco (Johann Holzel) (singer). As T 1042. Multicoloured.

| | | | |
|---|---|---|---|
| 2368 | 6s. "Rock Me Amadeus" (record sleeve) | 1·40 | 1·10 |



**1063** "Reclining Lady" (detail, Herbert Boeckl)

**1994.** Birth Centenary of Herbert Boeckl (painter).

| | | | | |
|---|---|---|---|---|
| 2369 | **1063** | 5s.50 multicoloured | 1·20 | 1·10 |

**1064** N.W. Tower of City Wall

**1994.** 800th Anniv of Wiener Neustadt.
2370 **1064** 6s. multicoloured 1·20 1·10

**1065** Lurgrotte (caves), Styria

**1994.** Natural Beauty Spots.
2371 **1065** 6s. multicoloured 1·20 1·10

**1066** Lake Rudolf (Teleki–Hohnel expedition to Africa, 1887)

**1994.** Europa. Discoveries.
2372 **1066** 7s. multicoloured 3·75 1·80

**1067** "E" and "L" as Ruins in Landscape

**1994.** Stamp Day.
2373 **1067** 7s.+3s. multicoloured 2·20 2·00
See note below No. 2266.

**1068** "Allegory of Theology, Justice, Philosophy and Medicine" (detail of fresco, National Library)

**1994.** 300th Birth Anniv of Daniel Gran (artist).
2374 **1068** 20s. multicoloured 4·75 3·25

**1069** Scene from "The Prodigal Son" (opera, Benjamin Britten)

**1994.** 25th Anniv of Carinthian Summer Festival, Ossiach and Villach.
2375 **1069** 5s.50 gold and red 1·20 1·10

**1070** Steam Locomotive and Diesel Railcar (Gailtal)

**1994.** Railway Centenaries. Multicoloured.
2376 5s.50 Type **1070** 1·40 1·30
2377 6s. Steam locomotive and diesel railcar (Murtal) 1·60 1·50

**1071** Gmeiner and Children

**1994.** 75th Birth Anniv of Hermann Gmeiner (founder of S.O.S. children's villages).
2378 **1071** 7s. multicoloured 1·40 1·30

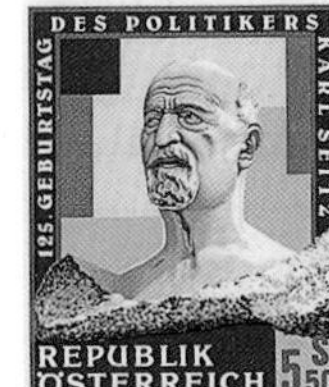


**1072** Seitz (bust, G. Ambrosi)

**1994.** 125th Birth Anniv of Karl Seitz (acting President, 1920).
2379 **1072** 5s.50 multicoloured 1·20 90

**1073** Bohm

**1994.** Birth Centenary of Karl Bohm (conductor).
2380 **1073** 7s. blue and gold 1·40 1·30

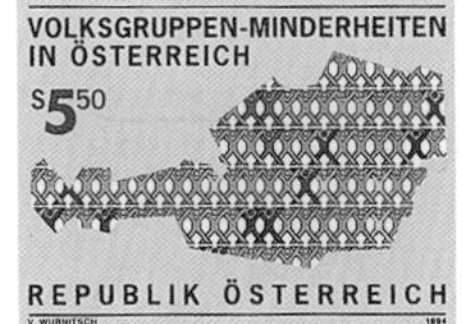


**1074** Ethnic Minorities on Map

**1994.** Legal and Cultural Protection of Ethnic Minorities.
2381 **1074** 5s.50 multicoloured 1·20 1·00

**1075** Franz Theodor Csokor (dramatist and poet)

**1994.** Writers' Anniversaries. Multicoloured.
2382 6s. Type **1075** (25th death anniv) 1·20 1·10
2383 7s. Joseph Roth (novelist, birth cent) 1·40 1·30

**1076** "Head" (Franz Ringel)

**1994.** Austrian Modern Art.
2384 **1076** 6s. multicoloured 1·40 1·10

**1077** Money Box

**1994.** 175th Anniv of Savings Banks in Austria.
2385 **1077** 7s. multicoloured 1·40 1·00

**1078** Air Hostess and Child

**1994.** Austrian World of Work (6th series).
2386 **1078** 6s. multicoloured 1·20 90

**1079** Coudenhove-Kalergi and Map of Europe

**1994.** Birth Cent of Richard Coudenhove-Kalergi (founder of Paneuropa Union).
2387 **1079** 10s. multicoloured 2·10 1·20

**1080** "Birth of Christ" (Anton Wollenek)

**1994.** Christmas.
2388 **1080** 6s. multicoloured 1·20 90

**1081** Map and Austrian and E.U. Flags

**1995.** Austria's Entry into E.U.
2389 **1081** 7s. multicoloured 1·40 90

**1082** Loos House, Michaelerplatz, Vienna

**1995.** 125th Birth Anniv of Adolf Loos (architect).
2390 **1082** 10s. multicoloured 1·90 1·50

**1083** Sporting Activities

**1995.** 50th Anniv of Austrian Gymnastics and Sports Association.
2391 **1083** 6s. multicoloured 1·20 90

**1084** Workers

**1995.** 75th Anniv of Workers' and Employees' Chambers (advisory body).
2392 **1084** 6s. multicoloured 1·20 80

**1995.** Folk Costumes and Art (5th series). As T 1005. Multicoloured.
2393 5s.50 Belt, Carinthia 1·20 1·10
2394 6s. Costume of Hiata (vineyard guard), Vienna 1·40 1·30
2395 7s. Gold bonnet, Wachau 1·60 1·50

**1085** State Seal

**1995.** 50th Anniv of Second Republic.
2396 **1085** 6s. multicoloured 1·20 90

**1086** Heft Ironworks

**1995.** Carinthian "History of Mining and Industry" Exhibition, Heft, Huttenberg.
2397 **1086** 5s.50 multicoloured 1·20 90

**1087** Hiker in Mountains

**1995.** Centenary of Friends of Nature.
2398 **1087** 5s.50 multicoloured 1·20 90

**1088** Heidenreichstein National Park

**1995.** Natural Beauty Spots.
2399 **1088** 6s. multicoloured 1·30 1·00

**1089** Woman and Barbed Wire around Skull

**1995.** Europa. Peace and Freedom.
2400 **1089** 7s. multicoloured 4·50 1·90

**1090** Map, Woman and Child and Transport

**1995.** Meeting of European Ministers of Transport Conference, Vienna.
2401 **1090** 7s. multicoloured 1·40 90

**1091** "F" and "A" on Vase of Flowers

**1995.** Stamp Day.
2402 **1091** 10s.+5s. mult 3·00 2·75
See note below No. 2266.

**1092** Set for "The Flying Dutchman"

**1995.** 50th Bregenz Festival.
2403 **1092** 6s. multicoloured 1·20 80

**1093** St. Gebhard (stained-glass window, Martin Hausle)

**1995.** Death Millenary of St. Gebhard, Bishop of Konstanz (patron saint of Vorarlberg chuches).
2404 **1093** 7s.50 multicoloured 1·40 90

**1094** Members' Flags

**1995.** 50th Anniv of U.N.O.
2405 **1094** 10s. multicoloured 2·10 1·20

**1095** Loschmidt

**1995.** Death Centenary of Josef Loschmidt (physical chemist).
2406 **1095** 20s. black, stone & brn 5·75 3·00

**1096** K. Leichter

**1995.** Birth Cent of Kathe Leichter (sociologist).
2407 **1096** 6s. cream, black & red 1·20 90

**1097** Scene from "Jedermann" (Hugo von Hofmannsthal)

**1995.** 75th Anniv of Salzburg Festival.
2408 **1097** 6s. multicoloured 1·20 90

**1098** "European Scene" (Adolf Frohner)

**1995.** Austrian Modern Art.
2409 **1098** 6s. multicoloured 1·20 90

**1099** Franz von Suppe and "The Beautiful Galatea"

**1995.** Composers' Anniversaries. Scenes from operettas. Multicoloured.
2410 6s. Type **1099** (death cent) 1·20 1·10
2411 7s. Nico Dostal and "The Hungarian Wedding" (birth centenary) 1·40 1·30

**1100** University Building

**1995.** 25th Anniv of Klagenfurt University.
2412 **1100** 5s.50 multicoloured 1·20 80

**1101** Hollenburg Castle

**1995.** 75th Anniv of Carinthian Referendum.
2413 **1101** 6s. multicoloured 1·20 80

**1102** Postman

**1995.** Austrian World of Work (7th series).
2414 **1102** 6s. multicoloured 1·20 80

**1103** Anton von Webern (50th death)

**1995.** Composers' Anniversaries.
2415 **1103** 6s. blue and orange 1·20 1·10
2416 - 7s. red and orange 1·40 1·30
DESIGN: 7s. Ludwig van Beethoven (225th birth).

**1104** Christ Child

**1995.** Christmas. 300th Anniv of Christkindl Church.
2417 **1104** 6s. multicoloured 1·20 80

**1996.** Folk Customs and Art (6th series). As T 1005.
2418 6s. multicoloured 1·30 1·20
DESIGN: 6s. Masked figures Roller and Scheller (Imst masquerades, Tyrol).

**1105** Empress Maria Theresia and Academy Building

**1996.** 250th Anniv of Theresian Academy, Vienna.
2419 **1105** 6s. multicoloured 1·30 1·20

**1106** Ski Jumping

**1996.** World Ski Jumping Championships, Tauplitz and Bad Mitterndorf.
2420 **1106** 7s. multicoloured 1·60 90

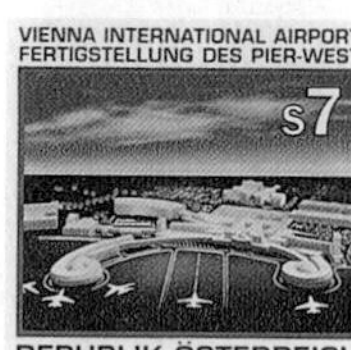


**1107** Terminal

**1996.** Completion of West Terminal, Vienna International Airport.
2421 **1107** 7s. multicoloured 1·60 90

**1108** Hohe Tauern National Park

**1996.** Natural Beauty Spots.
2422 **1108** 6s. multicoloured 1·40 80

**1109** "Mother and Child" (Peter Fendi)

**1996.** Artists' Birth Bicentenaries. Multicoloured.
2423 6s. Type **1109** 1·30 1·20
2424 7s. "Self-portrait" (Leopold Kupelwieser) 1·70 1·60

**1110** Organ and Music

**1996.** Death Cent of Anton Bruckner (composer).
2425 **1110** 5s.50 multicoloured 1·30 80

**1111** Kollmitz Castle (from copper engraving)

**1996.** 300th Death Anniv of Georg Vischer (cartographer and engraver).
2426 **1111** 10s. black and stone 2·20 1·30

**1112** Old Market Square

**1996.** 800th Anniv of Klagenfurt.
2427 **1112** 6s. multicoloured 1·60 90

**1113** Hotel Chef and Waitress

**1996.** Austrian World of Work (8th series).
2428 **1113** 6s. multicoloured 1·20 90

**1114** Paula von Preradovic (writer)

**1996.** Europa. Famous Women.
2429 **1114** 7s. stone, brown & grey 1·60 1·10

**1115** "M" and "T" and Bluebirds (mosaic)

**1996.** Stamp Day.
2430 **1115** 10s.+5s. mult 3·50 2·50
See note below No. 2266.

**1116** Mascot with Olympic Flag

**1996.** Olympic Games, Atlanta.
2431 **1116** 10s. multicoloured 2·20 1·50

**1996.** Folk Customs and Art (7th series). As T 1005.
2432 5s.50 Flower-bedecked poles, Salzburg 1·40 1·30
2433 7s. Tyrol militia 1·60 1·50

**1117** Landscape

**1996.** 75th Anniv of Burgenland.
2434 **1117** 6s. multicoloured 1·20 80

**1118** Mountaineers

**1996.** Cent of Austrian Mountain Rescue Service.
2435 **1118** 6s. multicoloured 1·20 80

**1119** Deed of Otto III, 996

**1996.** Millenary of Austria. Multicoloured.
2436 6s. Type **1119** 1·20 90
2437 6s. Archduke Joseph II (after Georg Weikert) and Archduchess Maria Theresia (after Martin van Meytens) 1·20 90
2438 7s. "Duke Heinrich II" (stained-glass window, Monastery of the Holy Cross) 1·30 1·10
2439 7s. Arms in flames (1848 Revolution) 1·30 1·10
2440 7s. Rudolf IV, the Founder 1·30 1·10
2441 7s. Karl Renner (first Federal Republic president) 1·30 1·10
2442 10s. Archduke Maximilian I (Holy Roman Emperor) (miniature from Statute Book of Order of the Golden Fleece) 2·20 1·60
2443 10s. Seal and signature of Leopold Figl (State Treaty of 1955) 2·20 1·60
2444 20s. Imperial crown of Rudolf II 4·25 3·25
2445 20s. State arms, stars of Europe and "The Horsebreaker" (bronze by Josef Lax) (Austria and Europe) 4·25 3·25

**1120** "Power Station" (Reinhard Artberg)

**1996.** Austrian Modern Art.
2446 **1120** 7s. multicoloured 1·60 1·10

**1121** Children of Different Nations

**1996.** 50th Anniv of UNICEF.
2447 **1121** 10s. multicoloured 2·20 1·30

**1122** Nativity and Vienna Town Hall

**1996.** Christmas.
2448 **1122** 6s. multicoloured 1·20 90

**1123** Kramer

**1997.** Birth Centenary of Theodor Kramer (poet).
2449 **1123** 5s.50 blue 1·20 80

**1997.** Folk Customs and Art (8th series). As T 1005. Multicoloured.
2450 7s. Epiphany carol singers, Eisenstadt Burgenland 1·60 1·50

**1124** Vineyards on the Nussberg, Vienna

**1997.** Natural Beauty Spots.
2451 **1124** 6s. multicoloured 1·30 90

**1125** Academy and Light

**1997.** 150th Anniv of Austrian Academy of Sciences, Vienna.
2452 **1125** 10s. multicoloured 2·30 1·30

**1126** Emblem

**1997.** 50th Anniv of Verbund Electricity Company.
2453 **1126** 6s. multicoloured 1·20 90

**1127** The Cruel Rosalia of Forchtenstein

**1997.** Myths and Legends.
2454 - 6s.50 grn, pink & blk 2·20 90
2455 **1127** 7s. black, stone & brn 2·40 65
2456 - 8s. orange, blk & lilac 2·20 1·10
2457 - 9s. black, stone & pur 3·00 1·70
2458 - 10s. black, grey & red 3·50 2·00
2459 - 13s. black, brn & pur 4·25 2·20
2460 - 14s. black, lt blue & bl 4·25 1·90
2461 - 20s. green, blk & stone 6·00 2·75
2462 - 22s. black, bl & stone 5·50 4·50
2463 - 23s. black, ochre and green 7·75 5·00
2464 - 25s. stone, black and yellow 7·25 3·25
2465 - 32s. black, brn & pink 11·00 5·50

DESIGNS: 6s.50, Lindworm of Klagenfurt; 8s. The Black Lady of Hardegg; 9s. Charming Augustin; 10s. Basilisk of Vienna; 13s. The Pied Piper of Korneuburg; 14s. The Strudengau Water-nymph; 20s. St. Notburga; 22s. Witches Whirl; 23s. Loaf Agony; 25s. St. Konrad and Altems Castle; 32s. The Discovery of Erzberg (Mountain of Ore).

**1128** Stage Set for "Die tote Stadt"

**1997.** Birth Cent of Erich Korngold (composer).
2470 **1128** 20s. black, blue & gold 5·75 2·75

**1129** Stadium, Badge and Players

**1997.** Rapid Vienna, National Football Champions, 1995–96.
2471 **1129** 7s. multicoloured 1·80 90

**1130** Red Deer

**1997.** Hunting and the Environment. Deer Feeding in Winter.
2472 **1130** 7s. multicoloured 1·60 90

**1131** Canisius and Children (altar by Josef Bachlechner in Innsbruck Seminary)

**1997.** 400th Death Anniv of St. Petrus Canisius (patron saint of Innsbruck).
2473 **1131** 7s.50 multicoloured 1·60 90

**1132** Johannes Brahms (after L. Michalek)

**1997.** Composers' Anniversaries.
2474 **1132** 6s. violet and gold 1·30 1·20
2475 - 10s. purple and gold 2·30 2·10

DESIGNS: 6s. Type **1132** (death centenary); 10s. Franz Schubert (birth bicentenary).

**1133** "A" and "E"

**1997.** Stamp Day.
2476 **1133** 7s. multicoloured 1·80 1·10
See note below No. 2266.

**1134** The Four Friends

**1997.** Europa. Tales and Legends. "The Town Band of Bremen" by the Brothers Grimm.
2477 **1134** 7s. multicoloured 4·25 1·10

**1135** 1850 9k. Stamp and Postman

**1997.** "WIPA 2000" International Stamp Exhibition, Vienna (1st issue).
2478 **1135** 27s.+13s. mult 9·00 6·75
See also Nos. 2521, 2543, **MS**2551 and **MS**2564.

**1136** Train on Hochschneeberg Line

**1997.** Railway Anniversaries. Multicoloured.
2479 6s. Type **1136** (centenary of Hochschneeberg rack-railway) 1·40 1·30
2480 7s.50 Steam locomotive "Licaon" and viaduct near Mattersburg (150th anniv of Odenburg–Wiener Neustadt line) 1·90 1·80

**1137** Cogwheels

**1997.** 125th Anniv of Austrian Technical Supervisory Association.
2481 **1137** 7s. multicoloured 1·70 90

**1997.** Folk Customs and Art (9th series). As T 1005. Multicoloured.
2482 6s.50 Tyrolean brass band 1·60 1·10

**1138** Waggerl (self-portrait)

**1997.** Birth Centenary of Karl Waggerl (writer).
2483 **1138** 7s. green, yellow & blue 1·70 90

**1139** Adolf Lorenz (founder of German Society of Orthopaedia)

**1997.** Orthopaedics Congress, Vienna.
2484 **1139** 8s. multicoloured 1·80 1·10

**1140** Emblem

**1997.** 125th Anniv of College of Agricultural Sciences, Vienna.
2485 **1140** 9s. multicoloured 2·10 1·30

**1141** Patient, Nurse and Doctor

**1997.** Austrian World of Work (9th series).
2486 **1141** 6s.50 multicoloured 1·40 90

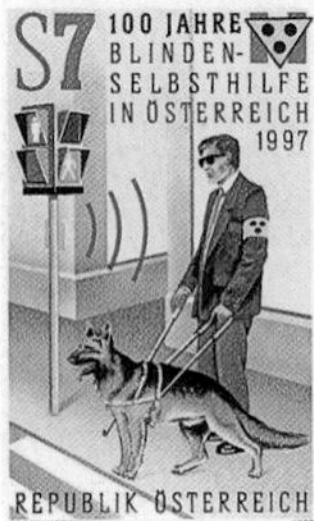


**1142** Blind Man with Guide Dog

**1997.** Cent of Austrian Association for the Blind.
2487 **1142** 7s. multicoloured 1·60 90

**1143** "House in Wind" (Helmut Schickhofer)

**1997.** Austrian Modern Art.
2488 **1143** 7s. multicoloured 1·80 1·10

**1144** Klestil

**1997.** 65th Birthday of Pres. Thomas Klestil.
2489 **1144** 7s. multicoloured 1·80 90

**1145** Werner

**1997.** 75th Birth Anniv of Oskar Werner (actor).
2490 **1145** 7s. black, orge & grey 1·80 90

**1997.** Folk Customs and Art (10th series). As T 1005. Multicoloured.
2491 6s.50 Tower wind-band, Upper Austria 1·40 1·10

**1146** Glowing Light

**1997.** 25th Anniv of Light in Darkness (umbrella organization of children's charities).
2492 **1146** 7s. blue 1·60 90

**1147** "Mariazell Madonna"

**1997.** Christmas.
2493 **1147** 7s. multicoloured 1·60 90

**1148** Kalkalpen National Park

**1998.** Natural Beauty Spots.
2494 **1148** 7s. multicoloured 1·40 90

**1149** Courting Pair

**1998.** Hunting and the Environment. Preservation of Breeding Habitat of the Black Grouse.
2495 **1149** 9s. multicoloured 1·80 1·30

**1150** Ice Skaters

**1998.** Winter Olympic Games, Nagano, Japan.
2496 **1150** 14s. multicoloured 2·75 2·00

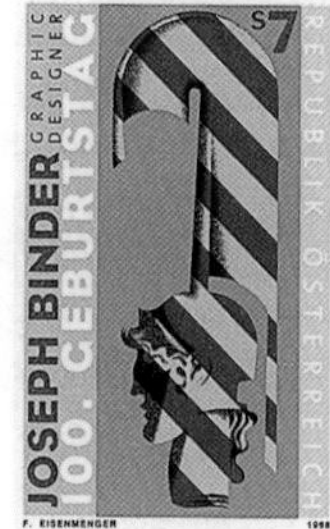


**1151** Austrian Poster Exposition Advertising Poster, 1928

**1998.** Birth Cent of Joseph Binder (designer).
2497 **1151** 7s. multicoloured 1·60 1·10

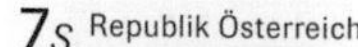

**1152** Alois Senefelder (inventor) on Lithographic Stone

**1998.** Bicentenary of Invention of Lithography (printing process).
2498 **1152** 7s. blue, yellow & black 1·40 90

**1153** Facade

**1998.** Centenary of Vienna Secession (exn hall).
2499 **1153** 8s. brown, gold & blue 1·80 1·10

**1998.** Folk Customs and Art (11th series). As T 1005. Multicoloured.
2500 6s.50 Fiacre, Vienna 1·40 1·30
2501 7s. Palm Sunday procession, Thaur, Tyrol 1·60 1·50

**1154** Player and Team Emblem

**1998.** Austria Memphis Football Club.
2502 **1154** 7s. multicoloured 1·80 1·00

**1155** "St. Florian" (glass painting)

**1998.** St. Florian, Patron Saint of Firemen.
2503 **1155** 7s. multicoloured 1·80 1·00

**1156** Rupertus Cross

**1998.** 1200th Anniv of Salzburg Archdiocese.
2504 **1156** 7s. multicoloured 1·80 1·00

**1157** Series Yv Locomotive No. 2, 1895

**1998.** Centenary of Completion of Ybbs Valley Railway.
2505 **1157** 6s.50 multicoloured 1·80 1·10

**1158** "Tyrolia" (Ferdinand Cosandier)

**1998.** 175th Anniv of Tyrol Ferdinandeum (state museum), Innsbruck.
2506 **1158** 7s. multicoloured 1·60 1·00

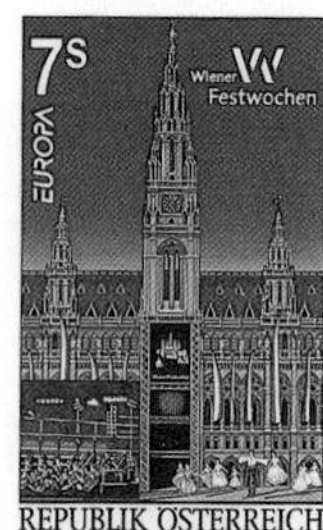


**1159** Vienna Town Hall (Viennese festive weeks)

**1998.** Europa. National Festivals.
2507 **1159** 7s. multicoloured 4·00 1·10

**1998.** Folk Customs and Art (12th series). As T 1005. Multicoloured.
2508 6s.50 Samson and the dwarves, Salzburg 1·80 1·10

25. TODESTAG DER LYRIKERIN CHRISTINE LAVANT
S7
REPUBLIK ÖSTERREICH

**1160** Christine Lavant

**1998.** 25th Death Anniv of Christine Lavant (poet).
2509 **1160** 7s. multicoloured 1·80 1·10

**1161** Electric Railcar No. 1

**1998.** Centenary of Postlingberg Railway.
2510 **1161** 6s.50 multicoloured 1·80 1·10

**1162** "R" and "L"

**1998.** Stamp Day.
2511 **1162** 7s. multicoloured 1·80 1·10
See note below No. 2266.

**1163** Presidency Emblem

**1998.** Austrian Presidency of E.U.
2512 **1163** 7s. multicoloured 1·80 1·10

**1164** Railcar No. 5090

**1998.** Centenary of Pinzgau Railway.
2513 **1164** 6s.50 multicoloured 1·80 1·10

**1165** Volksoper, Vienna

**1998.** Centenary of Volksoper (theatre) and 50th Death Anniv of Franz Lehar (composer).
2514 **1165** 6s.50 multicoloured 1·60 1·10

**1166** Empress Elisabeth (after Franz Winterhalter)

**1998.** Death Centenary of Empress Elisabeth.
2515 **1166** 7s. multicoloured 1·80 1·50

**1167** School Building

**1998.** Centenary of Vienna Business School.
2516 **1167** 7s. multicoloured 1·80 1·50

**1168** Kudlich and Farmers

**1998.** 175th Birth Anniv of Hans Kudlich (promoter of 1848 "Peasants' Liberation" Law).
2517 **1168** 6s.50 multicoloured 1·60 1·00

**1169** "My Garden" (Hans Staudacher)

**1998.** Austrian Modern Art.
2518 **1169** 7s. multicoloured 1·80 1·10

**1170** Town Hall and Arms

**1998.** 350th Anniv of Declaration of Eisenstadt as a Free Town.
2519 **1170** 7s. multicoloured 1·60 1·10

**1171** Photographer and Reporter

**1998.** Austrian World of Work (10th series). Art, Media and Freelances.
2520 **1171** 6s.50 multicoloured 1·40 1·00

**1172** 1929 2s. Stamp and Post Van

**1998.** "WIPA 2000" International Stamp Exhibition, Vienna (2nd issue).
2521 **1172** 32s.+13s. mult 9·75 7·75

**1173** "Nativity" (fresco, Tainach Church)

**1998.** Christmas.
2522 **1173** 7s. multicoloured 1·40 1·00

**1174** Cross-country Skiing

**1999.** World Nordic Skiing Championships, Ramsau.
2523 **1174** 7s. multicoloured 1·80 1·20

**1999.** Folk Customs and Art (13th series). As T 1005. Multicoloured.
2524 6s.50 Walking pilgrimage to Mariazell 1·40 1·10

**1175** Stingl Rock, Bohemian Forest

**1999.** Natural Beauty Spots.
2525 **1175** 7s. multicoloured 1·40 1·10

**1176** Books and Compact Disc

**1999.** Centenary of Austrian Patent Office.
2526 **1176** 7s. multicoloured 1·40 1·10

**1177** Player and Club Emblem

**1999.** SK Puntigamer Sturm Graz Football Club.
2527 **1177** 7s. multicoloured 1·80 1·10

**1178** Palace Facade

**1999.** World Heritage Site. Schonbrunn Palace, Vienna.
2528 **1178** 13s. multicoloured 2·75 2·20

**1179** Partridges

**1999.** Hunting and the Environment. Living Space for Grey Partridges.
2529 **1179** 6s.50 multicoloured 1·40 1·10

**1180** Snowboarder

**1999.** 50th Anniv of Austrian General Sport Federation.
2530 **1180** 7s. multicoloured 1·60 1·10

**1181** Council Building, Strasbourg

**1999.** 50th Anniv of Council of Europe.
2531 **1181** 14s. multicoloured 3·00 2·20
No. 2531 is denominated both in Austrian schillings and in euros.

**1182** Steyr Type 50 Baby Saloon

**1999.** Birth Centenary of Karl Jenschke (engineer and car manufacturer).
2532 **1182** 7s. multicoloured 1·60 1·20

**1183** "St. Martin" (marble relief, Peuerbach Church)

**1999.** Ancient Arts and Crafts (1st series).
2533 **1183** 8s. brown, blue & orange 1·80 1·30
See also Nos. 2542, 2575, 2600 and 2602.

**1184** Symbols of Aid and Emblem

**1999.** 125th Anniv of Diakonie (professional charitable services).
2534 **1184** 7s. multicoloured 1·40 1·10

**1185** Johann Strauss, the Younger

**1999.** Composers' Death Anniversaries. Mult.
2535 7s. Type **1185** (centenary) 1·70 1·60
2536 8s. Johann Strauss, the Elder (150th anniv) 1·80 1·70

**1186** Rural Gendarmes

**1999.** 150th Anniv of National Gendarmerie.
2537 **1186** 7s. multicoloured 1·60 1·10

**1187** Donau-auen National Park

**1999.** Europa. Parks and Gardens.
2538 **1187** 7s. multicoloured 1·80 1·10

1188 "K" and "I"

1999. Stamp Day.
2539 **1188** 7s. multicoloured 1·80 1·10
See note below No. 2266.

1189 Iron Stage Curtain

1999. Centenary of Graz Opera.
2540 **1189** 6s.50 multicoloured 1·80 1·10

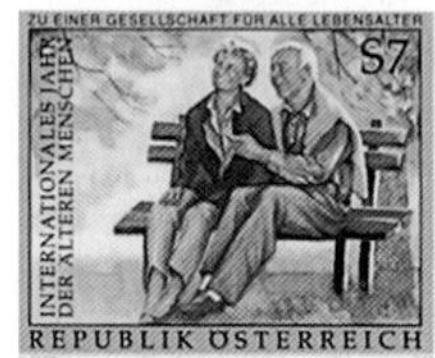
1190 Couple on Bench

1999. International Year of the Elderly.
2541 **1190** 7s. multicoloured 1·40 1·10

1191 "St. Anne with Mary and Child Jesus" (wood-carving, St. George's Church, Purgg)

1999. Ancient Arts and Crafts (2nd series).
2542 **1191** 9s. multicoloured 2·20 2·00

1192 1949 25g. Stamp and Vienna Airport

1999. "WIPA 2000" International Stamp Exhibition, Vienna (3rd issue).
2543 **1192** 32s.+16s. mult 11·50 8·50

1193 "Security throughout Life"

1999. 14th Congress of Federation of Austrian Trade Unions.
2544 **1193** 6s.50 multicoloured 1·40 1·10

1194 "Cafe Girardi" (Wolfgang Herzig)

1999. Austrian Modern Art.
2545 **1194** 7s. multicoloured 1·80 1·10

1999. Folk Customs and Art (14th series). As T 1005. Multicoloured.
2546 8s. Pumpkin Festival, Lower Austria 1·80 1·10

1999. Folk Customs and Art (15th series). As T 1005. Multicoloured.
2547 7s. The Pummerin (great bell of St. Stephen's Cathedral) ringing in the New Year 1·80 1·10

1195 Institute and Fossils

1999. 150th Anniv of National Institute of Geology.
2548 **1195** 7s. multicoloured 1·80 1·10

1196 "Nativity" (altar painting, Pinkafeld Church)

1999. Christmas.
2549 **1196** 7s. multicoloured 1·40 1·10

2000. Folk Customs and Art (16th series). As T 1005. Multicoloured.
2550 7s. Chapel procession, Carinthia 1·40 1·30

2000. "WIPA 2000" International Stamp Exhibition, Vienna (4th issue). Sheet 150×95 mm.
**MS**2551 27s.+13s. No. 2478; 32s.+13s. No. 2521; 32s.+16s. No. 2543 36·00 39·00

2000. Folk Customs and Art (17th series). As T 1005. Multicoloured.
2552 6s.50 Three men wearing masks (Cavalcade of Beautiful Masks, Telfs) 1·40 1·10

1197 *Zantadeschica aethiopica*

2000. International Garden Show, Graz.
2553 **1197** 7s. multicoloured 1·80 1·10

1198 Ibex

2000. Hunting and the Environment. Return of Ibex to Austrian Mountains.
2554 **1198** 7s. multicoloured 1·60 1·10

1199 Players

2000. F.C. Tirol Innsbruck, National Football Champion 2000.
2555 **1199** 7s. multicoloured 1·60 1·10

1200 Mt. Grossglockner and Viewing Point

2000. Bicentenary of First Ascent of Mt. Grossglockner.
2556 **1200** 7s. multicoloured 1·60 1·10

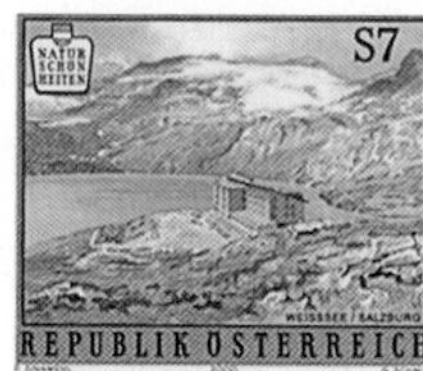
1201 Weisssee Lake

2000. Natural Beauty Spots.
2557 **1201** 7s. multicoloured 1·40 1·20

1202 "Building Europe"

2000. Europa.
2558 **1202** 7s. multicoloured 1·80 1·70

1203 Junkers F13 Airplane and Air Traffic Control Tower

2000. 75th Anniv of Civil Aviation at Klagenfurt Airport.
2559 **1203** 7s. multicoloured 1·40 1·30

1204 Madonna of Altenmarkt (statue) and Glass Roof, Palm House, Burggarten, Vienna

2000. 150th Anniv of Protection of Historic Monuments.
2560 **1204** 8s. multicoloured 1·80 1·50

1205 Illuminated Letter and Text

2000. Life of St. Malachy (treatise) by St. Bernard of Clairvaux.
2561 **1205** 9s. multicoloured 2·40 2·20

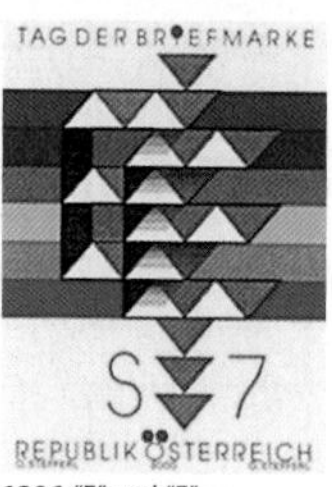
1206 "E" and "E"

2000. Stamp Day.
2562 **1206** 7s. multicoloured 1·80 1·30
See note below No. 2266.

1207 1850 9 Kreuzer and 2000 Stamp Day Stamps

2000. 150th Anniv of Austrian Stamps.
2563 **1207** 7s. multicoloured 1·80 1·30

2000. "WIPA 2000" International Stamp Exhibition, Vienna (5th series). Sheet 65×90 mm.
**MS**2564 10s. As No. 2458 36·00 34·00

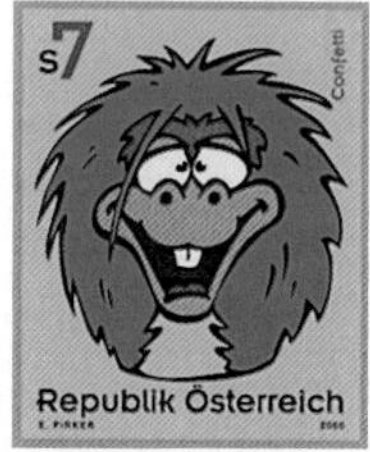
1208 "Confetti"

2000. Confetti (children's television programme).
2565 **1208** 7s. multicoloured 1·60 1·30

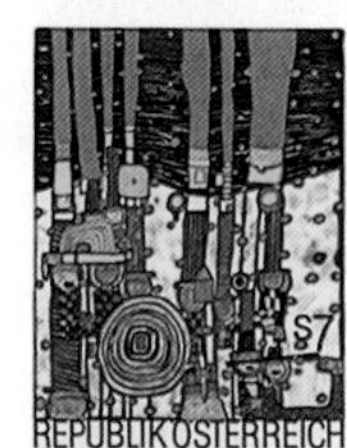
1209 "Blue Blues"

2000. Death Commemoration of Friedensreich Hundertwasser (artist). Sheet 129×126 mm, containing four versions of T 1209 identified by the colours of the vertical strips at the top of the design.
**MS**2566 7s. silver; 7s. red; 7s. mauve; 7s. black 9·75 9·00

1210 Blood Droplets

2000. Centenary of Discovery of Blood Groups by Karl Landsteiner (pathologist).
2567 **1210** 8s. pink, silver & black 1·60 1·50

1211 Daimler Cannstatter Bus

2000. Centenary of First Regular Bus Route between Purkersdorf and Gablitz.
2568 **1211** 9s. black, blue and light blue 2·40 2·00

2000. Folk Customs and Art (18th series). As T 1005. Multicoloured.
2569 7s. Men on raft (International Rafting Meeting, Carinthia) 1·40 1·30

**1212** Dachstein River and Hallstatt

**2000.** Natural Beauty Spots.
2570 **1212** 7s. multicoloured 1·40 1·30

**1213** String Instrument and Emblem

**2000.** Centenary of Vienna Symphony Orchestra.
2571 **1213** 7s. multicoloured 1·40 1·30

**1214** Dinghies

**2000.** Olympic Games, Sydney.
2572 **1214** 9s. multicoloured 2·20 1·80

**1215** Old and Modern Paper Production Methods

**2000.** Austrian World of Work (11th series). Printing and Paper.
2573 **1215** 6s.50 multicoloured 1·40 1·30

**1216** "Turf Turkey" (Ida Szigethy)

**2000.** Austrian Modern Art.
2574 **1216** 7s. multicoloured 1·40 1·30

**1217** Codex 965 (National Library)

**2000.** Ancient Arts and Crafts (3rd series).
2575 **1217** 8s. multicoloured 1·80 1·70

See also Nos. 2600 and 2602.

**1218** Child receiving Vaccination

**2000.** Bicentenary of Vaccination in Austria.
2576 **1218** 7s. black and cinnamon 1·40 1·30

**1219** Urania Building, Vienna

**2000.** 50th Anniv of Adult Education Association.
2577 **1219** 7s. brown, grey & gold 1·40 1·30

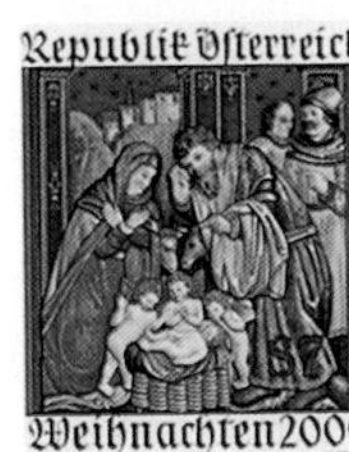


**1220** The Nativity (altar piece, Ludesch Church)

**2000.** Christmas.
2578 **1220** 7s. multicoloured 1·40 1·30

**1221** Downhill Skier

**2000.** World Skiing Championship (2001), St. Anton am Arlberg.
2579 **1221** 7s. multicoloured 1·60 1·50

**1222** Pair of Mallards

**2001.** Hunting and the Environment. Protection of Wetlands.
2580 **1222** 7s. multicoloured 1·60 1·50

**2001.** Folk Customs and Art (19th series). As T 1005. Multicoloured.
2581 8s. Boat mill, Mureck, Styria 1·80 1·50

**1223** Steam Locomotive No. 3

**2001.** Centenary of Zillertal Railway.
2582 **1223** 7s. multicoloured 1·60 1·50

**1224** Players and Club Emblem

**2001.** SV Casino Salzburg, National Football Champion.
2583 **1224** 7s. multicoloured 1·80 1·30

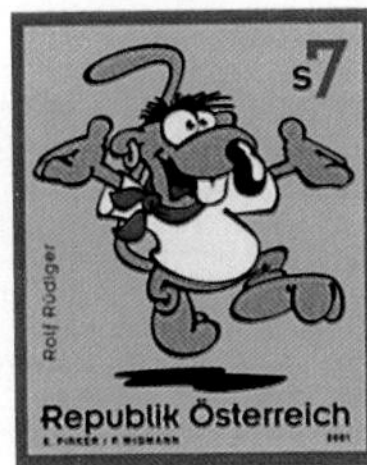


**1225** Rolf Rudiger

**2001.** Confetti (children's television programme).
2584 **1225** 7s. multicoloured 1·80 1·30

**1226** Fieseler Fi-156 Storch and Airport

**2001.** 75th Anniv of Salzburg Airport.
2585 **1226** 14s. multicoloured 3·25 2·75

**1227** Baerenschuetz Gorge

**2001.** Natural Beauty Spots.
2586 **1227** 7s. multicoloured 1·60 1·50

**2001.** Folk Customs and Art (20th series). As T 1005. Multicoloured.
2587 7s. Lent season cloth from Eastern Tyrol 1·60 1·50

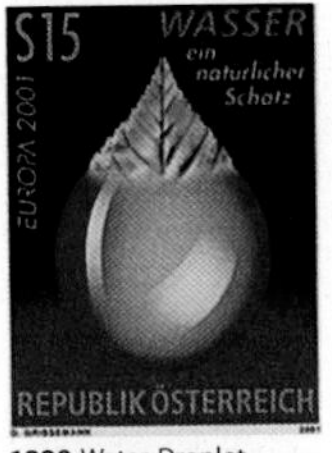


**1228** Water Droplet

**2001.** Europa. Water Resources.
2588 **1228** 15s. multicoloured 4·75 3·25

**1229** Post Office Railway Car

**2001.** Stamp Day.
2589 **1229** 20s.+10s. mult 11·00 10·00

**1230** Air Balloon

**2001.** Centenary of Austrian Flying Club.
2590 **1230** 7s. multicoloured 1·80 1·50

**1231** Refugee

**2001.** 50th Anniv of United Nations High Commissioner for Refugees.
2591 **1231** 21s. multicoloured 4·75 4·50

**1232** Kalte Rinne Viaduct

**2001.** UNESCO World Heritage Site. The Semmering Railway.
2592 **1232** 35s. multicoloured 11·00 10·00

**1233** "Seppl" (mascot) (Michelle Schneeweiss)

**2001.** 7th International Hiking Olympics, Seefeld.
2593 **1233** 7s. multicoloured 1·60 1·50

**1234** Field Post Office at Famagusta

**2001.** Army Postal Services Abroad.
2594 **1234** 7s. multicoloured 1·60 1·50

**2001.** Folk Customs and Art (21st series). As T 1005. Multicoloured.
2595 7s. Rifle and Clubhouse, Preberschiessen, Salzburg (Rifleman's gathering) 1·60 1·50

**1235** "Taurus" (Railway Engine)

**2001.** Conversion of East–West Railway to Four-tracked Railway.
2596 **1235** 7s. multicoloured 1·80 1·70

**1236** 19th-century Theatrical Scene

**2001.** Birth Bicentenary of Johann Nestroy (playwright and actor).
2597 **1236** 7s. multicoloured 1·60 1·50

**1237** "The Continents" (detail Helmut Leherb)

**2001.** Austrian Modern Art.
2598 **1237** 7s. multicoloured 1·60 1·50

**1238** "False Friends" (Von Fuehrich)

**2001.** 125th Death Anniv of Joseph Ritter von Fuehrich (artist and engraver).
2599 **1238** 8s. deep green & green 1·70 1·60

**1239** Pluviale (embroidered religious robe)

**2001.** Ancient Arts and Crafts (4th series).
2600 **1239** 10s. multicoloured 2·40 2·20

**1240** Dobler

**2001.** Birth Bicentenary of Leopold Ludwig Dobler (magician and inventor).
2601 **1240** 7s. multicoloured 1·60 1·50

**1241** Dalmatik (religious vestment) (Carmelite Monastery, Silbergrasse, Vienna)

**2001.** Ancient Arts and Crafts (5th series).
2602 **1241** 7s. multicoloured 1·60 1·50

**1242** Building and Scientific Equipment

**2001.** 150th Anniv of the Central Institute for Meteorology and Geodynamics, Vienna.
2603 **1242** 12s. multicoloured 3·00 2·20

**1243** Cat

**2001**
2604 **1243** 19s. multicoloured 6·00 5·50

**1244** Civil Servants

**2001.** Austrian World of Work (12th series). Civil Service.
2605 **1244** 7s. multicoloured 1·60 1·50

**1245** Figure of Infant Jesus

**2001.** Christmas. Glass Shrine, Fitzmoos Church.
2606 **1245** 7s. multicoloured 1·40 1·30

**New Currency**

**1246** House of the Basilisk, Vienna

**2002.** Tourism.

| | | | | |
|---|---|---|---|---|
| 2607 | - | 4c. multicoloured | 25 | 10 |
| 2608 | - | 7c. blue and black | 35 | 20 |
| 2609 | - | 13c. multicoloured | 50 | 35 |
| 2610 | - | 17c. violet and black | 60 | 45 |
| 2611 | - | 20c. multicoloured | 70 | 65 |
| 2612 | - | 25c. multicoloured | 85 | 80 |
| 2613 | - | 27c. blue and black | 95 | 90 |
| 2614 | - | 45c. multicoloured | 1·20 | 1·10 |
| 2615 | **1246** | 51c. multicoloured | 1·40 | 1·30 |
| 2616 | - | 55c. multicoloured | 1·40 | 1·20 |
| 2617 | - | 58c. multicoloured | 1·60 | 1·50 |
| 2618 | - | 73c. multicoloured | 1·80 | 1·70 |
| 2619 | - | 75c. multicoloured | 2·10 | 1·80 |
| 2620 | - | 87c. multicoloured | 2·40 | 2·20 |
| 2621 | - | €1 multicoloured | 2·75 | 2·20 |
| 2622 | - | €1.25 multicoloured | 3·25 | 2·50 |
| 2623 | - | €2.03 multicoloured | 6·00 | 5·50 |
| 2626 | - | €3.75 multicoloured | 9·25 | 8·50 |

DESIGNS: 4c. As No. 2615; 7c. As No. 2623; 13c. As No. 2620; 17c. As No. 2617; 20c. Yachts, Worthersee, Carintha; 25c. Crucifixes on rock, Mondsee, Upper Austria; 27c. As No. 2618; 45c. Snow covered chalet, Jungholz, Kleinwasler; 55c. Gothic houses, Steyr, Upper Austria; 58c. Wine cellars, Hadres, Lower Austria; 73c. Alpine chalet, Salzburg; 75c. Boat on Bodensee, Voralberg; 87c. Alpach Valley, Tyrol; €1 Farmhouse, Rossegg, Styria; €1.25 Wine press building, Eisenburg, Burgenland; €2.03 Heligenkreuz, Lower Austria; €3.75 Gothic shrine, Hochhosterwitz, Carinthia.

**1247** Stars, Map of Europe and €1 Coin

**2002.** Euro Currency.
2630 **1247** €3.27 multicoloured 9·75 9·00
No. 2630 is printed on the back under the gum with examples of Austrian schilling coins.

**1248** Skiers and Olympic Rings

**2002.** Winter Olympic Games, Salt Lake City, U.S.A.
2631 **1248** 73c. multicoloured 2·20 2·00

**1249** Bouquet of Flowers

**2002**
2632 **1249** 87c. multicoloured 2·30 2·10

**1250** Woman and Skyline

**2002.** Women's Day.
2633 **1250** 51c. multicoloured 3·50 3·25

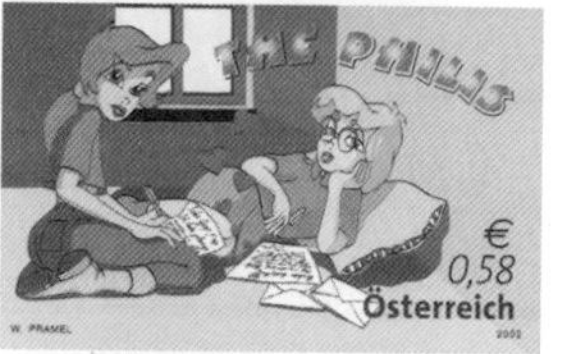

**1251** Mel and Lucy

**2002.** "Philis" (children's stamp awareness programme) (1st issue).
2634 **1251** 58c. multicoloured 2·20 2·00
See also Nos. 2639 and 2662.

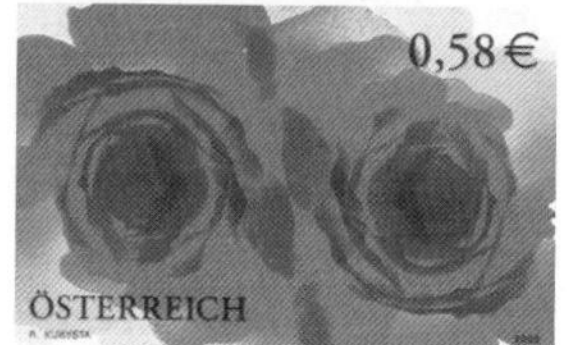

**1252** Red Roses

**2002.** Greetings Stamp.
2635 **1252** 58c. multicoloured 1·80 1·70

**1253** Kubin

**2002.** 125th Birth Anniv of Alfred Kubin (artist).
2636 **1253** 87c. black and buff 2·30 2·10

**1254** St. Elizabeth of Thuringia and Sick Man

**2002.** Caritas (Catholic charity organization).
2637 **1254** 51c. multicoloured 1·90 1·80

**1255** Tiger, Clown and Circus Tent

**2002.** Europa. The Circus.
2638 **1255** 87c. multicoloured 3·50 3·25

**1256** Sisko and Mauritius

**2002.** "Philis" (children's stamp awareness programme) (2nd issue).
2639 **1256** 58c. multicoloured 1·90 1·80

**1257** The Nativity

**2002.** 800th Anniv of Lilienfeld Abbey.
2640 **1257** €2.03 multicoloured 5·75 5·50

**1258** Mimi

**2002.** Confetti (children's television programme).
2641 **1258** 51c. multicoloured 1·80 1·70

**1259** Railway Carriage, 1919

**2002.** Stamp Day.
2642 **1259** €1.60+80c. multicoloured 8·50 7·75

**1260** Cheetah, Zebra and Orang-utan

**2002.** 250th Anniv of Schonbrunn Zoo. Mult.

| | | | |
|---|---|---|---|
| 2643 | 51c. Type **1260** | 1·70 | 1·60 |
| 2644 | 58c. Gulls, flamingos and pelicans | 1·80 | 1·70 |
| 2645 | 87c. Lion, turtle and crocodile | 2·40 | 2·20 |
| 2646 | €1.38 Elephant, birds and fish | 3·50 | 3·25 |

Nos. 2643/6 were issued together, se-tenant, forming a composite design.

**1261** Teddy Bears

**2002.** Centenary of the Teddy Bear.
2647 **1261** 51c. multicoloured 1·90 1·80

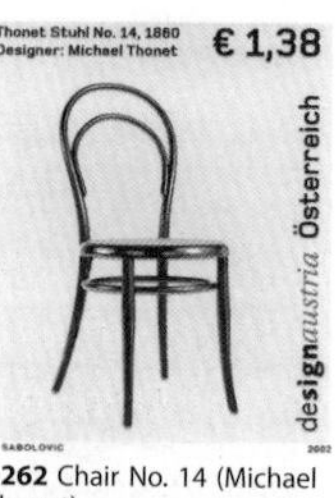

**1262** Chair No. 14 (Michael Thonet)

**2002.** 75th Anniv of "Design Austria" (design group) (1st issue).
2648 **1262** €1.38 multicoloured 3·50 3·25
See also Nos. 2661 and 2670.

**1263** Crystal Cup

**2002.** Ancient Arts and Crafts.
2649 **1263** €1.60 multicoloured 4·25 4·00

**1264** Museum Buildings

**2002.** Museumsquartier (MQ), Messepalast, Vienna.
2650 **1264** 58c. multicoloured 2·20 2·00

**1265** Figures supporting Emblem

**2002.** 50th Anniv of Union of Austrians Abroad.
2651 **1265** €2.47 multicoloured 6·75 6·25

**1266** Clown Doctor

**2002.** "Rote Nasen" (Red Noses (charity)).
2652 **1266** 51c. multicoloured 1·80 1·70

**1267** Head

**2002.** Linzer Klangwolke (sound and light performance), Linz.
2653 **1267** 58c. multicoloured 1·90 1·80

**1268** Graf & Stift Typ 40/45

**2002**
2654 **1268** 51c. multicoloured 1·60 1·50

**1269** Dog

**2002**
2655 **1269** 51c. multicoloured 1·60 1·50

**1270** Steam Locomotive 109

**2002**
2656 **1270** 51c. multicoloured 1·80 1·70

**1271** "Schutzenhaus" (Karl Goldammer)

**2002.** Austrian Modern Art.
2657 **1271** 51c. multicoloured 1·80 1·70

**1272** Lottery Ball

**2002.** 250th Anniv of Austrian Lottery. Sheet 72×90 mm.
**MS**2658 **1272** 87c. multicoloured 3·00 2·75

**1273** Thayatal National Park

**2002**
2659 **1273** 58c. multicoloured 1·80 1·70

**1274** Puch 175 SV

**2002**
2660 **1274** 58c. multicoloured 1·90 1·80

**1275** "Eye"

**2002.** 75th Anniv of "Design Austria" (design group) (2nd issue). Winning Entry in Design Competition.
2661 **1275** €1.38 multicoloured 4·25 4·00

**1276** Edison and Gogo

**2002.** "Philis" (children's stamp awareness programme) (3rd issue).
2662 **1276** 58c. multicoloured 2·20 2·00

**1277** Crib Aureola, Thaur, Tyrol

**2002.** Christmas.
2663 **1277** 51c. multicoloured 1·60 1·50

**1278** Emblem

**2003.** Make-up Rate Stamp.
2664 **1278** 45c. yellow, silver and black 6·75 4·50

**1279** Amphitheatre on River Mur

**2003.** Graz, Cultural Capital of Europe, 2003.
2665 **1279** 58c. multicoloured 1·80 1·70

**1280** Billy Wilder

**2003.** 1st Death Anniv of Billy Wilder (film director).
2666 **1280** 58c. multicoloured 1·90 1·80

**1281** Heart, Linked Rings and Doves

**2003.** Greetings Stamp. Wedding.
2667 **1281** 58c. multicoloured 1·90 1·80

**1282** Kasperl

**2003.** Confetti (children's television programme). 45th Anniv of Kasperl (puppet).
2668 **1282** 51c. multicoloured 1·60 1·50

**1283** Emblem

**2003.** 10th Anniv of Recycling Enterprise.
2669 **1283** 55c. multicoloured 1·40 1·30

**1284** Carafe and Glasses (Adolf Loos)

**2003.** 75th Anniv of "Design Austria" (design group) (3rd issue).
2670 **1284** €1.38 blue, black and orange 3·50 3·25

**1285** Seated Pandas

**2003.** Schönbrunn Zoo's Acquisition of Pandas from People's Republic of China. Sheet 110×76 mm containing T 1285 and similar multicoloured design.
**MS**2671 75c. Pandas nuzzling (40×34 mm) (horiz); €1 Type **1285** 8·50 6·75

**1286** St. George's Monastery

**2003.** Millenary of St. George's Monastery, Carinthia.
2672 **1286** 87c. multicoloured 2·20 2·00

**1287** Marcel Prawy

**2003.** Marcel Prawy Commemoration (musician). Sheet 100×100 mm.
**MS**2673 **1287** €1.75 multicoloured 6·75 6·75

**1288** Face

**2003.** Europa. Poster Art.
2674 **1288** €1.02 multicoloured 3·00 2·75

**1289** Siemmens M 320 Postal Wagon

**2003.** Stamp Day.
2675 **1289** €2.54+€1.26 multicoloured 11·00 10·00

**1290** Series 5045 Locomotive "Blue Flash"

**2003**
2676 **1290** 75c. multicoloured 2·30 2·10

**1291** Bridge over Salzach River

**2003.** Centenary of Oberndorf–Laufen Bridge.
2677 **1291** 55c. multicoloured 2·40 2·20

A stamp of the same design was issued by Germany.

**1292** Ford Model T

**2003.** Centenary of Ford Motor Company. Sheet 150×81 mm containing T 1292 and similar horiz designs. Multicoloured.
**MS**2678 Type **1292**; 55c. Henry Ford; 55c. Ford Streetka 6·75 6·25

**1293** Keith Richards

**2003.** Rolling Stones. Sheet 101×101 mm containing T 1291 and similar vert designs. Multicoloured.
**MS**2679 Type **1293**; 55c. Mick Jagger; 55c. Charlie Watts; 55c. Ronnie Woods 9·00 8·50

**1294** Panther Airport Fire Appliance

**2003**
2688 **1294** 55c. multicoloured 1·80 1·70

**1295** Apostle and Scribe

**2003.** Year of the Bible.
2689 **1295** 55c. multicoloured 1·40 1·30

**1296** "Prenez le temps d'aimer" (Take time to enjoy) (Kiki Kogelnik)

**2003**
2690 **1296** 55c. multicoloured 1·80 1·70

**1297** Lake

**2003.** UNESCO World Heritage Site. Lake Neusiedlersee.
2691 **1297** €1 multicoloured 3·00 2·75

**1298** Geisha and Samurai

**2003.** Japan Exhibition, Leoben.
2692 **1298** 55c. multicoloured 1·80 1·70

**1299** Princess Turandot

**2003.** Performance of Puccini's Opera Turandot, St. Margarethen Roman Quarry.
2693 **1299** 55c. multicoloured 1·80 1·70

**1300** Family (Eva Wallner)

**2003.** Children's Stamp.
2694 **1300** 55c. multicoloured 1·80 1·70

**1301** Water Tower

**2003.** 50th Anniv Local Government Conference, Wiener Neustadt.
2695 **1301** 55c. multicoloured 1·60 1·50

**1302** TomTom (cartoon character) and Bouquet

**2003.** Greetings stamp.
2696 **1302** 55c. multicoloured 2·20 2·00

**1303** TomTom throwing Parcel from Hot Air Balloon

**2003**
2697 **1303** 55c. multicoloured 2·20 2·00

**1304** Werner Schlager

**2003.** Werner Schlager, World Table Tennis Champion, 2003.
2698 **1304** 55c. multicoloured 2·40 2·20

**1305** Stylized Head (Cornelia Zell)

**2003.** Jugend-Phila '03 International Youth Stamp Exhibition, Graz.
2699 **1305** 55c. multicoloured 1·40 1·30

**1306** Fan and "Elisabeth"

**2003.** Elisabeth, the Musical (musical based on life of Empress Elisabeth).
2700 **1306** 55c. multicoloured 1·90 1·80

**1307** "Judith"

**2003.** 185th Death Anniv of Gustav Klimt (artist). Sheet 80×100 mm.
**MS**2701 **1307** €2.10 multicoloured 7·75 7·25

**1308** Hands enclosing Light

**2003.** 30th Anniv of "Licht ins Dunkel" (Bringing light into darkness) (fund raising campaign).
2702 **1308** 55c. multicoloured 1·40 1·30

**1309** Grand Piano

**2003.** 175th Anniv of Bosendorfer (piano manufacturer).
2703 **1309** 75c. multicoloured 2·20 2·00

**1310** Oscar Peterson

**2003.** 78th Birth Anniv of Oscar Peterson (pianist).
2704 **1310** €1.25 multicoloured 3·50 3·25

**1311** Stained Glass Window

**2003.** Christmas.
2705 **1311** 55c. multicoloured 1·90 1·80

**1312** Postal Emblem

**2003.** Greeting Stamps. T 1312 and similar design. Each yellow, black and gold.
2706 55c. Type **1312** 1·40 1·30
2707 55c. Postal emblem (horiz) 1·40 1·30

Nos. 2706/7 could be personalised by the addition of photograph or logo, replacing the design shown on the stamp.

**1313** Ricardo Muti

**2004.** Vienna Philharmonic Orchestra's New Year Concert conducted by Ricardo Muti (principal conductor, La Scala Milan).
2708 **1313** €1 multicoloured 3·50 3·25

**1314** Seiji Ozawa

**2004.** 2nd Anniv of Seija Ozawa's Appointment as Musical Director of Vienna State Opera House.
2709 **1314** €1 multicoloured 3·50 3·25

**1315** Jose Carreras

**2004.** 30th Anniv of Jose Carreras Association with Vienna State Opera House.
2710 **1315** €1 multicoloured 3·50 3·25

**1316** Gerard Hanappi

**2004.** Centenary of Austrian Football. Sheet 196×113 mm containing T 1316 and similar vert designs. Multicoloured.
**MS**2711 55c.×10, Type **1316**; Mathias Sindelar; Football and anniversary emblem; Bruno Pezzey; Ernst Ocwirk; Walter Zeman; Herbert Prohaska; Hans Krankl; Andreas Herzog; Anton Polster 16·00 16·00

**1317** Crucifixion (Werner Berg)

**2004.** Easter.
2712 **1317** 55c. multicoloured 1·40 1·30

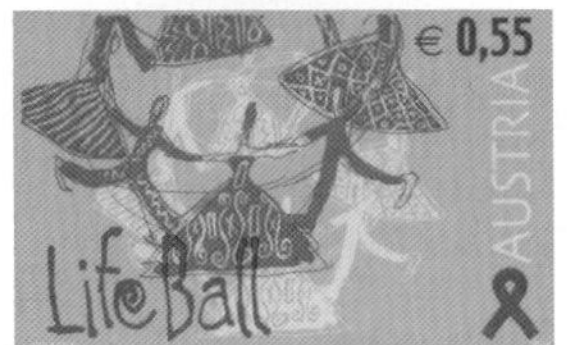


**1318** Dancers

**2004.** Life Ball (AIDS charity).
2713 **1318** 55c. multicoloured 1·60 1·30

**1319** Cardinal Franz Konig

**2004.** Cardinal Franz Konig Commemoration.
2714 **1319** €1 multicoloured 3·00 2·75

**1320** Emperor Franz Joseph and Empress Elisabeth

**2004.** 150th Anniv of the Marriage of Emperor Franz Joseph and Empress Elisabeth. Sheet 157×109 mm containing T 1320 and similar vert designs. Multicoloured.
**MS**2715 €1.25 Type **1320**; €1.50 Wedding procession; €1.75 Emperor Franz Joseph and Empress Elisabeth (35×42 mm) 13·50 13·50

**1321** Catholics' Day Emblem

**2004.** Catholics' Day. Sheet 110×160 mm containing T 1321 and similar vert designs. Multicoloured.
**MS**2716 55c. Type **1321**; €1.25 Pope John Paul II; €1.25 Magna Mater Austriae (Romanesque statue) (Chapel of Grace, Basilica, Mariazell); €1.25 Mother of God on Column of the Blessed Virgin (Basilica, Mariazell); €1.25 Virgin Mary (Treasury Altar, Basilica, Mariazell); €1.25 Crucifix (High Altar, Basilica, Mariazell) 19·00 19·00

**1322** Oeffag C.11 Mail Plane

**2004.** Stamp Day.
2717 **1322** €2.65+€1.30 multicoloured 11·50 10·50

**2004.** Folk Customs and Art (22nd series). As T 1005. Multicoloured.
2718 55c. Barrel sliding, Kosterneuburgs 1·80 1·70

**1323** Joe Zawinul (musician)

**2004**
2719 **1323** 55c. multicoloured 1·80 1·70

**1324** Sun and Flowers

**2004.** Europa. Holidays.
2720 **1324** 75c. multicoloured 2·10 1·90

**1325** Holy Sepulchre, Jerusalem

**2004.** Papal Order of the Holy Sepulchre.
2721 **1325** 125c. multicoloured 3·25 3·00

**1326** Imperial and Royal Southern State Railway Locomotive *Engerth*

**2004**
2722 **1326** 55c. multicoloured 1·70 1·60

**1327** Fireworks and Bubbles

**2004.** Danube Island Festival, Vienna.
2723 **1327** 55c. multicoloured 1·40 1·30

**1328** Theodor Herzl

**2004.** Death Centenary of Theodor Herzl (writer and Zionist pioneer).
2724 **1328** 55c. multicoloured 2·30 2·10

A stamp of the same design was issued by Israel and Hungary.

**1329** Arnold Schwarzenegger (governor of California)

**2004**
2725 **1329** 100c. multicoloured 5·50 5·00

**1330** Ernst Happel

**2004.** 12th Death Anniv of Ernst Happel (football trainer).
2726 **1330** 100c. black and scarlet 5·50 5·00

**1331** Tom Turbo (bicycle) (Andreas Wolkerstorfer)

**2004.** Tom Turbo (character from children's television series). Winning Entry in Children's Drawing Competition.
2727 **1331** 55c. multicoloured 1·70 1·60

**1332** TomTom (cartoon character) greeting Snail

**2004.** Greetings Stamp.
2728 **1332** 55c. multicoloured 1·90 1·80

**1333** Town Hall and Steam Tram

**2004.** Incorporation of Floridsdorf into Vienna.
2729 **1333** 55c. multicoloured 1·90 1·80

**1334** Crystal

**2004.** Crystal Worlds (tourist attraction), Wattens. Sheet 147×85 mm containing T 1334 and similar horiz design. Multicoloured.
**MS**2730 375c.×2, Type **1334**; Swan 21·00 21·00

The stamps of **MS**2730 have crystals applied to the surface.

**1335** Hermann Maier

**2004.** Hermann Maier—World Champion Giant Slalom Skier.
2731 **1335** 55c. multicoloured 2·40 2·20

**1336** "Kaspar Winterbild" (Josef Bramer)

**2004**
2732 **1336** 55c. multicoloured 1·60 1·50

**2004.** No. 2607 surch BASILISK.
2733 55c. on 51c. multicoloured 1·80 1·70

**1338** "Die Wartende" (Sylvia Gredenberg)

**2004**
2734 **1338** 55c. multicoloured 1·40 1·30

**1339** "Junge Sonnenblume" (Max Weiler)

**2004.** Sheet 80×100 mm.
**MS**2735 **1339** multicoloured 6·75 6·75

**1340** Campaign Poster (Friednsreich Hundertwasser)

**2004.** 20th Anniv of Campaign to save Danube Meadows (now National Park).
2736 **1340** 55c. multicoloured 3·50 3·25

**1341** Soldier and National Arms

**2004.** 50th Anniv of Federal Army.
2737 **1341** 55c. multicoloured 1·60 1·50

**1342** Nikolaus Harnoncourt

**2004.** 75th Birthday of Nikolaus Harnoncourt (musician).
2738 **1342** €1 multicoloured 2·75 2·50

**1343** Salzburg Christmas Market

**2004.** Christmas.
2739 **1343** 55c. multicoloured 1·40 1·30

**1344** Lorin Maazel

**2005.** Vienna Philharmonic Orchestra's New Year Concert conducted by Lorin Maazel.
2740 **1344** €1 multicoloured 2·75 2·50

**1345** Herbert von Karajan

**2005.** 10th Anniv of Herbert von Karajan Centre.
2741 **1345** 55c. blue, black and deep blue 1·40 1·30

**1346** Stephan Eberharter

**2005.** Stephan Eberharter—World Champion Skier.
2742 **1346** 55c. multicoloured 1·90 1·80

**2005.** Nos. 2607, 2609/10, 2613, 2617/18, 2620 and 2623 variously surch.
2743 55c. on 4c. multicoloured 1·40 1·30
2744 55c. on 13c. multicoloured 1·40 1·30
2745 55c. on 17c. multicoloured 1·40 1·30
2746 55c. on 27c. multicoloured 1·40 1·30
2747 55c. on 58c. multicoloured 1·40 1·30
2748 55c. on 73c. multicoloured 1·40 1·30
2749 55c. on 87c. multicoloured 1·40 1·30
2750 55c. on €2.03 multicoloured 1·40 1·30

**1355** Globe and Rotary Emblem

**2005.** Centenary of Rotary International (charitable organization).
2751 **1355** 55c. multicoloured 1·60 1·50

**1356** Max Schmeling

**2005.** Death Centenary of Max Schmeling (boxer).
2752 **1356** 100c. multicoloured 2·75 2·50

**1357** "Venus in Front of the Mirror" (Peter Paul Rubens)

**2005.** Liechtenstein Museum, Garden Palace, Vienna.
2753 **1357** 125c. multicoloured 3·50 3·25

**1358** Carl Djerassi

**2005.** 82nd Birth Anniv of Carl Djerassi (chemist and writer). Sheet 60×80 mm.
**MS**2754 **1358** multicoloured 3·50 3·50

**1359** Pope John Paul II

**2005.** Pope John Paul II Commemoration.
2755 **1359** €1 multicoloured 2·75 2·50

**1360** Taurus

**2005.** Astrology (1st issue). Multicoloured. Self-adhesive gum.
2756 55c. Type **1360** 1·60 1·50
2757 55c. Gemini 1·60 1·50
2758 55c. Cancer 1·60 1·50
2759 55c. Rooster (Year of the Rooster) (Chinese astrology) (red) 1·60 1·50

See also Nos. 2772/5, 2784/7 and 2799/2802.

**1361** Post Office Building and Carriages

**2005.** Imperial Post Office in Jerusalem (1859–1914).
2760 **1361** 100c. multicoloured 2·75 2·50

**1362** Saint Florian

**2005.** Saints (1st issue). Saint Florian (National Patron Saint).
2761 **1362** 55c. multicoloured 1·60 1·50

See also Nos. 2767, 2829, 2857, 2890, 2932 and 2959.

**1363** Tracks

**2005.** 60th Anniv of Liberation of Mauthausen Concentration Camp.
2762 **1363** 55c. multicoloured 1·60 1·50

**1364** State Arms

**2005.** 60th Anniv of Second Republic and 50th Anniv of State Treaty. Sheet 120×80 mm containing T **1364** and similar multicoloured design.
**MS**2763 55c.×2, Type **1364**; Seals and signatures on treaty (42×35 mm) 3·50 3·50

**1365** Heidi Klum

**2005.** Life Ball (AIDS charity).
2764 **1365** 75c. multicoloured 2·20 2·00

**1366** Junkers F13 Flying Boat

**2005.** Stamp Day.
2765 **1366** 265c.+130c. mult 11·00 11·00

**1367** Waiter in Cup of Coffee

**2005.** Europa. Gastronomy.
2766 **1367** 75c. multicoloured 2·30 2·10

**1368** Saint Joseph

**2005.** Saints (2nd issue).
2767 **1368** 55c. multicoloured 1·60 1·50

**1369** Jochen Rindt

**2005.** 25th Death Anniv of Karl Jochen Rindt (1970—Formula 1 World Champion).
2768 **1369** 55c. multicoloured 1·80 1·70

**1370** Melman, Marty, Alex and Gloria (characters)

**2005.** Madagascar (animated film).
2769 **1370** 55c. multicoloured 1·60 1·50

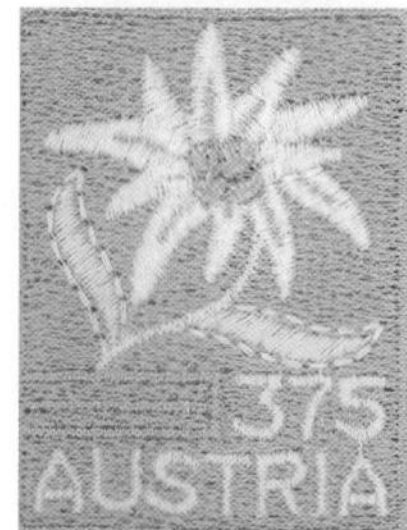


**1371** Peacock Butterfly (*Inachis io*)

**2005**
2770 **1371** 55c. multicoloured 1·60 1·50

**1372** Edelweiss

**2005.** Vorarlberg Embroidery.
2771 **1372** 375c. green 9·75 9·50

**2005.** Astrology (2nd issue). As T 1360. Multicoloured. Self-adhesive.
2772 55c. Leo 1·60 1·50
2773 55c. Virgo 1·60 1·50
2774 55c. Libra 1·60 1·50
2775 55c. As No. 2759 (yellow) 1·60 1·50

**2005.** Customs and Art (23rd series). As T 1005. Multicoloured.
2776 55c. Game of dice, Frankenburg 1·60 1·50

1373 Nikki Lauda

2005. Nikki Lauda (Formula 1 World Champion—1975, 1977 and 1984).
2777 1373 55c. multicoloured 1·70 1·60

1374 Pumpkin

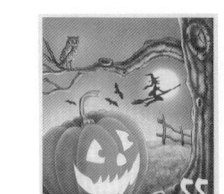

2005. Halloween.
2778 1374 55c. multicoloured 1·60 1·50

1375 "Houses" (Egon Schiele)

2005. Art. Sheet 100×80 mm.
MS2779 1375 210c. multicoloured 6·75 6·75

1376 ET 10.103 Railcar

2005. Centenary of Montafon Railway.
2780 1376 55c. multicoloured 1·60 1·50

1377 Presentation of Deed

2005. Landhaus (provincial government building), Klagenfurt.
2781 1377 75c. multicoloured 2·10 1·90

1378 "Master of the Woods" (Karl Hodina)

2005
2782 1378 55c. multicoloured 1·60 1·50

1379 Adalbert Stifter

2005. Birth Bicentenary of Adalbert Stifter (writer).
2783 1379 55c. multicoloured 2·40 2·20

2005. Astrology (3rd issue). As T 1360. Multicoloured. Self-adhesive.

| | | | |
|---|---|---|---|
| 2784 | 55c. Scorpio | 1·60 | 1·50 |
| 2785 | 55c. Sagittarius | 1·60 | 1·50 |
| 2786 | 55c. Capricorn | 1·60 | 1·50 |
| 2787 | 55c. As No. 2759 (orange) | 1·60 | 1·50 |

1380 National Theatre

2005. 50th Anniv of Re-opening of National Theatre and Opera House. Sheet 130×60 mm containing T 1380 and similar horiz design.
MS2788 55c. sepia and agate; 55c. indigo and black 4·75 4·75
DESIGNS: 55c.×2, Type 1380; State Opera House.

1381 Hills

2005. Restoration of Sattler's Cyclorama of Salzburg. Sheet 155×56 mm containing T 381 and similar horiz design. Multicoloured.
MS2789 125c.×2, Type 1381; Townscape 7·75 7·75

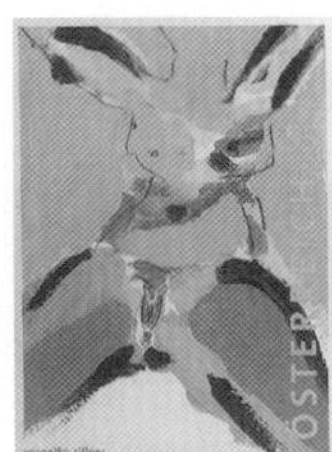
1382 "Nude" (Veronika Zillner)

2005
2790 1382 55c. multicoloured 1·60 1·50

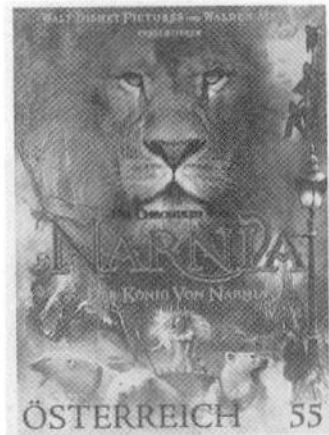
1383 Aslan (character)

2005. The Chronicles of Narnia (film of book by C. S. Lewis).
2791 1383 55c. multicoloured 1·60 1·50

1384 "Maria Heimsuchung" (Reinhold Stecher)

2005. Advent.
2792 1384 55c. multicoloured 1·40 1·30

1385 Shields

2005. 800th Anniv of Order of Teutonic Knights.
2793 1385 55c. multicoloured 1·40 1·30

1386 Snow-covered Houses

2005. Christmas.
2794 1386 55c. multicoloured 1·40 1·30

1387 Mariss Jansons

2006. Vienna Philharmonic Orchestra's New Year Concert conducted by Mariss Jansons.
2795 1387 75c. multicoloured 1·90 1·80

1388 Building Facade

2006. Austria's Presidency of European Union.
2796 1388 75c. multicoloured 1·90 1·80

1389 "Post" Philatelic Shop

2006. Greeting Stamp.
2797 1389 55c. multicoloured 1·40 1·30

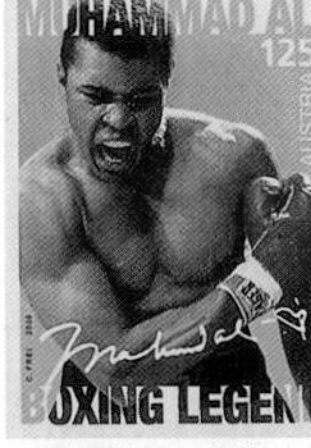
1390 Muhammad Ali

2006. Muhammad Ali (boxer).
2798 1390 €1.25 multicoloured 3·50 3·25

1391 Dog ("Year of the Dog")

2006. Astrology (4th issue). Multicoloured. Self-adhesive.

| | | | |
|---|---|---|---|
| 2799 | 55c. Type 1391 | 1·60 | 1·50 |
| 2800 | 55c. Aquarius | 1·60 | 1·50 |
| 2801 | 55c. Pisces | 1·60 | 1·50 |
| 2802 | 55c. Aries | 1·60 | 1·50 |

1392 Wolfgang Mozart

2006. 250th Birth Anniv of Wolfgang Amadeus Mozart (composer and musician).
2803 1392 55c. red and silver 1·60 1·50

1393 Europa (sculpture) (R. Chavanon)

2006. 50th Anniv of Europa Stamps.
2804 1393 125c. multicoloured 3·50 3·25

1394 "Lost in her Dreams" (Friedrich von Amerling)

2006. Liechtenstein Museum, Garden Palace, Vienna.
2805 1394 125c. multicoloured 3·50 3·25
A stamp of the same design was issued by Liechtenstein.

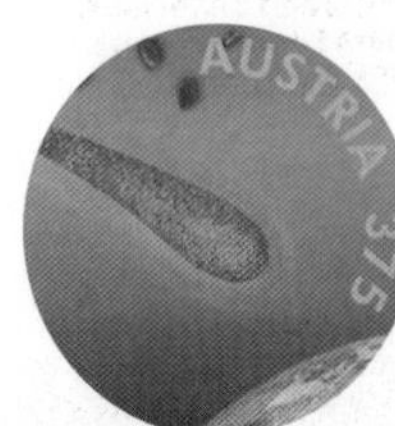
1395 Meteorite

2006. Post from another World. Meteorite H-chondrite on Stamps. Sheet 81×60 mm.
MS2806 1395 375c. multicoloured 11·00 11·00
No. MS2806 contains ground meteorite dust and is sold in a folder.

1396 Almaz and Karl Heinz Bohm (founders)

2006. 25th Anniv of Menschen fur Menschen (charity).
2807 1396 100c. multicoloured 2·50 2·40

1397 Initiation

2006. Freemasonry in Austria. Sheet 81×61 mm.
MS2808 1397 100c. multicoloured 3·50 3·50

**1398** Couch

**2006.** 150th Birth Anniv of Sigmund Freud (psychoanalysis).

2809 **1398** 55c. multicoloured 1·30 1·20

**1399** Franz Beckenbauer (Andy Warhol)

**2006.** Franz Beckenbauer (footballer).

2810 **1399** 75c. multicoloured 1·90 1·80

**2006.** Flood Relief. No. 2612 surch 75+425 HOCH WASSER HILFE 2006.

2811 75c.+425c. on 25c. multicoloured 9·75 9·50

The surcharge was for the victims of the Marchfeld floods.

**2006.** No. 2608 surch HEILIGENKREUZ NIEDEROSTERRICH and tree.

2812 55c. on 7c. multicoloured 1·40 1·30

**1402** Falco

**2006.** Hans Holzl (Falco) (rock musician) Commemoration.

2813 **1402** 55c. multicoloured 1·60 1·50

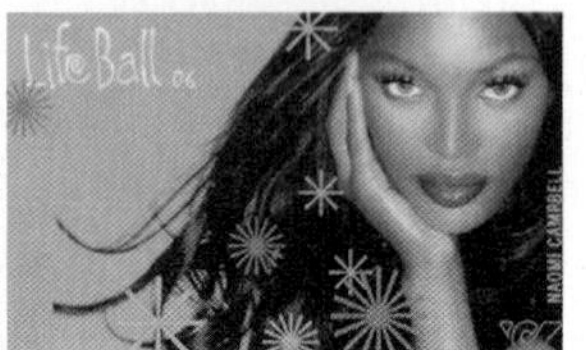

**1403** Naomi Campbell

**2006.** Life Ball (AIDS charity).

2814 **1403** 75c. multicoloured 2·30 2·10

**2006.** Customs and Art (24th series). As T 1005. Multicoloured.

2815 55c. Weitensfeld Kranzlreiten (race) 1·40 1·30

**1404** Emblem

**2006.** Privatization of Post Office.

2816 **1404** 55c. multicoloured 1·40 1·30

**1405** Jim Clark

**2006.** Formula I Motor Racing Legends. Sheet 140×185 mm containing T 1405 and similar horiz designs. Multicoloured.

**MS**2817 55c.×4, Type **1405**; Jacky Ickx; Jackie Stewart; Alain Prost; 75c.×2, Stirling Moss; Mario Andretti; 100c. Bruce McLaren; 125c. Jack Brabham 16·00 16·00

See also No. **MS**2868.

**1406** Saint Hemma

**2006**

2818 **1406** 55c. multicoloured 1·40 1·30

**1407** Emblem (image scaled to 73% of original size)

**2006.** 60th Anniv of Federal Chamber of Industry and Commerce.

2819 **1407** 55c. silver, vermilion and black 1·80 1·70

**1408** Mozart

**2006.** 250th Birth Anniv of Wolfgang Amadeus Mozart (composer and musician). Viva Mozart Exhibition, Salzburg.

2820 **1408** 55c. multicoloured 1·40 1·30

**1409** Ottfried Fischer

**2006.** Ottfried Fischer (actor).

2821 **1409** 55c. multicoloured 1·40 1·30

**1410** Figures

**2006.** Europa. Integration.

2822 **1410** 75c. multicoloured 1·90 1·80

**1411** Airbus A310-300

**2006.** Stamp Day.

2823 **1411** 265c.+130c. multicoloured 10·50 10·50

**1412** St. Anne's Column, Innsbruck

**2006**

2824 **1412** 55c. multicoloured 1·40 1·30

**1413** K. K. STB Reihe 106 Locomotive

**2006.** Centenary of Pyhrn Railway.

2825 **1413** 55c. multicoloured 1·40 1·30

**1414** Fireworks over Victoria Harbour, Hong Kong

**2006.** Fireworks. Sheet 146×85 mm containing T 1414 and similar horiz design. Multicoloured.

**MS**2826 €3.75×2, Type **1414**; Fireworks over Giant Ferris Wheel, Vienna, Austria 21·00 21·00

**MS**2826 has crystals applied to the surface of the stamps and was sold in a folder.

Stamps of a similar design were issued by Hong Kong.

**1415** European Lynx (*Lynx lynx*)

**2006.** Fauna.

2827 **1415** 55c. multicoloured 1·40 1·30

**1416** Emblem

**2006.** WIPA 2008 International Stamp Exhibition.

2828 **1416** 55c.+20c. multicoloured 2·20 2·00

**1417** Saint Gebhard

**2006.** Saints (3rd issue).

2829 **1417** 55c. multicoloured 1·40 1·30

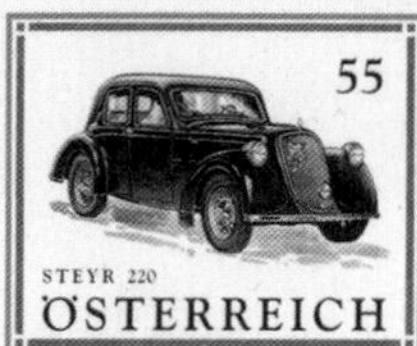


**1418** Steyr 220 Motor Car

**2006**

2830 **1418** 55c. multicoloured 1·40 1·30

**1419** KTM R 125 Tarzan Motorbike

**2006**

2831 **1419** 55c. multicoloured 1·40 1·30

**1420** Benjamin Raich

**2006.** Benjamin Raich—World Champion Skier.

2832 **1420** 55c. multicoloured 1·40 1·30

**1421** Piano

**2006.** Musical Instruments. Multicoloured.

2833 55c. Type **1421** 1·40 1·30

2834 55c. Guqin 1·40 1·30

Stamps of a similar design were issued by China.

**1422** "Young Boy" (Cornelia Schlesinger)

**2006**

2835 **1422** 55c. multicoloured 1·40 1·30

**1423** Alte Saline (salt refinery) and Saint Rupert

**2006.** German and Austrian Philatelic Exhibition, Bad Reichenhall.

2836 **1423** 55c.+20c. multicoloured 1·90 1·80

**1424** "Homo sapiens" (detail) (Valentin Oman)

**2006.** Modern Art.

2837 **1424** 55c. multicoloured 1·40 1·30

**1425** Pond Turtle

**2006.** Self-adhesive.

| | | | | |
|---|---|---|---|---|
| 2838 | **1425** | 55c. multicoloured | 1·40 | 1·30 |

**1426** Bald Ibis

**2006.** Fauna. Multicoloured. Self-adhesive.

| | | | |
|---|---|---|---|
| 2839 | 55c. Type **1426** | 1·40 | 1·30 |
| 2840 | 55c. Brown bear | 1·40 | 1·30 |

**1427** "The Holy Family at Rest" (Franz Weiss)

**2006.** Christmas (1st issue).

| | | | | |
|---|---|---|---|---|
| 2841 | **1427** | 55c. multicoloured | 1·40 | 1·30 |

**1428** "Christkindl Pilgrimage Church" (Reinhold Stecher)

**2006.** Christmas (2nd issue).

| | | | | |
|---|---|---|---|---|
| 2842 | **1428** | 55c. multicoloured | 1·40 | 1·30 |

**1429** "Ferdinand Square" (T. Chyshkovskii)

**2006.** 750th Anniv of Lvov.

| | | | | |
|---|---|---|---|---|
| 2843 | **1429** | 55c. multicoloured | 1·40 | 1·30 |

A stamp of a similar design was issued by Ukraine.

**1430** Michael Schumacher **1430a** Michael Schumacher

**2006.** Michael Schumacher (Formula 1 World Champion–1994/5 and 2000/4).

| | | | | |
|---|---|---|---|---|
| 2844 | **1430** | 75c. multicoloured | 2·20 | 2·00 |
| 2844a | **1430a** | 75c. multicoloured | 3·25 | 3·00 |

No. 2844a has different (incorrect) championship year dates and includes designer and year of issue at lower margin.

**1431** "Zinnoberroten Merkur" (No. N13 "Mercury")

**2006.** Centenary of National Stamp and Coin Dealers' Association.

| | | | | |
|---|---|---|---|---|
| 2845 | **1431** | 55c. cerise and gold | 1·40 | 1·30 |

**1432** Zubin Mehta

**2007.** Vienna Philharmonic Orchestra's New Year Concert conducted by Zubin Mehta.

| | | | | |
|---|---|---|---|---|
| 2846 | **1432** | 75c. multicoloured | 1·90 | 1·80 |

**1433** Alpine Flowers

**2007.** Flowers. Multicoloured.

| | | | |
|---|---|---|---|
| 2847 | 55c. Type **1433** | 1·30 | 1·20 |
| 2848 | 75c. Hellebores | 1·80 | 1·70 |
| 2849 | €1.25 Spring flowers | 3·00 | 2·75 |

**1434** Symbols of Technology and Figure

**2007.** Mankind and Technology. Self-adhesive.

| | | | | |
|---|---|---|---|---|
| 2850 | **1434** | 55c. multicoloured | 1·40 | 1·30 |

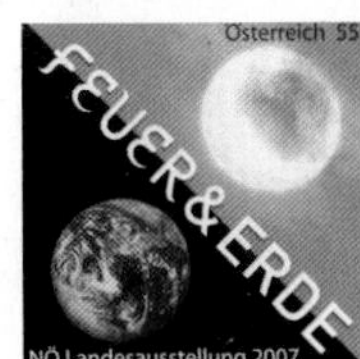

**1435** Fire and Earth

**2007.** Lower Austrian Provincial Exhibition.

| | | | | |
|---|---|---|---|---|
| 2851 | **1435** | 55c. multicoloured | 1·40 | 1·30 |

**1436** Outline of Robert Baden-Powell

**2007.** Centenary of Scouting. Sheet 170×130 mm containing T 1436 and similar horiz designs. Multicoloured.

**MS**2852 55c.×4, Type **1436**; Campfire; Tent; Guitar 6·00 6·00

**1437** Roe Deer

**2007**

| | | | | |
|---|---|---|---|---|
| 2853 | **1437** | 75c. multicoloured | 1·90 | 1·80 |

**1438** "Portrait of a Lady" (Bernardino Zaganelli da Cottignola)

**2007**

| | | | | |
|---|---|---|---|---|
| 2854 | **1438** | €1.25 multicoloured | 3·25 | 3·00 |

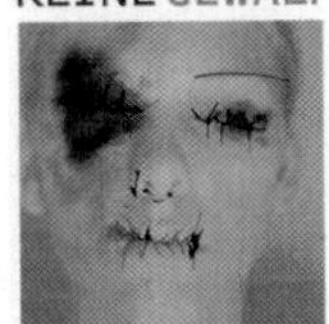

**1439** Injured Woman

**2007.** Stop Violence against Women Campaign.

| | | | | |
|---|---|---|---|---|
| 2855 | **1439** | 55c. multicoloured | 1·40 | 1·30 |

**1440** Easter Rattles

**2007.** Traditional Customs.

| | | | | |
|---|---|---|---|---|
| 2856 | **1440** | 55c. multicoloured | 1·40 | 1·30 |

**1441** Saint Klemens Maria Holbauer

**2007.** Saints (4th issue).

| | | | | |
|---|---|---|---|---|
| 2857 | **1441** | 55c. multicoloured | 1·40 | 1·30 |

**1442** Emblem

**2007.** WIPA 2008 International Stamp Exhibition.

| | | | | |
|---|---|---|---|---|
| 2858 | **1442** | 55c.+20c. multicoloured | 2·20 | 2·00 |

**1443** Roses

**2007.** Mourning Stamp. No value expressed.

| | | | | |
|---|---|---|---|---|
| 2859 | **1443** | (55c.) multicoloured | 1·40 | 1·30 |

**1444** Flowers

**2007.** Greetings Stamp. No value expressed.

| | | | | |
|---|---|---|---|---|
| 2860 | **1444** | (55c.) multicoloured | 1·40 | 1·30 |

**1445** Salamander (*Salamandra salamandra*)

**2007.** Fauna. Multicoloured. Self-adhesive.

| | | | |
|---|---|---|---|
| 2861 | 55c. Type **1445** | 1·40 | 1·30 |
| 2862 | 55c. Crayfish (*Astacus astacus*) | 1·40 | 1·30 |

**1446** Pope Benedict XVI

**2007.** 80th Birth Anniv of Pope Benedict XVI.

| | | | | |
|---|---|---|---|---|
| 2863 | **1446** | 100c. multicoloured | 2·75 | 2·50 |

**1447** Inscr "Myotis brandtii"

**2007.** Whiskered Bat. Self-adhesive.

| | | | | |
|---|---|---|---|---|
| 2864 | **1447** | 55c. multicoloured | 1·40 | 1·30 |

No. 2864 is described as "Whiskered Bat", that is Myotis mystacinus but is inscribed "Myotis brandtii", that is Brandt's Bat.

**1448** Violet

**2007**

| | | | | |
|---|---|---|---|---|
| 2865 | **1448** | 100c. multicoloured | 2·40 | 2·20 |

**1449** 'The Good Samaritan' (fresco, Franciscan Monastery, Schwaz)

**2007.** 80th Anniv of Austrian Workers Samaritan Federation (medical assistance organization).

| | | | | |
|---|---|---|---|---|
| 2866 | **1449** | 55c. multicoloured | 1·40 | 1·30 |

**1450** 'Untitled' (painting by Hermann Nitsch) (Illustration reduced. Actual size 60×80 mm)

**2007.** Modern Art. Sheet 61×80 mm. Imperf.
**MS**2867 **1450** scarlet and black 3·00 3·00

**2007.** Formula I Motor Racing Legends. Sheet 140×185 mm containing horiz designs (size 50×32 mm) as T 1405. Multicoloured.
**MS**2868 55c.×8, Phil Hill; Clay Regazzoni; Gerhard Berger; Juan Manuel Fangio; John Surtees; Mika Hakkinen; Graham Hill; Emerson Fittipaldi 11·50 11·50

**1451** Krause & Comp Electric Locomotive

**2007.** Centenary of Mariazell Narrow Gauge Railway.
2869 **1451** 55c. multicoloured 1·40 1·30

**1452** Church Facade and Tower

**2007.** 850th Anniv of Mariazell Basilica.
2870 **1452** 55c. multicoloured 1·40 1·30

**1453** Trix and Flix

**2007.** European Football Championships (Euro 2008), Austria and Switzerland. Sheet 100×80 mm containing T 1453 and similar horiz designs. Multicoloured.
**MS**2871 20c. Type **1453**; 25c. Holding trophy; 30c.Tackling for the ball; 35c. With arms around each other 3·00 3·00

**1454** 'Self-portrait' (painting by Angelika Kauffmann)

**2007.** Modern Art. Sheet 81×101 mm.
**MS**2872 210c. scarlet and black 6·00 6·00

**1455** *Wien* (steamer) (painting by Harry Heusser)

**2007.** Stamp Day.
2873 **1455** 265c.+130c. multicoloured 9·75 9·00

**1456** Globe as Scout

**2007.** Europa. Centenary of Scouting.
2874 **1456** 55c. multicoloured 1·40 1·30

**1457** Ignaz Pleyel

**2007.** 250th Birth Anniv of Ignaz Joseph Pleyel (composer).
2875 **1457** £1 multicoloured 2·40 2·20

**1458** Shrek and Fiona

**2007.** 'Shrek the Third' (animated film).
2876 **1458** 55c. multicoloured 1·40 1·30

**1459** Museum Building

**2007.** Essel Museum. Self-adhesive.
2877 **1459** 55c. multicoloured 1·40 1·30

**1460** Wilhelm Kienzl

**2007.** 150th Birth Anniv of Wilhelm Kienzl (composer).
2878 **1460** 75c. multicoloured 1·80 1·70

**1461** U Series Steam Locomotive

**2007.** Bregenz Forest Railway.
2879 **1461** 75c. multicoloured 1·90 1·80

**1462** 'Man' (Astrid Bernhart)

**2007**
2880 **1462** 55c. multicoloured 1·40 1·30

**1463** Dandelion

**2007.** Flora. Multicoloured.

| | | | |
|---|---|---|---|
| 2881 | 4c. Type **1463** | 25 | 20 |
| 2882 | 10c. Scottish laburnum | 35 | 35 |
| 2883 | 65c. Gelder rose | 1·60 | 1·50 |
| 2884 | 115c. *Gentiana ciliate* | 2·75 | 2·50 |
| 2885 | 140c. Clematis | 3·50 | 3·25 |

**1464** *Haliaeetus albicilla* (white-tailed eagle)

**2007**
2886 **1464** 55c. multicoloured 1·40 1·30

**1465** Ivory and Gold Medallions (Necklace, 1916) (image scaled to 60% of original size)

**2007.** Josef Hoffman (designer and architect) Commemoration. Sheet 81×51 mm. Imperf.
**MS**2887 **1465** multicoloured 7·75 7·75

**1466** Oil Derrick

**2007.** 75th Anniv of Austrian Oil Production.
2888 **1466** 75c. multicoloured 1·90 1·80
No. 2888 was impregnated with scent of oil which was released by rubbing part of the design.

**1467** Stag and Hind

**2007.** Birth Bicentenary of Friedrich Gauermann (artist).
2889 **1467** 55c. multicoloured 1·40 1·30

**1468** Saint Rupert

**2007.** Saints (5th issue).
2890 **1468** 55c. multicoloured 1·40 1·30

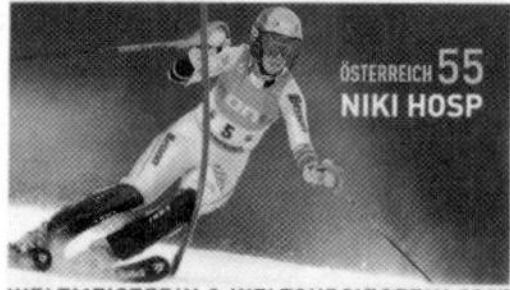

**1469** Niki Hosp

**2007.** Niki Hosp–Women's World Cup Alpine Ski Champion, 2006–2007.
2891 **1469** 55c. multicoloured 1·40 1·30

**1470** *Lucanus cervus* (stag beetle)

**2007.** Self-adhesive.
2892 **1470** 75c. multicoloured 2·10 1·90

**1471** Key

**2007.** Michel Blumelhuber (iron and steel carver) Commemoration.
2893 **1471** 75c. multicoloured 2·10 1·90

**1472** Christiane Horbiger

**2007.** Christiane Horbiger (actress and recipient of Cross of Honour for Science and Art).
2894 **1472** 55c. multicoloured 1·40 1·30

**1473** Scene from 'Queen of Spades' (Peter Illyich Tchaikovsky)

**2007.** Vienna State Opera Opening Nights (1st issue).
2895 **1473** 55c. multicoloured 1·40 1·30
See also No. 2914.

**1474** Nativity (altar painting, Oberwollan)

**2007.** Christmas. Multicoloured.

| | | | |
|---|---|---|---|
| 2896 | 55c. Type **1474** | 1·40 | 1·30 |
| 2897 | 65c. Nativity (icon, Church of St. Barbara) | 1·60 | 1·50 |

**1475** Clownfish

**2007.** 50th Anniv of Haus des Meeres (Aqua Terra Zoo).
2898 **1475** 55c. multicoloured 1·40 1·30

**1476** Thomas Gottschalk

**2007.** Thomas Gottschalk and 'Wetten dass?' (TV presenter and game show).
2899 **1476** 65c. multicoloured 1·70 1·60

**1477** *Cypripedium calceolus* (lady's slipper orchid)

**2008**
2900 **1477** 15c. multicoloured 35 35

**1478** Vienna

**2008.** EURO 2008 Football Championships (1st issue). Venues. Sheet 150×90 mm containing T 1478 and similar square designs. Multicoloured.
**MS**2901 55c.×4, Type **1478**; Salzburg; Klagenfurt; Innsbruck, 65c.×4, Zurich; Basel; Bern; Geneva 12·00 12·00

The stamps of No. **MS**2901 share a common background design.

See also Nos. 2903/4, 2906/7, 2909, 2910, 2917, 2918, 2919, 2912, 2922, 2926, 2925, **MS**2929, 2930, **MS**2931 and 2951.

**1479** Emblem and St Stephen's Cathedral

**2008.** WIPA 2008 International Stamp Exhibition.
2902 **1479** 55c.+20c. multicoloured 2·20 2·00

See also Nos. 2828 and 2858.

**1480** Trix and Flix (mascots)

**2008.** EURO 2008 Football Championships (2nd issue). Multicoloured. Self-adhesive.
2903 55c. Type **1480** 1·40 1·30
2904 65c. Emblem 1·60 1·50

**1481** *Portrait of Martina* (Hans Robert Pippal)

**2008.** Modern Art.
2905 **1481** 65c. multicoloured 1·60 1·50

**1482** Trix and Flix (Alexandra Payer)

**2008.** EURO 2008 Football Championships (3rd issue). Children's Drawings. Multicoloured.
2906 55c. Type **1482** 1·40 1·30
2907 55c. Footballs as map of Europe (Corina Payr) 1·40 1·30

**2008.** WIPA 2008 International Stamp Exhibition. Gold. Sheet 126×73 mm containing triangular designs as T 1479. Multicoloured.
**MS**2908 55c. As No. 2828; 55c. As No. 2858; 65c. As No. 2902 5·75 5·75

**1483** Map of Europe, Football and Euro Stars (Saskia Puchegger)

**2008.** EURO 2008 Football Championships (4th issue). Children's Drawings.
2909 **1483** 65c. multicoloured 1·60 1·50

**1484** *Defence* (Maria Lassnig)

**2008.** EURO 2008 Football Championships (5th issue).
2910 **1484** 55c. multicoloured 1·40 1·30

**1485** *Hyla arborea* (tree frog)

**2008.** Fauna. Multicoloured. Self-adhesive.
2911 65c. Type **1485** 1·70 1·60
2912 65c. *Alcedo atthis* (kingfisher) 1·70 1·60

**1486** Airbus A320

**2008.** 50th Anniv of Austrian Airlines.
2913 **1486** 140c. multicoloured 3·50 3·25

No. 2913 includes an area, which when scratched, could win a prize.

**1487** Scene from *La Forza del Destino* (Giuseppe Verdi)

**2008.** Vienna State Opera Opening Nights (2nd issue).
2914 **1487** 55c. multicoloured 1·40 1·30

**1488** *Princess Marie Franziska von Liechtenstein* (Friedrich von Amerling)

**2008**
2915 **1488** 125c. multicoloured 3·50 3·25

A stamp of a similar design was issued by Liechtenstein.

**1489** Imaginary Landscape

**2008.** Modern Art. Sysanne Sculler (Soshana).
2916 **1489** 55c. multicoloured 1·40 1·30

**1490** Football

**2008.** EURO 2008 Football Championships (6th issue). Self-adhesive.
2917 **1490** 375c. multicoloured 9·75 9·25

No. 2917 is made from a synthetic mixture containing polyurethane, as the original ball used for the EURO 2008 (known as the 'Europass').

**1491** Football Field, Ball and Player's Legs

**2008.** EURO 2008 Football Championships (7th issue).
2918 **1491** 55c. multicoloured 1·40 1·30

**1492** Lindwurm (symbol of Klagenfurt) on Football and Karawanken Mountains (Bolona Jencic)

**2008.** EURO 2008 Football Championships (8th issue). Children's Drawings.
2919 **1492** 125c. multicoloured 3·00 2·75

**1493** View from River

**2008.** World Heritage Site. Wachau.
2920 **1493** 100c. multicoloured 2·40 2·20

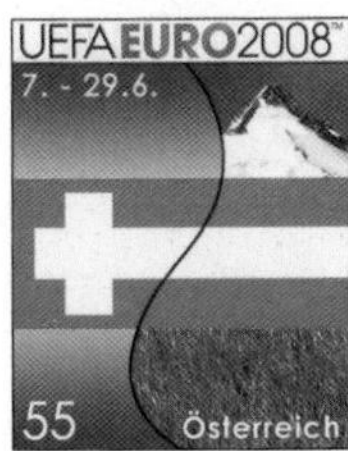

**1494** Austrian and Swiss Flags, Alps and Turf (Stefan Gritsch)

**2008.** EURO 2008 Football Championships (9th issue). Children's Drawings.
2921 **1494** 55c. multicoloured 1·40 1·30

**1495** Football wearing Lederhosen (Vanessa Schennach)

**2008.** EURO 2008 Football Championships (10th issue). Children's Drawings.
2922 **1495** 100c. multicoloured 2·40 2·20

**1496** Traditional Clothes

**2008.** Centenary of Tyrolean Federation of Traditional Provincial Costumes.
2923 **1496** 75c. multicoloured 2·00 1·90

**1497** *Erinaceus concolor* (southern white-breasted hedgehog)

**2008.** Fauna. Multicoloured. Self-adhesive.
2924 55c. Type **1497** 1·40 1·30
2925 55c. *Lepus europaeus* (hare) 1·40 1·30

**1498** Preparation and Goal

**2008.** EURO 2008 Football Championships (11th issue). Andreas Herzog's Winning Goal—World Cup Qualifier, 1997. Self-adhesive.
2926 **1498** 545c. multicoloured 14·00 14·00

**1499** Mare and Foal

**2008.** Federal Lipizzaner Stud, Piber.
2927 **1499** 55c. multicoloured 1·50 1·40

**1500** Turf (Silvia Holemar, Denise Prossegger and Guso Aldijana)

**2008.** EURO 2008 Football Championships (12th issue). Children's Drawings.
2928 **1500** 75c. multicoloured 2·00 1·90

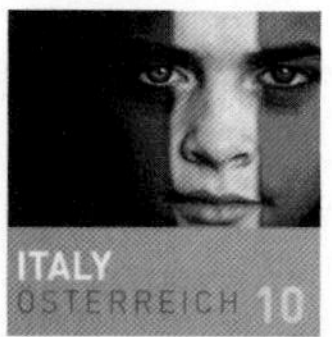

**1501** Italy

**2008.** EURO 2008 Football Championships (13th issue). Participating Teams. Two sheets 150×90 mm containing T 1501 and similar square designs showing faces painted with team flag.
**MS**2929 (a) 10c. Type **1501**; 10c. Croatia; 15c. Sweden; 15c. Greece; 20c. Austria; 20c. Portugal; 65c. Spain; 65c. Czech Republic. (b) 25c. Switzerland; 25c. Germany; 30c. Romania; 30c. Turkey; 35c. Netherlands; 35c. Poland; 55c. Russia; 55c. France 12·50 12·50

**1502** Ball and Chairs (Andrea Kastrun)

**2008.** EURO 2008 Football Championships (14th issue). Children's Drawings.
2930 **1502** 55c. multicoloured 1·50 1·40

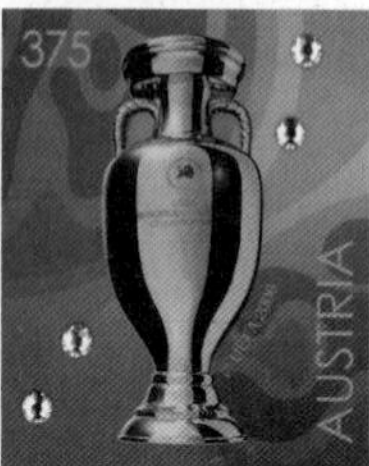

**1503** Henri Delaunay Cup (EURO 2008 trophy)

**2008.** EURO 2008 Football Championships (15th issue). Sheet 65×75 mm.
**MS**2931 **1503** multicoloured 10·00 10·00

No. **MS**2931 contains four crystals and was issued contained in a folder.

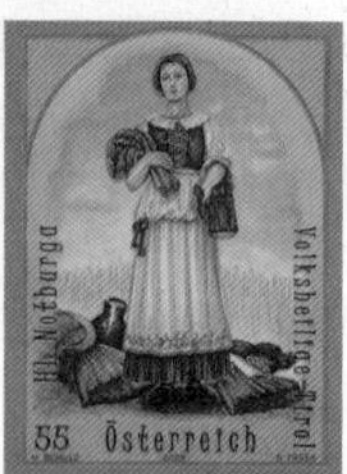

**1504** Saint Notburga

**2008.** Saints (6th issue).
2932 **1504** 55c. multicoloured 1·50 1·40

**1505** Script, Hand, Pen and Ink

**2008.** Europa. The Letter.
2933 **1505** 65c. multicoloured 1·80 1·60

**1506** *Upupa epops* (hoopoe)

**2008.** Fauna. Multicoloured. Self-adhesive.
2934 75c. Type **1506** 1·90 1·70
2935 75c. *Hemaris fuciformis* (broad-bordered bee hawk-moth ) 1·90 1·70

**1507** Steam Locomotive

**2008.** 110th Anniv of Vienna Urban Railway.
2936 **1507** 75c. multicoloured 2·00 1·90

**1508** Letterbox

**2008.** Death Centenary of Josef Maria Olbrich (artist and architect).
2937 **1508** 65c. multicoloured 1·80 1·60

**1509** Statuette

**2008.** Centenary of Discovery of Willendorf Venus. Self-adhesive.
2938 **1509** 375c. multicoloured 10·00 9·75

**1510** Columbine

**2008.** Flowers.
2939 **1510** 50c. multicoloured 1·40 1·30

**1511** Ranunculus

**2008.** Flowers.
2940 **1511** 55c. multicoloured 1·50 1·40

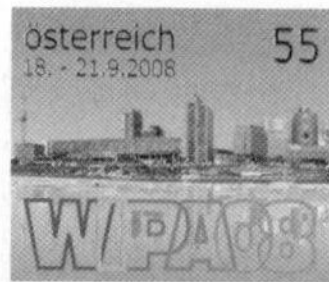

**1512** Skyline

**2008.** WIPA 2008 International Stamp Exhibition. Self-adhesive.
2941 **1512** 55c. multicoloured 1·50 1·40

See also No. 2828, 2858 and 2902.

**1513** Series 4130 Rail Car Set

**2008.** 150th Anniv of Empress Elizabeth Western Railway.
2942 **1513** 100c. multicoloured 2·75 2·50

**1514** Express Mail (detail) (painting by K. Schorpfeil)

**2008.** Praga 2008 and WIPA 2008, International Stamp Exhibitions. Sheet 120×80 mm.
**MS**2943 multicoloured 7·25 7·00

Stamp of the same design was issued by Czech Republic.

**1515** Maze

**2008.** 80th Birth Anniv of Friedensreich Hundertwasser (artist). Sheet 97×127 mm containing T 1515 and similar vert designs. Multicoloured.
**MS**2944 55c. Type **1515**; 75c. House; 100c. Stylized lamps; 125c. Maze (different) 10·00 10·00

**2008.** WIPA 2008 International Stamp Exhibition. Silver. Sheet 126×73 mm containing triangular designs as T 1479. Multicoloured.
**MS**2945 55c.+20c.×3, As No. 2828; As No. 2902; As No. 2858 6·25 6·25

**1516** *Schonbrunn* (paddle steamer)

**2008.** Stamp Day.
2946 **1516** 265c.+130c. multicoloured 10·50 10·00

**1517** Nude (Dina Larot)

**2008**
2947 **1517** 55c. multicoloured 1·50 1·40

**1518** Gentian

**2008.** Vorarlberg Embroidery. Self-adhesive.
2948 **1518** 375c. blue 10·00 9·75

**1519** *Maximilian Schell* ((Arnulf Rainer)

**2008.** Maximilian Schell (actor).
2949 **1519** 100c. multicoloured 2·75 2·50

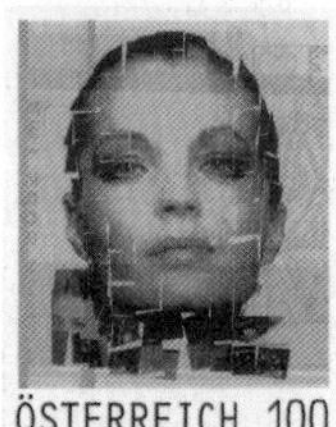

**1520** Romy Schneider

**2008.** 70th Birth Anniv of Romy Schneider (actress).
2950 **1520** 100c. multicoloured 2·75 2·50

**1521** Iker Casillas (winning Spanish team captain) holding Trophy

**2008.** Euro 2008 Football Championships (16th issue).
2951 **1521** 65c. multicoloured 1·80 1·60

**1522** Thomas Morgenstern

**2008.** Thomas Morgenstern—World Champion Ski-jumper, 2007 and Olympic Gold Medallist.
2952 **1522** 100c. multicoloured 2·75 2·50

**1523** Markus Rogan

**2008.** Markus Rogan—World Champion Backstroke Swimmer, 2008.
2953 **1523** 100c. multicoloured 2·75 2·50

**1524** Heinz Fischer

**2008.** 70th Birth Anniv of Heinz Fischer (federal president 2004—present).
2954 **1524** 55c. multicoloured 1·50 1·40

**1525** Manner Neapolitan Biscuits

**2008.** Classic Trademarks.
2955 **1525** 55c. multicoloured 1·50 1·40

**1526** Koloman Moser

**2008.** Koloman Moser (artist and stamp designer) Commemoration.
2956 **1526** 130c. multicoloured 3·75 3·50

**1527** Trieste Imperial and Royal Post Office Building

**2008.** Old Austria.
2957 **1527** 65c. multicoloured 2·00 1·90

**1528** *First Christmas Tree in Ried* (Felix Ignaz Pollingger)

**2008.** Art History.
2958 **1528** 65c. multicoloured 2·00 1·90

**1529** Saint Martin

**2008.** Saints (7th issue).
2959 **1529** 55c. multicoloured 1·50 1·40

**1530** Karl Schranz

**2008.** 70th Birth Anniv of Karl Schranz (World Champion skier).
2960 **1530** 65c. multicoloured 2·00 1·90

**1531** Adoration of the Magi (ceiling fresco, Collegiate Monastery and Parish Church of St Michael, Flachgau)

**2008.** Christmas.
2961 **1531** 55c. multicoloured 1·80 1·60

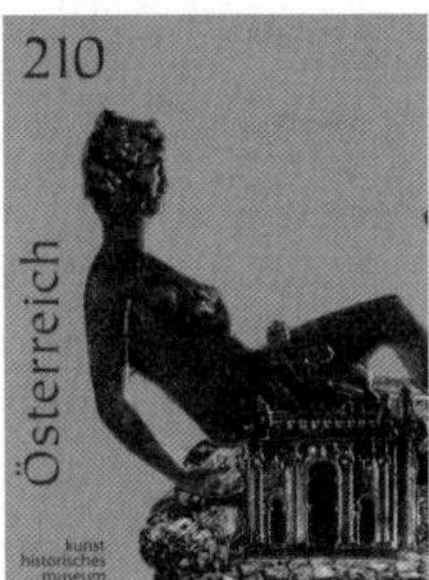
**1532** Female Figure

**2009.** Saliera (salt cellar) by Benvento Cellini. Sheet 110×75 mm containing T 1532 and similar vert design. Multicoloured.
**MS**2962 210c.×2, Type **1532**; Male figure 14·00 14·00

The stamps of **MS**2962 form a composite design of the salt cellar.

**1533** Landskron Castle

**2009.** Self-adhesive.
2963 **1533** 55c. multicoloured 1·90 1·70

**1534** Pez Peppermint Sweets

**2009.** Classic Trademarks.
2964 **1534** 55c. multicoloured 1·90 1·70

**1535** Post Building, Cracow

**2009.** Old Austria.
2965 **1535** 100c. multicoloured 3·00 2·75

**1536** Raimondo Montecuccoli

**2009.** 400th Birth Anniv of Raimondo Montecuccoli (soldier and writer).
2966 **1536** 130c. multicoloured 4·00 3·75

**1537** Girl

**2009.** 60th Anniv of SOS Children's Villages.
2967 **1537** 55c. multicoloured 1·90 1·70

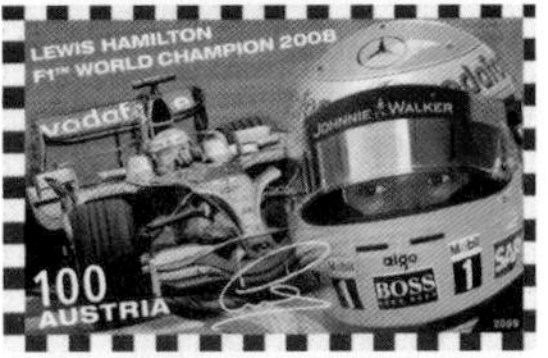
**1538** Lewis Hamilton and McLaren Race Car

**2009.** Lewis Hamilton (Formula I World Champion–2008).
2968 **1538** 100c. multicoloured 3·00 2·75

**1539** Mercedes W 196 Silver Arrow

**2009.** Centenary of Technical Museum, Vienna. Self-adhesive.
2969 **1539** 265c. multicoloured 8·00 8·00

**1540** Schonbrunn Imperial Palace

**2009**
2970 **1540** 65c. multicoloured 2·00 1·90

**1541** Venediger Glacier

**2009.** Preserve Polar Regions and Glaciers.
2971 **1541** 65c. multicoloured 2·00 1·90

**1542** Haflinger

**2009.** 50th Anniv of Steyr Daimler Puch Haflinger All Terrain Vehicle.
2972 **1542** 55c. murlticoloured 1·90 1·70

**1543** Joseph Haydn

**2009.** Death Bicentenary of Franz Joseph Haydn (composer).
2973 **1543** 65c. multicoloured 2·00 1·90

**1544** *Tyto alba* (barn owl)

**2009.** Self-adhesive.
2974 **1544** 55c. multicoloured 1·90 1·70

**1545** Wrapped Flak Tower

**2009.** Art. Works by Christo Vladimirov Javashev (Christo, the packaging artist). Sheet 78×80 mm containing T 1545 and similar vert design. Multicoloured.
**MS**2975 55c.×2, Type **1545**; The 21st Century Collection 3·75 3·75

**1546** Fred Zinnemann

**2009.** Fred Zinnemann (director) Commemoration
2976 **1546** 55c. multicoloured 1·60 1·40

**1547** Old Town

**2009.** 850th Anniv of St Pölten
2977 **1547** 55c. multicoloured 1·60 1·40

**1548** Burning Ring

**2009.** *The Ring of the Nibelungen* (opera) performed at Vienna State Opera House
2978 **1548** 100c. multicoloured 1·60 1·40

**1549** *Thalia*

**2009.** Centenary of *Thalia* (pleasure steamer)
2979 **1549** 55c. multicoloured 1·60 1·60

**1550** Baptismal Font, Old Cathedral, Linz

**2009.** Religious Art
2980 **1550** 55c. multicoloured 6·25 6·00

**1551** State Opera House

**2009.** 140th Anniv of Vienna State Opera House
2981 **1551** 100c. multicoloured 3·00 2·75

**1552** Wolfgang Graf Berghe von Trips

**2009.** Formula I Motor Racing Legends. Multicoloured.
**MS**2982 55c.×4, Type **1552**; Gilles Villeneuve; James Hunt; Bernie Ecclestone 6·25 6·25

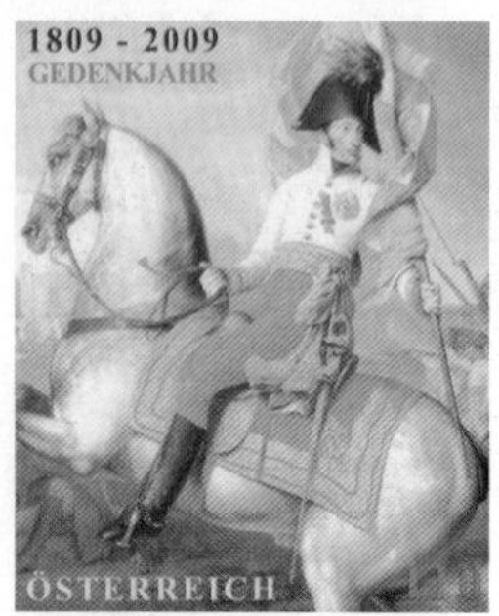

**1553** Napoleon

**2009.** Bicentenary of Battle of Aspern and Essling. Sheet 73×87 mm
**MS**2983 110c. multicoloured 3·00 3·00

**1554** TUGSAT-1 (nano-satellite)

**2009**
2984 **1554** 65c. multicoloured 2·10 1·90

**1555** Graz

**2009.** Old Town, Graz–World Heritage Site
2985 **1555** 100c. multicoloured 3·00 2·75

**1556** Early Aircraft

**2009.** Centenary of Wiener Neustadt Airfield
2986 **1556** 140c. multicoloured 4·00 3·75

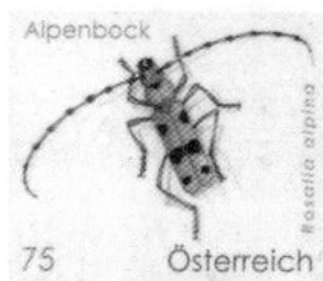

**1557** *Rosalia alpina* (longhorn beetle)

**2009.** Longhorn Beetle
2987 **1557** 75c. multicoloured 2·10 1·90

**1558** Steam Locomotive

**2009.** Centenary of Wachau Railway
2988 **1558** 75c. multicoloured 2·10 1·90

**1559** *Apis mellifera* (honeybee)

**2009.** Fauna. Multicoloured.
2989 55c. Type **1559** 1·60 1·40
2990 55c. *Merops apiaster* (bee-eater) 1·60 1·40

Nos. 2989/90 were issued in *se-tenant* 'hang sell' sheetlets of ten stamps

**1560** Anemones

**2009.** Flowers
2991 **1560** 55c. multicoloured 1·60 1·40

**1561** Film Poster

**2009.** 60th Anniv of *The Third Man* (film by Carol Reed, based on book by Graham Greene)
2992 **1562** 65c. multicoloured 1·90 1·70

**1562** '20'

**2009.** 20th Anniv of Opening of Border between Austria and Hungary
2993 **1562** 65c. multicoloured 1·90 1·70

**1563** Gateway and Soldier, Carnuntum

**2009.** Archaeology. Multicoloured.
**MS**2994 55c. Type **1563**; 65c. Bas-relief and mounted soldier, Gerulata 5·00 5·00

Stamps of a similar design were issued by Slovakia.

**1564** *MS Österreich* (oldest motor powered passenger ship on Lake Constance)

**2009.** Stamp Day
2995 **1564** 265c.+130c. multicoloured 11·50 10·00

**1565** Berta von Suttner

**2009.** 120th Anniv of *Lay Down Your Arms!* (antiwar novel by Berta von Suttner)
2996 **1565** 55c. multicoloured 1·60 1·40

**1566** *The Glorious Rosary*

**2009.** Tenth Anniv of the Return of Rosary Triptych (painted by Ernst Fuchs), Parish Church of Hetzendorf, Vienna. Multicoloured.
**MS**2997 55c. Type **1566**; 75c. *The Joyful Rosary*; 100c. *The Sorrowful Rosary* 6·75 6·75

**1567** Wolfgang Loitzl (Four Hills Champion)

**2009.** Champion Ski Jumpers. Multicoloured.
2998 100c. Type **1567** 3·00 2·75
2999 100c. Gregor Schlierenzauer (World Cup winner 2008–9) 3·00 2·75

**1568** 5042 Series Rail Car in Zistersdorf Station

**2009.** 120th Anniv of Drösing–Zistersdorf Local Railway
3000 **1568** 100c. multicoloured 3·00 2·75

**1569** *Woman rocking on a Chair* (Leander Kaiser)

**2009.** Modern Art
3001 **1569** 55c. multicoloured 1·90 1·70

**1570** *Emilie Flöge* (Gustav Klimt)

**2009.** Austria–Japan Year. Multicoloured.
**MS**3002 140c.×2, Type **1570**; *Autumn Clothes* (Shoen Uemura) 8·50 8·50

**1571** *Las Meninas (The Royal Family of Felipe IV)*

**2009.** Diego Rodríguez de Silva y Velázquez (artist) Commemoration. Multicoloured.
**MS**3003 55c. Type **1571**; 65c.*The Infanta Margarita Teresa in a Blue Dress* 4·25 4·25

Stamps of the same design were issued by Spain

**1572** Ranui Church, Vilnös Valley, South Tyrol

**2009.** Christmas
3004 **1572** 65c. multicoloured 2·00 1·90

**1573** Palmers Underwear

**2009.** Classic Trademarks
3005 **1573** 55c. multicoloured 1·90 1·70


**1574** St. Leopold

**2009.** Patron Saints
3006 **1574** 55c. multicoloured 1·90 1·70

**1575** Zum gnadenreichen Christkindl (Blessed Holy Child)

**2009.** Christmas

| | | | | |
|---|---|---|---|---|
| 3007 | **1575** | 55c. multicoloured | 1·90 | 1·70 |

**1576** *Tribute to Vedova* (George Baselitz)

**2009.** Tenth Anniv of Essl Art Museum

| | | | | |
|---|---|---|---|---|
| 3008 | **1576** | 55c. multicoloured | 1·90 | 1·70 |

**1577** Ape holding Book

**2009.** Birth Bicentenary of Charles Darwin (naturalist and evolutionary theorist). Multicoloured.

| | | | |
|---|---|---|---|
| **MS**3009 | 55c.×3, Type **1577**; Cherub with head in hands and mirror; Ape holding mirror to cherub | 5·75 | 5·75 |

The stamps and margins of **MS**3009 form a composite design

**1578** *Lutra lutra* (otter)

**2010.** Fauna (1st issue). Multicoloured.

| | | | |
|---|---|---|---|
| 3010 | 75c. Type **1578** | 2·10 | 2·00 |
| 3011 | 75c. *Salmo trutta fario* (brown trout) | 2·10 | 2·00 |

**1579** *Felis silvestris* (wild cat)

**2010.** Fauna (2nd issue)

| | | | | |
|---|---|---|---|---|
| 3012 | **1579** | 65c. multicoloured | 2·00 | 1·90 |

**1580** View from Salzach River

**2010.** World Heritage Site

| | | | | |
|---|---|---|---|---|
| 3013 | **1580** | 100c. multicoloured | 3·00 | 2·75 |

**1581** *Annual Rings of Scent and Bliss* (Helmut Kand)

**2010.** Modern Art

| | | | | |
|---|---|---|---|---|
| 3014 | **1581** | 55c. multicoloured | 1·90 | 1·70 |

**1582** *Prince Eugene as Victor over the Turks* (Jacob van Schuppen)

**2010.** Prince Eugene of Savoy Exhibition, Belvedere, Vienna

| | | | | |
|---|---|---|---|---|
| 3015 | **1582** | 65c. multicoloured | 2·00 | 1·90 |

**1583** Kleinbahn Model Railways

**2010.** Classic Trade Marks

| | | | | |
|---|---|---|---|---|
| 3016 | **1583** | 55c. multicoloured | 1·90 | 1·70 |

**1584** *The Tyrolean Land Army Year Nine* (Joseph Anton Koch)

**2010.** Death Bicentenary of Andreas Hofer (revolutionary leader)

| | | | |
|---|---|---|---|
| **MS**3017 | 175c. multicoloured | 5·75 | 5·75 |

**1585** Stage Setting for *Medea* (by Marco Auturo Marelli)

**2010.** Vienna State Opera House

| | | | | |
|---|---|---|---|---|
| 3018 | **1585** | 100c. multicoloured | 3·00 | 2·75 |

**1586** Otto Preminger

**2010.** Otto Ludwig Preminger (film director) Commemoration

| | | | | |
|---|---|---|---|---|
| 3019 | **1586** | 55c. multicoloured | 1·90 | 1·70 |

**1587** Roger Federer

**2010.** Roger Federer (world champion tennis player)

| | | | | |
|---|---|---|---|---|
| 3020 | **1587** | 65c. multicoloured | 2·00 | 1·90 |

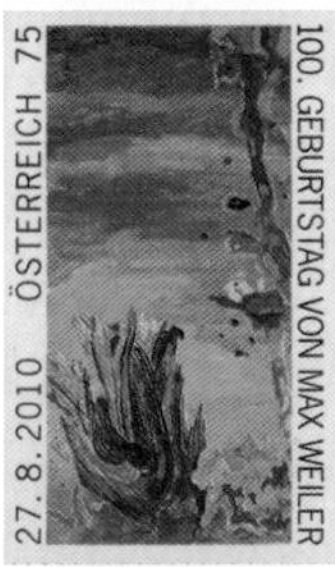


**1588** *Soon the Sun will rise*

**2010.** Birth Centenary of Max Weiler (artist)

| | | | | |
|---|---|---|---|---|
| 3021 | **1588** | 75c. multicoloured | 2·10 | 2·00 |

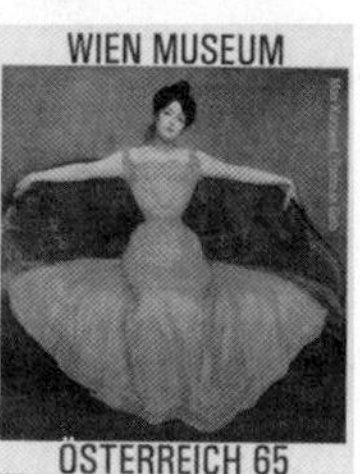


**1589** *Lady in Yellow* (Max Kurzwell)

**2010.** Wien Museum

| | | | | |
|---|---|---|---|---|
| 3022 | **1589** | 65c. multicoloured | 2·00 | 1·90 |

**1590** Upper Belvedere

**2010.** Belvedere Palace, Vienna

| | | | | |
|---|---|---|---|---|
| 3023 | **1590** | 65c. multicoloured | 2·00 | 1·90 |

**1591** 671 Steam Locomotive (1860 (oldest operational steam locomotive in the world)

**2010.** 150th Anniv of Graz Köflach Railway

| | | | | |
|---|---|---|---|---|
| 3024 | **1591** | 100c. multicoloured | 3·00 | 2·75 |

**1592** Prague Castle and St Vitus Cathedral.

**2010.** Old Austria

| | | | | |
|---|---|---|---|---|
| 3025 | **1592** | 65c. multicoloured | 2·00 | 1·90 |

**1593** Empress Elisabeth (Sisi)

**2010.** Expo 2010, Shanghai

| | | | |
|---|---|---|---|
| **MS**3026 | 55c. multicoloured | 1·50 | 1·50 |

**1594** Railway

**2010.** Centenary (2003) of Mendel (Mendola) Railway (first electric funicular railway)

| | | | | |
|---|---|---|---|---|
| 3027 | **1594** | 65c. multicoloured | 1·90 | 1·80 |

**1595** Post Box on Legs

**2010.** Post-Publicity Campaign 2010

| | | | | |
|---|---|---|---|---|
| 3028 | **1595** | 55c. multicoloured | 1·90 | 1·80 |

**1596** Palace during Early 19th Century

**2010.** Imperial Festival Palace Hof

| | | | | |
|---|---|---|---|---|
| 3029 | **1596** | 55c. multicoloured | 1·50 | 1·40 |

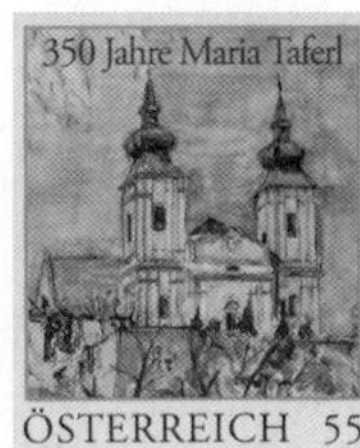


**1597** Baroque Church (painting by Franz Knapp

**2010.** 350th Anniv of Maria Taferl

| | | | | |
|---|---|---|---|---|
| 3030 | **1597** | 55c. multicoloured | 1·50 | 1·40 |

**1598** Gustav Mahler

**2010.** 150th Birth Anniv of Gustav Mahler (composer and conductor)

| | | | | |
|---|---|---|---|---|
| 3031 | **1598** | 100c. multicoloured | 3·00 | 2·75 |

**Type** Festival Poster, 1928 (by Leopoldine (Poldi) Wojtek)

**2010.** 90th Anniv of Salzburg Festival

| | | | | |
|---|---|---|---|---|
| 3032 | **1599** | 55c. multicoloured | 1·50 | 1·50 |

**1600** Coracias garrulus (European roller)

**2010.** Fauna. Multicoloured.

| | | | |
|---|---|---|---|
| 3033 | 55c. Type **1600** | 1·50 | 1·40 |
| 3034 | 75c. *Aquila chrysaetos* (golden eagle) | 2·10 | 2·00 |

**1601** Crozier

**2010.** Religious Art

| | | | | |
|---|---|---|---|---|
| 3035 | **1601** | 75c. multicoloured | 2·10 | 2·00 |

**1602** Fridolin Fuchs (post fox) on Skateboard (illustration by Carola Holland)

**2010.** Europa

| | | | | |
|---|---|---|---|---|
| 3036 | **1602** | 65c. multicoloured | 1·90 | 1·80 |

**1603** Self Portrait with Black Vase

**2010.** 120th Birth Anniv of Egon Schiele (artist)

| | | | | |
|---|---|---|---|---|
| 3037 | **1603** | 140c. multicoloured | 4·00 | 3·75 |

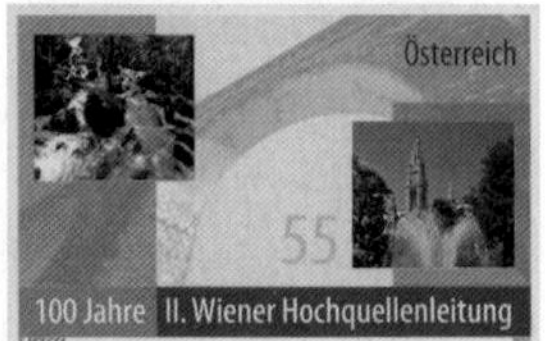

**1604** Mountain Spring and Fountain in Front of Vienna City Hall

**2010.** Centenary of Second Pipeline carrying Mountain Spring Water to Vienna

| | | | | |
|---|---|---|---|---|
| 3038 | **1604** | 55c. multicoloured | 2·10 | 2·00 |

**1605** Simon Wiesenthal in Star of David

**2010.** Simon Wiesenthal (holocaust survivor and pursuer of war criminals) Commemoration

| | | | | |
|---|---|---|---|---|
| 3039 | **1605** | 75c. multicoloured | 2·10 | 2·00 |

**1606** Opera House Interior and Ioan Holender

**2010.** 75th Birth Anniv of Ioan Holender (director of Vienna State Opera)

| | | | | |
|---|---|---|---|---|
| 3040 | **1606** | 100c. multicoloured | 2·75 | 2·50 |

**1607** Karnburg Church

**2010.** Churches

| | | | | |
|---|---|---|---|---|
| 3041 | **1607** | 100c multicoloured | 2·75 | 2·50 |

**1608** Johann Flux

**2010.** 350th Birth Anniv of Johann Joseph Fux (composer and musical theorist)

| | | | | |
|---|---|---|---|---|
| 3042 | **0608** | 100c. multicoloured | 3·00 | 2·75 |

**1609** Grete Rehor and Parliament Building, Vienna

**2010.** Birth Centenary of Grete Rehor (politician and first female Federal Minister)

| | | | | |
|---|---|---|---|---|
| 3043 | **1609** | 55c. multicoloured | 1·50 | 1·40 |

**1610** 'PARADE'

**2010.** 15th Anniv of Rainbow Parade

| | | | | |
|---|---|---|---|---|
| 3044 | **1610** | 55c. multicoloured | 3·00 | 2·75 |

**1611** Steam Locomotive

**2010.** 125th Anniv of Spielfeld Strass-Bad Radkersburg Railway

| | | | | |
|---|---|---|---|---|
| 3045 | **1611** | 65c. multicoloured | 1·90 | 1·80 |

**1612** Castle and Grounds

**2010.** Grafennegg Castle

| | | | | |
|---|---|---|---|---|
| 3046 | **1612** | 55c. multicoloured | 1·50 | 1·40 |

**1613** Zodiac

**2010.** 150th Birth Anniv of Alfons Maria Mucha (artist)

| | | | | |
|---|---|---|---|---|
| 3047 | **1613** | 115c. multicoloured | 3·25 | 3·00 |

**1614** Church

**2010.** 50th Anniv of Eisenstadt Diocese

| | | | | |
|---|---|---|---|---|
| 3048 | **1614** | 55c. multicoloured | 1·50 | 1·40 |

**1615** Mother Teresa

**2010.** Birth Centenary of Agnes Gonxha Bojaxhiu (Mother Teresa) (founder of Missionaries of Charity)

| | | | | |
|---|---|---|---|---|
| 3049 | **1615** | 130c. multicoloured | 3·50 | 3·25 |

**1616** Railjet Train and Gmunden

**2010.** Stamp Day

| | | | | |
|---|---|---|---|---|
| 3050 | **1616** | 265c.+130c. multicoloured | 11·00 | 10·50 |

**1617** Rosa centifolia Bullata

**2010.** Flowers

| | | | | |
|---|---|---|---|---|
| 3051 | **1617** | 55c. multicoloured | 1·50 | 1·40 |

**1618** Steam Locomotive, Salzburg, Austria

**2010.** Orient Express. Multicoloured.

| | | | |
|---|---|---|---|
| **MS**3052 | 65c.×2, Type **1618**; Steam locomotive, Sinaia, Romania | 3·50 | 3·50 |

**1619** Crucifix (Jakob Adhart), ArchAbbey of St. Peter, Salzburg

**2010.** Sacred Art

| | | | | |
|---|---|---|---|---|
| 3052a | **1619** | 100c. multicoloured | 2·75 | 2·50 |

**1620** Anniversary Emblem and Members Flags

**2010.** 50th Anniv of OPEC (Organization of Petroleum Exporting Countries)

| | | | | |
|---|---|---|---|---|
| 3053 | **1620** | 140c. multicoloured | 4·00 | 4·00 |

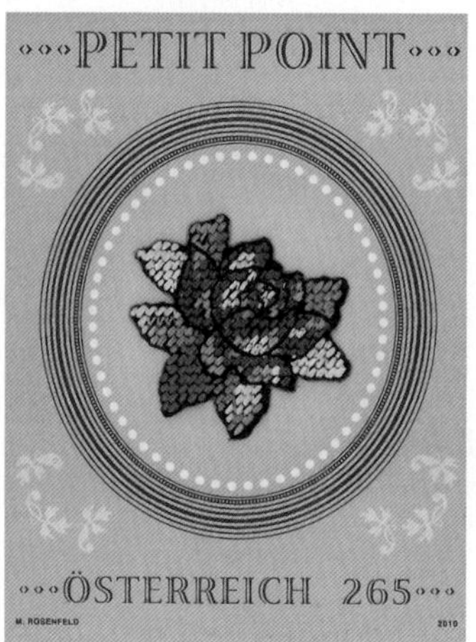

**1621** Rose

**2010.** Petit Point

| | | | |
|---|---|---|---|
| **MS**3054 | multicoloured | 7·25 | 7·25 |

**1622** Imperial and Royal State Railways Series 199 Locomotive

**2010.** Centenary of Wechsel Railway

| | | | | |
|---|---|---|---|---|
| 3055 | **1622** | 100c. multicoloured | 2·75 | 2·50 |

**1623** Andreas and Wolfgang Linger

**2010.** Andreas and Wolfgang Linger–Winners of Luge Olympic Gold Medal at Winter Olympic Games, Vancouver

| | | | | |
|---|---|---|---|---|
| 3056 | **1623** | 100c. multicoloured | 2·75 | 2·50 |

**1624** Desk

**2010.** Austrian Design

| | | | | |
|---|---|---|---|---|
| 3057 | **1624** | 65c. multicoloured | 1·90 | 1·80 |

**1625** Maria Theresa (Martin van Meytens)

**2010.** 230th Death Anniv of Archduchess Maria Theresia Walburga Amalia Christina von Österreich (Maria Theresa of Austria) (Archduchess of Austria and Queen of Hungary and Bohemia)

| | | | |
|---|---|---|---|
| 3058 | 65c. multicoloured | 1·90 | 1·80 |

**1626** Weather Station, City Park, Vienna

**2010.** Meteorological Architecture. Multicoloured.

| | | | | |
|---|---|---|---|---|
| **MS**3059 | 65c. Type **1626**; 140c. Austria-Hungarian community meteorological station, Botanical Garden, Buenos Aires | | 5·50 | 5·50 |

**1627** Ornithopter (first controlled flight, November 1808)

**2010.** 250th Birth Anniv of Jakob Degen (inventor)

| | | | | |
|---|---|---|---|---|
| 3060 | **1627** | 125c multicoloured | 1·90 | 1·80 |

**1628** Flag and Soldier

**2010.** 50th Anniv of Austrian Armed Forces International Assignments

| | | | | |
|---|---|---|---|---|
| 3061 | **1628** | 65c. multicoloured | 1·90 | 1·80 |

**1629** St Stephen's Cathedral and St Peter's Church, Vienna

**Cultural** Heritage

| | | | | |
|---|---|---|---|---|
| 3062 | **1629** | 199c. multicoloured | 3·00 | 2·75 |

**1630** Goldenes Dachl, Innsbruck

**2010.** Advent

| | | | | |
|---|---|---|---|---|
| 3063 | **1630** | 65c. multicoloured | 2·00 | 1·90 |

**1631** Three Wise Men (detail from 12th-century missal), St Florian's Monastery

**2010.** Christmas (1st issue)

| | | | | |
|---|---|---|---|---|
| 3064 | **1631** | (55c.) multicoloured | 1·50 | 1·40 |

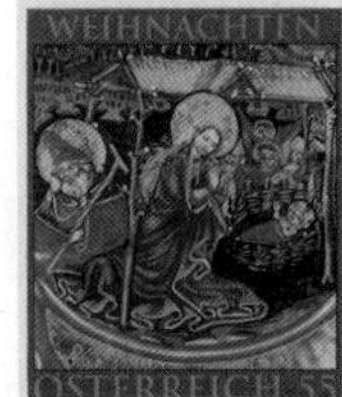


**1632** The Nativity (detail of antiphonal from Cistercian monastery, Rein, Styria)

**2010.** Christmas (2nd issue)

| | | | | |
|---|---|---|---|---|
| 3065 | **1632** | 55c. multicoloured | 1·50 | 1·40 |

**1632a** Emperor Franz Joseph and Dr. Anton Freiherr von Eiselsberg

**2011.** Centenary of Austrian Cancer Aid

| | | | | |
|---|---|---|---|---|
| 3065a | **1632a** | 55c. multicoloured | 1·50 | 1·40 |

**1633** Post Office

**2011.** Old Austria

| | | | | |
|---|---|---|---|---|
| 3066 | **1633** | 65c. multicoloured | 1·90 | 1·80 |

**1634** Violin

**2011.** Musical Instruments

| | | | | |
|---|---|---|---|---|
| 3067 | **1634** | 75c. multicoloured | 2·20 | 2·10 |

**1635** Bruno Kreisky

**2011.** Birth Centenary of Bruno Kreisky (politician)

| | | | | |
|---|---|---|---|---|
| 3068 | **1635** | 55c. multicoloured | 1·60 | 1·50 |

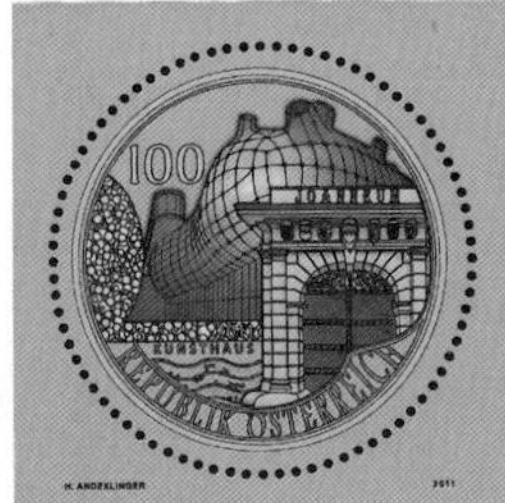


**1636** Stylized Joanneum Graz and Kunsthaus Graz

**2011.** Bicentenary of Joanneum Graz Museum

| | | | | |
|---|---|---|---|---|
| 3069 | **1636** | 100c. multicoloured | 3·00 | 2·75 |

**1637** Franz Liszt

**2011.** Birth Bicentenary of Franz Liszt

| | | | | |
|---|---|---|---|---|
| 3070 | **1637** | 65c. multicoloured | 1·90 | 1·90 |

**1638** Hedy Lamarr

**2011.** Hedwig Eva Maria Kiesler (Hedy Lamarr) (film actor) Commemoration

| | | | | |
|---|---|---|---|---|
| 3071 | **1638** | 55c. multicolured | 1·60 | 1·50 |

**1639** Niemetz Confectioners

**2010.** Classic Trade Marks

| | | | | |
|---|---|---|---|---|
| 3072 | | 55c. muulticoloured | 1·90 | 1·80 |

## IMPERIAL JOURNAL STAMPS

**J18**

**1853.** Imperf.

| | | | | |
|---|---|---|---|---|
| J67 | | 1k. blue | 15·00 | 2·10 |
| J15 | **J18** | 2k. green | £4250 | £120 |
| J68 | | 2k. brown | 13·50 | 3·00 |
| J32 | | 4k. brown | £550 | £1600 |

The 2k. green has different corner ornaments.

For similar values in black or red, see Lombardy and Venetia Imperial Journal stamps, Nos. J22/4.

**J21** Arms of Austria

**1890.** Imperf.

| | | | | |
|---|---|---|---|---|
| J76 | **J21** | 1k. brown | 15·00 | 2·10 |
| J77 | **J21** | 2k. green | 13·50 | 3·00 |

**J22** Arms of Austria

**1890.** Perf.

| | | | | |
|---|---|---|---|---|
| J78 | **J22** | 25k. red | £140 | £300 |

## NEWSPAPER STAMPS

**N2** Mercury

**1851.** Imperf.

| | | | | |
|---|---|---|---|---|
| N11b | **N 2** | (0.6k.) blue | £225 | £160 |

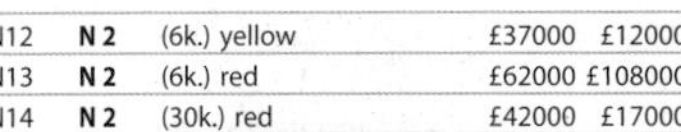

| | | | | |
|---|---|---|---|---|
| N12 | **N 2** | (6k.) yellow | £37000 | £12000 |
| N13 | **N 2** | (6k.) red | £62000 | £108000 |
| N14 | **N 2** | (30k.) red | £42000 | £17000 |

**N8** Francis Joseph I

**1858.** Imperf.

| | | | | |
|---|---|---|---|---|
| N28 | **N8** | (1k.05) blue | £800 | £900 |
| N29 | **N8** | (1k.05) lilac | £1100 | £425 |

**N11** Francis Joseph I

**1861.** Imperf.

| | | | | |
|---|---|---|---|---|
| N38 | **N11** | (1k.05) grey | £250 | £225 |

**N13** Arms of Austria

**1863.** Imperf.

| | | | | |
|---|---|---|---|---|
| N44 | **N13** | (1k.05) lilac | 55·00 | 21·00 |

**AHN17** Mercury

**1867.** Imperf.

| | | | | |
|---|---|---|---|---|
| AHN58b | **AHN17** | (1k.) lilac | 50 | 30 |

**N19** Mercury

**1880.** Imperf.

| | | | | |
|---|---|---|---|---|
| N69 | **N19** | ½k. green | 11·50 | 1·60 |

**N31** Mercury

**1899.** Imperf.

| | | | | |
|---|---|---|---|---|
| N122 | **N31** | 2h. blue | 30 | 20 |
| N123 | **N31** | 6h. orange | 3·00 | 3·00 |
| N124 | **N31** | 10h. brown | 2·10 | 1·60 |
| N125 | **N31** | 20h. pink | 2·10 | 3·00 |

**N43** Mercury

**1908.** Imperf.

| | | | | |
|---|---|---|---|---|
| N207C | **N43** | 2h. blue | 1·50 | 45 |
| N208C | **N43** | 6h. orange | 6·75 | 1·10 |
| N209C | **N43** | 10h. red | 6·75 | 85 |
| N210C | **N43** | 20h. brown | 6·75 | 85 |

**N53** Mercury

**1916.** Imperf.

| | | | | |
|---|---|---|---|---|
| N266 | **N53** | 2h. brown | 10 | 20 |
| N267 | **N53** | 4h. green | 50 | 1·60 |
| N268 | **N53** | 6h. blue | 40 | 1·70 |
| N269 | **N53** | 10h. orange | 1·00 | 2·10 |

| | | | | |
|---|---|---|---|---|
| N270 | **N53** | 30h. red | 50 | 1·90 |

**N54** Mercury

**1916.** For Express. Perf.

| | | | | |
|---|---|---|---|---|
| N271 | **N54** | 2h. red on yellow | 1·50 | 4·25 |
| N272 | **N54** | 5h. green on yellow | 1·50 | 4·25 |

**N61** Mercury

**1917.** For Express. Perf.

| | | | | |
|---|---|---|---|---|
| N294 | **N61** | 2h. red on yellow | 20 | 55 |
| N295 | **N61** | 5h. green on yellow | 20 | 55 |

**1919.** Optd Deutschosterreich. Imperf.

| | | | | |
|---|---|---|---|---|
| N318 | **N53** | 2h. brown | 20 | 1·10 |
| N319 | **N53** | 4h. green | 50 | 8·50 |
| N320 | **N53** | 6h. blue | 30 | 10·50 |
| N321 | **N53** | 10h. orange | 1·20 | 16·00 |
| N322 | **N53** | 30h. red | 60 | 21·00 |

**1919.** For Express. Optd Deutschosterreich. Perf.

| | | | | |
|---|---|---|---|---|
| N334 | **N61** | 2h. red on yellow | 10 | 30 |
| N335 | **N61** | 5h. green on yellow | 10 | 30 |

**N68** Mercury

**1920.** Imperf.

| | | | | |
|---|---|---|---|---|
| N365A | **N68** | 2h. violet | 10 | 20 |
| N366A | **N68** | 4h. brown | 10 | 30 |
| N367A | **N68** | 5h. slate | 10 | 20 |
| N368A | **N68** | 6h. blue | 15 | 20 |
| N369A | **N68** | 8h. green | 10 | 55 |
| N370A | **N68** | 9h. bistre | 10 | 20 |
| N371A | **N68** | 10h. red | 10 | 20 |
| N372A | **N68** | 12h. blue | 10 | 55 |
| N373A | **N68** | 15h. mauve | 10 | 25 |
| N374A | **N68** | 18h. turquoise | 10 | 30 |
| N375A | **N68** | 20h. orange | 10 | 30 |
| N376A | **N68** | 30h. brown | 10 | 20 |
| N377A | **N68** | 45h. green | 10 | 55 |
| N378A | **N68** | 60h. red | 10 | 30 |
| N379A | **N68** | 72h. brown | 20 | 55 |
| N380A | **N68** | 90h. violet | 30 | 85 |
| N381A | **N68** | 1k.20 red | 30 | 1·10 |
| N382A | **N68** | 2k.40 green | 30 | 1·10 |
| N383A | **N68** | 3k. grey | 30 | 1·10 |

**1921.** For Express. No. N334 surch 50 50.

| | | | | |
|---|---|---|---|---|
| N450 | **N 61** | 50 on 2h. red on yell | 10 | 45 |

**N78** Mercury

**1921.** Imperf.

| | | | | |
|---|---|---|---|---|
| N452 | **N78** | 45h. grey | 20 | 20 |
| N453 | **N78** | 75h. red | 10 | 55 |
| N454 | **N78** | 1k.50 green | 10 | 75 |
| N455 | **N78** | 1k.80 blue | 10 | 95 |
| N456 | **N78** | 2k.25 brown | 10 | 1·30 |
| N457 | **N78** | 3k. green | 10 | 1·10 |
| N458 | **N78** | 6k. purple | 10 | 1·20 |
| N459 | **N78** | 7k.50 brown | 20 | 1·60 |

**N79** Posthorn and Arrow

**1921.** For Express. Perf.

| | | | | |
|---|---|---|---|---|
| N460 | **N79** | 50h. lilac on yellow | 20 | 2·10 |

## POSTAGE DUE STAMPS

**D26**

**1894.** Perf.

| | | | | |
|---|---|---|---|---|
| D96 | **D26** | 1k. brown | 6·25 | 2·10 |
| D97 | **D26** | 2k. brown | 8·25 | 4·25 |
| D98 | **D26** | 3k. brown | 10·50 | 2·10 |
| D99 | **D26** | 5k. brown | 10·50 | 75 |
| D100 | **D26** | 6k. brown | 8·25 | 9·25 |
| D101 | **D26** | 7k. brown | 4·25 | 9·25 |
| D102 | **D26** | 10k. brown | 8·25 | 85 |
| D103 | **D26** | 20k. brown | 4·25 | 9·25 |
| D104 | **D26** | 50k. brown | 90·00 | £120 |

**1899.** As Type D 26, but value in heller. Perf or imperf.

| | | | | |
|---|---|---|---|---|
| D126 | | 1h. brown | 75 | 30 |
| D127 | | 2h. brown | 75 | 20 |
| D128d | | 3h. brown | 75 | 20 |
| D129 | | 4h. brown | 95 | 20 |
| D130 | | 5h. brown | 1·00 | 20 |
| D131d | | 6h. brown | 75 | 75 |
| D132 | | 10h. brown | 1·20 | 10 |
| D133 | | 12h. brown | 1·50 | 75 |
| D134 | | 15h. brown | 1·20 | 1·40 |
| D135 | | 20h. brown | 1·70 | 45 |
| D136 | | 40h. brown | 3·00 | 75 |
| D137d | | 100h. brown | 8·25 | 4·25 |

**D44**

**1908.** Perf.

| | | | | |
|---|---|---|---|---|
| D210B | **D44** | 1h. red | 1·00 | 2·10 |
| D211C | **D44** | 2h. red | 60 | 45 |
| D212C | **D44** | 4h. red | 40 | 20 |
| D213C | **D44** | 6h. red | 40 | 20 |
| D214C | **D44** | 10h. red | 60 | 20 |
| D215C | **D44** | 14h. red | 7·25 | 3·00 |
| D216C | **D44** | 20h. red | 15·00 | 20 |
| D217C | **D44** | 25h. red | 19·00 | 6·75 |
| D218C | **D44** | 30h. red | 10·50 | 45 |
| D219C | **D44** | 50h. red | 35·00 | 55 |
| D220C | **D44** | 100h. red | 29·00 | 75 |
| D221C | **D44** | 5k. violet | 85·00 | 20·00 |
| D222C | **D44** | 10k. violet | £300 | 5·25 |

**D55**

**D56**

**1916**

| | | | | |
|---|---|---|---|---|
| D273 | **D55** | 5h. red | 10 | 20 |
| D274 | **D55** | 10h. red | 10 | 20 |
| D275 | **D55** | 15h. red | 10 | 20 |
| D276 | **D55** | 20h. red | 10 | 20 |
| D277 | **D55** | 25h. red | 25 | 1·30 |
| D278 | **D55** | 30h. red | 30 | 55 |
| D279 | **D55** | 40h. red | 20 | 85 |
| D280 | **D55** | 50h. red | 1·20 | 3·75 |
| D281 | **D 56** | 1k. blue | 1·00 | 55 |
| D282 | **D 56** | 5k. blue | 3·00 | 4·25 |
| D283 | **D 56** | 10k. blue | 4·25 | 2·30 |

**1916.** Nos. 189/90 optd PORTO or surch 15 15 also.

| | | | | |
|---|---|---|---|---|
| D284 | | 1h. black | 10 | 20 |
| D285 | | 15 on 2h. violet | 35 | 75 |

**1917.** Unissued stamps as T 50 surch PORTO and value.

| | | | | |
|---|---|---|---|---|
| D286 | **50** | 10 on 24h. blue | 2·10 | 75 |
| D287 | **50** | 15 on 36h. violet | 60 | 30 |
| D288 | **50** | 20 on 54h. orange | 35 | 55 |
| D289 | **50** | 50 on 42h. brown | 40 | 30 |

The above differ from Type **50** by showing a full-face portrait.

**1919.** Optd Deutschosterreich.

| | | | | |
|---|---|---|---|---|
| D323 | **D55** | 5h. red | 10 | 20 |
| D324 | **D55** | 10h. red | 10 | 20 |
| D325 | **D55** | 15h. red | 30 | 55 |
| D326 | **D55** | 20h. red | 30 | 55 |
| D327 | **D55** | 25h. red | 10·50 | 32·00 |
| D328 | **D55** | 30h. red | 30 | 55 |
| D329 | **D55** | 40h. red | 30 | 1·10 |
| D330 | **D55** | 50h. red | 35 | 1·60 |
| D331 | **D 56** | 1k. blue | 5·75 | 19·00 |
| D332 | **D 56** | 5k. blue | 11·50 | 19·00 |
| D333 | **D 56** | 10k. blue | 13·50 | 5·25 |

**D69**

**D70**

**1920.** Imperf or perf (D 69), perf (D 70).

| | | | | |
|---|---|---|---|---|
| D384A | **D69** | 5h. pink | 20 | 45 |
| D385A | **D69** | 10h. pink | 10 | 20 |
| D386A | **D69** | 15h. pink | 10 | 1·60 |
| D387A | **D69** | 20h. pink | 10 | 20 |
| D388A | **D69** | 25h. pink | 20 | 1·60 |
| D389A | **D69** | 30h. pink | 10 | 45 |
| D390A | **D69** | 40h. pink | 10 | 45 |
| D391A | **D69** | 50h. pink | 10 | 30 |
| D392A | **D69** | 80h. pink | 10 | 55 |
| D393A | **D 70** | 1k. blue | 10 | 40 |
| D394A | **D 70** | 1½k. blue | 10 | 40 |
| D395A | **D 70** | 2k. blue | 10 | 40 |
| D396Aa | **D 70** | 3k. blue | 10 | 65 |
| D397Aa | **D 70** | 4k. blue | 10 | 85 |
| D398A | **D 70** | 5k. blue | 10 | 40 |
| D399A | **D 70** | 8k. blue | 10 | 1·10 |
| D400A | **D 70** | 10k. blue | 10 | 55 |
| D401A | **D 70** | 20k. blue | 50 | 2·75 |

**1921.** No. 343a surch Nachmarke 7½ K. Perf.

| | | | | |
|---|---|---|---|---|
| D451 | **64** | 7½k. on 15h. brown | 10 | 55 |

**D83**

**1921**

| | | | | |
|---|---|---|---|---|
| D510 | **D83** | 1k. brown | 20 | 45 |
| D511 | **D83** | 2k. brown | 20 | 55 |
| D512 | **D83** | 4k. brown | 20 | 95 |
| D513 | **D83** | 5k. brown | 20 | 45 |
| D514 | **D83** | 7½k. brown | 20 | 1·30 |
| D515 | - | 10k. blue | 20 | 55 |
| D516 | - | 15k. blue | 20 | 75 |
| D517 | - | 20k. blue | 20 | 85 |
| D518 | - | 50k. blue | 20 | 75 |

The 10k. to 50k. are larger (22×30 mm).

**D86**

**1922**

| | | | | |
|---|---|---|---|---|
| D526 | **D83** | 10k. turquoise | 10 | 65 |
| D527 | **D83** | 15k. turquoise | 10 | 95 |
| D528 | **D83** | 20k. turquoise | 10 | 75 |
| D529 | **D83** | 25k. turquoise | 10 | 1·60 |
| D530 | **D83** | 40k. turquoise | 10 | 55 |
| D531 | **D83** | 50k. turquoise | 10 | 1·90 |
| D532 | **D 86** | 100k. purple | 10 | 20 |
| D533 | **D 86** | 150k. purple | 10 | 20 |
| D534 | **D 86** | 200k. purple | 10 | 20 |
| D535 | **D 86** | 400k. purple | 10 | 20 |
| D536 | **D 86** | 600k. purple | 25 | 65 |
| D537 | **D 86** | 800k. purple | 10 | 20 |
| D538 | **D 86** | 1000k. purple | 10 | 20 |
| D539 | **D 86** | 1200k. purple | 1·50 | 9·25 |
| D540 | **D 86** | 1500k. purple | 10 | 55 |
| D541 | **D 86** | 1800k. purple | 4·25 | 18·00 |
| D542 | **D 86** | 2000k. purple | 50 | 1·30 |
| D543 | **D 86** | 3000k. purple | 9·25 | 37·00 |
| D544 | **D 86** | 4000k. purple | 6·25 | 30·00 |
| D545 | **D 86** | 6000k. purple | 10·50 | 47·00 |

**D94**

**1925**

| | | | | |
|---|---|---|---|---|
| D589 | **D94** | 1g. red | 10 | 10 |
| D590 | **D94** | 2g. red | 10 | 10 |
| D591 | **D94** | 3g. red | 10 | 10 |
| D592 | **D94** | 4g. red | 10 | 10 |
| D593 | **D94** | 5g. red | 10 | 10 |
| D594 | **D94** | 6g. red | 30 | 45 |
| D595 | **D94** | 8g. red | 20 | 20 |
| D596 | **D94** | 10g. blue | 30 | 10 |
| D597 | **D94** | 12g. blue | 10 | 10 |
| D598 | **D94** | 14g. blue | 10 | 10 |
| D599 | **D94** | 15g. blue | 10 | 10 |
| D600 | **D94** | 16g. blue | 30 | 25 |
| D601 | **D94** | 18g. blue | 2·10 | 3·75 |
| D602 | **D94** | 20g. blue | 20 | 10 |
| D603 | **D94** | 23g. blue | 60 | 20 |
| D604 | **D94** | 24g. blue | 3·00 | 10 |
| D605 | **D94** | 28g. blue | 2·75 | 25 |
| D606 | **D94** | 30g. blue | 1·30 | 10 |
| D607 | **D94** | 31g. blue | 3·00 | 25 |
| D608 | **D94** | 35g. blue | 3·00 | 20 |
| D609 | **D94** | 39g. blue | 3·50 | 10 |
| D610 | **D94** | 40g. blue | 1·50 | 2·10 |
| D611 | **D94** | 60g. blue | 1·50 | 1·90 |
| D612 | - | 1s. green | 6·75 | 95 |
| D613 | - | 2s. green | 36·00 | 3·75 |
| D614 | - | 5s. green | £140 | 60·00 |
| D615 | - | 10s. green | 55·00 | 5·25 |

DESIGN: 1 to 10s. Horiz bands of colour.

**D120**

**1935**

| | | | | |
|---|---|---|---|---|
| D746 | **D120** | 1g. red | 10 | 20 |
| D747 | **D120** | 2g. red | 10 | 20 |
| D748 | **D120** | 3g. red | 10 | 20 |
| D749 | **D120** | 5g. red | 10 | 20 |
| D750 | - | 10g. blue | 10 | 10 |
| D751 | - | 12g. blue | 10 | 10 |
| D752 | - | 15g. blue | 30 | 65 |
| D753 | - | 20g. blue | 30 | 20 |
| D754 | - | 24g. blue | 35 | 20 |
| D755 | - | 30g. blue | 35 | 20 |
| D756 | - | 39g. blue | 40 | 20 |
| D757 | - | 60g. blue | 85 | 1·60 |
| D758 | - | 1s. green | 1·00 | 45 |
| D759 | - | 2s. green | 2·10 | 1·30 |
| D760 | - | 5s. green | 4·25 | 4·00 |
| D761 | - | 10s. green | 6·25 | 85 |

DESIGNS: 10 to 60g. As Type D **120** but with background of horizontal lines; 1 to 10s. As last, but with positions of figures, arms and inscriptions reversed.

**D143**

**1945**

| | | | | |
|---|---|---|---|---|
| D891 | **D143** | 1pf. red | 20 | 20 |
| D892 | **D143** | 2pf. red | 20 | 20 |
| D893 | **D143** | 3pf. red | 20 | 20 |
| D894 | **D143** | 5pf. red | 20 | 20 |
| D895 | **D143** | 10pf. red | 20 | 20 |
| D896 | **D143** | 12pf. red | 20 | 25 |
| D897 | **D143** | 20pf. red | 20 | 25 |
| D898 | **D143** | 24pf. red | 20 | 45 |
| D899 | **D143** | 30pf. red | 20 | 50 |
| D900 | **D143** | 60pf. red | 20 | 55 |
| D901 | **D143** | 1rm. violet | 20 | 60 |
| D902 | **D143** | 2rm. violet | 20 | 95 |
| D903 | **D143** | 5rm. violet | 30 | 1·10 |
| D904 | **D143** | 10rm. violet | 30 | 1·30 |

**1946.** Optd PORTO.

| | | | | |
|---|---|---|---|---|
| D956 | **145** | 3g. orange | 10 | 10 |
| D957 | **145** | 5g. green | 10 | 10 |
| D958 | **145** | 6g. purple | 10 | 10 |
| D959 | **145** | 8g. red | 10 | 10 |
| D960 | **145** | 10g. grey | 10 | 20 |
| D961 | **145** | 12g. brown | 10 | 10 |
| D962 | **145** | 15g. red | 10 | 20 |
| D963 | **145** | 20g. brown | 10 | 10 |
| D964 | **145** | 25g. blue | 20 | 20 |
| D965 | **145** | 30g. mauve | 10 | 10 |
| D966 | **145** | 40g. blue | 10 | 10 |
| D967 | **145** | 60g. green | 10 | 10 |
| D968 | **145** | 1s. violet | 20 | 20 |
| D969 | **145** | 2s. yellow | 70 | 1·20 |
| D970 | **145** | 5s. blue | 30 | 95 |

**D162**

**1947**

| | | | | |
|---|---|---|---|---|
| D1035 | **D162** | 1g. brown | 10 | 10 |
| D1036 | **D162** | 2g. brown | 10 | 10 |
| D1037 | **D162** | 3g. brown | 10 | 20 |
| D1038 | **D162** | 5g. brown | 10 | 10 |
| D1039 | **D162** | 8g. brown | 10 | 10 |
| D1040 | **D162** | 10g. brown | 10 | 10 |
| D1041 | **D162** | 12g. brown | 10 | 10 |
| D1042 | **D162** | 15g. brown | 10 | 10 |
| D1043 | **D162** | 16g. brown | 50 | 95 |
| D1044 | **D162** | 17g. brown | 40 | 95 |
| D1045 | **D162** | 18g. brown | 40 | 95 |
| D1046 | **D162** | 20g. brown | 95 | 10 |
| D1047 | **D162** | 24g. brown | 40 | 1·10 |
| D1048 | **D162** | 30g. brown | 20 | 30 |
| D1049 | **D162** | 36g. brown | 95 | 1·60 |
| D1050 | **D162** | 40g. brown | 10 | 10 |
| D1051 | **D162** | 42g. brown | 1·10 | 1·60 |
| D1052 | **D162** | 48g. brown | 1·10 | 1·60 |
| D1053 | **D162** | 50g. brown | 95 | 30 |
| D1054 | **D162** | 60g. brown | 20 | 30 |
| D1055 | **D162** | 70g. brown | 20 | 25 |
| D1056 | **D162** | 80g. brown | 6·00 | 2·75 |
| D1057 | **D162** | 1s. blue | 20 | 10 |
| D1058 | **D162** | 1s.15 blue | 4·25 | 55 |
| D1059 | **D162** | 1s.20 blue | 4·50 | 2·20 |
| D1060 | **D162** | 2s. blue | 40 | 30 |
| D1061 | **D162** | 5s. blue | 50 | 40 |
| D1062 | **D162** | 10s. blue | 60 | 45 |

**D184**

**1949**

| | | | | |
|---|---|---|---|---|
| D1178 | **D184** | 1g. red | 20 | 20 |
| D1179 | **D184** | 2g. red | 20 | 20 |
| D1180 | **D184** | 4g. red | 65 | 65 |
| D1181 | **D184** | 5g. red | 2·75 | 75 |
| D1182 | **D184** | 8g. red | 2·75 | 2·20 |
| D1183 | **D184** | 10g. red | 45 | 10 |
| D1184 | **D184** | 20g. red | 45 | 10 |
| D1185 | **D184** | 30g. red | 45 | 10 |
| D1186 | **D184** | 40g. red | 45 | 10 |
| D1187 | **D184** | 50g. red | 45 | 10 |
| D1188 | **D184** | 60g. red | 14·00 | 75 |
| D1189 | **D184** | 63g. red | 6·75 | 4·25 |
| D1190 | **D184** | 70g. red | 45 | 10 |
| D1191 | **D184** | 80g. red | 45 | 20 |
| D1192 | **D184** | 90g. red | 75 | 55 |
| D1193 | **D184** | 1s. violet | 75 | 10 |
| D1194 | **D184** | 1s.20 violet | 75 | 30 |
| D1195 | **D184** | 1s.35 violet | 45 | 20 |
| D1196 | **D184** | 1s.40 violet | 75 | 45 |
| D1197 | **D184** | 1s.50 violet | 75 | 25 |
| D1198 | **D184** | 1s.65 violet | 65 | 45 |
| D1199 | **D184** | 1s.70 violet | 65 | 45 |
| D1200 | **D184** | 2s. violet | 1·10 | 20 |
| D1201 | **D184** | 2s.50 violet | 75 | 20 |
| D1202 | **D184** | 3s. violet | 75 | 30 |
| D1203 | **D184** | 4s. violet | 1·20 | 1·10 |
| D1204 | **D184** | 5s. violet | 1·60 | 45 |
| D1205 | **D184** | 10s. violet | 1·80 | 60 |

**D817**

**1985**

| | | | | |
|---|---|---|---|---|
| D2074 | **D817** | 10g. yellow & black | 10 | 10 |
| D2075 | **D817** | 20g. red and black | 10 | 10 |
| D2076 | **D817** | 50g. orange & black | 10 | 10 |
| D2077 | **D817** | 1s. blue and black | 20 | 20 |
| D2078 | **D817** | 2s. brown & black | 40 | 30 |
| D2079 | **D817** | 3s. violet and black | 50 | 40 |
| D2080 | **D817** | 5s. yellow & black | 90 | 60 |
| D2081 | **D817** | 10s. green & black | 1·80 | 90 |

Pt. 2

# AUSTRIAN TERRITORIES ACQUIRED BY ITALY

Italian territory acquired from Austria at the close of the war of 1914-18, including Trentino and Trieste.

1918. 100 heller = 1 krone.
1918. 100 centesimi = 1 lira.
1919. 100 centesimi = 1 corona.

## TRENTINO

**1918.** Stamps of Austria optd Regno d'Italia Trentino 3 nov 1918.

| | | | | |
|---|---|---|---|---|
| 1 | **49** | 3h. purple | 6·25 | 12·50 |
| 2 | **49** | 5h. green | 4·25 | 6·25 |
| 3 | **49** | 6h. orange | 70·00 | £110 |
| 4 | **49** | 10h. red | 4·25 | 9·25 |
| 5 | **49** | 12h. green | £200 | £300 |
| 6 | **60** | 15h. brown | 6·25 | 11·50 |
| 7 | **60** | 20h. green | 3·00 | 10·50 |
| 8 | **60** | 25h. blue | 55·00 | 70·00 |
| 9 | **60** | 30h. violet | 17·00 | 26·00 |
| 10 | **51** | 40h. green | 60·00 | £100 |
| 11 | **51** | 50h. green | 36·00 | 50·00 |
| 12 | **51** | 60h. blue | 50·00 | 90·00 |
| 13 | **51** | 80h. brown | 85·00 | £130 |
| 14 | **51** | 90h. red | £1700 | £3000 |
| 15 | **51** | 1k. red on yellow | 85·00 | £120 |
| 16 | **52** | 2k. blue | £500 | £850 |
| 17 | **52** | 4k. green | £2000 | £4000 |
| 18 | **52** | 10k. violet | £94000 | |

**1918.** Stamps of Italy optd Venezia Tridentina.

| | | | | |
|---|---|---|---|---|
| 19 | **30** | 1c. brown | 3·00 | 10·50 |
| 20 | **31** | 2c. brown | 3·00 | 10·50 |
| 21 | **37** | 5c. green | 3·00 | 10·50 |
| 22 | **37** | 10c. red | 3·00 | 10·50 |
| 23 | **41** | 20c. orange | 3·00 | 10·50 |
| 24 | **39** | 40c. brown | 65·00 | 90·00 |
| 25 | **33** | 45c. olive | 37·00 | 90·00 |
| 26 | **39** | 50c. mauve | 37·00 | 90·00 |
| 27 | **34** | 1l. brown and green | 37·00 | 90·00 |

**1919.** Stamps of Italy surch Venezia Tridentina and value.

| | | | | |
|---|---|---|---|---|
| 28 | **37** | 5h. on 5c. green | 3·00 | 5·25 |
| 29 | **37** | 10h. on 10c. red | 3·00 | 5·25 |
| 30 | **41** | 20h. on 20c. orange | 3·00 | 5·25 |

## VENEZIA GIULIA

For use in Trieste and territory, Gorizia and province, and in Istria.

**1918.** Stamps of Austria optd Regno d'Italia Venezia Giulia 3. XI. 18.

| | | | | |
|---|---|---|---|---|
| 31 | **49** | 3h. purple | 1·60 | 3·00 |
| 32 | **49** | 5h. green | 1·60 | 3·00 |
| 33 | **49** | 6h. orange | 1·80 | 4·25 |
| 34 | **49** | 10h. red | 5·25 | 5·25 |
| 35 | **49** | 12h. green | 2·50 | 5·25 |
| 36 | **60** | 15h. brown | 1·60 | 3·00 |
| 37 | **60** | 20h. green | 1·60 | 3·00 |
| 38 | **60** | 25h. blue | 8·25 | 13·50 |
| 39 | **60** | 30h. purple | 3·00 | 6·25 |
| 40 | **51** | 40h. green | £100 | £300 |
| 41 | **51** | 50h. green | 8·25 | 12·50 |
| 42 | **51** | 60h. blue | 29·00 | 36·00 |
| 43 | **51** | 80h. brown | 18·00 | 23·00 |
| 44 | **51** | 1k. red on yellow | 18·00 | 23·00 |
| 45 | **52** | 2k. blue | £275 | £500 |
| 46 | **52** | 3k. red | £350 | £600 |
| 47 | **52** | 4k. green | £550 | £1200 |
| 48 | **52** | 10k. violet | £65000 | £69000 |

**1918.** Stamps of Italy optd Venezia Giulia.

| | | | | |
|---|---|---|---|---|
| 49 | **30** | 1c. brown | 3·00 | 7·25 |
| 50 | **31** | 2c. brown | 3·00 | 7·25 |
| 51 | **37** | 5c. green | 2·10 | 3·00 |
| 52 | **37** | 10c. red | 2·10 | 3·00 |
| 53 | **41** | 20c. orange | 2·10 | 4·25 |
| 54 | **39** | 25c. blue | 2·10 | 5·25 |
| 55 | **39** | 40c. brown | 16·00 | 31·00 |
| 56 | **33** | 45c. green | 5·25 | 11·50 |
| 57 | **39** | 50c. mauve | 10·50 | 14·50 |
| 58 | **39** | 60c. red | 90·00 | £180 |
| 59 | **34** | 1l. brown and green | 41·00 | 70·00 |

**1919.** Stamps of Italy surch Venezia Giulia and value.

| | | | | |
|---|---|---|---|---|
| 60 | **37** | 5h. on 5c. green | 2·10 | 4·25 |
| 61 | **41** | 20h. on 20c. orange | 2·10 | 4·25 |

### EXPRESS LETTER STAMPS

**1919.** Express Letter stamp of Italy optd Venezia Giulia.

| | | | | |
|---|---|---|---|---|
| E60 | **E35** | 25c. red | 70·00 | £120 |

### POSTAGE DUE STAMPS

**1918.** Postage Due Stamps of Italy optd Venezia Giulia.

| | | | | |
|---|---|---|---|---|
| D60 | **D 12** | 5c. mauve and orange | 1·00 | 2·10 |
| D61 | **D 12** | 10c. mauve & orange | 1·00 | 2·10 |
| D62 | **D 12** | 20c. mauve & orange | 1·60 | 4·25 |
| D63 | **D 12** | 30c. mauve & orange | 4·25 | 8·25 |
| D64 | **D 12** | 40c. mauve & orange | 36·00 | 55·00 |
| D65 | **D 12** | 50c. mauve & orange | 60·00 | £160 |
| D66 | **D 12** | 1l. mauve and blue | £200 | £500 |

## GENERAL ISSUE

For use throughout the liberated area of Trentino, Venezia Giulia and Dalmatia.

**1919.** Stamps of Italy surch in new currency.

| | | | | |
|---|---|---|---|---|
| 62 | **30** | 1ce. di cor on 1c. brown | 2·10 | 3·00 |
| 64 | **31** | 2ce. di cor on 2c. brown | 2·10 | 3·00 |
| 65 | **37** | 5ce. di cor on 5c. green | 2·10 | 2·10 |
| 67 | **37** | 10ce. di cor on 10c. red | 2·10 | 2·10 |
| 68 | **41** | 20ce. di cor on 20c. orange | 2·10 | 2·10 |
| 70 | **39** | 25ce. di cor on 25c. blue | 2·10 | 5·25 |
| 71 | **39** | 40ce. di cor on 40c. brown | 2·10 | 5·25 |
| 72 | **33** | 45ce. di cor on 45c. green | 2·10 | 5·25 |
| 73 | **39** | 50ce. di cor on 50c. mauve | 2·10 | 5·25 |
| 74 | **39** | 60ce. di cor on 60c. red | 2·10 | 9·25 |
| 75 | **34** | 1cor. on 1l. brown & green | 4·25 | 8·25 |
| 76 | **34** | una corona on 1l. brn & grn | 5·25 | 21·00 |
| 82 | **34** | 5cor. on 5l. blue and red | 50·00 | £120 |
| 83 | **34** | 10cor. on 10l. green & red | 50·00 | £120 |

### EXPRESS LETTER STAMPS

**1919.** Express Letter stamps of Italy surch in new currency.

| | | | | |
|---|---|---|---|---|
| E76 | **E35** | 25ce. di cor on 25c. red | 2·10 | 4·25 |
| E77 | **E41** | 30ce. di cor on 30c. red and blue | 3·00 | 8·25 |

### POSTAGE DUE STAMPS

**1919.** Postage Due stamps of Italy surch in new currency.

| | | | | |
|---|---|---|---|---|
| D76 | **D12** | 5ce. di cor on 5c. mauve and orange | 1·00 | 3·00 |
| D77 | **D12** | 10ce. di cor. on 10c. mauve and orange | 1·00 | 3·00 |
| D78 | **D12** | 20ce. di cor on 20c. mauve and orange | 2·10 | 3·00 |
| D79 | **D12** | 30ce. di cor on 30c. mauve and orange | 2·30 | 5·25 |
| D80 | **D12** | 40ce. di cor on 40c. mauve and orange | 2·30 | 5·25 |
| D81 | **D12** | 50ce. di cor on 50c. mauve and orange | 5·25 | 10·50 |
| D82 | **D12** | una corona on 1l. mauve and blue | 5·25 | 12·50 |
| D83 | **D12** | due corona on 2l. mauve and blue | 80·00 | £180 |
| D84 | **D12** | cinque corona on 5l. mauve and blue | 80·00 | £180 |
| D86 | **D12** | 1cor. on 1l. mve & blue | 5·25 | 14·50 |
| D87 | **D12** | 2cor. on 2l. mve & blue | 50·00 | £110 |
| D88 | **D12** | 5cor. on 5l. mve & blue | 50·00 | £110 |

Pt. 2

# AUSTRO-HUNGARIAN MILITARY POST

A. General Issues.
100 heller = 1 krone.

B. Issues for Italy.
100 centesimi = 1 lira.

C. Issues for Montenegro.
100 heller = 1 krone.

D. Issues for Romania.
100 bani = 1 leu.

Issues for Serbia.
100 heller = 1 krone.

## A. GENERAL ISSUES

**1915.** Stamps of Bosnia and Herzegovina optd **K.U.K. FELDPOST.**

| | | | | |
|---|---|---|---|---|
| 1 | **25** | 1h. olive | 50 | 55 |
| 2 | **25** | 2h. blue | 50 | 55 |
| 3 | **25** | 3h. lake | 50 | 55 |
| 4 | **25** | 5h. green | 40 | 30 |
| 5 | **25** | 6h. black | 50 | 55 |
| 6 | **25** | 10h. red | 30 | 30 |
| 7 | **25** | 12h. olive | 50 | 75 |
| 8 | **25** | 20h. brown | 60 | 1·10 |
| 9 | **25** | 25h. blue | 50 | 75 |
| 10 | **25** | 30h. red | 4·25 | 8·50 |
| 11 | **26** | 35h. green | 3·00 | 7·50 |
| 12 | **26** | 40h. violet | 3·00 | 7·50 |
| 13 | **26** | 45h. brown | 3·00 | 7·50 |
| 14 | **26** | 50h. blue | 3·00 | 7·50 |
| 15 | **26** | 60h. purple | 60 | 1·40 |
| 16 | **26** | 72h. blue | 3·00 | 6·25 |
| 17 | **25** | 1k. brown on cream | 3·00 | 7·00 |
| 18 | **25** | 2k. indigo on blue | 3·00 | 7·00 |
| 19 | **26** | 3k. red on green | 31·00 | 70·00 |
| 20 | **26** | 5k. lilac on grey | 28·00 | 47·00 |
| 21 | **26** | 10k. blue on grey | £200 | £375 |

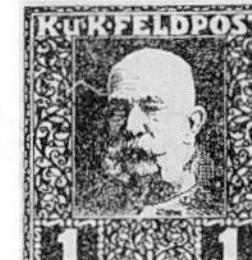

**2**

**1915**

| | | | | |
|---|---|---|---|---|
| 22 | **2** | 1h. green | 10 | 30 |
| 23 | **2** | 2h. blue | 10 | 45 |
| 24 | **2** | 3h. red | 10 | 30 |
| 25 | **2** | 5h. green | 10 | 30 |
| 26 | **2** | 6h. black | 10 | 45 |
| 27 | **2** | 10h. red | 10 | 30 |
| 28 | **2** | 10h. blue | 10 | 45 |
| 29 | **2** | 12h. green | 10 | 55 |
| 30 | **2** | 15h. red | 10 | 30 |
| 31 | **2** | 20h. brown | 40 | 55 |
| 32 | **2** | 20h. green | 40 | 65 |
| 33 | **2** | 25h. blue | 20 | 45 |
| 34 | **2** | 30h. red | 20 | 65 |
| 35 | **2** | 35h. green | 40 | 95 |
| 36 | **2** | 40h. violet | 40 | 95 |
| 37 | **2** | 45h. brown | 40 | 95 |
| 38 | **2** | 50h. deep green | 40 | 95 |
| 39 | **2** | 60h. purple | 40 | 95 |
| 40 | **2** | 72h. blue | 40 | 95 |
| 41 | **2** | 80h. brown | 40 | 45 |
| 42 | **2** | 90h. red | 1·10 | 1·80 |
| 43 | - | 1k. purple on cream | 2·10 | 3·25 |
| 44 | - | 2k. green on blue | 1·20 | 2·40 |
| 45 | - | 3k. red on green | 1·10 | 7·50 |
| 46 | - | 4k. violet on grey | 1·10 | 12·00 |
| 47 | - | 5k. violet on grey | 27·00 | 49·00 |
| 48 | - | 10k. blue on grey | 4·75 | 22·00 |

The kronen values are larger, with profile portrait.

**1917.** As 1917 issue of Bosnia, but inscr "K.u.K. FELDPOST".

| | | | | |
|---|---|---|---|---|
| 49 | | 1h. blue | 10 | 20 |
| 50 | | 2h. orange | 10 | 20 |
| 51 | | 3h. grey | 10 | 20 |
| 52 | | 5h. green | 10 | 20 |
| 53 | | 6h. violet | 10 | 20 |
| 54 | | 10h. brown | 10 | 20 |
| 55 | | 12h. blue | 10 | 20 |
| 56 | | 15h. red | 10 | 20 |
| 57 | | 20h. brown | 10 | 20 |
| 58 | | 25h. blue | 40 | 65 |
| 59 | | 30h. grey | 10 | 20 |
| 60 | | 40h. bistre | 10 | 20 |
| 61 | | 50h. green | 10 | 20 |
| 62 | | 60h. red | 10 | 55 |
| 63 | | 80h. blue | 10 | 30 |
| 64 | | 90h. purple | 40 | 95 |
| 65 | | 2k. red on buff | 20 | 55 |
| 66 | | 3k. green on blue | 1·40 | 5·50 |
| 67 | | 4k. red on green | 22·00 | 38·00 |
| 68 | | 10k. violet on grey | 2·30 | 16·00 |

The kronen values are larger and the border is different.

**1918.** Imperial and Royal Welfare Fund. As 1918 issue of Bosnia, but inscr "K. UND K. FELDPOST".

| | | | | |
|---|---|---|---|---|
| 69 | **40** | 10h. (+10h.) green | 50 | 1·10 |
| 70 | - | 20h. (+10h.) red | 50 | 1·10 |
| 71 | **40** | 45h. (+10h.) blue | 50 | 1·10 |

### NEWSPAPER STAMPS

**N4** Mercury

**1916**

| | | | | |
|---|---|---|---|---|
| N49 | **N4** | 2h. blue | 20 | 45 |
| N50 | **N4** | 6h. orange | 60 | 1·60 |
| N51 | **N4** | 10h. red | 60 | 1·60 |
| N52 | **N4** | 20h. brown | 60 | 1·60 |

## B. ISSUES FOR ITALY

**1918.** General Issue stamps of 1917 surch in figs and words.

| | | | |
|---|---|---|---|
| 1 | 2c. on 1h. blue | 10 | 55 |
| 2 | 3c. on 2h. orange | 10 | 55 |
| 3 | 4c. on 3h. grey | 10 | 55 |
| 4 | 6c. on 5h. green | 10 | 55 |
| 5 | 7c. on 6h. violet | 20 | 55 |
| 6 | 11c. on 10h. brown | 10 | 55 |
| 7 | 13c. on 12h. blue | 10 | 55 |
| 8 | 16c. on 15h. red | 10 | 55 |
| 9 | 22c. on 20h. brown | 10 | 55 |
| 10 | 27c. on 25h. blue | 40 | 1·60 |
| 11 | 32c. on 30h. grey | 20 | 1·50 |
| 12 | 43c. on 40h. bistre | 30 | 1·20 |
| 13 | 53c. on 50h. green | 20 | 1·10 |
| 14 | 64c. on 60h. red | 30 | 1·60 |
| 15 | 85c. on 80h. blue | 20 | 1·10 |
| 16 | 95c. on 90h. purple | 20 | 1·10 |

| | | | |
|---|---|---|---|
| 17 | 2l.11 on 2k. red on buff | 30 | 2·20 |
| 18 | 3l.16 on 3k. green on blue | 70 | 3·25 |
| 19 | 4l.22 on 4k. red on green | 85 | 4·25 |

**NEWSPAPER STAMPS**

**1918.** Newspaper stamps of General Issue surch in figs and words.

| | | | |
|---|---|---|---|
| N20 | 3c. on 2h. blue | 20 | 45 |
| N21 | 7c. on 6h. orange | 40 | 1·40 |
| N22 | 11c. on 10h. red | 40 | 1·40 |
| N23 | 22c. on 20h. brown | 50 | 1·40 |

**1918.** For Express. Newspaper stamps of Bosnia surch in figs and words.

| | | | | |
|---|---|---|---|---|
| N24 | **N 35** | 3c. on 2h. red on yell | 7·25 | 26·00 |
| N25 | **N 35** | 6c. on 5h. green on yell | 7·25 | 26·00 |

**POSTAGE DUE STAMPS**

**1918.** Postage Due stamps of Bosnia surch in figs and words.

| | | | | |
|---|---|---|---|---|
| D20 | **D 35** | 6c. on 5h. red | 4·25 | 11·00 |
| D21 | **D 35** | 11c. on 10h. red | 2·50 | 13·00 |
| D22 | **D 35** | 16c. on 15h. red | 1·00 | 5·50 |
| D23 | **D 35** | 27c. on 25h. red | 1·00 | 5·50 |
| D24 | **D 35** | 32c. on 30h. red | 1·00 | 5·50 |
| D25 | **D 35** | 43c. on 40h. red | 1·00 | 5·50 |
| D26 | **D 35** | 53c. on 50h. red | 1·00 | 5·50 |

**C. ISSUES FOR MONTENEGRO**

**1917.** Nos. 28 and 30 of General Issues optd **K.U.K. MILIT. VERWALTUNG MONTENEGRO**.

| | | | | |
|---|---|---|---|---|
| 1 | **2** | 10h. blue | 20·00 | 16·00 |
| 2 | **2** | 15h. red | 20·00 | 16·00 |

**D. ISSUES FOR ROMANIA**

**1917.** General Issue stamps of 1917 optd **BANI** or **LEI**.

| | | | |
|---|---|---|---|
| 1 | 3b. grey | 3·50 | 5·75 |
| 2 | 5b. green | 3·50 | 4·00 |
| 3 | 6b. violet | 3·50 | 4·00 |
| 4 | 10b. brown | 60 | 1·20 |
| 5 | 12b. blue | 2·30 | 4·00 |
| 6 | 15b. red | 2·30 | 4·00 |
| 7 | 20b. brown | 60 | 1·20 |
| 8 | 25b. blue | 60 | 1·20 |
| 9 | 30b. grey | 1·20 | 1·70 |
| 10 | 40b. bistre | 1·20 | 1·70 |
| 11 | 50b. green | 1·20 | 1·70 |
| 12 | 60b. red | 1·20 | 1·70 |
| 13 | 80b. blue | 60 | 1·20 |
| 14 | 90b. purple | 1·20 | 2·30 |
| 15 | 2l. red on buff | 1·70 | 3·00 |
| 16 | 3l. green on blue | 1·70 | 3·50 |
| 17 | 4l. red on green | 2·30 | 4·00 |

**3** Charles I

**1918**

| | | | | |
|---|---|---|---|---|
| 18 | **3** | 3b. grey | 60 | 1·20 |
| 19 | **3** | 5b. green | 60 | 1·20 |
| 20 | **3** | 6b. violet | 60 | 1·70 |
| 21 | **3** | 10b. brown | 60 | 1·70 |
| 22 | **3** | 12b. blue | 60 | 1·70 |
| 23 | **3** | 15b. red | 60 | 1·20 |
| 24 | **3** | 20b. brown | 60 | 1·20 |
| 25 | **3** | 25b. blue | 60 | 1·20 |
| 26 | **3** | 30b. grey | 60 | 1·20 |
| 27 | **3** | 40b. bistre | 60 | 1·20 |
| 28 | **3** | 50b. green | 60 | 1·20 |
| 29 | **3** | 60b. red | 60 | 1·70 |
| 30 | **3** | 80b. blue | 60 | 1·70 |
| 31 | **3** | 90b. purple | 60 | 1·20 |
| 32 | **3** | 2l. red on buff | 60 | 1·70 |
| 33 | **3** | 3l. green on blue | 1·20 | 4·00 |
| 34 | **3** | 4l. red on green | 1·70 | 4·00 |

**E. ISSUES FOR SERBIA**

**1916.** Stamps of Bosnia optd **SERBIEN**.

| | | | | |
|---|---|---|---|---|
| 22 | **25** | 1h. olive | 2·75 | 6·50 |
| 23 | **25** | 2h. blue | 2·75 | 6·50 |
| 24 | **25** | 3h. lake | 2·75 | 6·50 |
| 25 | **25** | 5h. green | 45 | 95 |
| 26 | **25** | 6h. black | 1·90 | 4·75 |
| 27 | **25** | 10h. red | 45 | 95 |
| 28 | **25** | 12h. olive | 95 | 2·75 |
| 29 | **25** | 20h. brown | 95 | 95 |
| 30 | **25** | 25h. blue | 95 | 2·75 |
| 31 | **25** | 30h. red | 95 | 1·90 |
| 32 | **26** | 35h. green | 95 | 1·90 |
| 33 | **26** | 40h. violet | 95 | 1·90 |
| 34 | **26** | 45h. brown | 95 | 1·90 |
| 35 | **26** | 50h. blue | 95 | 1·90 |
| 36 | **26** | 60h. brown | 95 | 1·90 |
| 37 | **26** | 72h. blue | 95 | 1·90 |
| 38 | **25** | 1k. brown on cream | 1·90 | 2·75 |
| 39 | **25** | 2k. indigo on blue | 1·90 | 2·75 |
| 40 | **26** | 3k. red on green | 1·90 | 2·75 |
| 41 | **26** | 5k. lilac on grey | 1·90 | 2·75 |
| 42 | **26** | 10k. blue on grey | 19·00 | 37·00 |

Pt. 2

# AUSTRO-HUNGARIAN POST OFFICES IN THE TURKISH EMPIRE

A. Lombardy and Venetia Currency.
100 soldi = 1 florin.

B. Turkish Currency.
40 paras = 1 piastre.

C. French Currency.
100 centimes = 1 franc.

**A. LOMBARDY AND VENETIA CURRENCY**

**1**

**2**

**1867**

| | | | | |
|---|---|---|---|---|
| 1 | **1** | 2s. yellow | 3·25 | 38·00 |
| 9 | **1** | 3s. green | 1·60 | 38·00 |
| 10 | **1** | 5s. red | 55 | 27·00 |
| 11 | **1** | 10s. blue | £140 | 1·70 |
| 5 | **1** | 15s. brown | 36·00 | 11·00 |
| 6 | **1** | 25s. lilac | 37·00 | 55·00 |
| 7a | **2** | 50s. brown | 1·60 | 85·00 |

**3**

**1883**

| | | | | |
|---|---|---|---|---|
| 14 | **3** | 2s. black and brown | 20 | £225 |
| 15 | **3** | 3s. black and green | 1·60 | 49·00 |
| 16 | **3** | 5s. black and red | 30 | 28·00 |
| 17 | **3** | 10s. black and blue | 1·10 | 85 |
| 18 | **3** | 20s. black and grey | 8·00 | 13·00 |
| 19 | **3** | 50s. black and mauve | 1·60 | 28·00 |

**B. TURKISH CURRENCY**

**1886.** Surch 10 PARA 10.

| | | | |
|---|---|---|---|
| 21a | 10p. on 3s. green | 45 | 11·00 |

**1888.** Nos. 71/75a of Austria surch.

| | | | | |
|---|---|---|---|---|
| 22 | **20** | 10pa. on 3k. green | 5·50 | 17·00 |
| 23 | **20** | 20pa. on 5k. red | 65 | 13·00 |
| 24 | **20** | 1pi. on 10k. blue | 95·00 | 2·20 |
| 25 | **20** | 2pi. on 20k. grey | 2·40 | 6·50 |
| 26 | **20** | 5pi. on 50k. purple | 2·75 | 27·00 |

**1890.** Stamps of Austria of 1890, the kreuzer values with lower figures of value removed, surch at foot.

| | | | | |
|---|---|---|---|---|
| 27 | **23** | 8pa. on 2k. brown | 20 | 85 |
| 28 | **23** | 10pa. on 3k. green | 75 | 85 |
| 29 | **23** | 20pa. on 5k. red | 45 | 85 |
| 30 | **23** | 1pi. on 10k. blue | 55 | 30 |
| 31 | **23** | 2pi. on 20k. olive | 11·00 | 43·00 |
| 32 | **23** | 5pi. on 50k. mauve | 16·00 | 95·00 |
| 33 | **24** | 10pi. on 1g. blue | 14·00 | 60·00 |
| 37 | **24** | 10pi. on 1g. lilac | 27·00 | 32·00 |
| 34 | **24** | 20pi. on 2g. red | 22·00 | 90·00 |
| 38 | **24** | 20pi. on 2g. green | 55·00 | £110 |

**1890.** Stamps of Austria of 1891, with lower figures of value removed, surch at foot.

| | | | | |
|---|---|---|---|---|
| 35 | **25** | 2pi. on 20k. green | 8·50 | 2·20 |
| 36 | **25** | 5pi. on 50k. mauve | 3·25 | 4·25 |

**1900.** Stamps of Austria of 1899, the heller values with lower figures of value removed, surch at foot.

| | | | | |
|---|---|---|---|---|
| 46 | **27** | 10pa. on 5h. green | 3·25 | 4·00 |
| 40 | **28** | 20pa. on 10h. red | 7·50 | 1·20 |
| 48 | **28** | 1pi. on 25h. blue | 2·20 | 1·10 |
| 49 | **29** | 2pi. on 50h. blue | 5·50 | 8·50 |
| 43d | **30** | 5pi. on 1k. red | 75 | 55 |
| 44d | **30** | 10pi. on 2k. lavender | 3·25 | 4·75 |
| 45d | **30** | 20pi. on 4k. green | 3·25 | 13·00 |

**1903.** Stamps of Austria of 1899, with all figures of value removed, surch at top and at foot.

| | | | | |
|---|---|---|---|---|
| 55 | **27** | 10pa. green | 75 | 2·75 |
| 56 | **28** | 20pa. red | 1·60 | 1·60 |
| 57 | **28** | 30pa. mauve | 75 | 5·50 |
| 58 | **28** | 1pi. blue | 1·10 | 55 |
| 59 | **29** | 2pi. blue | 1·10 | 1·20 |

**11** Francis Joseph I

**12** Francis Joseph I

**1908.** 60th Anniv of Emperor's Accession.

| | | | | |
|---|---|---|---|---|
| 60 | **11** | 10pa. green on yellow | 20 | 55 |
| 61 | **11** | 20pa. red on pink | 30 | 55 |
| 62 | **11** | 30pa. brown on buff | 55 | 75 |
| 63 | **11** | 60pa. purple on blue | 1·10 | 6·50 |
| 70 | **11** | 1pi. ultramarine on blue | 45 | 75 |
| 65 | **12** | 2pi. red on yellow | 1·10 | 20 |
| 66 | **12** | 5pi. brown on grey | 1·10 | 1·30 |
| 67 | **12** | 10pi. green on yellow | 1·60 | 2·75 |
| 68 | **12** | 20pi. blue on grey | 3·75 | 5·50 |

**POSTAGE DUE STAMPS**

**1902.** Postage Due stamps as Type D 32 of Austria, but with value in heller, surch with new value.

| | | | | |
|---|---|---|---|---|
| D50 | **D32** | 10pa. on 5h. green | 1·60 | 4·25 |
| D51 | **D32** | 20pa. on 10h. green | 1·60 | 5·50 |
| D52 | **D32** | 1pi. on 20h. green | 2·20 | 6·25 |
| D53 | **D32** | 2pi. on 40h. green | 2·20 | 6·25 |
| D54 | **D32** | 5pi. on 100h. green | 2·20 | 6·00 |

**D13**

**1908**

| | | | | |
|---|---|---|---|---|
| D71A | **D13** | ¼pi. green | 4·25 | 16·00 |
| D72A | **D13** | ½pi. green | 2·75 | 13·00 |
| D73A | **D13** | 1pi. green | 3·25 | 13·00 |
| D74A | **D13** | 1½pi. green | 1·60 | 30·00 |
| D75A | **D13** | 2pi. green | 2·20 | 27·00 |
| D76A | **D13** | 5pi. green | 3·25 | 19·00 |
| D77A | **D13** | 10pi. green | 23·00 | £190 |
| D78A | **D13** | 20pi. green | 15·00 | £225 |
| D79A | **D13** | 30pi. green | 23·00 | 19·00 |

**C. FRENCH CURRENCY**

**1903.** Stamps of Austria surch CENTIMES or FRANC.

| | | | | |
|---|---|---|---|---|
| F1A | **27** | 5c. on 5h. green and black | 1·60 | 6·50 |
| F2A | **28** | 10c. on 10h. red and black (No. 143) | 1·20 | 6·50 |
| F3A | **28** | 25c. on 25h. blue and black (No. 145) | 55·00 | 43·00 |
| F4A | **29** | 50c. on 50h. blue and black | 14·00 | £225 |
| F5 | **30** | 1f. on 1k. red | 1·60 | £190 |
| F6 | **30** | 2f. on 2k. lilac | 14·00 | £550 |
| F7 | **30** | 4f. on 4k. green | 16·00 | £850 |

**1904.** Stamps of Austria surch CENTIMES.

| | | | | |
|---|---|---|---|---|
| F14 | **33** | 5c. on 5h. green | 1·10 | 6·00 |
| F13 | **28** | 10c. on 10h. red and black (No. 160) | 75 | 22·00 |
| F10B | **28** | 25c. on 25h. blue and black (No. 176) | 75 | £170 |
| F11A | **35** | 50c. on 50h. blue | 75 | £750 |

**1906.** Type of Austria surch CENTIMES.

| | | | | |
|---|---|---|---|---|
| F15 | **28** | 10c. on 10h. red (No. 184) | 1·60 | 55·00 |
| F16 | **28** | 15c. on 15h. violet and black (as No. 185) | 1·10 | 55·00 |

No. F16 was not issued without the surch.

**1908.** 60th Anniv of Emperor's Accession. As T 11/12 but in centimes or franc.

| | | | | |
|---|---|---|---|---|
| F17 | **11** | 5c. green on yellow | 20 | 1·30 |
| F18 | **11** | 10c. red on pink | 45 | 1·60 |
| F19 | **11** | 15c. brown on buff | 65 | 9·75 |
| F20 | **11** | 25c. blue on blue | 19·00 | 8·50 |
| F21 | **12** | 50c. red on yellow | 5·50 | 49·00 |
| F22 | **12** | 1f. brown on grey | 7·50 | 75·00 |

Pt. 10

# AZERBAIJAN

Formerly part of the Russian Empire. Became independent on 27 May 1918, following the Russian Revolution. Soviet troops invaded the country on 27 April 1920, and a Soviet Republic followed. From 1 October 1923 stamps of the Transcaucasian Federation were used but these were superseded by those of the Soviet Union in 1924.

With the dissolution of the Soviet Union in 1991, Azerbaijan once again became an independent state.

1919. 100 kopeks = 1 rouble.
1992. 100 qopik = 1 manat.
2006. 1 manat = 100 qepik.

**1** Standard-bearer

**1919.** Imperf. Various designs.

| No. | Type | Description | Unused | Used |
|---|---|---|---|---|
| 1B | 1 | 10k. multicoloured | 20 | 20 |
| 2B | - | 20k. multicoloured | 20 | 20 |
| 3B | - | 40k. olive, black and yellow | 20 | 20 |
| 4B | - | 60k. orange, black & yellow | 20 | 25 |
| 5B | - | 1r. blue, black and yellow | 30 | 30 |
| 6B | - | 2r. red, black and yellow | 30 | 30 |
| 7B | - | 5r. blue, black and yellow | 40 | 55 |
| 8B | - | 10r. olive, black & yellow | 60 | 60 |
| 9B | - | 25r. blue, black and red | 1·00 | 1·00 |
| 10B | - | 50r. olive, black and red | 1·30 | 1·10 |

DESIGNS—HORIZ: 40k. to 1r. Reaper; 2r. to 10r. Citadel, Baku; 25r., 50r. Temple of Eternal Fires.

**3** "Labour"

**4** Petroleum Well

**1921.** Imperf.

| No. | Type | Description | Unused | Used |
|---|---|---|---|---|
| 11 | 3 | 1r. green | 35 | 75 |
| 12 | 4 | 2r. brown | 50 | 80 |
| 13 | - | 5r. brown | 35 | 75 |
| 14 | - | 10r. grey | 50 | 85 |
| 15 | - | 25r. orange | 35 | 75 |
| 16 | - | 50r. violet | 35 | 75 |
| 17 | - | 100r. orange | 40 | 80 |
| 18 | - | 150r. blue | 40 | 80 |
| 19 | - | 250r. violet and buff | 40 | 80 |
| 20 | - | 400r. blue | 40 | 80 |
| 21 | - | 500r. black and lilac | 40 | 80 |
| 22 | - | 1000r. red and blue | 40 | 80 |
| 23 | - | 2000r. black and blue | 40 | 80 |
| 24 | - | 3000r. brown and blue | 40 | 80 |
| 25 | - | 5000r. green on olive | 55 | 50 |

DESIGNS—HORIZ: 5r., 3000r. Bibi Eibatt Oilfield; 100r., 5000r. Goukasoff House (State Museum of Arts); 400r., 1000r. Hall of Judgment, Khan's Palace. VERT: 10r., 2000r. Minaret of Friday Mosque, Khan's Palace; 25r., 250r. Globe and Workers; 50r. Malden's Tower, Baku; 150r., 500r. Blacksmiths.

**6** Famine Supplies

**1921.** Famine Relief. Imperf.

| No. | Type | Description | Unused | Used |
|---|---|---|---|---|
| 26 | 6 | 500r. blue | 50 | 1·50 |
| 27 | - | 1000r. brown | 85 | 2·50 |

DESIGN—VERT: 1000r. Starving family.

For stamps of the above issues surch with new values, see Stanley Gibbons Part 10 (Russia) Catalogue.

**13** Azerbaijan Map and Flag

**1992.** Independence.

| No. | Type | Description | Unused | Used |
|---|---|---|---|---|
| 83 | 13 | 35q. multicoloured | 90 | 90 |

**1992.** Unissued stamp showing Caspian Sea surch **AZARBAYCAN** and new value.

| No. | Description | Unused | Used |
|---|---|---|---|
| 84B | 25q. on 15k. multicoloured | 45 | 45 |
| 85B | 35q. on 15k. multicoloured | 65 | 65 |
| 86B | 50q. on 15k. multicoloured | 85 | 85 |
| 87B | 1m.50 on 15k. multicoloured | 2·75 | 2·75 |
| 88B | 2m.50 on 15k. multicoloured | 4·25 | 4·25 |

**16** Maiden's Tower, Baku

**1992.** Dated "1992".

| No. | Type | Description | Unused | Used |
|---|---|---|---|---|
| 89 | 16 | 10q. green and black | 15 | 15 |
| 90 | 16 | 20q. red and black | 15 | 15 |
| 91 | 16 | 50q. yellow and black | 20 | 20 |
| 92 | 16 | 1m.50 blue and black | 85 | 85 |

See also Nos. 101/4.

**17** Akhalteka Horse

**1993.** Horses. Multicoloured.

| No. | Description | Unused | Used |
|---|---|---|---|
| 93 | 20q. Type **17** | 10 | 10 |
| 94 | 30q. Kabarda horse | 10 | 10 |
| 95 | 50q. Qarabair horse | 10 | 10 |
| 96 | 1m. Don horse | 10 | 10 |
| 97 | 2m.50 Yakut horse | 45 | 45 |
| 98 | 5m. Orlov horse | 85 | 85 |
| 99 | 10m. Diliboz horse | 1·70 | 1·70 |
| **MS**100 | 80×60 mm. 8m. Qarabag horse | 1·70 | 1·70 |

**1993.** Dated "1993".

| No. | Description | Unused | Used |
|---|---|---|---|
| 101 | 50q. blue and black | 25 | 25 |
| 102 | 1m. mauve and black | 15 | 15 |
| 103 | 2m.50 yellow and black | 30 | 30 |
| 104 | 5m. green and black | 55 | 55 |

**18** "Tulipa eichleri"

**1993.** Flowers. Multicoloured.

| No. | Description | Unused | Used |
|---|---|---|---|
| 105 | 25q. Type **18** | 10 | 10 |
| 106 | 50q. "Puschkinia scilloides" | 10 | 10 |
| 107 | 1m. "Iris elegantissima" | 15 | 15 |
| 108 | 1m.50 "Iris acutiloba" | 20 | 20 |
| 109 | 5m. "Tulipa florenskyii" | 70 | 70 |
| 110 | 10m. "Iris reticulata" | 1·30 | 1·30 |
| **MS**111 | 78×58 mm. 10m. *Muscari elecostomum* (31×39 mm) | 1·20 | 1·20 |

**19** Russian Sturgeon

**1993.** Fishes. Multicoloured.

| No. | Description | Unused | Used |
|---|---|---|---|
| 112 | 25q. Type **19** | 10 | 10 |
| 113 | 50q. Stellate sturgeon | 10 | 10 |
| 114 | 1m. Iranian roach | 15 | 10 |
| 115 | 1m.50 Caspian roach | 25 | 25 |
| 116 | 5m. Caspian trout | 90 | 90 |
| 117 | 10m. Black-backed shad | 1·80 | 1·80 |
| **MS**118 | 76×58 mm. 10m. Beluga (*Huso huso*) (39×31 mm) | 1·60 | 1·20 |

**20** Map of Nakhichevan

**1993.** 70th Birthday of President Heydar Aliev.

| No. | Type | Description | Unused | Used |
|---|---|---|---|---|
| 119 | - | 25m. black and red | 1·50 | 1·50 |
| 120 | 20 | 25m. multicoloured | 1·50 | 1·50 |
| **MS**121a | | 110×90 mm. Nos. 119/20 (map inscr "Naxcivan") | 9·50 | 9·50 |

DESIGN: No. 119, President Aliev.

**21** Government Building, Baku

**1993**

| No. | Type | Description | Unused | Used |
|---|---|---|---|---|
| 122 | 21 | 25q. black and yellow | 15 | 15 |
| 123 | 21 | 30q. black and green | 15 | 15 |
| 124 | 21 | 50q. black and blue | 30 | 30 |
| 125 | 21 | 1m. black and red | 60 | 60 |

**22** Flags, and Dish Aerials on Maps

**1993.** Azerbaijan–Iran Telecommunications Co-operation.

| No. | Type | Description | Unused | Used |
|---|---|---|---|---|
| 126 | 22 | 15q. multicoloured | 80 | 80 |

**23** National Colours and Islamic Crescent

**1994.** National Day.

| No. | Type | Description | Unused | Used |
|---|---|---|---|---|
| 127 | 23 | 5m. multicoloured | 35 | 35 |

**24** State Arms

**1994**

| No. | Type | Description | Unused | Used |
|---|---|---|---|---|
| 128 | 24 | 8m. multicoloured | 65 | 65 |

**25** Sirvan Palace

**1994.** Baku Architecture.

| No. | Type | Description | Unused | Used |
|---|---|---|---|---|
| 129 | 25 | 2m. red, silver and black | 15 | 15 |
| 130 | - | 4m. green, silver and black | 25 | 25 |
| 131 | - | 8m. blue, silver and black | 55 | 55 |

DESIGNS: 4m. 15th-century tomb; 8m. Divan-Khana.

**26** Fuzuli

**1994.** 500th Birth Anniv (1992) of Mohammed ibn Suleiman Fuzuli (poet).

| No. | Type | Description | Unused | Used |
|---|---|---|---|---|
| 132 | 26 | 10m. multicoloured | 45 | 45 |

**1994.** No. 126 surch **IRAN–AZERBAYGAN** and value.

| No. | Type | Description | Unused | Used |
|---|---|---|---|---|
| 133 | 22 | 2m. on 15q. multicoloured | 30 | 30 |
| 134 | 22 | 20m. on 15q. multicoloured | 85 | 85 |
| 135 | 22 | 25m. on 15q. multicoloured | 1·00 | 1·00 |
| 136 | 22 | 50m. on 15q. multicoloured | 2·40 | 2·40 |

**1994.** Nos. 122/5 surch.

| No. | Type | Description | Unused | Used |
|---|---|---|---|---|
| 137 | 21 | 5m. on 1m. black and red | 30 | 30 |
| 138 | 21 | 10m. on 30q. black & grn | 30 | 30 |
| 139 | 21 | 15m. on 30q. black & grn | 30 | 30 |
| 140 | 21 | 20m. on 50q. black & blue | 30 | 30 |
| 141 | 21 | 25m. on 1m. black & red | 35 | 35 |
| 142 | 21 | 40m. on 50q. black & blue | 65 | 65 |
| 143 | 21 | 50m. on 25q. black & yell | 85 | 85 |
| 144 | 21 | 100m. on 25q. black & yell | 1·70 | 1·70 |

**29** Rasulzade

**1994.** 110th Birth Anniv of Mammed Amin Rasulzade (politician).

| No. | Type | Description | Unused | Used |
|---|---|---|---|---|
| 145 | 29 | 15m. brown, ochre & black | 85 | 85 |

**30** Mamedquluzade

**1994.** 125th Birth Anniv of Jalil Mamedquluzade (writer).

| No. | Type | Description | Unused | Used |
|---|---|---|---|---|
| 146 | 30 | 20m. black, gold and blue | 85 | 85 |

**31** Temple of the Fire Worshippers of Atashgah

**1994.** 115th Anniv of Nobel Partnership to Exploit Black Sea Oil. Multicoloured.

| No. | Description | Unused | Used |
|---|---|---|---|
| 147 | 15m. Type **31** | 25 | 25 |
| 148 | 20m. Oil wells | 35 | 35 |
| 149 | 25m. "Zoroastr" (first oil tanker in Caspian Sea) | 40 | 40 |

| | | | |
|---|---|---|---|
| 150 | 50m. Nobel brothers and Petr Bilderling (partners) | 1·00 | 1·00 |
| **MS**151 | 110×73 mm. No. 150 | 1·10 | 1·10 |

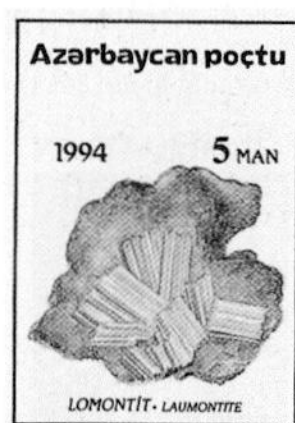


**32** Laumontite

**1994.** Minerals. Multicoloured.

| | | | |
|---|---|---|---|
| 152 | 5m. Type **32** | 25 | 25 |
| 153 | 10m. Epidot calcite | 40 | 40 |
| 154 | 15m. Andradite | 65 | 65 |
| 155 | 20m. Amethyst | 85 | 85 |
| **MS**156 | 120×110 mm. Nos. 152/5 | 2·10 | 2·10 |

**33** Players

**1994.** World Cup Football Championship, U.S.A.

| | | | | |
|---|---|---|---|---|
| 157 | **33** | 5m. multicoloured | 10 | 10 |
| 158 | - | 10m. multicoloured | 10 | 10 |
| 159 | - | 20m. multicoloured | 25 | 25 |
| 160 | - | 25m. multicoloured | 35 | 35 |
| 161 | - | 30m. multicoloured | 40 | 40 |
| 162 | - | 50m. multicoloured | 70 | 70 |
| 163 | - | 80m. multicoloured | 1·10 | 1·10 |
| **MS**164 | | 90×65 mm. 100m. multicoloured (31×39 mm) | 1·30 | 1·30 |

DESIGNS: 10m. to 100m. Match scenes.

**34** Posthorn

**1994**

| | | | | |
|---|---|---|---|---|
| 165 | **34** | 5m. red and black | 10 | 10 |
| 166 | **34** | 10m. green and black | 10 | 10 |
| 167 | **34** | 20m. blue and black | 30 | 20 |
| 168 | **34** | 25m. yellow and black | 30 | 30 |
| 169 | **34** | 40m. brown and black | 55 | 55 |

**35** Coelophysis and Segisaurus

**1994.** Prehistoric Animals. Multicoloured.

| | | | |
|---|---|---|---|
| 170 | 5m. Type **35** | 10 | 15 |
| 171 | 10m. Pentaceratops and tyrannosaurids | 10 | 15 |
| 172 | 20m. Segnosaurus and oviraptor | 40 | 40 |
| 173 | 25m. Albertosaurus and corythosaurus | 50 | 50 |
| 174 | 30m. Igaunodons | 60 | 60 |
| 175 | 50m. Stegosaurus and allosaurus | 1·10 | 1·10 |
| 176 | 80m. Tyrannosaurus and saurolophus | 1·70 | 1·70 |
| **MS**177 | 81×61 mm. 100m. Phobetor (39×31 mm) | 1·80 | 1·80 |

**36** Nesting Grouse

**1994.** The Caucasian Black Grouse. Multicoloured.

| | | | |
|---|---|---|---|
| 178 | 50m. Type **36** | 60 | 60 |
| 179 | 80m. Grouse on mountain | 95 | 95 |
| 180 | 100m. Pair of grouse | 1·40 | 1·40 |
| 181 | 120m. Grouse in spring meadow | 2·00 | 2·00 |

**1994.** No. 84 further surch 400 M.

| | | | |
|---|---|---|---|
| 182 | 400m. on 25q. on 15k. mult | 1·60 | 1·60 |

**38** "Kapitan Razhabov" (tug)

**1994.** Ships. Multicoloured.

| | | | |
|---|---|---|---|
| 183 | 50m. Type **38** | 30 | 30 |
| 184 | 50m. "Azerbaijan" (ferry) | 30 | 30 |
| 185 | 50m. "Merkuri 1" (ferry) | 30 | 30 |
| 186 | 50m. "Tovuz" (container ship) | 30 | 30 |
| 187 | 50m. "Ganzha" (tanker) | 30 | 30 |

Nos. 183/7 were issued together, se-tenant, the backgrounds of which form a composite design of a map.

**39** Pres. Aliev

**1994.** President Haidar Aliev. Sheet 102×72 mm.

| | | | |
|---|---|---|---|
| **MS**188 | **39** 150m. multicoloured | 2·40 | 2·40 |

**40** White-tailed Sea Eagle

**1994.** Birds of Prey. Multicoloured.

| | | | |
|---|---|---|---|
| 189 | 10m. Type **40** | 60 | 60 |
| 190 | 15m. Imperial eagle | 70 | 70 |
| 191 | 20m. Tawny eagle | 85 | 85 |
| 192 | 25m. Lammergeier (vert) | 1·00 | 1·00 |
| 193 | 50m. Saker falcon (vert) | 2·40 | 2·40 |
| **MS**194 | 83×64 mm. 100m. Golden eagle (*Aquila chrysaetos*) (39×31 mm) | 1·60 | 1·60 |

Nos. 190/1 and **MS**194 are wrongly inscr "Aguila".

**41** "Felis libica caudata"

**1994.** Wild Cats. Multicoloured.

| | | | |
|---|---|---|---|
| 195 | 10m. Type **41** | 60 | 60 |
| 196 | 15m. Manul cat | 70 | 70 |
| 197 | 20m. Lynx | 85 | 85 |
| 198 | 25m. Leopard (horiz) | 1·00 | 1·00 |
| 199 | 50m. Tiger (horiz) | 2·40 | 2·40 |
| **MS**200 | 64×56 mm. 100m. Tiger with cub (31×39 mm) | 1·60 | 1·60 |

No. 197 is wrongly inscribed "Felis lyns lyns".

**42** Ancient Greek and Modern Javelin Throwers

**1994.** Centenary of Int Olympic Committee. Mult.

| | | | |
|---|---|---|---|
| 201 | 100m. Type **42** | 60 | 60 |
| 202 | 100m. Ancient Greek and modern discus throwers | 60 | 60 |
| 203 | 100m. Baron Pierre de Coubertin (founder of modern games) and flame | 60 | 60 |

**1995.** Nos. 89/92 and 101/4 surch.

| | | | | |
|---|---|---|---|---|
| 204 | **15** | 250m. on 10q. green & blk | 50 | 50 |
| 205 | **15** | 250m. on 20q. red & black | 50 | 50 |
| 206 | **15** | 250m. on 50q. yell & blk | 50 | 50 |
| 207 | **15** | 250m. on 1m.50 bl & blk | 50 | 50 |
| 208 | **15** | 500m. on 50q. blue & blk | 1·10 | 1·10 |
| 209 | **15** | 500m. on 1m. mve & blk | 1·10 | 1·10 |
| 210 | **15** | 500m. on 2m.50 yellow and black | 1·10 | 1·10 |
| 211 | **15** | 500m. on 5m. green & blk | 1·10 | 1·10 |

**44** Apollo

**1995.** Butterflies. Multicoloured.

| | | | |
|---|---|---|---|
| 212 | 10m. Type **44** | 30 | 30 |
| 213 | 25m. "Zegris menestho" | 70 | 70 |
| 214 | 50m. "Manduca atropos" | 1·40 | 1·40 |
| 215 | 60m. "Pararge adrastoides" | 1·80 | 1·80 |
| **MS**216 | 103×157 mm. Nos. 212/15 | 4·25 | 4·25 |

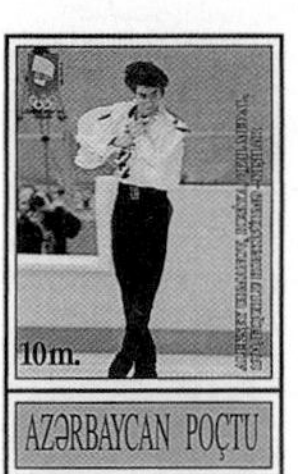


**45** Aleksei Urmanov (Russia) (gold, men's figure skating)

**1995.** Winter Olympic Games, Lillehammer, Norway, Medal Winners. Multicoloured.

| | | | |
|---|---|---|---|
| 217 | 10m. Type **45** | 10 | 10 |
| 218 | 25m. Nancy Kerrigan (U.S.A.) (silver, women's figure skating) | 25 | 25 |
| 219 | 40m. Bonnie Blair (U.S.A.) (gold, women's 500m. speed skating) (horiz) | 40 | 45 |
| 220 | 50m. Takanori Kano (Japan) (gold, men's ski jumping) (horiz) | 40 | 40 |
| 221 | 80m. Philip Laros (Canada) (silver, men's freestyle skiing) | 75 | 75 |
| 222 | 100m. German team (gold, three-man bobsleigh) | 1·00 | 1·00 |
| **MS**223 | 102×71 mm. 200m. Katya Seizinger (Germany) (gold, women's skiing) | 2·20 | 2·20 |

**46** Mary Cleave

**1995.** 25th Anniv (1994) of First Manned Moon Landing. Female Astronauts. Two sheets, each 137×78 mm, containing T 46 and similar vert designs. Multicoloured.

| | | | |
|---|---|---|---|
| **MS**224 | (a) 100m. Type **46**; 100m. Valentina Tereshkova; 100m. Tamara Jernigen; 100m. Wendy Lawrence. (b) 100m. Mae Jemison; 100m. Cathy Coleman; 100m. Ellen Shulman; 100m. Mary Weber | 3·75 | 3·75 |

**1995.** Nos. 165/7 surch.

| | | | | |
|---|---|---|---|---|
| 225 | **34** | 100m. on 5m. red & black | 15 | 15 |
| 226 | **34** | 250m. on 10m. grn & blk | 45 | 45 |
| 227 | **34** | 500m. on 20m. blue & blk | 90 | 90 |

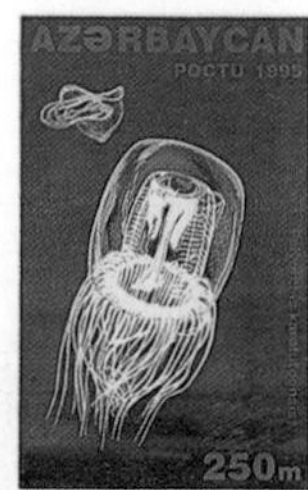


**48** "Polyorchis karafutoensis"

**1995.** Marine Animals. Multicoloured.

| | | | |
|---|---|---|---|
| 228 | 50m. "Loligo vulgaris" (horiz) | 15 | 15 |
| 229 | 100m. "Orchistoma pileus" (horiz) | 40 | 40 |
| 230 | 150m. "Pegea confoederata" (horiz) | 60 | 60 |
| 231 | 250m. Type **48** | 1·00 | 1·00 |
| 232 | 300m. "Agalma okeni" | 1·20 | 1·20 |
| **MS**233 | 89×60 mm. 500m. *Corolla spectabilis* (39×31 mm) | 3·00 | 2·00 |

**49** Matamata Turtle

**1995.** Tortoises and Turtles. Multicoloured.

| | | | |
|---|---|---|---|
| 234 | 50m. Type **49** | 15 | 15 |
| 235 | 100m. Loggerhead turtle | 40 | 40 |
| 236 | 150m. Leopard tortoise | 60 | 60 |
| 237 | 250m. Indian star tortoise | 1·00 | 1·00 |
| 238 | 300m. Hermann's tortoise | 1·20 | 1·20 |
| **MS**239 | 79×65 mm. 500m. Alligator-snapping turtle (*Macroclemys temmincki*) (31×39 mm) | 1·70 | 1·70 |

**50** Uzeyir Hacibeyov (composer, 110th)

**1995.** Birth Anniversaries.

| | | | | |
|---|---|---|---|---|
| 240 | **50** | 250m. silver and black | 40 | 40 |
| 241 | - | 400m. gold and black | 60 | 60 |

DESIGN: 400m. Vakhid (poet, centenary).

**1995.** Nos. 84/88 surch.

| | | | |
|---|---|---|---|
| 242 | 200m. on 2m.50 on 15k. mult | 60 | 60 |
| 243 | 400m. on 25q. on 15k. mult | 1·00 | 1·00 |
| 244 | 600m. on 35q. on 15k. mult | 1·80 | 1·80 |
| 245 | 800m. on 50q. on 15k. mult | 2·30 | 2·30 |
| 246 | 1000m. on 1m.50 on 15k. multicoloured | 3·00 | 3·00 |

**1995.** Nos. 168/9 surch.

| | | | | |
|---|---|---|---|---|
| 247 | **34** | 400m. on 25m. yell & blk | 1·10 | 1·10 |
| 248 | **34** | 900m. on 40m. brn & blk | 2·50 | 2·50 |

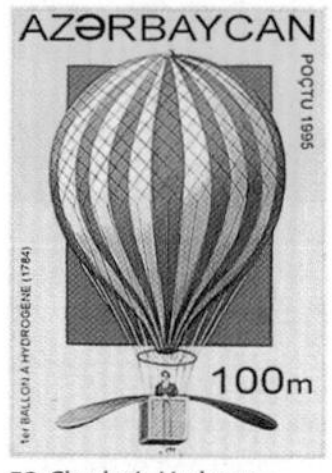


**53** Charles's Hydrogen Balloon, 1783

**1995.** History of Airships. Multicoloured.

| | | | |
|---|---|---|---|
| 249 | 100m. Type **53** | 15 | 15 |
| 250 | 150m. Tissandier Brothers' electrically-powered airship, 1883 | 30 | 30 |
| 251 | 250m. J.-B. Meusnier's elliptical balloon design, 1784 (horiz) | 50 | 50 |
| 252 | 300m. Baldwin's dirigible airship, 1904 (horiz) | 60 | 60 |
| 253 | 400m. U.S. Navy dirigible airship, 1917 (horiz) | 85 | 85 |
| 254 | 500m. Pedal-powered airship, 1909 (horiz) | 1·00 | 1·00 |
| **MS**255 | 79×62 mm. 800m. First rigid dirigible airship by Hugo Eckener, 1924 (horiz) | 1·70 | 1·70 |

No. 249 is wrongly dated.

**54** "Gymnopilus spectabilis"

**1995.** Fungi. Multicoloured.

| | | | |
|---|---|---|---|
| 256 | 100m. Type **54** | 35 | 35 |
| 257 | 250m. Fly agaric | 95 | 95 |
| 258 | 300m. Parasol mushroom | 1·10 | 1·10 |
| 259 | 400m. "Hygrophorus spectosus" | 1·40 | 1·40 |

| | | | |
|---|---|---|---|
| **MS**260 | 110×80 mm. 500m. Fly agaric (different) | 2·40 | 2·40 |

The 250m. and 500m. are wrongly inscr "agaris".

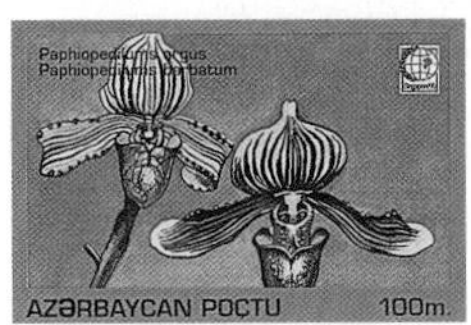

**55** "Paphiopedilum argus" and "Paphiopedilum barbatum"

**1995.** "Singapore '95" International Stamp Exhibition. Orchids. Multicoloured.

| | | | |
|---|---|---|---|
| 261 | 100m. Type **55** | 35 | 35 |
| 262 | 250m. "Maxillaria picta" | 95 | 95 |
| 263 | 300m. "Laeliocattleya" | 1·10 | 1·10 |
| 264 | 400m. "Dendrobium nobile" | 1·40 | 1·40 |
| **MS**265 | 110×80 mm. 500m. *Cattleya gloriette* | 1·30 | 1·30 |

**56** Pres. Aliev and U.N. Secretary-General Boutros Boutros Ghali

**1995.** 50th Anniv of U.N.O.

| | | | | |
|---|---|---|---|---|
| 266 | **56** | 250m. multicoloured | 2·10 | 2·10 |

**57** Players

**1995.** World Cup Football Championship, France (1998). Multicoloured.

| | | | |
|---|---|---|---|
| 267 | 100m. Type **57** | 35 | 35 |
| 268 | 150m. Dribbling | 50 | 50 |
| 269 | 250m. Tackling | 85 | 85 |
| 270 | 300m. Preparing to kick ball | 1·00 | 1·00 |
| 271 | 400m. Contesting for ball | 1·30 | 1·30 |
| **MS**272 | 79×60 mm. 600m. Goalkeeper diving for ball | 2·20 | 2·20 |

**58** American Bald Eagle

**1995.** Air.

| | | | | |
|---|---|---|---|---|
| 273 | **58** | 2200m. multicoloured | 2·50 | 2·50 |

**59** Persian

**1995.** Cats. Multicoloured.

| | | | |
|---|---|---|---|
| 274 | 100m. Type **59** | 15 | 15 |
| 275 | 150m. Chartreux | 30 | 30 |
| 276 | 250m. Somali | 50 | 50 |
| 277 | 300m. Longhair Scottish fold | 60 | 60 |
| 278 | 400m. Cymric | 85 | 85 |
| 279 | 500m. Turkish angora | 1·00 | 1·00 |
| **MS**280 | 85×75 mm. 800m. Birman (31×39 mm) | 1·70 | 1·70 |

**60** Horse

**1995.** Flora and Fauna. Multicoloured.

| | | | |
|---|---|---|---|
| 281 | 100m. Type **60** | 15 | 15 |
| 282 | 200m. Grape hyacinths (vert) | 40 | 40 |
| 283 | 250m. Beluga | 50 | 50 |
| 284 | 300m. Golden eagle | 60 | 60 |
| 285 | 400m. Tiger | 75 | 75 |
| 286 | 500m. Georgian black grouse nesting | 1·00 | 1·00 |
| 287 | 1000m. Georgian black grouse in meadow | 2·00 | 2·00 |

**61** Lennon and Signature

**1995.** 15th Death Anniv of John Lennon (entertainer).

| | | | | |
|---|---|---|---|---|
| 288 | **61** | 500m. multicoloured | 1·10 | 1·10 |

**62** Early Steam Locomotive, U.S.A.

**1996.** Railway Locomotives. Multicoloured.

| | | | |
|---|---|---|---|
| 289 | 100m. Type **62** | 45 | 45 |
| 290 | 100m. New York Central Class J3 locomotive | 45 | 45 |
| 291 | 100m. Steam locomotive on bridge | 45 | 45 |
| 292 | 100m. Steam locomotive No. 1959, Germany | 45 | 45 |
| 293 | 100m. Steam locomotive No. 4113, Germany | 45 | 45 |
| 294 | 100m. Steam locomotive, Italy | 45 | 45 |
| 295 | 100m. Class 59 steam locomotive, Japan | 45 | 45 |
| 296 | 100m. Class QJ steam locomotive, China | 45 | 45 |
| 297 | 100m. Class Sn 23 steam locomotive, China | 45 | 45 |
| **MS**298 | 110×80 mm. 500m. Electric train (vert) | 2·75 | 2·75 |

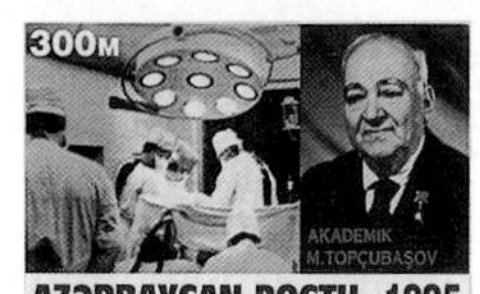

**63** Operating Theatre and Topcubasov

**1996.** Birth Centenary of M. Topcubasov (surgeon).

| | | | | |
|---|---|---|---|---|
| 299 | **63** | 300m. multicoloured | 1·00 | 1·00 |

**64** Feast and Woman wearing Traditional Costume

**1996.** New Year.

| | | | | |
|---|---|---|---|---|
| 300 | **64** | 250m. multicoloured | 90 | 90 |

**65** Carl Lewis (athletics, Los Angeles, 1984)

**1996.** Olympic Games, Atlanta. Previous Gold Medallists. Multicoloured.

| | | | |
|---|---|---|---|
| 301 | 50m. Type **65** (wrongly inscr "1994") | 15 | 15 |
| 302 | 100m. Mohammed Ali (Cassius Clay) (boxing, Rome, 1960) | 35 | 35 |
| 303 | 150m. Li Ning (gymnastics, Los Angeles, 1984) | 55 | 55 |
| 304 | 200m. Said Aouita (5000m, Los Angeles, 1984) | 70 | 70 |
| 305 | 250m. Olga Korbut (gymnastics, Munich, 1972) | 90 | 90 |
| 306 | 300m. Nadia Comaneci (gymnastics, Montreal, 1976) | 1·10 | 1·10 |
| 307 | 400m. Greg Louganis (diving, Los Angeles, 1984) | 1·30 | 1·30 |
| **MS**308 | 74×104 mm. 500m. Nazim Goussinev (bantamweight boxing, Barcelona, 1992) (vert) | 1·80 | 1·80 |

**66** "Maral-Gol"

**1996.** 5th Death Anniv of G. Aliev (painter). Mult.

| | | | |
|---|---|---|---|
| 309 | 100m. "Reka Cura" | 55 | 55 |
| 310 | 200m. Type **66** | 1·10 | 1·10 |

**67** Behbudov and Globe

**1996.** 7th Death Anniv of Resid Behbudov (singer).

| | | | | |
|---|---|---|---|---|
| 311 | **67** | 100m. multicoloured | 95 | 95 |

**68** Mammadaliev and Flasks

**1996.** 1st Death Anniv of Yusif Mammadaliev (scientist).

| | | | | |
|---|---|---|---|---|
| 312 | **68** | 100m. multicoloured | 95 | 95 |

**69** National Flag and Government Building

**1996.** 5th Anniv of Republic.

| | | | | |
|---|---|---|---|---|
| 313 | **69** | 250m. multicoloured | 90 | 90 |

**70** Dome of the Rock

**1996.** 3000th Anniv of Jerusalem. Multicoloured.

| | | | |
|---|---|---|---|
| 314 | 100m. Praying at the Wailing Wall | 70 | 70 |
| 315 | 250m. Interior of church | 1·70 | 1·70 |
| 316 | 300m. Type **70** | 2·00 | 2·00 |
| **MS**317 | 73×104 mm. 500m. Montefiore Windmill | 3·50 | 3·50 |

**71** German Shepherd

**1996.** Dogs. Multicoloured.

| | | | |
|---|---|---|---|
| 318 | 50m. Type **71** | 10 | 10 |
| 319 | 100m. Basset hounds | 40 | 40 |
| 320 | 150m. Collies | 60 | 60 |
| 321 | 200m. Bull terriers | 85 | 85 |
| 322 | 300m. Boxers | 1·30 | 1·30 |
| 323 | 400m. Cocker spaniels | 1·70 | 1·70 |
| **MS**324 | 70×80 mm. 500m. Shar-pei (38×30 mm) | 2·10 | 2·10 |

**72** Shaft-tailed Whydah

**1996.** Birds. Multicoloured.

| | | | |
|---|---|---|---|
| 325 | 50m. Type **72** | 10 | 10 |
| 326 | 100m. Blue-naped mousebird | 40 | 40 |
| 327 | 150m. Asian black-headed oriole | 60 | 60 |
| 328 | 200m. Golden oriole | 85 | 85 |
| 329 | 300m. Common starling | 1·30 | 1·30 |
| 330 | 400m. Yellow-fronted canary | 1·70 | 1·70 |
| **MS**331 | 60×80 mm. 500m. European bee eater (*Merops apaister*) (31×39 mm) | 2·10 | 2·10 |

**73** "Burgundy"

**1996.** Roses. Multicoloured.

| | | | |
|---|---|---|---|
| 332 | 50m. Type **73** | 10 | 10 |
| 333 | 100m. "Virgo" | 40 | 40 |
| 334 | 150m. "Rose Gaujard" | 60 | 60 |
| 335 | 200m. "Luna" | 85 | 85 |
| 336 | 300m. "Lady Rose" | 1·30 | 1·30 |
| 337 | 400m. "Landora" | 1·70 | 1·70 |
| **MS**338 | 90×70 mm. 500m. "Luxor" (39×31 mm) | 2·10 | 2·10 |

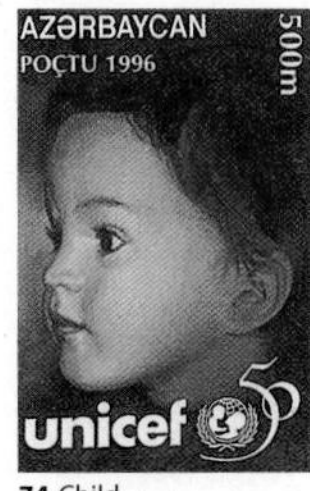

**74** Child

**1996.** 50th Anniv of UNICEF.

| | | | | |
|---|---|---|---|---|
| 339 | **74** | 500m. multicoloured | 90 | 90 |

**75** Spain v. Bulgaria

**1996.** European Football Championship, England. Multicoloured.

| | | | |
|---|---|---|---|
| 340 | 100m. Type **75** | 25 | 25 |
| 341 | 150m. Rumania v. France | 40 | 40 |

342 200m. Czech Republic v. Germany 50 50
343 250m. England v. Switzerland 70 70
344 300m. Croatia v. Turkey 75 75
345 400m. Italy v. Russia 1·10 1·10
**MS**346 110×80 mm. 500m. Detail of cup 1·40 1·40

**76** Chinese Junk

**1996.** Ships. Multicoloured.
347 100m. Type **76** 25 25
348 150m. "Danmark" (Danish full-rigged cadet ship) 40 40
349 200m. "Nippon-Maru II" (Japanese cadet ship) 60 60
350 250m. "Mircea" (Rumanian barque) 75 75
351 300m. "Kruzenshtern" (Russian cadet barque) 95 95
352 400m. "Ariadne" (German cadet schooner) 1·30 1·30
**MS**353 107×77 mm. 500m. *Tovarishch* (Russian four-masted cadet barque) (vert) 2·75 2·75

**77** Baxram Gur killing Dragon (fountain by A. Shulgin at Baku)

**1997**
354 **77** 100m. purple and black 35 35
356 **77** 250m. black and yellow 40 40
357 **77** 400m. black and red 55 55
358 **77** 500m. black and green 65 65
359 **77** 1000m. black and blue 1·30 1·30

**78** Nariman Narimanov (politician and writer)

**1997.** Anniversaries. Multicoloured.
365 250m. Type **78** (125th birth anniv (1995)) 80 80
366 250m. Fatali Xoyskin (politician, 120th birth anniv (1995)) 80 80
367 250m. Aziz Mammed-Kerim ogli Aliyev (politician, birth centenary) 80 80
368 250m. Ilyas Afendiyev (writer, 1st death anniv) 80 80

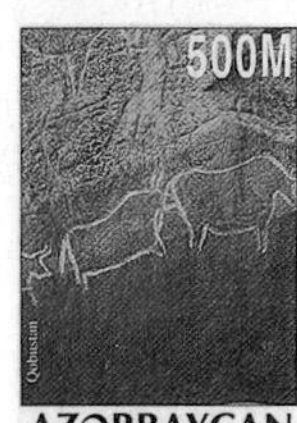


**79** Bulls

**1997.** Qobustasn Rock Carvings. Sheet 127×84 mm containing T **79** and similar vert designs. Multicoloured.
**MS**369 500m. Type **79**; 500m. Goats; 500m. Dancers 4·50 4·50

**1997.** Red Cross. Various stamps optd Red Cross and cross. (a) Nos. 93/99.
370 20q. multicoloured 10 10
371 30q. multicoloured 10 10
372 50q. multicoloured 10 10
373 1m. multicoloured 35 35
374 2m.50 multicoloured 1·00 1·00
375 5m. multicoloured 2·00 2·00
376 10m. multicoloured 4·25 4·25
**MS**377 80×60 mm. 8m. multicoloured 4·25 4·25

(b) Nos. 195/9.
378 10m. multicoloured 40 40
379 15m. multicoloured 70 70
380 20m. multicoloured 95 95
381 25m. multicoloured 1·20 1·20
382 50m. multicoloured 2·40 2·40
**MS**383 64×56 mm. 100m. multicoloured 4·25 4·25

**1997.** 50th Anniv of Rotary Club International in Azerbaijan. Various stamps optd 50th Anniversary of the Rotary Club and emblem. (a) Nos. 314/16.
384 100m. multicoloured 95 95
385 250m. multicoloured 2·20 2·20
386 300m. multicoloured 2·75 2·75
**MS**387 74×103 mm. 500m. multicoloured 2·50 2·50

(b) Nos. 347/52.
388 100m. multicoloured 40 40
389 150m. multicoloured 70 70
390 200m. multicoloured 85 85
391 250m. multicoloured 1·10 1·10
392 300m. multicoloured 1·30 1·30
393 400m. multicoloured 1·70 1·70
**MS**394 106×76 mm. 500m. multicoloured 4·50 4·50

**82** Dog

**1997.** "The Town Band of Bremen" by the Brothers Grimm. Multicoloured.
395 250m. Type **82** 1·50 1·50
396 250m. Donkey and cat 1·50 1·50
397 250m. Rooster 1·50 1·50
**MS**398 125×96 mm. 500m. Animals frightening robbers from hideaway 3·50 3·50
Nos. 395/7 were issued together, se-tenant, forming a composite design.

**83** Seal Pup

**1997.** The Caspian Seal. Multicoloured.
399 250m. Type **83** 65 65
400 250m. Bull and mountain peak 65 65
401 250m. Bull and gull 65 65
402 250m. Cow (profile) 65 65
403 250m. Cow (full face) 65 65
404 250m. Young seal (three-quarter face) 65 65
**MS**405 106×77 mm. 500m. Cow (vert) 3·50 3·50
Nos. 399/404 were issued together, se-tenant, forming a composite design.

**84** Tanbur

**1997.** Traditional Musical Instruments. Mult.
406 250m. Type **84** 60 60
407 250m. Gaval (tambourine) 60 60
408 500m. Jang (harp) 1·20 1·20

**85** 19th-century Oil Derricks, Aspheron Peninsula

**1997.** 125th Anniv of First Industrial Oil Well in Azerbaijan. Sheet 115×91 mm containing T **85** and similar vert design. Multicoloured.
**MS**409 500m. Type **85**; 500m. Modern drilling platform, Caspian Sea 2·50 2·50

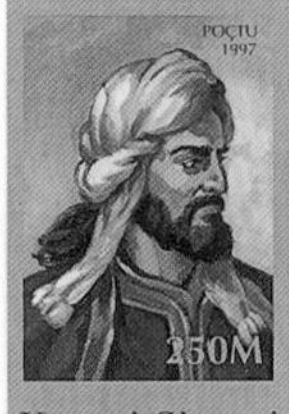


**86** Sirvani

**1997.** 870th Birth Anniv (1996) of Xanqani Sirvani (poet).
410 **86** 250m. multicoloured 85 85

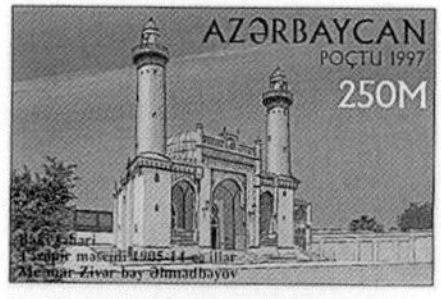


**87** Taza-pir Mosque, Baku

**1997.** Mosques. Multicoloured.
411 250m. Type **87** 75 75
412 250m. Momuna-Xatun Mosque, Nakhichevan 75 75
413 250m. Govharaga Mosque, Shusha 75 75

**88** Rasulbekov and Baku T.V. Tower

**1997.** 80th Birth Anniv of G. D. Rasulbekov (former Minister of Telecommunications).
414 **88** 250m. multicoloured 75 75

**89** Italy, 1938

**1997.** World Cup Football Championship, France (1998).
415 **89** 250m. black 70 70
416 - 250m. multicoloured 70 70
417 - 250m. black 70 70
418 - 250m. multicoloured 70 70
419 - 250m. multicoloured 70 70
420 - 250m. multicoloured 70 70
**MS**421 85×90 mm. 1500m. black and blue (Tofiq Bahramov (referee)) 3·25 3·25

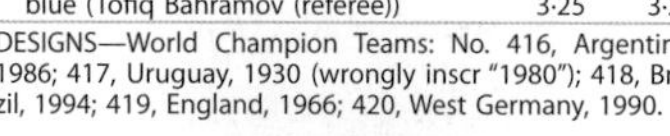
DESIGNS—World Champion Teams: No. 416, Argentina, 1986; 417, Uruguay, 1930 (wrongly inscr "1980"); 418, Brazil, 1994; 419, England, 1966; 420, West Germany, 1990.

**90** Katarina Wit, East Germany

**1997.** Winter Olympic Games, Nagano, Japan. Mult.
422 250m. Type **90** (figure skating gold medal, 1984 and 1988) 3·75 50
423 250m. Elvis Stoyko, Canada (figure skating silver medal, 1994) 50 50
424 250m. Midori Ito, Japan (figure skating silver medal, 1992) 50 50
425 250m. Azerbaijan flag and silhouettes of sports 50 50
426 250m. Olympic torch and mountain 50 50
427 250m. Kristin Yamaguchi, U.S.A. (figure skating gold medal, 1992) 50 50
428 250m. John Curry, Great Britain (figure skating gold medal, 1976) 50 50
429 250m. Cen Lu, China (figure skating bronze medal, 1994) 50 50
**MS**430 76×106 mm. 500m. Yekaterina Gordeyeva and Sergi Grinkov, Russia (figure skating gold medal, 1984 and 1988) 3·00 3·00

**91** Diana, Princess of Wales

**1998.** Diana, Princess of Wales Commem. Mult.
431 400m. Type **91** 50 50
432 400m. Wearing black polo-neck jumper 50 50

**92** Aliyev and Mountain Landscape

**1998.** 90th Birth Anniv of Hasan Aliyev (ecologist).
433 **92** 500m. multicoloured 85 85

**93** Tourist Map, Flag and Pres. Aliev

**1998.** 75th Birthday of President Haidar Aliev. Sheet 114×89 mm.
**MS**434 **93** 500m. multicoloured 2·10 2·10

**1998.** "Israel 98" International Stamp Exhibition, Tel Aviv. No. MS369 optd 98 and emblem on each stamp and "Israel 98–WORLD STAMP EXHIBITION TEL-AVIV 13–21 MAY 1998" in margin.
**MS**435 500m. ×3 multicoloured 5·50 5·50

**95** Ashug Alesker (singer)

**1998.** Birth Anniversaries. Multicoloured.
436 250m. Type **95** (175th anniv) 60 60
437 250m. Magomedhuseyn Shakhriyar (poet, 90th anniv) 60 60
438 250m. Qara Qarayev (composer, 80th anniv) 60 60

**96** Bul-Bul

**1998.** Birth Centenary of Bul-Bul (Murtuz Meshadirza ogli Mamedov) (singer).
439 **96** 500m. multicoloured 85 85

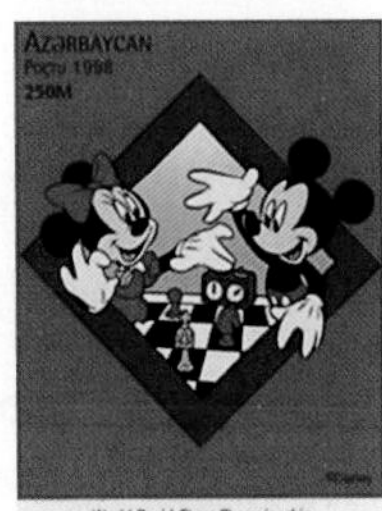

**97** Mickey and Minnie Mouse playing Chess

**1998.** World Rapid Chess Championship, Georgia. Multicoloured.
440 250m. Type **97** 2·10 2·10
441 500m. Mickey, Minnie, pawn and rook 2·40 2·40
442 500m. Goofy, bishop and knight 2·40 2·40
443 500m. Donald Duck, king and bishop 2·40 2·40
444 500m. Pluto, rook, pawn and clockwork pawn 2·40 2·40
445 500m. Minnie and queen 2·40 2·40
446 500m. Daisy Duck, bishop and king 2·40 2·40
447 500m. Goofy, Donald and pawn 2·40 2·40
448 500m. Mickey, queen and rook 2·40 2·40
**MS**449 Two sheets, each 127×101 mm. (a) 4000m. Mickey, Minnie, Pluto and queen; (b) 4000m. Donald, Mickey and pawn 19·00 19·00

**98** Preparing Pastries

**1998.** Europa. National Festivals: New Year. Mult.
450 1000m. Type **98** 1·20 1·20
451 3000m. Acrobat and wrestlers 3·00 3·00

**1999.** "iBRA" International Stamp Exhibition, Nuremberg, Germany. Nos. 450/1 optd with exhibition emblem.
452 1000m. multicoloured 75 75
453 3000m. multicoloured 2·30 2·30

**100** Greater Flamingo, Gizilagach National Park

**1999.** Europa. Parks and Gardens. Multicoloured.
454 1000m. Type **100** 1·20 1·20
455 3000m. Stag, Girkan National Park 3·00 3·00

**101** 14th-century Square Tower

**1999.** Towers at Mardakyan.
456 **101** 1000m. black and blue 60 60
457 - 3000m. black and red 2·30 1·90
DESIGN: 3000m. 13th-century round tower.
See also Nos. 547 and 557.

**102** President Aliev and Flag

**1999.** 75th Anniv of Nakhichevan Autonomous Region. Multicoloured.
460 1000m. Type **102** 1·00 1·00
461 1000m. Map of Nakhichevan 1·00 1·00
**MS**462 110×90 mm. Nos. 460/1 1·90 1·90

**103** Cabbarli

**1999.** Birth Centenary of Cafar Cabbarli (dramatist).
463 **103** 250m. multicoloured 75 75

**104** 40k. Stamp

**1999.** 80th Anniv of First Azerbaijani Stamps. Sheet 131×106 mm containing T 104 and similar multicoloured designs showing stamps of 1919.
**MS**464 500m. 10k. stamp (Type **1**) (25×35 mm); 500m. Type **104**; 500m. 5r. stamp; 500m. 50r. stamp (Type **2**) 3·25 3·25

**105** Flag, Pigeon and Emblem on Scroll

**1999.** 125th Anniv of Universal Postal Union. Multicoloured.
465 250m. Type **105** 10 10
466 300m. Satellite, computer and emblem 3·00 3·00

**106** Caravanserai Inner Court and Maiden's Tower, Baku

**1999.** 19th-century Caravanserais. Multicoloured.
467 500m. Type **106** 1·30 1·30
468 500m. Camels outside caravanserai, Sheki 1·30 1·30


**107** Anniversary Emblem

**1999.** 50th Anniv of Council of Europe.
469 **107** 1000m. multicoloured 95 95


**108** Beybur Khan's Son fighting Camel

**1999.** 1300th Anniv of Kitabi Dada Qorqud (folk epic). Sheet 90×125 mm containing T 108 and similar horiz designs. Multicoloured.
**MS**470 1000m. Type **108**; 1000m. Wounded Tural slumped on horse; 1000m. Gaza Khan asleep beside horse 2·75 2·75

**109** "Building Europe"

**2000.** Europa.
471 **109** 1000m. multicoloured 90 90
472 **109** 3000m. multicoloured 3·25 3·25

**110** Phaeton

**2000.** Baku City Transport. Sheet 111×88 mm containing T 110 and similar horiz designs. Multicoloured.
**MS**473 500m. Type **110**; 500m. Konka; 500m. Electric tram; 500m. Trolleybus 3·50 3·50

**111** 14th-century Square Tower, Ramana

**2000.** Towers of Mardakyan.
474 **111** 100m. black and orange 40 40
475 - 250m. black and green 1·00 1·00
DESIGN: 250m. 14th-century round tower, Nardaran.
See also Nos. 499/500.

**112** Wrestling

**2000.** Olympic Games, Sydney. Multicoloured.
476 500m. Type **112** 95 95
477 500m. Weightlifting 95 95
478 500m. Boxing 95 95
479 500m. Relay 95 95

**113** Duck flying

**2000.** The Ferruginous Duck. Multicoloured.
480 500m. Type **113** 70 70
481 500m. Ducks in water and standing on rocks 70 70
482 500m. Duck standing on rock and others swimming by grasses 70 70
483 500m. Ducks at sunset 70 70

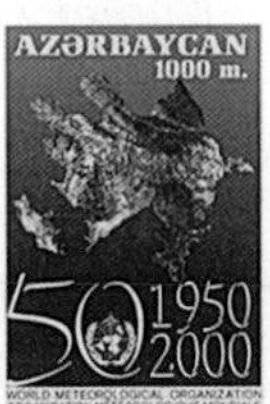

**114** Satellite Picture of Azerbaijan and Emblem

**2000.** 50th Anniv of World Meteorological Organization.
484 **114** 1000m. multicoloured 85 85

**115** Quinces

**2000.** Fruits. Multicoloured.
485 500m. Type **115** 75 75
486 500m. Pomegranates (*Punica granatum*) 75 75
487 500m. Peaches (*Persica*) 75 75
488 500m. Figs (*Ficus carica*) 75 75

**116** Ringed-necked Pheasant

**2000.** The Ringed-necked Pheasant (Phasanus colchicus). Sheet 102×72 mm.
**MS**489 **116** 2000m. multicoloured 2·50 2·50

**117** Rasul-Rza

**2000.** 90th Birth Anniv of Rasul-Rza (poet).
490 **117** 250m. multicoloured 80 80

**118** Levantine Viper

**2000.** Reptiles. Multicoloured.
491 500m. Type **118** 1·10 1·10
492 500m. Rock lizard (*Lacerta saxicola*) (wrongly inscr "Laserta saxcola") 1·10 1·10
493 500m. Ottoman viper (*Vipera xanthina*) 1·10 1·10
494 500m. Toad-headed agama (*Phrynocephalus mystaceus*) 1·10 1·10
**MS**495 90×63 mm. 500m. Watersnake (*Natrix tessellate*) and sunwatcher (*Phrynocephalus helioscopus*) (vert) 1·30 1·30

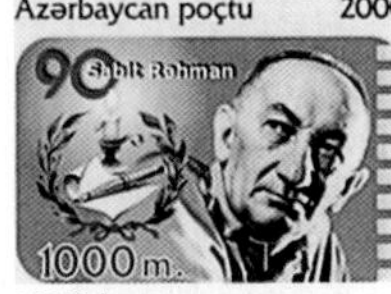

**119** Rahman

**2000.** 90th Birth Anniv of Sabit Rahman (writer).
496 **119** 1000m. multicoloured 1·40 1·40

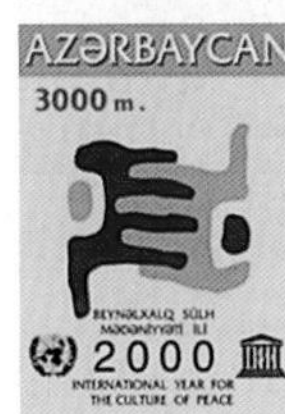

**120** Emblem

**2000.** UNESCO International Year of Culture and Peace.
497 **120** 3000m. multicoloured 2·75 2·75

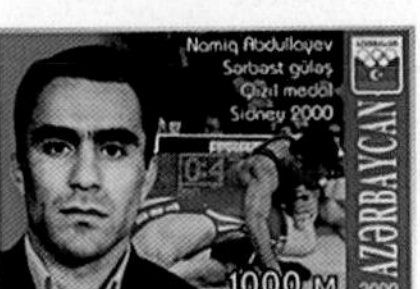

**121** Namig Abullayev (gold, freestyle flyweight wrestling)

**2001.** Olympic Games, Sydney. Medal Winners. Sheet 99×127 mm containing T 121 and similar horiz designs. Multicoloured.

| | | | |
|---|---|---|---|
| **MS**498 | 1000m. Type **121**; 1000m. Zemifira Meftahaddinova (gold, skeet shooting); 1000m. Vugar Alakbarov (bronze, middle-weight boxing) | 3·00 | 3·00 |

**122** Seal, Lesser White-fronted Goose and Oil Rig

**2001.** Europa. Water Resources. The Caspian Sea. Multicoloured.

| | | | |
|---|---|---|---|
| 499 | 1000m. Type **122** | 1·00 | 1·00 |
| 500 | 3000m. Sturgeon, crab and oil rig | 3·25 | 3·25 |

**123** Building and Flags

**2001.** Admission of Azerbaijan to Council of Europe.

| | | | | |
|---|---|---|---|---|
| 501 | **123** | 1000m. multicoloured | 1·00 | 1·00 |

**2001.** Towers of Sheki. As T 111.

| | | | |
|---|---|---|---|
| 502 | 100m. black and lilac | 30 | 30 |
| 503 | 250m. black and yellow | 80 | 80 |

DESIGNS: 100m. 18th-century round tower; 250m. Ruin of 12th-century tower.

**124** Refugee Camp

**2001.** 50th Anniv of United Nations High Commissioner for Refugees. Sheet 100×73 mm.

| | | | |
|---|---|---|---|
| **MS**504 | **124** 3000m. black and blue | 2·50 | 2·50 |

**125** Tusi, Globe and Books

**2001.** 800th Birth Anniv of Nasraddin Tusi (mathematician and astronomer). Sheet 110×78 mm.

| | | | |
|---|---|---|---|
| **MS**505 | **125** 3000m. multicoloured | 2·50 | 2·50 |

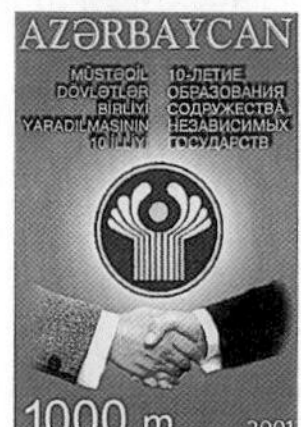


**126** Handshake and Emblem

**2001.** 10th Anniv of Union of Independent States.

| | | | | |
|---|---|---|---|---|
| 506 | **126** | 1000m. multicoloured | 1·00 | 1·00 |

**127** Yuri Gagarin, "Vostok 1" and Globe

**2001.** 40th Anniv of First Manned Space Flight. Sheet 83×56 mm.

| | | | |
|---|---|---|---|
| **MS**507 | **127** 3000m. multicoloured | 2·20 | 2·20 |

**128** Short-eared Owl (*Asio flammeus*)

**2001.** Owls. Multicoloured.

| | | | |
|---|---|---|---|
| 508 | 1000m. Type **128** | 75 | 75 |
| 509 | 1000m. Tawny owl (*Strix aluco*) | 75 | 75 |
| 510 | 1000m. Scops owl (*Otus scops*) | 75 | 75 |
| 511 | 1000m. Long-eared owl (*Asio otus*) | 75 | 75 |
| 512 | 1000m. Eagle owl on branch (*Bubo bubo*) | 75 | 75 |
| 513 | 1000m. Little owl (*Athene noctua*) | 75 | 75 |
| **MS**514 | 91×68 mm. 1000m. Eagle owl (*Bubo bubo*) in flight | 1·90 | 1·90 |

**129** Pres. Heydar Aliyev

**2001.** 10th Anniv of Independence.

| | | | | |
|---|---|---|---|---|
| 515 | **129** | 5000m. multicoloured | 7·75 | 7·75 |

**130** Pres. Vladimir Putin and Pres. Heydar Aliyev

**2001.** Visit of President Putin to Azerbaijan.

| | | | | |
|---|---|---|---|---|
| 516 | **130** | 1000m. multicoloured | 85 | 80 |

**131** Emblem and Athletes

**2002.** 10th Anniv of National Olympic Committee.

| | | | | |
|---|---|---|---|---|
| 517 | **131** | 3000m. multicoloured | 2·20 | 2·20 |

**132** Circus Performers

**2002.** Europa. Circus. Multicoloured.

| | | | |
|---|---|---|---|
| 518 | 1000m. Type **132** | 1·00 | 1·00 |
| 519 | 3000m. Equestrian juggler and trapeze artist | 3·25 | 3·25 |

**133** Presidents Heydar Aliyev and Jiang Zemin

**2002.** 10th Anniv of Azerbaijan–China Diplomatic Relations.

| | | | | |
|---|---|---|---|---|
| 520 | **133** | 1000m. multicoloured | 90 | 90 |

**134** Molla Panah Vagif's Mausoleum, Susa

**2002.** Towers of Karabakh.

| | | | | |
|---|---|---|---|---|
| 521 | **134** | 100m. black and green | 20 | 20 |
| 522 | - | 250m. black and cinnamon | 50 | 50 |

DESIGNS: 250m. 19th-century mosque, Aghdam.

**2002.** 10th Anniv of Azermarka Stamp Company. No. 83 surch Azermarka 1992–2002 1000m.

| | | | | |
|---|---|---|---|---|
| 523 | **13** | 1000m. on 35q. multicoloured | 85 | 85 |

**136** Emblem

**2002.** 10th Anniv of New Azerbaijan Party.

| | | | | |
|---|---|---|---|---|
| 524 | **136** | 3000m. multicoloured | 2·20 | 2·20 |

**137** African Monarch (*Danaus chrysippus*)

**2002.** Butterflies and Moths. Multicoloured.

| | | | |
|---|---|---|---|
| 525 | 1000m. Type **137** (inscr "Danais") | 95 | 95 |
| 526 | 1000m. Southern swallowtail (*Papilio alexanor*) | 95 | 95 |
| 527 | 1000m. *Thaleropis jonia* | 95 | 95 |
| 528 | 1000m. Red admiral (*Vanessa atalanta*) | 95 | 95 |
| 529 | 1000m. *Argynnis alexandra* | 95 | 95 |
| 530 | 1000m. *Brahmaea christoph* (moth) | 95 | 95 |

**138** Pres. Heydar Aliyev and Pope John Paul II

**2002.** Pope John Paul II's Visit to Azerbaijan. Sheet 80×65 mm.

| | | | |
|---|---|---|---|
| **MS**531 | **138** 1500m. multicoloured | 2·00 | 2·00 |

**139** Telegraph Machine, Building Facade and Emblem

**2002.** 70th Anniv of Baku Telegraph Office.

| | | | | |
|---|---|---|---|---|
| 532 | **139** | 3000m. multicoloured | 2·00 | 2·00 |

**140** Gadjiyev and Piano

**2002.** 80th Birth Anniv of Ruaf Gadjiyev (composer).

| | | | | |
|---|---|---|---|---|
| 533 | **140** | 5000m. multicoloured | 2·50 | 2·50 |

**141** Bearded Men with Swords, Black Pawns, White Pawn and White Rook

**2002.** European Junior Chess Championships, Baku. Showing chess board and views of Baku. Multicoloured.

| | | | |
|---|---|---|---|
| 534 | 1500m. Type **141** | 1·20 | 1·20 |
| 535 | 1500m. Two knights on horseback | 1·20 | 1·20 |
| 536 | 1500m. Two elephants | 1·20 | 1·20 |
| 537 | 1500m. Black rook, black pawn, bearded men with swords and fallen knight | 1·20 | 1·20 |

Nos. 534/7 were issued together, se-tenant, forming a composite design showing a chess game and views of ancient Baku.

**142** World Trade Centre, New York, U.S.A. and Azerbaijan Flags and Globe

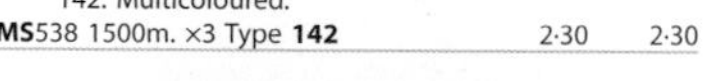

**2002.** 1st Anniv of Attack on World Trade Centre, New York. Sheet 130×65 mm containing vert design as T 142. Multicoloured.

| | | | |
|---|---|---|---|
| **MS**538 | 1500m. ×3 Type **142** | 2·30 | 2·30 |

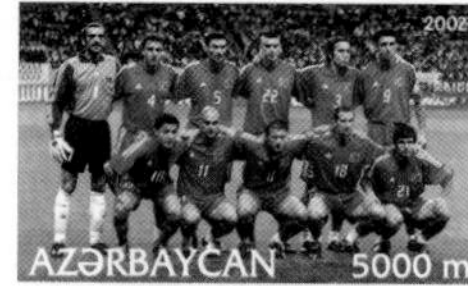


**143** Turkish Football Team

**2002.** Football World Cup Championship, Japan and South Korea. Sheet 102×110 mm.

| | | | |
|---|---|---|---|
| **MS**539 | **143** 5000m. multicoloured | 3·50 | 3·50 |

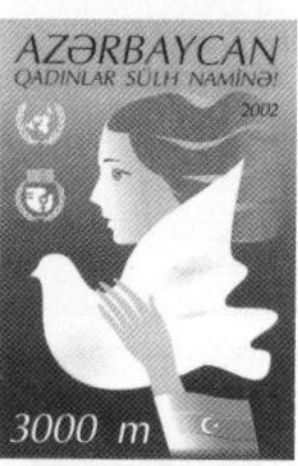


**144** Dove, Woman, Flag and Emblems

**2002.** United Nations Development Fund for Women.

| | | | | |
|---|---|---|---|---|
| 540 | **144** | 3000m. multicoloured | 2·10 | 2·10 |

**145** Siamese Fighting Fish (*Betta splendens*)

**2002.** Aquarium Fish. Multicoloured.

| | | | |
|---|---|---|---|
| 541 | 100m. Type **145** | 75 | 75 |
| 542 | 100m. Blue discus (*Symphysodon aequifasciatus*) | 75 | 75 |
| 543 | 100m. Freshwater angelfish (*Pterophyllum scalare*) | 75 | 75 |
| 544 | 100m. Black moor (*Carassius auratus auratus*) | 75 | 75 |
| 545 | 100m. Boeseman's rainbowfish (*Melanotaenia boesemani*) | 75 | 75 |
| 546 | 1000m. Firemouth cichlid (*Cichlasoma meeki*) | 75 | 75 |

**2003.** Towers of Karabakh. As T 101.

| | | | |
|---|---|---|---|
| 547 | 250m. black and blue | 45 | 45 |

DESIGN: No. 547, Askeran tower and fortress.

**146** Bomb and Scissors ("Stop Terrorism")

**2003.** Europa. Poster Art. Multicoloured.

| | | | |
|---|---|---|---|
| 548 | 1000m. Type **146** | 85 | 85 |
| 549 | 3000m. Wrestlers ("Sport is the Health of the Nation") | 2·50 | 2·50 |

**147** Flag and UPU Emblem

**2003.** 10th Anniv of Azerbaijan Membership of Universal Postal Union.

| | | | | |
|---|---|---|---|---|
| 550 | **147** | 3000m. multicoloured | 2·10 | 2·10 |

**148** H. Djavid Mausoleum and Hacha Mountain

**2003.** Nakhichevan.

| | | | | |
|---|---|---|---|---|
| 551 | **148** | 3000m. multicoloured | 2·10 | 2·10 |

**149** Map and Pipeline

**2003.** Baku–Tbilisi–Jeychan Oil Pipeline.

| | | | | |
|---|---|---|---|---|
| 552 | **149** | 3000m. multicoloured | 2·10 | 2·10 |

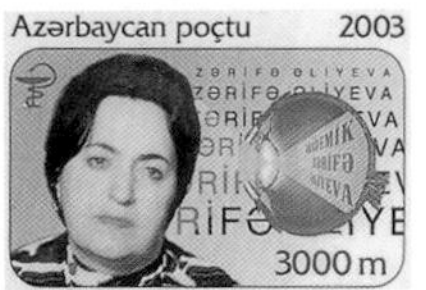


**150** Zarifa Aliyeva and Eye

**2003.** 80th Birth Anniv of Zarifa Aliyeva (ophthalmologist).

| | | | | |
|---|---|---|---|---|
| 553 | **150** | 3000m. multicoloured | 2·10 | 2·10 |

**151** Heydar Aliyev

**2003.** 80th Birth Anniv of Pres. Heydar Aliyev. Sheet 130×160 mm.

| | | | | |
|---|---|---|---|---|
| **MS**554 | **151** | 10000m. multicoloured | 6·00 | 6·00 |

**2003.** Nos. 131 and 168 surch.

| | | | |
|---|---|---|---|
| 555 | 500m. on 25m. yellow and black | 50 | 50 |
| 556 | 1000m. on 8m. blue, silver and black | 1·00 | 1·00 |

**2003.** Towers of Karabakh. As T 101.

| | | | |
|---|---|---|---|
| 557 | 1000m. black | 75 | 75 |

DESIGN: No. 557, Archway, walls and tower, Shusha Town.

**153** QAZ-11-73 Saloon Car

**2003.** Cars. Sheet 100×77 mm containing T 153 and similar horiz designs. Multicoloured.

| | | | |
|---|---|---|---|
| **MS**558 | 500m.×4 Type **153**; QAZ-M-20 Pobeda; QAZ 12 Zim; QAZ-21 Volga (inscr "Volqa") | 2·40 | 2·00 |

**154** Textile Seller

**2003.** 90th Anniv of U. Hajibekov's Musical Comedy "Arshin Mal Alan".

| | | | | |
|---|---|---|---|---|
| 559 | **154** | 10000m. multicoloured | 5·00 | 5·00 |

**2003.** Nos. 91, 129, 130, 152/5, 165 and 169 surch.

| | | | |
|---|---|---|---|
| 560 | 500m. on 50q. yellow and black | 40 | 40 |
| 561 | 500m. on 2m. red, silver and black | 40 | 40 |
| 562 | 500m. on 4m. green, silver and black | 40 | 40 |
| 563 | 500m. on 5m. multicoloured | 40 | 40 |
| 567 | 500m. on 5m. red and black | 40 | 40 |
| 564 | 500m. on 10m. multicoloured | 40 | 40 |
| 565 | 500m. on 15m. multicoloured | 40 | 40 |
| 566 | 500m. on 20m. multicoloured | 40 | 40 |
| 568 | 500m. on 40m. brown and black | 40 | 40 |

**155** Bear (*Ursus arctos*) (inscr "arctors")

**2003.** Sheki National Park. Sheet 106×84 mm containing T 155 and similar horiz designs. Multicoloured.

| | | | |
|---|---|---|---|
| **MS**569 | 3000m. Type **155**; Racoon (*Procyon lotor*); Wild boar (*Sus scrofa*); Fox (*Vulpes vulpes*) | 6·75 | 6·75 |

**156** Map and Monument

**2004.** 80th Anniversary of Nakhichevan Autonomous Republic.

| | | | | |
|---|---|---|---|---|
| 570 | **156** | 3000m. multicoloured | 1·70 | 1·70 |

**157** Dove of Peace (sculpture)

**2004.** Samgayit Town.

| | | | | |
|---|---|---|---|---|
| 571 | **157** | 500m. blue and black | 60 | 60 |

**158** Geygel Lake

**2004.** Europa. Holidays. Multicoloured.

| | | | |
|---|---|---|---|
| 572 | 1000m. Type **158** | 85 | 85 |
| 573 | 3000m. Baku at night | 2·50 | 2·50 |

**159** Molla Cuma

**2004.** 150th Birth Anniversary of Molla Cuma (singer).

| | | | | |
|---|---|---|---|---|
| 574 | **159** | 500m. multicoloured | 75 | 75 |

**160** High Jump

**2004.** Olympic Games, 2004, Greece. Multicoloured.

| | | | |
|---|---|---|---|
| 575 | 500m. Type **160** | 70 | 70 |
| 576 | 500m. Wrestlers | 70 | 70 |
| 577 | 500m. Runner | 70 | 70 |
| 578 | 500m. Greek vase | 70 | 70 |

Nos. 575/8 were issued together, se-tenant, forming a composite design.

**161** World Cup Trophy

**2004.** Centenary of FIFA (Federation Internationale de Football Association). Multicoloured.

| | | | |
|---|---|---|---|
| 579 | 500m. Type **161** | 70 | 70 |
| 580 | 500m. Player facing left | 70 | 70 |
| 581 | 500m. Player facing right | 70 | 70 |
| 582 | 500m. Goalkeeper | 70 | 70 |

Nos. 579/82 were issued together, se-tenant, forming a composite design.

**162** Heydar Aliyev

**2004.** Heydar Aliyev Commemoration (president, 1993–2003) (1st issue).

| | | | | |
|---|---|---|---|---|
| 583 | **162** | 500m. multicoloured | 60 | 60 |

See also Nos. **MS**590, 607 and 632.

**163** Mosques and Camels

**2004.** The Great Silk Route.

| | | | | |
|---|---|---|---|---|
| 584 | **163** | 3000m. multicoloured | 2·10 | 2·10 |

**164** Carpet and Couple wearing 19th-century Costume, Baku

**2004.** Traditional Costumes. Carpets and 19th-century costumes.

| | | | |
|---|---|---|---|
| 585 | 500m. Type **164** | 65 | 65 |
| 586 | 500m. Couple holding instruments, Karabakh | 65 | 65 |
| 587 | 500m. Woman wearing long headdress, man with cane, Nakhichevan | 65 | 65 |

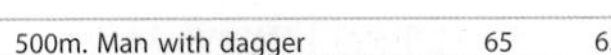

| | | | |
|---|---|---|---|
| 588 | 500m. Man with dagger | 65 | 65 |

**165** Globe, Honeywell DDP 516 and Modern Computer

**2004.** 35th Anniv of the Internet.

| | | | | |
|---|---|---|---|---|
| 589 | **165** | 3000m. multicoloured | 1·80 | 1·80 |

**166** Heydar Aliyev

**2004.** Heydar Aliyev Commemoration (president, 1993–2003) (2nd issue). Sheet 60×80 mm.

| | | | | |
|---|---|---|---|---|
| **MS**590 | **166** | 1000m. multicoloured | 5·50 | 5·50 |

**167** Leopard in Tree

**2005.** Endangered Species. Leopards. Multicoloured.

| | | | |
|---|---|---|---|
| 591 | 1000m. Type **167** | 80 | 80 |
| 592 | 1000m. Two cubs | 80 | 80 |
| 593 | 1000m. Adult | 80 | 80 |
| 594 | 1000m. Mother and cubs | 80 | 80 |

**2005.** Nos. 212/15 surch 1000 mm.

| | | | |
|---|---|---|---|
| 595 | 1000m. on 10m. multicoloured | 60 | 60 |
| 596 | 1000m. on 25m. multicoloured | 60 | 60 |
| 597 | 1000m. on 50m. multicoloured | 60 | 60 |
| 598 | 1000m. on 60m. multicoloured | 60 | 60 |

**169** Ministry Building and Emblem

**2005.** 5th Anniv of Ministry of Taxes.

| | | | | |
|---|---|---|---|---|
| 599 | **169** | 3000m. multicoloured | 2·50 | 1·80 |

**170** Observatory

**2005.** Shemakha Town.

| | | | | |
|---|---|---|---|---|
| 600 | **170** | 500m. mauve and black | 1·40 | 45 |

**171** *Cephalanthera rubra*

**2005.** Orchids. Multicoloured.

| | | | |
|---|---|---|---|
| 601 | 500m. Type **171** | 40 | 40 |
| 602 | 1000m. *Orchis papilionacea* | 85 | 85 |
| 603 | 1500m. *Epipactis atrorubens* | 1·30 | 1·30 |
| 604 | 3000m. *Orchis purpurea* | 3·00 | 3·00 |
| **MS**605 | 135×190 mm. Nos. 601/4 | 3·75 | 3·75 |

**172** Aircraft, Tanks and Oil Tankers

**2005.** 60th Anniv of the End of World War II.

| | | | | |
|---|---|---|---|---|
| 606 | **172** | 1000m. multicoloured | 60 | 60 |

**173** Heydar Aliyev

**2005.** Heydar Aliyev (president, 1993–2003) Commemoration (3rd issue).

| | | | | |
|---|---|---|---|---|
| 607 | **173** | 1000m. multicoloured | 60 | 60 |

**174** Pilaf

**2005.** Europa. Gastronomy. Multicoloured.

| | | | |
|---|---|---|---|
| 608 | 1000m. Type **174** | 70 | 70 |
| 609 | 3000m. Dolmasi | 3·00 | 3·00 |

**175** Rock Paintings and Academy Building

**2005.** 60th Anniv of Academy of Science.

| | | | | |
|---|---|---|---|---|
| 610 | **175** | 1000m. multicoloured | 45 | 45 |

**176** Astronaut

**2005.** 40th Anniv of First Space Walk. Sheet 86×58 mm.

| | | | |
|---|---|---|---|
| **MS**611 **176** | 3000m. multicoloured | 2·00 | 2·00 |

**177** Computers and Emblem

**2005.** Tunis 2005 (World Summit on Information Society).

| | | | | |
|---|---|---|---|---|
| 612 | **177** | 1000m. multicoloured | 45 | 45 |

**178** Pope John Paul II

**2005.** Pope John Paul II Commemoration.

| | | | | |
|---|---|---|---|---|
| 613 | **178** | 3000m. multicoloured | 2·00 | 2·00 |

**179** *Paravespula germanica*

**2005.** Insects. Sheet 101×80 mm containing T 179 and similar horiz designs. Multicoloured.

| | | |
|---|---|---|
| **MS**614 500m. Type **179**; 1000m. *Bombus terrestris*; 1500m. *Vespa crabro*; 3000m. *Apis mellifera caucasica* | 3·25 | 3·25 |

**180** Emblem and Nos. 450/1

**2005.** 50th Anniv of Europa Stamps. Showing previous Europa stamps. Multicoloured.

| | | | |
|---|---|---|---|
| 615 | 3000m. Type **180** | 1·40 | 1·40 |
| 616 | 3000m. Emblem and Nos. 471/2 | 1·40 | 1·40 |
| 617 | 3000m. Emblem and Nos. 548/9 | 1·40 | 1·40 |
| 618 | 3000m. Emblem and Nos. 1167/8 of West Germany | 1·40 | 1·40 |

| | | |
|---|---|---|
| **MS**619 Four sheets, each 88×88 mm. (a) As No. 615; (b) As No. 616; (c) As No. 617; (d) As No. 618 | 5·00 | 5·00 |

Note: On 1 January 2006 the manat was re-valued at the rate 1 new manat = 5000 old manat.

**2006.** Nos. 131, 110, 114, 168, 521, 113, 457, 146 and 127/8 surch.

| | | | |
|---|---|---|---|
| 620 | 5q. on 8m. blue, silver and black (No. 131) | 1·00 | 1·00 |
| 621 | 10q. on 1m. multicoloured (No. 110) | 1·30 | 1·30 |
| 622 | 10q. on 1m. multicoloured (No. 114) | 1·30 | 1·30 |
| 623 | 10q. on 25m. yellow and black (No. 168) | 1·30 | 1·30 |
| 624 | 10q. on 100m. black and green (No. 521) | 1·30 | 1·30 |
| 625 | 20q. on 50q. multicoloured (No. 113) | 1·75 | 1·75 |
| 627 | 20q. on 20m. black, gold and blue (No. 146) | 1·75 | 1·75 |
| 626 | 20q. on 3000m. black and scarlet (No. 457) | 1·75 | 1·75 |
| 628 | 60q. on 5m. multicoloured (No. 127) | 2·50 | 2·50 |
| 629 | 60q. on 8m. multicoloured (No. 128) | 2·50 | 2·50 |

**182** 19th-century Mosque, Lankaran

**2006.** Towns.

| | | | | |
|---|---|---|---|---|
| 630 | **182** | 10q. blue and black | 1·00 | 1·00 |
| 631 | - | 20q. buff and brown | 1·50 | 1·50 |

DESIGNS: Type **182**; 20q. 9th-century fortress, Lachin.
See also Nos. 652/3.

**2006.** Heydar Aliyev (president, 1993–2003) Commemoration (4th issue).

| | | | | |
|---|---|---|---|---|
| 632 | **162** | 60q. multicoloured | 4·25 | 4·25 |

**183** Emblem

**2006.** 30th Anniv of OPEC Fund for International Development.

| | | | | |
|---|---|---|---|---|
| 633 | **183** | 5q. multicoloured | 1·00 | 1·00 |

**184** Hands from Many Nations

**2006.** Europa. Integration. Multicoloured.

| | | | |
|---|---|---|---|
| 634 | 20q. Type **184** | 2·50 | 2·50 |
| 635 | 60q. Globe enclosed in star | 7·50 | 7·50 |

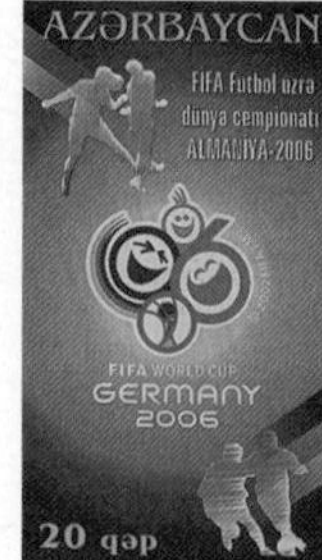


**185** Emblem

**2006.** World Cup Football Championship, Germany. Multicoloured.

| | | | |
|---|---|---|---|
| 636 | 20q. Type **185** | 1·50 | 1·50 |
| 637 | 60q. Player and map of Germany | 1·40 | 1·40 |

**186** Samad Vurgun

**2006.** Writers Birth Centenaries. Multicoloured.

| | | | |
|---|---|---|---|
| 638 | 10q. Type **186** | 80 | 80 |
| 639 | 60q. Suleyman Rustam | 2·40 | 2·40 |

**187** Russian Flag and Arms and St. Basil's Cathedral, Moscow

**2006.** Year of Russia in Azerbaijan. Multicoloured.

| | | | |
|---|---|---|---|
| 640 | 10q. Type **187** | 1·00 | 1·00 |
| 641 | 20q. Azerbaijan flag and arms and Taza Pir mosque, Baku | 1·30 | 1·30 |
| 642 | 30q. Azerbaijan flag and arms and Maiden Tower, Baku | 1·50 | 1·50 |
| 643 | 60q. Russian flag and arms and Kremlin, Moscow | 2·50 | 2·50 |

**188** Gulustan Mausoleum, Nakhichivan (13th-century)

**2006**

| | | | | |
|---|---|---|---|---|
| 644 | **188** | 20q. multicoloured | 1·40 | 1·40 |

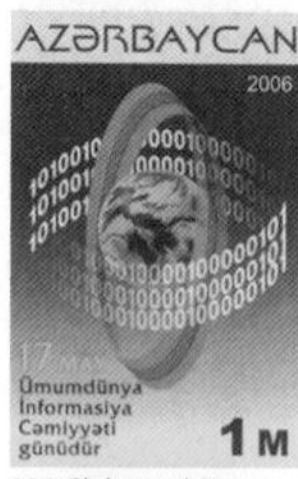


**189** Globe and Binary Code

**2006.** World Information Organization Day.

| | | | | |
|---|---|---|---|---|
| 645 | **189** | 1m. multicoloured | 6·00 | 6·00 |

**190** Khan (1867)

**2006.** Karabakh Horses. Multicoloured.

| | | | |
|---|---|---|---|
| 646 | 20q. Type **190** | 1·50 | 1·50 |
| 647 | 20q. Zaman (1952) | 1·50 | 1·50 |
| 648 | 20q. Sarvan (1987) | 1·50 | 1·50 |
| 649 | 20q. Gar-gar (2001) | 1·50 | 1·50 |

| | | |
|---|---|---|
| **MS**650 122×94 mm. Size 52×37 mm. Nos. 646/9 | 9·00 | 9·00 |
| **MS**651 82×65 mm. 60q. Rearing horse (vert) | 6·50 | 6·50 |

**2006.** Towns. As T 182. Multicoloured.

| | | | |
|---|---|---|---|
| 652 | 10q. lilac and black | 1·00 | 1·00 |
| 653 | 20q. pink and black | 1·50 | 1·50 |

DESIGNS: 10q. Sumuggala tower, Gakh; 20q. Nizami's mausoleum, Ganja.

**2006.** 50th Anniv of Europa Stamps. Nos. 608/609 surch. Multicoloured.

| | | | |
|---|---|---|---|
| 654 | 20q. on 1000m. multicoloured (Type **174**) | 2·50 | 2·50 |
| 655 | 60q. on 3000m. multicoloured (Dolmasi) | 8·00 | 8·00 |

**192** Emblem

**2006.** 15th Anniv of Regional Concord of Communication.

| | | | | |
|---|---|---|---|---|
| 656 | **192** | 20q. multicoloured | 1·60 | 1·60 |

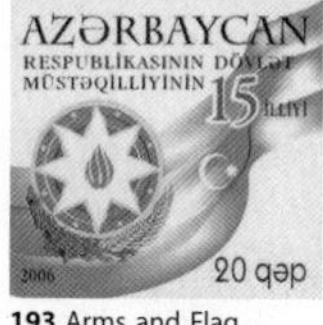


**193** Arms and Flag

**2006.** 15th Anniv of Independence.

| | | | | |
|---|---|---|---|---|
| 657 | **193** | 20q. multicoloured | 1·60 | 1·60 |

**194** Fire Appliance AMO-F15 (1926)

**2006.** Fire Engines. Sheet 101×76 mm containing T 194 and similar horiz designs showing fire engines. Multicoloured.

| | | |
|---|---|---|
| **MS**658 10q. Type **194**; 20q. PMQ-1 (1932); 60q. PMQ-9 (1950); 1m. ATS 2,5 (1998) | 10·50 | 10·50 |

**195** Pigeons and Tower

**2007.** Pigeons. Multicoloured.

| | | | |
|---|---|---|---|
| 659 | 20q. Type **195** | 1·60 | 1·60 |
| 660 | 20q. Iridescent pigeons and domes | 1·60 | 1·60 |
| 661 | 20q. Brown and white pigeons and oil derricks | 1·60 | 1·60 |
| 662 | 20q. White pigeon, brown and white pigeon and buildings | 1·60 | 1·60 |
| 663 | 20q. Dark pigeons and gateways | 1·60 | 1·60 |
| 664 | 20q. Spotted pigeons and windmills | 1·60 | 1·60 |

| | | |
|---|---|---|
| **MS**665 54×78 mm. 1m. White pigeon with feathered feet (vert) | 5·00 | 5·00 |

The stamp and margins of **MS**665 form a composite design.

**196** Baku Customs' Building

**2007.** Bicentenary of Baku Customs Services (20q.) or 15th Anniv of Azerbaijan Customs Services (60q.). Multicoloured.

| | | | |
|---|---|---|---|
| 666 | 20q. Type **196** | 1·60 | 1·60 |
| 667 | 60q. Azerbaijan Customs' building | 4·50 | 4·50 |

**197** Monument to Victims

**2007.** 15th Anniv of Khojali Tragedy. Sheet 99×72 mm.
**MS**668 **197** multicoloured 6·25 6·25

**198** Emblem

**2007.** Europa. Centenary of Scouting. Multicoloured.
669 20q. Type **198** 2·50 2·50
670 60q. Emblem on kite 7·00 7·00

**199** Symbols of Azerbaijan and Japan

**2007.** Azerbaijan—Japan Friendly Relations.
671 **199** 1m. multicoloured 5·50 5·50

**200** Mosque, Goycay

**2007.** Towns.
672 **200** 10q. yellow and black 1·00 1·00

2007 60qəp

**(201)**

60qəp 60qəp

**(202)** **(203)**

**2007.** Nos. 551 and 613 surch as T 201, 615/18 surch as T 202 and 570 surch as T 203.
673 60q. on 3000m. multicoloured (No. 551) 4·50 4·50
674 60q. on 3000m. multicoloured (No. 570) 4·50 4·50
675 60q. on 3000m. multicoloured (No. 613) 4·50 4·50
676 60q. on 3000m. multicoloured (No. 615) 3·75 3·75
677 60q. on 3000m. multicoloured (No. 616) 3·75 3·75
678 60q. on 3000m. multicoloured (No. 617) 3·75 3·75
679 60q. on 3000m. multicoloured (No. 618) 3·75 3·75

**204** Dog Fight

**2007.** Azim Azimzade (artist) Commemoration. Paintings. Multicoloured.
680 20q. Type **204** 1·50 1·50
681 20q. Wedding 1·50 1·50

**205** Emblem

**2007.** 15th Anniv of Azermarka (postal company).
682 **205** 50q. multicoloured 3·75 3·75

**206** Polar Bear Cub

**2007.** Polar Bear (Ursus maritimus). Multicoloured.
683 60q. Type **206** 4·50 4·50
**MS**684 76×122 mm 1m. Cub with stick (*vert*) 8·50 8·50

No. **MS**684 was cut around in the shape of a bear cub.

**207** *Gagea alexeenkoana*

**2007.** Local Flora. Two sheets containing T 207 and similar horiz designs. Multicoloured.
**MS**685 182×50 mm 10q. Type **207**; 20q. *Centaurea ficher*; 40q. *Galanthus caucasica*; 60q. *Ophrys caucasica* 7·00 7·00
**MS**686 50×54 mm 1m. *Ophrys caucasica* (different) 6·50 6·50

The stamp and margin of No. **MS**686 form a composite design.

**208** Huseyn Cavid

**2007.** 160th Birth Anniv of Huseyn Cavid.
687 **208** 20q. multicoloured 1·60 1·60

**209** Khudafarin Bridge, Jabrail

**2007.** Azim Azimzade (artist) Commemoration. Bridges. Multicoloured.
688 10q. Type **209** 80 80
689 20q. Gazanchi, Nakhchivan 1·60 1·60
690 30q. Gudyalchay, Guba 2·40 2·40
691 50q. Ganjachay, Ganja 3·00 3·00
**MS**692 74×58 mm 60q. 11th century bridge, Jabrail 4·00 4·00

The stamps and margin of No. **MS**692 form a composite design.

10 qəp

**(210)**

**2007.** No. 145 surch as T 210.
693 10q. on 15m. brown, ochre and black 1·20 1·20

**211** 11th-century Bridge, Jabrail

**2007.** Towns.
694 **211** 10q. pink and black 90 90
695 - 20q. emerald and black 1·00 1·00

DESIGNS: 10q. Type **211**; 20q. Fortress, Kalbajar.

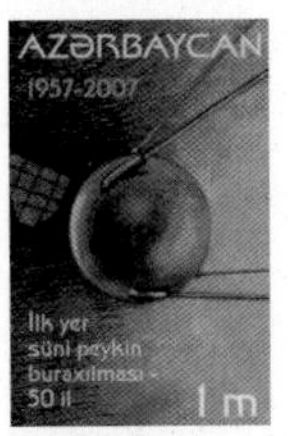


**212** Sputnik

**2007.** 50th Anniv of Space Exploration. Sheet 100×72 mm.
**MS**696 **212** multicoloured 6·75 6·75

**213** Karim Karimov

**2007.** 90th Birth Anniv of Karim Karimov (Chairman of the Aeronautics Commission). Sheet 61×76 mm.
**MS**697 **213** multicoloured 6·25 6·25

**214** Judo

**2008.** Olympic Games, Beijing. Showing stylized athletes. Multicoloured.
698 20q. Type **214** 1·60 1·60
699 30q. Weight lifting 2·20 2·20
700 40q. Wrestling 3·25 3·25
701 60q. Boxing 4·00 4·00

**215** Stylized Envelope

**2008.** Europa. The Letter. Multicoloured.
702 20q. Type **215** 2·50 2·50
703 60q. Stylized computer screen 6·75 6·75
**MS**704 110×65 mm. 1m. Dove (20×27 mm) 10·00 10·00

**216** 17th-century Tower, Gazakh

**2008.** Towns.
705 **216** 10q. pink and black 1·50 1·50

**217** Theatre Facade

**2008.** 125th Anniv of Musical Drama Theatre, Nakhchivan.
706 **217** 20q. multicoloured 2·50 2·50

**218** Zafira Aliyeva

**2008.** 85th Birth Anniv of Zafira Aliyeva (ophthalmologist). Multicoloured.
707 1m. Type **218** 6·50 6·50
708 1m. Zafira Aliyeva (painting) 6·50 6·50

**219** Heydar Aliyev

**2008.** 85th Birth Anniv of Heydar Aliyev (president, 1993–2003). Multicoloured.
709 1m. Type **219** 7·50 7·50
710 1m. Heydar Aliyev with national flag 7·50 7·50

**220** Map as Flag and Meeting

**2008.** 90th Anniv of Independence.
711 **220** 20q. multicoloured 1·50 1·50

**221** Mikayil Mushvig and Shirvan-Shakh Palace

**2008.** Birth Centenary of Mikayil Mushvig (writer).
712 **221** 20q. multicoloured 1·50 1·50

**222** Lev Davidovich Landau

**2008.** Academicians. Multicoloured.
713 20q. Type **222** (physicist, winner of 1962 Nobel Prize for Physics) (birth centenary) 1·50 1·50
714 20q. Hasan Abdullayev (President of Academy of Science, 1970–1983) (90th birth anniv) 1·50 1·50

**223** *Heydar Aliyev* (tanker)

**2008.** 150th Anniv of Caspian Shipping Company. Sheet 175×110 mm containing T 223 and similar horiz designs. Multicoloured.
**MS**715 20q. Type **223**; 30q. *Azerbaijan* (ferry); 50q. *Composer G. Garayev* (cargo boat); 60q. *Maestro Niyazi* (cargo); 1m. *Vandal* (tanker) 16·00 16·00

**224** Earring (12th—13th century)

**2008.** Jewellery. Multicoloured.

| | | | |
|---|---|---|---|
| 716 | 60q. Type **224** | 5·00 | 5·00 |
| 717 | 60q. Pendant (19th century) | 5·00 | 5·00 |

Stamps of a similar design were issued by Ukraine.

**225** Khanagah Mausoleum, Djulfa

**2008.** Towns.

| | | | |
|---|---|---|---|
| 718 | 10q. brown and black | 1·25 | 1·25 |
| 719 | 20q. bgrey and black (vert) | 2·00 | 2·00 |

DESIGNS: Type **225**; 20q. Garabaglar Mausoleum, Sharur.

**226** *Galeodes araneoides*

**2008.** Arachnids. Two sheets containing T 226 and similar multicoloured designs.

| | | |
|---|---|---|
| **MS**720 100×106 mm. 5q. Type **226**; 10q. *Buthus occitanus*; 20q. *Pisaura mirabilis*; 30q. *Latrodectus tredecim-guttatus*; 40q. *Araneus diadematus*; 60q. *Tegenaria domestica* | | |
| **MS**721 40×28 mm. 1m. *Argyroneta aquatica* (horiz) | 6·50 | 6·50 |

**227** Mir Jalal Pashayev

**2008.** Birth Centenary of Mir Jalal Pashayev (writer).

| | | | | |
|---|---|---|---|---|
| 722 | **227** | 60q. multicoloured | 15·00 | 15·00 |

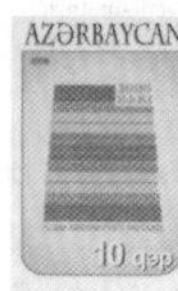

**228** Huseyn Javid Mausoleum

**2009.** 85th Anniv of Nakhchivan Autonomous Republic. Multicoloured.

| | | | |
|---|---|---|---|
| 723 | 20q. Type **228** | 1·60 | 1·60 |
| 724 | 20q. Heydar Aliev School | 1·60 | 1·60 |
| 725 | 20q. Ministry of Finance | 1·60 | 1·60 |
| 726 | 20q. Nahchivan State University Library | 1·60 | 1·60 |
| 727 | 20q. Nahchivan State University Conservatoire | 1·60 | 1·60 |
| 728 | 20q. Physiotherapy Centre | 1·60 | 1·60 |
| 729 | 20q. Tebriz Hotel | 1·60 | 1·60 |
| 730 | 20q. Diagnostic Medical Centre | 1·60 | 1·60 |


**229** Emblem

**2009.** Baku–Islamic Cultural Centre–2009. Multicoloured.

| | | | |
|---|---|---|---|
| 731 | 10q. Type **229** | 1·50 | 1·50 |
| 732 | 20q. Maiden Tower and emblem | 2·50 | 2·50 |

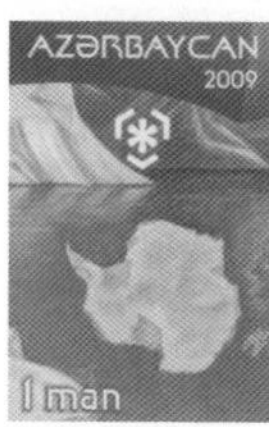

**230** Ice Cliffs, Emblem Antarctica Outline

**2009.** Preserve Polar Regions and Glaciers. Sheet 120×72 mm containing T 230 and similar vert design. Multicoloured.

| | | |
|---|---|---|
| **MS**733 1m.×2, Type **230**; Arctic outline | 13·00 | 13·00 |

The stamps and margins of **MS**733 form a composite polar design.

**231** Emblem and Map

**2009.** 10th Economic Cooperation Organization Summit, Tehran.

| | | | | |
|---|---|---|---|---|
| 734 | **231** | 1m. multicoloured | 6·50 | 6·50 |

**232** Nasiruddin Tusi (astronomer)

**2009.** Europa. Astronomy. Multicoloured.

| | | | |
|---|---|---|---|
| 735 | 20q. Type **232** | 2·50 | 2·50 |
| 736 | 60q. Observatory, Shamakhi region | 7·50 | 7·50 |
| **MS**737 80×80 mm. 1m. First telescope invented by Galileo Galilei, 1609 | | 10·00 | 10·00 |

**233** Flags

**2009.** 15th Anniv of Azerbaijan–NATO Co-operation.

| | | | | |
|---|---|---|---|---|
| 738 | **233** | 20q. multicoloured | 1·90 | 1·90 |

**234** '60', European Stars and Council Building

**2009.** 60th Anniv of Council of Europe.

| | | | | |
|---|---|---|---|---|
| 739 | **234** | 60q. multicoloured | 5·00 | 5·00 |

**235** Court Building

**2009.** 50th Anniv of European Court of Human Rights.

| | | | | |
|---|---|---|---|---|
| 740 | **235** | 60q. multicoloured | 5·00 | 5·00 |

**236** '60'

**2009.** 60th Anniv of Sumgait.

| | | | | |
|---|---|---|---|---|
| 741 | **236** | 10q. multicoloured | 1·00 | 1·00 |

**237** *Vanessa atalanta*

**2009.** Butterflies. Multicoloured.

| | | | |
|---|---|---|---|
| 742 | 10q. Type **237** | 1·00 | 1·00 |
| 743 | 20q. *Papilio alexanor* | 1·10 | 1·10 |

**238** Anniversary Emblem

**2009.** 90th Anniv of Diplomatic Service.

| | | | | |
|---|---|---|---|---|
| 744 | **238** | 60q. multicoloured | 5·00 | 5·00 |

**239** Jalil Mammadguluzadeh

**2009.** 140th Birth Anniv of Jalil Huseyngulu oglu Mammadguluzadeh (writer).

| | | | | |
|---|---|---|---|---|
| 745 | **239** | 20q. multicoloured | 1·60 | 1·60 |

**240** Leyla Mammadbekova

**2009.** Birth Centenary of Leyla Mammadbekova (first Azerbaijani woman pilot).

| | | | | |
|---|---|---|---|---|
| 746 | **240** | 20q. multicoloured | 5·75 | 5·75 |

**241** Anniversary Emblem

**2009.** 10th Anniv of State Oil Fund

| | | | | |
|---|---|---|---|---|
| 747 | **241** | 60q. multicoloured | 5·00 | 5·00 |

**242** Anniversary Emblem

**2009.** 135th Anniv of Universal Postal Union.

| | | | | |
|---|---|---|---|---|
| 748 | **242** | 20q. multicoloured | 2·50 | 2·50 |
| 749 | **242** | 60q. multicoloured | 7·50 | 7·50 |

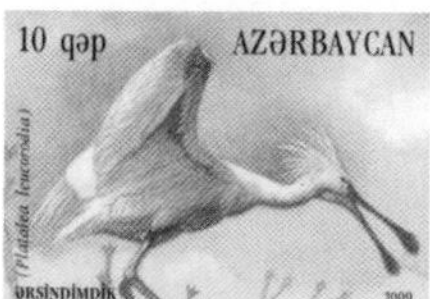

**243** *Platalea leucorodia* (spoonbill)

**2009.** Marsh Waterfowl. Sheet 100×72 mm containing T 243 and similar horiz designs. Multicoloured.

| | | |
|---|---|---|
| **MS**750 10q. Type **243**; 20q. *Phalacrocorax pygmaeus* (pygmy cormorant); 60q. *Numenius tenuirostris* (slender-billed curlew); 1m. *Porphyrio porphyrio* (gallinule) | 11·50 | 11·50 |

**244** Chess Pieces on Map of Europe and Azerbaijan

**2009.** Azerbaijan–European Chess Champion 2009. Sheet 92×70 mm containing T 244 and similar square design. Multicoloured.

| | | |
|---|---|---|
| **MS**751 50q. Type **244**; 1m. Chess pieces on map of Azerbaijan | 12·00 | 12·00 |

**245** Ancient Shamakha

**2009.** Azerbaijan Art. Paintings by Sattar Bahlulzade. Sheet 135×100 mm containing T 245 and similar horiz designs. Multicoloured.

| | | |
|---|---|---|
| **MS**752 20q.×6, Type **245**; *Still-life with Pomegranates*; *Buzovna. Shore*; *Landscape*; *Poppies*; *Red View* | 11·00 | 11·00 |

**246** *Thaleropis jonia fisch*

**2010.** Butterflies. Multicoloured.

| | | | |
|---|---|---|---|
| 753 | 10q. Type **246** | 70 | 70 |
| 754 | 20q. *Danais chrysippus* | 1·40 | 1·40 |

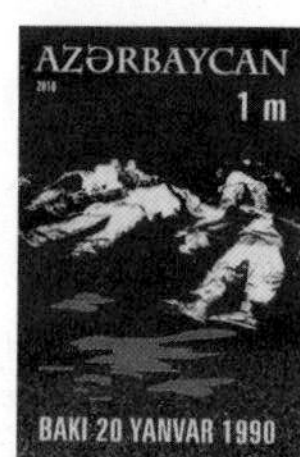

**247** Bodies

**2010.** 20th Anniv of 20 January 1990–National Day of Mourning Sheet 99×74 mm

| | | |
|---|---|---|
| **MS**755 **247** black and bright rose-red | 1·90 | 1·90 |

**248** Sunrise over Sea

**2010.** 10th Anniv of Ministry of Taxes.

| | | | | |
|---|---|---|---|---|
| 756 | **248** | 60q. multicoloured | 5·00 | 5·00 |

**249** Tiger

**2010.** Chinese New Year. Year of the Tiger.

| | | | | |
|---|---|---|---|---|
| 757 | **249** | 60q. multicoloured | 5·00 | 5·00 |

**250** Hands

**2010.** 90th Anniv of Azerbaijan Red Crescent Society.
758 **250** 60q. multicoloured 5·00 5·00

**251** *Bear's Dream*

**2010.** Europa. Children's Books. Multicoloured.
759 20q. Type **251** 1·40 1·40
760 60q. *Lion and Fox* 5·00 5·00
**MS**761 175×110 mm. Size 32×42 mm. 1m. *Jirtdan* 2·20 2·20

**252** Yellow Peony

**2010.** Peonies. Two sheets containing T 252 and similar square designs. Multicoloured.
**MS**762 152×104 mm. 10q.×4, Type **252**; Pink peony; White peony; Magenta peony 4·75 4·75
**MS**763 104×72 mm. 20q. Vase of Peonies 5·00 5·00

**253** Soldiers celebrating Victory in Berlin

**2010.** 65th Anniv of End of World War II. Multicoloured.
**MS**764 10q. Type **253**×2; 20q. Hoisting Soviet Flag over Reichstag×2; 60q. Oil container inscribed 'Baku - for front'×2 7·00 7·00

**254** Player and Championship Emblem

**2010.** World Cup Football Championships, South Africa. Multicoloured.
765 Type **254** 1·50 1·50
766 60q. Horiz pair. Nos. 765/6 5·50 5·50

**255** Shanghai Skyline

**2010.** Expo 2010, Shanghai
**MS**767 60q. multicoloured 4·75 4·75

**256** Cinefilm and A. Alekperov

**2010.** Birth Centenary of Alesker Gadzhi Aga ogly Alekperov (actor)
768 **256** 20q. multicoloured 2·20 2·20

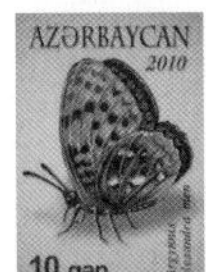


**257** Argynnis alexandra

**2010.** Butterflies. Multicoloured.
769 10q. Type **257** 1·00 1·00
770 20q. *Brahmaea christophi* 1·00 1·10

**258** Noah's Mausoleum, Nakhchivan

**2010.** Architectural Heritage
771 **258** 60q. multicoloured 4·75 4·75

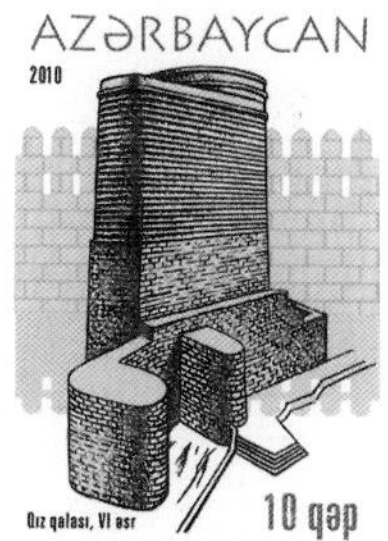


**259** Maiden Tower (6th century)

**2010.** Icheri Sheher Fortress, Baku Old City. Multicoloured.
**MS**772 10q. Type **259**; 20q. Mahammad mosque (11th century); 30q. Fortress walls (12th century); 40q. Palace Mosque (15th century); 50q. Shirvanshahlar tomb (15th century); 60q. Court-house (15th century) 9·25 9·25
**MS**773 Horiz. 10q. Palace building (12th-15th centuries); 20q. Bazar square (15th century); 30q. Two fortress archways (6th century); 40q. Jame mosque (14th century); 50q. Gasim Bay bathhouse (15th century); 60q. Multam and Bukhara Caravan-saries (15th century) 9·25 9·25
**MS**774 Horiz. 1m. Shirvanshahlar Palace complex (12th–16th centuries) 6·50 6·50

**260** Ateshgah (Zoroastrian fire temple), Baku

**2010.** Ancient Architecture. Multicoloured.
**MS**775 60q.×2, Type **260**; Pyramid of the Moon, Teotinakau (Mexico) 7·50 7·50
Stamps of a similar design were issued by Mexico.

**261** Shafaat Mehdiyev

**2010.** Birth Centenary of Shafaat Farhad Mehdiyev (academician)
776 **261** 60q. multicoloured 5·00 5·00

**262** Scottish Fold Kitten

**2010.** Cats. Multicoloured.
**MS**777 104×104 mm. 10q. Type **262**; 20q. Persian kitten; 30q. Somali kitten; 40q. British Shorthair kitten; 50q. Birman kitten; 60q. Maine coon kitten 9·25 9·25
**MS**778 28×40 mm. 1m. Turkish Angora cat with kitten (28×40 mm) 6·50 6·50

**263** *Phoenicopterus roseus* (greater flamingo)

**2010.** Ecology of Caspian Sea. Multicoloured.
779 60q. Type **263** 5·00 5·00
780 60q. *Ardeola ralloides* (Squacco heron) 5·00 5·00
Stamps of a similar design were issued by Kazakhstan.

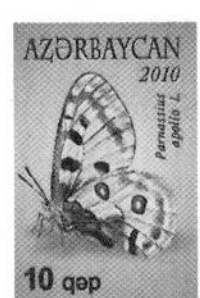


**264** *Parnassius apollo*

**2010.** Butterflies
781 **264** 10q. multicoloured 1·00 1·00

**265** *Centaurea* (inscr 'Centaurea Ficher')

**2011.** Garabagh Flora. Multicoloured.
782 20q. Type **265** 1·60 1·60
783 50q. *Gagea* (inscr 'Gagea alekxeenkoana') 3·50 3·50

**266** Samani and Fire (symbols of Novruz)

**2011.** Novruz Holiday
784 **266** 30q. multicoloured 2·20 2·20

**267** Rabbit

**2011.** Chinese New Year
785 **267** 1m. multicoloured 6·25 6·25

**268** '10'

**2011.** Tenth Anniversary of Azerbaijan Republic Joining to the Council of Europe
786 **268** 1m. multicoloured 6·25 6·25

Pt. 9

# AZORES

A group of islands in the Atlantic Ocean.

1868. 1000 reis = 1 milreis.
1912. 100 centavos = 1 escudo.
2002. 100 cents = 1 euro.

**NOTE.** Except where otherwise stated, Nos. 1/393 are all stamps of Portugal optd **ACORES**.

**1868.** Curved value labels. Imperf.

| | | | | |
|---|---|---|---|---|
| 1 | **14** | 5r. black | £4250 | £2500 |
| 2 | **14** | 10r. yellow | £1800 | £12000 |
| 3 | **14** | 20r. bistre | £250 | £200 |
| 4 | **14** | 50r. green | £250 | £200 |
| 5 | **14** | 80r. orange | £275 | £225 |
| 6 | **14** | 100r. purple | £275 | £225 |

**1868.** Curved value labels. Perf.

| | | | |
|---|---|---|---|
| 7 | 5r. black | 85·00 | 85·00 |
| 9 | 10r. yellow | £110 | 85·00 |
| 10 | 20r. bistre | 85·00 | 75·00 |
| 11 | 25r. pink | 85·00 | 13·00 |
| 12 | 50r. green | £250 | £225 |
| 13 | 80r. orange | £250 | £225 |
| 14 | 100r. lilac | £250 | £225 |
| 16 | 120r. blue | £225 | £140 |
| 17 | 240r. lilac | £750 | £475 |

**1871.** Straight value labels.

| | | | | |
|---|---|---|---|---|
| 38 | **15** | 5r. black | 16·00 | 10·50 |
| 39 | **15** | 10r. yellow | 65·00 | 40·00 |
| 73 | **15** | 10r. green | £100 | 80·00 |
| 29 | **15** | 15r. brown | 21·00 | 19·00 |
| 31 | **15** | 20r. bistre | 36·00 | 21·00 |
| 109 | **15** | 20r. red | £170 | £140 |
| 32 | **15** | 25r. pink | 21·00 | 5·00 |
| 33 | **15** | 50r. green | £110 | 40·00 |
| 54 | **15** | 50r. blue | £190 | £100 |
| 101b | **15** | 80r. orange | 90·00 | 70·00 |
| 103 | **15** | 100r. mauve | 70·00 | 60·00 |
| 25 | **15** | 120r. blue | £200 | £170 |
| 49 | **15** | 150r. blue | £225 | £190 |
| 104 | **15** | 150r. yellow | 70·00 | 60·00 |
| 26 | **15** | 240r. lilac | £1100 | £800 |
| 50 | **15** | 300r. lilac | £110 | 70·00 |
| 94 | **15** | 1000r. black | £170 | £140 |

**1880**

| | | | | |
|---|---|---|---|---|
| 58 | **16** | 5r. black | 29·00 | 12·50 |
| 60 | **17** | 25r. grey | £170 | 50·00 |
| 61 | **16** | 25r. grey | 65·00 | 10·00 |
| 61b | **16** | 25r. brown | 65·00 | 10·00 |
| 67 | **16** | 50r. blue | £200 | 55·00 |

**1882**

| | | | | |
|---|---|---|---|---|
| 136 | **19** | 5r. grey | 17·00 | 6·25 |
| 125 | **19** | 10r. green | 34·00 | 15·00 |
| 139 | **19** | 20r. red | 38·00 | 20·00 |
| 126 | **19** | 25r. brown | 34·00 | 5·00 |
| 141 | **19** | 25r. mauve | 38·00 | 3·25 |
| 142 | **19** | 50r. blue | 30·00 | 5·00 |
| 128 | **19** | 500r. black | £200 | £180 |
| 129 | **19** | 500r. mauve | £170 | £110 |

**1894.** Prince Henry the Navigator.

| | | | | |
|---|---|---|---|---|
| 143 | **32** | 5r. orange | 3·75 | 3·25 |
| 144 | **32** | 10r. red | 3·75 | 3·25 |
| 145 | **32** | 15r. brown | 4·75 | 4·25 |
| 146 | **32** | 20r. lilac | 5·00 | 4·50 |
| 147 | **32** | 25r. green | 5·50 | 4·75 |
| 148 | **32** | 50r. blue | 13·50 | 7·25 |
| 149 | **32** | 75r. red | 25·00 | 10·00 |
| 150 | **32** | 80r. green | 29·00 | 11·00 |
| 151 | **32** | 100r. brown on buff | 29·00 | 8·75 |
| 152 | **32** | 150r. red | 39·00 | 29·00 |
| 153 | **32** | 300r. blue on buff | 45·00 | 32·00 |
| 154 | **32** | 500r. purple | 85·00 | 48·00 |
| 155 | **32** | 1000r. black on buff | £180 | 90·00 |

**1895.** St. Anthony of Padua.

| | | | | |
|---|---|---|---|---|
| 156 | **35** | 2½r. black | 3·25 | 1·30 |
| 157 | - | 5r. orange | 10·50 | 3·25 |
| 158 | - | 10r. mauve | 10·50 | 4·75 |
| 159 | - | 15r. brown | 16·00 | 7·25 |
| 160 | - | 20r. grey | 18·00 | 10·50 |
| 161 | - | 25r. purple and green | 11·00 | 3·25 |

| No. | Type | Description | Mint | Used |
|---|---|---|---|---|
| 162 | 37 | 50r. brown and blue | 37·00 | 16·00 |
| 163 | 37 | 75r. brown and red | 55·00 | 45·00 |
| 164 | 37 | 80r. brown and green | 60·00 | 50·00 |
| 165 | 37 | 100r. black and brown | 60·00 | 46·00 |
| 166 | - | 150r. red and brown | £130 | £110 |
| 167 | - | 200r. blue and brown | £130 | £110 |
| 168 | - | 300r. black and brown | £160 | £120 |
| 169 | - | 500r. brown & green | £225 | £160 |
| 170 | - | 1000r. lilac and green | £375 | £275 |

**1898.** Vasco da Gama stamps as Nos. 378/385 of Portugal but inscr "ACORES".

| No. | Description | Mint | Used |
|---|---|---|---|
| 171 | 2½r. green | 3·75 | 1·40 |
| 172 | 5r. red | 3·75 | 1·70 |
| 173 | 10r. purple | 7·50 | 3·25 |
| 174 | 25r. green | 7·50 | 3·25 |
| 175 | 50r. blue | 11·00 | 10·00 |
| 176 | 75r. brown | 23·00 | 15·00 |
| 177 | 100r. brown | 29·00 | 16·00 |
| 178 | 150r. bistre | 46·00 | 32·00 |

**1906.** "King Carlos" key-type inscr "ACORES" and optd with letters A, H and PD in three of the corners.

| No. | Type | Description | Mint | Used |
|---|---|---|---|---|
| 179 | S | 2½r. grey | 45 | 40 |
| 180 | S | 5r. orange | 45 | 40 |
| 181 | S | 10r. green | 45 | 40 |
| 182 | S | 20r. lilac | 75 | 55 |
| 183 | S | 25r. red | 75 | 40 |
| 184 | S | 50r. blue | 6·75 | 5·00 |
| 185 | S | 75r. brown on yellow | 2·30 | 1·40 |
| 186 | S | 100r. blue on blue | 2·30 | 1·40 |
| 187 | S | 200r. purple on pink | 2·40 | 1·40 |
| 188 | S | 300r. blue on pink | 7·25 | 6·00 |
| 189 | S | 500r. black on blue | 17·00 | 15·00 |

7 King Manoel

**1910**

| No. | Type | Description | Mint | Used |
|---|---|---|---|---|
| 190 | 7 | 2½r. lilac | 50 | 40 |
| 191 | 7 | 5r. black | 50 | 40 |
| 192 | 7 | 10r. green | 50 | 40 |
| 193 | 7 | 15r. brown | 1·00 | 70 |
| 194 | 7 | 20r. red | 1·40 | 1·10 |
| 195 | 7 | 25r. brown | 50 | 50 |
| 196 | 7 | 50r. blue | 3·25 | 1·70 |
| 197 | 7 | 75r. brown | 3·25 | 1·70 |
| 198 | 7 | 80r. grey | 3·25 | 1·70 |
| 199 | 7 | 100r. brown on green | 5·25 | 4·00 |
| 200 | 7 | 200r. green on pink | 5·25 | 4·00 |
| 201 | 7 | 300r. black on blue | 3·25 | 3·00 |
| 202 | 7 | 500r. brown and olive | 10·50 | 11·00 |
| 203 | 7 | 1000r. black and blue | 24·00 | 20·00 |

**1910.** Optd REPUBLICA.

| No. | Description | Mint | Used |
|---|---|---|---|
| 204 | 2½r. lilac | 40 | 35 |
| 205 | 5r. black | 40 | 35 |
| 206 | 10r. green | 45 | 35 |
| 207 | 15r. brown | 2·00 | 1·40 |
| 208b | 20r. red | 2·00 | 1·40 |
| 209 | 25r. brown | 40 | 30 |
| 210a | 50r. blue | 1·40 | 1·30 |
| 211 | 75r. brown | 1·50 | 1·00 |
| 212 | 80r. grey | 1·50 | 1·00 |
| 213 | 100r. brown on green | 1·40 | 1·10 |
| 214 | 200r. green on orange | 1·40 | 1·10 |
| 215 | 300r. black on blue | 4·00 | 2·50 |
| 216 | 500r. brown and green | 4·75 | 3·50 |
| 217 | 1000r. black and blue | 12·00 | 7·00 |

**1911.** Vasco da Gama stamps of Azores optd REPUBLICA, some surch also.

| No. | Description | Mint | Used |
|---|---|---|---|
| 218 | 2½r. green | 70 | 50 |
| 219 | 15r. on 5r. red | 70 | 50 |
| 220 | 25r. green | 70 | 50 |
| 221 | 50r. blue | 2·40 | 1·60 |
| 222 | 75r. brown | 2·00 | 1·90 |
| 223 | 80r. on 150r. brown | 2·10 | 2·00 |
| 224 | 100r. brown | 2·40 | 2·10 |
| 225 | 1000r. on 10r. purple | 22·00 | 16·00 |

**1911.** Postage Due stamps optd or surch REPUBLICA ACORES.

| No. | Type | Description | Mint | Used |
|---|---|---|---|---|
| 226 | D48 | 5r. black | 1·40 | 1·20 |
| 227 | D48 | 10r. mauve | 3·00 | 1·20 |
| 228 | D48 | 20r. orange | 5·75 | 4·00 |
| 229 | D48 | 200r. brown on buff | 25·00 | 22·00 |
| 230 | D48 | 300r. on 50r. grey | 24·00 | 21·00 |
| 231 | D48 | 500r. on 100r. red on pink | 24·00 | 20·00 |

**1912.** "Ceres" type.

| No. | Type | Description | Mint | Used |
|---|---|---|---|---|
| 250 | 56 | ¼c. brown | 60 | 45 |
| 273 | 56 | ½c. black | 60 | 60 |
| 252 | 56 | 1c. green | 1·20 | 85 |
| 274 | 56 | 1c. brown | 60 | 60 |
| 254 | 56 | 1½c. brown | 1·20 | 85 |
| 255 | 56 | 1½c. green | 60 | 60 |
| 256 | 56 | 2c. red | 85 | 70 |
| 257 | 56 | 2c. orange | 60 | 60 |
| 258 | 56 | 2½c. lilac | 85 | 70 |
| 259 | 56 | 3c. red | 60 | 60 |
| 278 | 56 | 3c. blue | 45 | 35 |
| 260 | 56 | 3½c. green | 60 | 60 |
| 261 | 56 | 4c. green | 60 | 60 |
| 401 | 56 | 4c. orange | 75 | 60 |
| 262 | 56 | 5c. blue | 85 | 70 |
| 280 | 56 | 5c. brown | 60 | 60 |
| 264 | 56 | 6c. purple | 60 | 60 |
| 282 | 56 | 6c. brown | 65 | 55 |
| 403 | 56 | 6c. red | 50 | 35 |
| 265 | 56 | 7½c. brown | 7·25 | 4·00 |
| 266 | 56 | 7½c. blue | 2·00 | 1·80 |
| 267 | 56 | 8c. grey | 85 | 70 |
| 283 | 56 | 8c. green | 85 | 60 |
| 284 | 56 | 8c. orange | 1·10 | 1·00 |
| 268 | 56 | 10c. brown | 7·25 | 3·00 |
| 285 | 56 | 10c. red | 60 | 60 |
| 286 | 56 | 12c. blue | 3·00 | 1·90 |
| 287 | 56 | 12c. green | 1·00 | 80 |
| 288 | 56 | 13½c. blue | 3·00 | 1·90 |
| 249 | 56 | 14c. blue on yellow | 2·50 | 2·50 |
| 269 | 56 | 15c. purple | 90 | 70 |
| 289 | 56 | 15c. black | 60 | 60 |
| 290 | 56 | 16c. blue | 1·00 | 95 |
| 243 | 56 | 20c. brown on green | 13·50 | 7·75 |
| 291 | 56 | 20c. brown | 1·00 | 80 |
| 292 | 56 | 20c. green | 1·30 | 1·00 |
| 293 | 56 | 20c. drab | 85 | 70 |
| 294 | 56 | 24c. blue | 1·00 | 65 |
| 295 | 56 | 25c. pink | 75 | 60 |
| 244 | 56 | 30c. brown on pink | 85·00 | 65·00 |
| 245 | 56 | 30c. brown on yellow | 2·50 | 2·50 |
| 296 | 56 | 30c. brown | 2·10 | 1·80 |
| 406 | 56 | 32c. green | 3·50 | 2·40 |
| 298 | 56 | 36c. red | 90 | 70 |
| 299 | 56 | 40c. blue | 1·10 | 70 |
| 300 | 56 | 40c. brown | 2·00 | 1·10 |
| 407 | 56 | 40c. green | 1·90 | 95 |
| 408 | 56 | 48c. pink | 4·50 | 3·75 |
| 246 | 56 | 50c. orange on orange | 7·00 | 3·00 |
| 247 | 56 | 50c. orange on yellow | 7·00 | 3·00 |
| 302 | 56 | 50c. yellow | 2·00 | 1·60 |
| 410 | 56 | 50c. red | 6·00 | 4·50 |
| 303 | 56 | 60c. blue | 2·00 | 1·60 |
| 304 | 56 | 64c. blue | 5·25 | 2·40 |
| 411 | 56 | 64c. red | 6·00 | 4·50 |
| 305 | 56 | 75c. pink | 5·50 | 4·25 |
| 412 | 56 | 75c. red | 6·00 | 4·50 |
| 306 | 56 | 80c. purple | 2·75 | 2·20 |
| 307 | 56 | 80c. lilac | 3·00 | 2·10 |
| 413 | 56 | 80c. green | 6·00 | 3·75 |
| 308 | 56 | 90c. blue | 2·75 | 2·20 |
| 309 | 56 | 96c. red | 8·25 | 3·75 |
| 248 | 56 | 1e. green on blue | 7·75 | 6·50 |
| 310 | 56 | 1e. lilac | 2·75 | 2·20 |
| 314 | 56 | 1e. purple | 4·00 | 3·50 |
| 414 | 56 | 1e. red | 55·00 | 36·00 |
| 311 | 56 | 1e.10 brown | 3·00 | 2·20 |
| 312 | 56 | 1e.20 green | 3·50 | 2·20 |
| 315 | 56 | 1e.20 buff | 9·00 | 6·50 |
| 415 | 56 | 1e.25 blue | 3·50 | 3·00 |
| 316 | 56 | 1e.50 purple | 10·50 | 7·00 |
| 317 | 56 | 1e.50 lilac | 9·25 | 7·25 |
| 400 | 56 | 1e.60 blue | 5·25 | 2·20 |
| 313 | 56 | 2e. green | 11·50 | 7·00 |
| 319 | 56 | 2e.40 green | 80·00 | 50·00 |
| 320 | 56 | 3e. pink | 90·00 | 55·00 |
| 321 | 56 | 3e.20 green | 10·50 | 10·50 |
| 322 | 56 | 5e. green | 20·00 | 11·00 |
| 323 | 56 | 10e. pink | 55·00 | 30·00 |
| 324 | 56 | 20e. blue | £130 | 90·00 |

**1925.** C. C. Branco Centenary.

| No. | Type | Description | Mint | Used |
|---|---|---|---|---|
| 325 | 65 | 2c. orange | 25 | 25 |
| 326 | 65 | 3c. green | 25 | 25 |
| 327 | 65 | 4c. blue | 25 | 25 |
| 328 | 65 | 5c. red | 25 | 25 |
| 329 | - | 10c. blue | 25 | 25 |
| 330 | - | 16c. orange | 40 | 30 |
| 331 | 67 | 25c. red | 40 | 30 |
| 332 | - | 32c. green | 60 | 55 |
| 333 | 67 | 40c. black and green | 60 | 55 |
| 334 | 67 | 48c. purple | 1·30 | 1·30 |
| 335 | - | 50c. green | 1·30 | 1·10 |
| 336 | - | 64c. brown | 1·30 | 1·10 |
| 337 | - | 75c. grey | 1·30 | 1·10 |
| 338 | 67 | 80c. brown | 1·30 | 1·10 |
| 339 | - | 96c. red | 1·50 | 1·30 |
| 340 | - | 1e.50 blue on blue | 1·50 | 1·30 |
| 341 | 67 | 1e.60 blue | 1·70 | 1·50 |
| 342 | - | 2e. green on green | 2·75 | 2·40 |
| 343 | - | 2e.40 red on orange | 3·75 | 2·50 |
| 344 | - | 3e.20 black on green | 6·50 | 5·75 |

**1926.** 1st Independence Issue.

| No. | Type | Description | Mint | Used |
|---|---|---|---|---|
| 345 | 76 | 2c. black and orange | 45 | 35 |
| 346 | - | 3c. black and blue | 45 | 35 |
| 347 | 76 | 4c. black and green | 45 | 35 |
| 348 | - | 5c. black and brown | 45 | 35 |
| 349 | 76 | 6c. black and orange | 45 | 35 |
| 350 | - | 15c. black and green | 80 | 75 |
| 351 | 77 | 20c. black and violet | 80 | 75 |
| 352 | - | 25c. black and red | 80 | 75 |
| 353 | 77 | 32c. black and green | 80 | 75 |
| 354 | - | 40c. black and brown | 80 | 75 |
| 355 | - | 50c. black and olive | 1·80 | 1·70 |
| 356 | - | 75c. black and red | 1·90 | 1·80 |
| 357 | - | 1e. black and violet | 2·40 | 2·30 |
| 358 | - | 4e.50 black and green | 9·50 | 9·50 |

**1927.** 2nd Independence Issue.

| No. | Type | Description | Mint | Used |
|---|---|---|---|---|
| 359 | 80 | 2c. black and brown | 35 | 35 |
| 360 | - | 3c. black and blue | 35 | 35 |
| 361 | 80 | 4c. black and orange | 35 | 35 |
| 362 | - | 5c. black and brown | 35 | 35 |
| 363 | - | 6c. black and brown | 35 | 35 |
| 364 | - | 15c. black and brown | 45 | 35 |
| 365 | 80 | 25c. black and grey | 1·70 | 1·70 |
| 366 | - | 32c. black and green | 1·70 | 1·70 |
| 367 | - | 40c. black and green | 95 | 95 |
| 368 | - | 96c. black and red | 4·25 | 4·00 |
| 369 | - | 1e.60 black and blue | 4·50 | 4·25 |
| 370 | - | 4e.50 black and yellow | 11·50 | 11·50 |

**1928.** 3rd Independence Issue.

| No. | Type | Description | Mint | Used |
|---|---|---|---|---|
| 371 | | 2c. black and blue | 45 | 35 |
| 372 | 84 | 3c. black and green | 45 | 35 |
| 373 | - | 4c. black and red | 45 | 35 |
| 374 | - | 5c. black and olive | 45 | 35 |
| 375 | - | 6c. black and brown | 45 | 35 |
| 376 | 84 | 15c. black and grey | 85 | 80 |
| 377 | - | 16c. black and purple | 95 | 95 |
| 378 | - | 25c. black and blue | 95 | 95 |
| 379 | - | 32c. black and green | 1·00 | 1·00 |
| 380 | - | 40c. black and brown | 1·00 | 1·00 |
| 381 | - | 50c. black and red | 2·20 | 2·10 |
| 382 | 84 | 80c. black and grey | 2·20 | 2·10 |
| 383 | - | 96c. black and red | 4·25 | 4·00 |
| 384 | - | 1e. black and mauve | 4·25 | 4·00 |
| 385 | - | 1e.60 black and blue | 4·25 | 4·00 |
| 386 | - | 4e.50 black and yellow | 11·00 | 10·50 |

**1929.** "Ceres" type surch ACORES and new value.

| No. | Type | Description | Mint | Used |
|---|---|---|---|---|
| 387 | 56 | 4c. on 25c. pink | 95 | 95 |
| 388 | 56 | 4c. on 60c. blue | 1·90 | 1·80 |
| 389 | 56 | 10c. on 25c. pink | 1·90 | 1·80 |
| 390 | 56 | 12c. on 25c. pink | 1·90 | 1·80 |
| 391 | 56 | 15c. on 25c. pink | 1·90 | 1·80 |
| 392 | 56 | 20c. on 25c. pink | 3·25 | 3·00 |
| 393 | 56 | 40c. on 1e.10 brown | 6·25 | 6·00 |

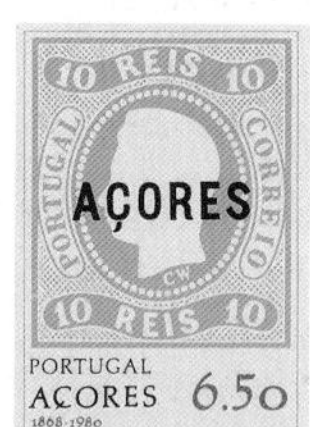

**14** 10r. Stamp of 1868

**1980.** 112th Anniv of First Azores Stamps.

| No. | Type | Description | Mint | Used |
|---|---|---|---|---|
| 416 | 14 | 6e.50 black, yellow & red | 45 | 25 |
| 417 | - | 19e.50 blk, purple & blue | 1·50 | 1·00 |
| **MS**418 | | 140×115 mm. Nos. 416/17 (sold at 30e.) | 6·75 | 6·75 |

DESIGN: 19e.50, 100r. stamp of 1868.

**15** Map of the Azores

**1980.** World Tourism Conference, Manila, Philippines. Multicoloured.

| No. | Description | Mint | Used |
|---|---|---|---|
| 419 | 50c. Type **15** | 20 | 15 |
| 420 | 1e. Church | 30 | 20 |
| 421 | 5e. Windmill | 75 | 40 |
| 422 | 6e.50 Traditional costume | 95 | 45 |
| 423 | 8e. Coastal scene | 1·40 | 65 |
| 424 | 30e. Coastal village | 2·75 | 1·10 |

**16** St. Peter's Cavalcade, Sao Miguel Island

**1981.** Europa. Folklore.

| No. | Type | Description | Mint | Used |
|---|---|---|---|---|
| 425 | 16 | 22e. multicoloured | 1·90 | 95 |
| **MS**426 | | 140×116 mm. No. 425×2 | 8·50 | 8·50 |

**17** Bulls attacking Spanish Soldiers

**1981.** 400th Anniv of Battle of Salga. Mult.

| No. | Description | Mint | Used |
|---|---|---|---|
| 427 | 8e.50 Type **17** | 80 | 10 |
| 428 | 33e.50 Friar Don Pedro leading attack | 3·00 | 1·40 |

**18** "Myosotis azorica"

**1981.** Regional Flowers. Multicoloured.

| No. | Description | Mint | Used |
|---|---|---|---|
| 429 | 4e. Type **18** | 20 | 10 |
| 430 | 7e. "Tolpis azorica" | 45 | 30 |
| 431 | 8e.50 "Ranunculus azoricus" | 60 | 30 |
| 432 | 10e. "Lactuca watsoniana" | 85 | 30 |
| 433 | 12e.50 "Hypericum foliosum" | 40 | 10 |
| 434 | 20e. "Platanthera micranta" | 1·00 | 70 |
| 435 | 27e. "Vicia dennesiana" | 1·90 | 1·20 |
| 436 | 30e. "Rubus hochstetterorum" | 1·20 | 50 |
| 437 | 33e.50 "Azorina vidalii" | 2·10 | 1·40 |
| 438 | 37e.50 "Vaccinium cylin-draceum" | 1·70 | 1·00 |
| 439 | 50e. "Laurus azorica" | 2·75 | 1·50 |
| 440 | 100e. "Juniperus brevifolia" | 3·50 | 1·60 |

**19** Embarkation of the Heroes of Mindelo

**1982.** Europa. Multicoloured.

| No. | Type | Description | Mint | Used |
|---|---|---|---|---|
| 445 | 19 | 33e.50 multicoloured | 2·75 | 1·40 |
| **MS**446 | | 140×113 mm. No. 445×3 | 21·00 | 21·00 |

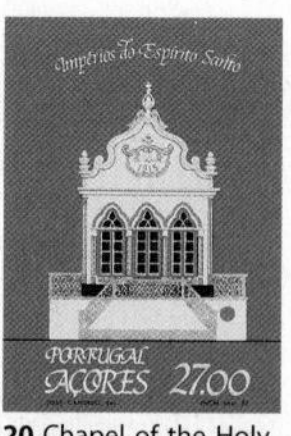

**20** Chapel of the Holy Ghost

**1982.** Regional Architecture. Multicoloured.

| No. | Description | Mint | Used |
|---|---|---|---|
| 447 | 27e. Type **20** | 2·00 | 1·20 |
| 448 | 33e.50 Chapel of the Holy Ghost (different) | 2·75 | 1·60 |

**21** Geothermal Power Station, Pico Vermeilho, São Miguel

**1983.** Europa.

| No. | Type | Description | Mint | Used |
|---|---|---|---|---|
| 449 | 21 | 37e.50 multicoloured | 2·75 | 1·10 |
| **MS**450 | | 114×140 mm. No. 449×3 | 23·00 | 23·00 |

**22** Flag of Azores

**1983.** Flag.

| | | | | |
|---|---|---|---|---|
| 451 | **22** | 12e.50 multicoloured | 1·10 | 20 |

**23** Two "Holy Ghost" Jesters, São Miguel

**1984.** Traditional Costumes. Multicoloured.

| | | | |
|---|---|---|---|
| 452 | 16e. Type **23** | 85 | 20 |
| 453 | 51e. Two women wearing Terceira cloak | 3·00 | 2·10 |

**23a** Bridge

**1984.** Europa.

| | | | | |
|---|---|---|---|---|
| 454 | **23a** | 51e. multicoloured | 4·00 | 1·90 |
| **MS**455 | | 114×139 mm. No. 454×3 | 20·00 | 20·00 |

**24** "Megabombus ruderatus"

**1984.** Insects (1st series). Multicoloured.

| | | | |
|---|---|---|---|
| 456 | 16e. Type **24** | 50 | 10 |
| 457 | 35e. Large white (butterfly) | 1·50 | 1·00 |
| 458 | 40e. "Chrysomela banksi" (leaf beetle) | 2·20 | 1·00 |
| 459 | 51e. "Phlogophora interrupta" (moth) | 2·50 | 1·60 |

**1985.** Insects (2nd series). As T 24. Multicoloured.

| | | | |
|---|---|---|---|
| 460 | 20e. "Polyspilla polyspilla" (leaf beetle) | 55 | 10 |
| 461 | 40e. "Sphaerophoria nigra" (hover fly) | 1·60 | 85 |
| 462 | 46e. Clouded yellow (butterfly) | 2·30 | 1·20 |
| 463 | 60e. Southern grayling (butterfly) | 2·50 | 1·40 |

**25** Drummer

**1985.** Europa. Music Year.

| | | | | |
|---|---|---|---|---|
| 464 | **25** | 60e. multicoloured | 4·00 | 1·70 |
| **MS**465 | | 140×114 mm. No. 464×3 | 25·00 | 25·00 |

**26** Jeque

**1985.** Traditional Boats. Multicoloured.

| | | | |
|---|---|---|---|
| 466 | 40e. Type **26** | 2·10 | 1·20 |
| 467 | 60e. Bote | 2·75 | 1·50 |

**27** Northern Bullfinch

**1986.** Europa.

| | | | | |
|---|---|---|---|---|
| 468 | **27** | 68e.50 multicoloured | 4·75 | 1·90 |
| **MS**469 | | 140×114 mm. No. 468×3 | 21·00 | 21·00 |

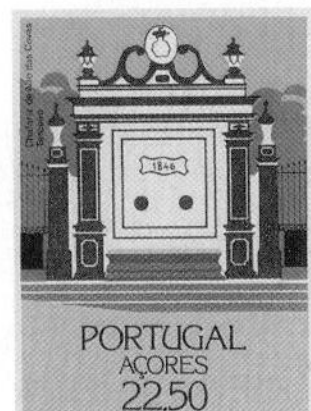

**28** Alto das Covas Fountain, Terceira

**1986.** Regional Architecture. Drinking Fountains. Multicoloured.

| | | | |
|---|---|---|---|
| 470 | 22e.50 Type **28** | 90 | 20 |
| 471 | 52e.50 Faja de Baixo, Sao Miguel | 2·75 | 1·40 |
| 472 | 68e.50 Portoes de S. Pedro, Terceira | 4·00 | 1·80 |
| 473 | 100e. Agua d'Alto, Sao Miguel | 5·50 | 1·60 |

**29** Ox Cart, Santa Maria

**1986.** Traditional Carts. Multicoloured.

| | | | |
|---|---|---|---|
| 474 | 25e. Type **29** | 90 | 10 |
| 475 | 75e. Ram cart, Sao Miguel | 4·00 | 2·30 |

**30** Regional Assembly Building (Correia Fernandes and Luis Miranda)

**1987.** Europa. Architecture.

| | | | | |
|---|---|---|---|---|
| 476 | **30** | 74e.50 multicoloured | 4·25 | 1·90 |
| **MS**477 | | 140×114 mm. No. 476×4 | 25·00 | 25·00 |

**31** Santa Cruz, Graciosa

**1987.** Windows and Balconies. Multicoloured.

| | | | |
|---|---|---|---|
| 478 | 51e. Type **31** | 2·50 | 1·40 |
| 479 | 74e.50 Ribeira Grande, São Miguel | 3·00 | 1·40 |

**32** A. C. Read's Curtiss NC-4 Flying Boat, 1919

**1987.** Historic Airplane Landings in the Azores. Multicoloured.

| | | | |
|---|---|---|---|
| 480 | 25e. Type **32** | 75 | 10 |
| 481 | 57e. E. F. Christiansen's Dornier Do-X flying boat, 1932 | 2·75 | 1·90 |
| 482 | 74e.50 Italo Balbo's Savoia Marchetti S-55X flying boat, 1933 | 4·00 | 1·70 |
| 483 | 125e. Charles Lindbergh's Lockheed 8 Sirius seaplane "Tingmissartoq", 1933 | 4·50 | 2·40 |

**33** 19th-century Mule-drawn Omnibus

**1988.** Europa. Transport and Communications.

| | | | | |
|---|---|---|---|---|
| 484 | **33** | 80e. multicoloured | 5·00 | 1·50 |
| **MS**485 | | 140×112 mm. As No. 484 ×4 but with cream background | 25·00 | 25·00 |

**34** Wood Pigeon

**1988.** Nature Protection. Birds (1st series). Mult.

| | | | |
|---|---|---|---|
| 486 | 27e. Type **34** | 90 | 30 |
| 487 | 60e. Eurasian woodcock | 2·75 | 1·40 |
| 488 | 80e. Roseate tern | 3·00 | 1·60 |
| 489 | 100e. Common buzzard | 3·75 | 1·60 |

See also Nos. 492/5 and 500/3.

**35** Azores Arms

**1988.** Coats-of-arms. Multicoloured.

| | | | |
|---|---|---|---|
| 490 | 55e. Type **35** | 2·30 | 1·20 |
| 491 | 80e. Bettencourt family arms | 3·00 | 1·60 |

**1989.** Nature Protection (2nd series). Goldcrest. As T 34. Multicoloured.

| | | | |
|---|---|---|---|
| 492 | 30e. Goldcrest perched on branch | 1·30 | 40 |
| 493 | 30e. Pair | 1·30 | 40 |
| 494 | 30e. Goldcrest on nest | 1·30 | 40 |
| 495 | 30e. Goldcrest with outspread wings | 1·30 | 40 |

**36** Boy in Boat

**1989.** Europa. Children's Games and Toys.

| | | | | |
|---|---|---|---|---|
| 496 | **36** | 80e. multicoloured | 3·75 | 1·60 |
| **MS**497 | | 139×112 mm. 80e. ×2, Type **36**; 80e. ×2, Boy with toy boat | 25·00 | 25·00 |

**37** Pioneers

**1989.** 550th Anniv of Portuguese Settlement in Azores. Multicoloured.

| | | | |
|---|---|---|---|
| 498 | 29e. Type **37** | 85 | 30 |
| 499 | 87e. Settler breaking land | 3·50 | 1·90 |

**1990.** Nature Protection (3rd series). Northern Bullfinch. As T 34. Multicoloured.

| | | | |
|---|---|---|---|
| 500 | 32e. Two bullfinches | 1·70 | 55 |
| 501 | 32e. Bullfinch on branch | 1·70 | 55 |
| 502 | 32e. Bullfinch landing on twig | 1·70 | 55 |
| 503 | 32e. Bullfinch on nest | 1·70 | 55 |

**38** Vasco da Gama P.O.

**1990.** Europa. P.O. Buildings.

| | | | | |
|---|---|---|---|---|
| 504 | **38** | 80e. multicoloured | 3·00 | 1·50 |
| **MS**505 | | 139×111 mm. 80e. ×2, Type **38**; 80e. ×2, Maia Post Office | 23·00 | 23·00 |

**39** Cart Maker

**1990.** Traditional Occupations. Multicoloured.

| | | | |
|---|---|---|---|
| 506 | 5e. Type **39** | 20 | 15 |
| 507 | 10e. Viol maker | 20 | 15 |
| 508 | 32e. Potter | 80 | 40 |
| 509 | 35e. Making roof tiles | 75 | 30 |
| 510 | 38e. Carpenter | 75 | 35 |
| 511 | 60e. Tinsmith | 2·30 | 1·20 |
| 512 | 65e. Laying pavement mosaics | 1·80 | 1·10 |
| 513 | 70e. Quarrying | 2·00 | 1·20 |
| 514 | 85e. Basket maker | 1·90 | 1·00 |
| 515 | 100e. Cooper | 3·25 | 1·80 |
| 516 | 110e. Shaping stones | 3·00 | 1·40 |
| 517 | 120e. Boat builders | 2·50 | 1·20 |

**40** "Hermes" Spaceplane

**1991.** Europa. Europe in Space.

| | | | | |
|---|---|---|---|---|
| 520 | **40** | 80e. multicoloured | 5·25 | 4·00 |
| **MS**521 | | 140×112 mm. 80e. ×2, Type **40**; 80e. ×2, "Sanger" spaceplane | 20·00 | 20·00 |

**41** "Helena" (schooner)

**1991.** Inter-island Transport. Multicoloured.

| | | | |
|---|---|---|---|
| 522 | 35e. Type **41** | 75 | 25 |
| 523 | 60e. Beech Model 18 airplane, 1947 | 1·50 | 85 |
| 524 | 80e. "Cruzeiro do Canal" (ferry), 1987 | 2·30 | 1·40 |
| 525 | 110e. British Aerospace ATP airliner, 1991 | 2·75 | 1·60 |

**42** "Santa Maria" off Azores

**1992.** Europa. 500th Anniv of Discovery of America by Columbus.

| | | | | |
|---|---|---|---|---|
| 526 | **42** | 85e. multicoloured | 2·40 | 1·10 |

**43** "Insulano" (steamer, 1868)

**1992.** The Empresa Insulana de Navegacao Shipping Fleet. Multicoloured.

| | | | |
|---|---|---|---|
| 527 | 38e. Type **43** | 75 | 30 |
| 528 | 65e. "Carvalho Araujo" (ferry, 1930) | 1·50 | 1·00 |
| 529 | 85e. "Funchal" (ferry, 1961) | 1·90 | 1·20 |
| 530 | 120e. "Terceirense" (freighter, 1948) | 2·50 | 1·40 |

**44** Ox-mill

**1993.** Traditional Grinders. Multicoloured.

| | | | |
|---|---|---|---|
| 531 | 42e. Type **44** | 75 | 35 |
| 532 | 130e. Hand-mill | 3·00 | 1·80 |

**45** "Two Sirens at the Entrance of a Grotto" (Antonio Dacosta)

**1993.** Europa. Contemporary Art.

| | | | |
|---|---|---|---|
| 533 **45** | 90e. multicoloured | 2·75 | 1·20 |
| **MS**534 | 140×112 mm. 90e. ×2, Type **45**; 90e. ×2, "Acorinan III" | 15·00 | 15·00 |

**46** Main Entrance, Praia da Vitoria Church, Terceira

**1993.** Doorways. Multicoloured.

| | | | |
|---|---|---|---|
| 535 | 42e. Type **46** | 75 | 35 |
| 536 | 70e. South door, Praia da Vitoria Church | 1·40 | 85 |
| 537 | 90e. Main door, Ponta Delgada Church, Sao Miguel | 1·80 | 1·10 |
| 538 | 130e. South door, Ponta Delgada Church | 2·75 | 1·40 |

**47** Floral Decoration, Our Lady of Sorrows, Caloura, Sao Miguel

**1994.** Tiles. Multicoloured.

| | | | |
|---|---|---|---|
| 539 | 40e. Type **47** | 60 | 35 |
| 540 | 70e. Decoration of crosses, Our Lady of Sorrows, Caloura, Sao Miguel | 1·40 | 80 |
| 541 | 100e. "Adoration of the Wise Men", Our Lady of Hope Monastery, Ponta Delgada, Sao Miguel | 1·80 | 1·10 |
| 542 | 150e. "St. Bras" (altar frontal), Our Lady of Anjos, Santa Maria | 2·75 | 1·70 |

**48** Monkey and Explorer with Model Caravel

**1994.** Europa. Discoveries. Multicoloured.

| | | | |
|---|---|---|---|
| 543 **48** | 100e. multicoloured | 2·20 | 1·10 |
| **MS**544 | 140×112 mm. 100e. ×2, Type **48**; 100e. ×2, Armadilo and explorer with model caravel | 12·50 | 12·50 |

**49** Doorway, St. Barbaras Church, Cedros, Faial

**1994.** Manoeline Architecture. Multicoloured.

| | | | |
|---|---|---|---|
| 545 | 45e. Type **49** | 65 | 35 |
| 546 | 140e. Window, Ribeira Grande, Sao Miguel | 2·40 | 1·60 |

**50** Aristides Moreira da Motta

**1995.** Centenary of Decree decentralizing Government of the Azores and Madeira Islands. Pro-autonomy activists. Multicoloured.

| | | | |
|---|---|---|---|
| 547 | 42e. Type **50** | 65 | 35 |
| 548 | 130e. Gil Mont' Alverne de Sequeira | 2·20 | 1·40 |

**51** Santana Palace, Ponta Delgada

**1995.** Architecture of Sao Miguel. Multicoloured.

| | | | |
|---|---|---|---|
| 549 | 45e. Type **51** | 65 | 35 |
| 550 | 80e. Chapel of Our Lady of the Victories, Furnas | 1·30 | 75 |
| 551 | 95e. Hospital, Ponta Delgada | 1·50 | 80 |
| 552 | 135e. Ernesto do Canto's villa, Furnas | 1·80 | 1·10 |

**52** Contendas Lighthouse, Terceira (image scaled to 63% of original size)

**1996.** Lighthouses. Multicoloured.

| | | | |
|---|---|---|---|
| 553 | 47e. Type **52** | 60 | 35 |
| 554 | 78e. Molhe Lighthouse, Sao Miguel | 1·30 | 85 |
| 555 | 98e. Arnel Lighthouse, Sao Miguel | 1·50 | 1·00 |
| 556 | 140e. Santa Clara Lighthouse, Sao Miguel | 2·10 | 1·30 |
| **MS**557 | 110×140 mm. 200e. Ponta da Barca Lighthouse, Graciosa | 3·00 | 3·00 |

**53** Natalia Correia (poet)

**1996.** Europa. Famous Women.

| | | | |
|---|---|---|---|
| 558 **53** | 98e. multicoloured | 1·70 | 85 |
| **MS**559 | 140×112 mm. No. 558×3 | 5·75 | 5·75 |

**54** Bird eating Grapes (St. Peter's Church, Ponta Delgada)

**1997.** Gilded Wooden Altarpieces. Multicoloured.

| | | | |
|---|---|---|---|
| 560 | 49e. Type **54** | 65 | 35 |
| 561 | 80e. Cherub (St. Peter of Alcantara Convent, Sao Roque) | 1·20 | 55 |
| 562 | 100e. Cherub with wings (All Saints Church, Jesuit College, Ponta Delgada) | 1·40 | 1·00 |
| 563 | 140e. Caryatid (St. Joseph's Church, Ponta Delgada) | 2·00 | 1·20 |

**55** Island of the Seven Cities

**1997.** Europa. Tales and Legends.

| | | | |
|---|---|---|---|
| 564 **55** | 100e. multicoloured | 1·70 | 85 |
| **MS**565 | 140×106 mm. No. 564×3 | 5·50 | 5·50 |

**56** Emperor and Empress and young Bulls (Festival of the Holy Spirit)

**1998.** Europa. National Festivals.

| | | | |
|---|---|---|---|
| 566 **56** | 100e. multicoloured | 1·60 | 85 |
| **MS**567 | 140×109 No. 566×3 | 4·75 | 4·75 |

**57** Spotted Dolphin

**1998.** "Expo '98" World's Fair, Lisbon. Marine Life. Multicoloured.

| | | | |
|---|---|---|---|
| 568 | 50e. Type **57** | 65 | 35 |
| 569 | 140e. Sperm whale (79×30 mm) | 1·90 | 1·20 |

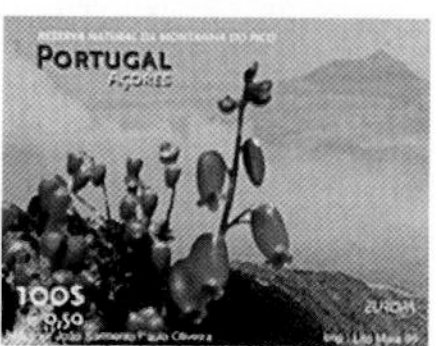


**58** Mt. Pico Nature Reserve

**1999.** Europa. Parks and Gardens.

| | | | |
|---|---|---|---|
| 570 **58** | 100e. multicoloured | 1·40 | 85 |
| **MS**571 | 154×109 mm. No. 570×3 | 4·75 | 4·75 |

**59** "Emigrants" (Domingos Rebelo)

**1999.** Paintings. Multicoloured.

| | | | |
|---|---|---|---|
| 572 | 51e. Type **59** | 65 | 35 |
| 573 | 95e. "Portrait of Vitorino Nemesio" (Antonio Dacosta) (vert) | 1·30 | 85 |
| 574 | 100e. "Cattle loose on the Alto das Covas" (Ze van der Hagen Bretao) | 1·30 | 85 |
| 575 | 140e. "Vila Franca Island" (Duarte Maia) | 1·70 | 1·20 |

**60** "Building Europe"

**2000.** Europa.

| | | | |
|---|---|---|---|
| 576 **60** | 100e. multicoloured | 1·70 | 95 |
| **MS**577 | 154×108 mm. No. 576×3 | 5·25 | 5·25 |

**61** Fishermen retrieving Mail Raft

**2000.** History of Mail Delivery in the Azores. Mult.

| | | | |
|---|---|---|---|
| 578 | 85e. Type **61** | 1·30 | 80 |
| 579 | 140e. Zeppelin airship dropping mail sacks | 2·10 | 1·40 |

**62** Coast Line

**2001.** Europa. Water Resources.

| | | | |
|---|---|---|---|
| 580 **62** | 105e. multicoloured | 1·70 | 95 |
| **MS**581 | 140×110 mm. No. 580×3 | 5·25 | 5·25 |

**63** Arch and Town

**2001.** UNESCO World Heritage Site, Angra do Heroismo. Multicoloured.

| | | | |
|---|---|---|---|
| 582 | 53e. Type **63** | 70 | 35 |
| 583 | 85e. Monument and town | 1·30 | 85 |
| 584 | 140e. Balcony and view over town | 2·00 | 1·30 |
| **MS**585 | 140×112 mm. 350e. Map of town | 5·00 | 5·00 |

**64** Clown

**2002.** Europa. Circus.

| | | | |
|---|---|---|---|
| 586 **64** | 54c. multicoloured | 1·70 | 1·90 |
| **MS**587 | 140×110 mm. No. 586×3 | 5·00 | 5·00 |

**65** Faial Island, Azores

**2002.** Windmills. Multicoloured.

| | | | |
|---|---|---|---|
| 588 | 43c. Type **65** | 1·10 | 70 |
| 589 | 54c. Onze-Lieve-Vrouw-Lombeek, Roosdaal | 1·50 | 85 |

Stamps of a similar design were issued by Belgium.

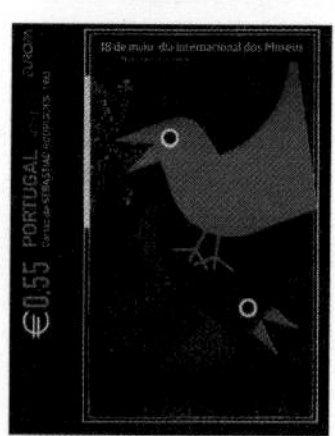


**66** Birds (Sebastiao Rodrigues)

**2003.** Europa. Poster Art.

| | | | |
|---|---|---|---|
| 590 **66** | 55c. multicoloured | 1·80 | 95 |
| **MS**591 | 140×113 mm. No. 591×2 | 3·25 | 3·25 |

**67** Pineapple Groves

**2003.** Sao Miguel Island. Multicoloured.

| | | | |
|---|---|---|---|
| 592 | 30c. Type **67** | 80 | 30 |
| 593 | 43c. Vineyards and grapes | 1·10 | 70 |
| 594 | 55c. Date growing | 1·40 | 90 |
| 595 | 70c. Coffee growing | 1·80 | 1·20 |
| **MS**596 | 140×112 mm. €1 Dancers and ceramic figure; €2 Fruit and ceramic bird (Espirito Santos festival) | 8·00 | 8·00 |

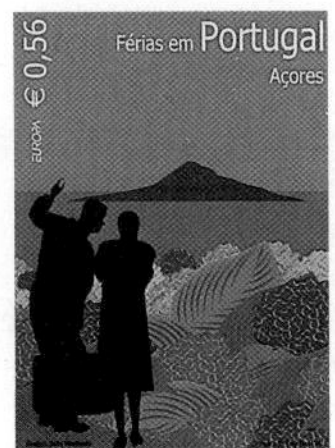

68 Figures, Flowers and Island

2004. Europa. Holidays.

| No. | Type | Description | Unused | Used |
|---|---|---|---|---|
| 597 | 68 | 56c. multicoloured | 1·60 | 90 |
| MS598 | | 141×112 mm. No. 597×2 | 3·25 | 3·25 |

69 Blue Marlin (*Makaira nigricans*)

2004. Endangered Species. Atlantic Marlin. Multicoloured.

| No. | Description | Unused | Used |
|---|---|---|---|
| 599 | 30c. Type 69 | 80 | 55 |
| 600 | 30c. Fin, body and tail | 80 | 55 |
| 601 | 30c. White marlin (*Tetrapturus albidus*) | 80 | 55 |
| 602 | 30c. Back and tail | 80 | 55 |

Nos. 599/602 were issued together, se-tenant, forming a composite design.

70 Torresmos (marinated pork)

2005. Europa. Gastronomy. Multicoloured.

| No. | Description | Unused | Used |
|---|---|---|---|
| 603 | 57c. Type 70 | 1·60 | 90 |
| MS604 | 125×95 mm. 57c.×2, *Polvo guisado* (octopus)×2 | 4·25 | 4·25 |

71 Cow

2005. Tourism. Multicoloured.

| No. | Description | Unused | Used |
|---|---|---|---|
| 605 | 30c. Type 71 | 70 | 50 |
| 606 | 30c. Arched window and lake | 70 | 50 |
| 607 | 45c. Decorated house | 1·10 | 75 |
| 608 | 45c. Windmill | 1·10 | 75 |
| 609 | 57c. Whale's tail | 1·40 | 90 |
| 610 | 74c. Pineapple and hot spring | 1·80 | 1·30 |
| MS611 | 125×95 mm. 30c. Santo Cristo dos Milagres (statue); €1.55 Bird | 4·50 | 4·50 |

Nos. 605/10 were issued together, se-tenant, forming a composite design.

72 Figures standing on Head (Joao Dinis)

2006. Europa. Integration. Winning Entries in ANACED (association for art and creativity by and for people with disabilities) Painting Competition. Multicoloured.

| No. | Description | Unused | Used |
|---|---|---|---|
| 612 | 60c. Type 72 | 1·50 | 85 |
| MS613 | 125×95 mm. 60c.×2, One legged figure; Figures with irregular outlines | 3·00 | 3·00 |

73 Crabs, Lucky Strike

2006. Hydrothermal Springs. Multicoloured.

| No. | Description | Unused | Used |
|---|---|---|---|
| 614 | 20c. Type 73 | 45 | 30 |
| 615 | 30c. Fish, Lucky Strike | 70 | 45 |
| 616 | 75c. Plumes, Rainbow | 1·70 | 1·10 |
| 617 | €2 Fish tower, Rainbow | 4·50 | 3·00 |
| MS618 | 125×95 mm. €2 No. 617 | 4·75 | 4·75 |

74 Mountain

2006. Wine from Pico Island. Multicoloured.

| No. | Description | Unused | Used |
|---|---|---|---|
| 619 | 30c. Type 74 | 70 | 45 |
| 620 | 60c. Terraces | 1·30 | 85 |
| 621 | 75c. Wine barrel | 1·70 | 1·10 |
| 622 | €1 Harvesting | 2·20 | 1·50 |
| MS623 | 125×95 mm. 45c. Young vines; 60c. Harvesting; 75c. Winery; €1 Barrels | 6·50 | 6·50 |

75 Scarf

2007. Europa. Centenary of Scouting. Multicoloured.

| No. | Description | Unused | Used |
|---|---|---|---|
| 624 | 61c. Type 75 | 1·40 | 85 |
| MS625 | 125×95 mm. 61c.×2, Reef knot; Scouts in camp | 3·00 | 3·00 |

The stamps of MS625 form a composite design.

76 Sao Miguel

2007. Windmills. Multicoloured.

| No. | Description | Unused | Used |
|---|---|---|---|
| 626 | 30c. Type 76 | 65 | 45 |
| 627 | 45c. Sao Jorge | 95 | 65 |
| 628 | 61c. Corvo | 1·30 | 85 |
| 629 | 75c. Blue windmill, Sao Jorge | 1·70 | 1·10 |
| MS630 | 125×95 mm. 45c. Sao Miguel (different); €2 Red windmill, Sao Jorge | 5·50 | 5·50 |

77 Capelinhos Volcano

2007. 50th Anniv of Eruption of Capelinhos Volcano, Faial Island. Multicoloured.

| No. | Description | Unused | Used |
|---|---|---|---|
| 631 | 30c. Type 77 | 65 | 45 |
| 632 | 75c. Erupting volcano and lighthouse | 1·70 | 1·10 |
| MS633 | 125×95 mm. €2.45 Island showing lighthouse (80×30 mm) | 5·75 | 5·75 |

The stamp and margin of MS633 form a composite design.

78 Envelope as Boat

2008. Europa. The Letter. Multicoloured.

| No. | Description | Unused | Used |
|---|---|---|---|
| 634 | 61c. Type 78 | 1·50 | 85 |
| MS635 | 125×95 mm. 61c.×2, Windmill and envelopes; As Type 78 | 3·00 | 3·00 |

The stamps of MS635 each form a composite design.

79 Cock Bird

2008. Azores Bullfinch (Pyrrhula murina). Multicoloured.

| No. | Description | Unused | Used |
|---|---|---|---|
| 636 | 30c. Type 79 | 75 | 45 |
| 637 | 61c. Female | 1·50 | 85 |
| 638 | 75c. Male facing right | 1·80 | 1·00 |
| 639 | €1 Male facing left | 2·50 | 1·40 |
| MS640 | Two sheets, each 125×95 mm. (a) €2.45 Head of male eating seed. (b) €2.95 Head of male with open beak | 14·00 | 14·00 |

The stamps and margins of MS640a/b form a composite design.

80 Ponta do Arnel

2008. Lighthouse.

| No. | Type | Description | Unused | Used |
|---|---|---|---|---|
| 641 | 80 | 61c. multicoloured | 1·50 | 85 |

81 Woodcock (Lagoa Comprida )

2009. Biodiversity. Lakes. Multicoloured.

| No. | Description | Unused | Used |
|---|---|---|---|
| 642 | 32c. Type 81 | 95 | 45 |
| 643 | 68c. Brown butterfly (Lagoa do Caldeirao ) | 2·10 | 1·00 |
| 644 | 80c. Dragonfly (Lagoa do Capitao) | 2·40 | 1·20 |
| 645 | €2 Azores juniper (Lagoinha) | 6·00 | 3·00 |
| MS646 | 125×95 mm. €2.50 Tessellate moray (80×30 mm) | 7·50 | 7·50 |
| MS647 | 125×95 mm. €2.50 Tufted duck, teal and capped heron (80×30 mm) | 7·50 | 7·50 |

82 European Space Agency Satellite Tracking Station, Santa Maria Island, Azores

2009. Europa. Astronomy. Multicoloured.

| No. | Description | Unused | Used |
|---|---|---|---|
| 648 | 68c. Type 82 | 2·10 | 1·00 |
| MS649 | 125×95 mm. 68c.×2, Ribeira Grande Astronomical Observatory, Sao Miguel Island, Azores; As Type 82 | 4·25 | 4·25 |

The stamps and margins of MS649 form a composite design.

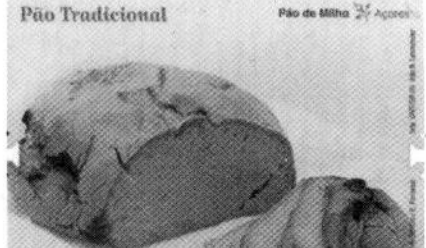

83 Milho (maize bread)

2009. Bread. Sheet 125×95 mm.

| No. | Type | Description | Unused | Used |
|---|---|---|---|---|
| MS650 | 83 | €2 multicoloured | 6·00 | 6·00 |

84 Girl

2010. Europa. Children's Books. Multicoloured.

| No. | Description | Unused | Used |
|---|---|---|---|
| 651 | 68c. Type 84 | 2·10 | 1·00 |
| MS652 | 125×96 mm. 68c.× 2 King on horseback; As Type 84 | 4·25 | 4·25 |

85 Dardanus callidus

2010. Invertebrates. Multicoloured.

| No. | Description | Unused | Used |
|---|---|---|---|
| 653 | 32c. Type 85 | 95 | 45 |
| 654 | 68c. Alicia mirabilis | 2·10 | 1·00 |
| 655 | 80c. Orphidiaster orphidianus | 2·40 | 1·20 |
| MS656 | 125×95 mm. €2 Grapsus adscencionis | 6·00 | 6·00 |
| MS657 | 125×95 mm. €2 Sphaerechinus granularis | 6·00 | 6·00 |

## CHARITY TAX STAMPS

Used on certain days of the year as an additional postal tax on internal letters. The proceeds were devoted to public charities. If one was not affixed in addition to the ordinary postage, postage due stamps were used to collect the deficiency and the fine.

1911. No. 206 optd ASSISTENCIA.

| No. | Type | Description | Unused | Used |
|---|---|---|---|---|
| C218a | 7 | 10r. green | 1·50 | 1·20 |

1913. No. 252 optd ASSISTENCIA.

| No. | Type | Description | Unused | Used |
|---|---|---|---|---|
| C250 | 56 | 1c. green | 5·25 | 4·00 |

1915. For the Poor. Charity stamp of Portugal optd ACORES.

| No. | Type | Description | Unused | Used |
|---|---|---|---|---|
| C251 | C58 | 1c. red | 70 | 35 |

1925. No. C251 surch 15 ctvs.

| No. | Description | Unused | Used |
|---|---|---|---|
| C325 | 15c. on 1c. red | 1·20 | 95 |

1925. Portuguese Army in Flanders issue of Portugal optd ACORES.

| No. | Type | Description | Unused | Used |
|---|---|---|---|---|
| C345 | C71 | 10c. red | 1·20 | 1·20 |
| C346 | C71 | 10c. green | 1·20 | 1·20 |
| C347 | C71 | 10c. blue | 1·20 | 1·20 |
| C348 | C71 | 10c. brown | 1·20 | 1·20 |

1925. As Marquis de Pombal issue of Portugal, inscr "ACORES".

| No. | Type | Description | Unused | Used |
|---|---|---|---|---|
| C349 | C73 | 20c. green | 1·20 | 1·20 |
| C350 | - | 20c. green | 1·20 | 1·20 |
| C351 | C75 | 20c. green | 1·20 | 1·20 |

## NEWSPAPER STAMPS

1876. Stamps of Portugal optd ACORES.

| No. | Type | Description | Unused | Used |
|---|---|---|---|---|
| N146 | N16 | 2r. black | 7·00 | 3·25 |
| N150a | N17 | 2½r. brown | 6·50 | 1·90 |
| N150b | N17 | 2½r. green | 6·50 | 1·90 |

## PARCEL POST STAMPS

1921. Stamps of Portugal optd ACORES.

| No. | Type | Description | Unused | Used |
|---|---|---|---|---|
| P325 | P59 | 1c. brown | 60 | 50 |
| P326 | P59 | 2c. orange | 60 | 50 |
| P327 | P59 | 5c. brown | 60 | 50 |
| P328 | P59 | 10c. brown | 80 | 50 |
| P329 | P59 | 20c. blue | 80 | 50 |
| P330 | P59 | 40c. red | 80 | 50 |
| P331 | P59 | 50c. black | 1·60 | 1·10 |
| P332 | P59 | 60c. blue | 1·60 | 1·10 |
| P333 | P59 | 70c. brown | 3·00 | 2·50 |
| P334 | P59 | 80c. blue | 3·00 | 2·50 |
| P335 | P59 | 90c. violet | 3·00 | 2·50 |
| P336 | P59 | 1e. green | 3·00 | 2·50 |
| P337 | P59 | 2e. lilac | 4·75 | 3·75 |
| P338 | P59 | 3e. olive | 8·50 | 4·00 |
| P339 | P59 | 4e. blue | 10·00 | 4·00 |
| P340 | P59 | 5e. lilac | 10·50 | 8·00 |
| P341 | P59 | 10e. brown | 43·00 | 24·00 |

## POSTAGE DUE STAMPS

Nos. D179/351 are stamps of Portugal overprinted **ACORES**.

1904

| No. | Type | Description | Unused | Used |
|---|---|---|---|---|
| D179 | D49 | 5r. brown | 1·40 | 1·20 |
| D180 | D49 | 10r. orange | 1·50 | 1·20 |
| D181 | D49 | 20r. mauve | 2·50 | 1·40 |
| D182 | D49 | 30r. green | 2·50 | 1·90 |
| D183 | D49 | 40r. lilac | 4·25 | 2·50 |
| D184 | D49 | 50r. red | 7·25 | 4·75 |
| D185 | D49 | 100r. blue | 9·00 | 8·75 |

1911. As last, optd REPUBLICA.

| No. | Description | Unused | Used |
|---|---|---|---|
| D218 | 5r. brown | 80 | 70 |
| D219 | 10r. orange | 80 | 70 |
| D220 | 20r. mauve | 1·00 | 90 |
| D221 | 30r. green | 1·00 | 90 |
| D222 | 40r. lilac | 1·60 | 1·20 |
| D223 | 50r. red | 8·50 | 8·00 |
| D224 | 100r. blue | 3·00 | 3·00 |

1918. Value in centavos.

| No. | Description | Unused | Used |
|---|---|---|---|
| D325 | ½c. brown | 85 | 80 |
| D326 | 1c. orange | 85 | 80 |
| D327 | 2c. purple | 85 | 85 |
| D328 | 3c. green | 85 | 80 |
| D329 | 4c. lilac | 85 | 80 |
| D330 | 5c. red | 85 | 80 |
| D331 | 10c. blue | 85 | 80 |

1922

| No. | Description | Unused | Used |
|---|---|---|---|
| D332 | ½c. green | 40 | 40 |
| D333 | 1c. green | 65 | 50 |
| D334 | 2c. green | 65 | 50 |
| D335 | 3c. green | 1·10 | 50 |
| D336 | 8c. green | 1·10 | 50 |
| D337 | 10c. green | 1·10 | 50 |
| D338 | 12c. green | 1·10 | 50 |
| D339 | 16c. green | 1·10 | 50 |
| D340 | 20c. green | 1·10 | 50 |
| D341 | 24c. green | 1·10 | 50 |
| D342 | 32c. green | 1·10 | 50 |
| D343 | 36c. green | 1·10 | 70 |
| D344 | 40c. green | 1·10 | 70 |
| D345 | 48c. green | 1·10 | 70 |
| D346 | 50c. green | 1·10 | 70 |
| D347 | 60c. green | 1·20 | 75 |

| | | | | |
|---|---|---|---|---|
| D348 | | 72c. green | 1·20 | 75 |
| D349 | | 80c. green | 5·50 | 4·50 |
| D350 | | 1e.20 green | 6·25 | 5·00 |

**1925.** Portuguese Army in Flanders.

| | | | | |
|---|---|---|---|---|
| D351 | **D72** | 20c. brown | 1·20 | 1·20 |

**1925.** As Nos. C349/51, optd MULTA.

| | | | | |
|---|---|---|---|---|
| D352 | **D73** | 40c. green | 1·20 | 1·20 |
| D353 | - | 40c. green | 1·20 | 1·20 |
| D354 | **D75** | 40c. green | 1·20 | 1·20 |

Pt. 7

## BADEN

In S.W. Germany. Formerly a Grand Duchy, now part of the German Federal Republic.

60 kreuzer = 1 gulden.

1

**1851.** Imperf.

| | | | | |
|---|---|---|---|---|
| 1 | 1 | 1k. black on buff | £650 | £350 |
| 8 | 1 | 1k. black on white | £200 | 34·00 |
| 3 | 1 | 3k. black on yellow | £325 | 21·00 |
| 9 | 1 | 3k. black on green | £200 | 10·50 |
| 10 | 1 | 3k. black on blue | £900 | 42·00 |
| 5 | 1 | 6k. black on green | £1100 | 65·00 |
| 11 | 1 | 6k. black on orange | £350 | 34·00 |
| 6 | 1 | 9k. black on red | £275 | 32·00 |

2

**1860.** Shaded background behind Arms. Perf.

| | | | | |
|---|---|---|---|---|
| 13 | 2 | 1k. black | £110 | 37·00 |
| 16 | 2 | 3k. blue | £120 | 26·00 |
| 17 | 2 | 6k. orange | £140 | 95·00 |
| 22 | 2 | 6k. blue | £200 | £140 |
| 19 | 2 | 9k. red | £350 | £250 |
| 25 | 2 | 9k. brown | £140 | £170 |

**1862.** Uncoloured background behind Arms.

| | | | |
|---|---|---|---|
| 27 | 1k. black | 65·00 | 19·00 |
| 28 | 3k. red | 65·00 | 5·25 |
| 30 | 6k. blue | 15·00 | 34·00 |
| 33 | 9k. brown | 21·00 | 37·00 |
| 36 | 18k. green | £550 | £750 |
| 38 | 30k. orange | 42·00 | £3000 |

**1868.** "K R." instead of "KREUZER".

| | | | |
|---|---|---|---|
| 39 | 1k. green | 5·25 | 11·50 |
| 41 | 3k. red | 3·25 | 5·25 |
| 44 | 7k. blue | 27·00 | 48·00 |

**RURAL POSTAGE DUE STAMPS**

D4

**1862**

| | | | | |
|---|---|---|---|---|
| D39 | **D4** | 1k. black on yellow | 4·50 | £350 |
| D40 | **D4** | 3k. black on yellow | 2·75 | £160 |
| D41 | **D4** | 12k. black on yellow | 40·00 | £15000 |

For later issues of 1947 to 1964 see Germany: Allied Occupation (French Zone).

Pt. 1

## BAGHDAD

A city in Iraq. Special stamps issued during British occupation in the War of 1914–18.

1917. 16 annas = 1 rupee.

**1917.** Various issues of Turkey surch **BAGHDAD IN BRITISH OCCUPATION** and new value in annas. A. Pictorial issues of 1913.

| | | | | |
|---|---|---|---|---|
| 1 | **32** | ¼a. on 2pa. red | £275 | £325 |
| 2 | **34** | ¼a. on 5pa. purple | £180 | £190 |
| 3 | - | ½a. on 10pa. green (No. 516) | £1000 | £1200 |
| 4 | **31** | ½a. on 10pa. green | £1900 | £2250 |
| 5 | - | 1a. on 20pa. red (No. 504) | £700 | £800 |
| 6 | - | 2a. on 1pi. blue (No. 518) | £325 | £350 |

B. As last, but optd with small star.

| | | | | |
|---|---|---|---|---|
| 7 | | 1a. on 20pa. red | £450 | £500 |
| 8 | | 2a. on 1pi. blue | £5500 | £6000 |

C. Postal Jubilee issue.

| | | | | |
|---|---|---|---|---|
| 9 | **60** | ½a. on 10pa. red | £750 | £850 |
| 10b | **60** | 1a. on 20pa. blue | £1600 | £1900 |
| 11b | **60** | 2a. on 1pi. black & violet | £190 | £200 |

D. Optd with Turkish letter "B".

| | | | | |
|---|---|---|---|---|
| 12 | **30** | 2a. on 1pi. blue | £750 | £900 |

E. Optd with star and Arabic date within crescent.

| | | | | |
|---|---|---|---|---|
| 13 | | ½a. on 10pa. green | £180 | £190 |
| 14 | | 1a. on 20pa. red | £700 | £750 |
| 15 | **23** | 1a. on 20pa. red | £750 | £850 |
| 16 | **21** | 1a. on 20pa. red (No. N185) | £6500 | £8000 |
| 17 | **30** | 2a. on 1pi. blue | £190 | £200 |
| 18 | **21** | 2a. on 1pi. blue | £325 | £375 |

F. Optd as last, but with date between star and crescent.

| | | | | |
|---|---|---|---|---|
| 19 | **23** | ½a. on 10pa. green | £200 | £250 |
| 20 | **60** | ½a. on 10pa. red | £325 | £350 |
| 21 | **30** | 1a. on 20pa. red | £200 | £250 |
| 22 | **28** | 1a. on 20pa. red | £750 | £800 |
| 23 | **15** | 1a. on 10pa. on 20pa. red | £375 | £400 |
| 24 | **30** | 2a. on 1pi. blue | £325 | £375 |
| 25 | **28** | 2a. on 1pi. blue | £2500 | £2750 |

Pt. 1

## BAHAMAS

A group of islands in the Br. W. Indies, S.E. of Florida. Self-Government introduced on 7 January 1964. The islands became an independent member of the British Commonwealth on 10 July 1973.

1859. 12 pence = 1 shilling; 20 shillings = 1 pound.
1966. 100 cents = 1 dollar.

1

**1859.** Imperf.

| | | | | |
|---|---|---|---|---|
| 2 | 1 | 1d. red | 65·00 | £1500 |

2

3

**1860.** Perf.

| | | | | |
|---|---|---|---|---|
| 33 | 1 | 1d. red | 65·00 | 15·00 |
| 26 | 2 | 4d. red | £300 | 60·00 |
| 31 | 2 | 6d. violet | £160 | 60·00 |
| 39ba | 3 | 1s. green | 8·00 | 9·50 |

**1883.** Surch **FOURPENCE**.

| | | | | |
|---|---|---|---|---|
| 45 | 2 | 4d. on 6d. violet | £550 | £400 |

5

**1884**

| | | | | |
|---|---|---|---|---|
| 48 | 5 | 1d. red | 7·50 | 2·00 |
| 52 | 5 | 2½d. blue | 10·00 | 1·75 |
| 53 | 5 | 4d. yellow | 9·50 | 4·00 |
| 54 | 5 | 6d. mauve | 6·00 | 35·00 |
| 56 | 5 | 5s. green | 75·00 | 85·00 |
| 57 | 5 | £1 red | £275 | £225 |

**6** Queen's Staircase, Nassau

**1901**

| | | | | |
|---|---|---|---|---|
| 111 | 6 | 1d. black and red | 2·75 | 2·50 |
| 76a | 6 | 3d. purple on buff | 6·00 | 7·50 |
| 77 | 6 | 3d. black and brown | 2·00 | 2·25 |
| 59 | 6 | 5d. black and orange | 8·50 | 48·00 |
| 78 | 6 | 5d. black and mauve | 2·75 | 5·50 |
| 113 | 6 | 2s. black and blue | 21·00 | 22·00 |
| 61 | 6 | 3s. black and green | 45·00 | 65·00 |

7

**1902**

| | | | | |
|---|---|---|---|---|
| 71 | 7 | ½d. green | 5·00 | 3·25 |
| 62 | 7 | 1d. red | 1·50 | 1·50 |
| 63 | 7 | 2½d. blue | 7·00 | 1·25 |
| 64 | 7 | 4d. yellow | 15·00 | 60·00 |
| 66 | 7 | 6d. brown | 4·00 | 26·00 |
| 67 | 7 | 1s. black and red | 22·00 | 55·00 |
| 69 | 7 | 5s. purple and blue | 70·00 | 90·00 |
| 70 | 7 | £1 green and black | £275 | £325 |

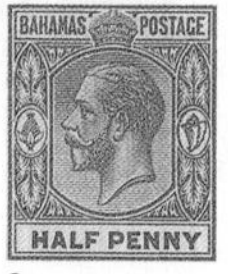


8

**1912**

| | | | | |
|---|---|---|---|---|
| 115 | 8 | ½d. green | 50 | 40 |
| 116 | 8 | 1d. red | 1·00 | 15 |
| 117 | 8 | 1½d. brown | 11·00 | 1·00 |
| 118 | 8 | 2d. grey | 1·50 | 2·25 |
| 119 | 8 | 2½d. blue | 1·00 | 2·25 |
| 120 | 8 | 3d. purple on yellow | 6·50 | 16·00 |
| 121 | 8 | 4d. yellow | 1·50 | 3·25 |
| 122 | 8 | 6d. brown | 70 | 1·25 |
| 123 | 8 | 1s. black and red | 4·00 | 5·50 |
| 124 | 8 | 5s. purple and blue | 40·00 | 65·00 |
| 125 | 8 | £1 green and black | £170 | £325 |

**1917.** Optd **1.1.17.** and Red Cross.

| | | | | |
|---|---|---|---|---|
| 90 | 6 | 1d. black and red | 40 | 2·00 |

**1918.** Optd **WAR TAX** in one line.

| | | | | |
|---|---|---|---|---|
| 96 | 8 | ½d. green | 1·75 | 1·75 |
| 93 | | 1d. black and red | 3·50 | 7·50 |
| 97 | 8 | 1d. red | 3·00 | 35 |
| 98 | 6 | 3d. purple on yellow | 1·00 | 1·50 |
| 100 | 6 | 3d. black and brown | 60 | 4·50 |
| 99 | 8 | 1s. black and red | 10·00 | 4·25 |

**1919.** Optd **WAR CHARITY 3.6.18.**

| | | | |
|---|---|---|---|
| 101 | 1d. black and red | 30 | 2·50 |

**1919.** Optd **WAR TAX** in two lines.

| | | | | |
|---|---|---|---|---|
| 102 | 8 | ½d. green | 30 | 1·25 |
| 103 | 8 | 1d. red | 1·50 | 1·50 |
| 105 | 6 | 3d. black and brown | 75 | 8·00 |
| 104 | 8 | 1s. black and red | 25·00 | 50·00 |

16

**1920.** Peace Celebration.

| | | | | |
|---|---|---|---|---|
| 106 | 16 | ½d. green | 1·00 | 5·50 |
| 107 | 16 | 1d. red | 2·75 | 1·00 |
| 108 | 16 | 2d. grey | 2·75 | 7·50 |
| 109 | 16 | 3d. brown | 2·75 | 9·00 |
| 110 | 16 | 1s. green | 14·00 | 38·00 |

**17** Seal of the Colony

**1930.** Tercentenary of the Colony.

| | | | | |
|---|---|---|---|---|
| 126 | 17 | 1d. black and red | 3·50 | 2·75 |
| 127 | 17 | 3d. black and brown | 5·50 | 15·00 |
| 128 | 17 | 5d. black and violet | 5·50 | 15·00 |
| 129 | 17 | 2s. black and blue | 18·00 | 50·00 |
| 130 | 17 | 3s. black and green | 48·00 | 85·00 |

**1931.** As T **17**, but without dates at top.

| | | | |
|---|---|---|---|
| 131b | 2s. black and blue | 14·00 | 8·00 |
| 132a | 3s. black and green | 11·00 | 4·50 |

**1935.** Silver Jubilee. As T **13** of Antigua.

| | | | |
|---|---|---|---|
| 141 | 1½d. blue and red | 1·00 | 3·50 |
| 142 | 2½d. brown and blue | 5·00 | 9·50 |
| 143 | 6d. blue and olive | 7·00 | 15·00 |
| 144 | 1s. grey and purple | 7·00 | 14·00 |

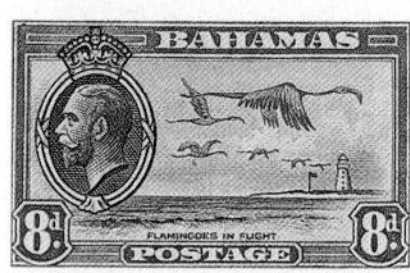


**19** Greater Flamingo (in flight)

**1935**

| | | | | |
|---|---|---|---|---|
| 145 | 19 | 8d. blue and red | 7·50 | 3·25 |

**1937.** Coronation. As T **2** of Aden.

| | | | |
|---|---|---|---|
| 146 | ½d. green | 15 | 15 |
| 147 | 1½d. brown | 30 | 1·10 |
| 148 | 2½d. blue | 50 | 1·10 |

**20** King George VI

**21** Sea Garden, Nassau

**1938**

| | | | | |
|---|---|---|---|---|
| 149 | 20 | ½d. green | 2·25 | 1·25 |
| 149e | 20 | ½d. purple | 1·00 | 3·25 |
| 150 | 20 | 1d. red | 8·50 | 2·50 |
| 150ab | 20 | 1d. grey | 60 | 70 |
| 151 | 20 | 1½d. brown | 1·50 | 1·25 |
| 152 | 20 | 2d. grey | 18·00 | 4·00 |
| 152b | 20 | 2d. red | 1·00 | 65 |
| 152c | 20 | 2d. green | 2·00 | 80 |
| 153 | 20 | 2½d. blue | 3·25 | 1·50 |
| 153a | 20 | 2½d. violet | 1·25 | 1·25 |
| 154 | 20 | 3d. violet | 16·00 | 3·00 |
| 154a | 20 | 3d. blue | 2·00 | 1·25 |
| 154b | 20 | 3d. red | 1·75 | 3·25 |
| 158 | 21 | 4d. blue and orange | 1·25 | 1·00 |
| 159 | - | 6d. green and blue | 1·25 | 1·00 |
| 160 | - | 8d. blue and red | 13·00 | 3·50 |
| 154c | 20 | 10d. orange | 2·50 | 20 |
| 155c | 20 | 1s. black and red | 18·00 | 75 |
| 156b | 20 | 5s. purple and blue | 35·00 | 25·00 |
| 157a | 20 | £1 green and black | 60·00 | 55·00 |

DESIGNS—As Type **21**: 6d. Fort Charlotte; 8d. Greater flamingos.

**1940.** Surch **3d.**

| | | | | |
|---|---|---|---|---|
| 161 | 20 | 3d. on 2½d. blue | 1·50 | 2·50 |

**1942.** 450th Anniv of Landing of Columbus. Optd **1492 LANDFALL OF COLUMBUS 1942.**

| | | | | |
|---|---|---|---|---|
| 162 | | ½d. green | 30 | 60 |
| 163 | | 1d. grey | 30 | 60 |
| 164 | | 1½d. brown | 40 | 60 |
| 165 | | 2d. red | 50 | 65 |
| 166 | | 2½d. blue | 50 | 65 |
| 167 | | 3d. blue | 30 | 65 |
| 168 | 21 | 4d. blue and orange | 40 | 90 |
| 169 | - | 6d. green & blue (No. 159) | 40 | 1·75 |
| 170 | - | 8d. blue and red (No. 160) | 2·50 | 70 |
| 171 | 20 | 1s. black and red | 11·00 | 5·00 |
| 172a | 17 | 2s. black and blue | 8·00 | 10·00 |
| 173 | 17 | 3s. black and green | 8·50 | 6·50 |
| 174a | 20 | 5s. purple and blue | 23·00 | 14·00 |
| 175a | 20 | £1 green and black | 30·00 | 25·00 |

**1946.** Victory. As T **9** of Aden.

| | | | |
|---|---|---|---|
| 176 | 1½d. brown | 10 | 60 |
| 177 | 3d. blue | 10 | 60 |

**26** Infant Welfare Clinic

**1948.** Tercentenary of Settlement of Island of Eleuthera. Inscr as in T **26**.

| | | | | |
|---|---|---|---|---|
| 178 | 26 | ½d. orange | 40 | 1·75 |
| 179 | - | 1d. olive | 40 | 35 |
| 180 | - | 1½d. yellow | 40 | 80 |
| 181 | - | 2d. red | 40 | 40 |
| 182 | - | 2½d. brown | 70 | 75 |
| 183 | - | 3d. blue | 2·50 | 85 |
| 184 | - | 4d. black | 60 | 70 |
| 185 | - | 6d. green | 2·50 | 80 |
| 186 | - | 8d. violet | 1·25 | 70 |
| 187 | - | 10d. red | 1·25 | 35 |
| 188 | - | 1s. brown | 3·00 | 50 |
| 189 | - | 2s. purple | 5·00 | 8·50 |
| 190 | - | 3s. blue | 13·00 | 8·50 |
| 191 | - | 5s. mauve | 20·00 | 5·50 |
| 192 | - | 10s. grey | 17·00 | 13·00 |

193 - £1 red 17·00 17·00

DESIGNS: 1d. Agriculture; 1½d. Sisal; 2d. Straw work; 2½d. Dairy; 3d. Fishing fleet; 4d. Island settlement; 6d. Tuna fishing; 8d. Paradise Beach; 10d. Modern hotels; 1s. Yacht racing; 2s. Water sports—skiing; 3s. Shipbuilding; 5s. Transportation; 10s. Salt production; £1 Parliament Buildings.

**1948.** Silver Wedding. As T **10/11** of Aden.

194 1½d. brown 20 25
195 £1 grey 42·00 32·00

**1949.** 75th Anniv of U.P.U. As T **20/23** of Antigua.

196 2½d. violet 35 75
197 3d. blue 2·25 3·50
198 6d. blue 55 3·25
199 1s. red 55 75

**1953.** Coronation. As T **13** of Aden.

200 6d. black and blue 1·50 60

**42** Infant Welfare Clinic

**1954.** Designs as Nos. 178/93 but with portrait of Queen Elizabeth II and without commemorative inscr as in T **42**.

201 **42** ½d. black and red 10 1·50
202 - 1d. olive and brown 10 30
203 - 1½d. blue and black 15 80
204 - 2d. brown and green 15 30
205 - 3d. black and red 65 1·25
206 - 4d. turquoise and purple 30 30
207 - 5d. brown and blue 1·40 2·25
208 - 6d. blue and black 2·25 20
209 - 8d. black and lilac 70 40
210 - 10d. black and blue 30 10
211 - 1s. blue and brown 1·50 10
212 - 2s. orange and black 2·00 70
213 - 2s.6d. black and blue 3·50 2·00
214 - 5s. green and orange 20·00 75
215 - 10s. black and slate 29·00 2·50
216 - £1 black and violet 27·00 7·00

DESIGNS: 1½d. Hatchet Bay, Eleuthera; 4d. Water sports—skiing; 5d. Dairy; 6d. Transportation; 2s. Sisal; 2s.6d. Ship-building; 5s. Tuna fishing. Other values the same as for the corresponding values in Nos. 178/93.

**43** Queen Elizabeth II

**1959.** Centenary of 1st Bahamas Postage Stamp.

217 **43** 1d. black and red 50 20
218 **43** 2d. black and green 50 1·00
219 **43** 6d. black and blue 60 40
220 **43** 10d. black and brown 60 1·00

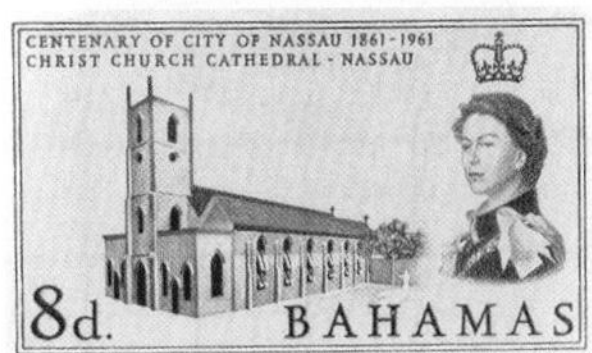


**44** Christ Church Cathedral

**1962.** Centenary of Nassau.

221 **44** 8d. green 65 55
222 - 10d. violet 65 25

DESIGN: 10d. Nassau Public Library.

**1963.** Freedom from Hunger. As T **28** of Aden.

223 8d. sepia 40 40

**1963.** Bahamas Talks. Nos. 209/10 optd **BAHAMAS TALKS 1962.**

224 8d. black and lilac 50 75
225 10d. black and blue 50 75

**1963.** Centenary of Red Cross. As T **33** of Antigua.

226 1d. red and black 50 50
227 10d. red and blue 1·75 2·50

**1964.** New Constitution. Nos. 201/16 optd **NEW CONSTITUTION 1964.**

228 **42** ½d. black and red 15 1·50
229 - 1d. olive and brown 15 15
230 - 1½d. blue and black 70 1·50
231 - 2d. brown and green 15 20
232 - 3d. black and red 2·00 1·75
233 - 4d. turquoise and purple 70 55
234 - 5d. brown and blue 70 1·50
235 - 6d. blue and black 3·25 30
236 - 8d. black and lilac 70 30
237 - 10d. black and blue 30 15
238 - 1s. blue and brown 1·50 15
239 - 2s. brown and black 2·00 1·75
240 - 2s.6d. black and blue 3·00 2·75
241 - 5s. green and orange 7·00 3·25
242 - 10s. black and slate 7·00 5·50
243 - £1 black and violet 7·50 25·00

**1964.** 400th Birth Anniv of Shakespeare. As T **34** of Antigua.

244 6d. turquoise 30 10

**1964.** Olympic Games, Tokyo. No. 211 surch **8d.** and Olympic rings.

245 8d. on 1s. blue and brown 45 15

**49** Colony's Badge

**1965**

247 **49** ½d. multicoloured 15 2·25
248 - 1d. slate, blue and orange 30 1·00
249 - 1½d. red, green and brown 15 3·50
250 - 2d. slate, green and blue 15 10
251 - 3d. red, blue and purple 4·50 20
252 - 4d. green, blue and brown 5·00 3·50
253 - 6d. green, blue and red 1·25 10
254 - 8d. purple, blue & bronze 50 30
255 - 10d. brown, green and violet 25 10
256a - 1s. multicoloured 40 10
257 - 2s. brown, blue and green 1·00 1·25
258 - 2s.6d. olive, blue and red 2·50 3·00
259 - 5s. brown, blue and green 2·75 1·00
260 - 10s. red, blue and brown 16·00 3·50
261 - £1 brown, blue and red 21·00 11·00

DESIGNS: 1d. Out Island regatta; 1½d. Hospital; 2d. High School; 3d. Greater flamingo; 4d. R.M.S. "Queen Elizabeth"; 6d. "Development"; 8d. Yachting; 10d. Public square; 1s. Sea garden; 2s. Old cannons at Fort Charlotte; 2s.6d. Sikorsky S-38 flying boat, 1929, and Boeing 707 airliner; 5s. Williamson film project, 1914, and undersea post office, 1939; 10s. Queen or pink conch; £1 Columbus's flagship.

**1965.** Centenary of I.T.U. As T **36** of Antigua.

262 1d. green and orange 15 10
263 2s. purple and olive 65 45

**1965.** No. 254 surch **9d.**

264 9d. on 8d. purple, blue & bronze 30 15

**1965.** I.C.Y. As T **37** of Antigua.

265 ½d. purple and turquoise 10 1·10
266 1s. green and lavender 30 40

**1966.** Churchill Commemoration. As T **38** of Antigua.

267 ½d. blue 10 75
268 2d. green 50 30
269 10d. brown 85 85
270 1s. violet 85 1·40

**1966.** Royal Visit. As T **39** of Antigua but inscr "to the Caribbean" omitted.

271 6d. black and blue 1·00 50
272 1s. black and mauve 1·25 1·25

**1966.** Decimal currency. Nos. 247/61 surch.

273 **49** 1c. on ½d. multicoloured 10 30
274 - 2c. on 1d. slate, blue and orange 75 30
275 - 3c. on 2d. slate, green and blue 10 10
276 - 4c. on 3d. red, blue and purple 2·00 20
277 - 5c. on 4d. green, blue and brown 2·00 3·00
278 - 8c. on 6d. green, blue and red 20 20
279 - 10c. on 8d. purple, blue and bronze 30 75
280 - 11c. on 1½d. red, green and brown 15 30
281 - 12c. on 10d. brown, green and violet 15 10
282 - 15c. on 1s. multicoloured 25 10
283 - 22c. on 2s. brown, blue and green 60 1·25
284 - 50c. on 2s.6d. olive, blue and red 1·00 1·40
285 - $1 on 5s. brown, blue and green 1·75 1·50
286 - $2 on 10s. red, blue and brown 7·50 4·50
287 - $3 on £1 brown, blue and red 7·50 4·50

**1966.** World Cup Football Championships. As T **40** of Antigua.

288 8c. multicoloured 35 15
289 15c. multicoloured 40 25

**1966.** Inauguration of W.H.O. Headquarters, Geneva. As T **41** of Antigua.

290 11c. black, green and blue 50 90
291 15c. black, purple and ochre 50 50

**1966.** 20th Anniv of UNESCO As T **54/6** of Antigua.

292 3c. multicoloured 10 10
293 15c. yellow, violet and olive 35 20
294 $1 black, purple and orange 1·10 2·00

**1967.** As Nos. 247/51, 253/9 and 261 but values in decimal currency, and new designs for 5c. and $2.

295 **49** 1c. multicoloured 10 3·25
296 - 2c. slate, blue and green 50 60
297 - 3c. slate, green and violet 10 10
298 - 4c. red, light blue and blue 4·75 50
299 - 5c. black, blue and purple 1·00 3·50
300 - 8c. green, blue and brown 1·50 10
301 - 10c. purple, blue and red 30 70
302 - 11c. red, green and blue 25 80
303 - 12c. brown, green and olive 25 10
304 - 15c. multicoloured 55 10
305 - 22c. brown, blue and red 70 65
306 - 50c. olive, blue and green 2·25 1·00
307 - $1 maroon, blue and purple 2·00 60
308 - $2 multicoloured 13·00 3·00
309 - $3 brown, blue and purple 3·75 2·00

NEW DESIGNS: 5c. "Oceanic"; $2 Conch shell (different).

**69** Bahamas Crest

**1967.** Diamond Jubilee of World Scouting. Mult.

310 3c. Type **69** 35 15
311 15c. Scout badge 40 15

**71** Globe and Emblem

**1968.** Human Rights Year. Multicoloured.

312 3c. Type **71** 10 10
313 12c. Scales of Justice and emblem 20 10
314 $1 Bahamas Crest and emblem 70 80

**74** Golf

**1968.** Tourism. Multicoloured.

315 5c. Type **74** 1·75 1·75
316 11c. Yachting 1·25 50
317 15c. Horse-racing 1·75 55
318 50c. Water-skiing 2·50 7·00

**78** Racing Yacht and Olympic Monument

**1968.** Olympic Games, Mexico City.

319 **78** 5c. brown, yellow and green 40 75
320 - 11c. multicoloured 40 25
321 - 50c. multicoloured 60 1·75
322 **78** $1 grey, blue and violet 2·00 3·75

DESIGNS: 11c. Long jumping and Olympic Monument; 50c. Running and Olympic Monument.

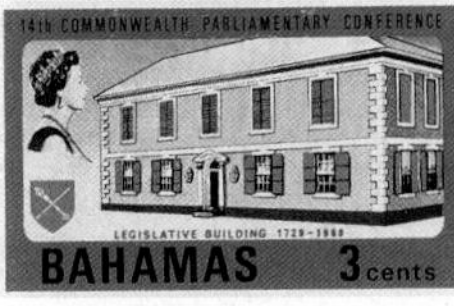


**81** Legislative Building

**1968.** 14th Commonwealth Parliamentary Conference. Multicoloured.

323 3c. Type **81** 10 30
324 10c. Bahamas Mace and West-minster Clock Tower (vert) 15 30
325 12c. Local straw market (vert) 15 25
326 15c. Horse-drawn surrey 20 35

**85** Obverse and reverse of $100 Gold Coin

**1968.** Gold Coins commemorating the first General Election under the New Constitution.

327 **85** 3c. red on gold 40 40
328 - 12c. green on gold 45 50
329 - 15c. purple on gold 50 60
330 - $1 black on gold 1·25 4·00

OBVERSE AND REVERSE OF: 12c. $50 gold coin; 15c. $20 gold coins; $1, $10 gold coin.

**89** First Flight Postcard of 1919

**1969.** 50th Anniv of Bahamas Airmail Services.

331 **89** 12c. multicoloured 50 50
332 - 15c. multicoloured 60 1·75

DESIGN: 15c. Sikorsky S-38 flying boat of 1929.

**91** Game-fishing Boats

**1969.** Tourism. One Millionth Visitor to Bahamas. Multicoloured.

333 3c. Type **91** 25 10
334 11c. Paradise Beach 35 15
335 12c. "Sunfish" sailing boats 35 15
336 15c. Rawson Square and parade 45 25
**MS**337 130×96 mm. Nos. 333/6 2·75 4·00

**92** "The Adoration of the Shepherds" (Louis le Nain)

**1969.** Christmas. Multicoloured.

338 3c. Type **92** 10 20
339 11c. "The Adoration of the Shepherds" (Poussin) 15 30
340 12c. "The Adoration of the Kings" (Gerard David) 15 20
341 15c. "The Adoration of the Kings" (Vincenzo Foppa) 20 65

**93** Badge of Girl Guides

**1970.** Diamond Jubilee of Girl Guides' Association. Multicoloured.

| | | | |
|---|---|---|---|
| 342 | 3c. Type **93** | 30 | 30 |
| 343 | 12c. Badge of Brownies | 45 | 40 |
| 344 | 15c. Badge of Rangers | 50 | 50 |

**94** New U.P.U. Headquarters and Emblem

**1970.** New U.P.U. Headquarters Building.

| | | | | |
|---|---|---|---|---|
| 345 | **94** | 3c. multicoloured | 10 | 40 |
| 346 | **94** | 15c. multicoloured | 20 | 60 |

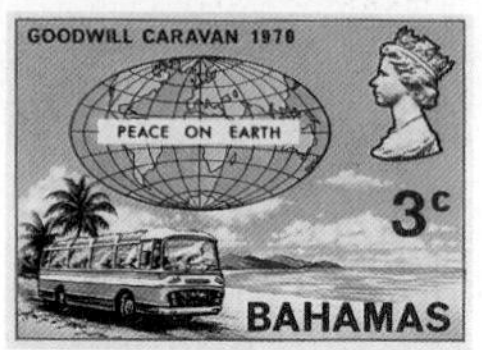

**95** Coach and Globe

**1970.** "Goodwill Caravan". Multicoloured.

| | | | |
|---|---|---|---|
| 347 | 3c. Type **95** | 75 | 20 |
| 348 | 11c. Diesel train and globe | 1·50 | 60 |
| 349 | 12c. "Canberra" (liner), yacht and globe | 1·50 | 60 |
| 350 | 15c. B.A.C. One Eleven airliner and globe | 1·50 | 1·75 |
| **MS**351 | 165×125 mm. Nos. 347/50 | 9·50 | 17·00 |

**96** Nurse, Patients and Greater Flamingo

**1970.** Centenary of British Red Cross. Multicoloured.

| | | | |
|---|---|---|---|
| 352 | 3c. Type **96** | 75 | 50 |
| 353 | 15c. Hospital and blue marlin | 75 | 1·75 |

**97** "The Nativity" (detail, Pittoni)

**1970.** Christmas. Multicoloured.

| | | | |
|---|---|---|---|
| 354 | 3c. Type **97** | 15 | 15 |
| 355 | 11c. "The Holy Family" (detail, Anton Raphael Mengs) | 20 | 25 |
| 356 | 12c. "The Adoration of the Shepherds" (detail, Giorgione) | 20 | 20 |
| 357 | 15c. "The Adoration of the Shepherds" (detail, School of Seville) | 30 | 75 |
| **MS**358 | 114×140 mm. Nos. 354/7 | 1·40 | 4·25 |

**98** International Airport

**1971.** Multicoloured.. Multicoloured..

| | | | |
|---|---|---|---|
| 359 | 1c. Type **98** | 10 | 30 |
| 360 | 2c. Breadfruit | 15 | 35 |
| 361 | 3c. Straw market | 15 | 30 |
| 362 | 4c. Hawksbill turtle | 1·75 | 10·00 |
| 363 | 5c. Nassau grouper | 60 | 60 |
| 364 | 6c. As 4c. | 45 | 1·25 |
| 365 | 7c. Hibiscus | 2·00 | 5·00 |
| 366 | 8c. Yellow elder | 60 | 1·50 |
| 367 | 10c. Bahamian sponge boat | 55 | 30 |
| 368 | 11c. Greater flamingos | 2·50 | 3·25 |
| 369 | 12c. As 7c. | 2·00 | 3·00 |
| 370 | 15c. Bonefish | 55 | 55 |
| 466 | 16c. As 7c. | 1·25 | 35 |
| 371 | 18c. Royal poinciana | 65 | 65 |
| 467a | 21c. As 2c. | 80 | 1·25 |
| 372 | 22c. As 18c. | 2·75 | 15·00 |
| 468 | 25c. As 4c. | 90 | 40 |
| 469 | 40c. As 10c. | 8·00 | 75 |
| 470 | 50c. Post Office, Nassau | 1·50 | 1·75 |
| 471 | $1 Pineapple (vert) | 1·50 | 2·50 |
| 399 | $2 Crawfish (vert) | 1·50 | 6·00 |
| 473 | $3 Junkanoo (vert) | 1·50 | 9·00 |

**99** Snowflake

**1971.** Christmas.

| | | | | |
|---|---|---|---|---|
| 377 | **99** | 3c. purple, orange and gold | 10 | 10 |
| 378 | - | 11c. blue and gold | 20 | 15 |
| 379 | - | 15c. multicoloured | 20 | 20 |
| 380 | - | 18c. blue, ultram & gold | 25 | 25 |
| **MS**381 | | 126×95 mm. Nos. 377/80 | 1·25 | 1·50 |

DESIGNS: 11c. "Peace on Earth" (doves); 15c. Arms of Bahamas and holly; 18c. Starlit lagoon.

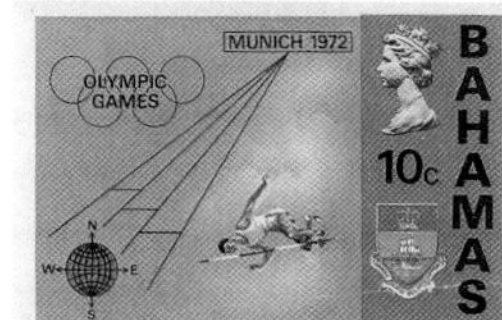

**100** High Jumping

**1972.** Olympic Games, Munich. Multicoloured.

| | | | |
|---|---|---|---|
| 382 | 10c. Type **100** | 35 | 60 |
| 383 | 11c. Cycling | 1·75 | 75 |
| 384 | 15c. Running | 60 | 75 |
| 385 | 18c. Sailing | 95 | 1·25 |
| **MS**386 | 127×95 mm. Nos. 382/5 | 3·25 | 3·00 |

**101** Shepherd

**1972.** Christmas. Multicoloured.

| | | | |
|---|---|---|---|
| 387 | 3c. Type **101** | 10 | 10 |
| 388 | 6c. Bells | 10 | 10 |
| 389 | 15c. Holly and Cross | 15 | 20 |
| 390 | 20c. Poinsettia | 25 | 45 |
| **MS**391 | 108×140 mm. Nos. 387/90 | 80 | 3·00 |

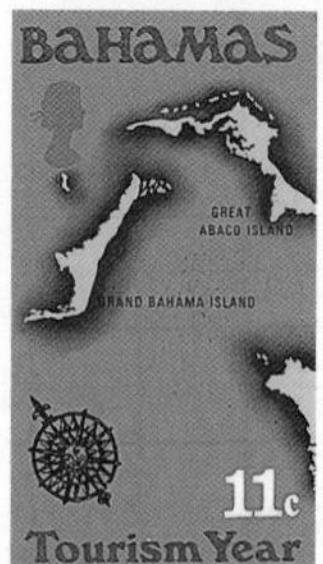

**102** Northerly Bahama Islands

**1972.** Tourism Year of the Americas. Sheet 133×105 mm, containing T **102**.

| | | | |
|---|---|---|---|
| **MS**392 | 11, 15, 18 and 50c. multicoloured | 3·75 | 3·25 |

The four designs are printed, se-tenant in **MS**392, forming a composite map design of the Bahamas.

**1972.** Royal Silver Wedding. As T **52** of Ascension, but with mace and galleon in background.

| | | | |
|---|---|---|---|
| 393 | 11c. pink | 15 | 15 |
| 394 | 18c. violet | 15 | 20 |

**104** Weather Satellite

**1973.** Centenary of I.M.O./W.M.O. Multicoloured.

| | | | |
|---|---|---|---|
| 410 | 15c. Type **104** | 50 | 25 |
| 411 | 18c. Weather radar | 60 | 35 |

**105** C. A. Bain (national hero)

**1973.** Independence. Multicoloured.

| | | | |
|---|---|---|---|
| 412 | 3c. Type **105** | 10 | 10 |
| 413 | 11c. Coat of arms | 15 | 10 |
| 414 | 15c. Bahamas flag | 20 | 15 |
| 415 | $1 Governor-General, M. B. Butler | 65 | 1·00 |
| **MS**416 | 86×121 mm. Nos. 412/15 | 1·75 | 1·75 |

**106** "The Virgin in Prayer" (Sassoferrato)

**1973.** Christmas. Multicoloured.

| | | | |
|---|---|---|---|
| 417 | 3c. Type **106** | 10 | 10 |
| 418 | 11c. "Virgin and Child with St. John" (Filippino Lippi) | 15 | 15 |
| 419 | 15c. "A Choir of Angels" (Simon Marmion) | 15 | 15 |
| 420 | 18c. "The Two Trinities" (Murillo) | 25 | 25 |
| **MS**421 | 120×99 mm. Nos. 417/20 | 1·75 | 1·40 |

**107** "Agriculture and Sciences"

**1974.** 25th Anniv of University of West Indies. Multicoloured.

| | | | |
|---|---|---|---|
| 422 | 15c. Type **107** | 20 | 25 |
| 423 | 18c. "Arts, Engineering and General Studies" | 25 | 30 |

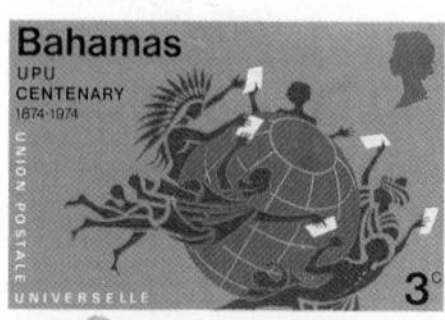

**108** U.P.U. Monument, Berne

**1974.** Centenary of U.P.U.

| | | | | |
|---|---|---|---|---|
| 424 | **108** | 3c. multicoloured | 10 | 15 |
| 425 | - | 13c. multicoloured (vert) | 20 | 25 |
| 426 | - | 14c. multicoloured | 20 | 30 |
| 427 | - | 18c. multicoloured (vert) | 25 | 40 |
| **MS**428 | | 128×95 mm. Nos. 424/7 | 80 | 1·60 |

DESIGNS—As Type **108** but showing different arrangements of the U.P.U. Monument.

**109** Roseate Spoonbills

**1974.** 15th Anniv of Bahamas National Trust. Mult.

| | | | |
|---|---|---|---|
| 429 | 13c. Type **109** | 1·60 | 1·10 |
| 430 | 14c. White-crowned pigeon | 1·60 | 75 |
| 431 | 21c. White-tailed tropic birds | 2·00 | 1·25 |
| 432 | 36c. Cuban amazon ("Bahamian parrot") | 2·00 | 5·00 |
| **MS**433 | 123×120 mm. Nos. 429/32 | 9·50 | 13·00 |

**110** "The Holy Family" (Jacques de Stella)

**1974.** Christmas. Multicoloured.

| | | | |
|---|---|---|---|
| 434 | 8c. Type **110** | 10 | 10 |
| 435 | 10c. "Madonna and Child" (16th-century Brescian School) | 15 | 15 |
| 436 | 12c. "Virgin and Child with St. John the Baptist and St. Catherine" (Previtali) | 15 | 15 |
| 437 | 21c. "Virgin and Child with Angels" (Previtali) | 25 | 30 |
| **MS**438 | 126×105 mm. Nos. 434/7 | 1·00 | 1·40 |

**111** "Anteos maerula"

**1975.** Butterflies. Multicoloured.

| | | | |
|---|---|---|---|
| 439 | 3c. Type **111** | 25 | 15 |
| 440 | 14c. "Eurema nicippe" | 80 | 50 |
| 441 | 18c. "Papilio andraemon" | 95 | 65 |
| 442 | 21c. "Euptoieta hegesia" | 1·10 | 85 |
| **MS**443 | 194×94 mm. Nos. 439/42 | 7·50 | 6·50 |

**112** Sheep Husbandry

**1975.** Economic Diversification. Multicoloured.

| | | | |
|---|---|---|---|
| 444 | 3c. Type **112** | 10 | 10 |
| 445 | 14c. Electric-reel fishing (vert) | 20 | 15 |
| 446 | 18c. Farming | 25 | 20 |
| 447 | 21c. Oil refinery (vert) | 80 | 35 |
| **MS**448 | 127×94 mm. Nos. 444/7 | 1·25 | 1·50 |

**113** Rowena Rand (evangelist)

**1975.** International Women's Year.

| | | | | |
|---|---|---|---|---|
| 449 | **113** | 14c. brown, lt blue & bl | 20 | 50 |
| 450 | - | 18c. yellow, grn & brn | 25 | 75 |

DESIGN: 18c. I.W.Y. symbol and harvest symbol.

**114** "Adoration of the Shepherds" (Perugino)

**1975.** Christmas. Multicoloured.

451 3c. Type **114** 15 60
452 8c. "Adoration of the Magi" (Ghirlandaio) 20 10
453 18c. As 8c. 55 90
454 21c. Type **114** 60 95
**MS**455 142×107 mm. Nos. 451/4 2·25 4·50

**115** Telephones, 1876 and 1976

**1976.** Centenary of Telephone. Multicoloured.

456 3c. Type **115** 20 50
457 16c. Radio-telephone link, Deleporte 40 50
458 21c. Alexander Graham Bell 50 65
459 25c. Satellite 60 1·00

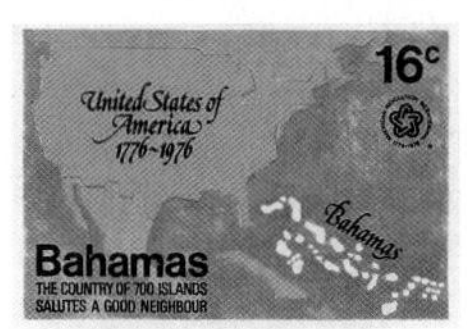


**116** Map of North America

**1976.** Bicentenary of American Revolution. Mult.

475 16c. Type **116** 30 30
476 $1 John Murray, Earl of Dunmore 1·50 1·75
**MS**477 127×100 mm. Nos. 476×4 6·00 7·50

**117** Cycling

**1976.** Olympic Games, Montreal.

478 **117** 8c. mauve, blue and light blue 1·60 20
479 - 16c. orange, brown and light blue 35 30
480 - 25c. blue, mauve and light blue 45 50
481 - 40c. brown, orange and blue 55 1·60
**MS**482 100×126 mm. Nos. 478/81 3·00 3·25

DESIGNS: 16c. Jumping; 25c. Sailing; 40c. Boxing.

**118** "Virgin and Child" (detail, Lippi)

**1976.** Christmas. Multicoloured.

483 3c. Type **118** 10 10
484 21c. "Adoration of the Shepherds" (School of Seville) 30 15
485 25c. "Adoration of the Kings" (detail, Foppa) 30 20
486 40c. "Virgin and Child" (detail, Vivarini) 40 40
**MS**487 107×127 mm. Nos. 483/6 1·00 2·00

**119** Queen beneath Cloth of Gold Canopy

**1977.** Silver Jubilee. Multicoloured.

488 8c. Type **119** 10 10
489 16c. The Crowning 15 15
490 21c. Taking the Oath 15 15
491 40c. Queen with sceptre and orb 25 30
**MS**492 122×90 mm. Nos. 488/91 80 1·25

**120** Featherduster

**1977.** Marine Life. Multicoloured.

493 3c. Type **120** 40 15
494 8c. Porkfish and cave 60 20
495 16c. Elkhorn coral 70 40
496 21c. Soft coral and sponge 80 55
**MS**497 119×93 mm. Nos. 493/6 2·75 4·50

**121** Scouts around Campfire and Home-made Shower

**1977.** 6th Caribbean Scout Jamboree. Multicoloured.

498 16c. Type **121** 75 30
499 21c. Boating scenes 85 35

**1977.** Royal Visit. Nos. 488/91 optd **Royal Visit October 1977**.

500 8c. Type **119** 15 10
501 16c. The Crowning 20 15
502 21c. Taking the Oath 25 25
503 40c. Queen with sceptre and orb 30 40
**MS**504 122×90 mm. Nos. 500/3 1·25 1·50

**123** Virgin and Child

**1977.** Christmas. Multicoloured.

505 3c. Type **123** 10 10
506 16c. The Magi 30 25
507 21c. Nativity scene 30 40
508 25c. The Magi and star 40 45
**MS**509 136×74 mm. Nos. 505/8 1·00 1·75

**124** Public Library, Nassau (Colonial)

**1978.** Architectural Heritage.

510 **124** 3c. black and green 10 10
511 - 8c. black and blue 15 10
512 - 16c. black and mauve 20 20
513 - 18c. black and pink 25 30
**MS**514 91×91 mm. Nos. 510/13 70 1·60

DESIGNS: 8c. St. Matthew's Church (Gothic); 16c. Government House (Colonial); 18c. Hermitage, Cat Island (Spanish).

**125** Sceptre, St. Edward's Crown and Orb

**1978.** 25th Anniv of Coronation. Multicoloured.

515 16c. Type **125** 15 10
516 $1 Queen in Coronation regalia 50 65
**MS**517 147×96 mm. Nos. 515/16 1·25 1·00

**126** Coat of Arms within Wreath and Three Ships

**1978.** Christmas.

532 **126** 5c. gold, lake and red 15 10
533 - 21c. gold, deep blue and blue 30 25
**MS**534 95×95 mm. Nos. 532/3 1·75 5·50

DESIGN: 21c. Three angels with trumpets.

**127** Child reaching for Adult

**1979.** International Year of the Child. Multicoloured.

535 5c. Type **127** 20 15
536 16c. Boys playing leapfrog 40 45
537 21c. Girls skipping 50 60
538 25c. Bricks with I.Y.C. emblem 50 75
**MS**539 101×125 mm. Nos. 535/8 1·40 3·25

**128** Sir Rowland Hill and Penny Black

**1979.** Death Centenary of Sir Rowland Hill. Multicoloured.

540 10c. Type **128** 30 10
541 21c. Printing press, 1840, and 6d. stamp of 1862 40 30
542 25c. Great Britain 1856 6d. with "A 05" (Nassau) cancellation, and 1840 2d. Blue 40 50
543 40c. Early mailboat and 1d. stamp of 1859 45 70
**MS**544 115×80 mm. Nos. 540/3 2·00 3·25

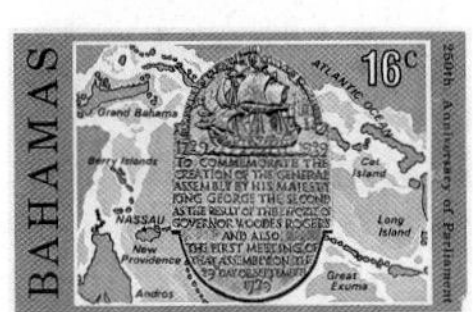


**129** Commemorative Plaque and Map of Bahamas

**1979.** 250th Anniv of Parliament. Multicoloured.

545 16c. Type **129** 35 10
546 21c. Parliament buildings 40 15
547 25c. Legislative Chamber 40 15
548 $1 Senate Chamber 80 1·00
**MS**549 116×89 mm. Nos. 545/8 2·50 3·75

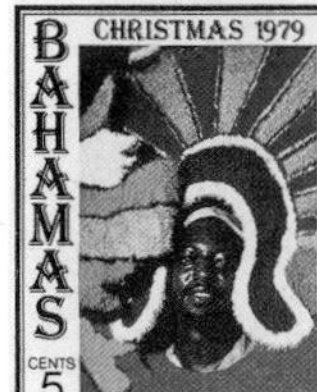


**130** Goombay Carnival Headdress

**1979.** Christmas.

550 **130** 5c. multicoloured 10 10
551 - 10c. multicoloured 15 10
552 - 16c. multicoloured 20 10
553 - 21c. multicoloured 20 20
554 - 25c. multicoloured 25 20
555 - 40c. multicoloured 30 45
**MS**556 50×88 mm. Nos. 550/5 2·00 3·00

DESIGNS: 10c. to 40c. Various Carnival costumes.

**131** Landfall of Columbus, 1492

**1980.** Multicoloured.. Multicoloured..

557 1c. Type **131** 1·25 2·50
558 3c. Blackbeard the pirate 30 2·50
559 5c. Eleutheran Adventurers (Articles and Orders, 1647) 30 1·25
560 10c. Ceremonial mace 20 40
561 12c. The Loyalists, 1783–88 30 2·25
562 15c. Slave trading, Vendue House 5·50 1·25
563 16c. Wrecking in the 1800s 1·75 1·25
564 18c. Blockade running (American Civil War) 2·50 2·50
565 21c. Bootlegging, 1919–29 60 2·50
566 25c. Pineapple cultivation 40 2·50
567 40c. Sponge clipping 70 1·50
568 50c. Tourist development 75 1·50
569 $1 Modern agriculture 75 4·25
570 $2 Boeing 737 and sea transport 4·25 5·50
571 $3 Banking (Central Bank) 1·25 4·00
572 $5 Independence, 10 July 1973 1·50 6·00

**132** Virgin and Child

**1980.** Christmas. Straw-work. Multicoloured.

573 5c. Type **132** 10 10
574 21c. Three Kings 25 10
575 25c. Angel 25 15
576 $1 Christmas tree 75 85
**MS**577 168×105 mm. Nos. 573/6 1·25 2·25

**133** Disabled Persons with Walking Stick

**1981.** International Year of Disabled People. Mult.

578 5c. Type **133** 10 10
579 $1 Disabled person in wheelchair 1·25 1·25
**MS**580 120×60 mm. Nos. 578/9 1·40 2·50

**134** Grand Bahama Tracking Site

**1981.** Space Exploration. Multicoloured.

581 10c. Type **134** 30 15
582 20c. Satellite view of Bahamas (vert) 60 50

| | | | |
|---|---|---|---|
| 583 | 25c. Satelite view of Eleuthera | 65 | 60 |
| 584 | 50c. Satellite view of Andros and New Province (vert) | 1·00 | 1·25 |
| **MS**585 | 115×99 mm. Nos. 581/4 | 2·25 | 2·25 |

**135** Prince Charles and Lady Diana Spencer

**1981.** Royal Wedding. Multicoloured.

| | | | |
|---|---|---|---|
| 586 | 30c. Type **135** | 1·50 | 30 |
| 587 | $2 Prince Charles and Prime Minister Pindling | 1·50 | 1·25 |
| **MS**588 | 142×120 mm. Nos. 586/7 | 5·00 | 1·25 |

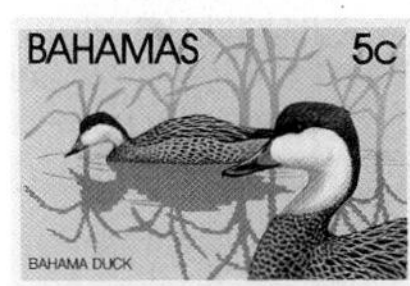


**136** Bahamas Pintail ("Bahama Duck")

**1981.** Wildlife (1st series). Birds. Multicoloured.

| | | | |
|---|---|---|---|
| 589 | 5c. Type **136** | 1·50 | 60 |
| 590 | 20c. Reddish egret | 2·00 | 60 |
| 591 | 25c. Brown booby | 2·00 | 65 |
| 592 | $1 Black-billed whistling duck ("West Indian Tree Duck") | 4·00 | 7·50 |
| **MS**593 | 100×74 mm. Nos. 589/92 | 8·50 | 8·50 |

See also Nos. 626/30, 653/7 and 690/4.

**1981.** Commonwealth Finance Ministers' Meeting. Nos. 559/60, 566 and 568 optd **COMMONWEALTH FINANCE MINISTERS' MEETING 21–23 SEPTEMBER 1981**.

| | | | |
|---|---|---|---|
| 594 | 5c. Eleutheran Adventures (Articles and Orders, 1647) | 15 | 15 |
| 595 | 10c. Ceremonial mace | 20 | 20 |
| 596 | 25c. Pineapple cultivation | 50 | 60 |
| 597 | 50c. Tourist development | 85 | 1·50 |

**138** Poultry

**1981.** World Food Day. Multicoloured.

| | | | |
|---|---|---|---|
| 598 | 5c. Type **138** | 20 | 10 |
| 599 | 20c. Sheep | 35 | 35 |
| 600 | 30c. Lobsters | 45 | 50 |
| 601 | 50c. Pigs | 75 | 1·50 |
| **MS**602 | 115×63 mm. Nos. 598/601 | 1·50 | 3·25 |

**139** Father Christmas

**1981.** Christmas. Multicoloured.

| | | | |
|---|---|---|---|
| 603 | 5c. Type **139** | 55 | 85 |
| 604 | 5c. Mother and child | 55 | 85 |
| 605 | 5c. St. Nicholas, Holland | 55 | 85 |
| 606 | 25c. Lussibruden, Sweden | 70 | 95 |
| 607 | 25c. Mother and child (different) | 70 | 95 |
| 608 | 25c. King Wenceslas, Czechoslovakia | 70 | 95 |
| 609 | 30c. Mother with child on knee | 70 | 95 |
| 610 | 30c. Mother carrying child | 70 | 95 |
| 611 | $1 Christkindl Angel, Germany | 1·00 | 1·50 |

**140** Robert Koch

**1982.** Centenary of Discovery of Tubercle Bacillus by Robert Koch.

| | | | | |
|---|---|---|---|---|
| 612 | **140** | 5c. black, brown and lilac | 75 | 50 |
| 613 | - | 16c. black, brown & orge | 1·40 | 50 |
| 614 | - | 21c. multicoloured | 1·60 | 55 |
| 615 | - | $1 multicoloured | 3·00 | 7·50 |
| **MS**616 | | 94×97 mm. Nos. 612/15 | 6·00 | 7·50 |

DESIGNS: 16c. Stylised infected person; 21c. Early and modern microscopes; $1 Mantoux test.

**141** Greater Flamingo (male)

**1982.** Greater Flamingos. Multicoloured.

| | | | |
|---|---|---|---|
| 617 | 25c. Type **141** | 1·60 | 1·00 |
| 618 | 25c. Female | 1·60 | 1·00 |
| 619 | 25c. Female with nestling | 1·60 | 1·00 |
| 620 | 25c. Juvenile | 1·60 | 1·00 |
| 621 | 25c. Immature bird | 1·60 | 1·00 |

**142** Lady Diana Spencer at Ascot, June, 1981

**1982.** 21st Birthday of Princess of Wales. Mult.

| | | | |
|---|---|---|---|
| 622 | 16c. Bahamas coat of arms | 20 | 10 |
| 623 | 25c. Type **142** | 45 | 15 |
| 624 | 40c. Bride and Earl Spencer arriving at St. Paul's | 60 | 20 |
| 625 | $1 Formal portrait | 1·00 | 1·25 |

**1982.** Wildlife (2nd series). Mammals. As T **136**. Multicoloured.

| | | | |
|---|---|---|---|
| 626 | 10c. Buffy flower bat | 1·00 | 15 |
| 627 | 16c. Bahamian hutia | 1·25 | 25 |
| 628 | 21c. Common racoon | 1·50 | 55 |
| 629 | $1 Common dolphin | 3·00 | 1·90 |
| **MS**630 | 115×76 mm. Nos. 626/9 | 6·00 | 3·50 |

**143** House of Assembly Plaque

**1982.** 28th Commonwealth Parliamentary Association Conference. Multicoloured.

| | | | |
|---|---|---|---|
| 631 | 5c. Type **143** | 15 | 10 |
| 632 | 25c. Association coat of arms | 50 | 35 |
| 633 | 40c. Coat of arms | 80 | 60 |
| 634 | 50c. House of Assembly | 1·10 | 75 |

**144** Wesley Methodist Church, Baillou Hill Road

**1982.** Christmas. Churches. Multicoloured.

| | | | |
|---|---|---|---|
| 635 | 5c. Type **144** | 10 | 20 |
| 636 | 12c. Centreville Seventh Day Adventist Church | 15 | 20 |
| 637 | 15c. The Church of God of Prophecy, East Street | 15 | 30 |
| 638 | 21c. Bethel Baptist Church, Meeting Street | 15 | 30 |
| 639 | 25c. St. Francis Xavier Catholic Church, Highbury Park | 15 | 50 |
| 640 | $1 Holy Cross Anglican Church, Highbury Park | 60 | 3·00 |

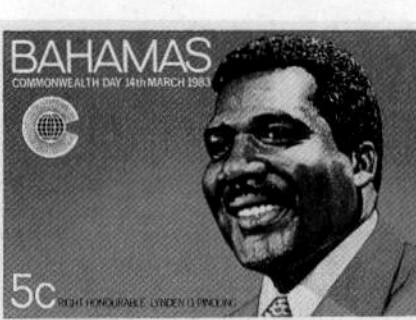


**145** Prime Minister Lyndon O. Pindling

**1983.** Commonwealth Day. Multicoloured.

| | | | |
|---|---|---|---|
| 641 | 5c. Type **145** | 10 | 10 |
| 642 | 25c. Bahamian and Commonwealth flags | 50 | 40 |
| 643 | 35c. Map showing position of Bahamas | 50 | 50 |
| 644 | $1 Ocean liner | 1·10 | 1·40 |

**1983.** Nos. 562/5 surch.

| | | | |
|---|---|---|---|
| 645 | 20c. on 15c. Slave trading, Vendue House | 50 | 35 |
| 646 | 31c. on 21c. Bootlegging, 1919–29 | 60 | 55 |
| 647 | 35c. on 16c. Wrecking in the 1800s | 70 | 60 |
| 648 | 80c. on 18c. Blockade running (American Civil War) | 80 | 1·40 |

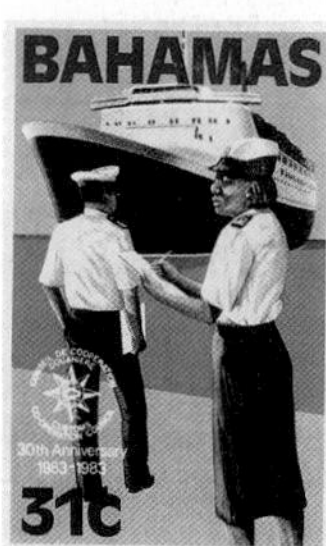


**147** Customs Officers and "Queen Elizabeth 2" (liner)

**1983.** 30th Anniv of Customs Co-operation Council. Multicoloured.

| | | | |
|---|---|---|---|
| 649 | 31c. Type **147** | 1·50 | 45 |
| 650 | $1 Customs officers and Lockheed L.1329 JetStar airliner | 3·50 | 2·75 |

**148** Raising the National Flag

**1983.** 10th Anniv of Independence.

| | | | | |
|---|---|---|---|---|
| 651 | **148** | $1 multicoloured | 1·00 | 1·40 |
| **MS**652 | | 105×65 mm. No. 651 | 1·00 | 1·40 |

**1983.** Wildlife (3rd series). Butterflies. As T **136**.

| | | | |
|---|---|---|---|
| 653 | 5c. multicoloured | 1·50 | 20 |
| 654 | 25c. multicoloured | 2·25 | 40 |
| 655 | 31c. black, yellow and red | 2·25 | 55 |
| 656 | 50c. multicoloured | 2·50 | 85 |
| **MS**657 | 120×80 mm. Nos. 653/6 | 7·50 | 6·00 |

DESIGNS: 5c. "Atalopedes carteri"; 25c. "Ascia monuste"; 31c. "Phoebis agarithe"; 50c. "Dryas julia".

**149** "Loyalist Dreams"

**1983.** Bicentenary of Arrival of American Loyalists in the Bahamas. Multicoloured.

| | | | |
|---|---|---|---|
| 658 | 5c. Type **149** | 10 | 10 |
| 659 | 31c. New Plymouth, Abaco (horiz) | 30 | 50 |
| 660 | 35c. New Plymouth Hotel (horiz) | 40 | 70 |
| 661 | 50c. "Island Hope" | 45 | 90 |
| **MS**662 | 111×76 mm. Nos. 658/61 | 1·25 | 2·50 |

**150** Consolidated PBY-5 Catalina flying boatf

**1983.** Air. Bicentenary of Manned Flight. Mult.

| | | | |
|---|---|---|---|
| 663 | 10c. Type **150** | 55 | 15 |
| 664 | 25c. Avro Tudor IV "Star Lion" | 75 | 30 |
| 665 | 31c. Avro Lancastrian | 85 | 45 |
| 666 | 35c. Consolidated Commodore flying boat | 1·00 | 50 |

For these stamps without the Manned Flight logo, see Nos. 699/702.

**151** "Christmas Bells" (Monica Pinder)

**1983.** Christmas. Children's Paintings. Multicoloured.

| | | | |
|---|---|---|---|
| 667 | 5c. Type **151** | 15 | 10 |
| 668 | 20c. "Flamingo" (Cory Bullard) | 35 | 30 |
| 669 | 25c. "Yellow Hibiscus with Christmas Candle" (Monique Bailey) | 45 | 40 |
| 670 | 31c. "Santa goes-a-sailing" (Sabrina Seiler) (horiz) | 55 | 45 |
| 671 | 35c. "Silhouette scene with Palm Trees" (James Blake) | 60 | 50 |
| 672 | 50c. "Silhouette scene with Pelicans" (Erik Russell) (horiz) | 70 | 70 |

**152** 1861 4d. Stamp

**1984.** 125th Anniv of First Bahamas Postage Stamp. Multicoloured.

| | | | |
|---|---|---|---|
| 673 | 5c. Type **152** | 25 | 10 |
| 674 | $1 1859 1d. stamp | 1·75 | 1·50 |

**153** "Trent I" (paddle-steamer)

**1984.** 250th Anniv of "Lloyd's List" (newspaper). Multicoloured.

| | | | |
|---|---|---|---|
| 675 | 5c. Type **153** | 50 | 10 |
| 676 | 31c. "Orinoco II" (mail ship), 1886 | 1·00 | 60 |
| 677 | 35c. Cruise liners in Nassau harbour | 1·10 | 75 |
| 678 | 50c. "Oropesa" (container ship) | 1·40 | 1·60 |

**154** Running

**1984.** Olympic Games, Los Angeles.

| | | | | |
|---|---|---|---|---|
| 679 | **154** | 5c. green, black and gold | 15 | 20 |
| 680 | - | 25c. blue, black and gold | 50 | 50 |
| 681 | - | 31c. red, black and gold | 55 | 60 |
| 682 | - | $1 brown, black and gold | 6·00 | 7·00 |
| **MS**683 | | 115×80 mm. Nos. 679/82 | 6·50 | 8·00 |

DESIGNS: 25c. Shot-putting; 31c. Boxing; $1 Basketball.

**155** Bahamas and Caribbean Community Flags

**1984.** 5th Conference of Caribbean Community Heads of Government.
684 **155** 50c. multicoloured 1·00 1·00

**156** Bahama Woodstar

**1984.** 25th Anniv of National Trust. Multicoloured.
685 31c. Type **156** 3·75 3·75
686 31c. Belted kingfishers, greater flamingos and "Eleutherodactylus planirostris" (frog) 3·75 3·75
687 31c. Black-necked stilts, greater flamingos and "Phoebis sennae" (butterfly) 3·75 3·75
688 31c. "Urbanus proteus" (butterfly) and "Chelonia mydas" (turtle) 3·75 3·75
689 31c. Osprey and greater flamingos 3·75 3·75

Nos. 685/9 were printed together in horiz strips of 5 forming a composite design.

**1984.** Wildlife (4th series). Reptiles and Amphibians. As T **136**.
690 5c. Allens' Cay iguana 85 20
691 25c. Curly-tailed lizard 1·75 60
692 35c. Greenhouse frog 2·00 85
693 50c. Atlantic green turtle 2·25 3·50
**MS**694 112×82 mm. Nos. 690/3 6·25 7·50

**157** "The Holy Virgin with Jesus and Johannes" (19th-century porcelain plaque after Titian)

**1984.** Christmas. Religious Paintings. Multicoloured.
695 5c. Type **157** 30 10
696 31c. "Madonna with Child in Tropical Landscape" (aquarelle, Anais Colin) 1·00 60
697 35c. "The Holy Virgin with the Child" (miniature on ivory, Elena Caula) 1·25 65
**MS**698 116×76 mm. Nos. 695/7 2·50 4·25

**1985.** Air. As Nos. 663/6, but without Manned Flight logo.
699 10c. Type **150** 80 50
700 25c. Avro Tudor IV "Star Lion" 95 50
701 31c. Avro Lancastrian 95 60
702 35c. Consolidated Commodore flying boat 1·40 1·10

**158** Brownie Emblem and Queen or Pink Conch

**1985.** International Youth Year. 75th Anniv of Girl Guide Movement. Multicoloured.
703 5c. Type **158** 60 50
704 25c. Tents and coconut palm 1·25 1·00
705 31c. Guide salute and greater flamingos 1·90 1·50
706 35c. Ranger emblem and marlin 1·90 1·50
**MS**707 95×74 mm. Nos. 703/6 5·50 7·50

**159** Killdeer Plover

**1985.** Birth Bicent of John J. Audubon (ornithologist). Multicoloured.
708 5c. Type **159** 1·00 60
709 31c. Mourning dove (vert) 2·25 60
710 35c. "Mourning dove" (John J. Audubon) (vert) 2·25 65
711 $1 "Killdeer Plover" (John J. Audubon) 4·00 4·50

**160** The Queen Mother at Christening of Peter Phillips, 1977

**1985.** Life and Times of Queen Elizabeth the Queen Mother. Multicoloured.
712 5c. Visiting Auckland, New Zealand, 1927 45 20
713 25c. Type **160** 70 40
714 35c. The Queen Mother attending church 75 55
715 50c. With Prince Henry at his christening (from photo by Lord Snowdon) 1·50 2·00
**MS**716 91×73 mm. $1.25, In horse-drawn carriage, Sark 2·75 1·90

**161** Ears of Wheat and Emblems

**1985.** 40th Anniv of U.N.O. and F.A.O.
717 **161** 25c. multicoloured 1·25 70

**162** Queen Elizabeth II

**1985.** Commonwealth Heads of Government Meeting, Nassau. Multicoloured.
718 31c. Type **162** 3·00 3·75
719 35c. Bahamas Prime Minister's flag and Commonwealth emblem 3·00 3·75

**163** "Grandma's Christmas Bouquet" (Alton Roland Lowe)

**1985.** Christmas. Paintings by Alton Roland Lowe. Multicoloured.
736 5c. Type **163** 60 40
737 25c. "Junkanoo Romeo and Juliet" (vert) 1·50 1·00
738 31c. "Bunce Gal" (vert) 1·75 1·50
739 35c. "Home for Christmas" 1·75 2·75
**MS**740 110×68 mm. Nos. 736/9 2·75 3·25

**1986.** 60th Birthday of Queen Elizabeth II. As T **110** of Ascension. Multicoloured.
741 10c. Princess Elizabeth aged one, 1927 15 15
742 25c. The Coronation, 1953 30 30
743 35c. Queen making speech at Commonwealth Banquet, Bahamas, 1985 35 40
744 40c. In Djakova, Yugoslavia, 1972 35 45
745 $1 At Crown Agents Head Office, London, 1983 80 1·40

**164** 1980 1c. and 18c. Definitive Stamps

**1986.** "Ameripex '86" International Stamp Exn, Chicago.
746 **164** 5c. multicoloured 85 50
747 - 25c. multicoloured 2·00 50
748 - 31c. multicoloured 2·25 60
749 - 50c. multicoloured 3·00 5·00
750 - $1 black, green and blue 3·25 6·00
**MS**751 80×80 mm. No. 750 4·00 4·00

DESIGNS—HORIZ: (showing Bahamas stamps)—25c. 1969 50th Anniv of Bahamas Airmail Service pair; 31c. 1976 Bicentenary of American Revolution 16c., 50c. 1981 Space Exploration miniature sheet. VERT: $1 Statue of Liberty.

No. 750 also commemorates the Centenary of the Statue of Liberty.

**1986.** Royal Wedding. As T **112** of Ascension. Mult.
756 10c. Prince Andrew and Miss Sarah Ferguson 20 20
757 $1 Prince Andrew 1·25 2·10

**165** Rock Beauty (juvenile)

**1986.** Fish. Multicoloured.
758A 5c. Type **165** 75 75
759A 10c. Stoplight parrotfish 80 1·00
760A 15c. Jackknife-fish 1·50 1·50
761A 20c. Flamefish 1·25 1·25
762A 25c. Peppermint basslet ("Swissguard basslet") 1·50 1·50
763A 30c. Spot-finned butterflyfish 1·10 1·50
764A 35c. Queen triggerfish 1·10 2·75
765B 40c. Four-eyed butterflyfish 1·10 1·60
766A 45c. Royal gramma ("Fairy basslet") 1·50 1·25
767A 50c. Queen angelfish 2·00 3·75
797 60c. Blue chromis 2·25 5·50
769B $1 Spanish hogfish 2·75 3·00
799 $2 Harlequin bass 3·00 8·50
771A $3 Black-barred soldierfish 6·00 7·00
772A $5 Cherub angelfish ("Pygmy angelfish") 6·50 8·00
773A $10 Red hind 18·00 25·00

**166** Christ Church Cathedral, Nassau, 1861

**1986.** 125th Anniv of City of Nassau. Diocese and Cathedral. Multicoloured.
774 10c. Type **166** 30 20
775 40c. Christ Church Cathedral, 1986 70 80
**MS**776 75×100 mm. Nos. 774/5 4·25 6·50

**167** Man and Boy looking at Crib

**1986.** Christmas. International Peace Year. Mult.
777 10c. Type **167** 35 20
778 40c. Mary and Joseph journeying to Bethlehem 85 75
779 45c. Children praying and Star of Bethlehem 95 1·00
780 50c. Children exchanging gifts 1·00 2·50
**MS**781 95×90 mm. Nos. 777/80 8·50 11·00

**168** Great Isaac Lighthouse

**1987.** Lighthouses. Multicoloured.
782 10c. Type **168** 3·00 85
783 40c. Bird Rock lighthouse 6·00 1·75
784 45c. Castle Island lighthouse 6·00 2·00
785 $1 "Hole in the Wall" lighthouse 9·00 12·00

**169** Anne Bonney

**1987.** Pirates and Privateers of the Caribbean. Multicoloured.
786 10c. Type **169** 3·50 1·25
787 40c. Edward Teach ("Blackbeard") 6·00 3·50
788 45c. Captain Edward England 6·00 3·50
789 50c. Captain Woodes Rogers 6·50 7·50
**MS**790 75×95 mm. $1.25, Map of Bahamas and colonial coat of arms 13·00 7·50

**170** Boeing 737

**1987.** Air. Aircraft. Multicoloured.
800 15c. Type **170** 3·25 1·50
801 40c. Boeing 757-200 4·25 2·25
802 45c. Airbus Industrie A300 B4-200 4·25 2·25
803 50c. Boeing 747-200 4·75 4·50

**171** "Norway" (liner) and Catamaran

**1987.** Tourist Transport. Multicoloured.
804 40c. Type **171** 2·00 2·00
805 40c. Liners and speedboat 2·00 2·00
806 40c. Game fishing boat and cruising yacht 2·00 2·00
807 40c. Game fishing boat and racing yachts 2·00 2·00
808 40c. Fishing boat and schooner 2·00 2·00
809 40c. Hawker Siddeley H.S.748 airliner 2·00 2·00
810 40c. Boeing 737 and Boeing 727-200 airliners 2·00 2·00
811 40c. Beech 200 Super King Air aircraft and radio beacon 2·00 2·00
812 40c. Aircraft and Nassau control tower 2·00 2·00
813 40c. Helicopter and parked aircraft 2·00 2·00

Nos. 804/8 and 809/13 were each printed together, se-tenant, forming composite design.

**172** "Cattleyopsis lindenii"

**1987.** Christmas. Orchids. Multicoloured.
814 10c. Type **172** 1·75 60
815 40c. "Encyclia lucayana" 3·00 1·50

816 45c. "Encyclia hodgeana" 3·00 1·50
817 50c. "Encyclia lleidae" 3·00 3·00
**MS**818 120×92 mm. Nos. 814/17 11·00 12·00

**173** King Ferdinand and Queen Isabella of Spain

**1988.** 500th Anniv (1992) of Discovery of America by Columbus (1st issue). Multicoloured.
819 10c. Type **173** 85 60
820 40c. Columbus before Talavera Committee 1·75 1·75
821 45c. Lucayan village 1·90 1·90
822 50c. Lucayan potters 2·00 3·50
**MS**823 65×50 mm. $1.50, Map of Antilles, c. 1500 6·00 3·75
See also Nos. 844/8, 870/4, 908/12 and 933/7.

**174** Whistling Ducks in Flight

**1988.** Black-billed Whistling Duck. Multicoloured.
824 5c. Type **174** 2·25 1·75
825 10c. Whistling duck in reeds 2·25 1·75
826 20c. Pair with brood 4·00 2·75
827 45c. Pair wading 6·00 3·25

**175** Grantstown Cabin, c.1820

**1988.** 150th Anniv of Abolition of Slavery. Multicoloured.
828 10c. Type **175** 50 30
829 40c. Basket-making, Grantstown 1·25 95

**176** Olympic Flame, High Jumping, Hammer throwing, Basketball and Gymnastics

**1988.** Olympic Games, Seoul. Designs taken from painting by James Martin. Multicoloured.
830 10c. Type **176** 90 50
831 40c. Athletics, archery, swimming, long jumping, weightlifting and boxing 90 60
832 45c. Javelin throwing, gymnastics, hurdling and shot put 90 60
833 $1 Athletics, hurdling, gymnastics and cycling 3·50 5·00
**MS**834 113×85 mm. Nos. 830/3 6·00 3·25

**1988.** 300th Anniv of Lloyd's of London. As T **123** of Ascension. Multicoloured.
835 10c. "Lloyd's List" of 1740 30 15
836 40c. Freeport Harbour (horiz) 2·00 60
837 45c. Space shuttle over Bahamas (horiz) 2·00 60
838 $1 "Yarmouth Castle" (freighter) on fire 3·00 2·50

**177** "Oh Little Town of Bethlehem"

**1988.** Christmas. Carols. Multicoloured.
839 10c. Type **177** 55 30
840 40c. "Little Donkey" 1·50 75
841 45c. "Silent Night" 1·50 90
842 50c. "Hark the Herald Angels Sing" 1·60 2·25
**MS**843 88×108 mm. Nos. 839/42 2·75 2·75

**1989.** 500th Anniv (1992) of Discovery of America by Columbus (2nd issue). As T **173**. Multicoloured.
844 10c. Columbus drawing chart 2·25 85
845 40c. Types of caravel 3·25 1·75
846 45c. Early navigational instruments 3·25 1·75
847 50c. Arawak artefacts 3·25 5·00
**MS**848 64×64 mm. $1.50, Caravel under construction (from 15th-cent "Nuremburg Chronicles") 2·50 2·50

**178** Cuban Emerald

**1989.** Hummingbirds. Multicoloured.
849 10c. Type **178** 1·75 1·25
850 40c. Ruby-throated hummingbird 3·00 2·00
851 45c. Bahama woodstar 3·00 2·00
852 50c. Rufous hummingbird 3·25 4·50

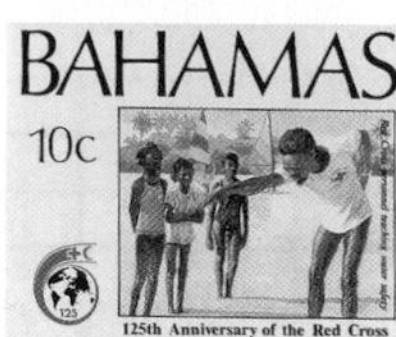


**179** Teaching Water Safety

**1989.** 125th Anniv of Int Red Cross. Mult.
853 10c. Type **179** 1·75 50
854 $1 Henri Dunant (founder) and Battle of Solferino 3·75 5·00

**1989.** 20th Anniv of First Manned Landing on Moon. As T **126** of Ascension. Multicoloured.
855 10c. "Apollo 8" Communications Station, Grand Bahama 1·25 50
856 40c. Crew of "Apollo 8" (30×30 mm) 2·00 90
857 45c. "Apollo 8" emblem (30×30 mm) 2·00 90
858 $1 The Earth seen from "Apollo 8" 2·75 5·00
**MS**859 100×83 mm. $2 "Apollo 11" astronauts in training, Manned Spacecraft Centre, Houston 5·00 6·00

**180** Church of the Nativity, Bethlehem

**1989.** Christmas. Churches of the Holy Land. Multicoloured.
860 10c. Type **180** 1·50 30
861 40c. Basilica of the Annunciation, Nazareth 2·50 70
862 45c. Tabgha Church, Galilee 2·50 70
863 $1 Church of the Holy Sepulchre, Jerusalem 4·50 7·00
**MS**864 92×109 mm. Nos. 860/3 10·00 11·00

**181** 1974 U.P.U. Centenary 13c. Stamp and Globe

**1989.** "World Stamp Expo '89" International Stamp Exhibition, Washington. Multicoloured.
865 10c. Type **181** 70 40
866 40c. New U.P.U. Headquarters Building 3c. and building 1·40 85
867 45c. 1986 "Ameripex '86" $1 and Capitol, Washington 1·40 90
868 $1 1949 75th anniv of U.P.U. 2½d. and Boeing 737 airliner 5·50 7·00
**MS**869 107×80 mm. $2 Map showing route of Columbus, 1492 (30×38 mm) 10·00 14·00

**1990.** 500th Anniv (1992) of Discovery of America by Columbus (3rd issue). As T **173**. Multicoloured.
870 10c. Launching caravel 1·75 80
871 40c. Provisional ship 2·75 2·00
872 45c. Shortening sail 2·75 2·00
873 50c. Lucayan fisherman 2·75 4·00
**MS**874 70×61 mm. $1.50, Departure of Columbus, 1492 5·50 7·00

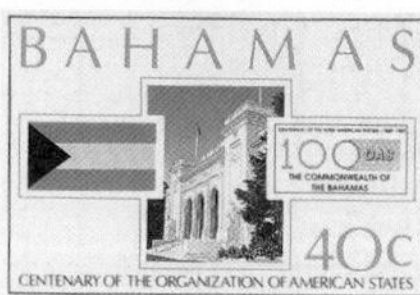


**182** Bahamas Flag, O.A.S. Headquarters and Centenary Logo

**1990.** Centenary of Organization of American States.
875 **182** 40c. multicoloured 2·00 2·25

**183** Supermarine Spitfire Mk I "Bahamas I"

**1990.** "Stamp World London 90" International Stamp Exhibition, London. Presentation Fighter Aircraft. Sheet 107×78 mm. containing T **183**. Multicoloured.
**MS**876 $1 Type **183**; $1 Hawker Hurricane Mk IIC "Bahamas V" 8·50 7·50

**184** Teacher with Boy

**1990.** International Literacy Year. Multicoloured.
877 10c. Type **184** 1·00 50
878 40c. Three boys in class 1·75 1·25
879 50c. Teacher and children with books 1·75 5·00

**1990.** 90th Birthday of Queen Elizabeth the Queen Mother. As T **134** of Ascension.
880 40c. multicoloured 1·50 50
881 $1.50 black and ochre 2·75 6·00
DESIGNS—21×36 mm: 40c. "Queen Elizabeth 1938" (Sir Gerald Kelly); 29×37 mm: $1.50, Queen Elizabeth at garden party, France, 1938.

**185** Cuban Amazon preening

**1990.** Cuban Amazon ("Bahamian Parrot"). Mult.
882 10c. Type **185** 1·25 85
883 40c. Pair in flight 2·25 1·50
884 45c. Cuban amazon's head 2·25 1·50
885 50c. Perched on branch 2·50 3·75
**MS**886 73×63 mm. $1.50, Feeding on berries 8·00 10·00

**186** The Annunciation

**1990.** Christmas. Multicoloured.
887 10c. Type **186** 65 50
888 40c. The Nativity 1·25 70
889 45c. Angel appearing to Shepherds 1·25 70
890 $1 The Three Kings 3·00 6·00
**MS**891 94×110 mm. Nos. 887/90 14·00 14·00

**187** Green-backed Heron ("Green Heron")

**1991.** Birds. Multicoloured.
892 5c. Type **187** 80 1·25
893 10c. Turkey vulture 1·50 1·50
976 15c. Osprey 1·00 70
895 20c. Clapper rail 1·00 80
978 25c. Royal tern 1·00 70
979 30c. Key West quail dove 5·50 1·25
898 40c. Smooth-billed ani 1·75 55
899 45c. Burrowing owl 3·00 80
900 50c. Hairy woodpecker 2·50 80
983 55c. Mangrove cuckoo 2·00 80
902 60c. Bahama mockingbird 2·50 1·75
903 70c. Red-winged blackbird 2·50 1·75
904 $1 Thick-billed vireo 3·00 1·50
905 $2 Bahama yellowthroat 6·00 6·50
988 $5 Stripe-headed tanager 6·50 9·00
907 $10 Greater Antillean bullfinch 13·00 16·00

**1991.** 500th Anniv (1992) of Discovery of America by Columbus (4th issue). As T **173**. Multicoloured.
908 15c. Columbus navigating by stars 1·75 85
909 40c. Fleet in mid-Atlantic 2·50 2·25
910 55c. Lucayan family worshiping at night 2·50 2·50
911 60c. Map of First Voyage 3·25 5·00
**MS**912 56×61 mm. $1.50, "Pinta"'s look-out sighting land 6·00 7·00

**1991.** 65th Birthday of Queen Elizabeth II and 70th Birthday of Prince Philip. As T **139** of Ascension. Multicoloured.
913 15c. Prince Philip 1·00 1·50
914 $1 Queen Elizabeth II 1·75 2·00

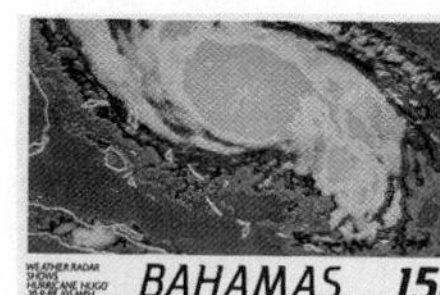


**188** Radar Plot of Hurricane Hugo

**1991.** International Decade for Natural Disaster Reduction. Multicoloured.
915 15c. Type **188** 1·25 65
916 40c. Diagram of hurricane 1·75 1·50
917 55c. Flooding caused by Hurricane David, 1979 2·00 2·25
918 60c. U.S. Dept of Commerce weather reconnaissance Lockhead WP-3D Orion 2·75 4·00

**189** The Annunciation

**1991.** Christmas. Multicoloured.
919 15c. Type **189** 1·25 30
920 55c. Mary and Joseph travelling to Bethlehem 2·25 1·00
921 60c. Angel appearing to the shepherds 2·25 1·50
922 $1 Adoration of the kings 3·75 4·50
**MS**923 92×108 mm. Nos. 919/22 10·00 11·00

**190** First Progressive Liberal Party Cabinet

**1992.** 25th Anniv of Majority Rule. Multicoloured.
924 15c. Type **190** 75 40
925 40c. Signing of Independence Constitution 1·60 1·10

| | | | |
|---|---|---|---|
| 926 | 55c. Prince of Wales handing over Constitutional Instrument (vert) | 1·75 | 1·50 |
| 927 | 60c. First Bahamian Governor-General, Sir Milo Butler (vert) | 2·00 | 3·50 |

**1992.** 40th Anniv of Queen Elizabeth II's Accession. As T **143** of Ascension. Multicoloured.

| | | | |
|---|---|---|---|
| 928 | 15c. Queen Elizabeth with bouquet | 60 | 30 |
| 929 | 40c. Queen Elizabeth with flags | 1·10 | 70 |
| 930 | 55c. Queen Elizabeth at display | 1·10 | 90 |
| 931 | 60c. Three portraits of Queen Elizabeth | 1·25 | 1·50 |
| 932 | $1 Queen Elizabeth II | 1·50 | 2·50 |

**1992.** 500th Anniv of Discovery of America by Columbus (5th issue). As T **173**. Multicoloured.

| | | | |
|---|---|---|---|
| 933 | 15c. Lucayans sighting fleet | 2·00 | 1·00 |
| 934 | 40c. "Santa Maria" and dolphins | 2·75 | 1·75 |
| 935 | 55c. Lucayan canoes approaching ships | 2·75 | 2·25 |
| 936 | 60c. Columbus giving thanks for landfall | 3·25 | 4·25 |
| **MS**937 | 61×57 mm. $1.50, Children at Columbus Monument | 3·50 | 6·00 |

**191** Templeton, Galbraith and Hansberger Ltd Building

**1992.** 20th Anniv of Templeton Prize for Religion.

| | | | | |
|---|---|---|---|---|
| 938 | **191** | 55c. multicoloured | 1·50 | 1·75 |

**192** Pole Vaulting

**1992.** Olympic Games, Barcelona. Multicoloured.

| | | | |
|---|---|---|---|
| 939 | 15c. Type **192** | 60 | 50 |
| 940 | 40c. Javelin | 1·00 | 90 |
| 941 | 55c. Hurdling | 1·10 | 1·25 |
| 942 | 60c. Basketball | 7·00 | 5·00 |
| **MS**943 | 70×50 mm. $2 Sailing | 7·50 | 9·00 |

**193** Arid Landscape and Starving Child

**1992.** International Conference on Nutrition, Rome. Multicoloured.

| | | | |
|---|---|---|---|
| 944 | 15c. Type **193** | 1·25 | 75 |
| 945 | 55c. Seedling, cornfield and child | 2·00 | 2·00 |

**1992.** 500th Anniv of Discovery of America by Columbus (6th issue). Sheet 65×65 mm, containing vert design as T **173**. Multicoloured.

| | | | |
|---|---|---|---|
| **MS**946 | $2 Columbus landing in Bahamas | 7·50 | 8·00 |

**194** Mary visiting Elizabeth

**1992.** Christmas. Multicoloured.

| | | | |
|---|---|---|---|
| 947 | 15c. Type **194** | 40 | 20 |
| 948 | 55c. The Nativity | 1·10 | 1·00 |
| 949 | 60c. Angel and shepherds | 1·25 | 1·50 |
| 950 | 70c. Wise Men and star | 1·40 | 2·50 |
| **MS**951 | 95×110 mm. Nos. 947/50 | 6·50 | 7·50 |

**1992.** Hurricane Relief. No. **MS**876 showing each stamp surch **HURRICANE RELIEF+$1**.

| | | | |
|---|---|---|---|
| **MS**952 | $1+$1 Type **183**; $1+$1 Hawker Hurricane Mk IIc "Bahamas V" | 12·00 | 15·00 |

**196** Flags of Bahamas and U.S.A. with Agricultural Worker

**1993.** 50th Anniv of The Contract (U.S.A.–Bahamas farm labour programme). Each including national flags. Multicoloured.

| | | | |
|---|---|---|---|
| 953 | 15c. Type **196** | 1·75 | 70 |
| 954 | 55c. Onions | 2·25 | 1·50 |
| 955 | 60c. Citrus fruit | 2·50 | 2·50 |
| 956 | 70c. Apples | 2·75 | 3·25 |

**1993.** 75th Anniv of Royal Air Force. As T **149** of Ascension. Multicoloured.

| | | | |
|---|---|---|---|
| 957 | 15c. Westland Wapiti IIA | 1·75 | 85 |
| 958 | 40c. Gloster Gladiator I | 2·25 | 1·00 |
| 959 | 55c. de Havilland Vampire F.3 | 2·50 | 1·75 |
| 960 | 70c. English Electric Lightning F.3 | 3·00 | 5·00 |
| **MS**961 | 110×77 mm. 60c. Avro Shackleton M.R.2; 60c. Fairey Battle; 60c. Douglas Boston III; 60c. De Havilland D.H.9a | 8·75 | 7·75 |

**197** 1978 Coronation Anniversary Stamps

**1993.** 40th Anniv of Coronation. Multicoloured.

| | | | |
|---|---|---|---|
| 962 | 15c. Type **197** | 70 | 50 |
| 963 | 55c. Two examples of 1953 Coronation stamp | 1·75 | 1·75 |
| 964 | 60c. 1977 Silver Jubilee 8c. and 16c. stamps | 1·75 | 2·00 |
| 965 | 70c. 1977 Silver Jubilee 21c. and 40c. stamps | 2·00 | 2·75 |

**198** "Lignum vitae" (national tree)

**1993.** 20th Anniv of Independence. Mult.

| | | | |
|---|---|---|---|
| 966 | 15c. Type **198** | 30 | 20 |
| 967 | 55c. Yellow elder (national flower) | 90 | 90 |
| 968 | 60c. Blue marlin (national fish) | 1·25 | 1·25 |
| 969 | 70c. Greater flamingo (national bird) | 2·00 | 3·00 |

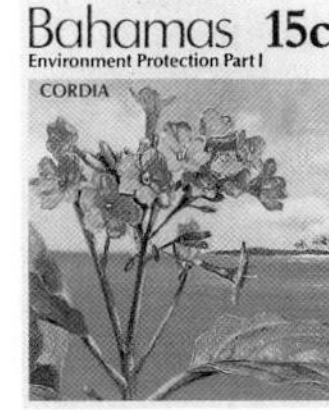


**199** Cordia

**1993.** Environment Protection (1st series). Wild-flowers. Multicoloured.

| | | | |
|---|---|---|---|
| 970 | 15c. Type **199** | 1·50 | 50 |
| 971 | 55c. Seaside morning glory | 3·00 | 1·25 |
| 972 | 60c. Poinciana | 3·25 | 2·25 |
| 973 | 70c. Spider lily | 3·75 | 4·50 |

See also Nos. 1017/21, 1035/8, 1084/7, 1121/4, 1149/53 and 1193/6.

**200** The Annunciation

**1993.** Christmas. Multicoloured.

| | | | |
|---|---|---|---|
| 990 | 15c. Type **200** | 75 | 50 |
| 991 | 55c. Angel and shepherds | 2·25 | 1·75 |
| 992 | 60c. Holy Family | 2·25 | 2·00 |
| 993 | 70c. Three Kings | 2·75 | 3·75 |
| **MS**994 | 86×106 mm. $1 Virgin Mary and Child | 5·50 | 7·50 |

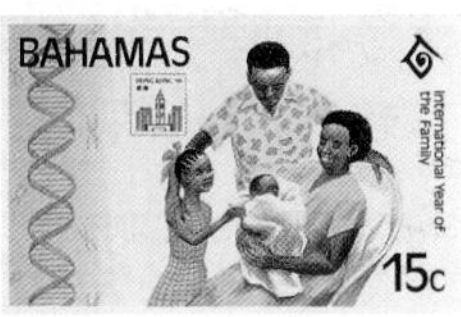


**201** Family

**1994.** "Hong Kong '94" International Stamp Exhibition. International Year of the Family. Multicoloured.

| | | | |
|---|---|---|---|
| 995 | 15c. Type **201** | 1·50 | 40 |
| 996 | 55c. Children doing homework | 2·50 | 1·25 |
| 997 | 60c. Grandfather and grandson fishing | 2·75 | 1·75 |
| 998 | 70c. Grandmother teaching grandchildren the Lord's Prayer | 3·25 | 5·00 |

**202** Flags of Bahamas and Great Britain

**1994.** Royal Visit. Multicoloured.

| | | | |
|---|---|---|---|
| 999 | 15c. Type **202** | 1·25 | 50 |
| 1000 | 55c. Royal Yacht "Britannia" | 2·50 | 1·75 |
| 1001 | 60c. Queen Elizabeth II | 2·50 | 1·75 |
| 1002 | 70c. Queen Elizabeth and Prince Philip | 2·50 | 4·50 |

**203** Yachts

**1994.** 40th Anniv of National Family Island Regatta. Multicoloured.

| | | | |
|---|---|---|---|
| 1003 | 15c. Type **203** | 80 | 40 |
| 1004 | 55c. Dinghies racing | 1·75 | 1·25 |
| 1005 | 60c. Working boats | 1·75 | 1·75 |
| 1006 | 70c. Sailing sloop | 2·25 | 4·00 |
| **MS**1007 | 76×54 mm. $2 Launching sloop (vert) | 8·00 | 9·00 |

**204** Logo and Bahamas 1968 Olympic Games Stamp

**1994.** Centenary of International Olympic Committee. Multicoloured.

| | | | |
|---|---|---|---|
| 1008 | 15c. Type **204** | 1·75 | 50 |
| 1009 | 55c. 1976 Olympic Games stamps (vert) | 2·75 | 1·25 |
| 1010 | 60c. 1984 Olympic Games stamps | 2·75 | 2·25 |
| 1011 | 70c. 1992 Olympic Games stamps (vert) | 3·00 | 4·50 |

**205** Star of Order

**1994.** First Recipients of Order of the Caribbean Community. Sheet 90×69 mm.

| | | | | |
|---|---|---|---|---|
| **MS**1012 | **205** | $2 multicoloured | 5·50 | 6·50 |

**206** "Calpodes ethlius" and Canna

**1994.** Butterflies and Flowers. Multicoloured.

| | | | |
|---|---|---|---|
| 1013 | 15c. Type **206** | 1·10 | 55 |
| 1014 | 55c. "Phoebis sennae" and cassia | 2·00 | 1·50 |
| 1015 | 60c. "Anartia jatrophae" and passion flower | 2·25 | 2·25 |
| 1016 | 70c. "Battus devilliersi" and calico flower | 2·25 | 3·00 |

**207** Spot-finned Hogfish and Spanish Hogfish

**1994.** Environment Protection (2nd series). Marine Life. Multicoloured.

| | | | |
|---|---|---|---|
| 1017 | 40c. Type **207** | 1·00 | 1·25 |
| 1018 | 40c. Tomate and long-spined squirrelfish | 1·00 | 1·25 |
| 1019 | 40c. French angelfish | 1·00 | 1·25 |
| 1020 | 40c. Queen angelfish | 1·00 | 1·25 |
| 1021 | 40c. Rock beauty | 1·00 | 1·25 |
| **MS**1022 | 57×55 mm. $2 Rock beauty, Queen angelfish and windsurfer | 6·00 | 7·00 |

Nos. 1017/21 were printed together, se-tenant, with the backgrounds forming a composite design.

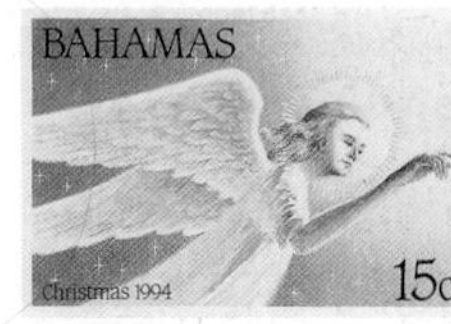


**208** Angel

**1994.** Christmas. Multicoloured.

| | | | |
|---|---|---|---|
| 1023 | 15c. Type **208** | 30 | 30 |
| 1024 | 55c. Holy Family | 90 | 1·10 |
| 1025 | 60c. Shepherds | 1·10 | 1·40 |
| 1026 | 70c. Wise Men | 1·25 | 2·50 |
| **MS**1027 | 73×85 mm. Jesus in manger | 3·50 | 5·00 |

**209** Lion and Emblem

**1995.** 20th Anniv of the College of the Bahamas. Multicoloured.

| | | | |
|---|---|---|---|
| 1028 | 15c. Type **209** | 30 | 30 |
| 1029 | 70c. Queen Elizabeth II and College building | 1·25 | 1·75 |

**1995.** 50th Anniv of End of Second World War. As T **161** of Ascension. Multicoloured.

| | | | |
|---|---|---|---|
| 1030 | 15c. Bahamian infantry drilling | 75 | 50 |
| 1031 | 55c. Consolidated PBY-5A Catalina flying boat | 2·00 | 1·25 |
| 1032 | 60c. Bahamian women in naval operations room | 2·00 | 2·25 |
| 1033 | 70c. Consolidated B-24 Liberator bomber | 2·50 | 3·75 |
| **MS**1034 | 75×85 mm. $2 Reverse of 1939–45 War Medal (vert) | 3·00 | 4·00 |

**210** Kirtlands Warbler on Nest

**1995.** Environment Protection (3rd series). Endangered Species. Kirtland's Warbler. Mult.

| | | | |
|---|---|---|---|
| 1035 | 15c. Type **210** | 55 | 75 |
| 1036 | 15c. Singing on branch | 55 | 75 |
| 1037 | 25c. Feeding chicks | 55 | 75 |
| 1038 | 25c. Catching insects | 55 | 75 |
| **MS**1039 | 73×67 mm. $2 On branch | 7·50 | 8·50 |

No. **MS**1039 does not show the W.W.F. Panda emblem.

**211** Eleuthera Cliffs

**1995.** Tourism. Multicoloured.

| | | | |
|---|---|---|---|
| 1040 | 15c. Type **211** | 1·50 | 50 |
| 1041 | 55c. Clarence Town, Long Island | 2·50 | 1·25 |
| 1042 | 60c. Albert Lowe Museum | 2·75 | 2·50 |
| 1043 | 70c. Yachts | 3·00 | 5·00 |

**212** Pigs and Chick

**1995.** 50th Anniv of F.A.O. Multicoloured.

| | | | |
|---|---|---|---|
| 1044 | 15c. Type **212** | 1·50 | 50 |
| 1045 | 55c. Seedling and hand holding seed | 2·00 | 1·10 |
| 1046 | 60c. Family with fruit and vegetables | 2·50 | 2·25 |
| 1047 | 70c. Fishes and crustaceans | 3·50 | 4·50 |

**213** Sikorsky S-55 Helicopter, Sinai, 1957

**1995.** 50th Anniv of United Nations. Multicoloured.

| | | | |
|---|---|---|---|
| 1048 | 15c. Type **213** | 70 | 50 |
| 1049 | 55c. Ferret armoured car, Sinai, 1957 | 1·25 | 1·25 |
| 1050 | 60c. Fokker F.27 Friendship (airliner), Cambodia, 1991–93 | 1·50 | 2·00 |
| 1051 | 70c. Lockheed C-130 Hercules (transport) | 1·60 | 2·75 |

**214** St. Agnes Anglican Church

**1995.** Christmas. Churches. Multicoloured.

| | | | |
|---|---|---|---|
| 1052 | 15c. Type **214** | 30 | 25 |
| 1053 | 55c. Church of God, East Street | 90 | 90 |
| 1054 | 60c. Sacred Heart Roman Catholic Church | 95 | 1·25 |
| 1055 | 70c. Salem Union Baptist Church | 1·10 | 1·75 |

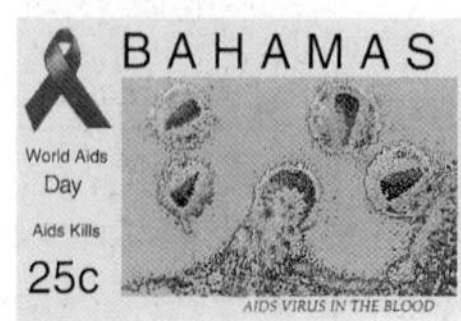

**215** Microscopic View of AIDS Virus

**1995.** World AIDS Day. Multicoloured.

| | | | |
|---|---|---|---|
| 1056 | 25c. Type **215** | 60 | 50 |
| 1057 | 70c. Research into AIDS | 1·00 | 1·50 |

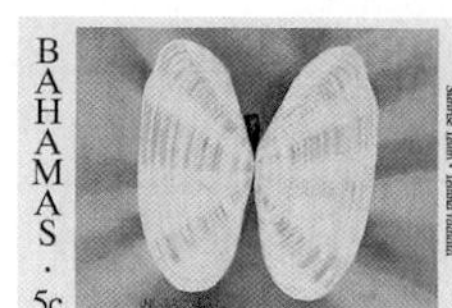

**216** Sunrise Tellin

**1996.** Sea Shells. Multicoloured.

| | | | |
|---|---|---|---|
| 1058 | 5c. Type **216** | 40 | 1·00 |
| 1059 | 10c. Queen conch | 45 | 1·00 |
| 1060 | 15c. Angular triton | 65 | 40 |
| 1061 | 20c. True tulip | 80 | 60 |
| 1062 | 25c. Reticulated cowrie-helmet | 80 | 60 |
| 1063 | 30c. Sand dollar | 1·00 | 60 |
| 1063a | 35c. As 30c. | 1·50 | 55 |
| 1064 | 40c. Lace short-frond murex | 1·25 | 60 |
| 1065 | 45c. Inflated sea biscuit | 1·50 | 60 |
| 1066 | 50c. West Indian top shell | 1·50 | 70 |
| 1067 | 55c. Spiny oyster | 1·50 | 75 |
| 1068 | 60c. King helmet | 1·50 | 80 |
| 1068a | 65c. As 45c. | 2·50 | 1·25 |
| 1069 | 70c. Lion's paw | 1·60 | 1·00 |
| 1069a | 80c. As 55c. | 2·50 | 1·50 |
| 1070 | $1 Crown cone | 2·50 | 1·75 |
| 1071 | $2 Atlantic partridge tun | 3·75 | 4·00 |
| 1072 | $5 Wide-mouthed purpura | 8·00 | 9·50 |
| 1073 | $10 Atlantic trumpet triton | 22·00 | 22·00 |

**217** East Goodwin Lightship with Marconi Apparatus on Mast

**1996.** Centenary of Radio. Multicoloured.

| | | | |
|---|---|---|---|
| 1074 | 15c. Type **217** | 1·75 | 80 |
| 1075 | 55c. Newspaper headline concerning Dr. Crippen | 2·50 | 1·25 |
| 1076 | 60c. "Philadelphia" (liner) and first readable transatlantic message | 2·50 | 2·00 |
| 1077 | 70c. Guglielmo Marconi and "Elettra" (yacht) | 2·75 | 3·50 |
| **MS**1078 | 80×47 mm. $2 "Titanic" and "Carpathia" (liners) | 8·50 | 8·50 |

**218** Swimming

**1996.** Centenary of Modern Olympic Games. Multicoloured.

| | | | |
|---|---|---|---|
| 1079 | 15c. Type **218** | 40 | 35 |
| 1080 | 55c. Running | 90 | 90 |
| 1081 | 60c. Basketball | 2·00 | 1·75 |
| 1082 | 70c. Long jumping | 1·40 | 2·50 |
| **MS**1083 | 73×86 mm. $2 Javelin throwing | 3·00 | 4·00 |

**219** Green Anole

**1996.** Environment Protection (4th series). Reptiles. Multicoloured.

| | | | |
|---|---|---|---|
| 1084 | 15c. Type **219** | 55 | 50 |
| 1085 | 55c. Little Bahama bank boa | 1·10 | 1·00 |
| 1086 | 60c. Inagua freshwater turtle | 1·50 | 1·75 |
| 1087 | 70c. Acklins rock iguana | 1·75 | 2·75 |
| **MS**1088 | 85×105 mm. Nos. 1084/7 | 5·00 | 6·00 |

**220** The Annunciation

**1996.** Christmas. Multicoloured.

| | | | |
|---|---|---|---|
| 1089 | 15c. Type **220** | 1·25 | 40 |
| 1090 | 55c. Joseph and Mary travelling to Bethlehem | 2·50 | 1·00 |
| 1091 | 60c. Shepherds and angel | 2·50 | 1·50 |
| 1092 | 70c. Adoration of the Magi | 2·75 | 4·00 |
| **MS**1093 | 70×87 mm. $2 Presentation in the Temple | 3·25 | 4·00 |

**221** Department of Archives Building

**1996.** 25th Anniv of Archives Department.

| | | | |
|---|---|---|---|
| 1094 | **221** 55c. multicoloured | 1·50 | 1·00 |
| **MS**1095 | 83×54 mm. $2 multicoloured | 4·75 | 6·50 |

**1997.** "HONG KONG '97" International Stamp Exhibition. Sheet 130×90 mm, containing design as No. 1070, but with "1997" imprint date. Multicoloured.

| | | | |
|---|---|---|---|
| **MS**1096 | $1 Crown cone | 3·00 | 3·50 |

**1997.** Return of Hong Kong to China. Sheet 130×90 mm, containing design as No. 1069, but with "1997" imprint date.

| | | | |
|---|---|---|---|
| **MS**1097 | 70c. Lion's paw | 2·00 | 2·50 |

**1997.** Golden Wedding of Queen Elizabeth and Prince Philip. As T **173** of Ascension. Multicoloured.

| | | | |
|---|---|---|---|
| 1114 | 50c. Queen Elizabeth II in Bonn, 1992 | 2·00 | 2·25 |
| 1115 | 50c. Prince Philip and Prince Charles at Trooping the Colour | 2·00 | 2·25 |
| 1116 | 60c. Prince Philip | 2·00 | 2·25 |
| 1117 | 60c. Queen at Trooping the Colour | 2·00 | 2·25 |
| 1118 | 70c. Queen Elizabeth and Prince Philip at polo, 1970 | 2·00 | 2·25 |
| 1119 | 70c. Prince Charles playing polo | 2·00 | 2·25 |
| **MS**1120 | 110×70 mm. $2 Queen Elizabeth and Prince Philip in landau (horiz) | 6·50 | 7·00 |

**222** Underwater Scene

**1997.** Environment Protection (5th series). International Year of the Reefs.

| | | | |
|---|---|---|---|
| 1121 | **222** 15c. multicoloured | 1·25 | 60 |
| 1122 | - 55c. multicoloured | 2·25 | 1·00 |
| 1123 | - 60c. multicoloured | 2·25 | 1·75 |
| 1124 | - 70c. multicoloured | 2·50 | 3·00 |

DESIGNS: 55c. to 70c. Different children's paintings of underwater scenes.

**223** Angel

**1997.** Christmas. Multicoloured.

| | | | |
|---|---|---|---|
| 1125 | 15c. Type **223** | 1·50 | 40 |
| 1126 | 55c. Mary and Baby Jesus | 2·25 | 80 |
| 1127 | 60c. Shepherd | 2·25 | 1·25 |
| 1128 | 70c. King | 2·75 | 3·75 |
| **MS**1129 | 74×94 mm. $2 Baby Jesus wrapped in swaddling-bands. | 8·00 | 8·50 |

**223a** Wearing Grey Jacket, 1988

**1998.** Diana, Princess of Wales Commemoration.

| | | | |
|---|---|---|---|
| 1130 | **223a** 15c. multicoloured | 50 | 50 |
| **MS**1131 | 145×70 mm. 15c. As No. 1130; 55c. Wearing striped jacket, 1983; 60c. In evening dress, 1983; 70c. Meeting crowds, 1993 | 2·50 | 2·75 |

**1998.** 80th Anniv of the Royal Air Force. As T **178** of Ascension. Multicoloured.

| | | | |
|---|---|---|---|
| 1132 | 15c. Handley Page Hyderabad | 55 | 40 |
| 1133 | 55c. Hawker Demon | 1·00 | 85 |
| 1134 | 60c. Gloster Meteor F8 | 1·10 | 1·25 |
| 1135 | 70c. Lockheed P2 Neptune | 1·40 | 2·25 |
| **MS**1136 | 110×76 mm. 50c. Sopwith Camel; 50c. Short 184 (seaplane); 50c. Supermarine Spitfire PR.19; 50c. North American Mitchell III | 4·00 | 4·25 |

**224** Newsletters

**1998.** 50th Anniv of Organization of American States. Multicoloured.

| | | | |
|---|---|---|---|
| 1137 | 15c. Type **224** | 30 | 30 |
| 1138 | 55c. Headquarters building and flags, Washington | 70 | 80 |

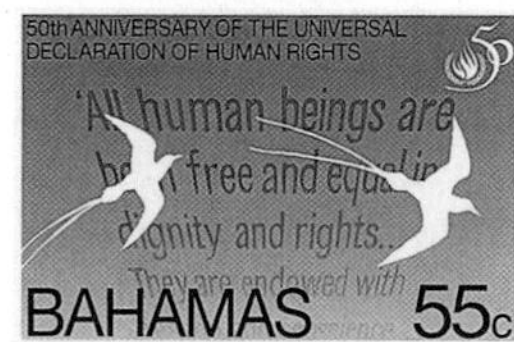

**225** Start of Declaration and Birds

**1998.** 50th Anniv of Universal Declaration of Human Rights.

| | | | |
|---|---|---|---|
| 1139 | **225** 55c. blue and black | 1·75 | 1·00 |

**226** University Arms and Graduates

**1998.** 50th Anniv of University of the West Indies.

| | | | |
|---|---|---|---|
| 1140 | **226** 55c. multicoloured | 1·50 | 1·00 |

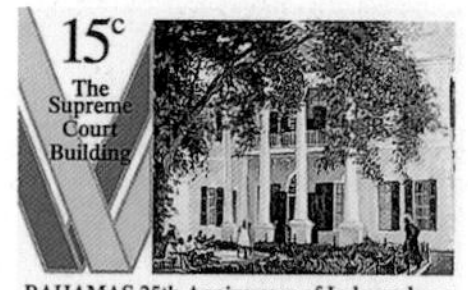

**227** Supreme Court Building

**1998.** 25th Anniv of Independence. Multicoloured.

| | | | |
|---|---|---|---|
| 1141 | 15c. Type **227** | 1·00 | 50 |
| 1142 | 55c. Nassau Library | 1·75 | 1·00 |
| 1143 | 60c. Government House | 1·90 | 1·50 |
| 1144 | 70c. Gregory Arch | 2·00 | 3·00 |
| **MS**1145 | 70×55 mm. $2 Island Regatta, George Town | 3·50 | 5·00 |

**228** "Disney Magic" (cruise liner) at Night

**1998.** Disney Cruise Line's Castaway Cay Holiday Development. Multicoloured.

| | | | |
|---|---|---|---|
| 1146 | 55c. Type **228** | 2·00 | 2·00 |
| 1147 | 55c. "Disney Magic" by day | 2·00 | 2·00 |

**229** "Ryndam" (cruise liner)

**1998.** Holland America Line's Half Moon Cay Holiday Development.

| | | | | |
|---|---|---|---|---|
| 1148 | **229** | 55c. multicoloured | 2·75 | 1·25 |

**230** Barrel Pink Rose

**1998.** Environment Protection (6th series). Roses. Multicoloured.

| | | | |
|---|---|---|---|
| 1149 | 55c. Type **230** | 1·50 | 1·60 |
| 1150 | 55c. Yellow cream | 1·50 | 1·60 |
| 1151 | 55c. Seven sisters | 1·50 | 1·60 |
| 1152 | 55c. Big red | 1·50 | 1·60 |
| 1153 | 55c. Island beauty | 1·50 | 1·60 |
| **MS**1154 | 100×70 mm. No. 1153 | 1·50 | 1·75 |

**231** The Annunciation

**1998.** Christmas. Multicoloured.

| | | | |
|---|---|---|---|
| 1155 | 15c. Type **231** | 50 | 30 |
| 1156 | 55c. Shepherds | 1·00 | 70 |
| 1157 | 60c. Three Kings | 1·25 | 1·10 |
| 1158 | 70c. The Flight into Egypt | 1·50 | 2·75 |
| **MS**1159 | 87×67 mm. The Nativity | 3·00 | 4·00 |

**232** Killer Whale and other Marine Life

**1998.** International Year of the Ocean. Multicoloured.

| | | | |
|---|---|---|---|
| 1160 | 15c. Type **232** | 65 | 50 |
| 1161 | 55c. Tropical fish | 85 | 90 |

**233** Timothy Gibson (composer)

**1998.** 25th Anniv of "March on Bahamaland" (national anthem).

| | | | | |
|---|---|---|---|---|
| 1162 | **233** | 60c. multicoloured | 1·00 | 1·25 |

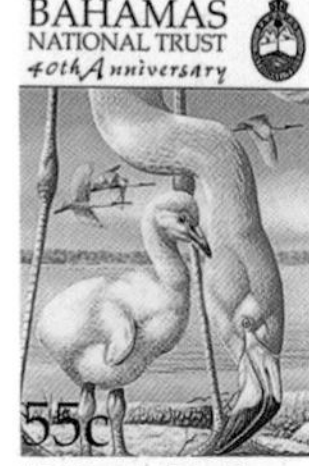

**234** Head of Greater Flamingo and Chick

**1999.** 40th Anniv of National Trust (1st issue). Inagua National Park. Multicoloured.

| | | | |
|---|---|---|---|
| 1163 | 55c. Type **234** | 1·50 | 1·60 |
| 1164 | 55c. Pair with two chicks | 1·50 | 1·60 |
| 1165 | 55c. Greater flamingos asleep or stretching wings | 1·50 | 1·60 |
| 1166 | 55c. Greater flamingos feeding | 1·50 | 1·60 |
| 1167 | 55c. Greater flamingos in flight | 1·50 | 1·60 |

Nos. 1163/7 were printed together, se-tenant, with the backgrounds forming a composite design.

See also Nos. 1173/7, 1198/1202 and 1207/11.

**235** Arawak Indian Canoe

**1999.** "Australia '99" World Stamp Exhibition, Melbourne. Maritime History. Multicoloured.

| | | | |
|---|---|---|---|
| 1168 | 15c. Type **235** | 55 | 30 |
| 1169 | 55c. "Santa Maria" (Columbus), 1492 | 1·75 | 1·10 |
| 1170 | 60c. "Queen Anne's Revenge" (Blackbeard), 1716 | 1·90 | 1·60 |
| 1171 | 70c. "The Banshee" (Confederate paddle-steamer) running blockade | 2·00 | 3·25 |
| **MS**1172 | 110×66 mm. $2 Firing on American ships, 1776 | 5·50 | 5·50 |

**1999.** 40th Anniv of National Trust (2nd issue). Exuma Cays Land and Sea Park. As T **234**. Mult.

| | | | |
|---|---|---|---|
| 1173 | 55c. Dolphin | 1·50 | 1·75 |
| 1174 | 55c. Angelfish and parrotfish | 1·50 | 1·75 |
| 1175 | 55c. Queen triggerfish | 1·50 | 1·75 |
| 1176 | 55c. Turtle | 1·50 | 1·75 |
| 1177 | 55c. Lobster | 1·50 | 1·75 |

Nos. 1173/7 were printed together, se-tenant, with the backgrounds forming a composite design.

**236** Society Headquarters Building

**1999.** 40th Anniv of Bahamas Historical Society.

| | | | | |
|---|---|---|---|---|
| 1178 | **236** | $1 multicoloured | 1·50 | 2·25 |

**1999.** 30th Anniv of First Manned Landing on Moon. As T **186** of Ascension. Multicoloured.

| | | | |
|---|---|---|---|
| 1179 | 15c. Constructing ascent module | 45 | 40 |
| 1180 | 65c. Diagram of command and service module | 1·25 | 1·25 |
| 1181 | 70c. Lunar module descending | 1·25 | 1·75 |
| 1182 | 80c. Lunar module preparing to dock with service module | 1·25 | 2·50 |
| **MS**1183 | 90×80 mm. $2 Earth as seen from Moon (circular, 40 mm diam) | 3·25 | 4·25 |

**1999.** "Queen Elizabeth the Queen Mother's Century". As T **187** of Ascension. Multicoloured.

| | | | |
|---|---|---|---|
| 1184 | 15c. Visiting Herts Hospital, 1940 | 60 | 35 |
| 1185 | 65c. With Princess Elizabeth, Hyde Park, 1944 | 1·50 | 1·00 |
| 1186 | 70c. With Prince Andrew, 1997 | 1·50 | 1·50 |
| 1187 | 80c. With Irish Guards' mascot, 1997 | 1·50 | 1·75 |
| **MS**1188 | 145×70 mm. $2 Lady Elizabeth Bowes-Lyon with her brother David, 1904, and England World Cup team celebrating, 1966. | 4·50 | 5·00 |

**237** "Delaware" (American mail ship), 1880

**1999.** 125th Anniv of U.P.U. Ships. Multicoloured.

| | | | |
|---|---|---|---|
| 1189 | 15c. Type **237** | 1·50 | 50 |
| 1190 | 65c. "Atlantis" (liner), 1923 | 2·50 | 1·25 |
| 1191 | 70c. "Queen of Bermuda 2" (liner), 1937 | 2·50 | 2·25 |
| 1192 | 80c. U.S.S. "Saufley (destroyer), 1943 | 3·00 | 3·25 |

**238** "Turtle Pond" (Green Turtle)

**1999.** Environment Protection (7th series). Marine Life Paintings by Ricardo Knowles. Multicoloured.

| | | | |
|---|---|---|---|
| 1193 | 15c. Type **238** | 50 | 35 |
| 1194 | 65c. "Turtle Cliff" (Loggerhead turtle) | 1·25 | 1·00 |
| 1195 | 70c. "Barracuda" | 1·40 | 1·40 |
| 1196 | 80c. "Coral Reef" | 1·50 | 2·25 |
| **MS**1197 | 90×75 mm. $2 "Atlantic Bottle-nosed Dolphins" | 3·25 | 4·50 |

The 65c. is inscribed "GREEN TURTLES" in error.

**1999.** 40th Anniv of National Trust (3rd issue). Birds. As T **234**. Multicoloured.

| | | | |
|---|---|---|---|
| 1198 | 65c. Bridled tern and white-tailed tropic bird | 1·75 | 1·75 |
| 1199 | 65c. Louisiana heron | 1·75 | 1·75 |
| 1200 | 65c. Bahama woodstar | 1·75 | 1·75 |
| 1201 | 65c. Black-billed whistling duck | 1·75 | 1·75 |
| 1202 | 65c. Cuban amazon | 1·75 | 1·75 |

Nos. 1198/1202 were printed together, se-tenant, with the backgrounds forming a composite design.

**239** Man on Elephant Float

**1999.** Christmas. Junkanoo Festival. Multicoloured.

| | | | |
|---|---|---|---|
| 1203 | 15c. Type **239** | 50 | 30 |
| 1204 | 65c. Man in winged costume | 1·00 | 1·00 |
| 1205 | 70c. Man in feathered mask | 1·25 | 1·25 |
| 1206 | 80c. Man blowing conch shell | 1·50 | 2·00 |

**1999.** 40th Anniv of National Trust (4th issue). Flora and Fauna. As T **234**. Multicoloured.

| | | | |
|---|---|---|---|
| 1207 | 65c. Foxglove | 2·25 | 2·25 |
| 1208 | 65c. Vole | 2·25 | 2·25 |
| 1209 | 65c. Cuban amazon | 2·25 | 2·25 |
| 1210 | 65c. Lizard | 2·25 | 2·25 |
| 1211 | 65c. Red hibiscus | 2·25 | 2·25 |

Nos. 1207/11 were printed together, se-tenant, with the backgrounds forming a composite design.

**240** New Plymouth

**2000.** Historic Fishing Villages. Multicoloured.

| | | | |
|---|---|---|---|
| 1212 | 15c. Type **240** | 1·25 | 40 |
| 1213 | 65c. Cherokee Sound | 2·25 | 1·00 |
| 1214 | 70c. Hope Town | 2·50 | 2·00 |
| 1215 | 80c. Spanish Wells | 2·75 | 3·25 |

**241** Gold Medal Winning Bahamas Women's Relay Team

**2000.** "The Golden Girls" winners of 4×100 metre Relay at I.A.A.F. World Track and Field Championship '99, Spain. Sheet 100×55 mm.

| | | | | |
|---|---|---|---|---|
| **MS**1216 | **241** | $2 multicoloured | 3·00 | 3·50 |

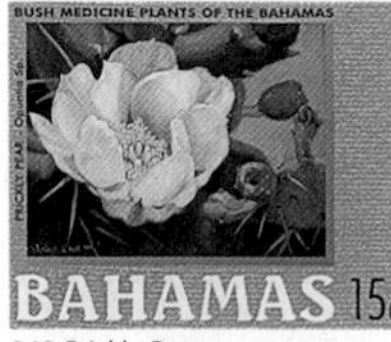

**242** Prickly Pear

**2000.** Medicinal Plants (1st series). Multicoloured.

| | | | |
|---|---|---|---|
| 1217 | 15c. Type **242** | 35 | 30 |
| 1218 | 65c. Buttercup | 1·25 | 1·25 |
| 1219 | 70c. Shepherd's needle | 1·25 | 1·50 |
| 1220 | 80c. Five fingers | 1·40 | 2·25 |

See also Nos. 1282/5 and 1324/7.

**243** Re-arming and Re-fuelling Supermarine Spitfire

**2000.** "The Stamp Show 2000" International Stamp Exhibition, London. 60th Anniv of Battle of Britain. Multicoloured.

| | | | |
|---|---|---|---|
| 1221 | 15c. Type **243** | 70 | 45 |
| 1222 | 65c. Sqdn. Ldr. Stanford-Tuck's Hurricane Mk I | 1·40 | 1·40 |
| 1223 | 70c. Dogfight between Spitfires and Heinkel IIIs | 1·60 | 1·75 |
| 1224 | 80c. Flight of Supermarine Spitfires attacking | 1·60 | 2·25 |
| **MS**1225 | 90×70 mm. $2 Presentation Spitfire Bahamas | 3·50 | 4·00 |

**244** Teachers' and Salaried Workers' Co-operative Credit Union Building

**2000.** Co-operatives Movement in Bahamas. Sheet 90×50 mm.

| | | | |
|---|---|---|---|
| **MS**1226 | $2 multicoloured | 3·50 | 4·00 |

**245** Swimming

**2000.** Olympic Games, Sydney. Each inscribed with details of previous Bahamian participation. Mult.

| | | | |
|---|---|---|---|
| 1227 | 15c. Type **245** | 50 | 30 |
| 1228 | 65c. Triple jump | 1·40 | 1·25 |
| 1229 | 70c. Women's 4×100 m relay | 1·40 | 1·40 |
| 1230 | 80c. Sailing | 1·50 | 2·25 |

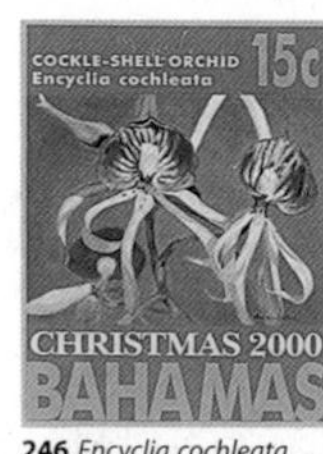

**246** *Encyclia cochleata*

**2000.** Christmas. Orchids. Multicoloured.

| | | | |
|---|---|---|---|
| 1231 | 15c. Type **246** | 70 | 30 |
| 1232 | 65c. *Encyclia plicata* | 1·60 | 1·25 |
| 1233 | 70c. *Bletia purpurea* | 1·75 | 1·60 |
| 1234 | 80c. *Encyclia gracilis* | 1·90 | 2·25 |

**247** Cuban Amazon and Primary School Class

**2000.** Bahamas Humane Society. Multicoloured.

| | | | |
|---|---|---|---|
| 1235 | 15c. Type **247** | 1·50 | 50 |
| 1236 | 65c. Cat and Society stall | 2·50 | 1·25 |
| 1237 | 70c. Dogs and veterinary surgery | 3·00 | 2·50 |
| 1238 | 80c. Goat and animal rescue van | 3·00 | 3·25 |

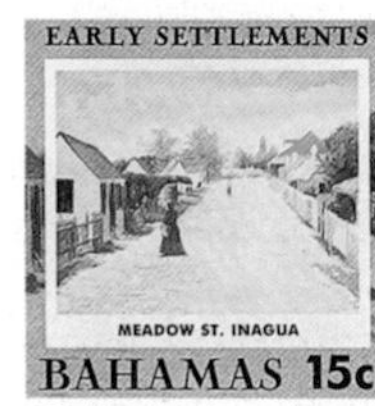

**248** "Meadow Street, Inagua"

**2001.** Early Settlements. Paintings by Ricardo Knowles. Multicoloured.

| | | | |
|---|---|---|---|
| 1239 | 15c. Type **248** | 40 | 30 |
| 1240 | 65c. "Bain Town" | 1·25 | 1·00 |
| 1241 | 70c. "Hope Town, Abaco" | 1·40 | 1·40 |
| 1242 | 80c. "Blue Hills" | 1·50 | 2·25 |

**249** Lynden Pindling presenting Independence Constitution, 1972

**2001.** Sir Lynden Pindling (former Prime Minister) Commemoration. Multicoloured.

| | | | |
|---|---|---|---|
| 1243 | 15c. Type **249** | 50 | 40 |
| 1244 | 65c. Sir Lynden Pindling with Bahamas flag | 1·40 | 1·50 |

**250** "Cocoaplum"

**2001.** Edible Wild Fruits. Paintings by Alton Roland Lowe. Multicoloured.

| | | | |
|---|---|---|---|
| 1245 | 15c. Type **250** | 35 | 25 |
| 1246 | 65c. "Guana Berry" | 1·25 | 1·10 |
| 1247 | 70c. "Mastic" | 1·25 | 1·25 |
| 1248 | 80c. "Seagrape" | 1·50 | 2·25 |

**251** Reddish Egret

**2001.** Birds and their Eggs. Multicoloured.

| | | | |
|---|---|---|---|
| 1249 | 5c. Type **251** | 60 | 1·25 |
| 1250 | 10c. American purple gallinule | 60 | 1·25 |
| 1251 | 15c. Antillean nighthawk | 70 | 40 |
| 1252 | 20c. Wilson's plover | 80 | 70 |
| 1253 | 25c. Killdeer plover | 80 | 70 |
| 1254 | 30c. Bahama woodstar | 85 | 70 |
| 1255 | 40c. Bahama swallow | 90 | 80 |
| 1256 | 50c. Bahama mockingbird | 1·25 | 80 |
| 1257 | 60c. Black-cowled oriole | 1·50 | 1·25 |
| 1258 | 65c. Great lizard cuckoo | 1·50 | 1·00 |
| 1259 | 70c. Audubon's shearwater | 1·75 | 1·25 |
| 1260 | 80c. Grey kingbird | 1·75 | 1·25 |
| 1261 | $1 Bananaquit | 2·50 | 2·50 |
| 1262 | $2 Yellow warbler | 4·50 | 4·75 |
| 1263 | $5 Greater Antillean bullfinch | 10·00 | 11·00 |
| 1264 | $10 Roseate spoonbill | 18·00 | 19·00 |

**252** H.M.S. *Norfolk* (cruiser), 1933

**2001.** Royal Navy Ships connected to Bahamas. Multicoloured.

| | | | |
|---|---|---|---|
| 1265 | 15c. Type **252** | 1·00 | 40 |
| 1266 | 25c. H.M.S. *Scarborough* (sloop), 1930s | 1·25 | 65 |
| 1267 | 50c. H.M.S. *Bahamas* (frigate), 1944 | 1·75 | 1·50 |
| 1268 | 65c. H.M.S. *Battleaxe* (frigate), 1979 | 2·00 | 1·50 |
| 1269 | 70c. H.M.S. *Invincible* (aircraft carrier), 1997 | 2·00 | 2·00 |
| 1270 | 80c. H.M.S. *Norfolk* (frigate), 2000 | 2·00 | 2·75 |

**253** "Adoration of the Shepherds"

**2001.** Christmas. Paintings by Rubens. Mult.

| | | | |
|---|---|---|---|
| 1271 | 15c. Type **253** | 55 | 25 |
| 1272 | 65c. "Adoration of the Magi" (with Van Dyck) | 1·40 | 1·10 |
| 1273 | 70c. "Holy Virgin in Wreath of Flowers" (with Breughel) | 1·50 | 1·40 |
| 1274 | 80c. "Holy Virgin adored by Angels" | 1·60 | 2·00 |

**2002.** Golden Jubilee. As T **200** of Ascension.

| | | | |
|---|---|---|---|
| 1275 | 15c. black, green and gold | 45 | 25 |
| 1276 | 65c. multicoloured | 1·25 | 1·00 |
| 1277 | 70c. multicoloured | 1·40 | 1·50 |
| 1278 | 80c. multicoloured | 1·40 | 2·00 |
| **MS**1279 | 162×95 mm. Nos. 1275/8 and $2 multicoloured | 6·50 | 6·50 |

DESIGNS—HORIZ: 15c. Princess Elizabeth; 65c. Queen Elizabeth in Bonn, 1992; 70c. Queen Elizabeth with Prince Edward, 1965; 80c. Queen Elizabeth at Sandringham, 1996. VERT (38×51 mm)—$2 Queen Elizabeth after Annigoni.

**254** Avard Moncur (athlete)

**2002.** Award of BAAA Most Outstanding Male Athlete Title to Avard Moncur. Sheet 65×98 mm.

| | | | |
|---|---|---|---|
| **MS**1280 | **254** $2 multicoloured | 3·25 | 3·50 |

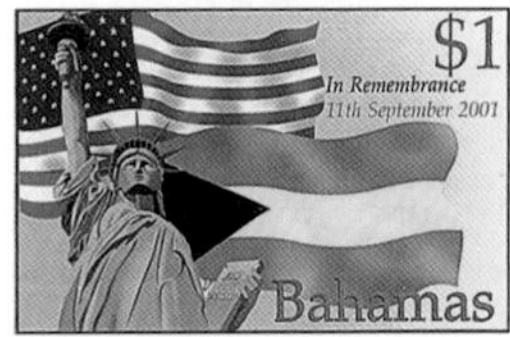

**255** Statue of Liberty with U.S. and Bahamas Flags

**2002.** In Remembrance. Victims of Terrorist Attacks on U.S.A. (11 September 2001).

| | | | |
|---|---|---|---|
| 1281 | **255** $1 multicoloured | 3·00 | 3·00 |

**2002.** Medicinal Plants (2nd series). As T **242**. Multicoloured.

| | | | |
|---|---|---|---|
| 1282 | 15c. Wild sage | 50 | 35 |
| 1283 | 65c. Seaside maho | 1·40 | 1·10 |
| 1284 | 70c. Sea ox-eye | 1·50 | 1·60 |
| 1285 | 80c. Mexican poppy | 1·50 | 2·00 |

**2002.** Queen Elizabeth the Queen Mother Commemoration. As T **202** of Ascension.

| | | | |
|---|---|---|---|
| 1286 | 15c. brown, gold and purple | 75 | 40 |
| 1287 | 65c. multicoloured | 1·75 | 1·50 |
| **MS**1288 | 145×70 mm. 70c. black and gold; 80c. multicoloured | 3·75 | 3·75 |

DESIGNS: 15c. Queen Elizabeth at American Red Cross Club, London, 1944; 65c. Queen Mother at Remembrance Service, 1989; 70c. Queen Elizabeth, 1944; 80c. Queen Mother at Cheltenham Races, 2000.

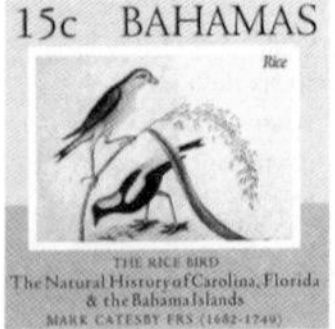

**256** Rice Bird and Rice

**2002.** Illustrations from The Natural History of Carolina, Florida and the Bahama Islands by Mark Catesby (1747). Multicoloured.

| | | | |
|---|---|---|---|
| 1289 | 15c. Type **256** | 85 | 45 |
| 1290 | 25c. Alligator and red mangrove | 1·00 | 60 |
| 1291 | 50c. Parrot fish | 1·40 | 1·10 |
| 1292 | 65c. Ilathera duck and sea ox-eye | 1·75 | 1·50 |
| 1293 | 70c. Flamingo and gorgonian coral | 1·90 | 2·00 |
| 1294 | 80c. Crested bittern and inkberry | 2·00 | 2·25 |

**257** "While Shepherds watched their Flocks"

**2002.** Christmas. Scenes from Carols. Multicoloured.

| | | | |
|---|---|---|---|
| 1295 | 15c. Type **257** | 60 | 25 |
| 1296 | 65c. "We Three Kings" | 1·40 | 1·10 |
| 1297 | 70c. "Once in Royal David's City" | 1·50 | 1·50 |
| 1298 | 80c. "I saw Three Ships" | 1·60 | 2·25 |

**258** Flamingo on Nest

**2003.** Inagua National Park Wetlands. Flamingos. Multicoloured.

| | | | |
|---|---|---|---|
| 1299 | 15c. Type **258** | 70 | 45 |
| 1300 | 25c. Flock of flamingos feeding | 95 | 65 |
| 1301 | 50c. Group of flamingos | 1·50 | 1·10 |
| 1302 | 65c. Group of flamingos walking | 1·75 | 1·50 |
| 1303 | 70c. Flamingos taking-off | 1·90 | 1·90 |
| 1304 | 80c. Flamingos in flight | 2·00 | 2·25 |

**259** Captain Edward Teach ("Blackbeard")

**2003.** Pirates. Multicoloured.

| | | | |
|---|---|---|---|
| 1305 | 15c. Type **259** | 75 | 45 |
| 1306 | 25c. Captain "Calico Jack" Rackham | 1·10 | 65 |
| 1307 | 50c. Anne Bonney | 1·75 | 1·40 |
| 1308 | 65c. Captain Woodes Rogers | 2·00 | 1·75 |
| 1309 | 70c. Sir John Hawkins | 2·25 | 2·25 |
| 1310 | 80c. Captain Bartholomew Roberts ("Black Bart") | 2·25 | 2·50 |

**260** Dinghies

**2003.** 50th Anniv of Family Island Regatta. Multicoloured.

| | | | |
|---|---|---|---|
| 1311 | 15c. Type **260** | 75 | 40 |
| 1312 | 65c. *New Courageous* (racing sloop) | 2·00 | 1·50 |
| 1313 | 70c. *New Susan Chase* (racing sloop) | 2·25 | 2·00 |
| 1314 | 80c. *Tida Wave* (racing sloop) | 2·40 | 2·75 |

**2003.** 50th Anniv of Coronation. As T **206** of Ascension. Multicoloured.

| | | | |
|---|---|---|---|
| 1315 | 65c. Queen with crown, orb and sceptre | 1·50 | 1·40 |
| 1316 | 80c. Royal family on Buckingham Palace balcony | 2·00 | 2·25 |
| **MS**1317 | 95×115 mm. 15c. As 65c.; 70c. As 80c. | 2·25 | 2·50 |

Nos. 1315/16 have red frame; stamps from **MS**1317 have no frame and country name in mauve panel.

**2003.** Medicinal Plants (3rd series). As T **242**.

| | | | |
|---|---|---|---|
| 1318 | 15c. *Asystasia* | 40 | 25 |
| 1319 | 65c. *Cassia* | 1·40 | 1·25 |
| 1320 | 70c. *Lignum vitae* | 1·50 | 1·60 |
| 1321 | 80c. Snowberry | 1·60 | 2·00 |

**2003.** Centenary of Powered Flight. As T **209** of Ascension. Multicoloured.

| | | | |
|---|---|---|---|
| 1322 | 15c. Piper Cub | 65 | 45 |
| 1323 | 25c. de Havilland Tiger Moth | 85 | 70 |
| 1324 | 50c. Lockheed SR-71A Blackbird | 1·60 | 1·50 |
| 1325 | 65c. Supermarine S6B | 1·75 | 1·60 |
| 1326 | 70c. North American P-51D Mustang "Miss America" | 1·90 | 1·90 |
| 1327 | 80c. Douglas DC-3 Dakota | 2·25 | 2·50 |

**261** Interior with Stained Glass Window

**2003.** Christmas. St. Matthew's Church, Nassau. Multicoloured.

| | | | |
|---|---|---|---|
| 1328 | 15c. Type **261** | 60 | 25 |
| 1329 | 65c. Church interior (horiz) | 1·50 | 1·10 |
| 1330 | 70c. St. Matthew's Church (horiz) | 1·75 | 1·60 |
| 1331 | 80c. Church tower | 2·00 | 2·00 |

**262** "Crawfishin"

**2003.** "Waters of Life". Paintings by Alton Lowe. Multicoloured.

| | | | |
|---|---|---|---|
| 1332 | 15c. Type **262** | 60 | 30 |
| 1333 | 65c. "Summer" | 1·50 | 1·25 |
| 1334 | 70c. "The Whelkers" | 1·75 | 1·75 |
| 1335 | 80c. "Annual Visit" | 2·00 | 2·00 |

**263** Egrets on Dead Tree

**2004.** Wetlands (2nd series). Harrold and Wilson Ponds, New Providence Island. Multicoloured.

| | | | |
|---|---|---|---|
| 1336 | 15c. Type **263** | 60 | 40 |
| 1337 | 25c. Green-backed heron and duck | 80 | 65 |
| 1338 | 50c. Birdwatchers in canoes | 1·50 | 1·40 |
| 1339 | 65c. Egret and Bahama pintail ducks | 1·75 | 1·60 |
| 1340 | 70c. Egret and Louisiana heron | 2·00 | 2·00 |
| 1341 | 80c. Birdwatchers with binoculars and telescope | 2·25 | 2·50 |

**264** Methodist Church, Cupid's Cay, Governor's Harbour

**2004.** 300th Birth Anniv of John Wesley (founder of Methodist Church) (2003). Multicoloured.

| | | | |
|---|---|---|---|
| 1342 | 15c. Type **264** | 60 | 30 |
| 1343 | 25c. Church, Grants Town, Nassau | 80 | 45 |
| 1344 | 50c. Wooden Chapel, Marsh Harbour (vert) | 1·50 | 1·40 |
| 1345 | 65c. Ebeneezer Methodist Church | 1·75 | 1·75 |
| 1346 | 70c. Trinity Methodist Church | 2·00 | 2·25 |
| 1346a | 80c. Portrait by Antonius Roberts (vert) | 2·25 | 2·50 |

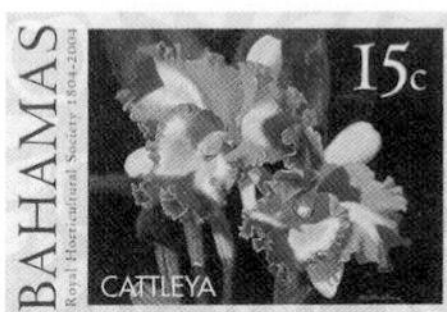

**265** Cattleya

**2004.** Bicentenary of the Royal Horticultural Society. Multicoloured.

| | | | |
|---|---|---|---|
| 1347 | 15c. Type **265** | 75 | 30 |
| 1348 | 65c. Hibiscus | 1·40 | 1·10 |
| 1349 | 70c. Canna | 1·50 | 1·60 |
| 1350 | 80c. Thunbergia | 1·60 | 2·00 |

**266** Elbow Reef Lighthouse

**2004.** Lighthouses (1st series). Multicoloured.

| | | | |
|---|---|---|---|
| 1351 | 15c. Type **266** | 1·00 | 50 |
| 1352 | 50c. Great Stirrup | 1·75 | 1·25 |
| 1353 | 65c. Great Isaac | 2·00 | 1·50 |
| 1354 | 70c. Hole in the Wall | 2·25 | 2·00 |
| 1355 | 80c. Hog Island | 2·50 | 2·50 |

See also Nos. 1396/1400.

**267** Boxing

**2004.** Olympic Games, Athens. Multicoloured.

| | | | |
|---|---|---|---|
| 1356 | 15c. Type **267** | 50 | 30 |
| 1357 | 50c. Swimming | 1·25 | 1·10 |
| 1358 | 65c. Tennis | 1·40 | 1·40 |
| 1359 | 70c. Relay racing | 1·40 | 1·75 |

**268** "Anticipation"

**2004.** Christmas. Junkanoo Festival. Multicoloured.

| | | | |
|---|---|---|---|
| 1360 | 15c. Type **268** | 40 | 20 |
| 1361 | 25c. "First Time" | 50 | 25 |
| 1362 | 50c. "On The Move" (vert) | 1·00 | 60 |
| 1363 | 65c. "I'm Ready" (vert) | 1·10 | 1·00 |
| 1364 | 70c. "Trumpet Player" (vert) | 1·25 | 1·40 |
| 1365 | 80c. "Drummer Boy" (vert) | 1·40 | 1·60 |

**269** RMS *Mauretania*

**2004.** Merchant Ships. Multicoloured.

| | | | |
|---|---|---|---|
| 1366 | 15c. Type **269** | 65 | 40 |
| 1367 | 25c. MV *Adonia* | 85 | 55 |
| 1368 | 50c. MS *Royal Princess* | 1·50 | 1·10 |
| 1369 | 65c. SS *Queen of Nassau* | 1·60 | 1·40 |
| 1370 | 70c. RMS *Transvaal Castle* | 1·75 | 1·75 |
| 1371 | 80c. SS *Norway* | 1·90 | 2·25 |

**2005.** Medicinal Plants (4th series). As T **242**. Multicoloured.

| | | | |
|---|---|---|---|
| 1372 | 15c. Aloe vera | 35 | 25 |
| 1373 | 25c. Red stopper | 45 | 35 |
| 1374 | 50c. Blue flower | 80 | 80 |
| 1375 | 65c. Bay lavender | 1·10 | 1·25 |

**270** Commando Squadron

**2005.** 25th Anniv of the Royal Bahamas Defence Force. Multicoloured.

| | | | |
|---|---|---|---|
| 1376 | 15c. Type **270** | 55 | 30 |
| 1377 | 25c. HMBS *Abaco* | 75 | 45 |
| 1378 | 50c. HMBS *Bahamas* | 1·40 | 1·10 |
| 1379 | 65c. Officers and marines in uniform | 1·60 | 1·60 |

**2005.** Bicentenary of Battle of Trafalgar. Multicoloured (except MS1386) designs as T **216** of Ascension.

| | | | |
|---|---|---|---|
| 1380 | 15c. Tower Sea Service pistols, 1801 RN Pattern (vert) | 50 | 30 |
| 1381 | 25c. Royal Marine, 1805 (vert) | 70 | 45 |
| 1382 | 50c. HMS *Boreas* off Bahamas, 1787 | 1·25 | 1·10 |
| 1383 | 65c. "Death of Nelson" (A. W. Devis) | 1·40 | 1·25 |
| 1384 | 70c. HMS *Victory* | 1·60 | 1·60 |
| 1385 | 80c. *Achille* surrendering to HMS *Polyphemus* | 1·75 | 2·00 |
| **MS**1386 | 120×78 mm. $1 Admiral Collingwood (brown, black and grey) (vert); $1 HMS *Polyphemus* (vert) | 6·00 | 6·50 |

No. 1384 contains traces of powdered wood from HMS *Victory*.

**271** William Curry

**2005.** Abaco—Key West Connections. Mult.

| | | | |
|---|---|---|---|
| 1387 | 15c. Type **271** | 45 | 25 |
| 1388 | 25c. Captain John Bartlum's House (horiz) | 60 | 40 |
| 1389 | 50c. Captain John Bartlum | 1·25 | 1·10 |
| 1390 | 65c. Captain Tuggy Roberts' House (horiz) | 1·50 | 1·60 |

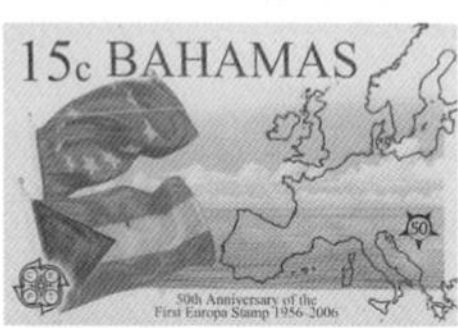

**272** Flags of EU and Bahamas and Map

**2005.** 50th Anniv of First Europa Stamp. Designs, all showing flags of EU and Bahamas, outline Map of Western Europe and different seascapes. Multicoloured.

| | | | |
|---|---|---|---|
| 1391 | 15c. Type **272** | 45 | 45 |
| 1392 | 25c. Seascape with bands of thin high cloud | 65 | 65 |
| 1393 | 50c. Seascape with small island | 1·25 | 1·40 |
| 1394 | $5 Seascape with clouds | 9·00 | 11·00 |
| **MS**1395 | 120×77 mm. Nos. 1391/4 | 10·00 | 12·00 |

**2005.** Lighthouses (2nd series). As T **266**. Multicoloured.

| | | | |
|---|---|---|---|
| 1396 | 15c. Bird Rock | 80 | 40 |
| 1397 | 50c. Castle Island | 1·75 | 1·10 |
| 1398 | 65c. San Salvador | 2·00 | 1·40 |
| 1399 | 70c. Great Inagua | 2·25 | 2·25 |
| 1400 | 80c. Cay Lobos | 2·50 | 2·75 |

**2005.** Pope John Paul II Commemoration. As T **219** of Ascension.

| | | | |
|---|---|---|---|
| 1401 | $1 multicoloured | 2·25 | 2·50 |

**273** College Entrance, Nassau

**2005.** 30th Anniv of the College of the Bahamas. Sheet 81×88 mm.

| | | | |
|---|---|---|---|
| **MS**1402 | **273** $2 multicoloured | 3·25 | 3·75 |

**2005.** Christmas. Birth Bicentenary of Hans Christian Andersen (writer). As T **220** of Ascension. Multicoloured.

| | | | |
|---|---|---|---|
| 1403 | 15c. *The Little Fir Tree* | 30 | 20 |
| 1404 | 25c. *The Princess and the Pea* | 45 | 35 |
| 1405 | 50c. *The Tin Soldier* | 90 | 90 |
| 1406 | 65c. *Thumbelina* | 1·10 | 1·25 |

**274** Bahama Nuthatch

**2006.** BirdLife International. Bahama Nuthatch (Sitta insularis). Multicoloured.

| | | | |
|---|---|---|---|
| 1407 | 15c. Type **274** | 65 | 30 |
| 1408 | 25c. On thick branch (facing left) | 80 | 45 |
| 1409 | 50c. On tree trunk (facing right) | 1·40 | 1·10 |
| 1410 | 65c. On thin branch among pine needles | 1·75 | 1·40 |
| 1411 | 70c. Nuthatch seen from underside | 1·90 | 1·90 |
| 1412 | 80c. On tree trunk near hole (facing left) | 2·00 | 2·25 |
| **MS**1413 | 170×85 mm. Nos. 1407/12 | 7·75 | 7·75 |

The stamps within No. **MS**1413 form a composite design showing nuthatches in Caribbean pine trees.

**2006.** 80th Birthday of Queen Elizabeth II. As T **223** of Ascension. Multicoloured.

| | | | |
|---|---|---|---|
| 1414 | 15c. Princess Elizabeth | 55 | 30 |
| 1415 | 25c. Queen Elizabeth II, c. 1952 | 75 | 40 |
| 1416 | 50c. Wearing blue feathered hat | 1·25 | 1·10 |
| 1417 | 65c. Wearing hat with brim raised at one side | 1·60 | 1·75 |
| **MS**1418 | 144×75 mm. $1.50 As No. 1415; $1.50 As No. 1416 | 6·00 | 6·50 |

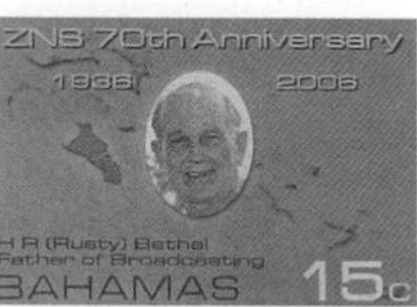

**275** H. R. (Rusty) Bethel (Manager, ZNS Radio 1945–70)

**2006.** 70th Anniv of Broadcasting in the Bahamas. Multicoloured.

| | | | |
|---|---|---|---|
| 1419 | 15c. Type **275** | 45 | 25 |
| 1420 | 25c. New Broadcasting Corporation of the Bahamas logo | 65 | 30 |
| 1421 | 50c. National Headquarters of Broadcasting Corporation of the Bahamas | 1·10 | 80 |
| 1422 | 65c. ZNS Nassau Radio stations building | 1·40 | 1·25 |
| 1423 | 70c. Radio mast and map of Bahamas | 1·50 | 1·50 |
| 1424 | 80c. "ZNS Radio" (70th anniv) and microphone | 1·60 | 1·75 |

**276** Amaryllis (*Hippeastrum puniceum*)

**2006.** Flowers of the Bahamas. Paintings by Alton Roland Lowe. Multicoloured.

| | | | |
|---|---|---|---|
| 1425 | 5c. Type **276** | 20 | 30 |
| 1426 | 10c. *Barleria cristata* | 25 | 30 |
| 1495a | 15c. Yesterday, today, tomorrow (*Brunfelsia solanaceae*) | 30 | 15 |
| 1427 | 25c. Desert rose (*Adenium obesum*) | 40 | 20 |
| 1428 | 35c. Poor man's orchid (*Bauhinia* sp.) | 55 | 25 |
| 1429 | 40c. Frangipani (*Plumeria* sp.) | 85 | 50 |
| 1430 | 55c. Herald's trumpet (*Beaumontia grandiflora*) | 1·25 | 1·00 |
| 1431 | 65c. Oleander (*Nerium oleander*) | 1·40 | 1·00 |
| 1432 | 75c. Bird of Paradise (*Strelitzia reginae*) | 1·60 | 1·25 |
| 1433 | 80c. *Plumbago capensis* | 1·75 | 1·40 |
| 1434 | 90c. Rose (*Rosa* sp.) | 1·90 | 1·50 |
| 1435 | $1 Rubber vine (*Cryptostegia madagascariensis*) | 2·25 | 2·00 |
| 1436 | $2 Star of Bethlehem (*Jatropha integerrima*) | 4·25 | 4·50 |
| 1437 | $5 Angel's trumpet (*Brugmansia suaveolens*) | 11·00 | 12·00 |
| 1438 | $10 Wine lily (*Crinum* sp.) | 22·00 | 24·00 |

**277** *Centrosema virginianum* (blue pea)

**2006.** Wild Flowering Vines. Paintings by Alton Roland Lowe. Multicoloured.

| | | | |
|---|---|---|---|
| 1439 | 15c. Type **277** | 40 | 25 |
| 1440 | 50c. *Urechites lutea* (allamanda) | 90 | 60 |
| 1441 | 65c. *Ipomoea indica* (morning glory) | 1·10 | 1·10 |
| 1442 | 70c. *Ipomoea microdactyla* (sky vine) | 1·25 | 1·50 |

**278** Christmas Sunday

**2006.** Christmas. Multicoloured.

| | | | |
|---|---|---|---|
| 1443 | 15c. Type **278** | 40 | 25 |
| 1444 | 25c. Christmas dinner | 60 | 30 |
| 1445 | 50c. Bay Street shopping | 1·00 | 1·60 |
| 1446 | 65c. Boxing Day Junkanoo | 1·25 | 85 |
| 1447 | 70c. Watch Night service | 1·40 | 1·40 |
| 1448 | 80c. New Year's Day Junkanoo | 1·50 | 1·75 |

**279** Blainville's Beaked Whale

**2007.** Endangered Species. Blainville's Beaked Whale (Mesoplodon densirostris). Multicoloured.

| | | | |
|---|---|---|---|
| 1449 | 15c. Type **279** | 40 | 40 |
| 1450 | 25c. Three whales | 60 | 60 |
| 1451 | 50c. Whales just beneath surface | 1·00 | 1·00 |
| 1452 | 60c. Two whales | 1·10 | 1·10 |

**280** Princess Elizabeth and Lt. Philip Mountbatten, 1949

**2007.** Diamond Wedding of Queen Elizabeth II and Prince Philip. Multicoloured.

| | | | |
|---|---|---|---|
| 1453 | 15c. Type **280** | 30 | 15 |
| 1454 | 25c. Princess Elizabeth riding in carriage on her wedding day, 1949 | 50 | 35 |
| 1455 | 50c. Princess Elizabeth and Prince Philip waving from balcony on wedding day, 1949 | 1·00 | 1·00 |
| 1456 | 65c. Princess Elizabeth, Prince Philip and Queen Mary | 1·40 | 1·50 |
| **MS**1457 | 125×85 mm. $5 Wedding portrait (42×56 mm) | 11·00 | 11·00 |

**281** Bahamas Scouts at Church Service

**2007.** Centenary of Scouting. Multicoloured.

| | | | |
|---|---|---|---|
| 1458 | 15c. Type **281** | 50 | 30 |
| 1459 | 25c. Scout in adventure playground | 75 | 45 |
| 1460 | 50c. Scout barbecue | 1·25 | 1·00 |
| 1461 | 65c. Bahamas girl scouts on parade | 1·50 | 1·60 |
| **MS**1462 | 90×65 mm. 70c. Scouts playing ball (*vert*); 80c. Lord Baden-Powell (*vert*) | 2·40 | 2·40 |

**282** Scouts repairing Causeway ('Service')

**2007.** 20th Anniv of Governor-General's Youth Award. Multicoloured.

| | | | |
|---|---|---|---|
| 1463 | 15c. Type **282** | 30 | 20 |
| 1464 | 25c. Painting ('Skills') | 45 | 30 |
| 1465 | 50c. Kayaking ('Physical Recreation') | 90 | 90 |
| 1466 | 65c. Hiking ('Adventurous Journey') | 1·25 | 1·25 |
| 1467 | 70c. Conch shell emblem | 1·50 | 1·75 |

**283** Flower Decoration

**2007.** Christmas. Tree Decorations. Multicoloured.

| | | | |
|---|---|---|---|
| 1468 | 15c. Type **283** | 25 | 15 |
| 1469 | 25c. Sea shells decoration | 40 | 25 |

1470 50c. Sea shells decoration (different) 90 70
1471 65c. Bow and sea shells decoration 1·25 90
1472 70c. Gold woven decoration 1·40 1·40
1473 80c. 'Angel' made from sea shells 1·60 1·75

**284** Choir

**2007.** 300th Birth Anniv of Charles Wesley. Multicoloured.
1474 15c. Type **284** 30 20
1475 50c. Charles and John Wesley (evangelists) (vert) 90 65
1476 65c. Revd. Charles Wesley and *Hymns and Sacred Poems* (vert) 1·10 90
1477 70c. Harbour Island Methodist Church (horiz) 1·50 1·60

**285** *Heliconius charitonius* (zebra longwing)

**2008.** Bahamas Butterflies. Multicoloured.
1478 15c. Type **285** 30 20
1479 25c. *Dryas julia carteri* (Julia) 45 30
1480 50c. *Phoebis sennae* (cloudless sulphur) 1·10 85
1481 65c. *Danaus gilippus berenice* (The Queen) 1·40 1·10
1482 70c. *Urbanus proteus* (long-tailed skipper) 1·60 1·75
1483 80c. *Dione vanillae insularis* (Gulf fritillary) 1·75 2·00
**MS**1484 170×75 mm. Nos. 1478/83 5·50 6·00

**286** His Majesty's Independant Company

**2008.** Military Uniforms. Multicoloured.
1485 15c. Type **286** 30 20
1486 25c. 47th Regiment of Foot 45 30
1487 50c. 99th Regiment of Foot 90 80
1488 65c. Royal Artillery 1·25 1·25
1489 70c. Black Garrison Companies 1·50 1·60

**287** Athlete breaking Finish Tape

**2008.** Olympic Games, Beijing. Multicoloured.
1490 15c. Type **287** 25 15
1491 50c. High jump 90 80
1492 65c. Javelin thrower 1·25 1·25
1493 70c. Triple jump 1·40 1·60

**288** Centenary Emblem

**2008.** Centenary of the Royal Bank of Canada in the Bahamas. Multicoloured.
1506 15c. Type **288** 40 25
1507 25c. Regional Head Office 55 40
1508 50c. Main Branch, Bay Street, Nassau, early 1900s 1·25 90
1509 65c. Artist's rendering of new Carmichael Road Branch, Nassau 1·50 1·60
1510 70c. Ross McDonald, Head of Caribbean Banking, and Nathaniel Beneby Jr., Vice President and Country Head 1·75 2·00

**289** Launch of Space Shuttle *Discovery* in STS-26 'Return to Flight' Mission

**2008.** 50th Anniv of NASA. Multicoloured.
1511 15c. Type **289** 30 20
1512 25c. Apollo 16 Command and Service Module over the Moon, 1972 50 35
1513 50c. *Skylab 3*, 1973 1·10 80
1514 65c. Hubble Space Telescope 1·40 1·25
1515 70c. Gasses in the Swan Nebula 1·50 1·60
1516 80c. Star forming region in the Carina Nebula 1·75 1·90

**290** The Three Kings worshipping Jesus

**2008.** Christmas. Book Illustrations by Leonhard Diefenbach from The First Christmas for Our Dear Little Ones by Rosa Mulholland. Multicoloured.
1517 15c. Type **290** 30 15
1518 50c. The Three Kings at the court of King Herod 1·10 70
1519 65c. Shepherds telling the news of the birth of Jesus 1·40 1·40
1520 70c. The shepherds visit the Baby Jesus 1·50 1·75

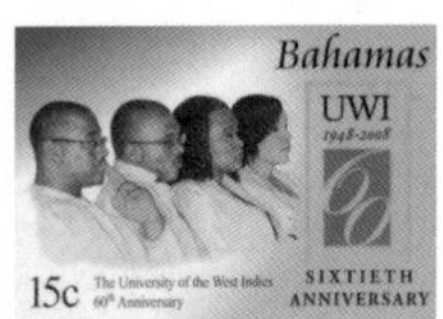

**291** Students

**2008.** 60th Anniv of the University of the West Indies. Multicoloured.
1521 15c. Type **291** 50 30
1522 25c. Plaque marking Bahamas Clinical Training Programme becoming part of University of the West Indies, 2007 1·00 55
1523 65c. Scroll 3·00 2·00

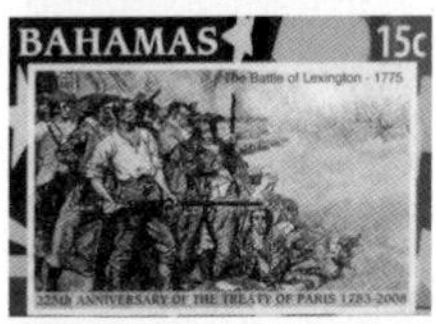

**292** Battle of Lexington, 1775

**2008.** 225th Anniv of the Treaty of Paris (recognising US Independence). Multicoloured.
1524 15c. Type **292** 40 30
1525 50c. Washington crossing the Delaware, 1776 1·25 90
1526 65c. American signatories of Treaty of Paris, 1783 (Benjamin West) 1·50 1·50
1527 70c. Detail of Treaty of Paris showing signatures 1·75 1·90

**293** Bahamas Oriole (*Icterus northropi*)

**2009.** Endangered Species–Resident Breeders. Multicoloured.
1528 15c. Type **293** 65 25
1529 50c. Rose throated parrot (*Amazona leucocephala bahamensis*) 1·50 1·10
1530 65c. Great lizard cuckoo (*Saurothera merlini bahamensis*) 1·75 1·60
1531 70c. Audubon's shearwater (*Puffinus lherminieri*) 1·90 1·90

**294** Peony

**2009.** China 2009 World Stamp Exhibition and Peony Festival, Luoyang. Sheet 180×110 mm. Multicoloured; colours of right-hand borders given.
**MS**1532 Type **294**×8 (colours of right-hand borders cream, white, pale pink, pale blue, pale flesh, pale green, pale yellow and pale azure) 8·25 8·25

**295** 'Tripod'

**2009.** Potcake Dogs. Multicoloured.
1533 15c. Type **295** 30 20
1534 50c. 'Amigo' 95 70
1535 65c. 'Turtle' 1·30 1·10
1536 70c. 'Oreo' 1·70 1·50

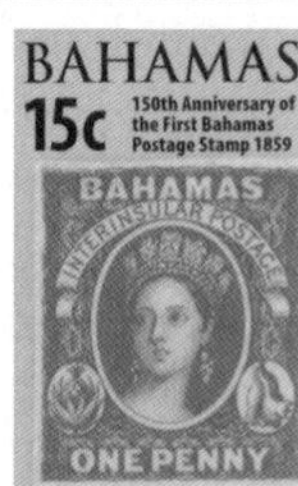

**296** Bahamas 1859 1d Stamp

**2009.** 150th Anniv of the First Bahamas Stamp. Multicoloured, background colour given.
1537 **296** 15c. pink 35 25
1538 **296** 15c. azure 35 25
1539 **296** 15c. dull green 35 25
1540 **296** 15c. dull reddish lilac 35 25
**MS**1541 130×100 mm. Nos. 1537/40 1·40 1·40

**2009.** Centenary of Naval Aviation. As T **87** of British Antarctic Territory. Multicoloured.
1542 15c. Hawker Sea Hurricane 35 25
1543 65c. Hawker Sea Fury 1·20 1·00
1544 70c. Fairey Gannet 1·30 1·10
1545 80c. de Havilland Sea Vampire 1·60 1·40
**MS**1546 110×70 mm. $2 Aircraft on deck of merchant aircraft carrier MV *Empire MacKendrick* 4·25 4·25

**297** East Street Tabernacle of Church of God of Prophecy

**2009.** Christmas. Churches. Multicoloured.
1547 15c. Type **297** 25 15
1548 25c. The Mission Baptist Church 40 30
1549 50c. Grant's Town Seventh-Day Adventist Church 85 65
1550 65c. Wesley Methodist Church, Harbour Island 1·40 1·20
1551 70c. St. Francis Xavier Cathedral 1·50 1·30
1552 80c. St. Ambrose Anglican Church 1·70 1·50

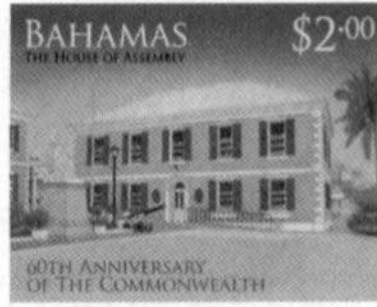

**298** The House of Assembly

**2009.** 60th Anniv of the Commonwealth. Sheet 120×85 mm.
**MS**1553 **298** $2 multicoloured 4·00 4·00

**299** Dolphin and Whale

**2010.** Friends of the Environment. Multicoloured.
1554 15c. Type **299** 25 15
1555 50c. Parrot and island map 85 65
1556 65c. Lizard and turtle 1·40 1·20
1557 70c. Bird and tree 1·50 1·30

**300** Winston Churchill

**2010.** 70th Anniv of the Battle of Britain. Multicoloured.
1558 15c. Type **300** ("...we shall never surrender...") 25 15
1559 25c. ..the Battle of Britain is about to begin... 45 25
1560 50c. "...never in the field of human conflict was so much owed by so many to so few..." 85 65
1561 65c. ...this was their finest hour... 1·40 1·20
1562 70c. ...upon this battle depends the survival of Christian civilization... 1·50 1·30
1563 80c. ...we shall fight on the beaches... 1·70
**MS**1563a 110×70 mm. $2 Sir Douglas Bader 4·00 4·00

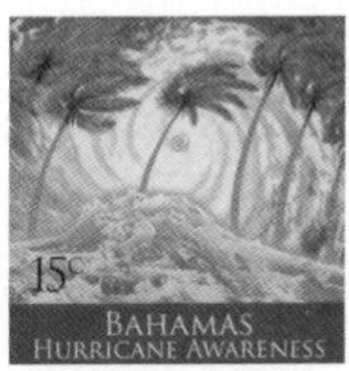

**301** Palm Trees in High Wind

**2010.** Hurricane Awareness. Multicoloured.
1564 15c. Type **301** 60 40
1565 50c. Map tracking hurricane across Bahamas 1·40 1·20
1566 65c. Reconnaissance aircraft flying through storm to measure intensity 2·00 1·80
1567 70c. Hurricane and NEMA (National Emergency Management Agency) logo 2·40 2·20

**302** Cruise Ship and Fireworks

**2010.** Christmas. 'Tourist Winter Escapes'. Multicoloured.
1568 15c. Type **302** 60 40
1569 50c. Atlantis Hotel, Paradise Island and fireworks 1·40 1·20
1570 65c. Aircraft tailfin and fireworks 2·00 1·80
1571 70c. Fort Fincastle and Water Tower and fireworks 2·30 2·10

**303** The Annual Heart Ball

**2011.** 50th Anniv of the Sir Victor Sassoon Heart Foundation. Multicoloured.
1572 15c. Type **303** 65 55
1573 50c. Doctor with young child 1·50 1·30
1574 65c. Doctor and young girl 2·10 1·90
1575 70c. Sir Victor Sassoon 2·50 2·30

**2011.** Queen Elizabeth II and Prince Philip. 'A Lifetime of Service'. Multicoloured.

| | | | |
|---|---|---|---|
| 1576 | 15c. Queen Elizabeth II, Balmoral, 6 February 1982 | 60 | 40 |
| 1577 | 50c. Queen Elizabeth II and Prince Philip, Windsor Castle, June 1959 | 1·60 | 1·40 |
| 1578 | 65c. Queen Elizabeth II and Prince Philip, Thames Valley University, London, 20 February 2009 | 2·00 | 1·80 |
| 1579 | 70c. Queen Elizabeth II and Prince Philip, Westminster Abbey, 8 March 2010 | 2·40 | 2·20 |
| 1580 | $1 Queen Elizabeth II and Prince Philip, Buckingham Palace, 19 July 1957 | 3·50 | 3·25 |
| 1581 | $2 Prince Philip, Balmoral, 6 February 1982 | 6·00 | 5·50 |
| **MS**1582 | 175×164 mm. Nos. 1576/81 and three stamp-size labels | 16·00 | 16·00 |
| **MS**1583 | 110×70 mm. $2.50 Queen Elizabeth II and Prince Philip, Sandringham House, Norfolk, 1992 | 8·00 | 8·00 |

**SPECIAL DELIVERY STAMPS**

**1916.** Optd **SPECIAL DELIVERY**.

| | | | | |
|---|---|---|---|---|
| S2 | **6** | 5d. black and orange | 50 | 9·50 |
| S3 | **6** | 5d. black and mauve | 30 | 3·75 |

Pt. 1

# BAHAWALPUR

A former Indian Feudatory state which joined Pakistan in 1947 and continued to use its own stamps until 1953.

12 pies = 1 anna, 16 annas = 1 rupee.

**(1)**

**1947.** Nos. 265/8, 269a/77 and 259/62 of India optd with Type 1.

| | | | |
|---|---|---|---|
| 1 | **100a** | 3p. slate | 35·00 |
| 3 | **100a** | 9p. green | 35·00 |
| 2 | **100a** | ½a. purple | 35·00 |
| 4 | **100a** | 1a. red | 35·00 |
| 5 | **101** | 1½a. violet | 35·00 |
| 6 | **101** | 2a. red | 35·00 |
| 7 | **101** | 3a. violet | 35·00 |
| 8 | **101** | 3½a. blue | 35·00 |
| 9 | **102** | 4a. brown | 35·00 |
| 10 | **102** | 6a. green | 35·00 |
| 11 | **102** | 8a. violet | 35·00 |
| 12 | **102** | 12a. lake | 35·00 |
| 13 | - | 14a. purple | 85·00 |
| 14 | **93** | 1r. grey and brown | 42·00 |
| 15 | **93** | 2r. purple and brown | £3250 |
| 16 | **93** | 5r. green and blue | £3250 |
| 17 | **93** | 10r. purple and red | £3250 |

**2** Amir Muhammad Bahawal Khan I Abbasi

**1948.** Bicentenary Commemoration.

| | | | | |
|---|---|---|---|---|
| 18 | **2** | ½a. black and red | 3·50 | 6·50 |

**4** H. H. the Amir of Bahawalpur

**5** The Tombs of the Amirs

**1948**

| | | | | |
|---|---|---|---|---|
| 19 | **4** | 3p. black and blue | 2·50 | 20·00 |
| 21 | **4** | 9p. black and green | 2·25 | 20·00 |
| 20 | **4** | ½a. black and red | 2·25 | 20·00 |
| 22 | **4** | 1a. black and red | 2·25 | 20·00 |
| 23 | **4** | 1½a. black and violet | 3·25 | 16·00 |
| 24 | **5** | 2a. green and red | 3·25 | 20·00 |
| 25 | - | 4a. orange and brown | 3·25 | 20·00 |
| 26 | - | 6a. violet and blue | 3·50 | 20·00 |
| 27 | - | 8a. red and violet | 4·25 | 20·00 |
| 28 | - | 12a. green and red | 5·00 | 30·00 |
| 29 | - | 1r. violet and brown | 19·00 | 45·00 |
| 35 | - | 1r. green and orange | 1·75 | 20·00 |
| 30 | - | 2r. green and red | 55·00 | 75·00 |
| 36 | - | 2r. black and red | 1·75 | 24·00 |
| 31 | - | 5r. black and violet | 55·00 | 95·00 |
| 37 | - | 5r. brown and blue | 1·90 | 42·00 |
| 32 | - | 10r. red and black | 32·00 | £120 |
| 38 | - | 10r. brown and green | 2·00 | 55·00 |

DESIGNS—HORIZ: 6a. Fort Derawar from the lake; 8a. Nur-Mahal Palace; 12a. Sadiq-Garh Palace. 46×32 mm: 10r. Three generations of Rulers. VERT (As Type **5**): 4a. Mosque in Sadiq-Garh; 1, 2, 5r. H.H. the Amir of Bahawalpur.

**12** H.H. the Amir of Bahawalpur and Mohammed Ali Jinnah

**1948.** 1st Anniv of Union with Pakistan.

| | | | | |
|---|---|---|---|---|
| 33 | **12** | 1½a. red and green | 1·75 | 5·50 |

**13** Soldiers of 1848 and 1948

**1948.** Centenary of Multan Campaign.

| | | | | |
|---|---|---|---|---|
| 34 | **13** | 1½a. black and red | 1·25 | 12·00 |

**14** Irrigation

**1949.** Silver Jubilee of Accession of H.H. the Amir of Bahawalpur.

| | | | | |
|---|---|---|---|---|
| 39 | **14** | 3p. black and blue | 10 | 8·00 |
| 41 | - | 9p. black and green | 10 | 8·00 |
| 40 | - | ½a. black and orange | 10 | 8·00 |
| 42 | - | 1a. black and red | 10 | 8·00 |

DESIGNS: ½a. Wheat; 9p. Cotton; 1a. Sahiwal bull.

**18** UPU Monument, Berne

**1949.** 75th Anniv of U.P.U.

| | | | | |
|---|---|---|---|---|
| 43 | **17** | 9p. black and green | 20 | 2·00 |
| 44 | **17** | 1a. black and mauve | 20 | 2·00 |
| 45 | **17** | 1½a. black and orange | 20 | 2·00 |
| 46 | **17** | 2½a. black and blue | 20 | 2·00 |

**OFFICIAL STAMPS**

**O4** Eastern White Pelicans

**1945.** As Type O **4** with Arabic opt.

| | | | | |
|---|---|---|---|---|
| O1 | - | ½a. black and green | 8·00 | 14·00 |
| O2 | - | 1a. black and red | 3·75 | 14·00 |
| O7 | - | 1a. black and brown | 80·00 | 80·00 |
| O3 | - | 2a. black and violet | 3·25 | 12·00 |
| O4 | **O 4** | 4a. black and olive | 12·00 | 26·00 |
| O5 | - | 8a. black and brown | 30·00 | 18·00 |
| O6 | - | 1r. black and orange | 30·00 | 18·00 |

DESIGNS: ½a. Panjnad Weir; 1a. (No. O2), Camel and calf; 1a. (No. O7), Baggage camels; 2a. Blackbuck antelopes; 8a. Friday Mosque, Fort Derawar; 1r. Temple at Pattan Munara.

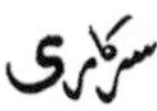

**(O8)**

**1945.** Types as Nos. O1, etc., in new colours and without Arabic opt. (a) Surch as Type O **8**.

| | | | |
|---|---|---|---|
| O11 | ½a. on 8a. black and purple (as No. O5) | 5·50 | 7·00 |
| O12 | 1½a. on 5r. black and orange (as No. O6) | 40·00 | 11·00 |
| O13 | 1½a. on 2r. black and blue (as No. O1) | £140 | 8·50 |

(b) Optd **SERVICE** and Arabic inscription.

| | | | |
|---|---|---|---|
| O14 | ½a. black and red (as No. O1) | 1·25 | 11·00 |
| O15 | 1a. black and red (as No. O2) | 2·00 | 13·00 |
| O16 | 2a. black and orange (as No. O3) | 3·25 | 50·00 |

**1945.** As Type **4** but inscr "**SERVICE**" at left.

| | | | |
|---|---|---|---|
| O17 | 3p. black and blue | 6·00 | 14·00 |
| O18 | 1½a. black and violet | 23·00 | 8·00 |

**O11** Allied Banners

**1946.** Victory.

| | | | | |
|---|---|---|---|---|
| O19 | **O11** | 1½a. green and grey | 4·50 | 4·25 |

**1948.** Stamps of 1948 with Arabic opt as in Type O **4**.

| | | | | |
|---|---|---|---|---|
| O20 | **4** | 3p. black and blue | 80 | 13·00 |
| O21 | **4** | 1a. black and red | 80 | 12·00 |
| O22 | **5** | 2a. green and red | 80 | 13·00 |
| O23 | - | 4a. orange and brown | 80 | 18·00 |
| O24 | - | 1r. green and orange | 80 | 20·00 |
| O25 | - | 2r. black and red | 80 | 26·00 |
| O26 | - | 5r. chocolate and blue | 80 | 42·00 |
| O27 | - | 10r. brown and green | 80 | 42·00 |

**1949.** 75th Anniv of U.P.U. optd as in Type O **4**.

| | | | | |
|---|---|---|---|---|
| O28 | **17** | 9p. black and green | 15 | 4·50 |
| O29 | **17** | 1a. black and mauve | 15 | 4·50 |
| O30 | **17** | 1½a. black and orange | 15 | 4·50 |
| O31 | **17** | 2½a. black and blue | 15 | 4·50 |

Pt. 1, Pt. 19

# BAHRAIN

An archipelago in the Persian Gulf on the Arabian coast. An independent shaikhdom with Indian and later British postal administration. The latter was closed on 1 January 1966, when the Bahrain Post Office took over.

1933. 12 pies = 1 anna; 16 annas = 1 rupee.
1957. 100 naya paise = 1 rupee.

Stamps of India optd **BAHRAIN**.

**1933.** King George V.

| | | | | |
|---|---|---|---|---|
| 1 | **55** | 3p. grey | 3·50 | 45 |
| 3 | **80** | 9p. green | 3·75 | 3·75 |
| 2 | **56** | ½a. green | 7·50 | 3·50 |
| 15 | **79** | ½a. green | 6·50 | 1·75 |
| 4 | **57** | 1a. brown | 7·00 | 2·50 |
| 16 | **81** | 1a. brown | 11·00 | 40 |
| 5 | **82** | 1a.3p. mauve | 13·00 | 3·50 |
| 6 | **70** | 2a. orange | 10·00 | 19·00 |
| 17 | **59** | 2a. orange | 45·00 | 7·50 |
| 7 | **62** | 3a. blue | 19·00 | 65·00 |
| 18 | **62** | 3a. red | 4·75 | 60 |
| 8 | **83** | 3a.6p. blue | 3·75 | 40 |
| 9 | **71** | 4a. green | 18·00 | 65·00 |
| 19 | **63** | 4a. olive | 5·00 | 40 |
| 10 | **65** | 8a. mauve | 6·00 | 30 |
| 11 | **66** | 12a. red | 7·50 | 1·50 |
| 12 | **67** | 1r. brown and green | 16·00 | 13·00 |
| 13 | **67** | 2r. red and orange | 29·00 | 35·00 |
| 14w | **67** | 5r. blue and violet | £140 | £160 |

**1938.** King George VI.

| | | | | |
|---|---|---|---|---|
| 20 | **91** | 3p. slate | 18·00 | 7·00 |
| 22 | **91** | 9p. green | 14·00 | 12·00 |
| 21 | **91** | ½a. brown | 7·50 | 20 |
| 23 | **91** | 1a. red | 13·00 | 20 |
| 24 | **92** | 2a. red | 5·00 | 5·00 |
| 26 | - | 3a. green (No. 253) | 12·00 | 11·00 |
| 27 | - | 3a.6p. blue (No. 254) | 6·00 | 8·50 |
| 28 | - | 4a. brown (No. 255) | £170 | 70·00 |
| 30 | - | 8a. violet (No. 257) | £250 | 35·00 |
| 31 | - | 12a. red (No. 258) | £140 | 45·00 |
| 32 | **93** | 1r. slate and brown | 7·00 | 1·75 |
| 33 | **93** | 2r. purple and brown | 17·00 | 9·50 |
| 34 | **93** | 5r. green and blue | 15·00 | 13·00 |
| 35 | **93** | 10r. purple and red | 85·00 | 50·00 |
| 36w | **93** | 15r. brown and green | 85·00 | 85·00 |
| 37 | **93** | 25r. slate and purple | £120 | £100 |

**1942.** King George VI.

| | | | | |
|---|---|---|---|---|
| 38 | **100a** | 3p. slate | 3·50 | 2·50 |
| 40 | **100a** | 9p. green | 18·00 | 20·00 |
| 39 | **100a** | ½a. mauve | 4·75 | 3·75 |
| 41 | **100a** | 1a. red | 8·00 | 1·00 |
| 42 | **101** | 1a.3p. bistre | 10·00 | 24·00 |
| 43 | **101** | 1½a. violet | 7·00 | 8·00 |
| 44 | **101** | 2a. red | 7·00 | 1·50 |
| 45 | **101** | 3a. violet | 22·00 | 7·50 |
| 46 | **101** | 3½a. blue | 6·50 | 21·00 |
| 47 | **102** | 4a. brown | 5·50 | 2·00 |
| 48 | **102** | 6a. green | 20·00 | 12·00 |
| 49 | **102** | 8a. violet | 9·00 | 5·50 |
| 50 | **102** | 12a. purple | 14·00 | 6·00 |

Stamps of Great Britain surch **BAHRAIN** and new value in Indian currency.

**1948.** King George VI.

| | | | | |
|---|---|---|---|---|
| 71 | **128** | ½a. on ½d. orange | 2·50 | 3·25 |
| 51 | **128** | ½a. on 1d. green | 50 | 1·25 |
| 52 | **128** | 1a. on 1d. red | 50 | 3·00 |
| 72 | **128** | 1a. on 1d. blue | 3·00 | 20 |
| 53 | **128** | 1½a. on 1½d. brown | 50 | 4·00 |
| 73 | **128** | 1½a. on 1½d. green | 3·00 | 13·00 |
| 54 | **128** | 2a. on 2d. orange | 50 | 20 |
| 74 | **128** | 2a. on 2d. brown | 1·50 | 30 |
| 55 | **128** | 2½a. on 2½d. blue | 50 | 4·75 |
| 75 | **128** | 2½a. on 2½d. red | 3·00 | 15·00 |
| 56 | **128** | 3a. on 3d. violet | 50 | 10 |
| 76 | **129** | 4a. on 4d. blue | 4·75 | 1·50 |
| 57 | **129** | 6a. on 6d. purple | 50 | 10 |
| 58 | **130** | 1r. on 1s. brown | 1·25 | 10 |
| 59 | **131** | 2r. on 2s.6d. green | 5·50 | 5·50 |
| 60 | **131** | 5r. on 5s. red | 5·50 | 5·50 |
| 60a | - | 10r. on 10s. blue (No. 478a) | 90·00 | 75·00 |

**1948.** Silver Wedding.

| | | | | |
|---|---|---|---|---|
| 61 | **137** | 2½a. on 2½d. blue | 1·00 | 2·75 |
| 62 | **138** | 15r. on £1 blue | 30·00 | 48·00 |

**1948.** Olympic Games.

| | | | | |
|---|---|---|---|---|
| 63 | **139** | 2½a. on 2½d. blue | 1·00 | 4·75 |
| 64 | **140** | 3a. on 3d. violet | 1·00 | 4·25 |
| 65 | - | 6a. on 6d. purple | 1·50 | 4·25 |
| 66 | - | 1r. on 1s. brown | 2·50 | 4·25 |

**1949.** U.P.U.

| | | | | |
|---|---|---|---|---|
| 67 | **143** | 2½a. on 2½d. blue | 60 | 2·50 |
| 68 | **144** | 3a. on 3d. violet | 70 | 4·50 |
| 69 | - | 6a. on 6d. purple | 60 | 3·00 |
| 70 | - | 1r. on 1s. brown | 1·25 | 3·50 |

**1951.** Pictorial stamps (Nos. 509/11).

| | | | | |
|---|---|---|---|---|
| 77 | **147** | 2r. on 2s.6d. green | 35·00 | 15·00 |
| 78 | - | 5r. on 5s. red | 15·00 | 5·00 |
| 79 | - | 10r. on 10s. blue | 35·00 | 9·00 |

**1952.** Queen Elizabeth II.

| | | | | |
|---|---|---|---|---|
| 97 | **154** | ½a. on ½d. orange | 10 | 15 |
| 81 | **154** | 1a. on 1d. blue | 10 | 10 |
| 82 | **154** | 1½a. on 1½d. green | 10 | 30 |
| 83 | **154** | 2a. on 2d. brown | 30 | 10 |
| 84 | **155** | 2½a. on 2½d. red | 20 | 1·75 |
| 85 | **155** | 3a. on 3d. lilac | 3·00 | 10 |
| 86 | **155** | 4a. on 4d. blue | 16·00 | 30 |
| 99 | **157** | 6a. on 6d. purple | 50 | 75 |
| 88 | **160** | 12a. on 1s.3d. green | 3·25 | 20 |
| 89 | **160** | 1r. on 1s.6d. blue | 3·25 | 10 |

**1953.** Coronation.

| | | | | |
|---|---|---|---|---|
| 90 | **161** | 2½a. on 2½d. red | 1·25 | 75 |
| 91 | - | 4a. on 4d. blue | 2·25 | 7·50 |
| 92 | **163** | 12a. on 1s.3d. green | 6·00 | 6·00 |
| 93 | - | 1r. on 1s.6d. blue | 7·50 | 50 |

**1955.** Pictorial stamps (Nos. 595a/598a).

| | | | | |
|---|---|---|---|---|
| 94 | **166** | 2r. on 2s.6d. brown | 5·50 | 2·00 |
| 95 | - | 5r. on 5s. red | 15·00 | 2·75 |
| 96 | - | 10r. on 10s. blue | 20·00 | 2·75 |

**1957.** Queen Elizabeth II.

| | | | | |
|---|---|---|---|---|
| 102 | **157** | 1n.p. on 5d. brown | 10 | 10 |
| 103 | **154** | 3n.p. on ½d. orange | 50 | 3·00 |
| 104 | **154** | 6n.p. on 1d. blue | 50 | 3·00 |
| 105 | **154** | 9n.p. on 1½d. green | 50 | 3·25 |
| 106 | **154** | 12n.p. on 2d. pale brown | 30 | 70 |
| 107 | **155** | 15n.p. on 2½d. red | 30 | 15 |
| 108 | **155** | 20n.p. on 3d. lilac | 30 | 10 |
| 109 | **155** | 25n.p. on 4d. blue | 1·25 | 2·50 |
| 110 | **157** | 40n.p. on 6d. purple | 40 | 10 |
| 111 | **157** | 50n.p. on 9d. olive | 3·75 | 4·50 |
| 112 | **157** | 75n.p. on 1s.3d. green | 2·50 | 50 |

**1957.** World Scout Jubilee Jamboree.

| | | | | |
|---|---|---|---|---|
| 113 | **170** | 15n.p. on 2½d. red | 35 | 35 |
| 114 | **171** | 25n.p. on 4d. blue | 35 | 35 |
| 115 | - | 75n.p. on 1s.3d. green | 40 | 45 |

**16** Shaikh Sulman bin Hamed al-Khalifa

**1960**

| | | | | |
|---|---|---|---|---|
| 117 | **16** | 5n.p. blue | 20 | 10 |
| 118 | **16** | 15n.p. orange | 20 | 10 |
| 119 | **16** | 20n.p. violet | 20 | 10 |
| 120 | **16** | 30n.p. bistre | 20 | 10 |
| 121 | **16** | 40n.p. grey | 20 | 10 |
| 122 | **16** | 50n.p. green | 20 | 10 |
| 123 | **16** | 75n.p. brown | 30 | 15 |
| 124 | - | 1r. black | 3·00 | 30 |
| 125 | - | 2r. red | 3·00 | 2·25 |
| 126 | - | 5r. blue | 5·00 | 3·00 |
| 127 | - | 10r. green | 13·00 | 5·50 |

The rupee values are larger, 27×32½ mm.

**18** Shaikh Isa bin Sulman al-Khalifa

**19** Air Terminal, Muharraq

**1964**

| | | | | |
|---|---|---|---|---|
| 128 | **18** | 5n.p. blue | 10 | 10 |
| 129 | **18** | 15n.p. orange | 10 | 1·00 |
| 130 | **18** | 20n.p. violet | 10 | 10 |
| 131 | **18** | 30n.p. bistre | 10 | 10 |
| 132 | **18** | 40n.p. slate | 15 | 10 |
| 133 | **18** | 50n.p. green | 15 | 1·50 |
| 134 | **18** | 75n.p. brown | 25 | 10 |
| 135 | **19** | 1r. black | 11·00 | 2·25 |
| 136 | **19** | 2r. red | 11·00 | 4·00 |
| 137 | - | 5r. blue | 14·00 | 17·00 |
| 138 | - | 10r. myrtle | 14·00 | 17·00 |

DESIGN—As Type **19**: 5r., 10r. Deep water harbour.

**21** Sheikh Isa bin Sulman al-Khalifa

**22** Ruler and Bahrain Airport

**1966**

| | | | | |
|---|---|---|---|---|
| 139 | **21** | 5f. green | 20 | 20 |
| 140 | **21** | 10f. red | 20 | 20 |
| 141 | **21** | 15f. blue | 20 | 20 |
| 142 | **21** | 20f. purple | 30 | 20 |
| 143 | **22** | 30f. black and green | 45 | 20 |
| 144 | **22** | 40f. black and blue | 55 | 20 |
| 145 | - | 50f. black and red | 75 | 30 |
| 146 | - | 75f. black and violet | 95 | 45 |
| 147 | - | 100f. blue and yellow | 3·25 | 1·30 |
| 148 | - | 200f. green and orange | 14·00 | 2·75 |
| 149 | - | 500f. brown and yellow | 12·00 | 4·75 |
| 150 | - | 1d. multicoloured | 21·00 | 10·50 |

DESIGNS—As Type **22**: 50f., 75f. Ruler and Mina Sulman deep-water harbour. VERT (26½×42½ mm): 100f. Pearl-diving; 200f. Lanner falcon and horse-racing; 500f. Serving coffee, and ruler's palace. LARGER (37×52½ mm): 1d. Ruler, crest, date palm, horse, dhow, pearl necklace, mosque, coffee-pot and Bab-al-Bahrain (gateway).

**23** Produce

**1966.** Trade Fair and Agricultural Show.

| | | | | |
|---|---|---|---|---|
| 151 | **23** | 10f. turquoise and red | 55 | 10 |
| 152 | **23** | 20f. lilac and green | 75 | 10 |
| 153 | **23** | 40f. blue and brown | 2·10 | 55 |
| 154 | **23** | 200f. red and blue | 10·00 | 4·75 |

**24** W.H.O. Emblem and Map of Bahrain

**1968.** 20th Anniv of W.H.O.

| | | | | |
|---|---|---|---|---|
| 155 | **24** | 20f. black and grey | 95 | 65 |
| 156 | **24** | 40f. black and turquoise | 3·25 | 1·70 |
| 157 | **24** | 150f. black and red | 14·00 | 6·50 |

**25** View of Isa Town

**1968.** Inauguration of Isa New Town. Mult.

| | | | | |
|---|---|---|---|---|
| 158 | | 50f. Type **25** | 4·75 | 1·40 |
| 159 | | 80f. Shopping centre | 7·00 | 2·75 |
| 160 | | 120f. Stadium | 10·50 | 5·00 |
| 161 | | 150f. Mosque | 13·00 | 6·50 |

**26** Symbol of Learning

**1969.** 50th Anniv of School Education in Bahrain.

| | | | | |
|---|---|---|---|---|
| 162 | **26** | 40f. multicoloured | 1·90 | 1·20 |
| 163 | **26** | 60f. multicoloured | 3·75 | 1·90 |
| 164 | **26** | 150f. multicoloured | 10·00 | 5·00 |

**27** Dish Aerial and Map of Persian Gulf

**1969.** Opening of Satellite Earth Station, Ras Abu Jarjour. Multicoloured.

| | | | | |
|---|---|---|---|---|
| 165 | | 20f. Type **27** | 2·75 | 65 |
| 166 | | 40f. Dish aerial and palms (vert) | 6·00 | 1·10 |
| 167 | | 100f. Type **27** | 13·00 | 4·75 |
| 168 | | 150f. As 40f. | 21·00 | 7·00 |

**28** Arms, Map and Manama Municipality Building

**1970.** 2nd Arab Cities Organization Conf, Manama.

| | | | | |
|---|---|---|---|---|
| 169 | **28** | 30f. multicoloured | 2·75 | 2·75 |
| 170 | **28** | 150f. multicoloured | 15·00 | 15·00 |

**29** Copper Bull's Head, Barbar

**1970.** 3rd International Asian Archaeology Conference, Bahrain. Multicoloured.

| | | | | |
|---|---|---|---|---|
| 171 | | 60f. Type **29** | 4·75 | 2·50 |
| 172 | | 80f. Palace of Dilmun excavations | 7·50 | 3·25 |
| 173 | | 120f. Desert gravemounds | 9·00 | 4·25 |
| 174 | | 150f. Dilmun seal | 10·50 | 5·25 |

**30** Vickers Super VC-10 Airliner, Big Ben, London, and Bahrain Minaret

**1970.** 1st Gulf Aviation Vickers Super VC-10 Flight, Doha–London.

| | | | | |
|---|---|---|---|---|
| 175 | **30** | 30f. multicoloured | 3·25 | 95 |
| 176 | **30** | 60f. multicoloured | 6·50 | 2·10 |
| 177 | **30** | 120f. multicoloured | 12·00 | 6·50 |

**31** I.E.Y. Emblem and Open Book

**1970.** International Education Year. Multicoloured.

| | | | | |
|---|---|---|---|---|
| 178 | | 60f. Type **31** | 5·25 | 5·25 |
| 179 | | 120f. Emblem and Bahraini children | 10·50 | 10·50 |

**32** Allegory of Independence

**1971.** Independence Day and 10th Anniv of Ruler's Accession. Multicoloured.

| | | | | |
|---|---|---|---|---|
| 180 | | 30f. Type **32** | 2·40 | 1·30 |
| 181 | | 60f. Government House | 4·75 | 2·40 |
| 182 | | 120f. Arms of Bahrain | 12·00 | 6·00 |
| 183 | | 150f. Arms of Bahrain (gold background) | 16·00 | 8·00 |

**33** Arab Dhow with Arab League and U.N. Emblems

**1972.** Bahrain's Membership of Arab League and U.N. Multicoloured.

| | | | | |
|---|---|---|---|---|
| 184 | | 30f. Type **33** | 6·00 | 6·00 |
| 185 | | 60f. Type **33** | 9·75 | 9·75 |
| 186 | | 120f. Dhow sails (vert) | 13·00 | 13·00 |
| 187 | | 150f. As 120f. | 24·00 | 24·00 |

**34** Human Heart

**1972.** World Health Day.

| | | | | |
|---|---|---|---|---|
| 188 | **34** | 30f. multicoloured | 6·00 | 6·00 |
| 189 | **34** | 60f. multicoloured | 12·00 | 12·00 |

**35** F.A.O. and U.N. Emblems

**1973.** 10th Anniv of World Food Programme.

| | | | | |
|---|---|---|---|---|
| 190 | **35** | 30f. brown, red and green | 5·25 | 5·25 |
| 191 | **35** | 60f. brown, lt brown & grn | 10·00 | 10·00 |

**36** "Races of the World"

**1973.** 25th Anniv of Declaration of Human Rights.

| | | | | |
|---|---|---|---|---|
| 192 | **36** | 30f. blue, brown and black | 6·50 | 6·50 |
| 193 | **36** | 60f. red, brown and black | 9·75 | 9·75 |

**38** Flour Mill

**1973.** National Day. "Progress in Bahrain". Mult.

| | | | | |
|---|---|---|---|---|
| 195 | | 30f. Type **38** | 2·40 | 65 |
| 196 | | 60f. Muharraq Airport | 3·25 | 1·20 |
| 197 | | 120f. Sulmaniya Medical Centre | 6·50 | 3·50 |
| 198 | | 150f. Aluminium Smelter | 6·50 | 3·75 |

**39** U.P.U. Emblem within Letters

**1974.** Admission of Bahrain to U.P.U. Mult.

| | | | | |
|---|---|---|---|---|
| 199 | | 30f. Type **39** | 2·40 | 2·40 |
| 200 | | 60f. U.P.U. emblem on letters | 4·00 | 4·00 |
| 201 | | 120f. Ruler and emblem on dove with letter in beak (37×28 mm) | 4·00 | 4·00 |
| 202 | | 150f. As 120f. (37×28 mm) | 6·00 | 6·00 |

**40** Traffic Lights and Directing Hands

**1974.** International Traffic Day.

| | | | | |
|---|---|---|---|---|
| 203 | **40** | 30f. multicoloured | 4·75 | 4·75 |
| 204 | **40** | 60f. multicoloured | 8·50 | 8·50 |

**41** U.P.U. "Stamp" and Mail Transport

**1974.** Centenary of U.P.U.

| | | | | |
|---|---|---|---|---|
| 205 | **41** | 30f. multicoloured | 1·30 | 1·30 |
| 206 | **41** | 60f. multicoloured | 1·50 | 1·50 |
| 207 | **41** | 120f. multicoloured | 4·00 | 4·00 |
| 208 | **41** | 150f. multicoloured | 5·25 | 5·25 |

**42** Emblem and Sitra Power Station

**1974.** National Day. Multicoloured.

| | | | | |
|---|---|---|---|---|
| 209 | | 30f. Type **42** | 85 | 30 |
| 210 | | 60f. Type **42** | 2·75 | 1·40 |
| 211 | | 120f. Emblem and Bahrain Dry Dock | 4·50 | 2·75 |
| 212 | | 150f. As 120f. | 6·00 | 3·75 |

**43** Costume and Headdress

**1975.** Bahrain Women's Costumes.

| | | | | |
|---|---|---|---|---|
| 213 | **43** | 30f. multicoloured | 85 | 85 |
| 214 | - | 60f. multicoloured | 2·00 | 2·00 |
| 215 | - | 120f. multicoloured | 4·00 | 4·00 |
| 216 | - | 150f. multicoloured | 4·75 | 4·75 |

DESIGNS: Nos. 214/16, Costumes as Type **43**.

**44** Jewelled Pendant

**1975.** Costume Jewellery. Multicoloured.

| | | | |
|---|---|---|---|
| 217 | 30f. Type **44** | 1·10 | 1·10 |
| 218 | 60f. Gold crown | 2·50 | 2·50 |
| 219 | 120f. Jewelled necklace | 5·00 | 5·00 |
| 220 | 150f. Gold necklace | 6·50 | 6·50 |

**45** Women planting "Flower"

**1975.** International Women's Year. Multicoloured.

| | | | |
|---|---|---|---|
| 221 | 30f. Type **45** | 2·40 | 1·10 |
| 222 | 60f. Woman holding I.W.Y. emblem | 6·50 | 2·40 |

**46** Head of Horse

**1975.** Horses. Multicoloured.

| | | | |
|---|---|---|---|
| 223a | 60f. Type **46** | 7·50 | 7·50 |
| 223b | 60f. Grey | 7·50 | 7·50 |
| 223c | 60f. Grey with foal (horiz) | 7·50 | 7·50 |
| 223d | 60f. Close-up of Arab with grey | 7·50 | 7·50 |
| 223e | 60f. Grey and herd of browns (horiz) | 7·50 | 7·50 |
| 223f | 60f. Grey and brown (horiz) | 7·50 | 7·50 |
| 223g | 60f. Arabs riding horses (horiz) | 7·50 | 7·50 |
| 223h | 60f. Arab leading grey beside sea (horiz) | 7·50 | 7·50 |

**47** National Flag

**48** Map of Bahrain within Cog and Laurel

**1976**

| | | | | |
|---|---|---|---|---|
| 224 | **47** | 5f. red, pink and blue | 30 | 30 |
| 225 | **47** | 10f. red, pink & green | 30 | 30 |
| 226 | **47** | 15f. red, pink & black | 30 | 30 |
| 227 | **47** | 20f. red, pink & brown | 55 | 30 |
| 227b | **48** | 25f. black and grey | 65 | 30 |
| 228 | **48** | 40f. black and blue | 65 | 45 |
| 228a | **48** | 50f. green, black & olive | 65 | 55 |
| 228b | **48** | 60f. black and green | 1·10 | 65 |
| 229 | **48** | 80f. black and mauve | 1·70 | 75 |
| 229b | **48** | 100f. black and red | 1·70 | 95 |
| 230 | **48** | 150f. black and yellow | 3·25 | 1·50 |
| 231 | **48** | 200f. black and yellow | 3·75 | 1·80 |

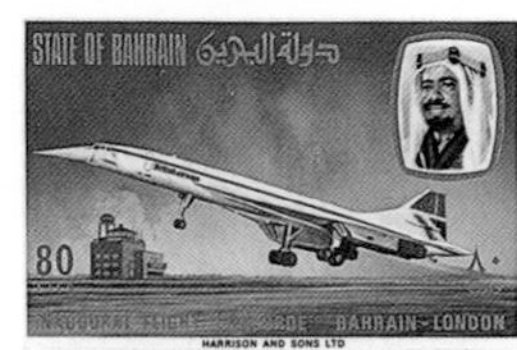


**49** Concorde Taking off

**1976.** 1st Commercial Flight of Concorde. Mult.

| | | | |
|---|---|---|---|
| 232 | 80f. Type **49** | 4·00 | 3·00 |
| 233 | 80f. Concorde landing | 4·00 | 3·00 |
| 234 | 80f. Concorde en route | 4·00 | 3·00 |
| 235 | 80f. Concorde on runway | 4·00 | 3·00 |
| **MS**236 | 154×115 mm. Nos. 232/5. Imperf | 18·00 | 18·00 |

**50** Soldier, Crest and Flag

**1976.** Defence Force Cadets' Day.

| | | | | |
|---|---|---|---|---|
| 237 | **50** | 40f. multicoloured | 3·00 | 3·00 |
| 238 | **50** | 80f. multicoloured | 5·25 | 5·25 |

**51** King Khalid of Saudi Arabia and Shaikh of Bahrain with National Flags

**1976.** Visit to Bahrain of King Khalid of Saudi Arabia.

| | | | | |
|---|---|---|---|---|
| 239 | **51** | 40f. multicoloured | 2·40 | 1·70 |
| 240 | **51** | 80f. multicoloured | 4·75 | 3·75 |

**52** Shaikh Isa bin Sulman al-Khalifa

**1976**

| | | | | |
|---|---|---|---|---|
| 241 | **52** | 300f. green and pale green | 5·25 | 2·75 |
| 242 | **52** | 400f. purple and pink | 7·50 | 3·75 |
| 243 | **52** | 500f. blue and pale blue | 9·00 | 4·75 |
| 244 | **52** | 1d. black and grey | 16·00 | 8·50 |
| 244a | **52** | 2d. violet and lilac | 20·00 | 10·50 |
| 244b | **52** | 3d. brown and pink | 48·00 | 32·00 |

**53** Ministry of Housing Emblem, Designs for Houses and Mosque

**1976.** National Day.

| | | | | |
|---|---|---|---|---|
| 245 | **53** | 40f. multicoloured | 2·10 | 95 |
| 246 | **53** | 80f. multicoloured | 4·75 | 1·90 |

**54** A.P.U. Emblem

**1977.** 25th Anniv of Arab Postal Union.

| | | | | |
|---|---|---|---|---|
| 247 | **54** | 40f. multicoloured | 2·10 | 1·60 |
| 248 | **54** | 80f. multicoloured | 4·75 | 3·25 |

**55** Dogs on Beach

**1977.** Saluki Dogs. Multicoloured.

| | | | |
|---|---|---|---|
| 249a | 80f. Type **55** | 3·75 | 3·75 |
| 249b | 80f. Dog and dromedaries | 3·75 | 3·75 |
| 249c | 80f. Dog and antelope | 3·75 | 3·75 |
| 249d | 80f. Dog on lawn of building | 3·75 | 3·75 |
| 249e | 80f. Head of dog | 3·75 | 3·75 |
| 249f | 80f. Heads of two dogs | 3·75 | 3·75 |
| 249g | 80f. Dog in scrubland | 3·75 | 3·75 |
| 249h | 80f. Dogs fighting | 3·75 | 3·75 |

**56** Arab Students and Candle

**1977.** International Literacy Day.

| | | | | |
|---|---|---|---|---|
| 250 | **56** | 40f. multicoloured | 2·10 | 1·60 |
| 251 | **56** | 80f. multicoloured | 4·75 | 3·25 |

**57** Shipyard Installations and Arab Flags

**1977.** Inauguration of Arab Shipbuilding and Repair Yard Co.

| | | | | |
|---|---|---|---|---|
| 252 | **57** | 40f. multicoloured | 2·10 | 1·60 |
| 253 | **57** | 80f. multicoloured | 4·75 | 3·25 |

**58** Microwave Antenna

**1978.** 10th World Telecommunications Day.

| | | | | |
|---|---|---|---|---|
| 254 | **58** | 40f. multicoloured | 2·10 | 1·60 |
| 255 | **58** | 80f. silver, dp blue & blue | 4·75 | 3·25 |

**59** Child being helped to Walk

**1979.** International Year of the Child. Mult.

| | | | |
|---|---|---|---|
| 256 | 50f. Type **59** | 2·10 | 1·50 |
| 257 | 100f. Hands protecting child | 4·50 | 2·75 |

**60** Boom Dhow

**1979.** Dhows. Multicoloured.

| | | | |
|---|---|---|---|
| 258 | 100f. Type **60** | 6·50 | 6·50 |
| 259 | 100f. Baghla | 6·50 | 6·50 |
| 260 | 100f. Shu'ai (horiz) | 6·50 | 6·50 |
| 261 | 100f. Ghanja (horiz) | 6·50 | 6·50 |
| 262 | 100f. Kotia | 6·50 | 6·50 |
| 263 | 100f. Sambuk | 6·50 | 6·50 |
| 264 | 100f. Jaliboot (horiz) | 6·50 | 6·50 |
| 265 | 100f. Zarook (horiz) | 6·50 | 6·50 |

**61** Dome of Mosque, Mecca

**1980.** 1400th Anniv of Hejira.

| | | | | |
|---|---|---|---|---|
| 266 | **61** | 50f. multicoloured | 1·10 | 55 |
| 267 | **61** | 100f. multicoloured | 2·40 | 1·80 |
| 268 | **61** | 150f. multicoloured | 2·75 | 2·10 |
| 269 | **61** | 200f. multicoloured | 3·75 | 3·00 |
| **MS**270 | | 84×91 mm. No. 267 (sold at 200f.) | 10·00 | 10·00 |

**62** Arab with Gyr Falcon

**1980.** Falconry. Multicoloured.

| | | | |
|---|---|---|---|
| 271 | 100f. Type **62** | 4·25 | 2·40 |
| 272 | 100f. Arab looking at Lanner falcon on wrist | 4·25 | 2·40 |
| 273 | 100f. Peregrine falcon resting with outstretched wings | 4·25 | 2·40 |
| 274 | 100f. Peregrine falcon in flight | 4·25 | 2·40 |
| 275 | 100f. Gyr falcon on pillar (with camels in background) (vert) | 4·25 | 2·40 |
| 276 | 100f. Gyr falcon on pillar (closer view) (vert) | 4·25 | 2·40 |
| 277 | 100f. Close-up of gyr falcon facing right (vert) | 4·25 | 2·40 |
| 278 | 100f. Close-up of Lanner falcon full-face (vert) | 4·25 | 2·40 |

**63** Map and I.Y.D.P. Emblem

**1981.** International Year for Disabled Persons.

| | | | | |
|---|---|---|---|---|
| 279 | **63** | 50f. multicoloured | 2·75 | 75 |
| 280 | **63** | 100f. multicoloured | 5·25 | 2·75 |

64 Jubilee Emblem

1981. 50th Anniv of Electrical Power in Bahrain.

| | | | | |
|---|---|---|---|---|
| 281 | 64 | 50f. multicoloured | 1·90 | 85 |
| 282 | 64 | 100f. multicoloured | 4·50 | 2·40 |

65 Carving

1981. Handicrafts. Multicoloured.

| | | | |
|---|---|---|---|
| 283 | 50f. Type **65** | 1·60 | 65 |
| 284 | 100f. Pottery | 2·10 | 1·20 |
| 285 | 150f. Weaving | 2·75 | 2·10 |
| 286 | 200f. Basket-making | 4·25 | 2·75 |

66 Mosque

1981. Mosques.

| | | | | |
|---|---|---|---|---|
| 287 | 66 | 50f. multicoloured | 1·60 | 65 |
| 288 | - | 100f. multicoloured | 2·10 | 1·20 |
| 289 | - | 150f. multicoloured | 2·75 | 2·10 |
| 290 | - | 200f. multicoloured | 4·25 | 2·75 |

DESIGNS: 100f. to 200f. As Type **66** but showing different mosques.

67 Shaikh Isa bin Sulman al-Khalifa

1981. 20th Anniv of Coronation of Shaikh Isa bin Sulman al-Khalifa.

| | | | | |
|---|---|---|---|---|
| 291 | 67 | 15f. gold, grey and mauve | 75 | 75 |
| 292 | 67 | 50f. gold, grey and red | 1·50 | 1·50 |
| 293 | 67 | 100f. gold, grey and brown | 2·50 | 2·50 |
| 294 | 67 | 150f. gold, grey and blue | 4·00 | 4·00 |
| 295 | 67 | 200f. gold, grey and blue | 4·75 | 4·75 |

68 Dorcas Gazelle

1982. Al-Areen Wildlife Park. Multicoloured.

| | | | |
|---|---|---|---|
| 296 | 100f. Goitred gazelle | 2·75 | 2·75 |
| 297 | 100f. Type **68** | 2·75 | 2·75 |
| 298 | 100f. Dhub lizard | 2·75 | 2·75 |
| 299 | 100f. Brown hares | 2·75 | 2·75 |
| 300 | 100f. Arabian oryx | 2·75 | 2·75 |
| 301 | 100f. Addax | 2·75 | 2·75 |

69 Flags and Clasped Hands encircling Emblem

1982. 3rd Supreme Council Session of Gulf Co-operation Council.

| | | | | |
|---|---|---|---|---|
| 302 | 69 | 50f. multicoloured | 1·20 | 1·20 |
| 303 | - | 100f. multicoloured | 3·25 | 3·25 |

70 Madinat Hamad

1983. Opening of Madinat Hamad New Town. Multicoloured.

| | | | |
|---|---|---|---|
| 304 | 50f. Type **70** | 2·10 | 65 |
| 305 | 100f. View of Madinat Hamad (different) | 3·75 | 2·10 |

71 Shaikh Isa bin Sulman al-Khalifa

1983. Bicentenary of Al-Khalifa Dynasty. Mult.

| | | | |
|---|---|---|---|
| 306 | 100f. Type **71** | 1·30 | 1·30 |
| 307 | 100f. Cartouche of Ali bin Khalifa al-Khalifa | 1·30 | 1·30 |
| 308 | 100f. Isa bin Ali al-Khalifa | 1·30 | 1·30 |
| 309 | 100f. Hamad bin Isa al-Khalifa | 1·30 | 1·30 |
| 310 | 100f. Salman bin Hamad al-Khalifa | 1·30 | 1·30 |
| 311 | 100f. Cartouche of Ahmed bin Mohammed al-Khalifa | 1·30 | 1·30 |
| 312 | 100f. Cartouche of Salman bin Ahmed al-Khalifa | 1·30 | 1·30 |
| 313 | 100f. Cartouche of Abdullah bin Ahmed al-Khalifa | 1·30 | 1·30 |
| 314 | 100f. Cartouche of Mohammed bin Khalifa al-Khalifa | 1·30 | 1·30 |
| **MS**315 | 109×83 mm. 500f. Type **71** (60×38 mm) | 8·50 | 8·50 |

72 G.C.C. and Traffic and Licensing Directorate Emblems

1984. Gulf Co-operation Council Traffic Week.

| | | | | |
|---|---|---|---|---|
| 316 | 72 | 15f. multicoloured | 55 | 20 |
| 317 | 72 | 50f. multicoloured | 1·60 | 55 |
| 318 | 72 | 100f. multicoloured | 2·40 | 1·10 |

73 Hurdling

1984. Olympic Games, Los Angeles. Multicoloured.

| | | | |
|---|---|---|---|
| 319 | 15f. Type **73** | 30 | 30 |
| 320 | 50f. Show-jumping | 1·10 | 1·10 |
| 321 | 100f. Swimming | 2·10 | 2·10 |
| 322 | 150f. Fencing | 2·75 | 2·75 |
| 323 | 200f. Shooting | 4·50 | 4·50 |

74 Manama and Emblem

1984. Centenary of Postal Services.

| | | | | |
|---|---|---|---|---|
| 324 | 74 | 15f. multicoloured | 55 | 20 |
| 325 | 74 | 50f. multicoloured | 1·60 | 55 |
| 326 | 74 | 100f. multicoloured | 2·75 | 1·40 |

75 Narrow-barred Spanish Mackerel

1985. Fishes. Multicoloured.

| | | | |
|---|---|---|---|
| 327 | 100f. Type **75** | 2·10 | 2·10 |
| 328 | 100f. Crocodile needlefish (three fishes) | 2·10 | 2·10 |
| 329 | 100f. Sombre sweetlips (fish swimming to left, blue and lilac background) | 2·10 | 2·10 |
| 330 | 100f. White-spotted rabbitfish (two fishes, blue and lilac background) | 2·10 | 2·10 |
| 331 | 100f. Grey mullet (two fishes, green and pink background) | 2·10 | 2·10 |
| 332 | 100f. Two-banded seabream (green and grey background) | 2·10 | 2·10 |
| 333 | 100f. River seabream (blue background) | 2·10 | 2·10 |
| 334 | 100f. Malabar grouper (green background) | 2·10 | 2·10 |
| 335 | 100f. Small-toothed emperor (pink anemone background) | 2·10 | 2·10 |
| 336 | 100f. Golden trevally (fish swimming to right, blue and lilac background) | 2·10 | 2·10 |

76 Hands cupping Emblem

1985. Arabian Gulf States Social Work Week.

| | | | | |
|---|---|---|---|---|
| 337 | 76 | 15f. multicoloured | 45 | 45 |
| 338 | 76 | 50f. multicoloured | 1·30 | 1·30 |
| 339 | 76 | 100f. multicoloured | 2·75 | 2·75 |

77 I.Y.Y. Emblem

1986. International Youth Year.

| | | | | |
|---|---|---|---|---|
| 340 | 77 | 15f. multicoloured | 45 | 45 |
| 341 | 77 | 50f. multicoloured | 1·30 | 1·30 |
| 342 | 77 | 100f. multicoloured | 2·75 | 2·75 |

78 Aerial View of Causeway

1986. Opening of Saudi–Bahrain Causeway. Mult.

| | | | |
|---|---|---|---|
| 343 | 15f. Type **78** | 45 | 45 |
| 344 | 50f. Aerial view of island | 1·30 | 1·30 |
| 345 | 100f. Aerial view of road bridge | 2·10 | 2·10 |

79 Shaikh Isa bin Sulman al-Khalifa

1986. 25th Anniv of Accession of Shaikh Isa bin Sulman al-Khalifa.

| | | | | |
|---|---|---|---|---|
| 346 | 79 | 15f. multicoloured | 45 | 45 |
| 347 | 79 | 50f. multicoloured | 1·30 | 1·30 |
| 348 | 79 | 100f. multicoloured | 2·10 | 2·10 |
| **MS**349 | | 148×110 mm. Nos. 346/8 | 8·50 | 8·50 |

80 Emblem

1988. 40th Anniv of W.H.O.

| | | | | |
|---|---|---|---|---|
| 350 | 80 | 50f. multicoloured | 75 | 75 |
| 351 | 80 | 150f. multicoloured | 2·10 | 2·10 |

81 Centre

1988. Opening of Ahmed al-Fateh Islamic Centre.

| | | | | |
|---|---|---|---|---|
| 352 | 81 | 50f. multicoloured | 75 | 75 |
| 353 | 81 | 150f. multicoloured | 2·10 | 2·10 |

82 Running

1988. Olympic Games, Seoul. Multicoloured.

| | | | |
|---|---|---|---|
| 354 | 50f. Type **82** | 45 | 30 |
| 355 | 80f. Dressage | 85 | 55 |
| 356 | 150f. Fencing | 1·80 | 1·30 |
| 357 | 200f. Football | 2·75 | 2·10 |

83 Emblem in "1988"

1988. 9th Supreme Council Meeting of Gulf Co-operation Council.

| | | | | |
|---|---|---|---|---|
| 358 | 83 | 50f. multicoloured | 75 | 75 |
| 359 | 83 | 150f. multicoloured | 2·10 | 2·10 |

84 Arab leading Camel

1989. Camels. Multicoloured.

| | | | |
|---|---|---|---|
| 360 | 150f. Type **84** | 1·60 | 1·60 |
| 361 | 150f. Arab leading camel (different) | 1·60 | 1·60 |
| 362 | 150f. Head of camel and pump-head | 1·60 | 1·60 |
| 363 | 150f. Close-up of Arab on camel | 1·60 | 1·60 |
| 364 | 150f. Arab riding camel | 1·60 | 1·60 |
| 365 | 150f. Two Arab camel-riders | 1·60 | 1·60 |
| 366 | 150f. Head of camel and camel-rider (horiz) | 1·60 | 1·60 |
| 367 | 150f. Camels at rest in camp (horiz) | 1·60 | 1·60 |
| 368 | 150f. Camels with calf (horiz) | 1·60 | 1·60 |
| 369 | 150f. Heads of three camels (horiz) | 1·60 | 1·60 |
| 370 | 150f. Camel in scrubland (horiz) | 1·60 | 1·60 |
| 371 | 150f. Arab on camel (horiz) | 1·60 | 1·60 |

85 Shaikh Isa bin Sulman al-Khalifa

1989. Multicoloured, colour of frame given.

| | | | | |
|---|---|---|---|---|
| 372 | 85 | 25f. green | 30 | 20 |
| 373 | 85 | 40f. grey | 45 | 20 |

| | | | | |
|---|---|---|---|---|
| 374 | **85** | 50f. pink | 45 | 20 |
| 375 | **85** | 60f. brown | 55 | 20 |
| 376 | **85** | 75f. mauve | 75 | 20 |
| 377 | **85** | 80f. green | 75 | 20 |
| 378 | **85** | 100f. orange | 1·10 | 30 |
| 379 | **85** | 120f. violet | 1·20 | 30 |
| 380 | **85** | 150f. grey | 1·50 | 55 |
| 381 | **85** | 200f. blue | 1·80 | 75 |
| **MS**382 | | 167×132 mm. Nos. 372/81 | 9·00 | 9·00 |

**86** Houbara Bustards

**1990.** The Houbara Bustard. Multicoloured.

| | | | |
|---|---|---|---|
| 383 | 150f. Type **86** | 1·50 | 1·50 |
| 384 | 150f. Two bustards (facing each other) | 1·50 | 1·50 |
| 385 | 150f. Chicks and eggs | 1·50 | 1·50 |
| 386 | 150f. Adult and chick | 1·50 | 1·50 |
| 387 | 150f. Adult (vert) | 1·50 | 1·50 |
| 388 | 150f. In flight | 1·50 | 1·50 |
| 389 | 150f. Adult (facing right) | 1·50 | 1·50 |
| 390 | 150f. Young bird (vert) | 1·50 | 1·50 |
| 391 | 150f. Adult (facing left) | 1·50 | 1·50 |
| 392 | 150f. Bird in display plumage | 1·50 | 1·50 |
| 393 | 150f. Two bustards in display plumage | 1·50 | 1·50 |
| 394 | 150f. Two bustards with bridge in background | 1·50 | 1·50 |

**87** Anniversary Emblem

**1990.** 40th Anniv of Gulf Air.

| | | | | |
|---|---|---|---|---|
| 395 | **87** | 50f. multicoloured | 55 | 30 |
| 396 | **87** | 80f. multicoloured | 85 | 55 |
| 397 | **87** | 150f. multicoloured | 1·60 | 1·10 |
| 398 | **87** | 200f. multicoloured | 2·40 | 1·50 |

**88** Anniversary Emblem

**1990.** 50th Anniv of Bahrain Chamber of Commerce and Industry.

| | | | | |
|---|---|---|---|---|
| 399 | **88** | 50f. multicoloured | 55 | 30 |
| 400 | **88** | 80f. multicoloured | 75 | 55 |
| 401 | **88** | 150f. multicoloured | 1·40 | 95 |
| 402 | **88** | 200f. multicoloured | 1·80 | 1·30 |

**89** I.L.Y. Emblem

**1990.** International Literacy Year.

| | | | | |
|---|---|---|---|---|
| 403 | **89** | 50f. multicoloured | 55 | 30 |
| 404 | **89** | 80f. multicoloured | 75 | 55 |
| 405 | **89** | 150f. multicoloured | 1·40 | 95 |
| 406 | **89** | 200f. multicoloured | 1·90 | 1·30 |

**90** Crested Lark

**1991.** Birds. Multicoloured.

| | | | |
|---|---|---|---|
| 407 | 150f. Type **90** | 1·30 | 1·30 |
| 408 | 150f. Hoopoe ("Upupa epops") | 1·30 | 1·30 |
| 409 | 150f. White-cheeked bulbul ("Pycnonotus leucogenys") | 1·30 | 1·30 |
| 410 | 150f. Turtle dove ("Streptopelia turtur") | 1·30 | 1·30 |
| 411 | 150f. Collared dove ("Streptopelia decaocto") | 1·30 | 1·30 |
| 412 | 150f. Common kestrel ("Falco tinnunculus") | 1·30 | 1·30 |
| 413 | 150f. House sparrow ("Passer domesticus") (horiz) | 1·30 | 1·30 |
| 414 | 150f. Great grey shrike ("Lanius excubitor") (horiz) | 1·30 | 1·30 |
| 415 | 150f. Rose-ringed parakeet ("Psittacula krameri") | 1·30 | 1·30 |

**91** Shaikh Isa bin Sulman al-Khalifa

**1991.** 30th Anniv of Amir's Coronation.

| | | | | |
|---|---|---|---|---|
| 416 | **91** | 50f. multicoloured | 45 | 30 |
| 417 | **A** | 50f. multicoloured | 45 | 30 |
| 418 | **91** | 80f. multicoloured | 65 | 45 |
| 419 | **A** | 80f. multicoloured | 65 | 45 |
| 420 | **91** | 150f. multicoloured | 1·40 | 85 |
| 421 | **A** | 150f. multicoloured | 1·40 | 85 |
| 422 | **91** | 200f. multicoloured | 1·80 | 1·10 |
| 423 | **A** | 200f. multicoloured | 1·80 | 1·10 |
| **MS**424 | | 134×114 mm. **91** 500f. multicoloured; A 500f. multicoloured | 10·50 | 10·50 |

DESIGN: A, The Amir and sunburst.

**92** White Stork ("Ciconia ciconia")

**1992.** Migratory Birds. Multicoloured.

| | | | |
|---|---|---|---|
| 425 | 150f. Type **92** | 1·20 | 1·20 |
| 426 | 150f. European bee eater ("Merops apiaster") | 1·20 | 1·20 |
| 427 | 150f. Common starling ("Sturnus vulgaris") | 1·20 | 1·20 |
| 428 | 150f. Grey hypocolius ("Hypocolius ampelinus") | 1·20 | 1·20 |
| 429 | 150f. European cuckoo ("Cuculus canorus") | 1·20 | 1·20 |
| 430 | 150f. Mistle thrush ("Turdus viscivorus") | 1·20 | 1·20 |
| 431 | 150f. European roller ("Coracias garrulus") | 1·20 | 1·20 |
| 432 | 150f. Eurasian goldfinch ("Carduelis carduelis") | 1·20 | 1·20 |
| 433 | 150f. Red-backed shrike ("Lanius collurio") | 1·20 | 1·20 |
| 434 | 150f. Redwing ("Turdus iliacus") (horiz) | 1·20 | 1·20 |
| 435 | 150f. Pied wagtail ("Motacilla alba") (horiz) | 1·20 | 1·20 |
| 436 | 150f. Golden oriole ("Oriolus oriolus") (horiz) | 1·20 | 1·20 |
| 437 | 150f. European robin ("Erithacus rubecula") | 1·20 | 1·20 |
| 438 | 150f. Nightingale ("Luscinia luscinia") | 1·20 | 1·20 |
| 439 | 150f. Spotted flycatcher ("Muscicapa striata") | 1·20 | 1·20 |
| 440 | 150f. Barn swallow ("Hirundo rustica") | 1·20 | 1·20 |

**93** Start of Race

**1992.** Horse-racing. Multicoloured.

| | | | |
|---|---|---|---|
| 441 | 150f. Type **93** | 1·30 | 1·30 |
| 442 | 150f. Parading in paddock | 1·30 | 1·30 |
| 443 | 150f. Galloping around bend | 1·30 | 1·30 |
| 444 | 150f. Galloping past national flags | 1·30 | 1·30 |
| 445 | 150f. Galloping past spectator stand | 1·30 | 1·30 |
| 446 | 150f. Head-on view of horses | 1·30 | 1·30 |
| 447 | 150f. Reaching winning post | 1·30 | 1·30 |
| 448 | 150f. A black and a grey galloping | 1·30 | 1·30 |

**94** Show-jumping

**1992.** Olympic Games, Barcelona. Multicoloured.

| | | | |
|---|---|---|---|
| 449 | 50f. Type **94** | 45 | 45 |
| 450 | 80f. Running | 85 | 85 |
| 451 | 150f. Karate | 1·60 | 1·60 |
| 452 | 200f. Cycling | 2·10 | 2·10 |

**95** Airport

**1992.** 60th Anniv of Bahrain International Airport.

| | | | | |
|---|---|---|---|---|
| 453 | **95** | 50f. multicoloured | 45 | 45 |
| 454 | **95** | 80f. multicoloured | 85 | 85 |
| 455 | **95** | 150f. multicoloured | 1·60 | 1·60 |
| 456 | **95** | 200f. multicoloured | 2·10 | 2·10 |

**96** Girl skipping

**1992.** Children's Paintings. Multicoloured.

| | | | |
|---|---|---|---|
| 457 | 50f. Type **96** | 45 | 30 |
| 458 | 80f. Women | 65 | 45 |
| 459 | 150f. Women preparing food (horiz) | 1·30 | 85 |
| 460 | 200f. Pearl divers (horiz) | 1·70 | 1·20 |

**97** Cable-cars and Pylons

**1992.** Expansion of Aluminium Industry. Mult.

| | | | |
|---|---|---|---|
| 461 | 50f. Type **97** | 45 | 45 |
| 462 | 80f. Worker in aluminium plant | 85 | 85 |
| 463 | 150f. Aerial view of aluminium plant | 1·60 | 1·60 |
| 464 | 200f. Processed aluminium | 2·10 | 2·10 |

**98** Artillery Gun Crew

**1993.** 25th Anniv of Bahrain Defence Force. Mult.

| | | | |
|---|---|---|---|
| 465 | 50f. Type **98** | 45 | 45 |
| 466 | 80f. General Dynamics Fighting Falcon jet fighters, tanks and patrol boat | 75 | 75 |
| 467 | 150f. "Ahmed al Fatah" (missile corvette) (horiz) | 1·50 | 1·50 |
| 468 | 200f. Fighting Falcon over Bahrain (horiz) | 1·90 | 1·90 |

**99** Satellite View of Bahrain

**1993.** World Meteorological Day. Multicoloured.

| | | | |
|---|---|---|---|
| 469 | 50f. Type **99** | 65 | 65 |
| 470 | 150f. Satellite picture of world (horiz) | 1·60 | 1·60 |
| 471 | 200f. Earth seen from space | 2·50 | 2·50 |

**100** Purple Heron

**1993.** Water Birds. Multicoloured.

| | | | |
|---|---|---|---|
| 472 | 150f. Type **100** | 1·60 | 1·60 |
| 473 | 150f. Moorhen ("Gallinula chloropus") | 1·60 | 1·60 |
| 474 | 150f. Socotra cormorant ("Phalacrocorax nigrogularis") | 1·60 | 1·60 |
| 475 | 150f. Crab plover ("Dromas ardeola") | 1·60 | 1·60 |
| 476 | 150f. River kingfisher ("Alcedo atthis") | 1·60 | 1·60 |
| 477 | 150f. Northern lapwing ("Vanellus vanellus") | 1·60 | 1·60 |
| 478 | 150f. Oystercatcher ("Haematopus ostralegus") (horiz) | 1·60 | 1·60 |
| 479 | 150f. Black-crowned night heron ("Nycticorax nycticorax") | 1·60 | 1·60 |
| 480 | 150f. Caspian tern ("Sterna caspia") (horiz) | 1·60 | 1·60 |
| 481 | 150f. Ruddy turnstone ("Arenaria interpres") (horiz) | 1·60 | 1·60 |
| 482 | 150f. Water rail ("Rallus aquaticus") (horiz) | 1·60 | 1·60 |
| 483 | 150f. Mallard ("Anas platyrhyncos") (horiz) | 1·60 | 1·60 |
| 484 | 150f. Lesser black-backed gull ("Larus fuscus") (horiz) | 1·60 | 1·60 |

**101** Fawn

**1993.** The Goitered Gazelle. Multicoloured.

| | | | |
|---|---|---|---|
| 485 | 25f. Type **101** | 1·20 | 1·20 |
| 486 | 50f. Doe walking | 2·40 | 2·40 |
| 487 | 50f. Doe with ears pricked | 2·40 | 2·40 |
| 488 | 150f. Male gazelle | 7·00 | 7·00 |

**102** "Lycium shawii"

**1993.** Wild Flowers. Multicoloured.

| | | | |
|---|---|---|---|
| 489 | 150f. Type **102** | 1·10 | 1·10 |
| 490 | 150f. "Alhagi maurorum" | 1·10 | 1·10 |
| 491 | 150f. Caper-bush ("Caparis spinosa") | 1·10 | 1·10 |
| 492 | 150f. "Cistanche phelypae" | 1·10 | 1·10 |
| 493 | 150f. "Asphodelus tenuifolius" | 1·10 | 1·10 |
| 494 | 150f. "Limonium axillare" | 1·10 | 1·10 |
| 495 | 150f. "Cynomorium coccineum" | 1·10 | 1·10 |
| 496 | 150f. "Calligonum polygonoides" | 1·10 | 1·10 |

**103** Children and Silhouettes of Parents' Heads

**1994.** International Year of the Family.

| | | | | |
|---|---|---|---|---|
| 497 | **103** | 50f. multicoloured | 45 | 45 |
| 498 | **103** | 80f. multicoloured | 75 | 75 |
| 499 | **103** | 150f. multicoloured | 1·50 | 1·50 |
| 500 | **103** | 200f. multicoloured | 1·90 | 1·90 |

**104** "Lepidochrysops arabicus"

**1994.** Butterflies. Multicoloured.

| | | | |
|---|---|---|---|
| 501 | 50f. Type **104** | 30 | 30 |
| 502 | 50f. "Ypthima bolanica" | 30 | 30 |
| 503 | 50f. Desert grass yellow ("Eurema brigitta") | 30 | 30 |
| 504 | 50f. "Precis limnoria" | 30 | 30 |
| 505 | 50f. Small tortoiseshell ("Aglais urticae") | 30 | 30 |
| 506 | 50f. Protomedia ("Colotis protomedia") | 30 | 30 |
| 507 | 50f. Clouded mother-of-pearl (Salamis anacardii") | 30 | 30 |
| 508 | 50f. "Byblia ilithyia" | 30 | 30 |
| 509 | 150f. Swallowtail ("Papilio machaon") (horiz) | 95 | 95 |
| 510 | 150f. Blue ("Agrodiaetus loewii") (horiz) | 95 | 95 |
| 511 | 150f. Painted lady ("Vanessa cardui") (horiz) | 95 | 95 |
| 512 | 150f. Chequered swallowtail ("Papilio demoleus") (horiz) | 95 | 95 |
| 513 | 150f. Guineafowl ("Hamanumida daedalus") (horiz) | 95 | 95 |
| 514 | 150f. "Funonia orithya" (horiz) | 95 | 95 |
| 515 | 150f. "Funonia chorimine" (horiz) | 95 | 95 |
| 516 | 150f. "Colias croceus" (horiz) | 95 | 95 |

**105** Anniversary Emblem

**1994.** 75th Anniv of International Red Cross and Red Crescent.

| | | | | |
|---|---|---|---|---|
| 517 | **105** | 50f. multicoloured | 45 | 45 |
| 518 | **105** | 80f. multicoloured | 75 | 75 |
| 519 | **105** | 150f. multicoloured | 1·50 | 1·50 |
| 520 | **105** | 200f. multicoloured | 1·90 | 1·90 |

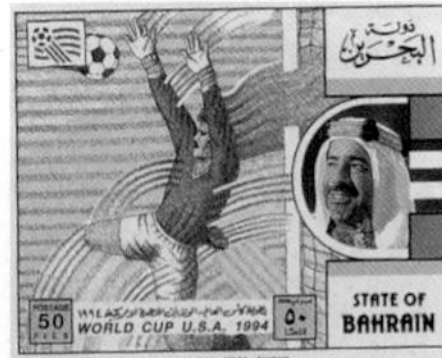


**106** Goalkeeper

**1994.** World Cup Football Championship, U.S.A. Multicoloured.

| | | | |
|---|---|---|---|
| 521 | 50f. Type **106** | 55 | 55 |
| 522 | 80f. Players | 85 | 85 |
| 523 | 150f. Players' legs | 1·60 | 1·60 |
| 524 | 200f. Player on ground | 2·10 | 2·10 |

**107** Earth Station

**1994.** 25th Anniv of Ras Abu Jarjour Satellite Earth Station.

| | | | | |
|---|---|---|---|---|
| 525 | **107** | 50f. multicoloured | 45 | 45 |
| 526 | **107** | 80f. multicoloured | 75 | 75 |
| 527 | **107** | 150f. multicoloured | 1·50 | 1·50 |
| 528 | **107** | 200f. multicoloured | 1·90 | 1·90 |

**108** Children on Open Book, Pen as Torch and School

**1994.** 75th Anniv of Education in Bahrain.

| | | | | |
|---|---|---|---|---|
| 529 | **108** | 50f. multicoloured | 45 | 45 |
| 530 | **108** | 80f. multicoloured | 75 | 75 |
| 531 | **108** | 150f. multicoloured | 1·50 | 1·50 |
| 532 | **108** | 200f. multicoloured | 1·90 | 1·90 |

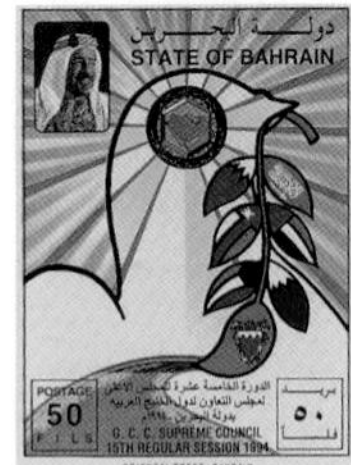


**109** Dove with "Olive Branch" of Members' Flags

**1994.** 15th Gulf Co-operation Council Supreme Council Session, Bahrain.

| | | | | |
|---|---|---|---|---|
| 533 | **109** | 50f. multicoloured | 45 | 45 |
| 534 | **109** | 80f. multicoloured | 75 | 75 |
| 535 | **109** | 150f. multicoloured | 1·40 | 1·40 |
| 536 | **109** | 200f. multicoloured | 1·80 | 1·80 |

**110** Date Palm in Bloom

**1995.** The Date Palm.

| | | | |
|---|---|---|---|
| 537 | 80f. Type **110** | 75 | 75 |
| 538 | 100f. Date palm with unripened dates | 85 | 85 |
| 539 | 200f. Dates ripening | 1·80 | 1·80 |
| 540 | 250f. Date palm trees with ripened dates | 2·10 | 2·10 |
| **MS**541 | 134×126 mm. 500f. Dates, coffee pot, cups and date palms (65×47 mm) | 4·25 | 4·25 |

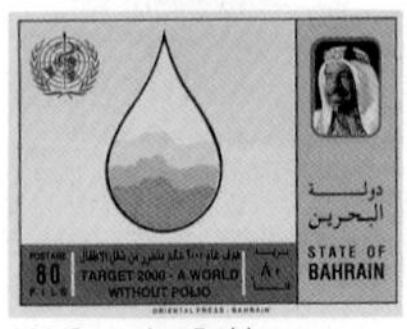


**111** Campaign Emblem

**1995.** World Health Day. Anti-poliomyelitis Campaign.

| | | | | |
|---|---|---|---|---|
| 542 | **111** | 80f. multicoloured | 55 | 55 |
| 543 | **111** | 200f. multicoloured | 1·50 | 1·50 |
| 544 | **111** | 250f. multicoloured | 2·00 | 2·00 |

**112** Exhibition Emblem

**1995.** 1st National Industries Exhibition.

| | | | | |
|---|---|---|---|---|
| 545 | **112** | 80f. multicoloured | 55 | 55 |
| 546 | **112** | 200f. multicoloured | 1·50 | 1·50 |
| 547 | **112** | 250f. multicoloured | 2·00 | 2·00 |

**113** Crops

**1995.** 50th Anniv of F.A.O. Multicoloured.

| | | | |
|---|---|---|---|
| 548 | 80f. Type **113** | 55 | 55 |
| 549 | 200f. Field of crops | 1·50 | 1·50 |
| 550 | 250f. Field of cabbages | 2·00 | 2·00 |

**114** Headquarters, Cairo

**1995.** 50th Anniv of Arab League.

| | | | | |
|---|---|---|---|---|
| 551 | **114** | 80f. multicoloured | 55 | 55 |
| 552 | **114** | 200f. multicoloured | 1·50 | 1·50 |
| 553 | **114** | 250f. multicoloured | 2·00 | 2·00 |

**115** U.N. Headquarters and Map of Bahrain

**1995.** 50th Anniv of U.N.O.

| | | | | |
|---|---|---|---|---|
| 554 | **115** | 80f. multicoloured | 55 | 55 |
| 555 | **115** | 100f. multicoloured | 75 | 75 |
| 556 | **115** | 200f. multicoloured | 1·60 | 1·60 |
| 557 | **115** | 250f. multicoloured | 2·00 | 2·00 |

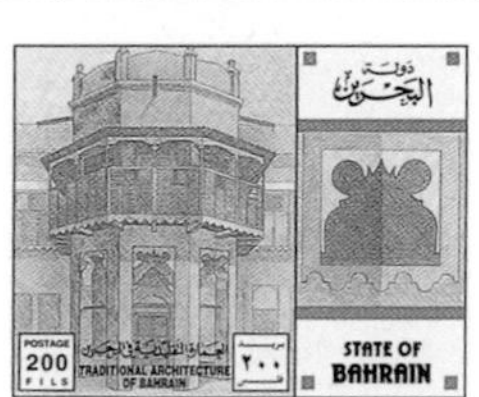


**116** Tower

**1995.** Traditional Architecture. Multicoloured.

| | | | |
|---|---|---|---|
| 558 | 200f. Type **116** | 1·30 | 1·30 |
| 559 | 200f. Balcony | 1·30 | 1·30 |
| 560 | 200f. Doorway | 1·30 | 1·30 |
| 561 | 200f. Multi-storied facade | 1·30 | 1·30 |
| 562 | 200f. Entrance flanked by two windows | 1·30 | 1·30 |
| 563 | 200f. Three arched windows | 1·30 | 1·30 |

**117** National Flag and Shaikh Isa Bin Sulman al-Khalifa

**1995.** National Day.

| | | | | |
|---|---|---|---|---|
| 564 | **117** | 80f. multicoloured | 55 | 55 |
| 565 | **117** | 100f. multicoloured | 75 | 75 |
| 566 | **117** | 200f. multicoloured | 1·60 | 1·60 |
| 567 | **117** | 250f. multicoloured | 2·00 | 2·00 |

**118** Bookcase and Open Book

**1996.** 50th Anniv of Public Library.

| | | | | |
|---|---|---|---|---|
| 568 | **118** | 80f. multicoloured | 55 | 55 |
| 569 | **118** | 200f. multicoloured | 1·60 | 1·60 |
| 570 | **118** | 250f. multicoloured | 2·00 | 2·00 |

**119** Divers on Dhow

**1996.** Pearl Diving. Multicoloured.

| | | | |
|---|---|---|---|
| 571 | 80f. Type **119** | 55 | 55 |
| 572 | 100f. Divers | 65 | 65 |
| 573 | 200f. Diver on sea-bed and dhow | 1·30 | 1·30 |
| 574 | 250f. Diver with net | 1·80 | 1·80 |
| **MS**575 | 119×119 mm. 500f. Diving equipment (70×70 mm) | 4·25 | 4·25 |

**120** Globe, Ship and Olympic Rings

**1996.** Olympic Games, Atlanta.

| | | | | |
|---|---|---|---|---|
| 576 | **120** | 80f. multicoloured | 55 | 55 |
| 577 | **120** | 100f. multicoloured | 65 | 65 |
| 578 | **120** | 200f. multicoloured | 1·30 | 1·30 |
| 579 | **120** | 250f. multicoloured | 1·80 | 1·80 |

**121** Interpol Emblem and Map, Arms and Flag of Bahrain

**1996.** 24th Anniv of Membership of International Criminal Police (Interpol).

| | | | | |
|---|---|---|---|---|
| 580 | **121** | 80f. multicoloured | 55 | 55 |
| 581 | **121** | 100f. multicoloured | 75 | 75 |
| 582 | **121** | 200f. multicoloured | 1·60 | 1·60 |
| 583 | **121** | 250f. multicoloured | 2·00 | 2·00 |

**122** Anniversary Emblems in English and Arabic

**1996.** 25th Anniv of Aluminium Bahrain.

| | | | | |
|---|---|---|---|---|
| 584 | **122** | 80f. multicoloured | 45 | 45 |
| 585 | **122** | 100f. multicoloured | 55 | 55 |
| 586 | **122** | 200f. multicoloured | 1·30 | 1·30 |
| 587 | **122** | 250f. multicoloured | 1·60 | 1·60 |

**123** National Flag, Map and Shaikh Isa bin Sulman al-Khalifa

**1996.** 35th Anniv of Amir's Accession.

| | | | | |
|---|---|---|---|---|
| 588 | **123** | 80f. multicoloured | 55 | 55 |
| 589 | **123** | 100f. multicoloured | 75 | 75 |
| 590 | **123** | 200f. multicoloured | 1·60 | 1·60 |
| 591 | **123** | 250f. multicoloured | 2·00 | 2·00 |

**124** Tanker, Refinery and Storage Tanks

**1997.** 60th Anniv of Bahrain Refinery.

| | | | | |
|---|---|---|---|---|
| 592 | **124** | 80f. multicoloured | 55 | 55 |
| 593 | **124** | 200f. multicoloured | 1·40 | 1·40 |
| 594 | **124** | 250f. multicoloured | 1·90 | 1·90 |

**125** Kuheilaan Weld umm Zorayr

**1997.** Arab Horses at Amiri Stud. Multicoloured.

| | | | |
|---|---|---|---|
| 595 | 200f. Musannaan (white horse), Al-Jellabieh and Rabdaan | 1·40 | 1·40 |
| 596 | 200f. Type **125** | 1·40 | 1·40 |
| 597 | 200f. Al-Jellaby | 1·40 | 1·40 |
| 598 | 200f. Musannaan (brown horse) | 1·40 | 1·40 |
| 599 | 200f. Kuheilaan Aladiyat | 1·40 | 1·40 |
| 600 | 200f. Kuheilaan Aafas | 1·40 | 1·40 |
| 601 | 200f. Al-Dhahma | 1·40 | 1·40 |
| 602 | 200f. Mlolshaan | 1·40 | 1·40 |
| 603 | 200f. Al-Kray | 1·40 | 1·40 |
| 604 | 200f. Krush | 1·40 | 1·40 |
| 605 | 200f. Al Hamdaany | 1·40 | 1·40 |
| 606 | 200f. Hadhfaan | 1·40 | 1·40 |
| 607 | 200f. Rabda | 1·40 | 1·40 |
| 608 | 200f. Al-Suwaitieh | 1·40 | 1·40 |
| 609 | 200f. Al-Obeyah | 1·40 | 1·40 |
| 610 | 200f. Al-Shuwaimeh | 1·40 | 1·40 |
| 611 | 200f. Al-Ma'anaghieh | 1·40 | 1·40 |
| 612 | 200f. Al-Tuwaisah | 1·40 | 1·40 |
| 613 | 200f. Wadhna | 1·40 | 1·40 |
| 614 | 200f. Al-Saqlawieh | 1·40 | 1·40 |
| 615 | 200f. Al-Shawafah | 1·40 | 1·40 |

**126** Championship Emblem

**1997.** 9th World Men's Junior Volleyball Championship.

| | | | | |
|---|---|---|---|---|
| 616 | **126** | 80f. multicoloured | 55 | 55 |
| 617 | **126** | 100f. multicoloured | 75 | 75 |
| 618 | **126** | 200f. multicoloured | 1·40 | 1·40 |
| 619 | **126** | 250f. multicoloured | 1·80 | 1·80 |

**127** Emblem

**1997.** 10th Anniv of Montreal Protocol (on reduction of use of chlorofluorocarbons).

| | | | | |
|---|---|---|---|---|
| 620 | **127** | 80f. multicoloured | 55 | 55 |
| 621 | **127** | 100f. multicoloured | 75 | 75 |
| 622 | **127** | 200f. multicoloured | 1·40 | 1·40 |
| 623 | **127** | 250f. multicoloured | 1·80 | 1·80 |

**128** Close-up of Support

**1997.** Inauguration of Shaikh Isa bin Salman Bridge between Manama and Muharraq. Multicoloured.

| | | | |
|---|---|---|---|
| 624 | 80f. Type **128** | 55 | 55 |
| 625 | 200f. Distant view of middle section | 1·50 | 1·50 |
| 626 | 250f. View of complete bridge (75×26 mm) | 1·80 | 1·80 |
| **MS**627 | 137×116 mm. 500f. As No. 626 | 3·75 | 3·75 |

**129** Complex at Night

**1998.** Inauguration of Urea Plant at Gulf Petrochemical Industries Co Complex. Mult.

| | | | |
|---|---|---|---|
| 628 | 80f. Type **129** | 55 | 55 |
| 629 | 200f. Refining towers | 1·50 | 1·50 |
| 630 | 250f. Aerial view of complex | 1·80 | 1·80 |

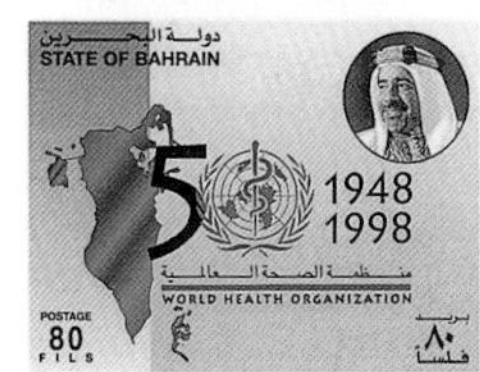

**130** Map of Bahrain and Anniversary Emblem

**1998.** 50th Anniv of W.H.O.

| | | | | |
|---|---|---|---|---|
| 631 | **130** | 80f. multicoloured | 55 | 55 |
| 632 | **130** | 200f. multicoloured | 1·50 | 1·50 |
| 633 | **130** | 250f. multicoloured | 1·80 | 1·80 |

**131** Emblem

**1998.** World Cup Football Championship, France. Multicoloured.

| | | | |
|---|---|---|---|
| 634 | 80f. Type **131** | 55 | 55 |
| 635 | 200f. Globes and football forming "98" (vert) | 1·50 | 1·50 |
| 636 | 250f. Footballers and globe (vert) | 1·80 | 1·80 |

**132** Football

**1998.** 14th Arabian Gulf Cup Football Championship, Bahrain. Multicoloured.

| | | | |
|---|---|---|---|
| 637 | 80f. Type **132** | 55 | 55 |
| 638 | 200f. Close-up of football | 1·50 | 1·50 |
| 639 | 250f. As No. 638 | 1·80 | 1·80 |

**133** Emblem and Koran

**1999.** Holy Koran Reading Competition.

| | | | | |
|---|---|---|---|---|
| 640 | **133** | 100f. multicoloured | 75 | 75 |
| 641 | **133** | 200f. multicoloured | 1·60 | 1·60 |
| 642 | **133** | 250f. multicoloured | 1·80 | 1·80 |

**134** Shaikh Isa bin Sulman al-Khalifa and State Flag

**1999.** Shaikh Isa bin Sulman al-Khalifa Commemoration. Multicoloured.

| | | | |
|---|---|---|---|
| 643 | 100f. Type **134** | 75 | 75 |
| 644 | 200f. Shaikh and map of Bahrain (41×31 mm) | 1·60 | 1·60 |
| 645 | 250f. Shaikh, map of Bahrain and state flag | 1·80 | 1·80 |
| **MS**646 | 125×170 mm. 500f. Type **134** (67×102 mm) | 4·25 | 4·25 |

**135** Emblem

**1999.** International Year of the Elderly. Mult.

| | | | |
|---|---|---|---|
| 647 | 100f. Type **135** | 75 | 75 |
| 648 | 200f. Emblem and flame | 1·60 | 1·60 |
| 649 | 250f. Emblem (different) | 1·80 | 1·80 |

**136** Emblem

**1999.** 10th Anniv of Bahrain Stock Exchange. Multicoloured.

| | | | |
|---|---|---|---|
| 650 | 100f. Type **136** | 75 | 75 |
| 651 | 200f. Shaikh Isa bin Salman Bridge and emblem | 1·60 | 1·60 |
| 652 | 250f. Globe and emblem | 1·80 | 1·80 |

**137** Shaikh Isa bin Salman and Shaikh Hamad bin Isa holding Flag

**1999.** National Day. Multicoloured.

| | | | |
|---|---|---|---|
| 653 | 100f. Type **137** | 75 | 75 |
| 654 | 200f. Shaikh Hamad bin Isa and flag | 1·60 | 1·60 |
| 655 | 250f. Shaikh Hamad bin Isa and globe | 1·80 | 1·80 |
| **MS**656 | 115×155 mm. 500f. As Type **137** (56×96 mm) | 3·75 | 3·75 |

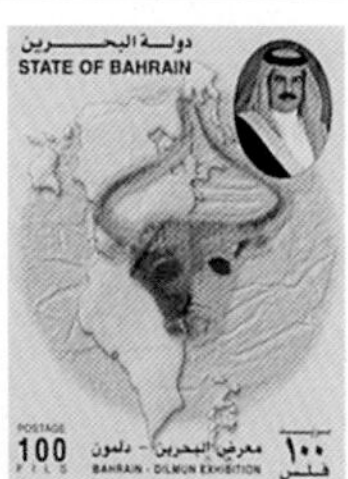

**138** Map of Bahrain and Animal Skull

**2000.** Dilmun Exhibition. Multicoloured.

| | | | |
|---|---|---|---|
| 657 | 100f. Type **138** | 75 | 75 |
| 658 | 200f. Map of Bahrain superimposed over animal skull | 1·60 | 1·60 |
| 659 | 250f. Map of Bahrain and artefact | 1·80 | 1·80 |

**139** Map of Bahrain and Emblem

**2000.** 50th Anniv of Gulf Air. Multicoloured.

| | | | |
|---|---|---|---|
| 660 | 100f. Type **139** | 1·20 | 1·20 |
| 661 | 200f. Map of Bahrain and emblem in circle | 2·40 | 2·40 |
| 662 | 250f. Map of Bahrain, emblem and eagles | 2·75 | 2·75 |

**140** Emblem

**2000.** "Made in Bahrain 2000" Exhibition. Multicoloured.

| | | | |
|---|---|---|---|
| 663 | 100f. Type **140** | 1·20 | 1·20 |
| 664 | 200f. Type **140** | 2·40 | 2·40 |
| 665 | 250f. Oil refinery | 2·75 | 2·75 |

**141** Minarets and Fort

**2000.** Millennium. Multicoloured.

| | | | |
|---|---|---|---|
| 666 | 100f. Type **141** | 1·30 | 1·30 |
| 667 | 100f. Dhows and factories | 1·30 | 1·30 |
| 668 | 100f. Man harvesting dates | 1·30 | 1·30 |
| 669 | 100f. Fort, globe and dish aerial | 1·30 | 1·30 |
| 670 | 200f. Lake and bridge | 1·80 | 1·80 |
| 671 | 200f. Modern building and woman | 1·80 | 1·80 |
| 672 | 200f. Dhows, jug and wicker basket | 1·80 | 1·80 |
| 673 | 200f. Horseman and falconer | 1·80 | 1·80 |
| 674 | 250f. Pearl divers | 2·20 | 2·20 |
| 675 | 250f. Opening clams | 2·20 | 2·20 |
| 676 | 250f. Fishermen | 2·20 | 2·20 |
| 677 | 250f. Man mending fishing nets | 2·20 | 2·20 |

**142** Emblem

**2000.** 21st Gulf Co-operation Council Supreme Council Session, Bahrain. Multicoloured.

| | | | |
|---|---|---|---|
| 678 | 100f. Type **142** | 1·20 | 1·20 |
| 679 | 200f. Members' flags | 2·40 | 2·40 |

**143** Stained-glass Window

**2001.** 10th Anniv of Beit Al Qur'an (Islamic institution). Multicoloured.

| | | | |
|---|---|---|---|
| 680 | 100f. Type **143** | 75 | 75 |
| 681 | 200f. Beit Al Qur'an by night | 1·50 | 1·50 |
| 682 | 250f. Facade | 2·00 | 2·00 |
| **MS**683 | 170×80 mm. 500f. Subjects as Nos. 680/2 but forming composite design. Imperf | 3·75 | 3·75 |

**144** Building

**2001.** 25th Anniv of Ministry of Housing and Agriculture. Multicoloured.

| | | | |
|---|---|---|---|
| 684 | 100f. Type **144** | 75 | 75 |
| 685 | 150f. Sculpture and building | 1·20 | 1·20 |
| 686 | 200f. Building viewed through arch | 1·50 | 1·50 |
| 687 | 250f. Tall, arched building | 2·00 | 2·00 |

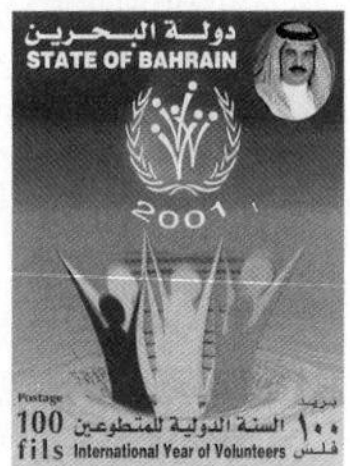

**145** Emblem and Stylized Figures

**2001.** International Year of Volunteers. Multicoloured.

| | | | |
|---|---|---|---|
| 688 | 100f. Type **145** | 75 | 75 |
| 689 | 150f. Hands encircling emblem | 1·20 | 1·20 |
| 690 | 200f. Star pattern and emblem | 1·50 | 1·50 |
| 691 | 250f. Paper cut figures | 2·00 | 2·00 |

**146** Emblem

**2002.** Arab Women's Day. Multicoloured.

| | | | |
|---|---|---|---|
| 692 | 100f. Type **146** | 75 | 75 |
| 693 | 200f. Elliptical shapes and emblem | 1·60 | 1·60 |
| 694 | 250f. Women (horiz) | 2·00 | 2·00 |

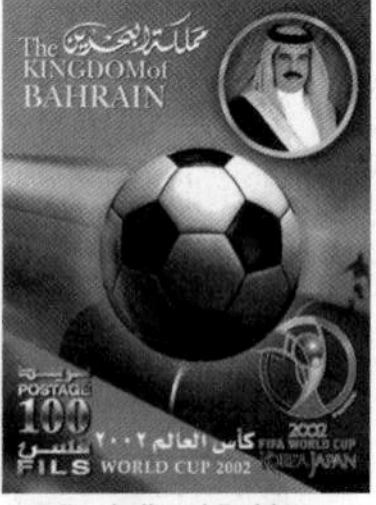

**147** Football and Emblem

**2002.** World Cup Football Championship, Japan and South Korea. Sheet 124×64 mm containing T 147 and similar vert designs. Multicoloured.

| | | | |
|---|---|---|---|
| **MS**695 | 100f. Type **147**; 200f. Earth, football and emblem; 250f. Football and white peaks | 4·25 | 4·25 |

**148** Shaikh Hamad Bin Isa Al Khalifa

**2002.** Multicoloured, background colour given. (a) Size 22×28 mm.

| | | | | |
|---|---|---|---|---|
| 696 | **148** | 25f. brown | 10 | 10 |
| 697 | **148** | 40f. purple | 30 | 30 |
| 698 | **148** | 50f. grey | 40 | 40 |
| 699 | **148** | 60f. blue | 50 | 50 |
| 700 | **148** | 80f. blue | 65 | 65 |
| 701 | **148** | 100f. orange | 75 | 75 |
| 702 | **148** | 125f. mauve | 95 | 95 |
| 703 | **148** | 150f. orange | 1·10 | 1·10 |
| 704 | **148** | 200f. green | 1·60 | 1·60 |
| 705 | **148** | 250f. pink | 2·00 | 2·00 |
| 706 | **148** | 300f. brown | 2·40 | 2·40 |
| 707 | **148** | 400f. green | 3·25 | 3·25 |

(b) 26×36 mm.

| | | | |
|---|---|---|---|
| 708 | 500f. mauve | 3·75 | 3·75 |
| 709 | 1d. orange | 8·00 | 8·00 |
| 710 | 2d. blue | 16·00 | 16·00 |
| 711 | 3d. brown | 24·00 | 24·00 |
| **MS**712 | 246×162 mm. Nos. 696/711 | 65·00 | 65·00 |

**149** Stylized Teacher, Child and Symbols of Communication

**2002.** World Teacher's Day.

| | | | | |
|---|---|---|---|---|
| 713 | **149** | 100f. multicoloured | 65 | 65 |
| 714 | **149** | 200f. multicoloured | 1·30 | 1·30 |

**150** Emblem

**2002.** Parliamentary Election, 2002. Multicoloured.

| | | | |
|---|---|---|---|
| 715 | 100f. Type **150** | 65 | 65 |
| 716 | 200f. Hand posting voting slip (vert) | 1·30 | 1·30 |

**151** Shaikh Hamad Bin Isa Al Khalifa and Flag

**2002.** National Day. Multicoloured.

| | | | |
|---|---|---|---|
| 717 | 100f. Type **151** | 65 | 65 |
| 718 | 200f. Shaikh Hamad Bin Isa and flag (different) (vert) | 1·30 | 1·30 |
| 719 | 250f. As No. 718 but with maroon background (vert) | 1·60 | 1·60 |

**152** Bahrain

**2003.** Arab Summit Conference, Sharm el-Sheikh, Egypt. Designs representing landmarks from each state.

| | | | |
|---|---|---|---|
| 720 | 100f. Type **152** | 65 | 65 |
| 721 | 100f. Sudan | 65 | 65 |
| 722 | 100f. Saudi Arabia | 65 | 65 |
| 723 | 100f. Djibouti | 65 | 65 |
| 724 | 100f. Algeria | 65 | 65 |
| 725 | 100f. Tunisia | 65 | 65 |
| 726 | 100f. UAE | 65 | 65 |
| 727 | 100f. Jordan | 65 | 65 |
| 728 | 200f. Comoros | 1·30 | 1·30 |
| 729 | 200f. Qatar | 1·30 | 1·30 |
| 730 | 200f. Palestine | 1·30 | 1·30 |
| 731 | 200f. Oman | 1·30 | 1·30 |
| 732 | 200f. Iraq | 1·30 | 1·30 |
| 733 | 200f. Somalia | 1·30 | 1·30 |
| 734 | 200f. Syria | 1·30 | 1·30 |
| 735 | 250f. Yemen | 1·60 | 1·60 |
| 736 | 250f. Mauritania | 1·60 | 1·60 |
| 737 | 250f. Egypt | 1·60 | 1·60 |
| 738 | 250f. Libya | 1·60 | 1·60 |
| 739 | 250f. Lebanon | 1·60 | 1·60 |
| 740 | 250f. Kuwait | 1·60 | 1·60 |
| **MS**741 | 120×103 mm. 500f. Buildings surrounding Holy Kabba. Imperf | 3·25 | 3·25 |

**153** Children, Emblem and Flowers

**2003.** World Health Day. Multicoloured.

| | | | |
|---|---|---|---|
| 742 | 100f. Type **153** | 75 | 75 |
| 743 | 200f. Stylized figures and emblem | 1·60 | 1·60 |

**154** Swan

**2003.** World Environment Day. Flora and Fauna. Multicoloured.

| | | | |
|---|---|---|---|
| 744 | 100f. Type **154** | 75 | 75 |
| 745 | 100f. Peacock | 75 | 75 |
| 746 | 100f. Flamingos | 75 | 75 |
| 747 | 100f. Ostrich | 75 | 75 |
| 748 | 200f. *Rumex vesicarius* | 1·50 | 1·50 |
| 749 | 200f. *Arnebia hispidissima* | 1·50 | 1·50 |
| 750 | 200f. *Capparis spinosa* | 1·50 | 1·50 |
| 751 | 200f. *Cassia italica* | 1·50 | 1·50 |
| 752 | 250f. Crab | 1·80 | 1·80 |
| 753 | 250f. Turtle | 1·80 | 1·80 |
| 754 | 250f. Sting ray | 1·80 | 1·80 |
| 755 | 250f. Shark | 1·80 | 1·80 |

**155** Girl Writing

**2003.** Children's Day. Multicoloured.

| | | | |
|---|---|---|---|
| 756 | 100f. Type **155** | 60 | 60 |
| 757 | 150f. Girl painting | 80 | 80 |
| 758 | 200f. Children playing (horiz) | 1·20 | 1·20 |
| 759 | 250f. School class (horiz) | 1·40 | 1·40 |

**156** Shaikh Hamad Bin Isa Al Khalifa on Horseback

**2003.** National Day.

| | | | | |
|---|---|---|---|---|
| 760 | **156** | 100f. multicoloured | 60 | 60 |
| 761 | **156** | 200f. multicoloured | 1·20 | 1·20 |
| 762 | **156** | 250f. multicoloured | 1·40 | 1·40 |
| **MS**763 | | 125×167 mm. **156** 500f. multicoloured (57×87 mm) | 2·75 | 2·75 |

**157** Mother and Baby

**2004.** Mothers' Day. Multicoloured.

| | | | |
|---|---|---|---|
| 764 | 100f. Type **157** | 55 | 55 |
| 765 | 200f. Mother and child reading | 1·10 | 1·10 |

**158** Computer Model of Formula One Car (image scaled to 56% of original size)

**2004.** Bahrain Formula One Grand Prix. Sheet 180×180 mm containing T 158 and similar multicoloured designs.

| | | | |
|---|---|---|---|
| **MS**766 | 100f. Type **158**; 150f. Model facing right; 200f. Side view; 250f. Rear view; 500f. Shakir tower, Bahrain International Circuit (40×40 mm) | 6·50 | 6·50 |

**159** Healthy Figures reaching for Drug Abuser

**2004.** International Day against Drug Abuse. Multicoloured.

| | | | |
|---|---|---|---|
| 767 | 100f. Type **159** | 55 | 55 |
| 768 | 150f. Shrunken arm | 70 | 70 |
| 769 | 200f. Needles and seated figure | 1·10 | 1·10 |
| 770 | 250f. Healthy hands reaching to diseased hand | 1·30 | 1·30 |

**160** Running

**2004.** Olympic Games, Athens 2004. Sheet 211×65 mm containing T 160 and similar horiz designs. Multicoloured.

| | | | |
|---|---|---|---|
| **MS**771 | 100f. Type **160**; 150f. Swimming; 200f. Windsurfing; 250f. Pistol Shooting | 3·50 | 3·50 |

**161** Hands holding Emblem

**2004.** 25th Session of Arabian Gulf States Co-operation Supreme Council. Multicoloured.

| | | | |
|---|---|---|---|
| 772 | 100f. Type **161** | 55 | 55 |
| 773 | 200f. Emblem with flags as ribbons | 1·10 | 1·10 |
| 774 | 250f. Emblem on background of flags | 1·30 | 1·30 |
| **MS**775 | 201×100 mm. 500f. Symbols of Gulf States (175×34 mm) | 2·30 | 2·30 |

**162** Amaryllis Flower and Fair Emblem

**2005.** Bahrain Garden Fair. Multicoloured.

| | | | |
|---|---|---|---|
| 776 | 100f. Type **162** | 55 | 55 |
| 777 | 200f. Rose | 1·10 | 1·10 |
| 778 | 250f. Jasmine | 1·30 | 1·30 |

**163** Scales and Court Building

**2005.** Inauguration of Constitutional Court.

| | | | | |
|---|---|---|---|---|
| 779 | **163** | 100f. multicoloured | 55 | 55 |
| 780 | **163** | 200f. multicoloured | 1·10 | 1·10 |
| 791 | **163** | 250f. multicoloured | 70 | 70 |

**164** Statuette

**2005.** 50th Anniv of Discovery of Dilmon Civilization. Multicoloured.

| | | | |
|---|---|---|---|
| 782 | 100f. Type **164** | 55 | 55 |
| 783 | 100f. Engraved seals | 55 | 55 |
| 784 | 100f. Horseman (statue) | 55 | 55 |
| 785 | 200f. pot spilling jewellery | 1·10 | 1·10 |
| 786 | 200f. Two decorated pots | 1·10 | 1·10 |
| 787 | 200f. Cylindrical vase and pot with lid | 1·10 | 1·10 |
| 788 | 250f. Walls and gateway (horiz) | 1·30 | 1·30 |
| 789 | 250f. Aerial view (horiz) | 1·30 | 1·30 |
| 790 | 250f. Walls and steps (horiz) | 1·30 | 1·30 |

**MS**791 Two sheets. (a) 195×155 mm. Nos. 782/90. (b) 140×105 mm. 500f. Sheikh Salman Bin Hamad Al Khalifa and archaeologists (88×58 mm) 10·50 10·50

**165** King Hamad bin Isa Al Khalifa

**2005.** National Day. Multicoloured.

| | | | |
|---|---|---|---|
| 792 | 100f. Type **165** | 55 | 55 |
| 793 | 200f. Flag and King Al Khalifa (vert) | 1·10 | 1·10 |
| 794 | 250f. Towers and King Al Khalifa | 1·30 | 1·30 |

**166** Flag

**2006.** 25th Anniv of Gulf Co-operation Council. Multicoloured.

| | | | |
|---|---|---|---|
| 795 | 100f. Type **166** | 1·00 | 1·00 |

**MS**796 165×105 mm. 500f. Flags of member states. Imperf 2·40 2·40

Stamps of similar designs were issued by Kuwait, Oman, Qatar, Saudi Arabia and United Arab Emirates.

**167** Emblem

**2006.** World Cup Football Championship, Germany. Multicoloured.

| | | | |
|---|---|---|---|
| 797 | 100f. Type **167** | 55 | 55 |
| 798 | 200f. Globe and balls | 1·10 | 1·10 |
| 799 | 250f. Emblem (different) | 1·30 | 1·30 |

**168** King Hamad Bin Isa Al Khalifa

**2006.** National Day. Accession of King Hamad Bin Isa Al Khalifa. Multicoloured.

| | | | |
|---|---|---|---|
| 800 | 100f. Type **168** | 55 | 55 |
| 801 | 200f. Facing front | 1·10 | 1·10 |
| 802 | 250f. Facing left | 1·30 | 1·30 |
| 803 | 500f. As Type **168** (40×54 mm) | 2·40 | 2·40 |

**169** Figures under Umbrella

**2007.** Consumer Protection Day. Multicoloured.

| | | | |
|---|---|---|---|
| 804 | 100f. Type **169** | 50 | 50 |
| 805 | 200f. Flags as umbrella | 1·00 | 1·00 |

**170** King Hamad Bin Isa Al Khalifa

**2007.** National Day. Multicoloured.

| | | | |
|---|---|---|---|
| 806 | 100f. Type **170** | 55 | 55 |
| 807 | 200f. Seated (horiz) | 1·10 | 1·10 |
| 808 | 250f. King Hamad Bin Isa Al Khalifa and previous rulers (horiz) | 1·30 | 1·30 |

**MS**809 125×201 mm. 100f.×2, No. 806×2; Horiz. 200f.×2, No. 807×2 2·75 2·75

**171** Clay Carving and Basket Work

**2008.** Arab Productive Families Day. Multicoloured.

| | | | |
|---|---|---|---|
| 810 | 100f. Type **171** | 50 | 50 |
| 811 | 200f. Stud work and embroiderey | 1·00 | 1·00 |

**172** Operating Theatre

**2008.** International Nurses Day. Multicoloured.

| | | | |
|---|---|---|---|
| 812 | 100f. Type **172** | 50 | 50 |
| 813 | 200f. Neo-natal nurses | 1·00 | 1·00 |

**173** Symbols of Bahrain and China

**2008.** Arab–Chinese Cooperation Forum Ministerial Meeting, Manama. Multicoloured.

| | | | |
|---|---|---|---|
| 814 | 100f. Type **173** | 50 | 50 |
| 815 | 200f. Great Wall and Bahrain World Trade Centre towers | 1·00 | 1·00 |

**174** 'BUSINESS friendly'

**2008.** Economic Developement Board. Multicoloured.

| | | | |
|---|---|---|---|
| 816 | 100f. Type **174** | 60 | 60 |
| 817 | 200f. BUSINESS FRIENDLY | 1·20 | 1·20 |

**175** Athletics

**2008.** Olympic Games, Beijing. Sheet 145×64 mm containing T 175 and similar square design. Multicoloured.

**MS**818 100f. Type **175**; 200f. Show jumping 1·80 1·80

**176** Dancers

**2008.** National Day. Bahraini Ardha (dance). Two sheets containing T 176 and similar horiz designs. Multicoloured.

**MS**819 210×151 mm. 100f.×8, Type **176**; Dancer with lowered sword and two rows of dancers facing each other; Dancer with out-stretched sword and four dancers wearing blue and yellow costumes; Dancer with raised sword and large square of dancers; Unarmed dancer and men with raised swords; Dancer with rifle and three others; Dancer with sword to his left and three men; Dancer with sword to his right and drummers 4·50 4·50

**MS**820 210×151 mm. Size 54×40 mm. 200f.×3, Dancer holding flag and sword and dancers with flag; Dancer holding scabard and dancers wearing blue and yellow costumes; Dancer with raised sword and dancers 2·75 2·75

**177** Dhow

**2009.** 1st GCC–ASEAN Ministerial Meeting, Manama. Multicoloured.

| | | | |
|---|---|---|---|
| 821 | 100f. Type **177** | 60 | 60 |
| 822 | 200f. As Type **177** | 1·00 | 1·00 |

**178** Pigeon (image scaled to 70% of original size)

**2009.** Arab Post Day. Sheet 170×60 mm containing T 178 and similar horiz design. Multicoloured.

**MS**823 500f.×2, Type **178**; Camels 5·25 5·25

**179** Emblems

**2009.** Palm Tree–Life and Civilization Symposium.

| | | | | |
|---|---|---|---|---|
| 824 | **179** | 100f. multicoloured | 60 | 60 |

**180** Emblem

**2009.** National Women's Day. Multicoloured.

| | | | |
|---|---|---|---|
| 825 | 100f. Type **180** | 60 | 60 |
| 826 | 200f. Emblem and flag | 1·00 | 1·00 |

**181** Students

**2009.** 90th Anniv of Education in Bahrain. Sheet 160×99 mm containing T 181 and similar horiz designs. Multicoloured.

**MS**827 100f. Type **181**; 100f. Classroom, teacher at whiteboard; 200f. Students in laboratory; 200f. Graduating students; 250f. Students, teacher wearing blue lab coat; 250f. Classroom, female teacher with student 6·25 6·25

**182** King Hamad Bin Isa Al Khalifa

**2009.** National Day. 10th Anniv of Accession of King Hamad Bin Isa Al Khalifa. Multicoloured.

| | | | |
|---|---|---|---|
| 828 | 100f. Type **182** | 60 | 60 |
| 829 | 200f. As Type **182** | 1·00 | 1·00 |
| 830 | 250f. King Hamad Bin Isa Al Khalifa, Isa bin Salman Al Khalifa, Salman Bin Hamad Al Khalifa, Hamad Bin Isa Al Khalifa and Isa bin Ali Al Khalifa | 1·50 | 1·50 |

**MS**831 126×101 mm. 500f. As No. 830. Imperf 5·25 5·25

**183** King Hamad Bin Isa Al Khalifa and Jet Fighter Aircraft

**2010.** International Airshow, Bahrain. Multicoloured.

| | | | |
|---|---|---|---|
| 832 | 100f. Type **183** | 65 | 65 |
| 833 | 200f. Emblem | 1·10 | 1·10 |

**184** Championship Emblem

**2010.** World Cup Football Championship, South Africa

| | | | |
|---|---|---|---|
| 834 | 100f. Type **184** | | |
| 835 | 200f. Championship mascot | | |
| 836 | 250f. Football, emblem and globe (39×29 mm) | | |

**WAR TAX STAMPS**

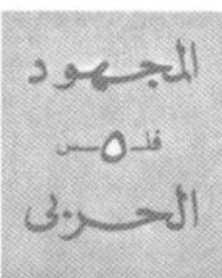
**T36** "War Effort"

**1973**

| | | | | |
|---|---|---|---|---|
| T192 | **T36** | 5f. blue and cobalt | £130 | 85·00 |

**T37** "War Effort"

**1973**

| | | | | |
|---|---|---|---|---|
| T194a | **T37** | 5f. blue | 5·25 | 45 |

Pt. 1

# BAMRA

A state in India. Now uses Indian stamps.

12 pies = 1 anna; 16 annas = 1 rupee.

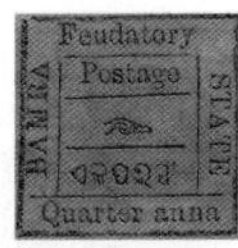


1

**1888**

| | | | | |
|---|---|---|---|---|
| 1 | 1 | ¼a. black on yellow | £600 | |
| 2 | 1 | ½a. black on red | £100 | |
| 3 | 1 | 1a. black on blue | 80·00 | |
| 4 | 1 | 2a. black on green | £110 | £500 |
| 5 | 1 | 4a. black on yellow | 95·00 | £500 |
| 6 | 1 | 8a. black on red | 60·00 | |

8

**1890.** Imperf.

| | | | | |
|---|---|---|---|---|
| 10 | 8 | ¼a. black on red | 2·00 | 2·75 |
| 11 | 8 | ½a. black on green | 5·00 | 5·00 |
| 30 | 8 | 1a. black on yellow | 4·75 | 3·25 |
| 16 | 8 | 2a. black on red | 5·00 | 5·00 |
| 19 | 8 | 4a. black on red | 16·00 | 11·00 |
| 22 | 8 | 8a. black on red | 14·00 | 22·00 |
| 25 | 8 | 1r. black on red | 21·00 | 22·00 |

Pt. 1

# BANGLADESH

Formerly the Eastern wing of Pakistan. Following a landslide victory at the Pakistan General Election in December 1970 by the Awami League party the National Assembly was suspended. Unrest spread throughout the eastern province culminating in the intervention of India on the side of the East Bengalis. The new state became effective after the surrender of the Pakistan army in December 1971.

1971. 100 paisa = 1 rupee.
1972. 100 paisa = 1 taka.

1 Map of Bangladesh

**1971**

| | | | | |
|---|---|---|---|---|
| 1 | 1 | 10p. indigo, orange and blue | 20 | 10 |
| 2 | - | 20p. multicoloured | 20 | 10 |
| 3 | - | 50p. multicoloured | 20 | 10 |
| 4 | - | 1r. multicoloured | 30 | 10 |
| 5 | - | 2r. turquoise, blue and red | 30 | 35 |
| 6 | - | 3r. light green, green and blue | 30 | 65 |
| 7 | - | 5r. multicoloured | 50 | 1·25 |
| 8 | - | 10r. gold, red and blue | 1·00 | 2·25 |

DESIGNS: 20p. "Dacca University Massacre"; 50p. "75 Million People"; 1r. Flag of Independence; 2r. Ballot box; 3r. Broken chain; 5r. Shaikh Majibur Rahman; 10r. "Support Bangla Desh" and map.

**1971.** Liberation. Nos. 1 and 7/8 optd BANGLADESH LIBERATED.

| | | | |
|---|---|---|---|
| 9 | 10p. indigo, orange and blue | 20 | 10 |
| 10 | 5r. multicoloured | 2·00 | 2·25 |
| 11 | 10r. gold, red and blue | 3·00 | 3·75 |

The remaining values of the original issue were also overprinted and placed on sale in Great Britian but were not issued in Bangladesh.

On 1 February 1972 the Agency placed on sale a further issue in the flag, map and Sheikh Mujib designs in new colours and new currency (100 paisa = 1 taka). This issue proved to be unacceptable to the Bangladesh authorities who declared them to be invalid for postal purposes, no supplies being sold within Bangladesh. The values comprise 1, 2, 3, 5, 7, 10, 15, 20, 25, 40, 50, 75p., 1, 2 and 5t.

3 "Martyrdom"

**1972.** In Memory of the Martyrs.

| | | | | |
|---|---|---|---|---|
| 12 | 3 | 20p. green and red | 30 | 50 |

4 Flames of Independence

**1972.** 1st Anniv of Independence.

| | | | | |
|---|---|---|---|---|
| 13 | 4 | 20p. lake and red | 25 | 10 |
| 14 | 4 | 60p. blue and red | 40 | 45 |
| 15 | 4 | 75p. violet and red | 45 | 55 |

5 Doves of Peace

**1972.** Victory Day.

| | | | | |
|---|---|---|---|---|
| 16 | 5 | 20p. multicoloured | 20 | 10 |
| 17 | 5 | 60p. multicoloured | 30 | 55 |
| 18 | 5 | 75p. multicoloured | 30 | 55 |

6 "Homage to Martyrs"

**1973.** In Memory of the Martyrs.

| | | | | |
|---|---|---|---|---|
| 19 | 6 | 20p. multicoloured | 15 | 10 |
| 20 | 6 | 60p. multicoloured | 30 | 40 |
| 21 | 6 | 1t.35 multicoloured | 65 | 1·75 |

7 Embroidered Quilt 8 Court of Justice

**1973**

| | | | | |
|---|---|---|---|---|
| 22 | 7 | 2p. black | 10 | 1·00 |
| 23 | - | 3p. green | 30 | 1·00 |
| 24 | - | 5p. brown | 30 | 10 |
| 25 | - | 10p. black | 30 | 10 |
| 26 | - | 20p. green | 50 | 10 |
| 27 | - | 25p. mauve | 3·25 | 10 |
| 28 | - | 50p. purple | 2·25 | 30 |
| 29 | - | 60p. grey | 1·75 | 1·25 |
| 30 | - | 75p. orange | 1·25 | 1·25 |
| 31 | - | 90p. brown | 1·50 | 2·00 |
| 32 | 8 | 1t. violet | 6·00 | 30 |
| 33 | - | 2t. green | 6·00 | 1·00 |
| 34 | - | 5t. blue | 7·50 | 2·50 |
| 35 | - | 10t. pink | 10·00 | 5·00 |

DESIGNS—As Type **7**: 3p. Jute field; 5p. Jack fruit; 10p. Bullocks ploughing; 20p. Rakta jaba (flower); 25p. Tiger; 60p. Bamboo grove; 75p. Plucking tea; 90p. Handicrafts. (28×22 mm): 50p. Hilsa (fish). As Type **8**. VERT: 2t. Date tree. HORIZ: 5t. Fishing boat; 10t. Sixty-dome mosque, Bagerhat.

See also Nos. 49/51a, 64/75 and 711.

9 Flame Emblem

**1973.** 25th Anniv of Declaration of Human Rights.

| | | | | |
|---|---|---|---|---|
| 36 | 9 | 10p. multicoloured | 10 | 10 |
| 37 | 9 | 1t.25 multicoloured | 20 | 20 |

10 Family, Map and Graph

**1974.** First Population Census.

| | | | | |
|---|---|---|---|---|
| 38 | 10 | 20p. multicoloured | 10 | 10 |
| 39 | 10 | 25p. multicoloured | 10 | 10 |
| 40 | 10 | 75p. multicoloured | 20 | 20 |

11 Copernicus and Heliocentric System

**1974.** 500th Birth Anniv of Copernicus.

| | | | | |
|---|---|---|---|---|
| 41 | 11 | 25p. orange, violet and black | 10 | 10 |
| 42 | 11 | 75p. orange, green and black | 25 | 50 |

12 U.N. H.Q. and Bangladesh Flag

**1974.** Bangladesh's Admission to the U.N.

| | | | | |
|---|---|---|---|---|
| 43 | 12 | 25p. multicoloured | 10 | 10 |
| 44 | 12 | 1t. multicoloured | 35 | 40 |

13 U.P.U. Emblem

**1974.** Centenary of Universal Postal Union. Mult.

| | | | |
|---|---|---|---|
| 45 | 25p. Type **13** | 10 | 10 |
| 46 | 1t.25 Mail runner | 20 | 15 |
| 47 | 1t.75 Type **13** | 20 | 25 |
| 48 | 5t. As 1t.25 | 80 | 1·60 |

14 Courts of Justice

**1974.** As Nos. 32/5 with revised inscriptions.

| | | | | |
|---|---|---|---|---|
| 49 | 14 | 1t. violet | 1·50 | 10 |
| 50 | - | 2t. olive | 2·00 | 2·00 |
| 51 | - | 5t. blue | 7·00 | 70 |
| 51a | - | 10t. pink | 23·00 | 15·00 |

For these designs redrawn to 32×20 mm or 20×32 mm, see Nos. 72/5 and, to 35×22 mm, see No. 711.

15 Tiger

**1974.** Wildlife Preservation. Multicoloured.

| | | | |
|---|---|---|---|
| 52 | 25p. Type **15** | 70 | 10 |
| 53 | 50p. Tiger cub | 1·00 | 70 |
| 54 | 2t. Tiger in stream | 1·75 | 3·50 |

16 Symbolic Family

**1974.** World Population Year. "Family Planning for All". Multicoloured.

| | | | |
|---|---|---|---|
| 55 | 25p. Type **16** | 15 | 10 |
| 56 | 70p. Village family | 25 | 50 |
| 57 | 1t.25 Heads of family (horiz) | 40 | 1·10 |

17 Radar Antenna

**1975.** Inauguration of Betbunia Satellite Earth Station.

| | | | | |
|---|---|---|---|---|
| 58 | 17 | 25p. black, silver and red | 10 | 10 |
| 59 | 17 | 1t. black, silver and blue | 20 | 70 |

18 Woman's Head

**1975.** International Women's Year.

| | | | | |
|---|---|---|---|---|
| 60 | 18 | 50p. multicoloured | 10 | 10 |
| 61 | 18 | 2t. multicoloured | 25 | 1·00 |

**1976.** As Nos. 24/31 and 49/51a but redrawn in smaller size.

| | | | | |
|---|---|---|---|---|
| 64 | - | 5p. green | 20 | 10 |
| 65 | - | 10p. black | 20 | 10 |
| 66 | - | 20p. green | 1·50 | 10 |
| 67 | - | 25p. mauve | 5·00 | 10 |
| 68 | - | 50p. purple | 3·75 | 10 |
| 69 | - | 60p. grey | 40 | 40 |
| 70 | - | 75p. green | 1·75 | 3·25 |
| 71 | - | 90p. brown | 40 | 60 |
| 72 | 14 | 1t. violet | 2·00 | 10 |
| 73 | - | 2t. green | 9·00 | 10 |
| 74 | - | 5t. blue | 3·25 | 3·00 |
| 75 | - | 10t. red | 11·00 | 4·50 |

Nos. 64/71 are 23×18 mm (50p.) or 18×23 mm (others) and Nos. 72/75 are 20×32 mm (2t.) or 32×20 mm (others).

For the 10t. redrawn to 35×22 mm, see No. 711.

19 Telephones of 1876 and 1976

**1976.** Centenary of Telephone.

| | | | | |
|---|---|---|---|---|
| 76 | **19** | 2t.25 multicoloured | 25 | 20 |
| 77 | - | 5t. red, green and black | 55 | 65 |

DESIGN: 5t. Alexander Graham Bell.

**20** Eye and Nutriments

**1976.** Prevention of Blindness.

| | | | | |
|---|---|---|---|---|
| 78 | **20** | 30p. multicoloured | 50 | 10 |
| 79 | **20** | 2t.25 multicoloured | 1·40 | 2·75 |

**21** Liberty Bell

**1976.** Bicentenary of American Revolution. Mult.

| | | | |
|---|---|---|---|
| 80 | 30p. Type **21** | 10 | 10 |
| 81 | 2t.25 Statue of Liberty | 20 | 25 |
| 82 | 5t. "Mayflower" | 40 | 40 |
| 83 | 10t. Mount Rushmore | 40 | 70 |
| **MS**84 | 167×95 mm. No. 83 | 1·00 | 2·50 |

**22** Industry, Science, Agriculture and Education

**1976.** 25th Anniv of Colombo Plan.

| | | | | |
|---|---|---|---|---|
| 85 | **22** | 30p. multicoloured | 15 | 10 |
| 86 | **22** | 2t.25 multicoloured | 35 | 1·00 |

**23** Hurdling

**1976.** Olympic Games, Montreal. Multicoloured.

| | | | |
|---|---|---|---|
| 87 | 25p. Type **23** | 10 | 10 |
| 88 | 30p. Running (horiz) | 10 | 10 |
| 89 | 1t. Pole vaulting | 15 | 10 |
| 90 | 2t.25 Swimming (horiz) | 30 | 45 |
| 91 | 3t.50 Gymnastics | 55 | 1·25 |
| 92 | 5t. Football | 1·00 | 2·00 |

**24** The Blessing

**1977.** Silver Jubilee. Multicoloured.

| | | | |
|---|---|---|---|
| 93 | 30p. Type **24** | 10 | 10 |
| 94 | 2t.25 Queen Elizabeth II | 20 | 25 |
| 95 | 10t. Queen Elizabeth and Prince Philip | 70 | 85 |
| **MS**96 | 114×127 mm. Nos. 93/5 | 80 | 1·50 |

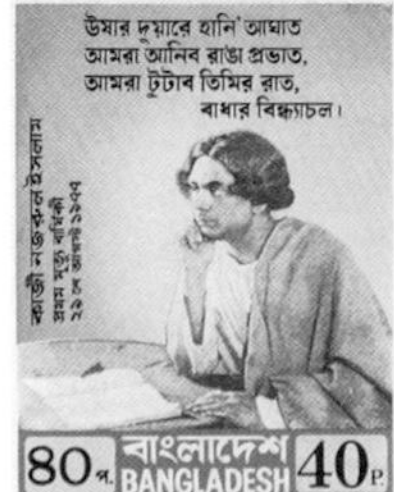


**25** Qazi Nazrul Islam (poet)

**1977.** Qazi Nazrul Islam Commemoration.

| | | | | |
|---|---|---|---|---|
| 97 | **25** | 40p. green and black | 10 | 10 |
| 98 | - | 2t.25 brown, red & lt brn | 50 | 30 |

DESIGN—HORIZ: 2t.25, Head and shoulders portrait.

**26** Bird with Letter

**1977.** 15th Anniv of Asian–Oceanic Postal Union.

| | | | | |
|---|---|---|---|---|
| 99 | **26** | 30p. red, blue and grey | 10 | 10 |
| 100 | **26** | 2t.25 red, blue and grey | 20 | 25 |

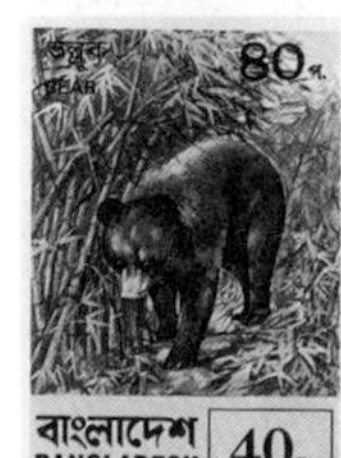


**27** Sloth Bear

**1977.** Animals. Multicoloured.

| | | | |
|---|---|---|---|
| 101 | 40p. Type **27** | 15 | 10 |
| 102 | 1t. Spotted deer | 15 | 10 |
| 103 | 2t.25 Leopard (horiz) | 30 | 20 |
| 104 | 3t.50 Gaur (horiz) | 30 | 35 |
| 105 | 4t. Indian elephant (horiz) | 80 | 50 |
| 106 | 5t. Tiger (horiz) | 90 | 75 |

The Bengali numerals on the 40p. resemble "80", and that on the 4t. resembles "8".

**28** Campfire and Tent

**1978.** First National Scout Jamboree.

| | | | | |
|---|---|---|---|---|
| 107 | **28** | 40p. red, blue and pale blue | 25 | 10 |
| 108 | - | 3t.50 lilac, green and blue | 80 | 30 |
| 109 | - | 5t. green, blue and red | 95 | 45 |

DESIGNS—HORIZ: 3t.50, Scout stretcher-team. VERT: 5t. Scout salute.

**29** "Michelia champaca"

**1978.** Flowers. Multicoloured.

| | | | |
|---|---|---|---|
| 110 | 40p. Type **29** | 20 | 10 |
| 111 | 1t. "Cassia fistula" | 25 | 15 |
| 112 | 2t.25 "Delonix regia" | 30 | 30 |
| 113 | 3t.50 "Nymphaea nouchali" | 35 | 60 |
| 114 | 4t. "Butea monosperma" | 35 | 80 |
| 115 | 5t. "Anthocephalus indicus" | 35 | 85 |

**30** St. Edward's Crown and Sceptres

**1978.** 25th Anniv of Coronation. Multicoloured.

| | | | |
|---|---|---|---|
| 116 | 40p. Type **30** | 10 | 10 |
| 117 | 3t.50 Balcony scene | 15 | 30 |
| 118 | 5t. Queen Elizabeth and Prince Philip | 25 | 50 |
| 119 | 10t. Coronation portrait by Cecil Beaton | 45 | 80 |
| **MS**120 | 89×121 mm. Nos. 116/19 | 1·10 | 1·50 |

**31** Sir Alan Cobham's de Havilland D.H.50

**1978.** 75th Anniv of Powered Flight.

| | | | | |
|---|---|---|---|---|
| 121 | **31** | 40p. multicoloured | 15 | 10 |
| 122 | - | 2t.25 brown and blue | 25 | 45 |
| 123 | - | 3t.50 brown and yellow | 25 | 65 |
| 124 | - | 5t. multicoloured | 2·50 | 3·50 |

DESIGNS: 2t.25, Captain Hans Bertram's seaplane "Atlantis"; 3t.50, Wright brothers' Flyer III; 5t. Concorde.

**32** Fenchuganj Fertiliser Factory

**1978**

| | | | | |
|---|---|---|---|---|
| 125 | | 5p. brown | 10 | 10 |
| 126 | **32** | 10p. blue | 10 | 10 |
| 127 | - | 15p. orange | 10 | 10 |
| 128 | - | 20p. red | 10 | 10 |
| 129 | - | 25p. blue | 15 | 10 |
| 130 | - | 30p. green | 3·00 | 10 |
| 131 | - | 40p. purple | 30 | 10 |
| 132 | - | 50p. black | 5·50 | 1·50 |
| 134 | - | 80p. brown | 20 | 10 |
| 136 | - | 1t. violet | 9·00 | 10 |
| 137 | - | 2t. blue | 3·00 | 3·25 |

DESIGNS—HORIZ: 5p. Lalbag Fort; 25p. Jute on a boat; 40, 50p. Baitul Mukarram Mosque; 1t. Dotara (musical instrument); 2t. Karnaphuli Dam. VERT: 15p. Pineapple; 20p. Bangladesh gas; 30p. Banana tree; 80p. Mohastan Garh.

**33** Tawaf-E-Ka'aba, Mecca

**1978.** Pilgrimage to Mecca. Multicoloured.

| | | | |
|---|---|---|---|
| 140 | 40p. Type **33** | 20 | 10 |
| 141 | 3t. Pilgrims in Wuquf, Arafat (horiz) | 60 | 45 |

**34** Jasim Uddin

**1979.** 3rd Death Anniv of Jasim Uddin (poet).

| | | | | |
|---|---|---|---|---|
| 142 | **34** | 40p. multicoloured | 20 | 50 |

**35** Moulana Abdul Hamid Khan Bhashani

**1979.** 3rd Death Anniv of Moulana Abdul Hamid Khan Bhashani (national leader).

| | | | | |
|---|---|---|---|---|
| 143 | **35** | 40p. multicoloured | 40 | 30 |

**36** Sir Rowland Hill

**1979.** Death Centenary of Sir Rowland Hill.

| | | | | |
|---|---|---|---|---|
| 144 | **36** | 40p. blue, red and light blue | 10 | 10 |
| 145 | - | 3t.50 multicoloured | 35 | 30 |
| 146 | - | 10t. multicoloured | 80 | 1·00 |
| **MS**147 | | 176×96 mm. Nos. 144/6 | 2·25 | 2·75 |

DESIGNS: 3t.50, Sir Rowland Hill and first Bangladesh stamp; 10t. Sir Rowland Hill and Bangladesh U.P.U. stamp.

**37** Children with Hoops

**1979.** International Year of the Child. Multicoloured.

| | | | |
|---|---|---|---|
| 148 | 40p. Type **37** | 10 | 10 |
| 149 | 3t.50 Boy with kite | 35 | 35 |
| 150 | 5t. Children jumping | 50 | 50 |
| **MS**151 | 170×120 mm. Nos. 148/50 | 1·50 | 2·75 |

**38** Rotary International Emblem

**1980.** 75th Anniv of Rotary International.

| | | | | |
|---|---|---|---|---|
| 152 | **38** | 40p. black, red and yellow | 20 | 10 |
| 153 | - | 5t. gold and blue | 65 | 1·00 |

DESIGN: 5t. Rotary emblem (different).

**39** Canal Digging

**1980.** Mass Participation in Canal Digging.

| | | | | |
|---|---|---|---|---|
| 154 | **39** | 40p. multicoloured | 40 | 30 |

**40** A. K. Fazlul Huq

**1980.** 18th Death Anniv of A. K. Fazlul Huq (national leader).

| | | | | |
|---|---|---|---|---|
| 155 | **40** | 40p. multicoloured | 30 | 30 |

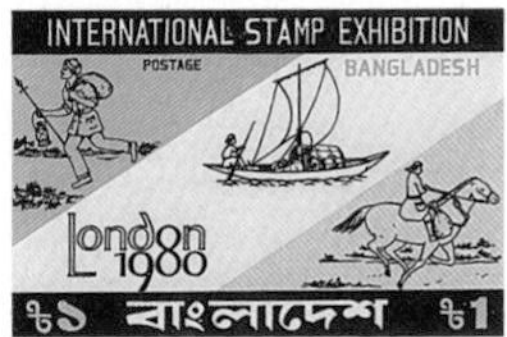


**41** Early Forms of Mail Transport

**1980.** "London 1980" International Stamp Exhibition. Multicoloured.

| | | | |
|---|---|---|---|
| 156 | 1t. Type **41** | 15 | 10 |
| 157 | 10t. Modern forms of mail transport | 1·25 | 1·40 |
| **MS**158 | 140×95 mm. Nos. 156/7 | 1·40 | 2·00 |

**42** Dome of the Rock

**1980.** Palestinian Welfare.

| | | | | |
|---|---|---|---|---|
| 159 | **42** | 50p. lilac | 1·00 | 30 |

**43** Outdoor Class

**1980.** Education.

| | | | | |
|---|---|---|---|---|
| 160 | **43** | 50p. multicoloured | 40 | 30 |

**44** Beach Scene

**1980.** World Tourism Conference, Manila. Mult.

| | | | |
|---|---|---|---|
| 161 | 50p. Type **44** | 35 | 50 |
| 162 | 5t. Beach scene (different) | 65 | 1·10 |
| **MS**163 | 140×88 mm. Nos. 161/2 | 1·00 | 1·60 |

**45** Mecca

**1980.** Moslem Year 1400 A. H. Commemoration.

| | | | | |
|---|---|---|---|---|
| 164 | **45** | 50p. multicoloured | 50 | 20 |

**46** Begum Roquiah

**1980.** Birth Centenary of Begum Roquiah (campaigner for women's rights).

| | | | | |
|---|---|---|---|---|
| 165 | **46** | 50p. multicoloured | 10 | 10 |
| 166 | **46** | 2t. multicoloured | 35 | 20 |

**47** Spotted Deer and Scout Emblem

**1981.** 5th Asia–Pacific and 2nd Bangladesh Scout Jamboree.

| | | | | |
|---|---|---|---|---|
| 167 | **47** | 50p. multicoloured | 25 | 15 |
| 168 | **47** | 5t. multicoloured | 1·00 | 2·00 |

**1981.** 2nd Population Census. Nos. 38/40 optd 2nd. CENSUS 1981.

| | | | | |
|---|---|---|---|---|
| 169 | **10** | 20p. multicoloured | 10 | 10 |
| 170 | **10** | 25p. multicoloured | 10 | 10 |
| 171 | **10** | 75p. multicoloured | 20 | 30 |

**49** Queen Elizabeth the Queen Mother

**1981.** 80th Birthday of the Queen Mother.

| | | | | |
|---|---|---|---|---|
| 172 | **49** | 1t. multicoloured | 15 | 15 |
| 173 | **49** | 15t. multicoloured | 1·75 | 2·50 |
| **MS**174 | | 95×73 mm. Nos. 172/3 | 1·75 | 2·50 |

**50** Revolutionary with Flag and Sub-machine-gun

**1981.** 10th Anniv of Independence. Mult.

| | | | |
|---|---|---|---|
| 175 | 50p. Type **50** | 15 | 10 |
| 176 | 2t. Figures on map symbolizing Bangladesh life style | 25 | 45 |

**51** Bangladesh Village and Farm Scenes

**1981.** U.N. Conference on Least Developed Countries, Paris.

| | | | | |
|---|---|---|---|---|
| 177 | **51** | 50p. multicoloured | 45 | 15 |

**52** Kemal Ataturk in Civilian Dress

**1981.** Birth Centenary of Kemal Ataturk (Turkish statesman).

| | | | |
|---|---|---|---|
| 178 | 50p. Type **52** | 45 | 30 |
| 179 | 1t. Kemal Ataturk in uniform | 80 | 1·25 |

**53** Deaf People using Sign Language

**1981.** Int Year for Disabled Persons. Mult.

| | | | |
|---|---|---|---|
| 180 | 50p. Type **53** | 40 | 20 |
| 181 | 2t. Disabled person writing (horiz) | 85 | 2·50 |

**54** Farm Scene and Wheat Ear

**1981.** World Food Day.

| | | | | |
|---|---|---|---|---|
| 182 | **54** | 50p. multicoloured | 50 | 1·00 |

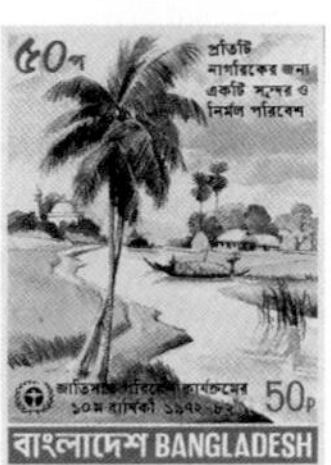


**55** River Scene

**1982.** 10th Anniv of Human Environment Conference.

| | | | | |
|---|---|---|---|---|
| 183 | **55** | 50p. multicoloured | 50 | 1·00 |

**56** Dr. M. Hussain

**1982.** 1st Death Anniv of Dr. Motahar Hussain (educationist).

| | | | | |
|---|---|---|---|---|
| 184 | **56** | 50p. multicoloured | 50 | 1·00 |

**57** Knotted Rope surrounding Bengali "75"

**1982.** 75th Anniv of Boy Scout Movement and 125th Birth Anniv of Lord Baden-Powell. Multicoloured.

| | | | |
|---|---|---|---|
| 185 | 50p. Type **57** | 50 | 30 |
| 186 | 2t. Lord Baden-Powell (vert) | 2·00 | 4·50 |

সম্মিলিত
সশস্ত্র বাহিনী দিবস
২১ নভেম্বর,৮২

**(58)**

**1982.** Armed Forces' Day. No. 175 optd with T 58.

| | | | |
|---|---|---|---|
| 187 | 50p. Type **50** | 3·50 | 3·00 |

**59** Captain Mohiuddin Jahangir

**1983.** Heroes and Martyrs of the Liberation. Multicoloured, background colour of commemorative plaque given.

| | | | |
|---|---|---|---|
| 188 | 50p. Type **59** (orange) | 30 | 50 |
| 189 | 50p. Sepoy Hamidur Rahman (green) | 30 | 50 |
| 190 | 50p. Sepoy Mohammed Mustafa Kamal (red) | 30 | 50 |
| 191 | 50p. Muhammed Ruhul Amin (yellow) | 30 | 50 |
| 192 | 50p. Flt. Lt. M. Matiur Rahman (brown) | 30 | 50 |
| 193 | 50p. Lance-Naik Munshi Abdur Rob (brown) | 30 | 50 |
| 194 | 50p. Lance-Naik Nur Mouhammad (green) | 30 | 50 |

**60** Metric Scales

**1983.** Introduction of Metric Weights and Measures. Multicoloured.

| | | | |
|---|---|---|---|
| 195 | 50p. Type **60** | 40 | 30 |
| 196 | 2t. Weights, jug and tape measure (horiz) | 1·40 | 2·75 |

**61** Dr. Robert Koch

**1983.** Centenary (1982) of Robert Koch's Discovery of Tubercle Bacillus. Multicoloured.

| | | | |
|---|---|---|---|
| 197 | 50p. Type **61** | 1·00 | 40 |
| 198 | 1t. Microscope, slide and X-ray | 2·25 | 3·50 |

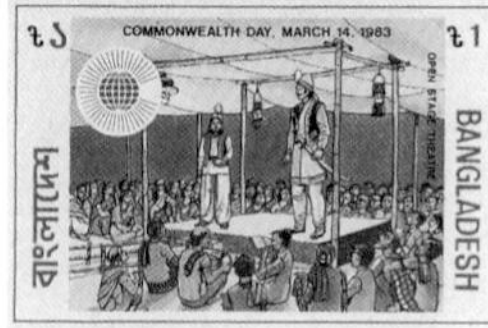


**62** Open Stage Theatre

**1983.** Commonwealth Day. Multicoloured.

| | | | |
|---|---|---|---|
| 199 | 1t. Type **62** | 10 | 15 |
| 200 | 3t. Boat race | 20 | 30 |
| 201 | 10t. Snake dance | 35 | 90 |
| 202 | 15t. Picking tea | 50 | 1·50 |

**63** Dr. Muhammed Shahidulla

**1983.** Dr. Muhammed Shahidulla (Bengali scholar) Commemoration.

| | | | | |
|---|---|---|---|---|
| 203 | **63** | 50p. multicoloured | 75 | 1·00 |

**64** Magpie Robin

**1983.** Birds of Bangladesh. Multicoloured.

| | | | |
|---|---|---|---|
| 204 | 50p. Type **64** | 75 | 40 |
| 205 | 2t. White-throated kingfisher (vert) | 1·00 | 2·00 |
| 206 | 3t.75 Lesser flame-backed woodpecker (vert) | 1·25 | 2·50 |
| 207 | 5t. White-winged wood duck | 1·40 | 2·75 |

| | | | |
|---|---|---|---|
| MS208 | 165×110 mm. Nos. 240/7 (sold at 13t.) | 4·00 | 11·00 |

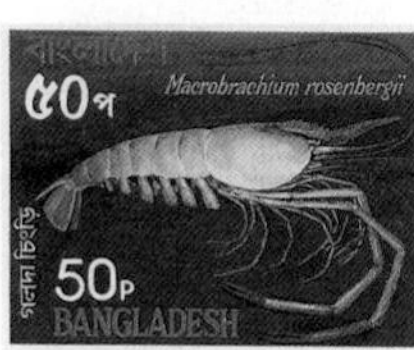

65 "Macrobrachium rosenbergii"

**1983.** Marine Life. Multicoloured.

| | | | |
|---|---|---|---|
| 209 | 50p. Type **65** | 40 | 30 |
| 210 | 2t. White pomfret | 60 | 1·50 |
| 211 | 3t.75 Rohu | 75 | 1·75 |
| 212 | 5t. Climbing perch | 90 | 2·50 |
| MS213 | 119×98 mm. Nos. 209/12 (sold at 13t.) | 2·50 | 6·00 |

**1983.** Visit of Queen Elizabeth II. No. 95 optd Nov. '83 Visit of Queen.

| | | | |
|---|---|---|---|
| 214 | 10t. Queen Elizabeth and Prince Philip | 7·00 | 7·50 |

67 Conference Hall, Dhaka

**1983.** 14th Islamic Foreign Ministers' Conference, Dhaka. Multicoloured.

| | | | |
|---|---|---|---|
| 215 | 50p. Type **67** | 35 | 30 |
| 216 | 5t. Old Fort, Dhaka | 1·25 | 3·00 |

68 Early Mail Runner

**1983.** World Communications Year. Multicoloured.

| | | | |
|---|---|---|---|
| 217 | 50p. Type **68** | 30 | 15 |
| 218 | 5t. Sailing ship, steam train and Boeing 707 airliner | 2·00 | 1·50 |
| 219 | 10t. Mail runner and dish aerial (horiz) | 2·75 | 4·50 |

69 Carrying Mail by Boat

**1983.** Postal Communications.

| | | | | |
|---|---|---|---|---|
| 220 | 69 | 5p. blue | 10 | 40 |
| 221 | - | 10p. purple | 10 | 40 |
| 222 | - | 15p. blue | 20 | 40 |
| 223 | - | 20p. black | 1·25 | 40 |
| 224 | - | 25p. grey | 30 | 40 |
| 225 | - | 30p. brown | 30 | 40 |
| 226 | - | 50p. brown | 1·00 | 10 |
| 227 | - | 1t. blue | 1·25 | 10 |
| 228 | - | 2t. green | 1·25 | 10 |
| 228a | - | 3t. brown | 4·00 | 70 |
| 229 | - | 5t. purple | 2·00 | 1·00 |

DESIGNS—HORIZ (22×17 mm): 10p. Counter, Dhaka G.P.O.; 15p. I.W.T.A. Terminal, Dhaka; 20p. Inside railway travelling post office; 30p. Emptying pillar box; 50p. Mobile post office van. (30×19 mm): 1t. Kamalapur Railway Station, Dhaka; 2t. Zia International Airport; 3t. Sorting mail by machine; 5t. Khulna G.P.O. VERT (17×22 mm): 25p. Delivering a letter.

প্রথম বাংলাদেশ জাতীয় ডাকটিকিট প্রদর্শনী-১৯৮৪

**(70)**

**1984.** 1st National Stamp Exhibition (1st issue). Nos. 161/2 optd with T 70 (5t.) or First Bangladesh National Philatelic Exhibition—1984 (50p.).

| | | | | |
|---|---|---|---|---|
| 230 | 44 | 50p. multicoloured | 1·50 | 2·00 |
| 231 | - | 5t. multicoloured | 2·00 | 2·75 |

**71** Girl with Stamp Album (image scaled to 73% of original size)

**1984.** 1st National Stamp Exhibition (2nd issue). Multicoloured.

| | | | |
|---|---|---|---|
| 232 | 50p. Type **71** | 65 | 1·25 |
| 233 | 7t.50 Boy with stamp album | 1·10 | 2·25 |
| MS234 | 98×117 mm. Nos. 232/3 (sold at 10t.) | 3·00 | 4·25 |

**72** Sarus Crane and Gavial

**1984.** Dhaka Zoo. Multicoloured.

| | | | |
|---|---|---|---|
| 235 | 1t. Type **72** | 1·75 | 85 |
| 236 | 2t. Common peafowl and tiger | 2·50 | 4·25 |

**73** Eagle attacking Hen with Chicks

**1984.** Centenary of Postal Life Insurance. Mult.

| | | | |
|---|---|---|---|
| 237 | 1t. Type **73** | 50 | 25 |
| 238 | 5t. Bangladesh family and postman's hand with insurance cheque | 1·50 | 2·25 |

**74** Abbasuddin Ahmad

**1984.** Abbasuddin Ahmad (singer) Commemoration.

| | | | | |
|---|---|---|---|---|
| 239 | 74 | 3t. multicoloured | 1·00 | 1·25 |

খুলনাপেক্স—৮৪

**(75)**

**1984.** "Khulnapex-84" Stamp Exhibition. No. 86 optd with T 75.

| | | | | |
|---|---|---|---|---|
| 240 | 22 | 2t.25 multicoloured | 1·00 | 1·75 |

**76** Cycling

**1984.** Olympic Games, Los Angeles. Multicoloured.

| | | | |
|---|---|---|---|
| 241 | 1t. Type **76** | 1·75 | 30 |
| 242 | 5t. Hockey | 2·50 | 2·25 |
| 243 | 10t. Volleyball | 2·75 | 4·25 |

**77** Farmer with Rice and Sickle

**1985.** 9th Annual Meeting of Islamic Development Bank, Dhaka. Multicoloured.

| | | | |
|---|---|---|---|
| 244 | 1t. Type **77** | 35 | 15 |
| 245 | 5t. Citizens of four races | 1·25 | 2·25 |

**78** Mother and Baby

**1985.** Child Survival Campaign. Multicoloured.

| | | | |
|---|---|---|---|
| 246 | 1t. Type **78** | 30 | 10 |
| 247 | 10t. Young child and growth graph | 2·00 | 3·25 |

উপজেলা নির্বাচন ১৯৮৫

**(79) (image scaled to 67% of original size)**

**1985.** Local Elections. Nos. 110/15 optd with T **79**.

| | | | |
|---|---|---|---|
| 248 | 40p. Type **29** | 40 | 50 |
| 249 | 1t. "Cassia fistula" | 50 | 30 |
| 250 | 2t.25 "Delonix regia" | 70 | 75 |
| 251 | 3t.50 "Nymphaea nouchali" | 80 | 1·25 |
| 252 | 4t. "Butea monosperma" | 80 | 1·25 |
| 253 | 5t. "Anthocephalus indicus" | 85 | 1·50 |

**80** Women working at Traditional Crafts

**1985.** U.N. Decade for Women. Multicoloured.

| | | | |
|---|---|---|---|
| 254 | 1t. Type **80** | 25 | 10 |
| 255 | 10t. Women with microscope, computer terminal and in classroom | 1·25 | 2·25 |

**81** U.N. Building, New York, Peace Doves and Flags

**1985.** 40th Anniv of United Nations Organization and 11th Anniv of Bangladesh Membership. Multicoloured.

| | | | |
|---|---|---|---|
| 256 | 1t. Type **81** | 10 | 10 |
| 257 | 10t. Map of world and Bangladesh flag | 1·40 | 1·75 |

**82** Head of Youth, Flowers and Symbols of Commerce and Agriculture

**1985.** International Youth Year. Multicoloured.

| | | | |
|---|---|---|---|
| 258 | 1t. Type **82** | 10 | 10 |
| 259 | 5t. Head of youth, flowers and symbols of industry | 40 | 60 |

**83** Emblem and Seven Doves

**1985.** 1st Summit Meeting of South Asian Association for Regional Co-operation, Dhaka. Multicoloured.

| | | | |
|---|---|---|---|
| 260 | 1t. Type **83** | 10 | 10 |
| 261 | 5t. Flags of member nations and lotus blossom | 1·75 | 1·25 |

**84** Zainul Abedin

**1985.** 10th Death Anniv of Zainul Abedin (artist).

| | | | | |
|---|---|---|---|---|
| 262 | 84 | 3t. multicoloured | 1·00 | 55 |

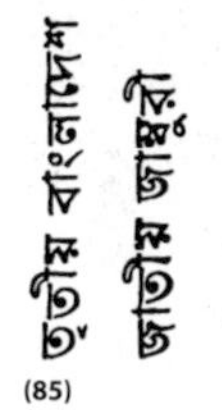
**(85)**

**1985.** 3rd National Scout Jamboree. No. 109 optd with T 85.

| | | | |
|---|---|---|---|
| 263 | 5t. green, blue and red | 2·50 | 3·50 |

**86** "Fishing Net" (Safiuddin Ahmed)

**1986.** Bangladesh Paintings. Multicoloured.

| | | | |
|---|---|---|---|
| 264 | 1t. Type **86** | 15 | 10 |
| 265 | 5t. "Happy Return" (Quamrul Hassan) | 40 | 50 |
| 266 | 10t. "Levelling the Ploughed Field" (Zainul Abedin) | 70 | 80 |

**87** Two Players competing for Ball

**1986.** World Cup Football Championship, Mexico. Multicoloured.

| | | | |
|---|---|---|---|
| 267 | 1t. Type **87** | 50 | 10 |
| 268 | 10t. Goalkeeper and ball in net | 2·25 | 3·00 |
| MS269 | 105×75 mm. 20t. Four players (60×44 mm) Imperf | 5·50 | 6·50 |

**88** General M. A. G. Osmani

**1986.** General M. A. G. Osmani (army commander-in-chief) Commemoration.

| | | | | |
|---|---|---|---|---|
| 270 | 88 | 3t. multicoloured | 1·75 | 1·00 |

**1986.** South Asian Association for Regional Co-operation Seminar. No. 183 optd SAARC SEMINAR '86.

| | | | | |
|---|---|---|---|---|
| 271 | 55 | 50p. multicoloured | 3·25 | 3·75 |

**90** Butterflies and Nuclear Explosion

**1986.** International Peace Year. Multicoloured.

272 1t. Type **90** 50 25
273 10t. Flowers and ruined buildings 2·75 4·00
**MS**274 109×80 mm. 20t. Peace dove and soldier 1·50 2·00

**1987.** Conference for Development. Nos. 152/3 optd CONFERENCE FOR DEVELOPMENT '87, No. 275 also surch TK. 1.00.

275 **38** 1t. on 40p. black, red and yellow 10 20
276 - 5t. gold and blue 55 1·75

**92** Demonstrators with Placards

**1987.** 35th Anniv of Bangla Language Movement. Multicoloured.

277 3t. Type **92** 1·40 2·50
278 3t. Martyrs' Memorial 1·40 2·50

Nos. 277/8 were printed together, se-tenant, forming a composite design.

**93** Nurse giving Injection

**1987.** World Health Day.

279 **93** 1t. black and blue 1·75 2·00

See also No 295.

**94** Pattern and Bengali Script

**1987.** Bengali New Year Day. Multicoloured.

280 1t. Type **94** 10 10
281 10t. Bengali woman 40 60

**95** Jute Shika

**1987.** Export Products. Multicoloured.

282 1t. Type **95** 10 10
283 5t. Jute carpet (horiz) 30 35
284 10t. Cane table lamp 45 70

**96** Ustad Ayet Ali Khan and Surbahar

**1987.** 20th Death Anniv of Ustad Ayet Ali Khan (musician and composer).

285 **96** 5t. multicoloured 1·50 1·00

**97** Palanquin

**1987.** Transport. Multicoloured.

286 2t. Type **97** 20 15
287 3t. Bicycle rickshaw 1·00 35
288 5t. River steamer 1·25 65
289 7t. Express diesel train 3·25 1·25
290 10t. Bullock cart 60 1·50

**98** H. S. Suhrawardy

**1987.** Hossain Shadid Suhrawardy (politician) Commemoration.

291 **98** 3t. multicoloured 20 30

**99** Villagers fleeing from Typhoon

**1987.** International Year of Shelter for the Homeless. Multicoloured.

292 5t. Type **99** 50 70
293 5t. Villagers and modern houses 50 70

**100** President Ershad addressing Parliament

**1987.** 1st Anniv of Return to Democracy.

294 **100** 10t. multicoloured 65 1·00

**1988.** World Health Day. As T **93**.

295 25p. brown 60 20

DESIGN: 25p. Oral rehydration.

**101** Woman planting Palm Saplings

**1988.** I.F.A.D. Seminar on Agricultural Loans for Rural Women. Multicoloured.

296 3t. Type **101** 15 25
297 5t. Village woman milking cow 20 75

**102** Basketball

**1988.** Olympic Games, Seoul. Multicoloured.

298 5t. Type **102** 1·25 80
299 5t. Weightlifting 1·25 80
300 5t. Tennis 1·25 80
301 5t. Rifle-shooting 1·25 80
302 5t. Boxing 1·25 80

**103** Interior of Shait Gumbaz Mosque, Bagerhat

**1988.** Historical Buildings. Multicoloured.

303 1t. Type **103** 40 10
304 4t. Paharpur Monastery 80 30
305 5t. Kantanagar Temple, Dinajpur 80 30
306 10t. Lalbag Fort, Dhaka 1·25 1·00

**104** Henri Dunant (founder), Red Cross and Crescent

**1988.** 125th Anniv of International Red Cross and Red Crescent. Multicoloured.

307 5t. Type **104** 1·40 30
308 10t. Red Cross workers with patient 2·00 1·10

**105** Dr. Qudrat-i-Khuda in Laboratory

**1988.** Dr. Qudrat-i-Khuda (scientist) Commem.

309 **105** 5t. multicoloured 50 40

**106** Wicket-keeper

**1988.** Asia Cup Cricket. Multicoloured.

310 1t. Type **106** 80 90
311 5t. Batsman 1·00 1·25
312 10t. Bowler 1·75 2·25

**107** Labourers, Factory and Technician

**1988.** 32nd Meeting of Colombo Plan Consultative Committee, Dhaka.

313 **107** 3t. multicoloured 10 10
314 **107** 10t. multicoloured 40 45

**108** Dhaka G.P.O. Building

**1988.** 25th Anniv of Dhaka G.P.O. Building. Multicoloured.

315 1t. Type **108** 15 10
316 5t. Post Office counter 30 30

৫ম জাতীয় রোভার মুট
১৯৮৮-৮৯
**(109)**

**1988.** 5th National Rover Scout Moot. No. 168 optd with T **109**.

317 **47** 5t. multicoloured 3·50 3·00

**110** Bangladesh Airport

**1989.** Bangladesh Landmarks.

318 **110** 3t. black and blue 40 10
318a - 4t. blue 40 10
710 - 5t. black and brown 60 15
320 - 10t. red 4·00 35
321 - 20t. multicoloured 1·00 40

DESIGNS—VERT (22×33 mm): 5t. Curzon Hall. (19½×31½ mm): 10t. Fertiliser factory, Chittagong. HORIZ (33×23 mm): 4t. Chittagong port; 20t. Postal Academy, Rajshahi.

চতুর্থ দ্বিবার্ষিক এশীয়
চারুকলা প্রদর্শনী
বাংলাদেশ ১৯৮৯
**(111)**

**1989.** 4th Biennial Asian Art Exhibition. No. 266 optd with T **111**.

322 10t. "Levelling the Ploughed Field" (Zainul Abedin) 75 1·00

**112** Irrigation Methods and Student with Telescope

**1989.** 12th National Science and Technology Week.

323 **112** 10t. multicoloured 50 60

**113** Academy Logo

**1989.** 75th Anniv of Police Academy, Sardah.

324 **113** 10t. multicoloured 75 60

**114** Rejoicing Crowds, Paris, 1789

**1989.** Bicentenary of French Revolution. Mult.

| | | | |
|---|---|---|---|
| 325 | 17t. Type **114** | 70 | 75 |
| 326 | 17t. Storming the Bastille, 1789 | 70 | 75 |
| **MS**327 | 125×125 mm 5t. Men with pickaxes; 10t. "Liberty guiding the People" (detail) (Delacroix); 10t. Crowd with cannon. P 14 | 2·00 | 3·00 |
| **MS**328 | 152×88 mm. 25t. Storming the Bastille. Imperf | 2·00 | 3·00 |

The design of No. **MS**328 incorporates the three scenes featured on No. **MS**327.

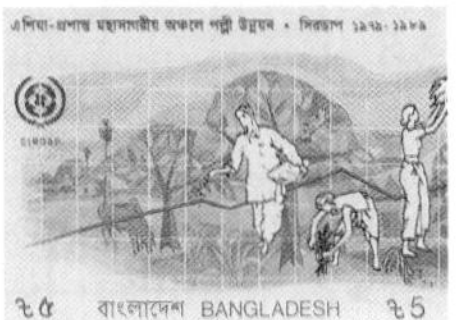

**115** Sowing and Harvesting

**1989.** 10th Anniv of Asia–Pacific Integrated Rural Development Centre. Multicoloured.

| | | | |
|---|---|---|---|
| 329 | 5t. Type **115** | 65 | 65 |
| 330 | 10t. Rural activities | 65 | 65 |

Nos. 329/30 were printed together, se-tenant, forming a composite design.

**116** Helper and Child playing with Baby

**1989.** 40th Anniv of S.O.S. International Children's Village. Multicoloured.

| | | | |
|---|---|---|---|
| 331 | 1t. Type **116** | 15 | 10 |
| 332 | 10t. Foster mother with children | 85 | 90 |

**117** U.N. Soldier on Watch

**1989.** 1st Anniv of Bangladesh Participation in U.N. Peace-keeping Force. Multicoloured.

| | | | |
|---|---|---|---|
| 333 | 4t. Type **117** | 50 | 30 |
| 334 | 10t. Two soldiers checking positions | 1·00 | 70 |

**118** Festival Emblem

**1989.** 2nd Asian Poetry Festival, Dhaka.

| | | | | |
|---|---|---|---|---|
| 335 | 118 | 2t. red, deep red and green | 15 | 10 |
| 336 | - | 10t. multicoloured | 85 | 90 |

DESIGN: 10t. Festival emblem and hall.

**119** State Security Printing Press

**1989.** Inauguration of State Security Printing Press, Gazipur.

| | | | | |
|---|---|---|---|---|
| 337 | 119 | 10t. multicoloured | 65 | 65 |

**120** Water Lilies and T.V. Emblem

**1989.** 25th Anniv of Bangladesh Television. Multicoloured.

| | | | |
|---|---|---|---|
| 338 | 5t. Type **120** | 35 | 30 |
| 339 | 10t. Central emblem and water lilies | 65 | 80 |

**121** Gharial in Shallow Water

**1990.** Endangered Wildlife. Gharial. Multicoloured.

| | | | |
|---|---|---|---|
| 340 | 50p. Type **121** | 80 | 45 |
| 341 | 2t. Gharial feeding | 1·00 | 60 |
| 342 | 4t. Gharials basking on sand bank | 1·40 | 70 |
| 343 | 10t. Two gharials resting | 1·75 | 95 |

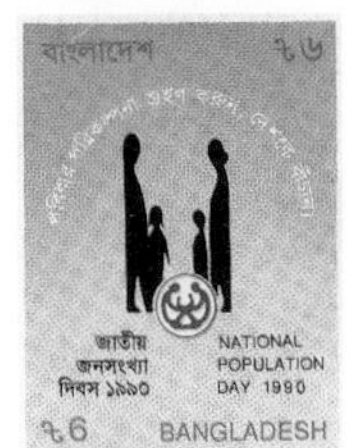

**122** Symbolic Family

**1990.** Population Day.

| | | | | |
|---|---|---|---|---|
| 344 | 122 | 6t. multicoloured | 55 | 35 |

**123** Justice S. M. Murshed

**1990.** 10th Death Anniv of Justice Syed Mahbub Murshed.

| | | | | |
|---|---|---|---|---|
| 345 | 123 | 5t. multicoloured | 2·25 | 1·25 |

**124** Boy learning Alphabet

**1990.** International Literacy Year. Multicoloured.

| | | | |
|---|---|---|---|
| 346 | 6t. Type **124** | 1·00 | 50 |
| 347 | 10t. Boy teaching girl to write | 1·50 | 1·25 |

**125** Penny Black with "Stamp World London 90" Exhibition Emblem

**1990.** 150th Anniv of the Penny Black. Multicoloured.

| | | | |
|---|---|---|---|
| 348 | 7t. Type **125** | 1·50 | 2·00 |
| 349 | 10t. Penny Black, 1983 World Communications Year stamp and Bengali mail runner | 1·75 | 2·50 |

**126** Goalkeeper and Ball

**1990.** World Cup Football Championship, Italy. Multicoloured.

| | | | |
|---|---|---|---|
| 350 | 8t. Type **126** | 1·75 | 1·75 |
| 351 | 10t. Footballer with ball | 2·00 | 2·25 |
| **MS**352 | 104×79 mm. 25t. Colosseum, Rome, with football. Imperf | 12·00 | 12·00 |

**127** Mango

**1990.** Fruit. Multicoloured.

| | | | |
|---|---|---|---|
| 353 | 1t. Type **127** | 30 | 20 |
| 354 | 2t. Guava | 30 | 20 |
| 355 | 3t. Water melon | 35 | 25 |
| 356 | 4t. Papaya | 40 | 30 |
| 357 | 5t. Bread fruit | 65 | 65 |
| 358 | 10t. Carambola | 1·25 | 1·50 |

**128** Man gathering Wheat

**1990.** U.N. Conference on Least Developed Countries, Paris.

| | | | | |
|---|---|---|---|---|
| 359 | 128 | 10t. multicoloured | 1·25 | 1·25 |

**129** Map of Asia with Stream of Letters

**1990.** 20th Anniv of Asia–Pacific Postal Training Centre. Multicoloured.

| | | | |
|---|---|---|---|
| 360 | 2t. Type **129** | 1·75 | 1·75 |
| 361 | 6t. Map of Pacific with stream of letters | 1·75 | 1·75 |

Nos. 360/1 were printed together, se-tenant, forming a composite map design.

**130** Canoe Racing

**1990.** Asian Games, Beijing. Multicoloured.

| | | | |
|---|---|---|---|
| 362 | 2t. Type **130** | 1·00 | 30 |
| 363 | 4t. Kabaddi | 1·25 | 30 |
| 364 | 8t. Wrestling | 1·75 | 1·50 |
| 365 | 10t. Badminton | 3·00 | 2·00 |

**131** Lalan Shah

**1990.** 1st Death Anniv of Lalan Shah (poet).

| | | | | |
|---|---|---|---|---|
| 366 | 131 | 6t. multicoloured | 1·50 | 1·00 |

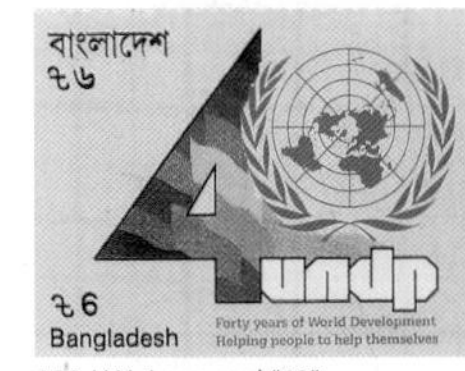

**132** U.N. Logo and "40"

**1990.** 40th Anniv of United Nations Development Programme.

| | | | | |
|---|---|---|---|---|
| 367 | 132 | 6t. multicoloured | 1·00 | 70 |

**133** Baby

**1990.** Immunization.

| | | | | |
|---|---|---|---|---|
| 368 | 133 | 1t. green | 50 | 50 |
| 369 | 133 | 2t. brown | 50 | 25 |

**134** "Danaus chrysippus"

**1990.** Butterflies. Multicoloured.

| | | | |
|---|---|---|---|
| 370 | 6t. Type **134** | 1·60 | 1·60 |
| 371 | 6t. "Precis almana" | 1·60 | 1·60 |
| 372 | 10t. "Ixias pyrene" | 1·75 | 1·75 |
| 373 | 10t. "Danaus plexippus" | 1·75 | 1·75 |

**135** Drugs attacking Bangladesh

**1991.** U.N. Anti-drugs Decade. Multicoloured.

| | | | |
|---|---|---|---|
| 374 | 2t. Type **135** | 1·25 | 50 |
| 375 | 4t. "Drug" snake around globe | 1·75 | 1·25 |

**136** Salimullah Hall

**1991**

| | | | | |
|---|---|---|---|---|
| 376 | 136 | 6t. blue and yellow | 20 | 15 |

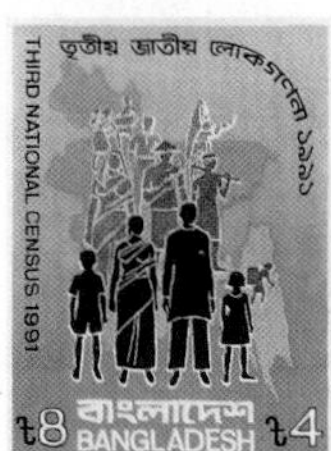

**137** Silhouetted People on Map

**1991.** 3rd National Census.

| | | | | |
|---|---|---|---|---|
| 382 | 137 | 4t. multicoloured | 1·50 | 1·50 |

**138** "Invincible Bangla" (statue)

**1991.** 20th Anniv of Independence. Multicoloured.

| | | | |
|---|---|---|---|
| 383 | 4t. Type **138** | 85 | 1·00 |
| 384 | 4t. "Freedom Fighter" (statue) | 85 | 1·00 |

| | | | |
|---|---|---|---|
| 385 | 4t. Mujibnagar Memorial | 85 | 1·00 |
| 386 | 4t. Eternal flame | 85 | 1·00 |
| 387 | 4t. National Martyrs' Memorial | 85 | 1·00 |

Nos. 383/7 were issued together, se-tenant, forming a composite design.

**139** President Rahman Seated

**1991.** 10th Death Anniv of President Ziaur Rahman. Multicoloured.

| | | | |
|---|---|---|---|
| 388 | 50p. Type **139** | 30 | 15 |
| 389 | 2t. President Rahman's head in circular decoration | 1·00 | 1·10 |
| **MS**390 | 146×75 mm. Nos. 388/9 (sold at 10t.) | 1·90 | 2·75 |

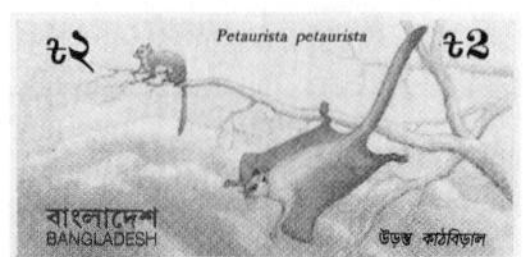


**140** Red Giant Flying Squirrel

**1991.** Endangered Species. Multicoloured.

| | | | |
|---|---|---|---|
| 391 | 2t. Type **140** | 2·00 | 2·25 |
| 392 | 4t. Black-faced monkey (vert) | 2·00 | 2·25 |
| 393 | 6t. Great Indian hornbill (vert) | 2·00 | 2·25 |
| 394 | 10t. Armoured pangolin | 2·00 | 2·25 |

**141** Kaikobad

**1991.** 40th Death Anniv of Kaikobad (poet).

| | | | | |
|---|---|---|---|---|
| 395 | **141** | 6t. multicoloured | 1·60 | 1·25 |

**142** Rabindranath Tagore and Temple

**1991.** 50th Death Anniv of Rabindranath Tagore (poet).

| | | | | |
|---|---|---|---|---|
| 396 | **142** | 4t. multicoloured | 1·00 | 65 |

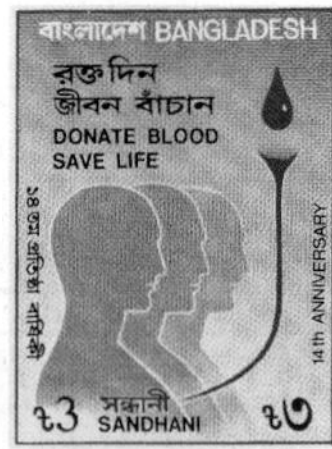


**143** Voluntary Blood Programme

**1991.** 14th Anniv of "Sandhani" (medical students' association).

| | | | | |
|---|---|---|---|---|
| 397 | **143** | 3t. black and red | 1·00 | 50 |
| 398 | - | 5t. multicoloured | 2·00 | 2·25 |

DESIGN: 5t. Blind man and eye.

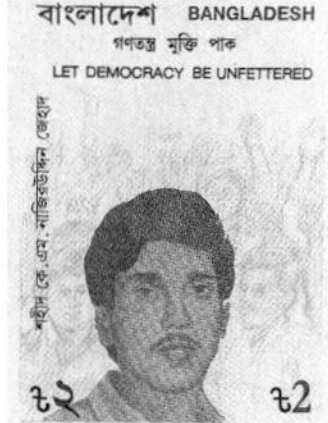


**144** Shahid Naziruddin and Crowd

**1991.** 1st Death Anniv of Shahid Naziruddin Jahad (democrat).

| | | | | |
|---|---|---|---|---|
| 399 | **144** | 2t. black, green and brown | 1·00 | 60 |

**145** Shaheed Noor Hossain with Slogan on Chest

**1991.** 4th Death Anniv of Shaheed Noor Hossain (democrat).

| | | | | |
|---|---|---|---|---|
| 400 | **145** | 2t. multicoloured | 1·00 | 55 |

**146** Bronze Stupa

**1991.** Archaeological Relics from Mainamati. Multicoloured.

| | | | |
|---|---|---|---|
| 401 | 4t. Type **146** | 1·50 | 1·60 |
| 402 | 4t. Earthenware and bronze pitchers | 1·50 | 1·60 |
| 403 | 4t. Remains of Salban Vihara Monastery | 1·50 | 1·60 |
| 404 | 4t. Gold coins | 1·50 | 1·60 |
| 405 | 4t. Terracotta plaque | 1·50 | 1·60 |

**147** Demostrators

**1991.** 1st Anniv of Mass Uprising.

| | | | | |
|---|---|---|---|---|
| 406 | **147** | 4t. multicoloured | 1·25 | 80 |

**148** Munier Chowdhury

**1991.** 20th Anniv of Independence. Martyred Intellectuals (1st series). Each black and brown.

| | | | |
|---|---|---|---|
| 407 | 2t. Type **148** | 50 | 55 |
| 408 | 2t. Ghyasuddin Ahmad | 50 | 55 |
| 409 | 2t. Rashidul Hasan | 50 | 55 |
| 410 | 2t. Muhammad Anwar Pasha | 50 | 55 |
| 411 | 2t. Dr. Muhammad Mortaza | 50 | 55 |
| 412 | 2t. Shahid Saber | 50 | 55 |
| 413 | 2t. Fazlur Rahman Khan | 50 | 55 |
| 414 | 2t. Ranada Prasad Saha | 50 | 55 |
| 415 | 2t. Adhyaksha Joges Chandra Ghose | 50 | 55 |
| 416 | 2t. Santosh Chandra Bhattacharyya | 50 | 55 |
| 417 | 2t. Dr. Gobinda Chandra Deb | 50 | 55 |
| 418 | 2t. A. Muniruzzaman | 50 | 55 |
| 419 | 2t. Mufazzal Haider Chaudhury | 50 | 55 |
| 420 | 2t. Dr. Abdul Alim Choudhury | 50 | 55 |
| 421 | 2t. Sirajuddin Hossain | 50 | 55 |
| 422 | 2t. Shahidulla Kaiser | 50 | 55 |
| 423 | 2t. Altaf Mahmud | 50 | 55 |
| 424 | 2t. Dr. Jyotirmay Guha Thakurta | 50 | 55 |
| 425 | 2t. Dr. Muhammad Abul Khair | 50 | 55 |
| 426 | 2t. Dr. Serajul Haque Khan | 50 | 55 |
| 427 | 2t. Dr. Mohammad Fazle Rabbi | 50 | 55 |
| 428 | 2t. Mir Abdul Quyyum | 50 | 55 |
| 429 | 2t. Golam Mostafa | 50 | 55 |
| 430 | 2t. Dhirendranath Dutta | 50 | 55 |
| 431 | 2t. S. Mannan | 50 | 55 |
| 432 | 2t. Nizamuddin Ahmad | 50 | 55 |
| 433 | 2t. Abul Bashar Chowdhury | 50 | 55 |
| 434 | 2t. Selina Parveen | 50 | 55 |
| 435 | 2t. Dr. Abul Kalam Azad | 50 | 55 |
| 436 | 2t. Saidul Hassan | 50 | 55 |

See also Nos. 483/92, 525/40, 568/83, 620/35, 656/71, 691/706, 731/46 and 779/94.

**149** "Penaeus monodon"

**1991.** Shrimps. Multicoloured.

| | | | |
|---|---|---|---|
| 437 | 6t. Type **149** | 2·00 | 2·25 |
| 438 | 6t. "Metapenaeus monoceros" | 2·00 | 2·25 |

**150** Death of Raihan Jaglu

**1992.** 5th Death Anniv of Shaheed Mirze Abu Raihan Jaglu.

| | | | | |
|---|---|---|---|---|
| 439 | **150** | 2t. multicoloured | 1·50 | 60 |

**151** Rural and Urban Scenes

**1992.** World Environment Day. Multicoloured.

| | | | |
|---|---|---|---|
| 440 | 4t. Type **151** | 75 | 25 |
| 441 | 10t. World Environment Day logo (horiz) | 2·00 | 2·75 |

**152** Nawab Sirajuddaulah

**1992.** 235th Death Anniv of Nawab Sirajuddaulah of Bengal.

| | | | | |
|---|---|---|---|---|
| 442 | **152** | 10t. multicoloured | 1·50 | 2·00 |

**153** Syed Ismail Hossain Sirajee

**1992.** 61st Death Anniv of Syed Ismail Hossain Sirajee.

| | | | | |
|---|---|---|---|---|
| 443 | **153** | 4t. multicoloured | 1·25 | 60 |

**154** Couple planting Seedling

**1992.** Plant Week. Multicoloured.

| | | | |
|---|---|---|---|
| 444 | 2t. Type **154** | 1·00 | 80 |
| 445 | 4t. Birds on tree (vert) | 2·00 | 1·25 |

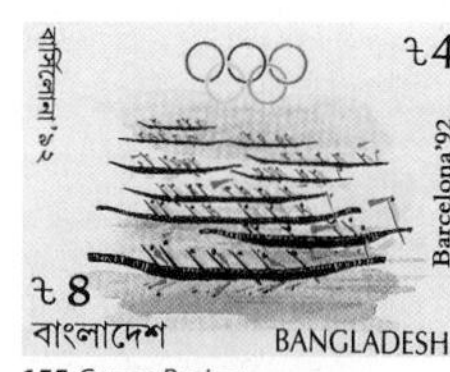


**155** Canoe Racing

**1992.** Olympic Games, Barcelona. Multicoloured.

| | | | |
|---|---|---|---|
| 446 | 4t. Type **155** | 1·40 | 1·75 |
| 447 | 6t. Hands holding torch with Olympic rings | 1·40 | 1·75 |
| 448 | 10t. Olympic rings and doves | 1·40 | 1·75 |
| 449 | 10t. Olympic rings and multiracial handshake | 1·40 | 1·75 |

**1992.** "Banglapex '92", National Philatelic Exhibition (1st issue). No. 290 optd Banglapex '92 in English and Bengali.

| | | | |
|---|---|---|---|
| 450 | 10t. Bullock cart | 2·25 | 2·75 |

See also Nos. 452/3.

**157** Masnad-e-Ala Isa Khan

**1992.** 393rd Death Anniv of Masnad-e-Ala Isa Khan.

| | | | | |
|---|---|---|---|---|
| 451 | **157** | 4t. multicoloured | 1·00 | 60 |

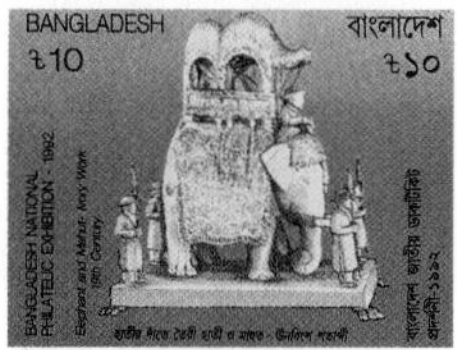


**158** Ceremonial Elephant (19th-century ivory carving)

**1992.** "Banglapex '92" National Philatelic Exhibition (2nd issue). Multicoloured.

| | | | |
|---|---|---|---|
| 452 | 10t. Type **158** | 1·60 | 2·25 |
| 453 | 10t. Victorian pillarbox between early and modern postmen | 1·60 | 2·25 |
| **MS**454 | 145×92 mm. Nos. 452/3. Imperf (sold at 25t.) | 4·50 | 5·00 |

**159** Star Mosque

**1992.** Star Mosque, Dhaka.

| | | | | |
|---|---|---|---|---|
| 455 | **159** | 10t. multicoloured | 2·00 | 2·00 |

**160** Meer Nisar Ali Titumeer and Fort

**1992.** 161st Death Anniv of Meer Nisar Ali Titumeer.

| | | | | |
|---|---|---|---|---|
| 456 | **160** | 10t. multicoloured | 1·75 | 1·75 |

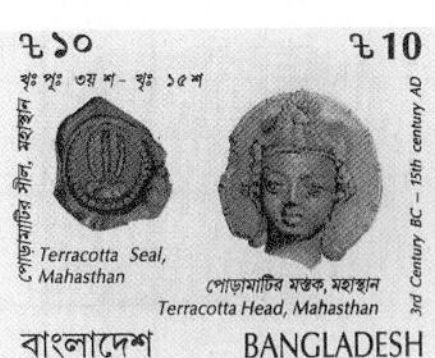


**161** Terracotta Head and Seal

**1992.** Archaeological Relics from Mahasthangarh. Multicoloured.

| | | | |
|---|---|---|---|
| 457 | 10t. Type **161** | 1·75 | 1·90 |
| 458 | 10t. Terracotta panel showing swan | 1·75 | 1·90 |
| 459 | 10t. Terracotta statue of Surya | 1·75 | 1·90 |
| 460 | 10t. Gupta stone column | 1·75 | 1·90 |

**162** Young Child and Food

**1992.** Int Conference on Nutrition, Rome.

| | | | | |
|---|---|---|---|---|
| 461 | **162** | 4t. multicoloured | 1·00 | 55 |

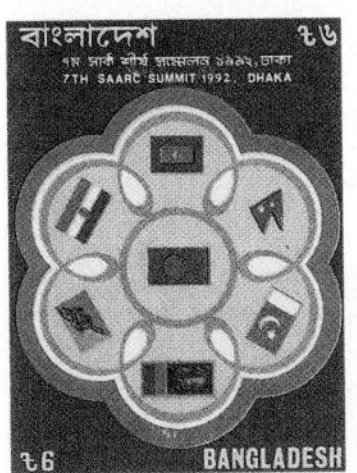


**163** National Flags

**1992.** 7th South Asian Association for Regional Co-operation Summit Conference, Dhaka. Mult.

| | | | |
|---|---|---|---|
| 462 | 6t. Type **163** | 1·40 | 75 |
| 463 | 10t. S.A.A.R.C. emblem | 1·60 | 2·00 |

**164** Syed Abdus Samad

**1993.** Syed Abdus Samad (footballer) Commem.

| | | | | |
|---|---|---|---|---|
| 464 | **164** | 2t. multicoloured | 1·50 | 70 |

**165** Haji Shariat Ullah

**1993.** Haji Shariat Ullah Commemoration.

| | | | | |
|---|---|---|---|---|
| 465 | **165** | 2t. multicoloured | 1·50 | 70 |

**166** People digging Canal

**1993.** Irrigation Canals Construction Project. Mult.

| | | | |
|---|---|---|---|
| 466 | 2t. Type **166** | 80 | 80 |
| 467 | 2t. Completed canal and paddy-fields | 80 | 80 |

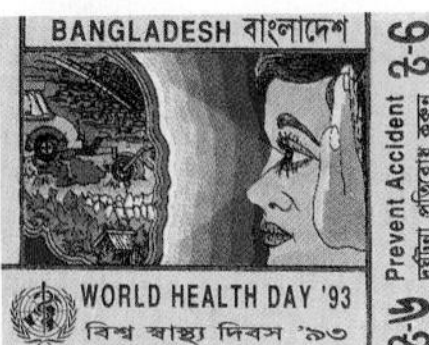


**167** Accident Prevention

**1993.** World Health Day. Multicoloured.

| | | | |
|---|---|---|---|
| 468 | 6t. Type **167** | 2·00 | 75 |
| 469 | 10t. Satellite photograph and symbols of trauma (vert) | 2·25 | 2·75 |

**168** National Images

**1993.** 1400th Year of Bengali Solar Calendar.

| | | | | |
|---|---|---|---|---|
| 470 | **168** | 2t. multicoloured | 1·00 | 50 |

**169** Schoolchildren and Bengali Script

**1993.** Compulsory Primary Education. Mult.

| | | | |
|---|---|---|---|
| 471 | 2t. Type **169** | 80 | 80 |
| 472 | 2t. Books and slate (horiz) | 80 | 80 |

**170** Nawab Sir Salimullah and Palace

**1993.** 122nd Birth Anniv of Nawab Sir Salimullah.

| | | | | |
|---|---|---|---|---|
| 473 | **170** | 4t. multicoloured | 1·25 | 70 |

**171** Fish Production

**1993.** Fish Fortnight.

| | | | | |
|---|---|---|---|---|
| 474 | **171** | 2t. multicoloured | 50 | 40 |

**172** Sunderban

**1993.** Natural Beauty of Bangladesh. Mult.

| | | | |
|---|---|---|---|
| 475 | 10t. Type **172** | 1·00 | 1·40 |
| 476 | 10t. Kuakata beach | 1·00 | 1·40 |
| 477 | 10t. Madhabkunda waterfall (vert) | 1·00 | 1·40 |
| 478 | 10t. River Piyain, Jaflang (vert) | 1·00 | 1·40 |
| **MS**479 | 174×102 mm. Nos. 475/8. Imperf (sold at 50t.) | 3·50 | 4·25 |

**173** Exhibition Emblem

**1993.** 6th Asian Art Biennale.

| | | | | |
|---|---|---|---|---|
| 480 | **173** | 10t. multicoloured | 80 | 1·00 |

**174** Foy's Lake

**1993.** Tourism Month.

| | | | | |
|---|---|---|---|---|
| 481 | **174** | 10t. multicoloured | 1·00 | 1·25 |

**175** Burdwan House

**1993.** Foundation Day, Bangla Academy.

| | | | | |
|---|---|---|---|---|
| 482 | **175** | 2t. brown and green | 1·25 | 40 |

**1993.** Martyred Intellectuals (2nd series). As T **148**. Each black and brown.

| | | | |
|---|---|---|---|
| 483 | 2t. Lt. Cdr. Moazzam Hussain | 20 | 30 |
| 484 | 2t. Muhammad Habibur Rahman | 20 | 30 |
| 485 | 2t. Khandoker Abu Taleb | 20 | 30 |
| 486 | 2t. Moshiur Rahman | 20 | 30 |
| 487 | 2t. Md. Abdul Muktadir | 20 | 30 |
| 488 | 2t. Nutan Chandra Sinha | 20 | 30 |
| 489 | 2t. Syed Nazmul Haque | 20 | 30 |
| 490 | 2t. Dr. Mohammed Amin Uddin | 20 | 30 |
| 491 | 2t. Dr. Faizul Mohee | 20 | 30 |
| 492 | 2t. Sukha Ranjan Somaddar | 20 | 30 |

**176** Throwing the Discus

**1993.** 6th South Asian Federation Games, Dhaka. Multicoloured.

| | | | |
|---|---|---|---|
| 493 | 2t. Type **176** | 20 | 20 |
| 494 | 4t. Running (vert) | 35 | 35 |

**177** Tomb of Sultan Ghiyasuddin Azam Shah

**1993.** Muslim Monuments.

| | | | | |
|---|---|---|---|---|
| 495 | **177** | 10t. multicoloured | 75 | 1·00 |

**178** Scouting Activities and Jamboree Emblem

**1994.** 14th Asian–Pacific and 5th Bangladesh National Scout Jamboree.

| | | | | |
|---|---|---|---|---|
| 496 | **178** | 2t. multicoloured | 40 | 30 |

**179** Emblem and Mother giving Solution to Child

**1994.** 25th Anniv of Oral Rehydration.

| | | | | |
|---|---|---|---|---|
| 497 | **179** | 2t. multicoloured | 65 | 30 |

**180** Interior of Chhota Sona Mosque, Nawabgonj

**1994.** Ancient Mosques. Multicoloured.

| | | | |
|---|---|---|---|
| 498 | 4t. Type **180** | 40 | 20 |
| 499 | 6t. Exterior of Chhota Sona Mosque | 50 | 65 |
| 500 | 6t. Exterior of Baba Adam's Mosque, Munshigonj | 50 | 65 |

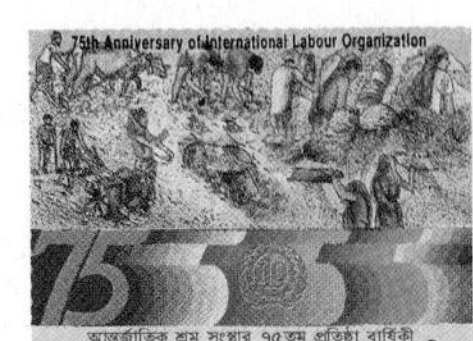


**181** Agricultural Workers and Emblem

**1994.** 75th Anniv of I.L.O. Multicoloured.

| | | | |
|---|---|---|---|
| 501 | 4t. Type **181** | 25 | 20 |
| 502 | 10t. Worker turning cog (vert) | 1·00 | 1·00 |

**182** Priest releasing Peace Doves

**1994.** 1500th Year of Bengali Solar Calendar.

| | | | | |
|---|---|---|---|---|
| 503 | **182** | 2t. multicoloured | 55 | 30 |

**183** Scenes from Baishakhi Festival

**1994.** Folk Festivals. Multicoloured.

| | | | |
|---|---|---|---|
| 504 | 4t. Type **183** | 35 | 35 |
| 505 | 4t. Scenes from Nabanna and Paush Parvana Festivals | 35 | 35 |

**184** Family, Globe and Logo

**1994.** International Year of the Family.

| | | | | |
|---|---|---|---|---|
| 506 | **184** | 10t. multicoloured | 1·00 | 1·50 |

**185** People planting Saplings

**1994.** Tree Planting Campaign. Multicoloured.

| | | | |
|---|---|---|---|
| 507 | 4t. Type **185** | 50 | 25 |
| 508 | 6t. Hands holding saplings | 75 | 60 |

**186** Player kicking Ball

**1994.** World Cup Football Championship, U.S.A. Multicoloured.

| | | | |
|---|---|---|---|
| 509 | 20t. Type **186** | 2·25 | 3·00 |
| 510 | 20t. Player heading ball | 2·25 | 3·00 |

**187** Traffic on Bridge

**1994.** Inauguration of Jamuna Multi-purpose Bridge Project.

| | | | | |
|---|---|---|---|---|
| 511 | **187** | 4t. multicoloured | 2·00 | 60 |

**188** Asian Black-headed Oriole

**1994.** Birds. Multicoloured.

| | | | |
|---|---|---|---|
| 512 | 4t. Type **188** | 40 | 40 |
| 513 | 6t. Greater racquet-tailed drongo | 60 | 80 |
| 514 | 6t. Indian tree pie | 60 | 80 |
| 515 | 6t. Red junglefowl | 60 | 80 |
| **MS**516 | 165×110 mm. Nos. 512/15 (sold at 25t.) | 2·00 | 2·75 |

**189** Dr. Mohammad Ibrahim and Hospital

**1994.** 5th Death Anniv of Dr. Mohammad Ibrahim (diabetes treatment pioneer).

| | | | | |
|---|---|---|---|---|
| 517 | **189** | 2t. multicoloured | 40 | 20 |

**190** Nawab Faizunnessa Chowdhurani

**1994.** 160th Birth Anniv of Nawab Faizunnessa Chowdhurani (social reformer).

| | | | | |
|---|---|---|---|---|
| 518 | **190** | 2t. multicoloured | 50 | 20 |

**191** Boxing

**1994.** Asian Games, Hiroshima, Japan.

| | | | | |
|---|---|---|---|---|
| 519 | **191** | 4t. multicoloured | 1·50 | 60 |

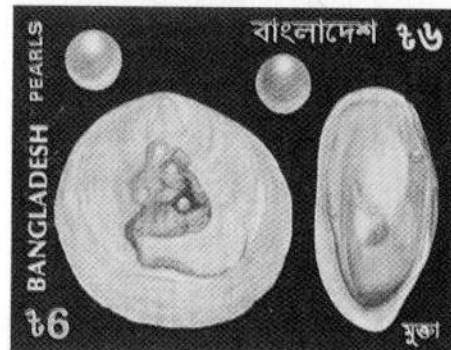


**192** Pink and White Pearls with Windowpane Oysters

**1994.** Sea Shells. Multicoloured.

| | | | |
|---|---|---|---|
| 520 | 6t. Type **192** | 1·40 | 1·60 |
| 521 | 6t. Tranquelous scallop and other shells | 1·40 | 1·60 |
| 522 | 6t. Lister's conch, Asiatic Arabian cowrie, bladder moon and woodcock murex | 1·40 | 1·60 |
| 523 | 6t. Spotted tun, spiny frog shell, spiral melongena and gibbous olive (vert) | 1·40 | 1·60 |

**193** Dr. Milon and Demonstrators

**1994.** 4th Death Anniv of Dr. Shamsul Alam Khan Milon (medical reformer).

| | | | | |
|---|---|---|---|---|
| 524 | **193** | 2t. multicoloured | 25 | 20 |

**1994.** Martyred Intellectuals (3rd series). As T **148**. Each black and brown.

| | | | |
|---|---|---|---|
| 525 | 2t. Dr. Harinath Dey | 25 | 30 |
| 526 | 2t. Dr. A. F. Ziaur Rahman | 25 | 30 |
| 527 | 2t. Mamun Mahmud | 25 | 30 |
| 528 | 2t. Mohsin Ali Dewan | 25 | 30 |
| 529 | 2t. Dr. N. A. M. Jahangir | 25 | 30 |
| 530 | 2t. Shah Abdul Majid | 25 | 30 |
| 531 | 2t. Muhammad Akhter | 25 | 30 |
| 532 | 2t. Meherunnesa | 25 | 30 |
| 533 | 2t. Dr. Kasiruddin Talukder | 25 | 30 |
| 534 | 2t. Fazlul Haque Choudhury | 25 | 30 |
| 535 | 2t. Md. Shamsuzzaman | 25 | 30 |
| 536 | 2t. A. K. M. Shamsuddin | 25 | 30 |
| 537 | 2t. Lt. Mohammad Anwarul Azim | 25 | 30 |
| 538 | 2t. Nurul Amin Khan | 25 | 30 |
| 539 | 2t. Mohammad Sadeque | 25 | 30 |
| 540 | 2t. Md. Araz Ali | 25 | 30 |

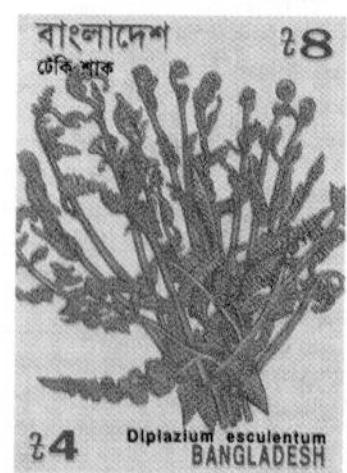


**194** "Diplazium esculentum"

**1994.** Vegetables. Multicoloured.

| | | | |
|---|---|---|---|
| 541 | 4t. Type **194** | 70 | 50 |
| 542 | 4t. "Momordica charantia" | 70 | 50 |
| 543 | 6t. "Lagenaria siceraria" | 90 | 70 |
| 544 | 6t. "Trichosanthes dioica" | 90 | 70 |
| 545 | 10t. "Solanum melongena" | 1·40 | 2·00 |
| 546 | 10t. "Cucurbita maxima" (horiz) | 1·40 | 2·00 |

**195** Sonargaon

**1995.** 20th Anniv of World Tourism Organization.

| | | | | |
|---|---|---|---|---|
| 547 | **195** | 10t. multicoloured | 1·75 | 1·75 |

**196** Exports

**1995.** Dhaka International Trade Fair '95. Mult.

| | | | |
|---|---|---|---|
| 548 | 4t. Type **196** | 20 | 20 |
| 549 | 6t. Symbols of industry | 45 | 65 |

**197** Soldiers of Ramgarh Battalion (1795) and of Bangladesh Rifles (1995)

**1995.** Bicentenary of Bangladesh Rifles. Mult.

| | | | |
|---|---|---|---|
| 550 | 2t. Type **197** | 1·25 | 50 |
| 551 | 4t. Riflemen on patrol | 1·60 | 90 |

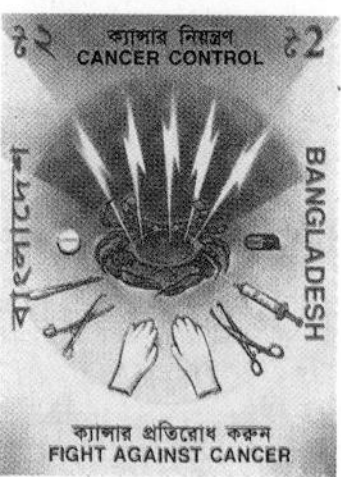


**198** Surgical Equipment and Lightning attacking Crab (cancer)

**1995.** Campaign against Cancer.

| | | | | |
|---|---|---|---|---|
| 552 | **198** | 2t. multicoloured | 40 | 25 |

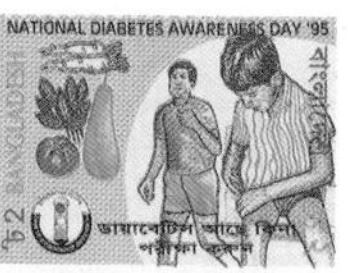


**199** Fresh Food and Boy injecting Insulin

**1995.** National Diabetes Awareness Day.

| | | | | |
|---|---|---|---|---|
| 553 | **199** | 2t. multicoloured | 1·00 | 30 |

**200** Munshi Mohammad Meherullah

**1995.** Munshi Mohammad Meherullah (Islamic educator) Commemoration.

| | | | | |
|---|---|---|---|---|
| 554 | **200** | 2t. multicoloured | 30 | 25 |

রাজশাহীপেক্স-৯৫

**(201)**

**1995.** "Rajshahipex '95" National Philatelic Exhibition. No. 499 optd with T 201.

| | | | |
|---|---|---|---|
| 555 | 6t. Exterior of Chhota Sona Mosque | 2·25 | 2·50 |

**202** "Lagerstroemia speciosa"

**1995.** Flowers. Multicoloured.

| | | | |
|---|---|---|---|
| 556 | 6t. Type **202** | 90 | 90 |
| 557 | 6t. "Bombax ceiba" (horiz) | 90 | 90 |
| 558 | 10t. "Passiflora incarnata" | 1·25 | 1·40 |
| 559 | 10t. "Bauhina purpurea" | 1·25 | 1·40 |
| 560 | 10t. "Canna indica" | 1·25 | 1·40 |
| 561 | 10t. "Gloriosa superba" | 1·25 | 1·40 |

**203** Aspects of Farming

**1995.** 50th Anniv of F.A.O.

| | | | | |
|---|---|---|---|---|
| 562 | **203** | 10t. multicoloured | 1·00 | 1·25 |

**204** Anniversary Emblem, Peace Dove and U.N. Headquarters

**1995.** 50th Anniv of United Nations. Multicoloured.

| | | | |
|---|---|---|---|
| 563 | 2t. Type **204** | 30 | 20 |
| 564 | 10t. Peace doves circling dates and Globe | 90 | 1·40 |
| 565 | 10t. Clasped hands and U.N. Headquarters | 90 | 1·40 |

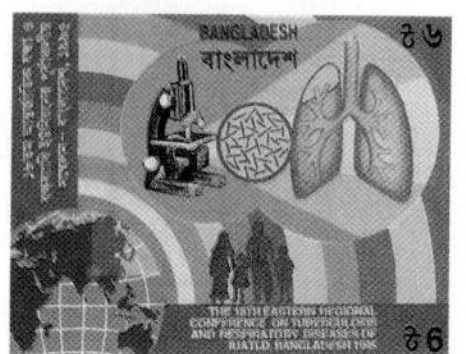


**205** Diseased Lungs, Microscope, Family and Map

**1995.** 18th Eastern Regional Conference on Tuberculosis, Dhaka.

| | | | | |
|---|---|---|---|---|
| 566 | **205** | 6t. multicoloured | 1·50 | 1·00 |

**206** Peace Doves, Emblem and National Flags

**1995.** 10th Anniv of South Asian Association for Regional Co-operation.

| | | | | |
|---|---|---|---|---|
| 567 | **206** | 2t. multicoloured | 1·40 | 55 |

**1995.** Martyred Intellectuals (4th series). As T **148**. Each black and brown.

| | | | |
|---|---|---|---|
| 568 | 2t. Abdul Ahad | 25 | 30 |
| 569 | 2t. Lt. Col. Mohammad Qadir | 25 | 30 |
| 570 | 2t. Mozammel Hoque Chowdhury | 25 | 30 |
| 571 | 2t. Rafiqul Haider Chowdhury | 25 | 30 |
| 572 | 2t. Dr. Azharul Haque | 25 | 30 |
| 573 | 2t. A. K. Shamsuddin | 25 | 30 |
| 574 | 2t. Anudwaipayan Bhattacharjee | 25 | 30 |
| 575 | 2t. Lutfunnahar Helena | 25 | 30 |

| | | | |
|---|---|---|---|
| 576 | 2t. Shaikh Habibur Rahman | 25 | 30 |
| 577 | 2t. Major Naimul Islam | 25 | 30 |
| 578 | 2t. Md. Shahidullah | 25 | 30 |
| 579 | 2t. Ataur Rahman Khan Khadim | 25 | 30 |
| 580 | 2t. A. B. M. Ashraful Islam Bhuiyan | 25 | 30 |
| 581 | 2t. Dr. Md. Sadat Ali | 25 | 30 |
| 582 | 2t. Sarafat Ali | 25 | 30 |
| 583 | 2t. M. A. Sayeed | 25 | 30 |

**207** Aspects of COMDECA Projects

**1995.** 2nd Asia–Pacific Community Development Scout Camp.

| | | | | |
|---|---|---|---|---|
| 584 | **207** | 2t. multicoloured | 70 | 35 |

**208** Volleyball Players

**1995.** Centenary of Volleyball.

| | | | | |
|---|---|---|---|---|
| 585 | **208** | 6t. multicoloured | 1·00 | 55 |

**209** Man in Punjabi and Lungi

**1995.** Traditional Costumes. Multicoloured.

| | | | |
|---|---|---|---|
| 586 | 6t. Type **209** | 1·00 | 1·00 |
| 587 | 6t. Woman in sari | 1·00 | 1·00 |
| 588 | 10t. Christian bride and groom | 1·40 | 1·50 |
| 589 | 10t. Muslim bride and groom | 1·40 | 1·50 |
| 590 | 10t. Buddhist bride and groom (horiz) | 1·40 | 1·50 |
| 591 | 10t. Hindu bride and groom (horiz) | 1·40 | 1·50 |

**210** Shaheed Amanullah Mohammad Asaduzzaman

**1996.** 27th Death Anniv of Shaheed Amanullah Mohammad Asaduzzaman (student leader).

| | | | | |
|---|---|---|---|---|
| 592 | **210** | 2t. multicoloured | 40 | 25 |

**211** Bowler and Map

**1996.** World Cup Cricket Championship. Multicoloured.

| | | | |
|---|---|---|---|
| 593 | 4t. Type **211** | 1·25 | 55 |
| 594 | 6t. Batsman and wicket keeper | 1·50 | 80 |
| 595 | 10t. Match in progress (horiz) | 2·00 | 2·25 |

**212** Liberation Struggle, 1971

**1996.** 25th Anniv of Independence. Multicoloured.

| | | | |
|---|---|---|---|
| 596 | 4t. Type **212** | 70 | 70 |
| 597 | 4t. National Martyrs Memorial | 70 | 70 |
| 598 | 4t. Education | 70 | 70 |
| 599 | 4t. Health | 70 | 70 |
| 600 | 4t. Communications | 70 | 70 |
| 601 | 4t. Industry | 70 | 70 |

**213** Michael Madhusudan Dutt

**1996.** Michael Madhusudan Dutt (poet) Commemoration.

| | | | | |
|---|---|---|---|---|
| 602 | **213** | 4t. multicoloured | 50 | 20 |

**214** Gymnastics

**1996.** Olympic Games, Atlanta. Multicoloured.

| | | | |
|---|---|---|---|
| 603 | 4t. Type **214** | 30 | 20 |
| 604 | 6t. Judo | 40 | 35 |
| 605 | 10t. Athletics (horiz) | 45 | 70 |
| 606 | 10t. High jumping (horiz) | 45 | 70 |
| **MS**607 | 165×110 mm. Nos. 603/6 (sold at 40t.) | 1·50 | 2·00 |

**1996.** 25th Anniv of Bangladesh Stamps. No. **MS**234 optd "Silver Jubilee Bangladesh Postage Stamps 1971-96" on sheet margin.

| | | | |
|---|---|---|---|
| **MS**608 | 98×117 mm. Nos. 232/3 (sold at 10t.) | 1·40 | 1·75 |

**215** Bangabandhu Sheikh Mujibur Rahman

**1996.** 21st Death Anniv of Bangabandhu Sheikh Mujibur Rahman.

| | | | | |
|---|---|---|---|---|
| 609 | **215** | 4t. multicoloured | 40 | 25 |

**216** Maulana Mohammad Akrum Khan

**1996.** 28th Death Anniv of Maulana Mohammad Akrum Khan.

| | | | | |
|---|---|---|---|---|
| 610 | **216** | 4t. multicoloured | 40 | 20 |

**217** Ustad Alauddin Khan

**1996.** 24th Death Anniv of Ustad Alauddin Khan (musician).

| | | | | |
|---|---|---|---|---|
| 611 | **217** | 4t. multicoloured | 70 | 30 |

**218** "Kingfisher" (Mayeesha Robbani)

**1996.** Children's Paintings. Multicoloured.

| | | | |
|---|---|---|---|
| 612 | 2t. Type **218** | 60 | 45 |
| 613 | 4t. "River Crossing" (Iffat Panchlais) (horiz) | 80 | 45 |

**219** Syed Nazrul Islam

**1996.** 21st Death Anniv of Jail Martyrs. Multicoloured.

| | | | |
|---|---|---|---|
| 614 | 4t. Type **219** | 30 | 40 |
| 615 | 4t. Tajuddin Ahmad | 30 | 40 |
| 616 | 4t. M. Monsoor Ali | 30 | 40 |
| 617 | 4t. A. H. M. Quamaruzzaman | 30 | 40 |

**220** Children receiving Medicine

**1996.** 50th Anniv of UNICEF Multicoloured.

| | | | |
|---|---|---|---|
| 618 | 4t. Type **220** | 50 | 25 |
| 619 | 10t. Mother and child | 1·10 | 1·40 |

**1996.** Martyred Intellectuals (5th series). As T **148**. Each black and brown.

| | | | |
|---|---|---|---|
| 620 | 2t. Dr. Jekrul Haque | 45 | 45 |
| 621 | 2t. Munshi Kabiruddin Ahmed | 45 | 45 |
| 622 | 2t. Md. Abdul Jabbar | 45 | 45 |
| 623 | 2t. Mohammad Amir | 45 | 45 |
| 624 | 2t. A. K. M. Shamsul Huq Khan | 45 | 45 |
| 625 | 2t. Dr. Siddique Ahmed | 45 | 45 |
| 626 | 2t. Dr. Soleman Khan | 45 | 45 |
| 627 | 2t. S. B. M. Mizanur Rahman | 45 | 45 |
| 628 | 2t. Aminuddin | 45 | 45 |
| 629 | 2t. Md. Nazrul Islam | 45 | 45 |
| 630 | 2t. Zahirul Islam | 45 | 45 |
| 631 | 2t. A. K. Lutfor Rahman | 45 | 45 |
| 632 | 2t. Afsar Hossain | 45 | 45 |
| 633 | 2t. Abul Hashem Mian | 45 | 45 |
| 634 | 2t. A. T. M. Alamgir | 45 | 45 |
| 635 | 2t. Baser Ali | 45 | 45 |

**221** Celebrating Crowds

**1996.** 25th Anniv of Victory Day. Multicoloured.

| | | | |
|---|---|---|---|
| 636 | 4t. Type **221** | 35 | 30 |
| 637 | 6t. Soldiers and statue (vert) | 65 | 70 |

**222** Paul P. Harris

**1997.** 50th Death Anniv of Paul Harris (founder of Rotary International).

| | | | | |
|---|---|---|---|---|
| 638 | **222** | 4t. multicoloured | 35 | 25 |

**223** Shaikh Mujibur Rahman making Speech

**1997.** 25th Anniv of Shaikh Mujibur's Speech of 7 March (1996).

| | | | | |
|---|---|---|---|---|
| 639 | **223** | 4t. multicoloured | 35 | 25 |

**224** Sheikh Mujibur Rahman

**1997.** 77th Birth Anniv of Sheikh Mujibur Rahman (first President).

| | | | | |
|---|---|---|---|---|
| 640 | **224** | 4t. multicoloured | 50 | 25 |

**225** Sheikh Mujibur Rahman and Crowd with Banners

**1997.** 25th Anniv (1996) of Independence.

| | | | | |
|---|---|---|---|---|
| 641 | **225** | 4t. multicoloured | 35 | 25 |

**226** Heinrich von Stephan

**1997.** Death Centenary of Heinrich von Stephan (founder of U.P.U.).

| | | | | |
|---|---|---|---|---|
| 642 | **226** | 4t. multicoloured | 35 | 25 |

**227** Sheep

**1997.** Livestock. Multicoloured.

| | | | |
|---|---|---|---|
| 643 | 4t. Type **227** | 75 | 75 |
| 644 | 4t. Goat | 75 | 75 |
| 645 | 6t. Buffalo bull | 90 | 90 |
| 646 | 6t. Cow | 90 | 90 |

**228** "Tilling the Field - 2" (S. Sultan)

**1997.** Bangladesh Paintings. Multicoloured.

| | | | |
|---|---|---|---|
| 647 | 6t. Type **228** | 40 | 30 |
| 648 | 10t. "Three Women" (Quamrul Hassan) | 60 | 1·25 |

**229** Trophy, Flag and Cricket Ball

**1997.** 6th International Cricket Council Trophy Championship, Malaysia.

| | | | | |
|---|---|---|---|---|
| 649 | **229** | 10t. multicoloured | 3·25 | 2·75 |

**230** Kusumba Mosque, Naogaon

**1997.** Historic Mosques. Multicoloured.

| | | | |
|---|---|---|---|
| 650 | 4t. Type **230** | 65 | 35 |
| 651 | 6t. Atiya Mosque, Tangail | 85 | 45 |
| 652 | 10t. Bagha Mosque, Rajshahi | 1·25 | 1·75 |

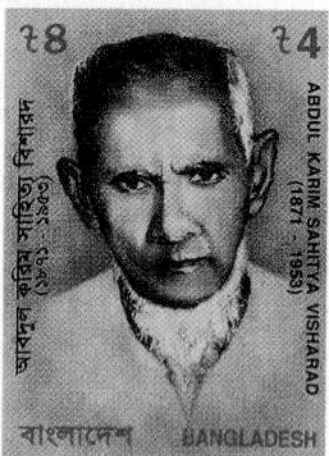
**231** Adul Karim Sahitya Vishard

**1997.** 126th Birth Anniv of Abdul Karim Sahitya Vishard (scholar).

| | | | | |
|---|---|---|---|---|
| 653 | **231** | 4t. multicoloured | 40 | 25 |

**232** River Moot Emblem and Scouts standing on top of World

**1997.** 9th Asia-Pacific and 7th Bangladesh Rover Moot, Lakkatura.

| | | | | |
|---|---|---|---|---|
| 654 | **232** | 2t. multicoloured | 50 | 25 |

**233** Officers and Flag

**1997.** 25th Anniv of Armed Forces.

| | | | | |
|---|---|---|---|---|
| 655 | **233** | 2t. multicoloured | 1·50 | 60 |

**1997.** Martyred Intellectuals (6th series). As T **148**. Each black and brown.

| | | | |
|---|---|---|---|
| 656 | 2t. Dr. Shamsuddin Ahmed | 65 | 65 |
| 657 | 2t. Mohammad Salimullah | 65 | 65 |
| 658 | 2t. Mohiuddin Haider | 65 | 65 |
| 659 | 2t. Abdur Rahin | 65 | 65 |
| 660 | 2t. Nitya Nanda Paul | 65 | 65 |
| 661 | 2t. Abdel Jabber | 65 | 65 |
| 662 | 2t. Dr. Humayun Kabir | 65 | 65 |
| 663 | 2t. Khaja Nizamuddin Bhuiyan | 65 | 65 |
| 664 | 2t. Gulam Hossain | 65 | 65 |
| 665 | 2t. Ali Karim | 65 | 65 |
| 666 | 2t. Md. Moazzem Hossain | 65 | 65 |
| 667 | 2t. Rafiqul Islam | 65 | 65 |
| 668 | 2t. M. Nur Husain | 65 | 65 |
| 669 | 2t. Captain Mahmood Hossain Akonda | 65 | 65 |
| 670 | 2t. Abdul Wahab Talukder | 65 | 65 |
| 671 | 2t. Dr. Hasimoy Hazra | 65 | 65 |

**234** Mohammad Mansooruddin

**1998.** Professor Mohammad Mansooruddin (folklorist) Commemoration.

| | | | | |
|---|---|---|---|---|
| 672 | **234** | 4t. multicoloured | 1·40 | 60 |

**235** Standard-bearer and Soldiers

**1998.** 50th Anniv of East Bengal Regiment.

| | | | | |
|---|---|---|---|---|
| 673 | **235** | 2t. multicoloured | 1·00 | 55 |

**236** Bulbul Chowdhury

**1998.** Bulbul Chowdhury (traditional dancer) Commemoration.

| | | | | |
|---|---|---|---|---|
| 674 | **236** | 4t. multicoloured | 40 | 25 |

**237** World Cup Trophy

**1998.** World Cup Football Championship, France. Multicoloured.

| | | | |
|---|---|---|---|
| 675 | 6t. Type **237** | 75 | 30 |
| 676 | 18t. Footballer and trophy | 2·00 | 2·50 |

**238** Eastern Approach Road, Bangabandhu Bridge

**1998.** Opening of Bangabandhu Bridge. Mult.

| | | | |
|---|---|---|---|
| 677 | 4t. Type **238** | 65 | 30 |
| 678 | 6t. Western approach road | 75 | 40 |
| 679 | 8t. Embankment | 95 | 1·40 |
| 680 | 10t. Main span, Bangabandhu Bridge | 1·25 | 1·60 |

**239** Diana, Princess of Wales

**1998.** Diana, Princess of Wales Commemoration. Multicoloured.

| | | | |
|---|---|---|---|
| 681 | 8t. Type **239** | 1·40 | 1·40 |
| 682 | 18t. Wearing pearl choker | 1·75 | 1·75 |
| 683 | 22t. Wearing pendant necklace | 1·75 | 2·00 |

**240** Means of collecting Solar Energy

**1998.** World Solar Energy Programme Summit.

| | | | | |
|---|---|---|---|---|
| 684 | **240** | 10t. multicoloured | 1·50 | 1·50 |

**241** World Habitat Day Emblem and City Scene

**1998.** World Habitat Day.

| | | | | |
|---|---|---|---|---|
| 685 | **241** | 4t. multicoloured | 1·25 | 60 |

**242** Farmworkers, Sunflower and "20"

**1998.** 20th Anniv of International Fund for Agricultural Development. Multicoloured.

| | | | |
|---|---|---|---|
| 686 | 6t. Type **242** | 65 | 35 |
| 687 | 10t. Farmworker with baskets and harvested crops | 1·10 | 1·40 |

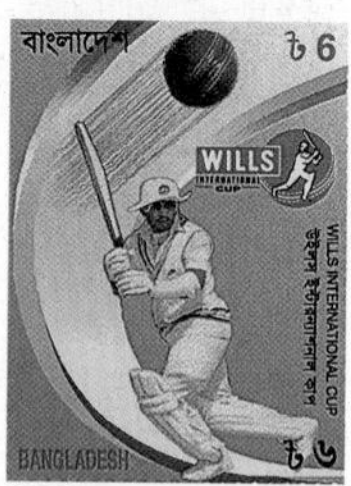
**243** Batsman

**1998.** Wills International Cricket Cup, Dhaka.

| | | | | |
|---|---|---|---|---|
| 688 | **243** | 6t. multicoloured | 1·75 | 1·25 |

**244** Begum Rokeya

**1998.** Begum Rokeya (campaigner for women's education) Commemoration.

| | | | | |
|---|---|---|---|---|
| 689 | **244** | 4t. multicoloured | 1·25 | 60 |

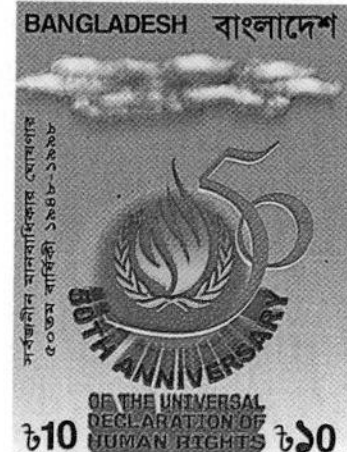
**245** Anniversary Logo

**1998.** 50th Anniv of Universal Declaration of Human Rights.

| | | | | |
|---|---|---|---|---|
| 690 | **245** | 10t. multicoloured | 1·25 | 1·25 |

**1998.** Martyred Intellectuals (7th series). As T **148**. Each black and brown.

| | | | |
|---|---|---|---|
| 691 | 2t. Md. Khorshed Ali Sarker | 50 | 50 |
| 692 | 2t. Abu Yakub Mahfuz Ali | 50 | 50 |
| 693 | 2t. S. M. Nural Huda | 50 | 50 |
| 694 | 2t. Nazmul Hoque Sarker | 50 | 50 |
| 695 | 2t. Md. Taslim Uddin | 50 | 50 |
| 696 | 2t. Gulam Mostafa | 50 | 50 |
| 697 | 2t. A. H. Nural Alam | 50 | 50 |
| 698 | 2t. Timir Kanti Dev | 50 | 50 |
| 699 | 2t. Altaf Hossain | 50 | 50 |
| 700 | 2t. Aminul Hoque | 50 | 50 |
| 701 | 2t. S. M. Fazlul Hoque | 50 | 50 |
| 702 | 2t. Mozammel Ali | 50 | 50 |
| 703 | 2t. Syed Akbar Hossain | 50 | 50 |
| 704 | 2t. Sk. Abdus Salam | 50 | 50 |
| 705 | 2t. Abdur Rahman | 50 | 50 |
| 706 | 2t. Dr. Shyamal Kanti Lala | 50 | 50 |

**246** Dove of Peace and U.N. Symbols

**1998.** 50th Anniv of U.N. Peace-keeping Operations.

| | | | | |
|---|---|---|---|---|
| 707 | **246** | 10t. multicoloured | 1·25 | 1·50 |

**247** Kazi Nazrul Islam

**1998.** Birth Centenary (1999) of Kazi Nazrul Islam (poet).

| | | | | |
|---|---|---|---|---|
| 708 | **247** | 6t. multicoloured | 1·25 | 70 |

**248** Jamboree Emblem and Scout Activities

**1999.** 6th Bangladesh National Scout Jamboree.

| | | | | |
|---|---|---|---|---|
| 709 | **248** | 2t. multicoloured | 1·00 | 50 |

**1999.** As No. 75 but redrawn. Size 35×22 mm.

| | | | |
|---|---|---|---|
| 711 | 10t. red | 1·10 | 30 |

No. 711 has been redrawn so that "SIXTY-DOME MOSQUE" appears above the face value at bottom right instead of below the main inscription at top left.

**249** Surjya Sen and Demonstrators

**1999.** Surjya Sen (revolutionary) Commemoration.

| | | | | |
|---|---|---|---|---|
| 715 | **249** | 4t. multicoloured | 1·25 | 60 |

**250** Dr. Fazlur Rahman Khan and Sears Tower

**1999.** 70th Birth Anniv of Dr. Fazlur Rahman Khan (architect).

| | | | | |
|---|---|---|---|---|
| 716 | **250** | 4t. multicoloured | 1·00 | 55 |

**251** National Team Badges

**1999.** Cricket World Cup, England. Multicoloured.

| | | | |
|---|---|---|---|
| 717 | 8t. Type **251** | 1·75 | 2·00 |
| 718 | 10t. Bangladesh cricket team badge and flag | 2·50 | 2·50 |
| **MS**719 | 139×89 mm. Nos. 717/18 (sold at 30t.) | 4·50 | 4·75 |

**252** Mother Teresa

**1999.** Mother Teresa Commemoration.

| | | | | |
|---|---|---|---|---|
| 720 | **252** | 4t. multicoloured | 1·50 | 65 |

**253** Sheikh Mujibur Rahman, New York Skyline and Dove

**1999.** 25th Anniv of Bangladesh's Admission to U.N.

| | | | | |
|---|---|---|---|---|
| 721 | **253** | 6t. multicoloured | 1·00 | 65 |

**254** Shaheed Mohammad Maizuddin

**1999.** 15th Death Anniv of Shaheed Mohammad Maizuddin (politician).

| | | | | |
|---|---|---|---|---|
| 722 | **254** | 2t. multicoloured | 60 | 30 |

**255** Faces in Tree

**1999.** International Year of the Elderly.

| | | | | |
|---|---|---|---|---|
| 723 | **255** | 6t. multicoloured | 1·00 | 60 |

**256** Shanty Town and Modern Buildings between Hands

**1999.** World Habitat Day.

| | | | | |
|---|---|---|---|---|
| 724 | **256** | 4t. multicoloured | 1·00 | 50 |

**257** Mobile Post Office

**1999.** 125th Anniv of U.P.U. Multicoloured.

| | | | |
|---|---|---|---|
| 725 | 4t. Type **257** | 80 | 65 |
| 726 | 4t. Postman on motorcycle | 80 | 65 |
| 727 | 6t. Postal motor launch | 1·00 | 90 |
| 728 | 6t. Douglas DC-10 and Boeing 737 | 1·00 | 90 |
| **MS**729 | 141×90 mm. Nos. 725/8 (sold at 25t.) | 3·25 | 3·25 |

**258** Sir Jagadis Chandra Bose

**1999.** Sir Jagadis Chandra Bose (physicist and botanist) Commemoration.

| | | | | |
|---|---|---|---|---|
| 730 | **258** | 4t. multicoloured | 1·50 | 60 |

**1999.** Martyred Intellectuals (8th series). As T **148**. Each black and brown.

| | | | |
|---|---|---|---|
| 731 | 2t. Dr. Mohammad Shafi | 50 | 50 |
| 732 | 2t. Maulana Kasimuddin Ahmed | 50 | 50 |
| 733 | 2t. Quazi Ali Imam | 50 | 50 |
| 734 | 2t. Sultanuddin Ahmed | 50 | 50 |
| 735 | 2t. A. S. M. Ershadullah | 50 | 50 |
| 736 | 2t. Mohammad Fazlur Rahman | 50 | 50 |
| 737 | 2t. Captain A. K. M. Farooq | 50 | 50 |
| 738 | 2t. Md. Latafot Hossain Joarder | 50 | 50 |
| 739 | 2t. Ram Ranjan Bhattacharjya | 50 | 50 |
| 740 | 2t. Abani Mohan Dutta | 50 | 50 |
| 741 | 2t. Sunawar Ali | 50 | 50 |
| 742 | 2t. Abdul Kader Miah | 50 | 50 |
| 743 | 2t. Major Rezaur Rahman | 50 | 50 |
| 744 | 2t. Md. Shafiqul Anowar | 50 | 50 |
| 745 | 2t. A. A. M. Mozammel Hoque | 50 | 50 |
| 746 | 2t. Khandkar Abul Kashem | 50 | 50 |

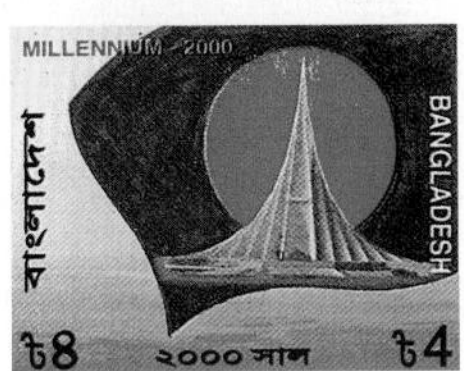


**259** Bangladesh Flag and Monument

**2000.** New Millennium. Multicoloured.

| | | | |
|---|---|---|---|
| 747 | 4t. Type **259** | 75 | 45 |
| 748 | 6t. Satellite, computer and dish aerial (vert) | 1·00 | 1·10 |

**260** Cub Scouts, Globe and Flag

**2000.** 5th Bangladesh Cub Camporee.

| | | | | |
|---|---|---|---|---|
| 749 | **260** | 2t. multicoloured | 70 | 40 |

**261** Jibananada Das

**2000.** Death Centenary (1999) of Jibananada Das (poet).

| | | | | |
|---|---|---|---|---|
| 750 | **261** | 4t. multicoloured | 70 | 40 |

**2000.** 30th Death Anniv (1999) of Dr. Muhammad Shamsuzzoha.

| | | | | |
|---|---|---|---|---|
| 751 | **262** | 4t. multicoloured | 1·00 | 40 |

**263** Shafiur Rahman

**2000.** International Mother Language Day. Mult.

| | | | |
|---|---|---|---|
| 752 | 4t. Type **263** | 65 | 75 |
| 753 | 4t. Abul Barkat | 65 | 75 |
| 754 | 4t. Abdul Jabbar | 65 | 75 |
| 755 | 4t. Rafiq Uddin Ahmad | 65 | 75 |

**264** Meteorological Equipment

**2000.** 50th Anniv of World Meteorological Organization.

| | | | | |
|---|---|---|---|---|
| 756 | **264** | 10t. multicoloured | 1·75 | 1·75 |

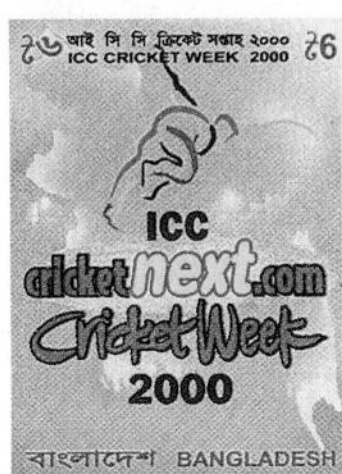


**265** Cricket Week Logo and Web Site Address

**2000.** International Cricket Week.

| | | | | |
|---|---|---|---|---|
| 757 | **265** | 6t. multicoloured | 1·75 | 1·25 |

**266** Wasp

**2000.** Insects. Multicoloured.

| | | | |
|---|---|---|---|
| 758 | 2t. Type **266** | 50 | 30 |
| 759 | 4t. Grasshopper | 70 | 35 |
| 760 | 6t. Bumble bee | 90 | 65 |
| 761 | 10t. Silkworms | 1·50 | 2·25 |

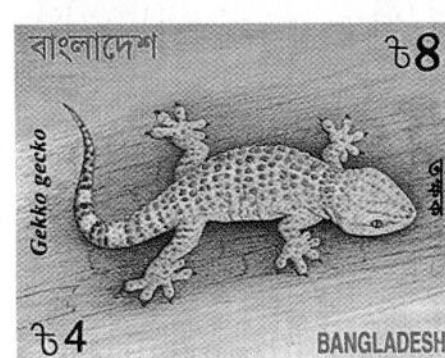


**267** Gecko

**2000.** Native Fauna. Multicoloured.

| | | | |
|---|---|---|---|
| 762 | 4t. Type **267** | 70 | 70 |
| 763 | 4t. Indian crested porcupine | 70 | 70 |
| 764 | 6t. Indian black-tailed python | 95 | 95 |
| 765 | 6t. Bengal monitor | 95 | 95 |

**268** Batsman

**2000.** Pepsi 7th Asia Cricket Cup.

| | | | | |
|---|---|---|---|---|
| 766 | **268** | 6t. multicoloured | 1·75 | 1·25 |

**269** Water Cock

**2000.** Birds. Multicoloured.

| | | | |
|---|---|---|---|
| 767 | 4t. Type **269** | 90 | 80 |
| 768 | 4t. White-breasted waterhen (*Amaurornis phoenicurus*) | 90 | 80 |
| 769 | 6t. Javanese cormorant (*Phalacrocorax niger*) (vert) | 1·25 | 1·10 |
| 770 | 6t. Indian pond heron (*Ardeola grayii*) (vert) | 1·25 | 1·10 |

**270** Women's Shotput

**2000.** Olympic Games, Sydney. Multicoloured.

| | | | |
|---|---|---|---|
| 771 | 6t. Type **270** | 1·00 | 50 |
| 772 | 10t. Men's Shotput | 1·50 | 1·75 |

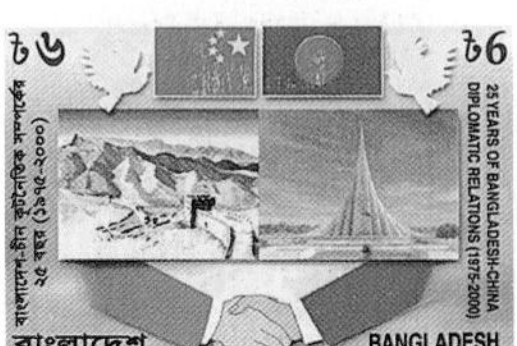


**271** Clasped Hands, Landmarks and Flags

**2000.** 25th Anniv of Diplomatic Relations with People's Republic of China.

| | | | | |
|---|---|---|---|---|
| 773 | **271** | 6t. multicoloured | 1·50 | 75 |

**272** Idrakpur Fort, Munshigonj

**2000.** Archaeology. Multicoloured.

| | | | |
|---|---|---|---|
| 774 | 4t. Type **272** | 75 | 40 |
| 775 | 6t. Statue of Buddha, Mainamati (vert) | 1·25 | 1·00 |

**273** Year Emblem

**2000.** International Volunteers' Year.

| | | | | |
|---|---|---|---|---|
| 776 | **273** | 6t. multicoloured | 1·25 | 65 |

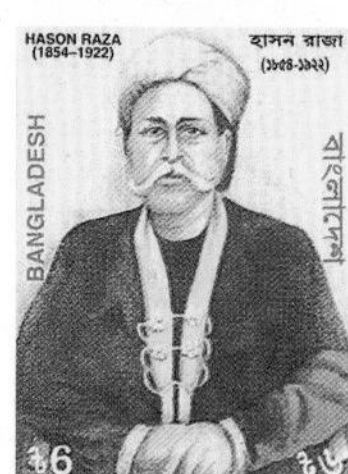

**274** Hason Raza

**2000.** 80th Death Anniv of Hason Raza (mystic poet).

| | | | | |
|---|---|---|---|---|
| 777 | **274** | 6t. multicoloured | 1·50 | 75 |

**275** U.N.H.C.R. Logo

**2000.** 50th Anniv of United Nations High Commissioner for Refugees (U.N.H.C.R.).

| | | | | |
|---|---|---|---|---|
| 778 | **275** | 10t. multicoloured | 1·50 | 2·00 |

**2000.** Martyred Intellectuals (9th series). As T **148**. Each black and brown.

| | | | |
|---|---|---|---|
| 779 | 2t. M. A. Gofur | 55 | 55 |
| 780 | 2t. Faizur Rahman Ahmed | 55 | 55 |
| 781 | 2t. Muslimuddin Miah | 55 | 55 |
| 782 | 2t. Sgt. Shamsul Karim Khan | 55 | 55 |
| 783 | 2t. Bhikku Zinananda | 55 | 55 |
| 784 | 2t. Abdul Jabber | 55 | 55 |
| 785 | 2t. Sekander Hayat Chowdhury | 55 | 55 |
| 786 | 2t. Chishty Shah Helalur Rahman | 55 | 55 |
| 787 | 2t. Birendra Nath Sarker | 55 | 55 |
| 788 | 2t. A. K. M. Nurul Haque | 55 | 55 |
| 789 | 2t. Sibendra Nath Mukherjee | 55 | 55 |
| 790 | 2t. Zahir Raihan | 55 | 55 |
| 791 | 2t. Ferdous Dowla Bablu | 55 | 55 |
| 792 | 2t. Capt A. K. M. Nurul Absur | 55 | 55 |
| 793 | 2t. Mizanur Rahman Miju | 55 | 55 |
| 794 | 2t. Dr. Shamshad Ali | 55 | 55 |

**276** Map of Faces

**2001.** Population and Housing Census.

| | | | | |
|---|---|---|---|---|
| 795 | **276** | 4t. multicoloured | 1·25 | 55 |

**277** Producing Food

**2001.** "Hunger-free Bangladesh" Campaign.

| | | | | |
|---|---|---|---|---|
| 796 | **277** | 6t. multicoloured | 1·25 | 65 |

**278** "Peasant Women" (Rashid Chowdbury)

**2001.** Bangladesh Paintings.

| | | | | |
|---|---|---|---|---|
| 797 | **278** | 10t. multicoloured | 2·00 | 2·00 |

**279** Lalbagh Kella Mosque

**2001.** Historic Buildings. Multicoloured.

| | | | |
|---|---|---|---|
| 798 | 6t. Type **279** | 85 | 85 |
| 799 | 6t. Uttara Ganabhavan, Natore | 85 | 85 |
| 800 | 6t. Armenian Church, Armanitola | 85 | 85 |
| 801 | 6t. Panam Nagar, Sonargaon | 85 | 85 |

**280** Smoking Accessories, Globe and Paper People

**2001.** World No Tobacco Day.

| | | | | |
|---|---|---|---|---|
| 802 | **280** | 10t. multicoloured | 1·75 | 1·75 |

**281** Ustad Gul Mohammad Khan

**2001.** Artists. Multicoloured.

| | | | |
|---|---|---|---|
| 803 | 6t. Type **281** | 80 | 80 |
| 804 | 6t. Ustad Khadem Hossain Khan | 80 | 80 |
| 805 | 6t. Gouhar Jamil | 80 | 80 |
| 806 | 6t. Abdul Alim | 80 | 80 |

**282** Begum Sufia Kamal

**2001.** Begum Sufia Kamal (poet) Commemoration.

| | | | | |
|---|---|---|---|---|
| 807 | **282** | 4t. multicoloured | 75 | 40 |

**283** Hilsa

**2001.** Fish. Multicoloured.

| | | | |
|---|---|---|---|
| 808 | 10t. Type **283** | 1·10 | 1·10 |
| 809 | 10t. Tengra | 1·10 | 1·10 |
| 810 | 10t. Punti | 1·10 | 1·10 |
| 811 | 10t. Khalisa | 1·10 | 1·10 |

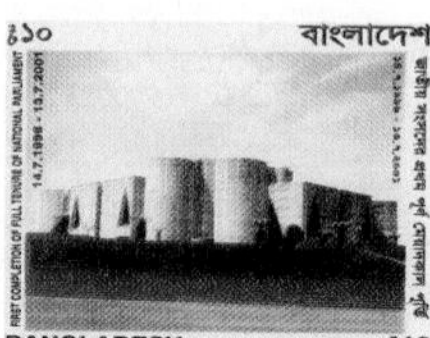

**284** Parliament House, Dhaka

**2001.** Completion of First Full National Parliamentary Term.

| | | | | |
|---|---|---|---|---|
| 812 | **284** | 10t. multicoloured | 2·25 | 2·25 |

**285** Parliament House, Dhaka

**2001.** 8th Parliamentary Elections.

| | | | | |
|---|---|---|---|---|
| 813 | **285** | 2t. multicoloured | 70 | 45 |

**286** "Children encircling Globe" (Urska Golob)

**2001.** U.N. Year of Dialogue among Civilizations.

| | | | | |
|---|---|---|---|---|
| 814 | **286** | 10t. multicoloured | 1·25 | 1·50 |
| **MS**815 95×65 mm. **286** 10t. multicoloured (sold at 30t.) | | | 1·75 | 3·00 |

**287** Meer Mosharraf Hossain

**2001.** Meer Mosharraf Hossain (writer) Commemoration.

| | | | | |
|---|---|---|---|---|
| 816 | **287** | 4t. black, red and crimson | 65 | 40 |

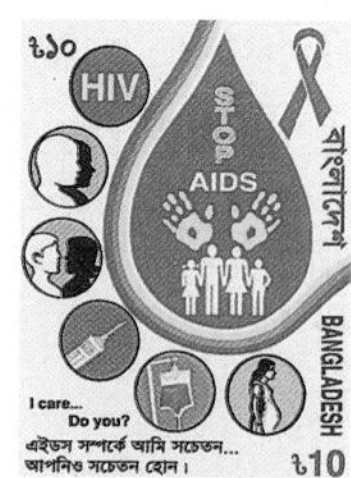

**288** Drop of Blood surrounded by Images

**2001.** World AIDS Day.

| | | | | |
|---|---|---|---|---|
| 817 | **288** | 10t. multicoloured | 1·75 | 1·75 |

**289** Sreshto Medal

**2001.** 30th Anniv of Independence. Gallantry Medals. Multicoloured.

| | | | |
|---|---|---|---|
| 818 | 10t. Type **289** | 1·25 | 1·50 |
| 819 | 10t. Uttom medal | 1·25 | 1·50 |
| 820 | 10t. Bikram medal | 1·25 | 1·50 |
| 821 | 10t. Protik medal | 1·25 | 1·50 |

**290** Publicity Poster

**2002.** 10th Asian Art Biennale, Dhaka.

| | | | | |
|---|---|---|---|---|
| 822 | **290** | 10t. multicoloured | 1·00 | 1·25 |

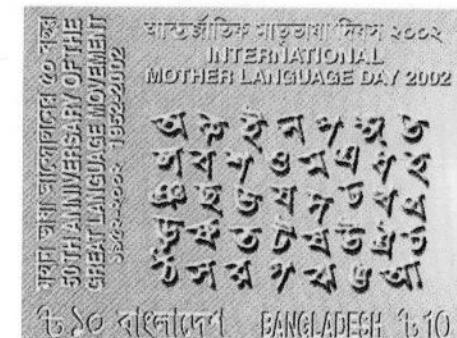

**291** Letters from Bengali Alphabet

**2002.** 50th Anniv of Amar Ekushey (language movement). International Mother Language Day.

| | | | | |
|---|---|---|---|---|
| 823 | **291** | 10t. black, gold and red | 80 | 1·10 |
| 824 | - | 10t. black, gold and red | 80 | 1·10 |
| 825 | - | 10t. black, gold and red | 80 | 1·10 |
| **MS**826 96×64 mm. 30t. multicoloured | | | 2·00 | 2·25 |

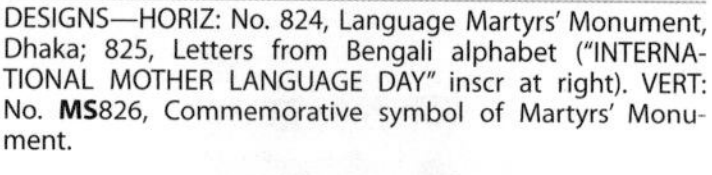
DESIGNS—HORIZ: No. 824, Language Martyrs' Monument, Dhaka; 825, Letters from Bengali alphabet ("INTERNATIONAL MOTHER LANGUAGE DAY" inscr at right). VERT: No. **MS**826, Commemorative symbol of Martyrs' Monument.

**292** Rokuon-Ji Temple, Japan

**2002.** 30th Anniv of Diplomatic Relations with Japan.

| | | | | |
|---|---|---|---|---|
| 827 | **292** | 10t. multicoloured | 1·00 | 1·25 |

**293** Silhouetted Goats

**2002.** Goat Production.

| | | | | |
|---|---|---|---|---|
| 828 | **293** | 2t. multicoloured | 45 | 25 |

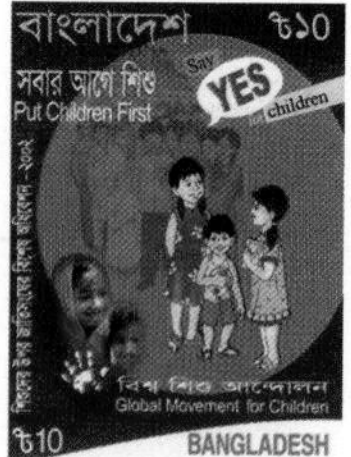

**294** Children

**2002.** U.N. Special Session on Children.

| | | | | |
|---|---|---|---|---|
| 829 | **294** | 10t. multicoloured | 1·25 | 1·25 |

**295** Mohammad Nasiruddin

**2002.** Mohammad Nasiruddin (journalist) Commemoration.

| | | | | |
|---|---|---|---|---|
| 830 | **295** | 4t. black and brown | 75 | 40 |

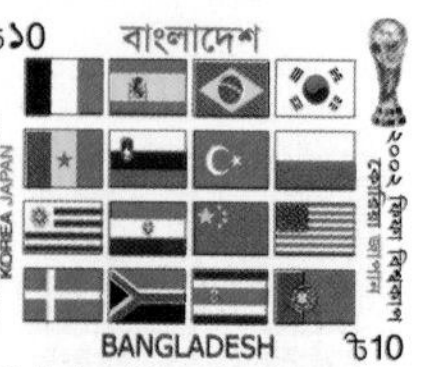

**296** National Flags (trophy at top right)

**2002.** World Cup Football Championship, Japan and Korea. Multicoloured.

| | | | |
|---|---|---|---|
| 831 | 10t. Type **296** | 1·00 | 1·25 |
| 832 | 10t. Pitch markings on world map | 1·00 | 1·25 |
| 833 | 10t. National flags (trophy at top left) | 1·00 | 1·25 |

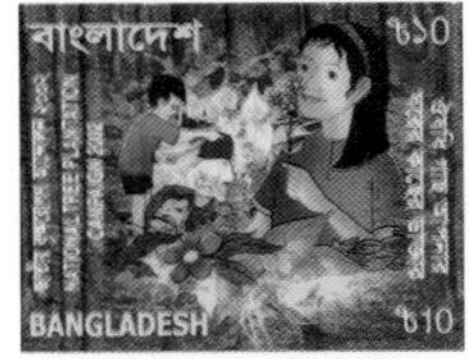

**297** Children tending Saplings

**2002.** National Tree Planting Campaign. Mult.

| | | | |
|---|---|---|---|
| 834 | 10t. Type **297** | 90 | 1·00 |
| 835 | 10t. Citrus fruit | 90 | 1·00 |
| 836 | 10t. Trees within leaf symbol (vert) | 90 | 1·00 |

**298** Children inside Symbolic House

**2002.** 30th Anniv of S.O.S. Children's Village in Bangladesh.

| | | | | |
|---|---|---|---|---|
| 837 | **298** | 6t. multicoloured | 80 | 45 |

**299** Rural Family

**2002.** World Population Day.

| | | | | |
|---|---|---|---|---|
| 838 | **299** | 6t. multicoloured | 80 | 45 |

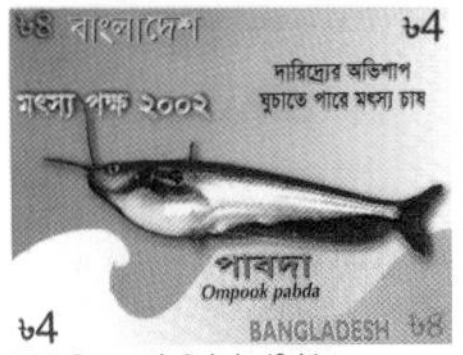

**300** Ompook Pabda (fish)

**2002.** Fish. Multicoloured.

| | | | |
|---|---|---|---|
| 839 | 4t. Type **300** | 50 | 50 |
| 840 | 4t. *Labeo gonius* | 50 | 50 |

**301** Bangladesh–U.K. Friendship Bridge, Bhairab

**2002.** Opening of Bangladesh–U.K. Friendship Bridge, Bhairab.

| | | | | |
|---|---|---|---|---|
| 841 | **301** | 4t. multicoloured | 1·00 | 45 |

**302** Dhaka City Centre

**2002.** World Habitat Day.

| | | | | |
|---|---|---|---|---|
| 842 | **302** | 4t. multicoloured | 70 | 35 |

**303** Dariabandha (Tag)

**2002.** Rural Games. Multicoloured.

| | | | |
|---|---|---|---|
| 843 | 4t. Type **303** | 70 | 70 |
| 844 | 4t. Kanamachee (Blind-man's buff) | 70 | 70 |

**304** Jasimuddin

**2003.** Birth Centenary of Jasimuddin (poet).

| | | | | |
|---|---|---|---|---|
| 845 | **304** | 5t. multicoloured | 50 | 35 |

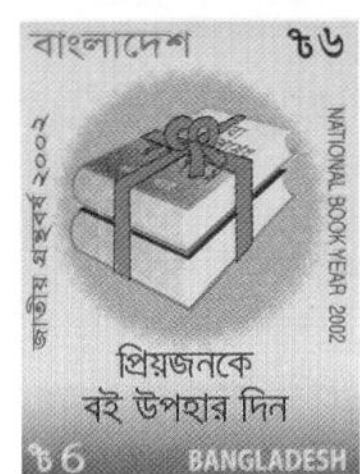

**305** Books

**2003.** National Book Year.

| | | | | |
|---|---|---|---|---|
| 846 | **305** | 6t. multicoloured | 60 | 35 |

**306** Footballers and Flags of Participating Countries

**2003.** 3rd SAFF Championship, Bangladesh.

| | | | | |
|---|---|---|---|---|
| 847 | **306** | 10t. multicoloured | 1·75 | 1·75 |

**ইফাদ-এর ২৫ বছর**

**25 Years of IFAD**

**(307)**

**2003.** 25th Anniv of International Fund for Agricultural Development. No. 687 optd with T **307**.

| | | | |
|---|---|---|---|
| 848 | 10t. Farmworker with baskets and harvested crops | 1·75 | 1·75 |

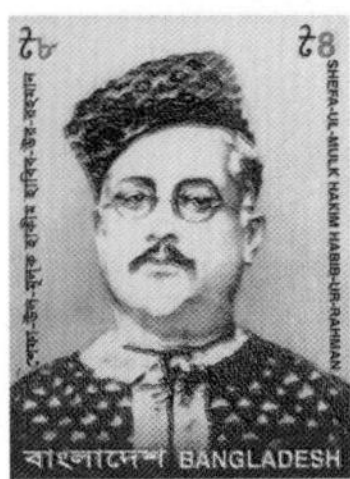

**308** Shefa-ul-Mulk Hakim Habib-ur-Rahman

**2003.** 56th Death Anniv of Shefa-ul-Mulk Hakim Habib-ur-Rahman.

| | | | | |
|---|---|---|---|---|
| 849 | **308** | 4t. multicoloured | 45 | 25 |

**309** Ziaur Rahman

**2003.** 22nd Death Anniv of Ziaur Rahman (President 1977–1981).

| | | | | |
|---|---|---|---|---|
| 850 | **309** | 4t. multicoloured | 45 | 25 |

**310** Sapling in Cupped Hands and Family

**2003.** National Tree Plantation Campaign. Multicoloured.

| | | | |
|---|---|---|---|
| 851 | 8t. Type **310** | 1·00 | 60 |
| 852 | 12t. Trees, plant, fruit and adult with children inside "petals" | 1·25 | 1·50 |

**311** Fruit

**2003.** Fruit Tree Plantation Fortnight.

| | | | | |
|---|---|---|---|---|
| 853 | **311** | 6t. multicoloured | 1·25 | 60 |

**312** *Labeo Calbasu* (Orange-fin labeo)

**2003.** Fish Fortnight.

| | | | | |
|---|---|---|---|---|
| 854 | **312** | 2t. multicoloured | 60 | 30 |

**313** Train on Jamuna Bridge and Signals

**2003.** Inauguration of Direct Train Communication between Rajshahi and Dhaka.

| | | | | |
|---|---|---|---|---|
| 855 | **313** | 10t. multicoloured | 1·50 | 1·50 |

**314** Jatiya Sangsad Bhaban (Parliament House)

**2003.** 49th Commonwealth Parliamentary Conference.

| | | | | |
|---|---|---|---|---|
| 856 | **314** | 10t. multicoloured | 1·25 | 1·40 |

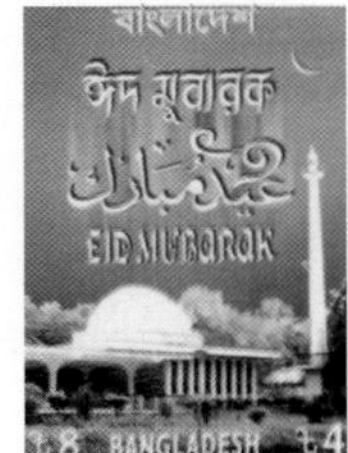

**315** Mosque

**2003.** Eid Mubarak.

| | | | | |
|---|---|---|---|---|
| 857 | **315** | 4t. multicoloured | 1·00 | 65 |

**316** Emblem

**2003.** International Centre for Diarrhoeal Disease Research, Bangladesh.

| | | | | |
|---|---|---|---|---|
| 858 | **316** | 10t. multicoloured | 1·25 | 1·40 |

**317** Rajshahi University

**2003.** 50th Anniv of Rajshahi University.

| | | | | |
|---|---|---|---|---|
| 859 | **317** | 4t. multicoloured | 1·00 | 55 |

**318** Books

**2004.** National Library Year (2003).

| | | | | |
|---|---|---|---|---|
| 860 | **318** | 6t. multicoloured | 1·00 | 70 |

**319** Tents inside Emblem and Member Flags

**2004.** 7th Bangladesh and Fourth South Asian Association for Regional Co-operation Jamboree.

| | | | | |
|---|---|---|---|---|
| 861 | **319** | 2t. multicoloured | 1·00 | 45 |

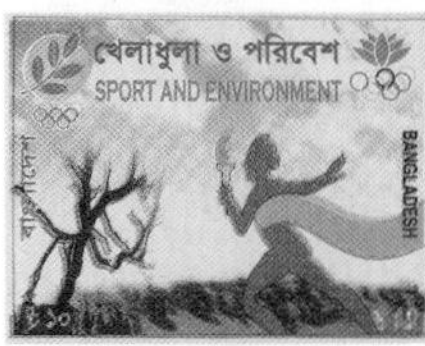

**320** Runner with Olympic Torch

**2004.** Sport and Environment.

| | | | | |
|---|---|---|---|---|
| 862 | **320** | 10t. multicoloured | 1·00 | 1·00 |

**321** Emblems

**2004.** 11th Asian Art Biennale.

| | | | | |
|---|---|---|---|---|
| 863 | **321** | 5t. multicoloured | 45 | 25 |

**322** Ziaur Rahman

**2004.** 33rd Anniv of Independence and National Day.

| | | | | |
|---|---|---|---|---|
| 864 | **322** | 5t. multicoloured | 45 | 25 |

**323** Road and Emblems

**2004.** World Health Day.

| | | | | |
|---|---|---|---|---|
| 865 | **323** | 6t. multicoloured | 45 | 25 |

**2004.** 25th Anniv of Bangladesh National Philatelic Association. No. 843 optd Silver Jubilee Bangladesh National Philatelic Association and emblem.

| | | | |
|---|---|---|---|
| 866 | 4t. Type **303** | 45 | 30 |

**325** Stylized Tree, Fruits and Berries

**2004.** National Tree Plantation Campaign. Multicoloured.

| | | | |
|---|---|---|---|
| 867 | 10t. Type **325** | 65 | 70 |
| 868 | 10t. Trees and saplings | 65 | 70 |

**326** Hafez Shirazi, Iranian Flag and Banay-e Azadi (Freedom Monument), Tehran

**2004.** Commemoration of Diplomatic Relations with Iran. Multicoloured.

| | | | |
|---|---|---|---|
| 869 | 10t. Type **326** | 80 | 90 |
| 870 | 10t. Nazrul Islam, Bangladeshi flag and War memorial, Dhaka | 80 | 90 |

**327** Woman Planting Tree and Fruit

**2004.** Fruit Tree Plantation Campaign.

| | | | | |
|---|---|---|---|---|
| 871 | **327** | 10t. multicoloured | 75 | 75 |

**328** Workers carrying Rice Harvest

**2004.** International Year of Rice.

| | | | | |
|---|---|---|---|---|
| 872 | **328** | 5t. multicoloured | 60 | 60 |

**329** Man feeding Child and Two Women

**2004.** World Population Day.

| | | | | |
|---|---|---|---|---|
| 873 | **329** | 6t. multicoloured | 45 | 30 |

**330** UN Headquarters and Flags

**2004.** 30th Anniv of United Nations Membership.

| | | | | |
|---|---|---|---|---|
| 874 | **330** | 4t. multicoloured | 30 | 20 |

**331** Bhasani Novo Theatre, Dhaka

**2004.** Bhasani Novo Theatre, Dhaka.

| | | | | |
|---|---|---|---|---|
| 875 | **331** | 4t. multicoloured | 30 | 20 |

**332** Centennial Bell

**2004.** Centenary of Rotary International.

| | | | | |
|---|---|---|---|---|
| 876 | **332** | 4t. multicoloured | 30 | 20 |

**333** *Argemone mexicana*

**2004.** Wild Flowers. Multicoloured.

| | | | |
|---|---|---|---|
| 877 | 5t. Type **333** | 70 | 70 |
| 878 | 5t. *Cyanotis axillaries* | 70 | 70 |
| 879 | 5t. *Thevetia Peruvians* | 70 | 70 |
| 880 | 5t. *Pentapetes phoenicea* | 70 | 70 |
| 881 | 5t. *Aegle marmelos* | 70 | 70 |
| 882 | 5t. *Datura stramonium* | 70 | 70 |

**2004.** 13th SAARC (South Asian Association for Regional Co-operation) Summit, Dhaka (2005).

| | | | | |
|---|---|---|---|---|
| 883 | **334** | 6t. multicoloured | 40 | 25 |

**335** *Sperata aor*

**2004.** Fish Fortnight. Multicoloured.

| | | | |
|---|---|---|---|
| 884 | 10t. Type **335** | 80 | 95 |
| 885 | 10t. *Notopterus notepturus* | 80 | 95 |

**336** Cub in Sunflower

**2004.** 6th National Cub Camporee.

| | | | | |
|---|---|---|---|---|
| 886 | **336** | 6t. multicoloured | 40 | 25 |

**337** Woman Farmer and Microcredit Symbol

**2005.** United Nations International Year of Microcredit. Multicoloured.

| | | | |
|---|---|---|---|
| 887 | 4t. Type **337** | 30 | 30 |
| 888 | 10t. Woman turning lever on coin and microcredit symbol pulley | 70 | 80 |

**338** Beach at Sunset

**2005.** South Asia Tourism Year.

| | | | | |
|---|---|---|---|---|
| 889 | **338** | 4t. multicoloured | 30 | 20 |

**339** Major Ziaur Rahman and War Memorial, Dhaka

**2005.** Independence and National Day.

| | | | | |
|---|---|---|---|---|
| 890 | **339** | 10t. multicoloured | 75 | 75 |

**340** Sewing Machinist, Fish in Net, Dairy Cattle, Hens and Goats

**2005.** Centenary of Co-operative Movement in Bangladesh.

| | | | | |
|---|---|---|---|---|
| 891 | **340** | 5t. multicoloured | 40 | 25 |

**341** Family Planting Tree

**2005.** National Tree Plantation Campaign. Multicoloured.

| | | | |
|---|---|---|---|
| 892 | 6t. Type **341** | 70 | 75 |
| 893 | 6t. Three types of different varieties | 70 | 75 |

**342** G. A. Mannan (choreographer)

**2005.** Talented Artists. Multicoloured.

| | | | |
|---|---|---|---|
| 894 | 6t. Type **342** | 60 | 70 |
| 895 | 6t. Unstad Phuljhuri Khan (musician) | 60 | 70 |
| 896 | 6t. Ustad Abed Hossian Khan (musician and composer) | 60 | 70 |
| 897 | 6t. Ustad Munshi Raisuddin (musician) | 60 | 70 |

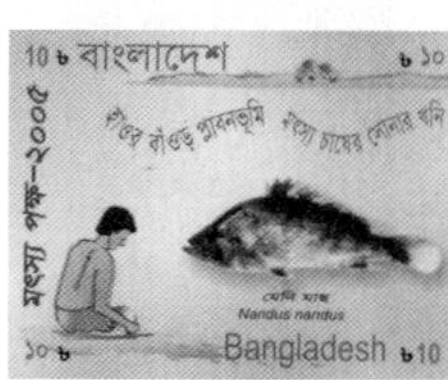


**343** *Nandus nandus*

**2005.** Fish Fortnight.

| | | | | |
|---|---|---|---|---|
| 898 | **343** | 10t. multicoloured | 1·00 | 75 |

**344** Dr. Nawab Ali

**2005.** Dr. Nawab Ali (physician) Commemoration.

| | | | | |
|---|---|---|---|---|
| 899 | **344** | 8t. multicoloured | 60 | 60 |

**345** Books, Compass and Dividers

**2006.** Science Book Year (2005).

| | | | | |
|---|---|---|---|---|
| 900 | **345** | 10t. multicoloured | 75 | 75 |

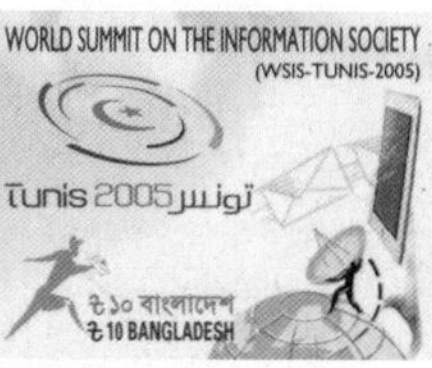


**346** Emblems, Globe and Computer Screen

**2006.** World Summit on the Information Society, Tunis (2005).

| | | | | |
|---|---|---|---|---|
| 901 | **346** | 10t. multicoloured | 1·00 | 75 |

**347** Verwaltungssitz, Vienna and Emblem

**2006.** 30th Anniv of OPEC Fund for International Development (2005).

902 **347** 10t. multicoloured 75 75

**348** Palace of Heavenly Peace, Beijing

**2006.** 30th Anniv of Bangladesh–China Diplomatic Relations (2005). Multicoloured.

903 10t. Type **348** 70 70
904 10t. Parliament Building, Dhaka 70 70
905 10t. 5th Bangladesh–China Friendship Bridge over Gabkhan River 70 70
906 10t. Great Wall of China 70 70
**MS**907 140×90 mm. Nos. 903/6 2·50 2·50

**349** Major Ziaur Rahman and War Memorial, Dhaka

**2006.** 35th Anniversary of Independence and National Day.

908 **349** 10t. multicoloured 1·00 75

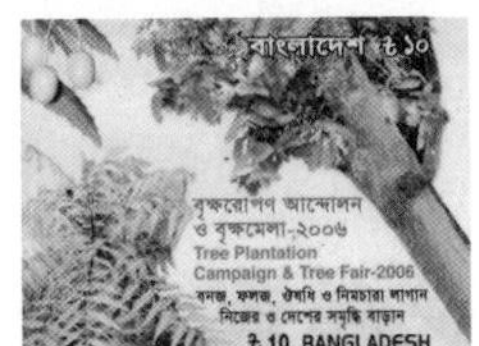


**350** Palm Tree

**2006.** National Tree Plantation Campaign and Tree Fair.

909 **350** 10t. multicoloured 1·00 75

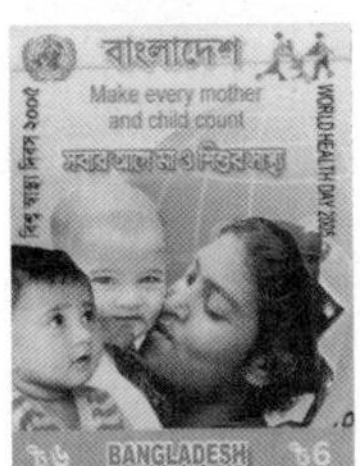


**351** Mother with Baby and Toddler

**2006.** World Health Day.

910 **351** 6t. multicoloured 1·25 1·00

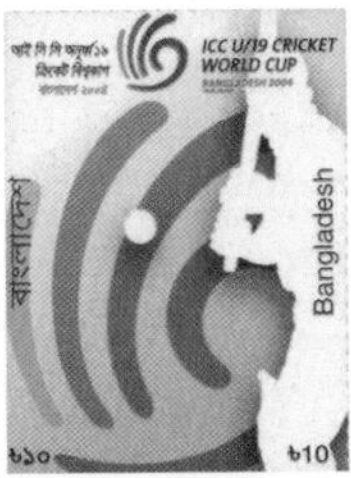


**352** Silhouette of Batsman

**2006.** ICC Under 19 Cricket World Cup (2004), Bangladesh.

911 **352** 10t. multicoloured 1·50 1·25

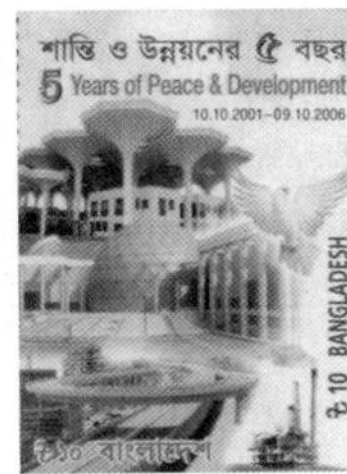


**353** Peace Dove and Modern Buildings and Roads

**2006.** Five Years of Peace and Development.

912 **353** 10t. multicoloured 1·00 1·00

**354** AIDS Ribbon and Globe

**2006.** World AIDS Day.

913 **354** 10t. multicoloured 1·00 1·00

**355** Profiles

**2006.** International Women's Day.

914 **355** 10t. multicoloured 1·00 1·00

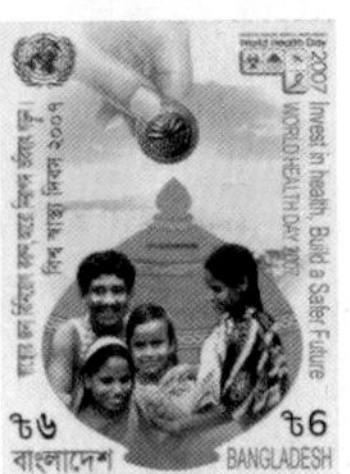


**356** Family and Jar of Coins ('Invest in health')

**2007.** World Health Day.

915 **356** 6t. multicoloured 1·00 1·00

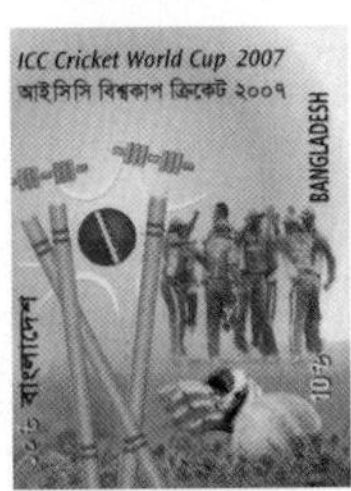


**357** Falling Wicket

**2007.** World Cup Cricket, West Indies. Multicoloured.

916 10t. Type **357** 1·00 1·00
917 10t. Tiger, bowler and trophy (horiz) 1·00 1·00
918 10t. Bangladesh team and Cricket World Cup trophy 1·00 1·00
919 10t. Batsman and trophy (horiz) 1·00 1·00

**358** House and Girls in Plantation

**2007.** National Tree Plantation Campaign.

920 **358** 10t. multicoloured 1·00 1·00

**359** Md. Habibullah Bahar Choudhury

**2007.** Birth Centenary (2006) of Md. Habibullah Bahar Choudhury (politician and writer).

921 **359** 10t. multicoloured 1·00 1·00

**360** Boy and Girl Scouts

**2007.** Centenary of World Scouting. Multicoloured.

922 10t. Type **360** 1·00 1·00
923 10t. Lord Baden-Powell (founder) 1·00 1·00

**(361)**

**2007.** 20th Anniv of Philatelic Association of Bangladesh. No. 768 optd with T 361.

924 4t. White-breasted waterhen (*Amaurornis phoenicurus*) 1·50 1·00

**362** Dr. Muhammad Yunus and Peace Medal

**2007.** Dr. Muhammad Yunus and Grameen Bank–winner of Nobel Peace Prize (2006).

925 **362** 10t. multicoloured 1·50 1·50

**363** Children standing in Flood Water

**2008.** In Charity of Flood Victims

926 2t. Type **363** 70 80
927 2t. Children and sheep in flood water 70 80
928 2t. People and goats taking refuge on corrugated iron roof 70 80
929 2t. Women queuing for food 70 80
930 2t. Woman and children with food bowls and flooded houses 70 80

**364** Cricket Match

**2007.** ICC World Twenty20 2007 Cricket Cup, South Africa. Multicoloured.

931 4t. Type **364** 80 80
932 4t. Cricketer and map of South Africa 80 80

**365** Emblem and Globe

**2008.** International Migrants Day.

933 **365** 10t. multicoloured 1·50 1·50

**366** Soldiers with Flag

**2008.** Independence and National Day.

934 **366** 10t. multicoloured 1·50 1·50

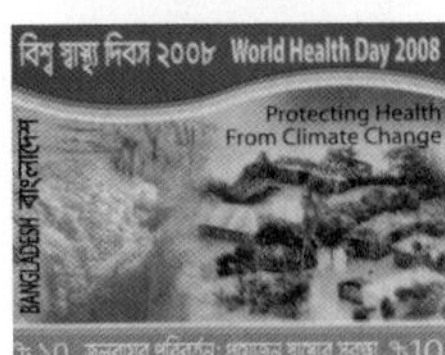


**367** Melting Glacier and Flooded Village

**2008.** World Health Day. 'Protecting Health From Climate Change'.

935 **367** 10t. multicoloured 1·50 1·50

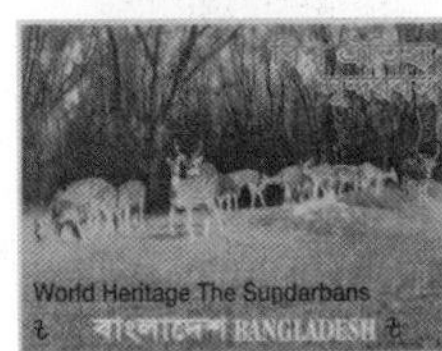


**368** Herd of Spotted Deer

**2008.** The Sundarbans World Heritage Site. Multicoloured.

936 10t. Type **368** 1·50 1·50
937 10t. Waterway and mangrove forest 1·50 1·50
938 10t. Collecting bee nests for honey 1·50 1·50
939 10t. Tiger 1·50 1·50
**MS**940 167×95 mm. Nos. 936/9 6·50 6·50

No. **MS**940 also exists imperforate.

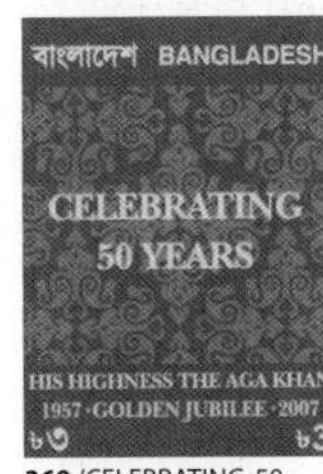


**369** 'CELEBRATING 50 YEARS' and Pattern

**2008.** Golden Jubilee of the Aga Khan (2007).

941 **369** 3t. emerald and green 55 55
942 **369** 3t. red and rose 55 55
943 – 3t. gold pattern on white 55 55
944 – 3t. white pattern on gold 55 55

DESIGN: Nos. 943/4 'CELEBRATING 50 YEARS' in circle surrounded by pattern.

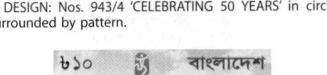

**370** Athletes on Training Run

**2008.** Olympic Games, Beijing. Multicoloured.

945 10t. Type **370** 1·00 1·00
946 15t. Rifle shooting 1·25 1·25
947 20t. Olympic mascots Beibei, Jingjing, Huanhuan, Yingying and Nini 1·40 1·40

948 25t. Pierre de Coubertin (founder of modern Olympics) and Olympic stamps of Greece (1876) and Bangladesh (1976) 1·60 1·60

**371** The First Stamps of Bangladesh, 1971

**2008.** Stamp Day. Sheet 140×90 mm.
**MS**949 **371** multicoloured 3·75 4·50

**372** Khepupara Radar Station, Patuakhali

**2008.** Japanese International Cooperation Agency ('Friends from the Birth of Bangladesh'). Sheet 123×75 mm containing T 372 and similar horiz designs. Multicoloured.
**MS**950 3t. Type **372**; 7t. Vocational training programme; 10t. Jamuna Multi-purpose Bridge; 10t. Polio vaccination programme 2·50 2·75

**373** Emblem

**2008.** 50th Anniv of Dhaka Chamber of Commerce and Industry.
951 **373** 10t. multicoloured 1·50 1·50

**374** Farmer and Workers in Rice Field

**2008.** First National Agriculture Day.
952 **374** 4t. multicoloured 70 50

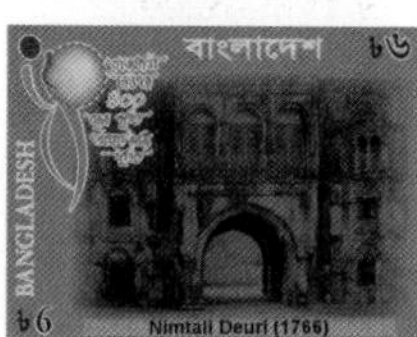

**375** Nimtali Deuri (gateway of Nimtali Palace)

**2008.** 400th Anniv of Dhaka.
953 **375** 6t. multicoloured 80 60

**376** Cox's Bazar

**2008.** Cox's Bazar (world's longest unbroken sea beach).
954 **376** 10t. multicoloured 1·00 1·00

**377** Disabled Man

**2008.** International Day of Persons with Disabilities.
955 **377** 3t. multicoloured 70 45

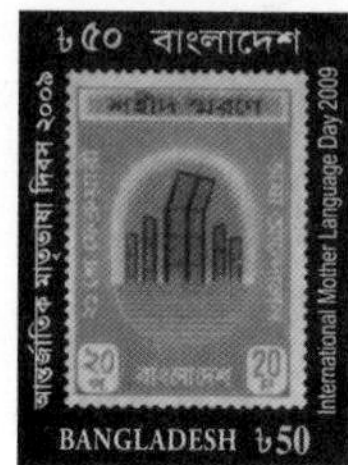

**378** Women and Child and Emblem

**2008.** International Year of Sanitation.
956 **378** 3t. multicoloured 70 45

**379** 1972 'In Memory of the Martyrs' 20p. Stamp

**2009.** International Mother Language Day. Sheet 180×119 mm.
**MS**957 multicoloured 6·00 6·00

**380** Sheikh Mujibur Rahman and Children

**2009.** Sheikh Mujibur Rahman Commemoration and National Children's Day.
958 **380** 10t. multicoloured 1·25 1·25

**381** Ziaur Rahman, National Flag and Painting

**2009.** Independence and National Day.
959 **381** 3t. multicoloured 1·00 45

**382** Doctors and Nurses with Patients and Hospital Building

**2009.** World Health Day.
960 **382** 3t. multicoloured 1·00 55

**383** China 2009 Emblem

**2009.** China 2009 World Stamp Exhibition, Luoyang. Sheet 100×70 mm containing T 383 and similar horiz designs. Multicoloured.
**MS**961 10t. Type **383**; 10t. China 2009 'Tree Peony Messenger' mascot; 20t. Ox 4·75 4·75

No. **MS**5961 contains three stamps and a stamp size label.

**384** Shamsun Nahar Mahmud

**2009.** Birth Centenary (2008) of Shamsun Nahar Mahmud (writer).
962 **384** 4t. multicoloured 70 50

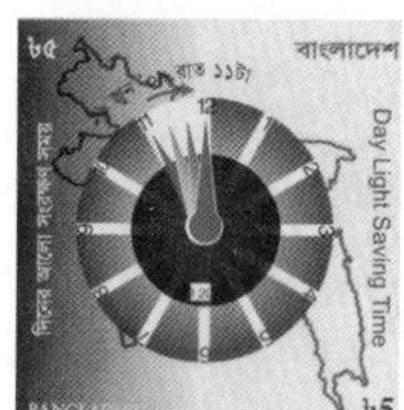

**385** Couple holding Tree Seedlings

**2009.** National Tree Plantation Campaign and Tree Fair.
963 **385** 3t. multicoloured 50 35

**386** Clock

**2009.** Day Light Saving Time.
964 **386** 5t. multicoloured 65 65

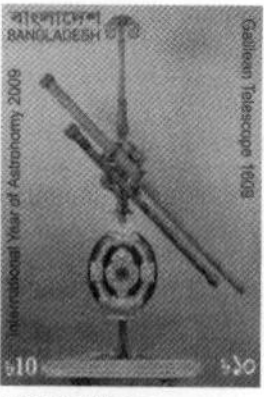

**387** Silhouette of Family

**2009.** World Population Day.
965 **387** 6t. multicoloured 70 70

**388** Galilean Telescope, 1609

**2009.** International Year of Astronomy. Multicoloured.
966 10t. Type **388** 1·50 1·50
967 10t. Andromeda Galaxy 1·50 1·50

**389** Begum Fazilatunnessa Mujib

**2009.** National Mourning Day. Sheikh Mujibur Rahman and his Family. Multicoloured.
968 3t. Type **389** 35 35
969 3t. Sheikh Kamal 35 35
970 3t. Sheikh Jamal 35 35
971 3t. Sheikh Russel 35 35
972 3t. Sheikh Abu Naser 35 35
973 3t. Sultana Kamal Khuku 35 35
974 3t. Parveen Jamal Rosy 35 35
975 3t. Abdur Rab Serniabat 35 35
976 3t. Sheikh Fazlul Haque Moni 35 35
977 3t. Begum Arju Moni 35 35
978 3t. Colonel Jamiluddin Ahmed 35 35
979 3t. Baby Serniabat 35 35
980 3t. Arif Serniabat 35 35
981 3t. Sukanto Abdullah Babu 35 35
982 3t. Shahid Serniabat 35 35
983 3t. Abdul Nayeem Khan Rintu 35 35
984 15t. Sheikh Mujibur Rahman 35 35

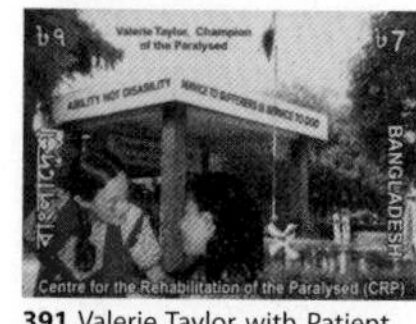

**390** Coin

**2009.** World Food Day. Multicoloured.
985 3t. Type **390** 45 45
986 3t. Bread and agricultural produce 45 45
987 3t. Boat loaded with produce 45 45
988 3t. Fishermen with catch 45 45

**391** Valerie Taylor with Patient

**2009.** 30th Anniv of Centre for the Rehabilitation of the Paralysed, Dhaka.
989 7t. Type **391** 90 90
990 7t. Rehabilitation 90 90

**392** Professor Abdul Moktader

**2009.** Birth Centenary of Professor Abdul Moktader.
991 **392** 4t. multicoloured 50 50

**393** Scouts saluting

**2010.** Eighth National Scout Jamboree
992 **393** 10t. multicoloured 3·25 3·25

**394** 'Alec's Red'

**2010.** Roses: Cultivated Varieties in Bangladesh. Multicoloured.
993 10t. Type **394** 2·75 2·75
994 10t. Royal Highness 2·75 2·75
995 10t. Queen Elizabeth 2·75 2·75
996 10t. Ballerina 2·75 2·75
997 10t. Alexander 2·75 2·75
998 10t. Blue Moon 2·75 2·75
999 10t. Papa Meilland 2·75 2·75
1000 10t. Double Delight 2·75 2·75
1001 10t. Iceberg 2·75 2·75
1002 10t. Sonia 2·75 2·75
1003 10t. Sunblest 2·75 2·75
1004 10t. Piccadilly 2·75 2·75
1005 10t. Pascali 2·75 2·75

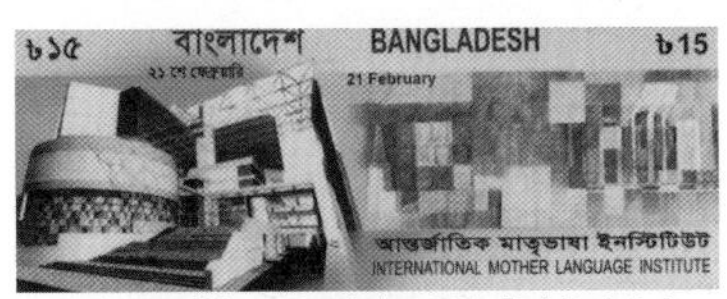

**395** 'Alec's Red' (image scaled to 61% of original size)

**2010.** Inauguration of International Mother Language Institute, Dhaka

| | | | | |
|---|---|---|---|---|
| 1006 | **395** | 15t. multicoloured | 4·25 | 4·25 |

**396** Women with Raised Fists

**2010.** Centenary of International Women's Day

| | | | | |
|---|---|---|---|---|
| 1007 | **396** | 5t. multicoloured | 2·00 | 2·00 |

**397** 1997 4t. Sheikh Mujibur Rahman Stamp

**2010.** National Children's Day. Sheet 140×100 mm.

| | | | | |
|---|---|---|---|---|
| **MS**1008 | **397** | 10t. multicoloured (sold at 25t.) | 8·50 | 8·50 |

**398** Liberation Monument, Public Library Campus, Brahman Baria

**2010.** Independence and National Day. Multicoloured.

| | | |
|---|---|---|
| **MS**1009 5t.×4, Type **398**; Liberation Monument, Shafipur, Gazipur; Liberation Monument, Jagannath Hall, Dhaka University; Liberation Monument, Vocational Training Institute, Rangpur | 7·00 | 7·00 |

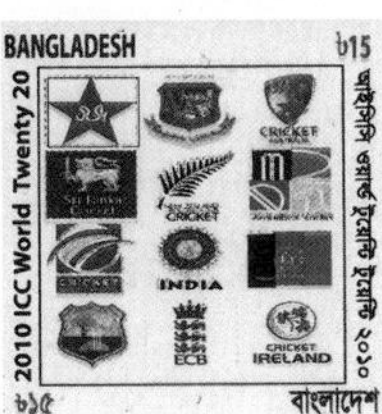

**399** Cricket Badges

**2010.** ICC World Twenty20 2010 Cricket Cup

| | | | | |
|---|---|---|---|---|
| 1010 | **398** | 15t. multicoloured | 4·25 | 4·25 |

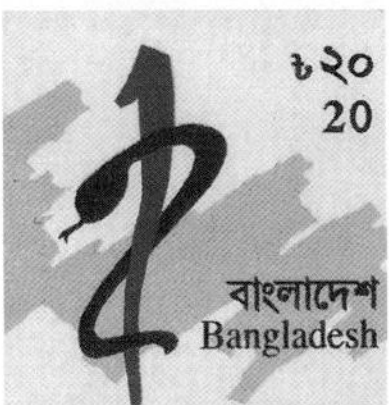

**400** Emblem

**2010.** 12th Anniv of Bangabandhu Sheikh Mujib Medical University

| | | | | |
|---|---|---|---|---|
| **MS**1011 | **400** | 20t. multicoloured | 7·25 | 7·25 |

**401** City Park

**2010.** National Tree Plantation Campaign and Tree Fair

| | | | | |
|---|---|---|---|---|
| 1012 | **401** | 6t. multicoloured | 1·50 | 1·50 |

**402** Bara Katra (Mughal Dhaka)

**2010.** 400th Anniv (2008) of Dhaka (2nd issue). Multicoloured.

| | | | |
|---|---|---|---|
| 1013 | 10t. Type **402** | 3·00 | 3·00 |
| 1014 | 10t. Buriganga River and Buckland Bund (embankment) (British Dhaka) | 3·00 | 3·00 |
| 1015 | 10t. Kamlapur Railway Station (Pakistan Period) | 3·00 | 3·00 |
| 1016 | 10t. Dhaka City Corporation building and modern Dhaka | 3·00 | 3·00 |

**403** Anniversary Emblem

**2010.** 50th Anniv of ICDDR'B (International Centre for Diarrhoeal Disease Research, Bangladesh)

| | | | | |
|---|---|---|---|---|
| 1017 | **403** | 5t. gold and black | 1·75 | 1·75 |

**404** Two Players

**2010.** World Cup Football Championships, South Africa. Multicoloured.

| | | | |
|---|---|---|---|
| 1018 | 10t. Type **404** | 1·50 | 1·50 |
| 1019 | 10t. Three players pursuing headed ball | 1·50 | 1·50 |
| 1020 | 20t. Zakumi mascot | 3·00 | 3·00 |

### OFFICIAL STAMPS

**1973.** Nos. 22, etc. optd SERVICE.

| | | | | |
|---|---|---|---|---|
| O1 | **7** | 2p. black | 10 | 1·50 |
| O2 | - | 3p. green | 10 | 1·50 |
| O3 | - | 5p. brown | 20 | 10 |
| O4 | - | 10p. black | 20 | 10 |
| O5 | - | 20p. green | 1·75 | 10 |
| O6 | - | 25p. mauve | 4·00 | 10 |
| O7 | - | 60p. grey | 4·00 | 2·25 |
| O8 | - | 75p. orange | 1·50 | 30 |
| O9 | **8** | 1t. violet | 17·00 | 6·50 |
| O10 | - | 5t. blue | 5·00 | 9·00 |

**1974.** Nos. 49/51 optd SERVICE.

| | | | | |
|---|---|---|---|---|
| O11 | **14** | 1t. violet | 5·00 | 50 |
| O12 | - | 2t. olive | 7·00 | 2·25 |
| O13 | - | 5t. blue | 18·00 | 14·00 |

**1976.** Nos. 64/70 and 72/4 optd SERVICE.

| | | | | |
|---|---|---|---|---|
| O14 | | 5p. green | 1·50 | 1·00 |
| O15 | | 10p. black | 3·00 | 1·00 |
| O16 | | 20p. green | 3·25 | 1·25 |
| O17 | | 25p. mauve | 3·50 | 1·00 |
| O18 | | 50p. purple | 5·00 | 60 |
| O19 | | 60p. grey | 30 | 3·00 |
| O20 | | 75p. olive | 30 | 3·75 |
| O21 | **14** | 1t. blue | 3·25 | 70 |
| O22 | - | 2t. green | 35 | 2·50 |
| O23 | - | 5t. blue | 30 | 2·75 |

**32** Fenchuganj Fertiliser Factory

**1981.** Nos. 125/37 optd SERVICE.

| | | | | |
|---|---|---|---|---|
| O24 | | 5p. brown | 2·75 | 2·50 |
| O25 | **32** | 10p. blue | 2·75 | 3·00 |
| O26 | - | 15p. orange | 2·75 | 2·75 |
| O27 | - | 20p. red | 1·50 | 2·75 |
| O28 | - | 25p. blue | 80 | 2·75 |
| O29 | - | 30p. green | 5·00 | 3·00 |
| O30 | - | 40p. purple | 2·75 | 2·75 |
| O31 | - | 50p. black | 30 | 10 |
| O32 | - | 80p. brown | 2·25 | 50 |
| O33 | - | 1t. violet | 30 | 10 |
| O34 | - | 2t. blue | 35 | 3·25 |

**1983.** Nos. 220/9, 318a and 710 (1989) optd Service.

| | | | | |
|---|---|---|---|---|
| O35 | **69** | 5p. blue | 20 | 60 |
| O36 | - | 10p. purple | 20 | 30 |
| O37 | - | 15p. blue | 20 | 45 |
| O38 | - | 20p. black | 20 | 30 |
| O39 | - | 25p. grey | 20 | 40 |
| O40 | - | 30p. brown | 25 | 40 |
| O41 | - | 50p. brown | 25 | 20 |
| O42 | - | 1t. blue | 50 | 20 |
| O43 | - | 2t. green | 1·75 | 30 |
| O44 | - | 3t. black and blue | 50 | 50 |
| O45 | - | 4t. blue | 55 | 55 |
| O46 | - | 5t. purple | 2·25 | 1·00 |

— সার্ভিস
**(O5)**

**1989.** Nos. 227 and 710 (1989) optd with Type O 5.

| | | | |
|---|---|---|---|
| O47 | 1t. blue | 50 | 20 |
| O48 | 5t. black and brown | 1·00 | 1·00 |

**(O6)**

**1990.** Nos. 368/9 (Immunization) optd with Type O 6.

| | | | | |
|---|---|---|---|---|
| O49 | **133** | 1t. green | 25 | 50 |
| O50 | **133** | 2t. brown | 25 | 50 |

**1992.** No. 376 optd as Type O **6** but horiz.

| | | | | |
|---|---|---|---|---|
| O51 | **136** | 6t. blue and yellow | 50 | 50 |

**1995.** No. 553 (National Diabetes Awareness Day) optd as Type O 6 but horiz.

| | | | | |
|---|---|---|---|---|
| O52 | **199** | 2t. multicoloured | 1·00 | 1·00 |

**(O7)**

**1996.** Nos. 221 and 223 optd with Type O **7**.

| | | | |
|---|---|---|---|
| O53 | 10p. purple | 75 | 75 |
| O54 | 20p. black | 1·25 | 1·25 |

**1999.** No. 710 optd as Type O **5** but vert.

| | | | |
|---|---|---|---|
| O56 | 5t. black and brown | 1·00 | 1·00 |

Pt. 1

# BARBADOS

An island in the Br. West Indies, E. of the Windward Islands, attained self-government on 16 October 1961 and achieved independence within the Commonwealth on 30 November 1966.

1852. 12 pence = 1 shilling; 20 shillings = 1 pound.
1950. 100 cents = 1 West Indian, later Barbados, dollar.

**1** Britannia

**2**

**1852.** Imperf.

| | | | | |
|---|---|---|---|---|
| 8 | **1** | (½d.) green | £180 | £200 |
| 10 | **1** | (1d.) blue | 75·00 | 60·00 |
| 4a | **1** | (2d.) slate | £300 | £1200 |
| 5 | **1** | (4d.) red | £120 | £275 |
| 11 | **2** | 6d. red | £750 | £120 |
| 12a | **2** | 1s. black | £225 | 75·00 |

**1860.** Perf.

| | | | | |
|---|---|---|---|---|
| 21 | **1** | (½d.) green | 25·00 | 27·00 |
| 24 | **1** | (1d.) blue | 60·00 | 3·75 |
| 25 | **1** | (4d.) red | £130 | 60·00 |
| 31 | **2** | 6d. red | £130 | 28·00 |
| 33 | **2** | 6d. orange | £170 | 48·00 |
| 35 | **2** | 1s. black | 65·00 | 9·00 |

**1873.** Perf.

| | | | |
|---|---|---|---|
| 72 | ½d. green | 19·00 | 50 |
| 74 | 1d. blue | £110 | 1·50 |
| 63 | 3d. brown | £325 | £110 |
| 75 | 3d. mauve | £150 | 12·00 |
| 76 | 4d. red | £150 | 14·00 |
| 79 | 6d. yellow | £150 | 2·25 |
| 81 | 1s. purple | £160 | 6·50 |

**3**

**1873**

| | | | | |
|---|---|---|---|---|
| 64 | **3** | 5s. red | £950 | £300 |

**1878.** Half of No. 64 surch **1D.**

| | | | |
|---|---|---|---|
| 86 | 1d. on half 5s. red | £5000 | £650 |

**4**

**1882**

| | | | | |
|---|---|---|---|---|
| 90 | **4** | ½d. green | 24·00 | 2·00 |
| 92 | **4** | 1d. red | 38·00 | 1·25 |
| 93 | **4** | 2½d. blue | £100 | 1·50 |
| 96 | **4** | 3d. purple | 6·00 | 25·00 |
| 97 | **4** | 4d. grey | £350 | 4·50 |
| 99 | **4** | 4d. brown | 10·00 | 2·00 |
| 100 | **4** | 6d. black | 75·00 | 48·00 |
| 102 | **4** | 1s. brown | 29·00 | 21·00 |
| 103 | **4** | 5s. bistre | £160 | £200 |

**1892.** Surch **HALF-PENNY**.

| | | | |
|---|---|---|---|
| 104 | ½d. on 4d. brown | 2·25 | 6·00 |

**6** Seal of Colony

**1892**

| | | | | |
|---|---|---|---|---|
| 105 | **6** | ¼d. grey and red | 2·50 | 10 |
| 163 | **6** | ¼d. brown | 10·00 | 30 |
| 106 | **6** | ½d. green | 2·50 | 10 |
| 107 | **6** | 1d. red | 4·75 | 10 |
| 108 | **6** | 2d. black and orange | 8·00 | 75 |
| 166 | **6** | 2d. grey | 8·00 | 18·00 |
| 139 | **6** | 2½d. blue | 25·00 | 15 |
| 110 | **6** | 5d. olive | 7·50 | 4·50 |
| 111 | **6** | 6d. mauve and red | 16·00 | 2·00 |
| 168 | **6** | 6d. deep purple and purple | 19·00 | 27·00 |
| 112 | **6** | 8d. orange and blue | 4·00 | 28·00 |
| 113 | **6** | 10d. green and red | 8·50 | 8·50 |
| 169 | **6** | 1s. black on green | 14·00 | 15·00 |
| 114 | **6** | 2s.6d. black and orange | 48·00 | 65·00 |
| 144 | **6** | 2s.6d. violet and green | 65·00 | £150 |

**7**

**1897.** Diamond Jubilee.

| | | | | |
|---|---|---|---|---|
| 116 | **7** | ¼d. grey and red | 8·00 | 60 |
| 117 | **7** | ½d. green | 8·00 | 60 |
| 118 | **7** | 1d. red | 8·00 | 60 |
| 119 | **7** | 2½d. blue | 11·00 | 85 |
| 120 | **7** | 5d. brown | 28·00 | 20·00 |
| 121 | **7** | 6d. mauve and red | 38·00 | 25·00 |
| 122 | **7** | 8d. orange and blue | 20·00 | 27·00 |
| 123 | **7** | 10d. green and red | 55·00 | 55·00 |
| 124 | **7** | 2s.6d. black and orange | 90·00 | 60·00 |

8 Nelson Monument

**1906.** Death Centenary of Nelson.

| 145 | 8 | ¼d. black and grey | 15·00 | 1·75 |
|---|---|---|---|---|
| 146 | 8 | ½d. black and green | 11·00 | 15 |
| 147 | 8 | 1d. black and red | 12·00 | 15 |
| 148 | 8 | 2d. black and yellow | 2·00 | 4·50 |
| 149 | 8 | 2½d. black and blue | 3·75 | 1·25 |
| 150 | 8 | 6d. black and mauve | 18·00 | 27·00 |
| 151 | 8 | 1s. black and red | 22·00 | 50·00 |

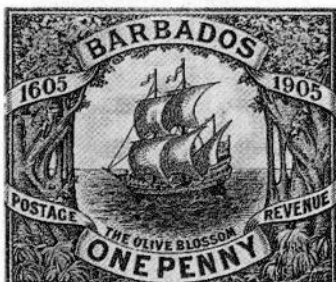

9 "Olive Blossom", 1650

**1906.** Tercentenary of Annexation of Barbados.

| 152 | 9 | 1d. black, blue and green | 15·00 | 25 |
|---|---|---|---|---|

**1907.** Surch **Kingston Relief Fund. 1d.**

| 153 | 6 | 1d. on 2d. black and orange | 4·75 | 11·00 |
|---|---|---|---|---|

11

**1912**

| 170 | 11 | ¼d. brown | 1·50 | 1·50 |
|---|---|---|---|---|
| 171 | 11 | ½d. green | 3·75 | 10 |
| 172 | 11 | 1d. red | 11·00 | 10 |
| 173 | 11 | 2d. grey | 5·50 | 18·00 |
| 174 | 11 | 2½d. blue | 1·50 | 65 |
| 175 | 11 | 3d. purple on yellow | 1·50 | 14·00 |
| 176 | 11 | 4d. black and red on yellow | 3·75 | 23·00 |
| 177 | 11 | 6d. deep purple and purple | 12·00 | 12·00 |

Larger type, with portrait at top centre.

| 178 | 1s. black on green | 11·00 | 22·00 |
|---|---|---|---|
| 179 | 2s. purple and blue on blue | 60·00 | 65·00 |
| 180 | 3s. green and violet | £110 | £120 |

14

**1916**

| 181 | 14 | ¼d. brown | 75 | 40 |
|---|---|---|---|---|
| 182 | 14 | ½d. green | 2·75 | 15 |
| 183a | 14 | 1d. red | 2·50 | 15 |
| 184 | 14 | 2d. grey | 10·00 | 30·00 |
| 185 | 14 | 2½d. blue | 5·00 | 3·50 |
| 186 | 14 | 3d. purple on yellow | 7·50 | 12·00 |
| 187 | 14 | 4d. red on yellow | 1·00 | 14·00 |
| 199 | 14 | 4d. black and red | 1·00 | 3·75 |
| 188 | 14 | 6d. purple | 8·00 | 6·50 |
| 189 | 14 | 1s. black on green | 9·00 | 12·00 |
| 190 | 14 | 2s. purple on blue | 16·00 | 7·50 |
| 191 | 14 | 3s. violet | 70·00 | £170 |
| 200 | 14 | 3s. green and violet | 24·00 | £110 |

**1917.** Optd **WAR TAX.**

| 197 | 11 | 1d. red | 50 | 15 |
|---|---|---|---|---|

16

**1920.** Victory. Inscr "VICTORY 1919".

| 201 | 16 | ¼d. black and brown | 30 | 70 |
|---|---|---|---|---|
| 202 | 16 | ½d. black and green | 1·00 | 15 |
| 203 | 16 | 1d. black and red | 4·00 | 10 |
| 204 | 16 | 2d. black and grey | 2·25 | 13·00 |
| 205 | 16 | 2½d. indigo and blue | 2·75 | 25·00 |
| 206 | 16 | 3d. black and purple | 3·00 | 6·50 |
| 207 | 16 | 4d. black and green | 3·25 | 7·00 |
| 208 | 16 | 6d. black and orange | 3·75 | 20·00 |
| 209 | - | 1s. black and green | 17·00 | 45·00 |
| 210 | - | 2s. black and brown | 45·00 | 65·00 |
| 211 | - | 3s. black and orange | 48·00 | 85·00 |

The 1s. to 3s. show Victory full-face.

18

**1921**

| 217 | 18 | ¼d. brown | 25 | 10 |
|---|---|---|---|---|
| 219 | 18 | ½d. green | 1·50 | 10 |
| 220 | 18 | 1d. red | 80 | 10 |
| 221 | 18 | 2d. grey | 1·75 | 20 |
| 222 | 18 | 2½d. blue | 1·50 | 9·00 |
| 213 | 18 | 3d. purple on yellow | 2·00 | 8·00 |
| 214 | 18 | 4d. red on yellow | 1·75 | 20·00 |
| 225 | 18 | 6d. purple | 3·50 | 6·00 |
| 215 | 18 | 1s. black on green | 5·50 | 21·00 |
| 227 | 18 | 2s. purple on blue | 10·00 | 20·00 |
| 228 | 18 | 3s. violet | 20·00 | 80·00 |

19

**1925.** Inscr "POSTAGE & REVENUE".

| 229 | 19 | ¼d. brown | 25 | 10 |
|---|---|---|---|---|
| 230 | 19 | ½d. green | 60 | 10 |
| 231 | 19 | 1d. red | 60 | 10 |
| 231ca | 19 | 1½d. orange | 4·00 | 1·00 |
| 232 | 19 | 2d. grey | 75 | 3·25 |
| 233 | 19 | 2½d. blue | 50 | 80 |
| 234 | 19 | 3d. purple on yellow | 1·00 | 45 |
| 235 | 19 | 4d. red on yellow | 75 | 1·00 |
| 236 | 19 | 6d. purple | 1·00 | 90 |
| 237 | 19 | 1s. black on green | 2·00 | 8·00 |
| 238 | 19 | 2s. purple on blue | 7·00 | 7·50 |
| 238a | 19 | 2s.6d. red on blue | 28·00 | 38·00 |
| 239 | 19 | 3s. violet | 11·00 | 18·00 |

20 King Charles I and King George V

**1927.** Tercentenary of Settlement of Barbados.

| 240 | 20 | 1d. red | 1·00 | 75 |
|---|---|---|---|---|

**1935.** Silver Jubilee. As T **13** of Antigua.

| 241 | 1d. blue and red | 1·75 | 20 |
|---|---|---|---|
| 242 | 1½d. blue and grey | 5·00 | 8·50 |
| 243 | 2½d. brown and blue | 2·75 | 6·50 |
| 244 | 1s. grey and purple | 23·00 | 29·00 |

**1937.** Coronation. As T **2** of Aden.

| 245 | 1d. red | 30 | 15 |
|---|---|---|---|
| 246 | 1½d. brown | 55 | 75 |
| 247 | 2½d. blue | 1·25 | 75 |

21 Badge of the Colony

**1938.** "POSTAGE & REVENUE" omitted.

| 248 | 21 | ½d. green | 6·00 | 15 |
|---|---|---|---|---|
| 248c | 21 | ½d. bistre | 15 | 30 |
| 249a | 21 | 1d. red | 16·00 | 10 |
| 249c | 21 | 1d. green | 15 | 10 |
| 250 | 21 | 1½d. orange | 15 | 40 |
| 250c | 21 | 2d. purple | 50 | 2·50 |
| 250d | 21 | 2d. red | 20 | 70 |
| 251 | 21 | 2½d. blue | 50 | 60 |
| 252b | 21 | 3d. brown | 20 | 60 |
| 252c | 21 | 3d. blue | 20 | 1·75 |
| 253 | 21 | 4d. black | 20 | 10 |
| 254 | 21 | 6d. violet | 80 | 40 |
| 254a | 21 | 8d. mauve | 55 | 2·00 |
| 255a | 21 | 1s. olive | 1·00 | 10 |
| 256 | 21 | 2s.6d. purple | 7·50 | 1·50 |
| 256a | 21 | 5s. blue | 7·50 | 12·00 |

22 Kings Charles I, George VI, Assembly Chamber and Mace

**1939.** Tercentenary of General Assembly.

| 257 | 22 | ½d. green | 2·75 | 1·00 |
|---|---|---|---|---|
| 258 | 22 | 1d. red | 2·75 | 1·25 |
| 259 | 22 | 1½d. orange | 2·75 | 60 |
| 260 | 22 | 2½d. blue | 4·00 | 8·50 |
| 261 | 22 | 3d. brown | 4·00 | 5·50 |

**1946.** Victory. As T **9** of Aden.

| 262 | 1½d. orange | 15 | 50 |
|---|---|---|---|
| 263 | 3d. brown | 15 | 50 |

**1947.** Surch **ONE PENNY.**

| 264 | 17 | 1d. on 2d. red | 2·25 | 4·00 |
|---|---|---|---|---|

**1948.** Silver Wedding. As T **10/11** of Aden.

| 265 | 1½d. orange | 30 | 50 |
|---|---|---|---|
| 266 | 5s. blue | 17·00 | 12·00 |

**1949.** U.P.U. As T **22/03** of Antigua.

| 267 | 1½d. orange | 50 | 2·00 |
|---|---|---|---|
| 268 | 3d. blue | 2·50 | 6·50 |
| 269 | 4d. grey | 50 | 3·25 |
| 270 | 1s. olive | 50 | 60 |

24 Dover Fort

35 Seal of Barbados

**1950**

| 271 | 24 | 1c. indigo | 35 | 4·50 |
|---|---|---|---|---|
| 272 | - | 2c. green | 15 | 3·00 |
| 273 | - | 3c. brown and green | 1·25 | 4·00 |
| 274 | - | 4c. red | 15 | 40 |
| 275 | - | 6c. blue | 15 | 2·25 |
| 276 | - | 8c. blue and brown | 1·50 | 3·75 |
| 277 | - | 12c. blue and olive | 1·00 | 1·50 |
| 278 | - | 24c. red and black | 1·00 | 50 |
| 279 | - | 48c. violet | 9·00 | 7·00 |
| 280 | - | 60c. green and lake | 10·00 | 11·00 |
| 281 | - | $1.20 red and olive | 11·00 | 4·50 |
| 282 | 35 | $2.40 black | 25·00 | 38·00 |

DESIGNS—As Type **24**: HORIZ: 2c. Sugar cane breeding; 3c. Public buildings; 6c. Casting net; 8c. "Frances W. Smith" (schooner); 12c. Four-winged flyingfish; 24c. Old Main Guard Garrison; 60c. Careenage. VERT: 4c. Statue of Nelson; 48c. St. Michael's Cathedral; $1.20, Map and wireless mast.

**1951.** Inauguration of B.W.I. University College. As T **24/25** of Antigua.

| 283 | 3c. brown and blue | 30 | 40 |
|---|---|---|---|
| 284 | 12c. blue and olive | 1·00 | 2·25 |

36 King George VI and Stamp of 1852

**1952.** Centenary of Barbados Stamps.

| 285 | 36 | 3c. green and slate | 40 | 40 |
|---|---|---|---|---|
| 286 | 36 | 4c. blue and red | 40 | 1·00 |
| 287 | 36 | 12c. slate and green | 40 | 1·00 |
| 288 | 36 | 24c. brown and sepia | 50 | 55 |

37 Harbour Police

**1953.** As 1950 issue but with portrait or cypher (No. 301) of Queen Elizabeth II as in T **37**.

| 289 | 24 | 1c. indigo | 10 | 80 |
|---|---|---|---|---|
| 290 | - | 2c. orange and turquoise | 15 | 1·50 |
| 291 | - | 3c. black and green | 1·00 | 1·00 |
| 292 | - | 4c. black and orange | 20 | 20 |
| 293 | 37 | 5c. blue and red | 1·00 | 60 |
| 294 | - | 6c. brown | 2·50 | 60 |
| 314 | - | 8c. black and blue | 60 | 35 |
| 296 | - | 12c. blue and olive | 1·00 | 10 |
| 297 | - | 24c. red and black | 1·00 | 10 |
| 317 | - | 48c. violet | 5·00 | 1·50 |
| 318 | - | 60c. green and purple | 10·00 | 4·00 |
| 300 | - | $1.20 red and olive | 19·00 | 6·50 |
| 319 | 35 | $2.40 black | 1·25 | 1·75 |

**1953.** Coronation. As T **13** of Aden.

| 302 | 4c. black and orange | 1·00 | 20 |
|---|---|---|---|

**1958.** British Caribbean Federation. As T **28** of Antigua.

| 303 | 3c. green | 45 | 20 |
|---|---|---|---|
| 304 | 6c. blue | 60 | 2·25 |
| 305 | 12c. red | 60 | 30 |

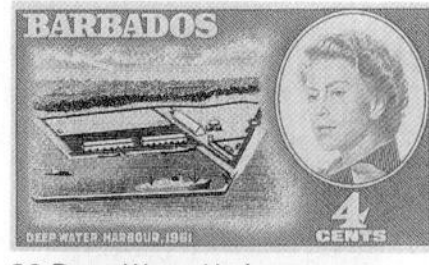

38 Deep Water Harbour, Bridgetown

**1961.** Opening of Deep Water Harbour.

| 306 | 38 | 4c. black and orange | 25 | 50 |
|---|---|---|---|---|
| 307 | 38 | 8c. black and blue | 25 | 60 |
| 308 | 38 | 24c. red and black | 25 | 60 |

39 Scout Badge and Map of Barbados

**1962.** Golden Jubilee of Barbados Boy Scout Association.

| 309 | 39 | 4c. black and orange | 85 | 10 |
|---|---|---|---|---|
| 310 | 39 | 12c. blue and brown | 1·25 | 15 |
| 311 | 39 | $1.20 red and green | 1·90 | 3·75 |

**1965.** Centenary of I.T.U. As T **36** of Antigua.

| 320 | 2c. lilac and red | 20 | 40 |
|---|---|---|---|
| 321 | 48c. yellow and drab | 45 | 1·00 |

40 Deep Sea Coral

**1965**

| 342 | 40 | 1c. black, pink and blue | 10 | 20 |
|---|---|---|---|---|
| 323 | - | 2c. brown, yell & mve | 20 | 15 |
| 324 | - | 3c. brown and orange | 45 | 60 |
| 344 | - | 3c. brown and orange | 30 | 2·75 |
| 325 | - | 4c. blue and green | 15 | 10 |
| 326 | - | 5c. sepia, red and lilac | 30 | 20 |
| 327 | - | 6c. multicoloured | 45 | 20 |
| 328 | - | 8c. multicoloured | 25 | 10 |
| 329 | - | 12c. multicoloured | 35 | 10 |
| 330 | - | 15c. black, yellow and red | 3·50 | 30 |
| 331 | - | 25c. blue and ochre | 1·00 | 30 |
| 332 | - | 35c. red and green | 1·50 | 15 |
| 333 | - | 50c. blue and green | 2·00 | 40 |
| 334 | - | $1 multicoloured | 3·50 | 2·00 |
| 335 | - | $2.50 multicoloured | 2·75 | 6·00 |
| 355a | - | $5 multicoloured | 21·00 | 13·00 |

DESIGNS—HORIZ: 2c. Lobster; 3c. (No. 324) Lined seahorse (wrongly inscribed "Hippocanpus"); 3c. (No. 344) (correctly inscribed "Hippocampus"); 4c. Sea urchin; 5c. Staghorn coral; 6c. Spot-finned butterflyfish; 8c. Rough file shell; 12c. Porcupinefish ("Balloon fish"); 15c Grey angel-fish; 25c. Brain coral; 35c. Brittle star; 50c. Four-winged flyingfish: $1 Queen or pink conch shell; $2.50, Fiddler crab. VERT: $5 Dolphin.

**1966.** Churchill Commemoration. As T **38** of Antigua.

| 336 | 1c. blue | 10 | 3·25 |
|---|---|---|---|
| 337 | 4c. green | 45 | 10 |
| 338 | 25c. brown | 1·10 | 50 |
| 339 | 35c. violet | 1·25 | 70 |

**1966.** Royal Visit. As T **39** of Antigua.

| 340 | 3c. black and blue | 65 | 1·00 |
|---|---|---|---|
| 341 | 35c. black and mauve | 1·60 | 1·00 |

**54** Arms of Barbados

**1966.** Independence. Multicoloured.

| | | | |
|---|---|---|---|
| 356 | 4c. Type **54** | 10 | 10 |
| 357 | 25c. Hilton Hotel (horiz) | 15 | 10 |
| 358 | 35c. G. Sobers (Test cricketer) | 1·50 | 65 |
| 359 | 50c. Pine Hill Dairy (horiz) | 70 | 1·10 |

**1967.** 20th Anniv of U.N.E.S.C.O. As T **54/56** of Antigua.

| | | | |
|---|---|---|---|
| 360 | 4c. multicoloured | 20 | 10 |
| 361 | 12c. yellow, violet and olive | 45 | 50 |
| 362 | 25c. black, purple and orange | 75 | 1·25 |

**58** Policeman and Anchor

**1967.** Centenary of Harbour Police. Multicoloured.

| | | | |
|---|---|---|---|
| 363 | 4c. Type **58** | 25 | 10 |
| 364 | 25c. Policeman and telescope | 40 | 15 |
| 365 | 35c. "BPI" (police launch) (horiz) | 45 | 15 |
| 366 | 50c. Policeman outside H.Q. | 60 | 1·60 |

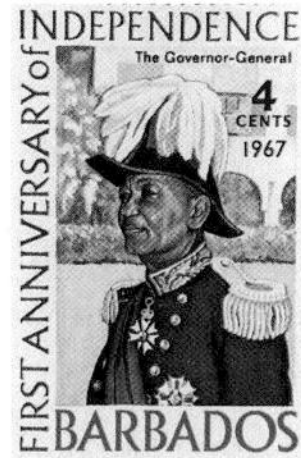

**62** Governor-General Sir Winston Scott G.C.M.G

**1967.** 1st Anniv of Independence. Multicoloured.

| | | | |
|---|---|---|---|
| 367 | 4c. Type **62** | 15 | 10 |
| 368 | 25c. Independence Arch (horiz) | 25 | 10 |
| 369 | 35c. Treasury Building (horiz) | 30 | 10 |
| 370 | 50c. Parliament Building (horiz) | 40 | 90 |

**66** U.N. Building, Santiago, Chile

**1968.** 20th Anniv of Economic Commission for Latin America.

| | | | | |
|---|---|---|---|---|
| 371 | **66** | 15c. multicoloured | 10 | 10 |

**67** Radar Antenna

**1968.** World Meteorological Day. Multicoloured.

| | | | |
|---|---|---|---|
| 372 | 3c. Type **67** | 10 | 10 |
| 373 | 25c. Meteorological Institute (horiz) | 25 | 10 |
| 374 | 50c. Harp Gun and Coat of Arms | 30 | 90 |

**70** Lady Baden-Powell and Guide at Campfire

**1968.** Golden Jubilee of Girl Guiding in Barbados.

| | | | | |
|---|---|---|---|---|
| 375 | **70** | 3c. blue, black and gold | 20 | 60 |
| 376 | - | 25c. blue, black and gold | 30 | 60 |
| 377 | - | 35c. yellow, black and gold | 35 | 60 |

DESIGNS: 25c. Lady Baden-Powell and Pax Hill; 35c. Lady Baden-Powell and Guides' Badge.

**73** Hands breaking Chain, and Human Rights Emblem

**1968.** Human Rights Year.

| | | | | |
|---|---|---|---|---|
| 378 | **73** | 4c. violet, brown and green | 10 | 20 |
| 379 | - | 25c. black, blue and yellow | 10 | 25 |
| 380 | - | 35c. multicoloured | 15 | 25 |

DESIGNS: 25c. Human Rights emblem and family enchained; 35c. Shadows of refugees beyond opening fence.

**76** Racehorses in the Paddock

**1969.** Horse Racing. Multicoloured.

| | | | |
|---|---|---|---|
| 381 | 4c. Type **76** | 25 | 15 |
| 382 | 25c. Starting-gate | 25 | 15 |
| 383 | 35c. On the flat | 30 | 15 |
| 384 | 50c. The winning-post | 35 | 2·40 |
| **MS**385 | 117×85 mm. Nos. 381/4 | 2·00 | 2·75 |

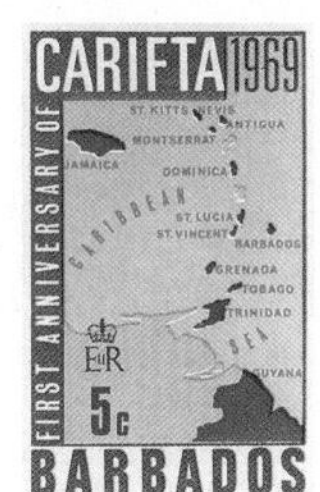

**80** Map showing "CARIFTA" Countries

**1969.** 1st Anniv of "CARIFTA". Multicoloured.

| | | | |
|---|---|---|---|
| 386 | 5c. Type **80** | 10 | 10 |
| 387 | 12c. "Strength in Unity" (horiz) | 10 | 10 |
| 388 | 25c. Type **80** | 10 | 10 |
| 389 | 50c. As 12c. | 15 | 20 |

**82** I.L.O. Emblem and "1919–1969"

**1969.** 50th Anniv of I.L.O.

| | | | | |
|---|---|---|---|---|
| 390 | **82** | 4c. black, green and blue | 10 | 10 |
| 391 | **82** | 25c. black, mauve and red | 20 | 10 |

**1969.** No. 363 surch **ONE CENT**.

| | | | | |
|---|---|---|---|---|
| 392 | **58** | 1c. on 4c. multicoloured | 10 | 10 |

**84** National Scout Badge

**1969.** Independence of Barbados Boy Scouts Association and 50th Anniv of Barbados Sea Scouts. Multicoloured.

| | | | |
|---|---|---|---|
| 393 | 5c. Type **84** | 15 | 10 |
| 394 | 25c. Sea Scouts rowing | 45 | 10 |
| 395 | 35c. Scouts around campfire | 55 | 10 |
| 396 | 50c. Scouts and National Scout H.Q. | 80 | 1·25 |
| **MS**397 | 155×115 mm. Nos. 393/6 | 15·00 | 13·00 |

**1970.** No. 326 surch **4**.

| | | | |
|---|---|---|---|
| 398 | 4c. on 5c. sepia, red and lilac | 10 | 10 |

**89** Lion at Gun Hill

**1970.** Multicoloured.. Multicoloured..

| | | | |
|---|---|---|---|
| 399 | 1c. Type **89** | 10 | 1·75 |
| 400 | 2c. Trafalgar Fountain | 30 | 1·25 |
| 401 | 3c. Montefiore Drinking Fountain | 10 | 1·00 |
| 402a | 4c. St. James' Monument | 30 | 10 |
| 403 | 5c. St. Ann's Fort | 10 | 10 |
| 404 | 6c. Old Sugar Mill, Morgan Lewis | 35 | 3·00 |
| 405 | 8c. The Cenotaph | 10 | 10 |
| 406a | 10c. South Point Lighthouse | 1·25 | 15 |
| 407 | 12c. Barbados Museum (horiz) | 1·50 | 10 |
| 408 | 15c. Sharon Moravian Church (horiz) | 30 | 15 |
| 409 | 25c. George Washington House (horiz) | 25 | 15 |
| 410 | 35c. Nicholas Abbey (horiz) | 30 | 85 |
| 411 | 50c. Bowmanston Pumping Station (horiz) | 40 | 1·00 |
| 412 | $1 Queen Elizabeth Hospital (horiz) | 70 | 2·50 |
| 413 | $2.50 Suger Factory (horiz) | 1·50 | 4·00 |
| 467 | $5 Seawell International Airport (horiz) | 6·50 | 5·50 |

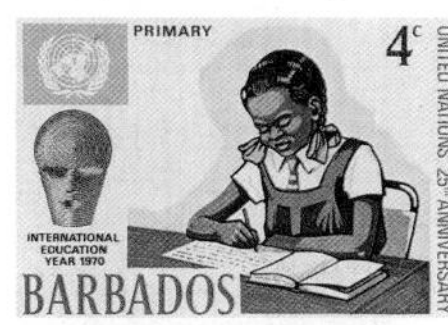

**105** Primary Schoolgirl

**1970.** 25th Anniv of U.N. Multicoloured.

| | | | |
|---|---|---|---|
| 415 | 4c. Type **105** | 10 | 10 |
| 416 | 5c. Secondary schoolboy | 10 | 10 |
| 417 | 25c. Technical student | 35 | 10 |
| 418 | 50c. University building | 55 | 1·50 |

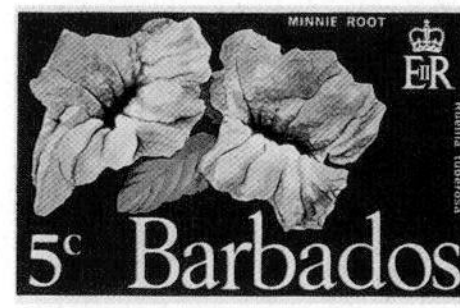

**106** Minnie Root

**1970.** Flowers of Barbados. Multicoloured.

| | | | |
|---|---|---|---|
| 419 | 1c. Barbados Easter lily (vert) | 10 | 2·00 |
| 420 | 5c. Type **106** | 40 | 10 |
| 421 | 10c. Eyelash orchid | 1·75 | 30 |
| 422 | 25c. Pride of Barbados (vert) | 1·25 | 75 |
| 423 | 35c. Christmas hope | 1·25 | 85 |
| **MS**424 | 162×101 mm. Nos. 419/23. Imperf | 2·00 | 6·50 |

**107** "Via Dolorosa" Window, St. Margaret's Church, St. John

**1971.** Easter. Multicoloured.

| | | | |
|---|---|---|---|
| 425 | 4c. Type **107** | 10 | 10 |
| 426 | 10c. "The Resurrection" (Benjamin West) | 10 | 10 |
| 427 | 35c. Type **107** | 15 | 10 |
| 428 | 50c. As 10c. | 30 | 1·50 |

**108** "Sailfish" Dinghy

**1971.** Tourism. Multicoloured.

| | | | |
|---|---|---|---|
| 429 | 1c. Type **108** | 10 | 50 |
| 430 | 5c. Tennis | 40 | 10 |
| 431 | 12c. Horse-riding | 60 | 10 |
| 432 | 25c. Water-skiing | 40 | 20 |
| 433 | 50c. Scuba-diving | 50 | 90 |

**109** S. J. Prescod (politician)

**1971.** Death Centenary of Samuel Jackman Prescod.

| | | | | |
|---|---|---|---|---|
| 434 | **109** | 3c. multicoloured | 10 | 15 |
| 435 | **109** | 35c. multicoloured | 15 | 15 |

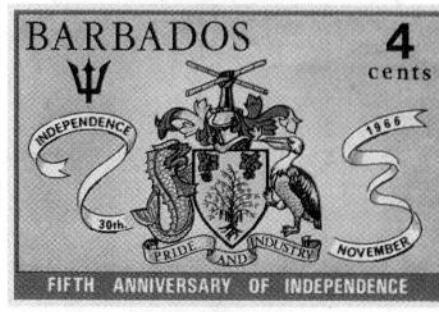

**110** Arms of Barbados

**1971.** 5th Anniv of Independence. Multicoloured.

| | | | |
|---|---|---|---|
| 436 | 4c. Type **110** | 20 | 10 |
| 437 | 15c. National flag and map | 45 | 10 |
| 438 | 25c. Type **110** | 45 | 10 |
| 439 | 50c. As 15c. | 90 | 1·60 |

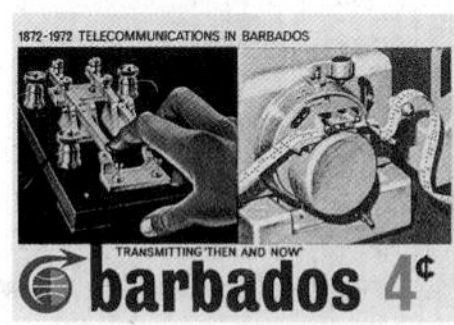

**111** Transmitting "Then and Now"

**1972.** Centenary of Cable Link. Multicoloured.

| | | | |
|---|---|---|---|
| 440 | 4c. Type **111** | 10 | 10 |
| 441 | 10c. Cable Ship "Stanley Angwin" | 20 | 10 |
| 442 | 35c. Barbados Earth Station and "Intelsat 4" | 35 | 20 |
| 443 | 50c. Mt. Misery and Tropospheric Scatter Station | 50 | 1·75 |

**112** Map and Badge

**1972.** Diamond Jubilee of Scouts. Multicoloured.

| | | | |
|---|---|---|---|
| 444 | 5c. Type **112** | 15 | 10 |
| 445 | 15c. Pioneers of scouting (horiz) | 15 | 10 |
| 446 | 25c. Scouts (horiz) | 30 | 15 |
| 447 | 50c. Flags (horiz) | 60 | 1·00 |

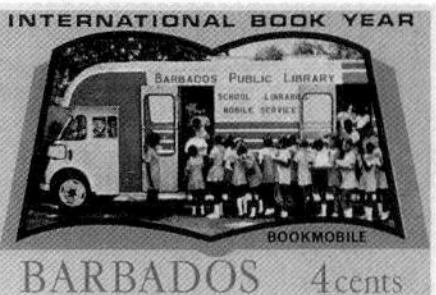

**113** Mobile Library

**1972.** Int Book Year. Multicoloured.

| | | | |
|---|---|---|---|
| 448 | 4c. Type **113** | 20 | 10 |
| 449 | 15c. Bedford mobile cinema truck | 25 | 10 |
| 450 | 25c. Public library | 25 | 10 |
| 451 | $1 Codrington College | 1·00 | 1·50 |

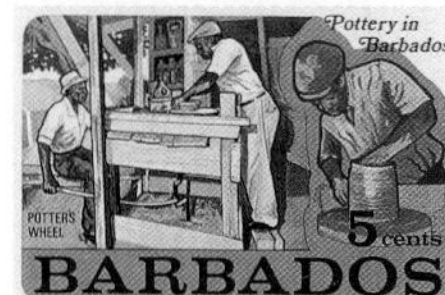

**114** Potter's Wheel

**1973.** Pottery in Barbados. Multicoloured.

| | | | |
|---|---|---|---|
| 468 | 5c. Type **114** | 10 | 10 |
| 469 | 15c. Kilns | 20 | 10 |
| 470 | 25c. Finished products | 25 | 10 |
| 471 | $1 Market scene | 90 | 1·10 |

**115** Wright Type B First Flight, 1911

**1973.** Aviation.

| | | | | |
|---|---|---|---|---|
| 472 | **115** | 5c. multicoloured | 30 | 10 |
| 473 | - | 15c. multicoloured | 90 | 10 |
| 474 | - | 25c. blue, blk & cobalt | 1·25 | 20 |
| 475 | - | 50c. multicoloured | 2·00 | 1·90 |

DESIGNS: 15c. de Havilland Cirrus Moth on first flight to Barbados, 1928; 25c. Lockheed 14 Super Electra, 1939; 50c. Vickers Super VC-10 airliner, 1973.

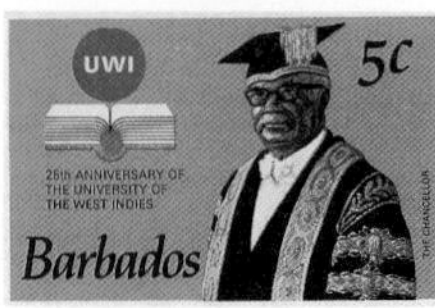

**116** University Chancellor

**1973.** 25th Anniv of University of West Indies. Multicoloured.

| | | | |
|---|---|---|---|
| 476 | 5c. Type **116** | 10 | 10 |
| 477 | 25c. Sherlock Hall | 25 | 15 |
| 478 | 35c. Cave Hill Campus | 30 | 25 |

**1974.** No. 462 surch **4c.**

| | | | |
|---|---|---|---|
| 479 | 4c. on 25c. multicoloured | 15 | 15 |

**118** Old Sail Boat

**1974.** Fishing Boats of Barbados. Multicoloured.

| | | | |
|---|---|---|---|
| 480 | 15c. Type **118** | 30 | 15 |
| 481 | 35c. Rowing-boat | 55 | 25 |
| 482 | 50c. Motor fishing-boat | 70 | 70 |
| 483 | $1 "Calamar" (fishing boat) | 1·10 | 1·40 |
| **MS**484 | 140×140 mm. Nos. 480/3 | 3·50 | 3·00 |

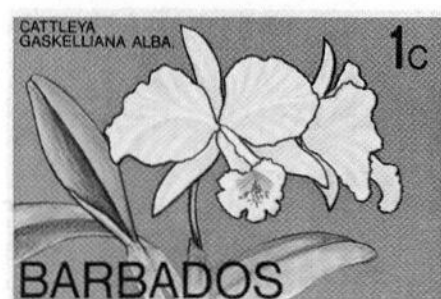

**119** "Cattleya gaskelliana alba"

**1974.** Orchids. Multicoloured.

| | | | |
|---|---|---|---|
| 510 | 1c. Type **119** | 15 | 1·25 |
| 511 | 2c. "Renanthera storiei" (vert) | 15 | 1·25 |
| 512 | 3c. "Dendrobium" "Rose Marie" (vert) | 15 | 1·00 |
| 488 | 4c. "Epidendrum ibaguense" (vert) | 1·75 | 90 |
| 514 | 5c. "Schomburgkia humboldtii" (vert) | 35 | 15 |
| 490 | 8c. "Oncidium ampliatum" (vert) | 1·75 | 90 |
| 515 | 10c. "Arachnis maggie oei" (vert) | 35 | 10 |
| 492 | 12c. "Dendrobium aggregatum" (vert) | 45 | 2·75 |
| 517 | 15c. "Paphiopedilum puddle" (vert) | 70 | 15 |
| 493b | 20c. "Spathoglottis" "The Gold" | 5·00 | 4·75 |
| 518 | 25c. "Epidendrum ciliare" (Eyelash) | 70 | 10 |
| 550 | 35c. "Bletia patula" (vert) | 2·00 | 1·75 |
| 519 | 45c. "Phalaenopsis schilleriana" "Sunset Glow" (vert) | 60 | 15 |
| 496 | 50c. As 45c. (vert) | 7·00 | 4·50 |
| 497 | $1 "Ascocenda" "Red Gem" (vert) | 10·00 | 3·25 |
| 498 | $2.50 "Brassolaeliocattleya" "Nugget" | 2·50 | 7·00 |
| 499 | $5 "Caularthron bicornutum" | 2·50 | 6·00 |
| 500 | $10 "Vanda" "Josephine Black" (vert) | 2·75 | 13·00 |

**120** 4d. Stamp of 1882, and U.P.U. Emblem

**1974.** Centenary of Universal Postal Union.

| | | | | |
|---|---|---|---|---|
| 501 | **120** | 8c. mauve, orange & grn | 10 | 10 |
| 502 | - | 35c. red, orge & brown | 20 | 10 |
| 503 | - | 50c. ultram, bl & silver | 25 | 35 |
| 504 | - | $1 blue, brown & black | 55 | 1·00 |
| **MS**505 | | 126×101 mm. Nos. 501/4 | 1·75 | 2·50 |

DESIGNS: 35c. Letters encircling the globe; 50c. U.P.U. emblem and arms of Barbados; $1 Map of Barbados, sailing ship and Boeing 747 airliner.

**121** Royal Yacht "Britannia"

**1975.** Royal Visit. Multicoloured.

| | | | |
|---|---|---|---|
| 506 | 8c. Type **121** | 85 | 30 |
| 507 | 25c. Type **121** | 1·40 | 30 |
| 508 | 35c. Sunset and palms | 60 | 35 |
| 509 | $1 As 35c. | 1·75 | 5·00 |

**122** St. Michael's Cathedral

**1975.** 150th Anniv of Anglican Diocese. Mult.

| | | | |
|---|---|---|---|
| 526 | 5c. Type **122** | 10 | 10 |
| 527 | 15c. Bishop Coleridge | 15 | 10 |
| 528 | 50c. All Saints' Church | 45 | 50 |
| 529 | $1 "Archangel Michael and Satan" (stained glass window, St. Michael's Cathedral, Bridgetown) | 70 | 80 |
| **MS**530 | 95×96 mm. Nos. 526/9 | 1·40 | 2·00 |

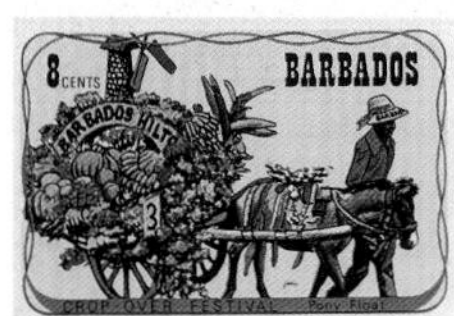

**123** Pony Float

**1975.** Crop-over Festival. Multicoloured.

| | | | |
|---|---|---|---|
| 531 | 8c. Type **123** | 10 | 10 |
| 532 | 25c. Man on stilts | 10 | 10 |
| 533 | 35c. Maypole dancing | 15 | 10 |
| 534 | 50c. Cuban dancers | 30 | 80 |
| **MS**535 | 127×85 mm. Nos. 531/4 | 1·00 | 1·60 |

**124** Barbados Coat of Arms

**1975.** Coil Definitives.

| | | | | |
|---|---|---|---|---|
| 536 | **124** | 5c. blue | 15 | 80 |
| 537 | **124** | 25c. violet | 25 | 1·10 |

**125** 17th-Century Sailing Ship

**1975.** 350th Anniv of First Settlement. Multicoloured.

| | | | |
|---|---|---|---|
| 538 | 4c. Type **125** | 50 | 20 |
| 539 | 10c. Bearded fig tree and fruit | 30 | 15 |
| 540 | 25c. Ogilvy's 17th-century map | 1·00 | 30 |
| 541 | $1 Captain John Powell | 1·00 | 5·00 |
| **MS**542 | 105×115 mm. Nos. 538/41 | 2·50 | 7·00 |

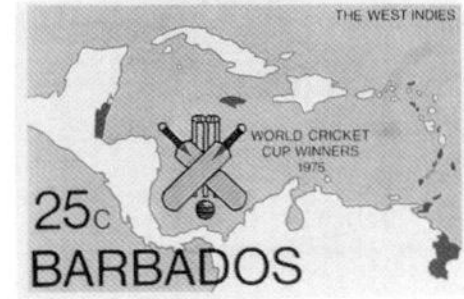

**126** Map of Caribbean

**1976.** West Indian Victory in World Cricket Cup.

| | | | | |
|---|---|---|---|---|
| 559 | **126** | 25c. multicoloured | 1·00 | 1·00 |
| 560 | - | 45c. black and purple | 1·00 | 2·00 |

DESIGN—VERT: 45c. The Prudential Cup.

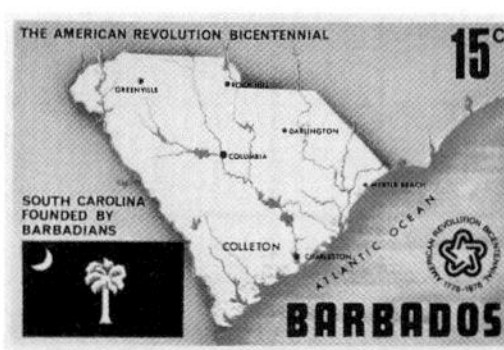

**127** Flag and Map of South Carolina

**1976.** Bicentenary of American Revolution. Mult.

| | | | |
|---|---|---|---|
| 561 | 15c. Type **127** | 75 | 15 |
| 562 | 25c. George Washington and map of Bridgetown | 75 | 15 |
| 563 | 50c. Independence Declaration | 60 | 1·00 |
| 564 | $1 Prince Hall | 75 | 3·00 |

**128** Early Postman

**1976.** 125th Anniv of Post Office Act. Multicoloured.

| | | | |
|---|---|---|---|
| 565 | 8c. Type **128** | 10 | 10 |
| 566 | 35c. Modern postman | 25 | 10 |
| 567 | 50c. Early letter | 30 | 75 |
| 568 | $1 Delivery van | 50 | 1·75 |

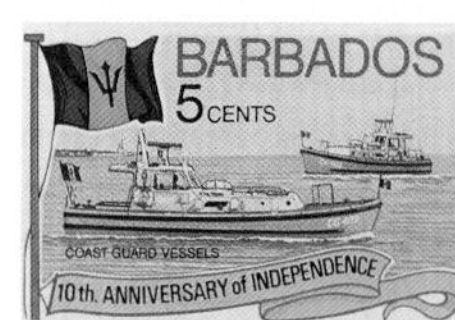

**129** Coast Guard "Commander Marshall" and "T. T. Lewis" launches

**1976.** 10th Anniv of Independence. Multicoloured.

| | | | |
|---|---|---|---|
| 569 | 5c. Type **129** | 30 | 20 |
| 570 | 15c. Reverse of currency note | 30 | 10 |
| 571 | 25c. Barbados national anthem | 30 | 20 |
| 572 | $1 Independence Day parade | 1·10 | 3·00 |
| **MS**573 | 90×125 mm. Nos. 569/72 | 2·75 | 3·75 |

**130** Arrival of Coronation Coach at Westminster Abbey

**1977.** Silver Jubilee. Multicoloured.

| | | | |
|---|---|---|---|
| 574 | 15c. Queen knighting Garfield Sobers, 1975 | 30 | 25 |
| 575 | 50c. Type **130** | 30 | 40 |
| 576 | $1 Queen entering Abbey | 30 | 70 |

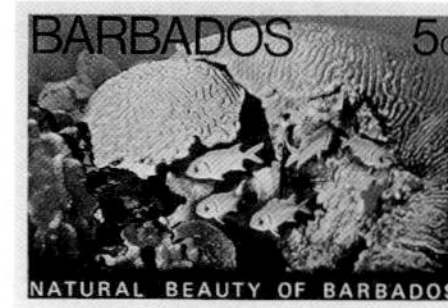

**131** Underwater Park

**1977.** Natural Beauty of Barbados. Multicoloured.

| | | | |
|---|---|---|---|
| 577 | 5c. Type **131** | 15 | 10 |
| 578 | 35c. Royal palms (vert) | 30 | 10 |
| 579 | 50c. Underwater caves | 40 | 50 |
| 580 | $1 Stalagmite in Harrison's Cave (vert) | 70 | 1·10 |
| **MS**581 | 138×92 mm. Nos. 577/80 | 2·50 | 2·75 |

**132** Maces of the House of Commons

**1977.** 13th Regional Conference of Commonwealth Parliamentary Association.

| | | | | |
|---|---|---|---|---|
| 582 | **132** | 10c. orange, yellow & brn | 10 | 10 |
| 583 | - | 25c. green, orge & dp grn | 10 | 10 |
| 584 | - | 50c. multicoloured | 20 | 20 |
| 585 | - | $1 blue, orange and dp bl | 55 | 75 |

DESIGNS—VERT: 25c. Speaker's Chair; 50c. Senate Chamber. HORIZ: $1 Sam Lord's Castle.

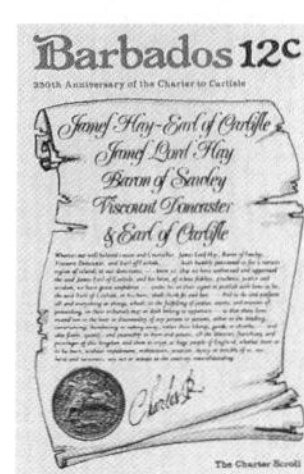

**133** The Charter Scroll

**1977.** 350th Anniv of Granting of Charter to Earl of Carlisle. Multicoloured.

| | | | |
|---|---|---|---|
| 586 | 12c. Type **133** | 15 | 10 |
| 587 | 25c. The earl receiving charter | 15 | 10 |
| 588 | 45c. The earl and Charles I (horiz) | 30 | 35 |
| 589 | $1 Ligon's map, 1657 (horiz) | 50 | 1·00 |

**1977.** Royal Visit. As Nos. 574/6 but inscr "SILVER JUBILEE ROYAL VISIT".

| | | | |
|---|---|---|---|
| 590 | 15c. Garfield Sobers being knighted, 1975 | 60 | 50 |
| 591 | 50c. Type **130** | 20 | 75 |
| 592 | $1 Queen entering Abbey | 30 | 1·25 |

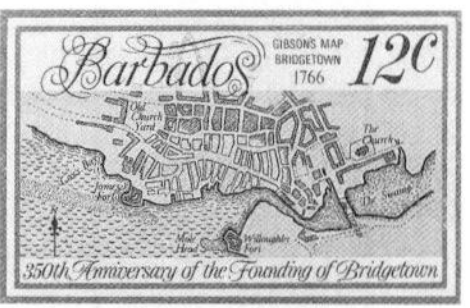

**134** Gibson's Map of Bridgtown, 1766

**1978.** 350th Anniv of Founding of Bridgetown.

| | | | | |
|---|---|---|---|---|
| 593 | **134** | 12c. multicoloured | 15 | 10 |
| 594 | - | 25c. black, green & gold | 15 | 10 |
| 595 | - | 45c. multicoloured | 20 | 15 |
| 596 | - | $1 multicoloured | 30 | 60 |

DESIGNS: 25c. "A Prospect of Bridgetown in Barbados" (engraving by S. Copens, 1695); 45c. "Trafalgar Square, Bridgetown" (drawing by J. M. Carter, 1835); $1 The Bridges, 1978.

**135** Brown Pelican

**1978.** 25th Anniv of Coronation.

| | | | | |
|---|---|---|---|---|
| 597 | | 50c. olive, black & blue | 25 | 50 |
| 598 | | 50c. multicoloured | 25 | 50 |
| 599 | **135** | 50c. olive, black & blue | 25 | 50 |

DESIGNS: No. 597, Griffin of Edward III. No. 598, Queen Elizabeth II.

**136** Barbados Bridge League Logo

**1978.** 7th Regional Bridge Tournament, Barbados. Multicoloured.

| | | | |
|---|---|---|---|
| 600 | 5c. Type **136** | 10 | 10 |
| 601 | 10c. Emblem of World Bridge Federation | 15 | 10 |
| 602 | 45c. Central American and Caribbean Bridge Federation emblem | 25 | 10 |
| 603 | $1 Playing cards on map of Caribbean | 40 | 60 |
| **MS**604 | 134×83 mm. Nos. 600/3 | 2·00 | 2·75 |

**137** Camp Scene

**1978.** Diamond Jubilee of Guiding. Multicoloured.

| | | | |
|---|---|---|---|
| 605 | 12c. Type **137** | 25 | 15 |
| 606 | 28c. Community work | 40 | 15 |
| 607 | 50c. Badge and "60" (vert) | 55 | 30 |
| 608 | $1 Guide badge (vert) | 75 | 1·00 |

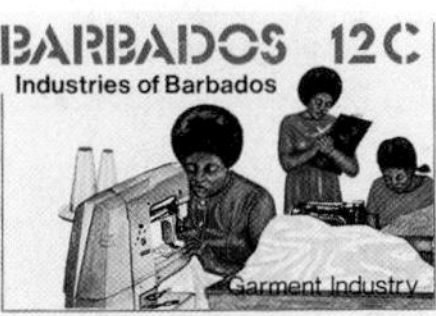

**138** Garment Industry

**1978.** Industries of Barbados. Multicoloured.

| | | | |
|---|---|---|---|
| 609 | 12c. Type **138** | 15 | 10 |
| 610 | 28c. Cooper (vert) | 25 | 25 |
| 611 | 45c. Blacksmith (vert) | 35 | 95 |
| 612 | 50c. Wrought iron working | 40 | 1·50 |

**139** "Forth" (early mail steamer)

**1979.** Ships. Multicoloured.

| | | | |
|---|---|---|---|
| 613 | 12c. Type **139** | 35 | 10 |
| 614 | 25c. "Queen Elizabeth 2" in Deep Water Harbour | 55 | 15 |
| 615 | 50c. "Ra II" nearing Barbados | 75 | 1·00 |
| 616 | $1 Early mail paddle-steamer | 1·00 | 2·50 |

**140** 1953 1c. Definitive Stamp

**1979.** Death Cent of Sir Rowland Hill. Mult.

| | | | |
|---|---|---|---|
| 617 | 12c. Type **140** | 15 | 15 |
| 618 | 28c. 1975 350th anniv of first settlement 25c. commemorative (vert) | 20 | 30 |
| 619 | 45c. Penny Black with Maltese Cross postmark (vert) | 30 | 45 |
| **MS**620 | 137×90 mm. 50c. Unissued "Brittannia" blue | 55 | 50 |

**1979.** St. Vincent Relief Fund. No. 495 surch **28c+4c ST. VINCENT RELIEF FUND**.

| | | | |
|---|---|---|---|
| 621 | 28c.+4c. on 35c. "Bletia patula" | 50 | 60 |

**142** Grassland Yellow Finch ("Grass Canary")

**1979.** Birds. Multicoloured.

| | | | |
|---|---|---|---|
| 622 | 1c. Type **142** | 10 | 1·25 |
| 623 | 2c. Grey kingbird ("Rainbird") | 10 | 1·25 |
| 624 | 5c. Lesser Antillean bullfinch ("Sparrow") | 10 | 70 |
| 625 | 8c. Magnificent frigate bird ("Frigate Bird") | 75 | 2·25 |
| 626 | 10c. Cattle egret | 10 | 40 |
| 627 | 12c. Green-backed heron ("Green Gaulin") | 50 | 1·50 |
| 627a | 15c. Carib grackle ("Blackbird") | 4·50 | 5·00 |
| 628 | 20c. Antillean crested hummingbird ("Humming Bird") | 20 | 55 |
| 629 | 25c. Scaly-breasted ground dove ("Ground Dove") | 20 | 60 |
| 630 | 28c. As 15c. | 2·00 | 2·00 |
| 631 | 35c. Green-throated carib | 70 | 70 |
| 631b | 40c. Red-necked pigeon ("Ramier") | 4·50 | 5·50 |
| 632 | 45c. Zenaida dove ("Wood Dove") | 1·50 | 1·50 |
| 633 | 50c. As 40c. | 1·50 | 2·00 |
| 633a | 55c. American golden plover ("Black breasted Plover") | 4·00 | 3·50 |
| 633b | 60c. Bananaquit ("Yellow Breasted") | 4·50 | 6·00 |
| 634 | 70c. As 60c. | 2·00 | 3·50 |
| 635 | $1 Caribbean elaenia ("Peer whistler") | 2·00 | 1·50 |
| 636 | $2.50 American redstart ("Christmas Bird") | 2·00 | 6·00 |
| 637 | $5 Belted kingfisher ("Kingfisher") | 3·25 | 9·00 |
| 638 | $10 Moorhen ("Red-seal Coot") | 4·50 | 14·00 |

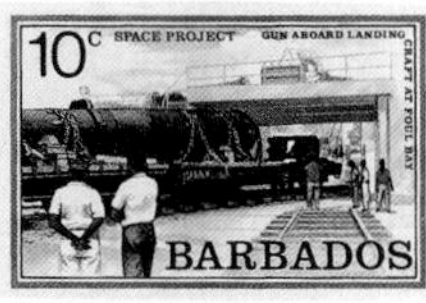

**143** Unloading H.A.R.P. Gun on Railway Wagon at Foul Bay

**1979.** Space Projects Commemorations. Mult.

| | | | |
|---|---|---|---|
| 639 | 10c. Type **143** | 30 | 10 |
| 640 | 12c. H.A.R.P. gun on railway wagon under tow (vert) | 30 | 15 |
| 641 | 20c. Firing launcher (vert) | 30 | 20 |
| 642 | 28c. Bath Earth Station and "Intelsat" | 30 | 30 |
| 643 | 45c. "Intelsat" over Caribbean | 35 | 50 |
| 644 | 50c. "Intelsat" over Atlantic (vert) | 35 | 60 |
| **MS**645 | 118×90 mm. $1 Lunar module descending on to Moon | 1·50 | 1·00 |

**144** Family

**1979.** International Year of the Child. Multicoloured.

| | | | |
|---|---|---|---|
| 646 | 12c. Type **144** | 10 | 10 |
| 647 | 28c. Ring of children and map of Barbados | 15 | 15 |
| 648 | 45c. Child with teacher | 20 | 20 |
| 649 | 50c. Children playing | 20 | 20 |
| 650 | $1 Children and kite | 35 | 45 |

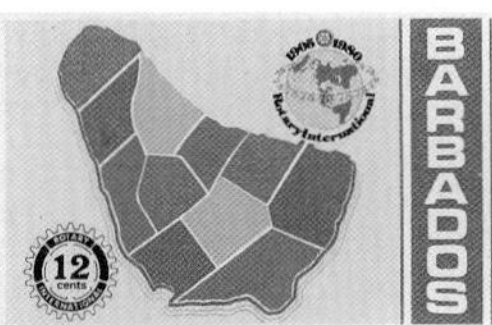

**145** Map of Barbados

**1980.** 75th Anniv of Rotary International. Multicoloured.

| | | | |
|---|---|---|---|
| 651 | 12c. Type **145** | 15 | 10 |
| 652 | 28c. Map of Caribbean | 15 | 15 |
| 653 | 50c. Rotary anniversary emblem | 20 | 35 |
| 654 | $1 Paul P. Harris (founder) | 30 | 95 |

**146** Private, Artillery Company, Barbados Volunteer Force, c.1909

**1980.** Barbados Regiment. Multicoloured.

| | | | |
|---|---|---|---|
| 655 | 12c. Type **146** | 25 | 10 |
| 656 | 35c. Drum Major, Zouave uniform | 35 | 15 |
| 657 | 50c. Sovereign's and Regimental Colours | 40 | 30 |
| 658 | $1 Barbados Regiment Women's Corps | 55 | 70 |

**147** Early Postman

**1980.** "London 1980" International Stamp Exhibition. Two sheets each 122×125 mm containing T 147 or similar vert design. Multicoloured.

| | | | |
|---|---|---|---|
| **MS**659 | (a) 28c.×6, Type **147**. (b) 50c.×6, Modern postwoman and Inspector Set of 2 sheets | 1·00 | 1·25 |

**148** Yellow-tailed Snapper

**1980.** Underwater Scenery. Multicoloured.

| | | | |
|---|---|---|---|
| 660 | 12c. Type **148** | 20 | 10 |
| 661 | 28c. Banded butterflyfish | 35 | 15 |
| 662 | 50c. Male and female blue-headed wrasse and princess parrotfish | 45 | 25 |
| 663 | $1 French grunt and French angelfish | 70 | 70 |
| **MS**664 | 136×110 mm. Nos. 660/3 | 2·50 | 3·75 |

**149** Bathsheba Railway Station

**1981.** Early Transport. Multicoloured.

| | | | |
|---|---|---|---|
| 665 | 12c. Type **149** | 30 | 10 |
| 666 | 28c. Cab stand at The Green | 20 | 15 |
| 667 | 45c. Animal-drawn tram | 30 | 30 |
| 668 | 70c. Horse-drawn bus | 45 | 60 |
| 669 | $1 Railway Station, Fairchild Street | 70 | 95 |

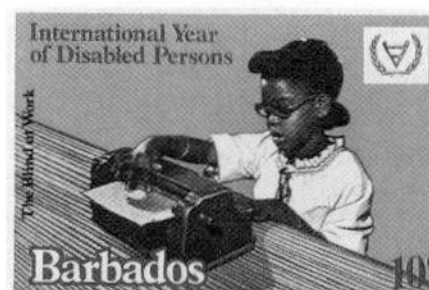

**150** The Blind at Work

**1981.** Int Year for Disabled Persons. Mult.

| | | | |
|---|---|---|---|
| 670 | 10c. Type **150** | 20 | 10 |
| 671 | 25c. Sign Language (vert) | 25 | 15 |
| 672 | 45c. "Be alert to the white cane" (vert) | 40 | 25 |
| 673 | $2.50 Children at play | 80 | 3·00 |

**151** Prince Charles dressed for Polo

**1981.** Royal Wedding. Multicoloured.

| | | | |
|---|---|---|---|
| 674 | 28c. Wedding bouquet from Barbados | 15 | 10 |
| 675 | 50c. Type **151** | 20 | 15 |
| 676 | $2.50 Prince Charles and Lady Diana Spencer | 55 | 1·25 |

**152** Landship Manoeuvre

**1981.** Carifesta (Caribbean Festival of Arts), Barbados. Multicoloured.

| | | | |
|---|---|---|---|
| 677 | 15c. Type **152** | 15 | 15 |
| 678 | 20c. Yoruba dancers | 15 | 15 |
| 679 | 40c. Tuk band | 20 | 25 |
| 680 | 55c. Sculpture by Frank Collymore | 25 | 35 |
| 681 | $1 Harbour scene | 50 | 75 |

**1981.** Nos. 630, 632 and 634 surch.

| | | | |
|---|---|---|---|
| 682 | 15c. on 28c. Carib grackle | 30 | 15 |
| 683 | 40c. on 45c. Zenaida dove | 30 | 35 |
| 684 | 60c. on 70c. Bananaquit | 30 | 45 |

**154** Satellite View of Hurricane

**1981.** Hurricane Season.

| | | | | |
|---|---|---|---|---|
| 685 | **154** | 35c. black and blue | 35 | 20 |
| 686 | - | 50c. multicoloured | 45 | 35 |
| 687 | - | 60c. multicoloured | 70 | 50 |
| 688 | - | $1 multicoloured | 85 | 90 |

DESIGNS: 50c. Hurricane "Gladys" from "Apollo 7"; 60c. Police Department on hurricane watch; $1 McDonnell Banshee "hurricane chaser" aircraft.

**155** Twin Falls

**1981.** Harrison's Cave. Multicoloured.

| | | | |
|---|---|---|---|
| 689 | 10c. Type **155** | 10 | 10 |
| 690 | 20c. Stream in Rotunda Room | 20 | 15 |
| 691 | 55c. Formations in Rotunda Room | 25 | 30 |
| 692 | $2.50 Cascade Pool | 60 | 2·25 |

**156** Black Belly Ram

**1982.** Black Belly Sheep. Multicoloured.

| | | | |
|---|---|---|---|
| 693 | 40c. Type **156** | 15 | 20 |
| 694 | 50c. Black belly ewe | 15 | 20 |
| 695 | 60c. Ewe with lambs | 20 | 45 |
| 696 | $1 Ram and ewe, with map of Barbados | 35 | 1·50 |

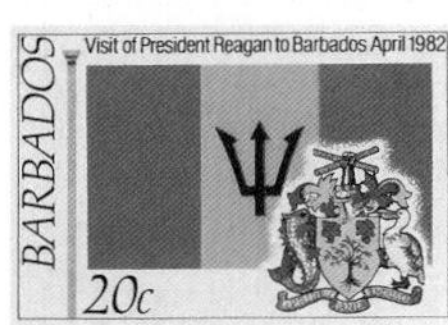


**157** Barbados Coat of Arms and Flag

**1982.** President Reagan's Visit. Multicoloured.

| | | | |
|---|---|---|---|
| 697 | 20c. Type **157** | 40 | 1·25 |
| 698 | 20c. U.S.A. coat of arms and flag | 40 | 1·25 |
| 699 | 55c. Type **157** | 50 | 1·50 |
| 700 | 55c. As No. 698 | 50 | 1·50 |

**158** Lighter

**1982.** Early Marine Transport. Multicoloured.

| | | | |
|---|---|---|---|
| 701 | 20c. Type **158** | 20 | 15 |
| 702 | 35c. Rowing boat | 35 | 25 |
| 703 | 55c. Speightstown schooner | 50 | 40 |
| 704 | $2.50 Inter-colonial schooner | 1·75 | 2·50 |

**159** Bride and Earl Spencer Proceeding up the Aisle

**1982.** 21st Birthday of Princess of Wales. Mult.

| | | | |
|---|---|---|---|
| 705 | 20c. Barbados coat of arms | 20 | 15 |
| 706 | 60c. Princess at Llanelwedd, October, 1981 | 45 | 50 |
| 707 | $1.20 Type **159** | 75 | 1·10 |
| 708 | $2.50 Formal portrait | 1·25 | 1·90 |

**160** "To Help other People"

**1982.** 75th Anniv of Boy Scout Movement. Mult.

| | | | |
|---|---|---|---|
| 709 | 15c. Type **160** | 50 | 10 |
| 710 | 40c. "I Promise to do my Best" (horiz) | 80 | 30 |
| 711 | 55c. "To do my Duty to God, the Queen and my Country" (horiz) | 90 | 65 |
| 712 | $1 National and Troop flags | 1·40 | 1·75 |
| **MS**713 | 119×93 mm. $1.50, The Scout Law | 3·50 | 3·00 |

**161** Arms of George Washington

**1982.** 250th Birth Anniv of George Washington. Multicoloured.

| | | | |
|---|---|---|---|
| 714 | 10c. Type **161** | 10 | 10 |
| 715 | 55c. Washington House, Barbados | 25 | 30 |
| 716 | 60c. Washington with troops | 25 | 35 |
| 717 | $2.50 Washington taking Oath | 75 | 1·60 |

**162** "Agraulis vanillae"

**1983.** Butterflies. Multicoloured.

| | | | |
|---|---|---|---|
| 718 | 20c. Type **162** | 1·00 | 40 |
| 719 | 40c. "Danaus plexippus" | 1·50 | 40 |
| 720 | 55c. "Hypolimnas misippus" | 1·50 | 45 |
| 721 | $2.50 "Hemiargus hanno" | 3·25 | 3·75 |

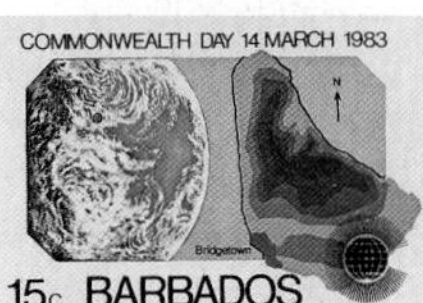


**163** Map of Barbados and Satellite View

**1983.** Commonwealth Day. Multicoloured.

| | | | |
|---|---|---|---|
| 722 | 15c. Type **163** | 20 | 10 |
| 723 | 40c. Tourist beach | 25 | 20 |
| 724 | 60c. Sugar cane harvesting | 35 | 40 |
| 725 | $1 Cricket match | 1·25 | 1·10 |

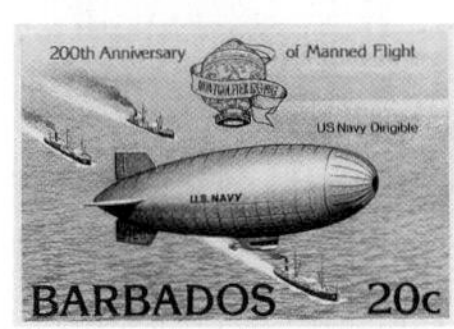


**164** U.S. Navy "M" Class Airship M-20

**1983.** Bicentenary of Manned Flight.

| | | | |
|---|---|---|---|
| 726 | 20c. Type **164** | 35 | 15 |
| 727 | 40c. Douglas DC-3 | 40 | 40 |
| 728 | 55c. Vickers Viscount 837 | 40 | 50 |
| 729 | $1 Lockheed TriStar 500 | 65 | 2·50 |

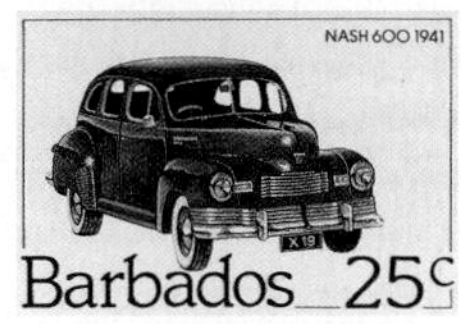


**165** Nash 600, 1934 (inscr "1941")

**1983.** Classic Cars. Multicoloured.

| | | | |
|---|---|---|---|
| 730 | 25c. Type **165** | 35 | 20 |
| 731 | 45c. Dodge D-8 coupe, 1938 | 40 | 30 |
| 732 | 75c. Ford Model A tourer, 1930 | 60 | 1·50 |
| 733 | $2.50 Dodge Four tourer, 1918 | 1·25 | 4·50 |

**166** Game in Progress

**1983.** Table Tennis World Cup Competition. Multicoloured.

| | | | |
|---|---|---|---|
| 734 | 20c. Type **166** | 25 | 20 |
| 735 | 65c. Map of Barbados | 50 | 55 |
| 736 | $1 World Table Tennis Cup | 75 | 1·00 |

**167** Angel playing Lute (detail "The Virgin and Child") (Masaccio)

**1983.** Christmas. 50th Anniv of Barbados Museum.

| | | | | |
|---|---|---|---|---|
| 737 | **167** | 10c. multicoloured | 30 | 10 |
| 738 | - | 25c. multicoloured | 60 | 20 |
| 739 | - | 45c. multicoloured | 90 | 40 |
| 740 | - | 75c. black and gold | 1·40 | 1·60 |
| 741 | - | $2.50 multicoloured | 4·50 | 6·00 |
| **MS**742 | | 59×98 mm. $2 multicoloured | 1·75 | 2·00 |

DESIGNS—HORIZ: 45c. "The Barbados Museum" (Richard Day); 75c. "St. Ann's Garrison" (W. S. Hedges); $2.50, Needham's Point, Carlisle Bay. VERT: 25c., $2 Different details from "The Virgin and Child" (Masaccio).

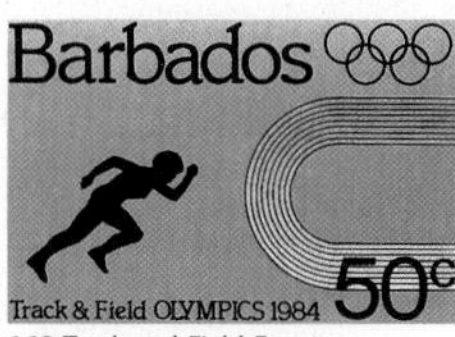


**168** Track and Field Events

**1984.** Olympic Games, Los Angeles.

| | | | | |
|---|---|---|---|---|
| 745 | **168** | 50c. green, black and brown | 60 | 45 |
| 746 | - | 65c. orange, blk & brn | 80 | 60 |
| 747 | - | 75c. blue, black & dp bl | 1·00 | 85 |
| 748 | - | $1 brown, black and yellow | 2·50 | 2·00 |
| **MS**749 | | 115×97 mm. Nos. 745/8 | 8·00 | 9·00 |

DESIGNS: 65c. Shooting; 75c. Sailing; $1 Cycling.

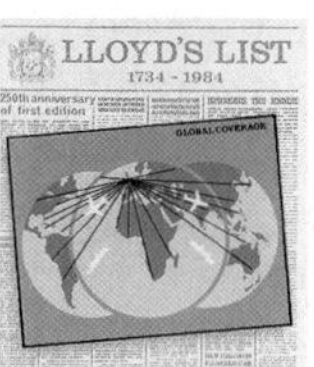


**169** Global Coverage

**1984.** 250th Anniv of "Lloyd's List" (newspaper). Multicoloured.

| | | | |
|---|---|---|---|
| 750 | 45c. Type **169** | 80 | 40 |
| 751 | 50c. Bridgetown harbour | 90 | 50 |
| 752 | 75c. "Philosopher" (full-rigged ship), 1857 | 1·40 | 1·25 |
| 753 | $1 "Sea Princess" (liner), 1984 | 1·40 | 1·60 |

**170** U.P.U. 1943 3d. Stamp and Logo

**1984.** Universal Postal Union Congress, Hamburg. Sheet 90×75 mm.

| | | | | |
|---|---|---|---|---|
| **MS**754 | **170** | $2 multicoloured | 2·50 | 2·50 |

**171** Local Junior Match

**1984.** 60th Anniv of International Chess Federation. Multicoloured.

| | | | |
|---|---|---|---|
| 755 | 25c. Type **171** | 1·50 | 30 |
| 756 | 45c. Staunton and 19th-century knights | 1·75 | 50 |
| 757 | 65c. Staunton queen and 18th-century queen from Macao | 2·00 | 1·75 |
| 758 | $2 Staunton and 17th-century rooks | 3·75 | 6·50 |

**172** Poinsettia

**1984.** Christmas. Flowers. Multicoloured.

| | | | |
|---|---|---|---|
| 759 | 50c. Type **172** | 1·75 | 90 |
| 760 | 65c. Snow-on-the-Mountain | 2·00 | 1·75 |
| 761 | 75c. Christmas Candle | 2·25 | 3·25 |
| 762 | $1 Christmas Hope | 2·50 | 3·75 |

**173** Pink-tipped Anemone

**1985.** Marine Life. Multicoloured.

| | | | |
|---|---|---|---|
| 794B | 1c. Bristle worm | 30 | 2·50 |
| 795B | 2c. Spotted trunkfish | 30 | 2·50 |
| 796A | 5c. Coney | 1·00 | 1·50 |
| 797B | 10c. Type **173** | 30 | 30 |
| 798B | 20c. Christmas tree worm | 30 | 40 |
| 799B | 25c. Hermit crab | 40 | 40 |
| 800A | 35c. Animal flower | 1·50 | 1·50 |
| 801B | 40c. Vase sponge | 50 | 50 |
| 802B | 45c. Spotted moray | 60 | 50 |
| 803B | 50c. Ghost crab | 60 | 60 |
| 804B | 65c. Flamingo tongue snail | 65 | 70 |
| 805B | 75c. Sergeant major | 70 | 75 |
| 806B | $1 Caribbean warty anemone | 85 | 85 |
| 807B | $2.50 Green turtle | 1·25 | 6·00 |
| 808B | $5 Rock beauty (fish) | 1·50 | 8·00 |
| 809B | $10 Elkhorn coral | 2·00 | 8·00 |

**174** The Queen Mother at Docks

**1985.** Life and Times of Queen Elizabeth the Queen Mother. Multicoloured.

| | | | |
|---|---|---|---|
| 779 | 25c. In the White Drawing Room, Buckingham Palace, 1930s | 50 | 20 |
| 780 | 65c. With Lady Diana Spencer at Trooping the Colour, 1981 | 2·50 | 1·00 |
| 781 | 75c. Type **174** | 80 | 1·00 |
| 782 | $1 With Prince Henry at his christening (from photo by Lord Snowdon) | 85 | 1·25 |
| **MS**783 | 91×73 mm. $2 In Land Rover Series I opening Syon House Garden Centre | 2·50 | 1·50 |

**175** Peregrine Falcon

**1985.** Birth Bicentenary of John J. Audubon (ornithologist). Designs showing original paintings. Multicoloured.

| | | | |
|---|---|---|---|
| 784 | 45c. Type **175** | 2·25 | 80 |
| 785 | 65c. Prairie warbler (vert) | 2·50 | 2·25 |
| 786 | 75c. Great blue heron (vert) | 2·75 | 3·00 |
| 787 | $1 Yellow warbler (vert) | 3·00 | 4·00 |

**176** Intelsat Satellite orbiting Earth

**1985.** 20th Anniv of Intelsat Satellite System.

| | | | | |
|---|---|---|---|---|
| 788 | **176** | 75c. multicoloured | 1·00 | 70 |

**177** Traffic Policeman

**1985.** 150th Anniv of Royal Barbados Police. Multicoloured.

| | | | |
|---|---|---|---|
| 789 | 25c. Type **177** | 80 | 20 |
| 790 | 50c. Police band on bandstand | 1·40 | 80 |
| 791 | 65c. Dog handler | 1·60 | 1·40 |
| 792 | $1 Mounted policeman in ceremonial uniform | 1·75 | 2·00 |
| **MS**793 | 85×60 mm. $2 Police Band on parade (horiz). | 1·50 | 2·75 |

**1986.** 60th Birthday of Queen Elizabeth II. As T **110** of Ascension. Multicoloured.

| | | | |
|---|---|---|---|
| 810 | 25c. Princess Elizabeth aged two, 1928 | 40 | 20 |
| 811 | 50c. At University College of West Indies, Jamaica, 1953 | 50 | 40 |
| 812 | 65c. With Duke of Edinburgh, Barbados, 1985 | 70 | 50 |
| 813 | 75c. At banquet in Sao Paulo, Brazil, 1968 | 70 | 60 |
| 814 | $2 At Crown Agents Head Office, London, 1983 | 1·10 | 1·50 |

**178** Canadair DC-4M2 North Star of Trans-Canada Airlines

**1986.** "Expo '86" World Fair, Vancouver. Mult.

| | | | |
|---|---|---|---|
| 815 | 50c. Type **178** | 75 | 50 |
| 816 | $2.50 "Lady Nelson" (cargo liner) | 2·00 | 2·50 |

**1986.** "Ameripex '86" International Stamp Exhibition, Chicago. As T **164** of Bahamas, showing Barbados stamps. Multicoloured.

| | | | |
|---|---|---|---|
| 817 | 45c. 1976 Bicentenary of American Revolution 25c. | 70 | 35 |
| 818 | 50c. 1976 Bicentenary of American Revolution 50c. | 80 | 55 |
| 819 | 65c. 1981 Hurricane Season $1 | 90 | 1·00 |
| 820 | $1 1982 Visit of President Reagan 55c. | 1·00 | 1·75 |
| **MS**821 | 90×80 mm. $2 Statue of Liberty and liner "Queen Elizabeth 2" | 10·00 | 12·00 |

No. **MS**821 also commemorates the Centenary of the Statue of Liberty.

**1986.** Royal Wedding. As T **112** of Ascension. Multicoloured.

| | | | |
|---|---|---|---|
| 822 | 45c. Prince Andrew and Miss Sarah Ferguson | 75 | 35 |
| 823 | $1 Prince Andrew in midshipman's uniform | 1·25 | 75 |

**179** Transporting Electricity Poles, 1923

**180** "Alpinia purpurata" and Church Window

**1986.** 75th Anniv of Electricity in Barbados. Multicoloured.

| | | | |
|---|---|---|---|
| 824 | 10c. Type **179** | 15 | 10 |
| 825 | 25c. Heathman Ladder, 1935 (vert) | 25 | 20 |
| 826 | 65c. Transport fleet, 1941 | 60 | 60 |
| 827 | $2 Bucket truck, 1986 (vert) | 1·60 | 2·00 |

**180** "Alpinia purpurata" and Church Window

**1986.** Christmas. Multicoloured.

| | | | |
|---|---|---|---|
| 828 | 25c. Type **180** | 20 | 20 |
| 829 | 50c. "Anthurium andraeanum" | 45 | 45 |
| 830 | 75c. "Heliconia rostrata" | 75 | 80 |
| 831 | $2 "Heliconia × psittacorum" | 1·50 | 4·25 |

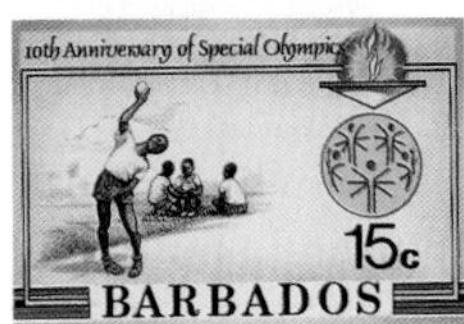

**181** Shot Putting

**1987.** 10th Anniv of Special Olympics. Multicoloured.

| | | | |
|---|---|---|---|
| 832 | 15c. Type **181** | 25 | 15 |
| 833 | 45c. Wheelchair racing | 45 | 30 |
| 834 | 65c. Long jumping | 60 | 65 |
| 835 | $2 Logo and slogan | 1·25 | 2·50 |

**182** Barn Swallow

**1987.** "Capex '87" International Stamp Exhibition, Toronto. Birds. Multicoloured.

| | | | |
|---|---|---|---|
| 836 | 25c. Type **182** | 2·00 | 50 |
| 837 | 50c. Yellow warbler | 2·25 | 1·75 |
| 838 | 65c. Audubon's shearwater | 2·25 | 1·75 |
| 839 | 75c. Black-whiskered vireo | 2·50 | 3·25 |
| 840 | $1 Scarlet tanager | 2·75 | 4·00 |

**183** Sea Scout saluting

**1987.** 75th Anniv of Scouting in Barbados. Multicoloured.

| | | | |
|---|---|---|---|
| 841 | 10c. Type **183** | 20 | 10 |
| 842 | 25c. Scout jamboree | 30 | 20 |
| 843 | 65c. Scout badges | 65 | 45 |
| 844 | $2 Scout band | 1·60 | 1·75 |

**184** Bridgetown Synagogue

**1987.** Restoration of Bridgetown Synagogue. Multicoloured.

| | | | |
|---|---|---|---|
| 845 | 50c. Type **184** | 2·00 | 1·75 |
| 846 | 65c. Interior of Synagogue | 2·25 | 2·25 |
| 847 | 75c. Ten Commandments (vert) | 2·50 | 2·50 |
| 848 | $1 Marble laver (vert) | 2·75 | 3·75 |

**185** Arms and Colonial Seal

**1987.** 21st Anniv of Independence. Mult.

| | | | |
|---|---|---|---|
| 849 | 25c. Type **185** | 50 | 20 |
| 850 | 45c. Flags of Barbados and Great Britain | 1·25 | 35 |
| 851 | 65c. Silver dollar and one penny coins | 1·25 | 55 |
| 852 | $2 Colours of Barbados Regiment | 2·50 | 2·75 |
| **MS**853 | 94×56 mm. $1.50, Prime Minister E. W. Barrow (vert) | 1·50 | 1·75 |

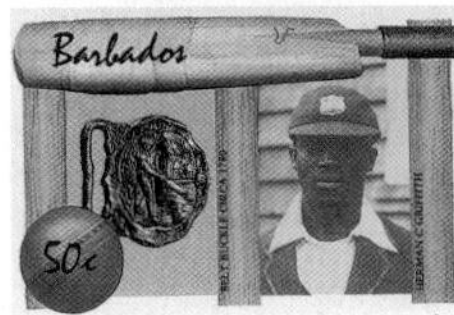

**186** Herman C. Griffith

**1988.** West Indian Cricket. Each showing portrait, cricket equipment and early belt buckle. Multicoloured.

| | | | |
|---|---|---|---|
| 854 | 15c. E. A. (Manny) Martindale | 2·50 | 75 |
| 855 | 45c. George Challenor | 3·25 | 75 |
| 856 | 50c. Type **186** | 3·50 | 2·25 |
| 857 | 75c. Harold Austin | 3·75 | 3·50 |
| 858 | $2 Frank Worrell | 4·50 | 11·00 |

**187** "Kentropyx borckianus"

**1988.** Lizards of Barbados. Multicoloured.

| | | | |
|---|---|---|---|
| 859 | 10c. Type **187** | 1·75 | 50 |
| 860 | 50c. "Hemidactylus mabouia" | 3·00 | 70 |
| 861 | 65c. "Anolis extremus" | 3·00 | 1·25 |
| 862 | $2 "Gymnophthalmus underwoodii" | 6·00 | 10·00 |

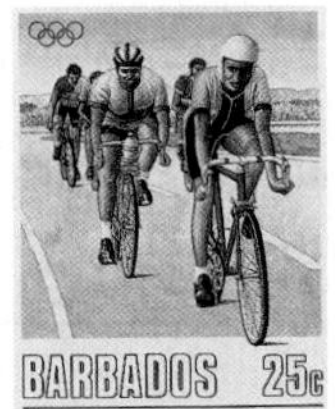

**188** Cycling

**1988.** Olympic Games, Seoul. Multicoloured.

| | | | |
|---|---|---|---|
| 863 | 25c. Type **188** | 1·75 | 40 |
| 864 | 45c. Athletics | 70 | 30 |
| 865 | 75c. Relay swimming | 85 | 65 |
| 866 | $2 Yachting | 2·00 | 2·75 |
| **MS**867 | 114×63 mm. Nos. 863/6 | 4·25 | 3·00 |

**1988.** 300th Anniv of Lloyd's of London. As T **123** of Ascension.

| | | | |
|---|---|---|---|
| 868 | 40c. multicoloured | 55 | 30 |
| 869 | 50c. multicoloured | 65 | 35 |
| 870 | 65c. multicoloured | 1·50 | 45 |
| 871 | $2 blue and red | 6·50 | 3·00 |

DESIGNS—VERT: 40c. Royal Exchange, 1774; $2 Sinking of "Titanic", 1912. HORIZ: 50c. Early sugar mill; 65c. "Author" (container ship).

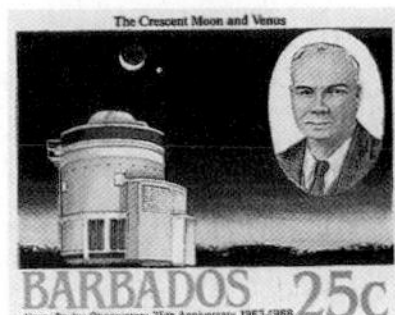

**189** Harry Bayley and Observatory

**1988.** 25th Anniv of Harry Bayley Observatory. Multicoloured.

| | | | |
|---|---|---|---|
| 872 | 25c. Type **189** | 60 | 20 |
| 873 | 65c. Observatory with North Star and Southern Cross constellations | 1·40 | 75 |
| 874 | 75c. Andromeda galaxy | 1·60 | 90 |
| 875 | $2 Orion constellation | 3·00 | 6·00 |

**190** L.I.A.T. Hawker Siddeley H.S.748

**1989.** 50th Anniv of Commercial Aviation in Barbados. Multicoloured.

| | | | |
|---|---|---|---|
| 876 | 25c. Type **190** | 2·50 | 40 |
| 877 | 65c. Pan Am Douglas DC-8-62 | 3·25 | 1·25 |
| 878 | 75c. British Airways Concorde at Grantley Adams Airport | 3·75 | 1·75 |
| 879 | $2 Caribbean Air Cargo Boeing 707-351C | 6·00 | 9·50 |

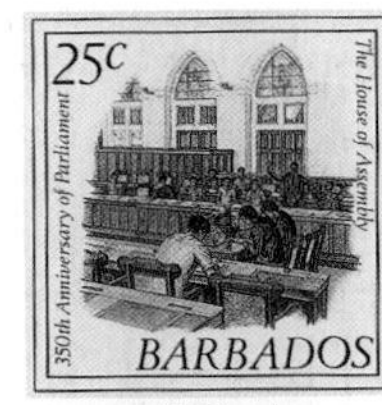

**191** Assembly Chamber

**1989.** 350th Anniv of Parliament.

| | | | | |
|---|---|---|---|---|
| 880 | **191** | 25c. multicoloured | 40 | 20 |
| 881 | - | 50c. multicoloured | 60 | 35 |
| 882 | - | 75c. blue and black | 1·00 | 50 |
| 883 | - | $2.50 multicoloured | 2·50 | 2·25 |

DESIGNS: 50c. The Speaker; 75c. Parliament Buildings, c. 1882; $2.50, Queen Elizabeth II and Prince Philip in Parliament.

**192** Brown Hare

**1989.** Wildlife Preservation. Multicoloured.

| | | | |
|---|---|---|---|
| 884 | 10c. Type **192** | 80 | 30 |
| 885 | 50c. Red-footed tortoise (horiz) | 2·00 | 70 |
| 886 | 65c. Savanna ("Green") monkey | 2·25 | 1·25 |
| 887 | $2 "Bufo marinus" (toad) (horiz) | 4·00 | 8·00 |
| **MS**888 | 87×97 mm. $1 Small Indian mongoose | 1·25 | 1·50 |

**1989.** 35th Commonwealth Parliamentary Conference. Square design as T **191**. Mult.

| | | | |
|---|---|---|---|
| **MS**889 | 108×69 mm. $1 Barbados Mace | 1·00 | 1·50 |

**193** Bread 'n Cheese

**1989.** Wild Plants. Multicoloured.

| | | | |
|---|---|---|---|
| 921 | 2c. Type **193** | 50 | 1·75 |
| 891 | 5c. Scarlet cordia | 50 | 1·00 |
| 892 | 10c. Columnar cactus | 50 | 30 |
| 893 | 20c. Spiderlily | 50 | 30 |
| 925 | 25c. Rock balsam | 65 | 20 |
| 895 | 30c. Hollyhock | 70 | 25 |
| 895a | 35c. Red sage | 1·25 | 1·00 |
| 927 | 45c. Yellow shak-shak | 75 | 35 |
| 928 | 50c. Whitewood | 80 | 40 |
| 898 | 55c. Bluebell | 1·00 | 55 |
| 930 | 65c. Prickly sage | 90 | 55 |
| 900 | 70c. Seaside samphire | 1·25 | 1·25 |
| 901 | 80c. Flat-hand dildo | 1·75 | 1·40 |
| 901a | 90c. Herringbone | 1·75 | 2·25 |
| 902 | $1.10 Lent tree | 1·50 | 2·25 |
| 934 | $2.50 Rodwood | 1·90 | 4·00 |
| 935 | $5 Cowitch | 3·75 | 7·00 |
| 936 | $10 Maypole | 7·00 | 10·00 |

**194** Water Skiing

**1989.** "World Stamp Expo '89" International Stamp Exn., Washington. Watersports. Mult.

| | | | |
|---|---|---|---|
| 906 | 25c. Type **194** | 1·50 | 40 |
| 907 | 50c. Yachting | 2·50 | 1·00 |
| 908 | 65c. Scuba diving | 2·50 | 1·75 |
| 909 | $2.50 Surfing | 6·50 | 11·00 |

**195** Barbados 1852 1d. Stamp

**1990.** 150th Anniv of the Penny Black and "Stamp World London '90" International Stamp Exn.

| | | | | |
|---|---|---|---|---|
| 910 | **195** | 25c. green, black and yellow | 1·50 | 40 |
| 911 | - | 50c. multicoloured | 2·00 | 1·00 |
| 912 | - | 65c. multicoloured | 2·00 | 1·50 |
| 913 | - | $2.50 multicoloured | 5·00 | 9·00 |
| **MS**914 | | 90×86 mm. 50c. multicoloured; 50c. multicoloured | 1·75 | 2·75 |

DESIGNS: 50c. 1882 1d. Queen Victoria stamp; 65c. 1899 2d. stamp; $2.50, 1912 3d. stamp; miniature sheet, 50c. Great Britain Penny Black, 50c. Barbados "1906" Nelson Centenary 1s.

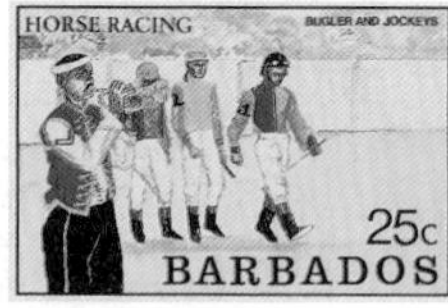

**196** Bugler and Jockeys

**1990.** Horse Racing. Multicoloured.

| | | | |
|---|---|---|---|
| 915 | 25c. Type **196** | 60 | 30 |
| 916 | 45c. Horse and jockey in parade ring | 85 | 50 |
| 917 | 75c. At the finish | 1·25 | 85 |
| 918 | $2 Leading in the winner (vert) | 2·75 | 6·00 |

**1990.** 90th Birthday of Queen Elizabeth the Queen Mother. As T **134** of Ascension.

| | | | |
|---|---|---|---|
| 919 | 75c. multicoloured | 75 | 60 |
| 920 | $2.50 black and green | 2·25 | 3·25 |

DESIGNS—21×36 mm: 75c. Lady Elizabeth Bowes-Lyon, April 1923 (from painting by John Lander). 29×37 mm: $2.50, Lady Elizabeth Bowes-Lyon on her engagement, January 1923.

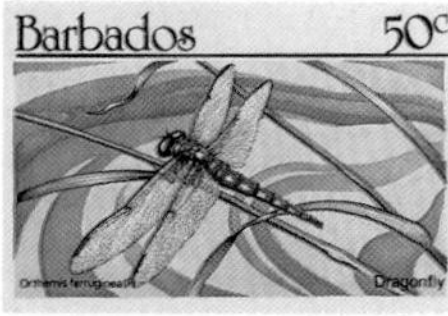

**197** "Orthemis ferruginea" (dragonfly)

**1990.** Insects. Multicoloured.

| | | | |
|---|---|---|---|
| 937 | 50c. Type **197** | 1·50 | 80 |
| 938 | 65c. "Ligyrus tumulosus" (beetle) | 1·75 | 1·00 |
| 939 | 75c. "Neoconocephalus sp." (grasshopper) | 2·00 | 1·25 |
| 940 | $2 "Bostra maxwelli" (stick-insect) | 3·50 | 5·50 |

**1990.** Visit of the Princess Royal. Nos. 925, 901 and 903 optd **VISIT OF HRH THE PRINCESS ROYAL OCTOBER 1990.**

| | | | |
|---|---|---|---|
| 941 | 25c. Rock balsam | 2·25 | 50 |
| 942 | 80c. Flat-hand dildo | 3·50 | 2·00 |
| 943 | $2.50 Rodwood | 8·50 | 12·00 |

**199** Star

**1990.** Christmas. Multicoloured.

| | | | |
|---|---|---|---|
| 944 | 20c. Type **199** | 65 | 20 |
| 945 | 50c. Figures from crib | 1·00 | 50 |
| 946 | $1 Stained glass window | 2·00 | 1·50 |
| 947 | $2 Angel (statue) | 3·00 | 5·50 |

**200** Adult Male Yellow Warbler

**1991.** Endangered Species. Yellow Warbler. Multicoloured.

| | | | |
|---|---|---|---|
| 948 | 10c. Type **200** | 1·40 | 80 |
| 949 | 20c. Pair feeding chicks in nest | 2·00 | 80 |
| 950 | 45c. Female feeding chicks in nest | 2·50 | 80 |
| 951 | $1 Male with fledgeling | 4·00 | 5·25 |

**201** Sorting Daily Catch

**1991.** Fishing in Barbados. Multicoloured.

| | | | |
|---|---|---|---|
| 952 | 5c. Type **201** | 50 | 50 |
| 953 | 50c. Line fishing (horiz) | 1·75 | 90 |
| 954 | 75c. Fish cleaning (horiz) | 2·25 | 1·25 |
| 955 | $2.50 Game fishing | 4·50 | 6·50 |

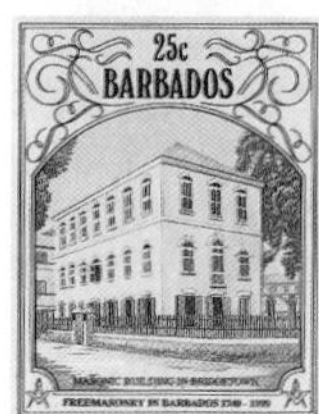

**202** Masonic Building, Bridgetown

**1991.** 250th Anniv of Freemasonry in Barbados (1990).

| | | | | |
|---|---|---|---|---|
| 956 | **202** | 25c. multicoloured | 1·75 | 50 |
| 957 | - | 65c. multicoloured | 2·50 | 1·25 |
| 958 | - | 75c. black, yellow & brn | 2·50 | 1·25 |
| 959 | - | $2.50 multicoloured | 5·00 | 7·00 |

DESIGNS: 65c. Compass and square (masonic symbols); 75c. Royal Arch jewel; $2.50, Ceremonial apron, columns and badge.

**203** "Battus polydamus"

**1991.** "Phila Nippon '91" International Stamp Exhibition, Tokyo. Butterflies. Multicoloured.

| | | | |
|---|---|---|---|
| 960 | 20c. Type **203** | 1·00 | 40 |
| 961 | 50c. "Urbanus proteus" (vert) | 1·50 | 65 |
| 962 | 65c. "Phoebis sennae" | 1·60 | 95 |
| 963 | $2.50 "Junonia evarete" (vert) | 4·00 | 6·00 |
| **MS**964 | 87×86 mm. $4 "Vanessa cardui" | 9·00 | 10·00 |

**204** School Class

**1991.** 25th Anniv of Independence. Multicoloured.

| | | | |
|---|---|---|---|
| 965 | 10c. Type **204** | 30 | 20 |
| 966 | 25c. Barbados Workers' Union Labour College | 45 | 30 |
| 967 | 65c. Building a house | 1·00 | 90 |
| 968 | 75c. Sugar cane harvesting | 1·00 | 1·00 |
| 969 | $1 Health clinic | 1·25 | 2·00 |
| **MS**970 | 123×97 mm. $2.50, Gordon Greenidge and Desmond Haynes (cricketers) (vert) | 12·00 | 12·00 |

**205** Jesus carrying Cross

**1992.** Easter. Multicoloured.

| | | | |
|---|---|---|---|
| 971 | 35c. Type **205** | 80 | 30 |
| 972 | 70c. Crucifixion | 1·40 | 90 |
| 973 | 90c. Descent from the Cross | 1·50 | 1·25 |
| 974 | $3 Risen Christ | 4·00 | 6·50 |

**206** Cannon Ball

**1992.** Conservation. Flowering Trees. Multicoloured.

| | | | |
|---|---|---|---|
| 975 | 10c. Type **206** | 60 | 40 |
| 976 | 30c. Golden shower tree | 1·00 | 50 |
| 977 | 80c. Frangipani | 2·25 | 2·50 |
| 978 | $1.10 Flamboyant | 2·75 | 3·00 |

**207** "Epidendrum" "Costa Rica"

**1992.** Orchids. Multicoloured.

| | | | |
|---|---|---|---|
| 979 | 55c. Type **207** | 85 | 65 |
| 980 | 65c. "Cattleya guttaca" | 1·00 | 1·00 |
| 981 | 70c. "Laeliacattleya" "Splashing Around" | 1·00 | 1·00 |
| 982 | $1.40 "Phalaenopsis" "Kathy Saegert" | 1·60 | 3·00 |

**208** Mini Moke and Gun Hill Signal Station, St. George

**1992.** Transport and Tourism. Multicoloured.

| | | | |
|---|---|---|---|
| 983 | 5c. Type **208** | 65 | 60 |
| 984 | 35c. Tour bus and Bathsheba Beach, St. Joseph | 1·25 | 30 |
| 985 | 90c. B.W.I.A. McDonnell Douglas MD-83 over Grantley Adams Airport | 3·00 | 2·25 |
| 986 | $2 "Festivale" (liner) and Bridgetown harbour | 4·25 | 6·50 |

**209** Barbados Gooseberry

**1993.** Cacti and Succulents. Multicoloured.

| | | | |
|---|---|---|---|
| 987 | 10c. Type **209** | 55 | 30 |
| 988 | 35c. Night-blooming cereus | 1·25 | 35 |
| 989 | $1.40 Aloe | 3·00 | 3·50 |
| 990 | $2 Scrunchineel | 3·50 | 5·50 |

**1993.** 75th Anniv of Royal Air Force. As T **149** of Ascension. Multicoloured.

| | | | |
|---|---|---|---|
| 991 | 10c. Hawker Hunter F.6 | 75 | 40 |
| 992 | 30c. Handley Page Victor K2 | 1·25 | 40 |
| 993 | 70c. Hawker Typhoon IB | 1·75 | 1·50 |
| 994 | $3 Hawker Hurricane Mk I | 3·75 | 6·50 |
| **MS**995 | 110×77 mm. 50c. Armstrong Whitworth Siskin IIIA; 50c. Supermarine S6B; 50c. Supermarine Walrus Mk I; 50c. Hawker Hart | 2·50 | 2·75 |

**1993.** 14th World Orchid Conference, Glasgow. Nos. 979/82 optd **WORLD ORCHID CONFERENCE 1993.**

| | | | |
|---|---|---|---|
| 996 | 55c. Type **207** | 1·25 | 1·25 |
| 997 | 65c. "Cattleya guttaca" | 1·40 | 1·40 |
| 998 | 70c. "Laeliacattleya" "Splashing Around" | 1·40 | 1·40 |
| 999 | $1.40 "Phalaenopsis" "Kathy Saegert" | 2·25 | 3·50 |

**211** 18 pdr Culverin of 1625, Denmark Fort

**1993.** 17th-century English Cannon. Mult.

| | | | |
|---|---|---|---|
| 1000 | 5c. Type **211** | 30 | 50 |
| 1001 | 45c. 6 pdr of 1649–60, St. Ann's Fort | 85 | 50 |
| 1002 | $1 9 pdr demi-culverin of 1691, The Main Guard | 1·75 | 2·00 |
| 1003 | $2.50 32 pdr demi–cannon of 1693–94, Charles Fort | 2·75 | 4·50 |

**212** Sailor's Shell-work Valentine and Carved Amerindian

**1993.** 60th Anniv of Barbados Museum. Mult.

| | | | |
|---|---|---|---|
| 1004 | 10c. Type **212** | 50 | 50 |
| 1005 | 75c. "Barbados Mulatto Girl" (Agostino Brunias) | 1·50 | 1·50 |
| 1006 | 90c. Morris Cup and soldier of West India Regiment, 1858 | 2·25 | 2·50 |
| 1007 | $1.10 Ogilby's map of Barbados, 1679, and Ashanti gold weights | 2·75 | 3·25 |

**213** Plesiosaurus

**1993.** Prehistoric Aquatic Animals. Mult.

| | | | |
|---|---|---|---|
| 1008 | 90c. Type **213** | 2·25 | 3·00 |
| 1009 | 90c. Ichthyosaurus | 2·25 | 3·00 |
| 1010 | 90c. Elasmosaurus | 2·25 | 3·00 |
| 1011 | 90c. Mosasaurus | 2·25 | 3·00 |
| 1012 | 90c. Archelon | 2·25 | 3·00 |

Nos. 1008/12 were printed together, se-tenant, with the background forming a composite design.

**214** Cricket

**1994.** Sports and Tourism. Multicoloured.

| | | | |
|---|---|---|---|
| 1013 | 10c. Type **214** | 1·25 | 75 |
| 1014 | 35c. Rally driving | 1·40 | 50 |
| 1015 | 50c. Golf | 2·25 | 1·75 |
| 1016 | 70c. Long distance running | 1·75 | 2·50 |
| 1017 | $1.40 Swimming | 2·00 | 3·50 |

**215** Whimbrel

**1994.** "Hong Kong '94" Int Stamp Exhibition. Migratory Birds. Multicoloured.

| | | | |
|---|---|---|---|
| 1018 | 10c. Type **215** | 50 | 50 |
| 1019 | 35c. Pacific golden plover ("American Golden Plover") | 1·00 | 50 |
| 1020 | 70c. Ruddy turnstone | 1·50 | 1·50 |
| 1021 | $3 Louisiana heron ("Tricoloured Heron") | 3·50 | 5·50 |

**216** Bathsheba Beach and Logo

**1994.** 1st United Nations Conference of Small Island Developing States. Multicoloured.

| | | | |
|---|---|---|---|
| 1022 | 10c. Type **216** | 25 | 15 |
| 1023 | 65c. Pico Tenneriffe | 1·00 | 70 |
| 1024 | 90c. Ragged Point Lighthouse | 6·00 | 2·50 |
| 1025 | $2.50 Consett Bay | 3·00 | 5·50 |

**217** William Demas

**1994.** First Recipients of Order of the Caribbean Community. Multicoloured.

| | | | |
|---|---|---|---|
| 1026 | 70c. Type **217** | 70 | 1·00 |
| 1027 | 70c. Sir Shridath Ramphal | 70 | 1·00 |
| 1028 | 70c. Derek Walcott | 70 | 1·00 |

**218** Dutch Flyut, 1695

**1994.** Ships. Multicoloured.

| | | | |
|---|---|---|---|
| 1075 | 5c. Type **218** | 2·50 | 2·75 |
| 1076 | 10c. "Geestport" (freighter), 1994 | 75 | 50 |
| 1031B | 25c. H.M.S. "Victory" (ship of the line), 1805 | 75 | 40 |
| 1078 | 30c. "Royal Viking Queen" (liner), 1994 | 50 | 30 |
| 1079 | 35c. H.M.S. "Barbados" (frigate), 1945 | 50 | 30 |
| 1080 | 45c. "Faraday" (cable ship), 1924 | 50 | 35 |
| 1081 | 50c. U.S.C.G. "Hamilton" (coastguard cutter), 1974 | 6·50 | 75 |
| 1082 | 65c. H.M.C.S. "Saguenay" (destroyer), 1939 | 75 | 70 |
| 1083 | 70c. "Inanda" (cargo liner), 1928 | 75 | 70 |
| 1084 | 80c. H.M.S. "Rodney" (battleship), 1944 | 75 | 70 |
| 1085 | 90c. U.S.S. "John F. Kennedy" (aircraft carrier), 1982 | 75 | 70 |
| 1086 | $1.10 "William and John" (immigrant ship), 1627 | 1·00 | 1·00 |
| 1087 | $5 U.S.C.G. "Champlain" (coastguard cutter), 1931 | 4·00 | 5·00 |
| 1042B | $10 "Artist" (full-rigged ship), 1877 | 7·00 | 9·00 |

**219** Private, 2nd West India Regt, 1860

**1995.** Bicentenary of Formation of West India Regiment. Multicoloured.

| | | | |
|---|---|---|---|
| 1043 | 30c. Type **219** | 75 | 35 |
| 1044 | 50c. Light Company private, 4th West India Regt, 1795 | 90 | 55 |
| 1045 | 70c. Drum Major, 3rd West India Regt, 1860 | 1·25 | 1·40 |
| 1046 | $1 Privates in undress and working dress, 5th West India Regt, 1815 | 1·40 | 1·50 |
| 1047 | $1.10 Troops from 1st and 2nd West India Regts in Review Order, 1874 | 1·60 | 1·90 |

**1995.** 50th Anniv of End of Second World War. As T **161** of Ascension. Multicoloured.

| | | | |
|---|---|---|---|
| 1048 | 10c. Barbadian Bren gun crew | 60 | 50 |
| 1049 | 35c. Avro Type 683 Lancaster bomber | 90 | 50 |
| 1050 | 55c. Supermarine Spitfire | 1·25 | 75 |
| 1051 | $2.50 "Davisian" (cargo liner) | 3·00 | 4·75 |
| **MS**1052 | 75×85 mm. $2 Reverse of 1939–45 War Medal (vert) | 1·50 | 2·25 |

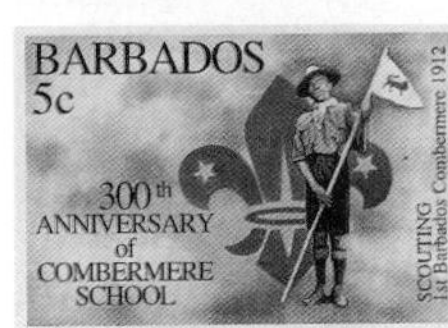


**220** Member of 1st Barbados Combermere Scout Troop, 1912

**1995.** 300th Anniv of Combermere School. Mult.

| | | | |
|---|---|---|---|
| 1053 | 5c. Type **220** | 25 | 40 |
| 1054 | 20c. Violin and sheet of music | 45 | 30 |
| 1055 | 35c. Sir Frank Worrell (cricketer) (vert) | 1·50 | 55 |
| 1056 | $3 Painting by pupil | 2·25 | 4·50 |
| **MS**1057 | 174×105 mm. Nos. 1053/6 and 90c. 1981 Carifesta 55c. stamp. | 4·00 | 4·75 |

**1995.** 50th Anniv of United Nations. As T **213** of Bahamas. Multicoloured.

| | | | |
|---|---|---|---|
| 1058 | 30c. Douglas C-124 Globemaster (transport), Korea, 1950–53 | 70 | 40 |
| 1059 | 45c. Royal Navy Sea King helicopter | 1·00 | 50 |
| 1060 | $1.40 Westland Wessex helicopter, Cyprus, 1964 | 1·50 | 2·00 |
| 1061 | $2 Sud Aviation SA 341 Gazelle helicopter, Cyprus, 1964 | 1·50 | 2·75 |

**221** Blue Beauty

**1995.** Water Lilies. Multicoloured.

| | | | |
|---|---|---|---|
| 1062 | 10c. Type **221** | 45 | 30 |
| 1063 | 65c. White water lily | 1·25 | 60 |
| 1064 | 70c. Sacred lotus | 1·25 | 60 |
| 1065 | $3 Water hyacinth | 3·00 | 5·00 |

**222** Magnifying Glass, Tweezers and 1896 Colony Seal ¼d. Stamp

**1996.** Centenary of Barbados Philatelic Society. Each showing magnifying glass, tweezers and stamp. Multicoloured.

| | | | |
|---|---|---|---|
| 1066 | 10c. Type **222** | 30 | 30 |
| 1067 | 55c. 1906 Tercentenary of Annexation 1d. | 65 | 45 |
| 1068 | $1.10 1920 Victory 1s. | 1·25 | 1·40 |

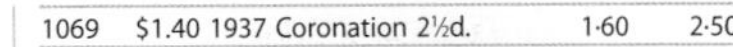

| | | | |
|---|---|---|---|
| 1069 | $1.40 1937 Coronation 2½d. | 1·60 | 2·50 |

**223** Football

**1996.** Cent of Modern Olympic Games. Mult.

| | | | |
|---|---|---|---|
| 1070 | 20c. Type **223** | 40 | 30 |
| 1071 | 30c. Relay running | 45 | 30 |
| 1072 | 55c. Basketball | 1·60 | 60 |
| 1073 | $3 Rhythmic gymnastics | 2·25 | 4·00 |
| **MS**1074 | 68×89 mm. $2.50, "The Discus Thrower" (Myron) | 2·00 | 3·25 |

**224** Douglas DC-10 of Canadian Airlines

**1996.** "CAPEX '96" International Stamp Exhibition, Toronto. Aircraft. Multicoloured.

| | | | |
|---|---|---|---|
| 1089 | 10c. Type **224** | 80 | 30 |
| 1090 | 90c. Boeing 767 of Air Canada | 1·75 | 80 |
| 1091 | $1 Airbus Industrie A320 of Air Canada | 1·75 | 1·25 |
| 1092 | $1.40 Boeing 767 of Canadian Airlines | 2·25 | 3·50 |

**225** Chattel House

**1996.** Chattel Houses.

| | | | | |
|---|---|---|---|---|
| 1093 | **225** | 35c. multicoloured | 40 | 25 |
| 1094 | - | 70c. multicoloured | 70 | 60 |
| 1095 | - | $1.10 multicoloured | 90 | 1·10 |
| 1096 | - | $2 multicoloured | 1·60 | 3·25 |

DESIGNS: 70c. to $2, Different houses.

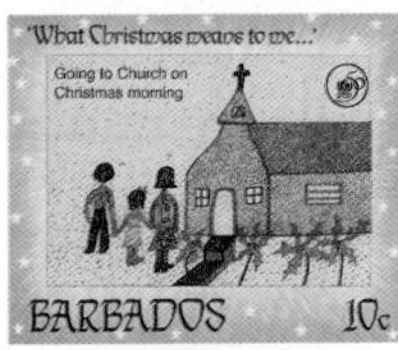


**226** "Going to Church"

**1996.** Christmas. 50th Anniv of U.N.I.C.E.F. Children's Paintings. Multicoloured.

| | | | |
|---|---|---|---|
| 1097 | 10c. Type **226** | 35 | 15 |
| 1098 | 30c. "The Tuk Band" | 55 | 25 |
| 1099 | 55c. "Singing carols" | 70 | 40 |
| 1100 | $2.50 "Decorated house" | 1·75 | 3·50 |

**227** Doberman Pinscher

**1997.** "HONG KONG '97" International Stamp Exhibition. Dogs. Multicoloured.

| | | | |
|---|---|---|---|
| 1101 | 10c. Type **227** | 1·00 | 50 |
| 1102 | 30c. German shepherd | 1·75 | 40 |
| 1103 | 90c. Japanese akita | 2·25 | 1·25 |
| 1104 | $3 Irish red setter | 4·75 | 7·00 |

**228** Barbados Flag and State Arms

**1997.** Visit of President Clinton of U.S.A. Multicoloured.

| | | | |
|---|---|---|---|
| 1105 | 35c. Type **228** | 1·00 | 75 |
| 1106 | 90c. American flag and arms | 1·50 | 1·25 |

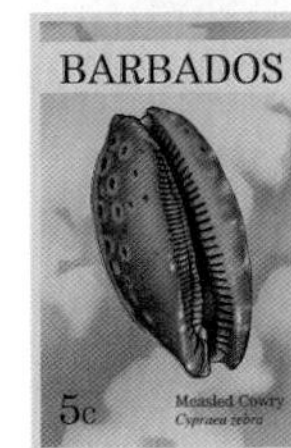


**229** Measled Cowrie

**1997.** Shells. Multicoloured.

| | | | |
|---|---|---|---|
| 1107 | 5c. Type **229** | 30 | 30 |
| 1108 | 35c. Trumpet triton | 75 | 25 |
| 1109 | 90c. Scotch bonnet | 1·40 | 90 |
| 1110 | $2 West Indian murex | 2·00 | 3·50 |
| **MS**1111 | 71×76 mm. $2.50, Underwater scene | 2·50 | 3·75 |

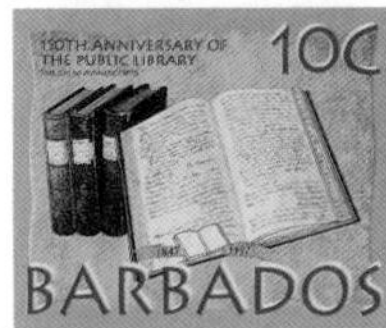


**230** Lucas Manuscripts

**1997.** 150th Anniv of the Public Library Service. Multicoloured.

| | | | |
|---|---|---|---|
| 1112 | 10c. Type **230** | 25 | 15 |
| 1113 | 30c. Librarian reading to children | 50 | 25 |
| 1114 | 70c. Mobile library van | 1·10 | 60 |
| 1115 | $3 Man using computer | 2·50 | 4·50 |

**231** Barbados Cherry

**1997.** Local Fruits. Multicoloured.

| | | | |
|---|---|---|---|
| 1116 | 35c. Type **231** | 45 | 30 |
| 1117 | 40c. Sugar apple | 50 | 30 |
| 1118 | $1.15 Soursop | 1·10 | 1·25 |
| 1119 | $1.70 Pawpaw | 1·75 | 2·75 |

**232** Arms of former British Caribbean Federation

**1998.** Birth Centenary of Sir Grantley Adams (statesman). Sheet 118×74 mm, containing T 232 and similar vert designs. Multicoloured.

| | | | |
|---|---|---|---|
| **MS**1120 | $1 Type **232**; $1 Sir Grantley Adams; $1 Flag of former British Caribbean Federation | 6·50 | 7·00 |

**1998.** Diana, Princess of Wales Commemoration. Sheet 145×70 mm, containing vert designs as T **177** of Ascension. Multicoloured.

| | | | |
|---|---|---|---|
| **MS**1121 | $1.15, Wearing blue hat, 1985; $1.15, Wearing red jacket, 1981; $1.15, Wearing tiara, 1987; $1.15, Wearing black jacket | 3·25 | 3·75 |

**233** Environment Regeneration

**1998.** 50th Anniv of Organization of American States. Multicoloured.

| | | | |
|---|---|---|---|
| 1122 | 15c. Type **233** | 20 | 15 |
| 1123 | $1 Stilt dancing | 70 | 80 |
| 1124 | $2.50 Judge and figure of Justice | 1·75 | 3·25 |

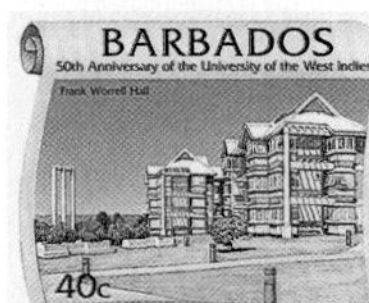

**234** Frank Worrell Hall

**1998.** 50th Anniv of University of West Indies. Multicoloured.

| | | | |
|---|---|---|---|
| 1125 | 40c. Type **234** | 50 | 30 |
| 1126 | $1.15 Student graduating | 1·25 | 1·25 |
| 1127 | $1.40 50th anniversary plaque | 1·50 | 2·00 |
| 1128 | $1.75 Quadrangle | 2·75 | 4·00 |

**235** Catamaran

**1998.** Tourism. Multicoloured.

| | | | |
|---|---|---|---|
| 1129 | 10c. Type **235** | 45 | 30 |
| 1130 | 45c. "Jolly Roger" (tourist schooner) (horiz) | 1·00 | 35 |
| 1131 | 70c. "Atlantis" (tourist submarine) (horiz) | 1·50 | 1·10 |
| 1132 | $2 "Harbour Master" (ferry) | 3·25 | 4·00 |

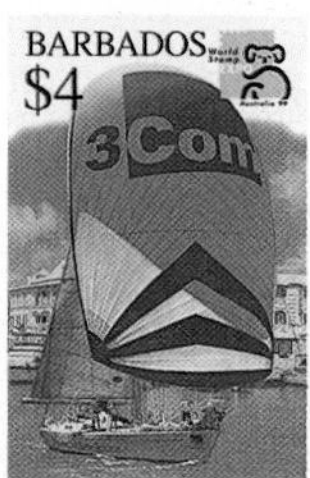

**236** Racing Yacht

**1999.** "Australia '99" World Stamp Exhibition, Melbourne. Sheet 90×90 mm.

| | | | |
|---|---|---|---|
| **MS**1133 | **236** $4 multicoloured | 3·50 | 5·00 |

**237** Juvenile Piping Plover in Shallow Water

**1999.** Endangered Species. Piping Plover. Mult.

| | | | |
|---|---|---|---|
| 1134 | 10c. Type **237** | 20 | 20 |
| 1135 | 45c. Female with eggs | 55 | 55 |
| 1136 | 50c. Male and female with fledglings | 55 | 75 |
| 1137 | 70c. Male in shallow water | 65 | 1·10 |

**1999.** 30th Anniv of First Manned Landing on Moon. As T **186** of Ascension. Multicoloured.

| | | | |
|---|---|---|---|
| 1138 | 40c. Astronaut in training | 55 | 45 |
| 1139 | 45c. 1st stage separation | 55 | 45 |
| 1140 | $1.15 Lunar landing module | 1·40 | 1·25 |
| 1141 | $1.40 Docking with service module | 1·50 | 2·25 |
| **MS**1142 | 90×80 mm. $2.50, Earth as seen from Moon (circular, 40 mm diam) | 2·25 | 3·25 |

**238** Hare running

**1999.** "China '99" International Stamp Exhibition, Beijing. Hares. Multicoloured.

| | | | |
|---|---|---|---|
| 1143 | 70c. Type **238** | 1·40 | 1·50 |
| 1144 | 70c. Head of hare | 1·40 | 1·50 |
| 1145 | 70c. Baby hares suckling | 1·40 | 1·50 |
| 1146 | 70c. Hares boxing | 1·40 | 1·50 |
| 1147 | 70c. Two leverets | 1·40 | 1·50 |

Nos. 1143/7 were printed together, se-tenant, forming a composite background design.

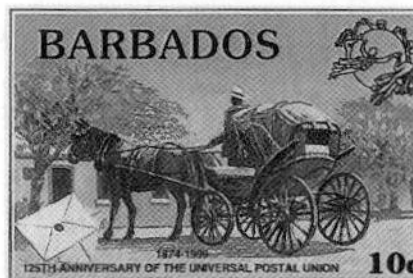

**239** Horse-drawn Mail Cart

**1999.** 125th Anniv of U.P.U. Multicoloured.

| | | | |
|---|---|---|---|
| 1148 | 10c. Type **239** | 1·25 | 35 |
| 1149 | 45c. Mail van | 1·50 | 40 |
| 1150 | $1.75 Sikorsky S42 flying boat | 2·00 | 2·25 |
| 1151 | $2 Computer and fax machine | 2·00 | 2·50 |

**240** Globe and Barbados Flag

**2000.** New Millennium. Sheet 90×80 mm.

| | | | |
|---|---|---|---|
| **MS**1152 | **240** $3 multicoloured | 3·50 | 4·00 |

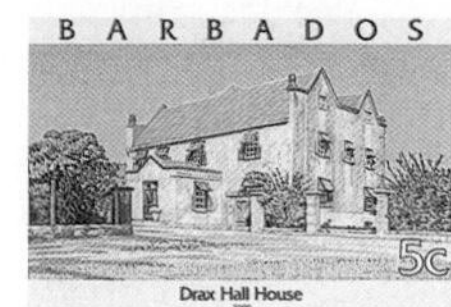

**241** Drax Hall House

**2000.** Pride of Barbados. Multicoloured.

| | | | |
|---|---|---|---|
| 1153 | 5c. Type **241** | 20 | 30 |
| 1154 | 10c. Reaping sugar cane (vert) | 20 | 30 |
| 1155 | 40c. Needham's Point Lighthouse (vert) | 1·50 | 60 |
| 1156 | 45c. Port St. Charles | 60 | 30 |
| 1157 | 65c. Interior of Jewish synagogue | 1·75 | 1·00 |
| 1158 | 70c. Bridgetown Port (I) | 1·50 | 2·00 |
| 1158a | 70c. Bridgetown Port (II) | 1·50 | 1·50 |
| 1159 | 90c. Harrison's Cave | 1·00 | 60 |
| 1160 | $1.15 Villa Nova | 1·10 | 85 |
| 1161 | $1.40 Cricket at Kensington Oval | 2·25 | 1·60 |
| 1162 | $1.75 Sunbury House | 1·50 | 1·75 |
| 1163 | $2 Bethel Methodist Church | 1·75 | 2·00 |
| 1164 | $3 Peacock, Barbados Wildlife Reserve (vert) | 2·75 | 3·00 |
| 1165 | $5 Royal Westmoreland Golf Course (vert) | 6·00 | 6·50 |
| 1166 | $10 Grantley Adams International Airport | 9·00 | 10·00 |

Two types of 70c.:

I. Central design reversed. The bows of three of the four liners shown point to the right.

II. Design corrected. The bows of three of the four liners point to the left.

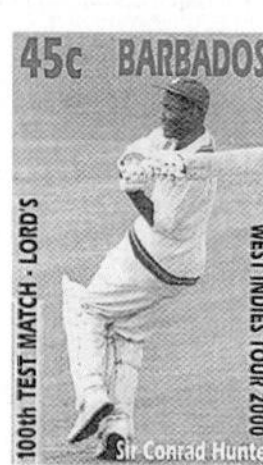

**242** Sir Conrad Hunte batting

**2000.** West Indies Cricket Tour and 100th Test Match at Lord's. Multicoloured.

| | | | |
|---|---|---|---|
| 1167 | 45c. Type **242** | 75 | 35 |
| 1168 | 90c. Malcolm Marshall bowling | 1·50 | 75 |
| 1169 | $2 Sir Garfield Sobers batting | 2·50 | 3·00 |
| **MS**1170 | 121×104 mm. $2.50, Lord's Cricket Ground (horiz) | 2·75 | 3·25 |

**243** Golf Clubs, Flag and Ball on Tee Peg

**2000.** "EXPO 2000" World Stamp Exhibition, Anaheim, U.S.A. Golf. Multicoloured.

| | | | |
|---|---|---|---|
| 1171 | 25c. Type **243** | 70 | 35 |
| 1172 | 40c. Golfer teeing off on top of giant ball | 90 | 35 |
| 1173 | $1.40 Golfer on green | 1·75 | 1·90 |
| 1174 | $2 Golfer putting | 2·25 | 3·00 |

**244** Bentley Mk VI Drophead Coupe, 1947

**2000.** Vintage Cars. Multicoloured.

| | | | |
|---|---|---|---|
| 1175 | 10c. Type **244** | 25 | 15 |
| 1176 | 30c. Vanden Plas Princess Limousine, 1964 | 50 | 25 |
| 1177 | 90c. Austin Atlantic, 1952 | 1·00 | 70 |
| 1178 | $3 Bentley Special, 1950 | 3·00 | 4·00 |

**245** Thread Snake

**2001.** "HONG KONG 2001" Stamp Exhibition. Sheet 125×80 mm.

| | | | |
|---|---|---|---|
| **MS**1179 | **245** $3 multicoloured | 3·50 | 4·00 |

**246** Lizardfish

**2001.** Deep Sea Creatures. Multicoloured.

| | | | |
|---|---|---|---|
| 1180 | 45c. Type **246** | 50 | 60 |
| 1181 | 45c. Golden-tailed moray | 50 | 60 |
| 1182 | 45c. Black-barred soldierfish | 50 | 60 |
| 1183 | 45c. Golden zoanthid | 50 | 60 |
| 1184 | 45c. Sponge brittle star | 50 | 60 |
| 1185 | 45c. Magnificent feather duster | 50 | 60 |
| 1186 | 45c. Bearded fireworm | 50 | 60 |
| 1187 | 45c. Lima shell | 50 | 60 |
| 1188 | 45c. Yellow tube sponge | 50 | 60 |

**247** Octagonal, Fish and Butterfly Kites

**2001.** "Philanippon '01" International Stamp Exhibition, Tokyo. Kites. Multicoloured.

| | | | |
|---|---|---|---|
| 1189 | 10c. Type **247** | 20 | 15 |
| 1190 | 65c. Hexagonal, bird and geometric kites | 60 | 45 |
| 1191 | $1.40 Policeman, Japanese and butterfly kites | 1·40 | 1·50 |
| 1192 | $1.75 Anti-drug, geisha and eagle kites | 1·60 | 1·75 |

**248** George Washington on the Quay, 1751

**2001.** 250th Anniv of George Washington's Visit to Barbados. Multicoloured.

| | | | |
|---|---|---|---|
| 1193 | 45c. Type **248** | 65 | 40 |
| 1194 | 50c. George Washington in Barbados | 65 | 40 |
| 1195 | $1.15 George Washington superimposed on Declaration of Independence, 1776 | 1·50 | 1·00 |
| 1196 | $2.50 Needham's Point Fort, 1750 | 2·50 | 3·25 |
| **MS**1197 | 110×90 mm. $3 George Washington as President of U.S.A. | 2·50 | 3·00 |

**249** Shaggy Bear(Traditional Carnival Character)

**2001.** 35th Anniv of Independence. Multicoloured.

| | | | |
|---|---|---|---|
| 1198 | 25c. Type **249** | 40 | 20 |
| 1199 | 45c. Tuk band | 70 | 30 |
| 1200 | $1 Landship Dancers | 1·25 | 80 |
| 1201 | $2 Guitar, saxophone and words of National Anthem | 2·25 | 2·75 |

**2002.** Golden Jubilee. As T **200** of Ascension.

| | | | |
|---|---|---|---|
| 1202 | 10c. black, violet and gold | 45 | 20 |
| 1203 | 70c. multicoloured | 1·00 | 60 |
| 1204 | $1 black, violet and gold | 1·25 | 1·00 |
| 1205 | $1.40 multicoloured | 1·50 | 2·00 |
| **MS**1206 | 162×95 mm. Nos. 1202/5 and $3 multicoloured | 4·75 | 5·50 |

DESIGNS—HORIZ: 10c. Princess Elizabeth; 70c. Queen Elizabeth in cerise hat; $1 Queen Elizabeth wearing Imperial State Crown, Coronation, 1953; $1.40, Queen Elizabeth in purple feathered hat. VERT (38×51 mm)—$3 Queen Elizabeth after Annigoni.

Designs as Nos. 1202/5 in **MS**1206 omit the gold frame around each stamp and "Golden Jubilee 1952–2002" inscription.

**250** 1852 (½d.) Britannia Stamp and Map

**2002.** 150th Anniv of Inland Postal Service. Multicoloured.

| | | | |
|---|---|---|---|
| 1207 | 10c. Type **250** | 30 | 15 |
| 1208 | 45c. Early twentieth-century postman delivering letter | 60 | 35 |
| 1209 | $1.15 *Esk* (mail steamer) | 1·50 | 1·25 |
| 1210 | $2 B.W.I.A. Tri-Star airliner | 2·00 | 2·50 |

**251** *Alpinia purpurata*

**2002.** Flowers. Multicoloured.

| | | | |
|---|---|---|---|
| 1211 | 10c. Type **251** | 20 | 20 |
| 1212 | 40c. *Heliconia caribaea* | 40 | 30 |
| 1213 | $1.40 *Polianthes tuberosa* (horiz) | 1·25 | 1·40 |
| 1214 | $2.50 *Anthurium* (horiz) | 2·00 | 2·75 |

**252** Drax Hall Windmill, St. George

**2002.** 375th Anniv of First Settlement.

| | | | | |
|---|---|---|---|---|
| 1215 | **252** | 10c. brown, agate and blue | 35 | 15 |
| 1216 | - | 45c. brown, agate and blue | 1·00 | 35 |
| 1217 | - | $1.15 multicoloured | 1·50 | 1·40 |
| 1218 | - | $3 multicoloured | 3·25 | 4·00 |

DESIGNS: 45c. Donkey cart; $1.15, Cattle Mill ruins, Gibbons; $3, Morgan Lewis windmill, St. Andrew.

**253** Traditional Christmas Fare

**2002.** Christmas. Multicoloured.

| | | | |
|---|---|---|---|
| 1219 | 45c. Type **253** | 60 | 35 |
| 1220 | $1.15 Christmas morning in the park | 1·25 | 1·25 |
| 1221 | $1.40 Nativity scene from float parade | 1·40 | 1·50 |

**254** AIDS Ribbon

**2002.** Centenary of Pan American Health Organization. Multicoloured.

| | | | |
|---|---|---|---|
| 1222 | 10c. Type **254** | 40 | 15 |
| 1223 | 70c. Amateur athletes | 85 | 50 |
| 1224 | $1.15 Sir George Alleyne (Director-General of P.A.H.O.) | 1·25 | 1·10 |
| 1225 | $2 Pregnant woman | 1·75 | 2·00 |

**255** H.M.S. *Tartar*, 1764

**2003.** Royal Navy Connections. Multicoloured.

| | | | |
|---|---|---|---|
| 1226 | 10c. Type **255** | 55 | 20 |
| 1227 | 70c. H.M.S. *Barbadoes*, 1803 | 1·10 | 55 |
| 1228 | $1.15 H.M.S. *Valerian*, 1926 | 1·40 | 1·25 |
| 1229 | $2.50 H.M.S. *Victorious*, 1941 | 2·50 | 3·25 |

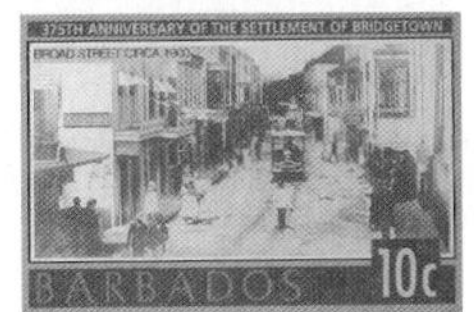

**256** Broad Street, c. 1900

**2003.** 375th Anniv of the Settlement of Bridgetown. Multicoloured.

| | | | |
|---|---|---|---|
| 1230 | 10c. Type **256** | 55 | 20 |
| 1231 | $1.15 Swan Street, 1900 | 1·40 | 90 |
| 1232 | $1.40 Roebuck Street, c. 1880 | 1·60 | 1·40 |
| 1233 | $2 Chamberlain Bridge | 2·25 | 3·00 |
| **MS**1234 | 160×120 mm. Nos. 1230/3 | 5·50 | 6·00 |

**2003.** Centenary of Powered Flight. As T **209** of Ascension. Multicoloured.

| | | | |
|---|---|---|---|
| 1235 | 10c. McDonnell F2H-2P Banshee | 40 | 20 |
| 1236 | 45c. Vickers Viscount 700 | 70 | 30 |
| 1237 | 50c. Douglas DC-9-30 | 80 | 30 |
| 1238 | $1.15 Short Sunderland Mk II | 1·10 | 70 |
| 1239 | $1.40 North American P-51D Mustang | 1·25 | 1·25 |
| 1240 | $2.50 Concorde | 2·75 | 3·50 |

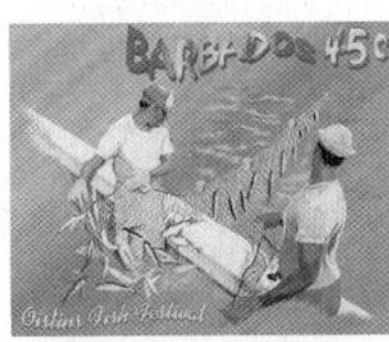

**257** Fishermen (Oistins Fish Festival)

**2003.** Barbados Festivals. Multicoloured.

| | | | |
|---|---|---|---|
| **MS**1241 | 127×105 mm. 45c. Type **257**; 45c. Saxophone player (Barbados Jazz Festival); 45c. Man and woman in traditional costume (Crop Over Festival); 45c. Actresses (National Independence Festival of Creative Arts); 45c. School choir (National Independence Festival of Creative Arts); 45c. Carnival dancers (Crop Over Festival); 45c. Bass player (Barbados Jazz Festival); 45c. Competitor in fish boning competition (Oistins Fish Festival) | 4·75 | 5·00 |

**258** Cadet Corps Banner

**2004.** Centenary of the Cadet Corps. Multicoloured.

| | | | |
|---|---|---|---|
| 1242 | 10c. Type **258** | 30 | 20 |
| 1243 | 25c. The Regular band marching | 50 | 25 |
| 1244 | 50c. The Toy Soldier band | 70 | 35 |
| 1245 | $1 The Sea Cadets | 1·00 | 80 |
| 1246 | $3 Map reading | 2·50 | 3·00 |

**259** Swimming

**2004.** Olympic Games, Athens. Multicoloured.

| | | | |
|---|---|---|---|
| 1247 | 10c. Type **259** | 35 | 20 |
| 1248 | 70c. Shooting | 70 | 45 |
| 1249 | $1.15 Running | 1·10 | 1·10 |
| 1250 | $2 Judo | 2·00 | 2·50 |

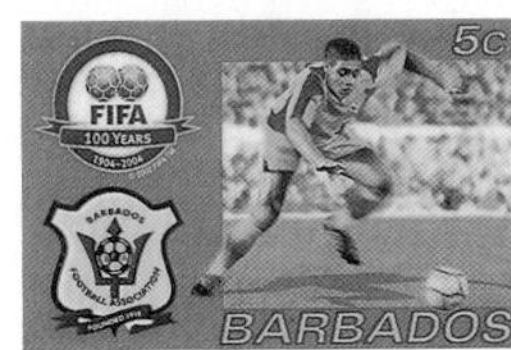

**260** Football Player

**2004.** Centenary of FIFA (Federation Internationale de Football Association). Multicoloured.

| | | | |
|---|---|---|---|
| 1251 | 5c. Type **260** | 15 | 30 |
| 1252 | 90c. Player in blue strip | 1·00 | 70 |
| 1253 | $1.40 Goal keeper | 1·25 | 1·25 |
| 1254 | $2.50 Player in yellow strip | 2·00 | 2·50 |

**261** Brain Coral

**2004.** Coral. Multicoloured.

| | | | |
|---|---|---|---|
| 1255 | $1 Type **261** | 1·40 | 1·50 |
| 1256 | $1 Pillar coral | 1·40 | 1·50 |
| 1257 | $1 Pillar coral (different) | 1·40 | 1·50 |
| 1258 | $1 Fan coral | 1·40 | 1·50 |
| 1259 | $1 Yellow pencil coral | 1·40 | 1·50 |
| **MS**1260 | 85×85 mm. $3.50 Maze coral (36×36 mm) | 3·50 | 3·75 |

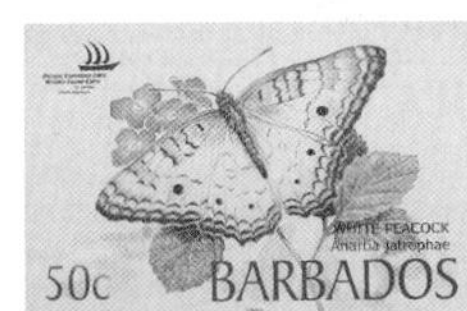

**262** White Peacock

**2005.** Pacific Explorer 2005 World Stamp Expo, Sydney, Australia. Butterflies. Multicoloured.

| | | | |
|---|---|---|---|
| 1261 | 50c. Type **262** | 70 | 35 |
| 1262 | $1 Great southern white | 1·25 | 80 |
| 1263 | $1.40 Orion | 1·60 | 1·40 |
| 1264 | $2.50 Mimic | 2·25 | 3·00 |
| **MS**1265 | 85×85 mm. $8 Monarch | 7·00 | 8·00 |

**263** Baobab

**2005.** Flowering Trees. Multicoloured.

| | | | |
|---|---|---|---|
| 1266 | 5c. Type **263** | 15 | 15 |
| 1267 | 10c. African tulip tree | 15 | 15 |
| 1268 | 25c. Rose of Sharon | 25 | 25 |
| 1269 | 45c. Black willow | 40 | 30 |
| 1270 | 50c. Black pearl tree | 45 | 35 |
| 1271 | 75c. Seaside mahoe | 70 | 50 |
| 1272 | 90c. Quickstick | 80 | 55 |
| 1273 | $1 Jerusalem Thorn | 90 | 65 |
| 1274 | $1.15 Pink cassia | 1·00 | 70 |
| 1275 | $1.40 Orchid tree | 1·25 | 70 |
| 1276 | $1.75 Yellow poui | 1·50 | 1·50 |
| 1277 | $2.10 Lignum vitae | 1·90 | 2·10 |
| 1278 | $3 Wild cinnamon | 2·50 | 2·75 |
| 1279 | $5 Pride of India | 4·25 | 4·50 |
| 1280 | $10 Immortelle | 7·50 | 8·00 |

**264** Firemen, c. 1955

**2005.** 50th Anniv of the Barbados Fire Service. Multicoloured.

| | | | |
|---|---|---|---|
| 1281 | 5c. Type **264** | 40 | 40 |
| 1282 | 10c. Fire Officers marching, Fire Service Headquarters, Bridgetown, 2003 | 40 | 40 |
| 1283 | 90c. Rosenbauer-Panther FL 6×6 Airport Rescue and Fire Fighting tender | 1·50 | 75 |
| 1284 | $1.15 Fire Service parade with Dennis Pump Escape, Garrison Savannah, 1975 | 1·75 | 1·10 |
| 1285 | $2.50 Scania 94G Water and Foam Tender | 3·75 | 4·00 |

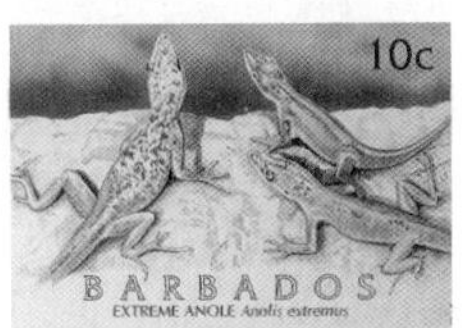

**265** Three Anoles

**2005.** Extreme Anole (Anolis extremus). Mult.

| | | | |
|---|---|---|---|
| 1286 | 10c. Type **265** | 30 | 15 |
| 1287 | 50c. Two anoles | 75 | 35 |
| 1288 | $1.75 One anole | 2·25 | 2·50 |
| 1289 | $2 Young anole hatching | 2·50 | 3·00 |

**266** Queen Triggerfish and Diver

**2006.** Endangered Species. Queen Triggerfish (Balistes vetula). Multicoloured.

| | | | |
|---|---|---|---|
| 1290 | 10c. Type **266** | 30 | 30 |
| 1291 | $1.15 Pair at edge of coral reef | 1·25 | 1·00 |
| 1292 | $1.40 Queen Triggerfish above sandy sea floor | 1·40 | 1·25 |
| 1293 | $2.10 Queen Triggerfish on coral reef | 2·00 | 2·25 |

**267** Girls reading

**2006.** Washington 2006 International Stamp Exhibition. "Children – they are the future". Multicoloured.

| | | | |
|---|---|---|---|
| 1294 | 10c. Type **267** | 30 | 20 |
| 1295 | 50c. Wheelchair basketball | 75 | 40 |
| 1296 | $2 Three children using computer | 2·00 | 2·25 |
| 1297 | $2.50 Two children playing violins | 2·25 | 2·50 |

**268** Cave Shepherd, c. 1911

**2006.** Centenary of Cave Shepherd Store, Bridgetown. Multicoloured.

| | | | |
|---|---|---|---|
| 1298 | 10c. Type **268** | 30 | 20 |
| 1299 | 50c. Cave Shepherd, c. 2000 | 60 | 35 |
| 1300 | $1.75 Cave Shepherd, c. 1975 | 1·75 | 2·00 |
| 1301 | $2 Cave Shepherd, c. 1920 | 2·00 | 2·25 |

**269** Old Town Hall, Bridgetown

**2006.** 175th Anniv of the Enfranchisement of Free Coloured and Black Barbadians. Multicoloured.

| | | | |
|---|---|---|---|
| 1302 | 10c. Type **269** | 30 | 20 |
| 1303 | 50c. Samuel Jackman Prescod, 1806–71 (campaigner for enfranchisement) | 60 | 35 |
| 1304 | $1.40 Voting in ballot box (introduced 1885) | 1·25 | 1·40 |
| 1305 | $2.50 Sir James Lyon (Governor of Barbados, 1829–33) | 2·00 | 2·50 |

**270** Joel 'Big Bird' Garner

**2007.** World Cup Cricket, West Indies. Multicoloured.

| | | | |
|---|---|---|---|
| 1306 | $1.75 Type **270** | 1·75 | 2·00 |
| 1307 | $2.10 Old Kensington Oval, Barbados (horiz) | 2·00 | 2·25 |
| 1308 | $3 New Kensington Oval, Barbados (horiz) | 2·50 | 2·75 |
| **MS**1309 | 161×121 mm. $10 World Cup Cricket trophy | 8·25 | 8·50 |

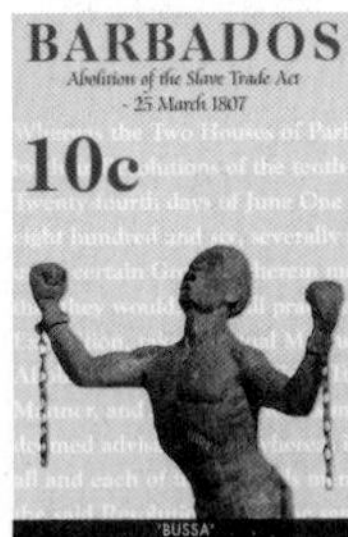

**271** Emancipation (Bussa) Statue

**2007.** Bicentenary of the Abolition of the Slave Trade Act. Multicoloured (except **MS**1314).

| | | | |
|---|---|---|---|
| 1310 | 10c. Type **271** | 15 | 10 |
| 1311 | $1 William Wilberforce (abolitionist) | 95 | 1·00 |
| 1312 | $1.75 Slave hut (horiz) | 1·25 | 1·40 |
| 1313 | $2 Freedom celebrations, 1838 (horiz) | 1·60 | 1·75 |
| **MS**1314 | 115×80 mm. $3 Slave ship (black and violet) | 2·50 | 2·75 |

**272** Interior of Nidhe Israel Synagogue, Bridgetown

**2007.** Opening of Nidhe Israel Museum, Bridgetown. Multicoloured.

| | | | |
|---|---|---|---|
| 1315 | 5c. Type **272** | 10 | 10 |
| 1316 | 10c. Nidhe Israel Museum (adjacent to synagogue) | 15 | 10 |
| 1317 | $1.40 Hanukiah (candelabra) | 1·00 | 1·10 |
| 1318 | $2.50 Stained glass window in synagogue | 2·00 | 2·25 |

**273** Green Turtle

**2007.** Turtles. Multicoloured.

| | | | |
|---|---|---|---|
| 1319 | 10c. Type **273** | 15 | 10 |
| 1320 | 50c. Loggerhead turtle | 40 | 45 |
| 1321 | $1 Hawksbill turtle | 70 | 75 |
| 1322 | $2.50 Leatherback turtle | 2·00 | 2·25 |

**274** *Padina gymnospora*

**2008.** Algae. Multicoloured.

| | | | |
|---|---|---|---|
| 1323 | 10c. Type **274** | 10 | 10 |
| 1324 | 50c. *Ulva lactuca* | 40 | 45 |
| 1325 | $1.75 *Sargassum platycarpum* | 1·25 | 1·40 |
| 1326 | $2 *Udotea conglutinata* | 1·75 | 1·90 |

**275** The Second Barbados Contingent of Volunteers for Armed Forces, 1940

**2008.** Airmen and Aircraft. Multicoloured.

| | | | |
|---|---|---|---|
| 1327 | 10c. Type **275** | 10 | 10 |
| 1328 | 50c. Warren Alleyne (Telegraphist 1) and Supermarine Spitfire Mk IX, 1944 | 40 | 45 |
| 1329 | $1.75 Wing Commander Aubrey Inniss and Bristol Beaufighter Mk VIC, 1943 | 1·25 | 1·40 |
| 1330 | $2 Flying Officer Errol Barrow and Avro Lancaster B Mk 1, 1945 | 1·75 | 1·90 |
| **MS**1331 | 100×73 mm. $6 Concorde over Barbados | 4·75 | 4·75 |

Nos. 1327/30 commemorate the 90th anniversary of the Royal Air Force.

**276** *Christmas Moon* (Alison Chapman-Andrews)

**2008.** Christmas. Designs showing paintings. Multicoloured.

| | | | |
|---|---|---|---|
| 1332 | 10c. Type **276** | 15 | 10 |
| 1333 | 50c. *Preparing for Christmas* (Virgil Broodhagen) | 60 | 45 |
| 1334 | $1.40 *Christmas Candles* (Darla Trotman) | 1·00 | 85 |
| 1335 | $3 *Poinsettia and Snow on the Mountain* (Darla Trotman) | 2·50 | 2·75 |

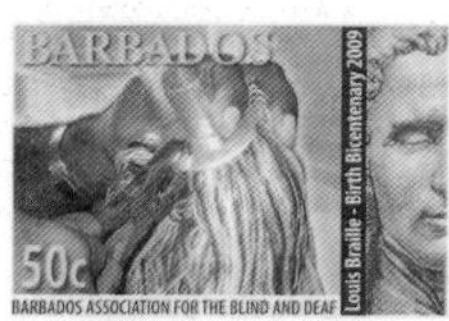


**277** Mop making

**2009.** Birth Bicentenary of Louis Braille (inventor of Braille writing for the blind) and Barbados Association for the Blind and Deaf. Multicoloured.

| | | | |
|---|---|---|---|
| 1336 | 50c. Type **277** | 60 | 45 |
| 1337 | $1.40 Chair caning | 1·00 | 85 |
| 1338 | $1.75 Girl using Braille typewriter | 1·25 | 1·40 |
| 1339 | $2 Louis Braille | 1·75 | 1·90 |

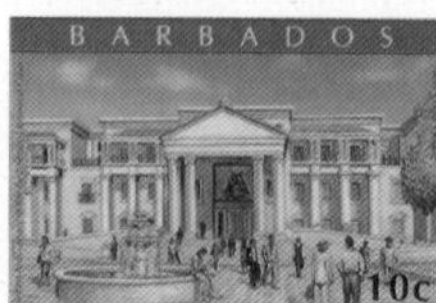


**278** New Court House

**2009.** 300th Anniv of the Restructured Criminal Court. Multicoloured.

| | | | |
|---|---|---|---|
| 1340 | 10c. Type **278** | 15 | 10 |
| 1341 | 50c. Handcuffs and seal of the Court | 65 | 45 |
| 1342 | $1.40 Judge's robe, wig and gavel | 1·00 | 45 |
| 1343 | $2.50 Old Court House | 2·00 | 2·25 |

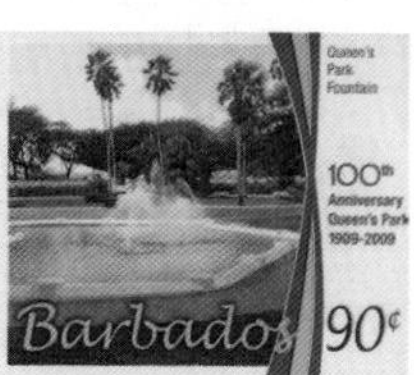


**279** Queen's Park Fountain

**2010.** Centenary (2009) of Queen's Park, Bridgetown. Multicoloured.

| | | | |
|---|---|---|---|
| 1344 | 90c. Type **279** | 85 | 90 |
| 1345 | $1 The Boaba Tree (baobab *Adansonia digitata*) | 90 | 95 |
| 1346 | $1.40 Queen's Park House | 1·50 | 1·60 |
| 1347 | $2 The Band Stand | 1·90 | 2·00 |
| **MS**1348 | 140x91 mm. $4 Queen's Park in 1909 | 4·00 | 4·00 |

**280** J 24 Keelboats flying Spinnakers

**2010.** Fireball International World Championships, Carlisle Bay. Multicoloured.

| | | | |
|---|---|---|---|
| 1349 | 10c. Type **280** | 15 | 10 |
| 1350 | 50c. J24 keelboats | 45 | 50 |
| 1351 | 90c. J24 keelboats | 85 | 90 |
| 1352 | $1.75 Laser dinghies | 1·90 | 2·00 |
| 1353 | $2 Racing keelboats | 2·10 | 2·20 |

**281** Guides camping

**2010.** Centenary of Girl Guiding. Multicoloured.

| | | | |
|---|---|---|---|
| 1354 | 10c. Type **281** | 15 | 10 |
| 1355 | 50c. Guides saluting ('The Promise') | 45 | 50 |
| 1356 | $1 Brownies and guides ('Guiding Uniforms') | 1·60 | 1·70 |
| 1357 | $2.50 Parade of guides | 2·10 | 2·00 |
| **MS**1358 | 94×64 mm. $3.50 Emblem | 3·50 | 3·50 |

**282** Golden Apple (*Spondias cytherea*)

**2011.** Local Fruits. Multicoloured.

| | | | |
|---|---|---|---|
| 1359 | 5c. Type **282** | 15 | 15 |
| 1360 | 10c. Coconut (*Cocos nucifera*) | 20 | 25 |
| 1361 | 35c. Cashew (*Anacardium occidentale*) | 40 | 45 |
| 1362 | 40c. Mammy apple (*Mammea americana*) | 45 | 50 |
| 1363 | 60c. Barbados cherry (*Malpighia emarginata*) | 70 | 75 |
| 1364 | 65c. Sugar apple (*Annona squamosa*) | 75 | 80 |
| 1365 | 80c. Sea grape (*Coccoloba uvifera*) | 90 | 95 |
| 1366 | $1 Tamarind (*Tamarindus indica*) | 1·10 | 1·20 |
| 1367 | $1.25 Carambola (*Averrhoa carambola*) | 1·20 | 1·30 |
| 1368 | $1.50 Mango (*Mangifera indica*) | 1·50 | 1·60 |
| 1369 | $1.80 Banana (*Musa X*) | 1·70 | 1·90 |
| 1370 | $2.20 Guava (*Psidium guajava*) | 2·10 | 2·20 |
| 1371 | $2.75 Avocado (*Persea americana*) | 2·40 | 2·50 |
| 1372 | $3 Gooseberry (*Phyllanthus acidus*) | 2·75 | 3·00 |
| 1373 | $5 Soursop (*Annona muricata*) | 5·25 | 5·50 |
| 1374 | $10 Pomegranate (*Punica granatum*) | 8·75 | 9·00 |

**283** 'Sailors' Valentine' from 1800s

**2011.** 'Sailors' Valentines' (collages of sea shells within octagonal wooden frames). Multicoloured.

| | | | |
|---|---|---|---|
| 1375 | 10c. Type **283** | 20 | 25 |
| 1376 | 65c. Modern 'sailors' valentine' by Daphne Hunte | 60 | 65 |
| 1377 | $2.20 'Sailors' valentine' with 'Live Today Hope Tomorrow' inscription | 2·20 | 2·30 |
| 1378 | $2.75 Modern 'sailors' valentine' by Pamela Boynton | 2·75 | 3·00 |

### POSTAGE DUE STAMPS

**D1**

**1934**

| | | | | |
|---|---|---|---|---|
| D1 | **D1** | ½d. green | 1·25 | 8·50 |
| D2 | **D1** | 1d. black | 1·25 | 1·25 |
| D3 | **D1** | 3d. red | 20·00 | 21·00 |

**1950.** Values in cents.

| | | | |
|---|---|---|---|
| D4a | 1c. green | 30 | 3·00 |
| D8 | 2c. black | 30 | 5·00 |
| D9 | 6c. red | 50 | 7·00 |

**D2**

**1976**

| | | | | |
|---|---|---|---|---|
| D14a | **D2** | 1c. mauve and pink | 10 | 10 |
| D15a | - | 2c. blue and light blue | 10 | 10 |
| D16a | - | 5c. brown and yellow | 10 | 15 |
| D17a | - | 10c. blue and lilac | 15 | 20 |
| D18a | - | 25c. deep green and green | 20 | 30 |
| D19 | - | $1 red and deep red | 75 | 1·25 |

DESIGNS: Nos. D15/19 show different floral backgrounds.

**Pt. 1**

## BARBUDA

One of the Leeward Is., Br. W. Indies. Dependency of Antigua. Used stamps of Antigua and Leeward Is. concurrently. The issues from 1968 are also valid for use in Antigua. From 1971 to 1973 the stamps of Antigua were again used.

1922. 12 pence = 1 shilling; 20 shillings = 1 pound.
1951. 100 cents = 1 West Indian dollar.

**1922.** Stamps of Leeward Islands optd **BARBUDA.**

| | | | | |
|---|---|---|---|---|
| 1 | **11** | ½d. green | 1·50 | 11·00 |
| 2 | **11** | 1d. red | 1·50 | 11·00 |
| 3 | **11** | 2d. grey | 1·50 | 7·00 |
| 4 | **11** | 2½d. blue | 1·50 | 7·50 |
| 9 | **11** | 3d. purple on yellow | 1·75 | 13·00 |
| 5 | **11** | 6d. purple | 2·00 | 18·00 |
| 10 | **11** | 1s. black on green | 1·50 | 8·00 |
| 6 | **11** | 2s. purple and blue on blue | 14·00 | 50·00 |
| 7 | **11** | 3s. green and violet | 35·00 | 80·00 |
| 8 | **11** | 4s. black and red | 42·00 | 80·00 |
| 11 | **11** | 5s. green and red on yellow | 65·00 | £130 |

**2** Map of Barbuda

**3** Greater Amberjack

**1968**

| | | | | |
|---|---|---|---|---|
| 12 | **2** | ½c. brown, black and pink | 35 | 3·00 |
| 13 | **2** | 1c. orange, black and flesh | 1·00 | 35 |
| 14 | **2** | 2c. brown, red and rose | 2·00 | 1·25 |
| 15 | **2** | 3c. brown, yellow and lemon | 1·00 | 55 |
| 16 | **2** | 4c. black, green & lt green | 2·50 | 3·00 |
| 17 | **2** | 5c. turquoise and black | 2·25 | 20 |
| 18 | **2** | 6c. black, purple and lilac | 1·00 | 3·25 |
| 19 | **2** | 10c. black, blue and cobalt | 1·50 | 1·25 |
| 20 | **2** | 15c. black, green & turq | 1·75 | 3·25 |
| 20a | - | 20c. multicoloured | 1·50 | 2·00 |
| 21 | **3** | 25c. multicoloured | 1·00 | 25 |
| 22 | - | 35c. multicoloured | 2·75 | 25 |
| 23 | - | 50c. multicoloured | 1·00 | 1·50 |
| 24 | - | 75c. multicoloured | 1·00 | 80 |
| 25 | - | $1 multicoloured | 50 | 1·50 |
| 26 | - | $2.50 multicoloured | 55 | 2·50 |
| 27 | - | $5 multicoloured | 65 | 2·75 |

DESIGNS: As T **3**—20c. Great barracuda; 35c. French angelfish; 50c. Porkfish; 75c. Princess parrotfish; $1, Long-spined squirrelfish; $2.50, Bigeye; $5, Blue chromis.

**10** Sprinting and Aztec Sun-stone

**1968.** Olympic Games. Mexico. Multicoloured.

| | | | |
|---|---|---|---|
| 28 | 25c. Type **10** | 50 | 30 |
| 29 | 35c. High-jumping and Aztec statue | 55 | 30 |
| 30 | 75c. Dinghy-racing and Aztec lion mask | 60 | 75 |
| **MS**31 | 87×76 mm. $1 Football and engraved plate | 2·00 | 3·25 |

**14** "The Ascension" (Orcagna)"

**1969.** Easter Commemoration.

| | | | | |
|---|---|---|---|---|
| 32 | **14** | 25c. black and blue | 15 | 45 |
| 33 | **14** | 35c. black and red | 15 | 50 |
| 34 | **14** | 75c. black and lilac | 15 | 55 |

**15** Scout Enrolment Ceremony

**1969.** 3rd Caribbean Scout Jamboree. Multicoloured.

| | | | |
|---|---|---|---|
| 35 | 25c. Type **15** | 35 | 55 |
| 36 | 35c. Scouts around camp fire | 45 | 65 |
| 37 | 75c. Sea Scouts rowing boat | 55 | 1·10 |

**18** "Sistine Madonna" (Raphael)

**1969.** Christmas.

| | | | | |
|---|---|---|---|---|
| 38 | **18** | ½c. multicoloured | 10 | 30 |
| 39 | **18** | 25c. multicoloured | 10 | 15 |
| 40 | **18** | 35c. multicoloured | 10 | 20 |
| 41 | **18** | 35c. multicoloured | 20 | 35 |

**19** William I (1066–87)

**1970.** English Monarchs. Multicoloured.

| | | | |
|---|---|---|---|
| 42 | 35c. Type **19** | 30 | 15 |
| 43 | 35c. William II (1087–1100) | 10 | 15 |
| 44 | 35c. Henry I (1100–35) | 10 | 15 |
| 45 | 35c. Stephen (1135–54) | 10 | 15 |
| 46 | 35c. Henry II (1154–89) | 10 | 15 |
| 47 | 35c. Richard I (1189–99) | 10 | 15 |
| 48 | 35c. John (1199–1216) | 10 | 15 |
| 49 | 35c. Henry III (1216–72) | 10 | 15 |
| 50 | 35c. Edward I (1272–1307) | 10 | 15 |
| 51 | 35c. Edward II (1307–27) | 10 | 15 |
| 52 | 35c. Edward III (1327–77) | 10 | 15 |
| 53 | 35c. Richard II (1377–99) | 10 | 15 |
| 54 | 35c. Henry IV (1399–1413) | 10 | 15 |
| 55 | 35c. Henry V (1413–22) | 10 | 15 |
| 56 | 35c. Henry VI (1422–61) | 10 | 15 |
| 57 | 35c. Edward IV (1462–83) | 10 | 15 |
| 58 | 35c. Edward V (April–June 1483) | 10 | 15 |
| 59 | 35c. Richard III (1483–85) | 10 | 15 |
| 60 | 35c. Henry VII (1485–1509) | 30 | 15 |
| 61 | 35c. Henry VIII (1509–47) | 30 | 15 |
| 62 | 35c. Edward VI (1547–53) | 30 | 15 |
| 63 | 35c. Lady Jane Grey (1553) | 30 | 15 |
| 64 | 35c. Mary I (1553–8) | 30 | 15 |
| 65 | 35c. Elizabeth I (1558–1603) | 30 | 15 |
| 66 | 35c. James I (1603–25) | 30 | 15 |
| 67 | 35c. Charles I (1625–49) | 30 | 15 |
| 68 | 35c. Charles II (1649–1685) | 30 | 15 |
| 69 | 35c. James II (1685–1688) | 30 | 15 |
| 70 | 35c. William III (1689–1702) | 30 | 15 |
| 71 | 35c. Mary II (1689–1694) | 30 | 15 |
| 72 | 35c. Anne (1702–1714) | 30 | 15 |
| 73 | 35c. George I (1714–1727) | 30 | 15 |
| 74 | 35c. George II (1727–1760) | 30 | 15 |
| 75 | 35c. George III (1760–1820) | 30 | 15 |
| 76 | 35c. George IV (1820–1830) | 30 | 15 |
| 77 | 35c. William IV (1830–1837) | 30 | 60 |
| 78 | 35c. Victoria (1837–1901) | 30 | 60 |

See also Nos. 710/5.

**1970.** No. 12 surch 20c.

| | | | | |
|---|---|---|---|---|
| 79 | **2** | 20c. on ½c. brn, blk & pink | 20 | 20 |

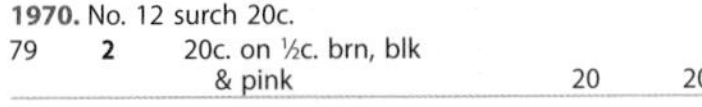

**21** "The Way to Calvary" (Ugolino)

**1970.** Easter. Paintings. Multicoloured.

| | | | |
|---|---|---|---|
| 80 | 25c. Type **21** | 15 | 30 |
| 81 | 35c. "The Deposition from the Cross" (Ugolino) | 15 | 30 |
| 82 | 75c. Crucifix (The Master of St. Francis) | 15 | 35 |

**22** Oliver is introduced to Fagin ("Oliver Twist")

**1970.** Death Centenary of Charles Dickens. Mult.

| | | | |
|---|---|---|---|
| 83 | 20c. Type **22** | 30 | 25 |
| 84 | 75c. Dickens and scene from "The Old Curiosity Shop" | 70 | 75 |

**23** "Madonna of the Meadows" (G. Bellini)

**1970.** Christmas. Multicoloured.

| | | | |
|---|---|---|---|
| 85 | 20c. Type **23** | 10 | 25 |
| 86 | 50c. "Madonna, Child and Angels" (from Wilton diptych) | 15 | 30 |
| 87 | 75c. "The Nativity" (della Francesca) | 15 | 35 |

**24** Nurse with Patient in Wheelchair

**1970.** Centenary of British Red Cross. Multicoloured.

| | | | |
|---|---|---|---|
| 88 | 20c. Type **24** | 15 | 30 |
| 89 | 35c. Nurse giving patient magazines (horiz) | 20 | 40 |
| 90 | 75c. Nurse and mother weighing baby (horiz) | 25 | 70 |

**25** "Angel with Vases"

**1971.** Easter. "Mond" Crucifixion by Raphael. Multicoloured.

| | | | |
|---|---|---|---|
| 91 | 35c. Type **25** | 15 | 85 |
| 92 | 50c. "Christ crucified" | 15 | £250 |
| 93 | 75c. "Angel with vase" | 15 | £375 |

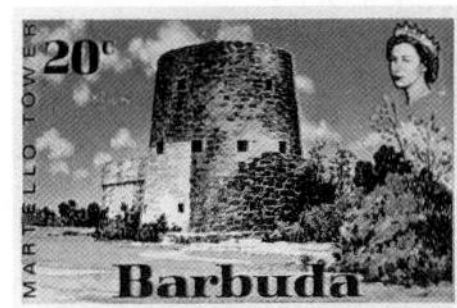


**26** Martello Tower

**1971.** Tourism. Multicoloured.

| | | | |
|---|---|---|---|
| 94 | 20c. Type **26** | 15 | 2·00 |
| 95 | 25c. "Sailfish" dinghy | 25 | 3·50 |
| 96 | 50c. Hotel bungalows | 25 | 2·50 |
| 97 | 75c. Government House and Mystery Stone | 25 | 40·00 |

**27** "The Granducal Madonna" (Raphael)

**1971.** Christmas. Multicoloured.

| | | | |
|---|---|---|---|
| 98 | ½c. Type **27** | 10 | 10 |
| 99 | 35c. "The Ansidei Madonna" (Raphael) | 10 | 30 |
| 100 | 50c. "The Madonna and Child" (Botticelli) | 15 | 50 |
| 101 | 75c. "The Madonna of the Trees" (Bellini) | 15 | 1·50 |

**1973.** Royal Wedding. Nos. 370/1 of Antigua optd **BARBUDA** twice.

| | | | | |
|---|---|---|---|---|
| 102 | **106** | 25c. multicoloured | 3·25 | 25 |
| 103 | **106** | $2 multicoloured | 1·25 | 2·50 |

Four stamps to commemorate the 500th Birth Anniv of Durer were prepared in late 1971, but their issue was not authorised by the Antigua Government.

**1973.** Ships. Nos. 269/85 of Antigua optd **BARBUDA**.

| | | | | |
|---|---|---|---|---|
| 116 | **92** | ½c. multicoloured | 15 | 15·00 |
| 104 | - | 1c. multicoloured | 15 | 10 |
| 105 | - | 2c. multicoloured | 25 | 15·00 |
| 117 | - | 3c. multicoloured | 25 | 13·00 |
| 106 | - | 4c. multicoloured | 30 | 10 |
| 107 | - | 5c. multicoloured | 40 | 1·50 |
| 108 | - | 6c. multicoloured | 40 | 1·75 |
| 109 | - | 10c. multicoloured | 45 | 1·75 |
| 118 | - | 15c. multicoloured | 45 | 35·00 |
| 110 | - | 20c. multicoloured | 55 | 20 |
| 111 | - | 25c. multicoloured | 55 | 1·50 |
| 112 | - | 35c. multicoloured | 55 | 9·00 |
| 113 | - | 50c. multicoloured | 55 | 1·25 |
| 114 | - | 75c. multicoloured | 55 | 4·25 |
| 119 | - | $1 multicoloured | 55 | £325 |
| 115 | - | $2.50 multicoloured | 75 | 50 |
| 121 | - | $5 multicoloured | 1·10 | £100 |

**1973.** Military Uniforms. Nos. 353, 355 and 357 of Antigua optd **BARBUDA**.

| | | | |
|---|---|---|---|
| 122 | ½c. multicoloured | 10 | 2·25 |
| 123 | 20c. multicoloured | 15 | 15 |
| 124 | 75c. multicoloured | 40 | 50 |
| **MS**125 | 127×145 mm. Nos. 353/7 of Antigua | 2·00 | 3·50 |

**1973.** Carnival. Nos. 360/3 of Antigua optd **BARBUDA**.

| | | | |
|---|---|---|---|
| 126 | 20c. multicoloured | 10 | 50·00 |
| 127 | 35c. multicoloured | 10 | 35 |
| 128 | 75c. multicoloured | 20 | 15 |
| **MS**129 | 134×95 mm. Nos. 359/62 of Antigua | 1·00 | 2·25 |

**1973.** Christmas. Nos. 364/69 of Antigua optd BARBUDA.

| | | | | |
|---|---|---|---|---|
| 130 | **105** | 3c. multicoloured | 10 | 2·00 |
| 131 | - | 5c. multicoloured | 10 | 1·25 |
| 132 | - | 20c. multicoloured | 10 | 75 |
| 133 | - | 35c. multicoloured | 15 | 1·50 |
| 134 | - | $1 multicoloured | 30 | 30 |
| **MS**135 | | 130×128 mm. Nos. 130/4 | 2·25 | 9·00 |

**1973.** Honeymoon Visit. Nos. 373/4 of Antigua additionally optd **BARBUDA**.

| | | | |
|---|---|---|---|
| 136 | 35c. multicoloured | 30 | 50 |
| 137 | $2 multicoloured | 70 | 10 |
| **MS**138 | 78×100 mm. Nos. 136/7 | 1·10 | 1·00 |

**1974.** University of West Indies. Nos. 376/9 of Antigua optd **BARBUDA**.

| | | | |
|---|---|---|---|
| 139 | 5c. multicoloured | 10 | 50 |
| 140 | 20c. multicoloured | 10 | 10 |
| 141 | 35c. multicoloured | 15 | 1·50 |
| 142 | 75c. multicoloured | 15 | 1·00 |

**1974.** Military Uniforms. Nos. 380/4 of Antigua optd **BARBUDA**.

| | | | |
|---|---|---|---|
| 143 | ½c. multicoloured | 10 | 60 |
| 144 | 10c. multicoloured | 15 | 15 |
| 145 | 20c. multicoloured | 25 | 30 |
| 146 | 35c. multicoloured | 25 | 85 |
| 147 | 75c. multicoloured | 45 | 45 |

**1974.** Centenary of U.P.U. (1st issue). Nos. 386/92 of Antigua optd with either a or b. (a) **BARBUDA 13 JULY 1992**.

| | | | |
|---|---|---|---|
| 148 | ½c. multicoloured | 10 | 85 |
| 150 | 1c. multicoloured | 10 | 21·00 |
| 152 | 2c. multicoloured | 20 | 10 |
| 154 | 5c. multicoloured | 50 | 45 |
| 156 | 20c. multicoloured | 80 | 15 |
| 158 | 35c. multicoloured | 30 | 50 |
| 160 | $1 multicoloured | 1·75 | 15 |

(b) **BARBUDA 15 SEPT. 1874 G.P.U.** ("General Postal Union").

| | | | |
|---|---|---|---|
| 149 | ½c. multicoloured | 16·00 | 6·50 |
| 151 | 1c. multicoloured | 60 | 20 |
| 153 | 2c. multicoloured | 10 | 10 |
| 155 | 5c. multicoloured | 20 | 55 |
| 157 | 20c. multicoloured | 25 | 10 |
| 159 | 35c. multicoloured | 35 | 55 |
| 161 | $1 multicoloured | 35 | 1·25 |
| **MS**162 | 141×164 mm. No. **MS**393 of Antigua optd **BARBUDA** | 3·50 | 6·00 |

**1974.** Antiguan Steel Bands. Nos. 394/98 of Antigua optd **BARBUDA**.

| | | | |
|---|---|---|---|
| 163 | 5c. deep red, red and black | 10 | 75 |
| 164 | 20c. brown, lt brown & blk | 10 | 35 |
| 165 | 35c. light green, green and black | 10 | 10 |
| 166 | 75c. deep blue, blue and black | 20 | 40 |
| **MS**167 | 115×108 mm. Nos. 163/6 | 65 | 80 |

**39** Footballers

**1974.** World Cup Football Championships (1st issue).

| | | | | |
|---|---|---|---|---|
| 168 | **39** | 35c. multicoloured | 10 | 30 |
| 169 | - | $1.20 multicoloured | 25 | 35 |
| 170 | - | $2.50 multicoloured | 35 | 60 |
| **MS**171 | | 70×128 mm. Nos. 168/70 | 85 | 90 |

DESIGNS: $1.20, $2.50, Footballers in action similar to Type **39**.

**1974.** World Cup Football Championships (2nd issue). Nos. 399/403 of Antigua optd **BARBUDA**.

| | | | | |
|---|---|---|---|---|
| 172 | **111** | 5c. multicoloured | 10 | 15 |
| 173 | - | 35c. multicoloured | 20 | 1·00 |
| 174 | - | 75c. multicoloured | 25 | 1·25 |
| 175 | - | $1 multicoloured | 25 | 6·50 |
| **MS**176 | | 135×130 mm. Nos. 172/5 | 75 | 1·25 |

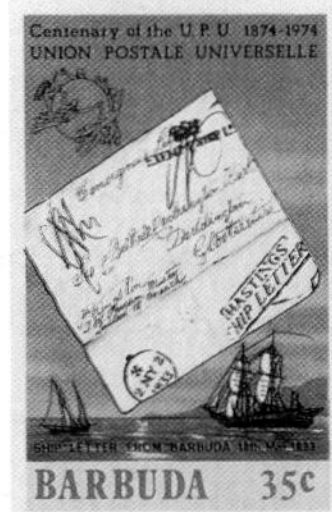


**41** Ship Letter of 1833

**1974.** Cent of Universal Postal Union (2nd issue). Multicoloured.

| | | | |
|---|---|---|---|
| 177 | 35c. Type **41** | 10 | 1·50 |
| 178 | $1.20 Stamps and postmarks of 1922 | 25 | 7·00 |
| 179 | $2.50 Britten Norman Islander mailplane over map of Barbuda | 35 | 14·00 |
| **MS**180 | 128×97 mm. Nos. 177/9 | 1·00 | 2·00 |

**42** Greater Amberjack

**1974.** Multicoloured.. Multicoloured..

| | | | |
|---|---|---|---|
| 181 | ½c. Oleander, Rose Bay (vert) | 10 | 25 |
| 182 | 1c. Blue petrea (vert) | 15 | 2·50 |
| 183 | 2c. Poinsettia (vert) | 15 | 10 |
| 184 | 3c. Cassia tree (vert) | 15 | 25 |
| 185 | 4c. Type **42** | 1·75 | 1·50 |
| 186 | 5c. Holy Trinity School | 15 | 50 |
| 187 | 6c. Snorkeling | 15 | 20 |
| 188 | 10c. Pilgrim Holiness Church | 15 | 80 |
| 189 | 15c. New Cottage Hospital | 15 | 20 |
| 190 | 20c. Post Office and Treasury | 15 | 1·00 |
| 191 | 25c. Island jetty and boats (vert) | 30 | 75 |
| 192 | 35c. Martello Tower | 30 | 2·50 |
| 193 | 50c. Warden's House | 30 | 15 |
| 194 | 75c. Britten Norman Islander aircraft | 2·50 | 1·25 |
| 195 | $1 Tortoise | 70 | 6·00 |
| 196 | $2.50 Spiny lobster | 80 | 1·50 |
| 197 | $5 Magnificent frigate bird | 4·00 | 60 |
| 197b | $10 Hibiscus (vert) | 1·50 | 4·50 |

The 50c. to $1 are 39×25 mm, $2.50 and $5 45×29 mm, $10 34×48 mm.

**1974.** Birth Centenary of Sir Winston Churchill (1st issue). Nos. 408/12 of Antigua optd **BARBUDA**.

| | | | | |
|---|---|---|---|---|
| 198 | **113** | 5c. multicoloured | 15 | 1·40 |
| 199 | - | 35c. multicoloured | 25 | 50 |
| 200 | - | 75c. multicoloured | 40 | 75 |
| 201 | - | $1 multicoloured | 75 | 15 |
| **MS**202 | | 107×82 mm. Nos. 198/201 | 7·00 | 14·00 |

**43** Churchill making Broadcast

**1974.** Birth Centenary of Sir Winston Churchill (2nd issue). Multicoloured.

| | | | |
|---|---|---|---|
| 203 | 5c. Type **43** | 10 | 1·10 |
| 204 | 35c. Churchill and Chartwell | 10 | 10 |
| 205 | 75c. Churchill painting | 20 | 10 |
| 206 | $1 Churchill making "V" sign | 25 | 25 |
| **MS**207 | 146×95 mm. Nos. 203/6 | 75 | 2·50 |

**1974.** Christmas. Nos. 413/21 of Antigua optd **BARBUDA**.

| | | | | |
|---|---|---|---|---|
| 208 | **114** | ½c. multicoloured | 10 | 10 |
| 209 | - | 1c. multicoloured | 10 | 10 |
| 210 | - | 2c. multicoloured | 10 | 25 |
| 211 | - | 3c. multicoloured | 10 | 70 |
| 212 | - | 5c. multicoloured | 10 | 10 |
| 213 | - | 20c. multicoloured | 10 | 10 |

214 - 35c. multicoloured 15 15
215 - 75c. multicoloured 30 25
**MS**216 139×126 mm. Nos. 208/15 80 1·40

**1975.** Nelson's Dockyard. Nos. 427/32 of Antigua optd **BARBUDA**.
217 **116** 5c. multicoloured 15 10
218 - 15c. multicoloured 35 20
219 - 35c. multicoloured 40 75
220 - 50c. multicoloured 45 10
221 - $1 multicoloured 50 10
**MS**222 130×134 mm. As Nos. 217/21, but larger format; 43×28 mm 1·75 2·75

**45** Ships of the Line

**1975.** Sea Battles. Battle of the Saints, 1782. Mult.
223 35c. Type **45** 40 1·40
224 50c. H.M.S. "Ramillies" 40 10
225 75c. "Bonhomme Richard" (American frigate) firing broadside 50 10
226 95c. "L'Orient" (French ship of the line) burning 50 40

**1975.** "Apollo–Soyuz" Space Project. No. 197 optd **U.S.A.-U.S.S.R SPACE COOPERATION 1975** with **APOLLO** (No. 227) or **SOYUZ** (No. 228).
227 $5 multicoloured 3·25 1·40
228 $5 multicoloured 3·25 10

**47** Officer, 65th Foot, 1763

**1975.** Military Uniforms. Multicoloured.
229 35c. Type **47** 60 15
230 50c. Grenadier, 27th Foot 1701–10 75 90
231 75c. Officer, 21st Foot, 1793–6 80 1·75
232 95c. Officer, Royal Regiment of Artillery, 1800 90 1·75

**1975.** 25th Anniv of United Nations. Nos. 203/6 optd **30TH ANNIVERSARY UNITED NATIONS 1945–1975**.
233 **43** 5c. multicoloured 10 10
234 - 35c. multicoloured 10 30
235 - 75c. multicoloured 15 10
236 - $1 multicoloured 20 2·25

**1975.** Christmas. Nos. 457/65 of Antigua optd **BARBUDA**.
237 **121** ½c. multicoloured 10 1·75
238 - 1c. multicoloured 10 2·75
239 - 2c. multicoloured 10 25
240 - 3c. multicoloured 10 1·25
241 - 5c. multicoloured 10 1·50
242 - 10c. multicoloured 10 65
243 - 35c. multicoloured 15 3·00
244 - $2 multicoloured 60 3·00
**MS**245 138×119 mm. Nos. 241/4 1·10 2·25

**1975.** World Cup Cricket Winners. Nos. 466/8 of Antigua optd **BARBUDA**.
246 **122** 5c. multicoloured 1·50 4·50
247 - 35c. multicoloured 2·75 15·00
248 - $2 multicoloured 4·25 19·00

**51** Surrender of Cornwallis at Yorktown (Trumbull)

**1976.** Bicentenary of American Revolution.
249 **51** 15c. multicoloured 10 20
250 - 15c. multicoloured 10 25
251 - 15c. multicoloured 10 10
252 - 35c. multicoloured 10 10
253 - 35c. multicoloured 10 20
254 - 35c. multicoloured 10 30
255 - $1 multicoloured 15 45
256 - $1 multicoloured 15 15
257 - $1 multicoloured 15 60
258 - $2 multicoloured 25 1·40
259 - $2 multicoloured 25 1·50
260 - $2 multicoloured 25 4·75
**MS**261 140×70 mm. Nos. 249/54 and 255/60 (two sheets) 1·40 9·00

DESIGNS—As Type **51**: Nos. 249/51; 252/4, The Battle of Princeton; 255/7, Surrender of General Burgoyne at Saratoga; 258/60, Jefferson presenting Declaration of Independence.

Type **51** shows the left-hand stamp of the 15c. design.

**52** Bananaquits

**1976.** Birds. Multicoloured.
262 35c. Type **52** 20 1·75
263 50c. Blue-hooded euphonia 20 1·50
264 75c. Royal tern 20 1·75
265 95c. Killdeer plover ("Killdeer") 25 4·00
266 $1.25 Shiney-headed cowbird ("Glossy Cowbird") 25 10
267 $2 American purple gallinule ("Purple Gallinule") 30 20

**1976.** Royal Visit to the U.S.A. Nos. 249/60 additionally inscr "H.M. QUEEN ELIZABETH ROYAL VISIT 6TH JULY 1976 H.R.H. DUKE OF EDINBURGH".
268 15c. multicoloured 10 25
269 15c. multicoloured 10 1·00
270 15c. multicoloured 10 15
271 35c. multicoloured 10 10
272 35c. multicoloured 10 65
273 35c. multicoloured 10 2·25
274 $1 multicoloured 15 2·50
275 $1 multicoloured 15 20
276 $1 multicoloured 15 1·75
277 $2 multicoloured 25 2·25
278 $2 multicoloured 25 2·50
279 $2 multicoloured 25 10
**MS**280 143×81 mm. Nos. 268/73 and 274/9 (two sheets) 1·50 9·00

**1976.** Christmas. Nos. 514/18 of Antigua optd **BARBUDA**.
281 **128** 8c. multicoloured 10 1·00
282 - 10c. multicoloured 10 2·00
283 - 15c. multicoloured 10 10
284 - 50c. multicoloured 15 20
285 - $1 multicoloured 25 65

**1976.** Olympic Games, Montreal. Nos. 495/502 of Antigua optd **BARBUDA**.
286 **125** ½c. brown, yellow and black 10 1·00
287 - 1c. violet and black 10 10
288 - 2c. green and black 10 50
289 - 15c. blue and black 10 75
290 - 30c. brown, yellow & blk 10 1·25
291 - $1 orange, red and black 20 10
292 - $2 red and black 35 50
**MS**293 88×138 mm. Nos. 289/92 1·75 2·40

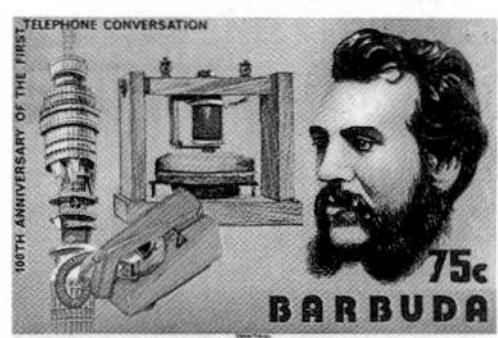

**55** P.O. Tower, Telephones and Alexander Graham Bell

**1977.** Cent of First Telephone Transmission. Mult.
294 75c. Type **55** 15 75
295 $1.25 T.V. transmission by satellite 20 1·25
296 $2 Globe showing satellite transmission scheme 30 1·60
**MS**297 96×144 mm. Nos. 294/6 70 2·00

**56** St. Margaret's Church, Westminster

**1977.** Silver Jubilee (1st issue). Multicoloured.
298 75c. Type **56** 10 15
299 75c. Street decorations 10 10
300 75c. Westminster Abbey 10 65
301 $1.25 Household Cavalry 15 1·75
302 $1.25 Coronation Coach 15 2·00
303 $1.25 Postillions 15 1·00
**MS**304 148×83 mm. As Nos. 298/303, but with silver borders. 75 1·50

Nos. 298/300 and 301/3 were printed together, se-tenant, forming composite designs.

See also Nos. 323/30 and 375/8.

**1977.** Nos. 469/86 of Antigua optd **BARBUDA**.
305 ½c. Antillean crested hummingbird 75 5·50
306 1c. Imperial amazon ("Imperial Parrot") 75 8·00
307 2c. Zenaida dove 75 75
308 3c. Loggerhead kingbird 75 75
309 4c. Red-necked pigeon 75 75
310 5c. Rufous throated solitaire 75 75
311 6c. Orchid tree 50 50
312 10c. Bougainvillea 30 20
313 15c. Geiger tree 30 25
314 20c. Flamboyant 30 25
315 25c. Hibiscus 30 25
316 35c. Flame of the Wood 35 30
317 50c. Cannon at Fort James 40 40
318 75c. Premier's Office 40 40
319 $1 Potworks Dam 50 60
320 $2.50 Irrigation scheme 75 10
321 $5 Government House 1·25 35
322 $10 Coolidge Airport 3·50 1·50

**1977.** Silver Jubilee (2nd issue). Nos. 526/31 of Antigua optd **BARBUDA**. (a) Ordinary gum.
323 10c. Royal Family 10 2·25
324 30c. Royal visit, 1966 10 10
325 50c. The Queen enthroned 15 50
326 90c. The Queen after Coronation 15 1·75
327 $2.50 The Queen and Prince Charles 45 2·50
**MS**328 116×78 mm. $5 Queen Elizabeth and Prince Philip 80 1·25

(b) Self-adhesive.
329 50c. Queen after Coronation 40 2·10
330 $5 The Queen and Prince Philip 3·00 10

**1977.** Caribbean Scout Jamboree, Jamaica. Nos. 534/40 of Antigua optd **BARBUDA**.
331 ½c. Type **131** 10 85
332 1c. Hiking 10 2·75
333 2c. Rock-climbing 10 3·50
334 10c. Cutting logs 10 10
335 30c. Map and sign reading 25 10
336 50c. First aid 25 40
337 $2 Rafting 55 1·40
**MS**338 127×114 mm. Nos. 335/7 2·50 4·00

**1977.** 21st Anniv of Carnival. Nos. 542/47 of Antigua optd **BARBUDA**.
339 10c. Type **312** 10 10
340 30c. Carnival Queen 10 4·00
341 50c. Butterfly costume 15 8·50
342 90c. Queen of the Band 20 35
343 $1 Calypso King and Queen 25 45
**MS**344 140×120 mm. Nos. 339/43 1·00 1·75

**61** Royal Yacht "Britannia"

**1977.** Royal Visit (1st issue). Multicoloured.
345 50c. Type **61** 10 20
346 $1.50 Jubilee emblem 25 35
347 $2.50 Union Jack and flag of Antigua 35 55
**MS**348 77×124 mm. Nos. 345/7 85 2·25

**1977.** Royal Visit (2nd issue). Nos. 548/53 of Antigua optd **BARBUDA**.
349A 10c. Royal Family 10 10
350B 30c. Queen Elizabeth and Prince Philip in car 10 15
351B 50c. Queen enthroned 15 20
352B 90c. Queen after Coronation 20 30
353B $2.50 The Queen and Prince Charles 45 80
**MS**354A 116×78 mm. $5 Queen and Prince Philip 1·75 4·00

**1977.** Christmas. Nos. 554/61 of Antigua optd **BARBUDA**.
355 ½c. Type **134** 10 10
356 1c. Crivelli 10 10
357 2c. Lotto 10 10
358 8c. Pontormo 10 60
359 10c. Tura (different) 10 2·25
360 25c. Lotto (different) 15 3·00
361 $2 Crivelli (different) 45 20
**MS**362 144×118 mm. Nos. 358/61 1·00 1·75

**64** Airship LZ-1

**1977.** Special Events, 1977. Multicoloured.
363 75c. Type **64** 30 1·50
364 75c. German battleship and German Navy airship L-31 30 1·75
365 75c. "Graf Zeppelin" in hangar 30 2·75
366 75c. Gondola of military airship 30 7·00
367 95c. Sputnik 1 35 10
368 95c. Vostok rocket 35 65
369 95c. Voskhod rocket 35 2·75
370 95c. Space walk 35 3·75
371 $1.25 Fuelling for flight 40 10
372 $1.25 Leaving New York 40 20
373 $1.25 "Spirit of St. Louis" 40 1·25
374 $1.25 Welcome to England 40 10
375 $2 Lion of England 50 50
376 $2 Unicorn of Scotland 50 50
377 $2 Yale of Beaufort 50 60
378 $2 Falcon of Plantagenets 50 1·10
379 $5 "Daniel in the Lion's Den" (Rubens) 50 10
380 $5 Different detail of painting 50 60
381 $5 Different detail of painting 50 60
382 $5 Different detail of painting 50 2·25
**MS**383 132×156 mm. Nos. 362/82 6·00 17·00

EVENTS: 75c. 75th anniv of navigable airships; 95c. 20th anniv of U.S.S.R. space programme; $1.25, 50th anniv of Lindbergh's transatlantic flight; $2 Silver Jubilee of Queen Elizabeth II; $5 400th birth anniv of Rubens.

Nos. 379/82 form a composite design.

**1978.** 10th Anniv of Statehood. Nos. 562/7 of Antigua optd **BARBUDA**.
384 10c. Type **135** 10 10
385 15c. State flag 15 30
386 50c. Police band 1·25 75
387 90c. Premier V. C. Bird 20 2·50
388 $2 State Coat of Arms 40 3·00
**MS**389 122×99 mm. Nos. 385/88 7·00 4·00

**66** "Pieta" (sculpture) (detail)

**1978.** Easter. Paintings and Sculptures by Michelangelo. Multicoloured.
390 75c. Type **66** 15 1·50
391 95c. "The Holy Family" 15 55
392 $1.25 "Libyan sibyl" (from the Sistine Chapel) 15 10
393 $2 "The Flood" (from the Sistine Chapel) 20 70
**MS**394 117×85 mm. Nos. 390/3 1·90 2·00

**1978.** 75th Anniv of Powered Flight. Nos. 568/75 of Antigua optd **BARBUDA**.
395 ½c. Wright Glider No. III, 1902 10 30
396 1c. Wright Flyer I, 1903 10 20
397 2c. Launch system and engine 10 2·50
398 10c. Orville Wright (vert) 10 1·75
399 50c. Wright Flyer III, 1905 25 1·50
400 90c. Wilbur Wright (vert) 35 1·75
401 $2 Wright Type B, 1910 60 2·25
**MS**402 90×75 mm. $2.50, Wright Flyer I on launch system 1·50 2·50

**1978.** Sailing Week. Nos. 576/80 of Antigua optd **BARBUDA**.
403 10c. Sunfish regatta 20 5·00
404 50c. Fishing and work boat race 40 10
405 90c. Curtain Bluff race 55 15
406 $2 Power boat rally 85 25
**MS**407 110×77 mm. $2.50, Guadeloupe–Antigua race 1·25 1·60

**68** St. Edward's Crown

**1978.** 25th Anniv of Coronation (1st issue). Multicoloured.
408 75c. Type **68** 15 80
409 75c. Imperial State Crown 15 10
410 $1.50 Queen Mary's Crown 20 55
411 $1.50 Queen Mother's Crown 20 65

| 412 | $2.50 Queen Consort's Crown | 35 | 1·50 |
|---|---|---|---|
| 413 | $2.50 Queen Victoria's Crown | 35 | 10 |
| **MS**414 | 123×117 mm. Nos. 408/13 | 1·10 | 1·75 |

**1978.** 25th Anniv of Coronation (2nd issue). Nos. 581/5 of Antigua optd **BARBUDA**.

| 415 | 10c. Queen Elizabeth and Prince Philip | 10 | 30 |
|---|---|---|---|
| 416 | 30c. The Crowning | 10 | 1·00 |
| 417 | 50c. Coronation procession | 10 | 15 |
| 418 | 90c. Queen seated in St. Edward's Chair | 15 | 35 |
| 419 | $2.50 Queen wearing Imperial State Crown | 30 | 1·10 |
| **MS**420 | 114×103 mm. $5 Queen Elizabeth and Prince Philip | 1·00 | 1·50 |

**1978.** 25th Anniv of Coronation (3rd issue). As Nos. 587/9 of Antigua, additionally inscr "BARBUDA".

| 421 | 25c. Glass Coach | 30 | 10 |
|---|---|---|---|
| 422 | 50c. Irish State Coach | 30 | 20 |
| 423 | $5 Coronation Coach | 1·00 | 35 |

**1978.** World Cup Football Championship, Argentina. Nos. 590/3 of Antigua optd **BARBUDA**.

| 424 | 10c. Player running with ball | 10 | 90 |
|---|---|---|---|
| 425 | 15c. Players in front of goal | 10 | 1·00 |
| 426 | $3 Referee and player | 1·00 | 10 |
| **MS**427 | 126×88 mm. 25c. Player crouching with ball; 30c. Players heading ball; 50c. Players running with ball; $2 Goalkeeper diving | 80 | 90 |

**1978.** Flowers. As Nos. 594/7 of Antigua optd **BARBUDA**.

| 428 | 25c. Petrea | 15 | 50 |
|---|---|---|---|
| 429 | 50c. Sunflower | 25 | 1·50 |
| 430 | 90c. Frangipani | 35 | 10 |
| 431 | $2 Passion flower | 60 | 35 |
| **MS**432 | 118×85 mm. $2.50, Hibiscus | 1·00 | 1·50 |

**1978.** Christmas. As Nos. 599/601 of Antigua optd **BARBUDA**.

| 433 | 8c. "St. Ildefonso receiving the Chasuble from the Virgin" | 10 | 80 |
|---|---|---|---|
| 434 | 25c. "The Flight of St. Barbara" | 15 | 90 |
| 435 | $2 "Madonna and Child, with St. Joseph, John the Baptist and Donor" | 60 | 2·50 |
| **MS**436 | 170×113 mm. $4 "The Annuciation" | 1·00 | 1·25 |

**70** Black-barred Soldierfish

**1978.** Flora and Fauna. Multicoloured.

| 437 | 25c. Type **70** | 1·25 | 40 |
|---|---|---|---|
| 438 | 50c. "Cynthia cardui" (butterfly) | 2·00 | 80 |
| 439 | 75c. Dwarf poinciana | 1·50 | 10 |
| 440 | 95c. "Heliconius charithonia" (butterfly) | 2·00 | 20 |
| 441 | $1.25 Bougainvillea | 1·50 | 30 |

**71** Footballers and World Cup

**1978.** Anniversaries and Events.

| 442 | 75c. Type **71** | 30 | 1·25 |
|---|---|---|---|
| 443 | 95c. Wright Brothers and Flyer I (horiz) | 30 | 10 |
| 444 | $1.25 Balloon "Double Eagle II" and map of Atlantic (horiz) | 40 | 55 |
| 445 | $2 Prince Philip paying homage to the Queen | 40 | 60 |
| **MS**446 | 122×90 mm. Nos. 442/5. Imperf | 5·00 | 6·00 |

EVENTS: 75c. Argentina—Winners of World Cup Football Championship; 95c. 75th anniv of powered flight; $1.25, First Atlantic crossing by balloon; $2 25th anniv of Coronation.

**72** Sir Rowland Hill

**1979.** Death Centenary of Sir Rowland Hill (1st issue). Multicoloured.

| 447 | 75c. Type **72** | 25 | 10 |
|---|---|---|---|
| 448 | 95c. Mail coach, 1840 (horiz) | 25 | 80 |
| 449 | $1.25 London's first pillar box, 1855 (horiz) | 30 | 1·40 |
| 450 | $2 Mail leaving St. Martin's Le Grand Post Office, London | 45 | 1·75 |
| **MS**451 | 129×104 mm. Nos. 447/50. Imperf | 1·40 | 2·25 |

**1979.** Death Centenary of Sir Rowland Hill (2nd issue). Nos. 603/6 of Antigua optd **BARBUDA**.

| 452 | 25c. 1d. Stamp of 1863 | 15 | 3·50 |
|---|---|---|---|
| 453 | 50c. Penny Black | 20 | 20 |
| 454 | $1 Stage-coach and woman posting letter, c. 1840 | 35 | 85 |
| 455 | $2 Modern mail transport | 80 | 1·25 |
| **MS**456 | 108×82 mm. $2.50, Sir Rowland Hill | 75 | 80 |

**1979.** Easter. Works of Durer. Nos. 608/11 of Antigua optd **BARBUDA**.

| 457 | 10c. multicoloured | 10 | 15 |
|---|---|---|---|
| 458 | 50c. multicoloured | 20 | 1·00 |
| 459 | $4 black, mauve and yellow | 90 | 3·75 |
| **MS**460 | 114×99 mm. $2.50, multicoloured | 55 | 75 |

**74** Passengers alighting from British Airways Boeing 747

**1979.** 30th Anniv of International Civil Aviation Organization. Multicoloured.

| 461 | 75c. Type **74** | 25 | 15 |
|---|---|---|---|
| 462 | 95c. Air traffic control | 25 | 75 |
| 463 | $1.25 Ground crew-man directing Douglas DC-8 on runway | 25 | 90 |

**1979.** International Year of the Child (1st issue). Nos. 612/15 of Antigua optd **BARBUDA**.

| 464 | 25c. Yacht | 20 | 3·25 |
|---|---|---|---|
| 465 | 50c. Rocket | 30 | 20 |
| 466 | 90c. Car | 40 | 1·25 |
| 467 | $2 Toy train | 80 | 1·75 |
| **MS**468 | 80×112 mm. $5 Airplane | 1·10 | 1·10 |

**1979.** Fish. Nos. 617/21 of Antigua optd **BARBUDA**.

| 469 | 30c. Yellow jack | 20 | 15 |
|---|---|---|---|
| 470 | 50c. Blue-finned tuna | 25 | 80 |
| 471 | 90c. Sailfish | 30 | 1·10 |
| 472 | $3 Wahoo | 65 | 3·25 |
| **MS**473 | 122×75 mm. $2.50, Great barracuda | 1·00 | 1·25 |

**1979.** Death Bicentenary of Captain Cook. Nos. 622/6 of Antigua optd **BARBUDA**.

| 474 | 25c. Cook's Birthplace, Marton | 25 | 1·25 |
|---|---|---|---|
| 475 | 50c. H.M.S. "Endeavour" | 70 | 1·25 |
| 476 | 90c. Marine chronometer | 70 | 6·00 |
| 477 | $3 Landing at Botany Bay | 1·50 | 1·25 |
| **MS**478 | 110×85 mm. $2.50, H.M.S. "Resolution" | 1·25 | 1·50 |

**77** "Virgin with the Pear"

**1979.** International Year of the Child (2nd issue). Paintings by Durer. Multicoloured.

| 479 | 25c. Type **77** | 15 | 75 |
|---|---|---|---|
| 480 | 50c. "Virgin with the Pink" (detail) | 20 | 1·25 |
| 481 | 75c. "Virgin with the Pear" (different detail) | 25 | 5·50 |
| 482 | $1.25 "Nativity" (detail) | 25 | 15 |
| **MS**483 | 86×118 mm. Nos. 479/82 | 1·00 | 1·75 |

**1979.** Christmas. Nos. 627/31 of Antigua optd **BARBUDA**.

| 484 | 8c. The Holy Family | 10 | 1·50 |
|---|---|---|---|
| 485 | 25c. Mary and Jesus on donkey | 15 | 4·50 |
| 486 | 50c. Shepherd looking at star | 25 | 15 |
| 487 | $4 The Three Kings | 85 | 70 |
| **MS**488 | 113×94 mm. $3 Angel with trumpet | 80 | 1·10 |

**1980.** Olympic Games, Moscow. Nos. 632/6 of Antigua optd **BARBUDA**.

| 489 | 10c. Javelin | 10 | 3·75 |
|---|---|---|---|
| 490 | 25c. Running | 15 | 65 |
| 491 | $1 Pole vault | 35 | 95 |
| 492 | $2 Hurdles | 55 | 1·25 |
| **MS**493 | 127×96 mm. $3 Boxing | 70 | 1·10 |

**1980.** "London 1980" International Stamp Exhibition. Nos. 452/5 optd **LONDON 1980**.

| 494 | 25c. 1d. stamp of 1863 | 35 | 15 |
|---|---|---|---|
| 495 | 50c. Penny Black | 45 | 50 |
| 496 | $1 Stage-coach and woman posting letter, c. 1840 | 85 | 60 |
| 497 | $2 Modern mail transport | 2·75 | 2·75 |

**80** "Apollo 11" Crew Badge

**1980.** 10th Anniv of "Apollo 11" Moon Landing. Multicoloured.

| 498 | 75c. Type **80** | 60 | 25 |
|---|---|---|---|
| 499 | 95c. Plaque left on Moon | 60 | 15 |
| 500 | $1.25 Rejoining the mother-ship | 70 | 80 |
| 501 | $2 Lunar module | 90 | 1·40 |
| **MS**502 | 118×84 mm. Nos. 498/501 | 1·60 | 2·50 |

**81** American Wigeon ("American Widgeon")

**1980.** Birds. Multicoloured.

| 503 | 1c. Type **81** | 70 | 25 |
|---|---|---|---|
| 504 | 2c. Snowy plover | 70 | 1·75 |
| 505 | 4c. Rose-breasted grosbeak | 75 | 2·50 |
| 506 | 6c. Mangrove cuckoo | 75 | 6·50 |
| 507 | 10c. Adelaide's warbler | 75 | 70 |
| 508 | 15c. Scaly-breasted thrasher | 80 | 70 |
| 509 | 20c. Yellow-crowned night heron | 80 | 70 |
| 510 | 25c. Bridled quail dove | 80 | 70 |
| 511 | 35c. Carib grackle | 85 | 1·25 |
| 512 | 50c. Northern pintail | 90 | 55 |
| 513 | 75c. Black-whispered vireo | 1·00 | 55 |
| 514 | $1 Blue-winged teal | 1·25 | 80 |
| 515 | $1.50 Green-throated carib (vert) | 1·50 | 80 |
| 516 | $2 Red-necked pigeon (vert) | 2·25 | 1·25 |
| 517 | $2.50 Wied's crested flycatcher ("Stolid Flycatcher") (vert) | 2·75 | 1·50 |
| 518 | $5 Yellow-bellied sapsucker (vert) | 3·50 | 3·50 |
| 519 | $7.50 Caribbean elaenia (vert) | 4·00 | 6·00 |
| 520 | $10 Great egret (vert) | 4·00 | 5·00 |

**1980.** Famous Works of Art. Nos. 651/8 of Antigua optd **BARBUDA**.

| 521 | 10c. "David" (statue, Donatello) | 10 | 10 |
|---|---|---|---|
| 522 | 30c. "The Birth of Venus" (painting, Sandro Botticelli) | 15 | 15 |
| 523 | 50c. "Reclining Couple" (sarcophagus), Cerveteri | 15 | 20 |
| 524 | 90c. "The Garden of Earthly Delights" (painting, Hieronymus Bosch) | 20 | 30 |
| 525 | $1 "Portinari Altarpiece" (painting, Hugo van der Goes) | 20 | 60 |
| 526 | $4 "Eleanora of Toledo and her Son Giovanni de'Medici" (painting, Agnolo Bronzino) | 60 | 75 |
| **MS**527 | 99×124 mm. $5 "The Holy Family" (painting, Rembrandt) | 1·50 | 1·75 |

**1980.** 75th Anniv of Rotary International. Nos. 658/62 of Antigua optd **BARBUDA**.

| 528 | 30c. Rotary Headquarters | 15 | 2·50 |
|---|---|---|---|
| 529 | 50c. Antigua Rotary banner | 20 | 30 |
| 530 | 90c. Map of Antigua | 25 | 70 |
| 531 | $3 Paul P. Harris (founder) | 65 | 1·00 |
| **MS**532 | 102×77 mm. $5 Antigua flags and Rotary emblems | 1·50 | 2·25 |

**1980.** 80th Birthday of the Queen Mother. Nos. 663/5 of Antigua optd **BARBUDA**.

| 533 | 10c. multicoloured | 50 | 15 |
|---|---|---|---|
| 534 | $2.50 multicoloured | 1·25 | 4·25 |
| **MS**535 | 68×88 mm. $3 multicoloured | 2·50 | 1·75 |

**1980.** Birds. Nos. 666/70 of Antigua optd **BARBUDA**.

| 536 | 10c. Ringed kingfisher | 3·25 | 90 |
|---|---|---|---|
| 537 | 30c. Plain pigeon | 3·75 | 1·50 |
| 538 | $1 Green-throated carib | 5·00 | 6·25 |
| 539 | $2 Black necked stilt | 6·00 | 25 |
| **MS**540 | 73×73 mm. $2.50, Roseate tern | 5·50 | 2·75 |

**1981.** Sugar Cane Railway Locomotives. Nos. 681/5 of Antigua optd **BARBUDA**.

| 541 | 25c. Diesel locomotive No. 15 | 1·00 | 55 |
|---|---|---|---|
| 542 | 50c. Narrow-gauge steam locomotive | 1·25 | 70 |
| 543 | 90c. Diesel locomotive Nos. 1 and 10 | 1·75 | 2·50 |
| 544 | $3 Steam locomotive hauling sugar cane | 3·25 | 1·75 |
| **MS**545 | 82×111 mm. $2.50, Antigua sugar factory, railway yard and sheds | 1·50 | 1·75 |

**84** Florence Nightingale

**1981.** Famous Women.

| 546 | **84** | 50c. multicoloured | 15 | 1·75 |
|---|---|---|---|---|
| 547 | - | 90c. multicoloured | 40 | 1·75 |
| 548 | - | $1 multicoloured | 35 | 1·75 |
| 549 | - | $4 black, brown and lilac | 50 | 15 |

DESIGNS: 90c. Marie Curie; $1 Amy Johnson; $4 Eleanor Roosevelt.

**85** Goofy in Motor-boat

**1981.** Walt Disney Cartoon Characters. Mult.

| 550 | 10c. Type **85** | 90 | 70 |
|---|---|---|---|
| 551 | 20c. Donald Duck reversing car into sea | 1·25 | 80 |
| 552 | 25c. Mickey Mouse asking tug-boat to take on more than it can handle | 1·40 | 3·50 |
| 553 | 30c. Porpoise turning tables on Goofy | 1·40 | 15 |
| 554 | 35c. Goofy in sailing boat | 1·40 | 60 |
| 555 | 40c. Mickey Mouse and boat being lifted out of water by fish | 1·40 | 70 |
| 556 | 75c. Donald Duck fishing for flying-fish with butterfly net | 2·00 | 5·75 |
| 557 | $1 Minnie Mouse in brightly decorated sailing boat | 2·00 | 15 |
| 558 | $2 Chip and Dale on floating ship-in-bottle | 2·50 | 55 |
| **MS**559 | 127×101 mm. $2.50, Donald Duck | 4·50 | 3·00 |

**1981.** Birth Centenary of Picasso. Nos. 697/701 of Antigua optd with **BARBUDA**.

| 560 | 10c. "Pipes of Pan" | 10 | 3·25 |
|---|---|---|---|
| 561 | 50c. "Seated Harlequin" | 25 | 25 |
| 562 | 90c. "Paulo as Harlequin" | 35 | 45 |
| 563 | $4 "Mother and Child" | 90 | 85 |
| **MS**564 | 115×140 mm. $5 "Three Musicians" (detail) | 1·40 | 1·50 |

**87/8** Buckingham Palace (image scaled to 73% of original size)

**1981.** Royal Wedding (1st issue). Buildings. Each printed in black on either pink, green or lilac backgrounds.

| | | | |
|---|---|---|---|
| 565 | $1 Type **87** | 25 | 6·50 |
| 566 | $1 Type **88** | 25 | 25 |
| 567 | $1.50 Caernarvon Castle (right) | 30 | 65 |
| 568 | $1.50 Caernarvon Castle (left) | 30 | 75 |
| 569 | $4 Highgrove House (right) | 55 | 4·00 |
| 570 | $4 Highgrove House (left) | 55 | 25 |
| **MS**571 | 75×90 mm. $5 black and yellow (St. Paul's Cathedral—26×32 mm) | 80 | 1·25 |

Same prices for any background colour. The two versions of each value form composite designs.

**1981.** Royal Wedding (2nd issue). Nos. 702/5 of Antigua optd **BARBUDA**.

| | | | |
|---|---|---|---|
| 572 | 25c. Prince Charles and Lady Diana Spencer | 15 | 1·25 |
| 573 | 50c. Glamis Castle | 25 | 8·00 |
| 574 | $4 Prince Charles skiing | 75 | 25 |
| **MS**575 | 95×85 mm. $5 Glass coach | 90 | 90 |

**89** "Integration and Travel"

**1981.** International Year of Disabled Persons (1st issue).

| | | | | |
|---|---|---|---|---|
| 576 | **89** | 50c. multicoloured | 25 | 75 |
| 577 | - | 90c. black, orange and green | 25 | 4·50 |
| 578 | - | $1 black, blue and green | 30 | 25 |
| 579 | - | $4 black, yellow and brown | 45 | 45 |

DESIGNS: 90c. Braille and sign language; $1 "Helping hands"; $4 "Mobility aids for disabled".

See also Nos. 603/6.

**1981.** Royal Wedding (3rd issue). Nos. 706/12 of Antigua optd **BARBUDA**.

| | | | |
|---|---|---|---|
| 580 | 25c. Prince of Wales at Investiture, 1969 | 40 | 1·25 |
| 581 | 25c. Prince Charles as baby, 1948 | 40 | 1·40 |
| 582 | $1 Prince Charles at R.A.F. College, Cranwell, 1971 | 50 | 2·50 |
| 583 | $1 Prince Charles attending Hill House School, 1956 | 50 | 3·50 |
| 584 | $2 Prince Charles and Lady Diana Spencer | 75 | 25 |
| 585 | $2 Prince Charles at Trinity College, 1967 | 75 | 60 |
| 586 | $5 Prince Charles and Lady Diana | 4·25 | 1·40 |

**1981.** Independence. No. 686/96 of Antigua additionally optd **BARBUDA**.

| | | | |
|---|---|---|---|
| 587 | 6c. Orchid tree | 50 | 1·60 |
| 588 | 10c. Bougainvillea | 55 | 6·00 |
| 589 | 20c. Flamboyant | 70 | 2·25 |
| 590 | 25c. Hibiscus | 80 | 2·25 |
| 591 | 35c. Flame of the wood | 90 | 2·25 |
| 592 | 50c. Cannon at Fort James | 1·10 | 2·25 |
| 593 | 75c. Premier's Office | 1·25 | 2·25 |
| 594 | $1 Potworks Dam | 1·50 | 2·25 |
| 595 | $2.50 Irrigation scheme, Diamond Estate | 2·50 | 2·25 |
| 596 | $5 Government House and Gardens | 2·75 | 2·25 |
| 597 | $10 Coolidge International Airport | 4·50 | 2·25 |

**1981.** 50th Anniv of Antigua Girl Guide Movement. Nos. 713/16 of Antigua optd **BARBUDA**.

| | | | |
|---|---|---|---|
| 598 | 10c. Irene Joshua (founder) | 55 | 2·25 |
| 599 | 50c. Campfire sing-song | 1·25 | 25 |
| 600 | 90c. Sailing | 1·75 | 65 |
| 601 | $2.50 Animal tending | 3·00 | 85 |
| **MS**602 | 170×113 mm. $4 "The Annunciation" (Rubens) | 3·50 | 1·50 |

**1981.** International Year of Disabled Persons (2nd issue). Sport for the Disabled. Nos. 728/32 of Antigua optd **BARBUDA**.

| | | | |
|---|---|---|---|
| 603 | 10c. Swimming | 15 | 15 |
| 604 | 50c. Discus throwing | 20 | 25 |
| 605 | 90c. Archery | 45 | 45 |
| 606 | $2 Baseball | 60 | 1·50 |
| **MS**607 | 108×84 mm. $4 Basketball | 2·00 | 1·75 |

**1981.** Christmas. Paintings. Nos. 723/7 of Antigua optd **BARBUDA**.

| | | | |
|---|---|---|---|
| 608 | 8c. "Holy Night" (Jacques Stella) | 10 | 10 |
| 609 | 30c. "Mary with Child" (Julius Schnorr von Carolfeld) | 20 | 20 |
| 610 | $1 "Virgin and Child" (Alsono Cano) | 40 | 40 |
| 611 | $3 "Virgin and Child" (Lorenzo di Credi) | 1·10 | 1·10 |
| **MS**612 | 77×111 mm. $5 "Holy Family" (Pieter von Avon) | 1·75 | 2·25 |

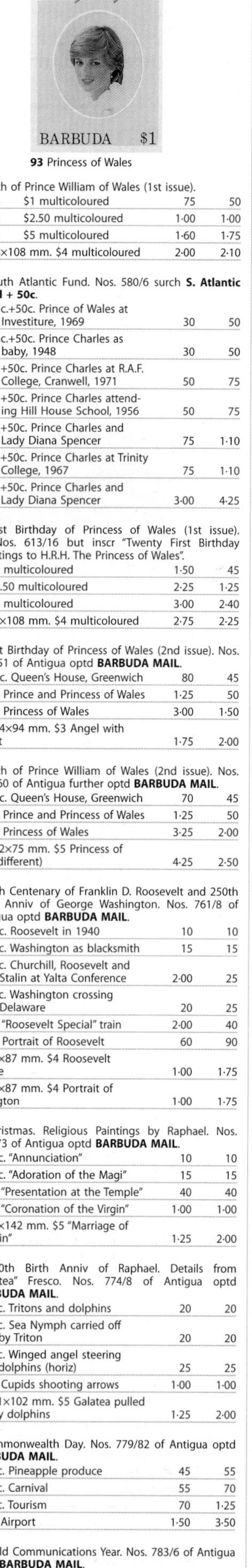

**93** Princess of Wales

**1982.** Birth of Prince William of Wales (1st issue).

| | | | | |
|---|---|---|---|---|
| 613 | **93** | $1 multicoloured | 75 | 50 |
| 614 | **93** | $2.50 multicoloured | 1·00 | 1·00 |
| 615 | **93** | $5 multicoloured | 1·60 | 1·75 |
| **MS**616 | | 88×108 mm. $4 multicoloured | 2·00 | 2·10 |

**1982.** South Atlantic Fund. Nos. 580/6 surch **S. Atlantic Fund + 50c**.

| | | | |
|---|---|---|---|
| 617 | 25c.+50c. Prince of Wales at Investiture, 1969 | 30 | 50 |
| 618 | 25c.+50c. Prince Charles as baby, 1948 | 30 | 50 |
| 619 | $1+50c. Prince Charles at R.A.F. College, Cranwell, 1971 | 50 | 75 |
| 620 | $1+50c. Prince Charles attending Hill House School, 1956 | 50 | 75 |
| 621 | $2+50c. Prince Charles and Lady Diana Spencer | 75 | 1·10 |
| 622 | $2+50c. Prince Charles at Trinity College, 1967 | 75 | 1·10 |
| 623 | $5+50c. Prince Charles and Lady Diana Spencer | 3·00 | 4·25 |

**1982.** 21st Birthday of Princess of Wales (1st issue). As Nos. 613/16 but inscr "Twenty First Birthday Greetings to H.R.H. The Princess of Wales".

| | | | |
|---|---|---|---|
| 624 | $1 multicoloured | 1·50 | 45 |
| 625 | $2.50 multicoloured | 2·25 | 1·25 |
| 626 | $5 multicoloured | 3·00 | 2·40 |
| **MS**627 | 88×108 mm. $4 multicoloured | 2·75 | 2·25 |

**1982.** 21st Birthday of Princess of Wales (2nd issue). Nos. 748/51 of Antigua optd **BARBUDA MAIL**.

| | | | |
|---|---|---|---|
| 628 | 90c. Queen's House, Greenwich | 80 | 45 |
| 629 | $1 Prince and Princess of Wales | 1·25 | 50 |
| 630 | $4 Princess of Wales | 3·00 | 1·50 |
| **MS**631 | 114×94 mm. $3 Angel with trumpet | 1·75 | 2·00 |

**1982.** Birth of Prince William of Wales (2nd issue). Nos. 757/60 of Antigua further optd **BARBUDA MAIL**.

| | | | |
|---|---|---|---|
| 632 | 90c. Queen's House, Greenwich | 70 | 45 |
| 633 | $1 Prince and Princess of Wales | 1·25 | 50 |
| 634 | $4 Princess of Wales | 3·25 | 2·00 |
| **MS**635 | 102×75 mm. $5 Princess of Wales (different) | 4·25 | 2·50 |

**1982.** Birth Centenary of Franklin D. Roosevelt and 250th Birth Anniv of George Washington. Nos. 761/8 of Antigua optd **BARBUDA MAIL**.

| | | | |
|---|---|---|---|
| 636 | 10c. Roosevelt in 1940 | 10 | 10 |
| 637 | 25c. Washington as blacksmith | 15 | 15 |
| 638 | 45c. Churchill, Roosevelt and Stalin at Yalta Conference | 2·00 | 25 |
| 639 | 60c. Washington crossing Delaware | 20 | 25 |
| 640 | $1 "Roosevelt Special" train | 2·00 | 40 |
| 641 | $3 Portrait of Roosevelt | 60 | 90 |
| **MS**642 | 92×87 mm. $4 Roosevelt and wife | 1·00 | 1·75 |
| **MS**643 | 92×87 mm. $4 Portrait of Washington | 1·00 | 1·75 |

**1982.** Christmas. Religious Paintings by Raphael. Nos. 769/73 of Antigua optd **BARBUDA MAIL**.

| | | | |
|---|---|---|---|
| 644 | 10c. "Annunciation" | 10 | 10 |
| 645 | 30c. "Adoration of the Magi" | 15 | 15 |
| 646 | $1 "Presentation at the Temple" | 40 | 40 |
| 647 | $4 "Coronation of the Virgin" | 1·00 | 1·00 |
| **MS**648 | 95×142 mm. $5 "Marriage of the Virgin" | 1·25 | 2·00 |

**1983.** 500th Birth Anniv of Raphael. Details from "Galatea" Fresco. Nos. 774/8 of Antigua optd **BARBUDA MAIL**.

| | | | |
|---|---|---|---|
| 649 | 45c. Tritons and dolphins | 20 | 20 |
| 650 | 50c. Sea Nymph carried off by Triton | 20 | 20 |
| 651 | 60c. Winged angel steering dolphins (horiz) | 25 | 25 |
| 652 | $4 Cupids shooting arrows | 1·00 | 1·00 |
| **MS**653 | 101×102 mm. $5 Galatea pulled along by dolphins | 1·25 | 2·00 |

**1983.** Commonwealth Day. Nos. 779/82 of Antigua optd **BARBUDA MAIL**.

| | | | |
|---|---|---|---|
| 654 | 25c. Pineapple produce | 45 | 55 |
| 655 | 45c. Carnival | 55 | 70 |
| 656 | 60c. Tourism | 70 | 1·25 |
| 657 | $3 Airport | 1·50 | 3·50 |

**1983.** World Communications Year. Nos. 783/6 of Antigua optd **BARBUDA MAIL**.

| | | | |
|---|---|---|---|
| 658 | 15c. T.V. satellite coverage of Royal Wedding | 2·00 | 25 |
| 659 | 50c. Police communications | 4·50 | 90 |
| 660 | 60c. House-to-diesel train telephone call | 3·00 | 90 |
| 661 | $3 Satellite earth station with planets Jupiter and Saturn | 3·75 | 2·50 |
| **MS**662 | 100×90 mm. $5 "Comsat" satellite over West Indies | 1·50 | 2·25 |

**97** Vincenzo Lunardi's Balloon Flight, London, 1785

**1983.** Bicent of Manned Flight (1st issue). Mult.

| | | | |
|---|---|---|---|
| 663 | $1 Type **97** | 25 | 35 |
| 664 | $1.50 Montgolfier brothers' balloon flight, Paris, 1783 | 40 | 55 |
| 665 | $2.50 Blanchard and Jeffries' Cross-Channel balloon flight, 1785 | 60 | 90 |
| **MS**666 | 111×111 mm. $5 Maiden flight of airship LZ-127 "Graf Zeppelin", 1928 | 2·00 | 2·75 |

See also Nos. 672/6.

**1983.** Whales. Nos. 788/93 of Antigua optd **BARBUDA MAIL**.

| | | | |
|---|---|---|---|
| 667 | 15c. Bottlenose dolphin | 1·25 | 40 |
| 668 | 50c. Finback whale | 4·00 | 1·60 |
| 669 | 60c. Bowhead whale | 4·50 | 1·75 |
| 670 | $3 Spectacled porpoise | 5·50 | 4·25 |
| **MS**671 | 122×101 mm. $5 Narwhal | 6·00 | 4·50 |

**1983.** Bicentenary of Manned Flight (2nd issue). Nos. 811/15 of Antigua optd **BARBUDA MAIL**.

| | | | |
|---|---|---|---|
| 672 | 30c. Dornier Do-X flying boat | 1·25 | 35 |
| 673 | 50c. Supermarine S6B seaplane | 1·50 | 60 |
| 674 | 60c. Curtiss Sparrowhawk biplane and airship U.S.S. "Akron" | 1·75 | 70 |
| 675 | $4 Hot-air balloon "Pro-Juventute" | 5·00 | 4·00 |
| **MS**676 | 80×105 mm. $5 Airship LZ-127 "Graf Zeppelin" | 3·75 | 4·25 |

**1983.** Nos. 565/70 surch.

| | | | |
|---|---|---|---|
| 677 | 45c. on $1 Type **87** | 25 | 45 |
| 678 | 45c. on $1 Type **88** | 25 | 45 |
| 679 | 50c. on $1.45 Caernarvon Castle (right) | 25 | 45 |
| 680 | 50c. on $1.45 Caernarvon Castle (left) | 25 | 45 |
| 681 | 60c. on $4 Highgrove House (left) | 25 | 45 |
| 682 | 60c. on $4 Highgrove House (right) | 25 | 45 |

**1983.** Nos. 793/810 of Antigua optd **BARBUDA MAIL**.

| | | | |
|---|---|---|---|
| 683 | 1c. Cashew nut | 10 | 10 |
| 684 | 2c. Passion fruit | 15 | 10 |
| 685 | 3c. Mango | 15 | 10 |
| 686 | 5c. Grapefruit | 15 | 10 |
| 687 | 10c. Pawpaw | 20 | 10 |
| 688 | 15c. Breadfruit | 40 | 10 |
| 689 | 20c. Coconut | 50 | 15 |
| 690 | 25c. Oleander | 50 | 15 |
| 691 | 30c. Banana | 55 | 20 |
| 692 | 40c. Pineapple | 65 | 25 |
| 693 | 45c. Cordia | 70 | 30 |
| 694 | 50c. Cassia | 80 | 30 |
| 695 | 60c. Poui | 80 | 30 |
| 696 | $1 Frangipani | 1·10 | 50 |
| 697 | $2 Flamboyant | 1·75 | 1·25 |
| 698 | $2.50 Lemon | 2·00 | 1·75 |
| 699 | $5 Lignum vitae | 3·00 | 2·75 |
| 700 | $10 National flag and coat of arms | 4·50 | 5·50 |

**1983.** Christmas. 500th Birth Anniv of Raphael. Nos. 816/20 of Antigua optd **BARBUDA MAIL**.

| | | | |
|---|---|---|---|
| 701 | 10c. multicoloured | 10 | 10 |
| 702 | 30c. multicoloured | 10 | 20 |
| 703 | $1 multicoloured | 30 | 50 |
| 704 | $4 multicoloured | 1·00 | 1·50 |
| **MS**705 | 101×131 mm. $5 multicoloured | 1·40 | 2·50 |

**1983.** Bicentenary (1984) of Methodist Church. Nos. 821/4 of Antigua optd **BARBUDA MAIL**.

| | | | |
|---|---|---|---|
| 706 | 15c. Type **181** | 20 | 15 |
| 707 | 50c. Nathaniel Gilbert (founder in Antigua) | 30 | 25 |
| 708 | 60c. St. John Methodist Church steeple | 30 | 30 |
| 709 | $3 Ebenezer Methodist Church, St John's | 80 | 1·00 |

**100** Edward VII

**1984.** Members of British Royal Family. Mult.

| | | | |
|---|---|---|---|
| 710 | $1 Type **100** | 70 | 1·50 |
| 711 | $1 George V | 70 | 1·50 |
| 712 | $1 George VI | 70 | 1·50 |
| 713 | $1 Elizabeth II | 70 | 1·50 |
| 714 | $1 Charles, Prince of Wales | 70 | 1·50 |
| 715 | $1 Prince William of Wales | 70 | 1·50 |

**1984.** Olympic Games, Los Angeles (1st issue). Nos. 825/9 of Antigua optd **BARBUDA MAIL**.

| | | | |
|---|---|---|---|
| 716 | 25c. Discus | 25 | 20 |
| 717 | 50c. Gymnastics | 40 | 40 |
| 718 | 90c. Hurdling | 50 | 60 |
| 719 | $3 Cycling | 2·75 | 1·50 |
| **MS**720 | 82×67 mm. $5 Volleyball | 2·25 | 3·25 |

**1984.** Ships. Nos. 830/4 of Antigua optd **BARBUDA MAIL**.

| | | | |
|---|---|---|---|
| 721 | 45c. "Booker Vanguard" (freighter) | 1·50 | 45 |
| 722 | 50c. "Canberra" (liner) | 1·50 | 50 |
| 723 | 60c. Yachts | 1·75 | 60 |
| 724 | $4 "Fairwind" (cargo liner) | 4·25 | 2·75 |
| **MS**725 | 101×80 mm. $5 18th-century British man-o-war (vert) | 4·50 | 4·25 |

**1984.** Universal Postal Union Congress, Hamburg. Nos. 835/8 of Antigua optd **BARBUDA MAIL**.

| | | | |
|---|---|---|---|
| 726 | 15c. Chenille | 25 | 15 |
| 727 | 50c. Shell flower | 30 | 30 |
| 728 | 60c. Anthurium | 40 | 40 |
| 729 | $3 Angels trumpet | 75 | 1·25 |
| **MS**730 | 100×75 mm. $5 Crown of Thorns | 2·00 | 2·50 |

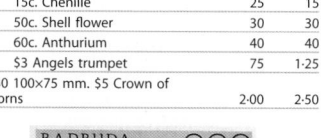

**101** Olympic Stadium, Athens, 1896

**1984.** Olympic Games, Los Angeles (2nd issue). Multicoloured.

| | | | |
|---|---|---|---|
| 731 | $1.50 Type **101** | 50 | 90 |
| 732 | $2.50 Olympic stadium, Los Angeles, 1984 | 70 | 1·50 |
| 733 | $5 Athlete carrying Olympic torch | 1·10 | 2·25 |
| **MS**734 | 121×95 mm. No. 733 | 1·50 | 2·50 |

**1984.** Presidents of the United States of America. Nos. 856/63 of Antigua optd **BARBUDA MAIL**.

| | | | |
|---|---|---|---|
| 735 | 10c. Abraham Lincoln | 10 | 10 |
| 736 | 20c. Harry Truman | 15 | 15 |
| 737 | 30c. Dwight Eisenhower | 20 | 25 |
| 738 | 40c. Ronald Reagan | 25 | 30 |
| 739 | 90c. Gettysburg Address, 1863 | 40 | 55 |
| 740 | $1.10 Formation of N.A.T.O., 1949 | 40 | 65 |
| 741 | $1.50 Eisenhower during Second World War | 45 | 70 |
| 742 | $2 Reagan and Caribbean Basin Initiative | 50 | 1·00 |

**1984.** Abolition of Slavery. Nos. 864/8 of Antigua optd **BARBUDA MAIL**.

| | | | |
|---|---|---|---|
| 743 | 40c. View of Moravian Mission | 30 | 30 |
| 744 | 50c. Antigua Courthouse, 1823 | 40 | 40 |
| 745 | 60c. Planting sugar-cane, Monks Hill | 45 | 45 |
| 746 | $3 Boiling house, Delaps' Estate | 1·40 | 1·40 |
| **MS**747 | 95×70 mm. $5 Loading sugar, Willoughby Bay | 2·00 | 2·50 |

**1984.** Songbirds. Nos. 869/74 of Antigua optd **BARBUDA MAIL**.

| | | | |
|---|---|---|---|
| 748 | 40c. Rufous-sided towhee | 2·25 | 55 |
| 749 | 50c. Parula warbler | 2·25 | 70 |
| 750 | 60c. House wren | 2·25 | 75 |
| 751 | $2 Ruby-crowned kinglet | 3·25 | 2·00 |
| 752 | $3 Common flicker ("Yellow-shafted Flicker") | 3·50 | 2·75 |
| **MS**753 | 76×76 mm. $5 Yellow-breasted chat | 4·00 | 4·50 |

**1984.** 450th Death Anniv of Correggio (painter). Nos. 878/82 of Antigua optd **BARBUDA MAIL**.

| | | | |
|---|---|---|---|
| 754 | 25c. "The Virgin and Infant with Angels and Cherubs" | 15 | 20 |
| 755 | 60c. "The Four Saints" | 40 | 45 |
| 756 | 90c. "St. Catherine" | 50 | 55 |
| 757 | $3 "The Campori Madonna" | 1·25 | 1·75 |

MS758 90×60 mm. $5 "St. John the Baptist" 1·75 3·25

**1984.** "Ausipex" International Stamp Exhibition Melbourne. Australian Sports. Nos. 875/7 of Antigua optd **BARBUDA MAIL**.

759 $1 Grass-skiing 50 60
760 $5 Australian Football 2·00 3·00
MS761 108×78 mm. Boomerang-throwing 2·00 3·25

**1984.** 150th Birth Anniv of Edgar Degas (painter). Nos. 883/7 of Antigua optd **BARBUDA MAIL**.

762 15c. "The Blue Dancers" 10 10
763 50c. "The Pink Dancers" 30 40
764 70c. "Two Dancers" 45 55
765 $4 "Dancers at the Bar" 1·25 3·50
MS766 90×60 mm. $5 "The Folk Dancers" (40×27 mm) 1·75 2·75

**1985.** Famous People. Nos. 888/96 of Antigua optd **BARBUDA MAIL**.

767 60c. Winston Churchill 5·50 2·50
768 60c. Mahatma Gandhi 5·50 2·50
769 60c. John F. Kennedy 5·50 2·50
770 60c. Mao Tse-tung 5·50 2·50
771 $1 Churchill with General De Gaulle, Paris, 1944 (horiz) 5·50 2·50
772 $1 Gandhi leaving London by train, 1931 (horiz) 5·50 2·50
773 $1 Kennedy with Chancellor Adenauer and Mayor Brandt, Berlin, 1963 (horiz) 5·50 2·50
774 $1 Mao Tse-tung with Lin Piao, Peking, 1969 (horiz) 5·50 2·50
MS775 114×80 mm. $5 Flags of Great Britain, India, the United States and China 9·00 8·00

**103** Lady Elizabeth Bowes-Lyon, 1907, and Camellias

**1985.** Life and Times of Queen Elizabeth the Queen Mother. Multicoloured.

776 15c. Type **103** 35 20
777 45c. Duchess of York, 1926, and "Elizabeth of Glamis" roses 45 25
778 50c. The Queen Mother after the Coronation, 1937 45 25
779 60c. In Garter robes, 1971, and dog roses 45 30
780 90c. Attending Royal Variety Show, 1967, and red Hibiscus 60 45
781 $1 The Queen Mother in 1982, and blue plumbago 75 1·10
782 $3 Receiving 82nd birthday gifts from children, and morning glory 95 2·50

**104** Roseate Tern

**1985.** Birth Bicentenary of John J. Audubon (ornithologist) (1st issue). Designs showing original paintings. Multicoloured.

783 45c. Type **104** 25 30
784 50c. Mangrove cuckoo 25 30
785 60c. Yellow-crowned night heron 30 40
786 $5 Brown pelican 1·00 3·50

See also Nos. 794/7 and 914/17.

**1985.** Centenary (1986) of Statue of Liberty (1st issue). Nos. 907/13 of Antigua optd **BARBUDA MAIL**.

787 25c. Torch from statue in Madison Square Park, 1885 20 20
788 30c. Statue of Liberty and scaffolding ("Restoration and Renewal") (vert) 20 20
789 50c. Frederic Bartholdi (sculpture) supervising construction, 1876 30 30
790 90c. Close-up of Statue 55 55
791 $1 Statue and sailing ship ("Operation Sail", 1976) (vert) 60 60
792 $3 Dedication ceremony, 1886 (vert) 1·75 1·75
MS793 110×80 mm. $5 Port of New York 5·75 4·75

See also Nos. 987/96.

**1985.** Birth Bicentenary of John J. Audubon (ornithologist) (2nd issue). Nos. 924/8 of Antigua optd **BARBUDA MAIL**.

794 90c. Slavonian grebe ("Horned Grebe") 9·00 4·25
795 $1 British storm petrel ("Least Petrel") 9·00 4·50
796 $1.50 Great blue heron 10·00 8·50
797 $3 Double-crested cormorant (white phase) 15·00 13·00
MS798 103×72 mm. $5 White-tailed tropic bird (vert) 28·00 11·00

**1985.** Butterflies. Nos. 929/33 of Antigua optd **BARBUDA MAIL**.

799 25c. "Anaea cyanea" 6·50 1·25
800 60c. "Leodonta dysoni" 8·50 2·00
801 90c. "Junea doraete" 9·50 2·50
802 $4 "Prepona pylene" 17·00 19·00
MS803 132×105 mm. $5 "Caervois gerdtrudtus" 16·00 9·00

**1985.** Centenary of Motorcycle. Nos. 919/23 of Antigua optd **BARBUDA MAIL**.

804 10c. Triumph 2hp "Jap", 1903 1·00 20
805 30c. Indian "Arrow", 1949 1·50 25
806 60c. BMW "R100RS", 1976 2·00 55
807 $4 Harley Davidson "Model II", 1916 5·00 4·50
MS808 90×93 mm. $5 Laverda "Jota", 1975 6·00 4·00

**1985.** 85th Birthday of Queen Elizabeth the Queen Mother. Nos. 776/82 optd **4TH AUG 1900–1985**.

809 15c. Type **103** 75 50
810 45c. Duchess of York, 1926 and "Elizabeth of Glamis" roses 1·10 60
811 50c. The Queen Mother after the Coronation, 1937 1·10 60
812 60c. In Garter robes, 1971, and dog roses 1·25 1·00
813 90c. Attending Royal Variey Show, 1967, and red hibiscus 1·25 1·25
814 $2 The Queen Mother in 1982, and blue plumbago 1·40 3·75
815 $3 Receiving 82nd birthday gifts from children, and morning glory 1·50 3·75

**1985.** Native American Artefacts. Nos. 914/18 of Antigua optd **BARBUDA MAIL**.

816 15c. Arawak pot sherd and Indians making clay utensils 15 10
817 50c. Arawak body design and Arawak Indians tattooing 25 25
818 60c. Head of the god "Yocahu" and Indians harvesting manioc 35 35
819 $3 Carib war club and Carib Indians going into battle 1·25 1·50
MS820 97×68 mm. $5 Taino Indians worshiping stone idol 2·00 3·00

**1985.** 40th Anniv of International Civil Aviation Organization. Nos. 934/8 of Antigua optd **BARBUDA MAIL**.

821 30c. Cessna Skyhawk 2·50 75
822 90c. Fokker D.VII 3·50 1·25
823 $1.50 SPAD VII 4·25 5·50
824 $3 Boeing 747 6·00 8·50
MS825 97×83 mm. De Havilland D.H.C.6 Twin Otter 3·25 3·50

**1985.** Life and Times of Queen Elizabeth the Queen Mother (2nd series). Nos. 946/9 of Antigua optd **BARBUDA MAIL**.

826 $1 The Queen Mother attending church 6·00 2·50
827 $1.50 Watching children playing in London garden 7·00 3·00
828 $2.50 The Queen Mother in 1979 8·00 3·50
MS829 56×85 mm. $5 With Prince Edward at Royal Wedding, 1981 17·00 11·00

**1985.** 850th Birth Anniv of Maimonides (physician philosopher and scholar). Nos. 939/40 of Antigua optd **BARBUDA MAIL**.

830 $2 green 4·50 3·75
MS831 70×84 mm. $5 brown 4·25 4·25

**1985.** Marine Life. Nos. 950/4 of Antigua optd **BARBUDA MAIL**.

832 15c. Magnificent frigate bird 7·00 1·25
833 45c. Brain coral 7·00 80
834 60c. Cushion star 7·00 1·25
835 $3 Spotted moray 15·00 5·50
MS836 110×80 mm. $5 Elkhorn coral 17·00 6·50

**1986.** International Youth Year. Nos. 941/5 of Antigua optd **BARBUDA MAIL**.

837 25c. Young farmers with produce 15 15
838 50c. Hotel management trainees 25 30
839 60c. Girls with goat and boys with football ("Environment") 30 35
840 $3 Windsurfing ("Leisure") 1·50 1·60
MS841 102×72 mm. $5 Young people with Antiguan flag 2·75 3·25

**1986.** Royal Visit. Nos. 965/8 of Antigua optd **BARBUDA MAIL**.

842 60c. Flags of Great Britain and Antigua 3·75 50
843 $1 Queen Elizabeth II (vert) 3·00 65
844 $4 Royal Yacht "Britannia" 8·50 2·50
MS845 110×83 mm. $5 Map of Antigua 11·00 4·00

**1986.** 75th Anniv of Girl Guide Movement. Nos. 955/9 of Antigua optd **BARBUDA MAIL**.

846 15c. Girl Guides nursing 1·50 80
847 45c. Open-air Girl Guide meeting 2·75 1·75
848 60c. Lord and Lady Baden-Powell 2·75 2·50
849 $3 Girl Guides gathering flowers 7·50 9·50
MS850 67×96 mm. $5 Barn swallow (Nature study) 32·00 22·00

**1986.** 300th Birth Anniv of Johann Sebastian Bach (composer). Nos. 960/4 of Antigua optd **BARBUDA MAIL**.

851 25c. multicoloured 3·50 70
852 50c. multicoloured 3·75 1·40
853 $1 multicoloured 5·00 2·00
854 $3 multicoloured 8·50 9·00
MS855 104×73 mm. $5 black and grey 26·00 12·00

**1986.** Christmas. Religious Paintings. Nos. 985/8 of Antigua optd **BARBUDA MAIL**.

856 10c. "Madonna and Child" (De Landi) 40 30
857 25c. "Madonna and Child" (Berlinghiero) 80 50
858 60c. "The Nativity" (Fra Angelico) 1·50 1·00
859 $4 "Presentation in the Temple" (Giovanni di Paolo) 4·00 7·00
MS860 113×81 mm. $5 "The Nativity" (Antoniazzo Romano) 4·25 5·50

**108** Queen Elizabeth II meeting Members of Legislature

**1986.** 60th Birthday of Queen Elizabeth II (1st issue). Multicoloured.

861 $1 Type **108** 50 1·00
862 $2 Queen with Headmistress of Liberta School 60 1·10
863 $2.50 Queen greeted by Governor-General of Antigua 60 1·25
MS864 95×75 mm. $5 Queen Elizabeth in 1928 and 1986 (33×27 mm) 6·50 8·50

See also Nos. 872/5.

**109** Halley's Comet over Barbuda Beach

**1986.** Appearance of Halley's Comet (1st issue). Multicoloured.

865 $1 Type **109** 60 1·25
866 $2.50 Early telescope and dish aerial (vert) 80 2·25
867 $5 Comet and world map 1·40 3·75

See also Nos. 886/9.

**1986.** 40th Anniv of United Nations Organization. Nos. 981/4 of Antigua optd **BARBUDA MAIL**.

868 40c. Benjamin Franklin and U.N. (New York) 1953 U.P.U. 5c. stamp 1·50 1·00
869 $1 George Washington Carver (agricultural chemist) and 1982 Nature Conservation 28c. stamp 2·25 2·25
870 $3 Charles Lindbergh (aviator) and 1978 I.C.A.O. 25c. stamp 4·00 5·00
MS871 101×77 mm. $5 Marc Chagell (artist) (vert) 11·00 12·00

**1986.** 60th Birthday of Queen Elizabeth II (2nd issue). Nos. 1005/8 of Antigua optd **BARBUDA MAIL**.

872 60c. black and yellow 2·50 1·25
873 $1 multicoloured 3·00 2·00
874 $4 multicoloured 4·75 4·50
MS875 120×85 mm. $5 black and brown 8·00 9·00

**1986.** World Cup Football Championship, Mexico. Nos. 995/9 of Antigua optd **BARBUDA MAIL**.

876 30c. Football, boots and trophy 4·00 1·00
877 60c. Goalkeeper (vert) 5·50 2·00
878 $1 Referee blowing whistle (vert) 6·00 2·25
879 $4 Ball in net 13·00 9·00
MS880 87×76 mm. $5 Two players competing for ball 23·00 15·00

**1986.** "Ameripex '86" International Stamp Exhibition, Chicago. Famous American Trains. Nos. 1014/18 of Antigua optd **BARBUDA MAIL**.

881 25c. "Hiawatha" express 2·00 1·50
882 50c. "Grand Canyon" express 2·75 2·25
883 $1 "Powhattan Arrow" express 3·50 3·00
884 $3 "Empire State" express 6·00 7·00
MS885 117×87 mm. $5 Southern Pacific "Daylight" express 9·00 9·50

**1986.** Appearance of Halley's Comet (2nd issue). Nos. 1000/4 of Antigua optd **BARBUDA MAIL**.

886 5c. Edmond Halley and Old Greenwich Observatory 2·50 1·00
887 10c. Messerschmitt Me 163B Komet (fighter aircraft), 1944 2·50 1·00
888 60c. Montezuma (Aztec Emperor) and Comet in 1517 (from "Historias de las Indias de Neuva Espana") 3·75 2·00
889 $4 Pocahontas saving Capt. John Smith and Comet in 1607 13·00 8·00
MS890 101×70 mm. $5 Halley's Comet over English Harbour, Antigua 6·00 5·00

**1986.** Royal Wedding. Nos. 1019/22 of Antigua optd **BARBUDA MAIL**.

891 45c. Prince Andrew and Miss Sarah Ferguson 75 50
892 60c. Prince Andrew 90 65
893 $4 Prince Andrew with Prince Philip 3·50 4·00
MS894 88×88 mm. $5 Prince Andrew and Miss Sarah Ferguson (different) 8·00 8·00

**1986.** Sea Shells. Nos. 1023/7 of Antigua optd **BARBUDA MAIL**.

895 15c. Fly-specked cerith 2·50 2·00
896 45c. Smooth Scotch bonnet 2·75 2·25
897 60c. West Indian crown conch 3·50 2·75
898 $3 Criboney murex 8·00 12·00
MS899 109×75 mm. $5 Colourful Atlantic moon (horiz) 20·00 18·00

**1986.** Flowers. Nos. 1028/36 of Antigua optd **BARBUDA MAIL**.

900 10c. "Nymphaea ampla" (water lily) 50 50
901 15c. Queen of the night 60 50
902 50c. Cup of gold 1·00 70
903 60c. Beach morning glory 1·10 70
904 70c. Golden trumpet 1·25 90
905 $1 Air plant 1·50 90
906 $3 Purple wreath 3·00 4·00
907 $4 Zephyr lily 3·50 4·25
MS908 Two sheets, each 102×72 mm. (a) $4 Dozakie. (b) $5 Four o'clock flower Set of 2 sheets 27·00 24·00

**1986.** Mushrooms. Nos. 1042/6 of Antigua optd **BARBUDA MAIL**.

909 10c. "Hygrocybe occidentalis var scarletina" 90 50
910 50c. "Trogia buccinalis" 3·25 1·75
911 $1 "Collybia subpruinosa" 4·75 2·75
912 $4 "Leucocoprinus brebissonii" 9·50 8·00
MS913 102×82 mm. $5 Pyrrhoglossum pyrrhum 25·00 18·00

**1986.** Birth Bicentenary of John J. Audubon (ornithologist) (3rd issue). Nos. 990/3 of Antigua optd **BARBUDA MAIL**.

914 60c. Mallard 6·50 2·50
915 90c. North American black duck ("Dusky Duck") 8·50 2·75
916 $1.50 American pintail ("Common Pintail") 11·00 8·50
917 $3 American wigeon ("Wigeon") 16·00 14·00

**1987.** Local Boats. Nos. 1009/13 of Antigua optd **BARBUDA MAIL**.

918 30c. Tugboat 1·00 1·50
919 60c. Game fishing boat 1·50 80
920 $1 Yacht 2·00 1·25
921 $4 Lugger with auxiliary sail 4·25 6·00
MS922 108×78 mm. $5 Boats under construction 22·00 17·00

**1987.** Centenary of First Benz Motor Car. Nos. 1052/60 of Antigua optd **BARBUDA MAIL**.

923 10c. Auburn "Speedster" (1933) 1·00 45
924 15c. Mercury "Sable" (1986) 1·25 50
925 50c. Cadillac (1959) 1·90 70
926 60c. Studebaker (1950) 1·90 70
927 70c. Lagonda "V-12" (1939) 2·00 1·00
928 $1 Adler "Standard" (1930) 2·50 1·00
929 $3 DKW (1956) 3·00 4·00
930 $4 Mercedes "500K" (1936) 3·00 4·00
MS931 Two sheets, each 99×70 mm. (a) $5 Daimler (1896). (b) $5 Mercedes "Knight" (1921) Set of 2 sheets 27·00 15·00

**1987.** World Cup Football Championship Winners, Mexico. Nos. 1037/40 of Antigua optd **BARBUDA MAIL**.

932 30c. Football, boots and trophy 4·00 1·00
933 60c. Goalkeeper (vert) 4·50 1·50

934 $1 Referee blowing whistle (vert) 5·50 2·25
935 $4 Ball in net 12·00 12·00

**1987.** America's Cup Yachting Championship. Nos. 1072/6 of Antigua optd **BARBUDA MAIL.**
936 30c. "Canada I" (1981) 90 40
937 60c. "Gretel II" (1970) 1·25 50
938 $1 "Sceptre" (1958) 1·60 80
939 $3 "Vigilant" (1893) 2·25 3·50
**MS**940 113×84 mm. $5 "Australia II" defeating "Liberty" (1983) (horiz) 4·50 5·00

**1987.** Marine Life. Nos. 1077/85 of Antigua optd **BARBUDA MAIL.**
941 15c. Bridled burrfish 6·50 1·50
942 30c. Common noddy ("Brown Noddy") 11·00 1·50
943 40c. Nassau grouper 8·00 1·50
944 50c. Laughing gull 13·00 2·25
945 60c. French angelfish 10·00 1·75
946 $1 Porkfish 10·00 2·50
947 $2 Royal tern 21·00 10·00
948 $3 Sooty tern 21·00 11·00
**MS**949 Two sheets, each 120×94 mm. (a) $5 Banded butterflyfish. (b) $5 Brown booby Set of 2 sheets 60·00 24·00

**1987.** Milestones of Transportation. Nos. 1100/9 of Antigua optd **BARBUDA MAIL.**
950 10c. "Spirit of Australia" (fastest powerboat), 1978 3·25 1·50
951 15c. Werner von Siemens's electric locomotive, 1879 4·25 1·25
952 30c. U.S.S. "Triton" (first submerged circumnavigation), 1960 4·25 1·25
953 50c. Trevithick's steam carriage (first passenger-carrying vehicle), 1801 4·75 2·00
954 60c. U.S.S. "New Jersey" (battleship), 1942 5·50 2·00
955 70c. Draisine bicycle, 1818 6·50 2·75
956 90c. "United States" (liner) (holder of the Blue Riband), 1952 6·50 2·25
957 $1.50 Cierva C.4 (first autogyro), 1923 6·50 7·00
958 $2 Curtiss NC-4 flying boat (first transatlantic flight), 1919 7·00 8·00
959 $3 "Queen Elizabeth 2" (liner), 1969 11·00 10·00

**110** Shore Crab

**1987.** Marine Life. Multicoloured.
960 5c. Type **110** 10 20
961 10c. Sea cucumber 10 20
962 15c. Stop-light parrotfish 10 20
963 25c. Banded coral shrimp 15 20
964 35c. Spotted drum 15 20
965 60c. Thorny starfish 20 40
966 75c. Atlantic trumpet triton 20 60
967 90c. Feather star and yellow beaker sponge 20 65
968 $1 Blue gorgonian (vert) 20 65
969 $1.25 Slender filefish (vert) 20 85
970 $5 Barred hamlet (vert) 45 3·50
971 $7.50 Royal gramma ("Fairy basslet") (vert) 60 4·50
972 $10 Fire coral and banded butterflyfish (vert) 75 5·00

**1987.** Olympic Games, Seoul (1988). Nos. 1086/90 of Antigua optd **BARBUDA MAIL.**
973 10c. Handball 1·00 50
974 60c. Fencing 2·00 80
975 $1 Gymnastics 2·50 1·40
976 $3 Football 4·25 5·50
**MS**977 100×77 mm. $5 Boxing gloves 8·50 4·75

**1987.** Birth Centenary of Marc Chagall (artist). Nos. 1091/9 of Antigua optd **BARBUDA MAIL.**
978 10c. "The Profile" 25 40
979 30c. "Portrait of the Artist's Sister" 35 20
980 40c. "Bride with Fan" 40 30
981 60c. "David in Profile" 45 30
982 90c. "Fiancee with Bouquet" 60 50
983 $1 "Self Portrait with Brushes" 70 55
984 $3 "The Walk" 2·00 2·50
985 $4 "Three Candles" 2·25 2·75
**MS**986 Two sheets, each 110×95 mm. (a) $5 "Fall of Icarus" (104×89 mm). (b) $5 "Myth of Orpheus" (104×89 mm) Set of 2 sheets 7·00 8·00

**1987.** Centenary (1986) of Statue of Liberty (2nd issue). Nos. 1110/19 of Antigua optd **BARBUDA MAIL.**
987 15c. Lee Iacocca at unveiling of restored statue 20 20
988 30c. Statue at sunset (side view) 30 20
989 45c. Aerial view of head 45 25
990 50c. Lee Iacocca and torch 50 30
991 60c. Workmen inside head of statue (horiz) 55 30
992 90c. Restoration work (horiz) 70 50
993 $1 Head of statue 80 75
994 $2 Statue at sunset (front view) 1·25 1·75
995 $3 Inspecting restoration work (horiz) 1·60 2·50
996 $5 Statue at night 2·50 3·50

**1987.** Entertainers. Nos. 1120/7 of Antigua optd **BARBUDA MAIL.**
997 15c. Grace Kelly 2·00 70
998 30c. Marilyn Monroe 5·00 1·25
999 45c. Orson Welles 2·00 75
1000 50c. Judy Garland 2·00 1·00
1001 60c. John Lennon 13·00 2·50
1002 $1 Rock Hudson 2·75 1·75
1003 $1 John Wayne 4·00 3·50
1004 $3 Elvis Presley 24·00 11·00

**1987.** "Capex '87" International Stamp Exhibition, Toronto. Reptiles and Amphibians. Nos. 1133/7 of Antigua optd **BARBUDA MAIL.**
1005 30c. Whistling frog 6·00 1·75
1006 60c. Croaking lizard 7·00 1·75
1007 $1 Antiguan anole 8·00 3·00
1008 $3 Red-footed tortoise 16·00 17·00
**MS**1009 106×76 mm. $5 Ground lizard 29·00 12·00

**1988.** Christmas. Religious Paintings. Nos. 1144/8 of Antigua optd **BARBUDA MAIL.**
1010 45c. "Madonna and Child" (Bernardo Daddi) 2·00 30
1011 60c. St. Joseph (detail, "The Nativity" (Sano di Pietro)) 2·00 55
1012 $1 Virgin Mary (detail, "The Nativity" (Sano di Pietro)) 2·25 1·25
1013 $4 "Music-making Angel" (Melozzo da Forli) 6·50 8·50
**MS**1014 90×70 mm. $5 "The Flight into Egypt" (Sano di Pietro) 9·00 6·50

**1988.** Salvation Army's Community Service. Nos. 1163/71 of Antigua optd **BARBUDA MAIL.**
1015 25c. First aid at daycare centre, Antigua 2·00 1·00
1016 30c. Giving penicillin injection, Indonesia 2·00 1·00
1017 40c. Children at daycare centre, Bolivia 2·00 1·00
1018 45c. Rehabilitation of the handicapped, India 2·00 1·00
1019 50c. Training blind man, Kenya 2·50 1·50
1020 60c. Weighing baby, Ghana 2·50 1·50
1021 $1 Training typist, Zambia 3·00 2·50
1022 $2 Emergency food kitchen, Sri Lanka 3·50 4·00
**MS**1023 152×83 mm. $5 General Eva Burrows 27·00 25·00

**1988.** Bicentenary of U.S. Constitution. Nos. 1139/43 of Antigua optd **BARBUDA MAIL.**
1024 15c. House of Burgesses, Virginia ("Freedom of Speech") 10 15
1025 45c. State Seal, Connecticut 20 25
1026 60c. State Seal, Delaware 25 40
1027 $4 Gouverneur Morris (Pennsylvania delegate) (vert) 1·75 3·25
**MS**1028 105×75 mm. $5 Roger Sherman (Connecticut delegate) (vert) 2·75 3·25

**1988.** Royal Ruby Wedding. Nos. 1149/53 of Antigua optd **BARBUDA MAIL.**
1029 25c. brown, black and blue 2·50 40
1030 60c. multicoloured 3·00 65
1031 $2 brown, black and green 6·50 2·50
1032 $3 multicoloured 7·50 3·00
**MS**1033 102×77 mm. $5 multicoloured 16·00 6·50

**1988.** Birds of Antigua. Nos. 1154/62 of Antigua optd **BARBUDA MAIL.**
1034 10c. Great blue heron 3·75 1·75
1035 15c. Ringed kingfisher (horiz) 4·00 1·75
1036 50c. Bananaquit (horiz) 5·50 1·75
1037 60c. American purple gallinule ("Purple Gallinule") (horiz) 5·50 1·75
1038 70c. Blue-hooded euphonia (horiz) 6·00 2·75
1039 $1 Brown-throated concure ("Caribbean Parakeet") 7·00 2·75
1040 $3 Troupial (horiz) 12·00 8·50
1041 $4 Purple-throated carib (horiz) 12·00 8·50
**MS**1042 Two sheets, each 115×86 mm. (a) $5 Greater flamingo. (b) $5 Brown pelican Set of 2 sheets 38·00 19·00

**1988.** 500th Anniv (1992) of Discovery of America by Columbus (1st issue). Nos. 1172/80 of Antigua optd **BARBUDA MAIL.**
1043 10c. Columbus's second fleet, 1493 3·25 1·00
1044 30c. Painos Indian village and fleet 3·25 80
1045 45c. "Santa Mariagalante" (flagship) and Painos village 4·00 80
1046 60c. Painos Indians offering Columbus fruit and vegetables 2·75 85
1047 90c. Painos Indian and Columbus with scarlet macaw 7·00 1·75
1048 $1 Columbus landing on island 5·50 1·75
1049 $3 Spanish soldier and fleet 7·00 4·50
1050 $4 Fleet under sail 7·00 4·50
**MS**1051 Two sheets, each 110×80 mm. (a) $5 Queen Isabella's cross. (b) $5 Gold coin of Ferdinand and Isabella Set of 2 sheets 15·00 13·00
See also Nos. 1112/16, 1177/85, 1285/93, 1374/80 and 1381/2.

**1988.** 500th Birth Anniv of Titian. Nos. 1181/9 of Antigua optd **BARBUDA MAIL.**
1052 30c. "Bust of Christ" 60 20
1053 40c. "Scourging of Christ" 75 25
1054 45c. "Madonna in Glory with Saints" 80 25
1055 50c. "The Averoldi Polyptych" (detail) 90 30
1056 $1 "Christ Crowned with Thorns" 1·60 55
1057 $2 "Christ Mocked" 2·50 1·50
1058 $3 "Christ and Simon of Cyrene" 3·00 2·50
1059 $4 "Crucifixion with Virgin and Saints" 3·00 3·00
**MS**1060 Two sheets, each 110×95 mm. (a) $5 "Ecce Homo" (detail). (b) $5 "Noli me Tangere" (detail) Set of 2 sheets 8·50 8·00

**1988.** 16th World Scout Jamboree, Australia. Nos. 1128/32 of Antigua optd **BARBUDA MAIL.**
1061 10c. Scouts around campfire and red kangaroo 2·50 1·00
1062 60c. Scouts canoeing and blue-winged kookaburra 7·50 1·50
1063 $1 Scouts on assault course and ring-tailed rock wallaby 4·00 1·75
1064 $3 Field kitchen and koala 7·50 6·50
**MS**1065 103×78 mm. $5 Flags of Antigua, Australia and Scout Movement 8·00 6·50

**1988.** Sailing Week. Nos. 1190/4 of Antigua optd **BARBUDA MAIL.**
1066 30c. Two yachts rounding buoy 60 35
1067 60c. Three yachts 1·00 70
1068 $1 British yacht under way 1·25 1·10
1069 $3 Three yachts (different) 2·25 2·75
**MS**1070 103×92 mm. $5 Two yachts 7·50 4·50

**1988.** Flowering Trees. Nos. 1213/21 of Antigua optd **BARBUDA MAIL.**
1071 10c. Jacaranda 15 20
1072 30c. Cordia 30 20
1073 50c. Orchid tree 40 25
1074 90c. Flamboyant 60 45
1075 $1 African tulip tree 70 60
1076 $2 Potato tree 1·25 1·50
1077 $3 Crepe myrtle 1·50 2·00
1078 $4 Pitch apple 1·75 2·50
**MS**1079 Two sheets, each 106×76 mm. (a) $5 Cassia. (b) $5 Chinaberry Set of 2 sheets 6·00 6·50

**1988.** Olympic Games, Seoul. Nos. 1222/6 of Antigua optd **BARBUDA MAIL.**
1080 40c. Gymnastics 1·50 40
1081 60c. Weightlifting 1·75 55
1082 $1 Water polo (horiz) 2·00 1·00
1083 $3 Boxing (horiz) 2·75 3·00
**MS**1084 114×80 mm. $5 Runner with Olympic torch 3·00 2·40

**1988.** Caribbean Butterflies. Nos. 1227/44 of Antigua optd **BARBUDA MAIL.**
1085 1c. "Danaus plexippus" 40 75
1086 2c. "Greta diaphanus" 40 75
1087 3c. "Calisto archebates" 50 75
1088 5c. "Hamadryas feronia" 50 75
1089 10c. "Mestra dorcas" 60 60
1090 15c. "Hypolimnas misippus" 75 40
1091 20c. "Dione juno" 90 50
1092 25c. "Heliconius charithonia" 90 50
1093 30c. "Eurema pyro" 95 50
1094 40c. "Papilio androgeus" 1·10 50
1095 45c. "Anteos maerula" 1·10 50
1096 50c. "Aphrissa orbis" 1·25 75
1097 60c. "Astraptes xagua" 1·25 60
1098 $1 "Heliopetes arsalte" 1·60 1·00
1099 $2 "Polites baracoa" 3·25 3·50
1100 $2.50 "Phocides pigmalion" 3·50 4·25
1101 $5 "Prepona amphitoe" 5·00 6·00
1102 $10 "Oarisma nanus" 8·00 9·50
1102a $20 "Parides lycimenes" 9·00 15·00

**1989.** 25th Death Anniv of John F. Kennedy (American statesman). Nos. 1245/53 of Antigua optd **BARBUDA MAIL.**
1103 1c. President Kennedy and family 10 75
1104 2c. Kennedy commanding "PT109" 10 75
1105 3c. Funeral cortege 10 75
1106 4c. In motorcade, Mexico 10 75
1107 30c. As 1c. 1·25 50
1108 60c. As 4c. 3·25 60
1109 $1 As 3c. 3·25 1·50
1110 $4 As 2c. 8·50 11·00
**MS**1111 105×75 mm. $5 Kennedy taking presidential oath of office 4·50 6·00

**1989.** 500th Anniv (1992) of Discovery of America by Columbus (2nd issue). Pre-Columbian Arawak Society. Nos. 1267/71 of Antigua optd **BARBUDA MAIL.**
1112 $1.50 Arawak warriors 4·00 4·25
1113 $1.50 Whip dancers 4·00 4·25
1114 $1.50 Whip dancers and chief with pineapple 4·00 4·25
1115 $1.50 Family and camp fire 4·00 4·25
**MS**1116 71×84 mm. $6 Arawak chief 5·50 6·50

**1989.** 50th Anniv of First Jet Flight. Nos. 1272/80 of Antigua optd **BARBUDA MAIL.**
1117 10c. Hawker Siddeley Comet 4 airliner 3·50 2·00
1118 30c. Messerschmitt Me 262 fighter 4·50 1·50
1119 40c. Boeing 707 airliner 4·75 2·25
1120 60c. Canadair CL-13 Sabre fighter 6·00 1·25
1121 $1 Lockheed Starfighters 7·00 2·50
1122 $2 Douglas DC-10 airliner 9·00 8·00
1123 $3 Boeing 747-300/400 airliner 10·00 11·00
1124 $4 McDonnell Douglas Phantom II fighter 10·00 11·00
**MS**1125 Two sheets, each 114×83 mm. (a) $7 Grumman F-14 Tomcat fighter. (b) $7 Concorde airliner Set of 2 sheets 50·00 40·00

**1989.** Caribbean Cruise Ships. Nos. 1281/9 of Antigua optd **BARBUDA MAIL.**
1126 25c. "Festivale" 3·75 1·50
1127 45c. "Southward" 4·00 1·50
1128 50c. "Sagafjord" 4·00 1·75
1129 60c. "Daphne" 4·00 1·75
1130 75c. "Cunard Countess" 4·25 2·75
1131 90c. "Song of America" 4·25 2·75
1132 $3 "Island Princess" 9·50 10·00
1133 $4 "Galileo" 9·50 10·00
**MS**1134 (a) 113×87 mm. $6 "Norway". (b) 111×82 mm. $6 "Oceanic" Set of 2 sheets 50·00 38·00

**1989.** Japanese Art. Paintings by Hiroshige. Nos. 1290/8 of Antigua optd **BARBUDA MAIL.**
1135 25c. "Fish swimming by Duck half-submerged in Stream" 4·00 1·00
1136 45c. "Crane and Wave" 4·75 1·00
1137 50c. "Sparrows and Morning Glories" 5·00 1·50
1138 60c. "Crested Blackbird and Flowering Cherry" 5·00 1·50
1139 $1 "Great Knot sitting among Water Grass" 5·50 1·75
1140 $2 "Goose on a Bank of Water" 7·50 4·25
1141 $3 "Black Paradise Fly-catcher and Blossoms" 9·00 5·00
1142 $4 "Sleepy Owl perched on a Pine Branch" 10·00 5·50
**MS**1143 Two sheets, each 102×75 mm. (a) $5 "Bullfinch flying near a Clematis Branch". (b) $5 "Titmouse on a Cherry Branch" Set of 2 sheets 48·00 23·00

**1989.** World Cup Football Championship, Italy (1990). Nos. 1308/12 of Antigua optd **BARBUDA MAIL.**
1144 15c. Goalkeeper 2·00 65
1145 25c. Goalkeeper moving towards ball 2·00 65
1146 $1 Goalkeeper reaching for ball 5·00 2·00
1147 $4 Goalkeeper saving goal 8·00 10·00
**MS**1148 Two sheets, each 75×105 mm. (a) $5 Three players competing for ball (horiz). (b) $5 Ball and players' legs (horiz) Set of 2 sheets 38·00 32·00

**1989.** Christmas. Paintings by Raphael and Giotto. Nos. 1351/9 of Antigua optd **BARBUDA MAIL.**
1149 10c. "The Small Cowper Madonna" (Raphael) 35 30
1150 25c. "Madonna of the Goldfinch" (Raphael) 45 20
1151 30c. "The Alba Madonna" (Raphael) 45 20
1152 50c. Saint (detail, "Bologna Altarpiece") (Giotto) 70 30
1153 60c. Angel (detail, "Bologna Altarpiece") (Giotto) 75 45
1154 70c. Angel slaying serpent (detail, "Bologna Altarpiece") (Giotto) 80 60
1155 $4 Evangelist (detail, "Bologna Altarpiece") (Giotto) 2·75 4·50
1156 $5 "Madonna of Foligno" (Raphael) 2·75 4·50
**MS**1157 Two sheets, each 71×96 mm. (a) $5 "The Marriage of the Virgin" (detail) (Raphael). (b) $5 Madonna and Child (detail, "Bologna Altarpiece") (Giotto) Set of 2 sheets 12·00 14·00

**1990.** Fungi. Nos. 1313/21 of Antigua optd **BARBUDA MAIL.**
1158 10c. "Mycena pura" 2·50 1·50
1159 25c. Psathyrella turberculata" (vert) 2·75 65
1160 50c. "Psilocybe cubenis" 3·25 1·00

1161 60c. "Leptonia caeruleocapitata" (vert) 3·25 1·00
1162 75c. "Xeromphalina tenuipes" (vert) 3·25 1·40
1163 $1 "Chlorophyllum molybdites" (vert) 3·50 1·40
1164 $3 "Marasmius haemato-cephalus" 6·00 7·50
1165 $4 "Cantharellus cinnabarinus" 6·00 7·50
**MS**1166 Two sheets, each 88×62 mm. (a) $6 "Leucopaxillus gracillimus" (vert). (b) $6 "Volvariella volvacea" Set of 2 sheets 38·00 23·00

**1990.** Local Fauna. Nos. 1322/6 optd **BARBUDA MAIL**.
1167 25c. Desmarest's hutia 1·00 60
1168 45c. Caribbean monk seal 2·50 1·25
1169 60c. Mustache bat (vert) 1·75 1·25
1170 $4 American manatee (vert) 4·25 6·50
**MS**1171 113×87 mm. $5 West Indian giant rice rat 22·00 22·00

**1990.** 20th Anniv of First Manned Landing on Moon. Nos. 1346/50 optd **BARBUDA MAIL**.
1172 10c. Launch of "Apollo 11" 3·00 1·50
1173 45c. Aldrin on Moon 5·50 80
1174 $1 Module "Eagle" over Moon (horiz) 7·00 2·75
1175 $4 Recovery of "Apollo 11" crew after splashdown (horiz) 13·00 13·00
**MS**1176 107×77 mm. $5 Astronaut Neil Armstrong 24·00 23·00

**1990.** 500th Anniv (1992) of Discovery of America by Columbus (3rd issue). New World Natural History – Marine Life. Nos. 1360/8 of Antigua optd **BARBUDA MAIL**.
1177 10c. Star-eyed hermit crab 1·75 1·75
1178 20c. Spiny lobster 2·25 1·75
1179 25c. Magnificent banded fanworm 2·25 1·75
1180 45c. Cannonball jellyfish 3·25 1·00
1181 60c. Red-spiny sea star 3·50 1·00
1182 $2 Peppermint shrimp 4·75 5·00
1183 $3 Coral crab 5·00 6·00
1184 $4 Branching fire coral 5·00 6·00
**MS**1185 Two sheets, each 101×69 mm. (a) $5 Common sea fan. (b) Portuguese man-o-war Set of 2 sheets 28·00 27·00

**1990.** "EXPO 90" International Gardens and Greenery Exhibition, Osaka. Orchids. Nos. 1369/77 of Antigua optd **BARBUDA MAIL**.
1186 15c. "Vanilla mexicana" 1·75 80
1187 45c. "Epidendrum ibaguense" 2·25 80
1188 50c. "Epidendrum secundum" 2·25 90
1189 60c. "Maxillaria conferta" 2·50 1·10
1190 $1 "Onicidium altissimum" 2·75 1·75
1191 $2 "Spiranthes lanceolata" 5·00 5·00
1192 $3 "Tonopsis utricularioides" 5·50 6·50
1193 $5 "Epidendrum nocturnum" 7·00 8·50
**MS**1194 Two sheets, each 101×69 mm. (a) $6 "Octomeria graminifolia". (b) $6 "Rodriguezia lanceolata" Set of 2 sheets 38·00 23·00

**1990.** Reef Fishes. Nos. 1386/94 of Antigua optd **BARBUDA MAIL**.
1195 10c. Flamefish 2·50 1·75
1196 15c. Coney 2·50 1·75
1197 50c. Long-spined squirrelfish 3·50 1·50
1198 60c. Sergeant major 3·50 1·50
1199 $1 Yellow-tailed snapper 4·25 2·50
1200 $2 Rock beauty 7·00 7·00
1201 $3 Spanish hogfish 9·00 10·00
1202 $4 Striped parrotfish 9·00 10·00
**MS**1203 Two sheets, each 99×70 mm. (a) $5 Black-barred soldierfish. (b) $5 Four-eyed butterflyfish Set of 2 sheets 38·00 32·00

**1990.** 1st Anniv of Hurricane Hugo. Nos. 971/2 surch **1st Anniversary Hurricane Hugo 16th September, 1989-1990** and new value.
1204 $5 on $7.50 Fairy basslet (vert) 12·00 14·00
1205 $7.50 on $10 Fire coral and butterfly fish (vert) 13·00 16·00

**1990.** 90th Birthday of Queen Elizabeth the Queen Mother. Nos. 1415/19 of Antigua optd **BARBUDA MAIL**.
1206 15c. multicoloured 8·00 1·75
1207 35c. multicoloured 11·00 1·50
1208 75c. multicoloured 17·00 3·25
1209 $3 multicoloured 30·00 19·00
**MS**1210 67×98 mm. $6 multicoloured 55·00 26·00

**1990.** Achievements in Space. Nos. 1395/414 of Antigua optd **BARBUDA MAIL**.
1211 45c. "Voyager 2" passing Saturn 3·25 2·25
1212 45c. "Pioneer 11" photographing Saturn 3·25 2·25
1213 45c. Astronaut in transporter 3·25 2·25
1214 45c. Space shuttle "Columbia" 3·25 2·25
1215 45c. "Apollo 10" command module on parachutes 3·25 2·25
1216 45c. "Skylab" space station 3·25 2·25
1217 45c. Astronaut Edward White in space 3·25 2·25
1218 45c. "Apollo" spacecraft on joint mission 3·25 2·25
1219 45c. "Soyuz" spacecraft on joint mission 3·25 2·25
1220 45c. "Mariner 1" passing Venus 3·25 2·25
1221 45c. "Gemini 4" capsule 3·25 2·25
1222 45c. "Sputnik 1" 3·25 2·25
1223 45c. Hubble space telescope 3·25 2·25
1224 45c. North American X-15 rocket plane 3·25 2·25
1225 45c. Bell XS-1 airplane 3·25 2·25
1226 45c. "Apollo 17" astronaut and lunar rock formation 3·25 2·25
1227 45c. Lunar rover 3·25 2·25
1228 45c. "Apollo 14" lunar module 3·25 2·25
1229 45c. Astronaut Buzz Aldrin on Moon 3·25 2·25
1230 45c. Soviet "Lunokhod" lunar vehicle 3·25 2·25

**1990.** Christmas. Paintings by Renaissance Masters. Nos. 1457/65 of Antigua optd **BARBUDA MAIL**.
1231 25c. "Madonna and Child with Saints" (detail, Sebastiano del Piombo) 2·25 60
1232 30c. "Virgin and Child with Angels" (detail, Grunewald) (vert) 2·25 60
1233 40c. "The Holy Family and a Shepherd" (detail, Titian) 2·25 60
1234 60c. "Virgin and Child" (detail, Lippi) (vert) 3·00 1·10
1235 $1 "Jesus, St. John and Two Angels" (Rubens) 3·75 1·50
1236 $2 "Adoration of the Shepherds" (detail, Vincenzo Catena) 5·50 6·00
1237 $4 "Adoration of the Magi" (detail, Giorgione) 8·50 9·50
1238 $5 "Virgin and Child adored by Warriors" (detail, Vincenzo Catena) 8·50 9·50
**MS**1239 Two sheets, each 71×101 mm. (a) $6 "Allegory of the Blessings of Jacob" (detail, Rubens) (vert). (b) $6 "Adoration of the Magi" (detail, Fra Angelico) (vert) Set of 2 sheets 25·00 26·00

**1991.** 150th Anniv of the Penny Black. Nos. 1378/81 of Antigua optd **BARBUDA MAIL**.
1240 45c. green 5·00 1·00
1241 60c. mauve 5·00 1·10
1242 $5 blue 15·00 15·00
**MS**1243 102×80 mm. $6 purple 18·00 12·00

**1991.** "Stamp World London 90" International Stamp Exhibition. Nos. 1382/4 of Antigua optd **BARBUDA MAIL**.
1244 50c. green and red 5·00 1·00
1245 75c. brown and red 5·00 1·50
1246 $4 blue and red 15·00 15·00
**MS**1247 104×81 mm. $6 black and red 21·00 23·00

**119** Troupial

**1991.** Wild Birds. Multicoloured.
1248 60c. Type **119** 2·25 65
1249 $2 Adelaide's warbler ("Christmas Bird") 3·75 3·00
1250 $4 Rose-breasted grosbeak 5·50 6·50
1251 $7 Wied's crested flycatcher ("Stolid Flycatcher") 7·50 11·00

**1991.** Olympic Games, Barcelona (1992). Nos. 1429/33 of Antigua optd **BARBUDA MAIL**.
1252 50c. Men's 20 kilometres walk 2·75 90
1253 75c. Triple jump 3·00 1·00
1254 $1 Men's 10,000 metres 3·25 1·75
1255 $5 Javelin 12·00 14·00
**MS**1256 100×70 mm. $6 Athlete lighting Olympic flame at Los Angeles Olympics 14·00 16·00

**1991.** Birds. Nos. 1448/56 of Antigua optd **BARBUDA MAIL**.
1257 10c. Pearly-eyed thrasher 2·75 1·50
1258 25c. Purple-throated carib 3·75 80
1259 50c. Common yellowthroat 4·50 1·00
1260 60c. American kestrel 4·50 1·10
1261 $1 Yellow-bellied sapsucker 4·75 2·00
1262 $2 American purple gallinule ("Purple Gallinule") 6·50 6·50
1263 $3 Yellow-crowned night heron 7·00 8·50
1264 $4 Blue-hooded euphonia 7·00 8·50
**MS**1265 Two sheets, each 76×60 mm. (a) $6 Brown pelican. (b) Magnificent frigate bird Set of 2 sheets 25·00 23·00

**1991.** 350th Death Anniv of Rubens. Nos. 1466/74 of Antigua optd **BARBUDA MAIL**.
1266 25c. "Rape of the Daughters of Leucippus" (detail) 2·25 70
1267 45c. "Bacchanal" (detail) 2·75 70
1268 50c. "Rape of the Sabine Women" (detail) 2·75 75
1269 60c. "Battle of the Amazons" (detail) 3·00 85
1270 $1 "Rape of the Sabine Women" (different detail) 3·50 1·75
1271 $2 "Bacchanal" (different detail) 5·50 6·00
1272 $3 "Rape of the Sabine Women" (different detail) 8·00 9·00
1273 $4 "Bacchanal" (different detail) 8·00 9·00
**MS**1274 Two sheets, each 111×71 mm. (a) $6 "Rape of Hippodameia" (detail). (b) "Battle of the Amazons" (different detail) Set of 2 sheets 28·00 30·00

**1991.** 50th Anniv of Second World War. Nos. 1475/88 of Antigua optd **BARBUDA MAIL**.
1275 10c. U.S. troops cross into Germany, 1944 3·25 2·25
1276 15c. Axis surrender in North Africa, 1943 3·75 2·00
1277 25c. U.S. tanks invade Kwalajalein, 1944 4·00 1·50
1278 45c. Roosevelt and Churchill meet at Casablanca, 1943 10·00 2·50
1279 50c. Marshall Badoglio, Prime Minister of Italian anti-facist government, 1943 3·75 1·75
1280 $1 Lord Mountbatten, Supreme Allied Commander South-east Asia, 1943 13·00 4·25
1281 $2 Greek victory at Koritza, 1940 10·00 10·00
1282 $4 Anglo-Soviet mutual assistance pact, 1941 12·00 12·00
1283 $5 Operation Torch landings, 1942 12·00 12·00
**MS**1284 Two sheets, each 108×80 mm. (a) $6 Japanese attack on Pearl Harbor, 1941. (b) $6 U.S.A.A.F. daylight raid on Schweinfurt, 1943 Set of 2 sheets 55·00 38·00

**1991.** 500th Anniv (1992) of Discovery of America by Columbus (4th issue). History of Exploration. Nos. 1503/11 of Antigua optd **BARBUDA MAIL**.
1285 10c. multicoloured 2·00 1·75
1286 15c. multicoloured 2·25 1·75
1287 45c. multicoloured 3·25 1·00
1288 60c. multicoloured 3·50 1·25
1289 $1 multicoloured 3·75 2·00
1290 $2 multicoloured 5·50 5·50
1291 $4 multicoloured 9·00 10·00
1292 $5 multicoloured 9·00 10·00
**MS**1293 Two sheets, each 106×76 mm. (a) $6 black and red. (b) $6 black and red Set of 2 sheets 32·00 27·00

**1991.** Butterflies. Nos. 1494/502 of Antigua optd **BARBUDA MAIL**.
1294 10c. "Heliconius charithonia" 3·00 1·75
1295 35c. "Marpesia petreus" 4·00 1·25
1296 50c. "Anartia amathea" 4·50 1·40
1297 75c. "Siproeta stelenes" 5·50 2·00
1298 $1 "Battus polydamas" 5·50 2·25
1299 $2 "Historis odius" 8·00 8·00
1300 $4 "Hypolimnas misippus" 10·00 11·00
1301 $5 "Hamadryas feronia" 10·00 11·00
**MS**1302 Two sheets. (a) 73×100 mm. $6 "Vanessa cardui" (caterpillar) (vert). (b) 100×73 mm. $6 "Danaus plexippus" (caterpillar) (vert) Set of 2 sheets 38·00 32·00

**1991.** 65th Birthday of Queen Elizabeth II. Nos. 1534/8 of Antigua optd **BARBUDA MAIL**.
1303 15c. Queen Elizabeth and Prince Philip in 1976 4·00 85
1304 20c. The Queen and Prince Philip in Portugal, 1985 4·00 85
1305 $2 Queen Elizabeth II 13·00 5·50
1306 $4 The Queen and Prince Philip at Ascot, 1986 21·00 15·00
**MS**1307 68×90 mm. $4 The Queen at National Theatre, 1986 and Prince Philip 40·00 17·00

**1991.** 10th Wedding Anniv of Prince and Princess of Wales. Nos. 1539/43 of Antigua optd **BARBUDA MAIL**.
1308 10c. Prince and Princess of Wales at party, 1986 3·50 1·75
1309 40c. Separate portraits of Prince, Princess and sons 9·00 1·25
1310 $1 Prince Henry and Prince William 10·00 3·50
1311 $5 Princess Diana in Australia and Prince Charles in Hungary 20·00 15·00
**MS**1312 68×90 mm. $4 Prince Charles in Hackney and Princess and sons in Majorca, 1987 38·00 17·00

**1991.** Christmas. Religious Paintings by Fra Angelico. Nos. 1595/1602 of Antigua optd **BARBUDA MAIL**.
1313 10c. "The Annunciation" 2·25 1·00
1314 30c. "Nativity" 2·75 70
1315 40c. "Adoration of the Magi" 2·75 70
1316 60c. "Presentation in the Temple" 3·50 70
1317 $1 "Circumcision" 4·50 1·75
1318 $3 "Flight into Egypt" 7·50 8·50
1319 $4 "Massacre of the Innocents" 7·50 9·00
1320 $5 "Christ teaching in the Temple" 7·50 9·00

**1992.** Death Centenary (1990) of Vincent van Gogh (artist). Nos. 1512/24 of Antigua optd **BARBUDA MAIL**.
1321 5c. "Camille Roulin" 1·75 2·00
1322 10c. "Armand Roulin" 2·00 2·00
1323 15c. "Young Peasant Woman with Straw Hat sitting in the Wheat" 2·25 2·00
1324 25c. "Adeline Ravoux" 2·25 2·00
1325 30c. "The Schoolboy" 2·25 1·25
1326 40c. "Doctor Gachet" 2·50 1·50
1327 50c. "Portrait of a Man" 2·50 1·75
1328 75c. "Two Children" 4·00 2·25
1329 $2 "The Postman Joseph Roulin" 7·50 7·50
1330 $3 "The Seated Zouave" 8·50 9·00
1331 $4 "L'Arlesienne" 9·00 10·00
1332 $5 "Self-Portrait, November/December 1888" 9·00 10·00
**MS**1333 Three sheets, each 102×76 mm. (a) $5 "Farmhouse in Provence" (horiz). (b) $5 "Flowering Garden" (horiz). (c) $6 "The Bridge at Trinquetaille" (horiz). Imperf Set of 3 sheets 38·00 38·00

**1992.** Birth Centenary of Charles de Gaulle (French statesman). Nos. 1562/70 of Antigua optd **BARBUDA MAIL**.
1334 10c. Pres. De Gaulle and Kennedy, 1961 2·75 1·75
1335 15c. General De Gaulle with Pres. Roosevelt, 1945 (vert) 2·75 1·75
1336 45c. President De Gaulle with Chancellor Adenauer, 1962 (vert) 3·50 80
1337 60c. De Gaulle at Arc de Triomphe, Liberation of Paris, 1944 (vert) 3·75 1·00
1338 $1 General De Gaulle crossing the Rhine, 1945 4·50 2·00
1339 $2 General De Gaulle in Algiers, 1944 7·50 7·50
1340 $4 Presidents De Gaulle and Eisenhower, 1960 10·00 12·00
1341 $5 De Gaulle returning from Germany, 1968 (vert) 10·00 12·00
**MS**1342 Two sheets. (a) 76×106 mm. $6 De Gaulle with crowd. (b) 106×76 mm. $6 De Gaulle and Churchill at Casablanca, 1943 Set of 2 sheets 38·00 32·00

**1992.** Easter. Religious Paintings. Nos. 1627/35 of Antigua optd **BARBUDA MAIL**.
1343 10c. "Supper at Emmaus" (Caravaggio) 1·75 1·25
1344 15c. "The Vision of St. Peter" (Zurbaran) 2·00 1·25
1345 30c. "Christ driving the Money-changers from the Temple" (Tiepolo) 2·25 80
1346 40c. "Martyrdom of St. Bartholomew" (detail) (Ribera) 2·25 80
1347 $1 "Christ driving the Money-changers from the Temple" (detail) (Tiepolo) 4·00 2·25
1348 $2 "Crucifixion" (detail) (Altdorfer) 6·00 6·50
1349 $4 "The Deposition" (detail) (Fra Angelico) 8·50 9·50
1350 $5 "The Deposition" (different detail) (Fra Angelico) 8·50 9·50
**MS**1351 Two sheets. (a) 102×71 mm. $6 "The Last Supper" (detail) (Masip). (b) 71×102 mm. $6 "Crucifixion" (detail) (vert) (Altdorfer) Set of 2 sheets 25·00 25·00

**1992.** Anniversaries and Events. Nos. 1573/83 of Antigua optd **BARBUDA MAIL**.
1352 25c. Germans celebrating Reunification 1·00 70
1353 75c. Cubs erecting tent 2·25 1·50
1354 $1.50 "Don Giovanni" and Mozart 12·00 4·25
1355 $2 Chariot driver and Gate at night 3·00 3·50
1356 $2 Lord Baden-Powell and members of the 3rd Antigua Methodist cub pack (vert) 3·00 3·50
1357 $2 Lilienthal's signature and glider "Flugzeug Nr. 5" 3·00 3·50
1358 $2.50 Driver in Class P36 steam locomotive (vert) 9·00 4·50
1359 $3 Statues from podium 3·00 4·50
1360 $3.50 Cubs and campfire 4·50 5·50
1361 $4 St. Peter's Cathedral, Salzburg 15·00 11·00
**MS**1362 Two sheets. (a) 100×72 mm. $4 Detail of chariot and helmet. (b) 89×117 mm. $5 Antiguan flag and Jamboree emblem (vert) Set of 2 sheets 42·00 32·00

**1992.** 50th Anniv of Japanese Attack on Pearl Harbor. Nos. 1585/94 of Antigua optd **BARBUDA MAIL**.
1364 $1 "Nimitz" class carrier and "Ticonderoga" class cruiser 6·00 3·50
1365 $1 Tourist launch 6·00 3·50
1366 $1 U.S.S. "Arizona" memorial 6·00 3·50
1367 $1 Wreaths on water and aircraft 6·00 3·50

1368 $1 White tern 6·00 3·50
1369 $1 Japanese torpedo bombers over Pearl City 6·00 3·50
1370 $1 Zeros attacking 6·00 3·50
1371 $1 Battleship Row in flames 6·00 3·50
1372 $1 U.S.S. "Nevada" (battleship) underway 6·00 3·50
1373 $1 Zeros returning to carriers 6·00 3·50

**1992.** 500th Anniv of Discovery of America by Columbus (5th issue). World Columbian Stamp "Expo '92", Chicago. Nos. 1654/60 of Antigua optd **BARBUDA MAIL**.
1374 15c. Memorial cross and huts, San Salvador 1·25 80
1375 30c. Martin Pinzon with telescope 1·50 90
1376 40c. Christopher Columbus 2·00 90
1377 $1 "Pinta" 6·00 2·75
1378 $2 "Nina" 8·00 7·50
1379 $4 "Santa Maria" 12·00 13·00
**MS**1380 Two sheets, each 108×76 mm. (a) $6 Ship and map of West Indies. (b) $6 Sea monster Set of 2 sheets 30·00 32·00

**1992.** 500th Anniv of Discovery of America by Columbus (6th issue). Organization of East Caribbean States. Nos. 1670/1 of Antigua optd BARBUDA MAIL.
1381 $1 Columbus meeting Amerindians 3·00 2·00
1382 $2 Ships approaching island 8·00 8·00

**1992.** Postage Stamp Mega Event, New York. No. MS1690 of Antigua optd **BARBUDA MAIL**.
**MS**1383 $6 multicoloured 15·00 16·00

**1992.** 40th Anniv of Queen Elizabeth II's Accession. Nos. 1604/8 of Antigua optd **BARBUDA MAIL**.
1384 10c. Queen Elizabeth II and bird sanctuary 6·50 1·75
1385 30c. Nelson's Dockyard 7·50 1·25
1386 $1 Ruins on Shirley Heights 9·50 2·75
1387 $5 Beach and palm trees 19·00 15·00
**MS**1388 Two sheets, each 75×98 mm. (a) $6 Beach. (b) $6 Hillside foliage Set of 2 sheets 45·00 26·00

**1992.** Prehistoric Animals. Nos. 1618/26 of Antigua optd **BARBUDA MAIL**.
1389 10c. Pteranodon 2·00 1·50
1390 15c. Brachiosaurus 2·50 1·50
1391 30c. Tyrannosaurus Rex 3·00 1·25
1392 50c. Parasaurolophus 3·00 2·25
1393 $1 Deinonychus (horiz) 3·75 2·25
1394 $2 Triceratops (horiz) 6·00 5·50
1395 $4 Protoceratops hatching (horiz) 7·00 8·50
1396 $5 Stegosaurus (horiz) 7·00 8·50
**MS**1397 Two sheets, each 100×70 mm. (a) $6 Apatosaurus (horiz). (b) $6 Allosaurus (horiz) Set of 2 sheets 35·00 26·00

**1992.** Christmas. Nos. 1691/9 of Antigua optd **BARBUDA MAIL**.
1398 10c. "Virgin and Child with Angels" (School of Piero della Francesca) 1·75 75
1399 25c. "Madonna degli Alberelli" (Giovanni Bellini) 1·75 75
1400 30c. "Madonna and Child with St. Anthony Abbot and St. Sigismund" (Neroccio) 1·75 75
1401 40c. "Madonna and the Grand Duke" (Raphael) 2·00 75
1402 60c. "The Nativity" (Georges de la Tour) 2·25 75
1403 $1 "Holy Family" (Jacob Jordaens) 2·75 1·50
1404 $4 "Madonna and Child Enthroned" (Magaritone) 6·50 8·50
1405 $5 "Madonna and Child on a Curved Throne" (Byzantine school) 6·50 8·50
**MS**1406 Two sheets, each 76×102 mm. (a) $6 "Madonna and Child" (Domenco Ghirlando). (b) $6 "The Holy Family" (Pontormo) Set of 2 sheets 25·00 25·00

**1993.** Fungi. Nos. 1645/53 of Antigua optd **BARBUDA MAIL**.
1407 10c. "Amanita caesarea" 1·75 1·25
1408 15c. "Collybia fusipes" 2·00 1·25
1409 30c. "Boletus aereus" 2·25 1·50
1410 40c. "Laccaria amethystina" 2·25 1·50
1411 $1 "Russula virescens" 3·25 2·00
1412 $2 "Tricholoma equestre" ("Tricholoma auratum") 4·50 4·00
1413 $4 "Calocybe gambosa" 5·50 6·50
1414 $5 "Lentinus tigrinus" ("Panus tigrinus") 5·50 6·50
**MS**1415 Two sheets, each 100×70 mm. (a) $6 "Clavariadelphus truncatus". (b) $6 "Auricularia auricula-judae" Set of 2 sheets 26·00 24·00

**1993.** "Granada '92" International Stamp Exhibition, Spain. Spanish Paintings. Nos. 1636/44 of Antigua optd **BARBUDA MAIL**.
1416 10c. "The Miracle at the Well" (Alonzo Cano) 1·25 1·00
1417 15c. "The Poet Luis de Goingora y Argote" (Velazquez) 1·50 1·00
1418 30c. "The Painter Francisco Goya" (Vincente Lopez Portana) 1·75 1·00
1419 40c. "Maria de las Nieves Michaela Fourdinier" (Luis Paret y Alcazar) 1·75 1·00
1420 $1 "Carlos III eating before his Court" (Alcazar) (horiz) 3·00 2·25
1421 $2 "Rain Shower in Granada" (Antonio Munoz Degrain) (horiz) 4·75 4·75
1422 $4 "Sarah Bernhardt" (Santiago Ruisnol i Prats) 6·50 7·50
1423 $5 "The Hermitage Garden" (Joaquim Mir Trinxet) 6·50 7·50
**MS**1424 Two sheets, each 120×95 mm. (a) $6 "The Ascent of Monsieur Boucle's Montgolfier Balloon in the Gardens of Aranjuez" (Antonio Carnicero) (112×87 mm). (b) $6 "Olympus: Battle with the Giants" (Francisco Bayeu y Subias) (112×87 mm). Imperf Set of 2 sheets 19·00 22·00

**1993.** "Genova '92" International Thematic Stamp Exhibition. Hummingbirds and Plants. Nos. 1661/9 of Antigua optd **BARBUDA MAIL**.
1425 10c. Antillean crested hummingbird and wild plantain 2·25 1·50
1426 25c. Green mango and parrot's plantain 2·50 1·00
1427 45c. Purple-throated carib and lobster claws 2·75 1·25
1428 60c. Antillean mango and coral plant 3·00 1·50
1429 $1 Vervain hummingbird and cardinal's guard 3·50 2·25
1430 $2 Rufous-breasted hermit and heliconia 5·00 5·00
1431 $4 Blue-headed hummingbird and reed ginger 6·50 7·50
1432 $5 Green-throated carib and ornamental banana 6·50 7·50
**MS**1433 Two sheets, each 100×70 mm. (a) $6 Bee humming-bird and jungle flame. (b) $6 Western streamertail and bignonia Set of 2 sheets 30·00 22·00

**1993.** Inventors and Inventions. Nos. 1672/80 of Antigua optd **BARBUDA MAIL**.
1434 10c. Ts'ai Lun and paper 65 85
1435 25c. Igor Sikorsky and "Bolshoi Baltiskii" (first four-engined airplane) 3·75 80
1436 30c. Alexander Graham Bell and early telephone 1·50 80
1437 40c. Johannes Gutenberg and early printing press 1·50 80
1438 60c. James Watt and stationary steam engine 8·50 2·25
1439 $1 Anton van Leeuwenhoek and early microscope 3·50 2·75
1440 $4 Louis Braille and hands reading braille 9·00 10·00
1441 $5 Galileo and telescope 9·00 10·00
**MS**1442 Two sheets, each 100×71 mm. (a) $6 Edison and Latimer's phonograph. (b) $6 "Clermont" (first commercial paddle-steamer) Set of 2 sheets 30·00 32·00

**1993.** Anniversaries and Events. Nos. 900/14 of Antigua optd **BARBUDA MAIL**.
1443 10c. Russian cosmonauts 1·75 1·40
1444 40c. "Graf Zeppelin" (airship), 1929 3·00 1·00
1445 45c. Bishop Daniel Davis 80 70
1446 75c. Konrad Adenauer making speech 1·00 1·00
1447 $1 Bus Mosbacher and "Weatherly" (yacht) 2·25 1·75
1448 $1.50 Rain forest 2·50 2·50
1449 $2 Tiger 9·00 5·50
1450 $2 National flag, plant and emblem (horiz) 5·50 3·50
1451 $2 Members of Community Players company (horiz) 3·50 3·50
1452 $2.25 Women carrying pots 3·50 4·00
1453 $3 Lions Club emblem 3·75 4·25
1454 $4 Chinese rocket on launch tower 5·50 5·50
1455 $4 West German and N.A.T.O. flags 5·50 5·50
1456 $6 Hugo Eckener (airship pioneer) 6·50 7·00
**MS**1457 Four sheets, each 100×71 mm. (a) $6 Projected European space station. (b) $6 Airship LZ-129 "Hindenburg", 1936. (c) $6 Brandenburg Gate on German flag. (d) $6 "Danaus plexippus" (butterfly) Set of 4 sheets 55·00 42·00

**1993.** Flowers. Nos. 1733/41 of Antigua optd **BARBUDA MAIL**.
1458 15c. Cardinal's guard 1·75 1·25
1459 25c. Giant granadilla 1·90 1·10
1460 30c. Spider flower 2·00 1·25
1461 40c. Gold vine 2·25 1·40
1462 $1 Frangipani 3·50 2·25
1463 $2 Bougainvillea 4·50 4·50
1464 $4 Yellow oleander 6·00 7·00
1465 $5 Spicy jatropha 6·00 7·00
**MS**1466 Two sheets, each 100×70 mm. (a) $6 Bird lime tree. (b) $6 Fairy lily Set of 2 sheets 30·00 30·00

**1993.** World Bird Watch. Nos. 1248/51 optd **WORLD BIRDWATCH 9-10 OCTOBER 1993**.
1467 60c. Type **119** 4·00 1·75
1468 $2 Adelaide's warbler 7·00 4·50
1469 $4 Rose-breasted grosbeak 9·50 10·00
1470 $7 Wied's crested flycatcher 12·00 13·00

**1993.** Endangered Species. Nos. 1759/71 of Antigua optd **BARBUDA MAIL**.
1471 $1 St. Lucia amazon ("St. Lucia Parrot") 5·50 4·00
1472 $1 Cahow 5·50 4·00
1473 $1 Swallow-tailed kite 5·50 4·00
1474 $1 Everglade kite ("Everglades Kite") 5·50 4·00
1475 $1 Imperial amazon ("Imperial Parrot") 5·50 4·00
1476 $1 Humpback whale 5·50 4·00
1477 $1 Plain pigeon ("Puerto Rican Plain Pigeon") 5·50 4·00
1478 $1 St. Vincent amazon ("St. Vincent Parrot") 5·50 4·00
1479 $1 Puerto Rican amazon ("Puerto Rican Parrot") 5·50 4·00
1480 $1 Leatherback turtle 5·50 4·00
1481 $1 American crocodile 5·50 4·00
1482 $1 Hawksbill turtle 5·50 4·00
**MS**1483 Two sheets, each 100×70 mm. (a) $6 As No. 1476. (b) $6 West Indian manatee Set of 2 sheets. 45·00 35·00

**1994.** Bicentenary of the Louvre, Paris. Paintings by Peter Paul Rubens. Nos. 1742/9 and MS1758 of Antigua optd **BARBUDA MAIL**.
1484 $1 "The Destiny of Marie de' Medici" (upper detail) 4·75 3·50
1485 $1 "The Birth of Marie de' Medici" 4·75 3·50
1486 $1 "The Education of Marie de' Medici" 4·75 3·50
1487 $1 "The Destiny of Marie de' Medici" (lower detail) 4·75 3·50
1488 $1 "Henry VI receiving the Portrait of Marie" 4·75 3·50
1489 $1 "The Meeting of the King and Marie at Lyons" 4·75 3·50
1490 $1 "The Marriage by Proxy" 4·75 3·50
1491 $1 "The Birth of Louis XIII" 4·75 3·50
**MS**1492 70×100 mm. $6 "Helene Fourment with a Coach" (52×85 mm) 22·00 23·00

**1994.** World Cup Football Championship, 1994, U.S.A. (1st Issue). Nos. 1816/28 of Antigua optd **BARBUDA MAIL**.
1493 $2 Paul Gascoigne 3·50 2·50
1494 $2 David Platt 3·50 2·50
1495 $2 Martin Peters 3·50 2·50
1496 $2 John Barnes 3·50 2·50
1497 $2 Gary Lineker 3·50 2·50
1498 $2 Geoff Hurst 3·50 2·50
1499 $2 Bobby Charlton 3·50 2·50
1500 $2 Bryan Robson 3·50 2·50
1501 $2 Bobby Moore 3·50 2·50
1502 $2 Nobby Stiles 3·50 2·50
1503 $2 Gordon Banks 3·50 2·50
1504 $2 Peter Shilton 3·50 2·50
**MS**1505 Two sheets, each 135×109 mm. (a) $6 Bobby Moore holding World Cup. (b) $6 Gary Lineker and Bobby Robson Set of 2 sheets 28·00 23·00
See also Nos. 1573/9.

**1994.** Anniversaries and Events. Nos. 1829/38, 1840 and 1842/7 of Antigua optd **BARBUDA MAIL**.
1506 10c. Grand Inspector W.Heath 4·50 2·00
1507 15c. Rodnina and Oulanov (U.S.S.R.) (pairs figure skating) (horiz) 2·00 1·50
1508 30c. Present Masonic Hall, St. John's (horiz) 5·50 1·50
1509 30c. Willy Brandt with Helmut Schmidt and George Leber (horiz) 1·50 1·00
1510 30c. "Cat and Bird" (Picasso) (horiz) 1·50 1·00
1511 40c. Previous Masonic Hall, St. John's (horiz) 5·50 1·50
1512 40c. "Fish on a Newspaper" (Picasso) (horiz) 1·50 1·00
1513 40c. Early astronomical equipment 1·50 1·00
1514 40c. Prince Naruhito and engagement photographs (horiz) 1·50 1·00
1515 60c. Grand Inspector J.Jeffery 6·50 1·75
1516 $3 Masako Owada and engagement photographs (horiz) 3·00 4·00
1517 $4 Willy Brandt and protest march (horiz) 4·00 4·50
1518 $4 Galaxy 4·00 4·50
1519 $5 Alberto Tomba (Italy) (giant slalom) (horiz) 4·00 4·50
1520 $5 "Dying Bull" (Picasso) (horiz) 4·00 4·50
1521 $5 Pres. Clinton and family (horiz) 4·00 4·50
**MS**1522 Six sheets. (a) 106×75 mm. $5 Copernicus. (b) 106×75 mm. $6 Womens' 1500 metre speed skating medallists (horiz). (c) 106×75 mm. $6 Willy Brandt at Warsaw Ghetto Memorial (horiz). (d) 106×75 mm. $6 "Woman with a Dog" (detail) (Picasso) (horiz). (e) 106×75 mm. $6 Masako Owada. (f) 106×75 mm. $6 Pres. Clinton taking the Oath (42½×57 mm) Set of 6 sheets 55·00 50·00

**1994.** Aviation Anniversaries. Nos. 1848/55 of Antigua optd **BARBUDA MAIL**.
1523 30c. Hugo Eckener and Dr. W. Beckers with airship "Graf Zeppelin" over Lake George, New York 3·25 1·75
1524 40c. Chicago World's Fair from "Graf Zeppelin" 3·25 1·75
1525 40c. Gloster Whittle E28/39, 1941 3·25 1·75
1526 40c. George Washington writing balloon mail letter (vert) 3·25 1·75
1527 $4 Pres. Wilson and Curtiss "Jenny" 9·00 10·00
1528 $5 Airship LZ-129 "Hindenburg" over Ebbets Field baseball stadium, 1937 9·00 10·00
1529 $5 Gloster Meteor in dogfight 9·00 10·00
**MS**1530 Three sheets. (a) 86×105 mm. $6 Hugo Eckener (vert). (b) 105×86 mm. $6 Consolidated Catalina PBY-5 flying boat (57×42½ mm). (c) 105×86 mm. $6 Alexander Hamilton, Washington and John Jay watching Blanchard's balloon, 1793 (horiz) Set of 3 sheets 40·00 35·00

**1994.** Centenaries of Henry Ford's First Petrol Engine (Nos. 1531, 1533, 1533a) and Karl Benz's First Four-wheeled Car (others). Nos. 1856/60 of Antigua optd **BARBUDA MAIL**.
1531 30c. Lincoln Continental 2·00 1·25
1532 40c. Mercedes racing car, 1914 2·00 1·25
1533 $4 Ford "GT40", 1966 7·00 7·50
1534 $5 Mercedes Benz "gull-wing" coupe, 1954 7·00 7·50
**MS**1535 Two sheets. (a) 114×87 mm. $6 Ford's Mustang emblem. (b) 87×114 mm. $6 Germany 1936 12pf. Benz and U.S.A. 1968 12c. Ford stamps Set of 2 sheets 23·00 21·00

**1994.** Famous Paintings by Rembrandt and Matisse. Nos. 1881/9 of Antigua optd **BARBUDA MAIL**.
1536 15c. "Hannah and Samuel" (Rembrandt) 2·25 1·75
1537 15c. "Guitarist" (Matisse) 2·25 1·75
1538 30c. "The Jewish Bride" (Rembrandt) 2·50 1·10
1539 40c. "Jacob wrestling with the Angel" (Rembrandt) 2·50 1·10
1540 60c. "Interior with a Goldfish Bowl" (Matisse) 3·00 1·25
1541 $1 "Mlle. Yvonne Landsberg" (Matisse) 3·75 1·75
1542 $4 "The Toboggan" (Matisse) 7·50 8·50
1543 $5 "Moses with the Tablets of the Law" (Rembrandt) 7·50 8·50
**MS**1544 Two sheets. (a) 124×99 mm. $6 "The Blinding of Samson by the Philistines" (detail) (Rembrandt). (b) 99×124 mm. $6 "The Three Sisters" (detail) (Matisse) Set of 2 sheets 22·00 22·00

**1994.** "Polska '93" International Stamp Exhibition, Poznan. Nos. 1839, 1841 and MS1847f of Antigua optd **BARBUDA MAIL**.
1545 $1 "Woman Combing her Hair" (W. Slewinski) (horiz) 5·00 2·50
1546 $3 "Artist's Wife with Cat" (Konrad Kryzanowski) (horiz) 9·00 10·00
**MS**1547 70×100 mm. $6 "General Confusion" (S. I. Witkiewicz) 10·00 12·00

**1994.** Orchids. Nos. 1949/56 of Antigua optd **BARBUDA MAIL**.
1548 10c. "Spiranthes lanceolata" 2·75 1·75
1549 20c. "Ionopsis utricularioides" 3·75 1·75
1550 30c. "Tetramicra canaliculata" 4·00 1·50
1551 50c. "Oncidium picturatum" 4·50 1·50
1552 $1 "Epidendrum difforme" 5·50 2·50
1553 $2 "Epidendrum ciliare" 8·00 6·50
1554 $4 "Epidendrum ibaguense" 9·00 10·00
1555 $5 "Epidendrum nocturnum" 9·00 10·00
**MS**1556 Two sheets, each 100×73 mm. (a) $6 "Rodriguezia lanceolata". (b) $6 "Encyclia cochleata" Set of 2 sheets 35·00 32·00

**1994.** Centenary of Sierra Club (environmental protection society) (1992). Endangered Species. Nos. 1907/22 of Antigua optd **BARBUDA MAIL**.
1557 $1.50 Sumatran rhinoceros lying down 3·00 2·50
1558 $1.50 Sumatran rhinoceros feeding 3·00 2·50
1559 $1.50 Ring-tailed lemur on ground 3·00 2·50
1560 $1.50 Ring-tailed lemur on branch 3·00 2·50
1561 $1.50 Red-fronted brown lemur on branch 3·00 2·50
1562 $1.50 Head of red-fronted brown lemur 3·00 2·50

1563 $1.50 Head of red-fronted brown lemur in front of trunk 3·00 2·50
1564 $1.50 Sierra Club Centennial emblem 1·75 1·60
1565 $1.50 Head of bactrian camel 3·00 2·50
1566 $1.50 Bactrian camel 3·00 2·50
1567 $1.50 African elephant drinking 3·00 2·50
1568 $1.50 Head of African elephant 3·00 2·50
1569 $1.50 Leopard sitting upright 3·00 2·50
1570 $1.50 Leopard in grass (emblem at right) 3·00 2·50
1571 $1.50 Leopard in grass (emblem at left) 3·00 2·50
**MS**1572 Four sheets. (a) 100×70 mm. $1.50, Sumatran rhinoceros (horiz). (b) 70×100 mm. $1.50, Ring-tailed lemur (horiz). (C) 70×100 mm. $1.50, Bactrian camel (horiz) (d) 100×70 mm. $1.50, African elephant (horiz) Set of 4 sheets 15·00 15·00

**1995.** World Cup Football Championship, U.S.A. (2nd issue). Nos. 2039/45 of Antigua optd **BARBUDA MAIL**.
1573 15c. Hugo Sanchez (Mexico) 2·25 1·25
1574 35c. Jurgen Klinsmann (Germany) 2·75 1·25
1575 65c. Antiguan player 3·00 1·25
1576 $1.20 Cobi Jones (U.S.A.) 4·00 2·75
1577 $4 Roberto Baggio (Italy) 8·00 8·50
1578 $5 Bwalya Kalusha (Zambia) 8·00 8·50
**MS**1579 Two sheets. (a) 72×105 mm. $6 Maldive Islands player (vert). (b) 107×78 mm. $6 World Cup trophy (vert) Set of 2 sheets 20·00 17·00

**1995.** Christmas. Religious Paintings. Nos. 2058/66 of Antigua optd **BARBUDA MAIL**.
1580 15c. "Virgin and Child by the Fireside" (Robert Campin) 1·75 75
1581 35c. "The Reading Madonna" (Giorgione) 2·25 70
1582 40c. "Madonna and Child" (Giovanni Bellini) 2·25 70
1583 45c. "The Little Madonna" (Da Vinci) 2·25 70
1584 65c. "The Virgin and Child under the Apple Tree" (Lucas Cranach the Elder) 2·75 1·00
1585 75c. "Madonna and Child" (Master of the Female Half-lengths) 2·75 1·25
1586 $1.20 "An Allegory of the Church" (Alessandro Allori) 4·25 4·00
1587 $5 "Madonna and Child wreathed with Flowers" (Jacob Jordaens) 8·50 12·00
**MS**1588 Two sheets. (a) 123×88 mm. $6 "Madonna and Child with Commissioners" (detail) (Palma Vecchio). (b) 88×123 mm. $6 "The Virgin Enthroned with Child" (detail) (Bohemian master) Set of 2 sheets 16·00 16·00

**1995.** "Hong Kong '94" International Stamp Exhibition (1st issue). Nos. 1890/1 of Antigua optd **BARBUDA MAIL**.
1589 40c. Hong Kong 1981 $1 Fish stamp and sampans, Shau Kei Wan 4·00 2·50
1590 40c. Antigua 1990 $2 Reef fish stamp and sampans, Shau Kei Wan 4·00 2·50
See also Nos. 1591/6.

**1995.** "Hong Kong '94" International Stamp Exhibition (2nd issue). Nos. 1892/7 of Antigua optd **BARBUDA MAIL**.
1591 40c. Terracotta warriors 1·25 1·00
1592 40c. Cavalryman and horse 1·25 1·00
1593 40c. Warriors in armour 1·25 1·00
1594 40c. Painted bronze chariot and team 1·25 1·00
1595 40c. Pekingese dog 1·25 1·00
1596 40c. Warriors with horses 1·25 1·00

**1995.** Centenary of International Olympic Committee. Nos. 1990/2 of Antigua optd **BARBUDA MAIL**.
1597 50c. Edwin Moses (U.S.A.) (400 metres hurdles), 1984 1·00 75
1598 $1.50 Steffi Graf (Germany) (tennis), 1988 8·50 4·25
**MS**1599 79×110 mm. $6 Johann Olav Koss (Norway) (500, 1500 and 10,000 metre speed skating), 1994 9·00 10·00

**1995.** Dogs of the World. Chinese New Year ("Year of the Dog"). Nos. 1923/47 of Antigua optd **BARBUDA MAIL**.
1600 50c. West Highland white terrier 1·50 95
1601 50c. Beagle 1·50 95
1602 50c. Scottish terrier 1·50 95
1603 50c. Pekingese 1·50 95
1604 50c. Dachshund 1·50 95
1605 50c. Yorkshire terrier 1·50 95
1606 50c. Pomeranian 1·50 95
1607 50c. Poodle 1·50 95
1608 50c. Shetland sheepdog 1·50 95
1609 50c. Pug 1·50 95
1610 50c. Shih tzu 1·50 95
1611 50c. Chihuahua 1·50 95
1612 50c. Mastiff 1·50 95
1613 50c. Border collie 1·50 95
1614 50c. Samoyed 1·50 95
1615 50c. Airedale terrier 1·50 95
1616 50c. English setter 1·50 95
1617 50c. Rough collie 1·50 95
1618 50c. Newfoundland 1·50 95
1619 50c. Weimarana 1·50 95
1620 50c. English springer spaniel 1·50 95
1621 50c. Dalmatian 1·50 95
1622 50c. Boxer 1·50 95
1623 50c. Old English sheepdog 1·50 95
**MS**1624 Two sheets, each 93×58 mm. (a) $6 Welsh corgi. (b) $6 Labrador retriever Set of 2 sheets 30·00 21·00

**1995.** Centenary of First English Cricket Tour to the West Indies (1995). Nos. 1994/7 of Antigua optd **BARBUDA MAIL**.
1625 35c. Mike Atherton (England) and Wisden Trophy 3·75 1·50
1626 75c. Viv Richards (West Indies) (vert) 5·50 2·75
1627 $1.20 Richie Richardson (West Indies) and Wisden Trophy 7·50 4·75
**MS**1628 80×100 mm. $3 English team, 1895 (black and brown) 13·00 11·00

**1995.** "Philakorea '94" International Stamp Exhibition (1st issue). Nos. 1998/2009 of Antigua optd **BARBUDA MAIL**.
1629 40c. Entrance bridge, Song-gwangsa Temple 1·00 80
1630 75c. Long-necked bottle 1·25 1·50
1631 75c. Punch'ong ware jar with floral decoration 1·25 1·50
1632 75c. Punch'ong ware jar with blue dragon pattern 1·25 1·50
1633 75c. Ewer in shape of bamboo shoot 1·25 1·50
1634 75c. Punch'ong ware green jar 1·25 1·50
1635 75c. Pear-shaped bottle 1·25 1·50
1636 75c. Porcelain jar with brown dragon pattern 1·25 1·50
1637 75c. Porcelain jar with floral pattern 1·25 1·25
1638 90c. Song-op Folk Village, Cheju 1·25 1·25
1639 $3 Port Sogwipo 3·00 3·75
**MS**1640 104×71 mm. $4 Ox herder playing flute (vert) 4·75 6·50

**1995.** 1st Recipients of Order of the Caribbean Community. Nos. 2046/8 of Antigua optd **BARBUDA MAIL**.
1641 65c. Sir Shridath Ramphal 60 75
1642 90c. William Demas 90 1·00
1643 $1.20 Derek Walcott 4·00 4·25

**1995.** 25th Anniv of First Moon Landing. Nos. 1977/89 of Antigua optd **BARBUDA MAIL**.
1644 $1.50 Edwin Aldrin (astronaut) 3·75 2·50
1645 $1.50 First lunar footprint 3·75 2·50
1646 $1.50 Neil Armstrong (astronaut) 3·75 2·50
1647 $1.50 Aldrin stepping onto Moon 3·75 2·50
1648 $1.50 Aldrin and equipment 3·75 2·50
1649 $1.50 Aldrin and U.S.A. flag 3·75 2·50
1650 $1.50 Aldrin at Tranquility Base 3·75 2·50
1651 $1.50 Moon plaque 3·75 2·50
1652 $1.50 "Eagle" leaving Moon 3·75 2·50
1653 $1.50 Command module in lunar orbit 3·75 2·50
1654 $1.50 First day cover of U.S.A. 1969 10c. First Man on Moon stamp 3·75 2·50
1655 $1.50 Pres. Nixon and astronauts 3·75 2·50
**MS**1656 72×102 mm. $6 Armstrong and Aldrin with postal official 21·00 16·00

**1995.** International Year of the Family. No. 1993 of Antigua optd **BARBUDA MAIL**.
1657 90c. Antiguan family 1·75 1·50

**1995.** 50th Anniv of D-Day. Nos. 2010/13 of Antigua optd **BARBUDA MAIL**.
1658 40c. Short S.25 Sunderland flying boat 3·50 1·25
1659 $2 Lockheed P-38 Lightning fighters attacking train 11·00 6·00
1660 $3 Martin B-26 Marauder bombers 11·00 7·00
**MS**1661 108×78 mm. $6 Hawker Typhoon fighter bomber 19·00 18·00

122 Queen Elizabeth the Queen Mother (95th birthday)

**1995.** Anniversaries. Multicoloured.
1662 $7.50 Type **122** 12·00 12·00
1663 $8 German bombers over St. Paul's Cathedral, London (horiz) (50th anniv of end of Second World War) 24·00 15·00
1664 $8 New York skyline with U.N. and national flags (horiz) (50th anniv of United Nations) 15·00 16·00

**1995.** Hurricane Relief. Nos. 1662/4 surch **HURRICANE RELIEF** and premium.
1665 $7.50+$1 Type **122** (90th birthday) 8·00 11·00
1666 $8+$1 German bombers over St. Paul's Cathedral, London (horiz) (50th anniv of end of Second World War) 18·00 16·00
1667 $8+$1 New York skyline with U.N. and national flags (horiz) (50th anniv of United Nations) 8·00 11·00

**1996.** Marine Life. Nos. 1967/76 of Antigua optd **BARBUDA MAIL**.
1668 50c. Bottlenose dolphin 1·40 1·40
1669 50c. Killer whale 1·40 1·40
1670 50c. Spinner dolphin 1·40 1·40
1671 50c. Oceanic sunfish 1·40 1·40
1672 50c. Caribbean reef shark and short fin pilot whale 1·40 1·40
1673 50c. Copper-banded butterflyfish 1·40 1·40
1674 50c. Mosaic moray 1·40 1·40
1675 50c. Clown triggerfish 1·40 1·40
1676 50c. Red lobster 1·40 1·40
**MS**1677 Two sheets, each 106×76 mm. (a) $6 Seahorse. (b) $6 Swordfish ("Blue Marlin") (horiz) Set of 2 sheets 17·00 18·00

**1996.** Christmas. Religious Paintings. Nos. 2267/73 of Antigua optd **BARBUDA MAIL**.
1678 15c. "Rest on the Flight into Egypt" (Paolo Veronese) 65 40
1679 35c. "Madonna and Child" (Van Dyck) 75 40
1680 65c. "Sacred Conversation Piece" (Veronese) 1·00 55
1681 75c. "Vision of St. Anthony" (Van Dyck) 1·25 60
1682 90c. "Virgin and Child" (Van Eyck) 1·40 75
1683 $6 "The Immaculate Conception" (Giovanni Tiepolo) 4·75 7·00
**MS**1684 Two sheets. (a) 101×127 mm. $5 "Christ appearing to his Mother" (detail) (Van der Weyden). (b) 127×101 mm. $6 "The Infant Jesus and the Young St. John" (Murillo) Set of 2 sheets 14·00 16·00

**1996.** Stars of Country and Western Music. Nos. 2014/38 of Antigua optd **BRBAUDA MAIL**.
1685 75c. Travis Tritt 80 75
1686 75c. Dwight Yoakam 80 75
1687 75c. Billy Ray Cyrus 80 75
1688 75c. Alan Jackson 80 75
1689 75c. Garth Brooks 80 75
1690 75c. Vince Gill 80 75
1691 75c. Clint Black 80 75
1692 75c. Eddie Rabbit 80 75
1693 75c. Patsy Cline 80 75
1694 75c. Tanya Tucker 80 75
1695 75c. Dolly Parton 80 75
1696 75c. Anne Murray 80 75
1697 75c. Tammy Wynette 80 75
1698 75c. Loretta Lynn 80 75
1699 75c. Reba McEntire 80 75
1700 75c. Skeeter Davis 80 75
1701 75c. Hank Snow 80 75
1702 75c. Gene Autry 80 75
1703 75c. Jimmie Rodgers 80 75
1704 75c. Ernest Tubb 80 75
1705 75c. Eddy Arnold 80 75
1706 75c. Willie Nelson 80 75
1707 75c. Johnny Cash 80 75
1708 75c. George Jones 80 75
**MS**1709 Three sheets. (a) 100×70 mm. $6 Hank Williams Jr. (b) 100×70 mm. $6 Hank Williams Sr. (c) 70×100 mm. $6 Kitty Wells (horiz) Set of 3 sheets 17·00 17·00

**1996.** Birds. Nos. 2067/81 of Antigua optd **BARBUDA MAIL**.
1710 15c. Magnificent frigate bird 1·25 90
1711 25c. Antillean euphonia ("Blue-hooded Euphonia") 1·40 60
1712 35c. Eastern meadowlark ("Meadowlark") 1·50 60
1713 40c. Red-billed tropic bird 1·50 60
1714 45c. Greater flamingo 1·50 60
1715 60c. Yellow-faced grassquit 1·75 1·00
1716 65c. Yellow-billed cuckoo 1·75 1·50
1717 70c. Purple-throated carib 1·75 1·50
1718 75c. Bananaquit 1·75 1·00
1719 90c. Painted bunting 1·90 1·00
1720 $1.20 Red-legged honeycreeper 2·25 2·00
1721 $2 Northern jacana ("Jacana") 3·25 3·25
1722 $5 Greater Antillean bullfinch 5·00 6·50
1723 $10 Caribbean elaenia 7·50 11·00
1724 $20 Brown trembler ("Trembler") 12·00 17·00

**1996.** Birds. Nos. 2050, 2052 and 2054/7 of Antigua optd **BARBUDA MAIL**.
1725 15c. Bridled quail dove 2·00 1·50
1726 40c. Purple-throated carib (vert) 2·50 1·00
1727 $1 Broad-winged hawk ("Antigua Broad-winged Hawk") (vert) 3·75 2·50
1728 $4 Yellow warbler 6·00 8·00
**MS**1729 Two sheets. (a) 70×100 mm. $6 Female magnificent frigate bird (vert). (b) 100×70 mm. $6 Black-billed whistling duck ducklings Set of 2 sheets 17·00 18·00

**1996.** Prehistoric Animals. Nos. 2082/100 of Antigua optd **BARBUDA MAIL**.
1730 15c. Head of pachycephalosaurus 2·00 2·00
1731 20c. Head of afrovenator 2·00 2·00
1732 65c. Centrosaurus 2·00 2·00
1733 75c. Kronosaurus (horiz) 2·00 2·00
1734 75c. Ichthyosaurus (horiz) 2·00 2·00
1735 75c. Plesiosaurus (horiz) 2·00 2·00
1736 75c. Archelon (horiz) 2·00 2·00
1737 75c. Pair of tyrannosaurus (horiz) 2·00 2·00
1738 75c. Tyrannosaurus (horiz) 2·00 2·00
1739 75c. Parasaurolophus (horiz) 2·00 2·00
1740 75c. Pair of parasaurolophus (horiz) 2·00 2·00
1741 75c. Oviraptor (horiz) 2·00 2·00
1742 75c. Protoceratops with eggs (horiz) 2·00 2·00
1743 75c. Pteranodon and protoceratops (horiz) 2·00 2·00
1744 75c. Pair of protoceratops (horiz) 2·00 2·00
1745 90c. Pentaceratops drinking 2·25 1·50
1746 $1.20 Head of tarbosaurus 2·75 2·00
1747 $5 Head of styracosaurus 6·50 7·50
**MS**1748 Two sheets, each 101×70 mm. (a) $6 Head of Corythosaurus (horiz). (b) $6 Head of Carnotaurus (horiz) Set of 2 sheets 20·00 21·00

**1996.** Olympic Games, Atlanta (1st issue). Previous Gold Medal Winners. Nos. 2101/7 of Antigua optd **BARBUDA MAIL**.
1749 15c. Al Oerter (U.S.A.) (discus – 1956, 1960, 1964, 1968) 1·50 1·00
1750 20c. Greg Louganis (U.S.A.) (diving – 1984, 1988) 1·50 1·00
1751 65c. Naim Suleymanoglu (Turkey) (weightlifting – 1988) 2·00 1·00
1752 90c. Louise Ritter (U.S.A.) (high jump – 1988) 2·50 1·25
1753 $1.20 Nadia Comaneci (Rumania) (gymnastics – 1976) 4·00 2·75
1754 $5 Olga Bondarenko (Russia) (10,000 m – 1988) 6·00 8·50
**MS**1755 Two sheets, each 106×76 mm. (a) $6 United States crew (eight-oared shell – 1964). (b) $6 Lutz Hessilch (Germany) (cycling – 1988) (vert) Set of 2 sheets 18·00 16·00
See also Nos. 1922/44.

**1996.** 18th World Scout Jamboree, Netherlands. Tents. Nos. 2203/9 of Antigua optd **BARBUDA MAIL**.
1756 $1.20 The Explorer Tent 1·25 1·50
1757 $1.20 Camper tent 1·25 1·50
1758 $1.20 Wall tent 1·25 1·50
1759 $1.20 Trail tent 1·25 1·50
1760 $1.20 Miner's tent 1·25 1·50
1761 $1.20 Voyager tent 1·25 1·50
**MS**1762 Two sheets, each 76×106 mm. (a) $6 Scout and camp fire. (b) $6 Scout with back pack Set of 2 sheets 8·00 10·00

**1996.** Centenary of Nobel Prize Trust Fund. Nos. 2226/44 of Antigua optd **BARBUDA MAIL**.
1763 $1 Dag Hammarskjold (1961 Peace) 1·40 1·00
1764 $1 Georg Wittig (1979 Chemistry) 1·40 1·00
1765 $1 Wilhelm Ostwold (1909 Chemistry) 1·40 1·00
1766 $1 Robert Koch (1905 Medicine) 1·40 1·00

1767 $1 Karl Ziegler (1963 Chemistry) 1·40 1·00
1768 $1 Alexander Fleming (1945 Medicine) 1·40 1·00
1769 $1 Hermann Staudinger (1953 Chemistry) 1·40 1·00
1770 $1 Manfred Eigen (1967 Chemistry) 1·40 1·00
1771 $1 Arno Penzias (1978 Physics) 1·40 1·00
1772 $1 Shumal Agnon (1966 Literature) 1·40 1·00
1773 $1 Rudyard Kipling (1907 Literature) 1·40 1·00
1774 $1 Aleksandr Solzhenitsyn (1970 Literature) 1·40 1·00
1775 $1 Jack Steinburger (1988 Physics) 1·40 1·00
1776 $1 Andrei Sakharov (1975 Peace) 1·40 1·00
1777 $1 Otto Stern (1943 Physics) 1·40 1·00
1778 $1 John Steinbeck (1962 Literature) 1·40 1·00
1779 $1 Nadine Gordimer (1991 Literature) 1·40 1·00
1780 $1 William Faulkner (1949 Literature) 1·40 1·00
**MS**1781 Two sheets, each 100×70 mm. (a) $6 Elie Wiesel (1986 Peace) (vert). (b) $6 Dalai Lama (1989 Peace) (vert) Set of 2 sheets 13·00 15·00

**1996.** 70th Birthday of Queen Elizabeth II. Nos. 2355/8 of Antigua optd **BARBUDA MAIL**.
1782 $2 Queen Elizabeth II in blue dress 2·50 2·50
1783 $2 With bouquet 2·50 2·50
1784 $2 In Garter robes 2·50 2·50
**MS**1785 96×111 mm. $6 Wearing white dress 7·00 6·00

**1997.** Christmas. Religious Paintings by Filippo Lippi. Nos. 2377/83 of Antigua optd **BARBUDA MAIL**.
1786 60c. "Madonna Enthroned" 60 35
1787 90c. "Adoration of the Child and Saints" 85 55
1788 $1 "The Annunciation" 1·00 80
1789 $1.20 "Birth of the Virgin" 1·25 1·10
1790 $1.60 "Adoration of the Child" 1·60 2·00
1791 $1.75 "Madonna and Child" 1·75 2·25
**MS**1792 Two sheets, each 76×106 mm. (a) $6 "Madonna and Child" (different). (b) $6 "The Circumcision" Set of 2 sheets 12·00 15·00

**1997.** 50th Anniv of F.A.O. Nos. 2121/4 of Antigua optd **BARBUDA MAIL**.
1793 75c. Woman buying produce from market 1·00 1·00
1794 90c. Women shopping 1·10 1·10
1795 $1.20 Women talking 1·40 1·75
**MS**1796 100×70 mm. $6 Tractor 5·50 7·00

**1997.** 90th Anniv of Rotary International (1995). No. 2126 of Antigua optd **BARBUDA MAIL**.
1797 $5 Beach and rotary emblem 3·25 4·25
**MS**1798 74×104 mm. $6 National flag and emblem 4·50 5·50

**1997.** 50th Anniv of End of Second World War in Europe and the Pacific. Nos. 2108/16 and 2132/8 of Antigua optd **BARBUDA MAIL**.
1799 $1.20 Map of Berlin showing Russian advance 90 90
1800 $1.20 Russian tank and infantry 90 90
1801 $1.20 Street fighting in Berlin 90 90
1802 $1.20 German tank exploding 90 90
1803 $1.20 Russian air raid 90 90
1804 $1.20 German troops surrendering 90 90
1805 $1.20 Hoisting the Soviet flag on the Reichstag 90 90
1806 $1.20 Captured German standards 90 90
1807 $1.20 Gen. Chiang Kai-shek and Chinese guerrillas 90 90
1808 $1.20 Gen. Douglas MacArthur and beach landing 90 90
1809 $1.20 Gen. Claire Chennault and U.S. fighter aircraft 90 90
1810 $1.20 Brig. Orde Wingate and supply drop 90 90
1811 $1.20 Gen. Joseph Stilwell and U.S. supply plane 90 90
1812 $1.20 Field-Marshal Bill Slim and loading cow onto plane 90 90
**MS**1813 Two sheets, each 100×70 mm. (a) $3 Admiral Nimitz and aircraft carrier. (b) $6 Gen. Konev (vert) Set of 2 sheets 9·00 10·00

**1997.** Bees. Nos. 2172/6 of Antigua optd **BARBUDA MAIL**.
1814 90c. Mining bees 1·00 50
1815 $1.20 Solitary bee 1·25 80
1816 $1.65 Leaf-cutter bee 1·60 1·75
1817 $1.75 Honey bees 1·75 2·00
**MS**1818 110×80 mm. $6 Solitary mining bird 5·50 6·50

**1997.** Flowers. Nos. 2177/89 of Antigua optd **BARBUDA MAIL**.
1819 75c. Narcissus 75 85
1820 75c. Camellia 75 85
1821 75c. Iris 75 85
1822 75c. Tulip 75 85
1823 75c. Poppy 75 85
1824 75c. Peony 75 85
1825 75c. Magnolia 75 85
1826 75c. Oriental lily 75 85
1827 75c. Rose 75 85
1828 75c. Pansy 75 85
1829 75c. Hydrangea 75 85
1830 75c. Azaleas 75 85
**MS**1831 80×110 mm. $6 Calla lily 6·50 8·00

**1997.** Cats. Nos. 2190/202 of Antigua optd **BARBUDA MAIL**.
1832 45c. Somali 70 70
1833 45c. Persian and butterflies 70 70
1834 45c. Devon rex 70 70
1835 45c. Turkish angora 70 70
1836 45c. Himalayan 70 70
1837 45c. Maine coon 70 70
1838 45c. Ginger non-pedigree 70 70
1839 45c. American wirehair 70 70
1840 45c. British shorthair 70 70
1841 45c. American curl 70 70
1842 45c. Black non-pedigree and butterfly 70 70
1843 45c. Birman 70 70
**MS**1844 104×74 mm. $6 Siberian kitten (vert) 8·00 9·00

**1997.** 95th Birthday of Queen Elizabeth the Queen Mother. Nos. 2127/31 of Antigua optd **BARBUDA MAIL**.
1845 $1.50 brown, lt brown & black 5·00 3·50
1846 $1.50 multicoloured 5·00 3·50
1847 $1.50 multicoloured 5·00 3·50
1848 $1.50 multicoloured 5·00 3·50
**MS**1849 102×27 mm. $6 multicoloured 14·00 11·00

**1997.** 50th Anniv of United Nations. Nos. 2117/18 of Antigua optd **BARBUDA MAIL**.
1850 75c. Signatures and Earl of Halifax 80 80
1851 90c. Virginia Gildersleeve 90 90
1852 $1.20 Harold Stassen 1·25 1·50
**MS**1853 100×70 mm. $6 Pres. Franklin D. Roosevelt 4·50 6·00

**1997.** Trains of the World. Nos. 2210/25 of Antigua optd **BARBUDA MAIL**.
1854 35c. Trans-Gabon diesel-electric train 90 30
1855 65c. Canadian Pacific diesel-electric locomotive 1·00 40
1856 75c. Santa Fe Railway diesel-electric locomotive, U.S.A. 1·00 50
1857 90c. High Speed Train, Great Britain 1·00 60
1858 $1.20 TGV express train, France 1·00 1·25
1859 $1.20 Diesel-electric locomotive, Australia 1·00 1·25
1860 $1.20 Pendolino "ETR 450" electric train, Italy 1·00 1·25
1861 $1.20 Diesel-electric locomotive, Thailand 1·00 1·25
1862 $1.20 Pennslyvania Railroad Type 4 steam locomotive, U.S.A. 1·00 1·25
1863 $1.20 Beyer-Garratt steam locomotive, East African Railways 1·00 1·25
1864 $1.20 Natal Govt steam locomotive 1·00 1·25
1865 $1.20 Rail gun, American Civil War 1·00 1·25
1866 $1.20 Locomotive "Lion" (red livery), Great Britain 1·00 1·25
1867 $1.20 William Hedley's "Puffing Billy" (green livery), Great Britain 1·00 1·25
1868 $6 Amtrak high speed diesel locomotive, U.S.A. 3·50 4·50
**MS**1869 Two sheets, each 110×80 mm. (a) $6 Locomotive "Iron Rooster", China (vert). (b) $6 "Indian-Pacific" diesel-electric locomotive, Australia (vert) Set of 2 sheets 13·00 15·00

**1997.** Golden Wedding of Queen Elizabeth II and Prince Philip (1st issue). Nos. 1662/3 optd **Golden Wedding of H.M. Queen Elizabeth II and Prince Philip 1947-1997**.
1870 $7.50 Type **122** 7·00 8·00
1871 $8 German bombers over St. Paul's Cathedral, London (horiz) 8·00 9·00
See also Nos. 1925/30.

**1997.** Fungi. Nos. 2274/82 of Antigua optd **BARBUDA MAIL**.
1872 75c. "Hygrophoropsis aurantiaca" 1·75 1·50
1873 75c. "Hygrophorus bakerensis" 1·75 1·50
1874 75c. "Hygrophorus conicus" 1·75 1·50
1875 75c. "Hygrophorus miniatus" ("Hygrocybe miniata") 1·75 1·50
1876 75c. "Suillus brevipes" 1·75 1·50
1877 75c. "Suillus luteus" 1·75 1·50
1878 75c. "Suillus granulatus" 1·75 1·50
1879 75c. "Suillus caerulescens" 1·75 1·50
**MS**1880 Two sheets, each 106×76 mm. (a) $6 "Conocybe filaris". (b) $6 "Hygrocybe flavescens" Set of 2 sheets 13·00 15·00

**1997.** Birds. Nos. 2140/64 of Antigua optd **BARBUDA MAIL**.
1881 75c. Purple-throated carib 70 75
1882 75c. Antilean crested hummingbird 70 75
1883 75c. Bananaquit 70 75
1884 75c. Mangrove cuckoo 70 75
1885 75c. Troupial 70 75
1886 75c. Green-throated carib 70 75
1887 75c. Yellow warbler 70 75
1888 75c. Antillean euphonia ("Blue-hooded Euphonia") 70 75
1889 75c. Scaly-breasted thrasher 70 75
1890 75c. Burrowing owl 70 75
1891 75c. Carib grackle 70 75
1892 75c. Adelaide's warbler 70 75
1893 75c. Ring-necked duck 70 75
1894 75c. Ruddy duck 70 75
1895 75c. Green-winged teal 70 75
1896 75c. Wood duck 70 75
1897 75c. Hooded merganser 70 75
1898 75c. Lesser scaup 70 75
1899 75c. Black-billed whistling duck ("West Indian Tree Duck") 70 75
1900 75c. Fulvous whistling duck 70 75
1901 75c. Bahama pintail 70 75
1902 75c. Northern shoveler ("Shoveler") 70 75
1903 75c. Masked duck 70 75
1904 75c. American wigeon 70 75
**MS**1905 Two sheets, each 104×74 mm. (a) $6 Head of purple gallinule. (b) $6 Heads of blue-winged teals Set of 2 sheets 12·00 12·00

**1997.** Sailing Ships. Nos. 2283/301 of Antigua optd **BARBUDA MAIL**.
1906 15c. H.M.S. "Resolution" (Cook) 1·25 1·00
1907 25c. "Mayflower" (Pilgrim Fathers) 1·00 50
1908 45c. "Santa Maria" (Columbus) 1·25 60
1909 75c. "Aemilia" (Dutch galleon) 1·00 60
1910 75c. "Sovereign of the Seas" (English galleon) 1·00 60
1911 90c. H.M.S. "Victory" (Nelson) 1·25 1·00
1912 $1.20 As No. 1909 1·25 1·25
1913 $1.20 As No. 1910 1·25 1·25
1914 $1.20 "Royal Louis" (French galleon) 1·25 1·25
1915 $1.20 H.M.S. "Royal George" (ship of the line) 1·25 1·25
1916 $1.20 "Le Protecteur" (French frigate) 1·25 1·25
1917 $1.20 As No. 1911 1·25 1·25
1918 $1.50 As No. 1908 1·25 1·40
1919 $1.50 "Victoria" (Magellan) 1·25 1·40
1920 $1.50 "Golden Hind" (Drake) 1·25 1·40
1921 $1.50 As No. 1907 1·25 1·40
1922 $1.50 "Griffin" (La Salle) 1·25 1·40
1923 $1.50 As No. 1906 1·25 1·40
**MS**1924 (a) 102×72 mm. $6 U.S.S. "Constitution" (frigate). (b) 98×67 mm. $6 "Grande Hermine" (Cartier) Set of 2 sheets 9·00 10·00

**1997.** Golden Wedding of Queen Elizabeth and Prince Philip (2nd issue). Nos. 2474/80 of Antigua optd **BARBUDA MAIL**.
1925 $1 Queen Elizabeth II 2·25 2·00
1926 $1 Royal coat of arms 2·25 2·00
1927 $1 Queen Elizabeth and Prince Philip at reception 2·25 2·00
1928 $1 Queen Elizabeth and Prince Philip in landau 2·25 2·00
1929 $1 Balmoral 2·25 2·00
1930 $1 Prince Philip 2·25 2·00
**MS**1931 100×71 mm. $6 Queen Elizabeth with Prince Philip in naval uniform 13·00 13·00

**1997.** Christmas. Religious Paintings. Nos. 2566/72 of Antigua optd **BARBUDA MAIL**.
1932 15c. "The Angel leaving Tobias and his Family" (Rembrandt) 80 35
1933 25c. "The Resurrection" (Martin Knoller) 90 35
1934 60c. "Astronomy" (Raphael) 1·25 65
1935 75c. "Music-making Angel" (Melozzo da Forli) 1·40 1·00
1936 90c. "Amor" (Parmigianino) 1·60 1·10
1937 $1.20 "Madonna and Child with Saints" (Rosso Fiorentino) 1·75 1·90
**MS**1938 Two sheets, each 105×96 mm. (a) $6 "The Wedding of Tobias" (Gianantonio and Francesco Guardi) (horiz). (b) $6 "The Portinari Altarpiece" (Hugo van der Goes) (horiz) Set of 2 sheets 9·00 10·00

**1998.** Sea Birds. Nos. 2325/33 of Antigua optd **BARBUDA MAIL**.
1939 75c. Black skimmer 1·50 1·50
1940 75c. Black-capped petrel 1·50 1·50
1941 75c. Sooty tern 1·50 1·50
1942 75c. Royal tern 1·50 1·50
1943 75c. Pomarine skua ("Pomarine Jaegger") 1·50 1·50
1944 75c. White-tailed tropic bird 1·50 1·50
1945 75c. Northern gannet 1·50 1·50
1946 75c. Laughing gull 1·50 1·50
**MS**1947 Two sheets, each 105×75 mm. (a) $5 Great frigate bird. (b) $6 Brown pelican Set of 2 sheets 9·00 10·00

**1998.** Centenary of Radio. Entertainers. Nos. 2372/6 of Antigua optd **BARBUDA MAIL**.
1948 65c. Kate Smith 90 65
1949 75c. Dinah Shore 1·00 80
1950 90c. Rudy Vallee 1·25 90
1951 $1.20 Bing Crosby 1·50 1·75
**MS**1952 72×104 mm. $6 Jo Stafford (28×42 mm) 5·50 7·00

**1998.** Olympic Games, Atlanta (2nd issue). Previous Medal Winners. Nos. 2302/23 of Antigua optd **BARBUDA MAIL**.
1953 65c. Florence Griffith Joyner (U.S.A.) (Gold – track, 1988) 85 75
1954 75c. Olympic Stadium, Seoul (1988) (horiz) 85 75
1955 90c. Allison Jolly and Lynne Jewell (U.S.A.) (Gold – yachting, 1988) (horiz) 1·00 1·00
1956 90c. Wolfgang Nordwig (Germany) (Gold – pole vaulting, 1972) 1·00 1·00
1957 90c. Shirley Strong (Great Britain) (Silver – 100 m hurdles, 1984) 1·00 1·00
1958 90c. Sergei Bubka (Russia) (Gold – pole vault, 1988) 1·00 1·00
1959 90c. Filbert Bayi (Tanzania) (Silver – 3000 m steeplechase, 1980) 1·00 1·00
1960 90c. Victor Saneyev (Russia) (Gold – triple jump, 1968, 1972, 1976) 1·00 1·00
1961 90c. Silke Renk (Germany) (Gold – javelin, 1992) 1·00 1·00
1962 90c. Daley Thompson (Great Britain) (Gold – decathlon, 1980, 1984) 1·00 1·00
1963 90c. Robert Richards (U.S.A.) (Gold – pole vault, 1952, 1956) 1·00 1·00
1964 90c. Parry O'Brien (U.S.A.) (Gold – shot put, 1952, 1956) 1·00 1·00
1965 90c. Ingrid Kramer (Germany) (Gold – Women's platform diving, 1960) 1·00 1·00
1966 90c. Kelly McCormick (U.S.A.) (Silver – Women's springboard diving, 1984) 1·00 1·00
1967 90c. Gary Tobian (U.S.A.) (Gold – Men's springboard diving, 1960) 1·00 1·00
1968 90c. Greg Louganis (U.S.A.) (Gold – Men's diving, 1984 and 1988) 1·00 1·00
1969 90c. Michelle Mitchell (U.S.A.) (Silver – Women's platform diving, 1984 and 1988) 1·00 1·00
1970 90c. Zhou Jihong (China) (Gold – Women's platform diving, 1984) 1·00 1·00
1971 90c. Wendy Wyland (U.S.A.) (Bronze – Women's platform diving, 1984) 1·00 1·00
1972 90c. Xu Yanmei (China) (Gold – Women's platform diving, 1988) 1·00 1·00
1973 90c. Fu Mingxia (China) (Gold – Women's platform diving, 1992) 1·00 1·00
1974 $1.20 2000 m tandem cycle race (horiz) 3·25 2·50
**MS**1975 Two sheets, each 106×76 mm. (a) $5 Bill Toomey (U.S.A.) (Gold – decathlon, 1968) (horiz). (b) $6 Mark Lenzi (U.S.A.) (Gold – Men's springboard diving, 1992) Set of 2 sheets 9·00 10·00

**1998.** World Cup Football Championship, France. Nos. 2525/39 of Antigua optd **BARBUDA MAIL**.
1976 60c. multicoloured 75 60
1977 75c. brown 75 60
1978 90c. multicoloured 80 65
1979 $1 brown 80 80
1980 $1 brown 80 80
1981 $1 brown 80 80
1982 $1 black 80 80
1983 $1 brown 80 80
1984 $1 brown 80 80
1985 $1 brown 80 80
1986 $1 brown 80 80
1987 $1.20 multicoloured 1·00 1·10
1988 $1.65 multicoloured 1·25 1·40
1989 $1.75 multicoloured 1·40 1·60
**MS**1990 Two sheets, each 102×127 mm. (a) $6 multicoloured. (b) $6 multicoloured Set of 2 sheets 9·00 10·00

**1998.** Cavalry through the Ages. Nos. 2359/63 of Antigua optd **BARBUDA MAIL**.
1991 60c. Ancient Egyptian cavalryman 1·50 1·25

| | | | |
|---|---|---|---|
| 1992 | 60c. 13th-century English knight | 1·50 | 1·25 |
| 1993 | 60c. 16th-century Spanish lancer | 1·50 | 1·25 |
| 1994 | 60c. 18th-century Chinese cavalryman | 1·50 | 1·25 |
| **MS**1995 | 100×70 mm. $6 19th-century French cuirassier (vert) | 6·50 | 8·00 |

**1998.** 50th Anniv of UNICEF Nos. 2364/7 of Antigua optd BARBUDA MAIL.

| | | | |
|---|---|---|---|
| 1996 | 75c. Girl in red sari | 90 | 90 |
| 1997 | 90c. South American mother and child | 1·10 | 1·10 |
| 1998 | $1.20 Nurse with child | 1·40 | 1·75 |
| **MS**1999 | 114×74 mm. $6 Chinese child | 4·75 | 6·00 |

**1998.** 3000th Anniv of Jerusalem. Nos. 2368/71 of Antigua optd **BARBUDA MAIL**.

| | | | |
|---|---|---|---|
| 2000 | 75c. Tomb of Zachariah and "Verbascum sinuatum" | 1·75 | 1·00 |
| 2001 | 90c. Pool of Siloam and "Hyacinthus orientalis" | 1·90 | 1·10 |
| 2002 | $1.20 Hurva Synagogue and "Ranunculus asiaticus" | 2·25 | 2·50 |
| **MS**2003 | 66×80 mm. $6 Model of Herod's Temple and "Cercis siliquastrum" | 6·50 | 6·50 |

**1998.** Diana, Princess of Wales Commemoration. Nos. 2573/85 of Antigua optd **BARBUDA MAIL**.

| | | | |
|---|---|---|---|
| 2004 | $1.65 Diana, Princess of Wales | 1·25 | 1·10 |
| 2005 | $1.65 Wearing hoop earrings (red and black) | 1·25 | 1·10 |
| 2006 | $1.65 Carrying bouquet | 1·25 | 1·10 |
| 2007 | $1.65 Wearing floral hat | 1·25 | 1·10 |
| 2008 | $1.65 With Prince Harry | 1·25 | 1·10 |
| 2009 | $1.65 Wearing white jacket | 1·25 | 1·10 |
| 2010 | $1.65 In kitchen | 1·25 | 1·10 |
| 2011 | $1.65 Wearing black and white dress | 1·25 | 1·10 |
| 2012 | $1.65 Wearing hat (brown and black) | 1·25 | 1·10 |
| 2013 | $1.65 Wearing floral print dress (brown and black) | 1·25 | 1·10 |
| 2014 | $1.65 Dancing with John Travolta | 1·25 | 1·10 |
| 2015 | $1.65 Wearing white hat and jacket | 1·25 | 1·10 |
| **MS**2016 | Two sheets, each 70×100 mm. (a) $6 Wearing red jumper. (b) $6 Wearing black dress for Papal audience (brown and black) Set of 2 sheets | 9·00 | 10·00 |

**1998.** Broadway Musical Stars. Nos. 2384/93 of Antigua optd **BARBUDA MAIL**.

| | | | |
|---|---|---|---|
| 2017 | $1 Robert Preston ("The Music Man") | 1·00 | 1·00 |
| 2018 | $1 Michael Crawford ("Phantom of the Opera") | 1·00 | 1·00 |
| 2019 | $1 Zero Mostel ("Fiddler on the Roof") | 1·00 | 1·00 |
| 2020 | $1 Patti Lupone ("Evita") | 1·00 | 1·00 |
| 2021 | $1 Raul Julia ("Threepenny Opera") | 1·00 | 1·00 |
| 2022 | $1 Mary Martin ("South Pacific") | 1·00 | 1·00 |
| 2023 | $1 Carol Channing ("Hello Dolly") | 1·00 | 1·00 |
| 2024 | $1 Yul Brynner ("The King and I") | 1·00 | 1·00 |
| 2025 | $1 Julie Andrews ("My Fair Lady") | 1·00 | 1·00 |
| **MS**2026 | 106×76 mm. $6 Mickey Rooney ("Sugar Babies") | 7·00 | 8·00 |

**1998.** 20th Death Anniv of Charlie Chaplin (film star). Nos. 2404/13 of Antigua optd **BARBUDA MAIL**.

| | | | |
|---|---|---|---|
| 2027 | $1 Charlie Chaplin as young man | 1·25 | 90 |
| 2028 | $1 Pulling face | 1·25 | 90 |
| 2029 | $1 Looking over shoulder | 1·25 | 90 |
| 2030 | $1 In cap | 1·25 | 90 |
| 2031 | $1 In front of star | 1·25 | 90 |
| 2032 | $1 In "The Great Dictator" | 1·25 | 90 |
| 2033 | $1 With movie camera and megaphone | 1·25 | 90 |
| 2034 | $1 Standing in front of camera lens | 1·25 | 90 |
| 2035 | $1 Putting on make-up | 1·25 | 90 |
| **MS**2036 | 76×106 mm. $6 Charlie Chaplin | 9·00 | 9·00 |

**1998.** Butterflies. Nos. 2414/36 of Antigua optd **BARBUDA MAIL**.

| | | | |
|---|---|---|---|
| 2037 | 90c. "Charaxes porthos" | 1·00 | 70 |
| 2038 | $1.10 "Charaxes protoclea protoclea" | 1·00 | 1·00 |
| 2039 | $1.10 "Byblia ilithyia" | 1·00 | 1·00 |
| 2040 | $1.10 Black-headed tchagra (bird) | 1·00 | 1·00 |
| 2041 | $1.10 "Charaxes nobilis" | 1·00 | 1·00 |
| 2042 | $1.10 "Pseudacraea boisduvali trimeni" | 1·00 | 1·00 |
| 2043 | $1.10 "Charaxes smaragdalis" | 1·00 | 1·00 |
| 2044 | $1.10 "Charaxes lasti" | 1·00 | 1·00 |
| 2045 | $1.10 "Pseudacraea poggei" | 1·00 | 1·00 |
| 2046 | $1.10 "Graphium colonna" | 1·00 | 1·00 |
| 2047 | $1.10 Carmine bee eater (bird) | 1·00 | 1·00 |
| 2048 | $1.10 "Pseudacraea eurytus" | 1·00 | 1·00 |
| 2049 | $1.10 "Hypolimnas monteironis" | 1·00 | 1·00 |
| 2050 | $1.10 "Charaxes anticlea" | 1·00 | 1·00 |
| 2051 | $1.10 "Graphium leonidas" | 1·00 | 1·00 |
| 2052 | $1.10 "Graphium illyris" | 1·00 | 1·00 |
| 2053 | $1.10 "Nephronia argia" | 1·00 | 1·00 |
| 2054 | $1.10 "Graphium policenes" | 1·00 | 1·00 |
| 2055 | $1.10 "Papilio dardanus" | 1·00 | 1·00 |
| 2056 | $1.20 "Aethiopana honorius" | 1·00 | 1·10 |
| 2057 | $1.60 "Charaxes hadrianus" | 1·25 | 1·40 |
| 2058 | $1.75 "Precis westermanni" | 1·40 | 1·60 |
| **MS**2059 | Three sheets, each 107×76 mm. (a) $6 "Charaxes lactincus" (horiz). (b) $6 "Eupheadra reophron". (c) "Euxantha tiberius") (horiz) Set of 3 sheets | 17·00 | 20·00 |

**1998.** Christmas. Dogs. Nos. 2771/8 of Antigua optd **BARBUDA MAIL**.

| | | | |
|---|---|---|---|
| 2060 | 15c. Border collie | 65 | 60 |
| 2061 | 25c. Dalmatian | 75 | 60 |
| 2062 | 65c. Weimaraner | 1·40 | 80 |
| 2063 | 75c. Scottish terrier | 1·40 | 85 |
| 2064 | 90c. Long-haired dachshund | 1·50 | 85 |
| 2065 | $1.20 Golden retriever | 1·75 | 1·75 |
| 2066 | $2 Pekingese | 2·25 | 2·75 |
| **MS**2067 | Two sheets, each 75×66 mm. (a) $6 Dalmatian. (b) $6 Jack Russell terrier Set of 2 sheets | 13·00 | 12·00 |

**1999.** Lighthouses of the World. Nos. 2612/20 of Antigua optd **BARBUDA MAIL**.

| | | | |
|---|---|---|---|
| 2068 | 45c. Europa Point Lighthouse, Gibraltar | 1·00 | 50 |
| 2069 | 65c. Tierra del Fuego, Argentina (horiz) | 1·25 | 70 |
| 2070 | 75c. Point Loma, California, U.S.A. (horiz) | 1·25 | 70 |
| 2071 | 90c. Groenpoint, Cape Town, South Africa | 1·40 | 80 |
| 2072 | $1 Youghal, Cork, Ireland | 1·50 | 1·10 |
| 2073 | $1.20 Launceston, Tasmania, Australia | 1·60 | 1·25 |
| 2074 | $1.65 Point Abino, Ontario, Canada (horiz) | 2·00 | 2·50 |
| 2075 | $1.75 Great Inagua, Bahamas (horiz) | 2·00 | 2·50 |
| **MS**2076 | 99×70 mm. $6 Cape Hatteras, North Carolina, U.S.A. | 9·00 | 9·00 |

**1999.** Endangered Species. Nos. 2457/69 of Antigua optd **BARBUDA MAIL**.

| | | | |
|---|---|---|---|
| 2077 | $1.20 Red bishop | 1·75 | 1·50 |
| 2078 | $1.20 Yellow baboon | 1·75 | 1·50 |
| 2079 | $1.20 Superb starling | 1·75 | 1·50 |
| 2080 | $1.20 Ratel | 1·75 | 1·50 |
| 2081 | $1.20 Hunting dog | 1·75 | 1·50 |
| 2082 | $1.20 Serval | 1·75 | 1·50 |
| 2083 | $1.65 Okapi | 2·00 | 1·75 |
| 2084 | $1.65 Giant forest squirrel | 2·00 | 1·75 |
| 2085 | $1.65 Lesser masked weaver | 2·00 | 1·75 |
| 2086 | $1.65 Small-spotted genet | 2·00 | 1·75 |
| 2087 | $1.65 Yellow-billed stork | 2·00 | 1·75 |
| 2088 | $1.65 Red-headed agama | 2·00 | 1·75 |
| **MS**2089 | Three sheets, each 106×76 mm. (a) $6 South African crowned crane. (b) $6 Bat-eared fox. (c) $6 Malachite kingfisher Set of 3 sheets | 16·00 | 18·00 |

**1999.** "Pacific 97" International Stamp Exhibition, San Francisco. Death Centenary of Heinrich von Stephan (founder of the U.P.U.). Nos. 2481/4 of Antigua optd **BARBUDA MAIL**.

| | | | |
|---|---|---|---|
| 2090 | $1.75 blue | 2·50 | 2·25 |
| 2091 | $1.75 brown | 2·50 | 2·25 |
| 2092 | $1.75 mauve | 2·50 | 2·25 |
| **MS**2093 | 82×119 mm. $6 violet | 4·50 | 5·50 |

DESIGNS: No. 2090, Kaiser Wilhelm I and Heinrich von Stephan; 2091, Von Stephan and Mercury; 2092, Carrier pigeon and loft; **MS**2093 Von Stephan and 15th-century Basel messenger.

**1999.** 175th Anniv of Brothers Grimm's Third Collection of Fairy Tales. Cinderella. Nos. 2485/8 of Antigua optd **BARBUDA MAIL**.

| | | | |
|---|---|---|---|
| 2094 | $1.75 The Ugly Sisters and their Mother | 2·75 | 2·50 |
| 2095 | $1.75 Cinderella and her Fairy Godmother | 2·75 | 2·50 |
| 2096 | $1.75 Cinderella and the Prince | 2·75 | 2·50 |
| **MS**2097 | 124×96 mm. $6 Cinderella trying on slipper | 6·00 | 7·00 |

**1999.** Orchids of the World. Nos. 2502/24 of Antigua optd **BARBUDA MAIL**.

| | | | |
|---|---|---|---|
| 2098 | 45c. *Odontoglossum cervantesii* | 1·25 | 45 |
| 2099 | 65c. *Phalaenopsis* Medford Star | 1·50 | 35 |
| 2100 | 75c. *Vanda* Motes Resplendent | 1·50 | 85 |
| 2101 | 90c. *Odontonia* Debutante | 1·75 | 1·00 |
| 2102 | $1 *Iwanagaara* Apple Blossom | 2·00 | 1·10 |
| 2103 | $1.65 *Cattleya* Sophia Martin | 2·00 | 2·00 |
| 2104 | $1.65 Dogface Butterfly | 2·00 | 2·00 |
| 2105 | $1.65 *Laeliocattleya* Mini Purple | 2·00 | 2·00 |
| 2106 | $1.65 *Cymbidium* Showgirl | 2·00 | 2·00 |
| 2107 | $1.65 *Brassolaeliocattleya* Dorothy Bertsch | 2·00 | 2·00 |
| 2108 | $1.65 *Disa blackii* | 2·00 | 2·00 |
| 2109 | $1.65 *Paphiopedilum leeanum* | 2·00 | 2·00 |
| 2110 | $1.65 *Paphiopedilum macranthum* | 2·00 | 2·00 |
| 2111 | $1.65 *Brassocattleya* Angel Lace | 2·00 | 2·00 |
| 2112 | $1.65 *Saphrolae liocattleya* Precious Stones | 2·00 | 2·00 |
| 2113 | $1.65 Orange Theope Butterfly | 2·00 | 2·00 |
| 2114 | $1.65 *Promenaea xanthina* | 2·00 | 2·00 |
| 2115 | $1.65 *Lycasle macrobulbon* | 2·00 | 2·00 |
| 2116 | $1.65 *Amestella philippinensis* | 2·00 | 2·00 |
| 2117 | $1.65 *Masdevallia* Machu Picchu | 2·00 | 2·00 |
| 2118 | $1.65 *Phalaenopsis* Zuma Urchin | 2·00 | 2·00 |
| 2119 | $2 *Dendrobium victoria-reginae* | 2·50 | 2·75 |
| **MS**2120 | Two sheets, each 76×106 mm. (a) $6 *Miltonia* Seine. (b) $6 *Paphiopedilum gratrixanum* Set of 2 sheets | 14·00 | 15·00 |

**1999.** 50th Death Anniv of Paul Harris (founder of Rotary International). No. 2472/3 of Antigua optd **BARBUDA MAIL**.

| | | | |
|---|---|---|---|
| 2121 | $1.65 Paul Harris and James Grant | 2·50 | 3·00 |
| **MS**2122 | 78×107 mm. $6 Group study exchange, New Zealand | 5·00 | 7·00 |

**1999.** Royal Wedding. Nos. 2912/16 of Antigua optd **BARBUDA MAIL**.

| | | | |
|---|---|---|---|
| 2123 | $3 Sophie Rhys-Jones | 2·50 | 2·75 |
| 2124 | $3 Sophie and Prince Edward | 2·50 | 2·75 |
| 2125 | $3 Prince Edward | 2·50 | 2·75 |
| **MS**2126 | 108×78 mm. $6 Prince Edward with Sophie Rhys-Jones and Windsor Castle | 6·00 | 7·00 |

All examples of Nos. 2123/5 show the incorrect country overprint as above.

**1999.** Fungi. Nos. 2489/501 of Antigua optd **BARBUDA MAIL**.

| | | | |
|---|---|---|---|
| 2127 | 45c. *Marasmius rotula* | 1·00 | 35 |
| 2128 | 65c. *Cantharellus cibarius* | 1·25 | 55 |
| 2129 | 70c. *Lepiota cristata* | 1·40 | 60 |
| 2130 | 90c. *Auricularia mesenterica* | 1·50 | 70 |
| 2131 | $1 *Pholiota alnicola* | 1·50 | 1·00 |
| 2132 | $1.65 *Leccinum aurantiacum* | 1·75 | 1·90 |
| 2133 | $1.75 *Entoloma serrulatum* | 1·75 | 1·90 |
| 2134 | $1.75 *Panaeolus sphinctrinus* | 1·75 | 1·90 |
| 2135 | $1.75 *Volvariella bombycina* | 1·75 | 1·90 |
| 2136 | $1.75 *Conocybe percincta* | 1·75 | 1·90 |
| 2137 | $1.75 *Pluteus cervinus* | 1·75 | 1·90 |
| 2138 | $1.75 *Russula foetens* | 1·75 | 1·90 |
| **MS**2139 | Two sheets, each 106×76 mm. (a) $6 *Amanita cothurnata*. (b) $6 *Panellus serotinus* Set of 2 sheets | 12·00 | 14·00 |

**1999.** 1st Death Anniv of Diana, Princess of Wales. No. 2753 of Antigua optd **BARBUDA MAIL**.

| | | | |
|---|---|---|---|
| 2140 | $1.20 Diana, Princess of Wales | 1·50 | 1·50 |

**1999.** Railway Locomotives of the World. Nos. 2553/65 of Antigua optd **BARBUDA MAIL**.

| | | | |
|---|---|---|---|
| 2141 | $1.65 Original drawing by Richard Trevithick, 1803 | 1·50 | 1·50 |
| 2142 | $1.65 William Hedley's *Puffing Billy*, (1813–14) | 1·50 | 1·50 |
| 2143 | $1.65 Crampton locomotive of French Nord Railway, 1858 | 1·50 | 1·50 |
| 2144 | $1.65 Lawrence Machine Shop locomotive, U.S.A., 1860 | 1·50 | 1·50 |
| 2145 | $1.65 Natchez and Hamburg Railway steam locomotive *Mississippi*, U.S.A., 1834 | 1·50 | 1·50 |
| 2146 | $1.65 Bury "Coppernob" locomotive, Furness Railway, 1846 | 1·50 | 1·50 |
| 2147 | $1.65 David Joy's *Jenny Lind*, 1847 | 1·50 | 1·50 |
| 2148 | $1.65 Schenectady Atlantic locomotive, U.S.A., 1899 | 1·50 | 1·50 |
| 2149 | $1.65 Kitson Class 1800 tank locomotive, Japan, 1881 | 1·50 | 1·50 |
| 2150 | $1.65 Pennsylvania Railroad express freight | 1·50 | 1·50 |
| 2151 | $1.65 Karl Goldsdorf's 4 cylinder locomotive, Austria | 1·50 | 1·50 |
| 2152 | $1.65 Series "E" locomotive, Russia, 1930 | 1·50 | 1·50 |
| **MS**2153 | Two sheets, each 72×100 mm. (a) $6 George Stephenson's "Patentee" Type locomotive, 1843. (b) $6 Brunel's trestle bridge over River Lynher, Cornwall | 9·50 | 10·00 |

**1999.** 175th Anniv of Cedar Hall Moravian Church. Nos. 2605/11 of Antigua optd **BARBUDA MAIL**.

| | | | |
|---|---|---|---|
| 2154 | 20c. First Church and Manse, 1822–40 | 45 | 35 |
| 2155 | 45c. Cedar Hall School, 1840 | 55 | 30 |
| 2156 | 75c. Hugh A. King, minister, 1945–53 | 75 | 45 |
| 2157 | 90c. Present Church building | 85 | 50 |
| 2158 | $1.20 Water tank, 1822 | 1·25 | 1·25 |
| 2159 | $2 Former Manse, demolished 1978 | 1·75 | 2·50 |
| **MS**2160 | 100×70 mm. $6 Present church building (different) (50×37 mm) | 4·25 | 5·50 |

**1999.** Christmas. Religious Paintings. Nos. 2945/51 of Antigua optd **BARBUDA MAIL**.

| | | | |
|---|---|---|---|
| 2161 | 15c. multicoloured | 35 | 30 |
| 2162 | 25c. black, stone and yellow | 40 | 30 |
| 2163 | 45c. multicoloured | 55 | 30 |
| 2164 | 60c. multicoloured | 80 | 35 |
| 2165 | $2 multicoloured | 1·75 | 2·50 |
| 2166 | $4 black, stone and yellow | 2·75 | 4·00 |
| **MS**2167 | 76×106 mm. $6 multicoloured | 4·25 | 5·50 |

**1999.** Centenary of Thomas Oliver Robinson Memorial School. Nos. 2634/40 of Antigua optd BARBUDA MAIL.

| | | | |
|---|---|---|---|
| 2168 | 20c. green and black | 35 | 25 |
| 2169 | 45c. multicoloured | 55 | 30 |
| 2170 | 65c. green and black | 75 | 40 |
| 2171 | 75c. multicoloured | 80 | 50 |
| 2172 | 90c. multicoloured | 90 | 60 |
| 2173 | $1.20 brown, green and black | 1·10 | 1·25 |
| **MS**2174 | 106×76 mm. $6 brown | 4·25 | 5·50 |

**2000.** Cats and Dogs. Nos. 2540/52 of Antigua optd **BARBUDA MAIL**.

| | | | |
|---|---|---|---|
| 2175 | $1.65 Scottish fold kitten | 1·25 | 1·25 |
| 2176 | $1.65 Japanese bobtail | 1·25 | 1·25 |
| 2177 | $1.65 Tabby manx | 1·25 | 1·25 |
| 2178 | $1.65 Bicolor American shorthair | 1·25 | 1·25 |
| 2179 | $1.65 Sorel Abyssinian | 1·25 | 1·25 |
| 2180 | $1.65 Himalayan blue point | 1·25 | 1·25 |
| 2181 | $1.65 Dachshund | 1·25 | 1·25 |
| 2182 | $1.65 Staffordshire terrier | 1·25 | 1·25 |
| 2183 | $1.65 Shar-pei | 1·25 | 1·25 |
| 2184 | $1.65 Beagle | 1·25 | 1·25 |
| 2185 | $1.65 Norfolk terrier | 1·25 | 1·25 |
| 2186 | $1.65 Golden retriever | 1·25 | 1·25 |
| **MS**2187 | Two sheets, each 107×77 mm. (a) $6 Red tabby (vert). (b) $6 Siberian husky (vert) | 11·50 | 11·50 |

**2000.** Fish. Nos. 2586/604 of Antigua optd **BARBUDA MAIL**.

| | | | |
|---|---|---|---|
| 2188 | 75c. Yellow damselfish | 75 | 50 |
| 2189 | 90c. Barred hamlet | 80 | 55 |
| 2190 | $1 Yellow-tailed damselfish ("Jewelfish") | 90 | 70 |
| 2191 | $1.20 Blue-headed wrasse | 1·10 | 1·00 |
| 2192 | $1.50 Queen angelfish | 1·25 | 1·25 |
| 2193 | $1.65 Jackknife-fish | 1·25 | 1·25 |
| 2194 | $1.65 Spot-finned hogfish | 1·25 | 1·25 |
| 2195 | $1.65 Sergeant major | 1·25 | 1·25 |
| 2196 | $1.65 Neon goby | 1·25 | 1·25 |
| 2197 | $1.65 Jawfish | 1·25 | 1·25 |
| 2198 | $1.65 Flamefish | 1·25 | 1·25 |
| 2199 | $1.65 Rock beauty | 1·25 | 1·25 |
| 2200 | $1.65 Yellow-tailed snapper | 1·25 | 1·25 |
| 2201 | $1.65 Creole wrasse | 1·25 | 1·25 |
| 2202 | $1.65 Slender filefish | 1·25 | 1·25 |
| 2203 | $1.65 Long-spined squirrelfish | 1·25 | 1·25 |
| 2204 | $1.65 Royal gramma ("Fairy Basslet") | 1·25 | 1·25 |
| 2205 | $1.75 Queen triggerfish | 1·40 | 1·40 |
| **MS**2206 | Two sheets, each 80×110 mm. (a) $6 Porkfish. (b) $6 Black-capped basslet | 15·00 | 15·00 |

**2000.** Ships of the World. Nos. 2679/85 of Antigua optd **BARBUDA MAIL**.

| | | | |
|---|---|---|---|
| 2207 | $1.75 *Savannah* (paddle-steamer) | 1·25 | 1·25 |
| 2208 | $1.75 Viking longship | 1·25 | 1·25 |
| 2209 | $1.75 Greek galley | 1·25 | 1·25 |
| 2210 | $1.75 Sailing clipper | 1·25 | 1·25 |
| 2211 | $1.75 Dhow | 1·25 | 1·25 |
| 2212 | $1.75 Fishing catboat | 1·25 | 1·25 |
| **MS**2213 | Three sheets, each 100×70 mm. (a) $6 13th-century English warship (41×22 mm). (b) $6 Sailing dory (22×41 mm). (c) $6 Baltimore clipper (41×22 mm) | 12·00 | 14·00 |

**2000.** Modern Aircraft. Nos. 2700/12 of Antigua optd **BARBUDA MAIL**.

| | | | |
|---|---|---|---|
| 2214 | $1.65 Lockheed-Boeing General Dynamics Yf-22 | 1·25 | 1·25 |
| 2215 | $1.65 Dassault-Breguet Rafale BO 1 | 1·25 | 1·25 |
| 2216 | $1.65 MiG 29 | 1·25 | 1·25 |
| 2217 | $1.65 Dassault-Breguet Mirage 2000D | 1·25 | 1·25 |
| 2218 | $1.65 Rockwell B-1B "Lancer" | 1·25 | 1·25 |
| 2219 | $1.65 McDonnell-Douglas C-17A | 1·25 | 1·25 |
| 2220 | $1.65 Space Shuttle | 1·25 | 1·25 |
| 2221 | $1.65 SAAB "Grippen" | 1·25 | 1·25 |
| 2222 | $1.65 Eurofighter EF-2000 | 1·25 | 1·25 |
| 2223 | $1.65 Sukhoi SU 27 | 1·25 | 1·25 |
| 2224 | $1.65 Northrop B-2 | 1·25 | 1·25 |
| 2225 | $1.65 Lockheed F-117 "Nighthawk" | 1·25 | 1·25 |
| **MS**2226 | Two sheets, each 110×85 mm. (a) $6 F18 Hornet. (b) $6 Sukhoi SU 35 | 11·00 | 12·00 |

**2000.** Classic Cars. Nos. 2687/**MS**2699 of Antigua optd **BARBUDA MAIL**.

| | | | |
|---|---|---|---|
| 2227 | $1.65 Ford (1896) | 1·25 | 1·25 |
| 2228 | $1.65 Ford A (1903) | 1·25 | 1·25 |
| 2229 | $1.65 Ford T (1928) | 1·25 | 1·25 |
| 2230 | $1.65 Ford T (1922) | 1·25 | 1·25 |
| 2231 | $1.65 Ford Blackhawk (1929) | 1·25 | 1·25 |
| 2232 | $1.65 Ford Sedan (1934) | 1·25 | 1·25 |
| 2233 | $1.65 Torpedo (1911) | 1·25 | 1·25 |
| 2234 | $1.65 Mercedes 22 (1913) | 1·25 | 1·25 |
| 2235 | $1.65 Rover (1920) | 1·25 | 1·25 |

| No. | Description | Mint | Used |
|---|---|---|---|
| 2236 | $1.65 Mercedes Benz (1956) | 1·25 | 1·25 |
| 2237 | $1.65 Packard V-12 (1934) | 1·25 | 1·25 |
| 2238 | $1.65 Opel (1924) | 1·25 | 1·25 |
| **MS**2239 | Two sheets, each 70×100 mm. (a) $6 Ford (1908) (60×40 mm). (b) $6 Ford (1929) (60×40 mm) Set of 2 sheets | 12·00 | 12·00 |

**2000.** 19th World Scout Jamboree, Chile. Nos. 2739/ MS2742 of Antigua optd **BARBUDA MAIL**.

| No. | Description | Mint | Used |
|---|---|---|---|
| 2240 | 90c. Scout handshake | 1·00 | 65 |
| 2241 | $1 Scouts hiking | 1·25 | 90 |
| 2242 | $1.20 Scout salute | 1·50 | 1·50 |
| **MS**2243 | 68×98 mm. $6 Lord Baden-Powell | 7·00 | 7·50 |

**2000.** 50th Anniv of Organisation of American States (1998). No. 2730 of Antigua optd **BARBUDA MAIL**.

| No. | Description | Mint | Used |
|---|---|---|---|
| 2244 | $1 Stylized Americas | 1·25 | 1·25 |

**2000.** International Year of the Ocean (1998). Nos. 2641/ **MS**2678a/b of Antigua optd **BARBUDA MAIL**.

| No. | Description | Mint | Used |
|---|---|---|---|
| 2245-2269 | 40c.×25 Spotted eagle ray; Manta ray; Hawksbill turtle; Jellyfish; Queen angelfish; Octopus; Emperor angelfish; Regal angelfish; Porkfish; Racoon butterflyfish; Atlantic barracuda; Sea horse; Nautilus; Trumpetfish; White tip shark; Sunken Spanish galleon; Black tip shark; Long-nosed butterflyfish; Green moray eel; Captain Nemo; Treasure chest; Hammerhead shark; Divers; Lionfish; Clownfish | 14·00 | 15·00 |
| 2270-2281 | 75c.×12 Maroon-tailed conure; Cocoi heron; Common tern; Rainbow lorikeet; Saddleback butterflyfish; Goatfish and cat shark; Blue shark and stingray; Majestic snapper; Nassau grouper; Black-cap gramma and blue tang; Stingrays; Stingray and giant starfish | 18·00 | 20·00 |
| **MS**2282 | Two sheets. (a) 68×98 mm. $6 Humpback whale. (b) 98×68 mm. $6 Fiddler ray Set of 2 sheets | 13·00 | 13·00 |

Nos. 2245/69 and 2270/81 were each printed together, se-tenant, with the backgrounds forming composite designs.

**2000.** Olympic Games, Sydney. Nos. 3109/12 of Antigua optd **BARBUDA MAIL**.

| No. | Description | Mint | Used |
|---|---|---|---|
| 2283 | $2 Marcus Latimer Hurley (cycling), St Louis (1904) | 2·25 | 2·25 |
| 2284 | $2 Diving | 2·25 | 2·25 |
| 2285 | $2 Flaminio Stadium, Rome (1960) and Italian flag | 2·25 | 2·25 |
| 2286 | $2 Ancient Greek javelin thrower | 2·25 | 2·25 |

**2000.** West Indies Cricket Tour and 100th Test Match at Lord's. Nos. 3113/MS3115 of Antigua optd **BARBUDA MAIL**.

| No. | Description | Mint | Used |
|---|---|---|---|
| 2287 | 90c. Richie Richardson | 1·50 | 1·40 |
| 2288 | $5 Viv Richards | 7·00 | 7·00 |
| **MS**2289 | 121×104 mm. $6 Lord's Cricket Ground | 8·00 | 8·50 |

**2000.** Satellites and Spacecraft. Nos. 2835/40 and **MS**2847b of Antigua optd **BARBUDA MAIL**.

| No. | Description | Mint | Used |
|---|---|---|---|
| 2290 | $1.65 "Luna 2" moon probe | 1·25 | 1·25 |
| 2291 | $1.65 "Mariner 2" space probe | 1·25 | 1·25 |
| 2292 | $1.65 Giotto space probe | 1·25 | 1·25 |
| 2293 | $1.65 Rosat satellite | 1·25 | 1·25 |
| 2294 | $1.65 International Ultraviolet Explorer | 1·25 | 1·25 |
| 2295 | $1.65 Ulysses space probe | 1·25 | 1·25 |
| **MS**2296 | 106×76 mm. $6 "MIR" space station | 7·00 | 7·50 |

**2000.** No. **MS**3233 of Antigua optd **BARBUDA MAIL**.

| No. | Description | Mint | Used |
|---|---|---|---|
| **MS**2313 | Two Sheets, each 90×60 mm. (a) $6 Junkers 87B (dive bomber). (b) $6 Supermarine Spitfires at dusk | 11·00 | 12·00 |

Pt. 1

## BARWANI

A State of Central India. Now uses Indian stamps.

12 pies = 1 anna; 16 annas = 1 rupee.

1 Rana Ranjit Singh

2

**1921**

| No. | Type | Description | Mint | Used |
|---|---|---|---|---|
| 5 | 1 | ¼a. green | 23·00 | £110 |
| 18 | 1 | ¼a. pink | 3·50 | 17·00 |
| 19 | 1 | ¼a. blue | 1·75 | 11·00 |
| 37B | 1 | ¼a. black | 5·00 | 45·00 |
| 4 | 1 | ½a. blue | 20·00 | £250 |
| 29 | 1 | ½a. green | 2·75 | 19·00 |
| 10 | 2 | 1a. red | 3·50 | 26·00 |
| 39B | 2 | 1a. brown | 15·00 | 35·00 |
| 11 | 2 | 2a. purple | 2·25 | 30·00 |
| 41B | 2 | 2a. red | 38·00 | £160 |
| 31 | 2 | 4a. orange | 85·00 | £300 |
| 42Ba | - | 4a. green | 16·00 | 55·00 |

DESIGN: 4a. Another portrait of Rana Ranjit Singh.

4 Rana Devi Singh

**1932**

| No. | Type | Description | Mint | Used |
|---|---|---|---|---|
| 32A | 4 | ¼a. slate | 3·50 | 26·00 |
| 33A | 4 | ½a. green | 4·75 | 27·00 |
| 34A | 4 | 1a. brown | 4·75 | 25·00 |
| 35A | 4 | 2a. purple | 3·75 | 50·00 |
| 36A | 4 | 4a. olive | 6·00 | 50·00 |

5

**1938**

| No. | Type | Description | Mint | Used |
|---|---|---|---|---|
| 43 | 5 | 1a. brown | 48·00 | 85·00 |

Pt. 1

## BASUTOLAND

An African territory under British protection, N.E. of Cape Province. Self-Government introduced on 1 April 1965. Attained independence on 4 October 1966, when the country was renamed Lesotho.

1933. 12 pence = 1 shilling; 20 shillings = 1 pound.
1961. 100 cents = 1 rand.

1 King George V, Nile Crocodile and Mountains

**1933**

| No. | Type | Description | Mint | Used |
|---|---|---|---|---|
| 1 | 1 | ½d. green | 1·00 | 1·75 |
| 2 | 1 | 1d. red | 75 | 1·25 |
| 3 | 1 | 2d. purple | 1·00 | 80 |
| 4 | 1 | 3d. blue | 75 | 1·25 |
| 5 | 1 | 4d. grey | 2·00 | 7·00 |
| 6 | 1 | 6d. yellow | 2·25 | 1·75 |
| 7 | 1 | 1s. orange | 3·00 | 4·50 |
| 8 | 1 | 2s.6d. brown | 32·00 | 50·00 |
| 9 | 1 | 5s. violet | 60·00 | 80·00 |
| 10 | 1 | 10s. olive | £170 | £180 |

**1935.** Silver Jubilee. As T **13** of Antigua.

| No. | Description | Mint | Used |
|---|---|---|---|
| 11 | 1d. blue and red | 55 | 3·00 |
| 12 | 2d. blue and grey | 65 | 3·00 |
| 13 | 3d. brown and blue | 3·75 | 7·00 |
| 14 | 6d. grey and purple | 3·75 | 7·00 |

**1937.** Coronation. As T **2** of Aden.

| No. | Description | Mint | Used |
|---|---|---|---|
| 15 | 1d. red | 35 | 1·25 |
| 16 | 2d. purple | 50 | 1·25 |
| 17 | 3d. blue | 60 | 1·25 |

**1938.** As T **1**, but portrait of King George VI.

| No. | Description | Mint | Used |
|---|---|---|---|
| 18 | ½d. green | 30 | 1·25 |
| 19 | 1d. red | 50 | 70 |
| 20 | 1½d. blue | 40 | 50 |
| 21 | 2d. purple | 30 | 60 |
| 22 | 3d. blue | 30 | 1·25 |
| 23 | 4d. grey | 1·50 | 3·75 |
| 24 | 6d. yellow | 2·50 | 1·50 |
| 25 | 1s. orange | 2·50 | 1·00 |
| 26 | 2s.6d. brown | 16·00 | 8·50 |
| 27 | 5s. violet | 40·00 | 9·50 |
| 28 | 10s. olive | 40·00 | 20·00 |

**1945.** Victory. Stamps of South Africa optd **Basutoland**. Alternate stamps inscr in English or Afrikaans.

| No. | Type | Description | Mint | Used |
|---|---|---|---|---|
| 29 | 55 | 1d. brown and red | 50 | 10 |
| 30 | 55 | 2d. blue and violet | 50 | 10 |
| 31 | 55 | 3d. blue | 50 | 15 |

Prices are for bi-lingual pairs.

5 King George VI and Queen Elizabeth

**1947.** Royal Visit.

| No. | Type | Description | Mint | Used |
|---|---|---|---|---|
| 32 | - | 1d. red | 10 | 10 |
| 33 | 5 | 2d. green | 10 | 10 |
| 34 | - | 3d. blue | 10 | 10 |
| 35 | - | 1s. mauve | 15 | 10 |

DESIGNS—VERT: 1d. King George VI. HORIZ: 3d. Queen Elizabeth II as Princess and Princess Margaret; 1s. The Royal Family.

**1948.** Silver Wedding. As T **10/11** of Aden.

| No. | Description | Mint | Used |
|---|---|---|---|
| 36 | 1½d. blue | 20 | 10 |
| 37 | 10s. green | 45·00 | 48·00 |

**1949.** U.P.U. As T **20/23** of Antigua.

| No. | Description | Mint | Used |
|---|---|---|---|
| 38 | 1½d. blue | 20 | 1·50 |
| 39 | 3d. blue | 2·00 | 2·00 |
| 40 | 6d. orange | 1·00 | 5·00 |
| 41 | 1s. brown | 50 | 1·40 |

**1953.** Coronation. As T **13** of Aden.

| No. | Description | Mint | Used |
|---|---|---|---|
| 42 | 2d. black and purple | 40 | 40 |

8 Qiloane

18 Mohair (Shearing Goats)

**1954**

| No. | Type | Description | Mint | Used |
|---|---|---|---|---|
| 43 | 8 | ½d. black and sepia | 40 | 10 |
| 44 | - | 1d. black and green | 30 | 10 |
| 45 | - | 2d. blue and orange | 1·00 | 10 |
| 46 | - | 3d. sage and red | 1·50 | 30 |
| 47 | - | 4½d. indigo and blue | 1·25 | 15 |
| 48 | - | 6d. brown and green | 1·75 | 15 |
| 49 | - | 1s. bronze and purple | 1·75 | 30 |
| 50 | - | 1s.3d. brown and turquoise | 25·00 | 8·50 |
| 51 | - | 2s.6d. blue and red | 25·00 | 11·00 |
| 52 | - | 5s. black and red | 10·00 | 11·00 |
| 53 | 18 | 10s. black and purple | 32·00 | 26·00 |

DESIGNS—HORIZ: 1d. Orange River; 2d. Mosuto horseman; 3d. Basuto household; 4½d. Maletsunyane Falls; 6d. Herd-boy playing lesiba; 1s. Pastoral scene; 1s.3d. De Havilland Comet 1 airplane over Lancers' Gap; 2s.6d. Old Fort, Leribe; 5s. Mission cave house.

**1959.** No. 45 Surch ½d. and bar.

| No. | Description | Mint | Used |
|---|---|---|---|
| 54 | ½d. on 2d. blue and orange | 10 | 15 |

20 "Chief Moshoeshoe I" (engraving by Delangle)

**1959.** Inauguration of National Council.

| No. | Type | Description | Mint | Used |
|---|---|---|---|---|
| 55 | 20 | 3d. black and olive | 60 | 10 |
| 56 | - | 1s. red and green | 60 | 20 |
| 57 | - | 1s.3d. blue and orange | 80 | 45 |

DESIGNS: 1s. Council house; 1s.3d. Mosuto horseman.

**1961.** Nos. 43/53 surch.

| No. | Type | Description | Mint | Used |
|---|---|---|---|---|
| 58 | 8 | ½c. on ½d. black and sepia | 10 | 30 |
| 59 | - | 1c. on 1d. black and green | 10 | 10 |
| 60 | - | 2c. on 2d. blue and orange | 60 | 1·00 |
| 61 | - | 2½c. on 3d. green and red | 10 | 10 |
| 62 | - | 3½c. on 4½d. indigo and blue | 20 | 10 |
| 63 | - | 5c. on 6d. brown and green | 30 | 10 |
| 64 | - | 10c. on 1s. green and purple | 20 | 10 |
| 65a | - | 12½c. on 1s.3d. brown and turquoise | 5·50 | 2·50 |
| 66 | - | 25c. on 2s.6d. blue and red | 1·00 | 60 |
| 67 | - | 50c. on 5s. black and red | 4·00 | 3·00 |
| 68b | 18 | 1r. on 10s. black and purple | 24·00 | 23·00 |

26 Basuto Household

**1961.** As 1954 but value in new currency as in T 26.

| No. | Type | Description | Mint | Used |
|---|---|---|---|---|
| 69 | 8 | ½c. black and brown | 20 | 20 |
| 70 | - | 1c. black and green (as 1d.) | 20 | 40 |
| 71 | - | 2c. blue and orange (as 2d.) | 2·75 | 1·40 |
| 86 | 26 | 2½c. green and red | 15 | 25 |
| 73 | - | 3½c. indigo and blue (as 4½d.) | 30 | 1·50 |
| 88 | - | 5c. brown and green (as 6d.) | 30 | 50 |
| 75 | - | 10c. green and purple (as 1s.) | 30 | 40 |
| 90 | - | 12½c. brown & grn (as 1s.3d.) | 8·00 | 1·50 |
| 77 | - | 25c. blue and red (as 2s.6d.) | 6·50 | 6·50 |
| 92 | - | 50c. black and red (as 5s.) | 7·25 | 11·00 |
| 79 | 18 | 1r. black and purple | 55·00 | 24·00 |

**1963.** Freedom from Hunger. As T **28** of Aden.

| No. | Description | Mint | Used |
|---|---|---|---|
| 80 | 12½c. violet | 40 | 15 |

**1963.** Centenary of Red Cross. As T **33** of Antigua.

| No. | Description | Mint | Used |
|---|---|---|---|
| 81 | 2½c. red and black | 20 | 10 |
| 82 | 12½c. red and blue | 80 | 60 |

28 Mosotho Woman and Child

**1965.** New Constitution. Inscr "SELF GOVERNMENT 1965". Multicoloured.

| No. | Description | Mint | Used |
|---|---|---|---|
| 94 | 2½c. Type **28** | 20 | 10 |
| 95 | 3½c. Maseru border post | 35 | 20 |
| 96 | 5c. Mountain scene | 35 | 20 |
| 97 | 12½c. Legislative Buildings | 60 | 70 |

**1965.** Centenary of I.T.U. As T **36** of Antigua.

| No. | Description | Mint | Used |
|---|---|---|---|
| 98 | 1c. red and purple | 15 | 10 |
| 99 | 20c. blue and brown | 50 | 30 |

**1965.** I.C.Y. As T **37** of Antigua.

| No. | Description | Mint | Used |
|---|---|---|---|
| 100 | ½c. purple and turquoise | 10 | 65 |
| 101 | 12½c. green and lavender | 45 | 35 |

**1966.** Churchill Commemoration. As T **38** of Antigua.

| No. | Description | Mint | Used |
|---|---|---|---|
| 102 | 1c. blue | 15 | 1·25 |
| 103 | 2½c. green | 50 | 10 |
| 104 | 10c. brown | 75 | 40 |
| 105 | 22½c. violet | 1·25 | 1·25 |

### OFFICIAL STAMPS

**1934.** Nos. 1/3 and 6 optd **OFFICIAL**.

| No. | Type | Description | Mint | Used |
|---|---|---|---|---|
| O1 | 1 | ½d. green | £12000 | £7000 |
| O2 | 1 | 1d. red | £4000 | £3250 |
| O3 | 1 | 2d. purple | £4500 | £1000 |
| O4 | 1 | 6d. yellow | £12000 | £4750 |

### POSTAGE DUE STAMPS

**1933.** As Type D **1** of Barbados.

| No. | Description | Mint | Used |
|---|---|---|---|
| D1b | 1d. red | 1·75 | 6·50 |
| D2a | 2d. violet | 30 | 22·00 |

D 2

**1956**

| No. | Type | Description | Mint | Used |
|---|---|---|---|---|
| D3 | D2 | 1d. red | 30 | 3·00 |
| D4 | D2 | 2d. violet | 30 | 6·00 |

**1961.** Surch.

| No. | Type | Description | Mint | Used |
|---|---|---|---|---|
| D5 | | 1c. on 1d. red | 10 | 35 |
| D6 | | 1c. on 2d. violet | 10 | 1·25 |
| D7 | | 5c. on 2d. violet | 15 | 45 |
| D8 | - | 5c. on 2d. violet (No. D2a) | 1·00 | 6·50 |

**1964.** As Type D **2**, but value in decimal currency.

| No. | Description | Mint | Used |
|---|---|---|---|
| D9 | 1c. red | 4·00 | 23·00 |
| D10 | 5c. violet | 4·00 | 23·00 |

For later issues see **LESOTHO**.

Pt. 1

# BATUM

Batum, a Russian port on the Black Sea, had been taken by Turkish troops during the First World War. Following the Armistice, British Forces occupied the town on 1 December 1918. Batum was handed over to the National Republic of Georgia on 7 July 1920.

100 kopeks = 1 rouble.

1 Aloe Tree

**1919.** Imperf.

| | | | | |
|---|---|---|---|---|
| 1 | 1 | 5k. green | 7·00 | 22·00 |
| 2 | 1 | 10k. blue | 7·00 | 22·00 |
| 3 | 1 | 50k. yellow | 6·00 | 9·50 |
| 4 | 1 | 1r. brown | 8·50 | 8·50 |
| 5 | 1 | 3r. violet | 9·50 | 18·00 |
| 6 | 1 | 5r. brown | 10·00 | 32·00 |

БАТУМ. ОБ.

Руб 10 Руб

(2)

**1919.** Arms types of Russia surch as T **2**. Imperf (Nos. 7/8), perf (Nos. 9/10).

| | | | |
|---|---|---|---|
| 7 | 10r. on 1k. orange | 70·00 | 80·00 |
| 8 | 10r. on 3k. red | 28·00 | 32·00 |
| 9 | 10r. on 5k. purple | £400 | £450 |
| 10 | 10r. on 10 on 7k. blue | £475 | £500 |

**1919.** T **1** optd **BRITISH OCCUPATION**.

| | | | |
|---|---|---|---|
| 11 | 5k. green | 26·00 | 18·00 |
| 12 | 10k. blue | 16·00 | 19·00 |
| 13 | 25k. yellow | 25·00 | 19·00 |
| 14 | 1r. blue | 7·00 | 19·00 |
| 15 | 2r. pink | 1·00 | 7·50 |
| 16 | 3r. violet | 1·00 | 7·50 |
| 17 | 5r. brown | 1·25 | 7·50 |
| 18 | 7r. red | 5·00 | 10·00 |

**1919.** Arms types of Russia surch with Russian inscr, **BRITISH OCCUPATION** and new value.

| | | | |
|---|---|---|---|
| 19 | 10r. on 3k. red | 24·00 | 27·00 |
| 20a | 15r. on 1k. orange | 75·00 | 95·00 |
| 29 | 25r. on 5k. purple | 48·00 | 65·00 |
| 30a | 25r. on 10 on 7k. blue | 80·00 | 90·00 |
| 31 | 25r. on 20 on 14k. red and blue | 90·00 | £110 |
| 32a | 25r. on 25k. purple and green | £100 | £130 |
| 33a | 25r. on 50k. green and purple | 85·00 | £110 |
| 21 | 50r. on 1k. orange | £550 | £650 |
| 34 | 50r. on 2k. green | £120 | £150 |
| 35 | 50r. on 3k. red | £120 | £150 |
| 36 | 50r. on 4k. red | £110 | £130 |
| 37 | 50r. on 5k. purple | 90·00 | £110 |
| 27 | 50r. on 10k. blue | £2000 | £2000 |
| 28 | 50r. on 15k. blue and brown | £750 | £900 |

**1920.** Romanov type of Russia surch with Russian inscr, **BRITISH OCCUPATION** and new value.

| | | | |
|---|---|---|---|
| 41 | 50r. on 4k. red | 90·00 | £110 |

**1920.** Nos. 11, 13 and 3 surch with new value (50r. with **BRITISH OCCUPATION** also).

| | | | |
|---|---|---|---|
| 42 | 25r. on 5k. green | 45·00 | 48·00 |
| 43 | 25r. on 25k. yellow | 35·00 | 38·00 |
| 44a | 50r. on 50k. yellow | 19·00 | 21·00 |

**1920.** T **1** optd **BRITISH OCCUPATION**.

| | | | |
|---|---|---|---|
| 45 | 1r. brown | 2·25 | 13·00 |
| 46 | 2r. blue | 2·25 | 13·00 |
| 47 | 3r. pink | 2·25 | 13·00 |
| 48 | 5r. black | 2·25 | 13·00 |
| 49 | 7r. yellow | 2·25 | 13·00 |
| 50 | 10r. green | 2·25 | 13·00 |
| 51 | 15r. violet | 2·75 | 17·00 |
| 52 | 25r. red | 2·50 | 16·00 |
| 53 | 50r. blue | 2·75 | 20·00 |

Pt. 7

# BAVARIA

In S. Germany. A kingdom till 1918, then a republic. Incorporated into Germany in 1920.

1849. 60 kreuzer = 1 gulden.
1874. 100 pfennig = 1 mark.

1

**1849.** Imperf.

| | | | | |
|---|---|---|---|---|
| 1 | | 1k. black | £1200 | £1700 |

2 (Circle cut)

**1849.** Imperf. Circle cut by labels.

| | | | | |
|---|---|---|---|---|
| 3 | 2 | 3k. blue | £300 | 4·75 |
| 23 | 2 | 3k. red | 70·00 | 6·50 |
| 7 | 2 | 6k. brown | £8500 | £300 |

**1850.** Imperf. As T **2**, but circle not cut.

| | | | | |
|---|---|---|---|---|
| 8a | | 1k. red | £250 | 30·00 |
| 21 | | 1k. yellow | 95·00 | 25·00 |
| 11 | | 6k. brown | 60·00 | 12·00 |
| 25 | | 6k. blue | 95·00 | 50·00 |
| 16 | | 9k. green | £275 | 20·00 |
| 28 | | 9k. brown | £150 | 20·00 |
| 18 | | 12k. red | £200 | £170 |
| 31 | | 12k. green | £130 | 80·00 |
| 19 | | 18k. yellow | £180 | £250 |
| 32 | | 18k. red | £200 | £600 |

3

6

**1867.** Imperf.

| | | | | |
|---|---|---|---|---|
| 34 | 3 | 1k. green | 85·00 | 15·00 |
| 37 | 3 | 3k. red | 90·00 | 3·00 |
| 39 | 3 | 6k. blue | 60·00 | 24·00 |
| 41 | 3 | 6k. brown | £110 | 60·00 |
| 43 | 3 | 7k. blue | £550 | 20·00 |
| 46 | 3 | 9k. brown | 60·00 | 46·00 |
| 48 | 3 | 12k. mauve | £475 | £120 |
| 50 | 3 | 18k. red | £180 | £225 |
| 65 | 6 | 1m. mauve | £850 | £100 |

**1870.** Perf.

| | | | | |
|---|---|---|---|---|
| 51A | 3 | 1k. green | 15·00 | 2·00 |
| 69 | 3 | 3k. red | 1·10 | 10·00 |
| 55A | 3 | 6k. brown | 42·00 | 41·00 |
| 56A | 3 | 7k. blue | 4·75 | 5·50 |
| 59A | 3 | 9k. brown | 5·75 | 5·00 |
| 60A | 3 | 10k. yellow | 7·50 | 17·00 |
| 61A | 3 | 12k. mauve | £1600 | £6000 |
| 63A | 3 | 18k. red | 16·00 | 18·00 |

8

**1876.** Perf.

| | | | | |
|---|---|---|---|---|
| 120 | 8 | 2pf. grey | 3·25 | 70 |
| 103 | 8 | 3pf. green | 13·50 | 2·50 |
| 121 | 8 | 3pf. brown | 40 | 80 |
| 107 | 8 | 5pf. mauve | 27·00 | 10·00 |
| 122 | 8 | 5pf. green | 40 | 80 |
| 123 | 8 | 10pf. red | 55 | 1·00 |
| 124 | 8 | 20pf. blue | 55 | 1·00 |
| 114 | 8 | 25pf. brown | 42·00 | 8·75 |
| 125 | 8 | 25pf. orange | 55 | 1·20 |
| 126 | 8 | 30pf. olive | 1·10 | 1·00 |
| 127 | 8 | 40pf. yellow | 1·10 | 1·40 |
| 86 | 8 | 50pf. red | 75·00 | 9·25 |
| 117 | 8 | 50pf. brown | 80·00 | 5·00 |
| 128 | 8 | 50pf. purple | 65 | 2·00 |
| 129 | 8 | 80pf. mauve | 4·25 | 5·00 |
| 100 | 6 | 1m. mauve | 6·25 | 5·00 |
| 101a | 6 | 2m. orange | 7·50 | 10·00 |
| 136 | 6 | 3m. brown | 11·50 | 46·00 |
| 137 | 6 | 5m. green | 11·50 | 55·00 |

11

13 Prince Luitpold

**1911.** Prince Regent Luitpold's 90th Birthday.

| | | | | |
|---|---|---|---|---|
| 138c | 11 | 3pf. brown on drab | 40 | 1·00 |
| 139c | 11 | 5pf. green on green | 40 | 1·00 |
| 140d | 11 | 10pf. red on buff | 40 | 1·00 |
| 141b | 11 | 20pf. blue on blue | 2·75 | 1·60 |
| 142a | 11 | 25pf. deep brown on buff | 4·25 | 3·00 |
| 143a | - | 30pf. orange on buff | 2·75 | 2·50 |
| 144a | - | 40pf. olive on buff | 4·25 | 2·50 |
| 145a | - | 50pf. red on drab | 4·25 | 13·00 |
| 146 | - | 60pf. green on buff | 4·25 | 4·25 |
| 147a | - | 80pf. violet on drab | 12·50 | 13·00 |
| 148a | 13 | 1m. brown on drab | 4·25 | 5·00 |
| 149a | 13 | 2m. green on green | 6·25 | 15·00 |
| 150a | 13 | 3m. red on buff | 17·00 | £100 |
| 151 | 13 | 5m. blue on buff | 34·00 | 60·00 |
| 152 | 13 | 10m. orange on yellow | 60·00 | 95·00 |
| 153 | 13 | 20m. brown on yellow | 34·00 | 50·00 |

The 30 pf. to 80 pf. values are similar to Type **11**, but larger.

14

**1911.** 25th Anniv of Regency of Prince Luitpold.

| | | | | |
|---|---|---|---|---|
| 154 | 14 | 5pf. yellow, green & black | 1·10 | 1·80 |
| 155 | 14 | 10pf. yellow, red & black | 1·60 | 3·00 |

15 King Ludwig III

16

**1914.** Imperf or perf.

| | | | | |
|---|---|---|---|---|
| 171A | 15 | 2pf. slate | 35 | 2·75 |
| 172A | 15 | 2½ on 2pf. slate | 35 | 2·75 |
| 173A | 15 | 3pf. brown | 35 | 2·75 |
| 175A | 15 | 5pf. green | 35 | 2·75 |
| 176A | 15 | 7½pf. green | 35 | 2·75 |
| 178A | 15 | 10pf. red | 35 | 2·75 |
| 179A | 15 | 15pf. red | 35 | 2·75 |
| 182A | 15 | 20pf. blue | 35 | 2·75 |
| 183A | 15 | 25pf. grey | 35 | 2·75 |
| 184A | 15 | 30pf. orange | 1·60 | 2·75 |
| 185A | 15 | 40pf. olive | 35 | 2·75 |
| 186A | 15 | 50pf. brown | 35 | 2·75 |
| 187A | 15 | 60pf. green | 1·60 | 2·75 |
| 188A | 15 | 80pf. violet | 35 | 2·75 |
| 189A | 16 | 1m. brown | 35 | 2·75 |
| 190A | 16 | 2m. violet | 45 | 3·75 |
| 191A | 16 | 3m. red | 55 | 7·50 |
| 192A | - | 5m. blue | 75 | 27·00 |
| 193A | - | 10m. green | 2·40 | 75·00 |
| 194A | - | 20m. brown | 4·50 | £110 |

The 5, 10 and 20m. are larger.

**1919.** Peoples' State Issue. Overprinted **Volksstaat Bayern**. Imperf or perf.

| | | | | |
|---|---|---|---|---|
| 195A | 15 | 3pf. brown | 35 | 2·75 |
| 196A | 15 | 5pf. green | 35 | 2·75 |
| 197A | 15 | 7½pf. green | 35 | 2·75 |
| 198A | 15 | 10pf. lake | 35 | 2·75 |
| 199A | 15 | 15pf. red | 35 | 2·75 |
| 200A | 15 | 20pf. blue | 35 | 2·75 |
| 201A | 15 | 25pf. grey | 35 | 2·75 |
| 202A | 15 | 30pf. orange | 35 | 2·75 |
| 203A | 15 | 35pf. orange | 35 | 3·25 |
| 204A | 15 | 40pf. olive | 35 | 2·75 |
| 205A | 15 | 50pf. brown | 35 | 2·75 |
| 206A | 15 | 60pf. turquoise | 35 | 2·75 |
| 207A | 15 | 75pf. brown | 35 | 2·75 |
| 208A | 15 | 80pf. violet | 35 | 2·75 |
| 209A | 16 | 1m. brown | 35 | 2·75 |
| 210A | 16 | 2m. violet | 65 | 2·75 |
| 211A | 16 | 3m. red | 65 | 6·25 |
| 212A | - | 5m. blue (No. 192) | 1·30 | 16·00 |
| 213A | - | 10m. green (No. 193) | 2·00 | 75·00 |
| 214A | - | 20m. brown (No. 194) | 3·25 | 70·00 |

**1919.** 1st Free State Issue. Stamps of Germany (inscr "DEUTSCHES REICH") optd **Freistaat Bayern**.

| | | | | |
|---|---|---|---|---|
| 215 | 24 | 2½pf. grey | 35 | 2·75 |
| 216 | 10 | 3pf. brown | 35 | 2·75 |
| 217 | 10 | 5pf. green | 35 | 2·75 |
| 218 | 24 | 7½pf. orange | 35 | 2·75 |
| 219 | 10 | 10pf. red | 35 | 2·75 |
| 220 | 24 | 15pf. violet | 35 | 2·75 |
| 221 | 10 | 20pf. blue | 35 | 2·75 |
| 222 | 10 | 25pf. black & red on yell | 35 | 2·75 |
| 223 | 24 | 35pf. brown | 35 | 2·75 |
| 224 | 10 | 40pf. black and red | 55 | 2·75 |
| 225 | 10 | 75pf. black and green | 75 | 3·25 |
| 226 | 10 | 80pf. black & red on rose | 75 | 4·25 |
| 227 | 12 | 1m. red | 1·80 | 6·25 |
| 228 | 13 | 2m. blue | 2·20 | 15·00 |
| 229 | 14 | 3m. black | 2·20 | 17·00 |
| 230 | 15 | 5m. red and black | 2·20 | 17·00 |

**1919.** 2nd Free State Issue. Stamps of Bavaria overprinted **Freistaat Bayern**. Imperf or perf.

| | | | | |
|---|---|---|---|---|
| 231A | | 3pf. brown | 35 | 2·75 |
| 232A | | 5pf. green | 35 | 2·75 |
| 233A | | 7½pf. green | 35 | 21·00 |
| 234A | | 10pf. lake | 35 | 2·75 |
| 235A | | 15pf. red | 35 | 2·75 |
| 236A | | 20pf. blue | 35 | 2·75 |
| 237A | | 25pf. grey | 35 | 2·75 |
| 238A | | 30pf. orange | 35 | 2·75 |
| 239A | | 40pf. olive | 35 | 19·00 |
| 240A | | 50pf. brown | 35 | 2·75 |
| 241A | | 60pf. turquoise | 35 | 19·00 |
| 242A | | 75pf. brown | 55 | 19·00 |
| 243A | | 80pf. violet | 35 | 4·75 |
| 244A | 16 | 1m. brown | 35 | 3·75 |
| 245A | 16 | 2m. violet | 35 | 7·50 |
| 246A | 16 | 3m. red | 90 | 9·50 |
| 247A | - | 5m. blue (No. 192) | 1·50 | 23·00 |
| 248A | - | 10m. green (No. 193) | 2·75 | 48·00 |
| 249A | - | 20m. brown (No. 194) | 3·25 | 80·00 |

**1919.** War Wounded. **Surch 5 Pf. fur Kriegs-beschadigte Freistaat Bayern.** Perf.

| | | | | |
|---|---|---|---|---|
| 250 | 15 | 10pf.+5pf. lake | 55 | 2·75 |
| 251 | 15 | 15pf.+5pf. red | 55 | 2·75 |
| 252 | 15 | 20pf.+5pf. blue | 55 | 3·25 |

**1920.** Surch **Freistaat Bayern** and value. Imperf or perf.

| | | | | |
|---|---|---|---|---|
| 253A | 16 | 1m.25pf. on 1m. green | 35 | 3·25 |
| 254A | 16 | 1m.50pf. on 1m. orange | 35 | 4·25 |
| 255A | 16 | 2m.50pf. on 1m. slate | 65 | 8·50 |

**1920.** No. 121 surch **20** in four corners.

| | | | | |
|---|---|---|---|---|
| 256 | 8 | 20 on 3pf. brown | 35 | 2·75 |

26

27

28

29

30

**1920**

| | | | | |
|---|---|---|---|---|
| 257 | 26 | 5pf. green | 20 | 3·25 |
| 258 | 26 | 10pf. orange | 20 | 3·25 |
| 259 | 26 | 15pf. red | 20 | 3·25 |
| 260 | 27 | 20pf. violet | 20 | 3·25 |
| 261 | 27 | 30pf. blue | 20 | 4·25 |
| 262 | 27 | 40pf. brown | 20 | 3·25 |
| 263 | 28 | 50pf. red | 20 | 3·25 |
| 264 | 28 | 60pf. turquoise | 20 | 3·25 |
| 265 | 28 | 75pf. red | 20 | 3·25 |
| 266 | 29 | 1m. red and grey | 45 | 3·25 |
| 267 | 29 | 1¼m. blue and brown | 35 | 3·25 |
| 268 | 29 | 1½m. green and grey | 35 | 4·25 |
| 269 | 29 | 2½m. black and grey | 35 | 42·00 |
| 270 | 30 | 3m. blue | 1·00 | 19·00 |
| 271 | 30 | 5m. orange | 1·00 | 19·00 |
| 272 | 30 | 10m. green | 1·60 | 32·00 |
| 273 | 30 | 20m. black | 2·20 | 44·00 |

### OFFICIAL STAMPS

O18

**1916**

| | | | | |
|---|---|---|---|---|
| O195 | O18 | 3pf. brown | 35 | 1·10 |
| O196 | O18 | 5pf. green | 35 | 1·10 |
| O197 | O18 | 7½pf. green on green | 35 | 65 |
| O198 | O18 | 7½pf. green | 35 | 1·10 |
| O199 | O18 | 10pf. red | 35 | 85 |
| O200 | O18 | 15pf. red on buff | 90 | 95 |
| O201 | O18 | 15pf. red | 35 | 1·10 |
| O202 | O18 | 20pf. blue on blue | 2·75 | 2·75 |
| O203 | O18 | 20pf. blue | 35 | 85 |
| O204 | O18 | 25pf. grey | 35 | 85 |
| O205 | O18 | 30pf. orange | 35 | 85 |
| O206 | O18 | 60pf. turquoise | 35 | 1·60 |
| O207 | O18 | 1m. purple on buff | 1·30 | 3·75 |
| O208 | O18 | 1m. purple | 3·75 | £650 |

**1919.** Optd **Volksstaat Bayern**.

| | | | |
|---|---|---|---|
| O215 | 3pf. brown | 35 | 18·00 |
| O216 | 5pf. green | 35 | 2·75 |
| O217 | 7½pf. green | 35 | 17·00 |
| O218 | 10pf. red | 35 | 3·00 |
| O219 | 15pf. red | 35 | 3·00 |
| O220 | 20pf. blue | 35 | 3·00 |
| O221 | 25pf. grey | 35 | 3·00 |
| O222 | 30pf. orange | 35 | 3·00 |
| O223 | 35pf. orange | 35 | 3·00 |
| O224 | 50pf. olive | 35 | 3·25 |
| O225 | 60pf. turquoise | 45 | 18·00 |
| O226 | 75pf. brown | 45 | 4·75 |
| O227 | 1m. purple on buff | 1·50 | 19·00 |
| O228 | 1m. purple | 5·50 | £500 |

O31

O32

O33

**1920**

| | | | | |
|---|---|---|---|---|
| O274 | O31 | 5pf. green | 35 | 8·50 |
| O275 | O31 | 10pf. orange | 35 | 8·50 |
| O276 | O31 | 15pf. red | 35 | 8·50 |
| O277 | O31 | 20pf. violet | 35 | 8·50 |
| O278 | O31 | 30pf. blue | 35 | 9·50 |
| O279 | O31 | 40pf. brown | 35 | 9·50 |
| O280 | O32 | 50pf. red | 35 | 30·00 |
| O281 | O32 | 60pf. green | 35 | 12·50 |
| O282 | O32 | 70pf. lilac | 35 | 38·00 |
| O283 | O32 | 75pf. red | 35 | 48·00 |
| O284 | O32 | 80pf. blue | 35 | 48·00 |
| O285 | O32 | 90pf. olive | 35 | 75·00 |
| O286 | O33 | 1m. brown | 35 | 65·00 |
| O287 | O33 | 1¼m. green | 35 | 85·00 |
| O288 | O33 | 1½m. red | 35 | 85·00 |
| O289 | O33 | 2½m. blue | 35 | 95·00 |
| O290 | O33 | 3m. lake | 75 | £140 |
| O291 | O33 | 5m. green | 3·25 | £160 |

### POSTAGE DUE STAMPS

D6

**1862.** Inscr "Bayer. Posttaxe" at top. Imperf.

| | | | | |
|---|---|---|---|---|
| D34 | D6 | 3k. black | £170 | £400 |

**1870.** As Type D **6**, but inscr "Bayr. Posttaxe" at top. Perf.

| | | | |
|---|---|---|---|
| D65B | 1k. black | 16·00 | £1100 |
| D66B | 3k. black | 16·00 | £600 |

**1876.** Optd **Vom Empfanger zahlbar**.

| | | | | |
|---|---|---|---|---|
| D130a | 8 | 2pf. grey | 1·10 | 3·00 |
| D131a | 8 | 3pf. grey | 1·10 | 5·00 |
| D132a | 8 | 5pf. grey | 1·50 | 4·50 |
| D133a | 8 | 10pf. grey | 1·10 | 2·50 |

**1895.** No. D131a surch 2 in each corner.

| | | | |
|---|---|---|---|
| D134 | 2 on 3pf. grey | † | £61000 |

**1908.** Stamps of 1876 optd **E**.

| | | | |
|---|---|---|---|
| R133 | 3pf. brown | 1·10 | 4·00 |
| R134 | 5pf. green | 30 | 50 |
| R135 | 10pf. red | 30 | 50 |
| R136 | 20pf. blue | 65 | 1·00 |
| R137 | 50pf. purple | 5·75 | 9·25 |

Pt. 1

# BECHUANALAND

A colony and protectorate in Central S. Africa. British Bechuanaland (colony) was annexed to Cape of Good Hope in 1895. Internal Self-Government in the protectorate was introduced on 1 March 1965. Attained independence on 30 September 1966, when the country was renamed Botswana.

1885. 12 pence = 1 shilling; 20 shillings = 1 pound.
1961. 100 cents = 1 rand.

## A. BRITISH BECHUANALAND

**1885.** Stamps of Cape of Good Hope ("Hope" seated) optd **British Bechuanaland**.

| | | | | |
|---|---|---|---|---|
| 4 | 6 | ½d. black | 10·00 | 23·00 |
| 38 | 6 | 1d. red | 3·00 | 2·25 |
| 32 | 6 | 2d. bistre | 4·25 | 2·25 |
| 2 | 6 | 3d. red | 40·00 | 55·00 |
| 3 | 6 | 4d. blue | 80·00 | 80·00 |
| 7 | 6 | 6d. purple | £150 | 38·00 |
| 8 | 6 | 1s. green | £300 | £170 |

**1887.** Stamp of Great Britain (Queen Victoria) optd **BRITISH BECHUANALAND**.

| | | | | |
|---|---|---|---|---|
| 9 | 71 | ½d. red | 1·25 | 1·25 |

3

4

**1887**

| | | | | |
|---|---|---|---|---|
| 10 | 3 | 1d. lilac and black | 20·00 | 3·00 |
| 11 | 3 | 2d. lilac and black | 90·00 | 2·25 |
| 12 | 3 | 3d. lilac and black | 6·00 | 5·50 |
| 13 | 3 | 4d. lilac and black | 50·00 | 2·50 |
| 14 | 3 | 6d. lilac and black | 60·00 | 2·50 |
| 15 | 4 | 1s. green and black | 30·00 | 8·50 |
| 16 | 4 | 2s. green and black | 55·00 | 48·00 |
| 17 | 4 | 2s.6d. green and black | 65·00 | 70·00 |
| 18 | 4 | 5s. green and black | £100 | £150 |
| 19 | 4 | 10s. green and black | £200 | £350 |
| 20 | - | £1 lilac and black | £850 | £750 |
| 21 | - | £5 lilac and black | £3750 | £1600 |

Nos. 20/1 are as Type **4** but larger, 23×39½ mm.

**1888.** Surch.

| | | | | |
|---|---|---|---|---|
| 22 | 3 | "1d." on 1d. lilac and black | 7·50 | 6·50 |
| 23 | 3 | "2d." on 2d. lilac and black | 42·00 | 3·50 |
| 25 | 3 | "4d." on 4d. lilac and black | £400 | £500 |
| 26 | 3 | "6d." on 6d. lilac and black | £140 | 12·00 |
| 28 | 4 | "1s." on 1s. green and black | £190 | 85·00 |

**1888.** Surch **ONE HALF PENNY** and bars.

| | | | | |
|---|---|---|---|---|
| 29 | 3 | ½d. on 3d. lilac and black | £225 | £275 |

**1891.** Stamps of Great Britain (Queen Victoria) optd **BRITISH BECHUANALAND**.

| | | | | |
|---|---|---|---|---|
| 33 | 57 | 1d. lilac | 7·00 | 1·50 |
| 34 | 73 | 2d. green and red | 19·00 | 4·00 |
| 35 | 76 | 4d. green and brown | 3·00 | 60 |
| 36 | 79 | 6d. purple on red | 5·50 | 2·00 |
| 37 | 82 | 1s. green | 13·00 | 16·00 |

## B. BECHUANALAND PROTECTORATE

**1888.** No. 9 to 19 optd **Protectorate** or surch also.

| | | | | |
|---|---|---|---|---|
| 40 | 71 | ½d. red | 9·00 | 45·00 |
| 41 | 3 | 1d. on 1d. lilac and black | 14·00 | 15·00 |
| 42 | 3 | 2d. on 2d. lilac and black | 32·00 | 17·00 |
| 43 | 3 | 3d. on 3d. lilac and black | £170 | £225 |
| 51 | 3 | 4d. on 4d. lilac and black | £100 | 50·00 |
| 45 | 3 | 6d. on 6d. lilac and black | 90·00 | 50·00 |
| 46 | 4 | 1s. green and black | £110 | 55·00 |
| 47 | 4 | 2s. green and black | £600 | £1000 |
| 48 | 4 | 2s.6s. green and black | £550 | £950 |
| 49 | 4 | 5s. green and black | £1300 | £2250 |
| 50 | 4 | 10s. green and black | £4250 | £6500 |

**1889.** Stamp of Cape of Good Hope ("Hope" seated) optd **Bechuanaland Protectorate**.

| | | | | |
|---|---|---|---|---|
| 52 | 6 | ½d. black | 4·75 | 55·00 |

**1889.** No. 9 surch **Protectorate Fourpence**.

| | | | | |
|---|---|---|---|---|
| 53 | 71 | 4d. on ½d. red | 35·00 | 5·00 |

**1897.** Stamp of Cape of Good Hope ("Hope" seated) optd **BRITISH BECHUANALAND**.

| | | | | |
|---|---|---|---|---|
| 56 | 6 | ½d. green | 2·50 | 17·00 |

**1897.** Queen Victoria stamps of Great Britain optd **BECHUANALAND PROTECTORATE**.

| | | | | |
|---|---|---|---|---|
| 59 | 71 | ½d. red | 1·50 | 2·25 |
| 60 | 71 | ½d. green | 1·40 | 3·50 |
| 61 | 57 | 1d. lilac | 4·00 | 75 |
| 62 | 73 | 2d. green and red | 8·50 | 3·50 |
| 63 | 75 | 3d. purple on yellow | 5·50 | 8·50 |
| 64 | 76 | 4d. green and brown | 22·00 | 20·00 |
| 65 | 79 | 6d. purple on red | 23·00 | 11·00 |

**1904.** King Edward VII stamps of Great Britain optd **BECHUANALAND PROTECTORATE**.

| | | | | |
|---|---|---|---|---|
| 66 | 83 | ½d. turquoise | 2·75 | 2·00 |
| 68 | 83 | 1d. red | 9·50 | 30 |
| 69 | 83 | 2½d. blue | 10·00 | 7·00 |
| 70 | - | 1s. green and red (No. 314) | 50·00 | £150 |

**1912.** King George V stamps of Great Britain optd **BECHUANALAND PROTECTORATE**.

| | | | | |
|---|---|---|---|---|
| 73 | 105 | ½d. green | 1·25 | 1·50 |
| 72 | 102 | 1d. red | 2·75 | 60 |
| 92 | 104 | 1d. red | 2·00 | 70 |
| 75 | 105 | 1½d. brown | 6·50 | 2·50 |
| 93 | 106 | 2d. orange | 1·75 | 1·00 |
| 78 | 104 | 2½d. blue | 3·50 | 26·00 |
| 79 | 106 | 3d. violet | 6·00 | 12·00 |
| 80 | 106 | 4d. grey | 6·50 | 27·00 |
| 81 | 107 | 6d. purple | 8·50 | 23·00 |
| 82 | 108 | 1s. brown | 17·00 | 32·00 |
| 88 | 109 | 2s.6d. brown | 90·00 | £160 |
| 89 | 109 | 5s. red | £110 | £275 |

**22** King George V, Baobab Tree and Cattle drinking

**1932**

| | | | | |
|---|---|---|---|---|
| 99 | 22 | ½d. green | 2·50 | 30 |
| 100 | 22 | 1d. red | 1·50 | 25 |
| 101 | 22 | 2d. brown | 1·50 | 30 |
| 102 | 22 | 3d. blue | 3·50 | 3·75 |
| 103 | 22 | 4d. orange | 3·50 | 8·50 |
| 104 | 22 | 6d. purple | 4·50 | 6·50 |
| 105 | 22 | 1s. black and olive | 3·75 | 7·00 |
| 106 | 22 | 2s. black and orange | 24·00 | 60·00 |
| 107 | 22 | 2s.6d. black and red | 22·00 | 45·00 |
| 108 | 22 | 3s. black and purple | 42·00 | 50·00 |
| 109 | 22 | 5s. black and blue | 95·00 | £100 |
| 110 | 22 | 10s. black and brown | £190 | £200 |

**1935.** Silver Jubilee. As T **13** of Antigua.

| | | | |
|---|---|---|---|
| 111 | 1d. blue and red | 1·75 | 6·50 |
| 112 | 2d. blue and black | 2·00 | 6·50 |
| 113 | 3d. brown and blue | 4·00 | 7·00 |
| 114 | 6d. grey and purple | 9·00 | 7·00 |

**1937.** Coronation. As T **2** of Aden.

| | | | |
|---|---|---|---|
| 115 | 1d. red | 45 | 40 |
| 116 | 2d. brown | 60 | 1·00 |
| 117 | 3d. blue | 60 | 1·25 |

**1938.** As T **22**, but portrait of King George VI.

| | | | |
|---|---|---|---|
| 118 | ½d. green | 3·75 | 3·75 |
| 119 | 1d. red | 75 | 50 |
| 120a | 1½d. blue | 1·00 | 1·00 |
| 121 | 2d. brown | 75 | 50 |
| 122 | 3d. blue | 1·00 | 2·50 |
| 123 | 4d. orange | 2·00 | 3·50 |
| 124a | 6d. purple | 4·25 | 2·50 |
| 125 | 1s. black and olive | 4·75 | 8·50 |
| 126 | 2s.6d. black and red | 14·00 | 18·00 |
| 127 | 5s. black and blue | 38·00 | 28·00 |
| 128 | 10s. black and brown | 25·00 | 32·00 |

**1945.** Victory. Stamps of South Africa optd **Bechuanaland**. Alternate stamps inscr in English or Afrikaans.

| | | | | |
|---|---|---|---|---|
| 129 | 55 | 1d. brown and red | 75 | 1·50 |
| 130 | 55 | 2d. blue and violet (No. 109) | 50 | 1·50 |
| 131 | 55 | 3d. blue (No. 110) | 50 | 1·75 |

Prices for bi-lingual pairs.

**1947.** Royal Visit. As Nos. 32/5 of Basutoland.

| | | | |
|---|---|---|---|
| 132 | 1d. red | 10 | 10 |
| 133 | 2d. green | 10 | 10 |
| 134 | 3d. blue | 10 | 10 |
| 135 | 1s. mauve | 10 | 10 |

**1948.** Silver Wedding. As T **10/11** of Aden.

| | | | |
|---|---|---|---|
| 136 | 1½d. blue | 30 | 10 |
| 137 | 10s. grey | 40·00 | 48·00 |

**1949.** U.P.U. As T **20/23** of Antigua.

| | | | |
|---|---|---|---|
| 138 | 1½d. blue | 30 | 1·25 |
| 139 | 3d. blue | 1·50 | 2·50 |
| 140 | 6d. mauve | 60 | 4·75 |
| 141 | 1s. olive | 60 | 1·50 |

**1953.** Coronation. As T **13** of Aden.

| | | | |
|---|---|---|---|
| 142 | 2d. black and brown | 1·50 | 30 |

**1955.** As T **22** but portrait of Queen Elizabeth II, facing right.

| | | | |
|---|---|---|---|
| 143 | ½d. green | 50 | 30 |
| 144 | 1d. red | 80 | 10 |
| 145 | 2d. brown | 1·25 | 30 |
| 146 | 3d. blue | 3·00 | 2·50 |
| 146b | 4d. orange | 11·00 | 12·00 |
| 147 | 4½d. blue | 1·50 | 35 |
| 148 | 6d. purple | 1·25 | 60 |
| 149 | 1s. black and olive | 1·25 | 1·00 |
| 150 | 1s.3d. black and lilac | 14·00 | 9·50 |
| 151 | 2s.6d. black and red | 12·00 | 10·00 |
| 152 | 5s. black and blue | 15·00 | 16·00 |
| 153 | 10s. black and brown | 38·00 | 18·00 |

**26** Queen Victoria. Queen Elizabeth II and Landscape

**1960.** 75th Anniv of Protectorate.

| | | | | |
|---|---|---|---|---|
| 154 | 26 | 1d. sepia and black | 40 | 50 |
| 155 | 26 | 3d. mauve and black | 40 | 30 |
| 156 | 26 | 6d. blue and black | 40 | 50 |

**1961.** Stamps of 1955 surch.

| | | | |
|---|---|---|---|
| 157 | 1c. on 1d. red | 30 | 10 |
| 158 | 2c. on 2d. brown | 30 | 10 |
| 159 | 2½c. on 2d. brown | 30 | 10 |
| 160 | 2½c. on 3d. blue | 4·50 | 8·00 |
| 161d | 3½c. on 4d. orange | 20 | 60 |
| 162a | 5c. on 6d. purple | 20 | 10 |
| 163 | 10c. on 1s. black and olive | 20 | 10 |
| 164 | 12½c. on 1s.3d. black and lilac | 65 | 20 |
| 165 | 25c. on 2s.6d. black and red | 1·50 | 50 |
| 166 | 50c. on 5s. black and blue | 2·00 | 2·25 |
| 167b | 1r. on 10s. black and brown | 15·00 | 10·00 |

**28** African Golden Oriole ("Golden Oriole")

**1961**

| | | | | |
|---|---|---|---|---|
| 168 | 28 | 1c. multicoloured | 1·50 | 50 |
| 169 | - | 2c. orange, black and olive | 2·00 | 4·50 |
| 170 | - | 2½c. multicoloured | 1·75 | 10 |
| 171 | - | 3½c. multicoloured | 2·50 | 4·75 |
| 172 | - | 5c. multicoloured | 3·25 | 1·00 |
| 173 | - | 7½c. multicoloured | 2·25 | 2·25 |
| 174 | - | 10c. multicoloured | 2·25 | 60 |
| 175 | - | 12½c. multicoloured | 18·00 | 6·00 |
| 176 | - | 20c. brown and drab | 3·75 | 4·00 |
| 177 | - | 25c. sepia and lemon | 4·75 | 2·25 |
| 178 | - | 35c. blue and orange | 4·00 | 4·25 |
| 179 | - | 50c. sepia and olive | 2·75 | 2·50 |
| 180 | - | 1r. black and brown | 9·00 | 2·50 |
| 181 | - | 2r. brown and turquoise | 24·00 | 13·00 |

DESIGNS—VERT: 2c. Hoopoe ("African Hoopoe"); 2½c. Scarlet-chested sunbird; 3½c. Yellow-rumped bishop ("Cape Widow-bird"); 5c. Swallow-tailed bee eater; 7½c. African grey hornbill ("Grey Hornbill"); 10c. Red-headed weaver; 12½c. Brown-hooded kingfisher; 20c. Woman musician; 35c. Woman grinding maize; 1r. Lion; 2r. Police camel patrol. HORIZ: 25c. Baobab tree; 50c. Bechuana ox.

**1963.** Freedom from Hunger. As T **28** of Aden.

| | | | |
|---|---|---|---|
| 182 | 12½c. green | 30 | 15 |

**1963.** Centenary of Red Cross. As T **33** of Antigua.

| | | | |
|---|---|---|---|
| 183 | 2½c. red and black | 20 | 10 |
| 184 | 12½c. red and blue | 40 | 50 |

**1964.** 400th Birth Anniv of Shakespeare. As T **34** of Antigua.

| | | | |
|---|---|---|---|
| 185 | 12½c. brown | 15 | 15 |

## C. BECHUANALAND

**42** Map and Gaberones Dam

**1965.** New Constitution.

| | | | | |
|---|---|---|---|---|
| 186 | 42 | 2½c. red and gold | 30 | 10 |
| 187 | 42 | 5c. blue and gold | 30 | 40 |
| 188 | 42 | 12½c. brown and gold | 40 | 40 |
| 189 | 42 | 25c. green and gold | 45 | 55 |

**1965.** Centenary of I.T.U. As T **36** of Antigua.

| | | | |
|---|---|---|---|
| 190 | 2½c. red and yellow | 20 | 10 |
| 191 | 12½c. mauve and brown | 45 | 30 |

**1965.** I.C.Y. As T **37** of Antigua.

| | | | |
|---|---|---|---|
| 192 | 1c. purple and turquoise | 10 | 45 |
| 193 | 12½c. green and lavender | 60 | 55 |

**1966.** Churchill Commemoration. As T **38** of Antigua.

| | | | |
|---|---|---|---|
| 194 | 1c. blue | 20 | 2·00 |
| 195 | 2½c. green | 35 | 10 |
| 196 | 12½c. brown | 70 | 35 |
| 197 | 20c. violet | 75 | 55 |

**43** Haslar Smoke Generator

**1966.** Bechuanaland Royal Pioneer Corps.

| | | | | |
|---|---|---|---|---|
| 198 | 43 | 2½c. blue, red and green | 25 | 10 |

| | | | | |
|---|---|---|---|---|
| 199 | - | 5c. brown and blue | 30 | 20 |
| 200 | - | 15c. blue, red and green | 1·00 | 25 |
| 201 | - | 35c. multicoloured | 30 | 1·00 |

DESIGNS: 5c. Bugler; 15c. Gun-site; 35c. Regimental cap badge.

### POSTAGE DUE STAMPS

**1926.** Postage Due stamps of Great Britain optd **BECHUANALAND PROTECTORATE**.

| | | | | |
|---|---|---|---|---|
| D1 | **D1** | ½d. green | 11·00 | £120 |
| D2 | **D1** | 1d. red | 11·00 | 75·00 |
| D3 | **D1** | 2d. black | 11·00 | 90·00 |

**D 3**

**1932**

| | | | | |
|---|---|---|---|---|
| D4 | **D3** | ½d. green | 6·00 | 60·00 |
| D5a | **D3** | 1d. red | 1·50 | 28·00 |
| D6c | **D3** | 2d. violet | 1·75 | 22·00 |

**1961.** Surch.

| | | | |
|---|---|---|---|
| D7 | 1c. on 1d. red | 25 | 50 |
| D8 | 2c. on 2d. violet | 25 | 1·50 |
| D9 | 5c. on ½d. green | 20 | 60 |

**1961.** As Type D **3** but value in decimal currency.

| | | | |
|---|---|---|---|
| D10 | 1c. red | 30 | 2·00 |
| D11 | 2c. violet | 30 | 2·00 |
| D12 | 5c. green | 50 | 2·00 |

For later issues see **BOTSWANA**.

Pt. 10

# BELARUS

Formerly a constituent republic of the Soviet Union, Belarus became independent in 1991.

100 kopeks = 1 rouble.
2000. Currency Revaluation.

**1** 12th-century Cross

**1992**

| | | | | |
|---|---|---|---|---|
| 1 | **1** | 1r. multicoloured | 1·30 | 75 |

**2** Shyrma

**1992.** Birth Cent of R. R. Shyrma (composer).

| | | | | |
|---|---|---|---|---|
| 2 | **2** | 20k. lt blue, blue and black | 50 | 30 |

**3** Arms of Polotsk

**1992**

| | | | | |
|---|---|---|---|---|
| 3 | **3** | 2r. multicoloured | 80 | 55 |

See also Nos. 63 and 89/90.

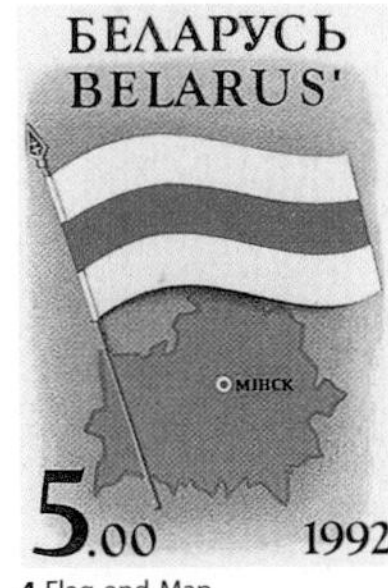

**4** Flag and Map

**1992**

| | | | | |
|---|---|---|---|---|
| 4 | **4** | 5r. multicoloured | 1·30 | 95 |
| 5 | - | 5r. black, yellow and red | 1·30 | 95 |

DESIGN: No. 5, State arms.

1000—ГОДДЗЕ БЕЛАРУСКАЙ
ПРАВАСЛАЎНАЙ ЦАРКВЫ

**(5)**

**1992.** Millenary of Orthodox Church in Belarus. (a) No. 1 optd with T 5.

| | | | | |
|---|---|---|---|---|
| 6 | **1** | 1r. multicoloured | 1·00 | 75 |

(b) Sheet 91×66 mm.

| | | |
|---|---|---|
| **MS**7 5r. multicoloured | 2·00 | 1·90 |

DESIGN: 24×36 mm—5r. Cross of Polotsk.

**6** Kamen Tower

**1992.** Ancient Buildings and Monuments. Mult.

| | | | |
|---|---|---|---|
| 8 | 2r. Type **6** | 50 | 30 |
| 9 | 2r. Calvinist church, Zaslavl | 50 | 30 |
| 10 | 2r. St. Euphrosyne's church, Polotsk | 50 | 30 |
| 11 | 2r. St. Boris Gleb church, Grodno (horiz) | 50 | 30 |
| 12 | 2r. Mir castle (horiz) | 50 | 30 |
| 13 | 2r. Nesvizh castle (horiz) | 50 | 30 |

**7** State Arms

**1992**

| | | | | |
|---|---|---|---|---|
| 14 | **7** | 30k. blue | 20 | 15 |
| 15 | **7** | 45k. green | 25 | 15 |
| 16 | **7** | 50k. green | 25 | 15 |
| 17 | **7** | 1r. brown | 25 | 15 |
| 18 | **7** | 2r. brown | 25 | 15 |
| 19 | **7** | 3r. yellow | 35 | 20 |
| 20 | **7** | 5r. blue | 40 | 20 |
| 21 | **7** | 10r. red | 95 | 55 |
| 22 | **7** | 15r. violet | 55 | 35 |
| 23 | **7** | 25r. green | 80 | 45 |
| 24 | **7** | 50r. mauve | 25 | 20 |
| 25 | **7** | 100r. red | 55 | 35 |
| 26 | **7** | 150r. purple | 80 | 45 |
| 27 | **7** | 200r. green | 20 | 20 |
| 28 | **7** | 300r. red | 20 | 20 |
| 29 | **7** | 600r. mauve | 25 | 20 |
| 30 | **7** | 1000r. red | 45 | 20 |
| 31 | **7** | 3000r. blue | 1·20 | 65 |

**8** Jug and Bowl

**1992.** Pottery. Multicoloured.

| | | | |
|---|---|---|---|
| 40 | 1r. Type **8** | 40 | 30 |
| 41 | 1r. Vases and jug on jug tree | 40 | 30 |
| 42 | 1r. Flagon | 40 | 30 |
| 43 | 1r. Jugs | 40 | 30 |

**9** Chickens

**1993.** Corn Dollies. Multicoloured.

| | | | |
|---|---|---|---|
| 44 | 5r. Type **9** | 20 | 10 |
| 45 | 10r. Woman and gunman (vert) | 30 | 20 |
| 46 | 15r. Woman (vert) | 50 | 40 |
| 47 | 25r. Man and woman (vert) | 1·00 | 75 |

**10** Harezki

**1993.** Birth Centenary of M. I. Harezki (author).

| | | | | |
|---|---|---|---|---|
| 48 | **10** | 50r. purple | 60 | 35 |

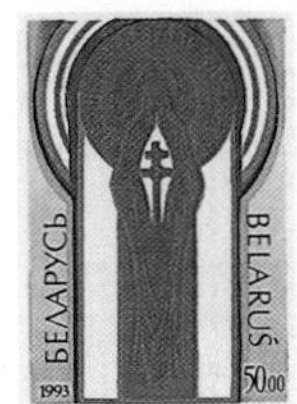

**11** Emblem

**1993.** World Belarussian Congress, Minsk.

| | | | | |
|---|---|---|---|---|
| 49 | **11** | 50r. red, gold and black | 2·00 | 1·60 |

**12** "Man Over Vitebsk"

**1993.** Europa. Contemporary Art. Paintings by Marc Chagall. Multicoloured.

| | | | |
|---|---|---|---|
| 50 | 1500r. Type **12** | 8·00 | 7·50 |
| 51 | 1500r. "Promenade" (vert) | 8·00 | 7·50 |
| **MS**52 | 142×103 mm. 2500r. "Allegory" (50×37 mm) | 70·00 | 65·00 |

**(13)**

ЧЭМПІЯНАТ СВЕТУ
ПА ФУТБОЛУ,
ЗША, 1994

**(14)**

**1993.** Sports Events. Nos. 4/5 variously surch. (a) Winter Olympic Games, Lillehammer, Norway (1994). Surch **Winter Pre-Olympic Games Lillehammer, Norway 1500** (in capitals on No. 44) or in Cyrillic as T **13**.

| | | | | |
|---|---|---|---|---|
| 53 | **4** | 1500r. on 5r. mult (in Cyrillic) | 5·00 | 4·75 |
| 54 | **4** | 1500r. on 5r. mult (in English) | 5·00 | 4·75 |
| 55 | - | 1500r. on 5r. black, yellow and red (in Cyrillic) | 5·00 | 4·75 |
| 56 | - | 1500r. on 5r. black, yellow and red (in English) | 5·00 | 4·75 |

| | | |
|---|---|---|
| **MS**57 Two sheets. (a) 1500r. on 5r. multicoloured (in Cyrillic); (b) 1500r. on 5r. (in English) | 20·00 | 19·00 |

(b) World Cup Football Championship, U.S.A. (1994). Surch WORLD CUP USA 94 1500 or in Cyrillic as T **14**.

| | | | | |
|---|---|---|---|---|
| 58 | **4** | 1500r. on 5r. mult (in Cyrillic) | 5·00 | 4·75 |
| 59 | **4** | 1500r. on 5r. mult (in English) | 5·00 | 4·75 |
| 60 | - | 1500r. on 5r. black, yellow and red (in Cyrillic) | 5·00 | 4·75 |
| 61 | - | 1500r. on 5r. black, yellow and red (in English) | 5·00 | 4·75 |

| | | |
|---|---|---|
| **MS**62 Two sheets. (a) 1500r. on 5r. multicoloured (in Cyrillic); (b) 1500r. on 5r. multicoloured (in English) | 20·00 | 19·00 |

**1993.** Town Arms. As T **3** . Multicoloured.

| | | | |
|---|---|---|---|
| 63 | 25r. Minsk | 50 | 30 |

**15** St. Stanislav's Church, Mogilev

**1993**

| | | | | |
|---|---|---|---|---|
| 64 | **15** | 150r. multicoloured | 80 | 60 |

**16** Kastus Kalinowski (leader)

**1993.** 130th Anniv of Peasants' Uprising.

| | | | | |
|---|---|---|---|---|
| 65 | **16** | 50r. multicoloured | 40 | 30 |

**17** Princess Ragneda

**1993.** 10th-century Rulers of Polotsk. Mult.

| | | | |
|---|---|---|---|
| 66 | 75r. Type **17** | 50 | 30 |
| 67 | 75r. Prince Ragvalod and map | 50 | 30 |

**18** Statue of Budny

**1993.** 400th Death Anniv of Simon Budny (poet).

| | | | | |
|---|---|---|---|---|
| 68 | **18** | 100r. multicoloured | 70 | 65 |

**19** Golden Eagle

**1994.** Birds in the Red Book. Multicoloured.

| | | | |
|---|---|---|---|
| 69 | 20r. Type **19** | 20 | 20 |
| 70 | 40r. Mute swan ("Cygnus olor") | 30 | 30 |
| 71 | 40r. River kingfisher ("Alcedo atthis") | 30 | 30 |

**1994.** Nos. 14/16 surch.

| | | | | |
|---|---|---|---|---|
| 72 | **7** | 15r. on 30k. blue | 20 | 10 |
| 73 | **7** | 25r. on 45k. green | 30 | 20 |
| 74 | **7** | 50r. on 50k. green | 50 | 30 |

See also Nos. 86/8.

**21** Map and Rocket Launchers (Liberation of Russia)

**1994.** 50th Anniv of Liberation. Multicoloured.

| | | | |
|---|---|---|---|
| 75 | 500r. Type **21** | 60 | 45 |
| 76 | 500r. Map and Ilyushin 11-2 Shturmovick airplanes (Ukraine) | 60 | 45 |
| 77 | 500r. Map, tank and soldiers (Byelorussia) | 60 | 45 |

**22** Yasev Drazdovich and "Persecution"

**1994.** Artists and Paintings. Multicoloured.

| | | | |
|---|---|---|---|
| 78 | 300r. Type **22** | 30 | 20 |
| 79 | 300r. Pyotr Sergievich and "The Path through Life" | 30 | 20 |
| 80 | 300r. Ferdinand Rushchyts and "The Land" | 30 | 20 |

**23** Figure Skating

**1994.** Winter Olympic Games, Lillehammer, Norway. Multicoloured.

| | | | |
|---|---|---|---|
| 81 | 1000r. Type **23** | 40 | 30 |
| 82 | 1000r. Biathlon | 40 | 30 |
| 83 | 1000r. Cross-country skiing | 40 | 30 |
| 84 | 1000r. Speed skating | 40 | 30 |
| 85 | 1000r. Ice hockey | 40 | 30 |

**1994.** Birds in the Red Book. As Nos. 69/71 but values changed. Multicoloured.

| | | | |
|---|---|---|---|
| 86 | 300r. As Type **19** | 50 | 30 |
| 87 | 400r. As No. 70 | 60 | 40 |
| 88 | 400r. As No. 71 | 60 | 40 |

**1994.** Town Arms. As T **3**. Multicoloured.

| | | | |
|---|---|---|---|
| 89 | 700r. Grodno | 30 | 20 |
| 90 | 700r. Vitebsk | 30 | 20 |

**25** Church, Synkavichai (16th-century)

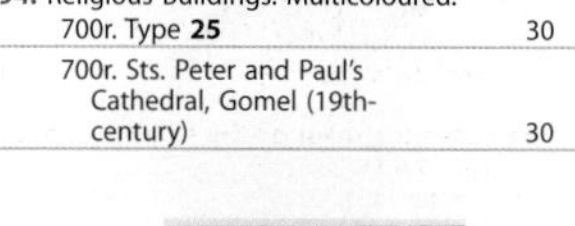

**1994.** Religious Buildings. Multicoloured.

| | | | |
|---|---|---|---|
| 91 | 700r. Type **25** | 30 | 20 |
| 92 | 700r. Sts. Peter and Paul's Cathedral, Gomel (19th-century) | 30 | 20 |

**26** "Belarus"

**1994.** 150th Birth Anniv of Ilya Repin (painter). Multicoloured.

| | | | |
|---|---|---|---|
| 93 | 1000r. Type **26** | 50 | 30 |
| 94 | 1000r. Repin Museum | 50 | 30 |

Nos. 93/4 were issued together, se-tenant, forming a composite design.

**27** Tomasz Wojshezki and Battle Scene

**1995.** Bicentenary (1994) of Polish Insurrection. Multicoloured.

| | | | |
|---|---|---|---|
| 95 | 600r. Type **27** | 45 | 35 |
| 96 | 600r. Jakub Jasinski | 45 | 35 |
| 97 | 1000r. Mikhail Aginski | 60 | 45 |
| 98 | 1000r. Tadeusz Kosciuszko | 60 | 45 |

**28** Memorial

**1995.** 50th Anniv of End of Second World War. Multicoloured.

| | | | |
|---|---|---|---|
| 99 | 180r. Type **28** | 20 | 15 |
| 100 | 600r. Clouds and memorial | 30 | 20 |

**29** Aleksandr Stepanovich Popov (radio pioneer)

**1995.** Centenary of First Radio Transmission (by Guglielmo Marconi).

| | | | |
|---|---|---|---|
| 101 | **29** 600r. multicoloured | 50 | 40 |

**30** Obelisk to the Fallen of the Red Army, Minsk

**1995**

| | | | |
|---|---|---|---|
| 102 | **30** 180r. bistre and red | 20 | 15 |
| 103 | **30** 200r. green and bistre | 30 | 20 |
| 104 | **30** 280r. green and blue | 40 | 30 |
| 107 | **30** 600r. purple and bistre | 50 | 40 |

**31** Cherski

**1995.** 150th Birth Anniv of Ivan Cherski (explorer).

| | | | |
|---|---|---|---|
| 115 | **31** 600r. multicoloured | 50 | 40 |

**32** Motal

**1995.** Traditional Costumes (1st series). Mult.

| | | | |
|---|---|---|---|
| 116 | 180r. Type **32** | 20 | 15 |
| 117 | 600r. Vaukavysk-Kamyanets | 40 | 30 |
| 118 | 1200r. Pukhavits | 70 | 55 |

See also Nos. 188/190, 256/8 and 460/1.

**33** Head of Beaver

**1995.** The Eurasian Beaver. Multicoloured.

| | | | |
|---|---|---|---|
| 119 | 300r. Type **33** | 30 | 20 |
| 120 | 450r. Beaver gnawing branch | 40 | 30 |
| 121 | 450r. Beaver (horiz) | 40 | 30 |
| 122 | 800r. Beaver swimming | 75 | 45 |

**34** Writer and Script

**1995.** Writers' Day.

| | | | |
|---|---|---|---|
| 123 | **34** 600r. multicoloured | 50 | 40 |

**35** Arms

**1995.** National Symbols. Multicoloured.

| | | | |
|---|---|---|---|
| 124 | 600r. Type **35** | 40 | 30 |
| 125 | 600r. Flag over map and arms | 40 | 30 |

**36** Anniversary Emblem

**1995.** 50th Anniv of U.N.O.

| | | | |
|---|---|---|---|
| 126 | **36** 600r. blue, black and gold | 50 | 40 |

**37** Mstislavl Church

**1995.** Churches. Multicoloured.

| | | | |
|---|---|---|---|
| 127 | 600r. Type **37** | 40 | 30 |
| 128 | 600r. Kamai Church | 40 | 30 |

See also Nos. 227/8.

**1995**
**125 год**
**з дня нараджэння**
**(38)**

**1995.** 125th Birth Anniv of Ferdinand Rushchyts (artist). No. 80 optd with T 38.

| | | | |
|---|---|---|---|
| 129 | 300r. multicoloured | 1·00 | 95 |

**39** Sukhoi and Aircraft

**1995.** Birth Centenary of P. V. Sukhoi (aircraft designer).

| | | | |
|---|---|---|---|
| 130 | **39** 600r. multicoloured | 40 | 30 |

**40** Red Deer (*Cervus elaphus*)

**1995.** Nature. Sheet 100×64 mm. Imperf.

| | | | |
|---|---|---|---|
| **MS**131 | **40** 10000r. multicoloured | 4·00 | 3·75 |

**41** Leu Sapega (statesman)

**1995.** 17th-century Belarussians. Multicoloured.

| | | | |
|---|---|---|---|
| 132 | 600r. Type **41** | 35 | 20 |
| 133 | 1200r. Kazimir Semyanovich (military scholar) | 50 | 30 |
| 134 | 1800r. Simyaon Polatski (writer) | 70 | 45 |

**42** Lynx

**1996.** Mammals. Multicoloured.

| | | | |
|---|---|---|---|
| 135 | 1000r. Type **42** | 45 | 30 |
| 136 | 2000r. Roe deer (vert) | 75 | 45 |
| 137 | 2000r. Brown bear | 75 | 45 |
| 138 | 3000r. Elk (vert) | 95 | 75 |
| 139 | 5000r. European bison | 1·50 | 1·30 |

**1996.** Nos. 17 and 23 optd with capital letter.

| | | | |
|---|---|---|---|
| 140 | **7** B (200r.) on 1r. brown | 30 | 20 |
| 141 | **7** A (400r.) on 25r. green | 30 | 20 |

**44** Krapiva

**1996.** Birth Centenary of Kandrat Krapiva (writer).

| | | | |
|---|---|---|---|
| 142 | **44** 1000r. multicoloured | 50 | 30 |

**45** Beaver

**1996.** The Eurasian Beaver (Castor fiber). Sheet 90×70 mm.

| | | | |
|---|---|---|---|
| **MS**143 | **45** 1200r. multicoloured | 70 | 45 |

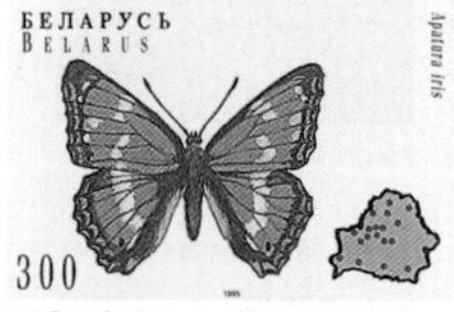

**46** Purple Emperor ("Apatura iris")

**1996.** Butterflies and Moths. Multicoloured.

| | | | |
|---|---|---|---|
| 144 | 300r. Type **46** | 1·20 | 95 |
| 145 | 300r. "Lopinga achine" | 1·20 | 95 |
| 146 | 300r. Scarlet tiger moth ("Callimorpha dominula") | 1·20 | 95 |
| 147 | 300r. Clifden's nonpareil ("Catocala fraxini") | 1·20 | 95 |
| 148 | 300r. Swallowtail ("Papilio machaon") | 1·20 | 95 |
| 149 | 300r. Apollo ("Parnassius apollo") | 1·20 | 95 |
| 150 | 300r. "Ammobiota hebe" | 1·20 | 95 |
| 151 | 300r. Palaeno sulphur yellow ("Colias palaeno") | 1·20 | 95 |

**MS**152 Two sheets, each 100×70 mm. (a) 1000r. *Vacciniina optilete*; (b) 1000r. Willow-herb hawk moth (*Proserpinus proserpina*) 16·00 15·00

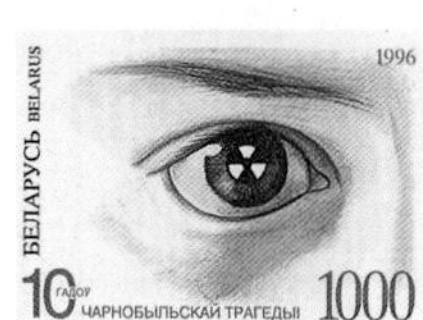


**47** Radioactivity Symbol within Eye

**1996.** 10th Anniv of Chernobyl Nuclear Disaster. Multicoloured.

| | | | | |
|---|---|---|---|---|
| 153 | | 1000r. Type **47** | 30 | 20 |
| 154 | | 1000r. Radioactivity symbol on diseased leaf | 30 | 20 |
| 155 | | 1000r. Radioactivity symbol on boarded-up window | 30 | 20 |

**48** State Arms

**1996.** Arms and value in black, background colours given.

| | | | | |
|---|---|---|---|---|
| 159 | **48** | 100r. blue | 15 | 10 |
| 160 | **48** | 200r. grey | 30 | 25 |
| 161 | **48** | 400r. brown | 20 | 15 |
| 162 | **48** | 500r. green | 15 | 10 |
| 163 | **48** | 600r. red | 15 | 10 |
| 164 | **48** | 800r. blue | 20 | 15 |
| 165 | **48** | 1000r. orange | 20 | 10 |
| 166 | **48** | 1500r. mauve | 25 | 15 |
| 167 | **48** | 1500r. blue | 25 | 25 |
| 168 | **48** | 1800r. violet | 25 | 15 |
| 169 | **48** | 2000r. green | 35 | 30 |
| 170 | **48** | 2200r. mauve | 30 | 20 |
| 171 | **48** | 2500r. blue | 35 | 30 |
| 172 | **48** | 3000r. brown | 30 | 30 |
| 173 | **48** | 3300r. yellow | 40 | 25 |
| 174 | **48** | 5000r. blue | 50 | 40 |
| 175 | **48** | 10000r. green | 1·00 | 75 |
| 176 | **48** | 30000r. brown | 3·00 | 2·30 |
| 177 | **48** | 50000r. purple | 5·25 | 3·75 |

**49** Russian and Belarussian Flags

**1996.** Russian–Belarussian Treaty.

| | | | | |
|---|---|---|---|---|
| 182 | **49** | 1500r. multicoloured | 70 | 45 |

**50** Gymnastics

**1996.** Olympic Games, Atlanta. Multicoloured.

| | | | | |
|---|---|---|---|---|
| 183 | | 3000r. Type **50** | 90 | 65 |
| 184 | | 3000r. Throwing the discus | 90 | 65 |
| 185 | | 3000r. Weightlifting | 90 | 65 |
| 186 | | 3000r. Wrestling | 90 | 65 |

**MS**187 100×71 mm. 5000r. Rifle-shooting. Imperf 1·50 1·10

**51** Kapyl-Kletski

**1996.** Traditional Costumes (2nd series). Mult.

| | | | | |
|---|---|---|---|---|
| 188 | | 1800r. Type **51** | 40 | 30 |
| 189 | | 2200r. David-Garadots Turau | 60 | 40 |
| 190 | | 3300r. Kobryn | 70 | 45 |

**MS**191 95×71 mm. 5000r. Naraulyanski. Imperf 1·50 1·10

See also Nos. 256/8 and 460/1.

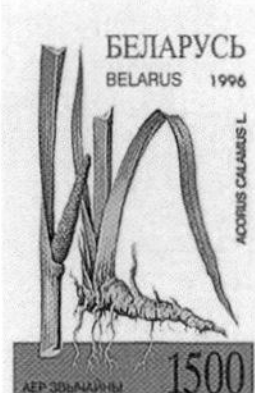


**52** "Acorus calamus"

**1996.** Medicinal Plants. Multicoloured.

| | | | | |
|---|---|---|---|---|
| 192 | | 1500r. Type **52** | 40 | 30 |
| 193 | | 1500r. "Sanguisorba officinalis" | 40 | 30 |
| 194 | | 2200r. "Potentilla erecta" | 60 | 40 |
| 195 | | 3300r. "Frangula alnus" | 70 | 45 |

**MS**196 96×71 mm. 5000r. *Menyanthes trifoliate*. Imperf 1·50 1·10

**53** Grey Heron ("Ardea cinerea")

**1996.** Birds. Multicoloured.

| | | | | |
|---|---|---|---|---|
| 197 | | 400r. Type **53** | 60 | 40 |
| 198 | | 400r. Black storks ("Ciconia nigra") | 60 | 40 |
| 199 | | 400r. Great cormorant ("Phalacrocorax carbo") | 60 | 40 |
| 200 | | 400r. White stork ("Ciconia ciconia") | 60 | 40 |
| 201 | | 400r. Black-headed gulls ("Larus ridibundus") | 60 | 40 |
| 202 | | 400r. Common snipe ("Gallinago gallinago") | 60 | 40 |
| 203 | | 400r. White-winged black tern ("Chlidonias leucopterus") | 60 | 40 |
| 204 | | 400r. Penduline tit ("Remiz pendulinus") | 60 | 40 |
| 205 | | 400r. Eurasian bittern ("Botaurus stellaris") | 60 | 40 |
| 206 | | 400r. Black coot ("Fulica atra") | 60 | 40 |
| 207 | | 400r. Little bittern ("Ixobrychus minutus") | 60 | 40 |
| 208 | | 400r. River kingfisher ("Alcedo atthis") | 60 | 40 |
| 209 | | 400r. Green-winged teals ("Anas crecca") | 60 | 40 |
| 210 | | 400r. Gadwalls ("Anas strepera") | 60 | 40 |
| 211 | | 400r. Northern pintails ("Anas acuta") | 60 | 40 |
| 212 | | 400r. Mallards ("Anas platyrhynchos") | 60 | 40 |
| 213 | | 400r. Greater scaups ("Aythya marila") | 60 | 40 |
| 214 | | 400r. Long-tailed duck ("Clangula hyemalis") | 60 | 40 |
| 215 | | 400r. Northern shovelers ("Anas clypeata") | 60 | 40 |
| 216 | | 400r. Garganeys ("Anas querquedula") | 60 | 40 |
| 217 | | 400r. European wigeon ("Anas penelope") | 60 | 40 |
| 218 | | 400r. Ferruginous ducks ("Aythya nyroca") | 60 | 40 |
| 219 | | 400r. Common goldeneyes ("Bucephala clangula") | 60 | 40 |
| 220 | | 400r. Goosander ("Mergus merganser") | 60 | 40 |
| 221 | | 400r. Smew ("Mergus albellus") | 60 | 40 |
| 222 | | 400r. Tufted duck ("Aythya fuligula") | 60 | 40 |
| 223 | | 400r. Red-breasted merganser ("Mergus serrator") | 60 | 40 |
| 224 | | 400r. Common pochard ("Aythya ferina") | 60 | 40 |

**MS**225 Two sheets, each 100×70 mm. (a) 1000r. Common snipe (*Gallinago gallinago*); (b) 1000r. European pochards (*Aythya farina*) 10·00 9·50

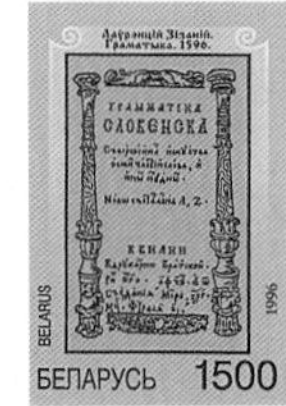


**54** Title Page

**1996.** 400th Anniv of Publication of First Belarussian Grammar.

| | | | | |
|---|---|---|---|---|
| 226 | **54** | 1500r. multicoloured | 80 | 55 |

**1996.** Churches. As T **37**. Multicoloured.

| | | | | |
|---|---|---|---|---|
| 227 | | 3300r. St. Nicholas's Church, Mogilev | 1·00 | 70 |
| 228 | | 3300r. Franciscan church, Pinsk | 1·00 | 70 |

**55** Shchakatsikhin

**1996.** Birth Centenary of Mikola Shchakatsikhin (artist).

| | | | | |
|---|---|---|---|---|
| 229 | **55** | 2000r. multicoloured | 75 | 45 |

**56** Old and New Telephones

**1996.** Cent of Telephone Service in Minsk.

| | | | | |
|---|---|---|---|---|
| 230 | **56** | 2000r. multicoloured | 75 | 45 |

**57** Lukashenka

**1996.** President Alyaksandr Rygoravich Lukashenka.

| | | | | |
|---|---|---|---|---|
| 231 | **57** | 2500r. multicoloured | 60 | 45 |

**58** Kiryla Turovski (12th-century Bishop of Turov)

**1996.** Multicoloured.. Multicoloured..

| | | | | |
|---|---|---|---|---|
| 232 | | 3000r. Type **58** | 65 | 45 |
| 233 | | 3000r. Mikolaj Radziwill (16th-century Chancellor of Lithuania) | 65 | 45 |
| 234 | | 3000r. Mikola Gusovski (15th-16th century writer) | 65 | 45 |

**59** Decorated Tree, Minsk

**1996.** New Year. Multicoloured.

| | | | | |
|---|---|---|---|---|
| 235 | | 1500r. Type **59** | 30 | 20 |
| 236 | | 2000r. Winter landscape (horiz) | 50 | 40 |

**60** "Paraskeva"

**1996.** Icons in National Museum, Minsk. Multicoloured.

| | | | | |
|---|---|---|---|---|
| 237 | | 3500r. Type **60** | 60 | 45 |
| 238 | | 3500r. "Illya" (17th-century) | 60 | 45 |
| 239 | | 3500r. "Three Holy Men" (Master of Sharashov) | 60 | 45 |
| 240 | | 3500r. "Madonna of Smolensk" | 60 | 45 |

**MS**241 70×100 mm. 5000r. "Birth of the Madonna" (Patr Yavseevich) 1·50 1·10

**61** Zhukov

**1997.** Birth Cent of Marshal G. K. Zhukov.

| | | | | |
|---|---|---|---|---|
| 242 | **61** | 2000r. black, gold and red | 50 | 40 |

**62** Theatre

**1997.** Kupala National Theatre, Minsk.

| | | | | |
|---|---|---|---|---|
| 243 | **62** | 3500r. black and gold | 70 | 55 |

**63** Byalnitsky-Birulya

**1997.** 125th Birth Anniv of W. K. Byalnitsky-Birulya (painter).

| | | | | |
|---|---|---|---|---|
| 244 | **63** | 2000r. black and brown | 50 | 40 |

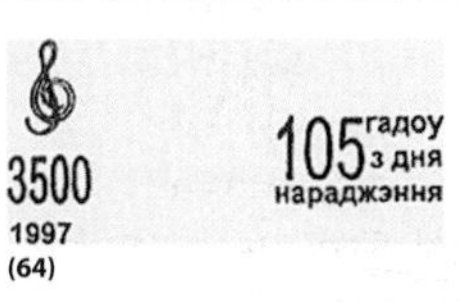


(**64**)

**1997.** 105th Birth Anniv of R. R. Shyrma (composer). No. 2 surch with T **64**.

| | | | | |
|---|---|---|---|---|
| 245 | **2** | 3500r. on 20k. light blue, blue and black | 60 | 55 |

**65** Salmon

**1997.** Fishes. Multicoloured.

| | | | | |
|---|---|---|---|---|
| 246 | | 2000r. Type **65** | 40 | 30 |
| 247 | | 3000r. Vimba | 60 | 45 |
| 248 | | 4500r. Barbel ("Barbus barbus") | 80 | 65 |
| 249 | | 4500r. European grayling ("Thymallus thymallus") | 80 | 65 |

**MS**250 90×60 mm. 5000r. Sterlet (*Acipenser ruthenus*) 1·50 1·10

**66** "SOS" on Globe

**1997.** International Conference on Developing Countries, Minsk. Multicoloured.

| | | | | |
|---|---|---|---|---|
| 251 | | 3000r. Type **66** | 50 | 40 |
| 252 | | 4500r. Protective hand over ecosystem | 70 | 55 |

Nos. 251/2 were issued together, se-tenant, with intervening label showing the Conference emblem, the whole strip forming a composite design.

**67** Emblem

**1997.** 50th Anniv of Belarussian Membership of Universal Postal Union.

| | | | | |
|---|---|---|---|---|
| 253 | **67** | 3000r. multicoloured | 60 | 45 |

**1997.** No. 18 surch 100 1997.

| | | | | |
|---|---|---|---|---|
| 254 | **7** | 100r. on 2r. brown | 30 | 20 |

**69** Map, National Flag and Monument to the Fallen of Second World War, Minsk

**1997.** Independence Day.

| | | | | |
|---|---|---|---|---|
| 255 | **69** | 3000r. multicoloured | 75 | 55 |

**1997.** Traditional Costumes (3rd series). As T **51**. Multicoloured.

| | | | | |
|---|---|---|---|---|
| 256 | | 2000r. Dzisensk | 35 | 35 |
| 257 | | 3000r. Navagrydsk | 60 | 55 |
| 258 | | 4500r. Bykhaisk | 85 | 80 |

**70** Page from Skorina Bible and Vilnius

**1997.** 480th Anniv of Printing in Belarus. Each red, black and grey.

| | | | | |
|---|---|---|---|---|
| 259 | | 3000r. Type **70** | 60 | 55 |
| 260 | | 3000r. Page from Skorina Bible and Prague | 60 | 55 |
| 261 | | 4000r. Franzisk Skorina and Polotsk | 60 | 55 |
| 262 | | 7500r. Skorina and Cracow | 1·30 | 1·20 |

**71** Jesuit College

**1997.** 900th Anniv of Pinsk.

| | | | | |
|---|---|---|---|---|
| 263 | **71** | 3000r. multicoloured | 60 | 55 |

**72** Books and Entrance

**1997.** 75th Anniv of National Library.

| | | | | |
|---|---|---|---|---|
| 264 | **72** | 3000r. multicoloured | 60 | 55 |

**73** Dark Glasses reflecting Hands reading Braille

**1997.** Cent of Schools for the Blind in Belarus.

| | | | | |
|---|---|---|---|---|
| 265 | **73** | 3000r. multicoloured | 50 | 45 |

**74** Child in Hand "Flower"

**1997.** World Children's Day.

| | | | | |
|---|---|---|---|---|
| 266 | **74** | 3000r. multicoloured | 60 | 55 |

**75** Red Ribbon and Crowd

**1997.** Red Ribbon AIDS Solidarity Campaign.

| | | | | |
|---|---|---|---|---|
| 267 | **75** | 4000r. multicoloured | 70 | 65 |

**76** Model 1221

**1997.** Belarussian Tractors. Multicoloured.

| | | | | |
|---|---|---|---|---|
| 268 | | 3300r. Type **76** | 60 | 55 |
| 269 | | 4400r. First Belarussian tractor, 1953 | 75 | 70 |
| 270 | | 7500r. Model 680 | 1·20 | 1·10 |
| 271 | | 7500r. Model 952 | 1·20 | 1·10 |

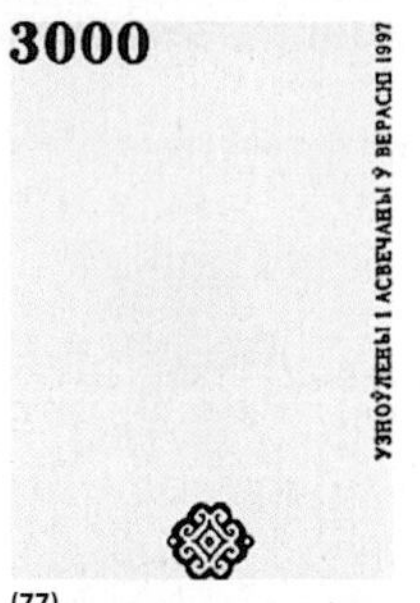


**(77)**

**1997.** Restoration of Cross of St. Ephrosina of Polotsk. No. 1 surch with T **77**.

| | | | | |
|---|---|---|---|---|
| 272 | **1** | 3000r. on 1r. multicoloured | 50 | 40 |

**78** St. Nicholas hang-gliding over Houses (New Year)

**1997.** Greetings Stamps. Multicoloured.

| | | | | |
|---|---|---|---|---|
| 273 | | 1400r. Type **78** | 30 | 20 |
| 274 | | 4400r. Procession of musicians (Christmas) | 60 | 45 |

**79** Cross-country Skiing

**1998.** Winter Olympic Games, Nagano, Japan. Multicoloured.

| | | | | |
|---|---|---|---|---|
| 275 | | 2000r. Type **79** | 40 | 30 |
| 276 | | 3300r. Ice hockey | 50 | 40 |
| 277 | | 4400r. Biathlon | 70 | 55 |
| 278 | | 7500r. Freestyle skiing | 90 | 75 |

**80** Mashcherov

**1998.** 80th Birth Anniv of P. M. Mashcherov (writer).

| | | | | |
|---|---|---|---|---|
| 279 | **80** | 2500r. multicoloured | 50 | 40 |

**81** MAZ-205 Lorry, 1947

**1998.** Tipper Trucks. Multicoloured.

| | | | | |
|---|---|---|---|---|
| 280 | | 1400r. Type **81** | 30 | 20 |
| 281 | | 2000r. MAZ-503, 1968 | 35 | 25 |
| 282 | | 3000r. MAZ-5549, 1977 | 40 | 30 |
| 283 | | 4400r. MAZ-5551, 1985 | 60 | 45 |
| 284 | | 7500r. MAZ-5516, 1994 | 85 | 70 |

**82** Entrance to Nyasvizh Castle

**1998.** Europa. National Festivals.

| | | | | |
|---|---|---|---|---|
| 285 | **82** | 15000r. multicoloured | 1·00 | 95 |

**83** Mickiewicz

**1998.** Birth Bicentenary of Adam Mickiewicz (political writer).

| | | | | |
|---|---|---|---|---|
| 286 | **83** | 8600r. multicoloured | 65 | 65 |

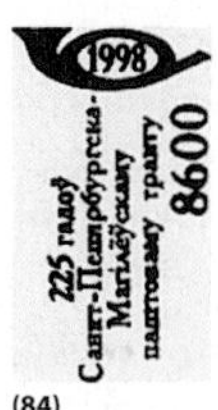


**(84)**

**1998.** 225th Anniv of Postal Service between Mogilov and St. Petersburg. No. 64 surch with T **84**.

| | | | | |
|---|---|---|---|---|
| 287 | **15** | 8600r. on 150r. mult | 65 | 65 |

**85** Bluethroat

**1998.** Birds. Multicoloured.

| | | | | |
|---|---|---|---|---|
| 288 | | 1500r. Type **85** | 20 | 10 |
| 289 | | 3200r. Penduline tit | 30 | 30 |
| 290 | | 3800r. Aquatic warbler | 40 | 35 |
| 291 | | 5300r. Savi's warbler | 50 | 45 |
| 292 | | 8600r. Azure tit | 85 | 80 |

**86** Watermill

**1998**

| | | | | |
|---|---|---|---|---|
| 293 | **86** | 100r. black and green | 20 | 15 |
| 294 | - | 200r. black and brown | 20 | 15 |
| 295 | - | 500r. black and blue | 20 | 15 |
| 296 | - | 800r. black and violet | 20 | 15 |
| 297 | - | 1000r. black and green | 20 | 15 |
| 298 | - | 1500r. black and brown | 30 | 30 |
| 299 | - | 2000r. black and blue | 20 | 15 |
| 300 | - | 3000r. black and yellow | 20 | 20 |
| 301 | - | 3200r. black and green | 30 | 20 |
| 302 | - | 5000r. black and blue | 25 | 30 |
| 303 | - | 5300r. black and yellow | 30 | 30 |
| 304 | - | 10000r. black and orange | 45 | 40 |
| 305 | **86** | 30000r. black and blue | 50 | 45 |
| 306 | - | 50000r. black, orange and deep orange | 60 | 55 |
| 308 | - | 100000r. black and mauve | 80 | 75 |
| 309 | - | 500000r. black and brown | 4·00 | 3·75 |

DESIGNS—VERT: 200, 50000r. Windmill; 500r. Stork; 800r. Cathedral of the Holy Trinity, Ishkold; 1000r. Bison; 1500, 3200r. Dulcimer; 2000r. Star; 3000, 5300r. Lute; 5000r. Church; 10000r. Flaming wheel; 500000r. Lyavoniha (folk dance). HORIZ: 100000r. Exhibition centre, Minsk.

**87** Bulldozer Model 7821

**1998.** 50th Anniv of Belaz Truck Works. Mult.

| | | | | |
|---|---|---|---|---|
| 310 | | 1500r. Type **87** | 20 | 15 |
| 311 | | 3200r. Tipper Model 75131 | 25 | 20 |
| 312 | | 3800r. Tipper Model 75303 | 30 | 25 |
| 313 | | 5300r. Tipper Model 75483 | 35 | 30 |
| 314 | | 8600r. Tipper Model 7555 | 40 | 40 |

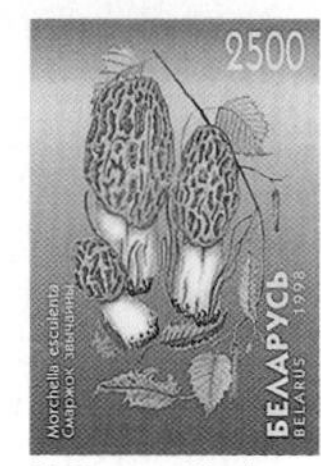


**88** Common Morel

**1998.** Fungi. Multicoloured.

| | | | | |
|---|---|---|---|---|
| 315 | | 2500r. Type **88** | 20 | 15 |
| 316 | | 3800r. "Morchella conica" | 25 | 20 |
| 317 | | 4600r. Shaggy parasol | 30 | 25 |
| 318 | | 5800r. Parasol mushroom | 35 | 30 |
| 319 | | 9400r. Shaggy ink cap | 65 | 50 |

**89** Lion's Head

**1998.** Wood Sculptures. Multicoloured.

| | | | | |
|---|---|---|---|---|
| 320 | | 3400r. Type **89** | 30 | 25 |
| 321 | | 3800r. Archangel Michael | 35 | 30 |
| 322 | | 5800r. Prophet Zacharias | 40 | 35 |
| 323 | | 9400r. Madonna and Child | 60 | 55 |

**90** Emblem and Belarussian Stamps

**1998.** World Post Day.

| | | | | |
|---|---|---|---|---|
| 324 | **90** | 5500r. multicoloured | 60 | 45 |

**91** "Kalozha" (V. K. Tsvirka)

**1998.** Paintings. Multicoloured.

| | | | | |
|---|---|---|---|---|
| 325 | | 3000r. Type **91** | 20 | 20 |
| 326 | | 3500r. "Hotel Lounge" (S. Yu. Zhukoiski) | 20 | 20 |

| | | | |
|---|---|---|---|
| 327 | 5000r. "Winter Sleep" (V. K. Byalynitski-Birulya) | 25 | 20 |
| 328 | 5500r. "Portrait of a Girl" (I. I. Alyashkevich) (vert) | 25 | 20 |
| 329 | 10000r. "Portrait of an Unknown Woman" (I. F. Khrutski) (vert) | 40 | 40 |

**92** Anniversary Emblem

**1998.** 50th Anniv of Universal Declaration of Human Rights.

| | | | | |
|---|---|---|---|---|
| 330 | **92** | 7100r. multicoloured | 50 | 40 |

**93** Girl, Rabbit and Fir Trees

**1998.** Christmas and New Year. Multicoloured.

| | | | |
|---|---|---|---|
| 331 | 5500r. Type **93** | 25 | 25 |
| 332 | 5500r. Girl, rabbit and house | 25 | 25 |

**94** Pushkin and Adam Mickiewicz Monument, St. Petersburg (A. Anikeichyk)

**1999.** Birth Bicentenary of Aleksandr Pushkin (writer).

| | | | | |
|---|---|---|---|---|
| 333 | **94** | 15300r. multicoloured | 80 | 75 |

**95** MAZ Model 8007 Truck and Excavator

**1999.** Minsk Truck and Military Works. Mult.

| | | | |
|---|---|---|---|
| 334 | 10000r. Type **95** | 25 | 20 |
| 335 | 15000r. MAZ model 543M and Smerch rocket system | 30 | 25 |
| 336 | 30000r. MAZ model 7907 crane | 45 | 40 |
| 337 | 30000r. MAZ model 543M Rubezh missile launcher | 45 | 40 |
| **MS**338 | 175×120 mm. Nos. 334/7; 5000r. Model 7917 and Topol missile; 150000r. Model 74135 low-loader | 6·00 | 5·75 |

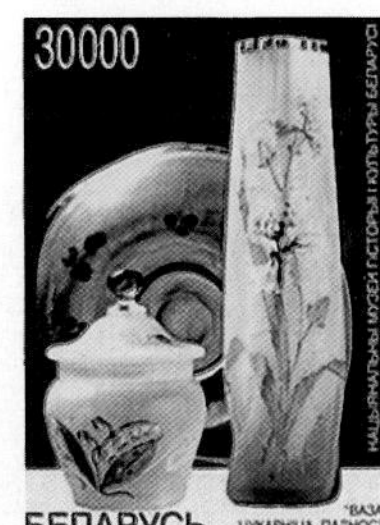

**96** Dish, Jar and Vase

**1999.** Glasswork. Multicoloured.

| | | | |
|---|---|---|---|
| 339 | 30000r. Type **96** | 50 | 45 |
| 340 | 30000r. Chalice | 50 | 40 |
| 341 | 100000r. Oil lamp | 1·00 | 95 |

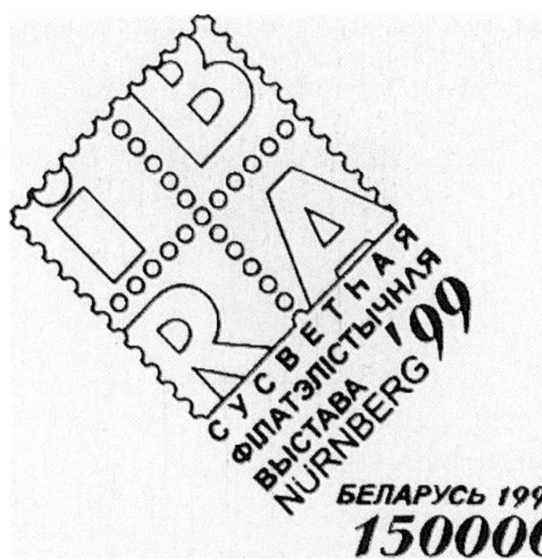

**(97)** **(image scaled to 74% of original size)**

**1999.** "iBRA '99" International Stamp Exhibition, Nuremberg. No. 69 surch with T **97**.

| | | | |
|---|---|---|---|
| 342 | 150000r. on 20r. multicoloured (Type **19**) | 2·00 | 1·90 |

**98** Belavezhskaya Pushcha Reserve

**1999.** Europa. Parks and Gardens. Multicoloured.

| | | | |
|---|---|---|---|
| 345 | 150000r. Type **98** | 1·50 | 1·40 |
| 346 | 150000r. Beaver in Byarezinski Reserve | 1·50 | 1·40 |

**99** Well

**1999.** Wooden Buildings. Multicoloured.

| | | | |
|---|---|---|---|
| 347 | 50000r. Type **99** | 70 | 45 |
| 348 | 50000r. Public house | 70 | 45 |
| 349 | 100000r. Windmill | 1·10 | 95 |

**100** "Portrait of Yu. M. Pen" (A. M. Brazer)

**1999.** Vitebsk Art School. Paintings. Multicoloured.

| | | | |
|---|---|---|---|
| 350 | 30000r. Type **100** | 30 | 20 |
| 351 | 60000r. "St. Anthony's Church, Vitebsk" (S. B.Yudovin) | 70 | 45 |
| 352 | 100000r. "Street in Vitebsk" (Yu. M. Pen) | 1·20 | 85 |
| 353 | 100000r. "Kryvaya Street, Vitebsk" (M. P. Mikhalap) (horiz) | 1·20 | 85 |
| **MS**354 | 104×82 mm. 200000r. "The World is a River without Banks" (Marc Chagall) | 2·00 | 1·90 |

**101** Karvat

**1999.** 3rd Death Anniv of Wing Commander Karvat.

| | | | | |
|---|---|---|---|---|
| 355 | **101** | 25000r. multicoloured | 1·20 | 95 |

**102** Main Post Office, Minsk, 1954

**1999.** 125th Anniv of Universal Postal Union. Mult.

| | | | |
|---|---|---|---|
| 356 | 150000r. Type **102** | 1·80 | 1·60 |
| 357 | 150000r. First post office in Minsk, 1800 | 1·80 | 1·60 |

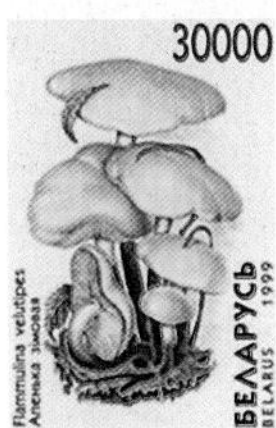

**103** Golden Mushroom

**1999.** Fungi. Multicoloured.

| | | | |
|---|---|---|---|
| 358 | 30000r. Type **103** | 30 | 20 |
| 359 | 50000r. Changeable agaric | 55 | 40 |
| 360 | 75000r. *Lyophyllum connatum* | 90 | 55 |
| 361 | 100000r. *Lyophyllum decastes* | 1·20 | 85 |
| **MS**362 | 97×79 mm. 150000r. Boot-lace fungus (*Armillariella mellea*) | 1·80 | 1·60 |

**104** East and West Belarussians Embracing

**1999.** 60th Anniv of Re-unification of Republic of Byelorussia.

| | | | | |
|---|---|---|---|---|
| 363 | **104** | 29000r. multicoloured | 40 | 30 |

**105** MAZ MA3-6430, 1998

**1999.** Minsk Truck and Military Works. Lorries. Multicoloured.

| | | | |
|---|---|---|---|
| 364 | 51000r. Type **105** | 50 | 30 |
| 365 | 86000r. Lorry Model MAZ MA3-4370 | 70 | 45 |

**106** Landscape (Olya Smantser)

**1999.** Children's Painting Competition Winners. Mult.

| | | | |
|---|---|---|---|
| 366 | 32000r. Type **106** | 30 | 20 |
| 367 | 59000r. Girl (Masha Dudarenko) (vert) | 50 | 30 |

**107** Teddybear in Snow (Mitya Kutas)

**1999.** Christmas and New Year. Children's Paintings. Multicoloured.

| | | | |
|---|---|---|---|
| 368 | 30000r. Type **107** | 40 | 30 |
| 369 | 30000r. Children building snow-man and ice-skating (Yulya Yakubovich) | 40 | 30 |

**108** Spasa-Praabrazhenskaya Church, Polatsk

**2000.** Birth Bimillenary of Jesus Christ (1st issue). Mult.

| | | | |
|---|---|---|---|
| 370 | 50r. Type **108** | 40 | 30 |
| 371 | 75r. St. Atsistratsiga Cathedral, Slutsk | 70 | 45 |
| 372 | 100r. The Reverend Serafim Sarovskaga Church, Belaazersk | 90 | 65 |

**109** Our Lady Oranta (mosaic, Spohia Catherdral, Kiev, Ukraine)

**2000.** Birth Bimillenary of Jesus Christ (2nd issue). Sheet 150×100 mm containing T 109 and similar vert designs. Multicoloured.

| | | | |
|---|---|---|---|
| **MS**373 | 100r. Type **109**; 100r. Jesus Christ (fresco, Spasa-Praabrazhenskaya Church, Polatsk); 100r. Our Lady Volodimirska (icon, National Tretyakov Gallery, Moscow, Russia) | 3·00 | 2·75 |

**110** Bison

**2000**

| | | | | |
|---|---|---|---|---|
| 374 | **110** | 1r. black and green | 20 | 10 |
| 375 | - | 2r. black and blue | 20 | 10 |
| 376 | - | 3r. black and yellow | 20 | 10 |
| 377 | - | 5r. black and blue | 20 | 10 |
| 378 | - | 10r. black and orange | 20 | 10 |
| 380 | - | 20r. black and mauve | 30 | 15 |
| 382 | - | 30r. black and green | 40 | 20 |
| 383 | - | 50r. black and yellow | 60 | 40 |
| 387 | - | 100r. black and mauve | 80 | 55 |

DESIGNS—VERT: 2r. Star; 3r. Lyre; 5r. Synkovichy Church; 10r. Flaming wheel; 20r. Type **111**; 30r. Watermill; 50r. Windmill. HORIZ: 100r. Exhibition Centre.

**111** Kryzhachok (folk dance)

**2000.** Self-adhesive.

| | | | | |
|---|---|---|---|---|
| 391 | **111** | 20r. black and red | 30 | 15 |

**112** Su-24 Bomber

**2000.** 25th Death Anniv of Pavel Sukhoi (aircraft designer). Multicoloured.

| | | | |
|---|---|---|---|
| 392 | 50r. Type **112** | 80 | 60 |
| 393 | 50r. Su-27 fighter | 80 | 60 |
| 394 | 50r. Su-25 battle fighter | 80 | 60 |
| **MS**395 | 120×83 mm. 150r. Type **112**; 150r. As No. 394; 150r. As No. 393 | 2·50 | 2·30 |

**113** Kupala Holiday

**2000**

| | | | | |
|---|---|---|---|---|
| 396 | **113** | A black and blue | 40 | 30 |

No. 396 was for Inland Letter Post rate.

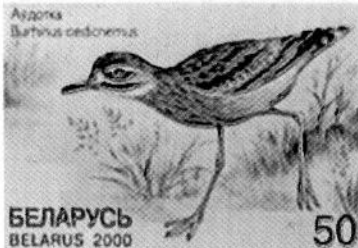

**114** Stone-Curlew

**2000.** Birds in the Red Book. Multicoloured.

| | | | |
|---|---|---|---|
| 397 | 50r. Type **114** | 60 | 40 |
| 398 | 50r. Smew (*Mergellus albellus*) | 60 | 40 |
| 399 | 75r. Willow grouse | 70 | 45 |
| 400 | 100r. Lesser spotted eagle (vert) | 90 | 65 |

**115** "The Partisan Madonna of Minsk" (M. Savitsky)

**2000.** 55th Anniv of End of Second World War.

| | | | | |
|---|---|---|---|---|
| 401 | **115** | 100r. multicoloured | 90 | 65 |

**116** "Building Europe"

**2000.** Europa.

| | | | | |
|---|---|---|---|---|
| 402 | **116** | 250r. multicoloured | 3·00 | 2·75 |

**117** Scene from "Creation of the World"

**2000.** National Ballet Company. Multicoloured.

| | | | |
|---|---|---|---|
| 403 | 100r. Type **117** | 1·00 | 75 |
| **MS**404 | 77×73 mm. 150r. Scene from "Passions" | 1·80 | 1·60 |

**118** Hands holding Lifebelt

**2000.** 50th Anniv of United Nations High Commission for Refugees.

| | | | | |
|---|---|---|---|---|
| 405 | **118** | 50r. multicoloured | 45 | 35 |

**119** Head of Lynx

**2000.** Endangered Species. The Lynx. Multicoloured.

| | | | |
|---|---|---|---|
| 406 | 100r. Type **119** | 80 | 65 |
| 407 | 100r. On branch | 80 | 65 |
| 408 | 150r. Walking through woodland | 1·20 | 95 |
| 409 | 150r. Adult and cub | 1·20 | 95 |

**120** People wearing National Costumes

**2000.** International Year of Culture.

| | | | | |
|---|---|---|---|---|
| 410 | **120** | 100r. multicoloured | 80 | 65 |

**121** Rings

**2000.** Olympic Games, Sydney. Multicoloured.

| | | | |
|---|---|---|---|
| 411 | 100r. Type **121** | 80 | 65 |
| 412 | 100r. Kayaking | 80 | 65 |
| 413 | 100r. Rhythmic gymnastics | 80 | 65 |
| **MS**414 | 77×74 mm. 400r. Athletes | 3·00 | 2·75 |

**122** Amber

**2000.** Minerals. Multicoloured.

| | | | |
|---|---|---|---|
| 415 | 200r. Type **122** | 1·30 | 1·10 |
| 416 | 200r. Galit | 1·30 | 1·10 |
| 417 | 200r. Flint | 1·30 | 1·10 |
| 418 | 200r. Silvin | 1·30 | 1·10 |

**123** People around decorated Tree

**2000.** New Year.

| | | | | |
|---|---|---|---|---|
| 419 | **123** | 200r. multicoloured | 1·50 | 1·30 |

**124** Nativity Scene

**2000.** Christmas.

| | | | | |
|---|---|---|---|---|
| 420 | **124** | 100r. multicoloured | 1·20 | 95 |

**125** "Connection of Times" (Roman Zabello)

**2000.** New Millennium. Children's Paintings. Multicoloured.

| | | | |
|---|---|---|---|
| 421 | 100r. Type **125** | 80 | 65 |
| 422 | 100r. "Festival of Life" (Alena Emeliyanova) | 80 | 65 |

**126** Euphrosiniya Polotskaya and Church (image scaled to 52% of original size)

**2001.** 900th Birth Anniv of St. Euphrosiniya Polotskaya (Saint Euphrosyne). Imperf.

| | | | | |
|---|---|---|---|---|
| 423 | **126** | 500r. multicoloured | 2·30 | 2·10 |

**127** Brest

**2001.** Town Arms. Multicoloured.

| | | | |
|---|---|---|---|
| 424 | 160r. Dubrovna | 50 | 30 |
| 424a | 200r. Type **127** | 60 | 40 |
| 425 | 200r. Gomel | 60 | 40 |
| 426 | 200r. Borisov | 60 | 40 |
| 427 | 300r. Minsk | 75 | 45 |
| 428 | 300r. David-Gorodok | 75 | 45 |
| 429 | 350r. Kamjanets | 80 | 55 |
| 430 | 460r. Slonim | 90 | 65 |
| 431 | 500r. Novogrudok | 95 | 75 |
| 432 | 500r. Turov | 95 | 75 |
| 433 | 780r. Zaslavl | 1·00 | 85 |
| 434 | 900r. Magilev | 1·20 | 95 |

**128** Runner

**2001.** Byelorussian Medal Winners, Olympic Games, Sydney. Sheet 78×75 mm.

| | | | | |
|---|---|---|---|---|
| **MS**435 | **128** | 1000r. multicoloured | 4·00 | 3·75 |

No. **MS**435 is as No. **MS**414 but with face value changed and design altered to include list of winners.

**129** Tupolev ANT-25 RD

**2001.** 25th Death Anniv of Pavel Sukhoy (aircraft designer). Multicoloured.

| | | | |
|---|---|---|---|
| 436 | 250r. Type **129** | 1·20 | 95 |
| 437 | 250r. Tupolev ANT-37 Rodina | 1·20 | 95 |

**2001.** As T **86**.

| | | | |
|---|---|---|---|
| 438 | 1r. black and green (inscr "2002") | 20 | 10 |
| 439 | 2r. black and blue (inscr "2002") | 20 | 10 |
| 440 | 3r. black and yellow (inscr "2002") | 20 | 10 |
| 441 | 5r. black and blue (inscr "2002") | 20 | 10 |
| 442 | 10r. black and brown (inscr "2002") | 20 | 10 |
| 442a | 20r. black and mauve (inscr "2002") | 30 | 15 |
| 442b | 30r. black and green (inscr "2002") | 40 | 20 |
| 442c | 50r. black and yellow (inscr "2002") | 60 | 40 |
| 442d | 100r. black and mauve (inscr "2002") | 80 | 55 |
| 442e | 100r. black and brown (inscr "2003") | 80 | 55 |
| 443 | 200r. black and green | 80 | 55 |
| 444 | 500r. black and brown | 1·80 | 1·40 |

DESIGNS: 1r. Bison; 2r. Star; 3r. Lyre; 5r. Synkovichy Church; 10r. Flaming wheel; 20r. Dancers; 50r. Windmill; 100r. Exhibition centre; 100r. (442e), Layavoniha folk dance; 200r. 18th-century town house, Vitebsk; 500r. As No. 309.

**130** Stag Beetle (*Lucanus cervus*)

**2001.** Beetles. Multicoloured.

| | | | |
|---|---|---|---|
| 445 | 300r. Type **130** | 1·50 | 1·20 |
| 446 | 300r. European rhinoceros beetle (*Oryctes nasicornis*) | 1·50 | 1·20 |

**2001.** As T **110**. Self-adhesive.

| | | | |
|---|---|---|---|
| 447 | 100r. black and mauve | 60 | 40 |
| 448 | 200r. black and green (vert) | 80 | 65 |

DESIGNS: 100r. As No. 387; 200r. As No. 438.

**131** *Nymphaea alba*

**2001.** Endangered Species. Flowers. Multicoloured.

| | | | |
|---|---|---|---|
| 455 | 200r. Type **131** | 80 | 65 |
| 456 | 400r. *Cypripedium calceolus* | 1·70 | 1·40 |

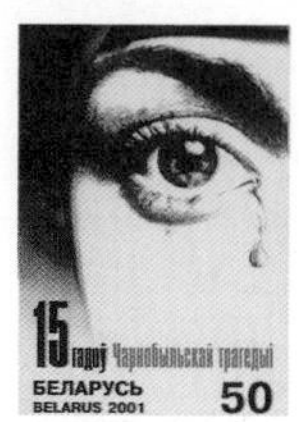

**132** Swans and Lake, Narochanskyi Nature Reserve

**2001.** Europa. Water Resources. Multicoloured.

| | | | |
|---|---|---|---|
| 457 | 400r. Geese and lake, Pripjatiskyi Nature Reserve | 2·00 | 1·40 |
| 458 | 1000r. Type **132** | 5·00 | 4·25 |

**133** Eye and Tear

**2001.** 15th Anniv of Chernobyl Nuclear Disaster.

| | | | | |
|---|---|---|---|---|
| 459 | **133** | 50r. black and rose | 50 | 30 |

**2001.** Traditional Costumes (4th series). As T **51**. Multicoloured.

| | | | |
|---|---|---|---|
| 460 | 200r. 19th-century, Slutsk region | 70 | 55 |
| 461 | 1000r. 19th-century, Pinsk region | 3·50 | 3·25 |

**134** National Arms

**2001.** 10th Anniv of State Sovereignty.

| | | | | |
|---|---|---|---|---|
| 462 | **134** | 500r. multicoloured | 2·00 | 1·90 |

**135** Union Emblem

**2001.** 10th Anniv of Union of Independent States.

| | | | | |
|---|---|---|---|---|
| 463 | **135** | 195r. multicoloured | 80 | 55 |

**2001.** No. 166 surch 400.

| | | | |
|---|---|---|---|
| 464 | 400r. on 1500r. mauve | 1·20 | 95 |



**137** King and Courtier ("The blue suit made inside out")

**2001.** Folk Tales. Multicoloured.

| | | | |
|---|---|---|---|
| 465 | 100r. Type **137** | 50 | 30 |
| 466 | 200r. Horse-drawn coach ("Okh and the golden snuff-box") | 90 | 65 |

DESIGNS—As Type **173**: VERT: 40c. "Rubens's Sons, Albert and Nicholas"; 1f. "Helene Fourment (2nd wife) and Children"; 1f.50, "Rubens and Isabella Brant" (1st wife); 1f.75, Rubens (after engraving by Pontius); 2f.50, "Straw Hat" (Suzanne Fourment). HORIZ: 75c. Arcade of Rubens's house. 35 ×45 mm: 5f. "The Descent from the Cross".

**175** Portrait by Memling

**1939.** Exn of Memling's Paintings, Bruges.

| | | | | |
|---|---|---|---|---|
| 855 | **175** | 75c.+75c. olive | 2·30 | 2·30 |

**177** Orval Abbey Cloisters and Belfry

**1939.** Orval Abbey Restoration Fund. Inscr "ORVAL".

| | | | | |
|---|---|---|---|---|
| 861 | - | 75c.+75c. olive | 5·25 | 5·25 |
| 862 | **177** | 1f.+1f. red | 2·50 | 2·50 |
| 863 | - | 1f.50+1f.50 brown | 2·50 | 2·50 |
| 864 | - | 1f.75+1f.75 blue | 3·50 | 3·50 |
| 865 | - | 2f.50+2f.50 mauve | 9·75 | 9·75 |
| 866 | - | 5f.+5f. purple | 11·00 | 11·00 |

DESIGNS—As Type **177**: VERT: 75c. Monks in laboratory. HORIZ: 1f.50, Monks harvesting; 1f.75, Aerial view of Orval Abbey; 52½×35½ mm: 2f.50, Cardinal Van Roey, Statue of the Madonna and Abbot of Orval; 5f. Kings Albert and Leopold III and shrine.

**180** Thuin

**1939.** Anti-tuberculosis Fund. Belfries.

| | | | | |
|---|---|---|---|---|
| 868 | | 10c.+5c. olive | 35 | 35 |
| 869 | **180** | 30c.+5c. brown | 35 | 35 |
| 870 | - | 40c.+5c. purple | 35 | 35 |
| 871 | - | 75c.+5c. grey | 35 | 35 |
| 872 | - | 1f.+25c. red | 1·50 | 1·50 |
| 873 | - | 1f.75+25c. blue | 1·20 | 1·20 |
| 874 | - | 2f.50+2f.50 brown | 11·00 | 11·00 |
| 875 | - | 5f.+5f. violet | 13·00 | 13·00 |

DESIGNS—As Type **180**: 10c. Bruges; 40c. Lier; 75c. Mons. LARGER (21½×34 mm): 1f. Furnes; 1f.75, Namur; 2f.50, Alost; 5f. Tournai.

**182** Arms of Mons

**1940.** Winter Relief Fund.

| | | | | |
|---|---|---|---|---|
| 901 | **182** | 10c.+5c. black, red and green | 35 | 35 |
| 902 | - | 30c.+5c. multicoloured | 35 | 35 |
| 903 | - | 40c.+10c. multicoloured | 35 | 35 |
| 904 | - | 50c.+10c. multicoloured | 35 | 35 |
| 905 | - | 75c.+15c. multicoloured | 35 | 35 |
| 906 | - | 1f.+25c. multicoloured | 45 | 45 |
| 907 | - | 1f.75c.+50c. mult | 70 | 70 |
| 908 | - | 2f.50c.+2f.50c. olive, red and black | 1·30 | 1·30 |
| 909 | - | 5f.+5f. multicoloured | 1·60 | 1·60 |
| **MS**910 | | 103×145 mm. Nos. 901/9 each in first colour given, together with red | 14·00 | 14·00 |

DESIGNS: 30c. to 5f. Arms of Ghent, Arlon, Bruges, Namur, Hasselt, Brussels, Antwerp and Liege, respectively.

**183** Painting

**184** Monks studying Plans of Orval Abbey

**1941.** Orval Abbey Restoration Fund.

| | | | | |
|---|---|---|---|---|
| 935 | **183** | 10c.+15c. brown | 50 | 50 |
| 936 | - | 30c.+30c. grey | 50 | 50 |
| 937 | - | 40c.+60c. brown | 50 | 50 |
| 938 | - | 50c.+65c. violet | 50 | 50 |
| 939 | - | 75c.+1f. mauve | 50 | 50 |
| 940 | - | 1f.+1f.50 red | 50 | 50 |
| 941 | **183** | 1f.25+1f.75 green | 50 | 50 |
| 942 | - | 1f.75+2f.50 blue | 50 | 50 |
| 943 | - | 2f.+3f.50 mauve | 50 | 50 |
| 944 | - | 2f.50+4f.50 brown | 50 | 50 |
| 945 | - | 3f.+5f. green | 50 | 50 |
| 946 | **184** | 5f.+10f. brown | 1·80 | 1·80 |
| **MS**947 | | 183×165 mm. 5f.+15f. blue (as 946) | 10·00 | 9·25 |

DESIGNS—As Type **183**. 30c., 1f., 2f.50, Sculpture; 40c., 2f. Goldsmiths (Monks carrying candlesticks and cross); 50c., 1f.75, Stained glass (Monk at prayer); 75c., 3f. Sacred music.

**1941.** Surch.

| | | | | |
|---|---|---|---|---|
| 955 | **152** | 10c. on 30c. brown | 10 | 10 |
| 956 | **152** | 10c. on 40c. lilac | 10 | 10 |
| 957 | **153** | 10c. on 70c. brown | 10 | 10 |
| 958 | **153** | 50c. on 75c. olive | 30 | 30 |
| 959 | **155** | 2f.25 on 2f.50 black | 65 | 65 |

**189** Maria Theresa

**1941.** Soldiers' Families Relief Fund.

| | | | | |
|---|---|---|---|---|
| 960 | **189** | 10c.+5c. black | 25 | 25 |
| 961 | - | 35c.+5c. green | 25 | 25 |
| 962 | - | 50c.+10c. brown | 25 | 25 |
| 963 | - | 60c.+10c. violet | 25 | 25 |
| 964 | - | 1f.+15c. red | 25 | 25 |
| 965 | - | 1f.50+1f. mauve | 25 | 25 |
| 966 | - | 1f.75+1f.75 blue | 25 | 25 |
| 967 | - | 2f.25+2f.25 brown | 30 | 30 |
| 968 | - | 3f.25+3f.25 brown | 50 | 50 |
| 969 | - | 5f.+5f. green | 1·00 | 1·00 |

PORTRAITS: 35c. to 5f. Charles of Lorraine, Margaret of Parma, Charles V, Johanna of Castile, Philip the Good, Margaret of Austria, Charles the Bold, Archduke Albert and Archduchess Isabella respectively.

**190** St. Martin, Dinant

**1941.** Winter Relief Fund. Statues.

| | | | | |
|---|---|---|---|---|
| 970 | **190** | 10c.+5c. brown | 30 | 30 |
| 971 | - | 35c.+5c. green | 30 | 30 |
| 972 | - | 50c.+10c. violet | 30 | 30 |
| 973 | - | 60c.+10c. brown | 30 | 30 |
| 974 | - | 1f.+15c. red | 30 | 30 |
| 975 | **190** | 1f.50+25c. green | 30 | 30 |
| 976 | - | 1f.75+50c. blue | 35 | 35 |
| 977 | - | 2f.25+2f.25 mauve | 35 | 35 |
| 978 | - | 3f.25+3f.25 brown | 45 | 45 |
| 979 | - | 5f.+5f. green | 85 | 85 |
| **MS**980 | | 105×139 mm. 5f.+20f. purple (as 979) | 27·00 | 27·00 |

DESIGNS (Statues of St. Martin in churches)—As Type **190**: 35c., 1f. Lennick, St. Quentin; 50c., 3f. Beck, Limberg; 60c., 2f.25, Dave on the Meuse; 1f.75, Hal, Brabant. 35×50 mm: 5f. St. Trond.

**192** Concert Hall, Argenteuil

**1941.** Fund for Queen Elisabeth's Concert Hall. Two sheets, each 103×133 mm.

| | | | | |
|---|---|---|---|---|
| **MS**981 | **192** | 10f.+15f. green | 8·25 | 7·50 |
| **MS**982 | | As last with perforated crown and monogram with violet control number on back | 8·25 | 7·50 |

**193** Mercator

**1942.** Anti-tuberculosis Fund. Portraits.

| | | | | |
|---|---|---|---|---|
| 986 | - | 10c.+5c. brown | 10 | 10 |
| 987 | - | 35c.+5c. green | 10 | 10 |
| 988 | - | 50c.+10c. brown | 10 | 10 |
| 989 | - | 60c.+10c. green | 10 | 10 |
| 990 | - | 1f.+15c. red | 10 | 10 |
| 991 | **193** | 1f.75+50c. blue | 10 | 10 |
| 992 | - | 3f.25+3f.25 purple | 10 | 10 |
| 993 | - | 5f.+5f. violet | 25 | 25 |
| 994 | - | 10f.+30f. orange | 1·70 | 1·70 |
| **MS**995 | | 77×59 mm. 3f.25+6f.75 green (as 968); 5f.+10f. red (as 969) | 14·00 | 14·00 |

SCIENTISTS—As T **193**: 10c. Bolland. 35c. Versale. 50c. S. Stevin. 60c. Van Helmont. 1f. Dodoens. 3f.25, Oertell. 5f. Juste Lipse. 25½×28½ mm: 10f. Plantin.

**198** Prisoner writing Letter

**1942.** Prisoners of War Fund.

| | | | | |
|---|---|---|---|---|
| 1000 | **198** | 5f.+45f. grey | 8·75 | 8·75 |



**199** St. Martin **200** St. Martin sharing his cloak

**1942.** Winter Relief Fund.

| | | | | |
|---|---|---|---|---|
| 1001 | **199** | 10c.+5c. orange | 25 | 25 |
| 1002 | - | 35c.+5c. green | 25 | 25 |
| 1003 | - | 50c.+10c. brown | 25 | 25 |
| 1004 | - | 60c.+10c. black (horiz) | 25 | 25 |
| 1005 | - | 1f.+15c. red | 25 | 25 |
| 1006 | - | 1f.50+25c. green | 30 | 30 |
| 1007 | - | 1f.75+50c. blue | 30 | 35 |
| 1008 | - | 2f.25+2f.25 brn (horiz) | 35 | 35 |
| 1009 | - | 3f.25+3f.25 purple (horiz) | 60 | 60 |
| 1010 | **200** | 5f.+10f. brown | 1·60 | 1·60 |
| 1011 | **200** | 10f.+20f. brown & vio | 1·70 | 1·70 |
| 1012 | **200** | 10f.+20f. red & violet | 1·50 | 1·50 |

**201** Soldiers and Vision of Home

**1943.** Prisoners of War Relief Fund.

| | | | | |
|---|---|---|---|---|
| 1013 | **201** | 1f.+30f. red | 3·50 | 3·50 |
| 1014 | - | 1f.+30f. brown | 2·30 | 2·30 |

DESIGN: No. 1014, Soldiers emptying parcel of books and vision of home.

**202** Tiler

**1943.** Anti-tuberculosis Fund. Trades.

| | | | | |
|---|---|---|---|---|
| 1015 | **202** | 10c.+5c. brown | 25 | 25 |
| 1016 | - | 35c.+5c. green | 25 | 25 |
| 1017 | - | 50c.+10c. brown | 25 | 25 |
| 1018 | - | 60c.+10c. green | 25 | 25 |
| 1019 | - | 1f.+15c. red | 30 | 25 |
| 1020 | - | 1f.75+75c. blue | 25 | 25 |
| 1021 | - | 3f.25+3f.25 purple | 35 | 35 |
| 1022 | - | 5f.+25f. violet | 1·20 | 1·20 |

DESIGNS: 35c. Blacksmith; 50c. Coppersmith; 60c. Gunsmith; 1f. Armourer; 1f.75, Goldsmith; 3f.25, Fishmonger; 5f. Clockmaker.

**203** Ornamental Letter

**204** Ornamental Letter (image scaled to 68% of original size)

**1943.** Orval Abbey Restoration Fund. Designs showing single letters forming "ORVAL".

| | | | | |
|---|---|---|---|---|
| 1023 | **203** | 50c.+1f. black | 45 | 45 |
| 1024 | - | 60c.+1f.90 violet | 35 | 35 |
| 1025 | - | 1f.+3f. red | 35 | 35 |
| 1026 | - | 1f.75+5f.25 blue | 35 | 35 |
| 1027 | - | 3f.25+16f.75 green | 65 | 65 |
| 1028 | **204** | 5f.+30f. brown | 1·10 | 1·10 |

**205** St. Leonard's Church, Leon, and St. Martin

**206** Church of Notre Dame, Hal, and St. Martin

**207** St. Martin and River Scheldt

**1943.** Winter Relief Fund.

| | | | | |
|---|---|---|---|---|
| 1029 | **205** | 10c.+5c. brown | 30 | 30 |
| 1030 | - | 35c.+5c. green | 30 | 30 |
| 1031 | - | 50c.+15c. green | 30 | 30 |
| 1032 | - | 60c.+20c. purple | 30 | 30 |
| 1033 | - | 1f.+1f. red | 35 | 35 |
| 1034 | - | 1f.75+4f.25 blue | 80 | 80 |
| 1035 | - | 3f.25+11f.75 mauve | 1·60 | 1·60 |
| 1036 | **206** | 5f.+25f. blue | 2·40 | 2·40 |
| 1037 | **207** | 10f.+30f. green | 1·90 | 1·90 |
| 1038 | - | 10f.+30f. brown | 1·90 | 1·90 |

DESIGNS: (Various churches and statues of St. Martin sharing his cloak). As Type **205**: HORIZ: 35c. Dion-le-Val; 50c. Alost; 60c. Liege; 3f.25, Loppem. VERT: 1f. Courtrai; 1f.75, Angre. As Type **207**: 10f. brown Meuse landscape.

**208** "Daedalus and Icarus"

**1944.** Red Cross.

| | | | | |
|---|---|---|---|---|
| 1039 | **208** | 35c.+1f.65 green | 40 | 40 |
| 1040 | - | 50c.+2f.50 grey | 40 | 40 |
| 1041 | - | 60c.+3f.40 brown | 40 | 40 |
| 1042 | - | 1f.+5f. red | 60 | 60 |
| 1043 | - | 1f.75+8f.25 blue | 60 | 60 |
| 1044 | - | 5f.+30f. brown | 95 | 95 |

DESIGNS: 50c. "The Good Samaritan" (Jacob Jordsen); 60c. "Christ healing the Paralytic" (detail); 1f. "Madonna and Child"; 1f.75, "Self-portrait"; 5f. "St. Sebastian".

Nos. 1039 and 1041/4 depict paintings by Anthony van Dyck.

**209** Jan van Eyck

**1944.** Prisoners of War Relief Fund.

| | | | | |
|---|---|---|---|---|
| 1045 | **209** | 10c.+15c. violet | 35 | 35 |
| 1046 | - | 35c.+15c. green | 35 | 35 |
| 1047 | - | 50c.+25c. brown | 35 | 35 |
| 1048 | - | 60c.+40c. olive | 35 | 35 |
| 1049 | - | 1f.+50c. red | 35 | 35 |
| 1050 | - | 1f.75+4f.25 blue | 35 | 35 |
| 1051 | - | 2f.25+8f.25 slate | 80 | 80 |
| 1052 | - | 3f.25+11f.25 brown | 40 | 40 |
| 1053 | - | 5f.+35f. grey | 85 | 85 |

PORTRAITS: 35c. "Godefroid de Bouillon". 50c. "Jacob van Maerlant". 60c. "Jean Joses de Dinant". 1f. "Jacob van Artevelde". 1f.75, "Charles Joseph de Ligne". 2f.25, "Andre Gretry". 3f.25, "Jan Moretus-Plantin". 5f. "Ruusbroeck".

**210** "Bayard and Four Sons of Aymon", Namur

**1944.** Anti-tuberculosis Fund. Provincial legendary types.

| | | | | |
|---|---|---|---|---|
| 1054 | **210** | 10c.+5c. brown | 10 | 10 |
| 1055 | - | 35c.+5c. green | 10 | 10 |
| 1056 | - | 50c.+10c. violet | 10 | 10 |
| 1057 | - | 60c.+10c. brown | 10 | 10 |
| 1058 | - | 1f.+15c. red | 10 | 10 |
| 1059 | - | 1f.75+5f.25 blue | 10 | 10 |
| 1060 | - | 3f.25+11f.75 green | 35 | 35 |
| 1061 | - | 5f.+25f. blue | 45 | 45 |

DESIGNS—VERT: 35c. "Brabo severing the giant's hand", Antwerp; 60c. "Thyl Ulenspiegel" and "Nele", Flanders; 1f. "St. George and the Dragon", Hainaut; 1f.75, "Genevieve of Brabant, with the Child and the Hind", Brabant. HORIZ: 50c. "St. Hubert encounters the Hind with the Cross", Luxemburg; 3f.25, "Tchantches wrestling with the Saracen", Liege; 5f. "St. Gertrude rescuing the Knight with the cards", Limburg.

**211** Lion Rampant

**1944.** Inscr "BELGIQUE-BELGIE" or "BELGIE-BELGIQUE".

| | | | | |
|---|---|---|---|---|
| 1062A | **211** | 5c. brown | 10 | 10 |
| 1063A | **211** | 10c. green | 10 | 10 |
| 1064A | **211** | 25c. blue | 10 | 10 |
| 1065A | **211** | 35c. brown | 10 | 10 |
| 1066A | **211** | 50c. green | 10 | 10 |
| 1067B | **211** | 75c. violet | 10 | 10 |
| 1068B | **211** | 1f. red | 10 | 10 |
| 1069B | **211** | 1f.25 brown | 25 | 25 |
| 1070B | **211** | 1f.50 orange | 40 | 40 |
| 1071A | **211** | 1f.75 blue | 10 | 10 |
| 1072B | **211** | 2f. blue | 1·70 | 1·70 |
| 1073A | **211** | 2f.75 mauve | 10 | 10 |
| 1074B | **211** | 3f. red | 25 | 25 |
| 1075B | **211** | 3f.50 grey | 15 | 10 |
| 1076B | **211** | 5f. brown | 3·50 | 3·50 |
| 1077B | **211** | 10f. black | 85 | 85 |

**1944.** Overprinted with large V.

| | | | | |
|---|---|---|---|---|
| 1078 | **152** | 2c. green | 10 | 10 |
| 1079 | **152** | 15c. blue | 10 | 10 |
| 1080 | **152** | 20c. violet | 10 | 10 |
| 1081 | **152** | 60c. grey | 10 | 10 |

**213** King Leopold III and "V"

**1944**

| | | | | |
|---|---|---|---|---|
| 1082 | **213** | 1f. red | 15 | 10 |
| 1083 | **213** | 1f.50 mauve | 15 | 10 |
| 1084 | **213** | 1f.75 blue | 45 | 45 |
| 1085 | **213** | 2f. violet | 60 | 35 |
| 1086 | **213** | 2f.25 green | 45 | 45 |
| 1087 | **213** | 3f.25 brown | 30 | 15 |
| 1088 | **213** | 5f. green | 1·20 | 35 |

**214** War Victims

**215** Rebuilding Homes

**1945.** War Victims' Relief Fund.

| | | | | |
|---|---|---|---|---|
| 1114 | **214** | 1f.+30f. red | 1·90 | 1·00 |
| 1115 | **215** | 1¾f.+30f. blue | 1·90 | 1·00 |

Nos. 1114/15 measure 50×35 mm.

**1945.** Post Office Employers' Relief Fund.

| | | | | |
|---|---|---|---|---|
| 1119 | **214** | 1f.+9f. red | 40 | 25 |
| 1120 | **215** | 1f.+9f. red | 45 | 25 |

**217** Resister

**218** Group of Resisters

**1945.** Prisoners of War Relief Fund.

| | | | | |
|---|---|---|---|---|
| 1121 | **217** | 10c.+15c. orange | 25 | 25 |
| 1122 | - | 20c.+20c. violet | 25 | 25 |
| 1123 | - | 60c.+25c. brown | 25 | 25 |
| 1124 | - | 70c.+30c. green | 25 | 25 |
| 1125 | **217** | 75c.+50c. brown | 25 | 25 |
| 1126 | - | 1f.+75c. green | 30 | 25 |
| 1127 | - | 1f.50+1f. red | 30 | 25 |
| 1128 | - | 3f.50+3f.50 blue | 2·00 | 1·30 |
| 1129 | **218** | 5f.+40f. brown | 2·50 | 1·50 |

DESIGNS—VERT: 20c., 1f. Father and child; 60c., 1f.50, Victim tied to stake. HORIZ: 70c., 3f.50, Rifleman.

**219** West Flanders

**1945.** Anti-tuberculosis Fund.

| | | | | |
|---|---|---|---|---|
| 1130 | **219** | 10c.+15c. green | 60 | 30 |
| 1131 | - | 20c.+20c. red | 35 | 30 |
| 1132 | - | 60c.+25c. brown | 35 | 30 |
| 1133 | - | 70c.+30c. green | 35 | 30 |
| 1134 | - | 75c.+50c. brown | 35 | 30 |
| 1135 | - | 1f.+75c. violet | 35 | 30 |
| 1136 | - | 1f.50+1f. red | 35 | 30 |
| 1137 | - | 3f.50+1f.50 blue | 75 | 75 |
| 1138 | - | 5f.+45f. mauve | 4·25 | 2·40 |

ARMS DESIGNS—VERT: 20c. to 5f. Arms of Luxemburg, East Flanders, Namur, Limburg Hainaut, Antwerp, Liege and Brabant respectively.

**222** Douglas DC-400-DAA

**1946.** Air.

| | | | | |
|---|---|---|---|---|
| 1165 | **222** | 6f. blue | 40 | 30 |
| 1166 | **222** | 8f.50 red | 75 | 60 |
| 1167 | **222** | 50f. green | 7·00 | 1·20 |
| 1168 | **222** | 100f. grey | 11·50 | 2·50 |

**1946.** Surch -10%, reducing the original value by 10%.

| | | | | |
|---|---|---|---|---|
| 1171 | **213** | "-10%" on 1f.50 mauve | 85 | 30 |
| 1172 | **213** | "-10%" on 2f. violet | 2·30 | 85 |
| 1173 | **213** | "-10%" on 5f. green | 2·00 | 30 |

**224** "Marie Henriette" (paddle-steamer)

**1946.** Ostend–Dover Mail-boat Service Centenary.

| | | | | |
|---|---|---|---|---|
| 1174a | - | 1f.35 blue | 45 | 25 |
| 1175 | **224** | 2f.25 green | 60 | 40 |
| 1176 | - | 3f.15 grey | 65 | 30 |

DESIGNS—21½×18½ or 21×17 mm: 1f.35, "Prince Baudouin" (mail steamer). As T **224**: 3f.15, "Diamant" (paddle-steamer), formerly "Le Chemin de Fer".

**225** Paratrooper

**1946.** Air. Bastogne Monument Fund.

| | | | | |
|---|---|---|---|---|
| 1177 | **225** | 17f.50+62f.50 green | 1·90 | 85 |
| 1178 | **225** | 17f.50+62f.50 purple | 1·90 | 85 |

**226** Father Damien **227** E. Vandervelde

**228** Francois Bovesse

**1946.** Belgian Patriots. (a) Father Damien.

| | | | | |
|---|---|---|---|---|
| 1179 | **226** | 65c.+75c. blue | 2·30 | 1·50 |
| 1180 | - | 1f.35+2f. brown | 2·30 | 1·50 |
| 1181 | - | 1f.75+18f. lake | 2·30 | 1·50 |

DESIGNS—HORIZ: 1f.35, Molokai Leper Colony. VERT: 1f.75, Damien's statue.

(b) Emile Vandervelde.

| | | | | |
|---|---|---|---|---|
| 1182 | **227** | 65c.+75c. green | 2·30 | 1·50 |
| 1183 | - | 1f.35+2f. blue | 2·30 | 1·50 |
| 1184 | - | 1f.75+18f. red | 2·30 | 1·50 |

DESIGNS—HORIZ: 1f.35, Vandervelde, miner, mother and child. VERT: 1f.75, Sower.

(c) Francois Bovesse.

| | | | | |
|---|---|---|---|---|
| 1185 | | 65c.+75c. violet | 2·30 | 1·50 |
| 1186 | **228** | 1f.35+2f. brown | 2·30 | 1·50 |
| 1187 | - | 1f.75+18f. red | 2·30 | 1·50 |

DESIGNS—VERT: 65c. Symbols of Patriotism and Learning; 1f.75, Draped memorial figures holding wreath and torch.

**229** Pepin d'Herstal

**1946.** War Victims' Relief Fund.

| | | | | |
|---|---|---|---|---|
| 1188 | **229** | 75c.+25c. green | 60 | 25 |
| 1189 | - | 1f.+50c. violet | 85 | 35 |
| 1190 | - | 1f.50+1f. purple | 85 | 45 |
| 1191 | - | 3f.50+1f.50 blue | 1·20 | 70 |
| 1192 | - | 5f.+45f. mauve | 15·00 | 14·00 |
| 1194 | - | 5f.+45f. orange | 13·00 | 13·00 |

DESIGNS: 1f. Charlemagne; 1f.50, Godfrey of Bouillon; 3f.50, Robert of Jerusalem; 5f. Baudouin of Constantinople.

See also Nos. 1207/11, 1258/9 and 1302/6.

**230** Allegory of "Flight"

**1946.** Air.

| | | | | |
|---|---|---|---|---|
| 1193 | **230** | 2f.+8f. violet | 65 | 60 |

**231** Malines

**1946.** Anti-tuberculosis Fund. No date.

| | | | | |
|---|---|---|---|---|
| 1195 | **231** | 65c.+35c. red | 70 | 25 |
| 1196 | - | 90c.+60c. olive | 80 | 25 |
| 1197 | - | 1f.35+1f.15 green | 80 | 25 |
| 1198 | - | 3f.15+1f.85 blue | 1·20 | 45 |
| 1199 | - | 4f.50+45f.50 brown | 19·00 | 16·00 |

DESIGNS—(Arms and Industries): 90c. Dinant; 1f.35, Ostend; 3f.15, Verviers; 4f.50, Louvain.

See also Nos. 1212/16.

**1947.** Air. "Cipex" International Stamp Exhibition, New York. Nos. 1179/87 surch LUCHTPOST POSTE AERIENNE or POSTE AERIENNE LUCHTPOST and new value. (a) Father Damien.

| | | | |
|---|---|---|---|
| 1199a | 1f.+2f. on 65c. +75c. blue | 95 | 60 |

1199b 1f.+50+2f.50 on 1f.35+2f. brown 95 60
1199c 2f.+45f. on 1f.75+18f. red 95 60

(b) Emile Vandervelde.

1199d 1f.+2f. on 65c.+75c. green 95 60
1199e 1f.50+2f.50 on 1f.35+2f. blue 95 60
1199f 2f.+45f. on 1f.75+18f. red 95 60

(c) Francois Bovesse.

1199g 1f.+2f. on 65c.+75c. vio 95 60
1199h 1f.50+2f.50 on 1f.35+2f. brown 95 60
1199i 2f.+45f. on 1f.75+18f. red 95 60

**232** Joseph Plateau

**1947.** Int Film and Belgian Fine Arts Festival.

1200 **232** 3f.15 blue 1·50 30

**233** Adrien de Gerlache
**234** Explorers landing from "Belgica"

**1947.** 50th Anniv of Belgian Antarctic Expedition.

1201 **233** 1f.35 red 30 10
1202 **234** 2f.25 grey 4·75 70

**1947.** War Victims' Relief Fund. Mediaeval Princes as T 229.

1207 65c.+35c. blue 1·30 60
1208 90c.+60c. green 1·90 85
1209 1f.35+1f.15 red 3·75 1·20
1210 3f.15+1f.85 blue 4·75 1·50
1211 20f.+20f. purple 60·00 48·00

DESIGNS: 65c. John II, Duke of Brabant; 90c. Philippe of Alsace; 1f.35, William the Good; 3f.15, Notger, Bishop of Liege; 20f. Philip the Noble.

**1947.** Anti-Tuberculosis Fund. Arms designs as T 231, but dated "1947".

1212 65c.+35c. orange 70 60
1213 90c.+60c. purple 80 70
1214 1f.35+1f.15 brown 95 75
1215 3f.15+1f.85 blue 3·25 1·50
1216 20f.+20f. green 31·00 20·00

DESIGNS (Arms and Industries): 65c. Nivelles; 90c. St. Truiden; 1f.35, Charleroi; 3f.15, St. Nicholas; 20f. Bouillon.

**237** Chemical Industry
**240** Textile Machinery

**239** Antwerp Docks

**1948.** National Industries.

1217 **237** 60c. blue 15 15
1218 **237** 1f.20 brown 3·00 30
1219 - 1f.35 brown 15 15
1220 - 1f.75 green 70 30
1221 - 1f.75 red 30 25
1222 **239** 2f.25 grey 85 60
1223 - 2f.50 mauve 9·50 65
1224 **239** 3f. purple 15·00 60
1225 **240** 3f.15 blue 1·40 70
1226 **240** 4f. blue 14·50 45
1227 - 6f. blue 36·00 65
1228 - 6f.30 purple 3·50 2·75

DESIGNS—As Type **237**: 1f.35, 1f.75 green, Woman making lace; 1f.75 red, 2f.50, Agricultural produce. As Type **239**: 6f., 6f.30, Steel works.

**242** St. Benedict and King Totila

**1948.** Achel Abbey Fund. Inscr "ACHEL".

1232 **242** 65c.+65c. brown 1·20 85
1233 - 1f.35+1f.35 green 1·70 1·20
1234 - 3f.15+2f.85 blue 4·00 1·50
1235 - 10f.+10f. purple 14·00 11·50

DESIGNS—HORIZ: 1f.35, Achel Abbey. VERT: 3f.15, St. Benedict as Law-Giver; 10f. Death of St. Benedict.

**243** St. Bega and Chevremont Castle

**1948.** Chevremont Abbey Fund. Inscr "CHEVREMONT".

1236 **243** 65c.+65c. blue 1·20 85
1237 - 1f.35+1f.35 red 1·70 1·20
1238 - 3f.15+2f.85 blue 3·50 1·50
1239 - 10f.+10f. brown 13·50 10·50

DESIGNS—HORIZ: 1f.35, Chevremont Basilica and Convent. VERT: 3f.15, Madonna of Chevremont and Chapel; 10f. Monk and Madonna of Mt. Carmel.

**244** Statue of Anseele
**245** Ghent and E. Anseele

**1948.** Inauguration of Edward Anseele (Socialist Leader) Statue.

1245 **244** 65c.+35c. red 3·00 1·70
1246 **245** 90c.+60c. grey 4·00 2·30
1247 - 1f.35+1f.15 brn 3·00 1·70
1248 - 3f.15+1f.85 blue 8·75 5·75
**MS**1249 82×145 mm. Nos. 1245/8 £250 £110

DESIGNS: 1f.35, Statue and Ed. Anseele; 3f.15, Reverse side of statue.

**247** "Liberty"
**248** "Resistance"

**1948.** Antwerp and Liege Monuments Funds.

1253 **247** 10f.+10f. green 60·00 29·00
1254 **248** 10f.+10f. brown 26·00 14·50

**249** Cross of Lorraine

**1948.** Anti-tuberculosis Fund.

1255 **249** 20c.+5c. green 60 30
1256 **249** 1f.20+30c. purple 2·00 60
1257 **249** 1f.75+25c. red 2·30 85
1258 - 4f.+3f.25 blue 9·50 5·75
1259 - 20f.+20f. green 50·00 35·00

DESIGNS—As Type **229**: 4f. Isabel of Austria; 20f. Albert, Archduke of Austria.

**250** "Madonna and Child"

**1949.** Social and Cultural Funds. Sheets 140×90 mm sold at 50f. each incl premium (a) Paintings by R. van der Weyden.

**MS**1260 90c. brown (T **250** "Madonna and Child"); 1f.75 purple ("Crucifixion"); 4f. blue ("Mary Magdalene") £225 £200

(b) Paintings by J. Jordaens.

**MS**1261 90c. violet ("Woman Reading"); 1f.75 red ("Flute-player"); 4f. blue ("Old Woman and Letter") £225 £200

**1949.** Surch 1-1-49 at top, 31-XII-49 and value at bottom with posthorn in between. (a) Arms type.

1262 **152** 5c. on 15c. blue 10 10
1263 **152** 5c. on 30c. brown 10 10
1264 **152** 5c. on 40c. lilac 10 10
1265 **152** 20c. on 70c. green 10 10
1266 **152** 20c. on 75c. mauve 10 10

(b) Anseele Statue.

1267 **244** 10c. on 65c.+35c. red 3·00 3·00
1268 **245** 40c. on 90c.+60c. grey 1·70 1·70
1269 - 80c. on 1f.35+1f.15 brown 85 90
1270 - 1f.20 on 3f.15+1f.85 blue 1·50 1·50

**251** King Leopold I

**252** Forms of Postal Transport

**1949.** Belgian Stamp Cent.

1271 **251** 90c. green (postage) 75 40
1272 **251** 1f.75 brown 40 30
1273 **251** 3f. red 11·00 3·50
1274 **251** 4f. blue 7·00 1·00
1275 **252** 50f. brown (air) 60·00 23·00

**253** St. Madeleine from "The Baptism of Christ"

**1949.** Exhibition of Paintings by Gerard David, Bruges.

1276 **253** 1f.75 brown 85 30

**255** Hemispheres and Allegorical Figure

**1949.** 75th Anniv of U.P.U.

1295 **255** 4f. blue 5·50 2·50

**256** Guido Gezelle

**1949.** 50th Death Anniv of Gezelle (poet).

1297 **256** 1f.75+75c. green 2·00 1·50

**257** Arnica

**1949.** Anti-tuberculosis and other Funds. (a) Flowers.

1298 **257** 20c.+5c. black, yellow and green 35 30
1299 - 65c.+10c. black, green and buff 1·40 45
1300 - 90c.+10c. black, blue and red 2·00 1·00
1301 - 1f.20+30c. mult 2·50 1·30

FLOWERS: 65c. Thistle. 90c. Periwinkle. 1f.20, Poppy.

(b) Portraits as T 229.

1302 1f.75+25c. orange 1·20 40
1303 3f.+1f.50 red 13·00 8·25
1304 4f.+2f. blue 13·50 8·25
1305 6f.+3f. brown 23·00 11·50
1306 8f.+4f. green 27·00 15·00

PORTRAITS: 1f.75, Philip the Good. 3f. Charles V. 4f. Maria Christina. 6f. Charles of Lorraine. 8f. Maria Theresa.

**260** Anglo-Belgian Monument, Hertain

**1950.** Anglo-Belgian Union and other Funds.

1307 - 80c.+20c. green 1·50 60
1308 - 2f.50+50c. red 6·75 4·00
1309 **260** 4f.+2f. blue 10·50 7·00

DESIGNS—HORIZ: 80c. Arms of Great Britain and Belgium; 2f.50, British tanks at Tournai.

**261** Allegory of Saving

**1950.** National Savings Bank Centenary.

1310 **261** 1f.75 sepia 60 30

**262** Hurdling

**1950.** European Athletic Championships. Inscr "HEYSEL 1950".

1311 **262** 20c.+5c. green 60 30
1312 - 90c.+10c. purple 4·75 2·30
1313 - 1f.75+25c. red 9·25 2·50
1314 - 4f.+2f. blue 44·00 23·00
1315 - 8f.+4f. green 46·00 30·00
**MS**1316 70×119 mm. 1f.75+25c. (+18f.) (No. 1313) 95·00 60·00

DESIGNS—HORIZ: 1f.75, Relay racing. VERT: 90c. Javelin throwing; 4f. Pole vaulting; 8f. Sprinting.

**263** Sikorsky S-51 Helicopter and Douglas DC-4 leaving Melsbroeck Airport

**1950.** Air. Inauguration of Helicopter Airmail Services and Aeronautical Committee's Fund.

1317 **263** 7f.+3f. blue 9·75 5·75

**265** Gentian **266** Sijsele Sanatorium

**1950.** Anti-tuberculosis and other Funds. Cross in red.

| | | | | |
|---|---|---|---|---|
| 1326 | **265** | 20c.+5c. blue, green and purple | 35 | 30 |
| 1327 | - | 65c.+10c. green and brown | 1·40 | 45 |
| 1328 | - | 90c.+10c. light green and green | 1·70 | 1·20 |
| 1329 | - | 1f.20+30c. blue, green and ultramarine | 2·00 | 1·30 |
| 1330 | **266** | 1f.75+25c. red | 2·50 | 1·70 |
| 1331 | - | 4f.+2f. blue | 23·00 | 1·70 |
| 1332 | - | 8f.+4f. green | 31·00 | 10·50 |

DESIGNS—Flowers as Type **265**: 65c. Rushes; 90c. Foxglove; 1f.20, Sea lavender. Sanatoria as Type **266**: HORIZ: 4f. Jauche. VERT: 8f. Tombeek.

**267** The Belgian Lion

**1951.** (a) 17½×20½ mm.

| | | | | |
|---|---|---|---|---|
| 1334 | **267** | 2c. brown | 10 | 10 |
| 1335 | **267** | 3c. violet | 10 | 10 |
| 1336 | **267** | 5c. lilac | 10 | 10 |
| 1336a | **267** | 5c. pink | 10 | 10 |
| 1337 | **267** | 10c. orange | 10 | 10 |
| 1338 | **267** | 15c. mauve | 10 | 10 |
| 1333 | **267** | 20c. blue | 30 | 10 |
| 1339 | **267** | 20c. red | 10 | 10 |
| 1340 | **267** | 25c. green | 1·70 | 15 |
| 1341 | **267** | 25c. blue | 10 | 10 |
| 1342 | **267** | 30c. green | 10 | 10 |
| 1343 | **267** | 40c. brown | 10 | 10 |
| 1344a | **267** | 50c. blue | 15 | 25 |
| 1345 | **267** | 60c. mauve | 10 | 10 |
| 1346 | **267** | 65c. purple | 13·50 | 60 |
| 1347 | **267** | 75c. lilac | 10 | 10 |
| 1348 | **267** | 80c. green | 85 | 35 |
| 1349 | **267** | 90c. blue | 1·30 | 35 |
| 1350 | **267** | 1f. red | 10 | 10 |
| 1351 | **267** | 1f.50 grey | 10 | 10 |
| 1353 | **267** | 2f. green | 25 | 10 |
| 1354 | **267** | 2f.50 brown | 25 | 10 |
| 1355 | **267** | 3f. mauve | 25 | 10 |
| 1355a | **267** | 4f. purple | 35 | 10 |
| 1355b | **267** | 4f.50 blue | 25 | 10 |
| 1355c | **267** | 5f. purple | 15 | 10 |

(b) 20½×24½ mm.

| | | | |
|---|---|---|---|
| 1356 | 50c. blue | 25 | 15 |
| 1357 | 60c. purple | 80 | 65 |
| 1358a | 1f. red | 10 | 10 |

(c) Size 17½×22 mm.

| | | | |
|---|---|---|---|
| 1359 | 50c. blue | 10 | 10 |
| 1360 | 1f. pink | 1·30 | 75 |
| 1361 | 2f. green | 50 | 25 |

**268** "Science"

**1951.** UNESCO Fund. Inscr "UNESCO".

| | | | | |
|---|---|---|---|---|
| 1365 | **268** | 80c.+20c. green | 1·70 | 60 |
| 1366 | - | 2f.50+50c. brown | 12·00 | 7·00 |
| 1367 | - | 4f.+2f. blue | 15·00 | 8·75 |

DESIGNS—HORIZ: 2f.50, "Education". VERT: 4f. "Peace".

**269** Fairey Tipsy Belfair Trainer I00-TIC

**1951.** Air. 50th Anniv of National Aero Club.

| | | | | |
|---|---|---|---|---|
| 1368 | | 6f. blue | 38·00 | 20·00 |
| 1369 | **269** | 7f. red | 38·00 | 20·00 |

DESIGN: 6f. Arsenal Air 100 glider.

**1951.** Air.

| | | | | |
|---|---|---|---|---|
| 1370 | - | 6f. brown (glider) | 7·25 | 30 |
| 1371 | **269** | 7f. green | 7·25 | 85 |

**270** Monument

**1951.** Political Prisoners' National Monument Fund.

| | | | | |
|---|---|---|---|---|
| 1372 | **270** | 1f.75+25c. brown | 3·50 | 60 |
| 1373 | - | 4f.+2f. blue | 37·00 | 20·00 |
| 1374 | - | 8f.+4f. green | 38·00 | 23·00 |

DESIGNS—HORIZ: 4f. Breendonk Fort. VERT: 8f. Side view of monument.

**272** Queen Elisabeth

**1951.** Queen Elisabeth Medical Foundation Fund.

| | | | | |
|---|---|---|---|---|
| 1376 | **272** | 90c.+10c. grey | 5·25 | 1·20 |
| 1377 | **272** | 1f.75+25c. red | 11·50 | 2·50 |
| 1378 | **272** | 3f.+1f. green | 38·00 | 17·00 |
| 1379 | **272** | 4f.+2f. blue | 41·00 | 19·00 |
| 1380 | **272** | 8f.+4f. sepia | 49·00 | 23·00 |

**273** Lorraine Cross and Dragon **274** Beersel Castle

**1951.** Anti-tuberculosis and other Funds.

| | | | | |
|---|---|---|---|---|
| 1381 | **273** | 20c.+5c. red | 45 | 30 |
| 1382 | **273** | 65c.+10c. blue | 70 | 35 |
| 1383 | **273** | 90c.+10c. brown | 85 | 40 |
| 1384 | **273** | 1f.20+30c. violet | 1·70 | 60 |
| 1385 | **274** | 1f.75+75c. brown | 5·25 | 1·70 |
| 1386 | - | 3f.+1f. green | 16·00 | 9·50 |
| 1387 | - | 4f.+2f. blue | 20·00 | 11·50 |
| 1388 | - | 8f.+4f. black | 30·00 | 16·00 |

CASTLES—As Type **274**: VERT: 3f. Horst Castle. 8f. Veves Castle. HORIZ: 4f. Lavaux St. Anne Castle.

For stamps as Type **273** but dated "1952" see Nos. 1416/19 and for those dated "1953" see Nos. 1507/10.

**276** Consecration of the Basilica

**1952.** 25th Anniv of Cardinalate of Primate of Belgium and Koekelberg Basilica Fund.

| | | | | |
|---|---|---|---|---|
| 1389 | | 1f.75+25c. brown | 1·70 | 60 |
| 1390 | | 4f.+2f. blue | 19·00 | 9·25 |
| 1391 | **276** | 8f.+4f. purple | 28·00 | 13·50 |
| **MS**1392 | | 120×72 mm. Nos. 1389/91 (10f.) | £475 | £200 |

DESIGNS—24×35 mm: 1f.75, Interior of Koekelberg Basilica; 4f. Exterior of Koekelberg Basilica.

**277** King Baudouin **278** King Baudouin

**1952**

| | | | | |
|---|---|---|---|---|
| 1393 | **277** | 1f.50 grey | 1·70 | 25 |
| 1394 | **277** | 2f. red | 60 | 25 |
| 1395 | **277** | 4f. blue | 8·75 | 30 |
| 1396a | **278** | 50f. purple | 4·00 | 25 |
| 1397a | **278** | 100f. red | 20·00 | 70 |

**279** Francis of Taxis

**1952.** 13th U.P.U. Congress, Brussels. Portraits of Members of the House of Thurn and Taxis.

| | | | | |
|---|---|---|---|---|
| 1398 | **279** | 80c. green | 35 | 30 |
| 1399 | - | 1f.75 orange | 35 | 30 |
| 1400 | - | 2f. brown | 70 | 45 |
| 1401 | - | 2f.50 red | 1·40 | 45 |
| 1402 | - | 3f. olive | 1·40 | 35 |
| 1403 | - | 4f. blue | 1·50 | 30 |
| 1404 | - | 5f. brown | 3·75 | 45 |
| 1405 | - | 5f.75 violet | 5·25 | 1·50 |
| 1406 | - | 8f. black | 23·00 | 4·00 |
| 1407 | - | 10f. purple | 29·00 | 9·25 |
| 1408 | - | 20f. grey | £120 | 55·00 |
| 1409 | - | 40f.+10f. turquoise | £180 | £150 |

DESIGNS—VERT: 1f.75, John Baptist; 2f. Leonard; 2f.50, Lamoral; 3f. Leonard Francis; 4f. Lamoral Claud; 5f. Eugene Alexander; 5f.75, Anselm Francis; 8f. Alexander Ferdinand; 10f. Charles Anselm; 20f. Charles Alexander; 40f. Beaulieu Chateau.

**281** A. Vermeylen

**1952.** Culture Fund. Writers.

| | | | | |
|---|---|---|---|---|
| 1410 | **281** | 65c.+30c. lilac | 7·25 | 3·00 |
| 1411 | - | 80c.+40c. green | 7·75 | 3·50 |
| 1412 | - | 90c.+45c. olive | 8·25 | 4·00 |
| 1413 | - | 1f.75+75c. lake | 17·00 | 5·75 |
| 1414 | - | 4f.+2f. blue | 46·00 | 21·00 |
| 1415 | - | 8f.+4f. sepia | 49·00 | 24·00 |

PORTRAITS: 80c. K. van de Woestijne. 90c. C. de Coster. 1f.75, M. Maeterlinck. 4f. E. Verhaeren. 8f. H. Conscience.

A 4f. blue as No. 1414 and an 8f. lake as No. 1415 each se-tenant with a label showing a laurel wreath and bearing a premium "+ 9 fr." were put on sale by subscription only.

**282** Arms, Malmedy

**1952.** Anti-tuberculosis and other Funds. As T 273 but dated "1952" and designs as T 282.

| | | | | |
|---|---|---|---|---|
| 1416 | **273** | 20c.+5c. brown | 35 | 30 |
| 1417 | **273** | 80c.+20c. green | 80 | 40 |
| 1418 | **273** | 1f.20+30c. purple | 2·00 | 1·20 |
| 1419 | **273** | 1f.50+50c. olive | 2·30 | 1·30 |
| 1420 | **282** | 2f.+75c. red | 3·25 | 1·50 |
| 1421 | - | 3f.+1f.50 brown | 27·00 | 16·00 |
| 1422 | - | 4f.+2f. blue | 25·00 | 15·00 |
| 1423 | - | 8f.+4f. purple | 27·00 | 17·00 |

DESIGNS—HORIZ: 3f. Ruins, Burgreuland. VERT: 4f. Dam, Eupen; 8f. Saint and lion, St. Vith.

**284** Dewe and Monument at Liege

**1953.** Walthere Dewe Memorial Fund.

| | | | | |
|---|---|---|---|---|
| 1435 | **284** | 2f.+1f. lake | 3·25 | 2·00 |

**285** Princess Josephine Charlotte

**1953.** Red Cross National Disaster Fund. Cross in red.

| | | | | |
|---|---|---|---|---|
| 1436 | **285** | 80c.+20c. green | 4·00 | 1·70 |
| 1437 | **285** | 1f.20+30c. brown | 3·75 | 1·50 |
| 1438 | **285** | 2f.+50c. lake | 3·25 | 1·50 |
| 1439 | **285** | 2f.50+50c. red | 20·00 | 11·50 |
| 1440 | **285** | 4f.+1f. blue | 22·00 | 10·50 |
| 1441 | **285** | 5f.+2f. black | 22·00 | 10·50 |

**286** Fishing Boats "Marcel", "De Meeuw" and "Jacqueline Denise"

**1953.** Tourist Propaganda and Cultural Funds.

| | | | | |
|---|---|---|---|---|
| 1442 | **286** | 80c.+20c. green | 2·30 | 1·20 |
| 1443 | - | 1f.20+30c. brown | 7·00 | 3·25 |
| 1444 | - | 2f.+50c. sepia | 8·25 | 3·25 |
| 1445 | - | 2f.50+50c. mauve | 19·00 | 9·25 |
| 1446 | - | 4f.+2f. blue | 30·00 | 15·00 |
| 1447 | - | 8f.+4f. green | 38·00 | 18·00 |

DESIGNS—HORIZ: 1f.20, Bridge Bouillon; 2f. Antwerp. VERT: 2f.50, Namur; 4f. Ghent; 8f. Freyr Rocks and River Meuse.

**289** King Baudouin

**1953.** (a) 21×24½ mm.

| | | | | |
|---|---|---|---|---|
| 1453 | **289** | 1f.50 black | 30 | 10 |
| 1454 | **289** | 2f. red | 9·25 | 30 |
| 1455 | **289** | 2f. green | 30 | 10 |
| 2188 | **289** | 2f.50 brown | 25 | 10 |
| 1457 | **289** | 3f. purple | 1·20 | 10 |
| 1458 | **289** | 3f.50 green | 60 | 10 |
| 1459 | **289** | 4f. blue | 4·00 | 25 |
| 2188A | **289** | 4f.50 brown | 80 | 50 |
| 1462 | **289** | 5f. violet | 1·50 | 10 |
| 1463 | **289** | 6f. mauve | 2·50 | 10 |
| 1464 | **289** | 6f.50 grey | £120 | 19·00 |
| 2189 | **289** | 7f. blue | 50 | 25 |
| 1466 | **289** | 7f.50 brown | £110 | 21·00 |
| 1467 | **289** | 8f. blue | 60 | 15 |
| 1468 | **289** | 8f.50 purple | 26·00 | 60 |
| 1469 | **289** | 9f. olive | £120 | 2·30 |
| 1470 | **289** | 12f. turquoise | 17·00 | 60 |
| 1471 | **289** | 30f. orange | 14·50 | 35 |

(b) 17½×22 mm.

| | | | |
|---|---|---|---|
| 1472 | 1f.50 black | 35 | 35 |
| 1473 | 2f.50 brown | 7·50 | 6·50 |
| 1474 | 3f. mauve | 25 | 10 |
| 1475 | 3f.50 green | 35 | 10 |
| 1476 | 4f.50 brown | 1·70 | 80 |

**290**

**1953.** European Child Welfare Fund.

| | | | | |
|---|---|---|---|---|
| 1482 | **290** | 80c.+20c. green | 5·75 | 3·50 |
| 1483 | **290** | 2f.50+1f. red | 35·00 | 23·00 |
| 1484 | **290** | 4f.+1f.50 blue | 37·00 | 26·00 |

**293** Ernest Malvoz

**1953.** Anti-tuberculosis and other Funds. As T 273 but dated "1953" and portraits as T 293.

| | | | | |
|---|---|---|---|---|
| 1507 | **273** | 20c.+5c. blue | 70 | 35 |
| 1508 | **273** | 80c.+20c. purple | 1·90 | 80 |
| 1509 | **273** | 1f.20+30c. brown | 3·00 | 1·20 |
| 1510 | **273** | 1f.50+50c. slate | 3·50 | 1·50 |
| 1511 | **293** | 2f.+75c. green | 4·25 | 2·00 |
| 1512 | - | 3f.+1f.50 red | 20·00 | 10·50 |
| 1513 | - | 4f.+2f. blue | 23·00 | 13·00 |
| 1514 | - | 8f.+4f. brown | 29·00 | 16·00 |

PORTRAITS—VERT: 3f. Carlo Forlanini. 4f. Albert Calmette. HORIZ: 8f. Robert Koch.

**1954.** Surch 20c and I-I-54 at top, 31-XII-54 at bottom and bars in between.

| | | | | |
|---|---|---|---|---|
| 1515 | **267** | 20c. on 65c. purple | 1·70 | 15 |
| 1516 | **267** | 20c. on 90c. blue | 1·70 | 15 |

See note below No. 480.

**296** King Albert Statue

**1954.** King Albert Memorial Fund.

| | | | | |
|---|---|---|---|---|
| 1520 | **296** | 2f.+50c. brown | 11·50 | 4·75 |
| 1521 | - | 4f.+2f. blue | 38·00 | 17·00 |
| 1522 | - | 9f.+4f.50 black | 31·00 | 17·00 |

DESIGNS—HORIZ: 4f. King Albert Memorial. VERT: 9f. Marche-les-Dames Rocks and medallion portrait.

**298** Monument **299** Breendonk Camp and Fort

**1954.** Political Prisoners' National Monument Fund.

| | | | | |
|---|---|---|---|---|
| 1531 | **298** | 2f.+1f. red | 27·00 | 24·00 |
| 1532 | **299** | 4f.+2f. brown | 55·00 | 26·00 |
| 1533 | - | 9f.+4f.50 green | 65·00 | 32·00 |

DESIGN—VERT: 9f. As Type **298** but viewed from different angle.

**300** Entrance to Beguinal House

**1954.** Beguinage of Bruges Restoration Fund.

| | | | | |
|---|---|---|---|---|
| 1534 | **300** | 80c.+20c. green | 1·20 | 60 |
| 1535 | - | 2f.+1f. red | 16·00 | 8·25 |
| 1536 | - | 4f.+2f. violet | 21·00 | 11·50 |
| 1537 | - | 7f.+3f.50 purple | 44·00 | 24·00 |
| 1538 | - | 8f.+4f. brown | 44·00 | 24·00 |
| 1539 | - | 9f.+4f.50 blue | 80·00 | 38·00 |

DESIGNS—HORIZ: 2f. River scene. VERT: 4f. Convent Buildings; 7f. Cloisters; 8f. Doorway; 9f. Statue of our Lady of the Vineyard (larger, 35×53 mm).

**302** Map of Europe and Rotary Symbol

**1954.** 50th Anniv of Rotary International and 5th Regional Conference, Ostend.

| | | | | |
|---|---|---|---|---|
| 1540 | **302** | 20c. red | 25 | 25 |
| 1541 | - | 80c. green | 35 | 25 |
| 1542 | - | 4f. blue | 1·70 | 35 |

DESIGNS: 80c. Mermaid, "Mercury" and Rotary symbol; 4f. Rotary symbol and hemispheres.

**303** Child **304** "The Blind Man and the Paralytic" (after Anto-Carte)

**1954.** Anti-T.B. and other Funds.

| | | | | |
|---|---|---|---|---|
| 1543 | **303** | 20c.+5c. green | 30 | 30 |
| 1544 | **303** | 80c.+20c. black | 85 | 35 |
| 1545 | **303** | 1f.20+30c. brown | 2·30 | 1·40 |
| 1546 | **303** | 1f.50+50c. violet | 4·75 | 2·50 |
| 1547 | **304** | 2f.+75c. red | 9·25 | 4·75 |
| 1548 | **304** | 4f.+1f. blue | 35·00 | 15·00 |

**305** Begonia and the Rabot

**1955.** Ghent Flower Show.

| | | | | |
|---|---|---|---|---|
| 1549 | **305** | 80c. red | 60 | 60 |
| 1550 | - | 2f.50 sepia | 10·50 | 3·00 |
| 1551 | - | 4f. lake | 6·00 | 80 |

DESIGNS—VERT: 2f.50, Azaleas and Chateau des Comtes; 4f. Orchid and the "Three Towers".

**306** "Homage to Charles V" (A. De Vriendt) **307** "Charles V" (Titian)

**1955.** Emperor Charles V Exhibition, Ghent.

| | | | | |
|---|---|---|---|---|
| 1552 | **306** | 20c. red | 25 | 25 |
| 1553 | **307** | 2f. green | 95 | 25 |
| 1554 | - | 4f. blue | 5·25 | 1·50 |

DESIGN—As Type **306**: 4f. "Abdication of Charles V" (L. Gallait).

**308** Emile Verhaeren (after C. Montald)

**1955.** Birth Centenary of Verhaeren (poet).

| | | | | |
|---|---|---|---|---|
| 1555 | **308** | 20c. black | 25 | 25 |

**309** "Textile Industry"

**1955.** 2nd Int Textile Exhibition, Brussels.

| | | | | |
|---|---|---|---|---|
| 1556 | **309** | 2f. purple | 1·30 | 30 |

**310** "The Foolish Virgin" (R. Wouters)

**1955.** 3rd Biennial Sculpture Exn, Antwerp.

| | | | | |
|---|---|---|---|---|
| 1557 | **310** | 1f.20 green | 1·20 | 40 |
| 1558 | **310** | 2f. violet | 2·00 | 30 |

**311** "The Departure of the Liege Volunteers in 1830" (Soubre)

**1955.** Liege Exn. 125th Anniv of 1830 Revolution.

| | | | | |
|---|---|---|---|---|
| 1559 | **311** | 20c. green | 30 | 30 |
| 1560 | **311** | 2f. brown | 85 | 30 |

**312** Ernest Solvay

**1955.** Cultural Fund. Scientists.

| | | | | |
|---|---|---|---|---|
| 1561 | **312** | 20c.+5c. brown | 35 | 35 |
| 1562 | - | 80c.+20c. violet | 1·40 | 50 |
| 1563 | - | 1f.20+30c. blue | 7·50 | 4·00 |
| 1564 | - | 2f.+50c. red | 7·00 | 3·75 |
| 1565 | - | 3f.+1f. green | 16·00 | 9·75 |
| 1566 | - | 4f.+2f. brown | 16·00 | 9·75 |

PORTRAITS—VERT: 80c. Jean-Jacques Dony. 2f. Leo H. Baekeland. 3f. Jean-Etienne Lenoir. HORIZ: 1f.20, Egide Walschaerts. 4f. Emile Fourcault and Emile Gobbe.

**313** "The Joys of Spring" (E. Canneel) **314** E. Holboll (Danish postal official)

**1955.** Anti-T.B. and other Funds.

| | | | | |
|---|---|---|---|---|
| 1567 | **313** | 20c.+5c. mauve | 35 | 35 |
| 1568 | **313** | 80c.+20c. green | 70 | 45 |
| 1569 | **313** | 1f.20+30c. brown | 3·25 | 1·20 |
| 1570 | **313** | 1f.50+50c. violet | 3·75 | 1·50 |
| 1571 | **314** | 2f.+50c. red | 12·00 | 5·75 |
| 1572 | - | 4f.+2f. blue | 30·00 | 14·50 |
| 1573 | - | 8f.+4f. sepia | 31·00 | 18·00 |

PORTRAITS—As Type **314**: 4f. J. D. Rockefeller (philanthropist). 8f. Sir R. W. Philip (physician).

**315** Blood Donors Emblem

**1956.** Blood Donors.

| | | | | |
|---|---|---|---|---|
| 1574 | **315** | 2f. red | 35 | 30 |

**316** Mozart when a Child

**317** Queen Elisabeth and Mozart Sonata

**1956.** Birth Bicentenary of Mozart. Inscr as in T 316.

| | | | | |
|---|---|---|---|---|
| 1575 | - | 80c.+20c. green | 60 | 30 |

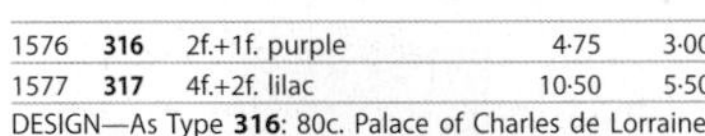

| | | | | |
|---|---|---|---|---|
| 1576 | **316** | 2f.+1f. purple | 4·75 | 3·00 |
| 1577 | **317** | 4f.+2f. lilac | 10·50 | 5·50 |

DESIGN—As Type **316**: 80c. Palace of Charles de Lorraine, Brussels.

**318**

**1956.** "Scaldis" Exhibitions in Tournai, Ghent and Antwerp.

| | | | | |
|---|---|---|---|---|
| 1578 | **318** | 2f. blue | 30 | 30 |

**319** Queen Elisabeth Medallion (Courtens)

**1956.** 80th Birthday of Queen Elisabeth and Foundation Fund.

| | | | | |
|---|---|---|---|---|
| 1579 | **319** | 80c.+20c. green | 60 | 40 |
| 1580 | **319** | 2f.+1f. lake | 4·75 | 2·40 |
| 1581 | **319** | 4f.+2f. sepia | 6·50 | 3·75 |

**320**

**1956.** Europa.

| | | | | |
|---|---|---|---|---|
| 1582 | **320** | 2f. green | 3·50 | 25 |
| 1583 | **320** | 4f. violet | 13·00 | 35 |

**321** Electric Train Type 122 and Railway Bridge

**1956.** Electrification of Brussels–Luxembourg Railway Line.

| | | | | |
|---|---|---|---|---|
| 1584 | **321** | 2f. blue | 30 | 25 |

**322** E. Anseele

**1956.** Birth Centenary of Anseele (statesman).

| | | | | |
|---|---|---|---|---|
| 1588 | **322** | 20c. purple | 25 | 25 |

**323** Medieval Ship **324** Weighing a Baby

**1956.** Anti-tuberculosis and other Funds.

| | | | | |
|---|---|---|---|---|
| 1589 | **323** | 20c.+5c. brown | 30 | 30 |
| 1590 | **323** | 80c.+20c. green | 60 | 40 |
| 1591 | **323** | 1f.20+30c. purple | 1·20 | 70 |
| 1592 | **323** | 1f.50+50c. slate | 1·50 | 95 |
| 1593 | **324** | 2f.+50c. green | 3·75 | 2·30 |
| 1594 | - | 4f.+2f. purple | 15·00 | 9·25 |
| 1595 | - | 8f.+4f. red | 17·00 | 11·50 |

DESIGNS—As Type **324**: HORIZ: 4f. X-ray examination. VERT: 8f. Convalescence and rehabilitation.

325 "Atomium" and Exhibition Emblem

1957. Brussels International Exhibition.

| | | | | |
|---|---|---|---|---|
| 1596 | 325 | 2f. red | 30 | 30 |
| 1597 | 325 | 2f.50 green | 35 | 30 |
| 1598 | 325 | 4f. violet | 70 | 25 |
| 1599 | 325 | 5f. purple | 1·60 | 70 |

327 Emperor Maximilian I, with Messenger

1957. Stamp Day.

| | | | | |
|---|---|---|---|---|
| 1603 | 327 | 2f. red | 40 | 30 |

328 Charles Plisnier and Albrecht Rodenbach (writers)

1957. Cultural Fund. Belgian Celebrities.

| | | | | |
|---|---|---|---|---|
| 1604 | 328 | 20c.+5c. violet | 30 | 30 |
| 1605 | - | 80c.+20c. brown | 40 | 30 |
| 1606 | - | 1f.20+30c. sepia | 95 | 70 |
| 1607 | - | 2f.+50c. red | 2·40 | 1·60 |
| 1608 | - | 3f.+1f. green | 3·50 | 2·30 |
| 1609 | - | 4f.+2f. blue | 4·00 | 3·00 |

DESIGNS: 80c. Professors Emiel Vliebergh and Maurice Wilmotte; 1f.20, Paul Pastur and Julius Hoste; 2f. Lodewijk de Raet and Jules Destree (politicians); 3f. Constantin Meunier and Constant Permeke (artists); 4f. Lieven Gevaert and Edouard Empain (industrialists).

329 Sikorsky S-58 Helicopter

1957. Conveyance of 100,000th Passenger by Belgian Helicopter Service.

| | | | | |
|---|---|---|---|---|
| 1610 | 329 | 4f. blue, green and grey | 95 | 45 |

330 Steamer entering Zeebrugge Harbour

1957. 50th Anniv of Completion of Zeebrugge Harbour.

| | | | | |
|---|---|---|---|---|
| 1611 | 330 | 2f. blue | 40 | 30 |

331 King Leopold I entering Brussels (after Simonau)

1957. 126th Anniv of Arrival of King Leopold I in Belgium.

| | | | | |
|---|---|---|---|---|
| 1612 | 331 | 20c. green | 30 | 30 |
| 1613 | - | 2f. mauve | 70 | 30 |

DESIGN—HORIZ: 2f. King Leopold I at frontier (after Wappers).

332 Scout and Guide Badges

1957. 50th Anniv of Boy Scout Movement and Birth Centenary of Lord Baden-Powell.

| | | | | |
|---|---|---|---|---|
| 1614 | 332 | 80c. brown | 30 | 30 |
| 1615 | - | 4f. green | 1·50 | 50 |

DESIGN—VERT: 4f. Lord Baden-Powell.

333 "Kneeling Woman" (after Lehmbruck)

1957. 4th Biennial Sculpture Exn, Antwerp.

| | | | | |
|---|---|---|---|---|
| 1616 | 333 | 2f.50 green | 1·20 | 60 |

334 "Agriculture and Industry"

1957. Europa.

| | | | | |
|---|---|---|---|---|
| 1617 | 334 | 2f. purple | 1·20 | 30 |
| 1618 | 334 | 4f. blue | 3·75 | 45 |

335 Sledge-dog Team

1957. Belgian Antarctic Expedition, 1957–58.

| | | | | |
|---|---|---|---|---|
| 1619 | 335 | 5f.+2f.50 orange, brown and grey | 4·00 | 3·00 |

MS1620 115×83 mm. Block of four of No. 1619 in new colours, brown, red and blue £200 £160

336 General Patton's Grave at Hamm

1957. General Patton Memorial Issue.

| | | | | |
|---|---|---|---|---|
| 1621 | 336 | 1f.+50c. black | 2·30 | 1·20 |
| 1622 | - | 2f.50+50c. green | 3·50 | 1·70 |
| 1623 | - | 3f.+1f. brown | 4·75 | 2·30 |
| 1624 | - | 5f.+2f.50 slate | 10·50 | 6·50 |
| 1625 | - | 6f.+3f. red | 14·00 | 9·25 |

DESIGNS—HORIZ: 2f.50, Patton Memorial project at Bastogne; 3f. Gen. Patton decorating Brig.-General A. MacAuliffe; 6f. (51×35½ mm) Tanks in action. VERT: 5f. General Patton.

337 Adolphe Max

1957. 18th Death Anniv of Burgomaster Adolphe Max (patriot).

| | | | | |
|---|---|---|---|---|
| 1626 | 337 | 2f.50+1f. blue | 1·50 | 65 |

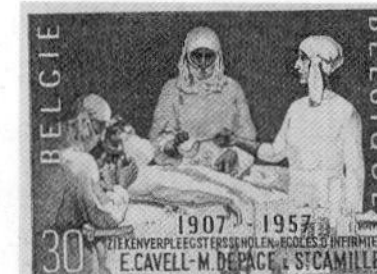
338 Queen Elisabeth with Doctors Depage and Debaisieux at a surgical operation

1957. 50th Anniv of "Edith Cavell-Marie Depage" and "St. Camille" Nursing Schools.

| | | | | |
|---|---|---|---|---|
| 1627 | 338 | 30c. red | 30 | 30 |

339 "Carnival Kings of Fosses" (Namur)

340 "Infanta Isabella with Crossbow" (Brussels)

1957. Anti-tuberculosis and other Funds. Provincial Legends.

| | | | | |
|---|---|---|---|---|
| 1628 | 339 | 30c.+20c. pur & yell | 30 | 30 |
| 1629 | - | 1f.+50c. sepia & blue | 35 | 35 |
| 1630 | - | 1f.50+50c. grey & red | 70 | 40 |
| 1631 | - | 2f.+1f. black & green | 1·00 | 45 |
| 1632 | 340 | 2f.50+1f. grn & mve | 2·30 | 1·70 |
| 1633 | - | 5f.+2f. black & blue | 4·75 | 3·75 |
| 1634 | - | 6f.+2f.50 lake & red | 5·75 | 4·75 |

DESIGNS: As Type 339—HORIZ: 1f.50, "St. Remacle and the Wolf" (Liege). VERT: 1f. "Op Signoorken" (Antwerp); 2f. "The Long Man and the Pea Soup" (Limburg). As Type 340—HORIZ: 6f. "Carnival Kings of Binche" (Hainaut). VERT: 5f. "The Virgin with the Inkwell" (West Flanders).

341 Posthorn and Postilion's Badges

1958. Postal Museum Day.

| | | | | |
|---|---|---|---|---|
| 1635 | 341 | 2f.50 grey | 30 | 30 |

342 Benelux Gate

1958. Inauguration of Brussels International Exhibition. Inscr as in T 342.

| | | | | |
|---|---|---|---|---|
| 1636 | 342 | 30c.+20c. sepia, brown and olive | 30 | 30 |
| 1637 | - | 1f.+50c. purple, slate and green | 30 | 30 |
| 1638 | - | 1f.50+50c. violet, turquoise and green | 35 | 30 |
| 1639 | - | 2f.50+1f. red, blue and vermilion | 35 | 30 |
| 1640 | - | 3f.+1f.50 blue, black and red | 85 | 60 |
| 1641 | - | 5f.+3f. mauve, black and blue | 1·90 | 1·50 |

DESIGNS—HORIZ: 1f. Civil Engineering Pavilion; 1f.50, Belgian Congo and Ruanda-Urundi Pavilion; 2f.50, "Belgium, 1900"; 3f. Atomium; 5f. (49×33½ mm) Telexpo Pavilion.

343 "Food and Agriculture Organization"

1958. United Nations Commemoration.

| | | | | |
|---|---|---|---|---|
| 1642 | | 50c. grey (postage) | 3·00 | 2·75 |
| 1643 | 343 | 1f. red | 35 | 35 |
| 1644 | - | 1f.50 blue | 40 | 35 |
| 1645 | - | 2f. purple | 60 | 50 |
| 1646 | - | 2f.50 green | 40 | 35 |
| 1647 | - | 3f. turquoise | 65 | 60 |
| 1648 | - | 5f. mauve | 40 | 35 |
| 1649 | - | 8f. brown | 75 | 60 |
| 1650 | - | 11f. lilac | 1·60 | 1·50 |
| 1651 | - | 20f. red | 3·25 | 2·75 |
| 1652 | - | 5f. blue (air) | 30 | 30 |
| 1653 | - | 6f. green | 35 | 30 |
| 1654 | - | 7f.50 violet | 45 | 35 |
| 1655 | - | 8f. sepia | 50 | 40 |
| 1656 | - | 9f. red | 60 | 45 |
| 1657 | - | 10f. brown | 70 | 50 |

DESIGNS (Emblems and symbols)—HORIZ: 50c. I.L.O. 2f.50, UNESCO 3f. U.N. Pavilion, Brussels Int Exn; 6f. World Meteorological Organization; 8f. (No. 1649), Int Monetary Fund; 8f. (No. 1655), General Agreement on Tariffs and Trade; 10f. Atomic Energy Agency; 11f. W.H.O. 20f. U.P.U. VERT: 1f.50, U.N.O. 2f. World Bank; 5f. (No. 1648), I.T.U. 5f. (No. 1652), I.C.A.O. 7f.50, Protection of Refugees; 9f. UNICEF.

344 Eugene Ysaye

1958. Birth Centenary of Ysaye (violinist).

| | | | | |
|---|---|---|---|---|
| 1658 | 344 | 30c. blue and red | 30 | 25 |

345 "Europa"

1958. Europa.

| | | | | |
|---|---|---|---|---|
| 1659 | 345 | 2f.50 blue and red | 3·50 | 25 |
| 1660 | 345 | 5f. red and blue | 7·75 | 35 |

346 "Marguerite Van Eyck" (after Jan Van Eyck)

1958. Cultural Relief Funds. Paintings as T 346. Frames in brown and yellow.

| | | | | |
|---|---|---|---|---|
| 1661 | 346 | 30c.+20c. myrtle | 60 | 30 |
| 1662 | - | 1f.+50c. lake | 85 | 60 |
| 1663 | - | 1f.+50+50c. blue | 1·50 | 85 |
| 1664 | - | 2f.50+1f. sepia | 3·00 | 2·00 |
| 1665 | - | 3f.+1f.50 red | 4·00 | 2·50 |
| 1666 | - | 5f.+3f. blue | 6·50 | 5·25 |

PAINTINGS—HORIZ: 1f. "Carrying the Cross" (Hieronymus Bosch). 3f. "The Rower" (James Ensor). VERT: 1f.50, "St. Donatien" (Jan Gossaert). 2f.50, Self-portrait (Lambert Lombard). 5f. "Henriette with the Large Hat" (Henri Evenepoel).

347 "Hoogstraten"

348 Pax—"Creche vivante"

1958. Anti-tuberculosis and other Funds. Provincial Legends.

| | | | | |
|---|---|---|---|---|
| 1667 | 347 | 40c.+10c. blue & grn | 30 | 30 |
| 1668 | - | 1f.+50c. sepia & yell | 35 | 35 |
| 1669 | - | 1f.50+50c. pur & grn | 65 | 35 |
| 1670 | - | 2f.+1f. brown & red | 70 | 45 |
| 1671 | 348 | 2f.50+1f. red and green | 2·10 | 1·20 |
| 1672 | - | 5f.+2f. purple & blue | 4·75 | 3·25 |
| 1673 | - | 6f.+2f. blue & red | 5·75 | 4·75 |

DESIGNS: As Type 347—VERT: 1f. "Jean de Nivelles"; 1f.50, "Jeu de Saint Evermare a Russon". HORIZ: 2f. "Les penitents de Furnes". As Type 348—HORIZ: "Marches de l'Entre Sambre et Meuse". VERT: 6f. "Pax—Vierge".

349 "Human Rights"

1958. 10th Anniv of Human Rights Declaration.

| | | | | |
|---|---|---|---|---|
| 1674 | 349 | 2f.50 slate | 40 | 25 |

**350** "Europe of the Heart"

**1959.** "Heart of Europe". Fund for Displaced Persons.

| | | | | |
|---|---|---|---|---|
| 1675 | **350** | 1f.+50c. purple | 45 | 35 |
| 1676 | **350** | 2f.50+1f. green | 1·00 | 80 |
| 1677 | **350** | 5f.+2f.50 brown | 1·70 | 1·20 |

**351** J. B. de Taxis taking the oath at the hands of Charles V (after J.-E. Van den Bussche)

**1959.** Stamp Day.

| | | | | |
|---|---|---|---|---|
| 1680 | **351** | 2f.50 green | 50 | 30 |

**352** N.A.T.O. Emblem

**1959.** 10th Anniv of N.A.T.O.

| | | | | |
|---|---|---|---|---|
| 1681 | **352** | 2f.50 blue and red | 45 | 30 |
| 1682 | **352** | 5f. blue and green | 1·30 | 60 |

On the 5f. value the French and Flemish inscriptions are transposed.

For similar design but inscr "1969", see No. 2112.

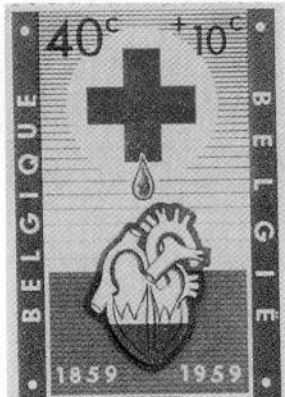

**353** "Blood Transfusion"

**354** J. H. Dunant and battle scene at Solferino, 1859

**1959.** Red Cross Commem. Inscr "1859 1959".

| | | | | |
|---|---|---|---|---|
| 1683 | **353** | 40c.+10c. red & grey | 35 | 35 |
| 1684 | **353** | 1f.+50c. red & sepia | 1·30 | 50 |
| 1685 | **353** | 1f.50+50c. red and lilac | 3·75 | 2·00 |
| 1686 | - | 2f.50+1f. red & grn | 4·25 | 2·30 |
| 1687 | - | 3f.+1f.50 red and blue | 7·75 | 4·75 |
| 1688 | **354** | 5f.+3f. red and sepia | 14·50 | 7·00 |

DESIGN—As Type **353**—HORIZ: 2f.50, 3f. Red Cross and broken sword ("Aid for the wounded").

**355** Philip the Good

**356** Arms of Philip the Good

**1959.** Royal Library of Belgium Fund. Mult.

| | | | | |
|---|---|---|---|---|
| 1689 | | 40c.+10c. Type **355** | 30 | 30 |
| 1690 | | 1f.+50c. Charles the Bold | 45 | 45 |
| 1691 | | 1f.50+50c. Maximillian of Austria | 1·60 | 1·00 |
| 1692 | | 2f.50+1f. Philip the Fair | 2·75 | 2·30 |
| 1693 | | 3f.+1f.50 Charles V | 5·00 | 3·50 |
| 1694 | | 5f.+3f. Type **356** | 6·75 | 5·00 |

**358** Town Hall, Oudenarde

**1959.** Oudenarde Town Hall Commem.

| | | | | |
|---|---|---|---|---|
| 1699 | **358** | 2f.50 purple | 40 | 30 |

**359** Pope Adrian VI

**1959.** 500th Birth Anniv of Pope Adrian VI.

| | | | | |
|---|---|---|---|---|
| 1700 | **359** | 2f.50 red | 30 | 30 |
| 1701 | **359** | 5f. blue | 40 | 30 |

**360** "Europa"

**1959.** Europa.

| | | | | |
|---|---|---|---|---|
| 1702 | **360** | 2f.50 red | 85 | 30 |
| 1703 | **360** | 5f. turquoise | 1·50 | 40 |

**361** Boeing 707

**1959.** Inauguration of Boeing 707 Airliners by SABENA.

| | | | | |
|---|---|---|---|---|
| 1704 | **361** | 6f. blue, grey and red | 2·10 | 75 |

**362** Antwerp fish (float)

**363** Stavelot "Blancs Moussis" (carnival figures)

**1959.** Anti-tuberculosis and other Funds. Carnival scenes.

| | | | | |
|---|---|---|---|---|
| 1705 | **362** | 40c.+10c. green, red and bistre | 30 | 30 |
| 1706 | - | 1f.+50c. green, violet and olive | 40 | 30 |
| 1707 | - | 2f.+50c. yellow, purple and brown | 50 | 35 |
| 1708 | **363** | 2f.50+1f. blue, violet and grey | 85 | 35 |
| 1709 | - | 3f.+1f. purple, yellow and grey | 2·30 | 1·20 |
| 1710 | - | 6f.+2f. blue, red and olive | 5·00 | 4·50 |
| 1711 | - | 7f.+3f. blk, yell, & bl | 6·50 | 5·25 |

DESIGNS—As Type **362**—HORIZ: 1f. Mons dragon (float); 2f. Eupen and Malmedy clowns in chariot. As Type **363**—VERT: 3f. Ypres jester. HORIZ: 6f. Holy Family; 7f. Madonna and child.

**364** Countess Alexandrine of Taxis (tapestry)

**1960.** Stamp Day.

| | | | | |
|---|---|---|---|---|
| 1712 | **364** | 3f. blue | 70 | 30 |

**365** Indian Azalea

**1960.** Ghent Flower Show. Inscr as in T 365.

| | | | | |
|---|---|---|---|---|
| 1713 | **365** | 40c. red and purple | 30 | 30 |
| 1714 | - | 3f. yellow, red and green | 70 | 30 |
| 1715 | - | 6f. red, green and blue | 1·70 | 60 |

FLOWERS: 3f. Begonia. 6f. Anthurium and bromelia.

**366** Refugee

**1960.** World Refugee Year. Inscr as in T 366.

| | | | | |
|---|---|---|---|---|
| 1716 | | 40c.+10c. purple | 30 | 30 |
| 1717 | **366** | 3f.+1f.50 sepia | 65 | 30 |
| 1718 | - | 6f.+3f. blue | 1·40 | 1·20 |
| **MS**1719 | | 121×93 mm. Nos. 1716/18 in new colours, violet, brown and red respectively | £100 | 85·00 |

DESIGNS: 40c. Child refugee; 6f. Woman refugee.

**367** "Labour" (after Meunier)

**1960.** 75th Anniv of Belgian Socialist Party. Inscr as in T 367.

| | | | | |
|---|---|---|---|---|
| 1720 | **367** | 40c. purple and red | 30 | 30 |
| 1721 | - | 3f. brown and red | 60 | 30 |

DESIGN—HORIZ: 3f. "Workers" (after Meunier).

**369** Parachutist on ground

**1960.** Parachuting. Designs bearing emblem of National Parachuting Club.

| | | | | |
|---|---|---|---|---|
| 1726 | | 40c.+10c. black & blue | 35 | 30 |
| 1727 | | 1f.+50c. black & blue | 1·90 | 85 |
| 1728 | | 2f.+50c. black, blue and green | 4·00 | 2·30 |
| 1729 | | 2f.50+1f. black, turquoise and green | 7·00 | 3·75 |
| 1730 | **369** | 3f.+1f. black, blue and green | 7·00 | 3·75 |
| 1731 | **369** | 6f.+2f. black, blue and green | 7·75 | 4·75 |

DESIGNS—HORIZ: 40c., 1f., Parachutists dropping from Douglas DC-4 aircraft. VERT: 2f., 2f.50, Parachutists descending.

**370** Ship's Officer and Helmsman

**1960.** Congo Independence.

| | | | | |
|---|---|---|---|---|
| 1732 | **370** | 10c. red | 30 | 30 |
| 1733 | - | 40c. red | 30 | 30 |
| 1734 | - | 1f. purple | 70 | 25 |
| 1735 | - | 2f. green | 70 | 30 |
| 1736 | - | 2f.50 blue | 1·30 | 30 |
| 1737 | - | 3f. blue | 1·30 | 35 |
| 1738 | - | 6f. violet | 3·25 | 80 |
| 1739 | - | 8f. brown | 10·50 | 6·75 |

DESIGNS—As Type **370**: 40c. Doctor and nurses with patient; 1f. Tree-planting; 2f. Sculptors; 2f.50, Sport (putting the shot); 3f. Broadcasting from studio. (52×35½ mm): 6f. Children with doll; 8f. Child with globe.

**371** Refugee Airlift

**1960.** Congo Refugees Relief Fund.

| | | | | |
|---|---|---|---|---|
| 1740 | **371** | 40c.+10c. turquoise | 30 | 30 |
| 1741 | - | 3f.+1f.50 red | 3·00 | 1·70 |
| 1742 | - | 6f.+3f. violet | 6·00 | 4·25 |

DESIGNS—As Type **371**: 3f. Mother and child. 35×51½ mm: 6f. Boeing 707 airplane spanning map of aircraft route.

**1960.** Surch.

| | | | | |
|---|---|---|---|---|
| 1743 | **267** | 15c. on 30c. green | 10 | 10 |
| 1744 | **267** | 15c. on 50c. blue | 10 | 10 |
| 1745 | **267** | 20c. on 30c. green | 10 | 10 |

**373** Conference Emblem

**1960.** 1st Anniv of E.P.T. Conference.

| | | | | |
|---|---|---|---|---|
| 1746 | **373** | 3f. lake | 1·00 | 35 |
| 1747 | **373** | 6f. green | 1·60 | 60 |

**374** Young Stamp Collectors

**1960.** "Philately for the Young" Propaganda.

| | | | | |
|---|---|---|---|---|
| 1748 | **374** | 40c. black and bistre | 30 | 30 |

**375** Pouring Milk for Child

**1960.** United Nations Children's Fund.

| | | | | |
|---|---|---|---|---|
| 1749 | **375** | 40c.+10c. yellow, green and brown | 30 | 30 |
| 1750 | - | 1f.+50c. red, blue and drab | 85 | 60 |
| 1751 | - | 2f.+50c. bistre, green and violet | 2·30 | 1·70 |
| 1752 | - | 2f.50+1f. sepia, blue and red | 2·50 | 1·70 |
| 1753 | - | 3f.+1f. violet, orange and turquoise | 3·25 | 2·00 |
| 1754 | - | 6f.+2f. brown, green and blue | 5·25 | 3·00 |

DESIGNS: 1f. Nurse embracing children; 2f. Child carrying clothes, and ambulance; 2f.50, Nurse weighing baby; 3f. Children with linked arms; 6f. Refugee worker and child.

**376** Frere Orban (founder)

**1960.** Centenary of Credit Communal (Co-operative Bank).

| | | | | |
|---|---|---|---|---|
| 1755 | **376** | 10c. brown and yellow | 30 | 30 |
| 1756 | **376** | 40c. brown and green | 35 | 30 |
| 1757 | **376** | 1f.50 brown and violet | 1·00 | 75 |
| 1758 | **376** | 3f. brown and red | 1·00 | 30 |

**377** Tapestry

**1960.** Anti-T.B. and other Funds. Arts and Crafts.

| | | | | |
|---|---|---|---|---|
| 1759 | **377** | 40c.+10c. ochre, brown and blue | 30 | 30 |
| 1760 | - | 1f.+50c. blue, brown and indigo | 95 | 85 |
| 1761 | - | 2f.+50c. green, black and brown | 1·70 | 1·20 |
| 1762 | - | 2f.50+1f. yellow and brown | 3·75 | 2·50 |
| 1763 | - | 3f.+1f. black, brown and blue | 4·25 | 3·00 |
| 1764 | - | 6f.+2f. lemon and black | 6·25 | 3·75 |

DESIGNS—VERT: 1f. Crystalware; 2f. Lace. HORIZ: 2f.50, Brassware; 3f. Diamond-cutting; 6f. Ceramics.

**378** King Baudouin and Queen Fabiola

**1960.** Royal Wedding.

| | | | | |
|---|---|---|---|---|
| 1765 | **378** | 40c. sepia and green | 35 | 30 |
| 1766 | **378** | 3f. sepia and purple | 1·00 | 30 |
| 1767 | **378** | 6f. sepia and blue | 2·75 | 35 |

**1961.** Surch in figs and 1961 at top, 1962 at bottom and bars in between.

| | | | | |
|---|---|---|---|---|
| 1768 | **267** | 15c. on 30c. green | 1·20 | 25 |
| 1769 | **267** | 20c. on 30c. green | 2·40 | 1·20 |

See note below No. 480.

**379** Nicolaus Rockox (after Van Dyck)

**1961.** 400th Birth Anniv of Nicolaus Rockox (Burgomaster of Antwerp).

| | | | | |
|---|---|---|---|---|
| 1770 | **379** | 3f. black, bistre & brn | 45 | 30 |

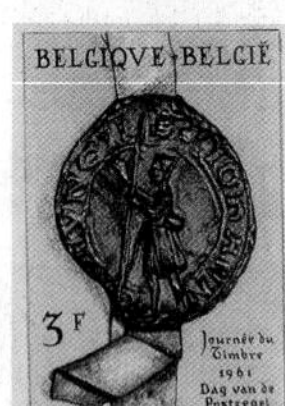

**380** Seal of Jan Bode

**1961.** Stamp Day.

| | | | | |
|---|---|---|---|---|
| 1771 | **380** | 3f. sepia and brown | 45 | 30 |

**381** K. Kats (playwright) and Father N. Pietkin (poet)

**1961.** Cultural Funds. Portrait in purple.

| | | | | |
|---|---|---|---|---|
| 1772 | | 40c.+10c. lake and pink | 60 | 35 |
| 1773 | | 1f.+50c. lake and brown | 2·50 | 1·40 |
| 1774 | | 2f.+50c. red and yellow | 4·50 | 3·50 |
| 1775 | | 2f.50+1f. myrtle and sage | 4·75 | 3·50 |
| 1776 | | 3f.+1f. blue and light blue | 5·00 | 3·50 |
| 1777 | | 6f.+2f. blue and lavender | 7·00 | 4·75 |

PORTRAITS: 40c. Type **381**. 1f. A. Mockel and J. F. Willems (writers). 2f. J. van Rijswijck and X. Neujean (politicians). 2f.50, J. Demarteau (journalist) and A. van de Perre (politician). 3f. J. David (litterateur) and A. du Bois (writer). 6f. H. Vieuxtemps (violinist) and W. de Mol (composer).

**382** White Rhinoceros

**1961.** Philanthropic Funds. Animals of Antwerp Zoo.

| | | | | |
|---|---|---|---|---|
| 1778 | | 40c.+10c. dp brown & brn | 35 | 35 |
| 1779 | | 1f.+50c. brown and green | 1·30 | 80 |
| 1780 | | 2f.+50c. sepia, red and black | 2·00 | 1·60 |
| 1781 | | 2f.50+1f. brown and red | 2·20 | 1·70 |
| 1782 | | 3f.+1f. brown and orange | 2·50 | 1·90 |
| 1783 | | 6f.+2f. ochre and blue | 3·25 | 2·30 |

ANIMALS—VERT: 40c. Type **382**; 1f. Wild horse and foal; 2f. Okapi. HORIZ: 2f.50, Giraffe; 3f. Lesser panda; 6f. Elk.

**383** Cardinal A.P. de Granville (first Archbishop)

**1961.** 400th Anniv of Archbishopric of Malines.

| | | | | |
|---|---|---|---|---|
| 1784 | **383** | 40c.+10c. brown, red and purple | 35 | 35 |
| 1785 | - | 3f.+1f.50 mult | 95 | 80 |
| 1786 | - | 6f.+3f. bistre, violet and purple | 1·60 | 1·50 |

DESIGNS: 3f. Cardinal's Arms; 6f. Symbols of Archbishopric and Malines.

**385** "Interparliamentary Union"

**1961.** 50th Interparliamentary Union Conference, Brussels.

| | | | | |
|---|---|---|---|---|
| 1791 | **385** | 3f. brown and turquoise | 70 | 30 |
| 1792 | **385** | 6f. purple and red | 1·00 | 60 |

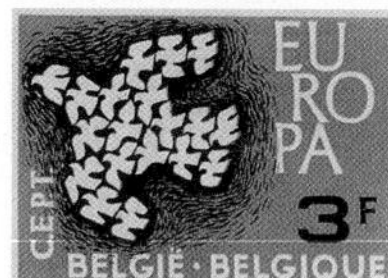

**386** Doves

**1961.** Europa.

| | | | | |
|---|---|---|---|---|
| 1793 | **386** | 3f. black and olive | 45 | 30 |
| 1794 | **386** | 6f. black and brown | 95 | 45 |

**387** Reactor BR 2, Mol

**1961.** Euratom Commemoration.

| | | | | |
|---|---|---|---|---|
| 1795 | **387** | 40c. green | 30 | 30 |
| 1796 | - | 3f. mauve | 35 | 30 |
| 1797 | - | 6f. blue | 50 | 45 |

DESIGNS—VERT: 3f. Heart of reactor BR 3, Mol. HORIZ: 6f. View of reactor BR 3, Mol.

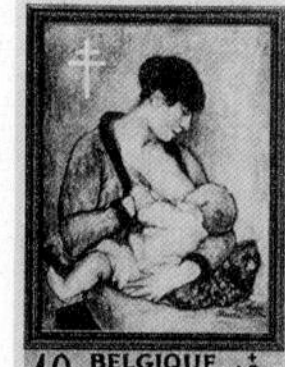

**388** "The Mother and Child" (after Paulus)

**1961.** Anti-T.B. and other Funds. Belgian paintings of mothers and children. Frames in gold.

| | | | | |
|---|---|---|---|---|
| 1798 | **388** | 40c.+10c. sepia | 30 | 30 |
| 1799 | - | 1f.+50c. blue | 75 | 70 |
| 1800 | - | 2f.+50c. red | 1·30 | 1·30 |
| 1801 | - | 2f.50+1f. lake | 1·40 | 1·30 |
| 1802 | - | 3f.+1f. violet | 1·30 | 1·20 |
| 1803 | - | 6f.+2f. myrtle | 1·90 | 1·60 |

PAINTINGS: 1f. "Maternal Love" (Navez). 2f. "Maternity" (Permeke). 2f.50, "The Virgin and the Child" (Van der Weyden). 3f. "The Virgin with the Apple" (Memling), 6f. "The Myosotis Virgin" (Rubens).

**389** Horta Museum

**1962.** Birth Cent of Victor Horta (architect).

| | | | | |
|---|---|---|---|---|
| 1804 | **389** | 3f. brown | 40 | 30 |

**390** Male Castle

**1962.** Cultural and Patriotic Funds. Buildings.

| | | | | |
|---|---|---|---|---|
| 1805 | **390** | 40c.+10c. green | 30 | 30 |
| 1806 | - | 90c.+10c. mauve | 35 | 35 |
| 1807 | - | 1f.+50c. lilac | 50 | 50 |
| 1808 | - | 2f.+50c. violet | 1·00 | 1·00 |
| 1809 | - | 2f.50+1f. brown | 1·40 | 1·40 |
| 1810 | - | 3f.+1f. turquoise | 1·50 | 1·50 |
| 1811 | - | 6f.+2f. red | 2·40 | 2·40 |

BUILDINGS—HORIZ: 90c. Royal Library, Brussels. 1f. Collegiate Church, Soignies. 6f. Ypres Halls. VERT: 1f. Notre-Dame Basilica, Tongres. 2f.50, Notre-Dame Church, Hanswijk, Malines. 3f. St. Denis-en-Broqueroie Abbey.

**391** 16th-Century Postilion

**1962.** Stamp Day.

| | | | | |
|---|---|---|---|---|
| 1812 | **391** | 3f. brown and green | 40 | 30 |

See also No. 1997.

**392** G. Mercator (after F. Hogenberg)

**1962.** 450th Birth Anniv of Mercator (geographer).

| | | | | |
|---|---|---|---|---|
| 1813 | **392** | 3f. sepia | 40 | 30 |

**393** Brother A. M. Gochet (scholar)

**1962.** Gochet and Triest Commemoration.

| | | | | |
|---|---|---|---|---|
| 1814 | **393** | 2f. blue | 30 | 30 |
| 1815 | - | 3f. brown | 35 | 30 |

PORTRAIT: 3f. Canon P.-J. Triest (benefactor of the aged).

**394** Guianan Cock of the Rock ("Coq de Roch, Rotshann")

**1962.** Philanthropic Funds. Birds of Antwerp Zoo. Birds, etc., in natural colours; colours of name panel and inscription given.

| | | | | |
|---|---|---|---|---|
| 1816 | **394** | 40c.+10c. blue | 35 | 35 |
| 1817 | - | 1f.+50c. blue and red | 60 | 60 |
| 1818 | - | 2f.+50c. mauve & blk | 1·00 | 95 |
| 1819 | - | 2f.50+1f. turq & red | 1·30 | 1·30 |
| 1820 | - | 3f.+1f. brown & grn | 1·70 | 1·60 |
| 1821 | - | 6f.+2f. blue and red | 2·00 | 1·90 |

BIRDS: 1f. Red lory ("Rode Lori, Lori Rouge"); 2f. Green turaco ("Touracou du Senegal, Senegal Toerakoe"); 2f.50, Keel-billed toucan ("Kortbek Toecan, Toucan a Bec Court"); 3f. Greater bird of paradise ("Grand Paradijsier, Grosse Paradisvogel"); 6f. Congo peafowl ("Kongo Pauw, Paon du Congo").

**395** Europa "Tree"

**1962.** Europa.

| | | | | |
|---|---|---|---|---|
| 1822 | **395** | 3f. black, yellow & red | 75 | 30 |
| 1823 | **395** | 6f. black, yellow & olive | 1·30 | 45 |

**396** "Captive Hands" (after sculpture by Ianchelivici)

**1962.** Concentration Camp Victims.

| | | | | |
|---|---|---|---|---|
| 1824 | **396** | 40c. blue and black | 30 | 30 |

**397** Reading Braille

**1962.** Handicapped Children Relief Funds.

| | | | | |
|---|---|---|---|---|
| 1825 | **397** | 40c.+10c. brown | 35 | 30 |
| 1826 | - | 1f.+50c. red | 60 | 60 |
| 1827 | - | 2f.+50c. mauve | 1·30 | 1·20 |
| 1828 | - | 2f.50+1f. green | 1·30 | 1·20 |
| 1829 | - | 3f.+1f. blue | 1·30 | 1·20 |
| 1830 | - | 6f.+2f. sepia | 1·60 | 1·50 |

DESIGNS—VERT: 1f. Girl solving puzzle; 2f.50, Crippled child with ball; 3f. Girl walking with crutches. HORIZ: 2f. Child with earphones; 6f. Crippled boys with football.

**398** "Adam" (after Michelangelo)

**1962.** "The Rights of Man".

| | | | | |
|---|---|---|---|---|
| 1831 | **398** | 3f. sepia and green | 35 | 30 |
| 1832 | **398** | 6f. sepia and brown | 60 | 40 |

**399** Queen Louise-Marie

**1962.** Anti-tuberculosis and other Funds. Belgian Queens in green and gold.

| | | | | |
|---|---|---|---|---|
| 1833 | | 40c.+10c. Type **399** | 30 | 30 |
| 1834 | | 40c.+10c. As T **399** but inscr "ML" | 30 | 30 |
| 1835 | | 1f.+50c. Marie-Henriette | 75 | 65 |
| 1836 | | 2f.+1f. Elisabeth | 1·50 | 1·40 |
| 1837 | | 3f.+1f.50 Astrid | 2·10 | 1·90 |
| 1838 | | 8f.+2f.50 Fabiola | 2·30 | 2·00 |

**400** Menin Gate, Ypres

**1962.** Ypres Millenary.

| | | | | |
|---|---|---|---|---|
| 1839 | **400** | 1f.+50c. multicoloured | 45 | 45 |
| **MS**1840 | | 113×137 mm. Block of eight | 7·00 | 7·00 |

**401** H. Pirenne

**1963.** Birth Cent of Henri Pirenne (historian).

| | | | | |
|---|---|---|---|---|
| 1841 | **401** | 3f. blue | 40 | 30 |

**402** "Peace Bell"

**1963.** Cultural Funds and Installation of "Peace Bell" in Koekelberg Basilica. Bell in yellow; "PAX" in black.

| | | | | |
|---|---|---|---|---|
| 1842 | **402** | 3f.+1f.50 green & bl | 1·90 | 1·90 |
| 1843 | **402** | 6f.+3f. chestnut & brn | 1·00 | 1·00 |
| **MS**1844 | | 82×116 mm. No. 1842 (block of four) | 9·25 | 9·25 |

**403** "The Sower" (after Brueghel)

**1963.** Freedom from Hunger.

| | | | | |
|---|---|---|---|---|
| 1845 | **403** | 2f.+1f. brown, black and green | 35 | 35 |
| 1846 | - | 3f.+1f. brown, black and purple | 40 | 40 |
| 1847 | - | 6f.+2f. yellow, black and brown | 70 | 70 |

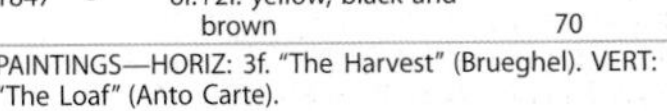

PAINTINGS—HORIZ: 3f. "The Harvest" (Brueghel). VERT: 6f. "The Loaf" (Anto Carte).

**404** 17th-century Duel

**1963.** 350th Anniv of Royal Guild and Knights of St. Michael.

| | | | | |
|---|---|---|---|---|
| 1848 | **404** | 1f. red and blue | 30 | 30 |
| 1849 | - | 3f. violet and green | 35 | 30 |
| 1850 | - | 6f. multicoloured | 80 | 45 |

DESIGNS—HORIZ: 3f. Modern fencing. VERT: 6f. Arms of the Guild.

**405** 19th-century Mail-coach

**1963.** Stamp Day.

| | | | | |
|---|---|---|---|---|
| 1851 | **405** | 3f. black and ochre | 35 | 30 |

See also No. 1998.

**406** Hotel des Postes, Paris, and Belgian 1c. Stamp of 1863

**1963.** Centenary of Paris Postal Conference.

| | | | | |
|---|---|---|---|---|
| 1852 | **406** | 6f. sepia, mauve & grn | 70 | 40 |

**407** Child in Wheatfield

**1963.** "8th May" Peace Movement.

| | | | | |
|---|---|---|---|---|
| 1853 | **407** | 3f. multicoloured | 40 | 30 |
| 1854 | **407** | 6f. multicoloured | 1·00 | 40 |

**408** "Transport"

**1963.** European Transport Ministers' Conference, Brussels.

| | | | | |
|---|---|---|---|---|
| 1855 | **408** | 6f. black and blue | 70 | 40 |

**409** Town Seal

**1963.** Int Union of Towns Congress, Brussels.

| | | | | |
|---|---|---|---|---|
| 1856 | **409** | 6f. multicoloured | 70 | 40 |

**410** Racing Cyclists

**1963.** Belgian Cycling Team's Participation in Olympic Games, Tokyo (1964).

| | | | | |
|---|---|---|---|---|
| 1857 | **410** | 1f.+50c. multicoloured | 30 | 30 |
| 1858 | - | 2f.+1f. multicoloured | 35 | 35 |
| 1859 | - | 3f.+1f.50 mult | 40 | 40 |
| 1860 | - | 6f.+3f. multicoloured | 70 | 70 |

DESIGNS—HORIZ: 2f. Group of cyclists; 3f. Cyclists rounding bend. VERT: 6f. Cyclists being paced by motorcyclists.

**411** Sud Aviation SE 210 Caravelle

**1963.** 40th Anniv of SABENA Airline.

| | | | | |
|---|---|---|---|---|
| 1861 | **411** | 3f. black and turquoise | 40 | 30 |

**412** "Co-operation"

**1963.** Europa.

| | | | | |
|---|---|---|---|---|
| 1862 | **412** | 3f. black, brown & red | 1·30 | 30 |
| 1863 | **412** | 6f. black, brown & blue | 2·40 | 45 |

No. 1863 is inscr with "6 F" on the left, "BELGIE" at foot and "BELGIQUE" on right.

**413** Princess Paola with Princess Astrid

**1963.** Centenary of Red Cross and Belgian Red Cross Fund. Cross in red.

| | | | | |
|---|---|---|---|---|
| 1864 | - | 40c.+10c. red & yell | 25 | 25 |
| 1865 | **413** | 1f.+50c. grey & yellow | 30 | 30 |
| 1866 | - | 2f.+50c. mauve & yell | 40 | 40 |
| 1867 | - | 2f.50+1f. blue & yell | 50 | 50 |
| 1868 | - | 3f.+1f. brown & yell | 80 | 80 |
| 1869 | - | 3f.+1f. bronze & yell | 2·50 | 2·50 |
| 1870 | - | 6f.+2f. green & yellow | 2·10 | 2·10 |

DESIGNS—As T **413**: 40c. Prince Philippe; 2f. Princess Astrid; 2f.50, Princess Paola; 6f. Prince Albert; 46×35 mm: 3f. (2), Prince Albert and family.

**414** J. Destree (writer)

**1963.** Jules Destree and H. Van de Velde Commems.

| | | | | |
|---|---|---|---|---|
| 1871 | **414** | 1f. purple | 25 | 25 |
| 1872 | - | 1f. green | 25 | 25 |

DESIGN: No. 1872, H. Van de Velde (architect).

**415** Bas-reliefs from Facade of Postal Cheques Office (after O. Jespars)

**1963.** 50th Anniv of Belgian Postal Cheques Office.

| | | | | |
|---|---|---|---|---|
| 1873 | **415** | 50c. black, blue & red | 25 | 25 |

**416** Balthasar Gerbier's Daughter

**1963.** T.B. Relief and Other Funds. Rubens's Drawings. Background buff; inscr in black: designs colour given.

| | | | | |
|---|---|---|---|---|
| 1874 | **416** | 50c.+10c. blue | 30 | 30 |
| 1875 | - | 1f.+40c. red | 35 | 35 |
| 1876 | - | 2f.+50c. violet | 40 | 40 |
| 1877 | - | 2f.50+1f. green | 80 | 80 |
| 1878 | - | 3f.+1f. brown | 70 | 70 |
| 1879 | - | 6f.+2f. black | 1·20 | 1·20 |

DRAWINGS—VERT: Rubens's children—1f. Nicolas (aged 2). 2f. Franz (aged 4). 2f.50, Nicolas (aged 6). 3f. Albert (aged 3). HORIZ: (46½×35½ mm): 6f. Infant Jesus, St. John and two angels.

**417** Dr. G. Hansen and Laboratory

**1964.** Leprosy Relief Campaign.

| | | | | |
|---|---|---|---|---|
| 1880 | **417** | 1f. black and brown | 30 | 30 |
| 1881 | - | 2f. brown and black | 30 | 30 |
| 1882 | - | 5f. black and brown | 60 | 45 |
| **MS**1883 | | 135×98 mm. Nos. 1880/2 (+4f.) | 3·50 | 3·50 |

DESIGNS: 2f. Leprosy hospital; 5f. Father Damien.

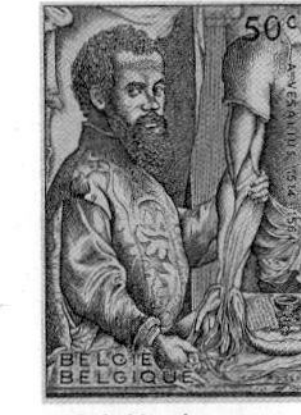


**418** A. Vesale (anatomist) with Model of Human Arm

**1964.** Belgian Celebrities.

| | | | | |
|---|---|---|---|---|
| 1884 | **418** | 50c. black and green | 30 | 30 |
| 1885 | - | 1f. black and green | 30 | 30 |
| 1886 | - | 2f. black and green | 30 | 30 |

DESIGNS—HORIZ: 1f. J. Boulvin (engineer) and internal combustion engine; 2f. H. Jaspar (statesman) and medallion.

**419** Postilion

**1964.** Stamp Day.

| | | | | |
|---|---|---|---|---|
| 1887 | **419** | 3f. grey | 35 | 30 |

**420** Admiral Lord Gambier and U.S. Ambassador J. Q. Adams after signing treaty (from painting by Sir A. Forestier)

**1964.** 150th Anniv of Signing of Treaty of Ghent.

| | | | | |
|---|---|---|---|---|
| 1888 | **420** | 6f.+3f. blue | 70 | 70 |

**421** Arms of Ostend

**1964.** Millenary of Ostend.

| | | | | |
|---|---|---|---|---|
| 1889 | **421** | 3f. multicoloured | 35 | 30 |

**422** Ida of Bure (Calvin's wife)

**1964.** "Protestantism in Belgium".

| | | | | |
|---|---|---|---|---|
| 1890 | - | 1f.+50c. blue | 30 | 30 |
| 1891 | **422** | 3f.+1f.50 red | 35 | 35 |
| 1892 | - | 6f.+3f. brown | 65 | 65 |

PORTRAITS: 1f. P. Marnix of St. Aldegonde (Burgomaster of Antwerp). 6f. J. Jordaens (painter).

**423** Globe, Hammer and Flame

**1964.** Centenary of Socialist International.

| No. | Type | Description | Mint | Used |
|---|---|---|---|---|
| 1893 | **423** | 50c. red and blue | 30 | 30 |
| 1894 | - | 1f. red and blue | 30 | 30 |
| 1895 | - | 2f. red and blue | 30 | 30 |

DESIGNS: 1f. "SI" on Globe; 2f. Flames.

**424** Infantryman of 1918

**1964.** 50th Anniv of German Invasion of Belgium. Multicoloured.

| No. | Description | Mint | Used |
|---|---|---|---|
| 1896 | 1f.+50c. Type **424** | 30 | 30 |
| 1897 | 2f.+1f. Colour sergeant of the Guides Regt, 1914 | 30 | 30 |
| 1898 | 3f.+1f.50 Trumpeter of the Grenadiers & Drummers of the Infantry and Carabiniers, 1914 | 45 | 45 |

**425** Soldier at Bastogne

**1964.** "Liberation–Resistance". Multicoloured.

| No. | Description | Mint | Used |
|---|---|---|---|
| 1899 | 3f.+1f. Type **425** | 35 | 35 |
| 1900 | 6f.+3f. Soldier at estuary of the Scheldt | 70 | 70 |

**426** Europa "Flower"

**1964.** Europa.

| No. | Type | Description | Mint | Used |
|---|---|---|---|---|
| 1901 | **426** | 3f. grey, red and green | 1·70 | 35 |
| 1902 | **426** | 6f. blue, green and red | 4·00 | 45 |

**427** "Philip the Good"

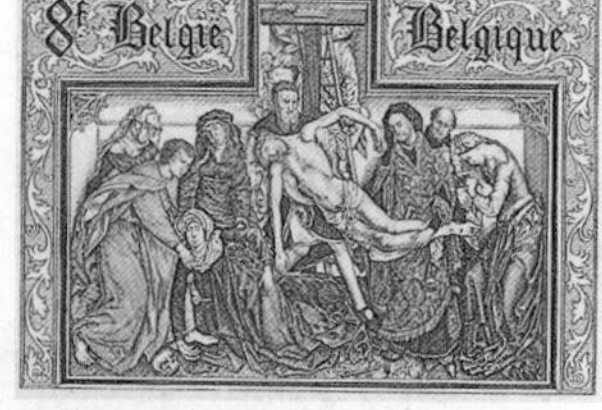

**428** "Descent from the Cross"

**1964.** Cultural Funds. 500th Death Anniv of R. van der Weyden. Two sheets each 153×114 mm showing paintings by Van der Weyden.

| No. | Description | Mint | Used |
|---|---|---|---|
| **MS**1903 | 1f. Type **427**; 2f. "Portrait of a Lady"; 3f. "The Man with the Arrow" (+8f.) | 5·00 | 5·00 |
| **MS**1904 | **428** 8f. (+8f.) brown | 4·75 | 4·75 |

**429** Pand Abbey, Ghent

**1964.** Pand Abbey Restoration Fund.

| No. | Type | Description | Mint | Used |
|---|---|---|---|---|
| 1905 | **429** | 2f.+1f. bl, turq & blk | 35 | 30 |
| 1906 | - | 3f.+1f. brown, blue and purple | 35 | 35 |

DESIGN: 3f. Waterside view of Abbey.

**430** King Baudouin, Queen Juliana and Grand Duchess Charlotte

**1964.** 20th Anniv of "BENELUX".

| No. | Type | Description | Mint | Used |
|---|---|---|---|---|
| 1907 | **430** | 3f. purple, blue and olive | 50 | 30 |

**431** "One of Charles I's Children" (Van Dyck)

**1964.** T.B. Relief and Other Funds. Paintings of Royalty.

| No. | Type | Description | Mint | Used |
|---|---|---|---|---|
| 1908 | **431** | 50c.+10c. purple | 30 | 30 |
| 1909 | - | 1f.+40c. red | 30 | 30 |
| 1910 | - | 2f.+1f. purple | 30 | 30 |
| 1911 | - | 3f.+1f. grey | 35 | 35 |
| 1912 | - | 4f.+2f. violet | 40 | 40 |
| 1913 | - | 6f.+3f. violet | 50 | 50 |

DESIGNS—VERT: 1f. "William of Orange and his fiancee, Marie" (Van Dyck); 2f. "Portrait of a Little Boy" (E. Quellin and Jan Fyt); 3f. "Alexander Farnese at the age of 12 Years" (A. Moro); 4f. "William II, Prince of Orange" (Van Dyck). HORIZ—LARGER (46×35 mm): 6f. "Two Children of Cornelis De Vos" (C. de Vos).

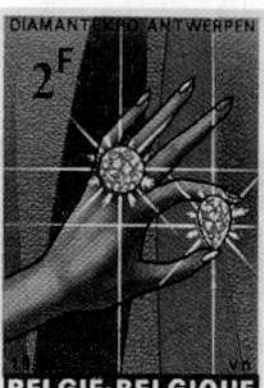

**432** "Diamonds"

**1965.** "Diamantexpo" (Diamonds Exn) Antwerp.

| No. | Type | Description | Mint | Used |
|---|---|---|---|---|
| 1914 | **432** | 2f. multicoloured | 30 | 25 |

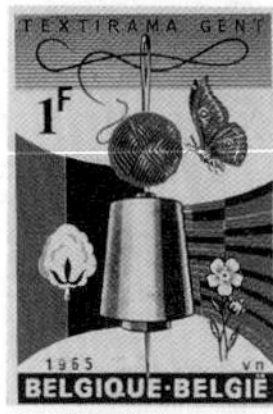

**433** "Textiles"

**1965.** "Textirama" (Textile Exn), Ghent.

| No. | Type | Description | Mint | Used |
|---|---|---|---|---|
| 1915 | **433** | 1f. black, red and blue | 30 | 25 |

**434** Vriesia

**1965.** Ghent Flower Show. Inscr "FLORALIES GANTOISES", etc. Multicoloured.

| No. | Description | Mint | Used |
|---|---|---|---|
| 1916 | 1f. Type **434** | 30 | 30 |
| 1917 | 2f. Echinocactus | 30 | 30 |
| 1918 | 3f. Stapelia | 30 | 30 |

**435** Paul Hymans

**1965.** Birth Cent of Paul Hymans (statesman).

| No. | Type | Description | Mint | Used |
|---|---|---|---|---|
| 1919 | **435** | 1f. violet | 30 | 30 |

**436** Rubens

**1965.** Centenary of General Savings and Pensions Funds. Painters.

| No. | Type | Description | Mint | Used |
|---|---|---|---|---|
| 1920 | **436** | 1f. sepia and mauve | 30 | 30 |
| 1921 | - | 2f. sepia and turquoise | 30 | 30 |
| 1922 | - | 3f. sepia and purple | 30 | 30 |
| 1923 | - | 6f. sepia and red | 60 | 35 |
| 1924 | - | 8f. sepia and blue | 75 | 60 |

PAINTERS: 2f. Franz Snyders. 3f. Adam van Noort. 6f. Anthony van Dyck. 8f. Jakob Jordaens.

**437** "Sir Rowland Hill with Young Collectors" (detail from mural by J. Van den Bussche)

**1965.** "Philately for the Young".

| No. | Type | Description | Mint | Used |
|---|---|---|---|---|
| 1925 | **437** | 50c. green | 30 | 30 |

**438** 19th-century Postmaster

**1965.** Stamp Day.

| No. | Type | Description | Mint | Used |
|---|---|---|---|---|
| 1926 | **438** | 3f. green | 30 | 30 |

**1965.** U.N.W.R.A. Commemoration. Sheet 123×89 mm. Nos. 1916/18 in new colours.

| No. | Description | Mint | Used |
|---|---|---|---|
| **MS**1927 | 1f., 2f., 3f. (+14f.) | 1·70 | 1·70 |

**439** Globe and Telephone

**1965.** Centenary of I.T.U.

| No. | Type | Description | Mint | Used |
|---|---|---|---|---|
| 1928 | **439** | 2f. black and purple | 30 | 30 |

**440** Handclasp

**1965.** 20th Anniv of Liberation of Prison Camps.

| No. | Type | Description | Mint | Used |
|---|---|---|---|---|
| 1929 | **440** | 50c.+50c. purple, black and bistre | 30 | 30 |
| 1930 | - | 1f.+50c. multicoloured | 30 | 30 |
| 1931 | - | 3f.+1f.50 black, purple and green | 40 | 35 |
| 1932 | - | 8f.+5f. multicoloured | 95 | 95 |

DESIGNS—VERT: 1f. Hand reaching for barbed wire. HORIZ: 3f. Tank entering prison camp; 8f. Rose within broken wall.

**441** Abbey Staircase

**1965.** Affligem Abbey.

| No. | Type | Description | Mint | Used |
|---|---|---|---|---|
| 1933 | **441** | 1f. blue | 30 | 30 |

**442** St. Jean Berchmans, Birthplace and Residence

**1965.** St. Jean Berchmans.

| No. | Type | Description | Mint | Used |
|---|---|---|---|---|
| 1934 | **442** | 2f. brown and purple | 30 | 30 |

**443** Toc H Lamp and Arms of Poperinge

**1965.** 50th Anniv of Founding of Toc H Movement at Talbot House, Poperinge.

| No. | Type | Description | Mint | Used |
|---|---|---|---|---|
| 1935 | **443** | 3f. multicoloured | 35 | 30 |

**444** Maison Stoclet, Brussels

**1965.** Josef Hoffman (architect) Commemoration.

| No. | Type | Description | Mint | Used |
|---|---|---|---|---|
| 1936 | **444** | 3f.+1f. grey and drab | 45 | 45 |
| 1937 | - | 6f.+3f. brown | 70 | 70 |
| 1938 | - | 8f.+4f. purple & drab | 1·00 | 1·00 |

DESIGNS—Maison Stoclet: VERT: 6f. Entrance hall. HORIZ: 8f. Rear of building.

**445** Tractor ploughing

**1965.** 75th Anniv of Boerenbond (Belgian Farmers' Association). Multicoloured.

| No. | Description | Mint | Used |
|---|---|---|---|
| 1939 | 50c. Type **445** | 30 | 30 |
| 1940 | 3f. Horse-drawn plough | 35 | 30 |

**446** Europa "Sprig"

**1965.** Europa.

| No. | Type | Description | Mint | Used |
|---|---|---|---|---|
| 1941 | **446** | 1f. black and pink | 40 | 30 |
| 1942 | **446** | 3f. black and green | 75 | 30 |

**447** Jackson's Chameleon

**1965.** Philanthropic Funds. Reptiles of Antwerp Zoo. Multicoloured.

| | | | | |
|---|---|---|---|---|
| 1943 | | 1f.+50c. Type **447** | 30 | 30 |
| 1944 | | 2f.+1f. Iguana | 30 | 30 |
| 1945 | | 3f.+1f.50 Nile lizard | 40 | 35 |
| 1946 | | 6f.+3f. Komodo lizard | 65 | 60 |
| **MS**1947 | | 118×98 mm. 8f.+4f. Soft-shelled turtle (larger) | 1·20 | 1·20 |

**448** J. Lebeau (after A. Schollaert)

**1965.** Death Cent of Joseph Lebeau (statesman).

| | | | | |
|---|---|---|---|---|
| 1948 | **448** | 1f. multicoloured | 30 | 30 |

**449** Leopold I (after 30c. and 1f. Stamps of 1865)

**1965.** Death Centenary of King Leopold I.

| | | | | |
|---|---|---|---|---|
| 1949 | **449** | 3f. sepia | 35 | 30 |
| 1950 | - | 6f. violet | 70 | 45 |

DESIGN: 6f. As 3f. but with different portrait frame.

**450** Huy

**1965.** Tourist Publicity. Multicoloured.

| | | | | |
|---|---|---|---|---|
| 1951 | | 50c. Type **450** | 10 | 10 |
| 1952 | | 50c. Hoeilaart (vert) | 10 | 10 |

See also Nos. 1995/6, 2025/6, 2083/4, 2102/3, 2123/4, 2159/60, 2240/1 and 2250/1.

**451** Guildhouse

**1965.** T.B. Relief and Other Funds. Public Buildings, Brussels.

| | | | | |
|---|---|---|---|---|
| 1953 | **451** | 50c.+10c. blue | 30 | 30 |
| 1954 | - | 1f.+40c. turquoise | 30 | 30 |
| 1955 | - | 2f.+1f. purple | 30 | 30 |
| 1956 | - | 3f.+1f.50 violet | 35 | 35 |
| 1957 | - | 10f.+4f.50 sepia and grey | 95 | 95 |

BUILDINGS—HORIZ: 1f. Brewers' House; 2f. Builders' House; 3f. House of the Dukes of Brabant. VERT: (24½×44½ mm): 10f. Tower of Town Hall.

**452** Queen Elisabeth (from medallion by A. Courtens)

**1965.** Queen Elisabeth Commem.

| | | | | |
|---|---|---|---|---|
| 1958 | **452** | 3f. black | 35 | 30 |

**453** "Peace on Earth"

**1966.** 75th Anniv of "Rerum Novarum" (papal encyclical). Multicoloured.

| | | | | |
|---|---|---|---|---|
| 1959 | | 50c. Type **453** | 30 | 30 |
| 1960 | | 1f. "Building for Tomorrow" (family and new building) | 30 | 30 |
| 1961 | | 3f. Arms of Pope Paul VI (vert 24½×45 mm) | 35 | 30 |

**1966.** Queen Elisabeth. Sheets 82×116 mm incorporating old designs, each with se-tenant label showing Crown over "E". (a) In brown, blue, gold and grey.

| | | | |
|---|---|---|---|
| **MS**1962 | 3f. T **125** and 3f. T **317** (sold at 20f.) | 1·60 | 1·60 |

(b) In brown, myrtle and green.

| | | | |
|---|---|---|---|
| **MS**1963 | 3f. T **160** and 3f. T **172** (sold at 20f.) | 1·60 | 1·60 |

**454** Rural Postman

**1966.** Stamp Day.

| | | | | |
|---|---|---|---|---|
| 1964 | **454** | 3f. black, lilac & buff | 35 | 30 |

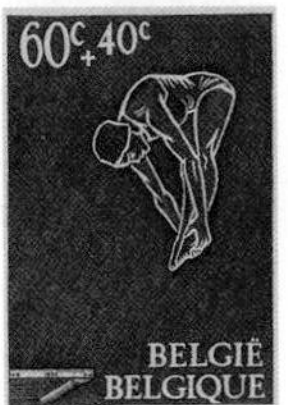

**455** High Diving

**1966.** Swimming.

| | | | | |
|---|---|---|---|---|
| 1965 | **455** | 60c.+40c. brown, green and blue | 30 | 30 |
| 1966 | - | 10f.+4f. brown, purple and green | 1·00 | 1·00 |

DESIGN: 10f. Diving from block.

**456** Iguanodon Fossil (Royal Institute of Natural Sciences)

**1966.** National Scientific Institutions.

| | | | | |
|---|---|---|---|---|
| 1967 | **456** | 1f. black and green | 30 | 30 |
| 1968 | - | 2f. black, orge & cream | 30 | 30 |
| 1969 | - | 2f. multicoloured | 30 | 30 |
| 1970 | - | 3f. multicoloured | 30 | 30 |
| 1971 | - | 3f. gold, black and red | 30 | 30 |
| 1972 | - | 6f. multicoloured | 40 | 30 |
| 1973 | - | 8f. multicoloured | 65 | 60 |

DESIGNS—HORIZ: No. 1968, Kasai head (Royal Central African Museum); No. 1969, Snow crystals (Royal Meteorological Institute). VERT: No. 1970, "Scholar" (Royal Library); No. 1971, Seal (General Archives); No. 1972, Arend-Roland comet and telescope (Royal Observatory); No. 1973, Satellite and rocket (Space Aeronomy Inst.).

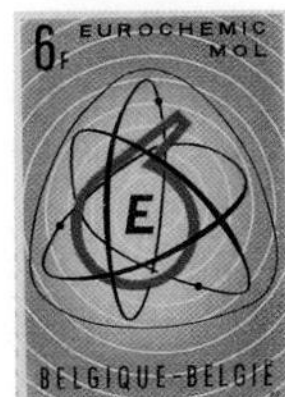

**457** Eurochemic Symbol

**1966.** European Chemical Plant, Mol.

| | | | | |
|---|---|---|---|---|
| 1974 | **457** | 6f. black, red and drab | 45 | 35 |

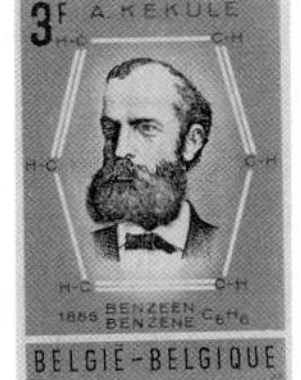

**458** A. Kekule

**1966.** Centenary of Professor August Kekule's Benzene Formula.

| | | | | |
|---|---|---|---|---|
| 1975 | **458** | 3f. brown, black & blue | 35 | 30 |

**1966.** 19th World I.P.T.T. Congress, Brussels. Optd XIXe CONGRES IPTT and emblem.

| | | | | |
|---|---|---|---|---|
| 1976 | **454** | 3f. black, lilac and buff | 35 | 30 |

**460** Rik Wouters (self-portrait)

**1966.** 50th Death Anniv of Rik Wouters (painter).

| | | | | |
|---|---|---|---|---|
| 1977 | **460** | 60c. multicoloured | 10 | 10 |

**461** Minorites Convent, Liege

**1966.** Cultural Series.

| | | | | |
|---|---|---|---|---|
| 1978 | **461** | 60c.+40c. purple, blue and brown | 30 | 30 |
| 1979 | - | 1f.+50c. blue, purple and turquoise | 30 | 30 |
| 1980 | - | 2f.+1f. red, purple and brown | 30 | 30 |
| 1981 | - | 10f.+4f.50 purple, turquoise and green | 85 | 85 |

DESIGNS: 1f. Val-Dieu Abbey, Aubel; 2f. Huy and town seal; 10f. Statue of Ambiorix and castle, Tongres.

**463** Europa "Ship"

**1966.** Europa.

| | | | | |
|---|---|---|---|---|
| 1989 | **463** | 3f. green | 45 | 25 |
| 1990 | **463** | 6f. purple | 1·00 | 40 |

**464** Surveying

**1966.** Antarctic Expeditions.

| | | | | |
|---|---|---|---|---|
| 1991 | **464** | 1f.+50c. green | 30 | 30 |
| 1992 | - | 3f.+1f.50 violet | 30 | 30 |
| 1993 | - | 6f.+3f. red | 60 | 60 |
| **MS**1994 | | 130×95 mm. 10f.+5f. multicoloured | 1·20 | 1·20 |

DESIGNS: 3f. Commander A. de Gerlache and "Belgica" (polar barque); 6f. "Magga Dan" (Antarctic supply ship) and meteorological operations. 52×35½ mm.—10f. "Magga Dan" and emperor penguins.

**1966.** Tourist Publicity. As T 450. Multicoloured.

| | | | | |
|---|---|---|---|---|
| 1995 | | 2f. Bouillon | 10 | 10 |
| 1996 | | 2f. Lier (vert) | 10 | 10 |

**1966.** 75th Anniv of Royal Federation of Belgian Philatelic Circles. Stamps similar to Nos. 1812 and 1851 but incorporating "1890 1996" and F.I.P. emblem.

| | | | | |
|---|---|---|---|---|
| 1997 | **391** | 60c. purple and green | 30 | 30 |
| 1998 | **405** | 3f. purple and ochre | 30 | 30 |

**466** Children with Hoops

**1966.** "Solidarity" (Child Welfare).

| | | | | |
|---|---|---|---|---|
| 1999 | - | 1f.+1f. black & pink | 30 | 30 |
| 2000 | - | 2f.+1f. black & green | 30 | 30 |
| 2001 | - | 3f.+1f.50 black & lav | 30 | 30 |
| 2002 | **466** | 6f.+3f. brown & flesh | 60 | 60 |
| 2003 | - | 8f.+3f.50 brown & grn | 70 | 70 |

DESIGNS—VERT: 1f. Boy with ball and dog; 2f. Girl with skipping-rope; 3f. Boy and girl blowing bubbles. HORIZ: 8f. Children and cat playing "Follow My Leader".

**467** Lions Emblem

**1967.** Lions International.

| | | | | |
|---|---|---|---|---|
| 2004 | **467** | 3f. sepia, blue and olive | 30 | 30 |
| 2005 | **467** | 6f. sepia, violet and green | 45 | 40 |

**468** Part of Cleuter Pistol

**1967.** Arms Museum, Liege.

| | | | | |
|---|---|---|---|---|
| 2006 | **468** | 2f. black, yellow & red | 30 | 30 |

**469** I.T.Y. Emblem

**1967.** International Tourist Year.

| | | | | |
|---|---|---|---|---|
| 2007 | **469** | 6f. blue, red and black | 60 | 35 |

**470** Young Refugee

**1967.** European Refugee Campaign Fund. Sheet 110×77 mm comprising T 470 and similar vert designs.

| | | | |
|---|---|---|---|
| **MS**2008 | 1f. black and yellow (Type **470**); 2f. black and blue; 3f. black and orange (sold at 20f.) | 1·20 | 1·20 |

**471** Woodland and Trientalis (flowers), Hautes Fagnes

**1967.** Nature Conservation. Multicoloured.

| | | | |
|---|---|---|---|
| 2009 | 1f. Type **471** | 30 | 30 |
| 2010 | 1f. Dunes and eryngium (flowers), Westhoek | 30 | 30 |

**472** Paul-Emile Janson (statesman)

**1967.** Janson Commemoration.

| | | | | |
|---|---|---|---|---|
| 2011 | **472** | 10f. blue | 85 | 60 |

**473** 19th-century Postman

**1967.** Stamp Day.

| | | | | |
|---|---|---|---|---|
| 2012 | **473** | 3f. purple and red | 30 | 30 |

**474** Cogwheels

**1967.** Europa.

| | | | | |
|---|---|---|---|---|
| 2013 | **474** | 3f. black, red and blue | 60 | 30 |
| 2014 | **474** | 6f. black, yellow & green | 1·20 | 45 |

**475** Flax Plant and Shuttle

**1967.** Belgian Linen Industry.

| | | | | |
|---|---|---|---|---|
| 2015 | **475** | 6f. multicoloured | 45 | 35 |

**476** Kursaal in 19th Century

**1967.** 700th Anniv of Ostend's Rank as Town.

| | | | | |
|---|---|---|---|---|
| 2016 | **476** | 2f. sepia, buff and blue | 30 | 30 |

**478** With F.I.T.C.E. Emblem

**1967.** European Telecommunications Day. "Stamp Day" design of 1967 incorporating F.I.T.C.E. emblem as T 478 in green.

| | | | | |
|---|---|---|---|---|
| 2021 | **478** | 10f. sepia and blue | 30 | 30 |

"F.I.T.C.E." "Federation des Ingenieurs des Tele-communications de la Communaute Europeenne."

**479** Robert Schuman (statesman)

**1967.** Charity.

| | | | | |
|---|---|---|---|---|
| 2022 | **479** | 2f.+1f. green | 30 | 30 |
| 2023 | - | 5f.+2f. brown, yellow and black | 50 | 50 |
| 2024 | - | 10f.+5f. multicoloured | 1·00 | 1·00 |

DESIGNS—HORIZ: 5f. Kongolo Memorial, Gentinnes (Congo Martyrs). VERT: 10f. "Colonial Brotherhood" emblem (Colonial Troops Memorial).

**1967.** Tourist Publicity. As T 450. Mult.

| | | | | |
|---|---|---|---|---|
| 2025 | | 1f. Ypres | 10 | 10 |
| 2026 | | 1f. Spontin | 10 | 10 |

**480** "Caesar Crossing the Rubicon" (Tournai Tapestry)

**1967.** Charles Plisnier and Lodewijk de Raet Foundations.

| | | | | |
|---|---|---|---|---|
| 2028 | **480** | 1f. multicoloured | 30 | 30 |
| 2029 | - | 1f. multicoloured | 30 | 30 |

DESIGN No. 2029, "Maximilian hunting boar" (Brussels tapestry).

**481** "Jester in Pulpit" (from Erasmus's "Praise of Folly")

**1967.** Cultural Series. "Erasmus and His Time".

| | | | |
|---|---|---|---|
| 2030 | 1f.+50c. multicoloured | 30 | 30 |
| 2031 | 2f.+1f. multicoloured | 30 | 30 |
| 2032 | 3f.+1f.50 multicoloured | 35 | 35 |
| 2033 | 5f.+2f. black, red & carmine | 60 | 60 |
| 2034 | 6f.+3f. multicoloured | 70 | 70 |

DESIGNS—VERT: 1f. Type **481**. 2f. "Jester declaiming" (from Erasmus' "Praise of Folly"); 3f. Erasmus; 6f. Pierre Gilles ("Aegidius" from painting by Metzijs). HORIZ: 5f. "Sir Thomas More's Family" (Holbein).

**482** "Princess Margaret of York" (from miniature)

**1967.** "British Week".

| | | | | |
|---|---|---|---|---|
| 2035 | **482** | 6f. multicoloured | 55 | 40 |

**483** Arms of Ghent University

**1967.** Universities of Ghent and Liege. Mult.

| | | | |
|---|---|---|---|
| 2036 | 3f. Type **483** | 30 | 30 |
| 2037 | 3f. Liege | 30 | 30 |

**484** Emblem of "Pro-Post" Association

**1967.** "Postphila" Stamp Exhibition, Brussels. Sheet 110×77 mm.

| | | | |
|---|---|---|---|
| **MS**2038 | **484** 10f.+5f. black, green, red and brown | 1·20 | 1·20 |

**485** Our Lady of Virga Jesse, Hasselt

**1967.** Christmas.

| | | | | |
|---|---|---|---|---|
| 2039 | **485** | 1f. blue | 30 | 30 |

**486** "Children's Games" (section of Brueghel's painting)

**1967.** "Solidarity".

| | | | | |
|---|---|---|---|---|
| 2040 | **486** | 1f.+50c. multicoloured | 30 | 30 |
| 2041 | - | 2f.+50c. multicoloured | 30 | 30 |
| 2042 | - | 3f.+1f. multicoloured | 40 | 30 |
| 2043 | - | 6f.+3f. multicoloured | 65 | 60 |
| 2044 | - | 10f.+4f. multicoloured | 1·00 | 90 |
| 2045 | - | 13f.+6f. multicoloured | 1·25 | 1·25 |

Nos. 2040/5 together form the complete painting.

**487** Worker in Protective Hand

**1968.** Industrial Safety Campaign.

| | | | | |
|---|---|---|---|---|
| 2046 | **487** | 3f. multicoloured | 30 | 30 |

**489** Army Postman (1916)

**1968.** Stamp Day.

| | | | | |
|---|---|---|---|---|
| 2068 | **489** | 3f. purple, brown & blue | 30 | 30 |

**490** Belgian 1c. "Small Lion" Stamp of 1866

**1968.** Cent of State Printing Works, Malines.

| | | | | |
|---|---|---|---|---|
| 2069 | **490** | 1f. olive | 30 | 30 |

**491** Grammont and Seal of Baudouin VI

**1968.** "Historical Series". Multicoloured.

| | | | |
|---|---|---|---|
| 2070 | 2f. Type **491** | 35 | 30 |
| 2071 | 3f. Theux-Franchimont Castle and battle emblems | 35 | 30 |
| 2072 | 6f. Archaeological discoveries, Spiennes | 55 | 35 |
| 2073 | 10f. Roman oil lamp and town crest, Wervik | 85 | 60 |

**492** Europa "Key"

**1968.** Europa.

| | | | | |
|---|---|---|---|---|
| 2074 | **492** | 3f. gold, black & green | 90 | 30 |
| 2075 | **492** | 6f. silver, black and red | 1·80 | 50 |

**493** Queen Elisabeth and Dr. Depage

**1968.** Belgian Red Cross Fund. Cross in red.

| | | | | |
|---|---|---|---|---|
| 2076 | **493** | 6f.+3f. sepia, black and green | 85 | 70 |
| 2077 | - | 10f.+5f. sepia, black and green | 1·20 | 1·10 |

DESIGN: 10f. Queen Fabiola and baby.

**494** Gymnastics

**1968.** Olympic Games, Mexico. Multicoloured.

| | | | |
|---|---|---|---|
| 2078 | 1f.+50c. Type **494** | 30 | 30 |
| 2079 | 2f.+1f. Weightlifting | 30 | 30 |
| 2080 | 3f.+1f.50 Hurdling | 35 | 30 |
| 2081 | 6f.+2f. Cycling | 70 | 60 |
| 2082 | 13f.+5f. Sailing (vert 24½×45 mm) | 1·30 | 1·20 |

Each design includes the Olympic "rings" and a Mexican cultural motif.

**1968.** Tourist Publicity. As Type 450.

| | | | |
|---|---|---|---|
| 2083 | 2f. multicoloured | 10 | 10 |
| 2084 | 2f. black, blue and green | 10 | 10 |

DESIGNS: No. 2083, Farm-house and windmill, Bokrijk; No. 2084, Bath-house and fountain, Spa.

**495** "Explosion"

**1968.** Belgian Disasters. Victims Fund. Mult.

| | | | |
|---|---|---|---|
| 2085 | 10f.+5f. Type **495** | 90 | 70 |
| 2086 | 12f.+5f. "Fire" | 1·20 | 1·10 |
| 2087 | 13f.+5f. "Typhoon" | 1·50 | 1·20 |

**496** St. Laurent Abbey, Liege

**1968.** "National Interest".

| | | | | |
|---|---|---|---|---|
| 2088 | **496** | 2f. black, bistre & blue | 30 | 30 |
| 2089 | - | 3f. brown, grey & lt brn | 35 | 30 |
| 2090 | - | 6f. black, blue & dp bl | 70 | 35 |
| 2091 | - | 10f. multicoloured | 95 | 40 |

DESIGNS: 3f. Church, Lissewege; 6f. "Mineral Seraing" and "Gand" (ore carriers), canal-lock, Zandvliet; 10f. Canal-lift, Ronquieres.

**497** Undulate Triggerfish

**1968.** "Solidarity" and 125th Anniv of Antwerp Zoo. Designs showing fish. Multicoloured.

2092 1f.+50c. Type **497** 25 25
2093 3f.+1f.50 Ear-spotted angelfish 35 30
2094 6f.+3f. Lionfish 70 55
2095 10f.+5f. Diagonal butterflyfish 1·10 85

**498** King Albert in Bruges (October, 1918)

**1968.** Patriotic Funds.

2096 **498** 1f.+50c. multicoloured 30 30
2097 - 3f.+1f.50 mult 35 30
2098 - 6f.+3f. multicoloured 60 55
2099 - 10f.+5f. multicoloured 90 85

DESIGNS—HORIZ: 3f. King Albert entering Brussels (November, 1918); 6f. King Albert in Liege (November, 1918). LARGER (46×35 mm): 10f. Tomb of the Unknown Soldier, Brussels.

**499** Lighted Candle

**1968.** Christmas.

2100 **499** 1f. multicoloured 30 30

**500** "Mineral Seraing" (ore carrier) in Ghent Canal

**1968.** Ghent Maritime Canal.

2101 **500** 6f. black brown, & blue 55 30

**1969.** Tourist Publicity. As Type 450.

2102 1f. black, blue & pur (vert) 10 10
2103 1f. black, olive and blue 10 10

DESIGNS. No. 2102, Town Hall, Louvain; No. 2103, Valley of the Ourthe.

**501** "Albert Magnis" (detail of wood carving by Quellin, Confessional, St. Paul's Church, Antwerp)

**1969.** St. Paul's Church, Antwerp, and Aulne Abbey Commemoration.

2104 **501** 2f. sepia 30 30
2105 - 3f. black and mauve 30 30

DESIGN: 3f. Aulne Abbey.

**502** "The Travellers" (sculpture, Archaeological Museum, Arlon)

**1969.** 2,000th Anniv of Arlon.

2106 **502** 2f. purple 30 30

**503** Broodjes Chapel, Antwerp

**1969.** "150 Years of Public Education in Antwerp".

2107 **503** 3f. black and grey 30 30

**504** Mail Train

**1969.** Stamp Day.

2108 **504** 3f. multicoloured 30 30

**505** Colonnade

**1969.** Europa.

2109 **505** 3f. multicoloured 50 30
2110 **505** 6f. multicoloured 85 35

**506** "The painter and the Amateur" (detail, Brueghel)

**1969.** "Postphila 1969" Stamp Exhibition, Brussels. Sheet 91×124 mm.

**MS**2111 **506** 10f.+5f. brown 1·40 1·20

**507** NATO Emblem

**1969.** 20th Anniv of N.A.T.O.

2112 **507** 6f. blue and brown 55 40

**508** "The Builders" (F. Leger)

**1969.** 50th Anniv of I.L.O.

2113 **508** 3f. multicoloured 35 30

**509** "Houses" (I. Dimitrova)

**1969.** UNICEF "Philanthropy" Funds. Mult.

2114 1f.+50c. Type **509** 30 30
2115 3f.+1f.50 "My Art" (C. Patric) 35 30
2116 6f.+3f. "In the Sun" (H. Rejchlova) 70 60
2117 10f.+5f. "Out for a Walk" (P. Sporn) (horiz) 1·10 85

**510** Racing Cyclist

**1969.** World Championship Cycle Races, Zolder.

2118 **510** 6f. multicoloured 60 30

**511** Mgr. V. Scheppers

**1969.** Monseigneur Victor Scheppers (founder of "Brothers of Mechlin") Commemoration.

2119 **511** 6f.+3f. purple 85 60

**512** National Colours

**1969.** 25th Anniv of BENELUX Customs Union.

2120 **512** 3f. multicoloured 35 30

**513** Pascali Rose and Annevoie Gardens

**1969.** Flowers and Gardens. Multicoloured.

2121 2f. Type **513** 25 30
2122 2f. Begonia and Lochristi Gardens 30 30

**1969.** Tourist Publicity. As Type 450.

2123 2f. brown, red and blue 25 10
2124 2f. black, green and blue 25 10

DESIGNS: No. 2123, Veurne Furnes; No. 2124, Vielsalm.

**514** "Feats of Arms" from "History of Alexander the Great" (Tournai, 15th century)

**1969.** "Cultural Works" Tapestries. Mult.

2125 1f.+50c. Type **514** 30 30
2126 3f.+1f.50 "The Violinist" from "Festival" (David Teniers II, Oudenarde, c.1700) 50 40
2127 10f.+4f. "The Paralytic", from "The Acts of the Apostles" (Brussels, c.1517) 1·20 1·10

**515** Astronauts and Location of Moon Landing

**1969.** 1st Man on the Moon.

2128 **515** 6f. sepia 50 35
**MS**2129 95×130 mm. 20f.+10f. blue 3·50 3·00

DESIGN: **MS**2129 is as T **515**, but in vert format.

**516** Wounded Soldier

**1969.** 50th Anniv of National War Invalids Works (O.N.I.G.).

2130 **516** 1f. green 30 30

**517** "The Postman" (Daniella Sainteney)

**1969.** "Philately for the Young".

2131 **517** 1f. multicoloured 30 30

**518** John F. Kennedy Motorway Tunnel, Antwerp

**1969.** Completion of Belgian Road-works. Mult.

2132 3f. Type **518** 35 30
2133 6f. Loncin flyover, Wallonie motorway 55 50

**519** Count H. Carton de Wiart (from painting by G. Geleyn)

**1969.** Birth Centenary of Count Henry Carton de Wiart (statesman).

2134 **519** 6f. sepia 65 50

**520** "Barbu d'Anvers" (Cockerel)

**1969.** "The Poultry-yard" (poultry-breeding).

| | | | | |
|---|---|---|---|---|
| 2135 | **520** | 10f.+5f. multicoloured | 1·30 | 1·10 |

**521** "Le Denombrement de Bethleem" (detail, Brueghel)

**1969.** Christmas.

| | | | | |
|---|---|---|---|---|
| 2136 | **521** | 1f.50 multicoloured | 30 | 30 |

**522** Emblem, "Coin" and Machinery

**1969.** 50th Anniv of National Credit Society (S.N.C.I.).

| | | | | |
|---|---|---|---|---|
| 2137 | **522** | 3f.50 brown and blue | 35 | 30 |

**523** Window, St. Waudru Church, Mons

**1969.** "Solidarity". Musicians in Stained-glass Windows. Multicoloured.

| | | | |
|---|---|---|---|
| 2138 | 1f.50+50c. Type **523** | 30 | 30 |
| 2139 | 3f.50+1f.50 s-Herenelderen Church | 35 | 30 |
| 2140 | 7f.+3f. St. Jacques Church, Liege | 80 | 70 |
| 2141 | 9f.+4f. Royal Museum of Art and History, Brussels | 1·20 | 1·10 |

No. 2141 is larger, 36×52 mm.

**524** Camellias

**1970.** Ghent Flower Show. Multicoloured.

| | | | |
|---|---|---|---|
| 2142 | 1f.50 Type **524** | 30 | 30 |
| 2143 | 2f.50 Water-lily | 30 | 30 |
| 2144 | 3f.50 Azaleas | 35 | 30 |
| **MS**2145 | 122×92 mm. Nos. 2142/4 in slightly different shades | 2·40 | 2·20 |

**525** Beech Tree in National Botanical Gardens

**1970.** Nature Conservation Year. Multicoloured.

| | | | |
|---|---|---|---|
| 2146 | 3f.50 Type **525** | 30 | 30 |
| 2147 | 7f. Birch | 60 | 35 |

**526** Young "Postman"

**1970.** "Philately for the Young".

| | | | | |
|---|---|---|---|---|
| 2148 | **526** | 1f.50 multicoloured | 30 | 30 |

**527** New U.P.U. Headquarters Building

**1970.** New U.P.U. Headquarters Building.

| | | | | |
|---|---|---|---|---|
| 2149 | **527** | 3f.50 green | 35 | 30 |

**528** "Flaming Sun"

**1970.** Europa.

| | | | | |
|---|---|---|---|---|
| 2150 | **528** | 3f.50 cream, blk & lake | 80 | 30 |
| 2151 | **528** | 7f. flesh, black and blue | 1·20 | 4·75 |

**529** Open-air Museum, Bokrijk

**1970.** Cultural Works. Multicoloured.

| | | | |
|---|---|---|---|
| 2152 | 1f.50+50c. Type **529** | 30 | 30 |
| 2153 | 3f.50+1f.50 Relay Post-house, Courcelles | 30 | 30 |
| 2154 | 7f.+3f. "The Reaper of Trevires" (bas-relief, Virton) | 65 | 60 |
| 2155 | 9f.+4f. Open-air Museum, Middelheim, (Antwerp) | 90 | 85 |

**530** Clock-tower, Virton

**1970.** Historic Towns of Virton and Zelzate.

| | | | | |
|---|---|---|---|---|
| 2156 | **530** | 2f.50 violet and ochre | 30 | 30 |
| 2157 | - | 2f.50 black and blue | 30 | 30 |

DESIGN—HORIZ: No. 2157, "Skaustand" (freighter), canal bridge, Zelzate.

**531** Co-operative Alliance Emblem

**1970.** 75th Anniv of Int Co-operative Alliance.

| | | | | |
|---|---|---|---|---|
| 2158 | **531** | 7f. black and orange | 60 | 30 |

**1970.** Tourist Publicity, As Type 450.

| | | | |
|---|---|---|---|
| 2159 | 1f.50 green, blue and black | 20 | 20 |
| 2160 | 1f.50 buff, blue & deep blue | 20 | 20 |

DESIGNS—HORIZ: No. 2159, Kasterlee. VERT: No. 2160, Nivelles.

**532** Allegory of Resistance Movements

**1970.** 25th Anniv of Prisoner of War and Concentration Camps Liberation.

| | | | | |
|---|---|---|---|---|
| 2161 | **532** | 3f.50+1f.50 black, red and green | 40 | 30 |
| 2162 | - | 7f.+3f. black, red and mauve | 80 | 60 |

DESIGN: 7f. Similar to Type **532**, but inscr "LIBERATION DES CAMPS", etc.

**533** King Baudouin

**1970.** King Baudouin's 40th Birthday.

| | | | | |
|---|---|---|---|---|
| 2163 | **533** | 3f.50 brown | 30 | 10 |

See also Nos. 2207/23c and 2335/9b.

**534** Fair Emblem

**1970.** 25th International Ghent Fair.

| | | | | |
|---|---|---|---|---|
| 2164 | **534** | 1f.50 multicoloured | 30 | 30 |

**535** U.N. Headquarters, New York

**1970.** 25th Anniv of United Nations.

| | | | | |
|---|---|---|---|---|
| 2165 | **535** | 7f. blue and black | 60 | 35 |

**536** Queen Fabiola

**1970.** Queen Fabiola Foundation.

| | | | | |
|---|---|---|---|---|
| 2166 | **536** | 3f.50 black and blue | 30 | 30 |

**537** Angler's Rod and Reel

**1970.** Sports. Multicoloured.

| | | | |
|---|---|---|---|
| 2167 | 3f.50+1f.50 Type **537** | 35 | 35 |
| 2168 | 9f.+4f. Hockey stick and ball (vert) | 85 | 70 |

**538** Belgian 8c. Stamp of 1870

**1970.** "Belgica 72" Stamp Exhibition, Brussels (1st issue).

| | | | |
|---|---|---|---|
| **MS**2169 | 1f.50+50c. violet and black; 3f.50+1f.50 lilac and black; 9f.+4f. brown and black | 4·25 | 3·50 |

DESIGNS: 3f.50, Belgian 1f. stamp of 1870; 9f. Belgian 5f. stamp of 1870.

**539** "The Mason" (sculpture by G. Minne)

**1970.** 50th Anniv of National Housing Society.

| | | | | |
|---|---|---|---|---|
| 2170 | **539** | 3f.50 brown & yell | 30 | 30 |

**540** Man, Woman and Hillside Town

**1970.** 25th Anniv of Belgian Social Security.

| | | | | |
|---|---|---|---|---|
| 2171 | **540** | 2f.50 multicoloured | 30 | 30 |

**541** "Madonna and Child" (Jan Gossaert)

**1970.** Christmas.

| | | | | |
|---|---|---|---|---|
| 2172 | **541** | 1f.50 brown | 30 | 30 |

**542** C. Huysmans (statesman)

**1970.** Cultural Works. Famous Belgians.

| | | | | |
|---|---|---|---|---|
| 2173 | **542** | 1f.50+50c. brown and red | 30 | 30 |
| 2174 | - | 3f.50+1f.50 brown and purple | 30 | 30 |
| 2175 | - | 7f.+3f. brown & green | 65 | 60 |
| 2176 | - | 9f.+4f. brown & blue | 1·90 | 1·80 |

PORTRAITS: 3f.50, Cardinal J. Cardijn. 7f. Maria Baers (Catholic social worker). 9f. P. Pastur (social reformer).

**543** Arms of Eupen, Malmedy and St. Vith

**1970.** 50th Anniv of Annexation of Eupen, Malmedy and St. Vith.

| | | | | |
|---|---|---|---|---|
| 2177 | **543** | 7f. brown and sepia | 50 | 35 |

**544** "The Uneasy Town" (detail, Paul Delvaux)

**1970.** "Solidarity". Paintings. Multicoloured.

| | | | |
|---|---|---|---|
| 2178 | 3f.50+1f.50 Type **544** | 35 | 35 |
| 2179 | 7f.+3f. "The Memory" (Rene Magritte) | 35 | 60 |

**545** Telephone

**1971.** Inaug of Automatic Telephone Service.
2183 **545** 1f.50 multicoloured 30 30

**546** "Auto" Car

**1971.** 50th Brussels Motor Show.
2184 **546** 2f.50 black and red 30 30

**547** Touring Club Badge

**1971.** 75th Anniv of Royal Touring Club of Belgium.
2185 **547** 3f.50 gold, red & blue 30 30

**548** Tournai Cathedral

**1971.** 800th Anniv of Tournai Cathedral.
2186 **548** 7f. blue 50 40

**549** "The Letter-box" (T. Lobrichon)

**1971.** "Philately for the Young".
2187 **549** 1f.50 brown 30 30


**550** Notre-Dame Abbey, Marche-les-Dames

**1971.** Cultural Works.
2190 **550** 3f.50+1f.50 black, green and brown 35 30
2191 - 7f.+3f. black, red and yellow 70 65

DESIGN: 7f. Convent, Turnhout.

**552** King Albert I, Jules Destree and Academy

**1971.** 50th Anniv of Royal Academy of French Language and Literature.
2201 **552** 7f. black and grey 30 10

**553** Postman of 1855 (from lithograph, J. Thiriar)

**1971.** Stamp Day.
2202 **553** 3f.50 multicoloured 30 30

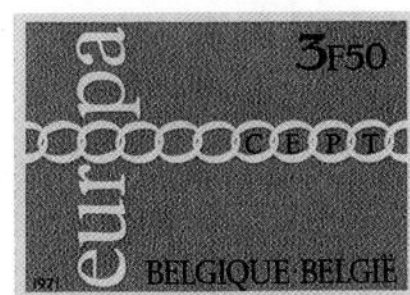

**554** Europa Chain

**1971.** Europa.
2203 **554** 3f.50 brown and black 90 30
2204 **554** 7f. green and black 1·50 50

**555** Satellite Earth Station

**1971.** World Telecommunications Day.
2205 **555** 7f. multicoloured 60 50

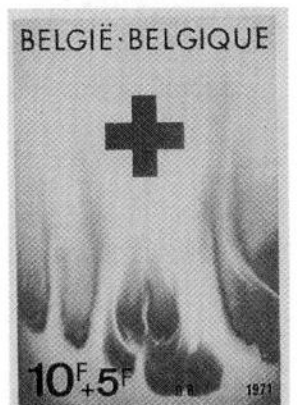

**556** Red Cross

**1971.** Belgian Red Cross.
2206 **556** 10f.+5f. red & black 1·00 70

**1971.** As T 533, but without dates.

| | | | |
|---|---|---|---|
| 2207 | 1f.75 green | 70 | 60 |
| 2208 | 2f.25 green | 30 | 10 |
| 2208a | 2f.50 green | 25 | 10 |
| 2209 | 3f. green | 30 | 10 |
| 2209a | 3f.25 plum | 30 | 25 |
| 2210 | 3f.50 brown | 50 | 10 |
| 2211 | 4f. blue | 40 | 10 |
| 2212 | 4f.50 purple | 95 | 10 |
| 2212a | 4f.50 blue | 40 | 10 |
| 2213 | 5f. violet | 50 | 10 |
| 2214 | 6f. red | 50 | 10 |
| 2214b | 6f.50 violet | 50 | 10 |
| 2215 | 7f. red | 65 | 10 |
| 2215ba | 7f.50 mauve | 40 | 10 |
| 2216a | 8f. black | 70 | 10 |
| 2217 | 9f. sepia | 95 | 10 |
| 2217a | 9f. brown | 90 | 10 |
| 2218a | 10f. mauve | 70 | 10 |
| 2218b | 11f. sepia | 1·00 | 10 |
| 2219 | 12f. blue | 3·00 | 30 |
| 2219b | 13f. blue | 1·20 | 10 |
| 2219c | 14f. green | 1·40 | 10 |
| 2220 | 15f. violet | 1·20 | 10 |
| 2220b | 16f. green | 2·10 | 10 |
| 2220c | 17f. purple | 1·40 | 10 |
| 2221 | 18f. blue | 1·40 | 10 |
| 2221a | 18f. turquoise | 2·10 | 25 |
| 2222 | 20f. blue | 1·60 | 10 |
| 2222b | 22f. black | 2·10 | 1·80 |
| 2222c | 22f. turquoise | 1·90 | 50 |
| 2222d | 25f. purple | 2·10 | 10 |
| 2223a | 30f. orange | 2·40 | 10 |
| 2223b | 35f. turquoise | 4·00 | 30 |
| 2223c | 40f. blue | 4·75 | 30 |
| 2223d | 45f. brown | 5·75 | 55 |

See also Nos. 2335/9.

**557** Scientist, Adelie Penguins and "Erika Dan" (polar vessel)

**1971.** 10th Anniv of Antarctic Treaty.
2230 **557** 10f. multicoloured 80 60

**558** "The Discus thrower" and Munich Cathedral

**1971.** Olympic Games, Munich (1972) Publicity.
2231 **558** 7f.+3f. black & blue 80 70

**559** G. Hubin (statesman)

**1971.** Georges Hubin Commemoration.
2232 **559** 1f.50 violet and black 30 30

**560** Notre-Dame Abbey, Orval

**1971.** 900th Anniv of Notre-Dame Abbey, Orval.
2233 **560** 2f.50 brown 30 30

**561** Processional Giants, Ath

**1971.** Historic Towns.
2234 **561** 2f.50 multicoloured 30 30
2235 - 2f.50 brown 30 30

DESIGN—HORIZ: (46×35 mm): No. 2235, View of Ghent.

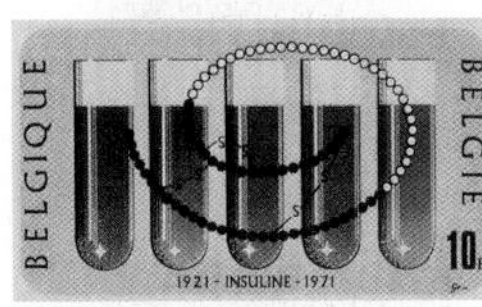

**562** Test-tubes and Diagram

**1971.** 50th Anniv of Discovery of Insulin.
2236 **562** 10f. multicoloured 85 60

**563** Flemish Festival Emblem

**1971.** Cultural Works. Festivals. Multicoloured.
2237 3f.50+1f.50 Type **563** 35 35
2238 7f.+3f. Walloon Festival emblem 85 70

**564** Belgian Family and "50"

**1971.** 50th Anniv of "League of Large Families".
2239 **564** 1f.50 multicoloured 30 30

**1971.** Tourist Publicity. Designs similar to T 450.
2240 2f.50 black, brown and blue 25 10
2241 2f.50 black, brown and blue 25 10

DESIGNS: No. 2240, St. Martin's Church, Alost; No. 2241, Town Hall and belfry, Mons.

**565** Dr. Jules Bordet (medical scientist)

**1971.** Belgian Celebrities.
2242 **565** 3f.50 green 35 30
2243 - 3f.50 brown 35 30

DESIGN: No. 2242, Type **565** (10th death anniv); No. 2243, "Stijn Streuvels" (Frank Lateur, writer, birth cent.).

**566** Achaemenid Tomb, Buzpar

**1971.** 2500th Anniv of Persian Empire.
2244 **566** 7f. multicoloured 60 50

**567** Elewijt Chateau

**1971.** "Belgica 72" Stamp Exhibition, Brussels (2nd issue).
2245 - 3f.50+1f.50 green 35 35
2246 **567** 7f.+3f. brown 85 85
2247 - 10f.+5f. blue 1·20 1·20

DESIGNS—HORIZ: (52×35½ mm): 3f. Attre Chateau; 10f. Royal Palace, Brussels.

**568** F.I.B./V.B.N. Emblem

**1971.** 25th Anniv of Federation of Belgian Industries.
2248 **568** 3f.50 gold, black & blue 35 30

569 "The Flight into Egypt" (15th-century Dutch School)

1971. Christmas.

| | | | | |
|---|---|---|---|---|
| 2249 | 569 | 1f.50 multicoloured | 30 | 30 |

1971. Tourist Publicity. Designs similar to T 450.

| | | | | |
|---|---|---|---|---|
| 2250 | | 1f.50 blue and buff | 10 | 10 |
| 2251 | | 2f.50 blue and buff | 25 | 10 |

DESIGNS—HORIZ: 1f.50, Town Hall, Malines. VERT: 2f.50, Basilica, St. Hubert.

570 "Actias luna"

1971. "Solidarity". Insects in Antwerp Zoo. Multicoloured.

| | | | | |
|---|---|---|---|---|
| 2252 | | 1f.50+50c. Type **570** | 30 | 30 |
| 2253 | | 3f.50+1f.50 "Tabanus bromius" (horiz) | 35 | 35 |
| 2254 | | 7f.+3f. "Polistes gallicus" (horiz) | 85 | 85 |
| 2255 | | 9f.+4f. "Cicindela campestris" | 95 | 95 |

572 Road Signs and Traffic Signals

1972. 20th Anniv of "Via Secura" Road Safety Organization.

| | | | | |
|---|---|---|---|---|
| 2263 | 572 | 3f.50 multicoloured | 30 | 30 |

573 Book Year Emblem

1972. International Book Year.

| | | | | |
|---|---|---|---|---|
| 2264 | 573 | 7f. blue, brown & black | 60 | 40 |

574 Coins of Belgium and Luxembourg

1972. 50th Anniv of Belgo–Luxembourgeoise Economic Union.

| | | | | |
|---|---|---|---|---|
| 2265 | 574 | 1f.50 silver, black and orange | 30 | 30 |

576 "Auguste Vermeylen" (I. Opsomer)

1972. Birth Centenary of Auguste Vemeylen (writer).

| | | | | |
|---|---|---|---|---|
| 2267 | 576 | 2f.50 multicoloured | 30 | 30 |

577 "Belgica 72" Emblem

1972. "Belgica 72" Stamp Exn., Brussels (3rd Issue).

| | | | | |
|---|---|---|---|---|
| 2268 | 577 | 3f.50 purple, blue & brn | 35 | 30 |

578 Heart Emblem

1972. World Heart Month.

| | | | | |
|---|---|---|---|---|
| 2269 | 578 | 7f. multicoloured | 60 | 40 |

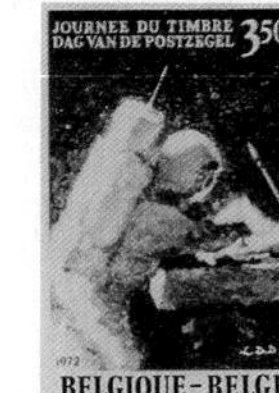
579 Astronaut cancelling Letter on Moon

1972. Stamp Day.

| | | | | |
|---|---|---|---|---|
| 2270 | 579 | 3f.50 multicoloured | 35 | 30 |

580 "Communications"

1972. Europa.

| | | | | |
|---|---|---|---|---|
| 2271 | 580 | 3f.50 multicoloured | 75 | 30 |
| 2272 | 580 | 7f. multicoloured | 1·20 | 60 |

581 Quill Pen and Newspaper

1972. "Liberty of the Press". 50th Anniv of Belga News Agency and 25th Congress of International Federation of Newspaper Editors (F.I.E.J.).

| | | | | |
|---|---|---|---|---|
| 2273 | 581 | 2f.50 multicoloured | 30 | 30 |

582 "UIC" on Coupled Wagons

1972. 50th Anniv of Int Railways Union (U.I.C.).

| | | | | |
|---|---|---|---|---|
| 2274 | 582 | 7f. multicoloured | 60 | 40 |

See also No. P2266.

583 Couvin

1972. Tourist Publicity.

| | | | | |
|---|---|---|---|---|
| 2275 | 583 | 2f.50 purple, blue & grn | 25 | 25 |
| 2276 | - | 2f.50 brown and blue | 25 | 25 |

DESIGN—VERT: No. 2276, Aldeneik Church, Maaseik.

584 Leopold I 10c. "Epaulettes" Stamp of 1849

1972. "Belgica 72" Stamp Exn, Brussels (4th issue).

| | | | | |
|---|---|---|---|---|
| 2277 | 584 | 1f.50+50c. brown, black and gold | 30 | 30 |
| 2278 | - | 2f.+1f. red, brown and gold | 35 | 35 |
| 2279 | - | 2f.50+1f. red, brown and gold | 40 | 40 |
| 2280 | - | 3f.50+1f.50 lilac, black and gold | 45 | 45 |
| 2281 | - | 6f.+3f. violet, black and gold | 60 | 60 |
| 2282 | - | 7f.+3f. red, black and gold | 70 | 70 |
| 2283 | - | 10f.+5f. blue, black and gold | 1·00 | 1·00 |
| 2284 | - | 15f.+7f.50 green, turquoise and gold | 1·60 | 1·60 |
| 2285 | - | 20f.+10f. chestnut, brown and gold | 2·10 | 2·10 |

DESIGNS: 2f. Leopold I 40c. "Medallion" of 1849; 2f.50, Leopold II 10c. of 1883. 3f.50, Leopold II 50c. of 1883; 6f. Albert I; 2f. "Tin Hat" of 1919; 7f. Albert I 50f. of 1929; 10f. Albert I 1f.75 of 1931; 15f. Leopold III 5f. of 1936; 20f. Baudouin 3f.50 of 1970.

585 "Beatrice" (G. de Smet)

1972. "Philately for the Young".

| | | | | |
|---|---|---|---|---|
| 2287 | 585 | 3f. multicoloured | 35 | 30 |

586 Emblem of Centre

1972. Inauguration of William Lennox Epileptic Centre, Ottignies.

| | | | | |
|---|---|---|---|---|
| 2288 | 586 | 10f.+5f. multicoloured | 1·20 | 1·20 |

587 Dish Aerial and "Intelstat 4" Satellite

1972. Inaug of Satellite Earth Station, Lessive.

| | | | | |
|---|---|---|---|---|
| 2289 | 587 | 3f.50 black, silver & bl | 35 | 30 |

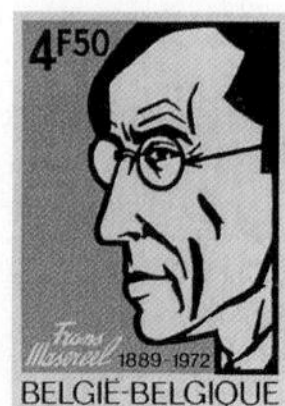
588 Frans Masereel (wood-carver and painter)

1972. Masereel Commem.

| | | | | |
|---|---|---|---|---|
| 2290 | 588 | 4f.50 black and green | 40 | 30 |

589 "Adoration of the Magi" (F. Timmermans)

1972. Christmas.

| | | | | |
|---|---|---|---|---|
| 2291 | 589 | 3f.50 multicoloured | 35 | 30 |

590 "Empress Maria Theresa" (unknown artist)

1972. Bicentenary of Belgian Royal Academy of Sciences, Letters and Fine Arts.

| | | | | |
|---|---|---|---|---|
| 2292 | 590 | 2f. multicoloured | 30 | 30 |

591 Greylag Goose

1972. "Solidarity". Birds from Zwin Nature Reserve. Multicoloured.

| | | | | |
|---|---|---|---|---|
| 2293 | | 2f.+1f. Type **591** | 35 | 35 |
| 2294 | | 4f.50+2f. Northern lapwing | 60 | 60 |
| 2295 | | 8f.+4f. White stork | 70 | 95 |
| 2296 | | 9f.+4f.50 Common kestrel (horiz) | 1·00 | 1·00 |

592 "Fire"

1973. Industrial Buildings Fire Protection Campaign.

| | | | | |
|---|---|---|---|---|
| 2297 | 592 | 2f. multicoloured | 30 | 30 |

593 W.M.O. Emblem and Meteorological Equipment

1973. Centenary of World Meteorological Organization.

| | | | | |
|---|---|---|---|---|
| 2298 | 593 | 9f. multicoloured | 80 | 45 |

594 Bijloke Abbey and Museum, Ghent

1973. Cultural Works. Religious Buildings.

| | | | | |
|---|---|---|---|---|
| 2299 | 594 | 2f.+1f. green | 40 | 40 |
| 2300 | - | 4f.50+2f. brown | 50 | 50 |
| 2301 | - | 8f.+4f. red | 95 | 95 |
| 2302 | - | 9f.+4f.50 blue | 1·20 | 1·20 |

DESIGNS: 4f.50, Collegiate Church of St. Ursmer, Lobbes; 8f. Park Abbey, Heverlee; 9f. Floreffe Abbey.

**595** W.H.O. Emblem as Man's "Heart"

**1973.** 25th Anniv of W.H.O.
2303 **595** 8f. black, yellow & red 60 45

**596** Ball in Hands

**1973.** 1st World Basketball Championships for the Handicapped, Bruges.
2304 **596** 10f.+5f. multicoloured 1·20 1·20

**597** Europa "Posthorn"

**1973.** Europa.
2305 **597** 4f.50 blue, yellow & brn 1·30 35
2306 **597** 8f. blue, yellow & green 2·50 35

**598** Thurn and Taxis Courier (17th-cent)

**1973.** Stamp Day.
2307 **598** 4f.50 brown and red 40 30

**599** Fair Emblem

**1973.** 25th International Fair, Liege.
2308 **599** 4f.50 multicoloured 40 30

**600** Arrows encircling Globe

**1973.** 5th World Telecommunications Day.
2309 **600** 3f.50 multicoloured 35 30

**601** "Sport" (poster for Ghent Exhibition, 1913)

**1973.** 60th Anniv of Workers' International Sports Organization.
2310 **601** 4f.50 multicoloured 40 30

**602** Douglas DC-10-30CF and De Havilland D.H.9

**1973.** 50th Anniv of SABENA.
2311 **602** 8f. black, blue and grey 70 45

**603** Ernest Tips's Biplane, 1908

**1973.** 35th Anniv (1972) of "Les Vieilles Tiges de Belgique" (pioneer aviators' association).
2312 **603** 10f. black, blue & green 85 50

**604** 15th-Century Printing-press

**1973.** Historical Events and Anniversaries.
2313 **604** 2f.+1f. blk, brn & red 40 40
2314 - 3f.50+1f.50 mult 40 40
2315 - 4f.50+2f. mult 45 45
2316 - 8f.+4f. multicoloured 85 85
2317 - 9f.+4f.50 mult 1·00 1·00
2318 - 10f.+5f. multicoloured 1·30 1·30

DESIGNS—VERT (As Type **604**): 2f. (500th anniv of first Belgian printed book, produced by Dirk Martens); 3f.50, Head of Amon (Queen Elisabeth Egyptological Foundation. 50th anniv.); 4f.50, "Portrait of a Young Girl" (Petrus Christus, 500th death anniv). HORIZ (36×25 mm): 8f. Gold coins of Hadrian and Marcus Aurelius (Discovery of Roman treasure at Luttre-Liberchies); (52×35 mm); 9f. "Members of the Great Council" (Coessaert) (Great Council of Malines, 500th anniv.). 10f. "Jong Jacob" (East Indiaman) (Ostend Merchant Company, 250th anniv).

**605** "Woman Bathing" (fresco by Lemaire)

**1973.** Thermal Treatment Year.
2319 **605** 4f.50 multicoloured 40 30

**606** Adolphe Sax and Tenor Saxophone

**1973.** Belgian Musical Instrument Industry.
2320 **606** 9f. multicoloured 70 40

**607** St. Nicholas Church, Eupen

**1973.** Tourist Publicity.
2321 **607** 2f. multicoloured 30 30

See also Nos. 2328/9, 2368/70, 2394/5, 2452/5, 2508/11, 2535/8, 2573/6, 2595/6 and 2614.

**608** "Little Charles" (Evenepoel)

**1973.** "Philately for the Young".
2322 **608** 3f. multicoloured 35 30

**609** J. B. Moens (philatelist) and Perforations

**1973.** 50th Anniv of Belgian Stamp Dealers Association.
2323 **609** 10f. multicoloured 80 60

**610** "Adoration of the Shepherds" (H. van der Goes)

**1973.** Christmas.
2324 **610** 4f. blue 40 30

**611** Motorway and Emblem

**1973.** 50th Anniv of "Vlaamse Automobilistenbond" (VAB) (motoring organization).
2325 **611** 5f. multicoloured 45 30

**612** L. Pierard (after sculpture by Ianchelevici)

**1973.** 21st Death Anniv of Louis Pierard (politician and writer).
2326 **612** 4f. red and cream 40 30

**613** Early Microphone

**1973.** 50th Anniv of Belgium Radio.
2327 **613** 4f. black and blue 40 30

**1973.** Tourist Publicity. As T 607.
2328 3f. grey, brown and blue 30 30
2329 4f. grey and green 40 35

DESIGNS—HORIZ: 3f. Town Hall, Leau; 4f. Chimay Castle.

**614** F. Rops (self-portrait)

**1973.** 75th Death Anniv of Felicien Rops (artist and engraver).
2330 **614** 7f. black and brown 60 35

**615** Jack of Diamonds

**1973.** "Solidarity". Old Playing Cards. Mult.
2331 5f.+2f.50 Type **615** 60 60
2332 5f.+2f.50 Jack of Spades 60 60
2333 5f.+2f.50 Queen of Hearts 60 60
2334 5f.+2f.50 King of Clubs 60 60

**1973.** As Nos. 2207/23 but smaller, 22×17 mm.
2335 **583** 3f. green 30 10
2336 **583** 4f. blue 35 25
2337 **583** 4f.50 blue 40 10
2338 **583** 5f. mauve 40 25
2338c **583** 6f. red 50 30
2339 **583** 6f.50 violet 50 30
2339b **583** 8f. grey 65 30

**616** King Albert (Baron Opsomer)

**1974.** 40th Death Anniv of King Albert I.
2340 **616** 4f. blue and black 35 30

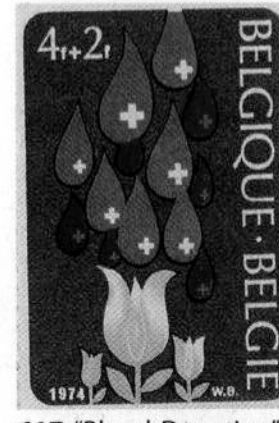


**617** "Blood Donation"

**1974.** Belgian Red Cross. Multicoloured.
2341 4f.+2f. Type **617** 45 45
2342 10f.+5f. "Traffic Lights" (Road Safety) 1·20 1·20

**618** "Protection of the Environment"

**1974.** Robert Schuman Association for the Protection of the Environment.
2343 **618** 3f. multicoloured 35 30

**619** "Armand Jamar" (Self-portrait)

**1974.** Belgian Cultural Celebrities. Multicoloured.
2344 4f.+2f. Type **619** 40 40

| | | | | |
|---|---|---|---|---|
| 2345 | | 5f.+2f.50 Tony Bergmann (author) and view of Lier | 45 | 45 |
| 2346 | | 7f.+3f.50 Henri Vieuxtemps (violinist) and view of Verviers | 70 | 70 |
| 2347 | | 10f.+5f. "James Ensor" (self-portrait with masks) (35×52 mm) | 1·00 | 1·00 |

**620** N.A.T.O. Emblem

**1974.** 25th Anniv of North Atlantic Treaty Organization.

| | | | | |
|---|---|---|---|---|
| 2348 | **620** | 10f. blue and light blue | 85 | 50 |

**621** Hubert Krains (Belgian postal administrator)

**1974.** Stamp Day.

| | | | | |
|---|---|---|---|---|
| 2349 | **621** | 5f. black and grey | 40 | 30 |

**622** "Destroyed Town" (O. Zadkine)

**1974.** Europa. Sculptures.

| | | | | |
|---|---|---|---|---|
| 2350 | **622** | 5f. black and red | 80 | 30 |
| 2351 | - | 10f. black and blue | 1·60 | 50 |

DESIGN: 10f. "Solidarity" (G. Minne).

**623** Heads of Boy and Girl

**1974.** 10th Lay Youth Festival.

| | | | | |
|---|---|---|---|---|
| 2352 | **623** | 4f. multicoloured | 40 | 30 |

**625** New Planetarium, Brussels

**1974.** Historical Buildings.

| | | | | |
|---|---|---|---|---|
| 2354 | **625** | 3f. brown and blue | 35 | 30 |
| 2355 | - | 4f. brown and red | 45 | 30 |
| 2356 | - | 5f. brown and green | 50 | 30 |
| 2357 | - | 7f. brown and yellow | 65 | 35 |
| 2358 | - | 10f. brown, orange & bl | 80 | 35 |

DESIGNS—As T **625**. HORIZ: 4f. Pillory, Braine-le-Chateau. VERT: 10f. Belfry, Bruges. 45×25 mm: 5f. Ruins of Soleilmont Abbey; 7f. "Procession" (fountain sculpture, Ghent).

**626** "BENELUX"

**1974.** 30th Anniv of Benelux Customs Union.

| | | | | |
|---|---|---|---|---|
| 2359 | **626** | 5f. blue, green & lt blue | 40 | 30 |

**627** "Jan Vekemans at the Age of Five" (Cornelis de Vos)

**1974.** "Philately for the Young".

| | | | | |
|---|---|---|---|---|
| 2360 | **627** | 3f. multicoloured | 35 | 30 |

**628** Self-portrait and Van Gogh House, Cuesmes

**1974.** Opening of Vincent Van Gogh House, Cuesmes.

| | | | | |
|---|---|---|---|---|
| 2361 | **628** | 10f.+5f. multicoloured | 1·20 | 85 |

**629** Corporal Tresignies and Brule Bridge

**1974.** 60th Death Anniv of Corporal Leon Tresignies (war hero).

| | | | | |
|---|---|---|---|---|
| 2362 | **629** | 4f. green and brown | 40 | 30 |

**630** Montgomery Blair and U.P.U. Emblem

**1974.** Centenary of U.P.U.

| | | | | |
|---|---|---|---|---|
| 2363 | **630** | 5f. black and green | 45 | 30 |
| 2364 | - | 10f. black and red | 80 | 50 |

DESIGN: 10f. H. von Stephan and U.P.U. Monument.

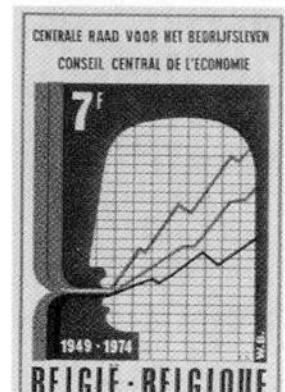


**631** Graph within Head

**1974.** 25th Anniv of Central Economic Council.

| | | | | |
|---|---|---|---|---|
| 2365 | **631** | 7f. multicoloured | 65 | 40 |

**632** Rotary Emblem on Belgian Flag

**1974.** 50th Anniv of Rotary Int in Belgium.

| | | | | |
|---|---|---|---|---|
| 2366 | **632** | 10f. multicoloured | 80 | 45 |

**633** Wild Boar

**1974.** 40th Anniv of Granting of Colours to Ardennes Regiment of Chasseurs.

| | | | | |
|---|---|---|---|---|
| 2367 | **633** | 3f. multicoloured | 35 | 30 |

**1974.** Tourist Publicity. As T 607.

| | | | | |
|---|---|---|---|---|
| 2368 | | 3f. brown and yellow | 40 | 30 |
| 2369 | | 4f. green and blue | 40 | 35 |
| 2370 | | 4f. green and blue | 40 | 35 |

DESIGNS—VERT: No. 2368, Aarschot. HORIZ: No. 2369, Meeting of three frontiers, Gemmenich; 2370, Nassogne.

**634** "Angel" (detail, "The Mystic Lamb", Brothers Van Eyck)

**1974.** Christmas.

| | | | | |
|---|---|---|---|---|
| 2371 | **634** | 4f. purple | 40 | 30 |

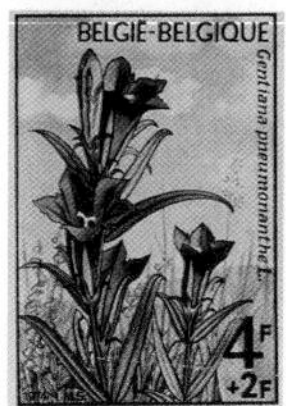


**635** Gentian

**1974.** "Solidarity". Flora and Fauna. Multicoloured.

| | | | |
|---|---|---|---|
| 2372 | 4f.+2f. Type **635** | 45 | 45 |
| 2373 | 5f.+2f.50 Eurasian badger (horiz) | 65 | 65 |
| 2374 | 7f.+3f.50 "Carabus auratus" (beetle) (horiz) | 75 | 75 |
| 2375 | 10f.+5f. Spotted cat's-ear | 1·20 | 1·20 |

**636** Adolphe Quetelet (after J. Odevaere)

**1974.** Death Centenary of Adolphe Quetelet. (scientist).

| | | | | |
|---|---|---|---|---|
| 2376 | **636** | 10f. black and brown | 80 | 50 |

**637** Exhibition Emblem

**1975.** "Themabelga" Stamp Exhibition, Brussels (1st issue).

| | | | | |
|---|---|---|---|---|
| 2377 | **637** | 6f.50 orange, blk & grn | 45 | 30 |

See also Nos. 2411/16.

**638** "Neoregelia carolinae"

**1975.** Ghent Flower Show. Multicoloured.

| | | | |
|---|---|---|---|
| 2378 | 4f.50 Type **638** | 40 | 35 |
| 2379 | 5f. "Tussilago petasites" | 45 | 30 |
| 2380 | 6f.50 "Azalea japonica" | 50 | 30 |

**639** Student and Young Boy

**1975.** Cent of Charles Buls Normal School.

| | | | | |
|---|---|---|---|---|
| 2381 | **639** | 4f.50 multicoloured | 40 | 30 |

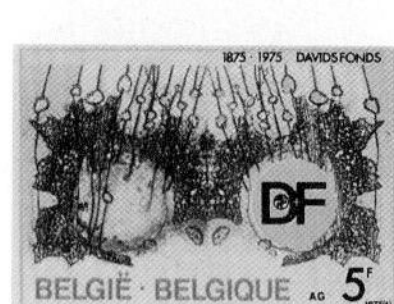


**640** Foundation Emblem

**1975.** Centenary of Davids Foundation (Flemish cultural organisation).

| | | | | |
|---|---|---|---|---|
| 2382 | **640** | 5f. multicoloured | 40 | 30 |

**641** King Albert I

**1975.** Birth Centenary of King Albert I.

| | | | | |
|---|---|---|---|---|
| 2383 | **641** | 10f. black and purple | 80 | 45 |

**642** Pesaro Palace, Venice

**1975.** Cultural Works.

| | | | | |
|---|---|---|---|---|
| 2384 | **642** | 6f.50+2f.50 brown | 65 | 65 |
| 2385 | - | 10f.+4f.50 purple | 1·00 | 1·00 |
| 2386 | - | 15f.+6f.50 blue | 1·50 | 1·50 |

DESIGNS—HORIZ: 10f. Sculpture Museum, St. Bavon Abbey, Ghent. VERT: 15f. "Virgin and Child" (Michelangelo, 500th Birth Anniv.).

**643** "Postman of 1840" (J. Thiriar)

**1975.** Stamp Day.

| | | | | |
|---|---|---|---|---|
| 2387 | **643** | 6f.50 purple | 50 | 30 |

**644** "An Apostle" (detail, "The Last Supper", Dirk Bouts)

**1975.** Europa. Paintings.

| | | | | |
|---|---|---|---|---|
| 2388 | **644** | 6f.50 black, blue & grn | 80 | 30 |
| 2389 | - | 10f. black, red & orange | 1·70 | 60 |

DESIGN: 10f. "The Suppliant's Widow" (detail, "The Justice of Otho", Dirk Bouts).

**645** Prisoners' Identification Emblems

**1975.** 30th Anniv of Concentration Camps' Liberation.

| | | | | |
|---|---|---|---|---|
| 2390 | **645** | 4f.50 multicoloured | 40 | 30 |

**646** St John's Hospice, Bruges

**1975.** European Architectural Heritage Year.

| | | | | |
|---|---|---|---|---|
| 2391 | **646** | 4f.50 purple | 45 | 30 |
| 2392 | - | 5f. green | 50 | 30 |
| 2393 | - | 10f. blue | 1·00 | 45 |

DESIGNS—VERT: 5f. St. Loup's Church, Namur. HORIZ: 10f. Martyrs Square, Brussels.

**1975.** Tourist Publicity. As T 607.

| | | | |
|---|---|---|---|
| 2394 | 4f.50 brown, buff and red | 40 | 30 |
| 2395 | 5f. multicoloured | 50 | 30 |

DESIGN—VERT: 4f.50, Church, Dottignies. HORIZ: 5f. Market Square, Saint Truiden.

**647** G. Ryckmans and L. Cerfaux (founders), and Louvain University Library

**1975.** 25th Anniv of Louvain Colloquium Biblicum (Biblical Scholarship Association).

| | | | | |
|---|---|---|---|---|
| 2396 | **647** | 10f. sepia and blue | 85 | 45 |

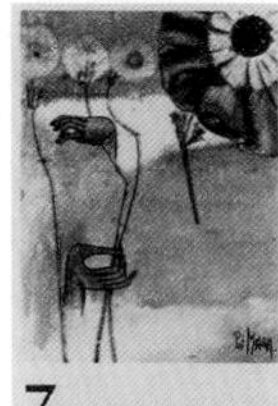


**648** "Metamorphosis" (P. Mara)

**1975.** Queen Fabiola Foundation for the Mentally Ill.

| | | | | |
|---|---|---|---|---|
| 2397 | **648** | 7f. multicoloured | 60 | 35 |

**649** Marie Popelin (women's rights pioneer) and Palace of Justice

**1975.** International Women's Year.

| | | | | |
|---|---|---|---|---|
| 2398 | **649** | 6f.50 purple and green | 65 | 30 |

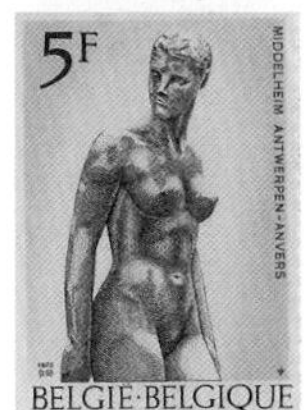


**650** "Assia" (Charles Despiau)

**1975.** 25th Anniv of Middelheim Open-air Museum, Antwerp.

| | | | | |
|---|---|---|---|---|
| 2399 | **650** | 5f. black and green | 40 | 30 |

**651** Dr. Hemerijckx and Leprosy Hospital, Zaire

**1975.** Dr. Frans Hemerijckx (treatment of leprosy pioneer) Commemoration.

| | | | | |
|---|---|---|---|---|
| 2400 | **651** | 20f.+10f. mult | 2·10 | 2·10 |

**652** Canal Map

**1975.** Opening of Rhine–Scheldt Canal.

| | | | | |
|---|---|---|---|---|
| 2401 | **652** | 10f. multicoloured | 85 | 40 |

**653** "Cornelia Vekemans at the Age of Seven" (Cornelis de Vos)

**1975.** "Philately for the Young".

| | | | | |
|---|---|---|---|---|
| 2402 | **653** | 4f.50 multicoloured | 45 | 30 |

**654** National Bank and F. Orban (founder)

**1975.** 125th Anniv of Belgian National Bank.

| | | | | |
|---|---|---|---|---|
| 2403 | **654** | 25f. multicoloured | 2·20 | 60 |

**655** Edmond Thieffry (pilot) and Hadley Page H.P.26 W.8e Hamilton OË-BAHO "Princess Marie-Jose"

**1975.** 50th Anniv of First Flight, Brussels–Kinshasa.

| | | | | |
|---|---|---|---|---|
| 2404 | **655** | 7f. purple and black | 60 | 40 |

**656** University Seal

**1975.** 550th Anniv of Louvain University.

| | | | | |
|---|---|---|---|---|
| 2405 | **656** | 6f.50 black, green & bl | 60 | 30 |

**657** "Angels", (detail, "The Nativity", R. de le Pasture)

**1975.** Christmas.

| | | | | |
|---|---|---|---|---|
| 2406 | **657** | 5f. multicoloured | 40 | 25 |

**658** Emile Moyson (Flemish Leader)

**1975.** "Solidarity".

| | | | | |
|---|---|---|---|---|
| 2407 | **658** | 4f.50+2f. purple | 45 | 45 |
| 2408 | - | 6f.50+3f. green | 70 | 70 |
| 2409 | - | 10f.+5f. vio, blk & bl | 1·00 | 1·00 |
| 2410 | - | 13f.+6f. multicoloured | 1·30 | 1·30 |

DESIGNS—VERT: 6f.50, Dr. Augustin Snellaert (Flemish literature scholar); 13f. Detail of retable, St. Dymphne Church, Geel. HORIZ: 10f. Eye within hand, and Braille characters (150th anniv of introduction of Braille).

**659** Cheese Seller

**1975.** "Themabelga" International Thematic Stamp Exhibition, Brussels (2nd issue). Traditional Belgian Trades. Multicoloured.

| | | | |
|---|---|---|---|
| 2411 | 4f.50+1f.50 Type **659** | 45 | 45 |
| 2412 | 6f.50+3f. Potato seller | 70 | 70 |
| 2413 | 6f.50+3f. Basket-carrier | 70 | 70 |
| 2414 | 10f.+5f. Prawn fisherman and pony (horiz) | 1·00 | 1·00 |
| 2415 | 10f.+5f. Knife-grinder and cart (horiz) | 1·00 | 1·00 |
| 2416 | 30f.+15f. Milk-woman with dog-cart (horiz) | 2·75 | 2·75 |

**660** "African" Collector

**1976.** Centenary of "Conservatoire Africain" (Charity Organization).

| | | | | |
|---|---|---|---|---|
| 2417 | **660** | 10f.+5f. multicoloured | 1·20 | 1·20 |

**661** Owl Emblem and Flemish Buildings

**1976.** 125th Anniv of Wilhems Foundation (Flemish cultural organization).

| | | | | |
|---|---|---|---|---|
| 2418 | **661** | 5f. multicoloured | 40 | 30 |

**662** Bicentennial Symbol

**1976.** Bicentenary of American Revolution.

| | | | | |
|---|---|---|---|---|
| 2419 | **662** | 14f. multicoloured | 1·20 | 65 |

**663** Cardinal Mercier

**1976.** 50th Death Anniv of Cardinal Mercier.

| | | | | |
|---|---|---|---|---|
| 2420 | **663** | 4f.50 purple | 40 | 30 |

**664** "Vlaams Ekonomisch Verbond"

**1976.** 50th Anniv of Flemish Economic Federation.

| | | | | |
|---|---|---|---|---|
| 2421 | **664** | 6f.50 multicoloured | 50 | 30 |

**665** Swimming

**1976.** Olympic Games, Montreal. Multicoloured.

| | | | |
|---|---|---|---|
| 2422 | 4f.50+1f.50 Type **665** | 45 | 45 |
| 2423 | 5f.+2f. Running (vert) | 45 | 45 |
| 2424 | 6f.50+2f.50 Horse jumping | 70 | 70 |

**666** Money Centre Building, Brussels

**1976.** Stamp Day.

| | | | | |
|---|---|---|---|---|
| 2425 | **666** | 6f.50 brown | 50 | 30 |

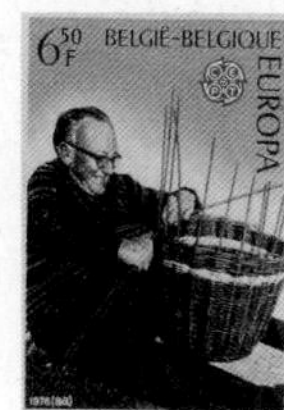


**667** Queen Elisabeth playing Violin

**1976.** 25th Anniv of Queen Elisabeth International Music Competitions.

| | | | | |
|---|---|---|---|---|
| 2426 | **667** | 14f.+6f. red & black | 1·40 | 1·40 |

**668** Basket-making

**1976.** Europa. Traditional Crafts. Multicoloured.

| | | | |
|---|---|---|---|
| 2427 | 6f.50 Type **668** | 95 | 25 |
| 2428 | 14f. Pottery (horiz) | 2·10 | 60 |

**669** Truck on Motorway

**1976.** 14th Congress of International Road Haulage Union, Brussels.

| | | | | |
|---|---|---|---|---|
| 2429 | **669** | 14f. black, red & yellow | 1·30 | 50 |

670 Queen Elisabeth

**1976.** Birth Centenary of Queen Elisabeth.

| | | | | |
|---|---|---|---|---|
| 2430 | **670** | 14f. green | 1·20 | 50 |

672 Jan Olieslagers (aviator), Bleriot XI Monoplane and club Badge

**1976.** 75th Anniv of Belgian Royal Aero Club. Sheet 82×116 mm.

| | | | |
|---|---|---|---|
| **MS**2435 **672** | 25f.+10f. black, yellow and blue | 2·50 | 2·50 |

673 Ardennes Horses

**1976.** 50th Anniv of Ardennes Draught Horses Society.

| | | | | |
|---|---|---|---|---|
| 2436 | **673** | 5f. multicoloured | 45 | 35 |

674 King Baudouin

**1976.** 25th Anniv of King Baudouin's Accession. Two sheets each 110×62 mm containing stamps as T 674.

| | | | |
|---|---|---|---|
| **MS**2437 | (a) 4f.50 grey; 6f.50 yellow; 10f. red (sold at 30f.). (b) 20f. green; 30f. blue (sold at 70f.) | 7·50 | 7·50 |

675 "Madonna and Child" (detail)

**1976.** 400th Birth Anniv of Peter Paul Rubens (artist) (1st issue). Multicoloured.

| | | | |
|---|---|---|---|
| 2438 | 4f.50+1f.50 "Descent from the Cross" (detail) | 60 | 60 |
| 2439 | 6f.50+3f. "Adoration of the Shepherds" (detail) (24½×35 mm) | 70 | 60 |
| 2440 | 6f.50+3f. "Virgin of the Parrot" (detail) (24½×35 mm) | 70 | 70 |
| 2441 | 10f.+5f. "Adoration of the Kings" (detail) (24½×35 mm) | 1·20 | 1·20 |
| 2442 | 10f.+5f. "Last Communion of St. Francis" (detail) (24½×35 mm) | 1·20 | 1·20 |
| 2443 | 30f.+15f. Type **675** | 3·00 | 3·00 |

See also Nos. 2459 and 2497.

676 William the Silent, Prince of Orange

**1976.** 400th Anniv of Pacification of Ghent.

| | | | | |
|---|---|---|---|---|
| 2444 | **676** | 10f. green | 85 | 45 |

678 Underground Train

**1976.** Opening of Brussels Metro (Underground) Service.

| | | | | |
|---|---|---|---|---|
| 2446 | **678** | 6f.50 multicoloured | 65 | 30 |

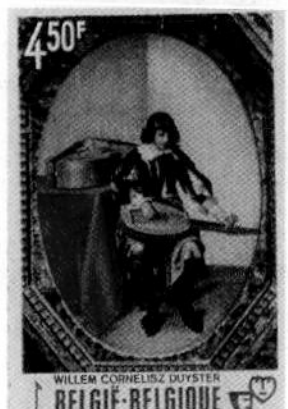
679 "The Young Musician" (W. C. Duyster)

**1976.** "Philately for the Young" and Young Musicians' Movement.

| | | | | |
|---|---|---|---|---|
| 2447 | **679** | 4f.50 multicoloured | 40 | 30 |

680 Charles Bernard (writer, birth cent)

**1976.** Cultural Anniversaries.

| | | | | |
|---|---|---|---|---|
| 2448 | **680** | 5f. purple | 45 | 30 |
| 2449 | - | 5f. red | 45 | 30 |
| 2450 | - | 6f.50 brown | 65 | 30 |
| 2451 | - | 6f.50 green | 65 | 30 |

DESIGNS—VERT: No. 2449, Fernand Toussaint van Boelaere (writer, birth cent 1975); No. 2450, "St. Jerome in Mountain Landscape" (J. le Patinier) (25th anniv of Charles Plisnier Foundation). HORIZ: No. 2451, "Story of the Blind" (P. Brueghel) (25th anniv of "Vereniging voor Beschaafde Omgangstaal" (Dutch language organisation)).

**1976.** Tourist Publicity. As T 607.

| | | | |
|---|---|---|---|
| 2452 | 4f.50 multicoloured | 45 | 35 |
| 2453 | 4f.50 multicoloured | 45 | 35 |
| 2454 | 5f. brown and blue | 45 | 35 |
| 2455 | 5f. brown and olive | 45 | 35 |

DESIGNS—HORIZ: No. 2452, Hunnegem Priory, Grammont; No. 2454, River Lys, Sint-Martens-Latem; No. 2455, Chateau, Ham-sur-Heure. VERT: No. 2453, Remouchamps Caves.

681 "Child with Impediment" (Velasquez)

**1976.** National Association for Aid to the Mentally Handicapped.

| | | | | |
|---|---|---|---|---|
| 2456 | **681** | 14f.+6f. multicoloured | 1·60 | 1·60 |

682 "The Nativity" (detail, Master of Flemalle)

**1976.** Christmas.

| | | | | |
|---|---|---|---|---|
| 2457 | **682** | 5f. violet | 45 | 30 |

683 Monogram

**1977.** 400th Birth Anniv of Peter Paul Rubens (2nd issue).

| | | | | |
|---|---|---|---|---|
| 2459 | **683** | 6f.50 black and lilac | 60 | 30 |

684 Belgian Lion

**1977.** (a) Size 17×20 mm.

| | | | | |
|---|---|---|---|---|
| 2460 | **684** | 50c. brown | 10 | 10 |
| 2461 | **684** | 65c. red | 10 | 10 |
| 2462 | **684** | 1f. mauve | 10 | 10 |
| 2463 | **684** | 1f.50 grey | 10 | 10 |
| 2464a | **684** | 2f. orange | 10 | 10 |
| 2465 | **684** | 2f.50 green | 35 | 25 |
| 2466 | **684** | 2f.75 blue | 35 | 35 |
| 2467a | **684** | 3f. violet | 25 | 10 |
| 2468 | **684** | 4f. brown | 25 | 10 |
| 2469 | **684** | 4f.50 blue | 45 | 25 |
| 2470 | **684** | 5f. green | 35 | 10 |
| 2471 | **684** | 6f. red | 45 | 10 |
| 2472 | **684** | 7f. red | 60 | 10 |
| 2473 | **684** | 8f. blue | 35 | 10 |
| 2474 | **684** | 9f. orange | 1·20 | 10 |

(b) 17×22 mm.

| | | | |
|---|---|---|---|
| 2475 | 1f. mauve | 25 | 25 |
| 2476 | 2f. orange | 45 | 35 |
| 2477 | 3f. violet | 50 | 40 |

685 Dr. Albert Hustin (pioneer of blood transfusion)

**1977.** Belgian Red Cross.

| | | | | |
|---|---|---|---|---|
| 2478 | **685** | 6f.50+2f.50 red and black | 75 | 75 |
| 2479 | - | 14f.+7f. red, blue and black | 1·40 | 1·40 |

DESIGN: 14f.+7f. Knee joint and red cross (World Rheumatism Year).

686 "50 Years of F.A.B.I."

**1977.** 50th Anniv of Federation of Belgian Engineers.

| | | | | |
|---|---|---|---|---|
| 2480 | **686** | 6f.50 multicoloured | 60 | 30 |

687 Jules Bordet School, Brussels (bicent)

**1977.** Cultural Anniversaries.

| | | | | |
|---|---|---|---|---|
| 2481 | **687** | 4f.50+1f. mult | 40 | 40 |
| 2482 | - | 4f.50+1f. mult | 40 | 40 |
| 2483 | - | 5f.+2f. multicoloured | 50 | 45 |
| 2484 | - | 6f.50+2f. mult | 60 | 60 |
| 2485 | - | 6f.50+2f. red & black | 60 | 60 |
| 2486 | - | 10f.+5 slate | 1·00 | 1·00 |

DESIGNS—VERT: 24×37 mm: No. 2482, Marie-Therese College, Herve (bicentenary); 2483, Detail from "La Grande Pyramide Musicale" (E. Tytgat) (50th anniv of Brussels Philharmonic Society). 35×45 mm: No. 2486, Camille Lemonnier (75th anniv of Society of Belgian Authors writing in French). HORIZ: 35×24 mm: No. 2484, Lucien van Obbergh and stage scene (50th anniv of Union of Artists). 37×24 mm: No. 2485, Emblem of Humanist Society (25th anniv).

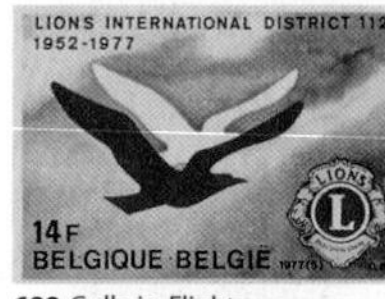
688 Gulls in Flight

**1977.** 25th Anniv of District 112 of Lions International.

| | | | | |
|---|---|---|---|---|
| 2487 | **688** | 14f. multicoloured | 1·20 | 35 |

689 Footballers

**1977.** 30th International Youth Tournament of European Football Association.

| | | | | |
|---|---|---|---|---|
| 2488 | **689** | 10f.+5f. multicoloured | 1·20 | 1·20 |

690 Pillar Box, 1852

**1977.** Stamp Day.

| | | | | |
|---|---|---|---|---|
| 2489 | **690** | 6f.50 olive | 65 | 30 |

691 Gileppe Dam, Jalhay

**1977.** Europa. Multicoloured.

| | | | |
|---|---|---|---|
| 2490 | 6f.50 Type **691** | 1·20 | 30 |
| 2491 | 14f. The Yser, Nieuport | 2·00 | 60 |

692 "Mars and Mercury Association Emblem"

**1977.** 50th Anniv of Mars and Mercury Association of Reserve and Retired Officers.

| | | | | |
|---|---|---|---|---|
| 2492 | **692** | 5f. green, black & brown | 40 | 30 |

**693** De Hornes Coat of Arms

**1977.** Historical Anniversaries.

| | | | | |
|---|---|---|---|---|
| 2493 | **693** | 4f.50 lilac | 40 | 30 |
| 2494 | - | 5f. red | 45 | 30 |
| 2495 | - | 6f.50 brown | 45 | 30 |
| 2496 | - | 14f. green | 1·20 | 60 |

DESIGNS AND EVENTS—VERT: 4f.50, Type **693** (300th anniv of creation of principality of Overijse under Eugene-Maximilien de Hornes); 6f.50, Miniature (600th anniv of Froissart's "Chronicles"); 14f. "The Conversion of St. Hubert" (1250th death anniv). HORIZ: (45×24 mm): 5f. Detail from "Oxford Chest" (675th anniv of Battle of Golden Spurs).

**694** "Self-Portrait"

**1977.** 400th Birth Anniv of Peter Paul Rubens (3rd issue).

| | | | | |
|---|---|---|---|---|
| 2497 | **694** | 5f. multicoloured | 45 | 30 |
| **MS**2498 | | 100×152 mm. As No. 2497 but larger (24×37 mm) ×3 (sold at 20f.) | 1·40 | 1·40 |

**695** "The Mystic Lamb" (detail, Brothers Van Eyck)

**1977.** 50th Anniv of International Federation of Library Associations and Congress, Brussels.

| | | | | |
|---|---|---|---|---|
| 2499 | **695** | 10f. multicoloured | 80 | 45 |

**696** Gymnast and Footballer

**1977.** Sports Events and Anniversaries.

| | | | | |
|---|---|---|---|---|
| 2500 | **696** | 4f.50 red, black & grn | 45 | 30 |
| 2501 | - | 6f.50 black, violet and brown | 50 | 30 |
| 2502 | - | 10f. turquoise, black and salmon | 85 | 45 |
| 2503 | - | 14f. green, blk & ochre | 1·30 | 60 |

DESIGNS—VERT: 4f.50, Type **696** (50th anniv of Workers' Central Sports Association); 10f. Basketball (20th European Championships); 14f. Hockey (International Hockey Cup competition). HORIZ: 6f.50, Disabled fencers (Rehabilitation through sport).

**697** Festival Emblem

**1977.** "Europalia '77" Festival.

| | | | | |
|---|---|---|---|---|
| 2504 | **697** | 5f. multicoloured | 45 | 30 |

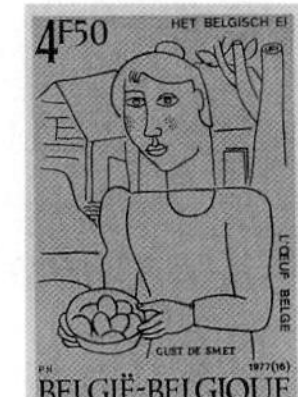

**699** "The Egg-seller" (Gustave de Smet)

**1977.** Promoting Belgian Eggs.

| | | | | |
|---|---|---|---|---|
| 2506 | **699** | 4f.50 black and ochre | 40 | 30 |

**700** "The Stamp Collectors" (detail, Constant Cap)

**1977.** "Philately for the Young".

| | | | | |
|---|---|---|---|---|
| 2507 | **700** | 4f.50 sepia | 40 | 30 |

**1977.** Tourist Publicity. As T 607.

| | | | |
|---|---|---|---|
| 2508 | 4f.50 multicoloured | 40 | 30 |
| 2509 | 4f.50 black, blue and green | 40 | 30 |
| 2510 | 5f. multicoloured | 40 | 30 |
| 2511 | 5f. multicoloured | 40 | 30 |

DESIGNS—VERT: No. 2508, Bailiff's House, Gembloux; No. 2509, St. Aldegone's Church. HORIZ: No. 2510, View of Liege and statue of Mother and Child; No. 2511, View and statue of St. Nicholas.

**701** "Nativity" (detail, R. de la Pasture)

**1977.** Christmas.

| | | | | |
|---|---|---|---|---|
| 2512 | **701** | 5f. red | 40 | 35 |

**702** Albert-Edouard Janssen (financier)

**1977.** "Solidarity".

| | | | | |
|---|---|---|---|---|
| 2513 | **702** | 5f.+2f.50 black | 45 | 45 |
| 2514 | - | 5f.+2f.50 red | 45 | 45 |
| 2515 | - | 10f.+5f. purple | 1·00 | 1·00 |
| 2516 | - | 10f.+5f. grey | 1·00 | 1·00 |

DESIGNS: No. 2514, Joseph Wauters (politician); No. 2516, Jean Capart (egyptologist); No. 2515, August de Boeck (composer).

**703** Distressed Girl (Deserted Children)

**1978.** Philanthropic Works. Multicoloured.

| | | | |
|---|---|---|---|
| 2517 | 4f.50+1f.50 Type **703** | 40 | 40 |
| 2518 | 6f.+3f. Blood pressure measurement (World Hypertension Month) | 60 | 60 |
| 2519 | 10f.+5f. De Mick Sanatorium, Brasschaat (Anti-tuberculosis) (horiz) | 1·00 | 1·00 |

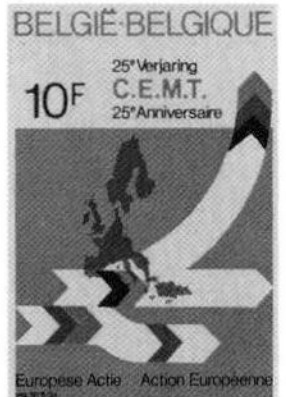

**704** Railway Signal as Arrows on Map of Europe

**1978.** "European Action". Multicoloured.

| | | | |
|---|---|---|---|
| 2520 | 10f. Type **704** (25th anniv of European Conference of Transport Ministers) | 85 | 35 |
| 2521 | 10f. European Parliament Building, Strasbourg (first direct elections) | 85 | 35 |
| 2522 | 14f. Campidoglio Palace, Rome and map of EEC countries (20th anniv of Treaties of Rome) (horiz) | 1·20 | 50 |
| 2523 | 14f. Paul Henri Spaak (Belgian Prime Minister) (horiz) | 1·20 | 50 |

**705** Grimbergen Abbey

**1978.** 850th Anniv of Premonstratensian Abbey, Grimbergen.

| | | | | |
|---|---|---|---|---|
| 2524 | **705** | 4f.50 brown | 40 | 30 |

**706** Emblem

**1978.** 175th Anniv of Ostend Chamber of Commerce and Industry.

| | | | | |
|---|---|---|---|---|
| 2525 | **706** | 8f. multicoloured | 60 | 30 |

**707** 5f. Stamp of 1878

**1978.** Stamp Day.

| | | | | |
|---|---|---|---|---|
| 2526 | **707** | 8f. brown, blk & drab | 60 | 30 |

**708** Antwerp Cathedral

**1978.** Europa. Multicoloured.

| | | | |
|---|---|---|---|
| 2527 | 8f. Type **708** | 1·20 | 35 |
| 2528 | 14f. Pont des Trous, Tournai (horiz) | 2·30 | 60 |

**709** Theatre and Characters from "The Brussels Street Singer"

**1978.** Cultural Anniversaries.

| | | | | |
|---|---|---|---|---|
| 2529 | **709** | 6f.+3f. multicoloured | 60 | 60 |
| 2530 | - | 6f.+3f. multicoloured | 60 | 60 |
| 2531 | - | 8f.+4f. brown | 75 | 75 |
| 2532 | - | 10f.+5f. brown | 1·00 | 1·00 |

DESIGNS AND EVENTS: No. 2529, (Type **709**) (Royal Flemish Theatre Cent.); 2530, Arquebusier with standard, arms and Company Gallery, Vise (Royal Company of Crossbowmen of Vise 400th anniv); 2531, Karel van der Woestijne (poet) (birth cent); 2532, Don John of Austria (signing of Perpetual Edict, 400th anniv).

**710** "Education"

**1978.** Teaching. Multicoloured.

| | | | |
|---|---|---|---|
| 2533 | 6f. Type **710** (Municipal education in Ghent, 150th anniv) | 45 | 35 |
| 2534 | 8f. Paul Pastur Workers' University, Charleroi (75th anniv) | 70 | 30 |

**1978.** Tourist Publicity. As T 607.

| | | | |
|---|---|---|---|
| 2535 | 4f.50 sepia, buff and blue | 40 | 35 |
| 2536 | 4f.50 multicoloured | 40 | 35 |
| 2537 | 6f. multicoloured | 50 | 35 |
| 2538 | 6f. multicoloured | 50 | 35 |

DESIGNS—VERT: No. 2535, Jonathas House, Enghien. HORIZ: No. 2536, View of Wetteren and couple in local costume; 2537, Brussels tourist hostess; 2538, Carnival Prince and church tower.

**711** "K.V.I."

**1978.** 50th Anniv of Royal Flemish Association of Engineers.

| | | | | |
|---|---|---|---|---|
| 2539 | **711** | 8f. black and red | 60 | 30 |

**712** Young Stamp Collector

**1978.** "Philately for the Young".

| | | | | |
|---|---|---|---|---|
| 2540 | **712** | 4f.50 violet | 40 | 30 |

**713** Mountain Scenery

**1978.** Olympic Games (1980) Preparation.

| | | | | |
|---|---|---|---|---|
| 2541 | **713** | 6f.+2f.50 mult | 65 | 65 |
| 2542 | - | 8f.+3f.50 green, brown and black | 75 | 75 |
| **MS**2543 | | 150×100 mm. 7f. + 3f., 14f.+6f. multicoloured | 2·30 | 2·30 |

DESIGNS: 7f. Ancient Greek athletes; 8f. Kremlin Towers, Moscow; 14f. Olympic flame.

**714** "The Nativity" (detail, Bethlehem Door, Notre Dame, Huy)

**1978.** Christmas.

| | | | | |
|---|---|---|---|---|
| 2544 | **714** | 6f. black | 50 | 35 |

**715** Tabernacle, Brussels Synagogue (centenary)

**1978.** "Solidarity". Anniversaries.

| | | | | |
|---|---|---|---|---|
| 2545 | **715** | 6f.+2f. brown, grey and black | 65 | 65 |
| 2546 | - | 8f.+3f. multicoloured | 80 | 80 |
| 2547 | - | 14f.+7f. multicoloured | 1·50 | 1·50 |

DESIGNS—HORIZ: (36×24 mm): 8f. Dancing figures (Catholic Students Action, 50th anniv); 14f. Father Dominique-Georges Pire and African Village (Award of Nobel Peace Prize, 20th anniv).

**716** Relief Workers giving First Aid

**1978.** Belgian Red Cross. Multicoloured.

| | | | |
|---|---|---|---|
| 2548 | 8f.+3f. Type **716** | 85 | 85 |
| 2549 | 16f.+8f. Skull smoking, bottle and syringe ("Excess kills") | 1·70 | 1·70 |

**717** "Till Eulenspiegel" (legendary character)

**1979.** 10th Anniv of Lay Action Centres.

| | | | | |
|---|---|---|---|---|
| 2550 | **717** | 4f.50 multicoloured | 40 | 30 |

**718** "European Dove"

**1979.** 1st Direct Elections to European Assembly.

| | | | | |
|---|---|---|---|---|
| 2551 | **718** | 8f. multicoloured | 70 | 30 |

**719** Millenary Emblem

**1979.** Brussels Millenary (1st issue).

| | | | | |
|---|---|---|---|---|
| 2552 | **719** | 4f.50 brown, blk & red | 35 | 30 |
| 2553 | **719** | 8f. turquoise, blk & grn | 80 | 30 |

See also Nos. 2559/62.

**720** Sculpture at N.A.T.O. Headquarters and Emblem

**1979.** 30th Anniv of North Atlantic Treaty Organization.

| | | | | |
|---|---|---|---|---|
| 2554 | **720** | 30f. blue, gold and light blue | 2·30 | 60 |

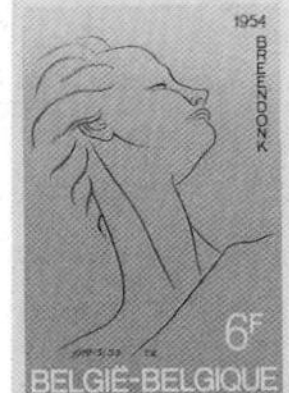

**721** Drawing of Monument

**1979.** 25th Anniv of Breendonk Monument.

| | | | | |
|---|---|---|---|---|
| 2555 | **721** | 6f. orange and black | 45 | 35 |

**722** Railway Parcels Stamp, 1879

**1979.** Stamp Day.

| | | | | |
|---|---|---|---|---|
| 2556 | **722** | 8f. multicoloured | 65 | 30 |

**723** Mail Coach and Renault R4 Post Van

**1979.** Europa. Multicoloured.

| | | | |
|---|---|---|---|
| 2557 | 8f. Type **723** | 1·70 | 30 |
| 2558 | 14f. Semaphore posts, satellite and dish aerial | 3·00 | 60 |

**724** "Legend of Our Lady of Sablon" (detail of tapestry, Town Museum of Brussels)

**1979.** Brussels Millenary (2nd issue). Multicoloured.

| | | | |
|---|---|---|---|
| 2559 | 6f.+2f. Type **724** | 60 | 60 |
| 2560 | 8f.+3f. Different detail of tapestry | 70 | 70 |
| 2561 | 14f.+7f. "Legend of Our Lady of Sablon" (tapestry) | 1·50 | 1·50 |
| 2562 | 20f.+10f. Different detail of tapestry | 2·20 | 2·20 |
| **MS**2563 | 100×150 mm. 20f.+10f. Different detail of Town Museum tapestry (48×37 mm) | 2·30 | 2·30 |

The tapestry shown on Nos. 2559/60 is from Brussels Town Museum and that on Nos. 2561/2 from the Royal Museum of Art and History.

**725** Caduceus and Factory

**1979.** 175th Anniv of Verviers Chamber of Commerce.

| | | | | |
|---|---|---|---|---|
| 2564 | **725** | 8f. multicoloured | 60 | 30 |

**726** "50" and Bank Emblem

**1979.** 50th Anniv of Professional Credit Bank.

| | | | | |
|---|---|---|---|---|
| 2565 | **726** | 4f.50 blue and gold | 40 | 30 |

**727** Bas-relief

**1979.** 50th Anniv of Chambers of Trade and Commerce.

| | | | | |
|---|---|---|---|---|
| 2566 | **727** | 10f. crimson, orange and red | 75 | 40 |

**728** Cambre Abbey

**1979.** Cultural Anniversaries.

| | | | | |
|---|---|---|---|---|
| 2567 | **728** | 6f.+2f. multicoloured | 60 | 60 |
| 2568 | - | 8f.+3f. multicoloured | 70 | 75 |
| 2569 | - | 14f.+7f. black, orange and green | 1·50 | 1·50 |
| 2570 | - | 20f.+10f. brown, red and grey | 2·20 | 2·20 |

DESIGNS: 6f. Type **728** (50th anniv of restoration); 8f. Beauvoorde Chateau; 14f. Barthelemy Dumortier (founder) and newspaper "Courrier de L'Escaut" (150th anniv); 20f. Crypt, shrine and Collegiate Church of St. Hermes, Renaix (850th anniv of consecration).

**729** "Tintin" with Dog, Stamps and Magnifier

**1979.** "Philately for the Young".

| | | | | |
|---|---|---|---|---|
| 2571 | **729** | 8f. multicoloured | 2·30 | 70 |

**730** Le Grand-Hornu

**1979.** Le Grand-Hornu Industrial Archaeological Site.

| | | | | |
|---|---|---|---|---|
| 2572 | **730** | 10f.+5f. black & grey | 1·00 | 1·00 |

**1979.** Tourist Publicity. As T 607.

| | | | |
|---|---|---|---|
| 2573 | 5f. multicoloured | 45 | 35 |
| 2574 | 5f. multicoloured | 45 | 35 |
| 2575 | 6f. black, turquoise & green | 60 | 35 |
| 2576 | 6f. multicoloured | 60 | 35 |

DESIGNS—HORIZ: No. 2573, Royal African Museum, Tervuren, and hunters with hounds; 2575, St. John's Church, Poperinge, and statue of Virgin Mary. VERT: No. 2574, Belfry, Thuin, and men carrying religious image; 2576, St. Nicholas's Church and cattle market, Ciney.

**731** Francois Auguste Gevaert

**1979.** Music. Each brown and ochre.

| | | | |
|---|---|---|---|
| 2577 | 5f. Type **731** (150th birth anniv) | 45 | 35 |
| 2578 | 6f. Emmanuel Durlet | 65 | 35 |
| 2579 | 14f. Grand piano and string instruments (40th anniv of Queen Elisabeth Musical Chapel) | 1·00 | 60 |

**732** Madonna and Child, Foy-Notre-Dame Church

**1979.** Christmas.

| | | | | |
|---|---|---|---|---|
| 2580 | **732** | 6f. black and blue | 40 | 30 |

**733** H. Heyman (politician, birth centenary)

**1979.** "Solidarity".

| | | | | |
|---|---|---|---|---|
| 2581 | **733** | 8f.+3f. brown, green and black | 60 | 60 |
| 2582 | - | 10f.+5f. multicoloured | 95 | 95 |
| 2583 | - | 16f.+8f. black, green and yellow | 1·60 | 1·60 |

DESIGNS—VERT: As Type **733**. 10f. War Invalids Organization medal (50th anniv). HORIZ: (44×24 mm): 16f. Child's head and International Year of the Child emblem.

**734** "1830–1980"

**1980.** 150th Anniv of Independence (1st issue).

| | | | | |
|---|---|---|---|---|
| 2584 | **734** | 9f. mauve & lt mauve | 70 | 30 |

See also Nos. 2597/2601.

**735** Frans Van Cauwelaert

**736** Spring Flowers

**1980.** Birth Centenary of Frans Van Cauwelaert (politician).

| | | | | |
|---|---|---|---|---|
| 2585 | **735** | 5f. black | 45 | 30 |

**736** Spring Flowers

**1980.** Ghent Flower Show. Multicoloured.

| | | | |
|---|---|---|---|
| 2586 | 5f. Type **736** | 45 | 35 |
| 2587 | 6f.50 Summer flowers | 60 | 35 |
| 2588 | 9f. Autumn flowers | 70 | 35 |

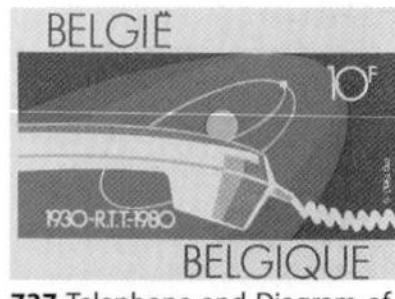

**737** Telephone and Diagram of Satellite Orbit

**1980.** 50th Anniv of Telegraph and Telephone Office.

| | | | | |
|---|---|---|---|---|
| 2589 | **737** | 10f. multicoloured | 80 | 35 |

**738** 5f. Airmail Stamp of 1930

**1980.** Stamp Day.

| | | | | |
|---|---|---|---|---|
| 2590 | **738** | 9f. multicoloured | 75 | 30 |

**739** St. Benedict of Nursia

**1980.** Europa. Multicoloured.
2591 9f. Type **739** 1·40 30
2592 14f. Marguerite of Austria 2·10 70

**740** Ivo van Damme

**1980.** Ivo van Damme (athlete) Commemoration.
2593 **740** 20f.+10f. mult 2·10 2·10

**741** Palais de la Nation

**1980.** 4th Interparliamentary Conference on European Co-operation and Security, Brussels.
2594 **741** 5f. blue, lilac and black 40 35

**742** Golden Carriage, Mons

**1980.** Tourist Publicity. Multicoloured.
2595 6f.50 Type **742** 50 35
2596 6f.50 Damme 50 35

**743** King Leopold I and Queen Louise-Marie

**1980.** 150th Anniv of Belgian Independence (2nd issue).
2597 **743** 6f.50+1f.50 pur & blk 65 65
2598 - 9f.+3f. blue & black 75 75
2599 - 14f.+6f. green & blk 1·40 1·40
2600 - 17f.+8f. orange. & blk 1·70 1·70
2601 - 25f.+10f. green & blk 2·40 2·40
**MS**2602 100×150 mm. 50f. black (sold at 75f.) 5·25 5·25

DESIGNS: 9f. King Leopold II and Queen Marie-Henriette; 14f. King Albert I and Queen Elisabeth; 17f. King Leopold III and Queen Astrid; 25f. King Baudouin and Queen Fabiola; 50f. Royal Mint Theatre, Brussels.

**744** King Baudouin

**1980.** King Baudouin's 50th Birthday.
2603 **744** 9f. red 75 25

**745** "Brewer" (detail, Reliquary of St. Lambert)

**1980.** Millenary of Liège. Multicoloured.
2604 9f.+3f. Type **745** 75 75
2605 17f.+6f. "The Miner" (sculpture by Constantin Meunier) (horiz) 1·70 1·70
2606 25f.+10f. "Seat of Wisdom" (Madonna, Collegiate Church of St. John, Liege) 2·40 2·40
**MS**2607 150×100 mm. 20f.+10f. Seal of Prince Bishop Notger (43×24 mm) 4·25 4·25

**746** Chiny

**1980.** Tourist Publicity.
2608 **746** 5f. multicoloured 45 30

**747** Emblem of Cardiological League of Belgium

**1980.** Heart Week.
2609 **747** 14f. light blue, red and blue 1·20 60

**748** Rodenbach (statue at Roulers)

**1980.** Death Cent of Albrecht Rodenbach (poet).
2610 **748** 9f. brown, blue and deep blue 75 30

**749** "Royal Procession" (children of Thyl Uylenspiegel Primary School)

**1980.** "Philately for the Young".
2611 **749** 5f. multicoloured 40 35

**750** Emblem

**1980.** 50th Anniv of Belgian Broadcasting Corporation.
2612 **750** 10f. black and grey 80 45

**751** "Garland of Flowers and Nativity" (attr. D. Seghers)

**1980.** Christmas.
2613 **751** 6f.50 multicoloured 50 35

**752** Gateway, Diest

**1980.** Tourist Publicity.
2614 **752** 5f. multicoloured 45 35

See also Nos. 2648/51 and 2787/92.

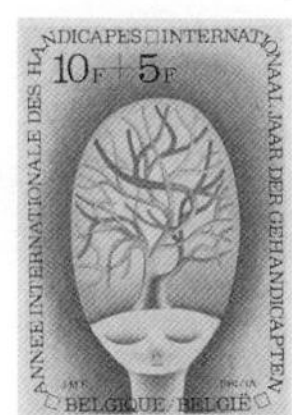


**754** Brain

**1981.** International Year of Disabled Persons. Multicoloured.
2637 10f.+5f. Type **754** 1·20 1·20
2638 25f.+10f. Eye (horiz) 2·50 2·50

**755** "Baron de Gerlache" (after F. J. Navez)

**1981.** Historical Anniversaries.
2639 **755** 6f. multicoloured 45 30
2640 - 9f. multicoloured 70 30
2641 - 50f. brown & yellow 3·75 70

DESIGNS—As T **755**: 6f. Type **755** (1st President of Chamber of Deputies) (150th anniv of Chamber); 9f. Baron de Stassart (1st President of Senate) (after F. J. Navez) (150th anniv of Senate). 35×51 mm: 50f. Statue of King Leopold I by Geefs (150th anniv of royal dynasty).

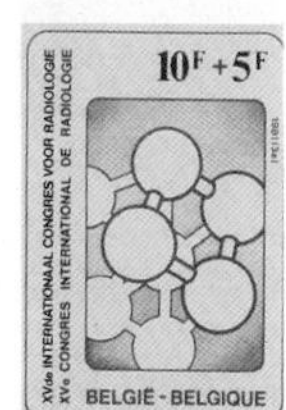


**756** Emblem of 15th International Radiology Convention

**1981.** Belgian Red Cross.
2642 **756** 10f.+5f. bl, blk & red 1·00 1·00
2643 - 25f.+10f. blue, red and black 2·40 2·40

DESIGN: 25f. Dove and globe symbolizing international emergency assistance.

**757** Tchantches and Op-Signoorke (puppets)

**1981.** Europa. Multicoloured.
2644 9f. Type **757** 1·50 30
2645 14f. D'Artagnan and Woltje (puppets) 2·50 85

**758** Stamp Transfer-roller depicting A. de Cock (founder of Postal Museum)

**1981.** Stamp Day.
2646 **758** 9f. multicoloured 75 30

**759** Ovide Decroly

**1981.** 110th Birth Anniv of Dr. Ovide Decroly (educational psychologist).
2647 **759** 35f.+15f. brown & bl 3·50 2·30

**1981.** Tourist Publicity. As T **752**. Multicoloured.
2648 6f. Statue of our Lady of Tongre 60 35
2649 6f. Egmont Castle, Zottegem 60 35
2650 6f.50 Dams on Eau d'Heure (horiz) 60 35
2651 6f.50 Tongerlo Abbey, Antwerp (horiz) 60 35

**760** Footballer

**1981.** Cent of Royal Antwerp Football Club.
2652 **760** 6f. red, brown & black 60 30

**761** Edouard Remouchamps (Walloon dramatist)

**1981.** 125th Anniv of Society of Walloon Language and Literature.
2653 **761** 6f.50 brown and stone 50 30

**762** French Horn

**1981.** Centenary of De Vredekring Band, Antwerp.
2654 **762** 6f.50 blue, mve & blk 50 30

**763** Audit Office

**1981.** 150th Anniv of Audit Office.

| | | | | |
|---|---|---|---|---|
| 2655 | **763** | 10f. purple | 80 | 30 |

**764** Pietà

**1981.** 25th Anniv of Bois du Cazier Mining Disaster. Sheet 150×100 mm.

| | | | |
|---|---|---|---|
| **MS**2656 **764** | 20f. multicoloured (sold at 30f.) | 2·30 | 2·30 |

**765** Tombs of Marie of Burgundy and Charles the Bold

**1981.** Relocation of Tombs of Marie of Burgundy and Charles the Bold in Notre-Dame Church, Bruges.

| | | | | |
|---|---|---|---|---|
| 2657 | **765** | 50f. multicoloured | 3·75 | 85 |

**766** Boy holding Globe in Tweezers

**1981.** "Philately for Youth".

| | | | | |
|---|---|---|---|---|
| 2658 | **766** | 6f. multicoloured | 45 | 30 |

**767** King Baudouin

**1981**

| | | | | |
|---|---|---|---|---|
| 2659 | **767** | 50f. light blue and blue | 5·50 | 30 |
| 2660 | **767** | 65f. mauve and black | 7·00 | 95 |
| 2661 | **767** | 100f. brown and blue | 11·50 | 60 |

**768** Max Waller (founder)

**1981.** Cultural Anniversaries.

| | | | | |
|---|---|---|---|---|
| 2672 | **768** | 6f. multicoloured | 45 | 30 |
| 2673 | - | 6f.50 multicoloured | 50 | 30 |
| 2674 | - | 9f. multicoloured | 70 | 30 |
| 2675 | - | 10f. multicoloured | 80 | 45 |
| 2676 | - | 14f. lt brn & brn | 1·30 | 60 |

DESIGNS: 6f. Type **768** (centenary of literary review "La Jeune Belgique"); 6f.50," Liqueur Drinkers" (detail, Gustave van de Woestijne (inscr "Woestyne") (birth centenary); 9f. Fernand Severin (poet, 50th death anniv); 10f. Jan van Ruusbroec (mystic, 600th death anniv); 14f. Owl (La Pensee et les Hommes organization, 25th anniv).

**769** Nativity (miniature from "Missale ad usum d. Leodensis")

**1981.** Christmas.

| | | | | |
|---|---|---|---|---|
| 2677 | **769** | 6f.50 brown and black | 45 | 30 |

**770** Mounted Gendarme, 1832

**1981.** "Solidarity". Multicoloured.

| | | | |
|---|---|---|---|
| 2678 | 9f.+4f. Type **770** | 1·00 | 1·00 |
| 2679 | 20f.+7f. Carabinier | 2·00 | 2·00 |
| 2680 | 40f.+20f. Mounted Guide, 1843 | 4·00 | 4·00 |

**771** Cellist and Royal Conservatory of Music, Brussels

**1982.** 150th Anniversaries. Multicoloured.

| | | | |
|---|---|---|---|
| 2681 | 6f.50 Type **771** | 45 | 30 |
| 2682 | 9f. Front of former Law Court, Brussels (anniv of judiciary) | 70 | 30 |

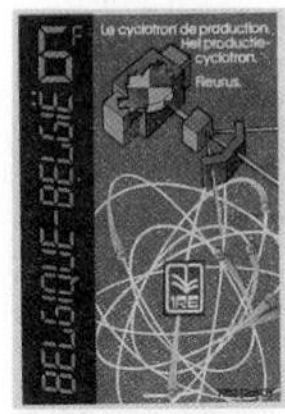


**772** Sectional View of Cyclotron

**1982.** Science. Multicoloured.

| | | | |
|---|---|---|---|
| 2683 | 6f. Type **772** (Installation of cyclotron at National Radio-elements Institute, Fleurus) | 45 | 35 |
| 2684 | 14f. Telescope and galaxy (Royal Observatory) | 1·00 | 45 |
| 2685 | 50f. Dr. Robert Koch and tubercle bacillus (centenary of discovery) | 3·50 | 80 |

**773** Billiards

**1982.** Sports. Multicoloured.

| | | | |
|---|---|---|---|
| 2686 | 6f.+2f. Type **773** | 95 | 95 |
| 2687 | 9f.+4f. Cycling | 1·30 | 1·30 |
| 2688 | 10f.+5f. Football | 1·40 | 1·40 |
| 2689 | 50f.+14f. "Treaty of Rome" (yacht) | 4·00 | 4·00 |
| **MS**2690 | 105×100 mm. 25f. multicoloured (Type **773**); 25f. brown, yellow and black (as No. 2687); 25f. red, yellow and black (as No. 2688); 25f. multicoloured (as No. 2689) | 8·75 | 8·25 |

**774** Joseph Lemaire (after Jean Maillard)

**1982.** Birth Centenary of Joseph Lemaire (Minister of State and social reformer).

| | | | | |
|---|---|---|---|---|
| 2691 | **774** | 6f.50 multicoloured | 50 | 30 |

**775** Voting (Universal Suffrage)

**1982.** Europa.

| | | | | |
|---|---|---|---|---|
| 2692 | **775** | 10f. multicoloured | 2·30 | 35 |
| 2693 | - | 17f. green, black and grey | 4·00 | 60 |

DESIGN: 17f. Portrait and signature of Emperor Joseph II (Edict of Toleration).

**1982.** Surch 1 F.

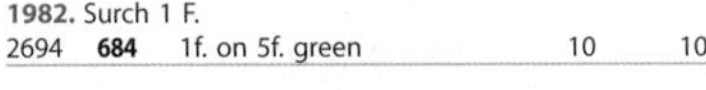

| | | | | |
|---|---|---|---|---|
| 2694 | **684** | 1f. on 5f. green | 10 | 10 |

**777** 17th-century Postal Messenger

**1982.** Stamp Day.

| | | | | |
|---|---|---|---|---|
| 2695 | **777** | 10f. multicoloured | 75 | 30 |

**778** "Tower of Babel" (Brueghel the Elder)

**1982.** World Esperanto Congress, Antwerp.

| | | | | |
|---|---|---|---|---|
| 2696 | **778** | 12f. multicoloured | 95 | 45 |

**1982.** Tourist Publicity. As T 752.

| | | | |
|---|---|---|---|
| 2697 | 7f. blue and light blue | 65 | 35 |
| 2698 | 7f. black and green | 65 | 35 |
| 2699 | 7f.50 brown and light brown | 65 | 35 |
| 2700 | 7f.50 violet and lilac | 65 | 35 |
| 2701 | 7f.50 black and grey | 65 | 35 |
| 2702 | 7f.50 black and pink | 65 | 35 |

DESIGNS—VERT: No. 2697, Gosselies Tower; 2698, Zwijveke Abbey, Termonde; 2701, Entrance gate, Grammont Abbey; 2702, Beveren pillory. HORIZ: No. 2699, Stavelot Abbey; 2700, Abbey ruins, Villers-la-Ville.

**780** Louis Paul Boon (writer)

**1982.** Cultural Anniversaries.

| | | | | |
|---|---|---|---|---|
| 2707 | **780** | 7f. black, red and grey | 45 | 30 |
| 2708 | - | 10f. multicoloured | 70 | 30 |
| 2709 | - | 12f. multicoloured | 95 | 45 |
| 2710 | - | 17f. multicoloured | 1·70 | 45 |

DESIGNS: 7f. Type **780** (70th birth anniv); 10f. "Adoration of the Shepherds" (detail of Portinari retable) (Hugo van der Goes, 500th death anniv); 12f. Michel de Ghelderode (dramatist, 20th death anniv); 17f. "Motherhood" (Pierre Paulus, birth centenary (1981)).

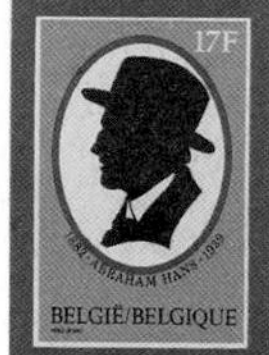


**781** Abraham Hans

**1982.** Birth Centenary of Abraham Hans (writer).

| | | | | |
|---|---|---|---|---|
| 2711 | **781** | 17f. black, turquoise and blue | 1·10 | 35 |

**782** Children playing Football

**1982.** "Philately for the Young". Scout Year.

| | | | | |
|---|---|---|---|---|
| 2712 | **782** | 7f. multicoloured | 65 | 35 |

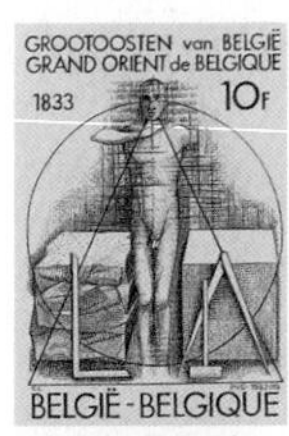


**783** Masonic Emblems

**1982.** 150th Anniv of Belgium Grand Orient (Freemasonry Lodge).

| | | | | |
|---|---|---|---|---|
| 2713 | **783** | 10f. yellow and black | 75 | 30 |

**784** Star over Village

**1982.** Christmas.

| | | | | |
|---|---|---|---|---|
| 2714 | **784** | 10f.+1f. multicoloured | 80 | 30 |

**785** Cardinal Cardijn

**1982.** Birth Centenary of Cardinal Joseph Cardijn.

| | | | | |
|---|---|---|---|---|
| 2715 | **785** | 10f. multicoloured | 80 | 10 |

**786** King Baudouin **787** King Baudouin

**1982**

| | | | | |
|---|---|---|---|---|
| 2716 | **786** | 10f. blue | 95 | 10 |
| 2717 | **786** | 11f. brown | 1·20 | 10 |
| 2718 | **786** | 12f. green | 3·00 | 60 |
| 2719 | **786** | 13f. red | 1·30 | 10 |
| 2720 | **786** | 14f. black | 1·20 | 10 |
| 2721 | **786** | 15f. red | 2·00 | 35 |
| 2722 | **786** | 20f. blue | 2·00 | 10 |
| 2723 | **786** | 22f. purple | 3·00 | 1·20 |
| 2724 | **786** | 23f. green | 3·00 | 60 |
| 2725 | **786** | 24f. grey | 2·30 | 35 |
| 2726 | **786** | 25f. blue | 2·50 | 30 |
| 2727 | **786** | 30f. brown | 2·40 | 10 |
| 2728 | **786** | 40f. red | 4·00 | 10 |
| 2729 | **787** | 50f. light brown, brown and black | 5·75 | 10 |
| 2730 | **787** | 100f. blue, deep blue and black | 16·00 | 25 |
| 2731 | **787** | 200f. light green, green and deep green | 34·00 | 85 |

**788** St. Francis preaching to the Birds

**1982.** 800th Birth Anniv of St. Francis of Assisi.

| | | | | |
|---|---|---|---|---|
| 2736 | **788** | 20f. multicoloured | 1·50 | 60 |

**789** Messenger handing Letter to King in the Field

**1982.** "Belgica 82" Postal History Exhibition. Multicoloured.

| | | | |
|---|---|---|---|
| 2737 | 7f.+2f. Type **789** | 60 | 60 |
| 2738 | 7f.50+2f.50 Messenger, Basel (vert) | 70 | 70 |
| 2739 | 10f.+3f. Messenger, Nuremburg (vert) | 85 | 85 |
| 2740 | 17f.+7f. Imperial courier, 1750 (vert) | 1·60 | 1·60 |
| 2741 | 20f.+9f. Imperial courier, 1800 | 1·90 | 1·90 |
| 2742 | 25f.+10f. Belgian postman, 1886 | 2·20 | 2·20 |
| **MS**2743 | 123×89 mm. 50f.+25f. Mail coach (48×37 mm) | 5·25 | 5·25 |

**790** Emblem

**1983.** 50th Anniv of Caritas Catholica Belgica.

| | | | | |
|---|---|---|---|---|
| 2744 | **790** | 10f.+2f. red and grey | 95 | 95 |

**791** Horse Tram

**1983.** Trams. Multicoloured.

| | | | |
|---|---|---|---|
| 2745 | 7f.50 Type **791** | 80 | 40 |
| 2746 | 10f. Electric tram | 1·20 | 35 |
| 2747 | 50f. Tram with trolley (invented by K. van de Poele) | 4·50 | 70 |

**792** Mountaineer

**1983.** Belgian Red Cross. Multicoloured.

| | | | |
|---|---|---|---|
| 2748 | 12f.+3f. Type **792** | 1·20 | 1·20 |
| 2749 | 20f.+5f. Walker | 2·00 | 2·00 |

**793** Brussels Buildings, Open Periodicals and Globe

**1983.** 24th International Periodical Press Federation World Congress, Brussels.

| | | | | |
|---|---|---|---|---|
| 2750 | **793** | 20f. multicoloured | 1·50 | 60 |

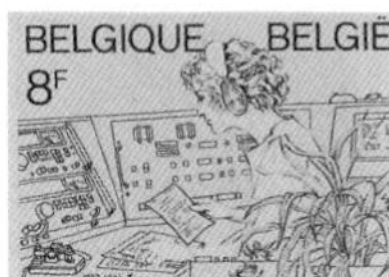

**794** Woman at Work

**1983.** Women.

| | | | | |
|---|---|---|---|---|
| 2751 | **794** | 8f. multicoloured | 80 | 35 |
| 2752 | - | 11f. multicoloured | 95 | 30 |
| 2753 | - | 20f. yellow, brown & bl | 1·70 | 60 |

DESIGNS: 11f. Woman at home; 20f. Woman manager.

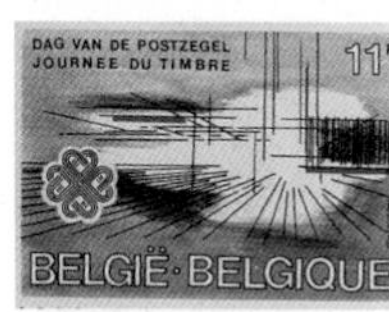

**795** Graphic Representation of Midi Railway Station, Brussels

**1983.** Stamp Day. World Communications Year.

| | | | | |
|---|---|---|---|---|
| 2754 | **795** | 11f. black, red and blue | 95 | 30 |

**796** Procession of the Holy Blood

**1983.** Procession of the Holy Blood, Bruges.

| | | | | |
|---|---|---|---|---|
| 2755 | **796** | 8f. multicoloured | 65 | 35 |

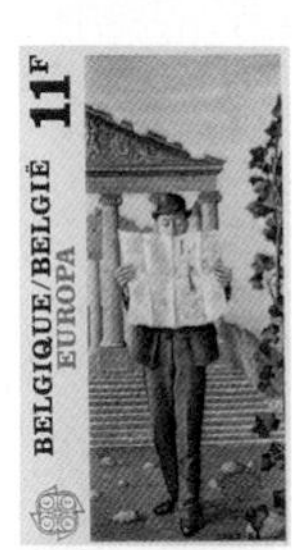

**797** "The Man in the Street"

**1983.** Europa. Paintings by Paul Delvaux. Mult.

| | | | |
|---|---|---|---|
| 2756 | 11f. Type **797** | 1·70 | 35 |
| 2757 | 20f. "Night Trains" (horiz) | 3·50 | 70 |

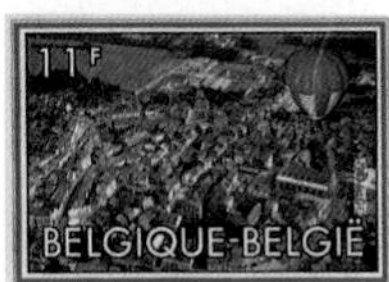

**798** Hot-air Balloon over Town

**1983.** Bicentenary of Manned Flight. Mult.

| | | | |
|---|---|---|---|
| 2758 | 11f. Type **798** | 80 | 30 |
| 2759 | 22f. Hot-air balloon over countryside | 1·70 | 70 |

**799** Church of Our Lady, Hastiere

**1983.** Tourist Publicity. Multicoloured.

| | | | |
|---|---|---|---|
| 2760 | 8f. Type **799** | 75 | 35 |
| 2761 | 8f. Tumulus, Landen | 75 | 35 |
| 2762 | 8f. Park, Mouscron | 75 | 35 |
| 2763 | 8f. Wijnendale Castle, Torhout | 75 | 35 |

**800** Milkmaid

**1983.** Tineke Festival, Heule.

| | | | | |
|---|---|---|---|---|
| 2764 | **800** | 8f. multicoloured | 65 | 35 |

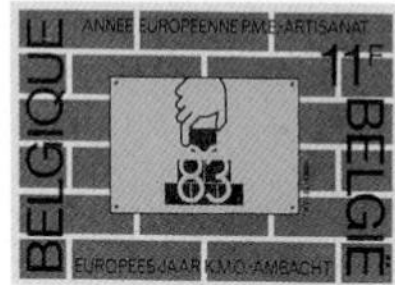

**801** Plaque on Wall

**1983.** European Small and Medium-sized Industries and Crafts Year.

| | | | | |
|---|---|---|---|---|
| 2765 | **801** | 11f. yellow, black & red | 85 | 30 |

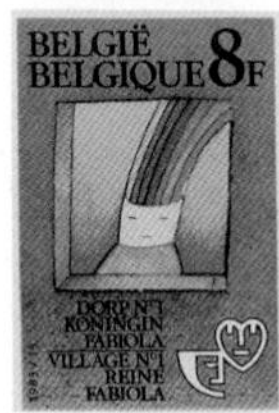

**802** Rainbow and Child

**1983.** "Philately for the Young". 20th Anniv of Queen Fabiola Village No. 1 (for handicapped people).

| | | | | |
|---|---|---|---|---|
| 2766 | **802** | 8f. multicoloured | 65 | 30 |

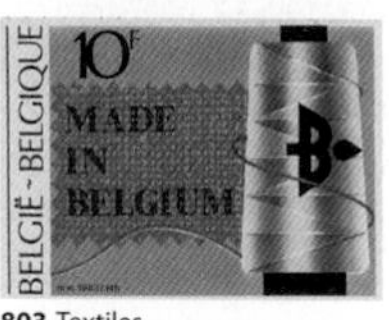

**803** Textiles

**1983.** Belgian Exports (1st series). Multicoloured.

| | | | |
|---|---|---|---|
| 2767 | 10f. Type **803** | 95 | 35 |
| 2768 | 10f. Steel beams (metallurgy) | 95 | 35 |
| 2769 | 10f. Diamonds | 95 | 35 |

See also Nos. 2777/80.

**804** Conscience (after wood engraving by Nelly Degouy)

**1983.** Death Centenary of Hendrik Conscience (writer).

| | | | | |
|---|---|---|---|---|
| 2770 | **804** | 20f. black and green | 1·60 | 45 |

**805** "Madonna" (Jef Wauters)

**1983.** Christmas.

| | | | | |
|---|---|---|---|---|
| 2771 | **805** | 11f.+1f. multicoloured | 95 | 95 |

**806** 2nd Foot Regiment

**1983.** "Solidarity". Military Uniforms. Mult.

| | | | |
|---|---|---|---|
| 2772 | 8f.+2f. Type **806** | 85 | 85 |
| 2773 | 11f.+2f. Lancer | 1·50 | 1·50 |
| 2774 | 50f.+12f. Grenadier | 4·25 | 4·25 |

**1983.** King Leopold III Commemoration.

| | | | | |
|---|---|---|---|---|
| 2775 | **155** | 11f. black | 85 | 30 |

**807** Free University of Brussels

**1984.** 150th Anniv of Free University of Brussels.

| | | | | |
|---|---|---|---|---|
| 2776 | **807** | 11f. multicoloured | 95 | 25 |

**1984.** Belgian Exports (2nd series). As T **803**. Multicoloured.

| | | | |
|---|---|---|---|
| 2777 | 11f. Retort and test tubes (chemicals) | 95 | 35 |
| 2778 | 11f. Combine harvester (agricultural produce) | 95 | 35 |
| 2779 | 11f. Ship, coach and electric commuter train (transport) | 95 | 35 |
| 2780 | 11f. Atomic emblem and computer terminal (new technology) | 95 | 35 |

**808** Albert I

**1984.** 50th Death Anniv of King Albert I.

| | | | | |
|---|---|---|---|---|
| 2781 | **808** | 8f. black and stone | 70 | 35 |

**809** Judo

**1984.** Olympic Games, Los Angeles. Multicoloured.

| | | | |
|---|---|---|---|
| 2782 | 8f.+2f. Type **809** | 70 | 70 |
| 2783 | 12f.+3f. Windsurfing (vert) | 1·20 | 1·20 |
| **MS**2784 | 125×90 mm. 10f. Archery; 24f. Dressage | 2·50 | 2·50 |

**810** Releasing Doves

**1984.** 25th Anniv of Movement without a Name.

| | | | | |
|---|---|---|---|---|
| 2785 | **810** | 12f. multicoloured | 95 | 30 |

**811** Clasped Hands

**1984.** 50th Anniv of National Lottery.

| | | | | |
|---|---|---|---|---|
| 2786 | **811** | 12f.+3f. multicoloured | 1·20 | 1·20 |

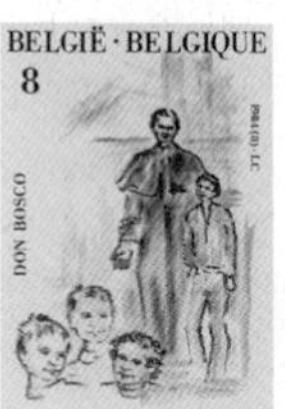

**812** St. John Bosco with Children

**1984.** 50th Anniv of Canonization of St. John Bosco (founder of Salesians).

| | | | | |
|---|---|---|---|---|
| 2787 | **812** | 8f. multicoloured | 70 | 30 |

**813** Bridge

**1984.** Europa. 25th Anniv of European Posts and Telecommunications Conference.

| | | | | |
|---|---|---|---|---|
| 2788 | **813** | 12f. red and black | 1·50 | 30 |
| 2789 | **813** | 22f. blue and black | 3·25 | 60 |

**814** Leopold II 1884 10c. Stamp

**1984.** Stamp Day.

| | | | | |
|---|---|---|---|---|
| 2790 | **814** | 12f. multicoloured | 1·00 | 30 |

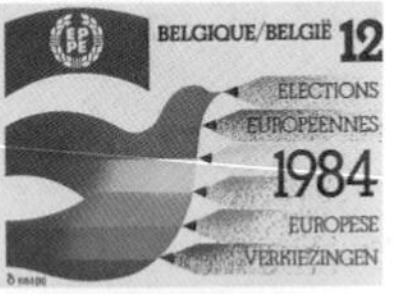


**815** Dove and Pencils

**1984.** 2nd European Parliament Elections.

| | | | | |
|---|---|---|---|---|
| 2791 | **815** | 12f. multicoloured | 1·00 | 30 |

**816** Shako

**1984.** 150th Anniv of Royal Military School.

| | | | | |
|---|---|---|---|---|
| 2792 | **816** | 22f. multicoloured | 1·70 | 50 |

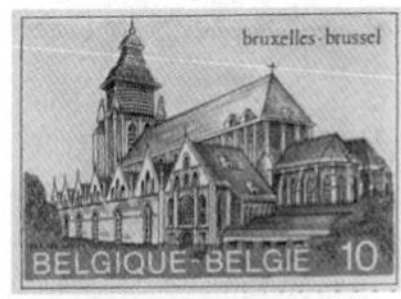


**817** Church of Our Lady of the Chapel, Brussels

**1984.** Tourist Publicity. Multicoloured.

| | | | |
|---|---|---|---|
| 2793 | 10f. Type **817** | 85 | 40 |
| 2794 | 10f. St. Martin's Church and lime tree, Montigny-le-Tilleul | 85 | 40 |
| 2795 | 10f. Belfry and Town Hall, Tielt (vert) | 85 | 40 |

**818** "Curious Masks" (detail, James Ensor)

**1984.** Inaug of Brussels Modern Art Museum.

| | | | | |
|---|---|---|---|---|
| 2796 | **818** | 8f.+2f. multicoloured | 85 | 85 |
| 2797 | - | 12f.+3f. multicoloured | 1·50 | 1·50 |
| 2798 | - | 22f.+5f. multicoloured | 2·00 | 2·00 |
| 2799 | - | 50f.+13f. grn, bl & blk | 4·75 | 4·75 |

DESIGNS: 12f. "The Empire of Lights" (detail, Rene Magritte); 22f. "The End" (detail, Jan Cox); 50f. "Rhythm No. 6" (Jo Delahaut).

**819** Symbolic Design

**1984.** 50th Anniv of Chirojeugd (Christian youth movement).

| | | | | |
|---|---|---|---|---|
| 2800 | **819** | 10f. yellow, violet & bl | 85 | 40 |

**820** Averbode Abbey

**1984.** Abbeys.

| | | | | |
|---|---|---|---|---|
| 2801 | **820** | 8f. green and brown | 65 | 40 |
| 2802 | - | 22f. brown & dp brown | 1·70 | 65 |
| 2803 | - | 24f. green & light green | 1·70 | 65 |
| 2804 | - | 50f. lilac and brown | 4·00 | 85 |

DESIGNS—VERT: 22f. Chimay; 24f. Rochefort. HORIZ: 50f. Affligem.

**821** Smurf as Postman

**1984.** "Philately for the Young".

| | | | | |
|---|---|---|---|---|
| 2805 | **821** | 8f. multicoloured | 1·50 | 45 |

**822** Child collecting Flowers

**1984.** Children.

| | | | |
|---|---|---|---|
| 2806 | 10f.+2f. Type **822** | 95 | 95 |
| 2807 | 12f.+3f. Children with globe | 1·20 | 1·20 |
| 2808 | 15f.+3f. Child on merry-go-round | 1·40 | 1·40 |

**823** Meulemans

**1984.** Birth Cent of Arthur Meulemans (composer).

| | | | | |
|---|---|---|---|---|
| 2809 | **823** | 12f. black and orange | 1·00 | 30 |

**824** Three Kings

**1984.** Christmas.

| | | | | |
|---|---|---|---|---|
| 2810 | **824** | 12f.+1f. multicoloured | 1·20 | 1·20 |

**825** St. Norbert

**1985.** 850th Death Anniv of St. Norbert.

| | | | | |
|---|---|---|---|---|
| 2811 | **825** | 22f. brown & lt brown | 1·80 | 60 |

**826** "Virgin of Louvain" (attr. Jan Gossaert)

**1985.** "Europalia 85 Espana" Festival.

| | | | | |
|---|---|---|---|---|
| 2812 | **826** | 12f. multicoloured | 1·00 | 30 |

**827** Press Card in Hatband

**1985.** Cent of Professional Journalists Association.

| | | | | |
|---|---|---|---|---|
| 2814 | **827** | 9f. multicoloured | 75 | 30 |

**828** Blood System as Tree

**1985.** Belgian Red Cross. Blood Donations.

| | | | | |
|---|---|---|---|---|
| 2815 | **828** | 9f.+2f. multicoloured | 95 | 95 |
| 2816 | - | 23f.+5f. red, blue and black | 2·20 | 2·20 |

DESIGN: 23f. Two hearts.

**829** "Sophrolaelio cattleya" "Burlingama"

**1985.** Ghent Flower Festival. Orchids. Mult.

| | | | |
|---|---|---|---|
| 2817 | 12f. Type **829** | 95 | 30 |
| 2818 | 12f. Phalaenopsis "Malibu" | 95 | 30 |
| 2819 | 12f. Tapeu orchid ("Vanda coerulea") | 95 | 30 |

**830** Pope John Paul II

**1985.** Visit of Pope John Paul II.

| | | | | |
|---|---|---|---|---|
| 2820 | **830** | 12f. multicoloured | 95 | 30 |

**831** Rising Sun behind Chained Gates

**1985.** Centenary of Belgian Workers' Party.

| | | | |
|---|---|---|---|
| 2821 | 9f. Type **831** | 70 | 40 |
| 2822 | 12f. Broken wall, flag and rising sun | 95 | 30 |

**832** Jean de Bast (engraver)

**1985.** Stamp Day.

| | | | | |
|---|---|---|---|---|
| 2823 | **832** | 12f. blue | 95 | 30 |

**834** Class 18 Steam Locomotive, 1896

**1985.** Public Transport Year. Multicoloured.

| | | | |
|---|---|---|---|
| 2826 | 9f. Type **834** | 80 | 35 |
| 2827 | 12f. Locomotive "Elephant", 1835 | 95 | 30 |
| 2828 | 23f. Class 23 tank engine, 1904 | 1·90 | 70 |
| 2829 | 24f. Class I Pacific locomotive, 1935 | 1·90 | 70 |
| **MS**2830 | 150×100 mm. 50f. Class 27 electric locomotive, 1979 | 4·75 | 4·75 |

**835** Cesar Franck and Score

**1985.** Europa. Music Year. Multicoloured.

| | | | |
|---|---|---|---|
| 2831 | 12f. Type **835** | 2·30 | 30 |
| 2832 | 23f. Queen and king with viola dressed in music score (Queen Elisabeth International Music Competition) | 4·00 | 70 |

**836** Planned Canal Lock, Strepy-Thieu

**1985.** Permanent International Navigation Congress Association Centenary Congress, Brussels. Multicoloured.

| | | | |
|---|---|---|---|
| 2833 | 23f. Type **836** | 1·90 | 70 |
| 2834 | 23f. Aerial view of Zeebrugge harbour | 1·90 | 70 |

**837** Church of Our Lady's Assumption, Avernas-le-Bauduin

**1985.** Tourist Publicity. Multicoloured.

| | | | |
|---|---|---|---|
| 2835 | 12f. Type **837** | 95 | 35 |
| 2836 | 12f. Saint Martin's Church, Marcinelle (horiz) | 95 | 35 |
| 2837 | 12f. Roman tower and Church of old beguinage, Tongres | 95 | 35 |
| 2838 | 12f. House, Wachtebeke (horiz) | 95 | 35 |

**838** Queen Astrid

**1985.** 50th Death Anniv of Queen Astrid.

| | | | | |
|---|---|---|---|---|
| 2839 | **838** | 12f. lt brown & brown | 1·00 | 30 |

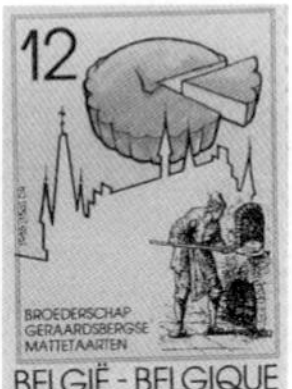


**839** Baking Matton Tart, Grammont

**1985.** Traditional Customs. Multicoloured.

| | | | |
|---|---|---|---|
| 2840 | 12f. Type **839** | 1·00 | 30 |

| | | | |
|---|---|---|---|
| 2841 | 24f. Young people dancing on trumpet filled with flowers (cent of Red Youths, St. Lambert Cultural Circle, Hermalle-sous-Argenteau) | 1·90 | 60 |

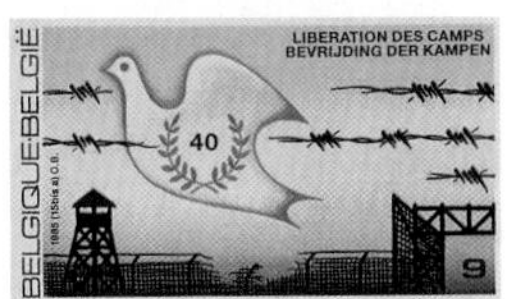

**840** Dove and Concentration Camp

**1985.** 40th Anniv of Liberation. Multicoloured.

| | | | |
|---|---|---|---|
| 2842 | 9f. Type **840** | 80 | 35 |
| 2843 | 23f. Battle of the Ardennes | 1·90 | 70 |
| 2844 | 24f. Troops landing at Scheldt estuary | 1·90 | 70 |

**841** Hawfinch ("Appelvink – Gros Bec")

**1985.** Birds (1st series). Multicoloured.

| | | | |
|---|---|---|---|
| 2845 | 1f. Lesser spotted woodpecker ("Pic epeichette") | 35 | 10 |
| 2846 | 2f. Eurasian tree sparrow ("Moineau friquet") | 30 | 10 |
| 2847 | 3f. Type **841** | 60 | 10 |
| 2847a | 3f.50 European robin ("Rouge-gorge") | 35 | 10 |
| 2848 | 4f. Bluethroat ("Gorge-bleue") | 45 | 10 |
| 2848a | 4f.50 Common stonechat ("Traquet patre") | 50 | 25 |
| 2849 | 5f. Eurasian nuthatch ("Sittelle torche-pot") | 45 | 10 |
| 2850 | 6f. Northern bullfinch ("Bou-vreuil") | 70 | 10 |
| 2851 | 7f. Blue tit ("Mesange bleue") | 70 | 25 |
| 2852 | 8f. River kingfisher ("Martin-pecheur") | 80 | 10 |
| 2853 | 9f. Eurasian goldfinch ("Char-donneret") | 1·20 | 10 |
| 2854 | 10f. Chaffinch ("Pinson") | 85 | 10 |

See also Nos. 3073/86 and 3306/23.

**842** Claes and Fictional Character

**1985.** Birth Centenary of Ernest Claes (writer).

| | | | | |
|---|---|---|---|---|
| 2855 | **842** | 9f. multicoloured | 75 | 30 |

**843** Youth

**1985.** "Philately for the Young". International Youth Year.

| | | | | |
|---|---|---|---|---|
| 2856 | **843** | 9f. multicoloured | 75 | 30 |

**844** Trazegnies Castle

**1985.** "Solidarity". Castles. Multicoloured.

| | | | |
|---|---|---|---|
| 2857 | 9f.+2f. Type **844** | 95 | 95 |
| 2858 | 12f.+3f. Laarne | 1·20 | 1·20 |
| 2859 | 23f.+5f. Turnhout | 2·00 | 2·00 |
| 2860 | 50f.+12f. Colonster | 4·00 | 4·00 |

**845** Miniature from "Book of Hours of Duc de Berry"

**1985.** Christmas.

| | | | | |
|---|---|---|---|---|
| 2861 | **845** | 12f.+1f. multicoloured | 1·00 | 1·00 |

**846** King Baudouin and Queen Fabiola

**1985.** Royal Silver Wedding.

| | | | | |
|---|---|---|---|---|
| 2862 | **846** | 12f. grey, blue and deep blue | 1·20 | 30 |

**847** Map and 1886 25c. Stamp

**1986.** Centenary of First Independent State of Congo Stamp.

| | | | | |
|---|---|---|---|---|
| 2863 | **847** | 10f. blue, grey & dp blue | 1·60 | 35 |

**848** Giants and Belfry, Alost

**1986.** Carnivals. Multicoloured.

| | | | |
|---|---|---|---|
| 2864 | 9f. Type **848** | 70 | 40 |
| 2865 | 12f. Clown, Binche | 1·00 | 30 |

**849** Dove as Hand holding Olive Twig

**1986.** International Peace Year.

| | | | | |
|---|---|---|---|---|
| 2866 | **849** | 23f. multicoloured | 2·00 | 60 |

**850** Emblem

**1986.** 10th Anniv of King Baudouin Foundation.

| | | | | |
|---|---|---|---|---|
| 2867 | **850** | 12f.+3f. blue, light blue and grey | 1·50 | 1·50 |

**851** Virgin Mary

**1986.** "The Mystic Lamb" (altarpiece, Brothers Van Eyck). Multicoloured.

| | | | |
|---|---|---|---|
| 2868 | 9f.+2f. Type **851** | 90 | 90 |
| 2869 | 13f.+3f. Christ in Majesty | 1·30 | 1·30 |
| 2870 | 24f.+6f. St. John the Baptist | 2·30 | 2·30 |
| **MS**2871 | 92×150 mm. 50f.+12f. The Lamb (central panel) (48×37 mm) | 9·00 | 9·00 |

**852** Exhibits

**1986.** Stamp Day. 50th Anniv of Postal Museum, Brussels.

| | | | | |
|---|---|---|---|---|
| 2872 | **852** | 13f. multicoloured | 1·10 | 30 |

**853** Living and Dead Fish and Graph

**1986.** Europa. Multicoloured.

| | | | |
|---|---|---|---|
| 2873 | 13f. Type **853** | 1·90 | 30 |
| 2874 | 24f. Living and dead trees and graph | 3·75 | 65 |

**854** Malinois Shepherd Dog

**1986.** Belgian Dogs. Multicoloured.

| | | | |
|---|---|---|---|
| 2875 | 9f. Type **854** | 85 | 40 |
| 2876 | 13f. Tervuren shepherd dog | 1·30 | 30 |
| 2877 | 24f. Groenendael cattle dog | 2·20 | 60 |
| 2878 | 26f. Flanders cattle dog | 2·30 | 60 |

**855** St. Ludger Church, Zele

**1986.** Tourist Publicity.

| | | | | |
|---|---|---|---|---|
| 2879 | **855** | 9f. brown and flesh | 70 | 35 |
| 2880 | - | 9f. red and pink | 70 | 35 |
| 2881 | - | 13f. green & light green | 1·10 | 35 |
| 2882 | - | 13f. black and green | 1·10 | 35 |
| 2883 | - | 13f. blue and azure | 1·10 | 35 |
| 2884 | - | 13f. brown & lt brown | 1·10 | 35 |

DESIGNS—VERT: No. 2880, Town Hall, Wavre; 2882, Chapel of Our Lady of the Dunes, Bredene. HORIZ: 2881, Water-mills, Zwalm; 2883, Chateau Licot, Viroinval; 2884, Chateau d'Eynebourg, La Calamine.

**856** Boy, Broken Skateboard and Red Triangle

**1986.** "Philately for the Young". 25th International Festival of Humour, Knokke.

| | | | | |
|---|---|---|---|---|
| 2885 | **856** | 9f. black, green & red | 70 | 40 |

**857** Constant Permeke (artist)

**1986.** Celebrities. Multicoloured.

| | | | |
|---|---|---|---|
| 2886 | 9f. Type **857** (birth centenary) | 70 | 35 |
| 2887 | 13f. Michael Edmond de Selys-Longchamps (naturalist) | 1·20 | 35 |
| 2888 | 24f. Felix Timmermans (writer) (birth cent) | 2·10 | 60 |
| 2889 | 26f. Maurice Careme (poet) | 2·20 | 60 |

**858** Academy Building, Ghent

**1986.** Centenary of Royal Academy for Dutch Language and Literature.

| | | | | |
|---|---|---|---|---|
| 2890 | **858** | 9f. blue | 70 | 35 |

**859** Hops, Glass of Beer and Barley

**1986.** Belgian Beer.

| | | | | |
|---|---|---|---|---|
| 2891 | **859** | 13f. multicoloured | 1·20 | 30 |

**860** Symbols of Provinces and National Colours

**1986.** 150th Anniv of Provincial Councils.

| | | | | |
|---|---|---|---|---|
| 2892 | **860** | 13f. multicoloured | 1·10 | 30 |

**861** Lenoir Hydrocarbon Carriage, 1863

**1986.** "Solidarity". Cars. Multicoloured.

| | | | |
|---|---|---|---|
| 2893 | 9f.+2f. Type **861** | 90 | 90 |
| 2894 | 13f.+3f. Pipe de Tourisme saloon, 1911 | 1·30 | 1·30 |
| 2895 | 24f.+6f. Minerva 22 h.p. coupe, 1930 | 2·40 | 2·40 |
| 2896 | 26f.+6f. FN 8 cylinder saloon, 1931 | 2·50 | 2·50 |

**862** Snow Scene

**1986.** Christmas.

| | | | | |
|---|---|---|---|---|
| 2897 | **862** | 13f.+1f. multicoloured | 1·20 | 1·20 |

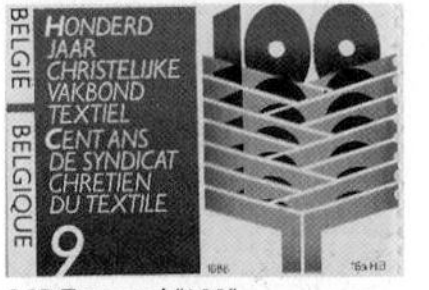

**863** Tree and "100"

**1986.** Centenaries. Multicoloured.

| | | | |
|---|---|---|---|
| 2898 | 9f. Type **863** (Textile Workers Christian Union) | 70 | 40 |

| | | | | |
|---|---|---|---|---|
| 2899 | | 13f. Tree and "100" (Christian Unions) | 1·10 | 30 |

**864** Corneel Heymans

**1987.** Belgian Red Cross. Nobel Physiology and Medicine Prize Winners. Each black, red and stone.

| | | | | |
|---|---|---|---|---|
| 2900 | | 13f.+3f. Type **864** | 1·50 | 1·50 |
| 2901 | | 24f.+6f. Albert Claude | 2·75 | 2·75 |

**865** Emblem

**1987.** "Flanders Technology International" Fair.

| | | | | |
|---|---|---|---|---|
| 2902 | **865** | 13f. multicoloured | 1·10 | 30 |

**866** Bee Orchid

**1987.** European Environment Year. Multicoloured.

| | | | | |
|---|---|---|---|---|
| 2903 | | 9f.+2f. Type **866** | 1·10 | 1·10 |
| 2904 | | 24f.+6f. Small horse-shoe bat | 2·40 | 2·40 |
| 2905 | | 26f.+6f. Peregrine falcon ("Slechtvalk–Faucan Pelerin") | 2·75 | 2·75 |

**867** "Waiting" (detail of mural, Gustav Klimt)

**1987.** "Europalia 87 Austria" Festival.

| | | | | |
|---|---|---|---|---|
| 2906 | **867** | 13f. multicoloured | 1·10 | 30 |

**868** Jakob Wiener (engraver)

**1987.** Stamp Day.

| | | | | |
|---|---|---|---|---|
| 2907 | **868** | 13f. deep green and green | 1·10 | 30 |

**869** Penitents' Procession, Furnes

**1987.** Folklore Festivals. Multicoloured.

| | | | | |
|---|---|---|---|---|
| 2908 | | 9f. Type **869** | 70 | 40 |
| 2909 | | 13f. "John and Alice" (play), Wavre | 1·10 | 30 |

**870** Louvain-la-Neuve Church (Jean Cosse)

**1987.** Europa. Architecture. Multicoloured.

| | | | | |
|---|---|---|---|---|
| 2910 | | 13f. Type **870** | 2·40 | 30 |
| 2911 | | 24f. St.-Maartensdal (Regional Housing Association tower block), Louvain (Braem, de Mol and Moerkerke) | 4·25 | 90 |

**871** Statue of Gretry and Stage Set

**1987.** 20th Anniv of Wallonia Royal Opera.

| | | | | |
|---|---|---|---|---|
| 2912 | **871** | 24f. multicoloured | 2·10 | 70 |

**872** Virelles Lake

**1987.** Tourist Publicity. Multicoloured.

| | | | | |
|---|---|---|---|---|
| 2913 | | 13f. St. Christopher's Church, Racour | 1·10 | 30 |
| 2914 | | 13f. Type **872** | 1·10 | 30 |
| 2915 | | 13f. Heimolen windmill, Keerbergen | 1·10 | 30 |
| 2916 | | 13f. Boondael Chapel | 1·10 | 30 |
| 2917 | | 13f. Statue of Jan Breydel and Pieter de Coninck, Bruges | 1·10 | 30 |

**873** Rowing

**1987.** Centenary of Royal Belgian Rowing Association (2918) and European Volleyball Championships (2919). Multicoloured.

| | | | | |
|---|---|---|---|---|
| 2918 | | 9f. Type **873** | 70 | 40 |
| 2919 | | 13f. Volleyball (27×37 mm) | 1·10 | 30 |

**874** Emblem

**1987.** Foreign Trade Year.

| | | | | |
|---|---|---|---|---|
| 2920 | **874** | 13f. multicoloured | 1·10 | 30 |

**875** "Leisure Time" (P. Paulus)

**1987.** Centenary of Belgian Social Law.

| | | | | |
|---|---|---|---|---|
| 2921 | **875** | 26f. multicoloured | 2·10 | 65 |

**876** Willy and Wanda (comic strip characters)

**1987.** "Philately for the Young".

| | | | | |
|---|---|---|---|---|
| 2922 | **876** | 9f. multicoloured | 2·10 | 60 |

**878** Rixensart Castle

**1987.** "Solidarity". Castles. Multicoloured.

| | | | | |
|---|---|---|---|---|
| 2928 | | 9f.+2f. Type **878** | 90 | 90 |
| 2929 | | 13f.+3f. Westerlo | 1·20 | 1·20 |
| 2930 | | 26f.+5f. Fallais | 2·40 | 2·40 |
| 2931 | | 50f.+12f. Gaasbeek | 4·50 | 4·50 |

**879** "Madonna and Child" (Remi Lens)

**1987.** Christmas.

| | | | | |
|---|---|---|---|---|
| 2932 | **879** | 13f.+1f. multicoloured | 1·20 | 1·20 |

**880** Cross and Road

**1987.** 50th Anniv of Yellow and White Cross (home nursing organization).

| | | | | |
|---|---|---|---|---|
| 2933 | **880** | 9f.+2f. multicoloured | 1·20 | 1·20 |

**881** Newsprint ("Le Soir")

**1987.** Newspaper Centenaries.

| | | | | |
|---|---|---|---|---|
| 2934 | **881** | 9f. multicoloured | 85 | 35 |
| 2935 | - | 9f. black and brown | 85 | 35 |

DESIGN—VERT: No. 2935, Type characters ("Het Laatste Nieuws" (1988)).

**882** Lighthouse, "Snipe" (trawler) and Horse Rider in Sea

**1988.** The Sea. Multicoloured.

| | | | | |
|---|---|---|---|---|
| 2936 | | 10f. Type **882** | 85 | 70 |
| 2937 | | 10f. "Asannot" (trawler) and people playing on beach | 85 | 70 |
| 2938 | | 10f. Cross-channel ferry, yacht and bathing huts | 85 | 70 |
| 2939 | | 10f. Container ship, spotted redshank and oystercatcher | 85 | 70 |

Nos. 2936/9 were issued together, se-tenant, forming a composite design.

**883** "Flanders Alive" (cultural activities campaign)

**1988.** Regional Innovations.

| | | | | |
|---|---|---|---|---|
| 2940 | **883** | 13f. multicoloured | 1·10 | 30 |
| 2941 | - | 13f. black, yellow & red | 1·10 | 30 |

DESIGN: No. 2941, "Operation Athena" emblem (technological advancement in Wallonia).

**884** 19th-century Postman (after James Thirian)

**1988.** Stamp Day.

| | | | | |
|---|---|---|---|---|
| 2942 | **884** | 13f. brown and cream | 1·10 | 30 |

**885** "Bengale Triomphant"

**1988.** Philatelic Promotion Fund. Illustrations from "60 Roses for a Queen" by Pierre-Joseph Redoute (1st series). Multicoloured.

| | | | | |
|---|---|---|---|---|
| 2943 | | 13f.+3f. Type **885** | 1·50 | 1·50 |
| 2944 | | 24f.+6f. "Centfeuille cristata" | 2·40 | 2·40 |
| **MS**2945 | | 150×100 mm. 50f.+12f. White tea rose | 8·50 | 8·50 |

See also Nos. 2979/**MS**2981, 3009/**MS**3011 and **MS**3025.

**886** Non-polluting Motor

**1988.** Europa. Transport and Communications. Multicoloured.

| | | | | |
|---|---|---|---|---|
| 2946 | | 13f. Dish aerial | 2·40 | 30 |
| 2947 | | 24f. Type **886** | 4·75 | 90 |

**887** Table Tennis

**1988.** Olympic Games, Seoul. Multicoloured.

| | | | | |
|---|---|---|---|---|
| 2948 | | 9f.+2f. Type **887** | 1·30 | 1·30 |
| 2949 | | 13f.+3f. Cycling | 1·50 | 1·50 |
| **MS**2950 | | 125×85 mm. 50f.+12f. Running | 8·50 | 8·50 |

**888** Amay Tower

**1988.** Tourist Publicity.

| | | | | |
|---|---|---|---|---|
| 2951 | **888** | 9f. black and brown | 85 | 35 |
| 2952 | - | 9f. black and blue | 85 | 35 |
| 2953 | - | 9f. black, green and pink | 85 | 35 |
| 2954 | - | 13f. black and pink | 1·10 | 30 |
| 2955 | - | 13f. black and grey | 1·10 | 30 |

DESIGNS—VERT: No. 2952, Lady of Hanswijk Basilica, Malines; 2954, Old Town Hall and village pump, Peer. HORIZ: No. 2953, St. Sernin's Church, Waimes; 2955, Basilica of Our Lady of Bon Secours, Peruwelz.

**889** Monnet

**1988.** Birth Centenary of Jean Monnet (statesman).
2956 **889** 13f. black and cream 1·10 30

**890** Tapestry (detail) and Academy Building

**1988.** 50th Annivs of Royal Belgian Academy of Medicine (2957) and Royal Belgian Academy of Sciences, Literature and Fine Arts (2958). Multicoloured.
2957 9f. Type **890** 70 35
2958 9f. Symbols of Academy and building 70 35

**891** Antwerp Ethnographical Museum Exhibits

**1988.** Cultural Heritage. Multicoloured.
2959 9f. Type **891** 85 35
2960 13f. Tomb of Lord Gilles Othon and Jacqueline de Lalaing, St. Martin's Church, Trazegnies 1·10 30
2961 24f. Organ, St. Bartholomew's Church, Geraardsbergen 2·10 70
2962 26f. St. Hadelin's reliquary, St. Martin's Church, Vise 2·30 70

**892** Spirou (comic strip character) and Stamp

**1988.** "Philately for the Young". 50th Anniv of "Spirou" (comic).
2963 **892** 9f. multicoloured 1·80 60

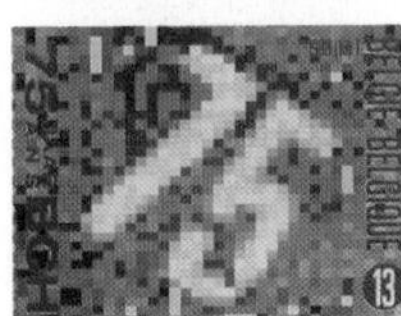

**893** Jacques Brel (songwriter)

**1988.** "Solidarity". Death Anniversaries. Mult.
2964 9f.+2f. Type **893** (10th) 1·50 1·50
2965 13f.+3f. Jef Denyn (carilloner) (47th) 1·50 1·50
2966 26f.+6f. Fr. Ferdinand Verbiest (astronomer) (300th) 2·40 2·40

**894** "75"

**1988.** 75th Anniv of Belgian Giro Bank.
2967 **894** 13f. multicoloured 1·20 30

**895** Winter Scene

**1988.** Christmas.
2968 **895** 9f. multicoloured 80 35

**896** Standard Bearer and Guards of Royal Mounted Escort

**1988.** 50th Anniv of Royal Mounted Escort.
2969 **896** 13f. multicoloured 1·10 30

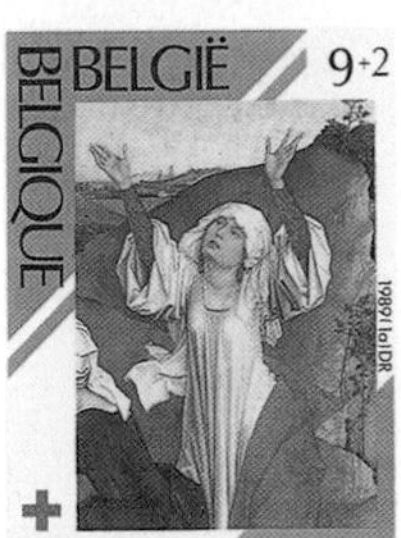

**897** Wooden Press, 1600

**1988.** Printing Presses.
2970 **897** 9f. black, pink and blue 85 30
2971 - 24f. brown, pink and deep brown 1·90 65
2972 - 26f. green, pink and light green 2·10 60

DESIGNS—VERT: 24f. 18th-cent Stanhope metal letterpress. HORIZ: 26f. 19th-cent Krause lithographic press.

**898** "Crucifixion of Christ" (detail, Rogier van der Weyden)

**1989.** Belgian Red Cross. Paintings. Mult.
2973 9f.+2f. Type **898** 1·20 1·20
2974 13f.+3f. "Virgin and Child" (Gerard David) 1·70 1·70
2975 24f.+6f. "The Good Samaritan" (detail, Denis van Alsloot) 2·50 2·50

**899** Marche en Famenne

**1989.** Lace-making Towns.
2976 **899** 9f. green, black & brown 85 40
2977 - 13f. blue, black & grey 1·10 30
2978 - 13f. red, black & grey 1·10 30

DESIGNS: No. 2977, Bruges; 2978, Brussels.

**1989.** Philatelic Promotion Fund. "60 Roses for a Queen" by Pierre-Joseph Redoute (2nd series). As T 885. Multicoloured.
2979 13f.+5f. "Centfeuille unique melee de rouge" 1·50 1·50
2980 24f.+6f. "Bengale a grandes feuilles" 2·40 2·40
MS2981 150×100 mm. 50f.+17f. "Aime vibere" 8·50 8·50

**900** Post-chaise and Mail Coach

**1989.** Stamp Day.
2982 **900** 13f. yellow, black & brn 1·00 30

**901** Marbles

**1989.** Europa. Children's Games and Toys. Multicoloured.
2983 13f. Type **901** 2·20 30
2984 24f. Jumping-jack 3·75 70

**902** Palette on Column

**1989.** 325th Anniv of Royal Academy of Fine Arts, Antwerp.
2985 **902** 13f. multicoloured 1·00 30

**903** Brussels (image scaled to 63% of original size)

**1989.** 3rd Direct Elections to European Parliament.
2986 **903** 13f. multicoloured 1·00 30

**904** Hand (detail, "Creation of Adam", Michelangelo)

**1989.** Bicentenary of French Declaration of Rights of Man.
2987 **904** 13f. black, red and blue 1·00 30

**905** St. Tillo's Church, Izegem

**1989.** Tourist Publicity. Multicoloured.
2988 9f. Type **905** 85 35
2989 9f. Logne Castle, Ferrieres (vert) 85 35
2990 13f. Antoing Castle (vert) 1·20 30
2991 13f. St. Laurentius's Church, Lokeren (vert) 1·20 30

**906** Mallard

**1989.** Ducks. Multicoloured.
2992 13f. Type **906** 1·50 60
2993 13f. Green-winged teal ("Sarcelle d'Hiver") 1·50 60
2994 13f. Common shoveler ("Canard Souchet") 1·50 60
2995 13f. Pintail ("Canard Pilet") 1·50 60

**907** "Shogun Uesugi Shigefusa" (Kamakura period wood figure)

**1989.** "Europalia 89 Japan" Festival.
2996 **907** 24f. multicoloured 1·90 70

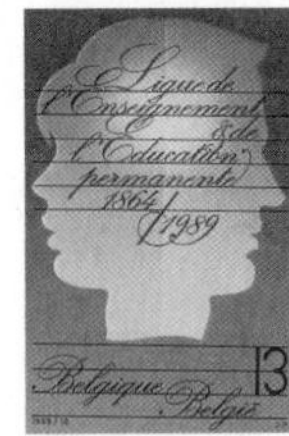

**908** Profiles

**1989.** 125th Anniv of League of Teaching and Permanent Education.
2997 **908** 13f. multicoloured 1·00 30

**909** Map

**1989.** 150th Anniv of Division of Limburg between Netherlands and Belgium.
2998 **909** 13f. multicoloured 1·00 30

**910** Nibbs (comic strip character)

**1989.** "Philately for the Young".
2999 **910** 9f. multicoloured 1·50 50

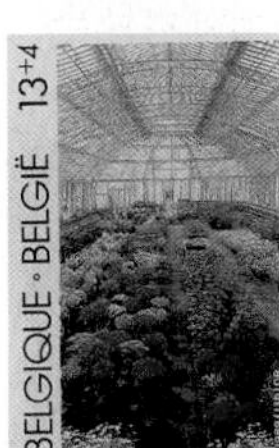

**911** Flower Beds in Greenhouse

**1989.** "Solidarity". Royal Greenhouses, Laeken. Multicoloured.
3000 9f.+3f. Statue and greenhouses (horiz) 1·20 1·20
3001 13f.+4f. Type **911** 1·60 1·60
3002 24f.+5f. External view of greenhouse 2·30 2·30
3003 26f.+6f. Trees in greenhouse 2·50 2·50

**912** Treble Clef

**1989.** 50th Anniv of Queen Elisabeth Musical Chapel, Waterloo.
3004 **912** 24f.+6f. multicoloured 2·40 2·40

**913** Army Musicians

**1989.** Christmas. Centenary of Salvation Army in Belgium.
3005 **913** 9f. multicoloured 80 30

**914** Fr. Damien and Church

**1989.** Death Cent of Fr. Damien (missionary).
3006 **914** 24f. multicoloured 2·10 65

**915** Fr. Daens

**1989.** 150th Birth Anniv of Fr. Adolf Daens (social reformer).
3007 **915** 9f. turquoise and green 70 30

**916** "Courier" (Albrecht Durer)

**1990.** 500th Anniv of Regular European Postal Services.
3008 **916** 14f. chocolate, buff and brown 1·10 30

**1990.** Philatelic Promotion Fund. "60 Roses for a Queen" by Pierre-Joseph Redoute (3rd series). As T 885. Multicoloured.
3009 14f.+7f. "Bengale Desprez" 1·80 1·80
3010 25f.+12f. "Bengale Philippe" 3·00 3·00
**MS**3011 151×100 mm. 50f.+20f. "Maria Leonida" 8·50 8·50

**917** "Iris florentina"

**1990.** Ghent Flower Show. Multicoloured.
3012 10f. Type **917** 85 50
3013 14f. "Cattleya harrisoniana" 1·20 35
3014 14f. "Lilium bulbiferum" 1·20 35

**918** Emilienne Brunfaut (women's rights activist)

**1990.** International Women's Day.
3015 **918** 25f. red and black 2·10 85

**919** Special Olympics

**1990.** Sporting Events. Multicoloured.
3016 10f. Type **919** 80 50
3017 14f. Football (World Cup football championship, Italy) 1·20 35
3018 25f. Disabled pictogram and ball (Gold Cup wheelchair basketball championship, Bruges) 1·90 70

**920** Water, Tap and Heart

**1990.** 75th Anniv of Foundation of National Water Supply Society (predecessor of present water-supply companies).
3019 **920** 14f. multicoloured 1·10 30

**921** "Postman Roulin" (Vincent van Gogh)

**1990.** Stamp Day.
3020 **921** 14f. multicoloured 1·10 30

**922** Worker and Crowd

**1990.** Centenary of Labour Day.
3021 **922** 25f. brown, pink & black 2·10 85

**923** Liege I Post Office

**1990.** Europa. Post Office Buildings.
3022 - 14f. black and blue 2·40 35
3023 **923** 25f. black and red 4·50 85
DESIGN—HORIZ: 14f. Ostend I Post Office.

**924** Monument of the Lys, Courtrai

**1990.** 50th Anniv of the 18 Days Campaign (resistance to German invasion).
3024 **924** 14f. black, yellow & red 1·20 30

**1990.** "Belgica 90" International Stamp Exhibition, Brussels. "60 Roses for a Queen" by Pierre-Joseph Rerdoute (4th series). Sheet 189×120 mm containing vert designs as T 885. Multicoloured.
**MS**3025 14f. Tricoloured rose; 14f. "Belle Rubanee"; 14f. "Mycrophylla"; 25f. "Amelie"; 25f. "Adelaide"; 25f. "Helene" (sold at 220f.) 36·00 36·00

**925** Battle Scene

**1990.** 175th Anniv of Battle of Waterloo.
3026 **925** 25f. multicoloured 2·10 1·80

**926** Berendrecht Lock, Antwerp

**1990.** Tourist Publicity. Multicoloured.
3027 10f. Type **926** 95 50
3028 10f. Procession of Bayard Steed, Termonde 95 50
3029 14f. St. Rolende's March, Gerpinnes (vert) 1·10 35
3030 14f. Lommel (1000th anniv) 1·10 35
3031 14f. St. Clement's Church, Watermael 1·10 35

**927** King Baudouin

**1990**
3032 **927** 14f. multicoloured 1·30 25

**928** Eurasian Perch

**1990.** Fishes. Multicoloured.
3033 14f. Type **928** 2·10 70
3034 14f. Eurasian minnow ("Vairon") 2·10 70
3035 14f. European bitterling ("Bouviere") 2·10 70
3036 14f. Three-spined stickle-back ("Epinoche") 2·10 70

**929** Orchestra and Children (image scaled to 63% of original size)

**1990.** "Solidarity". Multicoloured.
3037 10f.+2f. Type **929** (50th anniv of Jeunesses Musicales) 2·20 2·20
3038 14f.+3f. Count of Egmont (16th-century campaigner for religious tolerance) and Beethoven (composer of "Egmont" overture) 2·75 2·75
3039 25f.+6f. Jozef Cantre (sculptor) and sculptures (birth centenary) 3·75 3·75

**930** Lucky Luke (comic strip character)

**1990.** "Philately for the Young".
3040 **930** 10f. multicoloured 1·80 60

**931** St. Bernard

**1990.** 900th Birth Anniv of St. Bernard (Abbot of Clairvaux and Church mediator).
3041 **931** 25f. black and flesh 2·10 70

**932** "Pepingen, Winter 1977" (Jozef Lucas)

**1990.** Christmas.
3042 **932** 10f. multicoloured 85 30

**933** "Self-portrait"

**1990.** 300th Death Anniv of David Teniers, the Younger (painter). Multicoloured.
3043 10f. Type **933** 85 35
3044 14f. "Dancers" 1·20 35
3045 25f. "Peasants playing Bowls outside Village Inn" 2·20 70

**934** King Baudouin and Queen Fabiola (photograph by Valeer Vanbeckbergen)

**1990.** Royal 30th Wedding Anniversary.
3046 **934** 50f.+15f. mult 8·50 8·50

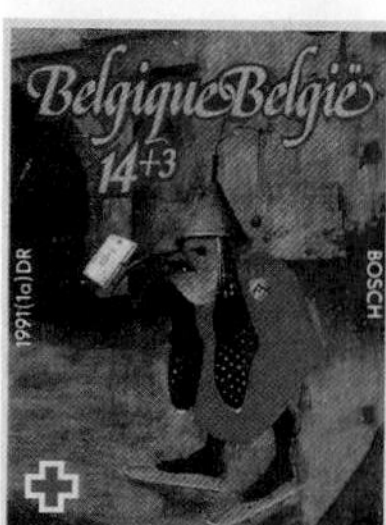

**935** "Temptation of St. Anthony" (detail, Hieronymus Bosch)

**1991.** Belgian Red Cross. Paintings. Mult.
3047 14f.+3f. Type **935** 2·75 2·75
3048 25f.+6f. "The Annunciation" (detail, Dirck Bouts) 4·00 4·00

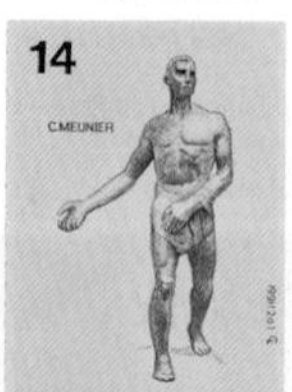

**936** "The Sower" (detail of "Monument to Labour", Brussels) (Constantin Meunier)

**1991.** 19th-Century Sculpture.
3049 **936** 14f. black & cinnamon 1·10 35

| | | | | |
|---|---|---|---|---|
| 3050 | - | 25f. black and blue | 1·80 | 70 |

DESIGN: 25f. Detail of Brabo Fountain, Antwerp (Jef Lambeaux).

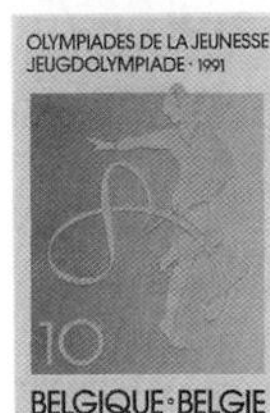
937 Rhythmic Gymnastics (European Youth Olympic Days, Brussels)

**1991.** Sports Meetings.

| | | | | |
|---|---|---|---|---|
| 3051 | 937 | 10f. grey, mauve & blk | 80 | 30 |
| 3052 | - | 10f. grey, green & black | 80 | 30 |

DESIGN: No. 3052, Korfball (Third World Championship, Belgium).

938 New Stamp Printing Office, Malines (Hugo van Hoecke)

**1991.** Stamp Day.

| | | | | |
|---|---|---|---|---|
| 3053 | 938 | 14f. multicoloured | 1·10 | 35 |

939 Cogwheels

**1991.** Centenary of Liberal Trade Union.

| | | | | |
|---|---|---|---|---|
| 3054 | 939 | 25f. blue, light blue and deep blue | 1·90 | 70 |

940 "Olympus 1" Communications Satellite

**1991.** Europa. Europe in Space. Multicoloured.

| | | | |
|---|---|---|---|
| 3055 | 14f. Type **940** | 2·40 | 30 |
| 3056 | 25f. "Ariane 5" rocket carrying space shuttle "Hermes" | 4·00 | 80 |

941 Leo XIII's Arms and Standard, and Christian Labour Movement Banners

**1991.** Centenary of "Rerum Novarum" (encyclical letter from Pope Leo XIII on workers' rights).

| | | | | |
|---|---|---|---|---|
| 3057 | 941 | 14f. multicoloured | 1·10 | 30 |

942 "Isabella of Portugal and Philip the Good" (anon)

**1991.** "Europalia 91 Portugal" Festival.

| | | | | |
|---|---|---|---|---|
| 3058 | 942 | 14f. multicoloured | 1·10 | 30 |

943 Neptune Grottoes, Couvin

**1991.** Tourist Publicity. Multicoloured.

| | | | |
|---|---|---|---|
| 3059 | 14f. Type **943** | 1·10 | 35 |
| 3060 | 14f. Dieleghem Abbey, Jette | 1·10 | 35 |
| 3061 | 14f. Niel Town Hall (vert) | 1·10 | 35 |
| 3062 | 14f. Hautes Fagnes nature reserve | 1·10 | 35 |
| 3063 | 14f. Giant Rolarius, Roeselare (vert) | 1·10 | 35 |

944 King Baudouin (photograph by Dimitri Ardelean)

**1991.** 60th Birthday (1990) and 40th Anniv of Accession to Throne of King Baudouin.

| | | | | |
|---|---|---|---|---|
| 3064 | 944 | 14f. multicoloured | 2·20 | 30 |

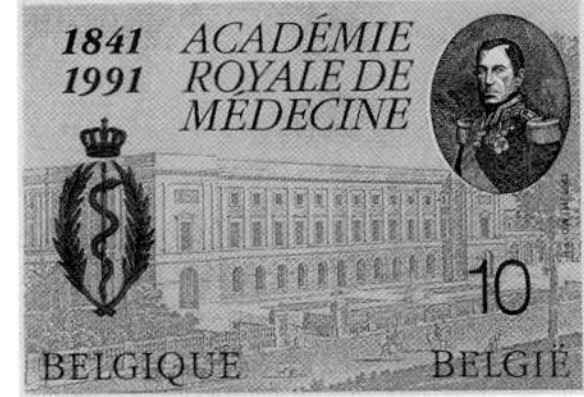
945 Academy Building, Caduceus and Leopold I

**1991.** 150th Anniv of Royal Academy of Medicine.

| | | | | |
|---|---|---|---|---|
| 3065 | 945 | 10f. multicoloured | 80 | 35 |

946 "The English Coast at Dover"

**1991.** 61st Death Anniv of Alfred Finch (painter and ceramic artist).

| | | | | |
|---|---|---|---|---|
| 3066 | 946 | 25f. multicoloured | 2·00 | 70 |

947 Death Cap

**1991.** Fungi. Multicoloured.

| | | | |
|---|---|---|---|
| 3067 | 14f. Type **947** | 2·10 | 85 |
| 3068 | 14f. The Blusher (inscr "Golmotte") | 2·10 | 85 |
| 3069 | 14f. Flaky-stemmed witches' mushroom (inscr "Bolet a pied rouge") | 2·10 | 85 |
| 3070 | 14f. "Hygrocybe persistens" (inscr "Hygrophore jaune conique") | 2·10 | 85 |

948 Hands reaching through Bars

**1991.** 30th Anniv of Amnesty International (3071) and 11th Anniv of Belgian Branch of Medecins sans Frontieres (3072). Multicoloured.

| | | | |
|---|---|---|---|
| 3071 | 25f. Type **948** | 2·00 | 70 |
| 3072 | 25f. Doctor examining baby | 2·00 | 70 |

**1991.** Birds (2nd series). As T 841. Mult.

| | | | |
|---|---|---|---|
| 3073 | 50c. Goldcrest ("Roitelet Huppe") | 15 | 15 |
| 3074 | 1f. Redpoll ("Sizerin Flamme") | 25 | 15 |
| 3075 | 2f. Blackbird ("Merle Noir") | 25 | 15 |
| 3076 | 3f. Reed bunting ("Bruant des Roseaux") | 50 | 15 |
| 3077 | 4f. Pied wagtail ("Bergeronette Grise") | 45 | 15 |
| 3078 | 5f. Barn swallow ("Hirondelle de Cheminee") | 45 | 15 |
| 3079 | 5f.50 Jay ("Geai des Chenes") | 65 | 25 |
| 3080 | 6f. White-throated dipper ("Cincle Plongeur") | 65 | 15 |
| 3081 | 6f.50 Sedge-warbler ("Phragmite des Jones") | 65 | 25 |
| 3082 | 7f. Golden oriole ("Loriot") | 75 | 15 |
| 3083 | 8f. Great tit ("Mesange Charbonniere") | 75 | 15 |
| 3084 | 9f. Song thrush ("Grive Musicienne") | 90 | 25 |
| 3085 | 10f. Western greenfinch ("Verdier") | 95 | 25 |
| 3086 | 11f. Winter wren ("Troglodyte Mignon") | 1·00 | 15 |
| 3087 | 13f. House sparrow ("Moineau Domestique") | 1·30 | 15 |
| 3088 | 14f. Willow warbler ("Pouillot Fitis") | 1·30 | 25 |
| 3088a | 16f. Bohemian waxwing ("Jaseur Boreal") | 1·60 | 15 |

949 Exhibition Emblem

**1991.** "Telecom 91" International Telecommunications Exhibition, Geneva.

| | | | | |
|---|---|---|---|---|
| 3089 | 949 | 14f. multicoloured | 1·10 | 30 |

950 Blake and Mortimer in "The Yellow Mark" (Edgar P. Jacobs)

**1991.** "Philately for the Young". Comic Strips. Multicoloured.

| | | | |
|---|---|---|---|
| 3090 | 14f. Type **950** | 2·00 | 1·30 |
| 3091 | 14f. Cori the ship boy in "The Ill-fated Voyage" (Bob de Moor) | 2·00 | 1·30 |
| 3092 | 14f. "Cities of the Fantastic" (Francois Schuiten) | 2·00 | 1·30 |
| 3093 | 14f. "Boule and Bill" (Jean Roba) | 2·00 | 1·30 |

951 Charles Dekeukeleire

**1991.** "Solidarity". Film Makers.

| | | | | |
|---|---|---|---|---|
| 3094 | 951 | 10f.+2f. black, brown and green | 1·30 | 1·30 |
| 3095 | - | 14f.+3f. black, orange and brown | 1·90 | 1·90 |
| 3096 | - | 25f.+6f. black, ochre and brown | 3·50 | 3·50 |

DESIGNS: 14f. Jacques Ledoux; 25f. Jacques Feyder.

952 Printing Press forming "100" ("Gazet van Antwerpen")

**1991.** Newspaper Centenaries. Multicoloured.

| | | | | |
|---|---|---|---|---|
| 3097 | 952 | 10f. black, lt grn & grn | 80 | 30 |
| 3098 | - | 10f. yellow, blue & blk | 80 | 30 |

DESIGN: No. 3098, Cancellation on "stamp" ("Het Volk").

953 "Our Lady rejoicing in the Child" (icon, Chevetogne Abbey)

**1991.** Christmas.

| | | | | |
|---|---|---|---|---|
| 3099 | 953 | 10f. multicoloured | 75 | 40 |

954 Mozart and Score

**1991.** Death Bicentenary of Wolfgang Amadeus Mozart (composer).

| | | | | |
|---|---|---|---|---|
| 3100 | 954 | 25f. purple, bl & ultram | 2·10 | 1·00 |

955 Speed Skating

**1992.** Olympic Games, Albertville and Barcelona. Multicoloured.

| | | | |
|---|---|---|---|
| 3101 | 10f.+2f. Type **955** | 1·40 | 1·40 |
| 3102 | 10f.+2f. Baseball | 1·40 | 1·40 |
| 3103 | 14f.+3f. Tennis (horiz) | 1·90 | 1·90 |
| 3104 | 25f.+6f. Clay-pigeon shooting | 3·50 | 3·50 |

956 Fire Hose and Service Emblem

**1992.** Fire Service.

| | | | | |
|---|---|---|---|---|
| 3105 | 956 | 14f. multicoloured | 1·10 | 30 |

957 Flames and Silhouette of Man

**1992.** The Resistance.

| | | | | |
|---|---|---|---|---|
| 3106 | 957 | 14f. yellow, black & red | 1·10 | 30 |

958 Tapestry and Carpet

**1992.** Prestige Occupations. Multicoloured.

| | | | |
|---|---|---|---|
| 3107 | 10f. Type **958** | 75 | 45 |
| 3108 | 14f. Chef's hat and cutlery (10th anniv (1991) of Association of Belgian Master Chefs) | 1·10 | 30 |

3109 27f. Diamond and "100" (centenary (1993) of Antwerp Diamond Club) 2·20 70

**959** Belgian Pavilion and Exhibition Emblem

**1992.** "Expo '92" World's Fair, Seville.

3110 **959** 14f. multicoloured 1·10 30

**960** King Baudouin **961**

**1992**

| | | | | |
|---|---|---|---|---|
| 3111 | **960** | 15f. red | 1·10 | 15 |
| 3115 | **960** | 28f. green | 2·50 | 70 |
| 3120 | **961** | 100f. green | 9·50 | 65 |

**962** Van Noten at Work

**1992.** Stamp Day. 10th Death Anniv of Jean van Noten (stamp designer).

3124 **962** 15f. black and red 1·10 30

**963** "White Magic No. VI"

**1992.** Original Art Designs for Stamps. Mult.

| | | | |
|---|---|---|---|
| 3125 | 15f. Type **963** | 1·10 | 40 |
| 3126 | 15f. "Colours" (horiz) | 1·10 | 40 |

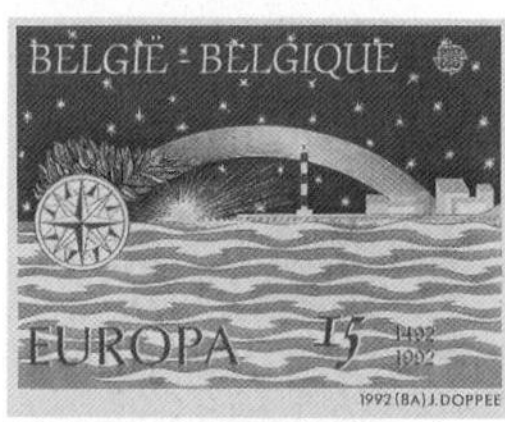


**964** Compass Rose, Setting Sun and Harbour

**1992.** Europa. 500th Anniv of Discovery of America. Multicoloured.

| | | | |
|---|---|---|---|
| 3127 | 15f. Type **964** | 2·50 | 45 |
| 3128 | 28f. Globe and astrolabe forming "500" | 5·00 | 95 |

**965** Faces of Different Colours

**1992.** Anti-racism.

3129 **965** 15f. grey, black & pink 1·10 30

**966** "The Hamlet" (Jacob Smits)

**1992.** Belgian Paintings in Orsay Museum, Paris. Multicoloured.

| | | | |
|---|---|---|---|
| 3130 | 11f. Type **966** | 80 | 40 |
| 3131 | 15f. "The Bath" (Alfred Stevens) | 1·40 | 30 |
| 3132 | 30f. "Man at the Helm" (Theo van Rysselberghe) | 2·50 | 90 |

**967** Proud Margaret

**1992.** Folk Tales. Multicoloured.

| | | | |
|---|---|---|---|
| 3133 | 11f.+2f. Type **967** | 1·60 | 1·60 |
| 3134 | 15f.+3f. Witches ("Les Macrales") | 2·20 | 2·20 |
| 3135 | 28f.+6f. Reynard the fox | 3·75 | 3·75 |

**968** Mannekin-Pis, Brussels

**1992.** Tourist Publicity. Multicoloured.

| | | | |
|---|---|---|---|
| 3136 | 15f. Type **968** | 1·10 | 30 |
| 3137 | 15f. Former Landcommandery of Teutonic Order, Alden Biesen (now Flemish cultural centre) (horiz) | 1·10 | 30 |
| 3138 | 15f. Andenne (1300th anniv) | 1·10 | 30 |
| 3139 | 15f. Carnival revellers on Fools' Monday, Renaix (horiz) | 1·10 | 30 |
| 3140 | 15f. Great Procession (religious festival), Tournai (horiz) | 1·10 | 30 |

**969** European Polecat

**1992.** Mammals. Multicoloured.

| | | | |
|---|---|---|---|
| 3141 | 15f. Type **969** | 1·90 | 80 |
| 3142 | 15f. Eurasian red squirrel | 1·90 | 80 |
| 3143 | 15f. Eurasian hedgehog | 1·90 | 80 |
| 3144 | 15f. Common dormouse | 1·90 | 80 |

**970** Henri van der Noot, Jean van der Meersch and Jean Vonck

**1992.** 203rd Anniv of Brabant Revolution.

3145 **970** 15f. multicoloured 1·10 30

**971** Arms of Thurn and Taxis

**1992.** 500th Anniv of Mention of Thurn and Taxis Postal Services in Lille Account Books.

3146 **971** 15f. multicoloured 1·10 30

**972** Gaston Lagaffe (cartoon character)

**1992.** "Philately for the Young".

3147 **972** 15f. multicoloured 1·50 45

**973** Star, "B" and Map

**1992.** European Single Market.

3148 **973** 15f. multicoloured 1·10 40

**974** Okapi

**1992.** 150th Anniv of Antwerp Zoo. Mult.

| | | | |
|---|---|---|---|
| 3149 | 15f. Type **974** | 1·10 | 40 |
| 3150 | 30f. Golden-headed tamarin | 2·30 | 50 |

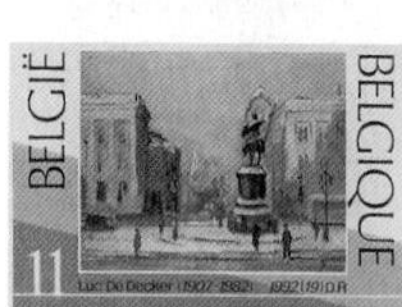


**975** "Place Royale in Winter" (Luc de Decker)

**1992.** Christmas.

3151 **975** 11f. multicoloured 75 30

**976** "Man with Pointed Hat" (Adriaen Brouwer)

**1993.** Belgian Red Cross. Paintings. Mult.

| | | | |
|---|---|---|---|
| 3152 | 15f.+3f. Type **976** | 2·40 | 2·40 |
| 3153 | 28f.+7f. "Nereid and Triton" (Peter Paul Rubens) (horiz) | 4·75 | 4·75 |

**977** Council of Leptines, 743

**1993.** Historical Events. Multicoloured.

| | | | |
|---|---|---|---|
| 3154 | 11f. Type **977** | 75 | 40 |
| 3155 | 15f. Queen Beatrix and King Matthias I Corvinus of Hungary (detail of "Missale Romanum") (77×24 mm) | 1·30 | 40 |
| 3156 | 30f. Battle scene (Battles of Neerwinden, 1673 and 1773) | 2·50 | 75 |
| **MS**3157 | 105×155 mm. 28f. Illustration from Matthias I Corvinus's *Missale Romanum*, 1485 (54×39 mm) | 2·50 | 2·50 |

**978** Town Hall

**1993.** Antwerp, European City of Culture. Mult.

| | | | |
|---|---|---|---|
| 3158 | 15f. Panorama of Antwerp (76×24 mm) | 1·30 | 30 |
| 3159 | 15f. Type **978** | 1·30 | 30 |
| 3160 | 15f. "Study of Women's Heads and Male Torso" (Jacob Jordaens) | 1·30 | 30 |
| 3161 | 15f. St. Job's altarpiece, Schoonbroek | 1·30 | 30 |
| 3162 | 15f. "Angels" (stained glass window by Eugeen Yoors, Mother of God Chapel, Marie-Josee Institute, Elisabethville) (vert) | 1·30 | 30 |

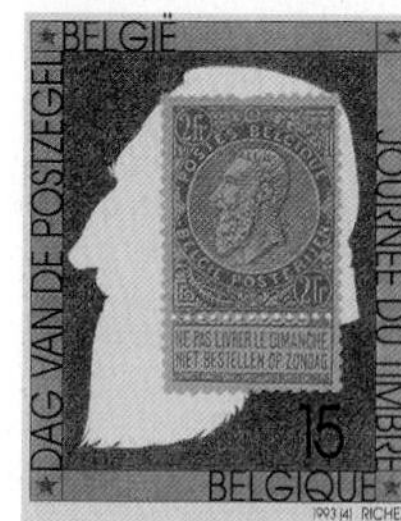


**979** 1893 2f. Stamp

**1993.** Stamp Day.

3163 **979** 15f. multicoloured 1·10 30

**980** "Florence 1960" (Gaston Bertrand)

**1993.** Europa. Contemporary Art. Multicoloured.

| | | | |
|---|---|---|---|
| 3164 | 15f. Type **980** | 1·30 | 30 |
| 3165 | 28f. "The Gig" (Constant Permeke) | 2·50 | 75 |

**981** Red Admiral ("Vanessa atalanta")

**1993.** Butterflies. Multicoloured.

| | | | |
|---|---|---|---|
| 3166 | 15f. Type **981** | 1·10 | 40 |
| 3167 | 15f. Purple emperor ("Apatura iris") | 1·10 | 40 |
| 3168 | 15f. Peacock ("Inachis io") | 1·10 | 40 |
| 3169 | 15f. Small tortoiseshell ("Aglais urticae") | 1·10 | 40 |

**982** Knot

**1993.** 150th Anniv of Alumni of Free University of Brussels Association.
3170 **982** 15f. blue and black 1·10 30

**983** Mayan Warrior (statuette)

**1993.** "Europalia 93 Mexico" Festival.
3171 **983** 15f. multicoloured 1·10 30

**984** Ommegang, Brussels

**1993.** Folklore Festivals. Multicoloured.
3172 11f. Type **984** 95 45
3173 15f. Royale Moncrabeau, Namur 1·10 30
3174 28f. Stilt-walkers, Merchtem (vert) 1·90 75

**985** La Hulpe Castle

**1993.** Tourist Publicity.
3175 **985** 15f. black and blue 1·10 30
3176 - 15f. black and lilac 1·10 30
3177 - 15f. black and grey 1·10 30
3178 - 15f. black and pink 1·10 30
3179 - 15f. black and green 1·10 30
DESIGNS—HORIZ: No. 3176, Cortewalle Castle, Beveren; 3177, Jehay Castle; 3179, Raeren Castle. VERT: No. 3178, Arenberg Castle, Heverlee.

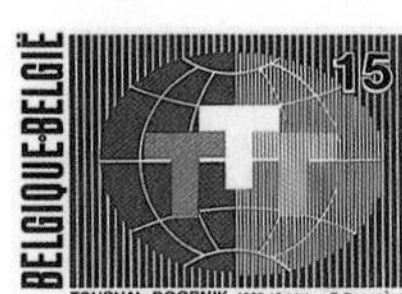

**986** Emblem

**1993.** 2nd International Triennial Textile Exhibition, Tournai.
3180 **986** 15f. blue, red and black 1·10 30

**987** Presidency Emblem

**1993.** Belgian Presidency of European Community Council.
3181 **987** 15f. multicoloured 1·10 30

**988** Magritte

**1993.** 25th Death Anniv (1992) of Rene Magritte (artist).
3182 **988** 30f. multicoloured 2·20 90

**989** King Baudouin

**1993.** King Baudouin Commemoration.
3183 **989** 15f. black and blue 1·30 25

**990** Red and White Cat

**1993.** Cats. Multicoloured.
3184 15f. Type **990** 1·40 75
3185 15f. Tabby and white cat standing on rock 1·40 75
3186 15f. Silver tabby lying on wall 1·40 75
3187 15f. Tortoiseshell and white cat sitting by gardening tools 1·40 75

**991** Highlighted Cancer Cell

**1993.** Anti-cancer Campaign.
3188 **991** 15f.+3f. multicoloured 1·90 1·90

**992** Frontispiece

**1993.** 450th Anniv of "De Humani Corporis Fabrica" (treatise on human anatomy) by Andreas Vesalius.
3189 **992** 15f. black, brown & red 1·10 30

**993** Natacha (cartoon character)

**1993.** "Philately for the Young".
3190 **993** 15f. multicoloured 1·40 50

**994** Sun's Rays

**1993.** 50th Anniv of Publication of "Le Faux Soir" (resistance newspaper).
3191 **994** 11f. multicoloured 80 50

**995** "Madonna and Child" (statue, Our Lady of the Chapel, Brussels)

**1993.** Christmas.
3192 **995** 11f. multicoloured 75 30

**996** Child looking at Globe

**1993.** Children's Town Councils.
3193 **996** 15f. multicoloured 1·10 30

**997** King Albert II **998** King Albert II

**1993**
3194 **997** 16f. multicoloured 1·70 15
3195 **997** 16f. turquoise and blue 1·30 20
3196 **997** 20f. brown and stone 1·70 25
3197 **997** 30f. purple and mauve 1·90 25
3198 **997** 32f. orange and yellow 2·20 15
3199 **997** 40f. red and mauve 3·00 15
3200 **997** 50f. myrtle and green 5·25 25
3201 **998** 100f. multicoloured 7·50 45
3202 **998** 200f. multicoloured 16·00 65

**999** "Ma Toute Belle" (Serge Vandercam)

**1994.** Painters' Designs. Multicoloured.
3210 16f. Type **999** 1·10 40
3211 16f. "The Malleable Darkness" (Octave Landuyt) (horiz) 1·10 40

**1000** Olympic Flames and Rings

**1994.** Sports. Multicoloured.
3212 16f.+3f. Type **1000** (cent of International Olympic Committee) 2·20 2·20
3213 16f.+3f. Footballers (World Cup Football Championship, U.S.A.) 2·20 2·20
3214 16f.+3f. Skater (Winter Olympic Games, Lillehammer, Norway) 2·20 2·20

**1001** Hanriot HD-1

**1994.** Biplanes. Multicoloured.
3215 13f. Type **1001** 1·10 45
3216 15f. Spad XIII 1·30 40

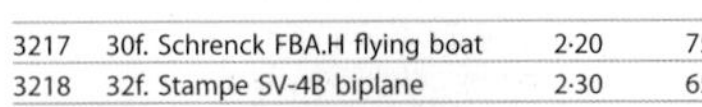
3217 30f. Schrenck FBA.H flying boat 2·20 75
3218 32f. Stampe SV-4B biplane 2·30 65

**1002** Masthead of "Le Jour-Le Courrier" (centenary)

**1994.** Newspaper Anniversaries. Multicoloured.
3219 16f. Type **1002** 1·10 40
3220 16f. Masthead of "La Wallonie" (75th anniv) (horiz) 1·10 40

**1003** "Fall of the Golden Calf" (detail, Fernand Allard l'Olivier)

**1994.** Centenary of Charter of Quaregnon (social charter).
3221 **1003** 16f. multicoloured 1·10 45

**1004** 1912 5f. Stamp

**1994.** Stamp Day. 60th Death Anniv of King Albert I.
3222 **1004** 16f. purple, mauve & bl 1·10 40

**1005** Reconciliation of Duke John I and Arnold, Squire of Wezemaal

**1994.** 700th Death Anniv of John I, Duke of Brabant. Illustrations from 15th-century "Brabantse Yeesten". Multicoloured.
3223 13f. Type **1005** 95 45
3224 16f. Tournament at wedding of his son John to Margaret of York, 1290 1·10 40
3225 30f. Battle of Woeringen (77×25 mm) 2·40 90

**1006** Georges Lemaitre (formulator of expanding Universe and of "big bang" theory)

**1994.** Europa. Discoveries and Inventions. Mult.
3226 16f. Type **1006** 1·30 40
3227 30f. Gerardus Mercator (inventor of Mercator projection in cartography) 2·50 90

**1007** Father Damien (missionary and leprosy worker)

**1994.** Visit of Pope John Paul II. Mult.

| | | | |
|---|---|---|---|
| 3228 | 16f. Type **1007** (beatification) | 1·10 | 30 |
| 3229 | 16f. St. Mutien-Marie (5th anniv of canonization) | 1·10 | 30 |

**1008** St. Peter's Church, Bertem

**1994.** Tourist Publicity. Multicoloured.

| | | | |
|---|---|---|---|
| 3230 | 16f. Type **1008** | 1·10 | 40 |
| 3231 | 16f. St. Bavo's Church, Kanegem (vert) | 1·10 | 40 |
| 3232 | 16f. Royal St. Mary's Church, Schaarbeek | 1·10 | 40 |
| 3233 | 16f. St. Gery's Church, Aubechies | 1·10 | 40 |
| 3234 | 16f. Sts. Peter and Paul's Church, St.-Severin en Condroz (vert) | 1·10 | 40 |

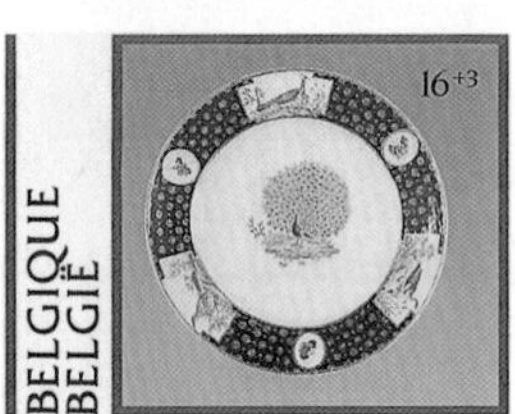


**1009** Tournai Porcelain Plate from Duke of Orleans Service (Mariemont Museum)

**1994.** Museum Exhibits. Multicoloured.

| | | | |
|---|---|---|---|
| 3235 | 16f.+3f. Type **1009** | 1·90 | 1·90 |
| 3236 | 16f.+3f. Etterbeek porcelain coffee cup and saucer (Louvain Municipal Museum) | 1·90 | 1·90 |
| **MS**3237 | 125×90 mm. 50f.+11f. Delft containers (Pharmacy Museum, Maaseik) | 9·50 | 9·50 |

**1010** Guillame Lekeu (composer)

**1994.** Anniversaries. Multicoloured.

| | | | |
|---|---|---|---|
| 3238 | 16f. Type **1010** (death cent) | 1·10 | 40 |
| 3239 | 16f. Detail of painting by Hans Memling (500th death anniv) | 1·10 | 40 |

**1011** Generals Crerar, Montgomery and Bradley and Allied Troops (image scaled to 61% of original size)

**1994.** 50th Anniv of Liberation.

| | | | | |
|---|---|---|---|---|
| 3240 | **1011** | 16f. multicoloured | 1·30 | 40 |

**1012** Marsh Marigold ("Caltha palustris")

**1994.** Flowers. Multicoloured.

| | | | |
|---|---|---|---|
| 3241 | 16f. Type **1012** | 1·60 | 75 |
| 3242 | 16f. White helleborine ("Cephalanthera damasonium") | 1·60 | 75 |
| 3243 | 16f. Sea bindweed ("Calystegia soldanella") | 1·60 | 75 |
| 3244 | 16f. Broad-leaved helleborine ("Epipactis helleborine") | 1·60 | 75 |

**1013** Cubitus (cartoon character)

**1994.** "Philately for the Young".

| | | | | |
|---|---|---|---|---|
| 3245 | **1013** | 16f. multicoloured | 1·60 | 50 |

**1014** Simenon and Bridge of Arches, Liege

**1994.** 5th Death Anniv of Georges Simenon (novelist).

| | | | | |
|---|---|---|---|---|
| 3246 | **1014** | 16f. multicoloured | 1·60 | 40 |

The depiction of the bridge alludes to Simenon's first novel "Au Pont des Arches".

**1015** Deaf Man and Butterfly

**1994.** "Solidarity".

| | | | | |
|---|---|---|---|---|
| 3247 | **1015** | 16f.+3f. mult | 1·50 | 1·50 |

**1016** Santa Claus on Rooftop

**1994.** Christmas.

| | | | | |
|---|---|---|---|---|
| 3248 | **1016** | 13f. multicoloured | 95 | 40 |

**1017** Field and Flax Knife (Flax Museum, Courtrai)

**1995.** Museums. Multicoloured.

| | | | |
|---|---|---|---|
| 3249 | 16f.+3f. Type **1017** | 1·40 | 1·40 |
| 3250 | 16f.+3f. River and pump (Water and Fountain Museum, Genval) | 1·40 | 1·40 |
| **MS**3251 | 125×90 mm. 34f.+6f. Mask (International Carnival and Mask Museum, Binche) | 3·75 | 3·75 |

The premium was for the promotion of philately.

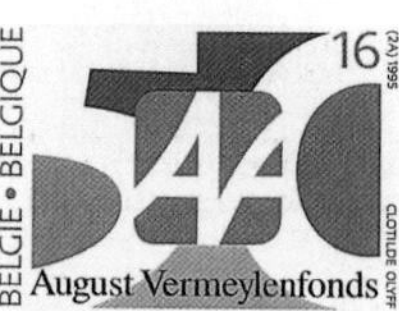


**1018** Emblem

**1995.** Anniversaries. Anniversary emblems.

| | | | | |
|---|---|---|---|---|
| 3252 | **1018** | 16f. red, blue & black | 1·10 | 40 |
| 3253 | - | 16f. multicoloured | 1·10 | 40 |
| 3254 | - | 16f. multicoloured | 1·10 | 40 |
| 3255 | - | 16f. red, black & brown | 1·10 | 40 |

ANNIVERSARIES: No. 3252, 50th anniv of August Vermeylen Fund; 3253, Centenary of Touring Club of Belgium; 3254, Centenary of Federation of Belgian Enterprises; 3255, 50th anniv of Social Security in Belgium.

**1019** "Hibiscus rosa-sinensis"

**1995.** Ghent Flower Show. Multicoloured.

| | | | |
|---|---|---|---|
| 3256 | 13f. Type **1019** | 95 | 50 |
| 3257 | 16f. Azalea | 1·30 | 40 |
| 3258 | 30f. Fuchsia | 2·20 | 75 |

**1020** Crossword Puzzle

**1995.** Games and Pastimes. Multicoloured.

| | | | |
|---|---|---|---|
| 3259 | 13f. Type **1020** | 95 | 45 |
| 3260 | 16f. King (chess piece) | 1·10 | 40 |
| 3261 | 30f. Scrabble | 2·20 | 75 |
| 3262 | 34f. Queen (playing cards) | 2·30 | 95 |

**1021** Frans de Troyer (promoter of thematic philately)

**1995.** Post Day.

| | | | | |
|---|---|---|---|---|
| 3263 | **1021** | 16f. black, stone & orge | 1·10 | 40 |

**1022** Watch Tower and Barbed Wire Fence

**1995.** Europa. Peace and Freedom. Mult.

| | | | |
|---|---|---|---|
| 3264 | 16f. Type **1022** (50th anniv of liberation of concentration camps) | 2·50 | 90 |
| 3265 | 30f. Nuclear cloud (25th anniv of Non-Proliferation Treaty) | 4·50 | 90 |

**1023** Soldiers of the Irish Brigade and Memorial Cross

**1995.** 250th Anniv of Battle of Fontenoy.

| | | | | |
|---|---|---|---|---|
| 3266 | **1023** | 16f. multicoloured | 1·30 | 30 |

**1024** U.N. Emblem

**1995.** 50th Anniv of U.N.O.

| | | | | |
|---|---|---|---|---|
| 3267 | **1024** | 16f. multicoloured | 1·10 | 40 |

**1025** "Sauvagemont, Maransart" (Pierre Alechinsky)

**1995.** Artists' Philatelic Creations.

| | | | | |
|---|---|---|---|---|
| 3268 | **1025** | 16f. red, black & yellow | 1·10 | 40 |
| 3269 | - | 16f. multicoloured | 1·10 | 40 |

DESIGN: No. 3269, "Telegram-style" (Pol Mara).

**1026** Paul Cauchie (Brussels)

**1995.** Tourist Publicity. Art nouveau house facades by named architects. Multicoloured.

| | | | |
|---|---|---|---|
| 3270 | 16f. Type **1026** | 1·10 | 40 |
| 3271 | 16f. Frans Smet-Verhas (Antwerp) | 1·10 | 40 |
| 3272 | 16f. Paul Jaspar (Liege) | 1·10 | 40 |

**1027** Anniversary Emblem

**1995.** Cent of Royal Belgian Football Assn.

| | | | | |
|---|---|---|---|---|
| 3273 | **1027** | 16f.+4f. mult | 1·60 | 1·60 |

**1028** "Mercator" (Belgian cadet barque)

**1995.** Sailing Ships. Multicoloured.

| | | | |
|---|---|---|---|
| 3274 | 16f. Type **1028** | 1·40 | 75 |
| 3275 | 16f. "Kruzenshern" (Russian cadet barque) (inscr "Kruzenstern") | 1·40 | 75 |
| 3276 | 16f. "Sagres II" (Portuguese cadet barque) | 1·40 | 75 |
| 3277 | 16f. "Amerigo Vespucci" (Italian cadet ship) | 1·40 | 75 |

**1029** Princess Astrid and Globe

**1995.** Red Cross. Multicoloured.

| | | | |
|---|---|---|---|
| 3278 | 16f.+3f. Type **1029** (Chairwoman) | 1·40 | 1·40 |
| 3279 | 16f.+3f. Wilhelm Rontgen (discoverer of X-rays) and X-ray of hand | 1·40 | 1·40 |
| 3280 | 16f.+3f. Louis Pasteur (chemist) and microscope | 1·40 | 1·40 |

**1030** 1908 Minerva

**1995.** Motorcycles. Multicoloured.

| | | | |
|---|---|---|---|
| 3281 | 13f. Type **1030** | 95 | 50 |
| 3282 | 16f. 1913 FN (vert) | 1·10 | 40 |
| 3283 | 30f. 1929 La Mondiale | 2·00 | 75 |
| 3284 | 32f. 1937 Gillet (vert) | 2·20 | 65 |

**1031** Sammy (cartoon character)

**1995.** "Philately for the Young".

| | | | | |
|---|---|---|---|---|
| 3285 | **1031** | 16f. multicoloured | 1·40 | 45 |

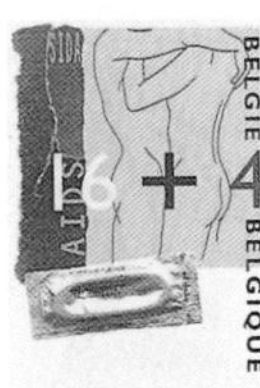

**1032** Couple and Condom in Wrapper

**1995.** "Solidarity". AIDS Awareness.

| | | | | |
|---|---|---|---|---|
| 3286 | **1032** | 16f.+4f. mult | 1·40 | 1·40 |

**1033** King Albert II and Queen Paola (photograph by Christian Louis)

**1995.** King's Day.

| | | | | |
|---|---|---|---|---|
| 3287 | **1033** | 16f. multicoloured | 1·30 | 40 |

**1034** "Nativity" (from 15th-century breviary)

**1995.** Christmas.

| | | | | |
|---|---|---|---|---|
| 3288 | **1034** | 13f. multicoloured | 95 | 40 |

**1035** Puppets, Walloon Museum, Liege

**1996.** Museums. Multicoloured.

| | | | |
|---|---|---|---|
| 3289 | 16f.+4f. Type **1035** | 1·40 | 1·40 |
| 3290 | 16f.+4f. National Gin Museum, Hasselt | 1·40 | 1·40 |
| **MS**3291 | 126×90 mm. 34f.+6f. "Fall of Saul" (detail of title panel), Butchers' Guild Hall Museum, Antwerp | 3·75 | 3·75 |

The premium was used for the promotion of philately.

**1036** "Emile Mayrisch"

**1996.** 70th Death Anniv of Theo van Rysselberghe (painter). No value expressed.

| | | | | |
|---|---|---|---|---|
| 3292 | **1036** | A (16f.) mult | 1·30 | 40 |

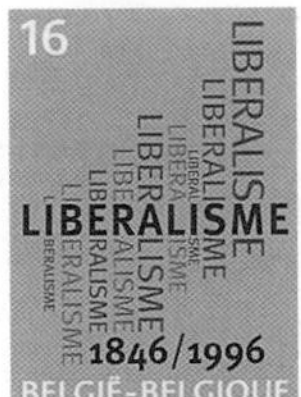

**1037** "LIBERALISME"

**1996.** 150th Anniv of Liberal Party.

| | | | | |
|---|---|---|---|---|
| 3293 | **1037** | 16f. dp blue, violet & bl | 1·30 | 40 |

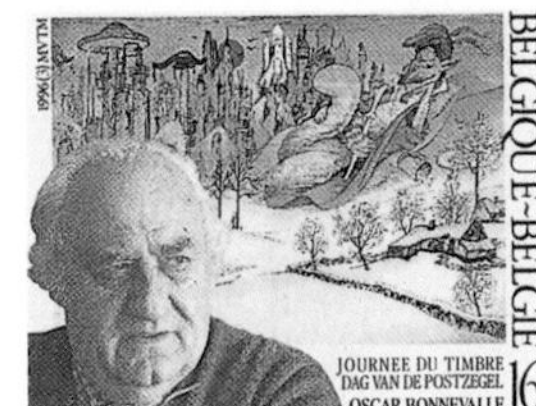

**1038** Oscar Bonnevalle (stamp designer) and "Gelatenheid"

**1996.** Stamp Day.

| | | | | |
|---|---|---|---|---|
| 3294 | **1038** | 16f. multicoloured | 1·30 | 40 |

**1039** Dragonfly ("Sympetrum sanguineum")

**1996.** 150th Anniv of Royal Institute of Natural Sciences of Belgium. Insects. Multicoloured.

| | | | |
|---|---|---|---|
| 3295 | 16f. Type **1039** | 90 | 70 |
| 3296 | 16f. Buff-tailed bumble bee ("Bombus terrestris") | 90 | 70 |
| 3297 | 16f. Stag beetle ("Lucanus cervus") | 90 | 70 |
| 3298 | 16f. May beetle ("Melolontha melolontha") | 90 | 70 |
| 3299 | 16f. European field cricket ("Gryllus campestris") | 90 | 70 |
| 3300 | 16f. Seven-spotted ladybird ("Coccinella septempunctata") | 90 | 70 |

**1040** Yvonne Nevejean (rescuer of Jewish children)

**1996.** Europa. Famous Women. Multicoloured.

| | | | |
|---|---|---|---|
| 3301 | 16f. Type **1040** | 1·00 | 40 |
| 3302 | 30f. Marie Gevers (poet) | 2·10 | 90 |

**1996.** Birds (3rd series). As T 841. Mult.

| | | | |
|---|---|---|---|
| 3303 | 1f. Crested tit ("Mesange Huppee") | 25 | 15 |
| 3304 | 2f. Redwing ("Grive mauvis") | 30 | 25 |
| 3305 | 3f. Eurasian skylark ("Alouette des champs") | 30 | 25 |
| 3306 | 4f. Pied flycatcher ("Gore-mouche noir") | 45 | 40 |
| 3307 | 5f. Common starling ("Etourneau sansonnet") | 45 | 25 |
| 3308 | 6f. Spruce siskin ("Tarin des aulnes") | 50 | 30 |
| 3309 | 7f. Yellow wagtail ("Bergeronnette printaniere") | 45 | 15 |
| 3310 | 7f.50 Great grey shrike ("Pie-Grieche Grise") | 50 | 40 |
| 3311 | 9f. Green woodpecker ("Pic Vert") | 65 | 50 |
| 3312 | 10f. Turtle dove ("Tourterelle des Bois") | 65 | 40 |
| 3313 | 15f. Willow tit ("Mesange boreale") | 1·20 | 25 |
| 3314 | 16f. Coal tit ("Mesange noire") | 1·00 | 30 |
| 3315 | 21f. Fieldfare ("Grive Litorne") (horiz) | 1·40 | 80 |
| 3316 | 150f. Black-billed magpie ("Pie bavarde") (35×25 mm) | 10·50 | 25 |

**1042** King Albert II

**1996.** 62nd Birthday of King Albert II.

| | | | | |
|---|---|---|---|---|
| 3327 | **1042** | 16f. multicoloured | 1·40 | 25 |

**1043** Han sur Lesse Grottoes

**1996.** Tourist Publicity. Multicoloured.

| | | | |
|---|---|---|---|
| 3328 | 16f. Type **1043** | 1·20 | 40 |
| 3329 | 16f. Statue of beguine, Begijnendijk (vert) | 1·20 | 40 |

**1044** Royal Palace

**1996.** Brussels, Heart of Europe. Mult.

| | | | |
|---|---|---|---|
| 3330 | 16f. Type **1044** | 1·30 | 40 |
| 3331 | 16f. St. Hubert Royal Galleries | 1·30 | 40 |
| 3332 | 16f. Le Petit Sablon, Egmont Palace (horiz) | 1·30 | 40 |
| 3333 | 16f. Jubilee Park (horiz) | 1·30 | 40 |

**1045** 1900 Germain 6CV Voiturette

**1996.** Cent of Motor Racing at Spa. Mult.

| | | | |
|---|---|---|---|
| 3334 | 16f. Type **1045** | 1·20 | 40 |
| 3335 | 16f. 1925 Alfa Romeo P2 | 1·20 | 40 |
| 3336 | 16f. 1939 Mercedes Benz W154 | 1·20 | 40 |
| 3337 | 16f. 1967 Ferrari 330P | 1·20 | 40 |

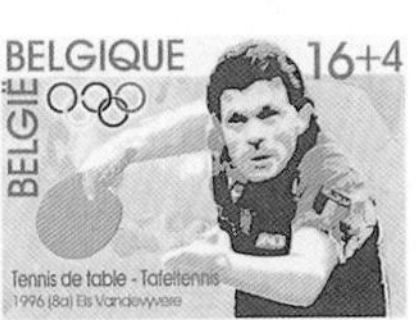

**1046** Table Tennis

**1996.** Olympic Games, Atlanta. Mult.

| | | | |
|---|---|---|---|
| 3338 | 16f.+4f. Type **1046** | 1·60 | 1·60 |
| 3339 | 16f.+4f. Swimming | 1·60 | 1·60 |
| **MS**3340 | 125×90 mm. 34f.+6f. High jumping (41×34 mm) | 3·50 | 3·50 |

**1996**

| | | | |
|---|---|---|---|
| 3341 | 16f. blue | 1·20 | 30 |
| 3342 | 17f. blue | 1·40 | 15 |
| 3343 | 18f. green | 1·30 | 50 |
| 3344 | 19f. lilac | 1·60 | 40 |
| 3344a | 20f. brown | 1·40 | 20 |
| 3345 | 25f. brown | 1·70 | 40 |
| 3346 | 28f. brown | 2·40 | 50 |
| 3347 | 32f. violet | 2·10 | 20 |
| 3348 | 34f. blue | 1·90 | 40 |
| 3349 | 36f. blue | 2·30 | 25 |
| 3350 | 50f. green | 4·00 | 30 |

**1047** "The Straw Hat" (Peter Paul Rubens)

**1996.** Paintings by Belgian Artists in the National Gallery, London. Multicoloured.

| | | | |
|---|---|---|---|
| 3351 | 14f. "St. Ivo" (Rogier van der Weyden) | 1·20 | 40 |
| 3352 | 16f. Type **1047** | 1·40 | 40 |
| 3353 | 30f. "Man in a Turban" (Jan van Eyck) | 2·75 | 65 |

**1048** Philip the Fair

**1996.** 500th Anniv of Marriage of Philip the Fair and Joanna of Castile and Procession into Brussels. Details of triptych by the Master of Affligem Abbey at Zierikzee Town Hall. Multicoloured.

| | | | |
|---|---|---|---|
| 3354 | 16f. Type **1048** | 4·00 | 40 |
| 3355 | 16f. Joanna of Castile | 1·30 | 40 |

**1049** Cloro (cartoon character)

**1996.** "Philately for the Young".

| | | | | |
|---|---|---|---|---|
| 3356 | **1049** | 16f. multicoloured | 1·40 | 40 |

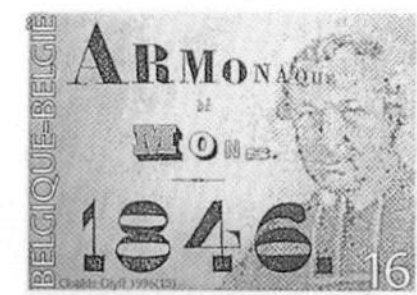

**1050** Title of First Issue and Charles Letellier (founder)

**1996.** 150th Anniv of "Mons Almanac".

| | | | | |
|---|---|---|---|---|
| 3357 | **1050** | 16f. black, yell & mve | 1·30 | 40 |

**1051** Arthur Grumiaux (violinist, 10th death anniv)

**1996.** Music and Literature Anniversaries.

| | | | | |
|---|---|---|---|---|
| 3358 | **1051** | 16f. multicoloured | 1·30 | 40 |
| 3359 | - | 16f. multicoloured | 1·30 | 40 |
| 3360 | - | 16f. black and brown | 1·30 | 40 |
| 3361 | - | 16f. multicoloured | 1·30 | 40 |

DESIGNS: No. 3359, Flor Peeters (organist, 10th death anniv); 3360, Christian Dotremont (poet, 5th death anniv); 3361, Paul van Ostaijen (writer, birth centenary) and cover drawing by Oscar Jespers for "Bezette Stad".

**1052** Globe and Children of Different Races

**1996.** "Solidarity". 50th Anniv of UNICEF.

| | | | | |
|---|---|---|---|---|
| 3362 | **1052** | 16f.+4f. mult | 1·40 | 1·40 |

**1053** Christmas Trees

**1996.** Christmas. Sheet 185×145 mm containing T 1053 and similar horiz designs. Multicoloured.

| | | | |
|---|---|---|---|
| **MS**3363 | 14f. Type **1053**; 14f. "Happy Christmas" in Flemish, German and French; 14f. Church; 14f. Cake stall; 14f. Stall with cribs; 14f. Meat stall; 14f. Father Christmas; 14f. Crowd including man smoking pipe; 14f. Crowd including man carrying holly | 9·25 | 9·25 |

**1054** Students

**1997.** Centenary of Catholic University, Mons.

| | | | | |
|---|---|---|---|---|
| 3364 | **1054** | 17f. multicoloured | 1·30 | 30 |

**1055** Barbed Wire and Buildings

**1997.** Museums. Multicoloured.

3365 17f.+4f. Type **1055** (Deportation and Resistance Museum, Dossin Barracks, Malines) 1·60 1·60
3366 17f.+4f. Foundryman pouring molten metal (Fourneau Saint-Michel Iron Museum) 1·60 1·60
**MS**3367 90×125 mm. 41f.+9f. Horta Museum, Saint-Giles 5·75 5·75

The premium was used for the promotion of philately.

**1056** Deer and Landscape (image scaled to 64% of original size)

**1997.** "Cantons of the East" (German-speaking Belgium).

3368 **1056** 17f. black and brown 1·30 40

**1057** Marie Sasse

**1997.** Opera Singers. Multicoloured.

3369 17f. Type **1057** 1·20 40
3370 17f. Ernest van Dijck 1·20 40
3371 17f. Hector Dufranne 1·20 40
3372 17f. Clara Clairbert 1·20 40

**1058** Soldier on Duty

**1997.** Belgian Involvement in United Nations Peacekeeping Forces.

3373 **1058** 17f. multicoloured 1·20 40

**1059** The Goat Riders

**1997.** Europa. Tales and Legends. Mult.

3374 17f. Type **1059** 1·40 40
3375 30f. Jean de Berneau 2·50 90

**1060** Spinoy working on Recess Plate

**1997.** Stamp Day. 4th Death Anniv of Constant Spinoy (engraver).

3376 **1060** 17f. brown, yell & blk 1·20 40

**1061** "The Man in the Street" (detail)

**1997.** Birth Centenary of Paul Delvaux (artist). Multicoloured.

3377 15f. Type **1061** 1·00 50
3378 17f. "The Public Voice" (horiz) 1·30 40
3379 32f. "The Messenger of the Night" 2·50 80

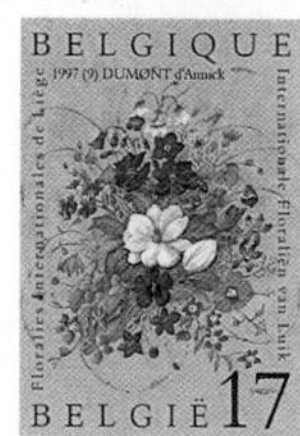


**1062** Flower Arrangement

**1997.** 2nd International Flower Show, Liege.

3380 **1062** 17f. multicoloured 1·30 40

**1063** Men's Judo

**1997.** Judo. Each black and red.

3381 17f.+4f. Type **1063** 1·40 1·30
3382 17f.+4f. Women's judo (showing female symbol) 1·40 1·30

**1064** Queen Paola and Belvedere Villa

**1997.** 60th Birthday of Queen Paola.

3383 **1064** 17f. multicoloured 1·30 40

**1065** Jommeke, Flip and Filiberke (comic strip characters)

**1997.** "Philately for the Young".

3384 **1065** 17f. multicoloured 1·60 45

**1066** "Rosa damascena" "Coccinea"

**1997.** Roses. Illustrations by Pierre-Joseph Redoute. Multicoloured.

3385 17f. Type **1066** 1·30 40
3386 17f. "Rosa sulfurea" 1·30 40
3387 17f. "Rosa centifolia" 1·30 40

**1067** St. Martin's Cathedral, Hal

**1997.** Tourist Publicity. Multicoloured.

3388 17f. Type **1067** 1·30 40
3389 17f. Notre-Dame Church, Laeken (horiz) 1·30 40
3390 17f. St. Martin's Cathedral, Liege 1·30 40

**1068** Stonecutter

**1997.** Trades. Multicoloured.

3391 17f. Type **1068** 1·30 30
3392 17f. Bricklayer 1·30 30
3393 17f. Carpenter 1·30 30
3394 17f. Blacksmith 1·30 30

**1069** Queen amidst Workers

**1997.** Centenary of Apimondia (International Apicultural Association) and 35th Congress, Antwerp. Bees. Multicoloured.

3395 17f. Type **1069** 1·30 90
3396 17f. Development of egg 1·30 90
3397 17f. Bees emerging from cells 1·30 90
3398 17f. Bee collecting nectar from flower 1·30 90
3399 17f. Bee fanning at hive entrance and worker arriving with nectar 1·30 90
3400 17f. Worker feeding drone 1·30 90

**1070** "Belgica" (polar barque) ice-bound

**1997.** Cent of Belgian Antarctic Expedition.

3401 **1070** 17f. multicoloured 1·30 50

**1071** Mask

**1997.** Centenary of Royal Central Africa Museum, Tervuren. Multicoloured.

3402 17f. Type **1071** 1·30 40
3403 17f. Museum (74×24 mm) 1·30 40
3404 34f. Statuette 2·50 1·00

**1073** "Fairon" (Pierre Grahame)

**1997.** Christmas.

3408 **1073** 15f. multicoloured 1·20 40

**1074** Disjointed Figure

**1997.** "Solidarity". Multiple Sclerosis.

3409 **1074** 17f.+4f. black & blue 1·60 1·60

**1997.** Willow Tit. As No. 3318 but horiz.

3410 15f. multicoloured 1·50 1·40

**1075** Azalea "Mrs. Haerens A"

**1997.** Self-adhesive.

3411 **1075** (17f.) multicoloured 1·30 20

**1076** Female Symbol

**1998.** 50th Anniv of Women's Suffrage in Belgium.

3412 **1076** 17f. red, brown & sepia 1·20 40

**1077** Thalys High Speed Train on Antoing Viaduct

**1998.** Paris–Brussels–Cologne–Amsterdam High Speed Rail Network.

3413 **1077** 17f. multicoloured 1·30 40

**1078** Gerard Walschap

**1998.** Writers' Birth Centenaries. Mult.

3414 17f. Type **1078** 1·20 40
3415 17f. Norge (Georges Mogin) 1·20 40

**1079** King Leopold III

**1998.** Kings of Belgium (1st series).

3416 **1079** 17f.+8f. green 1·70 1·70
3417 - 32f.+15f. brown 3·00 3·00
**MS**3418 125×90 mm. 50f.+25f. red 7·00 7·00

KINGS: 32f. Baudouin I; 50f. Albert II.

The premium was used for the promotion of philately.

See also Nos. 3466/8 and **MS**3508.

1080 "Black Magic"

1998. Birth Centenary of Rene-Ghislain Magritte (artist) (1st issue). Multicoloured.

| | | | |
|---|---|---|---|
| 3419 | 17f. Type **1080** | 1·30 | 40 |
| 3420 | 17f. "The Sensitive Chord" (horiz) | 1·30 | 40 |
| 3421 | 17f. "The Castle of the Pyrenees" | 1·30 | 40 |

See also No. 3432.

1081 "La Foire aux Amours" (Felicien Rops)

1998. Art Anniversaries. Multicoloured.

| | | | |
|---|---|---|---|
| 3422 | 17f. Type **1081** (death cent) | 1·20 | 1·00 |
| 3423 | 17f. "Hospitality for the Strangers" (Gustave van de Woestijne) (bicentenary of Museum of Fine Arts, Ghent) | 1·20 | 1·00 |
| 3424 | 17f. "Man with Beard" (self-portrait of Felix de Boeck, birth centenary) | 1·20 | 1·00 |
| 3425 | 17f. "black writing mixed with colours..." (Karel Appel and Christian Dotremont) (50th anniv of Cobra art movement) | 1·20 | 1·00 |

1082 Anniversary Emblem

1998. 75th Anniv of Belgian Postage Stamp Dealers' Association.

| | | | | |
|---|---|---|---|---|
| 3426 | **1082** | 17f. multicoloured | 1·20 | 40 |

1083 Avro RJ85 Airplane

1998. 75th Anniv of Sabena Airlines.

| | | | | |
|---|---|---|---|---|
| 3427 | **1083** | 17f. multicoloured | 1·30 | 40 |

1084 Fox

1998. Wildlife of the Ardennes. Mult.

| | | | |
|---|---|---|---|
| 3428 | 17f. Type **1084** | 1·30 | 50 |
| 3429 | 17f. Red deer ("Cervus elaphus") | 1·30 | 50 |
| 3430 | 17f. Wild boar ("Sus scrofa") | 1·30 | 50 |
| 3431 | 17f. Roe deer ("Capreolus capreolus") | 1·30 | 50 |

1085 "The Return" (Magritte)

1998. Birth Centenary of Rene-Ghislain Magritte (artist) (2nd issue).

| | | | | |
|---|---|---|---|---|
| 3432 | **1085** | 17f. multicoloured | 1·30 | 50 |

1086 Struyf

1998. Stamp Day. 2nd Death Anniv of Edmond Struyf (founder of Pro-Post (organization for promotion of philately)).

| | | | | |
|---|---|---|---|---|
| 3433 | **1086** | 17f. black, red & yellow | 1·20 | 40 |

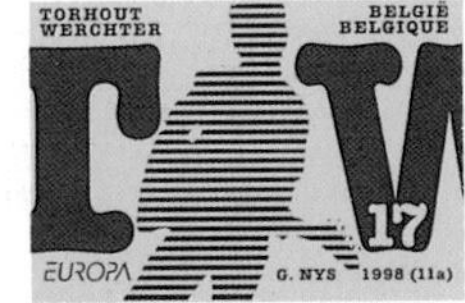

1087 Guitarist (Torhout and Werchter Festival)

1998. Europa. National Festivals.

| | | | | |
|---|---|---|---|---|
| 3434 | **1087** | 17f. violet and yellow | 1·40 | 40 |
| 3435 | - | 17f. violet and mauve | 1·40 | 40 |

DESIGN: No. 3435, Music conductor (Wallonie Festival).

1088 Pelote

1998. Sports. Multicoloured.

| | | | |
|---|---|---|---|
| 3436 | 17f.+4f. Type **1088** | 1·50 | 1·50 |
| 3437 | 17f.+4f. Handball | 1·50 | 1·50 |
| **MS**3438 | 123×88 mm. 30f.+7f. Goalkeeper (World Cup Football Championship, France) | 3·00 | 3·00 |

1089 Emblem

1998. European Heritage Days. Mult.

| | | | |
|---|---|---|---|
| 3439 | 17f. Type **1089** | 1·20 | 50 |
| 3440 | 17f. Bourla Theatre, Antwerp | 1·20 | 50 |
| 3441 | 17f. La Halle, Durbuy | 1·20 | 50 |
| 3442 | 17f. Halletoren, Kortrijk | 1·20 | 50 |
| 3443 | 17f. Louvain Town Hall | 1·20 | 50 |
| 3444 | 17f. Perron, Liege | 1·20 | 50 |
| 3445 | 17f. Royal Theatre, Namur | 1·20 | 50 |
| 3446 | 17f. Aspremont-Lynden Castle, Rekem | 1·20 | 50 |
| 3447 | 17f. Neo-Gothic kiosk, Saint Nicolas | 1·20 | 50 |
| 3448 | 17f. Saint-Vincent's Chapel, Tournai | 1·20 | 50 |
| 3449 | 17f. Villers-la-Ville Abbey | 1·20 | 50 |
| 3450 | 17f. Saint-Gilles Town Hall | 1·20 | 50 |

1090 Marnix van Sint-Aldegonde

1998. 400th Death Anniv of Philips van Marnix van St. Aldegonde (writer).

| | | | | |
|---|---|---|---|---|
| 3451 | **1090** | 17f. multicoloured | 1·20 | 40 |

1091 Face

1998. Bicentenary of "Amis Philanthropes" (circle of free thinkers).

| | | | | |
|---|---|---|---|---|
| 3452 | **1091** | 17f. black and blue | 1·20 | 40 |

1092 Mniszech Palace

1998. Belgium Embassy, Warsaw, Poland.

| | | | | |
|---|---|---|---|---|
| 3453 | **1092** | 17f. multicoloured | 1·20 | 40 |

1093 King Albert II

1998

| | | | | |
|---|---|---|---|---|
| 3454 | **1093** | 19f. lilac | 1·70 | 1·60 |

No. 3454 was for use on direct mail by large companies.

1094 "The Eighth Day" (dir. Jaco van Dormael)

1998. 25th Anniv of Brussels and Ghent Film Festivals. Multicoloured.

| | | | |
|---|---|---|---|
| 3455 | 17f. Type **1094** | 1·30 | 40 |
| 3456 | 17f. "Daens" (dir. Stijn Coninx) | 1·30 | 40 |

1096 Chick Bill and Ric Hochet

1998. "Philately for the Young". Comic Strip Characters.

| | | | | |
|---|---|---|---|---|
| 3460 | **1096** | 17f. multicoloured | 1·30 | 50 |

1097 "Youth and Space"

1998. 14th World Congress of Association of Space Explorers.

| | | | | |
|---|---|---|---|---|
| 3461 | **1097** | 17f. multicoloured | 1·30 | 45 |

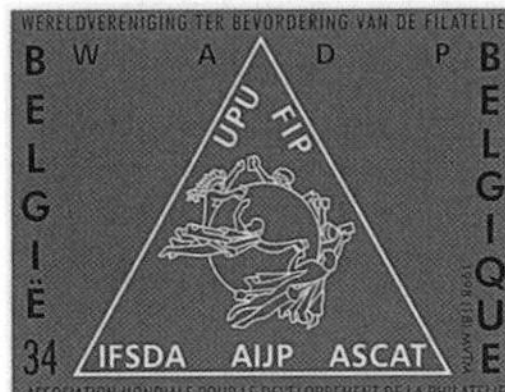

1098 Universal Postal Union Emblem

1998. World Post Day.

| | | | | |
|---|---|---|---|---|
| 3462 | **1098** | 34f. blue & ultramarine | 2·50 | 1·30 |

1099 "The Three Kings" (Michel Provost)

1998. Christmas. No value indicated.

| | | | | |
|---|---|---|---|---|
| 3463 | **1099** | (17f.) multicoloured | 1·20 | 40 |

1100 Detail of Triptych by Constant Dratz

1998. Cent of General Belgium Trade Union.

| | | | | |
|---|---|---|---|---|
| 3464 | **1100** | 17f. multicoloured | 1·20 | 40 |

1101 Blind Man with Guide Dog

1998. "Solidarity". Guide Dogs for the Blind.

| | | | | |
|---|---|---|---|---|
| 3465 | **1101** | 17f.+4f. multicoloured | 1·60 | 1·60 |

The face value is embossed in Braille.

1999. Kings of Belgium (2nd series). As T 1079.

| | | | |
|---|---|---|---|
| 3466 | 17f.+8f. deep green & green | 1·90 | 1·90 |
| 3467 | 32f.+15f. black | 3·25 | 3·25 |
| **MS**3468 | 125×90 mm. 50f.+25f. brown and purple | 5·75 | 5·75 |

KINGS: 17f. Albert I; 32f. Leopold II; 50f. Leopold I.
The premium was used for the promotion of philately.

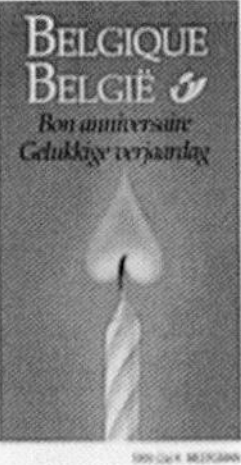

1102 Candle ("Happy Birthday")

1999. Greetings stamps. No value expressed. Mult.

| | | | |
|---|---|---|---|
| 3469 | (17f.) Type **1102** | 1·20 | 50 |
| 3470 | (17f.) Stork carrying heart ("Welcome" (new baby)) | 1·20 | 50 |
| 3471 | (17f.) Wristwatch ("Take your Time" (retirement)) | 1·20 | 50 |
| 3472 | (17f.) Four-leafed clover ("For your pleasure") | 1·20 | 50 |
| 3473 | (17f.) White doves ("Congratulations" (marriage)) | 1·20 | 50 |
| 3474 | (17f.) Arrow through heart ("I love you") | 1·20 | 50 |
| 3475 | (17f.) Woman with heart as head ("Happy Mother's Day") | 1·20 | 50 |
| 3476 | (17f.) Man with heart as head ("Happy Father's Day") | 1·20 | 50 |

**1103** Barn Owl

**1999.** Owls. Multicoloured.

| | | | |
|---|---|---|---|
| 3477 | 17f. Type **1103** | 1·30 | 40 |
| 3478 | 17f. Little owl ("Athene noctua") | 1·30 | 40 |
| 3479 | 17f. Tawny owl ("Strix aluco") | 1·30 | 40 |
| 3480 | 17f. Long-eared owl ("Asio otus") | 1·30 | 40 |

**1104** Leopard Tank (Army)

**1999.** 50th Anniv of North Atlantic Treaty Organization. Multicoloured.

| | | | |
|---|---|---|---|
| 3481 | 17f. Type **1104** | 1·20 | 40 |
| 3482 | 17f. Lockhead Martin F-16 Fighting Falcon (Air Force) | 1·20 | 40 |
| 3483 | 17f. "De Wandelaar" (frigate) (Navy) | 1·20 | 40 |
| 3484 | 17f. Field hospital (Medical Service) | 1·20 | 40 |
| 3485 | 17f. Display chart of military operations (General Staff) | 1·20 | 40 |

**1105** Envelopes and World Map

**1999.** 125th Anniv of U.P.U.

| | | | | |
|---|---|---|---|---|
| 3486 | **1105** | 34f. multicoloured | 2·30 | 65 |

**1106** De Bunt Nature Reserve, Hamme

**1999.** Europa. Parks and Gardens. Multicoloured.

| | | | |
|---|---|---|---|
| 3487 | 17f. Type **1106** | 1·40 | 40 |
| 3488 | 17f. Harchies Marsh | 1·40 | 40 |

**1107** 1849 10c. "Epaulettes" Stamp

**1999.** Stamp Day. 150th Anniv of First Belgian Postage Stamp. Multicoloured.

| | | | |
|---|---|---|---|
| 3489 | 17f. Type **1107** | 1·10 | 30 |
| 3490 | 17f. 1849 20c. "Epaulettes" stamp | 1·10 | 30 |

**1108** Racing

**1999.** Sport. Belgian Motor Cycling. Multicoloured.

| | | | |
|---|---|---|---|
| 3491 | 17f.+4f. Type **1108** | 1·60 | 1·60 |
| 3492 | 17f.+4f. Trial (vert) | 1·60 | 1·60 |
| **MS**3493 | 90×125 mm. 30f.+7f. Motocross (vert) | 3·25 | 3·25 |

**1109** "My Favourite Room"

**1999.** 50th Death Anniv of James Ensor (artist) (1st issue).

| | | | | |
|---|---|---|---|---|
| 3494 | **1109** | 17f. mullticoloured | 1·10 | 40 |

See also Nos. 3501/3.

**1110** Giant Family, Geraardsbergen

**1999.** Tourist Publicity. Multicoloured.

| | | | |
|---|---|---|---|
| 3495 | 17f. Type **1110** | 1·10 | 40 |
| 3496 | 17f. Members of Confrerie de la Misericorde in Car d'Or procession, Mons (horiz) | 1·10 | 40 |

**1111** Harvesting of Cocoa Beans

**1999.** Belgian Chocolate. Multicoloured.

| | | | |
|---|---|---|---|
| 3497 | 17f. Type **1111** | 1·10 | 40 |
| 3498 | 17f. Chocolate manufacture | 1·10 | 40 |
| 3499 | 17f. Selling product | 1·10 | 40 |

**1112** Photographs of 1959 and 1999

**1999.** 40th Wedding Anniv of King Albert and Queen Paola.

| | | | | |
|---|---|---|---|---|
| 3500 | **1112** | 17f. multicoloured | 1·30 | 40 |

**1113** "Woman eating Oysters"

**1999.** 50th Death Anniv of James Ensor (artist) (2nd issue).

| | | | | |
|---|---|---|---|---|
| 3501 | **1113** | 17f. multicoloured | 1·10 | 40 |
| 3502 | - | 30f. black, brown and grey | 1·90 | 80 |
| 3503 | - | 32f. multicoloured | 2·10 | 80 |

DESIGNS—30f. "Triumph of Death"; 32f. "Old Lady with Masks".

**1999.** "Bruphila '99" National Stamp Exhibition, Brussels. Kings of Belgium (3rd series). Sheet 191×121 mm containing vert designs as T 1079. Each deep blue and blue.

| | | | |
|---|---|---|---|
| **MS**3508 | 17f. As No. 3466; 17f. Type **1079**; 32f. As No. 3467; 32f. As No. 3417; 50f. As No. **MS**3468; 50f. As No. **MS**3418 | 26·00 | 26·00 |

**1115** Henri la Fontaine (President of International Peace Bureau), 1913

**1999.** Belgian Winners of Nobel Peace Prize.

| | | | | |
|---|---|---|---|---|
| 3509 | **1115** | 17f. red and gold | 1·10 | 40 |
| 3510 | - | 21f. blue and gold | 1·30 | 80 |

DESIGNS: 3510, Auguste Beernaert (Prime Minister 1884–94), 1909.

**DENOMINATION.** From No. 3511 Belgian stamps are denominated both in Belgian francs and in euros.

**1116** King Albert II **1116a** King Albert II

**1999**

| | | | | |
|---|---|---|---|---|
| 3511 | **1116** | 17f. multicoloured | 1·20 | 15 |
| 3512 | **1116** | 17f. blue | 1·20 | 15 |
| 3513 | **1116** | 19f. purple | 1·30 | 40 |
| 3514 | **1116** | 20f. brown | 1·30 | 30 |
| 3515 | **1116** | 25f. brown | 2·50 | 2·30 |
| 3516 | **1116** | 30f. purple | 2·10 | 25 |
| 3517 | **1116** | 32f. green | 1·90 | 25 |
| 3518 | **1116** | 34f. blue | 2·30 | 65 |
| 3519 | **1116** | 36f. brown | 2·30 | 15 |
| 3520 | **1116a** | 50f. blue | 3·25 | 65 |
| 3521 | **1116a** | 200f. lilac | 13·00 | 1·60 |

**1117** "Corentin" (Paul Cuvelier)

**1999.** "Philately for the Young". Comic Strips. Sheet 185×145 mm containing T 1117 and similar horiz designs. Multicoloured.

| | | | |
|---|---|---|---|
| **MS**3525 | 17f. Type **1117**; 17f. "Jerry Spring" (Jije); 17f. "Gil Jourdan" (Maurice Tillieux); 17f. "Beaver Patrol" (Mitacq); 17f. Entrance Hall, Belgian Comic Strip Centre; 17f. "Hassan and Kadour" (Jacques Laudy); 17f. "Buck Danny" (Victor Hubinon); 17f. "Tif and Tondu" (Fernand Dineur); 17f. "Les Timour" (Sirius) | 11·50 | 11·50 |

**1118** Geranium "Matador"

**1999.** Flowers. No value expressed (geranium) or inscr "ZONE A PRIOR" (tulip). Multicoloured. Self-adhesive.

| | | | |
|---|---|---|---|
| 3528 | (17f.) Type **1118** | 1·60 | 45 |
| 3529 | (21f.) Tulip (21×26 mm) | 1·20 | 40 |

The geranium design was for use on inland letters up to 20g. and the tulip design for letters within the European Union up to 20g.

**1119** Reindeer holding Glass of Champagne

**1999.** Christmas.

| | | | | |
|---|---|---|---|---|
| 3530 | **1119** | 17f. multicoloured | 1·20 | 40 |

**1120** Child bandaging Teddy Bear

**1999.** "Solidarity". Red Cross. Multicoloured.

| | | | |
|---|---|---|---|
| 3531 | 17f.+4f. Type **1120** | 1·50 | 1·50 |
| 3532 | 17f.+4f. Child and teddy bear cleaning teeth (vert) | 1·50 | 1·50 |

**1121** Prince Philippe and Mathilde d'Udekem d'Acoz

**1999.** Engagement of Prince Philippe and Mathilde d'Udekem d'Acoz.

| | | | |
|---|---|---|---|
| 3533 | 17f. Type **1121** | 1·60 | 50 |
| **MS**3534 | 120×89 mm. 21f. Prince Philippe and Mathilde d'Udekem d'Acoz (different) | 1·80 | 1·80 |

**1122** Pope John Paul XXIII

**1999.** The Twentieth Century (1st issue). Personalities, Sports and Leisure. Sheet 166×200 mm containing T 1122 and similar vert designs. Multicoloured.

| | | | |
|---|---|---|---|
| **MS**3535 | 17f. Type **1122**; 17f. King Baudouin; 17f. Willy Brandt (German statesman); 17f. John F. Kennedy (U.S. President, 1961–3); 17f. Mahatma Gandhi (Indian leader); 17f. Martin Luther King (civil rights leader); 17f. Vladimir Lenin (Prime Minister of Russia, 1917–24; 17f. Che Guevara (revolutionary); 17f. Golda Meir (Prime Minister of Israel, 1969–74); 17f. Nelson Mandela (Prime Minister of South Africa, 1994–99); 17f. Jesse Owens (American athlete) (modern Olympics); 17f. Football; 17f. Eddy Merckx (racing cyclist) (Tour de France); 17f. Edith Piaf (French singer); 17f. The Beatles (English pop band); 17f. Charlie Chaplin (English film actor and director); 17f. Postcards (tourism); 17f. Children around campfire (youth movements); 17f. Tintin and Snowy (comic strip); 17f. Magnifying glass over stamp (hobbies) | 23·00 | 23·00 |

See also Nos. **MS**3613 and **MS**3656.

**1123** Fireworks and Streamer forming "2000"

**2000.** New Year.

| | | | | |
|---|---|---|---|---|
| 3536 | **1123** | 17f. multicoloured | 1·30 | 25 |

**1124** Red-backed Shrike

**2000.** Birds. Multicoloured.

| | | | |
|---|---|---|---|
| 3537 | 50c. Goldcrest ("Roitelet Huppe") | 15 | 25 |
| 3538 | 1f. Red crossbill ("Beccroisé des Sapins") | 25 | 15 |
| 3539 | 2f. Short-toed treecreeper ("Grimpereau des Jardins") | 25 | 15 |

| | | | |
|---|---|---|---|
| 3540 | 3f. Meadow pipit ("Pipit Farlouse") | 25 | 15 |
| 3541 | 5f. Brambling ("Pinson du Nord") | 30 | 15 |
| 3542 | 7f.50 Great grey shrike ("Pie-Grieche Grise") | 50 | 50 |
| 3543 | 8f. Great tit ("Mesange Charbonniere") | 65 | 30 |
| 3544 | 10f. Wood warbler ("Pouillot Siffleur") | 65 | 40 |
| 3545 | 16f. Type **1124** | 1·10 | 40 |
| 3546 | 16f. Common tern ("Sterne Pierregarin") | 1·10 | 25 |
| 3547 | 21f. Fieldfare ("Grive Litorne") (horiz) | 1·30 | 50 |
| 3548 | 150f. Black-billed magpie ("Pie Bavarde") (36×25 mm) | 9·75 | 65 |

**1125** Brussels Skyline and Group of People

**2000.** Brussels, European City of Culture. Mult.

| | | | |
|---|---|---|---|
| 3555 | 17f. Type **1125** | 1·10 | 50 |
| 3556 | 17f. Toots Tielmans (jazz musician), Anne Teresa de Keersmaeker (gymnast) and skyline | 1·10 | 50 |
| 3557 | 17f. Lockhead L-1011 Tristar, train and skyline | 1·10 | 50 |

Nos. 3555/7 were issued together, se-tenant, forming a composite design showing the Brussels skyline.

**1126** Queen Astrid

**2000.** Queens of Belgium (1st series).

| | | | | |
|---|---|---|---|---|
| 3558 | **1126** | 17f.+8f. green and deep green | 1·90 | 1·90 |
| 3559 | - | 32f.+15f. brown and black | 3·25 | 3·25 |
| **MS**3560 | | 125×89 mm. 50f.+25f. deep purple and purple | 4·75 | 4·75 |

DESIGNS: 32f. Queen Fabiola; 50f. Queen Paola.

The premium was used for the promotion of philately.

See also Nos. 3615/**MS**3617 and **MS**3618.

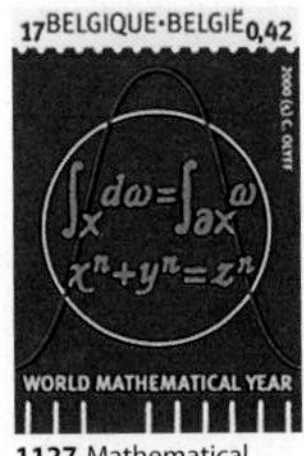
**1127** Mathematical Formulae

**2000.** World Mathematics Year.

| | | | | |
|---|---|---|---|---|
| 3561 | **1127** | 17f. multicoloured | 1·10 | 40 |

**1128** Globe and Technology (Joachim Beckers)

**2000.** "Stampin' the Future". Winning Entries in Children's International Painting Competition.

| | | | | |
|---|---|---|---|---|
| 3562 | **1128** | 17f. multicoloured | 1·10 | 40 |

**1129** "Charles V as Sovereign Master of the Order of the Golden Fleece" (anon)

**2000.** 500th Birth Anniv of Charles V, Holy Roman Emperor. Paintings of Charles V. Multicoloured.

| | | | |
|---|---|---|---|
| 3563 | 17f. Type **1129** | 1·10 | 40 |
| 3564 | 21f. "Charles V" (Corneille de la Haye) | 1·30 | 75 |
| **MS**3565 | 125×88 mm. 34f. "Charles V on Horseback" (Titian) | 2·50 | 2·50 |

**1130** Common Adder

**2000.** Amphibians and Reptiles. Multicoloured.

| | | | |
|---|---|---|---|
| 3566 | 17f. Type **1130** | 1·10 | 40 |
| 3567 | 17f. Sand lizard (*Lacerta agilis*) (vert) | 1·10 | 40 |
| 3568 | 17f. Common tree frog (*Hyla arborea*) (vert) | 1·10 | 40 |
| 3569 | 17f. Spotted salamander (*Salamander salamander*) | 1·10 | 40 |

**1131** Children flying Kites

**2000.** Red Cross and Red Crescent Movements.

| | | | | |
|---|---|---|---|---|
| 3570 | **1131** | 17f.+4f. multicoloured | 1·50 | 1·50 |

**1132** Players Celebrating

**2000.** European Football Championship, Belgium and The Netherlands. Multicoloured. (a) With face value. Size 26×38 mm.

| | | | |
|---|---|---|---|
| 3571 | 17f. Type **1132** | 1·30 | 25 |
| 3572 | 21f. Football | 1·60 | 40 |

(b) Size 20×26 mm. Self-adhesive.

| | | | |
|---|---|---|---|
| 3573 | (17f.) As Type **1132** | 1·60 | 40 |

Nos. 3571/3 were printed together, se-tenant, with the backgrounds forming the composite design of a crowd of spectators and the Belgian flag.

**1133** Cat and Rabbit reading Book

**2000.** Stamp Day. Winning Entry in Stamp Design Competition.

| | | | | |
|---|---|---|---|---|
| 3574 | **1133** | 17f. black, blue and red | 1·10 | 40 |

**1134** Francois de Tassis (detail of tapestry)

**2000.** "Belgica 2001" Int Stamp Exhibition, Brussels, (1st issue).

| | | | | |
|---|---|---|---|---|
| 3575 | **1134** | 17f. multicoloured | 1·10 | 50 |

See also Nos. 3629/33.

**1135** *Iris spuria*

**2000.** Ghent Flower Show. Multicoloured.

| | | | |
|---|---|---|---|
| 3576 | 16f. Type **1135** | 1·30 | 50 |
| 3577 | 17f. Rhododendron (horiz) | 1·50 | 40 |
| 3578 | 21f. Begonia (vert) | 1·60 | 75 |

**1136** Prince Philippe

**2000.** 2nd Anniv of Prince Philippe (cultural organization).

| | | | | |
|---|---|---|---|---|
| 3579 | **1136** | 17f. brn, grey & sil | 1·10 | 40 |

**1137** Harpsichord

**2000.** 250th Death Anniv of Johann Sebastian Bach. No value expressed. Multicoloured.

| | | | |
|---|---|---|---|
| 3580 | (17f.) Type **1137** | 1·30 | 1·00 |
| 3581 | (17f.) Violin | 1·30 | 1·00 |
| 3582 | (17f.) Two tenor lutes | 1·30 | 1·00 |
| 3583 | (17f.) Treble viol | 1·30 | 1·00 |
| 3584 | (17f.) Three trumpets | 1·30 | 1·00 |
| 3585 | (17f.) Bach | 1·30 | 1·00 |

**1138** Belgium Team Emblem and Olympic Rings

**2000.** Olympic Games, Sydney. Multicoloured.

| | | | |
|---|---|---|---|
| 3586 | 17f. Type **1138** | 1·00 | 50 |
| 3587 | 17f.+4f. Tae-kwon-do | 1·40 | 1·40 |
| 3588 | 17f.+4f. Paralympic athlete (horiz) | 1·40 | 1·40 |
| **MS**3589 | 125×90 mm. 30f.+7f. Swimmer (horiz) | 2·50 | 2·50 |

**1139** "Building Europe"

**2000.** Europa.

| | | | | |
|---|---|---|---|---|
| 3590 | **1139** | 21f. multicoloured | 1·50 | 75 |

**1140** Flemish Beguinages

**2000.** UNESCO World Heritage Sites in Belgium. Multicoloured.

| | | | |
|---|---|---|---|
| 3591 | 17f. Type **1140** | 1·10 | 30 |
| 3592 | 17f. Grand-Place, Brussels | 1·10 | 30 |
| 3593 | 17f. Four lifts, Centre Canal, Wallonia | 1·10 | 30 |

**1141** Baroque Organ, Norbertine Abbey Church, Grimbergen

**2000.** Tourism. Churches and Church Organs. Mult.

| | | | |
|---|---|---|---|
| 3594 | 17f. Type **1141** | 1·10 | 40 |
| 3595 | 17f. St. Wandru Abbey, Mons | 1·10 | 40 |
| 3596 | 17f. O.-L.-V. Hemelvaartkerk (former abbey church), Ninove | 1·10 | 40 |
| 3597 | 17f. St. Peter's Church, Bastogne | 1·10 | 40 |

**1142** Red-backed Shrike ("Pie grieche ecorcheur")

**2000**

| | | | | |
|---|---|---|---|---|
| 3598 | **1142** | 16f. multicoloured | 2·20 | 1·60 |
| 3599 | - | 17f. mult (51×21 mm) | 3·50 | 2·50 |
| 3600 | - | 23f. lilac | 2·50 | 2·00 |

DESIGNS: 17f. Francois de Tassis (detail of tapestry) and Belgica 2001 emblem; 23f. King Albert II.

**1143** Marcel, Charlotte, Fanny and Konstantinopel

**2000.** "Philately for the Young". Kiekeboe (cartoon series created by Robert Merhottein).

| | | | | |
|---|---|---|---|---|
| 3601 | **1143** | 17f. multicoloured | 1·10 | 50 |

**1144** "Springtime"

**2000.** Hainaut Flower Show.

| | | | | |
|---|---|---|---|---|
| 3602 | **1144** | 17f. multicoloured | 1·10 | 40 |

**1145** Pansies

**2000.** Flowers. No value expressed. Self-adhesive.
3603 **1145** (17f.) multicoloured 1·30 25

**1147** "Bing of the Ferro Lusto X" (Panamarenko)

**2000.** Modern Art. Multicoloured.
3608 17f. Type **1147** 1·10 65
3609 17f. "Construction" (Anne-Mie van Kerckhoven) (vert) 1·10 65
3610 17f. "Belgique eternelle" (Jacques Charlier) 1·10 65
3611 17f. "Les Belles de Nuit" (Marie Jo Lafontaine) 1·10 65

**1148** Postman

**2000.** Christmas.
3612 **1148** 17f. multicoloured 1·10 40

**1149** Soldiers at Yser Front, West Flanders (First World War, 1914–18)

**2000.** The Twentieth Century (2nd issue). War, Peace and Art. Sheet 200×166 mm containing T 1149 and similar horiz designs. Multicoloured.
**MS**3613 17f. Type **1149**; 17f. German concentration camp and prisoners (black and scarlet); 17f. Atomic cloud and Hiroshima (atomic bomb, 1945); 17f. Winston Churchill, Franklin D. Roosevelt and Joseph Stalin (Yalta conference, 1945); 17f. Headquarters (United Nations established, 1945); 17f. Joseph Kasavubu (first President) and map of Africa (independence of Belgian Congo, 1960); 17f. American soldiers and Boeing CH-14 Chinook(Vietnam War); 17f. Collapse of Berlin Wall, 1989; 17f. Campaign for Nuclear Disarmament emblem and crowd; 17f. Dome of the Rock (Middle East conflict); 17f. Rene Magritte (artist); 17f. Le Corbusier (architect) and building; 17f. Bertolt Brecht (dramatist and poet) and actors; 17f. James Joyce (novelist); 17f. Anne Teresa de Keersmaeker (choreographer); 17f. Bila Bartok (composer); 17f. Andy Warhol (artist); 17f. Maria Callas (opera singer); 17f. Henry Moore (sculptor) and sculpture; 17f. Charlie Parker (alto saxophonist and composer) and Toots Thielemans (composer and jazz musician) 23·00 23·00

**1150** Stars

**2000.** New Year.
3614 **1150** 17f. gold, blue & blk 1·30 50

**1150** Stars

**2001.** Queens of Belgium (2nd series). As T 1126.
3615 17f.+8f. green & dp green 1·90 1·90
3616 32f.+15f. black and green 3·25 3·25
**MS**3617 126×91 mm. 50f.+25f. deep brown and brown 4·75 4·75
DESIGNS: 17f. Queen Elisabeth; 32f. Queen Marie-Henriette; 50f. Queen Louise-Marie.
The premium was used for the promotion of philately.

**2001.** Queens of Belgium (3rd series). Vert designs as T 1126. Each blue, deep blue and ochre.
**MS**3618 190×121 mm. 17f. As No. 3615; 17f. As Type **1126**; 32f. As No. 3616; 32f. As No. 3559; 50f. As No. **MS**3617; 50f. As No. **MS**3560 23·00 23·00

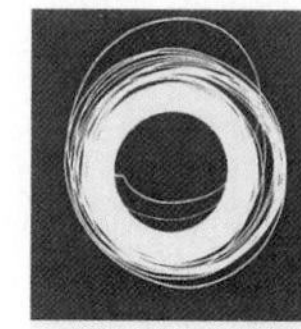

**1151** Movement of a Dynamo

**2001.** Death Centenary of Zenobe Gramme (physicist).
3619 **1151** 17f. black, red & black 1·10 40

**1152** Virgin and Child (statue)

**2001.** 575th Anniv of Louvain Catholic University.
3620 **1152** 17f. multicoloured 1·10 40

**2001.** As T 998 but with face value expressed in francs and euros.
3621 100f. multicoloured 6·25 55

**1153** Willem Elsschot (poet)

**2001.** Music and Literature.
3622 **1153** 17f. brown and black 1·10 40
3623 - 17f. grey and black 1·10 40
**MS**3624 125×90 mm. 21f. orange and brown 1·50 1·50
DESIGNS—VERT: No. 3623, Albert Ayguesparse (poet). HORIZ: **MS**3624 21f. Queen Elisabeth and emblem (50th anniv of Queen Elisabeth International Music Competition).

**1154** Boy washing Hands

**2001.** Europa. Water Resources.
3625 **1154** 21f. multicoloured 1·40 75

**1155** Type 12 Steam Locomotive

**2001.** 75th Anniv of National Railway Company. Multicoloured.
3626 17f. Type **1155** 1·10 65
3627 17f. Series 06 dual locomotive No. 671 1·10 65
3628 17f. Series 03 locomotive No. 328 1·10 65
Nos. 3626/8 were issued together, se-tenant, forming a composite design.

**1156** 16th-century Postman on horseback

**2001.** "Belgica 2001" International Stamp Exhibition, Brussels (2nd issue). 500th Anniv of European Post. Multicoloured.
3629 17f. Type **1156** 1·40 65
3630 17f. 17th-century postman with walking staff (vert) 1·40 65
3631 17f. 18th-century postman and hand using quill (vert) 1·40 65
3632 17f. Steam locomotive and 19th-century postman (vert) 1·40 65
3633 17f. 20th-century forms of communication (vert) 1·40 65
**MS**3634 190×120 mm. 150f. Female postal worker (35×46 mm) 20·00 20·00

**1157** Hassan II Mosque, Casablanca

**2001.** Places of Worship. Multicoloured.
3635 17f. Type **1157** 1·10 40
3636 34f. Koekelberg Basilica 2·30 1·00

**1158** "Winter Landscape with Skaters" (Pieter Bruegel the Elder)

**2001.** Art. Multicoloured.
3637 17f. Type **1158** 1·10 95
3638 17f. "Heads of Negros" (Peter Paul Rubens) 1·10 95
3639 17f. "Sunday" (Frits van den Berghe) 1·10 95
3640 17f. "Mussels" (Marcel Broodthaers) 1·10 95

**1159** Pottery Vase

**2001.** Chinese Pottery. Multicoloured.
3641 17f. Type **1159** 1·10 30
3642 34f. Teapot 2·30 80

**1160** Luc Orient

**2001.** "Philately for the Young". Cartoon Characters.
3643 **1160** 17f. multicoloured 1·10 50

**1161** Cyclists (World Cycling Championship, Antwerp)

**2001.** Sports. Multicoloured.
3644 17f.+4f. Type **1161** 1·40 1·40
3645 17f.+4f. Gymnast (World Gymnastics Championships, Ghent) 1·40 1·40

**1162** Emblem

**2001.** Belgian Presidency of European Union.
3646 **1162** 17f. multicoloured 1·10 50

**1163** Binche

**2001.** Town Hall Belfries.
3647 **1163** 17f. mauve and black 1·10 40
3648 - 17f. blue, mauve & blk 1·10 40
DESIGN: No. 3648, Diksmuide.

**1164** Damme

**2001.** Large Farmhouses. Multicoloured.
3649 17f. Type **1164** 1·10 40
3650 17f. Beauvechain 1·10 40
3651 17f. Louvain 1·10 40
3652 17f. Honnelles 1·10 40
3653 17f. Hasselt 1·10 40

**1165** Red Cross and Doctor

**2001.** Red Cross.
3654 **1165** 17f.+4f. multicoloured 1·40 1·40

**1166** Stam and Pilou

**2001.** Stamp Day. No value expressed. Self-adhesive.
3655 **1166** (17f.) multicoloured 1·40 50

No. 3655 was for use on inland standard letters up to 20g.

1167 Ovide Decroly (educational psychologist) and Road Sign

**2001.** The Twentieth Century. Science and Technology. Sheet 166×200 mm. Multicoloured.

**MS**3656 17f. Type **1167**; 17f. Dandelion and windmills (alternative energy sources); 17f. Globe, signature and map (first solo non-stop crossing of North Atlantic by Charles Lindbergh); 17f. Man with head on lap (Sigmund Freud, founder of psychoanalysis); 17f. Astronaut and foot print on moon surface (Neil Armstrong, first man on the moon, 1969); 17f. Claude Levi-Strauss (anthropologist); 17f. DNA double helix and athletes (human genetic code); 17f. Pierre Teilhard de Chardin (theologian palaeontologist and philosopher); 17f. Max Weber (sociologist) and crowd; 17f. Albert Einstein (physicist) (Theory of Relativity); 17f. Knight and jacket of pills (discovery of Penicillin, 1928); 17f. Ilya Prigogine (theoretical chemist and clock face; 17f. Text and Roland Barthes (writer and critic); 17f. Simone de Beauvoir (feminist writer); 17f. Globe and technology highway (computer science); 17f. John Maynard Keynes (economist) and folded paper; 17f. Marc Bloch (historian) and photographs; 17f. Tools and Julius Robert Oppenheimer (nuclear physicist); 17f. Marie and Pierre Curie, discoverers of radioactivity, 1896); 17f. Caricature of Ludwig Josef Wittgenstein (philosopher) 23·00 23·00

1168 Nativity

**2001.** Christmas.
3657 **1168** 15f. multicoloured 1·10 45

1169 Sunset

**2001.** Bereavement. No value expressed.
3658 **1169** (17f.) multicoloured 1·60 40

See also Nos. 3732 and 3856.

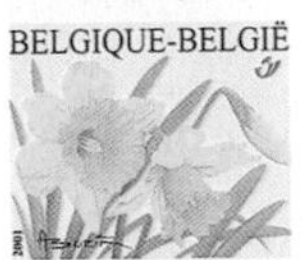

1170 Daffodil

**2001.** Flowers. No value expressed. Self-adhesive. (a) Without service indicator. Multicoloured.
3659 (17f.) Type **1170** 1·30 40

(b) Inscr "ZONE A PRIOR".
3660 (21f.) Tulip "Darwin" (vert) 1·40 50

No. 3659 was for use on inland letters up to 20g. and No. 3660 was for use on letters within the European Union up to 20g.

1171 Tintin

**2001.** 70th Anniv of Tintin in Congo (cartoon strip). Multicoloured.
3661 17f. Type **1171** 1·30 65

**MS**3662 123×88 mm. 34f. Tintin, Snowy and guide in car (48×37 mm) 3·25 3·25

1172 King Albert II 1173 King Albert II

**2002**

| | | | | |
|---|---|---|---|---|
| 3663 | **1173** | 7c. blue and red (postage) | 25 | 15 |
| 3666 | **1172** | 42c. red | 1·10 | 40 |
| 3667 | **1172** | 47c. green | 1·30 | 50 |
| 3668 | **1173** | 49c. red | 1·30 | 50 |
| 3669 | **1173** | 52c. blue | 1·40 | 50 |
| 3670 | **1172** | 59c. blue | 1·80 | 55 |
| 3671 | **1172** | 60c. blue | 1·20 | 90 |
| 3672 | **1173** | 79c. blue and red | 2·50 | 65 |
| 3674 | **1173** | €4.21 brown and red | 10·00 | 2·50 |
| 3674a | **1172** | 70c. blue (air) | 1·50 | 65 |
| 3674b | **1172** | 60c. blue | 1·80 | 65 |
| 3674c | **1172** | 80c. purple and red | 2·00 | 65 |

Nos. 3663, 3668 and 3672 are inscribed "PRIOR" at left.

1174 Female Tennis Player

**2002.** Centenary of Royal Belgian Tennis Federation. Multicoloured.
3675 42c. Type **1174** 1·30 50
3676 42c. Male tennis player 1·30 50

1175 Cyclist

**2002.** International Cycling Events held at Circuit Zolder. Multicoloured.
3677 42c. Type **1175** (World Cyclo-Cross Championships) 1·30 50
3678 42c. Cyclist with hand raised (Road Cycling Championships) 1·30 50

1176 Dinosaur

**2002.** Winning Entry in Children's Stamp Design Competition at "Belgica 2001".
3679 **1176** 42c.+10c. mult 1·50 1·50

The premium was used for the promotion of philately.

1177 Antwerp from River

**2002.** 150th Anniv of Antwerp University.
3680 **1177** 42c. blue and black 1·10 45

1178 Buildings and Architectural Drawing

**2002.** "Bruges 2002", European City of Culture. Multicoloured.
3681 42c. Type **1178** 1·30 45
3682 42c. Organ pipes and xylophone 1·30 45
3683 42c. Octopus 1·30 45

1179 16th-century Manuscript (poem, Anna Bijns)

**2002.** Women and Art. Multicoloured.
3684 42c. Type **1179** 1·30 45
3685 84c. Woman writing (painting, Anna Boch) (vert) 2·10 1·00

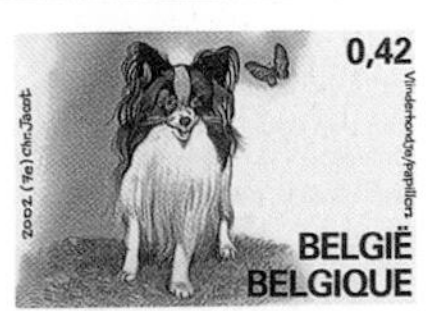

1180 Fountain Pen and Writing

**2002.** Stamp Day.
3686 **1180** 47c. multicoloured 1·40 55

1181 Papillon

**2002.** Centenary of Flanders Canine Society. Multicoloured.

| | | | |
|---|---|---|---|
| 3687 | 42c. Type **1181** | 1·30 | 65 |
| 3688 | 42c. Brussels griffon | 1·30 | 65 |
| 3689 | 42c. Bloodhounds | 1·30 | 65 |
| 3690 | 42c. Bouvier des Ardennes | 1·30 | 65 |
| 3691 | 42c. Schipperke | 1·30 | 65 |


1182 Stock Dove ("Pigeon Colombin-Holenduif")

**2002.** Birds. Multicoloured.

| | | | |
|---|---|---|---|
| 3692 | 1c. Nightingale ("Rossignol philomele-Nachtegaal") (postage) | 15 | 15 |
| 3693 | 2c. Snipe ("Becassine des Marais-Watersnip") | 15 | 15 |
| 3693a | 3c. Marsh tit ("Mesange Nonnette-Glanskopmees") | 15 | 15 |
| 3693aa | 5c. Little grebe ('Dodaars-Grebe castagneux') (23x27mm) | 20 | 15 |
| 3693b | 5c. Cirl bunting ("Bruant Zizi-Cirlors") | 20 | 15 |
| 3693c | 5c. Teal ("Wintertaling-Sarcelle D'Hiver") | 20 | 15 |
| 3693d | 6c. Little owl ('Steenuil-Chouette Cheveche') | 25 | 15 |
| 3694 | 7c. Type **1182** | 25 | 15 |
| 3694a | 10c. Tengmalm's owl ("Chouette De Tengmalm-Ruigpootuil") | 30 | 20 |
| 3694b | 10c. Hedge sparrow (Heggemus-Accentor Maichet) (air/prior) | 1·00 | 35 |
| 3694c | 15c. Spotted nutcracker (Cassenoix Mouchete-Notenkracker) (air/prior) | 1·00 | 35 |
| 3695 | 10c. Hedge Sparrow ('Heggemus-accenentor Mouchet') (AIRPRIOR) | 30 | 20 |
| 3696 | 15c. Spotted nutcracker ('Cassenoix Mouchete-Noutenkotenkrake')(AIRPRIOR) | 40 | 25 |
| 3697 | 20c. Mediterranean gull ("Zwartkopmeeuw-Mouette Melanocephale") | 50 | 30 |
| 3697a | 23c. Black-necked grebe ("Greb a Cou Noir - Geoorde Fuut") | 55 | 30 |
| 3697b | 23c. Jackdaw ("Kauw-Choucas des Tours") | 55 | 30 |
| 3698 | 25c. Oystercatcher ("Scholekster-Huitrier Pie") | 65 | 40 |
| 3698a | 27c. Eurasian woodcock ('Houtsnip-becasse des bois') | 70 | 40 |
| 3699 | 30c. Corncrake ("Rale des Genets—Kwartelkoning") | 95 | 40 |
| 3700 | 35c. Spotted woodpecker ("Pic Epeiche-Grote Bonte Specht") | 1·00 | 45 |
| 3700a | 40c. Spotted flycatcher ("Grauwe vliegenvanger-Gobemouche gris") | 1·00 | 50 |
| 3700b | Long-eared owl ("Hibou Moyen-Duc-Ransuil") | 1·00 | 50 |
| 3701 | 41c. Collared dove ("Tourterelle Turque") | 1·30 | 65 |
| 3701a | 44c. House martin ("Hirondelle de fenetre-Huiszwaluw") | 1·30 | 65 |
| 3701b | 44c. Wood pigeon ("Hourduif-Pigeon Ramier") | 1·30 | 65 |
| 3701c | 46c. Avocet ("Kluut—Avocette") | 1·30 | 70 |
| 3701d | 52c. Hoopoe ("Hop-Huppe Fasciee") | 1·40 | 75 |
| 3701e | 55c. Plover ("Kleine plevier-Petit gravelot") | 1·40 | 80 |
| 3702 | 57c. Black tern ("Guifette Noire") | 1·40 | 90 |
| 3702a | 60c. Partridge ("Perdrix Crise-Patrijs") | 1·50 | 1·00 |
| 3703 | 65c. Black-headed gull ("Mouette rieuse-Kapmeeuw") | 1·60 | 1·10 |
| 3704 | 70c. Redshank ("Chevalier Gambette") | 2·10 | 1·10 |
| 3704a | 70c. Swallow ('Aprus apus') | 1·90 | 1·20 |
| 3704aa | 75c. Golden plover ("Goudplevier-Pluvier dore") | 1·90 | 1·20 |
| 3704b | 75c. Firecrest ("Rottelet Triple-Bandeau Vuurgoudhaatje") | 1·90 | 1·20 |
| 3704ba | 75c. Kestrel ('Falco tinnunculus') | 1·90 | 1·20 |
| 3704c | 78c. Black-tailed godwit ("Gritto-Barge A Queue Noir") | 2·30 | 1·30 |
| 3705 | €1 Wheatear ("Traquet Motteux") (38x27 mm) | 3·00 | 1·50 |
| 3706 | €2 Ringed plover ("Grand Gravelot") (38x27 mm) | 6·00 | 2·50 |
| 3707 | €3.72 Moorhen ("Waterhoen-Poule d'eau") (38x27 mm) | 11·50 | 3·25 |
| 3708 | €4 Eagle owl ("Hibou grand-duc-Oehoe") (38x27 mm) | 13·00 | 5·25 |
| 3708a | €4.30 Grebe ("Fuut-Grebe Huppe") | 14·00 | 5·75 |
| 3708aa | €4.09 Pheasant ("Faisan de Colchide") (32x24 mm) (14.6.10) | 13·50 | 5·25 |
| 3708b | Peregrine falcon (Slechtwalk-Faucon Pelerin) (38x28 mm) | 14·50 | 6·00 |
| 3708c | € 4.60 Golden eagle | 15·00 | 6·25 |
| 3708ca | € 4.60 Barn owl ('Couette effraie-kerkuil') | 15·00 | 6·25 |
| 3709 | €5 Ruff ("Combattant Varie") (38x27 mm) | 16·00 | 7·00 |

1183 Big Top, Ringmaster, Seal and Clown

**2002.** Europa. Circus. Winning Entry in Children's Drawing Competition.
3710 **1183** 52c. multicoloured 2·50 1·00

1184 Paramedic, Patient and Damaged Buildings

**2002.** Red Cross.
3711 **1184** 84c.+12c. multicoloured 2·50 2·50

1185 Abbey Buildings

**2002.** 850th Anniv of Leffe Abbey.
3712 **1185** 42c. multicoloured 1·50 50

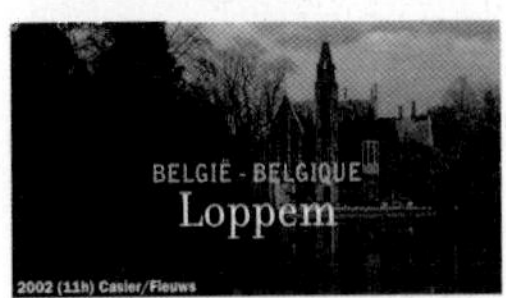

1186 Loppem Castle

**2002.** Tourism. Castles. Sheet 161×141 mm containing T 1186 and similar horiz designs showing castles. Multicoloured.

**MS**3713 42c. Type **1186**; 42c. Horst; 42c. Wissekerke; 42c. Chimay; 42c. Ecaussinnes-Lalaing; 42c. Reinhardstein; 42c. Modave; 42c. Ooidonk; 42c. Corroy-le-Chateau; 42c. Alden Biesen 11·50 11·50

1187 Show Jumping

**2002.** Horses. Designs showing equestrian events. Multicoloured.

| | | | |
|---|---|---|---|
| 3714 | 40c. Type **1187** | 1·00 | 45 |
| 3715 | 42c. Carriage driving (vert) | 1·10 | 50 |
| **MS**3716 | 126×91 mm. 52c. Two Brabant draught horses' heads (Centenary of St. Paul's horse procession, Opwijk) (37×48 mm) | 1·60 | 1·60 |

1188 Golden Spur and Battle Scene

**2002.** 700th Anniv of Battle of the Golden Spurs (Flemish–French battle), Kortrijk. Multicoloured.

| | | | |
|---|---|---|---|
| 3717 | 42c. Type **1188** | 1·10 | 40 |
| 3718 | 52c. Broel towers | 1·30 | 75 |
| **MS**3719 | 126×91 mm. 57c. Flemish and French soldiers, river and knight on horseback (48×38 mm) | 1·60 | 1·60 |

1189 Onze-Lieve-Vrouw-Lombeek, Roosdaal

**2002.** Windmills. Multicoloured.

| | | | |
|---|---|---|---|
| 3720 | 42c. Type **1189** | 1·10 | 40 |
| 3721 | 52c. Faial Island, Azores, Portugal | 1·40 | 75 |

Stamps of a similar design were issued by Portugal.

1190 Liedekerke Lacework and Statue of Lace-maker

**2002.** Lace-making. Multicoloured.

| | | | |
|---|---|---|---|
| 3722 | 42c. Type **1190** | 1·10 | 40 |
| 3723 | 74c. Pag lacework | 2·00 | 90 |

Stamps of a similar design were issued by Croatia.

1191 Bakelandt, Red Zita and Stagecoach

**2002.** "Philately for the Young". Bakelandt (comic strip created by Hec Leemans).

| | | | |
|---|---|---|---|
| 3724 | **1191** 42c. multicoloured | 1·30 | 65 |

1192 Teddy Bear

**2002.** "The Rights of the Child".

| | | | |
|---|---|---|---|
| 3725 | **1192** 42c. multicoloured | 1·30 | 40 |

1193 Rey

**2002.** Birth Centenary of Jean Rey (politician).

| | | | |
|---|---|---|---|
| 3726 | **1193** 52c. blue and cobalt | 1·60 | 75 |

1194 Princess Elisabeth

**2002.** 1st Birthday of Princess Elisabeth. Multicoloured.

| | | | |
|---|---|---|---|
| 3727 | 49c. Type **1194** | 1·60 | 50 |
| 3728 | 59c. Princess Elisabeth with parents (horiz) | 1·90 | 75 |
| **MS**3729 | 123×88 mm 84c. Princess Elisabeth (different) (59×38 mm) | 2·75 | 2·75 |

No. 3727 was issued with a se-tenant label inscribed "PRIOR".

1195 Church, Ice Cream Van and Family

**2002.** Christmas. Sheet 166×40 mm containing T 1195 and similar vert designs. Multicoloured.

| | | | |
|---|---|---|---|
| **MS**3730 | 41c. Type **1195**; 41c. Skier in snowy fir tree; 41c. Tobogganist and bird wearing hat; 41c. Skier wearing kilt; 41c. Skiers holding candles; 41c. Boy holding snowman-shaped ice cream; 41c. Children throwing snowballs; 41c. Children, snowman, and elderly man; 41c. Brazier, re-freshment hut and people; 41c. Hut, robbers, cow and policeman | 12·50 | 12·50 |

1196 Bricks

**2002.** The Twentieth Century. Society. Sheet 200×166 mm containing T 1196.

| | | | |
|---|---|---|---|
| **MS**3731 | 41c. purple, red and pink (Type **1196** (social housing)); 41c. deep purple, orange and purple ("MEI/MAI 68" and rubble (student protests)); 41c. slate, grey and green (telephone telecommunications)); 41c. red, orange and brown (slabs (gap between wealth and poverty)); 41c. brown, bistre and blue (broken crucifix (secularization of society)); 41c. multicoloured (towers of blocks (urbanization)); 41c. pink, violet and purple (combined female and male symbols (universal suffrage)); 41c. blue, orange and grey (enclosed circle (social security)); 41c. grey, green and bistre (schoolbag (equality in education)); 41c. grey, purple and deep purple (elderly man (ageing population)); 41c. blue, green and emerald ("E" (European Union)); 41c. chestnut, brown and yellow (stylized figure (declaration of Human Rights)); 41c. bistre, orange and light orange (pyramid of blocks (growth of consumer society)); 41c. blue, mauve and green (female symbol (feminism)); 41c. brown, sepia and light brown (mechanical arm (de-industrialization)); 41c. brown and green (dripping nozzle (oil crises)); 41c. multicoloured (vehicle (transportation)); 41c. lilac, brown and purple (sperm and egg (contraception)); 41c. green, red and grey (television (growth of television and radio)); 41c. pink, violet and blue (electric plug (increase in home appliances)) | 25·00 | 25·00 |

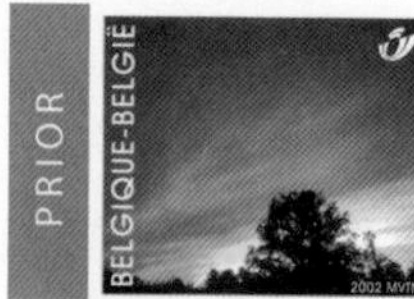
1197 Sunset

**2002.** Bereavement. No value expressed.

| | | | |
|---|---|---|---|
| 3732 | **1197** (49c.) multicoloured | 1·50 | 65 |

1198 Crocus

**2002.** Flowers. No value expressed. Ordinary or self-adhesive gum.

| | | | |
|---|---|---|---|
| 3733 | **1198** (49c.) multicoloured | 1·50 | 65 |

No. 3733 was for use on inland letters up to 50 g.

1199 Nero and Adhemar (cartoon characters)

**2003.** 80th (2002) Birth Anniv of Marc Sleen (cartoonist). Multicoloured.

| | | | |
|---|---|---|---|
| 3735 | 49c. Type **1199** | 1·60 | 60 |
| **MS**3736 | 121×91 mm 82c. Nero and Marc Sleen (49×38 mm) | 2·75 | 2·75 |

1200 Firefighters, Engine and Ladders

**2003.** Public Services (Nos. 3737/41) and St. Valentine (3742). Multicoloured.

| | | | |
|---|---|---|---|
| 3737 | 49c. Type **1200** | 1·60 | 60 |
| 3738 | 49c. Traffic police men and policewoman | 1·60 | 60 |
| 3739 | 49c. Civil defence workers mending flood defences | 1·60 | 60 |
| 3740 | 49c. Elderly woman wearing breathing mask, hand holding syringe and theatre nurse | 1·60 | 60 |
| 3741 | 49c. Postman riding bicycle and obtaining signature for parcel | 1·60 | 60 |
| 3742 | 49c. Hearts escaping from birdcage | 1·60 | 60 |

1201 Van de Velde and New House, Tervuren

**2003.** 140th Birth Anniv of Henry van de Velde (architect). Multicoloured.

| | | | |
|---|---|---|---|
| 3743 | 49c. Type **1201** | 1·60 | 60 |
| 3744 | 59c. Van de Velde and Belgian pavilion, Paris International Exhibition, 1937 (vert) | 1·90 | 70 |
| 3745 | 59c. Van de Velde and Book Tower, Central Library, Ghent University (vert) | 1·90 | 70 |
| **MS**3746 | 91×125 mm 84c. Woman and Art Nouveau newel post | 2·75 | 2·75 |

1202 Bowls

**2003.** Traditional Sports. Multicoloured.

| | | | |
|---|---|---|---|
| 3747 | 49c. Type **1202** | 1·80 | 65 |
| 3748 | 49c. Archery | 1·80 | 65 |
| **MS**3749 | 91×126 mm. 82c. Pigeon racing | 3·00 | 3·00 |

1203 Berlioz

**2003.** Birth Bicentenary of Hector Berlioz (composer).

| | | | |
|---|---|---|---|
| 3750 | **1203** 59c. multicoloured | 2·10 | 75 |

1204 Statue of Men Conversing

**2003.** Anniversaries. Multicoloured.

| | | | |
|---|---|---|---|
| 3751 | 49c. Type **1204** (150th anniv of engineers' association) | 1·80 | 65 |
| 3752 | 49c. Statue of seated man (centenary of Solvay Business School) | 1·80 | 65 |

1205 Papy Ferdinand

**2003.** Red Cross. Cartoon characters in rescue attempt. Multicoloured.

| | | | |
|---|---|---|---|
| 3753 | 41c. + 9c. Type **1205** | 2·10 | 1·30 |
| 3754 | 41c. + 9c. Pilou holding light | 2·10 | 1·30 |
| 3755 | 41c. + 9c. Stam running for help | 2·10 | 1·30 |

Nos. 3753/5 were issued together, se-tenant, forming a composite design.

1206 Bouquet

**2003.** 3rd International Flower Show, Liege.

| | | | |
|---|---|---|---|
| 3756 | **1206** 49c. multicoloured | 2·00 | 65 |

1207 "Maigret" (film poster)

**2002.** Birth Centenary of Georges Simenon (writer). Multicoloured.

| | | | |
|---|---|---|---|
| 3757 | 49c. Type **1207** | 2·00 | 65 |
| 3758 | 59c. "Le chat" (film poster) | 2·40 | 80 |
| **MS**3759 | 91×126 mm. 84c. Simenon (38×49 mm) | 3·25 | 3·25 |

1208 Bells of St. Rumbold's Cathedral, Maline

**2003.** 150th Anniv of Belgium–Russia Diplomatic Relations. Multicoloured.

| | | | |
|---|---|---|---|
| 3760 | 59c. Type **1208** | 2·40 | 80 |
| 3761 | 59c. Bells of St. Peter and Paul's Cathedral, St. Petersburg | 2·40 | 80 |

**1209** Eternity Symbol and "Mail Art"

**2003.** Stamp Day. Mail Art.
3762 **1209** 49c. multicoloured 2·10 65

**1210** Roland on Horseback

**2003.** "Philately for the Young". The Valiant Knight (comic strip created by Francois Craenhals).
3763 **1210** 49c. multicoloured 2·10 65

**1211** Calcite

**2003.** Minerals. Multicoloured.
3764 49c. Type **1211** 2·10 65
3765 49c. Quartz 2·10 65
3766 49c. Barytes 2·10 65
3767 49c. Galena 2·10 65
3768 49c. Turquoise 2·10 65

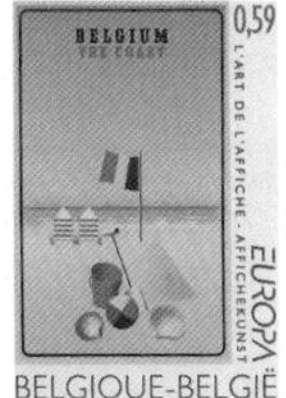

**1212** "Belgium, The Coast" ( Leo Marfut)

**2003.** Europa. Poster Art.
3769 **1212** 59c. multicoloured 2·75 1·40

**1213** "La Robe de Mariee" (Paul Delvaux, Koksijde)

**2003.** "This is Belgium" (1st series). Sheet 167×200 mm containing T 1213 and similar vert designs showing sites from smaller Belgian towns. Multicoloured.
**MS**3770 41c. Type **1213**; 41c. Mural, Town Hall, Oudenaarde; 41c. "De viust" (sculpture, Rik Poot) and Town Hall, Vilvoorde; 41c. Turnhout chateau; 41c. Ambiorix (sculpture), Gallo-Roman museum, Tongeren; 41c. Fountain (sculpture, Pol Bury), La Louviere; 41c. Town Hall, Braine; 52c. Mardasson Memorial, Bastogne; 52c. Tower and snow scene, Sankt Vith; 57c. Saxophone and Citadel, Dinant 20·00 11·00
See also Nos. **MS**3809, **MS**3943 and **MS**4033.

**1214** *Monument to the Seasonal Worker, Rillaar* (Jan Peirelinck)

**2003.** Tourism. Statues. Multicoloured.
3771 49c. Type **1214** 2·20 70
3772 49c. La Tionade, Treignes (Yves and Claude Rahir) 2·20 70
3773 49c. Textile Teut, Town Hall, Hamont-Achel (Teo Groenen) 2·20 70
3774 49c. The Canal Guy, Brussels (Tom Frantzen) 2·20 70
3775 49c. The Maca, Wavre (Jean Godart) 2·20 70

**1215** King Baudouin and Prince Albert

**2003.** 10th Anniv of the Accession of King Albert. Multicoloured.
3776 49c. Type **1215** 2·20 70
**MS**3777 90×125 mm. 59c. King Baudouin (38×48 mm); 84c. King Albert (38×48 mm) 6·75 5·50

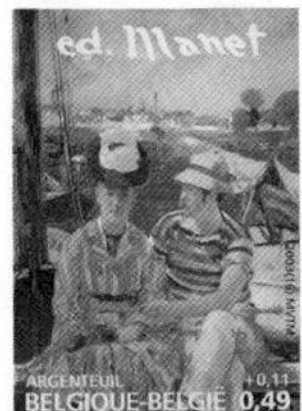

**1216** "Argenteuil" (Edouard Manet)

**2003.** Art.
3778 **1216** 49c. + 11c. multicoloured 2·75 1·80
No. 3778 was issued with a se-tenant label inscribed "PRIOR".

**1217** "Still Life" (Giorgio Morandi)

**2003.** "Europhalia 2003 Italy" Festival. Italian Presidency of European Union. Multicoloured.
3779 49c. Type **1217** 2·20 75
3780 59c. Cistalia 202 (1947) 2·75 90
No. 3779 was issued with a se-tenant label inscribed "PRIOR".
Stamps of the same design were issued by Italy.

**1218** Elderly Couple, Family and Young People

**2003.** Social Cohesion.
3781 **1218** 49c. multicoloured 2·20 80
No. 3781 was issued with a se-tenant label inscribed "PRIOR".

**1219** St. Nicholas

**2003.** Christmas.
3782 **1219** 49c. multicoloured 2·20 80
No. 3782 was issued with a se-tenant label inscribed "PRIOR".

**1220** King Albert II

**2003**
3783 **1220** 49c. red 2·20 80
3784 **1220** 50c. red 2·20 80
3785 **1220** 79c. blue and red 3·50 1·30
3786 **1220** 80c. violet and red 3·50 1·30
Nos. 3783/6 are inscribed "PRIOR" at left.

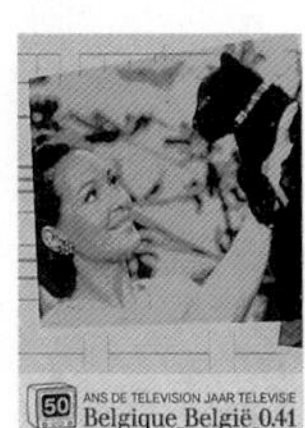

**1221** Woman holding Cat ("Jardin extraordinaire")

**2003.** 50th Anniv of Belgian Television. Sheet 166×140 mm containing T 1221 and similar vert designs. Multicoloured.
**MS**3795 41c.×5 Type **1221**; Cameraman and camera; Broadcasting tower; Brothers Cassiers and Jef Burm; Scene from "Schipper naast Mathide" 9·00 6·50

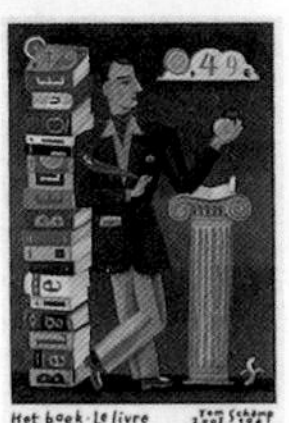

**1222** Man leaning against Pile of Books

**2003.** The Book. Multicoloured.
3796 49c. Type **1222** 2·20 80
3797 49c. Man rolling through printing machine (horiz) 2·20 80
3798 49c. Books on shelves 2·20 80
Nos. 3796/8 were each issued with an attached label inscribed "Prior".

**1223** Maurice Gilliams

**2003.** Writers.
3799 **1223** 49c. brown, sepia and light brown 2·20 80
3800 - 59c. brown and orange 2·75 95
DESIGN: 59c. Marguerite Yourcenar (Maugerite de Crayencour).
No. 3799 was issued with an attached label inscribed "Prior".

**1224** Tulip

**2003.** Flowers. No value expressed. Self-adhesive.
3801 **1224** (59c.) multicoloured 2·50 95
No. 3801 was for use on inland letters up to 50g.

**1225** Herbeumont Church

**2003.** Christmas and New Year.
3802 **1225** 41c. multicoloured 1·70 65

**1226** Justin Henin Hardenne

**2003.** Belgian Tennis Champions. Multicoloured.
3803 49c. Type **1226** (2003 Roland Garros and U.S. Open champion) 2·30 80
3804 49c. Kim Clijsters (2002 Masters Cup and 2003 WTA No. 1 champion) (horiz) 2·30 80
Nos. 3803/4 were each issued with an attached label inscribed "Prior", either at top or bottom (vert) or left or right (horiz).

**1227** XIII and Lighthouse

**2004.** "Philately for the Young". XIII (comic strip created by Jean van Damme and William Vance).
3805 **1227** 41c. multicoloured 1·80 65

**1228** "Portrait of Marguerite Khonopff"

**2004.** Fernand Khnopff (artist) Commemoration. Sheet 160×140 mm containing T 1228 and similar multicoloured designs.
**MS**3806 41c.×4, Type **1228**; "Caresses" (55×24 mm); "The Abandoned City"; "Brown Eyes and a Blue Flower" (55×24 mm) 5·25 4·75

**1229** Carnation

**2004.** Flowers. No value expressed. Self-adhesive.
3807 **1229** (49c.) multicoloured 1·80 80
No. 3807 was for use on inland letters up to 50g.

**1230** Profile, Stamp and Kiss

**2004.** Stamp Day.
3808 **1230** 41c. multicoloured 1·40 65

**1231** Peter Piot (AIDS agency director)

**2004.** "This is Belgium" (2nd series). Sheet 166×200 mm containing T 1231 and similar vert designs showing Belgian personalities. Multicoloured.

| | | |
|---|---|---|
| **MS**3809 57c.×10, Type **1231**; Nicole Van Goethem (film maker); Dirk Frimout and Frank de Winnie (astronaut and cosmonaut); Jaques Rogge (president, International Olympic Committee); Christian de Duve (winner, Nobel Prize for Medicine); Gabrielle Petit (war heroine); Catherine Verfaillie (director, Stem Cell Institute, Minnesota) and Christine Van Broeckhoven (director, Molecular Biology Laboratory, University of Antwerp); Jaques Stilbe (philatelist); Queen Fabiola; Adrien van der Burch (organizer, Brussels Exhibition, 1935) | 18·00 | 14·50 |

**1232** Herg and Models of Rocket and Tintin

**2004.** 75th Anniv of Tintin (cartoon character created by Georges Remi (Herge)). Sheet 163×126 mm containing T 1232 and similar vert designs. Multicoloured.

| | | |
|---|---|---|
| **MS**3810 41c.×5, Type **1232**; Technical sketch for Destination Moon; Tintin and Snowy (Bobbie); Tintin climbing up rocket (*Explorers on the Moon*); Tintin, Captain Haddock and Snowy on the moon (cover illustration, *Explorers on the Moon*) | 7·25 | 6·50 |

**1233** Sugar Beet

**2004.** Sugar Industry. Multicoloured.

| | | | | |
|---|---|---|---|---|
| 3811 | **49c.** | Type **1233** | 1·60 | 70 |
| 3812 | **49c.** | 49c. Sugar refinery | 1·60 | 70 |
| 3813 | **49c.** | 49c. Tienen city | 1·60 | 70 |

Nos. 3811/13 were each issued with a se-tenant label inscribed "Prior".

**1234** Stars

**2004.** European Elections.

| | | | | |
|---|---|---|---|---|
| 3814 | **1234** | 22c. cobalt, ultramarine and yellow | 80 | 35 |

**1235** "Temptation" (Salvador Dali)

**2004.** Birth Centenary of Salvador Dali (artist).

| | | | | |
|---|---|---|---|---|
| 3815 | **1235** | 49c.+11c. multicoloured | 2·10 | 1·90 |

No. 3815 was issued with a se-tenant label inscribed "Prior".

**1236** Chapel, Buggenhout

**2004.** Tourism. Places of Pilgrimage.

| | | | | |
|---|---|---|---|---|
| 3816 | **1236** | 49c. green | 1·60 | 70 |
| 3817 | - | 49c. agate | 1·60 | 70 |
| 3818 | - | 49c. purple | 1·60 | 70 |
| 3819 | - | 49c. indigo | 1·60 | 70 |

DESIGNS: No. 3817, Banneux; 3818, Scherpenheuvet; 3819, Beauraing (horiz).

Nos. 3816/19 were each issued with a se-tenant label inscribed "Prior".

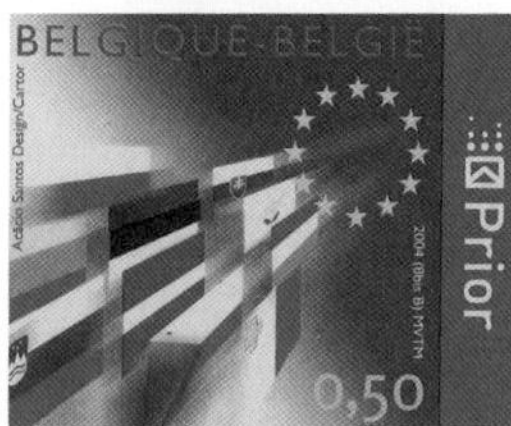


**1237** New Member's Flags and EU Emblem

**2004.** Enlargement of European Union (1st issue). Sheet 125×90 mm containing T 1237 and similar horiz designs. Multicoloured.

| | | |
|---|---|---|
| **MS**3820 50c.×2 Type **1237**×2; 60c.×2 Parliament building; As No. 3814 | 8·00 | 7·25 |

See also Nos. 3835/44.

**1238** Le Faune Mordu (sculpture) (Jef Lambeaux), Boverie Park

**2004.** Liege ("Lidje todi"). Multicoloured.

| | | | |
|---|---|---|---|
| 3821 | 49c. Type **1238** | 1·40 | 65 |
| 3822 | 49c. Bridge (Santiago Calatrava) | 1·40 | 65 |
| **MS**3823 90×125 mm. 75c. Blast furnace, Seraing (38×49 mm) | | 2·50 | 2·30 |

**1239** Earth showing Clouds and Ozone Layer (climate and CO2)

**2004.** Climatology. Multicoloured.

| | | | |
|---|---|---|---|
| 3824 | 50c. Type **1239** | 1·60 | 65 |
| 3825 | 65c. Sun and earth (earth–sun relationship) | 2·00 | 85 |
| 3826 | 80c. Earth showing continent and viewed from space (earth) | 2·50 | 1·00 |
| 3827 | 80c. Sun viewed through telescope and showing spots | 2·50 | 1·00 |

Nos. 3824 and 3826 were issued with a se-tenant label inscribed "Prior".

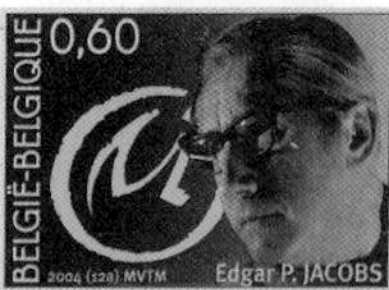


**1240** Edgar Jacobs

**2004.** Birth Centenary of Edgar Pierre Jacobs (creator of Blake and Mortimer (comic strip)). Black and yellow (60c.) or multicoloured (other).

| | | | |
|---|---|---|---|
| 3828 | 60c. Type **1240** | 2·20 | 90 |
| **MS**3829 125×90 mm. €1.20 Blake and Mortimer (45×36 mm) | | 3·75 | 3·00 |

Stamps of a similar design were issued by France.

**1241** Django Reinhardt

**2004.** Jazz Musicians. Multicoloured.

| | | | |
|---|---|---|---|
| 3830 | 50c. Type **1241** (guitarist) | 1·60 | 65 |
| 3831 | 50c. Fud Candrix (saxophonist) | 1·60 | 65 |
| 3832 | 50c. Rene Thomas (guitarist) | 1·60 | 65 |
| 3833 | 50c. Jack Sels (composer and saxophonist) | 1·60 | 65 |
| 3834 | 50c. Bobby Jaspar (flautist and saxophonist) | 1·60 | 65 |

Nos. 3830/4 were each issued with a se-tenant label inscribed "Prior".

**1242** EU Emblem and Cyprus Flag

**2004.** Enlargement of European Union (2nd issue). Designs showing emblem and new member flag. Multicoloured. Self-adhesive.

| | | | |
|---|---|---|---|
| 3835 | 44c. Type **1242** | 1·60 | 65 |
| 3836 | 44c. Estonia | 1·60 | 65 |
| 3837 | 44c. Hungary | 1·60 | 65 |
| 3838 | 44c. Latvia | 1·60 | 65 |
| 3839 | 44c. Lithuania | 1·60 | 65 |
| 3840 | 44c. Malta | 1·60 | 65 |
| 3841 | 44c. Poland | 1·60 | 65 |
| 3842 | 44c. Czech Republic | 1·60 | 65 |
| 3843 | 44c. Slovakia | 1·60 | 65 |
| 3844 | 44c. Slovenia | 1·60 | 65 |

**1243** King Albert II

**2004.** 70th Birthday of King Albert II. Each black and gold.

| | | | |
|---|---|---|---|
| 3845 | 50c. Type **1243** | 1·60 | 65 |
| **MS**3846 90×125 mm. 80c. As No. 3845 (38×48 mm) | | 2·50 | 2·10 |

No. 3845 was issued with a se-tenant label inscribed "Prior".

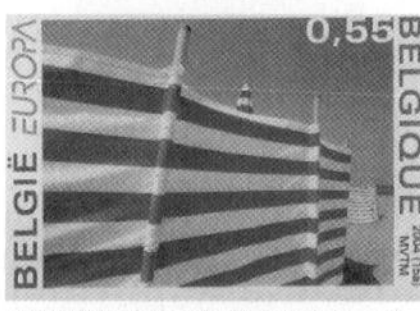


**1244** Wind Break (Belgian Coast)

**2004.** Europa. Holidays. Winning Designs in Photographic Competition. Multicoloured.

| | | | |
|---|---|---|---|
| 3847 | 55c. Type **1244** (Muriel Vekemans) | 1·70 | 1·40 |
| 3848 | 55c. Semois valley (Belgian Ardennes) (Freddy Deburghgraeve) | 1·70 | 1·40 |

**1245** Female Basketball Player

**2004.** Olympic Games, Athens 2004. Multicoloured.

| | | | |
|---|---|---|---|
| 3849 | 50c. Type **1245** | 1·70 | 65 |
| 3850 | 55c. Cyclist (horiz) | 1·80 | 75 |
| 3851 | 60c. Pole vaulter (horiz) | 2·00 | 80 |
| **MS**3852 136×90 mm. 80c. Olympic flame | | 2·75 | 2·10 |

No. 3849 was issued with a se-tenant label inscribed "Prior".

**1246** Red Cross Workers

**2004.** Red Cross.

| | | | | |
|---|---|---|---|---|
| 3853 | **1246** | 50c.+11c. multicoloured | 2·00 | 1·60 |

No. 3853 was issued with a se-tenant label inscribed "Prior".

**1247** "L'appel"

**2004.** 10th Death Anniv of Idel Ianchelevici (sculptor). Multicoloured.

| | | | |
|---|---|---|---|
| 3854 | 50c. Type **1247** | 1·70 | 65 |
| 3855 | 55c. "Perennis perdurat poeta" | 1·80 | 75 |

No. 3854 was issued with a se-tenant label inscribed "Prior".

Stamps of the same design were issued by Romania.

**2004.** Mourning Stamp. As T 1197.

| | | | | |
|---|---|---|---|---|
| 3856 | **1197** | 50c. multicoloured | 1·70 | 65 |

**1248** Squirrel and Blackcap

**2004.** Forest Week. Sheet 90×125 mm containing T 1248 and similar vert designs. Multicoloured.

| | | |
|---|---|---|
| **MS**3857 44c.×4, Type **1248**; Nightingale, robin and red admiral butterfly; Bee, vole and weasel; Jay and peacock butterfly | 6·50 | 5·25 |

The stamps and margin of **MS**3857 form a composite design of a forest scene.

**1249** Volunteer Medal

**2004.** War Volunteers.

| | | | | |
|---|---|---|---|---|
| 3858 | **1249** | 50c. multicoloured | 1·70 | 65 |

**1250** Impatiens

**2004.** Flowers. No value expressed. Self-adhesive.

| | | | | |
|---|---|---|---|---|
| 3859 | **1250** | (50c.) multicoloured | 1·70 | 65 |

No. 3859 was for use on inland letters up to 50g.

**1251** Foal

**2004.** Belgica 2006 International Stamp Exhibition, Brussels (1st issue). Sheet 166×140 mm containing T 1251 and similar vert designs. Multicoloured.

| | | |
|---|---|---|
| **MS**3860 44c.×5, Type **1251**; Robin; Cat; Puppy; Fish | 17·00 | 14·50 |

See also Nos. 3892/**MS**3897.

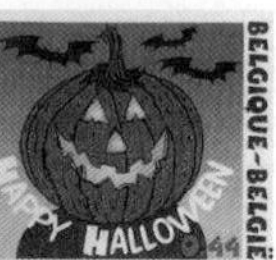


**1252** Jack O' Lantern

**2004.** Halloween. Self-adhesive. Multicoloured.

| | | | |
|---|---|---|---|
| 3861 | 44c. Type **1252** | 1·70 | 65 |
| 3862 | 44c. Witch, cat and bats | 1·70 | 65 |

**1253** Raymond Jean de Kramer

**2004.** Writers' Death Anniversaries. Multicoloured.

3863 50c. Type **1253** (writing as Jean Ray or John Flanders) (40th) 1·70 65
3864 75c. Johan Daisne (26th) 2·50 1·00
3865 80c. Thomas Owen (2nd) (vert) 2·75 1·10

Nos. 3863 and 3865 were issued with a se-tenant label inscribed "Prior".

**1254** Soldiers, Mother and Child on Snow-covered Street

**2004.** 60th Anniv of Attack on Bastogne. Multicoloured.

3866 44c. Type **1254** 1·70 65
3867 55c. Soldiers assisting wounded (vert) 1·80 75
3868 65c. Soldiers amongst trees 2·10 85

**1255** "Flight into Egypt"

**2004.** Christmas (1st issue). Paintings by Peter Paul Rubens. Multicoloured.

3869 44c. Type **1255** 1·70 65
3870 44c. "Adoration of the Magi" 1·70 65

Stamps of the same design were issued by Germany. See also No. 3872.

**1256** Rene Baeten

**2004.** Belgian International Motocross Champions. Sheet 151×166 mm containing T 1256 and similar horiz designs.

**MS**3871 50c.×12, (23bis a, d, e, f, g, i, j, k and l) multicoloured; (23bis b) green and brown; (23bis c) brown, lemon and deep brown; (23bis h) blue and brown 20·00 16·00

DESIGNS: Type **1256**; Jacky Martens; Georges Jobe; Joel Roberts; Eric Geboers; Roger de Coster; Stefan Everts; Gaston Rahier; Joel Smets; Harry Everts; Andre Malherbe and Steve Ramon.

The stamps of **MS**3871 were arranged around a central label, showing a motocross rider, each with a se-tenant label inscribed "Prior" attached at either left or right. The Belgium Post identification number is given in brackets to assist identification.

**2004.** Christmas (2nd issue). Paintings by Peter Rubens. Self-adhesive.

3872 44c. As No. 3870 (22×22 mm) 1·70 65

**1257** Stylized Posthorn

**2005**

3873 **1257** 6c. scarlet 35 15
3874 **1257** 10c. blue 85 40
3877 **1257** 1 (52c.) scarlet 1·00 90

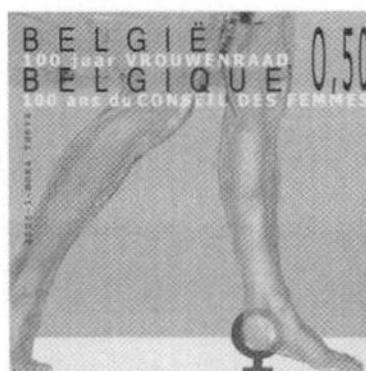


**1258** Woman's Legs

**2005.** Centenary of Women's Council.

3882 **1258** 50c. multicoloured 1·70 65

No. 3882 was issued with a se-tenant label inscribed "Prior".

**1259** Michel Vaillant

**2005.** "Philately for the Young". Michel Vaillant (comic strip created by Jean Graton).

3883 **1259** 50c. multicoloured 1·70 65

No. 3883 was issued with a se-tenant label inscribed "Prior".

**1260** "The Violinist" (Kees van Dongen)

**2005.** "Promotion of Philately".

3884 **1260** 50c.+12c. multicoloured 2·10 1·70

**1261** "www.175-25.be"

**2005.** 175th Anniv of Independence (1st issue). 25th Anniv of Federal State. No value expressed. Self-adhesive.

3885 **1261** (50c.) multicoloured 1·70 65

See also No. **MS**3889 and **MS**3891.

**1262** Johan Hendrick van Dale and "van Dale" (Dutch dictionary)

**2005.** Language. Multicoloured.

3886 55c. Type **1262** 1·80 75
3887 55c. Maurice Grevisse and "le bon usage" (French grammar) 1·80 75

**1263** Child receiving Polio Vaccine

**2005.** Centenary of Rotary International (charitable organization). Polio Eradication Campaign.

3888 **1263** 80c. multicoloured 2·75 1·30

**1264** First Railway Journey from Brussels to Malines (1835)

**2005.** 175th Anniv of Independence (2nd issue). Sheet 166×200 mm containing T 1264 and similar horiz designs. Multicoloured.

**MS**3889 44c.×10, Type **1264** (transport); Bakuba dancers, Congo; Early school children (education); Factory workers (industrialization); Family (social development); Bombardment of Edingen, 1940; Brussels Expo, 1958 (trade); Rue de la Loi, Wetstraat (federalization); Berlaymont building, Brussels (Europe); "The Shadow and its Shadow" (Rene Mgritte) (art) 15·00 13·50

**1265** "TSUNAMI" and Sea

**2005.** Red Cross. Support for Victims of Tsunami Disaster.

3890 **1265** 50c.+12c. multicoloured 2·10 1·70

No. 3890 was issued with a se-tenant label inscribed "Prior".

**1266** King Albert II and Queen Paola

**2005.** 175th Anniv of Independence (3rd issue). Sheet 126×90 mm.

**MS**3891 **1266** 75c. multicoloured 2·50 2·00

**1267** Go-Kart

**2005.** Belgica 2006 International Stamp Exhibition, Brussels (2nd issue). Multicoloured. (a) Self-adhesive.

3892 44c. Type **1267** 1·50 60
3893 44c. Motor boat 1·50 60
3894 44c. Train 1·50 60
3895 44c. Airplane 1·50 60
3896 44c. Spacecraft 1·50 60

(b) Size 27×39 mm. Miniature Sheet. Ordinary gum.

**MS**3897 166×131 mm. Nos. 3892/5 17·00 13·50

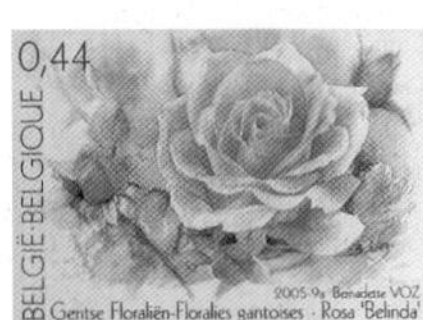


**1268** Rose "Belinda"

**2005.** Ghent Flower Show. Multicoloured.

3898 44c. Type **1268** 1·50 60
3899 70c. Rose "Pink Iceberg" (vert) 2·30 95
3900 80c. Rose "Old Master" 2·75 1·10

Nos. 3898/3900 were impregnated with the scent of roses.

No. 3900 was issued with a se-tenant label inscribed "Prior".

**1269** "The Children's Table" (Gustave van de Woestijne)

**2005.** Europa. Gastronomy. Multicoloured.

3901 60c. Type **1269** 2·00 1·60
3902 60c. "Still Life with Oysters, Fruit and Pastry" 2·00 1·60

**1270** Black Stork

**2005.** Stamp Day.

3903 **1270** €4 multicoloured 13·00 5·25

**1271** Soldiers

**2005.** 55th Anniv of Korean War.

3904 **1271** 44c. multicoloured 1·50 60

**1272** Celebration

**2005.** 60th Anniv of End of World War II. Multicoloured.

3905 44c. Type **1272** 1·50 60
3906 44c. Camp prisoner 1·50 60
3907 44c. Returning service men and prisoners 1·50 60

**1273** Zimmer Tower, Lier, Flanders

**2005.** Tourism. Clock Towers.

3908 **1273** 44c. black 1·50 60
3909 - 44c. agate 1·50 60
3910 - 44c. chocolate 1·50 60

DESIGNS: No. 3908 Type **1273**; 3909 Belfry, Mons, Wallonia; 3910 Mont des Arts Clock, Brussels.

**1274** Hiker (Ardennes)

**2005.** Holidays. Multicoloured.

3911 50c. Type **1274** 1·70 65
3912 50c. Sunbather 1·70 65

Nos. 3911/12 were each issued with a se-tenant label inscribed "Prior".

**1275** Hearts

**2005.** Greetings Stamps. Multicoloured. Self-adhesive.

3913 (50c.) Type **1275** 1·70 65
3914 80c. Doves (wedding) 2·75 1·10
3915 80c. Two rings (wedding) 2·75 1·10
3916 80c. Boy (birth) 2·75 1·10
3917 80c. Girl (birth) 2·75 1·10

No. 3913 was for use on inland letters up to 50g.

1276 Tulip

**2005.** Air. Flowers. No value expressed. Multicoloured. Self-adhesive.

| | | | | |
|---|---|---|---|---|
| 3918 | **1276** | (70c.) multicoloured | 2·30 | 95 |

1277 "L'humanitie assaillie par les sept Peches capiteux" (Seven Deadly Sins) (16th-century tapestry, Brussels)

**2005.** Carpets and Tapestries. Multicoloured.

| | | | |
|---|---|---|---|
| 3919 | 44c. Type **1277** | 1·50 | 60 |
| 3920 | 60c. Carpet, Hereke, Turkey | 2·00 | 80 |

Stamps of a similar design were issued by Turkey.

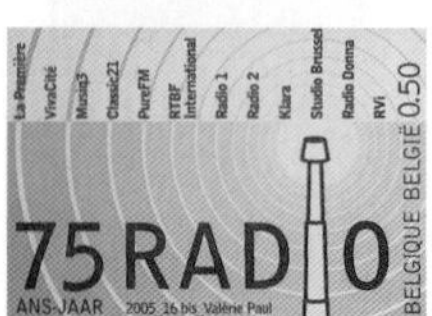

1278 Radio Waves

**2005.** 75th Anniv of Radio.

| | | | | |
|---|---|---|---|---|
| 3921 | **1278** | 50c. magenta and black | 1·70 | 65 |

No. 3921 was issued with a se-tenant label inscribed "Prior".

1279 Robert Van de Walle

**2005.** Belgian International Judo Champions. Sheet 100×167 mm containing T 1279 and similar horiz designs. Multicoloured.

**MS**3922 50c.×6, Type **1279**; Ingrid Berghmans; Ulla Werbrouck; Gella Vandecaveye; Christel Deliege; Johan Laats 10·00 8·00

The stamps of **MS**3922 were each issued with a se-tenant label inscribed "Prior" attached at either left or right.

1280 King Albert II

**2005**

| | | | | |
|---|---|---|---|---|
| 3923 | **1280** | 50c. multicoloured (postage) | 1·00 | 85 |
| 3923a | **1280** | 52c. multicoloured | 1·00 | 70 |
| 3928 | **1280** | 70c. blue and light (air) | 2·30 | 95 |
| 3928a | **1280** | 80c. blue, grey and black | 95 | 65 |
| 3928b | **1280** | 83c. multicoloured | 1·00 | 70 |
| 3929 | **1280** | 90c. blue, grey and black | 2·75 | 1·10 |

Nos. 3923 and 3928/9 were inscribed "Prior".

1281 *Buccinum undatum*

**2005.** Molluscs. Sheet 161×130 mm containing T 1281 and similar designs. Multicoloured. Self-adhesive.

**MS**3933 44c.×6, Type **1281**; *Epitonium clathrus; Cepea nemoralis* and *Arion rufus; Donax vittatus; Anodonta cygnea; Anodonta cygnea* (different) 9·00 7·25

1282 Centre for Comic Strip Art, Brussels

**2005.** Architecture. Multicoloured.

| | | | |
|---|---|---|---|
| 3934 | 44c. Type **1282** | 1·50 | 60 |
| 3935 | 44c. Museum of Musical Instruments, Brussels | 1·50 | 60 |
| 3936 | 65c. Bukit Pasoh Road, Singapore | 2·10 | 85 |
| 3937 | 65c. Kandahar Street, Singapore | 2·10 | 85 |

Stamps of the same design were issued by Singapore.

1283 Chrysanthemum

**2005.** Flowers. No value expressed. Self-adhesive.

| | | | | |
|---|---|---|---|---|
| 3938 | **1283** | (50c.) multicoloured | 1·70 | 65 |

No. 3938 was for use on inland letters up to 50g.

1284 "The Reaper" (Kasimir Malevich)

**2005.** "Europhalia 2005—Russia" Festival. Multicoloured.

| | | | |
|---|---|---|---|
| 3939 | 50c. Type **1284** | 1·70 | 65 |
| 3940 | 70c. "Allegory" (Sergei Sudeikin) | 2·30 | 95 |

No. 3939 was issued with a se-tenant label inscribed "Prior".

1285 Shrine of Our Lady, Tournai

**2005.** 800th Anniv of Shrine of Our Lady by Nicolas of Verdun.

| | | | | |
|---|---|---|---|---|
| 3941 | **1285** | 75c. bronze and gold | 2·50 | 1·00 |

1286 Asterix

**2005.** Asterix (comic strip written by Rene Goscinny and illustrated by Albert Uderzo). Sheet 161×130 mm containing T 1286 and similar designs showing characters. Multicoloured.

**MS**3942 60c.×6, Type **1286**; Cacofonix (27×41 mm.); Getafix (41×27 mm.); Obelix (41×27 mm.); Abraracourcix (27×41 mm.); Asterix feasting (39×34 mm.) 11·50 10·50

1287 "Objet" (Joelle Tuerlinckx)

**2005.** "This is Belgium" (3rd series). Art. Sheet 166×201 mm containing T 1287 and similar designs.

**MS**3943 44c.×10, black and claret (Type **1287**); multicoloured ("ABC" (Jef Geys)); multicoloured ("La Traviata" (Lili Dujourie)); multicoloured ("Representation d'un corps rond" (Ann Veronica Janssens)); black ("Portrait of an Artist by Himself (XIII)" (Jan Vercuysse)); multicoloured ("Donderwolk" (Panamarenko)); multicoloured ("Tournus" (Marthe Wery)); multicoloured ("Figuur op de rug gezien (la nuque)" (Luc Tuymans)); black and bright carmine ("Jeu de mains" (Michel Francois)); "Mur de la montee des Anges" (Jan Fabre)) 13·00 12·00

The stamps of No. **MS**3943 form a composite design.

1288 *The Princess and the Pea*

**2005.** Birth Bicentenary of Hans Christian Andersen (writer). Multicoloured. (a) Ordinary gum.

| | | | |
|---|---|---|---|
| 3944 | 50c. Type **1288b** | 1·70 | 65 |
| 3945 | 50c. *The Ugly Duckling* | 1·70 | 65 |
| 3946 | 50c. *Thumbelina* | 1·70 | 65 |
| 3947 | 50c. *The Little Mermaid* | 1·70 | 65 |
| 3948 | 50c. *The Emperor's New Clothes* | 1·70 | 65 |

(b) Size 28×22 mm. Self-adhesive.

| | | | |
|---|---|---|---|
| 3949 | 50c. As No. 3944 | 1·70 | 65 |
| 3950 | 50c. As No. 3945 | 1·70 | 65 |
| 3951 | 50c. As No. 3946 | 1·70 | 65 |
| 3952 | 50c. As No. 3947 | 1·70 | 65 |
| 3953 | 50c. As No. 3948 | 1·70 | 65 |

Nos. 3944/8 each have a label inscribed "Prior" attached at left.

1289 Father Christmas

**2005.** Christmas. (a) Ordinary gum.

| | | | | |
|---|---|---|---|---|
| 3954 | **1289** | 44c. multicoloured | 1·50 | 60 |

(b) Size 23×28 mm. Self-adhesive.

| | | | |
|---|---|---|---|
| 3955 | 44c. multicoloured | 1·50 | 60 |

1290 Maurits Sabbe

**2005.** Popular Literature. Writers. Multicoloured.

| | | | |
|---|---|---|---|
| 3956 | 44c. Type **1290** | 1·50 | 60 |
| 3957 | 44c. Arthur Masson | 1·50 | 60 |

1291 Queen Astrid

**2005.** Birth Centenary of Queen Astrid. Each black and gold.

| | | | |
|---|---|---|---|
| 3958 | 44c. Type **1291** | 1·50 | 60 |

**MS**3959 90×125 mm. 80c. Queen Astrid and Prince Albert (38×49 mm) 2·75 2·10

1292 Drum

**2005.** Music. Brass Bands. Multicoloured.

| | | | |
|---|---|---|---|
| 3960 | 50c. Type **1292** | 1·70 | 70 |
| 3961 | 50c. Cornet | 1·70 | 70 |
| 3962 | 50c. Sousaphone | 1·70 | 70 |
| 3963 | 50c. Clarinet | 1·70 | 70 |
| 3964 | 50c. Tuba | 1·70 | 70 |

Nos. 3960/4 each have a label inscribed "Prior" attached at foot.

1293 Donkey

**2006.** Farm Animals. Multicoloured. Self-adhesive.

| | | | |
|---|---|---|---|
| 3965 | 46c. Type **1293** | 1·40 | 65 |
| 3966 | 46c. Hens | 1·40 | 65 |
| 3967 | 46c. Ducks | 1·40 | 65 |
| 3968 | 46c. Pigs | 1·40 | 65 |
| 3969 | 46c. Cow | 1·40 | 65 |
| 3970 | 46c. Goat | 1·40 | 65 |
| 3971 | 46c. Rabbits | 1·40 | 65 |
| 3972 | 46c. Horses | 1·40 | 65 |
| 3973 | 46c. Sheep | 1·40 | 65 |
| 3974 | 46c. Geese | 1·40 | 65 |

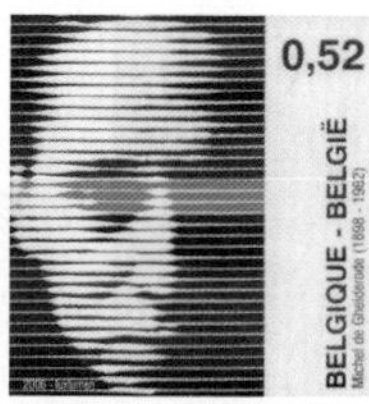

1294 Michel de Ghelderode

**2006.** Writers Commemorations.

| | | | | |
|---|---|---|---|---|
| 3975 | **1294** | 52c. black and blue | 1·60 | 70 |
| 3976 | - | 78c. black and magenta | 1·90 | 85 |

DESIGN: 78c. Herman Terlinck.

No. 3975 has a label inscribed "Prior" attached at left.

1295 Guillaume Dufay and Gilles Binchois

**2006.** Renaissance Polyphonists (part song writers). Multicoloured.

| | | | |
|---|---|---|---|
| 3977 | 60c. Type **1295** | 1·80 | 75 |
| 3978 | 60c. Johannes Ockeghem | 1·80 | 75 |
| 3979 | 60c. Jacob Obrecht | 1·80 | 75 |
| 3980 | 60c. Adriaan Willaert | 1·80 | 75 |
| 3981 | 60c. Orlandus Lassus | 1·80 | 75 |

1296 Musical Score and Mozart

**2006.** 250th Birth Anniv of Wolfgang Amadeus Mozart.

| | | | | |
|---|---|---|---|---|
| 3982 | **1296** | 70c. multicoloured | 2·30 | 1·00 |

**1297** Cross Bowman **1298** Cross Bowman

**2006.** Cross Bowmen. (a) Ordinary gum.

| | | | | |
|---|---|---|---|---|
| 3983 | **1297** | 46c. multicoloured | 1·50 | 65 |

(b) Size 24×32 mm. Self-adhesive gum.

| | | | | |
|---|---|---|---|---|
| 3984 | **1298** | (52c.) multicoloured | 1·70 | 70 |

**1299** Senate

**2006.** 175th Anniv of Democracy. Sheet 200×83 mm containing T 1299 and similar multicoloured designs.

**MS**3985 46c.×3, Type **1299**; King Leopold (vert); Chamber of representatives 4·50 3·75

**1300** Head with Open Mouth

**2006.** Freedom of the Press. Sheet 197×100 mm containing T 1300 and similar multicoloured designs.

**MS**3986 52c.×5, Type **1300** ×3; Blue sky ×2 (horiz) 8·25 7·25

The stamps of **MS**3986 each have a label inscribed "Prior" attached at foot. The stamp depicting a blue sky shows a woman's face when tilted.

**1301** Mouth and Script

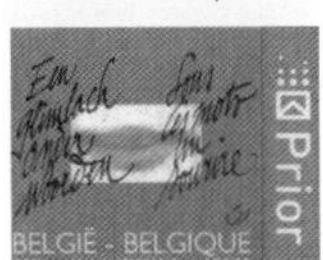


**1302** Mouth and Script

**2006.** Stamp Festival. Winning Entry in Design a Stamp Competition. (a) Ordinary gum.

| | | | | |
|---|---|---|---|---|
| 3987 | **1301** | 46c. multicoloured | 1·50 | 65 |

(b) Size 29×25 mm. Self-adhesive gum.

| | | | | |
|---|---|---|---|---|
| 3988 | **1302** | (52c.) multicoloured | 1·70 | 70 |
| 3988a | **1302** | (52c.) As Type **1302** but design reversed | 1·70 | 70 |

Nos. 3988/a were each issued with a se-tenant label inscribed "Prior".

**1303** Justus Lipsius

**2006.** 400th Death Anniv of Justus Lipsius (writer and scientist).

| | | | | |
|---|---|---|---|---|
| 3989 | **1303** | 70c. brown and cinnamon | 2·30 | 1·00 |

**1304** Winner and Trophy

**2006.** 1st Four Stages—Giro Italia (cycle race), Wallonia.

| | | | | |
|---|---|---|---|---|
| 3990 | **1304** | 52c. multicoloured | 1·70 | 70 |

**1305** John Walker

**2006.** 30th Anniv of Memorial Van Damme Track and Field Event. Sheet 167×100 mm containing T 1305 and similar vert designs. Multicoloured.

**MS**3991 52c.×5, Type **1305**; Alberto Juantorena; Ivo Van Damme; Sebastian Coe; Steve Ovett 8·25 7·25

The stamps of **MS**3991 were each issued with a label inscribed "Prior" at foot.

**1306** Clement Van Hassel

**2006.** Belgian World Champions—Billiards. Sheet 153×167 mm containing T 1306 and similar horiz designs. Multicoloured.

**MS**3992 52c.×12, Type **1306**; Tony Schrauwen; Leo Corin; Emile Wafflard; Ludo Dielis; Jos Vervest; Frederic Caudron; Laurent Boulanger; Paul Stroobants, Eddy Leppens and Peter De Backer; Raymond Ceulemans; Raymond Steylaerts; Jozef Philipoom 18·00 16·00

The stamps of **MS**3992 were each issued with a label inscribed "Prior" at either left or right.

The stamps of **MS**3992 were not for sale separately.

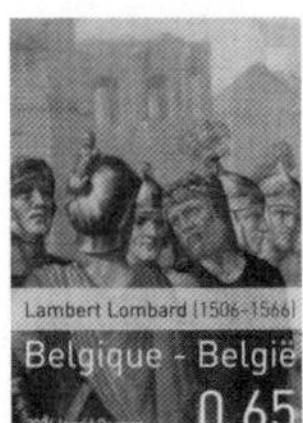


**1307** "L'offrande de Joachim Refusee" (Lambert Lombard)

**2006.** Art. 500th Birth Anniv of Lambert Lombard (3393/4) or 150th Birth Anniv of Leon Spilliaert (3395/6). Multicoloured.

| | | | |
|---|---|---|---|
| 3993 | 65c. Type **1307** | 2·10 | 90 |
| 3994 | 65c. "August et la Sybille de Tibur" (Lambert Lombard) | 2·10 | 90 |
| 3995 | 65c. "Duizeling" (Leon Spilliaert) | 2·10 | 90 |
| 3996 | 65c. "De Dame met de Hoed" (Leon Spilliaert) | 2·10 | 90 |

**1308** Ostend Lighthouse

**2006.** Lighthouses.Multicoloured.

| | | | |
|---|---|---|---|
| 3997 | 46c. Type **1308** | 1·50 | 65 |
| 3998 | 46c. Blankenberge | 1·50 | 65 |
| 3999 | 46c. Nieuwport | 1·50 | 65 |
| 4000 | 46c. Heist | 1·50 | 65 |

**1309** Dogfish

**2006.** North Sea Fish. Sheet 146×124 mm containing T 1309 and similar multicoloured designs.

**MS**4001 46c.×5, Type **1309**; Cod (47×26 mm); Thornback skate; Plaice (33×26 mm); Herring (33×26 mm) 7·50 6·50

The stamps and margins of **MS**4001 form a composite design.

**1310** Emblem **1311** Emblem

**2006.** Belgica 2006 International Stamp Exhibition. (a) Ordinary Gum.

| | | | | |
|---|---|---|---|---|
| 4002 | **1310** | 46c. multicoloured | 1·50 | 65 |

(b) Size 24×28 mm. Self-adhesive gum.

| | | | | |
|---|---|---|---|---|
| 4003 | **1311** | (52c.) multicoloured | 1·50 | 65 |

**1312** Nurse, Patients and Bandages

**1313** Nurse, Patients and Bandages

**2006.** Red Cross. Benjamin Secouriste (children's Red Cross certificate scheme). (a) Ordinary Gum.

| | | | | |
|---|---|---|---|---|
| 4004 | **1312** | 52c.+12c. multicoloured | 2·00 | 85 |

(b) Size 24×28 mm. Self-adhesive gum.

| | | | | |
|---|---|---|---|---|
| 4005 | **1313** | (52c.) multicoloured | 1·70 | 70 |
| 4005a | **1313** | (52c.) As Type **1313** but design reversed | 1·70 | 70 |

No. 4005/a were issued with a se-tenant label inscribed "Prior".

**1314** Emblem

**2006.** Centenary of BOIC (Belgian Olympic and Interfederal Committee).

| | | | | |
|---|---|---|---|---|
| 4006 | **1314** | 52c. multicoloured | 1·70 | 70 |

No. 4006 was issued with a se-tenant label inscribed "Prior".

**1315** Deigne

**2006.** Tourism. Wallonia. Showing village scenes. Multicoloured.

| | | | |
|---|---|---|---|
| 4007 | 52c. Type **1315** | 1·70 | 70 |
| 4008 | 52c. Mein | 1·70 | 70 |
| 4009 | 52c. Celles | 1·70 | 70 |
| 4010 | 52c. Lompret | 1·70 | 70 |
| 4011 | 52c. Ny | 1·70 | 70 |

Nos. 4007/11 were each issued with a se-tenant label inscribed "Prior".

**1316** Part of Football

**2006.** World Cup Football Championship, Germany. Sheet 126×90 mm.

**MS**4012 **1316** €1.30 multicoloured 4·25 3·75

**1317** *Centauria*

**2006.** Flowers. No value expressed. Self-adhesive.

| | | | | |
|---|---|---|---|---|
| 4013 | **1317** | (52c.) multicoloured | 1·70 | 70 |

No. 4013 was for use on inland letters up to 50g.

**1318** Miner

**2006.** 50th Anniv of Marcinelle Mine Disaster.

| | | | | |
|---|---|---|---|---|
| 4014 | **1318** | 70c. multicoloured | 2·30 | 1·00 |

**1319** Tulip

**2006.** Air. Flowers. No value expressed. Self-adhesive. Multicoloured.

| | | | | |
|---|---|---|---|---|
| 4015 | **1319** | (70c.) multicoloured | 2·30 | 1·00 |

No. 4015 was for use on letters of up to 50g. within Europe.

**1320** "Oosterlinghuis" (beguinage (religious community), Bruges) (painting)

**2006.** 650th Anniv of Hanseatic League. Multicoloured.

| | | | |
|---|---|---|---|
| 4016 | 70c. Type **1320** | 2·30 | 1·00 |
| 4017 | 80c. "Oosters Huis" (Bremen town hall) (painting) | 2·50 | 1·10 |

**1321** Institute Building

**2006.** Centenary of the Institute of Tropical Medicine.

| | | | | |
|---|---|---|---|---|
| 4018 | **1321** | 80c. multicoloured | 2·50 | 1·10 |

**1322** "ABA"

**2006.** Academie de Philatelie de Belgique.

4019 **1322** 52c. multicoloured 1·60 70

No. 4019 was issued with a se-tenant label inscribed "Prior" attached at top.

**1323** "Le Kleptomane" (Theodore Gericault)

**2006.** Foreign Masterpieces in Belgian Collections.

4020 **1323** 52c.+12c. multicoloured 2·10 95

No. 4020 was issued with a label inscribed "Prior" attached at left. The premium was for the promotion of philately.

**1324** Ying Yang Symbol

**2006.** Belgica 2006 International Stamp Exhibition. Young Philatelist World Championship. Two sheets containing T 1324 and similar vert designs. Multicoloured.

**MS**4021 (a) 166×133 mm. 46c.×5, Type **1324**; Tulips as wine glasses; Butterflies as four leaf clover; Tent at night; Comic page containing all designs. (b) 190×120 mm. €1.95 Emblem (38×49 mm) 29·00 26·00

Nos. **MS**4021a/b were each sold for €5, the premium for the promotion of philately.

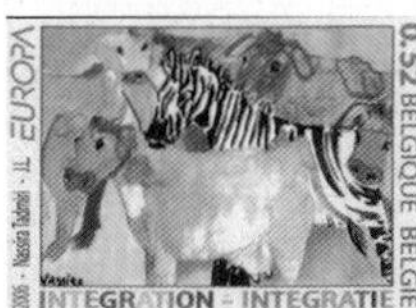


**1325** Animals (Nassira Tadmiri)

**2006.** Europa. Integration. Multicoloured.

4022 52c. Type **1325** 1·60 70

4023 52c. Children of many nations and rainbow (Lize-Maria Verhaeghe) 1·60 70

**1326** "New Skin" (Pierre Alechinsky)

**1327** "New Skin" (Pierre Alechinsky)

**2006.** CoBrA (artistic movement). Multicoloured. (a) Miniature sheet. Ordinary gum.

**MS**4024 125×90 mm. 46c. Type **1326**; 70c. "Untitled" (Asger Jorn) 3·75 3·25

(b) Size 28×25 mm. No value expressed. Self-adhesive gum.

4025 (52c.) Type **1327** 1·60 70

Stamps of similar design were issued by Denmark.

**1328** Rock and Roll **1329** Rock and Roll

**2006.** Dance. Multicoloured.

(a) Size 30×26 mm. No value expressed. Self-adhesive gum.

4026 (52c.) Type **1329** 1·60 70

4027 (52c.) Waltz 1·60 70

4028 (52c.) Tango 1·60 70

4029 (52c.) Cha-cha-cha 1·60 70

4030 (52c.) Samba 1·60 70

(b) Miniature sheet. Ordinary gum.

**MS**4031 166×125 mm. 60c.×5, Type **1328**; Waltz; Tango; Cha-cha-cha; Samba 8·75 8·75

**1330** Kramikske

**2006.** Youth Philately. Kramikske Briochon, cartoon character created by Jean-Pol Vandenbroek.

4032 **1330** 46c. multicoloured 1·50 70

**1331** Tomato and Shrimps

**2006.** "This is Belgium" (4th series). Food. Sheet 154×186 mm containing T 1331 and similar multicoloured designs.

**MS**4033 46c.×10, Type **1331**; Trappist beer (vert); Jenever (spirit) (vert); Chicory au gratin; Ham and sausages (vert); Waffles (vert); Stewed eels in chervil sauce; Chocolate; Mussels and fries (vert); Gueuze (beer) (vert) 13·50 13·00

**1332** Angel playing Psaltery (detail) **1333** Angel playing Psaltery (detail)

**2006.** Christmas. Altarpiece by Hans Memling. Showing angel musicians. Multicoloured. (a) Ordinary gum.

4034 46c. Type **1332** 1·50 70

4035 46c. Tromba marina 1·50 70

4036 46c. Lute 1·50 70

4037 46c. Trumpet 1·50 70

4038 46c. Shawn 1·50 70

(b) Size 25×29 mm. Self-adhesive.

4039 46c. Type **1333** 1·50 70

4040 46c. Tromba marina 1·50 70

4041 46c. Lute 1·50 70

4042 46c. Trumpet 1·50 70

4043 46c. Shawn 1·50 70

Nos. 4034/8 were issued together, se-tenant, forming a composite design.

**1334** "HAPPY BIRTHDAY TO YOU"

**2006.** Greetings Stamps. Self-adhesive. Multicoloured. No value expressed.

4044 (52c.) Type **1334** 1·50 70

4045 (52c.) Birthday cake (Prior at right) 1·50 70

4046 (52c.) As No. 4045 (Prior at left) 1·50 70

4047 (52c.) As No. 4044 (Prior at right) 1·50 70

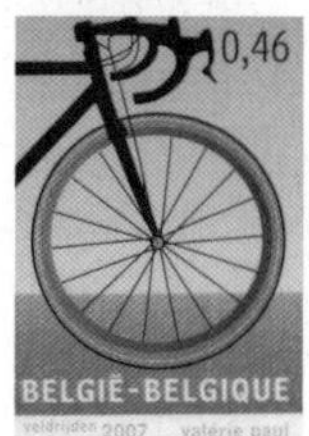


**1335** Cycle Wheel (cyclocross)

**2007.** Sport. Multicoloured. (a) Ordinary gum.

4048 46c. Type **1335** 1·40 65

4049 60c. Ball and skittles (bowling) 1·80 85

4050 65c. Club and ball (golf) 2·00 95

(b) Size 25×29 mm. Self-adhesive. No Value Expressed.

4051 (52c.) As Type **1335** 1·50 70

4052 (52c.) As No. 4049 1·50 70

4053 (52c.) As No. 4050 1·50 70

**1336** "Nu Assis" (Amedo Modigliani)

**2007.** Sheet 90×125 mm.

**MS**4054 **1336** 60c.+30c. multicoloured 2·75 2·50

The premium was for the promotion of philately.

**1337** Alix

**2007.** "Philately for the Young". Alix (comic strip created by Jacques Martin).

4055 **1337** 52c. multicoloured 1·70 80

**1338** Piano Accordion

**2007.** Bellows-driven Aerophones. Sheet 166×100 mm containing T 1338 and similar vert designs. Multicoloured.

**MS**4056 52c.×5 Type **1338**; Concertina; Button accordion; Melodeon; Melodeon (different) 7·50 7·25

The stamps of **MS**4056 each have a se-tenant label inscribed "Prior" attached at foot.

The stamps of **MS**4056 were not for sale separately.

**1339** Julia Tulkens

**2007.** Women in Literature. Sheet 166×100 mm containing T 1339 and similar vert designs. Multicoloured.

**MS**4057 52c.×5 Type **1339**; Madeleine Bourdhouxhe; Christine d'Haen; Jacqueline Harpman; Maria Rosseels 7·50 7·25

The stamps of **MS**4057 each have a se-tenant label inscribed "Prior" attached at foot and form a composite background design.

**1340** Hospital Librarian and Patient

**1341** Hospital Librarian and Patient

**2007.** Red Cross. Multicoloured. (a) Self-adhesive gum.

4058 (52c.) Type **1340** 1·50 70

4059 (52c.) As No. 4058 but with "Prior" at right 1·50 70

(b) Size 39×27 mm. Ordinary gum.

4060 52c.+25c. Type **1341** 2·40 1·10

No. 4060 has a label inscribed "Prior" attached at right.

**1342** "Tati l'periki" (Tati the hairdresser) (Edouard Remouchamps)

**2007.** Belgian Popular Theatre. Sheet 198×83 mm containing T 1342 and similar multicoloured designs.

**MS**4061 46c.×3, Type **1342**; Romain DeConinck (vert); "Le Mariage de Melle Beulemans" (Jean-Francois Fonson and Fernand Wicheler) 4·50 4·25

The stamps of **MS**4061 form a composite background design.

**1343** Stoclet Palace (interior) (Josef Hoffman)

**2007.** Architecture. Multicoloured.

4062 46c. Type **1343** 1·70 80

4063 80c. Stoclet Palace (exterior) 2·40 1·10

No. 4063 has a label inscribed "Prior" attached at top.

Stamps of a similar design were issued by Czech Republic.

**1344** Robert Baden-Powell (founder)

**2007.** Europa. Centenary of Scouting. Multicoloured.

4064 52c. Type **1344** 1·60 80

**MS**4065 90×125 mm. 75c. Scouts (38×48 mm) 2·50 2·50

The stamp and margins of **MS**4065 form a composite background design.

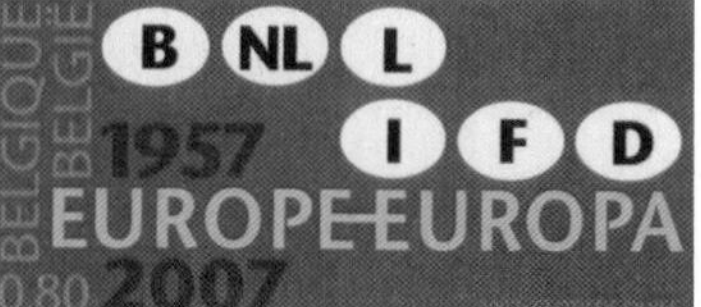


**1345** Country Identification Letters of Signatories (image scaled to 75% of original size)

**2007.** 50th Anniv of Treaty of Rome.

4066 **1345** 80c. multicoloured 2·50 1·30

BELGIQUE·BELGIË
LES AVENTURES DE
TINTIN
AU PAYS
DES SOVIETS
0,46

**1346** 'Tintin au pays de Soviets' (Tintin in the land of Soviets) (French)

**2007.** Birth Centenary of Georges Remi (Herge) (creator of Tintin). Designs showing Tintin book covers in different languages. Multicoloured.

| | | | |
|---|---|---|---|
| 4067 | 46c. Type **1346** | 1·60 | 80 |
| 4068 | 46c. Tintin in the Congo (Danish) | 1·60 | 80 |
| 4069 | 46c. Tintin in America | 1·60 | 80 |
| 4070 | 46c. Cigars of the Pharaoh (Luxembourg) | 1·60 | 80 |
| 4071 | 46c. The Blue Lotus (Chinese) | 1·60 | 80 |
| 4072 | 46c. The Broken Ear (Portuguese) | 1·60 | 80 |
| 4073 | 46c. The Black Island (Bengali) | 1·60 | 80 |
| 4074 | 46c. King Ottokar's Sceptre (Slovakian) | 1·60 | 80 |
| 4075 | 46c. The Crab with the Golden Claws (Russian) | 1·60 | 80 |
| 4076 | 46c. The Shooting Star (Icelandic) | 1·60 | 80 |
| 4077 | 46c. The Secret of the Unicorn (Polish) | 1·60 | 80 |
| 4078 | 46c. Red Rackham's Treasure (Afrikaans) | 1·60 | 80 |
| 4079 | 46c. Herge | 1·60 | 80 |
| 4080 | 46c. The Seven Crystal Balls (Arabic) | 1·60 | 80 |
| 4081 | 46c. Prisoners of the Sun (Spanish) | 1·60 | 80 |
| 4082 | 46c. Land of Black Gold (German) | 1·60 | 80 |
| 4083 | 46c. Destination Moon (Finnish) | 1·60 | 80 |
| 4084 | 46c. Explorers of the Moon (Swedish) | 1·60 | 80 |
| 4085 | 46c. The Calculus Affair (Japanese) | 1·60 | 80 |
| 4086 | 46c. The Red Sea Sharks (Turkish) | 1·60 | 80 |
| 4087 | 46c. Tintin in Tibet (Tibetan) | 1·60 | 80 |
| 4088 | 46c. The Castifiore Emerald (Italian) | 1·60 | 80 |
| 4089 | 46c. Flight 714 (Indonesian) | 1·60 | 80 |
| 4090 | 46c. Tintin and the Picaros (Greek) | 1·60 | 80 |
| 4091 | 46c. Tintin and the Alph-Art (Dutch) | 1·60 | 80 |

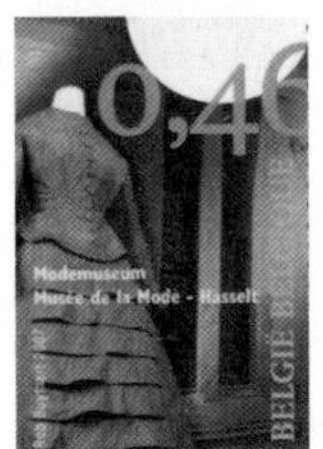

**1347** Dress (Museum of Fashion, Hasselt)

**2007.** Small Museums. Multicoloured.

| | | | |
|---|---|---|---|
| 4092 | 46c. Type **1347** | 1·60 | 80 |
| 4093 | 75c. Skeleton and woman (Notre-Dame a la Rose Hospital Cultural Museum, Lessines) | 2·40 | 1·20 |
| 4094 | 92c. Beaker (Jewish Museum, Brussels) | 3·00 | 1·50 |

**1348** Men carrying Canoe

**1349** Men carrying Canoe

**2007.** Summer Stamps. No Value Expressed. Multicoloured. (a) Self-adhesive.

| | | | |
|---|---|---|---|
| 4095 | (52c.) Type **1348** | 1·60 | 80 |
| 4096 | (52c.) As No. 4095 but with "Prior" at left | 1·60 | 80 |
| 4097 | (52c.) Couple with kite | 1·60 | 80 |
| 4098 | (52c.) As No. 4097 but with "Prior" at left | 1·60 | 80 |

(b) Ordinary gum.

| | | | |
|---|---|---|---|
| 4099 | 52c. Type **1349** | 1·60 | 80 |
| 4100 | 52c. As No. 4098 | 1·60 | 80 |

**1350** Building

**2007.** 50th Anniv of King Baudouin Antarctic Base (1st Belgian Antarctic research station). Sheet 90×125 mm.

| | | | |
|---|---|---|---|
| **MS**4101 | 75c. multicoloured | 2·50 | 2·50 |

**1351** Cyclists

**2007.** Tour de France Cycle Race.

| | | | |
|---|---|---|---|
| 4102 | **1351** 52c. multicoloured | 1·70 | 85 |

**1352** Ship in Port **1353** Ship in Port

**2007.** Centenary of Zeebrugge. No Value Expressed. Multicoloured. (a) Self-adhesive.

| | | | |
|---|---|---|---|
| 4103 | (52c.) Type **1352** | 1·70 | 85 |
| 4104 | (52c.) As No. 4103 but with 'Prior' at left | 1·70 | 85 |

(b) Ordinary gum.

| | | | |
|---|---|---|---|
| 4105 | €1.04 Type **1353** but with 'Prior' at left | 3·50 | 1·80 |

**1354** Athenee Royal Francois Bovesse, Namur

**2007.** Tourism. Multicoloured.

| | | | |
|---|---|---|---|
| 4106 | 52c. Type **1354** | 1·90 | 1·10 |
| 4107 | 52c. Saint Michel College, Brussels | 1·90 | 1·10 |
| 4108 | 52c. Heilig Hart College | 1·90 | 1·10 |

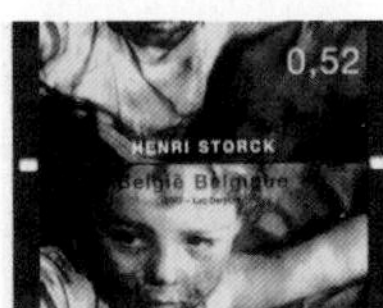

**1355** Scene from *Misere au Borinage* (film by Henri Storck)

**2007.** Belgium Cinema. Birth Centenary of Henri Storck (filmmaker). Sheet 98×167 mm containing T 1355 and similar horiz designs. Multicoloured.

| | | | |
|---|---|---|---|
| **MS**4109 | 52c.×5, Type **1355**; Boy sleeping (*Les Fils* by Luc and Jean-Pierre Dardenne); Haircut (*L'homme au crane rase* (Man who had his hair cut short) by Andre Delvaux); Bedside scene (*Malpertius* by Harry Kumel); Seated woman (*Dust* by Marion Hansel) | 8·50 | 8·50 |

**1356** Tombeau du Geant, Botassart

**2007.** Luxembourg European Capital of Culture–2007. Multicoloured.

| | | | |
|---|---|---|---|
| 4110 | 52c. Type **1356** | 1·90 | 1·10 |
| 4111 | 80c. Rotunda, Luxembourg Train Station | 3·00 | 1·70 |

Stamp of a similar design was issued by Luxembourg.

**1357** Queen Paola

**2007.** 70th Birth Anniv of Queen Paola. Sheet 125×90 mm.

| | | | |
|---|---|---|---|
| **MS**4112 | €1.04 multicoloured | 3·75 | 3·75 |

**1358** King Albert II

**2007**

| | | | |
|---|---|---|---|
| 4113 | **1358** 1 (52c.) red and vermilion | 1·80 | 1·10 |
| 4114 | **1358** 2 (€1.04) olive, green and slate | 3·50 | 2·10 |
| 4115 | **1358** 3 (€1.56) blue, indigo and slate | 5·25 | 3·25 |
| 4116 | **1358** 5 (€2.60) violet, purple and slate | 9·00 | 5·25 |
| 4117 | **1358** 7 (€3.64) brown, deep brown and slate | 12·50 | 7·50 |

This set is to introduce the new franking system which is in multiples of base price (currently 52c.). 1 (52c.) is for use on standard domestic mail from 0–50 grams, 2 (€1.04 (ie twice base rate of 52c.)) is for use on non-standard domestic mail from 0–100 grams, 3 (€1.56) is for use on non-standard domestic mail from 100–350 grams, 5 (€2.60) is for use on non-standard domestic mail from 350 grams–1 kilo, 7 (€3.64) is for use on non-standard domestic mail from 1–2 kilos.

**1359** Pears

**2007.** Fruit. Multicoloured. Self-adhesive.

| | | | |
|---|---|---|---|
| 4118 | 1 (52c.) Type **1359** | 1·80 | 1·10 |
| 4119 | 1 (52c.) Strawberries | 1·80 | 1·10 |
| 4120 | 1 (52c.) Red currants | 1·80 | 1·10 |
| 4121 | 1 (52c.) Apples | 1·80 | 1·10 |
| 4122 | 1 (52c.) Grapes | 1·80 | 1·10 |
| 4123 | 1 (52c.) Cherries | 1·80 | 1·10 |
| 4124 | 1 (52c.) Raspberries | 1·80 | 1·10 |
| 4125 | 1 (52c.) Peaches | 1·80 | 1·10 |
| 4126 | 1 (52c.) Plums | 1·80 | 1·10 |
| 4127 | 1 (52c.) Blackberries | 1·80 | 1·10 |

**1360** Remington (20th-century)

**1361** Remington (20th-century)

**2007.** Stamp Festival. Typewriters. Multicoloured. Self-adhesive.

| | | | |
|---|---|---|---|
| 4128 | 1 (52c.) Type **1360** | 1·80 | 1·10 |
| 4129 | 1 (52c.) Royal (1925) | 1·80 | 1·10 |
| 4130 | 1 (52c.) Olympia (1950) | 1·80 | 1·10 |
| 4131 | 1 (52c.) Olivetti (1972) | 1·80 | 1·10 |
| 4132 | 1 (52c.) Laptop word processor | 1·80 | 1·10 |

(b) Ordinary gum.

| | | | |
|---|---|---|---|
| **MS**4133 | 100×165 mm. 1 (52c.)×5, Type **1361**; As No. 4129; As No. 4130; As No. 4131; As No. 4132 | 9·00 | 9·00 |

**1362** Dahlia

**2007.** Flowers. Multicoloured. Self-adhesive.

| | | | |
|---|---|---|---|
| 4134 | 1 (52c.) Type **1362** | 1·80 | 1·10 |
| 4135 | 2 (€1.04) Petunia | 3·50 | 2·10 |

**1363** Marc Van Montagu (molecular genetics)

**2007.** This Belgium. Science. Sheet 166×193 mm containing T 1363 and similar circular designs. Multicoloured. Self-adhesive.

| | | | |
|---|---|---|---|
| **MS**4136 | 70c.×9, Type **1363**; Paul Janssen (medicine); Lise Thirly (microbiology/virology); Chris Van den Wyngaert (international criminal law); Peter Carmeliet (molecular medicine); Philippe Van Parijs (social philosophy); Marie-Claire Foblets (anthropology); Andre Berger (climate studies); Pierre Rene Deligne (mathematics) | 18·00 | 18·00 |

**1364** Tulip 'Peach Blossom'

**2007.** Self-adhesive.

| | | | |
|---|---|---|---|
| 4137 | **1364** A (80c.) multicoloured | 2·75 | 1·70 |

**1365** Sunset

**2007.** Bereavement. No value expressed.

| | | | |
|---|---|---|---|
| 4138 | **1365** 1 (52c.) multicoloured | 1·80 | 1·10 |

**1366** *Les chemins de la liberte* (*Le voyage*) (Thierry Merget)

**2007.** Postal Art.

| | | | |
|---|---|---|---|
| 4139 | **1366** 1 (52c.) multicoloured | 1·80 | 1·10 |

**1367** Couple in Wedding Outfits

**2007.** Greetings Stamps. Multicoloured. Self-adhesive.
4140 1 (52c.) Type **1367** 1·80 1·10
4141 1 (52c.) Father holding boy baby 1·80 1·10
4142 1 (52c.) Mother holding girl baby 1·80 1·10

**2007.** Belgian Billiards World Champions. Sheet 80×140 mm containing horiz designs as T 1306. Multicoloured.
**MS**4143 1 (52c.)×9, Piet J. Van Duppen; Albert Collette; Gustaaf Van Belle; Piet Sels; Gaston De Doncker; Theo Moons; Rene Gabriels; Victor Luypaerts; Rene Vingerhoerdt 14·50 14·50
See also **MS**3992.

**1368** Christmas Tree

**2007.** Christmas and New Year. (a) Ordinary gum.
4144 **1368** 1 (52c.) multicoloured (postage) 1·80 1·10

**1369** Christmas Tree

(b) Self-adhesive.
4145 **1369** 1 (52c.) multicoloured 1·80 1·10

**1370** Christmas Tree

(c) Self-adhesive.
4146 **1370** A (80c.) multicoloured (air) 2·75 1·70

**1371** *The Man From the Sea*

**2008.** Rene Magritte (artist) Commemoration. Sheet 80×140 mm containing T 1371 and similar multicoloured designs.
**MS**4147 1 (52c.)×5, Type **1371**; *Scheherazade*; *The Midnight Marriage*; *Georgette* (32×41 mm); *The Ignorant Fairy* (49×37 mm) 9·00 9·00

**1372** Give Blood

**2008.** Red Cross. Give Blood Campaign. (a) Self-adhesive.
4148 **1372** 1 (52c.) multicoloured 1·80 1·10

**1373** Give Blood

(b) Ordinary gum.
4149 **1373** 1 (52c.)+25c. multicoloured 2·75 1·70

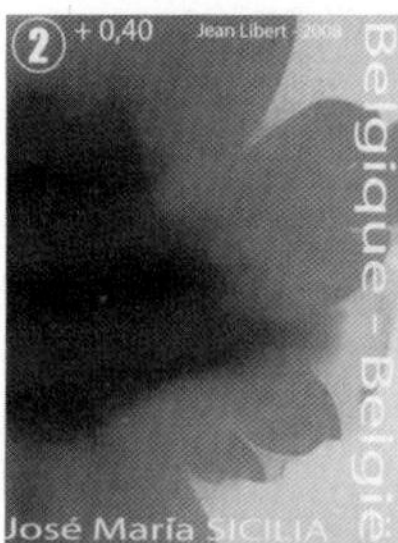


**1374** *La Luz que se Apaga* (Jose Maria Sicilia)

**2008.** Art. Sheet 90×125 mm.
**MS**4150 2 (€1.04)+40c. multicoloured 5·25 5·25

**1375** Jeremiah and Kurdy Malloy

**2008.** 'Philately for the Young'. Jeremiah (comic strip created by Hermann Huppen (Hermann)).
4151 **1375** 1 (52c.) multicoloured 2·10 1·30

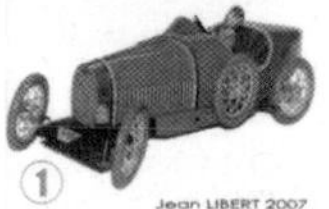


**1376** Car

**2008.** Toys. Self-adhesive. Multicoloured.
4152 1 (52c.) Type **1376** 2·10 1·30
4153 1 (52c.) Pram 2·10 1·30
4154 1 (52c.) Doll 2·10 1·30
4155 1 (52c.) Airplane 2·10 1·30
4156 1 (52c.) Horse 2·10 1·30
4157 1 (52c.) Tram 2·10 1·30
4158 1 (52c.) Diablo 2·10 1·30
4159 1 (52c.) Teddy 2·10 1·30
4160 1 (52c.) Top 2·10 1·30
4161 1 (52c.) Wooden scooter 2·10 1·30

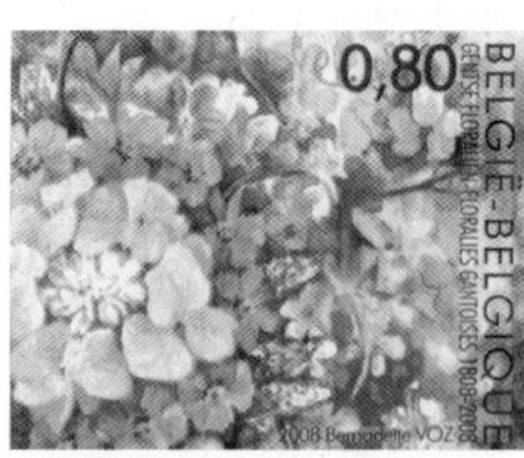


**1377** Flowers

**2008.** Bicentenary of Ghent Flower Show. Sheet 90×125 mm.
**MS**4162 80c. multicoloured 3·00 3·00

**1378** Suzy Delair as Mila Malou and Pierre Fresnay as Wens (scene from film *L'assassin habite au 21*)

**2008.** Detective Novels. Multicoloured.
4163 1 (52c.) Type **1378** (novel by Stanislas–Andre Steeman) 2·10 1·30
4164 1 (52c.) Jan Decleir as Angelo Ledda (scene from film *De zaak Alzheimer*) (novel by Jef Geeraerts) 2·10 1·30

**1379** Menorah

**2008.** Bicentenary of Belgian Jewish Community.
4165 **1379** 90c. blue and black 3·50 2·10

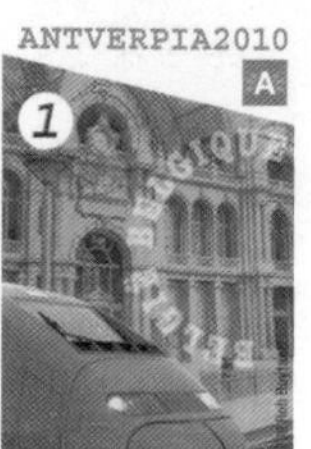


**1380** Central Station

**2008.** Antverpia 2010 European Philatelic Championship, Antwerp. 120th Anniv of Royal National Association of Stamp Collectors. Sheet 161×141 mm containing T 1380 and similar vert designs. Multicoloured.
**MS**4166 1 (54c.)×5, Type **1380**; Cathedral of Our Lady and Pieter Paul Rubens memorial; Port; Fashion; Diamond necklace by Reena Ahluwalia 17·00 17·00
No. **MS**4166 was sold for €5.

**1381** Comte de Champignac

**2008.** 70th Anniv of Spirou (cartoon character drawn by Andre Franquin). Sheet 166×100 mm containing T 1381 and similar vert designs. Multicoloured.
**MS**4167 1 (54c.)×5, Type **1381**; Fantasio; Spirou and Spip; Seccotine; Zorglub 10·50 10·50

**1382** Coastal Route

**2008.** Trams. Trams enroute. Multicoloured.
4168 1 (54c.) Type **1382** 2·10 1·30
4169 80c. Charleroi 3·00 1·90
4170 90c. Brussels 3·50 2·10

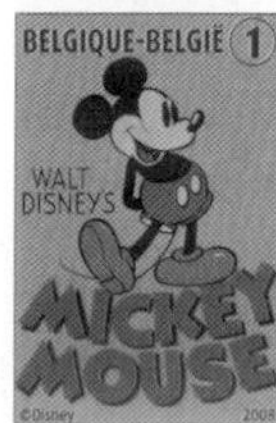


**1383** Mickey Mouse

**2008.** 80th Anniv of Mickey Mouse (cartoon character created by Walt Disney).
4171 **1383** 1 (54c.) multicoloured 2·10 1·30

**1384** Letterbox and Envelope

**1385** Letterbox and Envelope

**2008.** Europa. The Letter. (a) Self-adhesive gum.
4172 **1384** 1 (54c.) multicoloured 2·10 1·30

(b) Size 40×27 mm. Ordinary gum.
4173 **1385** 80c. multicoloured 3·00 1·90

**1386** *Tagetes portula*

**2008.** Flowers. Multicoloured. Self-adhesive.
4174 1 (54c.) Type **1386**(postage) 2·10 1·30

No value expressed.
4175 (80c.) Tulip 'Orange Favourite' (air) 3·00 1·90

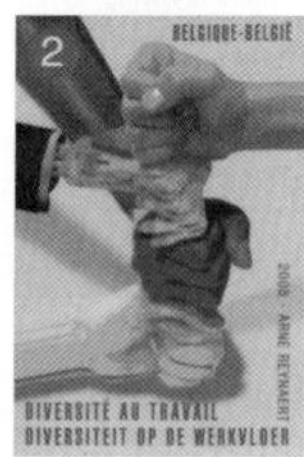


**1387** Artificial Hand and Hands of Many Nations

**2008.** Diversity in the Workplace.
4176 **1387** 2 (€1.08) multicoloured 4·25 2·50

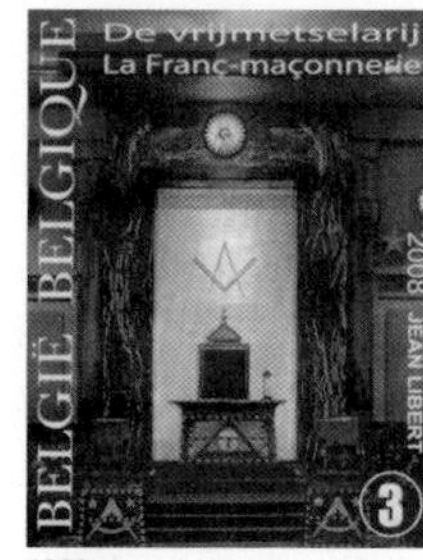


**1388**

**2008.** Freemasonry. Sheet 125×90 mm.
**MS**4177 multicoloured 6·25 6·25

**1389** Family hiking

**1390** Family hiking

**2008.** Summer Stamps. Multicoloured. (a) Ordinary gum.
4178 1 (52c.) Type **1389** 2·10 1·30
4179 1 (52c.) Family cycling 2·10 1·30

(b) Size 30×25 mm. Self-adhesive.
4180 1 (52c.) Type **1390** 2·10 1·30
4181 1 (52c.) Family cycling 2·10 1·30

**1391** Queen Fabiola and King Baudouin

**2008.** 80th Birth Anniv of Queen Fabiola. Sheet 170×120 mm containing T 1391 and similar vert designs. Multicoloured.
**MS**4182 1 (52c.)×3, Type **1391**; Portrait of Queen Fabiola; Queen Fabiola and King Baudouin, older, wearing casual dress 6·25 6·25

**1392** Woman (George Grard), Musee George Grard, Gijverinkhove

**2008.** Tourism. Multicoloured.

| | | | |
|---|---|---|---|
| 4183 | 1 (52c.) Type **1392** | 2·20 | 1·40 |
| 4184 | 80c. *Imago* (Emile Desmedt), Musee en Plein Air du Sart-Tilman, Liege | 3·25 | 2·00 |
| 4185 | 90c. *Autoportrait* (Gerald Dederen), Jardin de sculptures de l'UCL, Brussels | 3·50 | 2·30 |

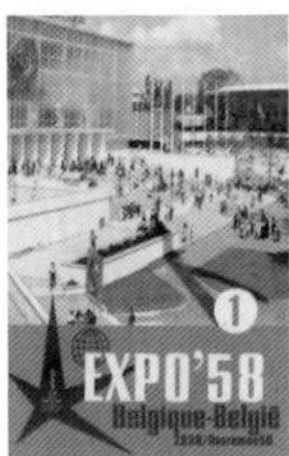

**1393** USSR Pavilion

**2008.** 50th Anniv of EXPO'58, Brussels. Multicoloured.

| | | | |
|---|---|---|---|
| **MS**4186 | 1 (54c.)×5, Type **1393**; Thailand pavilion; Hostesses carrying flags; Expo logo as lighting; Atomium | 10·50 | 10·50 |

The stamps of **MS**4186 were not for sale individually.

**1394** Planting of May Tree (tree of joy), Brussels (700th anniv)

**2008.** Folklore and Traditions. Multicoloured.

| | | | |
|---|---|---|---|
| 4187 | 1 (54c.) Type **1394** | 2·20 | 1·40 |
| 4188 | 1 (54c.) Hops, beer barrel, bonfire and hop devil, Asse (Hopduvelfeesten) (horiz) | 2·20 | 1·40 |
| 4189 | 1 (54c.) Jugglers (Eupen carnival) | 2·20 | 1·40 |
| 4190 | 1 (54c.) Men on stage (centenary (2007) of *La Royale Compagnie du Cabaret Wallon Tournaisien*) (philanthropic and literary company) | 2·20 | 1·40 |

**1395** BMX

**2008.** Olympic Games, Beijing. Multicoloured.

| | | | |
|---|---|---|---|
| 4191 | 1 (54c.) Type **1395** | 2·30 | 1·50 |
| 4192 | 90c. Relay (horiz) | 3·75 | 2·40 |
| **MS**4193 | 125×90 mm. (2) €1.08 Tennis (49×38 mm) | 4·50 | 4·50 |

**1396** Angel Gabriel

**2008.** Stamp Day. 50th Anniv of Cercle St-Gabriel. 50th Anniv of Thematic Philately in Belgium.

| | | | | |
|---|---|---|---|---|
| 4194 | **1396** | 1 (54c.) multicoloured | 2·30 | 1·50 |

**1397** Marten

**1398** Marten

**2008.** Nature. Mustelidae. Multicoloured. (a) Self-adhesive gum.

| | | | |
|---|---|---|---|
| 4195 | 1 (54c.) Type **1397** | 2·30 | 1·50 |
| 4196 | 1 (54c.) Stone marten | 2·30 | 1·50 |
| 4197 | 1 (54c.) Polecat | 2·30 | 1·50 |
| 4198 | 1 (54c.) Otter | 2·30 | 1·50 |
| 4199 | 1 (54c.) Badger | 2·30 | 1·50 |

(b) Ordinary gum. Sheet 178×146 mm.

| | | | |
|---|---|---|---|
| **MS**4200 | 1 (54c.)×6, Type **1398** (48×38 mm); Ermine (38×42 mm); Stone marten (48×38 mm); Polecat (38×42 mm); Otter (38×48 mm ); Badger (48×38 mm) | 12·00 | 12·00 |

**1399** Smurf

**1400** Smurf and Smurfette

**2008.** The Smurfs (characters created by Peyo (Pierre Culliford) ). Multicoloured. (a) Self-adhesive gum.

| | | | |
|---|---|---|---|
| 4201 | 1 (54c.) Type **1399** | 2·30 | 1·50 |
| 4202 | 1 (54c.) Smurfette | 2·30 | 1·50 |
| 4203 | 1 (54c.) Papa Smurf | 2·30 | 1·50 |
| 4204 | 1 (54c.) Smurf and drum (horiz) | 2·30 | 1·50 |
| 4205 | 1 (54c.) Poet Smurf | 2·30 | 1·50 |
| 4206 | 1 (54c.) Jokey Smurf | 2·30 | 1·50 |
| 4207 | 1 (54c.) Smurf carrying bag and envelope | 2·30 | 1·50 |
| 4208 | 1 (54c.) Brainy Smurf | 2·30 | 1·50 |
| 4209 | 1 (54c.) Gargamel | 2·30 | 1·50 |
| 4210 | 1 (54c.) Harmony Smurf (horiz) | 2·30 | 1·50 |

(b) Ordinary gum. Sheet 186×153 mm.

| | | | |
|---|---|---|---|
| **MS**4211 | 1 (54c.)×5, Type **1400** (42×33 mm); Smurf in party hat (42×33 mm); Two smurfs (42×33 mm); Smurf carrying cake (42×33 mm); Smurf eating cake (38×42 mm) | 12·00 | 12·00 |

**1401** Mothers and Children (Tim Driven)

**2008.** Belgian Photographers. Sheet 100×166 mm containing 1401 and similar horiz designs. Multicoloured.

| | | | |
|---|---|---|---|
| **MS**4212 | 80c.×5, Type **1401**; Jars (Paul Ausloos); Woman carrying pail (Leonard Misonne); Coloured lights in trees (Harry Gruyaert); Woman cycling (Stephan Vanfleteren) | 16·00 | 16·00 |

**1402** 1909 Belgian Congo 1f. Stamp (As No. 40B)

**2008.** Centenary of Belgian Congo.

| | | | | |
|---|---|---|---|---|
| 4213 | **1402** | 1 (54c.) multicoloured | 2·30 | 1·50 |

**1403** National Museum of Shoes, Izegem

**2008.** Museums. Multicoloured.

| | | | |
|---|---|---|---|
| 4214 | 1 (54c.) Type **1403** | 2·30 | 1·50 |
| 4215 | 80c. Piconrue Museum (religious museum), Bastogne | 3·25 | 2·10 |
| 4216 | 80c. David and Alice van Buuren Museum , Brussels | 3·25 | 2·10 |

**1404** Menin Gate, Ypres

**2008.** 90th Anniv of End of First World War. Sheet 201×85 mm containing T 1404 and similar vert designs. Multicoloured.

| | | | |
|---|---|---|---|
| **MS**4217 | 90c.×3, Type **1404**; King Albert I (statue); Poppies | 10·50 | 10·50 |

**1405** The Nativity **1406** The Nativity

**1407** Cardinal Mercier

**2008.** Christmas. Multicoloured. (a) Self-adhesive.

| | | | |
|---|---|---|---|
| 4218 | 1 (54c.) Type **1405** | 2·40 | 1·70 |
| 4219 | (80c.) Type **1406** | 3·50 | 2·40 |

(b) Ordinary gum. Sheet 127×124 mm.

| | | | |
|---|---|---|---|
| **MS**4220 | 1 (54c.)×5, Type **1407**; St. Francis; Mary and Joseph; Friar; Infant Jesus | 12·00 | 12·00 |

No. 4219 was inscribed 'INTERNATIONAL' and was originally on sale for 80c.

No. **MS**4220 includes four labels which, with the stamps form a composite design of a stained glass window.

**1408** Queen Elisabeth (Concours Reine Elisabeth (Queen Elisabeth International Music Competition))

**2008.** This Belgium. Music. Sheet 166×200 mm containing T 1408 and similar square designs. Multicoloured.

| | | | |
|---|---|---|---|
| **MS**4221 | 80c.×10, Type **1408**; Jose van Dam (bass-baritone); Rock Werchter Festival; Philippe Herreweghe and Collegium Vocale Gent (music ensemble); dEus (rock band); Il Novecento (orchestra) and Robert Groslot (conductor); Philip Catherine (jazz guitarist); Dani Klein (singer with Vaya con Dios); Salvatore Adamo (composer and ballad singer); Jaques Brel (singer–songwriter) | 32·00 | 32·00 |

The stamps of **MS**4136 were not for sale separately.

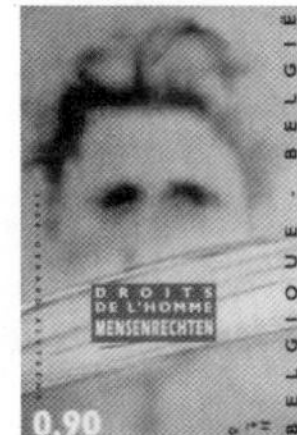

**1409** Face

**2008.** Universal Declaration of Human Rights.

| | | | | |
|---|---|---|---|---|
| 4222 | **1409** | 90c. multicoloured | 4·25 | 3·00 |

**1410** *Tulipa bakeri*

**2009.** Air. Flowers. Self-adhesive.

| | | | | |
|---|---|---|---|---|
| 4223 | **1410** | 1 (90c.) multicoloured | 4·25 | 3·00 |

**1411** King Albert II

**2009.** Air.

| | | | | |
|---|---|---|---|---|
| 4224 | **1411** | 1 (90c.) multicoloured | 4·25 | 3·00 |
| 4225 | **1411** | 1 (€1.05) multicoloured | 5·00 | 3·50 |
| 4226 | **1411** | 3 (€2.40) multicoloured | 11·00 | 7·75 |
| 4227 | **1411** | 3 (€2.70) multicoloured | 12·00 | 8·50 |

No. 4224 and 4225 were for use on airmail within Europe, Nos. 4226 and 4227 for use on international airmail.

See also 4113/17.

**1412** '€'

**2009.** 10th Anniv of European Union. Self-adhesive.

| | | | | |
|---|---|---|---|---|
| 4228 | **1412** | 1 (59c.) multicoloured | 2·75 | 2·00 |

**1413** Monument

**2009.** Regions. German Community. Sheet 150×183 mm containing T 1413 and similar multicoloured designs.

| | | | |
|---|---|---|---|
| **MS**4229 | 1 (90c.)×5, Type **1413**; Three handled pitcher; Lake Butgenbach; Eupen sanatorium (33×40 mm); Shooting (49×37 mm) | 19·00 | 19·00 |

The stamps of **MS**4229 were not for sale separately.

**1414** Hands 'reading' Braille

**2009.** Birth Bicentenary of Louis Braille (inventor of Braille writing for the blind).

| | | | | |
|---|---|---|---|---|
| 4230 | **1414** | 1 (59c.) multicoloured | 2·75 | 2·00 |

**1415** Child and Tap

**2009.** Red Cross. Water.

| | | | | |
|---|---|---|---|---|
| 4231 | **1415** | 1 (59c.) + 25c. black and vermillion | 4·00 | 2·75 |

**1416** Barge

**2009.** Transportation. Inland Waterways.

| | | | | |
|---|---|---|---|---|
| 4232 | **1416** | 2 (€1.18) multicoloured | 5·50 | 4·00 |

**1417** Figure and Postbox (Emitis Mohsenin)

**2009.** Post Day.

| | | | | |
|---|---|---|---|---|
| 4233 | **1417** | 1 (59c.) multicoloured | 2·75 | 2·00 |

**1418** Marthe Boel (promoter of women's issues)

**2009.** Women in Action. Multicoloured.

| | | | |
|---|---|---|---|
| 4234 | 1 (59c.) Type **1418** | 2·75 | 2·00 |
| 4235 | 1 (59c.) Lily Boeykens (lawyer and journalist) | 2·75 | 2·00 |

**1419** Penguins

**2009.** Preserve Polar Regions and Glaciers. Sheet 120×80 mm containing T 1419 and similar multicoloured design.

| | | |
|---|---|---|
| **MS**4236 2 (€1.05)×2, Type **1419**; Polar bear | 9·25 | 9·25 |

The stamps of **MS**4236 were for use on international priority mail and not for sale separately.

**1420** Bob

**2009.** Bob and Bobette (comic series created by Willy Vandersteen) in Les Diables du Texas (animated film).Showing characters from the film. Multicoloured. Self-adhesive.

| | | | |
|---|---|---|---|
| 4237 | 1 (59c.) Type **1420** | 2·75 | 2·00 |
| 4238 | 1 (59c.) Bobette | 2·75 | 2·00 |
| 4239 | 1 (59c.) Jerome | 2·75 | 2·00 |
| 4240 | 1 (59c.) Lambik | 2·75 | 2·00 |
| 4241 | 1 (59c.) Aunt Sidonie | 2·75 | 2·00 |

**1421** Telescope and Globe

**2009.** Europa. Astronomy. Sheet 125×90mm.

| | | |
|---|---|---|
| **MS**4242 multicoloured | 4·25 | 4·25 |

No. **MS**4242 was for use on mail within Europe.

**1422** Neolithic Flint Mines, Spiennes

**2009.** World Heritage Sites. Sheet 166×100 mm containing T 1422 and similar vert designs. Multicoloured.

| | | |
|---|---|---|
| **MS**4243 1 (€1.05)×5, Type **1422**; Notre Dame Cathedral, Tournai; Plantin-Moretus Museum, Antwerp; Historic Centre, Bruges; Maison de Maitre (Victor Horta), Brussels | 23·00 | 23·00 |

No. **MS**4243 was for use on International mail.

**1423** Girl with Camera

**2009.** Summer Stamps. Holidays in Wallonia and Flanders. Multicoloured. Self-adhesive.

| | | | |
|---|---|---|---|
| 4244 | 1 (59c.) Type **1423** | 2·75 | 2·00 |
| 4245 | 1 (59c.) Boy with camera | 2·75 | 2·00 |

**1424** Muhka and *Flemish Village* (Luc Tuymans)

**2009.** Antverpia 2010–International Stamp Exhibition, Antwerp. Artistic Antwerp (1st series). Sheet 180×64 mm containing T 1424 and similar vert designs. Multicoloured.

| | | |
|---|---|---|
| **MS**4246 1 (59c.)×5, Type **1424**; *Orbino* (Luc Deleu), Middelheim Sculpture Museum;Bourla Theater and Toneelhuis theatre company; *Hollywood on the Scheldt*, Robbe De Hert, Roma Cinema; *Willem Elschot* (writer) (sculpture by Wilfred Pas) and manuscript of *Kass* | 23·00 | 23·00 |

See also Nos. **MS**4290.

**1425** Henry Purcell (350th birth anniv)

**2009.** Composers Anniversaries. Sheet 180×64 mm containing T 1425 and similar vert designs. Multicoloured.

| | | |
|---|---|---|
| **MS**4247 1 (90c.)×5, Type **1425**; George Frideric Handel (250th death anniv); Franz Joseph Haydn (death bicentenary); Jakob Ludwig Felix Mendelssohn Bartholdy (birth bicentenary); Clara Schumann (nee Clara Josephine Wieck) (190th birth anniv) | 21·00 | 21·00 |

The stamps and margins of **MS**4247 form a composite design.

The stamps of **MS**4247 were for use on mail within Europe

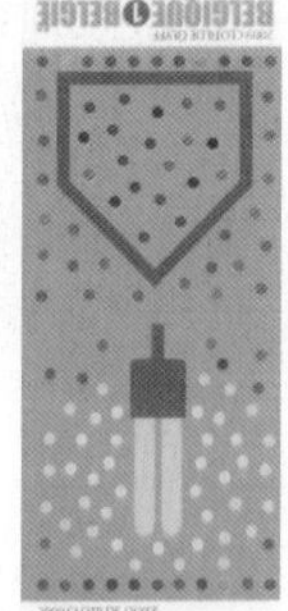

**1426** Low Energy Lightbulb

**2009.** Green Stamps. Environmental Preservation. Multicoloured. Self-adhesive.

| | | | |
|---|---|---|---|
| 4248 | 1 (59c.) Type **1426** | 2·75 | 2·00 |
| 4249 | 1 (59c.) Wind turbine | 2·75 | 2·00 |
| 4250 | 1 (59c.) Shared transport | 2·75 | 2·00 |
| 4251 | 1 (59c.) Solar panels | 2·75 | 2·00 |
| 4252 | 1 (59c.) Insulated house | 2·75 | 2·00 |

**1427** International Space Station, 2009

**2009.** Aviation, From Bleriot to De Winne. Multicoloured.

| | | | |
|---|---|---|---|
| 4253 | 1 (59c.) Type **1427** (Frank de Winne, first European Space Agency astronaut to command mission) | 2·75 | 2·00 |
| 4254 | 1 (59c.) Apollo 11, 1969 (first men on the moon) | 2·75 | 2·00 |
| 4255 | 1 (59c.) Concorde, 1969 (first supersonic flight) | 2·75 | 2·00 |
| 4256 | 1 (59c.) LZ 127 Graf Zeppelin, 1929 (flight around the world) | 2·75 | 2·00 |
| 4257 | 1 (59c.) *Bleriot XI*, 1909 (first flight over English Channel) | 2·75 | 2·00 |

**1428** Yoko Tsuno

**2009.** Youth Philately. Yoko Tsuno (comic created by Roger Leloup).

| | | | | |
|---|---|---|---|---|
| 4258 | **1428** | 1 (59c.) multicoloured | 2·75 | 2·00 |

**1429** King Albert and Queen Paola

**2009.** 50th Anniv of Wedding of King Albert and Queen Paola. Sheet 209×104 mm.

| | | |
|---|---|---|
| **MS**4259 multicoloured | 7·25 | 7·25 |

**1430** Citroen 2CV Delivery Van, c. 1959

**2009.** Postal Vehicles. Multicoloured.

| | | | |
|---|---|---|---|
| 4260 | 1 (59c.) Type **1430** | 2·75 | 2·00 |
| 4261 | 1 (59c.) Bedford van, c. 1960 | 2·75 | 2·00 |
| 4262 | 1 (59c.) Large Renault van, c. 1970 | 2·75 | 2·00 |
| 4263 | 1 (59c.) Renault 4 Fourgonnette van, c. 1980 | 2·75 | 2·00 |
| 4264 | 1 (59c.) Modern Citroen van | 2·75 | 2·00 |

**1431** Orchestra

**2009.** The Circus. Multicoloured. Self-adhesive.

| | | | |
|---|---|---|---|
| 4265 | 1 (59c.) Type **1431** | 2·75 | 2·00 |
| 4266 | 1 (59c.) Highwire artistes | 2·75 | 2·00 |
| 4267 | 1 (59c.) Illusionist | 2·75 | 2·00 |
| 4268 | 1 (59c.) Acrobat pyramid | 2·75 | 2·00 |
| 4269 | 1 (59c.) Trapeze artiste | 2·75 | 2·00 |
| 4270 | 1 (59c.) Clowns | 2·75 | 2·00 |
| 4271 | 1 (59c.) Acrobats balancing | 2·75 | 2·00 |
| 4272 | 1 (59c.) Illusionist with tophat, rabbit and doves | 2·75 | 2·00 |
| 4273 | 1 (59c.) Equestrian artiste | 2·75 | 2·00 |
| 4274 | 1 (59c.) Clown juggling on uni-cycle | 2·75 | 2·00 |

**1432** Maurice Bejart

**2009.** Maurice Bejart (dancer) Commemoration.

| | | | | |
|---|---|---|---|---|
| 4275 | **1432** | 1 (90c.) multicoloured | 4·00 | 3·00 |

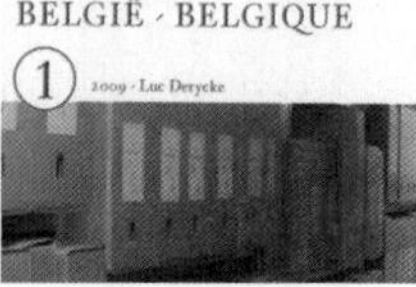

**1433** Archives of Belgium

**2009.** Monts des Arts. Sheet 200×166 mm containing T 1433 and similar multicoloured designs.

| | | |
|---|---|---|
| **MS**4276 1 (59c.)×10, Type **1433**; Royal Museum of Fine Arts; Royal Library; Square Meeting Centre; Brussels Palace (38×49 mm); Saint Jaques sur Coudenberg Church and Protestant Chapel (49×38 mm); Palace of Fine Arts; Royal Belgian Filmarchive (Cinematheque Royale de Belgique); Belvue Museum; Musical Instruments Museum | 25·00 | 25·00 |

**1434** Seven Sacraments Altarpiece (detail)

**2009.** Master of Passions

| | | | | |
|---|---|---|---|---|
| 4277 | **1434** | 2 (€1.18) multicoloured | 5·00 | 4·00 |

**1435** Lion Mask

**2009.** Europalia International Arts Festival, China. Self-adesive.

| | | | | |
|---|---|---|---|---|
| 4278 | **1435** | 1 (59c.) multicoloured | 2·75 | 2·00 |

**1436** Mettoy Streamline Train, 1950

**2009.** Miniature Trains. Sheet 160×200 mm containing T 1436 and similar square designs. Multicoloured.
**MS**4279 1 (59c.)×10, Type **1436**; Bavarian locomotive *Aloisus*; Locomotive tender; Diesel locomotive; Locomotive tender *Storchenbein*; Locomotive Type 16; Tin toy train; ICE Deutsche Bahn; Wooden toy train with waggon; Blue and red wooden toy train 28·00 28·00

1437 Pine Tree

**2009.** La Foret de Soignes (Sonian Forest ). Sheet 166×100 mm containing T 1437 and similar vert designs. Multicoloured.
**MS**4280 2 (€2.18)×5, Type **1437**; Beech; Birch; Larch; Oak 25·00 25·00

1438 Father Damien

**2009.** Canonization of Father Damien (Jozef De Veuster) (Roman Catholic missionary who ministered to lepers on the Hawaiian island of Molokai).
4281 **1438** 1 Europe (90c.) multicoloured 4·00 3·00

1439 Emblem

**2009.** 20th Anniv of Comic Strip Art Museum. Sheet 90×120 mm.
**MS**4282 multicoloured 4·50 3·25

1440 Tom Lanoye

**2009.** This is Belgium. Literature. Sheet 160×200 mm containing T 1440 and similar multicoloured designs.
**MS**4283 1 (59c.)×10, Type **1440**; Hugo Claus; Anne Provoost; Poeziezomers, Watou (summer poetry festival) (vert); Redu, Book Village (vert); Book Fair, Antwerp (vert); Book Fair, Brussels (vert); Pierre Mertens; Amelie Northomb; Henri Vernes 25·00 25·00

1441 Gold Baubles

**2009.** Christmas. Multicoloured. Self-adhesive.
4284 1 (59c.) Type **1441** 2·75 2·00
4285 1 (90c.) Blue baubles 2·75 2·00

No. 4284 were for use on domestic mail and were originally on sale for 59c.
No. 4285 were for use on international mail were originally on sale for 90c.

1442 1920 65c. Stamp (As No. 308b)

**2009.** Monacophil 2009. Promotion of Philately. Sheet 120×170 mm.
**MS**4286 multicoloured 5·75 4·25

The premium was for the promotion of philately.

1443 Sunset

**2010.** Bereavement. Self-adhesive.
4288 **1443** (59c.) multicoloured 2·75 2·00

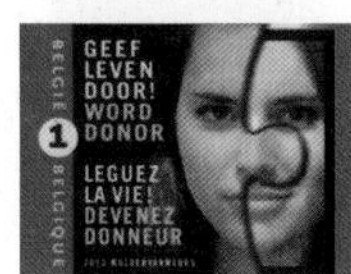
1444 Face as Jigsaw

**2010.** Organ Donation Awareness Campaign. Self-adhesive.
4289 **1444** (59c.) multicoloured 2·75 2·00

1445 Magnifying Glass

**2010.** Antverpia 2010–International Stamp Exhibition, Antwerp (2nd series). Sheet 160×140 mm containing T 1445 and similar vert designs. Multicoloured. Phosphorescent paper.
**MS**4290 (59c.)×6, Type **1445** (120th anniv of Royal Federation of Belgian Philatelic Circles); Commercial centre, Antwerp: Giraffes and Kai-Mook (elephant), Antwerp Zoo; painting by Eugeen van Mieghem and model, Museum aan de Stroom (MAS); *Self-portrait* and house of Peter Paul Rubens; City Hall and Cathedral, Old City Centre 15·00 15·00

No. **MS**4290 was on sale, above face value, at €6.50, the premium for the promotion of philately.

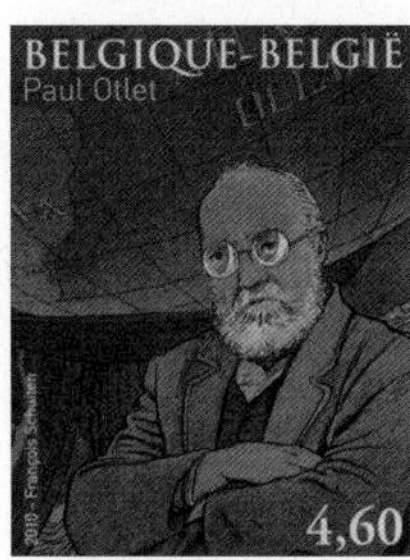
1446 Paul Otlet

**2010.** From Mundaneum (system for information storage, using Universal Decimal Classification, invented by Paul Otlet and Henri La Fontaine in 1910), the Internet. Sheet 90×125 mm.
**MS**4291 multicoloured 12·00 12·00

1447 Largo Winch

**2010.** Youth Philately. Largo Winch (comic created by Philip Francq and writer Jean Van Hamme).
4292 **1447** 1 (59c.) multicoloured 2·75 2·00

1448 Paul Verlane and Arthur Rimbaud

**2010.** Literary Walk through Brussels. Sheet 180×64 mm containing T 1448 and similar vert designs. Multicoloured.
**MS**4293 2 (€1.18)×5, Type **1448**; Charles Baudelaire; Multatuli (Eduard Douwes Dekker); Charlotte and Emily Bronte; Victor Hugo 9·00 9·00

The stamps and margins of **MS**4293 form a composite design.
The stamps of **MS**4293 were for use on mail within Europe

1449 *Nicotiana alata*

**2010.** Ghent Flower Show. Multicoloured.
4294 1 (59c.) Type **1449** 2·75 2·00
4295 1 (59c.) *Lychnis coronaria* 2·75 2·00

1450 Chicks

**2010.** Young Animals. Multicoloured. Self-adhesive.
4296 1 (59c.) Type **1450** 2·75 2·00
4297 1 (59c.) Rabbits 2·75 2·00
4298 1 (59c.) Kitten 2·75 2·00
4299 1 (59c.) Ducklings 2·75 2·00
4300 1 (59c.) Foal cantering 2·75 2·00
4301 1 (59c.) Labrador puppy 2·75 2·00
4302 1 (59c.) Long-haired dachshund puppy 2·75 2·00
4303 1 (59c.) Two kittens 2·75 2·00
4304 1 (59c.) Foal, head and shoulders 2·75 2·00
4305 1 (59c.) Two lambs 2·75 2·00

1451 Dog reading to Boy

**2010.** Europa. Childrens' Books. Sheet 80×120 mm containing T 1451 and similar vert design. Multicoloured.
**MS**4306 3 Europe (€2.70)×2, Type **1451**; Cat reading to girl 12·00 12·00

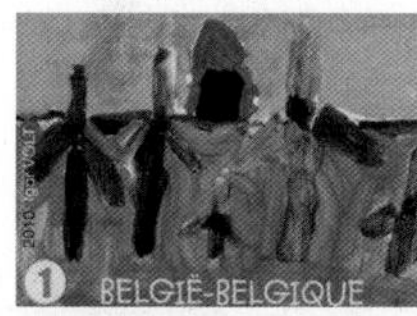
1452 Seas and Oceans (Igor Volt)

**2010.** Environmental Protection. Winning Designs in Childrens' Drawing Competition. Multicoloured.
4307 1 (59c.) Type **1452** 2·75 2·00
4308 1 (59c.) Forest (Lander Keyaerts) 2·75 2·00
4309 1 (59c.) Endangerd species (Eva Sterkens) 2·75 2·00
4310 1 (59c.) Climate (Lucie Octave) 2·75 2·00
4311 1 (59c.) Energy (Louise van Goylen) 2·75 2·00

1453 Natan

**2010.** This is Belgium. Fashion. Sheet 200×160 mm containing T 1453 and similar multicoloured designs.
**MS**4312 1 (59c.)×10, Type **1453**; Walter Van Beirendonck; Veronique Branquinho (43×35 mm); A.F. Vandevorst (33×44 mm); Ann Demeulemeester (44×26 mm); Olivier Theyskens (32×48 mm); Dirk Bikkembergs (48×38 mm); Cathy Pill (38×48 mm); Veronique Leroy (29×33 mm); Martin Margiela (48×38 mm) 6·50 6·50

1454 Exhibition Emblem

**2010.** Antverpia 2010–International Stamp Exhibition, Antwerp (3rd issue). Sheet 190×120 mm.
**MS**4313 multicoloured 7·75 7·75

1455 Gyrfalcon (inscr 'Buizerd–Buse Variable')

**2010.** 25th Anniv of Birds on Stamps drawn by André Buzin. Sheet 160×140 mm containing T 1455 and similar vert designs. Multicoloured.
**MS**4314 1 Europe (90c.)×5, Type **1455**; Hobby (Faucon hoberau–Boomvalk); Sparrow hawk (Sperwer–Epermer d'Europe); Red Kite (Milan Royal–Rode Wouw); Goshawk (Havik–Autour des Palombes) 25·00 25·00

See also No. 3692 etc.

1456 Prince Philippe

**2010.** 50th Birth Anniv of Prince Philippe, Duke of Brabant, Prince of Belgium.
4315 **1456** 2 (€1.18) multicoloured 5·00 4·00

1457 Early Steam and Modern High Speed Locomotives

**2010.** 175th Anniv of Belgian Railways
4316 **1457** 2 (€1.18) multicoloured 4·25 3·00

**1458** Profiles and Party Favours

**2010.** Greetings Stamps. Multicoloured.

| | | | |
|---|---|---|---|
| 4317 | 1 (59c.) Type **1458** | 2·75 | 2·00 |
| 4318 | 1 (59c.) Hands holding present and bouquet | 2·75 | 2·00 |
| 4319 | 1 (59c.) Hand holding lantern and profile wearing mask | 2·75 | 2·00 |
| 4320 | 1 (59c.) Hands holding tray of glasses and cake | 2·75 | 2·00 |
| 4321 | 1 (59c.) Children | 2·75 | 2·00 |

**1459** Zebra-striped Ball and Player's Boot

**2010.** World Cup Football Championships, South Africa

| | | | | |
|---|---|---|---|---|
| 4322 | **1459** | 1 (90c.) multicoloured | 3·75 | 2·75 |

**1460** Winners' Podiums and Athlete

**2010.** Youth Olympic Games, Singapore

| | | | | |
|---|---|---|---|---|
| 4323 | **1460** | 1 (€1.05) multicoloured | 4·25 | 3·00 |

**1461** Child and Map as Flag

**2010.** 50th Anniv of Congo Independence

| | | | | |
|---|---|---|---|---|
| 4324 | **1461** | 1 (€1.05) multicoloured | 4·25 | 3·00 |

**1462** Eddie Merckx

**2010.** 65th Birth Anniv of Edouard Louis Joseph Merckx (world champion cyclist)

| | | | | |
|---|---|---|---|---|
| 4325 | **1462** | 2 (€1.08) multicoloured | 5·00 | 3·50 |

**1463** 'eu'

**2010.** Belgium's Presidency of the European Union

| | | | | |
|---|---|---|---|---|
| 4326 | **1463** | 1 (90c.) multicoloured | 1·90 | 1·30 |

**1464** Cyclist riding on Fietsknooppunten

**2010.** Tourism. Multicoloured.

| | | | |
|---|---|---|---|
| 4327 | 1 (59c.) Type **1464** | 2·30 | 1·60 |
| 4328 | 1 (59c.) Tourist information board and cyclist, The Ravel | 2·30 | 1·60 |

**1465** Ford Bureau de Poste Vehicle (1953)

**2010.** Postal Transport. Multicoloured.

| | | | |
|---|---|---|---|
| 4329 | 1 (59c.) Type **1465** | 2·30 | 1·60 |
| 4330 | 1 (59c.) Independent postal train (1931) | 2·30 | 1·60 |
| 4331 | 1 (59c.) Bedford truck (1979) | 2·30 | 1·60 |
| 4332 | 1 (59c.) Independent postal train (1968) | 2·30 | 1·60 |
| 4333 | 1 (59c.) Volvo truck (2009) | 2·30 | 1·60 |

**1466** Le Tonneau, Brussels (S. Jasinsky)

**2010.** Pre-1960 Architecture. Multicoloured.

**MS**4334 1 (90c.)×5, Type **1466**; Saint-Maartensdal (Renaat Braem and A33 Architects), Louvain; Le fer à cheval (J. J. Eggericx and R.Verwilghen), Brussels; Boerentoren, Anvers (J. Vanhoenacker, J. Smolderen & E. Van Averbeke); Cité de Droixhe, Liège (EGAU architectural group) 18·00 18·00

**1467** Fruit Trees, Saint-Trond

**2010.** Regions. Multicoloured.

**MS**4335 1 (90c.)×5, Type **1467**; Fruit blossom; Wine and glasses; Building façade, Hélécine (33×40 mm); Ploughed field and farm buildings, Perwez (49×37 mm) 18·00 18·00

**1468** Leisure Centre, Rotselar (de Mena Brewery)

**2010.** Breweries, Change of Use. Multicoloured.

| | | | |
|---|---|---|---|
| 4336 | 1 (90c.) Type **1468** | 3·25 | 2·25 |
| 4337 | 1 (€1.05) Telematics Support Centre, Marche-en-Famenne (Carmelite monastery and brewery) | 4·00 | 2·75 |
| 4338 | 2 (€1.18) Weils Contemporary Art Centre, Brussels | 5·25 | 3·50 |

**1469** Shoe Making

**2010.** Craft Trades. Multicoloured.

| | | | |
|---|---|---|---|
| 4339 | 1 (59c.) Type **1469** | 2·50 | 1·70 |
| 4340 | 1 (59c.) Clog making | 2·50 | 1·70 |
| 4341 | 1 (59c.) Blacksmithing | 2·50 | 1·70 |
| 4342 | 1 (59c.) Spinning | 2·50 | 1·70 |
| 4343 | 1 (59c.) Laundry | 2·50 | 1·70 |

**1470** *Voyage dans la lune*

**2010.** Tenth Anniv of Folon Foundation. Multicoloured.

| | | | |
|---|---|---|---|
| 4344 | 1 (59c.) Type **1470** | 2·50 | 1·70 |
| 4345 | 1 (59c.) *Pays de connaissance* | 2·50 | 1·70 |
| 4346 | 1 (59c.) *Un cri* (horiz) | 2·50 | 1·70 |
| 4347 | 1 (59c.) *La mer ce grand sculpteur* (Knokke) (horiz) | 2·50 | 1·70 |
| 4348 | 1 (59c.) *L'étranger* (horiz) | 2·50 | 1·70 |
| 4349 | 1 (59c.) *Oiseau* (horiz) | 2·50 | 1·70 |
| 4350 | 1 (59c.) *Pluie* (La Hulpe) | 2·50 | 1·70 |
| 4351 | 1 (59c.) Stained glass window, Eglise de Waha (Marche-en-Famenne) | 2·50 | 1·70 |
| 4352 | 1 (59c.) *L'aube* | 2·50 | 1·70 |
| 4353 | 1 (59c.) *Un monde* | 2·50 | 1·70 |

**1471** Virgin and Child (Caen)

**2010.** Flemish Primitive Art in French and Belgian Collections. Multicoloured.

**MS**4354 3 (€2.07)×2, Type **1471**; *Portrait of Laurent Froimont* (Brussels) 18·00 18·00

Stamps of a similar design were issued by France

**1472** Santa in his Sleigh

**2010.** Christmas. Multicoloured.

| | | | |
|---|---|---|---|
| 4355 | 1 (59c.) Type **1472** | 2·75 | 2·00 |
| 4356 | 1 (90c.) Santa in his sleigh (different) | 5·25 | 3·50 |

**1473** '1-1-11'

**2011.** Liberalization of Postal Market from 1st January 2011

| | | | | |
|---|---|---|---|---|
| 4357 | **1473** | 1 (59c.) multicoloured | 2·75 | 2·00 |

## EXPRESS LETTER STAMPS

**E107** Ghent

**1929**

| | | | | |
|---|---|---|---|---|
| E530 | - | 1f.75 blue | 70 | 35 |
| E531 | **E107** | 2f.35 red | 2·20 | 50 |
| E581 | - | 2f.45 green | 23·00 | 3·00 |
| E532 | - | 3f.50 purple | 14·00 | 14·00 |
| E533 | - | 5f.25 olive | 13·50 | 13·00 |

DESIGNS: 1f.75, Town Hall, Brussels; 2f.45, Eupen; 3f.50, Bishop's Palace, Liege; 5f.25, Antwerp Cathedral.

**1932.** No. E581 surch 2 Fr 50 and cross.

| | | | |
|---|---|---|---|
| E608 | 2f.50 on 2f.45 green | 16·00 | 2·30 |

## MILITARY STAMPS

**1967.** As T 289 (Baudouin) but with letter "M" within oval at foot.

| | | | |
|---|---|---|---|
| M2027 | 1f.50 green | 25 | 20 |

**1971.** As No. 2207/8a and 2209a but with letter "M" within oval at foot.

| | | | |
|---|---|---|---|
| M2224 | 1f.75 green | 35 | 35 |
| M2225 | 2f.25 green | 30 | 40 |
| M2226 | 2f.50 green | 25 | 25 |
| M2227 | 3f.25 plum | 30 | 30 |

## NEWSPAPER STAMPS

**1928.** Railway Parcels stamps of 1923 optd JOURNAUX DAGBLADEN 1928.

| | | | | |
|---|---|---|---|---|
| N443 | **P 84** | 10c. red | 60 | 35 |
| N444 | **P 84** | 20c. green | 60 | 35 |
| N445 | **P 84** | 40c. olive | 60 | 35 |
| N446 | **P 84** | 60c. orange | 85 | 35 |
| N447 | **P 84** | 70c. brown | 85 | 35 |
| N448 | **P 84** | 80c. violet | 1·20 | 60 |
| N449 | **P 84** | 90c. slate | 10·50 | 3·50 |
| N450 | - | 1f. blue | 2·30 | 60 |
| N451 | - | 2f. olive | 4·75 | 85 |
| N452 | - | 3f. red | 4·75 | 85 |
| N453 | - | 4f. red | 4·75 | 85 |
| N454 | - | 5f. violet | 4·75 | 85 |
| N455 | - | 6f. brown | 7·25 | 2·00 |
| N456 | - | 7f. orange | 20·00 | 3·50 |
| N457 | - | 8f. brown | 14·50 | 2·30 |
| N458 | - | 9f. purple | 41·00 | 10·50 |
| N459 | - | 10f. green | 14·50 | 3·50 |
| N460 | - | 20f. pink | 41·00 | 14·50 |

**1929.** Railway Parcels stamps of 1923 optd JOURNAUX DAGBLADEN only.

| | | | | |
|---|---|---|---|---|
| N505 | **P 84** | 10c. red | 1·20 | 60 |
| N506 | **P 84** | 20c. green | 60 | 60 |
| N507 | **P 84** | 40c. olive | 60 | 60 |
| N508 | **P 84** | 60c. orange | 85 | 60 |
| N509 | **P 84** | 70c. brown | 60 | 60 |
| N510 | **P 84** | 80c. violet | 1·20 | 1·20 |
| N511 | **P 84** | 90c. slate | 7·75 | 6·50 |
| N512 | - | 1f. blue | 1·70 | 60 |
| N513 | - | 1f.10 brown | 5·75 | 1·70 |
| N514 | - | 1f.50 blue | 5·75 | 1·70 |
| N515 | - | 2f. olive | 3·75 | 1·20 |
| N516 | - | 2f.10 slate | 17·00 | 12·00 |
| N517 | - | 3f. red | 3·75 | 1·20 |
| N518 | - | 4f. red | 3·75 | 1·20 |
| N519 | - | 5f. violet | 3·75 | 1·20 |
| N520 | - | 6f. brown | 8·75 | 1·70 |
| N521 | - | 7f. orange | 26·00 | 1·70 |
| N522 | - | 8f. brown | 17·00 | 1·70 |
| N523 | - | 9f. purple | 35·00 | 19·00 |
| N524 | - | 10f. green | 20·00 | 4·75 |
| N525 | - | 20f. pink | 49·00 | 17·00 |

## PARCEL POST STAMPS

**1928.** Optd COLIS POSTAL POSTCOLLO.

| | | | | |
|---|---|---|---|---|
| B470 | **81** | 4f. brown | 8·75 | 2·00 |
| B471 | **81** | 5f. bistre | 8·75 | 2·00 |

**B106** G.P.O., Brussels

**1929**

| | | | | |
|---|---|---|---|---|
| B526 | **B106** | 3f. sepia | 1·50 | 30 |
| B527 | **B106** | 4f. slate | 1·50 | 30 |
| B528 | **B106** | 5f. red | 1·50 | 30 |
| B529 | **B106** | 6f. purple | 36·00 | 36·00 |

**1933.** Surch X4 4X.

| | | | |
|---|---|---|---|
| B645 | 4f. on 6f. purple | 32·00 | 45 |

## POSTAGE DUE STAMPS

**D21**

**1870**

| | | | | |
|---|---|---|---|---|
| D63 | **D21** | 10c. green | 4·75 | 3·00 |
| D64 | **D21** | 20c. blue | 95·00 | 5·75 |

**D35**

**1895**

| | | | | |
|---|---|---|---|---|
| D96a | **D35** | 5c. green | 15 | 15 |
| D97 | **D35** | 10c. brown | 26·00 | 2·30 |
| D101 | **D35** | 10c. red | 15 | 10 |
| D98a | **D35** | 20c. green | 15 | 15 |
| D102 | **D35** | 30c. blue | 20 | 15 |
| D99 | **D35** | 50c. brown | 26·00 | 7·00 |

| | | | | |
|---|---|---|---|---|
| D103 | D35 | 50c. grey | 45 | 45 |
| D100 | D35 | 1f. red | 23·00 | 13·00 |
| D104 | D35 | 1f. yellow | 5·75 | 5·75 |

**1919.** As Type D 35, but value in colour on white background.

| | | | |
|---|---|---|---|
| D251 | 5c. green | 60 | 30 |
| D323 | 5c. grey | 10 | 10 |
| D252b | 10c. red | 1·70 | 30 |
| D324 | 10c. green | 10 | 10 |
| D253b | 20c. green | 8·75 | 1·50 |
| D325 | 20c. brown | 10 | 10 |
| D254 | 30c. blue | 4·75 | 60 |
| D326 | 30c. red | 80 | 60 |
| D327 | 35c. green | 25 | 15 |
| D328 | 40c. brown | 25 | 15 |
| D329 | 50c. blue | 1·50 | 25 |
| D330 | 50c. grey | 25 | 10 |
| D331 | 60c. red | 30 | 15 |
| D1146 | 65c. green | 7·50 | 3·50 |
| D332 | 70c. brown | 30 | 15 |
| D333 | 80c. grey | 30 | 15 |
| D334 | 1f. violet | 50 | 25 |
| D335 | 1f. purple | 60 | 30 |
| D336 | 1f.20 olive | 65 | 25 |
| D337 | 1f.40 green | 65 | 60 |
| D338 | 1f.50 olive | 65 | 60 |
| D1147 | 1f.60 mauve | 14·50 | 7·00 |
| D1148 | 1f.80 red | 16·00 | 5·75 |
| D339 | 2f. mauve | 65 | 30 |
| D1149 | 2f.40 lavender | 9·25 | 3·50 |
| D1150 | 3f. red | 1·70 | 60 |
| D340 | 3f.50 blue | 65 | 30 |
| D1151 | 4f. blue | 11·00 | 60 |
| D1152 | 5f. brown | 3·50 | 30 |
| D1153 | 7f. violet | 3·50 | 1·70 |
| D1154 | 8f. purple | 13·00 | 10·50 |
| D1155 | 10f. violet | 7·50 | 3·25 |

**D218**

**1945.** Inscr "A PAYER" at top and "TE BETALEN" at bottom, or vice versa.

| | | | | |
|---|---|---|---|---|
| D1130A | D218 | 10c. olive | 10 | 10 |
| D1131A | D218 | 20c. blue | 10 | 10 |
| D1132A | D218 | 30c. red | 10 | 10 |
| D1133A | D218 | 40c. blue | 10 | 10 |
| D1134A | D218 | 50c. green | 10 | 10 |
| D1135A | D218 | 1f. brown | 10 | 10 |
| D1136A | D218 | 2f. orange | 10 | 10 |

**D462**

**1966**

| | | | | |
|---|---|---|---|---|
| D2812 | D462 | 1f. mauve | 10 | 10 |
| D2813 | D462 | 2f. green | 10 | 10 |
| D2814 | D462 | 3f. blue | 1·40 | 25 |
| D2815 | D462 | 4f. green | 25 | 25 |
| D1985ab | D462 | 5f. purple | 30 | 30 |
| D2816 | D462 | 5f. lilac | 30 | 30 |
| D1986 | D462 | 6f. brown | 85 | 15 |
| D1987 | D462 | 7f. red | 70 | † |
| D2818 | D462 | 7f. orange | 45 | 45 |
| D2819 | D462 | 8f. grey | 45 | 45 |
| D2820 | D462 | 9f. red | 50 | 50 |
| D2821 | D462 | 10f. brown | 60 | 60 |
| D1988 | D462 | 20f. green | 1·30 | 50 |
| D2822 | D462 | 20f. green | 1·20 | 1·20 |

On No. D1988 the "F" is outside the shield; on No. D2822 it is inside.

## RAILWAY PARCELS STAMPS

**P21**

**1879**

| | | | | |
|---|---|---|---|---|
| P63 | P21 | 10c. brown | £160 | 10·50 |
| P64 | P21 | 20c. blue | £400 | 29·00 |
| P65 | P21 | 25c. green | £550 | 17·00 |
| P66 | P21 | 50c. red | £2750 | 14·50 |
| P67 | P21 | 80c. yellow | £3000 | 85·00 |
| P68 | P21 | 1f. grey | £400 | † |

In Belgium the parcels service is largely operated by the Belgian Railways for which the following stamps were issued.

Certain stamps under this heading were also on sale at post offices in connection with a "small parcels" service. These show a posthorn in the design except for Nos. P1116/18.

**P22**

**1882**

| | | | | |
|---|---|---|---|---|
| P69 | P22 | 10c. brown | 35·00 | 3·00 |
| P73 | P22 | 15c. grey | 14·50 | 10·50 |
| P75 | P22 | 20c. blue | £100 | 5·75 |
| P77 | P22 | 25c. green | £100 | 6·00 |
| P78 | P22 | 50c. red | £100 | 1·20 |
| P81 | P22 | 80c. yellow | £110 | 3·00 |
| P84 | P22 | 80c. brown | £110 | 3·00 |
| P86 | P22 | 1f. grey | £600 | 4·75 |
| P87 | P22 | 1f. purple | £650 | 5·75 |
| P88 | P22 | 2f. buff | £350 | £100 |

**P35**

**1895.** Numerals in black except 1f. and 2f.

| | | | | |
|---|---|---|---|---|
| P96 | P35 | 10c. brown | 14·50 | 1·20 |
| P97 | P35 | 15c. slate | 14·50 | 11·50 |
| P98 | P35 | 20c. blue | 23·00 | 2·30 |
| P99 | P35 | 25c. green | 23·00 | 3·50 |
| P100 | P35 | 30c. orange | 28·00 | 2·50 |
| P101 | P35 | 40c. green | 41·00 | 2·50 |
| P102 | P35 | 50c. red | 41·00 | 1·20 |
| P103 | P35 | 60c. lilac | 75·00 | 1·20 |
| P104 | P35 | 70c. blue | 75·00 | 2·00 |
| P105 | P35 | 80c. yellow | 75·00 | 2·00 |
| P106 | P35 | 90c. red | £110 | 3·00 |
| P107 | P35 | 1f. purple | £300 | 4·75 |
| P108 | P35 | 2f. buff | £350 | 23·00 |

**P37** Winged Railway Wheel

**1902**

| | | | | |
|---|---|---|---|---|
| P109a | | 10c. slate and brown | 30 | 30 |
| P110 | | 15c. purple and slate | 30 | 30 |
| P111 | | 20c. brown and blue | 30 | 30 |
| P112 | | 25c. red and green | 30 | 30 |
| P113 | | 30c. green and orange | 30 | 30 |
| P114 | | 35c. green and brown | 30 | 30 |
| P115 | | 40c. mauve and green | 30 | 30 |
| P116 | | 50c. mauve and pink | 30 | 30 |
| P117 | | 55c. blue and purple | 30 | 30 |
| P118 | | 60c. red and lilac | 30 | 30 |
| P119 | | 70c. red and blue | 30 | 30 |
| P120 | | 80c. purple and yellow | 30 | 30 |
| P121 | | 90c. green and red | 30 | 30 |
| P122 | P37 | 1f. orange and purple | 30 | 30 |
| P123 | P37 | 1f.10 black and red | 30 | 30 |
| P124 | P37 | 2f. green and bistre | 30 | 30 |
| P125 | P37 | 3f. blue and black | 30 | 30 |
| P126 | P37 | 4f. red and green | 2·00 | 2·00 |
| P127 | P37 | 5f. green and orange | 1·20 | 1·20 |
| P128 | P37 | 10f. purple and yellow | 1·20 | 1·20 |

**1915.** Stamps of 1912–14 optd CHEMINS DE FER SPOORWEGEN and Winged Railway Wheel.

| | | | |
|---|---|---|---|
| P160 | 44 | 5c. green | £225 |
| P161 | 46 | 10c. red | £250 |
| P162 | 46 | 20c. green | £300 |
| P163 | 46 | 25c. blue | £300 |
| P164 | 45 | 35c. brown | £400 |
| P165 | 46 | 40c. green | £350 |
| P166 | 45 | 50c. grey | £375 |
| P167 | 45 | 1f. orange | £350 |
| P168 | 45 | 2f. violet | £2000 |
| P169 | - | 5f. purple (No. 143) | £4000 |

**P59** Winged Railway Wheel

**P60** Steam Locomotive

**1915**

| | | | | |
|---|---|---|---|---|
| P196 | P59 | 10c. blue | 1·20 | 60 |
| P197 | P59 | 15c. olive | 2·00 | 2·00 |
| P198 | P59 | 20c. red | 1·70 | 1·20 |
| P199 | P59 | 25c. brown | 1·70 | 1·20 |
| P200 | P59 | 30c. mauve | 1·70 | 1·20 |
| P201 | P59 | 35c. grey | 2·00 | 1·20 |
| P202 | P59 | 40c. orange | 3·25 | 3·00 |
| P203 | P59 | 50c. bistre | 3·00 | 1·20 |
| P204 | P59 | 55c. brown | 3·50 | 3·25 |
| P205 | P59 | 60c. lilac | 3·00 | 1·20 |
| P206 | P59 | 70c. green | 2·00 | 1·20 |
| P207 | P59 | 80c. brown | 2·00 | 1·20 |
| P208 | P59 | 90c. blue | 3·00 | 1·50 |
| P209 | P60 | 1f. grey | 2·00 | 1·20 |
| P210 | P60 | 1f.10 bl (FRANKEN) | 44·00 | 33·00 |
| P211 | P60 | 1f.10 blue (FRANK) | 3·00 | 1·20 |
| P212 | P60 | 2f. red | 65·00 | 1·70 |
| P213 | P60 | 3f. violet | 65·00 | 1·70 |
| P214 | P60 | 4f. green | 75·00 | 3·25 |
| P215 | P60 | 5f. brown | £150 | 4·25 |
| P216 | P60 | 10f. orange | £200 | 3·75 |

**P69** Winged Railway Wheel

**P70** Steam Train

**1920**

| | | | | |
|---|---|---|---|---|
| P259 | P69 | 10c. green | 2·30 | 1·20 |
| P280 | P69 | 10c. red | 60 | 30 |
| P281 | P69 | 15c. green | 60 | 30 |
| P261 | P69 | 20c. red | 2·30 | 1·20 |
| P282 | P69 | 20c. green | 2·00 | 30 |
| P262 | P69 | 25c. brown | 3·50 | 1·20 |
| P283 | P69 | 25c. blue | 85 | 30 |
| P263 | P69 | 30c. mauve | 38·00 | 34·00 |
| P284 | P69 | 30c. brown | 85 | 30 |
| P285 | P69 | 35c. brown | 85 | 45 |
| P286 | P69 | 40c. orange | 85 | 30 |
| P265 | P69 | 50c. bistre | 11·50 | 2·00 |
| P287 | P69 | 50c. red | 85 | 30 |
| P266 | P69 | 55c. brown | 13·00 | 9·50 |
| P288 | P69 | 55c. yellow | 7·00 | 5·75 |
| P267 | P69 | 60c. purple | 15·00 | 1·70 |
| P289 | P69 | 60c. red | 85 | 30 |
| P290 | P69 | 70c. green | 4·00 | 60 |
| P269 | P69 | 80c. brown | 65·00 | 2·00 |
| P291 | P69 | 80c. violet | 3·00 | 45 |
| P270 | P69 | 90c. blue | 17·00 | 1·70 |
| P292 | P69 | 90c. yellow | 46·00 | 43·00 |
| P293 | P69 | 90c. purple | 8·75 | 45 |
| P271 | P70 | 1f. grey | £120 | 2·00 |
| P272 | P70 | 1f.10 blue | 38·00 | 2·00 |
| P273 | P70 | 1f.20 green | 23·00 | † |
| P274 | P70 | 1f.40 brown | 23·00 | 1·70 |
| P275 | P70 | 2f. red | £170 | 1·70 |
| P276 | P70 | 3f. mauve | £200 | 1·20 |
| P277 | P70 | 4f. green | £200 | 1·70 |
| P278 | P70 | 5f. brown | £200 | 1·20 |
| P279 | P70 | 10f. orange | £200 | 1·70 |

On Nos. P271/9 the engine has one head lamp.

**1920.** Three head lamps on engine.

| | | | | |
|---|---|---|---|---|
| P294 | P70 | 1f. brown | 8·75 | 30 |
| P296 | P70 | 1f.10 blue | 3·00 | 30 |
| P297 | P70 | 1f.20 orange | 3·75 | 30 |
| P298 | P70 | 1f.40 yellow | 21·00 | 3·50 |
| P299 | P70 | 1f.60 green | 38·00 | 70 |
| P300 | P70 | 2f. red | 41·00 | 30 |
| P301 | P70 | 3f. red | 41·00 | 30 |
| P302 | P70 | 4f. green | 41·00 | 30 |
| P303 | P70 | 5f. violet | 41·00 | 30 |
| P304 | P70 | 10f. yellow | £225 | 23·00 |
| P305 | P70 | 10f. brown | 50·00 | 30 |
| P306 | P70 | 15f. red | 50·00 | 30 |
| P307 | P70 | 20f. blue | £600 | 3·75 |

**P75**

**1921**

| | | | | |
|---|---|---|---|---|
| P312 | P75 | 2f. black | 11·50 | 95 |
| P313 | P75 | 3f. brown | £100 | 95 |
| P314 | P75 | 4f. green | 26·00 | 95 |
| P315 | P75 | 5f. red | 26·00 | 95 |
| P316 | P75 | 10f. brown | 26·00 | 95 |
| P317 | P75 | 15f. red | 26·00 | 1·50 |
| P318 | P75 | 20f. blue | £190 | 3·75 |

**P84**

**1923**

| | | | | |
|---|---|---|---|---|
| P375 | P84 | 5c. brown | 25 | 25 |
| P376 | P84 | 10c. red | 10 | 10 |
| P377 | P84 | 15c. blue | 30 | 30 |
| P378 | P84 | 20c. green | 15 | 10 |
| P379 | P84 | 30c. purple | 15 | 10 |
| P380 | P84 | 40c. olive | 15 | 10 |
| P381 | P84 | 50c. red | 15 | 10 |
| P382 | P84 | 60c. orange | 15 | 10 |
| P383 | P84 | 70c. brown | 15 | 10 |
| P384 | P84 | 80c. violet | 15 | 10 |
| P385 | P84 | 90c. slate | 1·00 | 10 |

Similar type, but horiz.

| | | | |
|---|---|---|---|
| P386 | 1f. blue | 30 | 15 |
| P388 | 1f.10 orange | 2·30 | 85 |
| P389 | 1f.50 green | 2·30 | 60 |
| P390 | 1f.70 brown | 60 | 60 |
| P391 | 1f.80 red | 3·50 | 85 |
| P392 | 2f. olive | 30 | 30 |
| P393 | 2f.10 green | 6·50 | 1·70 |
| P394 | 2f.40 violet | 3·00 | 1·70 |
| P395 | 2f.70 grey | 45·00 | 1·70 |
| P396 | 3f. red | 30 | 25 |
| P397 | 3f.30 brown | 70·00 | 1·70 |
| P398 | 4f. red | 30 | 25 |
| P399 | 5f. violet | 60 | 25 |
| P400 | 6f. brown | 30 | 25 |
| P401 | 7f. orange | 60 | 25 |
| P402 | 8f. brown | 60 | 25 |
| P403 | 9f. purple | 2·00 | 85 |
| P404 | 10f. green | 85 | 25 |
| P405 | 20f. pink | 1·20 | 25 |
| P406 | 30f. green | 4·00 | 60 |
| P407 | 40f. slate | 55·00 | 1·70 |
| P408 | 50f. bistre | 7·75 | 60 |

See Nos. P911/34.

**1924.** No. P394 surch 2F30.

| | | | |
|---|---|---|---|
| P409 | 2f.30 on 2f.40 violet | 5·75 | 85 |

**P139** Type 5 Steam locomotive "Goliath", 1930

**1934**

| | | | | |
|---|---|---|---|---|
| P655 | P139 | 3f. green | 14·50 | 2·50 |
| P656 | P139 | 4f. mauve | 5·75 | 30 |
| P657 | P139 | 5f. red | 80·00 | 30 |

**P149** Diesel Locomotive

**1935.** Centenary of Belgian Railway.

| | | | | |
|---|---|---|---|---|
| P689 | P149 | 10c. red | 35 | 30 |
| P690 | P149 | 20c. violet | 35 | 30 |
| P691 | P149 | 30c. brown | 60 | 30 |
| P692 | P149 | 40c. blue | 60 | 30 |
| P693 | P149 | 50c. orange | 60 | 30 |
| P694 | P149 | 60c. green | 65 | 30 |
| P695 | P149 | 70c. blue | 65 | 30 |
| P696 | P149 | 80c. black | 65 | 30 |
| P697 | P149 | 90c. red | 1·20 | 60 |

Horiz type. Locomotive "Le Belge", 1835.

| | | | |
|---|---|---|---|
| P698 | 1f. purple | 85 | 30 |
| P699 | 2f. black | 2·30 | 30 |

| | | | |
|---|---|---|---|
| P700 | 3f. orange | 3·25 | 30 |
| P701 | 4f. purple | 3·25 | 30 |
| P702 | 5f. purple | 4·75 | 30 |
| P703 | 6f. green | 6·50 | 30 |
| P704 | 7f. violet | 26·00 | 30 |
| P705 | 8f. black | 26·00 | 35 |
| P706 | 9f. blue | 29·00 | 35 |
| P707 | 10f. red | 29·00 | 35 |
| P708 | 20f. green | 55·00 | 35 |
| P709 | 30f. violet | £150 | 5·75 |
| P710 | 40f. brown | £150 | 5·75 |
| P711 | 50f. red | £200 | 5·25 |
| P712 | 100f. blue | £375 | 85·00 |

**P162** Winged Railway Wheel and Posthorn

**1938**

| | | | | |
|---|---|---|---|---|
| P806 | **P162** | 5f. on 3f.50 green | 26·00 | 25 |
| P807 | **P162** | 5f. on 4f.50 purple | 30 | 10 |
| P808 | **P162** | 6f. on 5f.50 red | 60 | 10 |
| P1162 | **P162** | 8f. on 5f.50 brown | 60 | 15 |
| P1163 | **P162** | 10f. on 5f.50 blue | 85 | 15 |
| P1164 | **P162** | 12f. on 5f.50 violet | 1·50 | 25 |

**P176** Seal of the International Railway Congress

**1939.** International Railway Congress, Brussels.

| | | | | |
|---|---|---|---|---|
| P856 | **P176** | 20c. brown | 5·25 | 5·25 |
| P857 | **P176** | 50c. blue | 5·25 | 5·25 |
| P858 | **P176** | 2f. red | 5·25 | 5·25 |
| P859 | **P176** | 9f. green | 5·25 | 5·25 |
| P860 | **P176** | 10f. purple | 5·25 | 5·25 |

**1939.** Surch M. 3Fr.

| | | | | |
|---|---|---|---|---|
| P867 | **P162** | 3f. on 5f.50 red | 30 | 25 |

**1940.** Optd B in oval and two vert bars.

| | | | | |
|---|---|---|---|---|
| P878 | **P84** | 10c. red | 10 | 10 |
| P879 | **P84** | 20c. green | 10 | 10 |
| P880 | **P84** | 30c. purple | 10 | 10 |
| P881 | **P84** | 40c. olive | 10 | 10 |
| P882 | **P84** | 50c. red | 10 | 10 |
| P883 | **P84** | 60c. orange | 75 | 70 |
| P884 | **P84** | 70c. brown | 10 | 10 |
| P885 | **P84** | 80c. violet | 10 | 10 |
| P886 | **P84** | 90c. slate | 30 | 30 |
| P887 | **P84** | 1f. blue | 15 | 15 |
| P888 | **P84** | 2f. olive | 25 | 25 |
| P889 | **P84** | 3f. red | 25 | 25 |
| P890 | **P84** | 4f. red | 25 | 25 |
| P891 | **P84** | 5f. violet | 25 | 25 |
| P892 | **P84** | 6f. brown | 30 | 25 |
| P893 | **P84** | 7f. orange | 30 | 25 |
| P894 | **P84** | 8f. brown | 30 | 25 |
| P895 | **P84** | 9f. purple | 30 | 25 |
| P896 | **P84** | 10f. green | 30 | 25 |
| P897 | **P84** | 20f. pink | 75 | 45 |
| P898 | **P84** | 30f. green | 1·20 | 1·20 |
| P899 | **P84** | 40f. slate | 3·00 | 2·50 |
| P900 | **P84** | 50f. bistre | 1·70 | 1·70 |

**1940.** As Type P 84 but colours changed.

| | | | |
|---|---|---|---|
| P911 | 10c. olive | 10 | 10 |
| P912 | 20c. violet | 10 | 10 |
| P913 | 30c. red | 10 | 10 |
| P914 | 40c. blue | 10 | 10 |
| P915 | 50c. green | 10 | 10 |
| P916 | 60c. grey | 10 | 10 |
| P917 | 70c. green | 10 | 10 |
| P918 | 80c. orange | 30 | 10 |
| P919 | 90c. lilac | 3·00 | 10 |

Similar design, but horizontal.

| | | | |
|---|---|---|---|
| P920 | 1f. green | 30 | 10 |
| P921 | 2f. brown | 35 | 10 |
| P922 | 3f. grey | 35 | 10 |
| P923 | 4f. olive | 40 | 10 |
| P924 | 5f. lilac | 45 | 10 |
| P925 | 5f. black | 85 | 10 |
| P926 | 6f. red | 85 | 10 |
| P927 | 7f. violet | 85 | 10 |
| P928 | 8f. green | 85 | 10 |
| P929 | 9f. blue | 1·20 | 10 |
| P930 | 10f. mauve | 1·20 | 25 |
| P931 | 20f. blue | 3·50 | 50 |
| P932 | 30f. yellow | 5·75 | 1·00 |
| P933 | 40f. red | 7·25 | 1·00 |
| P934 | 50f. red | 11·50 | 85 |

No. P925 was for use as a railway parcels tax stamp.

**P195** Engine Driver

**1942.** Various designs.

| | | | | |
|---|---|---|---|---|
| P1090 | **P195** | 10c. grey | 30 | 25 |
| P1091 | **P195** | 20c. violet | 30 | 25 |
| P1092 | **P195** | 30c. red | 30 | 25 |
| P1093 | **P195** | 40c. blue | 30 | 25 |
| P1094 | **P195** | 50c. blue | 30 | 25 |
| P1095 | **P195** | 60c. black | 30 | 25 |
| P1096 | **P195** | 70c. green | 45 | 25 |
| P1097 | **P195** | 80c. orange | 45 | 25 |
| P1098 | **P195** | 90c. brown | 45 | 25 |
| P1099 | - | 1f. green | 30 | 25 |
| P1100 | - | 2f. purple | 30 | 25 |
| P1101 | - | 3f. black | 1·50 | 30 |
| P1102 | - | 4f. blue | 30 | 25 |
| P1103 | - | 5f. brown | 30 | 25 |
| P1104 | - | 6f. green | 1·50 | 60 |
| P1105 | - | 7f. violet | 30 | 25 |
| P1106 | - | 8f. red | 30 | 25 |
| P1107 | - | 9f. blue | 60 | 25 |
| P996 | - | 9f.20 red | 60 | 60 |
| P1108 | - | 10f. red | 3·25 | 35 |
| P1109 | - | 10f. brown | 2·30 | 45 |
| P997 | **P195** | 12f.30 green | 60 | 60 |
| P998 | - | 14f.30 red | 60 | 60 |
| P1110 | - | 20f. green | 1·20 | 25 |
| P1111 | - | 30f. violet | 1·20 | 25 |
| P1112 | - | 40f. red | 1·20 | 25 |
| P1113 | - | 50f. blue | 20·00 | 1·20 |
| P999 | - | 100f. blue | 24·00 | 24·00 |

DESIGNS—As Type P **195**: 1f. to 9f.20, Platelayer; 10f. and 14f.30 to 50f. Railway porter; 24½×34½ mm: 100f. Electric train.

No. P1109 was for use as a railway parcels tax stamp.

**P216** Mercury

**1945.** Inscribed "BELGIQUE-BELGIE" or vice-versa.

| | | | | |
|---|---|---|---|---|
| P1116A | **P216** | 3f. green | 30 | 15 |
| P1117A | **P216** | 5f. blue | 30 | 15 |
| P1118A | **P216** | 6f. red | 30 | 15 |

**P224** Level Crossing

**1947**

| | | | | |
|---|---|---|---|---|
| P1174 | **P224** | 100f. green | 7·25 | 30 |

**P230** Archer

**1947**

| | | | | |
|---|---|---|---|---|
| P1193 | **P230** | 8f. brown | 1·20 | 40 |
| P1194 | **P230** | 10f. blue and black | 1·20 | 30 |
| P1195 | **P230** | 12f. violet | 1·70 | 30 |

**1948.** Surch.

| | | | |
|---|---|---|---|
| P1229 | 9f. on 8f. brown | 1·50 | 25 |
| P1230 | 11f. on 10f. blue and black | 1·50 | 40 |
| P1231 | 13f.50 on 12f. violet | 2·00 | 25 |

**P246** "Parcel Post"

**1948**

| | | | | |
|---|---|---|---|---|
| P1250 | **P246** | 9f. brown | 8·75 | 35 |
| P1251 | **P246** | 11f. red | 7·50 | 25 |
| P1252 | **P246** | 13f.50 black | 13·00 | 25 |

**P 254** Type 1 Locomotive, 1867 (dated 1862)

**1949.** Locomotives.

| | | | | |
|---|---|---|---|---|
| P1277 | - | ½f. brown | 35 | 25 |
| P1278 | **P254** | 1f. red | 60 | 25 |
| P1279 | - | 2f. blue | 80 | 25 |
| P1280 | - | 3f. red (1884) | 2·50 | 25 |
| P1281 | - | 4f. green (1901) | 1·70 | 25 |
| P1282 | - | 5f. red (1902) | 1·70 | 25 |
| P1283 | - | 6f. purple (1904) | 2·50 | 25 |
| P1284 | - | 7f. green (1905) | 4·00 | 25 |
| P1285 | - | 8f. blue (1906) | 5·25 | 25 |
| P1286 | - | 9f. brown (1909) | 5·75 | 25 |
| P1287 | - | 10f. olive (1910) | 14·00 | 3·50 |
| P1288 | - | 10f. black and red (1905) | 7·00 | 25 |
| P1289 | - | 20f. orange (1920) | 13·00 | 25 |
| P1290 | - | 30f. blue (1928) | 23·00 | 25 |
| P1291 | - | 40f. red (1930) | 41·00 | 25 |
| P1292 | - | 50f. mauve (1935) | 70·00 | 25 |
| P1293 | - | 100f. red (1939) | £120 | 30 |
| P1294 | - | 300f. violet (1951) | £170 | 60 |

DESIGNS: 50c. Locomotive "Le Belge", 1835; 2f. Type 29 locomotive, 1875; 3f. Type 25 locomotive, 1884; 4f. Type 18 locomotive, 1901; 5f. Type 22 locomotive, 1902; 6f. Type 53 locomotive, 1904; 7f. Type 8 locomotive, 1905; 8f. Type 16 locomotive, 1906; 9f. Type 10 locomotive, 1909; 10f. (P1287) Type 36 locomotive, 1910; 10f. (P 1288) Type 38 locomotive, 1905; 20f. Type 38 locomotive, 1920; 30f. Type 48 locomotive, 1928; 40f. Type 5 locomotive, 1935; 50f. Type 1 Pacific locomotive, 1935; 100f. Type 12 locomotive, 1939; 300f. Two-car electric train, 1951.

The 300f. is larger (37½×25 mm).

**1949.** Electrification of Charleroi–Brussels Line. As Type P254.

| | | | |
|---|---|---|---|
| P1296 | 60f. brown | 2·00 | 1·50 |

DESIGN: 60f. Type 101 electric locomotive, 1945.

**P258** Loading Parcels

**1950**

| | | | | |
|---|---|---|---|---|
| P1307 | - | 11f. orange | 5·75 | 25 |
| P1308 | - | 12f. purple | 22·00 | 2·00 |
| P1309 | - | 13f. green | 7·50 | 25 |
| P1310 | - | 15f. blue | 16·00 | 30 |
| P1311 | **P258** | 16f. grey | 5·75 | 25 |
| P1312 | - | 17f. brown | 7·50 | 25 |
| P1313 | **P258** | 18f. red | 16·00 | 25 |
| P1314 | **P258** | 20f. orange | 7·50 | 30 |

DESIGNS—HORIZ: 11, 12, 17f. Dispatch counter; 13, 15f. Sorting compartment.

**P271** Mercury

**1951.** 25th Anniv of National Belgian Railway Society.

| | | | | |
|---|---|---|---|---|
| P1375 | **P271** | 25f. blue | 15·00 | 13·00 |

**1953.** Nos. P1307, P1310 and P1313 surch.

| | | | | |
|---|---|---|---|---|
| P1442 | - | 13f. on 15f. blue | 65·00 | 5·75 |
| P1443 | - | 17f. on 11f. orange | 32·00 | 1·20 |
| P1444 | **P258** | 20f. on 18f. red | 17·00 | 3·50 |

**P288** Electric Train and Brussels Skyline

**1953.** Inauguration of Nord-Midi Junction.

| | | | | |
|---|---|---|---|---|
| P1451 | **P288** | 200f. green | £250 | 85 |
| P1452 | **P288** | 200f. green & brown | £275 | 3·75 |

**P291** Nord Station

**P292** Central Station

**1953.** Brussels Railway Stations.

| | | | | |
|---|---|---|---|---|
| P1485 | **P291** | 1f. ochre | 30 | 25 |
| P1486 | **P291** | 2f. black | 45 | 25 |
| P1487 | **P291** | 3f. green | 60 | 30 |
| P1488 | **P291** | 4f. orange | 85 | 40 |
| P1489 | **P291** | 5f. brown | 3·00 | 25 |
| P1490 | - | 5f. brown | 10·50 | 25 |
| P1491 | **P291** | 6f. purple | 1·20 | 25 |
| P1492 | **P291** | 7f. green | 1·20 | 25 |
| P1493 | **P291** | 8f. red | 1·50 | 25 |
| P1494 | **P291** | 9f. blue | 2·00 | 25 |
| P1495 | - | 10f. green | 2·40 | 25 |
| P1496 | - | 10f. black | 1·50 | 30 |
| P1497 | - | 15f. red | 14·50 | 45 |
| P1498 | - | 20f. blue | 4·00 | 25 |
| P1498a | - | 20f. green | 2·30 | 45 |
| P1499 | - | 30f. purple | 6·50 | 25 |
| P1500 | - | 40f. mauve | 8·75 | 25 |
| P1501 | - | 50f. mauve | 10·50 | 25 |
| P1501a | - | 50f. blue | 3·50 | 70 |
| P1502 | - | 60f. violet | 22·00 | 25 |
| P1503 | - | 80f. purple | 35·00 | 25 |
| P1504 | **P292** | 100f. green | 20·00 | 50 |
| P1505 | **P292** | 200f. blue | £120 | 1·00 |
| P1506 | **P292** | 300f. mauve | £200 | 1·70 |

DESIGNS—VERT: 5f. (P1490), 10f. (P1496), 15, 20f. (P1498a), 50f. (P1501a), Congress Station; 10f. (P1495), 20f. (P1498) to 50f. (P1501), Midi Station. HORIZ: 60, 80f. Chapelle Station.

Nos. P1490, P1496/7, P1498a and P1501a were for use as railway parcels tax stamps.

**P295** Electric Train Type 121 and Nord Station, Brussels

**1953**

| | | | | |
|---|---|---|---|---|
| P1517 | **P295** | 13f. brown | 23·00 | 30 |
| P1518 | **P295** | 18f. blue | 23·00 | 30 |
| P1519 | **P295** | 21f. mauve | 23·00 | 30 |

**1956.** Surch in figures.

| | | | |
|---|---|---|---|
| P1585 | 14f. on 13f. brown | 8·25 | 30 |
| P1586 | 19f. on 18f. blue | 8·25 | 30 |
| P1587 | 22f. on 21f. mauve | 8·25 | 30 |

**P326** Mercury and Railway Winged Wheel

**1957**

| | | | | |
|---|---|---|---|---|
| P1600 | **P326** | 14f. green | 8·25 | 25 |
| P1601 | **P326** | 19f. sepia | 8·25 | 25 |
| P1602 | **P326** | 22f. red | 8·25 | 40 |

**1959.** Surch 20 F.

| | | | |
|---|---|---|---|
| P1678 | 20f. on 19f. sepia | 29·00 | 30 |
| P1679 | 20f. on 22f. red | 29·00 | 70 |

**P357** Brussels Nord Station, 1861–1954

**1959**

| | | | | |
|---|---|---|---|---|
| P1695 | **P357** | 20f. olive | 14·50 | 25 |
| P1696 | - | 24f. red | 5·75 | 30 |

| | | | | |
|---|---|---|---|---|
| P1697 | - | 26f. blue | 5·75 | 3·50 |
| P1698 | - | 28f. purple | 5·75 | 3·50 |

DESIGNS—VERT: 24f. Brussels Midi station, 1869–1949. HORIZ: 26f. Antwerp Central station, 1905; 28f. Ghent St. Pieter's station.

**P368** Congress Seal, Type 202 Diesel and Type 125 Electric Locomotives

**1960.** 75th Anniv of Int Railway Congress Assn.

| | | | | |
|---|---|---|---|---|
| P1722 | **P368** | 20f. red | 50·00 | 35·00 |
| P1723 | **P368** | 50f. blue | 50·00 | 35·00 |
| P1724 | **P368** | 60f. purple | 50·00 | 35·00 |
| P1725 | **P368** | 70f. green | 50·00 | 35·00 |

**1961.** Nos. P1695/8 surch.

| | | | | |
|---|---|---|---|---|
| P1787 | **P357** | 24f. on 20f. olive | 60·00 | 30 |
| P1788 | - | 26f. on 24f. red | 5·75 | 30 |
| P1789 | - | 28f. on 26f. blue | 5·75 | 30 |
| P1790 | - | 35f. on 28f. purple | 5·75 | 30 |

**P477** Arlon Station

**1967**

| | | | | |
|---|---|---|---|---|
| P2017 | **P477** | 25f. ochre | 9·25 | 45 |
| P2018 | **P477** | 30f. green | 2·30 | 45 |
| P2019 | **P477** | 35f. blue | 3·00 | 45 |
| P2020 | **P477** | 40f. red | 26·00 | 70 |

**P488** Type 122 Electric Train

**1968**

| | | | | |
|---|---|---|---|---|
| P2047 | **P488** | 1f. bistre | 30 | 30 |
| P2048 | **P488** | 2f. green | 30 | 30 |
| P2049 | **P488** | 3f. green | 60 | 30 |
| P2050 | **P488** | 4f. orange | 60 | 30 |
| P2051 | **P488** | 5f. brown | 60 | 30 |
| P2052 | **P488** | 6f. plum | 60 | 30 |
| P2053 | **P488** | 7f. green | 60 | 30 |
| P2054 | **P488** | 8f. red | 90 | 30 |
| P2055 | **P488** | 9f. blue | 1·50 | 30 |
| P2056 | - | 10f. green | 3·00 | 30 |
| P2057 | - | 20f. blue | 1·80 | 30 |
| P2058 | - | 30f. lilac | 5·50 | 30 |
| P2059 | - | 40f. violet | 6·00 | 30 |
| P2060 | - | 50f. purple | 7·50 | 30 |
| P2061 | - | 60f. violet | 11·00 | 30 |
| P2062 | - | 70f. brown | 48·00 | 30 |
| P2063 | - | 80f. purple | 7·50 | 30 |
| P2063a | - | 90f. green | 7·25 | 50 |
| P2064 | - | 100f. green | 12·00 | 30 |
| P2065 | - | 200f. violet | 15·00 | 60 |
| P2066 | - | 300f. mauve | 27·00 | 1·50 |
| P2067 | - | 500f. yellow | 42·00 | 2·10 |

DESIGNS: 10f. to 40f. Type 126 electric train; 50, 60, 70, 80, 90f. Type 160 electric train; 100, 200, 300f. Type 205 diesel-electric train; 500f. Type 210 diesel-electric train.

**1970.** Surch.

| | | | | |
|---|---|---|---|---|
| P2180 | **P477** | 37f. on 25f. ochre | 65·00 | 7·75 |
| P2181 | **P477** | 48f. on 35f. blue | 6·00 | 6·00 |
| P2182 | **P477** | 53f. on 40f. red | 6·00 | 6·00 |

**P551** Ostend Station

**1971.** Figures of value in black.

| | | | | |
|---|---|---|---|---|
| P2192 | **P551** | 32f. ochre | 1·80 | 1·50 |
| P2193 | **P551** | 37f. grey | 16·00 | 15·00 |
| P2194 | **P551** | 42f. blue | 2·40 | 1·80 |
| P2195 | **P551** | 44f. mauve | 2·40 | 1·80 |
| P2196 | **P551** | 46f. violet | 2·75 | 1·80 |
| P2197 | **P551** | 50f. red | 2·40 | 1·80 |
| P2198 | **P551** | 52f. brown | 17·00 | 16·00 |
| P2199 | **P551** | 54f. green | 6·75 | 6·00 |
| P2200 | **P551** | 61f. blue | 3·50 | 2·75 |

**1972.** Nos. P2192/5 and P2198/200 surch in figures.

| | | | |
|---|---|---|---|
| P2256 | 34f. on 32f. ochre | 2·75 | 1·20 |
| P2257 | 40f. on 37f. grey | 2·75 | 1·20 |
| P2258 | 47f. on 44f. mauve | 3·00 | 1·20 |
| P2259 | 53f. on 42f. blue | 4·00 | 1·20 |
| P2260 | 56f. on 52f. brown | 3·50 | 1·20 |
| P2261 | 59f. on 54f. green | 4·00 | 1·20 |
| P2262 | 66f. on 61f. blue | 4·25 | 1·20 |

**P575** Emblems within Bogie Wheels

**1972.** 50th Anniv of Int Railways Union (U.I.C.).

| | | | | |
|---|---|---|---|---|
| P2266 | **P575** | 100f. black, red and green | 9·00 | 2·40 |

See also No. 2274.

**P624** Global Emblem

**1974.** 4th International Symposium of Railway Cybernetics, Washington.

| | | | | |
|---|---|---|---|---|
| P2353 | **P624** | 100f. black, red and yellow | 7·00 | 2·30 |

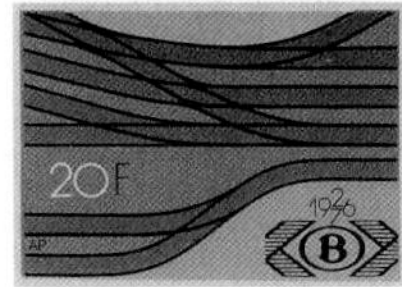


**P671** Railway Junction

**1976**

| | | | | |
|---|---|---|---|---|
| P2431 | **P671** | 20f. black, bl & lilac | 1·50 | 1·50 |
| P2432 | **P671** | 50f. black, green and turquoise | 2·50 | 1·50 |
| P2433 | **P671** | 100f. black & orange | 5·25 | 2·00 |
| P2434 | **P671** | 150f. black, mauve and deep mauve | 8·25 | 2·00 |

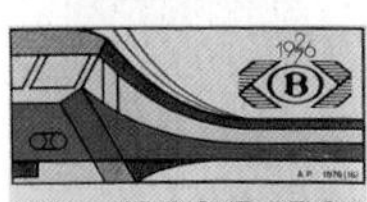


**P677** Modern Electric Train

**1976.** 50th Anniv of National Belgian Railway Company.

| | | | | |
|---|---|---|---|---|
| P2445 | **P677** | 6f.50 multicoloured | 50 | 15 |

**P698** Railway Station at Night

**1977**

| | | | | |
|---|---|---|---|---|
| P2505 | **P698** | 1000f. mult | 60·00 | 29·00 |

**P753** Goods Wagon, Type 2216 A8

**1980.** Values in black.

| | | | | |
|---|---|---|---|---|
| P2615 | **P753** | 1f. ochre | 30 | 30 |
| P2616 | **P753** | 2f. red | 30 | 30 |
| P2617 | **P753** | 3f. blue | 30 | 30 |
| P2618 | **P753** | 4f. blue | 30 | 30 |
| P2619 | **P753** | 5f. brown | 30 | 30 |
| P2620 | **P753** | 6f. orange | 45 | 45 |
| P2621 | **P753** | 7f. violet | 60 | 60 |
| P2622 | **P753** | 8f. black | 60 | 60 |
| P2623 | **P753** | 9f. green | 60 | 60 |
| P2624 | - | 10f. brown | 60 | 60 |
| P2625 | - | 20f. blue | 1·50 | 60 |
| P2626 | - | 30f. ochre | 2·30 | 60 |
| P2627 | - | 40f. mauve | 2·75 | 60 |
| P2628 | - | 50f. purple | 3·25 | 80 |
| P2629 | - | 60f. olive | 3·75 | 80 |
| P2630 | - | 70f. blue | 5·00 | 3·50 |
| P2631 | - | 80f. purple | 6·00 | 1·20 |
| P2632 | - | 90f. mauve | 6·50 | 4·00 |
| P2633 | - | 100f. red | 7·25 | 1·70 |
| P2634 | - | 200f. brown | 15·00 | 2·00 |
| P2635 | - | 300f. olive | 21·00 | 3·00 |
| P2636 | - | 500f. purple | 37·00 | 5·00 |

DESIGNS: 10f. to 40f. Packet wagon, Type 3614 A5; 50f. to 90f. Self-discharging wagon, Type 1000 D; 100f. to 500f. Tanker wagon, Type 2000 G.

**P833** Electric Train entering Station

**1985.** 150th Anniv of Belgian Railways. Paintings by P. Delvaux. Multicoloured.

| | | | |
|---|---|---|---|
| P2824 | 250f. Type P **833** | 17·00 | 11·50 |
| P2825 | 500f. Electric trains in station | 41·00 | 20·00 |

### RAILWAY PARCEL TAX STAMPS

**1940.** As Nos. P399 and P404 but colours changed.

| | | | | |
|---|---|---|---|---|
| P876 | **P84** | 5f. brown | 60 | 60 |
| P877 | **P84** | 10f. black | 6·50 | 6·50 |

**P779** Electric Locomotive at Station

**1982**

| | | | | |
|---|---|---|---|---|
| P2703 | **P779** | 10f. red & black | 2·00 | 30 |
| P2704 | **P779** | 20f. green & blk | 2·30 | 1·50 |
| P2705 | **P779** | 50f. brown & blk | 4·25 | 85 |
| P2706 | **P779** | 100f. blue & blk | 7·50 | 1·20 |

**P877** Buildings and Electric Locomotive

**1987**

| | | | | |
|---|---|---|---|---|
| P2923 | **P877** | 10f. red | 1·20 | 60 |
| P2924 | **P877** | 20f. green | 1·80 | 1·50 |
| P2925 | **P877** | 50f. brown | 5·50 | 2·10 |
| P2926 | **P877** | 100f. purple | 9·75 | 4·25 |
| P2927 | **P877** | 150f. brown | 15·00 | 5·50 |

### RAILWAY OFFICIAL STAMPS

**1929.** Stamps of 1922 optd with winged wheel.

| | | | | |
|---|---|---|---|---|
| O481 | **81** | 5c. slate | 35 | 30 |
| O482 | **81** | 10c. green | 35 | 30 |
| O483 | **81** | 35c. green | 45 | 30 |
| O484 | **81** | 60c. olive | 60 | 30 |
| O485 | **81** | 1f.50 blue | 19·00 | 9·25 |
| O486 | **81** | 1f.75 blue | 2·30 | 1·20 |

For use on the official mail of the Railway Company.

**1929.** Stamps of 1929 optd with winged wheel.

| | | | | |
|---|---|---|---|---|
| O534 | **104** | 5c. green | 30 | 15 |
| O535 | **104** | 10c. bistre | 30 | 15 |
| O536 | **104** | 25c. red | 2·50 | 45 |
| O537 | **104** | 35c. green | 80 | 25 |
| O538 | **104** | 40c. purple | 80 | 25 |
| O539 | **104** | 50c. blue | 40 | 25 |
| O540 | **104** | 60c. mauve | 23·00 | 11·50 |
| O541 | **104** | 70c. brown | 4·00 | 1·40 |
| O542 | **104** | 75c. blue | 8·25 | 1·20 |

**1932.** Stamps of 1931–34 optd with winged wheel.

| | | | | |
|---|---|---|---|---|
| O620 | **126** | 10c. green | 85 | 60 |
| O677 | **127** | 35c. green | 17·00 | 65 |
| O678 | **142** | 70c. green | 5·75 | 40 |
| O679 | **121** | 75c. brown | 2·50 | 50 |

**1936.** Stamps of 1936 optd with winged wheel.

| | | | | |
|---|---|---|---|---|
| O721 | **152** | 10c. olive | 15 | 15 |
| O722 | **152** | 35c. green | 15 | 15 |
| O723 | **152** | 40c. lilac | 25 | 25 |
| O724 | **152** | 50c. blue | 60 | 60 |
| O725 | **153** | 70c. brown | 4·75 | 4·75 |
| O726 | **153** | 75c. olive | 60 | 60 |

**1941.** Optd B in oval frame.

| | | | | |
|---|---|---|---|---|
| O948 | **152** | 10c. green | 15 | 15 |
| O949 | **152** | 40c. lilac | 15 | 15 |
| O950 | **152** | 50c. blue | 25 | 25 |
| O951 | **153** | 1f. red (No. 747) | 30 | 30 |
| O952a | **153** | 1f. red (No. 748) | 60 | 60 |
| O953 | **153** | 2f.25 black | 70 | 70 |
| O954 | **155** | 2f.25 violet | 35 | 35 |

**1942.** Nos. O722, O725 and O726 surch.

| | | | | |
|---|---|---|---|---|
| O983 | **152** | 10c. on 35c. green | 10 | 15 |
| O984 | **153** | 50c. on 70c. brown | 10 | 15 |
| O985 | **153** | 50c. on 75c. olive | 25 | 25 |

**O221**

**1946.** Designs incorporating letter "B".

| | | | | |
|---|---|---|---|---|
| O1156 | **O 221** | 10c. green | 10 | 10 |
| O1157 | **O 221** | 20c. violet | 3·75 | 1·20 |
| O1158 | **O 221** | 50c. blue | 10 | 10 |
| O1159 | **O 221** | 65c. purple | 5·25 | 1·50 |
| O1160 | **O 221** | 75c. mauve | 25 | 15 |
| O1161 | **O 221** | 90c. violet | 6·00 | 35 |
| O1240 | - | 1f.35 brn (as 1219) | 3·00 | 60 |
| O1241 | - | 1f.75 green (as 1220) | 7·50 | 60 |
| O1242 | **239** | 3f. purple | 35·00 | 10·50 |
| O1243 | **240** | 3f.15 blue | 14·00 | 8·75 |
| O1244 | **240** | 4f. blue | 28·00 | 11·50 |

**O283**

**1952**

| | | | | |
|---|---|---|---|---|
| O1424 | **O 283** | 10c. orange | 40 | 15 |
| O1425 | **O 283** | 20c. red | 4·25 | 85 |
| O1426 | **O 283** | 30c. green | 1·70 | 60 |
| O1427 | **O 283** | 40c. brown | 40 | 15 |
| O1428 | **O 283** | 50c. blue | 35 | 15 |
| O1429 | **O 283** | 60c. mauve | 85 | 30 |
| O1430 | **O 283** | 65c. purple | 35·00 | 29·00 |
| O1431 | **O 283** | 80c. green | 5·75 | 1·50 |
| O1432 | **O 283** | 90c. blue | 8·75 | 1·50 |
| O1433 | **O 283** | 1f. red | 60 | 15 |
| O1433a | **O 283** | 1f.50 grey | 25 | 25 |
| O1434 | **O 283** | 2f.50 brown | 30 | 15 |

**1954.** As T 289 (King Baudouin) but with letter "B" incorporated in design.

| | | | |
|---|---|---|---|
| O1523 | 1f.50 black | 40 | 15 |
| O1524 | 2f. red | 46·00 | 40 |
| O1525 | 2f. green | 45 | 15 |
| O1526 | 2f.50 brown | 37·00 | 85 |
| O1527 | 3f. mauve | 2·00 | 15 |
| O1528 | 3f.50 green | 85 | 15 |
| O1529 | 4f. blue | 1·20 | 35 |
| O1530 | 6f. red | 2·00 | 60 |

**1971.** As Nos. 2209/20 but with letter "B" incorporated in design.

| | | | |
|---|---|---|---|
| O2224 | 3f. green | 1·30 | 90 |
| O2225 | 3f.50 brown | 50 | 30 |
| O2226 | 4f. blue | 1·50 | 60 |
| O2227 | 4f.50 purple | 40 | 30 |
| O2228 | 4f.50 blue | 30 | 30 |
| O2229 | 5f. violet | 30 | 30 |
| O2230 | 6f. red | 50 | 30 |
| O2231 | 6f.50 violet | 60 | 30 |
| O2232a | 7f. red | 35 | 25 |
| O2233 | 8f. black | 60 | 30 |
| O2233a | 9f. brown | 60 | 30 |
| O2234 | 10f. red | 60 | 30 |
| O2235 | 15f. violet | 60 | 30 |
| O2236 | 25f. purple | 1·80 | 60 |
| O2237 | 30f. brown | 1·90 | 90 |

**1977.** As T 684 but with letter "B" incorporated in design.

| | | | |
|---|---|---|---|
| O2455 | 50c. brown | 25 | 25 |
| O2456 | 1f. mauve | 25 | 25 |
| O2457 | 2f. orange | 25 | 25 |
| O2458 | 4f. brown | 30 | 30 |
| O2459 | 5f. green | 30 | 30 |

Pt. 1

# BELIZE

British Honduras was renamed Belize on 1 June 1973 and the country became independent within the Commonwealth on 21 September 1981.

100 cents = 1 dollar.

**1973.** Nos. 256/66 and 277/8 of British Honduras optd **BELIZE** and two stars.

| No. | Type | Description | Mint | Used |
|---|---|---|---|---|
| 347 | - | ½c. multicoloured | 10 | 20 |
| 348 | 63 | 1c. black, brown and yellow | 10 | 20 |
| 349 | - | 2c. black, green and yellow | 10 | 20 |
| 350 | - | 3c. black, brown and lilac | 10 | 10 |
| 351 | - | 4c. multicoloured | 10 | 20 |
| 352 | - | 5c. black and red | 10 | 20 |
| 353 | - | 10c. multicoloured | 15 | 15 |
| 354 | - | 15c. multicoloured | 20 | 20 |
| 355 | - | 25c. multicoloured | 35 | 35 |
| 356 | - | 50c. multicoloured | 65 | 75 |
| 357 | - | $1 multicoloured | 75 | 1·50 |
| 358 | - | $2 multicoloured | 1·25 | 2·75 |
| 359 | - | $5 multicoloured | 1·40 | 4·75 |

**1973.** Royal Wedding. As T **47** of Anguilla. Background colours given. Multicoloured.

| No. | Description | Mint | Used |
|---|---|---|---|
| 360 | 26c. blue | 15 | 10 |
| 361 | 50c. brown | 15 | 20 |

**82** Mozambique Mouthbrooder

**1974.** As Nos. 256/66 and 276/78 of British Honduras. Multicoloured.

| No. | Description | Mint | Used |
|---|---|---|---|
| 362 | ½c. Type **82** | 10 | 50 |
| 363 | 1c. Spotted jewfish | 10 | 30 |
| 364 | 2c. White-lipped peccary ("Waree") | 10 | 30 |
| 365 | 3c. Misty grouper | 10 | 30 |
| 366 | 4c. Collared anteater | 10 | 30 |
| 367 | 5c. Bonefish | 10 | 30 |
| 368 | 10c. Paca ("Gibnut") | 15 | 15 |
| 369 | 15c. Dolphin | 20 | 20 |
| 370 | 25c. Kinkajou ("Night Walker") | 35 | 35 |
| 371 | 50c. Mutton snapper | 60 | 70 |
| 372 | $1 Tayra ("Bush Dog") | 75 | 1·50 |
| 373 | $2 Great barracuda | 1·25 | 2·50 |
| 374 | $5 Puma | 1·50 | 5·50 |

**83** Deer

**1974.** Mayan Artefacts (1st series). Pottery Motifs. Multicoloured.

| No. | Description | Mint | Used |
|---|---|---|---|
| 375 | 3c. Type **83** | 10 | 10 |
| 376 | 6c. Jaguar deity | 10 | 10 |
| 377 | 16c. Sea monster | 15 | 10 |
| 378 | 26c. Cormorant | 25 | 10 |
| 379 | 50c. Scarlet macaw | 40 | 40 |

See also Nos. 398/402.

**84** "Parides arcas"

**1974.** Butterflies of Belize. Multicoloured.

| No. | Description | Mint | Used |
|---|---|---|---|
| 380 | ½c. Type **84** | 1·00 | 5·00 |
| 381 | 1c. "Evenus regalis" | 1·00 | 1·75 |
| 405 | 2c. "Colobura dirce" | 50 | 70 |
| 406 | 3c. "Catonephele numilia" | 1·25 | 70 |
| 407 | 4c. "Battus belus" | 3·00 | 30 |
| 408 | 5c. "Callicore patelina" | 3·25 | 30 |
| 386 | 10c. "Diaethria astala" | 1·50 | 70 |
| 410 | 15c. "Nessaea aglaura" | 75 | 70 |
| 388 | 16c. "Prepona pseudojoiceyi" | 5·00 | 9·00 |
| 412 | 25c. "Papilio thoas" | 6·50 | 40 |
| 390 | 26c. "Hamadryas arethusa" | 2·00 | 4·25 |
| 413 | 35c. Type **84** | 13·00 | 4·50 |
| 391 | 50c. "Panthiades bathildis" | 3·25 | 65 |
| 392 | $1 "Caligo uranus" | 6·50 | 7·00 |
| 393 | $2 "Heliconius sapho" | 4·00 | 1·25 |
| 394 | $5 "Eurytides philolaus" | 5·50 | 6·00 |
| 395 | $10 "Philaethria dido" | 10·00 | 4·00 |

**85** Churchill when Prime Minister, and Coronation Scene

**1974.** Birth Centenary of Sir Winston Churchill. Multicoloured.

| No. | Description | Mint | Used |
|---|---|---|---|
| 396 | 50c. Type **85** | 20 | 20 |
| 397 | $1 Churchill in stetson, and Williamsburg Liberty Bell | 30 | 30 |

**86** The Actun Balam Vase

**1975.** Mayan Artefacts (2nd series). Multicoloured.

| No. | Description | Mint | Used |
|---|---|---|---|
| 398 | 3c. Type **86** | 10 | 10 |
| 399 | 6c. Seated figure | 10 | 10 |
| 400 | 16c. Costumed priest | 25 | 15 |
| 401 | 26c. Head with headdress | 35 | 20 |
| 402 | 50c. Layman and priest | 45 | 1·75 |

**87** Musicians

**1975.** Christmas. Multicoloured.

| No. | Description | Mint | Used |
|---|---|---|---|
| 435 | 6c. Type **87** | 10 | 10 |
| 436 | 26c. Children and "crib" | 20 | 10 |
| 437 | 50c. Dancer and drummers (vert) | 30 | 55 |
| 438 | $1 Family and map (vert) | 55 | 1·60 |

**88** William Wrigley Jr. and Chicle Tapping

**1976.** Bicent of American Revolution. Mult.

| No. | Description | Mint | Used |
|---|---|---|---|
| 439 | 10c. Type **88** | 10 | 10 |
| 440 | 35c. Charles Lindbergh | 20 | 40 |
| 441 | $1 J. L. Stephens (archaeologist) | 50 | 1·50 |

**89** Cycling

**1976.** Olympic Games, Montreal. Multicoloured.

| No. | Description | Mint | Used |
|---|---|---|---|
| 442 | 35c. Type **89** | 15 | 10 |
| 443 | 45c. Running | 20 | 15 |
| 444 | $1 Shooting | 35 | 1·40 |

**1976.** No. 390 surch 20c.

| No. | Description | Mint | Used |
|---|---|---|---|
| 445 | 20c. on 26c. multicoloured | 1·50 | 1·75 |

**1976.** West Indian Victory in World Cricket Cup. As Nos. 559/60 of Barbados.

| No. | Description | Mint | Used |
|---|---|---|---|
| 446 | 35c. multicoloured | 40 | 50 |
| 447 | $1 black and purple | 60 | 2·00 |

**1976.** No. 426 surch 5c.

| No. | Description | Mint | Used |
|---|---|---|---|
| 448 | 5c. on 15c. multicoloured | 1·10 | 2·75 |

**92** Queen and Bishops

**1977.** Silver Jubilee. Multicoloured.

| No. | Description | Mint | Used |
|---|---|---|---|
| 449 | 10c. Royal Visit, 1975 | 10 | 10 |
| 450 | 35c. Queen and Rose Window | 15 | 15 |
| 451 | $2 Type **92** | 45 | 90 |

**93** Red-capped Manakin

**1977.** Birds (1st series). Multicoloured.

| No. | Description | Mint | Used |
|---|---|---|---|
| 452 | 8c. Type **93** | 75 | 55 |
| 453 | 10c. Hooded oriole | 90 | 30 |
| 454 | 25c. Blue-crowned motmot | 1·25 | 55 |
| 455 | 35c. Slaty-breasted tinamou | 1·50 | 75 |
| 456 | 45c. Ocellated turkey | 1·75 | 1·25 |
| 457 | $1 White hawk | 3·00 | 5·50 |
| **MS**458 | 110×133 mm. Nos. 452/7 | 8·25 | 11·00 |

See also Nos. 467/78, 488/94 and 561/7.

**94** Laboratory Workers

**1977.** 75th Anniv of Pan-American Health Organization. Multicoloured.

| No. | Description | Mint | Used |
|---|---|---|---|
| 459 | 35c. Type **94** | 20 | 20 |
| 460 | $1 Mobile medical unit | 40 | 65 |
| **MS**461 | 126×95 mm. Nos. 459/60 | 85 | 1·40 |

**1978.** Nos. 386 and 413 optd **BELIZE DEFENCE FORCE 1ST JANUARY 1978.**

| No. | Description | Mint | Used |
|---|---|---|---|
| 462 | 10c. "Diaethria astala" | 75 | 1·50 |
| 463 | 35c. Type **84** | 1·50 | 2·25 |

**96** White Lion of Mortimer

**1978.** 25th Anniv of Coronation.

| No. | Type | Description | Mint | Used |
|---|---|---|---|---|
| 464 | 96 | 75c. brown, red and silver | 20 | 30 |
| 465 | - | 75c. multicoloured | 20 | 30 |
| 466 | - | 75c. brown, red and silver | 20 | 30 |

DESIGNS: No. 465, Queen Elizabeth II; 466, Jaguar (Maya god of Day and Night).

**1978.** Birds (2nd series). As T **93**. Multicoloured.

| No. | Description | Mint | Used |
|---|---|---|---|
| 467 | 10c. White-capped parrot("White-crowned Parrot") | 55 | 30 |
| 468 | 25c. Crimson-collared tanager | 80 | 45 |
| 469 | 35c. Black-headed trogon ("Citreoline Trogon") | 1·10 | 55 |
| 470 | 45c. American finfoot ("Sun-grebe") | 1·25 | 1·75 |
| 471 | 50c. Muscovy duck | 1·40 | 2·50 |
| 472 | $1 King vulture | 2·00 | 6·50 |
| **MS**473 | 111×133 mm. Nos. 467/72 | 8·00 | 11·00 |

**97** "Russelia sarmentosa"

**1978.** Christmas. Wild Flowers and Ferns. Mult.

| No. | Description | Mint | Used |
|---|---|---|---|
| 474 | 10c. Type **97** | 15 | 10 |
| 475 | 15c. "Lygodium polymorphum" | 20 | 15 |
| 476 | 35c. "Heliconia aurantiaca" | 20 | 20 |
| 477 | 45c. "Adiantum tetraphyllum" | 20 | 40 |
| 478 | 50c. "Angelonia ciliaris" | 35 | 50 |
| 479 | $1 "Thelypteris obliterata" | 50 | 1·25 |

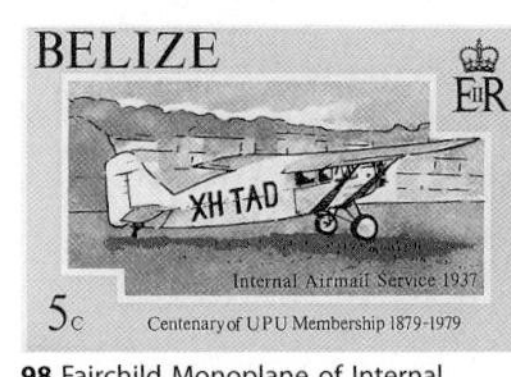


**98** Fairchild Monoplane of Internal Airmail Service, 1937

**1979.** Centenary of U.P.U. Membership. Mult.

| No. | Description | Mint | Used |
|---|---|---|---|
| 480 | 5c. Type **98** | 25 | 30 |
| 481 | 10c. "Heron H" (mail boat), 1949 | 25 | 10 |
| 482 | 35c. Internal mail service, 1920 (canoe) | 25 | 20 |
| 483 | 45c. Steam Creek Railway mail, 1910 | 45 | 55 |
| 484 | 50c. Mounted mail courier, 1882 | 45 | 60 |
| 485 | $2 "Eagle" (mail boat), 1856 | 80 | 2·50 |

**1979.** No. 413 surch **15c**.

| No. | Type | Description | Mint | Used |
|---|---|---|---|---|
| 487 | 84 | 15c. on 35c. multicoloured | 2·25 | 1·75 |

**1979.** Birds (3rd series). As T **93**. Multicoloured.

| No. | Description | Mint | Used |
|---|---|---|---|
| 488 | 10c. Boat-billed heron | 50 | 30 |
| 489 | 25c. Grey-necked wood rail | 75 | 30 |
| 490 | 35c. Lineated woodpecker | 85 | 55 |
| 491 | 45c. Blue-grey tanager | 90 | 70 |
| 492 | 50c. Laughing falcon | 90 | 1·25 |
| 493 | $1 Long-tailed hermit | 1·40 | 4·50 |
| **MS**494 | 113×136 mm. Nos. 488/93 | 4·75 | 7·00 |

**101** Paslow Building, Belize G.P.O.

**1979.** 25th Anniv of Coronation. Multicoloured.

| No. | Description | Mint | Used |
|---|---|---|---|
| 495 | 25c. Type **101** | 1·50 | 10 |
| 496 | 50c. Houses of Parliament | 2·00 | 10 |
| 497 | 75c. Coronation State Coach | 2·50 | 15 |
| 498 | $1 Queen on horseback (vert) | 3·25 | 20 |
| 499 | $2 Prince of Wales (vert) | 3·25 | 35 |
| 500 | $3 Queen and Duke of Edinburgh (vert) | 3·25 | 35 |
| 501 | $4 Portrait of Queen (vert) | 3·25 | 40 |
| 502 | $5 St. Edward's Crown (vert) | 3·50 | 40 |
| **MS**503 | Two sheets, both 126×95 mm: (a) $5 Princess Anne on horseback at Montreal Olympics (vert); $10 Queen at Montreal Olympics (vert). (b) $15 As Type **101** Set of 2 sheets | 25·00 | |

**102** Mortimer and Vaughan "Safety" Airplane, 1910

**1979.** Death Centenary of Sir Rowland Hill. 60th Anniv of I.C.A.O. (International Civil Aviation Organization), previously Int Commission for Air Navigation. Multicoloured.

| No. | Description | Mint | Used |
|---|---|---|---|
| 504 | 4c. Type **102** | 50 | 10 |
| 505 | 25c. Boeing 720 | 1·50 | 20 |
| 506 | 50c. Concorde | 4·25 | 30 |
| 507 | 75c. Handley Page H.P.18 W.8b (1922) | 2·00 | 30 |
| 508 | $1 Avro Type F (1912) | 2·00 | 30 |
| 509 | $1.50 Samuel Cody's biplane (1910) | 2·75 | 30 |
| 510 | $2 A.V. Roe Triplane I (1909) | 2·75 | 40 |
| 511 | $3 Santos Dumont's biplane "14 bis" (1906) | 2·75 | 45 |
| 512 | $4 Wright Type A | 3·00 | 65 |
| **MS**513 | Two sheets: (a) 115×95 mm. $5 Dunne D-5 (1910), $5 G.B. 1969 Concorde stamp; (b) 130×95 mm. $10 Boeing 720 (different) Set of 2 sheets | 21·00 | |

**103** Handball

**1979.** Olympic Games, Moscow (1980). Mult.

| | | | |
|---|---|---|---|
| 514 | 25c. Type **103** | 45 | 10 |
| 515 | 50c. Weightlifting | 65 | 10 |
| 516 | 75c. Athletics | 90 | 15 |
| 517 | $1 Football | 1·25 | 20 |
| 518 | $2 Yachting | 1·75 | 25 |
| 519 | $3 Swimming | 2·00 | 30 |
| 520 | $4 Boxing | 2·50 | 30 |
| 521 | $5 Cycling | 11·00 | 1·25 |

**MS**522 Two sheets: (a) 126×92 mm. $5 Athletics (different), $10 Boxing (different); (b) 92×126 mm. $15 As $5 Set of 2 sheets 16·00

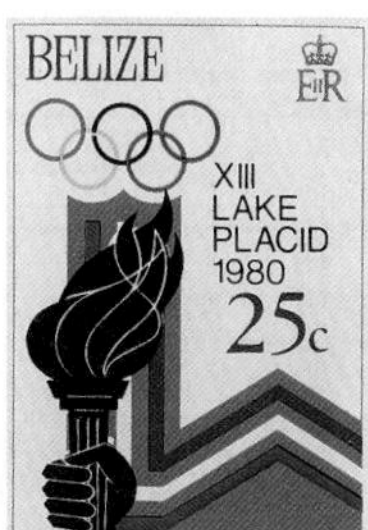


**104** Olympic Torch

**1979.** Winter Olympic Games, Lake Placid (1980). Multicoloured.

| | | | |
|---|---|---|---|
| 523 | 25c. Type **104** | 20 | 10 |
| 524 | 50c. Giant slalom | 45 | 15 |
| 525 | 75c. Figure-skating | 65 | 15 |
| 526 | $1 Downhill skiing | 80 | 15 |
| 527 | $2 Speed-skating | 1·60 | 20 |
| 528 | $3 Cross-country skiing | 2·50 | 30 |
| 529 | $4 Shooting | 3·00 | 40 |
| 530 | $5 Gold, Silver and Bronze medals | 3·50 | 45 |

**MS**531 Two sheets: (a) 127×90 mm. $5 Lighting the Olympic Flame, $10 Gold, Silver and Bronze medals (different); (b) 90×127 mm. $15 Olympic Torch (different) Set of 2 sheets 20·00

**105** Measled Cowrie

**1980.** Shells. Multicoloured.

| | | | |
|---|---|---|---|
| 532 | 1c. Type **105** | 65 | 10 |
| 533 | 2c. Callico clam | 80 | 10 |
| 534 | 3c. Altantic turkey wing (vert) | 90 | 10 |
| 535 | 4c. Leafy jewel box (vert) | 90 | 10 |
| 536 | 5c. Trochlear latirus | 90 | 10 |
| 537 | 10c. Alphabet cone (vert) | 1·25 | 10 |
| 538 | 15c. Cabrits murex (vert) | 1·75 | 10 |
| 539 | 20c. Stiff pen shell | 1·75 | 10 |
| 540 | 25c. Little knobbed scallop (vert) | 1·75 | 10 |
| 541 | 35c. Glory of the Atlantic cone (vert) | 2·00 | 10 |
| 542 | 45c. Sunrise tellin (vert) | 2·25 | 10 |
| 543 | 50c. "Leucozonia nassa leucozonalis" | 2·25 | 10 |
| 544 | 85c. Triangular typhis | 3·50 | 10 |
| 545 | $1 Queen or pink conch (vert) | 3·75 | 10 |
| 546 | $2 Rooster-tail conch (vert) | 6·00 | 30 |
| 547 | $5 True tulip | 8·50 | 50 |
| 548 | $10 Star arene | 10·00 | 90 |

**MS**549 Two sheets, each 125×90 mm. (a) Nos. 544 and 547. (b) Nos. 546 and 548 40·00 15·00

**106** Girl and Flower Arrangement

**1980.** International Year of the Child (1st issue). Multicoloured.

| | | | |
|---|---|---|---|
| 550 | 25c. Type **106** | 45 | 10 |
| 551 | 50c. Boy holding football | 70 | 10 |
| 552 | 75c. Boy with butterfly | 1·00 | 10 |
| 553 | $1 Girl holding doll | 1·00 | 10 |
| 554 | $1.50 Boy carrying basket of fruit | 1·50 | 15 |
| 555 | $2 Boy holding reticulated cowrie-helmet shell | 1·75 | 20 |
| 556 | $3 Girl holding posy | 2·25 | 25 |
| 557 | $4 Boy and girl wrapped in blanket | 2·50 | 30 |

**MS**558 130×95 mm. $5 Three children of different races. $5 "Madonna with Cat" (A. Dürer) (each 35×53 mm). 9·00

**MS**559 111×151 mm. $10 Children and Christmas tree (73×110 mm). 9·00

See also Nos. 583/91.

**1980.** No. 412 surch **10c**.

| | | | |
|---|---|---|---|
| 560 | 10c. on 25c. "Papilio thoas" | 1·25 | 1·25 |

**108** Jabiru

**1980.** Birds (4th series). Multicoloured.

| | | | |
|---|---|---|---|
| 561 | 10c. Type **108** | 7·00 | 2·75 |
| 562 | 25c. Barred antshrike | 8·00 | 2·75 |
| 563 | 35c. Northern royal flycatcher ("Royal Flycatcher") | 8·00 | 2·75 |
| 564 | 45c. White-necked puffbird | 8·00 | 3·00 |
| 565 | 50c. Ornate hawk-eagle | 8·00 | 3·00 |
| 566 | $1 Golden-masked tanager | 8·50 | 3·75 |

**MS**567 85×90 mm. $2 Type **108**, $3 As $1 32·00 18·00

**109** Speed Skating

**1980.** Winter Olympic Games, Lake Placid. Medal Winners. Multicoloured.

| | | | |
|---|---|---|---|
| 568 | 25c. Type **109** | 45 | 20 |
| 569 | 50c. Ice-hockey | 75 | 20 |
| 570 | 75c. Figure-skating | 80 | 20 |
| 571 | $1 Alpine-skiing | 1·10 | 20 |
| 572 | $1.50 Giant slalom (women) | 1·50 | 30 |
| 573 | $2 Speed-skating (women) | 1·75 | 40 |
| 574 | $3 Cross-country skiing | 2·25 | 50 |
| 575 | $5 Giant slalom | 3·50 | 65 |

**MS**576 Two sheets: (a) 126×91 mm. $5 Type **109**; $10 Type **109**; (b) 91×126 mm. $10 As 75 c. Set of 2 sheets 16·00

**1980.** "ESPAMER" International Stamp Exhibition, Madrid. Nos. 560/5 optd **BELIZE ESPAMER '80 MADRID 3-12 OCT 1980** and emblem (Nos. 577/9) or surch also.

| | | | |
|---|---|---|---|
| 577 | 10c. Type **107** | 7·50 | 2·75 |
| 578 | 25c. Barred antshrike | 8·00 | 3·00 |
| 579 | 35c. Northern royal flycatcher | 8·00 | 3·00 |
| 580 | 40c. on 45c. White-necked puffbird | 8·50 | 3·25 |
| 581 | 40c. on 50c. Ornate hawk eagle | 8·50 | 3·25 |

| | | | |
|---|---|---|---|
| 582 | 40c. on $1 Golden-masked tanager | 9·00 | 3·25 |

**111** Witch in Sky

**1980.** International Year of the Child (2nd issue). "Sleeping Beauty".

| | | | | |
|---|---|---|---|---|
| 583 | **111** | 25c. multicoloured | 2·25 | 15 |
| 584 | - | 40c. multicoloured | 2·50 | 15 |
| 585 | - | 50c. multicoloured | 2·75 | 15 |
| 586 | - | 75c. multicoloured | 3·00 | 20 |
| 587 | - | $1 multicoloured | 3·00 | 25 |
| 588 | - | $1.50 multicoloured | 3·50 | 40 |
| 589 | - | $3 multicoloured | 4·50 | 50 |
| 590 | - | $4 multicoloured | 4·50 | 55 |

**MS**591 Two sheets: (a) 82×110 mm. $8 "Paumgartner Altar-piece" (Dürer); (b) 110×82 mm. $5 Marriage ceremony, $5 Sleeping Beauty and Prince on horseback Set of 2 sheets 24·00

DESIGNS: 40c. to $4, Illustrations from the story.

**112** H.M. Queen Elizabeth the Queen Mother

**1980.** 80th Birthday of H.M. Queen Elizabeth the Queen Mother.

| | | | | |
|---|---|---|---|---|
| 592 | **112** | $1 multicoloured | 3·00 | 65 |

**MS**593 82×110 mm, $5 As Type **112** (41×32 mm) 14·00 4·75

**113** The Annunciation

**1980.** Christmas. Multicoloured.

| | | | |
|---|---|---|---|
| 594 | 25c. Type **113** | 65 | 10 |
| 595 | 50c. Bethlehem | 1·25 | 10 |
| 596 | 75c. The Holy Family | 1·50 | 10 |
| 597 | $1 The Nativity | 1·60 | 15 |
| 598 | $1.50 The Flight into Egypt | 1·75 | 25 |
| 599 | $2 Shepherds following the Star | 2·00 | 35 |
| 600 | $3 Virgin, Child and Angel | 2·25 | 40 |
| 601 | $4 Adoration of the Kings | 2·25 | 45 |

**MS**602 Two sheets, each 82×111 mm: (a) $5 As $1: (b) $10 As $3 Set of 2 sheets 14·00

**1981.** "WIPA" International Stamp Exhibition, Vienna. Nos. 598 and 601 surch.

| | | | |
|---|---|---|---|
| 603 | $1 on $1.50 The Flight into Egypt | 10·00 | 2·00 |
| 604 | $2 on $4 Adoration of the Kings | 11·00 | 3·00 |

**MS**605 82×111 mm. $2 on $10 Virgin, Child and Angel 18·00 6·00

**115** Paul Harris (founder)

**1981.** 75th Anniv of Rotary International. Mult.

| | | | |
|---|---|---|---|
| 606 | 25c. Type **115** | 2·50 | 25 |
| 607 | 50c. Emblems of Rotary activities | 3·00 | 35 |
| 608 | $1 75th Anniversary emblem | 3·50 | 65 |
| 609 | $1.50 Educational scholarship programme (horiz) | 4·25 | 1·00 |
| 610 | $2 "Project Hippocrates" | 4·75 | 1·40 |
| 611 | $3 Emblems | 6·50 | 2·00 |
| 612 | $5 Emblems and handshake (horiz) | 7·50 | 3·25 |

**MS**613 Two sheets: (a) 95×130 mm. $10 As 50c. (b) 130×95 mm, $5 As $1, $10 As $2 Set of 2 sheets 40·00

**116** Coat of Arms of Prince of Wales

**1981.** Royal Wedding. Mult. (a) Size 22×38 mm.

| | | | |
|---|---|---|---|
| 614 | 50c. Type **116** | 45 | 50 |
| 615 | $1 Prince Charles in military uniform | 80 | 90 |
| 616 | $1.50 Royal couple | 1·25 | 1·50 |

(b) Size 25×42 mm, with gold borders.

| | | | |
|---|---|---|---|
| 617 | 50c. Type **116** | 45 | 30 |
| 618 | $1 As No. 615 | 80 | 50 |
| 619 | $1.50 As No. 616 | 1·25 | 70 |

**MS**620 145×85 mm. $3×3 As Nos 614/16, but 30×47 mm. P 14 2·50 4·25

**1981.** No. 538 surch 10c.

| | | | |
|---|---|---|---|
| 621 | 10c. on 15c. "Murex cabritii" | 3·50 | 3·75 |

**118** Athletics

**1981.** History of the Olympics. Multicoloured.

| | | | |
|---|---|---|---|
| 622 | 85c. Type **118** | 2·50 | 30 |
| 623 | $1 Cycling | 9·00 | 50 |
| 624 | $1.50 Boxing | 3·25 | 50 |
| 625 | $2 1984 Games–Los Angeles and Sarajevo | 4·25 | 50 |
| 626 | $3 Baron de Coubertin | 5·00 | 60 |
| 627 | $5 Olympic Flame | 6·00 | 70 |

**MS**628 Two sheets, each 175×123 mm: (a) $5 As $3, $10 As $5 (each 35×53 mm). P13½; (b) $15 As $2 (45×67 mm). P 14½. Set of 2 sheets 45·00

**1981.** Independence Commemoration (1st issue). Optd **Independence 21 Sept., 1981.** (a) On Nos. 532/44 and 546/8.

| | | | |
|---|---|---|---|
| 629 | 1c. Type **105** | 1·00 | 10 |
| 630 | 2c. Callico clam | 1·00 | 10 |
| 631 | 3c. Atlantic turkey wing (vert) | 1·00 | 10 |
| 632 | 4c. Leafy jewel box (vert) | 1·00 | 10 |
| 633 | 5c. Trochlear latirus | 1·25 | 10 |
| 634 | 10c. Alphabet cone (vert) | 1·50 | 10 |
| 635 | 15c. Cabrits murex (vert) | 2·25 | 10 |
| 636 | 20c. Stiff pen shell | 2·25 | 15 |
| 637 | 25c. Little knobbed scallop (vert) | 2·50 | 25 |
| 638 | 35c. Glory of the Atlantic cone | 2·50 | 30 |
| 639 | 45c. Sunrise tellin (vert) | 3·00 | 40 |
| 640 | 50c. "Leucozonia nassa leucozonalis" | 3·00 | 40 |
| 641 | 85c. Triangular typhis | 4·75 | 90 |
| 642 | $2 Rooster-tail conch (vert) | 9·00 | 2·50 |
| 643 | $5 True tulip | 11·00 | 5·50 |
| 644 | $10 Star arene | 13·00 | 9·50 |

**MS**645 Two sheets, each 126×91 mm; (a) Nos. 641 and 643; (b) Nos. 642 and 644 Set of 2 sheets 40·00

(b) On Nos. 606/12.

| | | | |
|---|---|---|---|
| 646 | 25c. Type **115** | 2·75 | 25 |
| 647 | 50c. Emblems of Rotary activities | 3·00 | 35 |
| 648 | $1 75th Anniversary emblem | 3·50 | 65 |
| 649 | $1.50 Educational scholarship programme | 4·25 | 1·25 |
| 650 | $2 "Project Hippocrates" | 5·00 | 1·60 |

651 $3 Emblems 7·00 2·50
652 $5 Emblems and hand-shake 8·00 3·75
**MS**653 Two sheets: (a) 95×130 mm. $10 As 50c.; (b) 130×95 mm. $5 As $1, $10 As $2 Set of 2 sheets 40·00

See also Nos. 657/63.

**1981.** "ESPAMER" International Stamp Exhibition, Buenos Aires. No. 609 surch **$1 ESPAMER 81 BUENOS AIRES 13-22 NOV** and emblem.
654 $1 on $1.50 Educational scholarship programme 13·00 3·50
**MS**655 95×130 mm. $1 on $5 75th anniversary emblem, $1 on $10 "Project Hippocrates" 18·00 9·00

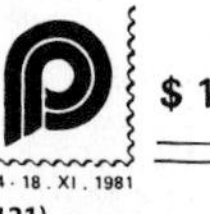

**(121)**

**1981.** "Philatelia 81" International Stamp Exhibition, Frankfurt. No. **MS**549 surch with T **121**.
**MS**656 Two sheets, each 125×90 mm: (a) $1 on 85c. "Tripterotyphis triangularis", $1 on $5 "Fasciolaria tulipa"; (b) $1 on $2 "Strombus gallus", $1 on $10 "Arene cruentata" Set of 2 sheets 65·00

**122** Black Orchid

**1981.** Independence Commemoration (2nd issue). Multicoloured.
657 10c. Belize Coat of Arms (horiz) 2·25 20
658 35c. Map of Belize 5·00 40
659 50c. Type **122** 9·50 1·25
660 85c. Baird's tapir (horiz) 3·00 1·25
661 $1 Mahogany tree 2·50 1·25
662 $2 Keel-billed toucan (horiz) 14·00 4·00
**MS**663 130×98 mm. $5 As 10c. 18·00 6·50

**123** Uruguayan Footballer

**1981.** World Cup Football Championship, Spain (1st issue). Multicoloured.
664 10c. Type **123** 2·25 20
665 25c. Italian footballer 3·25 20
666 50c. German footballer 4·00 45
667 $1 Brazilian footballer 5·00 70
668 $1.50 Argentinian footballer 6·50 1·50
669 $2 English footballer 7·00 1·75
**MS**670 Two sheets: (a) 145×115 mm. $2 "SPAIN '82" logo; (b) 155×115 mm. $3 Footballer (46×76 mm) Set of 2 sheets 30·00 7·50

See also Nos. 721/7.

**124** H.M.S. "Centurion" (frigate)

**1981.** Sailing Ships. Multicoloured.
671 10c. Type **124** 3·25 40
672 25c. "Madagascar" (1837) 4·75 50
673 35c. Brig "Whitby" (1838) 5·50 55
674 55c. "China" (1838) 6·00 85
675 85c. "Swiftsure" (1850) 7·50 1·25
676 $2 "Windsor Castle" (1857) 11·00 3·00
**MS**677 110×87 mm. $5 Ships in battle 32·00 8·50

**1982.** "ESSEN '82" Int Stamp Exn, West Germany. Nos. 662 and 669 surch **$1 ESSEN 82**.
678 $1 on $2 Keel-billed toucan 11·00 2·75
679 $1 on $2 English footballer 11·00 2·75

**126** Princess Diana

**1982.** 21st Birthday of Princess of Wales. (a) Size 22×38 mm.
680 **126** 50c. multicoloured 1·60 45
681 - $1 multicoloured 2·00 75
682 - $1.50 multicoloured 2·00 1·50

(b) Size 25×43 mm.
683 **126** 50c. multicoloured 1·60 30
684 - $1 multicoloured 2·00 60
685 - $1.50 multicoloured 2·00 1·10
**MS**686 145×85 mm. $3×3 As Nos. 680/2, but 30×47 mm. 2·75 3·00

DESIGNS: Portraits of Princess of Wales with different backgrounds.

**127** Lighting Campfire

**1982.** 125th Birth Anniv of Lord Baden-Powell. Multicoloured.
687 10c. Type **127** 1·75 20
688 25c. Bird watching 5·00 30
689 35c. Three scouts, one playing guitar 2·75 30
690 50c. Hiking 3·25 55
691 85c. Scouts with flag 4·50 1·00
692 $2 Saluting 5·00 2·50
**MS**693 Two sheets: each 85×115 mm: (a) $2 Scout with flag; (b) $3 Portrait of Lord Baden-Powell Set of 2 sheets 35·00 13·00

**128** "Gorgonia ventalina"

**1982.** 1st Anniv of Independence. Marine Life. Multicoloured.
694 10c. Type **128** 2·25 20
695 35c. "Carpiuis corallinus" 3·50 20
696 50c. "Plexaura flexuasa" 4·00 45
697 85c. "Candylactis gigantea" 4·25 60
698 $1 "Stenopus hispidus" 5·50 90
699 $2 Sergeant major 6·50 1·60
**MS**700 130×98 mm. $5 "Schyllarides aequinoclialis" 32·00 10·00

**1982.** "BELGICA 82" International Stamp Exhibition, Brussels. Nos. 687/92 optd BELGICA 82 INT. YEAR OF THE CHILD SIR ROWLAND HILL 1795 1879 Picasso CENTENARY OF BIRTH and emblems.
701 10c. Type **127** 2·75 40
702 25c. Bird watching 7·00 1·25
703 35c. Three scouts, one playing guitar 3·75 1·00
704 50c. Hiking 4·25 1·50
705 85c. Scouts with flag 10·00 2·75
706 $2 Saluting 11·00 7·50

**1982.** Birth of Prince William of Wales (1st issue). Nos. 680/5 optd **BIRTH OF H.R.H. PRINCE WILLIAM ARTHUR PHILIP LOUIS 21ST JUNE 1982**. (a) Size 22×38 mm.
707 50c. multicoloured 45 45
708 $1 multicoloured 55 60
709 $1.50 multicoloured 75 85

(b) Size 25×43 mm.
710 50c. multicoloured 45 45
711 $1 multicoloured 55 60
712 $1.50 multicoloured 75 85
**MS**713 145×85 mm. $3×3 as Nos. 707/9, but 30x477mm 3·25 3·50

**1982.** Birth of Prince William of Wales (2nd issue). Nos. 614/19 optd **BIRTH OF H.R.H. PRINCE WILLIAM ARTHUR PHILIP LOUIS 21ST JUNE 1982**. (a) Size 22×38 mm.
714 50c. Type **116** 3·25 1·00
715 $1 Prince Charles in military uniform 6·00 2·00
716 $1.50 Royal couple 8·50 3·00

(b) Size 25×42 mm.
717 50c. Type **116** 50 50
718 $1 As No. 715 70 70
719 $1.50 As No. 716 1·10 1·10
**MS**720 145×85 mm. $3×3 As Nos. 714/16 but 30×47 mm 7·50 7·00

**131** Scotland v New Zealand

**1982.** World Cup Football Championship, Spain (2nd issue). Multicoloured.
721 20c.+10c. Type **131** 2·75 1·50
722 30c.+15c. Scotland v New Zealand (different) 2·75 1·50
723 40c.+20c. Kuwait v France 3·00 1·50
724 60c.+50c. Italy v Brazil 3·50 1·75
725 $1+50c. France v Northern Ireland 4·25 2·00
726 $1.50+75c. Austria v Chile 5·00 2·50
**MS**727 Two sheets: (a) 91×137 mm. $1+50c. Germany v Italy (50×70 mm); (b) 122×116 mm. $2+$1 England v France (50×70 mm) Set of 2 sheets 20·00 9·50

**133** Belize Cathedral

**1983.** Visit of Pope John Paul II.
729 **133** 50c. multicoloured 2·75 1·50
**MS**730 135×110 mm. $2.50, Pope John Paul II (30×47 mm.) 23·00 8·00

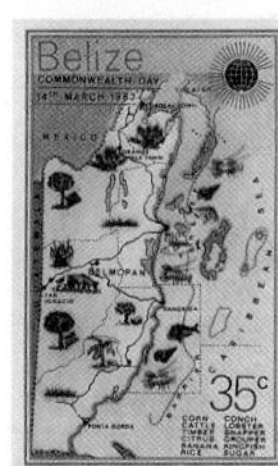

**134** Map of Belize

**1983.** Commonwealth Day. Multicoloured.
731 35c. Type **134** 35 35
732 50c. "Maya Stella" from Lamanai Indian church (horiz) 40 50
733 85c. Supreme Court Building (horiz) 50 75
734 $2 University Centre, Belize (horiz) 85 2·50

**1983.** No. 658 surch 10c.
735 10c. on 35c. Map of Belize 32·00

**136** De Lana-Terzis "Aerial Ship", 1670

**1983.** Bicentenary of Manned Flight. Multicoloured.
736 10c. Type **136** 2·50 65
737 25c. De Gusmao's "La Passarole", 1709 3·25 70
738 50c. Guyton de Morveau's balloon with oars, 1784 3·50 1·10
739 85c. Airship 4·25 1·25
740 $1 Airship "Clement Bayard" 4·50 1·60
741 $1.50 Beardmore airship R-34 5·00 3·25
**MS**742 Two sheets: (a) 125×84 mm. $3 Charles Green's balloon "Royal Vauxhall"; (b) 115×128 mm. $3 Montgolfier balloon, 1783 (vert) Set of 2 sheets 30·00 6·00

**1983.** Nos. 662 and 699 surch **$1.25**.
743 $1.25 on $2 Keel-billed toucan 18·00 12·00
744 $1.25 on $2 Sergeant major 6·00 8·50

**1983.** No. 541 surch **10c**.
746 10c. on 35c. Glory of the Atlantic cone 45·00

**141** Altun Ha

**1983.** Maya Monuments. Multicoloured.
747 10c. Type **141** 10 10
748 15c. Xunantunich 10 10
749 75c. Cerros 30 40
750 $3 Lamanal 70 1·75
**MS**751 102×72 mm. $3 Xunantunich (different) 1·00 1·75

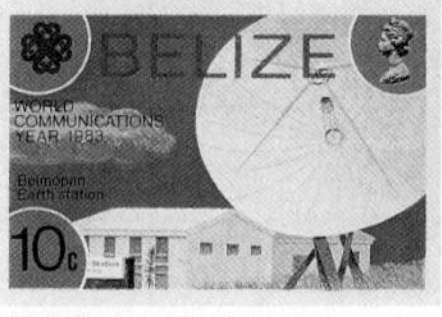

**142** Belmopan Earth Station

**1983.** World Communications Year. Multicoloured.
752 10c. Type **142** 30 10
753 15c. "Telstar 2" 40 25
754 75c. U.P.U. logo 70 1·75
755 $2 M.V. "Heron H" mail service 1·25 4·50

**143** Jaguar Cub

**1983.** The Jaguar. Multicoloured.
756 5c. Type **143** 30 75
757 10c. Adult jaguar 35 45
758 85c. Jaguar in river 1·40 3·00
759 $1 Jaguar on rock 1·50 3·25
**MS**760 102×72 mm. $3 Jaguar in tree (44×28 mm). P 13½×14 1·50 2·50

**144** Pope John Paul II

**1983.** Christmas.
761 **144** 10c. multicoloured 25 10
762 **144** 15c. multicoloured 25 10
763 **144** 75c. multicoloured 50 60
764 **144** $2 multicoloured 80 1·40
**MS**765 102×72 mm. $3 multicoloured 1·50 4·00

**145** Four-eyed Butterflyfish

**1984.** Marine Life from the Belize Coral Reef. Multicoloured.
766 1c. Type **145** 25 1·25
767 2c. Cushion star 30 1·00
768 3c. Flower coral 35 1·00
769 4c. Royal gramma ("Fairy basslet") 40 1·00
770 5c. Spanish hogfish 45 1·00
771 6c. Star-eyed hermit crab 45 1·25
772a 10c. Sea fans and fire sponge 50 35
773a 15c. Blue-headed wrasse 70 60
774a 25c. Blue-striped grunt 80 80
775a 50c. Coral crab 1·00 1·75
776a 60c. Tube sponge 1·00 1·75
777 75c. Brain coral 1·00 1·50
778 $1 Yellow-tailed snapper 1·00 1·25
779 $2 Common lettuce slug 1·00 55
780 $5 Three-spotted damselfish 1·25 70

781 $10 Rock beauty 1·50 1·10

**1984.** Visit of the Archbishop of Canterbury. Nos. 772 and 775 optd **VISIT OF THE LORD ARCHBISHOP OF CANTERBURY 8th-11th MARCH 1984**.

782 10c. Sea fans and fire sponge 1·00 50
783 50c. Coral crab 1·75 2·00

**147** Shooting

**1984.** Olympic Games, Los Angeles. Multicoloured. (a) As T 147.

784 25c. Type **147** 30 25
785 75c. Boxing 50 70
786 $1 Marathon 60 90
787 $2 Cycling 2·75 2·75
**MS**788 101×72 mm. $3 Statue of discus thrower 1·60 3·00

(b) Similar designs to T 147 but Royal cypher replaced by Queen's Head.

789 5c. Marathon 20 90
790 20c. Sprinting 25 90
791 25c. Shot-putting 25 90
792 $2 Olympic torch 35 1·25

**148** British Honduras 1866 1s. Stamp

**1984.** "Ausipex" International Stamp Exhibition, Melbourne. Multicoloured.

793 15c. Type **148** 25 15
794 30c. British mail coach, 1784 35 25
795 65c. Sir Rowland Hill and Penny Black 65 65
796 75c. British Honduras railway locomotive, 1910 70 75
797 $2 Royal Exhibition Buildings, Melbourne (46×28 mm) 1·00 2·25
**MS**798 103×73 mm. $3 Australia 1932 Sydney Harbour Bridge 5s. and British Honduras 1866 1s. stamps (44×28 mm). P 13½×14 1·10 2·00

**149** Prince Albert

**1984.** 500th Anniv (1985) of British Royal House of Tudor. Multicoloured.

799 50c. Type **149** 25 45
800 50c. Queen Victoria 25 45
801 75c. King George VI 30 55
802 75c. Queen Elizabeth the Queen Mother 30 55
803 $1 Princess of Wales 40 75
804 $1 Prince of Wales 40 75
**MS**805 147×97 mm. $1.50, Prince Philip; $1.50, Queen Elizabeth II 1·25 2·00

**150** White-fronted Amazon ("White-fronted Parrot")

**1984.** Parrots. Multicoloured.

806 $1 Type **150** 1·75 2·25
807 $1 White-capped parrot (horiz) 1·75 2·25
808 $1 Mealy amazon ("Mealy Parrot") (horiz) 1·75 2·25
809 $1 Red-lored amazon ("Red-lored Parrot") 1·75 2·25
**MS**810 102×73 mm. $3 Scarlet macaw 3·25 4·00

Nos. 806/9 were issued together, se-tenant, forming a composite design.

**151** Effigy Censer, 1450 (Santa Rita Site)

**1984.** Maya Artefacts. Multicoloured.

811 25c. Type **151** 30 25
812 75c. Vase, 675 (Actun Chapat) 60 80
813 $1 Tripod vase, 500 (Santa Rita site) 65 1·00
814 $2 Sun god Kinich Ahau, 600 (Altun Ha site) 90 2·50

**152** Governor-General inspecting Girl Guides

**1985.** International Youth Year and 75th Anniv of Girl Guides Movement. Multicoloured.

815 25c. Type **152** 30 15
816 50c. Girl Guides camping 45 30
817 90c. Checking map on hike 60 45
818 $1.25 Students in laboratory 70 60
819 $2 Lady Baden-Powell (founder) 90 75

**153** White-tailed Kite

**1985.** Birth Bicentenary of John J. Audubon (ornithologist). Designs showing original paintings. Multicoloured.

820 10c. Type **153** 50 60
821 15c. Ruby-crowned kinglet ("Cuvier's Kinglet") (horiz) 50 60
822 25c. Painted bunting 60 60
822a 60c. As 25c. 24·00 9·00
823 75c. Belted kingfisher 60 1·40
824 $1 Common cardinal ("Northern Cardinal") 60 2·25
825 $3 Long-billed curlew (horiz) 1·00 3·00
**MS**826 139×99 mm. $5 "John James Audubon" (John Syme) 2·50 2·00

**154** The Queen Mother with Princess Elizabeth, 1928

**1985.** Life and Times of Queen Elizabeth the Queen Mother. Multicoloured.

827 10c. Type **154** 10 10
828 15c. The Queen Mother, 1980 10 10
829 75c. Waving to the crowd, 1982 40 40
830 $5 Four generations of Royal Family at Prince William's Christening 1·50 2·75
**MS**831 Two sheets, each 138×98 mm. (a) $2 The Queen Mother with Prince Henry (from photo by Lord Snowdon) (38×50 mm): (b) $5 The Queen Mother, 1984 (38×50 mm) Set of 2 sheets 3·75 4·50

**1985.** Inauguration of New Government. Nos. 772/3 and 775 optd **INAUGURATION OF NEW GOVERNMENT – 21st. DECEMBER 1984.**

832 10c. Sea fans and fire sponge 1·50 60
833 15c. Blue-headed wrasse 1·50 60
834 50c. Coral crab 2·00 3·50

**156** British Honduras 1935 Silver Jubilee 25c. stamp and King George V with Queen Mary in Carriage

**1985.** 50th Anniv of First Commonwealth Omnibus Issue. Designs showing British Honduras/Belize stamps. Multicoloured.

835 50c. Type **156** 55 85
836 50c. 1937 Coronation 3c., and King George VI and Queen Elizabeth in Coronation robes 55 85
837 50c. 1946 Victory 3c. and Victory celebrations 55 85
838 50c. 1948 Royal Silver Wedding 4c. and King George VI and Queen Elizabeth at Westminster Abbey service 55 85
839 50c. 1953 Coronation 4c. and Queen Elizabeth II in Coronation robes 55 85
840 50c. 1966 Churchill 25c., Sir Winston Churchill and fighter aircraft 55 85
841 50c. 1972 Royal Silver Wedding 50c. and 1948 Wedding photograph 55 85
842 50c. 1973 Royal Wedding 50c. and Princess Anne and Capt. Mark Phillips at their Wedding 55 85
843 50c. 1977 Silver Jubilee $2 and Queen Elizabeth II during tour 55 85
844 50c. 1978 25th anniversary of Coronation 75c. and Imperial Crown 55 85
**MS**845 138×98 mm. $5 Queen Elizabeth in Coronation robes (38×50 mm) 4·50 4·50

**157** Mounted Postboy and Early Letter to Belize

**1985.** 350th Anniv of British Post Office. Mult.

846 10c. Type **157** 50 25
847 15c. "Hinchinbrook II" (sailing packet) engaging "Grand Turk" (American privateer) 70 25
848 25c. "Duke of Marlborough II" (sailing packet) 85 30
849 75c. "Diana" (packet) 1·40 1·50
850 $1 Falmouth packet ship 1·40 2·00
851 $3 "Conway" (mail paddle-steamer) 2·25 5·50

**1985.** Commonwealth Heads of Government Meeting, Nassau, Bahamas. Nos. 827/30 optd **COMMONWEALTH SUMMIT CONFERENCE, BAHAMAS 16th-22nd OCTOBER 1985.**

852 10c. Type **154** 30 30
853 15c. The Queen Mother, 1980 40 35
854 75c. Waving to the crowd, 1982 80 80
855 $4 Four generations of Royal Family at Prince William's christening 2·00 3·75
**MS**856 Two sheets, each 138×98 mm. (a) $2 The Queen Mother with Prince Henry (from photo by Lord Snowdon) (38×50 mm): (b) $5 The Queen Mother, 1984 (38×50 mm) Set of 2 sheets 2·75 3·50

**1985.** 80th Anniv of Rotary International. Nos. 815/19 optd **80TH ANNIVERSARY OF ROTARY INTERNATIONAL**.

857 25c. Type **152** 70 40
858 50c. Girl Guides camping 1·25 75
859 90c. Checking map on hike 1·75 2·00
860 $1.25 Students in laboratory 2·25 2·75
861 $2 Lady Baden-Powell (founder) 2·75 3·50

**160** Royal Standard and Belize Flag

**1985.** Royal Visit. Multicoloured.

862 25c. Type **160** 1·00 95
863 75c. Queen Elizabeth II 1·25 2·00
864 $4 Royal Yacht "Britannia" (81×39 mm) 4·50 4·00
**MS**865 138×98 mm. $5 Queen Elizabeth II (38×50 mm). 5·00 5·50

**161** Mountie in Canoe (Canada)

**1985.** Christmas. 30th Anniv of Disneyland, U.S.A. Designs showing dolls from "It's a Small World" exhibition. Multicoloured.

866 1c. Type **161** 10 15
867 2c. Indian chief and squaw (U.S.A.) 10 15
868 3c. Incas climbing Andes (South America) 10 15
869 4c. Africans beating drums (Africa) 10 15
870 5c. Snake-charmer and dancer (India and Far East) 10 15
871 6c. Boy and girl with donkey (Belize) 10 15
872 50c. Musician and dancer (Balkans) 1·75 1·50
873 $1.50 Boys with camel (Egypt and Saudi Arabia) 2·75 3·50
874 $3 Woman and girls playing with kite (Japan) 3·75 5·00
**MS**875 127×102 mm. $4 Beefeater and castle (Great Britain). P 13½×14 5·50 8·00

**1985.** World Cup Football Championship, Mexico (1986) (1st issue). Nos. 835/44 optd **PRE "WORLD CUP FOOTBALL" MEXICO 1986** and trophy.

876 50c. Type **156** 75 90
877 50c. 1937 Coronation 3c., and King George VI and Queen Elizabeth in Coronation robes 75 90
878 50c. Victory 3c., and Victory celebrations 75 90
879 50c. 1948 Royal Silver Wedding 4c., and King George VI and Queen Elizabeth at Westminster Abbey service 75 90
880 50c. 1953 Coronation 4c., and Queen Elizabeth II in Coronation robes 75 90
881 50c. 1966 Churchill 25c., Sir Winston Churchill and fighter aircraft 75 90
882 50c. 1972 Royal Silver Wedding 50c. and 1948 wedding photograph 75 90
883 50c. 1973 Royal Wedding 5c., and Princess Anne and Capt. Mark Phillips at their Wedding 75 90
884 50c. 1977 Silver Jubilee $2 and Queen Elizabeth II during tour 75 90
885 50c. 1978 25th anniv of Coronation 75c. and Imperial Crown 75 90
**MS**886 138×98 mm. $5 Queen Elizabeth II in Coronation robes 4·25 4·25

See also Nos. 936/40.

163 Indian Costume

**1986.** Costumes of Belize. Multicoloured.

| | | | |
|---|---|---|---|
| 887 | 5c. Type **163** | 75 | 30 |
| 888 | 10c. Maya | 80 | 30 |
| 889 | 15c. Garifuna | 1·00 | 35 |
| 890 | 25c. Creole | 1·25 | 35 |
| 891 | 50c. Chinese | 1·75 | 1·25 |
| 892 | 75c. Lebanese | 2·00 | 2·00 |
| 893 | $1 European c. 1900 | 2·00 | 2·50 |
| 894 | $2 Latin | 2·75 | 3·75 |
| **MS**895 | 139×98 mm. Amerindian (38×50 mm.) | 6·00 | 7·00 |

**164** Pope Pius X

**1986.** Easter. 20th-century Popes. Multicoloured.

| | | | |
|---|---|---|---|
| 896 | 50c. Type **164** | 1·40 | 1·50 |
| 897 | 50c. Benedict XV | 1·40 | 1·50 |
| 898 | 50c. Pius XI | 1·40 | 1·50 |
| 899 | 50c. Pius XII | 1·40 | 1·50 |
| 900 | 50c. John XXIII | 1·40 | 1·50 |
| 901 | 50c. Paul VI | 1·40 | 1·50 |
| 902 | 50c. John Paul I | 1·40 | 1·50 |
| 903 | 50c. John Paul II | 1·40 | 1·50 |
| **MS**904 | 147×92 mm. $4 Pope John Paul II preaching (vert). | 11·00 | 10·00 |

**165** Princess Elizabeth aged Three

**1986.** 60th Birthday of Queen Elizabeth II. Mult.

| | | | |
|---|---|---|---|
| 905 | 25c. Type **165** | 40 | 55 |
| 906 | 50c. Queen wearing Imperial State Crown | 60 | 75 |
| 907 | 75c. At Trooping the Colour | 75 | 85 |
| 908 | $3 Queen wearing diadem | 1·40 | 2·25 |
| **MS**909 | 147×93 mm. $4 Queen Elizabeth II (37×50 mm) | 3·25 | 4·50 |

**166** Halley's Comet and Japanese "Planet A" Spacecraft

**1986.** Appearance of Halley's Comet. Multicoloured.

| | | | |
|---|---|---|---|
| 910 | 10c. Type **166** | 55 | 80 |
| 911 | 15c. Halley's Comet, 1910 | 65 | 90 |
| 912 | 50c. Comet and European "Giotto" spacecraft | 70 | 1·00 |
| 913 | 75c. Belize Weather Bureau | 90 | 1·00 |
| 914 | $1 Comet and U.S.A. space telescope | 1·25 | 1·40 |
| 915 | $2 Edmond Halley | 1·60 | 1·90 |
| **MS**916 | 147×93 mm. $4 Computer enhanced photograph of Comet (37×50 mm) | 6·50 | 8·50 |

**167** George Washington

**1986.** United States Presidents. Multicoloured.

| | | | |
|---|---|---|---|
| **MS**923 | 147×93 mm. $4 George Washington (different) | 3·75 | 5·50 |
| 917 | 10c. Type **167** | 35 | 60 |
| 918 | 20c. John Adams | 35 | 65 |
| 916 | 30c. Thomas Jefferson | 40 | 70 |
| 920 | 50c. James Madison | 50 | 70 |
| 921 | $1.50 James Monroe | 80 | 1·25 |
| 922 | $2 John Quincy Adams | 1·00 | 1·50 |

**168** Auguste Bartholdi (sculptor) and Statue's Head

**1986.** Centenary of Statue of Liberty. Multicoloured.

| | | | |
|---|---|---|---|
| 924 | 25c. Type **168** | 40 | 65 |
| 925 | 50c. Statue's head at U.S. Centennial Celebration, Philadelphia, 1876 | 55 | 85 |
| 926 | 75c. Unveiling ceremony, 1886 | 55 | 90 |
| 927 | $4 Statue of Liberty and flags of Belize and U.S.A. | 1·50 | 2·50 |
| **MS**928 | 147×92 mm. $4 Statue of Liberty and New York skyline (37×50 mm.) | 3·75 | 5·50 |

**169** British Honduras 1866 1s. Stamp

**1986.** "Ameripex" International Stamp Exhibition, Chicago. Multicoloured.

| | | | |
|---|---|---|---|
| 929 | 10c. Type **169** | 40 | 55 |
| 930 | 15c. 1981 Royal Wedding $1.50 stamps | 55 | 75 |
| 931 | 50c. U.S.A. 1918 24c. airmail inverted centre error | 75 | 80 |
| 932 | 75c. U.S.S. "Constitution" (frigate) | 75 | 1·10 |
| 933 | $1 Liberty Bell | 80 | 1·40 |
| 934 | $2 White House | 90 | 1·60 |
| **MS**935 | 147×93 mm. $4 Capitol, Washington (37×50 mm) | 3·25 | 4·50 |

**170** English and Brazilian Players

**1986.** World Cup Football Championship, Mexico (2nd issue). Multicoloured.

| | | | |
|---|---|---|---|
| 936 | 25c. Type **170** | 1·50 | 1·75 |
| 937 | 50c. Mexican player and Maya statues | 1·75 | 2·00 |
| 938 | 75c. Two Belizean players | 2·00 | 2·25 |
| 939 | $3 Aztec stone calendar | 2·25 | 2·50 |
| **MS**940 | 147×92 mm. $4 Flags of competing nations on two footballs (37×50 mm) | 6·50 | 8·00 |

**171** Miss Sarah Ferguson

**1986.** Royal Wedding. Multicoloured.

| | | | |
|---|---|---|---|
| 941 | 25c. Type **171** | 65 | 40 |
| 942 | 75c. Prince Andrew | 1·00 | 90 |
| 943 | $3 Prince Andrew and Miss Sarah Ferguson (92×41 mm) | 1·75 | 2·75 |
| **MS**944 | 155×106 mm. $1 Miss Sarah Ferguson (different). $3 Prince Andrew (different) | 4·25 | 6·00 |

**1986.** World Cup Football Championship Winners, Mexico. Nos. 936/9 optd **ARGENTINA – WINNERS 1986.**

| | | | |
|---|---|---|---|
| 945 | 25c. Type **170** | 1·75 | 2·00 |
| 946 | 50c. Mexican player and Maya statues | 2·00 | 2·25 |
| 947 | 75c. Two Belizean players | 2·25 | 2·50 |
| 948 | $3 Aztec stone calendar | 3·25 | 3·50 |
| **MS**949 | 147×92 mm. $4 Flags of competing nations on two footballs (37×50 mm) | 8·00 | 10·00 |

**1986.** "Stockholmia '86" International Stamp Exhibition, Sweden. Nos. 929/34 optd **STOCKHOLMIA 86** and emblem.

| | | | |
|---|---|---|---|
| 950 | 10c. Type **169** | 50 | 75 |
| 951 | 15c. 1981 Royal Wedding $1.50 stamp | 65 | 90 |
| 952 | 50c. U.S.A. 1918 24c. airmail inverted centre error | 80 | 1·10 |
| 953 | 75c. U.S.S. "Constitution" | 1·00 | 1·50 |
| 954 | $1 Liberty Bell | 1·25 | 1·60 |
| 955 | $2 White House | 1·60 | 1·90 |
| **MS**956 | 147×93 mm. $4 Capitol, Washington (37×50 mm) | 5·00 | 7·00 |

**174** Amerindian Girl

**1986.** International Peace Year. Multicoloured.

| | | | |
|---|---|---|---|
| 957 | 25c. Type **174** | 65 | 80 |
| 958 | 50c. European boy and girl | 80 | 1·10 |
| 959 | 75c. Japanese girl | 1·00 | 1·60 |
| 960 | $3 Indian boy and European girl | 1·75 | 2·75 |
| **MS**961 | 132×106 mm. $4 As 25c. but vert (35×47 mm) | 5·50 | 7·00 |

**175** "Amanita lilloi"

**1986.** Fungi and Toucans. Multicoloured.

| | | | |
|---|---|---|---|
| 962 | 5c. Type **175** | 1·50 | 1·25 |
| 963 | 10c. Keel-billed toucan | 1·75 | 1·60 |
| 964 | 20c. "Boletellus cubensis" | 2·00 | 1·75 |
| 965 | 25c. Collared aracari | 2·00 | 1·75 |
| 966 | 75c. "Psilocybe caerulescens" | 2·25 | 2·00 |
| 967 | $1 Emerald toucanet | 2·25 | 2·00 |
| 968 | $1.25 Crimson-rumped toucanet ("Crimson-rumped Toucan") | 2·50 | 2·25 |
| 969 | $2 "Russula puiggarii" | 2·50 | 2·50 |

**176** Jose Carioca

**1986.** Christmas. Designs showing Walt Disney cartoon characters in scenes from "Saludos Amigos". Multicoloured.

| | | | |
|---|---|---|---|
| 970 | 2c. Type **176** | 20 | 20 |
| 971 | 3c. Jose Carioca, Panchito and Donald Duck | 20 | 20 |
| 972 | 4c. Daisy Duck as Rio Carnival dancer | 20 | 20 |
| 973 | 5c. Mickey and Minnie Mouse as musician and dancer | 20 | 20 |
| 974 | 6c. Jose Carioca using umbrella as flute | 20 | 20 |
| 975 | 50c. Donald Duck and Panchito | 1·00 | 1·75 |
| 976 | 65c. Joe Carioca and Donald Duck playing hide and seek | 1·25 | 2·00 |
| 977 | $1.35 Donald Duck playing maracas | 2·00 | 3·25 |
| 978 | $2 Goofy as matador | 2·75 | 3·75 |
| **MS**979 | 131×111 mm. $4 Donald Duck | 9·00 | 11·00 |

**177** Princess Elizabeth in Wedding Dress, 1947

**1987.** Royal Ruby Wedding. Multicoloured.

| | | | |
|---|---|---|---|
| 980 | 25c. Type **177** | 25 | 20 |
| 981 | 75c. Queen and Duke of Edinburgh, 1972 | 45 | 50 |
| 982 | $1 Queen on her 60th birthday | 50 | 60 |
| 983 | $4 In Garter robes | 1·00 | 2·00 |
| **MS**984 | 171×112 mm. $6 Queen and Duke of Edinburgh (44×50 mm) | 6·50 | 7·50 |

**178** "America II", 1983

**1987.** America's Cup Yachting Championship. Multicoloured.

| | | | |
|---|---|---|---|
| 985 | 25c. Type **178** | 30 | 25 |
| 986 | 75c. "Stars and Stripes", 1987 | 40 | 50 |
| 987 | $1 "Australia II", 1983 | 50 | 60 |
| 988 | $4 "White Crusader" | 1·00 | 2·00 |
| **MS**989 | 171×112 mm. $6 Sails of Australia II" (44×50 mm.) | 5·00 | 7·50 |

**179** "Mother and Child"

**1987.** Wood Carvings by George Gabb. Mult.

| | | | |
|---|---|---|---|
| 990 | 25c. Type **179** | 15 | 25 |
| 991 | 75c. "Standing Form" | 35 | 50 |
| 992 | $1 "Love-doves" | 40 | 60 |
| 993 | $4 "Depiction of Music" | 1·10 | 2·00 |
| **MS**994 | 173×114 mm. $6 "African Heritage" (44×50 mm.) | 4·25 | 7·00 |

**180** Black-handed Spider Monkey

**1987.** Primates. Multicoloured.

| | | | |
|---|---|---|---|
| 995 | 25c. Type **180** | 25 | 20 |
| 996 | 75c. Black howler monkey | 40 | 55 |
| 997 | $1 Spider monkeys with baby | 45 | 65 |
| 998 | $4 Two black howler monkeys | 1·10 | 2·25 |
| **MS**999 | 171×112 mm. $6 Young spider monkey (44×50 mm.) | 5·50 | 8·00 |

**181** Guides on Parade

**1987.** 50th Anniv of Girl Guide Movement in Belize. Multicoloured.

| | | | |
|---|---|---|---|
| 1000 | 25c. Type **181** | 45 | 20 |
| 1001 | 75c. Brownie camp | 80 | 1·00 |
| 1002 | $1 Guide camp | 1·00 | 1·25 |
| 1003 | $4 Olave, Lady Baden-Powell | 3·00 | 5·00 |
| **MS**1004 | 173×114 mm. $6 As $4 but vert (44×50 mm) | 4·00 | 6·50 |

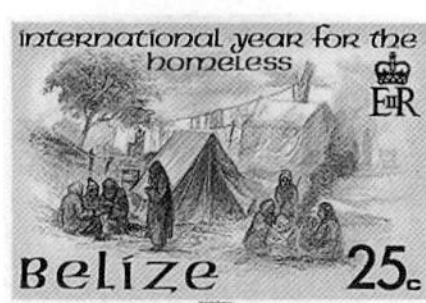

**182** Indian Refugee Camp

**1987.** Int Year of Shelter for the Homeless. Mult.

| | | | |
|---|---|---|---|
| 1005 | 25c. Type **182** | 50 | 25 |
| 1006 | 75c. Filipino family and slum | 90 | 90 |
| 1007 | $1 Family in Middle East shanty town | 1·10 | 1·25 |
| 1008 | $4 Building modern house in Belize | 2·00 | 4·50 |

**183** "Laelia euspatha"

**1987.** Christmas. Orchids. Illustrations from Sander's "Reichenbachia". Multicoloured.

| | | | |
|---|---|---|---|
| 1009 | 1c. Type **183** | 95 | 95 |
| 1010 | 2c. "Cattleya citrina" | 95 | 95 |
| 1011 | 3c. "Masdevallia backhousiana" | 95 | 95 |
| 1012 | 4c. "Cypripedium tautzianum" | 95 | 95 |
| 1013 | 5c. "Trichopilia suavis alba" | 95 | 95 |
| 1014 | 6c. "Odontoglossum hebraicum" | 95 | 95 |
| 1015 | 7c. "Cattleya trianaei schroederiana" | 95 | 95 |
| 1016 | 10c. "Saccolabium giganteum" | 95 | 95 |
| 1017 | 30c. "Cattleya warscewiczii" | 1·25 | 1·25 |
| 1018 | 50c. "Chysis bractescens" | 1·50 | 1·50 |
| 1019 | 70c. "Cattleya rochellensis" | 1·75 | 1·75 |
| 1020 | $1 "Laellia elegans schilleriana" | 1·90 | 1·90 |
| 1021 | $1.50 "Laelia anceps percivaliana" | 2·00 | 2·00 |
| 1022 | $3 "Laelia gouldiana" | 2·50 | 2·50 |
| **MS**1023 | Two sheets, each 171×112 mm. (a) $3 "Odontoglossum roezlii" (40×47 mm). (b) $5 "Cattleya dowiana aurea" (40×47 mm) Set of 2 sheets | 12·00 | 13·00 |

**184** Christ condemned to Death

**1988.** Easter. The Stations of the Cross. Mult.

| | | | |
|---|---|---|---|
| 1024 | 40c. Type **184** | 35 | 60 |
| 1025 | 40c. Christ carrying the Cross | 35 | 60 |
| 1026 | 40c. Falling for the first time | 35 | 60 |
| 1027 | 40c. Christ meets Mary | 35 | 60 |
| 1028 | 40c. Simon of Cyrene helping to carry the Cross | 35 | 60 |
| 1029 | 40c. Veronica wiping the face of Christ | 35 | 60 |
| 1030 | 40c. Christ falling a second time | 35 | 60 |
| 1031 | 40c. Consoling the women of Jerusalem | 35 | 60 |
| 1032 | 40c. Falling for the third time | 35 | 60 |
| 1033 | 40c. Christ being stripped | 35 | 60 |
| 1034 | 40c. Christ nailed to the Cross | 35 | 60 |
| 1035 | 40c. Dying on the Cross | 35 | 60 |
| 1036 | 40c. Christ taken down from the Cross | 35 | 60 |
| 1037 | 40c. Christ being laid in the sepulchre | 35 | 60 |

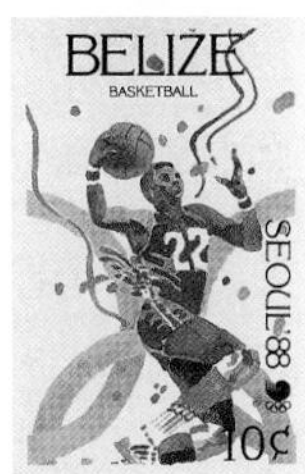

**185** Basketball

**1988.** Olympic Games, Seoul. Multicoloured.

| | | | |
|---|---|---|---|
| 1038 | 10c. Type **185** | 3·00 | 1·00 |
| 1039 | 25c. Volleyball | 1·00 | 30 |
| 1040 | 60c. Table tennis | 1·00 | 60 |
| 1041 | 75c. Diving | 1·00 | 70 |
| 1042 | $1 Judo | 1·25 | 1·10 |
| 1043 | $2 Hockey | 7·00 | 5·00 |
| **MS**1044 | 76×106 mm. $3 Gymnastics | 6·00 | 6·50 |

**186** Public Health Nurse, c. 1912

**1988.** 125th Anniv of Int Red Cross. Mult.

| | | | |
|---|---|---|---|
| 1045 | 60c. Type **186** | 3·25 | 1·25 |
| 1046 | 75c. "Aleda E. Lutz" (hospital ship) and ambulance launch, 1937 | 3·50 | 1·50 |
| 1047 | $1 Ambulance at hospital tent, 1956 | 4·00 | 2·00 |
| 1048 | $2 Auster ambulance plane, 1940 | 5·50 | 6·00 |

**187** Collared Anteater ("Ants Bear")

**1989.** Small Animals of Belize. Multicoloured.

| | | | |
|---|---|---|---|
| 1049 | 10c. Paca ("Gibnut") | 2·75 | 2·50 |
| 1050 | 25c. Four-eyed opossum (vert) | 2·75 | 1·75 |
| 1051 | 50c. Type **187** | 3·25 | 2·25 |
| 1052 | 60c. As 10c. | 3·25 | 2·50 |
| 1053 | 75c. Red brocket | 3·25 | 2·50 |
| 1054 | $1 Collared peccary | 4·50 | 6·50 |

**1989.** 20th Anniv of First Manned Landing on Moon. As T 126 of Ascension. Multicoloured.

| | | | |
|---|---|---|---|
| 1055 | 25c. Docking of "Apollo 9" modules | 2·00 | 30 |
| 1056 | 50c. "Apollo 9" command service module in Space (30×30 mm) | 2·50 | 75 |
| 1057 | 75c. "Apollo 9" emblem (30×30 mm) | 2·75 | 1·25 |
| 1058 | $1 "Apollo 9" lunar module in space | 3·00 | 2·25 |
| **MS**1059 | 83×100 mm. $5 "Apollo II" command service module undergoing test | 11·00 | 10·00 |

**1989.** No. 771 surch 5c.

| | | | |
|---|---|---|---|
| 1060 | 5c. on 6c. Star-eyed hermit crab | 15·00 | 2·50 |

**1989.** "World Stamp Expo '89" International Stamp Exhibition, Washington. No. **MS**1059 optd **WORLD STAMP EXPO '89, United States Postal Service Nov 17—20 and Nov 24—Dec 3. 1989 Washington Convention Center Washington, DC** and emblem.

| | | | |
|---|---|---|---|
| **MS**1061 | 83×100 mm. $5 "Apollo II" command service module undergoing tests | 9·50 | 10·00 |

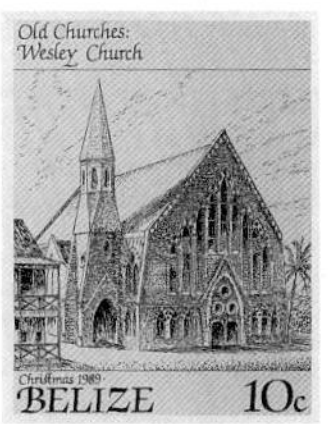

**190** Wesley Church

**1989.** Christmas. Belize Churches.

| | | | | |
|---|---|---|---|---|
| 1062 | **190** | 10c. black, pink and brown | 20 | 10 |
| 1063 | - | 25c. black, lilac and mauve | 25 | 20 |
| 1064 | - | 60c. black, turq & bl | 50 | 70 |
| 1065 | - | 75c. black, grn & lt grn | 65 | 90 |
| 1066 | - | $1 black, lt yell & yell | 80 | 1·25 |

DESIGNS: 25c. Baptist Church; 60c. St. John's Anglican Cathedral; 75c. St. Andrew's Presbyterian Church; $1 Holy Redeemer Roman Catholic Cathedral.

**191** White-winged Tanager and "Catonephele numilia"

**1990.** Birds and Butterflies. Multicoloured.

| | | | |
|---|---|---|---|
| 1067A | 5c. Type **191** | 60 | 1·00 |
| 1068B | 10c. Keel-billed toucan and "Nessaea aglaura" | 80 | 80 |
| 1069A | 15c. Magnificent frigate bird and "Eurytides philolaus" | 80 | 40 |
| 1070A | 25c. Jabiru and "Heliconius sapho" | 80 | 40 |
| 1071A | 30c. Great blue heron and "Colobura dirce" | 80 | 50 |
| 1072A | 50c. Northern oriole and "Hamadyras arethusia" | 1·00 | 60 |
| 1073A | 60c. Scarlet macaw and "Evenus regalis" | 1·25 | 70 |
| 1074A | 75c. Red-legged honey-creeper and "Callicore patelina" | 1·25 | 75 |
| 1075A | $1 Spectacled owl and "Caligo uranus" | 2·25 | 1·60 |
| 1076A | $2 Green jay and "Philaethria dido" | 2·75 | 3·50 |
| 1077A | $5 Turkey vulture and "Battus belus" | 4·50 | 6·50 |
| 1078A | $10 Osprey and "Papilio thoas" | 8·50 | 11·00 |

**1990.** First Belize Dollar Coin. No. 1075 optd **FIRST DOLLAR COIN 1990**.

| | | | |
|---|---|---|---|
| 1079 | $1 Spectacled owl and "Caligo uranus" | 4·75 | 2·75 |

**193** Green Turtle

**1990.** Turtles. Multicoloured.

| | | | |
|---|---|---|---|
| 1080 | 10c. Type **193** | 65 | 40 |
| 1081 | 25c. Hawksbill turtle | 1·00 | 40 |
| 1082 | 60c. Saltwater loggerhead turtle | 1·50 | 1·50 |
| 1083 | 75c. Freshwater loggerhead turtle | 1·60 | 1·60 |
| 1084 | $1 Bocatora turtle | 2·00 | 2·00 |
| 1085 | $2 Hicatee turtle | 2·75 | 5·50 |

**194** Fairey Battle

**1990.** 50th Anniv of the Battle of Britain. Multicoloured.

| | | | |
|---|---|---|---|
| 1086 | 10c. Type **194** | 1·00 | 50 |
| 1087 | 25c. Bristol Type 152 Beaufort | 1·60 | 50 |
| 1088 | 60c. Bristol Type 142 Blenheim Mk IV | 2·00 | 2·00 |
| 1089 | 75c. Armstrong-Whitworth Whitley | 2·00 | 2·00 |
| 1090 | $1 Vickers-Armstrong Wellington Mk 1c | 2·00 | 2·00 |
| 1091 | $1 Handley Page Hampden | 2·50 | 4·00 |

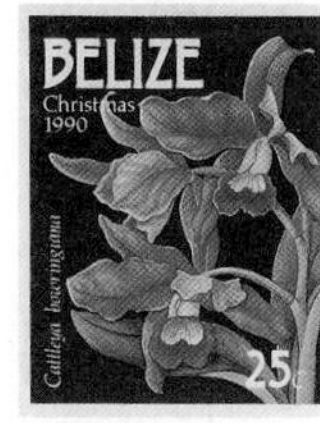

**195** "Cattleya bowringiana"

**1990.** Christmas. Orchids. Multicoloured.

| | | | |
|---|---|---|---|
| 1092 | 25c. Type **195** | 85 | 20 |
| 1093 | 50c. "Rhyncholaelia digbyana" | 1·25 | 50 |
| 1094 | 60c. "Sobralia macrantha" | 1·50 | 1·00 |
| 1095 | 75c. "Chysis bractescens" | 1·50 | 1·00 |
| 1096 | $1 "Vanilla planifolia" | 1·75 | 1·75 |
| 1097 | $2 "Epidendrum polyanthum" | 2·50 | 4·00 |

**196** Common Iguana

**1991.** Reptiles and Mammals. Multicoloured.

| | | | |
|---|---|---|---|
| 1098 | 25c. Type **196** | 80 | 35 |
| 1099 | 50c. Morelet's crocodile | 1·25 | 90 |
| 1100 | 60c. American manatee | 1·50 | 1·50 |
| 1101 | 75c. Boa constrictor | 1·75 | 1·75 |
| 1102 | $1 Baird's tapir | 2·00 | 2·00 |
| 1103 | $2 Jaguar | 2·75 | 3·75 |

**1991.** 65th Birthday of Queen Elizabeth II and 70th Birthday of Prince Philip. As T **139** of Ascension. Multicoloured.

| | | | |
|---|---|---|---|
| 1104 | $1 Queen Elizabeth II wearing tiara | 1·00 | 1·50 |
| 1105 | $1 Prince Philip wearing panama | 1·00 | 1·50 |

**197** Weather Radar

**1991.** International Decade for Natural Disaster Reduction.

| | | | | |
|---|---|---|---|---|
| 1106 | **197** | 60c. multicoloured | 1·50 | 1·25 |
| 1107 | - | 75c. multicoloured | 1·60 | 1·40 |
| 1108 | - | $1 blue and black | 1·75 | 1·75 |
| 1109 | - | $2 multicoloured | 2·50 | 3·25 |

DESIGNS: 75c. Weather station; $1 Floods in Belize after Hurricane Hattie, 1961; $2 Satellite image of Hurricane Gilbert.

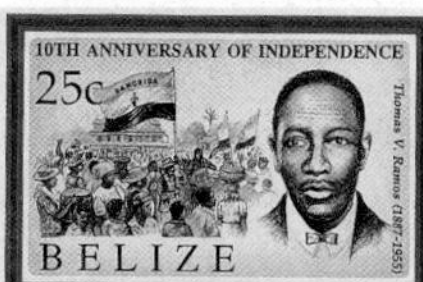

**198** Thomas Ramos and Demonstration

**1991.** 10th Anniv of Independence. Famous Belizeans (1st series). Multicoloured.

| | | | |
|---|---|---|---|
| 1110 | 25c. Type **198** | 60 | 30 |
| 1111 | 60c. Sir Isaiah Morter and palm trees | 1·25 | 1·50 |
| 1112 | 75c. Antonio Soberanis and political meeting | 1·25 | 1·75 |
| 1113 | $1 Santiago Ricalde and cutting sugar-cane | 1·50 | 2·00 |

See also Nos. 1126/9 and 1148/51.

**199** "Anansi the Spider"

**1991.** Christmas. Folklore. Multicoloured.

| | | | |
|---|---|---|---|
| 1114 | 25c. Type **199** | 1·75 | 20 |
| 1115 | 50c. "Jack-o-Lantern" | 2·25 | 55 |
| 1116 | 60c. "Tata Duende" (vert) | 2·50 | 1·25 |
| 1117 | 75c. "Xtabai" | 2·50 | 1·25 |
| 1118 | $1 "Warrie Massa" (vert) | 2·75 | 2·25 |
| 1119 | $2 "Old Heg" | 4·00 | 7·00 |

**200** "Gongora quinquenervis"

**1992.** Easter. Orchids. Multicoloured.

| | | | |
|---|---|---|---|
| 1120 | 25c. Type **200** | 1·25 | 20 |
| 1121 | 50c. "Oncidium sphacelatum" | 1·75 | 75 |
| 1122 | 60c. "Encyclia bratescens" | 2·00 | 1·75 |
| 1123 | 75c. "Epidendrum ciliare" | 2·00 | 1·75 |
| 1124 | $1 "Psygmorchis pusilla" | 2·25 | 2·25 |
| 1125 | $2 "Galeandra batemanii" | 3·75 | 4·50 |

**1992.** Famous Belizeans (2nd series). As T **198**, but inscr "EMINENT BELIZEANS" at top. Multicoloured.

| | | | |
|---|---|---|---|
| 1126 | 25c. Gwendolyn Lizarraga (politician) and High School | 75 | 30 |
| 1127 | 60c. Rafael Fonseca (civil servant) and Government Offices, Belize | 1·50 | 1·50 |
| 1128 | 75c. Vivian Seay (health worker) and nurses | 1·75 | 1·75 |
| 1129 | $1 Samuel Haynes (U.N.I.A. worker) and words of National Anthem | 2·00 | 2·50 |

**201** Xunantunich and National Assembly

**1992.** 500th Anniv of Discovery of America by Columbus. Mayan sites and modern buildings. Multicoloured.

| | | | |
|---|---|---|---|
| 1130 | 25c. Type **201** | 1·00 | 25 |
| 1131 | 60c. Altun Ha and Supreme Court | 1·50 | 1·00 |
| 1132 | 75c. Santa Rita and Tower Hill Sugar Factory | 1·60 | 1·25 |
| 1133 | $5 Lamanai and Citrus Company works | 8·00 | 11·00 |

**202** Hashishi Pampi

**1992.** Christmas. Folklore. Multicoloured.

| | | | |
|---|---|---|---|
| 1134 | 25c. Type **202** | 30 | 20 |
| 1135 | 60c. Cadejo | 60 | 60 |
| 1136 | $1 La Sucia (vert) | 90 | 1·00 |
| 1137 | $5 Sisimito | 4·00 | 7·00 |

**1993.** 75th Anniv of Royal Air Force. As T **149** of Ascension. Multicoloured.

| | | | |
|---|---|---|---|
| 1138 | 25c. Sud Aviation SA 330L Puma helicopter | 1·25 | 60 |
| 1139 | 50c. Hawker Siddeley Harrier GR3 | 1·50 | 80 |
| 1140 | 60c. de Havilland DH98 Mosquito Mk XVIII | 1·60 | 1·10 |
| 1141 | 75c. Avro Type 683 Lancaster | 1·60 | 1·10 |
| 1142 | $1 Consolidated Liberator I | 1·75 | 1·40 |
| 1143 | $3 Short Stirling Mk I | 3·50 | 6·00 |

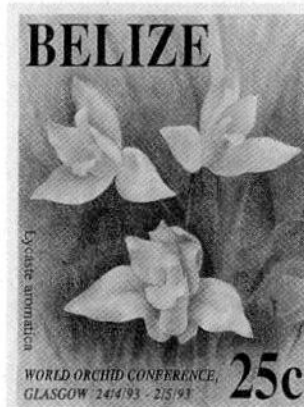


**203** "Lycaste aromatica"

**1993.** 14th World Orchid Conference, Glasgow. Multicoloured.

| | | | |
|---|---|---|---|
| 1144 | 25c. Type **203** | 40 | 25 |
| 1145 | 60c. "Sobralia decora" | 75 | 80 |
| 1146 | $1 "Maxillaria alba" | 1·00 | 1·25 |
| 1147 | $2 "Brassavola nodosa" | 1·75 | 3·00 |

**1993.** Famous Belizeans (3rd series). As T **198**, but inscr "EMINENT BELIZEANS" at top. Multicoloured.

| | | | |
|---|---|---|---|
| 1148 | 25c. Herbert Watkin Beaumont, Post Office and postmark | 40 | 25 |
| 1149 | 60c. Dr. Selvyn Walford Young and score of National Anthem | 75 | 85 |
| 1150 | 75c. Cleopatra White and health centre | 90 | 1·25 |
| 1151 | $1 Dr. Karl Heusner and early car | 1·10 | 1·40 |

**204** Boom and Chime Band

**1993.** Christmas. Local Customs. Mult.

| | | | |
|---|---|---|---|
| 1152 | 25c. Type **204** | 1·00 | 20 |
| 1153 | 60c. John Canoe dance | 2·00 | 75 |
| 1154 | 75c. Cortez dance | 2·00 | 80 |
| 1155 | $2 Maya musical group | 4·50 | 7·00 |

**1994.** "Hong Kong '94" International Stamp Exhibition. No. 1075 optd **HONG KONG '94** and emblem.

| | | | |
|---|---|---|---|
| 1156 | $1 Spectacled owl and "Caligo uranus" | 2·75 | 2·50 |

**1994.** Royal Visit. As T **202** of Bahamas. Mult.

| | | | |
|---|---|---|---|
| 1157 | 25c. Flags of Belize and Great Britain | 1·75 | 55 |
| 1158 | 60c. Queen Elizabeth II in yellow coat and hat | 2·25 | 1·25 |
| 1159 | 75c. Queen Elizabeth in evening dress | 2·50 | 1·50 |
| 1160 | $1 Queen Elizabeth, Prince Philip and Yeomen of the Guard | 2·75 | 2·50 |

**205** "Lonchorhina aurita" (bat)

**1994.** Bats. Multicoloured.

| | | | |
|---|---|---|---|
| 1161 | 25c. Type **205** | 45 | 20 |
| 1162 | 60c. "Vampyrodes caraccioli" | 75 | 65 |
| 1163 | 75c. "Noctilio leporinus" | 90 | 80 |
| 1164 | $2 "Desmodus rotundus" | 2·00 | 3·50 |

**1994.** 75th Anniv of I.L.O. No. 1074 surch **10c** and anniversary emblem.

| | | | |
|---|---|---|---|
| 1165 | 10c. on 75c. multicoloured | 2·00 | 1·75 |

**207** "Cycnoches chlorochilon"

**1994.** Christmas. Orchids. Multicoloured.

| | | | |
|---|---|---|---|
| 1166 | 25c. Type **207** | 45 | 20 |
| 1167 | 60c. "Brassavola cucullata" | 75 | 70 |
| 1168 | 75c. "Sobralia mucronata" | 90 | 90 |
| 1169 | $1 "Nidema boothii" | 1·10 | 1·50 |

**208** Ground Beetle

**1995.** Insects. Multicoloured.

| | | | |
|---|---|---|---|
| 1170A | 5c. Type **208** | 45 | 70 |
| 1171A | 10c. Harlequin beetle | 50 | 70 |
| 1172A | 15c. Giant water bug | 60 | 80 |
| 1173A | 25c. Peanut-head bug | 70 | 20 |
| 1174A | 30c. Coconut weevil | 70 | 25 |
| 1175A | 50c. Mantis | 85 | 40 |
| 1176B | 60c. Tarantula wasp | 1·10 | 50 |
| 1177B | 75c. Rhinoceros beetle | 1·40 | 60 |
| 1178B | $1 Metallic wood borer | 1·75 | 1·50 |
| 1179B | $2 Dobson fly | 4·00 | 4·50 |
| 1180B | $5 Click beetle | 7·00 | 8·50 |
| 1181B | $10 Long-horned beetle | 10·00 | 12·00 |

**1995.** 50th Anniv of End of Second World War. As T **161** of Ascension. Multicoloured.

| | | | |
|---|---|---|---|
| 1182 | 25c. War memorial | 35 | 25 |
| 1183 | 60c. Remembrance Day parade | 1·00 | 1·00 |
| 1184 | 75c. British Honduras forestry unit | 1·10 | 1·10 |
| 1185 | $1 Vickers Type **271** Wellington bomber | 1·40 | 1·75 |

**(209)**

**1995.** "Singapore '95" International Stamp Exhibition. Nos. 1166/9 optd with T **209**.

| | | | |
|---|---|---|---|
| 1186 | 25c. Type **207** | 1·00 | 30 |
| 1187 | 60c. "Brassavola cucullata" | 1·50 | 90 |
| 1188 | 75c. "Sobralia mucronata" | 1·75 | 1·25 |
| 1189 | $1 "Nidema boothii" | 2·00 | 2·25 |

**1995.** 50th Anniv of United Nations. As T 213 of Bahamas. Multicoloured.

| | | | |
|---|---|---|---|
| 1190 | 25c. M113-light reconnaisance vehicle | 25 | 20 |
| 1191 | 60c. Sultan armoured command vehicle | 60 | 65 |
| 1192 | 75c. Leyland-Daf 8×4 drop truck | 75 | 80 |
| 1193 | $2 Warrior infantry combat vehicle | 1·50 | 2·50 |

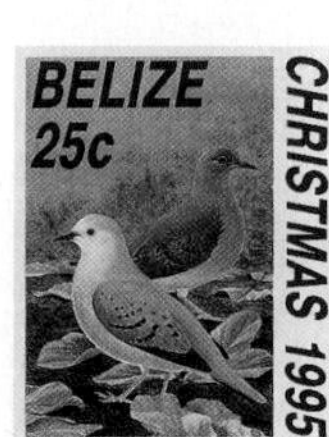


**210** Male and Female Blue Ground Dove

**1995.** Christmas. Doves. Multicoloured.

| | | | |
|---|---|---|---|
| 1194 | 25c. Type **210** | 35 | 20 |
| 1195 | 60c. White-fronted doves | 70 | 70 |
| 1196 | 75c. Pair of ruddy ground doves | 85 | 90 |
| 1197 | $1 White-winged doves | 1·25 | 1·50 |

**1996.** "CHINA '96" 9th Asian International Stamp Exhibition, Peking. Nos. 1172, 1174/5 and 1179 optd **'96 CHINA** and emblem.

| | | | |
|---|---|---|---|
| 1198 | 15c. Giant water bug | 20 | 15 |
| 1199 | 30c. Coconut weevil | 40 | 30 |
| 1200 | 50c. Mantis | 55 | 50 |
| 1201 | $2 Dobson fly | 1·75 | 2·50 |

**212** Unloading Banana Train, Commerce Bight Pier

**1996.** "CAPEX '96" International Stamp Exhibition, Toronto. Railways. Multicoloured.

| | | | |
|---|---|---|---|
| 1202 | 25c. Type **212** | 1·50 | 55 |
| 1203 | 60c. Locomotive No. 1 Stann Creek station | 2·00 | 1·25 |
| 1204 | 75c. Locomotive No. 4 pulling mahogany log train | 2·00 | 1·40 |
| 1205 | $3 L.M.S. No. 5602 "British Honduras" locomotive | 3·75 | 6·00 |

**213** "Epidendrum stamfordianum"

**1996.** Christmas. Orchids. Multicoloured.

| | | | |
|---|---|---|---|
| 1206 | 25c. Type **213** | 50 | 20 |
| 1207 | 60c. "Oncidium carthagenense" | 80 | 70 |
| 1208 | 75c. "Oerstedella verrucosa" | 90 | 90 |
| 1209 | $1 "Coryanthes speciosa" | 1·25 | 1·50 |

**214** Red Poll

**1997.** "HONG KONG '97" International Stamp Exhibition. Chinese New Year ("Year of the Ox"). Cattle Breeds. Multicoloured.

| | | | |
|---|---|---|---|
| 1210 | 25c. Type **214** | 60 | 25 |
| 1211 | 60c. Brahman | 95 | 1·00 |
| 1212 | 75c. Longhorn | 1·25 | 1·40 |
| 1213 | $1 Charbray | 1·40 | 1·90 |

**215** Coral Snake

**1997.** Snakes. Multicoloured.

| | | | |
|---|---|---|---|
| 1214 | 25c. Type **215** | 45 | 20 |
| 1215 | 60c. Green vine snake | 70 | 70 |
| 1216 | 75c. Yellow-jawed tommygoff | 80 | 80 |
| 1217 | $1 Speckled racer | 95 | 1·25 |

**216** Adult Male Howler Monkey

**1997.** Endangered Species. Howler Monkey. Multicoloured.

| | | | |
|---|---|---|---|
| 1218 | 10c. Type **216** | 25 | 25 |
| 1219 | 25c. Female feeding | 40 | 25 |
| 1220 | 60c. Female with young | 70 | 80 |
| 1221 | 75c. Juvenile monkey feeding | 90 | 1·10 |

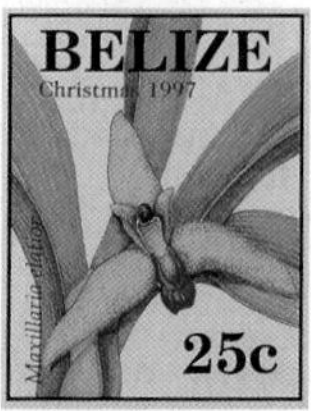


**217** "Maxillaria elatior"

**1997.** Christmas. Orchids. Multicoloured.

| | | | |
|---|---|---|---|
| 1222 | 25c. Type **217** | 65 | 25 |
| 1223 | 60c. "Dimmerandra emarginata" | 1·00 | 75 |
| 1224 | 75c. "Macradenia brassavolae" | 1·25 | 1·00 |
| 1225 | $1 "Ornithocephalus gladiatus" | 1·60 | 1·50 |

**1998.** Diana, Princess of Wales Commemoration. Sheet, 145×70 mm, containing vert designs as T **177** of Ascension. Multicoloured.

| | | | |
|---|---|---|---|
| **MS**1226 | $1 Wearing floral dress, 1988; $1 In evening dress, 1981; $1 Wearing pearl drop earrings, 1988; $1 Carrying bouquet, 1983 | 3·00 | 3·50 |

**218** School Children using the Internet

**1998.** 50th Anniv of Organization of American States. Multicoloured.

| | | | |
|---|---|---|---|
| 1227 | 25c. Type **218** | 25 | 20 |
| 1228 | $1 Map of Central America | 1·50 | 1·50 |

**219** University Arms

**1998.** 50th Anniv of University of West Indies.

| | | | | |
|---|---|---|---|---|
| 1229 | **219** | $1 multicoloured | 1·00 | 1·00 |

**220** Baymen Gun Flats

**1998.** Bicentenary of Battle of St. George's Cay. Multicoloured.

| | | | |
|---|---|---|---|
| 1230 | 10c. Boat moored at quayside (vert) | 30 | 50 |
| 1231 | 10c. Three sentries and cannon (vert) | 30 | 50 |
| 1232 | 10c. Cannon and rowing boats (vert) | 30 | 50 |
| 1233 | 25c. Type **220** | 60 | 25 |
| 1234 | 60c. Baymen sloops | 80 | 80 |
| 1235 | 75c. British schooners | 85 | 85 |
| 1236 | $1 H.M.S. "Merlin" (sloop) | 1·00 | 1·00 |
| 1237 | $2 Spanish flagship | 1·75 | 2·25 |

**221** "Brassia maculata"

**1998.** Christmas. Orchids. Multicoloured.

| | | | |
|---|---|---|---|
| 1238 | 25c. Type **221** | 35 | 20 |
| 1239 | 60c. "Encyclia radiata" | 50 | 40 |
| 1240 | 75c. "Stanhopea ecornuta" | 50 | 55 |
| 1241 | $1 "Isochilus carnosiflorus" | 60 | 80 |

**222** "Eucharis grandiflora"

**1999.** Easter. Flowers. Multicoloured.

| | | | |
|---|---|---|---|
| 1242 | 10c. Type **222** | 20 | 10 |
| 1243 | 25c. "Hippeastrum puniceum" | 30 | 20 |
| 1244 | 60c. "Zephyranthes citrina" | 50 | 50 |
| 1245 | $1 "Hymenocallis littoralis" | 60 | 80 |

**223** Postman on Bicycle

**1999.** 125th Anniv of UPU. Multicoloured.

| | | | |
|---|---|---|---|
| 1246 | 25c. Type **223** | 50 | 30 |
| 1247 | 60c. Postal truck | 65 | 55 |
| 1248 | 75c. "Dee" (mail ship) | 85 | 80 |
| 1249 | $1 Modern airliner | 1·00 | 1·25 |

**224** "Holy Family with Jesus and St. John" (School of Rubens)

**1999.** Christmas. Religious Paintings. Multicoloured.

| | | | |
|---|---|---|---|
| 1250 | 25c. Type **224** | 30 | 20 |
| 1251 | 60c. "Holy Family with St. John" (unknown artist) | 60 | 55 |
| 1252 | 75c. "Madonna and Child with St. John and Angel" (unknown artist) | 65 | 70 |
| 1253 | $1 "Madonna with Child and St. John" (Andrea del Salerno) | 90 | 1·10 |

**225** Iguana

**2000.** Wildlife. Multicoloured.

| | | | |
|---|---|---|---|
| 1254 | 5c. Type **225** | 15 | 40 |
| 1255 | 10c. Gibnut | 15 | 35 |
| 1256 | 15c. Howler monkey | 20 | 35 |
| 1257 | 25c. Collared anteater | 30 | 25 |
| 1258 | 30c. Hawksbill turtle | 30 | 25 |
| 1259 | 50c. Red brocket antelope | 50 | 40 |
| 1260 | 60c. Jaguar | 60 | 45 |
| 1261 | 75c. American manatee | 70 | 60 |
| 1262 | $1 Crocodile | 1·00 | 85 |
| 1263 | $2 Baird's tapir | 1·75 | 2·00 |
| 1264 | $5 Collared peccary | 4·50 | 6·00 |
| 1265 | $10 Boa constrictor | 8·50 | 11·00 |

**226** Mango

**2000.** Fruits. Multicoloured.

| | | | |
|---|---|---|---|
| 1266 | 25c. Type **226** | 35 | 25 |
| 1267 | 60c. Cashew | 65 | 60 |
| 1268 | 75c. Papaya | 80 | 75 |
| 1269 | $1 Banana | 1·10 | 1·40 |

**227** Meeting in Battlefield Park and Supreme Court, 1950

**2000.** 50th Anniv of People's United Party. Mult.

| | | | |
|---|---|---|---|
| 1270 | 10c. Type **227** | 20 | 15 |
| 1271 | 25c. Voters queuing, 1954 | 30 | 25 |
| 1272 | 60c. Legislative Council and Mace, 1964 | 55 | 50 |
| 1273 | 75c. National Assembly Building (under construction and completed), Belmopan, 1967–70 | 70 | 80 |
| 1274 | $1 Belizean flag in searchlights, Independence, 1981 | 2·25 | 1·75 |

**228** *Bletia purpurea*

**2000.** Christmas. Orchids. Multicoloured.

| | | | |
|---|---|---|---|
| 1275 | 25c. Type **228** | 55 | 25 |
| 1276 | 60c. *Cyrtopodium punctatum* | 85 | 50 |
| 1277 | 75c. *Cycnoches egertonianum* | 1·00 | 85 |
| 1278 | $1 *Catasetum integerrimum* | 1·40 | 1·60 |

**229** Children at Computers

**2001.** 20th Anniv of Independence. Multicoloured.

| | | | |
|---|---|---|---|
| 1279 | 25c. Type **229** | 35 | 25 |
| 1280 | 60c. Shrimp farm | 60 | 50 |
| 1281 | 75c. Privassion Cascade (vert) | 75 | 60 |
| 1282 | $2 Map of Belize (vert) | 3·00 | 3·50 |

**230** *Sobralia fragrans*

**2001.** Christmas. Orchids. Multicoloured.

| | | | |
|---|---|---|---|
| 1283 | 25c. Type **230** | 65 | 25 |
| 1284 | 60c. *Encyclia cordigera* | 1·00 | 60 |
| 1285 | 75c. *Maxillaria fulgens* | 1·25 | 1·00 |
| 1286 | $1 *Epidendrum nocturnum* | 1·60 | 1·75 |

**2002.** Golden Jubilee. As T **200** of Ascension.

| | | | |
|---|---|---|---|
| 1287 | 25c. black, violet and gold | 45 | 25 |
| 1288 | 60c. multicoloured | 75 | 60 |
| 1289 | 75c. black, violet and gold | 90 | 80 |
| 1290 | $1 multicoloured | 1·10 | 1·25 |
| **MS**1291 | 162×95 mm. Nos. 1287/90 and $5 multicoloured | 6·50 | 7·50 |

DESIGNS—Horiz: 25c. Princess Elizabeth in pantomime, Windsor, 1943; 60c. Queen Elizabeth in floral hat; 75c. Queen Elizabeth in garden with Prince Charles and Princess Anne, 1952; $1 Queen Elizabeth in South Africa, 1995. VERT (38×51 mm)—$5 Queen Elizabeth after Annigoni.

**231** *Dichaea neglecta*

**2002.** Christmas. Orchids. Multicoloured.

| | | | |
|---|---|---|---|
| 1292 | 25c. Type **231** | 65 | 25 |
| 1293 | 50c. *Epinendrum hawkesii* | 80 | 55 |
| 1294 | 60c. *Encyclia belizensis* | 90 | 60 |
| 1295 | 75c. *Eriopsis biloba* | 1·00 | 70 |
| 1296 | $1 *Harbenaria monorrhiza* | 1·25 | 1·50 |
| 1297 | $2 *Mormodes buccinator* | 1·75 | 2·75 |

**232** B.D.F. Emblem

**2003.** 25th Anniv of Belize Defence Force.

| | | | | |
|---|---|---|---|---|
| 1298 | **232** | 25c. multicoloured | 50 | 35 |

**233** Avro Shackleton MK 3

**2003.** Centenary of Powered Flight. Multicoloured.

| | | | |
|---|---|---|---|
| 1299 | 25c. Type **233** | 75 | 45 |
| 1300 | 60c. Lockheed L-749 Constellation | 1·00 | 70 |
| 1301 | 75c. Sepecat Jaguar GR. 1 | 1·25 | 80 |
| 1302 | $3 British Aerospace Harrier GR. 3 | 3·00 | 4·00 |
| **MS**1303 | 116×66 mm. $5 Ryan NYP *Spirit of St. Louis*, Belize, 1927 | 4·50 | 5·00 |

**234** Head of Scarlet Macaw

**2003.** Christmas. Scarlet Macaw. Multicoloured.

| | | | |
|---|---|---|---|
| 1304 | 25c. Type **234** | 80 | 45 |
| 1305 | 60c. Pair on tree | 1·25 | 65 |
| 1306 | 75c. Three macaws feeding on clay | 1·40 | 75 |
| 1307 | $5 Pair in flight | 4·75 | 6·50 |

**235** Whale Shark

**2004.** Whale Shark. Multicoloured.

| | | | |
|---|---|---|---|
| 1308 | 25c. Type **235** | 50 | 30 |
| 1309 | 60c. Near surface of water | 80 | 50 |
| 1310 | 75c. Whale shark and diver | 90 | 55 |
| 1311 | $5 Near coral reef | 4·50 | 5·50 |

**2004.** Wildlife. Nos. 1259/1261 surch.

| | | | |
|---|---|---|---|
| 1312 | 10c. on 50c. Red brocket antelope | 30 | 40 |
| 1313 | 10c. on 60c. Jaguar | 30 | 40 |
| 1314 | 15c. on 75c. American manatee | 40 | 40 |

**237** Woolly Opossum

**2005.** Endangered Species. Woolly Opossum. Showing the Woolly Opossum with the country name in different colours. Multicoloured.

| | | | |
|---|---|---|---|
| 1315 | 25c. Type **237** | 50 | 30 |
| 1316 | 60c. Bright new blue | 80 | 50 |
| 1317 | 75c. Dull orange (horiz) | 90 | 55 |
| 1318 | $5 Magenta (horiz) | 4·50 | 5·50 |

**2005.** No. 1300 surch.

| | | | |
|---|---|---|---|
| 1318a | 10c. on 60c. Lockheed L-749 Constellation | 80 | 80 |

**2005.** No. 1305 surch.

| | | | |
|---|---|---|---|
| 1318b | 10c. on 60c. Pair (of scarlet macaws) on tree | 10·00 | 10·00 |

**2005.** Pope John Paul II Commemoration. As T **219** of Ascension.

| | | | |
|---|---|---|---|
| 1319 | $1 multicoloured | 2·00 | 2·00 |

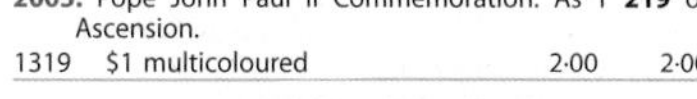

**239** Blue-crowned Motmot and Flower, Guanacaste National Park, Cayo District

**2005.** Ecological and Cultural Heritage. Multicoloured.

| | | | |
|---|---|---|---|
| 1320 | 5c. Type **239** | 15 | 15 |
| 1321 | 10c. Government House of Culture, Belize City | 15 | 15 |
| 1322 | 15c. Lubaantun Archaeological Reserve and ball court warriors, Toledo District | 20 | 20 |
| 1323 | 25c. Altun Ha Archaeological Reserve and jade head, Belize District | 30 | 30 |
| 1324 | 30c. Nohoch Che'n Archaeological Reserve and jar, Cayo District | 30 | 30 |
| 1325 | 50c. Goff's Caye, Belize District | 50 | 50 |
| 1326 | 60c. Blue Hole Natural Monument and diver, Belize District | 60 | 60 |

| | | | |
|---|---|---|---|
| 1327 | 75c. Lamanai Archaeological Reserve and crocodile effigy, Orange Walk District | 75 | 75 |
| 1328 | $1 Half Moon Caye, lighthouse and red footed booby (bird), Belize District | 1·25 | 1·25 |
| 1329 | $2 Beach and starfish, Placencia Peninsula, Stann Creek District | 2·25 | 2·50 |
| 1330 | $5 Museum of Belize, Belize City | 5·50 | 6·00 |
| 1331 | $10 Cerros Archaeological Reserve and Olmec jade pendant, Corozal District | 9·00 | 9·50 |

**240** 25c. Postman on Bicycle Stamp

**2006.** 50th Anniv of First Europa Stamp. Designs showing Belize 1999 125th Anniv of Universal Postal Union stamps. Multicoloured.

| | | | |
|---|---|---|---|
| 1332 | 25c. Type **240** | 75 | 40 |
| 1333 | 75c. 60c. Postal truck stamp | 1·50 | 75 |
| 1334 | $3 75c. Mail ship *Dee* stamp | 4·00 | 4·50 |
| 1335 | $5 $1 Airliner stamp | 7·00 | 8·00 |
| **MS**1336 | Nos. 1332/5 | 12·00 | 13·00 |

**241** George Price (Independence negotiator and first Prime Minister)

**2006.** 25th Anniv of Independence. Multicoloured.

| | | | |
|---|---|---|---|
| 1337 | 25c. Type **241** | 40 | 30 |
| 1338 | 30c. Black orchid, Baird's tapir, keel-billed toucan and mahogany tree (national symbols) (horiz) | 1·00 | 45 |
| 1339 | 60c. Map of Belize | 1·50 | 70 |
| 1340 | $1 1981 Independence logo | 1·50 | 1·40 |
| 1341 | $5 The Constitution of Belize (horiz) | 6·50 | 7·50 |

**242** Roman Goddess Diana reaching for Arrow

**2006.** Breast Cancer Research.

| | | | | |
|---|---|---|---|---|
| 1342 | **242** | $1 multicoloured | 1·75 | 1·75 |

A similar stamp was issued by the USA on 29 July 1998.

**243** *Sleeping Giant* sculpture (George Gabb)

**2007.** Belizean Artists. Multicoloured.

| | | | |
|---|---|---|---|
| 1343 | 25c. Type **243** | 15 | 10 |
| 1344 | 30c. *Market Scene* (Louis Belisle) (horiz) | 25 | 20 |
| 1345 | 60c. *The Original Turtle Shell Band* (Pen Cayetano) (horiz) | 50 | 45 |
| 1346 | 75c. *Have Some Coconut Water* (Benjamin Nicholas) | 65 | 65 |
| 1347 | $2 Woodcarving by Reuben Miguel | 1·75 | 1·75 |
| 1348 | $3 Mural of Corozal Town (Manuel Villamor) | 2·40 | 2·50 |

**244** Slave

**2007.** Bicentenary of the Abolition of the Slave Trade Act.

| | | | | |
|---|---|---|---|---|
| 1349 | **244** | $2 multicoloured | 2·40 | 3·00 |

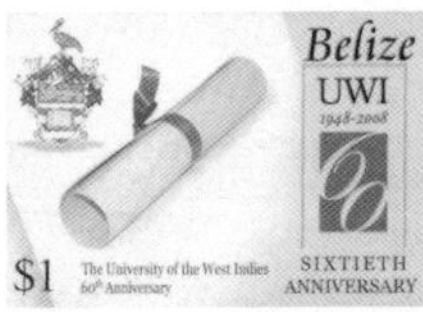

**245** Scroll

**2008.** 60th Anniv of the University of the West Indies.

| | | | | |
|---|---|---|---|---|
| 1350 | **245** | $1 multicoloured | 1·25 | 1·25 |

**2009.** As No. 1323

| | | | |
|---|---|---|---|
| 1351 | 25c. Altun Ha Archaeological Reserve and jade head, Belize District | 40 | 30 |

Nos. 1352/62 are left for possible additions.

**246** Yellow-headed Parrot (*Amazona oratrix*)

**2009.** Endangered Birds. Multicoloured.

| | | | |
|---|---|---|---|
| 1363 | 25c. Type **246** | 40 | 30 |
| 1364 | 60c. Harpy eagle (*Harpia harpyja*) | 50 | 45 |
| 1365 | $1 Slate-colored seedeater (*Sporophila schistacea*) | 1·25 | 1·25 |
| 1366 | $2 Green honeycreeper (*Chlorophanes spiza*) | 2·40 | 3·00 |
| 1367 | $5 Great curassow (*Crax rubra*) | 6·50 | 5·50 |

**247** Encyclia polybulbon

**2010.** Christmas. Orchids. Multicoloured.

| | | | |
|---|---|---|---|
| 1368 | 25c. Type **247** | 15 | 20 |
| 1369 | 60c. *Oncidium ensatum* | 45 | 35 |
| 1370 | $2 *Encyclia livida* | 2·40 | 2·50 |
| 1371 | $5 *Epidendrum difforme* | 5·75 | 6·00 |

### POSTAGE DUE STAMPS

**D2**

**1976**

| | | | | |
|---|---|---|---|---|
| D6 | **D2** | 1c. red and green | 10 | 1·00 |
| D7 | - | 2c. purple and violet | 15 | 1·00 |
| D8 | - | 5c. green and brown | 20 | 1·25 |
| D9 | - | 15c. green and red | 30 | 1·50 |
| D10 | - | 25c. orange and green | 40 | 1·75 |

DESIGNS: Nos. D7/10 as Type D **2** but with different frames.

Pt. 6, Pt. 12

# BENIN

A French possession on the west coast of Africa incorporated, in 1899, into the colony of Dahomey.

100 centimes = 1 franc.

### A. FRENCH COLONY

**1892.** Stamps of French Colonies. "Commerce" type, optd **BENIN**.

| | | | | |
|---|---|---|---|---|
| 1 | **J** | 1c. black on blue | £140 | £140 |
| 2 | **J** | 2c. brown on yellow | £130 | £130 |
| 3 | **J** | 4c. brown on grey | 75·00 | 75·00 |
| 4 | **J** | 5c. green on light green | 18·00 | 16·00 |
| 5 | **J** | 10c. black on lilac | £100 | 80·00 |
| 6 | **J** | 15c. blue on light blue | 60·00 | 26·00 |
| 7 | **J** | 20c. red on green | £225 | £200 |
| 8 | **J** | 25c. black on red | £120 | 70·00 |
| 9 | **J** | 30c. brown on drab | £180 | £160 |
| 10 | **J** | 35c. black on orange | £180 | £160 |
| 11 | **J** | 40c. red on yellow | £160 | £150 |
| 12 | **J** | 75c. red on pink | £300 | £275 |
| 13 | **J** | 1f. green | £325 | £275 |

**1892.** Nos. 4 and 6 surch.

| | | | |
|---|---|---|---|
| 14 | 01 on 5c. green on lt green | £275 | £225 |
| 15 | 40 on 15c. blue on lt blue | £170 | £120 |
| 16 | 75 on 15c. blue on lt blue | £750 | £450 |

**1893.** "Tablet" key-type inscr "GOLFE DE BENIN" in red (1, 5, 15, 25, 75c., 1f.) or blue (others).

| | | | | |
|---|---|---|---|---|
| 17 | **D** | 1c. black on blue | 3·00 | 8·75 |
| 18 | **D** | 2c. brown on buff | 3·75 | 4·50 |
| 19 | **D** | 4c. brown on grey | 3·25 | 8·50 |
| 20 | **D** | 5c. green on light green | 10·00 | 12·50 |
| 21 | **D** | 10c. black on lilac | 10·50 | 15·00 |
| 22 | **D** | 15c. blue | 40·00 | 50·00 |
| 23 | **D** | 20c. red on green | 7·25 | 11·00 |
| 24 | **D** | 25c. black on pink | 40·00 | 19·00 |
| 25 | **D** | 30c. brown on drab | 14·50 | 15·00 |
| 26 | **D** | 40c. red on yellow | 2·75 | 7·00 |
| 27 | **D** | 50c. red on pink | 3·75 | 5·50 |
| 28 | **D** | 75c. brown on orange | 11·50 | 22·00 |
| 29 | **D** | 1f. green | 75·00 | 80·00 |

**1894.** "Tablet" key-type inscr "BENIN" in red (1, 5, 15, 25, 75c., 1f.) or blue (others).

| | | | |
|---|---|---|---|
| 33 | 1c. black on blue | 2·75 | 3·25 |
| 34 | 2c. brown on buff | 3·75 | 4·50 |
| 35 | 4c. brown on grey | 2·75 | 4·25 |
| 36 | 5c. green on light green | 7·25 | 8·75 |
| 37 | 10c. black on lilac | 6·00 | 8·25 |
| 38 | 15c. blue | 18·00 | 3·25 |
| 39 | 20c. red on green | 14·00 | 17·00 |
| 40 | 25c. black on pink | 11·00 | 4·50 |
| 41 | 30c. brown on drab | 7·25 | 12·00 |
| 42 | 40c. red on yellow | 17·00 | 18·00 |
| 43 | 50c. red on pink | 25·00 | 29·00 |
| 44 | 75c. brown on orange | 18·00 | 8·75 |
| 45 | 1f. green | 7·00 | 12·50 |

### POSTAGE DUE STAMPS

**1894.** Postage Due stamps of French Colonies optd **BENIN**. Imperf.

| | | | | |
|---|---|---|---|---|
| D46 | **U** | 5c. black | £150 | 85·00 |
| D47 | **U** | 10c. black | £150 | 85·00 |
| D48 | **U** | 20c. black | £150 | 85·00 |
| D49 | **U** | 30c. black | £150 | 85·00 |

### B. PEOPLE'S REPUBLIC

The Republic of Dahomey was renamed the People's Republic of Benin on 30 November 1975.

**185** Celebrations

**1976.** Republic of Benin Proclamation. Mult.

| | | | |
|---|---|---|---|
| 603 | 50f. Type **185** | 75 | 30 |
| 604 | 60f. President Kerekou making Proclamation | 1·10 | 40 |
| 605 | 100f. Benin arms and flag | 1·80 | 70 |

**186** Skiing

**1976.** Air. Winter Olympic Games, Innsbruck. Multicoloured.

| | | | |
|---|---|---|---|
| 606 | 60f. Type **186** | 1·30 | 70 |
| 607 | 150f. Bobsleighing (vert) | 2·30 | 1·20 |
| 608 | 300f. Figure-skating | 4·75 | 2·30 |

**1976.** Various Dahomey stamps surch **POPULAIRE DU BENIN** and new value (609/11) or surch only (617/18).NIN

| | | | | |
|---|---|---|---|---|
| 609 | - | 135f. brown, purple and blue (No. 590) (air) | 2·00 | 90 |
| 610 | - | 210f. on 300f. brown, red and blue (No. 591) | 2·75 | 1·30 |
| 611 | - | 380f. on 500f. brown, red and green (No. 592) | 4·75 | 2·20 |
| 617 | **108** | 50f. on 1f. multicoloured (postage) | 70 | 30 |
| 618 | - | 60f. on 2f. multicoloured (No. 415) | 95 | 45 |

**188** Alexander Graham Bell, Early Telephone and Satellite

**1976.** Telephone Centenary.

| | | | | |
|---|---|---|---|---|
| 612 | **188** | 200f. red, violet & brown | 3·25 | 1·70 |

**189** Basketball

**1976.** Air. Olympic Games, Montreal. Mult.

| | | | |
|---|---|---|---|
| 613 | 60f. Long jump (horiz) | 1·00 | 45 |
| 614 | 150f. Type **189** | 2·00 | 95 |
| 615 | 200f. Hurdling (horiz) | 2·50 | 1·70 |
| **MS**616 | 150×120 mm. Nos. 613/15 | 7·50 | 6·75 |

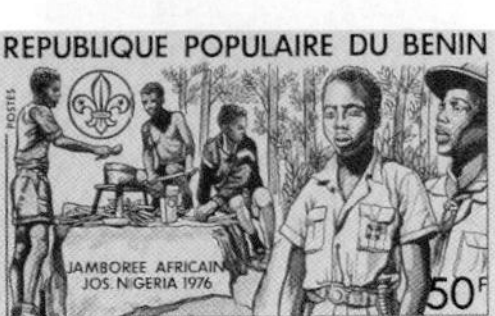

**191** Scouts and Camp-fire

**1976.** African Scout Jamboree, Jos, Nigeria.

| | | | | |
|---|---|---|---|---|
| 619 | **191** | 50f. purple, brown & blk | 75 | 35 |
| 620 | - | 70f. brown, green & blk | 1·00 | 55 |

DESIGN: 70f. "Comradeship".

**192** Konrad Adenauer

**1976.** Air. Birth Centenary of Konrad Adenauer (German statesman).

| | | | | |
|---|---|---|---|---|
| 621 | **192** | 90f. slate, blue and red | 1·50 | 65 |
| 622 | - | 250f. blue, red & lt blue | 4·00 | 1·50 |

DESIGN—HORIZ: 250f. Adenauer and Cologne Cathedral.

**193** Benin 1c. Stamp, 1893, and Lion Cub

**1976.** Air. "Juvarouen 76" Youth Stamp Exhibition, Rouen.

| | | | | |
|---|---|---|---|---|
| 623 | | 60f. blue and turquoise | 1·00 | 50 |
| 624 | **193** | 210f. red, brown & olive | 3·25 | 1·50 |

DESIGN—HORIZ: 60f. Dahomey 60f. Stamp of 1965, and children's silhouettes.

**194** Blood Bank, Cotonou

**1976.** National Days of Blood Transfusion Service. Multicoloured.

| | | | |
|---|---|---|---|
| 625 | 5f. Type **194** | 20 | 10 |
| 626 | 50f. Casualty and blood clinic | 70 | 40 |
| 627 | 60f. Donor, patient and ambulance | 1·10 | 55 |

**195** Manioc

**1976.** National Products Campaign Year. Mult.

| | | | |
|---|---|---|---|
| 628 | 20f. Type **195** | 50 | 15 |
| 629 | 50f. Maize cultivation | 75 | 25 |
| 630 | 60f. Cocoa trees | 1·00 | 40 |
| 631 | 150f. Cotton plantation | 2·30 | 80 |

**196** "Apollo" Emblem and Rocket

**1976.** Air. 5th Anniv of "Apollo 14" Space Mission.

| | | | | |
|---|---|---|---|---|
| 632 | **196** | 130f. lake, brown & blue | 1·50 | 70 |
| 633 | - | 270f. blue, turquoise & red | 3·00 | 1·50 |

DESIGN: 270f. Landing on Moon.

**197** Classroom

**1976.** 3rd Anniv of Bariba Periodical "Kparo".

| | | | | |
|---|---|---|---|---|
| 634 | **197** | 50f. multicoloured | 1·00 | 55 |

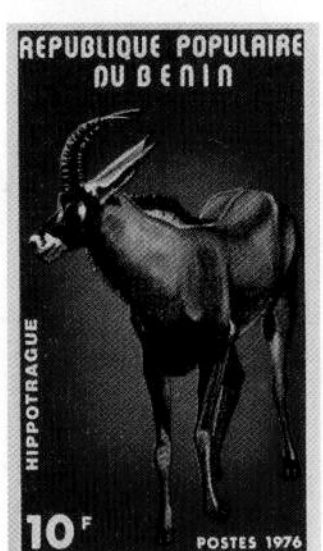

**198** Roan Antelope

**1976.** Mammals in Pendjari National Park. Multicoloured.

| | | | |
|---|---|---|---|
| 635 | 10f. Type **198** | 45 | 25 |
| 636 | 30f. African buffalo | 80 | 50 |
| 637 | 50f. Hippopotamus (horiz) | 1·60 | 85 |
| 638 | 70f. Lion | 1·80 | 1·00 |

**199** "Freedom"

**1976.** 1st Anniv of Proclamation of Republic. Multicoloured.

| | | | |
|---|---|---|---|
| 639 | 40f. Type **199** | 60 | 25 |
| 640 | 150f. Maize cultivation | 1·80 | 85 |

**200** "The Annunciation" (Master of Jativa)

**1976.** Air. Christmas. Multicoloured.

| | | | |
|---|---|---|---|
| 641 | 50f. Type **200** | 80 | 40 |
| 642 | 60f. "The Nativity" (David) | 90 | 50 |
| 643 | 270f. "Adoration of the Magi" (Dutch school) | 3·75 | 1·80 |
| 644 | 300f. "The Flight into Egypt" (Fabriano) (horiz) | 4·00 | 2·30 |

**201** Table Tennis and Games Emblem

**1976.** West African University Games, Cotonou. Multicoloured.

| | | | |
|---|---|---|---|
| 645 | 10f. Type **201** | 55 | 10 |
| 646 | 50f. Sports Hall, Cotonou | 80 | 25 |

**202** Loser with Ticket and Winner with Money

**1977.** Air. 10th Anniv of National Lottery.

| | | | | |
|---|---|---|---|---|
| 647 | **202** | 50f. multicoloured | 75 | 45 |

**203** Douglas DC-10 crossing Globe

**1977.** Europafrique.

| | | | | |
|---|---|---|---|---|
| 648 | **203** | 200f. multicoloured | 3·00 | 2·10 |

**204** Chateau Sassenage, Grenoble

**1977.** Air. 10th Anniv of International French Language Council.

| | | | | |
|---|---|---|---|---|
| 649 | **204** | 200f. multicoloured | 2·50 | 1·10 |

**205** Adder

**1977.** Reptiles and Domestic Animals. Mult.

| | | | |
|---|---|---|---|
| 650 | 2f. Type **205** | 45 | 10 |
| 651 | 3f. Tortoise | 45 | 10 |
| 652 | 5f. Zebus | 45 | 10 |
| 653 | 10f. Cats | 85 | 25 |

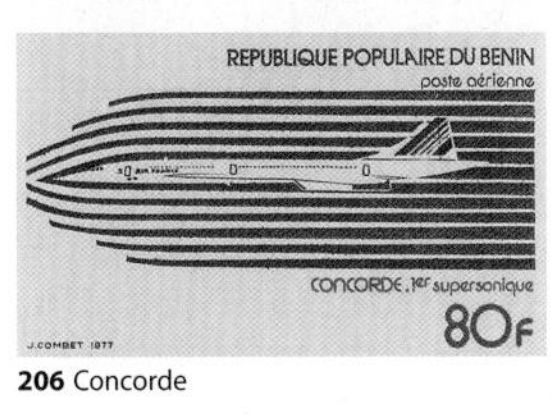

**206** Concorde

**1977.** Air. Aviation.

| | | | | |
|---|---|---|---|---|
| 654 | **206** | 80f. red and blue | 95 | 40 |
| 655 | - | 150f. red, violet & green | 2·10 | 90 |
| 656 | - | 300f. violet, red & mauve | 3·00 | 1·60 |
| 657 | - | 500f. red, blue & green | 6·25 | 3·25 |

DESIGNS: 150f. "Graf Zeppelin"; 300f. Charles Lindbergh and "Spirit of St. Louis"; 500f. Charles Nungesser and Francois Coli with "L'Oiseau Blanc".

**207** Footballer heading Ball

**1977.** Air. World Football Cup Eliminators. Multicoloured.

| | | | |
|---|---|---|---|
| 658 | 60f. Type **207** | 80 | 35 |
| 659 | 200f. Goalkeeper and players | 2·30 | 1·30 |

**208** Rheumatic Patients

**1977.** World Rheumatism Year.

| | | | | |
|---|---|---|---|---|
| 660 | **208** | 100f. multicoloured | 1·50 | 75 |

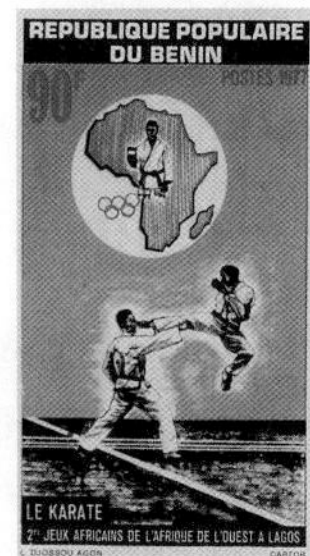

**209** Karate

**1977.** 2nd African Games, Lagos.

| | | | | |
|---|---|---|---|---|
| 661 | **209** | 90f. multicoloured | 1·40 | 70 |
| 662 | - | 100f. multicoloured | 1·40 | 90 |
| 663 | - | 150f. multicoloured | 2·30 | 1·10 |
| **MS**664 | | 144×92 mm. Nos. 661/3 | 6·75 | 6·50 |

DESIGNS—HORIZ: 100f. Javelin. VERT: 150f. Hurdles.

**210** Mao Tse-tung

**1977.** 1st Death Anniv of Mao Tse-tung.

| | | | | |
|---|---|---|---|---|
| 665 | **210** | 100f. multicoloured | 2·75 | 1·40 |

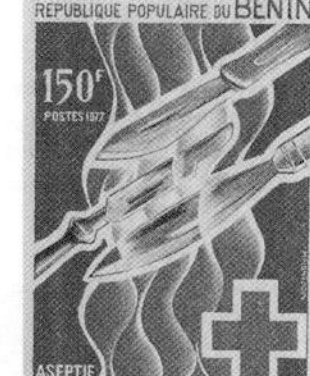

**211** Sterilising Scalpels

**1977.** 150th Birth Anniv of Joseph Lister.

| | | | | |
|---|---|---|---|---|
| 666 | **211** | 150f. grey, red & carmine | 2·00 | 90 |
| 667 | - | 210f. olive, green & red | 2·50 | 1·30 |

DESIGN: 210f. Lister and antiseptic spray.

**212** "Miss Haverfield" (Gainsborough)

**1977.** Air. Paintings.

| | | | | |
|---|---|---|---|---|
| 668 | **212** | 100f. green and brown | 2·40 | 60 |
| 669 | - | 150f. brown, bistre & red | 3·50 | 1·30 |
| 670 | - | 200f. red and bistre | 4·75 | 1·80 |

DESIGNS: 150f. "Self-Portrait" (Rubens); 200f. "Study of an Old Man" (da Vinci).

**213** "Jarre Trouee" Emblem of King Ghezo (D'Abomey Museum)

**1977.** Historic Museums of Benin. Mult.

| | | | |
|---|---|---|---|
| 671 | 50f. Type **213** | 75 | 40 |
| 672 | 60f. Mask (Porto-Novo Museum) (horiz) | 1·30 | 55 |
| 673 | 210f. D'Abomey Museum | 2·75 | 1·20 |

**214** Atacora Waterfall

**1977.** Tourism. Multicoloured.

| | | | |
|---|---|---|---|
| 674 | 50f. Type **214** | 70 | 40 |
| 675 | 60f. Stilt houses, Ganvie (horiz) | 95 | 55 |
| 676 | 150f. Hut village, Savalou | 2·30 | 1·10 |
| **MS**677 | 144×92 mm. Nos. 674/6 | 5·25 | 5·25 |

**1977.** Air. 1st Commercial Concorde Flight. Paris–New York. No. 654 optd **1er VOL COMMERCIAL 22.11.77 PARIS NEW-YORK**.

| | | | | |
|---|---|---|---|---|
| 678 | **206** | 80f. red and blue | 1·70 | 85 |

**216** "Viking" on Mars ("Operation Viking", 1977)

**1977.** Air. Space Conquest Anniversaries.

| | | | | |
|---|---|---|---|---|
| 679 | **216** | 100f. brown, olive & red | 1·00 | 60 |
| 680 | - | 150f. blue, turq & mve | 1·80 | 85 |

681 - 200f. brown, blue & red 2·75 1·10
682 - 500f. blue, brn & olive 6·50 3·00

DESIGNS AND EVENTS: 150f. Sir Isaac Newton, apple and stars (250th death anniv); 200f. Komarov and "Soyuz 2" over Moon (10th death anniv); 500f. Space dog "Laika" and rocket (20th anniv of ascent into Space).

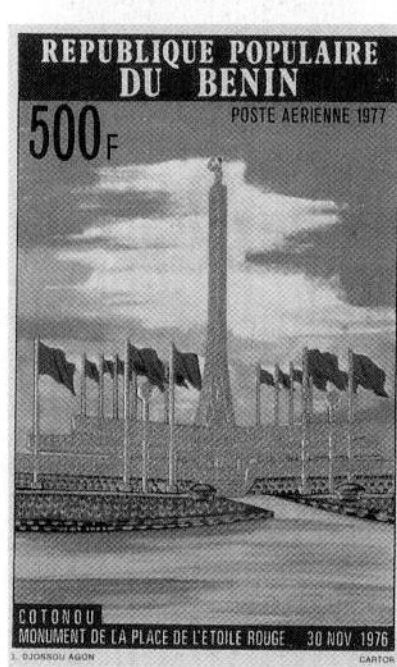

**217** Monument, Red Flag Square, Cotonou

**1977.** Air. 1st Anniv of Inauguration of Red Flag Square Monument.
683 **217** 500f. multicoloured 6·25 2·75

**218** Mother and Child with Owl of Wisdom

**1977.** Fight against Witchcraft. Multicoloured.
684 60f. Type **218** 1·30 55
685 150f. Felling the tree of sorcery 2·50 1·10

**219** "Suzanne Fourment"

**1977.** Air. 400th Birth Anniv of Rubens.
686 **219** 200f. brown, red & green 3·25 1·30
687 - 380f. orange and brown 5·50 2·20

DESIGN: 380f. "Albert Rubens".

**220** Battle Scene

**1978.** "Victory over Imperialism".
688 **220** 50f. multicoloured 1·20 45

**221** Benin Houses and Map of Heads

**1978.** General Population Census.
689 **221** 50f. multicoloured 80 35

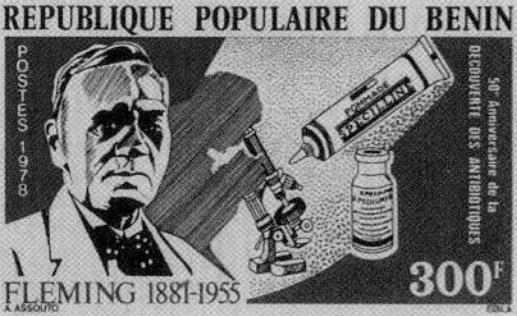

**222** Sir Alexander Fleming, Microscope and Drugs

**1978.** 50th Anniv of Discovery of Antibiotics.
690 **222** 300f. multicoloured 4·50 2·10

**223** Abdoulaye Issa

**1978.** 1st Death Anniv of Abdoulaye Issa.
691 **223** 100f. multicoloured 1·00 50

**224** El Hadj Omar

**1978.** Heroes of Anti-colonial Resistance.
692 - 90f. multicoloured 1·30 45
693 **224** 100f. green, grey & blue 1·30 65

DESIGN: 90f. Samory Toure.

**225** "Communications"

**1978.** 10th World Telecommunications Day.
694 **225** 100f. multicoloured 1·50 75

**226** Footballer and Stadium

**1978.** World Cup Football Championship, Argentina. Multicoloured.
695 200f. Type **226** 2·30 1·00
696 300f. Tackling (vert) 3·00 1·60
697 500f. Footballer and world map 5·50 2·50
**MS**698 190×121 mm. Nos. 695/7 in different colours 12·00 9·00

**1978.** Argentina's Victory in World Cup Football Championship. Nos. 695/7 optd.
699 **226** 200f. multicoloured 2·00 1·10
700 - 300f. multicoloured 3·00 1·90
701 - 500f. multicoloured 5·50 3·25
**MS**702 190×121 mm. Nos. 699/701 multicoloured 13·50 12·50

OPTS: 200f. **FINALE ARGENTINE: 3 HOLLANDE: 1**; 300f. **CHAMPION 1978 ARGENTINE**; 500f. **3e BRESIL 4e ITALIE**.

**228** Map, Olympic Flag and Basketball Players

**1978.** 3rd African Games, Algiers. Multicoloured.
703 50f. Type **228** 55 25
704 60f. African map and Volleyball 95 45
705 80f. Cyclists and map of Algeria 1·00 55
**MS**706 208×80 mm. Nos. 703/5 in different colours 4·00 3·75

**229** Martin Luther King

**1978.** 10th Anniv of Martin Luther King's Assassination.
707 **229** 300f. multicoloured 3·50 1·70

**230** Bicycle Taxi (Oueme)

**1978.** Benin Provinces. Multicoloured.
708 50f. Type **230** 1·20 40
709 60f. Leather work (Borgou) 1·10 40
710 70f. Drums (Oueme) 1·20 45
711 100f. Calabash with burnt-work ornamentation (Zou) 1·50 55

**231** "Stamps" and Magnifying Glass

**1978.** Philatelic Exhibition, Riccione, Italy.
712 **231** 200f. multicoloured 2·30 1·10

**232** Parthenon and Frieze showing Horsemen

**1978.** Air. UNESCO Campaign for the Preservation of the Acropolis. Multicoloured.
713 70f. Acropolis and Frieze showing Procession 80 25
714 250f. Type **232** 2·50 1·20
715 500f. The Parthenon (horiz) 5·00 2·20

**235** Turkeys

**1978.** Domestic Poultry. Multicoloured.
722 10f. Type **235** 35 10
723 20f. Ducks 60 25
724 50f. Chickens 1·70 50
725 60f. Helmeted guineafowl 1·90 70

**236** Post Runner and Boeing 747

**1978.** Centenary of UPU. Paris Congress. Mult.
726 50f. Messenger of the Dahomey Kings (horiz) 1·00 40
727 60f. Pirogue oarsman, boat and post car 1·10 40
728 90f. Type **236** 1·30 55

**237** Red-breasted Merganser and Baden 1851 1k. Stamp

**1978.** Air. "Philexafrique" Exhibition, Libreville (Gabon) (1st issue) and International Stamp Fair, Essen, West Germany. Multicoloured.
729 100f. Type **237** 4·00 1·50
730 100f. African Buffalo and Dahomey 1966 50f. African Pygmy Goose stamp 4·00 1·50

See also Nos. 747/8.

**238** Raoul Follereau

**1978.** 1st Death Anniv of Raoul Follereau (leprosy pioneer).
731 **238** 200f. multicoloured 2·00 95

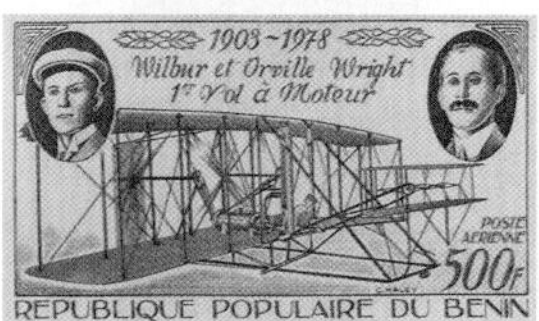

**239** Wilbur and Orville Wright and Wright Flyer 1

**1978.** Air. 75th Anniv of First Powered Flight.
732 **239** 500f. blue, yellow & brn 6·00 3·00

**240** I.Y.C. Emblem

**1979.** International Year of the Child. Mult.
733 10f. Type **240** 15 10
734 20f. Children in balloon 30 10
735 50f. Children dancing around globe 45 30

**241** Hydrangea

**1979.** Flowers. Multicoloured.

| | | | |
|---|---|---|---|
| 736 | 20f. Type **241** | 20 | 25 |
| 737 | 25f. Assangokan | 45 | 25 |
| 738 | 30f. Geranium | 70 | 35 |
| 739 | 40f. Water Lily (horiz) | 90 | 40 |

**242** Flags around Map of Africa

**1979.** OCAM Summit Meeting, Cotonou (1st series). Multicoloured.

| | | | |
|---|---|---|---|
| 740 | 50f. Type **242** | 55 | 40 |
| 741 | 60f. Flags and map of Benin | 85 | 45 |
| 742 | 80f. OCAM flag and map of member countries | 1·20 | 60 |

See also Nos. 754/6.

**1979.** Various stamps surch.

| | | | | |
|---|---|---|---|---|
| 743 | **205** | 50f. on 2f. multicoloured (postage) | £190 | 2·75 |
| 743a | - | 50f. on 3f. multicoloured (651) | 95·00 | 2·75 |
| 743b | - | 50f. on 70f. brown, green and black (620) | 95·00 | 2·75 |
| 744 | **207** | 50f. on 60f. mult (air) | 95·00 | 2·75 |
| 745 | **192** | 50f. on 90f. blue, deep blue and red | 95·00 | 2·75 |
| 746 | - | 50f. on 150f. mult (607) | 95·00 | 2·75 |
| 747 | **189** | 50f. on 150f. mult | 95·00 | 2·75 |

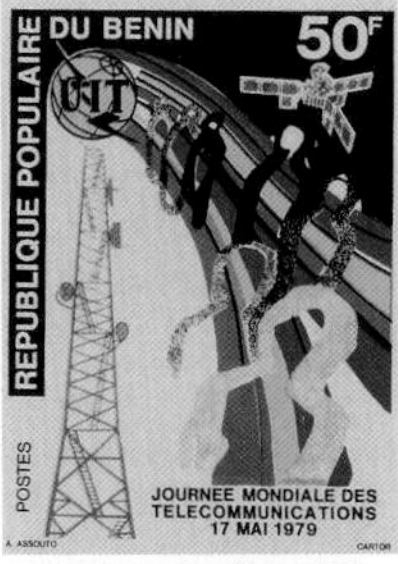


**244** Antenna, Satellite and Wave Pattern

**1979.** World Telecommunications Day.

| | | | | |
|---|---|---|---|---|
| 748 | **244** | 50f. multicoloured | 80 | 45 |

**245** Headquarters Building

**1979.** West African Savings Bank Building Opening.

| | | | | |
|---|---|---|---|---|
| 749 | **245** | 50f. multicoloured | 75 | 40 |

**246** "Resolution" and "Discovery" in Karakakoa Bay, Hawaii

**1979.** Air. Death Bicentenary of Capt. James Cook.

| | | | | |
|---|---|---|---|---|
| 750 | **246** | 20f. blue, green & brown | 1·30 | 40 |
| 751 | - | 50f. brown, green & blue | 1·00 | 45 |

DESIGN: 50f. Cook's death at Kowrowa.

**247** Guelede Mask, Abomey Tapestry and Fiery-breasted Bush Shrike

**1979.** "Philexafrique" Stamp Exhibition, Gabon (2nd issue).

| | | | | |
|---|---|---|---|---|
| 752 | **247** | 15f. multicoloured | 1·50 | 55 |
| 753 | - | 50f. orange, yellow & turq | 2·00 | 95 |

DESIGN: 50f. Lockheed L-1011 Tristar 500, satellite, U.P.U. emblem and canoe post.

**1979.** Common African and Mauritian Organization Summit Conference, Cotonou (2nd issue). Nos. 740/2 optd **26 Au 28 Juin 1979**.

| | | | |
|---|---|---|---|
| 754 | 50f. Type **242** | 80 | 40 |
| 755 | 60f. Map of Benin and flags of members | 95 | 50 |
| 756 | 80f. OCAM flag and map showing member countries | 1·10 | 55 |

**249** Olympic Flame, Benin Flags and Pictograms

**1979.** Pre-Olympic Year. Multicoloured.

| | | | |
|---|---|---|---|
| 757 | 10f. Type **249** | 30 | 10 |
| 758 | 50f. High jump | 1·00 | 45 |

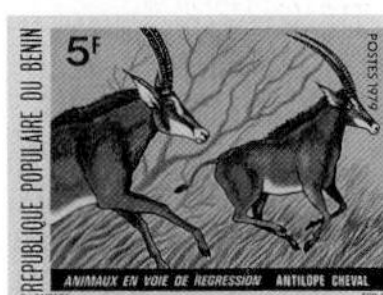


**250** Roan Antelope

**1979.** Endangered Animals. Multicoloured.

| | | | |
|---|---|---|---|
| 759 | 5f. Type **250** | 40 | 20 |
| 760 | 10f. Giraffes (vert) | 55 | 35 |
| 761 | 20f. Chimpanzee | 85 | 50 |
| 762 | 50f. African elephants (vert) | 1·80 | 75 |

**251** Emblem, Concorde and Map of Africa

**1979.** 20th Anniv of ASECNA (African Air Safety Organization). Multicoloured.

| | | | |
|---|---|---|---|
| 763 | 50f. Type **251** | 50 | 25 |
| 764 | 60f. As No. 763 but emblem at bottom right and without dates | 55 | 25 |

**252** Post Offices, Antenna, Telephone and Savings Book

**1979.** 20th Anniv of Posts and Telecommunications Office. Multicoloured.

| | | | |
|---|---|---|---|
| 765 | 50f. Type **252** | 50 | 25 |
| 766 | 60f. Collecting, sorting and delivering mail | 55 | 25 |

**253** Rotary Emblem, Symbols of Services and Globe

**1980.** 75th Anniv of Rotary International. Mult.

| | | | |
|---|---|---|---|
| 767 | 90f. Cotonou Rotary Club banner (vert) | 95 | 45 |
| 768 | 200f. Type **253** | 1·80 | 95 |

**254** Copernicus and Planetary System

**1980.** 50th Anniv of Discovery of Planet Pluto. Multicoloured.

| | | | |
|---|---|---|---|
| 769 | 70f. Kepler and astrolabe | 80 | 45 |
| 770 | 100f. Type **254** | 1·20 | 55 |

**255** Pharaonic Capital

**1980.** 20th Anniv of Nubian Monuments Preservation Campaign. Multicoloured.

| | | | |
|---|---|---|---|
| 771 | 50f. Type **255** | 55 | 30 |
| 772 | 60f. Rameses II, Abu Simbel | 95 | 45 |
| 773 | 150f. Temple, Abu Simbel (horiz) | 1·50 | 85 |

**256** Lenin in Library

**1980.** 110th Birth Anniv of Lenin. Mult.

| | | | |
|---|---|---|---|
| 774 | 50f. Lenin and globe | 75 | 25 |
| 775 | 150f. Type **256** | 2·00 | 85 |

**257** Monument

**1980.** Martyrs Square, Cotonou.

| | | | | |
|---|---|---|---|---|
| 776 | **257** | 50f. multicoloured | 45 | 10 |
| 777 | - | 60f. multicoloured | 55 | 25 |
| 778 | - | 70f. multicoloured | 75 | 25 |
| 779 | - | 100f. multicoloured | 1·20 | 40 |

DESIGNS—HORIZ: 60f. to 100f. Different views of the monument.

**258** Farmer using Telephone

**1980.** World Telecommunications Day. Mult.

| | | | |
|---|---|---|---|
| 780 | 50f. Type **258** | 45 | 25 |
| 781 | 60f. Telephone | 55 | 30 |

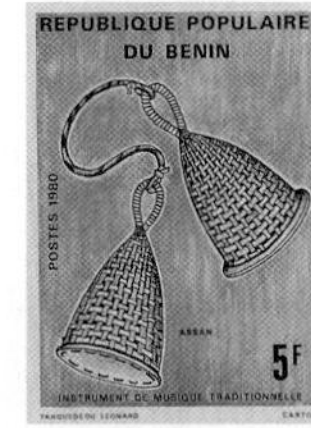


**259** Assan

**1980.** Traditional Musical Instruments. Mult.

| | | | |
|---|---|---|---|
| 782 | 5f. Type **259** | 25 | 10 |
| 783 | 10f. Tinbo (horiz) | 25 | 10 |
| 784 | 15f. Tam-tam sato | 55 | 25 |
| 785 | 20f. Kora (horiz) | 55 | 25 |
| 786 | 30f. Gangan (horiz) | 85 | 40 |
| 787 | 50f. Sinhoun (horiz) | 1·60 | 55 |

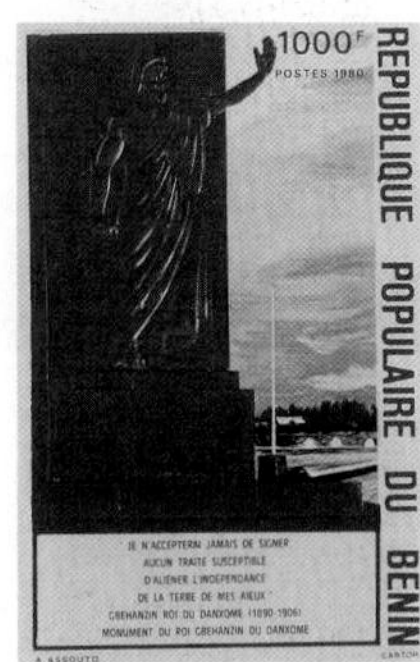


**260** Monument

**1980.** King Gbehanzin Monument.

| | | | | |
|---|---|---|---|---|
| 788 | **260** | 1000f. multicoloured | 13·00 | 8·50 |

**261** Dieudonne Costes, Maurice Bellonte and "Point d'Interrogation"

**1980.** 50th Anniv of First Paris–New York Non-stop Flight.

| | | | | |
|---|---|---|---|---|
| 789 | - | 90f. red, lt blue & blue | 1·00 | 45 |
| 790 | **261** | 100f. red, blue and flesh | 1·20 | 55 |

DESIGN: 90f. Airplane "Point d'Interrogation" and scenes of New York and Paris.

**262** "Lunokhod I"

**1980.** 10th Anniv of "Lunokhod I".

| | | | | |
|---|---|---|---|---|
| 791 | - | 90f. brown, blue and violet (postage) | 95 | 55 |
| 792 | **262** | 210f. purple, blue and yellow (air) | 2·75 | 1·30 |

DESIGN (48×36 mm): 90f. Rocket and "Lunokhod I".

**263** Show-jumping

**1980.** Olympic Games, Moscow. Multicoloured.

| | | | |
|---|---|---|---|
| 793 | 50f. Olympic Flame, running track, emblem and mascot Mischa the bear (horiz) | 50 | 25 |
| 794 | 60f. Type **263** | 55 | 40 |
| 795 | 70f. Judo (horiz) | 95 | 45 |
| 796 | 200f. Olympic flag and globe surrounded by sports pictogram | 2·00 | 90 |
| 797 | 300f. Weightlifting | 3·00 | 1·50 |

**264** OCAM Building

**1980.** Common African and Mauritian Organization Village, Cotonou. Multicoloured.

| | | | |
|---|---|---|---|
| 798 | 50f. Entrance to OCAM village | 60 | 25 |
| 799 | 60f. View of village | 75 | 25 |
| 800 | 70f. Type **264** | 95 | 55 |

**265** Dancers

**1980.** Agbadja Dance. Multicoloured.

| | | | |
|---|---|---|---|
| 801 | 30f. Type **265** | 55 | 25 |
| 802 | 50f. Singer and musicians | 95 | 45 |
| 803 | 60f. Dancers and musicians | 95 | 55 |

**266** Casting a Net

**1980.** Fishing. Multicoloured.

| | | | |
|---|---|---|---|
| 804 | 5f. Type **266** | 10 | 10 |
| 805 | 10f. Fisherman with catch (vert) | 30 | 10 |
| 806 | 15f. Line fishing | 30 | 25 |
| 807 | 20f. Fisherman emptying eel-pot | 35 | 25 |
| 808 | 50f. Hauling in a net | 95 | 45 |
| 809 | 60f. Fish farm | 95 | 45 |

**267** Philippines under Magnifying Glass

**1980.** World Tourism Conference, Manila. Mult.

| | | | |
|---|---|---|---|
| 810 | 50f. Type **267** | 55 | 25 |
| 811 | 60f. Conference flag on globe | 95 | 30 |

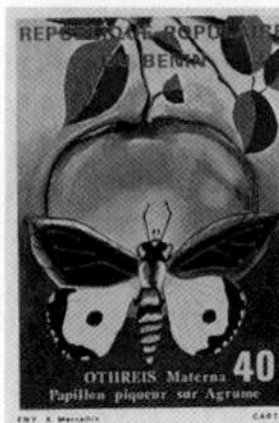


**268** "Othreis materna"

**1980.** Insects. Multicoloured.

| | | | |
|---|---|---|---|
| 812 | 40f. Type **268** | 80 | 35 |
| 813 | 50f. "Othreis fullonia" (butterfly) | 1·20 | 45 |
| 814 | 200f. "Oryctes" sp. (beetle) | 3·75 | 1·60 |

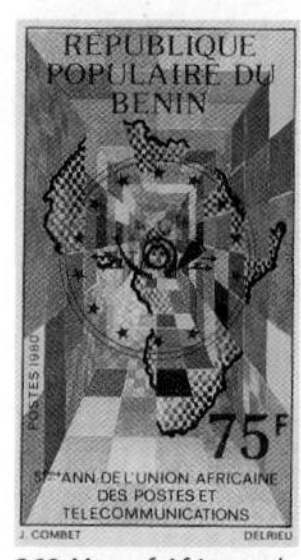


**269** Map of Africa and Posthorn

**1980.** 5th Anniv of African Posts and Telecommunications.

| | | | |
|---|---|---|---|
| 815 | **269** 75f. multicoloured | 75 | 25 |

**270** Hands freed from Chains

**1980.** 30th Anniv of Signing of Human Rights Convention. Multicoloured.

| | | | |
|---|---|---|---|
| 816 | 30f. Type **270** | 30 | 10 |
| 817 | 50f. African pushing through bars | 50 | 25 |
| 818 | 60f. Figure holding Human Rights flame | 75 | 25 |

**271** "Self-portrait"

**1980.** 90th Death Anniv of Van Gogh (artist). Multicoloured.

| | | | |
|---|---|---|---|
| 819 | 100f. Type **271** | 2·00 | 70 |
| 820 | 300f. "The Postman Roulin" | 5·00 | 2·20 |

**272** Offenbach and Scene from "Orpheus in the Underworld"

**1980.** Death Centenary of Jacques Offenbach (composer).

| | | | |
|---|---|---|---|
| 821 | **272** 50f. black, red and green | 1·30 | 50 |
| 822 | - 60f. blue, brown & dp brn | 1·90 | 75 |

DESIGN: 60f. Offenbach and scene from "La Vie Parisienne".

**273** Kepler and Astronomical Diagram

**1980.** 30th Death Anniv of Johannes Kepler (astronomer).

| | | | |
|---|---|---|---|
| 823 | **273** 50f. red, blue and grey | 75 | 25 |
| 824 | - 60f. blue, black and green | 95 | 45 |

DESIGN: 60f. Kepler, satellite and dish aerials.

**274** Footballers

**1981.** Air. World Cup Football Championship. Multicoloured.

| | | | |
|---|---|---|---|
| 825 | 200f. Football and globe | 1·80 | 70 |
| 826 | 500f. Type **274** | 5·00 | 1·90 |

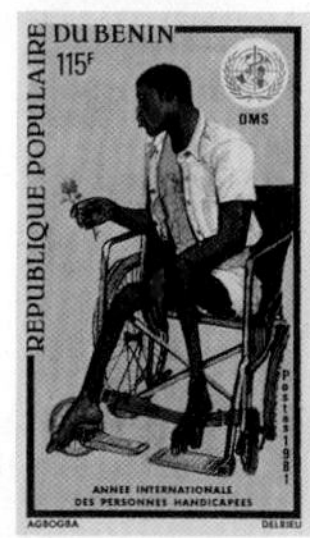


**275** Disabled Person holding Flower

**1981.** International Year of Disabled People.

| | | | |
|---|---|---|---|
| 827 | **275** 115f. multicoloured | 1·20 | 50 |

**276** Yuri Gagarin

**1981.** 20th Anniv of First Man in Space.

| | | | |
|---|---|---|---|
| 828 | **276** 500f. multicoloured | 5·50 | 2·75 |

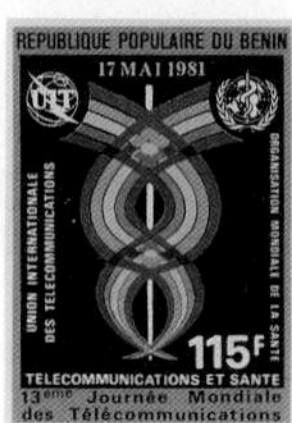


**277** ITU and WHO Emblems and Ribbons forming Caduceus

**1981.** World Telecommunications Day.

| | | | |
|---|---|---|---|
| 829 | **277** 115f. multicoloured | 1·20 | 45 |

**278** Amaryllis

**1981.** Flowers. Multicoloured.

| | | | |
|---|---|---|---|
| 830 | 10f. Type **278** | 20 | 15 |
| 831 | 20f. "Eischornia crassipes" | 45 | 30 |
| 832 | 80f. "Parkia biglobosa" | 1·50 | 50 |

**279** Hotel and Map

**1981.** Opening of Benin Sheraton Hotel.

| | | | |
|---|---|---|---|
| 833 | **279** 100f. multicoloured | 1·00 | 45 |

**1981.** Surch **50F**.

| | | | |
|---|---|---|---|
| 834 | **216** 50f. on 100f. brown, green and red | 85 | 25 |
| 835 | **193** 50f. on 210f. red, brown and green | 85 | 25 |

**281** Prince Charles, Lady Diana Spencer and Tower Bridge

**1981.** Air. British Royal Wedding.

| | | | |
|---|---|---|---|
| 836 | **281** 500f. multicoloured | 4·50 | 2·00 |

**282** Guinea Pig

**1981.** Domestic Animals. Multicoloured.

| | | | |
|---|---|---|---|
| 837 | 5f. Type **282** | 35 | 25 |
| 838 | 60f. Cat | 1·00 | 45 |
| 839 | 80f. Dogs | 1·40 | 70 |

**283** Heinrich von Stephan (founder of UPU)

**1981.** World Universal Postal Union Day.

| | | | |
|---|---|---|---|
| 840 | **283** 100f. slate and red | 95 | 45 |

**284** Heads, Quill, Paper Darts and U.P.U. Emblem

**1981.** International Letter Writing Week.

| | | | |
|---|---|---|---|
| 841 | **284** 100f. blue and purple | 95 | 45 |

**285** "The Dance"

**1981.** Air. Birth Centenary of Pablo Picasso. Multicoloured.

| | | | |
|---|---|---|---|
| 842 | 300f. Type **285** | 3·00 | 1·20 |
| 843 | 500f. "The Three Musicians" | 5·50 | 2·00 |

**286** Globe, Map of Member Countries and Communication Symbols

**1981.** 5th Anniv of ECOWAS (Economic Community of West African States).

| | | | |
|---|---|---|---|
| 844 | **286** 60f. multicoloured | 75 | 25 |

287 St. Theodore Stratilates (tile painting)

1981. Air. 1300th Anniv of Bulgarian State.

| | | | | |
|---|---|---|---|---|
| 845 | 287 | 100f. multicoloured | 95 | 45 |

288 Tractor and Map

1981. 10th Anniv of West African Rice Development Association.

| | | | | |
|---|---|---|---|---|
| 846 | 288 | 60f. multicoloured | 75 | 25 |

289 Pope John Paul II

1982. Air. Papal Visit.

| | | | | |
|---|---|---|---|---|
| 847 | 289 | 80f. multicoloured | 2·00 | 90 |

290 John Glenn

1982. Air. 20th Anniv of First United States Manned Space Flight.

| | | | | |
|---|---|---|---|---|
| 848 | 290 | 500f. multicoloured | 5·50 | 2·20 |

291 Dr. Robert Koch

1982. Centenary of Discovery of Tubercle Bacillus.

| | | | | |
|---|---|---|---|---|
| 849 | 291 | 115f. multicoloured | 1·80 | 70 |

292 Washington, U.S. Flag and Map

1982. 250th Birth Anniv of George Washington.

| | | | | |
|---|---|---|---|---|
| 850 | 292 | 200f. multicoloured | 2·30 | 85 |

1982. Red Cross. Surch **Croix Rouge 8 Mai 1982 60f.**

| | | | | |
|---|---|---|---|---|
| 851 | 266 | 60f. on 5f. multicoloured | 75 | 25 |

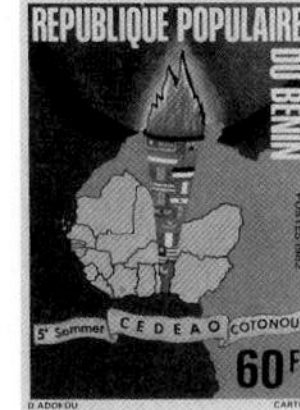
294 Map of Member Countries and Torch

1982. 5th Economic Community of West African States Summit, Cotonou.

| | | | | |
|---|---|---|---|---|
| 852 | 294 | 60f. multicoloured | 60 | 25 |

295 Scouts round Campfire

1982. Air. 75th Anniv of Boy Scout Movement.

| | | | | |
|---|---|---|---|---|
| 853 | 295 | 105f. multicoloured | 1·20 | 60 |

296 Footballers

1982. World Cup Football Championship, Spain. Multicoloured.

| | | | | |
|---|---|---|---|---|
| 854 | | 90f. Type **296** | 95 | 40 |
| 855 | | 300f. Leg with sock formed from flags of participating countries and globe/football | 3·00 | 1·20 |

1982. African Posts and Telegraph Union. Surch **UAPT 1982 60f.**

| | | | | |
|---|---|---|---|---|
| 856 | 282 | 60f. on 5f. multicoloured | 75 | 25 |

298 Stamp of Map of France and Magnifying Glass

1982. "Philexfrance 82" International Stamp Exhibition, Paris.

| | | | | |
|---|---|---|---|---|
| 857 | 298 | 90f. multicoloured | 95 | 45 |

1982. World Cup Football Championship Results. Nos. 854/5 optd.

| | | | | |
|---|---|---|---|---|
| 858 | | 90f. Type **296** | 1·20 | 45 |
| 859 | | 300f. Leg with flags of participating countries and football "globe" | 3·75 | 1·30 |

OVERPRINTS: 90f. **COUPE 82 ITALIE bat RFA 3-1**; 300f. **COUPE 82 1 ITALIE 2 RFA 3 POLOGNE.**

1982. Riccione Stamp Exhibition. Optd **RICCIONE 1982.**

| | | | | |
|---|---|---|---|---|
| 860 | 231 | 200f. multicoloured | 1·80 | 80 |

301 Laughing Kookaburra ("Dacelo Gigas")

1982. Birds. Multicoloured.

| | | | | |
|---|---|---|---|---|
| 861 | | 5f. Type **301** | 65 | 30 |
| 862 | | 10f. Bluethroat ("La Gorge Bleue") (horiz) | 1·00 | 30 |
| 863 | | 15f. Barn swallow ("L'Hirondelle") | 1·00 | 35 |
| 864 | | 20f. Woodland kingfisher ("Martin-Pecheur") and Village weaver ("Tisserin") | 1·60 | 40 |
| 865 | | 30f. Reed warbler ("La Rousserolle") (horiz) | 2·20 | 50 |
| 866 | | 60f. Warbler sp. ("Faurette Commoune") (horiz) | 3·00 | 75 |
| 867 | | 80f. Eagle owl ("Hibou Grand Doc") | 5·50 | 1·40 |
| 868 | | 100f. Sulphur-crested cockatoo ("Cacatoes") | 6·50 | 1·80 |

302 World Map and Satellite

1982. I.T.U. Delegates' Conference, Nairobi.

| | | | | |
|---|---|---|---|---|
| 869 | 302 | 200f. turq, blue & blk | 2·00 | 80 |

303 UPU Emblem and Heads

1982. UPU Day.

| | | | | |
|---|---|---|---|---|
| 870 | 303 | 100f. green, blue & brown | 1·00 | 45 |

305 "Claude Monet in his Studio"

1982. Air. 150th Birth Anniv of Edouard Manet (artist).

| | | | | |
|---|---|---|---|---|
| 876 | 305 | 300f. multicoloured | 6·75 | 2·40 |

306 "Virgin and Child" (Grunewald)

1982. Air. Christmas. Multicoloured.

| | | | | |
|---|---|---|---|---|
| 877 | | 200f. Type **306** | 2·20 | 1·10 |
| 878 | | 300f. "Virgin and Child with Angels and Cherubins" (Correggio) | 3·25 | 1·40 |

307 Pres. Mitterrand and Pres. Kerekou

1983. Visit of President Mitterrand.

| | | | | |
|---|---|---|---|---|
| 879 | 307 | 90f. multicoloured | 1·50 | 70 |

1983. Various stamps surch.

| | | | | |
|---|---|---|---|---|
| 880 | - | 60f. on 50f. multicoloured (No. 798) (postage) | 1·20 | 45 |
| 881 | - | 60f. on 70f. multicoloured (No. 778) | 1·20 | 45 |
| 882 | 279 | 60f. on 100f. mult | 47·00 | 2·75 |
| 883 | - | 75f. on 80f. multicoloured (No. 832) | 1·40 | 55 |
| 884 | - | 75f. on 80f. multicoloured (No. 839) | 1·50 | 85 |
| 885 | 262 | 75f. on 210f. red, blue and yellow (air) | 1·50 | 85 |

309 "Tender Benin" (tug) and "Amazone" (oil rig)

1983. Seme Oilfield.

| | | | | |
|---|---|---|---|---|
| 886 | 309 | 125f. multicoloured | 1·50 | 60 |

1983. Various stamps surch.

| | | | | |
|---|---|---|---|---|
| 887 | 267 | 5f. on 50f. multicoloured | 3·00 | 50 |
| 888 | 284 | 10f. on 100f. blue & pur | 3·00 | 50 |
| 889 | - | 10f. on 200f. mult (No. 659) | 3·00 | 50 |
| 890 | - | 15f. on 200f. red and bistre (No. 670) | 3·00 | 50 |
| 891 | - | 15f. on 200f. mult (No. 796) | 3·00 | 50 |
| 892 | - | 15f. on 210f. green, deep green and red (No. 667) | 3·00 | 50 |
| 893 | - | 15f. on 270f. mult (No. 643) | 3·00 | 50 |
| 894 | 219 | 20f. on 200f. brown, red and olive | 3·00 | 50 |
| 895 | - | 25f. on 70f. mult (No. 795) | 3·00 | 60 |
| 896 | - | 25f. on 210f. mult (No. 673) | 3·00 | 60 |
| 897 | - | 25f. on 270f. blue, turq & red (No. 633) | 3·00 | 50 |
| 898 | - | 25f. on 380f. brown and red (No. 687) | 3·00 | 50 |
| 899 | - | 30f. on 200f. brown, blue and red (No. 681) | 3·00 | 60 |
| 900 | 290 | 40f. on 500f. mult | 3·00 | 60 |
| 901 | 282 | 75f. on 5f. multicoloured | 3·25 | 65 |
| 902 | - | 75f. on 100f. red, blue and pink (No. 790) | 3·25 | 65 |
| 903 | - | 75f. on 150f. mult (No. 631) | 3·25 | 65 |
| 904 | - | 75f. on 150f. violet, red and green (No. 655) | 3·25 | 65 |
| 905 | 211 | 75f. on 150f. grey, orange and red | 3·25 | 65 |
| 906 | - | 75f. on 150f. dp brown, brown & red (No. 669) | 3·25 | 65 |

311 WCY Emblem

1983. World Communications Year.

| | | | | |
|---|---|---|---|---|
| 907 | 311 | 185f. multicoloured | 1·80 | 80 |

312 Stamps of Benin and Thailand and World Map

1983. Air. "Bangkok 1983" International Stamp Exhibition.

| | | | | |
|---|---|---|---|---|
| 908 | 312 | 300f. multicoloured | 3·00 | 1·40 |

313 Hand with Tweezers and Stamp

1983. "Riccione 83" Stamp Fair, San Marino.

| | | | | |
|---|---|---|---|---|
| 909 | 313 | 500f. multicoloured | 4·50 | 2·00 |

314 First Aid

1983. 20th Anniv of Benin Red Cross.

| | | | | |
|---|---|---|---|---|
| 910 | 314 | 105f. multicoloured | 1·20 | 60 |

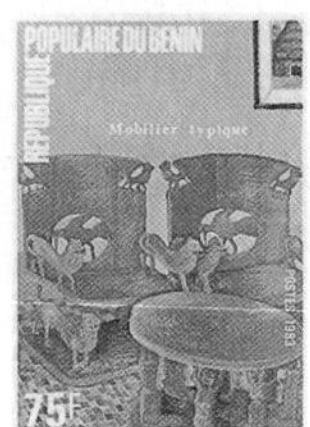

**315** Carved Table and Chairs

**1983.** Benin Woodwork. Multicoloured.

| | | | |
|---|---|---|---|
| 911 | 75f. Type **315** | 1·00 | 25 |
| 912 | 90f. Rustic table and chairs | 1·10 | 40 |
| 913 | 200f. Monkeys holding box | 2·00 | 75 |

**316** Boeing 747, World Map and UPU Emblem

**1983.** UPU Day.

| | | | | |
|---|---|---|---|---|
| 914 | **316** | 125f. green, blue & brown | 1·20 | 60 |

**317** Egoun

**1983.** Religious Cults. Multicoloured.

| | | | |
|---|---|---|---|
| 915 | 75f. Type **317** | 1·00 | 45 |
| 916 | 75f. Zangbeto | 1·00 | 45 |

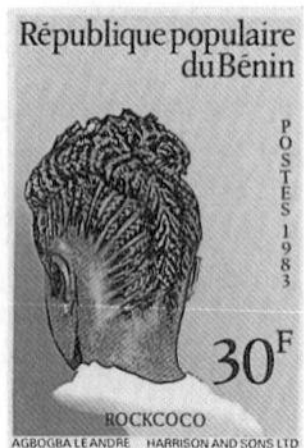

**318** Rockcoco

**1983.** Hair-styles. Multicoloured.

| | | | |
|---|---|---|---|
| 917 | 30f. Type **318** | 30 | 15 |
| 918 | 75f. Serpent | 75 | 45 |
| 919 | 90f. Songas | 1·30 | 55 |

**319** Alfred Nobel

**1983.** 150th Birth Anniv of Alfred Nobel.

| | | | | |
|---|---|---|---|---|
| 920 | **319** | 300f. multicoloured | 3·00 | 1·50 |

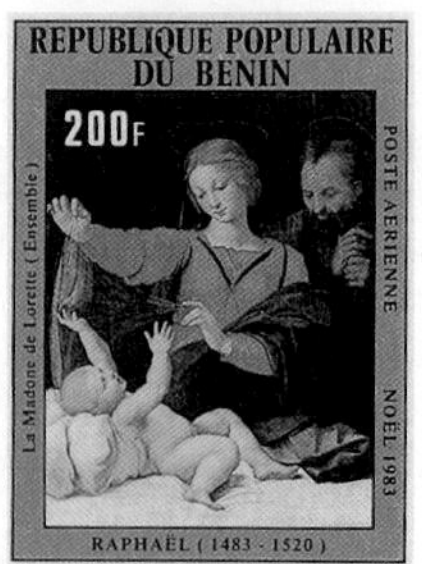

**320** "Madonna of Lorette" (Raphael)

**1983.** Air. Christmas.

| | | | | |
|---|---|---|---|---|
| 921 | **320** | 200f. multicoloured | 2·75 | 1·20 |

**1984.** Various stamps surch.

| | | | | |
|---|---|---|---|---|
| 922 | - | 5f. on 150f. mult (No. 685) (postage) | 3·25 | 75 |
| 923 | **316** | 5f. on 125f. green, blue and brown | 3·25 | 75 |
| 924 | **292** | 10f. on 200f. mult | 3·25 | 75 |
| 925 | - | 10f. on 200f. mult (No. 913) | 3·25 | 75 |
| 926 | - | 15f. on 300f. mult (No. 820) | 3·25 | 80 |
| 927 | - | 25f. on 300f. mult (No. 644) | 3·25 | 80 |
| 928 | **276** | 40f. on 500f. mult | 3·25 | 80 |
| 929 | **314** | 75f. on 105f. mult | 3·50 | 1·00 |
| 930 | **275** | 75f. on 115f. mult | 3·50 | 90 |
| 931 | **277** | 75f. on 115f. mult | 3·50 | 90 |
| 932 | **291** | 75f. on 115f. mult | 3·50 | 90 |
| 933 | **311** | 75f. on 185f. mult | 3·50 | 1·00 |
| 934 | **302** | 75f. on 200f. turquoise, blue and black | 3·50 | 1·00 |
| 935 | **320** | 15f. on 200f. mult (air) | 3·25 | 75 |
| 936 | **285** | 15f. on 300f. mult | 3·25 | 75 |
| 937 | **312** | 25f. on 300f. mult | 3·25 | 80 |
| 938 | **281** | 40f. on 500f. mult | 3·50 | 90 |
| 939 | **295** | 75f. on 105f. mult | 3·50 | 90 |
| 940 | **306** | 90f. on 200f. mult | 3·75 | 95 |
| 941 | **305** | 90f. on 300f. mult | 3·75 | 95 |

**322** Flags, Agriculture and Symbol of Unity and Growth

**1984.** 25th Anniv of Council of Unity.

| | | | | |
|---|---|---|---|---|
| 942 | **322** | 75f. multicoloured | 75 | 25 |
| 943 | **322** | 90f. multicoloured | 95 | 40 |

**323** UPU Emblem and Magnifying Glass

**1984.** 19th Universal Postal Union Congress, Hamburg.

| | | | | |
|---|---|---|---|---|
| 944 | **323** | 90f. multicoloured | 95 | 45 |

**324** Abomey-Calavi Ground Station

**1984.** Inauguration of Abomy-Calavi Ground Station.

| | | | | |
|---|---|---|---|---|
| 945 | **324** | 75f. multicoloured | 75 | 45 |

**325** Koumboro (Borgou)

**1984.** Traditional Costumes. Multicoloured.

| | | | |
|---|---|---|---|
| 946 | 5f. Type **325** | 15 | 10 |
| 947 | 10f. Taka (Borgou) | 30 | 25 |
| 948 | 20f. Toko (Atacora Province) | 30 | 25 |

**326** Olympic Mascot

**1984.** Air. Olympic Games, Los Angeles.

| | | | | |
|---|---|---|---|---|
| 949 | **326** | 300f. multicoloured | 3·00 | 1·40 |

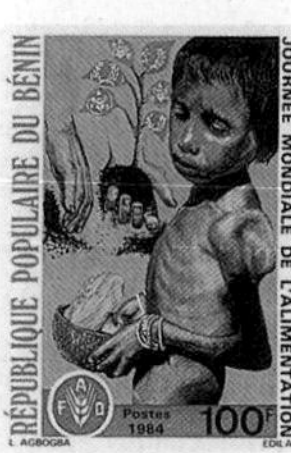

**327** Plant and Starving Child

**1984.** World Food Day.

| | | | | |
|---|---|---|---|---|
| 950 | **327** | 100f. multicoloured | 95 | 45 |

**328** Anatosaurus

**1984.** Prehistoric Animals. Multicoloured.

| | | | |
|---|---|---|---|
| 951 | 75f. Type **328** | 3·75 | 65 |
| 952 | 90f. Brontosaurus | 4·00 | 90 |

**329** "Virgin and Child" (detail, Murillo)

**1984.** Air. Christmas.

| | | | | |
|---|---|---|---|---|
| 953 | **329** | 500f. multicoloured | 5·50 | 2·20 |

**1984.** Various stamps surch.

| | | | | |
|---|---|---|---|---|
| 954 | **203** | 75f. on 200f. mult (post) | 6·00 | 1·30 |
| 955 | **226** | 75f. on 200f. mult | 6·00 | 1·30 |
| 956 | - | 75f. on 300f. mult (No. 696) | 6·00 | 1·30 |
| 957 | **229** | 75f. on 300f. mult | 6·00 | 1·30 |
| 958 | - | 90f. on 300f. mult (No. 855) | 6·25 | 1·40 |
| 959 | - | 90f. on 500f. mult (No. 697) | 6·25 | 1·40 |
| 960 | - | 90f. on 500f. mult (No. 701) | 6·75 | 1·40 |
| 961 | **204** | 75f. on 200f. mult (air) | 4·50 | 1·30 |
| 962 | - | 75f. on 200f. mult (No. 825) | 4·50 | 1·30 |
| 963 | - | 75f. on 300f. violet, red and mauve (No. 656) | 4·50 | 1·30 |
| 964 | - | 75f. on 300f. mult (No. 878) | 4·50 | 1·30 |
| 965 | **239** | 90f. on 500f. blue, yellow and brown | 4·50 | 1·40 |
| 966 | - | 90f. on 500f. mult (No. 715) | 4·50 | 1·40 |
| 967 | - | 90f. on 500f. mult (No. 843) | 4·50 | 1·40 |

**331** Sidon Merchant Ship (2nd century)

**1984.** Air. Ships.

| | | | | |
|---|---|---|---|---|
| 968 | **331** | 90f. black, green & blue | 1·30 | 60 |
| 969 | - | 125f. multicoloured | 2·00 | 85 |

DESIGN—VERT: 125f. Sail merchantman "Wavertree", 1895.

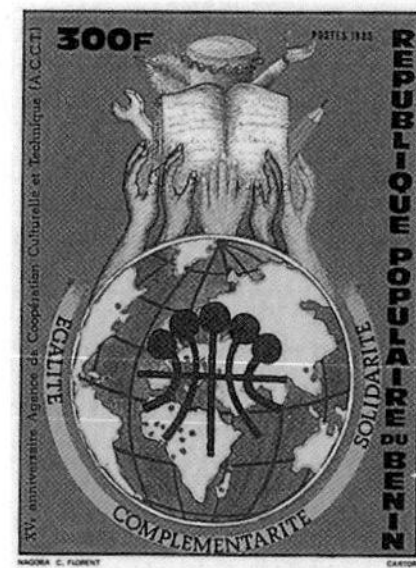

**332** Emblem on Globe and Hands reaching for Cultural Symbols

**1985.** 15th Anniv of Cultural and Technical Co-operation Agency.

| | | | | |
|---|---|---|---|---|
| 970 | **332** | 300f. multicoloured | 3·25 | 1·20 |

**333** Benin Arms

**1985.** Air. Postal Convention between Benin and Sovereign Military Order of Malta. Multicoloured.

| | | | |
|---|---|---|---|
| 971 | 75f. Type **333** | 75 | 25 |
| 972 | 75f. Arms of Sovereign Military Order | 75 | 25 |

**334** Soviet Flag, Soldier and Tank

**1985.** 40th Anniv of End of Second World War.

| | | | |
|---|---|---|---|
| 973 | **334** | 100f. multicoloured | |

**335** Teke Dance, Borgou

**1985.** Traditional Dances. Multicoloured.

| | | | |
|---|---|---|---|
| 974 | 75f. Type **335** | 1·00 | 40 |
| 975 | 100f. Tipen ti dance, Atacora | 1·30 | 60 |

**1985.** Various Dahomey Stamps optd **POPULAIRE DU BENIN** (985/6) or **REPUBLIQUE POPULAIRE DU BENIN** (others), Nos. 976/7 and 979/85 surch also.

| | | | | |
|---|---|---|---|---|
| 976 | **174** | 15f. on 40f. mult (post) | 2·75 | 60 |
| 977 | **182** | 25f. on 40f. brown, blue and violet (air) | 1·20 | 60 |
| 978 | **115** | 40f. black, purple & bl | 1·30 | 70 |
| 978a | - | 75f. on 85f. brown, blue and green (No. 468) | 48·00 | 1·60 |
| 979 | - | 75f. on 85f. brown, blue and green (No. 482) | 3·00 | 75 |
| 980 | **135** | 75f. on 100f. purple, violet and green | 3·00 | 75 |
| 981 | - | 75f. on 125f. green, blue and purple (No. 509) | 3·00 | 75 |
| 982 | **127** | 90f. on 20f. brown, blue and green | 3·00 | 80 |
| 983 | - | 90f. on 150f. purple, blue & brown (No. 456) | 3·00 | 80 |
| 984 | - | 90f. on 200f. green, red and blue (No. 438) | 3·00 | 80 |
| 985 | - | 90f. on 200f. mult (No. 563) | 3·00 | 80 |
| 986 | - | 150f. mult (No. 562) | 3·50 | 1·00 |

**338** Oil Rig

**1985.** Air. "Philexafrique" International Stamp Exhibition, Lome, Togo (1st issue). Mult.

| | | | |
|---|---|---|---|
| 987 | 200f. Type **338** | 2·30 | 1·50 |
| 988 | 200f. Footballers | 2·30 | 1·50 |

See also Nos. 999/1000.

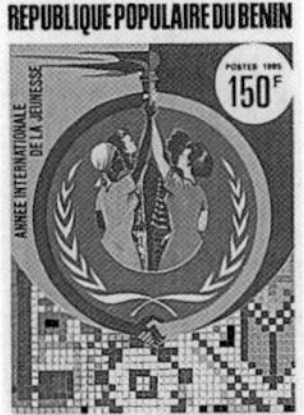


**339** Emblem

**1985.** International Youth Year.

| | | | | |
|---|---|---|---|---|
| 989 | **339** | 150f. multicoloured | 1·40 | 75 |

**340** Football between Globes

**1985.** World Cup Football Championship, Mexico (1986) (1st issue).

| | | | | |
|---|---|---|---|---|
| 990 | **340** | 200f. multicoloured | 1·80 | 95 |

See also No. 1015.

**341** Boeing 727, Map and Emblem

**1985.** 25th Anniv of Aerial Navigation Security Agency for Africa and Malagasy.

| | | | | |
|---|---|---|---|---|
| 991 | **341** | 150f. multicoloured | 1·80 | 75 |

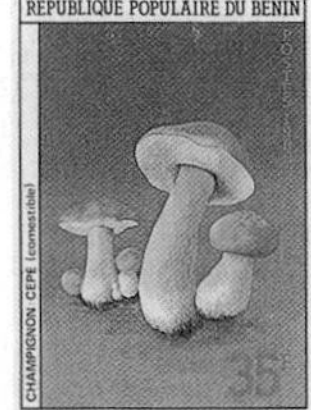


**342** "Boletus edulis"

**1985.** Fungi. Multicoloured.

| | | | |
|---|---|---|---|
| 992 | 35f. Type **342** | 1·50 | 45 |
| 993 | 40f. "Amanita phalloides" | 1·80 | 75 |
| 994 | 100f. "Paxillus involutus" | 4·50 | 1·70 |

**343** Audubon and Arctic Skua ("Labbe Parasite")

**1985.** Birth Bicentenary of John J. Audubon (ornithologist). Multicoloured.

| | | | |
|---|---|---|---|
| 995 | 150f. Type **343** | 3·00 | 1·50 |
| 996 | 300f. Audubon and oyster-catcher ("Huitrier Pie") | 7·00 | 2·20 |

**344** Emblem, Hands and Dove

**1985.** 40th Anniv of United Nations Organization and 25th Anniv of Benin's Membership.

| | | | | |
|---|---|---|---|---|
| 997 | **344** | 250f. multicoloured | 2·30 | 1·10 |

**345** Stamps and Globe

**1985.** "Italia '85" International Stamp Exhibition, Rome.

| | | | | |
|---|---|---|---|---|
| 998 | **345** | 200f. multicoloured | 1·80 | 95 |

**1985.** "Philexafrique" International Stamp Exhibition, Lome, Togo (2nd issue). As Type **338**. Multicoloured.

| | | | |
|---|---|---|---|
| 999 | 250f. Forest and hand holding tools | 4·25 | 1·80 |
| 1000 | 250f. Magnifying glass over judo stamp | 3·00 | 1·50 |

**1985.** Various Dahomey stamps optd **Republique Populaire du Benin**. Nos. 1001/9 and 1011 surch also.

| | | | | |
|---|---|---|---|---|
| 1001 | - | 75f. on 35f. mult (No. 596) (postage) | 2·50 | 60 |
| 1002 | - | 90f. on 70f. multicoloured (No. 419) | 2·50 | 65 |
| 1003 | - | 90f. on 140f. multicoloured (No. 446) | 2·50 | 65 |
| 1004 | **113** | 100f. on 40f. red, brown and green | 1·90 | 65 |
| 1005 | - | 150f. on 45f. multicoloured (No. 597) | 2·10 | 80 |
| 1006 | - | 75f. on 70f. multicoloured (No. 342) (air) | 4·25 | 90 |
| 1007 | - | 75f. on 100f. multicoloured (No. 251) | 4·25 | 90 |
| 1008 | **59** | 75f. on 200f. mult | 4·25 | 90 |
| 1009 | - | 90f. on 250f. multicoloured (No. 272) | 4·25 | 90 |
| 1010 | **110** | 100f. multicoloured | 2·75 | 90 |
| 1011 | - | 150f. on 500f. multicoloured (No. 252) | 2·75 | 90 |

No. 1010 is surcharged on the unoverprinted unissued stamp subsequently issued as No. 422.

**349** Church, Children playing and Nativity Scene

**1985.** Air. Christmas.

| | | | | |
|---|---|---|---|---|
| 1012 | **349** | 500f. multicoloured | 5·25 | 2·30 |

**350** Emblem

**1986.** 10th Anniv of African Parliamentary Union and Ninth Conference, Cotonou.

| | | | | |
|---|---|---|---|---|
| 1013 | **350** | 100f. multicoloured | 95 | 50 |

**351** Halley, Comet and "Giotto" Space Probe

**1986.** Appearance of Halley's Comet.

| | | | | |
|---|---|---|---|---|
| 1014 | **351** | 205f. multicoloured | 3·00 | 1·50 |

**352** Footballers

**1986.** World Cup Football Championship, Mexico (2nd issue). Multicoloured.

| | | | | |
|---|---|---|---|---|
| 1015 | **352** | 500f. Footballers | 4·50 | 2·30 |

**353** Dead and Healthy Trees

**1986.** Anti-desertification Campaign.

| | | | | |
|---|---|---|---|---|
| 1016 | **353** | 150f. multicoloured | 1·50 | 70 |

**354** Amazone

**1986**

| | | | | |
|---|---|---|---|---|
| 1017 | **354** | 100f. blue | 75 | 30 |
| 1018 | **354** | 150f. purple | 1·30 | 50 |

**355** "Haemanthus"

**1986.** Flowers. Multicoloured.

| | | | |
|---|---|---|---|
| 1019 | 100f. Type **355** | 1·10 | 70 |
| 1020 | 205f. "Hemerocallis" | 2·75 | 1·20 |

**356** "Inachis io", "Aglais urticae" and "Nymphalis antiopa"

**1986.** Butterflies. Multicoloured.

| | | | |
|---|---|---|---|
| 1021 | 150f. Type **356** | 3·00 | 1·30 |
| 1022 | 150f. "Anthocharis cardamines", "Papilio machaon" and "Cynthia cardui" | 3·00 | 1·30 |

**1986.** Various stamps of Dahomey surch **Republique Populaire du** Benin and new value.

| | | | | |
|---|---|---|---|---|
| 1024 | - | 150f. on 100f. mult (444) (postage) | 55·00 | 2·75 |
| 1025 | - | 15f. on 85f. mult (600) (air) | 33·00 | 2·75 |
| 1026 | - | 25f. on 200f. mult (432) | 55·00 | 2·75 |
| 1027 | **150** | 25f. on 200f. deep green, violet and green | 55·00 | 2·75 |
| 1030 | **175** | 100f. purple, indigo & bl | 55·00 | 2·75 |
| 1031 | **128** | 150f. on 100f. blue, violet and red | | |

**358** Statue and Buildings

**1986.** Centenary of Statue of Liberty.

| | | | | |
|---|---|---|---|---|
| 1032 | **358** | 250f. multicoloured | 3·00 | 1·20 |

**359** Bust of King Behanzin

**1986.** King Behanzin.

| | | | | |
|---|---|---|---|---|
| 1033 | **359** | 440f. multicoloured | 5·00 | 2·20 |

For design in smaller size, see Nos. 1101/4.

**360** Family with Crib, Church and Nativity Scene

**1986.** Air. Christmas.

| | | | | |
|---|---|---|---|---|
| 1034 | **360** | 300f. multicoloured | 5·25 | 1·80 |

**361** Rainbow and Douglas DC-10

**1986.** Air. 25th Anniv of Air Afrique.

| | | | | |
|---|---|---|---|---|
| 1035 | **361** | 100f. multicoloured | 1·00 | 50 |

**362** Emblem around Map in Cog

**1987.** Brazil Culture Week, Cotonou.

| | | | | |
|---|---|---|---|---|
| 1036 | **362** | 150f. multicoloured | 1·40 | 65 |

**363** Cotonou Centre for the Blind and Partially Sighted

**1987.** Rotary International 910 District Conference, Cotonou.

| | | | | |
|---|---|---|---|---|
| 1037 | **363** | 300f. multicoloured | 3·25 | 1·40 |

**1987.** Various stamps of Dahomey optd **Republique Populaire du Benin**. Nos. 1038/9 and 1042/53 surch also.

| | | | | |
|---|---|---|---|---|
| 1038 | **129** | 10f. on 65f. black, violet and red (postage) | | |
| 1039 | - | 15f. on 100f. red, blue and green (434) | 43·00 | 1·80 |
| 1040 | **98** | 40f. green, blue and brown | 55·00 | 2·75 |
| 1042 | - | 150f. on 200f. mult (560) | | |
| 1043 | **144** | 10f. on 65f. black, yellow & purple (air) | | |
| 1046 | - | 25f. on 150f. mult (487) | 55·00 | 2·75 |
| 1047 | - | 30f. on 300f. mult (602) | | |
| 1048 | **140** | 40f. on 15f. purple, green and blue | 47·00 | 2·75 |
| 1049 | - | 40f. on 100f. mult (453) | 43·00 | 2·75 |
| 1051 | - | 50f. on 140f. mult (601) | 55·00 | 2·75 |
| 1052 | - | 50f. on 500f. mult (252) | 55·00 | 2·75 |
| 1053 | - | 70f. on 250f. mult (462) | | |
| 1054 | - | 80f. mult (286) | 55·00 | 2·75 |
| 1055 | - | 100f. mult (429) | 55·00 | 2·75 |
| 1055a | - | 100f. mult (447) | 55·00 | 2·75 |

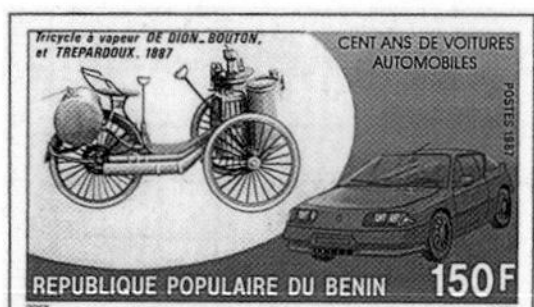


**365** De Dion-Bouton and Trepardoux Steam Tricycle and Ford Coupe

**1987.** Centenary of Motor Car. Multicoloured.

| | | | |
|---|---|---|---|
| 1058 | 150f. Type **365** | 1·50 | 70 |
| 1059 | 300f. Daimler motor carriage, 1886 and Mercedes Benz W124 series saloon | 3·25 | 1·40 |

**366** Baptism in the Python Temple

**1987.** Ritual Ceremonies.

| | | | | |
|---|---|---|---|---|
| 1060 | **366** | 100f. multicoloured | 1·50 | 70 |

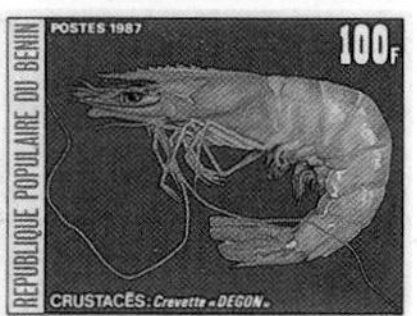


**367** Shrimp

**1987.** Shellfish. Multicoloured.

| | | | |
|---|---|---|---|
| 1061 | 100f. Type **367** | 1·30 | 75 |
| 1062 | 150f. Crab | 2·00 | 1·00 |

**368** G. Hansen and R. Follereau (leprosy pioneers) and Patients

**1987.** Anti-leprosy Campaign.

| | | | | |
|---|---|---|---|---|
| 1063 | **368** | 200f. multicoloured | 2·50 | 1·20 |

**369** Crop-spraying and Locusts

**1987.** Anti-locust Campaign.

| | | | | |
|---|---|---|---|---|
| 1064 | **369** | 100f. multicoloured | 1·20 | 65 |

**370** Fisherman and Farmer

**1987.** Air. 10th Anniv of International Agricultural Development Fund.

| | | | | |
|---|---|---|---|---|
| 1065 | **370** | 500f. multicoloured | 4·50 | 2·40 |

**371** Nativity Scene in Moon and Father Christmas giving Sweets to Crowd

**1987.** Christmas.

| | | | | |
|---|---|---|---|---|
| 1066 | **371** | 150f. multicoloured | 1·50 | 85 |

**372** Rally

**1988.** 15th Anniv (1987) of Start of Benin Revolution.

| | | | | |
|---|---|---|---|---|
| 1067 | **372** | 100f. multicoloured | £100 | 2·75 |

**1988.** Various stamps surch. (a) Stamps of Dahomey surch **Populaire du Benin** (1081c) or **Republique Populaire du Benin** (others).

| | | | | |
|---|---|---|---|---|
| 1068 | - | 5f. on 3f. black and blue (173) (postage) | 55·00 | 2·75 |
| 1069 | - | 20f. on 100f. mult (506) | 55·00 | 2·75 |
| 1071 | - | 25f. on 100f. mult (576) | 55·00 | 2·75 |
| 1073 | - | 50f. on 45f. mult (320) | 65·00 | 2·75 |
| 1074 | **178** | 55f. on 200f. olive, brown and green | 95·00 | 2·75 |
| 1075a | **178** | 125f. on 100f. mult (557) | | |
| 1076 | **116** | 10f. on 50f. black, orange and blue (air) | 55·00 | 2·75 |
| 1077 | **161** | 15f. on 150f. red and black | 55·00 | 2·75 |
| 1078 | - | 25f. on 100f. mult (526) | 75·00 | 2·75 |
| 1079 | **156** | 25f. on 100f. blue, brown and violet | 75·00 | 2·75 |
| 1079a | **153** | 40f. on 35f. mult | 55·00 | 2·75 |
| 1080 | - | 40f. on 100f. mult (495) | 55·00 | |
| 1081 | **162** | 40f. on 150f. red, brown and blue | 55·00 | 2·75 |
| 1081a | **148** | 100f. brown and green | 55·00 | 2·75 |
| 1081b | **181** | 125f. on 75f. lilac, red and green | 45·00 | 2·75 |
| 1081c | - | 125f. on 150f. blue and purple (541) | | 2·75 |
| 1082 | - | 125f. on 250f. mult (491) | 55·00 | 2·75 |
| 1082a | - | 125f. red and brown (540) | 55·00 | 2·75 |
| 1083 | - | 190f. on 250f. brown, green and red (594) | 90·00 | |
| 1084 | - | 1000f. on 150f. multicoloured (545) | 55·00 | 2·75 |

(b) No. 618 of Benin surch **Republique Populaire du Benin.**

| | | | |
|---|---|---|---|
| 1085 | 10f. on 60f. on 2f. mult | 55·00 | 2·75 |

(c) Stamps of Benin surch only.

| | | | | |
|---|---|---|---|---|
| 1086 | **359** | 125f. on 440f. mult (postage) | | |
| 1087 | **338** | 125f. on 200f. mult (air) | | |
| 1088 | - | 190f. on 250f. mult (999) | 90·00 | |
| 1089 | - | 190f. on 250f. mult (1000) | | |

**375** Hands holding Pot Aloft

**1988.** 25th Anniv of Organization of African Unity.

| | | | | |
|---|---|---|---|---|
| 1094 | **375** | 125f. multicoloured | 1·20 | 50 |

**376** Resuscitation of Man pulled from River

**1988.** 125th Anniv of Red Cross Movement.

| | | | | |
|---|---|---|---|---|
| 1095 | **376** | 200f. multicoloured | 3·25 | 1·60 |

**377** King

**1988.** 20th Death Anniv of Martin Luther King (Civil Rights leader).

| | | | | |
|---|---|---|---|---|
| 1096 | **377** | 200f. multicoloured | 2·00 | 95 |

**378** Scout and Camp

**1988.** 1st Benin Scout Jamboree, Savalou.

| | | | | |
|---|---|---|---|---|
| 1097 | **378** | 125f. multicoloured | 1·20 | 55 |

**379** Healthy Family and Health Care

**1988.** 40th Anniv of W.H.O. and 10th Anniv of "Health for All by 2000" Declaration.

| | | | | |
|---|---|---|---|---|
| 1098 | **379** | 175f. multicoloured | 1·50 | 80 |

**380** Dugout Canoes and Houses

**1988.** Ganvie (lake village). Multicoloured.

| | | | |
|---|---|---|---|
| 1099 | 125f. Type **380** | 1·20 | 55 |
| 1100 | 190f. Boatman and houses | 1·80 | 85 |

**1988.** As T **359** but smaller (17×24 mm).

| | | | | |
|---|---|---|---|---|
| 1101 | **359** | 40f. black | 30 | 15 |
| 1102 | **359** | 125f. red | 1·00 | 45 |
| 1103 | **359** | 190f. blue | 1·50 | 65 |
| 1104 | **359** | 220f. green | 1·80 | 80 |

**381** Adoration of the Magi

**1988.** Air. Christmas.

| | | | | |
|---|---|---|---|---|
| 1105 | **381** | 500f. multicoloured | 4·50 | 2·20 |

**382** Offering to Hebiesso, God of Thunder

**1988.** Ritual Ceremony.

| | | | | |
|---|---|---|---|---|
| 1106 | **382** | 125f. multicoloured | 1·20 | 55 |

**383** Roseate Tern

**1989.** Endangered Animals. Roseate Tern. Mult.

| | | | |
|---|---|---|---|
| 1107 | 10f. Type **383** | 1·10 | 70 |
| 1108 | 15f. Tern with fish | 1·10 | 70 |
| 1109 | 50f. Tern on rocks | 2·50 | 1·40 |
| 1110 | 125f. Tern flying | 5·00 | 2·75 |

**384** Eiffel Tower

**1989.** Centenary of Eiffel Tower.

| | | | | |
|---|---|---|---|---|
| 1111 | **384** | 190f. multicoloured | 2·50 | 1·10 |

**386** Tractor, Map and Pump

**1989.** 30th Anniv of Agriculture Development Council.

| | | | | |
|---|---|---|---|---|
| 1113 | **386** | 75f. multicoloured | 95·00 | |

**387** Symbols of Revolution and France 1950 National Relief Fund Stamps

**1989.** Bicentenary of French Revolution and "Philexfrance 89" International Stamp Exhibition, Paris.

| | | | | |
|---|---|---|---|---|
| 1114 | **387** | 190f. multicoloured | 2·50 | 1·50 |

**388** Burbot

**1989.** Fishes. Multicoloured.

| | | | |
|---|---|---|---|
| 1115 | 125f. Type **388** | 1·30 | 60 |
| 1116 | 190f. Northern pike and Atlantic salmon | 2·00 | 95 |

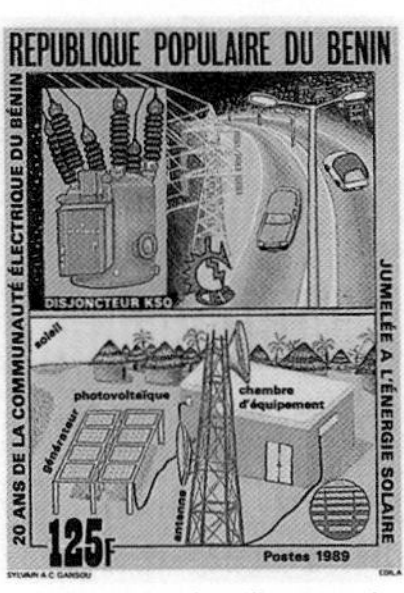

**389** Circuit Breaker, Illuminated Road and Solar Energy Complex

**1989.** 20th Anniv of Benin Electricity Community.

| | | | | |
|---|---|---|---|---|
| 1117 | **389** | 125f. multicoloured | 1·30 | 60 |

**390** Lion within Wreath

**1989.** Death Centenary of King Glele.

| | | | | |
|---|---|---|---|---|
| 1118 | **390** | 190f. multicoloured | 1·70 | 90 |

**391** Nativity

**1989.** Christmas.

| | | | | |
|---|---|---|---|---|
| 1119 | **391** | 200f. multicoloured | 1·80 | 95 |

**392** Anniversary Emblem and Means of Communications

**1990.** Centenary of Postal and Telecommunications Ministry (1st issue).

| | | | | |
|---|---|---|---|---|
| 1120 | **392** | 125f. multicoloured | 1·30 | 60 |

See also No. 1127.

**393** Oranges

**1990.** Fruit and Flowers. Multicoloured.

| | | | |
|---|---|---|---|
| 1121 | 60f. Type **393** | 75 | 40 |
| 1122 | 190f. Kaufmannia tulips (vert) | 2·00 | 95 |
| 1123 | 250f. Cashew nuts (vert) | 2·50 | 1·30 |

**394** Launch of "Apollo 11" and Footprint on Moon

**1990.** 21st Anniv of First Manned Moon Landing.

| | | | | |
|---|---|---|---|---|
| 1124 | **394** | 190f. multicoloured | 1·70 | 85 |

**395** Footballers

**1990.** World Cup Football Championship, Italy. Multicoloured.

| | | | |
|---|---|---|---|
| 1125 | 125f. Type **395** | 1·20 | 60 |
| 1126 | 190f. Mascot holding torch and pennant (vert) | 1·90 | 85 |

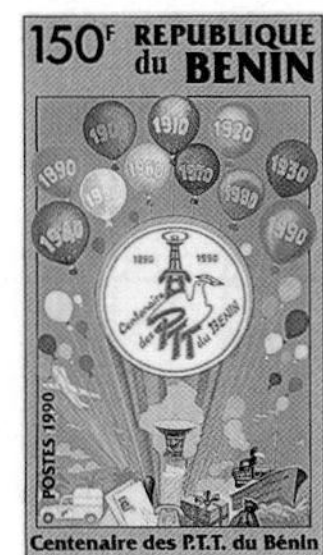

**396** Balloons, Emblem and Means of Communication

**1990.** Centenary of Postal and Telecommunications Ministry (2nd issue).

| | | | | |
|---|---|---|---|---|
| 1127 | **396** | 150f. multicoloured | 1·40 | 65 |

**1990.** World Cup Finalists. No. 1125 optd **FINALE R.F.A.-ARGENTINE 1-0**.

| | | | | |
|---|---|---|---|---|
| 1128 | **395** | 125f. multicoloured | 1·20 | 60 |

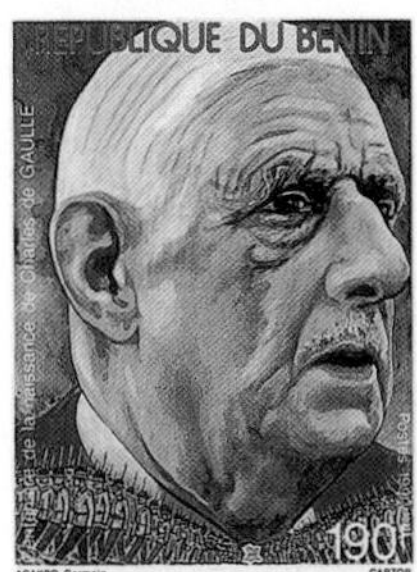

**398** De Gaulle

**1990.** Birth Centenary of Charles de Gaulle (French statesman) (1st issue).

| | | | | |
|---|---|---|---|---|
| 1129 | **398** | 190f. multicoloured | 2·00 | 1·20 |

See also No. 1160.

**399** "Galileo" Space Probe orbiting Jupiter

**1990.** Space Exploration.

| | | | | |
|---|---|---|---|---|
| 1130 | **399** | 100f. multicoloured | 1·00 | 60 |

**400** Nativity

**1990.** Christmas.

| | | | | |
|---|---|---|---|---|
| 1131 | **400** | 200f. multicoloured | 1·90 | 1·20 |

**401** Hands pointing to Scales of Justice

**1990.** National Conference of Active Forces.

| | | | | |
|---|---|---|---|---|
| 1132 | **401** | 125f. multicoloured | | |

**406** Different Cultures and Emblem

**1991.** African Tourism Year.

| | | | | |
|---|---|---|---|---|
| 1150 | **406** | 190f. multicoloured | 1·90 | 1·20 |

**407** Tennis Player

**1991.** Cent of French Open Tennis Championships.

| | | | | |
|---|---|---|---|---|
| 1151 | **407** | 125f. multicoloured | 1·50 | 95 |

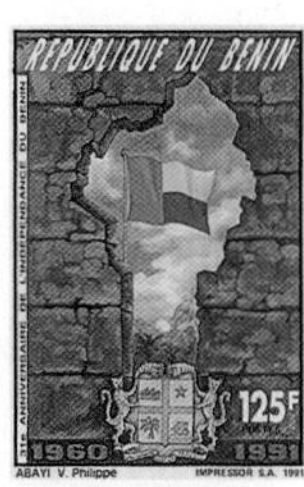

**408** Flag and Arms

**1991.** 31st Anniv of Independence.

| | | | | |
|---|---|---|---|---|
| 1152 | **408** | 125f. multicoloured | 1·30 | 50 |

**1991.** "Riccione 91" Stamp Fair. No. 1130 optd "**Riccione 91**".

| | | | | |
|---|---|---|---|---|
| 1153 | **399** | 100f. multicoloured | 95 | 70 |

**410** Adoration of the Magi

**1991.** Christmas.

| | | | | |
|---|---|---|---|---|
| 1154 | **410** | 125f. multicoloured | 1·30 | 60 |

**411** Guelede Dancer

**1991**

| | | | | |
|---|---|---|---|---|
| 1155 | **411** | 190f. multicoloured | 2·00 | 80 |

**412** Mozart

**1991.** Death Bicentenary of Wolfgang Amadeus Mozart (composer).

| | | | | |
|---|---|---|---|---|
| 1156 | **412** | 1000f. multicoloured | 10·00 | 5·75 |

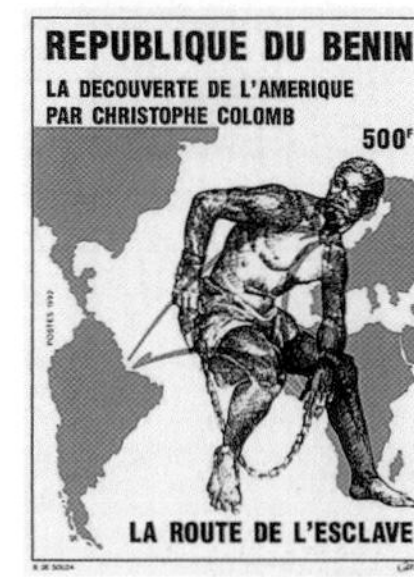

**413** Slave in Chains and Route Map

**1992.** 500th Anniv of Discovery of America by Columbus.

| | | | | |
|---|---|---|---|---|
| 1157 | **413** | 500f. black, brown & bl | 4·50 | 3·00 |
| 1158 | - | 1000f. multicoloured | 9·00 | 5·75 |
| **MS**1159 | | 133×93 mm. Nos. 1157/8 | 15·00 | 14·00 |

DESIGN—HORIZ: 1000f. Columbus landing at Guanahami, Bahamas.

**1992.** Birth Centenary (1990) of Charles de Gaulle (French statesman) (2nd issue). As No. 1129 but value changed.

| | | | | |
|---|---|---|---|---|
| 1160 | **398** | 300f. multicoloured | 3·00 | 1·60 |

**414** Child, Produce and Emblems

**1992.** International Nutrition Conference, Rome.

| | | | | |
|---|---|---|---|---|
| 1161 | **414** | 190f. multicoloured | 1·80 | 1·20 |

**415** Pope John Paul II

**1993.** Papal Visit.

| | | | | |
|---|---|---|---|---|
| 1162 | **415** | 190f. multicoloured | 2·00 | 1·10 |

**416** Emblem and Voodoo Culture

**1993.** "Ouidah 92" Voodoo Culture Festival.

| | | | | |
|---|---|---|---|---|
| 1163 | **416** | 125f. multicoloured | 1·20 | 60 |

417 Well and Blue-throated Roller

**1993.** Possotome Artesian Well.

| | | | | |
|---|---|---|---|---|
| 1164 | **417** | 125f. multicoloured | 2·20 | 1·40 |

418 Map, Clasped Hands and Flags of Member Countries

**1993.** 30th Anniv of Organization of African Unity.

| | | | | |
|---|---|---|---|---|
| 1165 | **418** | 125f. multicoloured | 1·20 | 70 |

419 John F. Kennedy (President of United States, 1961–63)

**1993.** Death Anniversaries. Multicoloured.

| | | | |
|---|---|---|---|
| 1166 | 190f. Type **419** (30th anniv) | 1·90 | 1·10 |
| 1167 | 190f. Dr. Martin Luther King (American civil rights campaigner, 25th anniv) (vert) | 2·00 | 1·10 |

**1993.** Stamps of Dahomey variously optd or surch. (a) **REPUBLIQUE DU BENIN**.

| | | | | |
|---|---|---|---|---|
| 1167a | **139** | 5f. multicoloured (postage) | 80·00 | 2·75 |
| 1170 | **108** | 50f. on 1f. multicoloured (617) | 55·00 | 2·75 |
| 1171 | **113** | 80f. on 40f. red, brown and green | 43·00 | 2·75 |
| 1173 | **113** | 135f. on 20f. black, green and red (190) | 95·00 | |
| 1175 | **113** | 135f. on 30f. black, brown and violet (472) | 55·00 | |
| 1177 | **107** | 135f. on 40f. mult | 38·00 | |
| 1179 | - | 135f. on 60f. olive, red and purple (181) | 55·00 | 2·75 |
| 1181 | - | 200f. on 100f. mult (322) | 65·00 | 2·75 |
| 1186 | - | 15f. on 40f. mult (458) (air) | 47·00 | 2·75 |
| 1190 | **126** | 100f. multicoloured | 55·00 | 2·75 |
| 1190a | **119** | 125f. on 40f. mult | 23·00 | 2·75 |
| 1191 | - | 125f. on 65f. red and blue (552) | 55·00 | 2·75 |
| 1201 | - | 200f. on 250f. mult (569) | 47·00 | |

(b) **DU BENIN**.

| | | | | |
|---|---|---|---|---|
| 1207 | **60** | 5f. on 1f. multicoloured (postage) | 65·00 | 2·75 |
| 1208 | - | 10f. on 3f. black and blue (173) | 55·00 | |
| 1211 | - | 25f. multicoloured (441) | 47·00 | 2·75 |
| 1220 | - | 135f. on 3f. mult (274) | 80·00 | |
| 1223 | - | 20f. on 200f. mult (451) (air) | 55·00 | |
| 1225 | - | 25f. on 85f. mult (600) | 47·00 | 2·75 |
| 1227 | **140** | 30f. on 15f. purple, green and blue | 38·00 | |
| 1231 | - | 125f. on 70f. mult (383) | 65·00 | 2·75 |
| 1235 | - | 150f. purple, blue and brown (456) | 80·00 | |
| 1236 | - | 150f. multicoloured (527) | 55·00 | 2·75 |
| 1239 | **150** | 200f. green, violet and emerald | 65·00 | 2·75 |
| 1242 | - | 200f. on 150f. mult (562) | 95·00 | |
| 1243 | **179** | 300f. multicoloured | 55·00 | 2·75 |

(c) **BENIN**.

| | | | | |
|---|---|---|---|---|
| 1257 | - | 25f. on 500f. brown, red and green (592) (air) | 47·00 | 2·75 |
| 1258 | - | 30f. on 200f. mult (528) | 24·00 | 2·75 |
| 1260a | - | 100f. brown, green and blue (522) | 55·00 | 2·75 |
| 1261 | **116** | 125f. on 50f. black, orange and blue | 43·00 | 2·75 |
| 1263a | - | 190f. on 200f. mult (478) | £190 | 2·75 |
| 1266 | - | 300f. brn, red & bl (591) | 70·00 | 2·75 |

**422** Conference Emblem

**1994.** UNESCO Conference on the Slave Route, Ouidah.

| | | | | |
|---|---|---|---|---|
| 1275 | **422** | 300f. multicoloured | 47·00 | 2·75 |

**423** World Map

**1994.** International Year of the Family.

| | | | | |
|---|---|---|---|---|
| 1276 | **423** | 200f. multicoloured | 75·00 | 2·75 |

**425** Water Polo

**1995.** Olympic Games, Atlanta (1996) (1st issue). Multicoloured.

| | | | |
|---|---|---|---|
| 1278 | 45f. Type **425** | 20 | 20 |
| 1279 | 50f. Throwing the javelin (vert) | 30 | 25 |
| 1280 | 75f. Weightlifting (vert) | 45 | 35 |
| 1281 | 100f. Tennis (vert) | 60 | 50 |
| 1282 | 135f. Baseball (vert) | 75 | 55 |
| 1283 | 200f. Synchronised swimming (vert) | 1·30 | 1·00 |
| **MS**1284 | 60×79 mm. 300f. Diving (31×39 mm) | 2·40 | 2·20 |

See also Nos. 1347/**MS**1353.

**426** Paddle-steamer

**1995.** Ships. Multicoloured.

| | | | |
|---|---|---|---|
| 1285 | 40f. Type **426** | 25 | 15 |
| 1286 | 50f. "Charlotte" (paddle steamer) | 30 | 15 |
| 1287 | 75f. "Citta di Catania" (Italian liner) | 45 | 20 |
| 1288 | 100f. "Mountbatten" SR-N4 (hovercraft) | 45 | 25 |
| 1289 | 135f. "Queen Elizabeth 2" (liner) | 85 | 30 |
| 1290 | 200f. "Matsu-Nef" (Japanese nuclear-powered freighter) | 1·30 | 60 |
| **MS**1291 | 72×58 mm. 300f. "Savannah" (sail/paddle-steamer) (39×31 mm) | 2·40 | 2·40 |

**427** Chimpanzee

**1995.** Primates. Multicoloured.

| | | | |
|---|---|---|---|
| 1292 | 50f. Type **427** | 30 | 15 |
| 1293 | 75f. Mandrill | 45 | 20 |
| 1294 | 100f. Colobus | 60 | 25 |
| 1295 | 135f. Barbary ape | 85 | 30 |
| 1296 | 200f. Hamadryas baboon | 1·30 | 70 |
| **MS**1297 | 93×72 mm. 300f. Yellow baboons (31×39 mm) | 2·50 | 2·10 |

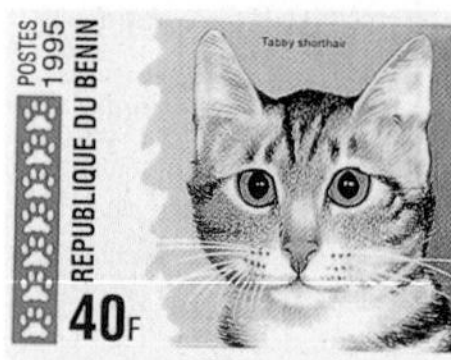

**428** Tabby Shorthair

**1995.** Cats. Multicoloured.

| | | | |
|---|---|---|---|
| 1298 | 40f. Type **428** | 25 | 15 |
| 1299 | 50f. Sorrel Abyssinian ("Ruddy red") | 30 | 15 |
| 1300 | 75f. White Persian long-hair | 45 | 20 |
| 1301 | 100f. Seal colourpoint | 60 | 25 |
| 1302 | 135f. Tabby point | 85 | 30 |
| 1303 | 200f. Black shorthair | 1·30 | 60 |
| **MS**1304 | 82×86 mm. 300f. Kitten climbing out of basket (38×31 mm) | 2·50 | 2·50 |

**429** German Shepherd

**1995.** Dogs. Multicoloured.

| | | | |
|---|---|---|---|
| 1305 | 40f. Type **429** | 25 | 15 |
| 1306 | 50f. Beagle | 30 | 15 |
| 1307 | 75f. Great dane | 45 | 20 |
| 1308 | 100f. Boxer | 60 | 25 |
| 1309 | 135f. Pointer | 85 | 30 |
| 1310 | 200f. Long-haired fox terrier | 1·30 | 60 |
| **MS**1311 | 80×70 mm. 300f. Schnauzer | 2·50 | 2·50 |

**430** Arms

**1995**

| | | | | |
|---|---|---|---|---|
| 1312 | **430** | 135f. multicoloured | 85 | 25 |
| 1313 | **430** | 150f. multicoloured | 95 | 55 |
| 1314 | **430** | 200f. multicoloured | 1·30 | 55 |

See also Nos. 1458 and 1480/2.

**431** Lion

**1995.** Mammals. Multicoloured.

| | | | |
|---|---|---|---|
| 1315 | 50f. Type **431** | 30 | 15 |
| 1316 | 75f. African buffalo | 45 | 20 |
| 1317 | 100f. Chimpanzee | 65 | 25 |
| 1318 | 135f. Impala | 85 | 30 |
| 1319 | 200f. Cape ground squirrel (horiz) | 1·30 | 70 |
| **MS**1320 | 80×60 mm. 300f. African elephant (31×39 mm) | 2·50 | 2·50 |

**432** Hawfinches

**1995.** Birds and their Young. Multicoloured.

| | | | |
|---|---|---|---|
| 1321 | 40f. Type **432** | 25 | 15 |
| 1322 | 50f. Spotted-necked doves | 30 | 15 |
| 1323 | 75f. Peregrine falcons | 45 | 20 |
| 1324 | 100f. Blackburnian warblers | 60 | 25 |
| 1325 | 135f. Black-headed gulls | 80 | 30 |
| 1326 | 200f. Eastern white pelican | 1·20 | 60 |

**433** "Dracunculus vulgaris"

**1995.** Flowers. Multicoloured.

| | | | |
|---|---|---|---|
| 1327 | 40f. Type **433** | 25 | 15 |
| 1328 | 50f. Daffodil | 30 | 15 |
| 1329 | 75f. Amaryllis | 45 | 20 |
| 1330 | 100f. Water-lily | 60 | 25 |
| 1331 | 135f. "Chrysanthemum carinatum" | 80 | 30 |
| 1332 | 200f. Iris | 1·20 | 60 |

**434** Lynx

**1995.** Big Cats and their Young. Mult.

| | | | |
|---|---|---|---|
| 1333 | 40f. Type **434** | 25 | 15 |
| 1334 | 50f. Pumas | 30 | 15 |
| 1335 | 75f. Cheetahs | 45 | 20 |
| 1336 | 100f. Leopards | 60 | 25 |
| 1337 | 135f. Tigers | 80 | 30 |
| 1338 | 200f. Lions | 1·30 | 60 |

**435** "Angraecum sesquipedale"

**1995.** Orchids. Multicoloured.

| | | | |
|---|---|---|---|
| 1339 | 40f. Type **435** | 25 | 15 |
| 1340 | 50f. "Polystachya virginea" | 30 | 15 |
| 1341 | 75f. "Disa uniflora" | 45 | 20 |
| 1342 | 100f. "Ansellia africana" | 60 | 25 |
| 1343 | 135f. "Angraecum eichlerianum" | 95 | 30 |
| 1344 | 200f. "Jumellea confusa" | 1·30 | 60 |

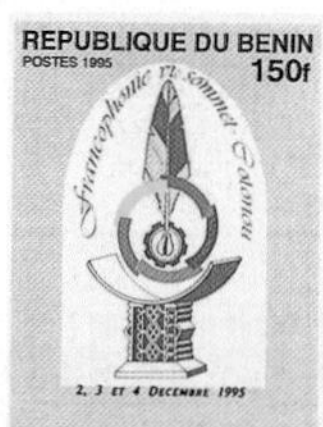

**436** Emblem

**1995.** 6th Francophone Summit, Cotonou.

| | | | | |
|---|---|---|---|---|
| 1345 | **436** | 150f. multicoloured | 85 | 55 |
| 1346 | **436** | 200f. multicoloured | 1·10 | 80 |

**437** Diving

**1996.** Olympic Games, Atlanta (2nd issue). Multicoloured.

| | | | |
|---|---|---|---|
| 1347 | 40f. Type **437** | 30 | 25 |
| 1348 | 50f. Tennis | 35 | 30 |
| 1349 | 75f. Running | 45 | 35 |
| 1350 | 100f. Gymnastics | 60 | 50 |
| 1351 | 135f. Weightlifting | 90 | 65 |

| | | | |
|---|---|---|---|
| 1352 | 200f. Shooting | 1·30 | 1·00 |
| MS1353 | 65×65 mm. 1000f. Water polo (31×39 mm) | 5·25 | 4·00 |

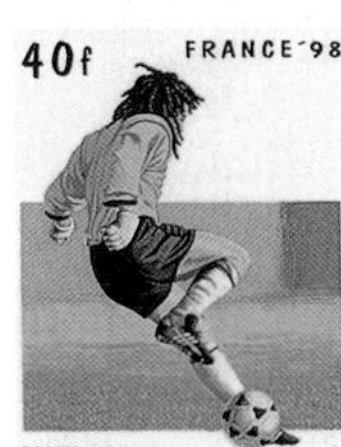

**438** Player with Ball

**1996.** World Cup Football Championship, France (1998) (1st issue).

| | | | | |
|---|---|---|---|---|
| 1354 | **438** | 40f. multicoloured | 25 | 20 |
| 1355 | - | 50f. multicoloured | 25 | 20 |
| 1356 | - | 75f. multicoloured | 50 | 40 |
| 1357 | - | 100f. multicoloured | 60 | 50 |
| 1358 | - | 135f. multicoloured | 1·00 | 65 |
| 1359 | - | 200f. multicoloured | 1·30 | 1·10 |
| **MS**1360 | | 88×63 mm. 1000f. Tackle (31×39 mm) | 4·75 | 4·00 |

DESIGNS: 50f. to 1000f. Different players.

See also Nos. 1614/**MS**1620.

**439** Small Striped Swallowtail

**1996.** Butterflies. Multicoloured.

| | | | |
|---|---|---|---|
| 1361 | 40f. Type **439** | 25 | 20 |
| 1362 | 50f. Red admiral | 25 | 20 |
| 1363 | 75f. Common blue | 45 | 35 |
| 1364 | 100f. African monarch | 55 | 45 |
| 1365 | 135f. Painted lady | 95 | 60 |
| 1366 | 200f. "Argus celbulina ortbitulus" | 1·30 | 1·00 |
| **MS**1367 | 60×70 mm. 1000f. Foxy charaxes ("Charaxes jasius") (31×39 mm) | 4·50 | 4·00 |

**440** Dancer

**1996.** "China '96" International Stamp Exhibition, Peking. Multicoloured.

| | | | |
|---|---|---|---|
| 1368 | 40f. Type **440** | 35 | 30 |
| 1369 | 50f. Exhibition emblem | 40 | 35 |
| 1370 | 75f. Water-lily | 60 | 50 |
| 1371 | 100f. Temple of Heaven, Peking | 85 | 75 |

Nos. 1368/71 were issued together, se-tenant, forming a composite design.

**441** Emblem

**1996.** 15th Convention of Lions Club International, Cotonou.

| | | | | |
|---|---|---|---|---|
| 1372 | **441** | 135f. multicoloured | 1·10 | 75 |
| 1373 | **441** | 150f. multicoloured | 1·10 | 80 |
| 1374 | **441** | 200f. multicoloured | 1·50 | 1·10 |
| 1457 | **441** | 100f. multicoloured | 55 | 25 |

**442** "Holy Family of Rouvre" (Raphael)

**1996.** Christmas. Multicoloured.

| | | | |
|---|---|---|---|
| 1375 | 40f. Type **442** | 25 | 20 |
| 1376 | 50f. "The Holy Family" (Raphael) | 25 | 20 |
| 1377 | 75f. "St. John the Baptist" (Bartolome Murillo) | 50 | 40 |
| 1378 | 100f. "The Virgin of the Scales" (Leonardo da Vinci) | 65 | 50 |
| 1379 | 135f. "The Virgin and Child" (Gerhard David) | 90 | 65 |
| 1380 | 200f. "Adoration of the Magi" (Juan Mayno) | 1·30 | 1·10 |
| **MS**1381 | 99×74 mm. 1000f. "Rest during the Flight into Egypt" (Murillo) (39×31 mm) | 5·25 | 3·75 |

**443** "Thermopylae" (clipper) (inscr "Thermopyles")

**1996.** Ships. Multicoloured.

| | | | |
|---|---|---|---|
| 1382 | 40f. Type **443** | 20 | 15 |
| 1383 | 50f. Barque | 25 | 20 |
| 1384 | 75f. "Nightingale" (full-rigged ship) | 45 | 30 |
| 1385 | 100f. Opium clipper | 50 | 40 |
| 1386 | 135f. "Torrens" (full-rigged ship) | 80 | 60 |
| 1387 | 200f. English tea clipper | 1·20 | 1·00 |
| **MS**1388 | 78×58 mm. 1000f. Opium clipper (31×39 mm) | 5·25 | 4·00 |

**444** Serval

**1996.** Big Cats. Multicoloured.

| | | | |
|---|---|---|---|
| 1389 | 40f. Type **444** | 25 | 20 |
| 1390 | 50f. Golden cat | 25 | 20 |
| 1391 | 75f. Ocelot | 45 | 35 |
| 1392 | 100f. Bobcat | 55 | 45 |
| 1393 | 135f. Leopard cat | 95 | 60 |
| 1394 | 200f. "Felis euptilura" | 1·30 | 1·00 |
| **MS**1395 | 80×64 mm. 1000f. Clouded leopard ("Neofelis nebulosa") (31×39 mm) | 5·25 | 4·00 |

**445** Hurdler and Gold Medal

**1996.** Centenary of Issue by Greece of First Olympic Stamps. Multicoloured.

| | | | |
|---|---|---|---|
| 1396 | 40f. Type **445** | 35 | 30 |
| 1397 | 50f. Hurdler and Olympic flames | 40 | 35 |
| 1398 | 75f. Pierre de Coubertin (founder of modern Olympics) and map showing south-west U.S.A. | 60 | 50 |
| 1399 | 100f. Map showing south-east U.S.A. | 85 | 75 |

Nos. 1396/9 were issued together, se-tenant, forming a composite design.

**446** Running

**1996.** "Olymphilex '96" Olympics and Sports Stamp Exhibition, Atlanta. Multicoloured.

| | | | |
|---|---|---|---|
| 1400 | 40f. Type **446** | 25 | 20 |
| 1401 | 50f. Canoeing | 25 | 20 |
| 1402 | 75f. Gymnastics | 50 | 40 |
| 1403 | 100f. Football | 60 | 50 |
| 1404 | 135f. Tennis | 1·00 | 65 |
| 1405 | 200f. Baseball | 1·40 | 1·10 |
| **MS**1406 | 65×95 mm. 1000f. Basketball (31×39 mm) | 5·25 | 4·00 |

**447** "Parodia subterranea"

**1996.** Flowering Cacti. Multicoloured.

| | | | |
|---|---|---|---|
| 1407 | 40f. Type **447** | 25 | 20 |
| 1408 | 50f. "Astrophytum senile" | 25 | 20 |
| 1409 | 75f. "Echinocereus melanocentrus" | 50 | 40 |
| 1410 | 100f. "Turbinicarpus klinkerianus" | 60 | 50 |
| 1411 | 135f. "Astrophytum capricorne" | 1·00 | 65 |
| 1412 | 200f. "Nelloydia grandiflora" | 1·40 | 1·10 |

**448** Chestnut Horse

**1996.** Horses. Multicoloured.

| | | | |
|---|---|---|---|
| 1413 | 40f. Type **448** | 25 | 20 |
| 1414 | 50f. Horse on hillside | 25 | 20 |
| 1415 | 75f. Foal by fence | 45 | 35 |
| 1416 | 100f. Mother and foal | 55 | 45 |
| 1417 | 135f. Pair of horses | 95 | 60 |
| 1418 | 200f. Grey horse (horiz) | 1·30 | 1·00 |

**449** Longisquama

**1996.** Prehistoric Animals. Multicoloured.

| | | | |
|---|---|---|---|
| 1419 | 40f. Type **449** | 25 | 20 |
| 1420 | 50f. Dimorphodon | 25 | 20 |
| 1421 | 75f. Dunkleosteus (horiz) | 45 | 35 |
| 1422 | 100f. Eryops (horiz) | 55 | 45 |
| 1423 | 135f. Peloneustes (horiz) | 85 | 60 |
| 1424 | 200f. Deinonychus (horiz) | 1·30 | 1·00 |

**450** Ivory-billed Woodpecker

**1996.** Birds. Multicoloured.

| | | | |
|---|---|---|---|
| 1425 | 40f. Type **450** | 25 | 20 |
| 1426 | 50f. Grey-necked bald crow | 25 | 20 |
| 1427 | 75f. Kakapo | 45 | 35 |
| 1428 | 100f. Puerto Rican amazon | 55 | 45 |
| 1429 | 135f. Japanese crested ibis | 95 | 60 |
| 1430 | 200f. California condor | 1·30 | 1·00 |
| **MS**1431 | 65×91 mm. 1000f. Blue bird of paradise ("Paradisaea rudolphi") (31×39 mm) | 5·25 | 4·00 |

**451** Golden Tops

**1996.** Fungi. Multicoloured.

| | | | |
|---|---|---|---|
| 1432 | 40f. Type **451** | 25 | 20 |
| 1433 | 50f. "Psilocybe zapotecorum" | 25 | 20 |
| 1434 | 75f. "Psilocybe mexicana" | 55 | 40 |
| 1435 | 100f. "Conocybe siligineoides" | 65 | 50 |
| 1436 | 135f. "Psilocybe caerulescens mazatecorum" | 1·00 | 65 |
| 1437 | 200f. "Psilocybe caerulescens nigripes" | 1·40 | 1·10 |
| **MS**1438 | 93×71 mm. 1000f. "Psilocybe aztecorum" (39×31 mm) | 5·25 | 4·00 |

**452** Impala

**1996.** Mammals. Multicoloured.

| | | | |
|---|---|---|---|
| 1439 | 40f. Type **452** | 25 | 20 |
| 1440 | 50f. Waterbuck | 25 | 20 |
| 1441 | 75f. African buffalo | 45 | 35 |
| 1442 | 100f. Blue wildebeest | 55 | 45 |
| 1443 | 135f. Okapi | 85 | 60 |
| 1444 | 200f. Greater kudu | 1·30 | 1·00 |

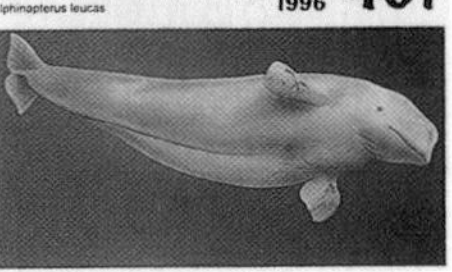

**453** White Whale

**1996.** Marine Mammals. Multicoloured.

| | | | |
|---|---|---|---|
| 1445 | 40f. Type **453** | 25 | 20 |
| 1446 | 50f. Bottle-nosed dolphin | 25 | 20 |
| 1447 | 75f. Blue whale | 45 | 35 |
| 1448 | 100f. "Eubalaena australis" | 55 | 45 |
| 1449 | 135f. "Gramphidelphis griseus" | 95 | 60 |
| 1450 | 200f. Killer whale | 1·30 | 1·00 |

**454** Grey Angelfish

**1996.** Fishes. Multicoloured.

| | | | |
|---|---|---|---|
| 1451 | 50f. Type **454** | 30 | 25 |
| 1452 | 75f. Sail-finned tang (horiz) | 40 | 35 |
| 1453 | 100f. Golden trevally (horiz) | 60 | 45 |

1454 135f. Pyramid butterflyfish (horiz) 85 60
1455 200f. Racoon butterflyfish (horiz) 1·30 1·00
**MS**1456 80×61 mm. 1000f. Parrotfish (horiz) 5·25 4·00

**1996.** Arms. Dated "1996".
1458 **430** 100f. multicoloured 65 25

**1996.** Stamps of Benin variously surch.
1469 **311** 15f. on 185f. mult (postage) 65·00 2·75
1470 **379** 25f. on 175f. mult
1473 **359** 50f. on 220f. green (1104) 65·00 2·75
1479 **414** 150f. on 190f. mult
1480 **415** 150f. on 190f. mult
1484 **412** 250f. on 1000f. mult 65·00 2·75
1494 **193** 40f. on 210f. red, brown and green (air) 65·00 2·75
1495 - 40f. on 210f. purple, blue and yellow (792)
1499 - 150f. on 500f. red, ultramarine and green (657)

**1996.** Stamps of Dahomey variously optd or surch. (a) **Republique de Benin** (1510, 1516, 1519, 1522, 1526/9, 1535, 1544, 1556, 1558 and 1568) or **REPUBLIQUE DU BENIN** (others).
1510 35f. on 85f. brown, orange and green (493) (postage)
1511 125f. on 100f. violet, red and black (510)
1516 **85** 150f. on 30f. mult
1519 **113** 150f. on 40f. red, brown and green
1522 - 150f. on 45f. mult (597)
1526 - 35f. on 100f. deep blue and blue (326) (air)
1527 - 35f. on 100f. on 200f. multicoloured (409)
1528 - 35f. on 125f. green, blue and light blue (553)
1529 - 35f. on 300f. brown, red and blue (591)
1535 - 150f. multicoloured (527)
1544 **112** 150f. on 40f. multicoloured
1556 - 150f. on 110f. mult (386)
1558 - 150f. on 120f. mult (404)
1568 - 200f. on 500f. mult (252)

(b) **DU BENIN**.
1578 35f. on 125f. brown and green (540) (air)
1579 125f. on 65f. mult (465)
1580 **168** 135f. on 35f. mult

(c) **BENIN**.
1587 **68** 150f. on 30f. mult (post) 75·00 2·75
1591 **68** 25f. on 85f. mult (600) (air)

**455** Grenadier, Glassenapps Regiment

**1997.** Military Uniforms. Multicoloured.
1600 135f. Type **455** 60 30
1601 150f. Officer, Von Groben's Regiment 80 35
1602 200f. Private, Dohna's Regiment 1·00 60
1603 270f. Artilleryman 1·30 70
1604 300f. Cavalry trooper 1·60 90
1605 400f. Trooper, Mollendorf's Dragoons 2·10 1·30
**MS**1606 90×108 mm. 1000f. Standard bearer (31×39 mm) 5·25 4·00

**456** Reid Macleod Gas-turbine Locomotive, 1920

**1997.** Railway Locomotives. Multicoloured.
1607 135f. Type **456** 60 30
1608 150f. Class O5 steam locomotive, 1935, Germany 80 40
1609 200f. Locomotive "Silver Fox", Great Britain 1·00 55
1610 270f. Class "Merchant Navy" locomotive, 1941, Great Britain 1·30 75
1611 300f. Diesel locomotive, 1960, Denmark 1·60 80
1612 400f. GM Type diesel locomotive, 1960 2·10 1·10
**MS**1613 94×64 mm. 1000f. "Coronation", 1937 (39×31 mm) 5·25 4·00
No. 1607 is wrongly inscr "Reid Maclead 1920".

**457** Footballer and Map

**1997.** World Cup Football Championship, France (1998) (2nd issue).
1614 **457** 135f. multicoloured 60 30
1615 - 150f. multicoloured 80 35
1616 - 200f. multicoloured 1·00 60
1617 - 270f. multicoloured 1·30 70
1618 - 300f. mult (horiz) 1·60 90
1619 - 400f. mult (horiz) 2·10 1·30
**MS**1620 107×83 mm. 1000f. multicoloured (39×31 mm) 5·25 4·00
DESIGNS: 135f. to 1000f. Each showing map of France and player.

**458** Arms

**1997.** T **430** redrawn as T **458**. Dated "1997".
1621 **458** 135f. multicoloured 70 25
1622 **458** 150f. multicoloured 1·00 60
1623 **458** 200f. multicoloured 1·20 60

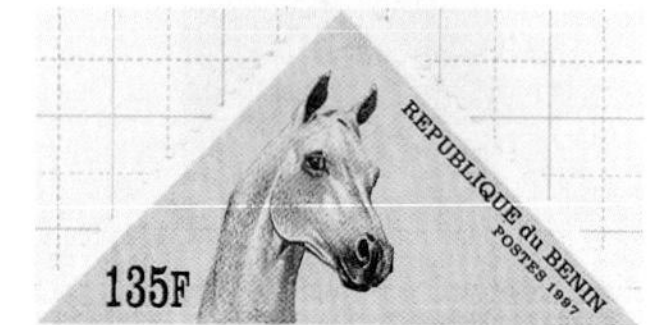

**459** Horse's Head

**1997.** Horses. Multicoloured.
1624 135f. Type **459** 70 30
1625 150f. Bay horse 80 45
1626 200f. Chestnut horse looking forward 1·00 55
1627 270f. Chestnut horse looking backwards 1·30 70
1628 300f. Black horse 1·70 80
1629 400f. Profile of horse 2·10 1·00
**MS**1630 84×109 mm. 1000f. Bay horse with white nose 5·25 4·00

**460** Irish Setter

**1997.** Dogs. Multicoloured.
1631 135f. Type **460** 60 30
1632 150f. Saluki 80 45
1633 200f. Dobermann pinscher 1·00 55
1634 270f. Siberian husky 1·60 70
1635 300f. Basenji 1·60 80
1636 400f. Boxer 2·30 1·00
**MS**1637 110×90 mm. 1000f. Rhodesian ridgeback (31×39 mm) 5·25 4·00

**461** "Phalaenopsis penetrate"

**1997.** Orchids. Multicoloured.
1638 135f. Type **461** 70 35
1639 150f. "Phalaenopsis" "Golden Sands" 80 45
1640 200f. "Phalaenopsis" "Sun Spots" 1·00 60
1641 270f. "Phalaenopsis fuscata" 1·70 70
1642 300f. "Phalaenopsis christi floyd" 1·70 85
1643 400f. "Phalaenopsis cayanne" 2·50 1·10
**MS**1644 99×99 mm. 1000f. "Phalaenopsis" "Janet Kuhn" (31×39 mm) 5·25 4·00

**462** Buick Model C Tourer, 1905

**1997.** Motor Cars. Multicoloured.
1645 135f. Type **462** 70 30
1646 150f. Ford model A tonneau, 1903 80 45
1647 200f. Stanley steamer tourer, 1913 1·00 60
1648 270f. Stoddar-Dayton tourer, 1911 1·30 70
1649 300f. Cadillac convertible sedan, 1934 1·70 85
1650 400f. Cadillac convertible sedan, 1931 2·10 1·10
**MS**1651 112×85 mm. 1000f. Ford, 1928 (39×31 mm) 5·25 4·00

**463** Northern Bullfinch

**1997.** Birds. Multicoloured.
1652 135f. Type **463** 60 30
1653 150f. Spruce siskin 80 40
1654 200f. Ring ousel 1·00 55
1655 270f. Crested tit 1·30 70
1656 300f. Spotted nutcracker 1·60 80
1657 400f. Nightingale 2·10 1·10
**MS**1658 107×87 mm. 1000f. Yellow wagtail (31×39 mm) 5·25 4·00

**464** "Faucaria lupina"

**1997.** Cacti. Multicoloured.
1659 135f. Type **464** 60 30
1660 150f. "Conophytum bilobun" 80 45
1661 200f. "Lithops aucampiae" 1·00 60
1662 270f. "Lithops helmutii" 1·30 75
1663 300f. "Stapelia grandiflora" 1·60 80
1664 400f. "Lithops fulviceps" 2·10 1·20
**MS**1665 109×90 mm. 1000f. "Pleiospilos willowmorensis" (31×38 mm) 5·25 4·00

**465** Egyptian Merchant Ship

**1997.** Ancient Sailing Ships. Multicoloured.
1666 135f. Type **465** 60 30
1667 150f. Greek merchant ship 80 40
1668 200f. Phoenician galley 1·00 55
1669 270f. Roman merchant ship 1·30 70
1670 300f. Norman knarr 1·60 80
1671 400f. Mediterranean sailing ship 2·10 1·00
**MS**1672 109×89 mm. 1000f. English kogge of Richard II's reign (28×36 mm) 5·25 4·00

**466** Black-tipped Grouper

**1997.** Fishes. Multicoloured.
1673 135f. Type **466** 60 30
1674 150f. Cardinal fish 75 40
1675 200f. Indo-Pacific humpheaded parrotfish 1·00 55
1676 270f. Regal angelfish 1·30 70
1677 300f. Wrasse 1·60 80
1678 400f. Hawkfish 2·10 1·00
**MS**1679 109×90 mm. 1000f. Hogfish (39×31 mm) 5·25 4·00

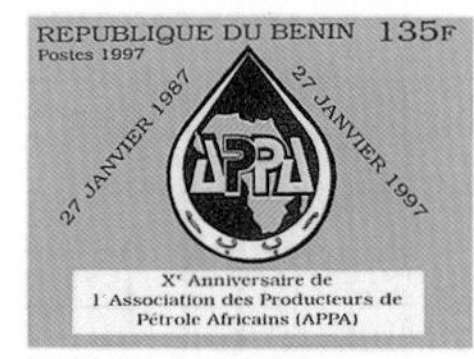

**467** Emblem

**1997.** 10th Anniv of African Petroleum Producers' Association.
1680 **467** 135f. multicoloured 60 30
1681 **467** 200f. multicoloured 1·00 55
1682 **467** 300f. multicoloured 1·50 80
1683 **467** 500f. multicoloured 2·75 1·40

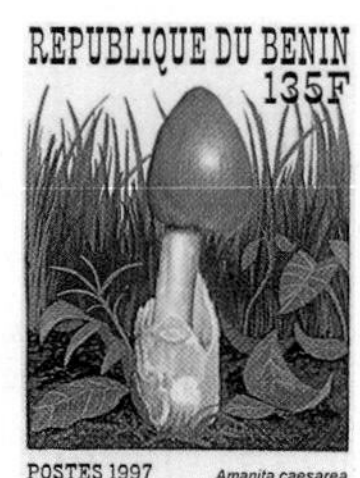

**468** Caesar's Mushroom

**1997.** Fungi. Multicoloured.
1684 135f. Type **468** 60 30
1685 150f. Slimy-banded cort 80 40
1686 200f. "Amanita bisporigera" 1·00 55
1687 270f. The blusher 1·30 70
1688 300f. Cracked green russula 1·60 80
1689 400f. Strangulated amanita 2·10 1·00
**MS**1690 90×110 mm. 1000f. Fly agaric (31×37 mm) 5·25 4·00

**469** "Puffing Billy", 1813

**1997.** Steam Railway Locomotives. Mult.
1691 135f. Type **469** 60 30
1692 150f. "Rocket", 1829 80 40
1693 200f. "Royal George", 1827 1·00 55
1694 270f. "Novelty", 1829 1·30 70
1695 300f. "Locomotion", 1825 (vert) 1·60 80
1696 400f. "Sans Pareil", 1829 (vert) 2·10 1·00
**MS**1697 110×89 mm. 1000f. Richard Trevithick's locomotive, 1803 (39×31 mm) 5·25 4·00

**470** "Tephrocybe carbonaria"

**1998.** Fungi. Multicoloured.

| | | | |
|---|---|---|---|
| 1698 | 135f. Type **470** | 55 | 30 |
| 1699 | 150f. Butter mushroom | 75 | 40 |
| 1700 | 200f. Oyster fungus | 95 | 55 |
| 1701 | 270f. "Hohenbuehelia geogenia" | 1·20 | 70 |
| 1702 | 300f. Bitter bolete | 1·50 | 80 |
| 1703 | 400f. "Lepiota leucothites" | 2·00 | 1·00 |
| **MS**1704 | 108×90 mm. 1000f. "Gymnopilus junonius" | 4·75 | 3·75 |

**471** Philadelphia or "Double Deck", 1885

**1998.** Fire Engines. Multicoloured.

| | | | |
|---|---|---|---|
| 1705 | 135f. Type **471** | 55 | 30 |
| 1706 | 150f. "Veteran", 1850 | 75 | 40 |
| 1707 | 200f. Merryweather, 1894 | 95 | 55 |
| 1708 | 270f. 19 th-century Hippomobile | 1·20 | 70 |
| 1709 | 300f. Jeep "Willy", 1948 | 1·50 | 80 |
| 1710 | 400f. Chevrolet 6400 | 2·00 | 1·00 |
| **MS**1711 | 110×89 mm. 1000f. Foamite, 1952 (38×30 mm) | 4·75 | 3·75 |

**472** Uranite

**1998.** Minerals. Multicoloured.

| | | | |
|---|---|---|---|
| 1712 | 135f. Type **472** | 55 | 30 |
| 1713 | 150f. Quartz | 75 | 40 |
| 1714 | 200f. Aragonite | 95 | 55 |
| 1715 | 270f. Malachite | 1·20 | 70 |
| 1716 | 300f. Turquoise | 1·50 | 80 |
| 1717 | 400f. Corundum | 2·00 | 1·00 |
| **MS**1718 | 89×109 mm. 1000f. Marble (short side as base) | 4·75 | 3·75 |

**473** Locomotive

**1998.** Steam Railway Locomotives. Multicoloured.

| | | | |
|---|---|---|---|
| 1719 | 135f. Type **473** | 55 | 30 |
| 1720 | 150f. Green locomotive | 75 | 40 |
| 1721 | 200f. Brown locomotive | 95 | 55 |
| 1722 | 270f. Lilac locomotive | 1·20 | 70 |
| 1723 | 300f. Toledo Furnace Co No. 1 | 1·50 | 80 |
| 1724 | 400f. No. 1 "Helvetia" | 2·00 | 1·00 |
| **MS**1725 | 109×86 mm. Shelby Steel Tube Co. Locomotive (39×31 mm) | 4·75 | 3·75 |

**474** Diana, Princess of Wales

**1998.** 1st Death Anniv of Diana, Princess of Wales. Multicoloured.

| | | | |
|---|---|---|---|
| 1726 | 135f. Type **474** | 55 | 35 |
| 1727 | 150f. Wearing pink dress | 75 | 40 |
| 1728 | 200f. Wearing beige jacket | 95 | 55 |
| 1729 | 270f. Wearing white jacket with revers | 1·20 | 75 |
| 1730 | 300f. Making speech | 1·50 | 80 |
| 1731 | 400f. Wearing collarless single-breasted white jacket | 2·00 | 1·10 |
| 1732 | 500f. Wearing red jacket | 2·40 | 1·40 |
| 1733 | 600f. Wearing black jacket | 2·75 | 1·70 |
| 1734 | 700f. Wearing double-breasted white jacket | 3·25 | 2·00 |

**475** Sordes

**1998.** Prehistoric Animals. Multicoloured.

| | | | |
|---|---|---|---|
| 1735 | 135f. Type **475** | 55 | 35 |
| 1736 | 150f. Scaphognatus | 70 | 40 |
| 1737 | 200f. Dsungaripterus | 95 | 55 |
| 1738 | 270f. Brontosaurus | 1·20 | 75 |
| 1739 | 300f. Diplodocus | 1·50 | 80 |
| 1740 | 400f. Coelurus and baryonyx | 2·00 | 1·10 |
| 1741 | 500f. Kronosaurus and ichthyosaurus | 2·40 | 1·40 |
| 1742 | 600f. Ceratosaurus | 2·75 | 1·70 |
| 1743 | 700f. Yangchuansaurus | 3·25 | 2·00 |

Nos. 1735/43 were issued together, se-tenant, forming a composite design.

**476** Beagle

**1998.** Dogs. Multicoloured.

| | | | |
|---|---|---|---|
| 1744 | 135f. Type **476** | 55 | 30 |
| 1745 | 150f. Dalmatians | 70 | 40 |
| 1746 | 200f. Dachshund | 95 | 55 |
| 1747 | 270f. Cairn terrier | 1·20 | 70 |
| 1748 | 300f. Shih-tzus | 1·50 | 80 |
| 1749 | 400f. Pug | 2·00 | 1·00 |
| **MS**1750 | 110×90 mm. 1000f. Springer spaniels (39×31 mm) | 4·75 | 3·75 |

**477** Abyssinian

**1998.** Cats. Multicoloured.

| | | | |
|---|---|---|---|
| 1751 | 135f. Type **477** | 55 | 30 |
| 1752 | 150f. Striped silver tabby | 70 | 40 |
| 1753 | 200f. Siamese | 95 | 55 |
| 1754 | 270f. Red tabby (horiz) | 1·20 | 70 |
| 1755 | 300f. Wild cat (horiz) | 1·50 | 80 |
| 1756 | 400f. Manx (horiz) | 2·00 | 1·00 |
| **MS**1757 | 110×89 mm. 1000f. Tortoise-shell and white (39×31 mm) | 4·75 | 3·75 |

**478** Bugatti 13 Torpedo, 1910

**1998.** Motor Cars. Multicoloured.

| | | | |
|---|---|---|---|
| 1758 | 135f. Type **478** | 55 | 30 |
| 1759 | 150f. Clement voiturette, 1903 | 70 | 40 |
| 1760 | 200f. Stutz Bearcat speedster, 1914 | 95 | 55 |
| 1761 | 270f. Darracq phaeton, 1907 | 1·20 | 70 |
| 1762 | 300f. Napier delivery car, 1913 | 1·50 | 80 |
| 1763 | 400f. Pierce Arrow roadster, 1911 | 2·00 | 1·00 |
| **MS**1764 | 109×91 mm. 1000f. Piccolo, 1904 (31×39 mm) | 4·75 | 3·75 |

**479** Apollo

**1998.** Butterflies. Multicoloured.

| | | | |
|---|---|---|---|
| 1765 | 135f. Type **479** | 55 | 30 |
| 1766 | 150f. Orange-tip | 70 | 40 |
| 1767 | 200f. Camberwell beauty | 95 | 55 |
| 1768 | 250f. Speckled wood | 1·20 | 70 |
| 1769 | 300f. Purple-edged copper | 1·50 | 80 |
| 1770 | 400f. Chequered skipper | 2·00 | 1·10 |
| **MS**1771 | 106×76 mm. 1000f. Small tortoiseshell (39×31 mm) | 4·75 | 3·75 |

**480** Gouldian Finch

**1999.** Birds. Multicoloured.

| | | | |
|---|---|---|---|
| 1772 | 135f. Type **480** | 55 | 30 |
| 1773 | 150f. Saffron finch | 70 | 40 |
| 1774 | 200f. Red-billed quelea | 95 | 55 |
| 1775 | 270f. Golden bishop | 1·20 | 70 |
| 1776 | 300f. Red-crested cardinal | 1·50 | 80 |
| 1777 | 400f. Golden-breasted bunting | 2·00 | 1·10 |
| **MS**1778 | 110×89 mm. 1000f. Green-backed twin-spot (31×39 mm) | 4·75 | 3·75 |

**481** Boat, Ceylon

**1999.** Sailing Boats. Multicoloured.

| | | | |
|---|---|---|---|
| 1779 | 135f. Type **481** | 55 | 30 |
| 1780 | 150f. Tanka-Tim, Canton, Macao | 70 | 40 |
| 1781 | 200f. Sampan, Hong Kong | 95 | 55 |
| 1782 | 270f. Outrigger sailing canoe, Polynesia | 1·20 | 70 |
| 1783 | 300f. Junk, Japan | 1·50 | 80 |
| 1784 | 400f. Dacca-Pulwar, Bengal | 2·00 | 1·10 |
| **MS**1785 | 84×109 mm. 1000f. Junk, China (39×31 mm) | 4·75 | 3·75 |

**482** White Rhinoceros

**1999.** Mammals.

| | | | | |
|---|---|---|---|---|
| 1786 | **482** | 50f. grey | 15 | 10 |
| 1787 | - | 100f. violet | 45 | 25 |
| 1788 | - | 135f. green | 50 | 25 |
| 1789 | - | 135f. black | 50 | 25 |
| 1790 | - | 150f. blue | 65 | 30 |
| 1791 | - | 150f. green | 65 | 30 |
| 1792 | - | 200f. blue | 85 | 45 |
| 1793 | - | 200f. brown | 85 | 45 |
| 1794 | - | 300f. brown | 1·40 | 70 |
| 1795 | - | 300f. red | 1·40 | 70 |
| 1796 | - | 400f. brown | 1·80 | 90 |
| 1797 | - | 500f. brown | 2·20 | 1·10 |

DESIGNS: No. 1787, Sable antelope; 1788, Warthog (*Phacochoerus aethiopicus*); 1789, Brown hyena (*Hyaena brunnea*); 1790, Eastern black-and-white colobus (*Colobus guereza*); 1791, Hippopotamus (*Hippopotamus amphibius*); 1792, Mountain zebra (*Equus zebra*); 1793, African buffalo (*Synceros caffer*) (wrongly inscr "Cyncerus"); 1794, Lion (*Panthera leo*); 1795, Cheetah (*Acinonyx jubatus*); 1796, Hunting dog; 1797, Potto.

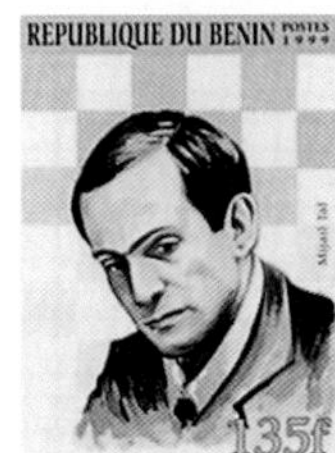


**483** Mikhail Tal

**1999.** Chess Players. Multicoloured.

| | | | |
|---|---|---|---|
| 1798 | 135f. Type **483** | 55 | 30 |
| 1799 | 150f. Emanuel Lasker | 70 | 40 |
| 1800 | 200f. Jose Raul Capablanca | 95 | 55 |
| 1801 | 270f. Aleksandr Alekhine | 1·20 | 70 |
| 1802 | 300f. Max Euwe | 1·50 | 80 |
| 1803 | 400f. Mikhail Botvinnik | 2·00 | 1·10 |
| **MS**1804 | 85×109 mm. 1000f. Wilhelm Steinitz (29×36 mm) | 4·75 | 3·75 |

**484** *Brassocattleya cliftonii*

**1999.** Orchids. Multicoloured.

| | | | |
|---|---|---|---|
| 1805 | 50f. Type **484** | 25 | 10 |
| 1806 | 100f. Wilsonara | 45 | 25 |
| 1807 | 150f. *Cypripedium paeony* | 70 | 40 |
| 1808 | 300f. *Cymbidium babylon* | 1·50 | 80 |
| 1809 | 400f. Cattleya | 2·00 | 1·10 |
| 1810 | 500f. *Miltonia minx* | 2·40 | 1·50 |
| **MS**1811 | 87×110 mm. 1000f. "Isis miltonia" (28×36 mm) | 4·75 | 3·75 |

**485** Royal Python

**1999.** Snakes. Multicoloured.

| | | | |
|---|---|---|---|
| 1812 | 135f. Type **485** | 55 | 35 |
| 1813 | 150f. Royal python (different) | 70 | 40 |
| 1814 | 200f. African rock python | 95 | 55 |
| 1815 | 2000f. Head of African rock python | 9·50 | 6·75 |

**486** Clown Knifefish

**1999.** Fishes. Multicoloured.

| | | | |
|---|---|---|---|
| 1816 | 135f. Type **486** | 55 | 30 |
| 1817 | 150f. Puntius filamentosus | 70 | 40 |
| 1818 | 200f. *Epalzeorhynchos bicolor* | 95 | 55 |
| 1819 | 270f. Spotted rasbora | 1·20 | 70 |
| 1820 | 300f. Tigernander | 1·50 | 80 |
| 1821 | 400f. Siamese fighting fish | 2·00 | 1·10 |
| **MS**1822 | 96×86 mm. 1000f. Three-spotted gourami (39×31 mm) | 4·75 | 3·75 |

**487** A. Murdock's Steam Tricycle, 1786

**1999.** Steam-powered Vehicles. Multicoloured.

| | | | |
|---|---|---|---|
| 1823 | 135f. Type **487** | 55 | 30 |
| 1824 | 150f. Richard Trevithick's locomotive, 1800 | 70 | 40 |
| 1825 | 200f. Trevithick's locomotive, 1803 | 95 | 55 |

| | | | |
|---|---|---|---|
| 1826 | 270f. John Blenkinsop's locomotive, 1811 | 1·20 | 70 |
| 1827 | 300f. Foster and Rastik's *Stourbridge Lion*, 1829 | 1·50 | 80 |
| 1828 | 400f. Peter Cooper's *Tom Thumb*, 1829 | 2·00 | 1·10 |
| **MS**1829 | 110×85 mm. 1000f. Isaac Newton's locomotive, 1760 (36×28 mm) | 4·75 | 3·75 |

**488** Aesculapian Snake

**1999.** Snakes. Multicoloured.

| | | | |
|---|---|---|---|
| 1830 | 135f. Type **488** | 55 | 30 |
| 1831 | 150f. Common pine snake | 70 | 40 |
| 1832 | 200f. Grass snake | 95 | 55 |
| 1833 | 270f. Green whip snake | 1·20 | 70 |
| 1834 | 300f. Jamaica boa | 1·50 | 80 |
| 1835 | 400f. Diamond-back rattlesnake | 2·00 | 1·10 |
| **MS**1836 | 109×86 mm. 1000f. Common European adder (39×29 mm) | 4·75 | 3·75 |

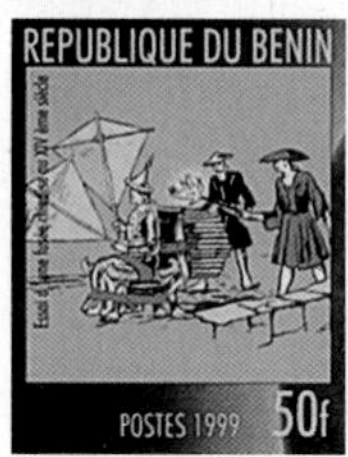


**489** Testing Chinese Lantern (14th-century)

**1999.** "China 1999" International Stamp Exhibition, Peking. Multicoloured.

| | | | |
|---|---|---|---|
| 1837 | 50f. Type **489** | 15 | 10 |
| 1838 | 100f. Satellite launching centre, Jiuquan | 45 | 25 |
| 1839 | 135f. DFH-3 communications satellite | 55 | 40 |
| 1840 | 150f. Satellite launch | 70 | 45 |
| 1841 | 200f. Launch of *Long March* (rocket) | 95 | 60 |
| 1842 | 300f. *Yuan Wang* (passenger ferry) at sea | 1·50 | 90 |
| 1843 | 400f. Dish aerial | 2·00 | 1·20 |
| 1844 | 500f. Items of space post | 2·40 | 1·80 |

Nos. 1837/44 were issued together, se-tenant, with the backgrounds forming a composite design of the Earth.

**490** Cheetah

**1999.** Big Cats. Multicoloured.

| | | | |
|---|---|---|---|
| 1845 | 135f. Type **490** | 55 | 30 |
| 1846 | 150f. Jaguar | 70 | 40 |
| 1847 | 200f. Snow leopard | 95 | 55 |
| 1848 | 270f. Leopard | 1·20 | 55 |
| 1849 | 300f. Puma | 1·50 | 65 |
| 1850 | 400f. Tiger | 2·00 | 90 |
| **MS**1851 | 110×85 mm. 2000f. Lion | 4·75 | 3·75 |

**490a** *Mammillaria lenta*

**1999.** Cacti. Multicoloured.

| | | | |
|---|---|---|---|
| 1856 | 135f. Type **490a** | | |
| 1857 | 150f. *Oehmea nelsonii* | | |
| 1858 | 200f. *Neobesseya rosiflora* | | |
| 1859 | 270f. *Opuntia gosseliniana* | | |
| 1860 | 300f. *Parodia nivosa* | | |
| 1861 | 400f. *Rebutia senilis* | | |
| **MS**1862 | 90×110 mm. 1000f. *Opuntia retrorsa* | | |

**492** Team Members

**1999.** Manchester United—Triple Cup Winners. Sheet 180×132 mm containing T **492** and similar horiz designs. Multicoloured.

**MS**1867 135f. Type **492**; 200f. Winning goal; 300f. Celebrating; 400f. Old Trafford football ground; 500f. Champions League, FA Cup and European Cup trophies; 1000f. Alex Ferguson (manager) and Champions League trophy

**493** Inscr 'Estrilda locustella'

**1999.** Birds. Multicoloured.

| | |
|---|---|
| 1868 | 135f. Type **493** |
| 1869 | 150f. *Estrilda melanotis* |
| 1870 | 200f. Inscr 'Pyrelia melba' |
| 1871 | 270f. *Uraeginthus bengalensis* |
| 1872 | 300f. *Pyromelana orix* |
| 1873 | 400f. *Ploceus cucullatus* |
| **MS**1874 | 90×110 mm. 1000f. *Steganura paradisea* |

### PARCEL POST STAMPS

**1982.** Optd or surch **Colis Postaux**.

| | | | | |
|---|---|---|---|---|
| P871 | - | 100f. multicoloured (No. 779) (postage) | 95 | 50 |
| P872 | **256** | 100f. on 150f. mult | 95 | 50 |
| P873 | - | 300f. mult (No. 797) | 2·75 | 1·40 |
| P874 | **260** | 1000f. multicoloured | 8·25 | 4·00 |
| P875 | **274** | 5000f. on 500f. mult (air) | 41·00 | 19·00 |

**1988.** No. 543 of Dahomey surch **Republique Populaire du Benin** colis postaux.

| | | | | |
|---|---|---|---|---|
| P1089 | **174** | 5f. on 40f. multicoloured (postage) | | |
| P1092 | - | 300f. on 200f. blue, yellow & brown (air) | | |
| P1093 | - | 500f. on 200f. mult | 5·25 | 2·30 |

### POSTAGE DUE STAMPS

**D 233** Pineapples

**1978.** Fruits. Multicoloured.

| | | | |
|---|---|---|---|
| D716 | 10f. Type **D 233** | 30 | 25 |
| D717 | 20f. Cashew nuts (vert) | 45 | 25 |
| D718 | 40f. Oranges | 95 | 55 |
| D719 | 50f. Breadfruit | 1·10 | 75 |

**D234** Village Postman on Bicycle

**1978.** Rural Post.

| | | | | |
|---|---|---|---|---|
| D720 | **D234** | 60f. brown, grn & red | 95 | 45 |
| D721 | - | 80f. blue, brn & red | 95 | 55 |

DESIGN: 80f. River village and postman in canoe.

### APPENDIX

The following stamps have either been issued in excess of postal needs, or have not been available to the public in reasonable quantities at face value. Such stamps may later be given full listings if there is evidence of regular postal use. Miniature sheets and imperforate stamps are excluded from this listing.

**2000**

Year of the Dragon. 135, 150, 200, 270, 300, 400f.
Dogs. 135, 150, 200, 270, 300, 400f.
Insects. 135, 150, 200, 270, 300, 400f.
Birds. 135×2, 150×2, 200×2, 270×2, 300×2, 400f.×2

Pt. 7

# BERGEDORF

A German city on the Elbe, governed by Hamburg and Lubeck until 1867 when it was purchased by the former. In 1868 became part of North German Confederation.

16 schilling = 1 Hamburg mark.

**1**

**1861.** Various sizes. Imperf.

| | | | | |
|---|---|---|---|---|
| 1 | **1** | ½s. black on lilac | £600 | |
| 2 | **1** | ½s. black on blue | 60·00 | £950 |
| 4 | **1** | 1s. black on white | 60·00 | £500 |
| 5 | **1** | 1½s. black on yellow | 26·00 | £1800 |
| 6 | **1** | 3s. black on red | £900 | |
| 7 | **1** | 3s. blue on red | 32·00 | £2750 |
| 8 | **1** | 4s. black on brown | 32·00 | £3000 |

Pt. 1

# BERMUDA

A group of islands in the W. Atlantic, E. of N. Carolina. Usually regarded by collectors as part of the Br. W. Indies group, though this is not strictly correct.

1865. 12 pence = 1 shilling; 20 shillings = 1 pound.
1970. 100 cents = 1 dollar (U.S.).

**9** Queen Victoria

**1865.** Portrait. Various frames.

| | | | | |
|---|---|---|---|---|
| 19 | **9** | ½d. stone | 6·50 | 4·75 |
| 21a | **9** | ½d. green | 4·00 | 80 |
| 24a | **9** | 1d. red | 14·00 | 20 |
| 25 | **9** | 2d. blue | 60·00 | 6·00 |
| 26a | **9** | 2d. purple | 4·00 | 1·50 |
| 27b | **9** | 2½d. blue | 12·00 | 40 |
| 10 | **9** | 3d. yellow | £180 | 60·00 |
| 28 | **9** | 3d. grey | 22·00 | 8·50 |
| 20 | **9** | 4d. red | 17·00 | 1·75 |
| 28a | **9** | 4d. brown | 35·00 | 60·00 |
| 7 | **9** | 6d. mauve | 23·00 | 12·00 |
| 11 | **9** | 1s. green | 15·00 | £120 |
| 29b | **9** | 1s. brown | 13·00 | 18·00 |

**1874.** Surch in words.

| | | | |
|---|---|---|---|
| 15 | 1d. on 2d. blue | £700 | £375 |
| 16 | 1d. on 3d. yellow | £450 | £350 |
| 17 | 1d. on 1s. green | £500 | £250 |
| 12 | 3d. on 1d. red | £18000 | |
| 14 | 3d. on 1s. green | £1500 | £650 |

**1901.** Surch **ONE FARTHING** and bar.

| | | | |
|---|---|---|---|
| 30 | ¼d. on 1s. grey | 4·00 | 50 |

**13** Dry Dock

**1902**

| | | | | |
|---|---|---|---|---|
| 34 | **13** | ¼d. brown and violet | 1·75 | 1·50 |
| 31 | **13** | ½d. black and green | 12·00 | 3·25 |
| 36 | **13** | ½d. green | 18·00 | 3·75 |
| 32 | **13** | 1d. brown and red | 8·00 | 10 |
| 38 | **13** | 1d. red | 19·00 | 10 |
| 39 | **13** | 2d. grey and orange | 7·50 | 10·00 |
| 40 | **13** | 2½d. brown and blue | 26·00 | 7·00 |
| 41 | **13** | 2½d. blue | 18·00 | 8·50 |
| 33 | **13** | 3d. mauve and green | 4·50 | 2·00 |
| 42 | **13** | 4d. blue and brown | 3·00 | 16·00 |

**14** Badge of the Colony

**15**

**1910**

| | | | | |
|---|---|---|---|---|
| 44a | **14** | ¼d. brown | 1·50 | 1·50 |
| 77 | **14** | ½d. green | 1·50 | 3·00 |
| 78 | **14** | 1d. red | 17·00 | 60 |
| 79b | **14** | 1½d. brown | 9·00 | 35 |
| 80 | **14** | 2d. grey | 1·50 | 1·50 |
| 81a | **14** | 2½d. green | 2·50 | 1·50 |
| 82b | **14** | 2½d. blue | 1·75 | 70 |
| 83 | **14** | 3d. blue | 17·00 | 26·00 |
| 84 | **14** | 3d. purple on yellow | 4·00 | 1·00 |
| 85 | **14** | 4d. red on yellow | 2·00 | 1·00 |
| 86 | **14** | 6d. purple | 1·25 | 80 |
| 51 | **14** | 1s. black on green | 4·50 | 4·50 |
| 51b | **15** | 2s. purple and blue on blue | 20·00 | 50·00 |
| 52 | **15** | 2s.6d. black and red on blue | 32·00 | 80·00 |
| 52b | **15** | 4s. black and red | 60·00 | £160 |
| 53d | **15** | 5s. green and red on yellow | 60·00 | £120 |
| 92 | **15** | 10s. green and red on green | £140 | £250 |
| 93 | **15** | 12s.6d. black and orange | £250 | £375 |
| 55 | **15** | £1 purple and black on red | £325 | £550 |

**1918.** Optd **WAR TAX**.

| | | | | |
|---|---|---|---|---|
| 56 | **14** | 1d. red | 50 | 1·25 |

**18** **19**

**1920.** Tercentenary of Representative Institutions. (a) 1st Issue.

| | | | | |
|---|---|---|---|---|
| 59 | **18** | ¼d. brown | 3·50 | 25·00 |
| 60 | **18** | ½d. green | 8·50 | 17·00 |
| 65 | **18** | 1d. red | 4·50 | 30 |
| 61 | **18** | 2d. grey | 15·00 | 50·00 |
| 66 | **18** | 2½d. blue | 19·00 | 20·00 |
| 62 | **18** | 3d. purple on yellow | 12·00 | 50·00 |
| 63 | **18** | 4d. black and red on yellow | 12·00 | 40·00 |
| 67 | **18** | 6d. purple | 28·00 | 90·00 |
| 64 | **18** | 1s. black on green | 16·00 | 48·00 |

(b) 2nd Issue.

| | | | | |
|---|---|---|---|---|
| 74 | **19** | ¼d. brown | 4·25 | 3·75 |
| 75 | **19** | ½d. green | 3·50 | 8·50 |
| 76 | **19** | 1d. red | 7·00 | 35 |
| 68 | **19** | 2d. grey | 10·00 | 45·00 |
| 69 | **19** | 2½d. blue | 13·00 | 5·00 |
| 70 | **19** | 3d. purple on yellow | 5·50 | 16·00 |
| 71 | **19** | 4d. red on yellow | 19·00 | 29·00 |
| 72 | **19** | 6d. purple | 19·00 | 60·00 |
| 73 | **19** | 1s. black on green | 25·00 | 60·00 |

**1935.** Silver Jubilee. As T **13** of Antigua.

| | | | |
|---|---|---|---|
| 94 | 1d. blue and red | 80 | 2·25 |
| 95 | 1½d. blue and grey | 80 | 3·50 |
| 96 | 2½d. brown and blue | 1·40 | 2·50 |
| 97 | 1s. grey and purple | 21·00 | 48·00 |

**20** Hamilton Harbour

**22** "Lucie" (yacht)

**1936**

| | | | | |
|---|---|---|---|---|
| 98 | **20** | ½d. green | 10 | 10 |
| 99 | - | 1d. black and red | 65 | 30 |
| 100 | - | 1½d. black and brown | 1·00 | 50 |
| 101 | **22** | 2d. black and blue | 5·00 | 1·50 |
| 102 | - | 2½d. blue | 1·00 | 25 |
| 103 | - | 3d. black and red | 3·00 | 2·75 |
| 104 | - | 6d. red and violet | 80 | 10 |
| 105 | - | 1s. green | 13·00 | 17·00 |
| 106 | **20** | 1s.6d. brown | 50 | 10 |

DESIGNS—HORIZ: 1d., 1½d. South Shore, near Spanish Rock; 3d. Point House, Warwick Parish. VERT: 2½d., 1s. Grape Bay, Paget Parish; 6d. House at Par-la-Ville, Hamilton.

The 1d., 1½d., 2½d. and 1s. values include a portrait of King George V.

**1937.** Coronation. As T **2** of Aden.

| | | | |
|---|---|---|---|
| 107 | 1d. red | 90 | 1·50 |
| 108 | 1½d. brown | 60 | 1·75 |
| 109 | 2½d. blue | 70 | 1·75 |

**26** Ships in Hamilton Harbour

**28** White-tailed Tropic Bird, Arms of Bermuda and Native Flower

**1938**

| | | | | |
|---|---|---|---|---|
| 110 | **26** | 1d. black and red | 2·25 | 20 |
| 111b | **26** | 1½d. blue and brown | 2·25 | 1·75 |
| 112 | **22** | 2d. blue and brown | 50·00 | 10·00 |
| 112a | **22** | 2d. blue and red | 2·50 | 2·00 |
| 113 | - | 2½d. blue and deep blue | 11·00 | 1·25 |
| 113b | - | 2½d. blue and black | 3·75 | 3·50 |
| 114 | - | 3d. black and red | 35·00 | 5·00 |
| 114a | - | 3d. black and blue | 1·75 | 40 |
| 114bc | **28** | 7½d. black, blue and green | 7·00 | 2·75 |
| 115 | - | 1s. green | 2·00 | 50 |

DESIGNS—VERT: 3d. St. David's Lighthouse. The 2½d. and 1s. are as 1935, but with King George VI portrait.

**1938.** As T **15**, but King George VI portrait.

| | | | |
|---|---|---|---|
| 116c | 2s. purple and blue on blue | 9·00 | 1·50 |
| 117d | 2s.6d. black and red on blue | 16·00 | 19·00 |
| 118f | 5s. green and red on yellow | 35·00 | 29·00 |
| 119e | 10s. green and red on green | 48·00 | 50·00 |
| 120b | 12s.6d. grey and orange | £110 | 55·00 |
| 121d | £1 purple and black on red | 55·00 | 85·00 |

**1940.** Surch **HALF PENNY**.

| | | | | |
|---|---|---|---|---|
| 122 | **26** | ½d. on 1d. black and red | 1·00 | 3·00 |

**1946.** Victory. As T **9** of Aden.

| | | | |
|---|---|---|---|
| 123 | 1½d. brown | 15 | 15 |
| 124 | 3d. blue | 40 | 65 |

**1948.** Silver Wedding. As T **10/11** of Aden.

| | | | |
|---|---|---|---|
| 125 | 1½d. brown | 30 | 50 |
| 126 | £1 red | 45·00 | 55·00 |

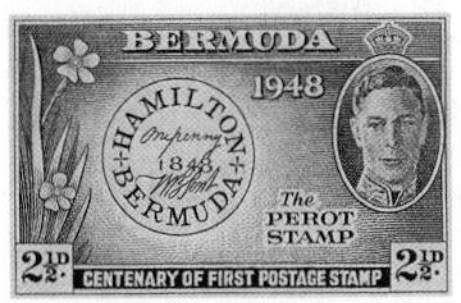


**31** Postmaster Perot's Stamp

**1949.** Centenary of Postmaster Perot's Stamp.

| | | | | |
|---|---|---|---|---|
| 127 | **31** | 2½d. blue and brown | 35 | 35 |
| 128 | **31** | 3d. black and blue | 35 | 15 |
| 129 | **31** | 6d. violet and green | 40 | 15 |

**1949.** U.P.U. As T **20/23** of Antigua.

| | | | |
|---|---|---|---|
| 130 | 2½d. black | 30 | 2·00 |
| 131 | 3d. blue | 1·75 | 1·25 |
| 132 | 6d. purple | 40 | 75 |
| 133 | 1s. green | 40 | 1·50 |

**1953.** Coronation. As T **13** of Aden.

| | | | |
|---|---|---|---|
| 134 | 1½d. black and blue | 1·00 | 40 |

**34** Easter Lily **43** Hog Coin

**1953**

| | | | | |
|---|---|---|---|---|
| 135a | - | ½d. olive | 40 | 2·00 |
| 136 | - | 1d. black and red | 2·00 | 50 |
| 137 | **34** | 1½d. green | 30 | 10 |
| 138 | - | 2d. blue and red | 50 | 40 |
| 139 | - | 2½d. red | 2·00 | 50 |
| 140 | - | 3d. purple | 30 | 10 |
| 141 | - | 4d. black and blue | 55 | 1·75 |
| 142 | - | 4½d. green | 1·50 | 1·00 |
| 143 | - | 6d. black and turquoise | 6·00 | 60 |
| 156 | - | 6d. black and mauve | 1·50 | 15 |
| 143a | - | 8d. black and red | 3·25 | 30 |
| 143b | - | 9d. violet | 11·00 | 2·50 |
| 144 | - | 1s. orange | 50 | 15 |
| 145 | - | 1s.3d. blue | 3·75 | 30 |
| 146 | - | 2s. brown | 4·00 | 85 |
| 147 | - | 2s.6d. red | 8·50 | 45 |
| 148 | **43** | 5s. red | 19·00 | 85 |
| 149 | - | 10s. blue | 16·00 | 7·50 |
| 150 | - | £1 multicoloured | 40·00 | 21·00 |

DESIGNS—HORIZ: ½d. Easter lilies; 1d., 4d. Postmaster Perot's stamp; 2d. "Victory II" (racing dinghy); 2½d. Sir George Somers and "Sea Venture"; 3d., 1s.3d. Map of Bermuda; 4½d. 9d. "Sea Venture" (galleon), coin and Perot stamp; 6d. (No. 143), 8d. White-tailed tropic bird; 6d. (No. 156), Perot's Post Office; 1s. Early Bermuda coins; 2s. Arms of St. George's 10s. Obverse and reverse of hog coin; £1 Arms of Bermuda. VERT: 2s.6d. Warwick Fort.

No. 156 commemorates the restoration and reopening of Perot's Post Office.

**1953.** Royal Visit. As No. 143a but inscr "ROYAL VISIT 1953".

| | | | |
|---|---|---|---|
| 151 | 6d. black and turquoise | 75 | 20 |

**1953.** Three Power Talks. Nos. 140 and 145 optd **Three Power Talks December, 1953.**

| | | | |
|---|---|---|---|
| 152 | 3d. purple | 10 | 10 |
| 153 | 1s.3d. blue | 10 | 10 |

**1956.** 50th Anniv of United States-Bermuda Yacht Race. Nos. 143a and 145 optd **50TH ANNIVERSARY US – BERMUDA OCEAN RACE 1956.**

| | | | |
|---|---|---|---|
| 154 | 8d. black and red | 20 | 45 |
| 155 | 1s.3d. blue | 20 | 55 |

**49** Arms of King James I and Queen Elizabeth II

**1959.** 350th Anniv of Settlement. Arms in red, yellow and blue. Frame colours given.

| | | | | |
|---|---|---|---|---|
| 157 | **49** | 1½d. blue | 30 | 10 |
| 158 | **49** | 3d. grey | 35 | 50 |
| 159 | **49** | 4d. purple | 40 | 55 |
| 160 | **49** | 8d. violet | 40 | 15 |
| 161 | **49** | 9d. olive | 40 | 1·25 |
| 162 | **49** | 1s.3d. brown | 40 | 30 |

**50** The Old Rectory, St George's, c.1730

**1962**

| | | | | |
|---|---|---|---|---|
| 163 | **50** | 1d. purple, black and orange | 10 | 75 |
| 164 | - | 2d. multicoloured | 1·00 | 35 |
| 165 | - | 3d. brown and blue | 10 | 10 |
| 166 | - | 4d. brown and mauve | 20 | 40 |
| 167 | - | 5d. blue and red | 75 | 3·00 |
| 168 | - | 6d. blue, green & lt blue | 30 | 30 |
| 169 | - | 8d. blue, green and orange | 30 | 35 |
| 170 | - | 9d. blue and brown | 30 | 60 |
| 197 | - | 10d. violet and ochre | 75 | 60 |
| 171 | - | 1s. multicoloured | 30 | 10 |
| 172 | - | 1s.3d. lake, grey and bistre | 75 | 15 |
| 173 | - | 1s.6d. violet and ochre | 75 | 1·00 |
| 199 | - | 1s.6d. blue and red | 1·00 | 50 |
| 200 | - | 2s. brown and orange | 1·00 | 75 |
| 175 | - | 2s.3d. sepia and green | 1·00 | 7·00 |
| 176 | - | 2s.6d. sepia, green & yell | 55 | 50 |
| 177 | - | 5s. purple and green | 1·25 | 1·50 |
| 178 | - | 10s. mauve, green and buff | 4·50 | 7·00 |
| 179 | - | £1 black, olive and orange | 14·00 | 14·00 |

DESIGNS: 2d. Church of St. Peter, St. George's; 3d. Government House, 1892; 4d. The Cathedral, Hamilton, 1894; 5d., 1s.6d. (No. 199) H.M. Dockyard, 1811; 6d. Perot's Post Office, 1848; 8d. G.P.O., Hamilton, 1869; 9d. Library, Par-la-Ville; 10d., 1s.6d. (No. 173) Bermuda cottage, c. 1705; 1s. Christ Church, Warwick, 1719; 1s.3d. City Hall, Hamilton, 1960; 2s. Town of St. George; 2s.3d. Bermuda house, c. 1710; 2s.6d. Bermuda house, early 18th century; 5s. Colonial Secretariat, 1833; 10s. Old Post Office, Somerset, 1890; £1 The House of Assembly, 1815.

**1963.** Freedom from Hunger. As T **28** of Aden.

| | | | |
|---|---|---|---|
| 180 | 1s.3d. sepia | 60 | 40 |

**1963.** Centenary of Red Cross. As T **33** of Antigua.

| | | | |
|---|---|---|---|
| 181 | 3d. red and black | 50 | 25 |
| 182 | 1s.3d. red and blue | 1·00 | 2·50 |

**67** "Tsotsi in the Bundu" (Finn class yacht)

**1964.** Olympic Games, Tokyo.

| | | | | |
|---|---|---|---|---|
| 183 | **67** | 3d. red, violet and blue | 10 | 10 |

**1965.** Centenary of ITU. As T **36** of Antigua.

| | | | |
|---|---|---|---|
| 184 | 3d. blue and green | 35 | 25 |
| 185 | 2s. yellow and blue | 65 | 1·50 |

**68** Scout Badge and St. Edward's Crown

**1965.** 50th Anniv of Bermuda Boy Scouts Association.

| | | | | |
|---|---|---|---|---|
| 186 | **68** | 2s. multicoloured | 50 | 50 |

**1965.** ICY. As T **37** of Antigua.

| | | | |
|---|---|---|---|
| 187 | 4d. purple and turquoise | 40 | 20 |
| 188 | 2s.6d. green and lavender | 60 | 80 |

**1966.** Churchill Commemoration. As T **38** of Antigua.

| | | | |
|---|---|---|---|
| 189 | 3d. blue | 30 | 20 |
| 190 | 6d. green | 70 | 1·00 |
| 191 | 10d. brown | 1·00 | 75 |
| 192 | 1s.3d. violet | 1·25 | 2·50 |

**1966.** World Cup Football Championship. As T **40** of Antigua.

| | | | |
|---|---|---|---|
| 193 | 10d. multicoloured | 1·00 | 15 |
| 194 | 2s.6d. multicoloured | 1·25 | 1·25 |

**1966.** 20th Anniv of UNESCO. As T **54/56** of Antigua.

| | | | |
|---|---|---|---|
| 201 | 4d. multicoloured | 45 | 15 |
| 202 | 1s.3d. yellow, violet and olive | 75 | 50 |
| 203 | 2s. black, purple and orange | 1·00 | 1·10 |

**69** GPO Building

**1967.** Opening of New General Post Office.

| | | | | |
|---|---|---|---|---|
| 204 | **69** | 3d. multicoloured | 10 | 10 |
| 205 | **69** | 1s. multicoloured | 10 | 10 |
| 206 | **69** | 1s.6d. multicoloured | 20 | 25 |
| 207 | **69** | 2s.6d. multicoloured | 20 | 70 |

**70** "Mercury" (cable ship) and Chain Links

**1967.** Inauguration of Bermuda–Tortola Telephone Service. Multicoloured.

| | | | |
|---|---|---|---|
| 208 | 3d. Type **70** | 15 | 10 |
| 209 | 1s. Map, telephone and microphone | 25 | 10 |
| 210 | 1s.6d. Telecommunications media | 25 | 25 |
| 211 | 2s.6d. "Mercury" (cable ship) and marine fauna | 40 | 70 |

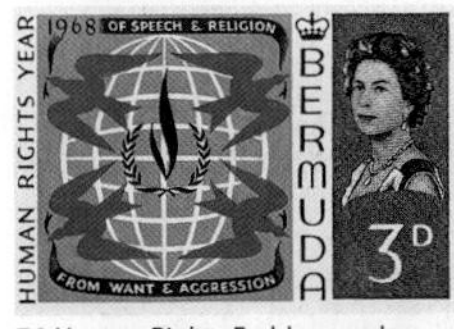


**74** Human Rights Emblem and Doves

**1968.** Human Rights Year.

| | | | | |
|---|---|---|---|---|
| 212 | **74** | 3d. indigo, blue and green | 10 | 10 |
| 213 | **74** | 1s. brown, blue and light blue | 10 | 10 |
| 214 | **74** | 1s.6d. black, blue and red | 10 | 15 |
| 215 | **74** | 2s.6d. green, blue and yellow | 15 | 25 |

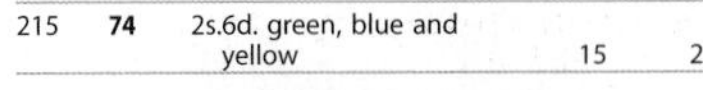

**75** Mace and Queen's Profile

**1968.** New Constitution.

| | | | | |
|---|---|---|---|---|
| 216 | **75** | 3d. multicoloured | 10 | 10 |
| 217 | **75** | 1s. multicoloured | 10 | 10 |
| 218 | - | 1s.6d. yellow, black and blue | 10 | 20 |
| 219 | - | 2s.6d. lilac, black and yellow | 15 | 75 |

DESIGNS: 1s.6d., 2s.6d., Houses of Parliament, and House of Assembly, Bermuda.

**77** Football, Athletics and Yachting

**1968.** Olympic Games, Mexico.

| | | | | |
|---|---|---|---|---|
| 220 | **77** | 3d. multicoloured | 15 | 10 |
| 221 | **77** | 1s. multicoloured | 25 | 10 |
| 222 | **77** | 1s.6d. multicoloured | 50 | 30 |
| 223 | **77** | 2s.6d. multicoloured | 50 | 1·40 |

**78** Brownie and Guide

**1969.** 50th Anniv of Girl Guides. Multicoloured.

| | | | |
|---|---|---|---|
| 224 | 3d. Type **78** | 10 | 10 |
| 225 | 1s. Type **78** | 20 | 10 |
| 226 | 1s.6d. Guides and Badge | 25 | 40 |
| 227 | 2s.6d. As 1s.6d. | 35 | 1·40 |

**80** Emerald-studded Gold Cross and Seaweed

**1969.** Underwater Treasure. Multicoloured.

| | | | |
|---|---|---|---|
| 228 | 4d. Type **80** | 20 | 10 |
| 229 | 1s.3d. Emerald-studded gold cross and sea-bed | 35 | 15 |
| 230 | 2s. As Type **80** | 45 | 90 |
| 231 | 2s.6d. As 1s.3d. | 45 | 1·75 |

**1970.** Decimal Currency. Nos. 163/79 surch.

| | | | |
|---|---|---|---|
| 232 | 1c. on 1d. purple, black & orge | 10 | 1·75 |
| 233 | 2c. on 2d. multicoloured | 10 | 10 |
| 234 | 3c. on 3d. brown and blue | 10 | 30 |
| 235 | 4c. on 4d. brown and mauve | 10 | 10 |
| 236 | 5c. on 8d. blue, green & orge | 15 | 2·25 |
| 237 | 6c. on 6d. blue, green & lt blue | 15 | 1·75 |
| 238 | 9c. on 9d. blue and brown | 30 | 2·75 |
| 239 | 10c. on 10d. violet and ochre | 30 | 25 |
| 240 | 12c. on 1s. multicoloured | 30 | 1·25 |
| 241 | 15c. on 1s.3d. lake, grey & bis | 2·00 | 1·75 |
| 242 | 18c. on 1s.6d. blue and red | 80 | 65 |
| 243 | 24c. on 2s. brown and orange | 85 | 3·50 |
| 244 | 30c. on 2s.6d. sepia, grn & yell | 1·00 | 3·00 |
| 245 | 36c. on 2s.3d. sepia and green | 1·75 | 8·00 |
| 246 | 60c. on 5s. purple and green | 2·25 | 4·50 |
| 247 | $1.20 on 10s. mve, grn & buff | 4·50 | 12·00 |
| 248 | $2.40 on £1 black, ol & orge | 5·50 | 15·00 |

**83** Spathiphyllum

**1970.** Flowers. Multicoloured.

| No. | Description | | |
|---|---|---|---|
| 249 | 1c. Type **83** | 10 | 20 |
| 250 | 2c. Bottlebrush | 20 | 25 |
| 251 | 3c. Oleander (vert) | 15 | 10 |
| 252 | 4c. Bermudiana | 15 | 10 |
| 253 | 5c. Poinsettia | 1·75 | 20 |
| 254 | 6c. Hibiscus | 30 | 30 |
| 255 | 9c. Cereus | 20 | 45 |
| 256 | 10c. Bougainvillea (vert) | 20 | 15 |
| 257 | 12c. Jacaranda | 60 | 60 |
| 258 | 15c. Passion flower | 90 | 1·40 |
| 258a | 17c. As 15c. | 2·75 | 4·75 |
| 259 | 18c. Coralita | 2·25 | 1·00 |
| 259a | 20c. As 18c. | 2·75 | 4·00 |
| 260 | 24c. Morning glory | 1·50 | 5·00 |
| 260a | 25c. As 24c. | 2·75 | 4·50 |
| 261 | 30c. Tecoma | 1·00 | 1·25 |
| 262 | 36c. Angel's trumpet | 1·25 | 1·50 |
| 262a | 40c. As 36c. | 2·75 | 5·50 |
| 263 | 60c. Plumbago | 1·75 | 1·50 |
| 263a | $1 As 60c. | 3·25 | 6·50 |
| 264 | $1.20 Bird of paradise flower | 2·25 | 1·75 |
| 264a | $2 As $1.20 | 9·00 | 10·00 |
| 265 | $2.40 Chalice cup | 5·50 | 2·50 |
| 265a | $3 As $2.40 | 11·00 | 11·00 |

**84** The State House, St. George's

**1970.** 350th Anniv of Bermuda Parliament. Multicoloured.

| No. | Description | | |
|---|---|---|---|
| 266 | 4c. Type **84** | 10 | 10 |
| 267 | 15c. The Sessions House, Hamilton | 25 | 20 |
| 268 | 18c. St. Peter's Church, St. George's | 25 | 25 |
| 269 | 24c. Town Hall, Hamilton | 35 | 1·00 |
| **MS**270 | 131×95 mm. Nos. 266/9 | 1·10 | 1·50 |

**85** Street Scene, St. George's

**1971.** "Keep Bermuda Beautiful". Multicoloured.

| No. | Description | | |
|---|---|---|---|
| 271 | 4c. Type **85** | 20 | 10 |
| 272 | 15c. Horseshoe Bay | 65 | 65 |
| 273 | 18c. Gibbs Hill Lighthouse | 1·50 | 2·25 |
| 274 | 24c. Hamilton Harbour | 1·25 | 2·50 |

**86** Building of the "Deliverance"

**1971.** Voyage of the "Deliverance". Multicoloured.

| No. | Description | | |
|---|---|---|---|
| 275 | 4c. Type **86** | 60 | 20 |
| 276 | 15c. "Deliverance" and "Patience" at Jamestown (vert) | 1·50 | 1·75 |
| 277 | 18c. Wreck of the "Sea Venture" (vert) | 1·50 | 2·25 |
| 278 | 24c. "Deliverance" and "Patience" on high seas | 1·75 | 2·50 |

**87** Green overlooking Ocean View

**1971.** Golfing in Bermuda. Multicoloured.

| No. | Description | | |
|---|---|---|---|
| 279 | 4c. Type **87** | 70 | 10 |
| 280 | 15c. Golfers at Port Royal | 1·25 | 65 |
| 281 | 18c. Castle Harbour | 1·25 | 1·00 |
| 282 | 24c. Belmont | 1·50 | 2·00 |

**1971.** Anglo-American Talks. Nos. 252, 258, 259 and 260 optd **HEATH-NIXON DECEMBER 1971**.

| No. | Description | | |
|---|---|---|---|
| 283 | 4c. Bermudiana | 10 | 10 |
| 284 | 15c. Passion flower | 10 | 20 |
| 285 | 18c. Coralita | 15 | 65 |
| 286 | 24c. Morning glory | 20 | 1·00 |

**89** Bonefish

**1972.** World Fishing Records. Multicoloured.

| No. | Description | | |
|---|---|---|---|
| 287 | 4c. Type **89** | 30 | 10 |
| 288 | 15c. Wahoo | 30 | 50 |
| 289 | 18c. Yellow-finned tuna | 35 | 75 |
| 290 | 24c. Greater amberjack | 40 | 1·25 |

**1972.** Silver Wedding. As T **52** of Ascension, but with "Admiralty Oar" and Mace in background.

| No. | Description | | |
|---|---|---|---|
| 291 | 4c. violet | 15 | 10 |
| 292 | 15c. red | 15 | 50 |

**91** Palmetto

**1973.** Tree Planting Year. Multicoloured.

| No. | Description | | |
|---|---|---|---|
| 293 | 4c. Type **91** | 25 | 10 |
| 294 | 15c. Olivewood bark | 65 | 75 |
| 295 | 18c. Bermuda cedar | 70 | 1·25 |
| 296 | 24c. Mahogany | 75 | 1·60 |

**1973.** Royal Wedding. As T **47** of Anguilla, background colour given. Multicoloured.

| No. | Description | | |
|---|---|---|---|
| 297 | 15c. mauve | 15 | 15 |
| 298 | 18c. blue | 15 | 15 |

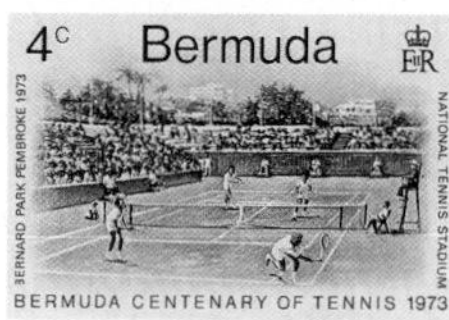

**92** Bernard Park, Pembroke, 1973

**1973.** Centenary of Lawn Tennis. Multicoloured.

| No. | Description | | |
|---|---|---|---|
| 299 | 4c. Type **92** | 30 | 10 |
| 300 | 15c. Clermont Court, 1873 | 40 | 65 |
| 301 | 18c. Leamington Spa Court, 1872 | 45 | 1·75 |
| 302 | 24c. Staten Island Courts, 1874 | 50 | 2·00 |

**93** Weather Vane, City Hall

**1974.** 50th Anniv of Rotary in Bermuda. Mult.

| No. | Description | | |
|---|---|---|---|
| 320 | 5c. Type **93** | 15 | 10 |
| 321 | 17c. St. Peter's Church, St. George's | 45 | 35 |
| 322 | 20c. Somerset Bridge | 50 | 1·50 |
| 323 | 25c. Map of Bermuda, 1626 | 60 | 2·25 |

**94** Jack of Clubs and "good bridge hand"

**1975.** World Bridge Championships, Bermuda. Multicoloured.

| No. | Description | | |
|---|---|---|---|
| 324 | 5c. Type **94** | 20 | 10 |
| 325 | 17c. Queen of Diamonds and Bermuda Bowl | 35 | 50 |
| 326 | 20c. King of Hearts and Bermuda Bowl | 40 | 1·75 |
| 327 | 25c. Ace of Spades and Bermuda Bowl | 40 | 2·50 |

**95** Queen Elizabeth II and the Duke of Edinburgh

**1975.** Royal Visit.

| No. | Type | Description | | |
|---|---|---|---|---|
| 328 | **95** | 17c. multicoloured | 60 | 65 |
| 329 | **95** | 20c. multicoloured | 65 | 2·10 |

**96** Short S.23 Flying Boat "Cavalier", 1937

**1975.** 50th Anniv of Air-mail Service to Bermuda. Multicoloured.

| No. | Description | | |
|---|---|---|---|
| 330 | 5c. Type **96** | 40 | 10 |
| 331 | 17c. U.S. Navy airship "Los Angeles", 1925 | 1·25 | 85 |
| 332 | 20c. Lockheed Constellation, 1946 | 1·40 | 2·75 |
| 333 | 25c. Boeing 747-100, 1970 | 1·50 | 3·50 |
| **MS**334 | 128×85 mm. Nos. 330/3 | 11·00 | 15·00 |

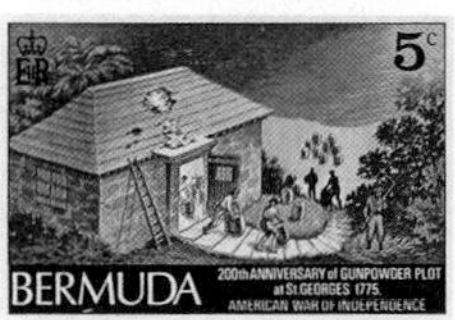

**97** Supporters of American Army raiding Royal Magazine

**1975.** Bicentenary of Gunpowder Plot, St. George's. Multicoloured.

| No. | Description | | |
|---|---|---|---|
| 335 | 5c. Type **97** | 15 | 10 |
| 336 | 17c. Setting off for raid | 30 | 40 |
| 337 | 20c. Loading gunpowder aboard American ship | 35 | 1·40 |
| 338 | 25c. Gunpowder on beach | 35 | 1·50 |
| **MS**339 | 165×138 mm. Nos. 335/8 | 2·75 | 7·00 |

**98** Launching "Ready" (bathysphere)

**1976.** 50th Anniv of Bermuda Biological Station. Multicoloured.

| No. | Description | | |
|---|---|---|---|
| 357 | 5c. Type **98** | 30 | 10 |
| 358 | 17c. View from the sea (horiz) | 60 | 60 |
| 359 | 20c. H.M.S. "Challenger", 1873 (horiz) | 65 | 2·25 |
| 360 | 25c. Beebe's Bathysphere descent, 1934 | 70 | 3·00 |

**99** "Christian Radich" (cadet ship)

**1976.** Tall Ships Race. Multicoloured.

| No. | Description | | |
|---|---|---|---|
| 361 | 5c. Type **99** | 75 | 20 |
| 362 | 12c. "Juan Sebastian de Elcano" (Spanish cadet schooner) | 80 | 2·25 |
| 363 | 17c. "Eagle" (U.S. coastguard cadet ship) | 80 | 1·50 |
| 364 | 20c. "Sir Winston Churchill" (cadet schooner) | 80 | 1·75 |
| 365 | 40c. "Kruzenshtern" (Russian cadet barque) | 1·00 | 2·75 |
| 366 | $1 "Cutty Sark" trophy | 1·25 | 7·00 |

**100** Silver Trophy and Club Flags

**1976.** 75th Anniv of St. George's v. Somerset Cricket Cup Match. Multicoloured.

| No. | Description | | |
|---|---|---|---|
| 367 | 5c. Type **100** | 30 | 10 |
| 368 | 17c. Badge and pavilion, St. George's Club | 50 | 65 |
| 369 | 20c. Badge and pavilion, Somerset Club | 65 | 2·75 |
| 370 | 25c. Somerset playing field | 1·00 | 3·75 |

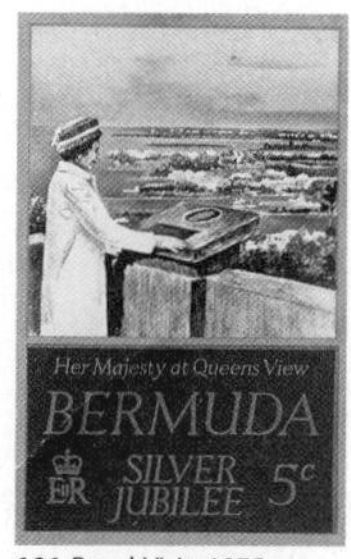

**101** Royal Visit, 1975

**1977.** Silver Jubilee. Multicoloured.

| No. | Description | | |
|---|---|---|---|
| 371 | 5c. Type **101** | 10 | 10 |
| 372 | 20c. St. Edward's Crown | 15 | 20 |
| 373 | $1 The Queen in Chair of Estate | 40 | 1·25 |

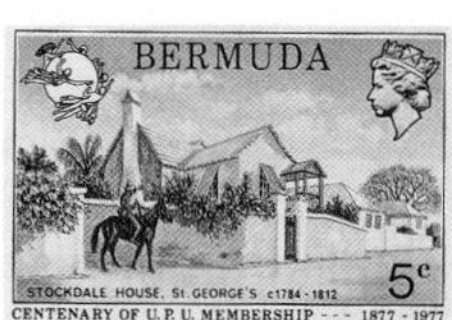

**102** Stockdale House, St. George's, 1784–1812

**1977.** Centenary of U.P.U. Membership. Mult.

| No. | Description | | |
|---|---|---|---|
| 374 | 5c. Type **102** | 15 | 10 |
| 375 | 15c. Perot Post Office and stamp | 25 | 50 |
| 376 | 17c. St. George's P.O. c. 1860 | 25 | 50 |
| 377 | 20c. Old G.P.O., Hamilton, c. 1935 | 30 | 60 |
| 378 | 40c. New G.P.O., Hamilton, 1967 | 45 | 1·10 |

**103** 17th-Century Ship approaching Castle Island

**1977.** Piloting. Multicoloured.

| No. | Description | | |
|---|---|---|---|
| 379 | 5c. Type **103** | 50 | 10 |
| 380 | 15c. Pilot leaving ship, 1795 | 70 | 60 |
| 381 | 17c. Pilots rowing out to paddle-steamer | 80 | 60 |
| 382 | 20c. Pilot gig and brig "Harvest Queen" | 85 | 2·25 |
| 383 | 40c. Modern pilot cutter and R.M.S. "Queen Elizabeth 2" | 1·60 | 3·75 |

**104** Great Seal of Queen Elizabeth I

**1978.** 25th Anniv of Coronation. Multicoloured.

| No. | Description | | |
|---|---|---|---|
| 384 | 8c. Type **104** | 10 | 10 |
| 385 | 50c. Great Seal of Queen Elizabeth II | 30 | 30 |
| 386 | $1 Queen Elizabeth II | 60 | 75 |

**105** White-tailed Tropic Bird

**1978.** Wildlife. Multicoloured.

| | | | |
|---|---|---|---|
| 387 | 3c. Type **105** | 2·50 | 2·50 |
| 388 | 4c. White-eyed vireo | 3·00 | 3·00 |
| 389 | 5c. Eastern bluebird | 1·25 | 1·75 |
| 390 | 7c. Whistling frog | 50 | 1·50 |
| 391 | 8c. Common cardinal ("Cardinal Redbird") | 1·25 | 55 |
| 392 | 10c. Spiny lobster | 20 | 10 |
| 393 | 12c. Land crab | 30 | 70 |
| 394 | 15c. Lizard (Skink) | 30 | 15 |
| 395 | 20c. Four-eyed butterflyfish | 30 | 30 |
| 396 | 25c. Red hind | 30 | 20 |
| 397 | 30c. "Danaus plexippus" (butterfly) | 2·25 | 2·50 |
| 398 | 40c. Rock beauty | 50 | 1·75 |
| 399 | 50c. Banded butterflyfish | 55 | 1·50 |
| 400 | $1 Blue angelfish | 2·50 | 1·75 |
| 401 | $2 Humpback whale | 2·00 | 2·25 |
| 402 | $3 Green turtle | 2·50 | 2·50 |
| 403 | $5 Cahow | 5·50 | 5·00 |

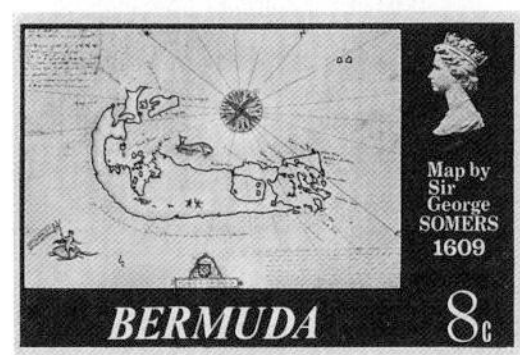

**106** Map by Sir George Somers, 1609

**1979.** Antique Maps. Multicoloured.

| | | | |
|---|---|---|---|
| 404 | 8c. Type **106** | 15 | 10 |
| 405 | 15c. Map by John Seller, 1685 | 20 | 15 |
| 406 | 20c. Map by H. Moll, 1729–40 (vert) | 25 | 25 |
| 407 | 25c. Map by Desbruslins, 1740 | 30 | 30 |
| 408 | 50c. Map by Speed, 1626 | 45 | 80 |

**107** Policeman and Policewoman

**1979.** Centenary of Police Force. Multicoloured.

| | | | |
|---|---|---|---|
| 409 | 8c. Type **107** | 30 | 10 |
| 410 | 20c. Policeman directing traffic (horiz) | 50 | 55 |
| 411 | 25c. "Blue Heron" (police launch) (horiz) | 60 | 65 |
| 412 | 50c. Police Morris Marina and motorcycle | 80 | 1·50 |

**108** 1d. "Perot" Stamp of 1848 and 1840 Penny Black

**1980.** Death Cent of Sir Rowland Hill. Mult.

| | | | |
|---|---|---|---|
| 413 | 8c. Type **108** | 20 | 10 |
| 414 | 20c. "Perot" and Sir Rowland Hill | 30 | 25 |
| 415 | 25c. "Perot" and early letter | 30 | 30 |
| 416 | 50c. "Perot" and "Paid 1" cancellation | 35 | 1·00 |

**109** Lockheed L-1011 TriStar 500 approaching Bermuda

**1980.** "London 1980" International Stamp Exhibition. Multicoloured.

| | | | |
|---|---|---|---|
| 417 | 25c. Type **109** | 30 | 15 |
| 418 | 50c. "Orduna I" (liner) at Grassy Bay, 1926 | 45 | 35 |
| 419 | $1 "Delta" (screw steamer) at St. George's Harbour, 1856 | 85 | 1·10 |
| 420 | $2 "Lord Sidmouth" (sailing packet) in Old Ship Channel, St. George's | 1·40 | 2·25 |

**110** Gina Swainson ("Miss World 1979–80")

**1980.** "Miss World 1979–80" Commem. Mult.

| | | | |
|---|---|---|---|
| 421 | 8c. Type **110** | 15 | 10 |
| 422 | 20c. Miss Swainson after crowning ceremony | 20 | 20 |
| 423 | 50c. Miss Swainson on Peacock Throne | 35 | 35 |
| 424 | $1 Miss Swainson in Bermuda carriage | 70 | 90 |

**111** Queen Elizabeth the Queen Mother

**1980.** 80th Birthday of The Queen Mother.

| | | | | |
|---|---|---|---|---|
| 425 | **111** | 25c. multicoloured | 30 | 1·00 |

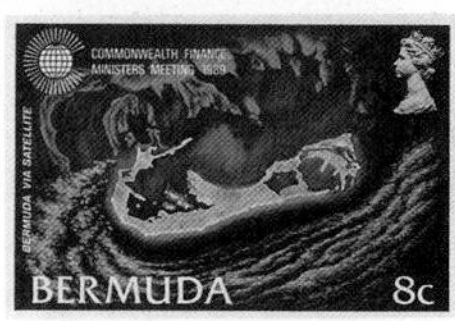

**112** Bermuda from Satellite

**1980.** Commonwealth Finance Ministers Meeting. Multicoloured.

| | | | |
|---|---|---|---|
| 426 | 8c. Type **112** | 10 | 10 |
| 427 | 20c. "Camden" | 20 | 40 |
| 428 | 25c. Princess Hotel, Hamilton | 20 | 50 |
| 429 | 50c. Government House | 35 | 1·50 |

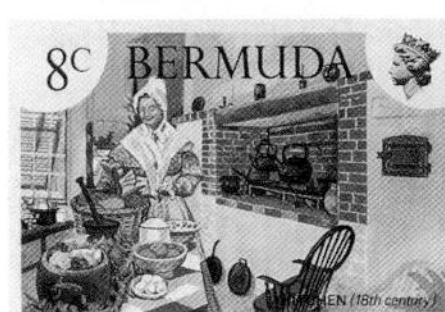

**113** Kitchen, 18th-century

**1981.** Heritage Week. Multicoloured.

| | | | |
|---|---|---|---|
| 430 | 8c. Type **113** | 15 | 10 |
| 431 | 25c. Gathering Easter lilies, 20th-century | 20 | 35 |
| 432 | 30c. Fishing, 20th-century | 30 | 50 |
| 433 | 40c. Stone cutting, 19th-century | 30 | 80 |
| 434 | 50c. Onion shipping, 19th-century | 50 | 90 |
| 435 | $1 Privateering, 17th-century | 1·10 | 2·50 |

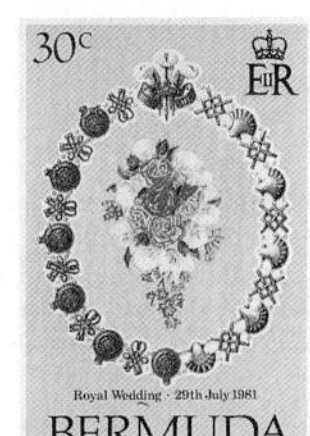

**114** Wedding Bouquet from Bermuda

**1981.** Royal Wedding. Multicoloured.

| | | | |
|---|---|---|---|
| 436 | 30c. Type **114** | 20 | 20 |
| 437 | 50c. Prince Charles as Royal Navy Commander | 35 | 40 |
| 438 | $1 Prince Charles and Lady Diana Spencer | 55 | 80 |

**115** "Service", Hamilton

**1981.** 25th Anniv of Duke of Edinburgh Award Scheme. Multicoloured.

| | | | |
|---|---|---|---|
| 439 | 10c. Type **115** | 15 | 10 |
| 440 | 25c. "Outward Bound", Paget Island | 20 | 20 |
| 441 | 30c. "Expedition", St. David's Island | 20 | 30 |
| 442 | $1 Duke of Edinburgh | 55 | 1·25 |

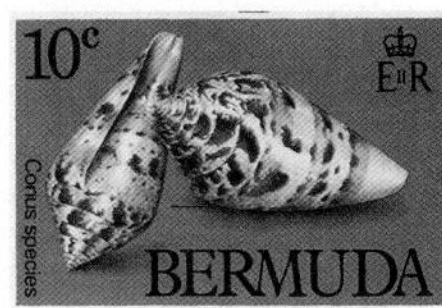

**116** Lightbourne's Cone

**1982.** Sea Shells. Multicoloured.

| | | | |
|---|---|---|---|
| 443 | 10c. Type **116** | 30 | 10 |
| 444 | 25c. Finlay's frog shell | 55 | 55 |
| 445 | 30c. Royal bonnet | 60 | 60 |
| 446 | $1 Lightbourne's murex | 1·75 | 3·25 |

**117** Regimental Colours and Colour Party

**1982.** Bermuda Regiment. Multicoloured.

| | | | |
|---|---|---|---|
| 447 | 10c. Type **117** | 60 | 10 |
| 448 | 25c. Queen's Birthday Parade | 80 | 80 |
| 449 | 30c. Governor inspecting Guard of Honour | 1·10 | 1·40 |
| 450 | 40c. Beating the Retreat | 1·25 | 1·75 |
| 451 | 50c. Ceremonial gunners | 1·25 | 2·00 |
| 452 | $1 Guard of Honour, Royal visit, 1975 | 1·75 | 3·50 |

**118** Charles Fort

**1982.** Historic Bermuda Forts. Multicoloured.

| | | | |
|---|---|---|---|
| 453 | 10c. Type **118** | 20 | 20 |
| 454 | 25c. Pembroks Fort | 50 | 85 |
| 455 | 30c. Southampton Fort (horiz) | 60 | 1·25 |
| 456 | $1 Smiths Fort and Pagets Fort (horiz) | 1·75 | 4·50 |

**119** Arms of Sir Edwin Sandys

**1983.** Coat of Arms (1st series). Multicoloured.

| | | | |
|---|---|---|---|
| 457 | 10c. Type **119** | 45 | 15 |
| 458 | 25c. Arms of the Bermuda Company | 1·10 | 1·00 |
| 459 | 50c. Arms of William Herbert, Earl of Pembroke | 1·90 | 3·75 |
| 460 | $1 Arms of Sir George Somers | 2·50 | 6·50 |

See also Nos. 482/5 and 499/502.

**120** Early Fitted Dinghy

**1983.** Fitted Dinghies. Multicoloured.

| | | | |
|---|---|---|---|
| 461 | 12c. Type **120** | 45 | 15 |
| 462 | 30c. Modern dinghy inshore | 60 | 75 |
| 463 | 40c. Early dinghy (different) | 70 | 90 |
| 464 | $1 Modern dinghy with red and white spinnaker | 1·40 | 3·25 |

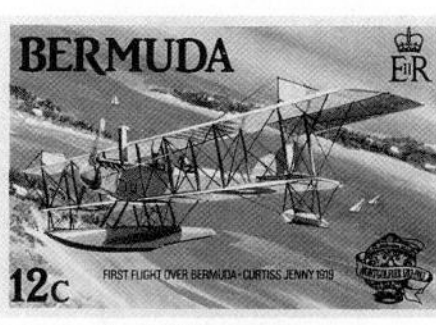

**121** Curtiss N-9 Seaplane

**1983.** Bicentenary of Manned Flight. Multicoloured.

| | | | |
|---|---|---|---|
| 465 | 12c. Type **121** (First flight over Bermuda) | 60 | 20 |
| 466 | 30c. Stinson Pilot Radio seaplane (First completed flight between U.S. and Bermuda) | 1·25 | 1·25 |
| 467 | 40c. S.23 Flying boat "Cavalier" (First scheduled passenger flight) | 1·50 | 1·75 |
| 468 | $1 U.S.N. "Los Angeles" (airship) moored to U.S.S. "Patoka" | 2·75 | 5·00 |

**122** Joseph Stockdale

**1984.** Bicentenary of Bermuda's First Newspaper and Postal Service. Multicoloured.

| | | | |
|---|---|---|---|
| 469 | 12c. Type **122** | 25 | 15 |
| 470 | 30c. "The Bermuda Gazette" | 45 | 80 |
| 471 | 40c. Stockdale's postal service (horiz) | 60 | 1·10 |
| 472 | $1 "Lady Hammond" (mail boat) (horiz) | 2·00 | 3·25 |

**123** Sir Thomas Gates and Sir George Somers

**1984.** 375th Anniv of First Settlement. Mult.

| | | | |
|---|---|---|---|
| 473 | 12c. Type **123** | 20 | 15 |
| 474 | 30c. Jamestown, Virginia | 50 | 1·25 |
| 475 | 40c. Wreck of "Sea Venture" | 90 | 1·25 |
| 476 | $1 Fleet leaving Plymouth, Devon | 2·00 | 6·00 |
| **MS**477 | 130×73 mm. Nos. 474 and 476 | 3·75 | 10·00 |

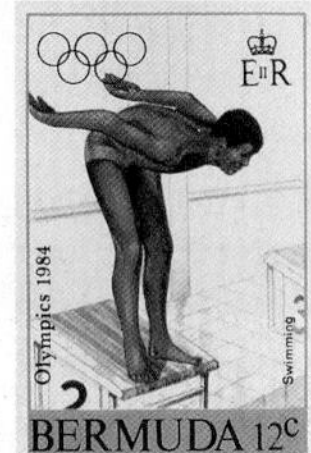

**124** Swimming

**1984.** Olympic Games, Los Angeles. Multicoloured.

| | | | |
|---|---|---|---|
| 478 | 12c. Type **124** | 40 | 15 |
| 479 | 30c. Track and field events (horiz) | 70 | 75 |
| 480 | 40c. Equestrian | 1·10 | 1·25 |
| 481 | $1 Sailing (horiz) | 2·00 | 5·50 |

**1984.** Coat of Arms (2nd series). As T **119**. Mult.

482 12c. Arms of Henry Wrothesley, Earl of Southampton 50 15
483 30c. Arms of Sir Thomas Smith 1·00 85
484 40c. Arms of William Cavendish, Earl of Devonshire 1·25 1·50
485 $1 Town arms of St. George 2·75 4·50

**125** Buttery

**1985.** Bermuda Architecture. Multicoloured.

486 12c. Type **125** 35 15
487 30c. Limestone rooftops (horiz) 80 70
488 40c. Chimneys (horiz) 95 1·00
489 $1.50 Entrance archway 3·00 3·75

**126** Osprey

**1985.** Birth Bicentenary of John J. Audubon (ornithologist). Designs showing original drawings. Multicoloured.

490 12c. Type **126** 2·00 65
491 30c. Yellow-crowned night heron 2·00 95
492 40c. Great egret (horiz) 2·25 1·25
493 $1.50 Eastern bluebird ("Bluebird") 3·75 6·50

**127** The Queen Mother with Grandchildren, 1980

**1985.** Life and Times of Queen Elizabeth the Queen Mother. Multicoloured.

494 12c. Queen Consort, 1937 35 15
495 30c. Type **127** 60 50
496 40c. At Clarence House on 83rd birthday 70 60
497 $1.50 With Prince Henry at his christening (from photo by Lord Snowdon) 2·00 2·75
**MS**498 91×73 mm. $1 With Prince Charles at 80th birthday celebrations 3·75 3·50

**1985.** Coats of Arms (3rd series). As T **119**. Mult.

499 12c. Hamilton 75 15
500 30c. Paget 1·40 80
501 40c. Warwick 1·60 1·40
502 $1.50 City of Hamilton 3·75 4·25

**128** Halley's Comet and Bermuda Archipelago

**1985.** Appearance of Halley's Comet. Multicoloured.

503 15c. Type **128** 85 25
504 40c. Halley's Comet, A.D. 684 (from Nuremberg Chronicles, 1493) 1·60 1·75
505 50c. "Halley's Comet, 1531" (from Peter Apian woodcut, 1532) 1·90 2·50
506 $1.50 "Halley's Comet, 1759" (Samuel Scott) 3·50 6·50

**129** "Constellation" (schooner) (1943)

**1986.** Ships Wrecked on Bermuda. Multicoloured.

507A 3c. Type **129** 70 2·00
508A 5c. "Early Riser" (pilot boat), 1876 20 20
509A 7c. "Madiana" (screw steamer), 1903 65 2·75
510A 10c. "Curlew" (sail/steamer), 1856 30 30
511A 12c. "Warwick" (galleon), 1619 60 80
512A 15c. H.M.S. "Vixen" (gun-boat), 1890 40 60
512cA 18c. As 7c. 6·00 4·25
513A 20c. "San Pedro" (Spanish galleon), 1594 1·10 80
514A 25c. "Alert" (fishing sloop), 1877 60 3·00
515A 40c. "North Carolina" (barque), 1880 65 1·25
516A 50c. "Mark Antonie" (Spanish privateer), 1777 1·50 3·25
517A 60c. "Mary Celestia" (Confederate paddle-steamer), 1864 1·50 1·75
517cA 70c. "Caesar" (brig), 1818 6·50 6·50
518B $1 "L'Herminie" (French frigate), 1839 1·50 1·60
519A $1.50 As 70c. 4·50 6·00
520B $2 "Lord Amherst" (transport), 1778 2·50 6·50
521B $3 "Minerva" (sailing ship), 1849 4·25 9·00
522A $5 "Caraquet" (cargo liner), 1923 4·50 11·00
523A $8 H.M.S. "Pallas" (frigate), 1783 6·00 13·00

**1986.** 60th Birthday of Queen Elizabeth II. As T **110** of Ascension. Multicoloured.

524 15c. Princess Elizabeth aged three, 1929 45 30
525 40c. With Earl of Rosebery at Oaks May Meeting, Epsom, 1954 80 60
526 50c. With Duke of Edinburgh, Bermuda, 1975 80 75
527 60c. At British Embassy, Paris, 1972 90 90
528 $1.50 At Crown Agents Head Office, London, 1983 2·00 2·50

**1986.** "Ameripex '86" International Stamp Exhibition, Chicago. As T **164** of Bahamas, showing Bermuda stamps. Multicoloured.

529 15c. 1984 375th Anniv of Settlement miniature sheet 1·50 30
530 40c. 1973 Lawn Tennis Centenary, 24c. 2·25 70
531 50c. 1983 Bicentenary of Manned Flight 12c. 2·25 1·00
532 $1 1976 Tall Ships Race 17c. 3·75 3·00
**MS**533 80×80 mm. $1.50, Statue of Liberty and "Monarch of Bermuda" 8·75 7·00

No. **MS**533 also commemorates the Centenary of the Statue of Liberty.

**1986.** 25th Anniv of World Wildlife Fund. No. 402 surch **90c.**

534 90c. on $3 Green turtle 3·00 4·25

**131** Train in Front Street, Hamilton, 1940

**1987.** Transport (1st series). Bermuda Railway. Multicoloured.

535 15c. Type **131** 2·00 25
536 40c. Train crossing Springfield Trestle 2·50 90
537 50c. "St. George Special" at Bailey's Bay Station 2·50 1·50
538 $1.50 Boat train at St. George 4·00 6·25

See also Nos. 557/60, 574/7 and 624/9.

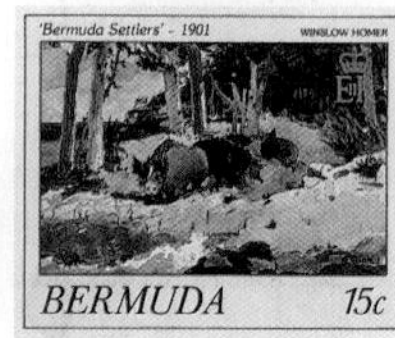

**132** "Bermuda Settlers", 1901

**1987.** Bermuda Paintings (1st series). Works by Winslow Homer. Multicoloured.

539 15c. Type **132** 60 25
540 30c. "Bermuda", 1900 85 45
541 40c. "Bermuda Landscape", 1901 (buff frame) 95 55
544 40c. Type **132** 1·00 1·75
545 40c. As No. 540 1·00 1·75
546 40c. As No. 541 (grey frame) 1·00 1·75
547 40c. As No. 542 1·00 1·75
548 40c. As No. 543 1·00 1·75
542 50c. "Inland Water", 1901 1·10 70
543 $1.50 "Salt Kettle", 1899 2·50 2·50

See also Nos. 607/10 and 630/3.

**133** Sikorsky S-42B Flying Boat "Bermuda Clipper"

**1987.** 50th Anniv of Inauguration of Bermuda–U.S.A. Air Service. Multicoloured.

549 15c. Type **133** 2·00 15
550 40c. Short S.23 flying boat "Cavalier" 3·00 70
551 50c. "Bermuda Clipper" in flight over signpost 3·25 80
552 $1.50 "Cavalier" on apron and "Bermuda Clipper" in flight 6·00 3·50

**134** 19th-century Wagon carrying Telephone Poles

**1987.** Centenary of Bermuda Telephone Company. Multicoloured.

553 15c. Type **134** 75 15
554 40c. Early telephone exchange 1·40 60
555 50c. Early and modern telephones 1·75 70
556 $1.50 Communications satellite orbiting Earth 2·75 5·75

**135** Mail Wagon, c. 1869

**1988.** Transport (2nd series). Horse-drawn Carts and Wagons. Multicoloured.

557 15c. Type **135** 25 15
558 40c. Open cart, c. 1823 55 55
559 50c. Closed cart, c. 1823 65 70
560 $1.50 Two-wheeled wagon, c. 1930 2·00 3·25

**136** "Old Blush"

**1988.** Old Garden Roses (1st series). Multicoloured.

561 15c. Type **136** 85 25
562 30c. "Anna Olivier" 1·25 45
563 40c. "Rosa chinensis semperflorens" (vert) 1·40 85
564 50c. "Archduke Charles" 1·50 1·25
565 $1.50 "Rosa chinensis viridiflora" (vert) 3·00 6·50

See also Nos. 584/8 and, for designs with the royal cypher instead of the Queen's head, Nos. 589/98 and 683/6.

**1988.** 300th Anniv of Lloyd's of London. As T **123** of Ascension. Multicoloured.

566 18c. Loss of H.M.S. "Lutine" (frigate), 1799 85 25
567 50c. "Sentinel" (cable ship) (horiz) 1·60 65
568 60c. "Bermuda" (liner), Hamilton, 1931 (horiz) 1·75 75
569 $2 Loss of H.M.S. "Valerian" (sloop) in hurricane, 1926 3·00 4·00

**137** Devonshire Parish Militia, 1812

**1988.** Military Uniforms. Multicoloured.

570 18c. Type **137** 1·50 25
571 50c. 71 st (Highland) Regiment, 1831–34 2·00 1·10
572 60c. Cameron Highlanders, 1942 2·25 1·25
573 $2 Troop of horse, 1774 4·75 8·00

**138** "Corona" (ferry)

**1989.** Transport (3rd series). Ferry Services. Mult.

574 18c. Type **138** 35 25
575 50c. Rowing boat ferry 75 65
576 60c. St. George's barge ferry 85 75
577 $2 "Laconia" 2·50 4·50

**139** Morgan's Island

**1989.** 150 Years of Photography. Multicoloured.

578 18c. Type **139** 85 25
579 30c. Front Street, Hamilton 1·10 45
580 50c. Waterfront, Front Street, Hamilton 1·60 1·25
581 60c. Crow Lane from Hamilton Harbour 1·75 1·40
582 70c. Shipbuilding, Hamilton Harbour 1·90 2·50
583 $1 Dockyard 2·25 3·50

**1989.** Old Garden Roses (2nd series). As T **136.** Multicoloured.

584 18c. "Agrippina" (vert) 90 25
585 30c. "Smith's Parish" (vert) 1·25 60
586 50c. "Champney's Pink Cluster" 1·75 1·40
587 60c. "Rosette Delizy" 1·75 1·60
588 $1.50 "Rosa bracteata" 2·75 6·00

**1989.** Old Garden Roses (3rd series). Designs as Nos. 561/5 and 584/8, but with royal cypher at top left instead of Queen's head. Multicoloured.

589 50c. As No. 565 (vert) 1·75 2·25
590 50c. As No. 563 (vert) 1·75 2·25
591 50c. Type **136** 1·75 2·25
592 50c. As No. 562 1·75 2·25
593 50c. As No. 564 1·75 2·25
594 50c. As No. 585 (vert) 1·75 2·25
595 50c. As No. 584 (vert) 1·75 2·25
596 50c. As No. 586 1·75 2·25
597 50c. As No. 587 1·75 2·25
598 50c. As No. 588 1·75 2·25

**140** Main Library, Hamilton

**1989.** 150th Anniv of Bermuda Library. Mult.

599 18c. Type **140** 60 25
600 50c. The Old Rectory, St. George's 1·25 65
601 60c. Somerset Library, Springfield 1·25 85
602 $2 Cabinet Building, Hamilton 3·25 4·50

**141** 1865 1d. Rose

**1989.** Commonwealth Postal Conference. Mult.

| | | | | |
|---|---|---|---|---|
| 603 | **141** | 18c. grey, pink and red | 1·50 | 25 |
| 604 | - | 50c. grey, blue & lt blue | 2·00 | 75 |
| 605 | - | 60c. grey, purple and mauve | 2·25 | 1·25 |
| 606 | - | $2 grey, green and emerald | 3·75 | 5·00 |

DESIGNS: 50c. 1866 2d. blue; 60c. 1865 6d. purple; $2 1865 1s. green.

**142** "Fairylands, c. 1890" (Ross Turner)

**1990.** Bermuda Paintings (2nd series). Multicoloured.

| | | | |
|---|---|---|---|
| 607 | 18c. Type **142** | 75 | 25 |
| 608 | 50c. "Shinebone Alley, c. 1953" (Ogden Pleissner) | 1·25 | 1·25 |
| 609 | 60c. "Salt Kettle, 1916" (Prosper Senat) | 1·25 | 1·50 |
| 610 | $2 "St. George's, 1934" (Jack Bush) | 3·25 | 7·00 |

**1990.** "Stamp World London 90" International Stamp Exhibition. Nos. 603/6 optd **Stamp World London 90** and logo.

| | | | |
|---|---|---|---|
| 611 | 18c. grey, pink and red | 1·25 | 25 |
| 612 | 50c. grey, blue and light blue | 1·75 | 1·50 |
| 613 | 60c. grey, purple and mauve | 2·00 | 1·75 |
| 614 | $2 grey, green and emerald | 3·50 | 6·00 |

**1990.** Nos. 511, 516 and 519 surch.

| | | | |
|---|---|---|---|
| 615 | 30c. on 12c. "Warwick" (galleon), (1619) | 1·75 | 1·25 |
| 616 | 55c. on 50c. "Mark Antonie" (Spanish privateer), 1777 | 2·25 | 2·25 |
| 617 | 80c. on $1.50 "Caesar" (brig), 1818 | 2·50 | 4·75 |

**145** The Halifax and Bermudas Cable Company Office, Hamilton

**1990.** Centenary of Cable and Wireless in Bermuda.

| | | | | |
|---|---|---|---|---|
| 618 | **145** | 20c. brown and black | 70 | 25 |
| 619 | - | 55c. brown and black | 2·00 | 1·25 |
| 620 | - | 70c. multicoloured | 2·00 | 2·75 |
| 621 | - | $2 multicoloured | 4·75 | 7·50 |

DESIGNS: 55c. "Westmeath" (cable ship), 1890; 70c. Wireless transmitter station, St. George's, 1928; $2 "Sir Eric Sharp" (cable ship).

**1991.** President Bush–Prime Minister Major Talks, Bermuda. Nos. 618/19 optd **BUSH-MAJOR 16 MARCH 1991**.

| | | | | |
|---|---|---|---|---|
| 622 | **145** | 20c. brown and black | 2·00 | 1·50 |
| 623 | - | 55c. brown and black | 3·00 | 3·50 |

**147** Two-seater Pony Cart, 1805

**1991.** Transport (4th series). Horse-drawn Carriages. Multicoloured.

| | | | |
|---|---|---|---|
| 624 | 20c. Type **147** | 80 | 30 |
| 625 | 30c. Varnished rockaway, 1830 | 90 | 60 |
| 626 | 55c. Vis-a-Vis victoria, 1895 | 1·60 | 1·10 |
| 627 | 70c. Semi-formal phaeton, 1900 | 2·25 | 2·50 |
| 628 | 80c. Pony runabout, 1905 | 2·50 | 3·75 |
| 629 | $1 Ladies phaeton, 1910 | 2·75 | 4·50 |

**148** "Bermuda, 1916" (Prosper Senat)

**1991.** Bermuda Paintings (3rd series). Multicoloured.

| | | | |
|---|---|---|---|
| 630 | 20c. Type **148** | 1·00 | 30 |
| 631 | 55c. "Bermuda Cottage" 1930 (Frank Allison) (horiz) | 2·00 | 1·40 |
| 632 | 70c. "Old Maid's Lane", 1934 (Jack Bush) | 2·50 | 3·25 |
| 633 | $2 "St. George's", 1953 (Ogden Pleissner) (horiz) | 5·00 | 8·50 |

**1991.** 65th Birthday of Queen Elizabeth II and 70th Birthday of Prince Philip. As T **139** of Ascension. Multicoloured.

| | | | |
|---|---|---|---|
| 634 | 55c. Prince Philip in tropical naval uniform | 1·25 | 1·75 |
| 635 | 70c. Queen Elizabeth II in Bermuda | 1·25 | 1·75 |

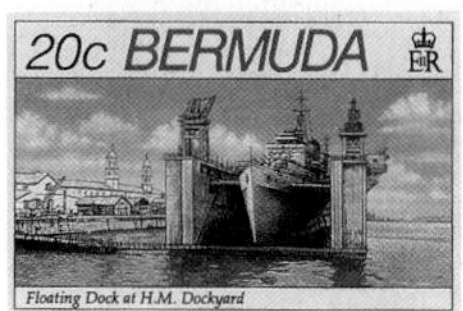

**149** H.M.S. "Argonaut" (cruiser) in Floating Dock

**1991.** 50th Anniv of Second World War. Mult.

| | | | |
|---|---|---|---|
| 636 | 20c. Type **149** | 1·50 | 40 |
| 637 | 55c. Kindley Airfield | 2·25 | 1·40 |
| 638 | 70c. Boeing 314A flying boat and map of Atlantic route | 2·75 | 3·25 |
| 639 | $2 Censored trans-Atlantic mail | 4·50 | 7·50 |

**1992.** 40th Anniv of Queen Elizabeth II's Accession. As T **143** of Ascension. Multicoloured.

| | | | |
|---|---|---|---|
| 640 | 20c. Old fort on beach | 60 | 30 |
| 641 | 30c. Public gardens | 75 | 55 |
| 642 | 55c. Cottage garden | 1·25 | 90 |
| 643 | 70c. Beach and hotels | 1·60 | 2·25 |
| 644 | $1 Queen Elizabeth II | 1·90 | 2·75 |

**150** Rings and Medallion

**1992.** 500th Anniv of Discovery of America by Columbus. Spanish Artifacts. Multicoloured.

| | | | |
|---|---|---|---|
| 645 | 25c. Type **150** | 1·25 | 35 |
| 646 | 35c. Ink wells | 1·40 | 75 |
| 647 | 60c. Gold ornaments | 2·25 | 2·00 |
| 648 | 75c. Bishop buttons and crucifix | 2·50 | 3·25 |
| 649 | 85c. Earrings and pearl buttons | 2·75 | 3·75 |
| 650 | $1 Jug and bowls | 3·00 | 4·25 |

**151** "Wreck of 'Sea Venture' "

**1992.** Stained Glass Windows. Multicoloured.

| | | | |
|---|---|---|---|
| 651 | 25c. Type **151** | 1·50 | 40 |
| 652 | 60c. "Birds in tree" | 2·75 | 2·00 |
| 653 | 75c. "St. Francis feeding bird" | 3·25 | 3·00 |
| 654 | $2 "Shells" | 7·00 | 10·00 |

**152** German Shepherd

**1992.** 7th World Congress of Kennel Clubs. Mult.

| | | | |
|---|---|---|---|
| 655 | 25c. Type **152** | 1·25 | 40 |
| 656 | 35c. Irish setter | 1·50 | 70 |
| 657 | 60c. Whippet (vert) | 2·25 | 2·25 |
| 658 | 75c. Border terrier (vert) | 2·25 | 3·25 |
| 659 | 85c. Pomeranian (vert) | 2·50 | 3·75 |
| 660 | $1 Schipperke (vert) | 2·50 | 4·25 |

**153** Policeman, Cyclist and Cruise Liner

**1993.** Tourism Posters by Adolph Treidler. Mult.

| | | | |
|---|---|---|---|
| 679 | 25c. Type **153** | 2·25 | 80 |
| 680 | 60c. Seaside golf course | 3·00 | 2·75 |
| 681 | 75c. Deserted beach | 2·50 | 2·75 |
| 682 | $2 Dancers in evening dress and cruise liner | 4·50 | 7·00 |

**154** "Duchesse de Brabant" and Bee

**1993.** Garden Roses (4th series).

| | | | | |
|---|---|---|---|---|
| 683 | **154** | 10c. multicoloured | 75 | 1·40 |
| 684 | **154** | 25c. multicoloured | 75 | 60 |
| 685 | **154** | 50c. multicoloured | 2·75 | 4·00 |
| 686 | **154** | 60c. multicoloured | 1·25 | 1·75 |

**1993.** 75th Anniv of Royal Air Force. As T **149** of Ascension. Multicoloured.

| | | | |
|---|---|---|---|
| 687 | 25c. Consolidated PBY-5 Catalina | 85 | 35 |
| 688 | 60c. Supermarine Spitfire Mk IX | 2·00 | 2·00 |
| 689 | 75c. Bristol Type 156 Beaufighter Mk X | 2·25 | 2·25 |
| 690 | $2 Handley Page Halifax Mk III | 3·75 | 6·00 |

**155** Hamilton from the Sea

**1993.** Bicentenary of Hamilton. Mult.

| | | | |
|---|---|---|---|
| 691 | 25c. Type **155** | 1·00 | 35 |
| 692 | 60c. Waterfront | 2·00 | 2·00 |
| 693 | 75c. Barrel warehouse | 2·00 | 2·50 |
| 694 | $2 Sailing ships off Hamilton | 5·00 | 7·00 |

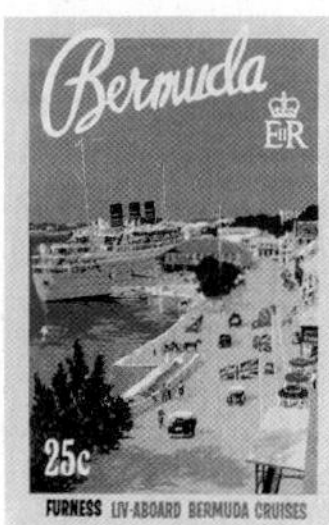

**156** "Queen of Bermuda" (liner) at Hamilton

**1994.** 75th Anniv of Furness Line's Bermuda Cruises. Adolphe Treidler Posters. Multicoloured.

| | | | |
|---|---|---|---|
| 695 | 25c. Type **156** | 65 | 35 |
| 696 | 60c. "Queen of Bermuda" entering port (horiz) | 1·50 | 1·60 |
| 697 | 75c. "Queen of Bermuda" and "Ocean Monarch" (liners) (horiz) | 1·60 | 1·75 |
| 698 | $2 Passengers on promenade deck at night | 3·50 | 6·00 |

**157** Queen Elizabeth II in Bermuda

**1994.** Royal Visit. Multicoloured.

| | | | |
|---|---|---|---|
| 699 | 25c. Type **157** | 1·00 | 35 |
| 700 | 60c. Queen Elizabeth and Prince Philip in open carriage | 2·50 | 1·75 |
| 701 | 75c. Royal Yacht "Britannia" | 5·00 | 3·50 |

**158** Peach

**1994.** Flowering Fruits. Multicoloured.

| | | | |
|---|---|---|---|
| 792 | 5c. Type **158** | 40 | 1·00 |
| 703A | 7c. Fig | 40 | 1·25 |
| 704A | 10c. Calabash (vert) | 35 | 35 |
| 795 | 15c. Natal plum | 65 | 35 |
| 796 | 18c. Locust and wild honey | 70 | 30 |
| 797 | 20c. Pomegranate | 70 | 35 |
| 798 | 25c. Mulberry (vert) | 70 | 40 |
| 709A | 35c. Grape (vert) | 70 | 55 |
| 710A | 55c. Orange (vert) | 1·00 | 80 |
| 711A | 60c. Surinam cherry | 1·25 | 1·40 |
| 802 | 75c. Loquat | 2·00 | 1·75 |
| 803 | 90c. Sugar apple | 2·25 | 2·00 |
| 804 | $1 Prickly pear (vert) | 2·50 | 3·50 |
| 715A | $2 Paw paw | 4·50 | 5·50 |
| 716A | $3 Bay grape | 5·00 | 6·00 |
| 717A | $5 Banana (vert) | 7·50 | 8·00 |
| 718A | $8 Lemon | 11·00 | 12·00 |

**159** Nurse with Mother and Baby

**1994.** Centenary of Hospital Care. Multicoloured.

| | | | |
|---|---|---|---|
| 719 | 25c. Type **159** | 1·00 | 35 |
| 720 | 60c. Patient on dialysis machine | 2·00 | 1·90 |
| 721 | 75c. Casualty on emergency trolley | 2·25 | 2·25 |
| 722 | $2 Elderly patient in wheelchair with physiotherapists | 4·75 | 7·00 |

**160** Gombey Dancers

**1994.** Cultural Heritage (1st series). Multicoloured.

| | | | |
|---|---|---|---|
| 723 | 25c. Type **160** | 75 | 35 |
| 724 | 60c. Christmas carol singers | 1·40 | 1·50 |
| 725 | 75c. Marching band | 2·50 | 2·00 |
| 726 | $2 National Dance Group performers | 4·75 | 7·50 |

See also Nos. 731/4.

**161** Bermuda 1970 Flower 1c. Stamps and 1c. Coin

**1995.** 25th Anniv of Decimal Currency. Mult.

| | | | |
|---|---|---|---|
| 727 | 25c. Type **161** | 75 | 35 |
| 728 | 60c. 1970 5c. stamps and coin | 1·40 | 1·50 |
| 729 | 75c. 1970 10c. stamps and coin | 1·75 | 2·00 |
| 730 | $2 1970 25c. stamps and coin | 4·50 | 6·50 |

**1995.** Cultural Heritage (2nd series). As T **160**. Multicoloured.

| | | | |
|---|---|---|---|
| 731 | 25c. Kite flying | 75 | 35 |
| 732 | 60c. Majorettes | 1·50 | 1·50 |
| 733 | 75c. Portuguese dancers | 1·75 | 2·00 |
| 734 | $2 Floral float | 4·00 | 6·00 |

**162** Bermuda Coat of Arms

**1995.** 375th Anniv of Bermuda Parliament.

| | | | | |
|---|---|---|---|---|
| 735 | **162** | 25c. multicoloured | 1·25 | 35 |
| 736 | **162** | $1 multicoloured | 2·50 | 3·25 |

For design as No. 736 but inscr "Commonwealth Finance Ministers Meeting", see No. 765.

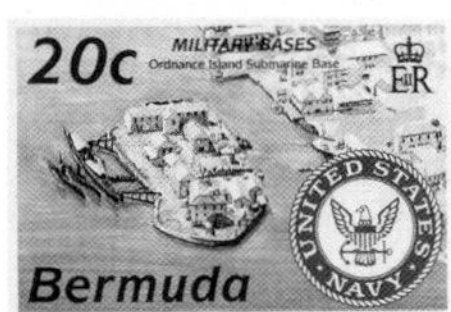


**163** U.S. Navy Ordnance Island Submarine Base

**1995.** Military Bases. Multicoloured.

| | | | |
|---|---|---|---|
| 737 | 20c. Type **163** | 70 | 60 |
| 738 | 25c. Royal Naval Dockyard | 75 | 35 |
| 739 | 60c. U.S.A.F. Fort Bell and Kindley Field | 1·60 | 1·25 |
| 740 | 75c. R.A.F. Darrell's Island flying boat base | 1·75 | 2·00 |
| 741 | 90c. U.S. Navy operating base | 1·90 | 2·75 |
| 742 | $1 Canadian Forces Communications Station, Daniel's Head | 1·90 | 2·75 |

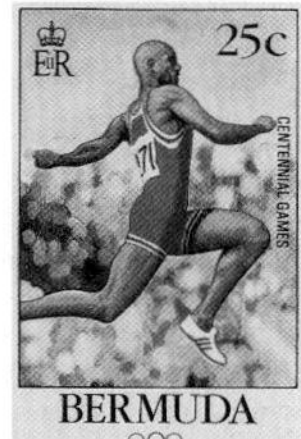


**164** Triple Jump

**1996.** Olympic Games, Atlanta. Multicoloured.

| | | | |
|---|---|---|---|
| 743 | 25c. Type **164** | 70 | 35 |
| 744 | 30c. Cycling | 3·00 | 1·00 |
| 745 | 65c. Yachting | 2·00 | 2·00 |
| 746 | 80c. Show jumping | 2·00 | 3·00 |

**165** Jetty and Islets, Hamilton

**1996.** Panoramic Paintings of Hamilton (Nos. 747/51) and St. George's (Nos. 752/6) by E. J. Holland. Multicoloured.

| | | | |
|---|---|---|---|
| 747 | 60c. Type **165** | 1·75 | 2·25 |
| 748 | 60c. End of island and buildings | 1·75 | 2·25 |
| 749 | 60c. Yachts and hotel | 1·75 | 2·25 |
| 750 | 60c. Islet, hotel and cathedral | 1·75 | 2·25 |
| 751 | 60c. Cliff and houses by shore | 1·75 | 2·25 |
| 752 | 60c. Islet and end of main island | 1·75 | 2·25 |
| 753 | 60c. Yacht and houses on hillside | 1·75 | 2·25 |
| 754 | 60c. Yacht and St. George's Hotel on hilltop | 1·75 | 2·25 |
| 755 | 60c. Shoreline and fishing boats | 1·75 | 2·25 |
| 756 | 60c. Entrance to harbour channel | 1·75 | 2·25 |

**166** Somerset Express Mail Cart, c. 1900

**1996.** "CAPEX '96" International Stamp Exhibition, Toronto. Local Transport. Multicoloured.

| | | | |
|---|---|---|---|
| 757 | 25c. Type **166** | 1·25 | 35 |
| 758 | 60c. Victoria carriage and railcar, 1930s | 2·75 | 1·75 |
| 759 | 75c. First bus, 1946 | 2·75 | 2·00 |
| 760 | $2 Sightseeing bus, c. 1947 | 5·00 | 7·50 |

**167** Hog Fish Beacon

**1996.** Lighthouses. Multicoloured.

| | | | |
|---|---|---|---|
| 761 | 30c. Type **167** | 1·50 | 50 |
| 762 | 65c. Gibbs Hill Lighthouse | 2·00 | 1·25 |
| 763 | 80c. St. David's Lighthouse | 2·50 | 2·00 |
| 764 | $2 North Rock Beacon | 4·50 | 7·00 |

See also Nos. 770/3.

**1996.** Commonwealth Finance Ministers' Meeting. As No. 736, but inscr "Commonwealth Finance Ministers Meeting" at top and with wider gold frame.

| | | | |
|---|---|---|---|
| 765 | $1 multicoloured | 2·50 | 3·00 |

**168** Waterville

**1996.** Architectural Heritage. Multicoloured.

| | | | |
|---|---|---|---|
| 766 | 30c. Type **168** | 1·00 | 45 |
| 767 | 65c. Bridge House | 1·40 | 1·50 |
| 768 | 80c. Fannie Fox's Cottage | 1·75 | 2·00 |
| 769 | $2.50 Palmetto House | 4·00 | 7·00 |

**1997.** "HONG KONG '97" International Stamp Exhibition. Designs as Nos. 761/4, but incorporating "HONG KONG '97" logo and with some values changed.

| | | | |
|---|---|---|---|
| 770 | 30c. As Type **167** | 2·00 | 65 |
| 771 | 65c. Gibbs Hill Lighthouse | 2·75 | 1·50 |
| 772 | 80c. St David's Lighthouse | 3·00 | 2·25 |
| 773 | $2.50 North Rock Beacon | 6·00 | 9·50 |

**169** White-tailed Tropic Bird

**1997.** Bird Conservation. Multicoloured.

| | | | |
|---|---|---|---|
| 774 | 30c. Type **169** | 60 | 50 |
| 775 | 60c. White-tailed tropic bird and chick (vert) | 1·25 | 1·25 |
| 776 | 80c. Cahow and chick (vert) | 1·75 | 2·00 |
| 777 | $2.50 Cahow | 4·00 | 6·50 |

**170** Queen Elizabeth II with Crowd

**1997.** Golden Wedding of Queen Elizabeth and Prince Philip. Multicoloured.

| | | | |
|---|---|---|---|
| 778 | 30c. Type **170** | 50 | 40 |
| 779 | $2 Queen Elizabeth and Prince Philip | 3·25 | 4·50 |
| **MS**780 | 90×56 mm. Nos. 778/9 | 3·75 | 4·50 |

**171** Father playing with Children

**1997.** Education. Multicoloured.

| | | | |
|---|---|---|---|
| 781 | 30c. Type **171** | 50 | 40 |
| 782 | 40c. Teacher and children with map | 60 | 55 |
| 783 | 60c. Boys holding sports trophy | 85 | 1·25 |
| 784 | 65c. Pupils outside Berkeley Institute | 90 | 1·25 |
| 785 | 80c. Scientific experiments | 1·25 | 2·00 |
| 786 | 90c. New graduates | 1·40 | 2·50 |

**1998.** Diana, Princess of Wales Commemoration. Sheet, 145×170 mm, containing vert designs as T **177** of Ascension. Multicoloured.

| | | | |
|---|---|---|---|
| **MS**787 | 30c. Wearing black hat, 1983; 40c. Wearing floral dress; 65c. Wearing blue evening dress, 1996; 80c. Carrying bouquets, 1993 (sold at $2.15 + 25c. charity premium) | 3·00 | 4·00 |

**172** "Fox's Cottage, St. Davids" (Ethel Tucker)

**1998.** Paintings by Catherine and Ethel Tucker. Multicoloured.

| | | | |
|---|---|---|---|
| 788 | 30c. Type **172** | 1·25 | 40 |
| 789 | 40c. "East Side, Somerset" | 1·40 | 70 |
| 790 | 65c. "Long Bay Road, Somerset" | 2·25 | 1·25 |
| 791 | $2 "Flatts Village" | 5·00 | 7·50 |

**173** Horse and Carriage

**1998.** Hospitality in Bermuda. Multicoloured.

| | | | |
|---|---|---|---|
| 809 | 25c. Type **173** | 1·25 | 40 |
| 810 | 30c. Golf club desk | 1·75 | 75 |
| 811 | 65c. Chambermaid preparing room | 1·50 | 1·25 |
| 812 | 75c. Kitchen staff under training | 1·50 | 2·00 |
| 813 | 80c. Waiter at beach hotel | 1·75 | 2·25 |
| 814 | 90c. Nightclub bar | 2·00 | 3·00 |

**174** "Agave attenuata"

**1998.** Centenary of Botanical Gardens. Multicoloured.

| | | | |
|---|---|---|---|
| 815 | 30c. Type **174** | 1·25 | 40 |
| 816 | 65c. Bermuda palmetto tree | 2·25 | 90 |
| 817 | $1 Banyan tree | 2·75 | 2·75 |
| 818 | $2 Cedar tree | 4·00 | 7·00 |

**175** Lizard with Fairy Lights (Claire Critchley)

**1998.** Christmas. Children's Paintings. Mult.

| | | | |
|---|---|---|---|
| 819 | 25c. Type **175** | 1·25 | 35 |
| 820 | 40c. "Christmas stairway" (Cameron Rowling) (horiz) | 1·50 | 1·25 |

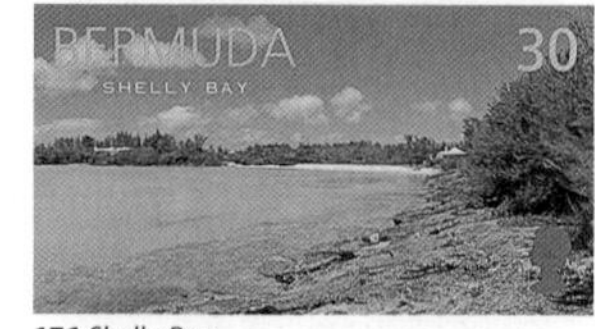


**176** Shelly Bay

**1999.** Bermuda Beaches. Multicoloured.

| | | | |
|---|---|---|---|
| 821 | 30c. Type **176** | 80 | 40 |
| 822 | 60c. Catherine's Bay | 1·10 | 1·00 |
| 823 | 65c. Jobson's Cove | 1·25 | 1·10 |
| 824 | $2 Warwick Long Bay | 3·50 | 5·50 |

**177** Tracking Station

**1999.** 30th Anniv of First Manned Landing on Moon. Multicoloured.

| | | | |
|---|---|---|---|
| 825 | 30c. Type **177** | 1·00 | 40 |
| 826 | 60c. Mission launch (vert) | 1·50 | 90 |
| 827 | 75c. Aerial view of tracking station, Bermuda | 1·75 | 1·25 |
| 828 | $2 Astronaut on Moon (vert) | 3·75 | 6·00 |
| **MS**829 | 90×80 mm. 65c. Earth as seen from Moon (circular, 40 mm diam) | 3·25 | 4·00 |

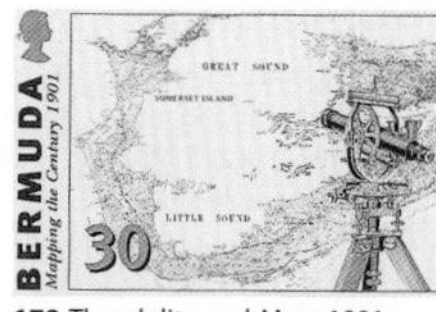


**178** Theodolite and Map, 1901

**1999.** Centenary of First Digital Map of Bermuda.

| | | | | |
|---|---|---|---|---|
| 830 | **178** | 30c. multicoloured | 1·50 | 40 |
| 831 | - | 65c. black, stone & silver | 2·25 | 1·50 |
| 832 | - | 80c. multicoloured | 2·75 | 2·50 |
| 833 | - | $1 multicoloured | 2·75 | 4·00 |

DESIGNS: 65c. Street map, 1901; 80c. Street plan and aerial photograph, 1999; $1 Satellite and Bermuda from Space, 1999.

**179** Victorian Pillar Box and Bermuda 1865 1s. Stamp

**1999.** Bermuda Postal History. Multicoloured.

| | | | |
|---|---|---|---|
| 834 | 30c. Type **179** | 1·00 | 40 |
| 835 | 75c. King George V pillar box and 1920 2s. stamp | 2·00 | 1·50 |
| 836 | 95c. King George VI wall box and 1938 3d. stamp | 2·25 | 2·75 |
| 837 | $1 Queen Elizabeth II pillar box and 1953 Coronation 1½d. stamp | 2·25 | 2·75 |

**180** Sir Henry Tucker and Meeting of House of Assembly

**2000.** Pioneers of Progress (1st series). Each brown, black and gold.

| | | | |
|---|---|---|---|
| 838 | 30c. Type **180** | 85 | 1·00 |
| 839 | 30c. Gladys Morrell and suffragettes | 85 | 1·00 |
| 840 | 30c. Dr. E. F. Gordon and workers | 85 | 1·00 |

See also Nos. 988/92 and 1018/1019.

**181** *Amerigo Vespucci* (full-rigged ship)

**2000.** Tall Ships Race. Multicoloured.

| | | | |
|---|---|---|---|
| 841 | 30c. Type **181** | 1·25 | 50 |
| 842 | 60c. *Europa* (barque) | 1·75 | 1·50 |
| 843 | 80c. *Juan Sebastian de Elcano* (schooner) | 2·00 | 2·50 |

**182** Prince William

**2000.** Royal Birthdays. Multicoloured.

| | | | |
|---|---|---|---|
| 844 | 35c. Type **182** | 1·25 | 45 |
| 845 | 40c. Duke of York | 1·25 | 50 |
| 846 | 50c. Princess Royal | 1·40 | 90 |
| 847 | 70c. Princess Margaret | 1·75 | 2·50 |
| 848 | $1 Queen Elizabeth the Queen Mother | 2·00 | 3·25 |
| **MS**849 | 169×90 mm. Nos. 844/8 | 8·00 | 8·50 |

**183** Santa Claus with Smiling Vegetable (Meghan Jones)

**2000.** Christmas. Children's Paintings. Mult.

| | | | |
|---|---|---|---|
| 850 | 30c. Type **183** | 1·00 | 45 |
| 851 | 45c. Christmas tree and presents (Carlita Lodge) | 1·25 | 80 |

**2001.** Endangered Species. Bird Conservation. Designs as Nos. 774/7, but with different face values, inscriptions redrawn and WWF panda emblem added. Multicoloured.

| | | | |
|---|---|---|---|
| 852 | 15c. As Type **169** | 90 | 1·00 |
| 853 | 15c. Cahow | 90 | 1·00 |
| 854 | 20c. White-tailed tropic bird with chick (vert) | 90 | 1·00 |
| 855 | 20c. Cahow with chick (vert) | 90 | 1·00 |
| **MS**856 | 200×190 mm. Nos. 852/5 each × 4 | 12·00 | 13·00 |

No. **MS**856 includes the "HONG KONG 2001" logo on the margin.

**184** King's Castle

**2001.** Historic Buildings, St. George's. Mult.

| | | | |
|---|---|---|---|
| 857 | 35c. Type **184** | 1·10 | 55 |
| 858 | 50c. Bridge House | 1·50 | 75 |
| 859 | 55c. Whitehall | 1·60 | 1·00 |
| 860 | 70c. Fort Cunningham | 1·90 | 2·25 |
| 861 | 85c. St. Peter's Church | 2·50 | 3·25 |
| 862 | 95c. Water Street | 2·50 | 3·25 |

**185** Boer Prisoners on Boat and Plough

**2001.** Centenary of Anglo-Boer War. Multicoloured.

| | | | |
|---|---|---|---|
| 863 | 35c. Type **185** | 85 | 55 |
| 864 | 50c. Prisoners in shelter and boot | 1·10 | 75 |
| 865 | 70c. Elderly Boer with children and jewellery | 1·60 | 1·75 |
| 866 | 95c. Bermuda residents and illustrated envelope of 1902 | 2·00 | 3·00 |

**186** Girl touching Underwater Environment

**2001.** 75th Anniv of Bermuda Aquarium. Multicoloured.

| | | | |
|---|---|---|---|
| 867 | 35c. Type **186** | 90 | 55 |
| 868 | 50c. Museum exhibits (horiz) | 1·25 | 75 |
| 869 | 55c. Feeding giant tortoise (horiz) | 1·25 | 95 |
| 870 | 70c. Aquarium building (horiz) | 1·75 | 1·75 |
| 871 | 80c. Lesson from inside tank | 1·75 | 2·25 |
| 872 | 95c. Turtle | 2·25 | 3·00 |

**187** "Fishing Boats" (Charles Lloyd Tucker)

**2001.** Paintings of Charles Lloyd Tucker. Multicoloured.

| | | | |
|---|---|---|---|
| 873 | 35c. Type **187** | 1·40 | 55 |
| 874 | 70c. "Bandstand and City Hall, Hamilton" | 2·00 | 1·50 |
| 875 | 85c. "Hamilton Harbour" | 2·25 | 2·50 |
| 876 | $1 "Train in Front Street, Hamilton" | 3·00 | 4·25 |

**2002.** Golden Jubilee. As T **200** of Ascension.

| | | | |
|---|---|---|---|
| 877 | 10c. black, violet and gold | 60 | 60 |
| 878 | 35c. multicoloured | 1·50 | 1·10 |
| 879 | 70c. black, violet and gold | 2·00 | 1·60 |
| 880 | 85c. multicoloured | 2·25 | 2·25 |
| **MS**881 | 162×95 mm. Nos. 887/80 and $1 multicoloured | 7·00 | 7·50 |

DESIGNS—HORIZ: 10c. Princess Elizabeth with corgi; 35c. Queen Elizabeth in evening dress, 1965; 70c. Queen Elizabeth in car, 1952; 85c. Queen Elizabeth on Merseyside, 1991. VERT (38×51 mm)—$2 Queen Elizabeth after Annigoni.

Designs as Nos. 877/80 in No. **MS**881 omit the gold frame around each stamp and the "Golden Jubilee 1952–2002" inscription.

**188** Fantasy Cave

**2002.** Caves. Multicoloured.

| | | | |
|---|---|---|---|
| 882 | 35c. Type **188** | 1·40 | 55 |
| 883 | 70c. Crystal Cave | 2·00 | 1·50 |
| 884 | 80c. Prospero's Cave | 2·25 | 2·50 |
| 885 | $1 Cathedral Cave | 2·75 | 4·00 |

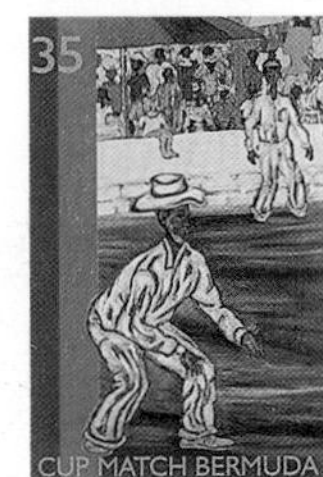

**189** Fielder and Somerset Club Colours

**2002.** Centenary of Bermuda Cup Cricket Match. Multicoloured.

| | | | |
|---|---|---|---|
| 886 | 35c. Type **189** | 1·25 | 1·00 |
| 887 | 35c. Batsman and wicket-keeper with St. George's Club colours | 1·25 | 1·00 |
| **MS**888 | 110×85 mm. $1 Batsman (48×31 mm) | 3·25 | 3·50 |

**2002.** Queen Elizabeth the Queen Mother Commemoration. As T **202** of Ascension.

| | | | |
|---|---|---|---|
| 889 | 30c. brown, gold and purple | 1·00 | 45 |
| 890 | $1.25 multicoloured | 2·50 | 3·00 |
| **MS**891 | 145×70 mm. Nos. 889/90 | 4·50 | 4·75 |

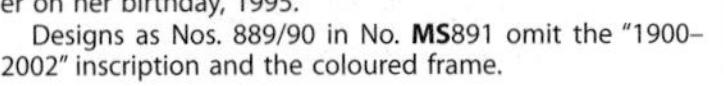
DESIGNS: 30c. Duchess of York, 1923; $1.25, Queen Mother on her birthday, 1995.

Designs as Nos. 889/90 in No. **MS**891 omit the "1900–2002" inscription and the coloured frame.

**190** Slit Worm-shell

**2002.** Shells. Multicoloured.

| | | | |
|---|---|---|---|
| 892 | 5c. Type **190** | 10 | 10 |
| 893 | 10c. Netted olive | 15 | 15 |
| 894 | 20c. Angular triton (horiz) | 35 | 30 |
| 895 | 25c. Frog shell (horiz) | 40 | 35 |
| 896 | 30c. Colourful atlantic moon (horiz) | 45 | 40 |
| 897 | 35c. Noble wentletrap | 50 | 45 |
| 898 | 40c. Atlantic trumpet triton (horiz) | 60 | 50 |
| 899 | 45c. Zigzag scallop | 70 | 55 |
| 900 | 50c. Bermuda cone | 80 | 65 |
| 901 | 75c. Very distorted distorsio (horiz) | 1·25 | 90 |
| 902 | 80c. Purple sea snail (horiz) | 1·40 | 95 |
| 903 | 90c. Flame helmet (horiz) | 1·40 | 1·10 |
| 904 | $1 Scotch bonnet (horiz) | 1·50 | 1·40 |
| 905 | $2 Gold mouth triton (horiz) | 2·75 | 2·50 |
| 906 | $3 Bermuda's slit shell (horiz) | 4·25 | 4·00 |
| 907 | $4 Reticulated cowrie-helmet (horiz) | 5·50 | 6·00 |
| 908 | $5 Dennison's morum (horiz) | 6·50 | 7·00 |
| 909 | $8 Sunrise tellin | 10·00 | 11·00 |

**191** Dove of Peace

**2002.** World Peace Day.

| | | | | |
|---|---|---|---|---|
| 910 | **191** | 35c. multicoloured | 1·25 | 50 |
| 911 | - | 70c. multicoloured | 2·00 | 2·25 |

DESIGN: 70c. Dove.

**192** Research Station and *Weatherbird II* (research ship)

**2003.** Centenary of Bermuda Biological Research Station. Multicoloured.

| | | | |
|---|---|---|---|
| 912 | 35c. Type **192** | 1·00 | 50 |
| 913 | 70c. Spotfin butterflyfish (horiz) | 1·75 | 1·50 |
| 914 | 85c. Collecting coral (horiz) | 1·90 | 2·25 |
| 915 | $1 Krill | 2·00 | 3·00 |

**193** Costume Dolls

**2003.** Heritage "Made in Bermuda". (1st Series). Multicoloured.

| | | | |
|---|---|---|---|
| 916 | 35c. Type **193** | 75 | 40 |
| 917 | 70c. Model sailing ship | 1·25 | 1·10 |
| 918 | 80c. Abstract sculpture in wood | 1·40 | 1·60 |
| 919 | $1 Silverware | 1·75 | 2·25 |

See also Nos. 934/7, 952/5 and 980/3.

**2003.** 50th Anniv of Coronation. As T **206** of Ascension. Multicoloured.

| | | | |
|---|---|---|---|
| 920 | 35c. Queen in Coronation Coach | 75 | 40 |
| 921 | 70c. Queen in Coronation chair, flanked by bishops of Durham and Bath & Wells | 1·25 | 1·50 |

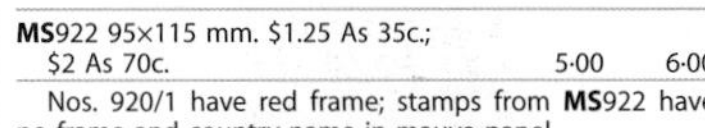

| | | | |
|---|---|---|---|
| **MS**922 | 95×115 mm. $1.25 As 35c.; $2 As 70c. | 5·00 | 6·00 |

Nos. 920/1 have red frame; stamps from **MS**922 have no frame and country name in mauve panel.

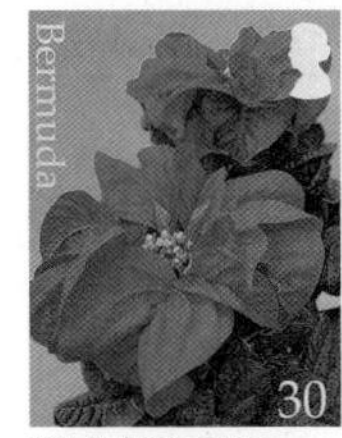

**194** Red Poinsettias

**2003.** Christmas Greetings. Poinsettias. Mult.

| | | | |
|---|---|---|---|
| 925 | 30c. Type **194** | 75 | 35 |
| 926 | 45c. White poinsettias | 1·10 | 55 |
| 927 | 80c. Pink poinsettias | 2·00 | 2·50 |

**195** Gateway

**2004.** Royal Naval Dockyard, Bermuda. Multicoloured.

| | | | |
|---|---|---|---|
| 928 | 25c. Type **195** | 65 | 50 |
| 929 | 35c. Fountain and Clock Tower | 90 | 80 |
| 930 | 70c. Waterside seat and Clock Tower | 1·75 | 1·50 |
| 931 | 85c. Marina | 1·90 | 2·00 |
| 932 | 95c. Window in ramparts | 2·25 | 2·50 |
| 933 | $1 Boats moored at pontoon and Clocktower Centre | 2·40 | 3·00 |

**2004.** Heritage "Made in Bermuda" (2nd series). As T **193**. Multicoloured.

| | | | |
|---|---|---|---|
| 934 | 35c. Carver chair | 65 | 45 |
| 935 | 70c. Ceramic jug and plate | 1·10 | 90 |
| 936 | 80c. Glass fish and glass plate with shell design | 1·25 | 1·40 |
| 937 | $1.25 Quilt | 1·75 | 2·50 |

**196** Bluefin Tuna

**2004.** Endangered Species. Bluefin Tuna. Multicoloured.

| | | | |
|---|---|---|---|
| 938 | 10c. Type **196** | 30 | 50 |
| 939 | 35c. Five bluefin tuna | 85 | 50 |
| 940 | 85c. Bluefin tuna near surface of water | 1·90 | 1·90 |
| 941 | $1.10 Bluefin tuna swimming left | 2·25 | 2·50 |

**197** Yellow Oncydium Orchids

**2004.** 50th Anniv of the Orchid Society. Multicoloured.

| | | | |
|---|---|---|---|
| 942 | 35c. Type **197** | 90 | 45 |
| 943 | 45c. *Encyclia radiate* | 1·10 | 55 |
| 944 | 85c. Purple and white orchids | 2·00 | 2·00 |
| 945 | $1.10 *Paphiopedilum spicerianum* | 2·50 | 2·75 |

**198** 1940 Map of Bermuda and Compass

**2005.** 500th Anniv of Discovery of Bermuda by Juan de Bermudez (Spanish navigator). Multicoloured.

| | | | |
|---|---|---|---|
| 946 | 25c. Type **198** | 1·00 | 50 |
| 947 | 35c. 1846 map and sextant | 1·10 | 55 |
| 948 | 70c. 1764 map and box compass | 1·90 | 1·40 |
| 949 | $1.10 1692 map and telescope | 2·75 | 3·00 |
| 950 | $1.25 1548 map and calipers | 2·75 | 3·25 |
| **MS**951 | 115×95 mm. $5 Aerial view of Bermuda | 11·00 | 12·00 |

**2005.** Heritage "Made in Bermuda" (3rd series). As T **193**. Multicoloured.

| | | | |
|---|---|---|---|
| 952 | 35c. Picture of Bermuda Gombey dancers | 70 | 45 |
| 953 | 70c. Papier-mache sculpture of parrotfish on tube coral | 1·25 | 1·25 |
| 954 | 85c. Stained glass picture of lion and lamb | 1·60 | 1·75 |
| 955 | $1 Earrings and pendant of silver, pearls and garnets | 1·90 | 2·50 |

**2005.** Bicentenary of Battle of Trafalgar. As T **216** of Ascension but horiz. Multicoloured.

| | | | |
|---|---|---|---|
| 956 | 10c. HMS *Victory* | 60 | 60 |
| 957 | 35c. HMS *Pickle* under construction in Bermuda | 1·00 | 50 |
| 958 | 70c. HMS *Pickle* picking up survivors from burning *Achille* | 1·60 | 1·50 |
| 959 | 85c. HMS *Pickle* racing back to England with news of victory | 1·90 | 2·25 |

No. 956 contains traces of powdered wood from HMS *Victory*.

**199** Ruddy Turnstone and Semipalmated Sandpiper

**2005.** Bermuda Habitats. Scenes from dioramas in Bermuda Natural History Museum. Multicoloured.

| | | | |
|---|---|---|---|
| 960 | 10c. Type **199** | 45 | 50 |
| 961 | 25c. Least bittern in reeds | 65 | 40 |
| 962 | 35c. White-tailed tropic bird | 85 | 45 |
| 963 | 70c. Eastern bluebird | 1·50 | 1·25 |
| 964 | 85c. Saw-whet owl | 2·00 | 2·00 |
| 965 | $1 Yellow-crowned night heron | 2·25 | 2·50 |

**200** Christmas Tree with Lights

**2005.** Christmas Greetings. Festival of Lights. Multicoloured.

| | | | |
|---|---|---|---|
| 966 | 30c. Type **200** | 50 | 50 |
| 967 | 45c. Dolphin | 65 | 60 |
| 968 | 80c. Snowman | 1·25 | 1·25 |

**201** Man working on Overhead Power Cables

**2006.** Centenary of the Bermuda Electric Light Company Ltd. Multicoloured.

| | | | |
|---|---|---|---|
| 969 | 35c. Type **201** | 70 | 45 |
| 970 | 70c. Engineer, power lines and vehicle | 1·40 | 1·10 |
| 971 | 85c. Power plant | 1·75 | 1·90 |
| 972 | $1 Office block | 1·90 | 2·50 |

**2006.** 80th Birthday of Queen Elizabeth II. As T **223** of Ascension. Multicoloured.

| | | | |
|---|---|---|---|
| 973 | 35p. Princess Elizabeth with corgi | 90 | 45 |
| 974 | 70p. Queen wearing tiara (black/white photo) | 1·40 | 1·10 |
| 975 | 85p. Wearing tiara and drop earrings (colour photo) | 1·75 | 1·75 |
| 976 | $1.25 Wearing blue hat | 2·75 | 3·25 |
| **MS**977 | 144×75 mm. $1.25 As No. 974; $2 As No. 975 | 6·00 | 7·00 |

**202** Map of Bermuda, 1747

**2006.** Washington 2006 International Stamp Exhibition.

| | | | |
|---|---|---|---|
| 978 | **202** $1.10 multicoloured | 1·90 | 2·00 |
| **MS**979 | 82×65 mm. No. 978 | 1·90 | 2·00 |

**2006.** Heritage "Made in Bermuda" (4th series). As T **193**. Multicoloured.

| | | | |
|---|---|---|---|
| 980 | 35c. Bees, honeycomb and honey | 90 | 45 |
| 981 | 70c. "Stonecutters" (detail) (Sharon Wilson) | 1·60 | 1·25 |
| 982 | 85c. "I've Caught Some Whoppers" (sculpture) by Desmond Fountain | 2·00 | 2·00 |
| 983 | $1.25 Flower and perfume (Bermuda Perfumery) | 2·75 | 3·25 |

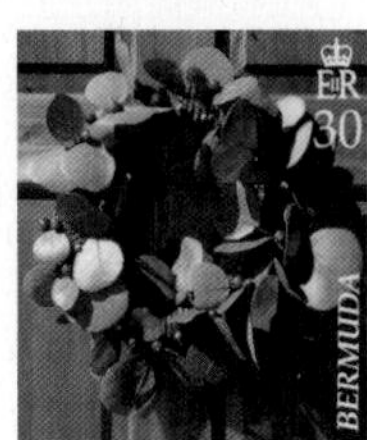

**203** Advent Wreath

**2006.** Christmas. Greetings. Advent Wreaths.

| | | | | |
|---|---|---|---|---|
| 984 | **203** | 30c. multicoloured | 80 | 45 |
| 985 | - | 35c. multicoloured | 90 | 30 |
| 986 | - | 45c. multicoloured | 1·10 | 40 |
| 987 | - | 80c. multicoloured | 2·00 | 2·25 |

DESIGNS: 35c. to 80c. Showing different advent wreaths.

**204** Francis L. Patton

**2007.** Pioneers of Progress (2nd series). Educators. Multicoloured.

| | | | |
|---|---|---|---|
| 988 | 35c. Type **204** | 65 | 70 |
| 989 | 35c. Adele Tucker | 65 | 70 |
| 990 | 35c. Edith and Matilda Crawford | 65 | 70 |
| 991 | 35c. Millie Neversen | 65 | 70 |
| 992 | 35c. May Francis | 65 | 70 |

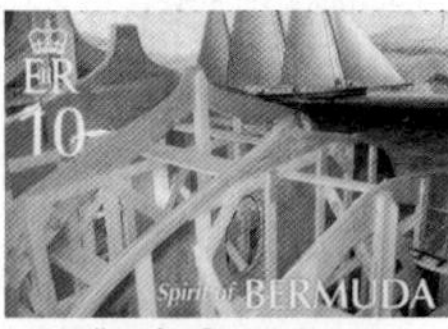

**205** Hull under Construction at Rockport, Maine, USA

**2007.** *Spirit of Bermuda*. Sail training schooner. Multicoloured.

| | | | |
|---|---|---|---|
| 993 | 10c. Type **205** | 50 | 40 |
| 994 | 35c. Close-up view | 85 | 40 |
| 995 | 70c. *Spirit of Bermuda* at sea | 1·50 | 1·10 |
| 996 | 85c. Off coast of Bermuda | 1·75 | 1·40 |
| 997 | $1.10 At Hamilton, Bermuda | 2·00 | 2·00 |
| 998 | $1.25 *Spirit of Bermuda* seen from stern | 2·25 | 2·50 |

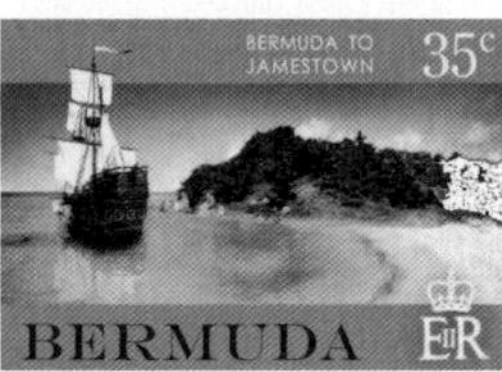

**206** *Deliverance* off Building Bay

**2007.** 400th Anniv of Jamestown, Virginia, USA. Voyage of the Deliverance from Bermuda to Jamestown, 1610. Multicoloured.

| | | | |
|---|---|---|---|
| 999 | 35c. Type **206** | 1·00 | 50 |
| 1000 | $1.10 *Deliverance* sailing from Building Bay, St. George's, Bermuda | 2·50 | 2·75 |

**2007.** Centenary of World Scouting. As T **281** of Bahamas. Multicoloured.

| | | | |
|---|---|---|---|
| 1001 | 35c. Bishop's Own Cubs, Government House, 22 February 1930 | 75 | 35 |
| 1002 | 70c. Lord Baden-Powell inspecting the Cubs, Hamilton, February 1930 | 1·25 | 85 |
| 1003 | 85c. Scout parade, Front Street, Hamilton, 25 February 1930 | 1·60 | 1·25 |
| 1004 | $1.10 Dance of Kaa, Government House, 25 February 1930 | 1·75 | 2·00 |
| **MS**1005 | 90×65 mm. $1.25 Bermuda Scouts emblem; $2 Lord Baden-Powell inspecting the Cubs, Hamilton, February 1930 (both vert) | 5·25 | 5·75 |

**207** *Celeste & Al Harris*

**2008.** Bermuda Calypso Music. Designs showing album covers. Multicoloured.

| | | | |
|---|---|---|---|
| 1006 | 35c. Type **207** | 75 | 35 |
| 1007 | 70c. *Bermuda Calypsos* | 1·25 | 90 |
| 1008 | 85c. *Calypso Varieties from Bermuda* | 1·50 | 1·25 |
| 1009 | $1.10 *The Talbot Brothers of Bermuda* | 1·75 | 2·00 |

**208** Perot Stamp, 1848

**2008.** 160th Anniv of the Perot Stamp (stamps prepared and issued by W. B. Perot, postmaster at Hamilton).

| | | | | |
|---|---|---|---|---|
| 1010 | **208** | 35c. brown and black | 80 | 35 |
| 1011 | **208** | 70c. blue and black | 1·50 | 1·10 |
| 1012 | **208** | 85c. sepia and black | 1·75 | 1·60 |
| 1013 | **208** | $1.25 silver and black | 2·50 | 2·75 |

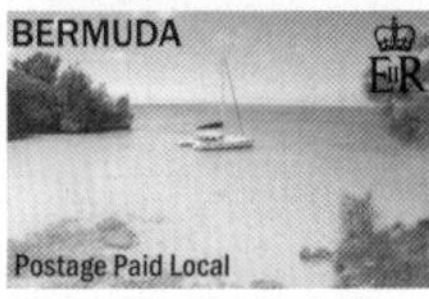

**209** Deep Bay, West Pembroke

**2008.** Bermuda Scenes. Multicoloured. Self-adhesive.

| | | | |
|---|---|---|---|
| 1014 | (35c.) Type **209** | 75 | 75 |
| 1015 | (70c.) Spanish Point Park | 1·40 | 1·40 |
| 1016 | (85c.) Flatts Inlet | 1·60 | 1·75 |
| 1017 | (95c.) Tucker's Town Bay | 1·75 | 2·00 |

No. 1014 is inscribed 'Postage Paid Local', No. 1015 'Postage Paid Zone 1', No. 1016 'Postage Paid Zone 2' and No. 1017 'Postage Paid Zone 3'.

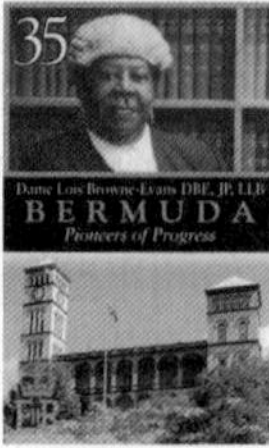

**210** Dame Lois Browne-Evans

**2008.** Pioneers of Progress (3rd series). Multicoloured.

| | | | |
|---|---|---|---|
| 1018 | 35c. Type **210** (barrister and PLP leader 1968–72, 1976–85) | 90 | 65 |
| 1019 | 35c. Dr. Pauulu Roosevelt Brown Kamarakafego (civil rights campaigner and rural technologist) | 90 | 65 |

**211** Sprinter at Start

**2008.** Olympic Games, Beijing. Multicoloured.

| | | | |
|---|---|---|---|
| 1020 | 10c. Type **211** | 40 | 40 |
| 1021 | 35c. Swimmer diving from start | 90 | 40 |
| 1022 | 70c. Horse and rider jumping | 1·75 | 1·50 |
| 1023 | 85c. Yachting | 1·90 | 2·00 |

**212** Reindeer Lights outside Houses

**2008.** Christmas. Greetings. Designs showing Christmas lights. Multicoloured.

| | | | |
|---|---|---|---|
| 1024 | 30c. Type **212** | 60 | 30 |
| 1025 | 35c. Lights on balcony and across street | 65 | 35 |
| 1026 | 45c. Horse and carriage and street lamp lights on roof | 85 | 40 |
| 1027 | 80c. Single storey house with lights around roof and verandah and in garden | 1·40 | 1·25 |

**213** Hamilton in 1930s and Modern Photographs

**2009.** 400th Anniv of Settlement of Bermuda. Each showing scene from past and modern photograph . Multicoloured.

| | | | |
|---|---|---|---|
| 1028 | 35c. Type **213** | 80 | 35 |
| 1029 | 70c. St. George's in 1830s painting by Thomas Driver and modern photograph | 1·60 | 1·10 |
| 1030 | 85c. Flatts Village in 1797 watercolour by Capt. George Tobin and modern photograph | 2·00 | 1·90 |
| 1031 | $1.25 17th-century map and aerial photograph of Bermuda | 3·00 | 2·75 |

**214** Aerial View of Cooper's Island

**2009.** International Year of Astronomy. 40th Anniv of First Moon Landing. Multicoloured.

| | | | |
|---|---|---|---|
| 1032 | 35c. Type **214** | 85 | 50 |
| 1033 | 70c. Tracking Station, Cooper's Island | 1·50 | 90 |
| 1034 | 85c. Apollo 11 Lunar Landing Module, 1969 | 1·90 | 1·10 |
| 1035 | 95c. STS 126, 2008 | 2·10 | 1·25 |
| 1036 | $1.25 International Space Station | 2·50 | 1·50 |
| **MS**1037 | 100×80 mm. $1.10 Lunar Landing Module on Moon (39×59 mm) | 2·25 | 2·25 |

**215** Winner and Trophy

**2009.** Centenary of Bermuda Marathon Derby.

| | | | | |
|---|---|---|---|---|
| 1038 | **215** | 35c. black, brown-red and brown | 75 | 45 |
| 1039 | - | 70c. black, orange-yellow and brown | 1·25 | 75 |
| 1040 | - | 85c. black, orange-yellow and brown | 1·60 | 95 |
| 1041 | - | $1.10 black, brown-red and brown | 2·40 | 1·50 |

DESIGNS: 70c. Winner with trophy (different); 85c. Runners and motorcycle; $1.10 Runners.

**216** *Concordia*

**2009.** Tall Ships Atlantic Challenge 2009. Multicoloured.

| | | | |
|---|---|---|---|
| 1042 | 35c. Type **216** | 75 | 45 |
| 1043 | 70c. *Picton Castle* | 1·25 | 75 |
| 1044 | 85c. *Jolie Brise* (horiz) | 1·50 | 90 |
| 1045 | 95c. *Tecla* | 1·90 | 1·10 |
| 1046 | $1.10 *Europa* | 2·10 | 1·25 |
| 1047 | $1.25 *Etoile* (horiz) | 2·40 | 1·50 |

**217** *Theatre Boycott, Upstairs Right, 1959* (Robert Barritt)

**2009.** 50th Anniv of Theatre Boycott (ended segregation in public buildings). Multicoloured.

| | | | |
|---|---|---|---|
| 1048 | 35c. Type **217** | 75 | 45 |
| 1049 | 70c. *Storm in a Teacup* (Charles Lloyd Tucker) (vert) | 1·25 | 75 |
| 1050 | 85c. Bronze statue of boycott leaders by Chesley Trott (vert) | 1·60 | 95 |
| 1051 | $1.25 Scene from documentary *When Voices Rise* | 2·40 | 1·50 |

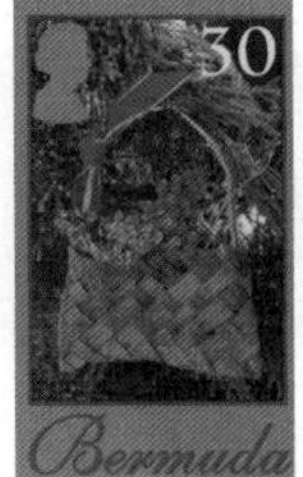


**218** Basket with Berries and Red Bow

**2009.** Christmas Greetings. Tree Decorations. Multicoloured.

| | | | |
|---|---|---|---|
| 1052 | 30c. Type **218** | 50 | 35 |
| 1053 | 35c. Angel | 60 | 45 |
| 1054 | 70c. Circular basket with red bow | 1·40 | 85 |
| 1055 | 85c. Gold bow and tassels | 1·60 | 95 |

**219** Guides and Leaders

**2010.** Centenary of Girlguiding. Multicoloured.

| | | | |
|---|---|---|---|
| 1056 | 35c. Type **219** | 75 | 45 |
| 1057 | 70c. Guide camp | 1·20 | 75 |
| 1058 | 85c. Parade of guides and brownies | 1·60 | 95 |
| 1059 | $1.10 Guides with carnival float carrying model galleon | 75 | 75 |
| **MS**1060 | 127x89 mm. $1.25 1st and 2nd Excelsior Gudies (Bermuda's first Black Unit) | 2·50 | 2·50 |

**220** Cobbs Hill Methodist Church

**2010.** African Diaspora Heritage Trail. Multicoloured.

| | | | |
|---|---|---|---|
| 1061 | 35c. Type **220** | 85 | 55 |
| 1062 | 70c. The Bermudian Heritage Museum | 1·40 | 85 |
| 1063 | 85c. St. Peter's Church | 1·80 | 1·10 |

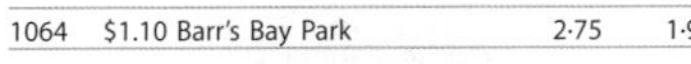

| | | | |
|---|---|---|---|
| 1064 | $1.10 Barr's Bay Park | 2·75 | 1·90 |

**221** Lined Seahorse

**2010.** Endangered Species. Multicoloured.

| | | | |
|---|---|---|---|
| 1065 | 35c. Type **221** | 85 | 55 |
| 1066 | 70c. Pair of seahorses | 1·40 | 85 |
| 1067 | 85c. Pair hiding in seaweed | 1·80 | 1·10 |
| 1068 | $1.25 Adults and young | 3·00 | 2·10 |

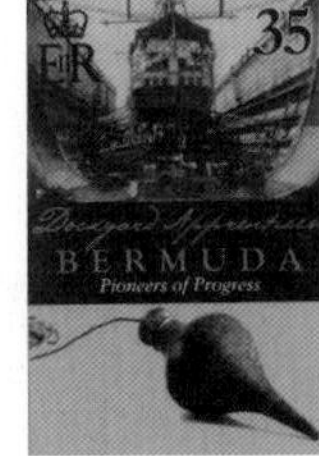


**222** HMS Urgent in Floating Dock, c.1880

**2010.** Pioneers of Progress (4th series). Dockyard Apprentices. Multicoloured.

| | | | |
|---|---|---|---|
| 1069 | 35c. Type **222** | 75 | 45 |
| 1070 | 70c. Dockyard Gate and part of dockyard clock | 2·00 | 75 |
| 1071 | 85c. George Dixon (senior ship-fitter) in front of power saw | 1·60 | 95 |
| 1072 | $1.10 Workmen outside chief constructor's shipfitting shop and tools | 2·40 | 1·50 |

**2011.** Queen Elizabeth II and Prince Philip 'A Lifetime of Service'. Multicoloured.

| | | | |
|---|---|---|---|
| 1073 | 10c. Queen Elizabeth II, c. 1952 | 15 | 20 |
| 1074 | 35c. Queen Elizabeth II and Prince Philip (black and white photo) | 80 | 55 |
| 1075 | 70c. Queen Elizabeth II (wearing red) and Prince Philip (in white uniform) | 1·40 | 95 |
| 1076 | 85c. Queen Elizabeth II (wearing blue) and Prince Philip | 1·50 | 1·10 |
| 1077 | $1.10 Princess Elizabeth and Prince Philip (in uniform) | 2·40 | 1·50 |
| 1078 | $1.25 Prince Philip, c. 1952 | 2·75 | 2·00 |
| **MS**1079 | 174x164 mm. Nos. 1073/8 and three stamp-size labels | 9·00 | 9·00 |
| **MS**1080 | 110x70 mm. $2.50 Queen Elizabeth II (wearing pale blue) and Prince Philip | 5·25 | 5·25 |

**EXPRESS LETTER STAMP**

**E1** Queen Elizabeth II

**1996**

| | | | | |
|---|---|---|---|---|
| E1 | **E1** | $22 orange and blue | 25·00 | 26·00 |

**2003.** As T **207** of Ascension.

| | | | |
|---|---|---|---|
| E2 | $25 black, blue and violet | 29·00 | 30·00 |

Pt. 1

# BHOPAL

A state of C. India. Now uses Indian stamps.

12 pies = 1 anna; 16 annas = 1 rupee.

**3**

**1876.** Imperf.

| | | | | |
|---|---|---|---|---|
| 5 | **3** | ¼a. black | 8·00 | 20·00 |
| 2 | **3** | ½a. red | 20·00 | 60·00 |

**4**

**1878.** Imperf or perf.

| | | | | |
|---|---|---|---|---|
| 7 | **4** | ¼a. green | 11·00 | 22·00 |
| 15 | **4** | ¼a. red | 7·00 | 4·50 |
| 8 | **4** | ½a. red | 7·00 | 20·00 |
| 9 | **4** | ½a. brown | 35·00 | 55·00 |

**1881.** As T **3**, but larger. Imperf or perf.

| | | | |
|---|---|---|---|
| 29 | ¼a. black | 2·25 | 2·50 |
| 37 | ½a. red | 2·00 | 3·75 |
| 46 | ½a. black | 1·75 | 1·75 |
| 30 | 1a. brown | 2·25 | 4·75 |
| 31 | 2a. blue | 2·00 | 2·75 |
| 32 | 4a. yellow | 2·50 | 3·75 |

**13**

**1884.** Perf.

| | | | | |
|---|---|---|---|---|
| 49 | **13** | ¼a. green | 6·00 | 22·00 |
| 76 | **13** | ¼a. black | 1·75 | 1·50 |

**15**

**1884.** Imperf or perf.

| | | | | |
|---|---|---|---|---|
| 64 | **15** | ¼a. green | 80 | 70 |
| 65 | **15** | ¼a. black | 50 | 50 |
| 53 | **15** | ½a. black | 1·00 | 3·50 |
| 56 | **15** | ½a. red | 65 | 1·75 |

**17**

**1890.** Imperf or perf.

| | | | | |
|---|---|---|---|---|
| 71 | **17** | 8a. greenish black | 23·00 | 23·00 |

**19**

**1902.** Imperf.

| | | | | |
|---|---|---|---|---|
| 90 | **19** | ¼a. red | 1·25 | 6·00 |
| 91 | **19** | ½a. black | 1·25 | 5·00 |
| 92 | **19** | 1a. brown | 4·00 | 9·00 |
| 94 | **19** | 2a. blue | 8·50 | 28·00 |
| 96 | **19** | 4a. yellow | 20·00 | 60·00 |
| 97 | **19** | 8a. lilac | 70·00 | £150 |
| 98 | **19** | 1r. red | £100 | £250 |

**20** State Arms

**1908.** Perf.

| | | | | |
|---|---|---|---|---|
| 100 | **20** | 1a. green | 3·75 | 5·50 |

**OFFICIAL STAMPS**

**1908.** As T 20 but inscr "H.H. BEGUM'S SERVICE" optd **SERVICE**.

| | | | |
|---|---|---|---|
| O301 | ½a. green | 2·25 | 10 |
| O302 | 1a. red | 4·25 | 40 |
| O307 | 2a. blue | 4·00 | 60 |
| O304 | 4a. brown | 15·00 | 55 |

**O4**

**1930.** Type O 4 optd **SERVICE**.

| | | | | |
|---|---|---|---|---|
| O309 | **O4** | ½a. green | 13·00 | 1·75 |
| O310 | **O4** | 1a. red | 14·00 | 15 |
| O311 | **O4** | 2a. blue | 9·50 | 45 |
| O312 | **O4** | 4a. brown | 13·00 | 90 |

**1932.** As T 20, but inscr "POSTAGE" at left and "BHOPAL STATE" at right, optd **SERVICE**.

| | | | |
|---|---|---|---|
| O313 | ¼a. orange | 2·50 | 75 |

**1932.** As T 20, but inscr "POSTAGE" at left and "BHOPAL GOVT" at right, optd SERVICE.

| | | | |
|---|---|---|---|
| O314 | ½a. green | 8·00 | 10 |
| O315 | 1a. red | 11·00 | 15 |
| O316 | 2a. blue | 14·00 | 45 |
| O317 | 4a. brown | 12·00 | 1·00 |

**1935.** Nos. O314, etc, surch.

| | | | |
|---|---|---|---|
| O319 | 3p. on ½a. green | 4·00 | 4·00 |
| O321 | 3p. on 2a. blue | 4·50 | 5·00 |
| O325 | 3p. on 4a. brown | 2·50 | 3·50 |
| O318 | ¼a. on ½a. green | 40·00 | 16·00 |
| O320 | ¼a. on 2a. blue | 38·00 | 23·00 |
| O323 | ¼a. on 4a. brown | £100 | 32·00 |
| O326 | 1a. on ½a. green | 5·00 | 1·50 |
| O328 | 1a. on 2a. blue | 70 | 2·50 |
| O329 | 1a. on 4a. brown | 7·50 | 5·00 |

**O8**

**1935**

| | | | | |
|---|---|---|---|---|
| O330 | **O8** | 1a.3p. blue and red | 3·50 | 1·75 |
| O331 | **O8** | 1a.6p. blue and red | 2·50 | 1·50 |
| O332 | **O8** | 1a.6p. red | 6·00 | 2·50 |

Nos. O331/2 are similar to Type O **8**, but inscr "BHOPAL STATE POSTAGE".

**O9**

**1936.** Type O 9 optd **SERVICE**.

| | | | | |
|---|---|---|---|---|
| O333 | **O9** | ¼a. yellow | 90 | 60 |
| O335 | **O9** | 1a. red | 1·50 | 10 |

**O10** The Moti Mahal

**1936.** As Type O 4 optd **SERVICE**.

| | | | | |
|---|---|---|---|---|
| O336d | **O10** | ½a. purple and green | 70 | 50 |
| O337 | - | 2a. brown and blue | 2·00 | 1·00 |
| O338 | - | 2a. green and violet | 15·00 | 30 |
| O339 | - | 4a. blue and brown | 3·75 | 50 |
| O340 | - | 8a. purple and blue | 5·50 | 2·50 |
| O341b | - | 1r. blue and purple | 18·00 | 4·50 |

DESIGNS: 2a. The Moti Masjid; 4a. Taj Mahal and Be-Nazir Palaces; 8a. Ahmadabad Palace; 1r. Rait Ghat.

Nos. O336 is inscr "BHOPAL GOVT" below the arms, other values have "BHOPAL STATE".

**1940.** Animal designs, as Type O **10** but inscr "SERVICE" in bottom panel.

| | | | |
|---|---|---|---|
| O344 | ¼a. blue (Tiger) | 5·50 | 1·75 |
| O345 | 1a. purple (Spotted deer) | 38·00 | 3·75 |

**1941.** As Type O **8** but "SERVICE" inscr instead of optd.

| | | | | |
|---|---|---|---|---|
| O346 | **O8** | 1a.3p. green | 2·75 | 3·00 |

**1944.** Palaces as Type O **10** but smaller.

| | | | |
|---|---|---|---|
| O347 | ½a. green (Moti Mahal) | 1·00 | 1·00 |
| O348 | 2a. violet (Moti Masjid) | 15·00 | 4·00 |
| O348c | 2a. purple (Moti Masjid) | 3·75 | 3·75 |
| O349 | 4a. brown (Be-Nazir) | 9·00 | 2·25 |

The 2a. and 4a. are inscr "BHOPAL STATE", and the other "BHOPAL GOVT".

**O14** Arms of Bhopal

**1944**.

| | | | | |
|---|---|---|---|---|
| O350 | **O14** | 3p. blue | 1·00 | 1·00 |
| O351b | **O14** | 9p. brown | 2·00 | 5·00 |
| O352 | **O14** | 1a. purple | 7·00 | 1·75 |
| O352b | **O14** | 1a. violet | 11·00 | 3·25 |
| O353 | **O14** | 1½a. red | 2·00 | 1·25 |
| O354 | **O14** | 3a. yellow | 19·00 | 20·00 |
| O354d | **O14** | 3a. brown | £110 | £130 |
| O355 | **O14** | 6a. red | 24·00 | 60·00 |

**1949**. Surch 2 As. and bars.

| | | | |
|---|---|---|---|
| O356 | 2a. on 1½a. red | 2·50 | 9·00 |

**1949**. Surch 2 As. and ornaments.

| | | | |
|---|---|---|---|
| O357 | 2a. on 1½a. red | £1500 | £1500 |

Pt. 1

# BHOR

A state of W. India, Bombay district. Now uses Indian stamps.

12 pies = 1 anna; 16 annas = 1 rupee.

**1**

**1879**. Imperf.

| | | | | |
|---|---|---|---|---|
| 1 | **1** | ½a. red | 4·50 | 6·50 |

Similar to T 1, but rectangular.

| | | | |
|---|---|---|---|
| 2 | 1a. red | 6·00 | 9·00 |

**3** Pandit Shankar Rao

**1901**. Imperf.

| | | | | |
|---|---|---|---|---|
| 3 | **3** | ½a. red | 18·00 | 45·00 |

Pt. 21

# BHUTAN

An independent territory in treaty relations with India and bounded by India, Sikkim and Tibet.

100 chetrum = 1 ngultrum.

**1** Postal Runner

**1962**.

| | | | | |
|---|---|---|---|---|
| 1 | **1** | 2ch. red and grey | 15 | 15 |
| 2 | - | 3ch. red and blue | 25 | 25 |
| 3 | - | 5ch. brown and green | 80 | 80 |
| 4 | - | 15ch. yellow, black and red | 15 | 30 |
| 5 | **1** | 33ch. green and violet | 25 | 25 |
| 6 | - | 70ch. ultramarine and blue | 50 | 35 |
| 7 | - | 1n.30 black and blue | 1·40 | 1·40 |

DESIGNS—HORIZ: 3, 70ch. Archer. 5ch., 1n.30, Yak. 15ch. Map of Bhutan, Maharaja Druk Gyalpo and Paro Dzong (fortress and monastery).

**2** "Uprooted Tree" Emblem and Crest of Bhutan

**1962**. World Refugee Year.

| | | | | |
|---|---|---|---|---|
| 8 | **2** | 1n. red and blue | 2·75 | 2·75 |
| 9 | **2** | 2n. violet and green | 2·50 | 2·50 |

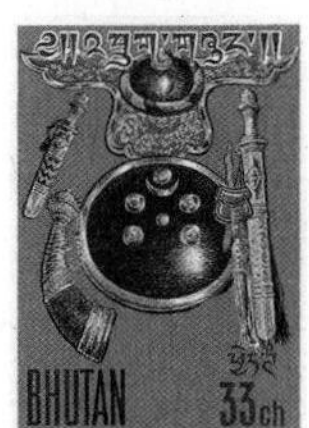

**3** Accoutrements of Ancient Warrior

**1962**. Membership of Colombo Plan.

| | | | | |
|---|---|---|---|---|
| 10 | **3** | 33ch. multicoloured | 25 | 25 |
| 11 | **3** | 70ch. multicoloured | 50 | 50 |
| 12 | **3** | 1n.30 red, brown & yellow | 75 | 75 |

**4** "Boy filling box" (with grain)

**1963**. Freedom from Hunger.

| | | | | |
|---|---|---|---|---|
| 13 | **4** | 20ch. brown, blue & yellow | 25 | 25 |
| 14 | **4** | 1n.50 purple, brown & blue | 65 | 65 |

**1964**. Winter Olympic Games, Innsbruck, and Bhutanese Winter Sports Committee Fund. Nos. 10/12 surch INNSBRUCK 1964 +50 ch, Olympic rings and emblem.

| | | | | |
|---|---|---|---|---|
| 15 | **3** | 33ch.+50ch. multicoloured | 2·40 | 2·40 |
| 16 | **3** | 70ch.+50ch. multicoloured | 2·40 | 2·40 |
| 17 | **3** | 1n.30+50ch. multicoloured | 2·40 | 2·40 |

**6** Dancer with upraised hands

**1964**. Bhutanese Dancers. Multicoloured.

| | | | |
|---|---|---|---|
| 18 | 2ch. Standing on one leg (vert) | 10 | 10 |
| 19 | 3ch. Type **6** | 10 | 10 |
| 20 | 5ch. With tambourine (vert) | 10 | 10 |
| 21 | 20ch. As 2ch. | 10 | 10 |
| 22 | 33ch. Type **6** | 10 | 10 |
| 23 | 70ch. With sword | 15 | 15 |
| 24 | 1n. With tasselled hat (vert) | 35 | 35 |
| 25 | 1n.30 As 5ch. | 65 | 65 |
| 26 | 2n. As 70ch. | 1·10 | 1·10 |

**7** Bhutanese Athlete

**1964**. Olympic Games, Tokyo. Multicoloured.

| | | | |
|---|---|---|---|
| 27 | 2ch. Type **7** | 15 | 10 |
| 28 | 5ch. Boxing | 10 | 10 |
| 29 | 15ch. Type **7** | 10 | 10 |
| 30 | 33ch. As 5ch. | 15 | 15 |
| 31 | 1n. Archery | 35 | 35 |
| 32 | 2n. Football | 70 | 70 |
| 33 | 3n. As 1n. | 1·30 | 1·30 |
| **MS**33a | 85×118 mm. Nos. 31/2 | 10·00 | 10·00 |

**8** Flags at Half-mast

**1964**. Pres. Kennedy Commemoration.

| | | | | |
|---|---|---|---|---|
| 34 | **8** | 33ch. multicoloured | 25 | 25 |
| 35 | **8** | 1n. multicoloured | 60 | 60 |
| 36 | **8** | 3n. multicoloured | 90 | 90 |
| **MS**36a | | 82×119 mm. Nos. 35/6 | 3·75 | 3·75 |

**9** Primula

**1965**. Flowers. Multicoloured.

| | | | |
|---|---|---|---|
| 37 | 2ch. Type **9** | 10 | 10 |
| 38 | 5ch. Gentian | 10 | 10 |
| 39 | 15ch. Type **9** | 10 | 10 |
| 40 | 33ch. As 5ch. | 15 | 15 |
| 41 | 50ch. Rhododendron | 25 | 25 |
| 42 | 75ch. Peony | 35 | 35 |
| 43 | 1n. As 50ch. | 35 | 35 |
| 44 | 2n. As 75ch. | 85 | 85 |

**1965**. Churchill Commemoration. Optd WINSTON CHURCHILL 1874 1965.

| | | | | |
|---|---|---|---|---|
| 45 | **1** | 33ch. green and violet | 35 | 35 |
| 46 | **8** | 1n. multicoloured | 55 | 55 |
| 47 | - | 1n. multicoloured (No. 43) | 50 | 50 |
| 48 | - | 2n. multicoloured (No. 44) | 85 | 85 |
| 49 | **8** | 3n. multicoloured | 1·30 | 1·30 |

**11** Pavilion and Skyscrapers

**1965**. New York World's Fair. Mult.

| | | | |
|---|---|---|---|
| 50 | 1ch. Type **11** | 10 | 10 |
| 51 | 10ch. Buddha and Michelangelo's "Pieta" | 10 | 10 |
| 52 | 20ch. Bhutan houses and New York skyline | 10 | 10 |
| 53 | 33ch. Bhutan and New York bridges | 10 | 10 |
| 54 | 1n.50 Type **11** | 50 | 50 |
| 55 | 2n. As 10ch. | 80 | 80 |
| **MS**55a | 120×86 mm. Nos. 54/5 | 3·50 | 5·50 |

**1965**. Surch.

| | | | | |
|---|---|---|---|---|
| 56 | **2** | 5ch. on 1n. (No. 8) | 28·00 | 28·00 |
| 57 | **2** | 5ch. on 2n. (No. 9) | 28·00 | 28·00 |
| 58 | - | 10ch. on 70ch. (No. 23) | 7·75 | 7·75 |
| 59 | - | 10ch. on 2n. (No. 26) | 7·75 | 7·75 |
| 60 | - | 15ch. on 70ch. (No. 6) | 6·50 | 6·50 |
| 61 | - | 15ch. on 1n.30 (No. 7) | 6·50 | 6·50 |
| 62 | - | 20ch. on 1n. (No. 24) | 9·25 | 9·25 |
| 63 | - | 20ch. on 1n.30 (No. 25) | 9·25 | 9·25 |

**13** "Telstar" and Portable Transmitter

**1966**. Centenary of I.T.U. Multicoloured.

| | | | |
|---|---|---|---|
| 64 | 35ch. Type **13** | 15 | 15 |
| 65 | 2n. "Telstar" & morse key | 40 | 40 |
| 66 | 3n. "Relay" and headphones | 75 | 75 |
| **MS**67 | 118×78 mm. Nos. 65/6 | 4·25 | 4·25 |

**14** Asiatic Black Bear

**1966**. Animals. Multicoloured.

| | | | |
|---|---|---|---|
| 68 | 1ch. Type **14** | 10 | 10 |
| 69 | 2ch. Snow leopard | 10 | 10 |
| 70 | 4ch. Pygmy hog | 10 | 10 |
| 71 | 8ch. Tiger | 10 | 10 |
| 72 | 10ch. Dhole | 10 | 10 |
| 73 | 75ch. As 8ch. | 25 | 25 |
| 74 | 1n. Takin | 40 | 40 |
| 75 | 1n.50 As 10ch. | 55 | 55 |
| 76 | 2n. As 4ch. | 70 | 70 |
| 77 | 3n. As 2ch. | 1·00 | 1·00 |
| 78 | 4n. Type **14** | 1·40 | 1·40 |
| 79 | 5n. As 1n. | 2·00 | 2·00 |

**15** Simtoke Dzong (fortress)

**1966**

| | | | | |
|---|---|---|---|---|
| 80 | - | 5c. brown | 15 | 10 |
| 81 | **15** | 15ch. brown | 15 | 15 |
| 82 | **15** | 20ch. green | 25 | 25 |

DESIGN: 5ch. Rinpung Dzong (fortress).

**16** King Jigme Dorji Wangchuck (obverse of 50n.p. coin)

**1966**. 40th Anniv of King Jigme Wangchuck's Accession (father of King Jigme Dorji Wangchuck). Circular designs, embossed on gold foil, backed with multicoloured patterned paper. Imperf. Sizes: (a) Diameter 38 mm; (b) Diameter 50 mm; (c) Diameter 63 mm. (i) 50n.p. Coin.

| | | | | |
|---|---|---|---|---|
| 83 | **16** | 10ch. green (a) | 15 | 15 |
| | | (ii) 1r. Coin. | | |
| 84 | | 25ch. green (b) | 25 | 25 |
| | | (iii) 3r. Coin. | | |
| 85 | | 50ch. green (c) | 45 | 45 |
| | | (iv) 1 sertum Coin. | | |
| 86 | | 1n. red (a) | 80 | 80 |
| 87 | - | 1n.30 red (a) | 1·20 | 1·20 |
| | | (v) 2 sertum Coin. | | |
| 88 | **16** | 2n. red (b) | 1·80 | 1·80 |
| 89 | - | 3n. red (b) | 2·50 | 2·50 |
| | | (vi) 5 sertum Coin. | | |
| 90 | **16** | 4n. red (c) | 3·25 | 3·25 |
| 91 | - | 5n. red (c) | 3·75 | 3·75 |

Nos. 87, 89 and 91 show the reverse side of the coins (Symbol).

**17** "Abominable Snowman"

**1966**. "Abominable Snowman". Various triangular designs.

| | | | | |
|---|---|---|---|---|
| 92 | **17** | 1ch. multicoloured | 10 | 10 |
| 93 | - | 2ch. multicoloured | 10 | 10 |
| 94 | - | 3ch. multicoloured | 10 | 10 |
| 95 | - | 4ch. multicoloured | 10 | 10 |
| 96 | - | 5ch. multicoloured | 10 | 10 |
| 97 | - | 15ch. multicoloured | 10 | 10 |
| 98 | - | 30ch. multicoloured | 10 | 10 |
| 99 | - | 40ch. multicoloured | 15 | 15 |
| 100 | - | 50ch. multicoloured | 15 | 15 |
| 101 | - | 1n.25 multicoloured | 30 | 30 |
| 102 | - | 2n.50 multicoloured | 50 | 50 |

| | | | | |
|---|---|---|---|---|
| 103 | - | 3n. multicoloured | 60 | 60 |
| 104 | - | 5n. multicoloured | 85 | 85 |
| 105 | - | 6n. multicoloured | 85 | 85 |
| 106 | - | 7n. multicoloured | 95 | 95 |

**1967.** Air. Optd AIR MAIL and Sikorsky S-55 helicopter.

| | | | | |
|---|---|---|---|---|
| 107 | **6** | 33ch. multicoloured | 10 | 15 |
| 108 | - | 50ch. mult (No. 41) | 25 | 25 |
| 109 | - | 70ch. mult (No. 23) | 30 | 30 |
| 110 | - | 75ch. mult (No. 42) | 25 | 25 |
| 111 | - | 1n. mult (No. 24) | 35 | 35 |
| 112 | - | 1n.50 mult (No. 75) | 55 | 55 |
| 113 | - | 2n. mult (No. 76) | 80 | 80 |
| 114 | - | 3n. mult (No. 77) | 1·20 | 1·20 |
| 115 | **14** | 4n. multicoloured | 1·80 | 1·80 |
| 116 | - | 5n. mult (No. 79) | 2·30 | 2·30 |

**20** "Lilium sherriffiae"

**1967.** Flowers. Multicoloured.

| | | | |
|---|---|---|---|
| 117 | 3ch. Type **20** | 10 | 10 |
| 118 | 5ch. "Meconopsis" | 10 | 10 |
| 119 | 7ch. "Rhododendron dhwoju" | 10 | 10 |
| 120 | 10ch. "Pleione hookeriana" | 10 | 10 |
| 121 | 50ch. Type **20** | 15 | 15 |
| 122 | 1n. As 5ch. | 30 | 30 |
| 123 | 2n.50 As 7ch. | 75 | 75 |
| 124 | 4n. As 10ch. | 1·00 | 1·00 |
| 125 | 5n. "Rhododendron giganteum" | 1·30 | 1·30 |

**21** Scouts planting Sapling

**1967.** Bhutanese Boy Scouts. Multicoloured.

| | | | |
|---|---|---|---|
| 126 | 5ch. Type **21** | 10 | 10 |
| 127 | 10ch. Scouts preparing meal | 10 | 10 |
| 128 | 15ch. Scout mountaineering | 15 | 15 |
| 129 | 50ch. Type **21** | 25 | 25 |
| 130 | 1n.25. As 10ch. | 70 | 70 |
| 131 | 4n. As 15ch. | 1·70 | 1·70 |
| **MS**132 | 93×93 mm. Nos. 130/1 | 6·25 | 6·25 |

**1967.** World Fair, Montreal. Nos. 53/5 optd expo67 and emblem.

| | | | | |
|---|---|---|---|---|
| 133 | - | 33ch. multicoloured | 30 | 30 |
| 134 | **11** | 1n.50 multicoloured | 40 | 40 |
| 135 | - | 2n. multicoloured | 45 | 45 |
| **MS**136 | | 120×86 mm. Nos. 134/5 | 2·00 | 2·00 |

**23** Avro Type **683** Lancaster

**1967.** Churchill and Battle of Britain Commemoration. Multicoloured.

| | | | |
|---|---|---|---|
| 137 | 45ch. Type **23** | 20 | 20 |
| 138 | 2n. Supermarine Spitfire Mk IIB | 45 | 45 |
| 139 | 4n. Hawker Hurricane Mk IIC | 90 | 90 |
| **MS**140 | 118×75 mm. Nos. 138/9 | 2·40 | 2·40 |

**1967.** World Scout Jamboree, Idaho. Nos. 126/31 optd WORLD JAMBOREE IDAHO, U.S.A. AUG. 1-9/67.

| | | | | |
|---|---|---|---|---|
| 141 | **21** | 5ch. multicoloured | 15 | 15 |
| 142 | - | 10ch. multicoloured | 20 | 20 |
| 143 | - | 15ch. multicoloured | 25 | 25 |
| 144 | - | 50ch. multicoloured | 35 | 35 |
| 145 | - | 1n.25 multicoloured | 70 | 75 |
| 146 | - | 4n. multicoloured | 1·80 | 1·80 |
| **MS**147 | | 93×93 mm. Nos. 145/6 | 3·75 | 3·75 |

**25** Painting

**1967.** Bhutan Girl Scouts. Multicoloured.

| | | | |
|---|---|---|---|
| 148 | 5ch. Type **25** | 10 | 10 |
| 149 | 10ch. Playing musical instrument | 10 | 10 |
| 150 | 15ch. Picking fruit | 10 | 10 |
| 151 | 1n.50 Type **25** | 45 | 45 |
| 152 | 2n.50 As 10ch. | 1·10 | 1·10 |
| 153 | 5n. As 15ch. | 2·50 | 2·50 |
| **MS**154 | 93×93 mm. Nos. 152/3 | 5·50 | 5·50 |

**26** Astronaut in Space

**1967.** Space Achievements. With laminated prismatic-ribbed plastic surface. Multicoloured.

| | | | |
|---|---|---|---|
| 155 | 3ch. Type **26** (postage) | 25 | 25 |
| 156 | 5ch. Space vehicle and astronaut | 25 | 25 |
| 157 | 7ch. Astronaut and landing vehicle | 45 | 45 |
| 158 | 10ch. Three astronauts in space | 50 | 50 |
| 159 | 15ch. Type **26** | 75 | 75 |
| 160 | 30ch. As 5ch. | 90 | 90 |
| 161 | 50ch. As 7ch. | 1·30 | 1·30 |
| 162 | 1n.25 As 10ch. | 2·75 | 2·75 |
| 163 | 2n.50 Type **26** (air) | 1·90 | 1·90 |
| 164 | 4n. As 5ch. | 2·75 | 2·75 |
| 165 | 5n. As 7ch. | 3·75 | 3·75 |
| 166 | 9n. As 10ch. | 6·50 | 6·50 |
| **MS**167 | Three sheets, each 130×111 mm. Nos. 155/8, 159/62 and 163/6. Imperf | 29·00 | 29·00 |

The laminated plastic surface gives the stamps a three-dimensional effect.

**27** Tashichho Dzong

**1968**

| | | | | |
|---|---|---|---|---|
| 168 | **27** | 10ch. purple and green | 20 | 10 |

**28** Elephant

**1968.** Mythological Creatures.

| | | | | |
|---|---|---|---|---|
| 169 | **28** | 2ch. red, blue and brown (postage) | 10 | 10 |
| 170 | - | 3ch. pink, blue & green | 10 | 10 |
| 171 | - | 4ch. orange, green & blue | 10 | 10 |
| 172 | - | 5ch. blue, yellow & pink | 10 | 10 |
| 173 | - | 15ch. green, purple & blue | 10 | 10 |
| 174 | **28** | 20ch. brown, blk & orge | 10 | 10 |
| 175 | - | 30ch. yellow, black & blue | 15 | 15 |
| 176 | - | 50ch. bistre, green & black | 15 | 15 |
| 177 | - | 1n.25 black, green & red | 15 | 15 |
| 178 | - | 2n. yellow, violet & black | 30 | 30 |
| 179 | **28** | 1n.50 green, purple and yellow (air) | 25 | 25 |
| 180 | - | 2n.50 red, black & blue | 35 | 35 |
| 181 | - | 4n. orange, green & black | 60 | 60 |
| 182 | - | 5n. brown, grey & orange | 80 | 80 |
| 183 | - | 10n. violet, grey & black | 1·50 | 1·50 |

DESIGNS: 3, 30ch., 2n.50, Garuda; 4, 50ch., 4n. Tiger; 5ch., 1n.25, 5n. Wind horse; 15ch., 2, 10n. Snow lion.

**29** Tongsa Dzong

**1968**

| | | | | |
|---|---|---|---|---|
| 184 | **29** | 50ch. green | 30 | 15 |
| 185 | - | 75ch. brown and blue | 35 | 20 |
| 186 | - | 1n. blue and violet | 40 | 25 |

DESIGNS: 75ch. Daga Dzong; 1n. Lhuntsi Dzong.

**30** Ward's Trogon

**1968.** Rare Birds.

| | | | |
|---|---|---|---|
| 187 | 2ch. Red-faced liocichla ("Crimson-winged Laughing Thrush") (horiz) (postage) | 10 | 10 |
| 188 | 3ch. Type **30** | 10 | 10 |
| 189 | 4ch. Burmese ("Grey") Peacock-pheasant (horiz) | 10 | 10 |
| 190 | 5ch. Rufous-necked hornbill | 10 | 10 |
| 191 | 15ch. Fire-tailed 'myzornis' ("Myzornis") (horiz) | 15 | 15 |
| 192 | 20ch. As No. 187 | 20 | 20 |
| 193 | 30ch. Type **30** | 20 | 20 |
| 194 | 50ch. As No. 189 | 25 | 25 |
| 195 | 1n.25 As No. 190 | 35 | 35 |
| 196 | 2n. As No. 191 | 45 | 45 |
| 197 | 1n.50 As No. 187 (air) | 50 | 50 |
| 198 | 2n.50 Type **30** | 60 | 55 |
| 199 | 4n. As No. 189 | 90 | 90 |
| 200 | 5n. As No. 190 | 1·20 | 1·20 |
| 201 | 10n. As No. 191 | 1·80 | 1·80 |

**31** Mahatma Gandhi

**1969.** Birth Centenary of Mahatma Gandhi.

| | | | | |
|---|---|---|---|---|
| 202 | **31** | 20ch. brown and blue | 15 | 15 |
| 203 | **31** | 2n. brown and yellow | 75 | 75 |

**1970.** Various stamps surch 5 CH or 20 CH. (a) Freedom from Hunger (No. 14).

| | | | |
|---|---|---|---|
| 223 | 20ch. on 1n.50 purple, brown and blue | 2·75 | 2·75 |

(b) Animals (Nos. 75/9).

| | | | |
|---|---|---|---|
| 224 | 20ch. on 1n.50 multicoloured | 2·75 | 2·75 |
| 225 | 20ch. on 2n. multicoloured | 2·75 | 2·75 |
| 204 | 20ch. on 3n. multicoloured | 2·10 | 2·10 |
| 205 | 20ch. on 4n. multicoloured | 2·10 | 2·10 |
| 206 | 20ch. on 5n. multicoloured | 2·10 | 2·10 |

(c) Abominable Snowmen (Nos. 101/6).

| | | | |
|---|---|---|---|
| 226 | 20ch. on 1n.25 multicoloured | 2·75 | 2·75 |
| 227 | 20ch. on 2n.50 multicoloured | 2·75 | 2·75 |
| 207 | 20ch. on 3n. multicoloured | 1·90 | 1·90 |
| 208 | 20ch. on 5n. multicoloured | 2·10 | 2·10 |
| 209 | 20ch. on 6n. multicoloured | 2·75 | 2·75 |
| 210 | 20ch. on 7n. multicoloured | 2·75 | 2·75 |

(d) Flowers (Nos. 124/5).

| | | | |
|---|---|---|---|
| 211 | 20ch. on 4n. multicoloured | 2·10 | 2·10 |
| 212 | 20ch. on 5n. multicoloured | 2·50 | 2·50 |

(e) Boy Scouts (Nos. 130/1).

| | | | |
|---|---|---|---|
| 228 | 20ch. on 1n.25 multicoloured | 2·75 | 2·75 |
| 213 | 20ch. on 4n. multicoloured | 17·00 | 17·00 |

(f) Churchill (Nos. 138/9).

| | | | |
|---|---|---|---|
| 229 | 20ch. on 2n. multicoloured | 2·75 | 2·75 |
| 230 | 20ch. on 4n. multicoloured | 2·75 | 2·75 |

(g) 1968 Pheasants (Appendix).

| | | | |
|---|---|---|---|
| 231 | 20ch. on 2n. multicoloured | 3·75 | 3·75 |
| 214 | 20ch. on 4n. multicoloured | 2·10 | 2·10 |
| 232 | 20ch. on 7n. multicoloured | 3·75 | 3·75 |

(h) Mythological Creatures (Nos. 175/80 and 182/3).

| | | | |
|---|---|---|---|
| 215 | 20ch. on 2n. yellow, violet and black | 3·75 | 3·75 |
| 216 | 20ch. on 5n. brown, grey and orange | 2·40 | 2·40 |
| 217 | 20ch. on 10n. violet, grey and black | 2·10 | 2·10 |
| 233 | 5ch. on 30ch. yellow, black and blue (postage) | 85 | 85 |
| 234 | 5ch. on 50ch. bistre, green and black | 85 | 85 |
| 235 | 5ch. on 1n.25 black, green and red | 85 | 85 |
| 236 | 5ch. on 2n. yellow, vio & blk | 85 | 85 |
| 237 | 5ch. on 1n.50 green, purple and brown (air) | 85 | 85 |
| 238 | 5ch. on 2n.50 red, black and blue | 85 | 85 |

(i) Rare Birds (Nos. 193/201).

| | | | |
|---|---|---|---|
| 218 | 20ch. on 2n. multicoloured | 2·75 | 2·75 |
| 219 | 20ch. on 2n.50. multicoloured | 2·75 | 2·75 |
| 220 | 20ch. on 4n. multicoloured | 2·10 | 2·10 |
| 221 | 20ch. on 5n. multicoloured | 2·50 | 2·50 |
| 222 | 20ch. on 10n. multicoloured | 3·50 | 3·50 |
| 239 | 20ch. on 30ch. mult (postage) | 3·75 | 3·75 |
| 240 | 20ch. on 50ch. multicoloured | 3·75 | 3·75 |
| 241 | 20ch. on 1n. 25. multicoloured | 3·75 | 3·75 |
| 242 | 20ch. on 1n.50. mult (air) | 3·75 | 3·75 |

(j) 1969 U.P.U. (Appendix).

| | | | |
|---|---|---|---|
| 243 | 20ch. on 1n.05. multicoloured | 2·75 | 2·75 |
| 244 | 20ch. on 1n.40. multicoloured | 2·75 | 2·75 |
| 245 | 20ch. on 4n. multicoloured | 2·75 | 2·75 |

For stamps surcharged with 55 or 90ch. values, see Nos. 253/65 and for 25ch. surcharges see Nos. 385/410.

**33** Wangdiphodrang Dzong and Bridge

**1971**

| | | | | |
|---|---|---|---|---|
| 246 | **33** | 2ch. grey | 25 | 10 |
| 247 | **33** | 3ch. mauve | 35 | 15 |
| 248 | **33** | 4ch. violet | 35 | 25 |
| 249 | **33** | 5ch. green | 10 | 10 |
| 250 | **33** | 10ch. brown | 15 | 10 |
| 251 | **33** | 15ch. blue | 20 | 15 |
| 252 | **33** | 20ch. purple | 30 | 15 |

**1971.** Various stamps surch 55 CH or 90 CH. I. Dancers (Nos. 25/6).

| | | | |
|---|---|---|---|
| 253 | 55ch. on 1n.30 multicoloured | 85 | 85 |
| 254 | 90ch. on 2n. multicoloured | 85 | 85 |

II. Animals (Nos. 77/8).

| | | | |
|---|---|---|---|
| 255 | 55ch. on 3n. multicoloured | 85 | 85 |
| 256 | 90ch. on 4n. multicoloured | 85 | 85 |

III. Boy Scouts (No. 131).

| | | | |
|---|---|---|---|
| 257 | 90ch. on 4n. multicoloured | 1·60 | 1·60 |

IV. 1968 Pheasants (Appendix).

| | | | |
|---|---|---|---|
| 258 | 55ch. on 5n. multicoloured | 3·00 | 3·00 |
| 259 | 90ch. on 9n. multicoloured | 3·00 | 3·00 |

V. Air. Mythological Creatures (No. 181).

| | | | |
|---|---|---|---|
| 260 | 55ch. on 4n. orange, green and black | 55 | 55 |

VI. 1968 Mexico Olympics (Appendix).

| | | | |
|---|---|---|---|
| 261 | 90ch. on 1n.05 multicoloured | 1·40 | 1·40 |

VII. Rare Birds (No. 196).

| | | | |
|---|---|---|---|
| 262 | 90ch. on 2n. multicoloured | 3·00 | 3·00 |

VIII. 1969 UPU (Appendix).

| | | | |
|---|---|---|---|
| 263 | 55ch. on 60ch. multicoloured | 85 | 85 |

IX. 1970 New UPU Headquarters (Appendix).

| | | | |
|---|---|---|---|
| 264 | 90ch. on 2n.50 gold and red | 2·75 | 2·75 |

X. 1971 Moon Vehicles (plastic-surfaced) (Appendix).

| | | | |
|---|---|---|---|
| 265 | 90ch. on 1n.70 multicoloured | 4·00 | 4·00 |

**34** Book Year Emblem

**1972.** International Book Year.

| | | | | |
|---|---|---|---|---|
| 266 | **34** | 2ch. green and blue | 10 | 10 |

| | | | | |
|---|---|---|---|---|
| 267 | **34** | 3ch. brown and yellow | 10 | 10 |
| 268 | **34** | 5ch. brown, orange & red | 10 | 10 |
| 269 | **34** | 20ch. brown and blue | 10 | 10 |

**35** Dochi

**1972.** Dogs. Multicoloured.

| | | | |
|---|---|---|---|
| 270 | 5ch. Apsoo standing on hind legs (vert) | 10 | 10 |
| 271 | 10ch. Type **35** | 10 | 10 |
| 272 | 15ch. Brown and white damci | 10 | 10 |
| 273 | 25ch. Black and white damci | 10 | 10 |
| 274 | 55ch. Apsoo lying down | 10 | 10 |
| 275 | 8n. Two damci | 1·40 | 1·40 |
| **MS**276 | 100×119 mm. Nos. 274/5 | 1·40 | 1·40 |

**36** King and Royal Crest

**1974.** Coronation of King Jigme Singye Wangchuck. Multicoloured.

| | | | |
|---|---|---|---|
| 277 | 10ch. Type **36** | 10 | 10 |
| 278 | 25ch. Bhutan Flag | 15 | 15 |
| 279 | 1n.25 Good Luck signs | 30 | 30 |
| 280 | 2n. Punakha Dzong | 45 | 45 |
| 281 | 3n. Royal Crown | 60 | 60 |
| **MS**282 | Two sheets, each 177×127 mm. (a) 5ch. As 10ch.; 5ch. As 3n.; (b) 90ch. As 1n.25; 4n. As 2n. Perf or imperf | 4·75 | 4·75 |

**37** Mail Delivery by Horse

**1974.** Centenary of UPU. Multicoloured.

| | | | |
|---|---|---|---|
| 283 | 1ch. Type **37** (postage) | 10 | 10 |
| 284 | 2ch. Early and modern locomotives | 10 | 10 |
| 285 | 3ch. "Hindoostan" (paddle-steamer) and "Iberia" (liner) | 10 | 10 |
| 286 | 4ch. Vickers FB-27 Vimy and Concorde aircraft | 10 | 10 |
| 287 | 25ch. Mail runner and four-wheel drive post car | 10 | 10 |
| 288 | 1n. As 25ch. (air) | 20 | 20 |
| 289 | 1n.40 As 2ch. | 45 | 45 |
| 290 | 2n. As 4ch. | 80 | 80 |
| **MS**291 | 91×78 mm. 10n. As 4 ch | 3·75 | 3·75 |

**38** Family and WPY Emblem

**1974.** World Population Year.

| | | | | |
|---|---|---|---|---|
| 292 | **38** | 25ch. multicoloured | 10 | 10 |
| 293 | **38** | 50ch. multicoloured | 10 | 10 |
| 294 | **38** | 90ch. multicoloured | 25 | 25 |
| 295 | **38** | 2n.50 multicoloured | 55 | 55 |
| **MS**296 | | 116×79 mm. **38** 10n. multicoloured | 2·10 | 2·10 |

**39** Eastern Courtier

**1975.** Butterflies. Multicoloured.

| | | | |
|---|---|---|---|
| 297 | 1ch. Type **39** | 10 | 10 |
| 298 | 2ch. Bamboo forester | 10 | 10 |
| 299 | 3ch. Tailed labyrinth | 10 | 10 |
| 300 | 4ch. Blue duchess | 10 | 10 |
| 301 | 5ch. Cruiser | 10 | 10 |
| 302 | 10ch. Bhutan glory | 10 | 10 |
| 303 | 3n. Bi-coloured commodore | 65 | 65 |
| 304 | 5n. Red-breasted jezebel | 1·40 | 1·40 |
| **MS**305 | 116×91 mm. 10n. Brown gorgon (*Dabasa gyas*) | 2·75 | 2·75 |

**40** King Jigme Singye Wangchuck

**1976.** King Jigme's 20th Birthday. Imperf. (a) Diameter 39 mm.

| | | | | |
|---|---|---|---|---|
| 306 | **40** | 15ch. green on gold | 10 | 10 |
| 307 | **40** | 1n. red on gold | 25 | 25 |
| 308 | - | 1n.30 red on gold | 25 | 25 |

(b) Diameter 50 mm.

| | | | | |
|---|---|---|---|---|
| 309 | **40** | 25ch. green on gold | 10 | 10 |
| 310 | **40** | 2n. red on gold | 45 | 45 |
| 311 | - | 3n. red on gold | 70 | 70 |

(c) Diameter 63 mm.

| | | | | |
|---|---|---|---|---|
| 312 | **40** | 90ch. green on gold | 75 | 75 |
| 313 | **40** | 4n. red on gold | 1·40 | 1·40 |
| 314 | - | 5n. red on gold | 1·70 | 1·70 |

DESIGN: 1n.30, 3, 5n. Decorative motif.

**41** "Apollo"

**1976.** "Apollo"–"Soyuz" Space Link. Mult.

| | | | |
|---|---|---|---|
| 315 | 10n. Type **41** | 2·40 | 2·40 |
| 316 | 10n. "Soyuz" | 2·40 | 2·40 |
| **MS**317 | 130×89 mm. 15n. Type **41**; 15n. As No. 316 | 6·75 | 6·75 |

**42** Jewellery

**1976.** Handicrafts and Craftsmen. Mult.

| | | | |
|---|---|---|---|
| 318 | 1ch. Type **42** | 10 | 10 |
| 319 | 2ch. Coffee-pot, hand bell and sugar dish | 10 | 10 |
| 320 | 3ch. Powder horns | 10 | 10 |
| 321 | 4ch. Pendants and inlaid box | 10 | 10 |
| 322 | 5ch. Painter | 10 | 10 |
| 323 | 15ch. Silversmith | 10 | 10 |
| 324 | 20ch. Wood carver with tools | 10 | 10 |
| 325 | 1n.50 Textile printer | 40 | 40 |
| 326 | 10n. Printer | 1·90 | 1·90 |
| **MS**327 | 105×79 mm. 5n. As No. 326 | 1·70 | 1·70 |

**43** "Rhododendron cinnabarinum"

**1976.** Rhododendrons. Multicoloured.

| | | | |
|---|---|---|---|
| 328 | 1ch. Type **43** | 10 | 10 |
| 329 | 2ch. "R. campanulatum" | 10 | 10 |
| 330 | 3ch. "R. fortunei" | 10 | 10 |
| 331 | 4ch. "R. arboreum" | 10 | 10 |
| 332 | 5ch. "R. arboreum" (different) | 25 | 10 |
| 333 | 1n. "R. falconeri" | 20 | 40 |
| 334 | 3n. "R. hodgsonii" | 55 | 55 |
| 335 | 5n. "R. keysii" | 1·10 | 1·10 |
| **MS**336 | 105×79 mm. 10n. *R. cinnabarinum* (different) | 2·75 | 2·75 |

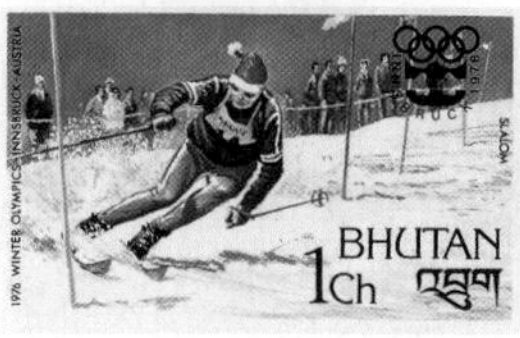

**44** Skiing

**1976.** Winter Olympic Games, Innsbruck. Mult.

| | | | |
|---|---|---|---|
| 337 | 1ch. Type **44** | 10 | 10 |
| 338 | 2ch. Bobsleighing | 10 | 10 |
| 339 | 3ch. Ice hockey | 10 | 10 |
| 340 | 4ch. Cross-country skiing | 10 | 10 |
| 341 | 5ch. Women's figure skating | 10 | 10 |
| 342 | 2n. Downhill skiing | 25 | 25 |
| 343 | 4n. Speed skating | 60 | 55 |
| 344 | 10n. Pairs figure skating | 1·90 | 1·70 |
| **MS**345 | 78×104 mm. 6n. Ski jumping | 1·60 | 1·60 |

**45** Dragon Mask

**1976.** Ceremonial Masks. Laminated prismatic-ribbed plastic surface.

| | | | | |
|---|---|---|---|---|
| 346 | **45** | 5ch. mult (postage) | 10 | 10 |
| 347 | - | 10ch. multicoloured | 10 | 10 |
| 348 | - | 15ch. multicoloured | 10 | 10 |
| 349 | - | 20ch. multicoloured | 10 | 10 |
| 350 | - | 25ch. multicoloured | 10 | 10 |
| 351 | - | 30ch. multicoloured | 10 | 10 |
| 352 | - | 35ch. multicoloured | 10 | 10 |
| 353 | - | 1n. multicoloured (air) | 25 | 25 |
| 354 | - | 2n. multicoloured | 45 | 45 |
| 355 | - | 2n.50 multicoloured | 75 | 75 |
| 356 | - | 3n. multicoloured | 90 | 90 |
| **MS**357 | | Two sheets, each 119×160 mm. (a) 5n. As No. 348; (b) 10n. As No. 351 | 4·00 | 4·00 |

DESIGNS:10ch. to 10n. Similar Bhutanese masks.

**46** Orchid

**1976.** Flowers. Multicoloured.

| | | | |
|---|---|---|---|
| 358 | 1ch. Type **46** | 10 | 10 |
| 359 | 2ch. Orchid (different) | 10 | 10 |
| 360 | 3ch. Orchid (different) | 10 | 10 |
| 361 | 4ch. "Primula denticulata" | 10 | 10 |
| 362 | 5ch. Arum | 10 | 10 |
| 363 | 2n. Orchid (different) | 35 | 35 |
| 364 | 4n. "Leguminosa" | 80 | 80 |
| 365 | 6n. Rhododendron | 1·20 | 1·20 |
| **MS**366 | 106×80 mm. 10n. Arum (*different*) | 3·75 | 3·75 |

**47** Double Carp Emblem

**1976.** 25th Anniv of Colombo Plan.

| | | | |
|---|---|---|---|
| 367 | 3ch. Type **47** | 10 | 10 |
| 368 | 4ch. Vase emblem | 10 | 10 |
| 369 | 5ch. Geometric design | 10 | 10 |
| 370 | 25ch. Design incorporating animal's face | 10 | 10 |
| 371 | 1n.25 Ornamental design | 25 | 25 |
| 372 | 2n. Floral design | 40 | 35 |
| 373 | 2n.50 Carousel design | 50 | 45 |
| 374 | 3n. Wheel design | 70 | 65 |

**48** Bandaranaike Conference Hall

**1976.** 5th Non-aligned Countries Summit Conference, Colombo.

| | | | | |
|---|---|---|---|---|
| 375 | **48** | 1n.25 multicoloured | 35 | 35 |
| 376 | **48** | 2n.50 multicoloured | 75 | 65 |

**49** Liberty Bell

**1978.** Anniversaries and Events. Mult.

| | | | |
|---|---|---|---|
| 377 | 20n. Type **49** (bicentenary of U.S. independence) | 4·00 | 4·00 |
| 378 | 20n. Alexander Graham Bell early telephone (telephone centenary) | 4·00 | 4·00 |
| 379 | 20n. Archer (Olympic Games, Montreal) | 4·00 | 4·00 |
| 380 | 20n. Alfred Nobel (75th anniv of Nobel Prizes) | 4·00 | 4·00 |
| 381 | 20n. "Spirit of St. Louis" (50th anniv of Lindbergh's transatlantic flight) | 4·00 | 4·00 |
| 382 | 20n. Airship LZ3 (75th anniv of Zeppelin) | 4·50 | 4·50 |
| 383 | 20n. Queen Elizabeth II (25th anniv of Coronation) | 4·00 | 4·00 |
| **MS**384 | Seven sheets, each 103×79 mm. (a) 25n. Flags of Bhutan and United States; (b) 25n. "Syncom II" communications satellite; (c) 25n. Shot putter; (d) 25n. Nobel medal; (e) 25n. "Spirit of St. Louis" landing at Le Bourget; (f) 25n. Airship "Viktoria Luise"; (g) 25n. Westminster Abbey | 42·00 | 42·00 |

**1978.** Provisionals. Various stamps surch 25 Ch (385, 394) or 25 CH (others). I. Girl Scouts (No. 153).

| | | | |
|---|---|---|---|
| 385 | 25ch. on 5n. mult (postage) | 12·50 | 10·00 |

II. Air. 1968 Mythological Creatures (Nos. 181 and 183).

| | | | |
|---|---|---|---|
| 386 | 25ch. on 4n. orange, green and black | 2·50 | 2·10 |
| 387 | 25ch. on 10n. violet, grey and black | 2·50 | 2·10 |

III. 1971 Admission to U.N. (Appendix).

| | | | |
|---|---|---|---|
| 388 | 25ch. on 3n. mult (postage) | 2·10 | 1·70 |
| 389 | 25ch. on 5n. mult (air) | 2·10 | 1·70 |
| 390 | 25ch. on 6n. multicoloured | 2·10 | 1·70 |

IV. Boy Scouts Anniv (Appendix).

| | | | |
|---|---|---|---|
| 391 | 25ch. on 6n. multicoloured | 13·00 | 11·00 |

V. 1972 Dogs (No. 275).

| | | | |
|---|---|---|---|
| 392 | 25ch. on 8n. multicoloured | 3·75 | 3·25 |

VI. 1973 Dogs (Appendix).

| | | | |
|---|---|---|---|
| 393 | 25ch. on 4n. multicoloured | 3·75 | 3·25 |

VII. 1973 "Indipex 73" (Appendix).

| | | | |
|---|---|---|---|
| 394 | 25ch. on 3n. mult (postage) | 3·25 | 3·00 |
| 395 | 25ch. on 5n. mult (air) | 3·25 | 3·00 |
| 396 | 25ch. on 6n. multicoloured | 3·25 | 3·00 |

VIII. U.P.U. (Nos. 289/90).

| | | | |
|---|---|---|---|
| 397 | 25ch. on 1n. 40 multicoloured | 3·00 | 2·50 |
| 398 | 25ch. on 2n. multicoloured | 3·00 | 2·50 |

IX. World Population Year (No. 295).

| | | | |
|---|---|---|---|
| 399 | 25ch. on 2n.50 multicoloured | 5·00 | 4·25 |

X. Butterflies (Nos. 303/4).

| | | | |
|---|---|---|---|
| 400 | 25ch. on 3n. multicoloured | 5·00 | 4·25 |
| 401 | 25ch. on 5n. multicoloured | 5·00 | 4·25 |

XI. "Apollo"–"Soyuz" (Nos. 315/16).

| | | | |
|---|---|---|---|
| 402 | 25ch. on 10n. mult (315) | 12·50 | 10·00 |
| 403 | 25ch. on 10n. mult (316) | 12·50 | 10·00 |

XII. Handicrafts (No. 326).

404 25ch. on 10n. multicoloured 2·50 2·10

XIII. Rhododendrons (No. 335).

405 25ch. on 5n. multicoloured 4·25 3·50

XIV. Winter Olympics (Nos. 343/4).

406 25ch. on 4n. multicoloured 5·75 5·00
407 25ch. on 10n. multicoloured 5·75 5·00

XV. Flowers (Nos. 364/5).

408 25ch. on 4n. multicoloured 2·10 1·80
409 25ch. on 6n. multicoloured 2·10 1·80

XVI. Colombo Plan (No. 373).

410 25ch. on 2n.50 multicoloured 2·50 2·10

**50** Mother and Child

**1979.** International Year of the Child. Mult.
411 2n. Type **50** 50 50
412 5n. Mother carrying two children 1·10 95
413 10n. Children at school 1·60 1·50
**MS**414 131×103 mm. Nos. 411/13 3·25 2·75

**51** Conference Emblem and Dove

**1979.** 6th Non-Aligned Countries Summit Conference, Havana. Multicoloured.
415 25ch. Type **51** 15 15
416 10n. Emblem and Bhutanese symbols 2·50 2·20

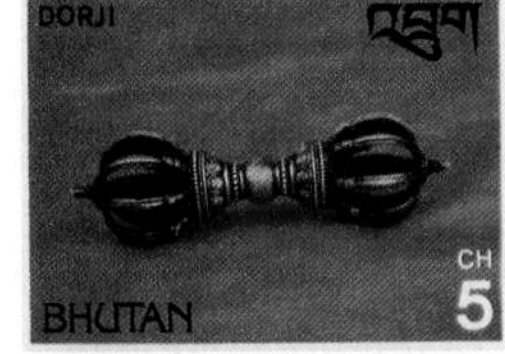

**52** Dorji (rattle)

**1979.** Antiquities. Multicoloured.
417 5ch. Type **52** 10 10
418 10ch. Dilbu (hand bell) (vert) 10 10
419 15ch. Jadum (cylindrical pot) (vert) 10 10
420 25ch. Jamjee (teapot) 10 10
421 1n. Kem (cylindrical container) (vert) 35 30
422 1n.25 Jamjee (different) 40 40
423 1n.70 Sangphor (ornamental vessel) (vert) 60 60
424 2n. Jamjee (different) (vert) 75 70
425 3n. Yangtho (pot with lid) (vert) 95 90
426 4n. Battha (circular case) 1·20 1·20
427 5n. Chhap (ornamental flask) (vert) 1·70 1·60

**53** Rinpiang Dzong, Bhutan Stamp and Rowland Hill Statue

**1980.** Death Cent of Sir Rowland Hill. Mult.
428 1n. Type **53** 45 40
429 2n. Dzong, Bhutan stamp and statue 80 75
430 5n. Ounsti Dzong, Bhutan stamp and statue 1·30 1·20
431 10n. Lingzi Dzong and British 1912 1d. stamp 2·75 2·50
**MS**432 102×103 mm. 20n. Rope bridge, British 1d. black stamp and statue 9·50 9·50

**54** Dungtse Lhakhang, Paro

**1981.** Monasteries. Multicoloured.
433 1n. Type **54** 20 15
434 2n. Kich Lhakhang, Paro (horiz) 40 35
435 2n.25 Kurjey Lhakhang (horiz) 55 50
436 3n. Tangu, Thimphu (horiz) 70 65
437 4n. Cheri, Thimphu (horiz) 95 85
438 5n. Chorten, Kora (horiz) 1·50 1·30
439 7n. Tak-Tsang, Paro 2·10 1·90

**55** St. Paul's Cathedral

**1981.** Wedding of Prince of Wales. Multicoloured.
440 1n. Type **55** 10 10
441 5n. Type **55** 90 75
442 20n. Prince Charles and Lady Diana Spencer 3·25 2·75
443 25n. As No. 442 4·00 3·75
**MS**444 69×90 mm. 20n. Wedding procession 4·00 3·50

**56** Orange-bellied Leafbird ("Orange-billed Chiropsis")

**1982.** Birds. Multicoloured.
445 2n. Type **56** 70 65
446 3n. Himalayan monal pheasant ("Monal Pheasant") 1·00 95
447 5n. Ward's trogon 2·00 1·80
448 10n. Mrs. Gould's sunbird 3·25 3·00
**MS**449 95×101 mm. 25n. Maroon oriole (*Oriolus trailii*) 6·75 6·00

**57** Footballers

**1982.** World Cup Football Championship, Spain.
450 **57** 1n. multicoloured 20 15
451 - 2n. multicoloured 45 40
452 - 3n. multicoloured 65 60
453 - 20n. multicoloured 3·75 3·25
**MS**454 79×108 mm. 25n. multicoloured (horiz) 6·75 5·25

DESIGNS: 2n. to 25n. Various football scenes.

No. **MS**454 exists in two versions, differing in the list of qualifying countries in the border.

**58** St. James's Palace

**1982.** 21st Birthday of Princess of Wales. Mult.
455 1n. Type **58** 40 35
456 10n. Prince and Princess of Wales 2·20 2·00
457 15n. Windsor Castle 3·75 4·00
458 25n. Princess in wedding dress 5·75 5·25
**MS**459 102×76 mm. 20n. Princess of Wales 5·00 4·50

**59** Lord Baden-Powell (founder)

**1982.** 75th Anniv of Boy Scout Movement. Multicoloured.
460 3n. Type **59** 55 50
461 5n. Scouts around campfire 1·10 95
462 15n. Map reading 2·75 2·50
463 20n. Pitching tents 4·00 3·75
**MS**464 91×70 mm. 25n. Scout 5·25 4·75

**60** Rama finds Mowgli

**1982.** "The Jungle Book" (cartoon film). Mult.
465 1ch. Type **60** 10 10
466 2ch. Bagheera leading Mowgli to Man-village 10 10
467 3ch. Kaa planning attack on Bagheera and Mowgli 10 10
468 4ch. Mowgli and elephants 10 10
469 5ch. Mowgli and Baloo 10 10
470 10ch. Mowgli and King Louie 10 10
471 30ch. Kaa and Shere Khan 10 10
472 2n. Mowgli, Baloo and Bagheera 45 35
473 20n. Mowgli carrying jug for girl 4·00 3·50
**MS**474 Two sheets, each 127×102 mm. (a) 20n. Mowgli and Baloo; (b) 20n. Mowgli and Baloo floating down river 8·75 7·75

**1982.** Birth of Prince William of Wales. Nos. 455/MS459 optd ROYAL BABY 21.6.82.
475 1n. multicoloured 40 40
476 10n. multicoloured 1·40 1·20
477 15n. multicoloured 2·75 2·50
478 25n. multicoloured 4·50 4·00
**MS**479 102×76 mm. 20n. multicoloured 5·00 4·75

**62** Washington surveying

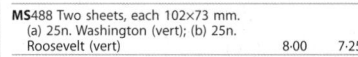

**1982.** 250th Birth Anniv of George Washington and Birth Centenary of Franklin D. Roosevelt. Mult.
480 50ch. Type **62** 10 10
481 1n. Roosevelt and Harvard University 10 10
482 2n. Washington at Valley Forge 30 30
483 3n. Roosevelt's mother and family 45 40
484 4n. Washington at Battle of Monmouth 55 50
485 5n. Roosevelt and the White House 80 75
486 15n. Washington and Mount Vernon 2·40 2·20
487 20n. Churchill, Roosevelt and Stalin at Yalta 3·25 3·00
**MS**488 Two sheets, each 102×73 mm. (a) 25n. Washington (vert); (b) 25n. Roosevelt (vert) 8·00 7·25

**1983.** "Druk Air" Bhutan Air Service. Various stamps optd DRUK AIR (491) or Druk Air (others), No. 489 surch also.
489 **42** 30ch. on 1n. multicoloured (postage) 1·30 1·30
490 - 5n. multicoloured (Scouts, Appendix) 2·40 2·10
491 - 8n. mult (No. 275) 2·50 2·20
492 - 5n. mult ("Indipex 73", Appendix) (air) 3·75 3·50
493 - 7n. mult (Munich Olympics, Appendix) 3·75 3·50

**64** "Angelo Doni"

**1983.** 500th Birth Anniv of Raphael (artist). Multicoloured.
494 1n. Type **64** 15 10
495 4n. "Maddalena Doni" 70 60
496 5n. "Baldassare Castiglione" 1·00 85
497 20n. "Woman with Veil" 4·00 3·50
**MS**498 Two sheets, each 127×101 mm. (a) 25n. Self-portrait (detail from "Mass of Bolsena"); (b) 25n. Self-portrait (detail from "Expulsion of Heliodorus") 10·50 9·75

**65** Ta-Gyad-Boom-Zu (the eight luck-bringing symbols)

**1983.** Religious Offerings. Multicoloured.
499 25ch. Type **65** 10 10
500 50ch. Doeyun Nga (the five sensory symbols) 15 15
501 2n. Norbu Chadun (the seven treasures) (47×41 mm) 35 35
502 3n. Wangpo Nga (the five sensory organs) 60 55
503 8n. Sha Nga (the five kinds of flesh) 1·30 1·10
504 9n. Men-Ra-Tor Sum (the sacrificial cake) (47×41 mm) 1·60 1·60
**MS**505 180×135 mm. Nos. 499/504 4·50 4·25

**66** Dornier Wal Flying Boat "Boreas"

**1983.** Bicentenary of Manned Flight. Mult.
506 50ch. Type **66** 10 10
507 3n. Savoia-Marchetti S.66 flying boat 60 55
508 10n. Hawker Osprey biplane 2·00 1·90
509 20n. Astra airship "Ville de Paris" 4·00 3·75
**MS**510 106×80 mm. 25n. Henri Giffard's balloon "Le Grand Ballon Captif" 5·00 4·50

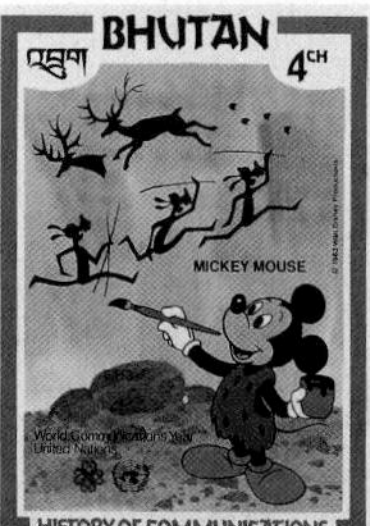

**67** Mickey Mouse as Caveman

**1984.** World Communications Year. Mult.
511 4ch. Type **67** 10 10
512 5ch. Goofy as printer 10 10
513 10ch. Chip 'n' Dale with morse key 10 10
514 20ch. Pluto talks to girlfriend on telephone 10 10
515 25ch. Minnie Mouse pulling record from bulldog 10 10
516 50ch. Morty and Ferdie with microphone and loudhailers 10 10
517 1n. Huey, Dewey, and Louie listening to radio 30 30
518 5n. Donald Duck watching television on buffalo 1·10 1·10
519 20n. Daisy Duck with computers and abacus 4·25 4·00
**MS**520 Two sheets, each 127×102 mm. (a) 20n. Mickey Mouse on television (horiz); (b) 20n. Donald Duck and satellite (horiz) 8·75 8·25

**68** Golden Langur

**1984.** Endangered Species. Multicoloured.
521 50ch. Type **68** 20 20
522 1n. Golden langur family in tree (horiz) 30 30
523 2n. Male and female Golden langurs with young (horiz) 70 70
524 4n. Group of langurs 1·40 1·30
**MS**525 Three sheets. (a) 88×121 mm. 20n. Snow leopard (horiz); (b) 121×88 mm. 25n. Yak; (c) 121×88 mm. 25n. Bharal (horiz) 14·50 12·00

**69** Downhill Skiing

**1984.** Winter Olympic Games, Sarajevo. Mult.
526 50ch. Type **69** 10 10
527 1n. Cross-country skiing 20 15
528 3n. Speed skating 70 65
529 20n. Four-man bobsleigh 3·50 3·25
**MS**530 108×76 mm. 25n. Ice hockey 4·75 4·00

**70** "Sans Pareil", 1829

**1984.** Railway Locomotives. Multicoloured.
531 50ch. Type **70** 10 10
532 1n. "Planet", 1830 15 15
533 3n. "Experiment" 1832 65 60
534 4n. "Black Hawk", 1835 85 80
535 5n.50 "Jenny Lind", 1847 (horiz) 1·10 1·10
536 8n. "Bavaria", 1851 (horiz) 1·60 1·50
537 10n. Great Northern locomotive No. 1, 1870 (horiz) 2·10 1·90
538 25n. Steam locomotive Type 110, Prussia, 1880 (horiz) 5·00 4·50
**MS**539 Four sheets, each 92×65 mm. (a) 20n. Crampton's locomotive, 1846 (horiz); (b) 20n. "Erzsebet", 1870 (horiz); (c) 20n. Sondermann freight, 1896 (horiz); (d) 20n. Darjeeling–Himalaya railway (horiz) 16·00 14·50

**71** Riley Sprite Sports Car, 1936

**1984.** Cars. Multicoloured.
540 50ch. Type **71** 10 10
541 1n. Lanchester Forty saloon, 1919 15 15
542 3n. Itala 35/45 racer, 1907 55 50
543 4n. Morris Oxford (Bullnose) tourer, 1913 80 70
544 5n.50 Lagonda LG6 drophead coupe, 1939 1·10 95
545 6n. Wolseley four seat tonneau, 1903 1·30 1·10
546 8n. Buick Super convertible, 1952 1·50 1·40
547 20n. Maybach Zeppelin limousine, 1933 4·00 3·50
**MS**548 Two sheets, each 126×99 mm. (a) 25n. Renault (1901); (b) 25n. Simplex (1912) 8·00 7·25

**72** Women's Archery

**1984.** Olympic Games, Los Angeles. Multicoloured.
549 15ch. Type **72** 10 10
550 25ch. Men's archery 15 10
551 2n. Table tennis 40 35
552 2n.25 Basketball 50 45
553 5n.50 Boxing 1·00 95
554 6n. Running 1·20 1·10
555 8n. Tennis 1·70 1·60
**MS**556 115×82 mm. 25n. Couple practising archery (72×43 mm) 4·50 4·00

**73** Domkhar Dzong

**1984.** Monasteries.
557 **73** 10ch. blue 10 10
558 - 25ch. red 10 10
559 - 50ch. violet 10 10
560 - 1n. brown 20 20
561 - 2n. red 35 35
562 - 5n. green 85 85
DESIGNS: 25ch. Shemgang Dzong; 50ch. Chapcha Dzong; 1n. Tashigang Dzong; 2n. Pungthang Dzong; 5n. Dechhenphoda Dzong.

**74** "Magician Mickey"

**1984.** 50th Anniv of Donald Duck. Scenes from films. Multicoloured.
563 4ch. Type **74** 10 10
564 5ch. "Slide, Donald, Slide" 10 10
565 10ch. "Donald's Golf Game" 10 10
566 20ch. "Mr. Duck Steps Out" 10 10
567 25ch. "Lion Around" 10 10
568 50ch. "Alpine Climbers" 10 10
569 1n. "Flying Jalopy" 10 10
570 5n. "Frank Duck brings 'Em Back Alive" 55 45
571 20n. "Good Scouts" 2·20 1·80
**MS**572 Two sheets, each 128×101 mm. (a) 20n. "Sea Scouts"; (b) 20n. "The Three Caballeros" 9·00 8·25

**1984.** Various stamps surch. (a) World Cup Football Championship, Spain (Nos. 450/3).
573 5n. on 1n. multicoloured 1·60 1·40
574 5n. on 2n. multicoloured 1·60 1·40
575 5n. on 3n. multicoloured 1·60 1·40
576 5n. on 20n. multicoloured 1·60 1·40
**MS**577 79×108 mm. 20n. on 25n. multicoloured 6·25 6·25
No. **MS**577 exists in two versions, differing in the list of qualifying countries in the border.

(b) 21st Birthday of Princess of Wales (Nos. 455/8).
578 5n. on 1n. multicoloured 1·40 1·30
579 5n. on 10n. multicoloured 1·40 1·30
580 5n. on 15n. multicoloured 1·40 1·30
581 40n. on 25n. multicoloured 11·00 10·00
**MS**582 102×76 mm. 25n. on 20n. multicoloured 7·50 7·50

(c) Birth of Prince William of Wales (Nos. 475/8).
583 5n. on 1n. multicoloured 1·30 1·30
584 5n. on 10n. multicoloured 1·30 1·30
585 5n. on 15n. multicoloured 1·30 1·30
586 40n. on 25n. multicoloured 11·00 10·50
**MS**587 102×76 mm. 25n. on 20n. multicoloured 10·00 10·00

(d) Wedding of Prince of Wales (Nos. 440/3).
588 10n. on 1n. multicoloured 2·40 2·20
589 10n. on 5n. multicoloured 2·40 2·20
590 10n. on 20n. multicoloured 2·40 2·20
591 10n. on 25n. multicoloured 2·40 2·20
**MS**592 69×90 mm. 30n. on 20n. multicoloured 10·00 10·00
On Nos. 588/**MS**592 the new value is surcharged twice.

(e) 75th Anniv of Boy Scout Movement (Nos. 460/3).
593 10n. on 3n. multicoloured 2·40 2·20
594 10n. on 5n. multicoloured 2·40 2·20
595 10n. on 15n. multicoloured 2·40 2·20
596 10n. on 20n. multicoloured 2·40 2·20
**MS**597 91×70 mm. 20n. on 25n. multicoloured 10·00 10·00

**76** Shinje Choegyel

**1985.** The Judgement of Death Mask Dance. Multicoloured.
598 5ch. Type **76** 10 10
599 35ch. Raksh Lango 10 10
600 50ch. Druelgo 10 10
601 2n.50 Pago 40 35
602 3n. Telgo 55 50
603 4n. Due Nakcung 75 70
604 5n. Lha Karpo 90 85
605 5n.50 Nyalbum 1·00 95
606 6n. Khimda Pelkyi 1·10 1·10
**MS**607 90×135 mm. Nos. 598/9 and 603/4 2·30 2·20

**77** Bhutan and UN Flags

**1985.** 40th Anniv of UNO.
608 **77** 50ch. multicoloured 20 20
609 - 15n. multicoloured 2·00 1·70
610 - 20n. black and blue 3·00 2·50
**MS**611 65×80 mm. 25n. black, yellow and scarlet 3·75 3·25
DESIGNS—VERT: 15n. UN building, New York; 25n. 1945 charter; HORIZ: 20n. Veterans' War Memorial Building San Francisco (venue of signing charter, 1945).

**78** Mickey Mouse tramping through Black Forest

**1985.** 150th Birth Anniv of Mark Twain (writer) and International Youth Year. Multicoloured.
612 50ch. Type **78** 10 10
613 2n. Mickey Mouse, Donald Duck and Goofy on steamboat trip on Lake Lucerne 35 30
614 5n. Mickey Mouse, Donald Duck and Goofy climbing Rigi-Kulm 85 75
615 9n. Mickey Mouse and Goofy rafting to Heidelberg on River Neckar 1·60 1·40
616 20n. Mickey Mouse leading Donald Duck on horse back up the Riffelberg 3·50 3·25
**MS**617 126×101 mm. 25n. Mickey Mouse and Goofy 4·75 4·25
Nos. 612/**MS**617 show scenes from "A Tramp Abroad" (cartoon film of Twain novel).

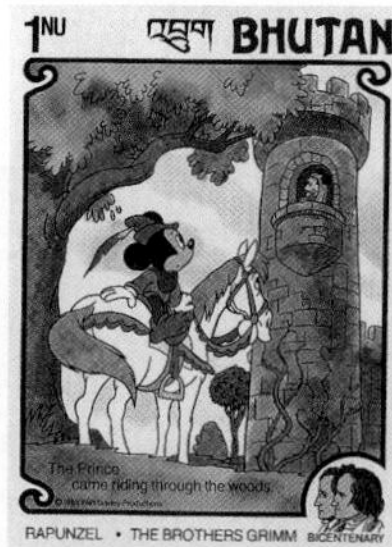

**79** Prince sees Rapunzel

**1985.** Birth Bicentenaries (1985 and 1986) of Grimm Brothers (folklorists). Multicoloured.
618 1n. Type **79** 10 10
619 4n. Rapunzel (Minnie Mouse) in tower 50 45
620 7n. Mother Gothel calling to Rapunzel to let down her hair 1·10 95
621 8n. Prince climbing tower using Rapunzel's hair 1·40 1·30
622 15n. Prince proposing to Rapunzel 2·40 2·10
**MS**623 126×101 mm. 25n. Prince riding away with Rapunzel 5·00 4·75

**80** "Brewers Duck" (mallard)

**1985.** Birth Bicentenary of John J. Audubon (ornithologist). Audubon illustrations. Mult.
624 50ch. Type **80** 10 10
625 1n. "Willow Ptarmigan" (Willow/red Grouse) 15 15
626 2n. "Mountain Plover" 35 30
627 3n. "Red-throated Loon" (Red-throated Diver) 50 50
628 4n. "Spruce Grouse" 80 70
629 5n. "Hooded Merganser" 95 90
630 15n. "Trumpeter Swan" (Whooper Swan) 2·75 2·50
631 20n. Common goldeneye 3·75 3·25
**MS**632 75×105 mm. 25n. "Sharp-shinned Hawk" 4·50 4·00
**MS**633 75×105 mm. 25n."Tufted Titmouse" 4·50 4·00

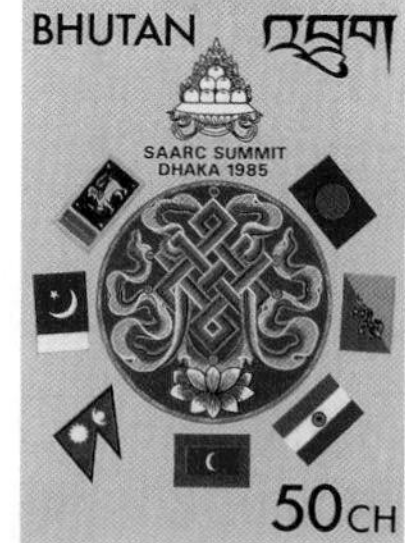

**81** Members' Flags around Buddhist Design

**1985.** South Asian Regional Co-operation Summit, Dhaka, Bangladesh.
634 **81** 50ch. multicoloured 15 15
635 **81** 5n. multicoloured 95 85

**82** Precious Wheel

**1986.** The Precious Symbols. Multicoloured.
636 30ch. Type **82** 10 10

| | | | |
|---|---|---|---|
| 637 | 50ch. Precious Gem | 10 | 10 |
| 638 | 1n.25 Precious Queen | 15 | 15 |
| 639 | 2n. Precious Minister | 30 | 30 |
| 640 | 4n. Precious Elephant | 55 | 55 |
| 641 | 6n. Precious Horse | 80 | 80 |
| 642 | 8n. Precious General | 1·10 | 1·10 |

**1986.** Olympic Games Gold Medal Winners. Nos. 549/50 and 552/5 optd.

| | | | | |
|---|---|---|---|---|
| 643 | 72 | 15ch. **GOLD HYANG SOON SEO SOUTH KOREA** | 10 | 10 |
| 644 | - | 25ch. **GOLD DARRELL PACE USA** | 10 | 10 |
| 645 | - | 2n.25 **GOLD MEDAL USA** | 35 | 35 |
| 646 | - | 5n.50 **GOLD MARK BRELAND USA** | 70 | 70 |
| 647 | - | 6n. **GOLD DALEY THOMPSON ENG-LAND** | 80 | 80 |
| 648 | - | 8n. **GOLD STEFAN EDBERG SWEDEN** | 1·10 | 1·10 |
| **MS**649 | | Two sheets, each 115×82 mm. (a) 25n. **HYANG SOON SEO, SOUTH KOREA**; (b) 25n. **DARRELL PACE, U.S.A.** | 7·50 | 6·25 |

**1986.** "Ameripex 86" International Stamp Exhibition, Chicago. Various stamps optd AMERIPEX 86. (a) Nos. 615/MS617.

| | | | |
|---|---|---|---|
| 650 | 8n. multicoloured | 2·20 | 1·80 |
| 651 | 20n. multicoloured | 3·25 | 3·00 |
| **MS**652 | 126×101 mm. 25n. multicoloured | 4·00 | 3·50 |

(b) Nos. 621/MS623.

| | | | |
|---|---|---|---|
| 653 | 8n. multicoloured | 1·40 | 1·20 |
| 654 | 15n. multicoloured | 1·90 | 1·70 |
| **MS**655 | 126×101 mm. 25n. multicoloured | 4·00 | 3·50 |

**85** Mandala of Phurpa (Ritual Dagger)

**1986.** Kilkhor Mandalas of Mahayana Buddhism. Multicoloured.

| | | | |
|---|---|---|---|
| 656 | 10ch. Type **85** | 10 | 10 |
| 657 | 25ch. Mandala of Amitayus in Wrathful Form | 10 | 10 |
| 658 | 50ch. Mandala of Overpowering Deities | 10 | 10 |
| 659 | 75ch. Mandala of the Great Wrathful One | 10 | 10 |
| 660 | 1n. Type **85** | 15 | 15 |
| 661 | 3n. As 25ch. | 45 | 45 |
| 662 | 5n. As 50ch. | 65 | 65 |
| 663 | 7n. As 75ch. | 85 | 85 |

**1986.** 75th Anniv of Girl Guides. Nos. 460/3 optd 75th ANNIVERSARY GIRL GUIDES.

| | | | |
|---|---|---|---|
| 664 | 3n. multicoloured | 40 | 40 |
| 665 | 5n. multicoloured | 1·00 | 1·00 |
| 666 | 15n. multicoloured | 3·00 | 3·00 |
| 667 | 20n. multicoloured | 4·00 | 4·00 |
| **MS**668 | 91×70 mm. 25n. multicoloured | 5·50 | 5·50 |

**87** Babylonian Tablet and Comet over Noah's Ark

**1986.** Appearance of Halley's Comet. Mult.

| | | | |
|---|---|---|---|
| 669 | 50ch. Type **87** | 10 | 10 |
| 670 | 1n. 17th-century print | 10 | 10 |
| 671 | 2n. 1835 French silhouette | 25 | 25 |
| 672 | 3n. Bayeux tapestry | 40 | 35 |
| 673 | 4n. Woodblock from "Nuremburg Chronicle" | 60 | 50 |
| 674 | 5n. Illustration of Revelation 6, 12–13 from 1650 Bible | 80 | 75 |
| 675 | 15n. Comet in constellation of Cancer | 2·30 | 2·10 |
| 676 | 20n. Decoration on Delft plate | 3·25 | 2·75 |
| **MS**677 | Two sheets, each 109×79 mm. (a) 25n. Comet over dzong in Himalayas; (b) 25n. Comet over shrine | 8·00 | 7·25 |

**88** Statue and "Libertad" (Argentine full-rigged cadet ship)

**1986.** Centenary of Statue of Liberty. Multicoloured.

| | | | |
|---|---|---|---|
| 678 | 50ch. Type **88** | 10 | 10 |
| 679 | 1n. "Shalom" (Israeli liner) | 10 | 10 |
| 680 | 2n. "Leonardo da Vinci" (Italian liner) | 25 | 25 |
| 681 | 3n. "Mircea" (Rumanian cadet barque) | 40 | 35 |
| 682 | 4n. "France" (French liner) | 55 | 50 |
| 683 | 5n. S.S. "United States" (American liner) | 80 | 75 |
| 684 | 15n. "Queen Elizabeth 2" (British liner) | 2·30 | 2·10 |
| 685 | 20n. "Europa" (West German liner) | 3·25 | 2·75 |
| **MS**686 | Two sheets, each 114×83 mm. (a) Statue (27×41 mm); (b) Statue and tower blocks (27×41 mm) | 7·50 | 6·75 |

The descriptions of the ships on Nos. 678 and 681 were transposed in error.

**89** "Santa Maria"

**1987.** 500th Anniv (1992) of Discovery of America by Columbus. Multicoloured.

| | | | |
|---|---|---|---|
| 687 | 20ch. Type **89** | 25 | 30 |
| 688 | 25ch. Queen Isabella of Spain | 25 | 25 |
| 689 | 50ch. Flying fish | 25 | 25 |
| 690 | 1n. Columbus's coat of arms | 50 | 40 |
| 691 | 2n. Christopher Columbus | 85 | 70 |
| 692 | 3n. Columbus landing with Spanish soldiers | 1·10 | 1·10 |
| **MS**693 | Seven sheets, each 97×65 mm. (a) 20ch. Pineapple; (b) 25ch. Indian hammock (horiz); (c) 50ch. Tobacco plant; (d) 1n. Greater flamingo; (e) 2n. Astrolabe; (f) 3n. Lizard (horiz); (g) 5n. Iguana (horiz) | 11·50 | 11·50 |
| **MS**694 | 170×144 mm. As Nos. 687/92 but with white backgrounds | 23·00 | 23·00 |

**90** Canadian National Class "U1-f" Steam Locomotive No. 6060

**1987.** "Capex '87" International Stamp Exhibition, Toronto. Canadian Railways. Multicoloured.

| | | | |
|---|---|---|---|
| 695 | 50ch. Type **90** | 10 | 10 |
| 696 | 1n. Via Rail "L.R.C." electric locomotive No. 6903 | 10 | 10 |
| 697 | 2n. Canadian National GM "GF30t" diesel locomotive No. 5341 | 35 | 30 |
| 698 | 3n. Canadian National steam locomotive No. 6157 | 45 | 40 |
| 699 | 8n. Canadian Pacific steam locomotive No. 2727 | 1·30 | 1·20 |
| 700 | 10n. Via Express diesel locomotive No. 6524 | 1·60 | 1·40 |
| 701 | 15n. Canadian National "Turbotrain" | 2·40 | 2·10 |
| 702 | 20n. Canadian Pacific diesel-electric locomotive No. 1414 | 3·00 | 2·75 |
| **MS**703 | Two sheets, each 102×75 mm. (a) 25n. Cab and tender of Royal Hudson steam locomotive (27×41 mm); (b) 25n. Canadian National steam locomotive (27×41 mm) | 7·50 | 6·75 |

**91** "Two Faces" (sculpture)

**1987.** Birth Centenary of Marc Chagall (artist). Multicoloured.

| | | | |
|---|---|---|---|
| 704 | 50ch. Type **91** | 15 | 15 |
| 705 | 1n. "At the Barber's" | 25 | 25 |
| 706 | 2n. "Old Jew with Torai" | 40 | 40 |
| 707 | 3n. "Red Maternity" | 65 | 65 |
| 708 | 4n. "Eve of Yom Kippur" | 1·00 | 1·00 |
| 709 | 5n. "The Old Musician" | 1·20 | 1·20 |
| 710 | 6n. "The Rabbi of Vitebsk" | 1·30 | 1·30 |
| 711 | 7n. "Couple at Dusk" | 1·50 | 1·50 |
| 712 | 9n. "The Artistes" | 1·80 | 1·80 |
| 713 | 10n. "Moses breaking the Tablets" | 2·00 | 2·00 |
| 714 | 12n. "Bouquet with Flying Lovers" | 2·30 | 2·30 |
| 715 | 20n. "In the Sky of the Opera" | 4·00 | 4·00 |
| **MS**716 | 12 sheets, each 95×110 mm (e) or 110×95 mm (others). Imperf. (a) 25n. "The Red Gateway". (b) 25n. "Romeo and Juliet". (c) 25n. "Maternity". (d) 25n. "The Carnival for Aleko, Scene II". (e) 25n. "Magician of Paris". (f) 25n. "Visit to the Grandparents". (g) 25n. "Cow with Parasol". (h) 25n. "Russian Village". (i) 25n. "Still Life". (j) 25n. "Composition with Goat". (k) 25n. "The Smolensk Newspaper". (l) 25n. "The Concert" | 47·00 | 47·00 |

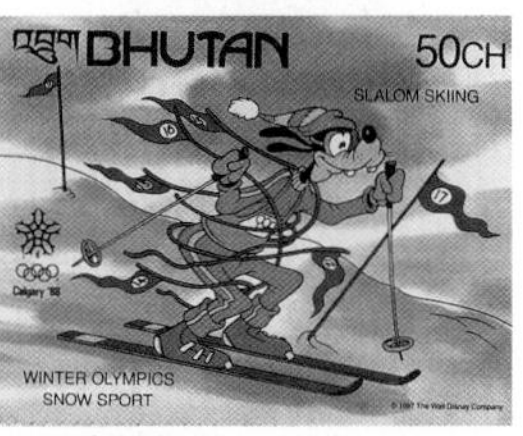

**92** Goofy (slalom)

**1988.** Winter Olympic Games, Calgary. Mult.

| | | | |
|---|---|---|---|
| 717 | 50ch. Type **92** | 10 | 10 |
| 718 | 1n. Donald Duck pushing Goofy at start (downhill skiing) | 15 | 15 |
| 719 | 2n. Goofy in goal (ice hockey) | 25 | 25 |
| 720 | 4n. Goofy (biathlon) | 55 | 50 |
| 721 | 7n. Goofy and Donald Duck (speed skating) | 1·10 | 95 |
| 722 | 8n. Minnie Mouse (figure skating) | 1·30 | 1·20 |
| 723 | 9n. Minnie Mouse (free-style skating) | 1·50 | 1·30 |
| 724 | 20n. Goofy and Mickey Mouse (two-man bobsleigh) | 3·00 | 2·75 |
| **MS**725 | Two sheets, each 127×101 mm. (a) 25n. Goofy (ski jumping); (b) 25n. Donald and Daisy Duck (ice skating) | 7·00 | 7·00 |

**93** Stephenson's Railway Locomotive "Rocket", 1829

**1988.** Transport. Multicoloured.

| | | | |
|---|---|---|---|
| 726 | 50ch. Pullman "Pioneer" sleeper, 1865 | 10 | 10 |
| 727 | 1n. Type **93** | 15 | 15 |
| 728 | 2n. Pierre Lallement's "Velocipede", 1866 | 25 | 25 |
| 729 | 3n. Benz "Patent Motor Wagon", 1866 | 45 | 35 |
| 730 | 4n. Volkswagen Beetle | 55 | 50 |
| 731 | 5n. Mississippi paddle-steamers "Natchez" and "Robert E. Lee", 1870 | 65 | 60 |
| 732 | 6n. American La France motor fire engine, 1910 | 80 | 75 |
| 733 | 7n. Frigate U.S.S. "Constitution", 1797 (vert) | 95 | 85 |
| 734 | 9n. Bell rocket belt, 1961 (vert) | 1·20 | 1·10 |
| 735 | 10n. Trevithick's railway locomotive, 1804 | 1·30 | 1·20 |
| **MS**736 | Four sheets, each 118×89 mm. (a) 25n. Steam locomotive "Mallard" (27×41 mm); (b) 25n. French "TGV" express train (41×27 mm); (c) 25n. Japanese Shinkansen "Tokaido" bullet train (41×27 mm); (d) 25n. Concorde supersonic airplane (41×27 mm) | 17·00 | 17·00 |

No. 731 is wrongly inscribed "Natches" and No. 733 is wrongly dated "1787".

**94** Dam and Pylon

**1988.** Chhukha Hydro-electric Project.

| | | | | |
|---|---|---|---|---|
| 737 | 94 | 50ch. multicoloured | 30 | 30 |

**1988.** World Aids Day. Nos. 411/13 optd WORLD AIDS DAY.

| | | | | |
|---|---|---|---|---|
| 738 | 50 | 2n. multicoloured | 40 | 35 |
| 739 | - | 5n. multicoloured | 1·00 | 90 |
| 740 | - | 10n. multicoloured | 2·10 | 1·90 |

**96** "Diana and Actaeon" (detail)

**1989.** 500th Birth Anniv of Titian (painter). Multicoloured.

| | | | |
|---|---|---|---|
| 741 | 50ch. "Gentleman with a Book" | 10 | 10 |
| 742 | 1n. "Venus and Cupid, with a Lute Player" (detail) | 15 | 15 |
| 743 | 2n. Type **96** | 30 | 30 |
| 744 | 3n. "Cardinal Ippolito dei Medici" | 50 | 45 |
| 745 | 4n. "Sleeping Venus" (detail) | 75 | 70 |
| 746 | 5n. "Venus risen from the Waves" (detail) | 90 | 85 |
| 747 | 6n. "Worship of Venus" (detail) | 1·20 | 1·10 |
| 748 | 7n. "Fete Champetre" (detail) | 1·40 | 1·30 |
| 749 | 10n. "Perseus and Andromeda" (detail) | 1·80 | 1·70 |
| 750 | 15n. "Danae" (detail) | 2·75 | 2·50 |
| 751 | 20n. "Venus at the Mirror" | 3·75 | 3·50 |
| 752 | 25n. "Venus and the Organ Player" (detail) | 4·50 | 4·25 |
| **MS**753 | 12 sheets, each 109×94 (a/d) or 94×109 mm (others). (a) 25n. "Bacchus and Ariadne"; (b) 25n. "Danae with the Shower of Gold" (horiz); (c) 25n. "The Pardo Venus" (horiz); (d) 25n. "Venus and Cupid with an Organist"; (e) 25n. "Diana and Callisto"; (f) 25n. "Mater Dolorosa with Raised Hands"; (g) 25n. "Miracle of the Irascible Son"; (h) 25n. "Portrait of Johann Friedrich"; (i) 25n. "Portrait of Laura Dianti"; (j) 25n. "St. John the Almsgiver"; (k) 25n. "Venus blindfolding Cupid"; (l) 25n. "Venus of Urbino" | 47·00 | 47·00 |

**97** Volleyball

**1989.** Olympic Games, Seoul (1988). Mult.

| | | | |
|---|---|---|---|
| 754 | 50ch. Gymnastics | 10 | 10 |
| 755 | 1n. Judo | 10 | 10 |
| 756 | 2n. Putting the shot | 25 | 25 |
| 757 | 4n. Type **97** | 55 | 50 |
| 758 | 7n. Basketball (vert) | 95 | 85 |
| 759 | 8n. Football (vert) | 1·10 | 95 |
| 760 | 9n. High jumping (vert) | 1·30 | 1·10 |
| 761 | 20n. Running (vert) | 2·75 | 2·50 |
| **MS**762 | Two sheets. (a) 109×79 mm. 25n. Fencing. (b) 79×109 mm. 25n. Archery (vert) | 7·00 | 7·00 |

**1989.** "Fukuoka '89" Asia-Pacific Exhibition. Nos. 598/606 optd ASIA-PACIFIC EXPOSITION FUKUOKA '89.

| | | | |
|---|---|---|---|
| 763 | 5ch. multicoloured | 10 | 10 |
| 764 | 35ch. multicoloured | 10 | 10 |
| 765 | 50ch. multicoloured | 10 | 10 |
| 766 | 2n.50 multicoloured | 25 | 25 |
| 767 | 3n. multicoloured | 40 | 35 |
| 768 | 4n. multicoloured | 50 | 45 |
| 769 | 5n. multicoloured | 60 | 55 |

770 5n.50 multicoloured 75 65
771 6n. multicoloured 85 80

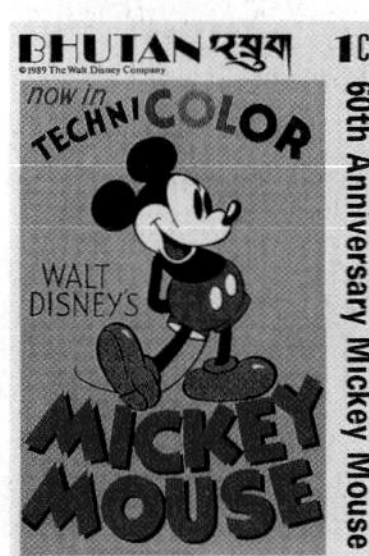


**99** Mickey Mouse

**1989.** 60th Anniv of Mickey Mouse. Film Posters. Multicoloured.

772 1ch. Type **99** 15 15
773 2ch. "Barnyard Olympics" 15 15
774 3ch. "Society Dog Show" 15 15
775 4ch. "Fantasia" 15 15
776 5ch. "The Mad Dog" 15 15
777 10ch. "A Gentleman's Gentleman" 15 15
778 50ch. "Symphony hour" 15 15
779 10n. "The Moose Hunt" 1·50 1·50
780 15n. "Wild Waves" 2·30 2·30
781 20n. "Mickey in Arabia" 3·25 3·25
782 25n. "Tugboat Mickey" 3·75 3·75
783 30n. "Building a Building" 4·75 4·75

**MS**784 12 sheets, each 127×101 mm. (a) 25n. *The Klondike Kid*; (b) 25n. "The Mad Doctoe" (c) 25n. "The Meller Drammer"; (d) 25n. "Mickey's Good Deed"; (e) 25n. "Mickey's Nightmare"; (f) 25n. "Mickey's Pal Pluto"; (g) 25n. "Steamboat Willie"; (h) 25n. "Touchdown Mickey"; (i) 25n. "Trader Mickey"; (j) 25n. "The Wayward Canary"; (k) 25n. "The Whoopee Party"; (l) 25n. "Ye Olden Days" 42·00 42·00

**100** "Tricholoma pardalotum"

**1989.** Fungi. Multicoloured.

785 50ch. Type **100** 10 10
786 1n. "Suillus placidus" 10 10
787 2n. Royal boletus 25 25
788 3n. "Gomphidius glutinosus" 45 35
789 4n. Scarlet-stemmed boletus 55 50
790 5n. Elegant boletus 70 65
791 6n. "Boletus appendiculatus" 85 80
792 7n. Griping toadstool 1·10 95
793 10n. "Macrolepiota rhacodes" 1·40 1·30
794 15n. The blusher 2·10 1·90
795 20n. Death cap 2·75 2·50
796 25n. False death cap 3·50 3·25

**MS**797 12 sheets, each 97×68 mm. (a) 25n. "Boletus rhodoxanthus"; (b) 25n.Chanterelle "Chanterelle repdandum"; (c) 25n. "Dentinum repandum"; (d) 25n. Chestnut boletus ("Gyroporus castaneus"); (e) 25n. Indigo boletus ("Gyroporus cyanescens"); (f) 25n. "Hydnum imbricatum"; (g) 25n. Blue leg ("Lepista nuda"); (h) 25n. "Lepista saeva"; (i) 25n. Brown roll-rim ("Paxillus involutus"); (j) 25n. Golden russula ("Russula aurata"); (k) 25n. "Russula olivacea"; (l) 25n. Downy boletus ("Xerocomus subtomentosus") 42·00 42·00

**101** "La Reale" (Spanish galley), 1680

**1989.** 30th Anniv of International Maritime Organization. Multicoloured.

798 50ch. Type **101** 10 10
799 1n. "Turtle" (submarine), 1776 15 15
800 2n. "Charlotte Dundas" (steamship), 1802 30 30
801 3n. "Great Eastern" (paddlesteamer), 1858 50 45
802 4n. H.M.S. "Warrior" (armoured ship), 1862 65 60
803 5n. Mississippi river steamer, 1884 85 75
804 6n. "Preussen" (full-rigged ship), 1902 1·00 90
805 7n. U.S.S. "Arizona" (battleship), 1915 1·20 1·10
806 10n. "Bluenose" (fishing schooner), 1921 1·60 1·50
807 15n. Steam trawler, 1925 2·50 2·20
808 20n. "Liberty" freighter, 1943 3·25 3·00
809 25n. "United States" (liner), 1952 4·00 3·50

**MS**810 12 sheets, each 100×70 mm. (a) 25n. Chinese junk, 1988; (b) 25n. "U.S.S. Constitution" (frigate); (c) 25n. VIIC type U-boat, 1942; (d) 25n. "Cutty Sark" (clipper), 1869; (e) 25n. H.M.S. "Dreadnought" (battleship), 1906; (f) 25n. U.S.S. "Monitor" (ironclad), 1862; (g) 25n. Moran Company tug, 1950; (h) 25n. "Normandie" (French liner), 1933; (i) 25n. H.M.S. "Resolution" (Capt. Cook); (j) 25n. "Titanic" (liner), 1912; (k) 25n. H.M.S. "Victory" (ship of the line), 1805; (l) 25n. "Yamato" (Japanese battleship), 1944 42·00 42·00

**102** Nehru

**1989.** Birth Centenary of Jawaharlal Nehru (Indian statesman).

811 **102** 1n. brown 30 30

No. 811 is erroneously inscribed "ch".

**103** Greater Flamed-backed Woodpecker

**1989.** Birds. Multicoloured.

812 50ch. Type **103** 10 10
813 1n. Black-naped blue monarch ("Black–naped Monarch") 15 15
814 2n. White-crested laughing thrush 30 30
815 3n. Blood pheasant 50 45
816 4n. Plum-headed ("Blossom-headed") parakeet 65 60
817 5n. Rosy minivet 85 75
818 6n. Chestnut-headed fulvetta ("Tit-Babbler") (horiz) 1·00 90
819 7n. Blue pitta (horiz) 1·20 1·10
820 10n. Black-naped oriole (horiz) 1·60 1·50
821 15n. Green magpie (horiz) 2·50 2·20
822 20n. Three-toed kingfisher ("Indian Three-toed Kingfisher") (horiz) 3·25 3·00
823 25n. Ibis bill (horiz) 4·00 3·50

**MS**824 12 sheets, each 76×104 mm (vert designs) or 104×76 mm (horiz). (a) 25n. Fire-tailed sunbird; (b) 25n. Crested tree swift (inscr "Indian Crested Swift"); (c) 25n. Greater (inscr "Large") racket-tailed drongo; (d) 25n. Little spider hunter; (e) 25n. Blue-backed fairy bluebird (horiz); (f) 25n. Great Indian (inscr "Pied") hornbill (horiz); (g) 25n. Red-legged (inscr "Himalayan Redbreasted") falconet (horiz); (h) 25n. Lammergeier (horiz); (i) 25n. Satyr tragopan (horiz); (j) 25n. Spotted forktail (horiz); (k) 25n. Wallcreeper (horiz); (l) 25n. White eared-pheasant (wrongly inscr "White-eared") (horiz) 42·00 42·00

**104** "Best Friend of Charleston", 1830, U.S.A.

**1990.** Steam Railway Locomotives. Mult.

825 50ch. Type **104** 10 10
826 1n. Class U locomotive, 1948, France 10 10
827 2n. Consolidation locomotive, 1866, U.S.A. 25 25
828 3n. Luggage engine, 1843, Great Britain 45 35
829 4n. Class 60-3 Shay locomotive No. 18, 1913, U.S.A. 55 50
830 5n. "John Bull", 1831, U.S.A. 70 65
831 6n. "Hercules", 1837, U.S.A. 85 80
832 7n. Locomotive No. 947, 1874, Great Britain 1·10 95
833 10n. "Illinois", 1852, U.S.A. 1·40 1·30
834 15n. Class O5 locomotive, 1935, Germany 2·10 1·90
835 20n. Standard locomotive, 1865, U.S.A. 2·75 2·50
836 25n. Class Ps-4 locomotive, 1936, U.S.A. 3·50 3·25

**MS**837 12 sheets, each 74×100 mm (horiz designs) or 100×74 mm (vert). (a) 25n. "The Cumberland" (U.S.A., 1845); (b) 25n. "Ariel" (U.S.A., 1877); (c) 25n. No. 22 Baldwin locomotive (U.S.A., 1873); (d) 25n. Class "A" (U.S.A., 1935) (vert); (e) 25n. Class "K-36" (U.S.A., 1923); (f) 25n. No. 999 "Empire State Express" (U.S.A., 1893); (g) 25n. "John Stevens" (U.S.A., 1849) (vert); (h) 25n. Class "A4" (Great Britain, 1935) (vert); (i) 25n. "Puffing Billy" (Great Britain, 1814) (vert); (j) 25n. "The Rocket" (Great Britain, 1829) (vert); (k) 25n. Class "P-1" (U.S.A., 1943) (vert); (l) 25n. No. 1301 Webb compound engine (Great Britain, 1889) 42·00 42·00

**105** "Charaxes harmodius"

**1990.** Butterflies. Multicoloured.

838 50ch. Type **105** 10 10
839 1n. "Prioneris thestylis" 10 10
840 2n. Eastern courtier 25 25
841 3n. "Penthema lisarda" (horiz) 45 35
842 4n. Golden birdwing 55 50
843 5n. Great nawab 70 65
844 6n. "Polyura dolon" (horiz) 85 80
845 7n. Tailed labyrinth (horiz) 1·10 95
846 10n. "Delias descombesi" 1·40 1·30
847 15n. "Childreni childrena" (horiz) 2·10 1·90
848 20n. Leaf butterfly (horiz) 2·75 2·50
849 25n. "Elymnias malelas" (horiz) 3·50 3·25

**MS**850 12 sheets, each 110×80 mm. (a) 25n. Bhutan glory; (b) 25n. Blue (inscr "Blue Banded") peacock; (c) 25n. Camberwell beauty; (d) 25n. Chequered swallowtail; (e) 25n. Chestnut tiger; (f) 25n. Common birdwing; (g) 25n. Common map butterfly; (h) 25n. Common (inscr "Great") eggfly; (i) 25n. Jungle glory; (j) 25n. Kaiser-i-hind; (k) 25n. Red lacewing; (l) 25n. Swallowtail 42·00 42·00

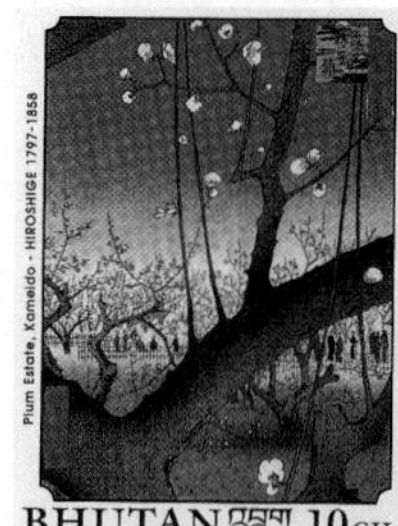


**107** "Plum Estate, Kameido"

**108** Thimphu Post Office

**109** Giant Panda

**106** "Renanthera monachica"

**1990.** "Expo '90" International Garden and Greenery Exposition, Osaka. Orchids. Mult.

851 10ch. Type **106** 10 10
852 50ch. "Vanda coerulea" 10 10
853 1n. "Phalaenopsis violacea" 15 15
854 2n. "Dendrobium nobile" 30 25
855 5n. "Vandopsis lissochiloides" 60 55
856 6n. "Paphiopedilum rothschildianum" 85 75
857 7n. "Phalaenopsis schilleriana" 1·00 90
858 9n. "Paphiopedilum insigne" 1·30 1·10
859 10n. "Paphiopedilum bellatulum" 1·40 1·30
860 20n. "Doritis pulcherrima" 2·75 2·50
861 25n. "Cymbidium giganteum" 4·25 3·25
862 35n. "Phalaenopsis mariae" 5·00 4·75

**MS**863 12 sheets, each 111×84 mm. (a) 30n. "Dendrobium aphyllum"; (b) 30n. "Dendrobium loddigesii"; (c) 30n. "Dendrobium margaritaceum"; (d) 30n. "Paphlopedilum haynaldianum"; (e) 30n. "Paphiopedilum niveum"; (f) 30n. "Phalaenopsis amabilis"; (g) 30n. "Phalaenopsis cornu-cervi"; (h) 30n"Phalaenopsis equestris"; (i) 30n. "Vanda alpine"; (j) 30n. "Vanda coerulescens"; (k) 30n. "Vanda cristata"; (l) 30n. "Vandopsis parishi" 50·00 50·00

**1990.** Death of Emperor Hirohito and Accession of Emperor Akihito of Japan. "100 Famous Views of Edo" by Ando Hiroshige. Multicoloured.

864 10ch. Type **107** 10 10
865 20ch. "Yatsumi Bridge" 10 10
866 50ch. "Ayase River and Kanegafuchi" 10 10
867 75ch. "View of Shiba Coast" 10 10
868 1n. "Grandpa's Teahouse, Meguro" 15 15
869 2n. "Inside Kameido Tenjin Shrine" 25 25
870 6n. "Yoroi Ferry, Koami-cho" 90 80
871 7n. "Sakasai Ferry" 1·10 95
872 10n. "Fukagawa Lumberyards" 1·50 1·40
873 15n. "Suido Bridge and Surugadai" 2·40 2·10
874 20n. "Meguro Drum Bridge and Sunset Hill" 3·00 2·75
875 25n. "Atagoshita and Yabu Lane" 3·75 3·25

**MS**876 12 sheets, each 102×76 mm. (a) 25n. "The City Flourishing, Tanabata Festival"; (b) 25n. "Fukagawa Susaki and Jumantsubo"; (c) 25n. "Horikiri Iris Garden"; (d) 25n. "Komakata Hall and Azuma Bridge"; (e) 25n. "Minowa, Kanasugi, Mikawashima"; (f) 25n. "New Year's Eve Foxfires at the Changing Tree, Oji"; (g) 25n. "Nihonbashi, Clearing after Snow"; (h) 25n. "Sudden Shower over Shin-Ohashi Bridge and Atake"; (i) 25n. "Suijin Shrine and Massaki on the Sumida River"; (j) 25n. "Suruga-cho"; (k) 25n. "Towboats along the Yotsugi-dori Canal"; (l) 25n. "View to the North from Asukayama" 42·00 38·00

**1990**

877 **108** 1n. multicoloured 15 15

**1990.** Mammals. Multicoloured.

878 50ch. Type **109** 10 10
879 1n. Giant panda in tree 15 15
880 2n. Giant panda with cub 30 30
881 3n. Giant panda (horiz) 50 45
882 4n. Giant panda eating (horiz) 65 60
883 5n. Tiger (horiz) 85 75
884 6n. Giant pandas pulling up bamboo (horiz) 1·00 90
885 7n. Giant panda and cub resting (horiz) 1·20 1·10
886 10n. Indian elephant (horiz) 1·60 1·50
887 15n. Giant panda beside fallen tree 2·50 2·20
888 20n. Indian muntjac (inscr "Barking deer") (horiz) 3·25 3·00

889 25n. Snow leopard (horiz) 4·00 3·50

**MS**890 12 sheets, each 100×73 mm. (a) 25n. Asiatic black bear; (b) 25n. Dhole (inscr "Asiatic wild dog"); (c) 25n. Clouded leopard; (d) 25n. Gaur; (e) 25n. Giant panda; (f) 25n. Golden cat; (g) 25n. Siberian musk deer (inscr "Himalayan"); (h) 25n. Redd deer (inscr "Himalayan shou"); (i) 25n. Pygmy hog; (j) 25n. Indian rhinoceros; (k) 25n. Sloth bear; (l) 25n. Wolf 45·00 45·00

**110** Roim

**1990.** Religious Musical Instruments. Mult.

891 10ch. Dungchen (large trumpets) 10 10
892 20ch. Dungkar (Indian chank shell) 10 10
893 30ch. Type **110** 10 10
894 50ch. Tinchag (cup cymbals) 10 10
895 1n. Dradu and drilbu (pellet drum and hand bell) 10 10
896 2n. Gya-ling (oboes) 20 15
897 2n.50 Nga (drum) 30 25
898 3n.50 Kang-dung (trumpets) 35 35

**MS**899 Two sheets, each 92×135 mm. (a) Nos. 891, 893, 895 and 898; (b) Nos. 892, 894 and 896/7 1·75 1·75

**111** Penny Black and Bhutan 1962 2ch. Stamp

**1990.** "Stamp World London 90" International Stamp Exhibition. 150th Anniv of the Penny Black. Multicoloured.

900 50ch. Type **111** 10 10
901 1n. Oldenburg 1852 1/30th. stamp 15 15
902 2n. Bergedorf 1861 1½s. stamp 25 25
903 4n. German Democratic Republic 1949 50pf. stamp 50 45
904 5n. Brunswick 1852 1 sgr. stamp 60 55
905 6n. Basel 1845 2½r. stamp 85 75
906 8n. Geneva 1843 5c.+5c. stamp 1·10 1·00
907 10n. Zurich 1843 4r. stamp 1·40 1·30
908 15n. France 1849 20c. stamp 2·10 1·90
909 20n. Vatican City 1929 5c. stamp 2·75 2·50
910 25n. Israel 1948 3m. stamp 3·50 3·25
911 30n. Japan 1871 48m. stamp 4·25 3·75

**MS**912 12 sheets, each 106×76 mm. (a) 15n. Baden 1851 1k. stamp, 15n. Wurttemberg 1851 1k. stamp; (b) 15n. Germany 1872 3k. and 2g. stamps, 15n. Prussia 1850 6pf. stamp; (c) 15n. Hamburg 1859 ½s. stamp, 15n. North German Confederation 1868 ¼g. and 1k. stamps; (d) 15n. Heligoland 1867 ½ch. stamp, 15n. Hanover 1850 1ggr. stamp; (e) 15n. Schleswig-Holstein 1850 1s. stamp; 15n. Lubeck 1859 4s. stamp; (f) 15n. Mecklenburg-Schwerin 1856 4/4s. stamp, 15n. Mecklenburg-Strelitz 1864 ¼sgr. stamp; (g) 15n. Thurn and Taxis (Northern District) 1852 ½sgr. stamp, 15n. Thurn and Taxis (Southern District) 1852 1k. stamp; (h) 30n. Bavaria 1849 1k. stamp; (i) 30n. West Berlin 1948 2pf. stamp; (j) 30n. Great Britain 1840 Penny Black; (k) 30n. Saxony 1850 3pf. stamp; (l) 30n. United States 1847 5c. stamp 48·00 48·00

Each value also depicts the Penny Black. No. 901 is wrongly inscribed "Oldenberg".

**112** Girls

**1990.** South Asian Association for Regional Co-operation Girl Child Year. Multicoloured.

913 50ch. Type **112** 20 20
914 20n. Girl 2·75 2·40

**113** Temple of Artemis, Ephesus

**1991.** Wonders of the World. Designs featuring Walt Disney cartoon characters. Multicoloured.

915 1ch. Type **113** 10 10
916 2ch. Statue of Zeus, Olympia 10 10
917 3ch. Pyramids of Egypt 10 10
918 4ch. Lighthouse of Alexandria, Egypt 10 10
919 5ch. Mausoleum, Halicarnassus 10 10
920 10ch. Colossus of Rhodes 10 10
921 50ch. Hanging Gardens of Babylon 10 10
922 5n. Mauna Loa Volcanoes, Hawaii (horiz) 70 65
923 6n. Carlsbad Caverns, New Mexico (horiz) 90 80
924 10n. Rainbow Bridge National Monument, Utah (horiz) 1·50 1·40
925 15n. Grand Canyon, Colorado (horiz) 3·25 1·90
926 20n. Old Faithful, Yellowstone National Park, Wyoming (horiz) 2·75 2·50
927 25n. Sequoia National Park, California (horiz) 3·75 3·25
928 30n. Crater Lake and Wizard Island, Oregon (horiz) 4·50 4·00

**MS**929 14 sheets, each 127×101 mm. (a) 25n. Alcan Highway, Alaska and Canada (horiz); (b) 25n. Catacombs of Alexandria; (c) 25n. Sears Tower, Chicago, Illinois (horiz); (d) 25n. Great Wall of China (horiz); (e) 25n. St. Sophia's Mosque, Constantinople; (f) 25n. Porcelain Tower, Nanking, China (horiz); (g) 25n. Hoover Dam, Nevada; (h) 25n. Empire State Building, New York City; (i) 25n. Panama Canal (horiz); (j) 25n. Leaning Tower of Pisa; (k) 25n. Colosseum Rome; (l) 25n. Gateway Arch, St. Louis, Missouri; (m) 25n. Golden Gate Bridge, San Francisco (horiz); (n) 25n. Stonehenge 42·00 42·00

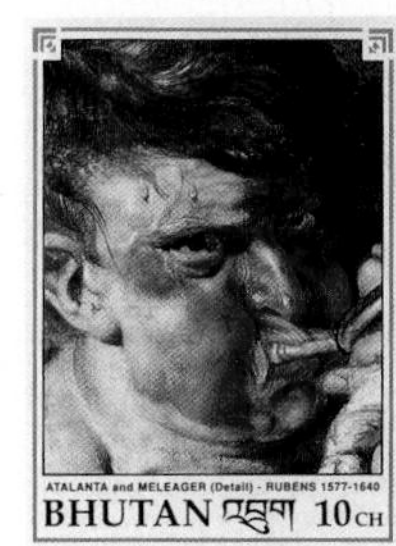


**114** "Atalanta and Meleager" (detail)

**1991.** 350th Death Anniv (1990) of Peter Paul Rubens (painter). Multicoloured.

930 10ch. Type **114** 10 10
931 50ch. "The Fall of Phaeton" (detail) 10 10
932 1n. "Feast of Venus Verticordia" (detail) 15 15
933 2n. "Achilles slaying Hector" (detail) 35 30
934 3n. "Arachne punished by Minerva" (detail) 50 35
935 4n. "Jupiter receives Psyche on Olympus" (detail) 75 55
936 5n. "Atalanta and Meleager" (different detail) 90 85
937 6n. "Atalanta and Meleager" (different detail) 1·10 1·00
938 7n. "Venus in Vulcan's Furnace" (detail) 1·30 1·20
939 10n. "Atalanta and Meleager" (different detail) 1·70 1·60
940 20n. "Briseis returned to Achilles" (detail) 3·50 3·25
941 30n. "Mars and Rhea Sylvia" (detail) 5·00 4·50

**MS**942 12 sheets, each 72×101 mm (a/e) or 101×72 mm (f/l). (a) 25n. "Atlanta and Meleager"; (b) 25n. "Feast of Venus Verticordia"; (c) 25n. "Ganymede and the Eagle"; (d) 25n. "Jupiter receives Psyche on Olympus"; (e) 25n. "Venus shivering"; (f) 25n. "Adonis and Venus" (horiz); (g) 25n. "Arachne punished by Minerva" (horiz); (h) 25n. "Briseis returned to Achilles" (horiz); (i) 25n. "The Fall of the Titans" (horiz); (j) 25n. "Hero and Leander" (horiz); (k) 25n. "Mars and Rhea Sylvia" (horiz); (l) 25n. "The Origin of the Milky Way" (horiz) 48·00 48·00

**115** "Cottages, Reminiscence of the North"

**1991.** Death Centenary (1990) of Vincent van Gogh (painter). Multicoloured.

943 10ch. Type **115** 10 10
944 50ch. "Head of a Peasant Woman with Dark Cap" 10 10
945 1n. "Portrait of a Woman in Blue" 15 15
946 2n. "Head of an Old Woman with White Cap (the Midwife)" 45 35
947 8n. "Vase with Hollyhocks" 1·20 1·10
948 10n. "Portrait of a Man with a Skull Cap" 1·40 1·30
949 12n. "Agostina Segatori sitting in the Cafe du Tambourin" 1·80 1·60
950 15n. "Vase with Daisies and Anemones" 2·20 2·00
951 18n. "Fritillaries in a Copper Vase" 2·75 2·40
952 20n. "Woman sitting in the Grass" 3·00 2·75
953 25n. "On the Outskirts of Paris" (horiz) 3·50 3·25
954 30n. "Chrysanthemums and Wild Flowers in a Vase" 4·25 3·75

**MS**955 12 sheets, each 76×101 mm (a/h) or 101×76 mm (i/l). (a) 30n. "Le Moulin de Blute-Fin"; (b) 30n. "Le Moulin de la Galette"; (c) 30n. "Le Moulin de la Galette" (with man in foreground); (d) 30n. "Poppies and Butterflies"; (e) 30n. "Trees in the Garden of St. Paul Hospital"; (f) 30n. "Vase with Peonies"; (g) 30n. "Vase with Red Poppies"; (h) 30n. "Vase with Zinnias"; (i) 30n. "Bowl with Sunflowers, Roses and Other Flowers" (horiz); (j) 30n. "Fishing in the Spring, Pont de Clichy" (horiz); (k) 30n. "Vase with Zinnias and Other Flowers" (horiz); (l) 30n. "Village Street in Auvers" (horiz) 48·00 48·00

**116** Winning Uruguay Team, 1930

**1991.** World Cup Football Championship. Mult.

956 50ch. Type **116** 10 10
957 1n. Italy, 1934 15 15
958 2n. Italy, 1938 25 20
959 3n. Uruguay, 1950 45 30
960 5n. West Germany, 1954 70 65
961 10n. Brazil, 1958 1·40 1·30
962 20n. Brazil, 1962 2·75 2·50
963 25n. England, 1966 3·50 3·25
964 29n. Brazil, 1970 4·00 3·50
965 30n. West Germany, 1974 4·25 3·75
966 31n. Argentina, 1978 4·25 3·75
967 32n. Italy, 1982 4·50 4·00
968 33n. Argentina, 1986 4·50 4·00
969 34n. West Germany, 1990 4·50 4·00
970 35n. Stadium, Los Angeles (venue for 1994 World Cup) 4·50 4·00

**MS**971 6 sheets, each 105×120 mm. (a) 30n. Roberto Baggio, Italy (vert); (b) 30n. Claudio Canniggia, Argentina (vert); (c) 30n. Paul Gascoigne, England (vert); (d) 30n. Lothar Matthaus, West Germany (vert); (e) 30n. Salvatore Schillaci, Italy (vert); (f) 30n. Peter Shilton, England 24·00 24·00

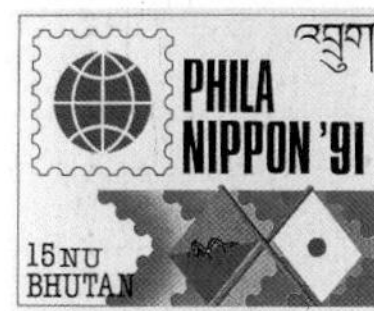


**117** Bhutan and Japan State Flags

**1991.** "Phila Nippon '91" International Stamp Exhibition, Tokyo.

972 **117** 15n. multicoloured 2·10 1·80

**118** Teachers, Pupils and Hemisphere

**1992.** "Education for All by Year 2000".

973 **118** 1n. multicoloured 10 10

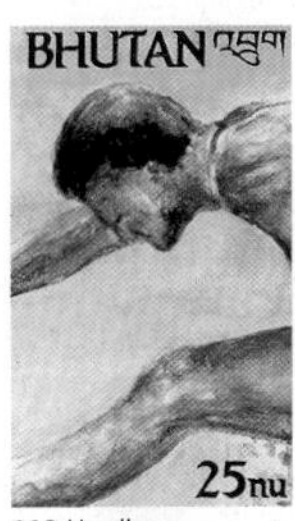


**119** Hurdler

**1992.** Olympic Games, Barcelona. Mult.

974 25n. Type **119** 3·25 3·25
975 25n. Body of hurdler 3·25 3·25
**MS**976 110×75 mm. 25n. Archery 4·75 4·75

Nos. 974/5 were issued together, se-tenant, forming a composite design.

**120** "Santa Maria"

**1992.** 500th Anniv of Discovery of America by Columbus. Multicoloured.

977 15n. Type **120** 1·10 1·10
978 20n. Columbus 1·40 1·40

**MS**979 78×118 mm. 25n. As No. 978 but without inscription at top (27×43 mm) 2·00 2·00

**121** Brandenburg Gate and rejoicing Couple

**1992.** 2nd Anniv of Reunification of Germany.

980 **121** 25n. multicoloured 1·80 1·80

**MS**981 110×82 mm. 25n. As No. 980 but without inscription at top (43×27 mm) 1·80 1·80

**122** British Aerospace BAe 146 and Post Van

**1992.** 30th Anniv of Bhutan Postal Organization. Multicoloured.

982 1n. Type **122** 10 10
983 3n. Rural letter courier 25 25
984 5n. Emptying post box 40 40

123 Industry and Agriculture

**1992.** 20th Anniv of Accession of King Jigme Singye Wangchuck. Multicoloured.

| | | | |
|---|---|---|---|
| 985 | 1n. Type **123** | 15 | 15 |
| 986 | 5n. British Aerospace RJ70 of National Airline | 35 | 35 |
| 987 | 10n. House with water-pump | 65 | 65 |
| 988 | 15n. King Jigme Singye Wangchuk | 1·20 | 1·20 |
| **MS**989 | 94×62 mm. 20n. King, flag and Bhutanese people (43×26 mm) | 1·70 | 1·70 |

Nos. 985/8 were issued together, se-tenant, each horizontal pair within the block forming a composite design.

124 Dragon

**1992.** International Volunteer Day.

| | | | | |
|---|---|---|---|---|
| 990 | 124 | 1n.50 multicoloured | 15 | 15 |
| 991 | 124 | 9n. multicoloured | 65 | 65 |
| 992 | 124 | 15n. multicoloured | 1·20 | 1·20 |

125 "Meconopsis grandis"

**1993.** Medicinal Flowers. Designs showing varieties of the Asiatic Poppy. Multicoloured.

| | | | |
|---|---|---|---|
| 993 | 1n.50 Type **125** | 15 | 15 |
| 994 | 7n. "Meconopsis" sp. | 60 | 60 |
| 995 | 10n. "Meconopsis wallichii" | 75 | 75 |
| 996 | 12n. "Meconopsis horridula" | 1·00 | 1·00 |
| 997 | 20n. "Meconopsis discigera" | 1·70 | 1·70 |
| **MS**998 | 74×107 mm. 25n. "Meconopsis horridula" (different) (27×43 mm) | 2·00 | 2·00 |

126 Rooster and Chinese Signs of the Zodiac (image scaled to 72% of original size)

**1993.** New Year. Year of the Water Rooster. Sheet 89×89 mm.

| | | | |
|---|---|---|---|
| **MS**999 | **126** 25n. multicoloured | 1·90 | 1·90 |

127 "The Love Letter" (Jean Honore Fragonard)

**1993.** Paintings. Multicoloured.

| | | | |
|---|---|---|---|
| 1000 | 1ch. Type **127** (postage) | 15 | 15 |
| 1001 | 2ch. "The Writer" (Vittore Carpaccio) | 15 | 15 |
| 1002 | 3ch. "Mademoiselle Lavergne" (Jean Etienne Liotard) | 15 | 15 |
| 1003 | 5ch. "Portrait of Erasmus" (Hans Holbein) | 15 | 15 |
| 1004 | 10ch. "Woman writing a Letter" (Gerard Terborch) | 15 | 15 |
| 1005 | 15ch. Type **127** | 15 | 15 |
| 1006 | 25ch. As No. 1001 | 15 | 15 |
| 1007 | 50ch. As No. 1002 | 15 | 15 |
| 1008 | 60ch. As No. 1003 | 15 | 15 |
| 1009 | 80ch. As No. 1004 | 15 | 15 |
| 1010 | 1n. Type **127** | 15 | 15 |
| 1011 | 1n.25 As No. 1001 | 15 | 15 |
| 1012 | 2n. As No. 1002 (air) | 15 | 15 |
| 1013 | 3n. As No. 1003 | 15 | 15 |
| 1014 | 6n. As No. 1004 | 15 | 15 |
| **MS**1015 | 135×97 mm. As Nos. 1012/14 but with copper borders | 1·70 | 1·70 |

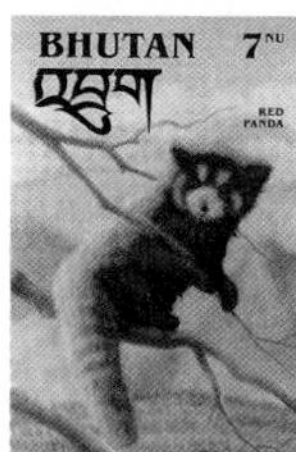

128 Lesser Panda

**1993.** Environmental Protection. Multicoloured.

| | | | |
|---|---|---|---|
| 1016 | 7n. Type **128** | 60 | 60 |
| 1017 | 10n. One-horned rhinoceros | 85 | 85 |
| 1018 | 15n. Black-necked crane and blue poppy | 1·20 | 1·20 |
| 1019 | 20n. Takin | 1·50 | 1·50 |

Nos. 1016/19 were issued together, se-tenant, forming a composite design.

**1993.** "Taipei'93" International Stamp Exhibition, Taiwan. No. MS999 surch TAIPEI'93 NU 30.

| | | | |
|---|---|---|---|
| **MS**1020 | **126** 30n. on 25n. multicoloured | 2·40 | 2·40 |

130 Namtheo-say

**1993.** Door Gods. Multicoloured.

| | | | |
|---|---|---|---|
| 1021 | 1n.50 Type **130** | 10 | 15 |
| 1022 | 5n. Pha-ke-po | 40 | 40 |
| 1023 | 10n. Chen-mi Jang | 80 | 80 |
| 1024 | 15n. Yul-khor-sung | 1·20 | 1·20 |

131 "Rhododendron mucronatum"

**1994.** Flowers. Multicoloured.

| | | | |
|---|---|---|---|
| 1025 | 1n. Type **131** | 15 | 15 |
| 1026 | 1n.50 "Anemone rupicola" | 15 | 15 |
| 1027 | 2n. "Polemonium coeruleum" | 15 | 15 |
| 1028 | 2n.50 "Rosa marophylla" | 15 | 15 |
| 1029 | 4n. "Paraquilegia microphylla" | 35 | 35 |
| 1030 | 5n. "Aquilegia nivalis" | 40 | 40 |
| 1031 | 6n. "Geranium wallichianum" | 50 | 50 |
| 1032 | 7n. "Rhododendron campanulatum" (wrongly inscr "Rhodendron") | 60 | 60 |
| 1033 | 9n. "Viola suavis" | 75 | 75 |
| 1034 | 10n. "Cyananthus lobatus" | 90 | 90 |
| **MS**1035 | 126×86 mm. 13n. Lily (horiz) | 1·00 | 1·00 |

132 Dog

**1994.** New Year. Year of the Dog. "Hong Kong '94" International Stamp Exhibition.

| | | | | |
|---|---|---|---|---|
| 1036 | 132 | 11n.50 multicoloured | 80 | 80 |
| **MS**1037 | | 118×178 mm. **132** 20n. multicoloured | 1·50 | 1·50 |

133 Trophy and Mascot

**1994.** World Cup Football Championship, U.S.A.

| | | | | |
|---|---|---|---|---|
| 1038 | 133 | 15n. multicoloured | 80 | 80 |

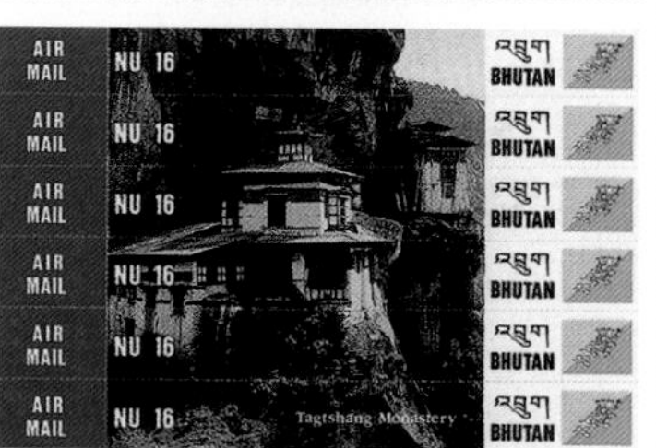

134 Tagtshang Monastery (image scaled to 57% of original size)

135 Relief Map of Bhutan (image scaled to 58% of original size)

**1994.** Air. Self-adhesive.

| | | | | |
|---|---|---|---|---|
| 1039 | 134 | 16n. multicoloured | 85 | 85 |
| 1040 | 135 | 20n. multicoloured | 1·00 | 1·00 |

The individual stamps are peeled directly from the card backing. Each card contains six different designs with the same face value forming the composite designs illustrated. Each stamp is a horizontal strip with a label indicating the main class of mail covered by the rate at the left, separated by a vertical line of rouletting. The outer edges of the cards are imperforate.

136 Tower Bridge, London (centenary)

**1994.** Bridges. Sheet 160×101 mm containing T 136 and similar horiz design. Multicoloured.

| | | | |
|---|---|---|---|
| **MS**1041 | 15n. Type **136**; 16n. "Wangdur Bridge, Bhutan" (Samuel Davies) (250th anniv) | 1·60 | 1·60 |

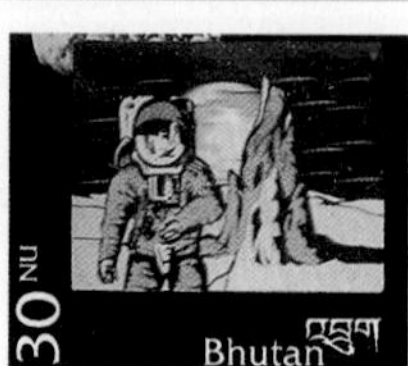

137 Astronaut on Moon

**1994.** 25th Anniv of First Manned Moon Landing. Sheet 114×57 mm containing T 137 and similar horiz design. Multicoloured.

| | | | |
|---|---|---|---|
| **MS**1042 | 30n. Type **137**; 36n. Space shuttle | 3·50 | 3·50 |

138 Horseman with raised Sword

**1994.** 350th Anniv of Victory over Tibet-Mongol Army. Multicoloured.

| | | | |
|---|---|---|---|
| 1043 | 15n. Type **138** | 80 | 80 |
| 1044 | 15n. Archers and hand-to-hand sword fighting | 80 | 80 |
| 1045 | 15n. Horseman with insignia on helmet amongst infantry | 80 | 80 |
| 1046 | 15n. Drummer, piper and troops | 80 | 80 |

Nos. 1043/6 were issued together, se-tenant, forming a composite design of a battle scene and the Drugyel Dzong.

139 Paro Valley

**1995.** World Tourism Year. Sheet 111×92 mm containing T **139** and similar horiz designs. Multicoloured.

| | | | |
|---|---|---|---|
| **MS**1047 | 1n.50 Type **139**; 5n. Chorton Kora; 10n. Thimphu Tshechu; 15n. Wangdue Tshechu | 2·40 | 2·40 |

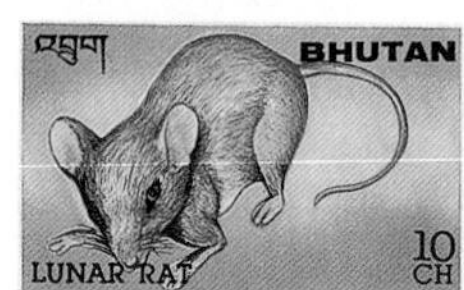

140 Lunar Rat

**1995.** New Year. Year of the Boar. Mult.

| | | | |
|---|---|---|---|
| 1048 | 10ch. Type **140** | 15 | 15 |
| 1049 | 20ch. Lunar ox | 15 | 15 |
| 1050 | 30ch. Lunar tiger | 15 | 15 |
| 1051 | 40ch. Lunar rabbit | 15 | 15 |
| 1052 | 1n. Lunar dragon | 15 | 15 |
| 1053 | 2n. Lunar snake | 15 | 15 |
| 1054 | 3n. Lunar horse | 15 | 15 |
| 1055 | 4n. Lunar sheep | 15 | 15 |
| 1056 | 5n. Lunar monkey | 15 | 15 |
| 1057 | 7n. Lunar rooster | 25 | 25 |
| 1058 | 8n. Lunar dog | 35 | 35 |
| 1059 | 9n. Lunar boar | 40 | 40 |
| **MS**1060 | 111×92 mm. 10n. Wood hogs | 55 | 55 |

141 "Pleione praecox"

**1995.** Flowers. Multicoloured.

| | | | |
|---|---|---|---|
| 1061 | 9n. Type **141** | 50 | 50 |
| 1062 | 10n. "Primula calderina" | 60 | 60 |
| 1063 | 16n. "Primula whitei" | 1·00 | 1·00 |
| 1064 | 18n. "Notholirion macrophyllum" | 1·10 | 1·10 |

142 Human Resources Development

**1995.** 50th Anniv of UNO. Multicoloured.

| | | | |
|---|---|---|---|
| 1065 | 1n.50 Type **142** | 15 | 15 |
| 1066 | 5n. Transport and Communications | 35 | 35 |
| 1067 | 9n. Health and Population | 50 | 50 |
| 1068 | 10n. Water and Sanitation | 60 | 60 |
| 1069 | 11n.50 UN in Bhutan | 65 | 65 |
| 1070 | 16n. Forestry and Environment | 90 | 90 |
| 1071 | 18n. Peace and Security | 1·00 | 1·00 |

143 Greater Pied Kingfisher ("Himalayan Pied Kingfisher")

**1995.** "Singapore '95" International Stamp Exhibition. Birds. Multicoloured.

| | | | |
|---|---|---|---|
| 1072 | 1n. Type **143** | 15 | 15 |
| 1073 | 2n. Blyth's tragopan | 15 | 15 |
| 1074 | 3n. Long-tailed minivets | 15 | 15 |
| 1075 | 10n. Red junglefowl | 60 | 60 |
| 1076 | 15n. Black-capped sibia | 85 | 85 |
| 1077 | 20n. Red-billed chough | 1·00 | 1·00 |
| **MS**1078 | 73×97 mm. 20n. Black-necked crane | 1·10 | 1·10 |

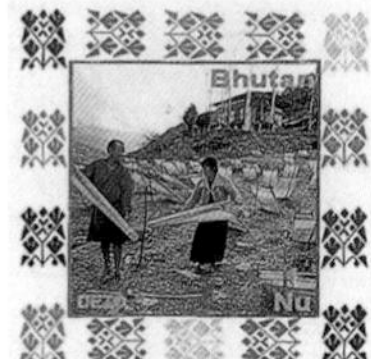


144 Making Paper

**1995.** Traditional Crafts. Multicoloured.

| | | | |
|---|---|---|---|
| 1079 | 1n. Type **144** | 15 | 15 |
| 1080 | 2n. Religious painting | 15 | 15 |
| 1081 | 3n. Clay sculpting | 15 | 15 |
| 1082 | 10n. Weaving | 60 | 60 |
| 1083 | 15n. Making boots | 85 | 85 |
| 1084 | 20n. Carving wooden bowls | 1·00 | 1·00 |
| **MS**1085 | 121×82 mm. 20n. Decorative carvings on wooden buildings | 1·00 | 1·00 |

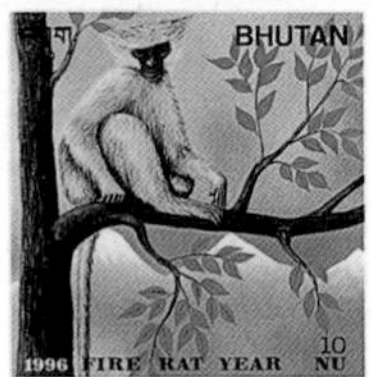


145 Golden Langer

**1996.** New Year. Year of the Rat. Sheet 111×176 mm containing T 145 and similar square designs. Multicoloured.

| | | | |
|---|---|---|---|
| **MS**1086 | 10n. Type **145**; 10n. Rat; 10n. Dragon | 1·60 | 1·60 |

146 "The White Bird"

**1996.** Folk Tales. Multicoloured.

| | | | |
|---|---|---|---|
| 1087 | 1n. Type **146** | 15 | 15 |
| 1088 | 2n. "Sing Sing Lhamo and the Moon" | 15 | 15 |
| 1089 | 3n. "The Hoopoe" | 15 | 15 |
| 1090 | 5n. "The Cloud Fairies" | 35 | 35 |
| 1091 | 10n. "The Three Wishes" | 60 | 60 |
| 1092 | 20n. "The Abominable Snowman" | 1·10 | 1·10 |
| **MS**1093 | 109×75 mm. 25n. As No. 1090 | 1·70 | 1·70 |

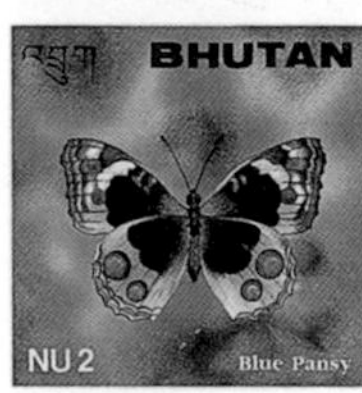


147 Blue Pansy

**1996.** Butterflies. Multicoloured.

| | | | |
|---|---|---|---|
| 1094 | 2n. Type **147** | 15 | 15 |
| 1095 | 3n. Blue peacock | 15 | 15 |
| 1096 | 5n. Great mormon | 25 | 25 |
| 1097 | 10n. Fritillary | 60 | 60 |
| 1098 | 15n. Blue duke | 85 | 85 |
| 1099 | 25n. Brown gorgon | 1·30 | 1·30 |
| **MS**1100 | Two sheets, each 108×75 mm. (a) 30n. Fivebar swordtail; (b) 30n. Xanthomelas | 3·00 | 3·00 |

148 300n. Football Coin

**1996.** Olympic Games, Atlanta. Mult.

| | | | |
|---|---|---|---|
| 1101 | 5n. Type **148** | 25 | 25 |
| 1102 | 7n. 300n. basketball coin | 40 | 40 |
| 1103 | 10n. 5s. judo coin | 60 | 60 |
| **MS**1104 | 102×80 mm. 15n. Archery | 85 | 85 |

149 Standard Goods Locomotive, India

**1996.** Trains. Multicoloured.

| | | | |
|---|---|---|---|
| 1105 | 20n. Type **149** | 1·00 | 1·00 |
| 1106 | 20n. Diesel-electric locomotive, Finland | 1·00 | 1·00 |
| 1107 | 20n. Shunting tank locomotive, Russia | 1·00 | 1·00 |
| 1108 | 20n. Alco PA-1 diesel-electric locomotive, U.S.A. | 1·00 | 1·00 |
| 1109 | 20n. Class C11 passenger tank locomotive, Japan | 1·00 | 1·00 |
| 1110 | 20n. Settebello high speed electric train, Italy | 1·00 | 1·00 |
| 1111 | 20n. Tank locomotive No. 191, Chile | 1·00 | 1·00 |
| 1112 | 20n. Pacific locomotive, France | 1·00 | 1·00 |
| 1113 | 20n. Steam locomotive No. 10, Norway | 1·00 | 1·00 |
| 1114 | 20n. Atlantic express locomotive, Germany | 1·00 | 1·00 |
| 1115 | 20n. Express steam locomotive, Belgium | 1·00 | 1·00 |
| 1116 | 20n. Type 4 diesel-electric locomotive, Great Britain | 1·00 | 1·00 |
| **MS**1117 | Two sheets, each 96×66 mm. (a) 70n. "Hikari" express train, Series 200, Japan; (b) Class KD steam goods locomotive, Sweden | 7·25 | 7·25 |

150 Penny Black

**1996**

| | | | | |
|---|---|---|---|---|
| 1118 | **150** | 140n. gold and black | 7·25 | 7·25 |

151 Vegard Ulvang, Norway

**1997.** Winter Olympic Gold Medallists. Multicoloured. (a) Without frame.

| | | | |
|---|---|---|---|
| 1119 | 10n. Type **151** (30km. cross-country skiing, 1992) | 60 | 60 |
| 1120 | 15n. Kristi Yamaguchi, U.S.A. (women's figure skating, 1992) | 85 | 85 |
| 1121 | 25n. Markus Wasmeier, Germany (men's super giant slalom, 1994) | 1·50 | 1·50 |
| 1122 | 30n. Georg Hackl, Germany (luge, 1992) | 1·70 | 1·70 |

(b) As T 151 but with black frame around design.

| | | | |
|---|---|---|---|
| 1123 | 15n. Andreas Ostler, West Germany (two-man bobsleighing, 1952) | 80 | 80 |
| 1124 | 15n. East German team (four-man bobsleighing, 1984) | 80 | 80 |
| 1125 | 15n. Stein Eriksen, Norway (men's giant slalom, 1952) | 80 | 80 |
| 1126 | 15n. Alberto Tomba, Italy (men's giant slalom, 1988) | 80 | 80 |
| **MS**1127 | Two sheets, each 106×76 mm. (a) 70n. Henri Oreiller, France (men's downhill skiing, 1948); (b) 70n. Swiss team (four-man bobsleighing, 1924) | 7·50 | 7·50 |

152 Bee

**1997.** Insects and Arachnidae. Multicoloured.

| | | | |
|---|---|---|---|
| 1128 | 1ch. Type **152** | 10 | 10 |
| 1129 | 2ch. "Neptunides polychromus" (beetle) | 10 | 10 |
| 1130 | 3ch. "Conocephalus maculctus" (grasshopper) | 10 | 10 |
| 1131 | 4ch. "Blattidae" sp. (beetle) | 10 | 10 |
| 1132 | 5ch. Great diving beetle | 10 | 10 |
| 1133 | 10ch. Hercules beetle | 10 | 10 |
| 1134 | 15ch. Ladybird | 10 | 10 |
| 1135 | 20ch. "Sarcophaga haemorrhoidalis" (fly) | 10 | 10 |
| 1136 | 25ch. Stag beetle | 10 | 10 |
| 1137 | 30ch. Caterpillar | 10 | 10 |
| 1138 | 35ch. "Lycia hirtaria" (moth) | 10 | 10 |
| 1139 | 40ch. "Clytarius pennatus" (beetle) | 10 | 10 |
| 1140 | 45ch. "Ephemera denica" (mayfly) | 10 | 10 |
| 1141 | 50ch. European field cricket | 10 | 10 |
| 1142 | 60ch. Elephant hawk moth | 10 | 10 |
| 1143 | 65ch. "Gerris" sp. (beetle) | 10 | 10 |
| 1144 | 70ch. Banded agrion | 10 | 10 |
| 1145 | 80ch. "Tachyta nana" (beetle) | 10 | 10 |
| 1146 | 90ch. "Eurydema pulchra" (shieldbug) | 10 | 10 |
| 1147 | 1n. "Hadrurus hirsutus" (scorpion) | 10 | 10 |
| 1148 | 1n.50 "Vespa germanica" (wasp) | 10 | 10 |
| 1149 | 2n. "Pyrops" sp. (beetle) | 10 | 10 |
| 1150 | 2n.50 Praying mantis | 10 | 10 |
| 1151 | 3n. "Araneus diadematus" (spider) | 10 | 10 |
| 1152 | 3n.50 "Atrophaneura" sp. (butterfly) | 10 | 10 |
| **MS**1153 | 76×111 mm. 15n. Cockchafer ("Melolontha" sp.) | 1·00 | 1·00 |

153 Polar Bears

**1997.** "Hong Kong '97" International Stamp Exhibition. Multicoloured.

| | | | |
|---|---|---|---|
| 1154 | 10n. Type **153** | 55 | 55 |
| 1155 | 10n. Koalas ("Phascolarctos cinereus") | 55 | 55 |
| 1156 | 10n. Asiatic black bear ("Selenarctos thibetanus") | 55 | 55 |
| 1157 | 10n. Lesser panda ("Ailurus fulgens") | 55 | 55 |
| **MS**1158 | 107×75 mm. 20n. Giant panda ("Ailuropoda melanoleuca") | 1·30 | 1·30 |

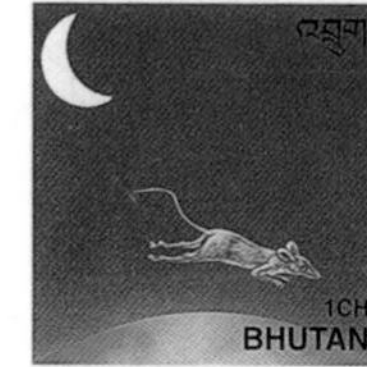


154 Rat

**1997.** New Year. Year of the Ox. Multicoloured.

| | | | |
|---|---|---|---|
| 1159 | 1ch. Type **154** | 15 | 15 |
| 1160 | 2ch. Ox | 15 | 15 |
| 1161 | 3ch. Tiger | 15 | 15 |
| 1162 | 4ch. Rabbit | 15 | 15 |
| 1163 | 90ch. Monkey | 15 | 15 |
| 1164 | 5n. Dragon | 25 | 25 |
| 1165 | 6n. Snake | 35 | 35 |
| 1166 | 7n. Horse | 40 | 40 |
| 1167 | 8n. Ram | 50 | 50 |
| 1168 | 10n. Cock | 65 | 65 |
| 1169 | 11n. Dog | 75 | 75 |
| 1170 | 12n. Boar | 85 | 85 |
| **MS**1171 | 70×66 mm. 20n. Ox | 2·75 | 2·75 |

155 Lynx

**1997.** Endangered Species. Multicoloured.

| | | | |
|---|---|---|---|
| 1172 | 10n. Type **155** | 55 | 55 |
| 1173 | 10n. Lesser ("Red") panda ("Ailurus fulgens") | 55 | 55 |
| 1174 | 10n. Takin ("Budorcas taxicolor") | 55 | 55 |
| 1175 | 10n. Forest musk deer ("Moschus chrysogaster") | 55 | 55 |
| 1176 | 10n. Snow leopard ("Panthera uncia") | 55 | 55 |
| 1177 | 10n. Golden langur ("Presbytis geei") | 55 | 55 |
| 1178 | 10n. Tiger ("Panthera tigris") | 55 | 55 |
| 1179 | 10n. Indian muntjac ("Muntiacus muntjak") | 55 | 55 |
| 1180 | 10n. Bobak marmot ("Marmota bobak") | 55 | 55 |
| 1181 | 10n. Dhole ("Cuon alpinis") running | 55 | 55 |
| 1182 | 10n. Dhole walking | 55 | 55 |
| 1183 | 10n. Mother dhole nursing cubs | 55 | 55 |
| 1184 | 10n. Two dhole | 55 | 55 |
| **MS**1185 | Two sheets, each 106×76 mm. (a) 70n. Bharal ("Pseudois nayaur"); (b) 70n. Asiatic black bear ("Ursus thibetanus") | 7·50 | 7·50 |

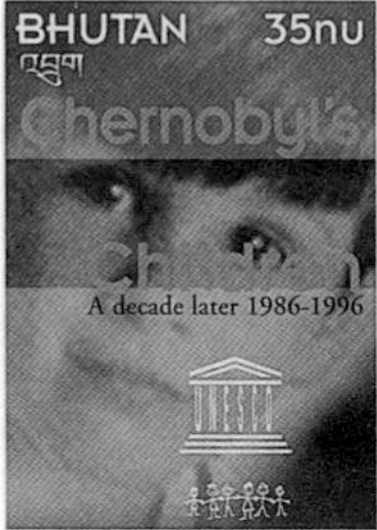


156 Child's Face and UNESCO Emblem

**1997.** 10th Anniv of Chernobyl Nuclear Disaster.

| | | | | |
|---|---|---|---|---|
| 1186 | **156** | 35n. multicoloured | 1·90 | 1·90 |

**157** Mount Huangshah, China

**1997.** 50th Anniv of UNESCO World Heritage Sites. Multicoloured.

1187 10n. Type **157** 65 65
1188 10n. Statue of Emperor Qin, China 65 65
1189 10n. Imperial bronze dragon, China 65 65
1190 10n. Pyramids, Tikal National Park, Guatemala 65 65
1191 10n. Fountain, Evora, Portugal 65 65
1192 10n. Forest path, Shirakami-Sanchi, Japan 65 65
1193 10n. View from Eiffel Tower, Paris, France 65 65
1194 10n. Wooden walkway, Valley Below the Falls, Croatia 65 65
1195 15n. Bamberg Cathedral, Germany 1·00 1·00
1196 15n. Aerial view of Bamberg 1·00 1·00
1197 15n. St. Michael's Church, Hildesheim, Germany 1·00 1·00
1198 15n. Potsdam Palace, Germany 1·00 1·00
1199 15n. Church, Potsdam 1·00 1·00
1200 15n. Waterfront, Lubeck, Germany 1·00 1·00
1201 15n. Quedlinberg, Germany 1·00 1·00
1202 15n. Benedictine church, Lorsch, Germany 1·00 1·00
**MS**1203 Two sheets, each 126×102 mm. (a) 60n. House, Goslar, Germany (horiz); (b) 60n. Comenzada Cathedral, Portugal (horiz) 6·25 6·25

**158** Turkish Angora

**1997.** Domestic Animals. Mult. (a) Cats.

1204 10n. Type **158** 65 65
1205 15n. Oriental shorthair 90 90
1206 15n. Japanese bobtail 85 85
1207 15n. Ceylon 85 85
1208 15n. Exotic 85 85
1209 15n. Rex 85 85
1210 15n. Ragdoll 85 85
1211 15n. Russian blue 85 85
1212 20n. British shorthair 1·20 1·20
1213 25n. Burmese 1·40 1·40

(b) Dogs.

1214 10n. Dalmatian 65 65
1215 15n. Siberian husky 90 90
1216 20n. Saluki 1·20 1·20
1217 20n. Dandie Dinmont terrier 1·20 1·20
1218 20n. Chinese crested 1·20 1·20
1219 20n. Norwich terrier 1·20 1·20
1220 20n. Basset hound 1·20 1·20
1221 20n. Cardigan Welsh corgi 1·20 1·20
1222 20n. French bulldog 1·20 1·20
1223 25n. Shar-Pei 1·40 1·40
**MS**1224 Two sheets, each 76×106 mm. (a) 60n. Tokinese (cat); (b) 60n. Hovawart (dog) 6·75 6·75

Nos. 1206/11 and 1217/22 respectively were issued together, se-tenant, forming composite designs.

**159** Stuart Pearce (England)

**1997.** World Cup Football Championship, France (1998). Black (Nos. 1225, 1231, 1235, 1237, 1241, 1243) or multicoloured (others).

1225 5n. Type **159** 35 35
1226 10n. Paul Gascoigne (England) 65 65
1227 10n. Diego Maradona (Argentina 1986) (horiz) 65 65
1228 10n. Carlos Alberto (Brazil 1970) (horiz) 65 65
1229 10n. Dunga (Brazil 1994) (horiz) 65 65
1230 10n. Bobby Moore (England 1966) (horiz) 65 65
1231 10n. Fritz Walter (West Germany 1954) (horiz) 65 65
1232 10n. Walter Matthaus (Germany 1990) (horiz) 65 65
1233 10n. Franz Beckenbauer (West Germany 1974) (horiz) 65 65
1234 10n. Daniel Passarella (Argentina 1978) (horiz) 65 65
1235 10n. Italy team, 1938 (horiz) 65 65
1236 10n. West Germany team, 1954 (horiz) 65 65
1237 10n. Uruguay team, 1958 (horiz) 65 65
1238 10n. England team, 1966 (horiz) 65 65
1239 10n. Argentina team, 1978 (horiz) 65 65
1240 10n. Brazil team, 1962 (horiz) 65 65
1241 10n. Italy team, 1934 (horiz) 65 65
1242 10n. Brazil team, 1970 (horiz) 65 65
1243 10n. Uruguay team, 1930 (horiz) 65 65
1244 10n. David Beckham (England) 1·00 1·00
1245 20n. Steve McManaman (England) 1·20 1·20
1246 25n. Tony Adams (England) 1·50 1·50
1247 30n. Paul Ince (England) 1·90 1·90
**MS**1248 Two sheets, each 102×127 mm. (a) 35n. Salvatore "Toto" Schillaci (Italy) (horiz); (b) 35n. Philippe Albert (Belgium) 4·75 4·75

**160** Buddha in Lotus Position

**1997.** "Indepex '97" International Stamp Exhibition, New Delhi. 50th Anniv of Independence of India. Multicoloured.

1249 3n. Type **160** 15 15
1250 7n. Mahatma Gandhi with hands together 35 35
1251 10n. Gandhi (three-quarter face portrait) 50 50
1252 15n. Buddha with feet on footstool 65 65
**MS**1253 Two sheets, each 75×106 mm. (a) 15n. Buddha with right hand raised; (b) 15n. Gandhi carrying stick 1·70 1·70

**161** Jawaharlal Nehru and King Jigme Dorji Wangchuck

**1997.** Int Friendship between India and Bhutan.

1254 **161** 3n. black and pink 15 15
**MS**1256 100×70 mm. 20n. multicoloured 2·30 2·30

DESIGNS: 10n. Prime Minister Rajiv Gandhi of India and King Jigme Singye Wangchuck. 76×34 mm—20n. President R Venkataraman of India and King Jigme Singye Wangchuck.

**162** Tiger

**1998.** New Year. Year of the Tiger. T 162 and similar square designs. Multicoloured.

1257 3n. Type **162** 10 10
**MS**1258 Two sheets. (a) 95×95 mm. 3n. Type **162**; 5n. Lying down; 15n. Hunting; 17n. On rocky outcrop; (b) 114×81 mm. 20n. Head of tiger 2·75 2·75

**163** Safe Motherhood and Anniversary Emblems

**1998.** 50th Anniv of WHO.

1259 **163** 3n. multicoloured 10 10
1260 **163** 10n. multicoloured 50 50
**MS**1261 100×60 mm. 15n. Safe Motherhood emblem (134×34 mm) 75 75

**164** Mother Teresa

**1998.** Mother Teresa (founder of Missionaries of Charity) Commemoration. Multicoloured.

1262 10n. Type **164** 50 50
1263 10n. With Diana, Princess of Wales 50 50
1264 10n. Holding child 50 50
1265 10n. Holding baby 50 50
1266 10n. With Sisters 50 50
1267 10n. Smiling 50 50
1268 10n. Praying 50 50
1269 10n. With Pope John Paul II 50 50
1270 10n. Close-up of face 50 50
**MS**1271 150×122 mm. 25n. As No. 1263 but 39×46 mm; 25n. As No. 1269 but different colour background and 39×46 mm 2·00 2·00

**165** Red-billed Chough

**1998.** Birds. Multicoloured.

1272 10ch. Type **165** 15 15
1273 30ch. Great Indian hornbill ("Great Hornbill") 15 15
1274 50ch. Western Singing bush lark ("Singing Lark") 15 15
1275 70ch. Chestnut-flanked white-eye 15 15
1276 90ch. Magpie robin (wrongly inscr "Megpie-robin") 15 15
1277 1n. Mrs. Gould's sunbird 15 15
1278 2n. Long-tailed tailor bird ("Tailorbird") 15 15
1279 3n. Mallard ("Duck") 15 15
1280 5n. Great spotted cuckoo ("Spotted Cuckoo") 15 15
1281 7n. Severtzov's tit warbler ("Goldcrest") 15 15
1282 9n. Common mynah 15 15
1283 10n. Green cochoa 15 15
**MS**1284 75×118 mm. 15n. Turtle dove (40×29 mm) 90 90

**166** Rabbit

**1999.** New Year. Year of the Rabbit. Multicoloured.

1285 4n. Type **166** 20 20
1286 16n. Rabbit on hillock 70 70
**MS**1287 83×114 mm. 20n. Rabbit beneath tree (34×34 mm) 1·00 1·00

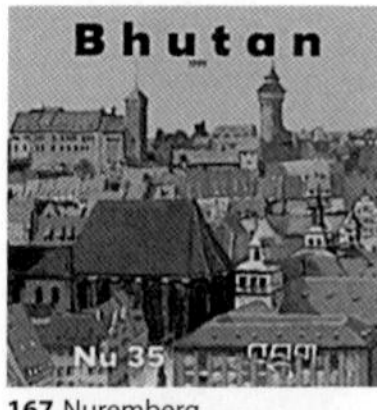

**167** Nuremberg

**1999.** "iBRA '99" International Stamp Exhibition, Nuremberg. Sheet 75×94 mm containing T 167 and similar square design. Multicoloured.

**MS**1288 35n. Type **167**; 40n. Exhibition emblem 1·00 1·00

**168** King Wangchuck

**1999.** 25th Anniv of Coronation of King Jigme Singye Wangchuck. Multicoloured.

1289 25n. Type **168** 1·20 1·20
1290 25n. Facing left (yellow background) 1·20 1·20
1291 25n. Facing forwards (orange background) 1·20 1·20
1292 25n. With arm raised (green background) 1·20 1·20
**MS**1293 180×140 mm. 25n. King Wangchuk (magenta background) 4·25 4·25

**169** Early German Steam Locomotive

**1999.** Trains. Multicoloured.

1294 5n. Type **169** 25 25
1295 10n. Electric locomotive 65 65
1296 10n. "Hikari" express train, Japan 60 60
1297 10n. Steam locomotive, South Africa, 1953 60 60
1298 10n. Super Chief locomotive, U.S.A., 1946 60 60
1299 10n. Magleus Magnet train, Japan, 1991 60 60
1300 10n. *Flying Scotsman*, Great Britain, 1992 60 60
1301 10n. Kodama locomotive, Japan, 1958 60 60
1302 10n. "Blue Train", South Africa, 1969 60 60
1303 10n. Intercity train, Germany, 1960 60 60
1304 10n. ET 403 high speed electric locomotive, Germany, 1973 60 60
1305 10n. 4-4-0 steam locomotive, U.S.A., 1855 60 60
1306 10n. Beyer-Garratt steam locomotive, South Africa, 1954 (wrongly inscr "BAYER GARRATT") 60 60
1307 10n. Settebello locomotive, Italy, 1953 60 60
1308 15n. Pacific Class 01 steam locomotive, Germany 85 85
1309 15n. Neptune Express, Germany 85 85
1310 15n. 4-6-0 steam locomotive, Great Britain 85 85
1311 15n. Shovelnose Streamliner diesel locomotive, U.S.A. 85 85

| | | | |
|---|---|---|---|
| 1312 | 15n. Electric locomotive, Germany | 85 | 85 |
| 1313 | 15n. Early steam locomotive, Germany | 85 | 85 |
| 1314 | 15n. Union Pacific diesel locomotive, U.S.A. | 85 | 85 |
| 1315 | 15n. 1881 Borsig steam locomotive, Germany | 85 | 85 |
| 1316 | 15n. Borsig 4-6-4 diesel locomotive, Germany | 85 | 85 |
| 1317 | 15n. Diesel-electric locomotive, France | 85 | 85 |
| 1318 | 15n. Pennsylvania Railroad locomotive, U.S.A. | 85 | 85 |
| 1319 | 15n. Steam locomotive, Germany | 85 | 85 |
| 1320 | 15n. Amtrak locomotive, U.S.A. | 85 | 85 |
| 1321 | 15n. 2-2-2 steam locomotive, Great Britain | 85 | 85 |
| 1322 | 15n. P class steam locomotive, Denmark | 85 | 85 |
| 1323 | 15n. Electric locomotive, France | 85 | 85 |
| 1324 | 15n. First Japanese locomotive | 85 | 85 |
| 1325 | 15n. 2-8-2 steam locomotive, Germany | 85 | 85 |
| 1326 | 20n. Steam locomotive | 1·20 | 1·20 |
| 1327 | 30n. Electric locomotive | 1·70 | 1·70 |

**MS**1328 Two sheets, each 110×85 mm. (a) 80n. City of Los Angeles, U.S.A.; (b) 80n. Great Northern diesel-electric Streamliner locomotive, U.S.A 9·75 9·75

**170** "Festive Dancers"

**1999.** 150th Death Anniv of Katsushika Hokusai (artist). Multicoloured.

| | | | |
|---|---|---|---|
| 1329 | 15n. Type **170** | 75 | 75 |
| 1330 | 15n. "Drawings of Women" (woman reading) | 75 | 75 |
| 1331 | 15n. "Festive Dancers" (man wearing pointed hat) | 75 | 75 |
| 1332 | 15n. "Festive Dancers" (man looking up) | 75 | 75 |
| 1333 | 15n. "Drawings of Women" (woman sitting on ground) | 75 | 75 |
| 1334 | 15n. "Festive Dancers" (woman) | 75 | 75 |
| 1335 | 15n. "Suspension Bridge between Hida and Etchu" | 75 | 75 |
| 1336 | 15n. "Drawings of Women" (woman dressing hair) | 75 | 75 |
| 1337 | 15n. "Exotic Beauty" | 75 | 75 |
| 1338 | 15n. "The Poet Nakamaro in China" | 75 | 75 |
| 1339 | 15n. "Drawings of Women" (woman rolling up sleeve) | 75 | 75 |
| 1340 | 15n. "Chinese Poet in Snow" | 75 | 75 |
| 1341 | 15n. "Mount Fuji seen above Mist on the Tama River" (horiz) | 75 | 75 |
| 1342 | 15n. "Mount Fuji seen from Shichirigahama" (horiz) | 75 | 75 |
| 1343 | 15n. "Sea Life" (turtle) (horiz) | 75 | 75 |
| 1344 | 15n. "Sea Life" (fish) (horiz) | 75 | 75 |
| 1345 | 15n. "Mount Fuji reflected in a Lake" (horiz) | 75 | 75 |
| 1346 | 15n. "Mount Fuji seen through the Piers of Mannenbashi" (horiz) | 75 | 75 |

**MS**1347 Three sheets (a) 100×71 mm 80n. "Peasants leading Oxen"; (b) 71×100 mm 80n. "The lotus Pedestal". (c) 71×100 mm 870n. "Kusunoki Masahige" 15·00 15·00

**171** Tyrannosaurus Rex

**1999.** Prehistoric Animals. Multicoloured.

| | | | |
|---|---|---|---|
| 1348 | 10n. Type **171** | 60 | 60 |
| 1349 | 10n. Dimorphodon | 60 | 60 |
| 1350 | 10n. Diplodocus | 60 | 60 |
| 1351 | 10n. Pterodaustro | 60 | 60 |
| 1352 | 10n. Tyrannosaurus Rex (different) | 60 | 60 |
| 1353 | 10n. Edmontosaurus | 60 | 60 |
| 1354 | 10n. Apatosaurus | 60 | 60 |
| 1355 | 10n. Deinonychus | 60 | 60 |
| 1356 | 10n. Hypsilophodon | 60 | 60 |
| 1357 | 10n. Oviraptor | 60 | 60 |
| 1358 | 10n. Stegosaurus beside lake | 60 | 60 |
| 1359 | 10n. Head of Triceratops | 60 | 60 |
| 1360 | 10n. Pterodactylus and Brachiosaurus | 60 | 60 |
| 1361 | 10n. Pteranodon | 60 | 60 |
| 1362 | 10n. Anurognathus and Tyrannosaurus Rex | 60 | 60 |
| 1363 | 10n. Brachiosaurus | 60 | 60 |
| 1364 | 10n. Corythosaurus | 60 | 60 |
| 1365 | 10n. Iguanodon | 60 | 60 |
| 1366 | 10n. Lesothosaurus | 60 | 60 |
| 1367 | 10n. Allosaurus | 60 | 60 |
| 1368 | 10n. Velociraptor | 60 | 60 |
| 1369 | 10n. Triceratops in water | 60 | 60 |
| 1370 | 10n. Stegosaurus in water | 60 | 60 |
| 1371 | 10n. Compsognathus | 60 | 60 |
| 1372 | 20n. Moeritherium | 90 | 90 |
| 1373 | 20n. Platybelodon | 90 | 90 |
| 1374 | 20n. Woolly mammoth | 90 | 90 |
| 1375 | 20n. African elephant | 90 | 90 |
| 1376 | 20n. Deinonychus | 90 | 90 |
| 1377 | 20n. Dimorphodon | 90 | 90 |
| 1378 | 20n. Archaeopteryx | 90 | 90 |
| 1379 | 20n. Common pheasant ("Ring-necked Pheasant") | 90 | 90 |

**MS**1380 Four sheets, each 110×85 mm. (a) 80n. Hoatzin (vert); (b) 80n. Icthyosaurus (wrongly inscr "Present Day Dolphin") (vert); (c) 80n. Triceratops (vert); (d) 80n. Pteranodon (wrongly inscr "Triceratops") 18·00 18·00

Nos. 1348/59 and 1360/71 were issued together, se-tenant, with the backgrounds forming a composite design.

**172** Siberian Musk Deer

**1999.** "China '99" World Philatelic Exhibition, Peking. Animals. Multicoloured.

| | | | |
|---|---|---|---|
| 1381 | 20n. Type **172** | 1·00 | 1·00 |
| 1382 | 20n. Takin (*Budorcas taxicolor*) | 1·00 | 1·00 |
| 1383 | 20n. Bharal ("Blue sheep") (*Pseudois nayur*) (wrongly inscr "nayour") | 1·00 | 1·00 |
| 1384 | 20n. Yak (*Bos gunniens*) | 1·00 | 1·00 |
| 1385 | 20n. Common goral (*Nemorhaedus goral*) | 1·00 | 1·00 |

**173** Sara Orange-tip

**1999.** Butterflies. Multicoloured.

| | | | |
|---|---|---|---|
| 1386 | 5n. Type **173** | 35 | 35 |
| 1387 | 10n. Pipe-vine swallowtail | 60 | 60 |
| 1388 | 15n. Longwings | 85 | 85 |
| 1389 | 20n. Viceroy | 1·10 | 1·10 |
| 1390 | 20n. Frosted skipper | 1·20 | 1·20 |
| 1391 | 20n. Fiery skipper | 1·20 | 1·20 |
| 1392 | 20n. Banded hairstreak | 1·20 | 1·20 |
| 1393 | 20n. Cloudless ("Clouded") sulphur | 1·20 | 1·20 |
| 1394 | 20n. Milbert's tortoiseshell | 1·20 | 1·20 |
| 1395 | 20n. Eastern tailed blue | 1·20 | 1·20 |
| 1396 | 20n. Jamaican kite ("Zebra") swallowtail | 1·20 | 1·20 |
| 1397 | 20n. Colorado hairstreak | 1·20 | 1·20 |
| 1398 | 20n. Pink-edged sulphur | 1·20 | 1·20 |
| 1399 | 20n. Barred sulphur (wrongly inscr "Fairy Yellow") | 1·20 | 1·20 |
| 1400 | 20n. Red-spotted purple | 1·20 | 1·20 |
| 1401 | 20n. Aphrodite | 1·20 | 1·20 |
| 1402 | 25n. Silver-spotted skipper (vert) | 1·40 | 1·40 |
| 1403 | 30n. Great spangled fritillary (vert) | 1·70 | 1·70 |
| 1404 | 35n. Little copper (vert) | 2·00 | 2·00 |

**MS**1405 Four sheets, each 98×68 mm. (a) 80n. Monarch (vert); (b) 80n. Checkered white; (c) 80n. Gulf fritillary (vert); (d) 80n. Grey hairstreak (vert) 14·50 14·50

Nos. 1390/95 and 1396/1401 were issued together, se-tenant, forming a composite design.

**174** Chestnut-breasted Chlorophonia

**1999.** Birds. Multicoloured.

| | | | |
|---|---|---|---|
| 1406 | 15n. Type **174** | 65 | 65 |
| 1407 | 15n. Yellow-faced amazon | 65 | 65 |
| 1408 | 15n. White ibis | 65 | 65 |
| 1409 | 15n. Parrotlet sp. ("Caique") | 65 | 65 |
| 1410 | 15n. Green jay | 65 | 65 |
| 1411 | 15n. Tufted coquette | 65 | 65 |
| 1412 | 15n. Troupial | 65 | 65 |
| 1413 | 15n. American purple gallinule ("Purple Gallinule") | 65 | 65 |
| 1414 | 15n. Copper-rumped hummingbird | 65 | 65 |
| 1415 | 15n. Great egret ("Common egret") | 65 | 65 |
| 1416 | 15n. Rufous-browed pepper shrike | 65 | 65 |
| 1417 | 15n. Glittering-throated emerald | 65 | 65 |
| 1418 | 15n. Great kiskadee | 65 | 65 |
| 1419 | 15n. Cuban green woodpecker | 65 | 65 |
| 1420 | 15n. Scarlet ibis | 65 | 65 |
| 1421 | 15n. Belted kingfisher | 65 | 65 |
| 1422 | 15n. Barred antshrike | 65 | 65 |
| 1423 | 15n. Brown-throated conure ("Caribbean Parakeet") | 65 | 65 |
| 1424 | 15n. Rufous-tailed jacamar (vert) | 65 | 65 |
| 1425 | 15n. Scarlet macaw (vert) | 65 | 65 |
| 1426 | 15n. Channel-billed toucan (vert) | 65 | 65 |
| 1427 | 15n. Louisiana heron ("Tri-colored heron") (vert) | 65 | 65 |
| 1428 | 15n. St. Vincent amazon ("St. Vincent Parrot") (vert) | 65 | 65 |
| 1429 | 15n. Blue-crowned motmot (vert) | 65 | 65 |
| 1430 | 15n. Horned screamer (vert) | 65 | 65 |
| 1431 | 15n. Grey plover ("Black-billed Plover") (vert) | 65 | 65 |
| 1432 | 15n. Eastern meadowlark ("Common meadowlark") (vert) | 65 | 65 |

**MS**1433 Three sheets, each 85×110 mm. (a) 80n. Military macaw (vert); (b) 80n. Toco toucan; (c) 80n. Red-billed scythebill (vert) 11·00 11·00

Nos. 1406/14, 1415/23 and 1424/32 were issued together, se-tenant, forming a composite design.

**175** Yuri Gagarin (first person in space, 1961)

**1999.** 30th Anniv of First Manned Moon Landing. Multicoloured.

| | | | |
|---|---|---|---|
| 1434 | 20n. Type **175** | 90 | 90 |
| 1435 | 20n. Alan Shepard (first American in space, 1961) | 90 | 90 |
| 1436 | 20n. John Glenn (first American to orbit Earth, 1962) | 90 | 90 |
| 1437 | 20n. Valentina Tereshkova (first woman in space, 1963) | 90 | 90 |
| 1438 | 20n. Edward White (first American to walk in space, 1965) | 90 | 90 |
| 1439 | 20n. Neil Armstrong (first person to set foot on Moon, 1969) | 90 | 90 |
| 1440 | 20n. Neil Armstrong (wearing N.A.S.A. suit) | 90 | 90 |
| 1441 | 20n. Michael Collins | 90 | 90 |
| 1442 | 20n. Edwin (Buzz) Aldrin | 90 | 90 |
| 1443 | 20n. *Columbia* (pointing upwards) | 90 | 90 |
| 1444 | 20n. *Eagle* on lunar surface | 90 | 90 |
| 1445 | 20n. Edwin Aldrin on lunar surface | 90 | 90 |
| 1446 | 20n. North American X-15 rocket (1960) | 90 | 90 |
| 1447 | 20n. Gemini 8 (1966) | 90 | 90 |
| 1448 | 20n. Saturn V rocket (1969) | 90 | 90 |
| 1449 | 20n. *Columbia* (pointing downwards) | 90 | 90 |
| 1450 | 20n. *Eagle* above Moon | 90 | 90 |
| 1451 | 20n. Edwin Aldrin descending ladder | 90 | 90 |

**MS**1452 Three sheets. (a) 111×85 mm. 80n. Neil Armstrong (different); (b) 111×85 mm. 80n. Gemini 8 docking with Agena target vehicle (56×41 mm); (c) 85×111 mm. 80n. Apollo 11 command module landing in Pacific Ocean (vert) 11·00 11·00

Nos. 1434/9, 1440/5 and 1446/51 were issued together, se-tenant, forming a composite design.

**176** Tortoiseshell Cat

**1999.** Animals. Multicoloured.

| | | | |
|---|---|---|---|
| 1453 | 5n. Type **176** | 75 | 75 |
| 1454 | 5n. Man watching blue and white cat | 75 | 75 |
| 1455 | 10n. Chinchilla golden longhair adult and kittens | 1·40 | 1·40 |
| 1456 | 12n. Russian blue adult and kitten | 65 | 65 |
| 1457 | 12n. Birman | 65 | 65 |
| 1458 | 12n. Devon rex | 65 | 65 |
| 1459 | 12n. Pewter longhair | 65 | 65 |
| 1460 | 12n. Bombay | 65 | 65 |
| 1461 | 12n. Sorrel somali | 65 | 65 |
| 1462 | 12n. Red tabby manx | 65 | 65 |
| 1463 | 12n. Blue smoke longhair | 65 | 65 |
| 1464 | 12n. Oriental tabby shorthair adult and kitten | 65 | 65 |
| 1465 | 12n. Australian silky terrier | 65 | 65 |
| 1466 | 12n. Samoyed | 65 | 65 |
| 1467 | 12n. Basset bleu de Gascogne | 65 | 65 |
| 1468 | 12n. Bernese mountain dog | 65 | 65 |
| 1469 | 12n. Pug | 65 | 65 |
| 1470 | 12n. Bergamasco | 65 | 65 |
| 1471 | 12n. Basenji | 65 | 65 |
| 1472 | 12n. Wetterhoun | 65 | 65 |
| 1473 | 12n. Drever | 65 | 65 |
| 1474 | 12n. Przewalski horse | 65 | 65 |
| 1475 | 12n. Shetland pony | 65 | 65 |
| 1476 | 12n. Dutch gelderlander horse | 65 | 65 |
| 1477 | 12n. Shire horse | 65 | 65 |
| 1478 | 12n. Arab | 65 | 65 |
| 1479 | 12n. Boulonnais | 65 | 65 |
| 1480 | 12n. Falabella | 65 | 65 |
| 1481 | 12n. Orlov trotter | 65 | 65 |
| 1482 | 12n. Suffolk punch | 65 | 65 |
| 1483 | 15n. Lipizzaner | 65 | 65 |
| 1484 | 20n. Andalusian | 1·20 | 1·20 |
| 1485 | 25n. Weimaraner (dog) | 1·70 | 1·70 |
| 1486 | 30n. German shepherd dog | 3·00 | 3·00 |

**MS**1487 Three sheets, each 115×91 mm. (a) 70n. Labrador retriever; (b) 70n. Norwegian forest cat; (c) 70n. Connemara horse 9·75 9·75

**177** Bharal

**1999.** Animals and Birds of the Himalayas. Multicoloured.

(a) Animals.

| | | | |
|---|---|---|---|
| 1489 | 20n. Type **177** | 90 | 90 |
| 1490 | 20n. Lynx | 90 | 90 |
| 1491 | 20n. Rat snake | 90 | 90 |
| 1492 | 20n. Indian elephant | 90 | 90 |
| 1493 | 20n. Langur | 90 | 90 |
| 1494 | 20n. Musk deer | 90 | 90 |
| 1495 | 20n. Otter | 90 | 90 |
| 1496 | 20n. Tibetan wolf | 90 | 90 |
| 1497 | 20n. Himalayan black bear | 90 | 90 |
| 1498 | 20n. Snow leopard | 90 | 90 |
| 1499 | 20n. Flying squirrel | 90 | 90 |
| 1500 | 20n. Red fox | 90 | 90 |
| 1501 | 20n. Ibex | 90 | 90 |
| 1502 | 20n. Takin | 90 | 90 |
| 1503 | 20n. Agama lizard | 90 | 90 |
| 1504 | 20n. Marmot | 90 | 90 |
| 1505 | 20n. Red panda | 90 | 90 |
| 1506 | 20n. Leopard cat | 90 | 90 |

**MS**1507 Three sheets, each 78×118 mm. (a) 100n. Cobra; (b) 100n. Tiger; (c) 100n. Rhinoceros (wrongly inscr "Rhinoerous") 16·00 16·00

(b) Birds.

1508 20n. Red-crested pochard 90 90
1509 20n. Satyr tragopan 90 90
1510 20n. Lammergeier ("Lammergeier Vulture") 90 90
1511 20n. Kalij pheasant 90 90
1512 20n. Great Indian hornbill 90 90
1513 20n. White stork ("Stork") 90 90
1514 20n. Rufous-necked hornbill (wrongly inscr "Rofous") 90 90
1515 20n. Black drongo ("Drongo") 90 90
1516 20n. Himalayan monal pheasant 90 90
1517 20n. Black-necked crane 90 90
1518 20n. Little green bee-eater 90 90
1519 20n. Oriental ibis ("Ibis") 90 90
1520 20n. Crested lark 90 90
1521 20n. Ferruginous duck 90 90
1522 20n. Blood pheasant 90 90
1523 20n. White-crested laughing thrush ("Laughing Thrush") 90 90
1524 20n. Golden eagle 90 90
1525 20n. Siberian rubythroat 90 90
**MS**1526 Three sheets, each 78×118 mm. (a) 100n. Siberian rubythroat (different); (b) 100n. Black-naped monarch; (c) 100n. Mountain peacock pheasant 16·00 16·00

**178** Elephant, Monkey, Rabbit and Bird (Four Friends)

**1999.** Year 2000.
1527 **178** 10n. multicoloured 60 60
1528 **178** 20n. multicoloured 1·10 1·10

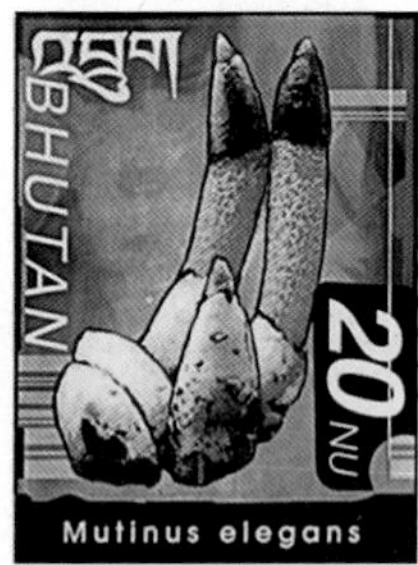


**179** Elegant Stink Horn

**1999.** Fungi. Multicoloured.
1529 20n. Type **179** 1·20 1·20
1530 20n. *Pholiota squarrosoides* 1·20 1·20
1531 20n. Scaly inky cap (*Coprinus quadrifidus*) 1·20 1·20
1532 20n. Golden spindles (*Clavulinopsis fusiformis*) 1·20 1·20
1533 20n. *Spathularia velutipes* 1·20 1·20
1534 20n. *Ganoderma lucidum* 1·20 1·20
1535 20n. *Microglossum rufum* 1·20 1·20
1536 20n. *Lactarius hygrophoroides* 1·20 1·20
1537 20n. *Lactarius speciosus complex* 1·20 1·20
1538 20n. *Calostoma cinnabarina* 1·20 1·20
1539 20n. *Clitocybe clavipes* 1·20 1·20
1540 20n. *Microstoma floccosa* 1·20 1·20
1541 20n. Frost's bolete (*Boletus frostii*) 1·20 1·20
1542 20n. Common morel (*Morchella esculenta*) (wrongly inscr "estculenta") 1·20 1·20
1543 20n. *Hypomyces lactifuorum* 1·20 1·20
1544 20n. *Polyporus auricularius* 1·20 1·20
1545 20n. *Cantharellus lateritius* 1·20 1·20
1546 20n. *Volvariella pusilla* 1·20 1·20
**MS**1547 Three sheets, each 78×118 mm. (a) 100n. *Pholiota aurivella*; (b) 100n. *Ramarai grandis*; (c) 100n. *Oudemansiella lucidum* 16·00 16·00

**180** Green Dragon with Red Flames

**2000.** New Year. Year of the Dragon. Multicoloured.
1548 3n. Type **180** 15 15
1549 5n. Green dragon encircling moon 25 25
1550 8n. Dragon and symbols of Chinese zodiac 50 50
1552 12n. Brown dragon encircling moon 75 75
**MS**1553 90×130 mm. 15n. Dragon head (29×40 mm) 85 85

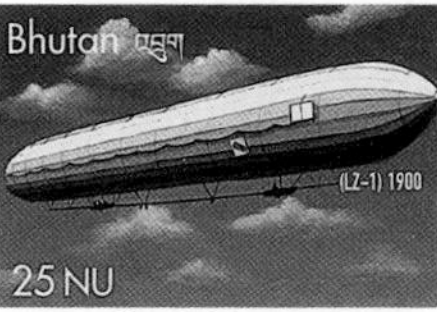


**181** LZ-1 (first flight), 1900

**2000.** Centenary of First Zeppelin Flight. Multicoloured.
1554 25n. Type **181** 1·30 1·30
1555 25n. LZ-2, 1906 1·30 1·30
1556 25n. LZ-3 over hills (first flight, 1906) 1·30 1·30
1557 25n. LZ-127 *Graf Zeppelin* (first flight, 1928) 1·30 1·30
1558 25n. LZ-129 *Hindenberg* (first flight, 1936) 1·30 1·30
1559 25n. LZ-130 *Graf Zeppelin II* (first flight, 1938) 1·30 1·30
1560 25n. LZ-1 over hill with tree 1·30 1·30
1561 25n. LZ-2 over mountains 1·30 1·30
1562 25n. LZ-3 against sky 1·30 1·30
1563 25n. LZ-4 (first flight, 1908) 1·30 1·30
1564 25n. LZ-5 (first flight, 1909) 1·30 1·30
1565 25n. LZ-6 (formation of Deutsche Liftschiffahrts Aktien Gesellschaft (DELAG) (world's first airline), 1909) 1·30 1·30
1566 25n. LZ-1 over grassy hills, 1900 1·30 1·30
1567 25n. Z11 *Ersatz*, 1913 1·30 1·30
1568 25n. LZ-6 exiting hangar, 1909 1·30 1·30
1569 25n. LZ-10 *Schwabein* (first flight, 1911) 1·30 1·30
1570 25n. LZ-7 *Deutschland* (inscr "Ersatz Deutschland") 1·30 1·30
1571 25n. LZ-11 *Viktoria Luise* 1·30 1·30
**MS**1572 Three sheets, each 106×80 mm. (a) 80n. Ferdinand von Zeppelin wearing white cap (vert); (b) 80n. Zeppelin wearing cap (vert); (c) 80n. Zeppelin (vert) 12·50 12·50

**182** Lunix III

**2000.** "WORLD STAMP EXPO 2000" International Stamp Exhibition, Anaheim, California. Space. Multicoloured.
1573 25n. Type **182** 1·30 1·30
1574 25n. Ranger 9 1·30 1·30
1575 25n. Lunar Orbiter 1·30 1·30
1576 25n. Lunar Prospector spacecraft 1·30 1·30
1577 25n. *Apollo 11* spacecraft 1·30 1·30
1578 25n. Selen satellite 1·30 1·30
1579 25n. Space shuttle *Challenger* 1·30 1·30
1580 25n. North American X-15 experimental rocket aircraft 1·30 1·30
1581 25n. Space shuttle *Buran* 1·30 1·30
1582 25n. Hermes (experimental space plane) 1·30 1·30
1583 25n. X-33 Venturi Star (reusable launch vehicle) 1·30 1·30
1584 25n. Hope (unmanned experimental spacecraft) 1·30 1·30
1585 25n. Victor Patsayev (cosmonaut) 1·30 1·30
1586 25n. Yladisloav Volkov (cosmonaut) 1·30 1·30
1587 25n. Georgi Dobrvolski (cosmonaut) 1·30 1·30
1588 25n. Virgil Grissom (astronaut) 1·30 1·30
1589 25n. Roger Chaffee (astronaut) 1·30 1·30
1590 25n. Edward White (astronaut) 1·30 1·30
**MS**1591 Three sheets. (a) 76×111 mm. 80n. Launch of space shuttle *Challenger* (vert); (b) 76×111 mm. 80n. Launch of space shuttle *Buran* (vert); (c) 116×85 mm. 80n. Edwin E. Aldrin on moon (first manned Moon landing, 1969) (vert) 12·50 12·50

**183** Trashigang Dzong

**2000.** "EXPO 2000" World's Fair, Hanover, Germany (1st issue). Monasteries. Multicoloured.
1592 3n. Type **183** 15 15
1593 4n. Lhuentse Dzong 15 15
1594 6n. Gasa Dzong 25 25
1595 7n. Punakha Dzong 35 35
1596 10n. Trashichhoe Dzong 40 40
1597 20n. Paro Dzong 85 85
**MS**1598 157×98 mm. 15n. Roof (29×40 mm) 65 65

**184** Snow Leopard

**2000.** "EXPO 2000" World's Fair, Hanover, Germany (2nd issue). Wildlife. Multicoloured.
1599 10n. Type **184** 40 40
1600 10n. Common raven ("Raven") 40 40
1601 10n. Golden langur 40 40
1602 10n. Rhododendron 40 40
1603 10n. Black-necked crane 40 40
1604 10n. Blue poppy 40 40

**185** Jesse Owens (U.S.A.) (Berlin, 1936)

**2000.** Olympic Games, Sydney. Multicoloured.
1605 20n. Type **185** 1·00 1·00
1606 20n. Kayaking (modern games) 1·00 1·00
1607 20n. Fulton County Stadium, Atlanta, Georgia (1996 games) 1·00 1·00
1608 20n. Ancient Greek athlete 1·00 1·00

**186** G. and R. Stephenson's *Rocket* (first steam locomotive)

**2000.** 175th Anniv of Opening of Stockton and Darlington Railway. Multicoloured.
1609 50n. Type **186** 2·50 2·50
1610 50n. Steam locomotive (opening of London and Birmingham railway, 1828) 2·50 2·50
1611 50n. Northumbrian locomotive, 1825 2·50 2·50
**MS**1612 118×79 mm. 100n. Inaugural run on Stockton and Darlington Railway, 1825 (56×42 mm) 4·00 4·00

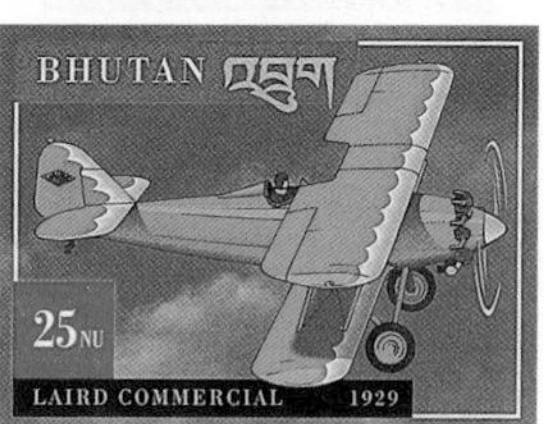


**187** Laird Commercial (biplane), 1929

**2000.** Airplanes. Multicoloured.
1613 25n. Type **187** 1·20 1·20
1614 25n. Ryan B-5 Brougham, 1927 (wrongly inscr "Broughm") 1·20 1·20
1615 25n. Cessna AW, 1928 1·20 1·20
1616 25n. Travel Air 4000 biplane, 1927 1·20 1·20
1617 25n. Fairchild F-71, 1927 1·20 1·20
1618 25n. Command Aire biplane, 1928 1·20 1·20
1619 25n. Waco YMF biplane, 1935 1·20 1·20
1620 25n. Piper J-4 Cub Coupe, 1938 1·20 1·20
1621 25n. Ryan ST-A, 1937 1·20 1·20
1622 25n. Spartan Executive, 1939 1·20 1·20
1623 25n. Luscombe 8, 1939 1·20 1·20
1624 25n. Stinson SR5 Reliant seaplane, 1935 1·20 1·20
1625 25n. Cessna 195 seaplane, 1949 1·20 1·20
1626 25n. Waco SRE biplane, 1940 1·20 1·20
1627 25n. Erco Ercope, 1948 1·20 1·20
1628 25n. Boeing Stearman biplane, 1941 1·20 1·20
1629 25n. Beech Staggerwing biplane, 1944 1·20 1·20
1630 25n. Republic Seabee, 1947 1·20 1·20
**MS**1631 Three sheets, each 77×108 mm. (a) 100n. Waco CSO seaplane, 1929; (b) 100n. Curtiss-Wright 19W, 1936; (c) 100n. Grumman G-44 Widgeon flying boat, 1941 12·00 12·00

**188** *A Kind of Loving*, 1962

**2000.** Berlin Film Festival. Winners of Golden Bear Award. Multicoloured.
1632 25n. Type **188** 1·20 1·20
1633 25n. *Bushido Zankoku Monogatari*, 1963 1·20 1·20
1634 25n. *Hobson's Choice*, 1954 1·20 1·20
1635 25n. *El Lazarillo de Tormes*, 1960 1·20 1·20
1636 25n. *In the Name of the Father*, 1997 1·20 1·20
1637 25n. *Les Cousins*, 1959 1·20 1·20
**MS**1638 96×102 mm. 100n. *Die Ratten*, 1962 4·00 4·00

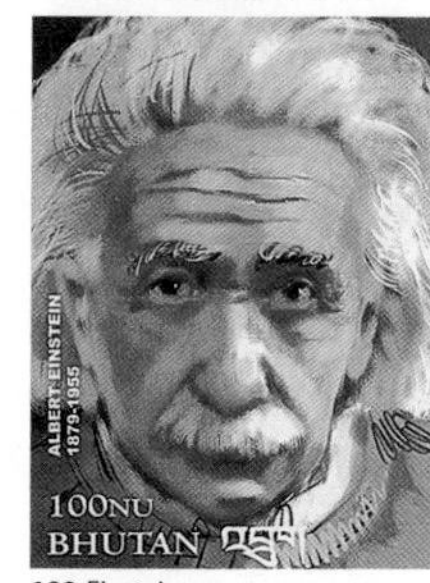


**189** Einstein

**2000.** Albert Einstein—Time Magazine Man of the Century. Sheet 113×83 mm.
**MS**1639 **189** 100n. multicoloured 4·50 4·50

**190** Aquinas

**2000.** 775th Birth Anniv of Thomas Aquinas (Catholic philosopher and theologian). Sheet 136×76 mm.
**MS**1640 **190** 25n.×4 multicoloured 4·00 4·00

**191** Pierre de Coubertin

**2000.** New Millennium. Multicoloured. (a) Centenary of the Modern Olympic Games.
1641 25n. Type **191** (founder of modern games) 1·20 1·20
1642 25n. Hand holding baton (first modern Games, Athens, 1896) 1·20 1·20
1643 25n. Jesse Owen (Berlin, 1936) 1·20 1·20
1644 25n. Handprint and white dove (Munich, 1972) 1·20 1·20
1645 25n. Sydney Opera House (Sydney, 2000) 1·20 1·20
1646 25n. Children wearing T-shirts (Greece, 2004) 1·20 1·20

(b) Breakthroughs in Modern Medicine.
1647 25n. Albert Calmette (bacteriologist, joint discoverer of B.C.G. vaccine) 1·20 1·20
1648 25n. Camillo Colgi and S. Ramon y Cajal (discovery of the neurone) 1·20 1·20
1649 25n. Alexander Fleming (bacteriologist, discoverer of penicillin) 1·20 1·20

1650 25n. Jonas Salk (virologist, developer of polio vaccine) 1·20 1·20
1651 25n. Christiaan Barnard (surgeon, performed first human heart transplant) 1·20 1·20
1652 25n. Luc Mantagnier (A.I.D.S. research) 1·20 1·20

**192** Paro Taktsang

**2000.** Sheet 86×49 mm.
**MS**1653 **192** 100n. multicoloured 4·00 4·00

**193** Christopher Columbus

**2000.** Explorers. Two sheets, each 66×83 mm. Multicoloured.
**MS**1654 (a) 100n. Type **193**; (b) 100n. Captain James Cook 8·00 8·00

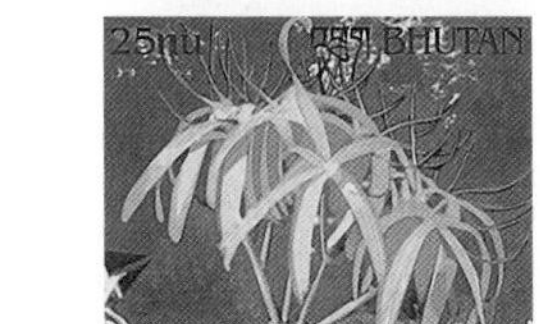

**194** *Crinum amoenum*

**2000.** Flowers of the Himalayan Mountains. Multicoloured.
1655 25n. Type **194** 1·20 1·20
1656 25n. *Beaumontia grandiflora* 1·20 1·20
1657 25n. *Trachelospermum lucidum* 1·20 1·20
1658 25n. *Curcuma aromatica* 1·20 1·20
1659 25n. *Barleria cristata* 1·20 1·20
1660 25n. *Holmskioldia sanguinea* 1·20 1·20
1661 25n. *Meconopsis villosa* 1·20 1·20
1662 25n. *Salva hians* 1·20 1·20
1663 25n. *Caltha palustris* 1·20 1·20
1664 25n. *Anemone polyanthes* 1·20 1·20
1665 25n. *Cypripedium cordigerum* 1·20 1·20
1666 25n. *Cryptochilus luteus* 1·20 1·20
1667 25n. *Androsace globifera* 1·20 1·20
1668 25n. *Tanacetum atkinsonii* 1·20 1·20
1669 25n. *Aster stracheyi* 1·20 1·20
1670 25n. *Arenaria glanduligera* 1·20 1·20
1671 25n. *Sibbaldia purpurea* 1·20 1·20
1672 25n. *Saxifraga parnassifolia* 1·20 1·20
**MS**1673 Three sheets, each 68×98 mm. (a) 100n. *Dendrobium densiflorum* (vert); (b) 100n. *Rhododendron arboreum* (vert); (c) 100n. *Gypsophila cerastioides* 14·50 14·50

Nos. 1655/60, 1661/6 and 1667/72 respectively were issued together, se-tenant, forming a composite design.

**195** "The Duke and Duchess of Osuna with their Children" (detail, Francisco de Goya)

**2000.** "Espana 2000" International Stamp Exhibition, Madrid. Prado Museum Exhibits. Multicoloured.
1674 25n. Type **195** 1·50 1·50
1675 25n. Young child (detail from "The Duke and Duchess of Osuna with their Children") 1·50 1·50
1676 25n. Duke (detail from "The Duke and Duchess of Osuna with their Children") 1·50 1·50
1677 25n. "Isidoro Maiquez" (Francisco de Goya) 1·50 1·50
1678 25n. "Dona Juana Galarza de Goicoechea" (Francisco de Goya) 1·50 1·50
1679 25n. "Ferdinand VII in an Encampment" (Francisco de Goya) 1·50 1·50
1680 25n. "Portrait of an Old Man" (Joos van Cleve) 1·50 1·50
1681 25n. "Mary Tudor" (Anthonis Mor) 1·50 1·50
1682 25n. "Portrait of a Man" (Jan van Scorel) 1·50 1·50
1683 25n. "The Court Jester Pejeron" (Anthonis Mor) 1·50 1·50
1684 25n. "Elizabeth of France" (Frans Pourbus the Younger) 1·50 1·50
1685 25n. "King James I" (Paul van Somer) 1·50 1·50
1686 25n. "The Empress Isabella of Portugal" (Titian) 1·50 1·50
1687 25n. "Lucrecia di Baccio del Fede, the Painter's Wife" (Andrea del Sarto) 1·50 1·50
1688 25n. "Self-Portrait" (Titian) 1·50 1·50
1689 25n. "Philip II" (Sofonisba Anguisciola) 1·50 1·50
1690 25n. "Portrait of a Doctor" (Lucia Anguisciola) 1·50 1·50
1691 25n. "Anna of Austria" (Sofonisba Anguisciola) 1·50 1·50
**MS**1692 Three sheets (a) 90×110 mm. 100n. Duchess and Duke (detail from "The Duke and Duchess of Osuna with their Children" (Francisco de Goya) (horiz); (b) 90×110 mm. 100n. "Charles V at Mühlberg" (Titian); (c) 110×90 mm. 100n. "The Relief of Genoa" (Antonio de Pereda) Set of 3 sheets 13·50 13·50

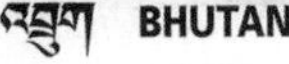

**196** Butterfly

**2000.** "Indepex Asiana 2000" International Stamp Exhibition, Calcutta. Multicoloured.
1693 5n. Type **196** 15 15
1694 8n. Red jungle fowl 40 40
1695 10n. *Zinnia elegans* 50 50
1696 12n. Tiger 60 60
**MS**1697 144×84 mm. 15n. Spotted deer (28×34 mm) 65 65

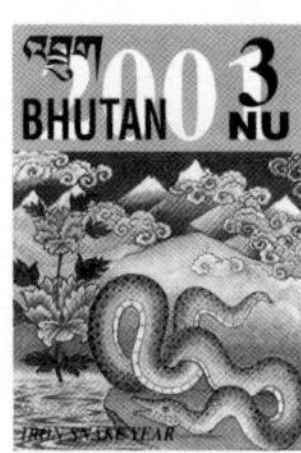


**197** Snake

**2001.** New Year. Year of the Snake. Multicoloured.
1698 3n. Type **197** 15 15
1699 20n. Snake 1·10 1·10
**MS**1700 135×135 mm. 3, 10n. As Type **197**; 15, 20n. As No. 1699 2·00 2·00

**198** Snow Leopard (*Uncia uncia*)

**2001.** "Hong Kong 2001" International Stamp Exhibition. Nature Protection. Sheet 195×138 mm containing T 198 and similar horiz designs. Multicoloured.
**MS**1701 15n. Type **198**; 15n. Rufous-necked hornbill (*Aceros nipalensis*); 15n. Black-necked crane (*Grus nigricollis*); 15n. Tiger (*Panthera tigris*) 2·75 2·75

**199** Working in Fields

**2001.** International Year of Volunteers. Mult.
1702 3n. Type **199** 15 15
1703 4n. Planting crops 25 25
1704 10n. Children and bucket 50 50
1705 15n. Planting seeds and making compost 75 75
**MS**1706 170×120 mm. Nos. 1702/5 1·30 1·30

**200** Chenrezig

**2001.** Buddhist Art, Taksang Monastery. Sheet 120×147 mm containing T 200 and similar vert designs. Multicoloured.
**MS**1707 10n. Type **200**; 15n. Guru Rimpoche; 20n. Sakyamuni 2·10 2·10

**2001.** Nos. 557/60 surch.
1708 4n. on 10ch. blue 40 40
1709 10n. on 25ch. red 50 50
1710 15n. on 50ch. violet 70 70
1711 20n. on 1n. brown 95 95

**202** Snow Leopard's Head

**2001.** Snow Leopard (Uncia uncial). Sheet 172×140 mm containing T 202 and similar multicoloured design.
**MS**1712 10n.×4, each ×2, Type **202**; Two adults; Three juveniles; Crouched adult 4·00 4·00

**203** Horse carrying Treasure Vase (Buddhist symbol)

**2002.** Year of the Horse. Multicoloured.
1713 20n. Type **203** 1·00 1·00
1714 20n. White horse 1·00 1·00
**MS**1715 94×94 mm. 25n. Horse and Dharma Wheel (horiz) 1·20 1·20

Nos. 1713/14 were issued together, se-tenant forming a composite design.

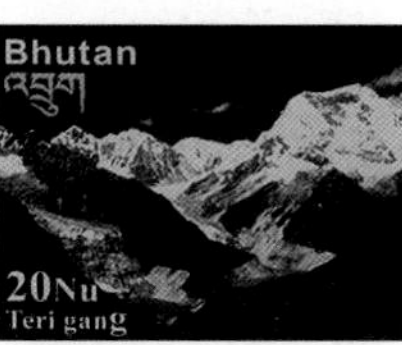


**204** Teri gang

**2002.** International Year of Mountains. Sheet 144×105 mm containing T 204 and similar horiz designs. Multicoloured.
**MS**1716 20n. Type **204**; 20n. Tsenda gang; 20n. Jomolhari; 20n. Gangeheytag; 20n. Jitchudrake; 20n. Tse-rim Gang 5·75 5·75

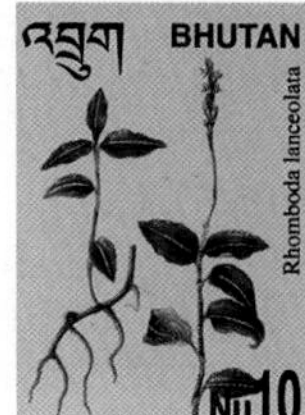


**205** *Rhomboda lanceolata*

**2002.** Orchids. Sheet 162×131 mm containing T 205 and similar vert designs. Multicoloured.
**MS**1717 10n. Type **205**; 10n. *Odontochilus lanceolatus*; 10n. *Zeuxine glandulosai*; 10n. *Goodyera schlechtendaliana*; 10n. *Anoectochilus lanceolatus*; 10n. *Goodyera hispida* 3·00 3·00

**206** *Rhododendron niveum*

**2002.** Rhododendrons. Sheet 132×132 mm containing T 206 and similar square designs. Multicoloured.
**MS**1718 15n. Type **206**; 15n. *Rhododendron glaucophyllum*; 15n. *Rhododendron arboreum*; 15n. *Rhododendron grande*; 15n. *Rhododendron dalhousiae*; 15n. *Rhododendron barbatum* 4·00 4·00

**207** Kapok Tree (*Bombax ceiba*)

**2002.** Medicinal Plants. Multicoloured.
1719 10n. Type **207** 25 25
1720 10n. Angel's trumpet (*Brugmansia suaveolens*) 25 25
1721 10n. Himalayan mayapple (*Podophyllum hexandrum*) 25 25
1722 10n. Himalayan pokeberry (*Photlacca acinosa*) 25 25
**MS**1723 85×106 mm. 10n.×4, Nos. 1719/22 1·20 1·20

**208** Fireman and Flags

**2002.** "United We Stand".
1724 **208** 25n. multicoloured 60 60

**209** Zinedine Zidane

**2002.** World Cup Football Championships, Japan and South Korea. Two sheets containing T 209 and similar vert designs. Multicoloured.
**MS**1725 (a) 167×118 mm. 25n. Type **209**; 25n. Michael Owen; 25n. Miyagi stadium, Japan; 25n. Cuauhtemoc Blanco (inscr "Cuahutemoc"); 25n. Gabriel Batistuta; 25n. Incheon stadium, South Korea; (b) 97×112 mm. 150n. Roberto Carlos 7·00 7·00

210 Queen Elizabeth

**2002.** Golden Jubilee of Queen Elizabeth II. Two sheets containing T 210 and similar square designs. Multicoloured.

**MS**1726 (a) 133×101 mm. 40n. Type **210**; 40n. Wearing green floral hat; 40n. With Duke of Edinburgh; 40n. Wearing white hat; (b) 79×108 mm. 90n. Wearing tiara 6·00 6·00

211 Ski Jumping

**2002.** Winter Olympic Games, Salt Lake City, USA. Sheet 89×120 mm containing T 211 and similar vert design. Multicoloured.

**MS**1727 50n. Type **211**; 50n. Cross country skiing 2·40 2·40

212 Lotus Flower

**2002.** United Nations Year of Eco-Tourism. Two sheets containing T 212 and similar vert designs. Multicoloured.

**MS**1728 (a) 117×75 mm. 50n. Type **212**; 50n. Northern jungle queen butterfly; 50n. Bengal tiger; (b) 72×95 mm. 90n. Peacock 5·75 5·75

213 Cub Scout

**2002.** World Scout Jamboree, Thailand. Two sheets containing T 213 and similar multicoloured designs.

**MS**1729 (a) 182×142 mm. 50n. Type **213**; 50n. Scouts of different nationalities; 50n. 1908 Scout; (b) 90×120 mm. 90n. Dan Beard (founder of American Boy Scouts) (vert) 5·75 5·75

214 Charles Lindbergh and *The Spirit of St Louis*

**2002.** 75th Anniv of First Solo Trans-Atlantic Flight. Two sheets containing T 214 and similar vert designs. Multicoloured.

**MS**1730 (a) 171×134 mm. 75n. Type **214**; 75n. Lindbergh; (b) 123×89 mm. 90n. Lindbergh (different) 5·75 5·75

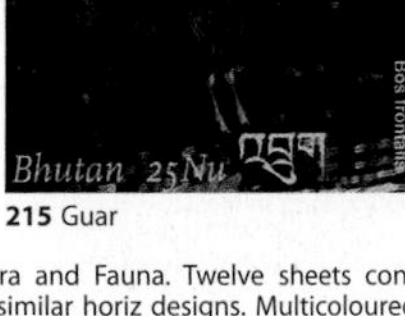
215 Guar

**2002.** Flora and Fauna. Twelve sheets containing T 215 and similar horiz designs. Multicoloured.

**MS**1731 (a) 132×155 mm. 25n. Type **215**; 25n. Hog badger; 25n. Indian cobra; 25n. Leopard gecko; 25n. Gavial; 25n. Hispid hare; (b) 132×155 mm. 25n. Yellow-legged gull; 25n. Sand martin; 25n. Asian open-bill stork; 25n. White stork; 25n. Eurasian oystercatcher; 25n. Indian pitta; (c) 132×155 mm. 25n. Blue oak-leaf butterfly (inscr "Dead leaf butterfly") (Kalima horsfieldi); 25n. Golden birdwing (*Troides aeacus*); 25n. *Atrophaneura latrellei*; 25n. Kaiser-I-Hind (*Teinopalpus imperialis*); 25n. *Zeuxidia aurelius*; 25n. *Euploea dufresne*; (d) 137×158 mm. 25n. *Primula cawdoriana*; 25n. *Meconopsis aculeate*; 25n. *Primula wigramiana*; 25n. *Primula stuartii*; 25n. *Saxifraga andersonii*; 25n. *Rheum nobile*; (e) 133×153 mm. 25n. *Russula integra*; 25n. *Hydgrophorus marzuolus*; 25n. *Trichloma fulvum*; 25n. *Hypholoma fasciculare*; 25n. *Tricholoma populinum*; 25n. *Cortinarius orellanus*; (f) 136×161 mm. 25n. *Coelogyne rhodeana*; 25n. *Coelogyne virescens*; 25n. *Phalanopsis schilleriana*; 25n. *Angraecum eburneum*; 25n. *Dendrobium aureum*; 25n. *Dendrobium Ceasar*; (g) 89×92 mm. 90n. Esturine crocodile; (h) 89×94 mm. 90n. Mandarin duck; (i) 93×94 mm. 90n. *Portia philota*; (j) 103×101 mm. 90n. *Paris polyphylla*; (k) 101×101 mm. 90n. *Clathrus archeri*; (l) 99×100 mm. 90n. *Dendrobium chrysotoxum* 35·00 35·00

216 Elvis Presley

**2003.** Anniversaries in 2002. 25th Death Anniv of Elvis Presley (entertainer) (MS1732a/b). 85th Birth Anniv of John Fitzgerald Kennedy (president USA, 1961–1963) (MS1732c/d). 5th Death Anniv of Diana, Princess of Wales (MS1732e/f). Six sheets containing T 216 and similar vert designs. Multicoloured.

**MS**1732 Six sheets (a) 110×178 mm. 25n.×4, Type **216**; Holding guitar at waist; Singing into microphone; Seated holding guitar to side; (b) 195×131 mm. 25n.×6, Wearing shirt and kerchief; (c) 132×146 mm. 25n.×6, College graduate, 1935; Walking with John F. Kennedy Jr.; As Congressman, 1946; At the White House, 1961; With Jacqueline Kennedy on tennis court; Jacqueline Kennedy and children at John F. Kennedy's funeral; (d) 76×108 mm. 90n. Head and shoulders; (e) 134×118 mm. 25n.×4, Wearing earrings and red dress; Wearing ballgown; Wearing jacket and blouse; Wearing tiara; (f) 65×98 mm. 90n. Wearing hat with feathers 17·00 17·00

**2003.** No. 659 surch 8NU.

1733 8n. on 75ch. multicoloured 20 20

218 Lamb

**2003.** Chinese New Year. ("Year of the Sheep"). Sheet 120×80 mm containing T 218 and similar multicoloured design.

**MS**1734 15n. Type **218**; 20n. Sheep's head (vert) 80 80

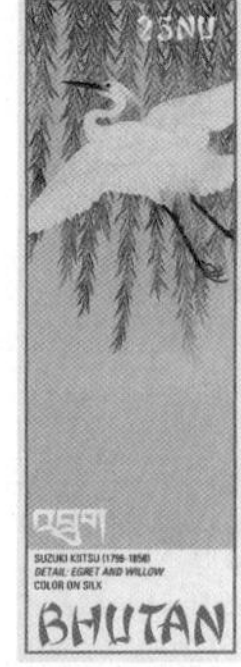
219 "Egret and Willow" (Suzuki Kitsu)

**2003.** Japanese Paintings. Six sheets containing T 219 and similar multicoloured designs.

**MS**1735 (a) 135×210 mm. 25n.×6, Type **219**; "White Cranes" (Ito Jakuchu); "Cranes" (Suzuki Kitsu); "Mandarin Ducks amid Snow-covered Reeds" (Ito Jakuchu); "Rooster, Hen and Hydrangea" (Ito Jakuchu); "Hawk on Snow-covered Branch" (Shibara Zeshin); (b) 135×210 mm. 25n.×6, "Beauty reading Letter" (Utagawa Kunisada); "Two Beauties" (Katsukawa Shunsho); "Beauty arranging her Hair" (Kaigetsudo Doshin); "Dancing" (Suzuki Kitsu); "Two Beauties" (Kitagawa Kikumaro); "Kambun Beauty"; (c) 159×140 mm. 25n.×6, Two seated men and one lying down (38×51 mm); Man holding fan, man holding lute and man facing left (38×51 mm); Man with raised arm and woman facing left (38×51 mm); Two men talking and two facing left (38×51 mm); Man wearing blue robe facing right and bald man (38×51 mm); Man with beard and two women (38×51 mm); (d) 90×90 mm. 90n. "Heads of Nine Beauties in a Roundel with Plum Blossom" (Hosoda Eishi); (e) 90×90 mm. 90n. "Hawk carrying Monkey" (Shibata Zeshin); (f) 92×92 mm. "Chrysanthemums by a Stream, with Rocks" (Ito Jakuchu) 17·00 17·00

The stamps of No. **MS**1735c form a composite design of "Thirty six Poets".

220 Lyonpo Sangay Ngedup

**2003.** Move for Health Walk (walk by Lyonpo Sangay Ngedup (Health Minister) from Trashigang to Thimphu). Sheet 120×80 mm.

**MS**1736 **220** 50n. multicoloured 1·20 1·20

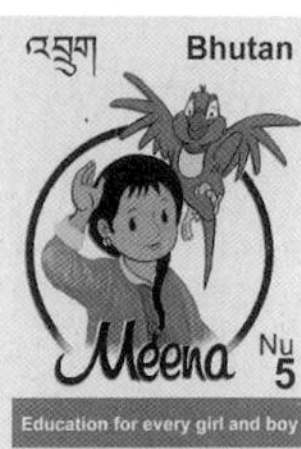

221 Girl and Parrot

**2003.** Education for All. Sheet 70×109 mm containing T 221 and similar vert designs. Multicoloured.

**MS**1737 5n. Type **221**; 5n. Girl reading; 10n. Boy and girl carrying books; 20n. Girl holding football 1·00 1·00

222 Kalij Pheasant (*Lophura leucomelana*) (inscr "leucomelanus")

**2003.** Endangered Species. Birds. Sheet 69×100 mm containing T 222 and similar vert designs. Multicoloured.

**MS**1738 2n. Type **222**; 5n. Blyth's tragopan (*Tragopan blythii*); 8n. Satyr tragopan (*Tragopan satyra*); 15n. Himalayan monal pheasant (*Lophophorus impeyanus*) (inscr "impejanus") 70 70

223 Monkey

**2004.** New Year. Year of the Monkey. Sheet 95×130 mm containing T 223 and similar vert designs. Multicoloured.

**MS**1739 10n.×4, Type **223**; Facing left; With raised back legs; Family 1·00 1·00

The stamps and margin of No. **MS**1739 were issued together, se-tenant, forming a composite design.

224 Brazil World Cup Champions Team, 2002

**2004.** Centenary of FIFA (Federation Internationale de Football Association). Multicoloured.

1740 10n. Type **224** 25 25

1741 10n. France World Cup Champions team, 1998 25 25

**2004.** No. 421 surch 5n.

1742 5n. on 1n. multicoloured 15 15

226 Traditional Ploughing

**2004.** 20th Anniv of Continuing Japanese Assistance with Food Production. Two sheets containing T 226 and similar multicoloured designs.

**MS**1743 (a) 155×105 mm. 5n.×6, Type **225**; Women transplanting; Traditional threshing; Modern ploughing; Modern transplanting; Modern threshing. (b) 130×85 mm. 30n. King Jigme Singe Wangchuk ploughing 1·50 1·50

The stamps and margin of No. **MS**1743a were issued together, se-tenant, forming a composite design.

227 Jungle Fowl

**2005.** New Year. "Year of the Rooster". Sheet 155×110 mm containing T 227 and similar horiz design. Multicoloured.

**MS**1744 15n. Type **227**; 20n. Domestic fowl 85 85

228 Dancer

**2005.** EXPO 2005 World Exposition, Aichi, Japan. Two sheets containing T 228 and similar vert designs. Multicoloured.

**MS**1745 126×201 mm. 10n. Type **228**; 10n. Dancer wearing skull mask; 20n. Dancer holding drum; 20n. Dancer wearing horned mask 1·50 1·50

**MS**1746 124×80 mm. 30n. Buddha (25×35 mm) 75 75

**229** Pope John Paul II

**2005.** Pope John Paul II Commemoration. Multicoloured.

1747 15n. Type **229** 40 40

1747a 15n. As No. 1747 40 40

1747b 15n. As No. 1747 40 40

1747c 15n. As No. 1747 40 40

**230** Locomotive P36 N 0097

**2005.** Bicentenary of Steam Locomotives (2004). Multicoloured.

1748-1751 30n.×4, Type **230**; Diesel locomotive VIA F 40 6428; InterRegio electric train, Amtrak 464 3·00 3·00

**MS**1752 100×71 mm. 85n. Locomotive P36N0032 (vert) 2·00 2·00

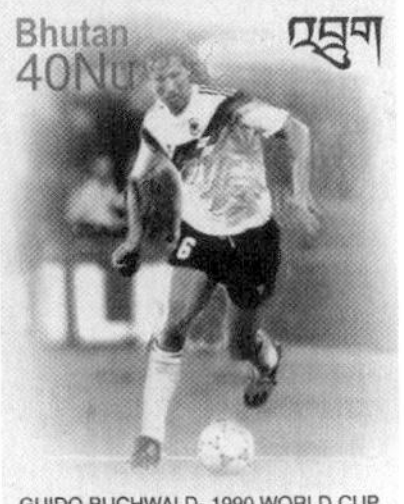


**231** Guido Buchwald

**2005.** 75th Anniv of World Cup Football Championships. Multicoloured.

1753-1755 40n.×3, Type **231**; Mario Basler; Torsten Frings 3·00 3·00

**MS**1756 124×105 mm. 85n. Fredi Bobic 2·00 2·00

**232** Linked Hands and Emblem

**2005.** Centenary of Rotary International. Sheet 95×113 mm.

**MS**1757 **232** 85n. multicoloured 2·00 2·00

**232a** Wachy Zam, Wangduephodrang

**2005.** Bridges. Sheet 200×160 mm containing T 232a and similar horiz designs. Multicoloured.

**MS**1758 10n. Type **232a**; 10n. Chain bridge, Doksam; 10n. Wooden cantilevered bridge, Mishi, Paro; 20n. Mo Chu bridge, Punakha; 20n. Langjo bridge, Thimphu; 20n. Punatshang Chu bridge, Wangduephodrang 2·20 2·20

**233** Children from Many Nations

**2005.** "My Dream of Peace One Day". Winning Designs in Children's Painting Competition. Multicoloured.

1759-1764 10n.×6, Type **233**; Candle of flags; Children holding jigsaw of family; Dove and light and dark hands holding globe; Hands holding children and dark globe releasing doves; Globe holding umbrella of flags 1·50 1·50

**234** King Jigme Singye Wangchuck

**2005.** 50th Birth Anniv of King Jigme Singye Wangchuck. Sheet 216×163 mm containing T 234 and similar vert designs. Multicoloured.

**MS**1765 20n.×5 Type **234**; Standing on podium (inauguration) (39×87 mm); Speaking with microphone; Seated on throne; With women 2·60 2·60

The stamps of **MS**1765 share a composite background design.

**234a** Raven

**2005.** National Symbols. Sheet 200×160 mm containing T 234a and similar square designs. Multicoloured.

**MS**1766 10n. Type **234a**; 10n. Takin (*Budorcas taxicolor*); 20n. Cypress tree; 20n. Blue poppy 1·30 1·30

**235** St. Bernard

**2006.** New Year. Year of the Dog. Multicoloured.

1767 5n. Type **235** 15 15

1768 10n. Lhasa Apso (Inscr 'Apsoo') 25 25

1769 15n. Maltese terrier (inscr 'Maltese') 40 40

1770 20n. Papillion (inscr 'Papillon') 50 50

**MS**1771 125×105 mm. 5n. As No. 1767; 10n. As No. 1768; 15n. As No. 1769; 20n. As No. 1770; 25n. Husky (36×70 mm) 1·90 1·90

**236** Jakur Dzong

**2006.** 50th Anniv of Europa Stamps. Multicoloured.

1772 150n. Type **236** 3·75

1773 250n. Archery 6·25

**MS**1774 100×72 mm. Nos. 1772/3 10·00 10·00

**237** Female Fire Hog

**2007.** New Year. Year of the Pig. Multicoloured.

1775 20n. Type **237** 50 50

**MS**1776 93×120 mm. 25n. Pig (35×33 mm) 2·00 2·00

**239** Ugyen Wangchuck (1907–1926)

**2008.** Centenary of Monarchy. Two sheets containing T 239 and similar multicoloured designs. Self-adhesive (MS1780) or ordinary gum (MS1779).

**MS**1779 170×122 mm. 5n. Type **239**; 10n. Jigme Wangchuck (1926–52); 15n. Jigme Dorji Wangchuck (1952–72); 20n. Jigme Singye Wangchuck (1972–2006); 25n. Jigme Khesar Namgyel Wangchuck (2006–) 1·80 1·80

**MS**1780 97×97 mm. 225n. Kings of Wangchuck dynasty 6·25 6·25

Nos. 1777/8 and Type **238** have been left for 'Year of the Rat', issued on 8 February 2008, not yet received.

No. **MS**1778 consists of a sleeve containing a CD ROM.

**240** (Illustration reduced. Actual size 97×97 mm) (image scaled to 50% of original size)

**2008.** In Harmony with Nature. Sheet 97×97 mm. Self-adhesive.

**MS**1781 multicoloured 6·25 6·25

No. **MS**1781 consists of a sleeve containing a CD ROM.

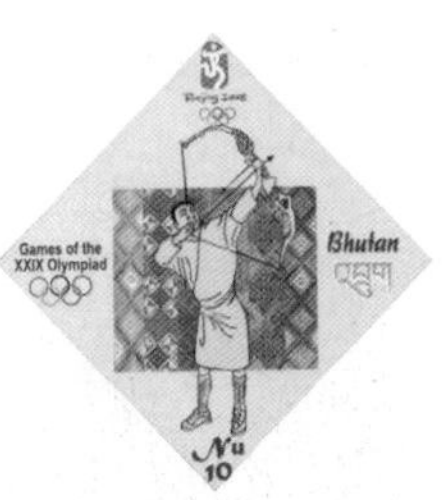


**241** Archer

**2008.** Olympic Games, Beijing. Sheet 130×130 mm containing T 241 and similar diamond shaped designs. Multicoloured.

**MS**1782 10n. Type **241**; 15n. Archer with leg raised; 25n. Auspicious symbols; 25n. Garuda in flight 1·80 1·80

**242** Masked Dancers

**2008.** Bhutan's Participation at Smithsonian Folklife Festival. Three sheets containing T 242 and similar multicoloured designs.

**MS**1783 230×168 mm. 20n.×5, Type **242**; Archer; Ploughing; Dancers; Wood carving 1·50 1·50

**MS**1784 100×90 mm. 50n. Pavillion (38×50 mm) 3·50 3·50

**MS**1785 100×90 mm. 50n. Fireworks (50×38 mm) 1·80 1·80

**243** Ox

**2009.** Chinese New Year

1786 20n. Type **243** 65 65

**MS**1787 162×210 mm. 30n. As Type **243** (40×30 mm) 1·10 1·10

**244** Cantilever Bridge

**2009.** Punakha Dzong Bridge. Multicoloured.

1788 20n. Type **244** 65 65

**MS**1789 170×118 mm. 25n.×2, Bridge, left; Bridge, right 1·40 1·40

The stamps and margins of **MS**1789 form a composite design of the bridge and environs.

**245** Eclipse (diamond ring effect)

**2009.** International Year of Astronomy. Multicoloured.

**MS**1790 25n.×2, Type **245**; Musicians and partial eclipse 1·70 1·70

**246** Child leading Yaks carrying Gifted Rice from Japan

**2009.** 35th Anniv of World Food Programme in Bhutan

**MS**1791 200×119mm. 10n. Type **246**; 10n.Yaks carrying gifted rice from Saudi Arabia; 10n. Gifted rice in store; 10n. Cultivating hillside; 10n. People on track; 10n. New dwelling; 20n. Mother and child; 20n. Feeding children; 20n. Children studying 3·75 3·75

**MS**1792 100×75mm. 25n. Children holding red 'fill the cup' mugs (46×46mm) 90 90

**247** Kushuthara

**2009.** Textiles. Multicoloured.

| | | | |
|---|---|---|---|
| **MS**1793 20n.x4, Type **245**; Mentse Mathra; Lungserma; Yathra | | 2·75 | 2·75 |

**248** Red Panda and Cub

**2009.** Red Panda (*Ailurus fulgens*). Multicoloured.

| | | | |
|---|---|---|---|
| 1794 | 20n. Type **248** | 1·20 | 1·20 |
| 1795 | 20n. Facing left | 1·20 | 1·20 |
| 1796 | 25n. Two pandas sleeping | 1·40 | 1·40 |
| 1797 | 25n. Eating bamboo shoots | | |

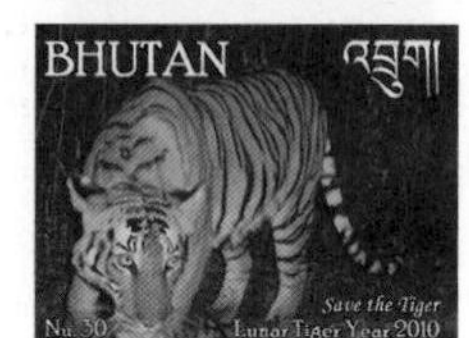

**249** Tiger

**2010.** Chinese New Year

| | | |
|---|---|---|
| **MS**1798 30n.×2, Type **249**; Laying facing right | 1·90 | 1·90 |
| **MS**1799 50n. Head and shoulders (vert) | 1·60 | 1·60 |

**APPENDIX**

The following stamps have either been issued in excess of postal needs or have not been available to the public in reasonable quantities at face value. Such stamps may later be given full listing if there is evidence of regular postal use.

**1968**

Bhutan Pheasants. 1, 2, 4, 8, 15ch., 2, 4, 5, 7, 9n.
Winter Olympic Games, Grenoble. Optd on 1966 Abominable Snowmen issue. 40ch., 1n.25, 3, 6n.
Butterflies (plastic-surfaced). Postage 15, 50ch., 1n.25, 2n.; Air 3, 4, 5, 6n.
Paintings (relief-printed). Postage 2, 4, 5, 10, 45, 80ch., 1n.05, 1n.40, 2, 3, 4, 5n.; Air 1n.50, 2n.50, 6, 8n.
Olympic Games, Mexico. 5, 45, 60, 80ch., 1n.05, 2, 3, 5n.
Human Rights Year. Die-stamped surch on unissued "Coins". 15ch. on 50n.p., 33ch. on 1r., 9n. on 3r.75.

**1969**

Flood Relief. Surch on 1968 Mexico Olympics issue. 5ch.+5ch., 80ch.+25ch., 2n.+50ch.
Fish (plastic-surfaced). Postage 15, 20, 30ch.; Air 5, 6, 7n.
Insects (plastic-surfaced). Postage 10, 75ch., 1n.25, 2n.; Air 3, 4, 5, 6n.
Admission of Bhutan to Universal Postal Union. 5, 10, 15, 45, 60ch., 1n.05, 1n.40, 4n.
5000 Years of Steel Industry. On steel foil. Postage 2, 5, 15, 45, 75ch., 1n.50, 1n.75, 2n.; Air 3, 4, 5, 6n.
Birds (plastic-surfaced). Postage 15, 50ch., 1n.25, 2n.; Air 3, 4, 5, 6n.
Buddhist Prayer Banners. On silk rayon. 15, 75ch., 2, 5, 6n.
Moon Landing of "Apollo 11" (plastic-surfaced). Postage 3, 5, 15, 20, 25, 45, 50ch., 1n.75; Air 3, 4, 5, 6n.

**1970**

Famous Paintings (plastic-surfaced). Postage 5, 10, 15ch., 2n.75; Air 3, 4, 5, 6n.
New U.P.U. Headquarters Building, Berne. 3, 10, 20ch., 2n.50.
Flower Paintings (relief-printed). Postage 2, 3, 5, 10, 15, 75ch., 1n., 1n.40; Air 80, 90ch., 1n.10, 1n.40, 1n.60, 1n.70, 3n., 3n.50.
Animals (plastic-surfaced). Postage 5, 10, 20, 25, 30, 40, 65, 75, 85ch.; Air 2, 3, 4, 5n.
Conquest of Space (plastic-surfaced). Postage 2, 5, 15, 25, 30, 50, 75ch., 1n.50; Air 2, 3, 6, 7n.

**1971**

History of Sculpture (plastic-moulded). Postage 10, 75ch., 1n.25, 2n.; Air 3, 4, 5, 6n.
Moon Vehicles (plastic-surfaced). Postage 10ch., 1n.70; Air 2n.50, 4n.
History of the Motor Car (plastic-surfaced). Postage 2, 5, 10, 15, 20, 30, 60, 75, 85ch., 1n., 1n.20, 1n.55, 1n.80, 2n., 2n.50; Air 4, 6, 7, 9, 10n.
Bhutan's Admission to United Nations. Postage 5, 10, 20ch., 3n.; Air 2n.50, 5, 6n.
60th Anniv of Boy Scout Movement. 10, 20, 50, 75ch., 2, 6n.
World Refugee Year. Optd on 1971 United Nations issue. Postage 5, 10, 20ch., 3n.; Air 2n.50, 5, 6n.

**1972**

Famous Paintings (relief-printed). Postage 15, 20, 90ch., 2n.50; Air 1n.70, 4n.60, 5n.40, 6n.
Famous Men (plastic-moulded). Postage 10, 15, 55ch.; Air 2, 6, 8n.
Olympic Games, Munich. Postage 10, 15, 20, 30, 45ch.; Air 35ch., 1n.35, 7n.
Space Flight of "Apollo 16" (plastic-surfaced). Postage 15, 20, 90ch., 2n.50; Air 1n.70, 4n.60, 5n.40, 6n.

**1973**

Dogs. 2, 3, 15, 20, 30, 99ch., 2n.50, 4n.
Roses (on scent-impregnated paper). Postage 15, 25, 30ch., 3n.; Air 6, 7n.
Moon Landing of "Apollo 17" (plastic-surfaced). Postage 10, 15, 55ch. 2n.; Air 7, 9n.
"Talking Stamps" (miniature records). Postage 10, 25ch., 1n.25, 7, 8n.; Air 3, 9n.
Death of King Jigme Dorji Wangchuck. Embossed on gold foil. Postage 10, 25ch., 3n.; Air 6, 8n.
Mushrooms. 15, 25, 30ch., 3, 6, 7n.
"Indipex 73" Stamp Exhibition, New Delhi. Postage 5, 10, 15, 25ch., 1n.25, 3n.; Air 5, 6n.

Pt. 1

## BIAFRA

The Eastern Region of Nigeria declared its Independence on 30 May 1967 as the Republic of Biafra. Nigerian military operations against the breakaway Republic commenced in July 1967.

The Biafran postal service continued to use Nigerian stamps when supplies of these became low. In July 1967 "Postage Paid" cachets were used pending the issue of Nos. 1/3.

12 pence = 1 shilling; 20 shillings = 1 pound.

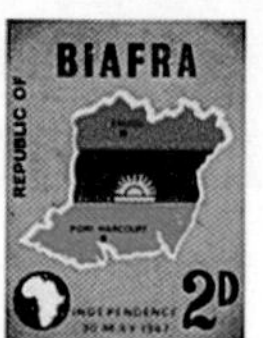

**1** Map of Republic

**1968.** Independence. Multicoloured.

| | | | | |
|---|---|---|---|---|
| 1 | | 2d. Type **1** | 10 | 70 |
| 2 | | 4d. Arms, flag and date of Independence | 10 | 70 |
| 3 | | 1s. Mother and child (17×22 mm) | 15 | 2·00 |

**1968.** Nos. 172/5 and 177/85 of Nigeria optd **SOVEREIGN BIAFRA** and arms.

| | | | |
|---|---|---|---|
| 4 | ½d. multicoloured (No. 172) | 2·00 | 5·00 |
| 5 | 1d. multicoloured (No. 173) | 3·25 | 8·00 |
| 6 | 1½d. multicoloured (No. 174) | 12·00 | 16·00 |
| 7 | 2d. multicoloured (No. 175) | 29·00 | 50·00 |
| 8 | 4d. multicoloured (No. 177) | 18·00 | 50·00 |
| 9 | 6d. multicoloured (No. 178) | 9·00 | 15·00 |
| 10 | 9d. blue and red (No. 179) | 3·25 | 3·50 |
| 11 | 1s. multicoloured (No. 180) | 60·00 | £110 |
| 12 | 1s.3d. multicoloured (No. 181) | 35·00 | 50·00 |
| 13 | 2s.6d. multicoloured (No. 182) | 3·00 | 16·00 |
| 14 | 5s. multicoloured (No. 183) | 3·50 | 15·00 |
| 15 | 10s. multicoloured (No. 184) | 10·00 | 40·00 |
| 16 | £1 multicoloured (No. 185) | 10·00 | 40·00 |

The overprint on No. 15 does not include **SOVEREIGN**.

**5** Flag and Scientist

**1968.** 1st Anniv of Independence. Multicoloured.

| | | | |
|---|---|---|---|
| 17 | 4d. Type **5** | 20 | 20 |
| 18 | 1s. Victim of atrocity | 20 | 30 |
| 19 | 2s.6d. Nurse and refugees | 55 | 4·50 |
| 20 | 5s. Biafran arms and banknote | 60 | 5·00 |
| 21 | 10s. Orphaned child | 1·00 | 5·50 |

**16** Child in Chains, and Globe

**1969.** 2nd Anniv of Independence. Multicoloured; frame colours given.

| | | | | |
|---|---|---|---|---|
| 35 | **16** | 2d. orange | 1·25 | 4·25 |
| 36 | **16** | 4d. red | 1·25 | 4·25 |
| 37 | **16** | 1s. blue | 1·75 | 7·00 |
| 38 | **16** | 2s.6d. green | 2·00 | 14·00 |

**17** Pope Paul VI, Africa, and Papal Arms

**1969.** Visit of Pope Paul to Africa. Multicoloured; background colours given.

| | | | | |
|---|---|---|---|---|
| 39 | **17** | 4d. orange | 60 | 3·00 |
| 40 | - | 6d. blue | 75 | 6·50 |
| 41 | - | 9d. green | 95 | 8·50 |
| 42 | - | 3s. mauve | 2·50 | 14·00 |

DESIGNS: Pope Paul VI, map of Africa and 6d. Arms of Vatican; 9d. St. Peter's Basilica; 3s. Statue of St. Peter.

Pt. 1

## BIJAWAR

A state of Central India. Now uses Indian stamps.

12 pies = 1 anna; 16 annas = 1 rupee.

**1** Maharaja Sarwant Singh

**1935**

| | | | | |
|---|---|---|---|---|
| 6 | **1** | 3p. brown | 6·00 | 8·50 |
| 2 | **1** | 6p. red | 8·00 | 6·00 |
| 3 | **1** | 9p. violet | 11·00 | 6·50 |
| 4 | **1** | 1a. blue | 12·00 | 6·00 |
| 5 | **1** | 2a. green | 11·00 | 6·00 |

**2** Maharaja Sarwant Singh

**1937**

| | | | | |
|---|---|---|---|---|
| 11 | **2** | 4a. orange | 19·00 | 95·00 |
| 12 | **2** | 6a. lemon | 19·00 | 95·00 |
| 13 | **2** | 8a. green | 20·00 | £140 |
| 14 | **2** | 12a. blue | 20·00 | £140 |
| 15 | **2** | 1r. violet | 42·00 | £190 |

Pt. 5

## BOHEMIA AND MORAVIA

Following the proclamation of Slovak Independence on 14 March, 1939, the Czech provinces of Bohemia and Moravia became a German Protectorate. The area was liberated in 1945 and returned to Czechoslovakia.

100 haleru = 1 koruna.

**1939.** Stamps of Czechoslovakia optd **BOHMEN u. MAHREN CECHY a MORAVA**.

| | | | | |
|---|---|---|---|---|
| 1 | **34** | 5h. blue | 55 | 2·40 |
| 2 | **34** | 10h. brown | 55 | 2·40 |
| 3 | **34** | 20h. red | 65 | 2·40 |
| 4 | **34** | 25h. green | 30 | 4·00 |
| 5 | **34** | 30h. purple | 55 | 2·40 |
| 6 | **59** | 40h. blue | 4·25 | 9·75 |
| 7 | **77** | 50h. green | 30 | 2·40 |
| 8 | **60a** | 60h. violet | 4·25 | 11·50 |
| 9 | **61** | 1k. purple (No. 348) | 80 | 4·00 |
| 10 | **61** | 1k. purple (No. 395) | 65 | 2·40 |
| 11 | - | 1k.20 purple (No. 354) | 3·75 | 9·75 |
| 12 | **64** | 1k.50 red | 3·25 | 13·00 |
| 13 | - | 1k.60 green (No. 355a) | 4·75 | 14·50 |
| 14 | - | 2k. green (No. 356) | 1·60 | 13·00 |
| 15 | - | 2k.50 blue (No. 357) | 3·75 | 9·75 |
| 16 | - | 3k. brown (No. 358) | 3·75 | 13·00 |
| 17 | **65** | 4k. violet | 5·75 | 14·50 |
| 18 | - | 5k. green (No. 361) | 5·75 | 18·00 |
| 19 | - | 10k. blue (No. 362) | 6·75 | 28·00 |

**2** Linden Leaves and Buds

**3** Karluv Tyn Castle

**5** Zlin

**1939**

| | | | | |
|---|---|---|---|---|
| 20 | **2** | 5h. blue | 20 | 40 |
| 21 | **2** | 10h. brown | 20 | 55 |
| 22 | **2** | 20h. red | 20 | 40 |
| 23 | **2** | 25h. green | 20 | 40 |
| 24 | **2** | 30h. purple | 20 | 40 |
| 25 | - | 40h. blue | 20 | 40 |
| 26 | **3** | 50h. green | 20 | 40 |
| 27 | - | 60h. violet | 20 | 40 |
| 28 | - | 1k. red | 20 | 40 |
| 29 | - | 1k.20 purple | 40 | 75 |
| 30 | - | 1k.50 red | 20 | 40 |
| 31 | - | 2k. green | 20 | 65 |
| 32 | - | 2k.50 blue | 20 | 40 |
| 33 | **5** | 3k. mauve | 20 | 40 |
| 34 | - | 4k. grey | 20 | 55 |
| 35 | - | 5k. green | 65 | 1·10 |
| 36 | - | 10k. blue | 55 | 1·30 |
| 37 | - | 20k. brown | 1·60 | 2·75 |

DESIGNS—As Type **3**: 40h. Svikov Castle; 60h. St. Barbara's Church, Kutna Hora; 1k. St. Vitus's Cathedral, Prague. As Type **5**—VERT: 1k.20, 1k.50, Brno Cathedral; 2k., 2k.50, Olomouc. HORIZ: 4k. Ironworks, Moravska-Ostrava; 5k., 10k., 20k. Karlsburg, Prague.

**1940.** As 1939 issue, but colours changed and new values.

| | | | | |
|---|---|---|---|---|
| 38 | **2** | 30h. brown | 20 | 20 |
| 39 | **2** | 40h. orange | 20 | 20 |
| 40 | **2** | 50h. green | 20 | 20 |
| 44 | - | 50h. green | 30 | 30 |
| 41 | **2** | 60h. violet | 20 | 20 |
| 42 | **2** | 80h. orange | 30 | 30 |
| 45 | - | 80h. blue | 20 | 40 |
| 43 | **2** | 1k. brown | 30 | 30 |
| 46 | - | 1k.20 brown | 40 | 30 |
| 47 | - | 1k.20 red | 30 | 30 |
| 48 | - | 1k.50 pink | 30 | 40 |
| 49 | - | 2k. green | 30 | 30 |
| 50 | - | 2k. blue | 30 | 40 |
| 51 | - | 2k.50 blue | 65 | 75 |
| 52 | - | 3k. green | 85 | 1·10 |
| 53 | - | 5k. green | 30 | 30 |
| 54 | - | 6k. brown | 30 | 75 |
| 55 | - | 8k. green | 30 | 40 |
| 56 | - | 10k. blue | 65 | 40 |
| 57 | - | 20k. brown | 1·30 | 3·25 |

DESIGNS—As Type **3**: 50h. (No. 44), Neuhaus Castle; 80h. (No. 45), 3k. Pernstyn Castle; 1k.20 (No. 46), 2k.50, Brno Cathedral; 1k.20 (No. 47), St. Vitus's Cathedral, Prague; 1k.50 St. Barbara's Church, Kutna Hora; 2k. Pardubitz Castle. As Type **5**—HORIZ: 5k. Bridge at Beching; 6k. Samson Fountain, Budweis; 8k. Kremsier; 10k. Wallenstein Palace, Prague; 20k. Karlsburg, Prague.

**6** Red Cross Nurse and Wounded Soldier

**1940.** Red Cross Relief Fund.

| | | | | |
|---|---|---|---|---|
| 58 | **6** | 60h.+40h. blue | 65 | 1·30 |
| 59 | **6** | 1k.20+80h. plum | 65 | 1·30 |

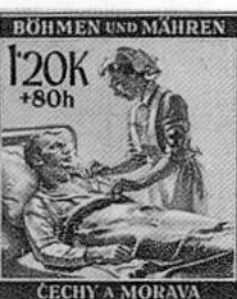

**7** Patient in Hospital

**1941.** Red Cross Relief Fund.

| | | | | |
|---|---|---|---|---|
| 60 | **7** | 60h.+40h. blue | 40 | 1·40 |
| 61 | **7** | 1k.20+80h. plum | 40 | 1·40 |

**8** Anton Dvorak

**1941.** Birth Centenary of Dvorak (composer).

| | | | | |
|---|---|---|---|---|
| 62 | **8** | 60h. violet | 40 | 75 |
| 63 | **8** | 1k.20 brown | 40 | 75 |

**9** Harvesting

**10** Blast furnace, Pilsen

**1941.** Prague Fair.

| | | | | |
|---|---|---|---|---|
| 64 | **9** | 30h. brown | 20 | 55 |
| 65 | **9** | 60h. green | 20 | 55 |
| 66 | **10** | 1k.20 plum | 20 | 55 |
| 67 | **10** | 2k.50 blue | 20 | 1·10 |

**11** "Ständetheater", Prague

**12** Mozart

**1941.** 150th Death Anniv of Mozart.

| | | | | |
|---|---|---|---|---|
| 68 | **11** | 30h.+30h. brown | 20 | 40 |
| 69 | **11** | 60h.+60h. green | 20 | 40 |
| 70 | **12** | 1k.20+1k.20 red | 20 | 40 |
| 71 | **12** | 2k.50+2k.50 blue | 40 | 85 |

**(13)**

**1942.** 3rd Anniv of German Occupation. Optd with T **13**

| | | | |
|---|---|---|---|
| 72 | 1k.20 red (No. 47) | 55 | 1·40 |
| 73 | 2k.50 blue (No. 51) | 55 | 1·40 |

**14** Adolf Hitler

**1942.** Hitler's 53rd Birthday.

| | | | | |
|---|---|---|---|---|
| 74 | **14** | 30h.+20h. brown | 20 | 40 |
| 75 | **14** | 60h.+40h. green | 20 | 40 |
| 76 | **14** | 1k.20+80h. purple | 20 | 40 |
| 77 | **14** | 2k.50+1k.50 blue | 30 | 1·40 |

**15** Adolf Hitler

**1942.** Various sizes.

| | | | | |
|---|---|---|---|---|
| 78 | **15** | 10h. black | 20 | 30 |
| 79 | **15** | 30h. brown | 20 | 30 |
| 80 | **15** | 40h. blue | 20 | 30 |
| 81 | **15** | 50h. green | 20 | 30 |
| 82 | **15** | 60h. violet | 20 | 30 |
| 83 | **15** | 80h. orange | 20 | 30 |
| 84 | **15** | 1k. brown | 20 | 30 |
| 85 | **15** | 1k.20 red | 25 | 40 |
| 86 | **15** | 1k.50 red | 25 | 40 |
| 87 | **15** | 1k.60 green | 25 | 40 |
| 88 | **15** | 2k. blue | 25 | 40 |
| 89 | **15** | 2k.40 brown | 25 | 40 |
| 90 | **15** | 2k.50 blue | 25 | 40 |
| 91 | **15** | 3k. olive | 25 | 40 |
| 92 | **15** | 4k. purple | 25 | 40 |
| 93 | **15** | 5k. green | 25 | 40 |
| 94 | **15** | 6k. brown | 25 | 55 |
| 95 | **15** | 8k. blue | 25 | 55 |
| 96 | **15** | 10k. green | 25 | 1·10 |
| 97 | **15** | 20k. violet | 30 | 1·10 |
| 98 | **15** | 30k. red | 55 | 2·50 |
| 99 | **15** | 50k. blue | 1·10 | 3·25 |

SIZES—17½×21½ mm: 10h. to 80h.; 18½×21 mm: 1k. to 2k.40; 19×24 mm: 2k.50 to 8k.; 24×30 mm: 10k. to 50k.

**16** Nurse and Patient

**1942.** Red Cross Relief Fund.

| | | | | |
|---|---|---|---|---|
| 100 | **16** | 60h.+40h. blue | 20 | 40 |
| 101 | **16** | 1k.20+80h. red | 20 | 40 |

**17** Mounted Postman

**1943.** Stamp Day.

| | | | | |
|---|---|---|---|---|
| 102 | **17** | 60h. purple | 25 | 75 |

**18** Peter Parler

**1943.** Winter Relief Fund.

| | | | | |
|---|---|---|---|---|
| 103 | - | 60h.+40h. violet | 20 | 30 |
| 104 | **18** | 1k.20+80h. red | 20 | 30 |
| 105 | - | 2k.50+1k.50 blue | 20 | 30 |

DESIGNS: 60h. Charles IV; 2k.50, King John of Luxembourg.

**19** Adolf Hitler

**1943.** Hitler's 54th Birthday.

| | | | | |
|---|---|---|---|---|
| 106 | **19** | 60h.+1k.40 violet | 20 | 85 |
| 107 | **19** | 1k.20+3k.80 red | 20 | 85 |

**20** Scene from "The Mastersingers of Nuremberg"

**21** Richard Wagner

**1943.** 130th Birth Anniv of Wagner.

| | | | | |
|---|---|---|---|---|
| 108 | **20** | 60h. violet | 10 | 55 |
| 109 | **21** | 1k.20 red | 10 | 55 |
| 110 | - | 2k.50 blue | 10 | 55 |

DESIGN: 2k.50, Blacksmith scene from "Siegfried".

**22** Reinhard Heydrich

**1943.** 1st Death Anniv of Reinhard Heydrich (German Governor).

| | | | | |
|---|---|---|---|---|
| 111 | **22** | 60h.+4k.40 black | 50 | 2·10 |

**23** Arms of Bohemia and Moravia and Red Cross

**1943.** Red Cross Relief Fund.

| | | | | |
|---|---|---|---|---|
| 112 | **23** | 1k.20+8k.80 blk & red | 30 | 65 |

**24** National Costumes

**25** Arms of Bohemia and Moravia

**1944.** 5th Anniv of German Occupation.

| | | | | |
|---|---|---|---|---|
| 113 | **24** | 1k.20+3k.80 red | 20 | 40 |
| 114 | **25** | 4k.20+18k.80 brown | 20 | 40 |
| 115 | **24** | 10k.+20k. blue | 20 | 40 |

**26** Adolf Hitler

**1944.** Hitler's 55th Birthday.

| | | | | |
|---|---|---|---|---|
| 116 | **26** | 60h.+1k.40 brown | 20 | 40 |
| 117 | **26** | 1k.20+3k.80 green | 20 | 40 |

**27** Smetana

**1944.** 60th Death Anniv of Bedrich Smetana (composer).

| | | | | |
|---|---|---|---|---|
| 118 | **27** | 60h.+1k.40 green | 20 | 40 |
| 119 | **27** | 1k.20+3k.80 red | 20 | 40 |

**28** St. Vitus's Cathedral, Prague

**1944**

| | | | | |
|---|---|---|---|---|
| 120 | **28** | 1k.50 purple | 20 | 40 |
| 121 | **28** | 2k.50 violet | 20 | 55 |

**29** Adolf Hitler

**1944**

| | | | | |
|---|---|---|---|---|
| 122 | **29** | 4k.20 green | 30 | 75 |

**NEWSPAPER STAMPS**

**N6** Dove

**1939.** Imperf.

| | | | | |
|---|---|---|---|---|
| N38 | **N6** | 2h. brown | 30 | 40 |
| N39 | **N6** | 5h. blue | 30 | 40 |
| N40 | **N6** | 7h. red | 30 | 40 |
| N41 | **N6** | 9h. green | 30 | 40 |
| N42 | **N6** | 10h. red | 30 | 40 |
| N43 | **N6** | 12h. blue | 30 | 40 |
| N44 | **N6** | 20h. green | 30 | 40 |
| N45 | **N6** | 50h. brown | 30 | 55 |
| N46 | **N6** | 1k. green | 55 | 1·10 |

**1940.** For bulk postings. No. N42 optd **GD-OT**.

| | | | |
|---|---|---|---|
| N60 | 10h. red | 25 | 75 |

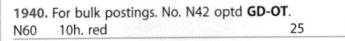

**N19** Dove

**1943.** Imperf.

| | | | | |
|---|---|---|---|---|
| N106 | **N19** | 2h. brown | 10 | 20 |
| N107 | **N19** | 5h. blue | 10 | 20 |
| N108 | **N19** | 7h. red | 10 | 20 |
| N109 | **N19** | 9h. green | 10 | 20 |
| N110 | **N19** | 10h. red | 10 | 20 |
| N111 | **N19** | 12h. blue | 10 | 20 |
| N112 | **N19** | 20h. green | 10 | 20 |
| N113 | **N19** | 50h. brown | 10 | 20 |
| N114 | **N19** | 1k. green | 10 | 20 |

**OFFICIAL STAMPS**

**O7** Numeral and Laurel Wreath

**1941**

| | | | | |
|---|---|---|---|---|
| O60 | **O7** | 30h. brown | 20 | 20 |
| O61 | **O7** | 40h. blue | 20 | 20 |
| O62 | **O7** | 50h. green | 20 | 20 |
| O63 | **O7** | 60h. green | 20 | 20 |
| O64 | **O7** | 80h. red | 55 | 20 |
| O65 | **O7** | 1k. brown | 25 | 20 |
| O66 | **O7** | 1k.20 red | 25 | 20 |
| O67 | **O7** | 1k.50 purple | 40 | 20 |
| O68 | **O7** | 2k. blue | 40 | 20 |
| O69 | **O7** | 3k. green | 40 | 20 |
| O70 | **O7** | 4k. purple | 55 | 65 |
| O71 | **O7** | 5k. yellow | 1·30 | 1·30 |

**O19** Eagle and Numeral

**1943**

| | | | | |
|---|---|---|---|---|
| O106 | **O19** | 30h. brown | 10 | 55 |
| O107 | **O19** | 40h. blue | 10 | 55 |
| O108 | **O19** | 50h. green | 10 | 55 |
| O109 | **O19** | 60h. violet | 10 | 55 |
| O110 | **O19** | 80h. red | 10 | 55 |
| O111 | **O19** | 1k. brown | 10 | 55 |
| O112 | **O19** | 1k.20 red | 10 | 55 |
| O113 | **O19** | 1k.50 brown | 10 | 55 |
| O114 | **O19** | 2k. blue | 10 | 55 |
| O115 | **O19** | 3k. green | 10 | 55 |
| O116 | **O19** | 4k. purple | 10 | 55 |
| O117 | **O19** | 5k. green | 10 | 55 |

**PERSONAL DELIVERY STAMPS**

**P6**

**1939**

| | | | | |
|---|---|---|---|---|
| P38 | **P6** | 50h. blue | 3·25 | 3·75 |
| P39 | **P6** | 50h. red | 2·10 | 4·25 |

**POSTAGE DUE STAMPS**

**D6**

**1939**

| | | | | |
|---|---|---|---|---|
| D38 | **D 6** | 5h. red | 30 | 40 |
| D39 | **D 6** | 10h. red | 30 | 40 |
| D40 | **D 6** | 20h. red | 30 | 40 |
| D41 | **D 6** | 30h. red | 30 | 40 |
| D42 | **D 6** | 40h. red | 30 | 40 |
| D43 | **D 6** | 50h. red | 30 | 40 |
| D44 | **D 6** | 60h. red | 30 | 40 |
| D45 | **D 6** | 80h. red | 30 | 40 |
| D46 | **D 6** | 1k. blue | 30 | 55 |
| D47 | **D 6** | 1k.20 blue | 40 | 55 |
| D48 | **D 6** | 2k. blue | 1·30 | 1·60 |
| D49 | **D 6** | 5k. blue | 1·50 | 2·10 |
| D50 | **D 6** | 10k. blue | 2·10 | 2·75 |
| D51 | **D 6** | 20k. blue | 3·75 | 4·25 |

Pt. 20

# BOLIVAR

One of the states of the Granadine Confederation. A department of Colombia from 1886, now uses Colombian stamps.

1863. 100 centavos = 1 peso.

1

**1863.** Imperf.

| | | | | |
|---|---|---|---|---|
| 1 | 1 | 10c. green | £1700 | £800 |
| 2 | 1 | 10c. red | 39·00 | 37·00 |
| 3 | 1 | 1p. red | 11·00 | 10·50 |

2

3

**1872.** Various frames. Imperf.

| | | | | |
|---|---|---|---|---|
| 4 | 2 | 5c. blue | 10·00 | 9·50 |
| 5 | 3 | 10c. mauve | 10·00 | 9·50 |
| 6 | - | 20c. green | 44·00 | 43·00 |
| 7 | - | 80c. red | 90·00 | 85·00 |

6

7

8

**1874.** Imperf.

| | | | | |
|---|---|---|---|---|
| 8 | 6 | 5c. blue | 33·00 | 18·00 |
| 9 | 7 | 5c. blue | 11·00 | 9·50 |
| 10 | 8 | 10c. mauve | 5·50 | 4·75 |

9 Simon Bolivar

**1879.** Various frames. Dated "1879". White or blue paper. Perf.

| | | | | |
|---|---|---|---|---|
| 14 | 9 | 5c. blue | 45 | 45 |
| 12 | 9 | 10c. mauve | 35 | 30 |
| 13 | 9 | 20c. red | 45 | 45 |

**1880.** Various frames. Dated "1880". White or blue paper.

| | | | |
|---|---|---|---|
| 19 | 5c. blue | 45 | 45 |
| 20 | 10c. mauve | 55 | 55 |
| 21 | 20c. red | 55 | 55 |
| 22 | 80c. green | 3·25 | 3·25 |
| 23 | 1p. orange | 3·50 | 3·50 |

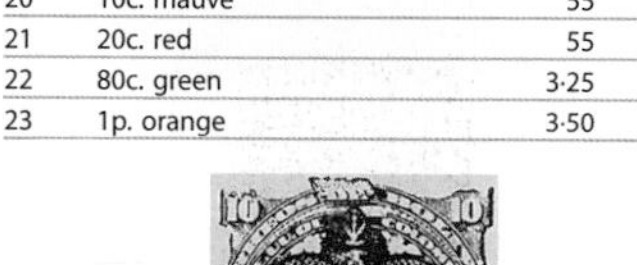

10 Simon Bolivar

**1882**

| | | | | |
|---|---|---|---|---|
| 30 | 10 | 5p. red and blue | 1·00 | 85 |
| 31 | 10 | 10p. blue and purple | 2·20 | 2·10 |

11 Simon Bolivar

**1882.** Various frames. Dated "1882".

| | | | | |
|---|---|---|---|---|
| 32A | 11 | 5c. blue | 45 | 45 |
| 33A | 11 | 10c. mauve | 35 | 30 |
| 34A | 11 | 20c. red | 45 | 45 |
| 35A | 11 | 80c. green | 90 | 85 |
| 36A | 11 | 1p. orange | 90 | 85 |

**1883.** Various frames. Dated "1883".

| | | | |
|---|---|---|---|
| 37B | 5c. blue | 35 | 30 |
| 38B | 10c. mauve | 45 | 45 |
| 39B | 20c. red | 45 | 45 |
| 40B | 80c. green | 45 | 45 |
| 41A | 1p. orange | 3·00 | 3·00 |

**1884.** Various frames. Dated "1884".

| | | | |
|---|---|---|---|
| 42B | 5c. blue | 45 | 45 |
| 43B | 10c. mauve | 35 | 30 |
| 44B | 20c. red | 35 | 30 |
| 45B | 80c. green | 45 | 45 |
| 46B | 1p. orange | 45 | 45 |

**1885.** Various frames. Dated "1885".

| | | | |
|---|---|---|---|
| 47B | 5c. blue | 20 | 20 |
| 48B | 10c. mauve | 20 | 20 |
| 49B | 20c. red | 20 | 20 |
| 50B | 80c. green | 35 | 30 |
| 51B | 1p. orange | 45 | 45 |

12 Simon Bolivar

**1891**

| | | | | |
|---|---|---|---|---|
| 56 | 12 | 1c. black | 45 | 45 |
| 57 | 12 | 5c. orange | 45 | 45 |
| 58 | 12 | 10c. red | 45 | 45 |
| 59 | 12 | 20c. blue | 90 | 85 |
| 60 | 12 | 50c. green | 1·30 | 1·30 |
| 61 | 12 | 1p. violet | 1·30 | 1·30 |

13 Simon Bolivar

**1903.** Various sizes and portraits. Imperf or perf. On paper of various colours.

| | | | | |
|---|---|---|---|---|
| 63A | 13 | 50c. green | 90 | 85 |
| 64Ab | 13 | 50c. blue | 75 | 75 |
| 65A | 13 | 50c. violet | 6·00 | 6·00 |
| 67A | - | 1p. red | 90 | 85 |
| 68A | - | 1p. green | 2·20 | 2·20 |
| 69A | - | 5p. red | 90 | 85 |
| 70Ab | - | 10p. blue | 1·90 | 1·80 |
| 71A | - | 10p. violet | 5·00 | 4·75 |

PORTRAITS: 1p. Fernandez Madrid. 5p. Rodriguez Torices. 10p. Garcia de Toledo.

20 J. M. del Castillo

**1904.** Various portraits. Imperf or perf.

| | | | | |
|---|---|---|---|---|
| 77A | 20 | 5c. black | 35 | 30 |
| 78A | - | 10c. brown (M. Anguiano) | 35 | 30 |
| 80A | - | 20c. red (P.G. Ribon) | 45 | 45 |

23

**1904.** Figures in various frames. Imperf.

| | | | | |
|---|---|---|---|---|
| 81 | 23 | ½c. black | 45 | 45 |
| 82 | 23 | 1c. blue (horiz) | 75 | 75 |
| 83 | 23 | 2c. violet | 90 | 85 |

### ACKNOWLEDGEMENT OF RECEIPT STAMPS

AR19

**1903.** Imperf. On paper of various colours.

| | | | | |
|---|---|---|---|---|
| AR75A | AR19 | 20c. orange | 1·90 | 1·80 |
| AR76A | AR19 | 20c. blue | 2·75 | 2·75 |

AR27

**1904.** Imperf.

| | | | | |
|---|---|---|---|---|
| AR85 | AR27 | 2c. red | 1·40 | 1·40 |

### LATE FEE STAMPS

L18

**1903.** Imperf. On paper of various colours.

| | | | | |
|---|---|---|---|---|
| L73A | L18 | 20c. red | 90 | 85 |
| L74B | L18 | 20c. violet | 90 | 85 |

### REGISTRATION STAMPS

**1879.** As T **9** but additionally inscr "CERTIFICADA".

| | | | | |
|---|---|---|---|---|
| R17 | 9 | 40c. brown | 45 | 45 |

**1880.** As previous issue dated "1880".

| | | | |
|---|---|---|---|
| R28 | 40c. brown | 45 | 45 |

**1882.** As T **11**, but additionally inscr "CERTIFICADA". Dated as shown.

| | | | | |
|---|---|---|---|---|
| R52B | 11 | 40c. brown ("1882") | 45 | 45 |
| R53B | 11 | 40c. brown ("1883") | 45 | 45 |
| R54B | 11 | 40c. brown ("1884") | 45 | 45 |
| R55B | 11 | 40c. brown ("1885") | 45 | 45 |

R17

**1903.** Imperf. On paper of various colours.

| | | | | |
|---|---|---|---|---|
| R72A | R17 | 20c. orange | 3·50 | 3·50 |

R26

**1904.** Imperf.

| | | | | |
|---|---|---|---|---|
| R84 | R26 | 5c. black | 2·30 | 2·30 |

Pt. 20

# BOLIVIA

A republic of Central South America.

1867. 100 centavos = 1 boliviano.
1963. 100 centavos = 1 peso boliviano.
1963. Currency reform. 1000 (old) pesos = 1 (new) peso
1987. 100 centavos = 1 boliviano.

1 Condor

**1867.** Imperf.

| | | | | |
|---|---|---|---|---|
| 3a | 1 | 5c. green | 2·50 | 5·00 |
| 10 | 1 | 5c. mauve | £200 | £150 |
| 7 | 1 | 10c. brown | £180 | £160 |
| 8 | 1 | 50c. yellow | 28·00 | 39·00 |
| 11 | 1 | 50c. blue | £400 | £350 |
| 9 | 1 | 100c. blue | 43·00 | 95·00 |
| 12 | 1 | 100c. green | £170 | £180 |

4 (9 Stars)

**1868.** Nine stars below Arms. Perf.

| | | | | |
|---|---|---|---|---|
| 32 | 4 | 5c. green | 22·00 | 12·50 |
| 33 | 4 | 10c. red | 39·00 | 15·00 |
| 34 | 4 | 50c. blue | 47·00 | 28·00 |
| 35 | 4 | 100c. orange | 55·00 | 28·00 |
| 36 | 4 | 500c. black | £750 | £750 |

**1871.** Eleven stars below Arms. Perf.

| | | | |
|---|---|---|---|
| 37 | 5c. green | 15·00 | 7·50 |
| 38 | 10c. red | 25·00 | 12·50 |
| 39 | 50c. blue | 39·00 | 22·00 |
| 40 | 100c. orange | 43·00 | 22·00 |
| 41 | 500c. black | £2250 | £2250 |

7

**1878.** Perf.

| | | | | |
|---|---|---|---|---|
| 42 | 7 | 5c. blue | 9·50 | 3·25 |
| 43 | 7 | 10c. orange | 8·75 | 2·40 |
| 44 | 7 | 20c. green | 24·00 | 4·75 |
| 45 | 7 | 50c. red | £120 | 20·00 |

**1887.** Eleven stars below Arms. Roul.

| | | | | |
|---|---|---|---|---|
| 46 | 4 | 1c. red | 3·25 | 3·00 |
| 47 | 4 | 2c. violet | 3·25 | 3·00 |
| 48 | 4 | 5c. blue | 10·50 | 5·25 |
| 49 | 4 | 10c. orange | 10·50 | 5·25 |

**1890.** Nine stars below Arms. Perf.

| | | | |
|---|---|---|---|
| 50 | 1c. red | 2·75 | 1·30 |
| 58 | 2c. violet | 7·00 | 4·00 |
| 52 | 5c. blue | 5·75 | 1·40 |
| 53 | 10c. orange | 14·00 | 1·40 |
| 54 | 20c. green | 20·00 | 2·75 |
| 55 | 50c. red | 9·00 | 2·50 |
| 56 | 100c. yellow | 18·00 | 5·25 |

**1893.** Eleven stars below Arms. Perf.

| | | | |
|---|---|---|---|
| 59 | 5c. blue | 8·50 | 2·75 |

11

**1894**

| | | | | |
|---|---|---|---|---|
| 63 | 11 | 1c. bistre | 2·00 | 1·80 |
| 64 | 11 | 2c. red | 2·75 | 2·50 |
| 65 | 11 | 5c. green | 2·00 | 1·80 |
| 66 | 11 | 10c. brown | 2·00 | 1·80 |
| 67 | 11 | 20c. blue | 8·00 | 5·75 |
| 68 | 11 | 50c. red | 17·00 | 11·50 |
| 69 | 11 | 100c. red | 40·00 | 29·00 |

12 Frias

13

**1897**

| | | | | |
|---|---|---|---|---|
| 77 | 12 | 1c. green | 2·10 | 1·50 |
| 78 | - | 2c. red (Linares) | 3·00 | 2·50 |
| 79 | - | 5c. green (Murillo) | 2·00 | 90 |
| 80 | - | 10c. purple (Monteagudo) | 2·30 | 1·50 |
| 81 | - | 20c. black and red (J. Ballivian) | 4·25 | 2·20 |
| 82 | - | 50c. orange (Sucre) | 6·50 | 3·75 |
| 83 | - | 1b. blue (Bolivar) | 8·00 | 5·25 |
| 84 | 13 | 2b. multicoloured | 48·00 | 75·00 |

18 Sucre

**1899**

| | | | | |
|---|---|---|---|---|
| 92 | 18 | 1c. blue | 2·75 | 1·70 |
| 93 | 18 | 2c. red | 2·50 | 1·70 |
| 94 | 18 | 5c. green | 4·00 | 1·70 |
| 95 | 18 | 5c. red | 2·75 | 90 |
| 96 | 18 | 10c. orange | 3·75 | 1·70 |
| 97 | 18 | 20c. red | 4·25 | 2·20 |
| 98 | 18 | 50c. brown | 10·00 | 3·75 |
| 99 | 18 | 1b. lilac | 3·25 | 3·50 |

19 A. Ballivian

24

**1901**

| | | | | |
|---|---|---|---|---|
| 100 | 19 | 1c. red | 45 | 25 |
| 101 | - | 2c. green (Camacho) | 55 | 35 |
| 102 | - | 5c. red (Campero) | 55 | 35 |
| 103 | - | 10c. blue (J. Ballivian) | 2·30 | 30 |
| 104 | - | 20c. black and purple (Santa Cruz) | 1·30 | 30 |
| 105 | 24 | 2b. brown | 7·00 | 4·00 |

25

26 Murillo

**1909.** Issued in La Paz. Centenary of Revolution of July, 1809. Centres in black.

| | | | | |
|---|---|---|---|---|
| 110 | 25 | 5c. blue | 16·00 | 12·50 |
| 111 | 26 | 10c. green | 16·00 | 12·50 |
| 112 | - | 20c. orange (Lanza) | 16·00 | 12·50 |
| 113 | - | 2b. red (Montes) | 16·00 | 12·50 |

37 P. D. Murillo

**1909.** Centenary of Beginning of War of Independence, 1809–25.

| | | | | |
|---|---|---|---|---|
| 115 | | 1c. black and brown | 65 | 40 |
| 116 | | 2c. black and green | 1·10 | 55 |
| 117 | 37 | 5c. black and red | 1·10 | 45 |
| 118 | - | 10c. black and blue | 1·30 | 35 |
| 119 | - | 20c. black and violet | 1·30 | 55 |
| 120 | - | 50c. black and bistre | 1·40 | 70 |
| 121 | - | 1b. black and brown | 1·80 | 1·30 |
| 122 | - | 2b. black and brown | 1·90 | 1·50 |

PORTRAITS: 1c. M. Betanzos. 2c. I. Warnes. 10c. B. Monteagudo. 20c. E. Arze. 50c. A. J. Sucre. 1b. S. Bolivar. 2b. M. Belgrano.

**1910.** Centenary of Liberation of Santa Cruz, Potosi and Cochabamba. Portraits as T 37.

| | | | |
|---|---|---|---|
| 123 | 5c. black and green | 55 | 25 |
| 124 | 10c. black and red | 55 | 35 |
| 125 | 20c. black and blue | 1·10 | 55 |

PORTRAITS: 5c. I. Warnes. 10c. M. Betanzos. 20c. E. Arze.

**1911.** Nos. 101 and 104 surch 5 Centavos 1911.

| | | | |
|---|---|---|---|
| 127 | 5c. on 2c. green | 65 | 35 |
| 128 | 5c. on 20c. black & purple | 23·00 | 25·00 |

F8 Figure of Justice

**1912.** Stamps similar to Type F 8 optd CORREOS 1912. or surch also.

| | | | | |
|---|---|---|---|---|
| 130 | F8 | 2c. green | 45 | 35 |
| 131 | F8 | 5c. orange | 75 | 55 |
| 132 | F8 | 10c. red | 1·50 | 70 |
| 129 | F8 | 10c. on 1c. blue | 75 | 35 |

**1913.** Portraits as 1901 and new types.

| | | | | |
|---|---|---|---|---|
| 133 | 19 | 1c. pink | 30 | 25 |
| 134 | - | 2c. red | 30 | 25 |
| 135 | - | 5c. green | 45 | 25 |
| 136 | - | 8c. yellow (Frias) | 1·30 | 45 |
| 137 | - | 10c. grey | 75 | 25 |
| 139 | - | 50c. purple (Sucre) | 1·90 | 55 |
| 140 | - | 1b. blue (Bolivar) | 3·25 | 1·50 |
| 141 | 24 | 2b. black | 8·00 | 5·25 |

46 Monolith

47 Mt. Potosi

**1916.** Various sizes.

| | | | | |
|---|---|---|---|---|
| 142 | 46 | ½c. brown | 35 | 30 |
| 143 | 47 | 1c. green | 45 | 30 |
| 144 | - | 2c. black and red | 50 | 30 |
| 145 | - | 5c. blue | 65 | 35 |
| 147 | - | 10c. blue and orange | 1·60 | 25 |

DESIGNS—HORIZ: 2c. Lake Titicaca; 5c. Mt. Illimani; 10c. Parliament Building, La Paz.

51

**1919**

| | | | | |
|---|---|---|---|---|
| 158a | 51 | 1c. lake | 30 | 15 |
| 158b | 51 | 2c. violet | 45 | 15 |
| 151 | 51 | 5c. green | 65 | 10 |
| 152 | 51 | 10c. red | 65 | 10 |
| 179 | 51 | 15c. blue | 1·20 | 35 |
| 180 | 51 | 20c. blue | 95 | 35 |
| 154 | 51 | 22c. blue | 1·60 | 1·50 |
| 155 | 51 | 24c. violet | 1·60 | 90 |
| 162 | 51 | 50c. orange | 3·50 | 80 |
| 163 | 51 | 1b. brown | 95 | 45 |
| 164 | 51 | 2b. brown | 65 | 45 |

See also Nos. 194/206.

**1923.** Surch Habilitada and value.

| | | | |
|---|---|---|---|
| 165 | 5c. on 1c. lake | 55 | 25 |
| 169 | 15c. on 10c. red | 1·30 | 45 |
| 168 | 15c. on 22c. blue | 95 | 45 |

54 Morane Saulnier Type P Airplane

**1924.** Air. Establishment of National Aviation School.

| | | | | |
|---|---|---|---|---|
| 170 | 54 | 10c. black and red | 55 | 45 |
| 171 | 54 | 15c. black and lake | 2·10 | 1·70 |
| 172 | 54 | 25c. black and blue | 1·10 | 80 |
| 173 | 54 | 50c. black and orange | 1·80 | 1·40 |
| 174 | - | 1b. black and brown | 2·30 | 1·90 |
| 175 | - | 2b. black and brown | 4·50 | 4·00 |
| 176 | - | 5b. black and violet | 6·50 | 6·25 |

Nos. 174/6 have a different view.

57 Andean Condor

**1925.** Centenary of Independence.

| | | | | |
|---|---|---|---|---|
| 184 | | 5c. red on green | 1·10 | 90 |
| 185 | | 10c. red on yellow | 1·20 | 1·10 |
| 186 | | 15c. red | 85 | 45 |
| 187 | 57 | 25c. blue | 1·90 | 80 |
| 188 | - | 50c. purple | 1·60 | 80 |
| 189 | - | 1b. red | 3·75 | 1·90 |
| 190 | - | 2b. yellow | 4·75 | 2·75 |
| 191 | - | 5b. brown | 5·00 | 3·00 |

DESIGNS—VERT: 5c. Torch of Freedom; 10c. Kantuta (national flower); 15c. Pres. B. Saavedra; 50c. Head of Liberty; 1b. Mounted archer; 5b. Marshal Sucre. HORIZ: 2b. Hermes.

**1927.** Surch 1927 and value.

| | | | | |
|---|---|---|---|---|
| 192 | 51 | 5c. on 1c. lake | 4·50 | 3·25 |
| 193 | 51 | 10c. on 24c. violet | 4·50 | 3·25 |

**1928**

| | | | |
|---|---|---|---|
| 194 | 2c. yellow | 55 | 35 |
| 195 | 3c. pink | 75 | 70 |
| 196 | 4c. red | 55 | 50 |
| 197 | 20c. olive | 95 | 35 |
| 198 | 25c. blue | 95 | 45 |
| 199 | 30c. violet | 1·20 | 1·00 |
| 200 | 40c. orange | 2·10 | 1·90 |
| 201 | 50c. brown | 2·10 | 1·90 |
| 202 | 1b. red | 2·50 | 1·90 |
| 203 | 2b. purple | 3·75 | 3·25 |
| 204 | 3b. green | 4·25 | 3·75 |
| 205 | 4b. lake | 5·75 | 4·75 |
| 206 | 5b. brown | 7·00 | 6·00 |

**1928.** Optd Octubre 1927 and star.

| | | | |
|---|---|---|---|
| 207 | 5c. green | 35 | 20 |
| 208 | 10c. grey | 45 | 20 |
| 209 | 15c. red | 60 | 35 |

**1928.** Surch 15 cts. 1928.

| | | | |
|---|---|---|---|
| 211 | 15c. on 20c. blue | 13·00 | 13·00 |
| 213 | 15c. on 24c. violet | 2·30 | 1·30 |
| 216 | 15c. on 50c. orange | 1·80 | 1·00 |

66 "L.A.B." (Lloyd Aereo Boliviano)

**1928.** Air.

| | | | | |
|---|---|---|---|---|
| 217 | 66 | 15c. green | 3·25 | 2·10 |
| 218 | 66 | 20c. blue | 5·25 | 4·25 |
| 219 | 66 | 35c. red | 4·25 | 3·25 |

68 Andean Condor

**1928**

| | | | | |
|---|---|---|---|---|
| 221 | 68 | 5c. green | 2·30 | 30 |
| 222 | - | 10c. blue | 45 | 20 |
| 223 | - | 15c. red | 75 | 20 |

DESIGNS: 10c. Pres. Siles; 15c. Map of Bolivia.

**1930.** Stamps of 1913 and 1916 surch R. S. 21-4 1930 and value.

| | | | | |
|---|---|---|---|---|
| 224 | | 0.01c. on 2c. (No. 134) | 1·30 | 1·30 |
| 225 | | 0.03c. on 2c. (No. 144) | 1·60 | 1·40 |
| 226 | 46 | 25c. on ½c. brown | 1·70 | 1·10 |
| 227 | - | 25c. on 2c. (No. 144) | 1·80 | 1·10 |

**1930.** Air. Optd CORREO AEREO R. S. 6-V-1930 or surch 5 Cts. also.

| | | | | |
|---|---|---|---|---|
| 228 | 54 | 5c. on 10c. black & red | 11·50 | 13·00 |
| 229 | 54 | 10c. black and red | 11·50 | 13·00 |
| 231 | 54 | 15c. black and lake | 11·50 | 13·00 |
| 232 | 54 | 25c. black and blue | 11·50 | 13·00 |
| 233 | 54 | 50c. black and orange | 11·50 | 13·00 |
| 235 | 54 | 1b. black and brown | £225 | £225 |

**1930.** "Graf Zeppelin" Air stamps. Stamps of 1928 surch Z 1930 and value.

| | | | | |
|---|---|---|---|---|
| 241 | 66 | 1b.50 on 15c. green | 75·00 | 85·00 |
| 242 | 66 | 3b. on 20c. blue | 75·00 | 85·00 |
| 243 | 66 | 6b. on 35c. red | £120 | £130 |

75 Junkers F-13 over Bullock Cart

**1930.** Air.

| | | | | |
|---|---|---|---|---|
| 244 | 75 | 5c. violet | 1·90 | 1·10 |
| 245 | - | 15c. red | 1·90 | 1·10 |
| 246 | - | 20c. yellow | 1·50 | 95 |
| 247 | 75 | 35c. green | 1·20 | 70 |
| 248 | - | 50c. blue | 2·30 | 1·60 |
| 249 | 75 | 1b. brown | 3·50 | 2·40 |
| 250 | - | 2b. red | 4·50 | 3·25 |
| 251 | 75 | 3b. grey | 7·00 | 4·50 |

DESIGN: 15, 20, 50c., 2b. Junkers F-13 seaplane over river boat.

77 Pres. Siles

78 Map of Bolivia

79 Marshal Sucre

**1930**

| | | | | |
|---|---|---|---|---|
| 252 | 77 | 1c. brown | 45 | 45 |
| 253 | - | 2c. green (Potosi) | 2·10 | 75 |
| 254 | - | 5c. blue (Illimani) | 2·10 | 30 |
| 255 | - | 10c. red (E. Abaroa) | 2·10 | 30 |
| 256 | 78 | 15c. violet | 2·10 | 30 |
| 257 | 78 | 35c. red | 3·25 | 1·30 |
| 258 | 78 | 45c. orange | 3·25 | 1·30 |
| 259 | 79 | 50c. slate | 1·30 | 60 |
| 260 | - | 1b. brown (Bolivar) | 1·90 | 1·50 |

80 Symbols of Revolution

**1931.** 1st Anniv of Revolution.

| | | | | |
|---|---|---|---|---|
| 263 | 80 | 15c. red | 3·75 | 65 |
| 264 | 80 | 50c. lilac | 1·60 | 85 |

81

**1932.** Air.

| | | | | |
|---|---|---|---|---|
| 265 | 81 | 5c. blue | 3·50 | 2·75 |
| 266 | 81 | 10c. grey | 1·90 | 1·50 |
| 267 | 81 | 15c. red | 2·30 | 1·80 |
| 268 | 81 | 25c. orange | 2·30 | 1·80 |
| 269 | 81 | 30c. green | 1·60 | 90 |
| 270 | 81 | 50c. purple | 3·50 | 2·75 |
| 271 | 81 | 1b. brown | 3·50 | 2·75 |

**1933.** Surch Habilitada D. S. 13-7-1933 and value.

| | | | | |
|---|---|---|---|---|
| 273 | 51 | 5c. on 1b. red | 95 | 55 |
| 274 | 78 | 15c. on 35c. red | 55 | 55 |
| 275 | 78 | 15c. on 45c. orange | 95 | 45 |
| 276 | 51 | 15c. on 50c. brown | 1·90 | 45 |
| 277 | 51 | 25c. on 40c. orange | 55 | 55 |

83

**1933**

| | | | | |
|---|---|---|---|---|
| 278 | 83 | 2c. green | 45 | 30 |
| 279 | 83 | 5c. blue | 35 | 25 |
| 280 | 83 | 10c. red | 75 | 45 |
| 281 | 83 | 15c. violet | 55 | 30 |
| 282 | 83 | 25c. blue | 1·10 | 85 |

84 M. Baptista

**1935.** Ex-President Baptista Commemoration.

| | | | | |
|---|---|---|---|---|
| 283 | 84 | 15c. violet | 75 | 30 |

85 Map of Bolivia

**1935**

| | | | | |
|---|---|---|---|---|
| 284 | 85 | 2c. blue | 45 | 20 |
| 285 | 85 | 3c. yellow | 45 | 20 |
| 286 | 85 | 5c. green | 45 | 20 |
| 287 | 85 | 5c. red | 45 | 20 |
| 288 | 85 | 10c. brown | 45 | 20 |
| 289 | 85 | 15c. blue | 45 | 20 |
| 290 | 85 | 15c. red | 45 | 20 |
| 291 | 85 | 20c. green | 55 | 20 |
| 292 | 85 | 25c. blue | 55 | 20 |
| 293 | 85 | 30c. red | 1·10 | 45 |
| 294 | 85 | 40c. orange | 1·10 | 30 |
| 295 | 85 | 50c. violet | 1·10 | 20 |
| 296 | 85 | 1b. yellow | 1·10 | 75 |
| 297 | 85 | 2b. brown | 2·30 | 1·40 |

**86** Fokker Super Universal

**1935.** Air.

| | | | | |
|---|---|---|---|---|
| 298 | **86** | 5c. brown | 20 | 20 |
| 299 | **86** | 10c. green | 20 | 20 |
| 300 | **86** | 20c. violet | 20 | 20 |
| 301 | **86** | 30c. blue | 20 | 20 |
| 302 | **86** | 50c. orange | 30 | 20 |
| 303 | **86** | 1b. brown | 30 | 45 |
| 304 | **86** | 1½b. yellow | 1·10 | 20 |
| 305 | **86** | 2b. red | 1·10 | 20 |
| 306 | **86** | 5b. green | 1·80 | 55 |
| 307 | **86** | 10b. brown | 3·75 | 1·30 |

**1937.** Surch Comunicaciones D.S. 25-2-37 and value in figures.

| | | | | |
|---|---|---|---|---|
| 308 | **83** | 5c. on 2c. green | 30 | 30 |
| 310 | **83** | 15c. on 25c. blue | 45 | 45 |
| 311 | **83** | 30c. on 25c. blue | 75 | 75 |
| 312 | **51** | 45c. on 1b. brown | 85 | 85 |
| 313 | **51** | 1b. on 2b. purple | 1·10 | 1·10 |
| 314 | **83** | 2b. on 25c. blue | 1·10 | 1·10 |
| 315 | **80** | 3b. on 50c. lilac | 1·50 | 1·50 |
| 316 | **80** | 5b. on 50c. lilac | 2·30 | 2·30 |

**1937.** Air. Surch Correo Aereo D. S. 25-2-37 and value in figures.

| | | | | |
|---|---|---|---|---|
| 321 | **75** | 5c. on 35c. green | 45 | 30 |
| 322 | **66** | 20c. on 35c. red | 55 | 45 |
| 323 | **66** | 50c. on 35c. red | 1·10 | 1·30 |
| 324 | **66** | 1b. on 35c. red | 1·10 | 95 |
| 325 | **54** | 2b. on 50c. black & orge | 1·70 | 1·40 |
| 317 | - | 3b. on 50c. pur (No. 188) | 2·30 | 1·40 |
| 318 | - | 4b. on 1b. red (No. 189) | 2·75 | 1·80 |
| 319 | **57** | 5b. on 2b. orange | 3·75 | 2·10 |
| 320 | **57** | 10b. on 5b. sepia (No. 191) | 7·00 | 4·50 |
| 326 | **54** | 12b. on 10c. black & red | 9·00 | 6·50 |
| 327 | **54** | 15b. on 10c. black & red | 9·00 | 3·75 |

**89** Native School

**92** Junkers Ju52/3m over Cornfield

**1938**

| | | | | |
|---|---|---|---|---|
| 328 | **89** | 2c. red (postage) | 85 | 65 |
| 329 | - | 10c. orange | 95 | 45 |
| 330 | - | 15c. green | 1·40 | 45 |
| 331 | - | 30c. yellow | 1·70 | 55 |
| 332 | - | 45c. red | 3·25 | 1·30 |
| 333 | - | 60c. violet | 2·50 | 65 |
| 334 | - | 75c. blue | 3·50 | 55 |
| 335 | - | 1b. brown | 5·00 | 55 |
| 336 | - | 2b. buff | 4·50 | 1·20 |

DESIGNS—VERT: 10c. Oil Wells; 15c. Industrial buildings; 30c. Pincers and torch; 75c. Indian and condor. HORIZ: 45c. Sucre-Camiri railway map; 60c. Natives and book; 1b. Machinery; 2b. Agriculture.

| | | | | |
|---|---|---|---|---|
| 337 | | 20c. red (air) | 30 | 25 |
| 338 | | 30c. grey | 30 | 25 |
| 339 | | 40c. yellow | 30 | 25 |
| 340 | **92** | 50c. green | 65 | 25 |
| 341 | - | 60c. blue | 65 | 25 |
| 342 | - | 1b. red | 85 | 25 |
| 343 | - | 2b. buff | 1·60 | 30 |
| 344 | - | 3b. brown | 1·60 | 30 |
| 345 | - | 5b. violet | 2·30 | 55 |

DESIGNS—VERT: 20c. Mint, Potosi; 30c. Miner; 40c. Symbolical of women's suffrage; 1b. Pincers, torch and slogan; 3b. New Government emblem; 5b. Junkers aircraft over map of Bolivia. HORIZ: 60c. Airplane and monument; 2b. Airplane over river.

**102** Llamas

**103** Arms

**1939**

| | | | | |
|---|---|---|---|---|
| 346 | **102** | 2c. green | 75 | 55 |
| 347 | **102** | 4c. brown | 75 | 55 |
| 348 | **102** | 5c. mauve | 75 | 45 |
| 349 | - | 10c. black | 95 | 55 |
| 350 | - | 15c. green | 95 | 60 |
| 351 | - | 20c. green | 95 | 45 |
| 352 | **103** | 25c. yellow | 1·10 | 45 |
| 353 | - | 30c. blue | 95 | 45 |
| 354 | - | 40c. red | 2·10 | 55 |
| 355 | - | 45c. black | 2·10 | 55 |
| 356 | - | 60c. red | 2·10 | 85 |
| 357 | - | 75c. slate | 3·25 | 85 |
| 358 | - | 90c. orange | 3·75 | 85 |
| 359 | - | 1b. blue | 3·75 | 85 |
| 360 | - | 2b. red | 4·50 | 85 |
| 361 | - | 3b. violet | 5·75 | 1·30 |
| 362 | - | 4b. brown | 6·50 | 1·80 |
| 363 | - | 5b. purple | 8·00 | 2·10 |

DESIGNS—HORIZ: 10, 15, 20c. Vicuna; 60, 75c. Mountain viscacha; 90c., 1b. Toco toucan; 2, 3b. Andean condor; 4, 5b. Jaguar. VERT: 40, 45c. Cocoi herons.

**107** Virgin of Copacabana

**1939.** Air. 2nd National Eucharistic Congress. Inscr "II° CONGRESO EUCARISTICO NACIONAL".

| | | | | |
|---|---|---|---|---|
| 364 | | 5c. violet | 75 | 45 |
| 365 | **107** | 30c. green | 1·10 | 30 |
| 366 | - | 45c. blue | 1·10 | 30 |
| 367 | - | 60c. red | 1·10 | 50 |
| 368 | - | 75c. red | 1·10 | 75 |
| 369 | - | 90c. blue | 1·10 | 30 |
| 370 | - | 2b. brown | 1·60 | 35 |
| 371 | - | 4b. mauve | 2·75 | 55 |
| 372 | **107** | 5b. blue | 6·50 | 1·10 |
| 373 | - | 10b. yellow | 9·00 | 1·60 |

DESIGNS—TRIANGULAR: 5c., 10b. Allegory of the Light of Religion. VERT: 45c., 4b. The "Sacred Heart of Jesus"; 75c., 90c. S. Anthony of Padua. HORIZ: 60c., 2b. Facade of St. Francis's Church, La Paz.

**111** Workman

**1939.** Obligatory Tax. Workers' Home Building Fund.

| | | | | |
|---|---|---|---|---|
| 374 | **111** | 5c. violet | 1·20 | 30 |

**112** Flags of 21 American Republics

**1940.** 50th Anniv of Pan-American Union.

| | | | | |
|---|---|---|---|---|
| 375 | **112** | 9b. red, blue & yellow | 2·40 | 1·20 |

**114** Urns of Murillo and Sagarnaga

**1941.** 130th Death Anniv of P. D. Murillo (patriot).

| | | | | |
|---|---|---|---|---|
| 376 | - | 10c. purple | 20 | 10 |
| 377 | **114** | 15c. green | 30 | 10 |
| 378 | - | 45c. red | 30 | 20 |
| 379 | - | 1b.05 blue | 65 | 30 |

DESIGNS—VERT: 10c. Murillo statue; 1b.05 Murillo portrait. HORIZ: 45c. "Murillo dreaming in Prison".

**117** Shadow of Aeroplane on Lake Titicaca

**1941.** Air.

| | | | | |
|---|---|---|---|---|
| 380 | **117** | 10b. green | 4·50 | 55 |
| 381 | **117** | 20b. blue | 5·25 | 85 |
| 382 | - | 50b. mauve | 10·50 | 1·40 |
| 383 | - | 100b. brown | 24·00 | 8·50 |

DESIGN: 50, 100b. Andean condor over Mt. Illimani.

**119** 1867 and 1941 Issues

**1942.** 1st Students' Philatelic Exn, La Paz.

| | | | | |
|---|---|---|---|---|
| 384 | **119** | 5c. mauve | 75 | 65 |
| 385 | **119** | 10c. orange | 75 | 65 |
| 386 | **119** | 20c. green | 1·60 | 1·10 |
| 387 | **119** | 40c. red | 2·00 | 1·30 |
| 388 | **119** | 90c. blue | 3·75 | 1·60 |
| 389 | **119** | 1b. violet | 4·75 | 2·50 |
| 390 | **119** | 10b. brown | 16·00 | 13·00 |

**120** "Union is Strength"

**1942.** Air. Chancellors' Meeting, Rio de Janeiro.

| | | | | |
|---|---|---|---|---|
| 391 | **120** | 40c. red | 45 | 30 |
| 392 | **120** | 50c. blue | 45 | 30 |
| 393 | **120** | 1b. brown | 1·70 | 1·10 |
| 394 | **120** | 5b. mauve | 1·10 | 45 |
| 395 | **120** | 10b. purple | 3·50 | 1·70 |

**121** Mt. Potosi

**122** Chaquiri Dam

**1943.** Mining Industry.

| | | | | |
|---|---|---|---|---|
| 396 | **121** | 15c. brown | 30 | 20 |
| 397 | - | 45c. blue | 65 | 30 |
| 398 | - | 1b.25 purple | 1·10 | 55 |
| 399 | - | 1b.50 green | 80 | 55 |
| 400 | - | 2b. brown | 1·10 | 55 |
| 401 | **122** | 2b.10 blue | 85 | 75 |
| 402 | - | 3b. orange | 3·50 | 1·40 |

DESIGNS—VERT: 45c. Quechisla (at foot of Mt. Choroloque); 1b.25, Miner Drilling. HORIZ: 1b.50, Dam; 2b. Truck Convoy; 3b. Entrance to Pulacayo Mine.

**125** Gen. Ballivian leading Cavalry Charge

**1943.** Centenary of Battle of Ingavi.

| | | | | |
|---|---|---|---|---|
| 403 | **125** | 2c. green | 30 | 10 |
| 404 | **125** | 3c. orange | 30 | 10 |
| 405 | **125** | 25c. purple | 45 | 15 |
| 406 | **125** | 45c. blue | 55 | 20 |
| 407 | **125** | 3b. red | 95 | 55 |
| 408 | **125** | 4b. purple | 1·30 | 65 |
| 409 | **125** | 5b. sepia | 1·50 | 85 |
| **MS**409a | | Two sheets each 139×100 mm. Nos. 403/6 and Nos. 407/9 | 14·00 | 18·00 |
| **MS**409b | | Do. Imperf | 14·00 | 18·00 |

**126** Gen. Ballivian and Trinidad Cathedral

**1943.** Centenary of Founding of El Beni. Centres in brown.

| | | | | |
|---|---|---|---|---|
| 410 | **126** | 5c. green (postage) | 30 | 15 |
| 411 | **126** | 10c. purple | 35 | 20 |
| 412 | **126** | 30c. red | 35 | 20 |
| 413 | **126** | 45c. blue | 45 | 30 |
| 414 | **126** | 2b.10 orange | 75 | 55 |
| 415 | - | 10c. violet (air) | 30 | 15 |

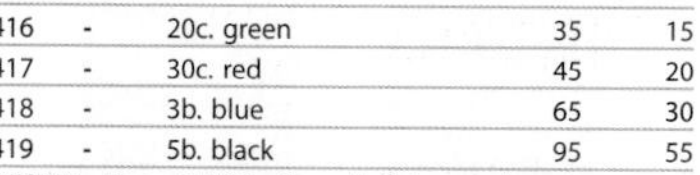

| | | | | |
|---|---|---|---|---|
| 416 | - | 20c. green | 35 | 15 |
| 417 | - | 30c. red | 45 | 20 |
| 418 | - | 3b. blue | 65 | 30 |
| 419 | - | 5b. black | 95 | 55 |

DESIGN: Nos. 415/19, Gen. Ballivian and mule convoy crossing bridge below airplane.

**127** Trans. "Honour-Work-Law/All for the Country"

**129** Allegory of "Flight"

**1944.** Revolution of 20th December, 1943.

| | | | | |
|---|---|---|---|---|
| 420 | **127** | 20c. orange (postage) | 20 | 10 |
| 421 | **127** | 20c. green | 20 | 10 |
| 422 | **127** | 90c. blue | 20 | 10 |
| 423 | **127** | 90c. red | 20 | 10 |
| 424 | - | 1b. purple | 25 | 10 |
| 425 | - | 2b.40 brown | 30 | 20 |

DESIGN—VERT: 1b., 2b.40, Clasped hands and flag.

**131** Posthorn and Envelope

**1944.** Obligatory Tax.

| | | | | |
|---|---|---|---|---|
| 430 | **131** | 10c. red | 1·10 | 30 |
| 432 | **131** | 10c. blue | 1·10 | 30 |

Smaller Posthorn and Envelope.

| | | | | |
|---|---|---|---|---|
| 469 | | 10c. red | 2·30 | 75 |
| 470 | | 10c. yellow | 2·30 | 75 |
| 471 | | 10c. green | 2·30 | 75 |
| 472 | | 10c. brown | 2·30 | 75 |

**132** Douglas DC-2 and National Airways Route Map

**1945.** Air. Panagra Airways, 10th Anniv of First La Paz–Tacna Flight.

| | | | | |
|---|---|---|---|---|
| 433 | **132** | 10c. red | 20 | 15 |
| 434 | **132** | 50c. orange | 25 | 15 |
| 435 | **132** | 90c. green | 30 | 20 |
| 436 | **132** | 5b. blue | 55 | 30 |
| 437 | **132** | 20b. brown | 1·90 | 65 |

**133** Lloyd-Aereo Boliviano Air Routes

**1945.** Air. 20th Anniv of First National Air Service.

| | | | | |
|---|---|---|---|---|
| 438 | **133** | 20c. blue, orange & vio | 20 | 10 |
| 439 | **133** | 30c. blue, orange & brn | 20 | 10 |
| 440 | **133** | 50c. blue, orange & grn | 20 | 10 |
| 441 | **133** | 90c. blue, orange & pur | 20 | 10 |
| 442 | **133** | 2b. blue and orange | 25 | 10 |
| 443 | **133** | 3b. blue, orange & red | 30 | 20 |
| 444 | **133** | 4b. blue, orange & bistre | 55 | 30 |

**134** L. B. Vincenti and J. I. de Sanjines, Composers of National Anthem

**1946.** Centenary of National Anthem.

| | | | | |
|---|---|---|---|---|
| 445 | **134** | 5c. black and mauve | 10 | 10 |
| 446 | **134** | 10c. black and blue | 10 | 10 |
| 447 | **134** | 15c. black and green | 10 | 10 |
| 448 | **134** | 30c. brown and red | 20 | 15 |
| 449 | **134** | 90c. brown and blue | 20 | 15 |
| 450 | **134** | 2b. brown and black | 75 | 55 |

**MS**450a Two sheets each 86×131 mm. (a) No. 448; (b) No. 450. Imperf. Each sold at 4b 7·00 7·00

**1947.** Surch 1947 Habilitada Bs. 1.40.

| | | | | |
|---|---|---|---|---|
| 451 | | 1b.40 on 75c. blue (No. 334) (postage) | 25 | 15 |
| 452 | | 1b.40 on 75c. slate (No. 357) | 25 | 15 |
| 455 | | 1b.40 on 75c. red (No. 368) (air) | 30 | 20 |

**136** Seizure of Government Palace

**137** Mt. Illimani

**1947.** Popular Revolution of 21 July 1946.

| | | | | |
|---|---|---|---|---|
| 456 | **136** | 20c. green (postage) | 10 | 10 |
| 457 | **136** | 50c. purple | 10 | 10 |
| 458 | **136** | 1b.40 blue | 10 | 10 |
| 459 | **136** | 3b.70 orange | 20 | 10 |
| 460 | **136** | 4b. violet | 30 | 20 |
| 461 | **136** | 10b. olive | 95 | 45 |
| 462 | **137** | 1b. red (air) | 10 | 10 |
| 463 | **137** | 1b.40 green | 10 | 10 |
| 464 | **137** | 2b.50 blue | 20 | 15 |
| 465 | **137** | 3b. orange | 30 | 20 |
| 466 | **137** | 4b. mauve | 45 | 20 |

**138** Arms of Bolivia and Argentina

**1947.** Meeting of Presidents of Bolivia and Argentina.

| | | | | |
|---|---|---|---|---|
| 467 | **138** | 1b.40 orange (postage) | 45 | 25 |
| 468 | **138** | 2b.90 blue (air) | 55 | 45 |

**140** Cross and Child

**1948.** 3rd Inter-American Catholic Education Congress.

| | | | | |
|---|---|---|---|---|
| 473 | - | 1b.40 bl & yell (postage) | 45 | 10 |
| 474 | **140** | 2b. green and orange | 55 | 20 |
| 475 | - | 3b. green and blue | 85 | 25 |
| 476 | - | 5b. violet and orange | 1·10 | 30 |
| 477 | - | 5b. brown and green | 1·50 | 30 |
| 478 | - | 2b.50 orange & yell (air) | 65 | 45 |
| 479 | **140** | 3b.70 red and buff | 75 | 45 |
| 480 | - | 4b. mauve and blue | 75 | 30 |
| 481 | - | 4b. blue and orange | 75 | 25 |
| 482 | - | 13b.60 blue and green | 95 | 45 |

DESIGNS: 1b.40, 2b.50, Christ the Redeemer, Monument; 3b., 4b. (No. 480), Don Bosco; 5b. (No. 476), 4b. (No. 481), Virgin of Copacabana; 5b. (No. 477), 13b.60, Pope Pius XII.

**141** Map of S. America and Bolivian Auto Club Badge

**1948.** Pan-American Motor Race.

| | | | | |
|---|---|---|---|---|
| 483 | **141** | 5b. blue & pink (postage) | 2·30 | 75 |
| 484 | **141** | 10b. green & cream (air) | 2·10 | 30 |

**142** Posthorn, Globe and Pres. G. Pacheco

**1950.** 75th Anniv of U.P.U.

| | | | | |
|---|---|---|---|---|
| 485 | **142** | 1b.40 blue (postage) | 25 | 10 |
| 486 | **142** | 4b.20 red | 30 | 10 |
| 487 | **142** | 1b.40 brown (air) | 25 | 10 |
| 488 | **142** | 2b.50 orange | 30 | 10 |
| 489 | **142** | 3b.30 purple | 25 | 10 |

**1950.** Air. Surch XV ANIVERSARIO PANAGRA 1935–1950 and value.

| | | | | |
|---|---|---|---|---|
| 490 | **132** | 4b. on 10c. red | 20 | 10 |
| 491 | **132** | 10b. on 20b. brown | 55 | 35 |

**1950.** No. 379 surch Bs. 2.- Habilitada D.S.6.VII.50.

| | | | | |
|---|---|---|---|---|
| 492 | | 2b. on 1b.05 blue | 45 | 20 |

**145** Apparition at Potosi

**1950.** 400th Anniv of Apparition at El Potosi.

| | | | | |
|---|---|---|---|---|
| 493 | **145** | 20c. violet | 30 | 15 |
| 494 | **145** | 30c. orange | 30 | 15 |
| 495 | **145** | 50c. purple | 30 | 15 |
| 496 | **145** | 1b. red | 30 | 15 |
| 497 | **145** | 2b. blue | 35 | 15 |
| 498 | **145** | 6b. brown | 45 | 15 |

**146** Douglas DC-2

**1950.** Air. 25th Anniv of Lloyd Aereo Boliviano.

| | | | | |
|---|---|---|---|---|
| 499 | **146** | 20c. orange | 20 | 10 |
| 500 | **146** | 30c. violet | 20 | 10 |
| 501 | **146** | 50c. green | 20 | 10 |
| 502 | **146** | 1b. yellow | 20 | 10 |
| 503 | **146** | 3b. blue | 20 | 10 |
| 504 | **146** | 15b. red | 65 | 20 |
| 505 | **146** | 50b. brown | 1·90 | 65 |

**1950.** Air. Surch Triunfo de la Democracia 24 de Sept. 49 Bs. 1.40.

| | | | | |
|---|---|---|---|---|
| 506 | **137** | 1b.40 on 3b. orange | 30 | 30 |

**148** UN Emblem and Globe

**1950.** 5th Anniv of UNO.

| | | | | |
|---|---|---|---|---|
| 507 | **148** | 60c. blue (postage) | 1·60 | 20 |
| 508 | **148** | 2b. green | 2·10 | 30 |
| 509 | **148** | 3b.60 red (air) | 75 | 20 |
| 510 | **148** | 4b.70 brown | 95 | 20 |

**150** St. Francis Gate

**149** Gate of the Sun, Tiahuanacu

**1951.** 4th Centenary of Founding of La Paz. Centres in black.

| | | | | |
|---|---|---|---|---|
| 511 | **149** | 20c. green (postage) | 20 | 10 |
| 512 | **150** | 30c. orange | 20 | 10 |
| 513 | **A** | 40c. brown | 20 | 10 |
| 514 | **B** | 50c. red | 20 | 10 |
| 515 | **C** | 1b. purple | 20 | 10 |
| 516 | **D** | 1b.40 violet | 30 | 15 |
| 517 | **E** | 2b. purple | 30 | 15 |
| 518 | **F** | 3b. mauve | 45 | 20 |
| 519 | **G** | 5b. red | 55 | 30 |
| 520 | **H** | 10b. sepia | 1·10 | 45 |

**MS**520a Three sheets each 150×100 mm. Nos. 511/12, 520; 513, 516, 519; 514/15, 517/18 8·50 8·50

**MS**520b Do. Imperf 8·50 8·50

| | | | | |
|---|---|---|---|---|
| 521 | **149** | 20c. red (air) | 20 | 10 |
| 522 | **150** | 30c. violet | 20 | 10 |
| 523 | **A** | 40c. slate | 20 | 10 |
| 524 | **B** | 50c. green | 20 | 10 |
| 525 | **C** | 1b. red | 30 | 20 |
| 526 | **D** | 2b. orange | 55 | 45 |
| 527 | **E** | 3b. blue | 75 | 65 |
| 528 | **F** | 4b. red | 80 | 65 |
| 529 | **G** | 5b. green | 85 | 75 |
| 530 | **H** | 10b. brown | 90 | 85 |

**MS**530a Three sheets each 150×100 mm. Nos. 521/2, 530; 523, 527, 529; 524/5, 526, 528 8·25 8·25

**MS**530b Do. Imperf 8·25 8·25

DESIGNS—HORIZ: As Type **149**: A, Camacho Avenue; B, Consistorial Palace; C, Legislative Palace; D, G.P.O. E, Arms; F, Pedro de la Casca authorizes plans of City; G, Founding the City; H, City Arms and Captain A. de Mendoza.

**151** Tennis

**1951.** Sports. Centres in black.

| | | | | |
|---|---|---|---|---|
| 531 | - | 20c. blue (postage) | 20 | 10 |
| 532 | **151** | 50c. red | 20 | 10 |
| 533 | - | 1b. purple | 25 | 10 |
| 534 | - | 1b.40 yellow | 30 | 20 |
| 535 | - | 2b. red | 65 | 45 |
| 536 | - | 3b. brown | 1·30 | 1·10 |
| 537 | - | 4b. blue | 1·60 | 1·40 |

**MS**537a Two sheets each 150×100 mm. Nos. 531/2, 535/6; 533/4, 537 6·50 6·50

**MS**537b Do. Imperf 6·50 6·50

| | | | | |
|---|---|---|---|---|
| 538 | | 20c. violet (air) | 30 | 10 |
| 539 | | 30c. purple | 45 | 15 |
| 540 | | 50c. orange | 75 | 20 |
| 541 | | 1b. brown | 75 | 20 |
| 542 | | 2b.50 orange | 1·20 | 45 |
| 543 | | 3b. sepia | 1·60 | 1·20 |
| 544 | | 5b. red | 3·25 | 2·30 |

**MS**544a 130×80 mm. Nos. 741/3 18·00 18·00

**MS**544b Do. Imperf 18·00 18·00

DESIGNS—Postage: 20c. Boxing; 1b. Diving; 1b.40, Football; 2b. Skiing; 3b. Pelota; 4b. Cycling. Air: 20c. Horse-jumping; 30c. Basketball; 50c. Fencing; 1b. Hurdling; 2b.50, Javelin; 3b. Relay race; 5b. La Paz Stadium.

**152** Andean Condor and Flag

**1951.** 100th National Flag Anniv. Flag in red, yellow and green.

| | | | | |
|---|---|---|---|---|
| 545 | **152** | 2b. green | 10 | 10 |
| 546 | **152** | 3b.50c. blue | 10 | 10 |
| 547 | **152** | 5b. violet | 20 | 15 |
| 548 | **152** | 7b.50c. grey | 55 | 20 |
| 549 | **152** | 15b. red | 75 | 45 |
| 550 | **152** | 30b. brown | 1·80 | 95 |

**153** Posthorn and Envelope

**1951.** Obligatory Tax.

| | | | | |
|---|---|---|---|---|
| 551 | - | 20c. orange | 75 | 30 |
| 551b | - | 20c. green | 75 | 30 |
| 552 | - | 20c. blue | 75 | 30 |
| 553 | **153** | 50c. green | 85 | 30 |
| 553d | **153** | 50c. red | 85 | 30 |
| 553e | **153** | 3b. green | 85 | 30 |
| 553f | **153** | 3b. bistre | 95 | 75 |
| 553g | **153** | 5b. violet | 1·10 | 75 |

DESIGN: 20c. Condor over posthorn and envelope.

**154** E. Abaroa

**1952.** 73rd Death Anniv of Abaroa (patriot).

| | | | | |
|---|---|---|---|---|
| 554 | **154** | 80c. red (postage) | 10 | 10 |
| 555 | **154** | 1b. orange | 10 | 10 |
| 556 | **154** | 2b. green | 20 | 10 |
| 557 | **154** | 5b. blue | 65 | 20 |
| 558 | **154** | 10b. mauve | 1·90 | 45 |
| 559 | **154** | 20b. brown | 3·25 | 75 |
| 560 | **154** | 70c. red (air) | 20 | 10 |
| 561 | **154** | 2b. yellow | 45 | 20 |
| 562 | **154** | 3b. green | 30 | 20 |
| 563 | **154** | 5b. blue | 65 | 20 |
| 564 | **154** | 50b. purple | 1·90 | 75 |
| 565 | **154** | 100b. black | 3·25 | 1·60 |

**155** Isabella the Catholic

**1952.** 500th Birth Anniv of Isabella the Catholic.

| | | | | |
|---|---|---|---|---|
| 566 | **155** | 2b. blue (postage) | 30 | 20 |
| 567 | **155** | 6b.30 red | 55 | 25 |
| 568 | **155** | 50b. green (air) | 95 | 30 |
| 569 | **155** | 100b. brown | 45 | 35 |

**156** Columbus Lighthouse

**1952.** Columbus Memorial Lighthouse. On tinted papers.

| | | | | |
|---|---|---|---|---|
| 570 | **156** | 2b. blue (postage) | 30 | 20 |
| 571 | **156** | 5b. red | 85 | 65 |
| 572 | **156** | 9b. green | 1·50 | 85 |
| 573 | **156** | 2b. purple (air) | 25 | 20 |
| 574 | **156** | 3b.70 turquoise | 25 | 20 |
| 575 | **156** | 4b.40 orange | 30 | 20 |
| 576 | **156** | 20b. brown | 65 | 30 |

**157** Miner

**1953.** Nationalization of Mining Industry.

| | | | | |
|---|---|---|---|---|
| 577 | **157** | 2b.50c. red | 20 | 10 |
| 578 | **157** | 8b. violet | 30 | 15 |

**158** Villarroel, Paz Estenssoro and Siles Zuazo

**159** Revolutionaries

**1953.** 1st Anniv of Revolution of April 9th, 1952.

| | | | | |
|---|---|---|---|---|
| 579 | **158** | 50c. mauve (postage) | 20 | 10 |
| 580 | **158** | 1b. red | 20 | 10 |
| 581 | **158** | 2b. blue | 20 | 10 |
| 582 | **158** | 3b. green | 20 | 10 |
| 583 | **158** | 4b. yellow | 20 | 10 |
| 584 | **158** | 5b. violet | 30 | 20 |
| 585 | **158** | 3b.70 brown (air) | 30 | 20 |
| 586 | **158** | 9b. red | 30 | 20 |
| 587 | **158** | 10b. turquoise | 30 | 20 |
| 588 | **158** | 16b. orange | 30 | 20 |
| 589 | **158** | 40b. grey | 65 | 20 |
| 590 | **159** | 6b. mauve | 30 | 20 |
| 591 | **159** | 22b.50 brown | 1·10 | 85 |

**1953.** Obligatory Tax. No. 551b and similar stamp surch 50 cts.

| | | | | |
|---|---|---|---|---|
| 592 | **158** | 50c. on 20c. mauve | 55 | 30 |
| 593 | **158** | 50c. on 20c. green | 45 | 20 |

**161**

**1954.** Obligatory Tax.

| | | | | |
|---|---|---|---|---|
| 594 | **161** | 1b. lake | 1·30 | 30 |
| 595 | **161** | 1b. brown | 30 | 30 |

**162** Ear of Wheat and Map

**1954.** 1st National Agronomical Congress.

| | | | | |
|---|---|---|---|---|
| 596 | **162** | 25b. blue | 30 | 10 |
| 597 | **162** | 85b. brown | 65 | 25 |

**163** Pres. Paz Estenssoro embracing Indian

**1954.** Air. 3rd Inter-American Indigenous Congress.

| | | | | |
|---|---|---|---|---|
| 598 | **163** | 20b. brown | 20 | 10 |
| 599 | **163** | 100b. turquoise | 80 | 10 |

**1954.** 1st Anniv of Agrarian Reform. As T 162, but designs inscr "REFORMA AGRARIA".

| | | | |
|---|---|---|---|
| 600 | 5b. red (postage) | 10 | 10 |
| 601 | 17b. turquoise | 15 | 10 |
| 602 | 27b. mauve (air) | 20 | 15 |
| 603 | 30b. orange | 30 | 20 |
| 604 | 45b. purple | 55 | 20 |
| 605 | 300b. green | 2·30 | 45 |

DESIGNS—5b., 17b. Cow's head and map; 27b. to 300b. Indian peasant woman.

**1955.** Obligatory Tax. Nos. 553e and 553f surch Bs. 5.—D. S. 21-IV-55.

| | | | | |
|---|---|---|---|---|
| 606 | **153** | 5b. on 3b. green | 55 | 20 |
| 607 | **153** | 5b. on 3b. bistre | 1·40 | 20 |

**166** Refinery

**167** Derricks

**1955.** Development of Petroleum Industry.

| | | | | |
|---|---|---|---|---|
| 608 | **166** | 10b. blue (postage) | 10 | 10 |
| 609 | **166** | 35b. red | 15 | 10 |
| 610 | **166** | 40b. green | 20 | 15 |
| 611 | **166** | 50b. purple | 30 | 20 |
| 612 | **166** | 80b. brown | 55 | 30 |
| 613 | **167** | 55b. blue (air) | 20 | 10 |
| 614 | **167** | 70b. black | 45 | 10 |
| 615 | **167** | 90b. green | 55 | 15 |
| 616 | **167** | 500b. mauve | 1·90 | 95 |
| 617 | **167** | 1000b. brown | 3·25 | 1·90 |

**168** Control Tower

**169** Douglas DC-6B Aircraft

**1957.** Obligatory Tax. Airport Building Fund.

| | | | | |
|---|---|---|---|---|
| 618 | **168** | 5b. blue | 55 | 20 |
| 619 | **169** | 10b. green | 45 | 20 |
| 620 | **168** | 5b. red | 9·50 | 9·50 |
| 620b | **169** | 20b. brown | 55 | 30 |

DESIGNS: 5b. (No. 620), Douglas DC-6B over runway; 20b. Lockheed Constellation in flight.

**1957.** Currency revaluation. Founding of La Paz stamps of 1951 surch. Centres in black.

| | | | | |
|---|---|---|---|---|
| 621 | **F** | 50b. on 3b. mauve (post) | 10 | 10 |
| 622 | **E** | 100b. on 2b. purple | 15 | 10 |
| 623 | **C** | 200b. on 1b. purple | 20 | 10 |
| 624 | **D** | 300b. on 1b.40 violet | 30 | 10 |
| 625 | **149** | 350b. on 20c. green | 45 | 15 |
| 626 | **A** | 400b. on 40c. brown | 45 | 15 |
| 627 | **150** | 600b. on 30c. orange | 65 | 20 |
| 628 | **B** | 800b. on 50c. red | 75 | 20 |
| 629 | **H** | 1000b. on 10b. sepia | 75 | 25 |
| 630 | **G** | 2000b. on 5b. red | 1·30 | 55 |
| 631 | **E** | 100b. on 3b. blue (air) | 10 | 10 |
| 632 | **D** | 200b. on 2b. orange | 15 | 10 |
| 633 | **F** | 500b. on 4b. red | 20 | 10 |
| 634 | **C** | 600b. on 1b. red | 25 | 15 |
| 635 | **149** | 700b. on 20c. red | 55 | 20 |
| 636 | **A** | 800b. on 40c. slate | 65 | 30 |
| 637 | **150** | 900b. on 30c. violet | 75 | 20 |
| 638 | **B** | 1800b. on 50c. green | 1·30 | 65 |
| 639 | **G** | 3000b. on 5b. green | 1·70 | 1·20 |
| 640 | **H** | 5000b. on 10b. brown | 3·25 | 2·10 |

**172** Congress Buildings (Santiago de Chile and La Paz)

**173** "Latin America" on Globe

**1957.** 7th Latin-America Economic Congress, La Paz.

| | | | | |
|---|---|---|---|---|
| 641 | **172** | 150b. bl & grey (postage) | 10 | 10 |
| 642 | **172** | 350b. grey and brown | 20 | 10 |
| 643 | **172** | 550b. sepia and blue | 25 | 10 |
| 644 | **172** | 750b. green and red | 35 | 15 |
| 645 | **172** | 900b. brown and green | 55 | 20 |
| 646 | **173** | 700b. violet & lilac (air) | 65 | 35 |
| 647 | **173** | 1200b. brown | 70 | 45 |
| 648 | **173** | 1350b. red and mauve | 1·10 | 65 |
| 649 | **173** | 2700b. olive and turq | 1·90 | 90 |
| 650 | **173** | 4000b. violet and blue | 3·75 | 1·50 |

**174** Steam Train and Presidents of Bolivia and Argentina

**1957.** Yacuiba-Santa Cruz Railway Inauguration.

| | | | | |
|---|---|---|---|---|
| 651 | **174** | 50b. orange (postage) | 35 | 35 |
| 652 | **174** | 350b. blue and light blue | 85 | 40 |
| 653 | **174** | 1000b. brown & cinna | 1·90 | 60 |
| 654 | **174** | 600b. purple & pink (air) | 80 | 40 |
| 655 | **174** | 700b. violet and blue | 1·40 | 60 |
| 656 | **174** | 900b. green | 1·90 | 45 |

**175** Presidents and Flags of Bolivia and Mexico

**1960.** Visit of Mexican President to Bolivia.

| | | | | |
|---|---|---|---|---|
| 657 | **175** | 350b. olive (postage) | 30 | 10 |
| 658 | **175** | 600b. brown | 45 | 20 |
| 659 | **175** | 1,500b. sepia | 95 | 30 |
| 660 | **175** | 400b. red (air) | 95 | 10 |
| 661 | **175** | 800b. blue | 1·30 | 30 |
| 662 | **175** | 2,000b. green | 1·90 | 75 |

The President's visit to Bolivia did not take place.

**176** Indians and Mt. Illimani

**177** "Gate of the Sun", Tiahuanacu

**1960.** Tourist Publicity.

| | | | | |
|---|---|---|---|---|
| 663 | **176** | 500b. bistre (postage) | 75 | 30 |
| 664 | **176** | 1000b. blue | 1·40 | 45 |
| 665 | **176** | 2000b. sepia | 3·25 | 75 |
| 666 | **176** | 4000b. green | 5·75 | 3·75 |
| 667 | **177** | 3000b. grey (air) | 3·25 | 1·70 |
| 668 | **177** | 5000b. orange | 4·75 | 1·80 |
| 669 | **177** | 10,000b. purple | 7·50 | 4·25 |
| 670 | **177** | 15,000b. violet | 10·50 | 7·00 |

**178** Refugees

**179** "Uprooted Tree"

**1960.** World Refugee Year.

| | | | | |
|---|---|---|---|---|
| 671 | **178** | 50b. brown (postage) | 10 | 10 |
| 672 | **178** | 350b. purple | 20 | 10 |
| 673 | **178** | 400b. blue | 30 | 15 |
| 674 | **178** | 1000b. sepia | 85 | 55 |
| 675 | **178** | 3000b. green | 1·90 | 1·20 |
| 676 | **179** | 600b. blue (air) | 55 | 20 |
| 677 | **179** | 700b. brown | 55 | 30 |
| 678 | **179** | 900b. turquoise | 65 | 35 |
| 679 | **179** | 1800b. violet | 1·30 | 85 |
| 680 | **179** | 2000b. black | 1·80 | 1·30 |

**180** Jaime Laredo (violinist) **181** Jaime Laredo (violinist)

**1960.** Jaime Laredo Commem.

| | | | | |
|---|---|---|---|---|
| 681 | **180** | 100b. green (postage) | 30 | 10 |
| 682 | **180** | 350b. lake | 65 | 10 |
| 683 | **180** | 500b. blue | 75 | 15 |
| 684 | **180** | 1000b. brown | 95 | 20 |
| 685 | **180** | 1500b. violet | 1·80 | 55 |
| 686 | **180** | 5000b. black | 5·75 | 1·60 |
| 687 | **181** | 600b. plum (air) | 1·30 | 45 |
| 688 | **181** | 700b. olive | 1·50 | 55 |
| 689 | **181** | 800b. brown | 1·50 | 55 |
| 690 | **181** | 900b. blue | 2·00 | 55 |
| 691 | **181** | 1800b. turquoise | 2·30 | 1·60 |
| 692 | **181** | 4000b. grey | 5·75 | 2·30 |

**182** Rotary Emblem and Nurse with Children

**1960.** Founding of Children's Hospital by La Paz Rotary Club. Wheel in blue and yellow, foreground in yellow; background given.

| | | | | |
|---|---|---|---|---|
| 693 | **182** | 350b. green (postage) | 30 | 10 |
| 694 | **182** | 500b. sepia | 45 | 10 |
| 695 | **182** | 600b. violet | 65 | 15 |
| 696 | **182** | 1000b. grey | 75 | 25 |
| 697 | **182** | 600b. brown (air) | 75 | 45 |
| 698 | **182** | 1000b. olive | 1·10 | 45 |
| 699 | **182** | 1800b. purple | 1·50 | 75 |
| 700 | **182** | 5000b. black | 4·75 | 2·10 |

**183**

**1960.** Air. Unissued stamp, surch as in T 183.

| | | | | |
|---|---|---|---|---|
| 701 | **183** | 1200b. on 10b. orange | 1·30 | 95 |

**184** Design from Gate of the Sun

**1960.** Unissued Tiahuanacu Excavation stamps surch as in T 184. Gold backgrounds.

| | | | |
|---|---|---|---|
| 702 | 50b. on ½c. red | 85 | 55 |
| 703 | 100b. on 1c. red | 55 | 20 |
| 704 | 200b. on 2c. black | 1·50 | 20 |
| 705 | 300b. on 5c. green | 30 | 20 |
| 706 | 350b. on 10c. green | 30 | 1·20 |
| 707 | 400b. on 15c. blue | 55 | 20 |
| 708 | 500b. on 20c. red | 55 | 20 |
| 709 | 500b. on 50c. red | 65 | 20 |
| 710 | 600b. on 22½c. green | 85 | 45 |
| 711 | 600b. on 60c. violet | 95 | 55 |
| 712 | 700b. on 25c. violet | 1·40 | 30 |
| 713 | 700b. on 1b. green | 1·90 | 1·20 |
| 714 | 800b. on 30c. red | 95 | 30 |
| 715 | 900b. on 40c. green | 85 | 45 |
| 716 | 1000b. on 2b. blue | 95 | 55 |
| 717 | 1800b. on 3b. grey | 9·50 | 6·50 |
| 718 | 4000b. on 4b. grey | 75·00 | 65·00 |
| 719 | 5000b. on 5b. grey | 19·00 | 14·00 |

DESIGNS: Various gods, motifs and ornaments. SIZES: Nos. 702/6, As Type **184**. Nos. 707/17, As Type **184** but horiz. No. 718, 49×23 mm. No. 719, 50×52½ mm.

**185** Flags of Argentina and Bolivia

**1961.** Air. Visit of Pres. Frondizi of Argentina.

| | | | | |
|---|---|---|---|---|
| 720 | **185** | 4000b. multicoloured | 1·40 | 1·30 |
| 721 | - | 6000b. sepia and green | 2·10 | 1·70 |

DESIGN: 6000b. Presidents of Argentina and Bolivia.

**186** Miguel de Cervantes (First Mayor of La Paz)

**1961.** M. de Cervantes Commem and 4th Centenary of Santa Cruz de la Sierra (1500b.).

| | | | | |
|---|---|---|---|---|
| 722 | **186** | 600b. violet and ochre (postage) | 65 | 30 |
| 723 | - | 1500b. blue and orange | 1·20 | 45 |
| 724 | - | 1400b. brown & green (air) | 85 | 30 |

DESIGNS: 1400b. Portrait as Type **186** (diamond shape, 30½×30½ mm); 1500b. Nuflo de Chaves (vert: as Type **186**).

See also Nos. 755/6.

**187** "United in Christ"

**1962.** 4th National Eucharistic Congress, Santa Cruz.

| | | | | |
|---|---|---|---|---|
| 725 | **187** | 1000b. yellow, red and green (postage) | 85 | 45 |
| 726 | - | 1400b. yellow, pink and brown (air) | 85 | 45 |

DESIGN: 1400b. Virgin of Cotoca.

**1962.** Nos. 671/80 surch.

| | | | | |
|---|---|---|---|---|
| 727 | **178** | 600b. on 50b. brown (postage) | 55 | 20 |
| 728 | **178** | 900b. on 350b. purple | 60 | 20 |
| 729 | **178** | 1000b. on 400b. blue | 65 | 25 |
| 730 | **178** | 2000b. on 1000b. brown | 75 | 55 |
| 731 | **178** | 3500b. on 3000b. green | 1·30 | 1·10 |
| 732 | **179** | 1200b. on 600b. blue (air) | 1·20 | 55 |
| 733 | **179** | 1300b. on 700b. brown | 1·20 | 55 |
| 734 | **179** | 1400b. on 900b. green | 1·20 | 55 |
| 735 | **179** | 2800b. on 1800b. violet | 1·90 | 75 |
| 736 | **179** | 3000b. on 2000b. black | 1·90 | 1·10 |

**189** Hibiscus

**1962.** Flowers in actual colours; background colours given.

| | | | | |
|---|---|---|---|---|
| 737 | **189** | 200b. green (postage) | 85 | 20 |
| 738 | - | 400b. brown | 1·30 | 20 |
| 739 | - | 600b. deep blue | 2·10 | 15 |
| 740 | - | 1000b. violet | 3·00 | 45 |
| 741 | - | 100b. blue (air) | 75 | 20 |

742 - 800b. green 1·40 30
743 - 1800b. violet 3·00 75
744 - 10,000b. deep blue 9·00 4·50
**MS**744a 130×80 mm. Nos. 741/3. Imperf 13·00 13·00
FLOWERS: Nos. 738, 740 Orchids; 739, St. James' lily; 741/4, Types of Kantuta (national flowers).

**190** Infantry

**1962.** Armed Forces Commemoration.
745 **190** 400b. mult (postage) 10 10
746 - 500b. multicoloured 20 10
747 - 600b. multicoloured 30 15
748 - 2000b. multicoloured 85 55
749 - 600b. mult (air) 55 20
750 - 1200b. multicoloured 65 30
751 - 2000b. multicoloured 95 55
752 - 5000b. multicoloured 2·10 1·40
DESIGNS: No. 746, Cavalry; 747, Artillery; 748, Engineers; 749, Parachutists and aircraft; 750, 752, "Overseas Flights" (Lockheed Super Electra airplane over oxen-cart); 751, "Aerial Survey" (Douglas DC-3 airplane photographing ground).

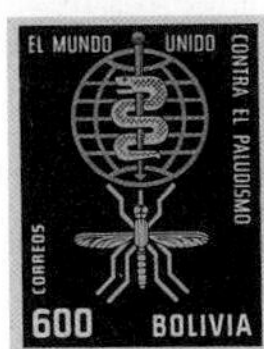

**191** Campaign Emblem

**1962.** Malaria Eradication.
753 **191** 600b. yellow, violet and lilac (postage) 65 45
754 - 2000b. yellow, green and blue (air) 2·00 95
DESIGN: 2000b. As No. 753 but with laurel wreath and inscription encircling emblem.

**1962.** Spanish Discoverers. As T 186 but inscribed "1548–1962".
755 600b. mauve on blue (postage) 45 20
756 1200b. brown on yellow (air) 65 30
PORTRAITS: 600b. A. de Mendoza. 1200b. P. de la Gasca.

**192** Goal-Keeper diving to save Goal

**1963.** 21st South American Football Championships, La Paz. Multicoloured.
757 **192** 60c. Type **192** (postage) 75 15
758 **192** 1p. Goalkeeper saving ball (vert) 1·20 30
759 **192** 1p.40 Andean condor on football (vert) (air) 1·90 1·30
760 **192** 1p.80 Ball in corner of net (vert) 2·00 1·40

**193** Globe and Emblem

**1963.** Freedom from Hunger.
761 **193** 60c. yellow, blue and indigo (postage) 55 15
762 - 1p.20 yellow, blue and myrtle (air) 1·30 1·20
DESIGN: 1p.20, Ear of wheat across Globe.

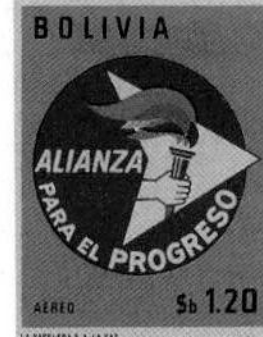

**194** Alliance Emblem

**1963.** Air. "Alliance for Progress".
763 **194** 1p.20 green, blue & bis 1·30 1·20

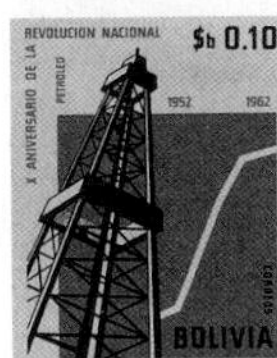

**195** Oil Derrick

**1963.** 10th Anniv of Revolution (1962).
764 **195** 10c. grn & brn (postage) 20 10
765 - 60c. sepia and orange 30 15
766 - 1p. yellow, violet & green 45 25
767 - 1p.20 pink, brown and grey (air) 65 30
768 - 1p.40 green and ochre 75 35
769 - 2p.80 buff and slate 1·60 1·40
DESIGNS: 60c. Map of Bolivia; 1p. Students; 1p.20, Ballot box and voters; 1p.40, Peasant breaking chain; 2p.80, Miners.

**196** Flags of Bolivia and Peru
**197** Marshal Santa Cruz

**1966.** Death Centenary of Marshal Santa Cruz.
770 **196** 10c. mult (postage) 20 10
771 **196** 60c. multicoloured 30 15
772 **196** 1p. multicoloured 55 30
773 **196** 2p. multicoloured 75 55
774 **197** 20c. blue (air) 20 10
775 **197** 60c. green 30 15
776 **197** 1p.20 brown 75 55
777 **197** 2p.80 black 1·30 1·10

**198** Generals Barrientos and Ovando, Bolivian Map and Flag

**1966.** Co-Presidents Commemoration.
778 **198** 60c. mult (postage) 55 10
779 **198** 1p. multicoloured 65 15
780 **198** 2p.80 mult (air) 1·70 1·10
781 **198** 10p. multicoloured 3·75 1·40
**MS**782 136×83 mm. Nos. 778/81. Imperf 10·00 10·00

**199** Needy Children

**1966.** Aid for Poor Children.
783 **199** 30c. brown, sepia and ochre (postage) 55 20
784 - 1p.40 black & blue (air) 2·50 65
DESIGN: 1p.40, Mother and needy children.

**1966.** Commemorative Issues. Various stamps surch with inscr (as given below) and value. (i) Red Cross Centenary. Surch Centenario de la Cruz Roja Internacional.
785 20c. on 150b. (No. 641) (post) 30 10
786 4p. on 4000b. (No. 650) (air) 2·10 1·60

(ii) General Azurduy de Padilla. Surch Homenaje a la Generala J. Azurduy de Padilla.
787 30c. on 550b. (No. 643) 45 20
788 2p.80 on 750b. (No. 644) 1·20 75

(iii) Air. Tupiza Cent. Surch Centenario de Tupiza.
789 60c. on 1350b. (No. 648) 75 30

(iv) Air. 25th Anniv of Bolivian Motor Club. Surch XXV Aniversario Automovil Club Boliviano.
790 2p.80 on 2700b. (No. 649) 3·25 2·30

(v) Air. Cochabamba Philatelic Society Anniv. Surch Aniversario Centro Filatelico Cochabamba.
791 1p.20 on 800b. (No. 742) 1·60 30
792 1p.20 on 1800b. (No. 743) 1·60 30

(vi) Rotary Help for Children's Hospital. Surch with value only. (a) Postage.
793 1p.60 on 350b. (No. 693) 1·20 75
794 2p.40 on 500b. (No. 694) 1·60 1·20

(b) Air.
795 1p.40 on 1000b. (No. 698) 85 75
796 1p.40 on 1800b. (No. 699) 85 75

(vii) 150th Anniv of Coronilla Heroines. Surch CL Aniversario Heroinas Coronilla. (a) Postage.
797 60c. on 350b. (No. 682) 75 20

(b) Air.
798 1p.20 on 800b. (No. 689) 1·20 75

(viii) Air. Centenary of Hymn La Paz. Surch Centenario Himno Paceno.
799 1p.40 on 4000b. (No. 692) 1·20 75

(ix) Air. 12th Anniv of Agrarian Reform. Surch XII Aniversario Reforma Agraria.
800 10c. on 27b. (No. 602) 30 20

(x) Air. 25th Anniv of Chaco Peace Settlement. Surch XXV Aniversario Paz del Chaco.
801 10c. on 55b. (No. 613) 30 20

(xi) Centenary of Rurrenabaque. Surch Centenario de Rurrenabaque.
802 1p. on 10b. brown 75 30

(xii) 25th Anniv of Busch Government. Surch XXV Aniversario Gobierno Busch.
803 20c. on 5b. red 30 20

(xiii) 20th Anniv of Villarroel Government. Surch XX Aniversario Gob. Villarroel.
804 60c. on 2b. green 45 20

(xiv) 25th Anniv of Pando Department. Surch XXV Aniversario Dpto. Pando. (a) Postage.
805 1p.60 on 50c. violet 75 30

(b) Air. Surch Aereo also.
806 1p.20 on 1b. blue 85 45

**201** Sower

**1967.** 50th Anniv of Lions International. Mult.
807 **201** 70c. Type **201** (postage) 55 20
808 **201** 2p. Lions emblem and Inca obelisks (horiz) (air) 1·30 95
**MS**809 129×80 mm. Nos. 807/8. Imperf 5·75 5·75

**202** "Macheteros"

**1968.** 9th Congress of the UPAE (Postal Union of the Americas and Spain). Bolivian Folklore. Designs showing costumed figures. Multicoloured.
810 **202** 30c. Type **202** (postage) 30 10
811 **202** 60c. "Chunchos" 45 20
812 **202** 1p. "Wiphala" 65 25
813 **202** 2p. "Diablada" 95 30
814 **202** 1p.20 "Pujllay" (air) 55 20
815 **202** 1p.40 "Ujusiris" 65 25
816 **202** 2p. "Morenada" 1·30 45
817 **202** 3p. "Auki-aukis" 1·70 55
**MS**818 Two sheets each 132×80 mm. Nos. 810/13 and 814/17. Imperf 27·00 27·00

**203** Arms of Tarija

**1968.** 150th Anniv of Battle of the Tablada (1817).
819 **203** 20c. mult (postage) 20 10
820 **203** 30c. multicoloured 20 10
821 **203** 40c. multicoloured 30 10
822 **203** 60c. multicoloured 45 15
823 - 1p. multicoloured (air) 55 20
824 - 1p.20 multicoloured 65 20
825 - 2p. multicoloured 1·20 55
826 - 4p. multicoloured 1·70 85
DESIGNS: Nos. 823/6, Moto Mendez.

**204** President G. Villarroel

**1968.** 400th Anniv of Cochabamba.
827 **204** 20c. brn & orge (postage) 80 20
828 **204** 30c. brown & turquoise 80 20
829 **204** 40c. brown and purple 80 20
830 **204** 50c. brown and green 80 20
831 **204** 1p. brown and bistre 95 20
832 - 1p.40 black & red (air) 1·10 45
833 - 3p. black and blue 1·50 55
834 - 4p. black and red 1·90 65
835 - 5p. black and green 2·40 65
836 - 10p. black and violet 4·25 1·30
DESIGN—HORIZ: 1p.40 to 10p. Similar portrait of President.

**205** Painted Clay Cup

**1968.** 20th Anniv of UNESCO (1966).
837 **205** 20c. mult (postage) 40 10
838 **205** 60c. multicoloured 75 45
839 **205** 1p.20 black & blue (air) 75 45
840 **205** 2p.80 black and green 1·40 95
DESIGNS: Nos. 839/40, UNESCO emblem.

**206** President J. F. Kennedy

**1968.** 5th Death Anniv of John F. Kennedy (U.S. President).
841 **206** 10c. black & grn (postage) 30 10
842 **206** 4p. black and violet 2·10 2·10
843 **206** 1p. black and green (air) 40 20
844 **206** 10p. black and red 4·25 4·25
**MS**845 Two sheets each 131×80 mm. (a) No. 842; (b) No. 843. Imperf 9·50 9·50

**207** ITU Emblem

**1968.** Centenary (1965) of ITU.
846 **207** 10c. black grey and yellow (postage) 30 10
847 **207** 60c. black, orange & bistre 55 30
848 **207** 1p.20 black, grey and yellow (air) 75 40
849 **207** 1p.40 black, blue & brn 85 30

**208** Tennis Player

**1968.** South American Tennis Championships, La Paz.
850 **208** 10c. black, brown and grey (postage) 40 15
851 **208** 20c. black, brown & yell 40 15
852 **208** 30c. black, brown & blue 40 15
853 **208** 1p.40 black, brown and orange (air) 1·30 45
854 **208** 2p.80 black, brown & bl 2·40 95

**MS**855 Two sheets each 132×81 mm. (a) Nos. 850/2; (b) No. 853. Imperf 17·00 17·00

**209** Unofficial 1r. Stamp of 1863

**1963.** Stamp Centenary.
856 **209** 10c. brown, black and green (postage) 90 15
857 **209** 30c. brown, black & blue 90 15
858 **209** 2p. brown, black & drab 90 15
859 - 1p.40 green, black and yellow (air) 1·30 70
860 - 2p.80 green, blk & pink 2·40 1·40
861 - 3p. green, black & lilac 2·40 1·40
**MS**862 Two sheets each 132×83 mm. (a) Nos. 856/8; (b) Nos. 859/61. Imperf 11·00 11·50
DESIGN: Nos. 859/61, First Bolivian stamp.

**210** Rifle-shooting

**1969.** Olympic Games, Mexico (1968).
863 **210** 40c. black, red and orange (postage) 55 25
864 - 50c. black, red and green 55 25
865 - 60c. black, blue & green 55 25
866 - 1p.20 black, green and ochre (air) 70 50
867 - 2p.80 black, red & yell 1·40 1·00
868 - 5p. multicoloured 2·20 2·10
**MS**869 Two sheets each 131×81 mm. (a) Nos. 863/5; (b) Nos. 866/8 17·00 17·00
DESIGNS—HORIZ: 50c. Horse-jumping; 60c. Canoeing; 5p. Hurdling. VERT: 1p.20, Running; 2p.80, Throwing the discus.

**211** F. D. Roosevelt

**1969.** Air. Franklin D. Roosevelt Commem.
870 **211** 5p. black, orange & brown 2·00 1·50

**212** "Temensis laothoe violetta"

**1970.** Butterflies. Multicoloured.
871 5c. Type **212** (postage) 90 80
872 10c. "Papilio crassus" 1·80 1·60
873 20c. "Catagramma cynosura" 1·80 1·60
874 30c. "Eunica eurota flora" 1·80 1·60
875 80c. "Ituna phenarete" 1·80 1·60
876 1p. "Metamorpha dido wernichei" (air) 2·00 1·70
877 1p.80 "Heliconius felix" 2·75 2·40
878 2p.80 "Morpho casica" 3·75 3·50
879 3p. "Papilio yuracares" 4·00 3·50
880 4p. "Heliconsus melitus" 5·00 4·50
**MS**881 Two sheets each 130×80 mm. (a) Nos. 871/3; (b) Nos. 876/8. Imerf 29·00 29·00

**213** Scout mountaineering

**1970.** Bolivian Scout Movement. Multicoloured.
882 **213** 5c. Type **213** (postage) 25 10
883 **213** 10c. Girl-scout planting shrub 25 10
884 **213** 50c. Scout laying bricks (air) 25 15
885 **213** 1p.20 Bolivian scout badge 55 45

**214** President A. Ovando and Revolutionaries

**1970.** Obligatory Tax. Revolution and National Day.
886 **214** 20c. blk & red (postage) 65 25
887 **214** 30c. black & green (air) 65 25
DESIGN: 30c. Pres. Ovando, oil derricks and laurel sprig.

**1970.** "Exfilca 70" Stamp Exhibition, Caracas, Venezuela. No. 706 further surch EXFILCA 70 and new value.
888 30c. on 350b. on 10c. 45 30

**1970.** Provisionals. Various stamps surch.
889 **178** 60c. on 900b. on 350b. (postage) 35 10
890 - 1p.20 on 1500b. (No. 723) 65 15
891 **185** 1p.20 on 4000b. (air) 45 15

**217** Pres. G. Busch and Oil Derrick

**1971.** 32nd Death Anniv of President G. Busch and 25th Death Anniv of Pres. Villarroel.
892 **217** 20c. blk & lilac (postage) 65 25
893 - 30c. black and blue (air) 65 25
DESIGN: 30c. Pres. Villarroel and oil refinery.

**218** "Amaryllis escobar uriae"

**1971.** Bolivian Flora. Multicoloured.
894 30c. Type **218** (postage) 35 15
895 40c. "Amaryllis evansae" 35 15
896 50c. "Amaryllis yungacensis" (vert) 55 25
897 2p. "Gymnocalycium chiquitanum" (vert) 1·40 55
898 1p.20 "Amaryllis pseudopardina" (air) 80 55
899 1p.40 "Rebutia kruegeri" (vert) 1·20 70
900 2p.80 "Lobivia pentlandii" 2·00 1·00
901 4p. "Rebutia tunariensis" (vert) 2·75 1·70
**MS**902 Two sheets each 130×80 mm. (a) Nos. 894/5, 898 and 900; (b) Nos. 896/7, 899 and 901. Imperf 27·00 27·00

**219** Sica Sica Cathedral

**1971.** "Exfilima" Stamp Exhibition, Lima, Peru.
903 **219** 20c. multicoloured 45 25

**220** Pres. H. Banzer

**1972.** "Bolivia's Development".
904 **220** 1p.20 multicoloured 1·80 25

**221** Chiriwano de Achocalla Dance

**1972.** Folk Dances. Multicoloured.
905 20c. Type **221** (postage) 25 10
906 40c. Rueda Chapaca 45 15
907 60c. Kena-Kena 65 25
908 1p. Waca Thokori 80 30
909 1p.20 Kusillo (air) 70 25
910 1p.40 Taquirari 90 25

**222** "Virgin and Child" (B. Bitti)

**1972.** Bolivian Paintings. Multicoloured.
911 10c. "The Washerwoman" (M. P. Holguín) (postage) 35 10
912 50c. "Coronation of the Virgin" (G. M. Berrio) 45 10
913 70c. "Arquebusier" (anon.) 65 10
914 80c. "St. Peter of Alcantara" (M. P. Holguín) 70 15
915 1p. Type **222** 1·00 20
916 1p.40 "Chola Pacena" (G. de Rojas) (air) 70 10
917 1p.50 "Adoration of the Kings" (G. Gamarra) 70 10
918 1p.60 "Pachamama Vision" (A. Borda) 70 10
919 2p. "Idol's Kiss" (G. de Rojas) 1·10 30

**223** Tarija Cathedral

**1972.** "EXFILIBRA 72" Stamp Exhibition, Rio de Janeiro.
920 **223** 30c. multicoloured 45 15

**224** National Arms

**1972.** Air.
921 **224** 4p. multicoloured 2·75 65

**225** Santos Dumont and "14 bis"

**1973.** Air. Birth Centenary of Alberto Santos Dumont (aviation pioneer).
922 **225** 1p.40 black and yellow 90 40

**226** "Echinocactus notocactus"

**1973.** Cacti. Multicoloured.
923 20c. Type **226** (postage) 55 25
924 40c. "Echinocactus lenninghaussii" 55 25
925 50c. "Mammillaria bocasana" 60 25
926 70c. "Echinocactus lenninghaussii" (different) 65 40
927 1p.20 "Mammillaria bocasana" (different) (air) 70 25
928 1p.90 "Opuntia cristata" 1·10 30
929 2p. "Echinocactus rebutia" 1·80 45

**227** Power Station, Santa Isabel

**1973.** Bolivian Development Multicoloured.
930 10c. Type **227** (postage) 1·30 25
931 20c. Tin foundry 1·30 25
932 90c. Bismuth plant 1·50 30
933 1p. Gas plant 1·50 30
934 1p.40 Road bridge, Highways 1 and 4 (air) 2·50 40
935 2p. Inspection car crossing bridge, Al Beni 3·75 45

**228** "Cattleya nobilior"

**1974.** Orchids. Multicoloured.
936 20c. Type **228** (postage) 1·30 25
937 50c. "Zygopetalum bolivianum" 1·30 25
938 1p. "Huntleya melagris" 1·30 25
939 2p.50 "Cattleya luteola" (horiz) (air) 2·30 40
940 3p.80 "Stanhopaea" 2·75 55
941 4p. "Catasetum" (horiz) 3·00 70
942 5p. "Maxillaria" 5·00 80

**1974.** Philatelic Exhibitions, 1975, 1976 and 1977. Four sheets each 130×80 mm showing reproductions of various stamps.
**MS**943 (a) Nos. 36, 911 and 942; (b) Nos. 36, 912 and 941; (c) Nos. 36, 914 and 939; (d) Nos. 36 and 921 16·00 16·00
See also No. **MS**954.

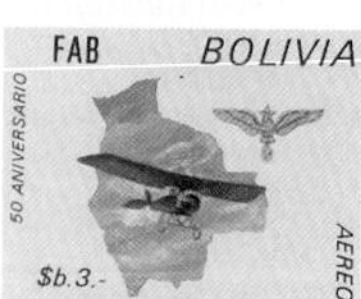

**229** Morane Saulnier Type P and Emblem

**1974.** Air. 50th Anniv of Bolivian Air Force. Multicoloured.
944 3p. Type **229** 80 65
945 3p.80 Douglas DC-3 crossing Andes 1·30 80
946 4p.50 Triplane trainer and Morane Saulnier Paris I aircraft 1·30 80
947 8p. Col. Rafael Pabon and biplane fighter 2·00 1·60
948 15p. Jet airliner on "50" 4·25 2·50

**230** General Sucre (after J. Wallpher)

**1974.** 150th Anniv of Battle of Avacucho.

| | | | | |
|---|---|---|---|---|
| 949 | **230** | 5p. multicoloured | 1·30 | 65 |

**231** UPU and Exhibition Emblems

**1974.** Centenary of UPU and Expo UPU (Montevideo) and Prenfil UPU (Buenos Aires) Stamp Exhibitions.

| | | | | |
|---|---|---|---|---|
| 950 | **231** | 3p.50 green, black & bl | 1·20 | 45 |

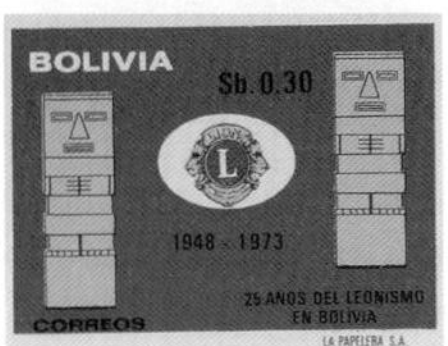


**232** Lions Emblem and Steles

**1975.** 50th Anniv of Lions International in Bolivia.

| | | | | |
|---|---|---|---|---|
| 951 | **232** | 30c. multicoloured | 45 | 40 |

**233** Exhibition Emblem

**1975.** "Espana 75" International Stamp Exhibition, Madrid.

| | | | | |
|---|---|---|---|---|
| 952 | **233** | 4p.50 multicoloured | 95 | 40 |

**234** Emblem of Meeting

**1975.** Cartagena Agreement. First Meeting of Postal Ministers, Quito, Ecuador.

| | | | | |
|---|---|---|---|---|
| 953 | **234** | 2p.50 silver, violet & blk | 80 | 30 |

**1975.** Philatelic Exhibitions 1975, 1976 and 1977. Four sheets as MS943.

| | | | |
|---|---|---|---|
| **MS**954 | (a) Nos. 36 and 950; (b) Nos. 36 and 951; (c) Nos. 36 and 952; (d) Nos. 36 and 953 | 17·00 | 17·00 |

**235** Arms of Pando

**1975.** 150th Anniv of Republic (1st issue). Provincial Arms. Multicoloured.

| | | | |
|---|---|---|---|
| 955 | 20c. Type **235** (postage) | 40 | 15 |
| 956 | 2p. Chuzuisaca | 85 | 45 |
| 957 | 3p. Cochabamba | 1·10 | 65 |
| 958 | 20c. Beni (air) | 40 | 15 |
| 959 | 30c. Tarija | 40 | 15 |
| 960 | 50c. Potosi | 55 | 25 |
| 961 | 1p. Oruro | 1·10 | 65 |
| 962 | 2p.50 Santa Cruz | 2·00 | 1·30 |
| 963 | 3p. La Paz | 2·00 | 1·30 |

See also Nos. 965/78.

**236** Presidents Perez and Banzer

**1975.** Air. Visit of Pres. Perez of Venezuela.

| | | | | |
|---|---|---|---|---|
| 964 | **236** | 3p. multicoloured | 85 | 65 |

**237** Pres. Victor Paz Estenssoro

**1975.** 150th Anniv of Republic (2nd issue).

| | | | |
|---|---|---|---|
| 965 | 30c. Type **237** (postage) | 10 | 10 |
| 966 | 60c. Pres. Thomas Frias | 15 | 10 |
| 966a | 1p. Ismael Montes | 25 | 15 |
| 967 | 2p.50 Aniceto Arce | 65 | 25 |
| 968 | 7p. Bautista Saavedra | 1·60 | 80 |
| 969 | 10p. Jose Manuel Pando | 2·50 | 1·30 |
| 970 | 15p. Jose Maria Linares | 3·25 | 1·60 |
| 971 | 50p. Simon Bolivar | 12·50 | 8·75 |
| 972 | 50c. Rene Barrientos Ortuno (air) | 15 | 10 |
| 973 | 2p. Francisco B. O'Connor | 80 | 25 |
| 973a | 3p.80 Gualberto Villaroel | 80 | 65 |
| 974 | 4p.20 German Busch | 1·30 | 80 |
| 975 | 4p.50 Pres. Hugo Banzer Suarez | 1·30 | 80 |
| 976 | 20p. Jose Ballivian | 5·00 | 3·25 |
| 977 | 30p. Pres. Andres de Santa Cruz | 6·00 | 4·25 |
| 978 | 40p. Pres. Antonio Jose de Sucre | 7·75 | 5·50 |

Nos. 965/70, 972/4 and 976/78 are smaller, 24×33 mm.

**238** Laurel Wreath and LAB Emblem

**1975.** Air. 50th Anniv of Lloyd-Aereo Boliviano (national airline). Multicoloured.

| | | | |
|---|---|---|---|
| 979 | 1p. Type **238** | 45 | 25 |
| 980 | 1p.50 Douglas DC-9 and L.A.B. route map (horiz) | 70 | 35 |
| 981 | 2p. Guillermo Kyllmann (founder) and Junkers F-13 aircraft (horiz) | 95 | 45 |

**1975.** Obligatory Tax. As No. 893 but inscr "XXV ANIVERSARIO DE SU GOBIERNO".

| | | | |
|---|---|---|---|
| 982 | 30c. black and blue | 3·50 | 3·25 |

**239** "EXFIVIA"

**1975.** "Exfivia 75". Stamp Exhibition.

| | | | | |
|---|---|---|---|---|
| 983 | **239** | 3p. multicoloured | 95 | 70 |

**240** UPU Emblem

**1975.** Air. Centenary (1974) of UPU.

| | | | | |
|---|---|---|---|---|
| 984 | **240** | 25p. multicoloured | 3·50 | 3·25 |

**241** Chiang Kai-shek

**1976.** 1st Death Anniv of President Chiang Kai-shek.

| | | | | |
|---|---|---|---|---|
| 985 | **241** | 2p.50 multicoloured | 3·50 | 1·30 |

**242** Geological Hammer, Lamp and Map

**1976.** Bolivian Geological Institute.

| | | | | |
|---|---|---|---|---|
| 986 | **242** | 4p. multicoloured | 1·00 | 45 |

**243** Naval Insignia

**1976.** Navy Day.

| | | | | |
|---|---|---|---|---|
| 987 | **243** | 50c. multicoloured | 45 | 30 |

**244** Douglas DC-10 and Divided Roundel

**1976.** 50th Anniv of Lufthansa Airline.

| | | | | |
|---|---|---|---|---|
| 988 | **244** | 3p. multicoloured | 1·20 | 45 |

**245** Bolivian Boy Scout and Badge

**1976.** 60th Anniv of Bolivian Boy Scouts.

| | | | | |
|---|---|---|---|---|
| 989 | **245** | 1p. multicoloured | 65 | 40 |

**246** Battle Scene

**1976.** Bicentenary of American Revolution.

| | | | | |
|---|---|---|---|---|
| 990 | **246** | 4p.50 multicoloured | 1·70 | 80 |
| **MS**991 | | 130×81 mm. No. 990 | 20·00 | 20·00 |

**247** Brother Vicente Bernedo (missionary)

**1976.** Brother Vincente Bernedo Commemoration.

| | | | | |
|---|---|---|---|---|
| 992 | **247** | 1p.50 multicoloured | 40 | 25 |

**248** Rainbow over La Paz, Police Handler with Dog

**1976.** 150th Anniv of Police Service.

| | | | | |
|---|---|---|---|---|
| 993 | **248** | 2p.50 multicoloured | 70 | 55 |

**249** Bolivian Family

**1976.** National Census.

| | | | | |
|---|---|---|---|---|
| 994 | **249** | 2p.50 multicoloured | 65 | 45 |

**250** Pedro Poveda (educator)

**1976.** Poveda Commemoration.

| | | | | |
|---|---|---|---|---|
| 995 | **250** | 1p.50 multicoloured | 45 | 25 |

**251** Arms, Bolivar and Sucre

**1976.** International Bolivarian Societies Congress.

| | | | | |
|---|---|---|---|---|
| 996 | **251** | 1p.50 multicoloured | 80 | 40 |

**252** "Numeral"

**1976**

| | | | | |
|---|---|---|---|---|
| 997 | **252** | 20c. brown | 30 | 10 |
| 998 | **252** | 1p. blue | 55 | 25 |
| 999 | **252** | 1p.50 green | 95 | 65 |

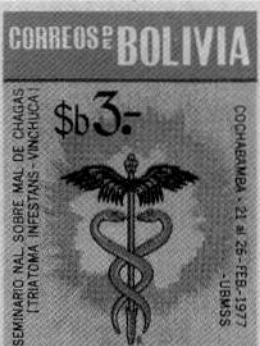


**253** Boy and Girl

**1977.** Christmas 1976 and 50th Anniv of Inter-American Children's Institute.

| | | | | |
|---|---|---|---|---|
| 1000 | **253** | 50c. multicoloured | 30 | 10 |

**254** Caduceus

**1977.** National Seminar on "Chagas Disease".

| | | | | |
|---|---|---|---|---|
| 1001 | **254** | 3p. multicoloured | 85 | 25 |

**255** Court Buildings, La Paz

**1977.** 150th Anniv of Bolivian Supreme Court. Multicoloured.

| | | | | |
|---|---|---|---|---|
| 1002 | | 2p.50 Type **255** | 40 | 10 |
| 1003 | | 4p. Dr. Manuel M. Urcullu, first President | 55 | 10 |
| 1004 | | 4p.50 Dr. Pantaleon Dalence, President, 1883–89 | 80 | 15 |

**256** Tower and Map

**1977.** 90th Anniv of Oruro Club.

| | | | | |
|---|---|---|---|---|
| 1005 | **256** | 3p. multicoloured | 65 | 25 |

**257** Newspaper Mastheads

**1977.** Bolivian Newspapers. Multicoloured.

| | | | | |
|---|---|---|---|---|
| 1006 | | 1p.50 Type **257** | 30 | 10 |
| 1007 | | 2p.50 "Ultima Hora" and Alfredo Alexander (horiz) | 40 | 15 |
| 1008 | | 3p. "El Diaro" and Jose Carrasco (horiz) | 45 | 25 |
| 1009 | | 4p. "Los Tiempos" and Demetrio Canelas | 65 | 30 |
| 1010 | | 5p.50 "Presencia" | 80 | 25 |

**258** Games Poster

**1977.** 8th Bolivarian Games, La Paz.

| | | | | |
|---|---|---|---|---|
| 1011 | **258** | 5p. multicoloured | 85 | 30 |

**259** Tin Miner and Mining Corporation Emblem

**1977.** 25th Anniv of Bolivian Mining Corporation.

| | | | | |
|---|---|---|---|---|
| 1012 | **259** | 3p. multicoloured | 85 | 25 |

**260** Miners, Globe and Chemical Symbol for Tin

**1977.** International Tin Symposium, La Paz.

| | | | | |
|---|---|---|---|---|
| 1013 | **260** | 6p. multicoloured | 1·20 | 45 |

**261** Map of Bolivia and Radio Masts

**1977.** 50th Anniv of Bolivian Radio.

| | | | | |
|---|---|---|---|---|
| 1014 | **261** | 2p.50 multicoloured | 65 | 40 |

**1977.** "Exfivia 77" Philatelic Exhibition, Cochabamba. No. 719 surch EXFIVIA — 77 $b. 5.—.

| | | | | |
|---|---|---|---|---|
| 1015 | | 5p. on 5,000b. on $b. 5 grey and gold | 2·40 | 1·60 |

**263** "Eye", Compass, Key and Law Book

**1978.** 50th Anniv of Audit Department.

| | | | | |
|---|---|---|---|---|
| 1016 | **263** | 5p. multicoloured | 85 | 25 |

**264** Aesculapius Staff and Map of Andean Countries

**1978.** 5th Meeting of Andean Countries' Health Ministers.

| | | | | |
|---|---|---|---|---|
| 1017 | **264** | 2p. orange and black | 45 | 25 |

**265** Map of the Americas

**1978.** World Rheumatism Year (1977).

| | | | | |
|---|---|---|---|---|
| 1018 | **265** | 2p.50 blue and red | 65 | 25 |

**266** Mt. Illimani

**1978**

| | | | | |
|---|---|---|---|---|
| 1019 | **266** | 50c. green and blue | 25 | 10 |
| 1020 | - | 1p. yellow and brown | 25 | 10 |
| 1021 | - | 1p.50 grey and red | 40 | 20 |

DESIGNS—HORIZ: 1p.50, Mt. Cerro de Potosi. VERT: 1p. Pre-Columbian monolith.

**267** Central Bank

**1978.** 50th Anniv of Bank of Bolivia.

| | | | | |
|---|---|---|---|---|
| 1022 | **267** | 7p. multicoloured | 1·20 | 30 |

**268** Jesus with Children

**1979.** International Year of the Child.

| | | | | |
|---|---|---|---|---|
| 1023 | **268** | 8p. multicoloured | 1·20 | 40 |

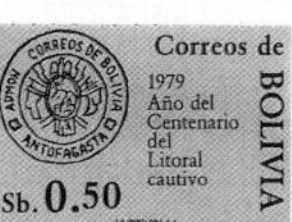

**269** Antofagasta Cancellation

**270** Antofagasta

**1979.** Centenary of Loss of Litoral Department to Chile.

| | | | | |
|---|---|---|---|---|
| 1024 | **269** | 50c. brown and black | 30 | 10 |
| 1025 | - | 1p. mauve and black | 55 | 10 |
| 1026 | - | 1p.50 green and black | 55 | 10 |
| 1027 | **270** | 5p.50 multicoloured | 80 | 15 |
| 1028 | - | 6p.50 multicoloured | 95 | 30 |
| 1029 | - | 7p. multicoloured | 95 | 30 |
| 1030 | - | 8p. multicoloured | 1·10 | 35 |
| 1031 | - | 10p. multicoloured | 1·50 | 40 |

DESIGNS—HORIZ: 1p. La Chimba cancel; 1p.50, Mejillonos cancel. VERT: (As Type **270**). 6p.50, Woman in chains; 7p. Eduardo Arbaroa; 8p. Map of Department, 1876; 10p. Arms of Litoral.

**271** Map and Radio Club Emblem

**1979.** Radio Club of Bolivia.

| | | | | |
|---|---|---|---|---|
| 1032 | **271** | 3p. multicoloured | 95 | 55 |

**272** Runner and Games Emblem

**1979.** 1st "Southern Cross" Games. Mult.

| | | | | |
|---|---|---|---|---|
| 1033 | | 6p.50 Type **272** | 1·00 | 25 |
| 1034 | | 10p. Gymnast | 1·60 | 40 |

**273** Bulgarian Stamp of 1879

**1979.** "Philaserdica 79" Philatelic Exhibition, Sofia, Bulgaria.

| | | | | |
|---|---|---|---|---|
| 1035 | **273** | 2p.50 black, yellow and light yellow | 45 | 30 |

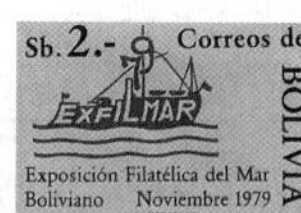

**274** "Exfilmar" Emblem

**1979.** "Exfilmar 79" Maritime Philatelic, Exhibition, La Paz.

| | | | | |
|---|---|---|---|---|
| 1036 | **274** | 2p. blue, black and light blue | 1·60 | 55 |

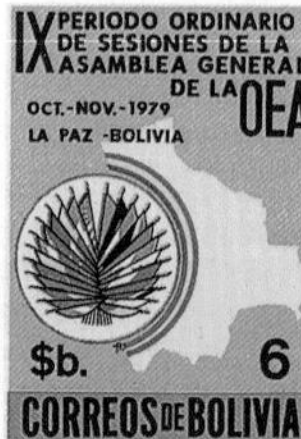

**275** OAS Emblem and Map

**1979.** 9th Congress of Organization of American States, La Paz.

| | | | | |
|---|---|---|---|---|
| 1037 | **275** | 6p. multicoloured | 95 | 30 |

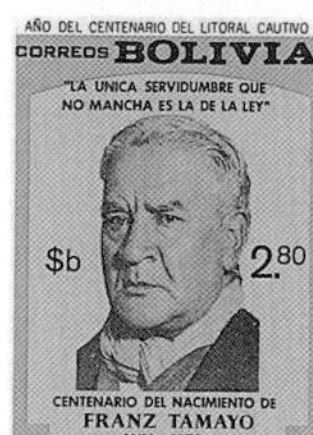

**276** Franz Tamayo (lawyer)

**1979.** Anniversaries and Events.

| | | | | |
|---|---|---|---|---|
| 1038 | **276** | 2p.80 light grey, black and grey | 45 | 40 |
| 1039 | - | 5p. multicoloured | 80 | 25 |
| 1040 | - | 5p. multicoloured | 80 | 25 |
| 1041 | - | 6p. multicoloured | 95 | 40 |
| 1042 | - | 9p.50 multicoloured | 2·75 | 80 |

DESIGNS—VERT: 2p.80, Type **276** (birth centenary); 5p. (No. 1039) U.N. emblem and delegates (18th CEPAL Sessions, La Paz); 5p. (No. 1042), Gastroenterological laboratory (Japanese health co-operation); 6p. Radio mast (50th anniv of national radio). HORIZ: 9p.50, Puerto Suarez iron ore deposits.

**277** 500c. Stamp of 1871, Exhibition Emblem and Flag

**1980.** "Exfilmar" Bolivian Maritime Stamp Exhibition, La Paz.

| | | | | |
|---|---|---|---|---|
| 1043 | **277** | 4p. multicoloured | 95 | 30 |

**278** Juana Azurduy de Padilla

**1980.** Birth Bicentenary of Juana Azurduy de Padilla (Independence heroine).

| | | | | |
|---|---|---|---|---|
| 1044 | **278** | 4p. multicoloured | 65 | 30 |

**279** Jean Baptiste de la Salle (founder)

**1980.** 300th Anniv of Brothers of Christian Schools.

| | | | | |
|---|---|---|---|---|
| 1045 | **279** | 9p. multicoloured | 1·40 | 55 |

**280** "Victory in a Chariot", Emblem and Flags

**1980.** "Espamer 80" International Stamp Exhibition, Madrid.

| | | | | |
|---|---|---|---|---|
| 1046 | **280** | 14p. multicoloured | 2·00 | 55 |

**281** Flags over Map of South America

**1980.** Meeting of Public Works and Transport Ministers of Argentina, Bolivia and Peru.

| | | | | |
|---|---|---|---|---|
| 1047 | **281** | 2p. multicoloured | 85 | 15 |

**282** Diesel Locomotive

**1980.** Inauguration of Santa Cruz-Trinidad Railway, Third Section.

| | | | | |
|---|---|---|---|---|
| 1048 | **282** | 3p. multicoloured | 55 | 25 |

**283** Soldier and Citizen with Flag destroying Communism

**1981.** 1st Anniv of 17 July Revolution. Mult.

| | | | |
|---|---|---|---|
| 1049 | 1p. Type **283** | 6·00 | 7·25 |
| 1050 | 3p. Flag shattering hammer and sickle on map | 6·00 | 7·25 |
| 1051 | 40p. Flag on map of Bolivia showing provinces | 4·00 | 1·50 |
| 1052 | 50p. Rejoicing crowd (horiz) | 5·75 | 1·20 |

**284** Scarlet Macaw

**1981.** Macaws. Multicoloured.

| | | | |
|---|---|---|---|
| 1053 | 4p. Type **284** | 65 | 25 |
| 1054 | 7p. Green-winged macaw | 1·10 | 40 |
| 1055 | 8p. Blue and yellow macaw | 1·30 | 45 |
| 1056 | 9p. Red-fronted macaw | 1·40 | 50 |
| 1057 | 10p. Yellow-collared macaw | 1·60 | 50 |
| 1058 | 12p. Hyacinth macaw | 2·00 | 85 |
| 1059 | 15p. Military macaw | 2·50 | 95 |
| 1060 | 20p. Chestnut-fronted macaw | 3·25 | 1·20 |

**285** Virgin and Child receiving Flower

**1981.** Christmas.

| | | | | |
|---|---|---|---|---|
| 1061 | **285** | 1p. pink and red | 15 | 10 |
| 1062 | - | 2p. light blue and blue | 30 | 10 |

DESIGN: 2p. Child and star (horiz).

See also No. 1080.

**286** Emblem

**1982.** 22nd American Air Force Commanders' Conference, Buenos Aires.

| | | | | |
|---|---|---|---|---|
| 1063 | **286** | 14p. multicoloured | 1·70 | 1·10 |

**287** Cobija

**1982.** 75th Anniv of Cobija City.

| | | | | |
|---|---|---|---|---|
| 1064 | **287** | 28p. multicoloured | 45 | 30 |

**288** Simon Bolivar

**1982.** Birth Bicentenary of Simon Bolivar.

| | | | | |
|---|---|---|---|---|
| 1065 | **288** | 18p. multicoloured | 30 | 25 |

**289** Dish Antenna

**1982.** World Communication Year.

| | | | | |
|---|---|---|---|---|
| 1066 | **289** | 26p. multicoloured | 45 | 30 |

**290** Footballers

**1982.** World Cup Football Championship, Spain. Multicoloured.

| | | | |
|---|---|---|---|
| 1067 | 4p. Type **290** | 25 | 10 |
| 1068 | 100p. "The Final Number" (Picasso) | 2·00 | 1·20 |

**291** Boy playing Football

**1982.** Bolivian Youth. Multicoloured.

| | | | |
|---|---|---|---|
| 1069 | 16p. Type **291** | 1·10 | 45 |
| 1070 | 20p. Girl playing piano (horiz) | 1·60 | 55 |

**292** Harvesting

**1982.** China-Bolivian Agricultural Co-operation.

| | | | | |
|---|---|---|---|---|
| 1071 | **292** | 30p. multicoloured | 95 | 55 |

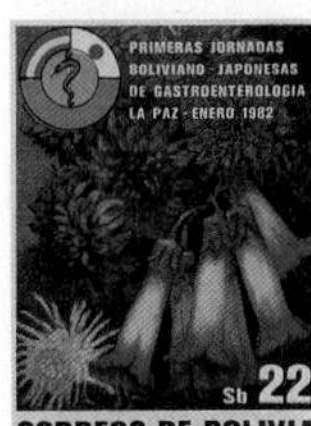

**293** Flowers

**1982.** 1st Bolivian-Japanese Gastroenterological Days.

| | | | | |
|---|---|---|---|---|
| 1072 | **293** | 22p. multicoloured | 1·20 | 80 |

**294** Bolivian Stamps

**1982.** 10th Anniv of Bolivian Philatelic Federation.

| | | | | |
|---|---|---|---|---|
| 1073 | **294** | 19p. multicoloured | 1·30 | 45 |

**295** Hernando Siles

**1982.** Birth Centenary of Hernando Siles (former President).

| | | | | |
|---|---|---|---|---|
| 1074 | **295** | 20p. buff and brown | 40 | 25 |

**296** Baden-Powell

**1982.** 125th Birth Anniv of Lord Baden-Powell and 75th Anniv of Boy Scout Movement.

| | | | | |
|---|---|---|---|---|
| 1075 | **296** | 5p. multicoloured | 30 | 10 |

**297** "Liberty", Cochabamba

**1982.** 25th Anniv of Cochabamba Philatelic Centre.

| | | | | |
|---|---|---|---|---|
| 1076 | **297** | 3p. buff, black & blue | 30 | 10 |

**298** High Court, Cochabamba

**1982.** 150th Anniv of High Court, Cochabamba.

| | | | | |
|---|---|---|---|---|
| 1077 | **298** | 10p. black, red and bronze | 40 | 15 |

**299** Virgin of Copacabana

**1982.** 400th Anniv of Enthronement of Virgin of Copacabana.

| | | | | |
|---|---|---|---|---|
| 1078 | **299** | 13p. multicoloured | 40 | 25 |

**300** Puerto Busch Naval Base

**1982.** Navy Day.

| | | | | |
|---|---|---|---|---|
| 1079 | **300** | 14p. multicoloured | 40 | 25 |

**1982.** Christmas. Design as Type 285, inscribed "NAVIDAD 1982".

| | | | | |
|---|---|---|---|---|
| 1080 | **285** | 10p. grey and green | 70 | 25 |

**301** Footballer and Emblem

**1983.** 10th American Youth Football Championships.

| | | | | |
|---|---|---|---|---|
| 1081 | **301** | 50p. multicoloured | 1·00 | 65 |

**302** Sun Gate

**1983.** "Exfivia 83" Stamp Exhibition.

| | | | | |
|---|---|---|---|---|
| 1082 | **302** | 150p. red | 1·30 | 65 |

**303** Presidents Figueiredo and Zuazo

**1984.** Visit of President of Brazil.

| | | | | |
|---|---|---|---|---|
| 1083 | **303** | 150p. multicoloured | 55 | 15 |

**1984.** Various stamps surch.

| | | | | |
|---|---|---|---|---|
| 1084 | **276** | 40p. on 2p.80 light grey, black and grey | 25 | 10 |
| 1085 | - | 60p. on 1p.50 green and black (1026) | 25 | 10 |
| 1086 | **265** | 60p. on 2p.50 blue and red | 25 | 10 |
| 1087 | **274** | 100p. on 2p. blue, black and light blue | 40 | 25 |
| 1088 | **174** | 200p. on 350b. blue and light blue | 80 | 30 |

**1984.** "Mladost 84" Youth Stamp Exn, Pleven, Bulgaria. No. 1035 surch.

| | | | | |
|---|---|---|---|---|
| 1089 | **273** | 40p. on 2p.50 black, yellow and light yellow | 25 | 10 |

**306** "Simon Bolivar" (Mulato Gil de Quesada)

**1984.** Birth Bicentenary of Simon Bolivar. Mult.

| | | | |
|---|---|---|---|
| 1090 | 50p. Type **306** | 25 | 10 |
| 1091 | 200p. "Simon Bolivar entering La Paz" (Carmen Baptista) | 70 | 30 |

**1984.** Various stamps surch.

| | | | | |
|---|---|---|---|---|
| 1092 | **297** | 500p. on 3p. buff, black and blue (postage) | 95 | 40 |
| 1093 | **290** | 1000p. on 4p. mult | 2·00 | 95 |
| 1094 | **285** | 2000p. on 10p. grey and green | 4·00 | 1·60 |
| 1095 | **296** | 5000p. on 5p. mult | 9·50 | 4·00 |

**308** Pedestrian walking in Road

**1984.** Road Safety Campaign. Multicoloured.

| | | | |
|---|---|---|---|
| 1096 | - 10000p. on 3p.80 mult (No. 940) (air) | 12·50 | 7·75 |
| 1097 | 80p. Type **308** | 40 | 25 |
| 1098 | 120p. Police motorcyclist and patrol car | 40 | 25 |

**309** "Mendezs Birthplace" (Jorge Campos)

**1984.** Birth Bicentenary of Jose Eustaquio Mendez. Multicoloured.

1099 300p. Type **309** 25 10

1100 500p. "Battle of La Tablada" (M. Villegas) 30 10

**310** Legs and Feet on Map and Bata Emblem

**1984.** World Footwear Festival. Mult.

1101 100p. Type **310** 40 15

1102 200p. Legs and feet on map and Power emblem 40 15

1103 600p. Football and globes (World Cup, Mexico, 1986) (horiz) 45 15

**311** Inca Postal Runner

**1985**

1104 **311** 11000p. blue 85 25

**312** Vicuna

**1985.** Endangered Animals.

1105 **312** 23000p. brown and deep brown 1·20 55

1106 - 25000p. brown, blue and orange 45 30

1107 - 30000p. red and green 60 40

DESIGNS—VERT: 25000p. Andean condor; 30000p. Marsh deer.

**313** National Work Education Service Emblem

**1985.** International Professional Education Year.

1108 **313** 2000p. blue and red 30 10

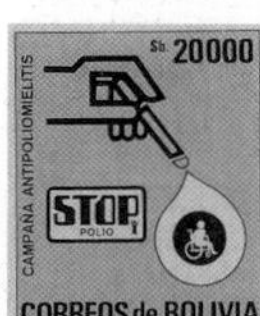


**314** Hand with Syringe, Victim in Droplet and Campaign Emblem

**1985.** Anti-polio Campaign.

1109 **314** 20000p. blue and violet 40 25

**315** Vicenta Juaristi Eguino

**1985.** Birth Bicentenary of Vicenta Juaristi Eguino (Independence heroine).

1110 **315** 300000p. multicoloured 95 55

**316** U.N. Emblem

**1985.** 40th Anniv of U.N.O.

1111 **316** 1000000p. blue and gold 3·25 40

**317** Emblem

**1985.** 75th Anniv of "The Strongest" Football Club.

1112 **317** 200000p. multicoloured 65 25

**318** Emblem, Envelope and Posthorn

**1986.** Cent of Bolivian U.P.U. Membership.

1113 **318** 800000p. multicoloured 1·20 65

**319** Bull and Rider

**1986.** 300th Anniv of Trinidad City.

1114 **319** 1400000p. multicoloured 2·00 1·20

**1986.** No. 1108 surch.

1115 **313** 200000p. on 2000p. blue and red 60 15

1116 **313** 5000000p. on 2000p. blue and red 6·00 3·25

**321** Football as Globes

**1986.** World Cup Football Championship, Mexico.

1117 **321** 300000p. red and black 45 20

1118 - 550000p. multicoloured 80 45

1119 - 1000000p. black and green (horiz) 1·30 70

1120 - 2500000p. green & yell 4·00 1·40

DESIGNS—VERT: 550000p. Pique (mascot); 2500000p. Trophy. HORIZ: 1000000p. Azteca Stadium, Mexico City.

**322** Alfonso Subieta Viaduct

**1986.** 25th Anniv of American Development Bank.

1121 **322** 400000p. blue 70 25

**323** Envelope

**1986.** 50th Anniv of Society of Postmen.

1122 **323** 2000000p. brown 4·75 1·40

**324** Emblem and Dove

**1986.** International Peace Year.

1123 **324** 200000p. green 50 20

**325** Emblem

**1986.** International Youth Year (1985).

1124 **325** 150000p. red 35 20

1125 **325** 500000p. green 1·00 45

1126 - 3000000p. multicoloured 6·50 2·20

DESIGNS: 3000000p. Child clutching trophy and flag (25th anniv of Enrique Happ Sports Club, Cochabamba).

**326** Zampa (after F. Diaz de Ortega)

**1986.** 50th Death Anniv of Friar Jose Antonio Zampa.

1127 **326** 400000p. multicoloured 95 45

**327** 1870 500c. Stamp

**1986.** 15th Anniv of Bolivian Philatelic Federation.

1128 **327** 600000p. brown 85 45

**328** Refinery

**1986.** 50th Anniv of National Petroleum Refining Corporation.

1129 **328** 1000000p. multicoloured 1·90 1·10

**329** Demon Mask

**1987.** Centenary of 10th February Society, Oruro.

1130 **329** 20c. multicoloured 95 25

**330** Flags

**1987.** State Visit of President Richard von Weizsacker of German Federal Republic.

1131 **330** 30c. multicoloured 85 45

**331** National Arms

**1987.** Visit of King Juan Carlos of Spain.

1132 **331** 60c. multicoloured 1·20 55

**332** Andean ("Condor")

**1987.** Endangered Animals. Multicoloured.

1133 20c. Type **332** 70 25

1134 20c. Tapir 70 25

1135 30c. Vicuna (new-born) 95 35

1136 30c. Armadillo 95 35

1137 40c. Spectacled bear 1·30 45

1138 60c. Keel-billed toucans ("Tucan") 1·90 65

**333** Modern View of Potosi

**1987.** "Exfivia 87" Stamp Exhibition, Potosi. Multicoloured.

1139 40c. Type **333** 80 45

1140 50c. 18th-century engraving of Potosi 1·90 55

**334** "Nina" and Stern of "Santa Maria"

**1987.** "Espamer '87" Stamp Exhibition, La Coruna. Multicoloured.

1141 20c. Type **334** 45 25

1142 20c. "Pinta" and bow of "Santa Maria" 45 25

Nos. 1141/2 were printed together, se-tenant, forming a composite design.

**335** Pan-pipes and Indian Flute

**1987.** Musical Instruments. Multicoloured.

1143 50c. Type **335** 1·10 45

1144 1b. Indian guitars 1·90 1·00

**336** Carabuco Church

**1988.** Visit of Pope John Paul II. Mult.

| No. | Type | Description | Mint | Used |
|---|---|---|---|---|
| 1145 | | 20c. Type **336** | 45 | 25 |
| 1146 | | 20c. Tihuanacu church | 45 | 25 |
| 1147 | | 20c. Cathedral of the Kings, Beni | 45 | 25 |
| 1148 | | 30c. St. Joseph church, Chiquitos | 70 | 25 |
| 1149 | | 30c. St. Francis's church, Sucre | 70 | 25 |
| 1150 | | 40c. Cobija chapel (vert) | 85 | 35 |
| 1151 | | 50c. Cochabamba cathedral (vert) | 1·10 | 35 |
| 1152 | | 50c. Jayu Kcota church | 1·10 | 35 |
| 1153 | | 60c. St. Francis's Basilica, La Paz (vert) | 1·30 | 45 |
| 1154 | | 70c. Church of Jesus, Machaca | 1·50 | 45 |
| 1155 | | 70c. St. Lawrence's church, Potosi (vert) | 1·50 | 45 |
| 1156 | | 80c. Vallegrande church | 1·70 | 65 |
| 1157 | | 80c. Copacabana Virgin (vert) | 1·70 | 65 |
| 1158 | | 80c. "The Holy Family" (Peter Paul Rubens) (vert) | 1·70 | 65 |
| 1159 | | 1b.30 Concepcion church | 2·75 | 1·10 |
| 1160 | | 1b.30 Tarija cathedral (vert) | 2·75 | 1·10 |
| 1161 | | 1b.50 Pope and Arms of John Paul II and Bolivia | 3·00 | 1·40 |

**337** Handshake and Flags

**1988.** Visit of President Jose Sarney of Brazil.

| No. | Type | Description | Mint | Used |
|---|---|---|---|---|
| 1162 | **337** | 50c. multicoloured | 85 | 45 |

**338** St. John Bosco

**1988.** Death Centenary of St. John Bosco (founder of Salesian Brothers).

| No. | Type | Description | Mint | Used |
|---|---|---|---|---|
| 1163 | **338** | 30c. multicoloured | 50 | 25 |

**339** La Paz–Beni Steam Locomotive

**1988.** Centenary of Bolivian Railways.

| No. | Type | Description | Mint | Used |
|---|---|---|---|---|
| 1164 | **339** | 1b. multicoloured | 2·30 | 80 |

**340** Aguirre

**1988.** Death Cent of Nataniel Aguirre (writer).

| No. | Type | Description | Mint | Used |
|---|---|---|---|---|
| 1165 | **340** | 1b. black and brown | 1·90 | 80 |

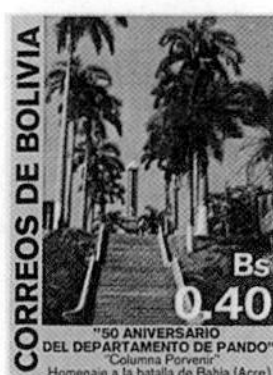

**341** "Column of the Future" (Battle of Bahia Monument)

**1988.** 50th Anniv of Pando Department. Mult.

| No. | Type | Description | Mint | Used |
|---|---|---|---|---|
| 1166 | | 40c. Type **341** | 75 | 25 |
| 1167 | | 60c. Rubber production | 1·00 | 45 |

**342** Athlete

**1988.** Olympic Games, Seoul.

| No. | Type | Description | Mint | Used |
|---|---|---|---|---|
| 1168 | **342** | 1b.50 multicoloured | 2·75 | 2·30 |

**343** Mother Rosa Gattorno

**1988.** 88th Death Anniv of Mother Rosa Gattorno (Founder of the Daughters of St. Anne).

| No. | Type | Description | Mint | Used |
|---|---|---|---|---|
| 1169 | **343** | 80c. multicoloured | 1·50 | 65 |

**344** Bernardino de Cardenas

**1988.** 220th Death Anniv of Br. Bernardino de Cardenas (first Bishop of La Paz).

| No. | Type | Description | Mint | Used |
|---|---|---|---|---|
| 1170 | **344** | 70c. black and brown | 1·30 | 60 |

**345** Ministry Building

**1988.** Ministry of Transport and Communications.

| No. | Type | Description | Mint | Used |
|---|---|---|---|---|
| 1171 | **345** | 2b. black, green & red | 3·50 | 1·70 |

**346** Arms

**1988.** 50th Anniv of Army Communications Corps.

| No. | Type | Description | Mint | Used |
|---|---|---|---|---|
| 1172 | **346** | 70c. multicoloured | 1·40 | 65 |

**347** Rally Car

**1988.** 50th Anniv of Bolivian Automobile Club.

| No. | Type | Description | Mint | Used |
|---|---|---|---|---|
| 1173 | **347** | 1b.50 multicoloured | 2·50 | 1·20 |

**348** Microphone and Emblem

**1989.** 50th Anniv of Radio Fides.

| No. | Type | Description | Mint | Used |
|---|---|---|---|---|
| 1174 | **348** | 80c. multicoloured | 1·30 | 65 |

**349** Obverse and Reverse of 1852 Gold Cuartillo

**1989.** Coins.

| No. | Type | Description | Mint | Used |
|---|---|---|---|---|
| 1175 | **349** | 1b. multicoloured | 1·80 | 70 |

**350** "Bulgaria 89" Stamp Exhibition Emblem and Orchid

**1989.** Events and Plants. Multicoloured.

| No. | Type | Description | Mint | Used |
|---|---|---|---|---|
| 1176 | | 50c. Type **350** | 1·60 | 35 |
| 1177 | | 60c. "Italia '90" World Cup football championship emblem and kantuta (national flower) (horiz) | 1·90 | 45 |
| 1178 | | 70c. "Albertville 1986" emblem and "Heliconia humilis" | 2·30 | 55 |
| 1179 | | 1b. Olympic Games, Barcelona emblem and "Hoffmanseggia" | 3·00 | 80 |
| 1180 | | 2b. Olympic Games, Seoul emblem and bromeliad | 6·25 | 1·50 |

**351** Birds

**1989.** Bicentenary of French Revolution.

| No. | Type | Description | Mint | Used |
|---|---|---|---|---|
| 1181 | **351** | 70c. multicoloured | 1·40 | 55 |

**352** Clock Tower and Steam Locomotive

**1989.** Centenary of Uyuni.

| No. | Type | Description | Mint | Used |
|---|---|---|---|---|
| 1182 | **352** | 30c. grey, black & blue | 85 | 25 |

**353** Federico Ahlfeld Waterfall, River Pauserna

**1989.** Noel Kempff Mercado National Park. Multicoloured.

| No. | Type | Description | Mint | Used |
|---|---|---|---|---|
| 1183 | | 1b.50 Type **353** | 3·00 | 1·20 |
| 1184 | | 3b. Pampas deer | 6·25 | 2·00 |

**354** Making Metal Articles

**1989.** America. Tiahuanacu Culture. Mult.

| No. | Type | Description | Mint | Used |
|---|---|---|---|---|
| 1185 | | 50c. Type **354** | 1·40 | 35 |
| 1186 | | 1b. Kalasasaya Temple | 2·75 | 70 |

**355** Dr. Carlos Perez and Jaime Zamora

**1989.** Meeting of Presidents of Bolivia and Venezuela.

| No. | Type | Description | Mint | Used |
|---|---|---|---|---|
| 1187 | **355** | 2b. multicoloured | 3·00 | 1·10 |

**356** Cobija Arch

**1989.** World Heritage Site, Potosi. Mult.

| No. | Type | Description | Mint | Used |
|---|---|---|---|---|
| 1188 | | 60c. Type **356** | 70 | 45 |
| 1189 | | 80c. Mint | 95 | 65 |

**357** "Andean Lake" (Arturo Borda)

**1989.** Christmas. Paintings. Multicoloured.

| No. | Type | Description | Mint | Used |
|---|---|---|---|---|
| 1190 | | 40c. Type **357** | 85 | 25 |
| 1191 | | 60c. "Virgin of the Roses" (anon) | 1·30 | 35 |
| 1192 | | 80c. "Conquistador" (Jorge de la Reza) | 1·80 | 55 |
| 1193 | | 1b. "Native Harmony" (Juan Rimsa) | 2·40 | 65 |
| 1194 | | 1b.50 "Woman with Pitcher" (Cecilio Guzman de Rojas) | 3·25 | 1·10 |
| 1195 | | 2b. "Flower of Tenderness" (Gil Imana) | 4·25 | 1·40 |

**358** Foot crushing Syringe

**1990.** Anti-drugs Campaign.

| No. | Type | Description | Mint | Used |
|---|---|---|---|---|
| 1196 | **358** | 80c. multicoloured | 1·20 | 70 |

**359** Map of Americas

**1990.** Centenary of Organization of American States.

| No. | Type | Description | Mint | Used |
|---|---|---|---|---|
| 1197 | **359** | 80c. blue and deep blue | 1·20 | 45 |

**360** Colonnade

**1990.** 450th Anniv of White City.

| No. | Type | Description | Mint | Used |
|---|---|---|---|---|
| 1198 | **360** | 1b.20 multicoloured | 1·80 | 80 |

**361** Penny Black, Sir Rowland Hill and Bolivian 5c. Condor Stamp

**1990.** 150th Anniv of the Penny Black.
1199 **361** 4b. multicoloured 6·25 2·40

**362** Giuseppe Meaza Stadium, Milan

**1990.** World Cup Football Championship, Italy. Multicoloured.
1200 2b. Type **362** 2·50 1·40
1201 6b. Match scene 8·00 3·50

**363** Emblem

**1990.** Cent of Bolivian Chamber of Commerce.
1202 **363** 50c. black, blue & gold 85 55

**364** Satellite, Map and Globe

**1990.** Telecommunications Development Year.
1203 **364** 70c. multicoloured 1·00 70

**365** Hall

**1990.** Centenary of Cochabamba Social Club.
1204 **365** 40c. multicoloured 65 35

**366** Chipaya Village, Oruro

**1990.** America. Multicoloured.
1205 80c. Type **366** 4·00 45
1206 1b. Nevado Huayna, Cordillera Real (mountain) (vert) 4·75 65

**367** Emblem

**1990.** "Meeting of Two Worlds. United towards Progress". 500th Anniv (1992) of Discovery of America by Columbus.
1207 **367** 2b. multicoloured 2·50 1·20

**368** Trees and Mountains

**1990.** 400th Anniv of Larecaja District.
1208 **368** 1b.20 multicoloured 1·50 70

**369** Dove and German National Colours

**1990.** Unification of Germany.
1209 **369** 2b. multicoloured 2·75 1·10

**370** Boys playing Football (Omar Espana)

**1990.** Christmas. Rights of the Child.
1210 **370** 50c. multicoloured 65 25

**371** Arms of Bolivia and Ecuador

**1990.** Visit of Pres. Rodrigo Borja Cevallos of Ecuador.
1211 **371** 80c. multicoloured 1·50 55

**372** Flags and Andes

**1990.** 4th Andean Presidents' Council, La Paz.
1212 **372** 1b.50 multicoloured 2·10 70

**373** Andes

**1990.** "Exfivia 90" National Stamp Exhibition.
1213 **373** 40c. blue 55 25

**374** Arms of Bolivia and Mexico

**1990.** Visit of Pres. Carlos Salinas de Gortari of Mexico.
1214 **374** 60c. multicoloured 1·30 55

**375** Emblem, Globe and Flags

**1990.** Express Mail Service.
1215 **375** 1b. multicoloured 1·30 45

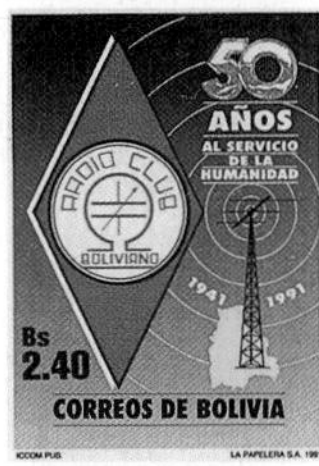

**376** Emblem

**1991.** 50th Anniv of Bolivian Radio Club.
1216 **376** 2b.40 multicoloured 2·75 1·10

**377** Head of Bear

**1991.** The Spectacled Bear. Multicoloured.
1217 30c. Type **377** 1·90 45
1218 30c. Bear on branch 1·90 45
1219 30c. Bear and cub at water's edge 1·90 45
1220 30c. Bear and cubs on branches 1·90 45

**378** National Museum of Archaeology

**1991.** "Espamer '91" Spain–Latin America Stamp Exhibition, Buenos Aires. Multicoloured.
1221 50c. Type **378** 55 20
1222 50c. National Art Museum 55 20
1223 1b. National Museum of Ethnography and Folklore 1·20 45

**379** Map

**1991.** 56th Anniv of Ending of Chaco War and Beginning of Construction of "Heroes of Chaco" Road.
1224 **379** 60c. multicoloured 75 35

**380** Statue of Our Lady of La Paz and Cathedral

**1991.** La Paz Cathedral.
1225 **380** 1b.20 multicoloured 1·90 65

**381** Presidents Lacalle and Paz Zamora

**1991.** Meeting of Uruguayan and Bolivian Presidents.
1226 **381** 1b. multicoloured 1·10 45

**382** Presidents Paz Zamora and Menem

**1991.** Meeting of Bolivian and Argentine Presidents.
1227 **382** 1b. multicoloured 1·10 45

**383** "Exfivia 83", "87" and "90" Stamps

**1991.** 20th Anniv of Bolivian Philatelic Federation.
1228 **383** 70c. multicoloured 1·00 35

**384** Presidents Fujimori and Paz Zamora

**1991.** Presidential Summit of Bolivia and Peru.
1229 **384** 50c. multicoloured 65 20

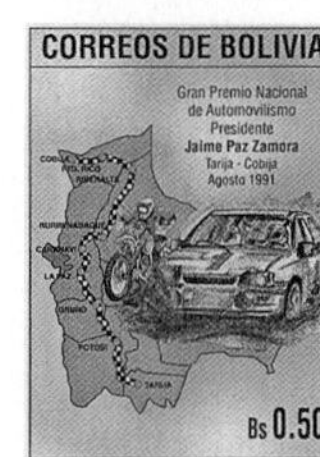

**385** Route Map, Motor Cycle and Rally Car

**1991.** Pres. Jaime Paz Zamora National Grand Prix Motor Rally, Tarija-Cobija.
1230 **385** 50c. multicoloured 65 20

**386** Data Retrieval Systems

**1991.** "Ecobol" Postal Security.
1231 **386** 1b.40 multicoloured 1·80 65

**387** "First Discovery of Chuquiago" (Arturo Reque)

**1991.** America. Voyages of Discovery. Mult.
1232 60c. Type **387** 2·10 35
1233 1b.20 "Foundation of City of Our Lady of La Paz" (J. Rimsa) (vert) 4·25 65

**388** Stylized Figures and City Skyline

**1991.** National Population and Housing Census.
1234 **388** 50c. multicoloured 65 20

**389** "Landscape" (Daniel Pena y Sarmiento)

**1991.** Christmas. Multicoloured.
1235 2b. Type **389** 2·50 80
1236 5b. "Fruit Seller" (Cecilio Guzman de Rojas) 6·25 2·00
1237 15b. "Native Mother" (Crespo Gastelu) 18·00 5·50

**390** Camp-site and Emblem

**1992.** 75th Anniv (1990) of Bolivian Scout Movement and Los Andes Jamboree, Cochabamba.
1238 **390** 1b.20 multicoloured 1·60 80

**391** Simon Bolivar

**1992.** "Exfilbo 92" National Stamp Exhibition, La Paz.
1239 **391** 1b.20 deep brown, brown and stone 1·60 80

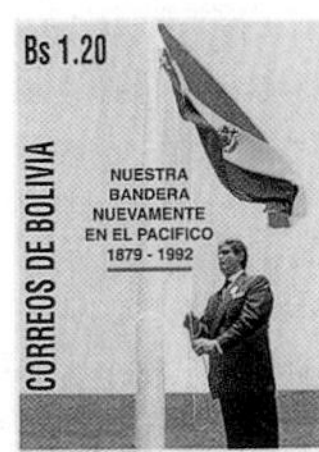

**392** Raising Flag

**1992.** Creation of Bolivian Free Zone in Ilo, Peru. Multicoloured.
1240 1b.20 Type **392** 1·40 80
1241 1b.50 Presidents Fujimori (Peru) and Paz Zamora (horiz) 1·60 90
1242 1b.80 Beach at Ilo (horiz) 2·10 1·00

**393** Logotype of Pavilion

**1992.** "Expo '92" World's Fair, Seville, and "Granada '92" Int Stamp Exhibition. Mult.
1243 30c. Type **393** 40 30
1244 50c. Columbus's fleet 70 40

**394** Rotary International Emblem and Prize

**1992.** Rotary Club Miraflores District 4690 "Illimani de Oro" Prize.
1245 **394** 90c. gold, blue & black 1·20 70

**395** School and Perez

**1992.** Birth Centenary of Elizardo Perez (founder of Ayllu School, Warisata).
1246 **395** 60c. blue, black & yellow 80 40

**396** Government Palace

**1992.** UNESCO World Heritage Site, Sucre.
1247 **396** 50c. multicoloured 1·30 30

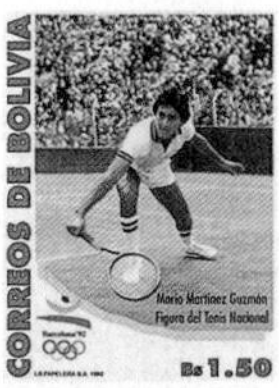

**397** Mario Martinez Guzman

**1992.** Olympic Games, Barcelona.
1248 **397** 1b.50 multicoloured 2·00 1·00

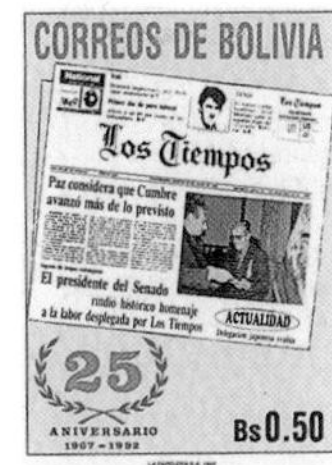

**398** Front Page

**1992.** 25th Anniv of "Los Tiempos" (newspaper).
1249 **398** 50c. multicoloured 70 40

**399** Canoeing

**1992.** 1st International River Bermejo Canoeing Championship.
1250 **399** 1b.20 multicoloured 2·00 90

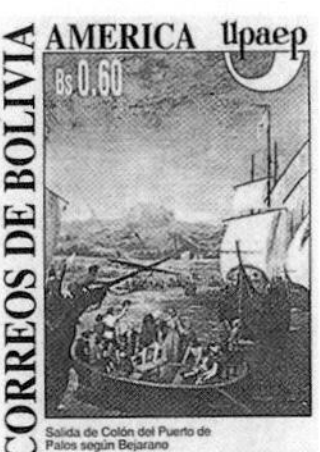

**400** Columbus leaving Palos (after Bejarano)

**1992.** America. 500th Anniv of Discovery of America by Columbus.
1251 **400** 60c. brown and black 1·20 50
1252 - 2b. multicoloured 4·25 1·50
DESIGN—HORIZ: 2b. "Columbus meeting the Caribisis Tribe" (Luis Vergara).

**401** Football Match

**1992.** World Cup Football Championship, U.S.A. (1994).
1253 **401** 1b.20 multicoloured 2·50 1·00

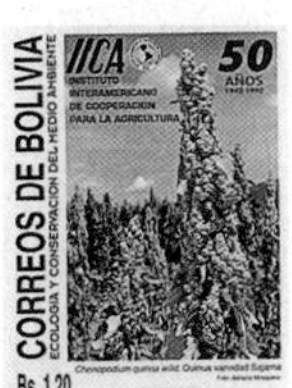

**402** "Chenopodium quinoa"

**1992.** 50th Anniv of Interamerican Institute for Agricultural Co-operation.
1254 **402** 1b.20 multicoloured 1·90 90

**403** University Arms and Minerals

**1992.** Cent of Oruro Technical University.
1255 **403** 50c. multicoloured 70 40

**404** Mascots

**1992.** 12th Bolivarian Games, Cochabamba and Santa Cruz (1st issue).
1256 **404** 2b. multicoloured 2·75 1·20
See also No. 1271.

**405** Cayman

**1992.** Ecology and Conservation. Multicoloured.
1257 20c. Type **405** 20 10
1258 50c. Spotted cavy 70 20
1259 1b. Chinchilla 1·40 60
1260 2b. Anteater 2·75 1·20
1261 3b. Jaguar 4·25 1·80
1262 4b. Long-tailed sylph ("Picaflor") (vert) 5·75 2·50
1263 5b. Piranhas 7·75 3·25
Each stamp also bears the emblem of an anniversary or event.

**406** Battle Scene

**1992.** 150th Anniv of Battle of Ingavi.
1264 **406** 1b.20 brown and black 2·75 70

**407** Man following Star in Boat

**1992.** Christmas. Multicoloured.
1265 1b.20 Type **407** 1·60 60
1266 2b.50 Star over church 3·50 1·30
1267 6b. Infant in manger and church 8·25 3·25

**408** Nicolas Copernicus (450th death anniv)

**1993.** Astronomy.
1268 - 50c. multicoloured 70 40
1269 **408** 2b. black 2·75 1·00
DESIGN—HORIZ: 50c. Santa Ana International Astronomical Observatory, Tarija (10th anniv (1992)).

**409** Mother Nazaria (after Victor Eusebio Choque)

**1993.** Beatification (1992) of Mother Nazaria Ignacia March Meza.
1270 **409** 60c. multicoloured 1·10 40

**410** Pictograms and Flags of Ecuador, Venezuela, Peru, Bolivia, Colombia and Panama

**1993.** 12th Bolivarian Games, Cochabamba and Santa Cruz (2nd issue).
1271 **410** 2b.30 multicoloured 2·75 1·20

**411** Bolivia 1962 10000b. Kantuta and Brazil 90r. "Bull's Eye" Stamps

**1993.** 150th Anniv of First Brazilian Stamps.
1272 **411** 2b.30 multicoloured 2·75 1·20

412 "Morpho sp."

**1993.** Butterflies. Multicoloured.

| | | | |
|---|---|---|---|
| 1273 | 60c. Type **412** | 1·10 | 30 |
| 1274 | 60c. "Archaeoprepona demophon" | 1·10 | 30 |
| 1275 | 80c. "Papilio sp." | 1·50 | 40 |
| 1276 | 80c. Orion ("Historis odius") | 1·50 | 40 |
| 1277 | 80c. Mexican fritillary ("Euptoieta hegesia") | 1·50 | 40 |
| 1278 | 1b.80 "Morpho deidamia" | 3·25 | 90 |
| 1279 | 1b.80 Orange swallowtail ("Papilio thoas") | 3·25 | 90 |
| 1280 | 1b.80 Monarch ("Danaus plexippus") | 3·25 | 90 |
| 1281 | 2b.30 Scarlet emperor ("Anaea marthesia") | 4·25 | 1·20 |
| 1282 | 2b.30 "Caligo sp." | 4·25 | 1·20 |
| 1283 | 2b.30 "Rothschildia sp." | 4·25 | 1·20 |
| 1284 | 2b.70 "Heliconius sp." | 5·00 | 1·40 |
| 1285 | 2b.70 "Marpesia corinna" | 5·00 | 1·40 |
| 1286 | 2b.70 "Prepona chromus" | 5·00 | 1·40 |
| 1287 | 3b.50 Rusty-tipped page ("Siproeta epaphus") | 6·75 | 1·90 |
| 1288 | 3b.50 "Heliconius sp." | 6·75 | 1·90 |

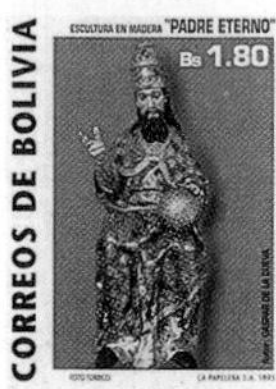

413 "Eternal Father" (wood statuette, Gaspar de la Cueva)

**1993**

| | | | | |
|---|---|---|---|---|
| 1289 | **413** | 1b.80 multicoloured | 2·75 | 90 |

414 "Virgin of Urkupina"

**1993.** 400th Anniv of Quillacollo.

| | | | | |
|---|---|---|---|---|
| 1290 | **414** | 50c. multicoloured | 1·10 | 40 |

415 Student, Machinery and Emblem

**1993.** 50th Anniv (1992) of Pedro Domingo Murillo Technical College.

| | | | | |
|---|---|---|---|---|
| 1291 | **415** | 60c. multicoloured | 70 | 30 |

416 Owl (painting, Chuquisaca)

**1993.** Cave Art. Multicoloured.

| | | | |
|---|---|---|---|
| 1292 | 80c. Type **416** | 2·30 | 40 |
| 1293 | 80c. Animals (painting, Cochabamba) | 2·30 | 40 |
| 1294 | 80c. Geometric patterns (engraving, Chuquisaca) (vert) | 2·30 | 40 |
| 1295 | 80c. Sun (engraving, Beni) (vert) | 2·30 | 40 |
| 1296 | 80c. Llama (painting, Oruro) | 2·30 | 40 |
| 1297 | 80c. Human figure (engraving, Potosi) | 2·30 | 40 |
| 1298 | 80c. Church and tower (painting, La Paz) (vert) | 2·30 | 40 |
| 1299 | 80c. Warrior (engraving, Tarija) (vert) | 2·30 | 40 |
| 1300 | 80c. Religious mask (engraving, Santa Cruz) (vert) | 2·30 | 40 |

417 Common Squirrel-monkeys

**1993.** America. Endangered Animals. Mult.

| | | | |
|---|---|---|---|
| 1301 | 80c. Type **417** | 1·40 | 40 |
| 1302 | 2b.30 Ocelot | 3·25 | 1·20 |

418 Emblems and Map

**1993.** 90th Anniv (1992) of Pan-American Health Organization. Anti-AIDS Campaign.

| | | | | |
|---|---|---|---|---|
| 1303 | **418** | 80c. multicoloured | 1·00 | 40 |

419 Yolanda Bedregal (poet)

**1993.** Personalities. Each brown.

| | | | |
|---|---|---|---|
| 1304 | 50c. Type **419** | 50 | 30 |
| 1305 | 70c. Simon Martinic (President of Cochabamba Philatelic Centre) | 80 | 40 |
| 1306 | 90c. Eugenio von Boeck (politician and President of Bolivian Philatelic Federation) | 1·00 | 45 |
| 1307 | 1b. Marina Nunez del Prado (sculptor) | 1·10 | 50 |

420 "Virgin with Child and Saints" (anonymous)

**1993.** Christmas. Multicoloured.

| | | | |
|---|---|---|---|
| 1308 | 2b.30 "Adoration of the Shepherds" (Leonardo Flores) | 5·00 | 1·20 |
| 1309 | 3b.50 Type **420** | 8·25 | 1·80 |
| 1310 | 6b. "Virgin of the Milk" (Melchor Perez de Holguin) | 13·50 | 3·00 |

421 Riberalta Square

**1994.** Centenary of Riberalta.

| | | | | |
|---|---|---|---|---|
| 1311 | **421** | 2b. multicoloured | 2·40 | 1·00 |

422 "Population and Our World" (Mayari Rodriguez)

**1994.** 2nd Prize-winning Design (6–8 year group) in United Nations Fund for Population Activities International Design Contest.

| | | | | |
|---|---|---|---|---|
| 1312 | **422** | 2b.30 multicoloured | 3·75 | 1·20 |

423 Sanchez de Lozada

**1994.** Presidency of Gonzalo Sanchez de Lozada.

| | | | | |
|---|---|---|---|---|
| 1313 | **423** | 2b. multicoloured | 2·40 | 1·00 |
| 1314 | **423** | 2b.30 multicoloured | 2·75 | 1·20 |

424 Mascot

**1994.** World Cup Football Championship, U.S.A. Multicoloured.

| | | | |
|---|---|---|---|
| 1315 | 80c. Type **424** | 1·00 | 40 |
| 1316 | 1b.80 Bolivia v Uruguay | 2·20 | 90 |
| 1317 | 2b.30 Bolivia v Venezuela | 2·75 | 1·20 |
| 1318 | 2b.50 Bolivian team (left half) | 2·75 | 1·30 |
| 1319 | 2b.50 Bolivian team (right half) | 2·75 | 1·30 |
| 1320 | 2b.70 Bolivia v Ecuador | 3·00 | 1·40 |
| 1321 | 3b.50 Bolivia v Brazil | 4·50 | 1·80 |

Nos. 1318/19 were issued together, se-tenant, forming a composite design.

425 Child

**1994.** S.O.S. Children's Villages.

| | | | | |
|---|---|---|---|---|
| 1322 | **425** | 2b.70 multicoloured | 3·00 | 1·30 |

426 St. Peter's Church and Mgr. Jorge Manrique Hurtado (Archbishop, 1967–87)

**1994.** 50th Anniv (1993) of Archdiocese of La Paz. Multicoloured.

| | | | |
|---|---|---|---|
| 1323 | 1b.80 Type **426** | 2·75 | 90 |
| 1324 | 2b. Church of the Sacred Heart of Mary and Mgr. Abel Antezana y Rojas (first Archbishop, 1943–67) (vert) | 3·25 | 1·00 |
| 1325 | 3b.50 Santo Domingo Church and Mgr. Luis Sainz Hinojosa (Archbishop since 1987) (vert) | 6·00 | 1·70 |

427 "Buddleja coriacea"

**1994.** Environmental Protection. Trees. Mult.

| | | | |
|---|---|---|---|
| 1326 | 60c. Type **427** | 65 | 30 |
| 1327 | 1b.80 "Bertholletia exelsa" | 1·90 | 90 |
| 1328 | 2b. "Schinus molle" (horiz) | 2·20 | 1·00 |
| 1329 | 2b.70 "Polylepis racemosa" | 2·75 | 1·30 |
| 1330 | 3b. "Tabebuia chrysantha" | 3·25 | 1·50 |
| 1331 | 3b.50 "Erythrina falcata" (horiz) | 3·75 | 1·70 |

428 Paz

**1994.** Dr. Victor Paz Estenssoro (former President).

| | | | | |
|---|---|---|---|---|
| 1332 | **428** | 2b. multicoloured | 2·20 | 90 |

429 Tramcar and Mail Van

**1994.** America. Postal Transport. Mult.

| | | | |
|---|---|---|---|
| 1333 | 1b. Type **429** | 1·10 | 40 |
| 1334 | 5b. Boeing 747 and ox cart | 5·50 | 2·30 |

430 Coral Tree

**1994.** 300th Anniv of San Borja.

| | | | | |
|---|---|---|---|---|
| 1335 | **430** | 1b.60 multicoloured | 1·70 | 70 |

431 Diagram of Eclipse

**1994.** Solar Eclipse.

| | | | | |
|---|---|---|---|---|
| 1336 | **431** | 3b.50 multicoloured | 3·75 | 1·50 |

432 1894 100c. Stamp

**1994.** Centenary of Arms Issue of 1894.

| | | | | |
|---|---|---|---|---|
| 1337 | **432** | 1b.80 multicoloured | 1·90 | 80 |

433 Col. Marzana and Soldiers

**1994.** 62nd Anniv of Defence of Fort Boqueron.

| | | | | |
|---|---|---|---|---|
| 1338 | **433** | 80c. multicoloured | 90 | 30 |

434 "Delicate Flower of Tarija"

**1994.** Christmas. Pastels of children by Maria Susana Castillo. Multicoloured.

| | | | |
|---|---|---|---|
| 1339 | 2b. Type **434** | 3·50 | 90 |
| 1340 | 5b. "Child of the High Plateau" | 8·75 | 2·30 |
| 1341 | 20b. "Shoot of the Bolivian East" | 25·00 | 9·25 |

**435** Emblem

**1994.** Pan-American Scout Jamboree, Cochabamba.

| | | | | |
|---|---|---|---|---|
| 1342 | **435** | 1b.80 multicoloured | 1·90 | 90 |

**436** Sucre

**1995.** Birth Bicentenary of General Antonio Jose de Sucre. Multicoloured.

| | | | |
|---|---|---|---|
| 1343 | 1b.80 Type **436** | 2·30 | 90 |
| 1344 | 3b.50 Sucre and national colours | 4·75 | 1·70 |

**437** Santa Ana Cathedral

**1995.** Centenary (1994) of Yacuma Province, Beni Department.

| | | | | |
|---|---|---|---|---|
| 1345 | **437** | 1b.90 multicoloured | 2·40 | 1·00 |
| 1346 | **437** | 2b.90 multicoloured | 3·50 | 1·50 |

**438** "Holy Virgin of Copacabana", Sanctuary and Franciscans

**1995.** Centenary of Franciscan Presence at Copacabana Sanctuary.

| | | | | |
|---|---|---|---|---|
| 1347 | **438** | 60c. multicoloured | 1·00 | 35 |
| 1348 | **438** | 80c. multicoloured | 1·40 | 55 |

**439** Anniversary Emblem

**1995.** 25th Anniv of Andean Development Corporation.

| | | | | |
|---|---|---|---|---|
| 1349 | **439** | 2b.40 multicoloured | 2·75 | 1·30 |

**440** Paraguay and Bolivia Flags (Chaco Peace Treaty, 1938)

**1995.** Visit of President Juan Carlos Wasmosy of Paraguay and 169th Anniv (1994) of Republic of Bolivia.

| | | | | |
|---|---|---|---|---|
| 1350 | **440** | 2b. multicoloured | 2·00 | 1·10 |

**441** Montenegro

**1995.** 50th Anniv of Publication of "Nationalism and Colonialism" by Carlos Montenegro.

| | | | | |
|---|---|---|---|---|
| 1351 | **441** | 1b.20 black and pink | 2·75 | 65 |

**442** Digging Potatoes

**1995.** 50th Anniv of FAO.

| | | | | |
|---|---|---|---|---|
| 1352 | **442** | 1b. multicoloured | 2·00 | 55 |

**443** Anniversary Emblem

**1995.** 50th Anniv of UNO.

| | | | | |
|---|---|---|---|---|
| 1353 | **443** | 2b.90 dp blue, gold & bl | 2·40 | 1·70 |

**444** Andean Condor ("Condor")

**1995.** America. Endangered Species. Mult.

| | | | |
|---|---|---|---|
| 1354 | 5b. Type **444** | 4·50 | 2·75 |
| 1355 | 5b. Llamas | 4·50 | 2·75 |

Nos. 1354/5 were issued together, se-tenant, forming a composite design.

**445** Airbus Industrie A320

**1995.** 50th Anniv (1994) of ICAO.

| | | | | |
|---|---|---|---|---|
| 1356 | **445** | 50c. multicoloured | 90 | 45 |

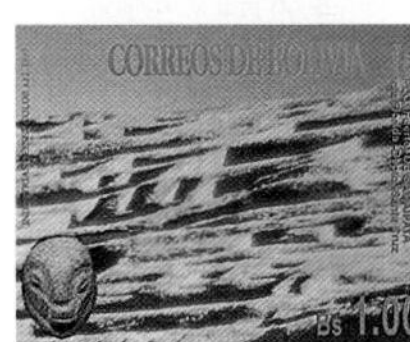

**446** Stone Head

**1995.** Archaeology. Samaipata Temple, Florida. Multicoloured.

| | | | |
|---|---|---|---|
| 1357 | 1b. Type **446** | 90 | 55 |
| 1358 | 1b.90 Stone head (different) | 1·70 | 1·10 |
| 1359 | 2b. Excavation and stone head | 1·70 | 1·10 |
| 1360 | 2b.40 Entrance and animal-shaped vessel | 2·00 | 1·30 |

Nos. 1357/60 were issued together, se-tenant, forming a composite design.

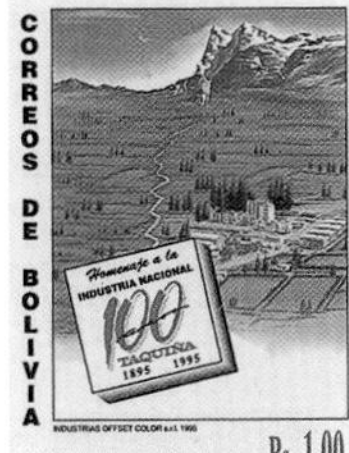

**447** Brewery Complex

**1995.** Centenary of Taquina Brewery.

| | | | | |
|---|---|---|---|---|
| 1361 | **447** | 1b. multicoloured | 2·40 | 55 |

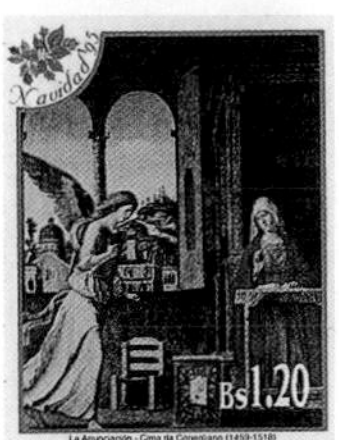

**448** "The Annunciation" (Cima da Conegliano)

**1995.** Christmas. Multicoloured.

| | | | |
|---|---|---|---|
| 1362 | 1b.20 Type **448** | 1·30 | 65 |
| 1363 | 3b. "The Nativity" (Hans Baldung) | 3·25 | 1·70 |
| 1364 | 3b.50 "Adoration of the Wise Men" (altarpiece, Rogier van der Weyden) | 4·00 | 2·00 |

**449** Jose de Sanjines (lyricist)

**1995.** 150th Anniv of National Anthem. Mult.

| | | | |
|---|---|---|---|
| 1365 | 1b. Type **449** | 90 | 55 |
| 1366 | 2b. Benedetto Vincenti (composer) | 1·70 | 1·10 |

Nos. 1365/6 were issued together, se-tenant, forming a composite design.

**450** Flats, Villarroel, Factories, Road and Railway

**1996.** 50th Anniv of Decree for Abolition of Enforced Amerindian Labour. Mult.

| | | | |
|---|---|---|---|
| 1367 | 1b.90 Type **450** | 1·70 | 1·10 |
| 1368 | 2b.90 Pres. Gualberto Villarroel addressing Congress and freed workers | 2·40 | 1·70 |

Nos. 1367/8 were issued together, se-tenant, forming a composite design.

**1996.** Various stamps surch.

| | | | | |
|---|---|---|---|---|
| 1369 | - | 50c. on 3000000p. multicoloured (No. 1126) (postage) | 45 | 35 |
| 1370 | **265** | 60c. on 2p.50 blue and red | 90 | 40 |
| 1371 | **313** | 60c. on 5000000p. on 2000p. blue and red (No. 1116) | 55 | 35 |
| 1372 | **319** | 60c. on 1400000p. mult | 55 | 35 |
| 1373 | **319** | 1b. on 2500000p. green and yellow (No. 1120) | 90 | 55 |
| 1374 | **311** | 1b.50 on 11000p. blue | 1·30 | 90 |
| 1375 | **312** | 2b.50 on 23000p. brown and sepia | 2·20 | 1·40 |
| 1376 | **316** | 3b. on 1000000p. blue and gold | 2·40 | 1·70 |
| 1377 | **272** | 3b.50 on 6p.50 mult | 3·25 | 2·00 |
| 1378 | **279** | 3b.50 on 9p. mult | 3·25 | 2·00 |
| 1379 | **323** | 3b.50 on 2000000p. brown | 3·25 | 2·00 |
| 1380 | **298** | 20b. on 10p. black, purple and bronze | 19·00 | 11·00 |
| 1381 | **299** | 20b. on 13p. mult | 19·00 | 11·00 |
| 1382 | - | 3b.80 on 3p.80 mult (No. 945) (air) | 3·25 | 2·10 |
| 1383 | - | 20b. on 3p.80 mult (No. 973a) | 19·00 | 11·00 |

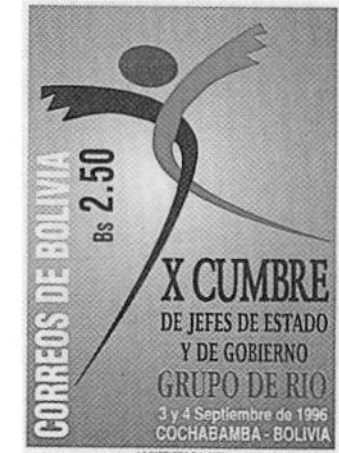

**452** Summit Emblem

**1996.** 10th Rio Group Summit Meeting, Cochabamba. Multicoloured.

| | | | |
|---|---|---|---|
| 1384 | 2b.50 Type **452** | 2·10 | 1·30 |
| 1385 | 3b.50 Rio Group emblem | 2·75 | 2·00 |

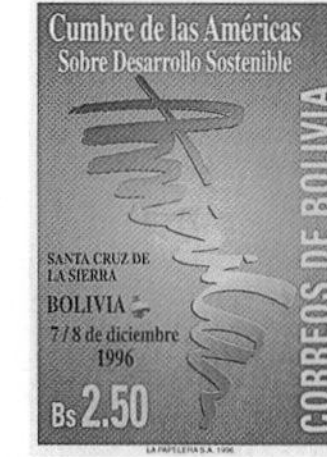

**453** Summit Emblem

**1996.** Summit of the Americas on Sustainable Development, Santa Cruz de la Sierra.

| | | | | |
|---|---|---|---|---|
| 1386 | **453** | 2b.50 multicoloured | 2·10 | 1·30 |
| 1387 | **453** | 5b. multicoloured | 4·25 | 2·75 |

**454** Facade

**1996.** National Bank.

| | | | | |
|---|---|---|---|---|
| 1388 | **454** | 50c. black and blue | 55 | 35 |

**455** De Lemoine

**1996.** 220th Birth Anniv of Jose Joaquin de Lemoine (first postal administrator).

| | | | | |
|---|---|---|---|---|
| 1389 | **455** | 1b. brown and stone | 1·20 | 65 |

**456** Family

**1997.** CARE (Co-operative for American Relief Everywhere). Multicoloured.

| | | | |
|---|---|---|---|
| 1390 | 60c. Type **456** (20th anniv in Bolivia) | 55 | 35 |
| 1391 | 70c. Hands cradling globe (50th anniv) (vert) | 65 | 45 |

**457** Musicians playing Piccolo and Saxophone

**1997.** 50th Anniv of National Symphony Orchestra. "Overture" by G. Rodo Boulanger. Multicoloured.

| | | | |
|---|---|---|---|
| 1392 | 1b.50 Type **457** | 1·40 | 1·00 |

| | | | |
|---|---|---|---|
| 1393 | 2b. Musicians playing violin and cello | 1·90 | 1·20 |

Nos. 1392/3 were issued together, se-tenant, forming a composite design of the complete painting.

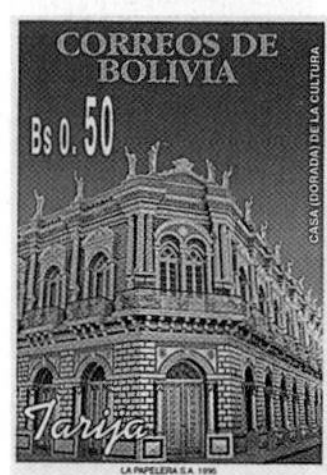

**458** Casa Dorada (cultural centre)

**1997.** Tarija. Multicoloured.

| | | | |
|---|---|---|---|
| 1394 | 50c. Type **458** | 45 | 35 |
| 1395 | 60c. Entre Rios Church and musician | 55 | 40 |
| 1396 | 80c. Narrows of San Luis (horiz) | 85 | 60 |
| 1397 | 1b. Memorial to the Fallen of the Chaco War (territorial dispute with Paraguay) (horiz) | 1·10 | 90 |
| 1398 | 3b. Virgin and shrine of Chaguaya (horiz) | 3·25 | 2·75 |
| 1399 | 20b. Birthplace and statue of Jose Eustaquio Mendez (Independence hero), San Lorenzo (horiz) | 20·00 | 18·00 |

**459** La Glorieta, Sucre

**1997.** Chuquisaca. Multicoloured.

| | | | |
|---|---|---|---|
| 1400 | 60c. Type **459** | 55 | 45 |
| 1401 | 1b. Government Palace, Sucre (vert) | 90 | 75 |
| 1402 | 1b.50 Footprints and drawing of dinosaur | 1·40 | 1·20 |
| 1403 | 1b.50 Interior of House of Freedom | 1·40 | 1·20 |
| 1404 | 2b. Man playing traditional wind instrument (vert) | 2·00 | 1·50 |
| 1405 | 3b. Statue of Juana Azurduy de Padilla (Independence heroine) (vert) | 2·75 | 2·50 |

**460** Miners' Monument

**1997.** Oruro. Multicoloured.

| | | | |
|---|---|---|---|
| 1406 | 50c. Type **460** | 55 | 45 |
| 1407 | 60c. Demon carnival mask | 85 | 55 |
| 1408 | 1b. Vigin of the Cave (statue) | 1·10 | 90 |
| 1409 | 1b.50 Sajama (volcano) (horiz) | 1·40 | 1·10 |
| 1410 | 2b.50 Chipaya child and belfry | 2·40 | 2·20 |
| 1411 | 3b. Moreno (Raul Shaw) (singer and musician) (horiz) | 2·75 | 2·50 |

**461** Pres. Gonzalo Sanchez de Lozada of Bolivia and Pres. Chirac

**1997.** Visit to Bolivia of President Jacques Chirac of France.

| | | | | |
|---|---|---|---|---|
| 1412 | **461** | 4b. multicoloured | 4·00 | 3·25 |

**462** Children playing (Pamela G. Villarroel)

**1997.** 50th Anniv of UNICEF Children's Drawings. Multicoloured.

| | | | |
|---|---|---|---|
| 1413 | 50c. Type **462** | 55 | 45 |
| 1414 | 90c. Boy leaping across clifftop (Lidia Acapa) | 1·00 | 90 |
| 1415 | 1b. Children of different races on top of world (Gabriela Philco) | 1·20 | 1·00 |
| 1416 | 2b.50 Children and swing (Jessica Grundy) | 2·75 | 2·40 |

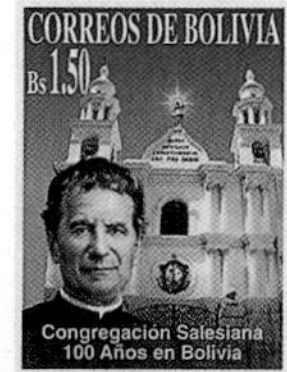

**463** St. John Bosco (founder)

**1997.** Centenary of Salesian Brothers in Bolivia. Multicoloured.

| | | | |
|---|---|---|---|
| 1417 | 1b.50 Type **463** | 1·40 | 1·20 |
| 1418 | 2b. Church and statue of Bosco with child | 2·00 | 1·70 |

**464** Chulumani

**1997.** La Paz. Multicoloured.

| | | | |
|---|---|---|---|
| 1419 | 50c. Type **464** | 45 | 35 |
| 1420 | 80c. Inca stone monolith | 75 | 65 |
| 1421 | 1b.50 La Paz and Mt. Illimani | 1·40 | 1·30 |
| 1422 | 2b. Gate of the Sun, Tiahuanaco (horiz) | 2·00 | 1·90 |
| 1423 | 2b.50 Dancers | 2·40 | 2·30 |
| 1424 | 10b. "Virgin of Copacabana" and balsa raft on Lake Titicaca (horiz) | 10·00 | 9·75 |

**465** Emblem

**1997.** Football Events. Multicoloured.

| | | | |
|---|---|---|---|
| 1425 | 3b. Type **465** (America Cup Latin-American Football Championship, Bolivia) | 2·75 | 2·75 |
| 1426 | 5b. Eiffel Tower and trophy (World Cup Football Championship, France (1998) Eliminating Rounds) | 5·00 | 4·75 |

**466** Parliamentary Session and Building

**1997.** National Congress.

| | | | | |
|---|---|---|---|---|
| 1427 | **466** | 1b. multicoloured | 90 | 75 |

**467** Valley

**1997.** America. Traditional Costumes. Mult.

| | | | |
|---|---|---|---|
| 1428 | 5b. Type **467** | 5·00 | 4·75 |
| 1429 | 15b. Eastern region | 14·50 | 14·00 |

**468** Members Flags and Southern Cross

**1997.** 6th Anniv of Mercosur (South American Common Market).

| | | | | |
|---|---|---|---|---|
| 1430 | **468** | 3b. multicoloured | 2·75 | 2·75 |

**469** "Virgin of the Hill" (anon)

**1997.** Christmas. Multicoloured.

| | | | |
|---|---|---|---|
| 1431 | 2b. Type **469** | 2·40 | 2·20 |
| 1432 | 5b. "Virgin of the Milk" (anon) | 5·50 | 5·00 |
| 1433 | 10b. "Holy Family" (Melchor Perez Holguin) | 11·00 | 10·00 |

**470** Diana, Princess of Wales

**1997.** Diana, Princess of Wales Commemoration. Multicoloured.

| | | | |
|---|---|---|---|
| 1434 | 2b. Type **470** | 2·20 | 2·00 |
| 1435 | 3b. Diana, Princess of Wales beside minefield warning sign (horiz) | 2·75 | 2·50 |

**471** Presidents of Boliva and Spain

**1998.** State Visit of Prime Minister Jose Maria Aznar of Spain.

| | | | | |
|---|---|---|---|---|
| 1436 | **471** | 6b. multicoloured | 5·50 | 5·00 |

**472** Juan Munoz Reyes (President) and Medallion

**1998.** 75th Anniv of Bolivian Engineers' Association.

| | | | | |
|---|---|---|---|---|
| 1437 | **472** | 3b.50 multicoloured | 3·25 | 2·75 |

**473** Linked Arms and Globe

**1998.** 70th Anniv of Rotary International in Bolivia.

| | | | | |
|---|---|---|---|---|
| 1438 | **473** | 5b. multicoloured | 4·75 | 4·25 |

**474** Delivering Letter, 1998

**1998.** America. The Postman. Multicoloured.

| | | | |
|---|---|---|---|
| 1439 | 3b. Type **474** | 2·75 | 2·50 |
| 1440 | 4b. Postmen on parade, 1942 (horiz) | 3·75 | 3·25 |

**475** Werner Guttentag Tichauer (35th anniv of his bibliography)

**1998.** Anniversaries.

| | | | | |
|---|---|---|---|---|
| 1441 | **475** | 1b.50 brown | 1·30 | 1·10 |
| 1442 | - | 2b. green | 1·90 | 1·60 |
| 1443 | - | 3b.50 black | 3·25 | 2·75 |

DESIGNS—VERT: 2b. Martin Cardenas Hermosa (botanist, birth centenary (1999)); 3b. Adrian Patino Carpio (composer, 47th death anniv).

**476** Amazon Water-lily

**1998.** Beni. Multicoloured.

| | | | |
|---|---|---|---|
| 1444 | 50c. Type **476** | 35 | 30 |
| 1445 | 1b. "Callandria" sp. | 90 | 75 |
| 1446 | 1b.50 White tajibo tree (vert) | 1·30 | 1·10 |
| 1447 | 3b.50 Ceremonial mask | 3·25 | 2·75 |
| 1448 | 5b. European otter | 4·75 | 4·00 |
| 1449 | 7b. King vulture ("Tropical Condor") | 6·50 | 5·75 |

**477** River Acre

**1998.** Pando. Multicoloured.

| | | | |
|---|---|---|---|
| 1450 | 50c. Type **477** | 45 | 40 |
| 1451 | 1b. Pale-throated sloth (vert) | 90 | 75 |
| 1452 | 1b.50 Arroyo Bahia (vert) | 1·30 | 1·10 |
| 1453 | 4b. Boa constrictor | 3·50 | 3·00 |
| 1454 | 5b. Capybara with young | 4·50 | 3·75 |
| 1455 | 7b. Palm trees, Cobija (vert) | 6·00 | 5·25 |

**478** Rural Activities and First Lady

**1998.** America. Women. Multicoloured.

| | | | |
|---|---|---|---|
| 1456 | 1b.50 Type **478** | 1·30 | 1·10 |
| 1457 | 2b. First Lady, girl at blackboard and woman using computer | 1·80 | 1·50 |

Nos. 1456/7 were issued together, se-tenant, forming a composite design.

**479** Town Arms and Church

**1998.** 450th Anniv of La Paz.

| | | | | |
|---|---|---|---|---|
| 1458 | **479** | 2b. multicoloured | 2·10 | 1·80 |

**480** Emblem

**1998.** 50th Anniv of Organization of American States.

| | | | | |
|---|---|---|---|---|
| 1459 | **480** | 3b.50 blue and yellow | 3·00 | 2·75 |

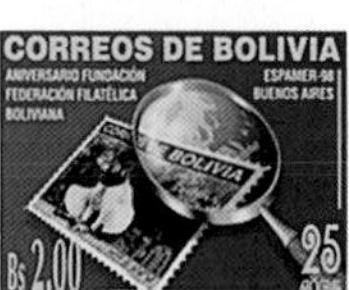


**481** Magnifying Glass and 1998 7b. Stamp

**1998.** "Espamer 98" Stamp Exhibition, Buenos Aires and 25th Anniv of Bolivian Philatelic Federation.

| | | | | |
|---|---|---|---|---|
| 1460 | **481** | 2b. multicoloured | 1·80 | 1·50 |

**482** "People going to Church" (Kathia Lucuy Saenz)

**1998.** Christmas. Multicoloured.

| | | | | |
|---|---|---|---|---|
| 1461 | | 2b. Type **482** | 1·70 | 1·40 |
| 1462 | | 6b. Pope John Paul II (vert) | 4·75 | 4·00 |
| 1463 | | 7b. Pope John Paul II with Mother Teresa (vert) | 5·50 | 4·75 |

**483** U.P.U. Monument, Berne

**1999.** 125th Anniv of Universal Postal Union.

| | | | | |
|---|---|---|---|---|
| 1464 | **483** | 3b.50 multicoloured | 2·75 | 2·50 |

**484** Statue of Football Player

**1999.** 75th Anniv of Cochabamba Football Association.

| | | | | |
|---|---|---|---|---|
| 1465 | **484** | 5b. multicoloured | 4·75 | 4·25 |

**485** Red Cross Lorries at Earthquake Site

**1999.** 50th Anniv of Geneva Conventions.

| | | | | |
|---|---|---|---|---|
| 1466 | **485** | 5b. multicoloured | 4·00 | 3·50 |

**486** Bernardo Guarachi and Mt. Everest

**1999.** 1st Ascent (1998) of Mt. Everest by a Bolivian.

| | | | | |
|---|---|---|---|---|
| 1467 | **486** | 6b. multicoloured | 5·50 | 4·75 |

**487** Winners on Podium

**1999.** 30th Anniv of First Special Olympics. Multicoloured.

| | | | | |
|---|---|---|---|---|
| 1468 | | 2b. Type **487** | 1·70 | 1·40 |
| 1469 | | 2b.50 Athletes on race track and winners on podium | 2·00 | 1·70 |

**488** Golden Palace

**1999.** Centenary of Japanese Immigration to Bolivia. Multicoloured.

| | | | | |
|---|---|---|---|---|
| 1470 | | 3b. Type **488** | 2·40 | 2·10 |
| 1471 | | 6b. View over lake and flags (vert) | 5·00 | 4·25 |

**489** Children dancing

**1999.** Anti-drugs Campaign.

| | | | | |
|---|---|---|---|---|
| 1472 | **489** | 3b.50 multicoloured | 2·75 | 2·40 |

**490** Route Map and Presidents Hugo Banzer Suarez of Bolivia and Fernando Cardoso of Brazil

**1999.** Inauguration of Gas Pipeline from Santa Cruz, Bolivia, to Campinas, Brazil. Multicoloured.

| | | | | |
|---|---|---|---|---|
| 1473 | | 3b. Type **490** | 2·40 | 2·10 |
| 1474 | | 6b. Presidents Hugo Banzer Suarez and Fernando Cardoso embracing | 4·75 | 3·75 |

**491** Village Scene

**1999.** 50th Anniv of SOS Children's Villages.

| | | | | |
|---|---|---|---|---|
| 1475 | **491** | 3b.50 multicoloured | 2·75 | 2·40 |

**492** "Hacia la Gloria" (directed Raul Duran, Mario Camacho and Jose Jimenez)

**1999.** Centenary of Motion Pictures in Bolivia. Multicoloured.

| | | | | |
|---|---|---|---|---|
| 1476 | | 50c. Type **492** | 35 | 30 |
| 1477 | | 50c. "Jonah and the Pink Whale" (dir. J. Carlos Valdivia) | 35 | 30 |
| 1478 | | 1b. "Wara Wara" (dir. Jose Velasco) | 65 | 55 |
| 1479 | | 1b. "Vuelve Sebastiana" (dir. Jorge Ruiz) | 65 | 55 |
| 1480 | | 3b. "The Chaco Campaign" (dir. Juan Penaranda, Jose Velasco and Mario Camacho) | 2·10 | 1·80 |
| 1481 | | 3b. "The Watershed" (dir. Jorge Ruiz) | 2·10 | 1·80 |
| 1482 | | 6b. "Yawar Mallku" (dir. Jorge Sanjines) | 4·25 | 3·50 |
| 1483 | | 6b. "Mi Socio" (dir. Paolo Agazzi) | 4·25 | 3·50 |

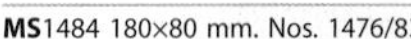

| | | | |
|---|---|---|---|
| **MS**1484 | 180×80 mm. Nos. 1476/83 | 14·50 | 14·00 |

**493** International Lions Emblem

**1999.** 50th Anniv (1998) of La Paz Lions Club.

| | | | | |
|---|---|---|---|---|
| 1485 | **493** | 3b.50 multicoloured | 2·75 | 2·40 |

**494** Mt. Tunari

**1999.** Cochabamba. Multicoloured.

| | | | | |
|---|---|---|---|---|
| 1486 | | 50c. Type **494** | 35 | 30 |
| 1487 | | 1b. Forest, Cochabamba Valley | 65 | 55 |
| 1488 | | 2b. Omereque vase and fertility goddess (vert) | 1·40 | 1·20 |
| 1489 | | 3b. Totora | 2·10 | 1·80 |
| 1490 | | 5b. Teofilo Vargas Candia (composer) and music score (vert) | 3·50 | 3·00 |
| 1491 | | 6b. "Christ of Harmony" (mountain-top statue) (vert) | 4·25 | 3·50 |

**495** Tarapaya Lagoon (Inca spa)

**1999.** Potosi. Multicoloured.

| | | | | |
|---|---|---|---|---|
| 1492 | | 50c. Type **495** | 35 | 30 |
| 1493 | | 1b. First republican coins, minted in 1827 (horiz) | 65 | 55 |
| 1494 | | 2b. Mt. Chorolque (horiz) | 1·40 | 1·20 |
| 1495 | | 3b. Green Lagoon (horiz) | 2·10 | 1·80 |
| 1496 | | 5b. "The Mestizo sitting on a Trunk" (Teofilo Loaiza) | 3·50 | 3·00 |
| 1497 | | 6b. Alfredo Dominguez Romeo (Tupiceno singer) | 4·25 | 3·50 |

**496** Globe with Children, Fish, Flower, Pencil, Heart and Stars

**1999.** America. A New Millennium without Arms. Multicoloured.

| | | | | |
|---|---|---|---|---|
| 1498 | | 3b.50 Type **496** | 2·40 | 2·10 |
| 1499 | | 3b.50 Globe emerging from flower | 2·40 | 2·10 |

**497** Children from S.O.S. Childrens Village

**1999.** Christmas. Multicoloured.

| | | | | |
|---|---|---|---|---|
| 1500 | | 2b. Type **497** | 1·30 | 1·10 |
| 1501 | | 6b. "The Birth of Jesus" (Gaspar Miguel de Berrios) (vert) | 4·00 | 3·50 |
| 1502 | | 7b. "Our Family in the World" (Omar Medina) (vert) | 5·00 | 4·25 |

**498** Ugarte

**2000.** 5th Death Anniv of Victor Agustin Ugarte (football player).

| | | | | |
|---|---|---|---|---|
| 1503 | **498** | 3b. grey, green and yellow | 2·20 | 1·90 |

**499** El Arenal Park

**2000.** Santa Cruz. Multicoloured.

| | | | | |
|---|---|---|---|---|
| 1504 | | 50c. Type **499** | 35 | 30 |
| 1505 | | 1b. Ox cart | 75 | 65 |
| 1506 | | 2b. Raul Otero Reiche, Gabriel Rene Moreno and Hernando Sanabria Fernandez (writers) | 1·50 | 1·30 |
| 1507 | | 3b. Cotoca Virgin (statue) (vert) | 2·20 | 1·90 |
| 1508 | | 5b. Anthropomorphic vase (vert) | 4·00 | 3·50 |
| 1509 | | 6b. Bush dog | 4·75 | 4·00 |

**500** "The Village of Serinhaem in Brazil" (Frans Post)

**2000.** 500th Anniv of Discovery of Brazil.

| | | | | |
|---|---|---|---|---|
| 1510 | **500** | 5b. multicoloured | 3·75 | 3·25 |

CORREOS DE BOLIVIA

**501** Granado

**2000.** Javier del Granado (poet) Commemoration.

| | | | | |
|---|---|---|---|---|
| 1511 | **501** | 3b. grey, blue and red | 3·00 | 2·75 |

**502** Cyclists

**2000.** "Double Copacabana" Cycle Race.

| | | | | |
|---|---|---|---|---|
| 1512 | **502** | 1b. multicoloured | 65 | 55 |
| 1513 | - | 3b. multicoloured | 2·20 | 1·90 |
| 1514 | - | 5b. multicoloured | 3·75 | 3·25 |
| 1515 | - | 7b. multicoloured | 5·00 | 4·25 |

DESIGNS: 3b. to 7b. Various race scenes.

**503** Oriental Clay Figure

**2000.** National Archaeology Museum Exhibits. Each brown and gold.

| | | | | |
|---|---|---|---|---|
| 1516 | | 50c. Type **503** | 35 | 30 |
| 1517 | | 50c. Clay figure, Potosi | 35 | 30 |
| 1518 | | 70c. Oriental clay head, Beni | 55 | 45 |
| 1519 | | 90c. Clay vase, Tarija | 65 | 55 |
| 1520 | | 1b. Clay head, Oruro | 70 | 60 |
| 1521 | | 1b. Yampara clay urn | 70 | 60 |
| 1522 | | 3b. Inca wood carving | 2·20 | 1·90 |
| 1523 | | 5b. Oriental anthropomorphic vase | 3·75 | 3·25 |
| 1524 | | 20b. Tiwanaku clay mask | 15·00 | 14·00 |

**504** Male and Female Symbols in Red Vortex

**2000.** America. Anti-AIDS Campaign. Mult.

1525 3b.50 Type **504** 2·75 2·50

1526 3b.50 Couple walking through wall 2·75 2·50

**505** Soldier's Head and Bird on Laurel Wreath

**2000.** Centenary of Maximiliano Parades Military School.

1527 **505** 2b.50 multicoloured 2·20 1·90

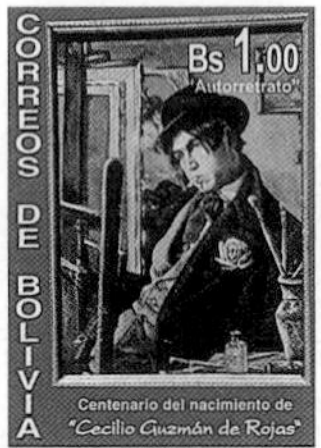


**506** "Self-portrait"

**2000.** Birth Centenary of Cecilio Guzman de Rojas (artist). Showing paintings. Multicoloured.

1528 1b. Type **506** 75 65

1529 2b.50 "Triumph of Nature" (horiz) 2·20 1·90

1530 5b. "Andina" 4·50 3·75

1531 6b. "Students' Quarrel" (horiz) 5·00 4·25

**507** Crowd and Brandenburg Gate

**2000.** 50th Anniv of German Federal Republic.

1532 **507** 6b. multicoloured 5·00 4·25

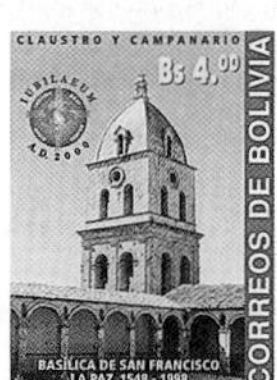


**508** San Francisco Basilica, La Paz

**2000.** Holy Year 2000. Bolivian Episcopal Conference. Multicoloured.

1533 4b. Type **508** 3·25 2·75

1534 6b. Stalks of grain breaking through barbed-wire 5·00 4·25

**509** Waterfall and Statue

**2000.** New Millennium.

1535 **509** 5b. multicoloured 4·00 3·50

**510** Archangel Gabriel

**2000.** Christmas. Showing 17th-century paintings of Angels from Calamarca Church. Multicoloured.

1536 3b. Type **510** 2·20 1·90

1537 5b. Angel of Virtue 4·50 3·75

1538 10b. Angel with ear of corn 7·75 6·50

**511** Painting of John the Baptist and Emblem

**2000.** 900th Anniv of Sovereign Military Order of St. John.

1539 **511** 6b. multicoloured 4·75 4·00

**512** Lobster Claw (*Heliconia rostrata*)

**2001.** Patriotic Symbols. Multicoloured.

1540 10b. Type **512** (designated national flower, 1990) 7·75 6·50

1541 20b. *Periphrangus dependens* (designated national flower 1924) 15·00 13·00

1542 30b. First Bolivian coat of arms (adopted 1825) 22·00 19·00

1543 50b. Second Bolivian coat of arms (adopted 1826) 40·00 34·00

1544 100b. Present day Bolivian coat of arms (adopted 1851) 75·00 65·00

**513** Map and Stars of European Union and Map of Bolivia

**2001.** 25th Anniv of Co-operation between Bolivia and European Union.

1550 **513** 6b. multicoloured 4·75 4·00

**514** Statue of Justice, Lion and Portico

**2001.** 171st Anniv of Faculty of Law and Political Sciences, Universidad de Mayor of San Andres, La Paz.

1551 **514** 6b. multicoloured 4·75 4·00

**515** Temple of San Francisco, Potosi

**2001.** America. UNESCO World Heritage Sites. Multicoloured.

1552 1b.50 Type **515** 1·20 1·00

1553 5b. "Fraile" and "Ponce" (monoliths) (horiz) 4·25 3·50

**516** Man carrying Envelopes up Stairs

**2001.** Philately. Each green.

1554 50c. Type **516** 35 30

1555 1b. Boy with six stamps 75 65

1556 1b.50 Man with glasses and stamp album 1·20 1·00

1557 2b. Child wearing hat, and three stamps 1·50 1·30

1558 2b.50 Humanized stamp lying in tray 2·00 1·70

**517** Devil's Molar (mountain)

**2001**

1559 **517** 1b.50 multicoloured 1·20 1·00

**518** Family

**2001.** National Census. Multicoloured.

1560 1b. Type **518** 90 75

1561 1b.50 People surrounding wheelchair user 1·20 1·00

1562 1b.50 Aboriginal woman and people of different races 1·20 1·00

1563 2b.50 People of different races 2·00 1·70

1564 3b. Children 2·40 2·10

**519** Silver Spot (*Dione juno*)

**2001.** Butterflies and Insects. Multicoloured.

1565 1b. Type **519** 75 65

1566 1b. *Orthoptera* sp. 75 65

1567 1b.50 Bamboo page (*Philaethria dido*) 1·20 1·00

1568 2b.50 Jewel butterfly (*Diaethria clymena*) (inscr "Diathria clymene") 2·00 1·70

1569 2b.50 *Mantis religiosa* 2·00 1·70

1570 3b. *Tropidacris latreillei* 2·40 2·10

1571 4b. Hercules beetle (*Dynastes hercules*) (inscr "Escarabajo Hercule") 3·25 2·75

1572 5b. *Arctiidae* sp. 4·25 3·50

1573 5b. *Acrocinus longimanus* 4·25 3·50

1574 5b. *Lucanidae* sp. 4·25 3·50

1575 6b. *Morpho godarti* 4·75 4·25

1576 6b. *Caligo idomeneus* ("inscr idomineus") 4·75 4·25

**520** Map of Americas and Emblem

**2001.** 21st Inter-America Scout Conference, Cochabamba.

1577 **520** 3b.50 multicoloured 2·75 2·50

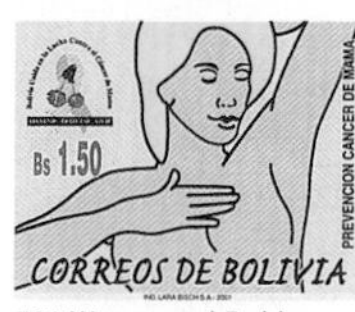


**521** Woman and Emblem

**2001.** Breast Cancer Prevention Campaign.

1578 **521** 1b.50 multicoloured 1·20 1·00

**522** St. Mary Magdalen

**2001.** Christmas. Showing sculptures by Gaspar of La Cueva from Convent of San Francisco, Potosí. Multicoloured.

1579 3b. Type **522** 2·40 2·10

1580 5b. St. Apolonia 4·25 3·50

1581 10b. St. Teresa of Avila 8·25 7·00

**523** Portrait and Casa La Laertad, Sucre

**2001.** Joaquin Gantier Valda Commemoration.

1582 **523** 4b. multicoloured 3·25 2·75

**524** Flags and Hands enclosing Farmer, Mother, Child and Doctor

**2001.** 25th Anniv of Co-operation between Bolivia and Belgium.

1583 **524** 6b. multicoloured 4·75 4·25

**525** Aerial Photograph and Bridge

**2002.** Bolivia–Peru Presidential Summit. Multicoloured.

1584 50c. Type **525** 45 40

1585 3b. Aerial photograph and bridge (different) 2·40 2·10

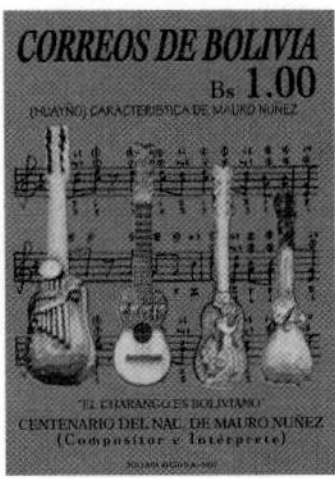

**526** Charangos (guitars) and Musical Score

**2001.** Birth Centenary of Mauro Nunez (musician). Multicoloured.

| | | | |
|---|---|---|---|
| 1586 | 1b. Type **526** | 90 | 75 |
| 1587 | 6b. Mauro Nunez | 4·75 | 4·25 |

**527** Dancers with Horned Head-dresses (Diablada)

**2001.** Cultural Heritage. Oruro Carnival. Multicoloured.

| | | | |
|---|---|---|---|
| 1588 | 50c. Type **527** | 45 | 40 |
| 1589 | 1b.50 Female dancer (Morenada) | 1·10 | 95 |
| 1590 | 2b.50 Female dancers and man in embroidered clothes (Caporales) | 1·80 | 1·50 |
| 1591 | 5b. Male dancers in multicoloured head-dresses (Tobas) | 3·50 | 3·00 |
| 1592 | 7b. Woman dancer in elaborate hat and yellow skirt (Suri Sikuri) (vert) | 5·00 | 4·25 |
| 1593 | 7b. Dancers wearing bonnets (Pujllay) (vert) | 5·00 | 4·25 |

**2002.** Butterflies and Insects (2nd series). As T 519. Multicoloured.

| | | | |
|---|---|---|---|
| 1594 | 3b. White-tailed page (*Urania leilus*) | 2·40 | 2·10 |
| 1595 | 3b. *Tropidacris latreilli* | 2·40 | 2·10 |
| 1596 | 3b. *Papilio cresphontes macho* | 2·40 | 2·10 |
| 1597 | 3b. Longhorn beetle (*Acrocinus longimanus*) | 2·40 | 2·10 |
| 1598 | 3b. *Prepona buckleyana* | 2·40 | 2·10 |
| 1599 | 3b. *Thysannia agripyna cramer* (left wings) | 2·40 | 2·10 |
| 1600 | 3b. *Thysannia agripyna cramer* (right wings) | 2·40 | 2·10 |
| 1601 | 3b. *Lucanus verde* (inscr "Lucano") | 2·40 | 2·10 |
| 1602 | 3b. Butterfly (inscr "Nymphalidae") | 2·40 | 2·10 |
| 1603 | 3b. *Escarabajo hercule* | 2·40 | 2·10 |
| 1604 | 3b. Butterfly (different) (inscr "Heliconinae") | 2·40 | 2·10 |
| 1605 | 3b. Grasshopper (inscr "Orthopterdae") | 2·40 | 2·10 |

Nos. 1599/1600 were issued in se-tenant pairs within the sheet, each pair forming a composite design.

**528** "El Kusillo" (folk character)

**2002.** 3rd International Theatre Festival, La Paz.

| | | | | |
|---|---|---|---|---|
| 1606 | **528** | 3b. multicoloured | 2·40 | 2·10 |

**529** Mountain Viscachas (rodent), Potosi

**2002.** International Year of Mountains and Eco-tourism. Multicoloured.

| | | | |
|---|---|---|---|
| 1607 | 80c. Type **529** | 65 | 55 |
| 1608 | 1b. Polylepis (tree), Cochabamba (vert) | 90 | 75 |
| 1609 | 1b.50 Huayna Potosi mountains, La Paz | 1·30 | 1·10 |
| 1610 | 2b.50 Payachatas mountains, Oruro | 2·20 | 1·90 |
| 1611 | 2b.50 Sajama mountain, Oruro (vert) | 2·20 | 1·90 |

**530** Anniversary Emblem and Rainbow

**2002.** Centenary of Pan-American Health Organization.

| | | | | |
|---|---|---|---|---|
| 1612 | **530** | 3b. multicoloured | 2·40 | 2·10 |

**531** Gunnar Mendoza

**2002.** Dr. Gunnar Mendoza (scientist) Commemoration.

| | | | | |
|---|---|---|---|---|
| 1613 | **531** | 4b. multicoloured | 3·00 | 2·75 |

**532** Gates Learget 25 over Mountains

**2002.** 50th Anniv of Military Aviation College, Gemán Busch. Multicoloured.

| | | | |
|---|---|---|---|
| 1614 | 4b. Type **532** | 3·00 | 2·75 |
| 1615 | 5b. Acrobatic aeroplanes (vert) | 4·00 | 3·50 |
| 1616 | 6b. Three helicopters | 4·75 | 4·00 |

**533** Orinoco Goose (*Neochen jubata*)

**2002.** Day of Natural Resources. Multicoloured.

| | | | |
|---|---|---|---|
| 1617 | 50c. Type **533** (CEFILCO philatelic association) | 45 | 40 |
| 1618 | 4b. Orange-breasted falcon (*Falco deiroleucus*) (30th anniv of Bolivian philatelic federation) | 3·25 | 2·75 |
| 1619 | 6b. Black-bodied woodpecker (*Dryocopus schulzi*) (PHILAKOREA 2002) | 4·75 | 4·25 |

**534** Thousand Year old Cedar Tree and Church Tower

**2002.** 400th Anniv of Sucre Monastery.

| | | | | |
|---|---|---|---|---|
| 1620 | **534** | 4b. multicoloured | 3·00 | 2·75 |

**535** Indian Madonna

**2002.** Twentieth-century Art. Multicoloured.

| | | | |
|---|---|---|---|
| 1621 | 70c. Type **535** (sculpture, Marina Nunez del Prado) | 55 | 45 |
| 1622 | 70c. Mountain (painting, Maria Luisa Pachero) | 55 | 45 |
| 1623 | 80c. Indian mother (sculpture, Marina Nunez del Prado) | 65 | 55 |
| 1624 | 80c. "Cordillera" (painting, Maria Luisa Pachero) | 65 | 55 |
| 1625 | 5b. Venus Negra (sculpture, Marina Nunez del Prado) | 4·00 | 3·50 |
| 1626 | 5b. "Cerros" (painting, Maria Luisa Pachero) (horiz) | 4·00 | 3·50 |

**536** Potosi and Armando Alba Zambrana

**2002.** Birth Centenary (2001) of Armando Alba Zambrana (historian).

| | | | | |
|---|---|---|---|---|
| 1627 | **536** | 3b. multicoloured | 2·40 | 2·10 |

**537** Couple wearing Traditional Costume

**2002.** Birth Bicentenary of Alcide d'Orbigny (naturalist and palaeontologist). Multicoloured.

| | | | |
|---|---|---|---|
| 1628 | 1b. Type **537** | 75 | 65 |
| 1629 | 4b. Boat on river (horiz) | 3·00 | 2·75 |
| 1630 | 6b. Alcide d'Orbigny | 4·75 | 4·00 |

**538** Teacher and Pupils

**2002.** America. Education and Literacy Campaign. Multicoloured.

| | | | |
|---|---|---|---|
| 1631 | 1b. Type **538** | 65 | 55 |
| 1632 | 2b.50 Indigenous children and computer | 1·50 | 1·30 |

**539** Mary and Jesus

**2002.** Christmas. Multicoloured.

| | | | |
|---|---|---|---|
| 1633 | 3b. Type **539** | 1·70 | 1·40 |
| 1634 | 5b. Nativity | 2·75 | 2·40 |
| 1635 | 6b. "The Adoration of the Kings" (painting, 18th-century) | 3·25 | 2·75 |

**540** Apolinar Camacho

**2003.** 1st Death Anniv of Apolinar Camacho (composer).

| | | | | |
|---|---|---|---|---|
| 1636 | **540** | 2b.50 multicoloured | 1·40 | 1·20 |

**541** Soldier (statue)

**2003.** Centenary of Battle of Bahia. Multicoloured.

| | | | |
|---|---|---|---|
| 1637 | 50c. Type **541** | 35 | 30 |
| 1638 | 1b. Three soldiers (statue) | 55 | 45 |

**542** Anniversary Emblem

**2003.** 25th Anniv of Culture of Peace Month (UN peace initiative). Bolivian Permanent Assembly of Human Rights.

| | | | | |
|---|---|---|---|---|
| 1639 | **542** | 6b. ultramarine | 3·25 | 2·75 |

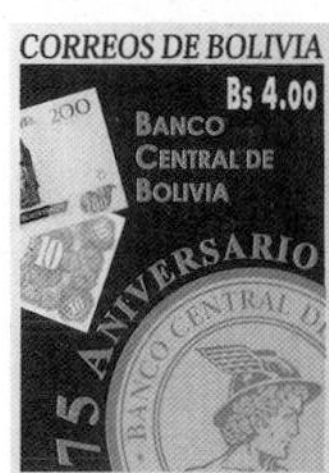

**543** Currency and Bank Emblem

**2003.** 75th Anniv of Central Bank.

| | | | | |
|---|---|---|---|---|
| 1640 | **543** | 4b. multicoloured | 2·20 | 1·90 |

**544** Court Emblem

**2003.** 5th Anniv of Sucre Constitutional Court.

| | | | | |
|---|---|---|---|---|
| 1641 | **544** | 1b.50 multicoloured | 90 | 75 |

**545** Quinoa (*Chenopodium quinoa*)

**2003.** America. Flora and Fauna Multicoloured.

| | | | |
|---|---|---|---|
| 1642 | 50c. Type **545** | 3·25 | 2·75 |
| 1643 | 1b. Llama | 3·75 | 3·25 |

**546** Anniversary Emblem

**2003.** Centenary of Panama Republic.

| | | | | |
|---|---|---|---|---|
| 1644 | **546** | 7b. multicoloured | 3·75 | 3·25 |

**547** Porfirio Diaz Machicao, Rosendo Villalobos and Monsignor Juan Quiros (writers)

**2003.** 75th Anniv of Language Academy.

| | | | | |
|---|---|---|---|---|
| 1645 | **547** | 6b. multicoloured | 3·25 | 2·75 |

**548** Flags and Latin America

**2003.** Latin American, Spanish and Portuguese Heads of Government Conference, Santa Cruz. Multicoloured.

| | | | |
|---|---|---|---|
| 1646 | 6b. Type **548** | 3·25 | 2·75 |
| 1647 | 6b. Eastern globe and flags | 3·25 | 2·75 |

Nos. 1646/7 were issued together, se-tenant, forming a composite design.

**549** Virgin of Guadeloupe (Brother Diego de Ocana)

**2003.** 450th Anniv of La Plata Archdiocese.
1648 **549** 6b. multicoloured 3·25 2·75

**550** "Adoration of the Shepherds" (Leonardo Flores) (Templo de Calamarca, La Paz)

**2003.** Christmas. Multicoloured.
1649 1b.50 Type **550** 90 75
1650 6b. "Adoration of the Shepherds" (Bernardo Bitti) (Cathedral museum, Sucre) 3·25 2·75
1651 7b. "Adoration of the Shepherds" (Melchor Perez de Holguin) (Santa Teresa museum, Potosi) (horiz) 3·75 3·25

**551** Pope John Paul II

**2004.** 25th Anniv of Pontificate of Pope John Paul II. Multicoloured.
1652 1b. Type **551** 55 45
1653 1b.50 Seated facing right (painting) 90 75
1654 5b. Giving blessing to native Bolivians 2·75 2·40
1655 6b. Wearing gold cope 3·25 2·75
1656 7b. Seated facing left 3·75 3·25
**MS**1657 150×110 mm. 10b.×2, Mary of Copacabana and balsa boat on the Lake Titicaca; Santa Tersa de Avila (statue) (Gaspar de la Cueva) 11·00 10·50

**552** Girl and Rainbow

**2004.** 10th Anniv of ARCO IRIS Foundation (street children's charitable organization).
1658 **552** 1b.80 multicoloured 1·40 1·20

**553** Battle Scene (painting)

**2004.** 25th Anniv of Military History Academy.
1659 **553** 1b. multicoloured 55 45

**554** Athens, 2004 Emblem, Rifle Shooting, Gymnastics and Judo

**2004.** Olympic Games, Athens. Multicoloured.
1660 1b.50 Type **554** 90 75
1661 7b. Emblem, running and swimming 3·75 3·25

**555** Holy Family

**2004.** Christmas. Multicoloured.
1662 1b.50 Type **555** 90 75
1663 3b. Child praying 2·40 2·10
1664 6b. Candle 3·25 2·75

**556** Typewriter on Wheels

**2004.** 75th Anniv of La Paz Journalists' Association.
1665 **556** 1b.50 multicoloured 2015 90 75

**557** Palm

**2004.** America. Environmental Protection. Mult.
1666 5b. Type **557** 2·75 2·40
1667 6b. Parrots (Gilka Wara Libermann) 3·25 2·75

**558** Map of Bolivia and Emblems

**2005.** Centenary of Rotary International (charitable organization). Multicoloured.
1668 3b. Type **558** 2·40 2·10
1669 3b. Paul Harris (founder), "100" and emblem 2·40 2·10

Nos. 1668/9 were issued together, se-tenant, forming a composite design.

**559** Water Pipe Outflow and Beach

**2005.** Environmental Projects. Multicoloured.
1670 5b. Type **559** (Pras Pando (water project)) 2·75 2·40
1671 6b. Seedling, European Union and Bolivian Flags (PRAEDAC (programme to support alternate development)) (vert) 3·25 2·75

**560** Striped Cloth

**2005.** Cultural Heritage. Textiles. Multicoloured.
1672 50c. Type **560** 45 40
1673 1b. Horizontal stripes and dark bands 55 45
1674 1b.50 Vertical decorated stripes and red bands 90 75
1675 6b. Wide black bands 3·25 2·75
1676 6b. Two decorated squares (horiz) 3·25 2·75

**561** Otto Felipe Braun

**2005.** 80th Anniv of Colegio Mariscal Braun, La Paz.
1677 **561** 6b. multicoloured 3·25 2·75

**562** *Harpia harpyja*

**2005.** Birds. Multicoloured.
1678 1b. Type **562** (Interexpo '05, Dominican Republic) 55 45
1679 1b.50 *Penelope dabbenei* (35th anniv of Filatelica Boliviana) 90 75
1680 7b. *Aulacorhynchus coeruleicinctus* (Washington 2006) 3·75 3·25

**563** Pope John Paul II and Children

**2005.** Pope John Paul II Commemoration (1681) and Inauguration of Pope Benedict XVI (1682). Multicoloured.
1681 5b. Type **563** 2·75 2·40
1682 5b. Pope Benedict XVI (vert) 2·75 2·40

**564** Sail Ship

**2005.** The Pacific War of 1879–1884.
1683 **564** 5b. multicoloured 2·75 2·40

**565** Don Quixote riding Rocinante

**2005.** 400th Anniv of the Publication of "Don Quixote de la Mancha" by Miguel de Cervantes.
1684 **565** 4b. multicoloured 2·20 1·90

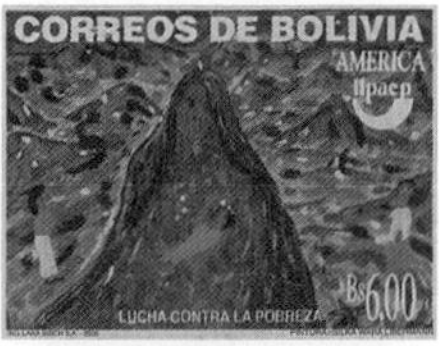


**566** Mother and Child

**2005.** America. Struggle against Poverty. Multicoloured.
1685 6b. Type **566** 3·25 2·75
1686 7b. Fisherman and fleshless fish 3·75 3·25

**567** Idelfonso Murguia

**2005.** 184th Anniv of Infanteria Colorado Regiment (presidential escort).
1687 **567** 2b. multicoloured 1·50 1·30

**568** Flamingos in Flight

**2005.** Tourism.
1688 **568** 6b. multicoloured 3·25 2·75

**569** Two-toed Sloth

**2005.** 20th Anniv of LIDEMA (conservation group).
1689 **569** 6b. multicoloured 3·25 2·75

**570** 1863 Un-issued 2r. Stamps

**2005.** Stamp Day. Sheet 91×110 mm containing T 570 and similar horiz designs. Multicoloured.
**MS**1690 2r.×3, Type **570**; 1924 5b. stamp; British 1840 Penny Black (1st stamp) and Brazil 1843 30r. ("Olho de Boi" ("Bull's Eye")) stamp; 4r.×3, 1867 5c. stamps (1st Bolivian stamps); 1930 3b. surch on 20c. ("Graf Zeppelin") stamp; 1987 60c. stamp 14·50 14·00

**571** Three Wise Men

**2005.** Christmas. Multicoloured.

| | | | |
|---|---|---|---|
| 1691 | 1b.50 Type **571** | 90 | 75 |
| 1692 | 3b. Holy family | 1·70 | 1·40 |

**2006.** Nos. 1119, 1115 and No. 1119 surch.

| | | | |
|---|---|---|---|
| 1693 | 1b. on 1000000p. black and green | 65 | 55 |
| 1694 | 2b. on 550000 multicoloured | 1·40 | 1·20 |
| 1695 | 2b.50 on 1000000 multicoloured | 2·30 | 2·00 |

**575** School Building, 1906

**2006.** Centenary of Engineering University.

| | | | | |
|---|---|---|---|---|
| 1696 | **575** | 6b. multicoloured | 3·25 | 2·75 |

**576** President Morales

**2006.** Election of President Juan Evo Morales Ayma (Evo Morales) (first indigenous South American President. Multicoloured.

| | | | |
|---|---|---|---|
| 1697 | 1b.50 Type **576** | 90 | 75 |
| 1698 | 5b. At inauguration | 2·75 | 2·40 |
| 1699 | 6b. Wearing tribal dress | 3·25 | 2·75 |

**577** Red Cross Worker

**2006.** Bolivian Red Cross.

| | | | | |
|---|---|---|---|---|
| 1700 | **577** | 5b. multicoloured | 2·75 | 2·40 |

**578** Inca Messenger and Envelopes

**2006.** 15th Anniv of ECOBOL.

| | | | | |
|---|---|---|---|---|
| 1701 | **578** | 1b. green | 55 | 45 |
| 1702 | **578** | 1b.50 ultramarine | 90 | 75 |

**579** Boy Scouts at Exfivia 75

**2006.** Stamp Collectors' Day. Sheet 90×105 mm containing T 579 and similar horiz designs. Multicoloured.

| | | | |
|---|---|---|---|
| **MS**1703 | 1b.50 Type **579**; 1b.50 Stamp album; 1b.50 Bird stamps of Boliva and Honduras; 6b. Exfilmar 80; 6b. Ship stamps of Bolivia and Iceland; 6b. Floral stamps of Bolivia and Dominican Republic | 15·00 | 14·00 |

**580** Legislative Palace and Second Adapted National Flag of 1851

**2006.** Flags. Multicoloured.

| | | | |
|---|---|---|---|
| 1704 | 1b.50 Type **580** | 55 | 45 |
| 1705 | 5b. Liberty House and first adapted national flag of 1826 | 2·75 | 2·40 |
| 1706 | 6b. Liberty House and first national flag of 1825 | 3·25 | 2·75 |

**581** Friar and Donkey

**2006.** 400th Anniv of Franciscan Order in Tarija. Multicoloured.

| | | | |
|---|---|---|---|
| 1707 | 2b. Type **581** | 1·40 | 1·20 |
| 1708 | 2b. Early church | 1·40 | 1·20 |
| 1709 | 6b. Basilica interior (vert) | 3·25 | 2·75 |
| 1710 | 6b. "La Inmaulada" (vert) | 3·25 | 2·75 |

**582** *14-bis*

**2006.** Centenary of First Flight by Alberto Santos Dumont.

| | | | | |
|---|---|---|---|---|
| 1711 | **582** | 1b.50 multicoloured | 90 | 75 |

**583** Sajama National Park

**2006.** 400th Anniv of Oruro.

| | | | | |
|---|---|---|---|---|
| 1712 | **583** | 4b. multicoloured | 2·20 | 1·90 |

**584** 9 February Avenue

**2006.** Centenary of Bahia Harbour. Multicoloured.

| | | | |
|---|---|---|---|
| 1713 | 1b. Type **584** | 55 | 45 |
| 1714 | 1b.50 German Busch Plaza | 90 | 75 |
| 1715 | 2b.50 Tree (vert) | 2·20 | 1·90 |
| 1716 | 3b. Potosi Plaza | 2·40 | 2·10 |
| 1717 | 4b. Bahia Pando river | 2·75 | 2·30 |
| 1718 | 6b. Friendship Bridge | 3·25 | 2·75 |
| 1719 | 7b. Port Avenue (vert) | 3·75 | 3·25 |

**585** Vicuna

**2006.** Endangered Species. Multicoloured.

| | | | |
|---|---|---|---|
| 1720 | 1b. Type **585** | 55 | 45 |
| 1721 | 1b.50 Head of Yacare caiman (Caiman yacare) (horiz) | 90 | 75 |
| 1722 | 5b. Yacare caiman (horiz) | 2·75 | 2·40 |
| 1723 | 7b. Vicuna (horiz) | 3·75 | 3·25 |

**586** Area damaged by Mining

**2006.** International Year of Deserts and Desertification. Multicoloured.

| | | | |
|---|---|---|---|
| 1724 | 1b.50 Type **586** | 90 | 75 |
| 1725 | 2b. Erosion, Tolomosa river basin | 1·40 | 1·20 |
| 1726 | 3b. Terraces | 2·40 | 2·10 |
| 1727 | 4b. Erosion, Caranavi | 2·75 | 2·30 |

**587** Low Energy Bulb as Flower

**2006.** America. Energy Conservation. Multicoloured.

| | | | |
|---|---|---|---|
| 1728 | 3b. Type **587** | 2·40 | 2·10 |
| 1729 | 4b. Light bulb containing cash | 2·75 | 2·30 |

**588** Virgin of Roses

**2006.** Christmas. Multicoloured.

| | | | |
|---|---|---|---|
| 1730 | 4b. Type **588** | 2·75 | 2·30 |
| 1731 | 5b. Adoration of the Magi | 3·00 | 2·50 |
| 1732 | 6b. Adoration of the shepherds | 3·25 | 2·75 |

**589** Rocks (astronomical observatory)

**2006.** Manco Kapac. Multicoloured.

| | | | |
|---|---|---|---|
| 1733 | 5b. Type **589** | 3·00 | 2·50 |
| 1734 | 6b. Copacabana Temple | 3·25 | 2·75 |
| 1735 | 7b. Boat on lake | 3·75 | 3·25 |

**590** Toucan

**2006.** Birds of Pando. Multicoloured.

| | | | |
|---|---|---|---|
| 1736 | 2b.50 Type **590** | 1·40 | 1·20 |
| 1737 | 6b. Inscr "Pajaro azul" | 3·25 | 2·75 |

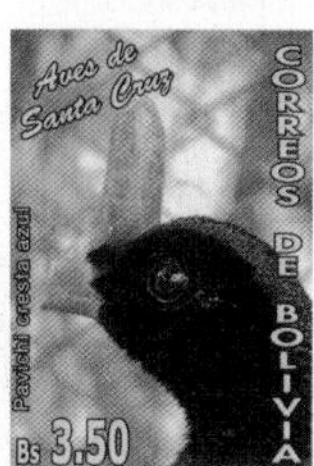


**591** Helmeted Curassow (inscr "Pavichi cresta azul")

**2006.** Birds of Santa Cruz. Multicoloured.

| | | | |
|---|---|---|---|
| 1738 | 3b.50 Type **591** | 2·75 | 2·40 |
| 1739 | 7b. Harpy eagle (inscr "Aguila arpia") | 3·75 | 3·25 |

**592** Miniature Schnauzer

**2006.** Dogs. Multicoloured.

| | | | |
|---|---|---|---|
| 1740 | 1b. Type **592** | 90 | 75 |
| 1741 | 2b. Husky | 1·40 | 1·20 |
| 1742 | 3b. American boxer | 2·40 | 2·10 |
| 1743 | 4b. Inscr "Criollo" | 2·75 | 2·40 |

**593** 14 September Plaza

**2007.** 'Latin America and Caribbean Lions' Forum, Cochabamba, Bolivia.

| | | | | |
|---|---|---|---|---|
| 1744 | **593** | 6b. multicoloured | 3·25 | 2·75 |

**594** Map of Europe

**2007.** 50th Anniv of Treaty of Rome. Multicoloured.

| | | | |
|---|---|---|---|
| 1745 | 3b.50 Type **594** | 2·75 | 2·30 |
| 1746 | 7b. Flag of stars | 3·75 | 3·25 |

Nos. 1745/6 were issued together, se-tenant, forming a composite design.

**595** Philatelic Magazines

**2007.** 50th Anniv of Philatelic Association. Multicoloured.

| | | | |
|---|---|---|---|
| 1747 | 50c. Type **595** | 45 | 40 |
| 1748 | 1b. Arnold Glaeser (first president) and overprinted stamp | 90 | 75 |
| 1749 | 2b.50 Simon Martinic and stamp catalogue | 2·00 | 1·70 |
| 1750 | 3b. Franz Steimbach and Oscar Roca | 2·40 | 2·10 |
| 1751 | 3b.50 Cathedral and 'Heroinas de la Coronilla' monument | 2·75 | 2·30 |
| 1752 | 6b. 'Christ of the Concord' (statue) and Cathedral, Cochabamba | 3·25 | 2·75 |

Nos. 1751/2 were issued together, se-tenant, forming a composite design.

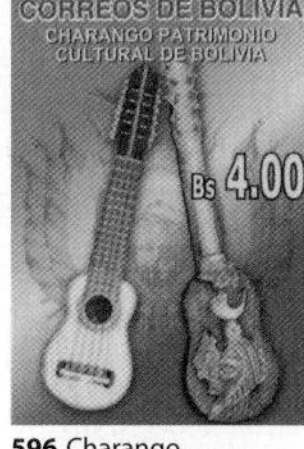


**596** Charango

**2007.** Cultural Heritage. Multicoloured.

| | | | |
|---|---|---|---|
| 1753 | 4b. Type **596** | 2·75 | 2·40 |
| 1754 | 6b. Charango (different) | 3·25 | 2·75 |

**597** Emblem and '90'

**2007.** 90th Anniv of Bolivian Red Cross.

| | | | | |
|---|---|---|---|---|
| 1755 | **597** | 2b.50 multicoloured | 2·00 | 1·70 |

**598** Francis Harrington (missionary and institute founder)

**2007.** Centenary of American Institute.
1756 **598** 7b.50 multicoloured 4·25 3·50

**599** Cog, Map and Emblems

**2007.** 75th Anniv of Chamber of Commerce. Multicoloured.
1757 9b. Type **599** 5·00 4·25
1758 12b. '75 Anos', emblems and cog 6·50 5·75

**599a** *Ara ararauna* (blue and gold macaw)

**2007.** Birds. Multicoloured.
1758a 5b.50 Type **599a** 3·00 2·75
1758b 7b.50 *Porphyrula martinica* (purple gallinule) 4·25 3·50

**600** Jaguar

**2007.** Santa Cruz Zoo. Multicoloured.
1759 6b. Type **600** 3·25 2·75
1760 9b. Puma 5·00 4·25

**601** Emblems

**2007.** Heads of the American Air Force Conference, Santa Cruz, Bolivia.
1761 **601** 10b.50 multicoloured 6·00 5·25

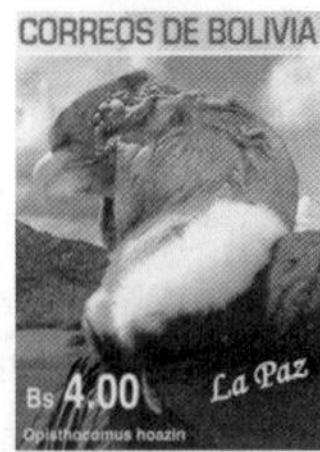

**602** Andean Condor (inscr 'Opisthocomus hoazin')

**2007.** Birds of La Paz. Multicoloured.
1762 4b. Type **602** 2·75 2·40
1763 5b.50 Andean cock-of-the rock (*Rupicola peruviana*) (inscr "Tunqui") (horiz) 3·00 2·75

**603** Robert Baden Powell (founder)

**2007.** Centenary of World Scouting. Multicoloured.
1764 7b.50 Type **603** 4·25 3·50
1765 8b.50 Emblem (vert) 4·75 4·00

**604** *Cyclarhis guyannensis*

**2007.** Birds. Multicoloured.
1766 3b.50 Type **604** 2·75 2·30
1767 4b. *Egretta alba* (vert) 2·75 2·40
1767a 5b.50 *Ramphastos toco* 3·00 2·75
1769 6b.50 *Bubo virgianus* (vert) 3·50 3·00
1770 6b.50 *Trogon melanurus* (vert) 3·50 3·00
1771 6b.50 *Falco sparverius* 3·50 3·00
1772 6b.50 *Hymantopus mexicanus* (vert) 3·50 3·00
1774 7b.50 *Platalea ajaja* 4·25 3·50
1774a 7b.50 *Opisthocomus hoazin* 4·25 3·50
1775 8b.50 *Sarcoramphus papa* 4·75 4·00
1776 8b.50 *Momotus momta* 4·75 4·00
1777 9b. *Tinamotis pentlandii* (vert) 5·00 4·25
1778 9b. *Chlorostilbon aureoventris* (vert) 5·00 4·25
1779 10b.50 *Ardea cocoi* (vert) 5·75 5·00

Nos. 1768 and 1773 have been left for stamps not yet received.

**605** Signature

**2007.** 40th Death Anniv of Ernesto (Che) Guevara (resistance fighter). Multicoloured.
1780 30b. Type **605** 22·00 19·00
1781 50b. Images of Che Guevara (vert) 40·00 34·00

**606** North American F-86 Sabres on Runway

**2007.** 50th Anniv of Bolivian Airforce. Multicoloured.
1782 7b.50 Type **606** 4·25 3·50
1783 9b. Aircraft in flight 5·00 4·25

**607** Globe and Aircraft

**2007.** International Day of Civil Aviation. Multicoloured
1784 6b.50 Type **607** 3·50 3·00
1785 8b.50 Map and aircraft 4·75 4·00

**608** School Pupils

**2007.** America. Education for All. Multicoloured.
1786 3b. Type **608** 2·40 2·10
1787 5b. Siembra, siembra no import que otro.....etc 3·00 2·50

1788 6b. Mother and child reading 3·25 2·75
1789 9b. Girl and flowers 5·00 4·25

**609** Syncline, Maragua

**2007.** Tourism. Multicoloured.
1790 2b. Type **609** 1·40 1·20
1791 2b.50 Fescue, Pasto Iro 2·00 1·70
1792 3b.50 Trees in lake 2·75 2·30
1793 5b. Beni river lake 3·00 2·50
1794 5b.50 Manuripi river 3·25 2·75
1795 5b.50 Serranias de Tarija valley 3·25 2·75
1796 5b.50 Zongo valley 3·25 2·75
1797 7b.50 Orthon river 4·25 3·50
1798 7b.50 Tornado in Sajama valley (vert) 4·25 3·50
1799 9b. Bridge over Pilcomayo river 5·00 4·25
1800 9b. Cactus, Isla del Pescador (vert) 5·00 4·25
1801 10b. Chapare river valley 5·50 4·75
1802 10b.50 Salar de Uyuni (world's largest salt flat) 5·75 5·00
1803 10b.50 *Trichocereus camarguensis* 5·75 5·00
1804 20b. Caiman lake 10·00 8·50
1805 30b. Zongo (vert) 12·00 10·50
1806 50b. Plaza Sucre 17·00 14·00
1807 100b. Acoiris waterfall (vert) 22·00 19·00

**610** *Holy Family* (Luca Cambiasso)

**2007.** Christmas. Multicoloured.
1808 3b.50 Type **610** 2·75 2·30
1809 4b. *Adoration of the Shepherds* (Pieter Aersten) 2·75 2·40
1810 6b.50 *The Nativity* (Gregoria Gamarra) 3·50 3·00

**611** Globe as Post Box

**2008.** World Post Day.
1811 **611** 1b. multicoloured 90 75

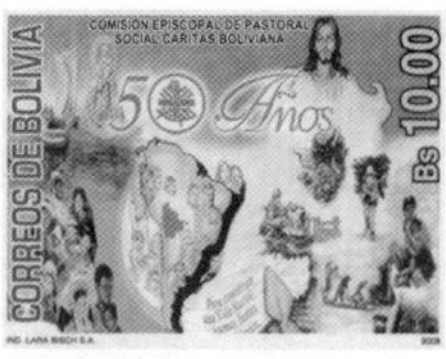

**612** Christ, Map and People

**2008.** 50th Anniv of ECOBOL (Episcopal social welfare commission). Multicoloured.
1812 10b. Type **612** 5·50 4·75
1813 15b. Indigenous inhabitants (vert) 8·25 7·00

**613** Church

**2008.** Jesuit Church, Santa Cruz. Multicoloured.
1814 5b. Type **613** 3·00 2·50
1815 9b. Church, veranda and tower 5·00 4·25

**614** '80' enclosing Emblem

**2008.** 80th Anniv (2007) of Rotary Club, Cochabamba.
1816 **614** 20b. multicoloured 10·00 8·50

**615** Justice and Court Building

**2008.** 150th Anniv (2005) of High Court of Justice.
1817 **615** 20b. multicoloured 10·00 8·50

**616** Centenary Emblem

**2008.** Centenary of 'The Strongest' Football Club. Multicoloured.
1818 1b.50 Type **616** 1·20 1·00
1819 2b.50 Arms 2·00 1·70
1820 5b.50 Model of *Quinteros* 3·25 2·75
1821 6b.50 Founding team 3·50 3·00

**617** Pope Benedict XVI

**2008.** Pope Benedict XVI. Multicoloured.
1822 12b. Type **617** 6·50 5·75
1823 15b. Wearing cope 8·25 7·00

**618** Stadium and Football

**2008.** Football—No Veto for Altitude.
1824 **618** 3b. multicoloured 2·40 2·10

**619** Clock Tower

**2008.** Sucre 2009–Bicentenary of Independence. Multicoloured.
1825 1b.50 Type **619** 1·20 1·00
1826 5b.50 Bell tower 3·25 2·75
1827 7b.50 Clock tower and '25 de Mayo' 4·25 3·50
1828 9b. White tower 5·00 4·25

**620** Emblem

**2008.** 80th Anniv of Supervision of Banks and Financial Institutions. Multicoloured.

1829 3b. Type **620** 2·40 2·10
1830 7b. Building facade (vert) 3·75 3·25

**621** MA 60 in Flight

**2008.** Air Force—Incorporation of MA 60. Multicoloured.

1831 1b.50 Type **621** 1·20 1·00
1832 9b. On ground 5·00 4·25

**622** Luk'i Negra

**2008.** International Year of the Potato. Multicoloured.

1833 1b.50 Type **622** 1·20 1·00
1834 5b.50 Sani Imilla 3·25 2·75
1835 7b.50 Saq'ampaya 4·25 3·50
1836 10b.50 Waych'a 5·75 4·50

**623** Emblem

**2009.** 1st Anniv of Nationalization of ENTEL (telecom company). Multicoloured.

1837 2b. Type **623** 1·10 85
1838 3b. Men and women (horiz) 2·40 2·10

**624** Children and Rainbow

**2009.** 15th Anniv of Fundacion Arcoiris (Rainbow Foundation) (charity for abandoned children).

1839 **624** 5b. multicoloured 2·75 2·20

**625** Building Facade

**2009.** Centenary of Mariscal Sucre National University.

1840 **625** 3b. multicoloured 2·40 2·10

**626** Detainees

**2009.** Freedom for Cuban Five.

1841 **626** 7b.50 multicoloured 4·25 3·50

**627** Children

**2009.** 50th Anniv of Inter-American Development Bank (IDB).

1842 **627** 5b. multicoloured 3·25 2·75

**628** Rebels

**2009.** Bicentenary of Bolivian Liberation.

1843 **628** 2b. multicoloured 1·10 85

**629** Building Facade

**2009.** 80th (2011) Anniv of School for Indigenous Pupils, Warisate.

1844 **629** 2b.50 multicoloured 2·00 1·70

**630** Institute of Bacteriology Building

**2009.** Centenary of National Institute of Health Laboratories (INLASA).

1845 **630** 1b.50 multicoloured 1·20 1·00

**631** Building Facade

**2009.** Centenary of Venezuela National High School.

1846 **631** 3b. multicoloured 2·40 2·10

**632** Palm Tree and Building

**2009.** 50th Anniv of Enrique Lindemann B Educational Unit.

1847 **632** 3b.50 multicoloured 2·50 2·20

**633** Bernardo Guarachi

**2009.** 10th Anniv of Bernardo Guarachi's Ascent of Mount Everest (first Bolivian ascent). Multicoloured.

1848 50c. Type **633** 40 30
1849 7b. Wearing mountain equipment (horiz) 3·75 3·25

**634** Elderly Couple

**2009.** Centenary of San Ramon Nursing Home.

1850 **634** 2b. multicoloured 1·10 85

**635** Games Emblem

**2009.** Sucre 2009. Multicoloured.

1851 1b.50 Type **635** 1·20 1·10
1852 9b. Emblem (different) 4·75 4·50

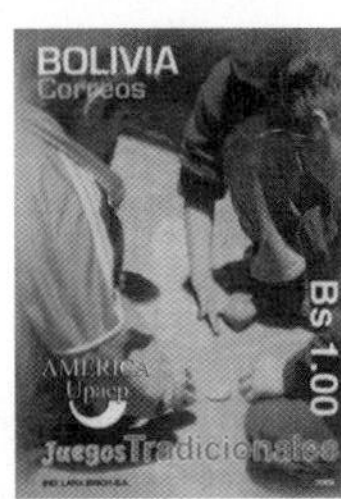


**636** Jacks

**2009.** America. Games. Multicoloured.

1853 1b. Type **636** 80 75
1854 7b. Kite flying 3·75 3·50

**637** Bromeliad

**2009.** 38th Anniv of Philatelic Federation.

1855 **637** 3b.50 multicoloured 2·50 2·20

**638** Holy Family

**2009.** Christmas. Multicoloured.

1856 7b. Type **638** 3·75 3·50
1857 9b. Infant Jesus 4·75 4·50

**639** Pres Evo Morales Ayma

**2010.** Second Term of President Evo Morales Ayma. Multicoloured.

1858 1b.50 Type **639** 80 60
1859 9b. Wearing presidential sash and formal dress 1·40 1·20

**640** Bi-plane (Potez 25 F-AJDZ) and Part of Envelope

**2010.** 80th Anniv of First Aeropostale Flight from the Pyrenees to Andes

1860 **640** 9b. multicoloured 2·00 1·80

**641** Nevado Chacaltaya Glacier showing Ice Shrinkage

**2010.** Global Warming Awareness Campaign. Multicoloured.

1861 2b.50 Type **641** 95 70
1862 10b. Nevado Chacaltaya before ice shrinkage 1·90 1·70

**642** Tupac Katari and Bartolina Sisa

**2010.** Tupac Katari and his Wife, Bartolina Sisa (Aymara anti-colonial rebels) Commemoration

1863 **642** 1b.50 reddish brown 45 30

**643** Pepino

**2010.** Folklore. Multicoloured.

1864 1b. Type **643** 35 20
1865 2b. Moreno 80 60
1866 9b. Chuncho 3·25 2·75
1867 10b. Kusillo 4·00 3·50

**644** Table set with Food for the Dead (All Saints)

**2010.** Traditions. Multicoloured.

1868 1b.50 Type **644** 80 60
1869 10b.50 Ekeko, God of Abundance and Wealth 1·40 1·20

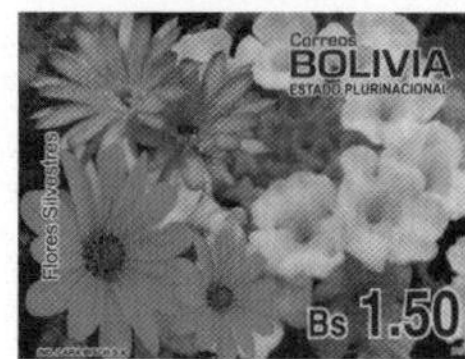

**645** Flowers

**2010.** Flowers. Multicoloured.

| | | | |
|---|---|---|---|
| 1870 | 1b.50 Type **645** | 70 | 50 |
| 1871 | 1b.50 Flowers, butterfly on pink flower at right | 70 | 50 |

Nos. 1870/1 were printed, *se-tenant*, each pair forming a composite design.

**646** Rainer and José Luis Ibsen

**2010.** Rainer Ibsen Cárdenas and José Luis Ibsen Peña (disappeared) Commemoration

| | | | | |
|---|---|---|---|---|
| 1872 | **646** | 3b. multicoloured | 70 | 50 |

**647** Tank, Modern Military Equipment and Soldiers

**2010.** Bicentenary of National Army. Multicoloured.

| | | | |
|---|---|---|---|
| 1873 | 3b.50 Type **647** | 1·30 | 1·00 |
| 1874 | 9b. Personalities and scene from early battle | 3·25 | 2·75 |

**648** Footballer, Cyclist and Games Emblem

**2010.** Youth Olympic Games, Singapore. Multicoloured.

| | | | |
|---|---|---|---|
| 1875 | 2b. Type **648** | 80 | 60 |
| 1876 | 9b. Swimmer, runner and games emblem | 3·25 | 2·75 |

**649** Revolutionary Statue, Cochabamba and Grupo Bicentenario Emblem

**2010.** Bicentenary of Latin American Freedom from Colonialism (1st issue)

| | | | | |
|---|---|---|---|---|
| 1877 | **649** | 9b. multicoloured | 3·25 | 2·75 |

**650** Oxen, Basílica Menor de San Lorenzo, Santa Cruz and Grupo Bicentenario Emblem

**2010.** Bicentenary of Latin American Freedom from Colonialism (2nd issue)

| | | | | |
|---|---|---|---|---|
| 1878 | **650** | 5b. multicoloured | 2·10 | 1·80 |

**651** Andean Condor (national bird)

**2010.** America. Multicoloured.

| | | | |
|---|---|---|---|
| 1879 | 2b.50 Type **651** | 1·30 | 1·00 |
| 1880 | 5b. Patuju (national flower) | 2·00 | 1·80 |

Nos. 1879/80 were printed, *se-tenant*, each pair forming a composite design.

**652** EMI Building

**2010.** 60th Anniv of Military School of Engineering (EMI)

| | | | | |
|---|---|---|---|---|
| 1881 | **652** | multicoloured | 2·60 | 2·40 |

**653** Adult Education

**2010.** 30th Anniv of JICA (Japan International Co-operation Agency) in Bolivia. Multicoloured.

| | | | |
|---|---|---|---|
| 1882 | 1b. Type **653** | 35 | 25 |
| 1883 | 1b.50 Children and teacher | 50 | 30 |
| 1884 | 3b. Drilling for water and children at stand pipe | 1·30 | 1·00 |
| 1885 | 9b. Martial arts class | 3·25 | 2·75 |

**POSTAGE DUE STAMPS**

**D81**

**1931**

| | | | | |
|---|---|---|---|---|
| D265 | **D81** | 5c. blue | 1·60 | 2·30 |
| D266 | **D81** | 10c. red | 1·80 | 2·50 |
| D267 | **D81** | 15c. yellow | 2·75 | 3·50 |
| D268 | **D81** | 30c. green | 2·75 | 3·50 |
| D269 | **D81** | 40c. violet | 4·00 | 5·50 |
| D270 | **D81** | 50c. sepia | 5·75 | 7·00 |

**D93** "Youth"

**1938.** Triangular designs.

| | | | | |
|---|---|---|---|---|
| D346 | **D93** | 5c. red | 75 | 75 |
| D347 | - | 10c. green | 75 | 75 |
| D348 | - | 30c. blue | 75 | 75 |

DESIGNS: 10c. Torch of Knowledge; 30c. Date and Symbol of 17 May 1936 Revolution.

**129** Allegory of "Flight"

**1944**

| | | | | |
|---|---|---|---|---|
| 426 | **129** | 40c. mauve (air) | 20 | 10 |
| 427 | - | 1b. violet | 25 | 10 |
| 428 | - | 1b.50 green | 25 | 10 |
| 429 | - | 2b.50 blue | 65 | 30 |

DESIGN—HORIZ: 1b.50, 2b.50, Lockheed 10 Electra airplane and sun.

Pt. 1

# BOPHUTHATSWANA

The republic of Bophuthatswana was established on 6 December 1977 as one of the "black homelands" constructed from the territory of the Republic of South Africa.

Although this independence did not receive international political recognition we are satisfied that the stamps had "de facto" acceptance as valid for the carriage of mail outside Bophuthatswana.

Bophuthatswana was formally re-incorporated into South Africa on 27 April 1994.

100 cents = 1 rand.

**1** Hand releasing Dove

**1977.** Independence. Multicoloured.

| | | | |
|---|---|---|---|
| 1 | 4c. Type **1** | 35 | 35 |
| 2 | 10c. Leopard (national emblem) | 75 | 60 |
| 3 | 15c. Coat of arms | 1·00 | 1·00 |
| 4 | 20c. National flag | 1·25 | 1·40 |

**2** African Buffalo

**1977.** Tribal Totems. Multicoloured.

| | | | |
|---|---|---|---|
| 5a | 1c. Type **2** | 20 | 15 |
| 6a | 2c. Bush pig | 20 | 15 |
| 7a | 3c. Chacma baboon | 20 | 15 |
| 8a | 4c. Leopard | 20 | 10 |
| 9a | 5c. Crocodile | 20 | 10 |
| 10 | 6c. Savanna monkey | 20 | 10 |
| 11a | 7c. Lion | 30 | 15 |
| 12a | 8c. Spotted hyena | 20 | 15 |
| 13 | 9c. Cape porcupine | 25 | 15 |
| 14 | 10c. Aardvark | 25 | 10 |
| 15 | 15c. Tilapia (fish) | 1·00 | 15 |
| 16 | 20c. Hunting dog | 25 | 20 |
| 17 | 25c. Common duiker | 40 | 30 |
| 18 | 30c. African elephant | 60 | 35 |
| 19 | 50c. Python | 70 | 40 |
| 20 | 1r. Hippopotamus | 1·10 | 1·00 |
| 21 | 2r. Greater kudu | 1·10 | 1·75 |

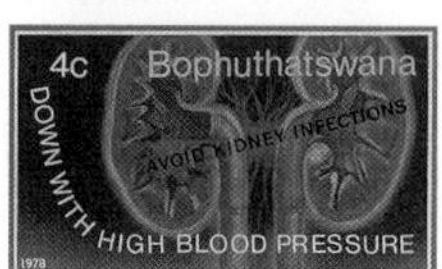

**3** Infected Kidney

**1978.** World Hypertension Month. Multicoloured.

| | | | |
|---|---|---|---|
| 22 | 4c. Type **3** | 50 | 25 |
| 23 | 10c. Heart and spoon of salt | 70 | 70 |
| 24 | 15c. Spoon reflecting skull, knife and fork | 1·25 | 1·25 |

**4** Skull behind Steering Wheel of Car

**1978.** Road Safety. Multicoloured.

| | | | |
|---|---|---|---|
| 25 | 4c. Type **4** | 70 | 40 |
| 26 | 10c. Child knocked off tricycle | 90 | 80 |
| 27 | 15c. Pedestrian stepping in front of car | 1·00 | 1·10 |
| 28 | 20c. Cyclist ignoring stop sign | 1·40 | 1·75 |

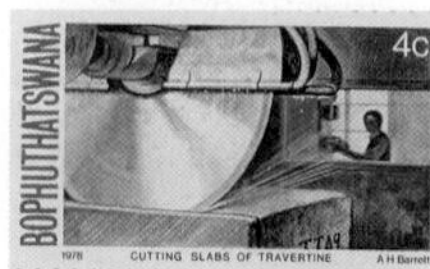

**5** Cutting slabs of Travertine

**1978.** Semi-precious Stones. Multicoloured.

| | | | |
|---|---|---|---|
| 29 | 4c. Type **5** | 65 | 25 |
| 30 | 10c. Polishing travertine | 1·25 | 85 |
| 31 | 15c. Sorting semi-precious stones | 1·50 | 1·25 |
| 32 | 20c. Factory at Taung | 2·25 | 1·60 |

**6** Wright Flyer I

**1978.** 75th Anniv of First Powered Flight by Wright Brothers.

| | | | | |
|---|---|---|---|---|
| 33 | **6** | 10c. black, blue and red | 1·00 | 1·00 |
| 34 | - | 15c. black, blue and red | 1·40 | 1·50 |

DESIGN: 15c. Orville and Wilbur Wright.

**7** Pres. Lucas M. Mangope

**1978.** 1st Anniv of Independence. Multicoloured.

| | | | |
|---|---|---|---|
| 35 | 4c. Type **7** | 25 | 20 |
| 36 | 15c. Full face portrait of President | 75 | 60 |

**8** Drying Germinated Wheat Sorghum

**1978.** Sorghum Beer-making. Multicoloured.

| | | | |
|---|---|---|---|
| 37 | 4c. Type **8** | 25 | 20 |
| 38 | 15c. Cooking the ground grain | 65 | 70 |
| 39 | 20c. Sieving the liquid | 70 | 75 |
| 40 | 25c. Drinking the beer | 80 | 1·00 |

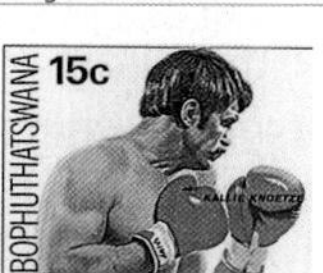

**9** Kallie Knoetze (South Africa)

**1979.** Knoetze–Tate Boxing Match. Multicoloured.

| | | | |
|---|---|---|---|
| 41 | 15c. Type **9** | 75 | 75 |
| 42 | 15c. John Tate (U.S.A.) | 75 | 75 |

**10** Emblem and Drawing of Local Fable (Hendrick Sebapo)

**1979.** International Year of the Child. Children's Drawings of Local Fables. Multicoloured.

| | | | |
|---|---|---|---|
| 43 | 4c. Type **10** | 20 | 20 |
| 44 | 15c. Family with animals (Daisy Morapedi) | 25 | 25 |
| 45 | 20c. Man's head and landscape (Peter Tladi) | 35 | 35 |
| 46 | 25c. Old man, boy and donkey (Hendrick Sebapo) | 45 | 60 |

**11** Miner and Molten Platinum

**1979.** Platinum Industry.

| | | | | |
|---|---|---|---|---|
| 47 | **11** | 4c. multicoloured | 25 | 10 |
| 48 | - | 15c. multicoloured | 35 | 30 |
| 49 | - | 20c. multicoloured | 45 | 45 |
| 50 | - | 25c. black and grey | 60 | 65 |

DESIGNS: 15c. Platinum granules and industrial use; 20c. Telecommunications satellite; 25c. Jewellery.

**12** Cattle

**1979.** Agriculture. Multicoloured.

| | | | |
|---|---|---|---|
| 51 | 5c. Type **12** | 20 | 20 |

| | | | |
|---|---|---|---|
| 52 | 15c. Picking cotton | 25 | 25 |
| 53 | 20c. Scientist examining maize | 30 | 30 |
| 54 | 25c. Catch of fish | 35 | 35 |

**13** Cigarettes forming Cross

**1979.** Anti-smoking Campaign.

| | | | | |
|---|---|---|---|---|
| 55 | **13** | 5c. multicoloured | 40 | 20 |

**14** "Landolphia capensis"

**1980.** Edible Wild Fruits. Multicoloured.

| | | | |
|---|---|---|---|
| 56 | 5c. Type **14** | 15 | 15 |
| 57 | 10c. "Vangueria infausta" | 30 | 30 |
| 58 | 15c. "Bequaertiodendron magalismontanum" | 40 | 40 |
| 59 | 20c. "Sclerocarya caffra" | 55 | 55 |

**15** Pied Babbler

**1980.** Birds. Multicoloured.

| | | | |
|---|---|---|---|
| 60 | 5c. Type **15** | 30 | 20 |
| 61 | 10c. Carmine bee eater | 40 | 35 |
| 62 | 15c. Shaft-tailed whydah | 60 | 60 |
| 63 | 20c. Brown parrot ("Meyer's Parrot") | 70 | 65 |

**16** Sun City Hotel

**1980.** Tourism. Sun City. Multicoloured.

| | | | |
|---|---|---|---|
| 64 | 5c. Type **16** | 10 | 15 |
| 65 | 10c. Gary Player Country Club | 40 | 30 |
| 66 | 15c. Casino | 45 | 50 |
| 67 | 20c. Extravaganza | 50 | 70 |

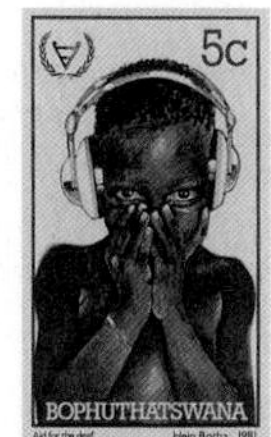


**17** Deaf Child

**1981.** Int Year of Disabled Persons. Mult.

| | | | |
|---|---|---|---|
| 68 | 5c. Type **17** | 15 | 10 |
| 69 | 15c. Blind child | 30 | 20 |
| 70 | 20c. Archer in wheelchair | 45 | 35 |
| 71 | 25c. Tuberculosis X-ray | 60 | 60 |

**18** "Behold the Lamb of God ..."

**1981.** Easter. Multicoloured.

| | | | |
|---|---|---|---|
| 72 | 5c. Type **18** | 10 | 10 |
| 73 | 15c. Bread ("I am the bread of life") | 25 | 25 |
| 74 | 20c. Shepherd ("I am the good shepherd") | 35 | 35 |
| 75 | 25c. Wheatfield ("Unless a grain of wheat falls into the earth and dies ...") | 45 | 45 |

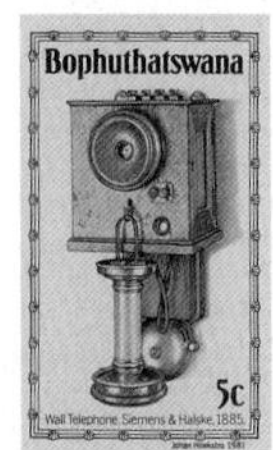


**19** Siemens and Halske Wall Telephone, 1885

**1981.** History of the Telephone (1st series). Multicoloured.

| | | | |
|---|---|---|---|
| 76 | 5c. Type **19** | 10 | 10 |
| 77 | 15c. Ericsson telephone, 1895 | 25 | 25 |
| 78 | 20c. Hasler telephone, 1900 | 35 | 35 |
| 79 | 25c. Mix and Genest wall telephone, 1904 | 45 | 45 |

See also Nos. 92/5, 108/11 and 146/9.

**20** "Themeda triandra"

**1981.** Indigenous Grasses (1st series). Multicoloured.

| | | | |
|---|---|---|---|
| 80 | 5c. Type **20** | 10 | 10 |
| 81 | 15c. "Rhynchelytrum repens" | 20 | 25 |
| 82 | 20c. "Eragrostis capensis" | 20 | 30 |
| 83 | 25c. "Monocymbium ceresii-forme" | 30 | 45 |

See also Nos. 116/19.

**21** Boy Scout

**1982.** 75th Anniv of Boy Scout Movement. Multicoloured.

| | | | |
|---|---|---|---|
| 84 | 5c. Type **21** | 15 | 10 |
| 85 | 15c. Mafeking siege stamps | 35 | 35 |
| 86 | 20c. Original cadet | 40 | 40 |
| 87 | 25c. Lord Baden-Powell | 45 | 45 |

**22** Jesus arriving at Bethany (John 12:1)

**1982.** Easter. Multicoloured.

| | | | |
|---|---|---|---|
| 88 | 15c. Type **22** | 25 | 25 |
| 89 | 20c. Jesus sending disciples for donkey (Matthew 21:1,2) | 30 | 30 |
| 90 | 25c. Disciples taking donkey (Mark 11:5,6) | 40 | 40 |
| 91 | 30c. Disciples with donkey and foal (Matthew 21:7) | 45 | 45 |

**23** Ericsson Telephone, 1878

**1982.** History of the Telephone (2nd series). Multicoloured.

| | | | |
|---|---|---|---|
| 92 | 8c. Type **23** | 15 | 10 |
| 93 | 15c. Ericsson telephone, 1885 | 20 | 20 |
| 94 | 20c. Ericsson telephone, 1893 | 20 | 20 |
| 95 | 25c. Siemens and Halske telephone, 1898 | 30 | 30 |

**24** Old Parliament Building

**1982.** 5th Anniv of Independence. Multicoloured.

| | | | |
|---|---|---|---|
| 96 | 8c. Type **24** | 10 | 10 |
| 97 | 15c. New government offices | 20 | 20 |
| 98 | 20c. University, Mmabatho | 25 | 25 |
| 99 | 25c. Civic Centre, Mmabatho | 30 | 30 |

**25** White Rhinoceros

**1983.** Pilanesberg Nature Reserve. Multicoloured.

| | | | |
|---|---|---|---|
| 100 | 8c. Type **25** | 30 | 10 |
| 101 | 20c. Common zebras | 40 | 30 |
| 102 | 25c. Sable antelope | 40 | 35 |
| 103 | 40c. Hartebeest | 60 | 60 |

**26** Disciples bringing Donkeys to Jesus (Matthew 21:7)

**1983.** Easter. Palm Sunday. Multicoloured.

| | | | |
|---|---|---|---|
| 104 | 8c. Type **26** | 10 | 10 |
| 105 | 20c. Jesus stroking colt (Mark 11:7) | 30 | 30 |
| 106 | 25c. Jesus enters Jerusalem on donkey (Matthew 21:8) | 35 | 35 |
| 107 | 40c. Crowd welcoming Jesus (Mark 11:9) | 60 | 60 |

**1983.** History of the Telephone (3rd series). As T **19** Multicoloured.

| | | | |
|---|---|---|---|
| 108 | 10c. A.T.M. table telephone c. 1920 | 15 | 10 |
| 109 | 20c. A/S Elektrisk wall telephone, c. 1900 | 30 | 30 |
| 110 | 25c. Ericsson wall telephone c. 1900 | 35 | 35 |
| 111 | 40c. Ericsson wall telephone c. 1900 (different) | 60 | 60 |

**27** Kori Bustard

**1983.** Birds of the Veld. Multicoloured.

| | | | |
|---|---|---|---|
| 112 | 10c. Type **27** | 30 | 20 |
| 113 | 20c. Black bustard ("Black Korhaan") | 45 | 45 |
| 114 | 25c. Crested bustard ("Red-crested Korhaan") | 55 | 55 |
| 115 | 40c. Denhan's ("Stanley Bustard") | 70 | 80 |

**1984.** Indigenous Grasses (2nd series). As T **20**. Multicoloured.

| | | | |
|---|---|---|---|
| 116 | 10c. "Panicum maximum" | 15 | 10 |
| 117 | 20c. "Hyparrhenia dregeana" | 20 | 20 |
| 118 | 25c. "Cenchrus ciliaris" | 25 | 35 |
| 119 | 40c. "Urochloa brachyura" | 50 | 70 |

**28** Money-lenders in the Temple (Mark 11:11)

**1984.** Easter. Multicoloured.

| | | | |
|---|---|---|---|
| 120 | 10c. Type **28** | 15 | 10 |
| 121 | 20c. Jesus driving the money-lenders from the Temple (Mark 11:15) | 25 | 20 |
| 122 | 25c. Jesus and fig tree (Matthew 21:9) | 35 | 35 |
| 123 | 40c. The withering of the fig tree (Matthew 21:9) | 60 | 70 |

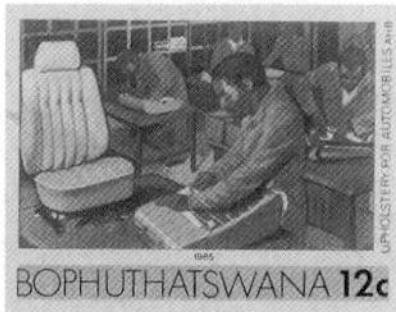


**29** Car Upholstery, Ga-Rankuwa

**1984.** Industries. Multicoloured.

| | | | |
|---|---|---|---|
| 124 | 1c. Textile mill | 10 | 10 |
| 125 | 2c. Sewing sacks, Selosesha | 10 | 10 |
| 126 | 3c. Ceramic tiles, Babelegi | 10 | 10 |
| 127 | 4c. Sheepskin car seat covers | 10 | 10 |
| 128 | 5c. Crossbow manufacture | 15 | 10 |
| 129 | 6c. Automobile parts, Babelegi | 15 | 10 |
| 130 | 7c. Hosiery, Babelegi | 15 | 10 |
| 131 | 8c. Specialised bicycle factory, Babelegi | 30 | 10 |
| 132 | 9c. Lawn mower assembly line | 30 | 15 |
| 133 | 10c. Dress factory, Thaba 'Nchu | 20 | 10 |
| 134 | 11c. Molten platinum | 60 | 20 |
| 135 | 12c. Type **29** | 40 | 15 |
| 136 | 14c. Maize mill, Mafeking | 50 | 15 |
| 137 | 15c. Plastic bags, Babelegi | 25 | 15 |
| 137b | 16c. Brick factory, Mmabatho | 60 | 15 |
| 137c | 18c. Cutlery manufacturing, Mogwase | 60 | 15 |
| 138 | 20c. Men's clothing, Babelegi | 25 | 15 |
| 138b | 21c. Welding bus chassis | 50 | 50 |
| 138c | 21c. Fitting engine to bus chassis | 50 | 50 |
| 138d | 21c. Bus body construction | 50 | 50 |
| 138e | 21c. Spraying and finishing bus | 50 | 50 |
| 138f | 21c. Finished bus | 50 | 50 |
| 139 | 25c. Chromium plating pram parts | 30 | 20 |
| 140 | 30c. Spray painting metal beds | 40 | 25 |
| 141 | 50c. Milk processing plant | 50 | 40 |
| 142 | 1r. Modern printing works | 60 | 75 |
| 143 | 2r. Industrial complex, Babelegi | 1·00 | 2·50 |

**1984.** History of the Telephone (4th series). As T **19.** Multicoloured.

| | | | |
|---|---|---|---|
| 146 | 11c. Schuchhardt table telephone, 1905 | 15 | 10 |
| 147 | 20c. Siemens wall telephone, 1925 | 25 | 20 |
| 148 | 25c. Ericsson table telephone, 1900 | 30 | 30 |
| 149 | 30c. Oki table telephone, 1930 | 40 | 50 |

**30** Yellow-throated Plated Lizard

**1984.** Lizards. Multicoloured.

| | | | |
|---|---|---|---|
| 150 | 11c. Type **30** | 20 | 10 |
| 151 | 25c. Transvaal girdled lizard | 30 | 30 |
| 152 | 30c. Ocellated sand lizard | 35 | 40 |
| 153 | 45c. Bibron's thick-toed gecko | 50 | 60 |

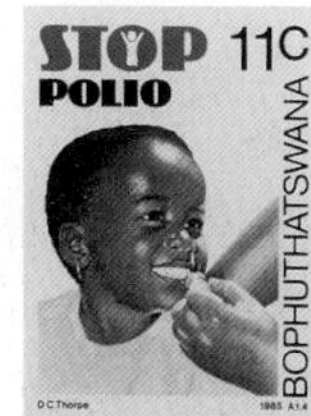


**31** Giving Oral Vaccine against Polio

**1985.** Health. Multicoloured.

| | | | |
|---|---|---|---|
| 154 | 11c. Type **31** | 40 | 10 |
| 155 | 25c. Vaccinating against measles | 50 | 30 |

| | | | |
|---|---|---|---|
| 156 | 30c. Examining child for diphtheria | 55 | 40 |
| 157 | 50c. Examining child for whooping cough | 80 | 90 |

**32** Chief Montshiwa of Barolong booRatshidi

**1985.** Centenary of Mafeking.

| | | | | |
|---|---|---|---|---|
| 158 | 32 | 11c. black, grey and orange | 20 | 10 |
| 159 | - | 25c. black, grey and blue | 40 | 30 |

DESIGN: 25c. Sir Charles Warren.

**33** The Sick flock to Jesus in the Temple (Matthew, 21:41)

**1985.** Easter. Multicoloured.

| | | | |
|---|---|---|---|
| 160 | 12c. Type **33** | 20 | 10 |
| 161 | 25c. Jesus cures the sick (Matthew 21:14) | 30 | 20 |
| 162 | 30c. Children praising Jesus (Matthew 21:15) | 35 | 30 |
| 163 | 50c. Community leaders discussing Jesus's acceptance of praise (Matthew 21:15, 16) | 50 | 60 |

**34** "Faurea saligna" and planting Sapling

**1985.** Tree Conservation. Multicoloured.

| | | | |
|---|---|---|---|
| 164 | 12c. Type **34** | 20 | 10 |
| 165 | 25c. "Boscia albitrunca" and kudu | 25 | 20 |
| 166 | 30c. "Erythrina lysistemon" and mariqua sunbird | 35 | 30 |
| 167 | 50c. "Bequaertiondendron magalismontanum" and bee | 55 | 50 |

**35** Jesus at Mary and Martha's, Bethany (John 12:2)

**1986.** Easter. Multicoloured.

| | | | |
|---|---|---|---|
| 168 | 12c. Type **35** | 25 | 10 |
| 169 | 20c. Mary anointing Jesus's feet (John 12:3) | 30 | 20 |
| 170 | 25c. Mary drying Jesus's feet with her hair (John 12:3) | 35 | 25 |
| 171 | 30c. Disciple condemns Mary for anointing Jesus's head with oil (Matthew 26:7) | 45 | 50 |

**36** "Wesleyan Mission Station and Residence of Moroka, Chief of the Barolong, 1834" (C. D. Bell)

**1986.** Paintings of Thaba 'Nchu. Multicoloured.

| | | | |
|---|---|---|---|
| 172 | 14c. Type **36** | 40 | 15 |
| 173 | 20c. "James Archbell's Congregation, 1834" (Charles Davidson Bell) | 60 | 60 |
| 174 | 25c. "Mission Station at Thaba 'Nchu, 1850" (Thomas Baines) | 65 | 80 |

**37** Farmer using Tractor (agricultural development)

**1986.** Temisano Development Project. Mult.

| | | | |
|---|---|---|---|
| 175 | 14c. Type **37** | 20 | 10 |
| 176 | 20c. Children at school (community development) | 30 | 20 |
| 177 | 25c. Repairing engine (training) | 35 | 30 |
| 178 | 30c. Grain elevator (secondary industries) | 50 | 50 |

**38** Stewardesses and Cessna Citation II

**1986.** "B.O.P." Airways. Multicoloured.

| | | | |
|---|---|---|---|
| 179 | 14c. Type **38** | 25 | 10 |
| 180 | 20c. Passengers disembarking from Boeing 707 | 40 | 20 |
| 181 | 25c. Mmabatho International Airport | 50 | 35 |
| 182 | 30c. Cessna Citation II | 60 | 50 |

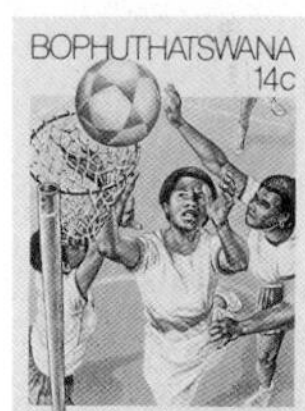


**39** Netball

**1987.** Sports. Multicoloured.

| | | | |
|---|---|---|---|
| 183 | 14c. Type **39** | 20 | 15 |
| 184 | 20c. Tennis | 30 | 30 |
| 185 | 25c. Football | 30 | 30 |
| 186 | 30c. Athletics | 45 | 50 |

**40** "Berkheya zeyheri"

**1987.** Wild Flowers. Multicoloured.

| | | | |
|---|---|---|---|
| 187 | 16c. Type **40** | 25 | 15 |
| 188 | 20c. "Plumbago auriculata" | 35 | 35 |
| 189 | 25c. "Pterodiscus speciosus" | 35 | 35 |
| 190 | 30c. "Gazania krebsiana" | 40 | 50 |

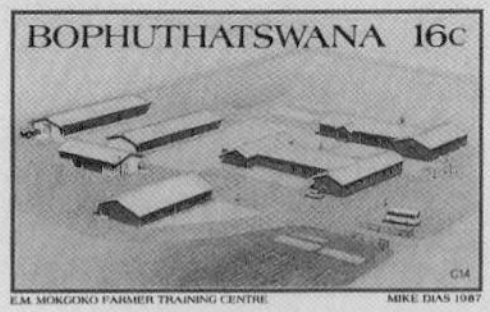


**41** E. M. Mokgoko Farmer Training Centre

**1987.** Tertiary Education. Multicoloured.

| | | | |
|---|---|---|---|
| 191 | 16c. Type **41** | 20 | 15 |
| 192 | 20c. Main lecture block, University of Bophuthatswana | 30 | 35 |
| 193 | 25c. Manpower Centre | 30 | 35 |
| 194 | 30c. Hotel Training School | 30 | 50 |

**42** Posts

**1987.** 10th Anniv of Independence. Communications. Multicoloured.

| | | | |
|---|---|---|---|
| 195 | 16c. Type **42** | 25 | 15 |
| 196 | 30c. Telephone | 35 | 35 |
| 197 | 40c. Radio | 35 | 35 |
| 198 | 50c. Television | 40 | 50 |

**43** Jesus entering Jerusalem on Donkey (John 12:12–14)

**1988.** Easter. Multicoloured.

| | | | |
|---|---|---|---|
| 199 | 16c. Type **43** | 25 | 15 |
| 200 | 30c. Judas negotiating with chief priests (Mark 14:10–11) | 35 | 35 |
| 201 | 40c. Jesus washing the disciples' feet (John 13:5) | 35 | 35 |
| 202 | 50c. Jesus handing bread to Judas (John 13:26) | 40 | 50 |

**44** Environment Education

**1988.** National Parks Board. Multicoloured.

| | | | |
|---|---|---|---|
| 203 | 16c. Type **44** | 25 | 15 |
| 204 | 30c. Rhinoceros (Conservation) | 40 | 40 |
| 205 | 40c. Catering workers | 40 | 40 |
| 206 | 50c. Cheetahs (Tourism) | 55 | 65 |

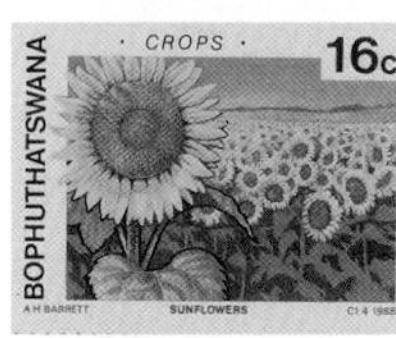


**45** Sunflowers

**1988.** Crops. Multicoloured.

| | | | |
|---|---|---|---|
| 207 | 16c. Type **45** | 25 | 15 |
| 208 | 30c. Peanuts | 35 | 35 |
| 209 | 40c. Cotton | 45 | 45 |
| 210 | 50c. Cabbages | 60 | 60 |

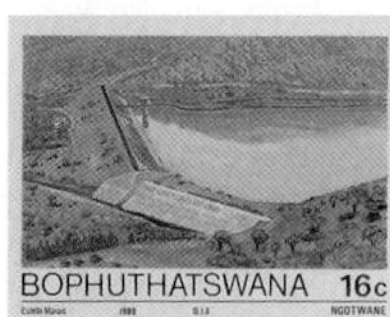


**46** Ngotwane Dam

**1988.** Dams. Multicoloured.

| | | | |
|---|---|---|---|
| 211 | 16c. Type **46** | 30 | 20 |
| 212 | 30c. Groothoek Dam | 50 | 50 |
| 213 | 40c. Sehujwane Dam | 50 | 50 |
| 214 | 50c. Molatedi Dam | 70 | 70 |

**47** The Last Supper (Matthew 26:26)

**1989.** Easter. Multicoloured.

| | | | |
|---|---|---|---|
| 215 | 16c. Type **47** | 40 | 20 |
| 216 | 30c. Jesus praying in Garden of Gethsemane (Matthew 26:39) | 60 | 55 |
| 217 | 40c. Judas kissing Jesus (Mark 14:45) | 70 | 70 |
| 218 | 50c. Peter severing ear of High Priest's slave (John 18:10) | 85 | 1·00 |

**48** Cock (Thembi Atong)

**1989.** Children's Art. Designs depicting winning entries in National Children's Day Art Competition.

| | | | |
|---|---|---|---|
| 219 | 18c. Type **48** | 30 | 20 |
| 220 | 30c. Traditional thatched hut (Muhammad Mahri) | 40 | 40 |
| 221 | 40c. Airplane, telephone wires and houses (Tshepo Mashokwi) | 45 | 45 |
| 222 | 50c. City scene (Miles Brown) | 50 | 60 |

**49** Black-shouldered Kite

**1989.** Birds of Prey. Paintings by Claude Finch-Davies. Multicoloured.

| | | | |
|---|---|---|---|
| 223 | 18c. Type **49** | 1·25 | 30 |
| 224 | 30c. Pale chanting goshawk | 1·40 | 75 |
| 225 | 40c. Lesser kestrel | 1·60 | 1·10 |
| 226 | 50c. Short-toed eagle | 1·75 | 1·50 |

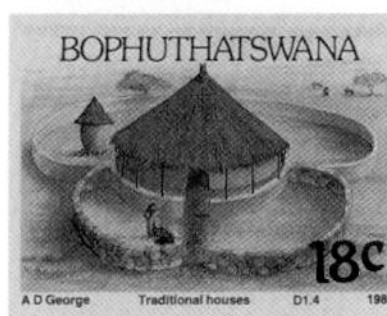


**50** Bilobial House

**1989.** Traditional Houses. Multicoloured.

| | | | |
|---|---|---|---|
| 227 | 18c. Type **50** | 25 | 20 |
| 228 | 30c. House with courtyards at front and side | 35 | 35 |
| 229 | 40c. House with conical roof | 35 | 35 |
| 230 | 50c. House with rounded roof | 40 | 50 |

**51** Early Learning Schemes

**1990.** Community Services. Multicoloured.

| | | | |
|---|---|---|---|
| 231 | 18c. Type **51** | 25 | 20 |
| 232 | 30c. Clinics | 35 | 35 |
| 233 | 40c. Libraries | 35 | 35 |
| 234 | 50c. Hospitals | 40 | 45 |

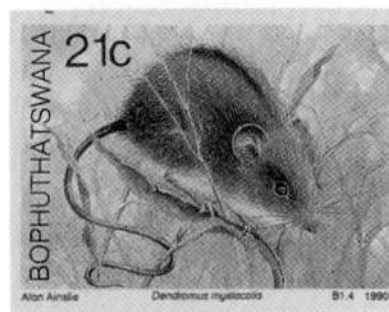


**52** Lesser Climbing Mouse

**1990.** Small Mammals. Multicoloured.

| | | | |
|---|---|---|---|
| 235 | 21c. Type **52** | 30 | 20 |
| 236 | 30c. Zorilla | 40 | 40 |
| 237 | 40c. Transvaal elephant shrew | 60 | 60 |
| 238 | 50c. Large-toothed rock hyrax | 80 | 85 |

**53** Variegated Sandgrouse

**1990.** Sandgrouse. Paintings by Claude Finch-Davies. Multicoloured.

| | | | |
|---|---|---|---|
| 239 | 21c. Type **53** | 90 | 30 |
| 240 | 35c. Double-banded sandgrouse | 1·10 | 75 |
| 241 | 40c. Namaqua sandgrouse | 1·10 | 90 |
| 242 | 50c. Yellow-throated sandgrouse | 1·40 | 1·40 |

**54** Basketry

**1990.** Traditional Crafts. Multicoloured.

| | | | |
|---|---|---|---|
| 243 | 21c. Type **54** | 40 | 20 |
| 244 | 35c. Training | 60 | 60 |
| 245 | 40c. Beer making | 60 | 65 |
| 246 | 50c. Pottery | 65 | 75 |

**55** Sud Aviation SE3130 Alouette II Helicopter

**1990**. Bophuthatswana Air Force. Multicoloured.

| | | | |
|---|---|---|---|
| 247 | 21c. Type **55** | 1·40 | 1·10 |
| 248 | 21c. MBB-Kawasaki BK-117 helicopter | 1·40 | 1·10 |
| 249 | 21c. Pilatus PC-7 turbo trainer | 1·40 | 1·10 |
| 250 | 21c. Pilatus PC-6 | 1·40 | 1·10 |
| 251 | 21c. CASA C-212 Aviocar | 1·40 | 1·10 |

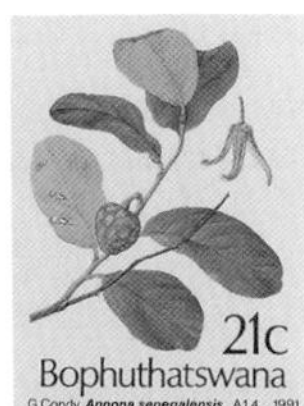


**56** Wild Custard Apple

**1991**. Edible Wild Fruit. Multicoloured.

| | | | |
|---|---|---|---|
| 252 | 21c. Type **56** | 50 | 25 |
| 253 | 35c. Spine-leaved monkey orange | 65 | 70 |
| 254 | 40c. Sycamore fig | 70 | 75 |
| 255 | 50c. Kei apple | 85 | 95 |

**57** Arrest of Jesus (Mark 14:46)

**1991**. Easter. Multicoloured.

| | | | |
|---|---|---|---|
| 256 | 21c. Type **57** | 45 | 25 |
| 257 | 35c. First trial by the Sanhedrin (Mark 14:53) | 60 | 55 |
| 258 | 40c. Assault and derision of Jesus after sentence (Mark 14:65) | 70 | 70 |
| 259 | 50c. Servant girl recognizing Peter (Mark 14:67) | 75 | 90 |

**58** Class 7A Locomotive No. 350, 1897

**1991**. Steam Locomotives. Multicoloured.

| | | | |
|---|---|---|---|
| 260 | 25c. Class 6A locomotive No. 194, 1897, trucks and caboose (71×25 mm) | 95 | 55 |
| 261 | 40c. Type **58** | 1·25 | 85 |
| 262 | 50c. Double-boiler Class 6Z locomotives pulling Cecil Rhodes's funeral train (71×25 mm) | 1·40 | 1·25 |
| 263 | 60c. Class 8 locomotive at Mafeking station, 1904 | 1·50 | 1·75 |

**59** Caneiro Chart, 1502

**1991**. Old Maps (1st series). Multicoloured.

| | | | |
|---|---|---|---|
| 264 | 25c. Type **59** | 1·10 | 40 |
| 265 | 40c. Cantino Chart, 1502 | 1·50 | 95 |
| 266 | 50c. Giovanni Contarini's map, 1506 | 1·75 | 1·40 |
| 267 | 60c. Martin Waldseemuller's map, 1507 | 1·75 | 1·90 |

See also Nos. 268/71 and 297/300.

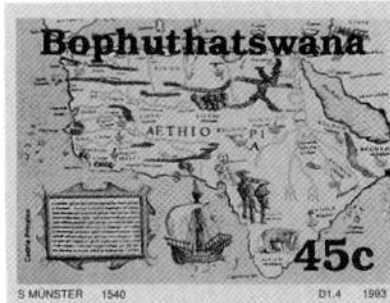


**60** Fracanzano Map, 1508

**1992**. Old Maps (2nd series). Multicoloured.

| | | | |
|---|---|---|---|
| 268 | 27c. Type **60** | 1·10 | 40 |
| 269 | 45c. Martin Waldseemuller's map (from edition of Ptolemy), 1513 | 1·50 | 95 |
| 270 | 65c. Section of Waldseemuller's woodcut "Carta Marina Navigatora Portugallan Navigationes", 1516 | 1·75 | 1·50 |
| 271 | 85c. Map from Laurent Fries's "Geographia", 1522 | 1·75 | 2·00 |

**61** Delivery of Jesus to Pilate (Mark 15:1)

**1992**. Easter. Multicoloured.

| | | | |
|---|---|---|---|
| 272 | 27c. Type **61** | 25 | 20 |
| 273 | 45c. Scourging of Jesus (Mark 15:15) | 40 | 40 |
| 274 | 65c. Placing crown of thorns on Jesus's head (Mark 15:17–18) | 50 | 70 |
| 275 | 85c. Soldiers mocking Jesus (Mark 15:19) | 60 | 90 |

**62** Sweet Thorn

**1992**. Acacia Trees. Multicoloured.

| | | | |
|---|---|---|---|
| 276 | 35c. Type **62** | 30 | 25 |
| 277 | 70c. Camel thorn | 50 | 60 |
| 278 | 90c. Umbrella thorn | 60 | 80 |
| 279 | 1r.05 Black thorn | 70 | 1·00 |

**63** View of Palace across Lake

**1992**. The Lost City Complex, Sun City. Mult.

| | | | |
|---|---|---|---|
| 280 | 35c. Type **63** | 35 | 45 |
| 281 | 35c. Palace facade | 35 | 45 |
| 282 | 35c. Palace porte cochere | 35 | 45 |
| 283 | 35c. Palace lobby | 35 | 45 |
| 284 | 35c. Tusk Bar, Palace | 35 | 45 |

**64** Light Sussex

**1993**. Chickens. Multicoloured.

| | | | |
|---|---|---|---|
| 285 | 35c. Type **64** | 40 | 25 |
| 286 | 70c. Rhode Island red | 55 | 50 |
| 287 | 90c. Brown leghorn | 60 | 80 |
| 288 | 1r.05 White leghorn | 70 | 1·10 |

**65** Pilate offering Release of Barabbas (Luke 23:25)

**1993**. Easter. Multicoloured.

| | | | |
|---|---|---|---|
| 289 | 35c. Type **65** | 60 | 30 |
| 290 | 70c. Jesus falling under cross (John 19:17) | 95 | 75 |
| 291 | 90c. Simon of Cyrene carrying cross (Mark 15:21) | 1·25 | 1·25 |
| 292 | 1r.05 Jesus being nailed to cross (Mark 15:23) | 1·40 | 1·75 |

**66** Mafeking Locomotive Shed, 1933 (image scaled to 64% of original size)

**1993**. Steam Locomotives (2nd series). Multicoloured.

| | | | |
|---|---|---|---|
| 293 | 45c. Type **66** | 65 | 55 |
| 294 | 65c. Rhodesian Railways steam locomotive No. 5, 1901 (34×25 mm) | 75 | 65 |
| 295 | 85c. Class 16B locomotive pulling "White Train" during visit of Prince George, 1934 | 95 | 95 |
| 296 | 1r.05 Class 19D locomotive, 1923 (34×25 mm) | 1·25 | 1·40 |
| **MS**297 | 127×113 mm. Nos. 293/6 | 2·75 | 3·25 |

**67** Sebastian Munster's Map (from edition of Ptolemy), 1540

**1993**. Old Maps (3rd series). Multicoloured.

| | | | |
|---|---|---|---|
| 298 | 45c. Type **67** | 50 | 50 |
| 299 | 65c. Jacopo Gastaldi's map, 1564 | 65 | 65 |
| 300 | 85c. Map from Mercator's "Atlas", 1595 | 75 | 90 |
| 301 | 1r.05 Map from Ortelius's "Theatrum Orbis Terrarum", 1570 | 90 | 1·25 |

**68** Crucifixion (Luke 23:33)

**1994**. Easter. Multicoloured.

| | | | |
|---|---|---|---|
| 302 | 35c. Type **68** | 65 | 45 |
| 303 | 65c. Soldiers and Jews mocking Jesus (Luke 23:35–36) | 95 | 80 |
| 304 | 85c. Soldier offering Jesus vinegar (Luke 23:36) | 1·10 | 1·25 |
| 305 | 1r.05 Jesus on cross and charge notice (Luke 23:38) | 1·60 | 1·75 |

Pt. 2, Pt. 3

# BOSNIA AND HERZEGOVINA

Turkish provinces administered by Austria from 1878 and annexed by her in 1908. In 1928 it became part of Yugoslavia.

In 1992 Bosnia and Herzegovina declared itself independent. Hostilities subsequently broke out between the Croat, Moslem and Serbian inhabitants, which ultimately led to the establishment of three de facto administrations: the mainly Moslem Bosnian government, based in Sarajevo ; the Croats in Mostar; and the Serbian Republic in Pale. Under the Dayton Agreement in November 1995 the Republic was split between a Moslem-Croat Federation and the Serbian Republic.

A. Austro-Hungarian Military Post.
1879. 100 kreuzer = 1 gulden.
1900. 100 heller = 1 krone.
1993. 100 paras = 1 dinar.
2002. 100 cents = 1 euro.

B. Independent Republic.
I. Sarajevo Government.
1993. 100 paras = 1 dinar.
1997. 100 fennig = 1 mark.

II. Croatian Posts.
1993. 100 paras = 1 Croatian dinar.
1994. 100 lipa = 1 kuna.
1999. 100 feninga (f) = 1 marka (m).

Republika Srpska.
1992. 100 paras = 1 dinar.
1998. 100 fennig = 1 mark.

## A. AUSTRO-HUNGARIAN MILITARY POST

1 Value at top

**1879**

| | | | | |
|---|---|---|---|---|
| 106 | 1 | ½k. black | 28·00 | 30·00 |
| 135 | 1 | 1k. grey | 6·50 | 1·50 |
| 136 | 1 | 2k. yellow | 4·00 | 65 |
| 137 | 1 | 3k. green | 6·50 | 1·60 |
| 146 | 1 | 5k. red | 6·50 | 80 |
| 139 | 1 | 10k. blue | 9·25 | 1·20 |
| 140 | 1 | 15k. brown | 8·25 | 4·50 |
| 141 | 1 | 20k. green | 9·00 | 5·25 |
| 142 | 1 | 25k. purple | 10·50 | 8·50 |

2 Value at bottom

**1900**

| | | | | |
|---|---|---|---|---|
| 148 | 2 | 1h. black | 45 | 15 |
| 149 | 2 | 2h. grey | 45 | 15 |
| 151 | 2 | 3h. yellow | 45 | 15 |
| 152 | 2 | 5h. green | 40 | 10 |
| 154 | 2 | 6h. brown | 60 | 20 |
| 155 | 2 | 10h. red | 40 | 10 |
| 156 | 2 | 20h. pink | £225 | 11·00 |
| 158 | 2 | 25h. blue | 1·70 | 40 |
| 160 | 2 | 40h. orange | £325 | 16·00 |
| 161 | 2 | 50h. purple | 1·20 | 80 |
| 173 | 2 | 30h. brown | £325 | 11·00 |

Larger stamps with value in each corner.

| | | | |
|---|---|---|---|
| 162 | 1k. red | 1·50 | 60 |
| 163 | 2k. blue | 2·40 | 1·90 |
| 164 | 5k. green | 5·00 | 5·75 |

**1901.** Black figures of value.

| | | | |
|---|---|---|---|
| 177 | 20h. pink and black | 75 | 55 |
| 178 | 30h. brown and black | 75 | 55 |
| 180 | 35h. blue and black | 1·20 | 85 |
| 181 | 40h. orange and black | 85 | 85 |
| 182 | 45h. turquoise and black | 95 | 85 |

4 View of Doboj

5 In the Carshija (business quarter) Sarajevo

**1906**

| | | | | |
|---|---|---|---|---|
| 186A | 4 | 1h. black | 15 | 15 |
| 187A | - | 2h. violet | 15 | 15 |
| 188A | - | 3h. yellow | 15 | 15 |
| 189A | - | 5h. green | 40 | 10 |
| 190A | - | 6h. brown | 25 | 30 |
| 191A | - | 10h. red | 45 | 10 |
| 192A | - | 20h. brown | 95 | 45 |
| 193A | - | 25h. blue | 2·30 | 1·60 |
| 194A | - | 30h. green | 2·30 | 80 |
| 195A | - | 35h. green | 2·30 | 80 |
| 196A | - | 40h. orange | 2·30 | 80 |
| 197A | - | 45h. red | 2·30 | 1·60 |
| 198A | - | 50h. brown | 2·30 | 1·60 |
| 199A | 5 | 1k. red | 7·00 | 3·75 |
| 200A | - | 2k. green | 7·75 | 16·00 |
| 201A | - | 5k. blue | 6·25 | 9·75 |

DESIGNS—As Type **4**: 2h. Mostar; 3h. The old castle, Jajce; 5h. Naretva pass and Prenz Planina; 6h. Valley of the Rama; 10h. Valley of the Vrbas; 20h. Old Bridge, Mostar; 25h. The Begova Djamia (Bey's Mosque), Sarajevo; 30h. Post by beast of burden; 35h. Village and lake, Jezero; 40h. Mail wagon; 45h. Bazaar at Sarajevo; 50h. Post car. As Type **5**: 2k. St. Luke's Campanile at Jajce; 5k. Emperor Francis Joseph I.

See also Nos. 359/61.

**1910.** 80th Birthday of Francis Joseph I. As stamps of 1906 but with date-label at foot.

| | | | |
|---|---|---|---|
| 343 | 1h. black | 70 | 40 |
| 344 | 2h. violet | 70 | 40 |
| 345 | 3h. yellow | 70 | 40 |
| 346 | 5h. green | 75 | 40 |
| 347 | 6h. brown | 1·00 | 40 |
| 348 | 10h. red | 80 | 15 |
| 349 | 20h. brown | 2·50 | 2·30 |
| 350 | 25h. blue | 4·25 | 3·75 |
| 351 | 30h. green | 4·00 | 3·75 |
| 352 | 35h. green | 4·00 | 3·75 |
| 353 | 40h. orange | 4·00 | 4·50 |
| 354 | 45h. red | 6·00 | 7·25 |
| 355 | 50h. brown | 7·50 | 7·25 |
| 356 | 1k. red | 7·50 | 7·75 |
| 357 | 2k. green | 31·00 | 29·00 |
| 358 | 5k. blue | 3·25 | 9·75 |

**1912.** As T 4 (new values and views).

| | | | |
|---|---|---|---|
| 359 | 12h. blue | 5·50 | 6·50 |
| 360 | 60h. grey | 3·00 | 5·50 |
| 361 | 72h. red | 14·50 | 27·00 |

DESIGNS: 12h. Jajce; 60h. Konjica; 72h. Vishegrad.

25 Francis Joseph I

26 Francis Joseph I

**1912.** Various frames. Nos. 378/82 are larger (27×22 mm).

| | | | | |
|---|---|---|---|---|
| 362 | 25 | 1h. olive | 40 | 15 |
| 363 | 25 | 2h. blue | 40 | 15 |
| 364 | 25 | 3h. lake | 40 | 15 |
| 365 | 25 | 5h. green | 40 | 15 |
| 366 | 25 | 6h. black | 40 | 15 |
| 367 | 25 | 10h. red | 40 | 15 |
| 368 | 25 | 12h. green | 55 | 35 |
| 369 | 25 | 20h. brown | 5·00 | 20 |
| 370 | 25 | 25h. blue | 2·50 | 20 |
| 371 | 25 | 30h. red | 2·50 | 20 |
| 372 | 26 | 35h. green | 2·50 | 20 |
| 373 | 26 | 40h. violet | 8·00 | 20 |
| 374 | 26 | 45h. brown | 5·00 | 35 |
| 375 | 26 | 50h. blue | 3·50 | 20 |
| 376 | 26 | 60h. brown | 2·50 | 20 |
| 377 | 26 | 72h. blue | 5·00 | 5·25 |
| 378 | 25 | 1k. brown on cream | 15·00 | 65 |
| 379 | 25 | 2k. blue on blue | 9·00 | 85 |
| 380 | 26 | 3k. red on green | 12·00 | 11·50 |
| 381 | 26 | 5k. lilac and grey | 25·00 | 29·00 |
| 382 | 26 | 10k. blue on grey | £100 | £130 |

**1914.** Nos. 189 and 191 surch 1914. and new value.

| | | | |
|---|---|---|---|
| 383 | 7h. on 5h. green | 60 | 75 |
| 384 | 12h. on 10h. red | 60 | 75 |

**1915.** Nos. 189 and 191 surch 1915. and new value.

| | | | |
|---|---|---|---|
| 385 | 7h. on 5h. green | 11·00 | 16·00 |
| 386 | 12h. on 10h. red | 40 | 55 |

**1915.** Surch 1915. and new value.

| | | | | |
|---|---|---|---|---|
| 387 | 25 | 7h. on 5h. green | 85 | 1·20 |
| 388 | 25 | 12h. on 10h. red | 1·90 | 3·50 |

**1916.** Surch 1916. and new value.

| | | | |
|---|---|---|---|
| 389 | 7h. on 5h. green | 80 | 80 |
| 390 | 12h. on 10h. red | 80 | 1·00 |

31

**1916.** War Invalids' Fund.

| | | | | |
|---|---|---|---|---|
| 391 | 31 | 5h. (+2h.) green | 1·10 | 1·80 |
| 392 | - | 10h. (+2h.) purple | 1·70 | 2·40 |

DESIGN: 10h. Blind soldier and girl.

See also Nos. 434/5.

33 Francis Joseph I

34 Francis Joseph I

**1916**

| | | | | |
|---|---|---|---|---|
| 393 | 33 | 3h. black | 45 | 35 |
| 394 | 33 | 5h. olive | 60 | 60 |
| 395 | 33 | 6h. violet | 60 | 60 |
| 396 | 33 | 10h. bistre | 2·50 | 3·00 |
| 397 | 33 | 12h. grey | 75 | 95 |
| 398 | 33 | 15h. red | 50 | 25 |
| 399 | 33 | 20h. brown | 90 | 95 |
| 400 | 33 | 25h. blue | 80 | 95 |
| 401 | 33 | 30h. green | 80 | 95 |
| 402 | 33 | 40h. red | 80 | 95 |
| 403 | 33 | 50h. green | 80 | 95 |
| 404 | 33 | 60h. lake | 80 | 95 |
| 405 | 33 | 80h. brown | 2·00 | 80 |
| 406 | 33 | 90h. purple | 2·00 | 1·40 |
| 407 | 34 | 2k. red on yellow | 1·20 | 2·75 |
| 408 | 34 | 3k. green on blue | 1·60 | 4·00 |
| 409 | 34 | 4k. red on green | 7·00 | 16·00 |
| 410 | 34 | 10k. violet on grey | 28·00 | 38·00 |

**1917.** War Widows' Fund. Optd WITWEN-UND WAISENWOCHE 1917.

| | | | | |
|---|---|---|---|---|
| 411 | 33 | 10h. (+2h.) bistre | 25 | 35 |
| 412 | 33 | 15h. (+2h.) pink | 25 | 35 |

36 Design for Memorial Church, Sarajevo

**1917.** Assassination of Archduke Ferdinand. Fund for Memorial Church at Sarajevo.

| | | | | |
|---|---|---|---|---|
| 413 | 36 | 10h. (+2h.) black | 25 | 40 |
| 414 | - | 15h. (+2h.) red | 25 | 40 |
| 415 | - | 40h. (+2h.) blue | 25 | 40 |

PORTRAITS—HORIZ: 40h. Francis Ferdinand and Sophie. VERT: 15h. Archduke Francis Ferdinand.

39 Emperor Charles

**1917**

| | | | | |
|---|---|---|---|---|
| 416 | 39 | 3h. grey | 40 | 30 |
| 417 | 39 | 5h. olive | 25 | 25 |
| 418 | 39 | 6h. violet | 1·00 | 90 |
| 419 | 39 | 10h. brown | 40 | 15 |
| 420 | 39 | 12h. blue | 1·10 | 90 |
| 421 | 39 | 15h. red | 25 | 15 |
| 422 | 39 | 20h. brown | 50 | 25 |
| 423 | 39 | 25h. blue | 1·60 | 80 |
| 424 | 39 | 30h. green | 70 | 40 |
| 425 | 39 | 40h. bistre | 60 | 40 |
| 426 | 39 | 50h. green | 1·60 | 80 |
| 427 | 39 | 60h. red | 1·60 | 80 |
| 428 | 39 | 80h. blue | 90 | 55 |
| 429 | 39 | 90h. lilac | 2·00 | 1·80 |
| 430 | - | 2k. red on yellow | 1·50 | 80 |
| 431 | - | 3k. green on blue | 21·00 | 29·00 |
| 432 | - | 4k. red on green | 8·00 | 20·00 |
| 433 | - | 10k. violet on grey | 4·00 | 21·00 |

The kronen values are larger (25×25 mm) and with different border.

**1918.** War Invalids' Fund.

| | | | | |
|---|---|---|---|---|
| 434 | | 10h. (+2h.) green (as No. 392) | 1·30 | 1·70 |
| 435 | 31 | 15h. (+2h.) brown | 1·30 | 1·70 |

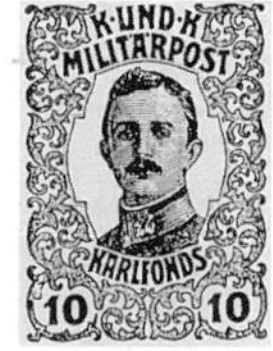

40 Emperor Charles

**1918.** Emperor's Welfare Fund.

| | | | | |
|---|---|---|---|---|
| 436 | 40 | 10h. (+10h.) green | 80 | 1·20 |
| 437 | - | 15h. (+10h.) brown | 80 | 1·20 |
| 438 | 40 | 40h. (+10h.) purple | 80 | 1·20 |

DESIGN—15h. Empress Zita.

**1918.** Optd 1918.

| | | | | |
|---|---|---|---|---|
| 439 | - | 2h. violet (No. 344) | 90 | 2·30 |
| 440 | 25 | 2h. blue | 90 | 1·80 |

## NEWSPAPER STAMPS

N27 Girl in Bosnian Costume

**1913.** Imperf.

| | | | | |
|---|---|---|---|---|
| N383 | N27 | 2h. blue | 65 | 1·10 |
| N384 | N27 | 6h. mauve | 2·30 | 3·50 |
| N385 | N27 | 10h. red | 2·75 | 3·50 |
| N386 | N27 | 20h. green | 3·00 | 3·75 |

For these stamps perforated see Yugoslavia, Nos. 25 to 28.

N35 Mercury

**1916.** For Express.

| | | | | |
|---|---|---|---|---|
| N411 | N35 | 2h. red | 55 | 65 |
| N412 | N35 | 5h. green | 80 | 1·00 |

## POSTAGE DUE STAMPS

D4

**1904.** Imperf. or perf.

| | | | | |
|---|---|---|---|---|
| D183 | D4 | 1h. black, red & yellow | 1·20 | 30 |
| D184 | D4 | 2h. black, red & yellow | 1·20 | 30 |
| D185 | D4 | 3h. black, red & yellow | 1·20 | 30 |
| D186 | D4 | 4h. black, red & yellow | 1·20 | 30 |
| D187 | D4 | 5h. black, red & yellow | 5·75 | 30 |
| D188 | D4 | 6h. black, red & yellow | 1·20 | 30 |
| D189 | D4 | 7h. black, red & yellow | 8·25 | 4·00 |
| D190 | D4 | 8h. black, red & yellow | 8·25 | 1·90 |
| D191 | D4 | 10h. black, red & yellow | 1·60 | 30 |
| D192 | D4 | 15h. black, red & yellow | 1·60 | 30 |
| D193 | D4 | 20h. black, red & yellow | 11·00 | 40 |
| D194 | D4 | 50h. black, red & yellow | 5·50 | 80 |
| D195 | D4 | 200h. black, red & grn | 27·00 | 2·75 |

D35

**1916**

| | | | | |
|---|---|---|---|---|
| D411 | D35 | 2h. red | 60 | 1·20 |
| D412 | D35 | 4h. red | 75 | 1·20 |
| D413 | D35 | 5h. red | 1·20 | 1·20 |
| D414 | D35 | 6h. red | 55 | 1·40 |
| D415 | D35 | 10h. red | 80 | 1·20 |

| | | | | |
|---|---|---|---|---|
| D416 | D35 | 15h. red | 6·25 | 9·00 |
| D417 | D35 | 20h. red | 80 | 1·40 |
| D418 | D35 | 25h. red | 2·75 | 3·50 |
| D419 | D35 | 30h. red | 2·75 | 3·50 |
| D420 | D35 | 40h. red | 31·00 | 22·00 |
| D421 | D35 | 50h. red | 70·00 | 65·00 |
| D422 | D35 | 1k. blue | 4·00 | 11·50 |
| D423 | D35 | 3k. blue | 16·00 | 43·00 |

**B. Independent Republic.**

**I. SARAJEVO GOVERNMENT**

The following issues were used for postal purposes in those areas controlled by the Sarajevo government.

**50** State Arms

**1993.** Imperf.

| | | | | |
|---|---|---|---|---|
| 450 | 50 | 100d. blue, lemon & yellow | 10 | 10 |
| 451 | 50 | 500d. blue, yellow & pink | 15 | 15 |
| 452 | 50 | 1000d. ultramarine, yellow and blue | 20 | 20 |
| 453 | 50 | 5000d. blue, yellow & grn | 85 | 85 |
| 454 | 50 | 10000d. blue, lemon & yell | 1·70 | 1·70 |
| 455 | 50 | 20000d. blue, yellow & bis | 3·25 | 3·25 |
| 456 | 50 | 50000d. blue, yellow & grey | 8·75 | 8·75 |

**51** Games Emblem

**1994.** 10th Anniv of Winter Olympic Games, Sarajevo. Imperf.

| | | | | |
|---|---|---|---|---|
| 457 | 51 | 50000d. black and orange | 1·20 | 1·20 |
| **MS**458 | | 78×65 mm. 100000d. black, orange and lilac; 200000d. black, orange and lilac | 9·75 | 9·75 |

DESIGNS: 45×27 mm—100000d. Four-man bobsleigh; 200000d. Ice hockey.

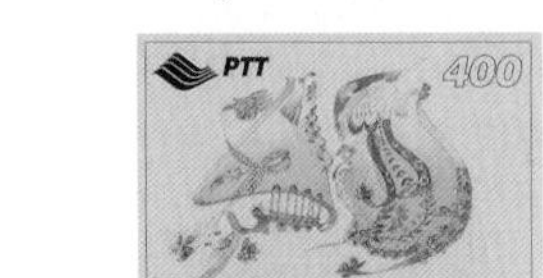

**52** Koran Illustration

**1995.** Bairam Festival. Sheet 105×50 mm containing T 52 and similar horiz design. Multicoloured.

| | | | |
|---|---|---|---|
| **MS**459 | 400d. Type **52**; 600d. Koran illustration (different) | 11·00 | 11·00 |

**53** Facade

**1995.** Sarajevo Head Post Office. Multicoloured.

| | | | |
|---|---|---|---|
| 460 | 10d. Type **53** | 10 | 10 |
| 461 | 20d. Interior | 20 | 20 |
| 462 | 30d. As No. 461 | 25 | 25 |
| 463 | 35d. Before conflict | 35 | 35 |
| 464 | 50d. As No. 463 | 55 | 55 |
| 465 | 100d. Present day | 1·20 | 1·20 |
| 466 | 200d. As No. 465 | 2·40 | 2·40 |

**54** Historical Map, 10th–15th Centuries

**1995.** Bosnian History. Multicoloured.

| | | | |
|---|---|---|---|
| 467 | 35d. Type **54** | 55 | 55 |
| 468 | 100d. 15th-century Bogomil tomb, Oplicici (vert) | 1·30 | 1·30 |
| 469 | 200d. Arms of Kotromanic Dynasty (14th-15th centuries) (vert) | 2·40 | 2·40 |
| 470 | 300d. Charter by Ban Kulin of Bosnia, 1189 | 3·50 | 3·50 |

**55** Postman and Globe

**1995.** World Post Day.

| | | | | |
|---|---|---|---|---|
| 471 | 55 | 100d. multicoloured | 1·10 | 1·10 |

**56** Dove with Olive Branch

**1995.** Europa. Peace and Freedom.

| | | | | |
|---|---|---|---|---|
| 472 | 56 | 200d. multicoloured | 3·50 | 3·50 |

**57** Children and Buildings (A. Softic)

**1995.** Children's Week.

| | | | | |
|---|---|---|---|---|
| 473 | 57 | 100d. multicoloured | 1·40 | 1·40 |

**58** Tramcar, 1895

**1995.** Centenary of Sarajevo Electric Tram System.

| | | | | |
|---|---|---|---|---|
| 474 | 58 | 200d. multicoloured | 2·75 | 2·75 |

**59** "Simphyandra hofmannii"

**1995.** Flowers. Multicoloured.

| | | | |
|---|---|---|---|
| 475 | 100d. Type **59** | 1·60 | 1·60 |
| 476 | 200d. Turk's-head lily | 2·75 | 2·75 |

**60** Dalmatian Barbel Gudgeon

**1995.** Fish. Multicoloured.

| | | | |
|---|---|---|---|
| 477 | 100d. Type **60** | 1·60 | 1·60 |
| 478 | 200d. Adriatic minnow | 2·75 | 2·75 |

**61** Kozija Bridge, Sarajevo

**1995.** Bridges. Multicoloured.

| | | | |
|---|---|---|---|
| 479 | 20d. Type **61** | 20 | 20 |
| 480 | 30d. Arslanagica Bridge, Trebinje | 35 | 35 |
| 481 | 35d. Latinska Bridge, Sarajevo | 45 | 45 |
| 482 | 50d. Old bridge, Mostar | 55 | 55 |
| 483 | 100d. Visegrad | 1·10 | 1·10 |

**62** Visiting Friends

**1995.** Christmas. Multicoloured.

| | | | |
|---|---|---|---|
| 484 | 100d. Type **62** | 1·10 | 1·10 |
| 485 | 200d. Madonna and Child (vert) | 2·20 | 2·20 |

**63** Queen Jelena of Bosnia and Tomb (600th death anniv)

**1995.** Multicoloured.. Multicoloured..

| | | | |
|---|---|---|---|
| 486 | 30d. Type **63** | 35 | 35 |
| 487 | 35d. Husein Kapetan Gradascevic "Dragon of Bosnia" (leader of 1831 uprising against Turkey) | 45 | 45 |
| 488 | 100d. Mirza Safvet Basagic (125th death anniv) (horiz) | 1·10 | 1·10 |

**64** Places of Worship and Graveyards

**1995.** Religious Pluralism.

| | | | | |
|---|---|---|---|---|
| 489 | 64 | 35d. multicoloured | 80 | 80 |

**65** Stadium and Sports

**1995.** Destruction of Olympic Stadium, Sarajevo. Multicoloured.

| | | | |
|---|---|---|---|
| 490 | 35d. Type **65** | 45 | 45 |
| 491 | 100d. Stadium ablaze (vert) | 1·60 | 1·60 |

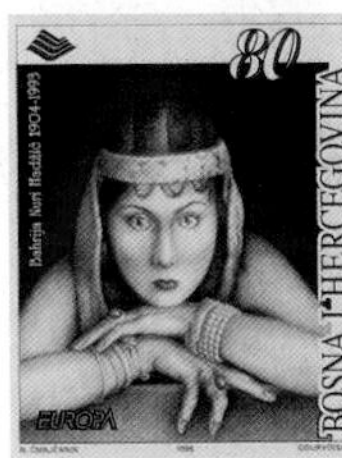

**66** Bahrija Hadzic (opera singer)

**1996.** Europa. Famous Women. Multicoloured.

| | | | |
|---|---|---|---|
| 492 | 80d. Type **66** | 1·30 | 1·30 |
| 493 | 120d. Nasiha Hadzic (children's writer and radio presenter) | 2·00 | 2·00 |

**67** Child's Handprint

**1996.** 50th Anniv of UNICEF. Multicoloured.

| | | | |
|---|---|---|---|
| 494 | 50d. Child stepping on landmine (P. Mirna and K. Princes) | 55 | 55 |
| 495 | 150d. Type **67** | 1·60 | 1·60 |

**68** Bobovac Castle

**1996**

| | | | | |
|---|---|---|---|---|
| 496 | 68 | 35d. black, blue and violet | 60 | 60 |

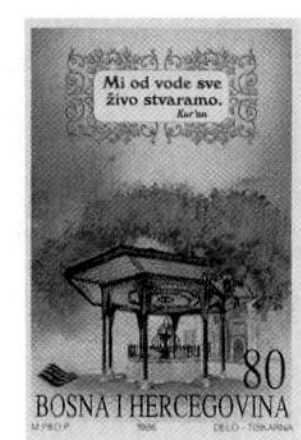

**69** Roofed Fountain and Extract from Holy Koran

**1996.** Bairam Festival.

| | | | | |
|---|---|---|---|---|
| 497 | 69 | 80d. multicoloured | 1·10 | 1·10 |

**70** Town Hall

**1996.** Centenary of Sarajevo Town Hall.

| | | | | |
|---|---|---|---|---|
| 498 | 70 | 80d. multicoloured | 1·10 | 1·10 |

**71** Hands on Computer Keyboard and Title Page of "Bosanki Prijatelj"

**1996.** 150th Anniv of Journalists' Association.

| | | | | |
|---|---|---|---|---|
| 499 | 71 | 100d. multicoloured | 1·30 | 1·30 |

**72** Essen

**1996.** "Essen 96" International Stamp Fair, Essen.

| | | | | |
|---|---|---|---|---|
| 500 | 72 | 200d. multicoloured | 2·50 | 2·50 |

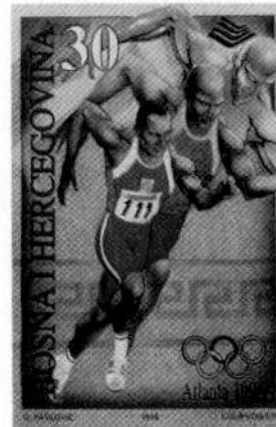

**73** Running

**1996.** Centenary of Modern Olympic Games and Olympic Games, Atlanta. Multicoloured.

| | | | |
|---|---|---|---|
| 501 | 30d. Type **73** | 35 | 35 |
| 502 | 35d. Games emblem | 40 | 40 |
| 503 | 80d. Torch bearer and Olympic flag | 85 | 85 |
| 504 | 120d. Pierre de Coubertin (founder) | 1·30 | 1·30 |

Nos. 501/4 were issued together, se-tenant, with the backgrounds forming a composite design of athletes.

**74** "Campanula hercegovina"

**1996.** Flowers. Multicoloured.

| | | | |
|---|---|---|---|
| 505 | 30d. Type **74** | 40 | 40 |
| 506 | 35d. "Iris bosniaca" | 45 | 45 |

**75** Barak

**1996.** Dogs. Multicoloured.

| | | | |
|---|---|---|---|
| 507 | 35d. Type **75** | 45 | 45 |
| 508 | 80d. Tornjak | 85 | 85 |

**76** Globe, Telephone and Alexander Bell

**1996.** Anniversaries. Multicoloured.

| | | | |
|---|---|---|---|
| 509 | 80d. Type **76** (120th anniv of Bell's invention of telephone) | 1·00 | 1·00 |
| 510 | 120d. 1910 50h. stamp (cent of post car in Bosnia and Herzegovina) | 1·40 | 1·40 |

**77** Charter with Seal

**1996.** Granting of Privileges to Dubrovnik by Ban Stepan II Kotromanic, 1333.

| | | | | |
|---|---|---|---|---|
| 511 | **77** | 100d. multicoloured | 1·20 | 1·20 |

**78** Hot-air Balloons

**1996.** SOS Children's Village, Sarajevo.

| | | | | |
|---|---|---|---|---|
| 512 | **78** | 100d. multicoloured | 1·20 | 1·20 |

**79** Muslim Costume of Bjelasnice

**1996.** Traditional Costumes. Multicoloured.

| | | | |
|---|---|---|---|
| 513 | 50d. Type **79** | 55 | 55 |
| 514 | 80d. Croatian | 1·10 | 1·10 |
| 515 | 100d. Muslim costume of Sarajevo | 1·60 | 1·60 |

**80** Bogomil Soldier

**1996.** Military Uniforms. Multicoloured.

| | | | |
|---|---|---|---|
| 516 | 35d. Type **80** | 45 | 45 |
| 517 | 80d. Austro-Hungarian rifleman | 85 | 85 |
| 518 | 100d. Turkish light cavalryman | 1·10 | 1·10 |
| 519 | 120d. Medieval Bosnian king | 1·40 | 1·40 |

**81** Mosque

**1996.** Winter Festival, Sarajevo.

| | | | | |
|---|---|---|---|---|
| 520 | **81** | 100d. multicoloured | 1·20 | 1·20 |

**82** Map and State Arms

**1996.** Bosnia Day.

| | | | | |
|---|---|---|---|---|
| 521 | **82** | 120d. multicoloured | 1·40 | 1·40 |

**83** Crowd around Baby Jesus

**1996.** Christmas.

| | | | | |
|---|---|---|---|---|
| 522 | **83** | 100d. multicoloured | 1·30 | 1·30 |

**84** Pope John Paul II

**1996.** Papal Visit.

| | | | | |
|---|---|---|---|---|
| 523 | **84** | 500d. multicoloured | 7·25 | 7·25 |

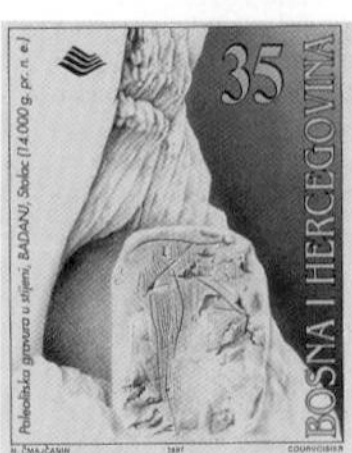

**85** Palaeolithic Rock Carving, Badanj

**1997.** Archaeological Finds. Multicoloured.

| | | | |
|---|---|---|---|
| 524 | 35d. Type **85** | 45 | 45 |
| 525 | 50d. Neolithic ceramic head, Butmir | 65 | 65 |
| 526 | 80d. Bronze Age "birds" wagon, Glasinac | 1·10 | 1·10 |
| **MS**527 | 100×72 mm. 100, 120d. Walls of Illyrian town of Daorson (composite design) | 2·75 | 2·75 |

**86** Ferhad Pasha Mosque, Banja Luka

**1997.** Bairam Festival.

| | | | | |
|---|---|---|---|---|
| 528 | **86** | 200d. multicoloured | 2·50 | 2·50 |

**87** "Clown" (Martina Nokto)

**1997.** Children's Week.

| | | | | |
|---|---|---|---|---|
| 529 | **87** | 100d. multicoloured | 1·20 | 1·20 |

**88** Komadina

**1997.** 72nd Death Anniv of Mujaga Komadina (developer and Mayor of Mostar).

| | | | | |
|---|---|---|---|---|
| 530 | **88** | 100d. multicoloured | 1·20 | 1·20 |

**89** Trojan Warriors and Map

**1997.** Europa. Tales and Legends. Mult.

| | | | |
|---|---|---|---|
| 531 | 100d. Type **89** (theory of Roberto Prays) | 1·60 | 1·60 |
| 532 | 120d. Man on prayer-mat and castle ("The Miraculous Spring of Ajvatovica") | 1·70 | 1·70 |

**90** "Rainbow Warrior"

**1997.** 26th Anniv of Greenpeace (environmental organization). Designs showing the "Rainbow Warrior". Multicoloured.

| | | | |
|---|---|---|---|
| 533 | 35d. Type **90** | 45 | 45 |
| 534 | 80d. inscr "Dorreboom" | 85 | 85 |
| 535 | 100d. inscr "Beltra" | 1·20 | 1·20 |
| 536 | 120d. inscr "Morgan" | 1·40 | 1·40 |

**91** Open Air Cinema, Sarajevo

**1997.** 3rd International Film Festival, Sarajevo.

| | | | | |
|---|---|---|---|---|
| 537 | **91** | 110d. multicoloured | 1·20 | 1·20 |

**92** Games Emblem

**1997.** Mediterranean Games, Bari. Mult.

| | | | |
|---|---|---|---|
| 538 | 40d. Type **92** | 45 | 45 |
| 539 | 130d. Boxing, basketball and kick boxing | 1·40 | 1·40 |

**93** Diagram of Electrons

**1997.** Anniversaries and Event. Mult.

| | | | |
|---|---|---|---|
| 540 | 40d. Type **93** (centenary of discovery of electrons) | 75 | 75 |
| 541 | 110d. Vasco da Gama (navigator) and map (500th anniv of science of navigation) (vert) | 1·60 | 1·60 |
| 542 | 130d. Airmail envelope and airplane (Stamp Day) | 1·80 | 1·80 |
| 543 | 150d. Steam locomotive "Bosna" (125th anniv of railway in Bosnia and Herzegovina) | 2·00 | 2·00 |

**94** Vole

**1997.** Flora and Fauna. Multicoloured.

| | | | |
|---|---|---|---|
| 544 | 40d. Type **94** | 55 | 55 |
| 545 | 40d. "Oxytropis prenja" | 55 | 55 |
| 546 | 80d. Alpine newt | 1·10 | 1·10 |
| 547 | 110d. "Dianthus freynii" | 1·60 | 1·60 |

**95** Map and Flags

**1997.** International Peace Day. Mult.

| | | | |
|---|---|---|---|
| 548 | 50d. Type **95** | 55 | 55 |
| 549 | 60d. Flags and right half of globe showing Europe and Africa | 65 | 65 |
| 550 | 70d. Flags and left half of globe showing the Americas | 75 | 75 |
| 551 | 110d. Map and flags (including U.S.A. and U.K.) | 1·20 | 1·20 |

Nos. 548/51 were issued together, se-tenant, Nos. 549/50 forming a composite design.

**96** House with Attic

**1997.** Architecture. Multicoloured.

| | | | |
|---|---|---|---|
| 552 | 40d. Type **96** | 45 | 45 |
| 553 | 50d. Tiled stove and door | 55 | 55 |
| 554 | 130d. Three-storey house | 1·40 | 1·40 |

**97** Sarajevo in 1697 and 1997

**1997.** 300th Anniv of Great Fire of Sarajevo.

| | | | | |
|---|---|---|---|---|
| 555 | **97** | 110d. multicoloured | 2·40 | 2·40 |

**98** Augustin Tin Ujevic

**1997.** Personalities. Multicoloured.

| | | | |
|---|---|---|---|
| 556 | 1m.30 Type **98** (lyricist and essayist) | 1·30 | 1·30 |
| 557 | 2m. Zaim Imanovic (singer) (vert) | 2·20 | 2·20 |

**99** Sarajevo and Corps Emblem

**1997.** Contribution of Italian Pioneer Corps in Reconstruction of Sarajevo.

| | | | | |
|---|---|---|---|---|
| 558 | **99** | 1m.40 multicoloured | 1·60 | 1·60 |

**100** Diana, Princess of Wales, and Roses

**1997.** Diana, Princess of Wales, Commem.

| | | | | |
|---|---|---|---|---|
| 559 | **100** | 2m.50 multicoloured | 5·50 | 5·50 |

**101** "Gnijezdo" (Fikret Libovac)

**1997.** Art. Multicoloured.

| | | | |
|---|---|---|---|
| 560 | 35f. Type **101** | 35 | 35 |
| 561 | 80f. "Sarajevo Library" (sculpture, Nusret Pasic) | 85 | 85 |

**102** Youth Builders Emblem attached to Route Map

**1997.** 50th Anniv of Samac-Sarajevo Railway.

| | | | | |
|---|---|---|---|---|
| 562 | **102** | 35f. multicoloured | 45 | 45 |

**103** Nativity (icon)

**1997.** Religious Events. Multicoloured.

| | | | |
|---|---|---|---|
| 563 | 50f. Type **103** (Orthodox Christmas) | 65 | 65 |
| 564 | 1m.10 Wreath on door (Christmas) | 1·30 | 1·30 |
| 565 | 1m.10 Pupils before teacher (14th-century miniature) (Haggadah) | 1·30 | 1·30 |

**104** Giant Slalom, Luge, Two-man Bobsleigh and Speed Skating

**1998.** Winter Olympic Games, Nagano, Japan. Sheet 78×60 mm containing T 104 and similar vert design. Multicoloured.

| | | | |
|---|---|---|---|
| **MS**566 | 35f. Type **104**; 1m. Games emblem | 1·60 | 1·60 |

**105** Mosque Fountain

**1998.** Bairam Festival.

| | | | | |
|---|---|---|---|---|
| 567 | **105** | 1m. multicoloured | 1·10 | 1·10 |

**106** Zvornik

**1998.** Old Fortified Towns. Multicoloured.

| | | | |
|---|---|---|---|
| 568 | 35f. Type **106** | 55 | 55 |
| 569 | 70f. Bihac | 1·10 | 1·10 |
| 570 | 1m. Pocitelj | 1·40 | 1·40 |
| 571 | 1m.20 Gradacac | 1·60 | 1·60 |

**107** Muradbegovic

**1998.** Birth Centenary of Ahmed Muradbegovic (dramatist and actor-director).

| | | | | |
|---|---|---|---|---|
| 572 | **107** | 1m.50 multicoloured | 1·60 | 1·60 |

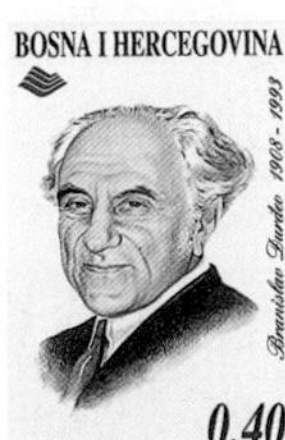

**108** Branislav Djurdjev

**1998.** Former Presidents of the University of Arts and Science. Multicoloured.

| | | | |
|---|---|---|---|
| 573 | 40f. Type **108** | 45 | 45 |
| 574 | 70f. Alojz Benac | 75 | 75 |
| 575 | 1m.30 Edhem Camo | 1·40 | 1·40 |

**109** White Storks

**1998.** Endangered Species. The White Stork. Multicoloured.

| | | | |
|---|---|---|---|
| 576 | 70f. Type **109** | 1·10 | 1·10 |
| 577 | 90f. Two storks flying | 1·40 | 1·40 |
| 578 | 1m.10 Two adult storks on nest | 1·50 | 1·50 |
| 579 | 1m.30 Adult stork with young | 1·60 | 1·60 |

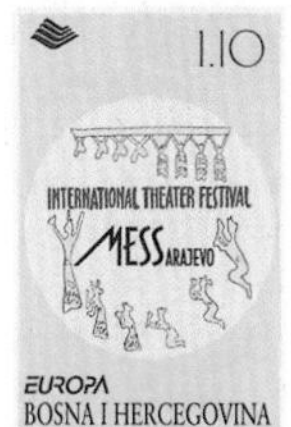

**110** International Theatre Festival, Sarajevo

**1998.** Europa. National Festivals.

| | | | | |
|---|---|---|---|---|
| 580 | **110** | 1m.10 multicoloured | 2·75 | 2·75 |

**111** Footballs

**1998.** World Cup Football Championship, France. Multicoloured.

| | | | |
|---|---|---|---|
| 581 | 50f. Type **111** | 55 | 55 |
| 582 | 1m. Map of Bosnia and ball | 1·10 | 1·10 |
| 583 | 1m.50 Asim Ferhatovic Hase (footballer) | 1·60 | 1·60 |

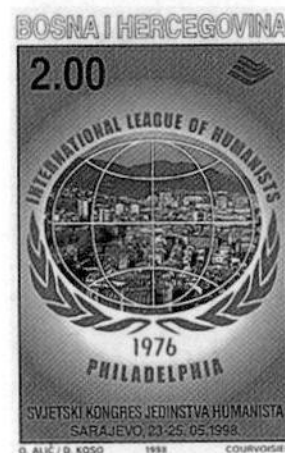

**112** Emblem

**1998.** International League of Humanists World Congress, Sarajevo. Sheet 104×61 mm containing T 112 and two labels.

| | | | |
|---|---|---|---|
| **MS**584 | **112** 2m. multicoloured | 2·20 | 2·20 |

**113** Common Morel

**1998.** Fungi. Multicoloured.

| | | | |
|---|---|---|---|
| 585 | 50f. Type **113** | 55 | 55 |
| 586 | 80f. Chanterelle | 85 | 85 |
| 587 | 1m.10 Edible mushroom | 1·20 | 1·20 |
| 588 | 1m.35 Caesar's mushroom | 1·40 | 1·40 |

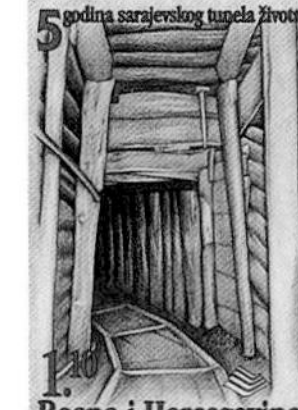

**114** Tunnel

**1998.** 5th Anniv of Sarajevo's Supply Tunnels.

| | | | | |
|---|---|---|---|---|
| 589 | **114** | 1m.10 multicoloured | 1·10 | 1·10 |

**115** Eiffel Tower and Underground Train

**1998.** Paris Metro.

| | | | | |
|---|---|---|---|---|
| 590 | **115** | 2m. multicoloured | 2·20 | 2·20 |

**116** Henri Dunant (founder of Red Cross)

**1998.** Anti-tuberculosis Week.

| | | | | |
|---|---|---|---|---|
| 591 | **116** | 50f. multicoloured | 55 | 55 |

**117** Vesna Misanovic

**1998.** Bosnian and Herzegovina Chess Teams. Sheet 109×88 mm containing T 117 and similar horiz designs. Multicoloured.

| | | | |
|---|---|---|---|
| **MS**592 | 20f. Type **117** (silver medal, tenth European Team championship, Debrecen, 1992); 40f. Men's team (silver medal winners, 31st Chess Olympiad, Moscow, 1994); 60f. Women's team (32nd Chess Olympiad, Yerevan, 1996); 80f. National team (11th European Team championship, Pula, 1997) | 2·20 | 2·20 |

**118** Travnik

**1998.** Old Towns.

| | | | | |
|---|---|---|---|---|
| 593 | **118** | 5f. black and green | 10 | 10 |
| 597 | - | 38f. black and brown | 45 | 45 |

DESIGN: 38f. Sarajevo.

**119** Postal Workers in New Uniforms

**1998.** World Post Day.

| | | | | |
|---|---|---|---|---|
| 605 | **119** | 1m. multicoloured | 1·10 | 1·10 |

**120** Lutes

**1998.** Musical Instruments.
606 **120** 80f. multicoloured 85 85

**121** "The Creation of Adam" (detail of fresco on ceiling of Sistine Chapel, Michelangelo)

**1998.** World Disabled Day.
607 **121** 1m. multicoloured 1·60 1·60

**122** Bjelasnica Mountain Range

**1998**
608 **122** 1m. multicoloured 1·10 1·10

**123** People

**1998.** 50th Anniv of Universal Declaration of Human Rights.
609 **123** 1m.35 multicoloured 1·60 1·60

**124** Christmas Tree (Lamija Pehilj)

**1998.** Christmas and New Year. Multicoloured.
610 1m. Type **124** 1·10 1·10
611 1m.50 Father Andeo Zvizdovic 1·60 1·60

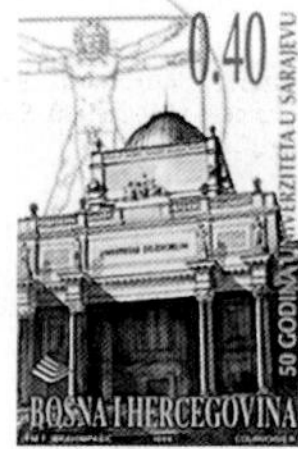


**125** Sarajevo University and "Proportion of Man" (Leonardo da Vinci)

**1999.** Anniversaries. Multicoloured.
612 40f. Type **125** (50th anniv) 45 45
613 40f. Sarajevo High School (120th anniv) (horiz) 45 45

**126** Feral Rock Pigeons

**1999.** Flora and Fauna. Multicoloured.
614 80f. Type **126** 1·10 1·10
615 1m.10 "Knautia sarajevensis" 1·60 1·60

**127** Astronaut, Earth and Moon

**1999.** 30th Anniv of First Manned Moon Landing.
616 **127** 2m. multicoloured 2·20 2·20

**128** Slapovi Une

**1999.** Europa. Parks and Gardens.
617 **128** 2m. multicoloured 3·25 3·25

**129** Gorazde

**1999**
618 **129** 40f. multicoloured 45 45

**130** Children playing Football in Sun (Pranjkovic Nenad)

**1999.** Children's Week.
619 **130** 50f. multicoloured 55 55

**131** House

**1999.** World Environment Day.
620 **131** 80f. multicoloured 85 85

**132** Church, Mosque and Emblem

**1999.** "Philexfrance 99" International Stamp Exhibition, Paris, France.
621 **132** 2m. multicoloured 2·20 2·20

**133** Sarajevo on Stamp

**1999.** 120th Anniv of First Bosnia and Herzegovina Stamps.
622 **133** 1m. multicoloured 1·10 1·10

**134** Letters encircling Globe and Telephones

**1999.** 125th Anniv of Universal Postal Union.
623 **134** 1m.50 multicoloured 1·60 1·60

**135** Tuzlait from Tuoanj

**1999.** Minerals. Multicoloured.
624 40f. Type **135** 45 45
625 60f. Siderit from Vitez 65 65
626 1m.20 Hijelofan from Busovaca 1·30 1·30
627 1m.80 Quartz from Srebrenica (vert) 2·00 2·00

**136** Dove and Cathedral

**1999.** Southern Europe Stability Pact, Sarajevo.
628 **136** 2m. multicoloured 2·20 2·20

**137** Kursum Medresa, Sarajevo, 1537 (site of library)

**1999.** Gazi-Husref Library. Multicoloured.
629 1m. Type **137** 1·10 1·10
630 1m.10 Miniature from Hval Codex, 1404 1·20 1·20

**138** Koran, 1550

**1999**
631 **138** 1m.50 multicoloured 1·60 1·60

**139** X-Ray and Thermal Image of Hands

**1999.** Centenary of Radiology in Bosnia and Herzegovina.
632 **139** 90f. multicoloured 1·00 1·00

**140** Kresevljakovic

**1999.** 40th Death Anniv of Hamdija Kresvljakovic (historian).
633 **140** 1m.30 multicoloured 1·40 1·40

**141** Chess Emblems and Stars

**1999.** 15th European Chess Clubs Championship Final, Bugojno.
634 **141** 1m.10 multicoloured 1·20 1·20

**142** Twipsy (exhibition mascot)

**1999.** "Expo 2000" World's Fair, Hanover, Germany.
635 **142** 1m. multicoloured 1·10 1·10

**143** Painting (Afan Ramic)

**1999**
636 **143** 1m.20 multicoloured 1·30 1·30

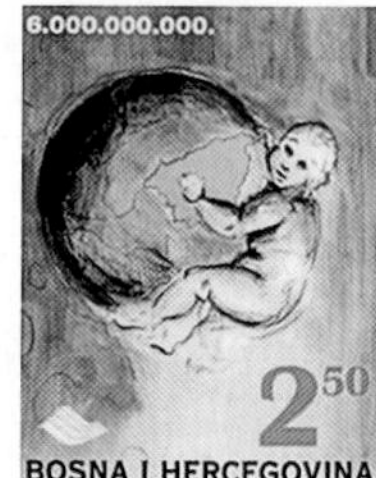


**144** Globe and Baby

**1999.** Birth of World's Six Billionth Inhabitant in Sarajevo.
637 **144** 2m.50 multicoloured 2·75 2·75

**145** Bjelasnica Observatory

**1999.** 105th Anniv of Bjelsnica Meteorological Observatory. Sheet 100×60 mm.
**MS**638 **145** 1m.10 multicoloured 1·20 1·20

**146** Philharmonic Orchestra Building, Sarajevo

**1999.** International Music Festival, Sarajevo.
639 **146** 40f. black and red 45 45
640 - 1m.10 multicoloured 1·20 1·20
DESIGN: 1m.10, Festival poster.

**147** Woman

**2000.** Bairam Festival.
641 **147** 1m.10 multicoloured 1·20 1·20

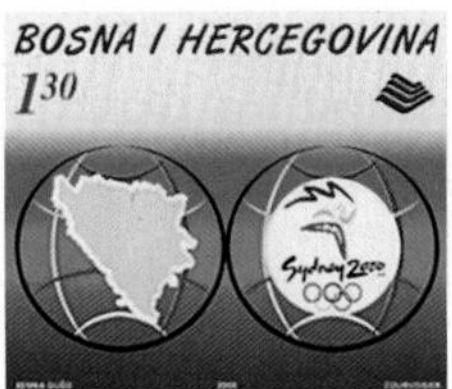

**148** Map of Bosnia and Herzegovina and Emblem

**2000.** Olympic Games, Sydney. Sheet 104×72 mm containing T 148 and similar horiz design. Multicoloured.
**MS**642 1m.30 Type **148**; 1m.70 Map of Australia and stylised sailing boats 3·25 3·25

**149** Spaho

**2000.** 60th (1999) Death Anniv of Mehmed Spaho (politician).
643 **149** 1m. multicoloured 1·10 1·10

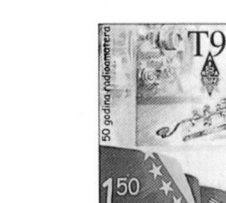

**150** Morse Apparatus

**2000.** 50th Anniv of Amateur Radio in Bosnia and Herzegovina.
644 **150** 1m.50 multicoloured 1·60 1·60

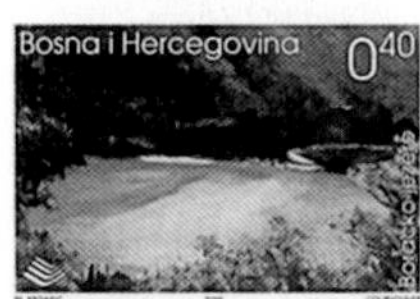

**151** Illuminated Manuscript

**2000.** 50th Anniv of Institute of Oriental Studies, Sarajevo University.
645 **151** 2m. multicoloured 2·20 2·20

**152** Boracko River

**2000.** 15th Anniv of Emerald River Nature Protection Organization. Multicoloured.
646 40f. Type **152** 65 65
647 1m. Figure of woman and river (vert) 1·70 1·70

**153** Scorpionfish

**2000.** Greenpeace (environmental organization). Sheet 100×72 mm containing T 153 and similar horiz design. Multicoloured.
**MS**648 50f. Type **153**; 60f. Crayfish; 90f. Crimson anemone; 1m.50 Wreck of *Rainbow Warrior* (campaign ship) 3·75 3·75

**154** Griffon Vulture

**2000.** Birds. Multicoloured.
649 1m. Type **154** 1·10 1·10
650 1m.50 White spoonbill 1·60 1·60

**155** "Building Europe"

**2000.** Europa.
651 **155** 2m. multicoloured 3·00 3·00

**156** Count Ferdinand von Zeppelin and LZ-1

**2000.** Centenary of 1st Zeppelin Flight.
652 **156** 1m.50 multicoloured 1·60 1·60

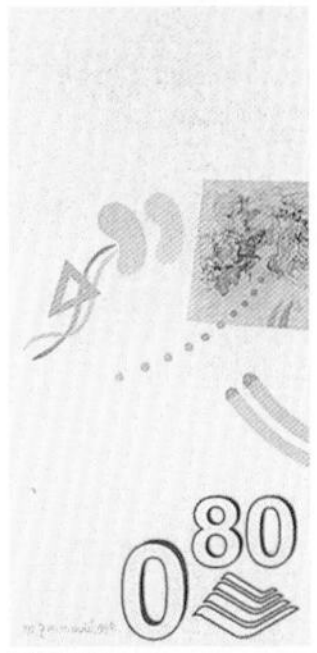

**157** Zenica

**2000.** Towns. Multicoloured.
653 50f. Type **157** 55 55
654 1m. Mostar 1·10 1·10
655 1m.10 Bihac 1·20 1·20
656 1m.50 Tuzla (vert) 1·60 1·60

**158** Millennium

**2000.** New Millennium. Sheet 100×72 mm containing T 158 and similar multicoloured design.
**MS**657 80f. Type **158**; 1m.20, Millennium (57×57 mm) 2·20 2·20

**159** Vranduk

**2000.** Towns. Multicoloured.
658 1m.30 Type **159** 1·50 1·50
659 1m.50 Franciscan Abbey, Kraljeva Sutjeska 1·70 1·70

**160** Tom Sawyer, Huckleberry Finn (characters) and Twain

**2000.** The Adventures of Tom Sawyer (children's book by Mark Twain).
660 **160** 1m.50 multicoloured 1·60 1·60

**161** People walking (Ismet Mujezinovic)

**2000.** Paintings. Multicoloured.
661 60f. Type **161** 65 65
662 80f. Trees (Ivo Seremet) 85 85

**162** Children and Globe

**2000.** International Children's Week.
663 **162** 1m.60 multicoloured 1·70 1·70

**163** Refugees

**2000.** 50th Anniv of United Nations Commissioner for Refugees.
664 **163** 1m. multicoloured 1·10 1·10

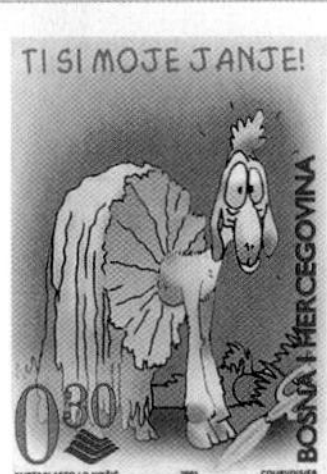

**164** Tesanj

**2001.** Towns. Multicoloured.
665 10f. Type **164** 10 10
666 20f. Bugojno (horiz) 20 20
667 30f. Konjic (horiz) 35 35
668 35f. Zivinice (horiz) 45 45
669 2m. Cazin (horiz) 2·20 2·20

**165** Horse wearing Skirt

**2001.** Thelma (cartoon character). Sheet 125×170 mm containing T 165 and similar vert designs. Multicoloured.
**MS**670 30f. Type **165**; 30f. Bear chased by bees; 30f. Cat and boot; 30f. Thelma wet from watering can; 30f. Roast turkey 1·60 1·60

**166** Kingfisher (*Alcedo athinis*)

**2001.** Fauna. Multicoloured.
671 90f. Type **166** 1·30 1·30
672 1m.10 Bohemian waxwing (*Bombycilla garrulous*) 1·40 1·40
673 1m.10 Serbian work horse (*Equus caballus*) 1·40 1·40
674 1m.90 Head of Serbian horse 2·40 2·40

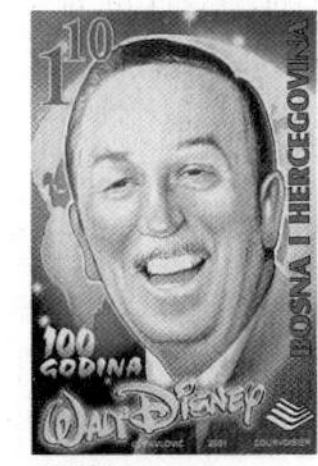

**167** Disney

**2001.** Birth Centenary of Walt Disney (film maker).
675 **167** 1m.10 multicoloured 1·20 1·20

**168** Sea Snail

**2001.** Fossils. Multicoloured.
676 1m.30 Type **168** 1·40 1·40
677 1m.80 Ammonite 1·80 1·80

**169** Land and Sea Sports

**2001.** 14th Mediterranean Games, Tunis.
678 **169** 1m.30 multicoloured 1·40 1·40

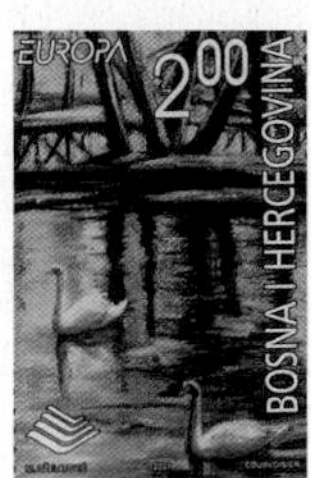

**170** Swans on Lake

**2001.** Europa. Water Resources. Sheet 60×81 mm.
**MS**679 **170** 2m. multicoloured 3·25 3·25

**171** Building

**2001.** Adil Zulfikarpasic Foundation Bosniak Institute (inter-denominational foundation). Sheet 81×50 mm.
**MS**680 **171** 1m.10 multicoloured 1·20 1·20

**172** Balic

**2001.** Emir Balic (bridge diving competition winner). Sheet 66×47 mm.
**MS**681 **172** 2m. multicoloured 2·20 2·20

**173** Ferrari 625 F1 (1954)

**2001.** Ferrari Racing Cars. Multicoloured.

| | | | |
|---|---|---|---|
| 682 | 40f. Type **173** | 45 | 45 |
| 683 | 60f. Ferrari 312 B (1970) | 65 | 65 |
| 684 | 1m.30 Ferrari 312 T3 (1978) | 1·40 | 1·40 |
| 685 | 1m.70 Ferrari 126 C3 (1983) | 1·80 | 1·80 |

**174** Zeljeznicar, Sarajevo Football Team

**2001.** National Football Champions, 2001.

| | | | | |
|---|---|---|---|---|
| 686 | **174** | 1m. multicoloured | 1·20 | 1·20 |

**175** Ink Well, Quill Pen, Medal and Dove

**2001.** Centenary of First Nobel Prize.

| | | | | |
|---|---|---|---|---|
| 687 | **175** | 1m.50 multicoloured | 1·70 | 1·70 |

**176** Charlie Chaplin

**2001.** Charlie Chaplin Commemoration.

| | | | | |
|---|---|---|---|---|
| 688 | **176** | 1m.60 multicoloured | 1·90 | 1·90 |

**177** "Traces" (Edin Numankadic)

**2001.** Art. Multicoloured.

| | | | |
|---|---|---|---|
| 689 | 80f. Type **177** | 1·20 | 1·20 |
| 690 | 2m. David (detail) (sculpture) | 2·30 | 2·30 |

**178** Feeding Bottle enclosed in Stop Sign and Baby at Breast

**2001.** International Breastfeeding Week.

| | | | | |
|---|---|---|---|---|
| 691 | **178** | 1m.10 multicoloured | 1·40 | 1·40 |

**179** Acropolis, Castle and Pyramid

**2001.** United Nations Year of Dialogue Among Civilizations.

| | | | | |
|---|---|---|---|---|
| 692 | **179** | 1m.30 multicoloured | 1·60 | 1·60 |

**180** Horse-drawn Tram

**2001.** Posteurop Plenary, Sarajevo.

| | | | | |
|---|---|---|---|---|
| 693 | **180** | 1m.10 multicoloured | 1·40 | 1·40 |

**181** Alija Bejtic and Monument

**2001.** 20th Death Anniv of Alija Bejtic (cultural historian).

| | | | | |
|---|---|---|---|---|
| 694 | **181** | 80f. multicoloured | 95 | 95 |

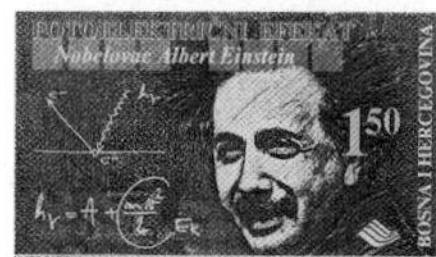


**182** Albert Einstein and Formula

**2001.** 80th Anniv of Albert Einstein's Nobel Prize for Physics (photoelectric effect).

| | | | | |
|---|---|---|---|---|
| 695 | **182** | 1m.50 multicoloured | 1·70 | 1·70 |

**183** Davorin Popovic

**2002.** 1st Death Anniv of Davorin Popovic (musician).

| | | | | |
|---|---|---|---|---|
| 696 | **183** | 38f. multicoloured | 60 | 60 |

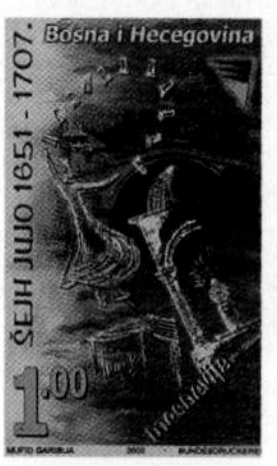


**184** Bridge, Figure and Books

**2002.** 350th Birth Anniv of Mustafa Ejubovic (Sejh Jujo) (writer).

| | | | | |
|---|---|---|---|---|
| 697 | **184** | 1m. multicoloured | 1·20 | 1·20 |

**185** Juraj Neidhardt

**2002.** Birth Centenary (2001) of Juraj Neidhardt (architect).

| | | | | |
|---|---|---|---|---|
| 698 | **185** | 1m. multicoloured | 1·20 | 1·20 |

**186** Sevala Zidzic

**2002.** Birth Centenary (2003) of Sevala Zidzic (first female Bosnian doctor).

| | | | | |
|---|---|---|---|---|
| 699 | **186** | 1m.30 multicoloured | 1·70 | 1·70 |

**187** Skier

**2002.** Sarajevo's Candidacy for Winter Olympic Games, 2010.

| | | | | |
|---|---|---|---|---|
| 700 | **187** | 1m.50 multicoloured | 1·80 | 1·80 |

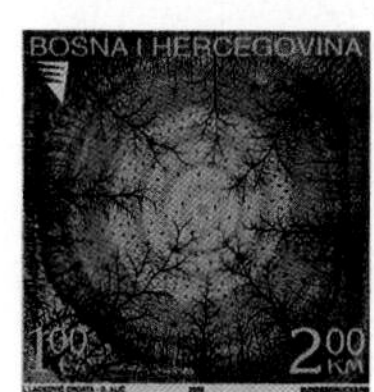


**188** Trees

**2002.** International Earth Day.

| | | | | |
|---|---|---|---|---|
| 701 | **188** | 2m. multicoloured | 2·40 | 2·40 |

**189** Scout Camp

**2002.** 80th Anniv of Bosnian Scouts.

| | | | | |
|---|---|---|---|---|
| 702 | **189** | 1m. multicoloured | 1·20 | 1·20 |

**190** Gentian (*Gentiana dinarica*)

**2002.** Flora. Multicoloured.

| | | | |
|---|---|---|---|
| 703 | 1m. Type **190** | 1·40 | 1·40 |
| 704 | 1m.50 Aquilegia (*Aquilegia dinarica*) | 2·20 | 2·20 |

**191** "War and Peace" (Asad Nuhanovic)

**2002.** 10th Anniv of Independence.

| | | | | |
|---|---|---|---|---|
| 705 | **191** | 2m.50 multicoloured | 3·50 | 3·50 |

**192** Apollo (*Parnassius Apollo*)

**2002.** Butterflies. Multicoloured.

| | | | |
|---|---|---|---|
| 706 | 1m.50 Type **192** | 1·80 | 1·80 |
| 707 | 2m.50 Scarce swallowtail (*Iphiclides podalirius*) | 3·50 | 3·50 |

**193** Firemen fighting Fire

**2002.** 120th Anniv of Sarajevo Fire Brigades. Sheet 68×48 mm.

| | | | | |
|---|---|---|---|---|
| MS708 | **193** | 2m.20 multicoloured | 3·00 | 3·00 |

**194** Clown

**2002.** Europa. Circus.

| | | | | |
|---|---|---|---|---|
| 709 | **194** | 2m.50 multicoloured | 3·50 | 3·50 |

**195** Boy wearing Gag

**2002.** Letter Writing Campaign. Sheet 120×105 mm containing T 195 and similar vert designs showing scenes from "Young Philatelists" (animated film). Multicoloured.

| | | | |
|---|---|---|---|
| MS710 | 40f. Type **195**; 40f. Boy with burnt face; 40f. Boy hit by frying pan; 40f. Boy hit by hammer; 40f. Boy hit with saucepan lids | 3·25 | 3·25 |

**196** Cevapcici (traditional dish)

**2002**

| | | | | |
|---|---|---|---|---|
| 711 | **196** | 1m.10 multicoloured | 1·70 | 1·70 |

**197** Galley

**2002.** Roman Ships. Sheet 90×54 mm containing T 197 and similar horiz design. Multicoloured.

| | | | |
|---|---|---|---|
| MS712 | 1m.20 Type **197**; 1m.80 Galleon | 4·00 | 4·00 |

**198** White Water Rafting

**2002.** 30th Anniv of Una International Regatta.
713 **198** 1m.30 multicoloured 1·90 1·90

**199** Association Emblem

**2002.** Centenary of Napredak (Croatian cultural association).
714 **199** 1m. multicoloured 1·50 1·50

**200** Mountaineer and Hut

**2002.** 110th Anniv of Mountaineering Association.
715 **200** 1m. multicoloured 1·50 1·50

**201** Synagogue

**2002.** Centenary of Ashkenazi Synagogue, Sarajevo.
716 **201** 2m. multicoloured 3·00 3·00

**202** Metal Worker

**2002.** Traditional Crafts. Sheet 110×75 mm containing T 202 and similar horiz designs. Multicoloured.
**MS**717 80f. Type **202**; 1m.10 Leather worker; 1m 20 Filigree jewellery; 1m.30 Lace work 6·50 6·50

**203** Bosnia and Herzegovina Flag

**2002**
718 **203** 1m. multicoloured 1·50 1·50

**204** Coin and Map of Europe

**2002.** "The Euro" (European currency).
719 **204** 2m. multicoloured 3·00 3·00

**205** Tvrtka I Coin (1376-1391)

**2002.** Old Coins.
720 **205** 20f. grey, red and black 25 25
721 - 30f. green, red and black 40 40
722 - 50f. blue, red and black 65 65
DESIGNS: 20f. Type **205**; 30f. Stepana Tomasa coin (1443-1461); 50f. Stepana Tomasevita coin (1461-1463).

**206** Mother and Child Institute, Sarajevo

**2002**
723 **206** 38f. multicoloured 65 65

**207** Horse's Head

**2002.** Art. Multicoloured.
724 40f. Type **207** 65 65
725 1m.10 Portrait of a woman (25×42 mm) 1·70 1·70
726 1m.50 Sculpture and portrait of two women (42×25 mm) 2·30 2·30

**208** Mak Dizdar

**2002.** 85th Birth Anniv of Mak Dizdar (poet).
727 **208** 1m. multicoloured 1·50 1·50

**209** Emaciated Man

**2002.** Anti-Drugs Campaign.
728 **209** 1m. multicoloured 25 25

**210** Josip Stadler

**2003.** 160th Birth Anniv of Josip Stadler (first archbishop).
729 **210** 50f. multicoloured 65 65

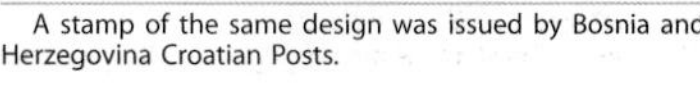

A stamp of the same design was issued by Bosnia and Herzegovina Croatian Posts.

**211** Musician

**2003.** Centenary of Bosnian Cultural Union "Preporod".
730 **211** 1m. multicoloured 1·30 1·30

**212** Stylized Skier

**2003.** European Nordic Skiing Competition, Sarajevo (2006).
731 **212** 1m. multicoloured 1·30 1·30

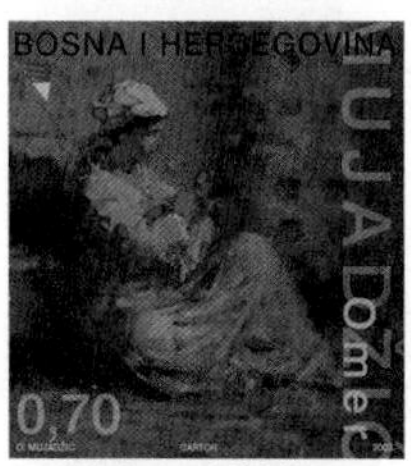


**213** "Mother and Child"

**2003.** Birth Centenary of Omer Mujadzic (artist).
732 **213** 70f. multicoloured 1·10 1·00

**214** Svetozar Zimonjic

**2003.** 75th Birth Anniv of Svetozar Zimonjic (president of Sciences and Arts Academy).
733 **214** 90f. multicoloured 1·30 1·30

**215** Edelweiss (*Leontopodium alpinium*)

**2003.** Flowers. Multicoloured.
734 90f. Type **215** 1·30 1·30
735 90f. Yellow gentian (*Gentiana symphyandra*) 1·30 1·30

**216** Team Members

**2003.** National Volleyball Team—World Champions, 2002.
736 **216** 1m. multicoloured 1·70 1·50

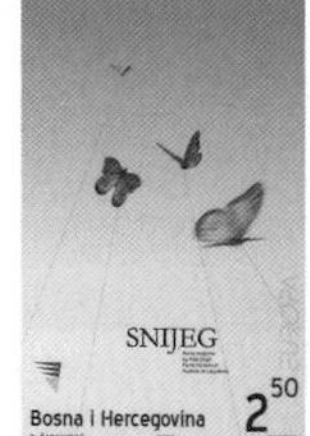


**217** Butterflies

**2003.** Europa. Poster Art.
737 **217** 1m. multicoloured 4·25 3·75

**218** Pope John Paul II and Ivan Merz

**2003.** 2nd Visit of Pope John Paul II.
738 **218** 1m.50 multicoloured 2·50 2·30

A stamp of the same design was issued by Bosnia and Herzegovina Croatian Posts.

**219** Stylized DNA

**2003.** 50th Anniv of the Discovery of DNA (genetic material).
739 **219** 50f. multicoloured 75 65

**220** Man on Rooftop

**2003.** Letter Writing Campaign. Sheet 116×73 mm containing T 220 and similar horiz designs showing scenes from "The Sleep of Monsters" (graphic novel by Enki Bilal). Multicoloured.
**MS**740 50f.×4, Type **220**; Flying taxi; Man and woman (37×25 mm); Faces (37×25 mm) 3·00 2·75

**221** Arches, Cekrelci Muslihudin Mosque

**2003.** Architecture. Multicoloured.
741 1m. Type **221** 2·30 2·30
742 2m. Hajji Sinan Dervish Convent, Sarajevo (30×30 mm) 4·75 4·75

**222** "Skakavac Waterfall" (Helena Skec)

**2003**
743 **222** 1m.50 multicoloured 3·50 3·50

**223** Children

**2003.** Children's Week. Ordinary gum or Self-adhesive gum.
744 **223** 50f. multicoloured 1·00 1·00

**224** Alija Izetbegovic

**2003.** Alija Izetbegovic (first president) Commemoration. Sheet 68×52 mm.
**MS**746 **224** 2m. multicoloured 4·75 4·75

**225** Lamps and Clock

**2003.** 90th Anniv of Post Building, Sarajevo. Sheet 80×65 mm.
**MS**747 **225** 3m. multicoloured 7·00 7·00

**226** Chamois (*Rupicapra rupicapra*)

**2003.** Fauna. Multicoloured.
748 30f. Type **226** 80 80
749 50f. Grizzly bear (*Ursus arctos*) 1·20 1·20

**227** "Plemenitas II" (Dzevad Hozo)

**2003**
750 **227** 10f. multicoloured 1·00 1·00

**228** Sleigh and Hands holding Present

**2003.** Christmas.
751 **228** 20f. multicoloured 1·00 1·00

**229** Orville and Wilbur Wright and Wright *Flyer I*

**2003.** Centenary of Powered Flight.
752 **229** 1m. multicoloured 2·40 2·40

**230** Allegorical Painting

**2003.** 65th Birth Anniv of Ibrahim Ljubovic (artist).
753 **230** 1m.50 multicoloured 3·75 3·75

**231** Bird

**2004.** Bayram Festival.
754 **231** 50f. multicoloured 1·30 1·30

**232** Kulin on Horseback

**2004.** 800th Anniv of Reign of Kulin Ban (king).
755 **232** 50f. multicoloured 1·20 1·20

**233** Aries

**2004.** Western Zodiac. Multicoloured. (a) Self-adhesive.
756 50f. Type **233** 95 95
757 50f. Taurus 95 95
758 50f. Gemini 95 95
759 50f. Cancer 95 95
760 50f. Leo 95 95
761 50f. Virgo 95 95
762 50f. Libra 95 95
763 50f. Scorpio 95 95
764 50f. Sagittarius 95 95
765 50f. Capricorn 95 95
766 50f. Aquarius 95 95
767 50f. Pisces 95 95

(b) Ordinary gum.
**MS**768 200×130 mm. 50f.×12, Nos. 756/67 14·00 14·00

**234** Hearts

**2004.** St. Valentine's Day.
769 **234** 2m. multicoloured 4·75 4·75

**235** Gloved Hand holding Torch

**2004.** 20th Anniv of Winter Olympics, Sarajevo.
770 **235** 1m.50 multicoloured 3·50 3·50

**236** Jajce

**2004.** Towns. Multicoloured.. Multicoloured..
770a 10f. Breko (horiz) 40 40
771 20f. Type **236** 60 60
771a 20f. Livno (horiz) 60 60
771b 30f. Vissoko 80 80
772 50f. Jablanica (horiz) 1·20 1·20
771c 1m. Sanski Most 2·30 2·30
773 2m. Stolac (horiz) 4·75 4·75
774 4m. Gradacac 9·25 9·25
775 5m. Fojinca (horiz) 11·50 11·50

**237** *Cattleya intermedia*

**2004.** Orchids. Multicoloured.
780 1m.50 Type **237** 4·00 4·00
781 2m. *Brassavola* 5·00 5·00

Nos. 780/1 were issued in se-tenant pairs within the sheet and were impregnated with the scent of orchid.

**238** *Aloe barbardensis*

**2004.** Succulents. Multicoloured.
782 1m.50 Type **238** 4·00 4·00
783 2m. *Carnegiea gigantean* 5·00 5·00

**239** Centenary Emblem

**2004.** Centenary of FIFA (Federation Internationale de Football Association).
784 **239** 2m. multicoloured 4·75 4·75

**240** Alarm Clock on Skis

**2004.** Europa. Holidays. Multicoloured.
785 1m. Type **240** 2·30 2·30
786 1m.50 Alarm clocks on beach 3·50 3·50

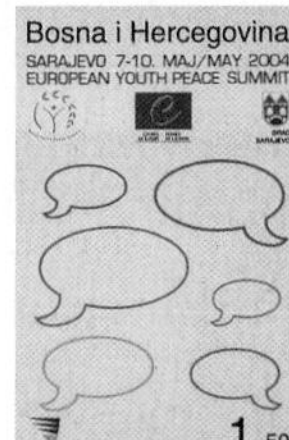

**241** Speech Bubbles

**2004.** European Youth Peace Conference, Sarajevo.
787 **241** 1m.50 multicoloured 3·75 3·75

**242** Clown holding Balloons

**2004.** Greetings Stamps. Multicoloured.
788 50f. Type **242** (birthday) 95 95
789 1m. Bride and bridegroom (wedding) 3·25 3·25

**243** Bee on Flower

**2004.** Bees. Sheet 100×50 mm containing T 243 and similar horiz design. Multicoloured.
**MS**790 2m.×2, Type **243**; Flying bee 8·75 8·75

**244** Old Bridge, Mostar (painting)

**2004.** Reconstruction of Mostar Bridge. Multicoloured.
791 50f. Type **244** 1·20 1·20
792 100f. Bridge (different) 2·30 2·30
**MS**793 287×110 mm. Nos. 791/2 3·50 3·50

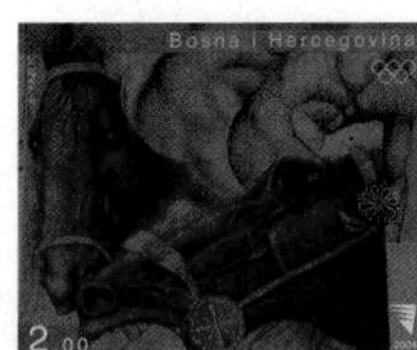

**245** Athlete and Horses' Heads

**2004.** Olympic Games, Athens. Sheet 101×71 mm.
**MS**794 **245** 2m. multicoloured 4·75 4·75

**246** "10" in Lights

**2004.** 10th International Film Festival, Sarajevo.
795 **246** 1m.50 vermilion, yellow and black 3·50 3·50

**247** Abstract

**2004.** New Year.
796 **247** 1m. multicoloured 2·30 2·30

**248** Svrzo House (18th-century Ottoman house)

**2004.** Cultural Heritage. Houses. Multicoloured.
797 1m. Type **248** 2·40 2·40
798 1m. Despic house (Serbian merchant's house) 2·40 2·40

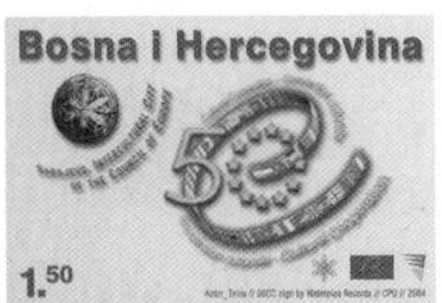

**249** Emblem, "50" and "@"

**2004.** 50th Anniv of European Cultural Convention.
799 **249** 1m.50 multicoloured 3·50 3·50

**250** "Prozori" (window) (Safet Zec)

**2004.** Art.
800 **250** 2m. multicoloured 4·75 4·75

**251** Nikola Sop

**2004.** Birth Centenary of Nikola Sop (writer).
801 **251** 3m. multicoloured 7·00 7·00

**252** Auditorium

**2005.** 50th Anniv of Chamber Theatre 55.
802 **252** 40f. multicoloured 1·00 1·00

**253** Dam

**2005.** 50th Anniv of Jablanica Hydroelectric Power Plant.
803 **253** 60f. multicoloured 1·40 1·40

**254** Electric Tram

**2005.** 110th Anniv of Electrification and First Electric Tram.
804 **254** 2m. multicoloured 4·75 4·75

**255** Izet Sarajlic

**2005.** 75th Birth Anniv of Izet Sarajlic (writer).
805 **255** 1m. multicoloured 2·30 2·30

**256** Hasan Kickic

**2005.** Birth Centenary of Hasan Kickic (writer).
806 **256** 1m.50 multicoloured 3·50 3·50

**257** *Rosa damascene*

**2005.** Roses. Multicoloured.
807 80f. Type **257** 1·60 1·60
808 1m.20 *Rosa alba* 2·30 2·30

**258** Baklava

**2005.** Europa. Gastronomy. Multicoloured.
809 2m. Type **258** 3·50 3·50
810 2m. Sogon Dolma (stuffed onions) 3·50 3·50
**MS**811 115×88 mm. Nos. 809/10 7·00 7·00

The stamps and margin of No. **MS**811 form a composite design of a table laid with food.

**259** Partridge (inscr "Tatro urogallus")

**2005.** Fauna. Multicoloured.
812 2m. Type **259** 3·50 3·50
813 3m. Beaver (*Castor fiber*) 5·25 5·25

**260** Sportsmen

**2005.** Mediterranean Games, Almeria.
814 **260** 1m. multicoloured 1·80 1·80

**261** Composers and Building Facade

**2005.** 50th Anniv of Sarajevo Music Academy.
815 **261** 1m. multicoloured 1·80 1·80

**262** Grieving Women

**2005.** 10th Anniv of Srebrenica Massacre.
816 **262** 1m. multicoloured 1·80 1·80

**263** Sarajevo and Doha

**2005**
817 **263** 2m. multicoloured 3·50 3·50

A stamp of the same design was issued by Qatar.

**264** Emblem and Post Van (EMS)

**2005.** Postal Service. Multicoloured.
818 10f. Type **264** 45 45
819 20f. Emblem and sorter (hybrid mail) 60 60
820 30f. Emblem and "IZBOR JE VAS!" (door to door) 75 75
821 50f. Emblem and pigeons (philately) 1·00 1·00

**265** *Pyrus communis*

**2005.** Fruit. Multicoloured.
822 1m. Type **265** 2·10 2·10
823 1m.50 Orange (inscr "Orange carica") 3·25 3·25
824 2m. *Ficus carica* 4·25 4·25
825 2m.50 *Prunus domestica* 5·25 5·25
826 5m. Cherry (inscr "Prunus avium") 10·50 10·50

**266** Column and Garden (Hakija Kulenovic)

**2005.** Birth Centenary of Hakija Kulenovic (artist).
827 **266** 2m. multicoloured 4·75 4·75

**267** Dogs and Girl

**2005.** Youth Stamps. Sheet 96×72 mm containing T **267** and similar vert design. Multicoloured.
**MS**828 50f.×2, Type **267**; Hedgehog windsurfing 2·40 2·40

**268** Trade Union Building

**2005.** Centenary of Trade Unions.
829 **268** 1m. multicoloured 2·40 2·40

**269** Stylized Buildings

**2005.** Plehan Monastery.
830 **269** 1m. multicoloured 2·40 2·40

**270** Aladza Mosque, Foca

**2005.** Cultural Heritage. Multicoloured.
831 1m. Type **270** 2·40 2·40
832 1m. Zitomislici Monastery 2·40 2·40

**271** King Tvrtko Kotromanic

**2005.** History. Bogomils. Multicoloured.
833 50f. Type **271** 1·20 1·20
834 50f. Kulin Ban 1·20 1·20
835 1m. Burning man (Inquisition) (stone plaque) 2·30 2·30
836 2m. Eugene IV's Papal Bull (1439) 4·75 4·75

**272** Decorated Salon

**2005.** Bosnia Institute. Multicoloured.
837 70f. Type **272** 1·60 1·60
838 4m. Exhibition 9·25 9·25

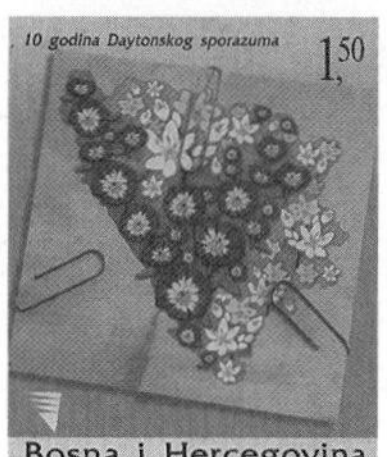

**273** Flowers over map

**2005.** 10th Anniv of Dayton Agreement.
839 **273** 1m.50 multicoloured 3·50 3·50

**274** Emblem

**2005.** 60th Anniv of End of World War II.
840 **274** 1m. multicoloured 2·40 2·40

**275** Members' Flags and Globe (left)

**2005.** 50th Anniv of Europa Stamps. Multicoloured.
841 3m. Type **275** 5·00 5·00
842 3m. Globe (right) and members flags 5·00 5·00
843 3m. Euro coin and map of Europe 5·00 5·00
844 3m. Stars and 1999 chess championships emblem 5·00 5·00
**MS**845 104×76 mm. Nos. 841/4 19·00 19·00

Nos. 841/2 were issued together, se-tenant, forming a composite design.

**276** Faces

**2005.** World Vision. People with Special Needs Week.
846 **276** 50f. multicoloured 1·60 1·60

**277** Slalom Skier

**2006.** Winter Olympic Games, Turin. Sheet 88×77 mm containing T 277 and similar horiz design. Multicoloured.
**MS**847 1m. Type **277**; 2m. Speed skaters 7·00 7·00

**278** Treskavica Mountains, Trnovo

**2006.** Tourism. Multicoloured.
848 1m. Type **278** 2·30 2·30
849 1m. Rafting, Goradzde (vert) 2·30 2·30

**279** Mercedes Benz 500K Cabriolet B, 1935

**2006.** Cars. Sheet 104×76 mm containing T 279 and similar horiz designs. Multicoloured.
**MS**850 50f.×2 Type **279**; Dodge D11 Graber Cabriolet, 1939; 1m. Mercedes Benz SS Schwarzer, 1929; 2m. Bugatti T 57 Ventoux, 1939 9·50 9·50

**280** Crowd

**2006.** Europa. Integration. Multicoloured.
851 2m. Type **280** 5·00 5·00
852 2m. Crowd (different) 5·00 5·00
**MS**853 115×87 mm. 2m.×2, As Type **280**; As No. 852 16·00 16·00

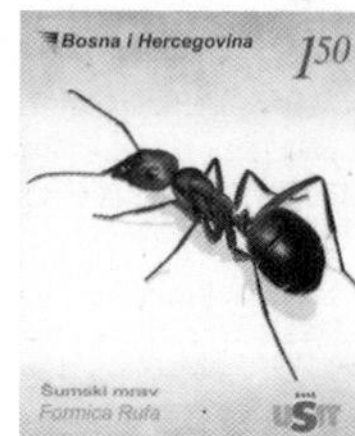

**281** *Formica rufa*

**2006.** Fauna and Flora. Multicoloured.
854 1m.50 Type **281** 3·50 3·50
855 3m. *Sarcosphaera crassa* 7·00 7·00

**282** Prisoners and Barbed Wire

**2006.** Prisoner of War Day.
856 **282** 1m. multicoloured 2·40 2·40

**283** Gallery Facade

**2006.** 60th Anniv of National Art Gallery.
857 **283** 1m. multicoloured 2·40 2·40

**284** Illustration from "Zenidba nosaca Samuela"

**2006.** Isak Samokovlija (writer) Commemoration.
858 **284** 1m. multicoloured 2·40 2·40

**284a** Mohamed Kadic

**2006.** Birth Centenaries. Multicoloured.
858a 1m. Type **284a** 2·40 2·40
858b 1m. Mustafa Kamaric 2·40 2·40

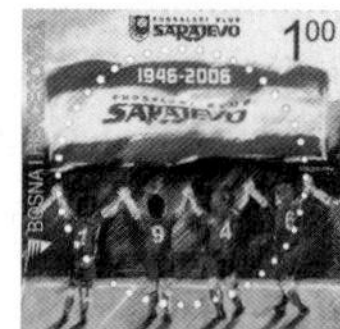

**285** Team Members

**2006.** Football Event and Anniversary. Multicoloured.
859 1m. Type **285** (60th anniv of Sarajevo Football Club) 2·40 2·40
860 3m. Player, globe and flags (World Cup Football Championship, Germany) 7·00 7·00

**286** Potatoes

**2006.** Vegetables. Multicoloured.
861 10f. Type **286** 60 60
862 20f. Cauliflower 80 80
863 30f. Savoy cabbage 95 95
864 40f. Green cabbage 1·20 1·20
865 1m. Carrots 2·50 2·50

**286a** *Lepus europaeus*

**2006.** Fauna. Multicoloured.
866 1m.50 Type **286a** 3·50 3·50
867 2m. *Capreolus capreolus* 4·75 4·75
868 2m.50 *Anas* (mallard) (horiz) 5·75 5·75
869 4m. *Vulpes vulpes* 9·25 9·25
870 5m. *Canis lupus* (horiz) 11·50 11·50

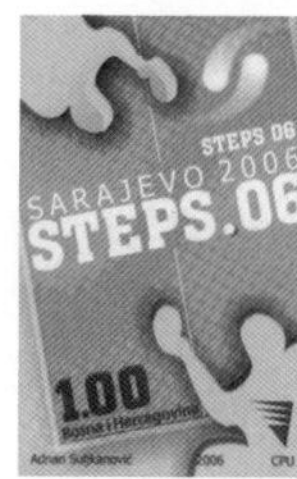

**287** Emblem

**2006.** European Junior Table Tennis Championship.
871 **287** 1m. multicoloured 2·40 2·40

**288** Basilica, Breza

**2006.** Cultural—Historical Heritage. Multicoloured.
872 1m. Type **288** 2·40 2·40
873 1m. Semiz Ali Pasha's Mosque, Praca (vert) 2·40 2·40

**289** Orange Bird

**2006.** Youth Philately. Sheet 115×88 mm containing T 289 and similar vert design. Multicoloured.
**MS**874 50f.×2, Type **289**; Yellow bird 4·75 4·75

**290** Girl

**2006.** Children's Week. Stop Violence against Children Campaign. Self-adhesive.
875 **290** 50f. multicoloured 1·20 1·20

**291** School Building

**2006.** 300th Anniv of Muslim Secondary School, Travnik.
876 **291** 1m. multicoloured 2·40 2·40

**292** Vladimir Prelog (Chemistry, 1975)

**2006.** Nobel Prize Winners. Multicoloured.
877 1m. Type **292** 2·40 2·40
878 2m.50 Iro Andric (Literature, 1961) 5·75 5·75

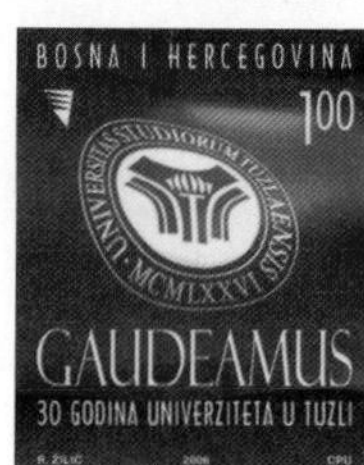

**293** Emblem

**2006.** 30th Anniv of Tuzli University.
879 **293** 1m. multicoloured 2·40 2·40

**294** Museum Exhibits

**2006**
880 **294** 1m. multicoloured 2·40 2·40

**296** Sheep

**295** Steam Locomotive

**2006.** Railways. Multicoloured.
881 50f. Type **295** 1·20 1·20
882 1m. Modern locomotive 2·40 2·40

**2007.** Domestic Animals. Multicoloured.

| | | | |
|---|---|---|---|
| 883 | 10f. Type **296** | 60 | 60 |
| 884 | 20f. Goat | 80 | 80 |
| 885 | 30f. Cow | 95 | 95 |
| 886 | 40f. Donkey | 1·20 | 1·20 |
| 887 | 70f. Horse (42×35 mm) | 1·90 | 1·90 |
| 888 | 1m. Cat (42×35 mm) | 2·40 | 2·40 |

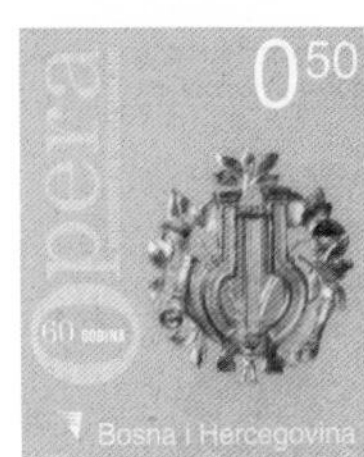


**297** Arms

**2007.** 60th Anniv of National Opera Theatre.

| | | | | |
|---|---|---|---|---|
| 889 | **297** | 50f. multicoloured | 1·30 | 1·30 |

**298** Scouts

**2007.** Europa. Centenary of Scouting. Multicoloured.

| | | | |
|---|---|---|---|
| 890 | 2m. Type **298** | 4·75 | 4·75 |
| 891 | 2m. Scouts by campfire | 4·75 | 4·75 |

**299** Prokos Lake

**2007.** Tourism.

| | | | | |
|---|---|---|---|---|
| 892 | **299** | 2m.50 multicoloured | 6·00 | 6·00 |

**300** *Knautia travnicensis*

**2007.** Fauna and Flora. Multicoloured.

| | | | |
|---|---|---|---|
| 893 | 80f. Type **300** | 1·70 | 1·70 |
| 894 | 1m.20 *Sciurus vulgaris* (horiz) | 3·00 | 3·00 |

**301** Kozarac

**2007.** Tourism.

| | | | | |
|---|---|---|---|---|
| 895 | **301** | 1m. multicoloured | 2·40 | 2·40 |

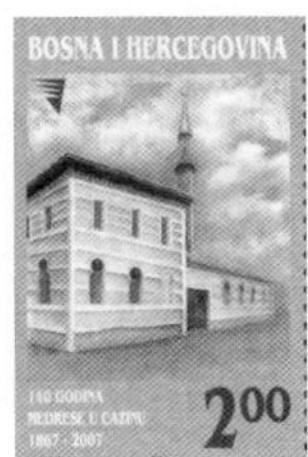


**302** Building Facade

**2007.** 140th Anniv of Cazin Madrasah (Islamic school).

| | | | | |
|---|---|---|---|---|
| 896 | **302** | 2m. multicoloured | 4·75 | 4·75 |

**302a** Fountain, Tuzla

**2007.** Fountains. Multicoloured.

| | | | |
|---|---|---|---|
| 897 | 1m.50 Type **302a** | 3·50 | 3·50 |
| 898 | 2m. Mostar | 4·75 | 4·75 |
| 899 | 2m.50 Sanski Most | 5·75 | 5·75 |
| 900 | 4m. Sebilj, Sarajevo (horiz) | 9·25 | 9·25 |
| 901 | 5m. Fountain, Bey's Mosque | 11·50 | 11·50 |

**303** Masthead

**2007.** Centenary of Gajret Periodical.

| | | | | |
|---|---|---|---|---|
| 902 | **303** | 1m. multicoloured | 2·40 | 2·40 |

**304** Courtyard

**2007.** 30th Anniv of Islamic Science Faculty, Sarajevo.

| | | | | |
|---|---|---|---|---|
| 903 | **304** | 2m. multicoloured | 4·75 | 4·75 |

**305** Front Elevation

**2007.** Gazi Husrev-Begova Library.

| | | | | |
|---|---|---|---|---|
| 904 | **305** | 1m.50 multicoloured | 3·50 | 3·50 |

**306** Landscape (Ismet Rizvic)

**2007.** Art. Multicoloured.

| | | | |
|---|---|---|---|
| 905 | 1m. Pocitelj Visual Art Colony | 2·40 | 2·40 |
| 906 | 1m.50 Type **306** | 3·50 | 3·50 |

**307** '140' and Stylised Building

**2007.** 140th Anniv of Abdulah Nakas Hospital.

| | | | | |
|---|---|---|---|---|
| 907 | **307** | 1m.50 red and silver | 3·50 | 3·50 |

**308** Bear Figurine

**2007.** Museum Exhibit.

| | | | | |
|---|---|---|---|---|
| 908 | **308** | 1m. multicoloured | 2·40 | 2·40 |

**309** Buildings and Karel Parik

**2007.** 150th Birth Anniv of Karel Parik (architect).

| | | | | |
|---|---|---|---|---|
| 909 | **309** | 2m.50 multicoloured | 6·00 | 6·00 |

**310** Combatants

**2007.** Karate.

| | | | | |
|---|---|---|---|---|
| 910 | **310** | 1m. multicoloured | 2·40 | 2·40 |

**311** *Self Portrait* (Zuko Dzumhur)

**2007.** Zuko Dzumhur (artist, writer and caricaturist).

| | | | | |
|---|---|---|---|---|
| 911 | **311** | 1m. multicoloured | 2·40 | 2·40 |

**312** Building Facade

**2007.** 60th Anniv of Medical Faculty of Sarajevo University.

| | | | | |
|---|---|---|---|---|
| 912 | **312** | 1m. multicoloured | 2·40 | 2·40 |

**313** Joseph Blatter

**2007.** Honorary Ambassadors for Sport and Culture of Peace. Multicoloured.

| | | | |
|---|---|---|---|
| 913 | 2m. Type **313** | 4·50 | 4·50 |
| 914 | 2m. Juan Antonio Samaranch (41×27 mm) | 4·50 | 4·50 |

**314** Heart (Amira Halilovic)

**2007.** Ecology. Children's Drawings. Multicoloured.

| | | | |
|---|---|---|---|
| 915 | 50f. Type **314** | 1·30 | 1·30 |
| 916 | 50f. Couple holding globe (Maida Hasanic) | 1·30 | 1·30 |
| **MS**916a | 75×95 mm. Nos. 915/16 | 2·50 | 2·50 |

**315** Fortress, Samobor

**2007.** Cultural Heritage.

| | | | | |
|---|---|---|---|---|
| 917 | **315** | 1m. multicoloured | 2·40 | 2·40 |

**316** Meat Pie

**2007.** Gastronomy.

| | | | | |
|---|---|---|---|---|
| 918 | **316** | 2m. multicoloured | 4·75 | 4·75 |

**317** Stegosaurus

**2007.** Pre-History. Dinosaurs.

| | | | | |
|---|---|---|---|---|
| 919 | **317** | 2m. multicoloured | 5·00 | 5·00 |

**318** Laika

**2007.** 50th Anniv of Space Exploration.

| | | | | |
|---|---|---|---|---|
| 920 | **318** | 3m. multicoloured | 7·00 | 7·00 |

**319** Emblem

**2007.** 60th Anniv of University Sports Association.

| | | | | |
|---|---|---|---|---|
| 921 | **319** | 50f. multicoloured | 1·40 | 1·40 |

**320** Player

**2007.** 60th Anniv of Bosnia Handball Club.

| | | | | |
|---|---|---|---|---|
| 922 | **320** | 50f. multicoloured | 1·30 | 1·30 |

**321** Emblem

**2008.** 95th Anniv of Merhamet (Muslim charitable society).

| | | | | |
|---|---|---|---|---|
| 923 | **321** | 70f. multicoloured | 1·80 | 1·80 |

**321a** College Campus (image scaled to 56% of original size)

**2008.** 35th Anniv of College of Pharmacy.

| | | | | |
|---|---|---|---|---|
| 923a | **321a** | 2m. multicoloured | 4·75 | 4·75 |

**322** Bosanska Krupa

**2008.** Tourism. Multicoloured.

| | | | |
|---|---|---|---|
| 924 | 70f. Type **322** | 4·75 | 4·75 |
| 925 | 1m. Velika Kladusa (horiz) | 7·00 | 7·00 |

**323** Shish-Kebab

**2008.** Gastronomy. Multicoloured.

| | | | |
|---|---|---|---|
| 926 | 1m. Type **323** | 2·40 | 2·40 |
| 927 | 2m. Stuffed apple | 4·75 | 4·75 |

**324** Building Facade

**2008.** 50th Anniv of Blood Transfusion Service.

| | | | | |
|---|---|---|---|---|
| 928 | **324** | 1m.50 multicoloured | 3·50 | 3·50 |

**325** Woman

**2008.** Centenary of International Women's Day.

| | | | | |
|---|---|---|---|---|
| 929 | **325** | 2m. multicoloured | 4·75 | 4·75 |

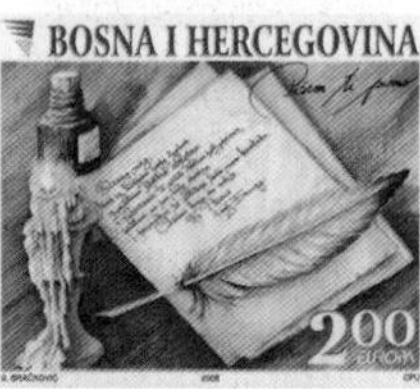
**326** Candle, Quill and Letter

**2008.** Europa. The Letter. Multicoloured.

| | | | |
|---|---|---|---|
| 930 | 2m. Type **326** | 4·75 | 4·75 |
| 931 | 3m. Postcard and hand holding pen | 7·00 | 7·00 |
| **MS**932 | 88×115 mm. Nos. 930/1 | 11·50 | 11·50 |

**327** Emblem

**2008.** Centenary of Esperanto.

| | | | | |
|---|---|---|---|---|
| 933 | **327** | 1m.50 multicoloured | 3·50 | 3·50 |

**328** Anniversary Emblem

**2008.** 60th Anniv of Shooting Club, Sarajevo.

| | | | | |
|---|---|---|---|---|
| 934 | **328** | 1m.50 multicoloured | 3·50 | 3·50 |

**329** Judo

**2008.** Olympic Games, Beijing. Multicoloured.

| | | | |
|---|---|---|---|
| 935 | 1m. Type **329** | 1·80 | 1·80 |
| 936 | 1m.50 Shot put and athletics | 3·50 | 3·50 |

**330** Oural-3 (M-66)

**2008.** Motorcycles. Multicoloured.

| | | | |
|---|---|---|---|
| 937 | 1m.50 Type **330** | 3·50 | 3·50 |
| 938 | 1m.50 Jawa Trail 90 | 3·50 | 3·50 |

**331** Vjetrenica Cave

**2008.** World Heritage Site.

| | | | | |
|---|---|---|---|---|
| 939 | **331** | 1m. multicoloured | 2·40 | 2·40 |

**332** Signing

**2008.** Bosnia Hergovina–European Union Stabilization and Association Agreement.

| | | | | |
|---|---|---|---|---|
| 940 | **332** | 70f. multicoloured | 1·80 | 1·80 |

**333** *Nymphaea alba*

**2008.** Flora and Fauna. Multicoloured.

| | | | |
|---|---|---|---|
| 941 | 1m.50 Type **333** | 3·50 | 3·50 |
| 942 | 2m. *Rana esculenta* | 4·75 | 4·75 |

**334** Krivaja Villa, Zavidovici

**2008.** Cultural Heritage (1st issue).

| | | | | |
|---|---|---|---|---|
| 943 | **334** | 2m.50 multicoloured | 5·75 | 5·75 |

**335** Musalla (place of prayer), Kamengrad

**2008.** Cultural Heritage (2nd issue). Multicoloured.

| | | | |
|---|---|---|---|
| 944 | 1m. Type **335** | 2·40 | 2·40 |
| 945 | 1m.50 Ostrovica (horiz) | 3·50 | 3·50 |

**336** Turritella turris

**2008.** Fossils.

| | | | | |
|---|---|---|---|---|
| 946 | **336** | 1m.50 multicoloured | 3·50 | 3·50 |

**337** Stylized Symbols of Kuwait and Bosnia Herzgovina (image scaled to 54% of original size)

**2008.** Bosnia Herzgovina–Kuwait Relations.

| | | | | |
|---|---|---|---|---|
| 947 | **337** | 3m. multicoloured | 7·00 | 7·00 |

**338** Skier

**2008.** 80th Anniv of Sarajevo Ski Club.

| | | | | |
|---|---|---|---|---|
| 948 | **338** | 2m. multicoloured | 4·75 | 4·75 |

**339** Lynx

**2008.** Flora and Fauna. Multicoloured.

| | | | |
|---|---|---|---|
| 949 | 5f. Type **339** | 1·30 | 1·30 |
| 950 | 70f. Goshawk (*Accipiter gentilis*) | 1·80 | 1·80 |
| 951 | 70f. Conifer and fields (horiz) | 1·80 | 1·80 |
| 952 | 70f. Birch grove (horiz) | 1·80 | 1·80 |
| 953 | 70f. Conifers and snow-covered chalet (horiz) | 1·80 | 1·80 |
| 954 | 5m. Owl | 11·50 | 11·50 |

**340** Family

**2009.** International Day of Missing Persons.

| | | | | |
|---|---|---|---|---|
| 955 | **340** | 20f. black and scarlet | 45 | 45 |

**341** *Hirundo rustica* (barn swallow)

**2009**

| | | | | |
|---|---|---|---|---|
| 956 | **341** | 70f. multicoloured | 1·80 | 1·80 |

**342** Documents (image scaled to 37% of original size)

**2009.** Cultural Heritage. Historical Archives.

| | | | | |
|---|---|---|---|---|
| 957 | **342** | 70f. multicoloured | 1·80 | 1·80 |

**343** Building Facade

**2009.** 60th Anniv of Arkus–Seljo Academic Cultural Centre, University of Sarajevo.

| | | | | |
|---|---|---|---|---|
| 958 | **343** | 1m. multicoloured | 2·40 | 2·40 |

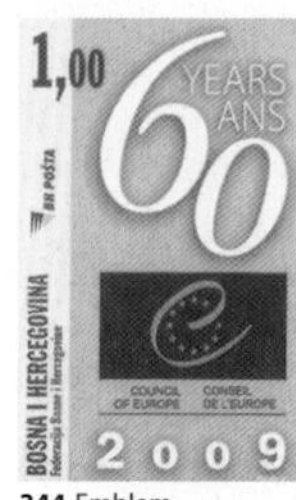
**344** Emblem

**2009.** 60th Anniv Council of Europe.

| | | | | |
|---|---|---|---|---|
| 959 | **344** | 1m. multicoloured | 2·40 | 2·40 |

**345** Coffee

**2009.** Bosnian Gastronomy.

| | | | | |
|---|---|---|---|---|
| 960 | **345** | 1m. multicoloured | 2·40 | 2·40 |

**346** Museum Emblem

**2009.** 60th Anniv of Sarajevo Museum.

| | | | | |
|---|---|---|---|---|
| 961 | **346** | 1m. multicoloured | 2·40 | 2·40 |

**347** Runners

**2009.** IAAF World Athletics Championships–Berlin 2009. Multicoloured.

| | | | |
|---|---|---|---|
| 962 | 1m.50 Type **347** | 3·50 | 3·50 |
| 963 | 2m. Stylized figures | 4·50 | 4·50 |
| **MS**964 | 106×50 mm. Nos. 962/3 | 8·00 | 8·00 |

**348** Charles Darwin and Progression of Humanoids

**2009.** Birth Bicentenary of Charles Darwin (naturalist and evolutionary theorist).

| | | | | |
|---|---|---|---|---|
| 965 | **348** | 2m. multicoloured | 4·50 | 4·50 |

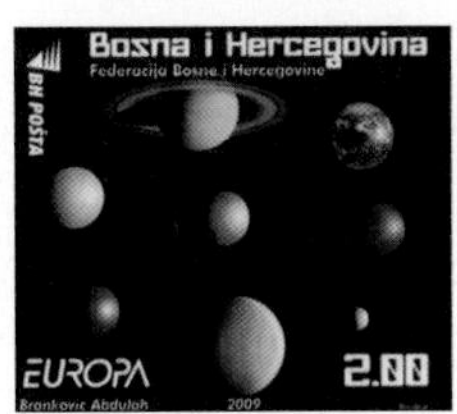

**349** Planets

**2009.** Europa. Astronomy. Multicoloured.

| | | | | |
|---|---|---|---|---|
| 966 | | 2m. Type **349** | 4·50 | 4·50 |
| 967 | | 3m. Satellite | 7·00 | 7·00 |
| **MS**968 | | 114×90 mm. Nos. 966/7 | 11·50 | 11·50 |

**350** Family Group

**2009.** Children's Week.

| | | | | |
|---|---|---|---|---|
| 969 | **350** | 70f. multicoloured | 1·80 | 1·80 |

**350a** Building Facade and Justice

**2009.** 130th Anniv of Canton Tribunal, Sarajevo.

| | | | | |
|---|---|---|---|---|
| 969a | **350a** | 1m. multicoloured | 2·40 | 2·40 |

**351** *Viola wittrockiana*

**2009.** Pansy.

| | | | | |
|---|---|---|---|---|
| 970 | **351** | 1m. multicoloured | 2·40 | 2·40 |

**352** Gazi Husrev-beg Mosque, Sarajevo and Selimiye Mosque, Edirne

**2009.** BH Post Sarajevo and Turkish Post Co-operation.

| | | | | |
|---|---|---|---|---|
| 971 | **352** | 2m. multicoloured | 5·00 | 5·00 |

**353** Strawberries

**2009.** Days of Berrylike Fruits Festival, Celic.

| | | | | |
|---|---|---|---|---|
| 972 | **353** | 5m. multicoloured | 11·50 | 11·50 |

**354** Hands

**2009.** Sign Language.

| | | | | |
|---|---|---|---|---|
| 973 | **354** | 1m.50 multicoloured | 3·50 | 3·50 |

**355** St Francis of Assissi

**2009.** 800th Anniv of Franciscan Order.

| | | | | |
|---|---|---|---|---|
| 974 | **355** | 1m.50 multicoloured | 3·50 | 3·50 |

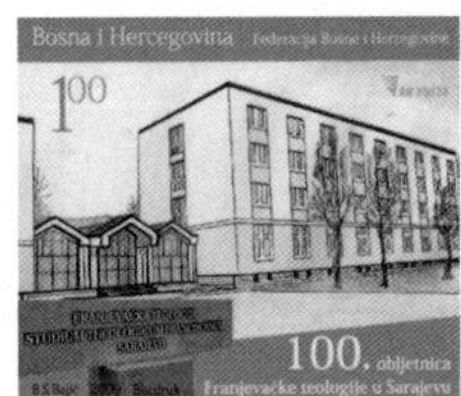

**356** Building Facade

**2009.** Centenary of Franciscan Theology Study Centre.

| | | | | |
|---|---|---|---|---|
| 975 | **356** | 1m. multicoloured | 2·40 | 2·40 |

**357** Speed Skater and Athletes

**2010.** Winter Olympic Games, Vancouver. Multicoloured.

| | | | | |
|---|---|---|---|---|
| **MS**976 | | 1m.50 Type **357**; 2m. Bobsleigh and other athletes | 8·50 | 8·50 |

**358** Old Town, Srebrenik

**2010.** Cultural Heritage. Multicoloured.

| | | | | |
|---|---|---|---|---|
| 977 | | 1m. Old Town and Castle, Ostrozac | 2·20 | 2·20 |
| 978 | | 70f. Type **358** | 2·75 | 2·75 |

**359** Taxus baccata (yew)

**2010.** Trees. Multicoloured.

| | | | | |
|---|---|---|---|---|
| 979 | | 1m. Type **359** | 3·50 | 3·50 |
| 980 | | 1m. *Aesculus hippocastanum* (horse chestnut) | 4·50 | 4·50 |

**360** Cynus olor (mute swan)

**2010.** Water Bird

| | | | | |
|---|---|---|---|---|
| **MS**981 | **360** | 2m. multicoloured | 5·50 | 5·50 |

**361** Wounded Chief watched over by his Sisters

**2010.** Ballad of Hasanaginica

| | | | | |
|---|---|---|---|---|
| 982 | **361** | 1m. multicoloured | 2·75 | 2·75 |

**362** Noch the little Dragon

**2010.** Europa. Multicoloured.

| | | | | |
|---|---|---|---|---|
| 983 | | 1m. Type **362** | 3·00 | 3·00 |
| 984 | | 1m.50 Little Blu | 4·00 | 4·00 |
| **MS**985 | | 67×103 mm. Nos. 982/3 | 7·00 | 7·00 |

Nos. 983/4 were printed, *se-tenant*, forming a composite design.

**363** Knight on Horseback (image scaled to 55% of original size)

**2010.** 500th Anniv of Ajvatovica (Prusac)

| | | | | |
|---|---|---|---|---|
| 986 | **363** | 1m.50 multicoloured | 3·50 | 3·50 |

**364** Robert Alexander Schumann

**2010.** Composers' Birth Bicentenaries. Multicoloured.

| | | | | |
|---|---|---|---|---|
| 987 | | 1m. Type **364** | 3·00 | 3·00 |
| 988 | | 1m.50 Fryderyk Franciszek (Frédéric) Chopin | 3·50 | 3·50 |

## II. CROATIAN POSTS

Issues made by the Croat administration in Mostar.

**C1** Statue and Church

**1993.** Sanctuary of Our Lady Queen of Peace Shrine, Medugorje.

| | | | | |
|---|---|---|---|---|
| C1 | **C1** | 2000d. multicoloured | 1·20 | 1·20 |

**C2** Silvije Kranjcevic (poet)

**1993.** Multicoloured.. Multicoloured..

| | | | | |
|---|---|---|---|---|
| C2 | | 200d. Type C **2** | 20 | 20 |
| C3 | | 500d. Jajce | 35 | 35 |
| C4 | | 1000d. Mostar (horiz) | 75 | 75 |

**C3** Medieval Gravestone

**1993.** 250th Anniv of Census in Bosnia and Herzegovina.

| | | | | |
|---|---|---|---|---|
| C5 | **C3** | 100d. multicoloured | 40 | 40 |

**C4** "Madonna of the Grand Duke" (Raphael)

**1993.** Christmas.

| | | | | |
|---|---|---|---|---|
| C6 | **C4** | 6000d. multicoloured | 2·30 | 2·30 |

**C5** "Uplands in Bloom"

**1993.** Europa. Contemporary Art. Paintings by Gabrijel Jurkic. Multicoloured.

| | | | | |
|---|---|---|---|---|
| C7 | | 3500d. Type C **5** | 4·75 | 4·75 |
| C8 | | 5000d. "Wild Poppy" | 5·25 | 5·25 |

**C6** Kravica Waterfall

**1993**

| | | | | |
|---|---|---|---|---|
| C9 | **C6** | 3000d. multicoloured | 1·30 | 1·30 |

**C7** Hrvoje (from "Hrvoje's Missal" by Butko)

**1993.** 577th Death Anniv of Hrvoje Vukcic Hrvatinic, Duke of Split, Viceroy of Dalmatia and Croatia and Grand Duke of Bosnia.

| | | | | |
|---|---|---|---|---|
| C10 | **C7** | 1500d. multicoloured | 80 | 80 |

**C8** Plehan Monastery

**1993**

| | | | | |
|---|---|---|---|---|
| C11 | **C8** | 2200d. multicoloured | 85 | 85 |

**C9** Arms

**1994.** Proclamation (August 1993) of Croatian Community of Herceg Bosna.

| | | | | |
|---|---|---|---|---|
| C12 | **C9** | 10000d. multicoloured | 4·00 | 4·00 |

**C10** Bronze Cross, Rama-Scit (Mile Blazevic)

**1994**
C13 **C10** 2m.80 multicoloured 1·20 1·20

**C 11** "Campanula hercegovina"

**1994.** Flora and Fauna. Multicoloured.
C14 3m.80 Type C **11** 1·60 1·60
C15 4m. Mountain dog 1·70 1·70

**C 12** Hutova Swamp

**1994**
C16 **C 12** 80f. multicoloured 45 45

**C 13** Penny Farthing Bicycles

**1994.** Europa. Discoveries and Inventions. Mult.
C17 8m. Type C **13** 4·75 4·75
C18 10m. Mercedes cars, 1901 5·75 5·75

**C14** Views of Town and Fortress

**1994.** 550th Anniv of First Written Record of Ljubuski.
C19 **C14** 1m. multicoloured 50 50

**C15** Hospital and Christ

**1994.** 2nd Anniv of Dr. Nikolic Franciscan Hospital, Nova Bila.
C20 **C15** 5m. multicoloured 2·00 2·00

**C16** Anniversary Emblem

**1995.** 50th Anniv of UNO. Self-adhesive. Rouletted.
C21 **C16** 1m.50 blue, red & black 60 60

**C17** Crib

**1995.** Christmas.
C22 **C17** 5m.40 multicoloured 2·20 2·20

**C18** Franciscan Monastery, Kraljeva Sutjeska

**1995**
C23 **C18** 3m. multicoloured 1·20 1·20

**C 19** Srebrenica

**1995.** Towns. Multicoloured.
C24 2m. Type C **19** 70 70
C25 4m. Franciscan Monastery, Mostar 1·40 1·40

**C20** Christ on the Cross

**1995.** Europa. Peace and Freedom.
C26 **C20** 6m.50 multicoloured 23·00 23·00

**C21** Statue and Church

**1996.** 15th Anniv of Sanctuary of Our Lady Queen of Peace Shrine, Medugorje.
C27 **C21** 10m. multicoloured 4·75 4·75

**C22** Queen Katarina Kosaca Kotromanic

**1996.** Europa. Famous Women.
C28 **C22** 2m.40 multicoloured 1·90 1·90

**C23** Monastery

**1996.** 150th Anniv of Franciscan Monastery and Church, Siroki Brijeg.
C29 **C23** 1m.40 multicoloured 55 55

**C24** Virgin Mary

**1996.** Self-adhesive. Rouletted.
C30 **C24** 2m. mult (postage) 60 60
C31 **C24** 9m. multicoloured (air) 3·00 3·00

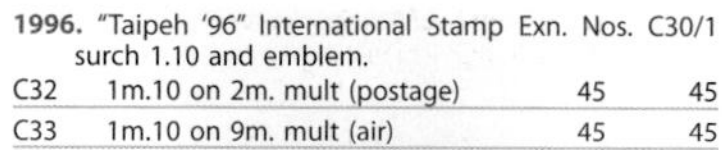

**1996.** "Taipeh '96" International Stamp Exn. Nos. C30/1 surch 1.10 and emblem.
C32 1m.10 on 2m. mult (postage) 45 45
C33 1m.10 on 9m. mult (air) 45 45

**C26** "Madonna and Child" (anon)

**1996.** Christmas.
C34 **C26** 2m.20 multicoloured 90 90

**C 27** St. George and the Dragon

**1997.** Europa. Tales and Legends. Mult.
C35 2m. Type C **27** 95 95
C36 5m. Zeus as bull and Europa (39×34 mm) 2·10 2·10

**C28** Pope John Paul II

**1997.** Papal Visit.
C37 **C28** 3m.60 multicoloured 1·50 1·50
**MS**C38 90×100 mm. No. 37×4 6·00 6·00

**C29** Chapel, Samatorje, Gorica

**1997**
C39 **C29** 1m.40 multicoloured 55 55

**C30** Purple Heron

**1997.** Flora and Fauna. Multicoloured.
C40 1m. Type C **30** 60 60
C41 2m.40 "Symphyandra hofmannii" (orchid) 1·00 1·00

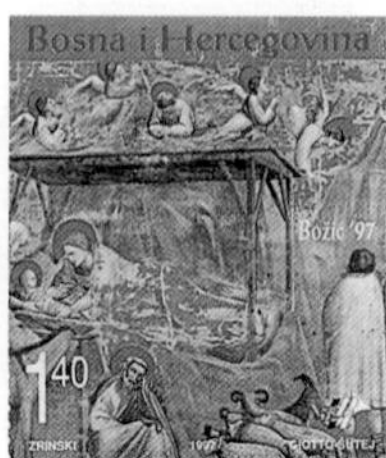


**C31** "Birth of Christ" (fresco, Giotto)

**1997.** Christmas.
C42 **C31** 1m.40 multicoloured 55 55

**C32** Cats

**1998.** Europa. Animated Film Festival.
C43 **C32** 6m.50 multicoloured 4·50 4·50

**C33** Seal

**1998.** 550th Anniv of Herzegovina.
C44 **C33** 2m.30 red, black and gold 90 90

**C34** Livno

**1998.** 1100th Anniv of Livno.
C45 **C34** 1m.20 multicoloured 55 55

**C35** "Sibiraea croatica"

**1998**
C46 **C35** 1m.40 multicoloured 80 80

**C36** Griffon Vulture

**1998**
C47 **C36** 2m.40 multicoloured 1·10 1·10

**C37** Adoration of the Wise Men

**1998.** Christmas.
C48 **C37** 5m.40 multicoloured 2·20 2·20

**C38** Woman, Posavina Region

**1999.** Regional Costumes.
C49 **C38** 40f. multicoloured 55 55

**C39** Ruins of Bobovac

**1999.** Old Towns.
C50 **C39** 10f. multicoloured 25 25

**C40** Simic

**1999.** Birth Centenary (1998) of Antun Simic (writer).
C51 **C40** 30f. multicoloured 55 55

**C41** Blidinje Nature Park

**1999.** Europa. Parks and Gardens.
C52 **C41** 1m.50 multicoloured 4·00 4·00

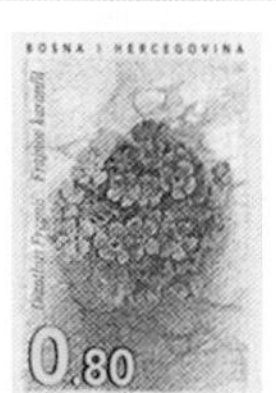

**C42** *Dianthus freynii*

**1999**
C53 **C42** 80f. multicoloured 1·30 1·30

**C43** Pine Marten

**1999**
C54 **C43** 40f. multicoloured 55 55

**C44** Gradina Osanici, Stolac

**1999.** Archaeology.
C55 **C44** 10f. multicoloured 25 25

**C45** The Nativity (mosaic)

**1999.** Christmas.
C56 **C45** 30f. multicoloured 55 55

**C46** Sop

**2000.** 96th Birth Anniv of Nikola Sop (poet).
C57 **C46** 40f. multicoloured 60 60

**C47** Emblem

**2000.** World Health Day.
C58 **C47** 40f. multicoloured 60 60

**C48** Ceramic Doves

**2000.** Europa.
C59 **C48** 1m.80 multicoloured 4·00 4·00

**C49** Chess Board and Emblem

**2000.** 40th Anniv of Bosnian Chess Association. Chess Events in 2000. Multicoloured.
C60 80f. Type C **49** (30th Chess Olympiad, Sarajevo) 1·30 1·30
C61 80f. Octopus holding pawn and emblem (16th European Chess Club Cup, Neum) 1·30 1·30

**C50** Brother Karaula

**2000.** Birth Bicentenary of Brother Lovro Karaula.
C62 **C50** 80f. multicoloured 1·30 1·30

**C51** Oak Tree (*Quercus sessilis*)

**2000.** Chestnut Oak of Siroki Brijeg.
C63 **C51** 1m.50 multicoloured 2·20 2·20

**C52** European Eel (*Anguilla anguilla*)

**2000**
C64 **C52** 80f. multicoloured 1·30 1·30

**C53** Franciscan Monastery, Tomislavgrad

**2000**
C65 **C53** 1m.50 multicoloured 2·20 2·20

**C54** Woman and Patterned Cloth

**2000.** Traditional Costume from Kraljeve Sutjeske.
C66 **C54** 40f. multicoloured 80 80

**C55** Man and Reflection

**2000.** A.I.D.S. Awareness Campaign.
C67 **C55** 80f. multicoloured 1·30 1·30

**C56** Nativity

**2000.** Christmas.
C68 **C56** 40f. multicoloured 65 65

**C57** *Chondrostoma phoxinus*

**2001.** Fishes. Multicoloured.
C69 30f. Type C **57** 40 40
C70 1m.50 *Salmo marmoratus* 2·20 2·20

**C58** Tihaljina Spring

**2001.** Europa. Water Resources. Multicoloured.
C71 1m.10 Type C **58** 2·00 2·00
C72 1m.80 Pliva Waterfall 3·25 3·25

**C59** Petar Zrinski

**2001.** 330th Death Anniversaries. Multicoloured.
C73 40f. Type C **59** 60 60
C74 40f. Fran Krsto Frankopan 60 60

**C60** 16th-century Galley Ship

**2001**
C75 **C60** 1m.80 multicoloured 2·75 2·75

**C61** Boat, Neretva River Valley

**2001**
C76 **C61** 80f. multicoloured 1·30 1·30

**C62** Queen of Peace of Medugorje

**2001.** 20th Anniv of Medugorje. Sheet 90×65 mm.
C77 **C62** 3m.80 multicoloured 5·25 5·25

**C63** Our Lady of Kondzilo (17th-century painting)

**2001**
C78 **C63** 80f. multicoloured 1·30 1·30

**C64** Binary Digits

**2001.** 50th Anniv of Computers. Each black and red.
C79 40f. Type C **64** 65 65
C80 40f. Binary forming "50" 65 65

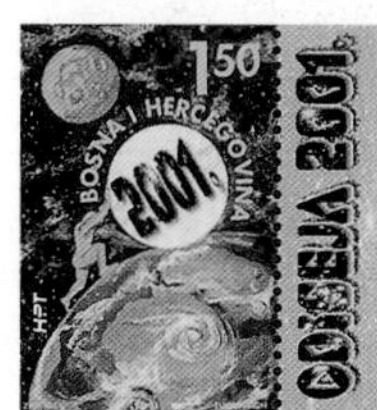

**C65** Mars, Globe and Sisyphus pushing Stone

**2001.** Millennium.
C81 **C65** 1m.50 multicoloured 2·00 2·00

**C66** Father Slavko Barbaric

**2001.** 1st Death Anniv of Father Slavko Barbaric.
C82 **C66** 80f. multicoloured 1·30 1·30

**C67** Minnie and Mickey Mouse (Danijela Nedic)

**2001.** Birth Centenary of Walt Disney (film maker).
C83 **C67** 1m.50 multicoloured 2·40 2·40

**C68** Nativity

**2001.** Christmas.

| | | | | |
|---|---|---|---|---|
| C84 | **C68** | 40f. multicoloured | 65 | 65 |

**C69** Alfred Nobel

**2001.** Centenary of the Nobel Prize.

| | | | | |
|---|---|---|---|---|
| C85 | **C69** | 1m.80 multicoloured | 3·00 | 3·00 |

**C70** Skier

**2002.** Winter Olympic Games, Salt Lake City, U.S.A.

| | | | | |
|---|---|---|---|---|
| C86 | **C70** | 80f. multicoloured | 1·40 | 1·40 |

**C71** Vran Mountain

**2002.** International Year of Mountains.

| | | | | |
|---|---|---|---|---|
| C87 | **C71** | 40f. multicoloured | 70 | 70 |

**C72** Bridge over River Neretva, Mostar

**2002.** 550th Anniv of First Written Record of Mostar.

| | | | | |
|---|---|---|---|---|
| C88 | **C72** | 30f. multicoloured | 55 | 55 |

**C73** Clown, Lion and Mouse

**2002.** Europa. Circus. Multicoloured.

| | | | |
|---|---|---|---|
| C89 | 80f. Type C **73** | 2·10 | 2·00 |
| C90 | 1m.50 Big Top and clowns | 3·50 | 3·50 |

**C74** Leonardo da Vinci and Designs

**2002.** 550th Birth Anniv of Leonardo da Vinci (artist and designer).

| | | | | |
|---|---|---|---|---|
| C91 | **C74** | 40f. brown and agate | 70 | 70 |

**C75** Players and Football

**2002.** World Cup Football Championships, Japan and South Korea.

| | | | | |
|---|---|---|---|---|
| C92 | **C75** | 1m.50 multicoloured | 2·50 | 2·40 |

**C76** Father Buntic and Children

**2002.** 60th Death Anniv of Father Didak Buntic (humanitarian).

| | | | | |
|---|---|---|---|---|
| C93 | **C76** | 80f. multicoloured | 1·40 | 1·40 |

**C77** Inscribed Tablet

**2002.** 11th-century Inscribed Tablet, Humac.

| | | | | |
|---|---|---|---|---|
| C94 | **C77** | 40f. multicoloured | 70 | 70 |

**C78** Marilyn Monroe

**2002.** 40th Death Anniv of Marilyn Monroe (actor).

| | | | | |
|---|---|---|---|---|
| C95 | **C78** | 40f. multicoloured | 70 | 70 |

**C79** Elvis Presley

**2002.** 25th Death Anniv of Elvis Presley (entertainer).

| | | | | |
|---|---|---|---|---|
| C96 | **C79** | 1m.50 multicoloured | 2·50 | 2·40 |

**C80** Transmitter Tower

**2002.** 50th Anniv of Television.

| | | | | |
|---|---|---|---|---|
| C97 | **C80** | 1m.50 multicoloured | 2·50 | 2·40 |

**C81** 1905 Postcard

**2002.** Stamp Day.

| | | | | |
|---|---|---|---|---|
| C98 | **C81** | 80f. multicoloured | 1·40 | 1·40 |

**C82** 1929 Calendar

**2002.** Centenary of "Naprodak" (cultural association).

| | | | | |
|---|---|---|---|---|
| C99 | **C82** | 40f. multicoloured | 70 | 70 |

**C83** Stylized Player

**2002.** European Bowling Championships, Grude.

| | | | | |
|---|---|---|---|---|
| C100 | **C83** | 1m.50 multicoloured | 2·50 | 2·40 |

**C84** *Viola beckiana*

**2002.** Flowers.

| | | | | |
|---|---|---|---|---|
| C101 | **C84** | 30f. multicoloured | 55 | 55 |

**C85** Red Admiral (*Vanessa atalanta*)

**2002.** Butterflies.

| | | | | |
|---|---|---|---|---|
| C102 | **C85** | 80f. multicoloured | 1·40 | 1·40 |

**C86** Madonna and Child (painting, Bernardino Luini)

**2002.** Christmas.

| | | | | |
|---|---|---|---|---|
| C103 | **C86** | 40f. multicoloured | 70 | 70 |

**C87** School Buildings

**2002.** 120th Anniv of Society of Jesuits High School, Travnik.

| | | | | |
|---|---|---|---|---|
| C104 | **C87** | 80f. multicoloured | 1·40 | 1·40 |

**C88** Josip Stadler

**2003.** 160th Birth Anniv (first archbishop).

| | | | | |
|---|---|---|---|---|
| C105 | **C88** | 50f. multicoloured | 85 | 85 |

**C89** Sirokom Brijegu High School

**2003**

| | | | | |
|---|---|---|---|---|
| C106 | **C89** | 40f. multicoloured | 80 | 80 |

**C90** Key Box and Letter Holder

**2003.** Europa. Poster Art.

| | | | | |
|---|---|---|---|---|
| C107 | **C90** | 1m.80 multicoloured | 4·75 | 4·75 |

**C91** Figures

**2003.** 800th Anniv of the Abjuration at Bilino Polje.

| | | | | |
|---|---|---|---|---|
| C108 | **C91** | 50f. multicoloured | 95 | 95 |

**C92** Mary and Angels

**2003.** 10th Anniv of HP Mostar.

| | | | | |
|---|---|---|---|---|
| C109 | **C92** | 980f. multicoloured | 1·60 | 1·60 |

**C93** Corkscrews

**2003.** World Wine Day.

| | | | | |
|---|---|---|---|---|
| C110 | **C93** | 1m.50 multicoloured | 2·75 | 2·75 |

**C94** *Oxytropis prenja*

**2003.** Flora and Fauna. Multicoloured.

| | | | |
|---|---|---|---|
| C111 | 50f. Type C **94** | 95 | 95 |
| C112 | 2m. Rock partridge (*Alectoris graeca*) | 3·75 | 3·75 |

**C95** Pope John Paul II and Ivan Merz

**2003.** 2nd Visit of Pope John Paul II.

| | | | | |
|---|---|---|---|---|
| C113 | **C95** | 1m.50 multicoloured | 2·75 | 2·75 |

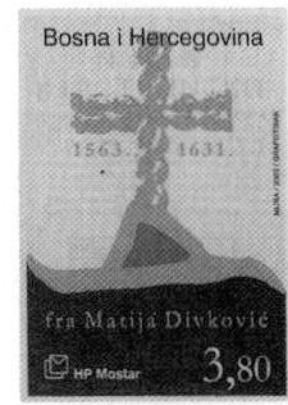
**C96** Crucifix

**2003.** 440th Birth Anniv of Matija Divkovic (writer).

| | | | | |
|---|---|---|---|---|
| C114 | **C96** | 3m.80 multicoloured | 7·00 | 7·00 |

**C97** Woman wearing Folk Costume, Rama

**2003.** Cultural Heritage. Multicoloured.

| | | | |
|---|---|---|---|
| C115 | 50f. Type C **97** | 95 | 95 |
| C116 | 70f. Jewellery, Neum (horiz) | 1·20 | 1·20 |

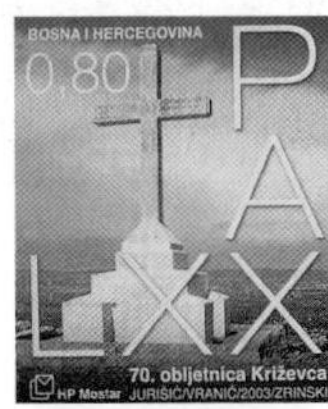
**C98** Summit Cross

**2003.** 70th Anniv of Summit Cross on Krizevac Mountain.

| | | | | |
|---|---|---|---|---|
| C117 | **C98** | 80f. multicoloured | 1·60 | 1·60 |

**C99** Stjepan Kotromanic

**2003.** 650th Death Anniv of Stjepan Kotromanic (King of Bosnia).

| | | | | |
|---|---|---|---|---|
| C118 | **C99** | 20f. multicoloured | 45 | 45 |

**C100** Tele-printer

**2003.** World Post Day.

| | | | | |
|---|---|---|---|---|
| C119 | **C100** | 1m.50 black and red | 3·25 | 3·25 |

**C101** Quill and Inkwell

**2003.** Birth Bicentenary of Alberto Fortis (writer).

| | | | | |
|---|---|---|---|---|
| C120 | **C101** | 50f. multicoloured | 1·00 | 1·00 |

**C102** Car and Bicycle

**2003.** Children.

| | | | | |
|---|---|---|---|---|
| C121 | **C102** | 1m. multicoloured | 2·10 | 2·10 |

**C103** Nativity

**2003.** Christmas.

| | | | | |
|---|---|---|---|---|
| C122 | **C103** | 50f. multicoloured | 1·00 | 1·00 |

**C104** "100"

**2003.** Centenary of Powered Flight.

| | | | | |
|---|---|---|---|---|
| C123 | **C104** | 2m. multicoloured | 4·25 | 4·25 |

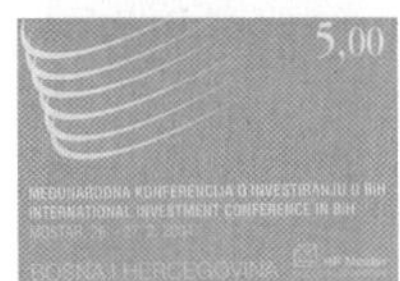
**C105** Emblem

**2004.** International Investment Conference.

| | | | | |
|---|---|---|---|---|
| C124 | **C105** | 5m. silver | 11·50 | 11·50 |

**C106** Hearts

**2004.** St. Valentine's Day.

| | | | | |
|---|---|---|---|---|
| C125 | **C106** | 10f. multicoloured | 1·00 | 1·00 |

**C107** Albert Einstein

**2004.** 125th Birth Anniv of Albert Einstein (physicist).

| | | | | |
|---|---|---|---|---|
| C126 | **C107** | 50f. multicoloured | 1·30 | 1·30 |

**C108** Decorated Hand

**2004.** Tattooing.

| | | | | |
|---|---|---|---|---|
| C127 | **C108** | 50f. multicoloured | 1·30 | 1·30 |

**C109** *Aquilegia dinarica*

**2004.** Flora and Fauna. Type C 109 and similar multicoloured design. P 14½.

| | | | |
|---|---|---|---|
| C128 | 1m. Type C **109** | 2·40 | 2·40 |
| C129 | 1m.50 *Salamandra atra prenjensis* (horiz) | 3·50 | 3·50 |

**C110** Skis and Snow Scene

**2004.** Europa. Holidays. Multicoloured.

| | | | |
|---|---|---|---|
| C130 | 1m.50 Type C **110** | 3·75 | 3·75 |
| C131 | 2m. Flippers and Beach Scene | 4·75 | 4·75 |

**C111** Andrije Kacica Miosica

**2004.** 300th Birth Anniv of Andrije Kacica Miosica (writer and theologian).

| | | | | |
|---|---|---|---|---|
| C132 | **C111** | 70f. yellow and brown | 1·80 | 1·80 |

**C112** Ball and Boots

**2004.** European Football Championship 2004, Portugal.

| | | | | |
|---|---|---|---|---|
| C133 | **C112** | 2m. multicoloured | 5·00 | 5·00 |

**C113** Kocerin Tablet (carved stone), Siroki Brijeg (c.1404)

**2004**

| | | | | |
|---|---|---|---|---|
| C134 | **C113** | 70f. multicoloured | 1·50 | 1·50 |

**C114** Footprint

**2004.** 35th Anniv of First Landing on Moon.

| | | | | |
|---|---|---|---|---|
| C135 | **C114** | 1m. multicoloured | 2·50 | 2·50 |

**C115** Old Bridge, Mostar

**2004.** Reconstruction of Mostar Bridge.

| | | | | |
|---|---|---|---|---|
| C136 | **C115** | 50f. multicoloured | 1·30 | 1·30 |

**C116** Water Wheel, Buna

**2004**

| | | | | |
|---|---|---|---|---|
| C137 | **C116** | 1m. Multicoloured | 2·50 | 2·50 |

**C117** Envelope and Earth

**2004.** World Post Day.

| | | | | |
|---|---|---|---|---|
| C138 | **C117** | 1m.50 multicoloured | 3·75 | 3·75 |

**C118** Money Box and Hippopotamus

**2004.** World Savings Day.

| | | | | |
|---|---|---|---|---|
| C139 | **C118** | 50f. multicoloured | 1·30 | 1·30 |

**C119** Karl Friedrich Benz

**2004.** 160th Birth Anniv of Karl Friedrich Benz (German motor pioneer).

| | | | | |
|---|---|---|---|---|
| C140 | **C119** | 1m.50 multicoloured | 3·75 | 3·75 |

**C120** Mary and Joseph

**2004.** Christmas. Multicoloured.

| | | | |
|---|---|---|---|
| C141 | 50f. Type C **120** | 1·30 | 1·30 |
| C142 | 1m. Postman carrying present | 2·50 | 2·50 |

**C121** Woman wearing Folk Costume, Kupres

**2005.** Cultural Heritage.

| | | | | |
|---|---|---|---|---|
| C143 | **C121** | 1m.50 multicoloured | 3·75 | 3·75 |

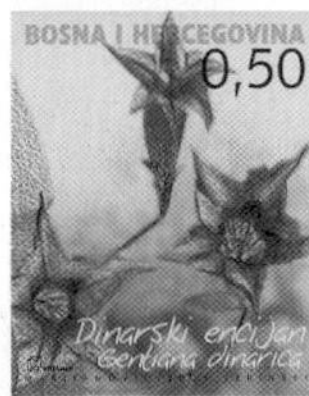
**C122** *Gentiana dinarica*

**2005.** Flora. Multicoloured.

| | | | |
|---|---|---|---|
| C144 | 50f. Type C **122** | 1·30 | 1·30 |
| C145 | 50f. *Petteria ramentacea* | 1·30 | 1·30 |

**C123** Little Egret (*Egretta garzetta*)

**2005.** Birds. Multicoloured.

| | | | |
|---|---|---|---|
| C146 | 1m. Type C **123** | 2·50 | 2·50 |
| C147 | 1m. Black-winged stilt (*Himantopus himantopus*) | 2·50 | 2·50 |
| C148 | 1m. Kingfisher (*Alcedo atthis*) | 2·50 | 2·50 |

C149 1m. European bee eater (*Merops apiaster*) 2·50 2·50

C124 Early Footballers

**2005.** Centenary of CSC Zrinjski Sports Club. Multicoloured.

C150 3m. Type C **124** 7·25 7·25
C151 3m. Modern footballers 7·25 7·25

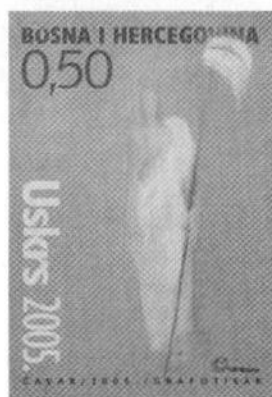


**C125** Figure holding Flag

**2005.** Easter.

C152 **C125** 50f. multicoloured 1·30 1·30

**C126** *Thumbelina* (Hans Christian Andersen)

**2005.** Writers Anniversaries. Multicoloured.

C153 20f. Type C **126** (birth bicentenary) 50 50
C154 20f. *Tintilinic* (Ivana Brlic Mazuranic) (130th (2004) birth anniv) 50 50

**C127** Bread, Grapes, Wine, Nuts and Soft Cheese

**2005.** Europa. Gastronomy. Multicoloured.

C155 2m. Type C **127** 5·00 5·00
C156 2m. Bread, garlic, meats, glass and flagon 5·00 5·00

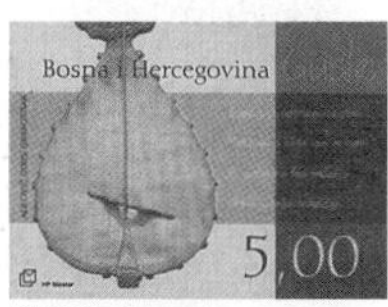


**C128** Gusle

**2005.** Musical Instruments.

C157 **C128** 5m. multicoloured 12·50 12·50

**C129** Vjetrenica Cave

**2005.** International Day of Water.

C158 **C129** 1m. multicoloured 2·50 2·50

**C130** Steam Locomotive

**2005.** 120th Anniv of Metkovic—Mostar Railway.

C159 **C130** 50f. multicoloured 1·30 1·30

**C131** Virgin Mary (statue) and Crowds

**2005.** Medjugorje Youth Festival.

C160 **C131** 1m. multicoloured 2·50 2·50

**C132** Father Grgo Martic

**2005.** Birth Centenary of Father Grgo Martic.

C161 **C132** 1m. multicoloured 2·50 2·50

**C133** Trumpet

**2005.** International Music Day.

C162 **C133** 50f. multicoloured 1·00 1·00

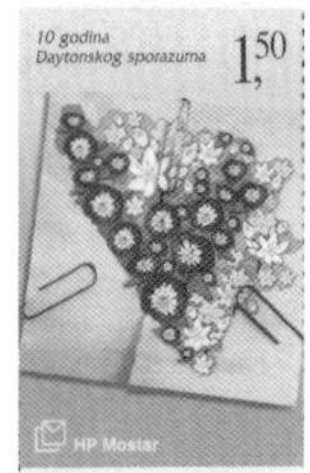


**C134** Flowers over map

**2005.** 10th Anniv of Dayton Agreement.

C163 **C134** 1m.50 multicoloured 3·75 3·75

**C135** Slavko Barbaric

**2005.** 5th Death Anniv of Slavko Barbaric (writer).

C164 **C135** 1m. multicoloured 2·50 2·50

**C136** Mary and Jesus

**2005.** Christmas. Multicoloured.

C165 50f. Type C **136** 1·30 1·30
C166 50f. Tree 1·30 1·30

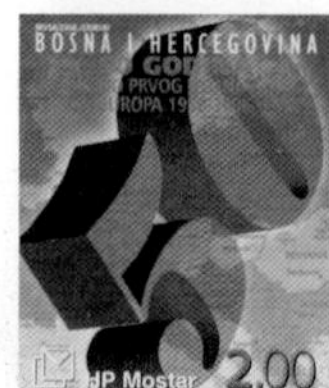


**C137** "50"

**2005.** 50th Anniv of Europa Stamps. Multicoloured.

C167 2m. Type C **137** 3·75 3·75
C168 2m. Sunflowers and envelope 3·75 3·75
C169 2m. Map and 2003 1k.80 stamp (No. C107) 3·75 3·75
C170 2m. European flags 3·75 3·75
**MS**C171 90×100 mm. Nos. 167/70 20·00 20·00

**C138** Lake and Bearded Tit

**2006.** International Swamp Protection Day.

C172 **C138** 1m. multicoloured 2·50 2·50

**C139** Faces

**2006.** Europa. Integration. Multicoloured.

C173 2m. Type C **139** 5·00 5·00
C174 2m. "Integration" 5·00 5·00

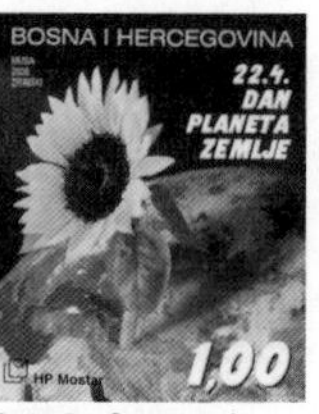


**C140** Sunflower and Globe

**2006.** Earth Day.

C175 **C140** 1m. multicoloured 2·50 2·50

**C141** Paper Birds

**2006.** World Press Freedom Day.

C176 **C141** 50f. multicoloured 1·30 1·30

**C142** Cable

**2006.** World Telecommunications Day.

C177 **C142** 1m. multicoloured 2·50 2·50

**C143** Queen of Peace (statue) and Church

**2006.** 25th Anniv of Medugorje. Multicoloured.

C178 1m. Type C **143** 2·40 2·40
C179 1m. Statue with multicoloured halo amongst rocks 2·40 2·40
C180 1m. Cross, Krizevac Hill and statue 2·40 2·40
C181 1m. Statue (detail) and church 2·40 2·40
C182 1m. Stylized church and crowd 2·40 2·40

**C144** Church

**2006.** 150th Anniv of Uzdol Parish.

C183 **C144** 50f. multicoloured 1·30 1·30

**C145** Nikola Tesla

**2006.** 150th Birth Anniv of Nikola Tesla (engineer).

C184 **C145** 2m. multicoloured 5·00 5·00

**C146** Archer and Stag

**2006.** Stecci (medieval tombstones).

C185 **C146** 20f. multicoloured 1·00 1·00

**C147** Car

**2006.** Car Free Day.

C186 **C147** 1m. black, vermilion and yellow 2·50 2·50

**C148** Crucifix from Woman's Rosary, Franciscan Monastery, Humac

**2006**

C187 **C148** 5m. multicoloured 12·50 12·50

**C149** *Upupa epops* (hoopoe)

**2006.** Birds of Hutovo. Multicoloured.

C188 70f. Type C **149** 1·80 1·80
C189 70f. *Alauda arvensis* (skylark) 1·80 1·80

Nos. C190/1 have been left for additions to this set.

**C150** *Papaver kerneri*

**2006.** Flora. Multicoloured.

C192 20f. Type C **150** 50 50
C193 20f. *Cerastium dinaricum* 50 50

**C151** Door with Wreath

**2006.** Christmas and New Year. Multicoloured.

C194 50f. Type C **151** 1·30 1·30

C195 1m. Grass and candles 2·50 2·50

**C152** Hearts and Birds

**2007.** St. Valentine's Day.
C196 **C152** 10f. multicoloured 1·00 1·00

**C153** Head of Dog

**2007.** Dogs. Tornjak. Multicoloured.
C197 70f. Type C **153** 1·70 1·70
C198 70f. Head of dog, black markings 1·70 1·70
C199 70f. Dog with black markings 1·70 1·70
C200 70f. Dog with brown markings 1·70 1·70

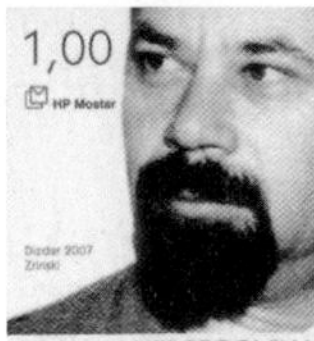

**C154** Mak Dizdar

**2007.** 90th Birth Anniv of Mehmedalija Mak Dizdar (poet).
C201 **C154** 1m. multicoloured 2·50 2·50

**C155** Clasped Hands

**2007.** Europa. Centenary of Scouting. Multicoloured.
C202 3m. Type C **155** 6·75 6·75
C203 3m. Reef knot 6·75 6·75

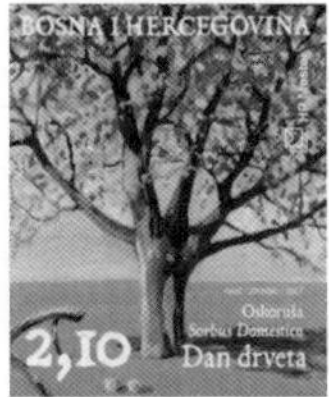

**C156** *Sorbus domestica*

**2007.** Tree Day. Sheet 68×91 mm.
**MS**C204 2k.10 multicoloured 5·25 5·25

**C157** Lion (bas relief) and Map

**2007.** Gabela Archaeological Site, Capljina.
C205 **C157** 1m.50 multicoloured 3·75 3·75

**C158** Iris

**2007.** Iris Illyrica. Multicoloured.
C206 2m. Type C **158** 5·00 5·00

**MS**C207 61×80 mm. 3k. Iris and trireme (24×58 mm) 7·75 7·75

**C159** Virgin Mary (statue)

**2007.** Medugorje. Multicoloured.
C208 1m. Type C **159** 2·40 2·40
C209 1m. Hands holding rosary 2·40 2·40
C210 1m. Virgin Mary and pilgrims 2·40 2·40
C211 1m. Bronze statue of Friar 2·40 2·40
C212 1m. Virgin Mary (statue) and tower 2·40 2·40

**C160** Friar Marko Dobretic

**2007.** 300th Birth Anniv of Friar Marko Dobretic.
C213 **C160** 60f. multicoloured 1·50 1·50

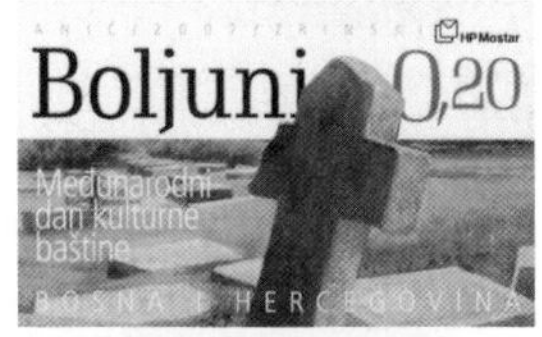

**C161** Duke Vlatko's Tombstone, Boljuni Necropolis

**2007.** Cultural Heritage Day.
C214 **C161** 20f. multicoloured 1·00 1·00

**C162** Emblem

**2007.** World Bowling Championship, Grude.
C215 **C162** 5m. black and scarlet 12·50 12·50

**C163** Hemp and Spindle

**2007.** Ethnological Treasures.
C216 **C163** 70f. multicoloured 1·80 1·80

**C164** *Fulica atra* (coot)

**2007.** Birds. Multicoloured.
C217 2m. Type C **164** 3·75 3·75
C218 2m. *Anas platyrhynchos* (mallard) 3·75 3·75
C219 2m. *Anas crecca* (common teal) 3·75 3·75
C220 2m. *Streptopelia turtur* (turtle dove) 3·75 3·75

**C165** *Gentiana lutea*

**2007.** Flora of Blidinje Park. Multicoloured.
C221 3m. Type C **165** 7·75 7·75
**MS**C222 80×60 mm. 3k. *Vaccinium vitis-idaea* 7·75 7·75

The stamp and margins **MS**C222 form a composite design.

**C166** Candles

**2007.** Christmas. Multicoloured.
C223 50f. Type **C166** 1·30 1·30
C224 70f. Decorated trees and doorway 1·90 1·90

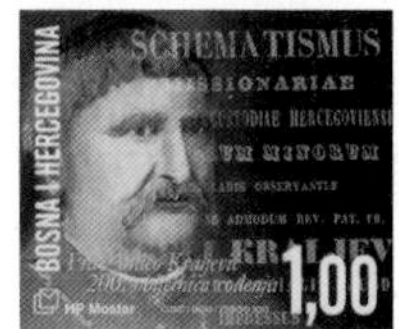

**C167** Friar Andeo Kraljevic

**2007.** Birth Bicentenary of Friar Ivan (Andeo) Kraljevic.
C225 **C167** 1m. multicoloured 2·75 2·75

**C168** Chick and Flowers

**2008.** Easter.
C226 **C168** 70f. multicoloured 1·90 1·90

**C169** Piano Keys

**2008.** 10th Anniv of Matica Hrvatska (cultural institution)'s Festival Week.
C227 **C169** 10f. black and vermilion 1·00 1·00

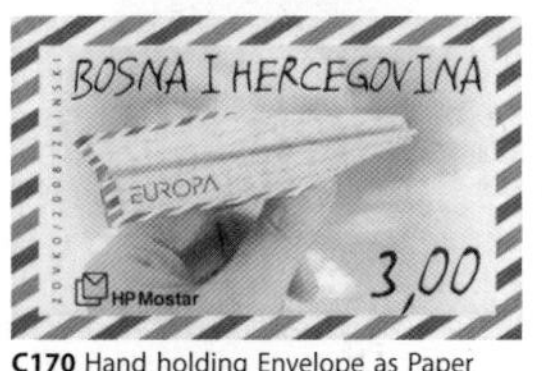

**C170** Hand holding Envelope as Paper Aeroplane

**2008.** Europa. The Letter. Multicoloured.
C228 3m. Type **C170** 7·00 7·00
C229 3m. Pen nib 7·00 7·00

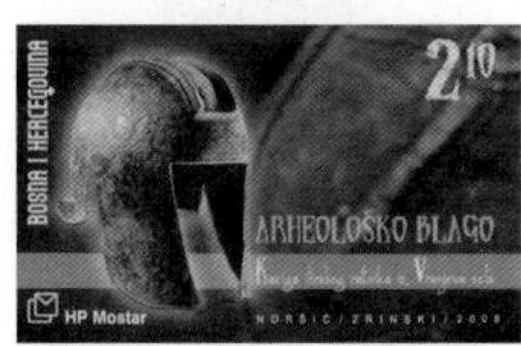

**C171** Illyrian Warrior's Helmet, Vranjevo Selo

**2008.** Archaeology.
C230 **C171** 2m.10 multicoloured 6·00 6·00

**C172** Grave of Mosha Danon, Rabbi of Sarajevo

**2008.** International Day of Diversity.
C231 **C172** 1m.50 multicoloured 4·25 4·25

**C173** *Achillea millefolium* (milfoil)

**2008.** Myth and Flora. Andrija Simic and Milfoil. Sheet 80×60 mm.
**MS**C232 **C173** multicoloured 8·25 8·25

**C174** Virgin Mary, Girl and Dove

**2008.** Medugorje. Multicoloured.
C233 1m. Type **C174** 2·75 2·75
C234 1m. Church of St. Jacob 2·75 2·75
C235 1m. Page, crucified Christ and praying hands 2·75 2·75
C236 1m. Virgin Mary (statue) 2·75 2·75
C237 1m. Summit Cross 2·75 2·75

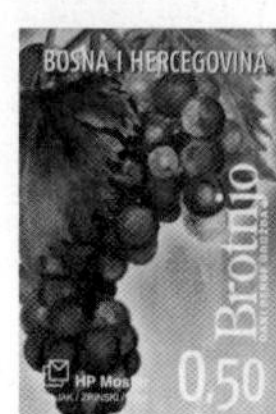

**C175** Grapes

**2008.** Vintage Days in Brotnjo, 2008. Multicoloured.
C238 50f. Type **C175** 1·30 1·30
C239 70f. White grapes 2·20 2·20

**C176** Building

**2008.** Zaostrog Monastery.
C240 **C176** 1m. multicoloured 3·00 3·00

**C177** Tobacco Cutter

**2008.** Cultural Heritage. Ethnological Treasures. Avan (tobacco cutter).
C241 **C177** 2m. multicoloured 3·75 3·75

**C178** Zepce

**2008.** 550th Anniv of Zepce.

| | | | | |
|---|---|---|---|---|
| C242 | **C178** | 1m.50 multicoloured | 4·50 | 4·50 |

**C179** Tubers

**2008.** International Year of the Potato. Multicoloured.

| | | | |
|---|---|---|---|
| C243 | 50f. Type **C179** | 1·75 | 1·75 |
| **MS**C244 | 80×60 mm. 5m. Flowers | 14·00 | 14·00 |

**C180** *Falco tinnunculus* (Kestrel)

**2008.** Birds. Multicoloured.

| | | | |
|---|---|---|---|
| C245 | 1m.50 Type **C180** | 90 | 90 |
| C246 | 1m.50 *Circactus gallicus* (short-toed eagle) | 90 | 90 |
| C247 | 1m.50 *Bubo bubo* (eagle owl) | 90 | 90 |
| C248 | 1m.50 *Accipiter gentilis* (goshawk) | 90 | 90 |

**C181** Leo Petrovic

**2008.** Father Leo Petrovic (professor of theology) Commemoration.

| | | | | |
|---|---|---|---|---|
| C249 | **C181** | 1m. multicoloured | 9·25 | 9·25 |

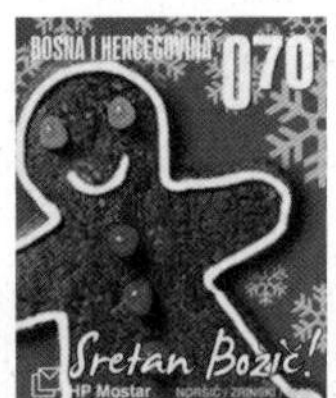

**C182** Gingerbread Man

**2008.** Christmas. Multicoloured.

| | | | |
|---|---|---|---|
| C250 | 70f. Type **C182** | 6·50 | 6·50 |
| C251 | 70f. Bow | 6·50 | 6·50 |

**C183** Early Players

**2008.** 60th Anniv of Siroki Brijeg Football Club. Multicoloured.

| | | | |
|---|---|---|---|
| C252 | 70f. Type **C183** | 6·50 | 6·50 |
| **MS**C253 | 80×60 mm. 2m.10 Modern players (35×30 mm) | 18·00 | 18·00 |

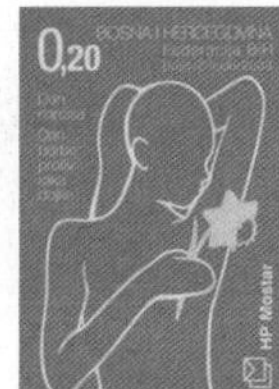

**C184** Woman holding Daffodil

**2009.** Daffodil Day (breast cancer awareness day).

| | | | | |
|---|---|---|---|---|
| C254 | **C184** | 20f. magenta and chrome yellow | 1·00 | 1·00 |

**C185** Waterfall, River Pliva

**2009.** International Water Day. Watermills in Pliva Lakes. Multicoloured.

| | | | |
|---|---|---|---|
| C255 | 70f. Type **C185** | 1·70 | 1·70 |
| C256 | 70f. Watermills | 1·70 | 1·70 |

**C186** '60'

**2009.** 60th Anniv of Council of Europe and European Court of Human Rights. Each new blue and lemon.

| | | | |
|---|---|---|---|
| C257 | 1m.50 Type **C186** | 4·50 | 4·50 |
| C258 | 1m.50 Court of Human Rights building (horiz) | 4·50 | 4·50 |

**C187** Earth and Planets

**2009.** Europa. Astronomy. Multicoloured.

| | | | |
|---|---|---|---|
| C259 | 3m. Type **C187** | 9·00 | 9·00 |
| C260 | 3m. Telescope and planets | 9·00 | 9·00 |

**C188** Arms of Herzeg Stipan Vukcic Kosaca

**2009.** Archaeology.

| | | | | |
|---|---|---|---|---|
| C261 | **C188** | 1m.50 multicoloured | 4·50 | 4·50 |

**C189** *Tanacetum balsamita* (costamary)

**2009.** Myths and Flora. Multicoloured.

| | | | |
|---|---|---|---|
| C262 | 2m.10 Type **C189** | 4·00 | 4·00 |
| **MS**C263 | 80×60 mm. 2m.10 Girl and flowers | 4·00 | 4·00 |

**C190** Building Facade

**2009.** 150th Anniv of Franciscan Monastery, Guca Gora.

| | | | | |
|---|---|---|---|---|
| C264 | **C190** | 70f. multicoloured | 1·70 | 1·70 |

**C191** Church of St. Jacob

**2009.** Medjugorje. Multicoloured.

| | | | |
|---|---|---|---|
| C265 | 1m. Type **C191** | 90 | 90 |
| C266 | 1m. Summit Cross | 90 | 90 |
| C267 | 1m. Crucified Christ | 90 | 90 |
| C268 | 1m. Virgin Mary and Church of St. Jacob | 90 | 90 |
| C269 | 1m. Virgin Mary | 90 | 90 |

**C192** Festival Emblem

**2009.** 10th Mediterranean Film Festival.

| | | | | |
|---|---|---|---|---|
| C270 | **C192** | 70f. multicoloured | 1·70 | 1·70 |

**C193** Chapel Entrance

**2009.** 800th Anniv of Franciscan Order.

| | | | | |
|---|---|---|---|---|
| C271 | | 1m. multicoloured | 1·20 | 1·20 |
| C272 | – | 1m. deep brown | 1·20 | 1·20 |

DESIGNS: Type C **193**; C272 Franciscan waist cord.

**C194** Decorated Chest

**2009.** Stamp Day. Ethnological Treasures.

| | | | | |
|---|---|---|---|---|
| C273 | **C194** | 70f. multicoloured | 1·70 | 1·70 |

**C195** Monastery

**2009.** 150th Anniv Franciscan Monastery, Gorica Livno.

| | | | | |
|---|---|---|---|---|
| C274 | **C195** | 60f. multicoloured | 1·70 | 1·70 |

**C196** *Nycticorax nycticorax* (black-crowned night heron)

**2009.** Birds of Hutovo Blato. Multicoloured.

| | | | |
|---|---|---|---|
| C275 | 1m.50 Type **C196** | 1·20 | 1·20 |
| C276 | 1m.50 *Cuculus canorus* (cuckoo) | 1·20 | 1·20 |
| C277 | 1m.50 *Coturnix coturnix* (quail) | 1·20 | 1·20 |
| C278 | 1m.50 *Rallus aquaticus* (water rail) | 1·20 | 1·20 |

**C197** Flowers and Fruit

**2009.** Prunus domestica (plum). Multicoloured.

| | | | |
|---|---|---|---|
| C279 | 5m. Type **C197** | 11·50 | 11·50 |
| **MS**C280 | 65×65 mm. 5m. Fruit | 11·50 | 11·50 |

**C198** Candles

**2009.** Christmas. Multicoloured.

| | | | |
|---|---|---|---|
| C281 | 70f. Type **C198** | 1·70 | 1·70 |
| C282 | 70f. Heart shaped cushion and parcels | 1·70 | 1·70 |

**C199** Maple Leaf

**2010.** Winter Olympic Games, Vancouver. Multicoloured.

| | | | |
|---|---|---|---|
| C283 | 70f. multicoloured | 1·60 | 1·70 |
| C284 | 1m.50 bright scarlet, black and gold | 2·10 | 2·10 |

Designs: 70f. Type **C199**; 1m.50 Stylized maple leaf on skis

**C200** Carnations

**2010.** Centenary of International Women's Day

| | | | | |
|---|---|---|---|---|
| C284a | **C200** | 20f. multicoloured | 1·00 | 1·00 |

**C201** Friar Martin Nedic

**2010.** Birth Bicentenary of Friar Martin Nedić (builder of monastery and church in Tolisa)

| | | | | |
|---|---|---|---|---|
| C285 | **C201** | 2m.10 multicoloured | 4·25 | 4·25 |

**C202** Open Book, Stylized Child standing on Rainbow and Kite

**2010.** Europa. Multicoloured.

| | | | |
|---|---|---|---|
| C286 | 3m. Type **C202** | 5·75 | 5·75 |
| C287 | 3m. Stylized child standing on open book holding windmill | 5·75 | 5·75 |

**C203** Cave Entrance and Pintadera

**2010.** Archeological Heritage

| | | | | |
|---|---|---|---|---|
| C288 | **C203** | 1m.50 multicoloured | 3·25 | 3·25 |

**C204** Linden Flower and Leaf

**2010.** Myths and Flora

| | | | | |
|---|---|---|---|---|
| MSC289 | **C204** | 5m. multicoloured | 8·25 | 8·25 |

**C205** Virgin Mary

**2010.** Medjugorje. Multicoloured.

| | | | |
|---|---|---|---|
| C290 | 1m. Type **C205** | 2·10 | 2·10 |
| C291 | 1m. Summit Cross | 2·10 | 2·10 |
| C292 | 1m. Hand holding rosary | 2·10 | 2·10 |
| C293 | 1m. Virgin Mary (head and shoulders) | 2·10 | 2·10 |
| C294 | 1m. Pilgrims and flags | 2·10 | 2·10 |

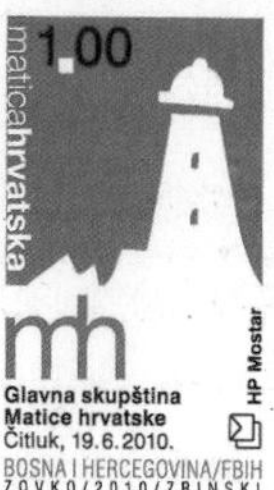


**C206** Lighthouse and Emblem

**2010.** General Assembly of Matrix Croatica

| | | | | |
|---|---|---|---|---|
| C295 | **C206** | 1m. scarlet-vermilion and black | 2·10 | 2·10 |

**C207** Mother Teresa and Child

**2010.** Birth Centenary of Agnes Gonxha Bojaxhiu (Mother Teresa) (founder of Missionaries of Charity in Calcutta)

| | | | | |
|---|---|---|---|---|
| C296 | **C207** | 2m.10 bright ultramarine | 4·25 | 4·25 |

**C208** Prokoško Lake

**2010.** Environmental Protection. Multicoloured.

| | | | |
|---|---|---|---|
| C297 | 1m. Type **C208** | 2·10 | 2·10 |
| C298 | 1m. *Triturus alpestris reiseri* (newt) | 2·10 | 2·10 |

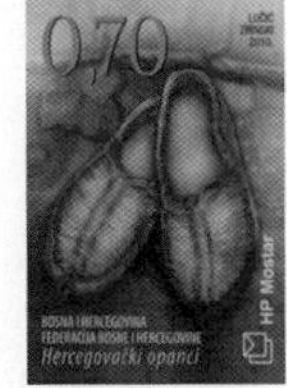


**C209** Peasant Shoes

**2010.** Ethnological Treasures

| | | | | |
|---|---|---|---|---|
| C299 | **C209** | 70f. multicoloured | 1·60 | 1·60 |

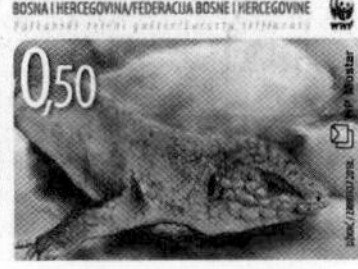


**C210** Balkan Green Lizard

**2010.** Balkan Green Lizard (*Lacerta trilineata*). Multicoloured.

| | | | |
|---|---|---|---|
| C300 | 50f. Type **C210** | 1·40 | 1·40 |
| C301 | 50f. Basking on rock | 1·40 | 1·40 |
| C302 | 50f. Climbing tree | 1·40 | 1·40 |
| C303 | 50f. Juvenile (brown striped) | 1·40 | 1·40 |

**C211** Fly Agaric (*Amanita muscaria*)

**2010.** Fungi. Multicoloured.

| | | | |
|---|---|---|---|
| C304 | 2m.10 Type **C211** | 4·25 | 4·25 |
| C305 | 2m.10 Puffball (*Lycoperdon perlatum*) | 4·25 | 4·25 |

## III. REPUBLIKA SRPSKA

Issued by the Serb administration based in Pale.

Република
Српска

(S 1)

**1992.** Nos. 2587/98 of Yugoslavia surch as Type S 1.

| | | | |
|---|---|---|---|
| S1 | 5d. on 10p. violet and green | 1·10 | 1·10 |
| S2 | 30d. on 3d. blue and red | £140 | £140 |
| S3a | 50d. on 40p. green & purple | 1·10 | 1·10 |
| S4 | 60d. on 20p. red and yellow | 1·20 | 1·20 |
| S5 | 60d. on 30p. green & orange | 1·20 | 1·20 |
| S6 | 100d. on 1d. blue and purple | 1·20 | 1·20 |
| S7a | 100d. on 2d. blue and red | 1·20 | 1·20 |
| S8 | 100d. on 3d. blue and red | 1·20 | 1·20 |
| S9a | 300d. on 5d. ultram & blue | 1·50 | 1·50 |
| S10 | 500d. on 50p. green & violet | 1·50 | 1·50 |
| S11 | 500d. on 60p. mauve & red | 1·50 | 1·50 |

**S2** Stringed Instrument

**1993.** Dated "1992".

| | | | | |
|---|---|---|---|---|
| S12 | **S2** | 10d. black and yellow | 4·50 | 4·50 |
| S13 | **S2** | 20d. black and blue | 20 | 20 |
| S14 | **S2** | 30d. black and pink | 50 | 50 |
| S15 | - | 50d. black and red | 60 | 60 |
| S16 | - | 100d. black and red | 1·50 | 1·50 |
| S17 | - | 500d. black and blue | 3·00 | 3·00 |

DESIGNS—VERT: 50, 100d. Coat of arms. HORIZ: 500d. Monastery.

**1993.** Dated "1993".

| | | | | |
|---|---|---|---|---|
| S18 | **S2** | 5000d. black and lilac | 10 | 10 |
| S19 | **S2** | 6000d. black and yellow | 20 | 20 |
| S20 | **S2** | 10000d. black and blue | 3·50 | 3·50 |
| S21 | - | 20000d. black and red | 95 | 95 |
| S22 | - | 30000d. black and red | 1·50 | 1·50 |
| S23 | - | 50000d. black and lilac | 1·50 | 1·50 |

DESIGNS—VERT: 20000, 30000d. Coat of arms. HORIZ: 50000d. Monastery.

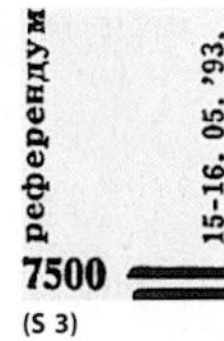


(S 3)

**1993.** Referendum. Nos. S15/16 surch as Type S 3.

| | | | |
|---|---|---|---|
| S24 | 7500d. on 50d. black and red | 2·00 | 2·00 |
| S25 | 7500d. on 100d. black and red | 2·00 | 2·00 |
| S26 | 9000d. on 50d. black and red | 2·75 | 2·75 |

**S4** Symbol of St. John the Evangelist

**1993.** No value expressed.

| | | | | |
|---|---|---|---|---|
| S27 | **S4** | A red | 70 | 70 |

No. S27 was sold at the rate for internal letters.

**S5** Icon of St. Stefan

**1994.** Republic Day.

| | | | | |
|---|---|---|---|---|
| S28 | **S5** | 1d. multicoloured | 7·00 | 7·00 |

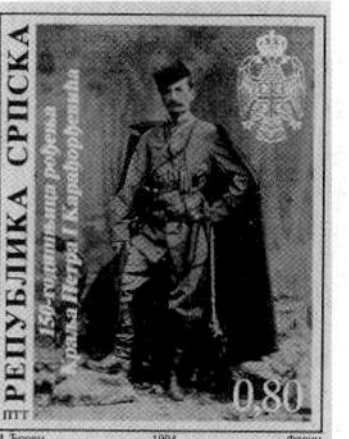


**S6** King Petar I

**1994.** 150th Birth Anniv of King Petar I of Serbia.

| | | | | |
|---|---|---|---|---|
| S29 | **S6** | 80p. sepia and brown | 3·50 | 3·50 |

**S7** Banja Luka

**1994.** 500th Anniv of Banja Luka.

| | | | | |
|---|---|---|---|---|
| S30 | **S7** | 1d.20 multicoloured | 4·00 | 4·00 |

**1994.** Issued at Doboj. Surch with letter. (a) On Nos. S13/16.

| | | | |
|---|---|---|---|
| S31 | **S2** | A on 20d. black and blue | |
| S32 | **S2** | R on 20d. black and blue | |
| S33 | **S2** | R on 30d. black and pink | |
| S34 | - | R on 50d. black and red | |
| S35 | - | R on 100d. black and red | |

(b) On Nos. S18/19 and S21/2.

| | | |
|---|---|---|
| S36 | **S2** | R on 5000d. black and lilac |
| S37 | **S2** | R on 6000d. black and yellow |
| S38 | - | A on 20000d. black and red |
| S39 | - | R on 20000d. black and red |
| S40 | - | R on 30000d. black and red |

Stamps surcharged "A" were sold at the current rate for internal letters and those surcharged "R" at the rate for internal registered letters. The "R" on No. S32 is reversed.

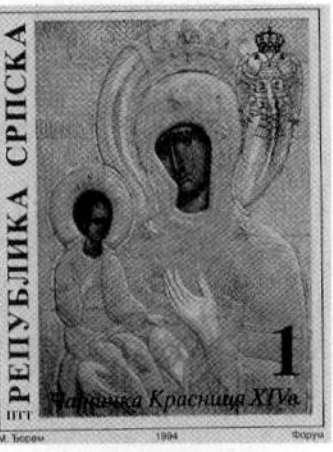


**S9** "Madonna and Child" (icon)

**1994.** Cajnicka Church.

| | | | | |
|---|---|---|---|---|
| S41 | **S9** | 1d. multicoloured | 3·50 | 3·50 |

**1994.** Nos. S18/20 and S23 surch (Nos. S42/3 with letter).

| | | | | |
|---|---|---|---|---|
| S42 | **S2** | A on 5000d. black & lilac | 2·00 | 2·00 |
| S43 | **S2** | R on 6000d. black & yell | 2·00 | 2·00 |
| S44 | **S2** | 40p. on 10000d. blk & bl | 2·00 | 2·00 |
| S45 | - | 2d. on 50000d. black and lilac | 2·00 | 2·00 |

No. S42 was sold at the current rate for internal letters and No. S43, which shows the surcharge as the cyrillic letter resembling "P", at the rate for internal registered letters.

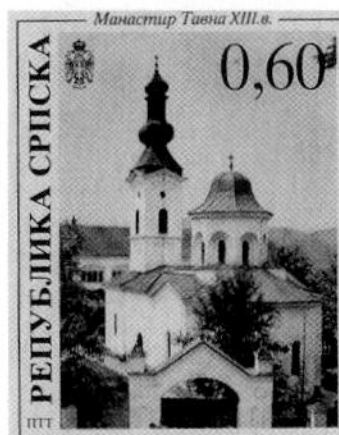


**S 11** Tavna Monastery

**1994.** Monasteries. Multicoloured.

| | | | |
|---|---|---|---|
| S46 | 60p. Type S **11** | 2·00 | 2·00 |
| S47 | 1d. Mostanica (horiz) | 3·00 | 3·00 |
| S48 | 1d.20 Zitomislic | 3·50 | 3·50 |

**S 12** "Aquilegia dinarica"

**1996.** Nature Protection. Multicoloured.

| | | | |
|---|---|---|---|
| S49 | 1d.20 Type S **12** | 2·00 | 2·00 |
| S50 | 1d.20 "Edraianthus niveus" (plant) | 2·00 | 2·00 |
| S51 | 1d.20 Shore lark | 2·00 | 2·00 |
| S52 | 1d.20 "Dinaromys bogdanovi" (dormouse) | 2·00 | 2·00 |

**1996.** Nos. S14/16, S19 and S22 surch.

| | | | | |
|---|---|---|---|---|
| S53 | **S2** | 70p. on 30d. black and pink | 60 | 60 |
| S54 | - | 1d. on 100d. black & red | 70 | 70 |
| S55 | - | 2d. on 30000d. blk & red | 1·30 | 1·30 |
| S56 | - | 3d. on 50d. black and red | 1·90 | 1·90 |
| S57 | **S2** | 5d. on 6000d. black and yellow | 3·25 | 3·25 |

**S14** Relay Station, Mt. Kozara

**1996**

| | | | | |
|---|---|---|---|---|
| S58 | **S14** | A green and bistre | 25 | 25 |
| S59 | - | R purple and brown | 60 | 60 |
| S60 | - | 1d.20 violet and blue | 65 | 65 |
| S61 | - | 2d. lilac and mauve | 1·30 | 1·30 |
| S62 | - | 5d. purple and blue | 2·75 | 2·75 |
| S63 | - | 10d. brown and sepia | 5·75 | 5·75 |

DESIGNS—VERT: R, Kraljica relay station, Mt. Ozren; 2d. Relay station, Mt. Romanija; 5d. Stolice relay station, Mt. Maljevica. HORIZ: 1d.20, Bridge over river Drina at Srbinje; 10d. Bridge at Visegrad.

No. S58 was sold at the current rate for an internal letter and No. S59 at the rate for an internal registered letter.

**S15** Orthodox Church, Bascarsiji

**1997**

| | | | | |
|---|---|---|---|---|
| S64 | **S15** | 2d.50 multicoloured | 1·40 | 1·40 |

**S16** Pupin

**1997.** 62nd Death Anniv of Michael Pupin (physicist and inventor).

| | | | | |
|---|---|---|---|---|
| S65 | **S16** | 2d.50 multicoloured | 1·40 | 1·40 |

S 17 "Primula kitaibeliana"

1997. Flowers. Multicoloured.

| | | | | |
|---|---|---|---|---|
| S66 | | 3d.20 Type S **17** | 1·50 | 1·50 |
| S67 | | 3d.20 "Pedicularis hoerman-niana" | 1·50 | 1·50 |
| S68 | | 3d.20 "Knautia sarajevensis" | 1·50 | 1·50 |
| S69 | | 3d.20 "Oxytropis campestris" | 1·50 | 1·50 |

S18 Robert Koch

1997. Obligatory Tax. Anti-tuberculosis Week. Self-adhesive.

| | | | | |
|---|---|---|---|---|
| S70 | **S18** | 15f. red and blue | 45 | 45 |

S 19 Branko Copic

1997. Writers. Each mauve and yellow.

| | | | |
|---|---|---|---|
| S71 | A (60p.) Type S **19** | 35 | 35 |
| S72 | R (90p.) Jovan Ducic | 60 | 60 |
| S73 | 1d.50 Mesa Selimovic | 60 | 60 |
| S74 | 3d. Aleksa Santic | 1·40 | 1·40 |
| S75 | 5d. Petar Kocic | 2·30 | 2·30 |
| S76 | 10d. Ivo Andric | 4·75 | 4·75 |

S20 European Otter

1997. Nature Protection. Multicoloured.

| | | | |
|---|---|---|---|
| S77 | 2d.50 Type S **20** | 60 | 60 |
| S78 | 4d.50 Roe deer | 1·70 | 1·70 |
| S79 | 6d.50 Brown bear | 3·50 | 3·50 |

S 21 Two Queens

1997. Europa. Tales and Legends. Multicoloured.

| | | | |
|---|---|---|---|
| S80 | 2d.50 Type S **21** | 9·25 | 9·25 |
| S81 | 6d.50 Prince on horseback | 20·00 | 20·00 |

S22 Diana, Princess of Wales

1998. Diana, Princess of Wales Commemoration.

| | | | | |
|---|---|---|---|---|
| S82 | **S22** | 3d.50 multicoloured ("DIANA" in Roman alphabet) | 5·75 | 5·75 |
| S83 | **S22** | 3d.50 multicoloured ("DIANA" in Cyrillic alphabet) | 5·75 | 5·75 |

S23 Cross and Globe

1998. Obligatory Tax. Red Cross. Self-adhesive.

| | | | | |
|---|---|---|---|---|
| S84 | **S23** | 90f. red, blue and ultram | 1·20 | 1·20 |

S 24 Brazil

1998. World Cup Football Championship, France. Showing flags and players of countries in final rounds. Multicoloured.

| | | | |
|---|---|---|---|
| S85 | 90f. Type S **24** | 1·90 | 1·90 |
| S86 | 90f. Morocco | 1·90 | 1·90 |
| S87 | 90f. Norway | 1·90 | 1·90 |
| S88 | 90f. Scotland | 1·90 | 1·90 |
| S89 | 90f. Italy | 1·90 | 1·90 |
| S90 | 90f. Chile | 1·90 | 1·90 |
| S91 | 90f. Austria | 1·90 | 1·90 |
| S92 | 90f. Cameroun | 1·90 | 1·90 |
| S93 | 90f. France | 1·90 | 1·90 |
| S94 | 90f. Saudi Arabia | 1·90 | 1·90 |
| S95 | 90f. Denmark | 1·90 | 1·90 |
| S96 | 90f. South Africa | 1·90 | 1·90 |
| S97 | 90f. Spain | 1·90 | 1·90 |
| S98 | 90f. Nigeria | 1·90 | 1·90 |
| S99 | 90f. Paraguay | 1·90 | 1·90 |
| S100 | 90f. Bulgaria | 1·90 | 1·90 |
| S101 | 90f. Netherlands | 1·90 | 1·90 |
| S102 | 90f. Belgium | 1·90 | 1·90 |
| S103 | 90f. Mexico | 1·90 | 1·90 |
| S104 | 90f. South Korea | 1·90 | 1·90 |
| S105 | 90f. Germany | 1·90 | 1·90 |
| S106 | 90f. United States of America | 1·90 | 1·90 |
| S107 | 90f. Yugoslavia | 1·90 | 1·90 |
| S108 | 90f. Iran | 1·90 | 1·90 |
| S109 | 90f. Romania | 1·90 | 1·90 |
| S110 | 90f. England (U.K. flag) | 1·90 | 1·90 |
| S111 | 90f. Tunisia | 1·90 | 1·90 |
| S112 | 90f. Colombia | 1·90 | 1·90 |
| S113 | 90f. Argentina | 1·90 | 1·90 |
| S114 | 90f. Jamaica | 1·90 | 1·90 |
| S115 | 90f. Croatia | 1·90 | 1·90 |
| S116 | 90f. Japan | 1·90 | 1·90 |

S25 Couple and Musical Instrument

1998. Europa. National Festivals. Multicoloured.

| | | | |
|---|---|---|---|
| S117 | 7m.50 Type S **25** | 9·25 | 9·25 |
| S118 | 7m.50 Couple from Neretva and musical instrument | 9·25 | 9·25 |

S26 Family walking in Countryside

1998. Obligatory Tax. Anti-tuberculosis Week.

| | | | | |
|---|---|---|---|---|
| S119 | **S26** | 75f. multicoloured | 1·20 | 1·20 |

S 27 St. Pantelejmon

1998. 800th Anniv of Hilandar Monastery. Icons. Multicoloured.

| | | | |
|---|---|---|---|
| S120 | 50f. Type S **27** | 80 | 80 |
| S121 | 70f. Jesus Christ | 1·20 | 1·20 |
| S122 | 1m.70 St. Nikola | 2·50 | 2·50 |
| S123 | 2m. St. John of Rila | 3·00 | 3·00 |

S 28 Bijelijna

1999. Towns. Multicoloured. (a) With face value.

| | | | |
|---|---|---|---|
| S124 | 15f. Type S **28** | 25 | 25 |
| S125 | 20f. Sokolac | 35 | 35 |
| S126 | 75f. Prijedor | 1·20 | 1·20 |
| S127 | 2m. Brcko | 3·00 | 3·00 |
| S128 | 4m.50 Zvornik | 6·50 | 6·50 |
| S129 | 10m. Doboj | 15·00 | 15·00 |

(b) Face value expressed by letter.

| | | | |
|---|---|---|---|
| S130 | A (50f.) Banja Luka | 70 | 70 |
| S131 | R (1m.) Trebinje | 1·50 | 1·50 |

No. S130 was sold at the current rate for an internal letter and No. S131 at the rate for an internal registered letter.

S 29 Avions de Transport Regional ATR 72 over Lake

1999. Founding of Air Srpska (state airline). Multicoloured.

| | | | |
|---|---|---|---|
| S132 | 50f. Type S **29** | 70 | 70 |
| S133 | 50f. Airliner above clouds | 70 | 70 |
| S134 | 75f. Airliner over beach | 1·20 | 1·20 |
| S135 | 1m.50 Airliner over lake (different) | 2·20 | 2·20 |

S30 Table Tennis Ball as Globe

1999. International Table Tennis Championships, Belgrade. Multicoloured.

| | | | |
|---|---|---|---|
| S136 | 1m. Type S **30** | 1·70 | 1·70 |
| S137 | 2m. Table tennis table, bat and ball | 3·50 | 3·50 |

S 31 Kozara National Park

1999. Europa. National Parks. Multicoloured.

| | | | |
|---|---|---|---|
| S138 | 1m.50 Type S **31** | 75·00 | 75·00 |
| S139 | 2m. Perucica National Park | 75·00 | 75·00 |

S 32 Open Hands

1999. Obligatory Tax. Red Cross.

| | | | | |
|---|---|---|---|---|
| S140 | **S32** | 10f. multicoloured | 45 | 45 |

S 33 Manuscript

1999. 780th Anniv of Bosnia and Herzegovina Archbishopric (S142, S144/8) and 480th Anniv of Garazole Printing Works (S141, S143). Mult.

| | | | |
|---|---|---|---|
| S141 | 50f. Type S **33** | 70 | 70 |
| S142 | 50f. Dobrun Monastery | 70 | 70 |
| S143 | 50f. "G" | 70 | 70 |
| S144 | 50f. Zhitomislib Monastery | 70 | 70 |
| S145 | 50f. Gomionitsa Monastery | 70 | 70 |
| S146 | 50f. Madonna and Child with angels and prophets (icon, 1578) | 70 | 70 |
| S147 | 50f. St. Nicolas (icon) | 70 | 70 |
| S148 | 50f. Wise Men (icon) | 70 | 70 |

S 34 Brown Trout

1999. Fishes. Multicoloured.

| | | | |
|---|---|---|---|
| S149 | 50f. Type S **34** | 6·75 | 1·20 |
| S150 | 50f. Lake trout (*Salmo trutta morpha lacustris*) | 1·20 | 1·20 |
| S151 | 75f. Huchen | 1·70 | 1·70 |
| S152 | 1m. European grayling | 2·30 | 2·30 |

S35 Lunar Module on Moon's Surface

1999. 30th Anniv of First Manned Landing on Moon. Multicoloured.

| | | | |
|---|---|---|---|
| S153 | 1m. Type S **35** | 1·90 | 1·90 |
| S154 | 2m. Astronaut on Moon | 3·00 | 3·00 |

S36 Pencil and Emblem

1999. 125th Anniv of Universal Postal Union. Mult.

| | | | |
|---|---|---|---|
| S155 | 75f. Type S **36** | 1·20 | 1·20 |
| S156 | 1m.25 Earth and emblem | 2·00 | 2·00 |

S 36a Roadway to '2000'

1999. Obligatory Tax. Tuberculosis Week. Ordinary or selfadhesive gum.

| | |
|---|---|
| S156a | 10f. Type **S 36a** |

S37 Madonna and Child

1999. Art. Icons. Multicoloured.

| | | | |
|---|---|---|---|
| S157 | 50f. Type S **37** | 75 | 75 |
| S158 | 50f. Madonna, Cajnice | 75 | 75 |
| S159 | 50f. Madonna Pelagonitisa | 75 | 75 |
| S160 | 50f. Holy Kirjak Otselnik | 75 | 75 |
| S161 | 50f. Pieta | 75 | 75 |
| S162 | 50f. Entry of Christ into Jerusalem | 75 | 75 |
| S163 | 50f. St. Jovan | 75 | 75 |
| S164 | 50f. Sava and Simeon | 75 | 75 |

**S 38** Ancient Egyptians

**1999.** Millennium (1st series). Sheet 137×86 mm containing Type S **38** and similar horiz designs. Multicoloured.

**MS**S170 50f.×5, Type S **38**; Inventions for time keeping; Iron working; Invention of steam engines; Transport; 1m. Space exploration. 10·00 10·00

**S 39** Postal Stage-Coach during Austro-Hungarian Occupation

**1999.** 135th Anniv of Postal Service. Multicoloured.

| | | | |
|---|---|---|---|
| S171 | 50f. Type S**39** | 75 | 75 |

**MS**S172 55×70 mm. 3m. Tatar postmen crossing bridge during Turkish regency 80·00 80·00

**S 40** Fresco of St. Simeon (Stefan Nemanja) holding Studenica Monastery

**2000.** 800th Death Anniv of Stefan Nemanja (Stephen II).

| | | | |
|---|---|---|---|
| S173 | **S 40** 1m.50 multicoloured | 2·20 | 2·20 |

**S 41** *Prunus domestica* (plum)

**2000.** Trees. Multicoloured.

| | | | |
|---|---|---|---|
| S174 | 1m. Type S**41** | 1·50 | 1·50 |
| S175 | 2m. *Corylus avellana* (hazel) | 3·00 | 3·00 |

**S 42** Bridge, Sepk

**2000.** Bridges on Drina River. Multicoloured.

| | | | |
|---|---|---|---|
| S176 | 1m. Type S**42** | 1·60 | 1·60 |
| S177 | 1m. Pavlovica Bridge, Bijeljina | 1·60 | 1·60 |
| S178 | 1m. Stag and iron bridge, Bratunac | 1·60 | 1·60 |
| S179 | 1m. Train crossing bridge, Zvornik | 1·60 | 1·60 |

**S 43** Jovan Ducic

**2000.** Jovan Ducic (writer) Commemoration.

| | | | |
|---|---|---|---|
| S180 | **S 43** 20f. multicoloured | 35 | 35 |

**S44** Construction of Europe

**2000.** Europa. Construction of Europe. Multicoloured.

| | | | |
|---|---|---|---|
| S181 | 1m.50 Type S **44** | 70·00 | 70·00 |
| S182 | 2m.50 Children and stars | 80·00 | 80·00 |

**S 45** Girl

**2000.** Obligatory Tax. Red Cross Week. Multicoloured. (a) Ordinary gum.

| | | | |
|---|---|---|---|
| S183 | 10f. Type S**45** | 50 | 50 |
| S183a | 10f. Symbols of care (30×41 mm) | 50 | 50 |

(b) Self-adhesive.

| | | | |
|---|---|---|---|
| S183b | 50f. As No. 183a (20×30 mm) | 50 | 50 |

**S 46** Basilica, Banja Luka (destroyed in 1941)

**2000.** Centenary of Banja Luka Province.

| | | | |
|---|---|---|---|
| S184 | **S 46** 1m.50 multicoloured | 2·20 | 2·20 |

**S 47** Footballers

**2000.** Euro 2000–European Football Championships, Belgium and the Netherlands. Multicoloured.

| | | | |
|---|---|---|---|
| S185 | 1m. Type S**47** | 1·50 | 1·50 |
| S186 | 2m. Footballers (different) | 3·00 | 3·00 |

**MS**S187 66×83 mm. 6m. Netherlands and Belgium flags as map and footballers (35×42 mm) 12·50 12·50

**S 48** Leaders of Herzegovina Uprising

**2000.** 125th Anniv of Herzegovina Rebellion (Nevesinje uprising).

| | | | |
|---|---|---|---|
| S188 | **S 48** 1m.50 multicoloured | 2·40 | 2·40 |

**S 49** Outline of Australia and Hurdling

**2000.** Olympic Games, Sydney. Multicoloured.

| | | | |
|---|---|---|---|
| S189 | 50f. Type S**49** | 75 | 75 |
| S190 | 50f. Australia and volleyball | 75 | 75 |
| S191 | 50f. Australia and basketball | 75 | 75 |
| S192 | 50f. Australia and handball | 75 | 75 |

**MS**S193 71×98 mm. 2m. Australia, emu and kangaroo 3·00 3·00

No. **MS**S193 also contains a stamp size label showing Sydney Opera House and Olympic Stadium, the whole forming a composite design.

**S50** Toddler

**2000.** Obligatory Tax. Tuberculosis Week. Multicoloured. (a) Ordinary gum.

| | | | |
|---|---|---|---|
| S194 | 10f. Type S**50** | 50 | 50 |

(b) Self-adhesive.

| | | | |
|---|---|---|---|
| S195 | 1m. As Type S**50** (20×30 mm) | 50 | 50 |

**S 51** Locomotive, 1848

**2000.** 175th Anniv of Railways. Multicoloured.

| | | | |
|---|---|---|---|
| S196 | 50f. Type S**51** | 2·50 | 2·50 |
| S197 | 50f. Steam locomotive, 1865 | 2·50 | 2·50 |
| S198 | 50f. Steam locomotive, 1930 | 2·50 | 2·50 |
| S199 | 1m. Electric locomotive, 1990 | 3·75 | 3·75 |

**S 52** *Leontopodium alpinum* (edelweiss)

**2000.** European Nature Protection. Multicoloured.

| | | | |
|---|---|---|---|
| S200 | 1m. Type S **52** | 1·50 | 1·50 |
| S201 | 2m. *Proteus anguinus* (olm) (horiz) | 3·00 | 3·00 |

**S 53** Columbus discovering America

**2000.** Millennium (2nd series). Two sheets, each 140×86 mm containing Type **S53** and similar horiz designs. Multicoloured.

**MS**S202 (a) 50f.×6, Type S**53**; Discovery of glass, iron and steel; First printing press; Industrial revolution; James Watt and steam engine; Hubble telescope and satellite (space exploration). (b) 3m. Exploration by sea (105×55 mm) 9·25 9·25

Nos. **MS**S202a/b were issued in a folder.

**S 54** The Assumption of Mary (fresco)

**2000.** Icons and Frescoes. Multicoloured.

| | | | |
|---|---|---|---|
| S203 | 50f. Type S**54** | 75 | 75 |
| S204 | 50f. Entry of Christ into Jerusalem (icon) | 75 | 75 |
| S205 | 1m. Madonna with Child and Angels (icon) | 1·50 | 1·50 |
| S206 | 1m. Christos Pantocrator (ceiling fresco) | 1·50 | 1·50 |

**S 55** Alexander Graham Bell and Development of Telephones

**2001.** 125th Anniv of Telephony.

| | | | |
|---|---|---|---|
| S207 | **S 55** 1m. multicoloured | 1·50 | 1·50 |

**S 56** Yuri Gagarin and *Vostok 1*

**2001.** 40th Anniv of First Manned Space Flight. Multicoloured.

| | | | |
|---|---|---|---|
| S208 | 1m. Type S**56** | 1·50 | 1·50 |

**MS**S209 86×66 mm. 3m. Yuri Gagarin, take off and first flight orbit (53×34 mm) 8·75 8·75

**S 57** Vlado Milosevic

**2001.** Birth Centenary of Vlado Milosevic (composer and ethnomusicologist).

| | | | |
|---|---|---|---|
| S210 | **S 57** 50f. multicoloured | 75 | 75 |

**S 58** Waterfall, Sutjeska River

**2001.** Europa. Water Conservation. Multicoloured.

| | | | |
|---|---|---|---|
| S211 | 1m. Type S **58** | 2·75 | 2·75 |
| S212 | 2m. Turjanica river | 5·50 | 5·50 |

**S 59** *Maniola jurtina*

**2001.** Butterflies. Multicoloured.

| | | | |
|---|---|---|---|
| S213 | 50f. Type S**59** | 75 | 75 |
| S214 | 50f. *Pyrgus malvae* | 75 | 75 |
| S215 | 1m. *Papilio machaon* | 1·50 | 1·50 |
| S216 | 1m. *Lycaena phlaeas* inscr 'Lycaena pylaeas ' | 1·50 | 1·50 |

**S60** Women's Costumes, Popovo

**2001.** Traditional Costumes. Multicoloured.

| | | | |
|---|---|---|---|
| S217 | 50f. Type S **60** | 75 | 75 |
| S218 | 50f. Bridal costume, Zmijanje | 75 | 75 |
| S219 | 1m. Woman's costume, Bileca mountains | 1·50 | 1·50 |
| S220 | 1m. Two women, Lijevce | 1·50 | 1·50 |

**S 61** Combatants

**2001.** Republic of Srpska–Karate World Champion, 2001.

| | | | | |
|---|---|---|---|---|
| S221 | **S 61** | 1m.50 multicoloured | 2·20 | 2·20 |

**S 62** Old Castle, Kostajnica

**2001.** Towns. Multicoloured.

| | | | |
|---|---|---|---|
| S222 | 25f. Type **S62** | 35 | 35 |
| S223 | A (50f.) As No. S130 (24×22 mm) | 75 | 75 |
| S224 | 1m. Square with monument dedicated to war victims, Srbinje | 1·50 | 1·50 |

No. S225 is vacant.

**S63** Emblem

**2001.** Obligatory Tax. Anti-Tuberculosis Week.

| | | | | |
|---|---|---|---|---|
| S226 | **S63** | 10f. multicoloured | 50 | 50 |

**S64** Rastusa Cave, Teslic

**2001.** Caves. Multicoloured.

| | | | |
|---|---|---|---|
| S227 | 50f. Type S **64** | 75 | 75 |
| S228 | 50f. Vagan cave, Vitorog | 75 | 75 |
| S229 | 50f. Pavlova cave, Petrovo | 75 | 75 |
| S230 | 50f. Orlovaca cave, Pale | 75 | 75 |
| S231 | 50f. Ledana cave, Bobija | 75 | 75 |
| S232 | 50f. Hole, Podovi plateau | 75 | 75 |

**S65** Alfred Nobel (founder)

**2001.** Centenary of Nobel Prizes. Multicoloured.

| | | | |
|---|---|---|---|
| S233 | 1m. Type S **65** | 1·50 | 1·50 |
| S234 | 2m. Ivo Andric (winner of Nobel prize for Literature, 1961) | 3·00 | 3·00 |

**S 66** Klinje Lake, Gacko

**2001.** European Nature Protection. Multicoloured.

| | | | |
|---|---|---|---|
| S235 | 1m. Type **S66** | 1·50 | 1·50 |
| S236 | 1m. Bardaca Lake, Srbac | 1·50 | 1·50 |

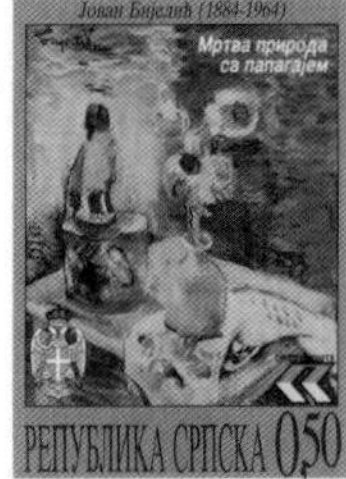

**S 67** *Still Life with Parrot* (Jovan Bijelic)

**2001.** Art. Multicoloured.

| | | | |
|---|---|---|---|
| S237 | 50f. Type **S67** | 75 | 75 |
| S238 | 50f. *Djerdap* (Todor Svrakic) | 75 | 75 |
| S239 | 50f. *Suburb of Belgrade* (Kosta Hakman) | 75 | 75 |
| S240 | 50f. *Adela* (Miodrag Vujacic Mirski) (vert) | 75 | 75 |

**S 68** Birth of Christ (icon, Studenica Monastery)

**2001.** Christmas.

| | | | | |
|---|---|---|---|---|
| S 241 | **S 68** | 1m. multicoloured | 1·50 | 1·50 |

**S 69** Player and Club Badge

**2001.** 75th Anniv of Borac Football Club.

| | | | | |
|---|---|---|---|---|
| S242 | **S 69** | 1m.50 multicoloured | 2·20 | 2·20 |

**S 70** National Arms

**2002.** 10th Anniv of Republic Srpska. Multicoloured.

| | | | |
|---|---|---|---|
| **MS**S243b | 71×64 mm. 2m. Map (42×35 mm) | 3·25 | 3·25 |
| S243 | 50f. Type **S70** | 80 | 80 |
| S243a | 1m. National flag (horiz) | 1·60 | 1·60 |

**S 71** Hand gripping Cobra

**2002.** Fight against Terrorism. Multicoloured.

| | | | |
|---|---|---|---|
| S244 | 1m. Type **S71** | 1·60 | 1·60 |
| **MS**S244a | 68×76 mm. 2m. Eyes enclosed in globe | 3·25 | 3·25 |

**S 72** Ski Jump

**2002.** Winter Olympic Games, Salt Lake City. Multicoloured.

| | | | |
|---|---|---|---|
| S245 | 50f. Type **S72** | 80 | 80 |
| S246 | 1m. Two man bobsleigh | 1·60 | 1·60 |

**S 73** Seated Woman with Cultural Symbols

**2002.** Centenary of Prosvjeta Cultural Association.

| | | | | |
|---|---|---|---|---|
| S247 | **S 73** | 1m. multicoloured | 1·60 | 1·60 |

**S 74** Vasilije Ostroski Church, Sarajevo

**2002.** Towns. Multicoloured.

| | | | |
|---|---|---|---|
| S248 | 50f. Type S **74** | 80 | 80 |
| S249 | 2m. Oil Refinery, Srpski Brod (horiz) | 3·25 | 32·00 |

NOTE: Due to the time lapse since Republika Srpska was last listed and the lack of stamps, several numbers have been left pending.

**S75** Charles Lindbergh and *Spirit of St. Louis*

**2002.** 75th Anniv of First Trans-Atlantic Flight.

| | | | | |
|---|---|---|---|---|
| S250 | **S75** | 1m. multicoloured | 1·60 | 1·60 |

**S 76** Horses and Clown

**2002.** Europa. Circus. Multicoloured.

| | | | |
|---|---|---|---|
| S251 | 1m. Type **S76** | 1·60 | 1·60 |
| S252 | 1m.50 Elephants | 2·40 | 2·40 |

**S 76a** Rescue Workers

**2002.** Obligatory Tax. Red Cross Week. Multicoloured. (a) Ordinary gum.

| | | | |
|---|---|---|---|
| S252a | 10f. Type **S76a** | 55 | 55 |

(b) Self-adhesive.

| | | | |
|---|---|---|---|
| S252b | 50f. As Type **S76a** plus emblem | 55 | 55 |

**S 77** Footballers

**2002.** World Cup Football Championships, Japan and South Korea.Multicoloured.

| | | | |
|---|---|---|---|
| S253 | 50f. Type **S77** | 80 | 80 |
| S254 | 1m. Footballers (different) | 1·60 | 1·60 |

**S 78** Slatina

**2002.** Spas. Multicoloured.

| | | | |
|---|---|---|---|
| S255 | 25f. Type **S78** | 40 | 40 |
| S256 | 50f. Mljecanica | 80 | 80 |
| S257 | 75f. Vilina Vlas | 1·30 | 1·30 |
| S258 | 1m. Laktasi | 1·70 | 1·70 |
| S259 | 1m.50 Vrucica | 2·50 | 2·50 |
| S260 | 5m. Dvorovi | 8·75 | 8·75 |

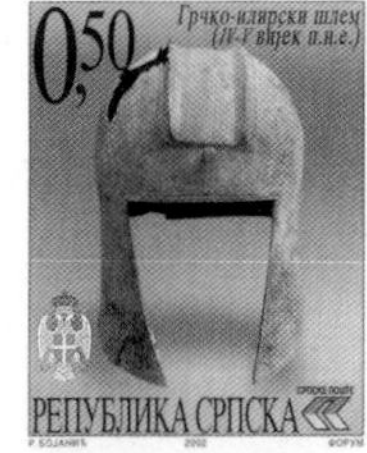

**S 79** Greek-Illyrian Helmet (4th—5th century BC)

**2002.** Museum Exhibits. Multicoloured.

| | | | |
|---|---|---|---|
| S261 | 50f. Type **S79** | 85 | 85 |
| S262 | 50f. Murano glass cup | 85 | 85 |
| S263 | 1m. Headstone of Grd (12th century parish priest) (horiz) | 1·70 | 1·70 |
| S264 | 1m. Silver bracelet (4th–5th century BC) (horiz) | 1·70 | 1·70 |

**S 79a** Waterfall and Lungs as Forest

**2002.** Obligatory Tax. Tuberculosis Week. Multicoloured. (a) Ordinary gum.

| | | | |
|---|---|---|---|
| S264a | 10f. Type **S79a** | 55 | 55 |

(b) Self-adhesive.

| | | | |
|---|---|---|---|
| S264b | 50f. As Type **S79a** (20×30 mm) | 55 | 55 |

**S80** *Boletus regius*

**2002.** Fungi. Multicoloured.

| | | | |
|---|---|---|---|
| S265 | 50f. Type S **80** | 85 | 85 |
| S266 | 50f. *Macrolepiota procera* | 85 | 85 |
| S267 | 1m. *Amanita caesarea* | 1·70 | 1·70 |
| S268 | 1m. *Craterellus cornucopoides* | 1·70 | 1·70 |

**S 81** Maglic Mountain

**2002.** European Nature Protection. Multicoloured.

| | | | |
|---|---|---|---|
| S269 | 50f. Type **S81** | 85 | 85 |
| S269a | 1m. Klekovaca Mountain | 1·70 | 1·70 |

**S 82** *Petar Popovic Pecija* (Spiro Bocaric) (1933)

**2002.** Art. Multicoloured.

| | | | |
|---|---|---|---|
| S270 | 50f. Type **S82** | 85 | 85 |
| S271 | 50f. *Black Lake beneath Durmitor* (Lazar Drljaca) (1935) (horiz) | 85 | 85 |
| S272 | 1m. *Zembilj Street* (Branko Sotra) (1937) (horiz) | 1·70 | 1·70 |
| S273 | 1m. *Birds and Landscape* (Milan Sovilj) (2000) (horiz) | 1·70 | 1·70 |

**S83** Vrbas Canyon (scene from film by Spiro Bocaric) (1937)

**2003.** Centenary of First Film shown in Republic Srpska. Sheet 92×73 mm.

**MS**S274 S **83** 3m. multicoloured 5·00 5·00

**S84** Alekse Santic

**2003.** 135th Birth Anniv of Alekse Santic (writer).

S275 **S84** 1m. multicoloured 1·80 1·80

**S 85** Crucifixion, Sretenje Monastery

**2003.** Easter. Multicoloured.

| | | | |
|---|---|---|---|
| S276 | 50f. Type S **85** | 90 | 90 |
| S277 | 1m. Resurrection (painting, Altarpiece, Eisenheim by Matias Greenwald) | 1·80 | 1·80 |

**S86** Everest Peaks

**2003.** 50th Anniv of First Ascent of Mount Everest. Sheet 82×58 mm containing Type S 86 and similar vert design. Multicoloured.

**MS**S278 1m.50 Type S **86**; 1m.50 Mountaineer through magnifying glass 7·25 7·25

The stamps and margin of **MS**S278 form a composite design.

**S87** Aviation Poster

**2003.** Europa. Poster Art. Multicoloured.

| | | | |
|---|---|---|---|
| S279 | 1m. Type S **87** | 1·80 | 1·80 |
| S280 | 1m.50 Naval poster | 2·75 | 2·75 |

**S 87a** Transfusion Equipment and Family

**2003.** Obligatory Tax. Red Cross Week.

S280a **S 87a** 10f. multicoloured 60 60

**S 88** Arab

**2003.** Horses. Multicoloured.

| | | | |
|---|---|---|---|
| S281 | 50f. Type S**88** | 90 | 90 |
| S282 | 50f. Lipizzaner | 90 | 90 |
| S283 | 1m. Inscr 'Bosanko' | 1·80 | 1·80 |
| S284 | 1m. Inscr 'Posavatz' | 1·80 | 1·80 |

**S 89** Pope John Paul II

**2003.** 2nd visit of Pope John Paul II to Bosnia Hercegovina. Multicoloured.

| | | | |
|---|---|---|---|
| S285 | 1m.50 Type S **89** | 8·25 | 8·25 |
| S285a | 1m.50 Pope John Paul II and Ivan Merz (Croatian lay academic, beatified by Pope John-Paul II on Sunday, June 22, 2003 at Banja Luka) (horiz) | 3·00 | 3·00 |

Stamps of the same design as No. S285a were issued by Bosnia Herzegovina (Sarajevo) and Bosnia Herzegovina (Croatia).

**S 90** Medal of Honour

**2003.** Medals. Multicoloured.

| | | | |
|---|---|---|---|
| S286 | 50f. Type S **90** | 1·00 | 1·00 |
| S287 | 1m. Njegos I medal | 2·00 | 2·00 |

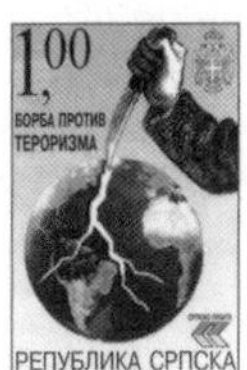

**S 91** Dagger piercing Globe

**2003.** Fight against Terrorism.

S288 **S 91** 1m. multicoloured 2·00 2·00

**S 91a** 'Stop TB'

**2003.** Obligatoery Tax. Tuberculosis Week. (a) Ordinary gum.

S288a **S 91a** 10f. multicoloured 65 65

(b) Self-adhesive.

S288b 50f. As No. S288a (30×20 mm) 65 65

**S 92** Leo Tolstoy

**2003.** 175th Birth Anniv of Count Lev Nikolayevich (Leo) Tolstoy (writer, pacifist, Christian anarchist and educational reformer).

S289 **S 92** 1m. multicoloured 2·10 2·10

**S 93** Ugar River Canyon

**2003.** European Nature Protection. Multicoloured.

| | | | |
|---|---|---|---|
| S290 | 50f. Type S**93** | 1·10 | 1·10 |
| S291 | 1m. Drina River canyon | 2·10 | 2·10 |

**S 94** *St. Sava and Martyr Varvara* (Radul)

**2003.** Religious Art. Multicoloured.

| | | | |
|---|---|---|---|
| S292 | 50f. Type S**94** | 1·30 | 1·30 |
| S293 | 50f. *St. Lazar* (Andrej Raicevic) | 1·30 | 1·30 |
| S294 | 1m. *Coronation of Madonna with Saints* (Dimitrije Bacevic) | 2·75 | 2·75 |
| S295 | 1m. *Deisis* (intercession of Madonna and Jovan Pretaca) | 2·75 | 2·75 |

**S 95** Child and Snowman

**2003.** Christmas and New Year. Multicoloured.

| | | | |
|---|---|---|---|
| S296 | 50f. Type S**95** | 1·30 | 1·30 |
| S297 | 1m. Santa Claus and reindeer | 2·75 | 2·75 |

**S 96** Wright Brothers and *Wright Flyer I*

**2003.** Centenary of Powered Flight. Multicoloured.

| | | | |
|---|---|---|---|
| S298 | 50f. Type S**96** | 1·30 | 1·30 |
| S299 | 1m. Ferdinand von Zeppelin and air ship LZ 127 *Graf Zeppelin* | 2·75 | 2·75 |

**S 97** *Oath of Rebels* (bas relief, memorial fountain, Orasac)

**2004.** Bicentenary of First Serbian Uprising. Sheet 78×62 mm containing Type S 97 and similar vert design. Multicoloured.

**MS**S300 1m.50×2, Type S **97**; *Oath of Rebels* (right) 8·00 8·00

The stamps of **MS**S300 form a composite design.

**S 98** Early Greek Chariot Race

**2004.** Olympic Games, Athens. Sheet 100×60 mm containing Type S 98 and similar vert design. Multicoloured.

**MS**S301 1m.50×2, Type S **98**; Early Greek chariot race (right) 8·50 8·50

The stamps of **MS**S301 form a composite design.

**S 99** Albert Einstein

**2004.** 125th Birth Anniv of Albert Einstein (physicist and 1921–Nobel Prize winner).

S 302 **S 99** 1m.50 multicoloured 4·25 4·25

**S100** Risen Christ

**2004.** Easter. Multicoloured.

| | | | |
|---|---|---|---|
| S303 | 50f. Type S **100** | 1·40 | 1·40 |
| S304 | 1m. Risen Christ (different) | 2·75 | 2·75 |

**S101** Canoeing

**2004.** Europa. Holidays. Multicoloured.

| | | | |
|---|---|---|---|
| S305 | 50f. Type S **101** | 2·75 | 2·75 |
| S306 | 1m. Hang-gliding | 4·25 | 4·25 |

**S102** Hands holding Blood Droplet as Gift

**2004.** Obligatory Tax. Red Cross.

S307 **S102** 10f. multicoloured 1·00 1·00

**S103** Kulasi

**2004.** Spas.

S308 **S103** 20f. multicoloured 1·00 1·00

**S104** Milutina Milankovica

**2004.** 125th Birth Anniv of Milutina Milankovica.

S309 **S104** 1m. multicoloured 2·75 2·75

**S 105** Football and Map

**2004.** European Football Championships, Portugal.

S310 **S 105** 1m.50 multicoloured 4·25 4·25

**S 106** Discus Thrower, Games Emblem and Temple Ruins

**2004.** Olympic Games, Greece. Multicoloured.

| | | | |
|---|---|---|---|
| S311 | 50f. Type S **106** | 1·40 | 1·40 |
| S312 | 50f. Hurdler, ruins and early runners | 1·40 | 1·40 |
| S313 | 1m. Early and modern runners and temple ruins | 2·75 | 2·75 |
| S314 | 1m. Runners and charioteers | 2·75 | 2·75 |

**S 107** *Arctostaphylos uva* (bear ears)

**2004.** European Nature Protection. Multicoloured.

| | | | |
|---|---|---|---|
| S315 | 50f. Type S **107** | 1·40 | 1·40 |
| S316 | 1m. *Monticola saxatilis* (rufous-tailed rock thrush) | 2·75 | 2·75 |

**S 107a** Stylized Lung

**2004.** Obligatory TaxX. Tuberculosis Week. (a) Ordinary gum.

| | | | |
|---|---|---|---|
| S316a | **S 107a** 10f. multicoloured | 1·00 | 1·00 |

(b) Self-adhesive.

| | | | |
|---|---|---|---|
| S316b | 10f. As Type S**107a** (20×30 mm) | 1·00 | 1·00 |

**S 108** Antimonite

**2004.** Minerals. Multicoloured.

| | | | |
|---|---|---|---|
| S317 | 50f. Type S **108** | 1·40 | 1·40 |
| S318 | 50f. Pyrites | 1·40 | 1·40 |
| S319 | 1m. Sphalerite | 2·75 | 2·75 |
| S320 | 1m. Quartz | 2·75 | 2·75 |

**S 109** Mihajlo Pupin

**2004.** 150th Birth Anniv of Mihajlo Pupin (scientist).

| | | | |
|---|---|---|---|
| S321 | **S 109** 1m. multicoloured | 2·75 | 2·75 |

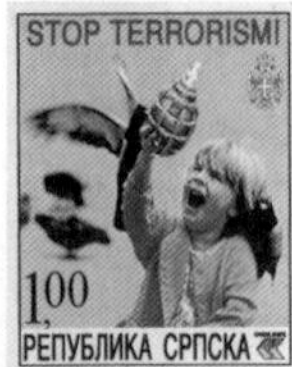

**S 110** Child, Grenade and Pigeons

**2004.** Struggle against Terrorism.

| | | | |
|---|---|---|---|
| S322 | **S 110** 1m. multicoloured | 2·75 | 2·75 |

**S 110a** *Digitalis grandiflora*

**2004.** Flora. Multicoloured.

| | | | |
|---|---|---|---|
| S322a | 50f. Type S **110a** | 1·40 | 1·40 |
| S322b | 50f. *Arnica montana* | 1·40 | 1·40 |
| S322c | 1m. *Rosa pendulina* | 2·75 | 2·75 |
| S322d | 1m. *Gentiana lutea* | 2·75 | 2·75 |

**S 111** Mljecanica near Kozarska Dubica

**2004.** Spas. Multicoloured.

| | | | |
|---|---|---|---|
| S323 | 50f. Type S **111** | 1·40 | 1·40 |
| S324 | 1m. Laktasi | 2·75 | 2·75 |

**S 112** The Nativity (icon)

**2004.** Christmas.

| | | | |
|---|---|---|---|
| S325 | **S 112** 1m. multicoloured | 2·75 | 2·75 |

**S 113** *Serbian Peasant from Semberija*

**2005.** Art. Paintings by Milenko Atanackovic. Multicoloured.

| | | | |
|---|---|---|---|
| S326 | 50f. Type S **113** | 1·40 | 1·40 |
| S327 | 1m. *Beledija–Old Community* (horiz) | 2·75 | 2·75 |

**S 114** Janj River

**2005.** International Day of Water Protection.

| | | | |
|---|---|---|---|
| S328 | **S 114** 1m. multicoloured | 2·75 | 2·75 |

**S115** Traditional Hearth

**2005.** Europa. Gastronomy. Multicoloured.

| | | | |
|---|---|---|---|
| S329 | 1m. Type S **115** | 2·75 | 2·75 |
| S330 | 1m.50 Table laid with food | 4·25 | 4·25 |

**S 116** *The Christ Guardian* (icon), Church of Madonna, Ljeviska

**2005.** Easter.

| | | | |
|---|---|---|---|
| S331 | **S 116** 50f. multicoloured | 1·50 | 1·50 |

**S117** Pope John Paul II

**2005.** Pope John Paul II Commemoration. Multicoloured.

| | | | |
|---|---|---|---|
| S332 | 1m.50 Type S **117** | 4·25 | 4·25 |
| **MS**S333 | 56×49 mm. 5m. St. Peters Basilica and Pope John Paul II | 14·00 | 14·00 |

**S118** Emblem

**2005.** Obligatory Tax. Red Cross. Self-adhesive.

| | | | |
|---|---|---|---|
| S334 | **S118** 10f. vermilion and black | 1·00 | 1·00 |

**S119** *Vipera berus berus*

**2005.** Snakes. Multicoloured.

| | | | |
|---|---|---|---|
| S335 | 50f. Type S **119** | 1·40 | 1·40 |
| S336 | 50f. *Vipera ursinii* | 1·40 | 1·40 |
| S337 | 1m. *Vipera berus bosniensis* | 2·75 | 2·75 |
| S338 | 1m. *Vipera ammodytes* | 2·75 | 2·75 |

**S 120** Castle

**2005.** 50th Anniv of Disneyland Theme Park, Florida. Multicoloured.

| | | | |
|---|---|---|---|
| S339 | 50f. Type S **120** | 1·40 | 1·40 |
| S340 | 1m. houses | 2·75 | 2·75 |

**S121** Fighting Bulls, Grmec

**2005.** Traditions.

| | | | |
|---|---|---|---|
| S341 | **S121** 1m.50 multicoloured | 4·25 | 4·25 |

**S122** *Prasuma Perucica*

**2005.** 50th Anniv of Europa Stamps. Multicoloured.

| | | | |
|---|---|---|---|
| S342 | 1m.95 Type S **122** | 5·50 | 5·50 |
| S343 | 1m.95 Rafting, Odmor | 5·50 | 5·50 |
| S344 | 1m.95 Mostar bridge | 5·50 | 5·50 |
| S345 | 1m.95 Drina river | 5·50 | 5·50 |

**S123** Landscape and Lungs

**2005.** Obligatory Tax. Anti-Tuberculosis Week.

| | | | |
|---|---|---|---|
| S346 | **S123** 10f. multicoloured | 1·00 | 1·00 |

**S124** Balls and Belgrade Arena

**2005.** European Basketball Championship, Belgrade. Multicoloured, colour wash given.

| | | | |
|---|---|---|---|
| S347 | **S124** 50f. lilac | 1·40 | 1·40 |
| S348 | **S124** 50f. yellow | 1·40 | 1·40 |
| S349 | **S124** 50f. green | 1·40 | 1·40 |
| S350 | **S124** 50f. lilac | 1·40 | 1·40 |
| S351 | **S124** 50f. blue | 1·40 | 1·40 |

**S125** National Museum

**2005.** 75th Anniversaries. Multicoloured.

| | | | |
|---|---|---|---|
| S352 | 1m. Type S **125** | 2·75 | 2·75 |
| S353 | 1m. National Theatre (horiz) | 2·75 | 2·75 |

**S126** Tunnel, Sargan

**2005.** Tourism. Makra Gora Railway, Visegard. Sheet 101×54 mm containing Type S **126** and similar vert design. Multicoloured.

| | | | |
|---|---|---|---|
| **MS**S354 | 50f. Type S **126**; 1m. Station, Makra Gora | 4·25 | 4·25 |

The stamps and margin of **MS**S354 form a composite design.

**S127** *Bleriot XI*

**2005.** Centenary of International Aviation Federation (FAI).

| | | | |
|---|---|---|---|
| S355 | **S127** 1m.50 multicoloured | 4·25 | 4·25 |

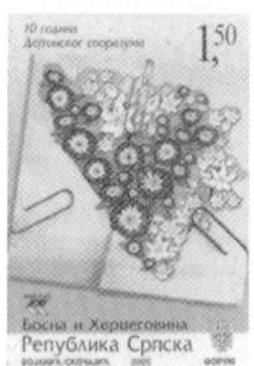

**S128** Flowers over map

**2005.** 10th Anniv of Dayton Agreement.

| | | | |
|---|---|---|---|
| S356 | **S128** 1m.50 multicoloured | 4·25 | 4·25 |

**S129** Guber

**2005.** Spas.

| | | | |
|---|---|---|---|
| S357 | **S129** 50f. multicoloured | 1·40 | 1·40 |

**S130** *Crex crex* (corncrake)

**2005.** European Nature Protection. Birds. Multicoloured.
S358 50f. Type S **130** 1·40 1·40
S359 1m. *Platalea leucorodia* (spoonbill) 2·75 2·75

**S131** Monument to Victims

**2005.** 60th Anniv of Liberation of Jasenovac Concentration Camp.
S360 **S131** 50f. multicoloured 1·40 1·40

**S132** Mozart

**2006.** 250th Birth Anniv of Wolfgang Amadeus Mozart (composer and musician).
S361 **S132** 1m.50 multicoloured 4·25 4·25

**S133** Branke Sotre

**2006.** Birth Centenary of Branke Sotre (artist).
S362 **S133** 1m. multicoloured 2·75 2·75

**S134** Biathlete

**2006.** Winter Olympic Games, Turin. Multicoloured.
S363 50f. Type S **134** 1·40 1·40
S364 1m. Alpine skier 2·75 2·75

**S135** Kulasi

**2006.** Spas.
S365 **S135** 20f. multicoloured 1·00 1·00
No. S365 is as No. S308 but redrawn.

**S136** Inscr "Saxifraga prenja"

**2006.** Flora. Multicoloured.
S366 50f. Type **S136** 1·40 1·40
S367 50f. *Asperula hercegovina* 1·40 1·40
S368 1m. *Campanula hercegovina* 2·75 2·75
S369 1m. Inscr "Oxtropis prenja" 2·75 2·75

**S137** Basket of Eggs

**2006.** Easter.
S370 **S137** 70f. multicoloured 2·10 2·10

**S138** "Tear" (Luja Kajkut)

**2006.** Europa. Integration. Multicoloured.
S371 1m. Type S **138** 2·75 2·75
S372 1m.50 "Country Dance" (Milica Popic) 4·25 4·25

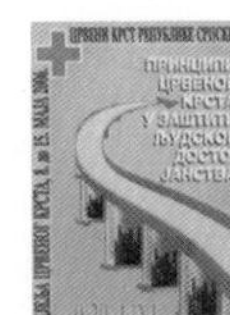
**S 139** Emblem

**2005.** Obligatory Tax. Red Cross.
S373 **S139** 20f. multicoloured 1·00 1·00

**S140** Legs and Ball

**2006.** World Cup Football Championship, Germany. Multicoloured.
S374 50f. Type S **140** 1·40 1·40
S375 1m. Stadium and ball 2·75 2·75
**MS**S376 65×49 mm. 3m.German player and ball 8·25 8·25

**S141** Runner

**2006.** 10th Anniv of Vidovdan Road Race.
S377 **S141** 1m. multicoloured 2·75 2·75

**S142** Nikola Tesla

**2006.** 150th Birth Anniv of Nikola Tesla (engineer) (1st issue). Sheet 66×60 mm.
**MS**S378 1m.50 multicoloured 4·25 4·25
The stamps and margin of **MS**S378 form a composite design.
See also No. S385.

**S143** "CTOH TB"

**2006.** Obligatory Tax. Anti-Tuberculosis Week.
S379 **S143** 20f. multicoloured 1·00 1·00

**S144** *Tetrao urogallus* (capercaille)

**2006.** European Nature Protection. Multicoloured.
S380 50f. Type S **144** 1·40 1·40
S381 1m. *Rupicapra rupicapra* (chamois) 2·75 2·75

No. S382 and Type S **145** have been left for "50th Anniv of Children's Theatre", issued on 14 October 2006, not yet received.

**S146** Buckle

**2006.** Museum Exhibits. Multicoloured.
S383 1m. Type S **146** 2·75 2·75
S384 1m. Curved buckle with red stones 2·75 2·75

**S147** Nikola Tesla

**2006.** 150th Birth Anniv of Nikola Tesla (engineer) (2nd issue).
S385 **S147** 70f. multicoloured 2·10 2·10

**S148** Johann von Goethe

**2007.** 175th Birth Anniv of Johann Wolfgang von Goethe (polymath).
S386 **S148** 1m.50 multicoloured 4·25 4·25

**S149** Decorated Egg

**2007.** Easter.
S387 **S149** 70f. multicoloured 2·10 2·10

**S150** Study for Isabella d'Este

**2007.** 555th Birth Anniv of Leonardo da Vinci (artist and polymath). Multicoloured.
S388 70f. Type S **150** 2·10 2·10
S389 1m. Study for The Last Supper 2·75 2·75

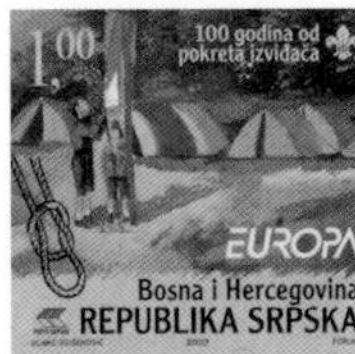

**S151** Campsite

**2007.** Europa. Centenary of Scouting. Multicoloured. (a) 26×41 mm.
S390 1m. Type S **151** 2·75 2·75
S391 1m.50 Scouts 4·25 4·25

(b) Size 35×45 mm.
S392 1m. As Type S **151**, with pink upper edge 2·75 2·75
S393 1m. As Type S **151**, with pink lower edge 'EUROPA 100 JAHRE PFADFINDERBEWEGUNG' 2·75 2·75
S394 1m. As Type S **151** with pink lower edge 'EUROPA 100 ANS DU SCOUTISME' 2·75 2·75
S395 1m.50 As No. S 391, with pink upper edge 4·25 4·25
S396 1m.50 As No. S 391, with pink upper edge 'EUROPA 100 YEARS OF SCOUTING' 4·25 4·25
S397 1m.50 As No. S 391, with pink lower edge 4·25 4·25

**S152** Clasped Hands

**2007.** Obligatory Tax. Red Cross.
S398 **S152** 20f. multicoloured 1·00 1·00

**S153** Liplje Monastery

**2007.** Monasteries. Multicoloured.
S399 70f. Type S **153** 1·90 1·90
S400 1m. Dobricevo 2·75 2·75

**S154** Koarac

**2007.** Cities. Multicoloured.
S401 20f. Type S **154** 70 70
S402 20f. Derventa 70 70
S403 20f. Prjedor 70 70
S404 20f. Laktasi 70 70
S405 20f. Foca 70 70
S406 20f. Bijelijina 70 70
S407 70f. Srebrenica 2·10 2·10
S408 1m.50 Sipovo 4·25 4·25
S409 1m.50 Mrkonjic Grad 4·25 4·25
S410 2m. Trebinje 5·50 5·50
S411 5m. Zvornik 14·00 14·00

**S155** Serbian Tri-colour Hound

**2007.** Dogs. Multicoloured.
S412 70f. Type S **155** 2·10 2·10
S413 70f. Istarski Ostrodlaki gonic (rough coated scent hound) 2·10 2·10
S414 70f. Srpski odbrambeni pas (Serbian guard dog) 2·10 2·10
S415 70f. Tornak (sheep dog) 2·10 2·10

**S156** Orthodox Church and Old Post Office

**2007.** Centenary of Post Office, Obudovac.
S416 **S156** 10f. multicoloured 1·00 1·00

**S157** Ban Milosavljevic (statue)

**2007.** 125th Birth Anniv of Ban Svetislav Milosavljevic (leader 1930–33).
S417 **S157** 1m.50 multicoloured 4·25 4·25

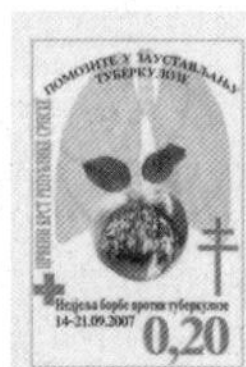
**S158** Apple containing People

**2007.** Obligatory Tax. Anti-Tuberculosis Week.
S418 **S158** 20f. multicoloured 1·20 1·20

**S159** Early Racquet and Balls

**2007.** Centenary of Banja Luca Tennis Club. Sheet 83×58 mm containing Type S 159 and similar horiz design. Multicoloured.
**MS**S419 1m.×2 Type S **159**; Modern racquet and ball 5·50 5·50

The stamps and margin of **MS**S342 form a composite design.

**S160** Sputnik and Globe

**2007.** 50th Anniv of Space Exploration.
S420 **S160** 1m.50 multicoloured 4·25 4·25

**S161** *Picea abies*

**2007.** European Nature Protection. Conifers. Multicoloured.
S421 70f. Type S **161** 1·90 1·90
S422 1m. *Picea omorica* 2·75 2·75

**S 162** Post Office Building

**2008.** 125th Anniv of Samac Post Office.
S422a **S 162** 1m.40 multicoloured 4·25 4·25

**S 163** *Self Portrait*

**2008.** 155th Birth Anniv of Vincent Van Gogh (artist).
S423 **S 163** 1m.50 multicoloured 4·25 4·25

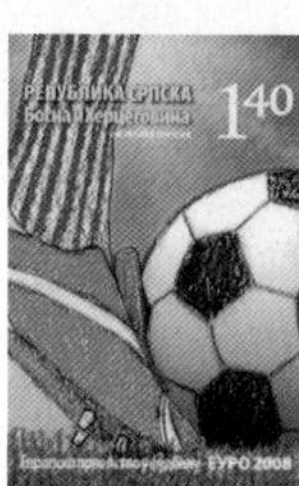
**S 164** Player's Foot and Ball

**2008.** Euro 2008–European Football Championships, Austria and Switzerland. Sheet 82×60 mm containing Type S **164** and similar vert design. Multicoloured.
**MS**S424 1m.40×2, Type **S 164**; Ball and red and white boot 8·25 8·25

The stamps and margins of **MS**S424 form a composite design.

**S 165** Quill and Ink Pot

**2008.** Europa. The Letter. Multicoloured.
S425 1m. Type **S 165** 2·75 2·75
S426 2m. Hand holding pencil 5·50 5·50
**MS**S427 108×82 mm. Nos. S425/6, each×3 26·00 26·00

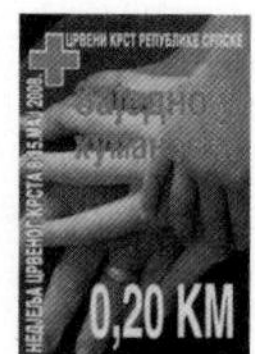
**S 166** Hands

**2008.** Obligatory Tax. Red Cross.
S428 **S 166** 20f. multicoloured 1·20 1·20

**S 167** Children and Microphone

**2008.** 15th Children's Song Festival, Djurdjerdan.
S429 **S 167** 1m.50 multicoloured 4·25 4·25

**S 168** Post Van

**2008.** Personal Stamps. Multicoloured. Self-adhesive.
S430 70f. Type S **168** 2·10 2·10
S431 70f. Post box (vert) 2·10 2·10
S432 70f. Hand stamp (vert) 2·10 2·10
S433 70f. Post horn 2·10 2·10

**S 169** Festival Mascot as Postman

**2008.** Banja Luka International Festival.
S434 **S 169** 1m.50 multicoloured 4·25 4·25

**S 170** *Gyromitra esculenta*

**2008.** Poisonous Fungi. Multicoloured.
S435 70f. Type S **170** 2·10 2·10
S436 70f. *Amanita muscaria* 2·10 2·10
S437 70f. *Amanita pantherina* 2·10 2·10
S438 70f. *Amanita phalloides* 2·10 2·10

**S 171** Charles Darwin

**2008.** 150th Anniv of Publication of Theory of Evolution by Charles Darwin.
S439 **S 171** 1m.50 multicoloured 4·25 4·25

**S 172** *Gentiana verna*

**2008.** Flowers. Multicoloured.
S440 50f. Type S **172** 1·60 1·60
S441 1m.50 *Galanthus nivalis* (vert) 4·75 4·75
S442 2m. *Viola odorata* 6·25 6·25
S443 5m. *Centaurea cyanus* 16·00 16·00

**S 173** High Jump and National Stadium

**2008.** Olympic Games, Beijing. Multicoloured.
S444 70f. Type **S 173** 2·40 2·40
S445 2m.10 Swimmer and National Aquatic Center, Beijing 6·50 6·50
**MS**S446 3m.10 Gymnast 10·00 10·00

No. S447 is vacant.

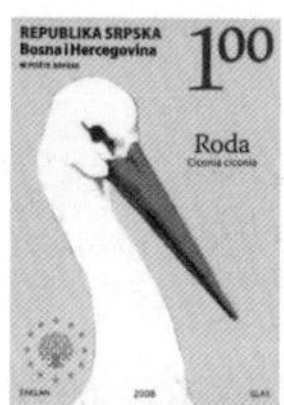
**S 174** *Ciconia ciconia* (white stork)

**2008.** European Nature Protection. Birds. Multicoloured.
S448 1m. Type S **174** 3·25 3·25
S449 1m. *Strix aluco* (Eurasian tawny owl) 3·25 3·25

**S 175** Tvrdos

**2008.** Monasteries. Multicoloured.
S450 1m. Type S **175** 3·25 3·25
S451 1m. Gracanica 3·25 3·25

**S 175a** Flowers

**2008.** Obligatory Tax. Tuberculosis Week.
S451a **S 175a** 20f. multicoloured 1·20 1·20

**S 176** Milan Jelic

**2008.** Milan Jelic (president 2006–7) Commemoration. Sheet 87×63 mm.
**MS**S452 multicoloured 6·50 6·50

**S 177** Train and Travellers

**2008.** 125th Anniv of Orient Express.
S453 **S 177** 1m.40 multicoloured 4·20 4·25

**S 178** Alfred Nobel

**2008.** 175th Birth Anniv of Alfred Nobel (chemist, engineer, inventor of dynamite instituted Nobel Prizes).
S454 **S 178** 1m.50 multicoloured 4·75 4·75

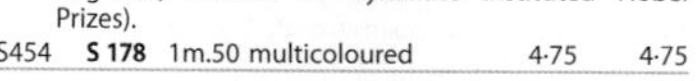

**S 179** Jovan Zmaj

**2008.** 125th Birth Anniv of Jovan Jovanovic Zmaj (writer).
S455 **S 179** 1m.50 multicoloured 4·25 4·25

**S 180** Celebratory Loaf of Bread

**2008.** Christmas.
S456 **S 180** 1m. multicoloured 3·00 3·00

**S 181** Vucko (games mascot)

**2009.** 25th Anniv of Winter Olympic Games, Sarajevo.
S457 **S 181** 1m.50 multicolured 4·75 4·75

**S 182** Amerigo Vespucci

**2009.** Explorers. Multicoloured.
S458 70f. Type S **182** 2·10 2·10
S459 1m.50 Marco Polo 4·75 4·75

**S 183** Triceratops

**2009.** Dinosaurs. Multicoloured.

| | | | |
|---|---|---|---|
| S460 | 70f. Type S **183** | 2·10 | 2·10 |
| S461 | 1m.50 Diplodocus | 4·75 | 4·75 |

**S 184** Court of Human Rights Building

**2009.** 50th Anniv of European Court of Human Rights (S462) or 60th Anniv of Council of Europe (S463). Multicoloured.

| | | | |
|---|---|---|---|
| S462 | 1m. Type S **184** | 3·75 | 3·75 |
| S463 | 1m.50 Council of Europe Building | 4·75 | 4·75 |

Nos. S464/6 and Type S **185** are left for Animals, issued on 15 April 2009, not yet received.

Nos. S467/9 and Type S **186** are left for Europa. Astronomy, issued on 23 April 2009, not yet received.

**S 187** Globe and Red Cross Flag

**2009.** Obligatory Tax.150th Anniv of Red Cross.

| | | | | |
|---|---|---|---|---|
| S470 | **S 187** | 20f. multicoloured | 1·00 | 1·00 |

Nos. S471 and Type S **188** are left for World Rafting Championship, issued on 15 May 2009, not yet received.

**S 189** Paje Jovanovic

**2009.** 150th Birth Anniv of Paje Jovanovic (artist).

| | | | | |
|---|---|---|---|---|
| S472 | **S 189** | 1m.50 multicoloured | 4·25 | 4·25 |

**S 190** Self and Other Portraits

**2009.** 125th Birth Anniv of Amedeo Clemente Modigliani (artist).

| | | | | |
|---|---|---|---|---|
| S473 | **S 190** | 1m.50 multicoloured | 4·25 | 4·25 |

**S 191** Siamese

**2009.** Cats. Multicoloured.

| | | | |
|---|---|---|---|
| S474 | 70f. Type S **191** | 2·10 | 2·10 |
| S475 | 70f. Tabby | 2·10 | 2·10 |
| S476 | 70f. Russian Blue | 2·10 | 2·10 |
| S477 | 70f. Persian | 2·10 | 2·10 |

**S 192** Dragonfly

**2009.** Insects. Multicoloured.

| | | | |
|---|---|---|---|
| S478 | 1m. Type S **192** | 2·75 | 2·75 |
| S479 | 1m. Ladybird | 2·75 | 2·75 |
| S480 | 1m. Staghorn beetle | 2·75 | 2·75 |

**S 193** Robert Koch (bacteriologist, Nobel Prize Winner for Physiology or Medicine, 1905)

**2009.** Obligatory Tax. Tuberculosis Week.

| | | | | |
|---|---|---|---|---|
| S481 | **S 193** | 20f. multicoloured | 4·75 | 4·75 |

**S 194** Zvornik

**2009.** Castles. Multicoloured.

| | | | |
|---|---|---|---|
| S482 | 70f. Type S **194** | 2·10 | 2·10 |
| S483 | 1m. Banja Luka | 3·25 | 3·25 |

**S 195** Locomotive SKODA 1937

**2009.** Narrow Gauge. Multicoloured.

| | | | |
|---|---|---|---|
| S484 | 70f. Type S **195** | 2·10 | 2·10 |
| S485 | 70f. Locomotive RAMA | 2·10 | 2·10 |
| S486 | 80f. Locomotive JZ 83-057 | 2·75 | 2·75 |
| S487 | 80f. Locomotive UNRRA 22 | 2·75 | 2·75 |

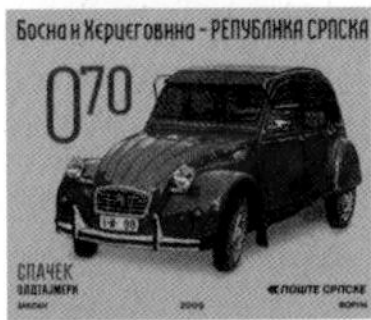
**S 196** Citroen 2 CV

**2009.** Classic Cars. Multicoloured.

| | | | |
|---|---|---|---|
| S488 | 70f. Type S **196** | 2·10 | 2·10 |
| S489 | 70f. Fiat Cinquecento | 2·10 | 2·10 |
| S490 | 80f. Volkswagen Beetle | 2·75 | 2·75 |

**S 197** Snowman

**2009.** Christmas and New Year. Multicoloured.

| | | | |
|---|---|---|---|
| S491 | 60f. Type S **197** | 1·70 | 1·70 |
| S492 | 60f. Santa Claus | 1·70 | 1·70 |

**S198** Badger

**2009.** Fauna

| | | | | |
|---|---|---|---|---|
| S493 | **S 198** | 20f. multicoloured | 75 | 75 |

**S199** Bridge and Tower

**2010.** 600th Anniv of Zvornik

| | | | | |
|---|---|---|---|---|
| S494 | **S 199** | 70f. multicoloured | | |

**S200** Games Emblem and Luge

**2010.** Winter Olympic Games, Vancouver. Multicoloured.

| | | | |
|---|---|---|---|
| S495 | 70f. Type S **200** | 1·60 | 1·60 |
| S496 | 1m.50 Ice dance | 3·25 | 3·25 |

**S201** Frédéric Chopin

**2010.** Birth Bicentenary of Frédéric François Chopin (composer)

| | | | | |
|---|---|---|---|---|
| S497 | **S201** | 1m.50 multicocloured | 4·75 | 4·75 |

No. S498 and Type S **202** are left for Birth Centenary of Mesa Selimovic, issued on 26 April 2010, not yet received.

Nos. S499/501 and Type S **203** are left for Europa, issued on 7 May 2010, not yet received.

**204** Player's Legs

**2010.** World Cup Football Championships, South Africa. Multicoloured.

| | | | |
|---|---|---|---|
| S502 | 1m.50 Type S **204** | 4·25 | 4·25 |
| S503 | 1m.50 No. 11 player with arms wide spread | 4·25 | £425 |

**S205** Hedgehog

**2010.** Fauna. Multicoloured.

| | | | |
|---|---|---|---|
| S504 | 10f. Type S**205** | 2·10 | 2·10 |
| S505 | 50f. Wild boar | 2·10 | 2·10 |
| S506 | 90f. Wolf | 2·10 | 2·10 |
| S507 | 1m. Brown bear | 2·10 | 2·10 |

**S206** Sword (yataghan)

**2010.** Weaponry. Multicoloured.

| | | | |
|---|---|---|---|
| S508 | 1m.80 Type S**206** | 6·25 | 6·25 |
| S509 | 2m. Flintlock pistol | 6·50 | 6·50 |
| S510 | 5m. Iron mace | 14·50 | 14·50 |

**S207** *Rhododendron hirsutum*

**2010.** Flora. Multicoloured.

| | | | |
|---|---|---|---|
| S511 | 70f. Type S **207** | 2·30 | 2·30 |
| S512 | 70f. *Edraianthus sutjeski* (inscr 'Edrainthus Sutjeski') | 2·30 | 2·30 |
| S513 | 70f. *Trollius europaeus* | 2·30 | 2·30 |
| S514 | 70f. *Pancicia serbica* | 2·30 | 2·30 |

**S208** Figures (bas-relief)

**2010.** Cultural Heritage. Multicoloured.

| | | | |
|---|---|---|---|
| S515 | 70f. Type S**208** | 1·60 | 1·60 |
| S516 | 1m.50 Inscribed tablet | 3·25 | 3·25 |

**S209** Trumpets and Trumpeter

**2010.** 50th Anniv of Trumpet Festival, Guca

| | | | | |
|---|---|---|---|---|
| S517 | **S 209** | 1m.50 multicoloured | 4·75 | 4·75 |

**S210** Empty Silhouette

**2010.** Day of Missing and Fallen Persons

| | | | | |
|---|---|---|---|---|
| S518 | **S 210** | 90f. scarlet-vermilion and black | 2·75 | 2·75 |

Nos. S519/20 and Type S **211** are left for Nature Protection, issued on 23 September 2010, not yet received.

**S212** '80' wearing Hats

**2010.** 80th Anniv of National Museum

| | | | | |
|---|---|---|---|---|
| S521 | **S 212** | 90f. multicoloured | 6·25 | 6·25 |

**S213** St. Nicholas and Stocking

**2010.** Christmas

| | | | | |
|---|---|---|---|---|
| S522 | **S213** | 1m. multicoloured | 3·25 | 3·25 |

Pt. 1

# BOTSWANA

Formerly Bechuanaland Protectorate, attained independence on 30 September 1966, and changed its name to Botswana.

1966. 100 cents = 1 rand.
1976. 100 thebe = 1 pula.

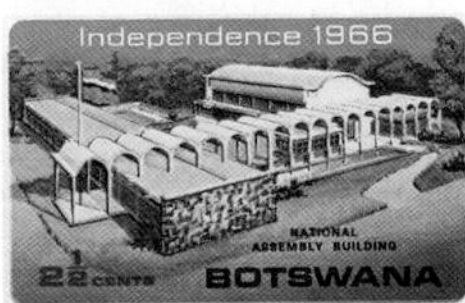

**47** National Assembly Building

**1966.** Independence. Multicoloured.

| | | | |
|---|---|---|---|
| 202 | 2½c. Type **47** | 15 | 10 |
| 203 | 5c. Abattoir, Lobatsi | 20 | 10 |
| 204 | 15c. National Airways Douglas DC-3 | 65 | 20 |
| 205 | 35c. State House, Gaberones | 40 | 30 |

**1966.** Nos. 168/81 of Bechuanaland optd **REPUBLIC OF BOTSWANA**.

| | | | | |
|---|---|---|---|---|
| 206 | **28** | 1c. multicoloured | 25 | 10 |
| 207 | - | 2c. orange, black and olive | 30 | 1·75 |
| 208 | - | 2½c. multicoloured | 30 | 10 |
| 209 | - | 3½c. multicoloured | 1·25 | 20 |
| 210 | - | 5c. multicoloured | 1·50 | 1·50 |
| 211 | - | 7½c. multicoloured | 50 | 1·75 |
| 212 | - | 10c. multicoloured | 1·00 | 20 |
| 213 | - | 12½c. multicoloured | 2·00 | 2·75 |
| 214 | - | 20c. brown and drab | 20 | 1·00 |
| 215 | - | 25c. sepia and lemon | 20 | 2·00 |

| | | | | |
|---|---|---|---|---|
| 216 | - | 35c. blue and orange | 30 | 2·25 |
| 217 | - | 50c. sepia and olive | 20 | 70 |
| 218 | - | 1r. black and brown | 40 | 1·25 |
| 219 | - | 2r. brown and turquoise | 60 | 2·50 |

**52** Golden Oriole

**1967.** Multicoloured.

| | | | |
|---|---|---|---|
| 220 | 1c. Type **52** | 30 | 15 |
| 221 | 2c. Hoopoe ("African Hoopoe") | 60 | 70 |
| 222 | 3c. Groundscraper thrush | 55 | 10 |
| 223 | 4c. Cordon-bleu ("Blue Waxbill") | 55 | 10 |
| 224 | 5c. Secretary bird | 55 | 10 |
| 225 | 7c. Southern yellow-billed hornbill ("Yellow-billed Hornbill") | 60 | 1·00 |
| 226 | 10c. Burchell's gonolek ("Crimson-breasted Shrike") | 60 | 15 |
| 227 | 15c. Malachite kingfisher | 7·50 | 3·00 |
| 228 | 20c. African fish eagle ("Fish Eagle") | 7·50 | 2·00 |
| 229 | 25c. Go-away bird ("Grey Loerie") | 4·00 | 1·50 |
| 230 | 35c. Scimitar-bill | 6·00 | 2·25 |
| 231 | 50c. Comb duck ("Knob-Billed Duck") | 2·75 | 2·75 |
| 232 | 1r. Levaillant's barbet ("Crested Barbet") | 5·00 | 3·50 |
| 233 | 2r. Didric cuckoo ("Diederick Cuckoo") | 7·00 | 17·00 |

**66** Students and University

**1967.** 1st Conferment of University Degrees.

| | | | | |
|---|---|---|---|---|
| 234 | **66** | 3c. sepia, blue and orange | 10 | 10 |
| 235 | **66** | 7c. sepia, blue and turquoise | 10 | 10 |
| 236 | **66** | 15c. sepia, blue and red | 10 | 10 |
| 237 | **66** | 35c. sepia, blue and violet | 20 | 20 |

**67** Bushbuck

**1967.** Chobe Game Reserve. Multicoloured.

| | | | |
|---|---|---|---|
| 238 | 3c. Type **67** | 10 | 20 |
| 239 | 7c. Sable Antelope | 15 | 30 |
| 240 | 35c. Fishing on the Chobe River | 90 | 1·10 |

**70** Arms of Botswana and Human Rights Emblem

**1968.** Human Rights Year.

| | | | | |
|---|---|---|---|---|
| 241 | **70** | 3c. multicoloured | 10 | 10 |
| 242 | - | 15c. multicoloured | 25 | 45 |
| 243 | - | 25c. multicoloured | 25 | 60 |

The designs of Nos. 242/3 are similar, but are arranged differently.

**73** Eland and Giraffe Rock Paintings, Tsodilo Hills

**1968.** Opening of National Museum and Art Gallery. Multicoloured.

| | | | |
|---|---|---|---|
| 244 | 3c. Type **73** | 20 | 20 |
| 245 | 7c. Girl wearing ceremonial beads (31×48 mm) | 25 | 40 |
| 246 | 10c. "Baobab Trees" (Thomas Baines) | 25 | 30 |
| 247 | 15c. National Museum and art gallery (72×19 mm) | 40 | 1·50 |
| MS248 | 132×82 mm. Nos. 244/7 | 1·00 | 2·25 |

**77** African Family, and Star over Village

**1968.** Christmas.

| | | | | |
|---|---|---|---|---|
| 249 | **77** | 1c. multicoloured | 10 | 10 |
| 250 | **77** | 2c. multicoloured | 10 | 10 |
| 251 | **77** | 5c. multicoloured | 10 | 10 |
| 252 | **77** | 25c. multicoloured | 15 | 50 |

**78** Scout, Lion and Badge in frame

**1969.** 22nd World Scout Conference, Helsinki. Mult.

| | | | |
|---|---|---|---|
| 253 | 3c. Type **78** | 30 | 30 |
| 254 | 15c. Scouts cooking over open fire (vert) | 35 | 1·00 |
| 255 | 25c. Scouts around camp fire | 35 | 1·00 |

**81** Woman, Child and Christmas Star

**1969.** Christmas.

| | | | | |
|---|---|---|---|---|
| 256 | **81** | 1c. blue and brown | 10 | 10 |
| 257 | **81** | 2c. olive and brown | 10 | 10 |
| 258 | **81** | 4c. yellow and brown | 10 | 10 |
| 259 | **81** | 35c. brown and violet | 20 | 20 |
| MS260 | | 86×128 mm. Nos. 256/9 | 70 | 1·10 |

**82** Diamond Treatment Plant, Orapa

**1970.** Developing Botswana. Multicoloured.

| | | | |
|---|---|---|---|
| 261 | 3c. Type **82** | 70 | 20 |
| 262 | 7c. Copper-nickel mining | 95 | 20 |
| 263 | 10c. Copper-nickel mine, Selebi-Pikwe (horiz) | 1·25 | 15 |
| 264 | 35c. Orapa Diamond mine and diamonds (horiz) | 2·75 | 1·25 |

**83** Mr. Micawber ("David Copperfield")

**1970.** Death Centenary of Charles Dickens. Mult.

| | | | |
|---|---|---|---|
| 265 | 3c. Type **83** | 25 | 10 |
| 266 | 7c. Scrooge ("A Christmas Carol") | 25 | 10 |
| 267 | 15c. Fagin ("Oliver Twist") | 45 | 40 |
| 268 | 25c. Bill Sykes ("Oliver Twist") | 70 | 60 |
| MS269 | 114×81 mm. Nos. 265/8 | 2·75 | 4·00 |

**84** U.N. Building and Emblem

**1970.** 25th Anniv of United Nations.

| | | | | |
|---|---|---|---|---|
| 270 | **84** | 15c. blue, brown and silver | 70 | 30 |

**85** Crocodile

**1970.** Christmas. Multicoloured.

| | | | |
|---|---|---|---|
| 271 | 1c. Type **85** | 10 | 10 |
| 272 | 2c. Giraffe | 10 | 10 |
| 273 | 7c. Elephant | 15 | 15 |
| 274 | 25c. Rhinoceros | 60 | 80 |
| MS275 | 128×90 mm. Nos. 271/4 | 1·00 | 3·00 |

**86** Sorghum

**1971.** Important Crops. Multicoloured.

| | | | |
|---|---|---|---|
| 276 | 3c. Type **86** | 15 | 10 |
| 277 | 7c. Millet | 20 | 10 |
| 278 | 10c. Maize | 20 | 10 |
| 279 | 35c. Groundnuts | 70 | 1·00 |

**87** Map and Head of Cow

**1971.** 5th Anniv of Independence.

| | | | | |
|---|---|---|---|---|
| 280 | **87** | 3c. black, brown and green | 10 | 10 |
| 281 | - | 4c. black, light blue and blue | 10 | 10 |
| 282 | - | 7c. black and orange | 20 | 15 |
| 283 | - | 10c. multicoloured | 20 | 15 |
| 284 | - | 20c. multicoloured | 55 | 2·50 |

DESIGNS: 4c. Map and cogs; 7c. Map and common zebra; 10c. Map and sorghum stalk crossed by tusk; 20c. Arms and map of Botswana.

**88** King bringing Gift of Gold

**1971.** Christmas. Multicoloured.

| | | | |
|---|---|---|---|
| 285 | 2c. Type **88** | 10 | 10 |
| 286 | 3c. King bringing frankincense | 10 | 10 |
| 287 | 7c. King bringing myrrh | 10 | 10 |
| 288 | 20c. Three Kings behold the star | 35 | 65 |
| MS289 | 85×128 mm. Nos. 285/8 | 1·00 | 3·50 |

**89** Orion

**1972.** "Night Sky".

| | | | | |
|---|---|---|---|---|
| 290 | **89** | 3c. blue, black and red | 75 | 30 |
| 291 | - | 7c. blue, black and yellow | 1·10 | 80 |
| 292 | - | 10c. green, black and orange | 1·25 | 85 |
| 293 | - | 20c. blue, black and green | 1·75 | 3·25 |

CONSTELLATIONS: 7c. The Scorpion; 10c. The Centaur; 20c. The Cross.

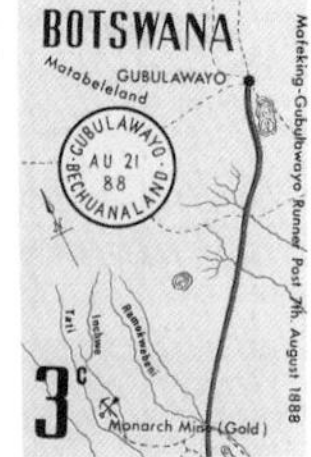

**90** Postmark and Map

**1972.** Mafeking-Gubulawayo Runner Post. Mult.

| | | | |
|---|---|---|---|
| 294 | 3c. Type **90** | 30 | 10 |
| 295 | 4c. Bechuanaland stamp and map | 30 | 35 |
| 296 | 7c. Runners and map | 45 | 50 |
| 297 | 20c. Mafeking postmark and map | 1·10 | 1·50 |
| MS298 | 84×216 mm. Nos. 294/7 vertically se-tenant, forming a composite map design | 11·00 | 15·00 |

For these designs with changed inscription see Nos. 652/5.

**91** Cross, Map and Bells

**1972.** Christmas. Each with Cross and Map. Mult.

| | | | |
|---|---|---|---|
| 299 | 2c. Type **91** | 10 | 75 |
| 300 | 3c. Cross, map and candle | 10 | 10 |
| 301 | 7c. Cross, map and Christmas tree | 15 | 25 |
| 302 | 20c. Cross, map, star and holly | 40 | 85 |
| MS303 | 96×119 mm. Nos. 299/302 | 1·25 | 3·25 |

**92** Thor

**1973.** Centenary of I.M.O./W.M.O. Norse Myths. Multicoloured.

| | | | |
|---|---|---|---|
| 304 | 3c. Type **92** | 20 | 10 |
| 305 | 4c. Sun God's chariot (horiz) | 25 | 15 |
| 306 | 7c. Ymir, the frost giant | 30 | 15 |
| 307 | 20c. Odin and Sleipnir (horiz) | 75 | 70 |

**93** Livingstone and River Scene

**1973.** Death Centenary of Dr. Livingstone. Mult.

| | | | |
|---|---|---|---|
| 308 | 3c. Type **93** | 20 | 10 |

| | | | |
|---|---|---|---|
| 309 | 20c. Livingstone meeting Stanley | 90 | 90 |

**94** Donkey and Foal at Village Trough

**1973.** Christmas. Multicoloured.

| | | | |
|---|---|---|---|
| 310 | 3c. Type **94** | 10 | 10 |
| 311 | 4c. Shepherd and flock (horiz) | 10 | 10 |
| 312 | 7c. Mother and Child | 10 | 10 |
| 313 | 20c. Kgotla meeting (horiz) | 40 | 85 |

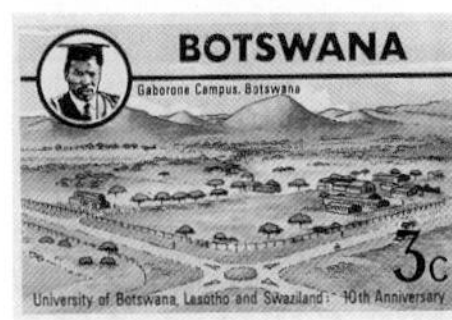


**95** Gaborone Campus

**1974.** 10th Anniv of University of Botswana, Lesotho and Swaziland. Multicoloured.

| | | | |
|---|---|---|---|
| 314 | 3c. Type **95** | 10 | 10 |
| 315 | 7c. Kwaluseni Campus | 10 | 10 |
| 316 | 20c. Roma Campus | 15 | 20 |
| 317 | 35c. Map and flags of the three countries | 20 | 35 |

**96** Methods of Mail Transport

**1974.** Centenary of U.P.U. Multicoloured.

| | | | |
|---|---|---|---|
| 318 | 2c. Type **96** | 55 | 35 |
| 319 | 3c. Post Office, Palapye, circa 1889 | 55 | 35 |
| 320 | 7c. Bechuanaland Police Camel Post, circa 1900 | 95 | 70 |
| 321 | 20c. Hawker Siddeley H.S.748 and De Havilland D.H.9 mail planes of 1920 and 1974 | 2·75 | 2·50 |

**97** Amethyst

**1974.** Botswana Minerals. Multicoloured.

| | | | |
|---|---|---|---|
| 322 | 1c. Type **97** | 60 | 2·00 |
| 323 | 2c. Agate-"Botswana Pink" | 60 | 2·00 |
| 324 | 3c. Quartz | 65 | 80 |
| 325 | 4c. Copper nickel | 70 | 60 |
| 326 | 5c. Moss agate | 70 | 1·00 |
| 327 | 7c. Agate | 80 | 1·25 |
| 328 | 10c. Stilbite | 1·60 | 65 |
| 329 | 15c. Moshaneng banded marble | 2·00 | 4·00 |
| 330 | 20c. Gem diamonds | 4·00 | 4·50 |
| 331 | 25c. Chrysotile | 5·00 | 2·50 |
| 332 | 35c. Jasper | 5·00 | 5·50 |
| 333 | 50c. Moss quartz | 4·50 | 7·00 |
| 334 | 1r. Citrine | 7·50 | 10·00 |
| 335 | 2r. Chalcopyrite | 20·00 | 20·00 |

**98** "Stapelia variegata"

**1974.** Christmas. Multicoloured.

| | | | |
|---|---|---|---|
| 336 | 2c. Type **98** | 20 | 40 |
| 337 | 7c. "Hibiscus lunarifolius" | 30 | 20 |
| 338 | 15c. "Ceratotheca triloba" | 45 | 1·00 |
| 339 | 20c. "Nerine laticoma" | 60 | 1·25 |

| | | | |
|---|---|---|---|
| **MS**340 | 85×130 mm. Nos. 336/9 | 2·00 | 4·25 |

**99** President Sir Seretse Khama

**1975.** 10th Anniv of Self-Government.

| | | | | |
|---|---|---|---|---|
| 341 | **99** | 4c. multicoloured | 10 | 10 |
| 342 | **99** | 10c. multicoloured | 15 | 10 |
| 343 | **99** | 20c. multicoloured | 25 | 25 |
| 344 | **99** | 35c. multicoloured | 45 | 50 |
| **MS**345 | | 93×130 mm. Nos. 341/4 | 1·00 | 1·50 |

**100** Ostrich

**1975.** Rock Paintings, Tsodilo Hills. Multicoloured.

| | | | |
|---|---|---|---|
| 346 | 4c. Type **100** | 60 | 10 |
| 347 | 10c. White rhinoceros | 1·00 | 10 |
| 348 | 25c. Spotted hyena | 2·00 | 55 |
| 349 | 35c. Scorpion | 2·00 | 1·10 |
| **MS**350 | 150×150 mm. Nos. 346/9 | 12·00 | 7·50 |

**101** Map of British Bechuanaland, 1885

**1975.** Anniversaries. Multicoloured.

| | | | |
|---|---|---|---|
| 351 | 6c. Type **101** | 30 | 20 |
| 352 | 10c. Chief Khama, 1875 | 40 | 15 |
| 353 | 25c. Chiefs Sebele, Bathoen and Khama, 1895 (horiz) | 80 | 75 |

EVENTS: 6c. 90th anniv of Protectorate; 10c. Centenary of Khama's accession; 25c. 80th anniv of Chiefs' visit to London.

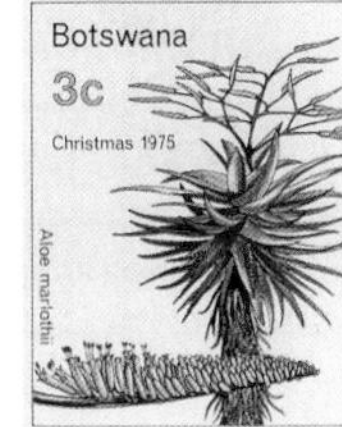


**102** "Aloe marlothii"

**1975.** Christmas. Aloes. Multicoloured.

| | | | |
|---|---|---|---|
| 354 | 3c. Type **102** | 20 | 10 |
| 355 | 10c. "Aloe lutescens" | 40 | 20 |
| 356 | 15c. "Aloe zebrina" | 60 | 1·50 |
| 357 | 25c. "Aloe littoralis" | 75 | 2·50 |

**103** Drum

**1976.** Traditional Musical Instruments. Mult.

| | | | |
|---|---|---|---|
| 358 | 4c. Type **103** | 15 | 10 |
| 359 | 10c. Hand piano | 20 | 10 |
| 360 | 15c. Segankuru (violin) | 25 | 50 |
| 361 | 25c. Kudu signal horn | 30 | 1·25 |

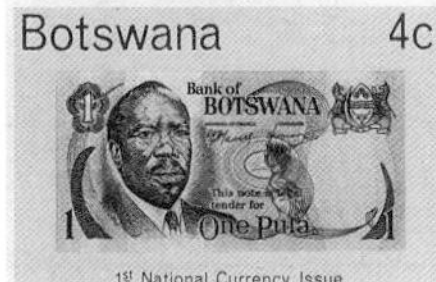


**104** One Pula Note

**1976.** 1st National Currency. Multicoloured.

| | | | |
|---|---|---|---|
| 362 | 4c. Type **104** | 15 | 10 |
| 363 | 10c. Two pula note | 20 | 10 |
| 364 | 15c. Five pula note | 35 | 20 |
| 365 | 25c. Ten pula note | 45 | 45 |
| **MS**366 | 163×107 mm. Nos. 362/5 | 1·00 | 3·50 |

**1976.** Nos. 322/35 surch in new currency.

| | | | |
|---|---|---|---|
| 367 | 1t. on 1c. multicoloured | 2·00 | 70 |
| 368 | 2t. on 2c. multicoloured | 2·00 | 1·75 |
| 369 | 3t. on 3c. multicoloured | 1·50 | 60 |
| 370 | 4t. on 4c. multicoloured | 2·50 | 40 |
| 371 | 5t. on 5c. multicoloured | 2·50 | 40 |
| 372 | 7t. on 7c. multicoloured | 1·25 | 2·75 |
| 373 | 10t. on 10c. multicoloured | 1·25 | 80 |
| 374 | 15t. on 15c. multicoloured | 4·25 | 3·25 |
| 375 | 20t. on 20c. multicoloured | 7·50 | 80 |
| 376 | 25t. on 25c. multicoloured | 5·00 | 1·25 |
| 377 | 35t. on 35c. multicoloured | 4·00 | 5·00 |
| 378 | 50t. on 50c. multicoloured | 5·50 | 9·00 |
| 379 | 1p. on 1r. multicoloured | 6·00 | 9·50 |
| 380 | 2p. on 2r. multicoloured | 8·00 | 11·00 |

**106** Botswana Cattle

**1976.** 10th Anniv of Independence. Multicoloured.

| | | | |
|---|---|---|---|
| 381 | 4t. Type **106** | 15 | 10 |
| 382 | 10t. Antelope, Okavango Delta (vert) | 20 | 10 |
| 383 | 15t. School and pupils | 20 | 40 |
| 384 | 25t. Rural weaving (vert) | 20 | 50 |
| 385 | 35t. Miner (vert) | 75 | 85 |

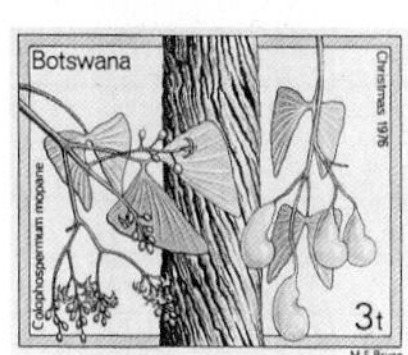


**107** "Colophospermum mopane"

**1976.** Christmas. Trees. Multicoloured.

| | | | |
|---|---|---|---|
| 386 | 3t. Type **107** | 15 | 10 |
| 387 | 4t. "Baikiaea plurijuga" | 15 | 10 |
| 388 | 10t. "Sterculia rogersii" | 20 | 10 |
| 389 | 25t. "Acacia nilotica" | 45 | 50 |
| 390 | 40t. "Kigelia africana" | 75 | 1·25 |

**108** Coronation Coach

**1977.** Silver Jubilee. Multicoloured.

| | | | |
|---|---|---|---|
| 391 | 4t. The Queen and Sir Seretse Khama | 10 | 10 |
| 392 | 25t. Type **108** | 20 | 15 |
| 393 | 40t. The Recognition | 35 | 90 |

**109** African Clawless Otter

**1977.** Diminishing Species. Multicoloured.

| | | | |
|---|---|---|---|
| 394 | 3t. Type **109** | 4·25 | 40 |
| 395 | 4t. Serval | 4·25 | 40 |
| 396 | 10t. Bat-eared fox | 4·75 | 40 |
| 397 | 25t. Temminck's ground pangolin | 11·00 | 2·00 |
| 398 | 40t. Brown hyena | 13·00 | 7·50 |

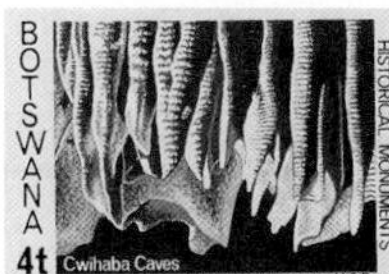


**110** Cwihaba Caves

**1977.** Historical Monuments. Multicoloured.

| | | | |
|---|---|---|---|
| 399 | 4t. Type **110** | 20 | 10 |
| 400 | 5t. Khama Memorial | 20 | 10 |
| 401 | 15t. Green's Tree | 30 | 40 |
| 402 | 20t. Mmajojo Ruins | 30 | 45 |
| 403 | 25t. Ancient morabaraba board | 30 | 50 |
| 404 | 35t. Matsieng's footprint | 40 | 60 |
| **MS**405 | 154×105 mm. Nos. 399/404 | 2·50 | 3·25 |

**111** "Hypoxis nitida"

**1977.** Christmas. Lilies. Multicoloured.

| | | | |
|---|---|---|---|
| 406 | 3t. Type **111** | 15 | 10 |
| 407 | 5t. "Haemanthus magnificus" | 15 | 10 |
| 408 | 10t. "Boophane disticha" | 20 | 10 |
| 409 | 25t. "Vellozia retinervis" | 40 | 55 |
| 410 | 40t. "Ammocharis coranica" | 55 | 1·25 |

**112** Black Bustard

**1978.** Birds. Multicoloured.

| | | | |
|---|---|---|---|
| 411 | 1t. Type **112** | 70 | 1·25 |
| 412 | 2t. Marabou stork | 90 | 1·25 |
| 413 | 3t. Green wood hoopoe ("Red Billed Hoopoe") | 70 | 85 |
| 414 | 4t. Carmine bee eater | 1·00 | 1·00 |
| 415 | 5t. African jacana | 1·00 | 40 |
| 416 | 7t. African paradise flycatcher ("Paradise Flycatcher") | 1·00 | 3·00 |
| 417 | 10t. Bennett's woodpecker | 2·00 | 60 |
| 418 | 15t. Red bishop | 1·50 | 3·00 |
| 419 | 20t. Crowned plover | 1·75 | 2·00 |
| 420 | 25t. Giant kingfisher | 70 | 3·00 |
| 421 | 30t. White-faced whistling duck ("White-faced Duck") | 70 | 70 |
| 422 | 35t. Green-backed heron | 70 | 3·25 |
| 423 | 45t. Black-headed heron | 1·00 | 3·00 |
| 424 | 50t. Spotted eagle owl | 5·00 | 4·50 |
| 425 | 1p. Gabar goshawk | 2·50 | 4·50 |
| 426 | 2p. Martial eagle | 3·00 | 8·00 |
| 427 | 5p. Saddle-bill stork | 6·50 | 16·00 |

**113** Tawana making Kaross

**1978.** Okavango Delta. Multicoloured.

| | | | |
|---|---|---|---|
| 428 | 4t. Type **113** | 10 | 30 |
| 429 | 5t. Tribe localities | 10 | 10 |
| 430 | 15t. Bushman collecting roots | 25 | 40 |
| 431 | 20t. Herero woman milking | 35 | 70 |
| 432 | 25t. Yei poling "mokoro" (canoe) | 40 | 60 |
| 433 | 35t. Mbukushu fishing | 45 | 1·75 |
| **MS**434 | 150×98 mm. Nos. 428/33 | 1·50 | 3·75 |

**114** "Caralluma lutea"

**1978.** Christmas. Flowers. Multicoloured.

| | | | |
|---|---|---|---|
| 435 | 5t. Type **114** | 35 | 10 |
| 436 | 10t. "Hoodia lugardii" | 50 | 15 |
| 437 | 15t. "Ipomoea transvaalensis" | 90 | 55 |
| 438 | 25t. "Ansellia gigantea" | 1·10 | 70 |

**115** Sip Well

**1979.** Water Development. Multicoloured.

| | | | |
|---|---|---|---|
| 439 | 3t. Type **115** | 10 | 10 |
| 440 | 5t. Watering pit | 10 | 10 |
| 441 | 10t. Hand dug well | 15 | 10 |
| 442 | 22t. Windmill | 20 | 30 |
| 443 | 50t. Drilling rig truck | 40 | 55 |

**116** Pottery

**1979.** Handicrafts. Multicoloured.

| | | | |
|---|---|---|---|
| 444 | 5t. Type **116** | 10 | 10 |
| 445 | 10t. Clay modelling | 10 | 10 |
| 446 | 25t. Basketry | 20 | 25 |
| 447 | 40t. Beadwork | 40 | 50 |
| **MS**448 | 123×96 mm. Nos. 444/7 | 1·00 | 2·50 |

**117** British Bechuanaland 1885 1d. Stamp and Sir Rowland Hill

**1979.** Death Centenary of Sir Rowland Hill. Mult.

| | | | |
|---|---|---|---|
| 449 | 5t. Type **117** | 20 | 10 |
| 450 | 25t. Bechuanaland Protectorate 1932 2d. stamp | 45 | 50 |
| 451 | 45t. 1967 Hoopoe 2c. definitive stamp | 55 | 1·25 |

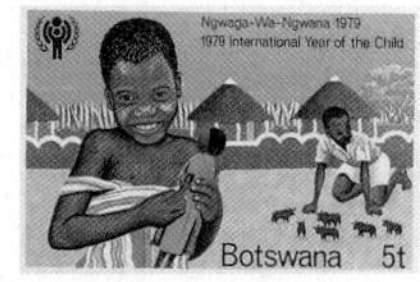

**118** Children Playing

**1979.** International Year of the Child. Multicoloured.

| | | | |
|---|---|---|---|
| 452 | 5t. Type **118** | 20 | 10 |
| 453 | 10t. Child playing with doll (vert) | 30 | 20 |

**119** "Ximenia caffra"

**1979.** Christmas. Flowers. Multicoloured.

| | | | |
|---|---|---|---|
| 454 | 5t. Type **119** | 10 | 10 |
| 455 | 10t. "Sclerocarya caffra" | 20 | 20 |
| 456 | 15t. "Hexalobus monopetalus" | 35 | 35 |
| 457 | 25t. "Ficus soldanella" | 45 | 45 |

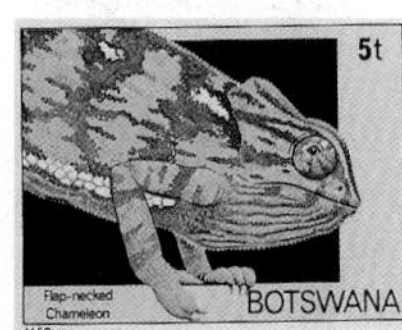

**120** Flap-necked Chameleon

**1980.** Reptiles. Multicoloured.

| | | | |
|---|---|---|---|
| 458 | 5t. Type **120** | 30 | 10 |
| 459 | 10t. Leopard tortoise | 30 | 15 |
| 460 | 25t. Puff adder | 50 | 65 |
| 461 | 40t. White-throated monitor | 60 | 2·50 |

**121** Rock Breaking

**1980.** Early Mining. Multicoloured.

| | | | |
|---|---|---|---|
| 462 | 5t. Type **121** | 25 | 15 |
| 463 | 10t. Ore hoisting | 30 | 15 |
| 464 | 15t. Ore transport | 70 | 60 |
| 465 | 20t. Ore crushing | 75 | 90 |
| 466 | 25t. Smelting | 80 | 90 |
| 467 | 35t. Tool and products | 1·00 | 1·75 |

**122** "Chiwele and the Giant"

**1980.** Folktales. Multicoloured.

| | | | |
|---|---|---|---|
| 468 | 5t. Type **122** | 10 | 10 |
| 469 | 10t. "Kgori is not deceived" (vert) | 15 | 10 |
| 470 | 30t. "Nyambi's wife and Crocodile" (vert) | 45 | 45 |
| 471 | 45t. "Clever Hare" (horiz) | 60 | 60 |

The 10t. and 30t. are 28×37 mm and the 45t. 44×27 mm.

**123** Game watching, Makgadikgadi Pans

**1980.** World Tourism Conference, Manila.

| | | | |
|---|---|---|---|
| 472 | **123** 5t. multicoloured | 45 | 20 |

**124** "Acacia gerrardii"

**1980.** Christmas. Multicoloured.

| | | | |
|---|---|---|---|
| 473 | 6t. Type **124** | 10 | 10 |
| 474 | 1t. "Acacia nilotica" | 20 | 10 |
| 475 | 25t. "Acacia erubescens" | 45 | 30 |
| 476 | 40t. "Dichrostachys cinerea" | 70 | 70 |

**125** Heinrich von Stephan and Botswana 3d. and 3c. U.P.U. Stamps

**1981.** 150th Birth Anniv of Heinrich von Stephan (founder of Universal Postal Union). Multicoloured.

| | | | |
|---|---|---|---|
| 477 | 6t. Type **125** | 50 | 30 |
| 478 | 20t. 6d. and 7c. U.P.U. stamps | 1·25 | 2·25 |

**126** "Anax imperator" (dragonfly)

**1981.** Insects. Multicoloured.

| | | | |
|---|---|---|---|
| 479 | 6t. Type **126** | 15 | 10 |
| 480 | 7t. "Sphodromantis gastrica" (mantid) | 15 | 20 |
| 481 | 10t. "Zonocerus elegans" (grasshopper) | 15 | 20 |
| 482 | 20t. "Kheper nigroaeneus" (beetle) | 25 | 50 |
| 483 | 30t. "Papilio demodocus" (butterfly) | 35 | 70 |
| 484 | 45t. "Acanthocampa belina" (moth larva) | 40 | 1·10 |
| **MS**485 | 180×89 mm. Nos. 479/84 | 3·00 | 8·50 |

**127** Camphill Community Rankoromane, Otse

**1981.** International Year for Disabled Persons. Multicoloured.

| | | | |
|---|---|---|---|
| 486 | 6t. Type **127** | 20 | 10 |
| 487 | 20t. Resource Centre for the Blind, Mochudi | 55 | 35 |
| 488 | 30t. Tlamelong Rehabilitation Centre, Tlokweng | 75 | 45 |

**128** Woman reading Letter

**1981.** Literacy Programme. Multicoloured.

| | | | |
|---|---|---|---|
| 489 | 6t. Type **128** | 20 | 10 |
| 490 | 7t. Man filling in form | 20 | 15 |
| 491 | 20t. Boy reading newspaper | 60 | 35 |
| 492 | 30t. Child being taught to read | 80 | 45 |

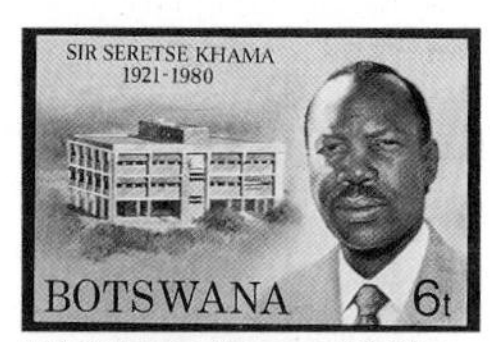

**129** Sir Seretse Khama and Building

**1981.** 1st Death Anniv of Sir Seretse Khama (former President). Multicoloured.

| | | | |
|---|---|---|---|
| 493 | 6t. Type **129** | 15 | 10 |
| 494 | 10t. Seretse Khama and building (different) | 25 | 15 |
| 495 | 30t. Seretse Khama and Botswana flag | 40 | 45 |
| 496 | 45t. Seretse Khama and building (different) | 55 | 70 |

**1981.** Nos. 417 and 422 surch.

| | | | |
|---|---|---|---|
| 497 | 25t. on 35t. Green-backed heron | 3·00 | 2·00 |
| 498 | 30t. on 10t. Bennett's woodpecker | 3·00 | 2·00 |

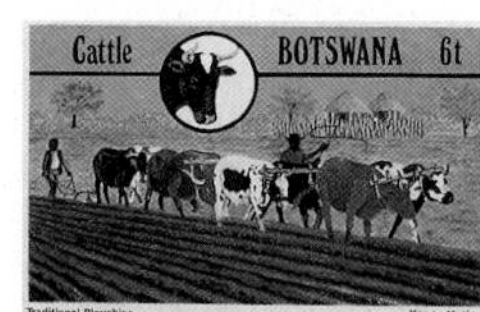

**131** Traditional Ploughing

**1981.** Cattle Industry. Multicoloured.

| | | | |
|---|---|---|---|
| 499 | 6t. Type **131** | 10 | 10 |
| 500 | 20t. Agricultural show | 30 | 50 |
| 501 | 30t. Botswana Meat Commission | 35 | 60 |
| 502 | 45t. Vaccine Institute, Botswana | 50 | 1·00 |

**132** "Nymphaea caerulea"

**1981.** Christmas. Flowers. Multicoloured.

| | | | |
|---|---|---|---|
| 503 | 6t. Type **132** | 20 | 10 |
| 504 | 10t. "Nymphoides indica" | 25 | 10 |
| 505 | 25t. "Nymphaea lotus" | 60 | 90 |
| 506 | 40t. "Ottelia kunenensis" | 80 | 2·25 |

**133** "Cattle Post Scene" (Boitumelo Golaakwena)

**1982.** Children's Art. Multicoloured.

| | | | |
|---|---|---|---|
| 507 | 6t. Type **133** | 40 | 10 |
| 508 | 10t. "Kgotla Meeting" (Reginald Klinck) | 50 | 15 |
| 509 | 30t. "Village Water Supply" (Keronmemang Matswiri) | 1·75 | 1·25 |
| 510 | 45t. "With the Crops" (Kennedy Balemoge) | 1·75 | 2·75 |

**134** Common Type

**1982.** Traditional House. Multicoloured.

| | | | |
|---|---|---|---|
| 511 | 6t. Type **134** | 40 | 15 |
| 512 | 10t. Kgatleng type | 50 | 15 |
| 513 | 30t. North Eastern type | 2·00 | 1·10 |
| 514 | 45t. Sarwa type | 2·00 | 3·00 |

**135** African Masked Weaver

**1982.** Birds. Multicoloured.

| | | | |
|---|---|---|---|
| 515 | 1t. Type **135** | 80 | 1·50 |
| 516 | 2t. Miombo double-collared sunbird ("Lesser double-collared Sunbird") | 90 | 1·60 |
| 517 | 3t. Red-throated bee eater | 1·00 | 1·60 |
| 518 | 4t. Ostrich | 1·00 | 1·60 |
| 519 | 5t. Grey-headed gull | 1·00 | 1·60 |
| 520 | 6t. African pygmy ("Pygmy Goose") | 1·00 | 40 |
| 521 | 7t. Cattle egret | 1·00 | 15 |
| 522 | 8t. Lanner falcon | 2·50 | 1·50 |
| 523 | 10t. Yellow-billed stork | 1·00 | 20 |
| 524 | 15t. Red-billed pintail ("Red-billed Teal") (horiz) | 2·75 | 25 |
| 525 | 20t. Barn owl (horiz) | 5·50 | 3·50 |
| 526 | 25t. Hammerkop ("Hammerkop") (horiz) | 3·25 | 70 |
| 527 | 30t. South African stilt ("Stilt") (horiz) | 3·75 | 90 |
| 528 | 35t. Blacksmith plover (horiz) | 3·75 | 80 |
| 529 | 45t. Senegal wattled plover ("Watted Plover") (horiz) | 3·75 | 1·75 |
| 530 | 50t. Helmeted guineafowl ("Crowned Guineafowl") (horiz) | 4·75 | 2·50 |
| 531 | 1p. Cape vulture (horiz) | 9·00 | 12·00 |
| 532 | 2p. Augur buzzard (horiz) | 11·00 | 16·00 |

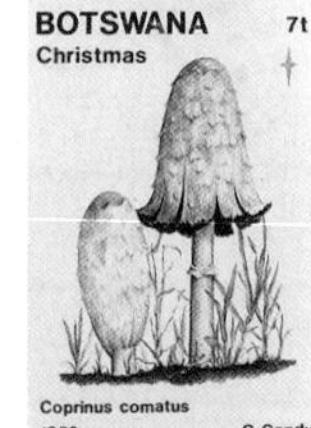

**136** "Coprinus comatus"

**1982.** Christmas. Fungi. Multicoloured.

| | | | |
|---|---|---|---|
| 533 | 7t. Type **136** | 2·50 | 20 |
| 534 | 15t. "Lactarius deliciosus" | 3·75 | 65 |
| 535 | 35t. "Amanita pantherina" | 6·00 | 2·00 |
| 536 | 50t. "Boletus edulis" | 7·50 | 8·00 |

**137** President Quett Masire

**1983.** Commonwealth Day. Multicoloured.

| | | | |
|---|---|---|---|
| 537 | 7t. Type **137** | 10 | 10 |
| 538 | 15t. Native dancers | 15 | 20 |
| 539 | 35t. Melbourne conference centre | 45 | 55 |
| 540 | 45t. Meeting of Heads of State, Melbourne | 55 | 80 |

**138** Wattled Crane

**1983.** Endangered Species. Multicoloured.

| | | | |
|---|---|---|---|
| 541 | 7t. Type **138** | 3·00 | 55 |
| 542 | 15t. "Aloe lutescens" | 2·50 | 80 |
| 543 | 35t. Roan antelope | 3·00 | 3·25 |
| 544 | 50t. Ivory palm | 3·50 | 7·00 |

**139** Wooden Spoons

**1983.** Traditional Artifacts. Multicoloured.

| | | | |
|---|---|---|---|
| 545 | 7t. Type **139** | 25 | 10 |
| 546 | 15t. Personal ornaments | 45 | 30 |
| 547 | 35t. Ox-hide milk bag | 75 | 65 |
| 548 | 50t. Decorated knives | 1·00 | 1·10 |
| **MS**549 | 115×102 mm. Nos. 545×8 | 4·25 | 5·00 |

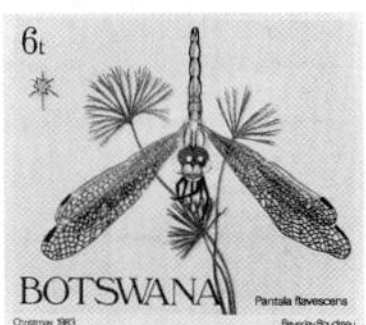

**140** "Pantala flavescens"

**1983.** Christmas. Dragonflies. Multicoloured.

| | | | |
|---|---|---|---|
| 550 | 6t. Type **140** | 85 | 10 |
| 551 | 15t. "Anax imperator" | 1·75 | 50 |
| 552 | 25t. "Trithemis arteriosa" | 2·00 | 85 |
| 553 | 45t. "Chlorolestes elegans" | 2·75 | 4·75 |

**141** Sorting Diamonds

**1984.** Mining Industry. Multicoloured.

| | | | |
|---|---|---|---|
| 554 | 7t. Type **141** | 2·00 | 50 |
| 555 | 15t. Lime kiln | 2·00 | 75 |
| 556 | 35t. Copper-nickel smelter plant (vert) | 3·25 | 3·25 |
| 557 | 60t. Stockpiled coal (vert) | 3·75 | 10·00 |

**142** Riding Cattle

**1984.** Traditional Transport. Multicoloured.

| | | | |
|---|---|---|---|
| 558 | 7t. Type **142** | 20 | 10 |
| 559 | 25t. Sledge | 65 | 60 |
| 560 | 35t. Wagon | 85 | 1·50 |
| 561 | 50t. Two-wheeled donkey cart | 1·25 | 4·50 |

**143** Avro 504 Aircraft

**1984.** 40th Anniv of International Civil Aviation Organization. Multicoloured.

| | | | |
|---|---|---|---|
| 562 | 7t. Type **143** | 75 | 20 |
| 563 | 10t. Westland Wessex trimotor | 1·00 | 35 |
| 564 | 15t. Junkers Ju 52/3m | 1·40 | 95 |
| 565 | 25t. de Havilland Dominie | 2·00 | 1·75 |
| 566 | 35t. Douglas DC-3 "Wenala" | 2·25 | 3·50 |
| 567 | 50t. Fokker Friendship | 2·50 | 7·00 |

**144** "Papilio demodocus"

**1984.** Christmas. Butterflies. Multicoloured.

| | | | |
|---|---|---|---|
| 568 | 7t. Type **144** | 2·00 | 30 |
| 569 | 25t. "Byblia anvatara" | 2·25 | 1·50 |
| 570 | 35t. "Danaus chrysippus" | 3·50 | 3·00 |
| 571 | 50t. "Graphium taboranus" | 4·75 | 11·00 |

No. 570 is incorrectly inscr "Hypolimnas misippus".

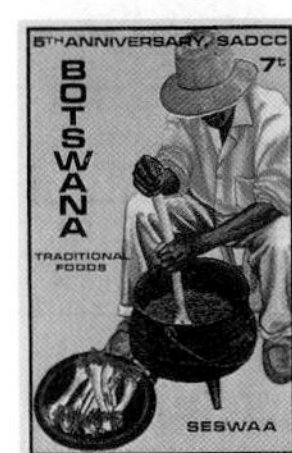

**145** Seswaa (meat dish)

**1985.** 5th Anniv of Southern African Development Co-ordination Conference. Traditional Foods. Multicoloured.

| | | | |
|---|---|---|---|
| 572 | 7t. Type **145** | 50 | 10 |
| 573 | 15t. Bogobe (cereal porridge) | 75 | 35 |
| 574 | 25t. Madila (soured coagulated cow's milk) | 1·00 | 55 |
| 575 | 50t. Phane (caterpillars) | 1·50 | 2·25 |
| **MS**576 | 117×103 mm. Nos. 572/5 | 7·00 | 10·00 |

**146** 1885 British Bechuanaland Overprint on Cape of Good Hope ½d.

**1985.** Centenary of First Bechuanaland Stamps.

| | | | | |
|---|---|---|---|---|
| 577 | **146** | 7t. black, grey and red | 1·00 | 20 |
| 578 | - | 15t. black, brown yell | 1·75 | 50 |
| 579 | - | 25t. black and red | 2·25 | 80 |
| 580 | - | 35t. black, blue and gold | 2·50 | 2·00 |
| 581 | - | 50t. multicoloured | 2·75 | 3·75 |

DESIGNS—VERT: 15t. 1897 Bechuanaland Protectorate overprint on G.B. 3d.; 25t. Bechuanaland Protectorate 1932 1d. definitive. HORIZ: 35t. Bechuanaland 1965 Internal Self-Government 5c.; 50t. Botswana 1966 Independence 2½c.

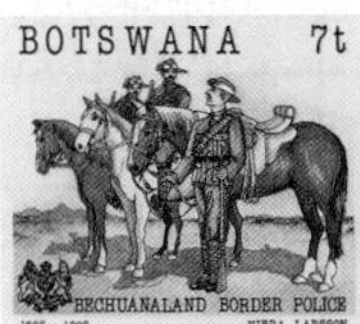

**147** Bechuanaland Border Police, 1885–95

**1985.** Centenary of Botswana Police. Multicoloured.

| | | | |
|---|---|---|---|
| 582 | 7t. Type **147** | 2·25 | 50 |
| 583 | 10t. Bechuanaland Mounted Police, 1895–1902 | 2·50 | 50 |
| 584 | 25t. Bechuanaland Protectorate Police, 1903–66 | 3·50 | 2·00 |
| 585 | 50t. Botswana Police, from 1966 | 5·00 | 7·50 |

**148** "Cucumis metuliferus"

**1985.** Christmas. Edible Wild Cucumbers. Mult.

| | | | |
|---|---|---|---|
| 586 | 7t. Type **148** | 1·25 | 10 |
| 587 | 15t. "Acanthosicyos naudinianus" | 2·25 | 70 |
| 588 | 25t. "Coccinia sessifolia" | 3·50 | 1·25 |
| 589 | 50t. "Momordica balsamina" | 5·00 | 9·50 |

**149** Mr. Shippard and Chief Gaseitsiwe of the Bangwaketse

**1985.** Centenary of Declaration of Bechuanaland Protectorate. Multicoloured.

| | | | |
|---|---|---|---|
| 590 | 7t. Type **149** | 35 | 10 |
| 591 | 15t. Sir Charles Warren and Chief Sechele of the Bakwena | 70 | 45 |
| 592 | 25t. Revd. Mackenzie and Chief Khama of the Bamangwato | 1·25 | 85 |
| 593 | 50t. Map showing Protectorate | 2·75 | 6·50 |
| **MS**594 | 130×133 mm. Nos. 590/3 | 12·00 | 14·00 |

**150** Halley's Comet over Serowe

**1986.** Appearance of Halley's Comet. Multicoloured.

| | | | |
|---|---|---|---|
| 595 | 7t. Type **150** | 80 | 15 |
| 596 | 15t. Comet over Bobonong at sunset | 1·50 | 70 |
| 597 | 35t. Comet over Gomare at dawn | 2·00 | 1·50 |
| 598 | 50t. Comet over Thamaga and Letlhakeng | 2·25 | 3·75 |

**151** Milk Bag

**1986.** Traditional Milk Containers. Multicoloured.

| | | | |
|---|---|---|---|
| 599 | 8t. Type **151** | 30 | 10 |
| 600 | 15t. Clay pot and calabashes | 45 | 30 |
| 601 | 35t. Wooden milk bucket | 75 | 65 |
| 602 | 50t. Milk churn | 1·00 | 1·40 |

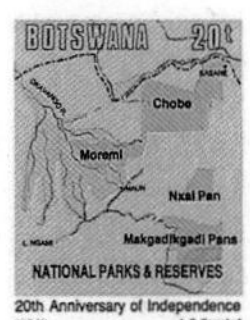

**152** Map showing National Parks and Reserves

**1986.** 20th Anniv of Independence. Sheet 100×120 mm. Multicoloured.

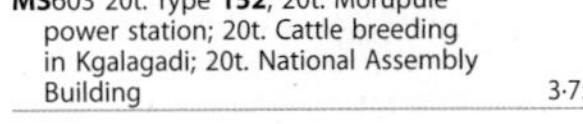

| | | | |
|---|---|---|---|
| **MS**603 | 20t. Type **152**; 20t. Morupule power station; 20t. Cattle breeding in Kgalagadi; 20t. National Assembly Building | 3·75 | 2·50 |

**153** "Ludwigia stogonifera"

**1986.** Christmas. Flowers of Okavango. Mult.

| | | | |
|---|---|---|---|
| 604 | 8t. Type **153** | 1·25 | 10 |
| 605 | 15t. "Sopubia mannii" | 2·25 | 1·10 |
| 606 | 35t. "Commelina diffusa" | 3·50 | 3·00 |
| 607 | 50t. "Hibiscus diversifolius" | 4·00 | 12·00 |

**154** Divining

**1987.** Traditional Medicine. Multicoloured.

| | | | |
|---|---|---|---|
| 608 | 8t. Type **154** | 80 | 10 |
| 609 | 15t. Lightning prevention | 1·50 | 80 |
| 610 | 35t. Rain making | 2·25 | 2·50 |
| 611 | 50t. Blood letting | 2·75 | 8·50 |

**1987.** Nos. 520, 523 and 530 surch.

| | | | |
|---|---|---|---|
| 612 | 3t. on 6t. African pygmy goose | 1·75 | 60 |
| 613 | 5t. on 10t. Yellow-billed stork | 1·75 | 60 |
| 614 | 20t. on 50t. Helmeted guineafowl (horiz) | 3·25 | 1·40 |

**156** Oral Rehydration Therapy

**1987.** UNICEF Child Survival Campaign. Multicoloured.

| | | | |
|---|---|---|---|
| 615 | 8t. Type **156** | 35 | 10 |
| 616 | 15t. Growth monitoring | 60 | 55 |
| 617 | 35t. Immunization | 1·25 | 2·00 |
| 618 | 50t. Breast feeding | 1·50 | 5·00 |

**157** Cape Fox

**1987.** Animals of Botswana. Multicoloured.

| | | | |
|---|---|---|---|
| 619 | 1t. Type **157** | 10 | 1·00 |
| 620 | 2t. Lechwe | 50 | 1·50 |
| 621 | 3t. Zebra | 15 | 1·00 |
| 622 | 4t. Duiker | 15 | 1·75 |
| 623 | 5t. Banded mongoose | 20 | 1·75 |
| 624 | 6t. Rusty-spotted genet | 20 | 1·75 |
| 625 | 8t. Hedgehog | 30 | 10 |
| 626 | 10t. Scrub hare | 30 | 10 |
| 627 | 12t. Hippopotamus | 3·00 | 3·50 |
| 628 | 15t. Suricate | 2·50 | 2·25 |
| 629 | 20t. Caracal | 70 | 65 |
| 630 | 25t. Steenbok | 70 | 1·50 |
| 631 | 30t. Gemsbok | 1·50 | 1·50 |
| 632 | 35t. Square-lipped rhinoceros | 2·00 | 2·50 |
| 633 | 40t. Mountain reedbuck | 1·75 | 1·50 |
| 634 | 50t. Rock dassie | 90 | 1·75 |
| 635 | 1p. Giraffe | 2·50 | 3·75 |
| 636 | 2p. Tsessebe | 2·50 | 5·50 |
| 637 | 3p. Side-striped jackal | 3·75 | 7·00 |
| 638 | 5p. Hartebeest | 6·00 | 9·00 |

**158** "Cyperus articulatus"

**1987.** Christmas. Grasses and Sedges of Okavango. Multicoloured.

| | | | |
|---|---|---|---|
| 639 | 8t. Type **158** | 40 | 10 |
| 640 | 15t. Broomgrass | 60 | 40 |
| 641 | 30t. "Cyperus alopurcides" | 1·25 | 75 |
| 642 | 1p. Bulrush sedge | 2·50 | 5·75 |
| **MS**643 | 88×99 mm. Nos. 639/42 | 4·25 | 5·75 |

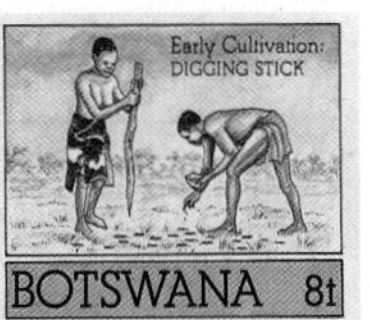

**159** Planting Seeds with Digging Stick

**1988.** Early Cultivation. Multicoloured.

| | | | |
|---|---|---|---|
| 644 | 8t. Type **159** | 40 | 10 |

645 15t. Using iron hoe 60 35
646 35t. Wooden ox-drawn plough 1·00 1·00
647 50t. Villagers working in lesotlas communal field 1·40 2·00

**160** Red Lechwe at Water-hole

**1988.** Red Lechwe. Multicoloured.
648 10t. Type **160** 90 15
649 15t. Red lechwe and early morning sun 1·75 65
650 35t. Female and calf 2·50 1·75
651 75t. Herd on the move 3·75 8·50

**161** Gubulawayo Postmark and Route Southwards to Tati

**1988.** Cent of Mafeking–Gubalawayo Runner Post. Designs as Nos. 294/7, but redrawn smaller with changed inscriptions as in T **161**. Multicoloured.
652 10t. Type **161** 35 10
653 15t. Bechuanaland 1888 6d. on 6d. stamp and route from Tati southwards 55 30
654 30t. Runners and twin routes south from Shoshong 95 75
655 60t. Mafeking postmark and routes to Bechuanaland and Transvaal 1·60 2·75
**MS**656 81×151 mm. Nos. 652/5 vertically se-tenant, forming a composite map design 6·00 6·50

**162** Pope John Paul II and Outline Map of Botswana

**1988.** Visit of Pope John Paul II. Multicoloured.
657 10t. Type **162** 2·00 20
658 15t. Pope John Paul II 2·25 30
659 30t. Pope giving blessing and outline map 2·75 70
660 80t. Pope John Paul II (different) 3·50 2·75

**163** National Museum and Art Gallery, Gaborone

**1988.** 20th Anniv of National Museum and Art Gallery, Gaborone. Multicoloured.
661 8t. Type **163** 15 10
662 15t. Pottery 20 25
663 30t. Blacksmith's buffalo bellows 35 40
664 60c. Children and land rover mobile museum van 70 1·00

**164** "Grewia flava"

**1988.** Flowering Plants of South-eastern Botswana. Multicoloured.
665 8t. Type **164** 20 10
666 15t. "Cienfuegosia digitata" 30 25
667 40t. "Solanum seaforthianum" 60 55
668 75t. "Carissa bispinosa" 1·00 1·40

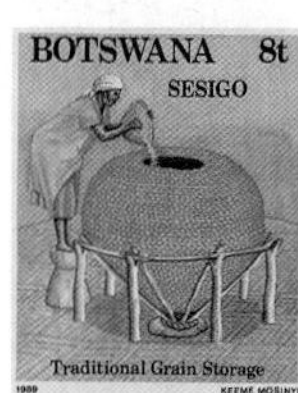


**165** Basket Granary

**1989.** Traditional Grain Storage. Multicoloured.
669 8t. Type **165** 75 10
670 15t. Large letlole granary 1·25 40
671 30t. Pot granary 1·75 60
672 60t. Two types of serala 2·50 2·25

**166** Female with Eggs

**1989.** Slaty Egret. Multicoloured.
673 8t. Type **166** 55 15
674 15t. Chicks in nest 75 40
675 30t. In flight 1·00 75
676 60t. Pair building nest 1·40 1·60
**MS**677 119×89 mm. Nos. 673/6 3·25 2·75

**167** "My Work at Home" (Ephraim Seeletso)

**1989.** Children's Paintings. Multicoloured.
678 10t. Type **167** 35 10
679 15t. "My Favourite Game" (hopscotch) (Neelma Bhatia) (vert) 50 35
680 30t. "My Favourite Toy" (clay animals) (Thabo Habana) 75 70
681 1p. "My School Day" (Thabo Olesitse) 2·00 3·25

**168** "Eulophia angolensis"

**1989.** Christmas. Orchids. Multicoloured.
682 8t. Type **168** 90 10
683 15t. "Eulophia hereroensis" 1·50 60
684 30t. "Eulophia speciosa" 2·00 1·00
685 60t. "Eulophia petersii" 3·50 7·00

**169** Bechuanaland 1965 New Constitution 25c. Stamp (25th anniv of Self-Government)

**1990.** Anniversaries.
686 **169** 8t. multicoloured 70 15
687 - 15t. multicoloured 75 50
688 - 30t. multicoloured 3·75 1·60
689 - 60t. black, blue and yellow 3·75 7·00

DESIGNS: 15t. Casting vote in ballot box (25th anniv of First Elections); 30t. Outline map and flags of Southern Africa Development Co-ordination Conference countries (10th anniv); 60t. Penny Black (150th anniv of first postage stamp).

**1990.** Nos. 619, 624 and 627 surch.
690 10t. on 1t. Type **157** 45 20
691 20t. on 6t. Rusty-spotted genet 60 80
692 50t. on 12t. Hippopotamus 2·00 3·50

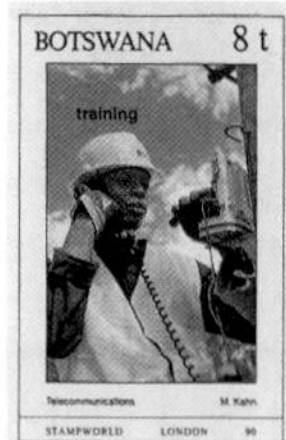


**171** Telephone Engineer

**1990.** "Stamp World London 90" International Stamp Exhibition. Multicoloured.
693 8t. Type **171** 35 10
694 15t. Transmission pylon 65 40
695 30t. Public telephone 1·00 75
696 2p. Testing circuit board 3·00 6·50

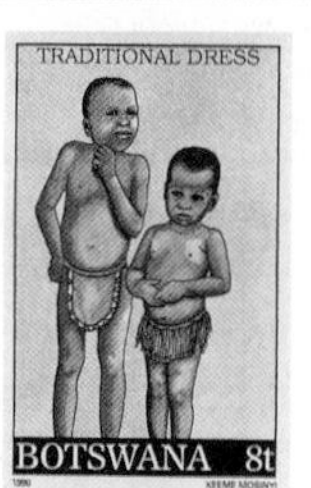


**172** Young Children

**1990.** Traditional Dress. Multicoloured.
697 8t. Type **172** 35 10
698 15t. Young woman 65 40
699 30t. Adult man 1·00 70
700 2p. Adult woman 3·00 6·50
**MS**701 104×150 mm. Nos. 697/700 5·00 7·50

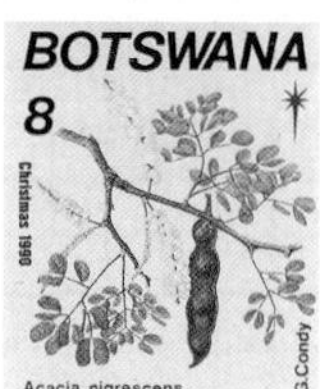


**173** "Acacia nigrescens"

**1990.** Christmas. Flowering Trees. Multicoloured.
702 8t. Type **173** 60 10
703 15t. "Peltophorum africanum" 95 35
704 30t. "Burkea africana" 1·75 75
705 2p. "Pterocarpus angolensis" 3·75 7·50

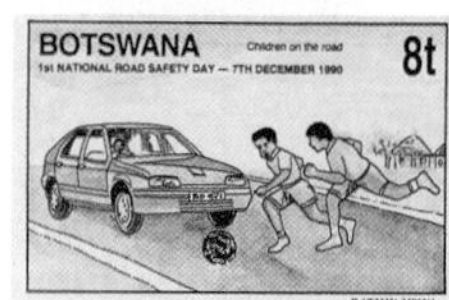


**174** Children running in front of Hatchback

**1990.** 1st National Road Safety Day. Multicoloured.
706 8t. Type **174** 2·50 30
707 15t. Careless overtaking 3·00 1·00
708 30t. Cattle on road 3·75 2·75

**175** Cattle

**1991.** Rock Paintings. Multicoloured.
709 8t. Type **175** 2·25 40
710 15t. Cattle, drying frames and tree 2·75 85
711 30t. Animal hides 3·25 1·50
712 2p. Family herding cattle 6·00 10·00

**176** Children

**1991.** National Census. Multicoloured.
713 8t. Type **176** 1·50 20
714a 15t. Village 2·00 55
715 30t. School 2·25 1·00
716 2p. Hospital 8·00 11·00

**177** Tourists viewing Elephants

**1991.** African Tourism Year. Okavango Delta. Mult.
717 8t. Type **177** 1·50 70
718 15t. Crocodiles basking on river bank 1·75 90
719 35t. Fish eagles and De Havilland D.H.C.7 Dash Seven aircraft 3·50 3·25
720 2p. Okavango wildlife (26×44 mm) 5·50 9·00

**178** "Harpagophytum procumbens"

**1991.** Christmas. Seed Pods. Multicoloured.
721 8t. Type **178** 60 10
722 15t. "Tylosema esculentum" 1·00 40
723 30t. "Abrus precatorius" 1·75 80
724 2p. "Kigelia africana" 4·50 8·50

**1992.** Nos. 621, 624 and 627 surch.
725 8t. on 12t. Hippopotamus 1·25 70
726 10t. on 12t. Hippopotamus 1·25 70
727 25t. on 6t. Rusty-spotted genet 1·25 1·50
728 40t. on 3t. Zebra 2·25 4·00

**179** "Cacosternum boettgeri"

**1992.** Climbing Frogs. Multicoloured.
729 8t. Type **179** 75 30
730 10t. "Hyperolius marmoratus angolensis" (vert) 75 30
731 40t. "Bufo fenoulheti" 2·50 1·50
732 1p. "Hyperolius sp." (vert) 5·00 7·00

**180** Air-conditioned Carriages

**1992.** Deluxe Railway Service. Multicoloured.
733 10t. Type **180** 1·50 40
734 25t. Diesel locomotive No. BD001 (vert) 2·25 80
735 40t. Carriage interior (vert) 2·50 1·25
736 2p. Diesel locomotive No. BD028 3·75 7·50
**MS**737 127×127 mm. Nos. 733/6 12·00 12·00

**181** Cheetah

**1992.** Animals. Multicoloured.
738 1t. Type **181** 30 1·75
739 2t. Spring hare 30 1·75
740 4t. Blackfooted cat 40 1·75
741 5t. Striped mouse 40 1·50
742 10t. Oribi 55 10
743 12t. Pangolin 1·00 2·50
744 15t. Aardwolf 1·00 40
745 20t. Warthog 1·00 40
746 25t. Ground squirrel 1·00 20
747 35t. Honey badger 1·25 30
748 40t. Common mole rat 1·25 30
749 45t. Wild dog 1·25 30

| | | | |
|---|---|---|---|
| 750 | 50t. Water mongoose | 1·25 | 35 |
| 751 | 80t. Klipspringer | 1·75 | 1·75 |
| 752 | 1p. Lesser bushbaby | 1·75 | 1·75 |
| 753 | 2p. Bushveld elephant shrew | 2·50 | 4·00 |
| 754 | 5p. Zorilla | 4·25 | 7·00 |
| 755 | 10p. Vervet monkey | 6·50 | 10·00 |

**182** Boxing

**1992.** Olympic Games, Barcelona. Multicoloured.

| | | | |
|---|---|---|---|
| 756 | 10t. Type **182** | 60 | 10 |
| 757 | 50t. Running | 1·50 | 50 |
| 758 | 1p. Boxing (different) | 2·00 | 2·50 |
| 759 | 2p. Running (different) | 2·50 | 5·00 |
| **MS**760 | 87×117 mm. Nos. 756/9 | 5·50 | 8·00 |

**183** "Adiantum incisum"

**1992.** Christmas. Ferns. Multicoloured.

| | | | |
|---|---|---|---|
| 761 | 10t. Type **183** | 40 | 10 |
| 762 | 25t. "Actiniopteris radiata" | 70 | 35 |
| 763 | 40t. "Ceratopteris cornuta" | 1·00 | 55 |
| 764 | 1p.50 "Pellaea calomelanos" | 3·00 | 7·00 |

**184** Helping Blind Person (Lions Club International)

**1993.** Charitable Organizations in Botswana. Mult.

| | | | |
|---|---|---|---|
| 765 | 10t. Type **184** | 80 | 20 |
| 766 | 15t. Nurse carrying child (Red Cross Society) (horiz) | 90 | 40 |
| 767 | 25t. Woman watering seedling (Ecumenical Decade) | 90 | 50 |
| 768 | 35t. Deaf children (Round Table) (horiz) | 1·25 | 1·50 |
| 769 | 40t. Crowd of people (Rotary International) | 1·25 | 1·75 |
| 770 | 50t. Hands at prayer (Botswana Christian Council) (horiz) | 1·50 | 2·50 |

**185** Bechuanaland Railways Class "6" Locomotive No. 1

**1993.** Railway Centenary. Multicoloured.

| | | | |
|---|---|---|---|
| 771 | 10t. Type **185** | 75 | 40 |
| 772 | 40t. Class "19" locomotive No. 317 | 1·40 | 75 |
| 773 | 50t. Class "12" locomotive No. 256 | 1·40 | 90 |
| 774 | 1p.50 Class "7" locomotive No. 71 | 2·00 | 5·00 |
| **MS**775 | 190×100 mm. Nos. 771/4 | 5·00 | 6·00 |

**186** Long-crested Eagle

**1993.** Endangered Eagles. Multicoloured.

| | | | |
|---|---|---|---|
| 776 | 10t. Type **186** | 70 | 35 |
| 777 | 25t. Short-toed eagle ("Snake eagle") | 1·25 | 65 |
| 778 | 50t. Bateleur ("Bateleur Eagle") | 1·60 | 1·75 |
| 779 | 1p.50 Secretary bird | 2·50 | 6·50 |

**187** "Aloe zebrina"

**1993.** Christmas. Flora. Multicoloured.

| | | | |
|---|---|---|---|
| 780 | 12t. Type **187** | 40 | 10 |
| 781 | 25t. "Croton megalobotrys" | 60 | 25 |
| 782 | 50t. "Boophane disticha" | 85 | 70 |
| 783 | 1p. "Euphoria davyi" | 1·25 | 3·50 |

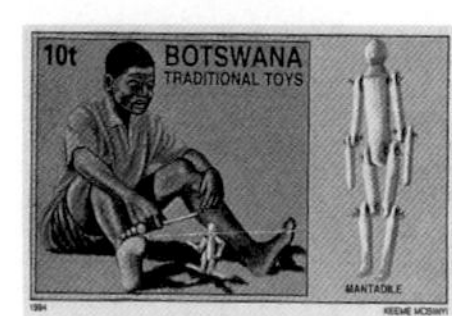

**188** Boy with String Puppet

**1994.** Traditional Toys. Multicoloured.

| | | | |
|---|---|---|---|
| 784 | 10t. Type **188** | 20 | 10 |
| 785 | 40t. Boys with clay cattle | 45 | 30 |
| 786 | 50t. Boy with spinner | 50 | 50 |
| 787 | 1p. Girls playing in make-believe houses | 1·10 | 3·00 |

**189** Interior of Control Tower, Gaborone Airport

**1994.** 50th Anniv of I.C.A.O. Multicoloured.

| | | | |
|---|---|---|---|
| 788 | 10t. Type **189** | 40 | 10 |
| 789 | 25t. Crash fire tender | 75 | 40 |
| 790 | 40t. Loading supplies onto airliner (vert) | 1·00 | 85 |
| 791 | 50t. Control tower, Gaborone (vert) | 1·00 | 1·75 |

**1994.** No. 743 surch 10t.

| | | | |
|---|---|---|---|
| 792 | 10t. on 12t. Pangolin | 6·50 | 75 |

**191** Lesser Flamingos at Sua Pan

**1994.** Environment Protection. Makgadikgadi Pans. Multicoloured.

| | | | |
|---|---|---|---|
| 793 | 10t. Type **191** | 1·00 | 40 |
| 794 | 35t. Baobab trees (horiz) | 50 | 40 |
| 795 | 50t. Zebra and palm trees | 65 | 80 |
| 796 | 2p. Map of area (horiz) | 3·00 | 6·00 |

**192** "Ziziphus mucronata"

**1994.** Christmas. Edible Fruits. Multicoloured.

| | | | |
|---|---|---|---|
| 797 | 10t. Type **192** | 25 | 10 |
| 798 | 25t. "Strychnos cocculoides" | 40 | 30 |
| 799 | 40t. "Bauhinia petersiana" | 60 | 70 |
| 800 | 50t. "Schinziphyton rautonenii" | 70 | 1·40 |

**193** Fisherman with Bow and Arrow

**1995.** Traditional Fishing. Multicoloured.

| | | | |
|---|---|---|---|
| 801 | 15t. Type **193** | 35 | 20 |
| 802 | 40t. Men in canoe and boy with fishing rod | 60 | 45 |
| 803 | 65t. Fisherman with net | 80 | 90 |
| 804 | 80t. Fisherman with basket fish trap | 1·00 | 2·00 |

**194** Boys watering Horses (FAO)

**1995.** 50th Anniv of United Nations. Multicoloured.

| | | | |
|---|---|---|---|
| 805 | 20t. Type **194** | 20 | 10 |
| 806 | 50t. Schoolchildren queueing for soup (WFP) | 35 | 30 |
| 807 | 80t. Policeman conducting census (UNDP) | 1·00 | 1·00 |
| 808 | 1p. Weighing baby (UNICEF) | 70 | 2·00 |

**195** Brown Hyena

**1995.** Endangered Species. Brown Hyena. Mult.

| | | | |
|---|---|---|---|
| 809 | 20t. Type **195** | 45 | 60 |
| 810 | 50t. Pair of hyenas | 65 | 75 |
| 811 | 80t. Hyena stealing ostrich eggs | 1·10 | 1·50 |
| 812 | 1p. Adult hyena and cubs | 1·25 | 2·25 |

**196** "Adenia glauca"

**1995.** Christmas. Plants. Multicoloured.

| | | | |
|---|---|---|---|
| 813 | 20t. Type **196** | 35 | 10 |
| 814 | 50t. "Pterodiscus ngamicus" | 60 | 30 |
| 815 | 80t. "Sesamothamnus lugardii" | 1·00 | 1·00 |
| 816 | 1p. "Fockea multiflora" | 1·10 | 2·00 |

**1996.** Nos. 738/40 surch.

| | | | |
|---|---|---|---|
| 817 | 20t. on 2t. Spring hare | 1·00 | 30 |
| 818 | 30t. on 1t. Type **181** | 1·25 | 30 |
| 819 | 70t. on 4t. Blackfooted cat | 2·00 | 3·25 |

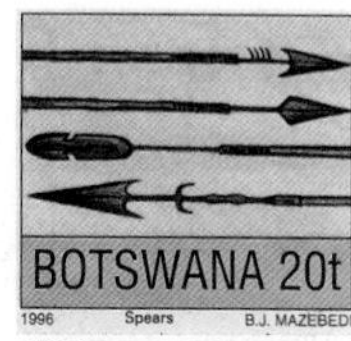

**198** Spears

**1996.** Traditional Weapons. Multicoloured.

| | | | |
|---|---|---|---|
| 820 | 20t. Type **198** | 20 | 10 |
| 821 | 50t. Axes | 35 | 30 |
| 822 | 80t. Shield and knobkerries | 55 | 65 |
| 823 | 1p. Knives and sheaths | 60 | 1·50 |

**199** Child with Basic Radio

**1996.** Centenary of Radio. Multicoloured.

| | | | |
|---|---|---|---|
| 824 | 20t. Type **199** | 25 | 10 |
| 825 | 50t. Radio Botswana's mobile transmitter | 40 | 30 |
| 826 | 80t. Police radio control | 1·50 | 1·10 |
| 827 | 1p. Listening to radio | 70 | 1·75 |

**200** Olympic Flame, Rings and Wreath

**1996.** Centenary of Modern Olympic Games. Mult.

| | | | |
|---|---|---|---|
| 828 | 20t. Type **200** | 30 | 10 |
| 829 | 50t. Pierre de Coubertin (founder of modern Olympics) | 45 | 30 |
| 830 | 80t. Map of Botswana with flags and athletes | 90 | 90 |
| 831 | 1p. Ruins of ancient stadium at Olympia | 90 | 1·60 |

**201** Family Planning Class (Botswana Family Welfare Association)

**1996.** Local Charities. Multicoloured.

| | | | |
|---|---|---|---|
| 832 | 20t. Type **201** | 20 | 10 |
| 833 | 30t. Blind workers (Pudulogong Rehabilitation Centre) | 20 | 15 |
| 834 | 50t. Collecting seeds (Forestry Association of Botswana) | 30 | 30 |
| 835 | 70t. Secretarial class (YWCA) | 40 | 70 |
| 836 | 80t. Children's day centre (Botswana Council of Women) | 50 | 80 |
| 837 | 1p. Children's village, Tlokweng (S.O.S. Children's village) | 60 | 1·50 |

**202** "Adansonia digitata" Leaf and Blossom

**1996.** Christmas. Parts of Life Cycle for "Adansonia digitata". Multicoloured.

| | | | |
|---|---|---|---|
| 838 | 20t. Type **202** | 25 | 10 |
| 839 | 50t. Fruit | 40 | 25 |
| 840 | 80t. Tree in leaf | 60 | 75 |
| 841 | 1p. Tree with bare branches | 70 | 1·60 |

**203** Tati Hotel

**1997.** Francistown Centenary. Multicoloured.

| | | | |
|---|---|---|---|
| 842 | 20t. Type **203** | 15 | 10 |
| 843 | 50t. Railway Station | 75 | 35 |
| 844 | 80t. Company Manager's House | 60 | 80 |
| 845 | 1p. Monarch Mine | 1·00 | 1·60 |

204 Steam Locomotive, Bechuanaland Railway, 1897

**1997.** Railway Centenary. Multicoloured.

| | | | |
|---|---|---|---|
| 846 | 35t. Type **204** | 40 | 20 |
| 847 | 50t. Elephants crossing railway line | 60 | 35 |
| 848 | 80t. First locomotive in Bechuanaland, 1897 | 70 | 45 |
| 849 | 1p. Beyer-Garratt type steam locomotive No. 352 | 75 | 75 |
| 850 | 2p. Diesel locomotive No. BD339 | 1·00 | 1·75 |
| 851 | 2p.50 Fantuzzi container stacker | 1·25 | 2·25 |

205 Pel's Fishing Owl

**1997.** Birds. Multicoloured.

| | | | |
|---|---|---|---|
| 852 | 5t. Type **205** | 50 | 75 |
| 853 | 10t. African harrier hawk ("Gymnogene") (horiz) | 50 | 75 |
| 854 | 15t. Brown parrot ("Meyer's Parrot") | 50 | 60 |
| 855 | 20t. Harlequin quail (horiz) | 60 | 60 |
| 856 | 25t. Mariqua sunbird ("Marico Sunbird") (horiz) | 60 | 60 |
| 857 | 30t. Kurrichane thrush (horiz) | 65 | 60 |
| 858 | 40t. Paradise sparrow ("Red-headed Finch") | 70 | 60 |
| 859 | 50t. Red-billed buffalo weaver ("Buffalo Weaver") | 80 | 40 |
| 860 | 60t. Sacred ibis (horiz) | 90 | 70 |
| 861 | 70t. Cape shoveler (horiz) | 90 | 80 |
| 862 | 80t. Black-throated honeyguide ("Greater Honeyguide") (horiz) | 90 | 70 |
| 863 | 1p. Woodland kingfisher (horiz) | 1·10 | 80 |
| 864 | 1p.25 Purple heron | 1·40 | 1·40 |
| 865 | 1p.50 Yellow-billed oxpecker (horiz) | 1·40 | 1·75 |
| 866 | 2p. Shaft-tailed whydah | 1·60 | 2·00 |
| 867 | 2p.50 White stork | 1·75 | 2·00 |
| 868 | 5p. Ovampo sparrow hawk ("Sparrowhawk") | 2·25 | 2·75 |
| 869 | 10p. Spotted crake | 3·25 | 4·50 |

No. 861 is inscribed "Shoveller" in error.

**1997.** Golden Wedding of Queen Elizabeth and Prince Philip. As T **173** of Ascension. Multicoloured.

| | | | |
|---|---|---|---|
| 870 | 35t. Prince Philip with carriage | 20 | 55 |
| 871 | 35t. Queen Elizabeth with binoculars | 20 | 55 |
| 872 | 2p. Queen Elizabeth with horse team | 90 | 1·50 |
| 873 | 2p. Prince Philip and horse | 90 | 1·50 |
| 874 | 2p.50 Queen Elizabeth and Prince Philip | 1·10 | 1·50 |
| 875 | 2p.50 Princess Anne and Prince Edward | 1·10 | 1·50 |
| **MS**876 | 110×70 mm. 10p. Queen Elizabeth and Prince Philip in landau (horiz) | 4·00 | 5·50 |

206 "Combretum zeyheri"

**1997.** Christmas. Plants. Multicoloured.

| | | | |
|---|---|---|---|
| 877 | 35t. Type **206** | 45 | 10 |
| 878 | 1p. "Combretum apiculatum" | 1·00 | 35 |
| 879 | 2p. "Combretum molle" | 1·75 | 1·90 |
| 880 | 2p.50 "Combretum imberbe" | 2·00 | 2·50 |

207 Baobab Trees

**1998.** Tourism (1st series). Multicoloured.

| | | | |
|---|---|---|---|
| 881 | 35t. Type **207** | 25 | 15 |
| 882 | 1p. Crocodile | 50 | 45 |
| 883 | 2p. Stalactites (vert) | 85 | 1·10 |
| 884 | 2p.50 Tourists and rock paintings (vert) | 1·10 | 1·60 |

See also Nos. 899/902.

**1998.** Diana, Princess of Wales Commemoration. As T **223a** of Bahamas. Multicoloured.

| | | | |
|---|---|---|---|
| 885 | 35t. Princess Diana, 1990 | 25 | 15 |
| 886 | 1p. In green hat, 1992 | 40 | 35 |
| 887 | 2p. In white blouse, 1993 | 75 | 1·10 |
| 888 | 2p.50 With crowd, Cambridge, 1993 | 90 | 1·50 |
| **MS**889 | 145×70 mm. As Nos. 885/8, but each with a face value of 2p.50 | 4·50 | 3·75 |

208 "Village Life" (tapestry)

**1998.** Botswana Weavers. Multicoloured.

| | | | |
|---|---|---|---|
| 890 | 35t. Type **208** | 30 | 15 |
| 891 | 55t. Weaver dyeing threads | 40 | 20 |
| 892 | 1p. "African wildlife" (tapestry) | 1·40 | 1·00 |
| 893 | 2p. Weaver at loom | 1·50 | 2·25 |
| **MS**894 | 68×58 mm. 2p.50, "Elephants" (tapestry) (horiz) | 3·00 | 3·25 |

209 "Ficus ingens"

**1998.** Christmas. Plants. Multicoloured.

| | | | |
|---|---|---|---|
| 895 | 35t. Type **209** | 40 | 10 |
| 896 | 55t. "Ficus pygmaea" | 60 | 20 |
| 897 | 1p. "Ficus abutilifolia" | 1·00 | 55 |
| 898 | 2p.50 "Ficus sycomorus" | 1·90 | 2·75 |

**1999.** Tourism (2nd series). As T **207**. Multicoloured.

| | | | |
|---|---|---|---|
| 899 | 35t. Rock painting of men and cattle | 70 | 25 |
| 900 | 55t. Expedition at Salt Pan | 1·00 | 30 |
| 901 | 1p. Rock painting of elephant and antelope (vert) | 1·40 | 1·40 |
| 902 | 2p. Tourists under Baobab tree (vert) | 1·60 | 2·25 |

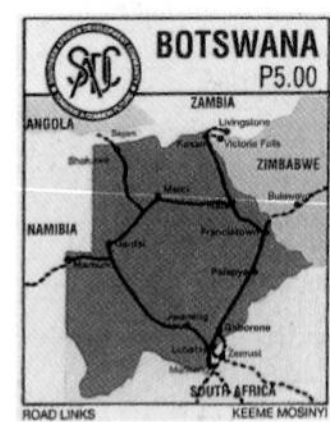
210 Road Map

**1999.** Southern African Development Community Day. Sheet 77×84 mm.

| | | | |
|---|---|---|---|
| **MS**903 | **210** 5p. multicoloured | 3·50 | 3·75 |

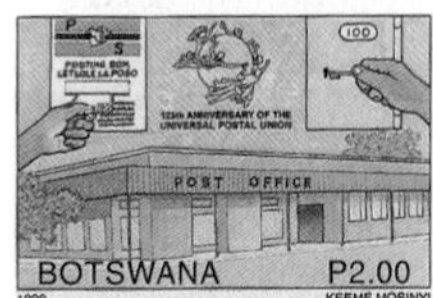
211 Modern Post Office

**1999.** 125th Anniv of Universal Postal Union.

| | | | | |
|---|---|---|---|---|
| 904 | **211** | 2p. multicoloured | 1·50 | 1·50 |

212 Mpule Kwelagobe winning contest

**1999.** Mpule Kwelagobe ("Miss Universe 1999"). Multicoloured.

| | | | |
|---|---|---|---|
| 905 | 35t. Type **212** | 35 | 10 |
| 906 | 1p. In traditional dress (horiz) | 75 | 30 |
| 907 | 2p. In traditional dancing costume with lion | 1·10 | 60 |
| 908 | 2p.50 Wearing "Botswana" sash (horiz) | 1·25 | 75 |
| 909 | 15p. With leopard in background (horiz) | 7·00 | 11·00 |
| **MS**910 | 175×80 mm. Nos. 905/9 | 9·50 | 12·00 |

213 Saddle-bill Stork and Limpopo River

**2000.** Scenic Rivers. Multicoloured.

| | | | |
|---|---|---|---|
| 911 | 35t. Type **213** | 40 | 20 |
| 912 | 1p. Hippopotamuses in water lilies (vert) | 70 | 60 |
| 913 | 2p. African skimmer and makoro (dugout canoe) | 1·25 | 1·50 |
| 914 | 2p.50 African elephant at sunset, Chobe River (vert) | 1·40 | 2·00 |

214 Mopane Moth

**2000.** Moths. Multicoloured.

| | | | |
|---|---|---|---|
| 915 | 35t. Type **214** | 15 | 10 |
| 916 | 70t. Wild silk moth | 25 | 20 |
| 917 | 1p. Crimson speckled footman ("Tiger Moth") | 35 | 30 |
| 918 | 2p. African lunar moth | 65 | 60 |
| 919 | 15p. Speckled emperor moth | 4·75 | 8·00 |
| **MS**920 | 175×135 mm. Nos. 915/19 | 7·50 | 9·50 |

No. **MS**920 is in the shape of a moth.

215 Mother reading Medicine Label with Child ("Protect Your Children")

**2000.** United Nations Literacy Decade. Mult.

| | | | |
|---|---|---|---|
| 921 | 35t. Type **215** | 20 | 10 |
| 922 | 70t. Adult literacy class ("Never Too Old To Learn") | 30 | 20 |
| 923 | 2p. Man smoking next to petrol pump ("Be Aware Of Danger") | 75 | 1·10 |
| 924 | 2p.50 Man at Automatic Teller Machine ("Be Independent") | 90 | 2·00 |

216 Pres. Sir Seretse Khama

**2000.** Chiefs and Presidents.

| | | | | |
|---|---|---|---|---|
| 925 | **216** | 35t. black, red and gold | 40 | 10 |
| 926 | - | 1p. multicoloured | 65 | 40 |
| 927 | - | 2p. multicoloured | 1·00 | 1·10 |
| 928 | - | 2p.50 multicoloured | 1·25 | 2·00 |

DESIGNS—HORIZ (60×40 mm): 35t. Chiefs Sebele I of Bakwena, Bathoen I of Bangwaketse and Khama III of Bangato, 1895. VERT (as T **216**): 2p. Pres. Sir Ketumile Masire; 2p.50, Pres. Festus Mogae.

217 Doctor giving Eye Test

**2000.** Airborne Medical Service. Multicoloured.

| | | | |
|---|---|---|---|
| 929 | 35t. Type **217** | 30 | 10 |
| 930 | 1p. Medical team and family | 65 | 40 |
| 931 | 2p. Aircraft over canoes | 1·25 | 1·40 |
| 932 | 2p.50 Donkeys and mule cart on airstrip | 1·50 | 2·25 |

218 Hippopotamus

**2000.** Wetlands (1st series). Okavango Delta. Mult.

| | | | |
|---|---|---|---|
| 933 | 35t. Type **218** | 50 | 20 |
| 934 | 1p. Tiger fish and tilapia | 55 | 30 |
| 935 | 1p.75 Painted reed frog and wattled crane (vert) | 1·50 | 1·50 |
| 936 | 2p. Pels fishing owl and vervet monkey (vert) | 1·75 | 1·75 |
| 937 | 2p.50 Nile crocodile, Sitatunga and red lechwe | 1·75 | 1·75 |
| **MS**938 | 175×80 mm. Nos. 933/7 | 5·50 | 5·50 |

See also Nos. 958/62, 994/**MS**999 and 1009/**MS**1014.

**2001.** "HONG KONG 2001" Stamp Exhibition. No. MS938 overprinted with exhibition logo on sheet margin.

| | | | |
|---|---|---|---|
| **MS**939 | 175×80 mm. Nos. 933/7 | 6·00 | 7·00 |

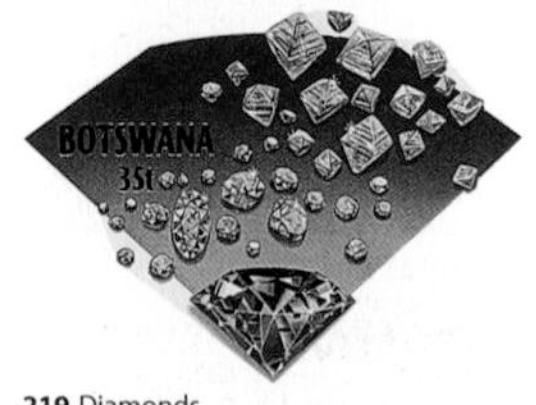
219 Diamonds

**2001.** Diamonds. Multicoloured. Self-adhesive.

| | | | |
|---|---|---|---|
| 940 | 35t. Type **219** | 55 | 20 |
| 941 | 1p.75 J.C.B. in open-cast mine | 1·50 | 1·60 |
| 942 | 2p. Quality inspector | 1·75 | 1·90 |
| 943 | 2p.50 Diamonds in jewellery | 2·00 | 2·25 |

220 African Pygmy Falcon

**2001.** Kgalagadi Transfrontier Wildlife Park. Joint Issue with South Africa. Multicoloured.

| | | | |
|---|---|---|---|
| 944 | 35t. Type **220** | 85 | 35 |
| 945 | 1p. Leopard | 1·00 | 70 |
| 946 | 2p. Gemsbok | 1·40 | 1·60 |
| 947 | 2p.50 Bat-eared fox | 1·60 | 2·25 |
| **MS**948 | 115×80 mm. Nos. 945 and 947 | 2·50 | 3·00 |

221 Shallow Basket

**2001.** Traditional Baskets. Multicoloured.

| | | | |
|---|---|---|---|
| 949 | 35t. Type **221** | 20 | 15 |
| 950 | 1p. Tall basket | 35 | 25 |

951 2p. Woman weaving basket 60 85
952 2p.50 Spherical basket 65 95
**MS**953 177×92 mm. Nos. 949/52 2·00 3·00

**222** Boys by River at Sunset

**2001**. Scenic Skies. Multicoloured.
954 50t. Type **222** 25 15
955 1p. Woman with baby at sunset 50 25
956 2p. Girls carrying firewood at sunset 75 75
957 10p. Traditional village at sunset near huts 2·50 3·50

**2001**. Wetlands (2nd series). Chobe River. As T **218**. Multicoloured.
958 50t. Water monitor and carmine bee-eater 65 20
959 1p.75 Buffalo 75 60
960 2p. Savanna baboons (vert) 90 1·00
961 2p.50 Lion (vert) 1·10 1·40
962 3p. African elephants in river 2·25 2·25
**MS**963 175×80 mm. Nos. 958/62 5·00 5·00

**223** Black Mamba

**2002**. Snakes. Multicoloured.
964 50t. Type **223** 45 15
965 1p.75 Spitting cobra (vert) 70 45
966 2p.50 Puff adder 80 1·25
967 3p. Boomslang (vert) 1·00 1·50

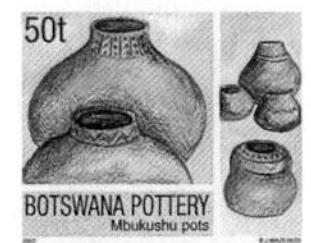


**224** Mbukushu Pots

**2002**. Botswana Pottery. Multicoloured.
968 50t. Type **224** 45 10
969 2p. Sekgatla pots 80 75
970 2p.50 Setswana pots 90 1·10
971 3p. Kalanga pots 1·10 1·50

**225** Queen Elizabeth in Evening Dress and Commonwealth Emblem

**2002**. Golden Jubilee. Multicoloured.
972 55t. Type **225** 65 15
973 2p.75 Queen Elizabeth with bouquet (vert) 1·75 2·00

**226** Tree Squirrel

**2002**. Mammals. Multicoloured.
974 5t. Type **226** 10 10
975 10t. Black-backed jackal 10 10
976 20t. African wild cat 10 10
977 30t. Slender mongoose (horiz) 15 10
978 40t. African civet (horiz) 15 10
979 55t. Elephant 20 15
980 90t. Reedbuck 30 25
981 1p. Kudu 35 35
982 1p.45 Waterbuck 50 50
983 1p.95 Sable (horiz) 60 65
984 2p.20 Sitatunga (horiz) 70 75
985 2p.75 Porcupine (horiz) 80 85
986 3p.30 Serval (horiz) 95 1·00
987 4p. Antbear (horiz) 1·25 1·40
988 5p. Bushpig (horiz) 1·40 1·50
989 15p. Chakma baboon 3·50 3·75

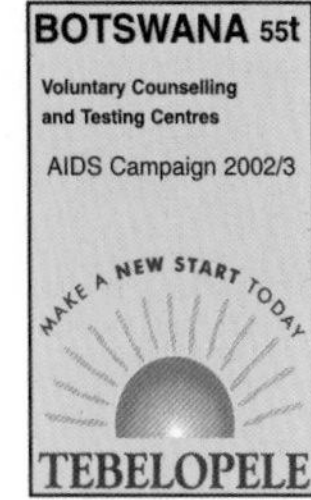


**227** Tebelopele (counselling and testing centres) Symbol

**2002**. AIDS Awareness. Multicoloured.
990 55t. Type **227** 60 15
991 1p.10 AIDS ribbon and mother and baby badge 1·10 40
992 2p.75 Hands and male gender symbol 1·75 1·90
993 3p.30 Orphans with foster parent 1·90 2·25

**2002**. Wetlands (3rd series). The Makgadikgadi Pans. As T **218**. Multicoloured.
994 55t. Aardwolf 50 15
995 1p.10 Blue wildebeest and zebra 85 30
996 2p.50 Zebra (vert) 1·40 1·40
997 2p.75 Flamingo (vert) 1·75 1·90
998 3p.30 Pelican in flight 1·90 2·25
**MS**999 175×80 mm. Nos. 994/8 5·75 5·75

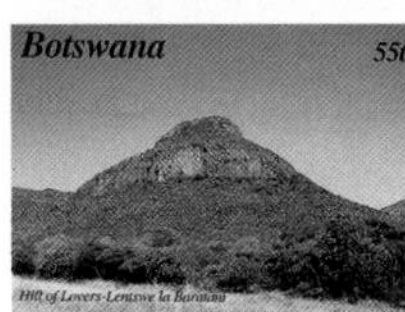


**228** Lentswe la Baratani ("Hill of Lovers")

**2003**. Natural Places of Interest. Multicoloured.
1000 55t. Type **228** 35 15
1001 2p.20 Sand dunes 1·00 90
1002 2p.75 Moremi Waterfalls (vert) 1·50 1·50
1003 3p.30 Gcwihaba Cave 1·75 1·90

**229** Ngwale

**2003**. Beetles. Multicoloured.
1004 55t. Type **229** 40 15
1005 2p.20 Kgomo-ya-buru 1·10 70
1006 2p.75 Kgomo-ya-pula 1·40 1·50
1007 3p.30 Lebitse 1·75 1·90
**MS**1008 69×59 mm. 5p.50 Kgaladuwa 3·00 3·50

**2003**. Wetlands (4th series). The Limpopo River. As Type **218**. Multicoloured.
1009 55t. Giraffe 70 35
1010 1p.45 Black eagle and Nile crocodile (vert) 1·50 85
1011 2p.50 Ostrich (vert) 2·00 1·50
1012 2p.75 Klipspringer 1·60 1·75
1013 3p.30 Serval cat 1·90 2·25
**MS**1014 175×80 mm. Nos. 1010/13 7·00 7·00

**230** San People with Birds (Cg'Ose Ntcox'o)

**2004**. Kuru Art Project. Multicoloured.
1015 55t. Type **230** 35 20
1016 1p.45 Tree with gum (Nxaedom Qhomatca) 75 55
1017 2p.75 Tree with berries (Nxaedom Qhomatca) 1·10 1·40
1018 3p.30 Snake (Qgoma Ncokg'o) 1·50 1·75

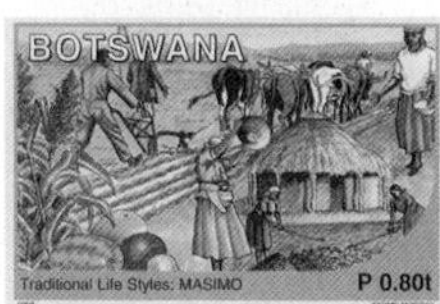


**231** Masimo (working the land)

**2004**. Traditional Life Styles. Multicoloured.
1019 80t. Type **231** 50 25
1020 2p.10 Kgotla (village meeting place) 1·25 85
1021 3p.90 Moraka (cattle post) 1·75 1·90
1022 4p.70 Legae (compound within village) 2·25 2·50

**232** Child posting Letter

**2004**. World Post Day. Multicoloured.
1023 80t. Type **232** 45 25
1024 2p.10 Children sharing a letter 1·00 85
1025 3p.90 Post man 1·60 1·90
1206 4p.70 Woman reading letter 2·00 2·50

**233** Peregrine Falcon (Angola)

**2004**. 1st Joint Issue of Southern Africa Postal Operators Association Members. Sheet 170×95 mm containing T **233** and similar hexagonal designs showing national birds of Association members. Multicoloured.
**MS**1027 40t. Type **233**; 50t. Two African Fish Eagles in flight (Zambia); 60t. Two African fish eagles perched (Zimbabwe); 70t. Bar-tailed trogon (Malawi) (inscribed "apaloderma vittatum"); 80t. Purple-crested turaco ("Lourie") (Swaziland); 1p. African fish eagle (Namibia); 2p. Stanley ("Blue") crane (South Africa); 5p. Cattle egret (Botswana) 7·00 7·50

The 70t. value stamp is not inscribed with the country of which the bird is a national symbol. Miniature sheets of similar designs were also issued by Namibia, Zimbabwe, Angola, Swaziland, South Africa, Malawi and Zambia.

**234** *Pterodiscus speciosus*

**2004**. Christmas. Flowers. Multicoloured.
1028 80t. Type **234** 45 25
1029 2p.10 *Bulbine narcissifolia* 85 60
1030 3p.90 *Bulbiana hypogea* 1·60 1·90
1031 4p.70 *Hibiscus micranthus* 2·00 2·50

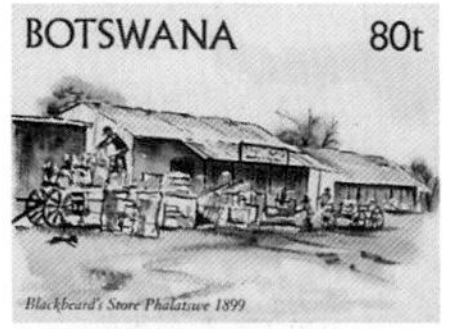


**235** Blackbeard's Store, Phalatswe

**2005**. Historical Buildings. Multicoloured.
1032 80t. Type **235** 45 25
1033 2p.10 Primary School 85 60
1034 3p.90 Telegraph Office, Phalatswe 1·60 1·90
1035 4p.70 Magistrate's Court, Phalatswe 2·00 2·50

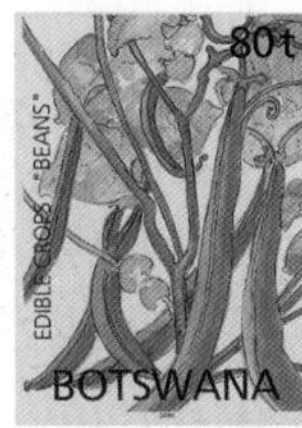


**236** Cowpeas ("beans")

**2005**. Edible Crops. Multicoloured.
1036 80t. Type **236** 35 20
1037 2p.10 Pearl millet 80 55
1038 3p.90 Sorghum 1·40 1·60
1039 4p.70 Watermelon 1·75 2·00

**237** Black-footed Cat with Prey

**2005**. Endangered Species. Black-footed Cat (Felis nigripes). Multicoloured.
1040 80t. Type **237** 45 20
1041 2p.10 Black-footed cat 85 60
1042 3p.90 With cub 1·60 1·75
1043 4p.70 In close-up 2·00 2·25
**MS**1044 160×185 mm. Nos. 1040/3, ×2 7·00 7·50

**238** Namaqua Dove

**2005**. Christmas. Doves and Pigeons. Multicoloured.
1045 80t. Type **238** 45 20
1046 2p.10 Red-eyed dove 85 60
1047 3p.90 Laughing doves (pair) 1·60 1·75
1048 4p.70 Green pigeons (pair) 2·00 2·25

**239** Nembwe

**2006**. Okavango Fish. Multicoloured.
1049 80t. Type **239** 25 30
1050 2p.10 Tiger fish 65 70
1051 3p.90 Pike 1·10 1·25
1052 4p.70 Spotted squeaker 1·50 1·75

**240** Oxen

**2006**. Tswana Cattle. Multicoloured.
1053 1p.10 Type **240** 40 35
1054 2p.60 Cows and calves 85 75
1055 4p.10 Bulls 1·25 1·40
1056 4p.90 Horn shapes 1·50 1·75

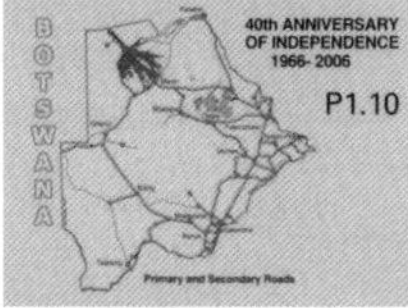


**241** Road Map

**2006**. 40th Anniv of Independence. Showing maps of Botswana. Multicoloured.
1057 1p.10 Type **241** 40 30
1058 2p.60 Population distribution 85 75
1059 4p.10 Mines and coal resources 1·50 1·60
1060 4p.90 National parks and game reserves 1·75 1·90

242 *Hyphaene petersiana*

**2006.** Christmas. Trees. Multicoloured.

| | | | |
|---|---|---|---|
| 1062 | 1p.10 Type **242** | 35 | 30 |
| 1063 | 2p.60 *Phoenix reclinata* | 80 | 70 |
| 1064 | 4p.10 *Hyphaene petersiana* | 1·25 | 1·40 |
| 1065 | 4p.90 *Phoenix reclinata* | 1·50 | 2·00 |

243 Pied Kingfisher

**2007.** Kingfishers. Multicoloured.

| | | | |
|---|---|---|---|
| 1066 | 1p.10 Type **243** | 25 | 30 |
| 1067 | 2p.60 Malachite kingfisher | 60 | 65 |
| 1068 | 4p.10 Woodland kingfisher | 1·00 | 1·10 |
| 1069 | 4p.90 Brown-hooded kingfisher | 1·40 | 1·50 |

244 *Chlorophyllum molybdites* (false parasol)

**2007.** Fungi. Multicoloured.

| | | | |
|---|---|---|---|
| 1070 | 1p.10 Type **244** | 25 | 30 |
| 1071 | 2p.60 *Phlebopus sudanicus* (bushveld bolete) | 60 | 65 |
| 1072 | 4p.10 *Ganoderma lucidum* (laquered bracket fungus) | 1·00 | 1·10 |
| 1073 | 4p.90 *Geastrum triplex* (collared earthstar) | 1·40 | 1·50 |

245 Nyala (pair) (Malawi)

**2007.** 2nd Joint Issue of Southern Africa Postal Operators Association Members. Designs showing national animals of association members. Multicoloured.

| | | | |
|---|---|---|---|
| 1074 | 1p.10 Type **245** | 25 | 30 |
| 1075 | 2p.60 Nyala (Zimbabwe) | 55 | 60 |
| 1076 | 4p.10 Oryx (Namibia) | 90 | 95 |
| 1077 | 4p.90 African buffalo (Zambia) | 1·25 | 1·40 |
| 1078 | 5p.50 Burchell's zebra (Botswana) | 1·50 | 1·75 |
| **MS**1079 | 135×170 mm. Nos. 1074/9 | 4·75 | 4·75 |

Miniature sheets containing similar designs were also issued by Malawi, Namibia, Zambia and Zimbabwe. Zambia also issued sheet stamps.

246 Students and Tutor (University of Botswana Library)

**2007.** 25th Anniv of University of Botswana. Multicoloured.

| | | | |
|---|---|---|---|
| 1080 | 1p.10 Type **246** | 25 | 30 |
| 1081 | 2p.60 Farmers and Sir Seretse Khama (first Botswana President) (BUCA campus appeal) | 60 | 65 |
| 1082 | 4p.10 Researcher, village and wetland (Okavango Research) | 1·00 | 1·10 |
| 1083 | 4p.90 Students and university buildings ('Infrastructure; old and new') | 1·40 | 1·50 |

247 Mimosa Sapphire (*Iolaus mimosae mimosae*)

**2007.** Butterflies. Multicoloured.

| | | | |
|---|---|---|---|
| 1084 | 10t. Type **247** | 10 | 10 |
| 1085 | 20t. Bushveld orange-tip (*Colotis pallene*) | 10 | 10 |
| 1086 | 30t. African monarch (*Danaus chrysippus aegyptius*) | 10 | 10 |
| 1087 | 40t. Common black-eye (*Gonatomyrina gorgias gorgias*) | 15 | 20 |
| 1088 | 50t. Brown playboy (*Virachola antalus*) | 25 | 30 |
| 1089 | 1p. Sapphire (*Lolaus silas*) | 50 | 55 |
| 1090 | (1p.10) Scarlet tip (*Colotis* (C) *danae annae*) | 55 | 60 |
| 1091 | 2p. Large blue emperor (*Charaxes bohemani*) | 65 | 70 |
| 1092 | (2p.60) Dwarf blue (*Oraidium barberae*)) | 70 | 75 |
| 1093 | 3p. Apricot playboy (*Virachola dinochares*) | 80 | 85 |
| 1094 | 4p. Blue pansy (*Junonia oenone oenone*) | 90 | 95 |
| 1095 | 5p. Black-striped hairtail (*Anthene amarah amarah*) | 1·10 | 1·25 |
| 1096 | 10p. Natal barred blue (*Spindasis natalensis*) | 2·25 | 2·40 |
| 1097 | 20p. Foxy charaxes (*C. jasius saturnus*) | 4·50 | 4·75 |

No. 1090 was inscr 'Standard Postage A' and sold for 1p.10. No. 1092 was inscr 'Standard Postage B' and sold for 2p.60.

248 Traditional Dancer (Boitshepo Lesego)

**2008.** Artists in Botswana. Designs showing winning entries in stamp design competition. Multicoloured.

| | | | |
|---|---|---|---|
| 1098 | 1p.10 Type **248** | 25 | 30 |
| 1099 | 2p.60 Baobab tree (Philip Huebsch) | 55 | 60 |
| 1100 | 4p.10 Girl playing with dolls (Giel Kgamane) | 90 | 95 |
| 1101 | 4p.90 Donkeys tired after hard work (Tineni Kepaletswe) (horiz) | 1·30 | 1·40 |
| 1102 | 5p.50 Donkeys in the city (Andrew Jones) (horiz) | 1·50 | 1·75 |

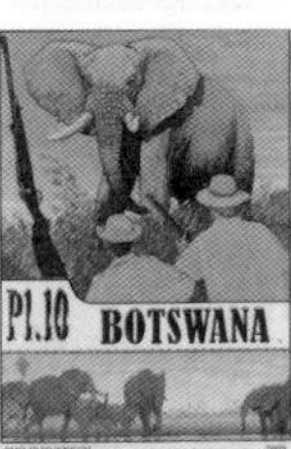
249 Hunter and Guide facing Bull Elephant

**2008.** Elephants in Botswana. Multicoloured.

| | | | |
|---|---|---|---|
| 1103 | 1p.10 Type **249** | 25 | 30 |
| 1104 | 2p.60 Tourists photographing female elephant with baby from dugout canoe | 60 | 65 |
| 1105 | 4p.10 Villagers chasing crop raiding elephant | 1·00 | 1·10 |
| 1106 | 4p.90 Elephant-back safari in Okavango Delta | 1·40 | 1·50 |

250 Athletes

**2008.** Olympic Games, Athens. Multicoloured.

| | | | |
|---|---|---|---|
| 1107 | 1p.10 Type **250** | 35 | 40 |
| 1108 | 2p.60 Boxers | 70 | 75 |

251 Pitse Ya Naga Launch

**2008.** 40th Anniv of Botswana National Museum. Multicoloured.

| | | | |
|---|---|---|---|
| 1109 | 1p.10 Type **251** | 25 | 30 |
| 1110 | 2p.60 Botanical Garden (vert) | 55 | 60 |
| 1111 | 4p.10 New Museum Galleries | 90 | 95 |
| 1112 | 4p.90 Rock painting, Tsodilo Hills | 1·40 | 1·50 |
| 1113 | 5p.50 Official opening (vert) | 1·50 | 1·75 |

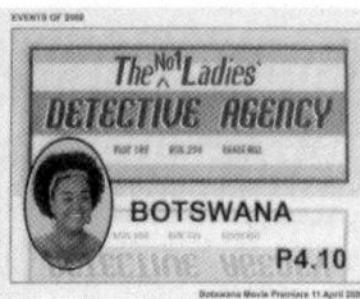
252 Plaque for 'The No. 1 Ladies Detective Agency' and Precious Ramotswe

**2008.** Events of Botswana 2008. Multicoloured.

| | | | |
|---|---|---|---|
| 1114 | 4p.10 Type **252** (Botswana Movie Premiere of *The No. 1 Ladies Detective Agency*) | 1·00 | 1·10 |
| 1115 | 4p.90 Heart within heart (launch of Heart Foundation) (vert) | 1·40 | 1·50 |
| 1116 | 5p.50 DTC Building (launch of Diamond Trading Company Botswana) | 1·50 | 1·75 |

253 *Gymnopleurus humanus* (small green dung beetle)

**2008.** Beetles of Botswana. Multicoloured.

| | | | |
|---|---|---|---|
| 1117 | 1p.10 Type **253** | 25 | 30 |
| 1118 | 2p.60 *Cheilomenes lunata* (lunate ladybird) | 55 | 60 |
| 1119 | 4p.10 *Pachnoda sinuata* (garden fruit chafer) | 1·00 | 1·10 |
| 1120 | 4p.90 *Eleodes* sp. (darkling beetle) | 1·40 | 1·50 |

254 Lesser Flamingo

**2009.** Endangered Birds of Botswana. Multicoloured.

| | | | |
|---|---|---|---|
| 1121 | 1p.10 Type **254** | 35 | 40 |
| 1122 | 2p.60 Grey crowned crane (horiz) | 70 | 75 |
| 1123 | 4p.10 Wattled crane (horiz) | 1·25 | 1·40 |
| 1124 | 4p.90 Blue crane (horiz) | 1·60 | 1·75 |

255 Boy and Girl reading ('Education')

**2009.** Children of Botswana

| | | | |
|---|---|---|---|
| 1125 | 1p.10 Type **255** | 35 | 40 |
| 1126 | 2p.60 Boy washing hands under tap ('Sanitation') (vert) | 70 | 75 |
| 1127 | 4p.10 Giving girl oral vaccine ('Inoculation') (vert) | 1·25 | 1·40 |
| 1128 | 4p.90 Woman with children ('Orphan Care') | 1·60 | 1·75 |

256 Southern Cross over Tsodilo World Heritage Site and Giraffes

**2009.** Night Skies. Multicoloured.

| | | | |
|---|---|---|---|
| 1129 | 1p.10 Type **256** | 35 | 40 |
| 1130 | 2p.60 Meteorite over Okavango Delta and Ju/'hoansi firing arrows | 70 | 75 |
| 1131 | 4p.10 Moon, Jupiter and Venus over central Kalahari and three Setswana women | 1·25 | 1·40 |
| 1132 | 4p.90 Solar eclipse over Setswana village and trickster lion from Naro story | 1·60 | 1·75 |

### POSTAGE DUE STAMPS

**1967.** Nos. D10/12 of Bechuanaland optd **REPUBLIC OF BOTSWANA**.

| | | | | |
|---|---|---|---|---|
| D13 | **D1** | 1c. red | 15 | 1·75 |
| D14 | **D1** | 2c. violet | 15 | 1·75 |
| D15 | **D1** | 5c. green | 20 | 1·75 |

D 5 African Elephant

**1971**

| | | | | |
|---|---|---|---|---|
| D16 | **D5** | 1c. red | 1·10 | 3·25 |
| D17 | **D5** | 2c. violet | 1·40 | 3·50 |
| D18 | **D5** | 6c. brown | 1·75 | 5·50 |
| D19 | **D5** | 14c. green | 2·00 | 7·50 |

D 6 Common Zebra

**1977**

| | | | | |
|---|---|---|---|---|
| D25a | **D6** | 1t. black and red | 40 | 1·25 |
| D26a | **D6** | 2t. black and green | 40 | 1·25 |
| D27a | **D6** | 4t. black and red | 40 | 1·25 |
| D28a | **D6** | 10t. black and blue | 40 | 1·25 |
| D29a | **D6** | 16t. black and brown | 50 | 1·50 |

Pt. 20

# BOYACA

One of the states of the Granadine Confederation. A Department of Colombia from 1886, now uses Colombian stamps.

100 centavos = 1 peso.

1 Mendoza Perez

**1899.** Imperf or perf.

| | | | | |
|---|---|---|---|---|
| 1 | **1** | 5c. green | 1·20 | 1·20 |

2

6 Battle of Boyaca Monument

**1903.** Imperf or perf.

| | | | | |
|---|---|---|---|---|
| 3A | **2** | 10c. grey | 35 | 30 |
| 4B | **2** | 10c. blue | 4·00 | 3·75 |
| 12 | - | 10c. orange | 35 | 30 |
| 5A | **2** | 20c. brown | 45 | 45 |
| 5Aa | **2** | 20c. lake | 45 | 45 |
| 6B | - | 50c. turquoise | 45 | 45 |
| 8A | - | 1p. red | 45 | 45 |
| 9B | - | 1p. red | 4·00 | 3·75 |
| 10B | **6** | 5p. black on red | 1·50 | 1·50 |
| 11A | - | 10p. black on buff | 1·50 | 1·50 |

DESIGNS—As Type **2**: 10c. orange, Building; 50c. Gen. Pinzon; 1p. Figure of value. As Type **6**: 10p. Pres. Marroquin.

Pt. 20

# BRAZIL

A country in the N.E. of S. America. Portuguese settlement, 1500. Kingdom, 1815. Empire, 1822. Republic from 1889.

1843. 1000 reis = 1 milreis.
1942. 100 centavos = 1 cruzeiro.
1986. 100 centavos = 1 cruzado.
1990. 100 centavos = 1 cruzeiro.
1994. 100 centavos = 1 real.
2008. 1st PCC = 1st porte Commercials.

1 "Bull's Eye"

**1843.** Imperf.

| | | | | |
|---|---|---|---|---|
| 4 | **1** | 30r. black | £1900 | £275 |
| 5 | **1** | 60r. black | £375 | £150 |
| 6 | **1** | 90r. black | £1800 | £750 |

2

**1844.** Imperf.

| | | | | |
|---|---|---|---|---|
| 10B | **2** | 10r. black | 70·00 | 13·50 |
| 11B | **2** | 30r. black | 90·00 | 20·00 |
| 12B | **2** | 60r. black | 70·00 | 13·50 |
| 13B | **2** | 90r. black | £550 | 70·00 |
| 14B | **2** | 180r. black | £2500 | £900 |
| 15B | **2** | 300r. black | £3750 | £1200 |
| 16B | **2** | 600r. black | £3500 | £1400 |

3

**1850.** Imperf.

| | | | | |
|---|---|---|---|---|
| 17A | **3** | 10r. black | 28·00 | 38·00 |
| 18A | **3** | 20r. black | 85·00 | £110 |
| 19A | **3** | 30r. black | 11·00 | 3·25 |
| 20A | **3** | 60r. black | 11·00 | 2·75 |
| 21A | **3** | 90r. black | 95·00 | 13·00 |
| 22A | **3** | 180r. black | 95·00 | 60·00 |
| 23A | **3** | 300r. black | £375 | 65·00 |
| 24A | **3** | 600r. black | £425 | £100 |

4

**1854.** Imperf.

| | | | | |
|---|---|---|---|---|
| 25 | | 10r. blue | 13·50 | 13·00 |
| 26 | | 30r. blue | 37·00 | 55·00 |
| 27 | **4** | 280r. red | £160 | £110 |
| 28 | **4** | 430r. yellow | £250 | £150 |

5

6

17 Emperor Dom Pedro II

**1866.** Various frames, but in T 5 the Emperor has a dark beard. Perf or roul.

| | | | | |
|---|---|---|---|---|
| 43 | **5** | 10r. red | 13·50 | 5·50 |
| 44a | **6** | 20r. purple | 24·00 | 3·25 |
| 45 | **5** | 50r. blue | 34·00 | 2·75 |
| 46a | **5** | 80r. purple | £170 | 19·00 |
| 47 | **5** | 100r. green | £534 | 1·70 |
| 55 | **6** | 200r. black | 95·00 | 8·50 |
| 56 | **5** | 500r. orange | £225 | 40·00 |
| 67 | **17** | 300r. green and orange | 95·00 | 23·00 |

12

13

**1878.** Various frames, but in T 13 the Emperor's beard is white. Roulette.

| | | | | |
|---|---|---|---|---|
| 57 | **12** | 10r. red | 13·50 | 3·25 |
| 58 | **13** | 20r. mauve | 19·00 | 2·75 |
| 59 | **12** | 50r. blue | 30·00 | 5·00 |
| 60 | **12** | 80r. red | 32·00 | 11·00 |
| 61 | **12** | 100r. green | 32·00 | 1·40 |
| 62 | **12** | 200r. black | £160 | 19·00 |
| 63 | **12** | 260r. brown | 95·00 | 25·00 |
| 64 | **12** | 300r. brown | 95·00 | 6·50 |
| 65 | **12** | 700r. red | £190 | 90·00 |
| 66 | **12** | 1000r. grey | £200 | 42·00 |

21

**1881.** Various frames. Perf.

| | | | | |
|---|---|---|---|---|
| 71 | **21** | 10r. black | 15·00 | 32·00 |
| 72 | **21** | 10r. orange | 3·75 | 3·25 |
| 73 | **21** | 50r. blue | 46·00 | 4·75 |
| 74 | **21** | 100r. olive | 55·00 | 4·50 |
| 77a | **21** | 100r. lilac | 70·00 | 7·00 |
| 75a | **21** | 200r. red | 60·00 | 15·00 |

No. 77 is inscr "CORREIO".

27 Pedro II

**1884**

| | | | | |
|---|---|---|---|---|
| 81 | **27** | 100r. lilac | £110 | 3·75 |

25 26 29

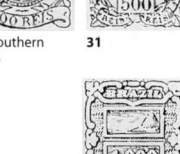

30 Southern Cross 31 32

33 Entrance to Bay of Rio de Janeiro

**1884**

| | | | | |
|---|---|---|---|---|
| 78 | **25** | 20r. green | 46·00 | 4·50 |
| 80 | **26** | 50r. blue | 44·00 | 6·50 |
| 83 | **29** | 100r. lilac | 95·00 | 2·30 |
| 84 | **30** | 300r. blue | £325 | 37·00 |
| 85a | **31** | 500r. olive | £180 | 18·00 |
| 86 | **32** | 700r. lilac | £100 | £150 |
| 87 | **33** | 1000r. blue | £375 | £150 |

35 Southern Cross

**1890**

| | | | | |
|---|---|---|---|---|
| 97a | **35** | 20r. green | 3·00 | 1·80 |
| 89 | **35** | 50r. green | 6·00 | 1·70 |
| 110a | **35** | 100r. purple | 50·00 | 2·00 |
| 91 | **35** | 200r. violet | 13·00 | 2·30 |
| 92 | **35** | 300r. blue | £120 | 15·00 |
| 100 | **35** | 300r. slate | £120 | 8·00 |
| 93 | **35** | 500r. buff | 20·00 | 13·00 |
| 94 | **35** | 500r. grey | 20·00 | 10·50 |
| 95 | **35** | 700r. brown | 28·00 | 32·00 |
| 96 | **35** | 1000r. yellow | 24·00 | 4·75 |

37 Head of Liberty

**1891**

| | | | | |
|---|---|---|---|---|
| 111d | **37** | 100r. red and blue | 39·00 | 1·70 |

38 Head of Liberty

**1893**

| | | | | |
|---|---|---|---|---|
| 114 | **38** | 100r. red | 70·00 | 1·50 |

39 Sugar-loaf Mountain

41 Head of Liberty

43 Head of Mercury

**1894**

| | | | | |
|---|---|---|---|---|
| 124 | **39** | 10r. blue and red | 2·40 | 85 |
| 125 | **39** | 20r. blue and orange | 1·60 | 55 |
| 126 | **39** | 50r. blue | 9·50 | 2·75 |
| 232 | **39** | 50r. green | 17·00 | 95 |
| 127 | **41** | 100r. black and red | 8·00 | 60 |
| 239 | **41** | 100r. red | 17·00 | 55 |
| 128 | **41** | 200r. black and orange | 1·20 | 45 |
| 234 | **41** | 200r. blue | 20·00 | 55 |
| 129 | **41** | 300r. black and green | 17·00 | 70 |
| 153 | **41** | 500r. black and blue | 35·00 | 2·50 |
| 131a | **41** | 700r. black and mauve | 20·00 | 2·20 |
| 132 | **43** | 1000r. mauve and green | 65·00 | 2·00 |
| 133 | **43** | 2000r. purple and grey | 75·00 | 18·00 |

**1897.** As T 39 but inscr "REIS REIS" instead of "DEZ REIS".

| | | | | |
|---|---|---|---|---|
| 165 | **43** | 10r. blue and red | 1·40 | 55 |

**1898.** Newspaper stamps of 1889 surch 1898 between value twice in figures.

| | | | | |
|---|---|---|---|---|
| 168 | **N34** | 100r. on 50r. orange | 2·40 | 50·00 |
| 169 | **N34** | 200r. on 100r. mauve | 4·25 | 1·40 |
| 170 | **N34** | 300r. on 200r. black | 4·25 | 1·40 |
| 171 | **N34** | 500r. on 300r. red | 7·50 | 5·50 |
| 172 | **N34** | 700r. on 500r. orange | 7·75 | 11·50 |
| 173 | **N34** | 700r. on 500r. green | 9·50 | 2·30 |
| 174 | **N34** | 1000r. on 700r. orange | 39·00 | 32·00 |
| 175 | **N34** | 1000r. on 700r. blue | 27·00 | 17·00 |
| 176 | **N34** | 2000r. on 1000r. orange | 33·00 | 17·00 |
| 177 | **N34** | 2000r. on 1000r. brown | 24·00 | 6·75 |

**1898.** Newspaper stamp of 1890 surch 200 over 1898.

| | | | | |
|---|---|---|---|---|
| 181 | **N37** | 200r. on 100r. mauve | 11·00 | 5·00 |

**1898.** Newspaper stamps of 1890 surch 1898 over new value.

| | | | | |
|---|---|---|---|---|
| 182 | **N38** | 20r. on 10r. blue | 3·25 | 6·00 |
| 183 | **N38** | 50r. on 20r. green | 8·50 | 10·00 |
| 184 | **N38** | 100r. on 50r. green | 18·00 | 20·00 |

**1899.** Postage stamps of 1890 surch 1899 over new value.

| | | | | |
|---|---|---|---|---|
| 194 | **35** | 50r. on 20r. green | 1·40 | 2·00 |
| 195 | **35** | 100r. on 50r. green | 1·40 | 2·00 |
| 196 | **35** | 300r. on 200r. violet | 5·25 | 8·00 |
| 190 | **35** | 500r. on 300r. blue | 12·50 | 5·00 |
| 190b | **35** | 500r. on 300r. slate | 12·50 | 5·00 |
| 191 | **35** | 700r. on 500r. buff | 17·00 | 4·00 |
| 192a | **35** | 1,000r. on 700r. brown | 12·50 | 4·00 |
| 193 | **35** | 2,000r. on 1,000r. yellow | 42·00 | 3·00 |

50 Discovery of Brazil

52 Emancipation of Slaves

**1900.** 400th Anniv of Discovery of Brazil.

| | | | | |
|---|---|---|---|---|
| 226 | **50** | 100r. red | 7·25 | 5·75 |
| 227 | - | 200r. green and yellow | 7·25 | 5·75 |
| 228 | **52** | 500r. blue | 7·25 | 5·75 |
| 229 | - | 700r. green | 7·25 | 5·75 |

DESIGNS—HORIZ: 200r. Declaration of Independence. VERT: 700r. Allegory of Republic.

56 Pan-American Congress

**1906**

| | | | | |
|---|---|---|---|---|
| 259a | **56** | 100r. red | 39·00 | 23·00 |
| 259b | **56** | 200r. blue | 95·00 | 10·50 |

57 Aristides Lobo

61 Liberty

**1906**

| | | | | |
|---|---|---|---|---|
| 260 | **57** | 10r. grey | 1·10 | 25 |
| 261 | - | 20r. violet | 65 | 15 |
| 262 | - | 50r. green | 1·10 | 25 |
| 264 | - | 100r. red | 1·40 | 15 |
| 265 | - | 200r. blue | 2·40 | 25 |
| 267 | - | 300r. brown | 3·75 | 75 |
| 268 | - | 400r. olive | 35·00 | 2·30 |
| 269 | - | 500r. violet | 7·00 | 65 |
| 272 | - | 600r. olive | 1·10 | 35 |
| 273 | - | 700r. brown | 7·00 | 3·50 |
| 274 | **61** | 1000r. red | 39·00 | 1·10 |
| 275 | - | 1000r. green | 4·75 | 45 |
| 276 | - | 1000r. grey | 28·00 | 75 |
| 277a | **61** | 2000r. green | 7·00 | 70 |
| 278 | **61** | 2000r. blue | 14·00 | 45 |
| 279 | **61** | 5000r. pink | 10·00 | 1·90 |
| 280 | - | 5000r. brown | 55·00 | 8·50 |
| 281 | - | 10000r. brown | 9·50 | 2·30 |

PORTRAITS: 20r. B. Constant. 50r. A. Cabral. 100r. Wandendkolk. 200r. D. da Fonseca. 300r. F. Peixoto. 400r., 600r. P. de Moraes. 500r. C. Salles. 700r., 5000r. (No. 280) R. Alves. 1000r. (Nos. 275/6) B. do Rio Branco. 10000r. N. Pecanha.

64 King Carlos and Pres. Affonso Penna and Emblems of Portuguese-Brazilian Amity

**1908.** Centenary of Opening of Brazilian Ports to Foreign Commerce.

| | | | | |
|---|---|---|---|---|
| 282 | **64** | 100r. red | 10·50 | 1·10 |

65 Emblems of Peace, Commerce and Industry

**1908.** National Exhibition, Rio de Janeiro.

| | | | | |
|---|---|---|---|---|
| 283 | **65** | 100r. red | 23·00 | 1·70 |

**66** Bonifacio, San Martin, Hidalgo, Washington, O'Higgins, Bolivar

**1909.** Pan-American Congress, Rio de Janeiro.

| | | | | |
|---|---|---|---|---|
| 284 | **66** | 200r. blue | 10·50 | 1·00 |

**67** Cape Frio

**1915.** 300th Anniv of Discovery of Cape Frio.

| | | | | |
|---|---|---|---|---|
| 285 | **67** | 100r. turquoise on yellow | 4·75 | 3·75 |

**69** Bay of Guajara

**1916.** 300th Anniv of City of Belem.

| | | | | |
|---|---|---|---|---|
| 286 | **69** | 100r. red | 10·50 | 5·25 |

**70** Revolutionary Flag

**1917.** Centenary of Pernambuco Revolution.

| | | | | |
|---|---|---|---|---|
| 287 | **70** | 100r. blue | 17·00 | 7·50 |

**71** Liberty **72** Liberty **74** Inscr "BRAZIL"

**1918.** Various frames.

| | | | | |
|---|---|---|---|---|
| 288A | **71** | 10r. brown | 60 | 30 |
| 289A | **71** | 20r. violet | 60 | 30 |
| 290A | **71** | 25r. grey | 60 | 30 |
| 291B | **71** | 50r. green | 1·70 | 60 |
| 292A | **72** | 100r. red | 2·00 | 30 |
| 293B | **72** | 200r. blue | 7·25 | 60 |
| 294A | **72** | 300r. orange | 23·00 | 3·75 |
| 295A | **72** | 500r. purple | 23·00 | 3·75 |
| 296B | **72** | 600r. orange | 3·00 | 9·50 |
| 297 | **74** | 1000r. blue | 8·00 | 30 |
| 298 | **74** | 2000r. brown | 35·00 | 8·50 |
| 299 | **74** | 5000r. lilac | 10·00 | 8·50 |
| 300a | **74** | 10,000r. red | 11·00 | 1·10 |

**77** Steam Locomotive **78** "Industry" **79** "Agriculture"

**80** "Aviation" **81** Mercury **82** "Shipping"

**1920.** T 74 inscr "BRASIL".

| | | | | |
|---|---|---|---|---|
| 317 | **77** | 10r. purple | 35 | 25 |
| 387A | **80** | 10r. brown | 20 | 15 |
| 318 | **77** | 20r. grey | 35 | 25 |
| 388A | **80** | 20r. violet | 20 | 15 |
| 389A | **78** | 25r. purple | 20 | 15 |
| 354 | **79** | 40r. brown | 60 | 35 |
| 306 | **78** | 50r. green | 1·10 | 45 |
| 355 | **78** | 50r. brown | 90 | 35 |
| 390 | **80** | 50r. purple | 20 | 15 |
| 391 | **80** | 50r. green | 20 | 15 |
| 308 | **79** | 80r. green | 35 | 2·20 |
| 309 | **80** | 100r. red | 3·75 | 45 |
| 367 | **80** | 100r. green | 45 | 20 |
| 392A | **80** | 100r. orange | 35 | 15 |
| 420 | **80** | 100r. yellow | 2·00 | 30 |
| 311 | **80** | 150r. violet | 1·30 | 25 |
| 312 | **80** | 200r. blue | 6·00 | 45 |
| 330 | **80** | 200r. red | 30 | 10 |
| 383 | **80** | 200r. green | 3·25 | 85 |
| 333 | **81** | 300r. red | 25 | 15 |
| 394A | **81** | 300r. green | 70 | 15 |
| 405 | **81** | 300r. grey | 20 | 15 |
| 335 | **81** | 400r. orange | 55 | 40 |
| 406 | **81** | 400r. blue | 25 | 20 |
| 385 | **81** | 500r. blue | 1·70 | 25 |
| 407 | **81** | 500r. brown | 4·00 | 15 |
| 341 | **82** | 600r. orange | 2·50 | 45 |
| 397 | **81** | 600r. brown | 4·00 | 15 |
| 422 | **81** | 600r. orange | 6·00 | 30 |
| 409 | **81** | 700r. violet | 4·25 | 15 |
| 342 | **82** | 1000r. purple | 6·75 | 30 |
| 410 | **81** | 1000r. blue | 12·00 | 35 |
| 362d | **74** | 2000r. blue | 7·00 | 40 |
| 411 | **74** | 2000r. violet | 32·00 | 1·40 |
| 363 | **74** | 5000r. brown | 20·00 | 5·25 |
| 364 | **74** | 10000r. purple | 21·00 | 1·00 |

**93** King Albert and Pres. Pessoa

**1920.** Visit of King of the Belgians.

| | | | | |
|---|---|---|---|---|
| 431 | **93** | 100r. red | 90 | 85 |

**94** Declaration of Ypiranga

**1922.** Centenary of Independence.

| | | | | |
|---|---|---|---|---|
| 432 | **94** | 100r. blue | 3·75 | 75 |
| 433 | - | 200r. red | 6·50 | 50 |
| 434 | - | 300r. green | 6·50 | 50 |

DESIGNS: 200r. Dom Pedro I and J. Bonifacio; 300r. National Exn. and Pres. Pessoa.

**97** Brazilian Army entering Bahia

**1923.** Centenary of Capture of Bahia from the Portuguese.

| | | | | |
|---|---|---|---|---|
| 435 | **97** | 200r. red | 10·50 | 6·50 |

**98** Arms of the Confederation

**1924.** Centenary of Confederation of the Equator.

| | | | | |
|---|---|---|---|---|
| 436 | **98** | 200r. multicoloured | 4·00 | 2·50 |

**99** Ruy Barbosa

**1927**

| | | | | |
|---|---|---|---|---|
| 438a | **99** | 1000r. red | 2·75 | 55 |

**100** "Justice"

**1927.** Centenary of Law Courses.

| | | | | |
|---|---|---|---|---|
| 439 | **100** | 100r. blue | 1·00 | 55 |
| 440 | - | 200r. red | 90 | 40 |

DESIGN: 200r. Map and Balances.

**1928.** Air. Official stamps of 1913, Type O 67, surch SERVICO AEREO and new value. Centres in black.

| | | | |
|---|---|---|---|
| 441 | 50r. on 10r. grey | 45 | 30 |
| 442 | 200r. on 1000r. brown | 2·40 | 4·75 |
| 443 | 200r. on 2000r. brown | 1·40 | 11·00 |
| 444 | 200r. on 5000r. bistre | 1·60 | 1·40 |
| 445 | 300r. on 500r. yellow | 1·60 | 2·30 |
| 446 | 300r. on 600r. purple | 85 | 85 |
| 447 | 500r. on 50r. grey | 1·60 | 75 |
| 448 | 1000r. on 20r. olive | 1·20 | 25 |
| 449 | 2000r. on 100r. red | 2·75 | 1·90 |
| 450 | 2000r. on 200r. blue | 3·50 | 1·90 |
| 451 | 2000r. on 10,000r. black | 3·25 | 70 |
| 452 | 5000r. on 20,000r. blue | 9·25 | 4·25 |
| 453 | 5000r. on 50,000r. green | 9·25 | 4·25 |
| 454 | 5000r. on 100,000r. red | 31·00 | 32·00 |
| 455 | 10,000r. on 500,000r. brown | 35·00 | 23·00 |
| 456 | 10,000r. on 1,000,000r. sepia | 33·00 | 30·00 |

**104** Liberty holding Coffee Leaves

**1928.** Bicent of Introduction of the Coffee Plant.

| | | | | |
|---|---|---|---|---|
| 457 | **104** | 100r. green | 1·60 | 65 |
| 458 | **104** | 200r. red | 1·00 | 50 |
| 459 | **104** | 300r. black | 8·75 | 40 |

**1928.** Official stamps of 1919 surch.

| | | | | |
|---|---|---|---|---|
| 460 | **O77** | 700r. on 500r. orange | 7·50 | 7·00 |
| 461 | **O77** | 1000r. on 100r. red | 4·50 | 50 |
| 462 | **O77** | 2000r. on 200r. blue | 6·25 | 1·00 |
| 463 | **O77** | 5000r. on 50r. green | 7·25 | 1·50 |
| 464 | **O77** | 10,000r. on 10r. brown | 27·00 | 1·90 |

**106** Ruy Barbosa

**1929**

| | | | | |
|---|---|---|---|---|
| 465 | **106** | 5000r. blue | 19·00 | 90 |

**108** Santos Dumonts Airship "Ballon No. 6" **109** Santos Dumont

**1929.** Air.

| | | | | |
|---|---|---|---|---|
| 469 | - | 50r. green | 30 | 25 |
| 470 | **108** | 200r. red | 1·40 | 15 |
| 471 | - | 300r. blue | 2·00 | 15 |
| 472 | - | 500r. purple | 2·50 | 15 |
| 473 | - | 1000r. brown | 8·50 | 30 |
| 479 | - | 2000r. green | 12·50 | 50 |
| 480 | - | 5000r. red | 14·50 | 1·30 |
| 481a | **109** | 10,000r. grey | 9·00 | 1·30 |

DESIGNS: 50r. De Gusmao's monument; 300r. A. Severo's airship "Pax"; 500r. Santos Dumont's biplane "14 bis"; 1000r. R. de Barros's flying boat "Jahu"; 2000r. De Gusmao; 5000r. A. Severo.

**110**

**1930.** Air.

| | | | | |
|---|---|---|---|---|
| 486 | **110** | 3000r. violet | 2·20 | 1·80 |

**112**

**1930.** 4th Pan-American Architectural Congress.

| | | | | |
|---|---|---|---|---|
| 487 | - | 100r. turquoise | 2·40 | 1·30 |
| 488 | **112** | 200r. grey | 4·25 | 95 |
| 489 | - | 300r. red | 6·50 | 1·70 |

DESIGNS: 100r. Sun rays inscr "ARCHITECTOS"; 300r. Architrave and Southern Cross.

**113** G. Vargas and J. Pessoa – "Redemption of Brazil" **114** O. Aranha – "What is the matter?"

**1931.** Charity. Revolution of 3 October 1930.

| | | | | |
|---|---|---|---|---|
| 490 | **113** | 10r.+10r. blue | 20 | 10·00 |
| 491 | **113** | 20r.+20r. brown | 20 | 7·50 |
| 492 | **114** | 50r.+50r. green, red and yellow | 20 | 35 |
| 493 | **113** | 100r.+50r. orange | 45 | 40 |
| 494 | **113** | 200r.+100r. green | 45 | 40 |
| 495 | - | 300r.+150r. mult | 45 | 40 |
| 496 | **113** | 400r.+200r. red | 1·50 | 1·20 |
| 497 | **113** | 500r.+250r. blue | 1·40 | 90 |
| 498 | **113** | 600r.+300r. purple | 90 | 10·50 |
| 499 | **113** | 700r.+350r. mult | 1·70 | 85 |
| 500 | **113** | 1$+500r. green, red and yellow | 3·00 | 45 |
| 501 | - | 2$+1$ grey and red | 12·50 | 80 |
| 502 | - | 5$+2$ 500r. black & red | 31·00 | 12·00 |
| 503 | - | 10$+5$ green & yellow | 75·00 | 22·00 |

DESIGNS: 300r., 700r. as Type **113**, but portraits in circles and frames altered. Milreis values as Type **114** with different portraits and frames.

**1931.** No. 333 surch 1931 200 Reis.

| | | | | |
|---|---|---|---|---|
| 507 | **81** | 200r. on 300r. red | 45 | 25 |

**1931.** Zeppelin Air Stamps. Surch ZEPPELIN and value.

| | | | | |
|---|---|---|---|---|
| 508 | **108** | 2$500 on 200r. red (No. 470) | 27·00 | 24·00 |
| 511 | **106** | 3$500 on 5000r. blue (No. 468b) | 28·00 | 27·00 |
| 509 | - | 5$000 on 300r. blue (No. 471) | 35·00 | 32·00 |
| 512 | **74** | 7$000 on 10,000r. red (No. 364) | 28·00 | 27·00 |

**1931.** Air. No. 486 surch 2.500 REIS.

| | | | | |
|---|---|---|---|---|
| 510 | **110** | 2500r. on 3000r. violet | 24·00 | 23·00 |

**121** Brazil

**1932.** 400th Anniv of Colonization of Sao Vicente.

| | | | | |
|---|---|---|---|---|
| 513 | **121** | 20r. purple | 25 | 40 |
| 514 | - | 100r. black | 55 | 45 |
| 515 | - | 200r. violet | 1·10 | 25 |
| 516 | - | 600r. brown | 1·90 | 1·90 |
| 517 | - | 700r. blue | 3·50 | 2·75 |

DESIGNS: 100r. Natives; 200r. M. Afonso de Souza; 600r. King John III of Portugal; 700r. Founding of Sao Vicente.

**125** Soldier and Flag **130** "Justice"

**1932.** Sao Paulo Revolutionary Government issue.

| | | | | |
|---|---|---|---|---|
| 518 | | 100r. brown | 55 | 2·75 |
| 519 | **125** | 200r. red | 45 | 95 |
| 520 | - | 300r. green | 2·75 | 5·00 |
| 521 | - | 400r. blue | 9·25 | 10·50 |
| 522 | - | 500r. sepia | 11·00 | 10·50 |
| 523 | - | 600r. red | 11·00 | 10·50 |
| 524 | **125** | 700r. violet | 5·00 | 10·50 |
| 525 | - | 1000r. orange | 2·40 | 10·50 |
| 526 | - | 2000r. brown | 21·00 | 28·00 |
| 527 | - | 5000r. green | 24·00 | 48·00 |
| 528 | **130** | 10,000r. purple | 29·00 | 55·00 |

DESIGNS—As Type **125**: 100, 500r. Map of Brazil; 300r., 600r. Symbolical of freedom, etc., 400, 1000r. Soldier in tin helmet. As Type **130**: 2000r. "LEX" and sword; 5000r. "Justice" and soldiers with bayonets.

**131** Campo Bello Square and memorial, Vassouras

**1933.** Centenary of Vassouras.

| | | | | |
|---|---|---|---|---|
| 529 | **131** | 200r. red | 1·30 | 1·10 |

**132** Flag and Dornier Wal Flying Boat

**1933.** Air.

| | | | | |
|---|---|---|---|---|
| 532 | **132** | 3500r. blue, green & yell | 4·00 | 2·00 |

**1933.** Surch 200 REIS.

| | | | | |
|---|---|---|---|---|
| 536 | **81** | 200r. on 300r. red | 55 | 50 |

**134** Flag of the Race

**1933.** 441st Anniv of Departure of Columbus from Polos.

| | | | | |
|---|---|---|---|---|
| 537 | **134** | 200r. red | 1·00 | 90 |

**135** Christian Symbols

**1933.** 1st Eucharistic Congress, Sao Salvador.

| | | | | |
|---|---|---|---|---|
| 538 | **135** | 200r. red | 1·00 | 90 |

**136** From Santos Dumont Statue, St. Cloud

**1933.** Obligatory Tax for Airport Fund.

| | | | | |
|---|---|---|---|---|
| 539 | **136** | 100r. purple | 75 | 25 |

**137** Faith and Energy

**1933**

| | | | | |
|---|---|---|---|---|
| 540 | **137** | 200r. red | 60 | 20 |
| 543 | **137** | 200r. violet | 1·40 | 30 |

**138** "Republic" and Flags

**1933.** Visit of Pres. Justo of Argentina.

| | | | | |
|---|---|---|---|---|
| 545 | **138** | 200r. blue | 55 | 55 |
| 546 | **138** | 400r. green | 1·80 | 1·70 |
| 547 | **138** | 600r. red | 6·50 | 9·00 |
| 548 | **138** | 1000r. violet | 9·25 | 6·50 |

**139** Santos Dumont Statue, St. Cloud

**1934.** 1st National Aviation Congress, Sao Paulo.

| | | | | |
|---|---|---|---|---|
| 549 | **139** | 200r. blue | 1·10 | 1·00 |

**140** Exhibition Building

**1934.** 7th International Sample Fair, Rio de Janeiro.

| | | | | |
|---|---|---|---|---|
| 550 | **140** | 200r. brown | 65 | 55 |
| 551 | **140** | 400r. red | 2·75 | 2·75 |
| 552 | **140** | 700r. blue | 2·75 | 1·90 |
| 553 | **140** | 1000r. orange | 7·75 | 1·30 |

**141** Brazilian Stamp of 1844

**1934.** National Philatelic Exhibition, Rio. Imperf.

| | | | | |
|---|---|---|---|---|
| 555 | **141** | 200r.+100r. purple | 1·80 | 5·50 |
| 556 | **141** | 300r.+100r. red | 1·80 | 5·50 |
| 557 | **141** | 700r.+100r. blue | 10·50 | 46·00 |
| 558 | **141** | 1000r.+100r. black | 10·50 | 46·00 |

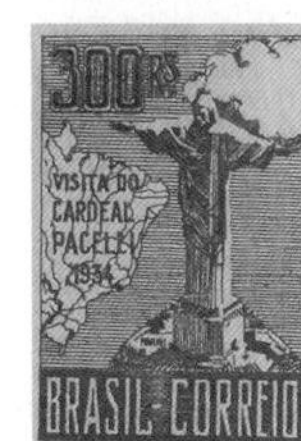


**142** Christ of Mt. Corcovado

**1934.** Visit of Cardinal Pacelli.

| | | | | |
|---|---|---|---|---|
| 559 | **142** | 300r. red | 5·50 | 5·50 |
| 560 | **142** | 700r. blue | 22·00 | 22·00 |

**143** Jose de Anchieta

**1934.** 400th Anniv of Founding of Sao Paulo by Anchieta.

| | | | | |
|---|---|---|---|---|
| 561 | **143** | 200r. brown | 90 | 75 |
| 562 | **143** | 300r. violet | 65 | 55 |
| 563 | **143** | 700c. blue | 4·00 | 4·00 |
| 564 | **143** | 1000r. green | 7·75 | 1·70 |

**145** "Brazil" and "Uruguay"

**1935.** Visit of President Terra of Uruguay.

| | | | | |
|---|---|---|---|---|
| 565 | - | 200r. orange | 1·30 | 75 |
| 566 | **145** | 300r. yellow | 1·70 | 1·40 |
| 567 | **145** | 700r. blue | 6·50 | 8·75 |
| 568 | - | 1000r. violet | 17·00 | 8·75 |

DESIGN—HORIZ: 200, 1000r. Female figures as in Type **145** and bridge.

**146** Town of Igarassu

**1935.** 400th Anniv of Founding of Pernambuco.

| | | | | |
|---|---|---|---|---|
| 569 | **146** | 200r. brown and red | 2·00 | 1·30 |
| 570 | **146** | 300r. olive and violet | 2·00 | 1·10 |

**147** Nurse and Patient

**1935.** 3rd Pan-American Red Cross Conference.

| | | | | |
|---|---|---|---|---|
| 571 | **147** | 200r.+100r. violet | 2·40 | 2·40 |
| 572 | **147** | 300r.+100r. brown | 2·40 | 2·00 |
| 573 | **147** | 700r.+100r. blue | 17·00 | 14·50 |

**149** Gen. da Silva

**1935.** Cent of Farroupilha "Ragged Revolution".

| | | | | |
|---|---|---|---|---|
| 574 | - | 200r. black | 1·80 | 1·80 |
| 575 | - | 300r. red | 1·80 | 1·10 |
| 576 | **149** | 700r. blue | 5·00 | 8·75 |
| 577 | - | 1000r. violet | 6·00 | 5·50 |

DESIGNS: 200, 300r. Mounted Gaucho; 1000r. Marshal Caxias.

**151** Gavea

**1935.** Children's Day.

| | | | | |
|---|---|---|---|---|
| 578 | **151** | 300r. violet and brown | 3·50 | 2·75 |
| 579 | **151** | 300r. turquoise and black | 3·50 | 2·75 |
| 580 | **151** | 300r. blue and green | 3·50 | 2·75 |
| 581 | **151** | 300r. black and red | 3·50 | 2·75 |

**152** Federal District Coat of Arms

**1935.** 8th International Fair.

| | | | | |
|---|---|---|---|---|
| 582 | **152** | 200r. blue | 5·00 | 5·25 |

**153** Coutinho's ship "Gloria", 1535

**1935.** 400th Anniv of Colonization of State of Espirito Santo.

| | | | | |
|---|---|---|---|---|
| 583 | **153** | 300r. red | 3·25 | 1·40 |
| 584 | - | 700r. blue | 7·25 | 4·25 |

DESIGN—VERT: 700r. Arms of Coutinho.

**154a** Viscount Cairu

**1936.** Death Centenary of Cairu.

| | | | | |
|---|---|---|---|---|
| 585 | **154a** | 1200r. violet | 12·00 | 8·75 |

**155** Cameta

**1936.** Tercentenary of Founding of Cameta.

| | | | | |
|---|---|---|---|---|
| 586 | **155** | 200r. buff | 2·20 | 2·00 |
| 587 | **155** | 500r. green | 2·20 | 1·10 |

**156** Coin Press

**1936.** Numismatic Congress, Sao Paulo.

| | | | | |
|---|---|---|---|---|
| 588 | **156** | 300r. brown | 2·00 | 2·00 |

**157** Scales of "Justice"

**1936.** 1st National Juridical Congress, Rio.

| | | | | |
|---|---|---|---|---|
| 589 | **157** | 300r. red | 2·40 | 90 |

**158** A. Carlos Gomes

**159** "Il Guarany"

**1936.** Birth Centenary of C. Gomes (composer).

| | | | | |
|---|---|---|---|---|
| 590 | **158** | 300r. red | 1·10 | 1·10 |
| 591 | **158** | 300r. brown | 1·10 | 1·10 |
| 592 | **159** | 700r. blue | 4·50 | 2·75 |
| 593 | **159** | 700r. buff | 5·00 | 4·00 |

**1936.** 9th International Sample Fair, Rio. As T **152** with inscription and date altered.

| | | | | |
|---|---|---|---|---|
| 594 | **152** | 200r. red | 1·50 | 90 |

**160** Congress Seal

**1936.** 2nd National Eucharistic Congress, Belo Horizonte.

| | | | | |
|---|---|---|---|---|
| 595 | **160** | 300r. multicoloured | 1·40 | 90 |

**161** Botafogo Bay

**1937.** Birth Centenary of Dr. Francisco Pereira Passos.

| | | | | |
|---|---|---|---|---|
| 596 | **161** | 700r. blue | 1·80 | 1·20 |
| 597 | **161** | 700r. black | 1·80 | 1·20 |

**162** Esperanto Star and National Flags

**1937.** 9th Brazilian Esperanto Congress, Rio de Janeiro.

| | | | | |
|---|---|---|---|---|
| 598 | **162** | 300r. green | 1·90 | 1·00 |

**163** Bay of Rio de Janeiro

**1937.** 2nd S. American Radio Conference.

| | | | | |
|---|---|---|---|---|
| 599 | **163** | 300r. black and orange | 1·10 | 1·10 |
| 600 | **163** | 700r. brown and blue | 3·00 | 1·10 |

**164** Globe

**1937.** Golden Jubilee of Esperanto.

| | | | | |
|---|---|---|---|---|
| 601 | **164** | 300r. green | 1·80 | 1·00 |

**166** Iguazu Falls

**1937.** Tourist Propaganda.

| | | | | |
|---|---|---|---|---|
| 602 | - | 200r. blue and brown | 1·30 | 1·30 |
| 603 | - | 300r. green and orange | 1·30 | 1·30 |
| 604 | **166** | 1000r. brown and sepia | 4·00 | 2·75 |
| 605 | - | 2000r. red and green | 17·00 | 18·00 |
| 606 | **166** | 5000r. green and black | 33·00 | 33·00 |
| 607 | - | 10,000r. blue and red | 65·00 | 65·00 |

DESIGNS—HORIZ: 200, 2000r. Monroe Palace, Rio. VERT: 300, 10,000r. Botanical Gardens, Rio.

**168** J. Da Silva Paes

**1937.** Bicent of Founding of Rio Grande do Sul.

| | | | | |
|---|---|---|---|---|
| 608 | **168** | 300r. blue | 1·30 | 65 |

**169** Eagle and Shield

**1937.** 150th Anniv of U.S. Constitution.

| | | | | |
|---|---|---|---|---|
| 609 | **169** | 400r. blue | 1·90 | 90 |

**170** Coffee

**1938.** Coffee Propaganda.

| | | | | |
|---|---|---|---|---|
| 610 | **170** | 1200r. multicoloured | 7·75 | 65 |

**171** "Grito" Memorial

**1938.** Commemoration of Abortive Proclamation of Republic.

| | | | | |
|---|---|---|---|---|
| 611 | **171** | 400r. brown | 1·30 | 65 |

**172** Arms of Olinda

**1938.** 4th Centenary of Olinda.

| | | | | |
|---|---|---|---|---|
| 612 | **172** | 400r. violet | 1·10 | 55 |

**173** Couto de Magalhaes

**1938.** Birth Centenary of De Magalhaes.

| | | | | |
|---|---|---|---|---|
| 613 | **173** | 400r. green | 1·00 | 55 |

**174** National Archives

**1938.** Centenary of Founding of National Archives.

| | | | | |
|---|---|---|---|---|
| 614 | **174** | 400r. brown | 1·00 | 55 |

**174a** Rowland Hill

**1938.** Brazilian International Philatelic Exhibition (BRAPEX), Rio de Janeiro. T 174a repeated ten times in sheet together with exhibition emblem.

| | | | |
|---|---|---|---|
| **MS**614a | 117×118 mm. 400r. green | 30·00 | 35·00 |

**174b** President Vargas

**1938.** 1st Anniv of Constitution issued by President Vargas. T 174b repeated ten times in sheet together with star emblem.

| | | | |
|---|---|---|---|
| **MS**614b | 115×138 mm. 400r. blue | 33·00 | 33·00 |

**175** Rio de Janeiro

**1939**

| | | | | |
|---|---|---|---|---|
| 615 | **175** | 1200r. purple | 2·75 | 20 |

**176** Santos

**1939.** Centenary of Santos City.

| | | | | |
|---|---|---|---|---|
| 616 | **176** | 400r. blue | 65 | 45 |

**177** Chalice-vine and Cup-of-gold Blossoms

**1939.** 1st S. American Botanical Congress, Rio.

| | | | | |
|---|---|---|---|---|
| 617 | **177** | 400r. green | 2·10 | 45 |

**178** Seal of Congress

**1939.** 3rd National Eucharistic Congress, Recife.

| | | | | |
|---|---|---|---|---|
| 618 | **178** | 400r. red | 65 | 65 |

**179** Duke of Caxias

**1939.** Soldiers' Day.

| | | | | |
|---|---|---|---|---|
| 619 | **179** | 400r. blue | 65 | 65 |

**180** Washington

**1939.** New York World's Fair. Inscr "FEIRA MUNDIAL DE NOVA YORK".

| | | | | |
|---|---|---|---|---|
| 620 | **180** | 400r. orange | 90 | 45 |
| 621 | - | 800r. green | 45 | 35 |
| 622 | - | 1200r. red | 1·00 | 35 |
| 623 | - | 1600r. blue | 1·00 | 45 |

DESIGNS—HORIZ: 1200r. Grover Cleveland. VERT: 800r. Dom Pedro II; 1m. Water lily; 1600r. Statue of Liberty, Rio de Janeiro; 5m. Bust of Pres. Vargas; 10m. Relief map of Brazil.

**184** Benjamin Constant

**1939.** 50th Anniv of Constitution.

| | | | | |
|---|---|---|---|---|
| 624 | **184** | 400r. green | 1·10 | 75 |
| 625 | - | 800r. black | 75 | 65 |
| 626 | - | 1200r. brown | 1·20 | 75 |

DESIGNS—VERT: 800r. Marshal da Fonseca. HORIZ: 1200r. Marshal da Fonseca and Pres. Vargas.

**188** Child and Southern Cross

**1940.** Child Welfare.

| | | | | |
|---|---|---|---|---|
| 627 | | 100r.+100r. violet | 1·30 | 1·30 |
| 628 | | 200r.+100r. blue | 1·80 | 1·80 |
| 629 | **188** | 400r.+200r. olive | 1·30 | 1·10 |
| 630 | - | 1200r.+400r. red | 5·50 | 2·40 |

DESIGNS: 100r. Three Wise Men; 200r. Angel and Child; 1200r. Mother and Child.

**189** Roosevelt, Vargas and American Continents

**1940.** 50th Anniv of Pan-American Union.

| | | | | |
|---|---|---|---|---|
| 631 | **189** | 400r. blue | 1·30 | 75 |

**190** Map of Brazil

**1940.** 9th National Geographical Congress, Florianopolis.

| | | | | |
|---|---|---|---|---|
| 632 | **190** | 400r. red | 65 | 65 |

**191** Water Lily **192** Map of Brazil

**1940.** New York World's Fair (2nd issue). No gum.

| | | | | |
|---|---|---|---|---|
| 633 | **191** | 1m. violet | 1·80 | 1·80 |
| 634 | — | 5m. red (Pres. Vargas) | 13·00 | 10·50 |
| 635 | **192** | 10m. blue | 15·00 | 5·00 |

| | | | |
|---|---|---|---|
| **MS**635a | Three sheets each 127×147 mm. Nos. 633/5 each in block of ten | £375 | £500 |

**1940.** Birth Centenary of Machado de Assis (poet and novelist). As T 173 but portrait of de Assis, dated "1839–1939".

| | | | |
|---|---|---|---|
| 636 | 400r. black | 90 | 45 |

**193** Two Workers

**1940.** Bicentenary of Colonization of Porto Alegre.

| | | | | |
|---|---|---|---|---|
| 637 | **193** | 400r. green | 75 | 45 |

**194** Acclaiming King John IV of Portugal

**1940.** Centenaries of Portugal (1140–1640-1940) (1st issue).

| | | | | |
|---|---|---|---|---|
| 638 | **194** | 1200r. grey | 3·25 | 55 |

See also Nos. 642/5.

**195** Brazilian Flags and Head of Liberty

**1940.** 10th Anniv of Govt. of President Vargas.

| | | | | |
|---|---|---|---|---|
| 639B | **195** | 400r. purple | 90 | 35 |

**196** Date of Fifth Census **197** Globe showing Spotlight on Brazil

**1941.** 5th General Census.

| | | | | |
|---|---|---|---|---|
| 640a | **196** | 400r. blue & red (postage) | 45 | 20 |
| 641 | **197** | 1200r. brown (air) | 4·75 | 90 |

**199** Father Antonio Vieira

**1941.** Centenaries of Portugal (2nd issue).

| | | | | |
|---|---|---|---|---|
| 642B | - | 200r. pink | 35 | 20 |
| 643B | **199** | 400r. blue | 35 | 10 |
| 644B | - | 800r. violet | 55 | 35 |
| 645B | - | 5400r. green | 2·75 | 75 |

DESIGNS—VERT: 200r. Alfonso Henriques; 800r. Governor-Gen. Benevides. HORIZ: 5,400r. Carmona and Vargas.

**202** Father Jose Anchieta

**1941.** 400th Anniv of Order of Jesuits.

| | | | | |
|---|---|---|---|---|
| 646 | **202** | 1m. violet | 2·20 | 1·30 |

**205** Oil Wells

**210** Count of Porto Alegre

**1941.** Value in reis.

| | | | | |
|---|---|---|---|---|
| 647A | **205** | 10r. orange | 55 | 40 |
| 648A | **205** | 20r. olive | 55 | 40 |
| 649A | **205** | 50r. brown | 55 | 40 |
| 650A | **205** | 100r. turquoise | 65 | 40 |
| 651B | - | 200r. brown | 2·00 | 65 |
| 652A | - | 300r. red | 65 | 40 |
| 653B | - | 400r. blue | 65 | 45 |
| 654A | - | 500r. red | 75 | 40 |
| 655B | - | 600r. violet | 90 | 55 |
| 656A | - | 700r. red | 65 | 40 |
| 657B | - | 1000r. grey | 3·25 | 65 |
| 658B | - | 1200r. blue | 4·00 | 65 |
| 659A | - | 2000r. purple | 6·00 | 65 |
| 660B | - | 5000r. blue | 7·75 | 65 |
| 661B | **210** | 10,000r. red | 17·00 | 2·75 |
| 662A | - | 20,000r. brown | 20·00 | 2·00 |
| 663D | - | 50m. red | 29·00 | 5·50 |
| 664D | - | 100m. blue | 2·00 | 6·50 |

DESIGNS: 200r. to 500r. Wheat harvesting machinery; 600r. to 1200r. Smelting works; 2000r. "Commerce"; 5000r. Marshal F. Peixoto; 20,000r. Admiral Maurity; 50m. "Armed Forces"; 100m. Pres. Vargas.

For stamps with values in centavos and cruzeiros see Nos. 751, etc.

**213** Amador Bueno

**1941.** 300th Anniv of Amador Bueno as King of Sao Paulo.

| | | | | |
|---|---|---|---|---|
| 665 | **213** | 400r. black | 1·10 | 65 |

**214** Brazilian Air Force Emblem

**1941.** Aviation Week.

| | | | | |
|---|---|---|---|---|
| 666 | **214** | 5400r. green | 6·00 | 4·50 |

**1941.** Air. 4th Anniv of President Vargas's New Constitution. Optd AEREO "10 Nov." 937-941.

| | | | | |
|---|---|---|---|---|
| 667a | | 5400r. green (No. 645) | 3·75 | 1·75 |

**215** Indo-Brazilian Cow

**1942.** 2nd Agriculture and Cattle Show, Uberaba.

| | | | | |
|---|---|---|---|---|
| 668 | **215** | 200r. blue | 1·00 | 65 |
| 669 | **215** | 400r. brown | 90 | 60 |

**216** Bernardino de Campos

**1942.** Birth Centenaries of B. de Campos and P. de Morais (lawyers and statesmen).

| | | | | |
|---|---|---|---|---|
| 670 | **216** | 1000r. red | 2·20 | 1·40 |
| 671 | - | 1200r. blue | 7·25 | 65 |

PORTRAIT: 1200r. Prudente de Morais.

**217** Torch of Learning

**1942.** 8th National Education Congress, Goiania.

| | | | | |
|---|---|---|---|---|
| 672 | **217** | 400r. brown | 90 | 55 |

**218** Map of Brazil showing Goiania

**1942.** Founding of Goiania City.

| | | | | |
|---|---|---|---|---|
| 673 | **218** | 400r. violet | 90 | 55 |

**219** Congressional Seal

**1942.** 4th National Eucharistic Congress, Sao Paulo.

| | | | | |
|---|---|---|---|---|
| 674 | **219** | 400r. brown | 1·10 | 40 |

**1942.** Air. 5th Anniv of President Vargas's New Constitution. No. 645 surch AEREO "10 Nov." 937-942 and value.

| | | | | |
|---|---|---|---|---|
| 675a | | 5cr.40 on 5400r. green | 4·50 | 2·40 |

**221** Tributaries of R. Amazon

**1943.** 400th Anniv of Discovery of River Amazon.

| | | | | |
|---|---|---|---|---|
| 676 | **221** | 40c. brown | 75 | 70 |

**222** Early Brazilian Stamp

**1943.** Centenary of Petropolis.

| | | | | |
|---|---|---|---|---|
| 677 | **222** | 40c. violet | 1·10 | 60 |

**223** Memorial Tablet

**1943.** Air. Visit of Pres. Morinigo of Paraguay.

| | | | | |
|---|---|---|---|---|
| 678 | **223** | 1cr.20 blue | 3·25 | 2·20 |

**224** Map of S. America showing Brazil and Bolivia

**1943.** Air. Visit of President Penaranda of Bolivia.

| | | | | |
|---|---|---|---|---|
| 679 | **224** | 1cr.20 multicoloured | 2·75 | 1·70 |

**225** "Bulls-eye"

**1943.** Centenary of 1st Brazilian Postage Stamps. (a) Postage. Imperf.

| | | | | |
|---|---|---|---|---|
| 680 | **225** | 30c. black | 1·10 | 1·00 |
| 681 | **225** | 60c. black | 1·20 | 45 |
| 682 | **225** | 90c. black | 75 | 75 |
| **MS**682a | | 127×95 mm. Nos. 680/2. No gum. Imperf | 29·00 | 33·00 |

**226**

(b) Air. Perf.

| | | | | |
|---|---|---|---|---|
| 683 | **226** | 1cr. black and yellow | 4·50 | 3·25 |
| 684 | **226** | 2cr. black and green | 6·00 | 3·25 |
| 685 | **226** | 5cr. black and red | 7·25 | 4·50 |
| **MS**685a | | 155×155 mm. Nos. 683/5. Imperf. No gum | 75·00 | 75·00 |

**227** Book of the Law

**1943.** Air. Inter-American Advocates Conference.

| | | | | |
|---|---|---|---|---|
| 686 | **227** | 1cr.20 red and brown | 1·70 | 65 |

**228** Ubaldino do Amaral

**1943.** Birth Centenary of Ubaldino do Amaral.

| | | | | |
|---|---|---|---|---|
| 687 | **228** | 40c. grey | 1·00 | 20 |

**229** Indo-Brazilian Cow

**1943.** 9th Cattle Show, Bahia.

| | | | | |
|---|---|---|---|---|
| 688 | **229** | 40c. brown | 1·40 | 90 |

**230** Justice and Seal

**1943.** Centenary of Institute of Brazilian Lawyers.

| | | | | |
|---|---|---|---|---|
| 689a | **230** | 2cr. red | 1·50 | 90 |

**231** Santa Casa de Misericordia Hospital

**1943.** 400th Anniv of Santa Casa de Misericordia de Santos.

| | | | | |
|---|---|---|---|---|
| 690 | **231** | 1cr. blue | 90 | 65 |

**232** Barbosa Rodrigues

**1943.** Birth Centenary of B. Rodrigues (botanist).

| | | | | |
|---|---|---|---|---|
| 691 | **232** | 40c. green | 90 | 45 |

**233** Pedro Americo

**1943.** Birth Cent of Americo (artist and author).

| | | | | |
|---|---|---|---|---|
| 692 | **233** | 40c. brown | 1·10 | 45 |

**1944.** Air. No. 629 surch. AEREO and value.

| | | | | |
|---|---|---|---|---|
| 693 | **188** | 20c. on 400r.+200r. | 1·80 | 1·00 |
| 694 | **188** | 40c. on 400r.+200r. | 2·75 | 1·00 |
| 695 | **188** | 60c. on 400r.+200r. | 4·00 | 70 |
| 696 | **188** | 1cr. on 400r.+200r. | 6·25 | 1·00 |
| 697 | **188** | 1cr.20 on 400r.+200r. | 6·00 | 65 |

**235** Gen. Carneiro and Defenders of Lapa

**1944.** 50th Anniv of Siege of Lapa.

| | | | | |
|---|---|---|---|---|
| 698 | **235** | 1cr.20c. red | 1·50 | 75 |

**236** Baron do Rio Branco

**1944.** Inauguration of Monument to Baron do Rio Branco.

| | | | | |
|---|---|---|---|---|
| 699 | **236** | 1cr. blue | 1·00 | 65 |

**237** Duke of Caxias

**1944.** Centenary of Pacification of Revolutionary Uprising of 1842.

| | | | | |
|---|---|---|---|---|
| 700 | **237** | 1cr.20 green and yellow | 1·60 | 65 |

**238** Emblems of YMCA

**1944.** Centenary of YMCA.

| | | | | |
|---|---|---|---|---|
| 701 | **238** | 40c. blue, red and yellow | 65 | 35 |

**239** Rio Grande Chamber of Commerce

**1944.** Centenary of Founding of Rio Grande Chamber of Commerce.

| | | | | |
|---|---|---|---|---|
| 702 | **239** | 40c. brown | 70 | 35 |

**240** "Bartolomeo de Gusmao and the Aerostat" (Bernardino de Souza Pereira)

**1944.** Air. Air Week.

| | | | | |
|---|---|---|---|---|
| 703 | **240** | 1cr.20 red | 75 | 45 |

**241** Ribeiro de Andrada

**1945.** Death Cent of M. de Andrada (statesman).

| | | | | |
|---|---|---|---|---|
| 704 | **241** | 40c. blue | 90 | 20 |

**242** Meeting between Caxias and Canabarro

**1945.** Cent of Pacification of Rio Grande do Sul.

| | | | | |
|---|---|---|---|---|
| 705 | **242** | 40c. blue | 90 | 20 |

**244** L. L. Zamenhof

**1945.** 10th Brazilian Esperanto Congress, Rio de Janeiro.

| | | | | |
|---|---|---|---|---|
| 706 | - | 40c. green (postage) | 1·20 | 65 |
| 707 | **244** | 1cr.20 brown (air) | 90 | 55 |

DESIGN: 40c. Woman and map.

**247** Baron do Rio Branco (statesman)

**1945.** Birth Centenary of Baron do Rio Branco.

| | | | | |
|---|---|---|---|---|
| 708 | - | 40c. blue (postage) | 1·20 | 55 |
| 709 | - | 1cr.20 purple (air) | 75 | 55 |
| 710 | **247** | 5cr. purple | 2·10 | 90 |

DESIGNS—HORIZ: 40c. Bookplate. VERT: 1cr.20, S. America.

**248** "Glory"

**250** "Co-operation"

**1945.** Victory of Allied Nations in Europe. Roul.

| | | | | |
|---|---|---|---|---|
| 711 | - | 20c. violet | 55 | 20 |
| 712 | **248** | 40c. red | 55 | 20 |
| 713 | - | 1cr. orange | 1·10 | 55 |
| 714 | - | 2cr. blue | 2·75 | 65 |
| 715 | **250** | 5cr. green | 5·50 | 90 |

SYMBOLICAL DESIGNS—VERT: 20c. Tranquility (inscr "SAUDADE"). HORIZ: 1cr. "Victory" (inscr "VITORIA"); 2cr. "Peace" (inscr "PAZ").

**251** F. M. da Silva

**1945.** 150th Birth Anniv of Francisco Manoel da Silva (composer of Brazilian National Anthem).

| | | | | |
|---|---|---|---|---|
| 716 | **251** | 40c. red | 1·30 | 60 |

**252** Bahia Institute

**1945.** 50th Anniv of Founding of Bahia Institute of Geography and History.

| | | | | |
|---|---|---|---|---|
| 717 | **252** | 40c. blue | 2·00 | 35 |

**253** Shoulder Flash

**255** "V" Sign and Flashes

**1945.** Return of Brazilian Expeditionary Force.

| | | | | |
|---|---|---|---|---|
| 718 | **253** | 20c. blue, red and green | 55 | 45 |
| 719 | - | 40c. multicoloured | 55 | 45 |
| 720 | - | 1cr. multicoloured | 1·50 | 90 |
| 721 | - | 2cr. multicoloured | 2·20 | 1·30 |
| 722 | **255** | 5cr. multicoloured | 6·50 | 1·50 |

DESIGNS (embodying shoulder flashes) As Type **253**: 40c. B.E.F. flash. As Type **255**. HORIZ: 1cr. U.S.A. flag; 2cr. Brazilian flag.

**256** Wireless Mast and Map

**1945.** 3rd Inter-American Radio Communication Conference.

| | | | | |
|---|---|---|---|---|
| 723 | **256** | 1cr.20 black | 1·40 | 20 |

**257** Admiral Saldanha da Gama

**1946.** Birth Centenary of Admiral S. da Gama.

| | | | | |
|---|---|---|---|---|
| 724 | **257** | 40c. grey | 90 | 1·40 |

**258** Princess Isabel d'Orleans-Braganza

**1946.** Birth Centenary of Princess Isabel d'Orleans-Braganza.

| | | | | |
|---|---|---|---|---|
| 725 | **258** | 40c. black | 90 | 1·90 |

**260** Lockheed 14 Super Electra over Bay of Rio de Janiero

**261** P.O., Rio de Janeiro

**1946.** 5th Postal Union. Congress of the Americas and Spain.

| | | | | |
|---|---|---|---|---|
| 726 | - | 40c. orange and black | 55 | 45 |
| 727 | **260** | 1cr.30 orange and green | 75 | 75 |
| 728 | **260** | 1cr.70 orange and red | 75 | 75 |
| 729 | **261** | 2cr. blue and slate | 1·10 | 45 |
| 730 | **260** | 2cr.20 orange and blue | 1·10 | 1·10 |
| 731 | **261** | 5cr. blue and brown | 5·50 | 1·90 |
| 732 | **261** | 10cr. blue and violet | 6·00 | 1·10 |

DESIGN (25×37 mm): 40c. Post-horn, V and envelope.

**262** Proposed Columbus Lighthouse

**1946.** Construction of Columbus Lighthouse, Dominican Republic.

| | | | | |
|---|---|---|---|---|
| 733 | **262** | 5cr. blue | 17·00 | 3·75 |

**263** "Liberty"

**1946.** New Constitution.

| | | | | |
|---|---|---|---|---|
| 734 | **263** | 40c. grey | 55 | 35 |

**264** Orchid

**1946.** 4th National Exn of Orchids, Rio de Janeiro.

| | | | | |
|---|---|---|---|---|
| 735 | **264** | 40c. blue, red and yellow | 1·20 | 35 |

**265** Gen. A. E. Gomes Carneiro

**1946.** Birth Cent of Gen. A. E. Gomes Carneiro.

| | | | | |
|---|---|---|---|---|
| 736 | **265** | 40c. green | 55 | 10 |

**266** Academy of Arts

**1946.** 50th Anniv of Brazilian Academy of Arts.

| | | | | |
|---|---|---|---|---|
| 737 | **266** | 40c. blue | 65 | 45 |

**267** Antonio de Castro Alves

**1947.** Birth Centenary of Castro Alves (poet).

| | | | | |
|---|---|---|---|---|
| 738 | **267** | 40c. turquoise | 55 | 10 |

**268** Pres. Gonzalez

**1947.** Visit of Chilean President.

| | | | | |
|---|---|---|---|---|
| 739 | **268** | 40c. brown | 55 | 10 |

**269** "Peace and Security"

**270** "Dove of Peace"

**1947.** Inter-American Defence Conference, Rio de Janeiro.

| | | | | |
|---|---|---|---|---|
| 740 | **269** | 1cr.20 blue (postage) | 55 | 45 |
| 741 | **270** | 2cr.20 green (air) | 75 | 55 |

**271** Pres. Truman, Map of S. America and Statue of Liberty

**1947.** Visit of President Truman.

| | | | | |
|---|---|---|---|---|
| 742 | **271** | 40c. blue | 65 | 10 |

**272** Pres. Enrico Gaspar Dutra

**1947.** Commemorating Pres. Dutra.

| | | | | |
|---|---|---|---|---|
| 743 | **272** | 20c. green (postage) | 20 | 10 |
| 744 | **272** | 40c. red | 35 | 10 |
| 745 | **272** | 1cr.20 blue | 65 | 10 |
| **MS**746a | | 130×75 mm. Nos. 743/5. No gum. Imperf (air) | £110 | £130 |

**273** Woman and Child

**1947.** Children's Week. 1st Brazilian Infant Welfare Convention and Paediatrics.

747 **273** 40c. blue 65 10

**274** Icarus

**1947.** Obligatory Tax. "Week of the Wing" Aviation Fund.

748 **274** 40c.+10c. orange 75 20

**275** Santos Dumont Monument, St. Cloud, France

**1947.** Air. Homage to Santos Dumont (aviation pioneer).

749 **275** 1cr.20c. brown & green 1·10 55

**276** Arms of Belo Horizonte

**1947.** 50th Anniv of Founding of City of Belo Horizonte.

750 **276** 1cr.20c. red 90 10

**1947.** As postage stamps of 1941, but values in centavos or cruzeiros.

751 **205** 2c. olive 35 10
752 **205** 5c. brown 35 10
753 **205** 10c. turquoise 45 10
754 - 20c. brown (No. 651) 55 10
755 - 30c. red (No. 652) 1·40 20
756 - 40c. blue (No. 653) 55 10
757 - 50c. red (No. 654) 1·40 20
758 - 60c. violet (No. 655) 2·20 20
759 - 70c. red (No. 656) 1·00 20
760 - 1cr. grey (No. 657) 4·50 20
761 - 1cr.20 blue (No. 658) 5·50 20
762 - 2cr. purple (No. 659) 7·75 20
763 - 5cr. blue (No. 660) 19·00 20
764 **210** 10cr. red 14·50 20
765 - 20cr. brown (No. 662) 26·00 20
766a - 50cr. red (No. 663) 31·00 5·50

**277** Rio de Janeiro and Rotary Emblem

**1948.** Air. 39th Rotary Congress Rio de Janeiro.

769 **277** 1cr.20 red 1·10 90
770 **277** 3cr.80 violet 2·20 95

**278** Globe **279** Quitandinha Hotel

**1948.** International Industrial and Commercial Exhibition, Quitandinha.

771 **278** 40c. grn & mve (postage) 65 30
772 **279** 1cr.20 brown (air) 55 55
773 **279** 3cr.80 violet 1·40 65

**280** Arms of Paranagua

**1948.** Tercentenary of Founding of Paranagua.

774 **280** 5cr. brown 4·50 1·10

**281** Girl Reading

**1948.** National Children's Campaign.

775 **281** 40c. green 55 20

**282** Three Muses (after Henrique Bernardelli)

**1948.** Air. Centenary of National School of Music.

776 **282** 1cr.20 blue 1·40 35

**283** President Berres

**1948.** Air. Visit of Uruguayan President.

777 **283** 1cr.70 blue 75 35

**284** Merino Ram

**1948.** Air. International Livestock Show, Bage.

778 **284** 1cr.20 orange 1·70 65

**285** Congress Seal

**1948.** Air. 5th National Eucharistic Congress, Porto Alegre.

779 **285** 1cr.20 purple 75 35

**286** "Tiradentes" (trans. "Tooth-puller")

**1948.** Birth Bicentenary of A. J. J. da Silva Xavier (patriot).

780 **286** 40c. orange 55 20

**287** Crab and Globe

**1948.** Anti-cancer Campaign.

781 **287** 40c. purple 55 55

**288** Adult Student

**1949.** Campaign for Adult Education.

782 **288** 60c. purple 55 10

**289** Battle of Guararapes

**1949.** 300th Anniv of 2nd Battle of Guararapes.

783 **289** 60c. blue (postage) 2·20 1·10
784 - 1cr.20 pink (air) 3·25 1·70

DESIGN: 1cr.20, View of Guararapes.

**290** St. Francis of Paula Church

**1949.** Bicentenary of Ouro Fino.

785 **290** 60c. brown 65 35
**MS**785a 70×89 mm. No. 785. Imperf 75·00 65·00

**291** Father Nobrega **292** De Souza meeting Indians

**1949.** 4th Centenary of Founding of Bahia. (a) Postage. Imperf.

786 **291** 60c. violet 65 35

(b) Air. Perf.

787 **292** 1cr.20 blue 75 40

**293** Franklin D. Roosevelt

**1949.** Air. Homage to Franklin D. Roosevelt. Imperf.

788 **293** 3cr.80 blue 2·20 1·50
**MS**788a 85×110 mm. No. 788 39·00 46·00

**294** Douglas DC-3 and Air Force Badge

**1949.** Homage to Brazilian Air Force. Imperf.

789 **294** 60c. violet 55 10

**295** Joaquim Nabuco

**1949.** Air. Birth Centenary of J. Nabuco (lawyer and author).

790 **295** 3cr.80 purple 1·70 45

**296** "Revelation"

**1949.** 1st Sacerdotal Vocational Congress, Bahia.

791 **296** 60c. purple 65 20

**297** Globe

**1949.** 75th Anniv of UPU.

792 **297** 1cr.50 blue 90 10

**298** Ruy Barbosa

**1949.** Birth Cent of Ruy Barbosa (statesman).

793 **298** 1cr.20 red 1·40 45

**299** Cardinal Arcoverde

**1950.** Birth Cent of Cardinal Joaquim Arcoverde.

| | | | | |
|---|---|---|---|---|
| 794 | **299** | 60c. pink | 75 | 15 |

**300** "Agriculture and Industry"

**1950.** 75th Anniv of Arrival of Italian Immigrants.

| | | | | |
|---|---|---|---|---|
| 795 | **300** | 60c. red | 65 | 10 |

**301** Virgin of the Globe

**1950.** Centenary of Establishment of Daughters of Charity of St. Vincent de Paul.

| | | | | |
|---|---|---|---|---|
| 796 | **301** | 60c. blue and black | 55 | 10 |

**302** Globe and Footballers **303** Stadium

**1950.** 4th World Football Championship, Rio de Janeiro.

| | | | | |
|---|---|---|---|---|
| 797 | **302** | 60c. grey & bl (postage) | 1·90 | 55 |
| 798 | **303** | 1cr.20 orange and blue (air) | 2·10 | 90 |
| 799 | - | 5cr.80 yellow, green and blue | 6·50 | 1·10 |

DESIGN—VERT: 5cr.80 Linesman and flag.

**304** Three Heads, Map and Graph **305** Line of People and Map

**1950.** 6th Brazilian Census, 1950.

| | | | | |
|---|---|---|---|---|
| 800 | **304** | 60c. red (postage) | 55 | 10 |
| 801 | **305** | 1cr.20 brown (air) | 85 | 20 |

**306** Oswaldo Cruz

**1950.** 5th International Microbiological Congress. Rio de Janeiro.

| | | | | |
|---|---|---|---|---|
| 802 | **306** | 60c. brown | 90 | 10 |

**307** Blumenau and Itajai River

**1950.** Centenary of Founding of Blumenau.

| | | | | |
|---|---|---|---|---|
| 803 | **307** | 60c. pink | 90 | 10 |

**308** Government Offices

**1950.** Centenary of Amazon Province.

| | | | | |
|---|---|---|---|---|
| 804 | **308** | 60c. red | 65 | 10 |

**309** Arms

**1950.** Centenary of Juiz de Fora City.

| | | | | |
|---|---|---|---|---|
| 805 | **309** | 60c. red | 75 | 35 |

**310** P.O. Building, Recife

**1951.** Inauguration of Head Post Office, Pernambuco Province.

| | | | | |
|---|---|---|---|---|
| 806 | **310** | 60c. red | 65 | 10 |
| 807 | **310** | 1cr.20 red | 70 | 10 |

**311** Arms of Joinville

**1951.** Centenary of Founding of Joinville.

| | | | | |
|---|---|---|---|---|
| 808 | **311** | 60c. brown | 70 | 15 |

**312** S. Romero

**1951.** Birth Centenary of Sylvio Romero (poet).

| | | | | |
|---|---|---|---|---|
| 809 | **312** | 60c. brown | 90 | 10 |

**313** De La Salle

**1951.** Birth Tricentenary of Jean-Baptiste de la Salle (educational reformer).

| | | | | |
|---|---|---|---|---|
| 810 | **313** | 60c. blue | 65 | 10 |

**314** Heart and Flowers

**1951.** Mothers' Day.

| | | | | |
|---|---|---|---|---|
| 811 | **314** | 60c. purple | 1·00 | 55 |

**315** J. Caetano and Stage

**1951.** 1st Brazilian Theatrical Congress.

| | | | | |
|---|---|---|---|---|
| 812 | **315** | 60c. blue | 65 | 10 |

**316** O. A. Derby

**1951.** Birth Centenary of Derby (geologist).

| | | | | |
|---|---|---|---|---|
| 813 | **316** | 2cr. slate | 1·00 | 55 |

**317** Crucifix and Congregation

**1951.** 4th Inter-American Catholic Education Congress, Rio de Janeiro.

| | | | | |
|---|---|---|---|---|
| 814 | **317** | 60c. brown and buff | 65 | 10 |

**318** E. P. Martins and Map

**1951.** 29th Anniv of First Rio–New York Flight.

| | | | | |
|---|---|---|---|---|
| 815 | **318** | 3cr.80 brown & lemon | 3·75 | 75 |

**319** Penha Convent

**1951.** 400th Anniv of Founding of Vitoria.

| | | | | |
|---|---|---|---|---|
| 816 | **319** | 60c. brown and buff | 75 | 15 |

**320** Santos Dumont and Boys with Model Aircraft

**1951.** "Week of the Wing" and 50th Anniv of Santos Dumont's Flight over Paris.

| | | | | |
|---|---|---|---|---|
| 817 | **320** | 60c. brn & orge (postage) | 1·00 | 35 |
| 818 | - | 3cr.80 violet (air) | 3·25 | 45 |

DESIGN: 3cr.80, "Ballon No. 6" airship over Eiffel Tower.

**321** Wheat Harvesters

**1951.** Wheat Festival, Bage.

| | | | | |
|---|---|---|---|---|
| 819 | **321** | 60c. green and grey | 90 | 75 |

**322** Bible and Map

**1951.** Bible Day.

| | | | | |
|---|---|---|---|---|
| 820 | **322** | 1cr.20 brown | 1·30 | 65 |

**323** Isabella the Catholic

**1952.** 500th Birth Anniv of Isabella the Catholic.

| | | | | |
|---|---|---|---|---|
| 821 | **323** | 3cr.80 blue | 1·60 | 55 |

**324** Henrique Oswald

**1952.** Birth Centenary of Oswald (composer).

| | | | | |
|---|---|---|---|---|
| 822 | **324** | 60c. brown | 65 | 10 |

**325** Map and Symbol of Labour

**1952.** 5th Conf of American Members of I.L.O.

| | | | | |
|---|---|---|---|---|
| 823 | **325** | 1cr.50 red | 65 | 10 |

**326** Dr. L. Cardoso

**1952.** Birth Centenary of Cardoso (scientist) and 4th Brazilian Homoeopathic Congress, Porto Alegre.

| | | | | |
|---|---|---|---|---|
| 824 | **326** | 60c. blue | 75 | 35 |

**327** Gen. da Fonseca

**1952.** Centenary of Telegraphs in Brazil.

| | | | | |
|---|---|---|---|---|
| 825 | **327** | 2cr.40 red | 1·00 | 20 |
| 826 | - | 5cr. blue | 5·00 | 35 |
| 827 | - | 10cr. turquoise | 5·00 | 35 |

PORTRAITS—VERT: 5cr. Baron de Capanema. 10cr. E. de Queiros.

**328** L. de Albuquerque

**1952.** Bicentenary of Mato Grosso City.

| | | | | |
|---|---|---|---|---|
| 828 | **328** | 1cr.20 violet | 65 | 10 |

**329** Olympic Flame and Athletes

**1952.** 50th Anniv of Fluminense Football Club.

| | | | | |
|---|---|---|---|---|
| 829 | **329** | 1cr.20 blue | 1·50 | 75 |

**330** Councillor J. A. Saraiva

**1952.** 100th Anniv of Terezina City.

| | | | | |
|---|---|---|---|---|
| 830 | **330** | 60c. mauve | 65 | 10 |

**331** Emperor Dom Pedro II

**1952.** Stamp Day and 2nd Philatelic Exhibition, Sao Paulo.

| | | | | |
|---|---|---|---|---|
| 831 | **331** | 60c. black and blue | 65 | 10 |

**332** Globe, Staff and Rio de Janeiro Bay

**1952.** 2nd American Congress of Industrial Medicine.

| | | | | |
|---|---|---|---|---|
| 832 | **332** | 3cr.80 green and brown | 1·90 | 65 |

**333** Dove, Globe and Flags

**1952.** United Nations Day.

| | | | | |
|---|---|---|---|---|
| 833 | **333** | 3cr.80 blue | 2·10 | 65 |

**334** Compasses and Modern Buildings, Sao Paulo

**1952.** City Planning Day.

| | | | | |
|---|---|---|---|---|
| 834 | **334** | 60c. yellow, green & blue | 65 | 10 |

**335** D. A. Feijo (Statesman)

**1952.** Homage to D. A. Feijo.

| | | | | |
|---|---|---|---|---|
| 835 | **335** | 60c. brown | 75 | 10 |

**336** Father Damien

**1952.** Obligatory Tax. Leprosy Research Fund.

| | | | | |
|---|---|---|---|---|
| 836 | **336** | 10c. brown | 90 | 35 |
| 837 | **336** | 10c. green | 40 | 15 |

**337** R. Bernardelli

**1952.** Birth Centenary of Bernardelli (sculptor).

| | | | | |
|---|---|---|---|---|
| 838 | **337** | 60c. blue | 65 | 10 |

**338** Arms of Sao Paulo and Settler **339** "Expansion"

**1953.** 400th Anniv of Sao Paulo (1st issue).

| | | | | |
|---|---|---|---|---|
| 839 | **338** | 1cr.20 black and brown | 2·20 | 55 |
| 840 | - | 2cr. green and yellow | 4·50 | 55 |
| 841 | - | 2cr.80 brown and orange | 3·25 | 35 |
| 842 | **339** | 3cr.80 brown and green | 3·25 | 35 |
| 843 | **339** | 5cr.80 blue and green | 2·10 | 35 |

DESIGNS—VERT: (Inscr as Type **339**): 2cr. Coffee blossom and berries; 2cr.80, Monk planting tree.

See also Nos. 875/9.

**340**

**1953.** 6th Brazilian Accountancy Congress, Port Alegre.

| | | | | |
|---|---|---|---|---|
| 844 | **340** | 1cr.20 brown | 65 | 10 |

**341** J. Ramalho

**1953.** 4th Centenary of Santo Andre.

| | | | | |
|---|---|---|---|---|
| 845 | **341** | 60c. blue | 65 | 10 |

**342** A. Reis and Plan of Belo Horizonte

**1953.** Birth Centenary of A. Reis (engineer).

| | | | | |
|---|---|---|---|---|
| 846 | **342** | 1cr.20 brown | 65 | 10 |

**343** "Almirante Saldanha" (cadet ship)

**1953.** 4th Voyage of Circumnavigation by Training Ship "Almirante Saldanha".

| | | | | |
|---|---|---|---|---|
| 847 | **343** | 1cr.50 blue | 1·00 | 35 |

**344** Viscount de Itaborahy

**1953.** Centenary of Bank of Brazil.

| | | | | |
|---|---|---|---|---|
| 848 | **344** | 1cr.20 violet | 65 | 10 |

**345** Lamp and Rio-Petropolis Highway

**1953.** 10th Int Nursing Congress, Petropolis.

| | | | | |
|---|---|---|---|---|
| 849 | **345** | 1cr.20 grey | 65 | 10 |

**346** Bay of Rio de Janeiro

**1953.** 4th World Conference of Young Baptists.

| | | | | |
|---|---|---|---|---|
| 850 | **346** | 3cr.80c. turquoise | 1·00 | 35 |

**347** Ministry of Health and Education

**1953.** Stamp Day and 1st National Philatelic Exhibition of Education, Rio de Janeiro.

| | | | | |
|---|---|---|---|---|
| 851 | **347** | 1cr.20 turquoise | 65 | 10 |

**348** Arms and Map

**1953.** Centenary of Jau City.

| | | | | |
|---|---|---|---|---|
| 852 | **348** | 1cr.20 violet | 65 | 10 |

**349** Maria Quiteria de Jesus

**1953.** Death Centenary of Maria Quiteria de Jesus.

| | | | | |
|---|---|---|---|---|
| 853 | **349** | 60c. blue | 40 | 10 |

**350** Pres. Odria

**1953.** Visit of President of Peru.

| | | | | |
|---|---|---|---|---|
| 854 | **350** | 1cr.40 purple | 65 | 10 |

**351** Caxias leading Troops

**1953.** 150th Birth Anniv of Duke of Caxias.

| | | | | |
|---|---|---|---|---|
| 855 | **351** | 60c. turquoise | 40 | 15 |
| 856 | - | 1cr.20 purple | 90 | 15 |
| 857 | - | 1cr.70 blue | 90 | 15 |
| 858 | - | 3cr.80 brown | 2·10 | 20 |
| 859 | - | 5cr.80 violet | 1·30 | 20 |

DESIGNS: 1cr.20, Tomb; 1cr.70, 5cr.80, Portrait of Caxias; 3cr.80, Coat of arms.

**352** Quill-pen and Map

**1953.** 5th National Congress of Journalists, Curitiba.

| | | | | |
|---|---|---|---|---|
| 860 | **352** | 60c. blue | 65 | 20 |

**353** H. Hora

**1953.** Birth Centenary of H. Hora (painter).

| | | | | |
|---|---|---|---|---|
| 861 | **353** | 60c. purple and orange | 65 | 10 |

**354** President Somoza

**1953.** Visit of President Somoza of Nicaragua.

| | | | | |
|---|---|---|---|---|
| 862 | **354** | 1cr.40 purple | 65 | 20 |

**355** A. de Saint-Hilaire

**1953.** Death Centenary of A. de Saint-Hilaire (explorer and botanist).

| | | | | |
|---|---|---|---|---|
| 863 | **355** | 1cr.20 lake | 75 | 30 |

**356** J. do Patrocinio and "Spirit of Emancipation" (after R. Amoedo)

**1953.** Death Centenary of J. do Patrocinio (slavery abolitionist).

| | | | | |
|---|---|---|---|---|
| 864 | **356** | 60c. slate | 65 | 20 |

**357** Clock Tower, Crato

**1953.** Centenary of Crato City.

| | | | | |
|---|---|---|---|---|
| 865 | **357** | 60c. green | 65 | 20 |

**358** C. de Abreu

**1953.** Birth Centenary of Abreu (historian).

| | | | | |
|---|---|---|---|---|
| 866 | **358** | 60c. blue | 40 | 10 |
| 867 | **358** | 5cr. violet | 2·40 | 35 |

**359** "Justice"

**1953.** 50th Anniv of Treaty of Petropolis.

| | | | | |
|---|---|---|---|---|
| 868 | **359** | 60c. blue | 65 | 10 |
| 869 | **359** | 1cr.20 purple | 65 | 10 |

**360** Harvesting

**1953.** 3rd National Wheat Festival, Erechim.

| | | | | |
|---|---|---|---|---|
| 870 | **360** | 60c. turquoise | 65 | 10 |

**361** Teacher and Pupils

**1953.** 1st National Congress of Elementary Schoolteachers, Salvador.

| | | | | |
|---|---|---|---|---|
| 871 | **361** | 60c. red | 65 | 20 |

**362** Porters with Trays of Coffee Beans

**1953.** Centenary of State of Parana.

| | | | | |
|---|---|---|---|---|
| 872a | - | 2cr. brown and black | 1·90 | 55 |
| 873 | **362** | 5cr. orange and black | 3·00 | 55 |

DESIGN: 2cr. Portrait of Z. de Gois e Vasconellos.

**363** A. de Gusmao

**1954.** Death Bicent of Gusmao (statesman).

| | | | | |
|---|---|---|---|---|
| 874 | **363** | 1cr.20 purple | 75 | 30 |

**364** Growth of Sao Paulo **365** Sao Paulo and Arms

**1954.** 400th Anniv of Sao Paulo (2nd issue).

| | | | | |
|---|---|---|---|---|
| 875 | **364** | 1cr.20 brown | 2·10 | 90 |
| 876 | - | 2cr. mauve | 3·25 | 65 |
| 877 | - | 2cr.80 violet | 3·75 | 55 |
| 878 | **365** | 3cr.80 green | 4·50 | 55 |
| 879 | **365** | 5cr.80 red | 4·50 | 55 |

DESIGNS—VERT: 2cr. Priest, pioneer and Indian; 2cr.80, J. de Anchieta.

**366** J. F. Vieira, A. V. de Negreiros, A. F. Camarao and H. Dias

**1954.** 300th Anniv of Recovery from the Dutch of Pernambuco.

| | | | | |
|---|---|---|---|---|
| 880 | **366** | 1cr.20 blue | 90 | 35 |

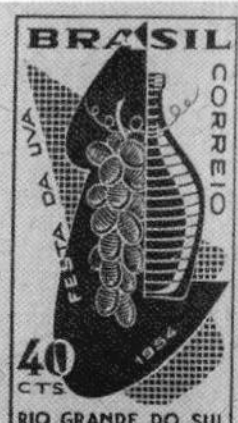


**367** Sao Paulo and Allegorical Figure

**1954.** 10th International Congress of Scientific Organization, Sao Paulo.

| | | | | |
|---|---|---|---|---|
| 881 | **367** | 1cr.50 purple | 75 | 35 |



**368** Grapes and Winejar

**1954.** Grape Festival, Rio Grande do Sul.

| | | | | |
|---|---|---|---|---|
| 882 | **368** | 40c. lake | 65 | 20 |

**369** Immigrants' Monument

**1954.** Immigrants' Monument, Caxias do Sul.

| | | | | |
|---|---|---|---|---|
| 883 | **369** | 60c. violet | 65 | 20 |

**370** "Baronesa", 1852 (first locomotive used in Brazil)

**1954.** Centenary of Brazilian Railways.

| | | | | |
|---|---|---|---|---|
| 884 | **370** | 40c. red | 1·30 | 40 |

**371** Pres. Chamoun

**1954.** Visit of President of Lebanon.

| | | | | |
|---|---|---|---|---|
| 885 | **371** | 1cr.50 lake | 75 | 30 |

**372** Sao Jose College, Rio de Janeiro **373** Vel Marcelino Champagnat

**1954.** 50th Anniv of Marists in Brazil.

| | | | | |
|---|---|---|---|---|
| 886 | **372** | 60c. violet | 50 | 20 |
| 887 | **373** | 1cr.20 blue | 50 | 20 |

**374** Apolonia Pinto

**1954.** Birth Centenary of Apolonia Pinto (actress).

| | | | | |
|---|---|---|---|---|
| 888 | **374** | 1cr.20 green | 65 | 20 |

**375** Admiral Tamandare

**1954.** Portraits.

| | | | | |
|---|---|---|---|---|
| 889 | **375** | 2c. blue | 35 | 20 |
| 890 | **375** | 5c. red | 35 | 10 |
| 891 | **375** | 10c. green | 35 | 10 |
| 892 | - | 20c. red | 35 | 15 |
| 893 | - | 30c. slate | 55 | 10 |
| 894 | - | 40c. red | 1·00 | 20 |
| 895 | - | 50c. lilac | 1·30 | 20 |
| 896 | - | 60c. turquoise | 50 | 15 |
| 897 | - | 90c. salmon | 1·00 | 20 |
| 904a | - | 1cr. brown | 1·90 | 55 |
| 899 | - | 1cr.50 blue | 35 | 10 |
| 904b | - | 2cr. green | 2·75 | 55 |
| 904c | - | 5cr. purple | 8·50 | 35 |
| 902 | - | 10cr. green | 2·50 | 30 |

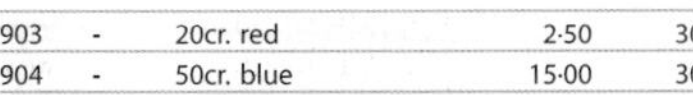

| | | | | |
|---|---|---|---|---|
| 903 | - | 20cr. red | 2·50 | 30 |
| 904 | - | 50cr. blue | 15·00 | 30 |

PORTRAITS—20, 30, 40c. O. Cruz; 50c. to 90c. J. Murtinho; 1cr., 1cr.50, 2cr. Duke of Caxias; 5, 10cr., R. Barbosa; 20, 50cr. J. Bonifacio.

**376** Boy Scout

**1954.** International Scout Encampment, Sao Paulo.

| | | | | |
|---|---|---|---|---|
| 905 | **376** | 1cr.20 blue | 1·60 | 35 |

**377** B. Fernandes

**1954.** Tercentenary of Sorocaba City.

| | | | | |
|---|---|---|---|---|
| 906 | **377** | 60c. red | 75 | 20 |

**378** Cardinal Piazza

**1954.** Visit of Cardinal Piazza (Papal Legate).

| | | | | |
|---|---|---|---|---|
| 907 | **378** | 4cr.20 red | 1·60 | 35 |

**379** Virgin and Map

**1954.** Marian Year. Inscr "ANO MARIANO".

| | | | | |
|---|---|---|---|---|
| 908 | **379** | 60c. lake | 90 | 30 |
| 909 | - | 1cr.20 blue | 1·10 | 45 |

DESIGN: 1cr.20, Virgin and globe.

No. 909 also commemorates the Centenary of the Proclamation of the Dogma of the Immaculate Conception.

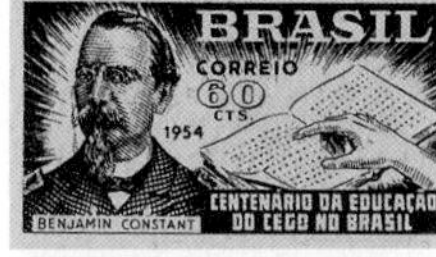


**380** Benjamin Constant and Braille Book

**1954.** Cent of Education for the Blind in Brazil.

| | | | | |
|---|---|---|---|---|
| 910 | **380** | 60c. green | 65 | 15 |

**381** River Battle of Riachuelo **382** Admiral Barroso

**1954.** 150th Birth Anniv of Admiral Barroso.

| | | | | |
|---|---|---|---|---|
| 911 | **381** | 40c. brown | 75 | 20 |
| 912 | **382** | 60c. violet | 50 | 20 |

**383** S. Hahnemann (physician)

**1954.** 1st World Congress of Homoeopathy.

| | | | | |
|---|---|---|---|---|
| 913 | **383** | 2cr.70 green | 75 | 35 |

**384** Nisia Floresta (suffragist)

**1954.** Removal of Ashes of Nisia Floresta (suffragist) from France to Brazil.

| | | | | |
|---|---|---|---|---|
| 914 | **384** | 60c. mauve | 75 | 20 |

**385** Ears of Wheat

**1954.** 4th Wheat Festival, Carazinho.

| | | | | |
|---|---|---|---|---|
| 915 | **385** | 60c. olive | 75 | 35 |

**386** Globe and Basketball Player

**1954.** 2nd World Basketball Championship.

| | | | | |
|---|---|---|---|---|
| 916 | **386** | 1cr.40 red | 1·00 | 45 |

**387** Girl, Torch and Spring Flowers

**1954.** 6th Spring Games.

| | | | | |
|---|---|---|---|---|
| 917 | **387** | 60c. brown | 75 | 35 |

**388** Father Bento

**1954.** Obligatory Tax. Leprosy Research Fund.

| | | | | |
|---|---|---|---|---|
| 918 | **388** | 10c. blue | 40 | 10 |
| 919 | **388** | 10c. mauve | 40 | 10 |
| 919a | **388** | 10c. salmon | 40 | 10 |
| 919b | **388** | 10c. green | 40 | 10 |
| 919c | **388** | 10c. lilac | 40 | 10 |
| 919d | **388** | 10c. brown | 40 | 10 |
| 919e | **388** | 10c. slate | 40 | 10 |
| 919f | **388** | 2cr. lake | 40 | 10 |
| 919g | **388** | 2cr. lilac | 40 | 10 |
| 919h | **388** | 2cr. orange | 40 | 10 |

See also Nos. 1239/40.

**389** Sao Francisco Power Station

**1955.** Inauguration of Sao Francisco Hydro-electric Station.

| | | | | |
|---|---|---|---|---|
| 920 | **389** | 60c. orange | 65 | 15 |

**390** Itutinga Power Plant

**1955.** Inaug of Itutinga Hydro-electric Station.

| | | | | |
|---|---|---|---|---|
| 921 | **390** | 40c. blue | 65 | 15 |

**391** Rotary Symbol and Rio Bay

**1955.** 50th Anniv of Rotary International.

| | | | | |
|---|---|---|---|---|
| 922 | **391** | 2cr.70 green and black | 3·25 | 55 |

**392** Aviation Symbols

**1955.** 3rd Aeronautical Congress, Sao Paulo.

| | | | | |
|---|---|---|---|---|
| 923 | **392** | 60c. grey and black | 65 | 15 |

**393** Fausto Cardoso Palace

**1955.** Centenary of Aracaiu.

| | | | | |
|---|---|---|---|---|
| 924 | **393** | 40c. brown | 65 | 20 |

**394** Arms of Botucatu

**1955.** Centenary of Botucatu.

| | | | | |
|---|---|---|---|---|
| 925 | **394** | 60c. brown | 50 | 10 |
| 926 | **394** | 1cr.20 green | 65 | 15 |

**395** Young Athletes

**1955.** 5th Children's Games, Rio de Janeiro.

| | | | | |
|---|---|---|---|---|
| 927 | **395** | 60c. brown | 75 | 15 |

**396** Marshal da Fonseca

**1955.** Birth Centenary of Marshal da Fonseca.

| | | | | |
|---|---|---|---|---|
| 928 | **396** | 60c. violet | 65 | 15 |

**397** Congress Altar, Sail and Sugar-loaf Mountain

**1955.** 36th International Eucharistic Congress.

| | | | | |
|---|---|---|---|---|
| 929 | **397** | 1cr.40 green | 50 | 10 |
| 930 | - | 2cr.70 lake (St. Pascoal) | 65 | 15 |

**398** Cardinal Masella

**1955.** Visit of Cardinal Masella (Papal Legate) to Eucharistic Congress.

| | | | | |
|---|---|---|---|---|
| 931 | **398** | 4cr.20 blue | 75 | 20 |

**399** Gymnasts

**1955.** 7th Spring Games.

| | | | | |
|---|---|---|---|---|
| 932 | **399** | 60c. mauve | 65 | 15 |

**400** Monteiro Lobato

**1955.** Honouring M. Lobato (author).

| | | | | |
|---|---|---|---|---|
| 933 | **400** | 40c. green | 65 | 15 |

**401** A. Lutz

**1955.** Birth Cent of Lutz (public health pioneer).

| | | | | |
|---|---|---|---|---|
| 934 | **401** | 60c. green | 65 | 15 |

**402** Lt.-Col. T. C. Vilagran Cabrita

**1955.** Centenary of 1st Battalion of Engineers.

| | | | | |
|---|---|---|---|---|
| 935 | **402** | 60c. blue | 65 | 15 |

**403** Salto Grande Dam

**1956.** Salto Grande Dam.

| | | | | |
|---|---|---|---|---|
| 936 | **403** | 60c. red | 65 | 15 |

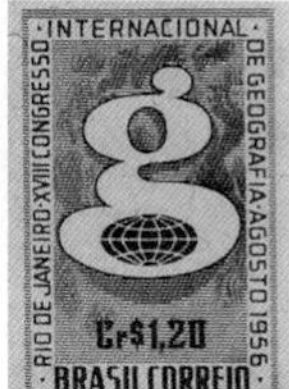

**404**

**1956.** 18th International Geographical Congress, Rio de Janeiro.

| | | | | |
|---|---|---|---|---|
| 937 | **404** | 1cr.20 blue | 1·60 | 20 |

**405** Arms of Mococa

**1956.** Centenary of Mococa, Sao Paulo.

| | | | | |
|---|---|---|---|---|
| 938 | **405** | 60c. red | 65 | 15 |

**406** Girls Running

**1956.** 6th Children's Games.

| | | | | |
|---|---|---|---|---|
| 939 | **406** | 2cr.50 blue | 1·00 | 15 |

**407** Douglas DC-3 and Map

**1956.** 25th Anniv of National Air Mail.

| | | | | |
|---|---|---|---|---|
| 940 | **407** | 3cr.30 blue | 1·10 | 45 |

**408** Rescue Work

**1956.** Centenary of Firemen's Corps, Rio de Janeiro.

| | | | | |
|---|---|---|---|---|
| 941 | **408** | 2cr.50 red | 1·10 | 55 |

**409** Franca Cathedral

**1956.** Centenary of City of Franca.

| | | | | |
|---|---|---|---|---|
| 942 | **409** | 2cr.50 blue | 75 | 20 |

**410** Open book with Inscription and Map

**1956.** 50th Anniv of Arrival of Marist Brothers in N. Brazil.

| | | | | |
|---|---|---|---|---|
| 943 | **410** | 2cr.50 blue (postage) | 75 | 20 |
| 944 | - | 3cr.30 purple (air) | 75 | 35 |

DESIGN—VERT: 3cr.30, Father J. B. Marcelino Champagnat.

**411** Hurdler

**1956.** 8th Spring Games.

945 **411** 2cr.50 red 1·50 20

**412** Forest and Map of Brazil

**1956.** Afforestation Campaign.

946 **412** 2cr.50 green 75 15

**413** Baron da Bocaina and Express Letter

**1956.** Birth Centenary of Baron da Bocaina.

947 **413** 2cr.50 brown 75 15

**414** Commemorative Stamp from Panama

**1956.** Pan-American Congress. Panama.

948 **414** 3cr.30 black and green 1·40 45

**415** Santos Dumont's Biplane "14 bis"

**1956.** Air. 50th Anniv of Dumont's First Heavier-than-air Flight.

**MS**948a 125×156 mm. **415** 3cr. red (in block of four) 18·00 15·00

**1956.** Air. Alberto Santos Dumont (aviation pioneer) Commemoration.

| | | | | |
|---|---|---|---|---|
| 949 | **415** | 3cr. green | 2·50 | 35 |
| 950 | **415** | 3cr.30 blue | 25 | 10 |
| 951 | **415** | 4cr. purple | 1·50 | 10 |
| 952 | **415** | 6cr.50 brown | 25 | 10 |
| 953 | **415** | 11cr.50 orange | 4·00 | 35 |

**416** Volta Redonda Steel Mill, and Molten Steel

**1957.** Nat Steel Company's Expansion Campaign.

955 **416** 2cr.50 brown 75 10

**417** J. E. Gomes da Silva (civil engineer)

**1957.** Birth Centenary of Gomes da Silva.

956 **417** 2cr.50 green 75 10

**418** Allan Kardec, Code and Globe

**1957.** Centenary of Spiritualism Code.

957 **418** 2cr.50 brown 65 15

**419** Young Gymnast

**1957.** 7th Children's Games.

958 **419** 2cr.50 lake 1·50 20

**420** Gen. Craveiro Lopes

**1957.** Visit of President of Portugal.

959 **420** 6cr.50 blue 1·50 20

**421** Stamp of 1932

**1957.** 25th Anniv of Sao Paulo Revolutionary Government.

960 **421** 2cr.50 red 75 10

**422** Lord Baden-Powell

**1957.** Air. Birth Centenary of Lord Baden-Powell.

961 **422** 3cr.30 lake 1·50 20

**423** Convent of Santo Antonio

**1957.** 300th Anniv of Emancipation of Santo Antonio Province.

962 **423** 2cr.50 purple 65 15

**424** Volleyball

**1957.** 9th Spring Games.

963 **424** 2cr.50 brown 1·50 20

**425** Basketball

**1957.** 2nd Women's World Basketball Championships.

964 **425** 3cr.30 green and brown 1·50 20

**426** U.N. Emblem, Map of Suez Canal and Soldier

**1957.** Air. United Nations Day.

965 **426** 5cr.30 blue 75 15

**427** Count of Pinhal (founder), Arms and Locomotive

**1957.** Centenary of City of San Carlos.

966 **427** 2cr.50 red 90 15

**428** Auguste Comte (philosopher)

**1957.** Death Centenary of Comte.

967 **428** 2cr.50 brown 75 15

**429** Sarapui Radio Station

**1957.** Inauguration of Sarapui Radio Station.

968 **429** 2cr.50 myrtle 75 15

**430** Admiral Tamandare (founder) and "Almirante Tamandare" (cruiser)

**1957.** 150th Anniv of Brazilian Navy.

| | | | | |
|---|---|---|---|---|
| 969 | **430** | 2cr.50 blue | 90 | 15 |
| 970 | - | 3cr.30 green | 1·80 | 45 |

DESIGN: 3cr.30, Aircraft-carrier "Minas Gerais".

**431** Coffee Beans and Emblem

**1957.** Centenary of City of Ribeirao Preto.

971a **431** 2cr.50 red 1·40 15

**432** King John VI of Portugal and Sail Merchantman

**1958.** 150th Anniv of Opening of Ports to Foreign Trade.

972 **432** 2cr.50 purple 1·00 20

**433** Bugler

**1958.** 150th Anniv of Corps of Brazilian Marines.

973 **433** 2cr.50 red 1·00 35

**434** Locomotive "Baronesa", 1852, and Dom Pedro II Station, Rio de Janeiro

**1958.** Centenary of Central Brazil Railway.

974 **434** 2cr.50 brown 1·00 35

**435** High Court Building

**1958.** 150th Anniv of Military High Courts.

975 **435** 2cr.50 green 75 15

**436** Brazilian Pavilion

**1958.** Brussels International Exhibition.

976 **436** 2cr.50 blue 90 35

**437** Marshal C. M. da Silva Ronden

**1958.** Rondon Commem and "Day of the Indian".

977 **437** 2cr.50 purple 75 20

438 Jumping

1958. 8th Children's Games, Rio de Janeiro.
978 438 2cr.50 red 75 20

439 Hydro-electric Station

1958. Inaug of Salto Grande Hydro-electric Station.
979 439 2cr.50 purple 75 20

440 National Printing Works

1958. 150th Anniv of National Printing Works.
980 440 2cr.50 brown 75 20

441 Marshal Osorio

1958. 150th Birth Anniv of Marshal Osorio.
981 441 2cr.50 violet 75 20

442 Pres. Morales of Honduras

1958. Visit of President of Honduras.
982 442 6cr.50 green 5·00 1·90

443 Botanical Gardens, Rio de Janeiro

1958. 150th Anniv of Botanical Gardens, Rio de Janeiro.
983 443 2cr.50 green 75 20

444 Hoe, Rice and Cotton

1958. 50th Anniv of Japanese Immigration.
984 444 2cr.50 red 75 20

445 Prophet Joel

1958. Bicentenary of Basilica of the Good Jesus, Matosinhos.
985 445 2cr.50 blue 75 20

446 Brazil on Globe

1958. Int Investments Conf, Belo Horizonte.
986 446 2cr.50 brown 75 20

447 Tiradentes Palace, Rio de Janeiro

1958. 47th Inter-Parliamentary Union Conf.
987 447 2cr.50 brown 75 20

448 J. B. Brandao (statesman)

1958. Centenary of Brandao.
988 448 2cr.50 brown 75 20

449 Dawn Palace, Brasilia

1958. Construction of Presidential Palace.
989 449 2cr.50 blue 75 20

450 Freighters

1958. Govt Aid for Brazilian Merchant Navy.
990 450 2cr.50 blue 75 20

451 J. C. da Silva

1958. Birth Centenary of Da Silva (author).
991 451 2cr.50 brown 75 20

452 Pres. Gronchi

1958. Visit of President of Italy.
992 452 7cr. blue 1·50 45

453 Archers

1958. 10th Spring Games, Rio de Janeiro.
993 453 2cr.50 orange 1·10 35

454 Old People within Hour-glass

1958. Old People's Day.
994 454 2cr.50 lake 75 20

455 Machado de Assis (writer)

1958. 50th Death Anniv of Machado de Assis.
995 455 2cr.50 brown 75 20

456 Pres. Vargas with oily Hand

1958. 5th Anniv of State Petroleum Law.
996 456 2cr.50 blue 75 20

457 Globe showing Brazil and the Americas

1958. 7th Inter-American Municipalities Congress, Rio de Janeiro.
997 457 2cr.50 blue 75 20

458 Gen. L. Sodre

1958. Birth Centenary of Sodre.
998 458 3cr.30 green 75 20

459 UN Emblem

1958. 10th Anniv of Human Rights Declaration.
999 459 2cr.50 blue 75 20

460 Footballer

1959. World Football Cup Victory, 1958.
1000 460 3cr.30 brown & green 1·10 45

461 Map and Railway Line

1959. Centenary of Opening of Patos-Campina Grande Railway.
1001 461 2cr.50 brown 75 20

462 Pres. Sukarno

1959. Visit of President of Indonesia.
1002 462 2cr.50 blue 75 20

463 Basketball Player

1959. Air. World Basketball Championships 1959.
1003 463 3cr.30 brown & blue 1·00 20

464 King John VI of Portugal

1959
1004 464 2cr.50 red 75 20

465 Polo Players

1959. Children's Games.
1005 465 2cr.50 brown 75 20

**466** Dockside Scene

**1959.** Rehabilitation of National Ports Law.

| 1006 | **466** | 2cr.50 green | 75 | 20 |
|---|---|---|---|---|

**467** Church Organ, Diamantina

**1959.** Bicent of Carmelite Order in Brazil.

| 1007 | **467** | 3cr.30 lake | 75 | 20 |
|---|---|---|---|---|

**468** Dom J. S. de Souza (First Archbishop)

**1959.** Birth Cent of Archbishop of Diamantina.

| 1008 | **468** | 2cr.50 brown | 75 | 20 |
|---|---|---|---|---|

**469** Sugar-loaf Mountain and Road

**1959.** 11th International Roads Congress.

| 1009 | **469** | 3cr.30 blue and green | 75 | 20 |
|---|---|---|---|---|

**470** Londrina and Parana

**1959.** 25th Anniv of Londrina.

| 1010 | **470** | 2cr.50 green | 75 | 20 |
|---|---|---|---|---|

**471** Putting the Shot

**1959.** Spring Games.

| 1011 | **471** | 2cr.50 mauve | 75 | 20 |
|---|---|---|---|---|

**472** Daedalus

**1959.** Air. Aviation Week.

| 1012 | **472** | 3cr.30 blue | 75 | 20 |
|---|---|---|---|---|

**473** Globe and "Snipe" Class Yachts

**1959.** World Sailing Championships, Porto Alegre.

| 1013 | **473** | 6cr.50 green | 75 | 20 |
|---|---|---|---|---|

**474** Lusignan Cross and Arms of Salvador, Bahia

**1959.** 4th International Brazilian–Portuguese Study Conference, Bahia University.

| 1014 | **474** | 6cr.50 blue | 75 | 20 |
|---|---|---|---|---|

**475** Gunpowder Factory

**1959.** 50th Anniv of President Vargas Gunpowder Factory.

| 1015 | **475** | 3cr.30 brown | 75 | 20 |
|---|---|---|---|---|

**476**

**1959.** Thanksgiving Day.

| 1016 | **476** | 2cr.50 blue | 75 | 20 |
|---|---|---|---|---|

**477** Sud Aviation SE 210 Caravelle

**1959.** Air. Inauguration of "Caravelle" Airliners by Brazilian National Airlines.

| 1017 | **477** | 6cr.50 blue | 75 | 20 |
|---|---|---|---|---|

**478** Burning Bush

**1959.** Centenary of Presbyterian Work in Brazil.

| 1018 | **478** | 3cr.30 green | 75 | 20 |
|---|---|---|---|---|

**479** P. da Silva and "Schistosoma mansoni"

**1959.** 50th Anniv of Discovery and Identification of "Schistosoma mansoni" (fluke).

| 1019 | **479** | 2cr.50 purple | 1·50 | 45 |
|---|---|---|---|---|

**480** L. de Matos and Church

**1960.** Birth Centenary of Luiz de Matos (Christian evangelist).

| 1020 | **480** | 3cr.30 brown | 75 | 20 |
|---|---|---|---|---|

**481** Pres. Lopez Mateos of Mexico

**1960.** Air. Visit of Mexican President.

| 1021 | **481** | 6cr.50 brown | 75 | 20 |
|---|---|---|---|---|

**482** Pres. Eisenhower

**1960.** Air. Visit of United States President.

| 1022 | **482** | 6cr.50 brown | 75 | 20 |
|---|---|---|---|---|

**483** Dr. L. Zamenhof

**1960.** Birth Centenary of Zamenhof (inventor of Esperanto).

| 1023 | **483** | 6cr.50 green | 75 | 20 |
|---|---|---|---|---|

**484** Adel Pinto (engineer)

**1960.** Birth Centenary of Adel Pinto.

| 1024 | **484** | 11cr.50 red | 1·00 | 35 |
|---|---|---|---|---|

**485** "Care of Refugees"

**1960.** Air. World Refugee Year.

| 1025 | **485** | 6cr.50 blue | 75 | 20 |
|---|---|---|---|---|

**486** Plan of Brasilia

**1960.** Inauguration of Brasilia as Capital.

| 1026 | - | 2cr.50 green (postage) | 75 | 35 |
|---|---|---|---|---|
| 1027 | - | 3cr.30 violet (air) | 50 | 20 |
| 1028 | - | 4cr. blue | 2·10 | 45 |
| 1029 | - | 6cr.50 mauve | 50 | 20 |
| 1030 | **486** | 11cr.50 brown | 50 | 20 |

**1960.** Miniature Sheet. Birthday of Pres. Kubitschek.

**MS**1031 110×52 mm. 27cr. Orange (postage) 2·20 1·90

DESIGNS—Outlines representing: HORIZ: 2cr.50 President's Palace of the Plateau; 3cr.30 Parliament Buildings; 4cr. Cathedral; 11cr.50, 27cr. T **486**. VERT: 6cr.50 Tower.

**487** Congress Emblem

**1960.** Air. 7th Nat Eucharistic Congress, Curitiba.

| 1032 | **487** | 3cr.30 mauve | 75 | 20 |
|---|---|---|---|---|

**488** Congress Emblem, Sugar-loaf Mountain and Cross

**1960.** Air. 10th Baptist World Alliance Congress, Rio de Janeiro.

| 1033 | **488** | 6cr.50 blue | 75 | 20 |
|---|---|---|---|---|

**489** Boy Scout

**1960.** Air. 50th Anniv of Scouting in Brazil.

| 1034 | **489** | 3cr.30 orange | 75 | 20 |
|---|---|---|---|---|

**490** "Agriculture"

**1960.** Cent of Brazilian Ministry of Agriculture.

| 1035 | **490** | 2cr.50 brown | 75 | 20 |
|---|---|---|---|---|

**491** Caravel

**1960.** Air. 5th Death Centenary of Prince Henry the Navigator.

| 1036 | **491** | 6cr.50 black | 75 | 20 |
|---|---|---|---|---|

**492** P. de Frontin

**1960.** Birth Cent of Paulo de Frontin (engineer).

| 1037 | **492** | 2cr.50 orange | 75 | 20 |
|---|---|---|---|---|

493 Locomotive Piston Gear

1960. 10th Pan-American Railways Congress.
1038 **493** 2cr.50 blue 1·50 55

494 Athlete

1960. 12th Spring Games.
1039 **494** 2cr.50 turquoise 75 20

495

1960. World Volleyball Championships.
1040 **495** 11cr. blue 25 10

496 Maria Bueno in play

1960. Air. Maria Bueno's Wimbledon Tennis Victories, 1959–60.
1041 **496** 6cr. brown 75 20

497 Exhibition Emblem

1960. International Industrial and Commercial Exhibition, Rio de Janeiro.
1042 **497** 2cr.50 brown & yellow 75 20

498 War Memorial, Rio de Janeiro

1960. Air. Return of Ashes of World War II Heroes from Italy.
1043 **498** 3cr.30 lake 75 20

499 Pylon and Map

1961. Air. Inauguration of Tres Marias Hydro-electric Station.
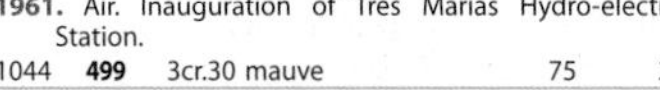
1044 **499** 3cr.30 mauve 75 20

500 Emperor Haile Selassie

1961. Visit of Emperor of Ethiopia.
1045 **500** 2cr.50 brown 75 20

501 Sacred Book and Map of Brazil

1961. 50th Anniv of Sacre-Coeur de Marie College.
1046 **501** 2cr.50 blue 75 20

502 Map of Guanabara State

1961. Promulgation of Guanabara Constitution.
1047 **502** 7cr.50 brown 75 20

503 Arms of Academy

1961. 150th Anniv of Agulhas Negras Military Academy.
1048 **503** 2cr.50 green 65 15
1049 - 3cr.30 red 65 15
DESIGN: 3cr.30, Military cap and sabre.

504 "Spanning the Atlantic Ocean"

1961. Visit of Foreign Minister to Senegal.
1050 **504** 27cr. blue 90 35

505 View of Ouro Preto

1961. 250th Anniv of Ouro Preto.
1051 **505** 1cr. orange 75 20

506 Arsenal, Rio de Janeiro

1961. 150th Anniv of Rio de Janeiro Arsenal.
1052 **506** 5cr. brown 75 20

507 Coffee Plant

1961. Int Coffee Convention, Rio de Janeiro.
1053 **507** 20cr. brown 3·00 30

508 Tagore

1960. Birth Cent of Rabindranath Tagore (poet).
1054 **508** 10cr. mauve 75 10

509 280r. Stamp of 1861 and Map of France

1961. "Goat's Eyes" Stamp Centenary.
1055 **509** 10cr. red 2·00 10
1056 - 20cr. orange 6·25 10
DESIGN: 20cr. 430r. stamp and map of the Netherlands.

510 Cloudburst

1962. World Meteorological Day.
1057 **510** 10cr. brown 2·30 55

511 Pinnacle, Rope and Haversack

1962. 50th Anniv of 1st Ascent of "Finger of God" Mountain.
1058 **511** 8cr. green 80 25

512 Dr. G. Vianna and parasites

1962. 50th Anniv of Vianna's Cure for Leishman's Disease.
1059 **512** 8cr. blue 70 25

513 Campaign Emblem

1962. Air. Malaria Eradication.
1060 **513** 21cr. blue 70 25

514 Henrique Dias (patriot)

1962. 300th Death Anniv of Dias.
1061 **514** 10cr. purple 80 30

515 Metric Measure

1962. Cent of Brazil's Adoption of Metric System.
1062 **515** 100cr. red 1·40 10

516 "Snipe" Sailing-boats

1962. 13th "Snipe" Class Sailing Championships, Rio de Janeiro.
1063 **516** 8cr. turquoise 70 25

517 J. Mesquita and Newspaper "O Estado de Sao Paulo"

1962. Birth Centenary of Mesquita (journalist and founder of "O Estado de Sao Paulo").
1064 **517** 8cr. bistre 95 25

518 Empress Leopoldina

1962. 140th Anniv of Independence.
1065 **518** 8cr. mauve 70 25

519 Brasilia

1962. 51st Interparliamentary Conference, Brasilia.
1066 **519** 10cr. orange 80 40

520 Foundry Ladle

1962. Inauguration of "Usiminas" (national iron and steel foundry).
1067 **520** 8cr. orange 70 25

**521** UPAE Emblem

**1962.** 50th Anniv of Postal Union of the Americas and Spain.

| | | | | |
|---|---|---|---|---|
| 1068 | **521** | 8cr. mauve | 70 | 25 |

**522** Emblems of Industry

**1962.** 10th Anniv of National Bank.

| | | | | |
|---|---|---|---|---|
| 1069 | **522** | 10cr. turquoise | 70 | 25 |

**523** Q. Bocaiuva

**1962.** 50th Death Anniv of Bocaiuva (journalist and patriot).

| | | | | |
|---|---|---|---|---|
| 1070 | **523** | 8cr. brown | 80 | 40 |

**524** Footballer

**1962.** Brazil's Victory in World Football Championships, 1962.

| | | | | |
|---|---|---|---|---|
| 1071 | **524** | 10cr. turquoise | 1·30 | 15 |

**525** Carrier Pigeon

**1962.** Tercentenary of Brazilian Posts.

| | | | | |
|---|---|---|---|---|
| 1072 | **525** | 8cr. multicoloured | 70 | 25 |
| **MS**1072a 145×58 mm. **525** 100cr. multicoloured | | | 4·75 | 4·25 |

**526** Dr. S. Neiva (first Brazilian P.M.G.)

**1963**

| | | | | |
|---|---|---|---|---|
| 1073 | **526** | 8cr. violet | 70 | 15 |
| 1073a | - | 30cr. turquoise (Euclides da Cunha) | 3·75 | 15 |
| 1073b | - | 50cr. brown (Prof. A. Moreira da Costa Lima) | 2·75 | 15 |
| 1073c | - | 100cr. blue (G. Dias) | 1·10 | 15 |
| 1073d | - | 200cr. red (Tiradentes) | 5·75 | 15 |
| 1073e | - | 500cr. brown (Emperor Pedro I) | 40·00 | 40 |
| 1073f | - | 1000cr. blue (Emperor Pedro II) | £100 | 1·00 |

**527** Rockets and "Dish" Aerial

**1963.** Int Aeronautics and Space Exn, Sao Paulo.

| | | | | |
|---|---|---|---|---|
| 1074 | **527** | 21cr. blue | 70 | 15 |

**528** Cross

**1963.** Ecumenical Council, Vatican City.

| | | | | |
|---|---|---|---|---|
| 1075 | **528** | 8cr. purple | 70 | 25 |

**529** "abc" Symbol

**1963.** National Education Week.

| | | | | |
|---|---|---|---|---|
| 1076 | **529** | 8cr. blue | 70 | 25 |

**530** Basketball

**1963.** 4th World Basketball Championships.

| | | | | |
|---|---|---|---|---|
| 1077 | **530** | 8cr. mauve | 70 | 10 |

**531** Torch Emblem

**1963.** 4th Pan-American Games, Sao Paulo.

| | | | | |
|---|---|---|---|---|
| 1078 | **531** | 10cr. red | 90 | 15 |

**532** "OEA" and Map

**1963.** 15th Anniv of Organization of American States.

| | | | | |
|---|---|---|---|---|
| 1079 | **532** | 10cr. orange | 90 | 40 |

**533** J. B. de Andrada e Silva

**1963.** Birth Bicentenary of Jose B. de Andrada e Silva ("Father of Independence").

| | | | | |
|---|---|---|---|---|
| 1080 | **533** | 8cr. bistre | 70 | 15 |

**534** Campaign Emblem

**1963.** Freedom from Hunger.

| | | | | |
|---|---|---|---|---|
| 1081 | **534** | 10cr. blue | 90 | 40 |

**535** Centenary Emblem

**1963.** Red Cross Centenary.

| | | | | |
|---|---|---|---|---|
| 1082 | **535** | 8cr. red and yellow | 70 | 15 |

**536** J. Caetano

**1963.** Death Centenary of Joao Caetano (actor).

| | | | | |
|---|---|---|---|---|
| 1083 | **536** | 8cr. black | 70 | 15 |

**537** "Atomic" Development

**1963.** 1st Anniv of National Nuclear Energy Commission.

| | | | | |
|---|---|---|---|---|
| 1084 | **537** | 10cr. mauve | 70 | 10 |

**538** Throwing the Hammer

**1963.** International Students' Games, Porto Alegre.

| | | | | |
|---|---|---|---|---|
| 1085 | **538** | 10cr. black and grey | 1·40 | 40 |

**539** Pres. Tito

**1963.** Visit of President Tito of Yugoslavia.

| | | | | |
|---|---|---|---|---|
| 1086 | **539** | 80cr. drab | 1·70 | 55 |

**540** Cross and Map

**1963.** 8th Int Leprology Congress, Rio de Janeiro.

| | | | | |
|---|---|---|---|---|
| 1087 | **540** | 8cr. turquoise | 70 | 15 |

**541** Petroleum Installations

**1963.** 10th Anniv of National Petroleum Industry.

| | | | | |
|---|---|---|---|---|
| 1088 | **541** | 8cr. green | 70 | 15 |

**542** "Jogos da Primavera"

**1963.** Spring Games.

| | | | | |
|---|---|---|---|---|
| 1089 | **542** | 8cr. yellow | 70 | 15 |

**543** A. Borges de Medeiros

**1963.** Birth Centenary of A. Borges de Medeiros (politician).

| | | | | |
|---|---|---|---|---|
| 1090 | **543** | 8cr. brown | 70 | 15 |

**544** Bridge of Sao Joao del Rey

**1963.** 250th Anniv of Sao Joao del Rey.

| | | | | |
|---|---|---|---|---|
| 1091 | **544** | 8cr. blue | 70 | 15 |

**545** Dr. A. Alvim

**1963.** Birth Cent of Dr. Alvaro Alvim (scientist).

| | | | | |
|---|---|---|---|---|
| 1092 | **545** | 8cr. slate | 70 | 15 |

**546** Viscount de Maua

**1963.** 150th Birth Anniv of Viscount de Maua (builder of Santos–Jundiai Railway).
1093 **546** 8cr. mauve 70 15

**547** Cactus

**1964.** 10th Anniv of North-East Bank.
1094 **547** 8cr. green 70 15

**548** C. Netto

**1964.** Birth Centenary of Coelho Netto (author).
1095 **548** 8cr. violet 70 15

**549** L. Muller

**1964.** Birth Cent of Lauro Muller (patriot).
1096 **549** 8cr. red 70 15

**550** Child with Spoon

**1964.** Schoolchildren's Nourishment Week.
1097 **550** 8cr. yellow and brown 70 15

**551** "Chalice" (carved rock), Vila Velha, Parana

**1964.** Tourism.
1098 **551** 80cr. red 90 15

**552** A. Kardec (author)

**1964.** Cent of Spiritual Code, "O Evangelho".
1099 **552** 30cr. green 1·60 40

**553** Pres. Lubke

**1964.** Visit of Pres. Lubke of West Germany.
1100 **553** 100cr. brown 1·70 45

**554** Pope John XXIII

**1964.** Pope John Commemoration.
1101 **554** 20cr. lake 70 15

**555** Pres. Senghor

**1964.** Visit of Pres. Senghor of Senegal.
1102 **555** 20cr. sepia 70 15

**556** "Visit Rio de Janeiro"

**1964.** 400th Anniv (1965) of Rio de Janeiro.
1103 **556** 15cr. blue and orange 90 45
1104 - 30cr. red and blue 80 15
1105 - 30cr. black and blue 80 40
1106 - 35cr. black and orange 55 30
1107 - 100cr. brn & grn on yell 70 30
1108 - 200cr. red and green 5·75 25
**MS**1109 Two sheets 129×76 mm. containing stamps similar to Nos. 1103, 1107/8 each in brown (sold at 320cr.) and 132×78 mm containing stamps similar to Nos. 1104/6 each in orange (sold at 100cr.) 22·00 24·00

DESIGNS: As Type **556**—HORIZ: 30cr. (No. 1105), Tramway viaduct; 200cr. Copacabana Beach. VERT: 35cr. Estacio de Sa's statue; 100cr. Church of Our Lady of the Rock. SMALLER (24½×37 mm): 30cr. (No. 1104), Statue of St. Sebastian.

**558** Pres. De Gaulle

**1964.** Visit of Pres. De Gaulle.
1110 **558** 100cr. brown 1·00 15

**559** Pres. Kennedy

**1964.** Pres. Kennedy Commemoration.
1111 **559** 100cr. black 70 30

**560** Nahum (statue)

**1964.** 150th Death Anniv of A. F. Lisboa (sculptor).
1112 **560** 10cr. black 70 15

**561** Cross and Sword

**1965.** 1st Anniv of Democratic Revolution.
1113 **561** 120cr. grey 80 30

**562** V. Brazil (scientist)

**1965.** Birth Cent of Vital Brazil.
1114 **562** 120cr. orange 80 30

**563** Shah of Iran

**1965.** Visit of Shah of Iran.
1115 **563** 120cr. red 70 15

**564** Marshal Rondon and Map

**1965.** Birth Cent of Marshal C. M. da S. Rondon.
1116 **564** 30cr. purple 70 15

**565** Lions Emblem

**1965.** Brazilian Lions Clubs National Convention, Rio de Janeiro.
1117 **565** 35cr. black and lilac 70 15

**566** I.T.U. Emblem and Symbols

**1965.** I.T.U. Centenary.
1118 **566** 120cr. green and yellow 90 15

**567** E. Pessoa

**1965.** Birth Centenary of Epitacio Pessoa.
1119 **567** 35cr. slate 70 15

**568** Barrosos Statue

**1965.** Centenary of Naval Battle of Riachuelo.
1120 **568** 30cr. blue 70 15

**569** Author and Heroine

**1965.** Centenary of Publication of Jose de Alencar's "Iracema".
1121 **569** 30cr. purple 70 15

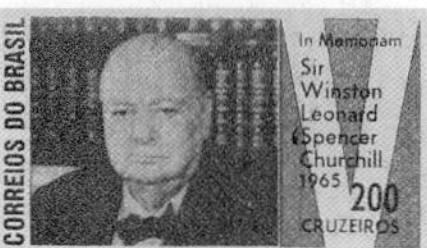

**570** Sir Winston Churchill

**1965.** Churchill Commemoration.
1122 **570** 200cr. slate 1·80 25

**571** Scout Badge and Emblem of Rio's 400th Anniv

**1965.** 1st Pan-American Scout Jamboree, Rio de Janeiro.
1123 **571** 30r. multicoloured 80 30

**572** ICY Emblem

**1965.** International Co-operation Year.
1124 **572** 120cr. black and blue 70 15

**573** L. Correia

**1965.** Birth Centenary of Leoncia Correia (poet).
1125 **573** 35cr. green 70 15

**574** Exhibition Emblem

**1965.** Sao Paulo Biennale (Art Exn).
1126 **574** 30cr. red 70 15

**575** President Saragat

**1965.** Visit of President of Italy.
1127 **575** 100cr. green on pink 70 15

**576** Grand Duke and Duchess of Luxembourg

**1965.** Visit of Grand Duke and Duchess of Luxembourg.
1128 **576** 100cr. brown 70 15

**577** Curtiss Fledgling on Map

**1965.** Aviation Week and 3rd Philatelic Exn.
1129 **577** 35cr. blue 70 15

**578** OEA Emblem

**1965.** Inter-American Conference, Rio de Janeiro.
1130 **578** 100cr. black and blue 70 15

**579** King Baudouin and Queen Fabiola

**1965.** Visit of King and Queen of the Belgians.
1131 **579** 100cr. slate 80 15

**580** Coffee Beans

**1965.** Brazilian Coffee.
1132 **580** 30cr. brown on cream 90 15

**581** F. A. Varnhagen

**1965.** Air. 150th Birth Anniv of Francisco Varnhagen (historian).
1133 **581** 45cr. brown 70 15

**582** Emblem and Map

**1966.** Air. 5th Anniv of "Alliance for Progress".
1134 **582** 120cr. blue & turquoise 1·40 15

**583** Sister and Globe

**1966.** Air. Centenary of Dorothean Sisters Educational Work in Brazil.
1135 **583** 35cr. violet 70 15

**584** Loading Ore at Quayside

**1966.** Inauguration of Rio Doce Iron-ore Terminal Tubarao, Espirito Santo.
1136 **584** 110cr. black and bistre 80 30

**585** "Steel"

**1966.** Silver Jubilee of National Steel Company.
1137 **585** 30cr. black on orange 70 15

**586** Prof. Rocha Lima

**1966.** 50th Anniv of Professor Lima's Discovery of the Characteristics of "Rickettsia prowazeki" (cause of typhus fever).
1138 **586** 30cr. turquoise 1·10 40

**587** Battle Scene

**1966.** Centenary of Battle of Tuiuti.
1139 **587** 30cr. green 90 15

**588** "The Sacred Face"

**1966.** Air. "Concilio Vaticano II".
1140 **588** 45cr. brown 70 15

**589** Mariz e Barros

**1966.** Air. Death Centenary of Commander Mariz e Barros.
1141 **589** 35cr. brown 70 15

**590** Decade Symbol

**1966.** International Hydrological Decade.
1142 **590** 100cr. blue and brown 90 15

**591** Pres. Shazar

**1966.** Visit of President Shazar of Israel.
1143 **591** 100cr. blue 80 40

**592** "Youth"

**1966.** Air. Birth Centenary of Eliseu Visconti (painter).
1144 **592** 120cr. brown 1·10 40

**593** Imperial Academy of Fine Arts

**1966.** 150th Anniv of French Art Mission's Arrival in Brazil.
1145 **593** 100cr. brown 2·20 25

**594** Military Service Emblem

**1966.** New Military Service Law.
1146 **594** 30cr. blue and yellow 70 15
**MS**1147 111×53 mm. No. 1146. No gum (sold at 100cr.) 2·30 2·40

**595** R. Dario

**1966.** 50th Death Anniv of Ruben Dario (Nicaraguan poet).
1148 **595** 100cr. purple 70 15

**596** Santarem Candlestick

**1966.** Centenary of Goeldi Museum.
1149 **596** 30cr. brown on salmon 70 15

**597** Arms of Santa Cruz do Sul

**1966.** 1st National Tobacco Exn, Santa Cruz.
1150 **597** 30cr. green 70 15

**598** UNESCO Emblem

**1966.** 20th Anniv of UNESCO.
1151 **598** 120cr. black 2·20 45
**MS**1152 110×52 mm. No. 1151. No gum (sold at 150cr.) 5·75 5·50

**599** Capt. A. C. Pinto and Map

**1966.** Bicentenary of Arrival of Captain A. C. Pinto.
1153 **599** 30cr. red 70 15

**600** Lusignan Cross and Southern Cross

**1966.** "Lubrapex 1966" Stamp Exn, Rio de Janeiro.
1154 **600** 100cr. green 80 30

**601** Madonna and Child

**1966.** Christmas.
1155 **601** 30cr. green 70 15
1156 - 35cr. blue and orange 70 15
1157 - 150cr. pink and blue 6·75 6·75
DESIGN—DIAMOND(34×34 mm). 35cr. Madonna and child (different). VERT (46×103 mm). 150cr. As 35cr. inscr "Pax Hominibus" but not "Brazil Correio".

**602** Arms of Laguna

**1967.** Centenary of Laguna Postal and Telegraphic Agency.
1158 **602** 60cr. sepia 70 15

**603** Grota Funda Viaduct and 1866 Viaduct

**1967.** Centenary of Santos–Jundiai Railway.
1159 **603** 50cr. orange 1·50 25

**604** Polish Cross and "Black Madonna"

**1967.** Polish Millennium.
1160 **604** 50cr. red, blue & yellow 1·30 30

**605** Research Rocket

**1967.** World Meteorological Day.
1161 **605** 50cr. black and blue 1·70 25

**606** Anita Garibaldi

**1967**
1162 - 1c. blue 55 10
1163 - 2c. red 55 10
1164 - 3c. green 55 10
1165 **606** 5c. black 1·00 15
1166 - 6c. brown 1·00 15
1167 - 10c. green 3·00 40
PORTRAITS: 1c. Mother Angelica. 2c. Marilia de Dirceu. 3c. Dr. R. Lobato. 6c. Ana Neri. 10c. Darci Vargas.

**607** "VARIG 40 Years"

**1967.** 40th Anniv of Varig Airlines.
1171 **607** 6c. black and blue 80 25

**608** Lions Emblem and Globes

**1967.** 50th Anniv of Lions International.
1172 **608** 6c. green 80 25
**MS**1173 130×80 mm. No. 1172. Imperf (sold at 15c.) 7·50 7·50

**609** "Madonna and Child"

**1967.** Mothers' Day.
1174 **609** 5c. violet 80 25
**MS**1175 130×76 mm. **609** 15c. violet. Imperf 7·50 7·50

**610** Prince Akihito and Princess Michiko

**1967.** Visit of Crown Prince and Princess of Japan.
1176 **610** 10c. black and red 80 25

**611** Radar Aerial and Pigeon

**1967.** Inaug of Communications Ministry, Brasilia.
1177 **611** 10c. black and mauve 70 15

**612** Brother Vicente do Salvador

**1967.** 400th Birth Anniv of Brother Vicente do Salvador (founder of Franciscan Brotherhood, Rio de Janeiro).
1178 **612** 5c. brown 70 15

**613** Emblem and Members

**1967.** National 4-S ("4-H") Clubs Day.
1179 **613** 5c. green and black 70 15

**614** Mobius Symbol

**1967.** 6th Brazilian Mathematical Congress. Rio de Janeiro.
1180 **614** 5c. black and blue 70 15

**615** Dorado (fish) and "Waves"

**1967.** Bicentenary of Piracicaba.
1181 **615** 5c. black and blue 80 25

**616** Papal Arms and "Golden Rose"

**1967.** Pope Paul's "Golden Rose" Offering to Our Lady of Fatima.
1182 **616** 20c. mauve and yellow 2·75 80

**617** General A. de Sampaio

**1967.** Gen. Sampaio Commem.
1183 **617** 5c. blue 70 15

**618** King Olav of Norway

**1967.** Visit of King Olav.
1184 **618** 10c. brown 70 15

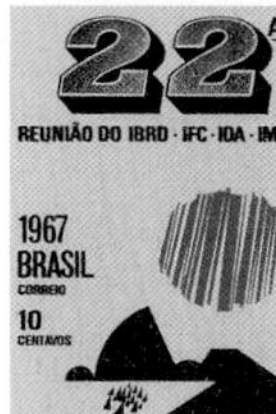

**619** Sun and Rio de Janeiro

**1967.** Meeting of International Monetary Fund, Rio de Janeiro.
1185 **619** 10c. black and red 70 15

**620** N. Pecanha (statesman)

**1967.** Birth Centenary of Nilo Pecanha.
1186 **620** 5c. purple 70 15

**621** Our Lady of the Apparition and Basilica

**1967.** 250th Anniv of Discovery of Statue of Our Lady of the Apparition.
1187 **621** 5c. blue and ochre 80 25
**MS**1188 80×130 mm. **621** 5c. and 10c. each blue and ochre. Imperf 10·50 10·50
No. **MS**1188 was issued for Christmas.

**622** "Song Bird"

**1967.** International Song Festival.

| | | | | |
|---|---|---|---|---|
| 1189 | **622** | 20c. multicoloured | 1·40 | 80 |

**623** Balloon, Rocket and Airplane

**1967.** Aviation Week.

| | | | | |
|---|---|---|---|---|
| 1190 | **623** | 10c. blue | 1·40 | 55 |
| **MS**1191 131×76 mm. **623** 15c. blue. Imperf | | | 17·00 | 17·00 |

**624** Pres. Venceslau Braz

**1967**

| | | | | |
|---|---|---|---|---|
| 1192 | - | 10c. blue | 70 | 15 |
| 1193 | - | 20c. brown | 2·20 | 15 |
| 1195 | **624** | 50c. black | 11·00 | 40 |
| 1198 | - | 1cr. purple | 17·00 | 40 |
| 1199 | - | 2cr. green | 3·50 | 25 |

Portraits of Brazilian Presidents: 10c. Arthur Bernardes. 20c. Campos Salles. 1cr. Washington Luiz. 2cr. Castello Branco.

**625** Rio Carnival

**1967.** International Tourist Year.

| | | | | |
|---|---|---|---|---|
| 1200 | **625** | 10c. multicoloured | 80 | 25 |
| **MS**1201 76×130 mm. **625** 15c. multi-coloured. Imperf | | | 10·50 | 11·00 |

**626** Sailor, Anchor and "Almirante Tamandare" (cruiser)

**1967.** Navy Week.

| | | | | |
|---|---|---|---|---|
| 1202 | **626** | 10c. blue | 80 | 25 |

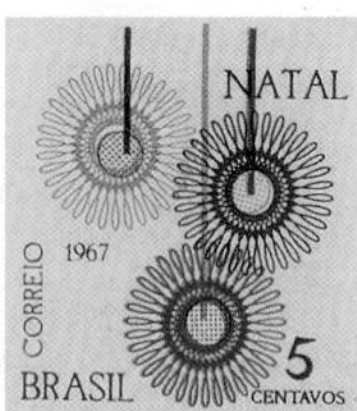

**627** Christmas Decorations

**1967.** Christmas.

| | | | | |
|---|---|---|---|---|
| 1203 | **627** | 5c. multicoloured | 70 | 15 |

**628** O. Bilac (poet), Aircraft, Tank and Aircraft carrier "Minas Gerais"

**1967.** Reservists Day.

| | | | | |
|---|---|---|---|---|
| 1204 | **628** | 5c. blue and yellow | 80 | 25 |

**629** J. Rodrigues de Carvalho

**1967.** Birth Centenary of Jose Rodriques de Carvalho (jurist and writer).

| | | | | |
|---|---|---|---|---|
| 1205 | **629** | 10c. green | 70 | 15 |

**630** O. Rangel

**1968.** Birth Cent of Orlando Rangel (chemist).

| | | | | |
|---|---|---|---|---|
| 1206 | **630** | 5c. black and blue | 1·00 | 45 |

**631** Madonna and Diver

**1968.** 250th Anniv of Paranagua Underwater Exploration.

| | | | | |
|---|---|---|---|---|
| 1207 | **631** | 10c. green and slate | 1·00 | 45 |

**632** Map of Free Zone

**1968.** Manaus Free Zone.

| | | | | |
|---|---|---|---|---|
| 1208 | **632** | 10c. red, green and yellow | 1·00 | 45 |

**633** Human Rights Emblem

**1968.** 20th Anniv of Declaration of Human Rights.

| | | | | |
|---|---|---|---|---|
| 1209 | **633** | 10c. red and blue | 1·00 | 45 |

**634** Paul Harris

**1968.** Birth Centenary of Paul Harris (founder of Rotary International).

| | | | | |
|---|---|---|---|---|
| 1210 | **634** | 20c. brown and green | 3·00 | 1·40 |

GUM. All the following issues to No.1425 are without gum, except where otherwise stated.

**635** College Arms

**1968.** Centenary of St. Luiz College. With gum.

| | | | | |
|---|---|---|---|---|
| 1211 | **635** | 10c. gold, blue and red | 1·60 | 70 |

**636** Cabral and his Fleet, 1500

**1968.** 500th Birth Anniv of Pedro Cabral (discoverer of Brazil).

| | | | | |
|---|---|---|---|---|
| 1212 | **636** | 10c. multicoloured | 2·30 | 85 |
| 1213 | - | 20c. multicoloured | 2·50 | 1·20 |

DESIGN: 20c. "The First Mass" (C. Portinari).

**637** "Maternity" (after H. Bernardeli)

**1968.** Mother's Day.

| | | | | |
|---|---|---|---|---|
| 1214 | **637** | 5c. multicoloured | 1·00 | 45 |

**638** Harpy Eagle

**1968.** 150th Anniv of National Museum. With gum.

| | | | | |
|---|---|---|---|---|
| 1215 | **638** | 20c. black and blue | 9·75 | 1·20 |

**639** Women of Brazil and Japan

**1968.** Inaug of "VARIG" Brazil–Japan Air Service.

| | | | | |
|---|---|---|---|---|
| 1216 | **639** | 10c. multicoloured | 1·70 | 80 |

**640** Horse-racing

**1968.** Centenary of Brazilian Jockey Club.

| | | | | |
|---|---|---|---|---|
| 1217 | **640** | 10c. multicoloured | 1·00 | 45 |

**641** Musician Wren

**1968.** Birds.

| | | | | |
|---|---|---|---|---|
| 1218 | - | 10c. multicoloured | 2·30 | 55 |
| 1219 | **641** | 20c. brown, green & bl | 2·50 | 55 |
| 1220 | - | 50c. multicoloured | 5·75 | 1·10 |

DESIGNS—VERT: 10c. Red-crested cardinal; 50c. Royal flycatcher.

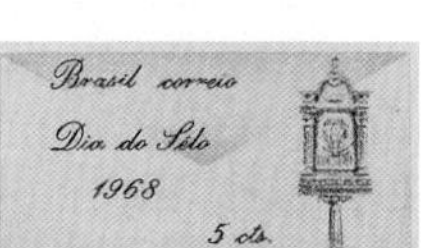

**642** Ancient Post-box

**1968.** Stamp Day. With gum.

| | | | | |
|---|---|---|---|---|
| 1221 | **642** | 5c. black, green & yellow | 70 | 15 |

**643** Marshal E. Luiz Mallet

**1968.** Mallet Commemoration. With gum.

| | | | | |
|---|---|---|---|---|
| 1222 | **643** | 10c. lilac | 70 | 15 |

**644** Map of South America

**1968.** Visit of Chilean President. With gum.

| | | | | |
|---|---|---|---|---|
| 1223 | **644** | 10c. orange | 70 | 15 |

**645** Lyceum Badge

**1968.** Centenary of Portuguese Literacy Lyceum (High School). With gum.

| | | | | |
|---|---|---|---|---|
| 1224 | **645** | 5c. green and pink | 70 | 15 |

**646** Map and Telex Tape

**1968.** "Telex Service for 25th City (Curitiba)". With gum.

| | | | | |
|---|---|---|---|---|
| 1225 | **646** | 20c. green and yellow | 1·40 | 45 |

**647** "Cock" shaped as Treble Clef

**1968.** 3rd Int Song Festival, Rio de Janeiro.

| | | | | |
|---|---|---|---|---|
| 1227 | **647** | 6c. multicoloured | 80 | 30 |

**648** Soldiers on Medallion

**1968.** 8th American Armed Forces Conference.

| | | | | |
|---|---|---|---|---|
| 1226 | **648** | 5c. black and blue | 1·40 | 55 |

**649** "Petrobras" Refinery

**1968.** 15th Anniv of National Petroleum Industry.

| | | | | |
|---|---|---|---|---|
| 1228 | **649** | 6c. multicoloured | 1·30 | 80 |

**650** Boy walking towards Rising Sun

**1968.** UNICEF.

| | | | | |
|---|---|---|---|---|
| 1229 | **650** | 5c. black and blue | 90 | 45 |
| 1230 | - | 10c. black, red & blue | 1·10 | 45 |
| 1231 | - | 20c. multicoloured | 1·40 | 45 |

DESIGNS—HORIZ: 10c. Hand protecting child. VERT: 20c. Young girl in plaits.

**651** Children with Books

**1968.** Book Week.

| | | | | |
|---|---|---|---|---|
| 1232 | **651** | 5c. multicoloured | 80 | 25 |

**652** WHO Emblem and Flags

**1968.** 20th Anniv of WHO.

| | | | | |
|---|---|---|---|---|
| 1233 | **652** | 20c. multicoloured | 1·70 | 70 |

**653** J. B. Debret (painter)

**1968.** Birth Bicentenary of Jean Baptiste Debret (1st issue).

| | | | | |
|---|---|---|---|---|
| 1234 | **653** | 10c. black and yellow | 1·00 | 45 |

See Nos. 1273/4.

**654** Queen Elizabeth II

**1968.** State Visit of Queen Elizabeth II.

| | | | | |
|---|---|---|---|---|
| 1235 | **654** | 70c. multicoloured | 4·50 | 2·00 |

**655** Brazilian Flag

**1968.** Brazilian Flag Day.

| | | | | |
|---|---|---|---|---|
| 1236 | **655** | 10c. multicoloured | 1·10 | 55 |

**656** F. Braga and part of "Hymn of National Flag"

**1968.** Birth Cent of Francisco Braga (composer).

| | | | | |
|---|---|---|---|---|
| 1237 | **656** | 5c. purple | 1·10 | 45 |

**657** Clasped Hands

**1968.** Blood Donors' Day.

| | | | | |
|---|---|---|---|---|
| 1238 | **657** | 5c. red, black and blue | 70 | 25 |

**1968.** Obligatory Tax. Leprosy Research Fund. Revalued currency. With gum.

| | | | | |
|---|---|---|---|---|
| 1239 | **388** | 5c. green | 2·10 | 85 |
| 1240 | **388** | 5c. red | 80 | 25 |

**658** Steam Locomotive No. 1 "Maria Fumaca", 1868

**1968.** Centenary of Sao Paulo Railway.

| | | | | |
|---|---|---|---|---|
| 1241 | **658** | 5c. multicoloured | 2·75 | 95 |

**659** Angelus Bell

**1968.** Christmas. Multicoloured.

| | | | |
|---|---|---|---|
| 1242 | 5c. Type **659** | 80 | 25 |
| 1243 | 6c. Father Christmas giving present | 80 | 25 |

**660** F.A.V. Caldas Jr

**1968.** Birth Centenary of Francisco Caldas Junior (founder of "Correio do Povo" newspaper).

| | | | | |
|---|---|---|---|---|
| 1244 | **660** | 10c. black, pink & red | 70 | 20 |

**661** Reservists Emblem and Memorial

**1968.** Reservists' Day. With gum.

| | | | | |
|---|---|---|---|---|
| 1245 | **661** | 5c. green and brown | 1·00 | 40 |

**662** Dish Aerial

**1969.** Inaug of Satellite Communications System.

| | | | | |
|---|---|---|---|---|
| 1246 | **662** | 30c. black and blue | 2·10 | 1·10 |

**663** Viscount do Rio Branco

**1969.** 150th Birth Anniv of Viscount do Rio Branco.

| | | | | |
|---|---|---|---|---|
| 1247 | **663** | 5c. sepia and drab | 80 | 30 |

**664** St. Gabriel

**1969.** St. Gabriel's Day (Patron Saint of Telecommunications).

| | | | | |
|---|---|---|---|---|
| 1248 | **664** | 5c. multicoloured | 1·10 | 40 |

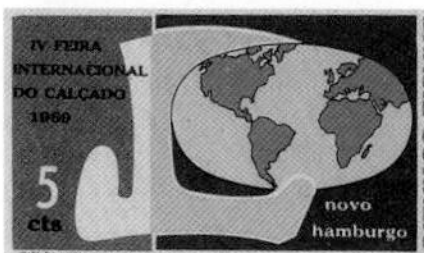

**665** Shoemaker's Last and Globe

**1969.** 4th Int Shoe Fair, Novo, Hamburgo.

| | | | | |
|---|---|---|---|---|
| 1249 | **665** | 5c. multicoloured | 70 | 30 |

**666** Kardec and Monument

**1969.** Death Centenary of "Allan Kardec" (Professor H. Rivail) (French educationalist and spiritualist).

| | | | | |
|---|---|---|---|---|
| 1250 | **666** | 5c. brown and green | 80 | 30 |

**667** Men of Three Races and Arms of Cuiaba

**1969.** 250th Anniv of Cuiaba (capital of Mato Grosso state).

| | | | | |
|---|---|---|---|---|
| 1251 | **667** | 5c. multicoloured | 80 | 30 |

**668** Mint and Banknote Pattern

**1969.** Opening of New State Mint Printing Works.

| | | | | |
|---|---|---|---|---|
| 1252 | **668** | 5c. bistre and orange | 1·30 | 70 |

**669** Society Emblem and Stamps

**1969.** 50th Anniv of Sao Paulo Philatelic Society.

| | | | | |
|---|---|---|---|---|
| 1253 | **669** | 5c. multicoloured | 80 | 30 |

**670** "Our Lady of Santana" (statue)

**1969.** Mothers' Day.

| | | | | |
|---|---|---|---|---|
| 1254 | **670** | 5c. multicoloured | 1·40 | 80 |

**671** ILO Emblem

**1969.** 50th Anniv of ILO. With gum.

| | | | | |
|---|---|---|---|---|
| 1255 | **671** | 5c. gold and red | 70 | 25 |

672 Diving Platform and Swimming Pool

**1969.** 40th Anniv of Cearense Water Sports Club, Fortaleza.

1256 **672** 20c. black, green & brn 1·70 85

673 "Mother and Child at Window" (after Di Cavalcanti)

**1969.** 10th Art Exhibition Biennale, Sao Paulo. Multicoloured.

1257 10c. Type **673** 1·80 45
1258 20c. Modern sculpture (F. Leirner) 1·80 1·00
1259 50c. "Sunset in Brasilia" (D. di Prete) 4·50 2·50
1260 1cr. "Angelfish" (A. Martins) 4·00 2·00

No. 1258 is square, size 33×33 mm and Nos. 1259/60 vertical, size 33×53 mm.

674 Freshwater Angelfish

**1969.** ACAPI Fish Preservation and Development Campaign.

1261 20c. Type **674** 1·70 80
**MS**1262 134×100 mm. Four designs each 38×22 mm. 10c. Tetra; 15c. Piranha; 20c. "Megalamphodus megalopterus"; 30c. Black tetra 17·00 17·00

675 I. O. Teles de Manezes (founder)

**1969.** Centenary of Spiritualist Press. With gum.

1263 **675** 50c. green and orange 3·00 2·00

676 Postman delivering Letter

**1969.** Stamp Day. With gum.

1264 **676** 30c. blue 2·75 1·70

677 General Fragoso

**1969.** Birth Centenary of General Tasso Fragoso. With gum.

1265 **677** 20c. green 2·30 95

678 Map of Army Bases

**1969.** Army Week. Multicoloured.

1266 10c. Type **678** 1·40 60
1267 20c. Monument and railway bridge (39×22 mm) 2·30 1·00

679 Jupia Dam

**1969.** Inauguration of Jupia Dam.

1268 **679** 20c. multicoloured 1·70 1·00

680 Mahatma Gandhi and Spinning-wheel

**1969.** Birth Centenary of Mahatma Gandhi.

1269 **680** 20c. black and yellow 1·20 60

681 Alberto Santos Dumont, "Ballon No. 6", Eiffel Tower and Moon Landing

**1969.** 1st Man on the Moon and Santos Dumont's Flight (1906). Commemoration.

1270 **681** 50c. multicoloured 4·25 1·90

682 Smelting Plant

**1969.** Expansion of USIMINAS Steel Consortium.

1271 **682** 20c. multicoloured 1·30 85

683 Steel Furnace

**1969.** 25th Anniv of ACESITA Steel Works.

1272 **683** 10c. multicoloured 1·30 85

684 "The Water Cart" (after Debrot)

**1969.** Birth Centenary of J. B. Debret (painter) (2nd issue). Multicoloured. No. 1274 dated "1970".

1273 20c. Type **684** 3·00 95
1274 30c. "Street Scene" 3·00 1·90

685 Exhibition Emblem

**1969.** "Abuexpo 69" Stamp Exn.

1275 **685** 10c. multicoloured 1·10 35

686 Embraer Bandeirante Airplane

**1969.** Brazilian Aeronautical Industry Expansion Year.

1276 **686** 50c. multicoloured 7·00 2·50

687 Pele scoring Goal

**1969.** Footballer Pele's 1,000th Goal.

1277 **687** 10c. multicoloured 1·30 95
**MS**1278 81×120 mm. **687** 75c. multi-coloured. Imperf 12·00 7·00

688 "Madonna and Child" (painted panel)

**1969.** Christmas.

1279 **688** 10c. multicoloured 1·20 35
**MS**1280 137×102 mm. **688** 75c. multi-coloured. Imperf 32·00 30·00

689 "Pernambuco" (destroyer) and "Bahia" (submarine)

**1969.** Navy Day. With gum.

1281 **689** 5c. blue 1·10 45

690 Dr. H. Blumenau

**1969.** 150th Birth Anniv of Dr. Hermann Blumenau (German immigrant leader). With gum.

1282 **690** 20c. green 2·20 80

691 Carnival Dancers

**1969.** Carioca Carnival, Rio de Janeiro (1970). Multicoloured.

1283 5c. Type **691** 1·10 60
1284 10c. Samba dancers (horiz) 1·10 60
1285 20c. Clowns (horiz) 1·30 80
1286 30c. Confetti and mask 7·00 5·25
1287 50c. Tambourine-player 7·00 4·75

692 Carlos Gomes conducting

**1970.** Centenary of Opera "O. Guarani" by A. Carlos Gomes.

1288 **692** 20c. multicoloured 1·70 80

693 Monastery

**1970.** 400th Anniv of Penha Monastery, Vilha Velha.

1289 **693** 20c. multicoloured 85 35

694 National Assembly Building

**1970.** 10th Anniv of Brasilia. Multicoloured.

1290 20c. Type **694** 2·50 1·40
1291 50c. Reflecting Pool 6·00 3·50
1292 1cr. Presidential Palace 6·00 3·50

**695** Emblem on Map

**1970.** Rondon Project (students' practical training scheme).
1293 **695** 50c. multicoloured 6·50 7·00

**696** Marshal Osorio and Arms

**1970.** Opening of Marshal Osorio Historical Park.
1294 **696** 20c. multicoloured 4·25 1·90

**697** "Madonna and Child" (San Antonio Monastery)

**1970.** Mothers' Day.
1295 **697** 20c. multicoloured 1·20 80

**698** Brasilia Cathedral (stylized)

**1970.** 8th National Eucharistic Congress, Brasilia. With gum.
1296 **698** 20c. green 85 45

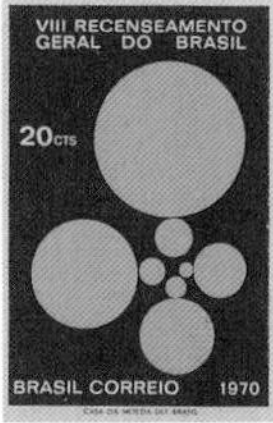


**699** Census Symbol

**1970.** 8th National Census.
1297 **699** 20c. yellow and green 1·70 1·70

**700** Jules Rimet Cup, and Map

**1970.** World Cup Football Championships Mexico.
1298 **700** 50c. black, gold & blue 2·40 2·20

**701** Statue of Christ

**1970.** Marist Students. 6th World Congress.
1299 **701** 50c. multicoloured 7·00 6·50

**702** Bellini and Swedish Flag (1958)

**1970.** Brazil's Third Victory in World Cup Football Championships. Multicoloured.
1300 1cr. Type **702** 4·75 3·50
1301 2cr. Garrincha and Chilean flag (1962) 9·25 3·50
1302 3cr. Pele and Mexican flag (1970) 7·75 2·50

**703** Pandia Calogeras

**1970.** Birth Centenary of Calogeras (author and politician).
1303 **703** 20c. green 1·40 95

**704** Brazilian Forces Badges and Map

**1970.** 25th Anniv of World War II. Victory.
1304 **704** 20c. multicoloured 1·30 95

**705** "The Annunciation" (Cassio M'Boy)

**1970.** St. Gabriel's Day (Patron Saint of Telecommunications).
1305 **705** 20c. multicoloured 3·00 1·90

**706** Boy in Library

**1970.** Book Week.
1306 **706** 20c. multicoloured 3·00 1·90

**707** U.N. Emblem

**1970.** 25th Anniv of United Nations.
1307 **707** 50c. blue, silver & ultram 3·00 2·30

**708** "Rio de Janeiro, circa 1820"

**1970.** 3rd Brazilian–Portuguese Stamp Exhibition "Lubrapex 70", Rio de Janeiro.
1308 **708** 20c. multicoloured 3·00 1·50
1309 - 50c. brown and black 7·00 3·00
1310 - 1cr. multicoloured 7·25 4·50
**MS**1311 60×80 mm. **708** 1cr. multicoloured. Imperf 24·00 26·00

DESIGNS: 50c. Post Office Symbol; 1cr. Rio de Janeiro (modern view).

**709** "The Holy Family" (C. Portinari)

**1970.** Christmas.
1312 **709** 50c. multicoloured 3·00 3·00
**MS**1313 107×52 mm. **709** 1cr. multicoloured. Imper 42·00 45·00

**710** "Graca Aranha" (destroyer)

**1970.** Navy Day.
1314 **710** 20c. multicoloured 3·00 1·70

**711** Congress Emblem

**1971.** 3rd Inter-American Housing Congress, Rio de Janeiro.
1315 **711** 50c. red and black 3·75 4·00

**712** Links and Globe

**1971.** Racial Equality Year.
1316 **712** 20c. multicoloured 1·80 1·10

**713** "Morpho melacheilus"

**1971.** Butterflies. Multicoloured.
1317 20c. Type **713** 2·40 1·40
1318 1cr. "Papilio thoas brasiliensis" 10·50 7·50

**714** Madonna and Child

**1971.** Mothers' Day.
1319 **714** 20c. multicoloured 2·10 90

**715** Hands reaching for Ball

**1971.** 6th Women's Basketball World Championships.
1320 **715** 70c. multicoloured 4·25 2·20

**716** Eastern Part of Highway Map

**1971.** Trans-Amazon Highway Project. Mult.
1321 40c. Type **716** 12·00 6·00
1322 1cr. Western part of Highway Map 12·00 9·75

Nos. 1321/2 were issued together se-tenant, forming a composite design.

**717** "Head of Man" (V. M. Lima)

**1971.** Stamp Day. Multicoloured.
1323 40c. Type **717** 4·25 1·80
1324 1cr. "Arab Violinist" (Pedro Americo) 9·50 3·75

**718** General Caxias and Map

**1971.** Army Week.
1325 **718** 20c. red and green 1·30 1·40

**719** Anita Garibaldi

**1971.** 150th Birth Anniv of Anita Garibaldi.

| | | | | |
|---|---|---|---|---|
| 1326 | **719** | 20c. multicoloured | 1·30 | 90 |

**720** Xavante and Santos Dumont's Biplane "14 bis"

**1971.** 1st Flight of Embraer Xavante Jet Fighter.

| | | | | |
|---|---|---|---|---|
| 1327 | **720** | 40c. multicoloured | 4·25 | 1·70 |

**721** Flags of Central American Republics

**1971.** 150th Anniv of Central American Republics' Independence.

| | | | | |
|---|---|---|---|---|
| 1328 | **721** | 40c. multicoloured | 3·00 | 1·40 |

**722** Exhibition Emblem

**1971.** "Franca 71" Industrial, Technical and Scientific Exhibition, Sao Paulo.

| | | | | |
|---|---|---|---|---|
| 1329 | **722** | 1cr.30 multicoloured | 4·25 | 2·50 |

**723** "The Black Mother" (L. de Albuquerque)

**1971.** Centenary of Slaves Emancipation Law.

| | | | | |
|---|---|---|---|---|
| 1330 | **723** | 40c. multicoloured | 2·00 | 1·10 |

**724** Archangel Gabriel

**1971.** St. Gabriel's Day (Patron Saint of Communications).

| | | | | |
|---|---|---|---|---|
| 1331 | **724** | 40c. multicoloured | 1·90 | 1·50 |

**725** "Couple on Bridge" (Marisa da Silva Chaves)

**1971.** Children's Day. Multicoloured.

| | | | |
|---|---|---|---|
| 1332 | 35c. Type **725** | 1·40 | 1·00 |
| 1333 | 45c. "Couple on Riverbank" (Mary Rosa e Silva) | 3·00 | 1·00 |
| 1334 | 60c. "Girl in Hat" (Teresa A. P. Ferreira) | 1·40 | 1·00 |

**726** "Laelia purpurata Werkhauserii superba"

**1971.** Brazilian Orchids.

| | | | | |
|---|---|---|---|---|
| 1335 | **726** | 40c. multicoloured | 5·25 | 2·30 |

**727** Eunice Weaver

**1971.** Obligatory Tax. Leprosy Research Fund.

| | | | | |
|---|---|---|---|---|
| 1336 | **727** | 10c. green | 1·70 | 55 |
| 1337 | **727** | 10c. purple | 60 | 20 |

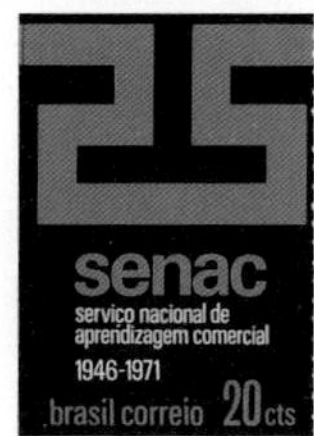


**728** "25 Senac"

**1971.** 25th Annivs of SENAC (apprenticeship scheme) and SESC (workers' social service).

| | | | | |
|---|---|---|---|---|
| 1338 | **728** | 20c. blue and black | 3·00 | 2·30 |
| 1339 | - | 40c. orange and black | 3·00 | 2·30 |

DESIGN: 40c. As Type **728**, but inscribed "25 SESC".

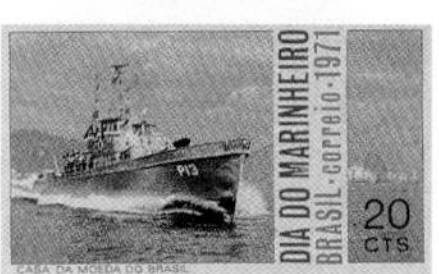


**729** "Parati" (gunboat)

**1971.** Navy Day.

| | | | | |
|---|---|---|---|---|
| 1340 | **729** | 20c. multicoloured | 2·00 | 1·20 |

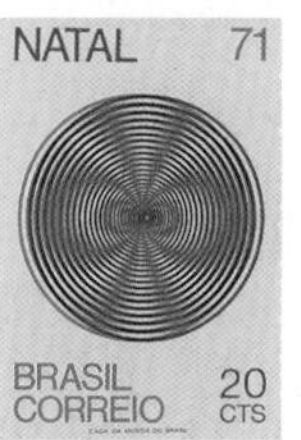


**730** Cruciform Symbol

**1971.** Christmas.

| | | | | |
|---|---|---|---|---|
| 1341 | **730** | 20c. lilac, red and blue | 1·00 | 80 |
| 1342 | **730** | 75c. black on silver | 2·10 | 6·25 |
| 1343 | **730** | 1cr.30 multicoloured | 10·50 | 4·75 |

**731** Washing Bomfim Church

**1972.** Tourism. Multicoloured.

| | | | |
|---|---|---|---|
| 1344 | 20c. Type **731** | 3·75 | 1·70 |
| 1345 | 40c. Cogwheel and grapes (Grape Festival, Rio Grande do Sul) | 5·75 | 1·20 |
| 1346 | 75c. Nazareth Festival procession, Belem | 6·00 | 5·50 |
| 1347 | 1cr.30 Street scene (Winter Festival of Ouro Preto) | 13·00 | 5·75 |

**732** Pres. Lanusse

**1972.** Visit of President Lanusse of Argentina.

| | | | | |
|---|---|---|---|---|
| 1348 | **732** | 40c. multicoloured | 4·75 | 5·75 |

**733** Presidents Castello Branco, Costa e Silva and Medici

**1972.** 8th Anniv of 1964 Revolution.

| | | | | |
|---|---|---|---|---|
| 1349 | **733** | 20c. multicoloured | 3·00 | 1·40 |

**734** Post Office Symbol

**1972**

| | | | | |
|---|---|---|---|---|
| 1350 | **734** | 20c. brown | 4·75 | 30 |

**735** Pres. Tomas

**1972.** Visit of Pres. Tomas of Portugal.

| | | | | |
|---|---|---|---|---|
| 1351 | **735** | 75c. multicoloured | 4·75 | 3·75 |

**736** Exploratory Borehole (C.P.R.M.)

**1972.** Mineral Resources. Multicoloured.

| | | | |
|---|---|---|---|
| 1352 | 20c. Type **736** | 3·00 | 1·20 |
| 1353 | 40c. Oil rig (PETROBRAS) (vert) | 7·25 | 1·90 |
| 1354 | 75c. Power station and dam (ELECTROBRAS) | 3·25 | 3·25 |
| 1355 | 1cr.30 Iron ore production (Vale do Rio Doce Co.) | 7·25 | 3·25 |

**737** "Female Nude" (1922 Catalogue cover by Di. Cavalcanti)

**1972.** 50th Anniv of 1st Modern Art Week, Sao Paulo. Sheet 79×111 mm. With gum.

| | | | | |
|---|---|---|---|---|
| **MS**1356 | **737** | 1cr. black and carmine | 70·00 | 65·00 |

**738** Postman and Map (Post Office)

**1972.** Communications. Multicoloured.

| | | | |
|---|---|---|---|
| 1357 | 35c. Type **738** | 3·25 | 85 |
| 1358 | 45c. Microwave Transmitter (Telecommunications) (vert) | 3·50 | 3·50 |
| 1359 | 60c. Symbol and diagram of Amazon microwave system | 3·50 | 2·75 |
| 1360 | 70c. Worker and route map (Amazon Basin development) | 4·50 | 2·75 |

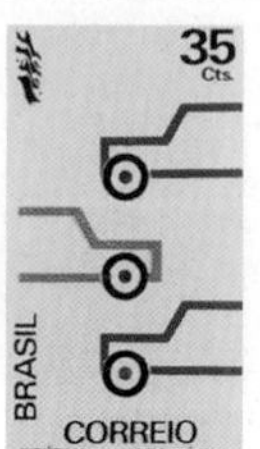


**739** Motor Cars

**1972.** Major Industries.

| | | | | |
|---|---|---|---|---|
| 1361 | **739** | 35c. orange, red & black | 2·50 | 1·20 |
| 1362 | - | 45c. multicoloured | 2·50 | 1·40 |
| 1363 | - | 70c. multicoloured | 2·50 | 1·20 |

DESIGNS—HORIZ: 45c. Three hulls (Shipbuilding); 70c. Metal Blocks (Iron and Steel Industry).

**740** Footballer (Independence Cup Championships)

**1972.** "Sports and Pastimes".

| | | | | |
|---|---|---|---|---|
| 1364 | **740** | 20c. black and brown | 2·40 | 1·20 |
| 1365 | - | 75c. black and red | 4·25 | 6·50 |
| 1366 | - | 1cr.30 black and blue | 8·00 | 6·50 |

DESIGNS: 75c. Treble clef in open mouth ("Popular Music"); 1cr.30, Hand grasping plastic ("Plastic Arts").

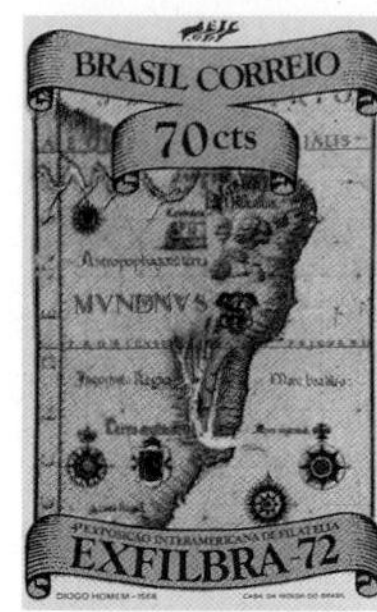


**741** Diego Homem's Map of Brazil, 1568

**1972.** "EXFILBRA 72" 4th International Stamp Exhibition, Rio de Janeiro. Multicoloured.

| | | | |
|---|---|---|---|
| 1367 | 70c. Type **741** | 1·30 | 1·20 |
| 1368 | 1cr. Nicolau Visscher's Map of Americas, c. 1652 | 18·00 | 2·30 |
| 1369 | 2cr. Lopo Homem's World Map, 1519 | 8·75 | 3·50 |
| **MS**1370 | 125×89 mm. 1cr. "Declaration of Ypiranga" (Pedro Americo) (horiz) | 10·50 | 11·00 |

**742** Figurehead, Sao Francisco River

**1972.** Brazilian Folklore. Multicoloured.

| | | | |
|---|---|---|---|
| 1371 | 45c. Type **742** | 2·10 | 85 |
| 1372 | 60c. Fandango, Rio Grande do Sul | 3·25 | 2·75 |
| 1373 | 75c. Capoeira (game), Bahia | 70 | 65 |
| 1374 | 1cr.15 Karaja statuette | 1·40 | 1·30 |
| 1375 | 1cr.30 "Bumba-Meu-Boi" (folk play) | 10·00 | 3·75 |

**743** "Institution of Brazilian Flag"

**1972.** 150th Anniv of Independence.

| | | | | |
|---|---|---|---|---|
| 1376 | **743** | 30c. green and yellow | 3·00 | 2·75 |
| 1377 | - | 70c. mauve and pink | 2·40 | 1·80 |
| 1378 | - | 1cr. red and brown | 14·50 | 2·75 |
| 1379 | - | 2cr. black and brown | 7·50 | 2·75 |
| 1380 | - | 3cr.50 black and grey | 14·00 | 7·00 |

DESIGNS—HORIZ: 70c. "Proclamation of Emperor Pedro I" (lithograph after Debret); 2cr. Commemorative gold coin of Pedro I; 3cr.50, Declaration of Ypiranga monument. VERT: 1cr. "Emperor Pedro I" (H. J. da Silva).

**744** Numeral and P.T.T. Symbol **745** Scroll

**1972**

| | | | | |
|---|---|---|---|---|
| 1383 | **744** | 5c. orange | 55 | 20 |
| 1384 | **744** | 10c. brown | 80 | 20 |
| 1394 | **744** | 15c. blue | 45 | 10 |
| 1385 | **744** | 20c. blue | 80 | 20 |
| 1396 | **744** | 25c. brown | 55 | 30 |
| 1386 | **744** | 30c. red | 90 | 20 |
| 1387 | **744** | 40c. green | 45 | 20 |
| 1388 | **744** | 50c. green | 70 | 20 |
| 1398 | **744** | 70c. purple | 70 | 10 |
| 1389 | **745** | 1cr. purple | 1·00 | 20 |
| 1390 | **745** | 2cr. blue | 1·60 | 20 |
| 1391 | **745** | 4cr. orange and lilac | 3·50 | 20 |
| 1392 | **745** | 5cr. brown, cinnamon and red | 5·25 | 20 |
| 1393 | **745** | 10cr. green, brown & blk | 11·00 | 65 |

Nos. 1392/3 have a background of multiple P.T.T. symbols.

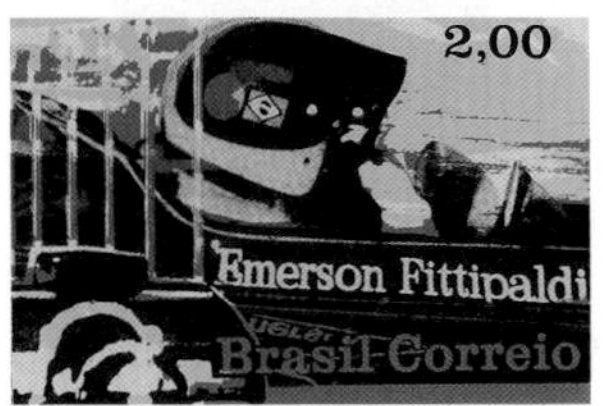


**746** Fittipaldi in Racing Car

**1972.** Emerson Fittipaldi's Victory in Formula 1 World Motor-racing Championship. Sheet 122×87 mm.

| | | | |
|---|---|---|---|
| **MS**1411 **746** 2cr. multicoloured | 22·00 | 25·00 |

**747** Writing Hand and People ("Mobral" Literacy Campaign)

**1972.** Social Development. Multicoloured.

| | | | |
|---|---|---|---|
| 1412 | 10c. Type **747** | 45 | 55 |
| 1413 | 20c. Graph and people (National Census Cent) | 2·50 | 1·70 |
| 1414 | 1cr. House in hand (Pension Fund system) | 17·00 | 65 |
| 1415 | 2cr. Workers and factory (Gross National Product) | 4·75 | 1·70 |

**748** Legislative Building, Brasilia

**1972.** National Congress Building, Brasilia.

| | | | | |
|---|---|---|---|---|
| 1416 | **748** | 1cr. black, orange & bl | 20·00 | 11·00 |

**749** Pottery Crib

**1972.** Christmas.

| | | | | |
|---|---|---|---|---|
| 1417 | **749** | 20c. black and brown | 2·10 | 1·20 |

**750** Farm-worker and Pension Book (Rural Social Security Scheme)

**1972.** Government Services.

| | | | | |
|---|---|---|---|---|
| 1418 | **750** | 10c. black, orange & bl | 1·30 | 1·20 |
| 1419 | - | 10c. multicoloured | 2·50 | 2·30 |
| 1420 | - | 70c. black, brown & red | 18·00 | 7·00 |
| 1421 | - | 2cr. multicoloured | 29·00 | 12·50 |

DESIGNS—VERT: 70c. Dr. Oswald Cruz, public health pioneer (birth cent.). HORIZ: 10c. (No. 1419), Children and traffic lights (Transport system development); 2cr. Bull, fish and produce (Agricultural exports).

**751** Brazilian Expeditionary Force Monument

**1972.** Armed Forces' Day.

| | | | | |
|---|---|---|---|---|
| 1422 | **751** | 10c. black, purple & brn | 3·75 | 2·50 |
| 1423 | - | 30c. multicoloured | 3·75 | 2·50 |
| 1424 | - | 30c. multicoloured | 3·75 | 2·50 |
| 1425 | - | 30c. black, brn & lilac | 3·75 | 2·50 |

DESIGNS: No. 1423, Sail-training ship (Navy); No. 1424, Trooper (Army); No. 1425, Dassault Mirage IIIC jet fighter (Air Force).

GUM. All the following issues are with gum, except where otherwise stated.

**752** Emblem and Cogwheels

**1973.** 50th Anniv of Rotary in Brazil.

| | | | | |
|---|---|---|---|---|
| 1426 | **752** | 1cr. blue, lt blue & yell | 4·00 | 3·50 |

**753** Swimming

**1973.** Sporting Events.

| | | | | |
|---|---|---|---|---|
| 1427 | **753** | 40c. brown and blue | 80 | 75 |
| 1428 | - | 40c. red and green | 5·50 | 2·10 |
| 1429 | - | 40c. brown and purple | 1·70 | 1·60 |

DESIGNS AND EVENTS—HORIZ: No. 1427, ("Latin Cup" Swimming Championships); No. 1428, Gymnast (Olympic Festival of Gymnastics, Rio de Janeiro). VERT: No. 1429, Volleyball player (Internation Volleyball Championships, Rio de Janeiro).

**754** Paraguayan Flag

**1973.** Visit of Pres. Stroessner of Paraguay.

| | | | | |
|---|---|---|---|---|
| 1430 | **754** | 70c. multicoloured | 4·00 | 2·75 |

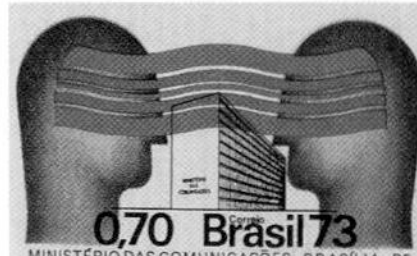


**755** "Communications"

**1973.** Inauguration of Ministry of Communications Building, Brasilia.

| | | | | |
|---|---|---|---|---|
| 1431 | **755** | 70c. multicoloured | 1·90 | 1·60 |

**756** Neptune and Map

**1973.** Inauguration of "Bracan I" Underwater Cable, Recife to Canary Islands.

| | | | | |
|---|---|---|---|---|
| 1432 | **756** | 1cr. multicoloured | 9·75 | 7·00 |

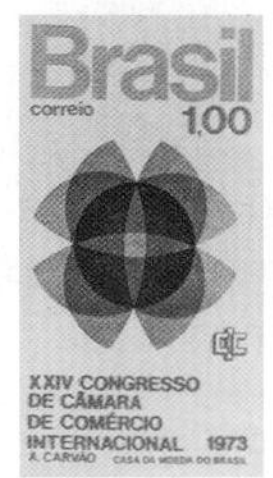


**757** Congress Emblem

**1973.** 24th Int Chamber of Commerce Congress.

| | | | | |
|---|---|---|---|---|
| 1433 | **757** | 1cr. purple and orange | 9·50 | 7·00 |

**758** Swallow-tailed Manakin and "Acacia decurrens"

**1973.** Tropical Birds and Plants. Mult.

| | | | |
|---|---|---|---|
| 1434 | 20c. Type **758** | 2·75 | 75 |
| 1435 | 20c. Troupial and "Cereus peruvianus" | 2·75 | 75 |
| 1436 | 20c. Brazilian ruby and "Tecoma umbellata" | 2·75 | 75 |

**759** "Tourism"

**1973.** National Tourism Year.

| | | | | |
|---|---|---|---|---|
| 1437 | **759** | 70c. multicoloured | 2·50 | 1·90 |

**760** "Caboclo" Festival Cart

**1973.** Anniversaries. Multicoloured.

| | | | |
|---|---|---|---|
| 1438 | 20c. Type **760** | 1·80 | 75 |
| 1439 | 20c. Arariboia (Indian chief) | 1·80 | 75 |
| 1440 | 20c. Convention delegates | 1·80 | 75 |
| 1441 | 20c. "The Graciosa Road" | 1·80 | 75 |

EVENTS: No. 1438, 150th anniv of Liberation Day; 1439, 400th anniv of Niteroi; 1440, Cent of Itu Convention; 1441, Cent of Nhundiaquara highway.

**761** "Institute of Space Research"

**1973.** Scientific Research Institute. Mult.

| | | | |
|---|---|---|---|
| 1442 | 20c. Type **761** | 90 | 65 |
| 1443 | 70c. "Federal Engineering School", Itajuba | 6·25 | 2·30 |
| 1444 | 1cr. "Institute for Pure and Applied Mechanics" | 8·00 | 2·30 |

**762** Santos Dumont and Biplane "14 bis"

**1973.** Birth Centenary of Alberto Santos Dumont (aviation pioneer).

| | | | | |
|---|---|---|---|---|
| 1445 | **762** | 20c. brown, grn & lt grn | 2·20 | 55 |
| 1446 | - | 70c. brown, red & yellow | 4·50 | 2·75 |
| 1447 | - | 2cr. brown, ultram & bl | 5·25 | 2·75 |

DESIGNS: 70c. Airship "Ballon No. 6"; 2cr. Monoplane No. 20 "Demoiselle".

**763** Map of the World

**1973.** Stamp Day.

| | | | | |
|---|---|---|---|---|
| 1448 | **763** | 40c. black and red | 5·75 | 4·75 |
| 1449 | - | 40c. black and red | 5·75 | 4·75 |

The design of No. 1449 differs from Type **763** in that the red portion is to the top and right, instead of to the top and left.

**764** G. Dias

**1973.** 150th Birth Anniv of Goncalves Dias (poet).

| | | | | |
|---|---|---|---|---|
| 1450 | **764** | 40c. black and violet | 2·10 | 85 |

See also Nos. 1459 and 1477.

**765** Copernicus and "Sun-god"

**1973.** 500th Anniv of Nicholas Copernicus (astronomer). Sheet 125×87 mm.

| | | | |
|---|---|---|---|
| **MS**1451 **765** 1cr. multicoloured | 14·00 | 13·00 |

**766** Festival Banner

**1973.** National Folklore Festival.

| | | | | |
|---|---|---|---|---|
| 1452 | **766** | 40c. multicoloured | 2·10 | 1·20 |

**767** Masonic Emblems

**1973.** 150th Anniv of Masonic Grand Orient Lodge of Brazil.

| | | | | |
|---|---|---|---|---|
| 1453 | **767** | 1cr. blue | 6·75 | 4·25 |

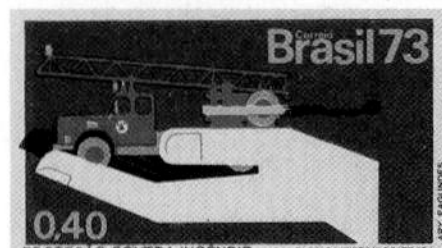

**768** Fire Protection

**1973.** National Protection Campaign. Mult.

| | | | |
|---|---|---|---|
| 1454 | 40c. Type **768** | 1·80 | 85 |
| 1455 | 40c. Cross and cornice (cultural protection) | 1·80 | 85 |
| 1456 | 40c. Winged emblem (protection in flight) | 1·80 | 85 |
| 1457 | 40c. Leaf (protection of nature) | 1·80 | 85 |

**769** St. Gabriel and Papal Bull

**1973.** 1st National Exhibition of Religious Philately, Rio de Janeiro. Sheet 125×87 mm.

| | | | |
|---|---|---|---|
| **MS**1458 **769** | 1cr. black and ochre | 17·00 | 18·00 |

**1973.** Birth Centenary of St. Theresa of Lisieux. As T 764.

| | | | |
|---|---|---|---|
| 1459 | 2cr. brown and orange | 8·50 | 5·75 |

DESIGN: Portrait of St. Theresa.

**770** M. Lobato and "Emilia"

**1973.** Monteiro Lobato's Children's Stories. Multicoloured.

| | | | |
|---|---|---|---|
| 1460 | 40c. Type **770** | 1·90 | 1·20 |
| 1461 | 40c. "Aunt Nastasia" | 1·90 | 1·20 |
| 1462 | 40c. "Nazarinho", "Pedrinho" and "Quindim" | 1·90 | 1·20 |
| 1463 | 40c. "Visconde de Sabugosa" | 1·90 | 1·20 |
| 1464 | 40c. "Dona Benta" | 1·90 | 1·20 |

**771** Father J. M. Nunes Garcia

**1973.** "The Baroque Age". Multicoloured.

| | | | |
|---|---|---|---|
| 1465 | 40c. Wood carving, Church of St. Francia, Bahia | 70 | 65 |
| 1466 | 40c. "Prophet Isaiah" (detail, sculpture by Aleijadinho) | 70 | 65 |
| 1467 | 70c. Type **771** | 3·75 | 3·25 |
| 1468 | 1cr. Portal, Church of Conceicao da Praia | 16·00 | 7·00 |
| 1469 | 2cr. "Glorification of Holy Virgin", ceiling, St. Francis Assisi Church, Ouro Preto | 8·50 | 7·00 |

**772** Early Telephone and Modern Instruments

**1973.** 50th Anniv of Brazilian Telephone Company.

| | | | |
|---|---|---|---|
| 1470 **772** | 40c. multicoloured | 80 | 65 |

**773** "Angel" (J. Kopke)

**1973.** Christmas.

| | | | |
|---|---|---|---|
| 1471 **773** | 40c. multicoloured | 80 | 65 |

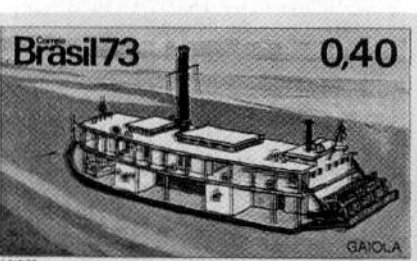

**774** "Gailora" (river steamboat)

**1973.** Brazilian Boats. Multicoloured.

| | | | |
|---|---|---|---|
| 1472 | 40c. Type **774** | 80 | 65 |
| 1473 | 70c. "Regatao" (river trading boat) | 2·75 | 2·50 |
| 1474 | 1cr. "Jangada" (coastal raft) | 9·75 | 4·50 |
| 1475 | 2cr. "Saveiro" (passenger boat) | 9·75 | 4·50 |

**775** Scales of Justice

**1973.** Judiciary Power.

| | | | |
|---|---|---|---|
| 1476 **775** | 40c. violet and mauve | 1·40 | 65 |

**1973.** Birth Centenary of Placido de Castro. As T 764.

| | | | |
|---|---|---|---|
| 1477 | 40c. black and red | 1·70 | 85 |

DESIGN: Portrait of Castro.

**776** Scarlet Ibis and "Victoria Regia" Lilies

**1973.** Brazilian Flora and Fauna. Mult.

| | | | |
|---|---|---|---|
| 1478 | 40c. Type **776** | 2·50 | 45 |
| 1479 | 70c. Jaguar and Indian tulip | 7·50 | 3·75 |
| 1480 | 1cr. Scarlet macaw and palm | 9·75 | 45 |
| 1481 | 2cr. Greater rhea and mulunga plant | 16·00 | 6·00 |

**777** Saci Perere (goblin)

**1974.** Brazilian Folk Tales. Multicoloured.

| | | | |
|---|---|---|---|
| 1482 | 40c. Type **777** | 90 | 55 |
| 1483 | 80c. Zumbi (warrior) | 1·80 | 1·30 |
| 1484 | 1cr. Chico Rei (African king) | 4·00 | 1·10 |
| 1485 | 1cr.30 Little black boy of the pasture (32×33 mm) | 6·25 | 1·90 |
| 1486 | 2cr.50 Iara, queen of the waters (32×33 mm) | 21·00 | 5·75 |

**778** View of Bridge

**1974.** Inauguration of President Costa e Silva (Rio de Janeiro–Niteroi) Bridge.

| | | | |
|---|---|---|---|
| 1487 **778** | 40c. multicoloured | 1·70 | 65 |

**779** "Press"

**1974.** Brazilian Communications Pioneers.

| | | | |
|---|---|---|---|
| 1488 **779** | 40c. red, blue & bistre | 1·10 | 65 |
| 1489 - | 40c. brown, blue & bistre | 1·10 | 65 |
| 1490 - | 40c. blue, pink & brown | 1·10 | 65 |

DESIGNS AND EVENTS: No. 1488, Birth bicentenary of Hipolito da Costa (founder of newspaper "Correio Braziliense", 1808); 1489, "Radio waves" (Edgar R. Pinto, founder of Radio Sociedade do Rio de Janeiro, 1923); 1490, "Television screen" (F. de Assis Chateaubriand, founder of first T.V. station, Sao Paulo, 1950).

**780** "Construction"

**1974.** 10th Anniv of March Revolution.

| | | | |
|---|---|---|---|
| 1491 **780** | 40c. multicoloured | 1·70 | 95 |

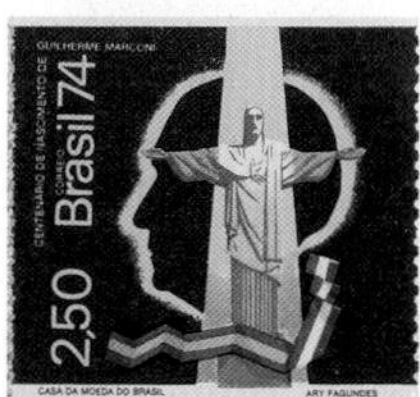

**781** Christ of the Andes

**1974.** Birth Cent of G. Marconi (radio pioneer).

| | | | |
|---|---|---|---|
| 1492 **781** | 2cr.50 multicoloured | 11·50 | 6·50 |

**782** Heads of Three Races

**1974.** Ethnical Origins and Immigration. Mult.

| | | | |
|---|---|---|---|
| 1493 | 40c. Type **782** | 80 | 65 |
| 1494 | 40c. Heads of many races | 45 | 45 |
| 1495 | 2cr.50 German immigration | 8·50 | 3·50 |
| 1496 | 2cr.50 Italian immigration | 12·50 | 3·50 |
| 1497 | 2cr.50 Japanese immigration | 3·00 | 2·10 |

**783** Artwork and Stamp-printing Press

**1974.** State Mint.

| | | | |
|---|---|---|---|
| 1498 **783** | 80c. multicoloured | 2·50 | 45 |

**784** Sete Cidades National Park

**1974.** Tourism. Multicoloured.

| | | | |
|---|---|---|---|
| 1499 | 40c. Type **784** | 1·80 | 1·20 |
| 1500 | 80c. Ruins of church of St. Michael of the Missions | 1·80 | 1·20 |

**785** Footballer

**1974.** World Cup Football Championship, West Germany. Sheet 125×87 mm.

| | | | |
|---|---|---|---|
| **MS**1501 **785** | 2cr.50 multicoloured | 9·75 | 9·75 |

See also No. 1506.

**786** Caraca College

**1974.** Bicentenary of Caraca College.

| | | | |
|---|---|---|---|
| 1502 **786** | 40c. multicoloured | 1·30 | 85 |

**787** Wave Pattern

**1974.** 3rd Brazilian Telecommunications Congress, Brasilia.

| | | | |
|---|---|---|---|
| 1503 **787** | 40c. black and blue | 70 | 65 |

**788** Fernao Dias Paes

**1974.** 300th Anniv of Paes Expedition.

| | | | |
|---|---|---|---|
| 1504 **788** | 20c. multicoloured | 70 | 65 |

**1974.** Visit of President Alvarez of Mexico. As T 754. Multicoloured.

| | | | |
|---|---|---|---|
| 1505 | 80c. Mexican Flag | 6·25 | 2·30 |

**789** Flags and Crowd in Stadium

**1974.** World Cup Football Championship, West Germany (2nd issue).

| | | | |
|---|---|---|---|
| 1506 **789** | 40c. multicoloured | 1·30 | 1·20 |

**790** Braille "Eye" and Emblem

**1974.** 5th General Assembly of World Council for Welfare of the Blind. Sheet 127×90 mm.

| | | | |
|---|---|---|---|
| **MS**1507 **790** | 1cr.30 multicoloured | 2·30 | 3·25 |

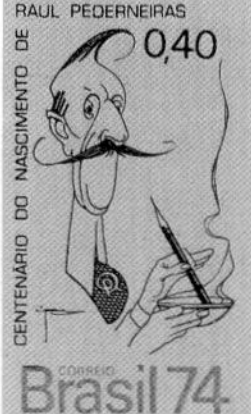

**791** Pederneiras (after J. Carlos)

**1974.** Birth Centenary of Raul Pederneiras (lawyer, author and artist).

1508 **791** 40c. black & yell on brn 70 65

**792** Emblem and Seascape

**1974.** 13th Int Union of Building Societies and Savings Associations Congress, Rio de Janeiro.

1509 **792** 1cr.30 multicoloured 3·50 2·00

**793** "Five Women of Guaratingueta" (E di Cavalcanti)

**1974.** Lubrapex 74 Stamp Exhibition, Sao Paulo (1st issue). Sheet 87×126 mm.

**MS**1510 **793** 2cr. multicoloured 6·75 10·50

See also No. 1522.

**794** "UPU" on World Map

**1974.** Centenary of UPU.

1511 **794** 2cr.50 black and blue 11·50 3·75

**795** Aruak Hammock

**1974.** "Popular Culture".

| | | | | |
|---|---|---|---|---|
| 1512 | **795** | 50c. purple | 4·50 | 85 |
| 1513 | - | 50c. light blue and blue | 5·75 | 85 |
| 1514 | - | 50c. brown, red & yellow | 1·40 | 85 |
| 1515 | - | 50c. brown and yellow | 1·80 | 85 |

DESIGNS—SQUARE: No. 1513, Bilro Lace. VERT: (24×37 mm), No. 1514, Guitar player (folk literature); 1515, Horseman (statuette by Vitalino).

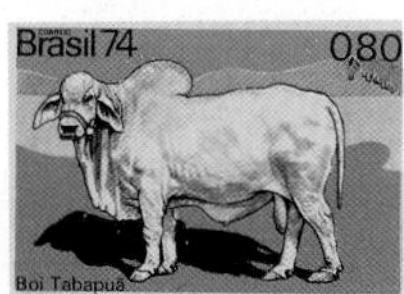


**796** Coffee Beans

**1974.** Bicentenary of City of Campinas.

1516 **796** 50c. multicoloured 2·30 1·30

**797** Hornless Tabapua

**1974.** Domestic Animals. Multicoloured.

| | | | |
|---|---|---|---|
| 1517 | 80c. Type **797** | 2·50 | 1·50 |
| 1518 | 1cr.30 Creole horse | 2·40 | 1·50 |
| 1519 | 2cr.50 Brazilian mastiff | 16·00 | 4·50 |

**798** Ilha Solteira Dam

**1974.** Ilha Solteira Hydro-electric Power Project.

1520 **798** 50c. brown, grey & yell 3·50 1·20

**799** Herald Angel

**1974.** Christmas.

1521 **799** 50c. multicoloured 1·70 65

**800** "The Girls" (Carlos Reis)

**1974.** "Lubrapex 74" Stamp Exhibition, Sao Paulo (2nd issue).

1522 **800** 1cr.30 multicoloured 1·70 1·20

**801** "Justice for Juveniles"

**1974.** 50th Anniv of Brazilian Juvenile Court.

1523 **801** 90c. multicoloured 70 65

**802** Athlete

**1974.** 50th Anniv of Sao Silvestre Long-distance Race.

1524 **802** 3cr.30 multicoloured 1·80 1·70

**803** Mounted Newsvendor and Newspaper Masthead

**1975.** Cent of Newspaper "O Estado de S. Paulo".

1525 **803** 50c. multicoloured 3·00 1·70

**804** Industrial Complex, Sao Paulo

**1975.** Economic Resources.

| | | | | |
|---|---|---|---|---|
| 1526 | **804** | 50c. yellow and blue | 3·25 | 85 |
| 1527 | - | 1cr.40 yellow & brown | 1·40 | 85 |
| 1528 | - | 4cr.50 yellow & black | 11·00 | 85 |

DESIGNS: 1cr.40 Rubber industry, Acre; 4cr.50, Manganese industry, Amapa.

**805** Santa Cruz Fortress, Rio de Janeiro

**1975.** Colonial Forts. Each brown on yellow.

| | | | |
|---|---|---|---|
| 1529 | 50c. Type **805** | 70 | 45 |
| 1530 | 50c. Reis Magos Fort, Rio Grande do Norte | 1·30 | 55 |
| 1531 | 50c. Monte Serrat Fort, Bahia | 2·30 | 55 |
| 1532 | 90c. Nossa Senhora dos Remedios Fort, Fernando de Noronha | 70 | 45 |

**806** "Palafita" House, Amazonas

**1975.** Brazilian Architecture. Multicoloured.

| | | | |
|---|---|---|---|
| 1533 | 50c. Modern Architecture, Brasilia | 2·75 | 2·50 |
| 1534 | 50c. Modern Architecture, Brasilia (yellow line at left) | 19·00 | 11·50 |
| 1535 | 1cr. Type **806** | 1·90 | 45 |
| 1536 | 1cr.40 Indian hut, Rondonia (yellow line at left) | 4·25 | 4·00 |
| 1537 | 1cr.40 As No. 1536 but yellow line at right | 1·10 | 1·00 |
| 1538 | 3cr.30 "Enxaimel" house, Santa Catarina (yellow line at right) | 1·80 | 1·70 |
| 1539 | 3cr.30 As No. 1538 but yellow line at left | 8·00 | 7·50 |

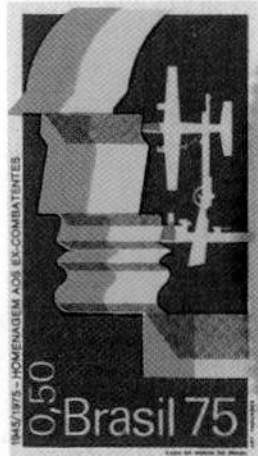


**807** Oscar ("Astronotus ocellatus")

**1975.** Freshwater Fishes. Multicoloured.

| | | | |
|---|---|---|---|
| 1540 | 50c. Type **807** | 3·75 | 45 |
| 1541 | 50c. South American pufferfish ("Colomesus psitacus") | 90 | 85 |
| 1542 | 50c. Tail-spot livebearer ("Phallocerus caudimaculatus") | 90 | 85 |
| 1543 | 50c. Red discus ("Symphysodon discus") | 1·40 | 55 |

**808** Flags forming Serviceman's Head

**1975.** Honouring Ex-Servicemen of Second World War.

1544 **808** 50c. multicoloured 90 65

**809** Brazilian Pines

**1975.** Fauna and Flora Preservation. Mult.

| | | | |
|---|---|---|---|
| 1545 | 70c. Type **809** | 4·00 | 75 |
| 1546 | 1cr. Giant otter (vert) | 2·50 | 1·10 |
| 1547 | 3cr.30 Marsh cayman | 2·50 | 1·10 |

**810** Inga Carved Stone, from Paraiba

**1975.** Archaeology. Multicoloured.

| | | | |
|---|---|---|---|
| 1548 | 70c. Type **810** | 1·40 | 85 |
| 1549 | 1cr. Marajoara pot from Para | 80 | 75 |
| 1550 | 1cr. Fossilized garfish from Ceara (horiz) | 80 | 75 |

**811** Statue of the Virgin Mary

**1975.** Holy Year. 300th Anniv of Franciscan Province of Our Lady of the Immaculate Conception.

1551 **811** 3cr.30 multicoloured 2·50 1·60

**812** Ministry of Communications Building, Rio de Janeiro

**1975.** Stamp Day.

1552 **812** 70c. red 1·70 65

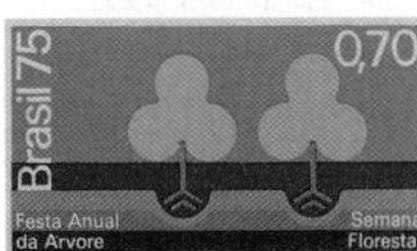


**813** "Congada" Sword Dance, Minas Gerais

**1975.** Folk Dances. Multicoloured.

| | | | |
|---|---|---|---|
| 1553 | 70c. Type **813** | 90 | 75 |
| 1554 | 70c. "Frevo" umbrella dance, Pernambuco | 90 | 75 |
| 1555 | 70c. "Warrior" dance, Alagoas | 90 | 75 |



**814** Stylized Trees

**1975.** Tree Festival.

1556 **814** 70c. multicoloured 70 55

**815** Dish Aerial and Globe

**1975.** Inauguration of Tangua Satellite Telecommunications Station.

1557 **815** 3cr.30 multicoloured 1·70 1·60

**816** Woman holding Globe

**1975.** International Women's Year.
1558 **816** 3cr.30 multicoloured 2·50 1·40

**817** Tile, Balcony Rail and Memorial Column, Alcantara

**1975.** Historic Towns. Multicoloured.
1559 70c. Type **817** 1·50 95
1560 70c. Belfry, weather vane and jug, Goias (26×38 mm) 1·50 95
1561 70c. Sao Francisco Convent, Sao Cristovao (40×22 mm) 1·50 95

**818** Crowd welcoming Walking Book

**1975.** Day of the Book.
1562 **818** 70c. multicoloured 55 55

**819** ASTA Emblem and Arrows

**1975.** 45th American Society of Travel Agents Congress.
1563 **819** 70c. multicoloured 55 55

**820** Two Angels

**1975.** Christmas.
1564 **820** 70c. brown and red 55 45

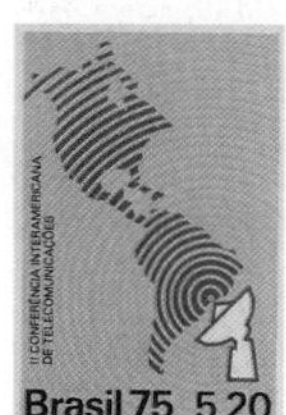


**821** Aerial, and Map of America

**1975.** 2nd International Telecommunications Conference, Rio de Janeiro.
1565 **821** 5cr.20 multicoloured 7·50 4·50

**822** Friar Nicodemus

**1975.** Obligatory Tax. Leprosy Research Fund.
1566 **822** 10c. brown 35 30

**823** People in front of Cross

**1975.** Thanksgiving Day.
1567 **823** 70c. turquoise and blue 90 85

**824** Emperor Pedro II in Naval Uniform (after P. P. da Silva Manuel)

**1975.** 150th Birth Anniv of Emperor Pedro II.
1568 **824** 70c. brown 2·10 95

**825** Sal Stone Beach, Piaui

**1975.** Tourism. Multicoloured.
1569 70c. Type **825** 70 65
1570 70c. Guarapari Beach, Espirito Santo 70 65
1571 70c. Torres Cliffs Rio Grande do Sul 70 65

**826** Triple Jump

**1975.** 7th Pan-American Games, Santo Domingo, Dominican Republic.
1572 **826** 1cr.60 turquoise & black 70 65

**827** UN Emblem and HQ Building, New York

**1975.** 30th Anniv of United Nations.
1573 **827** 1cr.30 violet on blue 55 55

**828** Light Bulbs and House

**1976.** "Preservation of Fuel Resources". Mult.
1574 70c. Type **828** 70 45
1575 70c. Drops of petrol and car 70 45

**829** Concorde

**1976.** Concorde's First Commercial Flight, Paris–Rio de Janeiro.
1576 **829** 5cr.20 black and grey 1·30 75

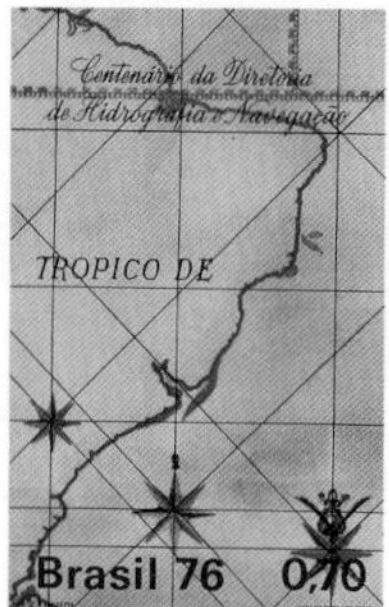


**830** Pinheiro's Nautical Map of 1776

**1976.** Cent of Hydrographical and Navigational Directorate. Sheet 88×124 mm.
**MS**1577 **830** 70c. multicoloured 2·75 2·75

**831** Early and Modern Telephone Equipment

**1976.** Telephone Centenary.
1578 **831** 5cr.20 black & orange 1·90 1·20

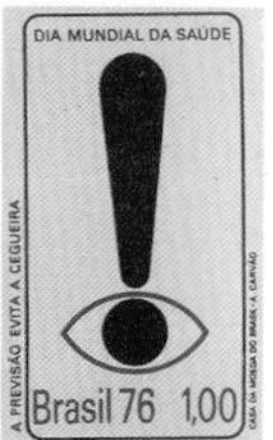


**832** "Eye"-part of Exclamation Mark

**1976.** World Health Day.
1579 **832** 1cr. red, brown & violet 1·30 1·20

**833** Kaiapo Body-painting

**1976.** Brazil's Indigenous Culture. Mult.
1580 1cr. Type **833** 45 30
1581 1cr. Bakairi ceremonial mask 45 30
1582 1cr. Karaja feather head-dress 45 30

**834** Itamaraty Palace, Brasilia

**1976.** Diplomats' Day.
1583 **834** 1cr. multicoloured 1·90 1·40

**835** "The Sprinkler" (3D composition by J. Tarcisio)

**1976.** Modern Brazilian Art. Multicoloured.
1584 1cr. Type **835** 55 45
1585 1cr. "Beribboned Fingers" (P. Checcacci) (horiz) 55 45

**836** Basketball

**1976.** Olympic Games, Montreal.
1586 **836** 1cr. black and green 45 45
1587 - 1cr.40 black and blue 45 45
1588 - 5cr.20 black and orange 1·60 1·30
DESIGNS: 1cr.40, Olympic yachts; 5cr.20, Judo.

**837** Golden Lion-Tamarin

**1976.** Nature Protection. Multicoloured.
1589 1cr. Type **837** 1·40 45
1590 1cr. Orchid ("Acacallis cyanea") 1·40 45

**838** Cine Camera on Screen

**1976.** Brazilian Cinematograph Industry.
1591 **838** 1cr. multicoloured 55 55

**839** Ox-cart Driver

**1976**

| | | | | |
|---|---|---|---|---|
| 1592 | **839** | 10c. red | 45 | 20 |
| 1593 | - | 15c. brown | 70 | 30 |
| 1594 | - | 20c. blue | 45 | 10 |
| 1595 | - | 30c. red | 45 | 10 |
| 1596 | - | 40c. orange | 55 | 20 |
| 1597a | - | 50c. brown | 45 | 20 |
| 1598 | - | 70c. black | 55 | 20 |
| 1599 | - | 80c. green | 1·90 | 30 |
| 1600a | - | 1cr. black | 45 | 20 |
| 1601 | - | 1cr.10 purple | 45 | 10 |
| 1602 | - | 1cr.30 red | 55 | 10 |
| 1603a | - | 1cr.80 violet | 55 | 20 |
| 1604a | - | 2cr. brown | 1·10 | 30 |
| 1605 | - | 2cr.50 brown | 55 | 20 |
| 1605a | - | 3cr.20 blue | 55 | 20 |
| 1606a | - | 5cr. lilac | 4·50 | 55 |
| 1607 | - | 7cr. violet | 8·00 | 30 |
| 1608a | - | 10cr. green | 4·50 | 55 |
| 1609 | - | 15cr. green | 2·75 | 30 |
| 1610 | - | 20cr. blue | 6·75 | 30 |
| 1611 | - | 21cr. purple | 1·60 | 30 |
| 1612 | - | 27cr. brown | 1·60 | 55 |

DESIGNS—HORIZ: 20c. Pirogue fisherman; 40c. Cowboy; 3cr.20, Sao Francisco boatman; 27cr. Muleteer. VERT: 15c. Bahia woman; 30c. Rubber gatherer; 50c. Gaucho; 70c. Women breaking Babacu chestnuts; 80c. Gold-washer; 1cr. Banana gatherer; 1cr.10, Grape harvester; 1cr.30, Coffee harvester; 1cr.80, Carnauba cutter; 2cr. Potter; 2cr.50, Basket maker; 5cr. Sugar-cane cutter; 7cr. Salt worker; 10cr. Fisherman; 15cr. Coconut vendor; 20cr. Lace maker; 21cr. Ramie cutter.

**840** Neon Tetra ("Paracheirodon innesi")

**1976.** Brazilian Freshwater Fishes. Mult.

| | | | | |
|---|---|---|---|---|
| 1613 | 1cr. Type **840** | | 1·40 | 85 |
| 1614 | 1cr. Splash tetra ("Copeina arnold") | | 1·40 | 85 |
| 1615 | 1cr. Prochilodus ("Prochilodus insignis") | | 1·40 | 85 |
| 1616 | 1cr. Spotted pike cichlid ("Crenicichla lepidota") | | 1·40 | 85 |
| 1617 | 1cr. Bottle-nosed catfish ("Ageneiosus sp.") | | 1·40 | 85 |
| 1618 | 1cr. Reticulated corydoras ("Corydoras reticulatus") | | 1·40 | 85 |

**841** Santa Marta Lighthouse

**1976.** 300th Anniv of Laguna.

| | | | | |
|---|---|---|---|---|
| 1619 | **841** | 1cr. blue | 45 | 20 |

**842** Postage Stamps as Magic Carpet

**1976.** Stamp Day.

| | | | | |
|---|---|---|---|---|
| 1620 | **842** | 1cr. multicoloured | 55 | 30 |

**843** Oil Lamp and Profile

**1976.** 50th Anniv of Brazilian Nursing Assn.

| | | | | |
|---|---|---|---|---|
| 1621 | **843** | 1cr. multicoloured | 55 | 30 |

**844** Puppet Soldier

**1976.** Mamulengo Puppet Theatre. Mult.

| | | | | |
|---|---|---|---|---|
| 1622 | 1cr. Type **844** | | 45 | 20 |
| 1623 | 1cr.30 Puppet girl | | 45 | 20 |
| 1624 | 1cr.60 Finger puppets (horiz) | | 45 | 20 |

**845** Winner's Medal

**1976.** 27th International Military Athletics Championships, Rio de Janeiro.

| | | | | |
|---|---|---|---|---|
| 1625 | **845** | 5cr.20 multicoloured | 1·70 | 1·20 |

**846** Family within "House"

**1976.** SESC and SENAC National Organizations for Appenticeship and Welfare.

| | | | | |
|---|---|---|---|---|
| 1626 | **846** | 1cr. blue | 55 | 20 |

**847** Rotten Tree

**1976.** Conservation of the Environment.

| | | | | |
|---|---|---|---|---|
| 1627 | **847** | 1cr. multicoloured | 55 | 20 |

**848** Electron Orbits and Atomic Agency Emblem

**1976.** 20th International Atomic Energy Conference, Rio de Janeiro.

| | | | | |
|---|---|---|---|---|
| 1628 | **848** | 5cr.20 multicoloured | 1·70 | 1·20 |

**849** Underground Train

**1976.** Inauguration of Sao Paulo Underground Railway.

| | | | | |
|---|---|---|---|---|
| 1629 | **849** | 1cr.60 multicoloured | 80 | 30 |

**850** St. Francis

**1976.** 750th Death Anniv of St. Francis of Assisi.

| | | | | |
|---|---|---|---|---|
| 1630 | **850** | 5cr.20 multicoloured | 1·70 | 85 |

**851** School Building

**1976.** Centenary of Ouro Preto Mining School.

| | | | | |
|---|---|---|---|---|
| 1631 | **851** | 1cr. violet | 90 | 1·10 |

**852** "Three Kings" (J. A. da Silva)

**1976.** Christmas. Multicoloured.

| | | | | |
|---|---|---|---|---|
| 1632 | 80c. Type **852** | | 70 | 45 |
| 1633 | 80c. "Father Christmas" (T. Onivaldo Cogo) | | 70 | 45 |
| 1634 | 80c. "Nativity Scene" (R. Yabe) | | 70 | 45 |
| 1635 | 80c. "Angels" (E. Folchini) | | 70 | 45 |
| 1636 | 80c. "Nativity" (A.L. Cintra) | | 70 | 45 |

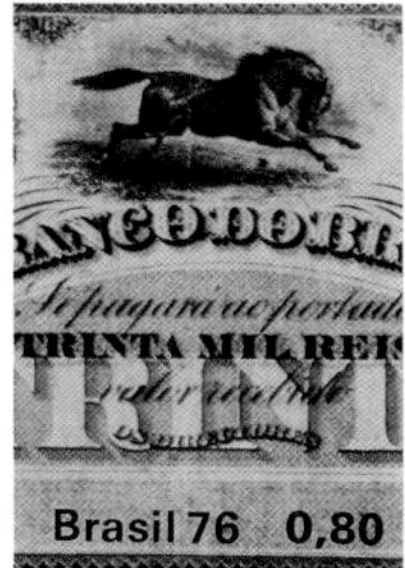

**853** Section of Brazilian 30,000-reis Banknote

**1976.** Opening of Bank of Brazil's Thousandth Branch at Barra do Bugres. Sheet 125×88 mm.

| | | | | |
|---|---|---|---|---|
| MS1637 | **853** | 80c. multicoloured | 1·70 | 2·75 |

**854** "Our Lady of Monte Serrat" (Friar A. da Piedade)

**1976.** Brazilian Sculpture. Multicoloured.

| | | | | |
|---|---|---|---|---|
| 1638 | 80c. Type **854** | | 45 | 45 |
| 1639 | 5cr. "St. Joseph" (unknown artist) (25×37 mm) | | 1·60 | 85 |
| 1640 | 5cr.60 "The Dance" (J. Bernardelli) (square) | | 1·60 | 85 |
| 1641 | 6cr.50 "The Caravel" (B. Giorgi) (As 5cr.) | | 1·60 | 85 |

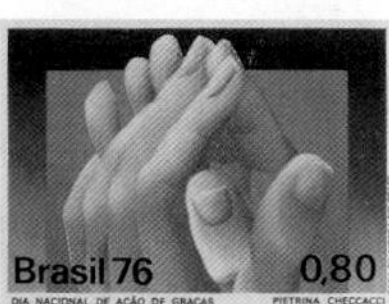

**855** Hands in Prayer

**1976.** Thanksgiving Day.

| | | | | |
|---|---|---|---|---|
| 1642 | **855** | 80c. multicoloured | 70 | 45 |

**856** Sailor of 1840

**1976.** Brazilian Navy Commemoration. Mult.

| | | | | |
|---|---|---|---|---|
| 1643 | 80c. Type **856** | | 70 | 30 |
| 1644 | 2cr. Marine of 1808 | | 90 | 55 |

**857** "Natural Resources"

**1976.** Brazilian Bureau of Standards.

| | | | | |
|---|---|---|---|---|
| 1645 | **857** | 80c. multicoloured | 55 | 30 |

**858** "Wheel of Life" (wood-carving, G. T. de Oliveira)

**1977.** 2nd World Black and African Festival of Arts and Culture, Lagos (Nigeria). Multicoloured.

| | | | | |
|---|---|---|---|---|
| 1646 | 5cr. Type **858** | | 1·40 | 75 |
| 1647 | 5cr.60 "The Beggar" (wood-carving, A. dos Santos) | | 1·40 | 75 |
| 1648 | 6cr.50 Benin pectoral mask | | 2·75 | 85 |

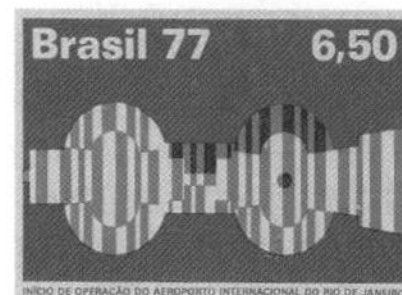

**859** Airport Layout

**1977.** Inauguration of Operation of International Airport, Rio de Janeiro.

| | | | | |
|---|---|---|---|---|
| 1649 | **859** | 6c.50 multicoloured | 2·10 | 1·40 |

**860** Seminar Emblem

**1977.** 6th InterAmerican Budget Seminar.

| | | | | |
|---|---|---|---|---|
| 1650 | **860** | 1cr.10 turq, bl & stone | 1·90 | 45 |

**861** Salicylic Acid Crystals

**1977.** World Rheumatism Year.

| | | | | |
|---|---|---|---|---|
| 1651 | **861** | 1cr.10 multicoloured | 70 | 30 |

**862** Emblem of Lions Clubs

**1977.** 25th Anniv of Brazilian Lions Clubs.

| | | | | |
|---|---|---|---|---|
| 1652 | **862** | 1cr.10 multicoloured | 70 | 30 |

**863** H. Villa-Lobos and Music

**1977.** Brazilian Composers. Multicoloured.

| | | | | |
|---|---|---|---|---|
| 1653 | 1cr.10 Type **863** | | 45 | 10 |
| 1654 | 1cr.10 Chiquinha Gonzaga and guitar | | 45 | 10 |
| 1655 | 1cr.10 Noel Rosa and guitar | | 45 | 10 |

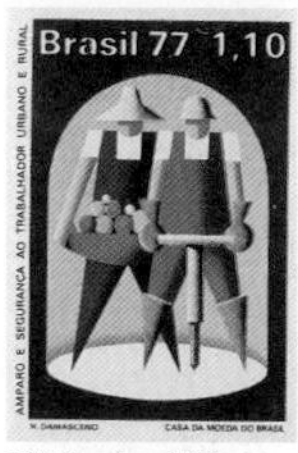

**864** Rural and Urban Workers

**1977.** Industrial Protection and Safety. Mult.

| | | | | |
|---|---|---|---|---|
| 1656 | 1cr.10 Type **864** | | 45 | 10 |
| 1657 | 1cr.10 Laboratory vessels | | 45 | 10 |

**865** Memorial, Porto Seguro

**1977.** Centenary of UPU Membership. Views of Porto Seguro. Multicoloured.

| | | | | |
|---|---|---|---|---|
| 1658 | 1cr.10 Type **865** | | 35 | 10 |
| 1659 | 5cr. Beach | | 2·75 | 65 |

1660 5cr.60 Old houses 1·50 65
1661 6cr.50 Post Office 2·00 65

**866** Newspaper Title in Linotype and Print

**1977.** 150th Anniv of Brazilian Newspaper "Diario de Porto Allegre".
1662 **866** 1cr.10 black & purple 55 30

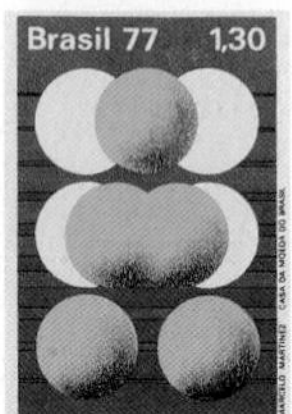


**867** Blue Whale

**1977.** Fauna Preservation.
1663 **867** 1cr.30 multicoloured 3·50 45

**868** "Cell System"

**1977.** 25th Anniv of National Economic Development Bank.
1664 **868** 1cr.30 multicoloured 55 30

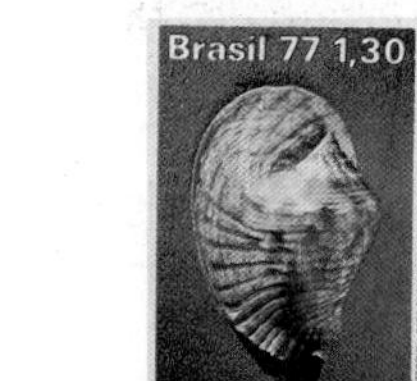


**869** Locomotive leaving Tunnel

**1977.** Centenary of Rio de Janeiro–Sao Paulo Railway.
1665 **869** 1c.30 black 1·10 45

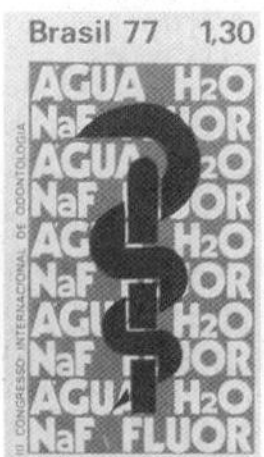


**870** Goliath Conch

**1977.** Brazilian Molluscs. Multicoloured.
1666 1cr.30 Type **870** 1·40 45
1667 1cr.30 Thin-bladed murex ("Murex tenuivaricosus") 1·40 45
1668 1cr.30 Helmet vase ("Vasum cassiforme") 1·40 45

**871** Caduceus

**1977.** 3rd International Congress of Odontology.
1669 **871** 1cr.30 brown, bis & orge 45 20

**872** Masonic Symbols

**1977.** 50th Anniv of Brazilian Grand Masonic Lodge.
1670 **872** 1cr.30 blue, dp bl & blk 55 30

**873** "Sailboat"

**1977.** Stamp Day.
1671 **873** 1cr.30 multicoloured 45 20

**874** Law Proclamation

**1977.** 150th Anniv of Juridical Courses.
1672 **874** 1cr.30 multicoloured 55 30

**875** "Cavalhada" (horsemen)

**1977.** Folklore. Multicoloured.
1673 1cr.30 Type **875** 45 20
1674 1cr.30 Horseman with flag 45 20
1675 1cr.30 Jousting (horiz) 45 20

**876** Doubloon

**1977.** Brazilian Colonial Coins. Multicoloured.
1676 1cr.30 Type **876** 45 20
1677 1cr.30 Pataca 45 20
1678 1cr.30 Vintem 45 20

**877** Toy Windmill

**1977.** National Day.
1679 **877** 1cr.30 multicoloured 55 30

**878** "Neoregelia carolinae"

**1977.** Nature Conservation.
1680 **878** 1cr.30 multicoloured 55 30

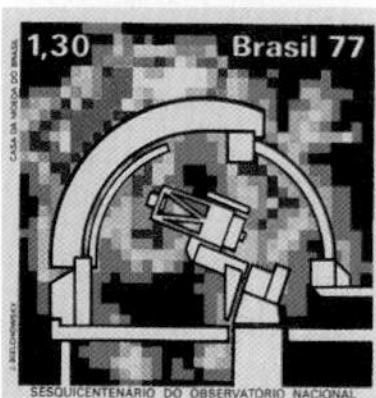


**879** Pen, Pencil and Writing

**1977.** 150th Anniv of Official Elementary Schooling.
1681 **879** 1cr.30 multicoloured 55 30

**880** Observatory and Electrochromograph of Supernova

**1977.** 150th Anniv of National Observatory.
1682 **880** 1cr.30 multicoloured 70 35

**881** Airship "Pax"

**1977.** Aviation Anniversaries. Multicoloured.
1683 1cr.30 Type **881** 80 55
1684 1cr.30 Savoia Marchetti flying boat "Jahu" 80 55

ANNIVERSARIES: No. 1683, 75th anniv of "Pax" flight; 1684, 50th anniv of "Jahu" South Atlantic crossing.

**882** Text from "O Guarani" and Ceci

**1977.** Day of the Book and Jose de Alencar Commemoration.
1685 **882** 1cr.30 multicoloured 55 20

**883** Radio Waves

**1977.** Amateur Radio Operators' Day.
1686 **883** 1cr.30 multicoloured 55 20

**884** Nativity (in carved gourd)

**1977.** Christmas. Multicoloured.
1687 1cr.30 Type **884** 55 20
1688 2cr. The Annunciation 70 30
1689 5cr. Nativity 1·50 45

**885** Emerald

**1977.** "Portucale 77" Thematic Stamp Exhibition. Multicoloured.
1690 1cr.30 Type **885** 70 45
1691 1cr.30 Topaz 70 45
1692 1cr.30 Aquamarine 70 45

**886** Angel holding Cornucopia

**1977.** Thanksgiving Day.
1693 **886** 1cr.30 multicoloured 55 30

**887** Curtiss Fledgling Douglas DC-3 and Badge (National Airmail Service)

**1977.** National Integration. Multicoloured.
1694 1cr.30 Type **887** 70 45
1695 1cr.30 Amazon River naval patrol boat and badge (Amazon Fleet) 70 45
1696 1cr.30 Train crossing bridge and badges (Engineering Corps and Railway Battalion) 70 45

**888** Douglas DC-10 and Varig Airline Emblems

**1977.** 50th Anniv of Varig State Airline.
1697 **888** 1cr.30 black, lt bl & bl 55 30

**889** Sts. Cosmus and Damian Church, Igaracu

**1977.** Regional Architecture, Churches. Mult.
1698 2cr.70 Type **889** 70 30
1699 7cr.50 St. Bento Monastery Church, Rio de Janeiro 2·10 75
1700 8cr.50 St. Francis Assisi Church, Ouro Preto 2·20 85
1701 9cr.50 St. Anthony Convent Church, Joao Pessoa 2·75 95

**890** Woman with Wheat Sheaf

**1977.** Diplomats' Day.
1702 **890** 1cr.30 multicoloured 55 30

**891** Scene from "Fosca" and Carlos Gomes (composer)

**1978.** Bicentenary of La Scala Opera House, Milan, and Carlos Gomes Commemoration.
1703 **891** 1cr.80 multicoloured 45 20

**892** Foot kicking Ball

**1978.** World Cup Football Championship, Argentina. Multicoloured.
1704 1cr.80 Type **892** 70 20
1705 1cr.80 Ball in net 70 20
1706 1cr.80 Stylized player with cup 70 20

**893** "Postal Efficiency"

**1978.** Postal Staff College.
1707 **893** 1cr.80 multicoloured 55 30

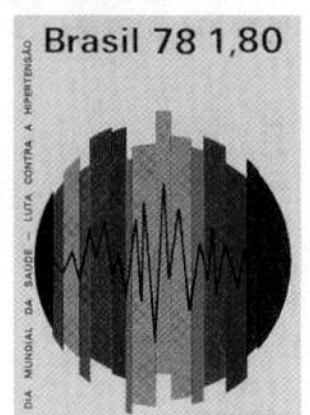


**894** Electrocardiogram

**1978.** World Hypertension Month.
1708 **894** 1cr.80 multicoloured 55 30

**895** World Map and Antenna

**1978.** World Telecommunications Day.
1709 **895** 1cr.80 multicoloured 55 30

**896** Saffron Finch

**1978.** Birds. Multicoloured.
1710 7cr.50 Type **896** 2·30 85
1711 8cr.50 Banded cotinga 2·40 1·10
1712 9cr.50 Seven-coloured tanager 2·75 1·30

**897** "Discussing the Opening Speech" (G. Mondin)

**1978.** 85th Anniv of Union Court of Audit.
1713 **897** 1cr.80 multicoloured 55 30

**898** Post and Telegraph Headquarters, Brasilia

**1978.** Opening of Post and Telegraph Headquarters.
1714 **898** 1cr.80 multicoloured 55 45

**1978.** Brapex III Third Brazilian Philatelic Exhibition. Sheet 70×90 mm.
**MS**1715 **898** 7cr. 50 multicoloured 2·30 3·25

**899** President Geisel

**1978.** President Geisel Commemoration.
1716 **899** 1cr.80 olive 55 30

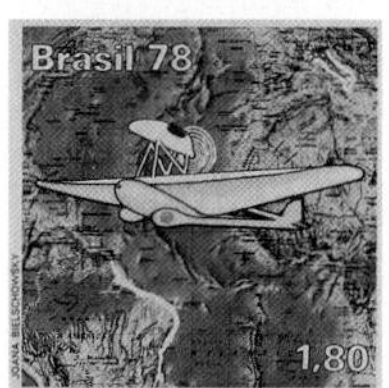


**900** Savoia Marchetti S-64 and Map

**1978.** 50th Anniv of South Atlantic Flight by del Prete and Ferrarin.
1717 **900** 1cr.80 multicoloured 55 30

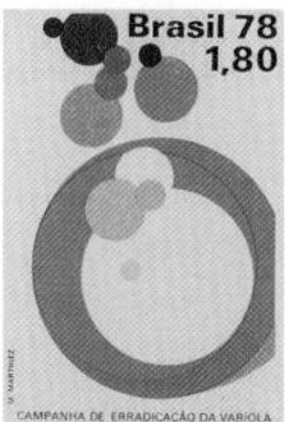


**901** "Smallpox"

**1978.** Global Eradication of Smallpox.
1718 **901** 1cr.80 multicoloured 55 30

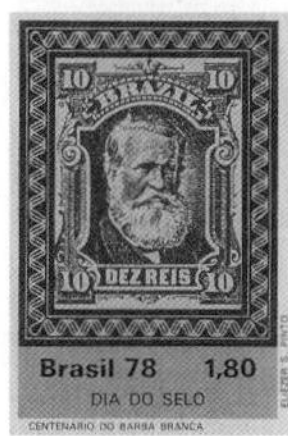


**902** 10r. Pedro II "White Beard" Stamp of 1878

**1978.** Stamp Day.
1719 **902** 1cr.80 multicoloured 45 20

**903** "Jangadeiros"

**1978.** Birth Centenary of Helios Seelinger (painter).
1720 **903** 1cr.80 multicoloured 55 30

**904** Musicians with Violas

**1978.** Folk Musicians. Multicoloured.
1721 1cr.80 Type **904** 45 20
1722 1cr.80 Two fife players 45 20
1723 1cr.80 Berimbau players 45 20

**905** Children playing Football

**1978.** National Week.
1724 **905** 1cr.80 multicoloured 55 30

**906** Patio de Colegio Church

**1978.** Restoration of Patio de Colegio Church, Sao Paulo.
1725 **906** 1cr.80 brown 55 30

**907** "Justice" (A. Ceschiatti)

**1978.** 150th Anniv of Federal Supreme Court.
1726 **907** 1cr.80 black and bistre 55 30

**908** Ipe (flowering tree)

**1978.** Environment Protection. Iguacu Falls National Park. Multicoloured.
1727 1cr.80 Type **908** 55 30
1728 1cr.80 Iguacu Falls 55 30

**909** Stages of "Intelsat" Assembly

**1978.** 3rd Assembly. Users of "Intelsat" Telecommunications Satellite.
1729 **909** 1cr.80 multicoloured 55 30

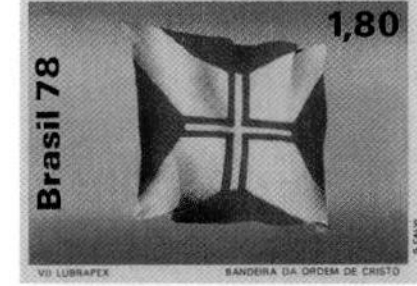


**910** Flag of the Order of Christ

**1978.** "Lubrapex 78" Stamp Exhibition. Flags. Multicoloured.
1730 1cr.80 Type **910** 1·30 1·10
1731 1cr.80 Principality of Brazil 1·30 1·10
1732 1cr.80 United Kingdom of Brazil 1·30 1·10
1733 8cr.50 Empire of Brazil 1·30 1·10
1734 8cr.50 National Flag of Brazil 1·30 1·10

**911** Postal Tramcar

**1978.** 18th U.P.U. Congress, Rio de Janeiro.
1735 **911** 1cr.80 brown, blk & bl 1·50 65
1736 - 1cr.80 brown, blk & bl 1·50 65
1737 - 1cr.80 grey, blk & rose 1·50 65
1738 - 7cr.50 grey, blk & rose 1·80 85
1739 - 8cr.50 brown, blk & grn 2·10 95
1740 - 9cr.50 brown, blk & grn 2·30 1·10

DESIGNS: No. 1736, Post container truck; 1737, Post van, 1914; 1738, Travelling post office; 1739, Mail coach; 1740, Mule caravan.

**912** Gaucho

**1978.** Day of the Book and J. Guimaraes Rosa Commemoration.
1741 **912** 1cr.80 multicoloured 45 30

**913** "Morro de Santo Antonio" (Nicolas Antoine Taunay)

**1978.** Landscape Paintings. Multicoloured.
1742 1cr.80 Type **913** 45 30
1743 1cr.80 "View of Pernambuco" (Frans Post) 45 30
1744 1cr.80 "Morro de Castelo" (Victor Meirelles) 45 30
1745 1cr.80 "Landscape at Sabara" (Alberto da Veiga Guignard) 45 30

**914** Angel with Lute

**1978.** Christmas. Multicoloured.
1746 1cr.80 Type **914** 45 30
1747 1cr.80 Angel with lyre 45 30
1748 1cr.80 Angel with trumpet 45 30

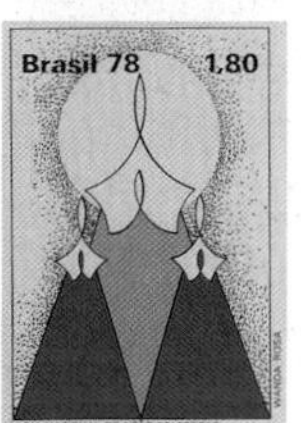


**915** "Thanksgiving"

**1978.** Thanksgiving Day.
1749 **915** 1cr.80 ochre, blk & red 55 30

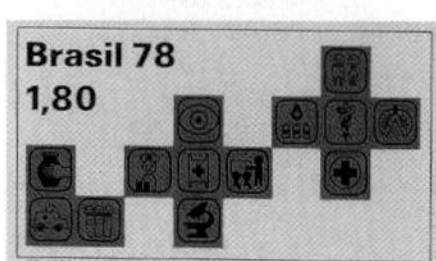


**916** Red Cross Services

**1978.** 70th Anniv of Brazilian Red Cross.
1750 **916** 1cr.80 red and black 55 30

**917** Peace Theatre, Belem

**1978.** Brazilian Theatres. Multicoloured.

| | | | |
|---|---|---|---|
| 1751 | 10cr.50 Type **917** | 1·50 | 55 |
| 1752 | 12cr. Jose de Alencar Theatre, Fortaleza | 1·60 | 65 |
| 1753 | 12cr.50 Rio de Janeiro Municipal Theatre | 1·90 | 75 |

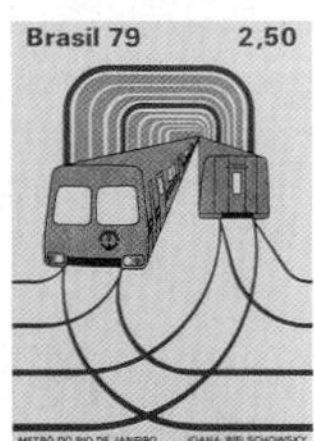


**918** Underground Trains

**1979.** Inauguration of Rio de Janeiro Underground Railway.

| | | | | |
|---|---|---|---|---|
| 1754 | **918** | 2cr.50 multicoloured | 1·10 | 45 |

**919** Old and New Post Offices

**1979.** 10th Anniv of Post & Telegraph Department and 18th U.P.U. Congress (2nd issue). Multicoloured.

| | | | |
|---|---|---|---|
| 1755 | 2cr.50 Type **919** | 55 | 30 |
| 1756 | 2cr.50 Mail boxes | 55 | 30 |
| 1757 | 2cr.50 Mail sorting | 55 | 30 |
| 1758 | 2cr.50 Mail planes | 55 | 30 |
| 1759 | 2cr.50 Telegraph and telex machines | 55 | 30 |
| 1760 | 2cr.50 Postmen | 55 | 30 |

**920** "O'Day 23" Class Yacht

**1979.** "Brasiliana 79" 3rd World Thematic Stamp Exhibition (1st issue). Multicoloured.

| | | | |
|---|---|---|---|
| 1761 | 2cr.50 Type **920** | 70 | 55 |
| 1762 | 10cr.50 "Penguin" class dinghy | 1·40 | 75 |
| 1763 | 12cr. "Hobie Cat" class catamaran | 1·60 | 65 |
| 1764 | 12cr.50 "Snipe" class dinghy | 1·90 | 75 |

See Nos. 1773/6 and 1785/90.

**921** Joao Bolinha (characters from children's story)

**1979.** Children's Book Day.

| | | | | |
|---|---|---|---|---|
| 1765 | **921** | 2cr.50 multicoloured | 55 | 30 |

**922** "Victoria amazonica"

**1979.** 18th U.P.U. Congress (3rd issue). Amazon National Park. Multicoloured.

| | | | |
|---|---|---|---|
| 1766 | 10cr.50 Type **922** | 1·60 | 85 |
| 1767 | 12cr. Amazon manatee | 1·80 | 1·10 |
| 1768 | 12cr.50 Tortoise | 1·90 | 1·20 |

**923** Bank Emblem

**1979.** 25th Anniv of Northeast Bank of Brazil.

| | | | | |
|---|---|---|---|---|
| 1769 | **923** | 2cr.50 multicoloured | 55 | 30 |

**924** Physicians and Patient (15th cent woodcut)

**1979.** 150th Anniv of National Academy of Medicine.

| | | | | |
|---|---|---|---|---|
| 1770 | **924** | 2cr.50 yellow and black | 55 | 30 |

**925** Clover with Hearts as Leaves

**1979.** 35th Brazilian Cardiology Congress.

| | | | | |
|---|---|---|---|---|
| 1771 | **925** | 2cr.50 multicoloured | 55 | 30 |

**926** Hotel Nacional, Rio de Janeiro

**1979.** Brasiliana 79 (2nd issue). Sheet 87×124 mm.

| | | | |
|---|---|---|---|
| **MS**1772 **926** | 12cr.50 multicoloured | 2·30 | 2·50 |

**927** "Cithaerias aurora"

**1979.** "Brasiliana 79" (2nd issue). Butterflies. Multicoloured.

| | | | |
|---|---|---|---|
| 1773 | 2cr.50 Type **927** | 45 | 20 |
| 1774 | 10cr.50 "Evenus regalis" | 1·70 | 45 |
| 1775 | 12cr. "Caligo eurilochus" | 1·70 | 65 |
| 1776 | 12cr.50 "Diaethria clymena janeira" | 1·90 | 75 |

**928** Embraer Xingu

**1979.** 10th Anniv of Brazilian Aeronautical Industry.

| | | | | |
|---|---|---|---|---|
| 1777 | **928** | 2cr.50 dp blue and blue | 55 | 30 |

**929** Globe illuminating Land

**1979.** National Week.

| | | | | |
|---|---|---|---|---|
| 1778 | **929** | 3cr.20 blue, green & yell | 55 | 30 |

**930** Our Lady Aparecida

**1979.** 75th Anniv of Coronation of Our Lady Aparecida.

| | | | | |
|---|---|---|---|---|
| 1779 | **930** | 2cr.50 multicoloured | 55 | 30 |

**931** Envelope and Transport

**1979.** 18th UPU Congress, Rio de Janeiro (4th issue). Multicoloured.

| | | | |
|---|---|---|---|
| 1780 | 2cr.50 Type **931** | 55 | 30 |
| 1781 | 2cr.50 Post Office emblems | 55 | 30 |
| 1782 | 10cr.50 Globe | 1·10 | 95 |
| 1783 | 12cr. Flags of Brazil and UPU | 1·60 | 1·30 |
| 1784 | 12cr.50 UPU emblem | 1·80 | 1·50 |

**932** "Igreja da Gloria"

**1979.** "Brasiliana 79" Third World Thematic Stamp Exhibition (3rd issue). Paintings by Leandro Joaquim. Multicoloured.

| | | | |
|---|---|---|---|
| 1785 | 2cr.50 Type **932** | 45 | 30 |
| 1786 | 12cr. "Fishing on Guanabara Bay" | 1·40 | 1·10 |
| 1787 | 12cr.50 "Boqueirao Lake and Carioca Arches" | 1·60 | 1·30 |

**933** Pyramid Fountain, Rio de Janeiro

**1979.** "Brasiliana 79" (4th issue). 1st International Exhibition of Classical Philately. Fountains.

| | | | | |
|---|---|---|---|---|
| 1788 | **933** | 2cr.50 black, grn & emer | 45 | 30 |
| 1789 | - | 10cr.50 black, turq & bl | 1·00 | 75 |
| 1790 | - | 12cr. black, red and pink | 1·40 | 1·10 |

DESIGNS—VERT: 12cr. Boa Vista, Recife. HORIZ: 10cr.50, Marilia Fountain, Ouro Preto.

**934** World Map

**1979.** 3rd World Telecommunications Exhibition, Geneva.

| | | | | |
|---|---|---|---|---|
| 1791 | **934** | 2cr.50 multicoloured | 55 | 30 |

**935** "UPU" and Emblem

**1979.** UPU Day.

| | | | | |
|---|---|---|---|---|
| 1792 | **935** | 2cr.50 multicoloured | 55 | 45 |
| 1793 | **935** | 10cr.50 multicoloured | 1·30 | 1·10 |
| 1794 | **935** | 12cr. multicoloured | 1·40 | 1·20 |
| 1795 | **935** | 12cr.50 multicoloured | 1·60 | 1·30 |

**936** "Peteca" (shuttlecock)

**1979.** International Year of the Child. Mult.

| | | | |
|---|---|---|---|
| 1796 | 2cr.50 Type **936** | 55 | 45 |
| 1797 | 3cr.20 Spinning top | 70 | 55 |
| 1798 | 3cr.20 Jumping Jack | 70 | 55 |
| 1799 | 3cr.20 Rag doll | 70 | 55 |

**937** "The Birth of Jesus"

**1979.** Christmas. Tiles from the Church of Our Lady of Health and Glory, Salvador. Multicoloured.

| | | | |
|---|---|---|---|
| 1800 | 3cr.20 Type **937** | 55 | 30 |
| 1801 | 3cr.20 "Adoration of the Kings" | 55 | 30 |
| 1802 | 3cr.20 "The Boy Jesus among the Doctors" | 55 | 30 |

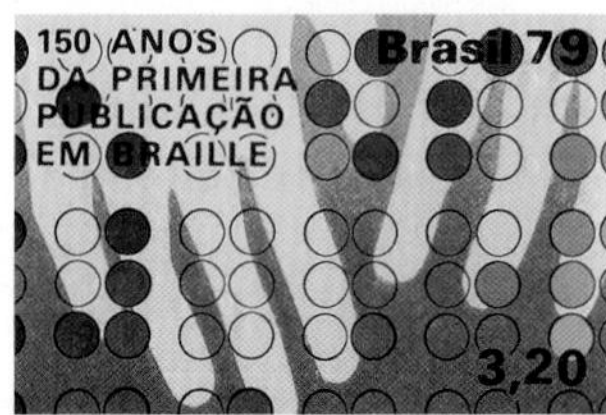


**938** Hands reading Braille

**1979.** 150th Anniv of First Braille Publication. Sheet 127×88 mm.

| | | | |
|---|---|---|---|
| **MS**1803 **938** | 3cr. 20 multicoloured | 1·10 | 1·10 |

**939** Woman with Wheat

**1979.** Thanksgiving Day.

| | | | | |
|---|---|---|---|---|
| 1804 | **939** | 3cr.20 multicoloured | 55 | 30 |



**940** Steel Mill

**1979.** 25th Anniv of Cosipa Steel Works, Sao Paulo.

| | | | | |
|---|---|---|---|---|
| 1805 | **940** | 3cr.20 multicoloured | 55 | 30 |

**941** Plant within Raindrop

**1980.** Energy Conservation. Multicoloured.

| | | | |
|---|---|---|---|
| 1806 | 3cr.20 Type **941** | 55 | 30 |
| 1807 | 17cr.+7cr. Sun and lightbulb | 2·75 | 1·30 |
| 1808 | 20cr.+8cr. Windmill and lightbulb | 3·50 | 1·60 |
| 1809 | 21cr.+9cr. Dam and lightbulb | 4·75 | 1·70 |

**942** Coal Trucks

**1980.** Coal Industry.

| | | | | |
|---|---|---|---|---|
| 1810 | **942** | 4cr. black, orge & red | 55 | 30 |

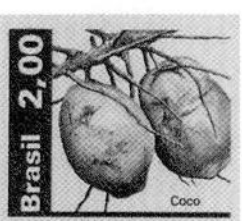


**943** Coconuts

**1980**

| | | | | |
|---|---|---|---|---|
| 1811 | **943** | 2cr. brown | 25 | 10 |
| 1812 | - | 3cr. red | 35 | 10 |
| 1813 | - | 4cr. orange | 55 | 10 |
| 1814 | - | 5cr. violet | 25 | 10 |
| 1815 | - | 7cr. orange | 55 | 20 |
| 1816 | - | 10cr. green | 25 | 10 |
| 1817 | - | 12cr. green | 45 | 20 |
| 1818 | - | 15cr. brown | 25 | 10 |
| 1819 | - | 17cr. red | 55 | 20 |
| 1820 | - | 20cr. brown | 25 | 10 |
| 1821 | - | 24cr. orange | 2·30 | 20 |
| 1822 | - | 30cr. black | 2·50 | 30 |
| 1823 | - | 34cr. brown | 9·75 | 1·50 |
| 1824 | - | 38cr. red | 3·50 | 85 |
| 1825 | - | 42cr. green | 17·00 | 1·70 |
| 1825a | - | 45cr. brown | 25 | 10 |
| 1826 | - | 50cr. orange | 55 | 20 |
| 1826a | - | 57cr. brown | 2·50 | 1·80 |
| 1826b | - | 65cr. purple | 45 | 20 |
| 1827 | - | 66cr. violet | 13·50 | 1·90 |
| 1827a | - | 80cr. red | 1·10 | 95 |
| 1828 | - | 100cr. brown | 4·75 | 30 |
| 1828a | - | 120cr. blue | 1·30 | 30 |
| 1829 | - | 140cr. red | 8·00 | 95 |
| 1829a | - | 150cr. green | 70 | 20 |
| 1830 | - | 200cr. green | 2·30 | 30 |
| 1830a | - | 300cr. purple | 2·50 | 45 |
| 1831 | - | 500cr. brown | 2·50 | 45 |
| 1832 | - | 800cr. green | 2·75 | 45 |
| 1833 | - | 1000cr. olive | 2·75 | 45 |
| 1834 | - | 2000cr. orange | 2·75 | 55 |

DESIGNS: 3cr. Mangoes; 4cr. Corn; 5cr. Onions; 7cr. Oranges; 10cr. Passion fruit; 12cr. Pineapple; 15cr. Bananas; 17cr. Guarana; 20cr. Sugar cane; 24cr. Bee and honeycomb; 30cr. Silkworm and mulberry; 34cr. Cocoa beans; 38cr. Coffee; 42cr. Soya bean; 45cr. Manioc; 50cr. Wheat; 57cr. Peanuts; 65cr. Rubber; 66cr. Grapes; 80cr. Brazil nuts; 100cr. Cashews; 120cr. Rice; 140cr. Tomatoes; 150cr. Eucalyptus; 200cr. Castor-oil bean; 300cr. Parana pine; 500cr. Cotton; 800cr. Carnauba palm; 1000cr. Babassu palm; 2000cr. Sunflower.

**944** Banknote with Development Symbols

**1980.** 21st Inter-American Bank of Development Directors' Annual Assembly Meeting, Rio de Janeiro.

| | | | | |
|---|---|---|---|---|
| 1836 | **944** | 4cr. blue, brown & blk | 55 | 30 |

**945** Tapirape Mask

**1980.** Indian Art. Ritual Masks. Mult.

| | | | |
|---|---|---|---|
| 1837 | 4cr. Type **945** | 55 | 30 |
| 1838 | 4cr. Tukuna mask (vert) | 55 | 30 |
| 1839 | 4cr. Kanela mask (vert) | 55 | 30 |

**946** Geometric Head

**1980.** 30th Anniv of Brazilian Television.

| | | | | |
|---|---|---|---|---|
| 1840 | **946** | 4cr. multicoloured | 55 | 30 |

**947** Duke of Caxias (after Miranda Junior)

**1980.** Death Centenary of Duke de Caxias (General and statesman).

| | | | | |
|---|---|---|---|---|
| 1841 | **947** | 4cr. multicoloured | 55 | 30 |

**948** "The Labourer" (Candido Portinari)

**1980.** Art in Brazilian Museums. Mult.

| | | | |
|---|---|---|---|
| 1842 | 24cr. Type **948** | 2·50 | 1·20 |
| 1843 | 28cr. "Mademoiselle Pogany" (statuette, Constantin Brancusi) | 2·75 | 1·30 |
| 1844 | 30cr. "The Glass of Water" (A. de Figueiredo) | 4·00 | 1·50 |

MUSEUMS. 24cr. Sao Paulo Museum of Art. 28cr. Rio de Janeiro Museum of Modern Art. 30cr. Rio de Janeiro Museum of Fine Art.

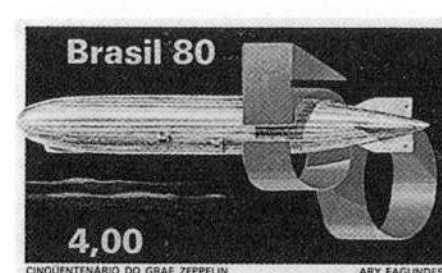


**949** "Graf Zeppelin" flying through "50"

**1980.** 50th Annivs of "Graf Zeppelin" and First South Atlantic Air Mail Flight.

| | | | | |
|---|---|---|---|---|
| 1845 | **949** | 4cr. black, blue & violet | 1·00 | 45 |
| 1846 | - | 4cr. multicoloured | 1·00 | 45 |

DESIGN: No. 1846, Latecoere seaplane "Comte de la Vaulx".

**950** Sail and Bone-lace "Sun"

**1980.** Brapex IV National Stamp Exhibition, Fortaleza. Sheet 125×87 mm.

| | | | | |
|---|---|---|---|---|
| MS1847 | **950** | 30cr. multicoloured | 2·30 | 3·25 |

**951** Pope John Paul II and Fortaleza Cathedral

**1980.** Papal Visit and 10th National Eucharistic Congress. Pope John Paul II and cathedrals. Multicoloured.

| | | | |
|---|---|---|---|
| 1848 | 4cr. Type **951** | 55 | 30 |
| 1849 | 4cr. St. Peter's, Rome (horiz) | 55 | 30 |
| 1850 | 24cr. Apericida (horiz) | 1·90 | 75 |
| 1851 | 28cr. Rio de Janeiro (horiz) | 2·10 | 85 |
| 1852 | 30cr. Brasilia (horiz) | 3·75 | 95 |

**952** Shooting

**1980.** Olympic Games, Moscow. Mult.

| | | | |
|---|---|---|---|
| 1853 | 4cr. Type **952** | 55 | 30 |
| 1854 | 4cr. Cycling | 55 | 30 |
| 1855 | 4cr. Rowing | 55 | 30 |

**953** Classroom

**1980.** Rondon Project (voluntary student work in rural areas).

| | | | | |
|---|---|---|---|---|
| 1856 | **953** | 4cr. multicoloured | 55 | 30 |

**954** Helen Keller and Anne Sullivan

**1980.** Birth Centenary of Helen Keller, and 4th Brazilian Congress on Prevention of Blindness, Belo Horizonte.

| | | | | |
|---|---|---|---|---|
| 1857 | **954** | 4cr. multicoloured | 55 | 30 |

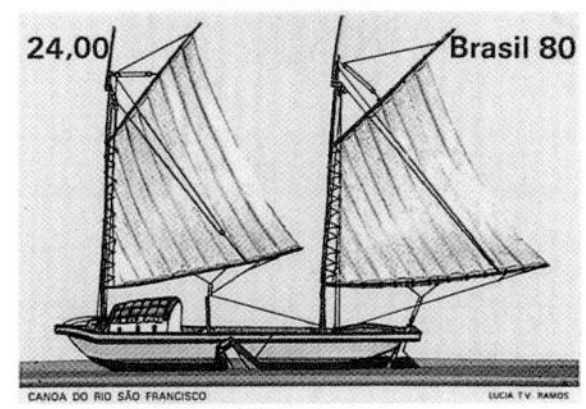


**955** Sao Francisco River Canoe

**1980.** Stamp Day. Sheet 125×86 mm.

| | | | | |
|---|---|---|---|---|
| MS1858 | **955** | 24cr. multicoloured | 2·30 | 2·40 |

**956** Houses and Microscope

**1980.** National Health Day. Campaign against Chagas Disease (barber bug fever).

| | | | | |
|---|---|---|---|---|
| 1859 | **956** | 4cr. multicoloured | 55 | 30 |

**957** Communications Equipment

**1980.** 15th Anniv of National Telecommunications System.

| | | | | |
|---|---|---|---|---|
| 1860 | **957** | 5cr. stone, blue & green | 55 | 30 |

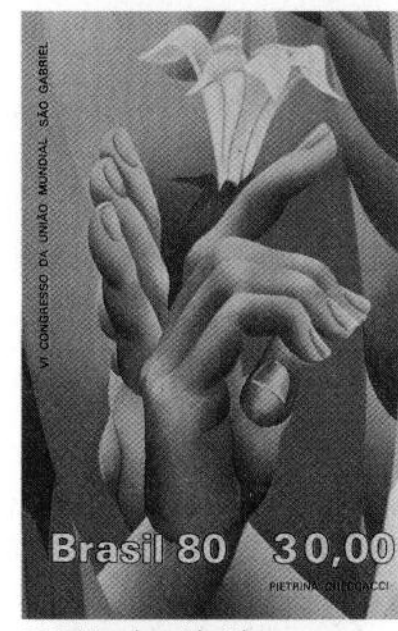


**958** Hands with Lily

**1980.** 6th World Union of St. Gabriel (Religious Philately Federation) Congress, Sao Paulo. Sheet 124×86 mm.

| | | | | |
|---|---|---|---|---|
| MS1861 | **958** | 30cr. multicoloured | 2·30 | 2·30 |

**959** "Cattleya amethystoglossa"

**1980.** "Espamer 80" International Stamp Exhibition, Madrid. Orchids. Multicoloured.

| | | | |
|---|---|---|---|
| 1862 | 5cr. Type **959** | 55 | 30 |
| 1863 | 5cr. "Laelia cinnabarina" | 55 | 30 |
| 1864 | 24cr. "Zygopetalum crinitum" | 2·30 | 1·20 |
| 1865 | 28cr. "Laelia tenebrosa" | 2·30 | 1·20 |

**960** Vinaceous Amazon

**1980.** "Lubrapex 80" Portuguese–Brazilian Stamp Exhibition, Lisbon. Parrots. Multicoloured.

| | | | |
|---|---|---|---|
| 1866 | 5cr. Type **960** | 80 | 50 |
| 1867 | 5cr. Red-tailed amazon | 80 | 50 |
| 1868 | 28cr. Red-spectacled amazon | 5·25 | 2·10 |
| 1869 | 28cr. Brown backed parrotlet | 5·25 | 2·10 |

**961** Captain Rodrigo (fictional character)

**1980.** Book Day and Erico Verissimo (writer). Commemoration.

| | | | | |
|---|---|---|---|---|
| 1870 | **961** | 5cr. multicoloured | 55 | 30 |

**962** Flight into Egypt

**1980.** Christmas.

| | | | | |
|---|---|---|---|---|
| 1871 | **962** | 5cr. multicoloured | 55 | 30 |

**963** Wave-form

**1980.** Inauguration of Telecommunications Centre for Research and Development, Campanas City.

| | | | | |
|---|---|---|---|---|
| 1872 | **963** | 5cr. multicoloured | 70 | 30 |

**964** Carvalho Viaduct, Paranagua–Curitiba Railway Line

**1980.** Centenary of Engineering Club.

| | | | | |
|---|---|---|---|---|
| 1873 | **964** | 5cr. multicoloured | 80 | 35 |

**965** Postal Chessboard

**1980.** Postal Chess.

| | | | | |
|---|---|---|---|---|
| 1874 | **965** | 5cr. multicoloured | 70 | 45 |

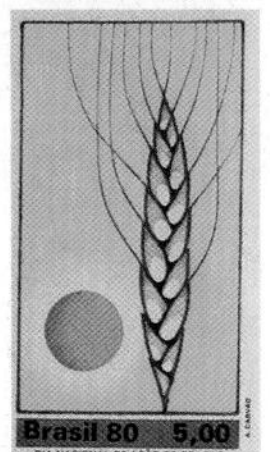

**966** Sun and Wheat

**1980.** Thanksgiving Day.

| | | | | |
|---|---|---|---|---|
| 1875 | **966** | 5cr. multicoloured | 55 | 30 |

**967** Father Anchieta writing Poem in Sand

**1980.** Beatification of Father Jose de Anchieta.

| | | | | |
|---|---|---|---|---|
| 1876 | **967** | 5cr. multicoloured | 55 | 30 |

**968** Christ on the Mount of Olives

**1980.** 250th Birth Anniv of Antonio Lisboa (Aleijadinho) (sculptor). Wood sculptures of Christ's head. Multicoloured.

| | | | |
|---|---|---|---|
| 1877 | 5cr. Type **968** | 70 | 45 |
| 1878 | 5cr. The Arrest in the Garden | 70 | 45 |
| 1879 | 5cr. Flagellation | 70 | 45 |
| 1880 | 5cr. Wearing Crown of Thorns | 70 | 45 |
| 1881 | 5cr. Carrying the cross | 70 | 45 |
| 1882 | 5cr. Crucifixion | 70 | 45 |

**969** Agricultural Produce

**1981.** Agricultural Development. Mult.

| | | | |
|---|---|---|---|
| 1883 | 30cr. Type **969** | 2·75 | 65 |
| 1884 | 35cr. Shopping | 2·30 | 65 |
| 1885 | 40cr. Exporting | 2·30 | 65 |

**970** Scout sitting by Camp Fire

**1981.** 4th Pan-American Jamboree. Multicoloured.

| | | | |
|---|---|---|---|
| 1886 | 5cr. Type **970** | 55 | 10 |
| 1887 | 5cr. Troop cooking | 55 | 10 |
| 1888 | 5cr. Scout with totem pole | 55 | 10 |

**971** First-class Mailman (Empire period)

**1981.** 50th Anniv of Integrated Post Office and Telegraph Department (DCT). Sheet 99×70 mm containing T 971 and similar vert designs. Multicoloured.

| | | | |
|---|---|---|---|
| **MS**1889 | 30cr. Type **971**; 35cr. DCT mailman; 40cr. Telegraph messenger (first republic) | 8·50 | 8·50 |

**972** "The Hunter and the Jaguar"

**1981.** Death Centenary of Felix Emile, Baron of Tauny (artist). Sheet 70×90 mm.

| | | | |
|---|---|---|---|
| **MS**1890 **972** | 30cr. multicoloured | 3·00 | 3·25 |

**973** Lima Barreto and Rio de Janeiro Street Scene

**1981.** Birth Centenary of Lima Barreto (author).

| | | | | |
|---|---|---|---|---|
| 1891 | **973** | 7cr. multicoloured | 60 | 25 |

**974** Tupi-Guarani Ceramic Funeral Urn

**1981.** Artefacts from Brazilian Museums. Mult.

| | | | |
|---|---|---|---|
| 1892 | 7cr. Type **974** (Archaeology and Popular Arts Museum, Paranagua) | 60 | 25 |
| 1893 | 7cr. Marajoara "tanga" ceramic loincloth (Emilio Goeldi Museum, Para) | 60 | 25 |
| 1894 | 7cr. Maraca tribe funeral urn (National Museum, Rio de Janeiro) | 60 | 25 |

**975** Ruby-topaz Hummingbird

**1981.** Hummingbirds. Multicoloured.

| | | | |
|---|---|---|---|
| 1895 | 7cr. Type **975** | 1·70 | 55 |
| 1896 | 7cr. Horned sungem | 1·70 | 55 |
| 1897 | 7cr. Frilled coquette | 1·70 | 55 |
| 1898 | 7cr. Planalto hermit | 1·70 | 55 |

**976** Hands and Cogwheels

**1981.** 72nd Int Rotary Convention, Sao Paulo.

| | | | | |
|---|---|---|---|---|
| 1899 | **976** | 7cr. red and black | 45 | 45 |
| 1900 | - | 35cr. multicoloured | 2·20 | 1·60 |

DESIGN: 35cr. Head and cogwheels.

**977** "Protection of the Water"

**1981.** Environment Protection. Multicoloured.

| | | | |
|---|---|---|---|
| 1901 | 7cr. Type **977** | 70 | 20 |
| 1902 | 7cr. "Protection of the forests" | 70 | 20 |
| 1903 | 7cr. "Protection of the air" | 70 | 20 |
| 1904 | 7cr. "Protection of the soil" | 70 | 20 |

**978** Curtiss Fledgling

**1981.** 50th Anniv of National Air Mail Service.

| | | | | |
|---|---|---|---|---|
| 1905 | **978** | 7cr. multicoloured | 1·00 | 45 |

**979** Locomotive "Colonel Church" and Map of Railway

**1981.** 50th Anniv of Madeira–Mamore Railway Nationalization.

| | | | | |
|---|---|---|---|---|
| 1906 | **979** | 7cr. multicoloured | 1·40 | 55 |

**980** Esperanto Star and Arches of Alvorada Governmental Palace, Brasilia

**1981.** 66th World Esperanto Congress, Brasilia.

| | | | | |
|---|---|---|---|---|
| 1907 | **980** | 7cr. green, grey & black | 45 | 20 |

**981** Pedro II and 50r. "Small Head" Stamp

**1981.** Cent of Pedro II "Small Head" Stamps.

| | | | | |
|---|---|---|---|---|
| 1908 | **981** | 50cr. brown, blk & bl | 2·75 | 55 |
| 1909 | - | 55cr. mauve and green | 2·75 | 55 |
| 1910 | - | 60cr. blue, black & orge | 2·75 | 55 |

DESIGNS: 55cr. Pedro II and 100r. "Small Head" stamp; 60r. Pedro II and 200r. "Small Head" stamp.

**982** Military Institute of Engineering

**1981.** 50th Anniv of Military Institute of Engineering.

| | | | | |
|---|---|---|---|---|
| 1911 | **982** | 12cr. multicoloured | 45 | 30 |

**983** Caboclinhos Folkdance

**1981.** Festivities. Multicoloured.

| | | | |
|---|---|---|---|
| 1912 | 50cr. Type **983** | 1·90 | 55 |
| 1913 | 55cr. Marujada folk festival | 1·90 | 55 |
| 1914 | 60cr. Resado parade | 1·90 | 55 |

**984** Sun and Erect, Drooping, and Supported Flowers

**1981.** International Year of Disabled Persons.

| | | | | |
|---|---|---|---|---|
| 1915 | **984** | 12cr. multicoloured | 45 | 10 |

**985** "Dalechampia capero-niodes"

**1981.** Flowers of the Central Plateau. Multicoloured.

| | | | |
|---|---|---|---|
| 1916 | 12cr. Type **985** | 1·10 | 45 |
| 1917 | 12cr. "Palicourea rigida" | 1·10 | 45 |
| 1918 | 12cr. "Eremanthus sphaerocephalus" (vert) | 1·10 | 45 |
| 1919 | 12cr. "Cassia clausseni" (vert) | 1·10 | 45 |

**986** Image of Our Lady of Nazareth

**1981.** Festival of Our Lady of Nazareth, Belem.

| | | | | |
|---|---|---|---|---|
| 1920 | **986** | 12cr. multicoloured | 45 | 30 |

**987** Christ the Redeemer Monument

**1981.** 50th Anniv of Christ the Redeemer Monument, Rio de Janeiro.

| | | | | |
|---|---|---|---|---|
| 1921 | **987** | 12cr. multicoloured | 45 | 30 |

**988** Farmhands seeding the Land

**1981.** World Food Day.

| | | | | |
|---|---|---|---|---|
| 1922 | **988** | 12cr. multicoloured | 45 | 30 |

**989** Santos Dumont and Biplane "14 bis" landing at Paris

**1981.** 75th Anniv of Santos Dumont's First Powered Flight.

| | | | | |
|---|---|---|---|---|
| 1923 | **989** | 60cr. multicoloured | 2·20 | 65 |

**990** Friar Santos Rita Durao, Title Page and Scene from "Caramuru"

**1981.** Book Day and Bicentenary of Publication of Epic Poem "Caramuru".

| | | | | |
|---|---|---|---|---|
| 1924 | **990** | 12cr. multicoloured | 45 | 30 |

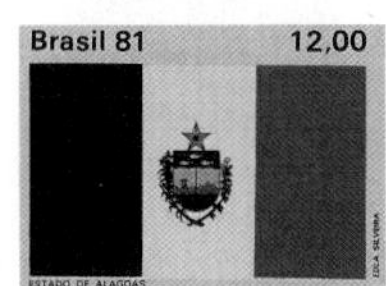

**991** Crib, Juazeiro de Norte (Cica)

**1981.** Christmas. Various designs showing Cribs. Multicoloured.

| | | | |
|---|---|---|---|
| 1925 | 12cr. Type **991** | 45 | 30 |
| 1926 | 50cr. Caruaru (Vitalino Filho) | 2·75 | 45 |
| 1927 | 55cr. Sao Jose dos Campos (Eugenia) (vert) | 2·75 | 45 |
| 1928 | 60cr. Taubate (Candida) (vert) | 2·75 | 55 |

**992** Alagoas

**1981.** State Flags (1st series). Multicoloured.

| | | | |
|---|---|---|---|
| 1929 | 12cr. Type **992** | 55 | 55 |
| 1930 | 12cr. Bahia | 55 | 55 |
| 1931 | 12cr. Federal District | 55 | 55 |
| 1932 | 12cr. Pernambuco | 55 | 55 |
| 1933 | 12cr. Sergipe | 55 | 55 |

See also Nos. 1988/92, 2051/5, 2113/17, 2204/7 and 3043/4.

**993** Girls with Wheat

**1981.** Thanksgiving Day.

| | | | | |
|---|---|---|---|---|
| 1934 | **993** | 12cr. multicoloured | 45 | 30 |

**994** Heads and Symbols of Occupations

**1981.** 50th Anniv of Ministry of Labour.

| | | | | |
|---|---|---|---|---|
| 1935 | **994** | 12cr. multicoloured | 55 | 30 |

**995** Federal Engineering School, Itajuba

**1981.** Birth Centenary of Theodomiro Carneiro Santiago (founder of Federal Engineering School).

| | | | | |
|---|---|---|---|---|
| 1936 | **995** | 15cr. green and mauve | 90 | 45 |

**996** Musician of Police Military Band and Headquarters

**1981.** 150th Anniv of Sao Paulo Military Police. Multicoloured.

| | | | |
|---|---|---|---|
| 1937 | 12cr. Type **996** | 45 | 10 |
| 1938 | 12cr. Lancers of Ninth of July Regiment, Mounted Police | 45 | 10 |

**997** Army Library "Ex Libris"

**1981.** Centenary of Army Library.

| | | | | |
|---|---|---|---|---|
| 1939 | **997** | 12cr. multicoloured | 45 | 30 |

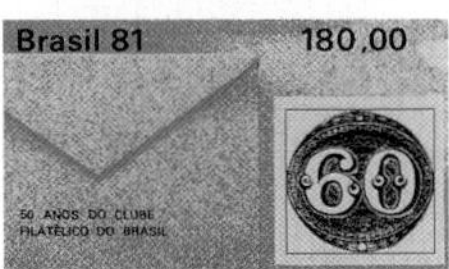

**998** Envelope and "Bull's Eye" Stamp

**1981.** 50th Anniv of Philatelic Club of Brazil. Sheet 89×69 mm.

**MS**1940 **998** 180cr. bistre, blue and black 9·75 9·75

**999** Brigadier Eduardo Gomes

**1982.** Brigadier Eduardo Gomes Commem.

| | | | | |
|---|---|---|---|---|
| 1941 | **999** | 12cr. blue and black | 70 | 45 |

**1000** Lage, Coal Trucks, "Ita" freighter and HL-1 Airplane

**1981.** Birth Cent of Henrique Lage (industrialist).

| | | | | |
|---|---|---|---|---|
| 1942 | **1000** | 17cr. multicoloured | 1·60 | 45 |

**1001** Tackle

**1982.** World Cup Football Championship, Spain. Multicoloured.

| | | | |
|---|---|---|---|
| 1943 | 75cr. Type **1001** | 2·30 | 65 |
| 1944 | 80cr. Kicking ball | 2·30 | 65 |
| 1945 | 85cr. Goalkeeper | 2·30 | 65 |

**MS**1946 125×87 mm. 100cr.×3. As Nos. 1943/5. Imperf 8·00 8·00

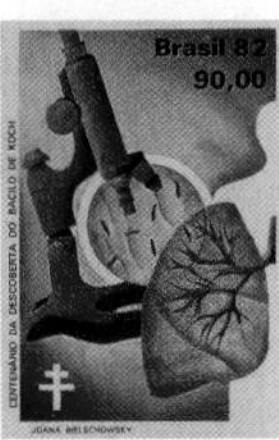

**1002** Microscope, Bacillus and Lung

**1982.** Centenary of Robert Koch's Discovery of Tubercle Bacillus. Multicoloured.

| | | | |
|---|---|---|---|
| 1947 | 90cr. Type **1002** | 5·25 | 1·90 |
| 1948 | 100cr. Flasks, tablets, syringe, bacillus and lung | 5·25 | 1·90 |

**1003** *Laelia purpurata*

**1982.** Brapex V National Stamp Exhibition, Santa Catarina. Sheet 100×70 mm containing T 1003 and similar vert designs showing orchids. Multicoloured.

**MS**1949 75cr. Type **1003**; 80cr. *Oncidium flexuosum*; 85cr. *Cleistes revolute* 13·50 13·50

**1004** Oil Rig Workers

**1982.** Birth Centenary of Monteiro Lobato (writer).

| | | | | |
|---|---|---|---|---|
| 1950 | **1004** | 17cr. multicoloured | 55 | 30 |

**1005** St. Vincent de Paul

**1982.** 400th Birth Anniv of St. Vincent de Paul.

| | | | | |
|---|---|---|---|---|
| 1951 | **1005** | 17cr. multicoloured | 55 | 30 |

**1006** Fifth Fall

**1982.** Guaira's Seven Falls. Multicoloured.

| | | | |
|---|---|---|---|
| 1952 | 17cr. Type **1006** | 55 | 30 |
| 1953 | 21cr. Seventh fall | 70 | 45 |

**1007** Envelope, Telephone, Antenna and Postcode

**1982.** 15th Anniv of Ministry of Communications.

| | | | | |
|---|---|---|---|---|
| 1954 | **1007** | 21cr. multicoloured | 65 | 35 |

**1008** The Old Arsenal (National Historical Museum)

**1982.** 50th Anniv of Museology Course.

| | | | | |
|---|---|---|---|---|
| 1955 | **1008** | 17cr. black and pink | 65 | 35 |

**1009** Cogwheels and Ore Mountains

**1982.** 40th Anniv of Vale do Rio Doce Company.

| | | | | |
|---|---|---|---|---|
| 1956 | **1009** | 17cr. multicoloured | 65 | 35 |

**1010** Martim Afonso de Souza proclaiming Sao Vicente a Town

**1982.** 450th Anniv of Sao Vicente.

| | | | | |
|---|---|---|---|---|
| 1957 | **1010** | 17cr. multicoloured | 70 | 45 |

**1011** Giant Anteater

**1982.** Animals. Multicoloured.

| | | | |
|---|---|---|---|
| 1958 | 17cr. Type **1011** | 1·30 | 45 |
| 1959 | 21cr. Maned wolf | 1·40 | 50 |
| 1960 | 30cr. Pampas deer | 3·75 | 55 |

**1012** Film and "Golden Palm"

**1982.** 20th Anniv of "Golden Palm" Film Award to "The Given World".

| | | | | |
|---|---|---|---|---|
| 1961 | **1012** | 17cr. multicoloured | 55 | 30 |

**1013** Obelisk with Reliefs illustrating Verses by Guilherme de Almeida

**1982.** 50th Anniv of Sao Paulo Revolutionary Government. Sheet 70×100 mm.

**MS**1962 **1013** 140cr. black and blue 5·25 5·25

**1014** Church of Our Lady of O, Sabara

**1982.** Baroque-style Architecture in Minas Gerais. Multicoloured.

| | | | |
|---|---|---|---|
| 1963 | 17cr. Type **1014** | 90 | 20 |
| 1964 | 17cr. Church of Our Lady of Carmo, Mariana (horiz) | 90 | 20 |
| 1965 | 17cr. Church of Our Lady of Rosary, Diamantina (horiz) | 90 | 20 |

**1015** St. Francis of Assisi

**1982.** 800th Birth Anniv of St. Francis of Assisi.

| | | | | |
|---|---|---|---|---|
| 1966 | **1015** | 21cr. multicoloured | 55 | 30 |

**1016** "Large Head" Stamp of 1882

**1982.** Centenary of Pedro II "Large Head" Stamps.

| | | | | |
|---|---|---|---|---|
| 1967 | **1016** | 21cr. yellow, brn & blk | 55 | 30 |

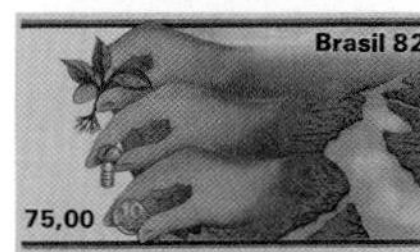

**1017** Amazon River and Hands holding Seedling, Screw and Coin

**1982.** Manaus Free Trade Zone.

| | | | | |
|---|---|---|---|---|
| 1968 | **1017** | 75cr. multicoloured | 2·10 | 65 |

**1018** Lord Baden-Powell

**1982.** 125th Birth Anniv of Lord Baden Powell and 75th Anniv of Boy Scout Movement. Sheet 100×70 mm containing T 1018 and similar vert design. Multicoloured.

| | | | |
|---|---|---|---|
| **MS**1969 | 85cr. Type **1018**; 185cr. Scout saluting | 10·50 | 10·50 |

**1019** Xango

**1982.** Orixas Religious Costumes. Mult.

| | | | |
|---|---|---|---|
| 1970 | 20cr. Type **1019** | 50 | 10 |
| 1971 | 20cr. Iemanja | 50 | 10 |
| 1972 | 20cr. Oxumare | 50 | 10 |

**1020** XII Florin

**1982.** 10th Anniv of Brazilian Central Bank Values Museum. Multicoloured.

| | | | |
|---|---|---|---|
| 1973 | 25cr. Type **1020** | 55 | 30 |
| 1974 | 25cr. Pedro I Coronation piece | 55 | 30 |

**1021** "Ipiranga Cry" (Dom Pedro proclaiming independence)

**1982.** Independence Week.

| | | | | |
|---|---|---|---|---|
| 1975 | **1021** | 25cr. multicoloured | 90 | 55 |

**1022** St. Theresa of Jesus

**1982.** 400th Death Anniv of St. Theresa of Jesus.

| | | | | |
|---|---|---|---|---|
| 1976 | **1022** | 85cr. multicoloured | 2·40 | 55 |

**1023** Musical Instrument Maker

**1982.** "Lubrapex 82" Brazilian–Portuguese Stamp Exhibition, Curitiba. The Paranaense Fandango. Multicoloured.

| | | | |
|---|---|---|---|
| 1977 | 75cr. Type **1023** | 2·00 | 1·10 |
| 1978 | 80cr. Dancers | 2·00 | 1·10 |
| 1979 | 85cr. Musicians | 2·00 | 1·10 |
| **MS**1980 | 100×70 mm. Nos. 1977/9 | 8·00 | 8·00 |

**1024** Embraer Tucano Trainers

**1982.** Aeronautical Industry Day.

| | | | | |
|---|---|---|---|---|
| 1981 | **1024** | 24cr. multicoloured | 55 | 25 |

**1025** Bastos Tigre and Verse from "Saudade"

**1982.** Day of the Book and Birth Centenary of Bastos Tigre (poet).

| | | | | |
|---|---|---|---|---|
| 1982 | **1025** | 24cr. multicoloured | 55 | 30 |

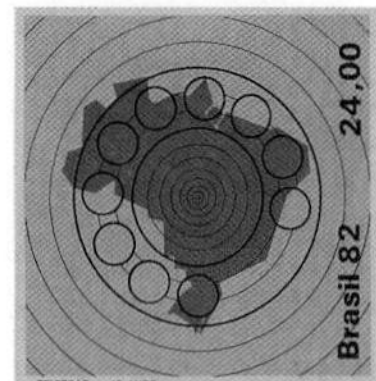

**1026** Telephone Dial on Map of Brazil

**1982.** 10th Anniv of Telebras (Brazilian Telecommunications Corporation).

| | | | | |
|---|---|---|---|---|
| 1983 | **1026** | 24cr. multicoloured | 55 | 30 |

**1027** "Nativity" (C.S. Miyaba)

**1982.** Christmas. Children's Paintings. Mult.

| | | | |
|---|---|---|---|
| 1984 | 24cr. Type **1027** | 2·10 | 10 |
| 1985 | 24cr. "Choir of Angels" (N. N. Aleluia) | 2·10 | 10 |
| 1986 | 30cr. "Holy Family" (F. T. Filho) | 2·10 | 20 |
| 1987 | 30cr. "Nativity with Angel" (N. Arand) | 2·10 | 20 |

**1982.** State Flags (2nd series). As T 992. Mult.

| | | | |
|---|---|---|---|
| 1988 | 24cr. Ceara | 2·30 | 65 |
| 1989 | 24cr. Espirito Santo | 2·30 | 65 |
| 1990 | 24cr. Paraiba | 2·30 | 65 |
| 1991 | 24cr. Rio Grande do Norte | 2·30 | 65 |
| 1992 | 24cr. Rondonia | 2·30 | 65 |

**1028** "Germination"

**1982.** Thanksgiving Day.

| | | | | |
|---|---|---|---|---|
| 1993 | **1028** | 24cr. multicoloured | 90 | 20 |

**1029** "Efeta" (S. Tempel)

**1982.** The Hard of Hearing.

| | | | | |
|---|---|---|---|---|
| 1994 | **1029** | 24cr. multicoloured | 70 | 45 |

**1030** "Benjamin Constant" (cadet ship)

**1982.** Bicentenary of Naval Academy. Mult.

| | | | |
|---|---|---|---|
| 1995 | 24cr. Type **1030** | 1·10 | 45 |
| 1996 | 24cr. "Almirante Saldanha" (cadet ship) | 1·10 | 45 |
| 1997 | 24cr. "Brasil" (training frigate) | 1·10 | 45 |

**1031** 300r. Stamp of 1845

**1982.** Brasiliana 83 International Stamp Exhibition, Rio de Janeiro (1st issue). Sheet 99×69 mm.

| | | | |
|---|---|---|---|
| **MS**1998 | **1031** 200cr. black, ochre and blue | 8·50 | 8·50 |

See Also Nos. 1999/2002, 2029/**MS**2032 and **MS**2033.

**1032** Samba Parade Drummers

**1983.** "Brasiliana 83" International Stamp Exhibition, Rio de Janeiro. Carnival. Multicoloured.

| | | | |
|---|---|---|---|
| 1999 | 24cr. Type **1032** | 1·10 | 45 |
| 2000 | 130cr. Masked clowns | 4·00 | 1·10 |
| 2001 | 140cr. Dancer | 4·00 | 1·10 |
| 2002 | 150cr. Indian | 4·00 | 1·10 |

**1033** Support Ship "Barao de Teffe" in Antarctic

**1983.** 1st Brazilian Antarctic Expedition.

| | | | | |
|---|---|---|---|---|
| 2003 | **1033** | 150cr. multicoloured | 4·50 | 1·20 |

**1034** Woman with Ballot Paper

**1983.** 50th Anniv of Women's Suffrage in Brazil.

| | | | | |
|---|---|---|---|---|
| 2004 | **1034** | 130cr. multicoloured | 2·75 | 95 |

**1035** Itaipu Dam

**1983.** Itaipu Brazilian–Paraguayan Hydro-electric Project.

| | | | | |
|---|---|---|---|---|
| 2005 | **1035** | 140cr. multicoloured | 4·50 | 85 |

**1036** Luther

**1983.** 500th Birth Anniv of Martin Luther (Protestant reformer).

| | | | | |
|---|---|---|---|---|
| 2006 | **1036** | 150cr. deep green, green and black | 3·50 | 65 |

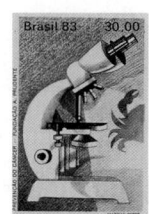

**1037** Microscope and Crab

**1983.** Cancer Prevention. 30th Anniv of Antonio Prudente Foundation and A.C. Camargo Hospital. Multicoloured.

| | | | |
|---|---|---|---|
| 2007 | 30cr. Type **1037** | 50 | 45 |
| 2008 | 38cr. Antonio Prudente, hospital and crab | 50 | 45 |

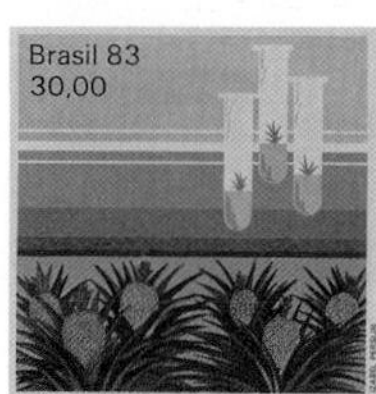

**1038** Tissue Culture

**1983.** Agricultural Research. Multicoloured.

| | | | |
|---|---|---|---|
| 2009 | 30cr. Type **1038** | 50 | 10 |
| 2010 | 30cr. Brazilian wild chestnut tree | 50 | 10 |
| 2011 | 38cr. Tropical soya beans | 55 | 15 |

**1039** Friar Rogerio Neuhaus before Altar

**1983.** Cent of Ordination of Friar Rogerio Neuhaus.

| | | | | |
|---|---|---|---|---|
| 2012 | **1039** | 30cr. multicoloured | 50 | 10 |

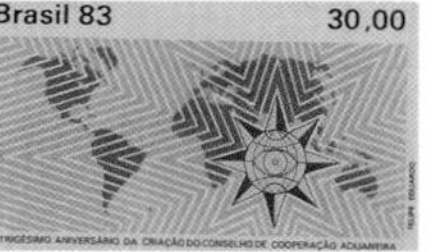

**1040** Council Emblem and World Map

**1983.** 30th Anniv of Customs Co-operation Council.

| | | | | |
|---|---|---|---|---|
| 2013 | **1040** | 30cr. multicoloured | 50 | 10 |

**1041** Satellite

**1983.** World Communications Year.

2014 **1041** 250cr. multicoloured 4·75 1·40

**1042** Toco Toucan

**1983.** Toucans. Multicoloured.

2015 30cr. Type **1042** 1·10 35

2016 185cr. Red-billed toucan 4·00 1·10

2017 205cr. Red-breasted toucan 4·25 1·20

2018 215cr. Channel-billed toucan 4·50 1·30

**1043** "The Resurrection"

**1983.** 500th Birth Anniv of Raphael (artist). Sheet 70×90 mm.

**MS**2019 **1043** 250cr. multicoloured 6·75 7·00

**1044** Baldwin Locomotive No. 1, 1881

**1983.** Locomotives. Multicoloured.

2020 30cr. Type **1044** 95 55

2021 30cr. Hohenzollern locomotive No. 980, 1875 95 55

2022 38cr. Locomotive No. 1 "Maria Fumaca", 1868 95 55

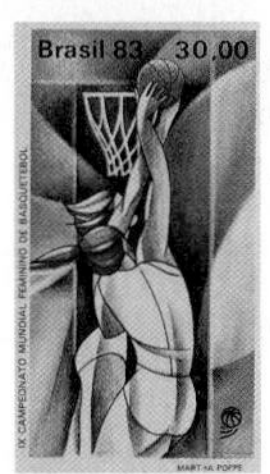

**1045** Basketball Players

**1983.** 9th Women's World Basketball Championship, Sao Paulo.

2023 30cr. Type **1045** 45 10

2024 30cr. Basketball players (different) 45 10

**1046** Bolivar (after Tito Salas)

**1983.** Birth Bicentenary of Simon Bolivar.

2025 **1046** 30cr. multicoloured 45 10

**1047** Boy with Kite and Boy waiting for Polio Vaccination

**1983.** Polio and Measles Vaccination Campaign. Multicoloured.

2026 30cr. Type **1047** 50 20

2027 30cr. Girl on bicycle and girl receiving measles vaccination 50 20

**1048** Minerva and Computer Punched Tape

**1983.** 20th Anniv of Post-graduate Master's Programmes in Engineering.

2028 **1048** 30cr. light brown, blue and brown 50 20

**1049** 30r. "Bulls Eye" Stamp and Rio de Janeiro Bay

**1983.** "Brasiliana 83" International Stamp Exhibition, Rio de Janeiro. 140th Anniv of "Bull's Eye" Stamps.

2029 **1049** 185cr. black and blue 2·50 85

2030 - 205cr. black and blue 2·50 85

2031 - 215cr. black and violet 2·50 85

**MS**2032 100×70 mm. 185cr., 205cr., 215cr. each black and blue 20·00 21·00

DESIGNS: Nos. 2030/1, As Type **1049** but showing 60r. and 90r. "Bull's-Eye" stamp respectively; No. **MS**2032, "Bull's-Eye" stamp on each value as for Nos. 2029/31, and composite design of Rio de Janeiro Bay across the three.

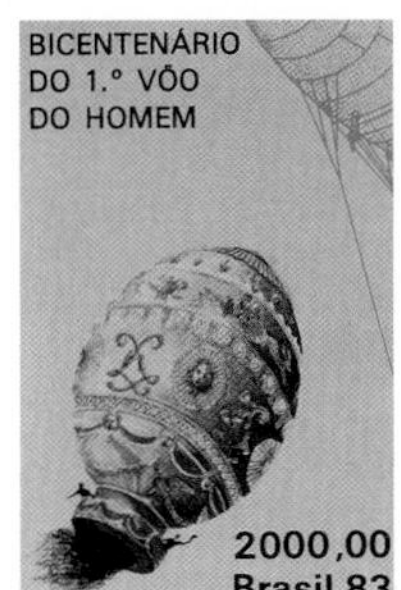

**1050** Montgolfier Balloon

**1983.** Brasiliana 83 International Stamp Exhibition, Rio de Janeiro (4th issue). Five sheets 105×149 mm (a, d) or 149×105 mm (others), each containing design as T 1050. Multicoloured.

**MS**2033 Five sheets (a) 2000cr. Type **1050** (Bicentenary of manned flight); (b) 2000cr. Racing car (Formula 1 champions 1972, 1974, 1981); (c) 2000cr. "Tornado" and "Class 470" sailing dinghies (Olympic sailing champion, 1980); (d) 2000cr. Triple jumper (Olympic triple jump champions, 1952, 1956); (e) 2000cr. World Cup and footballer (World Cup champions, 1958, 1962, 1970) £225 £225

**1051** "The First Mass in Brazil"

**1983.** 150th Birth Anniv (1982) of Victor Meireles (artist). Sheet 100×70 mm.

**MS**2034 **1051** 250cr. multicoloured 7·00 7·00

**1052** Embracer EMB-120 Brasilia

**1983.** Brazilian Aeronautics Industry.

2035 **1052** 30cr. multicoloured 50 20

**1053** Bosco and State Departments Esplanade, Brasilia

**1983.** Dom Bosco's Dream of Brazil.

2036 **1053** 130cr. multicoloured 1·60 45

**1054** "Council of State decides on Independence" (detail, Georgina de Albuquerque)

**1983.** National Week.

2037 **1054** 50cr. multicoloured 75 35

**1055** Iron and Steel Production

**1983.** 10th Anniv of Siderbras (Brazilian Steel Corporation).

2038 **1055** 45cr. multicoloured 65 15

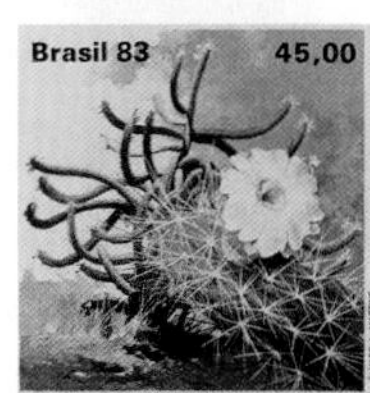

**1056** "Pilosocereus gounellei"

**1983.** Cacti. Multicoloured.

2039 45cr. Type **1056** 1·30 35

2040 45cr. "Melocactus bahiensis" 1·30 35

2041 57cr. "Cereus jamacari" 1·50 35

**1057** Monstrance

**1983.** 50th Anniv of National Eucharistic Congress.

2042 **1057** 45cr. multicoloured 1·00 35

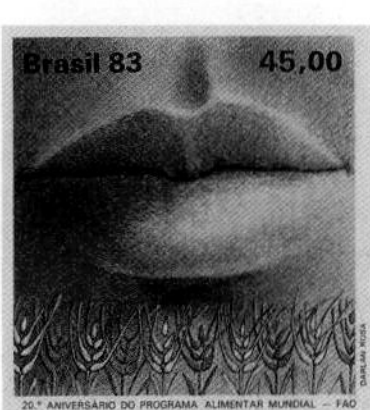

**1058** Mouth and Wheat

**1983.** 20th Anniv of World Food Programme. Fishery Resources. Multicoloured.

2043 45cr. Type **1058** 1·30 20

2044 57cr. Fish and fishing pirogue 2·50 45

**1059** Telegraph Key and Praca da Republica, Rio de Janeiro

**1983.** Death Centenary of Louis Breguet (telegraph pioneer). Sheet 70×99 mm.

**MS**2045 **1059** 376cr. multicoloured 11·50 11·50

**1060** "Our Lady of Angels" (wood, Franisco Xavier de Brito)

**1983.** Christmas. Statues of the Madonna. Multicoloured.

2046 45cr. Type **1060** 1·30 35

2047 315cr. "Our Lady of Birth" 3·50 1·20

2048 335cr. "Our Lady of Joy" (fired clay, Agostinho de Jesus) 3·50 1·30

2049 345cr. "Our Lady of Presentation" 3·50 1·40

**1061** Moraes and Map of Italian Campaign

**1983.** Birth Centenary of Marshal Mascarenhas de Moraes.

2050 **1061** 45cr. pink, green & pur 50 20

**1983.** State Flags (3rd series). As Type 992. Multicoloured.

2051 45cr. Amazonas 1·00 55

2052 45cr. Goias 1·00 55

2053 45cr. Rio de Janeiro 1·00 55

2054 45cr. Mato Grosso do Sul 1·00 55

2055 45cr. Parana 1·00 55

**1062** Praying Figure and Wheat

**1983.** Thanksgiving Day.

2056 **1062** 45cr. multicoloured 75 35

**1063** Friar Vincente Borgard

**1983.** Obligatory Tax. Anti-leprosy Week.

2057 **1063** 10cr. brown 3·25 1·60

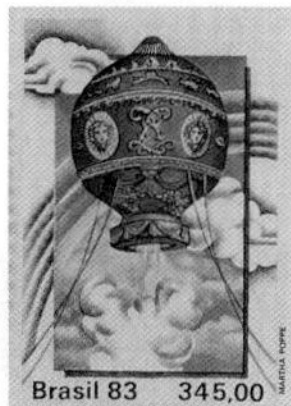

**1064** Montgolfier Balloon

**1983.** Bicentenary of Manned Flight.

2058 **1064** 345cr. multicoloured 10·00 3·00

**1065** Indian, Portuguese Navigator and Negro

**1984.** 50th Anniv of Publication of "Masters and Slaves" by Gilberto Freyre.

| | | | | |
|---|---|---|---|---|
| 2059 | **1065** | 45cr. multicoloured | 50 | 35 |

**1066** Crystal Palace

**1984.** Centenary of Crystal Palace, Petropolis.

| | | | | |
|---|---|---|---|---|
| 2060 | **1066** | 45cr. multicoloured | 50 | 35 |

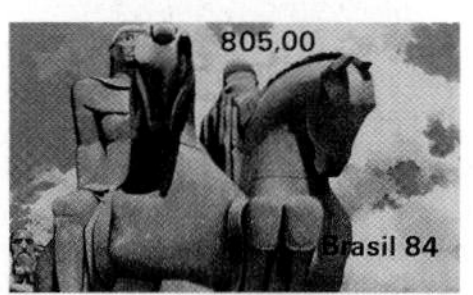


**1067** "Monument of the Flags", Sao Paulo

**1984.** 90th Birth Anniv of Victor Brecheret (sculptor). Sheet 100×70 mm.

| | | | | |
|---|---|---|---|---|
| **MS**2061 | **1067** | 805cr. multicoloured | 4·50 | 4·50 |

**1068** "Don Afonso" (sail/steam warship) and Figurehead

**1984.** Cent of Naval Oceanographic Museum.

| | | | | |
|---|---|---|---|---|
| 2062 | **1068** | 620cr. multicoloured | 3·25 | 1·10 |

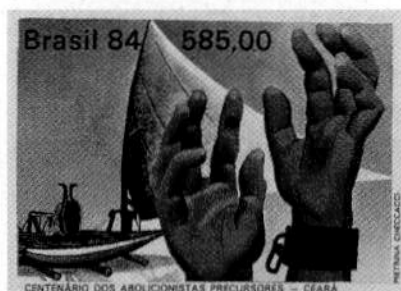


**1069** Manacled Hands and Beached Fishing Pirogue

**1984.** Centenary of Abolition of Slavery in Ceara and Amazonas. Multicoloured.

| | | | |
|---|---|---|---|
| 2063 | 585cr. Type **1069** | 2·30 | 60 |
| 2064 | 610cr. Emancipated slave | 2·40 | 65 |

**1070** King Carl XVI Gustaf and Pres. Figueiredo

**1984.** Visit of King of Sweden. Sheet 98×69 mm.

| | | | | |
|---|---|---|---|---|
| **MS**2065 | **1070** | 2105cr. mult | 8·25 | 8·25 |

**1071** Long Jumping

**1984.** Olympic Games, Los Angeles. Mult.

| | | | |
|---|---|---|---|
| 2066 | 65cr. Type **1071** | 1·30 | 45 |
| 2067 | 65cr. 100 metres | 1·30 | 45 |
| 2068 | 65cr. Relay | 1·30 | 45 |
| 2069 | 585cr. Pole vaulting | 1·50 | 75 |
| 2070 | 610cr. High jumping | 1·50 | 75 |
| 2071 | 620cr. Hurdling | 1·50 | 75 |

**1072** Oil Rigs and Blast Furnace

**1984.** Birth Cent (1983) of Getulio Vargas (President 1930–45 and 1951–54). Multicoloured.

| | | | |
|---|---|---|---|
| 2072 | 65cr. Type **1072** | 50 | 10 |
| 2073 | 65cr. Ballot boxes and symbols of professions and trades | 50 | 10 |
| 2074 | 65cr. Sugar refinery and electricity pylons | 50 | 10 |

**1073** Pedro Alvares Cabral

**1984.** "Espana 84" International Stamp Exhibition, Madrid. Explorers. Multicoloured.

| | | | |
|---|---|---|---|
| 2075 | 65cr. Type **1073** | 75 | 20 |
| 2076 | 610cr. Christopher Columbus | 3·25 | 65 |

**1074** Heads and Map of Americas

**1984.** 8th Pan-American Surety Association General Assembly.

| | | | | |
|---|---|---|---|---|
| 2077 | **1074** | 65cr. multicoloured | 50 | 35 |

**1075** Chinese Painting

**1984.** "Lubrapex 84" Brazilian-Portuguese Stamp Exhibition, Lisbon.

| | | | | |
|---|---|---|---|---|
| 2078 | **1075** | 65cr. multicoloured | 50 | 35 |
| 2079 | - | 585cr. multicoloured | 2·00 | 75 |
| 2080 | - | 610cr. multicoloured | 2·10 | 1·00 |
| 2081 | - | 620cr. multicoloured | 2·30 | 1·00 |

DESIGNS: 585 to 620cr. Chinese paintings from Mariana Cathedral.

**1076** FIFA Emblem

**1984.** 80th Anniv of International Federation of Football Associations. Sheet 98×68 mm.

| | | | | |
|---|---|---|---|---|
| **MS**2082 | **1076** | 2115cr. mult | 7·50 | 7·50 |

**1077** Marsh Deer and Great Egret

**1984.** Mato Grosso Flood Plain. Multicoloured.

| | | | |
|---|---|---|---|
| 2083 | 65cr. Type **1077** | 1·30 | 45 |
| 2084 | 65cr. Jaguar, capybara and roseate spoonbill | 1·30 | 45 |
| 2085 | 80cr. Alligator, jabiru and red-cowled cardinals | 1·40 | 55 |

**1078** "The First Letter Sent from Brazil" (Guido Mondin)

**1984.** 1st Anniv of Postal Union of the Americas and Spain H.Q., Montevideo, Uruguay.

| | | | | |
|---|---|---|---|---|
| 2086 | **1078** | 65cr. multicoloured | 50 | 20 |

**1079** Route Map and Dornier Wal Flying Boat

**1984.** 50th Anniv of First Trans-Oceanic Air Route. Multicoloured.

| | | | |
|---|---|---|---|
| 2087 | 610cr. Type **1079** | 2·50 | 1·00 |
| 2088 | 620cr. Support ship "Westfalen" and Dornier Wal | 2·75 | 1·10 |

**1080** Mother and Baby

**1984.** Wildlife Preservation. Woolley Spider Monkey. Multicoloured.

| | | | |
|---|---|---|---|
| 2089 | 65cr. Type **1080** | 2·50 | 75 |
| 2090 | 80cr. Monkey in tree | 1·90 | 75 |

**1081** Murrah Buffaloes

**1984.** Marajo Island Water Buffaloes. Designs showing different races. Multicoloured.

| | | | |
|---|---|---|---|
| 2091 | 65cr. Type **1081** | 1·30 | 35 |
| 2092 | 65cr. Carabao buffaloes | 1·30 | 35 |
| 2093 | 65cr. Mediterranean buffaloes | 1·30 | 35 |

Nos. 2091/3 were issued together, se-tenant, forming a composite design.

**1082** Headquarters, Salvador

**1984.** 150th Anniv of Economic Bank.

| | | | | |
|---|---|---|---|---|
| 2094 | **1082** | 65cr. multicoloured | 25 | 10 |

**1083** Da Luz Station, Sao Paulo

**1984.** Preservation of Historic Railway Stations. Multicoloured.

| | | | |
|---|---|---|---|
| 2095 | 65cr. Type **1083** | 1·30 | 35 |
| 2096 | 65cr. Japeri station Rio de Janeiro | 1·30 | 35 |
| 2097 | 80cr. Sao Joao del Rei station, Minas Gerais | 1·30 | 35 |

**1084** Girl Guide

**1984.** 65th Anniv of Girl Guides Movement in Brazil. Sheet 99×69 mm.

| | | | | |
|---|---|---|---|---|
| **MS**2098 | **1084** | 585cr. multicoloured | 6·25 | 6·25 |

**1086** "Pedro I" (Solano Peixoto Machado)

**1984.** 20th Anniv of National Housing Bank.

| | | | | |
|---|---|---|---|---|
| 2099 | **1085** | 65cr. multicoloured | 50 | 20 |

**1085** Roof protecting Couple

**1984.** National Week. Designs showing children's paintings. Multicoloured.

| | | | |
|---|---|---|---|
| 2100 | 100cr. Type **1086** | 40 | 10 |
| 2101 | 100cr. Girl painting word "BRASIL" (Juruce Maria Klein) | 40 | 10 |
| 2102 | 100cr. Children of different races under rainbow (Priscela Barreto da Fonseca Bara) | 40 | 10 |
| 2103 | 100cr. Caravels (Carlos Peixoto Mangueira) | 40 | 10 |

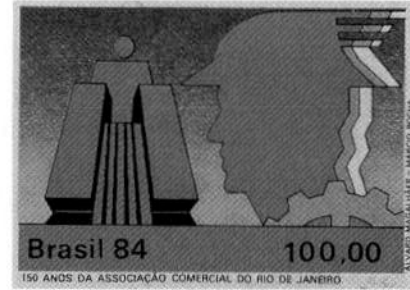


**1087** Headquarters, Mercury and Cogwheel

**1984.** 150th Anniv of Rio de Janeiro Commercial Association.

| | | | | |
|---|---|---|---|---|
| 2104 | **1087** | 100cr. multicoloured | 50 | 20 |

**1088** Pedro I

**1984.** 150th Death Anniv of Emperor Pedro I.

| | | | | |
|---|---|---|---|---|
| 2105 | **1088** | 1000cr. multicoloured | 4·50 | 2·40 |

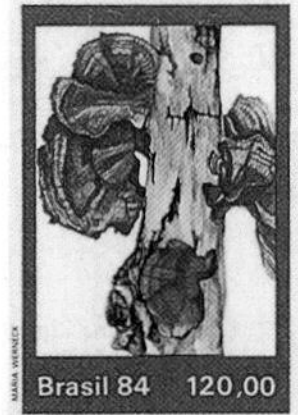


**1089** "Pycnoporus sanguineus"

**1984.** Fungi. Multicoloured.

| | | | |
|---|---|---|---|
| 2106 | 120cr. Type **1089** | 75 | 30 |
| 2107 | 1050cr. "Calvatia" sp. | 3·25 | 1·00 |
| 2108 | 1080cr. "Pleurotus" sp. (horiz) | 3·25 | 1·00 |

**1090** Child stepping from Open Book

**1984.** Book Day. Children's Literature.

| | | | | |
|---|---|---|---|---|
| 2109 | **1090** | 120cr. multicoloured | 65 | 10 |

**1091** New State Mint and 17th-century Minter

**1984.** Inauguration of New State Mint, Santa Cruz, Rio de Janeiro.

| | | | | |
|---|---|---|---|---|
| 2110 | **1091** | 120cr. blue & deep blue | 65 | 10 |

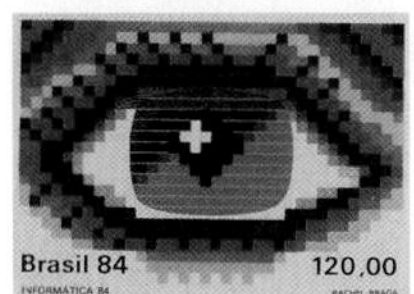

**1092** Computer Image of Eye

**1984.** "Informatica 84" 17th National Information Congress and 4th International Informatics Fair, Rio de Janeiro.

| | | | | |
|---|---|---|---|---|
| 2111 | **1092** | 120cr. multicoloured | 65 | 10 |

**1093** Sculpture by Bruno Giorgi and Flags

**1984.** 14th General Assembly of Organization of American States, Brasilia.

| | | | | |
|---|---|---|---|---|
| 2112 | **1093** | 120cr. multicoloured | 65 | 10 |

**1984.** State Flags (4th series). As T 992.

| | | | |
|---|---|---|---|
| 2113 | 120cr. red, black & buff | 1·00 | 65 |
| 2114 | 120cr. multicoloured | 1·00 | 65 |
| 2115 | 120cr. multicoloured | 1·00 | 65 |
| 2116 | 120cr. multicoloured | 1·00 | 65 |
| 2117 | 120cr. multicoloured | 1·00 | 65 |

DESIGNS: No. 2113, Minas Gerais; 2114, Mato Grosso; 2115, Piaui; 2116, Maranhao; 2117, Santa Catarina.

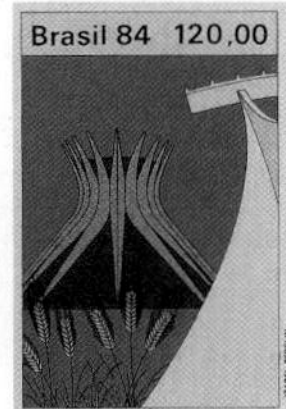

**1094** Brasilia Cathedral and Wheat

**1984.** Thanksgiving Day.

| | | | | |
|---|---|---|---|---|
| 2118 | **1094** | 120cr. multicoloured | 65 | 10 |

**1095** Father Bento Dias Pacheco

**1984.** Obligatory Tax. Anti-leprosy Week.

| | | | | |
|---|---|---|---|---|
| 2119 | **1095** | 30cr. blue | 75 | 35 |

See also Nos. 2208, 2263 and 2291.

**1096** "Nativity" (Djanira da Mota e Silva)

**1984.** Christmas. Paintings from Federal Savings Bank collection. Multicoloured.

| | | | |
|---|---|---|---|
| 2120 | 120cr. Type **1096** | 45 | 20 |
| 2121 | 120cr. "Virgin and Child" (Glauco Rodrigues) | 45 | 20 |
| 2122 | 1050cr. "Flight into Egypt" (Paul Garfunkel) | 2·50 | 75 |
| 2123 | 1080cr. "Nativity" (Emiliano Augusto di Cavalcanti) | 2·50 | 75 |

**1097** Airbus Industrie A300

**1984.** 40th Anniv of I.C.A.O.

| | | | | |
|---|---|---|---|---|
| 2124 | **1097** | 120cr. multicoloured | 65 | 20 |

**1098** Symbols of Agriculture and Industry on Hat

**1984.** 25th Anniv of North-east Development Office.

| | | | | |
|---|---|---|---|---|
| 2125 | **1098** | 120cr. multicoloured | 50 | 20 |

**1099** "Virgin of Safe Journeys Church" (detail)

**1985.** 77th Death Anniv of Emilio Rouede (artist).

| | | | | |
|---|---|---|---|---|
| 2126 | **1099** | 120cr. multicoloured | 50 | 20 |

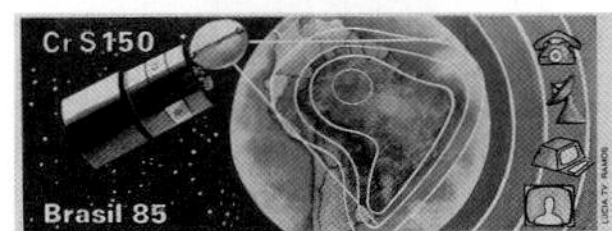

**1100** "Brasilsat" over Brazil

**1985.** Launch of "Brasilsat" (first Brazilian telecommunications satellite).

| | | | | |
|---|---|---|---|---|
| 2127 | **1100** | 150cr. multicoloured | 50 | 20 |

**1101** Electric Trains and Plan of Port Alegre Station

**1985.** Inauguration of Metropolitan Surface Railway, Recife and Porto Alegre.

| | | | | |
|---|---|---|---|---|
| 2128 | **1101** | 200cr. multicoloured | 1·30 | 35 |

**1102** Butternut Tree

**1985.** Opening of Botanical Gardens, Brasilia.

| | | | | |
|---|---|---|---|---|
| 2129 | **1102** | 200cr. multicoloured | 75 | 10 |

**1103** Parachutist

**1985.** 40th Anniv of Military Parachuting.

| | | | | |
|---|---|---|---|---|
| 2130 | **1103** | 200cr. multicoloured | 75 | 10 |

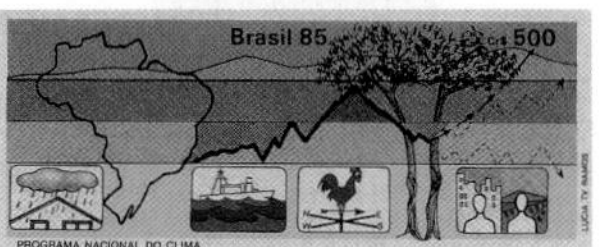

**1104** Map, Temperature Graph and Weather Scenes

**1985.** National Climate Programme.

| | | | | |
|---|---|---|---|---|
| 2131 | **1104** | 500cr. multicoloured | 80 | 20 |

**1105** Campolina

**1985.** Brazilian Horses. Multicoloured.

| | | | |
|---|---|---|---|
| 2132 | 1000cr. Type **1105** | 2·10 | 55 |
| 2133 | 1500cr. Marajoara | 2·75 | 65 |
| 2134 | 1500cr. Mangalarga pacer | 2·75 | 65 |

**1106** Ouro Preto

**1985.** UNESCO World Heritage Sites. Multicoloured.

| | | | |
|---|---|---|---|
| 2135 | 220cr. Type **1106** | 40 | 10 |
| 2136 | 220cr. Sao Miguel das Missoes | 40 | 10 |
| 2137 | 220cr. Olinda | 40 | 10 |

**1107** "Polyvolume" (Mary Vieira)

**1985.** 40th Anniv of Rio-Branco Institute (diplomatic training academy).

| | | | | |
|---|---|---|---|---|
| 2138 | **1107** | 220cr. multicoloured | 50 | 10 |

**1108** National Theatre

**1985.** 25th Anniv of Brasilia. Multicoloured.

| | | | |
|---|---|---|---|
| 2139 | 220cr. Type **1108** | 50 | 10 |
| 2140 | 220cr. Catetinho (home of former President Juscelino Keubitschek) and memorial | 50 | 10 |

**1109** Rondon and Morse Telegraph

**1985.** 120th Birth Anniv of Marshal Candido Mariano da Silva Rondon (military engineer and explorer).

| | | | | |
|---|---|---|---|---|
| 2141 | **1109** | 220cr. multicoloured | 50 | 10 |

**1110** Fontoura and Pharmaceutical Equipment

**1985.** Birth Centenary of Candido Fontoura (pharmacist).

| | | | | |
|---|---|---|---|---|
| 2142 | **1110** | 220cr. multicoloured | 50 | 10 |

**1111** Lizards

**1985.** Rock Paintings. Multicoloured.

| | | | |
|---|---|---|---|
| 2143 | 300cr. Type **1111** | 40 | 20 |
| 2144 | 300cr. Deer | 40 | 20 |
| 2145 | 2000cr. Various animals | 1·80 | 1·00 |
| **MS**2146 | 100×70 mm. Nos. 2143/5 | 4·00 | 4·00 |

Nos. **MS**2146 is inscribed for Brapex VI national stamp exhibition, Belo Horizonte.

**1112** Numeral **1113** Numeral

**1985**

| | | | | |
|---|---|---|---|---|
| 2147 | **1112** | 50cr. red | 30 | 10 |
| 2148 | **1112** | 100cr. purple | 30 | 10 |
| 2149 | **1112** | 150cr. lilac | 30 | 10 |
| 2150 | **1112** | 200cr. blue | 30 | 10 |
| 2151 | **1112** | 220cr. green | 1·10 | 55 |
| 2152 | **1112** | 300cr. blue | 30 | 10 |
| 2153 | **1112** | 500cr. black | 40 | 20 |
| 2154 | **1113** | 1000cr. brown | 30 | 10 |
| 2155 | **1113** | 2000cr. green | 40 | 20 |
| 2156 | **1113** | 3000cr. lilac | 45 | 20 |
| 2157 | **1113** | 5000cr. brown | 2·20 | 20 |

**1114** Common Noddies

**1985.** National Marine Park, Abrolhos. Mult.

| | | | |
|---|---|---|---|
| 2168 | 220cr. Type **1114** | 1·20 | 40 |
| 2169 | 220cr. Magnificent frigate birds and blue-faced booby | 1·20 | 40 |
| 2170 | 220cr. Blue-faced boobies and red-billed tropic bird | 1·20 | 40 |
| 2171 | 2000cr. Grey plovers | 3·50 | 75 |

**1115** Breast-feeding

**1985.** United Nations Children's Fund Child Survival Campaign. Multicoloured.

| | | | |
|---|---|---|---|
| 2172 | 220cr. Type **1115** | 35 | 15 |
| 2173 | 220cr. Growth chart and oral rehydration | 35 | 15 |

**1116** Bell 47J Ranger Helicopter rescuing Man, "Brasil" (corvette) and Diver

**1985.** International Sea Search and Rescue Convention, Rio de Janeiro.
2174 **1116** 220cr. multicoloured 60 40

**1117** World Cup and Ball

**1985.** World Cup Football Championship, Mexico (1986) (1st issue). Sheet 70×99 mm.
**MS**2175 **1117** 2000cr. mult 8·25 8·25
See also No.**MS**2213.

**1118** Children holding Hands

**1985.** International Youth Year.
2176 **1118** 220cr. multicoloured 45 25

**1119** Hands holding Host

**1985.** 11th Nat Eucharistic Congress, Aparecida.
2177 **1119** 2000cr. multicoloured 1·70 75

**1120** Scene from "Mineiro Blood", Camera and Mauro

**1985.** 60th Anniv of Humberto Mauro's Cataguases Cycle of Films.
2178 **1120** 300cr. multicoloured 45 25

**1121** Escola e Sacro Museum

**1985.** 400th Anniv of Paraiba State.
2179 **1121** 330cr. multicoloured 45 25

**1122** Inconfidencia Museum, Ouro Preto

**1985.** Museums. Multicoloured.
2180 300cr. Type **1122** 35 15
2181 300cr. Historical and Diplomatic Museum Itamaraty 35 15

**1123** "Cabano" (Guido Mondin)

**1985.** 150th Anniv of Cabanagem Insurrection, Belem City.
2182 **1123** 330cr. multicoloured 45 25

**1124** Aeritalia/Aermacchi AM-X Fighter

**1985.** AM-X (military airplane) Project.
2183 **1124** 330cr. multicoloured 45 25

**1125** Captain and Crossbowman (early 16th century)

**1985.** Military Dress. Multicoloured.
2184 300cr. Type **1125** 45 25
2185 300cr. Arquebusier and sergeant (late 16th cent) 45 25
2186 300cr. Musketeer and pikeman (early 17th century) 45 25
2187 300cr. Mulatto fusilier and pikeman with scimitar (early 17th century) 45 25

**1126** "Farroupilha Rebels" (Guido Mondin)

**1985.** 150th Anniv of Farroupilha Revolution.
2188 **1126** 330cr. multicoloured 45 25

**1127** Itaimbezinho Canyon

**1985.** Aparados da Serra National Park. Mult.
2189 3100cr. Type **1127** 2·00 55
2190 3320cr. Mountain range 2·00 55
2191 3480cr. Pine forest 2·00 55

**1128** Neves and Brasilia Buildings

**1985.** Tancredo Neves (President-elect) Commem.
2192 **1128** 330cr. black & orange 45 25

**1129** "FEB" on Envelope

**1985.** 40th Anniv (1984) of Brazilian Expeditionary Force Postal Service.
2193 **1129** 500cr. multicoloured 45 25

**1130** "Especuladora", 1835

**1985.** 150th Anniv of Rio de Janeiro–Niteroi Ferry Service. Multicoloured.
2194 500cr. Type **1130** 60 30
2195 500cr. "Segunda", 1862 60 30
2196 500cr. "Terceira", 1911 60 30
2197 500cr. "Urca", 1981 60 30

**1131** Muniz M-7

**1985.** 50th Anniv of Muniz M-7 Biplane's Maiden Flight.
2198 **1131** 500cr. multicoloured 45 25

**1132** Dove Emblem and Stylized Flags

**1985.** 40th Anniv of UNO.
2199 **1132** 500cr. multicoloured 45 25

**1133** Front Page of First Edition

**1985.** 160th Anniv of "Pernambuco Daily News".
2200 **1133** 500cr. multicoloured 45 25

**1134** Adoration

**1985.** Christmas. Multicoloured.
2201 500cr. Type **1134** 45 25
2202 500cr. Adoration of the Magi 45 25
2203 500cr. Flight into Egypt 45 25

**1985.** State Flags (5th series). As T 992. Mult.
2204 500cr. Para 55 25
2205 500cr. Rio Grande do Sul 55 25
2206 500cr. Acre 55 25
2207 500cr. Sao Paulo 55 25

**1985.** Obligatory Tax. Anti-leprosy Week.
2208 **1095** 100cr. red 55 35

**1135** Child holding Wheat

**1985.** Thanksgiving Day.
2209 **1135** 500cr. multicoloured 45 25

**1136** Transport, Mined Ore and Trees

**1985.** Carajas Development Programme.
2210 **1136** 500cr. multicoloured 45 25

**1137** Gusmao and Balloons

**1985.** 300th Birth Anniv of Bartolomeu Lourenco de Gusmao (inventor).
2211 **1137** 500cr. multicoloured 45 25

**1138** "The Trees"

**1985.** Birth Centenary of Antonio Francisco da Costa e Silva (poet).
2212 **1138** 500cr. multicoloured 45 25

**1139** Footballers

**1986.** World Cup Football Championship, Mexico (2nd issue) and Lubrepex 86 Brazilian—Portuguese Stamp Exhibition, Rio de Janeiro (1st issue). Sheet 69×99 mm.
**MS**2213 **1139** 10000cr. multicoloured 6·00 6·00
See also Nos. 2260/**MS**2262.

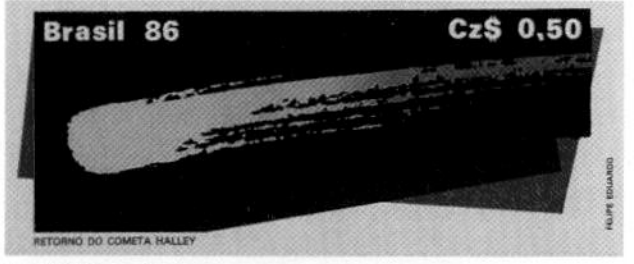


**1140** Comet

**1986.** Appearance of Halley's Comet.
2214 **1140** 50c. multicoloured 45 25

**1141** Flags and Station

**1986.** 2nd Anniv of Commander Ferraz Antarctic Station.
2215 **1141** 50c. multicoloured 45 25

**1142** Symbols of Industry, Agriculture and Commerce

**1986.** Labour Day.

| | | | | |
|---|---|---|---|---|
| 2216 | **1142** | 50c. multicoloured | 45 | 25 |

**1143** "Maternity"

**1986.** 50th Death Anniv of Henrique Bernardelli (artist).

| | | | | |
|---|---|---|---|---|
| 2217 | **1143** | 50c. multicoloured | 45 | 25 |

**1144** Broken Chain Links as Birds

**1986.** 25th Anniv of Amnesty International.

| | | | | |
|---|---|---|---|---|
| 2218 | **1144** | 50c. multicoloured | 45 | 25 |

**1145** "Pyrrhopyge ruficauda"

**1986.** Butterflies. Multicoloured.

| | | | |
|---|---|---|---|
| 2219 | 50c. Type **1145** | 85 | 35 |
| 2220 | 50c. "Pierriballia mandela molione" | 85 | 35 |
| 2221 | 50c. "Prepona eugenes diluta" | 85 | 35 |

**1146** Gomes Peri, and Score of "O Guarani"

**1986.** 150th Birth Anniv of Antonio Carlos Gomes (composer).

| | | | | |
|---|---|---|---|---|
| 2222 | **1146** | 50c. multicoloured | 45 | 25 |

**1147** Man in Safety Harness

**1986.** Prevention of Industrial Accidents.

| | | | | |
|---|---|---|---|---|
| 2223 | **1147** | 50c. multicoloured | 45 | 25 |

**1148** "Black Beard" 10r. Stamp

**1986.** Stamp Day. 120th Anniv of Pedro II Black Beard Stamps and 75th Anniv of Brazilian Philatelic Society. Sheet 69×99 mm.

| | | | | |
|---|---|---|---|---|
| MS2224 | **1148** | 5cz. red and ochre | 2·00 | 2·00 |

**1149** Garcia D'Avilas House Chapel, Nazare de Mata

**1986**

| | | | | |
|---|---|---|---|---|
| 2225 | **1149** | 10c. green | 35 | 10 |
| 2226 | - | 20c. blue | 35 | 10 |
| 2228 | - | 50c. orange | 1·10 | 25 |
| 2230 | - | 1cz. brown | 35 | 10 |
| 2231 | - | 2cz. red | 45 | 10 |
| 2233 | - | 5cz. green | 1·30 | 25 |
| 2235 | - | 10cz. blue | 1·10 | 25 |
| 2236 | - | 20cz. red | 1·50 | 25 |
| 2238 | - | 50cz. orange | 2·75 | 25 |
| 2240 | - | 100cz. green | 2·75 | 25 |
| 2241 | - | 200cz. blue | 2·75 | 25 |
| 2242 | - | 500cz. brown | 3·50 | 80 |

DESIGNS—HORIZ: 20c. Church of Our Lady of the Assumptiom, Anchieta; 50c. Reis Magos Fortress, Natal; 1cz. Pelourinho, Alcantara; 2cz. St. Francis's Monastery, Olinda; 5cz. St. Anthony's Chapel, Sao Roque; 10cz. St Lawrence of the Indians Church, Niteroi; 20cz. Principe da Beira Fortress, Costa Marques, Rondobua; 100cz. Church of Our Lady of Sorrows, Campanha; 200cz. Counting House, Ouro Preto; 500cz. Customs building, Belem. VERT: 50cz. Church of the Good Jesus, Matasinhos.

**1150** Kubitschek and Alvorada Palace

**1986.** 10th Death Anniv of Juscelino Kubitschek (President 1956–61).

| | | | | |
|---|---|---|---|---|
| 2244 | **1150** | 50c. multicoloured | 45 | 25 |

**1151** Mangabeira and Itamaraty Palace, Rio de Janeiro

**1986.** Birth Cent of Octavio Mangabeira (politician).

| | | | | |
|---|---|---|---|---|
| 2245 | **1151** | 50c. multicoloured | 45 | 25 |

**1152** Congress Emblem and Sao Paulo

**1986.** 8th World Gastroenterology Congress, Sao Paulo.

| | | | | |
|---|---|---|---|---|
| 2246 | **1152** | 50c. multicoloured | 45 | 25 |

**1153** Microphone and Radio Waves

**1986.** 50th Annivs. of National Radio and Education and Culture Ministry Radio.

| | | | | |
|---|---|---|---|---|
| 2247 | **1153** | 50c. multicoloured | 45 | 25 |

**1154** "Peace" (detail, Candido Portinari)

**1986.** International Peace Year.

| | | | | |
|---|---|---|---|---|
| 2248 | **1154** | 50c. multicoloured | 45 | 25 |

**1155** "Urera mitis"

**1986.** Flowers. Multicoloured.

| | | | |
|---|---|---|---|
| 2249 | 50c. Type **1155** | 35 | 15 |
| 2250 | 6cz.50 "Couroupita guyanensis" | 1·70 | 45 |
| 2251 | 6cz.90 Mountain ebony (horiz) | 1·80 | 45 |

**1156** Simoes Filho and Newspaper

**1986.** Birth Centenary of Ernesto Simoes Filho (politician and founder of "A Tarde").

| | | | | |
|---|---|---|---|---|
| 2252 | **1156** | 50c. multicoloured | 45 | 25 |

**1157** Title Page of Gregorio de Matto's MS

**1986.** Book Day. Poets' Birth Anniversaries.

| | | | | |
|---|---|---|---|---|
| 2253 | **1157** | 50c. brown & lt brown | 45 | 25 |
| 2254 | - | 50c. green and red | 45 | 25 |

DESIGNS: No. 2253, Type **1157** (350th anniv); 2254, Manuel Bandeira and last verse of "I'll Return to Pasargada" (centenary).

**1158** Head Office, Brasilia

**1986.** 125th Anniv of Federal Savings Bank.

| | | | | |
|---|---|---|---|---|
| 2255 | **1158** | 50c. multicoloured | 45 | 25 |

**1159** Birds around Baby lying in Nest

**1986.** Christmas. Multicoloured.

| | | | |
|---|---|---|---|
| 2256 | 50c. Type **1159** | 60 | 25 |
| 2257 | 6cz.50 Birds around tree with Christmas decorations | 2·20 | 55 |
| 2258 | 7cz.30 Birds wearing Santa Claus caps | 2·20 | 70 |

**1160** Rocha on Strip of Film

**1986.** 5th Death Anniv of Glauber Rocha (film producer).

| | | | | |
|---|---|---|---|---|
| 2259 | **1160** | 50c. multicoloured | 45 | 25 |

**1161** "History of Empress Porcina"

**1986.** "Lubrapex 86" Brazilian–Portuguese Stamp Exhibition, Rio de Janeiro. Design showing scenes from Cordel Literature. Multicoloured.

| | | | |
|---|---|---|---|
| 2260 | 6cz.90 Type **1161** | 1·40 | 70 |
| 2261 | 6cz.90 "Romance of the Mysterious Peacock" | 1·40 | 70 |
| MS2262 | 70×100 mm. Nos. 2260/2 | 4·25 | 4·25 |

**1986.** Obligatory Tax. Anti-leprosy Week.

| | | | | |
|---|---|---|---|---|
| 2263 | **1095** | 10c. brown | 35 | 25 |

**1162** Lieutenant Commander, 1930

**1986.** Military Uniforms. Multicoloured.

| | | | |
|---|---|---|---|
| 2264 | 50c. Type **1162** | 35 | 25 |
| 2265 | 50c. Military Aviation flight lieutenant, 1930 | 35 | 25 |

**1163** "Graf Zeppelin" over Hangar

**1986.** 50th Anniv of Bartolomeu de Gusmao Airport, Santa Cruz.
2266 **1163** 1cz. multicoloured 45 35

**1164** Museum

**1987.** 50th Anniv of National Fine Arts Museum, Rio de Janeiro.
2267 **1164** 1cz. multicoloured 45 35

**1165** Villa-Lobos conducting and Musical Motifs

**1987.** Birth Cent of Heitor Villa-Lobos (composer).
2268 **1165** 1cz.50 multicoloured 55 35

**1166** Flag, Lockheed C-130 Hercules Aircraft and Antarctic Landscape

**1987.** Air Force Participation in Brazilian Antarctic Programme.
2269 **1166** 1cz. multicoloured 95 25

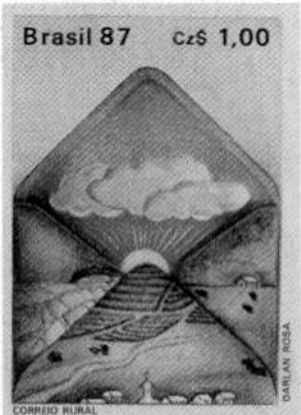

**1167** Landscape on Open Envelope (Rural Post Office Network)

**1987.** Special Mail Services. Multicoloured.
2270 1cz. Type **1167** 45 35
2271 1cz. Satchel and globe (International Express Mail Service) 45 35

**1168** "Brasilsat" Satellite, Radio Wave and Globe

**1987.** "Telecom 87" World Telecommunications Exhibition, Geneva.
2272 **1168** 2cz. multicoloured 45 35

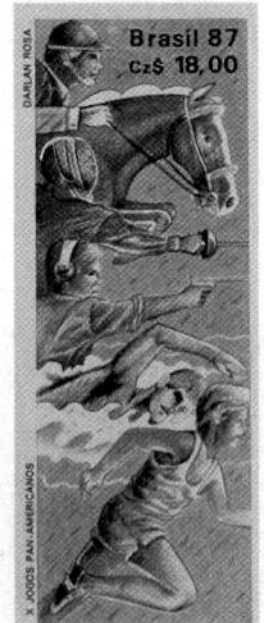

**1169** Modern Pentathlon

**1987.** 10th Pan-American Games, Indianapolis, U.S.A.
2273 **1169** 18cz. multicoloured 3·00 1·10

**1170** Hawksbill Turtle

**1987.** Endangered Animals. Multicoloured.
2274 2cz. Type **1170** 85 45
2275 2cz. Right whale 85 45

**1171** Old and New Court Buildings and Symbol of Justice

**1987.** 40th Anniv of Federal Appeal Court.
2276 **1171** 2cz. multicoloured 45 35

**1172** Arms

**1987.** Centenary of Military Club.
2277 **1172** 3cz. multicoloured 60 35

**1173** Institute and Foodstuffs

**1987.** Centenary of Agronomic Institute, Campinas.
2278 **1173** 2cz. multicoloured 45 35

**1174** "Fulgora servillei"

**1987.** 50th Anniv of Brazilian Entomology Society. Multicoloured.
2279 3cz. Type **1174** 85 35
2280 3cz. "Zoolea lopiceps" 85 35

**1175** Features of Northern and North-east Regions

**1987.** National Tourism Year. Multicoloured.
2281 3cz. Type **1175** 45 35
2282 3cz. Features of mid-west, south-east and south regions 45 35

**1176** Main Tower

**1987.** 150th Anniv of Royal Portuguese Reading Cabinet, Rio de Janeiro.
2283 **1176** 30cz. green and red 2·20 1·70

**1177** International Sport Club (1975, 1976, 1979)

**1987.** Brazilian Football Championship Gold Cup Winners (1st series). Designs showing footballers and Club emblems.
2284 **1177** 3cz. red, black & yellow 45 25
2285 - 3cz. red, yellow & black 45 25
2286 - 3cz. multicoloured 45 25
2287 - 3cz. red, black & yellow 45 25

DESIGNS: No. 2285, Sao Paulo Football Club (1977, 1986); 2286, Guarani Football Club (1978); 2287, Regatas do Flamengo Club (1980, 1982, 1983).

See also Nos. 2322/5, 2398 and 2408.

**1178** St. Francis's Church and Tiled Column

**1987.** 400th Anniv of St. Francis's Monastery, Salvador.
2288 **1178** 4cz. multicoloured 45 35

**1179** Almeida and Scenes from "A Bagaceira"

**1987.** Birth Centenary of Jose Americo de Almeida (writer).
2289 **1179** 4cz. multicoloured 35 25

**1180** Barra do Picao

**1987.** 450th Anniv of Recife.
2290 **1180** 5cz. multicoloured 35 10

**1987.** Obligatory Tax. Anti-leprosy Week.
2291 **1095** 30cz. green 35 25

**1181** Rainbow, Dove and Open Hands

**1987.** Thanksgiving Day.
2292 **1181** 5cz. multicoloured 35 25

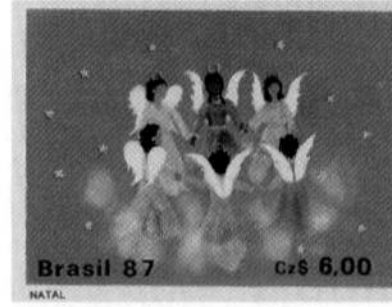

**1182** Angels

**1987.** Christmas. Multicoloured.
2293 6cz. Type **1182** 45 35
2294 6cz. Dancers on stage 45 35
2295 6cz. Shepherd playing flute 45 35

**1183** Bernardo Pereira de Vasconcelos (founder) and Pedro II

**1987.** 150th Anniv of Pedro II School, Rio de Janeiro.
2296 **1183** 6cz. yellow, blk & red 45 35

**1184** "Cattleya guttata"

**1987.** 50th Anniv of Brazilian Orchid Growers Society. Multicoloured.
2297 6cz. Type **1184** 85 25
2298 6cz. "Laelia lobata" 85 25

**1185** Statue and Fatima Basilica, Portugal

**1987.** Marian Year. Visit to Brazil of Statue of Our Lady of Fatima.
2299 **1185** 50cz. multicoloured 3·00 2·30

**1186** Sousa, Indians and Fauna

**1987.** 400th Anniv of "Descriptive Treaties of Brazil" by Gabriel Soares de Sousa.
2300 **1186** 7cz. multicoloured 45 35

**1187** Page from Book of Gregorian Chants and Computer Terminal

**1988.** 150th Anniv of National Archives.
2301 **1187** 7cz. multicoloured 45 35

**1188** National Colours, Caravel and Modern Ship

**1988.** 180th Anniv of Opening of Brazilian Ports to Free Trade.
2302 **1188** 7cz. multicoloured 45 35

**1189** Microscope and Map

**1988.** Antarctic Research. Sheet 99×69 mm.
**MS**2303 **1189** 80cz. multicoloured 4·25 4·25

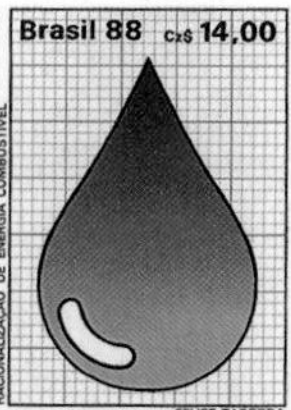

**1190** Petrol Droplet

**1988.** Energy Conservation. Multicoloured.
2304 14cz. Type **1190** 45 35
2305 14cz. Flash of electricity 45 35

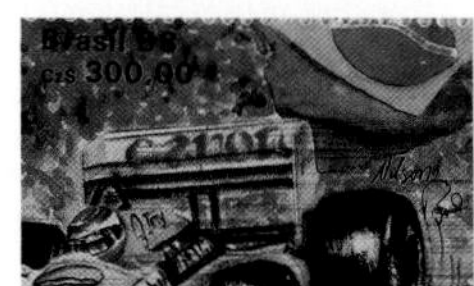

**1191** Williams-Honda Racing Car and Flag

**1988.** Nelson Piquet's Third Formula 1 Motor Racing World Championship Title (1987). Sheet 99×69 mm.

| | | | | |
|---|---|---|---|---|
| **MS**2306 | **1191** | 300cz. multicoloured | 9·50 | 9·50 |

**1192** Bonifacio and Emblems of his Life

**1988.** 150th Death Anniv of Jose Bonifacio de Andrada e Silva (scientist, writer and "Patriarch of the Independence").

| | | | | |
|---|---|---|---|---|
| 2307 | **1192** | 20cz. multicoloured | 60 | 45 |

**1193** Quill Pen on Page of Aurea Law

**1988.** Centenary of Abolition of Slavery. Mult.

| | | | |
|---|---|---|---|
| 2308 | 20cz. Type **1193** | 45 | 35 |
| 2309 | 50cz. Norris map of Africa, 1773, slave ship and plan of trading routes | 1·30 | 1·00 |

**1194** Church of the Good Jesus of Matosinhos

**1988.** UNESCO World Heritage Sites. Mult.

| | | | |
|---|---|---|---|
| 2310 | 20cz. Type **1194** | 45 | 35 |
| 2311 | 50cz. Brasilia | 1·30 | 90 |
| 2312 | 100cz. Pelourinho, Salvador | 2·40 | 1·80 |

**1195** Concentric Circles on Map of Americas

**1988.** "Americas Telecom 88" Telecommunications Exhibition, Rio de Janeiro.

| | | | | |
|---|---|---|---|---|
| 2313 | **1195** | 50cz. multicoloured | 1·90 | 90 |

**1196** "Kasato Maru" (first immigrant ship) and Japanese Family

**1988.** 80th Anniv of Japanese Immigration into Brazil.

| | | | | |
|---|---|---|---|---|
| 2314 | **1196** | 100cz. multicoloured | 1·90 | 1·00 |

**1197** Postal Authority Emblem

**1988.** No value expressed.

| | | | | |
|---|---|---|---|---|
| 2315 | **1197** | (–) blue | 1·40 | 25 |

No. 2315 was valid for use at the current first class inland letter rate. It could not be used to pay postage to foreign countries.

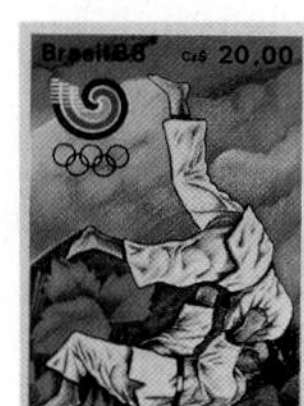

**1198** Judo

**1988.** Olympic Games, Seoul.

| | | | | |
|---|---|---|---|---|
| 2316 | **1198** | 20cz. multicoloured | 1·10 | 25 |

**1199** Giant Anteater

**1988.** Endangered Mammals. Multicoloured.

| | | | |
|---|---|---|---|
| 2317 | 20cz. Type **1199** | 60 | 35 |
| 2318 | 50cz. Thin-spined porcupine | 95 | 45 |
| 2319 | 100cz. Bush dog | 2·00 | 1·10 |

**1200** "Motherland" (Pedro Bruno)

**1988.** Stamp Day. Brasiliana 89 International Stamp Exhibition. Sheet 98×69 mm.

| | | | | |
|---|---|---|---|---|
| **MS**2320 | **1200** | 250cz. multicoloured | 6·50 | 6·50 |

**1201** Industrial Symbols

**1988.** 50th Anniv of National Confederation of Industry.

| | | | | |
|---|---|---|---|---|
| 2321 | **1201** | 50cz. multicoloured | 60 | 35 |

**1988.** Brazilian Football Championship Gold Cup Winners (2nd series). As T 1177. Multicoloured.

| | | | |
|---|---|---|---|
| 2322 | 50cz. Sport Club do Recife (1987) | 45 | 25 |
| 2323 | 50cz. Coritiba Football Club (1985) | 45 | 25 |
| 2324 | 100cz. Gremio Football Porto Alegrense (1981) | 70 | 35 |
| 2325 | 200cz. Fluminense Football Club (1984) | 1·20 | 80 |

**1202** Congress, Brasilia

**1988.** Promulgation of 1998 Consitution. Sheet 99×69 mm.

| | | | |
|---|---|---|---|
| **MS**2326 | 550cz. multicoloured | 5·00 | 5·00 |

**1203** Raul Pompeia and Lines from "O Ateneu"

**1988.** Book Day. Centenaries of Publication of "O Ateneu" and "Verses". Multicoloured.

| | | | |
|---|---|---|---|
| 2327 | 50cz. Type **1203** | 40 | 25 |
| 2328 | 100cz. Olavo Bilac and lines from "Verses" | 55 | 30 |

**1204** Church

**1988.** Christmas. Origami by Marcia Bloch. Multicoloured.

| | | | |
|---|---|---|---|
| 2329 | 50cz. Type **1204** | 60 | 35 |
| 2330 | 100cz. Nativity | 70 | 35 |
| 2331 | 200cz. Santa Claus and parcels | 1·40 | 80 |

**1205** Father Santiago Uchoa

**1988.** Obligatory Tax. Anti-leprosy Week.

| | | | | |
|---|---|---|---|---|
| 2332 | **1205** | 1cz.30 brown | 45 | 25 |

See also Nos. 2614 and 2686.

**1206** Mate and Rodeo Rider

**1988.** "Abrafex" Argentine–Brazilian Stamp Exhibition, Buenos Aires.

| | | | | |
|---|---|---|---|---|
| 2333 | **1206** | 400cz. multicoloured | 3·00 | 1·00 |

**1207** Hatchetfish ("Gasteropelecus sp.")

**1988.** Freshwater Fishes. Multicoloured.

| | | | |
|---|---|---|---|
| 2334 | 55cz. Type **1207** | 35 | 35 |
| 2335 | 55cz. Black arawana ("Osteoglossum ferreira") | 35 | 35 |
| 2336 | 55cz. Green moenkhausia ("Moenkhausia sp.") | 35 | 35 |
| 2337 | 55cz. Pearlfish ("Xavantei") | 35 | 35 |
| 2338 | 55cz. Armoured bristlemouth catfish ("Ancistrus hoplogenys") | 35 | 35 |
| 2339 | 55cz. Emerald catfish ("Brochis splendens") | 35 | 35 |

**1208** Red-tailed Amazon

**1988.** Brapex VII National Stamp Exhibition, Sao Paulo. Conservation of Jurelia. Sheet 99×68 mm containing T 1208 and similar vert designs. Multicoloured.

| | | | |
|---|---|---|---|
| **MS**2340 | 100cz. Type **1208**; 250cz. "Vriesia ensiformis" (bromelia); 400cz. Great egret | 17·00 | 17·00 |

**1209** Dish Aerials

**1988.** 10th Anniv of Ansat 10 (first Brazilian dish aerial), Macapa.

| | | | | |
|---|---|---|---|---|
| 2341 | **1209** | 70cz. multicoloured | 35 | 35 |

**1210** "Four Arts"

**1988.** Establishment of National Foundation of Scenic Arts.

| | | | | |
|---|---|---|---|---|
| 2342 | **1210** | 70cz. multicoloured | 45 | 35 |

**1211** Court Building

**1989.** 380th Anniv of Bahia Court of Justice.

| | | | | |
|---|---|---|---|---|
| 2343 | **1211** | 25c. multicoloured | 95 | 55 |

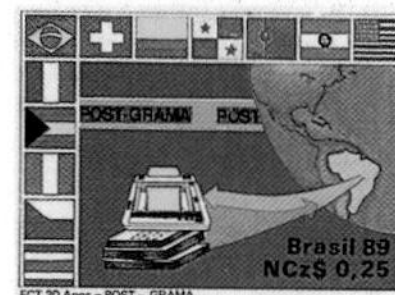

**1212** Library Building and Detail of Main Door

**1989.** Public Library Year. 178th Anniv of First Public Library, Bahia.

| | | | | |
|---|---|---|---|---|
| 2344 | **1212** | 25c. multicoloured | 95 | 55 |

**1213** Facsimile Machine

**1989.** 20th Anniv of Post and Telegraph Department. Postal Services. Multicoloured.

| | | | |
|---|---|---|---|
| 2345 | 25c. Type **1213** | 85 | 55 |
| 2346 | 25c. Hand holding parcel (Express Mail Service) | 85 | 55 |
| 2347 | 25c. Airbus Industrie 300 airplane on runway (SEDEX express parcel service) | 85 | 55 |
| 2348 | 25c. Putting coin in savings box (CEF postal savings) | 85 | 55 |

**1214** Senna

**1989.** Aryton Senna's Formula 1 Motor Racing World Championship Title (1988). Sheet 99×69 mm.

| | | | | |
|---|---|---|---|---|
| **MS**2349 | **1214** | 2cz. multicoloured | 15·00 | 15·00 |

1215 Emblem

1989. "Our Nature" Programme.

| | | | | |
|---|---|---|---|---|
| 2350 | 1215 | 25c. multicoloured | 70 | 45 |

1216 Hand reaching for Symbol of Freedom

1989. Bicentenary of Inconfidencia Mineira (independence movement). Multicoloured.

| | | | |
|---|---|---|---|
| 2351 | 30c. Type **1216** | 60 | 35 |
| 2352 | 30c. Man's profile and colonial buildings | 60 | 35 |
| 2353 | 40c. Baroque buildings in disarray | 95 | 45 |

1217 School

1989. Cent of Rio de Janeiro Military School.

| | | | | |
|---|---|---|---|---|
| 2354 | 1217 | 50c. multicoloured | 1·10 | 70 |

1218 "Pavonia alnifolia"

1989. Endangered Plants. Multicoloured.

| | | | |
|---|---|---|---|
| 2355 | 50c. Type **1218** | 1·40 | 1·00 |
| 2356 | 1cz. "Worsleya rayneri" (vert) | 3·00 | 2·20 |
| 2357 | 1cz.50 "Heliconia farinosa" (vert) | 4·25 | 3·50 |

1219 Barreto and Pedro II Square, Recife Law School

1989. 150th Birth Anniv of Tobias Barreto (writer).

| | | | | |
|---|---|---|---|---|
| 2358 | 1219 | 50c. multicoloured | 1·50 | 90 |

1220 "Quiabentia zehntneri"

1989. Flowers. Currency expressed as "NCz $". Multicoloured.

| | | | |
|---|---|---|---|
| 2359 | 10c. "Dichorisandra" sp. | 35 | 25 |
| 2360 | 20c. Type **1220** | 45 | 25 |
| 2361 | 50c. "Bougainvillea glabra" | 95 | 30 |
| 2363 | 1cz. "Impatiens" sp. | 2·10 | 40 |
| 2364 | 2cz. "Chorisia crispiflora" (vert) | 70 | 25 |
| 2366 | 5cz. "Hibiscus trilineatus" | 70 | 30 |

See also Nos. 2413/24.

1221 Shooting of "Revistinha"

1989. 20th Anniv of TV Cultura.

| | | | | |
|---|---|---|---|---|
| 2371 | 1221 | 50c. multicoloured | 1·40 | 90 |

1222 Postal Authority Emblem

1989. No value expressed.

| | | | | |
|---|---|---|---|---|
| 2372 | 1222 | (–) blue and orange | 1·40 | 30 |

No. 2372 was sold at the current rate for first class internal postage.

1223 Brasilia T.V. Tower and Microlight

1989. Aerosports and 80th Anniv of Santos Dumont's Flight in "Demoiselle". Mult.

| | | | |
|---|---|---|---|
| 2373 | 50c. Type **1223** | 95 | 80 |
| 2374 | 1cz.50 Eiffel Tower and "Demoiselle" | 3·25 | 2·20 |

1224 "Largo da Carioca" (detail, Nicolas Antoine Taunay)

1989. Philexfrance 89 International Stamp Exhibition, Paris and Bicentenary of French Revolution. Sheet 99×69 mm.

| | | |
|---|---|---|
| **MS**2375 **1224** 3cz. multicoloured | 6·00 | 6·00 |

1225 Tourmaline

1989. Precious Stones. Multicoloured.

| | | | |
|---|---|---|---|
| 2376 | 50c. Type **1225** | 95 | 55 |
| 2377 | 1cz.50 Amethyst | 2·40 | 1·80 |

1226 Imperial Palace, Rio de Janeiro

1989. Stamp Day. Brasiliana 89 International Stamp Exhibition, Rio de Janeiro. Sheet 99×69 mm.

| | | |
|---|---|---|
| **MS**2378 **1226** 5cz. multicoloured | 7·75 | 7·75 |

1227 Rainbow and Association H.Q. Mercury

1989. 150th Anniv of Pernambuco Trade Assn.

| | | | | |
|---|---|---|---|---|
| 2379 | 1227 | 50c. multicoloured | 85 | 55 |

1228 Pioneers' Names and 19th-century to Modern Photographs

1989. International Photography Year.

| | | | | |
|---|---|---|---|---|
| 2380 | 1228 | 1cz.50 multicoloured | 2·40 | 1·70 |

1229 Power Station

1989. Centenary of Marmelos-o Power Station (first South American hydro-electric power station).

| | | | | |
|---|---|---|---|---|
| 2381 | 1229 | 50c. multicoloured | 70 | 45 |

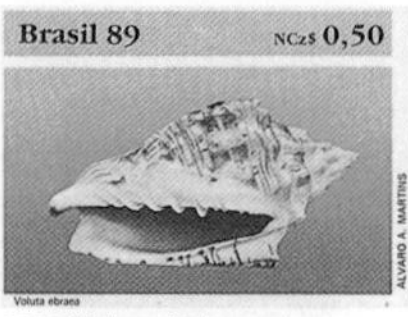
1230 Hebrew Volute

1989. Molluscs. Multicoloured.

| | | | |
|---|---|---|---|
| 2382 | 50c. Type **1230** | 35 | 25 |
| 2383 | 1cz. Matthew's morum | 85 | 45 |
| 2384 | 1cz.50 Travasso's ancilla | 1·20 | 70 |

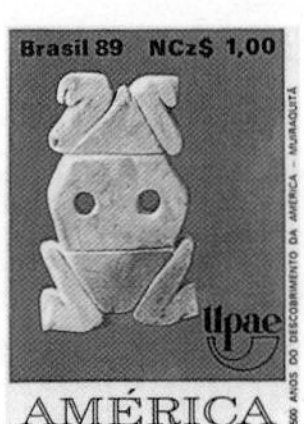
1231 Muiraquita

1989. America. Pre-Columbian Artefacts. Mult.

| | | | |
|---|---|---|---|
| 2385 | 1cz. Type **1231** | 95 | 6·75 |
| 2386 | 4cz. Caryatid vase (horiz) | 3·75 | 2·75 |

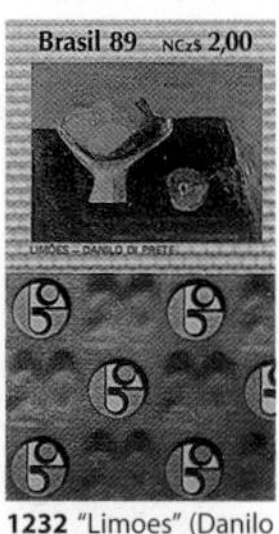
1232 "Limoes" (Danilo di Prete)

1989. 20th International Biennial Art Exhibition, Sao Paulo. Sheet 99×79 mm containing T 1232 and similar vert designs. Multicoloured.

| | | |
|---|---|---|
| **MS**2387 2cz. Type **1232**; 3cz. "O Indio e a Suacuaoara" (sculpture, Brecheret); 5cz. Francisco Matarazzo (exhibition founder) | 7·75 | 7·75 |

1233 Casimiro de Abreu

1989. Book Day. Writers' Birth Annivs. Mult.

| | | | |
|---|---|---|---|
| 2388 | 1cz. Type **1233** (150th anniv) | 1·10 | 80 |
| 2389 | 1cz. Machado de Assis (150th anniv) | 1·10 | 80 |
| 2390 | 1cz. Cora Coralina (cent) | 1·10 | 80 |

1234 Postal Authority Emblem

1989. No value expressed. Burelage in second colour.

| | | | | |
|---|---|---|---|---|
| 2391 | 1234 | (–) red and orange | 4·50 | 1·90 |

No. 2391 was sold at the current rate for first class international postage.

1235 Police Emblem

1989. 25th Anniv of Federal Police Department.

| | | | | |
|---|---|---|---|---|
| 2392 | 1235 | 1cz. multicoloured | 60 | 35 |

1236 "Deodoro presents the Flag of the Republic" (detail, anon)

1989. Centenary of Proclamation of Republic. Sheet 98×68 mm.

| | | |
|---|---|---|
| **MS**2393 **1236** 15cz. multicoloured | 8·75 | 8·75 |

1237 Angel

1989. Christmas. Multicoloured.

| | | | |
|---|---|---|---|
| 2394 | 70c. Type **1237** | 35 | 35 |
| 2395 | 1cz. Nativity | 45 | 35 |

1238 Candle Flame as Dove

1989. Thanksgiving Day.

| | | | | |
|---|---|---|---|---|
| 2396 | 1238 | 1cz. multicoloured | 45 | 35 |

1239 Fr. Damien de Veuster

1989. Obligatory Tax. Anti-leprosy Week.

| | | | | |
|---|---|---|---|---|
| 2397 | 1239 | 2c. red | 35 | 25 |

See also Nos. 2458, 2509 and 2565.

1989. Football Clubs. As T 1177. Multicoloured.

| | | | |
|---|---|---|---|
| 2398 | 50c. Bahia Sports Club | 45 | 35 |

1240 "The Yellow Man"

1989. Birth Cent of Anita Malfatti (painter).

| | | | | |
|---|---|---|---|---|
| 2399 | 1240 | 1cz. multicoloured | 45 | 35 |

1241 Archive and Proclamation by Bento Goncalves

1990. Cent of Bahia State Public Archive.

| | | | | |
|---|---|---|---|---|
| 2400 | 1241 | 2cz. multicoloured | 60 | 35 |

**1242** "Mimosa caesalpiniifolia"

**1990.** 40th Anniv of Brazilian Botanical Society. Multicoloured.

| | | | |
|---|---|---|---|
| 2401 | 2cz. Type **1242** | 45 | 35 |
| 2402 | 13cz. "Caesalpinia echinata" | 2·75 | 2·20 |

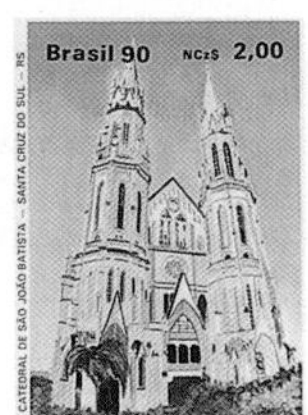

**1243** Cathedral of St. John the Baptist, Santa Cruz do Sul

**1990.** Churches. Multicoloured.

| | | | |
|---|---|---|---|
| 2403 | 2cz. Type **1243** | 35 | 25 |
| 2404 | 3cz. Our Lady of Victory Church, Oeiras (horiz) | 60 | 35 |
| 2405 | 5cz. Our Lady of the Rosary Church, Ouro Preto | 85 | 55 |

**1244** Sailing Barque and Modern Container Ship

**1990.** Cent of Lloyd Brasileiro Navigation Company.

| | | | | |
|---|---|---|---|---|
| 2406 | **1244** | 3cz. multicoloured | 45 | 25 |

**1245** Chinstrap Penguins and Map

**1990.** Brazilian Antarctic Programme. Sheet 98×68 mm.

| | | | |
|---|---|---|---|
| **MS**2407 | **1245** 20cz. multicoloured | 3·75 | 3·75 |

**1990.** Brazilian Football Clubs As T 1177. Multicoloured.

| | | | |
|---|---|---|---|
| 2408 | 10cz. Vasco da Gama Regatas Club | 95 | 80 |

**1246** Collor and Newspaper Mastheads

**1990.** Birth Cent of Lindolfo Collor (journalist).

| | | | | |
|---|---|---|---|---|
| 2409 | **1246** | 20cz. multicoloured | 1·90 | 1·40 |

**1247** Sarney

**1990.** Tribute to Jose Sarney (retiring President).

| | | | | |
|---|---|---|---|---|
| 2410 | **1247** | 20cz. blue | 2·00 | 1·40 |

**1248** Gold Coin, Anniversary Emblem and Bank Headquarters, Brasilia

**1990.** 25th Anniv of Brazil Central Bank.

| | | | | |
|---|---|---|---|---|
| 2411 | **1248** | 20cr. multicoloured | 1·80 | 90 |

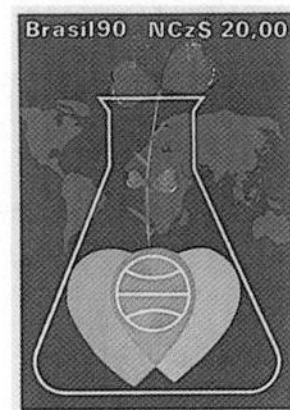

**1249** Hearts sprouting in Flask

**1990.** World Health Day. Anti-AIDS Campaign.

| | | | | |
|---|---|---|---|---|
| 2412 | **1249** | 20cr. multicoloured | 1·90 | 90 |

**1990.** Flowers. As T 1220 but with currency expressed as "Cr$".

| | | | |
|---|---|---|---|
| 2413 | 1cr. "Impatiens sp" | 25 | 10 |
| 2414 | 2cr. "Chorisia crispiflora" (vert) | 25 | 10 |
| 2415 | 5cr. "Hibiscus trilineatus" | 25 | 10 |
| 2417 | 10cr. "Tibouchina granulosa" (vert) | 35 | 25 |
| 2418 | 20cr. "Cassia micranthera" (vert) | 60 | 35 |
| 2419 | 50cr. *Tibouchina mutabillis* (vert) | 70 | 45 |
| 2420 | 50cr. "Clitoria fairchildiana" (vert) | 70 | 45 |
| 2421 | 50cr. "Tibouchina mutabilis" (vert) | 60 | 35 |
| 2422 | 100cr. "Erythrina crista-galli" (vert) | 1·30 | 55 |
| 2423 | 200cr. "Jacaranda mimosifolia" (vert) | 2·20 | 1·10 |
| 2424 | 500cr. "Caesalpinia peltophoroides" (vert) | 3·50 | 1·80 |
| 2424a | 1000cr. "Pachira aquatica" (vert) | 45 | 25 |
| 2424b | 2000cr. "Hibiscus pernambucensis" (vert) | 60 | 25 |
| 2424c | 5000cr. "Triplaris surinamensis" (vert) | 1·40 | 60 |
| 2424d | 10000cr. "Tabebuia heptaphylia" (vert) | 3·00 | 1·20 |
| 2424e | 20000cr. "Erythrina speciosa" (vert) | 3·75 | 1·40 |

**1250** Amazon Post Launch

**1990.** River Post Network.

| | | | | |
|---|---|---|---|---|
| 2425 | **1250** | 20cr. multicoloured | 1·90 | 1·00 |

**1251** Emperor Pedro LL and 30r. "Bull's-Eye"

**1990.** Stamp World London 90 International Stamp Exhibition and 150th Anniv of Penny Black. Sheet 100×70 mm containing T 1251 and similar vert design, each black and lemon.

| | | | |
|---|---|---|---|
| **MS**2426 | 20cz. Type **1251**; 100cr. Queen Victoria and Penny Black | 8·25 | 8·25 |

**1252** Map and Emblem

**1990.** World Cup Football Championship, Italy. Sheet 69×99 mm.

| | | | |
|---|---|---|---|
| **MS**2427 | **1252** 120cr. multicoloured | 8·75 | 8·75 |

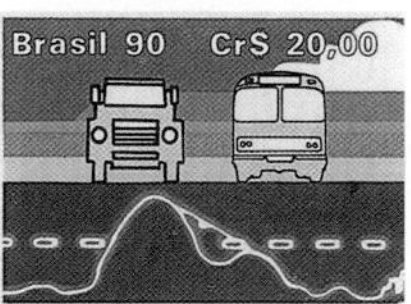

**1253** Truck and Coach

**1990.** 22nd World Congress of Int Road Transport Union, Rio de Janeiro. Multicoloured.

| | | | |
|---|---|---|---|
| 2428 | 20cr. Type **1253** | 1·30 | 90 |
| 2429 | 80cr. Volkswagen transporter van and car | 1·90 | 1·40 |

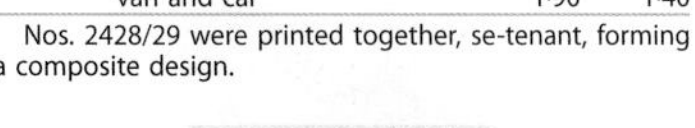
Nos. 2428/29 were printed together, se-tenant, forming a composite design.

**1254** Imperial Crown (Imperial Museum, Petropolis)

**1990.** Museum 50th Anniversaries. Multicoloured.

| | | | |
|---|---|---|---|
| 2430 | 20cr. Type **1254** | 1·40 | 90 |
| 2431 | 20cr. "Our Lady of the Immaculate Conception" (woodcarving) (Missionary Museum, Sao Miguel das Missoes) | 1·40 | 90 |

**1990.** Creation of State of Tocantins. As T 992, showing state flag.

| | | | |
|---|---|---|---|
| 2432 | 20cr. yellow, blue and black | 1·40 | 90 |

**1255** Service Building. Hildebrand Theodolite and Map of Rio de Janeiro

**1990.** Centenary of Army Geographic Service.

| | | | | |
|---|---|---|---|---|
| 2433 | **1255** | 20cr. multicoloured | 1·40 | 90 |

**1256** Adhemar Gonzaga (producer)

**1990.** Brazilian Film Industry. Each maroon and purple.

| | | | |
|---|---|---|---|
| 2434 | 25cr. Type **1256** | 1·20 | 70 |
| 2435 | 25cr. Carmen Miranda (actress) | 1·20 | 70 |
| 2436 | 25cr. Carmen Santos (actress) | 1·20 | 70 |
| 2437 | 25cr. Oscarito (actor) | 1·20 | 70 |

**1257** Aerial View of House

**1990.** 5th Anniv of France–Brazil House, Rio de Janeiro.

| | | | | |
|---|---|---|---|---|
| 2438 | **1257** | 50cr. multicoloured | 3·00 | 2·50 |

**1258** Ball and Net

**1990.** 12th World Men's Volleyball Championship, Brazil.

| | | | | |
|---|---|---|---|---|
| 2439 | **1258** | 10cr. multicoloured | 85 | 45 |

**1259** Embraer/FMA Vector

**1990.** Aeronautics Industry.

| | | | | |
|---|---|---|---|---|
| 2440 | **1259** | 10cr. multicoloured | 85 | 45 |

**1260** Globe, Pencil and Alphabet

**1990.** International Literacy Year.

| | | | | |
|---|---|---|---|---|
| 2441 | **1260** | 10cr. multicoloured | 85 | 45 |

**1261** Institute

**1990.** Cent of Granbery Institute, Juiz de Fora.

| | | | | |
|---|---|---|---|---|
| 2442 | **1261** | 13cr. multicoloured | 95 | 55 |

**1262** Map, Track and Diesel Locomotive

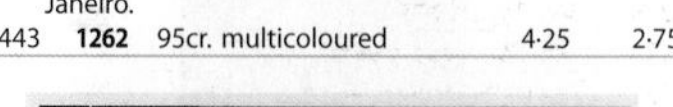
**1990.** 18th Pan-American Railways Congress, Rio de Janeiro.

| | | | | |
|---|---|---|---|---|
| 2443 | **1262** | 95cr. multicoloured | 4·25 | 2·75 |

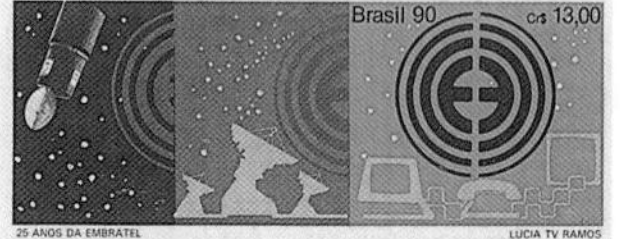

**1263** Satellite and Computer Communication

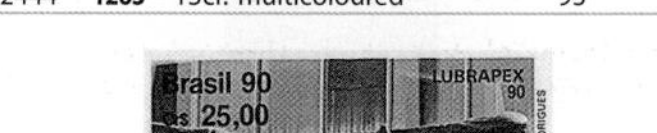
**1990.** 25th Anniv of Embratel (Telecommunications Enterprise).

| | | | | |
|---|---|---|---|---|
| 2444 | **1263** | 13cr. multicoloured | 95 | 55 |

**1264** "Bathers" (Alfredo Ceschiatti)

**1990.** "Lubrapex 90" Brazilian–Portuguese Stamp Exhibition, Brasilia. Brasilia Sculptures. Mult.

| | | | |
|---|---|---|---|
| 2445 | 25cr. Type **1264** | 1·20 | 90 |
| 2446 | 25cr. "Warriors" (Bruno Giorgi) | 1·20 | 90 |
| 2447 | 100cr. "St. John" (Ceschiatti) | 2·50 | 1·80 |
| 2448 | 100cr. "Justice" (Ceschiatti) | 2·50 | 1·80 |
| **MS**2449 | 150×89 mm. Nos. 2445/8 | 12·00 | 12·00 |

**1265** "Bromelia antiacantha"

**1990.** America. 500th Anniv of Discovery of America by Columbus. Praia do Sul Nature Reserve. Multicoloured.

| | | | |
|---|---|---|---|
| 2450 | 15cr. Type **1265** | 95 | 55 |

2451 105cr. Wooded shoreline of Lagoa do Sul 4·75 3·50

Nos. 2450/1 were printed together, se-tenant, forming a composite design.

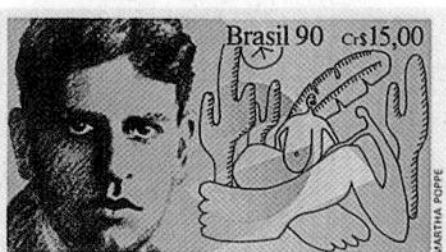


**1266** Oswald de Andrade (birth centenary) and Illustration from "Anthropophagic Manifesto"

**1990.** Book Day. Anniversaries. Mult.

2452 15cr. Type **1266** 85 55
2453 15cr. Guilherme de Almeida (birth cent) and illustration of "Greek Songs" 85 55
2454 15cr. National Library (180th anniv) and illuminated book 85 55

**1267** Emblem and Tribunal Offices, Brasilia

**1990.** Centenary of National Accounts Tribunal.

2455 **1267** 15cr. multicoloured 85 55

**1268** National Congress Building

**1990.** Christmas. Brasilia Lights. Mult.

2456 15cr. Type **1268** 85 55
2457 15cr. Television Tower 85 55

**1990.** Obligatory Tax. Anti-Leprosy Week. As No. 2397 but value and colour changed.

2458 **1239** 50c. blue 35 25

**1269** Fingers touching across Map of Americas

**1990.** Centenary of Organization of American States.

2459 **1269** 15cr. multicoloured 45 25

**1270** "Nike Apache" Rocket on Launch Pad

**1990.** 25th Anniv of Launch of "Nike Apache" Rocket.

2460 **1270** 15cr. multicoloured 45 25

**1271** Sao Cristovao City

**1990.** 400th Anniv of Colonization of Sergipe State.

2461 **1271** 15cr. multicoloured 45 25

**1272** Gymnasts

**1991.** World Congress on Physical Education, Sports and Recreation, Foz do Iguacu.

2462 **1272** 17cr. multicoloured 55 25

**1273** Cazuza

**1991.** "Rock in Rio" Concert. Multicoloured.

2463 25cr. Type **1273** 95 55
2464 185cr. Raul Seixas 3·50 90

Nos. 2463/4 were printed together, se-tenant, forming a composite design.

**1274** Aeritalia/Aermacchi AM-X and Republic Thunderbolt

**1991.** 50th Anniv of Aeronautics Ministry.

2465 **1274** 17cr. multicoloured 55 35

**1275** Effigies of Day Woman and Midnight Man, Olinda

**1991.** Carnival. Multicoloured.

2466 25cr. Type **1275** 35 30
2467 30cr. Electric trio on truck, Salvador 40 35
2468 280cr. Samba dancers, Rio de Janeiro 5·25 4·00

**1276** Antarctic Wildlife

**1991.** Visit of President Collor to Antarctica.

2469 **1276** 300cr. multicoloured 4·25 2·30

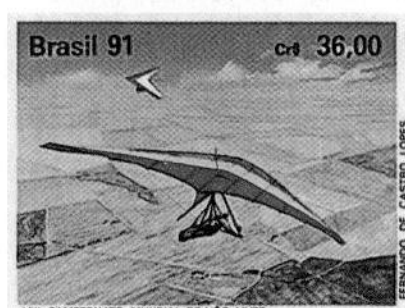


**1277** Hang-gliders

**1991.** 8th World Free Flight Championships, Governador Valadares.

2470 **1277** 36cr. multicoloured 85 55

**1278** Yachting

**1991.** 11th Pan-American Games, Cuba, and Olympic Games, Barcelona (1992). Mult.

2471 36cr. Type **1278** 70 45
2472 36cr. Rowing 70 45
2473 300cr. Swimming 4·75 3·75

**1279** Cross over Bottle (alcoholism)

**1991.** Anti-addiction Campaign. Mult.

2474 40cr. Type **1279** 85 55
2475 40cr. Cross over cigarette (smoking) 85 55
2476 40cr. Cross over syringe (drug abuse) 85 55

**1280** Old and Present Offices and Mastheads

**1991.** Cent of "Jornal do Brasil" (newspaper).

2477 **1280** 40cr. multicoloured 85 55

**1281** Yanomami Youth in Ceremonial Paint

**1991.** Indian Culture. The Yanomami. Mult.

2478 40cr. Type **1281** 70 55
2479 400cr. Hunter (horiz) 7·00 5·25

**1282** Orinoco Goose

**1991.** United Nations Conference on Environment and Development.

2480 **1282** 45cr. multicoloured 85 55

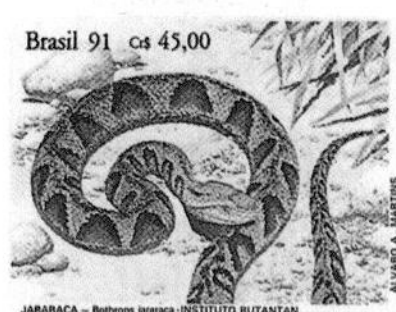


**1283** Jararaca

**1991.** 90th Anniv of Butantan Institute (2481/2) and 173rd Anniv of National Museum (others). Multicoloured.

2481 45cr. Type **1283** 70 45
2482 45cr. Green tree boa 70 45
2483 45cr. Theropoda (dinosaurs) 70 45
2484 350cr. Sauropoda (dinosaurs) 4·25 3·00

**1284** National Flag

**1991.** No value expressed.

2485a **1284** (–) multicoloured 45 25

**1285** Early Steam Pump and Santos City 6th Fire Group's Headquarters

**1991.** Fire Fighting.

2486 **1285** 45cr. multicoloured 60 45

**1286** Pedra Pintada, Boa Vista, Roraima

**1991.** Tourism. Centenaries of Boa Vista (1990) and Teresopolis. Multicoloured.

2487 45cr. Type **1286** 60 45
2488 350cr. God's Finger, Teresopolis, Rio de Janeiro 2·75 2·10

**1287** Welder, "Justice" and Farmer

**1991.** 50th Anniv of Labour Justice Legal System.

2489 **1287** 45cr. multicoloured 60 45

**1288** Folklore Characters, Singers and Mota

**1991.** 5th International Festival of Folklore and Birth Centenary of Leonardo Mota (folklorist).

2490 **1288** 45cr. red, ochre & black 60 45

**1289** Jose Basilio da Gama (poet)

**1991.** Writers' Birth Anniversaries. Mult.

2491 45cr. Type **1289** (250th anniv) 55 40
2492 50cr. Luis Nicolau Fagundes Varela (poet, 150th anniv) 60 45
2493 50cr. Jackson de Figueiredo (essayist and philosopher, centenary) 60 45

**1290** Pope John Paul II

**1991.** Papal Visit and 12th National Eucharistic Congress, Natal. Multicoloured.

2494 50cr. Type **1290** 60 45
2495 400cr. Congress emblem 1·80 1·10

Nos. 2494/5 were issued together, se-tenant, forming a composite design.

**1291** "The Constitutional Commitment" (Aurelio de Figueiredo)

**1991.** Centenary of 1891 Constitution.
2496 **1291** 50cr. multicoloured 85 35

**1292** Exhibition Emblem and dish Aerial

**1991.** "Telecom 91" International Telecommuni- cations Exhibition, Geneva.
2497 **1292** 50cr. multicoloured 85 35

**1293** Ferdinand Magellan

**1991.** America. Voyages of Discovery. Mult.
2498 50cr. Type **1293** 85 35
2499 400cr. Francisco de Orellana on River Amazon 2·75 2·10

**1294** White-vented Violetear and "Cattleya warneri"

**1991.** "Brapex 91" National Stamp Exhibition, Vitoria. Humming Birds and Orchids in Mata Atlantica Forest. Multicoloured.
2500 50cr. Type **1294** 60 35
2501 65cr. Glittering-bellied emerald and "Rodriguezia venusta" 70 45
2502 65cr. Brazilian ruby and "Zygop- etalum intermedium" 70 45
**MS**2503 99×69 mm. 50cr. White-vented violetear and "Cattelya warneri"; 50cr. Glittering-bellied emerald and tree trunk; 500cr. "Rodriguezia venusta" and Brazilian ruby 12·00 12·00

**1295** "Self-portrait III"

**1991.** Birth Cent of Lasar Segall (artist).
2504 **1295** 400cr. multicoloured 1·80 75

**1296** Agricultural Projects

**1991.** Centenary of Bureau of Agriculture and Provision, Sao Paulo.
2505 **1296** 70cr. multicoloured 60 35

**1297** Dr. Manuel Ferraz de Campos Salles (President, 1898–1902)

**1991.** 150th Birth Anniversaries. Mult.
2506 70cr. Type **1297** 60 35
2507 90cr. Dr. Prudente de Moraes (President, 1894–98) and Catete Palace, Rio de Janeiro (former Executive Headquarters) 70 45

Nos. 2506/7 were issued together, se-tenant, forming a composite design.

**1298** Madonna and Child

**1991.** Christmas.
2508 **1298** 70cr. multicoloured 1·20 35

**1991.** Obligatory Tax. Anti-leprosy Week.
2509 **1239** 3cr. green 35 25

**1299** Hand holding Prayer Book

**1991.** Thanksgiving Day.
2510 **1299** 70cr. multicoloured 60 35

**1300** Pedro II

**1991.** 150th Anniv of Coronation and Death Centenary of Emperor Pedro II. Sheet 99×69 mm containing T 1300 and similar vert design. Multicoloured.
**MS**2511 80cr. Type **1300**; 800cr. Pedro II at coronation 4·75 4·75

**1301** Policeman in Historic Uniform and Tobias de Aguiar Battalion Building, Sao Paulo

**1991.** Military Police.
2512 **1301** 80cr. multicoloured 60 35

**1302** First Baptist Church, Niteroi (centenary)

**1992.** Church Anniversaries. Multicoloured.
2513 250cr. Type **1302** 1·30 45

2514 250cr. Presbyterian Cathedral, Rio de Janeiro (130th anniv) 1·30 45

**1303** Afranio Costa (silver, free pistol)

**1992.** Olympic Games, Barcelona (1st issue). 1920 Olympics Shooting Medal Winners. Multicoloured.
2515 300cr. Type **1303** 1·80 85
2516 2500cr. Guilherme Paraense (gold, 30 m revolver) 14·00 3·50

See also No. 2526.

**1304** Old and Modern Views of Port

**1992.** Centenary of Port of Santos.
2517 **1304** 300cr. multicoloured 1·10 55

**1305** White-tailed Tropic Birds

**1992.** 2nd United Nations Conference on Environment and Development, Rio de Janeiro (1st issue). Multicoloured.
2518 400cr. Type **1305** 1·20 55
2519 2500cr. Spinner dolphins 4·25 2·00

See also Nos. 2532/5, 2536/8, 2539/42 and 2543/6.

**1306** Ipe

**1992.** No value expressed.
2520 **1306** (–) multicoloured 2·30 25

No. 2520 was valid for use at the second class inland letter rate.

**1307** Hunting using Boleadeira

**1992.** "Abrafex '92" Argentinian–Brazilian Stamp Exhibition, Porto Alegre. Multicoloured.
2521 250cr. Type **1307** 70 55
2522 250cr. Traditional folk dancing 70 55
2523 250cr. Horse and cart 70 55
2524 1000cr. Rounding-up cattle 1·40 1·10
**MS**2525 150×89 mm. 250cr. As No. 2522; 250cr. As No. 2523; 500cr. Type **1307**; 1500cr. As No. 2524 8·75 8·75

**1308** Sportsmen on Globe

**1992.** Olympic Games, Barcelona (2nd issue).
2526 **1308** 300cr. multicoloured 60 35

**1309** Tiradentes (sculpture, Bruno Giorgi)

**1992.** Death Bicentenary of Joaquim Jose da Silvaxavier (Independence fighter). Sheet 98×68 mm.
**MS**2527 **1309** 3500cr. mult 6·50 6·50

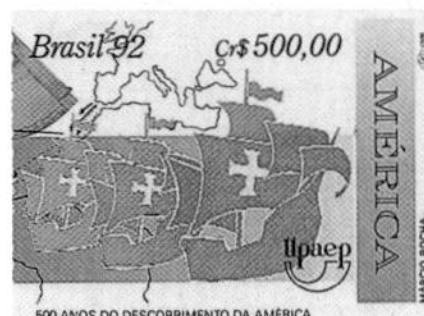

**1310** Columbus's Fleet

**1992.** America. 500th Anniv of Discovery of America by Columbus. Multicoloured.
2528 500cr. Type **1310** 70 45
2529 3500cr. Columbus, route map and quadrant 3·75 2·30

Nos. 2528/9 were issued together, se-tenant, forming a composite design.

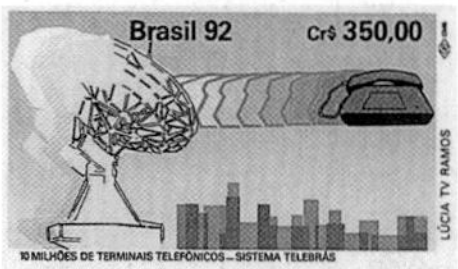

**1311** Dish Aerial, Telephone and City

**1992.** Installation of 10,000,000th Telephone Line in Brazil.
2530 **1311** 350cr. multicoloured 70 35

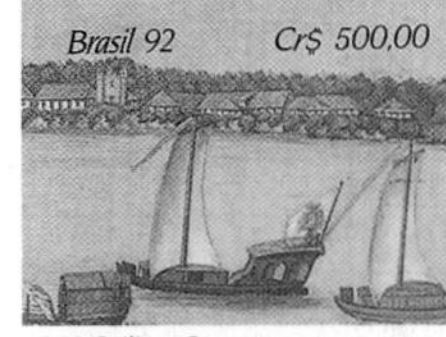

**1312** Sailing Canoes

**1992.** Lubrapex 92 Brazilian–Portuguese Stamp Exhibition, Lisbon. Bicentenary of "Philosophical Journey" by Alexandre Rodrigues Ferreira. Sheet 148×88 mm containing T 1312 and similar horiz designs.
**MS**2531 500cr., 1000cr., 2500cr. Com- posite design of watercolour by Jose Freire showing arrival of expedition's ship at Vila de Cameta 6·75 6·75

**1313** Hercule Florence (botanist)

**1992.** 2nd UN Conference on Environment and Development (2nd issue). 170th Anniv of Langsdorff Expedition. Multicoloured.
2532 500cr. Type **1313** 60 45
2533 500cr. Aime-Adrien Taunay (eth- nographer) and Amerindians 60 45
2534 500cr. Johann Moritz Rugendas (zoologist) 60 45
2535 3000cr. Gregory Ivanovich Langsdorff and route map 3·75 2·50

**1314** Urban and Rural Symbols

**1992.** 2nd UN Conference on Environment and Development (3rd issue). Multicoloured.
2536 450cr. Type **1314** 45 35
2537 450cr. Flags of Sweden (host of first conference) and Brazil around globe 45 35
2538 3000cr. Globe, map, flora and fauna 3·75 2·50

**1315** Monica sitting by Waterfall

**1992.** 2nd UN Conference on Environment and Development (4th issue). Ecology. Designs showing cartoon characters. Multicoloured.

| | | | |
|---|---|---|---|
| 2539 | 500cr. Type **1315** | 70 | 35 |
| 2540 | 500cr. Cebolinha in canoe | 70 | 35 |
| 2541 | 500cr. Cascao photographing wildlife | 70 | 35 |
| 2542 | 500cr. Magali picking wild fruit | 70 | 35 |

Nos. 2539/42 were issued together, se-tenant, forming a composite design.

**1316** "Nidularium innocentii"

**1992.** 2nd UN Conference on Environment and Development (5th issue). 3rd Anniv of Margaret Mee Brazilian Botanical Foundation. Flower paintings by Margaret Mee. Multicoloured.

| | | | |
|---|---|---|---|
| 2543 | 600cr. Type **1316** | 85 | 55 |
| 2544 | 600cr. "Canistrum exiguum" | 85 | 55 |
| 2545 | 700cr. "Nidularium rubens" | 90 | 65 |
| 2546 | 700cr. "Canistrum cyathiforme" | 90 | 65 |

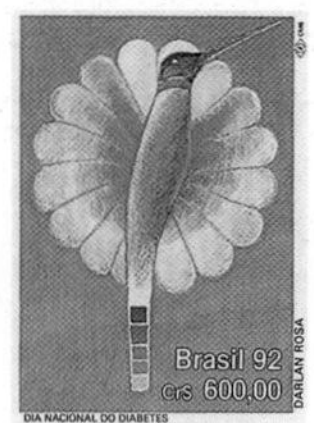

**1317** Humming-bird's Wings forming Flower

**1992.** National Diabetes Day.

| | | | | |
|---|---|---|---|---|
| 2547 | **1317** | 600cr. multicoloured | 85 | 35 |

**1318** Training Tower and First Manual Pump

**1992.** Centenary of Joinville Volunteer Fire Service.

| | | | | |
|---|---|---|---|---|
| 2548 | **1318** | 550cr. multicoloured | 60 | 35 |

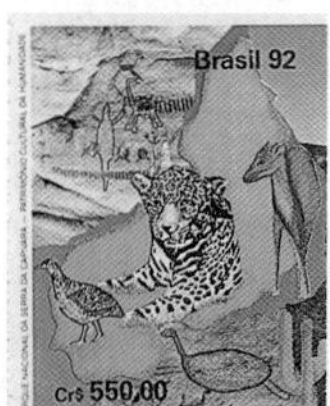

**1319** Animals, Cave Paintings and Map of Piaui State

**1992.** 13th Anniv of Capivara Mountain National Park. Multicoloured.

| | | | |
|---|---|---|---|
| 2549 | 550cr. Type **1319** | 60 | 35 |
| 2550 | 550cr. Canyons and map of Brazil | 60 | 35 |

Nos. 2549/50 were issued together, se-tenant, forming a composite design.

**1320** Projects within Flask

**1992.** 24th Anniv of Financing Agency for Studies and Projects.

| | | | | |
|---|---|---|---|---|
| 2551 | **1320** | 550cr. multicoloured | 60 | 35 |

**1321** Students at Work

**1992.** 50th Anniv of National Industrial Training Service.

| | | | | |
|---|---|---|---|---|
| 2552 | **1321** | 650cr. multicoloured | 60 | 55 |

**1322** Santa Cruz Fortress, Anhatomirim Island

**1992.** Santa Catarina Fortresses. Multicoloured.

| | | | |
|---|---|---|---|
| 2553 | 650cr. Type **1322** | 60 | 45 |
| 2554 | 3000cr. Santo Antonio Fort, Ratones Grande island | 2·20 | 1·80 |

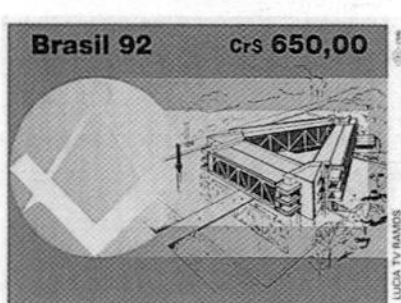

**1323** Masonic Emblem and Palace, Brasilia

**1992.** 170th Anniv of Grande Oriente (Federation of Brazil's Freemasonry Lodges).

| | | | | |
|---|---|---|---|---|
| 2555 | **1323** | 650cr. multicoloured | 60 | 35 |

**1324** Profiles of Child and Man forming Hourglass

**1992.** 50th Anniv of Brazilian Legion of Assistance.

| | | | | |
|---|---|---|---|---|
| 2556 | **1324** | 650cr. multicoloured | 60 | 35 |

**1325** Medical Equipment and Patients

**1992.** Sarah Locomotor Hospital, Brasilia.

| | | | | |
|---|---|---|---|---|
| 2557 | **1325** | 800cr. multicoloured | 60 | 45 |

**1326** Menotti del Picchia

**1992.** Book Day. Writers' Birth Centenaries. Multicoloured.

| | | | |
|---|---|---|---|
| 2558 | 900cr. Type **1326** | 60 | 45 |
| 2559 | 900cr. Graciliano Ramos | 60 | 45 |
| 2560 | 1000cr. Assis Chateaubriand (journalist) (horiz) | 65 | 50 |

**1327** Meridian Circle, Map, Cruls and Tent

**1992.** Centenary of Luiz Cruls's Exploration of Central Plateau.

| | | | | |
|---|---|---|---|---|
| 2561 | **1327** | 900cr. multicoloured | 60 | 45 |

**1328** Productivity Graph on Flag

**1992.** 2nd Anniv of Brazilian Quality and Productivity Programme.

| | | | | |
|---|---|---|---|---|
| 2562 | **1328** | 1200cr. multicoloured | 55 | 35 |

**1329** Pepino Beach, Rio de Janeiro

**1992.** Year of Tourism in the Americas. Sheet 70×100 mm containing T 1329 and similar horiz design. Multicoloured.

| | | |
|---|---|---|
| **MS**2563 1200cr. Type **1329**; 9000cr. Sugar Loaf, Rio de Janeiro | 3·75 | 3·75 |

**1330** Father Christmas

**1992.** Christmas. No value expressed.

| | | | | |
|---|---|---|---|---|
| 2564 | **1330** | (–) multicoloured | 75 | 45 |

**1992.** Obligatory Tax. Anti-leprosy Week.

| | | | | |
|---|---|---|---|---|
| 2565 | **1239** | 30cr. brown | 65 | 55 |

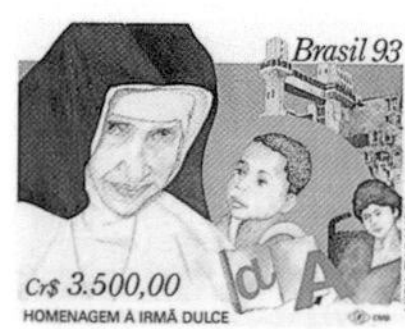

**1331** Sister Dulce, Patients and Lacerda Lift, Salvador

**1993.** Sister Dulce (founder of Santo Antonio Hospital and Simoes Filho Educational Centre) Commemoration.

| | | | | |
|---|---|---|---|---|
| 2566 | **1331** | 3500cr. multicoloured | 40 | 25 |

**1332** Diving

**1993.** South American Water Sports Championships, Goiania. Sheet 69×99 mm containing T 1332 and similar horiz designs. Multicoloured.

| | | |
|---|---|---|
| **MS**2567 3500cr. Type **1332**; 3500cr. Synchronized swimming; 25000cr. Water polo | 5·25 | 3·25 |

**1333** Tube Station, Pine Trees and Church of the Third Order of St. Francis of Assisi and Stigmata

**1993.** 300th Anniv of Curitiba.

| | | | | |
|---|---|---|---|---|
| 2568 | **1333** | 4500cr. multicoloured | 75 | 70 |

**1334** Heart dripping Blood onto Flowers

**1993.** Health and Preservation of Life. Mult.

| | | | |
|---|---|---|---|
| 2569 | 4500cr. Type **1334** (blood donation) | 50 | 35 |
| 2570 | 4500cr. Crab attacking healthy cell (anti-cancer campaign) | 50 | 35 |
| 2571 | 4500cr. Rainbow, head and encephalogram (mental health) | 50 | 35 |

**1335** "Night with the Geniuses of Study and Love"

**1993.** 150th Birth Anniv of Pedro Americo (painter). Multicoloured.

| | | | |
|---|---|---|---|
| 2572 | 5500cr. Type **1335** | 65 | 45 |
| 2573 | 36000cr. "David and Abizag" (horiz) | 4·50 | 2·75 |
| 2574 | 36000cr. "A Carioca" | 4·50 | 2·75 |

**1336** Flag

**1993.** No value expressed. Self-adhesive. Die-cut.

| | | | | |
|---|---|---|---|---|
| 2575 | **1336** | (–) blue, yellow & grn | 2·10 | 55 |

No. 2575 was valid for use at the current first class inland letter rate. It could not be used to pay postage to foreign countries.

**1337** "Dynastes hercules"

**1993.** World Environment Day. Beetles. Mult.

| | | | |
|---|---|---|---|
| 2576 | 8000cr. Type **1337** | 65 | 45 |
| 2577 | 55000cr. "Batus barbicornis" | 3·00 | 2·75 |

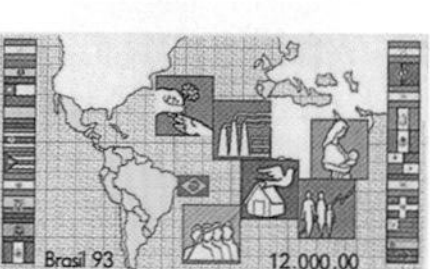

**1338** Map, Flags and Discussion Themes

**1993.** 3rd Iberian-American Summit Conference, Salvador.

| | | | | |
|---|---|---|---|---|
| 2578 | **1338** | 12000cr. multicoloured | 75 | 35 |

**1339** Lake, Congress Building and "Os Candangos" (statue), Brasilia

**1993.** Union of Portuguese-speaking Capital Cities. Multicoloured.

| | | | |
|---|---|---|---|
| 2579 | 15000cr. Type **1339** | 40 | 25 |
| 2580 | 71000cr. Copacabana beach and "Christ the Redeemer" (statue), Rio de Janeiro | 2·10 | 1·30 |

Nos. 2579/80 were issued together, se-tenant, forming a composite design.

**1340** 30r. "Bulls Eye" Stamp

**1993.** 150th Anniv of First Brazilian Stamps (1st issue) and "Brasiliana 93" International Stamp Exhibition, Rio de Janeiro. Each black, red and yellow.

| | | | |
|---|---|---|---|
| 2581 | 30000cr. Type **1340** | 90 | 45 |
| 2582 | 60000cr.60r. "Bull's Eye" stamp | 1·90 | 1·10 |
| 2583 | 90000cr.90r. "Bull's Eye" stamp | 2·50 | 1·60 |
| **MS**2584 | 132×99 mm. As Nos. 2581/3 but without engraver's name and commemorative inscription | 15·00 | 15·00 |

See also Nos. 2585/8.

**1341** Cebolinha designing Stamp

**1993.** 150th Anniv of First Brazilian Stamps (2nd issue). No value expressed. Cartoon characters. Multicoloured.

| | | | |
|---|---|---|---|
| 2585 | (–) Type **1341** | 75 | 25 |
| 2586 | (–) Cascao as King and 30r. "Bull's Eye" stamp | 75 | 25 |
| 2587 | (–) Monica writing letter and 60r. "Bull's Eye" stamp | 75 | 25 |
| 2588 | (–) Magali receiving letter and 90r. "Bull's Eye" stamp | 75 | 25 |

Nos. 2585/8 were issued together, se-tenant, forming a composite design.

Nos. 2585/8 were valid for use at the current first class inland letter rate. They could not be used to pay postage to other countries.

**1342** Imperial Palace (former postal H.Q.), Rio de Janeiro

**1993.** 330th Anniv of Postal Service. Mult.

| | | | |
|---|---|---|---|
| 2589 | 20000cr. Type **1342** | 65 | 35 |
| 2590 | 20000cr. Petropolis post office | 65 | 35 |
| 2591 | 20000cr. Main post office, Rio de Janeiro | 65 | 35 |
| 2592 | 20000cr. Niteroi post office | 65 | 35 |

**1343** Polytechnic School, Sao Paulo University

**1993.** Engineering Schools. Multicoloured.

| | | | |
|---|---|---|---|
| 2593 | 17cr. Type **1343** (centenary, 1994) | 90 | 55 |
| 2594 | 17cr. Old and new engineering schools, Rio de Janeiro Federal University (bicent, 1992) | 90 | 55 |

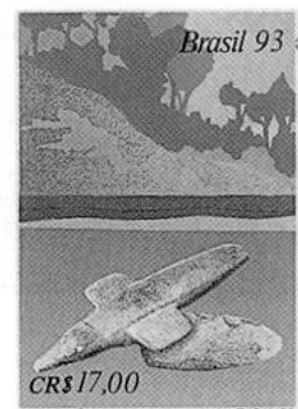

**1344** Forest Mound and Tools

**1993.** Preservation of Archaeological Sites. Mult.

| | | | |
|---|---|---|---|
| 2595 | 17cr. Type **1344** | 65 | 45 |
| 2596 | 17cr. Coastal mound, shells and tools | 65 | 45 |

**1345** Guimaraes and National Congress

**1993.** Ulysses Guimaraes (politician).

| | | | |
|---|---|---|---|
| 2597 | **1346** 22cr. Multicoloured. | 65 | 55 |

**1346** Hands holding Candles and Rope around Statue

**1993.** Bicentenary of Procession of "Virgin of Nazareth", Belem.

| | | | |
|---|---|---|---|
| 2598 | 22cr. multicoloured | 65 | 55 |

**1347** Hyacinth Macaw, Glaucous Macaw and Indige Macaw

**1993.** America. Endangered Macaws. Mult.

| | | | |
|---|---|---|---|
| 2599 | 22cr. Type **1347** | 75 | 45 |
| 2600 | 130cr. Spix's macaw | 2·50 | 75 |

**1348** Vinicius de Moraes

**1993.** Composers' Anniversaries. Mult.

| | | | |
|---|---|---|---|
| 2601 | 22cr. Type **1348** (80th birth anniv) | 40 | 25 |
| 2602 | 22cr. Alfredo da Rocha Vianna (pseud. Pixinguinha) and score of "Carinhoso" (20th death anniv) | 40 | 25 |

**1349** Liberty

**1993.** No value expressed.

| | | | |
|---|---|---|---|
| 2603 | **1349** (–) blue, turq & yell | 5·00 | 4·50 |

No. 2603 was sold at the current rate for first class international postage.

**1350** Mario de Andrade

**1993.** Book Day. Writers' Birth Centenaries. Multicoloured.

| | | | |
|---|---|---|---|
| 2604 | 30cr. Type **1350** | 40 | 25 |
| 2605 | 30cr. Alceu Amoroso Lima (pseud. Tristao de Athayde) | 40 | 25 |
| 2606 | 30cr. Gilka Machado (poet) | 40 | 25 |

**1351** Knot

**1993.** 40th Anniv of Brazil–Portugal Consultation and Friendship Treaty.

| | | | |
|---|---|---|---|
| 2607 | **1351** 30cr. multicoloured | 50 | 25 |

**1352** Nho-Quim

**1993.** 2nd International Comic Strip Biennial. No value expressed. Multicoloured.

| | | | |
|---|---|---|---|
| 2608 | (–) Type **1352** | 1·00 | 35 |
| 2609 | (–) Benjamin (Louneiro) | 1·00 | 35 |
| 2610 | (–) Lamparina | 1·00 | 35 |
| 2611 | (–) Reco-Reco, Bolao and Azeitona (Luiz Sa) | 1·00 | 35 |

See note below Nos. 2585/8.

**1353** Diagram and "Tamoio" (submarine)

**1993.** Launch of First Brazilian-built Submarine.

| | | | |
|---|---|---|---|
| 2612 | **1353** 240cr. multicoloured | 3·25 | 2·75 |

**1354** Nativity

**1993.** Christmas. No value expressed.

| | | | |
|---|---|---|---|
| 2613 | **1354** (–) multicoloured | 1·30 | 85 |

See note below Nos. 2585/8.

**1993.** Obligatory Tax. Anti-leprosy Week.

| | | | |
|---|---|---|---|
| 2614 | **1205** 50c. blue | 40 | 25 |

**1355** Republic P-47 Thunderbolt Fighters over Tarquinia Camp, Italy

**1993.** 50th Anniv of Formation of 1st Fighter Group, Brazilian Expeditionary Force.

| | | | |
|---|---|---|---|
| 2615 | **1355** 42cr. multicoloured | 90 | 55 |

**1356** Flag

**1994.** No value expressed. Self-adhesive. Imperf.

| | | | |
|---|---|---|---|
| 2616 | **1356** (–) blue, yellow & green | 1·20 | 70 |

See note below Nos. 2585/8.

**1357** Foundation of Republican Memory, Convent and Cloisters

**1994.** 340th Anniv of Convent of Merces (now Cultural Centre), Sao Luis.

| | | | |
|---|---|---|---|
| 2617 | **1357** 58cr. multicoloured | 65 | 35 |

**1358** "Mae Menininha"

**1994.** Birth Centenary of Mae Menininha do Gantois (Escolastica Maria da Conceiao Nazare).

| | | | |
|---|---|---|---|
| 2618 | **1358** 80cr. multicoloured | 75 | 70 |

**1359** Olympic Rings and Rower

**1994.** Centenaries of International Olympic Committee and Rowing Federation, Rio Grande do Sul. No value expressed.

| | | | |
|---|---|---|---|
| 2619 | **1359** (–) multicoloured | 4·00 | 2·30 |

See note below No. 2603.

**1360** Blue and White Swallow

**1994.** Birds. Multicoloured.

| | | | |
|---|---|---|---|
| 2620 | 10cr. Type **1360** | 65 | 10 |
| 2621 | 20cr. Roadside hawk | 65 | 10 |
| 2622 | 50cr. Rufous-bellied thrush | 65 | 10 |
| 2623 | 100cr. Ruddy ground dove | 65 | 10 |
| 2624 | 200cr. Southern lapwing | 65 | 10 |
| 2625 | 500cr. Rufous-collared sparrow | 1·90 | 35 |

See after Nos. 2649/61.

**1361** Map and Prince Henry

**1994.** 600th Birth Anniv of Prince Henry the Navigator.

| | | | |
|---|---|---|---|
| 2626 | **1361** 635cr. multicoloured | 5·00 | 2·50 |

**1362** Bicycle

**1994.** America. Postal Vehicles. Mult.

| | | | |
|---|---|---|---|
| 2627 | 110cr. Type **1362** | 65 | 35 |
| 2628 | 635cr. Post motor cycle | 5·75 | 1·70 |

**1363** Statue, Grain Store and Chapel of Help, Juazeiro do Norte

**1994.** 150th Anniv of Birth of Father Cicero Romao Batista. With service indicator.
2629 **1363** (-) multicoloured 1·20 85
See note below Nos. 2585/8.

**1364** Sabin and Children

**1994.** 1st Death Anniv of Albert Sabin (developer of oral polio vaccine).
2630 **1364** 160cr. multicoloured 1·00 55

**1365** Castello Branco and Brasilia

**1994.** Carlos Castello Branco (journalist).
2631 **1365** 160cr. multicoloured 1·00 55

**1366** "Euterpe oleracea"

**1994.** Birth Bicentenary of Karl Friedrich Phillip von Martius (botanist). With service indicator. Multicoloured. (a) Inscr "1. PORTE NACIONAL".
2632 (-) Type **1366** 1·30 55
2633 (-) "Jacaranda paucifoliolata" 1·30 55

(b) Inscr "1. PORTE INTERNACIONAL TAXE PERCUE".
2634 (-) "Barbacenia tomentosa" 3·50 1·70
Nos. 2632/3 were for use at the current first class inland letter rate and Nos. 2634 for first class international postage.

**1367** "Brazil"

**1994.** With service indicator. (a) Size 21×28 mm. Self-adhesive. Rouletted. (i) PRINTED MATTER. Inscr "1. PORTE IMPRESSO CATEGORIA II".
2635 **1367** (-) blue 55 45

(ii) INLAND POSTAGE. Inscr "3. PORTE NACIONAL".
2636 (3rd) red 1·00 75

(b) INLAND POSTAGE. Inscr "PORTE NACIONAL". Size 26×35 mm.
2637 (4th) green 2·00 1·50
2638 (5th) red 4·00 2·75
Nos. 2635/8 were valid for internal use in the category described.

**1368** Brazilian Player wearing "100"

**1994.** Centenary of Football in Brazil and World Cup Football Championship, U.S.A. With service indicator.
2639 **1368** (-) multicoloured 3·75 2·50
See note below No. 2603.

**1369** Emperor Tamarin ("Saguinus imperator")

**1994.** Endangered Mammals. With service indicator. Multicoloured.
2640 (-) Type **1369** 1·10 50
2641 (-) Bare-faced tamarin ("Saguinus bicolor") 1·10 50
2642 (-) Golden lion tamarin ("Leontopithecus rosalia") 1·10 50
See note below Nos. 2585/8.

**1370** Book and Disks

**1994.** 46th International Book Fair, Frankfurt, Germany. Sheet 99×69 mm.
**MS**2643 **1370** (-) multicoloured 4·25 4·25
No. **MS**2643 was sold at the currant rate for first class international postage.

**1371** Pencils Crossing over Fingerprint

**1994.** 10 Year Education Plan. With service indicator. Multicoloured.
2644 (-) Type **1371** (literacy campaign) 1·20 55
2645 (-) PRONAICA pencil and school (National Programme of Integral Care to Children and Teenagers) 1·20 55
2646 (-) Lecture scene and graph (increase in qualified teachers) 1·20 55
2647 (-) Pencil and "lecturers" on television (distance learning by video) 1·20 55
See note below Nos. 2585/8.

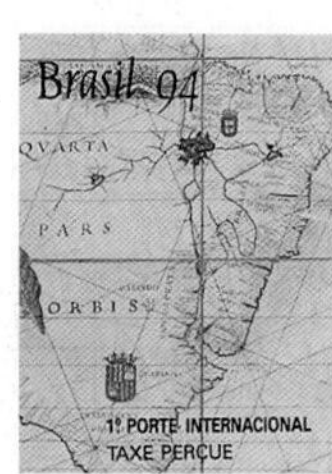

**1372** Map of the Americas (Bartholomeu Velho, 1561) and Treaty Boundaries

**1994.** 500th Anniv of the Treaty of Tordesillas (defining Portuguese and Spainsh spheres of influence). Sheet 67×99 mm.
**MS**2648 **1372** (-) multicoloured 4·00 4·00
No. **MS**2648 was sold at the currant rate for first class international postage.

**1994.** Birds. As T 1360 but with value expressed as "R$". Multicoloured.
2649 1c. Type **1360** 45 15
2650 2c. As No. 2621 45 15
2652 5c. As No. 2622 45 15
2654 10c. As No. 2623 45 15
2655 15c. Saffron finch 80 45
2656 20c. As No. 2624 1·00 50
2657 22c. Fork-tailed fly-catcher 80 50
2658 50c. As No. 2625 3·00 1·30
2661 1r. Rufous hornero 5·25 2·50

**1373** Edgard Santos (founder of Bahia University)

**1994.** Anniversaries. With service indicator. Multicoloured.
2662 (-) Type **1373** (birth centenary) 1·30 65
2663 (-) Oswaldo Aranha (politician, birth centenary) 1·30 65
2664 (-) Otto Lara Resende (author and journalist, 2nd death anniv) 1·30 65
See note below Nos. 2585/8.

**1374** "Petrobras X" (drilling platform), Campos Basin. Rio de Janeiro

**1994.** 40th Anniv of Petrobras (state oil company).
2665 **1374** 12c. multicoloured 80 50

**1375** 17th century Coin Production

**1994.** 300th Anniv of Brazilian Mint.
2666 **1375** 12c. multicoloured 80 65

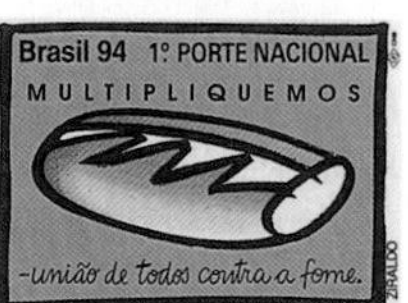

**1376** Loaf of Bread

**1994.** Campaign against Famine and Misery. With service indicator.
2667 **1376** (-) multicoloured 1·20 65
2668 - (-) black and blue 1·20 65
DESIGN: No. 2668, Fish.
See note below Nos. 2585/8.

**1377** Writing with Quill and Scales of Justice

**1994.** 150th Anniv of Brazilian Lawyers Institute.
2669 **1377** 12c. multicoloured 80 65

**1378** Family within Heart

**1994.** International Year of the Family.
2670 **1378** 84c. multicoloured 5·25 4·00

**1379** Hospital, White Stork and Babies forming "1000000"

**1994.** Centenary of Sao Paulo Maternity Hospital. Its Millionth Birth.
2671 **1379** 12c. multicoloured 85 65

**1380** Celestino performing and "Maternal Heart" (record sleeve)

**1994.** Birth Centenary of Vicente Celestino (singer).
2672 **1380** 12c. multicoloured 1·30 50

**1381** Fernando de Azevedo (educationist)

**1994.** Writers' Birth Anniversaries. Mult.
2673 12c. Type **1381** (cent) 65 40
2674 12c. Tomas Antonio Gonzaga (poet, 250th) 65 40

**1382** "Joao and Maria" (Hansel and Gretel)

**1994.** Centenary of Publication of "Fairy Tales" by Alberto Figueiredo Pimentel (first Brazilian children's book). Multicoloured.
2675 12c. Type **1382** 85 65
2676 12c. "Dona Baratinha" (Little Mrs Cockroach) 85 65
2677 84c. "Puss in Boots" 3·50 2·40
2678 84c. "Tom Thumb" 3·50 2·40

**1383** St. Clare, St. Damian's Convent and Statue of St. Francis

**1994.** 800th Birth Anniv of St. Clare of Assisi (founder of order of Poor Clares).
2679 **1383** 12c. multicoloured 65 40

**1384** McLaren–Honda F1 Racing Car and Brazilian Flag

**1994.** Ayrton Senna (racing driver) Commemoration. Multicoloured.
2680 12c. Type **1384** 1·10 60
2681 12c. Senna and crowd waving farewell 1·10 60
2682 84c. Brazilian and chequered flags, racing cars and Senna giving victory salute 3·50 2·20
Nos. 2680/2 were issued together, se-tenant, forming a composite design.

**1385** Books and Globe

**1994.** Centenary of Historical and Geographical Institute, Sao Paulo.
2683 **1385** 12c. multicoloured 65 50

**1386** Adoniran Barbosa and "11 o'Clock Train"

**1994.** Composers. Multicoloured.
2684 12c. Type **1386** 65 50
2685 12c. Score of "The Sea" (Dorival Caymmi) 65 50

**1994.** Obligatory Tax. Anti-Leprosy Week.
2686 **1205** 1c. purple 40 25

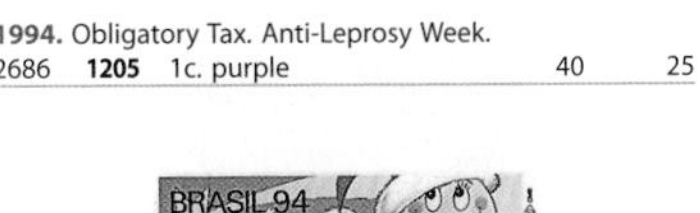

**1387** Maggot wearing Santa Claus Hat in Apple

**1994.** Christmas. Multicoloured.
2687 12c. Type **1387** 55 40
2688 12c. Carol singers 55 40
2689 12c. Boy smoking pipe and letter in boot 55 40
2690 84c. Boy wearing saucepan on head and Santa Claus cloak 3·75 2·30

**1388** Trophy

**1994.** Brazil, World Cup Football Championship (U.S.A.) Winners. Sheet 100×69 mm.
**MS**2691 **1388** 2r.14 multicoloured 10·50 10·00

**1389** Pasteur

**1995.** Death Centenary of Louis Pasteur (chemist).
2692 **1389** 84c. multicoloured 4·00 3·25

**1390** Duke of Caxias and Soldiers

**1995.** 150th Anniv of Peace of Ponche Verde (pacification of Farroupilha Revolution) (2693) and 50th Anniv of Battle of Monte Castello (2694). Multicoloured.
2693 12c. Type **1390** 65 40
2694 12c. Soldier, Brazilian flag and battle scene 65 40

**1391** Pres. Franco

**1995.** Itamar Franco (President 1992–94).
2695 **1391** 12c. multicoloured 65 40

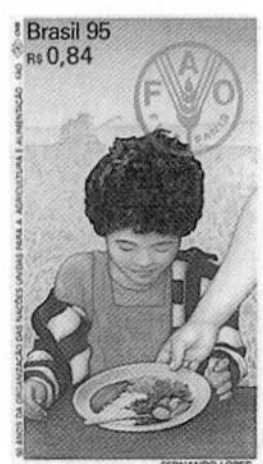

**1392** Meal before Child

**1995.** 50th Anniv of F.A.O.
2696 **1392** 84c. multicoloured 4·00 3·25

**1393** Alexandre de Gusmao (diplomat)

**1995.** Birth Anniversaries. Multicoloured.
2697 12c. Type **1393** (300th anniv) 65 40
2698 12c. Visconde (Viscount) de Jequitinhonha (lawyer, bicent (1994)) 65 40
2699 15c. Barao (Baron) do Rio Branco (diplomat, 150th anniv) 65 40

**1394** Guglielmo Marconi and his Transmitter

**1995.** Centenary of First Radio Transmission.
2700 **1394** 84c. multicoloured 4·00 3·25

**1395** Ipe-amarelo and Cherry Blossom

**1995.** Centenary of Brazil–Japan Friendship Treaty.
2701 **1395** 84c. multicoloured 4·00 3·25

**1396** Solitary Tinamou ("Tinamus solitarius")

**1995.** Birds. Multicoloured.
2702 12c. Type **1396** 1·00 50
2703 12c. Razor-billed curassow ("Mitu mitu") 1·00 50

**1397** St. John's Party, Campina Grande

**1995.** June Festivals. Multicoloured.
2704 12c. Type **1397** 65 40
2705 12c. Country wedding, Caruaru 65 40

**1398** St. Antony holding Child Jesus (painting, Vieira Lusitano)

**1995.** 800th Birth Anniv of St. Antony of Padua.
2706 **1398** 84c. multicoloured 4·25 3·25

**1399** Lumiere Brothers and Early Projection Equipment

**1995.** Centenary of Motion Pictures. Sheet 99×70 mm.
**MS**2707 **1399** 2r.14 multicoloured 10·50 10·00

**1400** Laurel and "Republic"

**1995.** 1st Anniv of Real Currency.
2708 **1400** 12c. brown, green & blk 65 40

**1401** Player, Net and Anniversary Emblem

**1995.** Centenary of Volleyball.
2709 **1401** 15c. multicoloured 1·10 65

**1402** "Angaturama limai"

**1995.** 14th Brazilian Palaeontology Society Congress, Uberaba. Dinosaurs. Multicoloured.
2710 15c. Type **1402** 65 45
2711 1r.50 Titanosaurus 3·25 3·00

**1403** Crash Test Dummies in Car

**1995.** Road Safety Campaign. Multicoloured.
2712 12c. Type **1403** 65 50
2713 71c. Car crashing into glass of whisky 4·00 2·75

**1404** "Calathea burle-marxii"

**1995.** "Singapore '95" International Stamp Exhibition. 10th Anniv of Donation to Nation by Roberto Burle Marx of his Botanical Collection. Multicoloured.
2714 15c. Type **1404** 20 15
2715 15c. "Vellozia burle-marxii" 20 15
2716 1r.50 "Heliconia aemygdiana" 2·00 1·75

**1405** Paratroopers and Lockheed C-130 Hercules

**1995.** 50th Anniv of Parachutist Infantry Brigade.
2717 **1405** 15c. multicoloured 80 65

**1406** Paulista Museum and "Fernao Dias Paes Leme" (statue, Luigi Brizzolara)

**1995.** Centenary of Paulista Museum of the University of Sao Paulo.
2718 **1406** 15c. multicoloured 80 65

**1407** Olinda

**1995.** Lighthouses. Multicoloured.
2719 15c. Type **1407** 80 65
2720 15c. Sao Joao 80 65
2721 15c. Santo Antonio da Barra 80 65

**1408** Scarlet Ibis and Stoat catching Fish

**1995.** "Lubrapex 95" Brazilian–Portuguese Stamp Exhibition, Sao Paulo. Fauna of the Tiete River Valley. Multicoloured.
2722 15c. Type **1408** 80 65
2723 84c. Great egret flying over canoe 4·00 2·50
**MS**2724 125×185 mm. 1r.50×2 Motifs as in Nos. 2722/3 forming a composite design 14·50 14·50

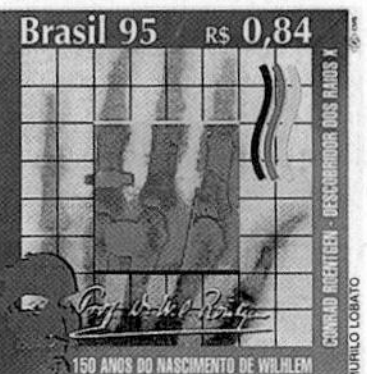

**1409** X-Ray of Hand

**1995.** 150th Birth Anniv of Wilhelm Rontgen and Centenary of his Discovery of X-Rays.

2725 **1409** 84c. multicoloured 4·25 3·25

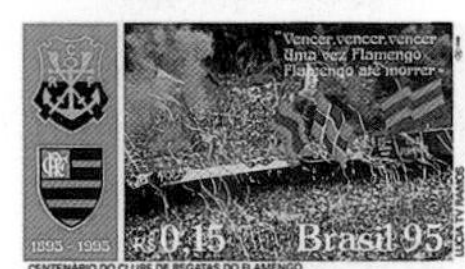


**1410** Arms and Crowd

**1995.** Centenary of Flamengo Regatta Club.

2726 **1410** 15c. multicoloured 95 65

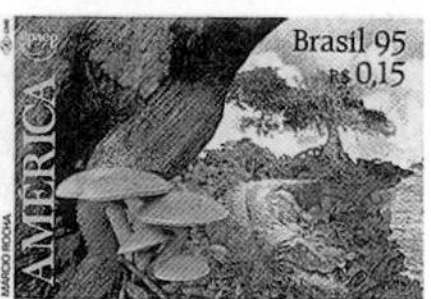


**1411** Fungi and Alligator

**1995.** America. Environmental Protection. Mult.

2727 15c. Type **1411** 80 65

2728 84c. Black-necked swans on lake 3·50 2·40

Nos. 2727/8 were issued together, se-tenant, forming a composite design.

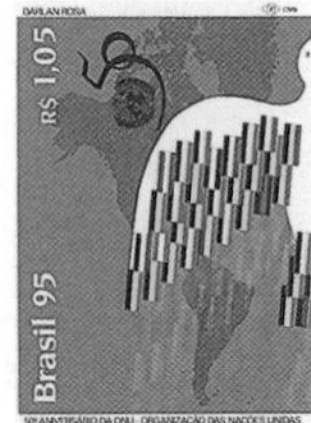


**1412** Dove over World Map (left detail)

**1995.** 50th Anniv of U.N.O. Multicoloured.

2729 1r.05 Type **1412** 4·50 4·25

2730 1r.05 Dove over world map (right detail) 4·50 4·25

Nos. 2729/30 were issued together, se-tenant, forming a composite design.

**1413** Jose Maria Eca de Queiroz

**1995.** Book Day. Writers' Anniversaries. Mult.

2731 15c. Type **1413** (150th birth) 65 50

2732 15c. Rubem Braga (5th death) 65 50

2733 23c. Carlos Drummond de Andrade (8th death) 1·10 65

**1414** Zumbi

**1995.** 300th Death Anniv of Zumbi (leader of Palmares (autonomous state formed by rebelled slaves)). Sheet 100×69 mm.

2734 **1414** 1r.05 multicoloured 5·00 5·00

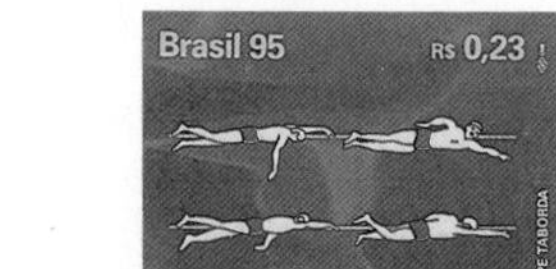


**1415** Front Crawl (Freestyle)

**1995.** 11th World Short-course Swimming Championships, Rio de Janeiro. Multicoloured.

2735 23c. Type **1415** 95 65

2736 23c. Backstroke 95 65

2737 23c. Butterfly 95 65

2738 23c. Breaststroke 95 65

Nos. 2735/8 were issued together, se-tenant, forming a composite design of a swimming pool.

**1416** Cherub

**1995.** Christmas. Multicoloured.

2739 15c. Type **1416** 80 50

2740 23c. Cherub (different) 95 65

Nos. 2739/40 were issued together, se-tenant, forming a composite design.

**1417** Flag, Former Headquarters and "Manequinho" (statue)

**1995.** Centenary (1994) of Botafogo Football and Regatta Club.

2741 **1417** 15c. multicoloured 80 65

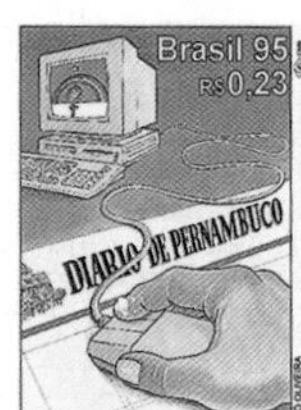


**1418** Computer, Mouse and Masthead

**1995.** 170th Anniv of "Diario de Pernambuco" (newspaper).

2742 **1418** 23c. multicoloured 95 65

**1419** Theatre Dome

**1996.** Centenary of Amazon Theatre, Manaus. Sheet 98×69 mm.

MS2743 **1419** 1r.23 multicoloured 6·00 6·00

**1420** Prestes Maia and Sao Paulo

**1996.** Birth Centenary of Francisco Prestes Maia (Mayor of Sao Paulo).

2744 **1420** 18c. multicoloured 80 40

**1421** Bornhausen and Santa Catarina

**1996.** Birth Centenary of Irineu Bornhausen (Governor of State of Santa Catarina).

2745 **1421** 27c. multicoloured 1·00 65

**1422** "Ouro Preto Landscape" (Alberto da Veiga Guignard)

**1996.** Artists' Birth Centenaries. Mult.

2746 15c. Type **1422** 60 40

2747 15c. "Boat with Little Flags and Birds" (Alfredo Volpi) 60 40

**1423** Doll

**1996.** 50th Anniv of United Nations Children's Fund. Campaign against Sexual Abuse.

2748 **1423** 23c. multicoloured 1·00 50

**1424** Anniversary Emblem

**1996.** 500th Anniv (2000) of Discovery of Brazil by the Portuguese.

2749 **1424** 1r.05 multicoloured 3·75 2·50

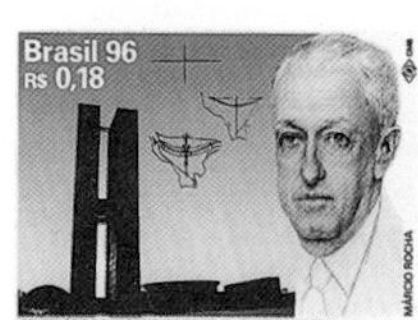


**1425** Pinheiro da Silva and National Congress

**1996.** Birth Centenary of Israel Pinheiro da Silva (politician).

2750 **1425** 18c. multicoloured 85 50

**1426** Pantanal

**1996.** Tourism. Multicoloured. Self-adhesive. Imperf (backing paper rouletted).

2751 23c. Amazon River 1·00 65

2752 23c. Type **1426** 1·00 65

2753 23c. Jangada raft 1·00 65

2754 23c. "The Sugarloaf", Guanabara Bay 1·00 65

2755 23c. Iguazu Falls 1·00 65

**1427** Crimson Topaz

**1996.** "Espamer 96" Spanish and Latin-American Stamp Exhibition, Seville, Spain. Hummingbirds. Multicoloured.

2756 15c. Type **1427** 85 40

2757 1r.05 Black-breasted plover-crest 5·00 2·50

2758 1r.15 Swallow-tailed hummingbird 5·00 2·50

**1428** Marathon Runners

**1996.** Cent of Modern Olympic Games. Mult.

2759 18c. Type **1428** 60 40

2760 23c. Gymnastics 65 50

2761 1r.05 Swimming 2·75 2·50

2762 1r.05 Beach volleyball 2·75 2·50

**1429** Cave Entrance

**1996.** National Heritage. Caverns. Sheet 99×68 mm.

MS2763 **1429** 2r.68 multicoloured 9·50 9·50

**1430** Dish Aerial, Satellite over Earth and Sports

**1996.** "Americas Telecom 96" International Telecommunications Exn, Rio de Janeiro.

2764 **1430** 1r.05 multicoloured 4·00 2·50

**1431** Sun and Raindrop replenishing Dry Tree

**1996.** World Anti-desertification Day. Sheet 70×96 mm.

MS2765 **1431** 1r.23 multicoloured 5·50 5·50

**1432** Addict and Drugs

**1996.** Anti-drug Abuse Campaign.

2766 **1432** 27c. multicoloured 3·50 1·10

**1433** Coloured Pencils

**1996.** Education Year.

2767 **1433** 23c. multicoloured 95 50

**1434** Princess Isabel and Aurea Law

**1996.** 150th Birth Anniv of Princess Isabel the Redeemer.

| | | | | |
|---|---|---|---|---|
| 2768 | **1434** | 18c. multicoloured | 80 | 40 |

The Aurea Law abolished slavery in Brazil.

**1435** Gomes and Peace Theatre

**1996.** Death Centenary of Carlos Gomes (opera composer).

| | | | | |
|---|---|---|---|---|
| 2769 | **1435** | 50c. multicoloured | 2·10 | 1·10 |

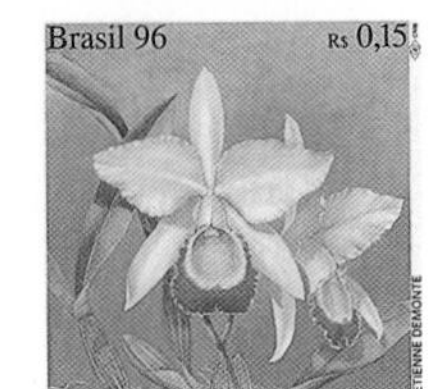


**1436** "Cattleya eldorado"

**1996.** 15th International Orchid Conference, Rio de Janeiro. Multicoloured.

| | | | |
|---|---|---|---|
| 2770 | 15c. Type **1436** | 1·30 | 45 |
| 2771 | 15c. "Cattleya loddigesii" | 1·30 | 45 |
| 2772 | 15c. "Promenaea stapellioides" | 1·30 | 45 |

**1437** Melania and Maximino and Virgin Mary

**1996.** 150th Anniv of Apparition of Our Lady at La Salette, France.

| | | | | |
|---|---|---|---|---|
| 2773 | **1437** | 1r. multicoloured | 3·25 | 2·75 |

**1438** Cuca

**1996.** BRAPEX 96 National Stamp Exhibition, Recife. Folk Legends. Sheet 72×100 mm containing T 1438 and similar horiz designs. Multicoloured.

| | | |
|---|---|---|
| **MS**2774 23c. Type **1438**; 1r.05 Boitata; 1r.15 Caipora | 7·50 | 7·50 |

**1439** "Marilyn Monroe" (Andy Warhol)

**1996.** 23rd International Biennale, Sao Paulo. Paintings. Multicoloured.

| | | | |
|---|---|---|---|
| 2775 | 55c. Type **1439** | 1·40 | 1·00 |
| 2776 | 55c. "The Scream" (Edvard Munch) | 1·40 | 1·00 |
| 2777 | 55c. "Mirror for the red Room" (Louise Bourgeois) | 1·40 | 1·00 |
| 2778 | 55c. "Lent" (Pablo Picasso) | 1·40 | 1·00 |

**1440** Emblem

**1996.** Defenders of Nature (environmental organization).

| | | | | |
|---|---|---|---|---|
| 2779 | **1440** | 10r. multicoloured | 14·50 | 12·00 |

**1441** Vaqueiro

**1996.** America. Traditional Costumes. Mult.

| | | | |
|---|---|---|---|
| 2780 | 50c. Type **1441** | 1·60 | 1·10 |
| 2781 | 1r. Baiana (seller of beancakes) | 3·25 | 2·30 |

**1442** Poinsettia and Lighted Candle

**1996.** Christmas.

| | | | | |
|---|---|---|---|---|
| 2782 | **1442** | (–) multicoloured | 1·40 | 50 |

See second note below No. 2588.

**1443** "Melindrosa" (cover of 1931 "O Cruzeiro" magazine)

**1996.** 46th Death Anniv of Jose Carlos (caricaturist).

| | | | | |
|---|---|---|---|---|
| 2783 | **1443** | (–) multicoloured | 1·40 | 50 |

See second note below No. 2588.

**1444** Ipiranga Monument

**1996.** Tourism. Multicoloured. Self-adhesive. Imperf (backing paper rouletted).

| | | | |
|---|---|---|---|
| 2784 | (–) Type **1444** | 80 | 55 |
| 2785 | (–) Hercilio Luz Bridge | 80 | 55 |
| 2786 | (–) National Congress building | 80 | 55 |
| 2787 | (–) Pelourinho | 80 | 55 |
| 2788 | (–) Ver-o-Peso market | 80 | 55 |

Nos. 2784/8 were valid for use at the current first stage inland letter rate.

**1445** Campaign Emblem and Guanabara Bay

**1997.** Bid by Rio de Janeiro for 2004 Olympic Games.

| | | | | |
|---|---|---|---|---|
| 2789 | **1445** | (–) multicoloured | 4·25 | 2·75 |

No. 2789 was valid for use at the current first stage international letter rate.

**1446** Postman and Letter Recipients

**1997.** America. The Postman.

| | | | | |
|---|---|---|---|---|
| 2790 | **1446** | (–) multicoloured | 1·30 | 60 |

No. 2790 was valid for use at the current first stage inland letter rate.

**1447** Alves, Flogging and Salvador Harbour

**1997.** 150th Birth Anniv of Antonio de Castro Alves (poet).

| | | | | |
|---|---|---|---|---|
| 2791 | **1447** | 15c. multicoloured | 65 | 40 |

**1448** Tamandare (after Miranda Junior) and "Rescue of 'Ocean Monarch' by Don Afonso" (Samuel Walters)

**1997.** Death Centenary of Marquis of Tamandare (naval reformer).

| | | | | |
|---|---|---|---|---|
| 2792 | **1448** | 23c. multicoloured | 65 | 50 |

**1449** "Joy. Joy"

**1997.** Winning Entry in "Art on Stamps" Competition.

| | | | | |
|---|---|---|---|---|
| 2793 | **1449** | 15c. multicoloured | 4·25 | 65 |

**1450** Globe in Glass of Water

**1997.** World Water Day.

| | | | | |
|---|---|---|---|---|
| 2794 | **1450** | 1r.05 multicoloured | 3·25 | 2·50 |

**1451** Embraer EMB-145

**1997.** Brazilian Aircraft. Multicoloured. Self-adhesive. Imperf (backing paper rouletted).

| | | | |
|---|---|---|---|
| 2795 | 15c. Type **1451** | 40 | 25 |
| 2796 | 15c. Aeritalia/Aermacchi AM-X jet fighter | 40 | 25 |
| 2797 | 15c. Embraer EMB-312 H Super Tucano | 40 | 25 |
| 2798 | 15c. Embraer EMB-120 Brasilia | 40 | 25 |
| 2799 | 15c. Embraer EMB-312 Tucano trainer | 40 | 25 |

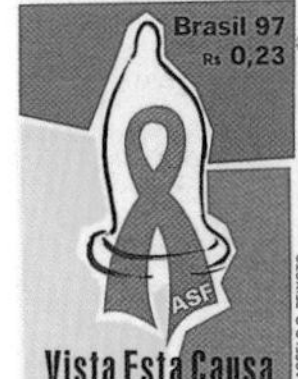


**1452** Red Ribbon inside Condom

**1997.** Family Health Association (A.S.F.) Anti-AIDS Campaign.

| | | | | |
|---|---|---|---|---|
| 2810 | **1452** | 23c. multicoloured | 75 | 45 |

**1453** Traditional Weapons and Tribesmen

**1997.** Indian Cultures. Sheet 70×100 mm.

| | | |
|---|---|---|
| **MS**2811 **1453** 1r.15 multicoloured | 3·50 | 3·25 |

**1454** Emblem

**1997.** 500th Anniv (2000) of Discovery of Brazil by the Portuguese.

| | | | | |
|---|---|---|---|---|
| 2812 | **1454** | 1r.05 multicoloured | 3·25 | 2·50 |

**1455** Pixinguinha

**1997.** Birth Centenary of Pixinguinha (musician).

| | | | | |
|---|---|---|---|---|
| 2813 | **1455** | 15c. multicoloured | 45 | 40 |

**1456** Landmark

**1997.** Centenary of Brazilian Sovereignty of Trinidade Island. Sheet 99×68 mm.

| | | |
|---|---|---|
| **MS**2814 **1456** 1r.23 multicoloured | 4·00 | 3·75 |

**1457** Inscription

**1997.** "Human Rights, Rights of All".

| | | | | |
|---|---|---|---|---|
| 2815 | **1457** | 18c. black and red | 65 | 40 |

**1458** Map

**1997.** Brazilian Antarctic Programme. Sheet 69×99 mm.

| | | | | |
|---|---|---|---|---|
| **MS**2816 | **1458** | 2r.68 multicoloured | 8·75 | 8·25 |

**1459** Melon

**1997.** Fruits. Self-adhesive. (a) Imperf (backing paper rouletted). (i) With service indicator.

| | | | | |
|---|---|---|---|---|
| 2817 | **1459** | (–) red and green | 55 | 50 |

(ii) With face values.

| | | | |
|---|---|---|---|
| 2818 | 1c. yellow, orange & grn | 15 | 15 |
| 2819 | 2c. yellow, brown & blk | 15 | 15 |
| 2820 | 5c. orange, yellow & blk | 15 | 15 |
| 2821 | 10c. yellow, brown & grn | 25 | 25 |
| 2822 | 20c. yellow, red & green | 55 | 50 |

(b) Die-cut wavy edge.

| | | | |
|---|---|---|---|
| 2823 | 1c. yellow, orange & grn | 15 | 15 |
| 2824 | 10c. yellow, brown & grn | 15 | 15 |
| 2825 | 20c. lt green, grn & blk | 55 | 50 |
| 2826 | 22c. red, purple & green | 55 | 40 |
| 2827 | 27c. orange, brown and green | 65 | 65 |
| 2828 | 40c. multicoloured | 80 | 75 |
| 2829 | 50c. multicoloured | 80 | 75 |
| 2830 | 51c. green, lt grn & brn | 1·30 | 1·30 |
| 2831 | 80c. red, green & yellow | 2·10 | 2·00 |
| 2832 | 82c. lt grn, grn & dp grn | 2·10 | 2·00 |
| 2833 | 1r. red, green & yellow | 2·75 | 1·60 |

DESIGNS—HORIZ: Nos. 2818, 2823, Oranges; 2819, Bananas; 2820, Mango. VERT: Nos. 2821, 2824, Pineapple; 2822, Cashew nuts; 2825, Sugar-apple; 2826, Grapes; 2827, Cupuacu; 2828, Soursop; 2829, Suriname cherry ("Pitanga"); 2830, Coconut; 2831, Apples; 2832, Limes; 2833, Strawberries.

No. 2817 was valid for use at the current first stage inland letter rate.

**1460** Mahogany ("Swietenia macropylla")

**1997.** World Environment Day. Amazon Flora and Fauna. Multicoloured.

| | | | |
|---|---|---|---|
| 2836 | 27c. Type **1460** | 80 | 65 |
| 2837 | 27c. Arapaima (55×22 mm) | 80 | 65 |

**1461** Antonio Vieira in Pulpit

**1997.** Death Anniversaries of Missionaries to Brazil. Multicoloured.

| | | | |
|---|---|---|---|
| 2838 | 1r.05 Type **1461** (300th) | 2·75 | 2·50 |
| 2839 | 1r.05 Indian children and Jose de Auchieta (400th) | 2·75 | 2·50 |

**1462** Parnaiba Delta and Sculpture (Mestre Dezinho)

**1997.** Tourism. With service indicator. Mult.

| | | | |
|---|---|---|---|
| 2840 | (–) Type **1462** | 2·75 | 2·50 |
| 2841 | (–) Lencois Maranhenses National Park and costume | 2·75 | 2·50 |

Nos. 2840/1 were valid for use at the current rate for first class international postage.

**1463** Blue-black Grassquit

**1997.** Birds. Multicoloured. Self-adhesive. Imperf (backing paper rouletted). (a) With service indicator.

| | | | |
|---|---|---|---|
| 2842 | (–) Type **1463** | 95 | 90 |

(b) With face value.

| | | | |
|---|---|---|---|
| 2843 | 22c. Social flycatcher ("Vermilion-crowned Flycatcher") | 55 | 50 |

No. 2842 was valid for use at the current first stage inland letter rate.

**1464** Academy

**1998.** Cent of Brazilian Literature Academy.

| | | | | |
|---|---|---|---|---|
| 2850 | **1464** | 22c. multicoloured | 95 | 50 |

**1465** "Gipsies" (Di Cavalcanti)

**1997.** Birth Centenary of Emiliano di Cavalcanti (artist).

| | | | | |
|---|---|---|---|---|
| 2851 | **1465** | 31c. multicoloured | 85 | 75 |

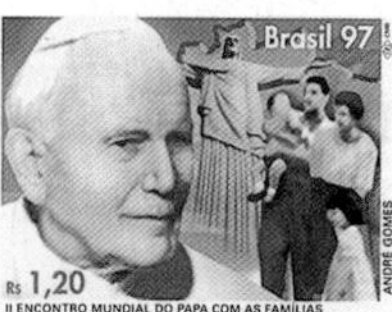


**1466** Pope John Paul II, "Christ the Redeemer" and Family

**1997.** 2nd World Meeting of Pope with Families, Rio de Janeiro.

| | | | | |
|---|---|---|---|---|
| 2852 | **1466** | 1r.20 multicoloured | 4·75 | 3·00 |

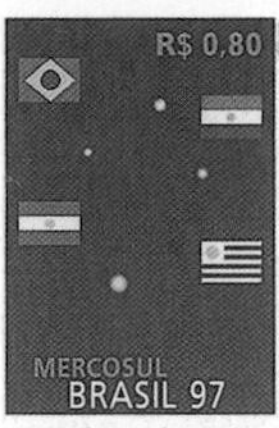


**1467** Flags of Member Countries

**1997.** Mercosur (South American Common Market).

| | | | | |
|---|---|---|---|---|
| 2853 | **1467** | 80c. multicoloured | 2·75 | 1·90 |

**1468** Antonio Conselheiro (religious leader)

**1997.** Centenary of End of Canudos War.

| | | | | |
|---|---|---|---|---|
| 2854 | **1468** | 22c. multicoloured | 70 | 50 |

**1469** Mercosur Members starred on Map of South America

**1997.** 25th Anniv of Telebras.

| | | | | |
|---|---|---|---|---|
| 2855 | **1469** | 80c. multicoloured | 3·25 | 1·90 |

**1470** Lorenzo Fernandez and Score of "Sonata Breve"

**1997.** Composers' Birth Centenaries. Each black and gold.

| | | | |
|---|---|---|---|
| 2856 | 22c. Type **1470** | 70 | 50 |
| 2857 | 22c. Francisco Mignone and score of "Second Brazilian Fantasia" | 70 | 50 |

**1471** "Our Good Mother" and Blackboard with Marist Motto

**1997.** Centenary of Marist Brothers in Brazil.

| | | | | |
|---|---|---|---|---|
| 2858 | **1471** | 22c. multicoloured | 70 | 50 |

**1472** Angel playing Trumpet

**1997.** Christmas.

| | | | | |
|---|---|---|---|---|
| 2859 | **1472** | 22c. multicoloured | 70 | 50 |

**1473** "Equality" (Gian Calvi)

**1997.** Children and Citizenship. Multicoloured.

| | | | |
|---|---|---|---|
| 2860 | 22c.+8c. Type **1473** | 85 | 75 |
| 2861 | 22c.+8c. "Love and Tenderness" (Alcy Linares) | 85 | 75 |
| 2862 | 22c.+8c. "Admission to School" (Ziraldo) | 85 | 75 |
| 2863 | 22c.+8c. "Healthy Pregnancy" (Claudio Martins) | 85 | 75 |
| 2864 | 22c.+8c. "Being Happy" (Cica Fittipaldi) | 85 | 75 |
| 2865 | 22c.+8c. "Work for Parents, School for Children" (Roger Mello) | 85 | 75 |
| 2866 | 22c.+8c. "Breast-feeding" (Angela Lago) | 85 | 75 |

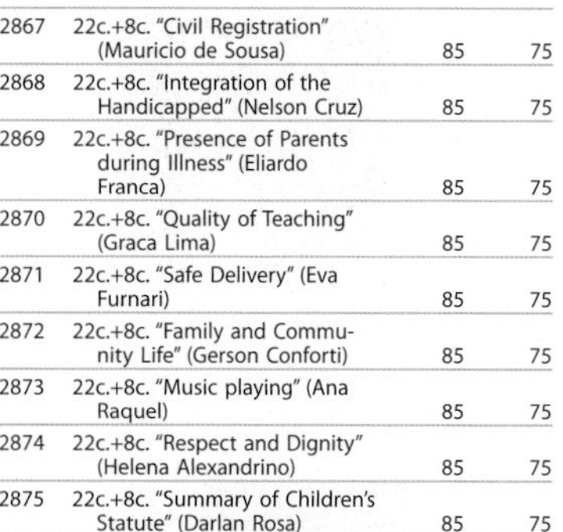

| | | | |
|---|---|---|---|
| 2867 | 22c.+8c. "Civil Registration" (Mauricio de Sousa) | 85 | 75 |
| 2868 | 22c.+8c. "Integration of the Handicapped" (Nelson Cruz) | 85 | 75 |
| 2869 | 22c.+8c. "Presence of Parents during Illness" (Eliardo Franca) | 85 | 75 |
| 2870 | 22c.+8c. "Quality of Teaching" (Graca Lima) | 85 | 75 |
| 2871 | 22c.+8c. "Safe Delivery" (Eva Furnari) | 85 | 75 |
| 2872 | 22c.+8c. "Family and Community Life" (Gerson Conforti) | 85 | 75 |
| 2873 | 22c.+8c. "Music playing" (Ana Raquel) | 85 | 75 |
| 2874 | 22c.+8c. "Respect and Dignity" (Helena Alexandrino) | 85 | 75 |
| 2875 | 22c.+8c. "Summary of Children's Statute" (Darlan Rosa) | 85 | 75 |

**1474** Children and Globe

**1997.** Education and Citizenship.

| | | | | |
|---|---|---|---|---|
| 2876 | **1474** | 31c. blue and yellow | 1·00 | 75 |

**1475** Belo Horizonte at Night

**1997.** Centenary of Belo Horizonte.

| | | | | |
|---|---|---|---|---|
| 2877 | **1475** | 31c. multicoloured | 1·00 | 75 |

**1476** Outline Map and Books (Education)

**1997.** Citizens' Rights. Mult. Self-adhesive.

| | | | |
|---|---|---|---|
| 2878 | 22c. Type **1476** | 1·40 | 50 |
| 2879 | 22c. Map and hand holding labour card (work) | 1·40 | 50 |
| 2880 | 22c. Map and fruit (agriculture) | 1·40 | 50 |
| 2881 | 22c. Map and stethoscope (health) | 1·40 | 50 |
| 2882 | 22c. Clapper-board and paint brush (culture) | 1·40 | 50 |

**1477** Alexandrite

**1998.** Minerals. Multicoloured.

| | | | |
|---|---|---|---|
| 2883 | 22c. Type **1477** | 85 | 50 |
| 2884 | 22c. Chrysoberyl cat's-eye | 85 | 50 |
| 2885 | 22c. Indicolite | 85 | 50 |

**1478** Elis Regina (singer)

**1998.** America. Famous Women. Multicoloured.

| | | | |
|---|---|---|---|
| 2886 | 22c. Type **1478** | 70 | 50 |
| 2887 | 22c. Clementina de Jesus (singer) | 70 | 50 |
| 2888 | 22c. Dulcina de Moraes (actress) | 70 | 50 |
| 2889 | 22c. Clarice Lispector (writer) | 70 | 50 |

**1479** Pupils

**1998.** Education. Multicoloured.
2890 31c. Type **1479** (universal schooling) 85 75
2891 31c. Teacher (teacher appraisal) 85 75

Nos. 2390/1 were issued together, se-tenant, forming a composite design of a classroom.

**1480** Cruze Sousa

**1998.** Death Centenary of Joao da Cruze Sousa (poet).
2892 **1480** 36c. multicoloured 1·10 90

**1481** Map, 1519

**1998.** 500th Anniv (2000) of Discovery of Brazil by the Portuguese. Multicoloured.
2893 1r.05 Type **1481** 2·75 2·50
2894 1r.05 Galleon 2·75 2·50

Nos. 2893/4 were issued together, se-tenant, forming a composite design.

**1482** Woman Caring for Elderly Man

**1998.** Voluntary Work. Multicoloured.
2895 31c. Type **1482** 85 75
2896 31c. Woman caring for child 85 75
2897 31c. Fighting forest fire 85 75
2898 31c. Adult's and child's hands 85 75

Nos. 2895/8 were issued together, se-tenant, forming a composite design.

**1483** Clown

**1998.** Circus. Multicoloured.
2899 31c. Type **1483** 85 75
2900 31c. Clown resting on stick 85 75
2901 31c. Clown (left half) and outside of Big Top 85 75
2902 31c. Clown (right half) and inside of Big Top 85 75

Nos. 2899/2902 were issued together, se-tenant, forming a composite design.

**1484** Turtle

**1998.** Expo '98 World's Fair, Lisbon. International Year of the Ocean. Multicoloured.
2903 31c. Type **1484** 85 75
2904 31c. Tail of whale 85 75
2905 31c. Barracuda 85 75
2906 31c. Jellyfish and fishes 85 75
2907 31c. Diver and school of fishes 85 75
2908 31c. Two dolphins 85 75
2909 31c. Angelfish (brown spotted fish) 85 75
2910 31c. Two whales 85 75
2911 31c. Two long-nosed butterflyfishes (with black stripe across eye) 85 75
2912 31c. Sea perch (red and yellow fish) 85 75
2913 31c. Manatee 85 75
2914 31c. Seabream (blue, yellow and white fish) 85 75
2915 31c. Emperor angelfish and coral 85 75
2916 31c. School of snappers (blue and yellow striped fishes) 85 75
2917 31c. Flying gurnard 85 75
2918 31c. Manta ray 85 75
2919 31c. Two butterflyfishes (black and green fishes) 85 75
2920 31c. Pipefish 85 75
2921 31c. Moray eel 85 75
2922 31c. Angelfish (blue, yellow and black) and coral 85 75
2923 31c. Red and yellow fish, starfish and coral 85 75
2924 31c. Crab and coral 85 75
2925 31c. Snapper and coral 85 75
2926 31c. Seahorse and coral 85 75

Nos. 2903/26 were issued together, se-tenant, forming a composite design.

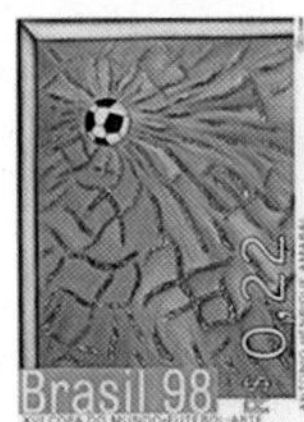

**1485** Ball breaking Net (Antonio Henrique Amaral)

**1998.** World Cup Football Championship, France. Designs depicting football art by named artists. Multicoloured.
2927 22c. Type **1485** 55 50
2928 22c. Aldemir Martins 55 50
2929 22c. Glauco Rodrigues 55 50
2930 22c. Marcia Grostein 55 50
2931 22c. Claudio Tozzi 55 50
2932 22c. Zelio Alves Pinto 55 50
2933 22c. Guto Lacaz 55 50
2934 22c. Antonio Peticov 55 50
2935 22c. Cildo Meireles 55 50
2936 22c. Mauricio Nogueira Lima 55 50
2937 22c. Roberto Magalhaes 55 50
2938 22c. Luiz Zerbine 55 50
2939 22c. Maciej Babinski (horiz) 55 50
2940 22c. Wesley Duke Lee (horiz) 55 50
2941 22c. Joao Camara (horiz) 55 50
2942 22c. Jose Zaragoza (horiz) 55 50
2943 22c. Mario Gruber (horiz) 55 50
2944 22c. Nelson Leirner (horiz) 55 50
2945 22c. Carlos Vergara (horiz) 55 50
2946 22c. Tomoshige Kusuno (horiz) 55 50
2947 22c. Gregorio Gruber (horiz) 55 50
2948 22c. Jose Roberto Aguilar (horiz) 55 50
2949 22c. Ivald Granato (horiz) 55 50
2950 22c. Leda Catunda (horiz) 55 50

**1486** Bean Casserole and Vegetables

**1998.** Cultural Dishes.
2951 **1486** 31c. multicoloured 1·00 75

**1487** "Araucaria angustifolia"

**1998.** Environmental Protection. Multicoloured.
2952 22c. Type **1487** 95 50
2953 22c. Azure jay ("Cyanocorax caeruleus") 95 50

Nos. 2952/3 were issued together, se-tenant, forming a composite design.

**1488** "Tapajo"

**1998.** Launching of Submarine "Tapajo".
2954 **1488** 51c. multicoloured 1·40 1·30

**1489** Bust of Queiroz and College Building

**1998.** Death Centenary of Luiz de Queiroz (founder of Agricultural College, Piracicaba).
2955 **1489** 36c. multicoloured 1·00 90

**1490** Statue of St. Benedict and Monastery

**1998.** 400th Anniv of St. Benedict's Monastery, Sao Paulo.
2956 **1490** 22c. multicoloured 85 50

**1491** Santos-Dumont and his First Balloon "Brasil"

**1998.** Aviation. Aircraft Designs by Alberto Santos-Dumont (aviator). Multicoloured.
2957 31c. Type **1491** 85 75
2958 31c. Santos-Dumont and Dirigible "No. 1" 85 75

**1492** Early Film of Guanabara Bay

**1998.** Centenary (1997) of Brazilian Cinema. Multicoloured.
2959 31c. Type **1492** 85 75
2960 31c. Taciana Reis (actress) in "Limite" (dir. Mario Peixoto, 1912) 85 75
2961 31c. Grande Otela and Oscarito in "A Dupla do Barulho" (dir. Carlos Manga, 1953) (inscr "Chanchada") 85 75
2962 31c. Mazzaropi (actor) and film titles (Vera Cruz film company) 85 75
2963 31c. Glauber Rocha (director) ("New Cinema") 85 75
2964 31c. Titles of prize-winning films, 1962–98 85 75

**1493** Andrade, Entrance to St. Antony's Church (Tiradentes) and Church of Our Lady of the Rosary (Ouro Preto)

**1998.** Birth Centenary of Rodrigo Melo Franco de Andrade (founder of Federal Institution for Preservation of the National Historic and Artistic Patrimony).
2965 **1493** 51c. multicoloured 1·40 1·10

**1494** Cascudo and Folk Characters

**1998.** Birth Centenary of Luis da Camara Cascudo (writer).
2966 **1494** 22c. multicoloured 90 50

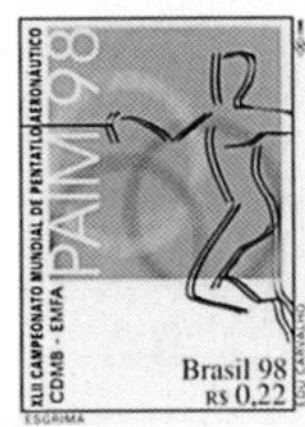

**1495** Fencing

**1998.** 42nd World Aeronautical Pentathlon Championships, Natal. Multicoloured.
2967 22c. Type **1495** 90 50
2968 22c. Running 90 50
2969 22c. Swimming 90 50
2970 22c. Shooting 90 50
2971 22c. Basketball 90 50

**1496** Missionary Cross and St. Michael of the Missions Church

**1998.** Mercosur. Missions.
2972 **1496** 80c. multicoloured 2·30 1·50

**1497** Untitled Work (Jose Leonilson) (Biennale emblem)

**1998.** 24th Art Biennale, Sao Paulo. Paintings. Mult.
2973 31c. Type **1497** 85 65
2974 31c. "Tapuia Dance" (Albert von Eckhout) 85 65
2975 31c. "The Schoolboy" (Vincent van Gogh) (vert) 85 65
2976 31c. "Portrait of Michel Leiris" (Francis Bacon) (vert) 85 65
2977 31c. "The King's Museum" (Rene Magritte) (vert) 85 65
2978 31c. "Urutu" (Tarsila do Amaral) 85 65
2979 31c. "Facade with Arcs, Circle and Fascia" (Alfredo Volpi) (vert) 85 65
2980 31c. "The Raft of the Medusa" (Asger Jorn) 85 65

**1498** "Citizenship" (Erika Albuquerque)

**1998.** Child and Citizenship.
2981 **1498** 22c. multicoloured 85 40

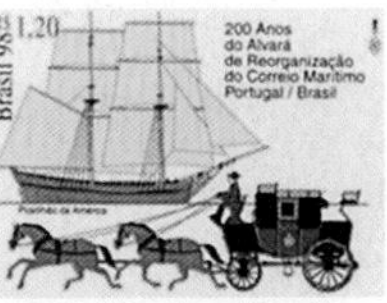

**1499** Mail Coach and "Postilhao da America" (brigantine)

**1998.** Bicentenary of Reorganization of Maritime Mail Service between Portugal and Brazil.
2982 **1499** 1r.20 multicoloured 2·75 2·50

**1500** "D. Pedro I" (Simplicio Rodrigues da Sa), Crown and Sceptre

**1998.** Birth Bicentenary of Emperor Pedro I.

| | | | | |
|---|---|---|---|---|
| 2983 | **1500** | 22c. multicoloured | 80 | 40 |

**1501** Mangoes and Glasses of Juice

**1998.** Frisco (fruit juice) Publicity Campaign. Self-adhesive.

| | | | | |
|---|---|---|---|---|
| 2984 | **1501** | 36c. multicoloured | 4·00 | 2·75 |

**1502** "Solanum lycocarpum"

**1998.** Cerrado Flowers. Multicoloured.

| | | | |
|---|---|---|---|
| 2985 | 31c. Type **1502** | 80 | 65 |
| 2986 | 31c. "Cattleya walkeriana" | 80 | 65 |
| 2987 | 31c. "Kielmeyera coriacea" | 80 | 65 |

**1503** Mother Teresa (founder of Missionaries of Charity)

**1998.** Peace and Fraternity. Multicoloured.

| | | | |
|---|---|---|---|
| 2988 | 31c. Type **1503** | 80 | 65 |
| 2989 | 31c. Friar Galvao (first Brazilian to be beatified, 1998) | 80 | 65 |
| 2990 | 31c. Betinho (Herbert Jose de Souza) | 80 | 65 |
| 2991 | 31c. Friar Damiao | 80 | 65 |

Nos. 2988/91 were issued together, se-tenant, forming a central composite design of the Earth.

**1504** Sergio Motta and Headquarters, Brasilia

**1998.** 1st Anniv of National Telecommunications Agency.

| | | | | |
|---|---|---|---|---|
| 2992 | **1504** | 31c. multicoloured | 95 | 65 |

Motta was Minister of Communications when the agency was established.

**1505** Tiles and Church of Our Lady of Fatima, Brasilia

**1998.** Christmas.

| | | | | |
|---|---|---|---|---|
| 2993 | **1505** | 22c. multicoloured | 90 | 40 |

**1506** Moxoto Goat

**1998.** Domestic Animals. Mult. Self-adhesive.

| | | | |
|---|---|---|---|
| 2994 | 22c. Type **1506** | 60 | 35 |
| 2995 | 22c. North-eastern donkey | 60 | 35 |
| 2996 | 22c. Junqueira ox | 60 | 35 |
| 2997 | 22c. Brazilian terrier (vert) | 60 | 35 |
| 2998 | 22c. Brazilian shorthair (vert) | 60 | 35 |

**1507** Man casting Winged Shadow

**1998.** 50th Anniv of Universal Declaration of Human Rights.

| | | | | |
|---|---|---|---|---|
| 2999 | **1507** | 1r.20 multicoloured | 4·00 | 1·90 |

**1508** Mother Luiza Lighthouse, Natal

**1999.** 400th Annivs of Natal (1999) and of Wise Men's Fortress (1998). Multicoloured.

| | | | |
|---|---|---|---|
| 3000 | 31c. Type **1508** | 1·00 | 40 |
| 3001 | 31c. Wise Men's Fortress, Natal (horiz) | 1·00 | 40 |

**1509** Extent of Economic Zone, Satellite and Belmonte Lighthouse

**1999.** Evaluation Programme of Sustainable Potential of Living Resources in the Exclusive Economic Zone (REVIZEE). Multicoloured.

| | | | |
|---|---|---|---|
| 3002 | 31c. Type **1509** (Sao Pedro and Sao Paulo Archipelago Research Programme) | 65 | 40 |
| 3003 | 31c. Blue-faced booby on buoy | 65 | 40 |
| 3004 | 31c. "Riobaldo" (research ship) | 65 | 40 |
| 3005 | 31c. Turtle | 65 | 40 |
| 3006 | 31c. Dolphin | 65 | 40 |
| 3007 | 31c. Diver | 65 | 40 |

Nos. 3002/7 were issued together, se-tenant, forming a composite design.

No. 3004 includes the emblem of "Australia 99" International Stamp Exhibition, Melbourne.

**1510** Stamp Vending Machines of 1940s and 1998

**1999.** 125th Anniv of Universal Postal Union. Multicoloured.

| | | | |
|---|---|---|---|
| 3008 | 31c. Type **1510** | 65 | 40 |
| 3009 | 31c. Postal products vending machines of 1906 and 1998 | 65 | 40 |
| 3010 | 31c. Postboxes of 1870 and 1973 | 65 | 40 |
| 3011 | 31c. Brazilian Quality and Productivity Programme silver award to Rio Grande postal region, 1998 | 65 | 40 |

Nos. 3008/11 were issued together, se-tenant, forming a composite design of the U.P.U. emblem.

**1511** Lacerda Lift, Barra Lighthouse and Church of Our Lady of the Rosary

**1999.** 450th Anniv of Salvador.

| | | | | |
|---|---|---|---|---|
| 3012 | **1511** | 1r.05 multicoloured | 3·50 | 1·60 |

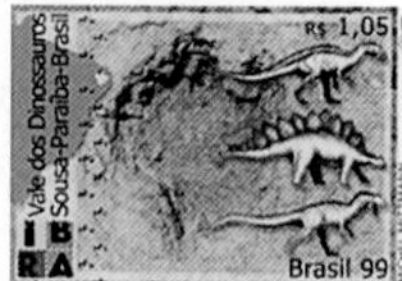

**1512** Footprint, Iguanodon, Stegosaurus and Allosaurus

**1999.** "iBRA 99" International Stamp Exhibition, Nuremberg, Germany. Valley of the Dinosaurs, Sousa.

| | | | | |
|---|---|---|---|---|
| 3013 | **1512** | 1r.05 multicoloured | 2·75 | 1·90 |

**1513** Fortress

**1999.** 415th Anniv of St. Amaro of Barra Grande Fortress, Guaruja.

| | | | | |
|---|---|---|---|---|
| 3014 | **1513** | 22c. multicoloured | 75 | 40 |

**1514** Children of Various Races

**1999.** 500th Anniv (2000) of Discovery of Brazil (4th issue). Sheet 69×99 mm.

| | | | | |
|---|---|---|---|---|
| **MS**3015 | **1514** | 2r.68 multicoloured | 6·25 | 6·25 |

**1515** Embracer EMB-110 Bandeirante, Emblem, Dove and Globe

**1999.** 30th Anniv of 6th Air Transportation Squadron.

| | | | | |
|---|---|---|---|---|
| 3016 | **1515** | 51c. multicoloured | 1·60 | 90 |

**1516** Banner and Revellers

**1999.** Feast of the Holy Spirit, Planaltina.

| | | | | |
|---|---|---|---|---|
| 3017 | **1516** | 22c. multicoloured | 70 | 40 |

**1517** Ouro Preto

**1999.** Philexfrance 99 International Stamp Exhibition. World Heritage Sites. Sheet 70×110 containing T 1517 and similar horiz designs. Multicoloured.

| | | | |
|---|---|---|---|
| **MS**3018 | 1r.05 Type **1517**; 1r.05 Olinda; 1r.05 Sao Lius | 7·00 | 7·00 |

**1518** Symbols of Computer Science, Chemistry, Engineering, Metallurgy and Geology

**1999.** Centenary of Institute for Technological Research, Sao Paulo.

| | | | | |
|---|---|---|---|---|
| 3019 | **1518** | 36c. multicoloured | 95 | 50 |

**1519** Santos-Dumont and Ballon No. 3

**1999.** Centenary of Flight of Alberto Santos-Dumont's Airship Ballon No. 3.

| | | | | |
|---|---|---|---|---|
| 3020 | **1519** | 1r.20 multicoloured | 3·50 | 1·80 |

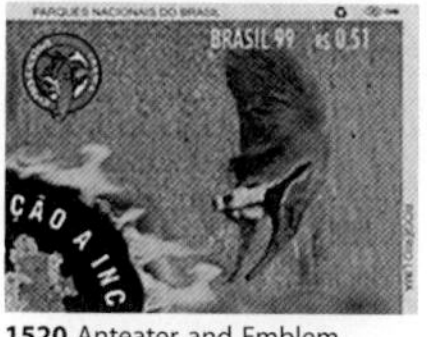
**1520** Anteater and Emblem

**1999.** National Campaign for Prevention and Combat of Forest Fires (PREVFOGO). Mult. Self-adhesive.

| | | | |
|---|---|---|---|
| 3021 | 51c. Type **1520** | 1·10 | 75 |
| 3022 | 51c. Flower and IBAMA emblem | 1·10 | 75 |
| 3023 | 51c. Leaf and IBAMA emblem | 1·10 | 75 |
| 3024 | 51c. Burnt tree trunk and PREVFOGO emblem | 1·10 | 75 |

Nos. 3021/4 were issued together, se-tenant, forming a composite design of a map and flames.

Nos. 3021/4 are also impregnated with the scent of burnt wood.

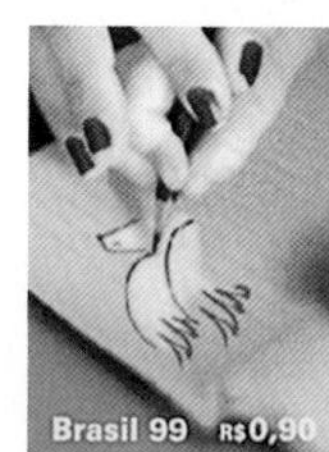

**1521** Hands drawing Dove

**1999.** America. A New Millennium without Arms. Sheet 109×69 mm containing T 1521 and similar vert design. Multicoloured.

| | | | |
|---|---|---|---|
| **MS**3025 | 90c. Type **1521**; 90c. Overturned tank | 4·25 | 4·25 |

**1522** Stitched Heart

**1999.** 20th Anniv of Political Amnesty in Brazil.

| | | | | |
|---|---|---|---|---|
| 3026 | **1522** | 22c. multicoloured | 65 | 25 |

**1523** Joaquim Nabuco (politician)

**1999.** 150th Birth Anniversaries. Multicoloured.

| | | | |
|---|---|---|---|
| 3027 | 22c. Type **1523** | 65 | 25 |
| 3028 | 31c. Rui Barbosa (politician) | 80 | 40 |

**1524** Dorado

**1999.** "China '99" International Stamp Exhibition, Peking. Fishes. Multicoloured.

| | | | |
|---|---|---|---|
| 3029 | 22c. Type **1524** | 30 | 25 |

| | | | |
|---|---|---|---|
| 3030 | 31c. *Brycon microlepis* | 45 | 40 |
| 3031 | 36c. *Acestrorhynchus pantaneiro* | 65 | 50 |
| 3032 | 51c. Tetra "*Hyphessobrycon eques*" | 95 | 75 |
| 3033 | 80c. *Rineloricaria* sp. | 1·40 | 1·10 |
| 3034 | 90c. *Leporinus macrocephalus* | 1·60 | 1·30 |
| 3035 | 1r.05 *Abramites* sp. | 1·90 | 1·50 |
| 3036 | 1r.20 Bristle-mouthed catfish | 2·20 | 1·80 |

Nos. 3029/36 were issued together, se-tenant, with the backgrounds forming a composite design.

No. 3036 also includes a hologram of the exhibition emblem.

**1525** Open Book and Flags of Member Countries

**1999.** Mercosur. The Book.

| | | | | |
|---|---|---|---|---|
| 3037 | **1525** | 80c. multicoloured | 2·50 | 1·30 |

**1526** Aguas Emendadas Ecological Station

**1999.** Water Resources. Multicoloured.

| | | | |
|---|---|---|---|
| 3038 | 31c. Type **1526** | 50 | 40 |
| 3039 | 31c. House and jetty | 50 | 40 |
| 3040 | 31c. Cedro Dam | 50 | 40 |
| 3041 | 31c. Oros Dam | 50 | 40 |

Nos. 3038/41 were issued together, se-tenant, forming a composite design of a whirlpool.

**1527** "Ex Libris" (Eliseu Visconti)

**1999.** National Library, Rio de Janeiro.

| | | | | |
|---|---|---|---|---|
| 3042 | **1527** | 22c. multicoloured | 55 | 25 |

**1999.** State Flags (6th series). As T 992.

| | | | |
|---|---|---|---|
| 3043 | 31c. Amapa | 65 | 50 |
| 3044 | 36c. Roraima | 65 | 50 |

**1528** Piano and Woman

**1999.** 5th Death Anniv of Antonio Carlos Jobim (composer).

| | | | | |
|---|---|---|---|---|
| 3045 | **1528** | 31c. multicoloured | 65 | 50 |

**1529** The Annunciation

**1999.** Christmas. Birth Bimillenary of Jesus Christ. Multicoloured.

| | | | |
|---|---|---|---|
| 3046 | 22c. Type **1529** | 35 | 25 |
| 3047 | 22c. Adoration of the Magi | 35 | 25 |
| 3048 | 22c. Presentation of Jesus in the Temple | 35 | 25 |
| 3049 | 22c. Baptism of Jesus by John the Baptist | 35 | 25 |
| 3050 | 22c. Jesus and the Twelve Apostles | 35 | 25 |
| 3051 | 22c. Death and resurrection of Jesus | 35 | 25 |

**1530** Open Book and Globe

**1999.** New Middle School Education Programme.

| | | | | |
|---|---|---|---|---|
| 3052 | **1530** | 31c. multicoloured | 70 | 50 |

**1531** Itamaraty Palace, Rio de Janeiro

**1999.** Centenary of Installation of Ministry of Foreign Relations Headquarters in Itamaraty Palace, Rio de Janeiro.

| | | | | |
|---|---|---|---|---|
| 3053 | **1531** | 1r.05 brown and stone | 2·75 | 1·60 |

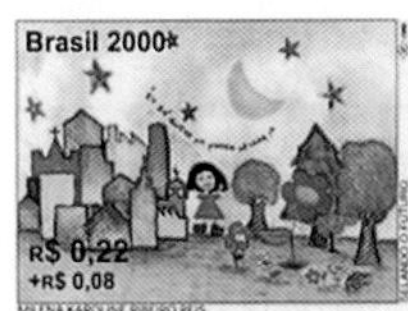

**1532** Buildings and Trees (Milena Karoline Ribeiro Reis)

**2000.** "Stampin the Future". Winning Entries in Children's International Painting Competition. Mult.

| | | | |
|---|---|---|---|
| 3054 | 22c.+8c. Type **1532** | 65 | 50 |
| 3055 | 22c.+8c. Globe, sun, trees, children and whale (Caio Ferreira Guimaraes de Oliveira) | 65 | 50 |
| 3056 | 22c.+8c. Woman with globe on dress (Clarissa Cazane) | 65 | 50 |
| 3057 | 22c.+8c. Children hugging globe (Jonas Sampaio de Freitas) | 65 | 50 |

**1533** "2000"

**2000.** New Millennium.

| | | | | |
|---|---|---|---|---|
| 3058 | **1533** | 90c. multicoloured | 2·00 | 1·50 |

**1534** Map of South America and Children holding Books

**2000.** National School Book Programme.

| | | | | |
|---|---|---|---|---|
| 3059 | **1534** | 31c. multicoloured | 85 | 65 |

**1535** Ada Rogato

**2000.** Women Aviators. Multicoloured.

| | | | |
|---|---|---|---|
| 3060 | 22c. Type **1535** | 50 | 40 |
| 3061 | 22c. Thereza de Marzo | 50 | 40 |
| 3062 | 22c. Anesia Pinheiro | 50 | 40 |

**1536** Moqueca Capixaba

**2000.** Cultural Dishes. Multicoloured.

| | | | |
|---|---|---|---|
| 3063 | 1r.05 Type **1536** | 2·75 | 2·10 |
| 3064 | 1r.05 Moqueca baiana | 2·75 | 2·10 |

**1537** Freyre and Institute Facade

**2000.** Birth Centenary of Gilberto Freyre (writer).

| | | | | |
|---|---|---|---|---|
| 3065 | **1537** | 36c. multicoloured | 1·00 | 75 |

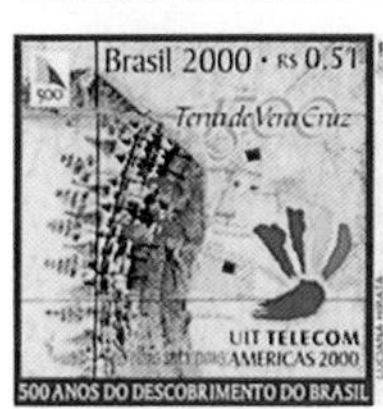

**1538** Painting and Emblem

**2000.** 500th Anniv of the Discovery of Brazil.

| | | | | |
|---|---|---|---|---|
| 3066 | **1538** | 51c. multicoloured | 1·30 | 1·00 |

**1539** Natives

**2000.** 500th Anniv of the Discovery of Brazil. Multicoloured.

| | | | |
|---|---|---|---|
| 3067 | 31c. Type **1539** | 85 | 65 |
| 3068 | 31c. Natives watching ships | 85 | 65 |
| 3069 | 31c. Sailors in rigging | 85 | 65 |
| 3070 | 31c. Ships sails and natives | 85 | 65 |

**1540** Sailing Ship and Brazilian Flag

**2000.** 500th Anniv of the Discovery of Brazil. Multicoloured.

| | | | |
|---|---|---|---|
| 3071 | 45c. Type **1540** | 1·30 | 1·00 |
| 3072 | 45c. Man dressed in red suit, pineapple and telephone dial | 1·30 | 1·00 |
| 3073 | 45c. Red-spectacled amazon and silhouettes of sailing ships | 1·30 | 1·00 |
| 3074 | 45c. Four babies | 1·30 | 1·00 |
| 3075 | 45c. Go-kart, Formula 1 racing car and Ayrton Senna | 1·30 | 1·00 |
| 3076 | 45c. Sloth, Toco toucan, crocodile, penguin and tiger | 1·30 | 1·00 |
| 3077 | 45c. Outline of Brazil and compass roses | 1·30 | 1·00 |
| 3078 | 45c. Peace dove | 1·30 | 1·00 |
| 3079 | 45c. Child with decorated face | 1·30 | 1·00 |
| 3080 | 45c. "500" emblem | 1·30 | 1·00 |
| 3081 | 45c. Man wearing feather headdress | 1·30 | 1·00 |
| 3082 | 45c. Man in boat, sails and town (Nataly M. N. Moriya) | 1·30 | 1·00 |
| 3083 | 45c. Wristwatch, balloon, Alberto Santos-Dumont and his biplane *14 bis* | 1·30 | 1·00 |
| 3084 | 45c. Sailing ship and document (first report of discovery) | 1·30 | 1·00 |
| 3085 | 45c. Jules Rimet Cup and World Cup trophies, player, football and year dates (Brazilian victories in World Cup Football Championship) | 1·30 | 1·00 |
| 3086 | 45c. Hand writing, street lights and fireworks | 1·30 | 1·00 |
| 3087 | 45c. Banners and Brazilian flag forming cow | 1·30 | 1·00 |
| 3088 | 45c. Golden conure perched on branch | 1·30 | 1·00 |
| 3089 | 45c. Bakairi masks | 1·30 | 1·00 |
| 3090 | 45c. Globe, ship and emblem | 1·30 | 1·00 |

**1541** Globe and Map of Brazil

**2000.** 2nd Anniv of BrazilTradeNet (business information web site).

| | | | | |
|---|---|---|---|---|
| 3091 | **1541** | 27c. multicoloured | 65 | 50 |

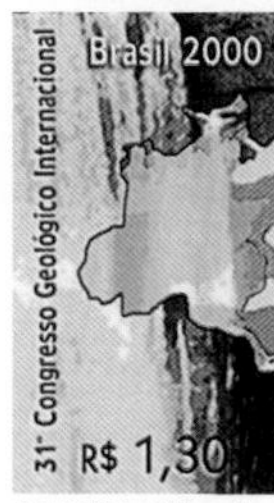

**1542** Turtle, Scarlet Macaw and Map

**2000.** National Coastal Management Programme (GERCO).

| | | | | |
|---|---|---|---|---|
| 3092 | **1542** | 40c. multicoloured | 1·00 | 75 |

**1543** Waterfall and Detail of Map

**2000.** EXPO 2000 World's Fair, Hanover, Germany and 31st International Geologic Congress, Rio de Janeiro. Sheet 109×69 mm containing T 1543 and similar vert design. Multicoloured.

| | | | |
|---|---|---|---|
| **MS**3093 | 1r.30 Type **1543**; 1r.30 Map of Brazil; 1r.30 Gold ingot and minerals | 10·00 | 10·00 |

**1544** Cruz, Students and Building Facade

**2000.** Centenary of the Oswaldo Cruz Foundation (medical research institution).

| | | | | |
|---|---|---|---|---|
| 3094 | **1544** | 40c. multicoloured | 1·00 | 75 |

**1545** Mask, Musical Instruments and Jewellery

**2000.** Africa Day.

| | | | | |
|---|---|---|---|---|
| 3095 | **1545** | 1r.10 multicoloured | 2·75 | 2·10 |

**1546** Klink in Rowing Boat and Portion of Globe showing Route

**2000.** Voyages by Amyr Klink (navigator). Multicoloured.

| | | | |
|---|---|---|---|
| 3096 | 1r. Type **1546** (first South Atlantic crossing by rowing boat (1984)) | 2·75 | 2·00 |
| 3097 | 1r. *Paratii* (polar sailing boat) in Antarctica and portion of globe showing route (first single-handed circumnavigation of Antarctica (1999)) | 2·75 | 2·00 |

Nos. 3096/7 were issued together, se-tenant, forming a composite design.

**1547** Flag, Buildings, Map and City Arms

**2000.** 150th Anniv of Juiz de Fora.

| | | | | |
|---|---|---|---|---|
| 3098 | **1547** | 60c. multicoloured | 1·70 | 1·30 |

**1548** Hang Gliding

**2000.** Outdoor Pursuits. Multicoloured. Self-adhesive.

3099 27c. Type **1548** 65 50
3100 27c. Surfing 65 50
3101 40c. Rock climbing 1·00 75
3102 40c. Skateboarding 1·00 75

**1549** Forest

**2000.** Environmental Protection. Multicoloured.

3103 40c. Type **1549** 1·20 90
3104 40c. Oncilla standing on branch in forest 1·20 90
3105 40c. Vegetation, adult oncilla and head of kitten 1·20 90
3106 40c. Vegetation, adult oncilla and body of kitten 1·20 90

Nos. 3103/6 were issued together, se-tenant, forming a composite design.

**1550** *Cisne Branco* (full-rigged cadet ship)

**2000.** Brazilian Navy. Cadet Ships. Multicoloured.

3107 27c. Type **1550** 85 65
3108 27c. *Brasil* (cadet frigate) 85 65

**1551** "Oswaldo Cruz" (hospital ship) and Birds

**2000.** Environment Protection. Sheet 137×84 mm.

**MS**3109 **1551** 1r.50 multicoloured 4·25 4·25

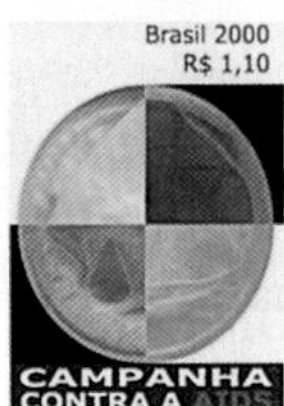

**1552** Emblem

**2000.** America. Health Campaigns. Sheet 84×137 mm containing T 1552 and similar vert design. Multicoloured.

**MS**3110 1r.10 Type **1552** (anti-AIDS); 1r.10 Glasses, pills, needles and Marijuana leaves (national anti-drugs week) 6·00 6·00

**1553** Teixeira, Carneiro Ribeiro Education Center, Salvador and Pupils

**2000.** Birth Centenary of Anisio Teixeira (education reformer).

3111 **1553** 45c. multicoloured 1·30 1·00

**1554** Child walking to School

**2000.** 10th Anniv of the Children and Teenagers Statute (3112) and 15th Anniv of National Movement of Street Boys and Girls (3113). Multicoloured.

3112 27c. Type **1554** 85 65
3113 40c. Rainbow with girl and boy holding star 1·20 90

**1555** Capanema

**2000.** Birth Centenary of Gustavo Capanema Filho (politician).

3114 **1555** 60c. multicoloured 1·70 1·30

**1556** Television and Hand writing in Notebook

**2000.** 5th Anniv of Telecourse 2000 (educational television programme).

3115 **1556** 27c. multicoloured 85 65

**1557** Campos

**2000.** Birth Centenary of Milton Campos (politician and lawyer).

3116 **1557** 1r. multicoloured 2·75 2·10

**1558** Hand protecting Globe

**2000.** World Day for Protection of the Ozone Layer.

3117 **1558** 1r.45 multicoloured 3·75 3·00

**1559** Archery

**2000.** Olympic Games, Sydney. Multicoloured.

3118 40c. Type **1559** 1·00 75
3119 40c. Beach volleyball 1·00 75
3120 40c. Boxing 1·00 75
3121 40c. Football 1·00 75
3122 40c. Canoeing 1·00 75
3123 40c. Handball 1·00 75
3124 40c. Diving 1·00 75
3125 40c. Rhythmic gymnastics 1·00 75
3126 40c. Badminton 1·00 75
3127 40c. Swimming 1·00 75
3128 40c. Hurdling 1·00 75
3129 40c. Pentathlon 1·00 75
3130 40c. Basketball 1·00 75
3131 40c. Tennis 1·00 75
3132 40c. Marathon 1·00 75
3133 40c. High-jump 1·00 75
3134 40c. Long-distance running 1·00 75
3135 40c. Triple jump 1·00 75
3136 40c. Triathlon 1·00 75
3137 40c. Sailing 1·00 75
3138 40c. Pommel horse (gymnastics) 1·00 75
3139 40c. Weightlifting 1·00 75
3140 40c. Discus 1·00 75
3141 40c. Rings (gymnastics) 1·00 75
3142 40c. Athletics 1·00 75
3143 40c. Javelin 1·00 75
3144 40c. Artistic gymnastics 1·00 75
3145 40c. Hockey 1·00 75
3146 40c. Volleyball 1·00 75
3147 40c. Synchronized swimming 1·00 75
3148 40c. Judo 1·00 75
3149 40c. Wrestling 1·00 75
3150 40c. Cycling 1·00 75
3151 40c. Rowing 1·00 75
3152 40c. Parallel bars (gymnastics) 1·00 75
3153 40c. Horse riding 1·00 75
3154 40c. Pole vault 1·00 75
3155 40c. Fencing 1·00 75
3156 40c. Rifle shooting 1·00 75
3157 40c. Taekwondo 1·00 75

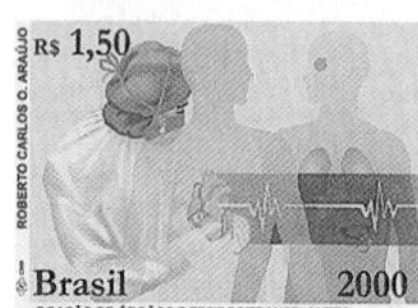

**1560** Surgeon and Electrocardiogram Graph

**2000.** Organ Donation. Multicoloured.

3158 1r.50 Type **1560** 4·00 3·00
3159 1r.50 Hands holding heart 4·00 3·00

Nos. 3158/9 were issued together, se-tenant, each pair forming a composite design.

**1561** Brazilian Clovis Mask

**2000.** Brazil–China Joint Issue. 25th Anniv of Diplomatic Relations between Brazil and China. Multicoloured.

3160 27c. Type **1561** 65 50
3161 27c. Chinese Monkey King puppet 65 50

**1562** Chico Landi and Ferrari 125 Formula 1 Racing Car

**2000.** Motor Racing Personalities. Multicoloured.

3162 1r.30 Type **1562** 3·25 2·40
3163 1r.45 Ayrton Senna and Formula 1 racing car 3·50 2·75

**1563** Embraer EMB 145 AEW

**2000.** Brazilian Aircraft. Multicoloured. Self-adhesive.

3164 27c. Type **1563** 65 50
3165 27c. Super Tucano 65 50
3166 27c. Embraer AMX-T 65 50
3167 27c. Embraer ERJ 135 65 50
3168 27c. Embraer ERJ 170 65 50
3169 27c. Embraer ERJ 145 65 50
3170 27c. Embraer ERJ 190 65 50
3171 27c. Embraer EMB 145 RS/MP 65 50
3172 27c. Embraer ERJ 140 65 50
3173 27c. Embraer EMB 120 65 50

**1564** Hand reaching for Star

**2000.** Christmas. Multicoloured.

3174 27c. Type **1564** 65 50
3175 27c. Mary and Jesus 65 50
3176 27c. Family and fishes 65 50
3177 27c. Jesus pointing to his heart 65 50
3178 27c. Trees, Globe and open hand 65 50
3179 27c. Jesus and Globe 65 50

Nos. 3174/5, 3176/7 and 3178/9 respectively were issued together, se-tenant, forming a composite design.

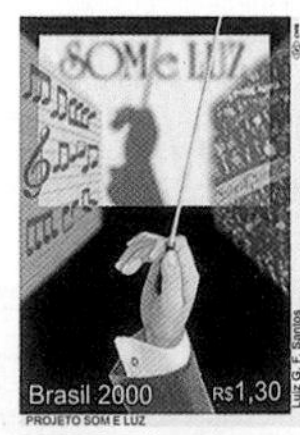

**1565** Conductor's Baton and Music Score

**2000.** Light and Sound Shows.

3180 **1565** 1r.30 multicoloured 3·25 2·50

**1566** Maps and Baron Rio Branco

**2000.** Centenary of Arbitration Ruling setting Boundary between Brazil and French Guiana.

3181 **1566** 40c. multicoloured 1·00 75

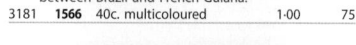

**1567** Three Wise Men, Chalice and Dove

**2001.** New Millennium. Multicoloured.

3182 40c. Type **1567** 1·00 75
3183 1r.30 Star of David, Menorah, scroll and stone tablets 3·25 2·50
3184 1r.30 Minaret, dome and Holy Kaaba 3·25 2·50

**MS**3185 68×113 mm. As Nos. 3182/4 7·50 7·50

No. **MS**3185 also has a barcode at the bottom of the sheet, separated from the miniature sheet by a line of rouletting.

**1568** Map of Americas, Flags, Emblems and Waterfall

**2001.** 11th Pan American Scout Jamboree, Foz do Iguacu. Multicoloured.

3186 1r.10 Type **1568** 2·75 2·10
3187 1r.10 Waterfall, canoeists and emblems 2·75 2·10

Nos. 3186/7 were issued together, se-tenant, forming a composite design.

**1569** Snake and Chinese Zodiac (image scaled to 64% of original size)

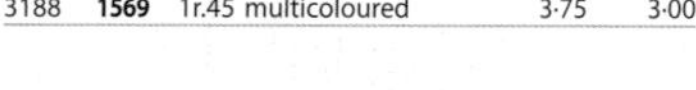

**2001.** "HONG KONG 2001" Stamp Exhibition. New Year. Year of the Snake.

3188 **1569** 1r.45 multicoloured 3·75 3·00

**1570** *Dirphya* sp. and Institute

**2001.** Centenary of Butantan Institute (vaccine research centre), Sao Paulo. Venomous Animals. Sheet 115×155 mm containing T 1570 and similar horiz designs showing Institute building. Multicoloured.

| | | | |
|---|---|---|---|
| 3189 | 40c. Type **1570** | 1·00 | 85 |
| 3190 | 40c. Puss caterpillar (*Megalopyge* sp.) | 1·00 | 85 |
| 3191 | 40c. *Phoneutria* sp. | 1·00 | 85 |
| 3192 | 40c. Brown scorpion (*Tityus bahiensis*) | 1·00 | 85 |
| 3193 | 40c. Brazilian rattle snake (*Crotalus durissus*) | 1·00 | 85 |
| 3194 | 40c. Coral snake (*Micrurus corallinus*) | 1·00 | 85 |
| 3195 | 40c. Bushmaster (*Lachesis muta*) | 1·00 | 85 |
| 3196 | 40c. Jararaca (*Bothrops jacaraca*) | 1·00 | 85 |

**1571** Old and Modern Printing Methods

**2001.** Publishing.
3197 **1571** 27c. multicoloured 65 55

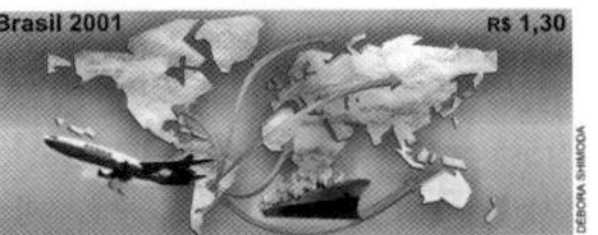


**1572** McDonnell Douglas DC-10, World Map and Ship

**2001.** Exports.
3198 **1572** 1r.30 multicoloured 3·00 2·50

**1573** Books and Library Facade

**2001.** 190th Anniv of National Library, Rio de Janeiro.
3199 **1573** 27c. multicoloured 65 55

**1574** Man, Microscope and Emblem

**2001.** Brazilian Council for Scientific and Technological Development (CNPq).
3200 **1574** 40c. blue 85 70

**1575** Footballer and Emblem

**2001.** 89th Anniv of Santos Football Club.
3201 **1575** 1r. multicoloured 2·20 1·80

**1576** Children

**2001.** International Decade for a Culture of Peace.
3202 **1576** 1r.10 multicoloured 2·50 2·10

**1577** Mendes and Halfeld Street

**2001.** Birth Centenary of Muriles Mendes (poet).
3203 **1577** 40c. multicoloured 85 70

**1578** Building Facade and View of Town

**2001.** Centenary of Minas Gerais Trade Association.
3204 **1578** 40c. multicoloured 85 70

**1579** Sunflower and No-Smoking Signs

**2001.** World No-Smoking Day.
3205 **1579** 40c. multicoloured 85 70

**1580** Do Rego and Illustrations from his Novels

**2001.** Birth Centenary of Jose Lins do Rego (writer).
3206 **1580** 60c. multicoloured 1·20 1·00

**1581** Hyacinth Macaw (*Anodorhynchus hyacinthinus*)

**2001.** Birds. Sheet 106×149 mm containing T 1581 and similar vert designs. Multicoloured.
**MS**3207 1r.30 Type **1581**; 1r.30 Sun conure (*Aratinga solititialis auricapilla*); 1r.30 Blue-throated conure (*Pyrrhura cruentata*); 1r.30 Yellow-faced amazon (*Amazona xanthops*) 10·00 10·00

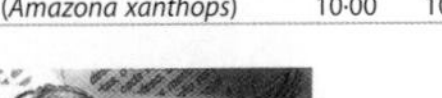

**1582** Sobrinho

**2001.** 1st Death Anniv of Alexandre Jose Barbosa Lima Sobrinho (journalist).
3208 **1582** 40c. multicoloured 85 70

**1583** Jericoacoara Beach, Ceara

**2001.** Beaches. Multicoloured.

| | | | |
|---|---|---|---|
| 3209 | 40c. Type **1583** | 85 | 70 |
| 3210 | 40c. Ponta Negra beach, Rio Grande do Norte | 85 | 70 |
| 3211 | 40c. Rosa beach, Santa Catarina | 85 | 70 |

**1584** Romi-Isetta, 1959 (½-size illustration)

**2001.** Cars. Sheet 159×115 mm containing T 1584 and similar horiz designs. Multicoloured.
**MS**3212 1r.10 Type **1584**; 1r.10 DKW-Vemag, 1965; 1r.10 Renault Gordini, 1962; 1r.10 Fusca-Volkswagen 1200, 1959; 1r.10 Simca Chambord, 1964; 1r.10 Aero Willys, 1961 13·00 13·00

**1585** Sayao

**2001.** Birth Centenary of Bernado Sayao (politician and construction pioneer).
3213 **1585** 60c. multicoloured 1·20 1·00

**1586** Eleazar de Carvalho, Musical Notation and Musicians

**2001.** Eleazar de Carvalho (composer and conductor) Commemoration.
3214 **1586** 45c. multicoloured 1·00 85

**1587** Racquet and Ball

**2001.** Roland Garros Tennis Championship. Sheet 70×112 mm.
**MS**3215 **1587** 1r.30 multicoloured 2·75 2·75

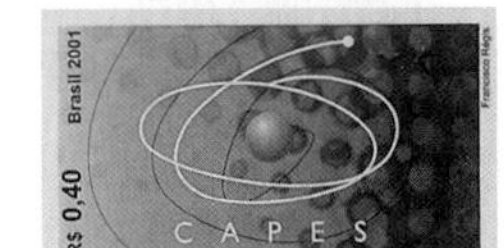


**1588** Emblem

**2001.** 50th Anniv of CAPES (training fund).
3216 **1588** 40c. multicoloured 85 70

**1589** Buildings, Symbols of Justice and Pedro Alexio

**2001.** Birth Centenary of Pedro Alexio (Judge and politician).
3217 **1589** 55c. multicoloured 1·20 1·00

**1590** Player and Ball

**2001.** Vasco da Gama Football Club.
3218 **1590** 70c. multicoloured 1·50 1·30

**1591** Figure enclosing Map of Brazil (½-size illustration)

**2001.** 5th Anniv of Solidarity Council. Multicoloured.

| | | | |
|---|---|---|---|
| 3219 | 55c. Type **1591** | 1·20 | 1·00 |
| 3220 | 55c. Map enclosing figure | 1·20 | 1·00 |

Nos. 3219/20 were issued together, se-tenant, forming a composite design.

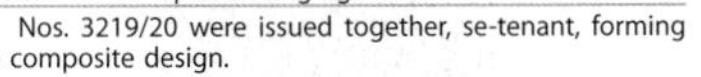

**1592** Player and Ball

**2001.** Palmeiras Football Club.
3221 **1592** 70c. multicoloured 1·50 1·30

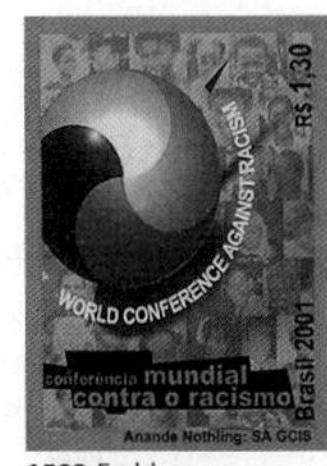


**1593** Emblem

**2001.** World Conference on Racism, Durban, South Africa.
3222 **1593** 1r.30 multicoloured 2·75 2·30

**1594** Player and Ball

**2001.** Gremio Football Porto Algrense (football club).
3223 **1594** 70c. multicoloured 1·50 1·30

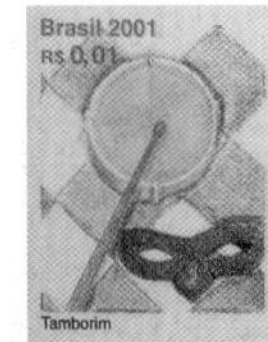


**1595** Tambourine

**2001.** Musical Instruments. Multicoloured. Self-adhesive.

| | | | |
|---|---|---|---|
| 3224 | 1c. Type **1595** | 15 | 15 |
| 3224a | 1c. Conga drum | 15 | 15 |
| 3225 | 5c. Saxophone | 15 | 15 |
| 3225a | 5c. Snare drum | 15 | 15 |
| 3226 | 10c. Cavaquinho (guitar) | 15 | 15 |
| 3226a | 10c. Trumpet | 15 | 15 |
| 3227 | 20c. Clarinet | 35 | 30 |
| 3228 | 40c. Flute | 85 | 70 |
| 3229 | 45c. Mandolin | 90 | 80 |
| 3230 | 50c. Fiddle | 1·00 | 85 |
| 3230a | 50c. Tambourine | 1·00 | 85 |
| 3231 | 55c. Viola (guitar) | 1·20 | 1·00 |
| 3232 | 60c. Zabumba | 1·30 | 1·10 |
| 3233 | 70c. Viola Caipira (guitar) | 1·50 | 1·30 |
| 3234 | 70c. Rattle | 1·50 | 1·30 |
| 3235 | 80c. Xylophone | 1·70 | 1·40 |
| 3236 | 1r. Trombone | 2·20 | 1·80 |
| 3236a | 1r. Berimbau | 2·20 | 1·80 |

**1596** Clóvis Beviláqua

**2001.** Clóvis Beviláqua (lawyer) Commemoration.
3250 **1596** 55c. multicoloured 1·20 1·00

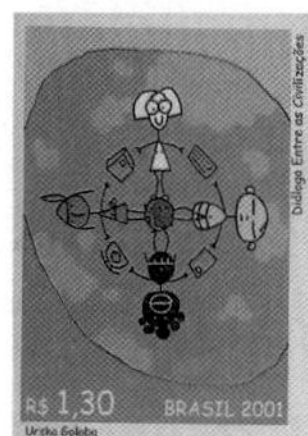


**1597** Children encircling Globe

**2001.** United Nations Year of Dialogue among Civilizations.
3251 **1597** 1r.30 multicoloured 2·75 2·30

**1598** Map of Brazil and Jewish and Dutch Flags

**2001.** 365th Anniv of First Jewish Synagogue in Recife.
3252 **1598** 1r.30 multicoloured 2·75 2·30

**1599** Junkers F13 Passenger Aircraft

**2001.** Commercial Aircraft. Sheet 107×149 mm containing T 1599 and similar horiz designs. Multicoloured.
**MS**3253 55c. Type **1599**; 55c. Douglas DC-3/C47; 55c. Dornier Do-J Wal flying boat; 55c. Lockheed Constellation; 55c. Convair CV 340; 55c. Caravelle V1-R jet airliner 6·50 6·50

**1600** Cecíla Meireles

**2001.** Birth Centenary of Cecíla Meireles (writer).
3254 **1600** 55c. multicoloured 1·20 1·00

**1601** Aleijadinho (sculptor) and Bom Jesus de Matosinhos Sanctuary

**2001.** America. UNESCO World Heritage Sites.
3255 **1601** 1r.30 multicoloured 2·75 2·30

**1602** Madalena Caramuru and Page

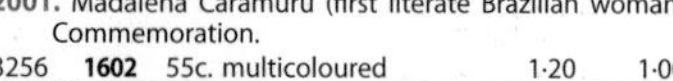

**2001.** Madalena Caramuru (first literate Brazilian woman) Commemoration.
3256 **1602** 55c. multicoloured 1·20 1·00

**1603** Face, Gavel, Book and Dove

**2001.** National Black Awareness Day.
3257 **1603** 40c. multicoloured 85 70

**1604** Caiman (*Caiman crocodilus*) and Roseate Spoonbill (*Platalea ajaja*) (inscr "*Plataleia*")

**2001.** Flora and Fauna. Multicoloured. Self-adhesive.

| | | | |
|---|---|---|---|
| 3258 | 55c. Type **1604** | 1·20 | 1·00 |
| 3259 | 55c. American darter (*Anhinga anhinga*) | 1·20 | 1·00 |
| 3260 | 55c. Cocoi heron (*Ardea cocoi*) | 1·20 | 1·00 |
| 3261 | 55c. Jabiru (*Ephippiorhynchus mycteria*) (inscr "Jabiru") | 1·20 | 1·00 |
| 3262 | 55c. *Pseudoplatystoma fasciatum* (fish) | 1·20 | 1·00 |
| 3263 | 55c. *Leporinus macrocephalus* (fish) | 1·20 | 1·00 |
| 3264 | 55c. Capybara (*Hydrochoerus hydrochaeris*) (inscr "hydrochoeris") | 1·20 | 1·00 |
| 3265 | 55c. Southern coati (*Nasua nasua*) | 1·20 | 1·00 |
| 3266 | 55c. Water hyacinth (*Eichornia crassipes*) | 1·20 | 1·00 |
| 3267 | 55c. Purple gallinule (*Porphyrula martinica*) | 1·20 | 1·00 |

**1605** Three Kings and Holy Family

**2001.** Christmas.
3268 **1605** 40c. multicoloured 85 70

**1606** Emblem, Player and Football

**2001.** Libertadores da America Football Championship Winners (1st issue). Flamengo Football Club (1981).
3269 **1606** 1r. multicoloured 2·00 1·70

See also No. 3275.

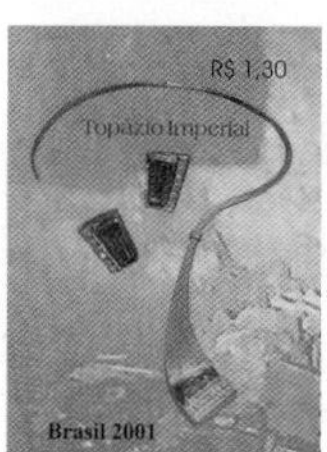


**1607** Imperial Topaz Necklace and Earrings

**2001.** Jewellery. Sheet 101×70 mm containing T 1607 and similar vert design. Multicoloured.
**MS**3270 1r.30 Type **1607**; 1r.30 Garnet ring 5·50 5·50

No. **MS**3270 was issued with a strip containing a bar-code separated by a line of rouletting.

**1608** Stylized Eye, Mouth, Hand and Ear (image scaled to 65% of original size)

**2001.** International Day of the Disabled.
3271 **1608** 1r.45 multicoloured 3·00 2·50

**1609** Cup of Coffee and Beans

**2001.** Coffee.
3272 **1609** 1r.30 multicoloured 2·75 2·40

**1610** *Copocabana*

**2001.** Merchant Ships. Multicoloured.
3273 55c. Type **1610** 1·20 1·00
3274 55c. *Flamengo* 1·20 1·00

Nos. 3273/4 were issued together, se-tenant, forming a composite design.

**1611** Emblem, Player and Football

**2001.** Libertadores da America Football Championship Winners (2nd issue). Sao Paulo Football Club (1992 and 1993).
3275 **1611** 70c. multicoloured 1·50 1·30

**1612** Water Hyacinth (*Eichornia crassipes*)

**2001.** Mercosur. Flora.
3276 **1612** 1r. multicoloured 2·00 1·70

**1613** Chinese Zodiac and Horse (image scaled to 65% of original size)

**2002.** New Year. Year of the Horse.
3277 **1613** 1r.45 multicoloured 3·00 2·50

**1614** Alpine skier

**2002.** Winter Olympic Games, Salt Lake City, USA. Multicoloured.

| | | | |
|---|---|---|---|
| 3278 | 1r.10 Type **1614** | 2·30 | 2·00 |
| 3279 | 1r.10 Cross country skier | 2·30 | 2·00 |
| 3280 | 1r.10 Luge | 2·30 | 2·00 |
| 3281 | 1r.10 Bobsled | 2·30 | 2·00 |

Nos. 3278/81 were issued together, se-tenant, forming a composite design.

**1615** Brasilia and Lucio Costa

**2002.** Birth Centenary of Lucio Costa (architect).
3282 **1615** 55c. multicoloured 1·20 1·00

**1616** Women encircling Globe

**2002.** International Women's Day.
3283 **1616** 40c. multicoloured 85 70

**1617** View of City from River

**2002.** 150th Anniv of Sao Jose do Rio Preto.
3284 **1617** 40c. multicoloured 85 70

**1618** Brasilia and Juscelino Kubitschek

**2002.** Birth Centenary of Juscelino Kubitschek (president, 1956–61).
3285 **1618** 55c. multicoloured 1·20 1·00

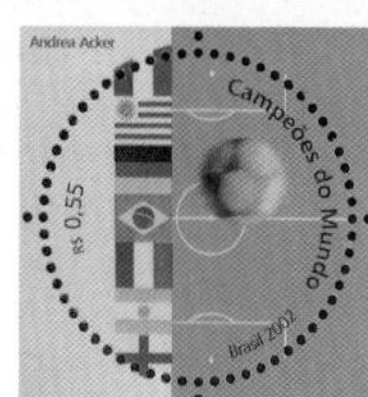


**1619** Winners' Flags and Football

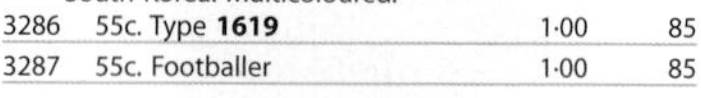

**2002.** World Cup Football Championship, Japan and South Korea. Multicoloured.
3286 55c. Type **1619** 1·00 85
3287 55c. Footballer 1·00 85

**1620** School Children and Alphabet

**2002.** Education. Multicoloured.
3288 40c. Type **1620** 85 70
3289 40c. Computer, globe and alphabet 85 70

**1621** Josemaria Escriva

**2002.** Birth Centenary of Josemaria Escriva de Balaguer (founder of Opus Dei (religious organization)).
3290 **1621** 55c. multicoloured 1·20 1·00

**1622** North American T6

**2002.** Smoke Air Squadron (air force display team). Sheet 105×150 mm containing T 1622 and similar horiz designs. Multicoloured.
**MS**3291 55c. ×6, Type **1622**; T-24 Fouga Magister; Neiva T-25 Universal (inscr "T-25 Universal"); Two Embraer EMB-312 Tucano (inscr "T-27 Tucano") and plateau; T-27 Tucano and heart-shape; T-27 Tucano over forest 6·50 6·50

**1623** Boy wearing Crown, Girls carrying Banners and Boy with Sword

**2002.** Cavalhadinha (children's festival). Multicoloured.

| | | | |
|---|---|---|---|
| 3292 | 40c. Type **1623** | 85 | 70 |
| 3293 | 40c. Boys riding hobby horses | 85 | 70 |
| 3294 | 40c. Children wearing masks | 85 | 70 |
| 3295 | 40c. Musicians and drinks vendor | 85 | 70 |

**1624** Cannonball Tree (*Couroupita guianensis*)

**2002.** Self-adhesive.
3296 **1624** 55c. multicoloured 1·00 85

**1625** Coral and Fish

**2002.** Coral Reefs. Sheet 105×150 mm containing T 1625 and similar square designs. Multicoloured.
**MS**3297 40c. ×4, Type **1625**; Seahorse; Corals and fish; Fish and starfish 2·75 2·75

**1626** Building Facade

**2002.** 150th Anniv of Sisterhood of Charity Hospital, Curitiba.
3298 **1626** 70c. multicoloured 1·00 85

**1627** Jules Rimet and World Cup Trophies

**2002.** Brasil, Football World Cup Championship Winners (1958, 1962, 1970, 1994, 2002).
3299 **1627** 55c. multicoloured 1·20 1·00

**1628** White-browed Guan (*Penelope jacucaca*)

**2002.** Conservation of North Eastern Caatinga Region. Sheet 70×111 mm.
**MS**3300 **1628** 1r.10 multicoloured 1·50 1·60

**1629** Footballer and Emblem

**2002.** Centenary of Santos Football Club.
3301 **1629** 55c. multicoloured 65 55

**1630** House Facade

**2002.** "The Enchanted House" Museum (house of Alberto Santos Dumont (aviation pioneer)), Rio De Janeiro. Sheet containing T 1630 and similar square design. Multicoloured.
**MS**3302 1r. ×2, Type **1630**; Alberto Santos Dumont 2·75 2·75

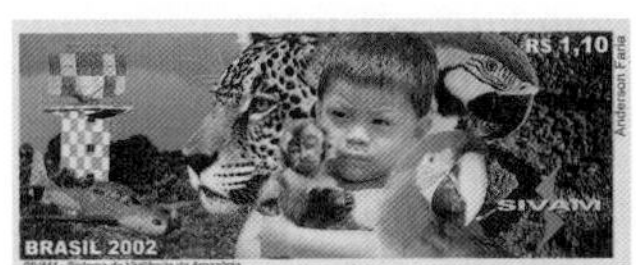


**1631** Radar, Airplane, Boy, Animals and Birds

**2002.** SIVAM (environmental monitoring of Amazon project).
3303 **1631** 1r.10 multicoloured 1·50 1·30

**1632** Families enclosed in Wheel

**2002.** Crianca Esperanca (Hope of the Child) Awareness Campaign. Multicoloured.

| | | | |
|---|---|---|---|
| 3304 | (1st Porto) Type **1632** (child development) | 85 | 70 |
| 3305 | (1st Porto) Children playing (eradication of child labour) | 85 | 70 |

**1633** Jorge Amado

**2002.** 1st Death Anniv of Jorge Amado (writer).
3306 **1633** 40c. multicoloured 50 45

**1634** Rio Branco Palace, Xapuri Village and Placido de Castro (revolutionary leader)

**2002.** Centenary of Acre River Revolution.
3307 **1634** 50c. multicoloured 65 55

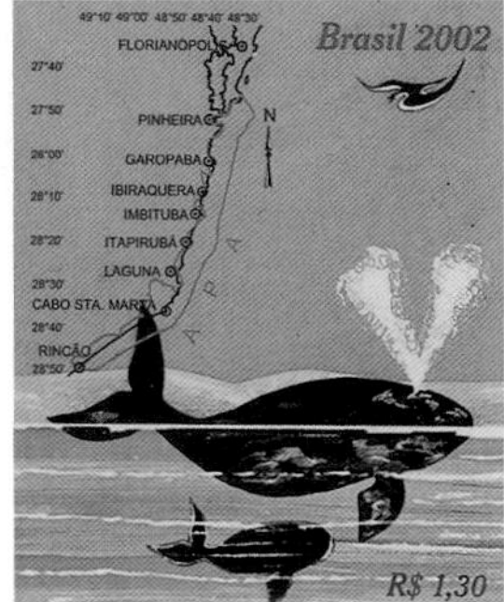


**1635** Whale and Calf

**2002.** Southern Right Whale Habitat Protection Project. Sheet 71×112 mm.
**MS**3308 1r.30. multicoloured 1·70 1·70

**1636** Rivers

**2002.** Watershed of Negro and Solimoes Rivers, Manaus.
3309 **1636** 45c. multicoloured 50 45

**1637** Adhelmar Ferreira da Silva

**2002.** 1st Death Anniv of Adhelmar Ferreira da Silva (Olympic triple jump champion).
3310 **1637** 40c. multicoloured 50 45

**1638** Yamaha 125cc. (1974) and YZF-R1

**2002.** Motorcycles. Sheet 105×149 mm containing T 1638 and similar horiz designs. Multicoloured.
**MS**3311 60c.×6 Type **1638**; Honda CB100 (1976) and CG125 Titan; Suzuki 1952 model and GSX-R1000; First Triumph model (1902) and Datona 955i; BMW R32 and R 1200C; First Harley Davidson model (1903) and V-Rod 4·25 4·25

**1639** Steam Locomotive "Baroneza" (1852)

**2002.** Trains. Multicoloured.

| | | | |
|---|---|---|---|
| 3312 | 55c. Type **1639** | 65 | 55 |
| 3313 | 55c. Locomotive "Zeze Leoni" (1922) | 65 | 55 |

**1640** Birds, Fish and Waterfall

**2002.** Mercosur (South American Common Market).
3314 **1640** 1r. multicoloured 1·40 1·20

**1641** Itabira, Carlos Drummond de Andrade and Rio de Janeiro

**2002.** Birth Centenary of Carlos Drummond de Andrade (writer).
3315 **1641** 55c. multicoloured 80 70

**1642** Fingerprint, Book, Globe and Figure Child

**2002.** America. Education and Literacy Campaign.
3316 **1642** 1r.30 multicoloured 1·80 1·60

**1643** Map and Building

**2002.** National Archives.
3317 **1643** 40c. multicoloured 60 50

**1644** Sergio Motta (founder) and Centre Building

**2002.** Sergio Motta Cultural Centre.
3318 **1644** 45c. multicoloured 60 50

**1645** "Nativity" (Candido Portinari)

**2002.** Christmas.
3319 **1645** 45c. multicoloured 60 50

**1646** "80"

**2002.** 80th Anniv of Social Security.
3320 **1646** 45c. multicoloured 60 50

**1647** "Dancing Tapuia"

**2002.** Art. Paintings by Albert Eckhout. Paintings. Multicoloured.

| | | | |
|---|---|---|---|
| 3321 | 45c. Type **1647** | 80 | 70 |
| 3322 | 45c. "Mameluca" | 80 | 70 |
| 3323 | 45c. "Tapuia Man" | 80 | 70 |
| 3324 | 45c. "Tupi Man" | 80 | 70 |
| 3325 | 45c. "Negro" | 80 | 70 |
| 3326 | 45c. "Tupi Woman" | 80 | 70 |
| 3327 | 45c. "West African Woman and Child" | 80 | 70 |
| 3328 | 45c. "Mestizo Man" | 80 | 70 |

**1648** Marajoara Pots, Brazil

**2002.** Centenary of Brazil–Iran Diplomatic Relations. Multicoloured.

3329 60c. Type **1648** 1·00 85
3330 60c. Iranian decorated pots 1·00 85

Stamps of a similar design were issued by Iran.

**1649** Anniversary Emblem

**2003.** 80th Anniv of Rotary Club (charitable organization).

3331 **1649** 60c. multicoloured 1·00 85

**1650** Salto do Itiquira, Formosa

**2003.** International Day of Freshwater. Waterfalls. Multicoloured.

3332 45c. Type **1650** 80 70
3333 45c. Salto do Rio Preto, Alto Paraiso 80 70

**1651** Winnowing and Building

**2003.** Coffee Production. Sheet 70×110 mm containing T 1651 and similar square design. Multicoloured.

**MS**3334 1r.×2, Type **1651**; Buildings, planting and picking 3·25 3·25

**1652** Flag, Hands, Dove and Map

**2003.** Timor Leste Independence.

3335 **1652** 1r.45 multicoloured 2·40 2·10

**1653** *Macrosiphonia velame*

**2003.** America. Flora and Fauna. Sheet 107×150 mm containing T 1653 and similar square designs. Multicoloured.

**MS**3336 60c.×6, Type **1653**; *Lychnophora ericoides; Lafoensia pacari; Tabebuia impetignosa;Xylopia aromatica; Himatanthus obovatus* 5·00 5·00

**1654** Decorated Bottles

**2003.** Mercosur. Recycling. Multicoloured.

3337 60c. Type **1654** 1·00 85
3338 60c. Paper dolls 1·00 85
3339 60c. Plastic flower pot 1·00 85
3340 60c. Decorated metal box 1·00 85

**1655** Saint Inacio, College Building and Students

**2003.** Centenary of St. Inacio College, Rio de Janeiro.

3341 **1655** 60c. multicoloured 1·00 85

**1656** Pluft and Maribel

**2003.** Pluft (cartoon character created by Maria Clara Machado).

3342 **1656** 80c. multicoloured 1·20 1·00

**1657** Sail Boat on Beach

**2003.** Centenary of Ceara State.

3343 **1657** 70c. multicoloured 1·20 1·00

**1658** Album, Tweezers and Stamps

**2003.** Philately. Sheet 110×71 mm containing T 1658 and similar square design. Multicoloured.

**MS**3344 1r.30×2, Type **1658**; Portuguese 25r. stamp 4·25 4·25

**1659** Dolphins

**2003.** 500th Anniv of Fernando de Noronha Island. Sheet 69×100 mm.

**MS**3345 2r.90 multicoloured 4·50 4·50

**1660** Emblem, Buildings and Antonio Maria Zaccaria (founder)

**2003.** Centenary of Barnabite Priests in Brazil.

3346 **1660** 45c. multicoloured 80 70

**1661** Duke of Caxias and Battle Scene

**2003.** Birth Bicentenary of Luis Alves de Lima y Silva, Duke of Caxias.

3347 **1661** 60c. multicoloured 1·00 85

**1662** Self-Portrait

**2003.** Birth Centenary of Candido Potinari (artist).

3348 **1662** 80l. multicoloured 1·40 1·20

**1663** Stop Sign enclosing Bottle

**2003.** Traffic Code Awareness. Multicoloured. Self-adhesive.

3349 (50c.) Type **1663** 80 70
3350 (74c.) Triangular traffic sign enclosing dove 1·20 1·00

**1664** Club Emblem

**2003.** Centenary of Gremio Football Porto Alegrense.

3351 **1664** 60c. multicoloured 90 80

**1665** Locomotive

**2003.** Preservation of Railways.

3352 **1665** 74c. multicoloured 1·20 1·00

**1666** Kite Flying

**2003.** Children's Games. Multicoloured.

3353 50c. Type **1666** 80 70
3354 50c. Ball games 80 70
3355 50c. Skipping 80 70
3356 50c. Hula hoop 80 70

**1667** Campaign Emblem

**2003.** Zero Hunger Campaign.

3357 **1667** 50c. multicoloured 80 70

**1668** Grapes, Bridge and Mask

**2003.** Export Campaign. Sheet 110×69 mm.

**MS**3358 1r.30 multicoloured 2·00 2·00

**1669** Decorated Tree

**2003.** Christmas. T 1669 and similar triangular design. Self-adhesive.

3359 **1669** 50c. multicoloured 80 70
3360 **1669** 50c. multicoloured 80 70

**Sao** Paulo Art Critcs Trophy and Auditing Court (building)

**2003.** Marcantonio Vilaca Cultural Space.

3361 **1670** 74c. multicoloured 1·20 1·00

**1671** Ary Barroso and Maracana Stadium

**2003.** Birth Centenary of Ary Barroso (conductor and sports commentator).

3362 **1671** 1r.50 multicoloured 2·40 2·10

**1672** Palacio des Arcos, Cadeia Velha and New Congress Building, Rio de Janeiro

**2003.** 180th Anniv of National Congress.

3363 **1672** 74c. multicoloured 1·20 1·00

**1673** Para-glider over Sao Conrado, Rio de Janeiro

**2003.** Adventurous Sports.

3364 **1673** 75c. multicoloured 1·20 1·00

**1674** Cedar Lebanon

**2003.** 60th Anniv of Diplomatic Relations with Lebanon.

3365 **1674** 1r.75 multicoloured 2·75 2·40

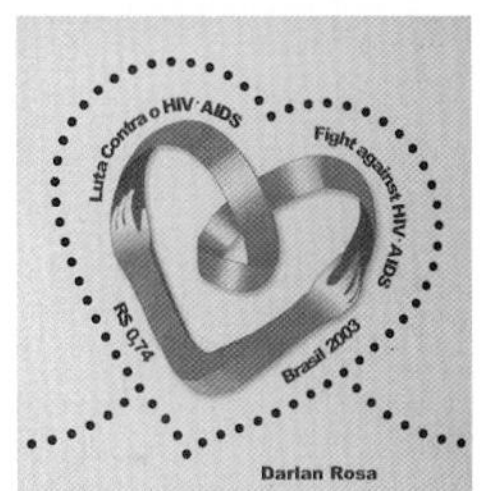

**1675** Heart-shaped Ribbon and Hands

**2003.** AIDS Awareness Campaign.
3366 **1675** 74c. multicoloured 1·20 1·00

**2003.** Birth Centenary of Candido Potinari. Lost Paintings (1st issue). As T 1662. Black. Self-adhesive.
3367 74c. "Menino de Brodoski" 1·20 1·00
3368 75c. "Cangaceiro" 1·20 1·00
See also Nos. 3382/6.

**1676** Capistrano de Abreu

**2003.** 150th Birth Anniv of Capistrano de Abreu (historian and ethnographer).
3369 **1676** 50c. multicoloured 80 70

**1677** Fernando Henrique Cardoso

**2003.** Fernando Henrique Cardoso (38th president).
3370 **1677** 74c. multicoloured 1·20 1·00

**1678** Archangel St. Michael Chapel, Sao Paulo

**2004.** Cultural Heritage. Sheet 100×70 mm. Litho.
**MS**3371 1r.50 multicoloured 2·20 2·20

**1679** Faces

**2004.** 450th Anniv of Sao Paulo. Multicoloured.
3372 74c. Type **1679** 1·20 1·00
3373 74c. Buildings surrounding roadway 1·20 1·00
3374 74c. Park and city buildings 1·20 1·00
3375 74c. "450" 1·20 1·00

**1680** Dom Vicente Scherer

**2004.** Birth Centenary of Cardinal Vicente Scherer.
3376 **1680** 50c. multicoloured 80 70

**1681** Musicians and Dancers

**2004.** Lapa District, Rio de Janeiro.
3377 **1681** 75c. multicoloured 1·20 1·00

**1682** Scarlet Ibis (*Eudocimus ruber*)

**2004**
3378 **1682** 74c. multicoloured 1·20 1·00

**1683** Figure holding Water Droplet

**2004.** Mercosur. Water Conservation Campaign.
3379 **1683** 1r.20 multicoloured 1·80 1·60

**1684** Orlando Villas Boas

**2004.** 90th Birth Anniv of Orlando Villas Boas (joint founder Xingu National Park and Nobel Peace Prize winner).
3380 **1684** 74c. multicoloured 1·20 1·00

**1685** Anniversary Emblem

**2004.** Centenary of FIFA (Federation Internationale de Football Association).
3381 **1685** 1r.60 multicoloured 2·50 2·30

**2004.** Birth Centenary of Candido Potinari. Lost Paintings (2nd issue). As T 1662. Self-adhesive.
3382 55c. multicoloured 90 80
3383 80c. multicoloured 1·20 1·00
3384 95c. multicoloured 1·50 1·30
3385 1r.15 black 1·70 1·50
3386 1r.50 multicoloured 2·40 2·10
DESIGNS: 55c. "Negrinha"; 80c. "Duas Criancas"; 95c. "Menino Sentado e Carneiro"; 1r.15 "Comosicao"; 1r.50 "Marcel Gontrau".

**1686** Emblem

**2004.** 92nd International Labour Conference (ILO).
3387 **1686** 50c. multicoloured 80 70

**1687** Roseate Spoonbill (*Ajaia ajaja*)

**2004.** Mangrove Swamps and Tidal Zones Preservation. Sheet 149×105 mm containing T 1687 and similar horiz designs. Multicoloured.
**MS**3388 1r.60×5, Type **1687**; Great kiskadee (*Pitangus sulphuratus*); *Chasmagnathus granulate*; *Aramides mangle*; *Goniopsis cruentata* 10·50 10·50

**1688** Runner holding Olympic Torch

**2004.** Olympic Games, Athens. Multicoloured 2004.
3389 1r.60 Type **1688** 2·50 2·30
3390 1r.60 Athens 2004 emblem 2·50 2·30
3391 1r.60 Dinghies and catamarans 2·50 2·30
3392 1r.60 Runner 2·50 2·30

**1689** Senhor Bom Jesus do Bonfim Church, Salvador

**2004.** Cultural Heritage.
3393 **1689** 74c. multicoloured 1·20 1·00

**1690** Caprichoso Bull

**2004.** Parintins Festival. Multicoloured.
3394 74c. Type **1690** 1·20 1·00
3395 74c. Garantido bull 1·20 1·00
Nos. 3394/5 were issued together, se-tenant, forming a composite design.

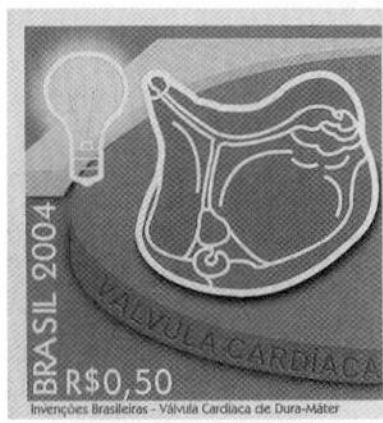

**1691** Dura-Mater Artificial Heart Valve

**2004.** Brazilian Inventions. Multicoloured.
3396 50c. Type **1691** 80 70
3397 50c. Telephone caller identification (BINA) 80 70
3398 50c. Telephone cards 80 70

**1692** Map of South America, Satellite and Brazilian and Chinese Flags as Clasped Hands

**2004.** CBER-2 (Brazilian—Chinese satellite).
3399 **1692** 1r.75 multicoloured 2·75 2·40

**1693** Columns, Square and Compass

**2004.** Masonic Philatelic Association.
3400 50c. Type **1693** 80 70
3401 50c. Stone mason 80 70
3402 50c. Jacob's ladder 80 70
3403 50c. Masonic tools 80 70

**1694** Nelson Rodrigues

**2004.** Nelson Rodrigues (writer) Commemoration.
3404 **1694** 50c. multicoloured 80 70

**1695** FAB Emblem, Republic P-47 Thunderbolt and Campaign Medals

**2004.** World War II. Multicoloured.
3405 50c. Type **1695** (Italian air campaign) 80 70
3406 50c. Navy emblem, destroyer and campaign medals (South Atlantic campaign) 80 70
3407 50c. FEB emblem, soldiers and campaign medals (Italian land campaign) 80 70
3408 50c. Soldier reading letter 80 70

**1696** Crowned Halo enclosing Statue

**2004.** Centenary of Coronation of Our Lady of Immaculate Conception ("Aparecida").
3409 **1696** 74c. multicoloured 1·20 1·00

**1697** Allan Kardec

**2004.** Birth Bicentenary of Allan Kardec (writer).
3410 **1697** 1r.60 multicoloured 2·50 2·30

**1698** Father Christmas

**2004.** Christmas. Self-adhesive.
3411 **1698** 1st class (50c.) multicoloured 80 70
No. 3406 was for use on internal non-commercial mail weighing 20 grams or less.

**1699** Post Office Building (museum)

**2004.** Porto Alegre Museum and Archive.
3412 **1699** 50c. multicoloured 80 70

**1700** *Cyperus articulatus*

**2004.** Aromatic Plants.
3413 **1700** 1r.60 multicoloured 2·50 2·30

**1701** Buildings and Statue

**2004.** Pampulha Architectural Complex.
3414 **1701** 80c. multicoloured 1·30 1·10

**1702** Cat, Art, Textiles and Nise da Silveira

**2005.** Birth Centenary of Nise da Silveira (psychiatrist).
3415 **1702** 55c. multicoloured 90 80

**1703** Rotary Emblem and Faces

**2005.** Centenary of Rotary International (charitable organization).
3416 **1703** 1r.45 multicoloured 2·40 2·10

**1704** Fruit on Tree

**2005.** Cupacu (Theobrome grandiflorum). Sheet 70×111 mm containing T 1704 and similar square design. Multicoloured.
**MS**3417 1r.90×2, Type **1704**; Open fruit 6·00 6·00

**1705** Brazilian and Lebanese Trees and Flags

**2005.** Lebanese Immigration to Brazil.
3418 **1705** 1r.75 multicoloured 2·75 2·40

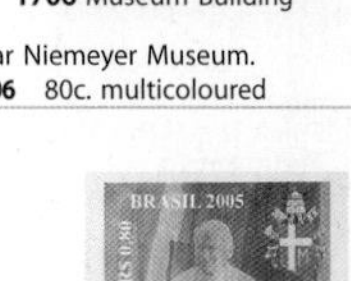

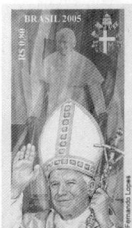

**1706** Museum Building

**2005.** Oscar Niemeyer Museum.
3419 **1706** 80c. multicoloured 1·30 1·10

**1707** Pope John Paul II

**2005.** Pope John Paul II Commemoration.
3420 **1707** 80c. multicoloured 1·30 1·10

**1708** Circle and Arrows

**2005.** World Information Society Summit, Tunis. Sheet 86×128 mm containing T 1708 and similar horiz designs. Multicoloured.
**MS**3421 80c.×3, Type **1708**; Figure enclosed in circle; Envelope contained in circle 3·50 3·50

The stamps and margins of No. **MS**3421 form a composite design.

**1709** Dancers (contemporary dance)

**2005.** Brazil Year in France. Multicoloured.
3422 80c. Type **1709** 1·30 1·10
3423 80c. Pankaranu Indians (indigenous art) 1·30 1·10
3424 80c. Pato no Tucupi (gastronomy) 1·30 1·10
3425 80c. Choro musicians (music) 1·30 1·10
3426 80c. String of pages (literature) 1·30 1·10
3427 80c. Vivaldo Lima Stadium (architecture) 1·30 1·10

**1710** Erico Verissimo

**2005.** Birth Centenary of Erico Verissimo (writer).
3428 **1710** 1r.25 multicoloured 1·90 1·60

**1711** Mario Quintana

**2005.** Birth Centenary (2006) of Mario Quintana (writer).
3429 **1711** 80c. green 1·30 1·10

**1712** Woman, Water Barrel, Cistern, Boy and Workmen

**2005.** America. Water Cisterns.
3430 **1712** 80c. multicoloured 1·30 1·10

**1713** Emblem

**2005.** 19th Congress of America, Spain and Portugal Postal Union. Self-adhesive.
3431 **1713** (80c.) multicoloured 1·30 1·10

**1714** Gold panning, Route and Caravan

**2005.** Tourism. Estrada Real (road from Diamantina to Parati and Rio De Janeiro). Multicoloured.
3432 80c. Type **1714** 1·30 1·10
3433 80c. Hikers 1·30 1·10
3434 80c. Horse riders 1·30 1·10

Nos. 3432/4 were issued together, se-tenant, forming a composite design.

**1715** Dancer

**2005.** Samba (dance).
3435 **1715** 55c. multicoloured 90 80

**1716** Brazilian Flag and Samba Dancers

**2005.** National Dances. Multicoloured.
3436 80c. Type **1716** 1·30 1·10
3437 80c. Cuban flag and Son dancers 1·30 1·10

Stamps of a similar design were issued by Cuba.

**1717** Sao Francisco River

**2005**
3438 **1717** 80c. multicoloured 1·30 1·10

**1718** School Building

**2005.** Centenary of Command and General Staff School.
3439 **1718** 80c. multicoloured 1·30 1·10

**1719** "ABC"

**2005.** Teachers' Day. Self-adhesive.
3440 **1719** (1st porte) multicoloured 90 80

**1720** Bell

**2005.** Christmas (1st issue). Self-adhesive.
3441 **1720** (1st porte) multicoloured 90 80

See also No. **MS**3444.

**1721** Referee and Players

**2005.** Women's Football.
3442 **1721** 85c. multicoloured 1·40 1·20

**1722** Fish Leaping (*Salminus maxillosus*)

**2005.** Piracema (fish reproduction). Sheet 101×71 mm.
**MS**3443 **1722** 3r.10 multicoloured 5·00 5·00

**1723** "Adoration of Shepherds" (Oscar Pereira da Silva)

**2005.** Christmas (2nd issue). Sheet 71×111 mm.
**MS**3444 **1723** 2r.90 multicoloured 4·50 4·50

**1724** Light "Luna" (Fernando Prado)

**2005.** Brazilian Design. Multicoloured.
3445 85c. Type **1724** 1·40 1·20

| | | | |
|---|---|---|---|
| 3446 | 85c. Ventilator "Spirit" (Indio da Costa design) | 1·40 | 1·20 |
| 3447 | 85c. Chair "Corallo" (Hemberto and Fernando Corallo) | 1·40 | 1·20 |
| 3448 | 85c. Table "Bandeirola" (Ivan Rezende) | 1·40 | 1·20 |

**1725** Hans Christian Andersen and "The Ugly Duckling"

**2005.** Birth Bicentenary of Hans Christian Andersen (writer).

| | | | | |
|---|---|---|---|---|
| 3449 | **1725** | 55c. multicoloured | 90 | 80 |

**1726** Dressmaker

**2005.** Professions. Multicoloured. Self-adhesive.

| | | | |
|---|---|---|---|
| 3450 | 5c. Type **1726** | 20 | 15 |
| 3451 | 20c. Cobbler | 40 | 35 |
| 3452 | 85c. Shoe shine | 1·40 | 1·20 |

**1727** Sambista

**2005.** Urban Art. Multicoloured.

| | | | |
|---|---|---|---|
| 3453 | 55c. Type **1727** | 90 | 80 |
| 3454 | 55c. Boy in pipe | 90 | 80 |
| 3455 | 55c. Graffiti artist (horiz) | 90 | 80 |

**1728** Santos-Dumont Biplane *14 bis*

**2005.** Centenarian Mission (Brazilian astronaut, Marcos Pontes's flight on Soyuz rocket to International Space Station). Multicoloured.

| | | | |
|---|---|---|---|
| 3456 | 85c. Type **1728** | 1·40 | 1·20 |
| 3457 | 85c. "Soyuz" | 1·40 | 1·20 |
| 3458 | 85c. International Space Station | 1·40 | 1·20 |

Nos. 3456/8 were issued together, se-tenant, forming a composite design.

**1729** Emblem

**2006.** World Cup Football Championship, Germany.

| | | | | |
|---|---|---|---|---|
| 3459 | **1729** | 85c. multicoloured | 1·40 | 1·20 |

**1730** Bidu Sayao

**2006.** Balduina de Oliveira Sayao (Bidu Sayao) (opera singer) Commemoration.

| | | | | |
|---|---|---|---|---|
| 3460 | **1730** | 55c. multicoloured | 90 | 80 |

**1731** World Map and Faces

**2006.** International Day of Cultural Diversity.

| | | | | |
|---|---|---|---|---|
| 3461 | **1731** | 1r.90 multicoloured | 3·25 | 2·75 |

**1732** Emblem

**2006.** RIO 2007—15th Pan American Games. Self-adhesive.

| | | | | |
|---|---|---|---|---|
| 3462 | **1732** | (1st Porte) multicoloured | 1·40 | 1·20 |

**1733** Stylized Athlete

**2006.** Brazilian Paralympics Committee.

| | | | | |
|---|---|---|---|---|
| 3463 | **1733** | 1r.35 multicoloured | 2·00 | 1·70 |

**1734** Viola de Cocho

**2006.** Mercosur. Musical Instruments.

| | | | | |
|---|---|---|---|---|
| 3464 | **1734** | 55c. multicoloured | 90 | 80 |

**1735** Rhea, Emas National Park

**2006.** National Parks. Multicoloured. Self-adhesive.

| | | | |
|---|---|---|---|
| 3465 | 85c. Type **1735** | 1·40 | 1·20 |
| 3466 | 85c. Uakari monkey, Sustainable Development Reserve, Mamiraua | 1·40 | 1·20 |
| 3467 | 85c. Maned wolf, Chapada dos Veadeiros National Park | 1·40 | 1·20 |
| 3468 | 85c. Squirrel, Itatiaia National Park | 1·40 | 1·20 |

**2006.** Urban Art (2nd issue). Sheet 111×70 mm containing vert designs as T 1727. Multicoloured.

| | | | |
|---|---|---|---|
| **MS**3468a | 1r.60×2, As No. 3454; As No. 3455 | 5·00 | 5·00 |

**1735a** Leaves and Fruit (image scaled to 67% of original size)

**2006.** Cajueiro (cashew nut tree). Sheet 111×70 mm.

| | | | |
|---|---|---|---|
| **MS**3468b | **1735a** 2r.90 multicoloured | 4·50 | 4·50 |

No. **MS**3468b was cut round in the shape of a tree.

**1736** Fernando de Noronha Archipelago

**2006.** Tourism.

| | | | | |
|---|---|---|---|---|
| 3469 | **1736** | 2r.50 multicoloured | 3·50 | 3·00 |

**1737** Santos-Dumont *14-bis*

**2006.** Centenary of Flight of Santos-Dumont 14-bis.

| | | | | |
|---|---|---|---|---|
| 3470 | **1737** | (90c.) multicoloured | 1·40 | 1·20 |

**1738** Star, House and Mail Box

**2006.** Christmas (1st issue). Self-adhesive.

| | | | | |
|---|---|---|---|---|
| 3471 | **1738** | (1st Porte) multicoloured | 1·00 | 85 |

**2006.** Professions. As T 1726. Multicoloured. Self-adhesive.

| | | | |
|---|---|---|---|
| 3471a | 1c. Popcorn seller | 20 | 15 |
| 3471b | 1r. Manicurist | 1·75 | 1·75 |

**1739** The Magi

**2006.** Christmas (2nd issue). Sheet 111×70 mm containing T 1739 and similar multicoloured designs.

| | | | |
|---|---|---|---|
| **MS**3472 | 1r.60×3, Type **1739** Angel (36×40 mm) (arched): Holy family | 7·00 | 7·00 |

**1740** Hydro-electric Dam and Street Lighting

**2006.** America. Energy Conservation.

| | | | | |
|---|---|---|---|---|
| 3473 | **1740** | 1r.75 multicoloured | 2·75 | 2·40 |

**1741** *Isurus oxyrinchus* and *Sphyrna lewini*

**2006.** Sharks. Sheet 70×111 mm containing T 1741 and similar square design. Multicoloured.

| | | | |
|---|---|---|---|
| **MS**3474 | 1r.90×2, Type **1741** *Mustelus schmitti* | 6·00 | 6·00 |

**1742** Diving

**2007.** Pan American Games, Rio de Janeiro. Multicoloured. Self-adhesive.

| | | | |
|---|---|---|---|
| 3477 | (1º Porte Carta Comercial) Type **1742** | 1·20 | 1·00 |
| 3478 | (1º Porte Carta Comercial) Swimming | 1·20 | 1·00 |
| 3479 | (1º Porte Carta Comercial) Synchronised Swimming | 1·20 | 1·00 |
| 3480 | (1º Porte Carta Comercial) Futsal | 1·20 | 1·00 |
| 3481 | (1º Porte Carta Comercial) Water polo | 1·20 | 1·00 |

**1743** Carimbo

**2007.** Dances. Multicoloured.

| | | | |
|---|---|---|---|
| 3482 | (1º Porte Carta Comercial) Type **1743** | 90 | 80 |
| 3483 | (1º Porte Carta Comercial) Frevo | 90 | 80 |

**1744** Research Vessel

**2007.** International Polar Year. Multicoloured.

| | | | |
|---|---|---|---|
| 3484 | (1º Porte Carta Comercial) Type **1744** | 1·40 | 1·20 |
| 3485 | (1º Porte Carta Comercial) Ferraz research station | 1·40 | 1·20 |
| 3486 | (1º Porte Carta Comercial) Penguin and map of Antarctica | 1·40 | 1·20 |

Nos. 3484/6 were issued together, setenant, forming a composite design.

**1745** First Church of Our Lady of Assumption

**2007.** Jose de Anchieta (Jesuit missionary) Commemoration. Multicoloured.

| | | | |
|---|---|---|---|
| 3487 | 90c. Type **1745** | 1·40 | 1·20 |
| 3488 | 90c. Founding of Espirito Santo | 1·40 | 1·20 |
| 3489 | 90c. Metropolitan Cathedral of Vitoria | 1·40 | 1·20 |

Nos. 3487/9 were issued together, setenant, forming a composite design.

**1746** Estadio Olimpico Edgard Proenca (Mangueirao), Belem

**2007.** Stadia. Multicoloured.

| | | | |
|---|---|---|---|
| 3490 | 60c. Type **1746** | 1·00 | 85 |
| 3491 | 60c. Estadio Municipal Paulo Machado de Carvalho, Pacaembu | 1·00 | 85 |
| 3492 | 90c. Estadio Serra Dourada, Goiania | 1·50 | 1·30 |
| 3493 | 2r.60 Estadio Jornalista Mario Filho (Maracana), Rio de Janeiro | 4·00 | 3·50 |

**1747** JK Bridge

**2007.** Mercosul. National Architecture.

| | | | |
|---|---|---|---|
| 3494 | **1747** (1º porte Carta Comercial) mult | 1·50 | 1·30 |

**1748** Robert Baden-Powell

**2007.** Centenary of Scouting.

| | | | |
|---|---|---|---|
| 3495 | **1748** 2r. multicoloured | 3·25 | 3·00 |

**1749** Pope Benedict XVI

**2007.** Pope Benedict XVI Visit to Brazil.

| | | | |
|---|---|---|---|
| 3496 | **1749** 90c. multicoloured | 1·50 | 1·30 |

**1750** *Cochlespira elongate*

**2007.** Shells. Sheet 126×84 mm containing T 1750 and similar vert designs. Multicoloured.

| | | |
|---|---|---|
| **MS**3497 2r.×3, Type **1750** *Charonia variegata*; *Chicoreus* | 9·75 | 9·75 |

The stamps and margins of **MS**3497 form a composite design of a seashore.

**1751** *My New Accordion* (Napachie Pootoogook)

**2007.** 140th Anniv of Brazil–Canada Diplomatic Relations.

| | | | |
|---|---|---|---|
| 3498 | **1751** 90c. multicoloured | 1·50 | 1·30 |

**1752** *Rio Pardo* and Giuseppe Garibaldi

**2007.** Birth Bicentenary of Giuseppe Garibaldi (soldier and nationalist). Multicoloured.

| | | | |
|---|---|---|---|
| 3499 | 1r.40 Type **1752** | 2·20 | 1·90 |
| 3500 | 1r.40 On horseback | 2·20 | 1·90 |

Stamps of a similar design were issued by Uruguay.

**1753** Metro Locomotive

**2007.** Transport. Multicoloured.

| | | | |
|---|---|---|---|
| 3501 | 1r.40 Type **1753** | 2·20 | 1·90 |
| 3502 | 1r.45 Steam locomotive No. 1 *Baroneza* | 2·30 | 2·00 |
| 3503 | 1r.90 Tram, Bonde Santa Teresa | 3·25 | 2·75 |

**1754** Teofilo Ottoni

**2007.** Birth Bicentenary of Teofilo Benedict Ottoni (politician and journalist).

| | | | |
|---|---|---|---|
| 3504 | **1754** 60c. multicoloured | 1·00 | 85 |

**1755** Children, Computers and 'abc'

**2007.** America. Education for All.

| | | | |
|---|---|---|---|
| 3505 | **1755** 60c. multicoloured | 1·00 | 85 |

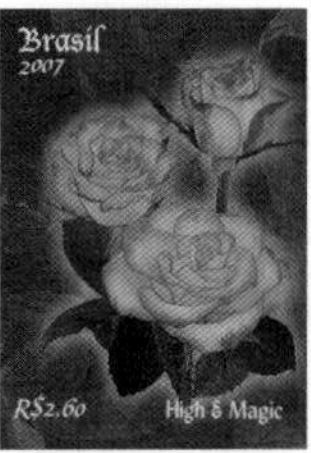
**1756** Inscr 'High & Magic'

**2007.** Roses. Sheet 85×128 mm containing T 1756 and similar vert designs.

| | | |
|---|---|---|
| **MS**3506 2r.60×3, Type **1756**; Inscr 'Caballero'; Inscr 'Avalanche' | 12·00 | 12·00 |

The stamps and margins of **MS**3506 form a composite design.

**1757** Giraffes

**2007.** Zoological Fauna. Multicoloured.

| | | | |
|---|---|---|---|
| 3507 | 60c. Type **1757** | 1·00 | 85 |
| 3508 | 60c. Tiger | 1·00 | 85 |
| 3509 | 60c. Elephant | 1·00 | 85 |
| 3510 | 60c. Lion | 1·00 | 85 |
| 3511 | 60c. Chimpanzees | 1·00 | 85 |
| 3512 | 60c. Macaw | 1·00 | 85 |

**1758** Candles

**2007.** Christmas. Multicoloured. Self-adhesive.

| | | | |
|---|---|---|---|
| 3513 | 1st (porte nao-Comercial) Type **1758** | 1·50 | 1·30 |
| 3514 | 1st (porte Comercial) The Nativity | 1·50 | 1·30 |

**1759** King Joao VI

**2008.** Bicentenary of Portuguese Royal Family's Arrival in Brazil (1st issue). Multicoloured.

| | | | |
|---|---|---|---|
| 3515 | 2r. Type **1759** | 3·25 | 2·75 |
| 3516 | 2r. Royal Family and Entourage | 3·25 | 2·75 |

Nos. 3515/16 were issued together, se-tenant, forming a composite design.

Stamps of the same design were issued by Portugal.

**1760** Ships (opening of ports to friendly nations)

**2008.** Bicentenary of Portuguese Royal Family's Arrival in Brazil (2nd issue). Bicentenary of External Relations. Multicoloured.

| | | | |
|---|---|---|---|
| 3517 | 1st Porte Carta Comercial Type 1760 | 3·00 | 2·50 |
| 3518 | 1st Porte Carta Comercial Globe (foreign trade) | 3·00 | 2·50 |

No. 3519 is left for stamp not yet received.

**1761** Dancer and Musicians (Tambor de Crioula)

**2008.** America. National Festivals. Self-adhesive.

| | | | |
|---|---|---|---|
| 3520 | **1761** 1st Porte Carta Nao Comercial multicoloured | 3·00 | 2·50 |

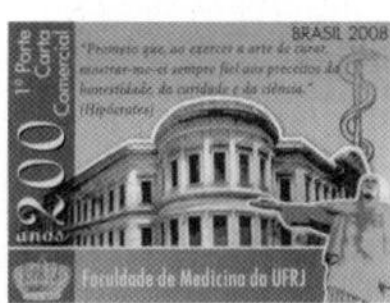
**1762** UFRJ Faculty of Medicine

**2008.** Bicentenary of Portuguese Royal Family's Arrival in Brazil (3rd issue). Bicentenary of Faculties of Medicine. Multicoloured.

| | | | |
|---|---|---|---|
| 3521 | 1st Porte Carta Nao Comercial Type **1762** | 3·00 | 2·50 |
| 3522 | 1st Porte Carta Nao Comercial Bahia Faculty of Medicine | 3·00 | 2·50 |

**1763** Stylized figures and Map as Jigsaw

**2008.** National Conference on Youth. Self-adhesive.

| | | | |
|---|---|---|---|
| 3523 | **1763** 1st Porte Carta Nao Comercial multicoloured | 3·00 | 2·50 |

**1764** Transport Ship, Helicopter and Soldiers

**2008.** Bicentenary of Portuguese Royal Family's Arrival in Brazil (4th issue). Bicentenary of Naval Fusiliers Corps.

| | | | |
|---|---|---|---|
| 3524 | **1764** 1st Porte Carta Comercial multicoloured | 3·00 | 2·50 |

**1765** Museum of Contemporary Art, Niteroi

**2008.** Designs by Oscar Niemeyer (architect). Sheet 112×72 mm containing T 1765 and similar vert design. Black, ultramarine and vermilion.

| | | |
|---|---|---|
| **MS**3525 2r.60×2, Type **1765**; Latin America Memorial | 7·75 | 7·75 |

**1766** Building and *A Justica* (Alfredo Ceschiatti)

**2008.** Bicentenary of Portuguese Royal Family's Arrival in Brazil (5th issue). Bicentenary of Independent Judiciary.

| | | | |
|---|---|---|---|
| 3526 | **1766** 1st Porte Carta Comercial multicoloured | 3·00 | 2·50 |

**1767** Flag and 'Justice'

**2008.** Bicentenary of Portuguese Royal Family's Arrival in Brazil (6th issue). Bicentenary of Supreme Military Court.

| | | | |
|---|---|---|---|
| 3527 | **1767** 1st Porte Carta Comercial multicoloured | 3·00 | 2·50 |

**1768** Headquarters and Gustavo de Lacerda (founder)

**2008.** Centenary of Press Association.

| | | | |
|---|---|---|---|
| 3528 | **1768** 1st Porte Carta Comercial multicoloured | 3·00 | 2·50 |

**1769** Dom Pedro I (first ruler of independent Brazil)

**2008.** National Heroes. Multicoloured.

| | | | |
|---|---|---|---|
| 3529 | 1st Porte Carta Comercial Type **1769** | 3·00 | 2·50 |
| 3530 | 1st Porte Carta Comercial Marechal Deodoro da Foncesca (first president of Republic of Brazil) | 3·00 | 2·50 |

3531 1st Porte Carta Comercial Luís Alves de Lima e Silva, Duke of Caxias (military leader, statesman and Prime Minister) 3·00 2·50

3532 1st Porte Carta Comercial Admiral Francisco Manuel Barroso da Silva (commander of victorious Brazilian Navy at Battle of Riachuelo) 3·00 2·50

3533 1st Porte Carta Comercial Joaquim Marques Lisbon, Admiral Tamandare 3·00 2·50

3534 1st Porte Carta Comercial Jose Bonifacio de Andrada e Silva (statesman and naturalist) 3·00 2·50

3535 1st Porte Carta Comercial Alberto Santos-Dumont (aviation pioneer) 3·00 2·50

3536 1st Porte Carta Comercial Zumbi dos Palmares (last leaders of Quilombo dos Palmares (runaway and free-born Black African slaves community)) 3·00 2·50

3537 1st Porte Carta Comercial Joaquim Jose da Silva Xavier (Triadentes) (nationalist) 3·00 2·50

3538 1st Porte Carta Comercial Placido de Castro 3·00 2·50

**1770** Policeman

**2008.** Bicentenary of Portuguese Royal Family's Arrival in Brazil (7th issue). Bicentenary of Civil Police (horiz) or bicentenary of Dragoons (vert). Multicoloured.

3539 1st Porte Carta Comercial Type **1770** 3·00 2·50

3540 1st Porte Carta Comercial Cavalry (vert) 3·00 2·50

**1771** Printing Press, Print and Building

**2008.** Bicentenary of Portuguese Royal Family's Arrival in Brazil (8th issue). Bicentenary of National Press.

3541 **1771** 1st Porte Carta Comercial multicoloured 3·00 2·50

**1772** *Tangara cayana* (burnished-buff tanager )

**2008.** Serra do Japi—São Paulo Natural Heritage. Sheet 111×70 mm containing T 1772 and similar horiz design. Multicoloured.

**MS**3542 2r.×2, Type **1772**; *Consul fabius drurii* 5·50 5·50

The stamps and margins of **MS**3542 form a composite design.

**1773** *Lippia alba* and *Copaifera lucens*

**2008.** Bicentenary of Portuguese Royal Family's Arrival in Brazil (9th issue). Bicentenary of Botanic Garden.

3543 **1773** 1st Porte Carta Comercial multicoloured 3·00 2·50

**1774** Ship

**2008.** Centenary of Japanese Immigration. Sheet 128×86 mm containing T 1774 and similar vert design. Multicoloured.

**MS**3544 3r.50×2, Type **1774**; Flags and origami 14·00 14·00

The stamps and margins of **MS**3544 form a composite design.

**1775** Mer de Glace

**2008.** Landscapes. Multicoloured.

3545 2r. Type **1775** 3·25 2·75

3546 2r. Serra do Araca 3·25 2·75

Nos. 3545/6 were issued together, se-tenant,forming a composite design.

Stamps of a similar design were issued by France.

**1776** Joao Guimaraes Rosa and Scene from *Grande Sertão: Veredas*

**2008.** Birth Centenary of Joao Guimaraes Rosa (writer).

3547 **1776** 60c. multicoloured 1·00 85

No. 3547 is embossed with Braille characters.

**1777** Headquarters

**2008.** Bicentenary of Portuguese Royal Family's Arrival in Brazil (10th issue). Bicentenary of Ministry of Finance.

3548 **1777** 1st Porte Carta Comercial multicoloured 3·00 2·50

**1778** Gymnastics

**2008.** Olympic Games, Beijing. Multicoloured.

3549 65c. Type **1778** 1·10 90

3550 65c. Equestrian 1·10 90

3551 65c. Swimming 1·10 90

3552 65c. Games emblem 1·10 90

**1779** Cozido Completo and Quindim

**2008.** Bicentenary of Portuguese Royal Family's Arrival in Brazil (11th issue). Brazilian Portuguese Cuisine.

3553 **1779** 90c. multicoloured 1·50 1·30

**1780** *Lontra longicaudis* (American river otter)

**2008.** Endangered Species. Multicoloured.

3554 1r. Type **1780** 1·50 1·30

3555 1r. *Trichechus inunguis* (Amazonian manatee) 1·50 1·30

3556 1r. *Pteronura brasiliensis* (giant otter) 1·50 1·30

**1781** *Strix virgata* (mottled owl)

**2008.** Mercosul. Birds. Multicoloured.

3557 1r.40 Type **1781** 2·20 1·90

3558 1r.40 *Celeus obrieni* (Kaempfer's woodpecker) 2·20 1·90

**1782** Nativity

**2008.** Christmas. Multicoloured. Self adhesive.

3559 1st Porte Carta Nao Comercial Type **1782** (800th anniv of Franciscans) 3·00 2·50

3560 1st Porte Carta Comercial San Antonio (400th anniv of Santo Antonio convent) 3·00 2·50

Nos. 3559/60 were for use on mail up to 20g., No. 3559 was originally on sale for 65c. and No. 3560 for 1r.

**1783** Map and Symbols of Post

**2008.** Bicentenary of Portuguese Royal Family's Arrival in Brazil (9th issue). Bicentenary of Postal Provision.

3561 **1783** 1r. multicoloured 2·75 2·20

**1784** Louis Braille

**2009.** Birth Bicentenary of Louis Braille (inventor of Braille writing for the blind).

3562 **1784** 2r.20 multicoloured 3·25 2·50

No. 3562 is embossed with Braille writing.

**1785** Globe as Green Fuel Pump

**2009.** Brazil–Leader in Renewable Fuel Production. Self-adhesive.

3563 **1785** 1r. multicoloured 1·50 1·20

**1786** Ox

**2009.** Chinese New Year. Year of the Ox.

3564 **1786** 2r.35 multicoloured 3·50 2·75

**1787** Sao Simao Dam, Paranaiba River

**2009.** Natural Heritage. Rivers. Centenary of Meteorological Office. Two sheets, 112×70 mm, containing T 1787 and similar horiz design. Multicoloured.

**MS**3565 2r.60 Type **1787** 4·00 3·25

**MS**3566 3r.85 *Cichla mirianae* (Amazon peacock bass) 5·75 4·50

**1789** *Hydrurga leptonyx* (leopard seal)

**2009.** Preserve Polar Regions and Glaciers. Multicoloured.

3568 1r. Type **1789** 1·50 1·20

3569 1r. *Ursus maritimus* (polar bear) 1·50 1·20

No. 3567 and Type **1788** are left for Birth Centenary of Dom Helder Camara, issued on 7 February 2009, not yet received.

Nos. 3568/9, were printed, se-tenant, each pair forming a composite design.

**1790** Emblem

**2009.** Centenary of Sports Club International.

3570 **1790** 1r. multicoloured 1·50 1·20

**1791** *Aechmea disticantha*, Atlantic Forest and Sao Pedro de Alcantara Cathedral

**2009.** Brazil–Thailand Diplomatic Relations. Multicoloured.

3571 2r.35 Type **1791** 3·50 2·75

3572 2r.35 *Rhynchostylis gigantea* and Dusit Maha Prasat Palace (Grand Palace) 3·50 2·75

**1792** Books, Tower Blocks and Kahlil Gibran (writer)

**2009.** Brazil–Lebanon Diplomatic Relations. Beirut–World Book Capital, 2009.

| 3573 | **1792** | 2r.35 multicoloured | 3·50 | 2·75 |
|---|---|---|---|---|

**1793** Musicians and Dancers

**2009.** Capoeira and Craft of the Masters of Capoeira. Self-adhesive.

| 3574 | **1793** | 65c. multicoloured | 1·00 | 80 |
|---|---|---|---|---|

**1794** Justice and Building Facade

**2009.** Escola Judicial Desembargador Edesio Fernandes (Judge Edesio Fernandes judicial school).

| 3575 | **1794** | 1r. multicoloured | 1·50 | 1·20 |
|---|---|---|---|---|

**1795** *Soyuz*

**2009.** Brazil–Russia Diplomatic Relations. Co-operation in Space.

| 3576 | **1795** | 2r.35 multicoloured | 3·50 | 2·75 |
|---|---|---|---|---|

**1796** Theatre Facade

**2009.** Centenary of Rio de Janeiro Municipal Theatre.

| 3577 | **1796** | 1st Porte Carta Comercial multicoloured | 3·00 | 2·50 |
|---|---|---|---|---|

**1797** Anniversary Emblem

**2009.** Bicentenary of Royal Charter.

| 3578 | **1797** | 1r. multicoloured | 1·50 | 1·20 |
|---|---|---|---|---|

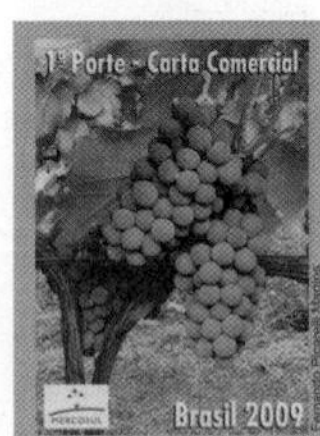

**1798** *Vitis labrusca*

**2009.** Mercosul. Exports. Fruit. Multicoloured.

| | | | |
|---|---|---|---|
| 3579 | 1st PCC Type **1798** | 3·50 | 2·50 |
| 3580 | 1st PCC *Prunus persica* (peach) | 3·00 | 2·50 |
| 3581 | 1st PCC *Prunus salicina* (Japanese plum) | 3·00 | 2·50 |
| 3582 | 1st PCC *Malpighia glabra* (Barbados cherry) | 3·00 | 2·50 |
| 3583 | 1st PCC *Vitus labrusca* (white grapes) | 3·00 | 2·50 |
| 3584 | 1st PCC *Fragaria×ananassa* (strawberry) | 3·00 | 2·50 |
| 3585 | 1st PCC *Pasiflora edulis* (passion fruit) | 3·00 | 2·50 |
| 3586 | 1st PCC *Vitis* (black grapes) | 3·00 | 2·50 |
| 3587 | 1st PCC *Ficus carica* (fig) | 3·00 | 2·50 |
| 3588 | 1st PCC *Diospyros kaki* (persimmon) | 3·00 | 2·50 |

1st PCC=Porte Carte Comercial

**1799** Mauricio de Nassau

**2009.** Dutch Presence in Brazil. Sheet 105×148 mm containing T 1799 and similar vert designs. Multicoloured.

**MS**3589 2r.20×6, Type **1799**; *Zutphen*; Dutch pipes; Palacio de Friburgo, Santo Antônio, Recife; Palacio do Campo das Princesas (state administrative headquarters), Santo Antônio, Recife; Rua Aurora 6·50 6·50

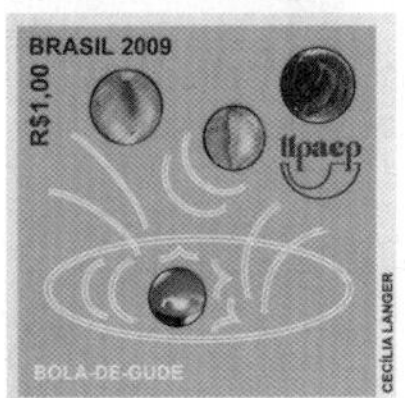

**1800** Marbles

**2009.** America. Games. Multicoloured.

| | | | |
|---|---|---|---|
| 3590 | 1r. Type **1800** | 1·50 | 1·20 |
| 3591 | 1r. Dominoes | 1·50 | 1·20 |
| 3592 | 1r. Chess | 1·50 | 1·20 |
| 3593 | 1r. Table tennis | 1·50 | 1·20 |

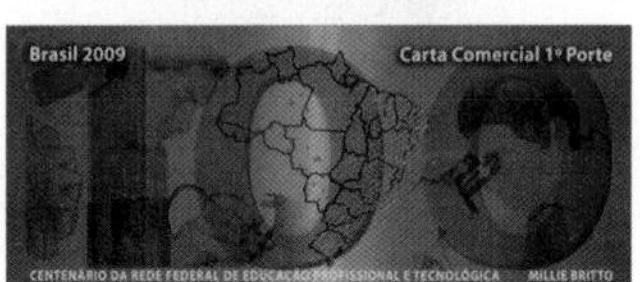

**1801** '100', Symbols of Education and Map showing Centres

**2009.** Centenary of Federal Network of Professional Technical Education.

| 3594 | **1801** | 1st PCC multicoloured | 3·00 | 2·50 |
|---|---|---|---|---|

**1802** Lookouts of Sao Luis

**2009.** Lookouts of Sao Luis

| 3595 | **1802** | 1st PCC multicoloured | 3·00 | 2·50 |
|---|---|---|---|---|

**1803** *Paroaria coronata* (red-crested cardinal)

**2009.** Brightly Coloured Birds. Multicoloured.

**MS**3596 1r.×6, Type **1803**; *Rupicola rupicola* (cock-of-the-rock); *Chlorophonia cyanea* (blue-naped chlorophonia); *Porphyrospiza caerulescens* (yellow-billed blue finch); *Tangara cyanocephala* (red-necked tanager); *Amblyramphus holosericeus* (scarlet-headed blackbird) 5·25 5·25

**1804** Carmen Miranda

**2009.** Brazil–Portugal Diplomatic Relations

| 3597 | **1804** | 2r.20 multicoloured | 2·20 | 1·70 |
|---|---|---|---|---|

Nos. 3599/600 and Type **1806** are left for Postal Services, issued on 9 October 2009, not yet received.

**1805** Carmen Miranda

**2009.** Brazil–France Diplomatic Relations. Year of France in Brazil. Multicoloured.

**MS**3598 2r.20×2, Type **1805**; Amerindian (Claude Levi-Strauss (anthropologist)) 4·25 4·25

The stamps and margins of **MS**3598 form a composite design.

**1807** Club Emblem

**2009.** Centenary of Coritiba Football Club

| 3601 | **1807** | 1r.05 multicoloured | 1·70 | 1·20 |
|---|---|---|---|---|

**1808** Garland

**2009.** Christmas (1st issue)

| 3602 | **1808** | 1st PCC multicoloured | 1·70 | 1·20 |
|---|---|---|---|---|

**1809** Roadside Crib

**2009.** Christmas (2nd issue). Multicoloured.

| | | | |
|---|---|---|---|
| 3603 | 1st PCC Type **1809** | 1·70 | 1·20 |
| 3604 | 1st PCC The Nativity | 1·70 | 1·20 |
| 3605 | 1st PCC Crib festooned with lights, amongst trees | 1·70 | 1·20 |
| 3606 | 1st PCC Ceramic crib showing The Nativity and Magi | 1·70 | 1·20 |
| 3607 | 1st PCC Thatched crib showing Magi, Infant Jesus, Mary and sheep | 1·70 | 1·20 |
| 3608 | 1st PCC Ceramic crib showing Holy Family, shepherd holding child, cow and donkey | 1·70 | 1·20 |

**1810** Angel

**2009.** Christmas (3rd issue). Multicoloured.

**MS**3609 2r.70×2, Type **1810**; Angel facing left 5·75 5·75

The stamps and margins of **MS**3609 form a composite design.

**1811** Incheon Bridge, South Korea

**2009.** Brazil–South Korea Diplomatic Relations. Multicoloured.

| | | | |
|---|---|---|---|
| 3610 | 1r.05 Type **1811** | 1·70 | 1·20 |
| 3611 | 1r.05 Octávio Frias de Oliveira bridge, Brazil | 1·70 | 1·20 |

Nos. 3610/11 were printed, *se-tenant*, each pair forming a composite design.

**1812** Brazil Player

**2009.** Brazil–Hong Kong Diplomatic Relations. Multicoloured.

| | | | |
|---|---|---|---|
| 3612 | 1r.05 Type **1812** | 1·70 | 1·20 |
| 3613 | 1r.05 Brazilian player (different) | 1·70 | 1·20 |
| 3614 | 1r.05 Hong Kong player | 1·70 | 1·20 |
| 3615 | 1r.05 Hong Kong goalkeeper | 1·70 | 1·70 |

Nos. 3612/15 were printed, *se-tenant*, forming a composite design.

Stamps of a similar design were issued by Hong Kong.

**1813** Runners

**2010.** Race of Kings (road race from Cuiabá–Mato Grosso).

| 3616 | **1813** | 70c. multicoloured | 1·10 | 80 |
|---|---|---|---|---|

**1814** Pres. Tancredo Neves

**2010.** Birth Centenary of Tancredo de Almeida Neves (politician and president March–April 1985 (who died before inauguration))

| 3617 | **1814** | 1r.05 multicoloured | 1·70 | 1·20 |
|---|---|---|---|---|

**1815** Zilda Arns

**2010.** Mercosur

| 3618 | **1815** | 1r.45 multicoloured | 2·40 | 2·00 |
|---|---|---|---|---|

**1816** Chico Xavier

**2010.** Birth Centenary of Francisco Cândido Xavier (Chico Xavier) (spritism medium)

| | | | | |
|---|---|---|---|---|
| 3619 | **1816** | 1st PCC multicoloured | 3·00 | 2·50 |

**1817** Memorial JK (memorial to President Juscelino Kubitschek)

**2010.** 50th Anniv of Brasilia as National Capital. Multicoloured.

| | | | |
|---|---|---|---|
| 3620 | 1st PCC Type **1817** | 3·00 | 2·50 |
| 3621 | 1st PCC *Dois Candangos* (two labourers) | 3·00 | 2·50 |
| 3622 | 1st PCC Cathedral of Brasília (horiz) | 3·00 | 2·50 |
| 3623 | 1st PCC Igrejinha de Fátima (little chapel of Fatima) (horiz) | 3·00 | 2·50 |
| 3624 | 1st PCC Sculpture (by Alfredo Ceschiatti), Palacio da Alvorada (Oscar Niemeyer, architect) | 3·00 | 2·50 |
| 3625 | 1st PCC National Congress Building and Ipe Amarelo (national flower) | 3·00 | 2·50 |

**1818** Monastery Façade

**2010.** Religious Architecture and Festivals

| | | | | |
|---|---|---|---|---|
| 3626 | **1818** | 1st PCC multicoloured | 3·00 | 2·50 |

**1819** Amerigo Vespucci and Caravel

**2010.** Brazil–Italy Diplomatic Relations. Multicoloured.

**MS**3627 2r.40×2, Type **1819**; In old age 4·25 4·25

The stamps and margins of **MS**3627 form a composite design.

**1820** 'RIO 2011' and Games Emblem

**2010.** Rio 2011, Fifth International Military Games, Rio de Janeiro

| | | | | |
|---|---|---|---|---|
| 3628 | **1820** | 2r. multicoloured | 3·00 | 2·50 |

**1821** Cathedral of Brasilia, Congress Emblem and Dois Candangos (two labourers)

**2010.** 50th Anniv of Brasilia as National Capital. Multicoloured.

**MS**3629 2r.70×2, Type **1821**; *Dois Candangos* (two labourers), *Memorial JK* and Catetinho (first official residence of the President in new capital) 5·50 5·50

The stamps and margins of **MS**3629 form a composite design.

**1822** Our Lady of the Rosary, Church Façade and St. Benedict

**2010.** Religious Architecture and Festivals

| | | | | |
|---|---|---|---|---|
| 3630 | **1822** | 1r.10 multicoloured | 1·70 | 1·20 |

**1823** The Holy Trinity, Mary, Shrine of Divine Eternal Father Basilica and Ox Cart

**2010.** Religious Architecture and Festivals

| | | | | |
|---|---|---|---|---|
| 3631 | **1823** | 70c. multicoloured | 1·40 | 1·00 |

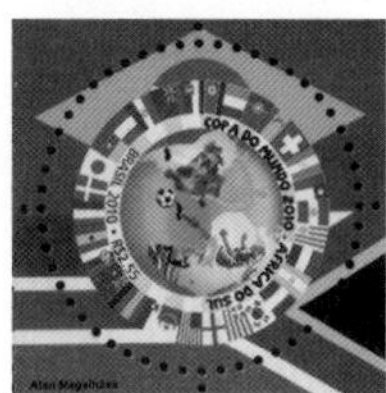
**1824** Flags surrounding Stylized Players

**2010.** World Cup Football Championships, South Africa

| | | | | |
|---|---|---|---|---|
| 3632 | **1824** | 2r.55 multicoloured | 4·25 | 3·75 |

**1825** Peter Lund and Cave at Lagoa Santa

**2010.** Peter Wilhelm Lund ('father' of Brazilian paleontology and discoverer of Pleistocene era remains at Lagoa Santa) Commemoration

| | | | | |
|---|---|---|---|---|
| 3633 | **1825** | 1r.50 multicoloured | 1·70 | 1·20 |

**1826** Abu Simbel Temples, Nubia

**2011.** Brazil–Egypt Diplomatic Relationships

| | | | | |
|---|---|---|---|---|
| 3634 | **1826** | 1r.05 multicoloured | 1·70 | 1·20 |

**1827** Rio de Janeiro, Brazil and Maalula, Syria

**2010.** Brazil–Syria Diplomatic Relationships

| | | | | |
|---|---|---|---|---|
| 3635 | **1827** | 2r. multicoloured | 2·20 | 1·70 |

No. 3636 is vacant.

**1828** *Nimbochromis venustus*

**2010.** Brazil–Malawi Diplomatic Relationships. Multicoloured.

**MS**3637 2r.×3, Type **1828**; *A. jacobfreibergi eureka*; *Cynotilapia* 6·50 6·50

**1829** Clock Tower and Village Skyline

**2010.** Paranapiacaba, Santo André (company town for employees of São Paulo Railway, privately owned British company)

| | | | | |
|---|---|---|---|---|
| 3638 | **1829** | 1r.05 multicoloured | 1·70 | 1·20 |

**1830** '150 ANOS' and Stylized Fields

**2010.** 150th Anniv of Ministry of Agriculture

| | | | | |
|---|---|---|---|---|
| 2639 | **1830** | 1r.05 multicoloured | 1·70 | 1·20 |

**1831** Barao de Maua (transport pioneer)

**2010.** 150th Anniv of Ministry of Transport

| | | | | |
|---|---|---|---|---|
| 3640 | **1831** | 1r.05 multicoloured | 1·70 | 1·20 |

**1832** *Gossyplum hirsutum*

**2010.** Textile Plants. Multicoloured.

| | | | |
|---|---|---|---|
| 3641 | 2r. Type **1832** | 2·20 | 1·70 |
| 3642 | 2r. *Cocos nucifera* (coir) | 2·20 | 1·70 |
| 3643 | 2r. *Corchorus capsularis* (jute) | 2·20 | 1·70 |
| 3644 | 2r. *Agave sisalana* (sisal) | 2·20 | 1·70 |

No. 3645 and Type **1833** are left for Centenary of Sport Club issued on 1 September 2010, not yet received.

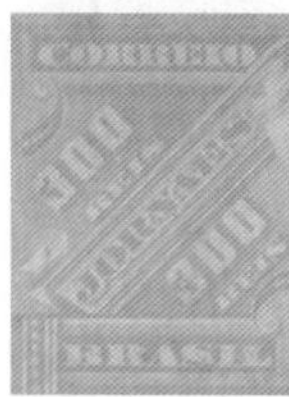

**1834** Arms

**2010.** America. Patriotic Symbols. Multicoloured.

| | | | |
|---|---|---|---|
| 3646 | 1r.05 Type **1834** | 1·70 | 1·20 |
| 3647 | 1r.05 Flag | 1·70 | 1·20 |
| 3648 | 1r.05 Seal | 1·70 | 1·20 |
| 3649 | 1r.05 National anthem score | 1·70 | 1·20 |

## EXPRESS STAMP

**1930.** Surch 1000 REIS EXPRESSO and bars.

| | | | | |
|---|---|---|---|---|
| E490 | **66** | 1000r. on 200r. blue | 6·25 | 2·30 |

## NEWSPAPER STAMPS

**N34**

**1889.** Roul.

| | | | | |
|---|---|---|---|---|
| N88 | **N34** | 10r. orange | 4·75 | 4·50 |
| N89 | **N34** | 20r. orange | 9·25 | 11·50 |
| N90 | **N34** | 50r. orange | 15·00 | 9·00 |
| N91 | **N34** | 100r. orange | 6·00 | 4·50 |
| N92 | **N34** | 200r. orange | 4·75 | 2·30 |
| N93 | **N34** | 300r. orange | 4·75 | 2·30 |
| N94 | **N34** | 500r. orange | 33·00 | 13·00 |
| N95 | **N34** | 700r. orange | 4·75 | 15·00 |
| N96 | **N34** | 1000r. orange | 4·75 | 15·00 |

**1889.** Roul.

| | | | |
|---|---|---|---|
| N97 | 10r. green | 2·20 | 80 |
| N98 | 20r. green | 2·20 | 80 |
| N99 | 50r. buff | 2·75 | 1·40 |
| N100 | 100r. mauve | 3·75 | 2·00 |
| N101 | 200r. black | 3·50 | 2·10 |
| N102 | 300r. red | 14·50 | 11·00 |
| N103 | 500r. green | 60·00 | 60·00 |
| N104 | 700r. blue | 32·00 | 37·00 |
| N105 | 1000r. brown | 14·50 | 34·00 |

**N37**

**1890.** Perf.

| | | | | |
|---|---|---|---|---|
| N111 | **N37** | 10r. blue | 19·00 | 11·50 |
| N112 | **N37** | 20r. green | 60·00 | 18·00 |
| N113 | **N37** | 100r. mauve | 21·00 | 15·00 |

**N38** Southern Cross and Sugar-loaf Mountain

**1890.** Perf.

| | | | | |
|---|---|---|---|---|
| N119 | **N38** | 10r. blue | 6·25 | 2·75 |
| N123a | **N38** | 20r. green | 5·00 | 80 |
| N127 | **N38** | 50r. green | 18·00 | 10·00 |

## OFFICIAL STAMPS

**O64** Pres. Affonso Penna

**1906.** Various frames.

| | | | | |
|---|---|---|---|---|
| O282 | **O64** | 10r. green & orange | 1·00 | 30 |
| O283 | **O64** | 20r. green & orange | 1·20 | 30 |
| O284 | **O64** | 50r. green & orange | 1·70 | 30 |
| O285 | **O64** | 100r. green & orange | 1·00 | 30 |
| O286 | **O64** | 200r. green & orange | 1·20 | 30 |
| O287 | **O64** | 300r. green & orange | 3·75 | 65 |
| O288 | **O64** | 400r. green & orange | 8·00 | 2·75 |
| O289 | **O64** | 500r. green & orange | 4·25 | 1·70 |
| O290 | **O64** | 700r. green & orange | 5·00 | 4·00 |
| O291 | **O64** | 1000r. green & orange | 4·00 | 1·30 |
| O292 | **O64** | 2000r. green & orange | 6·50 | 2·30 |
| O293 | **O64** | 5000r. green & orange | 12·50 | 1·60 |
| O294 | **O64** | 10000r. green & orange | 12·50 | 1·50 |

**O67** Pres. Hermes de Fonseca

**1913.** Various frames.

| | | | | |
|---|---|---|---|---|
| O295 | **O67** | 10r. black and grey | 40 | 60 |
| O296 | **O67** | 20r. black and olive | 40 | 60 |
| O297 | **O67** | 50r. black and grey | 40 | 60 |
| O298 | **O67** | 100r. black and red | 90 | 40 |
| O299 | **O67** | 200r. black and blue | 1·50 | 40 |
| O300 | **O67** | 500r. black & yellow | 3·50 | 50 |
| O301 | **O67** | 600r. black & purple | 4·25 | 2·75 |
| O302 | **O67** | 1000r. black & brown | 5·00 | 1·50 |
| O303 | **O67** | 2000r. black & brown | 7·50 | 1·50 |
| O304 | **O67** | 5000r. black & bistre | 9·75 | 3·75 |
| O305 | **O67** | 10000r. black | 16·00 | 8·50 |
| O306 | **O67** | 20000r. black & blue | 30·00 | 29·00 |
| O307 | **O67** | 50000r. black & green | 55·00 | 60·00 |
| O308 | **O67** | 100000r. black & red | £200 | £200 |
| O309 | **O67** | 500000r. black & brn | £350 | £350 |
| O310 | **O67** | 1000000r. black & brn | £375 | £375 |

**O77** Pres. Wenceslao Braz

**1919**

| | | | | |
|---|---|---|---|---|
| O311 | **O77** | 10r. brown | 45 | 4·50 |
| O312 | **O77** | 50r. green | 1·20 | 1·40 |
| O313 | **O77** | 100r. red | 2·10 | 90 |
| O314 | **O77** | 200r. blue | 3·50 | 90 |
| O315 | **O77** | 500r. orange | 9·25 | 24·00 |

**POSTAGE DUE STAMPS**

**D34**

**1889.** Roul.

| | | | | |
|---|---|---|---|---|
| D88 | **D34** | 10r. red | 2·75 | 2·10 |
| D89 | **D34** | 20r. red | 4·50 | 2·75 |
| D90 | **D34** | 50r. red | 7·75 | 5·75 |
| D91 | **D34** | 100r. red | 2·75 | 2·10 |
| D92 | **D34** | 200r. red | 90·00 | 21·00 |
| D93 | **D34** | 300r. red | 9·25 | 11·50 |
| D94 | **D34** | 500r. red | 9·25 | 11·50 |
| D95 | **D34** | 700r. red | 15·00 | 21·00 |
| D96 | **D34** | 1000r. red | 15·00 | 15·00 |

**1890.** Roul.

| | | | |
|---|---|---|---|
| D97 | 10r. orange | 90 | 45 |
| D98 | 20r. blue | 90 | 45 |
| D99 | 50r. olive | 2·00 | 45 |
| D100 | 200r. red | 9·25 | 85 |
| D101 | 300r. green | 4·50 | 2·10 |
| D102 | 500r. grey | 6·00 | 4·25 |
| D103 | 700r. violet | 7·25 | 11·50 |
| D104 | 1000r. purple | 8·75 | 7·50 |

**D45**

**1895.** Perf.

| | | | | |
|---|---|---|---|---|
| D172 | **D45** | 10r. blue | 2·10 | 1·40 |
| D173 | **D45** | 20r. green | 8·75 | 3·25 |
| D174 | **D45** | 50r. green | 11·00 | 6·00 |
| D175 | **D45** | 100r. red | 7·25 | 1·40 |
| D176b | **D45** | 200r. lilac | 5·50 | 3·50 |
| D177 | **D45** | 300r. blue | 4·00 | 2·50 |
| D178 | **D45** | 2000r. brown | 18·00 | 17·00 |

**D64**

**1906**

| | | | | |
|---|---|---|---|---|
| D282 | **D64** | 10r. slate | 25 | 25 |
| D283 | **D64** | 20r. violet | 25 | 25 |
| D284 | **D64** | 50r. green | 30 | 25 |
| D285 | **D64** | 100r. red | 2·00 | 65 |
| D286 | **D64** | 200r. blue | 1·10 | 30 |
| D287 | **D64** | 300r. grey | 40 | 65 |
| D288 | **D64** | 400r. green | 1·30 | 1·00 |
| D289 | **D64** | 500r. lilac | 40·00 | 38·00 |
| D290 | **D64** | 600r. purple | 1·40 | 3·25 |
| D291 | **D64** | 700r. brown | 35·00 | 32·00 |
| D292 | **D64** | 1000r. red | 1·60 | 3·50 |
| D293 | **D64** | 2000r. green | 5·25 | 6·00 |
| D294 | **D64** | 5000r. brown | 1·60 | 23·00 |

**D77**

**1919**

| | | | | |
|---|---|---|---|---|
| D345 | **D77** | 5r. brown | 25 | 25 |
| D403 | **D77** | 10r. mauve | 15 | 15 |
| D365 | **D77** | 20r. olive | 45 | 5·00 |
| D404 | **D77** | 20r. black | 15 | 15 |
| D405 | **D77** | 50r. green | 20 | 15 |
| D375 | **D77** | 100r. red | 1·00 | 95 |
| D407 | **D77** | 200r. blue | 30 | 20 |
| D408 | **D77** | 400r. brown | 1·40 | 1·40 |
| D350 | **D77** | 600r. orange | 65 | 55 |
| D401 | **D77** | 600r. violet | 25 | 15 |
| D409 | **D77** | 1000r. turquoise | 50 | 40 |
| D411 | **D77** | 5000r. blue | 90 | 70 |
| D439 | **D77** | 2000r. brown | 1·60 | 1·50 |

Pt. 7

# BREMEN

A free city of the Hanseatic League, situated on the R. Weser in northern Germany. Joined the North German Confederation in 1868.

72 grote = 1 thaler (internal).
22 grote = 10 silbergroschen (overseas mail)

1

**1855.** Imperf.

| | | | | |
|---|---|---|---|---|
| 1 | **1** | 3g. black on blue | £275 | £425 |

2

3

**1856.** Imperf.

| | | | | |
|---|---|---|---|---|
| 3 | **2** | 5g. black on red | £200 | £425 |
| 4 | **2** | 7g. black on yellow | £325 | £950 |
| 5 | **3** | 5sg. green | £200 | £475 |

4

5

**1861.** Zigzag roulette or perf.

| | | | | |
|---|---|---|---|---|
| 17 | **4** | 2g. orange | £130 | £425 |
| 19 | **1** | 3g. black on blue | £110 | £400 |
| 20 | **2** | 5g. black on red | £170 | £400 |
| 21 | **2** | 7g. black on yellow | £200 | £6000 |
| 22 | **5** | 10g. black | £250 | £1500 |
| 24 | **3** | 5sg. green | £700 | £275 |

Pt. 1

# BRITISH ANTARCTIC TERRITORY

Constituted in 1962 comprising territories south of latitude 60°S., from the former Falkland Island Dependencies.

1963. 12 pence = 1 shilling; 20 shillings = 1 pound.
1971. 100 (new) pence = 1 pound.

1 M.V. "Kista Dan"

**1963**

| No. | Type | Description | Mint | Used |
|---|---|---|---|---|
| 1 | 1 | ½d. blue | 1·25 | 1·75 |
| 2 | - | 1d. brown | 1·25 | 80 |
| 3 | - | 1½d. red and purple | 1·25 | 1·50 |
| 4 | - | 2d. purple | 1·50 | 80 |
| 5 | - | 2½d. myrtle | 3·25 | 1·25 |
| 6 | - | 3d. turquoise | 3·75 | 1·50 |
| 7 | - | 4d. sepia | 2·75 | 1·50 |
| 8 | - | 6d. olive and blue | 4·75 | 2·50 |
| 9 | - | 9d. green | 3·50 | 2·00 |
| 10 | - | 1s. turquoise | 4·25 | 1·50 |
| 11 | - | 2s. violet and brown | 20·00 | 10·00 |
| 12 | - | 2s.6d. blue | 22·00 | 15·00 |
| 13 | - | 5s. orange and red | 22·00 | 19·00 |
| 14 | - | 10s. blue and green | 45·00 | 26·00 |
| 15 | - | £1 black and blue | 48·00 | 48·00 |
| 15a | - | £1 red and black | £130 | £120 |

DESIGNS: 1d. Manhauling; 1½d. Muskeg (tractor); 2d. Skiing; 2½d. de Havilland D.H.C.2 Beaver (aircraft); 3d. R.R.S. "John Biscoe II"; 4d. Camp scene; 6d. H.M.S. "Protector"; 9d. Sledging; 1s. de Havilland D.H.C.3 Otter (aircraft); 2s. Huskies; 2s.6d. Westland Whirlwind helicopter; 5s. Snocat (tractor); 10s. R.R.S. "Shackleton"; £1 (No. 15), Antarctic map; £1 (No. 15a), H.M.S. "Endurance I".

**1966.** Churchill Commemoration. As T **38** of Antigua.

| No. | Description | Mint | Used |
|---|---|---|---|
| 16 | ½d. blue | 80 | 3·25 |
| 17 | 1d. green | 3·25 | 3·25 |
| 18 | 1s. brown | 23·00 | 6·50 |
| 19 | 2s. violet | 25·00 | 7·00 |

17 Lemaire Channel and Icebergs

**1969.** 25th Anniv of Continuous Scientific Work.

| No. | Type | Description | Mint | Used |
|---|---|---|---|---|
| 20 | 17 | 3½d. black, blue and ultram | 2·50 | 3·00 |
| 21 | - | 6d. multicoloured | 1·00 | 2·50 |
| 22 | - | 1s. black, blue and red | 1·00 | 2·00 |
| 23 | - | 2s. black, orange and turquoise | 1·00 | 3·00 |

DESIGNS: 6d. Radio Sonde balloon; 1s. Muskeg pulling tent equipment; 2s. Surveyors with theodolite.

**1971.** Decimal Currency. Nos. 1/14 surch.

| No. | Description | Mint | Used |
|---|---|---|---|
| 24 | ½p. on ½d. blue | 60 | 3·00 |
| 25 | 1p. on 1d. brown | 1·00 | 90 |
| 26 | 1½p. on 1½d. red and purple | 1·25 | 75 |
| 27 | 2p. on 2d. purple | 1·25 | 40 |
| 28 | 2½p. on 2½d. green | 3·00 | 2·25 |
| 29 | 3p. on 3d. blue | 2·50 | 75 |
| 30 | 4p. on 4d. brown | 2·25 | 75 |
| 31 | 5p. on 6d. green and blue | 4·75 | 3·50 |
| 32 | 6p. on 9d. green | 16·00 | 8·00 |
| 33 | 7½p. on 1s. blue | 18·00 | 8·50 |
| 34 | 10p. on 2s. violet and brown | 18·00 | 12·00 |
| 35 | 15p. on 2s.6d. blue | 18·00 | 12·00 |
| 36 | 25p. on 5s. orange and red | 20·00 | 15·00 |
| 37 | 50p. on 10s. blue and green | 24·00 | 25·00 |

19 Setting up Camp, Graham Land

**1971.** 10th Anniv of Antarctic Treaty. Multicoloured.

| No. | Description | Mint | Used |
|---|---|---|---|
| 38 | 1½p. Type **19** | 6·00 | 5·50 |
| 39 | 4p. Snow petrels | 16·00 | 8·00 |
| 40 | 5p. Weddell seals | 9·50 | 8·00 |
| 41 | 10p. Adelie penguins | 22·00 | 9·00 |

Nos. 38/41 each include Antarctic map and Queen Elizabeth in their design.

**1972.** Royal Silver Wedding. As T **52** of Ascension, but with Kerguelen fur seals and Emperor penguins in background.

| No. | Description | Mint | Used |
|---|---|---|---|
| 42 | 5p. brown | 2·00 | 3·00 |
| 43 | 10p. green | 2·00 | 3·00 |

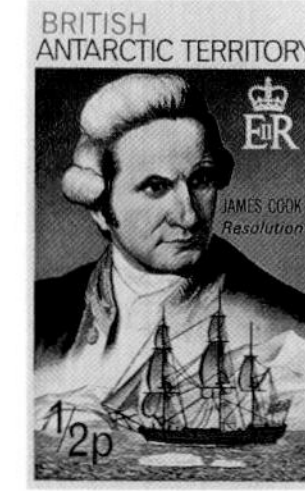

21 James Cook and H.M.S. "Resolution"

**1973.** Multicoloured.. Multicoloured..

| No. | Description | Mint | Used |
|---|---|---|---|
| 64a | ½p. Type **21** | 1·00 | 2·50 |
| 65 | 1p. Thaddeus von Bellingshausen and "Vostok" | 60 | 2·25 |
| 66 | 1½p. James Weddell and "Jane" | 60 | 2·25 |
| 67 | 2p. John Biscoe and "Tula" | 1·50 | 2·50 |
| 48 | 2½p. J. S. C. Dumont d'Urville and "L'Astrolabe" | 1·50 | 1·75 |
| 49 | 3p. James Clark Ross and H.M.S. "Erebus" | 1·00 | 1·75 |
| 50 | 4p. C. A. Larsen and "Jason" | 1·00 | 1·75 |
| 51 | 5p. Adrien de Gerlache and "Belgica" | 1·00 | 1·75 |
| 52 | 6p. Otto Nordenskjold and "Antarctic" | 1·25 | 2·75 |
| 53 | 7½p. W. S. Bruce and "Scotia" | 1·25 | 2·75 |
| 74a | 10p. Jean-Baptiste Charcot and "Pourquoi Pas?" | 50 | 3·00 |
| 75 | 15p. Ernest Shackleton and "Endurance" | 1·25 | 2·25 |
| 76 | 25p. Hubert Wilkins and Lockheed Vega "San Francisco" | 1·00 | 1·50 |
| 77b | 50p. Lincoln Ellsworth and Northrop Gamma "Polar Star" | 85 | 2·75 |
| 78 | £1 John Rymill and "Penola" | 2·75 | 2·00 |

The 25p. and 50p. show aircraft; the rest show ships.

**1973.** Royal Wedding. As T **47** of Anguilla. Background colour given. Multicoloured.

| No. | Description | Mint | Used |
|---|---|---|---|
| 59 | 5p. brown | 40 | 20 |
| 60 | 15p. blue | 70 | 30 |

22 Churchill and Churchill Peninsula, B.A.T.

**1974.** Birth Centenary of Sir Winston Churchill. Multicoloured.

| No. | Description | Mint | Used |
|---|---|---|---|
| 61 | 5p. Type **22** | 1·50 | 1·75 |
| 62 | 15p. Churchill and "Trepassey" | 1·75 | 2·25 |
| **MS**63 | 114×88 mm. Nos. 61/2 | 8·00 | 8·00 |

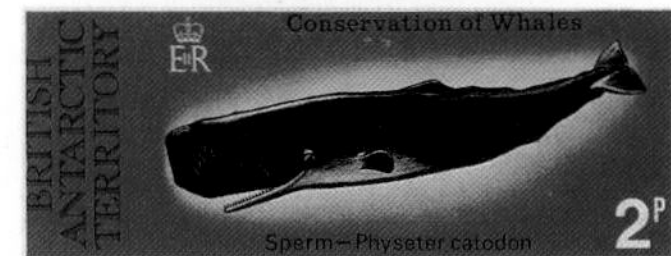

23 Sperm Whale

**1977.** Whale Conservation. Multicoloured.

| No. | Description | Mint | Used |
|---|---|---|---|
| 79 | 2p. Type **23** | 5·50 | 3·00 |
| 80 | 8p. Fin whale | 6·50 | 3·50 |
| 81 | 11p. Humpback whale | 7·00 | 3·50 |
| 82 | 25p. Blue whale | 7·50 | 4·50 |

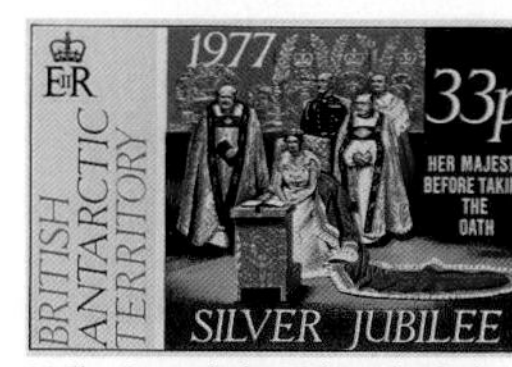

24 The Queen before Taking the Oath

**1977.** Silver Jubilee. Multicoloured.

| No. | Description | Mint | Used |
|---|---|---|---|
| 83 | 6p. Prince Philip's visit, 1956/7 | 70 | 40 |
| 84 | 11p. The Coronation Oath | 80 | 50 |
| 85 | 33p. Type **24** | 1·00 | 65 |

25 Emperor Penguin

**1978.** 25th Anniv of Coronation.

| No. | Type | Description | Mint | Used |
|---|---|---|---|---|
| 86 | - | 25p. green, deep green and silver | 60 | 1·00 |
| 87 | - | 25p. multicoloured | 60 | 1·00 |
| 88 | 25 | 25p. green, deep green and silver | 60 | 1·00 |

DESIGNS: No. 86, Black Bull of Clarence; 87, Queen Elizabeth II.

26 Macaroni Penguins

**1979.** Penguins. Multicoloured.

| No. | Description | Mint | Used |
|---|---|---|---|
| 89 | 3p. Type **26** | 9·00 | 10·00 |
| 90 | 8p. Gentoo penguins | 2·00 | 2·75 |
| 91 | 11p. Adelie penguins | 2·50 | 3·25 |
| 92 | 25p. Emperor penguins | 3·50 | 4·25 |

27 Sir John Barrow and "Tula"

**1980.** 150th Anniv of Royal Geographical Society. Former Presidents. Multicoloured.

| No. | Description | Mint | Used |
|---|---|---|---|
| 93 | 3p. Type **27** | 15 | 15 |
| 94 | 7p. Sir Clement Markham and "Discovery" | 15 | 25 |
| 95 | 11p. Lord Curzon and whaleboat "James Caird" | 20 | 30 |
| 96 | 15p. Sir William Goodenough | 20 | 35 |
| 97 | 22p. Sir James Wordie | 25 | 55 |
| 98 | 30p. Sir Raymond Priestley | 30 | 65 |

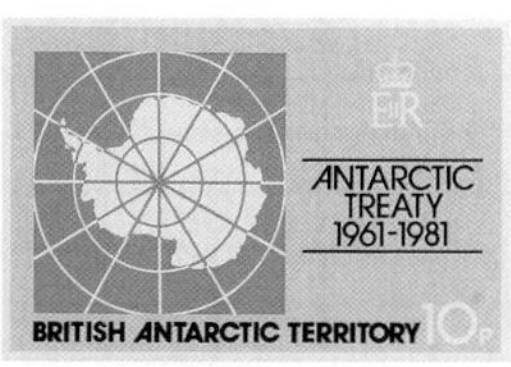

28 Map of Antarctic

**1981.** 20th Anniv of Antarctic Treaty.

| No. | Type | Description | Mint | Used |
|---|---|---|---|---|
| 99 | 28 | 10p. black, blue and light blue | 30 | 70 |
| 100 | - | 13p. black, blue and green | 35 | 80 |
| 101 | - | 25p. black, blue and mauve | 40 | 90 |
| 102 | - | 26p. black, brown and red | 40 | 90 |

DESIGNS: 13p. Conservation research ("scientific co-operation"); 25p. Satellite image mapping ("technical co-operation"); 26p. Global geophysics ("scientific co-operation").

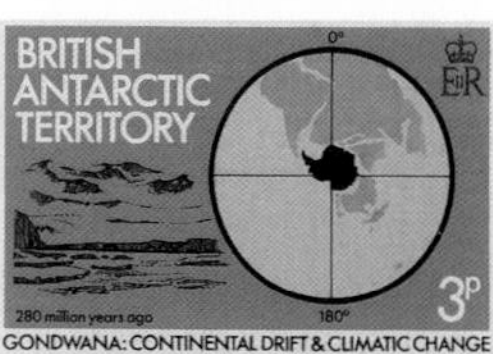

29 Map of Gondwana 280 million years ago and Contemporary Landscape Scene

**1982.** Gondwana – Continental Drift and Climatic Change. Maps of Gondwana showing position of continents, and contemporary landscapes. Mult.

| No. | Description | Mint | Used |
|---|---|---|---|
| 103 | 3p. Type **29** | 20 | 40 |
| 104 | 6p. 260 million years ago | 20 | 50 |
| 105 | 10p. 230 million years ago | 25 | 60 |
| 106 | 13p. 175 million years ago | 30 | 70 |
| 107 | 25p. 50 million years ago | 35 | 75 |
| 108 | 26p. Present day | 35 | 75 |

30 British Antarctic Territory Coat of Arms

**1982.** 21st Birthday of Princess of Wales. Multicoloured.

| No. | Description | Mint | Used |
|---|---|---|---|
| 109 | 5p. Type **30** | 15 | 30 |
| 110 | 17p. Princess of Wales (detail of painting by Bryan Organ) | 35 | 60 |
| 111 | 37p. Wedding ceremony | 50 | 90 |
| 112 | 50p. Formal portrait | 90 | 1·25 |

31 Leopard Seal

**1983.** 10th Anniv of Antarctic Seal Conservation Convention. Multicoloured.

| No. | Description | Mint | Used |
|---|---|---|---|
| 113 | 5p. Type **31** | 25 | 35 |
| 114 | 10p. Weddell seals | 30 | 40 |
| 115 | 13p. Southern elephant seals | 30 | 45 |
| 116 | 17p. Kerguelen fur seals | 30 | 55 |
| 117 | 25p. Ross seals | 30 | 65 |
| 118 | 34p. Crabeater seals | 35 | 85 |

32 de Havilland Twin Otter 200/300

**1983.** Bicentenary of Manned Flight. Multicoloured.

| No. | Description | Mint | Used |
|---|---|---|---|
| 119 | 5p. Type **32** | 25 | 30 |
| 120 | 13p. de Havilland DHC-3 Twin Otter | 35 | 45 |
| 121 | 17p. Consolidated PBY-5A Canso amphibian | 45 | 60 |
| 122 | 50p. Lockheed Vega "San Francisco" | 70 | 1·25 |

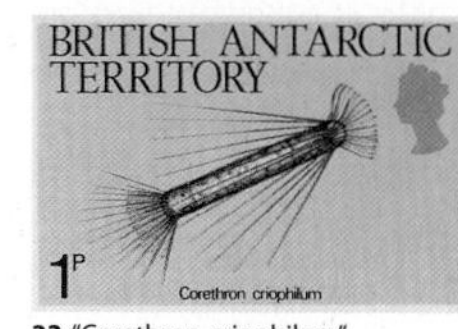

33 "Corethron criophilum"

**1984.** Marine Life. Multicoloured.

| No. | Description | Mint | Used |
|---|---|---|---|
| 123 | 1p. Type **33** | 60 | 1·75 |
| 124 | 2p. "Desmonema gaudichaudi" | 65 | 1·75 |
| 125 | 3p. "Tomopteris carpenteri" | 65 | 1·75 |
| 126 | 4p. "Pareuchaeta antarctica" | 70 | 1·75 |
| 127 | 5p. "Antarctomysis maxima" | 70 | 1·75 |
| 128 | 6p. "Antarcturus signiensis" | 70 | 1·75 |
| 129 | 7p. "Serolis cornuta" | 70 | 1·75 |
| 130 | 8p. "Parathemisto gaudichaudii" | 70 | 1·75 |
| 131 | 9p. "Bovallia gigantea" | 70 | 1·75 |
| 132 | 10p. "Euphausia superba" | 70 | 1·75 |
| 133 | 15p. "Colossendeis australis" | 70 | 1·75 |
| 134 | 20p. "Todarodes sagittatus" | 75 | 1·75 |
| 135 | 25p. Antarctic rockcod | 80 | 1·75 |
| 136 | 50p. Black-finned icefish | 1·25 | 2·00 |
| 137 | £1 Crabeater seal | 1·75 | 2·50 |
| 138 | £3 Antarctic marine food chain | 5·00 | 6·50 |

34 M.Y. "Penola" in Stella Creek

**1985.** 50th Anniv of British Graham Land Expedition. Multicoloured.

| No. | Description | Mint | Used |
|---|---|---|---|
| 139 | 7p. Type **34** | 40 | 75 |
| 140 | 22p. Northern Base, Winter Island | 70 | 1·40 |
| 141 | 27p. de Havilland DH.83 Fox Moth at Southern Base, Barry Island | 80 | 1·60 |
| 142 | 54p. Dog Team, near Ablation Point, George VI Sound | 1·50 | 2·25 |

**35** Robert McCormick and South Polar Skua

**1985.** Early Naturalists. Multicoloured.

| | | | |
|---|---|---|---|
| 143 | 7p. Type **35** | 80 | 1·25 |
| 144 | 22p. Sir Joseph Dalton Hooker and "Deschampsia antarctica" | 1·25 | 2·50 |
| 145 | 27p. Jean Rene C. Quoy and hourglass dolphin | 1·25 | 2·50 |
| 146 | 54p. James Weddell and Weddell seal | 1·75 | 3·50 |

**36** Dr. Edmond Halley

**1986.** Appearance of Halley's Comet. Multicoloured.

| | | | |
|---|---|---|---|
| 147 | 7p. Type **36** | 75 | 1·25 |
| 148 | 22p. Halley Station, Antarctica | 1·00 | 2·25 |
| 149 | 27p. "Halley's Comet, 1531" (from Peter Apian woodcut, 1532) | 1·25 | 2·50 |
| 150 | 44p. "Giotto" spacecraft | 2·25 | 4·50 |

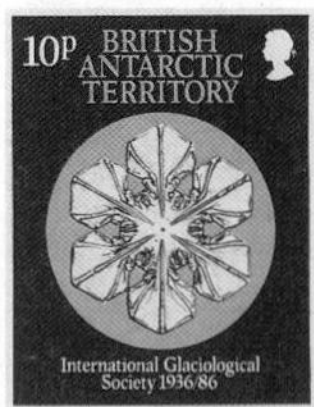

**37** Snow Crystal

**1986.** 50th Anniv of International Glaciological Society. Snow Crystals.

| | | | | |
|---|---|---|---|---|
| 151 | **37** | 10p. light blue and blue | 50 | 75 |
| 152 | - | 24p. green and deep green | 65 | 1·40 |
| 153 | - | 29p. mauve and deep mauve | 70 | 1·50 |
| 154 | - | 58p. blue and violet | 1·00 | 2·50 |

**38** Captain Scott, 1904

**1987.** 75th Anniv of Captain Scott's Arrival at South Pole. Multicoloured.

| | | | |
|---|---|---|---|
| 155 | 10p. Type **38** | 55 | 95 |
| 156 | 24p. Hut Point and "Discovery" Ross Island, 1902–4 | 90 | 2·00 |
| 157 | 29p. Cape Evans Hut, 1911–13 | 1·00 | 2·25 |
| 158 | 58p. Scott's expedition at South Pole, 1912 | 1·50 | 3·00 |

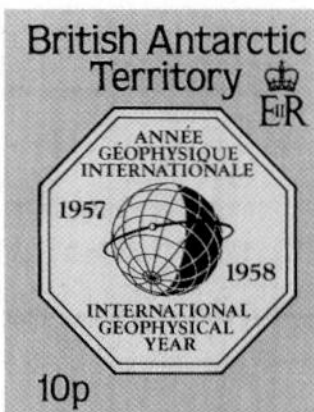

**39** IGY Logo

**1987.** 30th Anniv of International Geophysical Year.

| | | | | |
|---|---|---|---|---|
| 159 | **39** | 10p. black and green | 30 | 75 |
| 160 | - | 24p. multicoloured | 50 | 1·40 |
| 161 | - | 29p. multicoloured | 60 | 1·75 |
| 162 | - | 58p. multicoloured | 1·10 | 2·50 |

DESIGNS: 24p. Port Lockroy; 29p. Argentine Islands; 58p. Halley Bay.

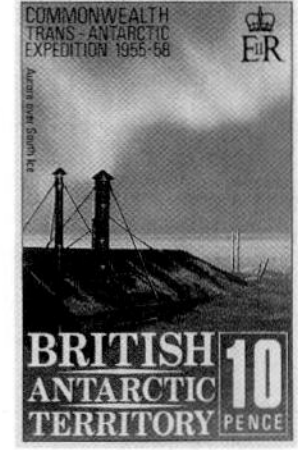

**40** Aurora over South Ice Plateau Station

**1988.** 30th Anniv of Commonwealth Trans-Antarctic Expedition. Multicoloured.

| | | | |
|---|---|---|---|
| 163 | 10p. Type **40** | 30 | 75 |
| 164 | 24p. de Havilland Canada DHC-3 Otter at Theron Mountains | 50 | 1·25 |
| 165 | 29p. Seismic ice-depth sounding | 60 | 1·40 |
| 166 | 58p. "Sno-cat" over crevasse | 1·00 | 2·00 |

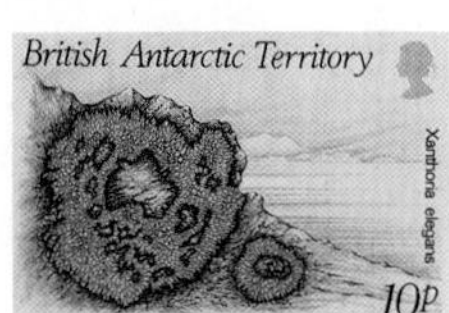

**41** "Xanthoria elegans"

**1989.** Lichens. Multicoloured.

| | | | |
|---|---|---|---|
| 167 | 10p. Type **41** | 90 | 1·00 |
| 168 | 24p. "Usnea aurantiaco-atra" | 1·60 | 2·00 |
| 169 | 29p. "Cladonia chlorophaea" | 1·75 | 2·25 |
| 170 | 58p. "Umbilicaria antarctica" | 2·50 | 3·25 |

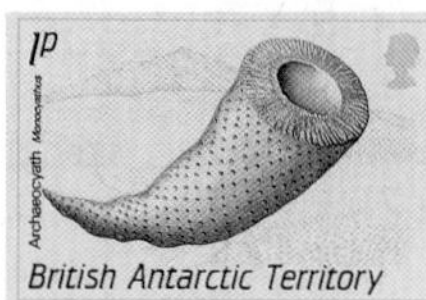

**42** "Monocyathus" (archaeocyath)

**1990.** Fossils. Multicoloured.

| | | | |
|---|---|---|---|
| 171 | 1p. Type **42** | 1·00 | 1·50 |
| 172 | 2p. "Lingulella" (brachiopod) | 1·00 | 1·50 |
| 173 | 3p. "Triplagnoslus" (trilobite) | 1·00 | 1·50 |
| 174 | 4p. "Lyriaspis" (trilobite) | 1·25 | 1·50 |
| 175 | 5p. "Glossopteris" leaf (gymnosperm) | 1·25 | 1·50 |
| 176 | 6p. "Gonatosorus" (fern) | 1·25 | 1·60 |
| 177 | 7p. "Belemnopsis aucklandica" (belemnite) | 1·25 | 1·60 |
| 178 | 8p. "Sanmartinoceras africanum insignicostatum" (ammonite) | 1·25 | 1·60 |
| 179 | 9p. "Pinna antarctica" (mussel) | 1·25 | 1·60 |
| 180 | 10p. "Aucellina andina" (mussel) | 1·25 | 1·60 |
| 181 | 20p. "Pterotrigonia malagninoi" (mussel) | 1·75 | 2·25 |
| 182 | 25p. "Perissoptera" (conch shell) | 1·75 | 2·25 |
| 183 | 50p. "Ainoceras sp." (ammonite) | 2·25 | 3·50 |
| 184 | £1 "Gunnarites zinsmeisteri" (ammonite) | 3·50 | 4·75 |
| 185 | £3 "Hoploparia" (crayfish) | 7·00 | 8·50 |

**1990.** 90th Birthday of Queen Elizabeth the Queen Mother. As T **134** of Ascension.

| | | | |
|---|---|---|---|
| 186 | 26p. multicoloured | 1·50 | 2·25 |
| 187 | £1 black and brown | 3·00 | 4·00 |

DESIGNS: 29×36 mm: 26p. Wedding of Prince Albert and Lady Elizabeth Bowes-Lyon, 1923. 29×37 mm: £1 The Royal Family, 1940.

**43** Late Cretaceous Forest and Southern Beech Fossil

**1991.** Age of the Dinosaurs. Multicoloured.

| | | | |
|---|---|---|---|
| 188 | 12p. Type **43** | 1·25 | 1·25 |
| 189 | 26p. Hypsilophodont dinosaurs and skull | 2·00 | 2·25 |
| 190 | 31p. Frilled sharks and tooth | 2·25 | 2·50 |
| 191 | 62p. Mosasaur, plesiosaur, and mosasaur vertebra | 3·50 | 4·00 |

**44** Launching Meteorological Balloon, Halley IV Station

**1991.** Discovery of Antarctic Ozone Hole. Mult.

| | | | |
|---|---|---|---|
| 192 | 12p. Type **44** | 90 | 1·75 |
| 193 | 26p. Measuring ozone with Dobson spectrophotometer | 1·60 | 2·75 |
| 194 | 31p. Satellite map showing ozone hole | 1·90 | 3·00 |
| 195 | 62p. Lockheed ER-2 aircraft and graph of chlorine monoxide and ozone levels | 3·25 | 4·50 |

**45** Researching Dry Valley

**1991.** 30th Anniv of Antarctic Treaty.

| | | | | |
|---|---|---|---|---|
| 196 | **45** | 12p. multicoloured | 90 | 90 |
| 197 | - | 26p. multicoloured | 1·60 | 1·75 |
| 198 | - | 31p. black and green | 1·75 | 1·90 |
| 199 | - | 62p. multicoloured | 3·00 | 3·25 |

DESIGNS: 26p. Relief map of ice sheet; 31p. BIOMASS logo; 62p. Ross seal.

**46** "H.M.S. 'Erebus' and H.M.S. 'Terror' in the Antarctic" (J. Carmichael)

**1991.** Maiden Voyage of "James Clark Ross" (research ship). Multicoloured.

| | | | |
|---|---|---|---|
| 200 | 12p. Type **46** | 90 | 1·50 |
| 201 | 26p. Launch of "James Clark Ross" | 1·60 | 2·50 |
| 202 | 31p. "James Clark Ross" in Antarctica | 1·75 | 2·75 |
| 203 | 62p. Scientific research | 3·00 | 3·75 |

**1991.** Birth Bicentenary of Michael Faraday (scientist). Nos. 200/3 additionally inscr "200th Anniversary M. Faraday 1791–1867".

| | | | |
|---|---|---|---|
| 204 | 12p. Type **46** | 90 | 1·75 |
| 205 | 26p. Launch of "James Clark Ross" | 1·60 | 2·75 |
| 206 | 31p. "James Clark Ross" in Antarctica | 1·75 | 3·00 |
| 207 | 62p. Scientific research | 3·00 | 4·50 |

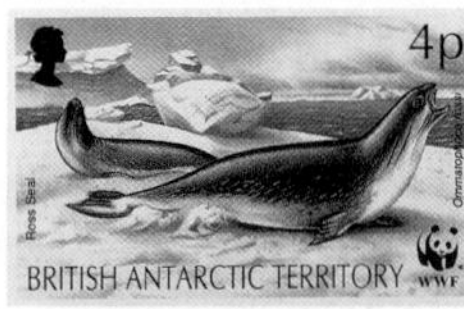

**47** Ross Seals

**1992.** Endangered Species. Seals and Penguins. Multicoloured.

| | | | |
|---|---|---|---|
| 208 | 4p. Type **47** | 1·00 | 1·25 |
| 209 | 5p. Adelie penguins | 1·00 | 1·25 |
| 210 | 7p. Weddell seal with pup | 1·00 | 1·25 |
| 211 | 29p. Emperor penguins with chicks | 2·25 | 2·25 |
| 212 | 34p. Crabeater seals with pup | 1·75 | 2·25 |
| 213 | 68p. Bearded penguins ("Chinstrap Penguin") with young | 2·50 | 2·75 |

**48** Sun Pillar at Faraday

**1992.** Lower Atmospheric Phenomena. Mult.

| | | | |
|---|---|---|---|
| 214 | 14p. Type **48** | 80 | 1·50 |
| 215 | 29p. Halo over iceberg | 1·40 | 1·90 |
| 216 | 34p. Lee Wave cloud | 1·75 | 2·25 |
| 217 | 68p. Nacreous clouds | 2·75 | 4·00 |

**49** "Fitzroy" (mail and supply ship)

**1993.** Antarctic Ships. Multicoloured.

| | | | |
|---|---|---|---|
| 218 | 1p. Type **49** | 2·00 | 2·50 |
| 219 | 2p. "William Scoresby" (research ship) | 2·25 | 2·50 |
| 220 | 3p. "Eagle" (sealer) | 2·25 | 2·50 |
| 221 | 4p. "Trepassey" (supply ship) | 2·25 | 2·50 |
| 222 | 5p. "John Biscoe I" (research ship) | 2·25 | 2·75 |
| 223 | 10p. "Norsel" (supply ship) | 2·50 | 2·75 |
| 224 | 20p. H.M.S. "Protector" (ice patrol ship) | 3·50 | 3·50 |
| 225 | 30p. "Oluf Sven" (supply ship) | 4·00 | 4·25 |
| 226 | 50p. "John Biscoe II" and "Shackleton" (research ships) | 5·00 | 5·50 |
| 227 | £1 "Tottan" (supply ship) | 6·00 | 7·00 |
| 228 | £3 "Perla Dan" (supply ship) | 9·50 | 11·00 |
| 229 | £5 H.M.S. "Endurance I" (ice patrol ship) | 14·00 | 15·00 |

**1994.** "Hong Kong '94", International Stamp Exhibition. Nos. 240/5 optd **HONG KONG '94** and emblem.

| | | | |
|---|---|---|---|
| 230 | 15p. Type **51** | 1·10 | 1·25 |
| 231 | 24p. de Havilland Turbo Beaver III aircraft | 1·60 | 1·90 |
| 232 | 31p. de Havilland Otter aircraft and dog team | 1·75 | 2·25 |
| 233 | 36p. de Havilland Twin Otter 200/300 aircraft and dog team | 1·90 | 2·50 |
| 234 | 62p. de Havilland Dash Seven aircraft over landing strip, Rothera Point | 2·75 | 3·00 |
| 235 | 72p. de Havilland Dash Seven aircraft on runway | 2·75 | 3·00 |

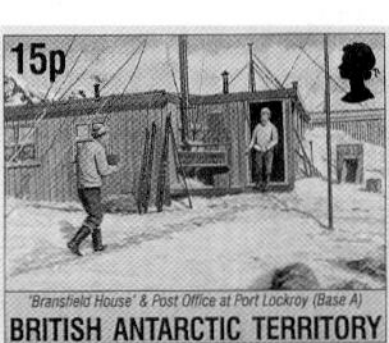

**50** Bransfield House Post Office, Port Lockroy

**1994.** 50th Anniv of Operation Tabarin. Multicoloured.

| | | | |
|---|---|---|---|
| 236 | 15p. Type **50** | 1·00 | 1·40 |
| 237 | 31p. Survey team, Hope Bay | 1·60 | 1·90 |
| 238 | 36p. Dog team, Hope Bay | 2·50 | 2·25 |
| 239 | 72p. "Fitzroy" (supply ship) and H.M.S. "William Scoresby" (minesweeper) | 3·25 | 4·25 |

**51** Huskies and Sledge

**1994.** Forms of Transportation. Multicoloured.

| | | | |
|---|---|---|---|
| 240 | 15p. Type **51** | 70 | 80 |
| 241 | 24p. de Havilland Turbo Beaver III aircraft | 90 | 1·00 |
| 242 | 31p. de Havilland Otter aircraft and dog team | 1·00 | 1·10 |
| 243 | 36p. de Havilland Twin Otter 200/300 aircraft and dog team | 1·10 | 1·40 |
| 244 | 62p. de Havilland Dash Seven aircraft over landing strip, Rothera Point | 2·00 | 2·50 |
| 245 | 72p. de Havilland Dash Seven aircraft on runway | 2·00 | 2·75 |

**52** Capt. James Cook and H.M.S. "Resolution"

**1994.** Antarctic Heritage Fund. Multicoloured.

| | | | |
|---|---|---|---|
| 246 | 17p.+3p. Type **52** | 2·50 | 3·00 |
| 247 | 35p.+15p. Sir James Clark Ross with H.M.S. "Erebus" and H.M.S. "Terror" | 2·75 | 3·25 |
| 248 | 40p.+10p. Capt. Robert Falcon Scott and interior of hut | 2·75 | 3·25 |
| 249 | 76p.+4p. Sir Ernest Shackleton and "Endurance" | 3·75 | 4·00 |

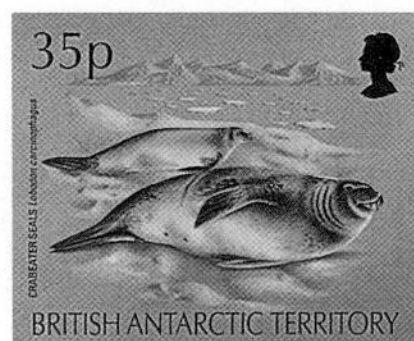


53 Pair of Crabeater Seals

**1994.** Antarctic Food Chain. Multicoloured.

| | | | |
|---|---|---|---|
| 250 | 35p. Type **53** | 2·00 | 2·50 |
| 251 | 35p. Blue whale | 2·00 | 2·50 |
| 252 | 35p. Wandering albatross | 2·00 | 2·50 |
| 253 | 35p. Mackerel icefish | 2·00 | 2·50 |
| 254 | 35p. Krill | 2·00 | 2·50 |
| 255 | 35p. Seven star flying squid | 2·00 | 2·50 |

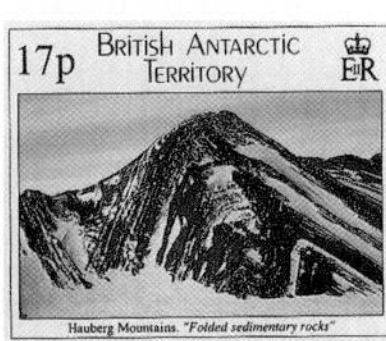


54 Hauberg Mountains

**1995.** Geological Structures. Multicoloured.

| | | | |
|---|---|---|---|
| 256 | 17p. Type **54** | 1·50 | 1·75 |
| 257 | 35p. Arrowsmith Peninsula | 2·25 | 2·75 |
| 258 | 40p. Colbert Mountains | 2·50 | 3·00 |
| 259 | 76p. Succession Cliffs | 3·75 | 4·75 |

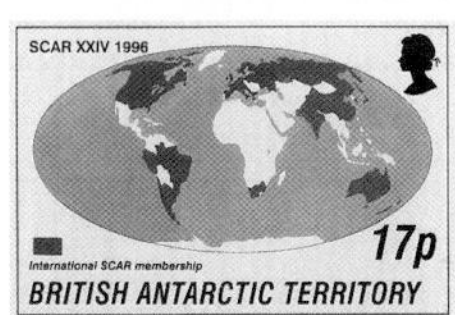


55 World Map showing Member Countries

**1996.** 24th Meeting of Scientific Committee on Antarctic Research. Multicoloured.

| | | | |
|---|---|---|---|
| 260 | 17p. Type **55** | 1·00 | 1·50 |
| 261 | 35p. Scientist analysing ice samples | 1·75 | 2·00 |
| 262 | 40p. Releasing balloon | 2·00 | 2·25 |
| 263 | 76p. Antarctic research ship catching marine life | 2·75 | 3·50 |
| **MS**264 | 100×90 mm. £1 S.C.A.R. logo | 6·50 | 8·00 |

56 Killer Whales

**1996.** Whales. Multicoloured.

| | | | |
|---|---|---|---|
| 265 | 17p. Type **56** | 80 | 1·00 |
| 266 | 35p. Sperm whales | 1·40 | 1·50 |
| 267 | 40p. Minke whales | 1·60 | 1·75 |
| 268 | 76p. Blue whale and calf | 2·50 | 2·75 |
| **MS**269 | 105×82 mm. £1 Humpback whale | 4·00 | 4·25 |

**1996.** 70th Birthday of Queen Elizabeth II. As T **165** of Ascension, each incorporating a different photograph of the Queen. Mult.

| | | | |
|---|---|---|---|
| 270 | 17p. At premiere of "Chaplin", Leicester Square, 1992 | 1·00 | 1·00 |
| 271 | 35p. At Buckingham Palace dinner, 1991 | 1·50 | 1·60 |
| 272 | 40p. In Aberdeen, 1993 | 1·75 | 1·75 |
| 273 | 76p. At Royal Military School of Music, 1990 | 2·25 | 3·25 |

**1997.** "HONG KONG '97" International Stamp Exhibition. Sheet 130×90 mm, containing design as No. 226. Multicoloured.

| | | | |
|---|---|---|---|
| **MS**274 | 50p. "John Biscoe II" and "Shackleton" (research ships) | 1·75 | 2·25 |

**1997.** Return of Hong Kong to China. Sheet 130×90 mm containing design as No. 227, but with "1997" imprint date.

| | | | |
|---|---|---|---|
| **MS**275 | £1 "Tottan" | 2·75 | 3·25 |

57 Chinstrap Penguins sledging

**1997.** Christmas. Multicoloured.

| | | | |
|---|---|---|---|
| 276 | 17p. Type **57** | 2·25 | 1·50 |
| 277 | 35p. Emperor penguins carol singing | 2·75 | 2·25 |
| 278 | 40p. Adelie penguins throwing snowballs | 3·00 | 2·50 |
| 279 | 76p. Gentoo penguins ice-skating | 4·25 | 5·50 |

**1998.** Diana, Princess of Wales Commemoration. Sheet 145×70 mm, containing vert designs as T **177** of Ascension. Multicoloured.

| | | | |
|---|---|---|---|
| **MS**280 | 35p. Wearing sunglasses; 35p. Wearing round-necked white blouse, 1993; 35p. Wearing white blouse and jacket, 1990; 35p. Wearing green jacket, 1992 (sold at £1.40+20p. charity premium) | 3·00 | 3·00 |

58 Chart of South Shetland Islands (Swedish South Polar Expedition, 1902–3)

**1998.** History of Mapping in Antarctica. Multicoloured.

| | | | |
|---|---|---|---|
| 281 | 16p. Type **58** | 2·00 | 1·75 |
| 282 | 30p. Map of Antarctic Peninsula (1949) | 2·50 | 2·25 |
| 283 | 35p. Map of AntarcticPeninsula (1964) | 2·75 | 2·50 |
| 284 | 40p. Map of Antarctic Peninsula from Landsat (1981) | 2·75 | 2·75 |
| 285 | 65p. Map of Antarctic Peninsula from satellite (1995) | 3·50 | 4·00 |

59 Antarctic Explorer and H.M.S. "Erebus", 1843

**1998.** Antarctic Clothing. Multicoloured.

| | | | |
|---|---|---|---|
| 286 | 30p. Type **59** | 2·50 | 1·75 |
| 287 | 35p. Explorer with dog, and "Discovery I", 1900 | 3·00 | 1·90 |
| 288 | 40p. Surveyor, and "Fitzroy", 1943 | 3·00 | 2·00 |
| 289 | 65p. Scientist with Adelie penguins, and "James Clark Ross", 1998 | 4·50 | 4·00 |

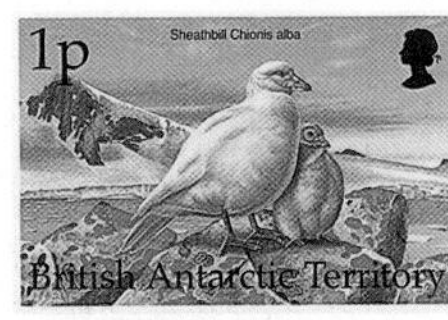


60 Snowy Sheathbill

**1998.** Antarctic Birds. Multicoloured.

| | | | |
|---|---|---|---|
| 290 | 1p. Type **60** | 2·00 | 2·00 |
| 291 | 2p. Dove prion ("Antarctic Prion") | 2·00 | 2·00 |
| 292 | 5p. Adelie penguin | 2·00 | 2·00 |
| 293 | 10p. Emperor penguin | 2·00 | 2·00 |
| 294 | 20p. Antarctic tern | 2·00 | 2·00 |
| 295 | 30p. Black-bellied storm petrel | 2·00 | 2·00 |
| 296 | 35p. Southern fulmar ("Antarctic Fulmar") | 2·25 | 2·00 |
| 297 | 40p. Blue-eyed cormorant ("Blue-eyed Shag") | 2·25 | 2·00 |
| 298 | 50p. South polar skua ("McCormick's Skua") | 2·50 | 2·25 |
| 299 | £1 Southern black-backed gull ("Kelp Gull") | 4·00 | 4·00 |
| 300 | £3 Wilson's storm petrel | 8·00 | 8·00 |
| 301 | £5 Antactic skua ("Brown Skua") | 11·00 | 12·00 |

61 Mackerel Icefish

**1999.** Fish of the Southern Ocean. Multicoloured.

| | | | |
|---|---|---|---|
| 302 | 10p. Type **61** | 1·75 | 1·75 |
| 303 | 20p. Blenny rockcod ("Toothfish") | 2·25 | 2·25 |
| 304 | 25p. Borch | 2·25 | 2·25 |
| 305 | 50p. Marbled rockcod ("Marbled notothen") | 3·75 | 3·75 |
| 306 | 80p. Bernacchi's rockcod ("Bernach") | 5·50 | 6·50 |

62 Map showing Crustal Microplates of West Antarctica

**1999.** British Antarctic Survey Discoveries. Mult.

| | | | |
|---|---|---|---|
| 307 | 15p. Type **62** | 2·25 | 1·75 |
| 308 | 30p. Testing lead levels in ice | 2·75 | 2·25 |
| 309 | 35p. Decolopodid sea spider (Gigantism in marine invertebrates) (horiz) | 2·75 | 2·25 |
| 310 | 40p. Scientist operating Dobson Spectrophotometer for testing ozone layer (horiz) | 2·75 | 2·50 |
| 311 | 70p. Radar antenna (aurora electric field research) (horiz) | 4·00 | 5·00 |

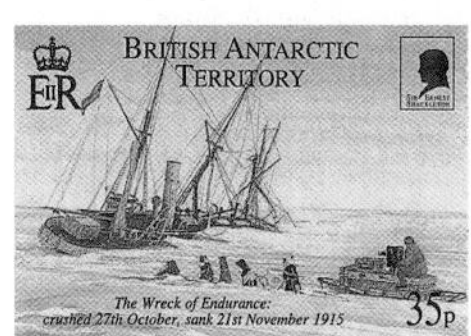


63 Wreck of "Endurance"

**2000.** Shackleton's Trans-Antarctic Expedition, 1914–17, Commemoration. Multicoloured.

| | | | |
|---|---|---|---|
| 312 | 35p. Type **63** | 4·25 | 3·50 |
| 313 | 40p. Ocean Camp on ice | 4·25 | 3·50 |
| 314 | 65p. Launching "James Caird" from Elephant Island | 6·00 | 7·50 |

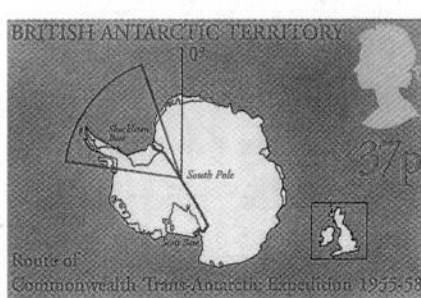


64 Iceberg and Opening Bars

**2000.** Composition of Antarctic Symphony by Sir Peter Maxwell Davies. Multicoloured.

| | | | |
|---|---|---|---|
| 315 | 37p. Type **64** | 2·75 | 3·00 |
| 316 | 37p. Stern of *James Clark Ross* and pack ice | 2·75 | 3·00 |
| 317 | 43p. de Havilland Canada DH-6 Twin Otter and camp on Jones Ice Self | 3·25 | 3·50 |
| 318 | 43p. Frozen sea | 3·25 | 3·50 |

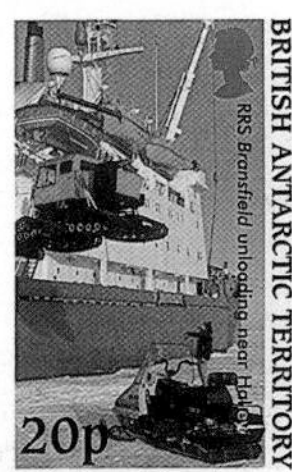


65 Route of Commonwealth Trans-Antarctic Expedition, 1955–58

**2000.** "Heroic Age of Antarctica" (1st series). Commonwealth Trans-Antarctic Expedition, 1955–8. Multicoloured.

| | | | |
|---|---|---|---|
| 319 | 37p. Type **65** | 4·00 | 3·75 |
| 320 | 37p. Expedition at South Pole, 1958 | 4·00 | 3·75 |
| 321 | 37p. *Magga Dan* (Antarctic supply ship) | 4·00 | 3·75 |
| 322 | 37p. "Sno-cat" repair camp | 4·00 | 3·75 |
| 323 | 37p. "Sno-cat" over crevasse | 4·00 | 3·75 |
| 324 | 37p. Seismic explosion | 4·00 | 3·75 |

See also Nos. 333/8 and 351/6.

66 *Bransfield* unloading "Sno-cat", Halley

**2000.** Survey Ships. Multicoloured.

| | | | |
|---|---|---|---|
| 325 | 20p. Type **66** | 2·50 | 2·00 |
| 326 | 33p. *Ernest Shackleton* unloading supplies into *Tula* | 3·75 | 2·50 |
| 327 | 37p. *Bransfield* in the ice (horiz) | 3·50 | 2·50 |
| 328 | 43p. *Ernest Shackleton* with Westland Lynx helicopter (horiz) | 5·00 | 5·00 |

67 Tourists at Port Lockroy

**2001.** Restoration of Port Lockroy Base. Multicoloured.

| | | | |
|---|---|---|---|
| 329 | 33p. Type **67** | 2·50 | 2·00 |
| 330 | 37p. Port Lockroy and cruise ship | 2·50 | 2·00 |
| 331 | 43p. Port Lockroy huts in 1945 | 3·00 | 2·25 |
| 332 | 65p. Interior of Port Lockroy laboratory in 1945 | 5·00 | 6·00 |

68 Map of Ross Sea Area

**2001.** "Heroic Age of Antarctica" (2nd series). Captain Scott's 1901–04 Expedition. Multicoloured.

| | | | |
|---|---|---|---|
| 333 | 33p. Type **68** | 2·25 | 2·25 |
| 334 | 37p. Captain Robert F. Scott | 2·50 | 2·50 |
| 335 | 43p. First Antarctic balloon ascent, 1902 (horiz) | 3·00 | 3·00 |
| 336 | 65p. "Emperor Penguin chick" (drawing by Edward Wilson) | 4·00 | 4·00 |
| 337 | 70p. Shackleton, Scott and Wilson and most southerly camp, 1902 (horiz) | 4·00 | 4·00 |
| 338 | 80p. *Discovery I* trapped in ice off Hut Point (horiz) | 4·50 | 4·50 |

**2002.** Golden Jubilee. As T **200** of Ascension.

| | | | |
|---|---|---|---|
| 339 | 20p. black, mauve and gold | 1·50 | 1·50 |
| 340 | 37p. multicoloured | 1·75 | 1·75 |
| 341 | 43p. black, mauve and gold | 2·00 | 2·00 |
| 342 | 50p multicoloured | 2·50 | 3·25 |
| **MS**343 | 162×95 mm. Nos. 339/42 and 50p. multicoloured | 7·50 | 9·00 |

DESIGNS—HORIZ: 20p. Princess Elizabeth and Princess Margaret making radio broadcast, 1940; 37p. Queen Elizabeth in Garter robes, 1998; 43p. Queen Elizabeth at Balmoral, 1952; 50p. Queen Elizabeth in London, 1996. VERT (38×51 mm)—50p. Queen Elizabeth after Annigoni.

Designs as Nos. 339/42 in No. **MS**343 omit the gold frame around each stamp and the "Golden Jubilee 1952–2002" inscription.

**2002.** Queen Elizabeth the Queen Mother Commemoration. As T **202** of Ascension.

| | | | |
|---|---|---|---|
| 344 | 40p. black, gold and purple | 1·50 | 1·50 |
| 345 | 45p. multicoloured | 1·50 | 1·50 |
| **MS**346 | 145×70 mm. 70p. black and gold; 95p. multicoloured | 7·50 | 7·50 |

DESIGNS: 40p. Lady Elizabeth Bowes-Lyon, 1913; 45p. Queen Mother on her birthday, 1996; 70p. Queen Elizabeth at niece's wedding, London, 1951; 95p. Queen Mother at Cheltenham Races, 1999.

Designs in No. **MS**346 omit the "1900–2002" inscription and the coloured frame.

69 Satellite and Antarctica

**2002.** 20th Anniv of Commission for Conservation of Antarctic Marine Living Resources (CCAMLR). Multicoloured.

| | | | |
|---|---|---|---|
| 347 | 37p. Type **69** | 2·50 | 3·00 |

348 37p. Trawler and wandering albatross 2·50 3·00
349 37p. Icefish, toothfish and crabeater seal 2·50 3·00
350 37p. Krill and phytoplankton 2·50 3·00

**2002.** "Heroic Age of Antarctica" (3rd series). Scottish National Antarctic Expedition, 1902–04. As T **68** but horiz. Multicoloured.
351 30p. Map of Weddell Sea 2·75 2·75
352 40p. Piper Gilbert Kerr and emperor penguin (horiz) 3·50 3·50
353 45p. *Scotia* (expedition ship) 3·50 3·50
354 70p. Weather station and meteorologist (horiz) 4·00 4·25
355 95p. William Speirs Bruce 4·25 4·50
356 £1 Omond House, Laurie Island (horiz) 4·50 4·75

**2003.** 50th Anniv of Coronation. As T **206** of Ascension. Multicoloured.
357 40p. Coronation Coach in procession 2·50 2·00
358 45p. Queen Elizabeth II with Prince Charles on Buckingham Palace balcony 2·50 2·00
**MS**359 95×115 mm. 95p. As 40p.; 95p. As 45p. 8·50 7·50
Nos. 357/8 have scarlet frame; stamps from **MS**359 have no frame and country name in mauve panel.

**2003.** As T **207** of Ascension.
360 £2 multicoloured 6·00 6·00

**70** Blue Whale

**2003.** Endangered Species. Blue Whale. Multicoloured.
361 40p. Type **70** 1·50 1·50
362 45p. Tail fluke 1·50 1·50
363 45p. Two blue whales 1·50 1·50
364 70p. Two blue whales at surface 2·00 2·00

**71** Emperor Penguins

**2003.** Penguins of the Antarctic (1st series). Multicoloured.
365 (–) Type **71** 1·90 1·90
366 (–) Head of macaroni penguin 1·90 1·90
367 (–) Gentoo penguin 1·90 1·90
368 (–) Pair of adelie penguins 1·90 1·90
369 (–) Chinstrap penguin 1·90 1·90
370 (–) Gentoo penguin chick 1·90 1·90
371 (–) Emperor penguins (different) 1·90 1·90
372 (–) Chinstrap penguin chick 1·90 1·90
373 (–) Group of adelie penguins 1·90 1·90
374 (–) Gentoo penguin and chick 1·90 1·90
375 (–) Pair of macaroni penguins 1·90 1·90
376 (–) Emperor penguin chick 1·90 1·90
Nos. 365/76, inscribed "AIRMAIL POSTCARD", were initially sold at 40p.
See also Nos. 424/47 and 474/485.

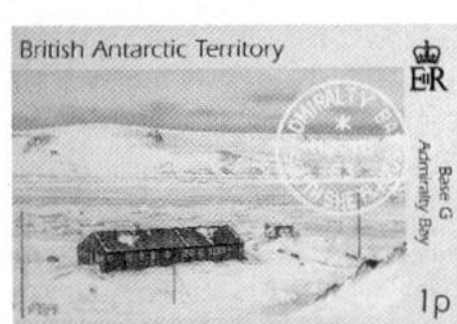

**72** Base G, Admiralty Bay

**2003.** Research Bases and Postmarks. Multicoloured.
377 1p. Type **72** 70 1·00
378 2p. Base B, Deception Island 80 1·00
379 5p. Base D, Hope Bay 1·00 1·50
380 22p. Base F, Argentine Islands 1·75 1·75
381 25p. Base E, Stonington Island 1·75 1·75
382 40p. Base A, Port Lockroy 2·00 2·00
383 45p. Base H, Signy 2·00 2·00
384 50p. Base N, Anvers Island 2·00 2·00
385 95p. Base P, Rothera 4·00 4·00
386 £1 Base T, Adelaide Island 4·25 4·25
387 £3 Base Y, Horseshoe Island 10·00 10·00
388 £5 Base Z, Halley Bay 16·00 16·00

**73** Annual Temperature Trends since 1950

**2004.** Climate Change. Multicoloured.
389 24p. Type **73** 1·50 1·50
390 24p. Larsen ice shelf 1·50 1·50
391 42p. Ice core measurements 2·25 2·25
392 42p. Ice core drilling 2·25 2·25
393 50p. Rise in air temperatures at Faraday Station 3·00 3·00
394 50p. Antarctic pearlwort 3·00 3·00

**74** Pintado ("Cape") Petrel

**2005.** Birdlife International. Petrels. Multicoloured.
395 25p. Type **74** 2·00 85
396 42p. Snow petrel 2·75 1·50
397 75p. Wilson's storm petrel 4·00 3·00
398 £1 Antarctic petrel 4·50 3·25
**MS**399 170×85 mm. 50p.×6 Southern giant petrel and glaciers; Southern giant petrel in flight (from side); Head of Southern giant petrel; Southern giant petrel standing over chick; Southern giant petrel roosting with chick; Southern giant petrel chick 16·00 14·00

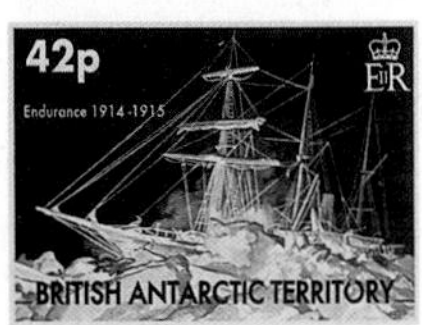

**75** *Endurance* 1914–15 (three masted barque)

**2005.** *Endurance*. Multicoloured.
400 42p. Type **75** 2·50 1·40
401 50p. HMS *Endurance*, 1968–90 (ice patrol and hydrographic survey ship) 3·25 2·00
402 £1 HMS *Endurance*, 1991 (class 1A1 ice-breaker ship) 4·75 4·00

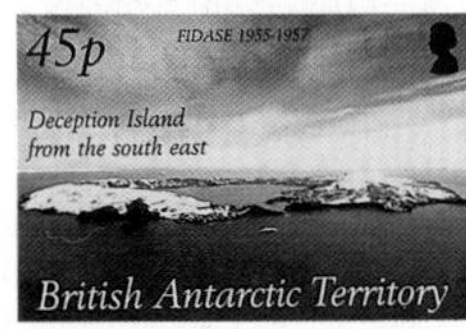

**76** Deception Island from the South East

**2005.** 50th Anniv of FIDASE (Falkland Islands and Dependencies Aerial Survey Expedition, 1955–7). Multicoloured.
403 45p. Type **76** 1·90 1·90
404 55p. Hunting Lodge, Deception Island 2·25 2·25
405 80p. Bell 47D helicopter with perspex bubble and flotation landing gear 4·00 4·00
406 £1 Canso flying boat 4·25 4·25

**77** Samson, Shakespeare and Surley

**2005.** Shackleton Expedition (1914—16) Dogs. Multicoloured.
407 45p. Type **77** 2·50 2·25
408 45p. Tom Crean holding puppies (vert) 2·50 2·25
409 55p. Dogs outside ice kennels and HMS *Endurance* 2·75 2·50
410 £1 Sled dog team training on sea ice and HMS *Endurance* (vert) 5·00 6·00

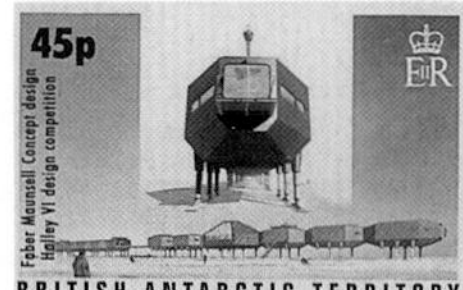

**78** Faber Maunsell's Winning Concept Design

**2005.** Halley VI Research Station International Design Competition. Multicoloured.
411 45p. Type **78** 1·75 1·75
412 45p. Buro Happold concept design 1·75 1·75
413 55p. Hopkins concept design 1·90 1·90
414 80p. Laws building at Halley V Research Station 3·00 3·00

**79** Sea and Icebergs (Erica Currie)

**2006.** ATCM XXIX Edinburgh (Tristan da Cunha) 2006 Stamp Design Competition. Children's Paintings. Multicoloured.
415 45p. Type **79** 1·75 1·75
416 45p. Penguins and icebergs (Meghan Joyce) 1·75 1·75
417 55p. Icebreaker (Lorna MacDonald) 1·90 1·90
418 £1 Penguin wearing Union Jack (Danielle Dalgleish) 3·50 3·50

**2006.** 80th Birthday of Queen Elizabeth II. As T **223** of Ascension. Multicoloured.
419 45p. Princess Elizabeth 2·25 2·00
420 55p. Queen wearing diadem, c. 1952 2·50 2·25
421 80p. Wearing red hat 3·50 3·50
422 £1 In evening dress 3·75 3·75
**MS**423 144×75 mm. Nos. 420/1 5·50 5·50
Stamps from **MS**423 do not have white borders.

**2006.** Penguins of the Antarctic (2nd series). As T **71**. Multicoloured. (a) Ordinary gum.
424 (–) Chinstrap penguin chick 1·75 1·75
425 (–) Head of emperor penguin 1·75 1·75
426 (–) Adelie penguin with wings outstretched 1·75 1·75
427 (–) Head of chinstrap penguin 1·75 1·75
428 (–) Macaroni penguin 1·75 1·75
429 (–) Gentoo penguin feeding chick 1·75 1·75
430 (–) Emperor penguin chick 1·75 1·75
431 (–) Adelie penguin on nest 1·75 1·75
432 (–) Emperor penguin 1·75 1·75
433 (–) Gentoo penguin 1·75 1·75
434 (–) Adelie penguin feeding chick 1·75 1·75
435 (–) Two emperor penguin chicks 1·75 1·75

(b) Self-adhesive. Size 24×29 mm.
436 (–) As No. 424 1·75 2·00
437 (–) As No. 425 1·75 2·00
438 (–) As No. 426 1·75 2·00
439 (–) As No. 430 1·75 2·00
440 (–) As No. 431 1·75 2·00
441 (–) As No. 432 1·75 2·00
442 (–) As No. 427 1·75 2·00
443 (–) As No. 428 1·75 2·00
444 (–) As No. 429 1·75 2·00
445 (–) As No. 433 1·75 2·00
446 (–) As No. 434 1·75 2·00
447 (–) As No. 435 1·75 2·00
Nos. 424/47 are inscribed "AIRMAIL POSTCARD" and were sold at 50p. each.

**80** Elephant Seals

**2006.** Seals. Multicoloured.
448 25p. Type **80** 1·25 1·25
449 50p. Crabeater seals 1·75 1·75
450 60p. Weddell seals 2·25 2·50
451 £1.05 Leopard seal 3·25 4·00

**81** *Marseniopsis molle* (sea lemon)

**2007.** Marine Invertebrates. Multicoloured.
452 25p. Type **81** 1·25 1·25
453 50p. *Isotealia antarctica* (Antarctic sea anemone) 2·00 2·00
454 60p. *Decolopoda australis* (sea spider) 2·50 2·50
455 £1.05 *Odontaster validus* (sea star) 4·50 5·00

**82** Pinnacle Iceberg

**2007.** Icebergs. Multicoloured.
456 25p. Type **82** 1·25 1·25
457 50p. Pinnacle and tabular icebergs and ice floes at sunset 2·00 2·00
458 60p. Wedge iceberg 2·50 2·50
459 £1.05 Tabular iceberg and ice floes 4·50 5·00

**83** Aerial View of Antarctica

**2007.** International Polar Year 2007–2008. Circular sheet 97×97 mm.
**MS**460 £2 multicoloured 6·50 7·50

**84** James Weddell, *Jane* and *Beaufoy*

**2008.** Explorers and Ships. Multicoloured.
461 1p. Type **84** 20 30
462 2p. Sir James Clark Ross, *Erebus* and *Terror* 35 40
463 5p. Neil Alison Mackintosh and *Discovery II* 55 65
464 27p. Sir Douglas Mawson and *Discovery* 1·25 1·00
465 55p. Captain James Cook and *Resolution* 2·50 2·00
466 65p. Carsten Egeberg Borchgrevink and *Southern Cross* 2·50 2·50
467 65p. Dr. William Speirs Bruce and *Scotia* 2·50 2·50
468 65p. Captain Robert Falcon Scott and *Discovery* 2·50 2·50
469 65p. Sir Ernest Shackleton and *Endurance* 2·50 2·50
470 £1.10 John Riddoch Rymill and *Penola* 4·25 4·50
471 £2.50 Captain Victor Marchesi and *William Scoresby* 8·25 8·50
472 £5 Sir Vivian Fuchs and *Magga Dan* 16·00 16·00
**MS**473 110×80 mm. As Nos. 466/9 but inscr 'AIRMAIL LETTER' 9·00 9·00
No. **MS**473 was sold for £2.60.

**2008.** Penguins of the Antarctic (3rd series). As T **71**. Multicoloured.
474 (–) Head of chinstrap penguin 2·25 2·25
475 (–) Gentoo penguin and two chicks 2·25 2·25
476 (–) Head of macaroni penguin, calling with beak open 2·25 2·25
477 (–) Chinstrap penguin, calling, with beak open and wings and tail raised 2·25 2·25
478 (–) Two emperor penguins 2·25 2·25
479 (–) Adelie penguin 2·25 2·25
480 (–) Chinstrap penguin, walking with wings outstretched 2·25 2·25
481 (–) Head of gentoo penguin, calling with beak open 2·25 2·25
482 (–) Macaroni penguin 2·25 2·25

| | | | |
|---|---|---|---|
| 483 | (–) Emperor penguin with chick | 2·25 | 2·25 |
| 484 | (–) Two adelie penguins | 2·25 | 2·25 |
| 485 | (–) Emperor penguin chick | 2·25 | 2·25 |

Nos. 474/85, inscribed 'AIRMAIL POSTCARD' and were sold at 55p. each.

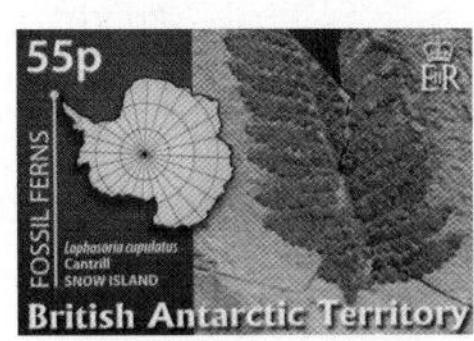


**85** *Lophosoria cupulatus*, Snow Island

**2008.** Fossil Ferns. Designs showing map of Antarctica and fossil ferns. Multicoloured.

| | | | |
|---|---|---|---|
| 486 | 55p. Type **85** | 2·00 | 1·75 |
| 487 | 65p. cf. *Cladophlebis oblonga*, Alexander Island | 2·50 | 2·00 |
| 488 | £1.10 *Pachypteris indica*, Snow Island | 4·25 | 4·50 |
| 489 | £1.10 *Aculea acicularis*, Alexander Island | 4·25 | 4·50 |

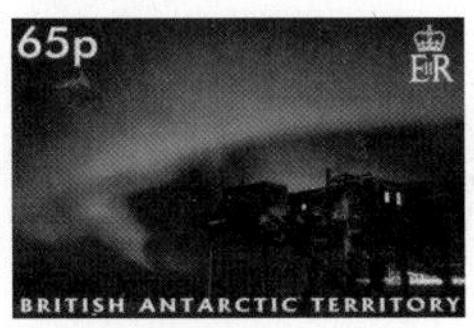


**86** Aurora Australis

**2008.** Aurora Australis. Multicoloured.

| | | | |
|---|---|---|---|
| 490 | 65p. Type **86** | 2·50 | 2·50 |
| 491 | 65p. Blue aurora | 2·50 | 2·50 |
| 492 | 65p. Red aurora | 2·50 | 2·50 |
| 493 | 65p. Turquoise-blue aurora | 2·50 | 2·50 |
| 494 | 65p. Green and white aurora | 2·50 | 2·50 |

**87** Fairey Seafox

**2009.** Centenary of Naval Aviation. Multicoloured.

| | | | |
|---|---|---|---|
| 495 | 10p. Type **87** | 60 | 70 |
| 496 | 10p. Westland Lynx helicopter | 60 | 70 |
| 497 | 90p. Supermarine Walrus | 4·00 | 4·25 |
| 498 | 90p. Westland Wasp helicopter | 4·00 | 4·25 |
| **MS**499 | 110×70 mm. £2 HMA No. 1 *Mayfly* (airship) | 7·50 | 8·00 |

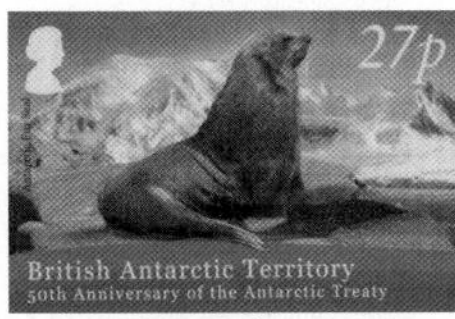


**88** Antarctic Fur Seal

**2009.** 50th Anniv of the Antarctic Treaty. Multicoloured.

| | | | |
|---|---|---|---|
| 500 | 27p. Type **88** | 1·10 | 1·25 |
| 501 | 27p. Humpback whale | 1·10 | 1·25 |
| 502 | 55p. Southern giant petrel | 2·00 | 1·75 |
| 503 | 55p. Gentoo penguin | 2·00 | 1·75 |
| 504 | 65p. Giant squid | 2·50 | 2·00 |
| 505 | 65p. Jellyfish | 2·50 | 2·00 |

Nos. 500/1, 502/3 and 504/5 were each printed together, se-tenant, each pair forming a composite background design.

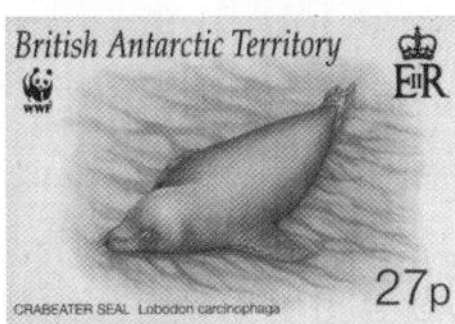


**89** Crabeater Seal

**2009.** Endangered Species. Crabeater Seal (Lobodon carcinophaga). Multicoloured.

| | | | |
|---|---|---|---|
| 506 | 27p. Type **89** | 1·25 | 1·00 |
| 507 | 65p. Crabeater seal (close-up of head) | 2·50 | 2·00 |
| 508 | £1.10 Two crabeater seals | 4·25 | 4·50 |
| 509 | £1.50 Crabeater seal (swimming to right) | 6·00 | 6·25 |

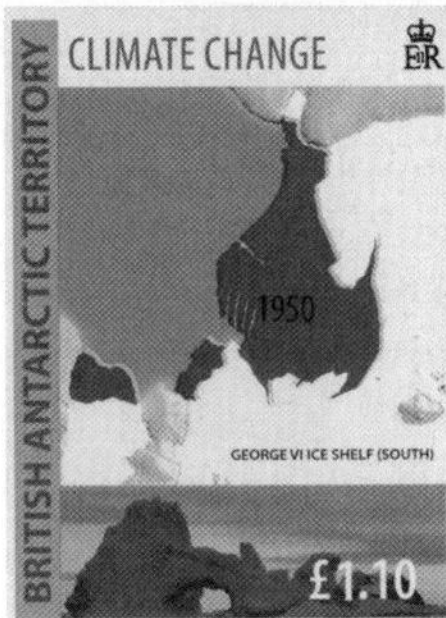


**90** George VI Ice Shelf (South)

**2009.** Climate Change. Sheet 165×130 mm containing T **90** and similar vert designs showing the extent of Antarctic ice shelves in 1950 and today. Multicoloured.

| | | | |
|---|---|---|---|
| **MS**510 | Type **90**; Larsen B Ice Shelf; Wilkins Ice Shelf; Larsen C Ice Shelf | 18·00 | 18·00 |

**91** Button Worm

**2010.** Marine Biodiversity

| | | | |
|---|---|---|---|
| 511 | 27p. Type **91** | 90 | 90 |
| 512 | 27p. Amphipod | 90 | 90 |
| 513 | 27p. Polychaete worm | 90 | 90 |
| 514 | 27p. Sponge | 90 | 90 |
| **MS**515 | 140×95 mm. £1.15×4 Solitary coral; Amphipod (different); Comb jelly; Basket star (all 36×36 mm) | 14·00 | 14·00 |

**92** *Terra Nova* on the Horizon

**2010.** Centenary of the British Antarctic Expedition (1910–13). Each black and grey.

| | | | |
|---|---|---|---|
| 516 | 27p. Type **92** | 90 | 90 |
| 517 | 27p. Expedition ponies | 90 | 90 |
| 518 | 27p. Cavern in the iceberg | 90 | 90 |
| 519 | 27p. The 'Tenements' bunks in Winterquarters Hut | 90 | 90 |
| 520 | 27p. Captain Scott's birthday dinner | 90 | 90 |
| 521 | 27p. Observing at the weather station | 90 | 90 |
| 522 | 27p. Captain Scott writing in his journal | 90 | 90 |
| 523 | 27p. *Terra Nova* in the ice | 90 | 90 |
| 524 | 60p. *Terra Nova* in harbour | 1·40 | 1·40 |
| 525 | 60p. Lieut. Rennick leading pony | 1·40 | 1·40 |
| 526 | 60p. The Matterhorn Berg | 1·40 | 1·40 |
| 527 | 60p. Nelson at work in the lab | 1·40 | 1·40 |
| 528 | 60p. Captain Scott on skis | 1·40 | 1·40 |
| 529 | 60p. Chris (dog) and the gramophone | 1·40 | 1·40 |
| 530 | 60p. Motor and load passing Inaccessible Island | 1·40 | 1·40 |
| 531 | 60p. The polar party at the South Pole | 1·40 | 1·40 |

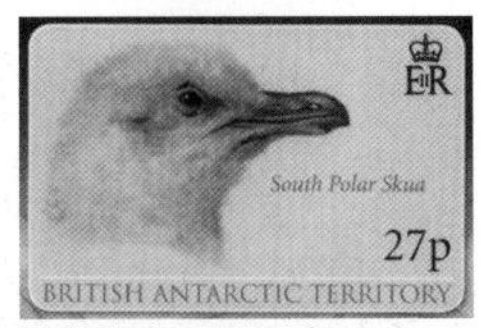


**93** South Polar Skua

**2010.** Antarctic Birds. Multicoloured.

| | | | |
|---|---|---|---|
| 532 | 27p. Type **93** | 90 | 90 |
| 533 | 27p. Adélie penguin | 90 | 90 |
| 533 | 70p. Grey-headed albatross | 2·10 | 2·10 |
| 535 | 70p. Emperor penguin | 2·10 | 2·10 |
| 536 | £1.15 Kelp gull | 4·00 | 4·00 |
| 537 | £1.15 Antarctic petrel | 4·00 | 4·00 |

Pt. 1

# BRITISH COLUMBIA AND VANCOUVER ISLAND

Former British colonies, now a Western province of the Dominion of Canada, whose stamps are now used.

1860. 12 pence = 1 shilling; 20 shillings = 1 pound.
1865. 100 cents = 1 dollar.

**1**

**1860.** Imperf or perf.

| | | | | |
|---|---|---|---|---|
| 2 | **1** | 2½d. pink | £425 | £200 |

## VANCOUVER ISLAND

**2**

**1865.** Imperf or perf. Various frames.

| | | | | |
|---|---|---|---|---|
| 13 | **2** | 5c. red | £350 | £190 |
| 14 | - | 10c. blue | £250 | £160 |

## BRITISH COLUMBIA

**4** Emblems of United Kingdom

**1865**

| | | | | |
|---|---|---|---|---|
| 22 | **4** | 3d. blue | £100 | 80·00 |

**1868.** Surch in words or figures and words.

| | | | |
|---|---|---|---|
| 28 | 2c. brown | £170 | £140 |
| 29 | 5c. red | £225 | £160 |
| 24 | 10c. red | £900 | £700 |
| 31 | 25c. yellow | £250 | £160 |
| 26 | 50c. mauve | £800 | £700 |
| 27 | $1 green | £1300 | £1400 |

Pt. 1

# BRITISH COMMONWEALTH OCCUPATION OF JAPAN

Stamps used by British Commonwealth Occupation Forces, 1946–49.

12 pence = 1 shilling; 20 shillings = 1 pound.

**1946.** Stamps of Australia optd **B.C.O.F. JAPAN 1946.**

| | | | | |
|---|---|---|---|---|
| J1 | **27** | ½d. orange | 6·00 | 10·00 |
| J2 | **46** | 1d. purple | 5·00 | 6·00 |
| J3 | **31** | 3d. brown | 2·75 | 4·25 |
| J4 | - | 6d. brown (No. 189a) | 24·00 | 19·00 |
| J5 | - | 1s. green (No. 191) | 18·00 | 21·00 |
| J6 | **1** | 2s. red | 45·00 | 60·00 |
| J7a | **38** | 5s. red | 95·00 | £150 |

Pt. 1

# BRITISH EAST AFRICA

Now incorporated in Kenya and Uganda.

16 annas = 100 cents = 1 rupee.

**1890.** Stamps of Great Britain (1881) surch **BRITISH EAST AFRICA COMPANY** and value in annas.

| | | | | |
|---|---|---|---|---|
| 1 | **57** | ½a. on 1d. lilac | £275 | £200 |
| 2 | **73** | 1a. on 2d. green and red | £475 | £275 |
| 3 | **78** | 4a. on 5d. purple and blue | £500 | £300 |

**3** Arms of the Company

**1890.** Nos. 16/19 are larger (24×25 mm).

| | | | | |
|---|---|---|---|---|
| 4b | **3** | ½a. brown | 70 | 8·00 |
| 5 | **3** | 1a. green | 7·50 | 11·00 |
| 6 | **3** | 2a. red | 4·00 | 4·75 |
| 7c | **3** | 2½a. black on yellow | 4·75 | 5·50 |
| 8a | **3** | 3a. black on red | 2·25 | 11·00 |
| 9 | **3** | 4a. brown | 2·50 | 10·00 |
| 11a | **3** | 4½a. purple | 2·50 | 17·00 |
| 29 | **3** | 5a. black on blue | 1·25 | 10·00 |
| 30 | **3** | 7½a. black | 1·25 | 16·00 |
| 12 | **3** | 8a. blue | 5·50 | 9·50 |
| 13 | **3** | 8a. grey | £275 | £225 |
| 14 | **3** | 1r. red | 6·00 | 9·00 |
| 15 | **3** | 1r. grey | £225 | £225 |
| 16 | - | 2r. red | 14·00 | 42·00 |
| 17 | - | 3r. purple | 11·00 | 50·00 |
| 18 | - | 4r. blue | 12·00 | 50·00 |
| 19 | - | 5r. green | 30·00 | 70·00 |

**1891.** With handstamped or pen surcharges. Initialled in black.

| | | | |
|---|---|---|---|
| 20 | ½a. on 2a. red | £8500 | £850 |
| 31 | ½a. on 3a. black on red | £425 | 50·00 |
| 32 | 1a. on 3a. black on red | £6500 | £3500 |
| 26 | 1a. on 4a. brown | £7500 | £1500 |

**1894.** Surch in words and figures.

| | | | |
|---|---|---|---|
| 27 | 5a. on 8a. blue | 70·00 | 85·00 |
| 28 | 7½a. on 1r. red | 70·00 | 85·00 |

**1895.** Optd **BRITISH EAST AFRICA.**

| | | | | |
|---|---|---|---|---|
| 33 | | ½a. brown | 80·00 | 29·00 |
| 34 | | 1a. green | £190 | £120 |
| 35 | | 2a. red | £190 | £100 |
| 36 | | 2½a. black on yellow | £200 | 60·00 |
| 37 | | 3a. black on red | 90·00 | 55·00 |
| 38 | | 4a. brown | 60·00 | 40·00 |
| 39 | | 4½a. purple | £200 | £100 |
| 40 | | 5a. black on blue | £275 | £150 |
| 41 | | 7½a. black | £140 | 85·00 |
| 42 | | 8a. blue | £100 | 80·00 |
| 43 | | 1r. red | 65·00 | 55·00 |
| 44 | - | 2r. red | £450 | £275 |
| 45 | - | 3r. purple | £225 | £140 |
| 46 | - | 4r. blue | £200 | £170 |
| 47 | - | 5r. green | £425 | £275 |

**1895.** Surch with large 2½.

| | | | | |
|---|---|---|---|---|
| 48 | **3** | 2½a. on 4½a. purple | £190 | 80·00 |

**1895.** Stamps of India (Queen Victoria) optd **British East Africa.**

| | | | | |
|---|---|---|---|---|
| 49 | **23** | ½a. turquoise | 7·00 | 5·50 |
| 50 | - | 1a. purple | 6·50 | 6·00 |
| 51 | - | 1½a. brown | 4·25 | 4·00 |
| 52 | - | 2a. blue | 8·00 | 3·00 |
| 53 | - | 2a.6p. green | 11·00 | 2·50 |
| 54 | - | 3a. orange | 18·00 | 11·00 |
| 55a | - | 4a. green (No. 96) | 28·00 | 24·00 |
| 56 | - | 6a. brown (No. 80) | 48·00 | 50·00 |
| 57c | - | 8a. mauve | 30·00 | 55·00 |
| 58 | - | 12a. purple on red | 22·00 | 35·00 |
| 59 | - | 1r. grey (No. 101) | £100 | 65·00 |
| 60 | **37** | 1r. green and red | 45·00 | £130 |
| 61 | **38** | 2r. red and orange | £110 | £170 |
| 62 | **38** | 3r. brown and green | £130 | £180 |
| 63 | **38** | 5r. blue and violet | £140 | £180 |

**1895.** No. 51 surch with small 2½.

| | | | |
|---|---|---|---|
| 64 | 2½ on 1½a. brown | £110 | 50·00 |

**11**

**1896**

| | | | | |
|---|---|---|---|---|
| 65 | **11** | ½a. green | 4·75 | 80 |
| 66 | **11** | 1a. red | 12·00 | 40 |
| 67 | **11** | 2a. brown | 9·50 | 6·50 |
| 68 | **11** | 2½a. blue | 15·00 | 1·75 |
| 69 | **11** | 3a. grey | 8·00 | 11·00 |
| 70 | **11** | 4a. green | 8·00 | 3·75 |
| 71 | **11** | 4½a. yellow | 14·00 | 16·00 |
| 72 | **11** | 5a. brown | 8·00 | 6·50 |
| 73 | **11** | 7½a. mauve | 8·50 | 22·00 |
| 74 | **11** | 8a. grey | 9·00 | 6·50 |
| 75 | **11** | 1r. blue | 70·00 | 25·00 |
| 76 | **11** | 2r. orange | 65·00 | 29·00 |
| 77 | **11** | 3r. violet | 65·00 | 32·00 |
| 78 | **11** | 4r. red | 60·00 | 75·00 |
| 79 | **11** | 5r. brown | 55·00 | 42·00 |

**1897.** Stamps of Zanzibar, 1896, optd **British East Africa.**

| | | | | |
|---|---|---|---|---|
| 80 | **13** | ½a. green and red | 60·00 | 50·00 |
| 81 | **13** | 1a. blue and red | £100 | 95·00 |
| 82 | **13** | 2a. brown and red | 42·00 | 21·00 |
| 83 | **13** | 4½a. orange and red | 60·00 | 30·00 |
| 84 | **13** | 5a. brown and red | 65·00 | 40·00 |
| 85 | **13** | 7½a. mauve and red | 60·00 | 42·00 |

**1897.** As last, surch 2½.

| | | | |
|---|---|---|---|
| 86 | 2½ on 1a. blue and red | £120 | 65·00 |

| | | | | |
|---|---|---|---|---|
| 89 | | 2½ on 3a. grey and red | £120 | 60·00 |

**1897.** As Type **11**, but larger.

| | | | | |
|---|---|---|---|---|
| 92a | | 1r. blue | 95·00 | 48·00 |
| 93 | | 2r. orange | £120 | £120 |
| 94 | | 3r. violet | £160 | £170 |
| 95 | | 4r. red | £450 | £550 |
| 96 | | 5r. brown | £400 | £475 |
| 97 | | 10r. brown | £400 | £500 |
| 98 | | 20r. green | £850 | £1900 |
| 99 | | 50r. mauve | £1800 | |

Pt. 1

# BRITISH FORCES IN EGYPT

SPECIAL SEALS AND STAMPS FOR THE USE OF BRITISH FORCES IN EGYPT

### A. SEALS

A1

**1932.** (a) Inscr "POSTAL SEAL".

| | | | | |
|---|---|---|---|---|
| A1 | **A1** | 1p. blue and red | 95·00 | 4·00 |

(b) Inscr "LETTER SEAL".

| | | | | |
|---|---|---|---|---|
| A2 | | 1p. blue and red | 42·00 | 85 |

A2

**1932.** Christmas Seals.

| | | | | |
|---|---|---|---|---|
| A3 | **A2** | 3m. black on blue | 50·00 | 70·00 |
| A4 | **A2** | 3m. lake | 7·50 | 50·00 |
| A5 | **A2** | 3m. blue | 7·00 | 29·00 |
| A6a | **A2** | 3m. red | 9·50 | 27·00 |

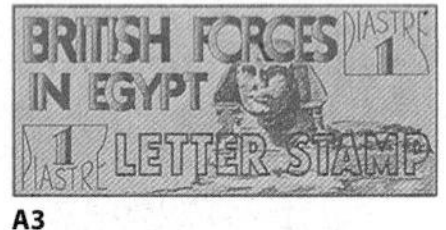

A3

**1934**

| | | | | |
|---|---|---|---|---|
| A8 | **A3** | 1p. green | 4·50 | 4·50 |
| A9 | **A3** | 1p. red | 3·50 | 3·50 |

**1935.** Silver Jubilee. Optd JUBILEE COMMEMORATION 1935.

| | | | | |
|---|---|---|---|---|
| A10 | | 1p. blue | £250 | £180 |

**1935.** Provisional Christmas Seal. Surch Xmas 1935 3 Milliemes.

| | | | | |
|---|---|---|---|---|
| A11 | | 3m. on 1p. red | 16·00 | 70·00 |

### B. POSTAGE STAMPS

**A6** King Fuad 1

**1936**

| | | | | |
|---|---|---|---|---|
| A12 | **A6** | 3m. green | 1·00 | 2·00 |
| A13 | **A6** | 10m. red | 6·50 | 10 |

**A7** King Farouk

**1939**

| | | | | |
|---|---|---|---|---|
| A14 | **A7** | 3m. green | 5·00 | 8·00 |
| A15 | **A7** | 10m. red | 7·00 | 10 |

Pt. 1

# BRITISH GUIANA

Situated on the N.E. coast of S. America. A British colony granted full internal self-government in August 1951. Attained independence on 26 May 1966, when the country was renamed Guyana.

100 cents = 1 dollar.

1

**1850.** Imperf.

| | | | | |
|---|---|---|---|---|
| 1 | **1** | 2c. black on red | | £200000 |
| 2 | **1** | 4c. black on orange | £55000 | £9500 |
| 4 | **1** | 8c. black on green | £38000 | £8500 |
| 5 | **1** | 12c. black on blue | £16000 | £6000 |

Prices are for used stamps cut round. Stamps cut square are worth much more.

2

**1852.** Imperf.

| | | | | |
|---|---|---|---|---|
| 9 | **2** | 1c. black on magenta | £9000 | £4250 |
| 10 | **2** | 4c. black on blue | £16000 | £9000 |

**3** Seal of the Colony

**1853.** Imperf.

| | | | | |
|---|---|---|---|---|
| 12 | **3** | 1c. red | £4250 | £1500 |
| 20 | **3** | 4c. blue | £1400 | £500 |

6

**1856.** Imperf.

| | | | | |
|---|---|---|---|---|
| 23 | **6** | 1c. black on magenta | † | |
| 24 | **6** | 4c. black on magenta | | £10000 |
| 25 | **6** | 4c. black on blue | £35000 | £15000 |

7

9

**1860.** Perf.

| | | | | |
|---|---|---|---|---|
| 29 | **7** | 1c. pink | £2750 | £250 |
| 40 | **7** | 1c. brown | £400 | £100 |
| 85 | **7** | 1c. black | 18·00 | 8·00 |
| 87 | **7** | 2c. orange | 48·00 | 4·75 |
| 89 | **7** | 4c. blue | £120 | 13·00 |
| 92 | **9** | 6c. blue | £170 | 35·00 |
| 95 | **7** | 8c. red | £225 | 32·00 |
| 98 | **7** | 12c. lilac | £225 | 22·00 |
| 99 | **7** | 12c. grey | £225 | 24·00 |
| 64 | **7** | 24c. green | £325 | 50·00 |
| 79 | **9** | 24c. green | £200 | 13·00 |
| 82 | **9** | 48c. red | £325 | 65·00 |

The prices quoted for Nos. 29/82 are for fine copies with four margins. Medium specimens can be supplied at much lower rates.

10

**1862.** Various borders. Roul.

| | | | | |
|---|---|---|---|---|
| 116 | **10** | 1c. black on red | £4500 | £750 |
| 119 | **10** | 2c. black on yellow | £4500 | £400 |
| 122 | **10** | 4c. black on blue | £4750 | £850 |

The above prices are for stamps signed in the centre by the Postmaster. Unsigned stamps are worth considerably less.

16

**1876**

| | | | | |
|---|---|---|---|---|
| 126 | **16** | 1c. grey | 2·75 | 1·40 |
| 171 | **16** | 2c. orange | 40·00 | 15 |
| 172 | **16** | 4c. blue | 95·00 | 5·00 |
| 173 | **16** | 6c. brown | 5·00 | 6·50 |
| 174 | **16** | 8c. red | £100 | 40 |
| 131 | **16** | 12c. violet | 65·00 | 1·75 |
| 132 | **16** | 24c. green | 70·00 | 3·25 |
| 133 | **16** | 48c. brown | £140 | 40·00 |
| 134 | **16** | 96c. olive | £475 | £250 |

**1878.** Optd with thick horiz or horiz and vert bars. (a) On postage stamps.

| | | | | |
|---|---|---|---|---|
| 137 | | 1c. on 6c. brown | 42·00 | £120 |
| 141 | **9** | 1c. on 6c. blue | £190 | 75·00 |

(b) On official stamps of 1875 and 1877.

| | | | | |
|---|---|---|---|---|
| 138 | **7** | 1c. black | £250 | 75·00 |
| 139 | **16** | 1c. grey | £200 | 70·00 |
| 140 | **16** | 2c. orange | £375 | 65·00 |
| 144 | **16** | 4c. blue | £350 | £110 |
| 145 | **16** | 6c. brown | £500 | £110 |
| 146 | **7** | 8c. red | £3750 | £325 |
| 148 | **16** | 8c. red | £475 | £120 |

**1881.** Surch with figure. Old value barred out in ink. (a) On postage stamps.

| | | | | |
|---|---|---|---|---|
| 152 | **9** | "1" on 48c. red | 45·00 | 5·00 |
| 149 | | "1" on 96c. olive | 4·00 | 8·00 |
| 150 | | "2" on 96c. olive | 11·00 | 15·00 |

(b) On stamps optd **OFFICIAL**.

| | | | | |
|---|---|---|---|---|
| 153 | **7** | "1" on 12c. lilac | £130 | 70·00 |
| 154 | **16** | "1" on 48c. brown | £180 | £120 |
| 155 | **16** | "2" on 12c. violet | 80·00 | 45·00 |
| 157 | **16** | "2" on 24c. green | 90·00 | 50·00 |

26

**1882**

| | | | | |
|---|---|---|---|---|
| 162 | **26** | 1c. black on red | 60·00 | 30·00 |
| 165 | **26** | 2c. black on yellow | 80·00 | 50·00 |

Each stamp is perforated with the word "SPECIMEN".

**1888.** T **16** without value in bottom tablet, surch **INLAND REVENUE** and value.

| | | | | |
|---|---|---|---|---|
| 175 | **16** | 1c. purple | 2·50 | 20 |
| 176 | **16** | 2c. purple | 1·75 | 1·75 |
| 177 | **16** | 3c. purple | 1·25 | 20 |
| 178 | **16** | 4c. purple | 11·00 | 30 |
| 179 | **16** | 6c. purple | 11·00 | 4·00 |
| 180 | **16** | 8c. purple | 1·50 | 30 |
| 181 | **16** | 10c. purple | 6·00 | 2·50 |
| 182 | **16** | 20c. purple | 21·00 | 19·00 |
| 183 | **16** | 40c. purple | 29·00 | 28·00 |
| 184 | **16** | 72c. purple | 65·00 | 65·00 |
| 185 | **16** | $1 green | £450 | £550 |
| 186 | **16** | $2 green | £225 | £250 |
| 187 | **16** | $3 green | £225 | £250 |
| 188 | **16** | $4 green | £500 | £650 |
| 189 | **16** | $5 green | £325 | £350 |

**1889.** No. 176 surch with additional **2**.

| | | | | |
|---|---|---|---|---|
| 192 | | "2" on 2c. purple | 4·25 | 15 |

30

**1889**

| | | | | |
|---|---|---|---|---|
| 193 | **30** | 1c. purple and grey | 6·00 | 2·75 |
| 213 | **30** | 1c. green | 75 | 10 |
| 194 | **30** | 2c. purple and orange | 4·00 | 10 |
| 234 | **30** | 2c. purple and red | 3·25 | 30 |
| 241a | **30** | 2c. purple & black on red | 4·00 | 10 |
| 253a | **30** | 2c. red | 8·50 | 10 |
| 195 | **30** | 4c. purple and blue | 4·50 | 3·50 |
| 254 | **30** | 4c. brown and purple | 2·50 | 1·25 |
| 214 | **30** | 5c. blue | 3·25 | 10 |
| 243a | **30** | 5c. purple & blue on blue | 3·50 | 6·50 |
| 198 | **30** | 6c. purple and brown | 7·00 | 19·00 |
| 236 | **30** | 6c. black and blue | 7·00 | 11·00 |
| 256 | **30** | 6c. grey and black | 13·00 | 7·00 |
| 199 | **30** | 8c. purple and red | 13·00 | 3·25 |
| 215 | **30** | 8c. purple and black | 5·00 | 1·50 |
| 200a | **30** | 12c. purple and mauve | 8·50 | 3·50 |
| 257 | **30** | 12c. orange and purple | 4·00 | 5·50 |
| 246a | **30** | 24c. purple and green | 3·75 | 4·50 |
| 202 | **30** | 48c. purple and red | 25·00 | 10·00 |
| 247a | **30** | 48c. grey and brown | 14·00 | 23·00 |
| 248a | **30** | 60c. green and red | 14·00 | 95·00 |
| 203 | **30** | 72c. purple and brown | 28·00 | 48·00 |
| 205 | **30** | 96c. purple and red | 65·00 | 70·00 |
| 250 | **30** | 96c. black & red on yellow | 35·00 | 45·00 |

**1890.** Nos. 185/8 surch **ONE CENT**.

| | | | | |
|---|---|---|---|---|
| 207 | **16** | 1 cent on $1 green | 2·00 | 35 |
| 208 | **16** | 1 cent on $2 green | 2·00 | 60 |
| 209 | **16** | 1 cent on $3 green | 2·25 | 1·25 |
| 210 | **16** | 1 cent on $4 green | 4·00 | 9·00 |

**32** Mount Roraima

**33** Kaieteur Falls

**1898.** Jubilee.

| | | | | |
|---|---|---|---|---|
| 216 | **32** | 1c. black and red | 7·50 | 2·25 |
| 217 | **33** | 2c. brown and blue | 29·00 | 4·25 |
| 219w | **32** | 5c. green and brown | 45·00 | 5·00 |
| 220 | **33** | 10c. black and red | 25·00 | 25·00 |
| 221 | **32** | 15c. brown and blue | 30·00 | 22·00 |

**1899.** Nos. 219/21 surch **TWO CENTS**.

| | | | | |
|---|---|---|---|---|
| 222 | | 2c. on 5c. green and brown | 3·25 | 2·75 |
| 223 | **33** | 2c. on 10c. black and red | 3·25 | 2·25 |
| 224 | **32** | 2c. on 15c. brown and blue | 3·00 | 1·25 |

**1905.** T **30** but inscr "REVENUE", optd **POSTAGE AND REVENUE**.

| | | | | |
|---|---|---|---|---|
| 251 | **30** | $2.40 green and violet | £180 | £400 |

37

**1913**

| | | | | |
|---|---|---|---|---|
| 259a | **37** | 1c. green | 1·75 | 25 |
| 260 | **37** | 2c. red | 1·50 | 10 |
| 274 | **37** | 2c. violet | 2·50 | 10 |
| 261b | **37** | 4c. brown and purple | 3·75 | 25 |
| 262 | **37** | 5c. blue | 1·75 | 1·00 |
| 263 | **37** | 6c. grey and black | 3·00 | 1·75 |
| 276 | **37** | 6c. blue | 3·00 | 30 |
| 264 | **37** | 12c. orange and violet | 1·25 | 1·00 |
| 278 | **37** | 24c. purple and green | 2·00 | 4·50 |
| 279 | **37** | 48c. grey and purple | 9·50 | 3·50 |
| 280 | **37** | 60c. green and red | 10·00 | 48·00 |
| 281 | **37** | 72c. purple and brown | 30·00 | 75·00 |
| 269a | **37** | 96c. black and red on yellow | 25·00 | 48·00 |

**1918.** Optd **WAR TAX**.

| | | | | |
|---|---|---|---|---|
| 271 | | 2c. red | 1·50 | 15 |

**39** Ploughing a Rice Field

**40** Indian shooting Fish

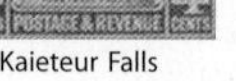

**41** Kaieteur Falls

**42** Public Buildings, Georgetown

**1931.** Centenary of County Union.

| | | | | |
|---|---|---|---|---|
| 283 | **39** | 1c. green | 2·50 | 1·25 |
| 284 | **40** | 2c. brown | 2·00 | 10 |
| 285 | **41** | 4c. red | 2·25 | 45 |
| 286 | **42** | 6c. blue | 2·25 | 1·75 |
| 287 | **41** | $1 violet | 45·00 | 55·00 |

**43** Ploughing a Rice Field

**44** Gold Mining

**1934**

| | | | | |
|---|---|---|---|---|
| 288 | **43** | 1c. green | 60 | 1·75 |
| 289 | **40** | 2c. brown | 1·50 | 1·50 |
| 290 | **44** | 3c. red | 30 | 10 |
| 291 | **41** | 4c. violet | 2·00 | 3·25 |
| 292 | - | 6c. blue | 4·25 | 6·50 |
| 293 | - | 12c. orange | 20 | 20 |
| 294 | - | 24c. purple | 3·50 | 10·00 |
| 295 | - | 48c. black | 8·00 | 8·50 |
| 296 | **41** | 50c. green | 11·00 | 19·00 |
| 297 | - | 60c. brown | 26·00 | 27·00 |
| 298 | - | 72c. purple | 1·25 | 2·25 |
| 299 | - | 96c. black | 27·00 | 32·00 |
| 300 | - | $1 violet | 40·00 | 40·00 |

DESIGNS—HORIZ: 6c. Shooting logs over falls; 12c. Stabroek Market; 24c. Sugar canes in punts; 48c. Forest road; 60c. Victoria Regia lilies; 72c. Mount Roraima; $1 Botanical Gardens. VERT: 96c. Sir Walter Raleigh and his son.

The 2c., 4c. and 50c. are without the dates shown in Types **40/44** and the 12, 48, 72 and 96c. have no portrait.

**1935.** Silver Jubilee. As T **13** of Antigua.

| | | | |
|---|---|---|---|
| 301 | 2c. blue and grey | 30 | 20 |
| 302 | 6c. brown and blue | 2·00 | 4·50 |
| 303 | 12c. green and blue | 7·50 | 8·50 |
| 304 | 24c. grey and purple | 12·00 | 14·00 |

**1937.** Coronation. As T **2** of Aden.

| | | | |
|---|---|---|---|
| 305 | 2c. brown | 15 | 10 |
| 306 | 4c. grey | 50 | 40 |
| 307 | 6c. blue | 60 | 1·75 |

**53** South America

**1938.** Designs as for same values of 1934 issue (except where indicated) but with portrait of King George VI (as in T **53**) where portrait of King George V previously appeared.

| | | | | |
|---|---|---|---|---|
| 308a | **43** | 1c. green | 30 | 10 |
| 309a | - | 2c. violet (As 4c.) | 30 | 10 |
| 310b | **53** | 4c. red and black | 50 | 15 |
| 311 | - | 6c. blue (As 2c.) | 70 | 10 |
| 312a | - | 24c. green | 2·50 | 10 |
| 313 | - | 36c. violet (As 4c.) | 3·50 | 20 |
| 314 | - | 48c. orange | 60 | 50 |
| 315 | - | 60c. brown (As 6c.) | 17·00 | 9·00 |
| 316 | - | 96c. purple | 7·00 | 2·75 |
| 317 | - | $1 violet | 22·00 | 35 |
| 318 | - | $2 purple (As 72c.) | 12·00 | 25·00 |
| 319 | - | $3 brown | 35·00 | 32·00 |

DESIGN—HORIZ: $3 Victoria Regia lilies.

**1946.** Victory. As T **9** of Aden.

| | | | |
|---|---|---|---|
| 320 | 3c. red | 10 | 40 |
| 321 | 6c. blue | 60 | 85 |

**1948.** Silver Wedding. As T **10/11** of Aden.

| | | | |
|---|---|---|---|
| 322 | 3c. red | 10 | 40 |
| 323 | $3 brown | 21·00 | 25·00 |

**1949.** UPU. As T **20/23** of Antigua.

| | | | |
|---|---|---|---|
| 324 | 4c. red | 10 | 50 |
| 325 | 6c. blue | 1·75 | 1·75 |
| 326 | 12c. orange | 15 | 50 |
| 327 | 24c. green | 15 | 70 |

**1951.** Inauguration of BWI University College. As T **24/25** of Antigua.

| | | | |
|---|---|---|---|
| 328 | 3c. black and red | 30 | 50 |
| 329 | 6c. black and blue | 30 | 65 |

**1953.** Coronation. As T **13** of Aden.

| | | | |
|---|---|---|---|
| 330 | 4c. black and red | 30 | 10 |

**55** G.P.O., Georgetown

**1954**

| | | | | |
|---|---|---|---|---|
| 331 | **55** | 1c. black | 20 | 10 |
| 332 | - | 2c. myrtle | 20 | 10 |
| 333 | - | 3c. olive and brown | 3·50 | 20 |
| 334 | - | 4c. violet | 1·50 | 10 |
| 335 | - | 5c. red and black | 1·75 | 10 |
| 336 | - | 6c. green | 1·00 | 10 |
| 337 | - | 8c. blue | 40 | 20 |
| 338a | - | 12c. black and brown | 1·00 | 10 |
| 360 | - | 24c. black and orange | 4·00 | 10 |
| 361 | - | 36c. red and black | 60 | 60 |
| 341 | - | 48c. blue and brown | 1·25 | 1·00 |
| 342 | - | 72c. red and green | 14·00 | 2·75 |
| 364 | - | $1 multicoloured | 7·00 | 90 |
| 344 | - | $2 mauve | 24·00 | 8·50 |
| 345 | - | $5 blue and black | 21·00 | 32·00 |

DESIGNS—HORIZ: 2c. Botanical Gardens; 3c. *Victoria Regia* lilies; 5c. Map of Caribbean; 6c. Rice combine-harvester; 8c. Sugar cane entering factory; 24c. Bauxite mining; 36c. Mount Roraima; $1 Channel-billed toucan; $2 Dredging gold. VERT: 4c. Amerindian shooting fish; 12c. Felling greenheart; 48c. Kaieteur Falls; 72c. Arapaima (fish); $5 Arms of British Guiana.

**70**

**1961.** History and Culture Week.

| | | | | |
|---|---|---|---|---|
| 346 | **70** | 5c. sepia and red | 20 | 10 |
| 347 | **70** | 6c. sepia and green | 20 | 15 |
| 348 | **70** | 30c. sepia and orange | 45 | 45 |

**1963.** Freedom from Hunger. As T **28** of Aden.

| | | | |
|---|---|---|---|
| 349 | 20c. violet | 30 | 10 |

**1963.** Centenary of Red Cross. As T **33** of Antigua.

| | | | |
|---|---|---|---|
| 350 | 5c. red and black | 20 | 20 |
| 351 | 20c. red and blue | 55 | 35 |

**71** Weightlifting

**1964.** Olympic Games, Tokyo.

| | | | | |
|---|---|---|---|---|
| 367 | **71** | 5c. orange | 10 | 10 |
| 368 | **71** | 8c. blue | 15 | 35 |
| 369 | **71** | 25c. mauve | 25 | 40 |

**1965.** Centenary of ITU. As T **36** of Antigua.

| | | | |
|---|---|---|---|
| 370 | 5c. green and olive | 10 | 15 |
| 371 | 25c. blue and mauve | 20 | 15 |

**1965.** ICY. As T **37** of Antigua.

| | | | |
|---|---|---|---|
| 372 | 5c. purple and turquoise | 15 | 10 |
| 373 | 25c. green and lavender | 30 | 20 |

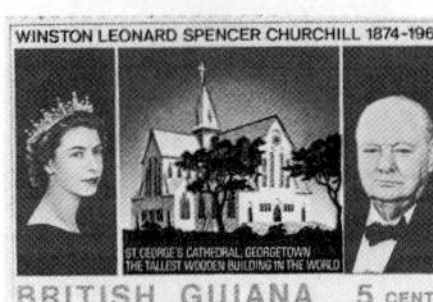


**72** St George's Cathedral, Georgetown

**1966.** Churchill Commemoration.

| | | | | |
|---|---|---|---|---|
| 374 | **72** | 5c. black, red and gold | 75 | 10 |
| 375 | **72** | 25c. black, blue and gold | 2·25 | 50 |

**1966.** Royal Visit. As T **39** of Antigua.

| | | | |
|---|---|---|---|
| 376 | 3c. black and blue | 75 | 15 |
| 377 | 25c. black and mauve | 1·50 | 60 |

**OFFICIAL STAMPS**

**1875.** Optd **OFFICIAL**.

| | | | | |
|---|---|---|---|---|
| O1 | **7** | 1c. black | 60·00 | 22·00 |
| O2 | **7** | 2c. orange | £200 | 14·00 |
| O3 | **7** | 8c. red | £325 | £120 |
| O4 | **7** | 12c. lilac | £3000 | £500 |
| O5 | **9** | 24c. green | £2250 | £225 |

**1877.** Optd **OFFICIAL**.

| | | | | |
|---|---|---|---|---|
| O6 | **16** | 1c. grey | £250 | 65·00 |
| O7 | **16** | 2c. orange | £130 | 15·00 |
| O8 | **16** | 4c. blue | £100 | 22·00 |
| O9 | **16** | 6c. brown | £5500 | £600 |
| O10 | **16** | 8c. red | £2000 | £450 |

**POSTAGE DUE STAMPS**

**1940.** As Type D **1** of Barbados, but inscr "BRITISH GUIANA".

| | | | |
|---|---|---|---|
| D1a | 1c. green | 2·00 | 19·00 |
| D2a | 2c. black | 4·25 | 7·50 |
| D3 | 4c. blue | 30 | 12·00 |
| D4 | 12c. red | 32·00 | 5·50 |

For later issues see **GUYANA**.

Pt. 1

# BRITISH HONDURAS

A British colony on the East coast of Central America. Self-government was granted on 1 January 1964. The country was renamed Belize from 1 June 1973.

1866. 12 pence = 1 shilling; 20 shillings = 1 pound.
1888. 100 cents = 1 dollar.

**1**

**1866**

| | | | | |
|---|---|---|---|---|
| 17 | **1** | 1d. blue | 70·00 | 19·00 |
| 18 | **1** | 1d. red | 23·00 | 13·00 |
| 13 | **1** | 3d. brown | £160 | 24·00 |
| 20 | **1** | 4d. mauve | 90·00 | 4·75 |
| 21 | **1** | 6d. yellow | £275 | £200 |
| 9 | **1** | 6d. red | £425 | 50·00 |
| 16 | **1** | 1s. green | £325 | 12·00 |
| 22 | **1** | 1s. grey | £250 | £160 |

**1888.** Surch as **2 CENTS**.

| | | | |
|---|---|---|---|
| 36 | 1c. on 1d. green | 80 | 1·50 |
| 37 | 2c. on 1d. red | 60 | 2·25 |
| 25 | 2c. on 6d. red | £190 | £160 |
| 38 | 3c. on 3d. brown | 3·25 | 1·40 |
| 39 | 6c. on 3d. blue | 4·25 | 22·00 |
| 40 | 10c. on 4d. mauve | 20·00 | 50 |
| 41 | 20c. on 6d. yellow | 17·00 | 14·00 |
| 42 | 50c. on 1s. grey | 32·00 | 85·00 |

**1888.** No. 42 surch **TWO**.

| | | | |
|---|---|---|---|
| 35 | "TWO" on 50c. on 1s. grey | 55·00 | 95·00 |

**1891.** No. 40 surch **6** and bar.

| | | | |
|---|---|---|---|
| 44 | 6c. on 10c. on 4d. mauve | 1·25 | 1·50 |

**1891.** Nos. 38 and 39 surch.

| | | | |
|---|---|---|---|
| 49 | "FIVE" on 3c. on 3d. brown | 1·25 | 1·40 |
| 50 | "15" on 6c. on 3d. blue | 13·00 | 28·00 |

**8**

**1891**

| | | | | |
|---|---|---|---|---|
| 51 | **8** | 1c. green | 2·50 | 1·25 |
| 52 | **8** | 2c. red | 4·00 | 20 |
| 53 | **8** | 3c. brown | 9·00 | 4·00 |
| 54 | **8** | 5c. blue | 12·00 | 75 |
| 55 | **8** | 5c. black and blue on blue | 18·00 | 2·50 |
| 56 | **8** | 6c. blue | 12·00 | 2·00 |
| 57 | **8** | 10c. mauve and green (A) | 13·00 | 14·00 |
| 58 | **8** | 10c. purple and green (B) | 11·00 | 7·50 |
| 59 | **8** | 12c. lilac and green | 2·50 | 3·00 |
| 60 | **8** | 24c. yellow and blue | 5·50 | 20·00 |
| 61 | **8** | 25c. brown and green | 85·00 | £130 |
| 62 | **8** | 50c. green and red | 28·00 | 65·00 |
| 63 | **8** | $1 green and red | 90·00 | £140 |
| 64 | **8** | $2 green and blue | £140 | £190 |
| 65 | **8** | $5 green and black | £325 | £425 |

NOTE: 10c. (A) inscr "POSTAGE POSTAGE"; (B) inscr "POSTAGE & REVENUE".

**1899.** Optd **REVENUE**.

| | | | | |
|---|---|---|---|---|
| 66 | | 5c. blue | 23·00 | 2·50 |
| 67 | | 10c. mauve and green | 12·00 | 16·00 |
| 68 | | 25c. brown and green | 3·50 | 35·00 |
| 69 | **1** | 50c. on 1s. grey | £200 | £350 |

**14**

**1902**

| | | | | |
|---|---|---|---|---|
| 84a | **14** | 1c. green | 2·25 | 2·25 |
| 85a | **14** | 2c. purple and black on red | 1·00 | 20 |
| 96 | **14** | 2c. red | 12·00 | 10 |
| 86 | **14** | 5c. black and blue on blue | 1·75 | 20 |
| 97 | **14** | 5c. blue | 1·75 | 10 |
| 87 | **14** | 10c. purple and green | 4·00 | 15·00 |
| 83 | **14** | 20c. purple | 10·00 | 17·00 |
| 89 | **14** | 25c. purple and orange | 8·50 | 50·00 |
| 100 | **14** | 25c. black on green | 4·75 | 45·00 |
| 90 | **14** | 50c. green and red | 22·00 | 85·00 |
| 91 | **14** | $1 green and red | 65·00 | 95·00 |
| 92 | **14** | $2 green and blue | £140 | £190 |
| 93 | **14** | $5 green and black | £325 | £375 |

**16**

**1913**

| | | | | |
|---|---|---|---|---|
| 101 | **16** | 1c. green | 3·75 | 1·50 |
| 102 | **16** | 2c. red | 4·25 | 1·00 |
| 103 | **16** | 3c. orange | 1·00 | 20 |
| 104 | **16** | 5c. blue | 2·00 | 85 |
| 105 | **16** | 10c. purple and green | 3·75 | 6·50 |
| 106 | **16** | 25c. black on green | 1·25 | 12·00 |
| 107 | **16** | 50c. purple and blue on blue | 23·00 | 15·00 |
| 108 | **16** | $1 black and red | 24·00 | 60·00 |
| 109 | **16** | $2 purple and green | 80·00 | 95·00 |
| 110 | **16** | $5 purple and black on red | £250 | £275 |

**1915.** Optd with pattern of wavy lines.

| | | | |
|---|---|---|---|
| 111a | 1c. green | 50 | 18·00 |
| 112 | 2c. red | 3·50 | 50 |
| 113 | 5c. blue | 30 | 6·00 |

**1916.** Optd **WAR**.

| | | | |
|---|---|---|---|
| 114 | 1c. green (No. 111a) | 10 | 2·75 |
| 119 | 1c. green (No. 101) | 20 | 30 |
| 120 | 3c. orange (No. 103) | 80 | 3·25 |

**21**

**1921.** Peace.

| | | | | |
|---|---|---|---|---|
| 121 | **21** | 2c. red | 4·50 | 50 |

**1921.** As No. 121 but without word "PEACE".

| | | | |
|---|---|---|---|
| 123 | 4c. grey | 11·00 | 50 |

**22**

**1922**

| | | | | |
|---|---|---|---|---|
| 126 | **22** | 1c. green | 14·00 | 6·50 |
| 127 | **22** | 2c. brown | 1·50 | 1·50 |
| 128 | **22** | 2c. red | 7·50 | 1·50 |
| 129 | **22** | 3c. orange | 30·00 | 4·00 |
| 130 | **22** | 4c. grey | 18·00 | 85 |
| 131 | **22** | 5c. blue | 1·50 | 55 |
| 132 | **22** | 10c. purple and olive | 3·50 | 30 |
| 133 | **22** | 25c. black on green | 1·75 | 8·50 |
| 134 | **22** | 50c. purple and blue on blue | 4·75 | 16·00 |
| 136 | **22** | $1 black and red | 15·00 | 26·00 |
| 137 | **22** | $2 green and purple | 45·00 | £120 |
| 125 | **22** | $5 purple and black on red | £200 | £250 |

**1932.** Optd **BELIZE RELIEF FUND PLUS** and value.

| | | | |
|---|---|---|---|
| 138 | 1c.+1c. green | 2·00 | 13·00 |
| 139 | 2c.+2c. red | 2·00 | 13·00 |
| 140 | 3c.+3c. orange | 2·00 | 26·00 |
| 141 | 4c.+4c. grey | 14·00 | 28·00 |
| 142 | 5c.+5c. blue | 6·50 | 14·00 |

**1935.** Silver Jubilee. As T **13** of Antigua.

| | | | | |
|---|---|---|---|---|
| 143 | | 3c. blue and black | 2·00 | 50 |
| 144 | | 4c. green and blue | 4·50 | 4·00 |
| 145 | | 5c. brown and blue | 2·00 | 2·50 |
| 146 | | 25c. grey and purple | 6·50 | 8·00 |

**1937.** Coronation. As T **2** of Aden.

| | | | | |
|---|---|---|---|---|
| 147 | | 3c. orange | 30 | 30 |
| 148 | | 4c. grey | 70 | 30 |
| 149 | | 5c. blue | 80 | 1·90 |

**24** Maya figures

**1938**

| | | | | |
|---|---|---|---|---|
| 150 | **24** | 1c. purple and green | 60 | 1·50 |
| 151 | - | 2c. black and red | 1·00 | 1·00 |
| 152 | - | 3c. purple and brown | 1·75 | 1·50 |
| 153 | - | 4c. black and green | 1·25 | 70 |
| 154 | - | 5c. purple and blue | 3·00 | 1·75 |
| 155 | - | 10c. green and brown | 3·75 | 60 |
| 156 | - | 15c. brown and blue | 6·50 | 1·25 |
| 157 | - | 25c. blue and green | 4·25 | 1·75 |
| 158 | - | 50c. black and purple | 23·00 | 4·50 |
| 159 | - | $1 red and olive | 40·00 | 10·00 |
| 160 | - | $2 blue and purple | 50·00 | 26·00 |
| 161 | - | $5 red and brown | 45·00 | 40·00 |

DESIGNS—VERT: 2c. Chicle tapping; 3c. Cohune palm; $1 Court House, Belize; $2 Mahogany felling; $5 Arms of Colony. HORIZ: 4c. Local products; 5c. Grapefruit; 10c. Mahogany logs in river; 15c. Sergeant's Cay; 25c. Dorey; 50c. Chicle industry.

**1946.** Victory. As T **9** of Aden.

| | | | | |
|---|---|---|---|---|
| 162 | | 3c. brown | 10 | 20 |
| 163 | | 5c. blue | 10 | 20 |

**1948.** Silver Wedding. As T **10** and **11** of Aden.

| | | | | |
|---|---|---|---|---|
| 164 | | 4c. green | 15 | 60 |
| 165 | | $5 brown | 22·00 | 48·00 |

**36** Island of Saint George's Cay

**1949.** 150th Anniv of Battle of Saint George's Cay.

| | | | | |
|---|---|---|---|---|
| 166 | **36** | 1c. blue and green | 10 | 1·25 |
| 167 | **36** | 3c. blue and brown | 10 | 1·50 |
| 168 | **36** | 4c. olive and violet | 10 | 1·75 |
| 169 | - | 5c. brown and blue | 1·75 | 75 |
| 170 | - | 10c. green and brown | 1·75 | 30 |
| 171 | - | 15c. green and blue | 1·75 | 30 |

DESIGNS: 5, 10 and 15c. H.M.S. "Merlin".

**1949.** U.P.U. As T **20/23** of Antigua.

| | | | | |
|---|---|---|---|---|
| 172 | | 4c. green | 30 | 50 |
| 173 | | 5c. blue | 1·50 | 50 |
| 174 | | 10c. brown | 40 | 3·25 |
| 175 | | 25c. blue | 35 | 50 |

**1951.** Inauguration of B.W.I. University College. As T **24/25** of Antigua.

| | | | | |
|---|---|---|---|---|
| 176 | | 3c. violet and brown | 45 | 1·50 |
| 177 | | 10c. green and brown | 45 | 30 |

**1953.** Coronation. As T **13** of Aden.

| | | | | |
|---|---|---|---|---|
| 178 | | 4c. black and green | 40 | 30 |

**39** Baird's Tapir

**49** Mountain Orchid

**1953**

| | | | | |
|---|---|---|---|---|
| 179 | - | 1c. green and black | 10 | 40 |
| 180a | **39** | 2c. brown and black | 1·75 | 30 |
| 181a | - | 3c. lilac and mauve | 20 | 10 |
| 182 | - | 4c. brown and green | 1·50 | 30 |
| 183 | - | 5c. olive and red | 20 | 20 |
| 184 | - | 10c. slate and blue | 50 | 10 |
| 185 | - | 15c. green and violet | 40 | 10 |
| 186 | - | 25c. blue and brown | 6·50 | 3·75 |
| 187 | - | 50c. brown and purple | 16·00 | 4·00 |
| 188 | - | $1 slate and brown | 9·00 | 5·00 |
| 189 | - | $2 red and grey | 9·00 | 4·50 |
| 190 | **49** | $5 purple and slate | 48·00 | 17·00 |

DESIGNS—HORIZ: 1c. Arms of British Honduras; 3c. Mace and Legislative Council Chamber; 4c. Pine industry; 5c. Spiny lobster; 10c. Stanley Field Airport; 15c. Maya frieze, Xunantunich; 25c. "Morpho peleides" (butterfly); $1 Nine-banded armadillo; $2 Hawkesworth Bridge. VERT: 50c. Maya indian.

**50** "Belize from Fort George, 1842" (C. J. Hullmandel)

**1960.** Post Office Centenary.

| | | | | |
|---|---|---|---|---|
| 191 | **50** | 2c. green | 45 | 1·25 |
| 192 | - | 10c. red | 45 | 10 |
| 193 | - | 15c. blue | 45 | 35 |

DESIGNS: 10c. Public seals, 1860 and 1960; 15c. Tamarind tree, Newtown Barracks.

**1961.** New Constitution. Stamps of 1953 optd **NEW CONSTITUTION 1960.**

| | | | | |
|---|---|---|---|---|
| 194 | **39** | 2c. brown and black | 25 | 40 |
| 195 | - | 3c. lilac and mauve | 30 | 40 |
| 196 | - | 10c. slate and blue | 30 | 10 |
| 197 | - | 15c. green and violet | 30 | 20 |

**1962.** Hurricane Hattie Relief Fund. Stamps of 1953 optd **HURRICANE HATTIE.**

| | | | | |
|---|---|---|---|---|
| 198 | | 1c. green and black | 10 | 65 |
| 199 | | 10c. slate and blue | 30 | 10 |
| 200 | | 25c. blue and brown | 1·75 | 80 |
| 201 | | 50c. brown and purple | 75 | 1·00 |

**55** Great Curassow

**1962.** Birds in natural colours; portrait and inscr in black; background colours given.

| | | | | |
|---|---|---|---|---|
| 239 | **55** | 1c. yellow | 10 | 50 |
| 240 | - | 2c. grey | 30 | 1·00 |
| 204 | - | 3c. green | 4·00 | 3·25 |
| 241 | - | 4c. grey | 1·75 | 2·00 |
| 242 | - | 5c. buff | 40 | 10 |
| 243 | - | 10c. stone | 40 | 10 |
| 244 | - | 15c. stone | 40 | 10 |
| 209 | - | 25c. slate | 4·50 | 30 |
| 210 | - | 50c. grey | 6·00 | 35 |
| 211 | - | $1 blue | 9·00 | 2·00 |
| 212 | - | $2 stone | 22·00 | 5·50 |
| 213 | - | $5 grey | 28·00 | 16·00 |

BIRDS: 2c. Red-legged honeycreeper; 3c. Northern jacana ("American Jacana"); 4c. Great kiskadee; 5c. Scarlet-rumped tanager; 10c. Scarlet macaw; 15c. Slaty-tailed trogon ("Massena Trogon"); 25c. Red-footed booby; 50c. Keel-billed toucan; $1 Magnificent frigate bird; $2 Rufous-tailed jacamar; $5 Montezuma oropendola.

**1963.** Freedom from Hunger. As T **28** of Aden.

| | | | | |
|---|---|---|---|---|
| 214 | | 22c. green | 30 | 15 |

**1963.** Centenary of Red Cross. As T **33** of Antigua.

| | | | | |
|---|---|---|---|---|
| 215 | | 4c. red and black | 20 | 1·00 |
| 216 | | 22c. red and blue | 40 | 1·25 |

**1964.** New Constitution. Nos. 202, 204, 205, 207 and 209 optd **SELF GOVERNMENT 1964.**

| | | | | |
|---|---|---|---|---|
| 217 | **55** | 1c. yellow | 10 | 30 |
| 218 | - | 3c. green | 45 | 30 |
| 219 | - | 4c. pale grey | 45 | 30 |
| 220 | - | 10c. stone | 45 | 10 |
| 221 | - | 25c. slate | 55 | 30 |

**1965.** Centenary of I.T.U. As T **36** of Antigua.

| | | | | |
|---|---|---|---|---|
| 222 | | 2c. red and green | 10 | 10 |
| 223 | | 50c. yellow and purple | 35 | 25 |

**1965.** I.C.Y. As T **37** of Antigua.

| | | | | |
|---|---|---|---|---|
| 224 | | 1c. purple and turquoise | 10 | 15 |
| 225 | | 22c. green and lavender | 20 | 15 |

**1966.** Churchill Commemoration. As T **38** of Antigua.

| | | | | |
|---|---|---|---|---|
| 226 | | 1c. blue | 10 | 75 |
| 227 | | 4c. green | 50 | 10 |
| 228 | | 22c. brown | 75 | 10 |
| 229 | | 25c. violet | 95 | 45 |

**1966.** Dedication of new Capital Site. Nos. 202, 204/5 207 and 209 optd **DEDICATION OF SITE NEW CAPITAL 9th OCTOBER 1965.**

| | | | | |
|---|---|---|---|---|
| 230 | **55** | 1c. yellow | 10 | 40 |
| 231 | - | 3c. green | 45 | 40 |
| 232 | - | 4c. grey | 45 | 40 |
| 233 | - | 10c. stone | 45 | 10 |
| 234 | - | 25c. slate | 55 | 35 |

**58** Citrus Grove

**1966.** Stamp Centenary. Multicoloured.

| | | | | |
|---|---|---|---|---|
| 235 | | 5c. Type **58** | 10 | 10 |
| 236 | | 10c. Half Moon Cay | 10 | 10 |
| 237 | | 22c. Hidden Valley Falls | 10 | 10 |
| 238 | | 25c. Maya ruins, Xunantunich | 15 | 45 |

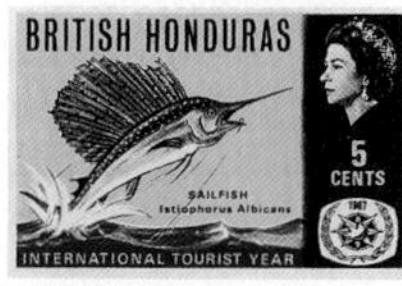


**59** Sailfish

**1967.** International Tourist Year.

| | | | | |
|---|---|---|---|---|
| 246 | **59** | 5c. blue, black and yellow | 15 | 30 |
| 247 | - | 10c. brown, black and red | 15 | 10 |
| 248 | - | 22c. orange, black and green | 30 | 10 |
| 249 | - | 25c. blue, black and yellow | 30 | 60 |

DESIGNS: 10c. Red brocket; 22c. Jaguar; 25c. Atlantic tarpon.

**60** "Schomburgkia tibicinis"

**1968.** 20th Anniv of Economic Commission for Latin America. Orchids. Multicoloured.

| | | | | |
|---|---|---|---|---|
| 250 | | 5c. Type **60** | 20 | 15 |
| 251 | | 10c. "Maxillaria tenuifolia" | 25 | 10 |
| 252 | | 22c. "Bletia purpurea" | 30 | 10 |
| 253 | | 25c. "Sobralia macrantha" | 40 | 20 |

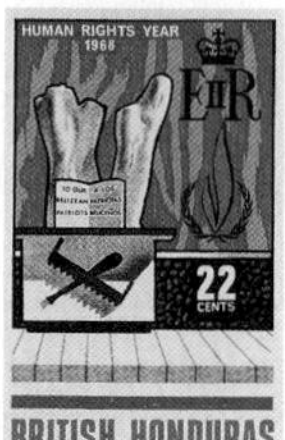


**61** Monument Belizean Patriots

**1968.** Human Rights Year. Multicoloured.

| | | | | |
|---|---|---|---|---|
| 254 | | 22c. Type **61** | 15 | 10 |
| 255 | | 50c. Monument at site of new capital | 15 | 20 |

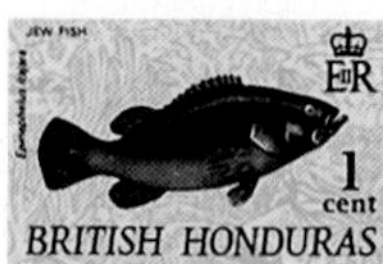


**63** Spotted Jewfish

**1968.** Wildlife.

| | | | | |
|---|---|---|---|---|
| 276 | - | ½c. multicoloured and blue | 10 | 10 |
| 277 | - | ½c. multicoloured and yellow | 2·50 | 1·00 |
| 256 | **63** | 1c. black, brown and yellow | 30 | 10 |
| 257 | - | 2c. black, green and yellow | 10 | 10 |
| 258 | - | 3c. black, brown and lilac | 20 | 10 |
| 259 | - | 4c. multicoloured | 15 | 1·25 |
| 260 | - | 5c. black and red | 15 | 1·25 |
| 261 | - | 10c. multicoloured | 15 | 10 |
| 262 | - | 15c. multicoloured | 2·00 | 20 |
| 263 | - | 25c. multicoloured | 30 | 20 |
| 264 | - | 50c. multicoloured | 70 | 1·25 |
| 265 | - | $1 multicoloured | 2·50 | 1·25 |
| 266 | - | $2 multicoloured | 2·50 | 2·00 |
| 278 | - | $5 multicoloured | 2·50 | 10·00 |

DESIGNS: ½c. (Nos. 276 and 277) Mozambique mouthbrooder ("Crana"); 2c. White-lipped peccary; 3c. Misty grouper; 4c. Collared anteater; 5c. Bonefish; 10c. Paca; 15c. Dolphin; 25c. Kinkajou; 50c. Mutton snapper; $1 Tayra; $2 Great barracuda; $5 Puma.

**64** "Rhyncholaelia digbyana"

**1969.** Orchids of Belize (1st series). Multicoloured.

| | | | | |
|---|---|---|---|---|
| 268 | | 5c. Type **64** | 60 | 20 |
| 269 | | 10c. "Cattleya bowringiana" | 65 | 15 |
| 270 | | 22c. "Lycaste cochleatum" | 95 | 15 |
| 271 | | 25c. "Coryanthes speciosum" | 1·10 | 1·10 |

See also Nos. 287/90.

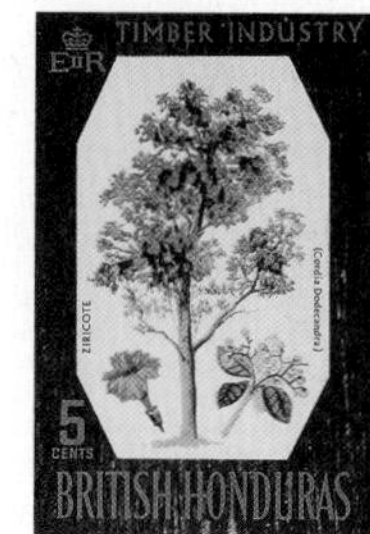


**65** Ziricote Tree

**1969.** Indigenous Hardwoods (1st series). Mult.

| | | | | |
|---|---|---|---|---|
| 272 | | 5c. Type **65** | 10 | 20 |
| 273 | | 10c. Rosewood | 10 | 10 |
| 274 | | 22c. Mayflower | 20 | 10 |
| 275 | | 25c. Mahogany | 20 | 45 |

See also Nos. 291/4, 315/18 and 333/7.

**66** "The Virgin and Child" (Bellini)

**1969.** Christmas. Paintings. Multicoloured.

| | | | | |
|---|---|---|---|---|
| 279 | | 5c. Type **66** | 10 | 10 |
| 280 | | 15c. Type **66** | 10 | 10 |
| 281 | | 22c. "The Adoration of the Magi" (Veronese) | 10 | 10 |
| 282 | | 25c. As No. 281 | 10 | 20 |

**1970.** Population Census. Nos. 260/3 optd **POPULATION CENSUS 1970.**

| | | | | |
|---|---|---|---|---|
| 283 | | 5c. multicoloured | 10 | 10 |
| 284 | | 10c. multicoloured | 15 | 10 |
| 285 | | 15c. multicoloured | 20 | 10 |
| 286 | | 25c. multicoloured | 20 | 15 |

**1970.** Orchids of Belize (2nd series). As T **64**. Mult.

| | | | | |
|---|---|---|---|---|
| 287 | | 5c. Black orchid | 35 | 15 |
| 288 | | 15c. White butterfly orchid | 50 | 10 |
| 289 | | 22c. Swan orchid | 70 | 10 |
| 290 | | 25c. Butterfly orchid | 70 | 40 |

**69** Santa Maria

**1970.** Indigenous Hardwoods (2nd series). Mult.

| | | | | |
|---|---|---|---|---|
| 291 | | 5c. Type **69** | 25 | 10 |
| 292 | | 15c. Nargusta | 40 | 10 |
| 293 | | 22c. Cedar | 45 | 10 |
| 294 | | 25c. Sapodilla | 45 | 35 |

70 "The Nativity" (A. Hughes)

**1970.** Christmas. Multicoloured.

| | | | |
|---|---|---|---|
| 295 | ½c. Type **70** | 10 | 10 |
| 296 | 5c. "The Mystic Nativity" (Botticelli) | 10 | 10 |
| 297 | 10c. Type **70** | 10 | 10 |
| 298 | 15c. As 5c. | 20 | 10 |
| 299 | 22c. Type **70** | 25 | 10 |
| 300 | 50c. As 5c. | 40 | 85 |

**71** Legislative Assembly House

**1971.** Establishment of New Capital, Belmopan. Multicoloured.

| | | | |
|---|---|---|---|
| 301 | 5c. Old capital, Belize | 10 | 10 |
| 302 | 10c. Government Plaza | 10 | 10 |
| 303 | 15c. Type **71** | 10 | 10 |
| 304 | 22c. Magistrates' Court | 15 | 10 |
| 305 | 25c. Police H.Q | 15 | 15 |
| 306 | 50c. New G.P.O | 25 | 40 |

The 5c. and 10c. are larger, 60×22 mm.

**72** "Tabebuia chrysantha"

**1971.** Easter. Flowers. Multicoloured.

| | | | |
|---|---|---|---|
| 307 | ½c. Type **72** | 10 | 10 |
| 308 | 5c. "Hymenocallis littorallis" | 10 | 10 |
| 309 | 10c. "Hippeastrum equestre" | 10 | 10 |
| 310 | 15c. Type **72** | 20 | 10 |
| 311 | 22c. As 5c. | 20 | 10 |
| 312 | 25c. As 10c. | 20 | 30 |

**1971.** Racial Equality Year. Nos. 261 and 264 optd **RACIAL EQUALITY YEAR–1971**.

| | | | |
|---|---|---|---|
| 313 | 10c. multicoloured | 25 | 10 |
| 314 | 50c. multicoloured | 55 | 20 |

**74** Tubroos

**1971.** Indigenous Hardwoods (3rd series). Mult.

| | | | |
|---|---|---|---|
| 315 | 5c. Type **74** | 60 | 10 |
| 316 | 15c. Yemeri | 80 | 30 |
| 317 | 26c. Billywebb | 1·10 | 35 |
| 318 | 50c. Logwood | 1·75 | 4·25 |
| **MS**319 | 96×171 mm. Nos. 315/18 | 3·50 | 7·50 |

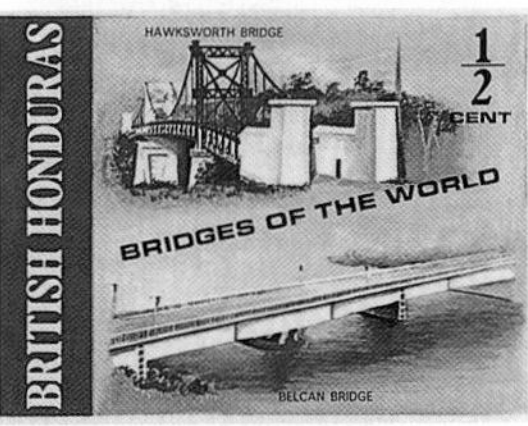
**75** Hawksworth and Belcan Bridges

**1971.** Bridges of the World. Multicoloured.

| | | | |
|---|---|---|---|
| 320 | ½c. Type **75** | 10 | 20 |
| 321 | 5c. Narrows Bridge, N.Y. and Quebec Bridge | 30 | 15 |
| 322 | 26c. London Bridge (1871) and reconstructed, Arizona (1971) | 80 | 15 |

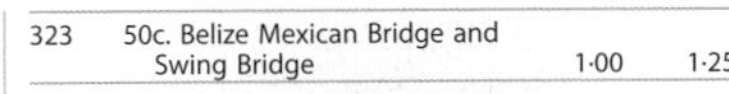

| | | | |
|---|---|---|---|
| 323 | 50c. Belize Mexican Bridge and Swing Bridge | 1·00 | 1·25 |

**76** "Petrae volubis"

**1972.** Easter. Wild Flowers. Multicoloured.

| | | | |
|---|---|---|---|
| 324 | 6c. Type **76** | 15 | 10 |
| 325 | 15c. Yemeri | 25 | 30 |
| 326 | 26c. Mayflower | 50 | 45 |
| 327 | 50c. Tiger's Claw | 80 | 1·40 |

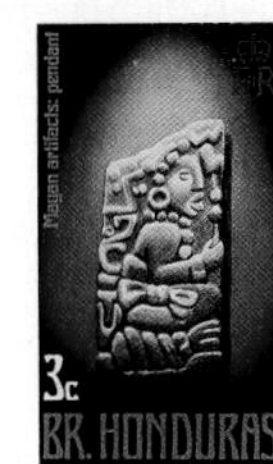
**77** Seated Figure

**1972.** Mayan Artefacts. Multicoloured.

| | | | |
|---|---|---|---|
| 328 | 3c. Type **77** | 25 | 10 |
| 329 | 6c. Priest in "dancing" pose | 25 | 10 |
| 330 | 16c. Sun God's head (horiz) | 50 | 15 |
| 331 | 26c. Priest and Sun God | 70 | 20 |
| 332 | 50c. Full-front figure | 1·40 | 3·75 |

**78** Banak

**1972.** Indigenous Hardwoods (4th series). Mult.

| | | | |
|---|---|---|---|
| 333 | 3c. Type **78** | 25 | 10 |
| 334 | 5c. Quamwood | 25 | 10 |
| 335 | 16c. Waika Chewstick | 55 | 15 |
| 336 | 26c. Mamee-Apple | 75 | 25 |
| 337 | 50c. My Lady | 1·60 | 3·25 |

**1972.** Royal Silver Wedding. As T **52** of Ascension, but with Orchids of Belize in background.

| | | | |
|---|---|---|---|
| 341 | 26c. green | 25 | 10 |
| 342 | 50c. violet | 40 | 65 |

**80** Baron Bliss Day

**1973.** Festivals of Belize. Multicoloured.

| | | | |
|---|---|---|---|
| 343 | 3c. Type **80** | 15 | 10 |
| 344 | 10c. Labour Day | 15 | 10 |
| 345 | 26c. Carib Settlement Day | 30 | 10 |
| 346 | 50c. Pan American Day | 50 | 85 |

### POSTAGE DUES

D1

**1923**

| | | | | |
|---|---|---|---|---|
| D1 | **D1** | 1c. black | 2·25 | 13·00 |
| D4 | **D1** | 2c. black | 2·75 | 6·00 |
| D5 | **D1** | 4c. black | 1·25 | 6·00 |

For later issues see **BELIZE**.

Pt. 1

# BRITISH INDIAN OCEAN TERRITORY

A Crown Colony, established 8 November 1965, comprising the Chagos Archipelago (previously administered by Mauritius) and Aldabra, Farquhar and Desroches, previously administered by Seychelles to which country they were returned on 29 June 1976.

The Chagos Archipelago has no indigenous population, but stamps were provided from 1990 for use by civilian workers at the U.S. Navy base on Diego Garcia.

1968. 100 cents = 1 rupee.
1990. 100 pence = 1 pound.

**1968.** Nos 196/200, 202/4 and 206/12 of Seychelles optd **B.I.O.T.**

| | | | | |
|---|---|---|---|---|
| 1 | **24** | 5c. multicoloured | 1·00 | 1·50 |
| 2 | - | 10c. multicoloured | 10 | 15 |
| 3 | - | 15c. multicoloured | 10 | 15 |
| 4 | - | 20c. multicoloured | 15 | 15 |
| 5 | - | 25c. multicoloured | 15 | 15 |
| 6 | - | 40c. multicoloured | 20 | 20 |
| 7 | - | 45c. multicoloured | 20 | 30 |
| 8 | - | 50c. multicoloured | 20 | 30 |
| 9 | - | 75c. multicoloured | 1·50 | 35 |
| 10 | - | 1r. multicoloured | 1·00 | 35 |
| 11 | - | 1r.50 multicoloured | 1·75 | 1·50 |
| 12 | - | 2r.25 multicoloured | 3·00 | 3·75 |
| 13 | - | 3r.50 multicoloured | 3·00 | 4·50 |
| 14 | - | 5r. multicoloured | 10·00 | 6·50 |
| 15 | - | 10r. multicoloured | 20·00 | 15·00 |

**2** Lascar

**1968.** Marine Life. Multicoloured.

| | | | |
|---|---|---|---|
| 16 | 5c. Type **2** | 1·00 | 2·00 |
| 17 | 10c. Smooth hammerhead (vert) | 30 | 1·25 |
| 18 | 15c. Tiger shark | 30 | 1·50 |
| 19 | 20c. Spotted eagle ray ("Bat ray") | 30 | 1·00 |
| 20 | 25c. Yellow-finned butterflyfish and ear-spot angelfish (vert) | 80 | 1·00 |
| 20a | 30c. Robber crab | 3·50 | 2·75 |
| 21 | 40c. Blue-finned trevalley ("Caranx") | 2·25 | 40 |
| 22 | 45c. Crocodile needlefish ("Garfish") (vert) | 2·25 | 2·50 |
| 23 | 50c. Pickhandle barracuda | 2·25 | 30 |
| 23a | 60c. Spotted pebble crab | 3·50 | 3·25 |
| 24 | 75c. Indian Ocean steep-headed parrotfish | 2·50 | 2·25 |
| 24a | 85c. Rainbow runner ("Dorade") | 4·50 | 3·00 |
| 25 | 1r. Giant hermit crab | 1·75 | 35 |
| 26 | 1r.50 Parrotfish ("Humphead") | 2·50 | 3·00 |
| 27 | 2r.25 Yellow-edged lyre-tail and Aredate grouper ("Rock cod") | 12·00 | 10·00 |
| 28 | 3r.50 Black marlin | 4·00 | 3·75 |
| 29 | 5r. black, green and blue (Whale shark) (vert) | 18·00 | 13·00 |
| 30 | 10r. Lionfish | 6·00 | 6·50 |

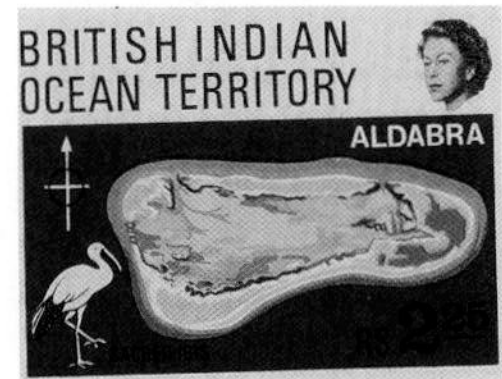
**3** Sacred Ibis and Aldabra Coral Atoll

**1969.** Coral Atolls.

| | | | | |
|---|---|---|---|---|
| 31 | **3** | 2r.25 multicoloured | 1·75 | 1·00 |

**4** Outrigger Canoe

**1969.** Ships of the Islands. Multicoloured.

| | | | |
|---|---|---|---|
| 32 | 45c. Type **4** | 55 | 75 |
| 33 | 75c. Pirogue | 55 | 80 |
| 34 | 1r. M.V. "Nordvaer" | 60 | 90 |
| 35 | 1r.50 "Isle of Farquhar" | 65 | 1·00 |

**5** Giant Land Tortoise

**1971.** Aldabra Nature Reserve. Multicoloured.

| | | | |
|---|---|---|---|
| 36 | 45c. Type **5** | 2·50 | 2·50 |
| 37 | 75c. Aldabra lily | 3·00 | 2·50 |
| 38 | 1r. Aldabra tree snail | 3·50 | 2·75 |
| 39 | 1r.50 Western reef heron ("Dimorphic Egrets") | 12·00 | 10·00 |

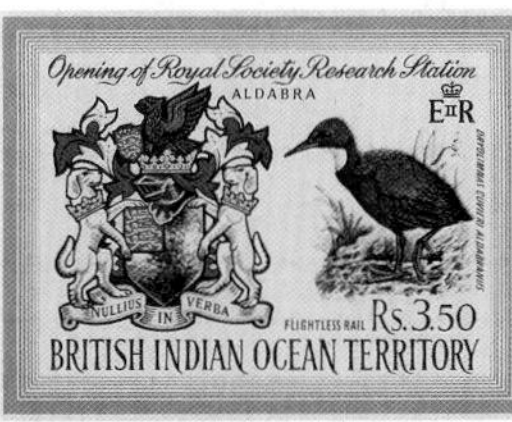
**6** Arms of Royal Society and White-throated Rail

**1971.** Opening of Royal Society Research Station, Aldabra.

| | | | | |
|---|---|---|---|---|
| 40 | **6** | 3r.50 multicoloured | 15·00 | 8·50 |

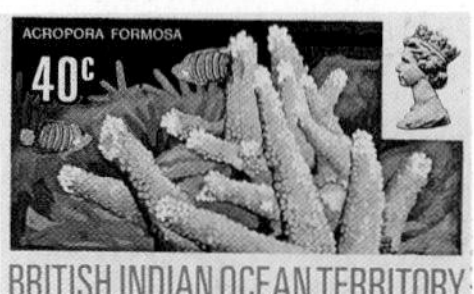
**7** Staghorn Coral

**1972.** Coral. Multicoloured.

| | | | |
|---|---|---|---|
| 41 | 40c. Type **7** | 3·50 | 4·00 |
| 42 | 60c. Brain coral | 4·00 | 4·25 |
| 43 | 1r. Mushroom coral | 4·00 | 4·25 |
| 44 | 1r.75 Organ pipe coral | 5·00 | 6·50 |

**1972.** Royal Silver Wedding. As T **52** of Ascension, but with White-throated rail and Sacred ibis in background.

| | | | |
|---|---|---|---|
| 45 | 95c. green | 50 | 40 |
| 46 | 1r.50 violet | 50 | 40 |

**9** "Christ on the Cross"

**1973.** Easter. Multicoloured.

| | | | |
|---|---|---|---|
| 47 | 45c. Type **9** | 20 | 40 |
| 48 | 75c. "Joseph and Nicodemus burying Jesus" | 30 | 55 |
| 49 | 1r. Type **9** | 30 | 60 |
| 50 | 1r.50 As 75c. | 30 | 70 |
| **MS**51 | 126×110 mm. Nos. 47/50 | 1·00 | 4·00 |

**10** Upsidedown Jellyfish

**1973.** Wildlife (1st series). Multicoloured.

| | | | |
|---|---|---|---|
| 53 | 50c. Type **10** | 3·50 | 3·00 |
| 54 | 1r. "Hypolimnas misippus" and "Belenois aldabrensis" (butterflies) | 4·00 | 3·00 |
| 55 | 1r.50 "Nephila madagascarienis" (spider) | 4·25 | 3·00 |

See also Nos. 58/61, 77/80 and 86/9.

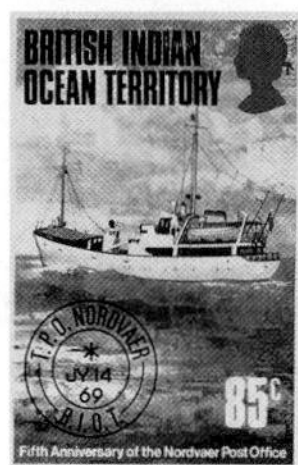


**11** M.V. "Nordvaer"

**1974.** 5th Anniv of "Nordvaer" Travelling Post Office. Multicoloured.

| | | | |
|---|---|---|---|
| 56 | 85c. Type **11** | 85 | 75 |
| 57 | 2r.50 "Nordvaer" off shore | 1·40 | 1·25 |

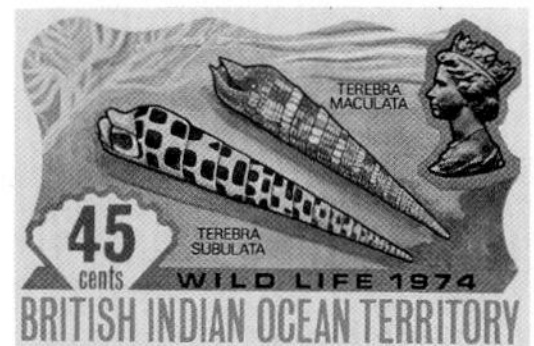


**12** Red-cloud Auger and Subulat Auger

**1974.** Wildlife (2nd series). Shells. Multicoloured.

| | | | |
|---|---|---|---|
| 58 | 45c. Type **12** | 2·25 | 1·25 |
| 59 | 75c. Great green turban | 2·50 | 1·50 |
| 60 | 1r. Strawberry drupe | 2·75 | 1·75 |
| 61 | 1r.50 Bull-mouth helmet | 3·00 | 2·00 |

**13** Aldabra Drongo

**1975.** Birds. Multicoloured.

| | | | |
|---|---|---|---|
| 62 | 5c. Type **13** | 1·25 | 2·75 |
| 63 | 10c. Black coucal ("Malagasy Coucal") | 1·25 | 2·75 |
| 64 | 20c. Mascarene fody ("Red-Headed Forest Foddy") | 1·25 | 2·75 |
| 65 | 25c. White tern | 1·25 | 2·75 |
| 66 | 30c. Crested tern | 1·25 | 2·75 |
| 67 | 40c. Brown booby | 1·25 | 2·75 |
| 68 | 50c. Common noddy ("Noddy Tern") (horiz) | 1·25 | 3·00 |
| 69 | 60c. Grey heron | 1·25 | 3·00 |
| 70 | 65c. Blue-faced booby (horiz) | 1·25 | 3·00 |
| 71 | 95c. Madagascar white eye ("Malagasy White-eye") (horiz) | 1·25 | 3·00 |
| 72 | 1r. Green-backed heron (horiz) | 1·25 | 3·00 |
| 73 | 1r.75 Lesser frigate bird (horiz) | 2·00 | 5·50 |
| 74 | 3r.50 White-tailed tropic bird (horiz) | 2·75 | 5·50 |
| 75 | 5r. Souimanga sunbird (horiz) | 3·00 | 5·00 |
| 76 | 10r. Madagascar turtle dove ("Malagasy Turtle Dove") (horiz) | 5·00 | 9·00 |

**14** "Grewia salicifolia"

**1975.** Wildlife (3rd series). Seashore Plants. Multicoloured.

| | | | |
|---|---|---|---|
| 77 | 50c. Type **14** | 50 | 1·40 |
| 78 | 65c. "Cassia aldabrensis" | 55 | 1·50 |
| 79 | 1r. "Hypoestes aldabrensis" | 65 | 1·60 |
| 80 | 1r.60 "Euphorbia pyrifolia" | 80 | 1·75 |

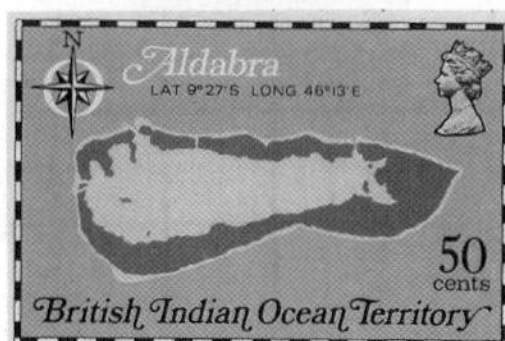


**15** Map of Aldabra

**1975.** 10th Anniv of Territory. Maps. Multicoloured.

| | | | |
|---|---|---|---|
| 81 | 50c. Type **15** | 80 | 65 |
| 82 | 1r. Desroches | 95 | 85 |
| 83 | 1r.50 Farquhar | 1·10 | 1·00 |
| 84 | 2r. Diego Garcia | 1·25 | 1·25 |
| **MS**85 | 147×147 mm. Nos. 81/4 | 7·00 | 14·00 |

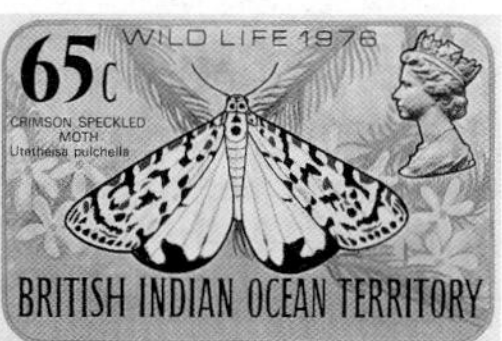


**16** "Utetheisa pulchella" (moth)

**1976.** Wildlife (4th series). Multicoloured.

| | | | |
|---|---|---|---|
| 86 | 65c. Type **16** | 60 | 1·10 |
| 87 | 1r.20 "Dysdercus fasciatus" (bug) | 75 | 1·25 |
| 88 | 1r.50 "Sphex torridus" (wasp) | 80 | 1·40 |
| 89 | 2r. "Oryctes rhinoceros" (beetle) | 85 | 1·40 |

**17** White-tailed Tropic Bird

**1990.** Birds. Multicoloured.

| | | | |
|---|---|---|---|
| 90 | 15p. Type **17** | 1·10 | 2·00 |
| 91 | 20p. Madagascar turtle dove ("Turtle Dove") | 1·25 | 2·00 |
| 92 | 24p. Great frigate bird ("Greater Frigate") | 1·40 | 2·00 |
| 93 | 30p. Green-backed heron ("Little Green Heron") | 1·50 | 2·25 |
| 94 | 34p. Great sand plover ("Greater Sand Plover") | 1·60 | 2·25 |
| 95 | 41p. Crab plover | 1·75 | 2·50 |
| 96 | 45p. Crested tern | 3·50 | 2·50 |
| 97 | 54p. Lesser crested tern | 2·25 | 2·75 |
| 98 | 62p. White tern ("Fairy Tern") | 2·25 | 2·75 |
| 99 | 71p. Red-footed booby | 2·25 | 3·00 |
| 100 | 80p. Common mynah ("Indian Mynah") | 2·50 | 3·25 |
| 101 | £1 Madagascar red fody ("Madagascar Fody") | 3·25 | 3·50 |

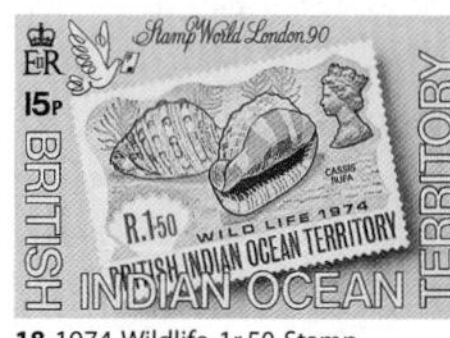


**18** 1974 Wildlife 1r.50 Stamp

**1990.** "Stamp World London 90" International Stamp Exhibition. Multicoloured.

| | | | |
|---|---|---|---|
| 102 | 15p. Type **18** | 4·75 | 3·25 |
| 103 | 20p. 1976 Wildlife 2r. stamp | 5·00 | 3·50 |
| 104 | 34p. 1975 Diego Garcia map 2r. stamp | 8·50 | 5·50 |
| 105 | 54p. 1969 "Nordvaer" 1r. stamp | 9·50 | 7·50 |

**1990.** 90th Birthday of Queen Elizabeth the Queen Mother. As T **34** of Ascension.

| | | | |
|---|---|---|---|
| 106 | 24p. multicoloured | 3·50 | 3·50 |
| 107 | £1 black and ochre | 6·50 | 6·50 |

DESIGNS—21×36 mm: Lady Elizabeth Bowes-Lyon, 1923. 29×37 mm: £1 Queen Elizabeth and her daughters, 1940.

**19** Territory Flag

**1990.** 25th Anniv of British Indian Ocean Territory. Multicoloured.

| | | | |
|---|---|---|---|
| 108 | 20p. Type **19** | 4·00 | 4·50 |
| 109 | 24p. Coat of arms | 4·00 | 4·50 |
| **MS**110 | 63×99 mm. £1 map of Chagos Archipelago | 9·50 | 12·00 |

**20** Postman emptying Pillar Box

**1991.** British Indian Ocean Territory Administration. Multicoloured.

| | | | |
|---|---|---|---|
| 111 | 20p. Type **20** | 1·50 | 2·50 |
| 112 | 24p. Commissioner inspecting guard of Royal Marines | 1·75 | 2·50 |
| 113 | 34p. Policeman outside station | 3·50 | 4·50 |
| 114 | 54p. Customs officers boarding yacht | 4·25 | 6·00 |

**21** "Experiment" (E.I.C. survey brig), 1786

**1991.** Visiting Ships. Multicoloured.

| | | | |
|---|---|---|---|
| 115 | 20p. Type **21** | 2·00 | 3·00 |
| 116 | 24p. "Pickering" (American brig), 1819 | 2·25 | 3·25 |
| 117 | 34p. "Emden" (German cruiser), 1914 | 3·00 | 4·25 |
| 118 | 54p. H.M.S. "Edinburgh" (destroyer), 1988 | 3·75 | 5·50 |

**1992.** 40th Anniv of Queen Elizabeth II's Accession. As T **143** of Ascension. Multicoloured.

| | | | |
|---|---|---|---|
| 119 | 15p. Catholic chapel, Diego Garcia | 1·25 | 1·25 |
| 120 | 20p. Planter's house, Diego Garcia | 1·40 | 1·40 |
| 121 | 24p. Railway tracks on wharf, Diego Garcia | 3·00 | 2·00 |
| 122 | 34p. Three portraits of Queen Elizabeth | 2·50 | 2·25 |
| 123 | 54p. Queen Elizabeth II | 2·50 | 2·50 |

**22** R.A.F. Consolidated PBY-5 Catalina (flying boat)

**1992.** Visiting Aircraft. Multicoloured.

| | | | |
|---|---|---|---|
| 124 | 20p. Type **22** | 1·50 | 2·50 |
| 125 | 24p. R.A.F. Hawker Siddeley Nimrod M.R.2 (maritime reconnaissance aircraft) | 1·75 | 2·50 |
| 126 | 34p. Lockheed P-3 Orion (transport aircraft) | 2·50 | 3·25 |
| 127 | 54p. U.S.A.A.F. Boeing B-52 Stratofortress (heavy bomber) | 3·00 | 4·50 |

**23** "The Mystical Marriage of St. Catherine" (Correggio)

**1992.** Christmas. Religious Paintings. Mult.

| | | | |
|---|---|---|---|
| 128 | 5p. Type **23** | 70 | 80 |
| 129 | 24p. "Madonna" (anon) | 1·25 | 1·60 |
| 130 | 34p. "Madonna" (anon) (different) | 1·40 | 2·25 |
| 131 | 54p. "The Birth of Jesus" (Kaspar Jele) | 1·75 | 3·50 |

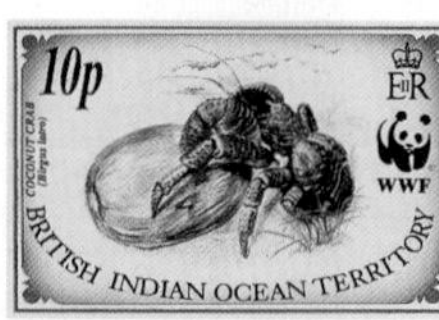


**24** Coconut Crab and Rock

**1993.** Endangered Species. Coconut Crab. Mult.

| | | | |
|---|---|---|---|
| 132 | 10p. Type **24** | 1·25 | 1·25 |
| 133 | 10p. Crab on beach | 1·25 | 1·25 |
| 134 | 10p. Two crabs | 1·25 | 1·25 |
| 135 | 15p. Crab climbing coconut tree | 1·50 | 1·50 |

**1993.** 75th Anniv of Royal Air Force. As T **149** of Ascension. Multicoloured.

| | | | |
|---|---|---|---|
| 136 | 20p. Vickers Virginia Mk X | 1·00 | 1·50 |
| 137 | 24p. Bristol Bulldog IIA | 1·10 | 1·50 |
| 138 | 34p. Short S.25 Sunderland Mk III | 1·25 | 2·00 |
| 139 | 54p. Bristol Blenheim Mk IV | 2·00 | 3·25 |
| **MS**140 | 110×77 mm. 20p. Douglas DC-3 Dakota; 20p. Gloster G.41 Javelin; 20p. Blackburn Beverley C1; 20p. Vickers VC-10 | 7·50 | 8·00 |

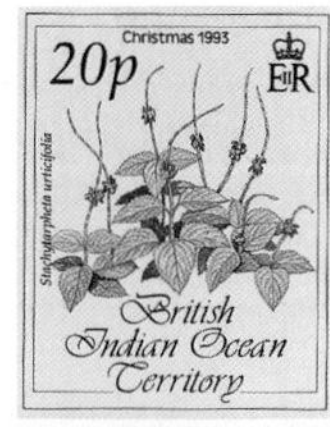


**25** "Stachytarpheta urticifolia"

**1993.** Christmas. Flowers. Multicoloured.

| | | | |
|---|---|---|---|
| 141 | 20p. Type **25** | 80 | 1·50 |
| 142 | 24p. "Ipomea pes-caprae" | 80 | 1·50 |
| 143 | 34p. "Sida pusilla" | 1·10 | 2·25 |
| 144 | 54p. "Catharanthus roseus" | 1·75 | 3·50 |

**1994.** "Hong Kong '94" International Stamp Exhibition. Nos. 92 and 101 optd **HONG KONG '94** and emblem.

| | | | |
|---|---|---|---|
| 145 | 24p. Great frigate bird ("Greater Frigate") | 4·00 | 3·00 |
| 146 | £1 Madagascar red fody ("Madagascar Fody") | 6·00 | 8·00 |

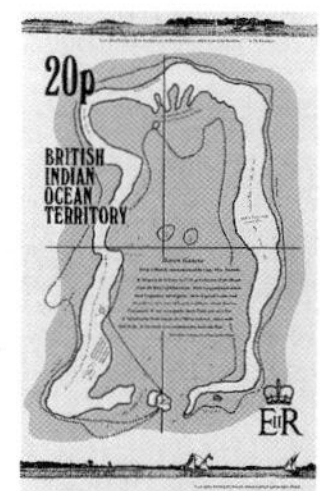


**26** Forrest's Map of Diego Garcia, 1778

**1994.** 18th-century Maps. Each black and blue.

| | | | |
|---|---|---|---|
| 147 | 20p. Type **26** | 70 | 1·50 |
| 148 | 24p. Blair's plan of Diego Garcia harbour, 1786–87 | 75 | 1·60 |
| 149 | 34p. Blair's chart of Chagos Archipelago, 1786–87 | 80 | 1·75 |
| 150 | 44p. Plan of part of Diego Garcia, 1774 | 90 | 1·90 |
| 151 | 54p. Fontaine's plan of Diego Garcia, 1770 | 1·10 | 2·00 |

**27** "Junonia villida"

**1994.** Butterflies. Multicoloured.

| | | | |
|---|---|---|---|
| 152 | 24p. Type **27** | 1·50 | 1·75 |
| 153 | 30p. "Petrelaea dana" | 1·75 | 2·50 |
| 154 | 56p. "Hypolimnas misippus" | 2·75 | 4·00 |

**28** Short-tailed Nurse Sharks

**1994.** Sharks. Multicoloured.

| | | | |
|---|---|---|---|
| 155 | 15p. Type **28** | 3·25 | 3·00 |
| 156 | 20p. Silver-tipped sharks | 3·25 | 3·00 |
| 157 | 24p. Black-finned reef shark | 3·25 | 3·00 |
| 158 | 30p. Oceanic white-tipped sharks | 3·75 | 3·50 |
| 159 | 35p. Black-tipped shark | 4·00 | 3·75 |
| 160 | 41p. Smooth hammerhead | 4·00 | 3·75 |
| 161 | 46p. Sickle-finned lemon shark | 4·00 | 3·75 |
| 162 | 55p. White-tipped reef shark | 4·75 | 4·25 |
| 163 | 65p. Tiger sharks | 4·75 | 4·25 |
| 164 | 74p. Indian sand tiger | 5·00 | 4·50 |

| | | | |
|---|---|---|---|
| 165 | 80p. Great hammerhead | 5·00 | 4·50 |
| 166 | £1 Great white shark | 5·50 | 5·00 |

**1995.** 50th Anniv of End of Second World War. As T **161** of Ascension. Multicoloured.

| | | | |
|---|---|---|---|
| 167 | 20p. Military cemetery | 1·50 | 1·75 |
| 168 | 24p. Rusty 6-inch naval gun at Cannon Point | 1·75 | 1·75 |
| 169 | 30p. Short S.25 Sunderland flying boat | 2·00 | 2·25 |
| 170 | 56p. H.M.I.S. "Clive" (sloop) | 3·00 | 3·75 |
| **MS**171 | 75×85 mm. £1 Reverse of 1939–45 War Medal (vert) | 2·50 | 3·00 |

**29** Dolphin (fish)

**1995.** Gamefish. Multicoloured.

| | | | |
|---|---|---|---|
| 172 | 20p. Type **29** | 1·50 | 1·60 |
| 173 | 24p. Sailfish | 1·60 | 1·60 |
| 174 | 30p. Wahoo | 2·25 | 2·50 |
| 175 | 56p. Striped marlin | 3·25 | 3·75 |

**30** "Terebra crenulata"

**1996.** Sea Shells. Multicoloured.

| | | | |
|---|---|---|---|
| 176 | 20p. Type **30** | 1·25 | 1·50 |
| 177 | 24p. "Bursa bufonia" | 1·25 | 1·50 |
| 178 | 30p. "Nassarius papillosus" | 1·75 | 2·00 |
| 179 | 56p. "Lopha cristagalli" | 3·00 | 3·25 |

**1996.** 70th Birthday of Queen Elizabeth II. As T **165** of Ascension, each incorporating a different photograph of the Queen. Multicoloured.

| | | | |
|---|---|---|---|
| 180 | 20p. View of lagoon from south | 75 | 1·00 |
| 181 | 24p. Manager's House, Peros Banhos | 80 | 1·00 |
| 182 | 30p. Wireless hut, Peros Banhos | 1·00 | 1·40 |
| 183 | 56p. Sunset | 1·50 | 2·00 |
| **MS**184 | 64×66 mm. £1 Queen Elizabeth II | 2·75 | 3·75 |

**31** Loggerhead Turtle

**1996.** Turtles. Multicoloured.

| | | | |
|---|---|---|---|
| 185 | 20p. Type **31** | 1·00 | 1·25 |
| 186 | 24p. Leatherback turtle | 1·10 | 1·25 |
| 187 | 30p. Hawksbill turtle | 1·40 | 1·60 |
| 188 | 56p. Green turtle | 2·00 | 2·50 |

**32** Commissioner's Representative (naval officer)

**1996.** Uniforms. Multicoloured.

| | | | |
|---|---|---|---|
| 189 | 20p. Type **32** | 1·00 | 1·10 |
| 190 | 24p. Royal Marine officer | 1·10 | 1·10 |
| 191 | 30p. Royal Marine in battle-dress | 1·50 | 1·75 |
| 192 | 56p. Police officers | 2·25 | 2·75 |

**1997.** "HONG KONG '97" International Stamp Exhibition. Sheet 130×90 mm, containing design as No. 163. Multicoloured.

| | | | |
|---|---|---|---|
| **MS**193 | 65p. Tiger sharks | 2·00 | 2·75 |

**1997.** Return of Hong Kong to China. Sheet 130×90 mm, containing design as No. 164, but with "1997" imprint date.

| | | | |
|---|---|---|---|
| **MS**194 | 74p. Indian sand tiger | 2·75 | 3·50 |

**1997.** Golden Wedding of Queen Elizabeth and Prince Philip. As T 173 of Ascension. Mult.

| | | | |
|---|---|---|---|
| 195 | 20p. Queen Elizabeth at Bristol, 1994 | 1·75 | 1·90 |
| 196 | 20p. Prince Philip competing in Royal Windsor Horse Show, 1996 | 1·75 | 1·90 |
| 197 | 24p. Queen Elizabeth in phaeton, Trooping the Colour, 1987 | 1·75 | 1·90 |
| 198 | 24p. Prince Philip | 1·75 | 1·90 |
| 199 | 30p. Queen Elizabeth and Prince Philip with Land Rover | 1·75 | 1·90 |
| 200 | 30p. Queen Elizabeth at Balmoral | 1·75 | 1·90 |
| **MS**201 | 110×71 mm. £1.50, Queen Elizabeth and Prince Philip in landau (horiz) | 10·00 | 10·00 |

Nos. 195/6, 197/8 and 199/20 respectively were printed together, se-tenant, with the backgrounds forming a compsite design.

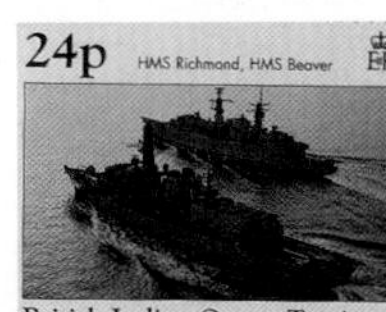


**33** H.M.S. "Richmond" (frigate) and H.M.S. "Beaver" (frigate)

**1997.** Exercise Ocean Wave. Multicoloured.

| | | | |
|---|---|---|---|
| 202 | 24p. Type **33** | 1·50 | 1·60 |
| 203 | 24p. H.M.S. "Illustrious" (aircraft carrier) launching BAe (Hawker) Sea Harrier | 1·50 | 1·60 |
| 204 | 24p. H.M.S. "Beaver" | 1·50 | 1·60 |
| 205 | 24p. Royal Yacht "Britannia", R.F.A. "Sir Percival" and H.M.S. "Beaver" | 1·50 | 1·60 |
| 206 | 24p. Royal Yacht "Britannia" | 1·50 | 1·60 |
| 207 | 24p. H.M.S. "Richmond", H.M.S. "Beaver" and H.M.S. "Gloucester" (destroyer) | 1·50 | 1·60 |
| 208 | 24p. H.M.S. "Richmond" | 1·50 | 1·60 |
| 209 | 24p. Aerial view of H.M.S. "Illustrious" | 1·50 | 1·60 |
| 210 | 24p. H.M.S. "Gloucester" (wrongly inscr "Sheffield") | 1·50 | 1·60 |
| 211 | 24p. H.M.S. "Trenchant" (submarine) and R.F.A. "Diligence" | 1·50 | 1·60 |
| 212 | 24p. R.F.A. "Fort George" replenishing H.M.S. "Illustrious" and H.M.S. "Gloucester" | 1·50 | 1·60 |
| 213 | 24p. Aerial view of H.M.S. "Richmond", H.M.S. "Beaver" and H.M.S. "Gloucester" | 1·50 | 1·60 |

**1998.** Diana, Princess of Wales Commemoration. Sheet 145×70 mm, containing vert designs as T **177** of Ascension. Multicoloured.

| | | | |
|---|---|---|---|
| **MS**214 | 26p. Wearing patterned jacket, 1993; 26p. Wearing heart-shaped earrings, 1988; 34p. Wearing cream jacket, 1993; 60p. Wearing blue blouse, 1982 (sold at £1.46 + 20p. charity premium) | 3·25 | 4·00 |

**1998.** 80th Anniv of the Royal Air Force. As T **178** of Ascension. Multicoloured.

| | | | |
|---|---|---|---|
| 215 | 26p. Blackburn Iris | 1·00 | 1·10 |
| 216 | 34p. Gloster Gamecock | 1·25 | 1·40 |
| 217 | 60p. North American SF-86 abre F.4 | 2·25 | 2·50 |
| 218 | 80p. Avro Type **694** Lincoln | 2·75 | 3·00 |
| **MS**219 | 110×77 mm. 34p. Sopwith Baby (seaplane); 34p. Martinsyde Elephant; 34p. de Havilland Tiger Moth; 34p. North American Mustang III | 6·00 | 7·00 |

**34** Bryde's Whale

**1998.** International Year of the Ocean. Multicoloured.

| | | | |
|---|---|---|---|
| 220 | 26p. Type **34** | 2·75 | 2·50 |
| 221 | 26p. Striped dolphin | 2·75 | 2·50 |
| 222 | 34p. Pilot whale | 2·75 | 2·50 |
| 223 | 34p. Spinner dolphin | 2·75 | 2·50 |

**35** "Westminster" (East Indiaman), 1837

**1999.** Ships. Multicoloured.

| | | | |
|---|---|---|---|
| 224 | 2p. Type **35** | 40 | 75 |
| 225 | 15p. "Sao Cristovao" (Spanish galleon), 1589 | 1·25 | 1·25 |
| 226 | 20p. "Sea Witch" (U.S. clipper), 1849 | 1·25 | 1·25 |
| 227 | 26p. H.M.S. "Royal George" (ship of the line), 1778 | 1·50 | 1·25 |
| 228 | 34p. "Cutty Sark" (clipper), 1883 | 2·00 | 1·50 |
| 229 | 60p. "Mentor" (East Indiaman), 1789 | 2·50 | 2·75 |
| 230 | 80p. H.M.S. "Trinculo" (brig), 1809 | 2·75 | 3·00 |
| 231 | £1 "Enterprise" (paddle-steamer), 1825 | 3·00 | 3·50 |
| 232 | £1.15 "Confiance" (French privateer), 1800 | 3·25 | 3·75 |
| 233 | £2 "Kent" (East Indiaman), 1820 | 5·50 | 6·50 |

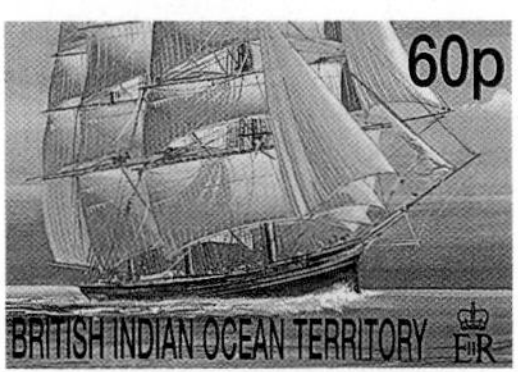


**36** Cutty Sark (clipper)

**1999.** "Australia '99" World Stamp Exhibition, Melbourne. Sheet 150×75 mm, containing T b and similar horiz design. Multicoloured.

| | | | |
|---|---|---|---|
| **MS**234 | 60p. Type **36**; 60p. "Thermopylae" (clipper) | 4·75 | 6·00 |

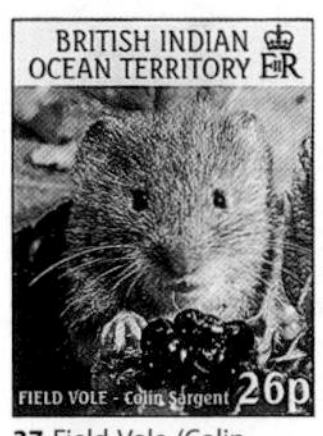


**37** Field Vole (Colin Sargent)

**2000.** "The Stamp Show 2000", International Stamp Exhibition, London. "Shoot a Stamp" Competition Winners. Sheet 150×100 mm, containing T 37 and similar vert designs. Multicoloured.

| | | | |
|---|---|---|---|
| **MS**235 | 26p. Type **37**; 34p. Atlantic puffin (P. J. Royal); 55p. Red fox (Jim Wilson); £1 European robin ("Robin") (Harry Smith) | 7·00 | 8·50 |

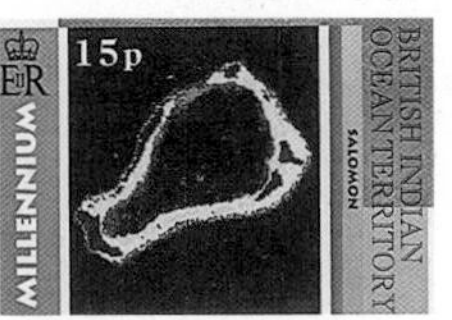


**38** Satellite Image of Salomon Island

**2000.** New Millennium. Satellite Images of Islands. Multicoloured.

| | | | |
|---|---|---|---|
| 236 | 15p. Type **38** | 1·60 | 1·40 |
| 237 | 20p. Egmont | 1·75 | 1·50 |
| 238 | 60p. Blenheim Reef | 2·75 | 2·75 |
| 239 | 80p. Diego Garcia | 3·00 | 3·00 |

**39** Queen Elizabeth the Queen Mother

**2000.** Queen Elizabeth the Queen Mother's 100th Birthday. Multicoloured.

| | | | |
|---|---|---|---|
| 240 | 26p. Type **39** | 1·40 | 1·40 |
| 241 | 34p. Wearing green hat and outfit | 1·40 | 1·40 |
| **MS**242 | 113×88 mm. 55p. In blue hat and outfit | 4·75 | 5·50 |

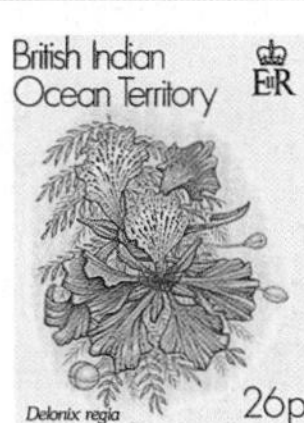


**40** *Delonix regia*

**2000.** Christmas Flowers. Multicoloured.

| | | | |
|---|---|---|---|
| 243 | 26p. Type **40** | 1·75 | 1·50 |
| 244 | 34p. *Barringtonia asiatica* | 2·00 | 1·75 |
| 245 | 60p. *Zephyranthes rosea* | 3·50 | 3·50 |

**2000.** "HONG KONG 2001" Stamp Exhibition. Sheet 150×90 mm, containing T **41** and similar design showing butterfly. Multicoloured.

| | | | |
|---|---|---|---|
| **MS**246 | 26p. Type **41**; 34p. "Junonia villida chagoensis" | 3·25 | 3·75 |

**42** H.M.S. *Turbulent*

**2001.** Centenary of Royal Navy Submarine Service. Multicoloured (except Nos. 248 and 250).

| | | | |
|---|---|---|---|
| 247 | 26p. Type **42** | 1·60 | 1·75 |
| 248 | 26p. H.M.S. *Churchill* (grey and black) | 1·60 | 1·75 |
| 249 | 34p. H.M.S. *Resolution* | 1·75 | 2·00 |
| 250 | 34p. H.M.S. *Vanguard* | 1·75 | 2·00 |
| 251 | 60p. H.M.S. *Otter* (73×27 mm) | 2·25 | 2·50 |
| 252 | 60p. H.M.S. *Oberon* (73×27 mm) (grey and black) | 2·25 | 2·50 |

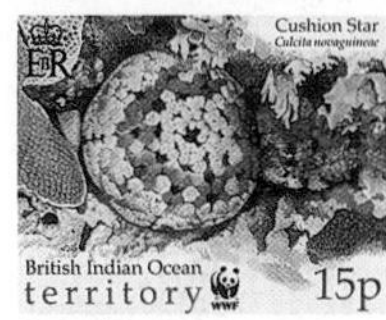


**43** Cushion Star

**2001.** Endangered Species. Seastars. Multicoloured.

| | | | |
|---|---|---|---|
| 253 | 15p. Type **43** | 1·50 | 1·25 |
| 254 | 26p. Azure sea star | 2·00 | 1·50 |
| 255 | 34p. Crown-of-Thorns | 2·25 | 1·75 |
| 256 | 56p. Banded bubble star | 3·25 | 3·50 |

**44** *Scadoxus multiflora*

**2001.** Plants (1st series). Flowers. Multicoloured.

| | | | |
|---|---|---|---|
| 257 | 26p. Type **44** | 1·75 | 1·75 |
| 258 | 34p. *Striga asiatica* | 1·75 | 1·75 |
| **MS**259 | 173×78 mm. Nos. 257/8 and 10p. "Catharanthus roseus" (horiz); 60p. "Argusia argentea" (horiz); 70p. "Euphorbia cyathophora" (horiz) | 5·50 | 6·50 |

In No. **MS**259 the 60p. is inscribed "argentia" in error.

**45** Crab Plovers on Beach

**2001.** Birdlife World Bird Festival. Crab Plovers. Sheet 175×80 mm, containing T **45** and similar multicoloured designs.

| | | | |
|---|---|---|---|
| **MS**260 | 50p. Type **45**; 50p. Crab plover catching crab (vert); 50p. Head of crab plover (vert); 50p. Crab plovers in flight; 50p. Crab plover standing on one leg | 6·50 | 7·00 |

**2002.** Golden Jubilee. As T **200** of Ascension.

| | | | |
|---|---|---|---|
| 261 | 10p. brown, blue and gold | 1·25 | 1·25 |
| 262 | 25p. multicoloured | 1·75 | 1·50 |
| 263 | 35p. black, blue and gold | 2·00 | 1·75 |
| 264 | 55p. multicoloured | 2·75 | 3·00 |
| **MS**265 | 162×95 mm. Nos. 261/4 and 75p. multicoloured | 6·50 | 7·00 |

DESIGNS—HORIZ: 10p. Princess Elizabeth in pantomime, Windsor, 1943; 25p. Queen Elizabeth in floral hat, 1967; 35p. Princess Elizabeth and Prince Philip on their engagement, 1947; 55p. Queen Elizabeth in evening dress. VERT (38×51 mm)—75p. Queen Elizabeth after Annigoni.

Designs as Nos. 261/4 in No. **MS**265 omit the gold frame around each stamp and the "Golden Jubilee 1952–2002" inscription.

**46** Adult Red-footed Booby

**2002.** Birdlife International. Red-footed Booby. Sheet 175×80 mm, containing T 46 and similar multicoloured designs.
**MS**266 50p. Type **46**; 50p. Head of dark morph red-footed booby; 50p. Adult bird in flight (vert); 50p. Dark morph on nest (vert); 50p. Fledgling on nest 9·00 9·50

**2002.** Queen Elizabeth the Queen Mother Commemoration. As T **202** of Ascension.
267 26p. brown, gold and purple 1·50 1·25
268 £1 multicoloured 3·00 3·25
**MS**269 145×70 mm. £1 black and gold; £1 multicoloured 8·00 9·00
DESIGNS: 26p. Lady Elizabeth Bowes-Lyon, 1921; £1 (No. 268) Queen Mother, 1986; £1 brownish black and gold (No. **MS**269) Queen Elizabeth at garden party, 1951; £1 multicoloured (No. **MS**269) Queen Mother at Cheltenham Races, 1994.
Designs in No. **MS**269 omit the "1900–2002" inscription and the coloured frame.

**47** Microgoby

**2002.** 10th Anniv of Friends of Chagos (conservation association). Reef Fish. Mult.
270 2p. Type **47** 40 60
271 15p. Angel fish 85 85
272 26p. Surgeonfish 1·25 1·25
273 34p. Trunkfish 1·50 1·50
274 58p. Soldierfish 2·50 3·00
275 £1 Chagos anemonefish 4·00 4·50

**48** *Halgerda tesselata*

**2003.** Sea Slugs. Multicoloured.
276 2p. Type **48** 40 60
277 15p. *Notodoris minor* 85 85
278 26p. *Nembrotha lineolata* 1·25 1·25
279 50p. *Chromodoris quadricolor* 2·00 2·25
280 76p. *Glossodoris cincta* 3·00 3·50
281 £1.10 *Chromodoris cf leopardus* 3·75 4·25

**2003.** 50th Anniv of Coronation. As T **206** of Ascension. Multicoloured.
282 £1 Queen Elizabeth II wearing Imperial State Crown in Coronation Coach 4·00 4·00
283 £2 Queen with members of Royal Family in Coronation robes 7·00 8·00
**MS**284 95×115 mm. £1 As No. 282; £2 As No. 283 10·00 11·00
Nos. 282/3 have red frame; stamps from **MS**284 have no frame and country name in mauve panel.

**2003.** As T **207** of Ascension.
285 £2.50 black, pink and red 7·00 7·50

**2003.** 21st Birthday of Prince William of Wales. As T **208** of Ascension. Multicoloured.
286 50p. Prince William at Cirencester Polo Club 2·25 2·25
287 £1 With Prince Charles on skiing holiday and at Cirencester Polo Club 3·75 4·00

**2003.** Centenary of Powered Flight. As Type **209** of Ascension. Multicoloured.
288 34p. Avro Type 683 Lancaster 1·50 1·50
289 34p. de Havilland D.H.98 Mosquito 1·50 1·50
290 58p. Hawker Hurricane 2·00 2·00
291 58p. Supermarine Spitfire 2·00 2·00
292 76p. Vickers-Armstrong Wellington 2·50 2·50
293 76p. Lockheed C-130 Hercules 2·50 2·50
**MS**294 233×85 mm. 26p. Boeing E-3A Sentry AWACS; 26p. Boeing B-17 Flying Fortress; 26p. Lockheed P-3 Orion; 26p. Consolidated B-24 Liberator; 26p. Lockheed C-141 StarLifter; 26p. Supermarine Walrus; 26p. Short S.25 Sunderland (flying boat); 26p. Supermarine Stranraer; 26p. PBY Catalina; 26p. Supermarine Sea Otter 9·00 10·00

**49** *Pacific Marlin* (fisheries patrol ship)

**2004.** Fisheries Patrol. Multicoloured.
**MS**295 150×110 mm. 34p. Type **49**; 34p. Marlin; 58p. Skipjack tuna; 58p. Yellowfin tuna; 76p. Swordfish; 76p. Bigeye tuna 11·00 11·00

**50** Madagascar Red Fody ("Madagascar Fody")

**2004.** Birds. Multicoloured.
296 2p. Type **50** 20 30
297 14p. Zebra dove ("Barred Ground Dove") 50 50
298 20p. Common mynah ("Indian Mynah") 70 70
299 26p. Cattle egret 80 70
300 34p. White tern ("Fairy Tern") 1·00 90
301 58p. Blue-faced booby ("Masked Booby") 1·75 1·75
302 76p. Great frigate bird 2·25 2·25
303 80p. White-tailed tropic bird 2·25 2·25
304 £1.10 Green-backed heron ("Little Green Heron") 3·25 3·50
305 £1.34 Pacific golden plover 4·00 4·25
306 £1.48 Garganey ("Garganey Teal") 4·50 4·75
307 £2.50 Bar-tailed godwit 7·00 7·50

**51** Coconut Crab

**2004.** Crabs. Multicoloured.
308 26p. Type **51** 90 80
309 34p. Land crab 1·25 1·00
310 76p. Rock crab 2·50 2·75
311 £1.10 Ghost crab 3·75 4·00

**52** Two Hawksbill Turtle Babies

**2005.** Turtles. Multicoloured.
312 26p. Type **52** 1·25 1·25
313 26p. Baby Green turtle 1·25 1·25
314 34p. Adult Hawksbill turtle 1·60 1·60
315 34p. Adult Green turtle 1·60 1·60
316 76p. Hawksbill turtle swimming 3·00 3·25
317 £1.10 Green turtle swimming 4·25 4·50
**MS**318 90×63 mm. £1.70 As No. 317 6·00 7·00
No. **MS**318 commemorates the Turtle Cove Clean-up operation sponsored by Cable and Wireless.

**2005.** Bicentenary of Battle of Trafalgar (1st issue). As T **216** of Ascension. Multicoloured.
319 26p. Tower Sea Service Pistol, 1796 1·10 1·10
320 26p. HMS *Phoebe* 1·10 1·10
321 34p. Boatswain RN, 1805 1·50 1·50
322 34p. HMS *Harrier* 1·50 1·50
323 76p. Portrait of Admiral Nelson 3·00 3·00
324 76p. HMS *Victory* (horiz) 3·00 3·00
**MS**325 120×79 mm. £1.10 HMS *Minotaur*; £1.10 HMS *Spartiate* 6·50 7·00
No. 324 contains traces of powdered wood from HMS *Victory*.
See also Nos. 344/6.

**53** HMAS *Wollongong*, September 1942

**2005.** 60th Anniv of the End of World War II. "Route to Victory". As T **53**. Multicoloured.
326 26p. Type **53** 90 90
327 26p. *Ondina* (Dutch tanker) and HMS *Bengal* attacked by Japanese surface raiders, 11 November 1942 90 90
328 26p. HMS *Pathfinder* (arrived at Diego Garcia, 4 April 1944) 90 90
329 26p. HMS *Lossie* (rescued survivors from Australian freighter *Nellore*, 29 June 1944) 90 90
330 26p. US Liberty Ship *Jean Nicolet* (sunk by Japanese, 2 July 1944) 90 90
331 34p. General Douglas MacArthur and landing party wading ashore 1·25 1·25
332 34p. General Bernard Montgomery and tanks in North African desert 1·25 1·25
333 34p. General George Patton and tanks 1·25 1·25
334 34p. Winston Churchill and St. Paul's Cathedral 1·25 1·25
335 34p. US Pres. Franklin Roosevelt and steelworks 1·25 1·25

**54** Blacktip Reef Shark

**2005.** Sharks and Rays. Multicoloured.
336 26p. Type **54** 90 90
337 26p. Grey reef shark 90 90
338 34p. Silvertip shark 1·25 1·25
339 34p. Tawny nurse shark 1·25 1·25
340 34p. Spotted eagle ray 1·25 1·25
341 34p. Manta ray 1·25 1·25
342 76p. Porcupine ray 2·50 2·75
343 £2 Feathertail stingray 6·00 6·50

**2005.** Bicentenary of the Battle of Trafalgar (2nd issue). As T **220** of Ascension. Multicoloured.
344 26p. HMS *Victory* 1·00 1·00
345 34p. Ships engaged in battle (horiz) 1·50 1·50
346 £2 Admiral Lord Nelson 6·50 6·50

**55** Crab on Beach

**2005.** 40th Anniv of British Indian Ocean Territory. T 55 and similar vert designs. Multicoloured.
**MS**347 205×129 mm. 34p. Type **55**; 34p. Two hermit crabs on beach; 34p. Blue-faced boobies at nest; 34p. Outline map of Indian Ocean and lesser frigate bird; 34p. Pair of imperial angelfish; 34p. Pair of racoon butterflyfish; 34p. Moorish idol (fish); 34p. Outline map of British Indian Ocean Territory and turtle 11·00 12·00
The stamps within No. **MS**347 form a composite background design showing a beach and coral reef.

**2006.** 80th Birthday of Queen Elizabeth II. As T **223** of Ascension. Multicoloured.
348 26p. Princess Elizabeth 1·25 1·25
349 34p. Queen Elizabeth II, c. 1952 1·50 1·50
350 76p. Wearing tiara 2·75 3·00
351 £1.10 Wearing headscarf 3·50 3·75
**MS**352 144×75 mm. £1 As No. 349; £1 As No. 350 7·00 7·50

**56** Dusky Angelfish

**2006.** Marine Life (1st series). Angelfish. Sheet 205×129 mm containing T 56 and similar horiz designs. Multicoloured.
**MS**353 26p. Type **56**; 26p. Two-spined angelfish; 26p. Bicolour angelfish; 34p. Orangeback angelfish; 34p. Emperor angelfish; £2 Threespot angelfish 11·00 12·00
The stamps and margins of No. **MS**353 form a composite design showing a coral reef.
See also Nos. **MS**354, **MS**356 and **MS**372.

**2006.** Marine Life (2nd series). Butterflyfish. Sheet 205×129 mm containing horiz designs as T **56**. Multicoloured.
**MS**354 26p. Melon butterflyfish; 26p. Raccoon butterflyfish; 26p. Scrawled butterflyfish; 34p. Longnose butterflyfish; 34p. Threadfin butterflyfish; £2 Masked bannerfish 11·00 12·00
The stamps and margins of No. **MS**354 form a composite design showing a coral reef.

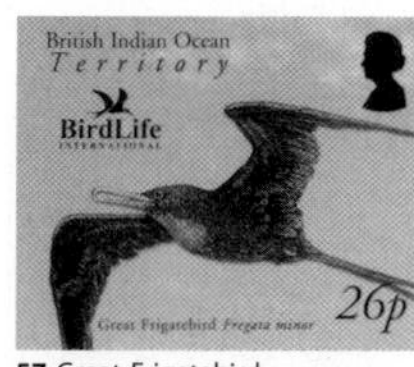
**57** Great Frigatebird

**2006.** BirdLife International. Barton Point Nature Reserve. Sheet 170×85 mm containing T 57 and similar horiz designs. Multicoloured.
**MS**355 26p. Type **57**; 26p. Black-naped tern; 26p. Yellow-billed tropicbird; 26p. White tern; 26p. Brown noddy; £2 Red-footed booby 10·50 11·50
The stamps within No. **MS**355 form a composite design.

**2007.** Marine Life (3rd series). Parrotfish. Sheet 205×129 mm containing horiz designs as T **56**. Multicoloured.
**MS**356 54p. Common parrotfish; 54p. Daisy parrotfish; 54p. Bicolour parrotfish; 54p. Bridled parrotfish; 90p. Indian Ocean steephead parrotfish; 90p. Ember parrotfish 8·50 9·50
The stamps and margins of No. **MS**356 form a composite design showing a coral reef.

**58** Princess Elizabeth and Lt. Philip Mountbatten, c. 1947

**2007.** Diamond Wedding of Queen Elizabeth II and Duke of Edinburgh. Multicoloured.
357 54p. Type **58** 1·60 1·60
358 54p. Wedding procession and crowds, 1949 1·60 1·60
359 90p. Princess Elizabeth and Lt. Philip Mountbatten arm in arm, c. 1947 3·00 3·00
360 90p. Wedding ceremony, 1949 3·00 3·00
**MS**361 125×85 mm. £2.14 Princess Elizabeth and Lt. Philip Mountbatten, c. 1947 (42×56 mm) 7·00 7·00

**59** Charles Darwin and Beach with Tropic Bird, Terns and Turtle

**2007.** 125th Death Anniv of Charles Darwin. Multicoloured.
362 54p. Type **59** 1·60 1·60
363 54p. HMS *Beagle* 1·60 1·60
364 90p. Turtles 3·00 3·00
365 90p. Coral reef 3·00 3·00

**60** Pomarine Skua pursuing Tropic Bird

**2007.** BirdLife International. Pomarine Skua (Stercorarius pomarinus). Multicoloured.
366 54p. Type **60** 1·75 1·75
367 54p. Pomarine skua pursuing booby 1·75 1·75
368 54p. Pair of pomarine skuas in flight 1·75 1·75
369 54p. Pair of pomarine skuas on beach 1·75 1·75

| | | | |
|---|---|---|---|
| 370 | 90p. Pomarine skua pursuing terns | 3·00 | 3·00 |
| 371 | 90p. Pomarine skua on sea | 3·00 | 3·00 |

**2008.** Marine Life (4th series). Damselfish. Sheet 205×129 mm containing horiz designs as T **56**. Multicoloured.

| | | | |
|---|---|---|---|
| **MS**372 | 54p. *Chrysiptera unimaculata* (onespot demoiselle); 54p. *Abudefdufseptemfasciatus* (banded sergeant); 54p. *Plectroglyphidodon johnstonianus* (Johnston Island damsel); 54p. *Amphiprion chagosensis* (Chagos anemonefish); 90p. *Chromisatripectoralis* (black-axil chromis); 90p. *Pomacentrus caeruleus* (caerulean damsel) | 9·50 | 9·50 |

The stamps and margins of No. **MS**372 form a composite design showing a coral reef.

**2008.** Military Uniforms. As T **286** of Bahamas. Multicoloured.

| | | | |
|---|---|---|---|
| 373 | 27p. Royal Marines | 90 | 90 |
| 374 | 27p. Royal Engineers | 90 | 90 |
| 375 | 54p. Sepoys, East India Company Army | 1·75 | 1·75 |
| 376 | 54p. Officer, East India Company Army | 1·75 | 1·75 |
| 377 | 54p. Artillery Corps | 1·75 | 1·75 |
| 378 | 54p. Sergeant, Royal Military Police | 1·75 | 1·75 |

61 Avro 504

**2008.** 90th Anniv of the Royal Air Force. Multicoloured.

| | | | |
|---|---|---|---|
| 379 | 27p. Type **61** | 90 | 90 |
| 380 | 27p. Short Sunderland | 90 | 90 |
| 381 | 27p. de Havilland Mosquito | 90 | 90 |
| 382 | 27p. Vickers VC10 | 90 | 90 |
| 383 | 54p. English Electric Canberra | 1·75 | 1·75 |
| **MS**384 | 70×110 mm. £1.72 King George V, Marshal of the RAF (vert). Wmk inverted | 5·50 | 5·50 |

63 Pte Harry Lamin, 1918

**2008.** 90th Anniv of the End of World War I. Designs showing soldiers and their letters home. Multicoloured.

| | | | |
|---|---|---|---|
| 385 | 50p. Type **63** | 1·60 | 1·60 |
| 386 | 50p. Second Lt. Eric Heaton, 1916 | 1·60 | 1·60 |
| 387 | 50p. Pte Dennis Harry Wilson, 1917 | 1·60 | 1·60 |
| 388 | 50p. Second Lt. Eric Rose, 1917 | 1·60 | 1·60 |
| 389 | 50p. Sgt.-Major Francis Proud, 1915 | 1·60 | 1·60 |
| 390 | 50p. Second Lt. Charles Roberts, 1917 | 1·60 | 1·60 |
| **MS**391 | 110×70 mm. £1 UK Overseas Territories Wreath of Remembrance | 3·25 | 3·25 |

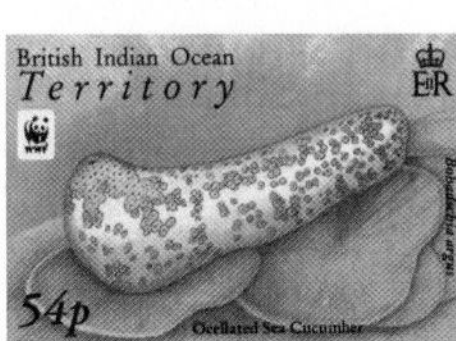


64 *Bohadschia argus* (ocellated sea cucumber)

**2008.** Endangered Species. Sea Cucumbers. Multicoloured.

| | | | |
|---|---|---|---|
| 392 | 54p. Type **64** | 1·75 | 1·75 |
| 393 | 54p. *Thelenota ananas* (pineapple sea cucumber) | 1·75 | 1·75 |
| 394 | 90p. *Pearsonothuria graeffei* (Graeffe's sea cucumber) | 2·75 | 2·75 |
| 395 | 90p. *Stichopus chloronotus* (dark green sea cucumber) | 2·75 | 2·75 |

65 HMS *Endeavour* (Cook)

**2009.** Seafaring and Exploration. Multicoloured.

| | | | |
|---|---|---|---|
| 396 | 54p. Type **65** | 1·75 | 1·75 |
| 397 | 54p. HMS *Victory* (Nelson) | 1·75 | 1·75 |
| 398 | 54p. HMS *Beagle* (Darwin) | 1·75 | 1·75 |
| 399 | 54p. SS *Windsor Castle* (landing of Captain Raymond, Diego Garcia, 1884) | 1·75 | 1·75 |
| 400 | 54p. SMS *Fürst Bismarck* (German armoured cruiser, 1900) | 1·75 | 1·75 |
| 401 | 54p. HMS *Edinburgh* (1983) | 1·75 | 1·75 |
| **MS**402 | 110×70 mm. £1.30 Vasco da Gama (Portuguese navigator, sighted Chagos Archipelago, early 16th century) (vert) | 3·75 | 3·75 |

**2009.** Centenary of Naval Aviation. Multicoloured (except **MS**407).

| | | | |
|---|---|---|---|
| 403 | 27p. Short S.38 | 1·00 | 1·00 |
| 404 | 27p. Sopwith Pup | 1·00 | 1·00 |
| 405 | 54p. Supermarine Scimitar | 1·75 | 1·75 |
| 406 | 54p. Westland Wessex helicopter | 1·75 | 1·75 |
| **MS**407 | 110×70 mm. £1.72 Sqn. Cdr. E. H. Dunning landing aircraft on HMS *Furious*, 1917 (black, deep ultramarine and rosine) | 5·50 | 5·50 |

**2009.** International Year of Astronomy. 40th Anniv of First Moon Landing. Multicoloured.

| | | | |
|---|---|---|---|
| 408 | 54p. Development of early rockets *Corporal* and *Private* | 2·50 | 2·50 |
| 409 | 54p. *Flying Bedstead*, 1964 | 2·50 | 2·50 |
| 410 | 54p. Apollo Launch Site, 1969 | 2·50 | 2·50 |
| 411 | 54p. Space Transportation System 71 launch, 1995 | 2·50 | 2·50 |
| 412 | 90p. ESA Columbus Laboratory STS 122, 2008 | 4·00 | 4·00 |
| **MS**413 | 100×80 mm. £1.50 *Savoring the Moment* (astronaut Jack Schmitt on Moon) (Alan Bean) (39×59 mm) | 6·50 | 6·50 |

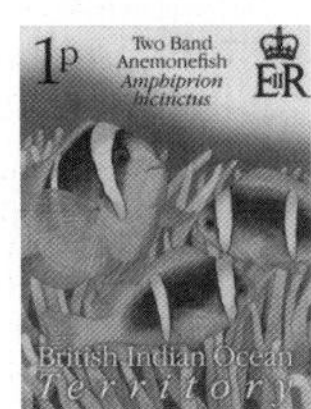


66 Two Band Anemonefish (*Amphiprion bicinctus*)

**2009.** Fish, Fauna, Flora and Coves. Multicoloured.

| | | | |
|---|---|---|---|
| 414 | 1p. Type **66** | 10 | 10 |
| 415 | 2p. Angelfish (*Centropyge bicolor*) | 15 | 15 |
| 416 | 5p. Royal poinciana (*Delonix regia*) | 25 | 25 |
| 417 | 12p. Beach morning glory (*Ipomoea pes-caprae*) | 55 | 55 |
| 418 | 27p. Bay cedar (*Suriana maritima*) | 1·25 | 1·25 |
| 419 | 45p. Scaevola bush (*Scaevola taccada*) | 2·00 | 2·00 |
| 420 | 54p. Madagascan red fody (*Foudia madagascariensis*) | 2·50 | 2·50 |
| 421 | 90p. Greater frigatebird (*Fregata minor*) | 4·00 | 4·00 |
| 422 | £1.30 Sharks Cove | 5·00 | 5·00 |
| 423 | £1.72 Turtle Cove | 6·25 | 6·25 |
| 424 | £2.64 Hawksbill turtle | 8·75 | 8·75 |
| 425 | £3.02 Sicklefin lemon shark (*Negaprion acutidens*) | 11·00 | 11·00 |
| **MS**426 | 194×134 mm. Nos. 414/25 | 38·00 | 38·00 |

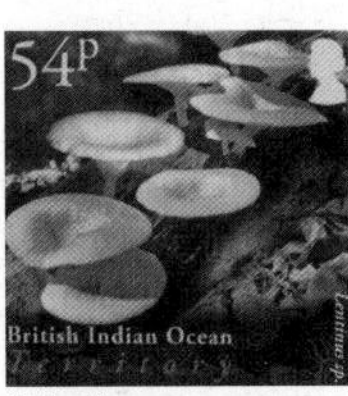


67 *Lentinus* sp.

**2009.** Fungi. Multicoloured.

| | | | |
|---|---|---|---|
| 427 | 54p. Type **67** | 2·50 | 2·50 |
| 428 | 54p. *Entoloma* sp. | 2·50 | 2·50 |
| 429 | 90p. *Leucocoprinus* sp. | 4·00 | 4·00 |
| 430 | 90p. *Pycnoporus* sp. | 4·00 | 4·00 |

68 Hugh Dowding

**2010.** 70th Anniv of the Battle of Britain. Aces and Leaders. Multicoloured.

| | | | |
|---|---|---|---|
| 431 | 50p. Type **68** | 1·60 | 1·60 |
| 432 | 50p. Bob Stanford-Tuck | 1·60 | 1·60 |
| 433 | 50p. Ginger Lacey | 1·60 | 1·60 |
| 434 | 50p. Eric Lock | 1·60 | 1·60 |
| 435 | 50p. Mike Crossley | 1·60 | 1·60 |
| 436 | 50p. Bob Doe | 1·60 | 1·60 |
| **MS**437 | 110×70mm. $1.50 Sir Douglas Bader | 4·75 | 4·75 |

69 Great Britain George V 1934 1½d. Stamp

**2010.** London 2010 Festival of Stamps and Centenary of Accession of King George V

| | | | |
|---|---|---|---|
| **MS**438 | **69** £1.50 multicoloured | 4·75 | 4·75 |

70 Archer and Mounted Knight, Battle of Hastings, 1066

**2010.** Great Battles. Multicoloured.

| | | | |
|---|---|---|---|
| 439 | 50p. Type **70** | 1·60 | 1·60 |
| 440 | 50p. Mounted knight carrying standard and archers, Battle of Agincourt, 1415 | 1·60 | 1·60 |
| 441 | 50p. Mounted knights, Battle of Bosworth, 1485 | 1·60 | 1·60 |
| 442 | 50p. Cavalry, Battle of Naseby, 1645 | 1·60 | 1·60 |
| 443 | 50p. Soldiers, Battle of Culloden, 1746 | 1·60 | 1·60 |
| 444 | 50p. Duke of Wellington on horseback and soldiers, Battle of Waterloo, 1815 | 1·60 | 1·60 |
| 445 | 50p. Soldiers and cavalryman, Battle of Alma, 1854 | 1·60 | 1·60 |
| 446 | 50p. British soldiers, Battle of Rorke's Drift, 1879 | 1·60 | 1·60 |
| 447 | 50p. Soldiers, Siege of Mafeking, 1899 | 1·60 | 1·60 |
| 448 | 50p. Soldiers, Battle of the Somme, 1916 | 1·60 | 1·60 |
| 449 | 50p. Soldiers, Battle of El Alamein, 1942 | 1·60 | 1·60 |
| 450 | 50p. Normandy Landings, 1944 | 1·60 | 1·60 |

Nos. 439/50 were each printed in sheetlets of six stamps with enlarged illustrated margins.

**2011.** Queen Elizabeth II and Prince Philip 'A Lifetime of Service'. Multicoloured.

| | | | |
|---|---|---|---|
| 451 | 54p. Queen Elizabeth II, c. 1952 | 1·80 | 1·80 |
| 452 | 54p. Queen Elizabeth II and Prince Philip (black/white photo), c. 1972 | 1·80 | 1·80 |
| 453 | 54p. Queen Elizabeth II and Prince Philip, c. 1955 | 1·80 | 1·80 |
| 454 | 54p. Queen Elizabeth II and Prince Philip (seen in profile), c. 2010 | 1·80 | 1·80 |
| 455 | 54p. Queen Elizabeth II and Prince Philip, c. 1970 | 1·80 | 1·80 |
| 456 | 54p. Prince Philip, c. 1955 | 1·80 | 1·80 |
| **MS**457 | 174×163 mm. Nos. 451/6 and three stamp-size labels | 10·50 | 10·50 |
| **MS**458 | 110×70 mm. £3.02 Queen Elizabeth II and Prince Philip, c. 2007 | 10·00 | 10·00 |

### PARCEL POST STAMPS

**2002.** 10th Anniv of Friends of Chagos (conservation association). Reef Fish. Sheet 115×95 mm, containing horiz design as T **47**. Multicoloured.

| | | | |
|---|---|---|---|
| PMS1 | £1.90 Parrotfish | 6·00 | 6·50 |

Pt. 1

# BRITISH LEVANT

Stamps used at British post offices in the Turkish Empire. These offices closed in 1914. The stamps were again in use after 1918, during the British Occupation of Turkey.

Stamps of Great Britain surcharged or overprinted.

40 paras = 1 piastre.

### A. BRITISH POST OFFICES IN TURKISH EMPIRE
### I. TURKISH CURRENCY

**1885.** Queen Victoria stamps surch in PARAS or PIASTRES.

| | | | | |
|---|---|---|---|---|
| 1 | **64** | 40pa. on 2½d. lilac | £130 | 1·25 |
| 4 | **74** | 40pa. on 2½d. purple on blue | 11·00 | 10 |
| 7 | **71** | 40pa. on ½d. red | £425 | £100 |
| 2 | **62** | 80pa. on 5d. green | £225 | 9·50 |
| 5 | **78** | 80pa. on 5d. purple & blue | 17·00 | 30 |
| 6 | **81** | 4pi. on 10d. purple and red | 42·00 | 8·00 |
| 3a | **58** | 12pi. on 2s.6d. lilac | 55·00 | 26·00 |

**1902.** King Edward VII stamps surch in PARAS or PIASTRES.

| | | | | |
|---|---|---|---|---|
| 29 | - | 30pa. on 1½d. purple & grn | 6·50 | 55 |
| 8 | **83** | 40pa. on 2½d. blue | 20·00 | 10 |
| 9 | - | 80pa. on 5d. purple and blue | 14·00 | 2·00 |
| 13 | **83** | 1pi. on 2½d. blue | 23·00 | 10 |
| 30 | - | 2pi. on 5d. purple and blue | 22·00 | 3·00 |
| 10 | - | 4pi. on 10d. purple and red | 18·00 | 4·00 |
| 21 | - | 5pi. on 1s. green and red | 4·25 | 15·00 |
| 11 | - | 12pi. on 2s.6d. purple | 38·00 | 38·00 |
| 12 | - | 24pi. on 5s. red | 32·00 | 42·00 |

**1906.** Surch 1 Piastre.

| | | | | |
|---|---|---|---|---|
| 15 | | 1pi. on 2d. green and red | £1400 | £650 |

**1909.** King Edward VII stamps surch in PIASTRE PARAS.

| | | | | |
|---|---|---|---|---|
| 17 | - | 1pi. 10pa. on 3d. pur on yell | 12·00 | 48·00 |
| 18 | - | 1pi. 30pa. on 4d. grn & brn | 5·00 | 17·00 |
| 19 | - | 1pi. 30pa. on 4d. orange | 20·00 | 70·00 |
| 20 | **83** | 2pi. 20pa. on 6d. purple | 26·00 | 70·00 |

**1910.** King Edward VII stamps surch in PIASTRES.

| | | | | |
|---|---|---|---|---|
| 22 | - | 1¼pi. on 3d. purple on yellow | 65 | 1·00 |
| 23 | - | 1¾pi. on 4d. orange | 50 | 60 |
| 24 | **83** | 2½pi. on 6d. purple | 2·25 | 65 |

**1913.** King George V stamps surch.

| | | | | |
|---|---|---|---|---|
| 35 | **105** | 30pa. on 1½d. brown | 3·50 | 14·00 |
| 41 | **105** | 30pa. on ½d. green | 75 | 15·00 |
| 36a | **104** | 1pi. on 2½d. blue | 12·00 | 15 |
| 37 | **106** | 1¼pi. on 3d. violet | 8·00 | 4·25 |
| 42 | **104** | 1½pi. on 1d. red | 1·75 | 1·50 |
| 38 | **106** | 1¾pi. on 4d. grey-green | 3·50 | 8·00 |
| 43 | **104** | 3¾pi. on 2½d. blue | 1·25 | 25 |
| 39 | **108** | 4pi. on 10d. blue | 10·00 | 26·00 |
| 44 | **106** | 4½pi. on 3d. violet | 2·00 | 3·75 |
| 40 | **108** | 5pi. on 1s. brown | 42·00 | 60·00 |
| 45 | **107** | 7½pi. on 5d. brown | 50 | 10 |
| 46 | **108** | 15pi. on 10d. blue | 70 | 15 |
| 47 | **108** | 18¾pi. on 1s. brown | 4·25 | 4·25 |
| 48 | **109** | 45pi. on 2s.6d. brown | 20·00 | 45·00 |
| 49 | **109** | 90pi. on 5s. red | 25·00 | 30·00 |
| 50 | **109** | 180pi. on 10s. blue | 45·00 | 40·00 |

### II. BRITISH CURRENCY

**1905.** King Edward VII stamps optd LEVANT.

| | | | | |
|---|---|---|---|---|
| L1 | **83** | ½d. green | 8·50 | 15 |
| L2 | **83** | 1d. red | 13·00 | 15 |
| L3 | - | 1½d. purple and green | 6·00 | 2·00 |
| L4a | - | 2d. green and red | 3·50 | 7·50 |
| L5 | **83** | 2½d. blue | 8·50 | 20·00 |
| L6 | - | 3d. purple and yellow | 7·00 | 12·00 |
| L7 | - | 4d. green and brown | 9·50 | 65·00 |
| L8 | - | 5d. purple and blue | 16·00 | 38·00 |
| L9 | **83** | 6d. purple | 12·00 | 25·00 |
| L10 | **83** | 1s. green and red | 42·00 | 50·00 |

**1911.** King George V stamps optd LEVANT.

| | | | | |
|---|---|---|---|---|
| L12 | **98** | ½d. green | 2·25 | 2·50 |
| L14 | **101** | ½d. green | 2·00 | 20 |
| L16 | **105** | ½d. green | 1·75 | 3·00 |
| L13 | **99** | 1d. red | 50 | 7·50 |
| L15 | **102** | 1d. red | 2·00 | 1·60 |
| L17 | **104** | 1d. red | 30 | 7·00 |
| L18 | **106** | 2d. orange | 2·25 | 38·00 |
| L19 | **106** | 3d. violet | 7·50 | 10·00 |
| L20 | **106** | 4d. green | 5·00 | 19·00 |
| L21 | **107** | 5d. brown | 12·00 | 28·00 |
| L22a | **107** | 6d. purple | 27·00 | 8·50 |
| L23 | **108** | 1s. brown | 17·00 | 8·50 |
| L24 | **109** | 2s.6d. brown | 38·00 | 90·00 |

### B. BRITISH FIELD OFFICE IN SALONICA

**1916.** King George V stamps of Great Britain optd Levant.

| | | | | |
|---|---|---|---|---|
| S1 | **105** | ½d. green | 65·00 | £300 |

| | | | | |
|---|---|---|---|---|
| S2 | 104 | 1d. red | 65·00 | £300 |
| S3 | 106 | 2d. orange | £180 | £425 |
| S4 | 106 | 3d. violet | £150 | £425 |
| S5 | 106 | 4d. green | £180 | £425 |
| S6 | 107 | 6d. purple | £100 | £375 |
| S7 | 108 | 9d. black | £375 | £700 |
| S8 | 108 | 1s. brown | £325 | £600 |

The above stamps were optd at Salonica during the war of 1914–18.

Pt. 1

# BRITISH OCCUPATION OF ITALIAN COLONIES

Issues for use in Italian colonies occupied by British Forces. Middle East Forces overprints were used in Cyrenaica, Dodecanese Islands, Eritrea, Italian Somaliland and Tripolitania.

Middle East Forces.
12 pence = 1 shilling; 20 shillings = 1 pound.

Cyrenaica.
10 milliemes = 1 piastre; 20 shillings = 1 pound.

Eritrea.
100 cents = 1 shilling.

### MIDDLE EAST FORCES

**1942.** Stamps of Great Britain optd M.E.F.

| | | | | |
|---|---|---|---|---|
| M11 | 128 | 1d. red | 1·50 | 10 |
| M12 | 128 | 2d. orange | 1·75 | 1·25 |
| M13 | 128 | 2½d. blue | 1·75 | 10 |
| M4 | 128 | 3d. violet | 1·50 | 30 |
| M5 | 129 | 5d. brown | 1·50 | 30 |
| M16 | 129 | 6d. purple | 40 | 10 |
| M17 | 130 | 9d. olive | 85 | 10 |
| M18 | 130 | 1s. brown | 50 | 10 |
| M19 | 131 | 2s.6d. green | 7·00 | 1·00 |
| M20 | 131 | 5s. red | 24·00 | 17·00 |
| M21 | 131 | 10s. blue (No. 478a) | 35·00 | 10·00 |

**PRICES.** Our prices for Nos. M1/21 in used condition are for stamps with identifiable postmarks of the territories in which they were issued. These stamps were also used in the United Kingdom with official sanction, from the summer of 1950 onwards, and with U.K. postmarks are worth about 25 per cent less.

### POSTAGE DUE STAMPS

**1942.** Postage Due stamps of Great Britain optd M.E.F.

| | | | | |
|---|---|---|---|---|
| MD1 | D1 | ½d. green | 30 | 13·00 |
| MD2 | D1 | 1d. red | 30 | 1·75 |
| MD3 | D1 | 2d. black | 1·25 | 1·25 |
| MD4 | D1 | 3d. violet | 50 | 4·25 |
| MD5 | D1 | 1s. blue | 3·75 | 13·00 |

### CYRENAICA

24 Mounted Warrior

25 Mounted Warrior

**1950**

| | | | | |
|---|---|---|---|---|
| 136 | 24 | 1m. brown | 3·75 | 7·00 |
| 137 | 24 | 2m. red | 3·75 | 7·00 |
| 138 | 24 | 3m. yellow | 3·75 | 6·50 |
| 139 | 24 | 4m. green | 3·75 | 7·00 |
| 140 | 24 | 5m. grey | 3·75 | 5·50 |
| 141 | 24 | 8m. orange | 3·75 | 3·25 |
| 142 | 24 | 10m. violet | 3·75 | 2·50 |
| 143 | 24 | 12m. red | 3·75 | 2·75 |
| 144 | 24 | 20m. blue | 3·75 | 2·50 |
| 145 | 25 | 50m. blue and brown | 12·00 | 8·50 |
| 146 | 25 | 100m. red and black | 20·00 | 10·00 |
| 147 | 25 | 200m. violet and blue | 28·00 | 30·00 |
| 148 | 25 | 500m. yellow and green | 55·00 | 75·00 |

### POSTAGE DUE STAMPS

D26

**1950**

| | | | | |
|---|---|---|---|---|
| D149 | D26 | 2m. brown | 60·00 | £110 |
| D150 | D26 | 4m. green | 60·00 | £110 |
| D151 | D26 | 8m. red | 60·00 | £120 |
| D152 | D26 | 10m. orange | 60·00 | £120 |
| D153 | D26 | 20m. yellow | 60·00 | £140 |
| D154 | D26 | 40m. blue | 60·00 | £180 |
| D155 | D26 | 100m. black | 60·00 | £200 |

### ERITREA BRITISH MILITARY ADMINISTRATION

**1948.** Stamps of Great Britain surch B.M.A. ERITREA and value in cents or shillings.

| | | | | |
|---|---|---|---|---|
| E1 | 128 | 5c. on ½d. green | 2·50 | 65 |
| E2 | 128 | 10c. on 1d. red | 2·00 | 2·50 |
| E3 | 128 | 20c. on 2d. orange | 2·50 | 2·25 |
| E4 | 128 | 25c. on 2½d. blue | 2·00 | 60 |
| E5 | 128 | 30c. on 3d. violet | 2·25 | 4·50 |
| E6 | 129 | 40c. on 5d. brown | 2·75 | 4·25 |
| E7 | 129 | 50c. on 6d. purple | 1·75 | 1·00 |
| E7a | 130 | 65c. on 8d. red | 7·00 | 2·00 |
| E8 | 130 | 75c. on 9d. olive | 3·00 | 75 |
| E9 | 130 | 1s. on 1s. brown | 2·50 | 50 |
| E10 | 131 | 2s.50 on 2s.6d. green | 9·00 | 10·00 |
| E11 | 131 | 5s. on 5s. red | 11·00 | 23·00 |
| E12 | - | 10s. on 10s. blue (No. 478a) | 24·00 | 23·00 |

### BRITISH ADMINISTRATION

**1950.** Stamps of Great Britain surch B.A. ERITREA and value in cents or shillings.

| | | | | |
|---|---|---|---|---|
| E13 | 128 | 5c. on ½d. green | 1·50 | 8·00 |
| E26 | 128 | 5c. on ½d. orange | 1·50 | 1·75 |
| E14 | 128 | 10c. on 1d. red | 40 | 3·00 |
| E27 | 128 | 10c. on 1d. blue | 1·25 | 75 |
| E15 | 128 | 20c. on 2d. orange | 1·00 | 80 |
| E28 | 128 | 20c. on 2d. brown | 1·50 | 30 |
| E16 | 128 | 25c. on 2½d. blue | 1·00 | 60 |
| E29 | 128 | 25c. on 2½d. red | 1·50 | 30 |
| E17 | 128 | 30c. on 3d. violet | 40 | 2·25 |
| E18 | 129 | 40c. on 5d. brown | 2·25 | 1·75 |
| E19 | 129 | 50c. on 6d. purple | 40 | 20 |
| E20 | 130 | 65c. on 8d. red | 5·00 | 1·50 |
| E21 | 130 | 75c. on 9d. olive | 1·50 | 25 |
| E22 | 130 | 1s. on 1s. brown | 40 | 15 |
| E23 | 131 | 2s.50 on 2s.6d. green | 8·00 | 4·75 |
| E24 | 131 | 5s. on 5s. red | 8·00 | 12·00 |
| E25 | - | 10s. on 10s. blue (No. 478a) | 70·00 | 65·00 |

**1951.** Nos. 509/11 of Great Britain surch B.A. ERITREA and value in cents and shillings.

| | | | | |
|---|---|---|---|---|
| E30 | 147 | 2s.50 on 2s.6d. green | 19·00 | 28·00 |
| E31 | - | 5s. on 5s. red | 22·00 | 28·00 |
| E32 | - | 10s. on 10s. blue | 25·00 | 30·00 |

### POSTAGE DUE STAMPS

**1948.** Postage Due stamps of Great Britain surch B.M.A ERITREA and new value in cents and shillings.

| | | | | |
|---|---|---|---|---|
| ED1 | D1 | 5c. on ½d. green | 10·00 | 22·00 |
| ED2 | D1 | 10c. on 1d. red | 10·00 | 24·00 |
| ED3 | D1 | 20c. on 2d. black | 17·00 | 16·00 |
| ED4 | D1 | 30c. on 3d. violet | 13·00 | 17·00 |
| ED5 | D1 | 1s. on 1s. blue | 21·00 | 32·00 |

**1950.** Postage Due stamps of Great Britain surch B.A. ERITREA and new value in cents or shillings.

| | | | |
|---|---|---|---|
| ED6 | 5c. on ½d. green | 15·00 | 55·00 |
| ED7 | 10c. on 1d. red | 15·00 | 20·00 |
| ED8 | 20c. on 2d. black | 15·00 | 24·00 |
| ED9 | 30c. on 3d. violet | 20·00 | 40·00 |
| ED10 | 1s. on 1s. blue | 20·00 | 40·00 |

### SOMALIA BRITISH OCCUPATION

**1943.** Stamps of Great Britain optd E.A.F. (East African Forces).

| | | | | |
|---|---|---|---|---|
| S1 | 128 | 1d. red | 1·50 | 70 |
| S2 | 128 | 2d. orange | 1·75 | 1·75 |
| S3 | 128 | 2½d. blue | 2·00 | 3·50 |
| S4 | 128 | 3d. violet | 1·75 | 15 |
| S5 | 129 | 5d. brown | 2·50 | 40 |
| S6 | 129 | 6d. purple | 2·25 | 1·25 |
| S7 | 130 | 9d. olive | 2·75 | 3·00 |
| S8 | 130 | 1s. brown | 3·75 | 15 |
| S9 | 131 | 2s.6d. green | 26·00 | 12·00 |

**PRICES.** Our prices for Nos. S1/9 in used condition are for stamps with identifiable postmarks of the territories in which they were issued. These stamps were also used in the United Kingdom with official sanction, from the summer of 1950, and with U.K. postmarks are worth about 25 per cent less.

### BRITISH MILITARY ADMINISTRATION

**1948.** Stamps of Great Britain surch B.M.A. SOMALIA and new value in cents and shillings.

| | | | | |
|---|---|---|---|---|
| S10 | 128 | 5c. on ½d. green | 1·25 | 2·00 |
| S11 | 128 | 15c. on 1½d. brown | 1·75 | 15·00 |
| S12 | 128 | 20c. on 2d. orange | 3·00 | 5·00 |
| S13 | 128 | 25c. on 2½d. blue | 2·25 | 4·50 |
| S14 | 128 | 30c. on 3d. violet | 2·25 | 9·00 |
| S15 | 129 | 40c. on 5d. brown | 1·25 | 20 |
| S16 | 129 | 50c. on 6d. purple | 50 | 2·00 |
| S17 | 130 | 75c. on 9d. olive | 2·00 | 24·00 |
| S18 | 130 | 1s. on 1s. brown | 1·25 | 20 |
| S19 | 131 | 2s.50 on 2s.6d. green | 5·50 | 25·00 |
| S20 | 131 | 5s. on 5s. red | 16·00 | 55·00 |

### BRITISH ADMINISTRATION

**1950.** Stamps of Great Britain surch B.A. SOMALIA and value in cents and shillings.

| | | | | |
|---|---|---|---|---|
| S21 | 128 | 5c. on ½d. green | 20 | 3·00 |
| S22 | 128 | 15c. on 1½d. brown | 75 | 17·00 |
| S23 | 128 | 20c. on 2d. orange | 75 | 7·50 |
| S24 | 128 | 25c. on 2½d. blue | 50 | 11·00 |
| S25 | 128 | 30c. on 3d. violet | 1·25 | 7·50 |
| S26 | 129 | 40c. on 5d. brown | 55 | 1·25 |
| S27 | 129 | 50c. on 6d. purple | 50 | 1·00 |
| S28 | 130 | 75c. on 9d. olive | 2·00 | 9·00 |
| S29 | 130 | 1s. on 1s. brown | 60 | 1·50 |
| S30 | 131 | 2s.50 on 2s.6d. green | 5·00 | 28·00 |
| S31 | 131 | 5s. on 5s. red | 15·00 | 48·00 |

### TRIPOLITANIA BRITISH MILITARY ADMINISTRATION

**1948.** Stamps of Great Britain surch B.M.A. TRIPOLITANIA and value in M.A.L. (Military Administration lire).

| | | | | |
|---|---|---|---|---|
| T1 | 128 | 1l. on ½d. green | 1·00 | 3·00 |
| T2 | 128 | 2l. on 1d. red | 50 | 15 |
| T3 | 128 | 3l. on 1½d. brown | 50 | 50 |
| T4 | 128 | 4l. on 2d. orange | 50 | 70 |
| T5 | 128 | 5l. on 2½d. blue | 50 | 20 |
| T6 | 128 | 6l. on 3d. violet | 50 | 40 |
| T7 | 129 | 10l. on 5d. brown | 50 | 15 |
| T8 | 129 | 12l. on 6d. purple | 50 | 20 |
| T9 | 130 | 18l. on 9d. olive | 1·25 | 1·25 |
| T10 | 130 | 24l. on 1s. brown | 2·00 | 2·25 |
| T11 | 131 | 60l. on 2s.6d. green | 6·50 | 15·00 |
| T12 | 131 | 120l. on 5s. red | 24·00 | 27·00 |
| T13 | 131 | 240l. on 10s. blue (No. 478a) | 29·00 | £130 |

### BRITISH ADMINISTRATION

**1950.** As Nos. T1/13 but surch B.A. TRIPOLITANIA and value in M.A.L.

| | | | | |
|---|---|---|---|---|
| T14 | 128 | 1l. on ½d. green | 5·00 | 13·00 |
| T27 | 128 | 1l. on ½d. orange | 30 | 8·00 |
| T15 | 128 | 2l. on 1d. red | 4·25 | 40 |
| T28 | 128 | 2l. on 1d. blue | 30 | 1·00 |
| T16 | 128 | 3l. on 1½d. brown | 3·25 | 13·00 |
| T29 | 128 | 3l. on 1½d. green | 30 | 8·00 |
| T17 | 128 | 4l. on 2d. orange | 3·75 | 4·50 |
| T30 | 128 | 4l. on 2d. brown | 30 | 1·25 |
| T18 | 128 | 5l. on 2½d. blue | 1·75 | 70 |
| T31 | 128 | 5l. on 2½d. red | 30 | 7·50 |
| T19 | 128 | 6l. on 3d. violet | 2·75 | 3·25 |
| T20 | 129 | 10l. on 5d. brown | 2·75 | 4·00 |
| T21 | 129 | 12l. on 6d. purple | 4·00 | 50 |
| T22 | 130 | 18l. on 9d. olive | 6·00 | 2·75 |
| T23 | 130 | 24l. on 1s. brown | 5·50 | 3·75 |
| T24 | 131 | 60l. on 2s.6d. green | 14·00 | 12·00 |
| T25 | 131 | 120l. on 5s. red | 29·00 | 32·00 |
| T26 | - | 240l. on 10s. blue (No. 478a) | 48·00 | 80·00 |

**1951.** Nos. 509/11 of Great Britain surch B.A. TRIPOLITANIA and value in M.A.L.

| | | | | |
|---|---|---|---|---|
| T32 | 147 | 60l. on 2s.6d. green | 14·00 | 30·00 |
| T33 | - | 120l. on 5s. red | 14·00 | 32·00 |
| T34 | - | 240l. on 10s. blue | 48·00 | 75·00 |

### POSTAGE DUE STAMPS

**1948.** Postage Due stamps of Great Britain surch B.M.A. TRIPOLITANIA and value in M.A.L.

| | | | | |
|---|---|---|---|---|
| TD1 | D1 | 1l. on ½d. green | 5·50 | 60·00 |
| TD2 | D1 | 2l. on 1d. red | 2·50 | 50·00 |
| TD3 | D1 | 4l. on 2d. black | 13·00 | 48·00 |
| TD4 | D1 | 6l. on 3d. violet | 7·50 | 25·00 |
| TD5 | D1 | 24l. on 1s. blue | 29·00 | £100 |

**1950.** As Nos. TD1/5 but surch B.A. TRIPOLITANIA and value in M.A.L.

| | | | |
|---|---|---|---|
| TD6 | 1l. on ½d. green | 13·00 | 95·00 |
| TD7 | 2l. on 1d. red | 8·50 | 28·00 |
| TD8 | 4l. on 2d. black | 9·50 | 42·00 |
| TD9 | 6l. on 3d. violet | 19·00 | 75·00 |
| TD10 | 24l. on 1s. blue | 50·00 | £160 |

Pt. 1

# BRITISH POST OFFICES IN CHINA

Stamps for use in Wei Hai Wei, and the neighbouring islands, leased to Great Britain from 1898 to 1 October 1930, when they were returned to China. The stamps were also used in the Treaty Ports from 1917 until 1922.

100 cents = 1 dollar.

**1917.** Stamps of Hong Kong (King George V) optd CHINA.

| | | | | |
|---|---|---|---|---|
| 18 | 24 | 1c. brown | 2·50 | 4·75 |
| 19 | 24 | 2c. green | 6·00 | 2·25 |
| 3 | 24 | 4c. red | 8·50 | 30 |
| 4 | 24 | 6c. orange | 8·50 | 1·00 |
| 5 | 24 | 8c. grey | 15·00 | 1·25 |
| 6 | 24 | 10c. blue | 15·00 | 30 |
| 7 | 24 | 12c. purple on yellow | 17·00 | 8·00 |
| 8 | 24 | 20c. purple and olive | 18·00 | 1·00 |
| 9 | 24 | 25c. purple | 9·00 | 15·00 |
| 11 | 24 | 30c. purple and orange | 45·00 | 7·50 |
| 12b | 24 | 50c. black on green | 45·00 | 5·50 |
| 13 | 24 | $1 purple and blue on blue | 75·00 | 2·50 |
| 14 | 24 | $2 red and black | £225 | 75·00 |
| 15 | 24 | $3 green and purple | £850 | £225 |
| 16 | 24 | $5 green and red on green | £350 | £325 |
| 17 | 24 | $10 purple and black on red | £950 | £650 |

Pt. 1

# BRITISH POST OFFICES IN CRETE

40 paras = 1 piastre.

B1

**1898**

| | | | | |
|---|---|---|---|---|
| B1 | B1 | 20pa. violet | £425 | £225 |

B2

**1898**

| | | | | |
|---|---|---|---|---|
| B2 | B2 | 10pa. blue | 9·00 | 22·00 |
| B4 | B2 | 10pa. brown | 11·00 | 29·00 |
| B3 | B2 | 20pa. green | 17·00 | 20·00 |
| B5 | B2 | 20pa. red | 20·00 | 17·00 |

Pt. 1

# BRITISH POST OFFICES IN SIAM

Used at Bangkok.

100 cents = 1 dollar.

**1882.** Stamps of Straits Settlements optd B on issue of 1867.

| | | | | |
|---|---|---|---|---|
| 1 | 19 | 32c. on 2a. yellow | £35000 | |
| | | On issues of 1867 to 1883. | | |
| 14 | 5 | 2c. brown | £600 | £375 |
| 15 | 5 | 2c. red | 70·00 | 50·00 |
| 13 | 9 | 2c. on 32c. red (No. 60) | £3500 | £3500 |
| 16 | 5 | 4c. red | £750 | £350 |
| 17 | 5 | 4c. brown | 90·00 | 80·00 |
| 4 | 18 | 5c. brown | £425 | £475 |
| 18 | 18 | 5c. blue | £325 | £190 |
| 5 | 5 | 6c. lilac | £300 | £130 |
| 20 | 5 | 8c. orange | £200 | 70·00 |
| 21 | 19 | 10c. grey | £200 | 90·00 |
| 8 | 5 | 12c. blue | £1100 | £500 |
| 22 | 5 | 12c. purple | £350 | £160 |
| 9 | 5 | 24c. green | £750 | £160 |
| 10 | 8 | 30c. red | £45000 | £30000 |
| 11 | 9 | 96c. grey | £7500 | £3000 |

Pt. 1

# BRITISH POST AGENICES IN EASTERN ARABIA

British stamps surcharged for use in parts of the Perisian Gulf.

The stamps were used in Muscat from 1 April 1948 to 29 April 1966; in Dubai from 1 April 1948 to 6 January 1961; In Qatar: Doho from August 1950, Umm Said from February 1956 to 31 March 1957; and in Abu Dhabi from 30 March 1963 (Das Islandfrom December 1960) to 29 March 1964.

Nos 21/2 were placed on sale in Kuwait Post Offices in 1951 and from February to November 1953 due to shortages of stamps "KUWAIT" overprinted. Isolated examples of other values can be found comercially used from Bahrain and Kuwait.

1948. 12 pies = 1 anna; 16 annas = 1 rupee.
1957. 100 naya paise = 1 rupee.

**Stamps of Great Britain surch in Indian currency.**

**1948.** King George VI.

| | | | | |
|---|---|---|---|---|
| 16 | 128 | ½a. on ½d. green | 2·75 | 7·50 |
| 35 | 128 | ½a. on ½d. orange | 70 | 9·00 |
| 17 | 128 | 1a. on 1d. red | 3·00 | 30 |
| 36 | 128 | 1a. on 1d. blue | 30 | 7·50 |
| 18 | 128 | 1½a. on 1½d. brown | 13·00 | 5·50 |
| 37 | 128 | 1½a. on 1½d. green | 15·00 | 35·00 |
| 19 | 128 | 2a. on 2d. orange | 2·00 | 3·25 |
| 38 | 128 | 2a. on 2d. brown | 30 | 8·50 |
| 20 | 128 | 2½a. on 2½d. blue | 3·50 | 8·00 |
| 39 | 128 | 2½a. on 2½d. red | 30 | 16·00 |
| 21 | 128 | 3a. on 3d. violet | 3·50 | 10 |
| 40 | 129 | 4a. on 4d. blue | 45 | 3·50 |
| 22 | 129 | 6a. on 6d. purple | 4·00 | 10 |
| 23 | 130 | 1r. on 1s. brown | 4·50 | 60 |
| 24 | 131 | 2r. on 2s.6d. green | 10·00 | 50·00 |

**1948.** Royal Silver Wedding.

| | | | | |
|---|---|---|---|---|
| 25 | 137 | 2½a. on 2½d. blue | 2·75 | 5·00 |
| 26 | 138 | 15r. on £1 blue | 25·00 | 35·00 |

**1948.** Olympic Games.

| 27 | 139 | 2½a. on 2½d. blue | 35 | 2·50 |
|---|---|---|---|---|
| 28 | 140 | 3a. on 3d. violet | 45 | 2·50 |
| 29 | - | 6a. on 6d. purple | 45 | 2·75 |
| 30 | - | 1r. on 1s. brown | 1·25 | 4·00 |

**1949.** 75th Anniv of U.P.U.

| 31 | 143 | 2½a. on 2½d. blue | 60 | 3·00 |
|---|---|---|---|---|
| 32 | 144 | 3a. on 3d. violet | 60 | 4·00 |
| 33 | - | 6a. on 6d. purple | 60 | 2·75 |
| 34 | - | 1r. on 1s. brown | 2·25 | 7·00 |

**1951.** Pictorial.

| 41 | 147 | 2r. on 2s.6d. green | 40·00 | 7·00 |
|---|---|---|---|---|

**1952.** Queen Elizabeth.

| 42 | 154 | ½a. on ½d. orange | 10 | 2·25 |
|---|---|---|---|---|
| 43 | 154 | 1a. on 1d. blue | 10 | 2·25 |
| 44 | 154 | 1½a. on 1½d. green | 10 | 2·25 |
| 45 | 154 | 2a. on 2d. brown | 20 | 10 |
| 46 | 155 | 2½a. on 2½d. red | 10 | 10 |
| 47 | 155 | 3a. on 3d. lilac | 20 | 1·25 |
| 48 | 155 | 4a. on 4d. blue | 2·00 | 4·00 |
| 49 | 157 | 6a. on 6d. purple | 35 | 10 |
| 50 | 160 | 12a. on 1s.3d. green | 7·00 | 30 |
| 51 | 160 | 1r. on 1s.6d. blue | 2·25 | 10 |

**1953.** Coronation.

| 52 | 161 | 2½a. on 2½d. red | 1·75 | 3·50 |
|---|---|---|---|---|
| 53 | - | 4a. on 4d. blue | 1·75 | 1·00 |
| 54 | 163 | 12a. on 1s.3d. green | 2·50 | 1·00 |
| 55 | - | 1r. on 1s.6d. blue | 2·75 | 50 |

**1955.** Pictorials.

| 56 | 166 | 2r. on 2s.6d. brown | 8·00 | 70 |
|---|---|---|---|---|
| 57 | - | 5r. on 5s. red | 10·00 | 2·25 |

**1957.** Value in naye paise. Queen Elizabeth II stamps surch NP twice (once only on 75n.p.) and value.

| 79 | 157 | 1n.p. on 5d. brown | 10 | 20 |
|---|---|---|---|---|
| 80 | 154 | 3n.p. on ½d. orange | 55 | 80 |
| 81 | 154 | 5n.p. on 1d. blue | 1·75 | 3·25 |
| 67 | 154 | 6n.p. on 1d. blue | 20 | 2·75 |
| 68 | 154 | 9n.p. on 1½d. green | 20 | 2·50 |
| 83 | 154 | 10n.p. on 1½d. green | 1·00 | 2·75 |
| 69 | 154 | 12n.p. on 2d. brown | 30 | 2·75 |
| 85 | 155 | 15n.p. on 2½d. red | 25 | 10 |
| 71 | 155 | 20n.p. on 3d. lilac | 20 | 10 |
| 72 | 155 | 25n.p. on 4d. blue | 70 | 7·50 |
| 87 | 155 | 30n.p. on 4½d. brown | 40 | 50 |
| 73 | 157 | 40n.p. on 6d. purple | 30 | 10 |
| 89 | 158 | 50n.p. on 9d. olive | 1·00 | 2·50 |
| 75 | 160 | 75n.p. on 1s.3d. green | 2·00 | 40 |
| 91 | 159 | 1r. on 1s.6d. blue | 27·00 | 7·00 |
| 92 | 166 | 2r. on 2s.6d. brown | 12·00 | 45·00 |
| 93 | 166 | 5r. on 5s. red | 28·00 | 55·00 |

DESIGN: No. 93 Caernarvon Castle.

**1957.** World Scout Jubilee Jamboree.

| 76 | 170 | 15n.p. on 2½d. red | 35 | 85 |
|---|---|---|---|---|
| 77 | 171 | 25n.p. on 4d. blue | 35 | 85 |
| 78 | - | 75n.p. on 3d. green | 40 | 85 |

Pt. 1

# BRITISH VIRGIN ISLANDS

A group of the Leeward Islands, Br. W. Indies. Used general issues for Leeward Islands concurrently with Virgin Islands stamps until 1 July 1956. A Crown Colony.

1951. 100 cents = 1 West Indian dollar.
1962. 100 cents = 1 U.S. dollar.

1 St. Ursula

2

3

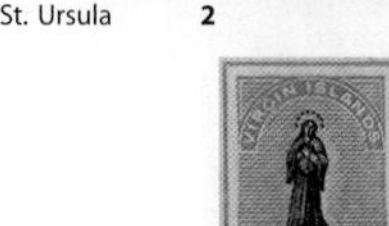

4

**1866**

| 1 | 1 | 1d. green | 45·00 | 60·00 |
|---|---|---|---|---|
| 16 | 3 | 4d. red | 42·00 | 60·00 |
| 7 | 2 | 6d. red | 60·00 | 90·00 |
| 11 | 4 | 1s. black and red | £275 | £375 |

No. 11 has a double-lined frame.

**1867.** With heavy coloured border.

| 19 | 4 | 1s. black and red | 65·00 | 75·00 |
|---|---|---|---|---|

6

**1880**

| 26 | 6 | ½d. yellow | 85·00 | 85·00 |
|---|---|---|---|---|
| 27 | 6 | ½d. green | 6·50 | 13·00 |
| 24 | 6 | 1d. green | 75·00 | 90·00 |
| 29 | 6 | 1d. red | 32·00 | 38·00 |
| 25 | 6 | 2½d. brown | £110 | £130 |
| 31 | 6 | 2½d. blue | 2·75 | 16·00 |

**1887**

| 32 | 1 | 1d. red | 3·75 | 9·00 |
|---|---|---|---|---|
| 35 | 3 | 4d. brown | 35·00 | 65·00 |
| 39 | 2 | 6d. violet | 19·00 | 50·00 |
| 41 | 4 | 1s. brown | 45·00 | 70·00 |

**1888.** No. 18 surch 4D.

| 42 | | 4d. on 1s. black and red | £130 | £160 |
|---|---|---|---|---|

8

**1899**

| 43 | 8 | ½d. green | 3·75 | 55 |
|---|---|---|---|---|
| 44 | 8 | 1d. red | 4·75 | 2·50 |
| 45 | 8 | 2½d. blue | 12·00 | 2·75 |
| 46 | 8 | 4d. brown | 4·00 | 18·00 |
| 47 | 8 | 6d. violet | 5·50 | 3·00 |
| 48 | 8 | 7d. green | 11·00 | 6·00 |
| 49 | 8 | 1s. yellow | 22·00 | 35·00 |
| 50 | 8 | 5s. blue | 70·00 | 85·00 |

9

**1904**

| 54 | 9 | ½d. purple and green | 1·00 | 40 |
|---|---|---|---|---|
| 55 | 9 | 1d. purple and red | 2·50 | 35 |
| 56 | 9 | 2d. purple and brown | 7·00 | 3·50 |
| 57 | 9 | 2½d. purple and blue | 3·00 | 2·00 |
| 58 | 9 | 3d. purple and black | 4·00 | 2·50 |
| 59 | 9 | 6d. purple and brown | 3·25 | 2·50 |
| 60 | 9 | 1s. green and red | 5·50 | 5·00 |
| 61 | 9 | 2s.6d. green and black | 32·00 | 55·00 |
| 62 | 9 | 5s. green and blue | 48·00 | 70·00 |

11

**1913**

| 69 | 11 | ½d. green | 3·50 | 5·00 |
|---|---|---|---|---|
| 70a | 11 | 1d. red | 2·25 | 14·00 |
| 71 | 11 | 2d. grey | 5·00 | 28·00 |
| 72 | 11 | 2½d. blue | 6·50 | 9·00 |
| 73 | 11 | 3d. purple on yellow | 2·75 | 6·50 |
| 74 | 11 | 6d. purple | 7·50 | 16·00 |
| 75 | 11 | 1s. black on green | 3·25 | 9·00 |
| 76 | 11 | 2s.6d. black and red on blue | 50·00 | 55·00 |
| 77 | 11 | 5s. green and red on yellow | 42·00 | £130 |

**1917.** Optd WAR STAMP.

| 78c | | 1d. red | 1·50 | 3·75 |
|---|---|---|---|---|
| 79a | | 3d. purple on yellow | 3·75 | 17·00 |

14

**1922**

| 86 | 14 | ½d. green | 85 | 2·75 |
|---|---|---|---|---|
| 87 | 14 | 1d. red | 60 | 60 |
| 88 | 14 | 1d. violet | 1·25 | 4·50 |
| 91 | 14 | 1½d. red | 2·00 | 1·50 |
| 92 | 14 | 2d. grey | 1·25 | 6·00 |
| 94 | 14 | 2½d. orange | 1·25 | 1·75 |
| 95 | 14 | 2½d. blue | 9·50 | 3·50 |
| 96 | 14 | 3d. purple on yellow | 2·25 | 11·00 |
| 97 | 14 | 5d. purple and olive | 5·50 | 45·00 |
| 98 | 14 | 6d. purple | 1·75 | 6·50 |
| 83 | 14 | 1s. black on green | 75 | 14·00 |
| 84 | 14 | 2s.6d. black and red on blue | 5·50 | 11·00 |
| 101 | 14 | 5s. green and red on yellow | 19·00 | 70·00 |

**1935.** Silver Jubilee. As T 13 of Antigua.

| 103 | 1d. blue and red | 1·25 | 7·50 |
|---|---|---|---|
| 104 | 1½d. blue and grey | 1·25 | 6·50 |
| 105 | 2½d. brown and blue | 3·25 | 5·50 |
| 106 | 1s. grey and purple | 18·00 | 30·00 |

**1937.** Coronation. As T 2 of Aden.

| 107 | 1d. red | 75 | 3·25 |
|---|---|---|---|
| 108 | 1½d. brown | 75 | 3·00 |
| 109 | 2½d. blue | 60 | 1·50 |

15 King George VI and Badge of Colony

**1938**

| 110a | 15 | ½d. green | 1·50 | 1·00 |
|---|---|---|---|---|
| 111a | 15 | 1d. red | 2·25 | 1·50 |
| 112a | 15 | 1½d. brown | 2·50 | 1·50 |
| 113a | 15 | 2d. grey | 2·50 | 1·50 |
| 114a | 15 | 2½d. blue | 3·25 | 2·50 |
| 115a | 15 | 3d. orange | 2·00 | 1·00 |
| 116a | 15 | 6d. mauve | 5·50 | 2·00 |
| 117a | 15 | 1s. brown | 3·75 | 2·00 |
| 118a | 15 | 2s.6d. brown | 17·00 | 5·00 |
| 119a | 15 | 5s. red | 16·00 | 6·00 |
| 120 | 15 | 10s. blue | 8·00 | 9·00 |
| 121 | 15 | £1 black | 9·50 | 23·00 |

**1946.** Victory. As T 9 of Aden.

| 122 | 1½d. brown | 10 | 10 |
|---|---|---|---|
| 123 | 3d. orange | 10 | 60 |

**1949.** Silver Wedding. As T 10/11 of Aden.

| 124 | 2½d. blue | 10 | 10 |
|---|---|---|---|
| 125 | £1 grey | 15·00 | 19·00 |

**1949.** 75th Anniv of U.P.U. As T 20/23 of Antigua.

| 126 | 2½d. blue | 30 | 2·00 |
|---|---|---|---|
| 127 | 3d. orange | 1·50 | 2·50 |
| 128 | 6d. mauve | 45 | 40 |
| 129 | 1s. olive | 35 | 50 |

**1951.** Inauguration of B.W.I. University College. As T 24/25 of Antigua.

| 130 | 3c. black and red | 40 | 2·50 |
|---|---|---|---|
| 131 | 12c. black and violet | 60 | 1·75 |

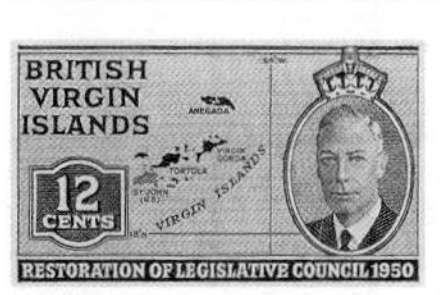

16 Map

**1951.** Restoration of Legislative Council.

| 132 | 16 | 6c. orange | 50 | 1·50 |
|---|---|---|---|---|
| 133 | 16 | 12c. purple | 75 | 50 |
| 134 | 16 | 24c. olive | 60 | 1·00 |
| 135 | 16 | $1.20 red | 2·00 | 1·00 |

18 Map of Jost Van Dyke

**1952**

| 136 | - | 1c. black | 80 | 3·25 |
|---|---|---|---|---|
| 137 | 18 | 2c. green | 70 | 30 |
| 138 | - | 3c. black and brown | 80 | 2·25 |
| 139 | - | 4c. red | 70 | 2·50 |
| 140 | - | 5c. red and black | 1·50 | 50 |
| 141 | - | 8c. blue | 1·00 | 1·75 |
| 142 | - | 12c. violet | 1·00 | 1·75 |
| 143 | - | 24c. brown | 70 | 50 |
| 144 | - | 60c. green and blue | 5·00 | 11·00 |
| 145 | - | $1.20 black and blue | 5·50 | 12·00 |
| 146 | - | $2.40 green and brown | 14·00 | 16·00 |
| 147 | - | $4.80 blue and red | 16·00 | 19·00 |

DESIGNS—VERT: 1c. Sombrero lighthouse; 24c. Badge of Presidency. HORIZ—VIEWS: 3c. Sheep industry; 5c. Cattle industry; 60c. Dead Man's Chest (Is); $1.20, Sir Francis Drake Channel; $2.40, Road Town. HORIZ—MAPS: 4c. Anegada Island; 8c. Virgin Gorda Island; 12c. Tortola Island; $4.80, Virgin Islands.

**1953.** Coronation. As T 13 of Aden.

| 148 | 2c. black and green | 30 | 1·25 |
|---|---|---|---|

29 Map of Tortola

30 Virgin Island Sloop

**1956**

| 149 | 29 | ½c. black and purple | 1·25 | 30 |
|---|---|---|---|---|
| 150 | - | 1c. turquoise and slate | 1·50 | 1·00 |
| 151 | - | 2c. red and black | 30 | 10 |
| 152 | - | 3c. blue and olive | 30 | 30 |
| 153 | - | 4c. brown and turquoise | 70 | 30 |
| 154 | - | 5c. black | 50 | 10 |
| 155 | - | 8c. orange and blue | 2·00 | 40 |
| 156 | - | 12c. blue and red | 4·00 | 75 |
| 157 | - | 24c. green and brown | 1·00 | 65 |
| 158 | - | 60c. blue and orange | 8·50 | 8·00 |
| 159 | - | $1.20 green and red | 3·50 | 9·50 |
| 160 | 30 | $2.40 yellow and purple | 42·00 | 13·00 |
| 161 | - | $4.80 sepia and turquoise | 42·00 | 13·00 |

DESIGNS—HORIZ: As Type **29**: 1c. Virgin Islands sloop; 2c. Nelthrop Red Poll bull; 3c. Road Harbour; 4c. Mountain travel; 5c. Badge of the Presidency; 8c. Beach scene; 12c. Boat launching; 24c. White cedar tree; 60c. Skipjack tuna ("Bonito"); $1.20, Treasury Square Coronation celebrations. As Type **30**: $4.80, Magnificent frigate bird ("Man-o'-War Bird").

**1962.** New Currency. Nos. 149/53, 155/61 surch in U.S. Currency.

| 162 | 29 | 1c. on ½c. black and purple | 30 | 10 |
|---|---|---|---|---|
| 163 | - | 2c. on 1c. turq & vio | 1·75 | 10 |
| 164 | - | 3c. on 2c. red and black | 70 | 10 |
| 165 | - | 4c. on 3c. blue and olive | 30 | 10 |
| 166 | - | 5c. on 4c. brown & turq | 30 | 10 |
| 167 | - | 8c. on 8c. orange and blue | 30 | 10 |
| 168 | - | 10c. on 12c. blue and red | 2·00 | 10 |
| 169 | - | 12c. on 24c. green & brn | 30 | 10 |
| 170 | - | 25c. on 60c. blue and orange | 2·75 | 45 |
| 171 | - | 70c. on $1.20 green and red | 35 | 45 |
| 172 | 30 | $1.40 on $2.40 yellow and purple | 9·50 | 4·00 |
| 173 | - | $2.80 on $4.80 sepia & turq | 9·50 | 4·00 |

**1963.** Freedom from Hunger. As T 28 of Aden.

| 174 | 25c. violet | 20 | 10 |
|---|---|---|---|

**1963.** Centenary of Red Cross. As T 33 of Antigua.

| 175 | 2c. red and black | 15 | 20 |
|---|---|---|---|
| 176 | 25c. red and blue | 50 | 20 |

**1964.** 400th Birth Anniv of Shakespeare. As T 34 of Antigua.

| 177 | 10c. blue | 20 | 10 |
|---|---|---|---|

43 Skipjack Tuna

44 Soper's Hole

**1964**

| 178 | 43 | 1c. blue and olive | 30 | 1·75 |
|---|---|---|---|---|
| 179 | 44 | 2c. olive and red | 15 | 30 |
| 180 | 44 | 3c. sepia and turquoise | 4·75 | 2·00 |
| 181 | - | 4c. black and red | 80 | 2·75 |
| 182 | - | 5c. black and green | 1·50 | 2·25 |
| 183 | - | 6c. black and orange | 30 | 85 |
| 184 | - | 8c. black and mauve | 30 | 50 |
| 185 | - | 10c. lake and lilac | 5·50 | 30 |
| 186 | - | 12c. green and blue | 2·00 | 3·00 |
| 187 | - | 15c. green and black | 1·50 | 2·75 |
| 188 | - | 25c. green and purple | 11·00 | 2·00 |
| 189 | - | 70c. black and brown | 4·25 | 8·50 |
| 190 | - | $1 green and brown | 3·00 | 2·00 |
| 191 | - | $1.40 blue and red | 24·00 | 10·00 |
| 192 | - | $2.80 black and purple | 26·00 | 11·00 |

DESIGNS—HORIZ (As Type **43**): 2c. Soper's Hole; 3c. Brown pelican; 4c. Dead Man's Chest; 5c. Road Harbour; 6c. Fallen Jerusalem; 8c. The Baths, Virgin Gorda; 10c. Map of Virgin Islands; 12c. "Youth of Tortola" (Tortola–St Thomas ferry); 15c. The Towers, Tortola; 25c. Beef Island Airfield. VERT (As Type **44**): $1 Virgin Gorda; $1.40, Yachts at anchor. (27½x37½ mm): $2.80, Badge of the Colony.

**1965.** Centenary of I.T.U. As T 36 of Antigua.
193 4c. yellow and turquoise 20 10
194 25c. blue and buff 45 20

**1965.** I.C.Y. As T 37 of Antigua.
195 1c. purple and turquoise 10 15
196 25c. green and lavender 30 15

**1966.** Churchill Commemoration. As T 38 of Antigua.
197 1c. blue 10 30
198 2c. green 30 30
199 10c. brown 65 10
200 25c. violet 1·25 25

**1966.** Royal Visit. As T 39 of Antigua.
201 4c. black and blue 40 10
202 70c. black and mauve 1·40 45

**58** "Atrato I" (paddle-steamer), 1866

**1966.** Stamp Centenary. Multicoloured.
203 5c. Type **58** 35 10
204 10c. 1d. and 6d. stamps of 1866 35 10
205 25c. Mail transport, Beef Island, and 6d. stamp of 1866 55 10
206 60c. Landing mail at Roadtown, 1866 and 1d. stamp of 1866 1·00 2·50

**1966.** Nos. 189 and 191/2 surch.
207 **44** 50c. on 70c. blk & brn 1·25 90
208 - $1.50 on $1.40 blue and red 2·25 2·00
209 - $3 on $2.80 black and purple 2·25 2·75

**1966.** 20th Anniv of UNESCO. As T 54/6 of Antigua.
210 2c. multicoloured 10 10
211 12c. yellow, violet and olive 30 10
212 60c. black, purple and orange 1·00 45

**63** Map of Virgin Islands

**1967.** New Constitution.
213 **63** 2c. multicoloured 10 10
214 **63** 10c. multicoloured 15 10
215 **63** 25c. multicoloured 15 10
216 **63** $1 multicoloured 55 40

**64** "Mercury" (cable ship) and Bermuda–Tortola Link

**1967.** Inauguration of Bermuda–Tortola Telephone Service. Multicoloured.
217 4c. Type **64** 30 10
218 10c. Chalwell Telecommunications Station 20 10
219 50c. "Mercury" (cable ship) 60 30

**67** Blue Marlin

**1968.** Game Fishing. Multicoloured.
220 2c. Type **67** 10 65
221 10c. Cobia 25 10
222 25c. Wahoo 55 10
223 40c. Fishing launch and map 85 75

**1968.** Human Rights Year. Nos. 185 and 188 optd 1968 INTERNATIONAL YEAR FOR HUMAN RIGHTS.
224 10c. lake and lilac 20 10
225 25c. green and purple 30 40

**72** Dr. Martin Luther King, Bible, Sword and Armour Gauntlet

**1968.** Martin Luther King Commemoration.
226 **72** 4c. multicoloured 25 20
227 **72** 25c. multicoloured 40 40

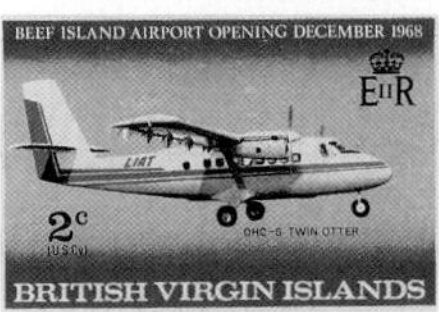

**73** de Havilland Canada DH-6 Twin Otter 100

**1968.** Opening of Beef Island Airport Extension. Multicoloured.
228 2c. Type **73** 20 1·25
229 10c. Hawker Siddeley H.S.748 airliner 35 10
230 25c. de Havilland Canada DH-114 Heron 2 airplane 40 10
231 $1 Royal Engineers' cap badge 50 2·00

**77** Long John Silver and Jim Hawkins

**1969.** 75th Death Anniv of Robert Louis Stevenson. Scenes from "Treasure Island".
232 **77** 4c. blue, yellow and red 20 15
233 - 10c. multicoloured 20 10
234 - 40c. brown, black and blue 25 30
235 - $1 multicoloured 45 1·00

DESIGNS—HORIZ: 10c. Jim Hawkins escaping from the pirates; $1 Treasure trove. VERT: 40c. The fight with Israel Hands.

**82** Yachts in Road Harbour, Tortola

**1969.** Tourism. Multicoloured.
236 2c. Tourist and yellow-finned grouper (fish) 15 50
237 10c. Type **82** 30 10
238 20c. Sun-bathing at Virgin Gorda National Park 40 20
239 $1 Tourist and Pipe Organ cactus at Virgin Gorda 90 1·50

Nos. 236 and 239 are vert.

**85** Carib Canoe

**1970**
240 **85** ½c. buff, brown and sepia 10 1·50
241 - 1c. blue and green 15 75
242 - 2c. orange, brown and slate 40 1·00
243 - 3c. red, blue and sepia 30 1·25
244 - 4c. turquoise, blue & brn 30 50
245 - 5c. green, pink and black 30 10
246 - 6c. violet, mauve and green 40 2·25
247 - 8c. green, yellow and sepia 50 4·75
248 - 10c. blue and brown 50 15
249 - 12c. yellow, red and brown 65 1·50
250 - 15c. green, orange and brown 6·00 85
251 - 25c. green, blue and purple 4·00 1·75
252 - 50c. mauve, green and brown 3·25 1·50
253 - $1 salmon, green and brown 4·00 3·75
254 - $2 buff, slate and grey 7·50 7·00
255 - $3 ochre, blue and sepia 2·75 4·50
256 - $5 violet and grey 2·75 5·00

DESIGNS: 1c. "Santa Maria" (Columbus's flagship); 2c. "Elizabeth Bonaventure" (Drake's flagship); 3c. Dutch buccaneer, c. 1660; 4c. "Thetis", 1827 (after etching by E. W. Cooke); 5c. Henry Morgan's ship (17th-century); 6c. H.M.S. "Boreas" (Captain Nelson, 1784); 8c. H.M.S. "Eclair", 1804; 10c. H.M.S. "Formidable", 1782; 12c. H.M.S. "Nymph", 1778; 15c. "Windsor Castle" (sailing packet) engaging "Jeune Richard" (French brig), 1807; 25c. H.M.S. "Astrea", 1808; 50c. Wreck of R.M.S. "Rhone", 1867; $1 Tortola sloop; $2 H.M.S. "Frobisher"; $3 "Booker Viking" (cargo liner), 1967; $5 Hydrofoil "Sun Arrow".

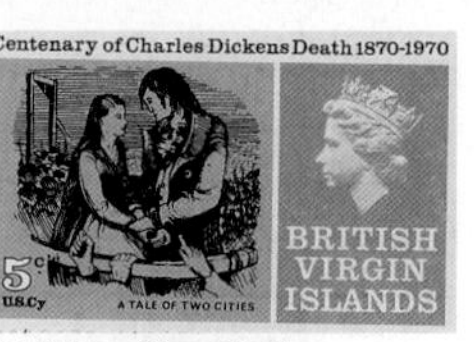

**102** "A Tale of Two Cities"

**1970.** Death Centenary of Charles Dickens.
257 **102** 5c. black, red and grey 15 1·00
258 - 10c. black, blue and green 25 10
259 - 25c. black, green and yellow 40 25

DESIGNS: 10c. "Oliver Twist"; 25c. "Great Expectations".

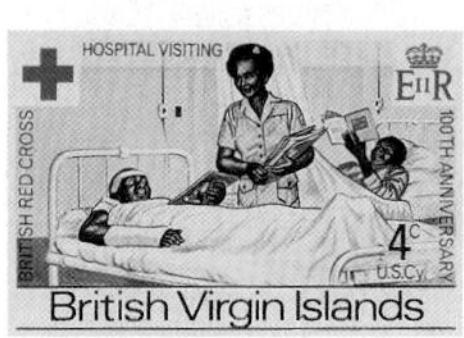

**103** Hospital Visit

**1970.** Centenary of British Red Cross. Multicoloured.
260 4c. Type **103** 20 45
261 10c. First Aid class 20 10
262 25c. Red Cross and coat of arms 50 55

**104** Mary Read

**1970.** Pirates. Multicoloured.
263 ½c. Type **104** 10 15
264 10c. George Lowther 30 10
265 30c. Edward Teach (Blackbeard) 60 25
266 60c. Henry Morgan 80 1·00

**105** Children and "UNICEF"

**1971.** 25th Anniv of UNICEF.
267 **105** 15c. multicoloured 10 10
268 **105** 30c. multicoloured 20 25

**1972.** Royal Visit of Princess Margaret. Nos 244 and 251 optd VISIT OF H.R.H. THE PRINCESS MARGARET 1972 1972.
269 4c. blue, light blue and brown 40 15
270 25c. green, blue and plum 60 45

**107** Seaman of 1800

**1972.** "Interpex" Stamp Exhibition, New York. Naval Uniforms. Multicoloured.
271 ½c. Type **107** 10 40
272 10c. Boatswain, 1787–1807 35 10
273 30c. Captain, 1795–1812 85 55
274 60c. Admiral, 1787–95 1·25 2·75

**1972.** Royal Silver Wedding. As T 52 of Ascension, but with sailfish and "Sir Winston Churchill" (cadet schooner) in background.
275 15c. blue 25 15
276 25c. blue 25 15

**109** Blue Marlin

**1972.** Game Fish. Multicoloured.
277 ½c. Type **109** 15 1·40
278 ½c. Wahoo 15 1·40
279 15c. Yellow-finned tuna ("Allison tuna") 65 25
280 25c. White marlin 75 30
281 50c. Sailfish 1·25 1·50
282 $1 Dolphin 2·00 2·75
**MS**283 194×158 mm. Nos. 277/82 8·50 8·50

**110** J. C. Lettsom

**1973.** "Interpex 1973" (Quakers). Multicoloured.
284 ½c. Type **110** 10 15
285 10c. Lettsom House (horiz) 15 10
286 15c. Dr. W. Thornton 20 10
287 30c. Dr. Thornton and Capitol, Washington (horiz) 25 20
288 $1 William Penn (horiz) 60 1·10

**111** Green-throated Carib and Antillean Crested Hummingbird

**1973.** First Issue of Coinage. Coins and local scenery. Multicoloured.
289 1c. Type **111** 10 30
290 5c. "Zenaida Dove" (5c. coin) 60 10
291 10c. "Ringed Kingfisher" (10c. coin) 75 10
292 25c. "Mangrove Cuckoo" (25c. coin) 95 15
293 50c. "Brown Pelican" (50c. coin) 1·10 1·00
294 $1 "Magnificent Frigate-bird ($1 coin) 1·40 2·00

**1973.** Royal Wedding. As T 47 of Anguilla. Multicoloured. Background colours given.
301 5c. brown 10 10
302 50c. blue 20 20

**112** "Virgin and Child" (Pintoricchio)

**1973.** Christmas. Multicoloured.
303 ½c. Type **112** 10 10
304 3c. "Virgin and Child" (Lorenzo di Credi) 10 10
305 25c. "Virgin and Child" (Crivelli) 15 10
306 50c. "Virgin and Child with St. John" (Luini) 30 40

**113** Crest of the "Canopus" (French)

**1974.** "Interpex 1974". Naval Crests. Multicoloured.

| | | | |
|---|---|---|---|
| 307 | 5c. Type **113** | 15 | 10 |
| 308 | 18c. U.S.S. "Saginaw" | 25 | 25 |
| 309 | 25c. H.M.S. "Rothesay" | 25 | 30 |
| 310 | 50c. H.M.C.S. "Ottawa" | 45 | 60 |
| **MS**311 | 196×128 mm. Nos. 307/10 | 1·25 | 4·50 |

**114** Christopher Columbus

**1974.** Historical Figures.

| | | | | |
|---|---|---|---|---|
| 312 | **114** | 5c. orange and black | 20 | 10 |
| 313 | - | 10c. blue and black | 20 | 10 |
| 314 | - | 25c. violet and black | 25 | 25 |
| 315 | - | 40c. brown and deep brown | 45 | 75 |
| **MS**316 | | 84×119 mm. Nos. 312/15 | 1·00 | 2·25 |

PORTRAITS: 10c. Sir Walter Raleigh; 25c. Sir Martin Frobisher; 40c. Sir Francis Drake.

**115** Atlantic Trumpet Triton (image scaled to 34% of original size)

**1974.** Seashells. Multicoloured.

| | | | |
|---|---|---|---|
| 317 | 5c. Type **115** | 30 | 15 |
| 318 | 18c. West Indian murex | 50 | 30 |
| 319 | 25c. Bleeding tooth | 60 | 35 |
| 320 | 75c. Virgin Islands latirus | 1·25 | 2·25 |
| **MS**321 | 146×95 mm. Nos. 317/20 | 3·00 | 6·50 |

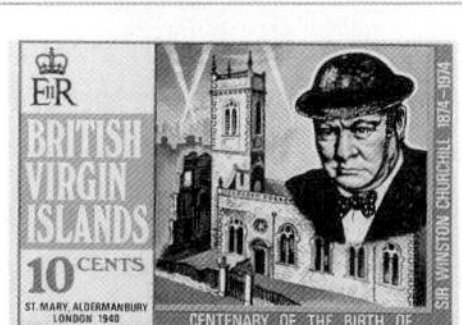

**116** Churchill and St. Mary, Aldermanbury, London

**1974.** Birth Centenary of Sir Winston Churchill. Multicoloured.

| | | | |
|---|---|---|---|
| 322 | 10c. Type **116** | 15 | 10 |
| 323 | 50c. St. Mary, Fulton, Missouri | 35 | 50 |
| **MS**324 | 141×108 mm. Nos. 322/3 | 80 | 1·40 |

**117** H.M.S. "Boreas"

**1975.** "Interpex 1975" Stamp Exhibition, New York. Ships' Figure-heads. Multicoloured.

| | | | |
|---|---|---|---|
| 325 | 5c. Type **117** | 20 | 10 |
| 326 | 18c. "Golden Hind" | 40 | 15 |
| 327 | 40c. H.M.S. "Superb" | 50 | 25 |
| 328 | 85c. H.M.S. "Formidable" | 1·00 | 1·50 |

| | | | |
|---|---|---|---|
| **MS**329 | 192×127 mm. Nos. 325/8 | 1·75 | 8·00 |

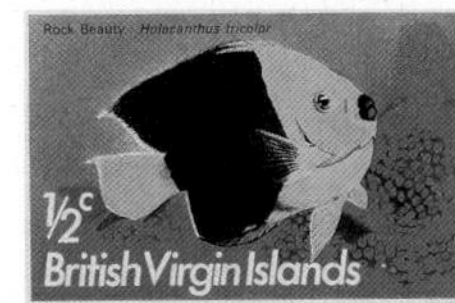

**118** Rock Beauty

**1975.** Fishes. Multicoloured.

| | | | |
|---|---|---|---|
| 330 | ½c. Type **118** | 15 | 50 |
| 331 | 1c. Long-spined squirrelfish | 40 | 2·75 |
| 332 | 3c. Queen triggerfish | 1·00 | 2·75 |
| 333 | 5c. Blue angelfish | 30 | 20 |
| 334 | 8c. Stoplight parrotfish | 30 | 25 |
| 335 | 10c. Queen angelfish | 30 | 25 |
| 336 | 12c. Nassau grouper | 40 | 30 |
| 337 | 13c. Blue tang | 40 | 30 |
| 338 | 15c. Sergeant major | 40 | 35 |
| 339 | 18c. Spotted jewfish | 80 | 1·50 |
| 340 | 20c. Bluehead wrasse | 60 | 80 |
| 341 | 25c. Grey angelfish | 1·00 | 60 |
| 342 | 60c. Glass-eyed snapper | 1·25 | 2·25 |
| 343 | $1 Blue chromis | 1·75 | 1·75 |
| 344 | $2.50 French angelfish | 2·00 | 4·50 |
| 345 | $3 Queen parrotfish | 2·50 | 4·50 |
| 346 | $5 Four-eyed butterflyfish | 2·75 | 6·00 |

**119** St. George's Parish School (first meeting-place, 1950)

**1975.** 25th Anniv of Restoration of Legislative Council. Multicoloured.

| | | | |
|---|---|---|---|
| 347 | 5c. Type **119** | 10 | 10 |
| 348 | 25c. Legislative Council Building | 20 | 10 |
| 349 | 40c. Mace and gavel | 25 | 15 |
| 350 | 75c. Commemorative scroll | 35 | 65 |

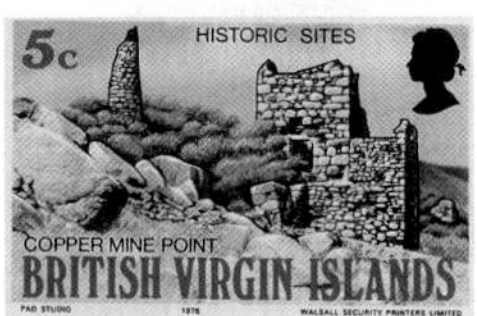

**120** Copper Mine Point

**1976.** Historic Sites. Multicoloured.

| | | | |
|---|---|---|---|
| 351 | 5c. Type **120** | 10 | 10 |
| 352 | 18c. Pleasant Valley | 20 | 10 |
| 353 | 50c. Callwood Distillery | 40 | 30 |
| 354 | 75c. The Dungeon | 60 | 65 |

**121** Massachusetts Brig "Hazard"

**1976.** Bicentenary of American Revolution. Mult.

| | | | |
|---|---|---|---|
| 355 | 8c. Type **121** | 30 | 15 |
| 356 | 22c. American privateer "Spy" | 45 | 20 |
| 357 | 40c. "Raleigh" (American frigate) | 55 | 60 |
| 358 | 75c. Frigate "Alliance" and H.M.S. "Trepassy" | 80 | 1·25 |
| **MS**359 | 114×89 mm. Nos. 355/8 | 2·75 | 11·00 |

**122** Government House, Tortola

**1976.** 5th Anniv of Friendship Day with U.S. Virgin Islands. Multicoloured.

| | | | |
|---|---|---|---|
| 360 | 8c. Type **122** | 10 | 10 |
| 361 | 15c. Government House, St. Croix (vert) | 10 | 10 |
| 362 | 30c. Flags (vert) | 15 | 10 |
| 363 | 75c. Government seals | 50 | 40 |

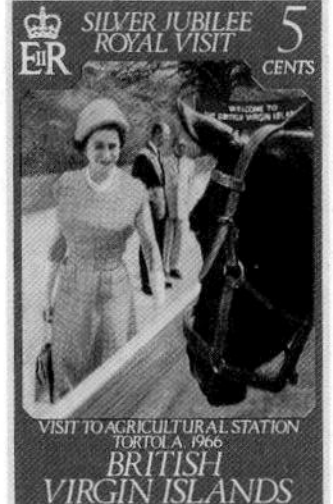

**123** Royal Visit, 1966

**1977.** Silver Jubilee. Multicoloured.

| | | | |
|---|---|---|---|
| 364 | 8c. Type **123** | 10 | 10 |
| 365 | 30c. The Holy Bible | 15 | 15 |
| 366 | 60c. Presentation of Holy Bible | 25 | 40 |

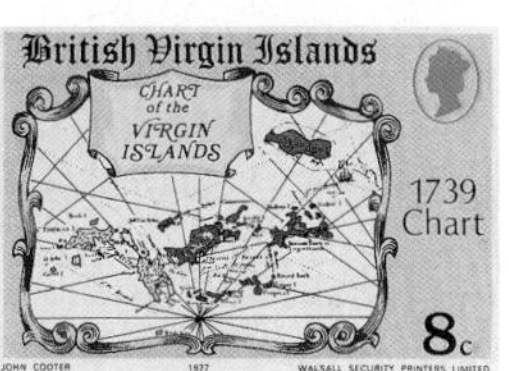

**124** Chart of 1739

**1977.** 18th-century Maps. Multicoloured.

| | | | |
|---|---|---|---|
| 367 | 8c. Type **124** | 40 | 10 |
| 368 | 22c. French map, 1758 | 55 | 30 |
| 369 | 30c. Map from English and Danish surveys, 1775 | 65 | 65 |
| 370 | 75c. Map of 1779 | 85 | 1·50 |

**1977.** Royal Visit. As Nos. 364/6 inscr "SILVER JUBILEE ROYAL VISIT".

| | | | |
|---|---|---|---|
| 371 | 5c. Type **123** | 10 | 10 |
| 372 | 25c. The Holy Bible | 20 | 10 |
| 373 | 50c. Presentation of Holy Bible | 35 | 25 |

**125** Divers checking Equipment

**1978.** Tourism. Multicoloured.

| | | | |
|---|---|---|---|
| 374 | ½c. Type **125** | 10 | 10 |
| 375 | 5c. Cup coral on wreck of "Rhone" | 20 | 10 |
| 376 | 8c. Sponge formation on wreck of "Rhone" | 25 | 10 |
| 377 | 22c. Cup coral and sponges | 45 | 15 |
| 378 | 30c. Sponges inside cave | 60 | 20 |
| 379 | 75c. Marine life | 90 | 85 |

**126** Fire Coral

**1978.** Corals. Multicoloured.

| | | | |
|---|---|---|---|
| 380 | 8c. Type **126** | 25 | 15 |
| 381 | 15c. Staghorn coral | 40 | 30 |
| 382 | 40c. Brain coral | 75 | 85 |
| 383 | 75c. Elkhorn coral | 1·50 | 1·60 |

**127** Iguana

**1978.** 25th Anniv of Coronation.

| | | | | |
|---|---|---|---|---|
| 384 | - | 50c. brown, green and silver | 20 | 40 |
| 385 | - | 50c. multicoloured | 20 | 40 |
| 386 | **127** | 50c. brown, green and silver | 20 | 40 |

DESIGNS: No. 384, Plantagenet Falcon; 385, Queen Elizabeth II.

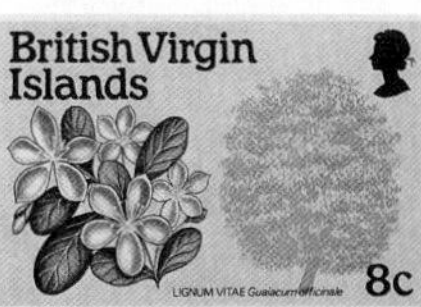

**128** Lignum Vitae

**1978.** Flowering Trees. Multicoloured.

| | | | |
|---|---|---|---|
| 387 | 8c. Type **128** | 15 | 10 |
| 388 | 22c. Ginger Thomas | 20 | 15 |
| 389 | 40c. Dog almond | 30 | 20 |
| 390 | 75c. White cedar | 45 | 70 |
| **MS**391 | 131×95 mm. Nos. 387/90 | 1·00 | 3·00 |

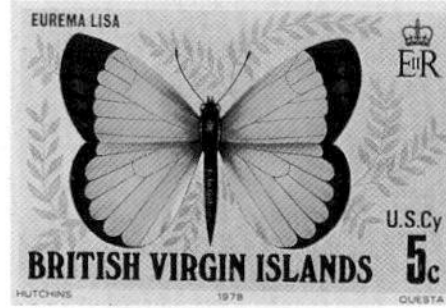

**129** "Eurema lisa"

**1978.** Butterflies. Multicoloured.

| | | | |
|---|---|---|---|
| 392 | 5c. Type **129** | 25 | 10 |
| 393 | 22c. "Agraulis vanillae" | 40 | 20 |
| 394 | 30c. "Heliconius charithonia" | 1·10 | 30 |
| 395 | 75c. "Hemiargus hanno" | 1·40 | 1·25 |
| **MS**396 | 159×113 mm. No. 392×6 and No. 393×3 | 2·50 | 5·50 |

**130** Spiny Lobster

**1978.** Wildlife Conservation. Multicoloured.

| | | | |
|---|---|---|---|
| 397 | 5c. Type **130** | 15 | 10 |
| 398 | 15c. Large iguana (vert) | 25 | 10 |
| 399 | 22c. Hawksbill turtle | 40 | 15 |
| 400 | 75c. Black coral (vert) | 75 | 90 |
| **MS**401 | 130×153 mm. Nos. 397/400 | 1·75 | 3·75 |

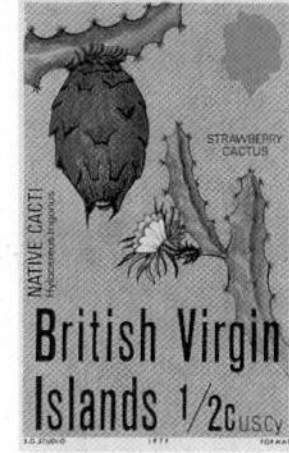

**131** Strawberry Cactus

**1979.** Native Cacti. Multicoloured.

| | | | |
|---|---|---|---|
| 402 | ½c. Type **131** | 10 | 10 |
| 403 | 5c. Snowy cactus | 15 | 10 |
| 404 | 13c. Barrel cactus | 20 | 20 |
| 405 | 22c. Tree cactus | 25 | 35 |
| 406 | 30c. Prickly pear | 30 | 40 |
| 407 | 75c. Dildo cactus | 40 | 1·00 |

**132** West Indian Girl

**1979.** International Year of the Child. Multicoloured.

| | | | |
|---|---|---|---|
| 408 | 5c. Type **132** | 10 | 10 |
| 409 | 10c. African boy | 10 | 10 |
| 410 | 13c. Asian girl | 10 | 10 |
| 411 | $1 European boy | 50 | 85 |
| **MS**412 | 91×114 mm. Nos. 408/11 | 70 | 1·50 |

**133** 1956 Road Harbour 3c. Definitive Stamp

**1979.** Death Centenary of Sir Rowland Hill.

| | | | | |
|---|---|---|---|---|
| 413 | **133** | 5c. dp blue, blue & green | 10 | 10 |
| 414 | - | 13c. blue and mauve | 10 | 10 |
| 415 | - | 75c. blue and purple | 45 | 50 |
| **MS**416 | | 37×91 mm. $1 blue and red | 70 | 1·25 |

DESIGNS (39×27 mm)—13c. 1880 2½d. red-brown; 75c. Great Britain 1910 unissued 2d. Tyrian plum. (40×28 mm)—$1 1867 1s. "Missing Virgin" error.

**134** Pencil Urchin

**1979.** Marine Life. Multicoloured.

| | | | |
|---|---|---|---|
| 417 | ½c. Calcified algae | 40 | 2·75 |
| 418 | 1c. Purple-tipped sea anemone | 55 | 2·75 |
| 419 | 3c. Common starfish | 1·25 | 2·75 |
| 420 | 5c. Type **134** | 1·25 | 2·25 |
| 421 | 8c. Atlantic trumpet triton | 1·25 | 1·75 |
| 422 | 10c. Christmas tree worms | 30 | 1·25 |
| 423a | 13c. Flamingo tongue snail | 1·50 | 75 |
| 424 | 15c. Spider crab | 40 | 1·00 |
| 425 | 18c. Sea squirts | 2·00 | 4·25 |
| 426 | 20c. True tulip | 55 | 1·50 |
| 427 | 25c. Rooster-tail conch | 1·25 | 4·00 |
| 428 | 30c. West Indian fighting conch | 2·50 | 1·50 |
| 429 | 60c. Mangrove crab | 1·50 | 3·00 |
| 430 | $1 Coral polyps | 1·25 | 4·25 |
| 431 | $2.50 Peppermint shrimp | 1·25 | 4·00 |
| 432 | $3 West Indian murex | 1·25 | 4·50 |
| 433 | $5 Carpet anemone | 1·75 | 5·50 |

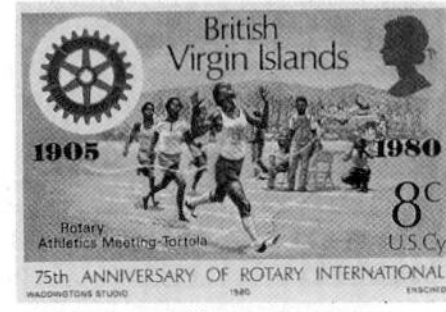


**135** Rotary Athletics Meeting, Tortola

**1980.** 75th Anniv of Rotary International. Mult.

| | | | |
|---|---|---|---|
| 434 | 8c. Type **135** | 10 | 10 |
| 435 | 22c. Paul P. Harris (founder) | 15 | 10 |
| 436 | 60c. Mount Saga, Tortola ("Creation of National Park") | 30 | 40 |
| 437 | $1 Rotary anniversary emblem | 55 | 75 |
| **MS**438 | 149×148 mm. Nos. 434/7 | 1·00 | 3·75 |

**136** Brown Booby

**1980.** "London 1980" International Stamp Exhibition. Birds. Multicoloured.

| | | | |
|---|---|---|---|
| 439 | 20c. Type **136** | 20 | 20 |
| 440 | 25c. Magnificent frigate bird | 25 | 25 |
| 441 | 50c. White-tailed tropic bird | 40 | 40 |
| 442 | 75c. Brown pelican | 55 | 55 |
| **MS**443 | 152×130 mm. Nos. 439/42 | 1·25 | 2·25 |

**1980.** Caribbean Commonwealth Parliamentary Association Meeting, Tortola. Nos. 414/15 optd CARIBBEAN COMMONWEALTH PARLIAMENTARY ASSOCIATION MEETING TORTOLA 11–19 JULY 1980.

| | | | |
|---|---|---|---|
| 444 | 13c. blue and red | 15 | 10 |
| 445 | 75c. deep blue and blue | 40 | 40 |

**138** Sir Francis Drake

**1980.** Sir Francis Drake Commemoration. Mult.

| | | | |
|---|---|---|---|
| 446 | 8c. Type **138** | 50 | 10 |
| 447 | 15c. Queen Elizabeth I | 70 | 15 |
| 448 | 30c. Drake receiving knighthood | 90 | 30 |
| 449 | 75c. "Golden Hind" and coat of arms | 1·75 | 1·25 |
| **MS**450 | 171×121 mm. Nos. 446/9 | 3·75 | 6·50 |

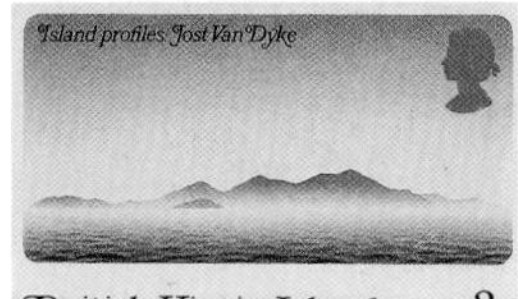


**139** Jost Van Dyke

**1980.** Island Profiles. Multicoloured.

| | | | |
|---|---|---|---|
| 451 | 2c. Type **139** | 10 | 10 |
| 452 | 5c. Peter Island | 10 | 10 |
| 453 | 13c. Virgin Gorda | 15 | 10 |
| 454 | 22c. Anegada | 20 | 10 |
| 455 | 30c. Norman Island | 25 | 15 |
| 456 | $1 Tortola | 70 | 1·00 |
| **MS**457 | 95×88 mm. No. 456 | 85 | 1·50 |

**140** Dancing Lady

**1981.** Flowers. Multicoloured.

| | | | |
|---|---|---|---|
| 458 | 5c. Type **140** | 10 | 10 |
| 459 | 20c. Love in the mist | 15 | 15 |
| 460 | 22c. "Pitcairnia angustifolia" | 15 | 15 |
| 461 | 75c. Dutchman's pipe | 35 | 65 |
| 462 | $1 Maiden apple | 35 | 80 |

**141** Wedding Bouquet from British Virgin Islands

**1981.** Royal Wedding. Multicoloured.

| | | | |
|---|---|---|---|
| 463 | 10c. Type **141** | 10 | 10 |
| 464 | 35c. Prince Charles and Queen Elizabeth the Queen Mother in Garter robes | 20 | 15 |
| 465 | $1.25 Prince Charles and Lady Diana Spencer | 60 | 80 |

**142** Stamp Collecting

**1981.** 25th Anniv of Duke of Edinburgh Award Scheme. Multicoloured.

| | | | |
|---|---|---|---|
| 466 | 10c. Type **142** | 10 | 10 |
| 467 | 15c. Athletics | 10 | 10 |
| 468 | 50c. Camping | 25 | 25 |
| 469 | $1 Duke of Edinburgh | 40 | 45 |

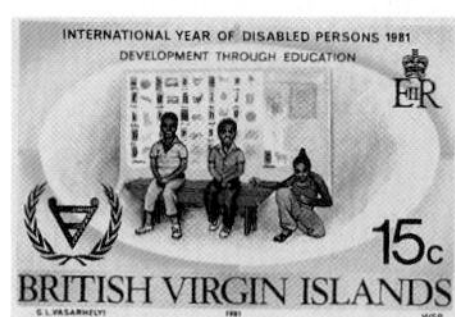


**143** "Development through Education"

**1981.** International Year for Disabled Persons. Multicoloured.

| | | | |
|---|---|---|---|
| 470 | 15c. Type **143** | 15 | 15 |
| 471 | 20c. Fort Charlotte Children's Centre | 15 | 20 |
| 472 | 30c. "Developing cultural awareness" | 20 | 30 |
| 473 | $1 Fort Charlotte Children's Centre (different) | 60 | 1·25 |

**144** Detail from "The Adoration of the Shepherds" (Rubens)

**1981.** Christmas.

| | | | | |
|---|---|---|---|---|
| 474 | **144** | 5c. multicoloured | 15 | 10 |
| 475 | - | 15c. multicoloured | 25 | 10 |
| 476 | - | 30c. multicoloured | 45 | 15 |
| 477 | - | $1 multicoloured | 1·10 | 1·10 |
| **MS**478 | | 117×90 mm. 50c. multicoloured (horiz) | 2·00 | 1·00 |

DESIGNS: 15c. to $1 Further details from "The Adoration of the Shepherds" by Rubens.

**145** Green-throated Caribs and Erythrina

**1982.** Hummingbirds. Multicoloured.

| | | | |
|---|---|---|---|
| 479 | 15c. Type **145** | 50 | 15 |
| 480 | 30c. Green-throated carib and bougainvillea | 60 | 45 |
| 481 | 35c. Antillean crested hummingbirds and "granadilla passiflora" | 70 | 55 |
| 482 | $1.25 Antillean crested hummingbirds and hibiscus | 1·75 | 3·00 |

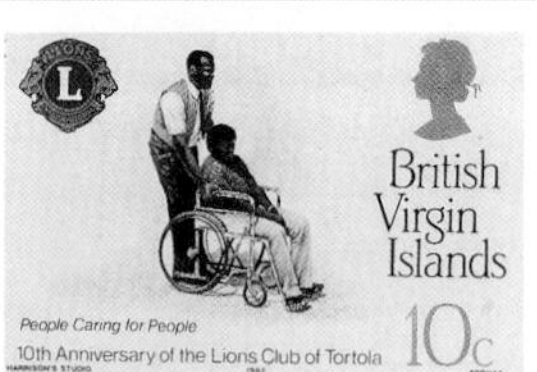


**146** "People caring for People"

**1982.** 10th Anniv of Lions Club of Tortola. Mult.

| | | | |
|---|---|---|---|
| 483 | 10c. Type **146** | 15 | 10 |
| 484 | 20c. Tortola Headquarters | 20 | 15 |
| 485 | 30c. "We Serve" | 25 | 15 |
| 486 | $1.50 "Lions" symbol | 60 | 1·00 |
| **MS**487 | 124×102 mm. Nos. 483/6 | 1·75 | 4·25 |

**147** Princess at Victoria and Albert Museum, November, 1981

**1982.** 21st Birthday of Princess of Wales. Mult.

| | | | |
|---|---|---|---|
| 488 | 10c. British Virgin Islands coat of arms | 15 | 10 |
| 489 | 35c. Type **147** | 30 | 15 |
| 490 | 50c. Bride and groom proceeding into Vestry | 45 | 35 |
| 491 | $1.50 Formal portrait | 1·10 | 1·10 |

**148** Douglas DC-3

**1982.** 10th Anniv of Air BVI. Multicoloured.

| | | | |
|---|---|---|---|
| 492 | 10c. Type **148** | 45 | 15 |
| 493 | 15c. Britten-Norman BN-2 Islander | 60 | 20 |
| 494 | 60c. Hawker Siddeley H.S.748 | 1·10 | 75 |
| 495 | 75c. Runway scene | 1·25 | 90 |

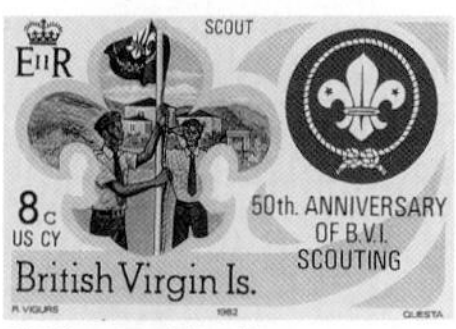


**149** Scouts raising Flag

**1982.** 75th Anniv of Boy Scout Movement and 50th Anniv of Scouting in B.V.I. Multicoloured.

| | | | |
|---|---|---|---|
| 496 | 8c. Type **149** | 20 | 10 |
| 497 | 20c. Cub Scout | 30 | 25 |
| 498 | 50c. Sea Scout | 40 | 55 |
| 499 | $1 First camp, Brownsea Island, and portrait of Lord Baden-Powell | 70 | 1·50 |

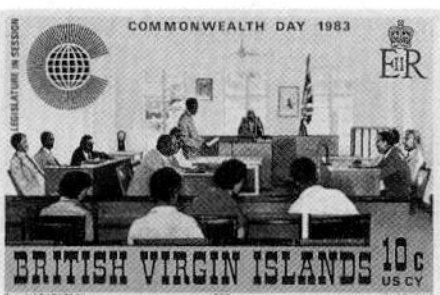


**150** Legislature in Session

**1983.** Commonwealth Day. Multicoloured.

| | | | |
|---|---|---|---|
| 500 | 10c. Type **150** | 10 | 10 |
| 501 | 30c. Tourism | 25 | 20 |
| 502 | 35c. Satellite view of Earth showing Virgin Islands | 25 | 25 |
| 503 | 75c. B.V.I. and Commonwealth flags | 70 | 90 |

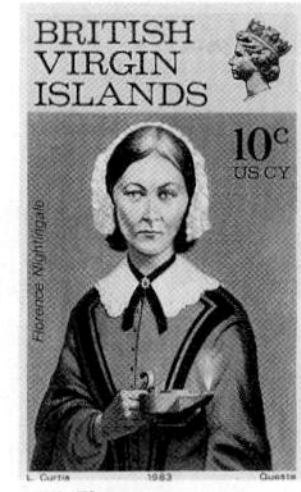


**151** Florence Nightingale

**1983.** Nursing Week. Multicoloured.

| | | | |
|---|---|---|---|
| 504 | 10c. Type **151** | 50 | 15 |
| 505 | 30c. Staff nurse and assistant nurse | 90 | 45 |
| 506 | 60c. Public Health nurses testing blood pressure (horiz) | 1·75 | 1·25 |
| 507 | 75c. Peebles Hospital (horiz) | 1·90 | 1·75 |

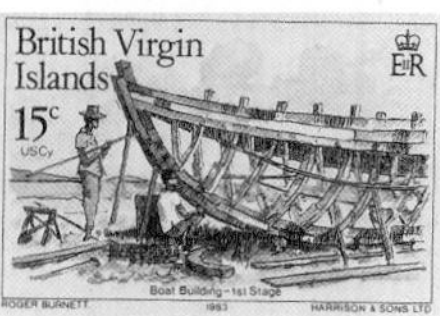


**152** Frame Construction

**1983.** Traditional Boat-building. Multicoloured.

| | | | |
|---|---|---|---|
| 508 | 15c. Type **152** | 25 | 25 |
| 509 | 25c. Planking | 30 | 45 |
| 510 | 50c. Launching | 50 | 80 |
| 511 | $1 Maiden voyage | 65 | 1·75 |
| **MS**512 | 127×101 mm. Nos. 508/11 | 1·50 | 3·75 |

**153** Grumman G21 Goose Amphibian

**1983.** Bicentenary of Manned Flight. Multicoloured.

513 10c. Type **153** 20 15
514 30c. Riley Turbo Skyliner 45 45
515 60c. Embraer EMB-110 Bandeirante 65 85
516 $1.25 Hawker Siddeley H.S.748 90 1·60

**154** "Madonna and Child with the Infant Baptist"

**1983.** Christmas. 500th Birth Anniv of Raphael. Multicoloured.

517 8c. Type **154** 10 10
518 15c. "La Belle Jardiniere" 20 15
519 50c. "Madonna del Granduca" 50 60
520 $1 "The Terranuova Madonna" 90 1·10
**MS**521 108×101 mm. Nos. 517/20 2·75 4·00

**155** Local Tournament

**1984.** 60th Anniv of International Chess Federation. Multicoloured.

522 10c. Type **155** 1·00 40
523 35c. Staunton king, rook and pawn (vert) 2·00 1·50
524 75c. Karpov's winning position against Jakobsen in 1980 Olympiad (vert) 3·75 4·25
525 $1 B.V.I. Gold Medal won by Bill Hook at 1980 Chess Olympiad 4·25 5·50

**156** Port Purcell

**1984.** 250th Anniv of "Lloyd's List" (newspaper). Multicoloured.

526 15c. Type **156** 25 30
527 25c. Boeing 747-100 45 50
528 50c. Wreck of "Rhone" (mail steamer), 1867 90 95
529 $1 "Booker Viking" (cargo liner) 1·50 1·60

**157** Mail Ship "Boyne", Boeing 747-100 and U.P.U. Logo

**1984.** Universal Postal Union Congress, Hamburg. Sheet 90×69 mm.

**MS**530 **157** $1 blue and black 2·25 2·50

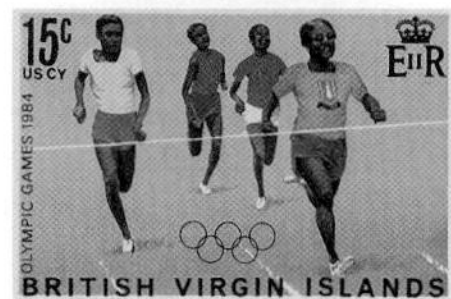


**158** Running

**1984.** Olympic Games, Los Angeles. Multicoloured.

531 15c. Type **158** 40 40
532 15c. Runner 40 40
533 20c. Wind-surfing 45 45
534 20c. Surfer 45 45
535 30c. Sailing 65 65
536 30c. Yacht 65 65
**MS**537 97×69 mm. Torch-bearer 1·50 1·90

**159** Steel Band

**1984.** 150th Anniv of Abolition of Slavery. Mult.

538 10c. Type **159** 30 35
539 10c. Dancing girls 30 35
540 10c. Men in traditional costumes 30 35
541 10c. Girl in traditional costumes 30 35
542 10c. Festival Queen 30 35
543 30c. Green and yellow dinghies 45 50
544 30c. Blue and red dinghies 45 50
545 30c. White and blue dinghies 45 50
546 30c. Red and yellow dinghies 45 50
547 30c. Blue and white dinghies 45 50

DESIGNS: Various aspects of Emancipation Festival.

Nos. 543/7 form a composite design, the sail colours of the dinghies being described.

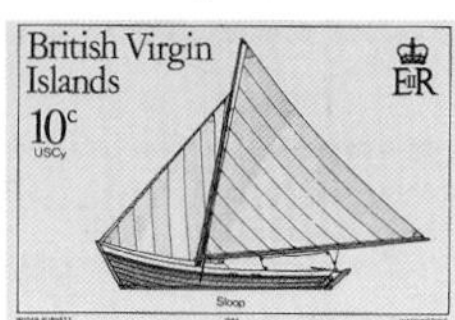


**160** Sloop

**1984.** Boats. Multicoloured.

548 10c. Type **160** 40 20
549 35c. Fishing boat 60 65
550 60c. Schooner 75 1·25
551 75c. Cargo boat 75 1·60
**MS**552 125×90 mm. Nos. 548/51 1·50 4·00

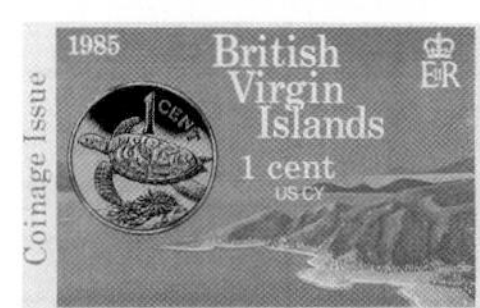


**161** One Cent Coin and Aerial View

**1985.** New Coinage. Coins and Local Scenery. Multicoloured.

553 1c. Type **161** 10 10
554 5c. Five cent coin and boulders on beach 10 10
555 10c. Ten cent coin and scuba diving 20 20
556 25c. Twenty-five cent coin and yachts 45 50
557 50c. Fifty cent coin and jetty 90 1·25
558 $1 One dollar coin and beach at night 1·75 2·25
**MS**559 103×159 mm. Nos. 553/8 3·00 7·00

**162** Red-billed Tropic Bird

**1985.** Birds of the British Virgin Islands. Multicoloured.

560 1c. Type **162** 1·00 2·50
561 2c. Yellow-crowned night heron ("Night Gaulin") 1·00 2·50
562 5c. Mangrove cuckoo ("Rain Bird") 1·50 2·00
563 8c. Northern mockingbird ("Mockingbird") 1·50 2·75
564 10c. Grey kingbird ("Chinchary") 1·50 40
565 12c. Red-necked pigeon ("Wild Pigeon") 2·25 1·50
649 15c. Least bittern ("Bittlin") 2·75 1·25
567 18c. Smooth-billed ani ("Black Witch") 2·75 3·25
651 20c. Clapper rail ("Pond Shakey") 2·75 1·25
652 25c. American kestrel ("Killy-killy") 2·75 1·25
570 30c. Pearly-eyed thrasher ("Thrushie") 2·75 1·75
654 35c. Bridled quail dove ("Marmi Dove") 2·75 1·25
572 40c. Green-backed heron ("Little Gaulin") 3·00 1·75
573 50c. Scaly-breasted ground dove ("Ground Dove") 3·25 3·50
574 60c. Little blue heron ("Blue Gaulin") 3·75 5·00
658 $1 Audubon's shearwater ("Pimleco") 5·00 5·50
576 $2 Blue-faced booby ("White Booby") 5·00 8·50
577 $3 Cattle egret ("Cow Bird") 6·50 12·00
578 $5 Zenaida dove ("Turtle Dove") 8·50 14·00

**163** The Queen Mother at Festival of Remembrance

**1985.** Life and Times of Queen Elizabeth the Queen Mother. Multicoloured.

579A 10c. Type **163** 10 20
580A 10c. At Victoria Palace Theatre, 1984 10 20
581A 25c. At the engagement of the Prince of Wales, 1981 15 40
582A 25c. Opening Celia Johnson Theatre, 1985 15 40
583A 50c. The Queen Mother on her 82nd birthday 20 70
584A 50c. At the Tate Gallery, 1983 20 70
585A 75c. At the Royal Smithfield Show, 1983 25 1·00
586A 75c. Unveiling Mountbatten Statue, 1983 25 1·00
**MS**587A 85×114 mm. $1 At Columbia University; $1 At a Wedding, St. Margaret's, Westminster, 1983 85 4·00

**164** Seaside Sparrow

**1985.** Birth Bicentenary of John J. Audubon (ornithologist). Designs showing original paintings. Multicoloured.

588 5c. Type **164** 30 20
589 30c. Passenger pigeon 40 70
590 50c. Yellow-breasted chat 45 1·75
591 $1 American kestrel 50 2·75

**165** S.V. "Flying Cloud"

**1986.** Visiting Cruise Ships. Multicoloured.

592 35c. Type **165** 80 85
593 50c. M.V. "Newport Clipper" 1·10 1·50
594 75c. M.V. "Cunard Countess" 1·10 2·50
595 $1 M.V. "Sea Goddess" 1·25 3·00

**1986.** Inaugural Flight of Miami–Beef Island Air Service. Nos 581/2 and 585/6 optd MIAMI B.V.I. INAUGURAL FLIGHT.

596A 25c. At the engagement of the Prince of Wales, 1981 40 50
597A 25c. Opening Celia Johnson Theatre, 1985 40 50
598A 75c. At the Royal Smithfield Show, 1983 1·25 1·50
599A 75c. Unveiling Mountbatten statue, 1983 1·25 1·50

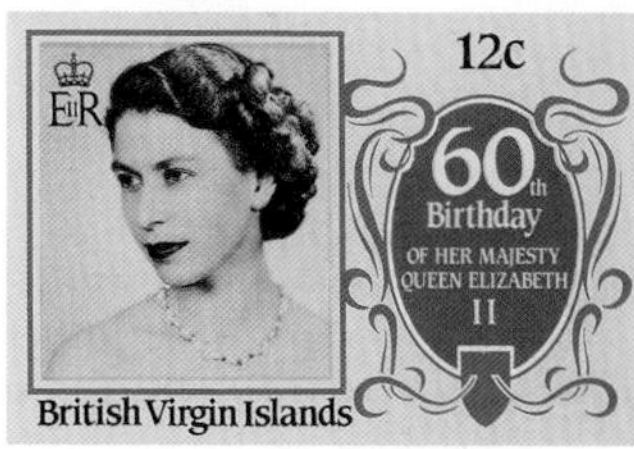


**167** Queen Elizabeth II in 1958

**1986.** 60th Birthday of Queen Elizabeth II. Multicoloured.

600 12c. Type **167** 15 20
601 35c. At a Maundy Service 20 45
602 $1.50 Queen Elizabeth 45 1·75
603 $2 During a visit to Canberra, 1982 (vert) 60 2·25
**MS**604 85×115 mm. $3 Queen with bouquet 3·50 6·00

**168** Miss Sarah Ferguson

**1986.** Royal Wedding. Multicoloured.

605 35c. Type **168** 30 70
606 35c. Prince Andrew and Miss Sarah Ferguson 30 70
607 $1 Prince Andrew in morning dress (horiz) 50 1·25
608 $1 Miss Sarah Ferguson (different) (horiz) 50 1·25
**MS**609 115×85 mm. $4 Duke and Duchess of York in carriage after wedding (horiz) 2·50 6·00

**169** Harvesting Sugar Cane

**1986.** History of Rum Making. Multicoloured.

610 12c. Type **169** 1·00 20
611 40c. Bringing sugar cane to mill 1·75 1·25
612 60c. Rum distillery 2·25 3·50
613 $1 Delivering barrels of rum to ship 5·50 5·50
**MS**614 115×84 mm. $2 Royal Navy rum issue 6·50 8·50

**170** "Sentinel"

**1986.** 20th Anniv of Cable and Wireless Caribbean Headquarters, Tortola. Cable Ships. Multicoloured.

615 35c. Type **170** 60 80
616 35c. "Retriever" (1961) 60 80
617 60c. "Cable Enterprise" (1964) 75 1·50
618 60c. "Mercury" (1962) 75 1·50
619 75c. "Recorder" (1955) 75 1·75
620 75c. "Pacific Guardian" (1984) 75 1·75
621 $1 "Great Eastern" (1860's) 80 2·00
622 $1 "Cable Venture" (1977) 80 2·00
**MS**623 Four sheets, each 102×131 mm. (a) 40c. × 2 As 35c. (b) 50c. × 2 As 60c. (c) 80c. × 2 As 75c. (d) $1.50 × 2 As $1 Set of 4 sheets 5·00 12·00

**1986.** Centenary of Statue of Liberty. T 17 and similar vert views of Statue in separate miniature sheets. Multicoloured.

**MS**624 Nine sheets, each 85×115 mm. 50c.; 75c.; 90c.; $1; $1.25; $1.50; $1.75; $2; $2.50 Set of 9 sheets 5·00 13·00

**172** 18th-century Spanish Galleon

**1987.** Shipwrecks. Multicoloured.

625 12c. Type **172** 2·50 55
626 35c. H.M.S. "Astrea" (frigate), 1808 3·75 1·40
627 75c. "Rhone" (mail steamer), 1867 5·50 4·50
628 $1.50 "Captain Rokos" (freighter), 1929 8·00 11·00
**MS**629 85×65 mm. $1.50, "Volvart", 1819 16·00 15·00

**173** Outline Map and Flag of Montserrat

**1987.** 11th Meeting of Organization of Eastern Caribbean States. Each showing map and flag. Multicoloured.

630 10c. Type **173** 70 70
631 15c. Grenada 80 75
632 20c. Dominica 85 80
633 25c. St. Kitts-Nevis 90 1·00
634 35c. St. Vincent and Grenadines 1·40 1·00
635 50c. British Virgin Islands 2·00 2·50
636 75c. Antigua and Barbuda 2·25 3·25
637 $1 St. Lucia 2·75 3·50

**174** Spider Lily

**1987.** Opening of Botanical Gardens. Multicoloured.

638 12c. Type **174** 80 35
639 35c. Barrel cactus 1·75 1·00
640 $1 Wild plantain 2·75 3·25
641 $1.50 Little butterfly orchid 8·00 8·50
**MS**642 139×104 mm. $2.50, White cedar 3·75 6·00

**175** Early Mail Packet and 1867 1s. Stamp

**1987.** Bicentenary of Postal Services. Multicoloured.

662 10c. Type **175** 1·50 65
663 20c. Map and 1899 1d. stamp 2·00 1·10
664 35c. Road Town Post Office and Customs House, c. 1913, and 1847 4d. stamp 2·25 1·75
665 $1.50 Piper PA-23 Apache mail plane and 1964 25c. definitive 7·00 10·00
**MS**666 70×60 mm. $2.50, Mail ship, 1880's, and 1880 1d. 6·00 9·50

**1988.** 500th Birth Anniv of Titian (artist). As T 238 of Antigua. Multicoloured.

667 10c. "Salome" 65 55
668 12c. "Man with the Glove" 70 60
669 20c. "Fabrizio Salvaresio" 90 80
670 25c. "Daughter of Roberto Strozzi" 1·00 90
671 40c. "Pope Julius II" 1·60 2·00
672 50c. "Bishop Ludovico Beccadelli" 1·75 2·00
673 60c. "King Philip II" 1·90 2·50
674 $1 "Empress Isabella of Portugal" 2·50 2·75
**MS**675 Two sheets, each 110×95 mm. (a) $2 "Emperor Charles V at Muhlberg" (detail). (b) $2 "Pope Paul III and his Grandsons" (detail) Set of 2 sheets 15·00 13·00

**176** de Havilland Canada DHC-5 Transporter over Sir Francis Drake Channel and Staunton Pawn

**1988.** 1st British Virgin Islands Open Chess Tournament. Multicoloured.

676 35c. Type **176** 4·50 1·50
677 $1 Jose Capablanca (former World Champion) and Staunton king 8·50 8·50
**MS**678 109×81 mm. $2 Chess match 9·00 11·00

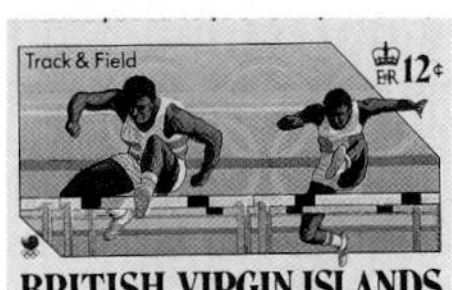

**177** Hurdling

**1988.** Olympic Games, Seoul. Multicoloured.

679 12c. Type **177** 35 25
680 20c. Windsurfing 60 45
681 75c. Basketball 3·75 3·25
682 $1 Tennis 3·75 3·75
**MS**683 71×102 mm. $2 Athletics 3·00 4·50

**178** Swimmer ("Don't Swim Alone")

**1988.** 125th Anniv of International Red Cross.

684 **178** 12c. black, red and blue 1·50 40
685 - 30c. black, red and blue 2·25 80
686 - 60c. black, red and blue 3·50 3·00
687 - $1 black, red and blue 4·25 4·00
**MS**688 68×96 mm. 50c. × 4 black and red 5·00 6·50

DESIGNS—HORIZ: 30c. Swimmers ("No swimming during electrical storms"); 60c. Beach picnic ("Don't eat before swimming"); $1 Boat and equipment ("Proper equipment for boating"). VERT: 50c.×4 Recovery position, clearing airway, mouth-to-mouth resuscitation, cardiac massage.

**179** Princess Alexandra

**1988.** Visit of Princess Alexandra. Designs showing different portraits.

689 **179** 40c. multicoloured 2·50 75
690 - $1.50 multicoloured 5·50 4·75
**MS**691 102×98 mm. $2 multicoloured 5·00 6·50

**180** Brown Pelican in Flight

**1988.** Wildlife (1st series). Aquatic Birds. Mult.

692 10c. Type **180** 1·60 50
693 12c. Brown pelican perched on post 1·60 55
694 15c. Brown pelican 1·75 1·10
695 35c. Brown pelican swallowing fish 2·75 3·00
**MS**696 106×76 mm. $2 Common shoveler (horiz) 11·00 9·00

No. **MS**696 is without the W.W.F. logo.

**181** Anegada Rock Iguana

**1988.** Wildlife (2nd series). Endangered Species. Multicoloured.

697 20c. Type **181** 1·25 75
698 40c. Virgin Gorda dwarf gecko 1·50 1·40
699 60c. Hawksbill turtle 2·50 3·50
700 $1 Humpback whale 7·00 8·00
**MS**701 106×77 mm. $2 Trunk turtle (vert) 6·50 8·50

**182** Yachts at Start

**1989.** Spring Regatta. Multicoloured.

702 12c. Type **182** 45 40
703 40c. Yacht tacking (horiz) 1·00 1·00
704 75c. Yachts at sunset 1·60 2·50
705 $1 Yachts rounding buoy (horiz) 2·00 2·75
**MS**706 83×69 mm. $2 Yacht under full sail 5·50 6·50

**1989.** 500th Anniv (1992) of Discovery of America by Columbus (1st issue). Pre-Columbian Arawak Society. As T 247 of Antigua. Multicoloured.

707 10c. Arawak in hammock 70 45
708 20c. Making fire 1·00 50
709 25c. Making implements 1·00 60
710 $1.50 Arawak family 4·50 7·00
**MS**711 85×70 mm. $2 Religious ceremony 9·00 11·00

See also Nos. 741/5, 793/7 and 818/26.

**183** "Apollo II" Emblem

**1989.** 20th Anniv of First Manned Landing on the Moon. Multicoloured.

712 15c. Type **183** 1·25 60
713 30c. Edwin Aldrin deploying scientific experiments 2·25 1·00
714 65c. Aldrin and U.S. flag on Moon 3·00 4·00
715 $1 "Apollo II" capsule after splashdown 4·00 4·25
**MS**716 102×77 mm. $2 Neil Armstrong (38×50 mm) 9·00 10·50

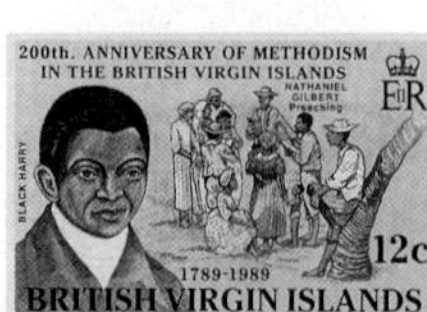

**184** Black Harry and Nathaniel Gilbert preaching to Slaves

**1989.** Bicentenary of Methodist Church in British Virgin Islands. Multicoloured.

717 12c. Type **184** 1·00 50
718 25c. Methodist school exercise book 1·40 75
719 35c. East End Methodist Church, 1810 1·60 85
720 $1.25 Reverend John Wesley (founder of Methodism) and church youth choir 3·25 6·50
**MS**721 100×69 mm. $2 Dr. Thomas Cole 4·75 9·00

**185** Player tackling

**1989.** World Cup Football Championship, Italy, 1990. Multicoloured.

722 5c. Type **185** 80 80
723 10c. Player dribbling ball 80 80
724 20c. Two players chasing ball 1·50 80
725 $1.75 Goalkeeper diving for ball 7·00 7·50
**MS**726 100×70 mm. $2 British Virgin Islands team captain 8·50 11·00

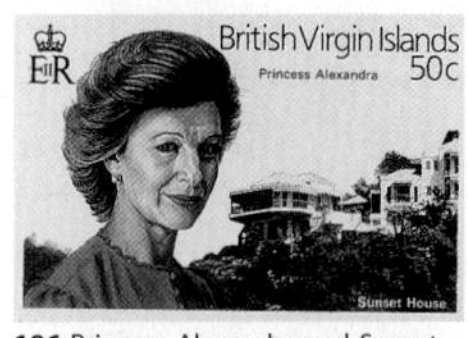

**186** Princess Alexandra and Sunset House

**1990.** "Stamp World London 90" International Stamp Exhibition. Royal Visitors. Multicoloured.

727 50c. Type **186** 3·50 3·50
728 50c. Princess Margaret and Government House 3·50 3·50
729 50c. Hon. Angus Ogilvy and Little Dix Bay Hotel 3·50 3·50
730 50c. Princess Diana with Princes William and Henry and Necker Island Resort 3·50 3·50
**MS**731 89×80 mm. $2 Royal Yacht "Britannia" 12·00 12·00

**187** Audubon's Shearwater

**1990.** Birds. Multicoloured.

732 5c. Type **187** 1·50 1·75
733 12c. Red-necked pigeon 2·00 60
734 20c. Moorhen ("Common Gallinule") 2·25 60
735 25c. Green-backed heron ("Green Heron") 2·25 60
736 40c. Yellow warbler 2·50 1·50
737 60c. Smooth-billed ani 2·75 2·75
738 $1 Antillean crested hummingbird 2·75 3·25
739 $1.25 Black-faced grassquit 2·75 4·50
**MS**740 Two sheets, each 98×70 mm. (a) $2 Royal tern egg (vert) (b) $2 Red-billed tropicbird egg (vert) Set of 2 sheets 9·50 7·00

**1990.** 500th Anniv (1992) of Discovery of America by Columbus (2nd issue). New World Natural History–Fishes. As T 260 of Antigua. Mult.

741 10c. Blue tang (horiz) 1·50 60
742 35c. Glass-eyed snapper (horiz) 2·50 70
743 50c. Slippery dick (horiz) 3·00 3·50
744 $1 Porkfish (horiz) 4·50 4·75
**MS**745 100×70 mm. $2 Yellow-tailed snapper 5·00 6·50

**188** Queen Elizabeth the Queen Mother

**1990.** 90th Birthday of Queen Elizabeth the Queen Mother.

746 **188** 12c. multicoloured 50 25
747 - 25c. multicoloured 90 55
748 - 60c. multicoloured 1·75 2·25
749 - $1 multicoloured 2·00 2·50
**MS**750 75×75 mm. $2 multicoloured 2·75 2·75

DESIGNS: 25, 60c., $2 Recent photographs.

**189** Footballers

**1990.** World Cup Football Championship, Italy.

751 **189** 12c. multicoloured 60 40
752 - 20c. multicoloured 90 50
753 - 50c. multicoloured 1·75 2·00
754 - $1.25 multicoloured 2·50 3·75
**MS**755 91×76 mm. $2 multicoloured 4·50 4·50

DESIGNS: 20, 50c., $2, Footballers.

**190** Judo

**1990.** Olympic Games, Barcelona (1992). Mult.

756 12c. Type **190** 1·50 45
757 40c. Yachting 2·25 1·60
758 60c. Hurdling 2·75 3·75
759 $1 Show jumping 4·00 4·50
**MS**760 78×105 mm. $2 Windsurfing 4·50 4·00

**191** Tree-fern, Sage Mountain National Park

**1991.** 30th Anniv of National Parks Trust. Multicoloured.

761 10c. Type **191** 80 1·00
762 25c. Coppermine ruins, Virgin Gorda (horiz) 1·50 80
763 35c. Ruined windmill, Mt. Healthy 1·50 80
764 $2 The Baths (rock formation), Virgin Gorda (horiz) 9·00 11·00

**192** Haiti Haiti

**1991.** Flowers. Multicoloured.

765 1c. Type **192** 20 1·25
766 2c. Lobster claw 20 1·25
767 5c. Frangipani 20 1·25
887 10c. Autograph tree 50 1·40
769 12c. Yellow allamanda 40 30
889 15c. Lantana 65 40
771 20c. Jerusalem thorn 50 30
772 25c. Turk's cap 55 40
892 30c. Swamp immortelle 70 50
893 35c. White cedar 85 55
775 40c. Mahoe tree 75 65
895 45c. Pinguin 95 80
896 50c. Christmas orchid 2·25 1·75
778 70c. Lignum vitae 1·10 2·00
779 $1 African tulip tree 1·25 2·00
899 $2 Beach morning glory 3·00 5·00
781 $3 Organ pipe cactus 4·00 7·00
901 $5 Tall ground orchid 8·50 12·00
783 $10 Ground orchid 14·00 18·00

**193** "Phoebis sennae"

**1991.** Butterflies. Multicoloured.

784 5c. Type **193** 90 1·25
785 10c. "Dryas iulia" 1·00 1·25
786 15c. "Junonia evarete" 1·50 75
787 20c. "Dione vanillae" 1·60 80
788 25c. "Battus polydamus" 1·60 1·00
789 30c. "Eurema lisa" 1·75 1·00
790 35c. "Heliconius charitonius" 1·75 1·10
791 $1.50 "Siproeta stelenes" 4·25 6·50
**MS**792 Two sheets. (a) 77×117 mm. $2 "Danaus plexippus" (horiz). (b) 117×77 mm. $2 "Biblis hyperia" (horiz) Set of 2 sheets 14·00 15·00

**1991.** 500th Anniv (1992) of Discovery of America by Columbus (3rd issue). History of Exploration. As T 277 of Antigua. Multicoloured.

793 12c. multicoloured 1·75 50
794 50c. multicoloured 3·25 2·00
795 75c. multicoloured 4·00 3·25
796 $1 multicoloured 4·50 4·00
**MS**797 105×76 mm. $2 black and orange 8·50 9·50

DESIGNS—HORIZ: 12c. "Vitoria" in Pacific (Magellan 1519–21); 50c. La Salle on the Mississippi, 1682; 75c. John Cabot landing in Nova Scotia, 1497–98; $1 Cartier discovering the St. Lawrence, 1534. VERT: $2 "Santa Maria" (woodcut).

**1991.** Death Centenary (1990) of Vincent Van Gogh (artist). As T 278 of Antigua. Multicoloured.

798 15c. "Cottage with Decrepit Barn and Stooping Woman" (horiz) 1·25 50
799 30c. "Paul Gauguin's Armchair" 1·75 80
800 75c. "Breton Women" (horiz) 3·00 3·00
801 $1 "Vase with Red Gladioli" 3·50 3·50
**MS**802 103×81 mm. $2 "Dance Hall in Arles" (detail) (horiz) 12·00 13·00

**1991.** Christmas. Religious Paintings by Quinten Massys. As T 291 of Antigua. Multicoloured.

803 15c. "The Virgin and Child Enthroned" (detail) 1·25 25
804 30c. "The Virgin and Child Enthroned" (different detail) 2·00 50
805 60c. "Adoration of the Magi" (detail) 3·50 3·75
806 $1 "Virgin in Adoration" 3·75 4·00
**MS**807 Two sheets, each 102×127 mm. (a) $2 "The Virgin standing with Angels". (b) $2 "The Adoration of the Magi" Set of 2 sheets 15·00 17·00

**194** "Agaricus bisporus"

**1992.** Fungi. Multicoloured.

808 12c. Type **194** 1·50 55
809 30c. "Lentinula edodes" (horiz) 2·25 85
810 45c. "Hygocybe acutoconica" 2·25 1·00
811 $1 "Gymnopilus chrysopellus" (horiz) 4·00 6·00
**MS**812 94×68 mm. $2 "Pleurotous ostreatus" (horiz) 12·00 13·00

**1992.** 40th Anniv of Queen Elizabeth II's Accession. As T 288 of Antigua. Multicoloured.

813 12c. Little Dix Bay, Virgin Gorda 1·00 30
814 25c. Deadchest Bay, Peter Island 2·00 90
815 60c. Pond Bay, Virgin Gorda 2·50 2·50
816 $1 Cane Garden Bay, Tortola 2·75 3·00
**MS**817 75×97 mm. $2 Long Bay, Beef Island 9·50 10·00

**195** Queen Isabella of Spain

**1992.** 500th Anniv of Discovery of America by Columbus (4th issue). Multicoloured.

818 10c. Type **195** 80 75
819 15c. Fleet of Columbus (horiz) 1·40 90
820 20c. Arms awarded to Columbus 1·40 90
821 30c. Landing Monument, Watling Island and Columbus's signature (horiz) 1·40 1·00
822 45c. Christopher Columbus 1·90 1·40
823 50c. Landing in New World and Spanish royal standard (horiz) 1·90 1·90
824 70c. Convent at La Rabida 2·25 3·25
825 $1.50 Replica of "Santa Maria" and Caribbean Pavilion, New York World's Fair (horiz) 3·50 4·75
**MS**826 Two sheets. (a) 116×86 mm. $2 Ships of second voyage at Virgin, Gorda (horiz). (b) 86×116 mm. $2 De la Cosa's map of New World (horiz) Set of 2 sheets 12·00 15·00

**196** Basketball

**1992.** Olympic Games, Barcelona. Multicoloured.

827 15c. Type **196** 2·50 75
828 30c. Tennis 2·50 90
829 60c. Volleyball 2·75 3·00
830 $1 Football 3·00 3·75
**MS**831 100×70 mm. $2 Olympic flame 11·00 13·00

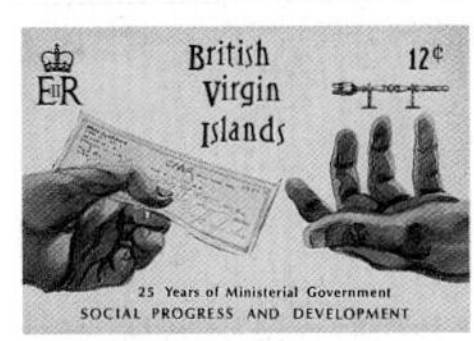


**197** Issuing Social Security Cheque

**1993.** 25th Anniv of Ministerial Government. Multicoloured.

832 12c. Type **197** 40 40
833 15c. Map of British Virgin Islands 1·25 70
834 45c. Administration building 80 70
835 $1.30 International currency abbreviations 2·25 4·25

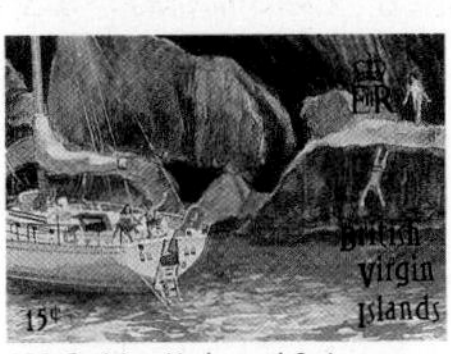

**198** Cruising Yacht and Swimmers, The Baths, Virgin Gorda

**1993.** Tourism. Multicoloured.

836 15c. Type **198** 1·50 50
837 30c. Cruising yacht under sail (vert) 1·75 60
838 60c. Scuba diving 2·50 2·75
839 $1 Cruising yacht at anchor and snorklers (vert) 2·75 3·25
**MS**840 79×108 mm. $1 "Promenade" (trimaran) (vert); $1 Scuba diving (different) (vert) 7·50 8·50

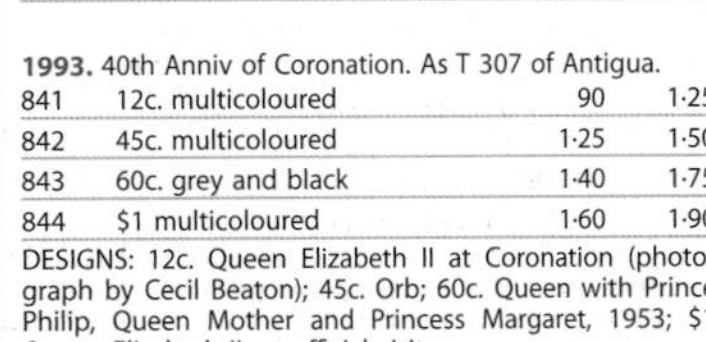

**1993.** 40th Anniv of Coronation. As T 307 of Antigua.

841 12c. multicoloured 90 1·25
842 45c. multicoloured 1·25 1·50
843 60c. grey and black 1·40 1·75
844 $1 multicoloured 1·60 1·90

DESIGNS: 12c. Queen Elizabeth II at Coronation (photograph by Cecil Beaton); 45c. Orb; 60c. Queen with Prince Philip, Queen Mother and Princess Margaret, 1953; $1 Queen Elizabeth II on official visit.

**200** Columbus with King Ferdinand and Queen Isabella

**1993.** 500th Anniv of Discovery of Virgin Islands by Columbus. Multicoloured.

846 3c. Type **200** 15 40
847 12c. Columbus's ship leaving port 40 40
848 15c. Blessing the fleet 45 45
849 25c. Arms and flag of B.V.I. 60 60
850 30c. Columbus and "Santa Maria" 70 70
851 45c. Ships of second voyage 95 95
852 60c. Columbus in ship's boat 1·50 2·25
853 $1 Landing of Columbus 2·00 2·50
**MS**854 Two sheets, each 120×80 mm. (a) $2 Amerindians sighting fleet. (b) $2 Christopher Columbus and ships Set of 2 sheets 11·00 13·00

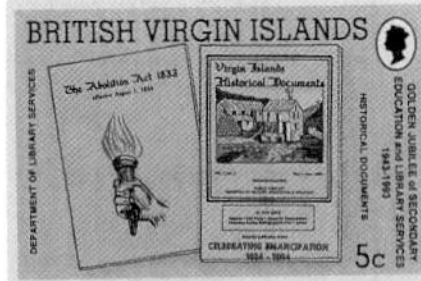


**201** Library Services Publications

**1993.** 50th Anniv of Secondary Education and Library Services. Multicoloured.

855 5c. Type **201** 60 1·00
856 10c. Secondary school sports 2·00 1·25
857 15c. Stanley Nibbs (school teacher) (vert) 1·00 60
858 20c. Mobile library 1·50 70
859 30c. Dr. Norwell Harrigan (adminstrator and lecturer) (vert) 1·50 70
860 35c. Children in library 1·50 70
861 70c. Commemorative inscription on book 2·50 3·50
862 $1 B.V.I. High School 2·75 3·50

**202** Anegada Ground Iguana

**1994.** Endangered Species. Anegada Ground Iguana.

863 **202** 5c. multicoloured 70 70
864 - 10c. multicoloured 70 70
865 - 15c. multicoloured 80 60
866 - 45c. multicoloured 1·25 1·25
**MS**867 106×77 mm. $2 multicoloured 5·00 6·00

DESIGNS: 10c. to $2 Different iguanas.

No. **MS**867 does not carry the W.W.F. Panda emblem.

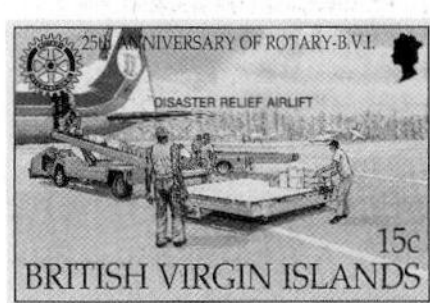


**203** Loading Disaster Relief HS748 Aircraft

**1994.** Centenary of Rotary International in B.V.I. Multicoloured.

868 15c. Type **203** 35 35
869 45c. Training children in marine safety 85 85
870 50c. Donated operating table 90 1·00
871 90c. Paul Harris (founder) and emblem 1·60 2·50

**1994.** 25th Anniv of First Manned Moon Landing. As T 326 of Antigua. Multicoloured.

872 50c. Anniversary logo 2·00 2·25
873 50c. Lunar landing training vehicle 2·00 2·25
874 50c. Launch of "Apollo 11" 2·00 2·25
875 50c. Lunar module "Eagle" in flight 2·00 2·25
876 50c. Moon's surface 2·00 2·25
877 50c. Neil Armstrong (astronaut) taking first step 2·00 2·25
**MS**878 106×76 mm. $2 Signatures and mission logo 14·00 14·00

**204** Argentina v. Netherlands, 1978

**1994.** World Cup Football Championship, U.S.A. Previous Winners. Multicoloured.

879 15c. Type **204** 1·25 50
880 35c. Italy v. West Germany, 1982 2·00 70
881 50c. Argentina v. West Germany, 1986 2·75 2·25
882 $1.30 West Germany v. Argentina, 1990 4·50 6·50
**MS**883 74×101 mm. $2 U.S. flag and World Cup trophy (horiz) 12·00 14·00

**1995.** 50th Anniv of United Nations. As T 213 of Bahamas. Multicoloured.

903 15c. Peugeot P4 all-purpose field cars 45 40
904 30c. Foden medium road tanker 75 60
905 45c. SISU all-terrain vehicle 1·00 90
906 $2 Westland Lynx AH7 helicopter 3·75 5·50

**205** Pair of Juvenile Greater Flamingos

**1995.** Anegada Flamingos Restoration Project. Multicoloured.

907 15c. Type **205** 85 50
908 20c. Pair of adults 85 55
909 60c. Adult feeding 1·40 2·00
910 $1.45 Adult feeding chick 2·50 4·00
**MS**911 80×70 mm. $2 Chicks 6·50 7·00

**206** "Tortola House with Christmas Tree" (Maureen Walters)

**1995.** Christmas. Children's Paintings. Mult.

912 12c. Type **206** 1·75 30
913 50c. "Father Christmas in Row-ing Boat" (Collin Collins) 3·00 1·40
914 70c. "Christmas Tree and Gifts" (Clare Wassell) 3·25 2·75
915 $1.30 "Peace Dove" (Nicholas Scott) 4·50 6·50

**207** Seine Fishing

**1996.** Island Profiles (1st series). Jost Van Dyke. Multicoloured.

916 15c. Type **207** 1·50 40
917 35c. Sandy Spit 1·75 55
918 90c. Map 4·00 3·50
919 $1.50 Foxy's Regatta 4·25 6·50

See also Nos. 1003/6 and 1105/10.

**1996.** 70th Birthday of Queen Elizabeth II. As T 165 of Ascension, each incorporating a different photograph of the Queen. Multicoloured.

920 10c. Government House, Tortola 30 20
921 30c. Legislative Council Building 65 55
922 45c. Liner in Road Harbour 1·50 70
923 $1.50 Map of British Virgin Islands 3·25 5·00
**MS**924 63×65 mm. $2 Queen Elizabeth II 3·00 3·75

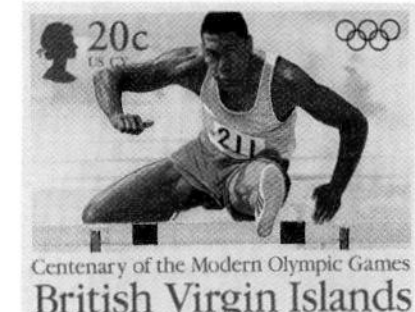


**208** Hurdling

**1996.** Centenary of Modern Olympic Games. Multicoloured.

925 20c. Type **208** 45 30
926 35c. Volley ball 70 60
927 50c. Swimming 1·10 1·75
928 $1 Yachting 2·00 2·75

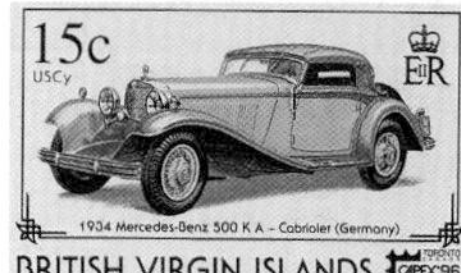


**209** Mercedes-Benz 500 K A, Cabriolet 1934

**1996.** "CAPEX '96" International Stamp Exhibition, Toronto. Early Motor Cars. Multicoloured.

929 15c. Type **209** 45 30
930 40c. Citroen 12 Traction saloon, 1934 1·00 70
931 60c. Cadillac V-8 Sport Phaeton, 1932 1·25 1·75
932 $1.35 Rolls Royce Phantom II saloon, 1934 2·75 4·00
**MS**933 79×62 mm. $2 Ford Sport Coupe, 1932 3·25 4·25

**210** Children with Computer

**1996.** 50th Anniv of UNICEF. Multicoloured.

934 10c. Type **210** 40 40
935 15c. Carnival costume 50 50
936 30c. Children on Scales of Justice 80 80
937 45c. Children on beach 1·25 1·25

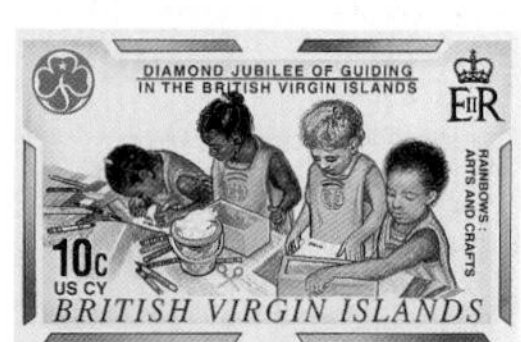


**211** Young Rainbows in Art Class

**1996.** 75th Anniv of Guiding in the British Virgin Islands. Multicoloured.

938 10c. Type **211** 20 20
939 15c. Brownies serving meals 30 25
940 30c. Guides around campfire 50 45
941 45c. Rangers on parade 65 70
942 $2 Lady Baden-Powell 2·75 4·00

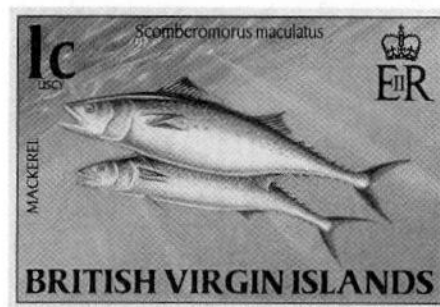


**212** Spanish Mackerel

**1997.** Game Fishes. Multicoloured.

943 1c. Type **212** 10 10
944 10c. Wahoo 15 50
945 15c. Great barracuda 40 40
946 20c. Tarpon 75 35
947 25c. Tiger shark 75 35
948 35c. Sailfish 70 30
949 40c. Dolphin 1·25 65
950 50c. Black-finned tuna 1·25 70
951 60c. Yellow-finned tuna 1·25 70
952 75c. King mackerel ("Kingfish") 1·40 85
953 $1.50 White marlin 2·50 2·00
954 $1.85 Amberjack 3·00 2·75
955 $2 Atlantic bonito 4·00 4·00
956 $5 Bonefish 7·50 8·50
957 $10 Blue marlin 13·00 14·00

**1997.** "HONG KONG '97" International Stamp Exhibition. Sheet 130×90 mm, containing design as No. 953, but with "1997" imprint date. Mult.

**MS**958 $1.50, White marlin 2·25 2·75

**1997.** Golden Wedding of Queen Elizabeth and Prince Philip. As T 173 of Ascension. Multicoloured.

959 30c. Prince Philip with horse 70 1·00
960 30c. Queen Elizabeth at Windsor, 1989 70 1·00
961 45c. Queen in phaeton, Trooping the Colour 90 1·25
962 45c. Prince Philip in Scots Guards uniform 90 1·25
963 70c. Queen Elizabeth and Prince Philip at the Derby, 1993 1·25 1·60
964 70c. Prince Charles playing polo, Mexico, 1993 1·25 1·60
**MS**965 110×70 mm. $2 Queen Elizabeth and Prince Philip in landau (horiz) 3·25 4·00

**213** Fiddler Crab

**1997.** Crabs. Multicoloured.

966 12c. Type **213** 55 50
967 15c. Coral crab 60 50
968 35c. Blue crab 85 60
969 $1 Giant hermit crab 1·75 2·75
**MS**970 76×67 mm. $2 Arrow crab 3·50 4·50

**214** "Psychilis macconnelliae"

**1997.** Orchids of the World. Multicoloured.

971 20c. Type **214** 80 85
972 50c. "Tolumnia prionochila" 1·25 1·10
973 60c. "Tetramicra canaliculata" 1·25 1·40
974 75c. "Liparis elata" 1·40 1·40
**MS**975 59×79 mm. $2 "Dendrobium crumenatum" (vert) 3·25 4·25

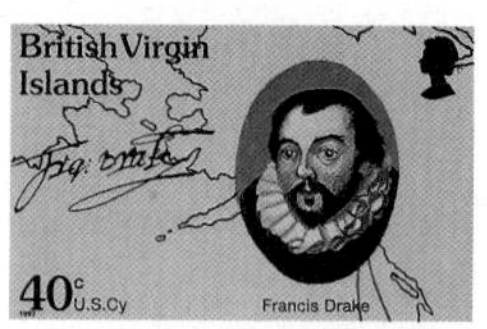


**215** Sir Francis Drake and Signature

**1997.** 420th Anniv of Drake's Circumnavigation of the World. Multicoloured.

976 40c. Type **215** 1·40 1·40
977 40c. Drake's coat of arms 1·40 1·40
978 40c. Queen Elizabeth I and signature 1·40 1·40
979 40c. "Christopher" and "Marigold" 1·40 1·40
980 40c. "Golden Hind" 1·40 1·40
981 40c. "Swan" 1·40 1·40
982 40c. "Cacafuego" (Spanish galleon) 1·40 1·40
983 40c. "Elizabeth" 1·40 1·40
984 40c. "Maria" (Spanish merchant ship) 1·40 1·40
985 40c. Drake's astrolabe 1·40 1·40
986 40c. "Golden Hind's" figurehead 1·40 1·40
987 40c. Compass rose 1·40 1·40
**MS**988 96×76 mm. $2 "Sir Francis Drake" (ketch) 3·75 4·50

Nos. 976/87 were printed together, se-tenant, with the backgrounds forming a composite map of Drake's route.

**1998.** Diana, Princess of Wales Commemoration. Sheet 145×70 mm, containing vert designs as T 177 of Ascension. Multicoloured.

**MS**989 15c. Wearing pink jacket, 1992; 45c. Holding child, 1991; 70c. Laughing, 1991; $1 Wearing high-collared blouse, 1986 (sold at $2.30 + 20c. charity premium) 3·50 4·00

**1998.** 80th Anniv of Royal Air Force. As T 178 of Ascension. Multicoloured.

990 20c. Fairey IIIF (seaplane) 60 40
991 35c. Supermarine Scapa (flying boat) 85 50
992 50c. Westland Sea King H.A.R. (helicopter) 1·40 1·10
993 $1.50 BAe Harrier GR7 2·50 3·25
**MS**994 110×77 mm. 75c. Curtiss H.16 (flying boat); 75c. Curtiss JN-4A; 75c. Bell Airacobra; 75c. Boulton-Paul Defiant 6·50 7·00

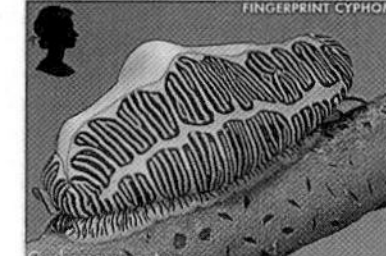


**216** Fingerprint Cyphoma

**1998.** Marine Life. Multicoloured.

995 15c. Type **216** 80 40
996 30c. Long-spined sea urchin 1·00 55
997 45c. Split crown feather duster worm 1·40 70
998 $1 Upside down jelly 2·25 3·00
**MS**999 77×56 mm. $2 Giant anemone 4·75 5·00

**217** "Carnival Reveller" (Rebecca Peck)

**1998.** Festival. Children's Paintings. Multicoloured.

1000 30c. Type **217** 1·00 50
1001 45c. "Leader of a Troupe" (Jehiah Maduro) 1·25 65
1002 $1.30 "Steel Pans" (Rebecca McKenzie) (horiz) 3·00 3·75

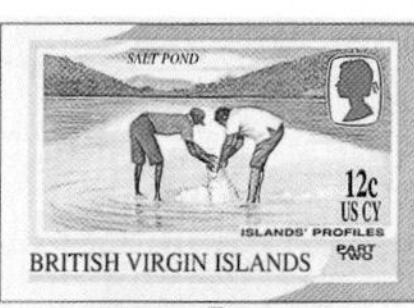


**218** Salt Pond

**1998.** Island Profiles (2nd series). Salt Island. Multicoloured.

1003 12c. Type **218** 1·25 60
1004 30c. Wreck of "Rhone" (mail steamer) 1·75 65
1005 70c. Traditional house 1·50 2·00
1006 $1.45 Salt Island from the air 3·00 4·00
**MS**1007 118×78 mm. $2 Collecting salt 6·00 7·00

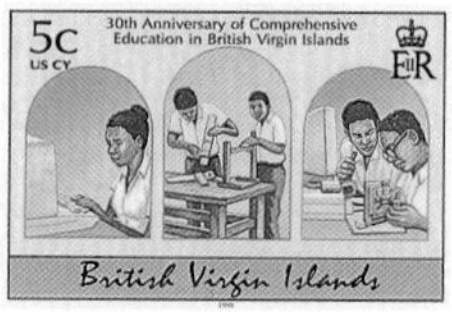


**219** Business Studies, Woodwork and Technology Students

**1998.** Anniversaries. Multicoloured.

1008 5c. Type **219** 25 50
1009 15c. Comprehensive school band 45 30
1010 30c. Chapel, Mona Campus, Jamaica 60 40
1011 45c. Anniversary plaque and University arms 75 60
1012 50c. Dr. John Coakley Lettsom and map of Little Jost Van Dyke 1·00 1·10
1013 $1 The Medical Society of London building and arms 1·50 2·25

EVENTS: 5, 15c. 30th anniv of Comprehensive Education in B.V.I.; 30, 45c. 50th anniv of University of West Indies; 50c., $1 250th anniv of Medical Society of London.

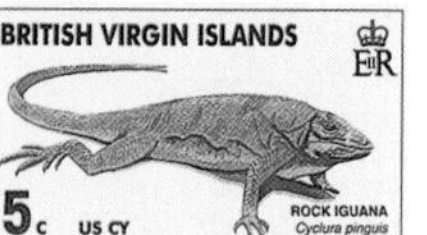


**220** Rock Iguana

**1999.** Lizards. Multicoloured.

1014 5c. Type **220** 30 40
1015 35c. Pygmy gecko 85 45
1016 60c. Slippery back skink 1·50 1·25
1017 $1.50 Wood slave gecko 2·25 3·25
**MS**1018 100×70 mm. 75c. Doctor lizard; 75c. Yellow-bellied lizard; 75c. Man lizard; 75c. Ground lizard 5·00 6·00

**1999.** Royal Wedding. As T 185 of Ascension. Multicoloured.

1019 20c. Photographs of Prince Edward and Miss Sophie Rhys-Jones 1·00 40

| | | | |
|---|---|---|---|
| 1020 | $3 Engagement photograph | 4·75 | 6·00 |

**1999.** 30th Anniv of First Manned Landing on Moon. As T 186 of Ascension. Multicoloured.

| | | | |
|---|---|---|---|
| 1021 | 10c. "Apollo 11" on launch pad | 45 | 35 |
| 1022 | 40c. Firing of second stage rockets | 1·00 | 65 |
| 1023 | 50c. Lunar module on Moon | 1·10 | 85 |
| 1024 | $2 Astronauts transfer to command module | 3·00 | 4·00 |
| **MS**1025 | 90×80 mm. $2.50, Earth as seen from moon (circular, 40 mm diam) | 3·75 | 4·50 |

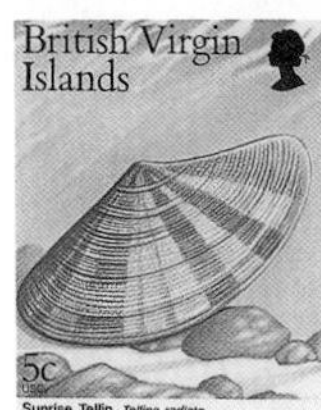

**221** Sunrise Tellin

**1999.** Sea Shells. Multicoloured.

| | | | |
|---|---|---|---|
| 1026A | 5c. Type **221** | 45 | 55 |
| 1027A | 10c. King helmet | 45 | 55 |
| 1028A | 25c. Measle cowrie | 65 | 75 |
| 1029A | 35c. West Indian top shell | 75 | 85 |
| 1030A | 75c. Zigzag scallop | 1·00 | 1·25 |
| 1031A | $1 West Indian fighting conch | 1·25 | 1·50 |

Nos. 1026A/31A were printed together, se-tenant, with the backgrounds forming a composite design.

**222** Zion Hill Methodist Church

**1999.** Christmas. Church Buildings. Multicoloured.

| | | | |
|---|---|---|---|
| 1032 | 20c. Type **222** | 45 | 35 |
| 1033 | 35c. Seventh Day Adventist Church, Fat Hogs Bay, 1982 | 60 | 45 |
| 1034 | 50c. Ruins of St. Phillip's Anglican Church, Kingstown | 85 | 1·00 |
| 1035 | $1 St. William's Catholic Church, Road Town | 1·60 | 2·25 |

**223** King Henry VII

**2000.** "Stamp Show 2000" International Stamp Exhibition, London. Kings and Queens of England. Multicoloured.

| | | | |
|---|---|---|---|
| 1036 | 60c. Type **223** | 1·10 | 1·25 |
| 1037 | 60c. Lady Jane Grey | 1·10 | 1·25 |
| 1038 | 60c. King Charles I | 1·10 | 1·25 |
| 1039 | 60c. King William III | 1·10 | 1·25 |
| 1040 | 60c. King George III | 1·10 | 1·25 |
| 1041 | 60c. King Edward VII | 1·10 | 1·25 |

**2000.** 18th Birthday of Prince William. As T 191 of Ascension. Multicoloured.

| | | | |
|---|---|---|---|
| 1042 | 20c. Prince William as baby (horiz) | 60 | 35 |
| 1043 | 40c. Prince William playing with ball, 1984 | 90 | 60 |
| 1044 | 50c. Skiing in British Columbia, 1998 | 1·25 | 1·00 |
| 1045 | $1 In evening dress, 1997 (horiz) | 2·00 | 2·50 |
| **MS**1046 | 175×95 mm. 60c. Prince William in 1999 (horiz) and Nos. 1042/5 | 8·50 | 8·50 |

**224** Duchess of York, 1920s

**2000.** 100th Birthday of Queen Elizabeth the Queen Mother. Multicoloured.

| | | | |
|---|---|---|---|
| 1047 | 15c. Type **224** | 50 | 25 |
| 1048 | 35c. As Queen Mother in 1957 | 1·00 | 1·50 |
| 1049 | 70c. In evening dress, 1970 | 1·50 | 1·50 |
| 1050 | $1.50 With family on 99th birthday | 2·50 | 3·25 |

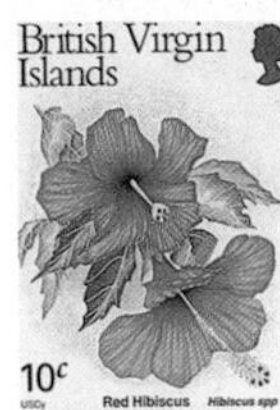

**225** Red Hibiscus

**2000.** Flowers. Multicoloured.

| | | | |
|---|---|---|---|
| 1051 | 10c. Type **225** | 30 | 30 |
| 1052 | 15c. Pink oleander | 35 | 30 |
| 1053 | 35c. Yellow bell | 75 | 55 |
| 1054 | 50c. Yellow and white frangipani | 1·00 | 75 |
| 1055 | 75c. Flamboyant | 1·50 | 2·00 |
| 1056 | $2 Bougainvillea | 3·25 | 4·50 |

**226** Sunday Morning Well (Site of Emancipation Proclamation)

**2000.** New Millennium. Multicoloured.

| | | | |
|---|---|---|---|
| 1057 | 5c. Type **226** | 15 | 25 |
| 1058 | 20c. Nurse Mary Louise Davies M.B.E. | 45 | 35 |
| 1059 | 30c. Cheyney University, U.S.A. | 60 | 45 |
| 1060 | 45c. Enid Leona Scatliffe (former chief education officer) | 80 | 70 |
| 1061 | 50c. H. Lavity Stoutt Community College | 90 | 1·00 |
| 1062 | $1 Sir J. Olva Georges | 1·60 | 2·00 |
| **MS**1063 | 69×59 mm. $2 Private Samuel Hodge's Victoria Cross (vert) | 3·75 | 4·25 |

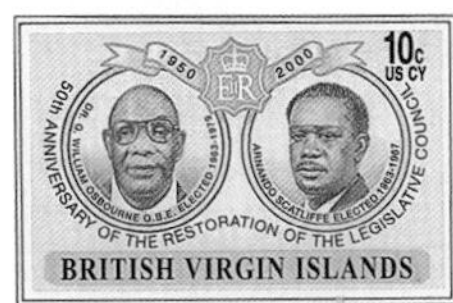

**227** Dr. Q. William Osborne and Arnando Scatliffe

**2000.** 50th Anniv of Restoration of Legislative Council. Multicoloured.

| | | | |
|---|---|---|---|
| 1064 | 10c. Type **227** | 25 | 30 |
| 1065 | 15c. H. Robinson O'Neal and A. Austin Henley | 35 | 30 |
| 1066 | 20c. Wilfred W. Smith and John C. Brudenell-Bruce | 45 | 35 |
| 1067 | 35c. Howard R. Penn and I. G. Fonseca | 65 | 55 |
| 1068 | 50c. Carlton L. de Castro and Theodolph H. Faulkner | 90 | 90 |
| 1069 | 60c. Willard W. Wheatley (Chief Minister, 1971–79) | 1·25 | 1·40 |
| 1070 | $1 H. Lavity Stoutt (Chief Minister, 1967–71, 1979–83 and 1986–95) | 1·60 | 2·00 |

**2001.** "HONG KONG 2001" Stamp Exhibition. Sheet 150×90 mm, containing T 228 and similar horiz design showing dove. Multicoloured.

| | | | |
|---|---|---|---|
| **MS**1071 | 50c. Type **41**; 50c. Bar-tailed cuckoo dove | 3·50 | 4·50 |

**229** H.M.S.*Wistaria* (sloop), 1923–30

**2001.** Royal Navy Ships connected to British Virgin Islands (1st series). Multicoloured.

| | | | |
|---|---|---|---|
| 1072 | 35c. Type **229** | 1·00 | 55 |
| 1073 | 50c. H.M.S. *Dundee* (sloop), 1934–35 | 1·25 | 75 |
| 1074 | 60c. H.M.S. *Eurydice* (frigate), 1787 | 1·50 | 1·40 |
| 1075 | 75c. H.M.S. *Pegasus* (frigate), 1787 | 1·75 | 1·60 |
| 1076 | $1 H.M.S. *Astrea* (frigate), 1807 | 2·25 | 2·25 |
| 1077 | $1.50 Royal Yacht *Britannia*, 1966 | 3·50 | 4·50 |

See also Nos. 1101/4.

**230** Fridtjof Nansen (Peace Prize, 1922)

**2001.** Centenary of Nobel Prize. Multicoloured.

| | | | |
|---|---|---|---|
| 1078 | 10c. Type **230** | 60 | 60 |
| 1079 | 20c. Albert Einstein (Physics Prize,1921) | 70 | 50 |
| 1080 | 25c. Sir Arthur Lewis (Economic Sciences Prize, 1979) | 60 | 50 |
| 1081 | 40c. Saint-John Perse (Literature Prize, 1960) | 70 | 70 |
| 1082 | 70c. Mother Teresa (Peace Prize, 1979) | 3·00 | 2·50 |
| 1083 | $2 Christian Lous Lange (Peace Prize, 1921) | 3·25 | 4·00 |

**2002.** Golden Jubilee. As T 200 of Ascension.

| | | | |
|---|---|---|---|
| 1084 | 15c. brown, mauve and gold | 70 | 25 |
| 1085 | 50c. multicoloured | 1·25 | 1·00 |
| 1086 | 60c. multicoloured | 1·25 | 1·40 |
| 1087 | 75c. multicoloured | 1·50 | 1·75 |
| **MS**1088 | 162×95 mm. Nos. 1084/7 and $1 multicoloured | 8·00 | 9·00 |

DESIGNS—HORIZ: 15c. Princess Elizabeth in A.T.S. uniform, changing wheel; 50c. Queen Elizabeth in fur hat, 1977; 60c. Queen Elizabeth carrying bouquet; 75c. Queen Elizabeth at banquet, Prague, 1996. VERT (38×51 mm)—$1 Queen Elizabeth after Annigoni.

Designs as Nos. 1084/7 in No. **MS**1088 omit the gold frame around each stamp and the "Golden Jubilee 1952–2002" inscription.

**231** Estuarine Crocodile

**2002.** Reptiles. Multicoloured.

| | | | |
|---|---|---|---|
| 1089 | 5c. Type **231** | 30 | 50 |
| 1090 | 20c. Reticulated python | 60 | 30 |
| 1091 | 30c. Komodo dragon | 80 | 45 |
| 1092 | 40c. Boa constrictor | 95 | 65 |
| 1093 | $1 Dwarf caiman | 2·25 | 2·25 |
| 1094 | $2 *Sphaerodactylus parthenopion* (gecko) | 4·00 | 4·50 |
| **MS**1095 | 89×68 mm. $1.50, Head of *Sphaerodactylus parthenopion* on finger | 3·75 | 4·50 |

**2002.** Queen Elizabeth the Queen Mother Commemoration. As T 202 of Ascension.

| | | | |
|---|---|---|---|
| 1096 | 20c. brown, gold and purple | 45 | 30 |
| 1097 | 60c. multicoloured | 1·25 | 1·00 |
| 1098 | $2 black, gold and purple | 3·50 | 3·75 |
| 1099 | $3 multicoloured | 4·75 | 5·50 |
| **MS**1100 | 145×70 mm. Nos. 1098/9 | 8·50 | 9·50 |

DESIGNS—20c. Duchess of York, 1920s; 60c. Queen Mother at Somerset House, 2000; $2 Lady Elizabeth Bowes-Lyon, 1920; $3 Queen Mother inspecting guard of honour.

Designs as Nos. 1098/9 in No. **MS**1100 omit the "1900–2002" inscription and the coloured frame.

**2002.** Royal Navy Ships connected to British Virgin Islands (2nd series). As T 229. Multicoloured.

| | | | |
|---|---|---|---|
| 1101 | 20c. H.M.S. Invincible (ship of the line) re-capturing H.M.S. *Argo* (frigate), 1783 | 85 | 40 |
| 1102 | 35c. H.M.S. *Boreas* and H.M.S. *Solebay* (sailing frigates) | 1·50 | 55 |
| 1103 | 50c. H.M.S. *Coventry* (frigate) | 1·75 | 1·00 |
| 1104 | $3 H.M.S. *Argyll* (frigate) | 7·50 | 8·00 |

**2002.** Island Profiles (3rd series). Virgin Gorda. As T 218. Multicoloured.

| | | | |
|---|---|---|---|
| 1105 | 5c. Spring Bay | 30 | 50 |
| 1106 | 40c. Devils Bay | 1·00 | 55 |
| 1107 | 60c. The Baths | 1·40 | 1·00 |
| 1108 | 75c. St. Thomas Bay | 1·50 | 1·40 |
| 1109 | $1 Savannah and Pond Bay | 1·75 | 1·75 |
| 1110 | $2 Trunk Bay | 3·50 | 4·50 |

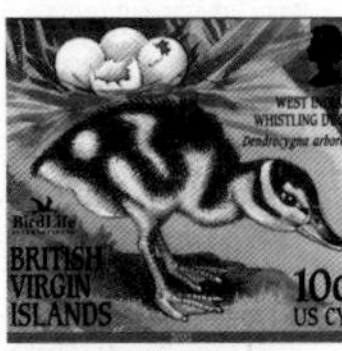

**232** Young West Indian Whistling Duck and Nest

**2002.** Birdlife International (1st series). West Indian Whistling Duck. Multicoloured.

| | | | |
|---|---|---|---|
| 1111 | 10c. Type **232** | 30 | 40 |
| 1112 | 35c. Adult bird on rock (vert) | 70 | 55 |
| 1113 | 40c. Adult bird landing on water (vert) | 75 | 70 |
| 1114 | 70c. Two adult birds | 1·25 | 1·75 |
| **MS**1115 | 175×80 mm. Nos. 1111/14 and $2 Head of duck | 6·00 | 7·00 |

See also Nos. 167/76.

**233** 200 Metres Race

**2003.** Anniversaries and Events. Multicoloured.

| | | | |
|---|---|---|---|
| 1116 | 10c. Type **233** | 50 | 70 |
| 1117 | 10c. Indoor cycling | 50 | 70 |
| 1118 | 35c. Laser class dinghy racing | 75 | 75 |
| 1119 | 35c. Women's long-jumping | 75 | 75 |
| 1120 | 50c. Bareboat class yachts | 1·00 | 1·25 |
| 1121 | 50c. Racing cruiser class yachts | 1·00 | 1·25 |
| 1122 | $1.35 Carlos and Esme Downing (founders) | 2·00 | 2·25 |
| 1123 | $1.35 Copies of newspaper and anniversary logo | 2·00 | 2·25 |

ANNIVERSARIES and EVENTS: 10c. Commonwealth Games, 2002; 35c. 20th anniv of British Virgin Islands' admission to Olympic Games; 50c. 30th anniv of Spring Regatta; $1.35, 40th anniv of *The Island Sun* (newspaper).

**2003.** 50th Anniv of Coronation. A T 206 of Ascension. Multicoloured.

| | | | |
|---|---|---|---|
| 1124 | 15c. Queen Elizabeth II | 75 | 30 |
| 1125 | $5 Queen and Royal Family on Buckingham Palace balcony | 8·50 | 9·00 |
| **MS**1126 | 95×115 mm. As Nos. 1124/5 | 8·00 | 8·50 |

Nos. 1124/5 have red frame; stamps from **MS**1126 have no frame and country name in mauve panel.

**2003.** As T 207 of Ascension.

| | | | |
|---|---|---|---|
| 1127 | $5 black, bistre and brown | 5·25 | 5·50 |

**2003.** 21st Birthday of Prince William of Wales. As T 208 of Ascension. (a) Multicoloured.

| | | | |
|---|---|---|---|
| 1128 | 50c. Prince William at Tidworth and Beaufort Polo Clubs, 2002 | 1·00 | 75 |
| 1129 | $2 Playing polo, 2002 and at Holyrood House, 2001 | 4·00 | 4·25 |

(b) As Nos. 1128/9 but with grey frame.

| | | | |
|---|---|---|---|
| 1130 | 50c. As No. 1128 | 1·00 | 75 |
| 1131 | $2 As No. 1129 | 4·00 | 4·25 |

**2003.** Centenary of Powered Flight. As T 209 of Ascension. Multicoloured.

| | | | |
|---|---|---|---|
| 1132 | 15c. Douglas DC-4 | 70 | 40 |
| 1133 | 20c. Boeing Stearman Kaydet | 75 | 40 |
| 1134 | 35c. North American B-25J Mitchell | 1·00 | 50 |
| 1135 | 40c. McDonnell Douglas F-4B Phantom | 1·10 | 55 |
| 1136 | 70c. Boeing-Vertol CH-47 Chinook helicopter | 2·00 | 1·50 |
| 1137 | $2 Hughes AH-64 Apache helicopter | 4·25 | 4·75 |

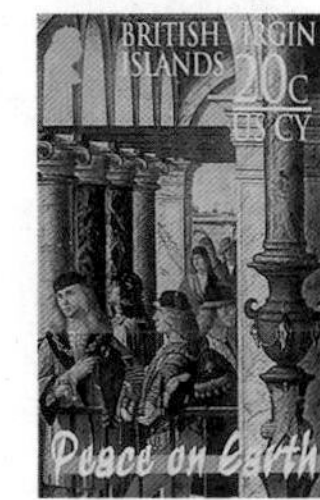

**234** Townsmen under Arcades

**2003.** Christmas. "Stories from the Life of St. Ursula: Arrival of the English Ambassadors" by Carpaccio. Multicoloured.

| | | | |
|---|---|---|---|
| 1138 | 20c. Type **234** | 60 | 25 |
| 1139 | 40c. English ambassadors | 1·00 | 50 |
| 1140 | $2.50 King Maurus of Brittany | 4·50 | 5·00 |
| **MS**1141 | 172×87 mm. $1 King Maurus receiving English ambassadors (35×35 mm) and Nos. 1138/40 | 7·00 | 7·50 |

Nos. 1138/40 show details of the painting and No. **MS**1141 the complete painting.

**2004.** Game Fish. Designs as Nos. 945/6 and 948/9. Self-adhesive. Size 23×19 mm.

| | | | |
|---|---|---|---|
| 1142 | 15c. Great barracuda | 15 | 20 |
| 1143 | 20c. Tarpon | 25 | 30 |
| 1144 | 35c. Sailfish | 40 | 45 |
| 1145 | 40c. Dolphin | 45 | 50 |

**235** Pomegranate

**2004.** Local Fruits. Multicoloured.

| | | | |
|---|---|---|---|
| 1146 | 1c. Hog plum | 10 | 15 |
| 1147 | 10c. Coco plum | 15 | 15 |
| 1148 | 15c. Type **235** | 25 | 20 |
| 1149 | 20c. Cashew | 30 | 30 |
| 1150 | 25c. Sugar apple | 40 | 35 |
| 1151 | 35c. Tamarind | 60 | 45 |
| 1152 | 40c. Soursop | 65 | 50 |
| 1153 | 50c. Mango | 80 | 65 |
| 1154 | 60c. Papaya | 90 | 75 |
| 1155 | 75c. Custard apple | 1·25 | 90 |
| 1156 | $1 Otaheite gooseberry | 1·60 | 1·75 |
| 1157 | $1.50 Guava | 2·50 | 2·25 |
| 1158 | $2 Guavaberry | 3·25 | 3·25 |
| 1159 | $5 Mamee apple | 7·50 | 8·00 |
| 1160 | $10 Passion fruit | 13·00 | 14·00 |

**236** Festival Parade

**2004.** Golden Jubilee of Island Festival. Multicoloured.

| | | | |
|---|---|---|---|
| 1161 | 10c. Type **236** | 30 | 30 |
| 1162 | 60c. Horse racing | 1·25 | 75 |
| 1163 | $1 Canoeing | 1·75 | 1·60 |
| 1164 | $2 Festival queen | 3·50 | 4·00 |

**237** Women's Football

**2004.** Centenary of FIFA (Federation Internationale de Football Association) and Olympic Games, Athens. Multicoloured.

| | | | |
|---|---|---|---|
| 1165 | 75c. Type **237** | 1·40 | 1·40 |
| 1166 | $1 Sprinting | 1·75 | 1·75 |

**238** Black and White Warbler

**2005.** Birdlife International (2nd series). Caribbean Endemic Bird Festival. Multicoloured.

| | | | |
|---|---|---|---|
| 1167 | 5c. Type **238** | 20 | 25 |
| 1168 | 10c. Prairie warbler | 20 | 25 |
| 1169 | 15c. Yellow-rumped warbler | 30 | 30 |
| 1170 | 25c. Worm-eating warbler | 50 | 50 |
| 1171 | 35c. Yellow warbler | 70 | 70 |
| 1172 | 40c. Black-throated warbler | 80 | 80 |
| 1173 | 50c. Prothonotary warbler | 1·00 | 1·00 |
| 1174 | 60c. Cape May warbler | 1·25 | 1·40 |
| 1175 | 75c. Parula warbler (inscr "Northern Parula") | 1·50 | 1·60 |
| 1176 | $2.75 Palm warbler | 5·50 | 6·50 |

**2005.** Pope John Paul II Commemoration. As T 219 of Ascension.

| | | | |
|---|---|---|---|
| 1177 | 75c. multicoloured | 2·00 | 1·75 |

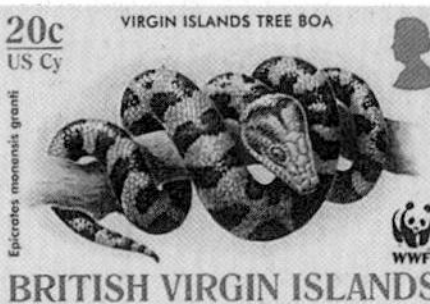

**239** Virgin Islands Tree Boa

**2005.** Endangered Species. Virgin Islands Tree Boa (Epicrates monensis grant). Multicoloured.

| | | | |
|---|---|---|---|
| 1178 | 20c. Type **239** | 60 | 40 |
| 1179 | 30c. Boa in plant (facing left) | 80 | 60 |
| 1180 | 70c. On leafy branch | 2·00 | 1·75 |
| 1181 | $1.05 In foliage (facing right) | 2·75 | 3·00 |

**2005.** Bicentenary of the Battle of Trafalgar. As T 220 of Ascension. Multicoloured.

| | | | |
|---|---|---|---|
| 1182 | 5c. HMS *Colossus* in action before breaking the line | 60 | 60 |
| 1183 | 25c. HMS *Boreas* off British Virgin Islands, 1787 | 1·25 | 60 |
| 1184 | 75c. "HMS Victory" (Francis Smitheman) | 2·50 | 2·00 |
| 1185 | $3 Admiral Lord Nelson (vert) | 7·50 | 8·50 |
| **MS**1186 | 120×79 mm. $2.50 HMS *Colossus* firing (44×44 mm) | 7·00 | 8·00 |

**240** Mr. Joshua Smith (first director of Social Security)

**2005.** Anniversaries. Multicoloured. Multicoloured.

| | | | |
|---|---|---|---|
| 1187 | 20c. Type **240** (25th anniv of Social Security) | 55 | 40 |
| 1188 | 40c. Transmitter on mast and world map (40th anniv of Radio Station ZBVI) | 1·00 | 80 |
| 1189 | 50c. Control tower (25th anniv of Beef Island airstrip) | 1·50 | 1·00 |
| 1190 | $1 Emblem (Centenary of Rotary International) | 2·25 | 2·75 |

**241** Decorated Century Plant

**2005.** Christmas. Plants and Flowers. Multicoloured.

| | | | |
|---|---|---|---|
| 1191 | 15c. Type **241** | 50 | 30 |
| 1192 | 35c. Poinsettia (horiz) | 95 | 70 |
| 1193 | 60c. Decorated ink-berry in pot | 1·60 | 1·25 |
| 1194 | $2.50 Snow-on-the-mountain (horiz) | 5·00 | 6·50 |

**2006.** 80th Birthday of Queen Elizabeth II. As T 223 of Ascension. Multicoloured.

| | | | |
|---|---|---|---|
| 1195 | 15c. Princess Elizabeth in Girl Guide uniform | 60 | 30 |
| 1196 | 75c. Queen Elizabeth II wearing white hat and green and white jacket | 1·75 | 1·25 |
| 1197 | $1.50 Wearing drop earrings | 3·25 | 3·50 |
| 1198 | $2 Wearing pale mauve hat and jacket | 4·50 | 5·00 |
| **MS**1199 | 144×75 mm. $1.50 As No. 1196; $2 As No. 1197 | 7·50 | 8·50 |

Stamps from **MS**1199 do not have white borders.

**242** New Red Cross Headquarters, Virgin Gorda

**2007.** Red Cross Buildings. Multicoloured.

| | | | |
|---|---|---|---|
| 1200 | 20c. Type **242** | 75 | 80 |
| 1201 | $3 Former Red Cross building | 4·50 | 5·00 |

**2008.** 90th Anniv of the Royal Air Force. As T 63 of British Indian Ocean Territory. Multicoloured.

| | | | |
|---|---|---|---|
| 1202 | 18c. Supermarine Spitfire | 25 | 25 |
| 1203 | 20c. Avro Lancaster | 45 | 45 |
| 1204 | 35c. Douglas C-47 Dakota | 55 | 55 |
| 1205 | 60c. Handley Page Halifax | 1·25 | 1·40 |
| 1206 | $1.75 Westland Lysander | 2·75 | 3·00 |
| **MS**1207 | 110×70 mm. $2.50 Spitfire patrolling D-Day beaches | 4·25 | 4·25 |

**243** Diana, Princess of Wales

**2008.** 10th Death Anniv of Diana, Princess of Wales. Multicoloured.

| | | | |
|---|---|---|---|
| 1208 | 60c. Type **243** | 1·00 | 1·00 |
| **MS**1209 | 120×85 mm. $3.50 Wearing red sleeveless dress (42×57 mm) | 6·00 | 6·00 |

**244** Shield

**2008.** 300th Birth Anniv of Charles Wesley (2007). Multicoloured.

| | | | |
|---|---|---|---|
| 1210 | 20c. Type **244** | 40 | 40 |
| 1211 | 50c. Rev. Charles Wesley | 1·10 | 1·25 |
| 1212 | $1.75 Rev. Charles Wesley (in half profile) | 2·75 | 3·00 |

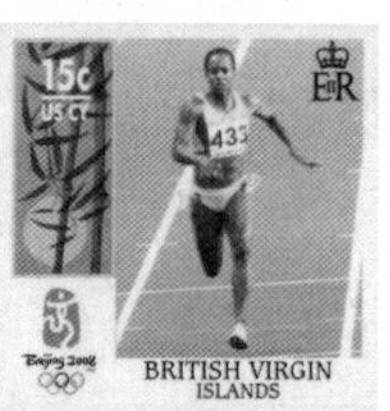

**245** Athlete running

**2008.** Olympic Games, Beijing. Multicoloured.

| | | | |
|---|---|---|---|
| 1213 | 15c. Type **245** | 15 | 20 |
| 1214 | 18c. Yachting | 20 | 25 |
| 1215 | 20c. Athlete in race | 35 | 40 |
| 1216 | $1 Dinghy sailing | 2·10 | 2·25 |

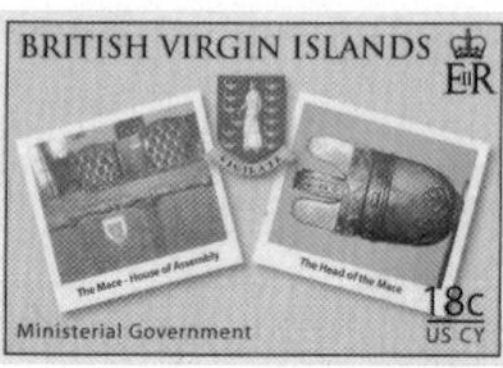

**246** Mace and Mace Head

**2008.** Ministerial Government. Multicoloured.

| | | | |
|---|---|---|---|
| 1217 | 18c. Type **246** | 25 | 25 |
| 1218 | 35c. Facade and entrance of House of Assembly | 55 | 55 |
| 1219 | 60c. Henry O. Creque and Ivan Dawson (legislators) | 1·40 | 1·50 |
| 1220 | $2 Paul Wattley and Terrance B. Lettsome (legislators) | 3·25 | 3·50 |

**247** Sanctuary Wood Cemetery, Ypres, Belgium

**2008.** 90th Anniv of the End of World War I. Multicoloured.

| | | | |
|---|---|---|---|
| 1221 | 75c. Type **247** | 1·40 | 1·50 |
| 1222 | 80c. Poppies growing on Somme Battlefield, France (horiz) | 1·50 | 1·75 |
| 1223 | 90c. Lone Pine Cemetery, Gallipoli (horiz) | 1·75 | 2·00 |
| 1224 | $1 War Memorial, Vauquois, France | 2·00 | 2·10 |
| 1225 | $1.15 Thiepval Memorial, France (horiz) | 2·10 | 2·25 |
| 1226 | $1.25 Menin Gate, Ypres, Belgium (horiz) | 2·25 | 2·40 |
| **MS**1227 | 110×70 mm. $2 UK Overseas Territories Wreath of Remembrance | 4·00 | 4·00 |

**248** Climbing Pandanus (*Freycinetia cumingiana*)

**2009.** J. R. O'Neal Botanic Gardens, Road Town, Tortola. Multicoloured.

| | | | |
|---|---|---|---|
| 1228 | 20c. Type **248** | 35 | 35 |
| 1229 | 35c. True aloe (*Aloe vera*) | 65 | 65 |
| 1230 | 50c. Crown of thorns (*Euphorbia milii*) | 1·25 | 1·25 |
| 1231 | $1 Red-eared slider (*Trachemys scripta elegans*) (terrapin) | 2·25 | 2·25 |
| **MS**1232 | 64×90 mm. $2.50 Fountain and royal palms | 4·00 | 4·00 |

**2009.** Seafaring and Exploration. As T 65 of British Indian Ocean Territory. Multicoloured.

| | | | |
|---|---|---|---|
| 1233 | 15c. HMS *Ark Royal* (English galleon) | 35 | 35 |
| 1234 | 20c. *Whydah* (three masted ship of galley design) | 45 | 45 |
| 1235 | 60c. *Santa Maria* (Columbus) | 1·40 | 1·40 |
| 1236 | 70c. RMS *Rhone* (steam packet) | 1·60 | 1·60 |
| 1237 | 90c. *Golden Hind* (Drake) | 1·75 | 1·75 |
| 1238 | $1.95 HMY *Britannia* (royal yacht) | 3·25 | 3·25 |
| **MS**1239 | 110×70 mm. $2 Christopher Columbus | 4·00 | 4·00 |

**249** Lt. Robert Hampton Gray, 9 August 1945

**2009.** Centenary of Naval Aviation. Designs showing Victoria Cross holders and aircraft. Multicoloured.

| | | | |
|---|---|---|---|
| 1240 | 18c. Type **249** | 25 | 25 |
| 1241 | 35c. Lt. Cdr. (A) Eugene Esmonde, 12 February 1942 | 55 | 55 |
| 1242 | 60c. Flt. SLt. Rex Warneford, 7 June 1915 | 1·40 | 1·40 |
| 1243 | 90c. Sqn. Cdr. Richard Bell Davies, 19 November 1915 | 1·75 | 1·75 |
| **MS**1244 | 110×70 mm. $2 Airplane on deck of HMS *Illustrious*, Taranto, 1940 | 4·00 | 4·00 |

**2009.** International Year of Astronomy. 40th Anniv of First Moon Landing. As T 214 of Bermuda. Multicoloured.

| | | | |
|---|---|---|---|
| 1245 | 50c. Goddard Rocket Shop, Roswell, 1940 | 1·50 | 1·50 |
| 1246 | 75c. Vertol VZ-2, 1960 | 1·75 | 1·75 |
| 1247 | $1 Apollo 11, 1969 | 2·10 | 2·10 |
| 1248 | $1.25 Space Transportation System 126, 2008 | 2·50 | 2·50 |
| 1249 | $2.30 Docking procedure, International Space Station | 2·50 | 2·50 |
| **MS**1250 | 100×80 mm. $3 *Tuning in Earth* (Dave Scott pointing antenna at Earth and Jim Irwin loading Lunar Rover) (Alan Bean) (39×59 mm) | 6·00 | 6·00 |

**250** Turtle

**2010.** Coral Reefs

| | | | |
|---|---|---|---|
| 1251 | 20c. Type **250** | 40 | 40 |
| 1252 | 35c. Fish | 55 | 60 |
| 1253 | 50c. Seahorse (vert) | 1·50 | 1·60 |
| 1254 | 60c. Conch shell (vert) | 1·60 | 1·70 |
| 1255 | $1.50 Coral reef | 3·75 | 4·00 |

**251** Mr. John E. George (sub-postmaster)

**2010.** North Sound Post Office. Multicoloured.

| | | | |
|---|---|---|---|
| 1256 | 20c. Type **251** | 90 | 95 |
| 1257 | 50c. New North Sound Sub Post Office (horiz) | 1·60 | 1·70 |
| 1258 | $2 Old North Sound Sub Post Office (horiz) | 3·75 | 4·00 |

**252** Church Bell

**2010.** Bicentenary of East End Methodist Church. Multicoloured.

| | | | |
|---|---|---|---|
| 1259 | 20c. Type **252** | 45 | 50 |
| 1260 | 50c. East End Methodist Church, 2010 | 1·50 | 1·60 |
| 1261 | 60c. East End Methodist Church, 1977 | 1·80 | 1·90 |
| 1262 | $2 East End Methodist Church in early 19th century | 3·75 | 4·00 |

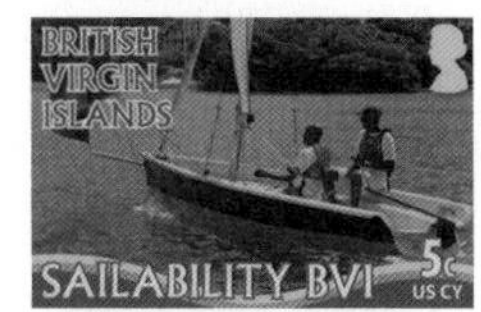

**253** Dinghy sailing

**2011.** Sailability BVI (sailing programme for the disabled). Multicoloured.

| | | | |
|---|---|---|---|
| 1263 | 5c. Type **253** | 10 | 10 |
| 1264 | 20c. Two sailors in dinghy with red sails | 50 | 55 |
| 1265 | 25c. Two sailors in blue dinghy | 65 | 70 |
| 1266 | 40c. Arrival of Geoff Holt (quadriplegic transatlantic sailor) in Tortola, 2010 | 1·20 | 1·30 |
| 1267 | 50c. Geoff Holt on board yacht *Impossible Dream*, arm raised in triumph | 1·50 | 1·60 |
| 1268 | $1.50 Geoff Holt on board yacht *Impossible Dream*, arm raised in triumph | 3·25 | 3·50 |

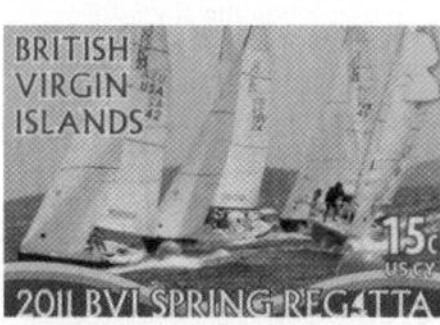

**254** IC24 (J24) racing, 2000

**2011.** 40th Anniv of British Virgin Islands Spring Regatta. Multicoloured.

| | | | |
|---|---|---|---|
| 1269 | 15c. Type **254** | 45 | 50 |
| 1270 | 35c. Mixed fleet (vert), 1980s | 1·50 | 1·60 |
| 1271 | 50c. Yachts flying spinnakers, 1990s | 1·80 | 1·90 |
| 1272 | $2 Clubhouse and moored dinghies, 1970s | 3·75 | 4·00 |

### OFFICIAL STAMPS

**1985.** Nos. 418/21 and 423/33 optd OFFICIAL.

| | | | |
|---|---|---|---|
| O1 | 1c. Purple-tipped sea anemone | 30 | 1·25 |
| O2 | 3c. Common starfish | 45 | 1·25 |
| O3 | 5c. Type **134** | 45 | 45 |
| O4 | 8c. Triton's trumpet (shell) | 55 | 60 |
| O5 | 13c. Flamingo tongue snail | 80 | 75 |
| O6 | 15c. Spider crab | 85 | 70 |
| O7 | 18c. Sea squirts | 90 | 1·75 |
| O8 | 20c. True tulip (shell) | 90 | 80 |
| O9 | 25c. Rooster tail conch (shell) | 1·25 | 2·00 |
| O10 | 30c. Fighting conch (shell) | 1·40 | 1·00 |
| O11 | 60c. Mangrove crab | 2·00 | 2·50 |
| O12 | $1 Coral polyps | 3·00 | 3·75 |
| O13 | $2.50 Peppermint shrimp | 4·50 | 9·00 |
| O14 | $3 West Indian murex (shell) | 5·50 | 10·00 |
| O15 | $5 Carpet anemone | 7·50 | 10·00 |

**1986.** Nos. 560/78 optd OFFICIAL.

| | | | |
|---|---|---|---|
| O16 | 1c. Type **162** | 40 | 1·50 |
| O17 | 2c. Yellow-crowned night heron | 40 | 1·50 |
| O18 | 5c. Mangrove cuckoo | 55 | 1·50 |
| O19 | 8c. Northern mockingbird | 55 | 2·25 |
| O20 | 10c. Grey kingbird | 70 | 1·50 |
| O21 | 12c. Red-necked pigeon | 70 | 40 |
| O22 | 15c. Least bittern | 70 | 40 |
| O23 | 18c. Smooth-billed ani | 70 | 75 |
| O24 | 20c. Clipper rail | 1·00 | 1·00 |
| O25 | 25c. American kestrel | 1·00 | 1·00 |
| O26 | 30c. Pearly-eyed thrasher | 1·25 | 1·00 |
| O27 | 35c. Bridled quail dove | 1·25 | 1·00 |
| O28 | 40c. Green-backed heron | 1·25 | 1·00 |
| O29 | 50c. Scaly-breasted ground dove | 1·40 | 1·75 |
| O30 | 60c. Little blue heron | 1·50 | 2·50 |
| O31 | $1 Audubon's shearwater | 2·25 | 3·50 |
| O32 | $2 Blue-faced booby | 2·50 | 4·00 |
| O33 | $3 Cattle egret | 6·00 | 7·00 |
| O34 | $5 Zenaida dove | 6·50 | 7·50 |

**1991.** Nos. 767/8, 771, 773/9 and 781 optd OFFICIAL.

| | | | |
|---|---|---|---|
| O35 | 5c. Frangipani | 45 | 1·25 |
| O36 | 10c. Autograph tree | 45 | 1·25 |
| O37 | 20c. Jerusalem thorn | 55 | 55 |
| O38 | 30c. Swamp immortelle | 70 | 55 |
| O39 | 35c. White cedar | 70 | 55 |
| O40 | 40c. Mahoe tree | 80 | 70 |
| O41 | 45c. Pinguin | 80 | 75 |
| O42 | 50c. Christmas orchid | 1·50 | 90 |
| O43 | 70c. Lignum vitae | 1·50 | 2·25 |
| O44 | $1 African tulip tree | 1·50 | 2·50 |
| O45 | $3 Organ pipe cactus | 4·00 | 6·50 |

Pt. 1

# BRUNEI

A Sultanate on the North Coast of Borneo.

100 cents = 1 dollar.

**1** Star and Local Scene

**1895**

| | | | | |
|---|---|---|---|---|
| 1 | **1** | ½c. brown | 5·00 | 20·00 |
| 2 | **1** | 1c. brown | 4·50 | 15·00 |
| 3 | **1** | 2c. black | 4·50 | 16·00 |
| 4 | **1** | 3c. blue | 4·50 | 14·00 |
| 5 | **1** | 5c. green | 6·50 | 17·00 |
| 6 | **1** | 8c. purple | 6·50 | 42·00 |
| 7 | **1** | 10c. red | 8·00 | 40·00 |
| 8 | **1** | 25c. green | 80·00 | £100 |
| 9 | **1** | 50c. green | 23·00 | £100 |
| 10 | **1** | $1 green | 25·00 | £120 |

**1906.** Stamps of Labuan optd BRUNEI. or surch also.

| | | | | |
|---|---|---|---|---|
| 11 | **18** | 1c. black and purple | 42·00 | 55·00 |
| 12 | **18** | 2c. on 3c. black and brown | 5·50 | 16·00 |
| 13 | **18** | 2c. on 8c. black and orange | 27·00 | 80·00 |
| 14 | **18** | 3c. black and brown | 38·00 | 85·00 |
| 15 | **18** | 4c. on 12c. black and yellow | 6·00 | 5·00 |
| 16 | **18** | 5c. on 16c. green and brown | 48·00 | 75·00 |
| 17 | **18** | 8c. black and orange | 12·00 | 32·00 |
| 18 | **18** | 10c. on 16c. green and brown | 6·50 | 22·00 |
| 19 | **18** | 25c. on 16c. green and brown | £100 | £120 |
| 20 | **18** | 30c. on 16c. green and brown | £100 | £120 |
| 21 | **18** | 50c. on 16c. green and brown | £110 | £130 |
| 22 | **18** | $1 on 8c. black and orange | £110 | £130 |

**5** View on Brunei River

**1907**

| | | | | |
|---|---|---|---|---|
| 23 | **5** | 1c. black and green | 2·25 | 11·00 |
| 24 | **5** | 2c. black and red | 2·50 | 3·75 |
| 25 | **5** | 3c. black and brown | 10·00 | 22·00 |
| 26 | **5** | 4c. black and mauve | 7·50 | 8·00 |
| 27 | **5** | 5c. black and blue | 50·00 | 90·00 |
| 28 | **5** | 8c. black and orange | 7·50 | 23·00 |
| 29 | **5** | 10c. black and green | 4·50 | 5·00 |
| 30 | **5** | 25c. blue and brown | 32·00 | 48·00 |
| 31 | **5** | 30c. violet and black | 27·00 | 22·00 |
| 32 | **5** | 50c. green and brown | 15·00 | 22·00 |
| 33 | **5** | $1 red and grey | 60·00 | 90·00 |

**1908**

| | | | |
|---|---|---|---|
| 35 | 1c. green | 60 | 2·00 |
| 60 | 1c. black | 1·00 | 75 |
| 79 | 1c. brown | 50 | 2·00 |
| 36 | 2c. black and brown | 4·00 | 1·25 |
| 61 | 2c. brown | 1·00 | 9·00 |
| 62 | 2c. green | 2·00 | 1·00 |
| 80 | 2c. grey | 60 | 7·00 |
| 37 | 3c. red | 6·50 | 1·25 |
| 63 | 3c. green | 1·50 | 6·50 |
| 64 | 4c. purple | 1·50 | 1·25 |
| 65 | 4c. orange | 2·00 | 1·00 |
| 40 | 5c. black and orange | 7·00 | 7·00 |
| 67 | 5c. grey | 20·00 | 12·00 |
| 68 | 5c. brown | 20·00 | 1·00 |
| 82 | 5c. orange | 80 | 2·00 |
| 41 | 8c. blue and indigo | 7·00 | 11·00 |
| 71 | 8c. blue | 6·00 | 5·00 |
| 72 | 8c. black | 16·00 | 75 |
| 84 | 8c. red | 50 | 1·75 |
| 42 | 10c. purple on yellow | 5·00 | 1·75 |
| 85 | 10c. violet | 2·25 | 30 |
| 86 | 15c. blue | 1·75 | 70 |
| 87 | 25c. purple | 2·75 | 1·75 |
| 44 | 30c. purple and yellow | 11·00 | 15·00 |
| 88 | 30c. black and orange | 2·50 | 1·00 |
| 77 | 50c. black on green | 15·00 | 15·00 |
| 89 | 50c. black | 5·00 | 1·00 |
| 46 | $1 black and red on blue | 25·00 | 48·00 |
| 90 | $1 black and red | 12·00 | 1·75 |
| 47 | $5 red on green | £180 | £275 |
| 91 | $5 green and orange | 18·00 | 23·00 |
| 92 | $10 black and purple | 85·00 | 30·00 |
| 48 | $25 black on red | £600 | £1100 |

**1922.** Optd MALAYA- BORNEO EXHIBITION. 1922.

| | | | |
|---|---|---|---|
| 51 | 1c. green | 9·00 | 45·00 |
| 52 | 2c. black and brown | 9·00 | 50·00 |
| 53 | 3c. red | 10·00 | 55·00 |
| 54 | 4c. red | 16·00 | 55·00 |
| 55 | 5c. orange | 21·00 | 60·00 |
| 56 | 10c. purple on yellow | 8·00 | 60·00 |
| 57 | 25c. lilac | 14·00 | 80·00 |
| 58 | 50c. black on green | 45·00 | £150 |
| 59 | $1 black and red on blue | 70·00 | £190 |

**7** Native Houses, Water Village

**1924**

| | | | | |
|---|---|---|---|---|
| 81 | **7** | 3c. green | 1·00 | 6·00 |
| 70 | **7** | 6c. red | 9·00 | 11·00 |
| 83 | **7** | 6c. black | 1·00 | 4·75 |
| 74 | **7** | 12c. blue | 4·50 | 9·00 |

**8** Sultan Ahmed Tajudin and Water Village

**1949.** Silver Jubilee of H.H. the Sultan.

| | | | | |
|---|---|---|---|---|
| 93 | **8** | 8c. black and red | 1·25 | 1·25 |
| 94 | **8** | 25c. purple and orange | 1·25 | 1·60 |
| 95 | **8** | 50c. black and blue | 1·25 | 1·60 |

**1949.** 75th Anniv of UPU. As T 20/23 of Antigua.

| | | | |
|---|---|---|---|
| 96 | 8c. red | 1·00 | 2·25 |
| 97 | 15c. blue | 3·50 | 1·50 |
| 98 | 25c. mauve | 1·00 | 1·50 |
| 99 | 50c. black | 1·00 | 1·25 |

**9** Sultan Omar Ali Saifuddin

**1952.** Dollar values as T 8, but with arms instead of portrait inset.

| | | | | |
|---|---|---|---|---|
| 100 | **9** | 1c. black | 10 | 50 |
| 101 | **9** | 2c. black and orange | 10 | 50 |
| 102 | **9** | 3c. black and lake | 15 | 30 |
| 103 | **9** | 4c. black and green | 15 | 20 |
| 104 | **9** | 6c. black and grey | 1·00 | 10 |
| 123 | **9** | 8c. black and red | 1·00 | 10 |
| 106 | **9** | 10c. black and sepia | 15 | 10 |
| 125 | **9** | 12c. black and violet | 1·50 | 10 |
| 126 | **9** | 15c. black and blue | 55 | 10 |
| 109 | **9** | 25c. black and purple | 2·50 | 10 |
| 110 | **9** | 50c. black and blue | 4·50 | 10 |
| 111 | **9** | $1 black and green (horiz) | 1·50 | 1·40 |
| 112 | **9** | $2 black and red (horiz) | 5·00 | 3·00 |
| 113 | **9** | $5 black and purple (horiz) | 27·00 | 9·50 |

**11** Brunei Mosque and Sultan Omar

**1958.** Opening of the Brunei Mosque.

| | | | | |
|---|---|---|---|---|
| 114 | **11** | 8c. black and green | 20 | 65 |
| 115 | **11** | 15c. black and red | 25 | 15 |
| 116 | **11** | 35c. black and lilac | 30 | 90 |

**12** "Protein Foods"

**1963.** Freedom from Hunger.

| | | | | |
|---|---|---|---|---|
| 117 | **12** | 12c. sepia | 2·75 | 1·00 |

**13** ITU Emblem

**1965.** Centenary of ITU.

| | | | | |
|---|---|---|---|---|
| 132 | **13** | 4c. mauve and brown | 35 | 10 |
| 133 | **13** | 75c. yellow and green | 1·00 | 75 |

**14** ICY Emblem

**1965.** International Co-operation Year.

| | | | | |
|---|---|---|---|---|
| 134 | **14** | 4c. purple and turquoise | 20 | 10 |
| 135 | **14** | 15c. green and lavender | 55 | 35 |

**15** Sir Winston Churchill and St. Paul's Cathedral in Wartime

**1966.** Churchill Commemoration. Designs in black, red and gold and with backgrounds in colours given.

| | | | | |
|---|---|---|---|---|
| 136 | **15** | 3c. blue | 30 | 1·50 |
| 137 | **15** | 10c. green | 1·50 | 20 |
| 138 | **15** | 15c. brown | 1·75 | 35 |
| 139 | **15** | 75c. violet | 4·25 | 3·50 |

**16** Footballer's Legs, Ball and Jules Rimet Cup

**1966.** World Cup Football Championships.

| | | | | |
|---|---|---|---|---|
| 140 | **16** | 4c. multicoloured | 20 | 15 |
| 141 | **16** | 75c. multicoloured | 80 | 60 |

**17** WHO Building

**1966.** Inauguration of WHO Headquarters, Geneva.

| | | | | |
|---|---|---|---|---|
| 142 | **17** | 12c. black, green and blue | 40 | 65 |
| 143 | **17** | 25c. black, purple and ochre | 60 | 1·25 |

**18** "Education"

**1966.** 20th Anniv of UNESCO.

| | | | | |
|---|---|---|---|---|
| 144 | **18** | 4c. multicoloured | 35 | 10 |
| 145 | - | 15c. yellow, violet and olive | 75 | 50 |
| 146 | - | 75c. black, purple and orange | 2·50 | 6·00 |

DESIGNS: 15c. "Science"; 75c. "Culture".

**21** Religious Headquarters Building

**1967.** 1400th Anniv of Revelation of the Koran.

| | | | | |
|---|---|---|---|---|
| 147 | **21** | 4c. multicoloured | 10 | 10 |
| 148 | **21** | 10c. multicoloured | 15 | 10 |
| 149 | - | 25c. multicoloured | 20 | 30 |
| 150 | - | 50c. multicoloured | 35 | 1·50 |

Nos. 149/50 have sprigs of laurel flanking the main design (which has a smaller circle) in place of flagpoles.

**22** Sultan of Brunei, Mosque and Flags

**1968.** Installation of Y.T.M. Seri Paduka Duli Pengiran Temenggong. Multicoloured.

| | | | |
|---|---|---|---|
| 151 | 4c. Type **22** | 15 | 80 |
| 152 | 12c. Sultan of Brunei, Mosque and Flags (different) (horiz) | 40 | 1·60 |
| 153 | 25c. Type **22** | 55 | 2·00 |

**23** Sultan of Brunei

**1968.** Birthday of Sultan.

| | | | | |
|---|---|---|---|---|
| 154 | **23** | 4c. multicoloured | 10 | 50 |
| 155 | **23** | 12c. multicoloured | 20 | 85 |
| 156 | **23** | 25c. multicoloured | 30 | 1·40 |

**24** Sultan of Brunei

**1968.** Coronation of Sultan of Brunei.

| | | | |
|---|---|---|---|
| 157 | 4c. multicoloured | 15 | 25 |
| 158 | 12c. multicoloured | 25 | 50 |
| 159 | 25c. multicoloured | 40 | 75 |

**25** New Building and Sultan's Portrait

**1968.** Opening of Hall of Language and Literature Bureau. Multicoloured.

| | | | |
|---|---|---|---|
| 160 | 10c. Type **25** | 20 | 1·75 |
| 161 | 15c. New Building and Sultan's portrait (48½×22 mm) | 20 | 35 |
| 162 | 30c. As 15c. | 45 | 90 |

**27** Human Rights Emblem and struggling Man

**1968.** Human Rights Year.

| | | | | |
|---|---|---|---|---|
| 163 | **27** | 12c. black, yellow and green | 10 | 20 |
| 164 | **27** | 25c. black, yellow and blue | 15 | 25 |
| 165 | **27** | 75c. black, yellow and purple | 45 | 1·75 |

**28** Sultan of Brunei and WHO Emblem

**1968.** 20th Anniv of World Health Organization.

| | | | | |
|---|---|---|---|---|
| 166 | **28** | 4c. yellow, black and blue | 30 | 30 |
| 167 | **28** | 15c. yellow, black and violet | 55 | 65 |
| 168 | **28** | 25c. yellow, black and olive | 65 | 1·25 |

**29** Deep Sea Oil-Rig, Sultan of Brunei and inset portrait of Pengiran Di-Gadong

**1969.** Installation (9th May, 1968) of Pengiran Shar-bandar as Y.T.M. Seri Paduka Duli Pengiran Di-Gadong Sahibol Mal.

| | | | | |
|---|---|---|---|---|
| 169 | **29** | 12c. multicoloured | 85 | 50 |
| 170 | **29** | 40c. multicoloured | 1·25 | 2·00 |
| 171 | **29** | 50c. multicoloured | 1·25 | 2·00 |

**30** Aerial View of Parliament Buildings

**1969.** Opening of Royal Audience Hall and Legislative Council Chamber.

| | | | | |
|---|---|---|---|---|
| 172 | **30** | 12c. multicoloured | 20 | 25 |
| 173 | **30** | 25c. multicoloured | 30 | 45 |
| 174 | - | 50c. red and violet | 60 | 3·50 |

DESIGN: 50c. Elevation of new buildings.

**32** Youth Centre and Sultan's Portrait

**1969.** Opening of New Youth Centre.

| | | | | |
|---|---|---|---|---|
| 175 | **32** | 6c. multicoloured | 20 | 1·00 |
| 176 | **32** | 10c. multicoloured | 25 | 10 |
| 177 | **32** | 30c. multicoloured | 70 | 1·00 |

**33** Soldier, Sultan and Badge

**1971.** 10th Anniv of Royal Brunei Malay Regiment. Multicoloured.

| | | | |
|---|---|---|---|
| 178 | 10c. Type **33** | 80 | 30 |
| 179 | 15c. Bell 205 Iroquois helicopter, Sultan and badge (horiz) | 1·75 | 70 |
| 180 | 75c. "Pahlawan" (patrol boat), Sultan and badge (horiz) | 3·25 | 7·00 |

**34** Badge, and Officer in Full-dress Uniform

**1971.** 50th Anniv of Royal Brunei Police Force. Multicoloured.

| | | | |
|---|---|---|---|
| 181 | 10c. Type **34** | 50 | 30 |
| 182 | 15c. Badge and Patrol constable | 60 | 90 |
| 183 | 50c. Badge and Traffic constable | 1·10 | 6·00 |

**35** Perdana Wazir, Sultan of Brunei and View of Water Village

**1971.** Installation of the Yang Teramat Mulia as the Perdana Wazir.

| | | | | |
|---|---|---|---|---|
| 184 | **35** | 15c. multicoloured | 40 | 50 |
| 185 | - | 25c. multicoloured | 70 | 1·00 |
| 186 | - | 50c. multicoloured | 1·40 | 5·00 |

Nos. 185/6 show various views of Brunei Town.

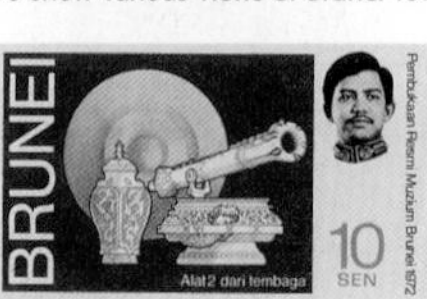


**36** Pottery

**1972.** Opening of Brunei Museum. Mult.

| | | | |
|---|---|---|---|
| 187 | 10c. Type **36** | 30 | 10 |
| 188 | 12c. Straw-work | 40 | 20 |
| 189 | 15c. Leather-work | 45 | 20 |
| 190 | 25c. Gold-work | 1·25 | 1·25 |
| 191 | 50c. Museum Building (58×21 mm) | 2·25 | 5·50 |

**37** Modern Building, Queen Elizabeth and Sultan of Brunei

**1972.** Royal Visit. Each design with portrait of Queen and Sultan. Multicoloured.

| | | | |
|---|---|---|---|
| 192 | 10c. Type **37** | 70 | 20 |
| 193 | 15c. Native houses | 95 | 55 |
| 194 | 25c. Mosque | 2·00 | 1·60 |
| 195 | 50c. Royal Assembly Hall | 3·75 | 7·00 |

**38** Secretariat Building

**1972.** Renaming of Brunei Town as Bandar Seri Begawan.

| | | | | |
|---|---|---|---|---|
| 196 | **38** | 10c. multicoloured | 20 | 15 |
| 197 | - | 15c. green, yellow and black | 25 | 15 |
| 198 | - | 25c. blue, yellow and black | 45 | 50 |
| 199 | - | 50c. red, blue and black | 75 | 2·25 |

VIEWS: 15c. Darul Hana Palace; 25c. Old Brunei Town; 50c. Town and Water Village.

**39** Blackburn Beverley C1 parachuting Supplies

**1972.** Opening of R.A.F. Museum, Hendon. Multicoloured.

| | | | |
|---|---|---|---|
| 200 | 25c. Type **39** | 1·75 | 1·25 |
| 201 | 75c. Blackburn Beverley C1 landing | 3·25 | 4·75 |

**1972.** Royal Silver Wedding. As T 52 of Ascension, but with girl with traditional flower-pot, and boy with bowl and pipe in background.

| | | | |
|---|---|---|---|
| 210 | 12c. red | 10 | 10 |
| 211 | 75c. green | 20 | 50 |

**41** Interpol H.Q., Paris

**1973.** 50th Anniv of Interpol.

| | | | | |
|---|---|---|---|---|
| 212 | **41** | 25c. green, purple and black | 1·50 | 1·25 |
| 213 | - | 50c. blue, ultram & red | 1·50 | 1·25 |

DESIGN: 50c. Different view of the H.Q.

**42** Sultan, Princess Anne and Captain Phillips

**1973.** Royal Wedding.

| | | | | |
|---|---|---|---|---|
| 214 | **42** | 25c. multicoloured | 15 | 10 |
| 215 | **42** | 50c. multicoloured | 15 | 25 |

**43** Churchill Painting

**1973.** Opening of Churchill Memorial Building. Multicoloured.

| No. | Description | Mint | Used |
|---|---|---|---|
| 216 | 12c. Type **43** | 10 | 20 |
| 217 | 50c. Churchill statue | 30 | 1·40 |

**44** Sultan Sir Hassanal Bolkiah Mu'izzaddin Waddaulah

**1975.** Multicoloured. Background colours given.

| No. | Type | Description | Mint | Used |
|---|---|---|---|---|
| 218 | **44** | 4c. green | 20 | 20 |
| 219 | **44** | 5c. blue | 20 | 30 |
| 220 | **44** | 6c. green | 3·25 | 6·50 |
| 221 | **44** | 10c. lilac | 30 | 10 |
| 222 | **44** | 15c. brown | 2·50 | 40 |
| 223 | **44** | 20c. stone | 30 | 20 |
| 224 | **44** | 25c. green | 40 | 15 |
| 225 | **44** | 30c. blue | 40 | 15 |
| 226 | **44** | 35c. grey | 40 | 20 |
| 227 | **44** | 40c. purple | 40 | 20 |
| 228 | **44** | 50c. brown | 40 | 20 |
| 229 | **44** | 75c. green | 60 | 3·50 |
| 256 | **44** | $1 orange | 1·50 | 3·50 |
| 231 | **44** | $2 yellow | 2·25 | 11·00 |
| 232 | **44** | $5 silver | 3·00 | 18·00 |
| 233 | **44** | $10 gold | 5·00 | 32·00 |

**45** Aerial View of Airport

**1974.** Inauguration of Brunei International Airport. Multicoloured.

| No. | Description | Mint | Used |
|---|---|---|---|
| 234 | 50c. Type **45** | 1·25 | 1·00 |
| 235 | 75c. Sultan in Army uniform, and airport (48×36 mm) | 1·50 | 1·50 |

**46** U.P.U. Emblem and Sultan

**1974.** Centenary of Universal Postal Union.

| No. | Type | Description | Mint | Used |
|---|---|---|---|---|
| 236 | **46** | 12c. multicoloured | 20 | 20 |
| 237 | **46** | 50c. multicoloured | 40 | 1·40 |
| 238 | **46** | 75c. multicoloured | 50 | 1·75 |

**47** Sir Winston Churchill

**1974.** Birth Centenary of Sir Winston Churchill.

| No. | Type | Description | Mint | Used |
|---|---|---|---|---|
| 239 | **47** | 12c. black, blue and gold | 25 | 20 |
| 240 | - | 75c. black, green and gold | 45 | 1·40 |

DESIGN: 75c. Churchill smoking cigar (profile).

**48** Boeing 737 and R.B.A. Crest

**1975.** Inauguration of Royal Brunei Airlines. Mult.

| No. | Description | Mint | Used |
|---|---|---|---|
| 241 | 12c. Type **48** | 1·00 | 25 |
| 242 | 35c. Boeing 737 over Bandar Seri Begawan Mosque | 1·75 | 1·75 |
| 243 | 75c. Boeing 737 in flight | 2·50 | 4·00 |

**1976.** Surch 10 sen.

| No. | Type | Description | Mint | Used |
|---|---|---|---|---|
| 263 | **44** | 10c. on 6c. brown | 1·75 | 1·75 |

**50** Royal Coat of Arms

**1977.** Silver Jubilee. Multicoloured.

| No. | Description | Mint | Used |
|---|---|---|---|
| 264 | 10c. Type **50** | 15 | 15 |
| 265 | 20c. Imperial State Crown | 20 | 20 |
| 266 | 75c. Queen Elizabeth (portrait by Annigoni) | 45 | 60 |

**51** The Moment of Crowning

**1978.** 25th Anniv of Coronation. Multicoloured.

| No. | Description | Mint | Used |
|---|---|---|---|
| 267 | 10c. Type **51** | 15 | 10 |
| 268 | 20c. Queen in Coronation regalia | 20 | 20 |
| 269 | 75c. Queen's departure from Abbey | 55 | 80 |

**52** Royal Crest

**1978.** 10th Anniv of Coronation of Sultan.

| No. | Type | Description | Mint | Used |
|---|---|---|---|---|
| 270 | **52** | 10c. black, red and yellow | 20 | 10 |
| 271 | - | 20c. multicoloured | 40 | 25 |
| 272 | - | 75c. multicoloured | 1·10 | 3·50 |
| **MS**273 | | 182×77 mm. Nos. 270/2 | 12·00 | 16·00 |

DESIGNS: 20c. Coronation; 75c. Sultan's Crown.

**53** Human Rights Emblem and Struggling Man

**1978.** Human Rights Year.

| No. | Type | Description | Mint | Used |
|---|---|---|---|---|
| 274 | **53** | 10c. black, yellow and red | 15 | 10 |
| 275 | **53** | 20c. black, yellow and violet | 20 | 35 |
| 276 | **53** | 75c. black, yellow and bistre | 40 | 2·50 |

Type **53** is similar to the design used for the previous Human Rights issue in 1968.

**54** Smiling Children

**1979.** International Year of the Child.

| No. | Type | Description | Mint | Used |
|---|---|---|---|---|
| 277 | **54** | 10c. multicoloured | 20 | 10 |
| 278 | - | $1 black and green | 80 | 2·50 |

DESIGN: $1 I.Y.C. emblem.

**55** Earth Satellite Station

**1979.** Telisai Earth Satellite Station. Multicoloured.

| No. | Description | Mint | Used |
|---|---|---|---|
| 279 | 10c. Type **55** | 20 | 15 |
| 280 | 20c. Satellite and antenna | 30 | 40 |
| 281 | 75c. Television camera, telex machine and telephone | 60 | 2·75 |

**56** Hegira Symbol

**1979.** Moslem Year 1400 A.H. Commemoration.

| No. | Type | Description | Mint | Used |
|---|---|---|---|---|
| 282 | **56** | 10c. black, yellow and green | 10 | 15 |
| 283 | **56** | 20c. black, yellow and blue | 15 | 30 |
| 284 | **56** | 75c. black, yellow and lilac | 45 | 2·25 |
| **MS**285 | | 178×200 mm. Nos. 282/4 | 3·00 | 7·50 |

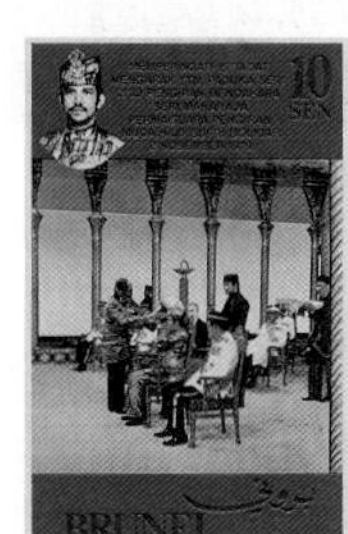

**57** Installation Ceremony

**1980.** 1st Anniv of Prince Sufri Bolkiah's Installation as First Wazir. Multicoloured. Blue borders.

| No. | Description | Mint | Used |
|---|---|---|---|
| 286 | 10c. Type **57** | 15 | 10 |
| 287 | 75c. Prince Sufri | 85 | 2·25 |

**1980.** 1st Anniv of Prince Jefri Bolkiah's Installation as Second Wazir. Designs similar to T 57. Multicoloured. Green borders.

| No. | Description | Mint | Used |
|---|---|---|---|
| 288 | 10c. Installation ceremony | 15 | 10 |
| 289 | 75c. Prince Jefri | 85 | 2·25 |

**58** Royal Umbrella and Sash

**1981.** Royal Regalia (1st series). Multicoloured.

| No. | Description | Mint | Used |
|---|---|---|---|
| 290 | 10c. Type **58** | 20 | 15 |
| 291 | 15c. Sword and Shield | 35 | 25 |
| 292 | 20c. Lance and Sheath | 40 | 40 |
| 293 | 30c. Betel Leaf Container | 60 | 1·25 |
| 294 | 50c. Coronation Crown (39×22 mm) | 1·25 | 5·00 |
| **MS**295 | 98×142 mm. Nos. 290/4 | 5·00 | 8·00 |

See Nos. 298/303, 314/19 and 320/5.

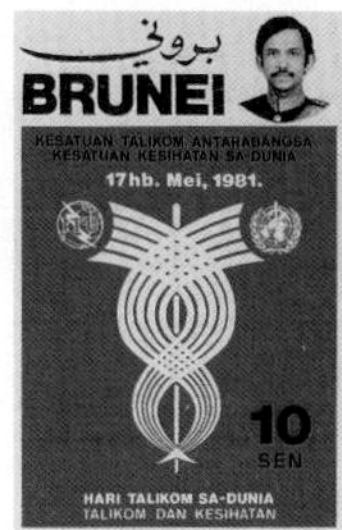

**59** ITU and WHO Emblems

**1981.** World Telecommunications and Health Day.

| No. | Type | Description | Mint | Used |
|---|---|---|---|---|
| 296 | **59** | 10c. black and red | 50 | 25 |
| 297 | **59** | 75c. black, blue and violet | 2·25 | 5·00 |

**60** Shield and Broadsword

**1981.** Royal Regalia (2nd series). Multicoloured.

| No. | Description | Mint | Used |
|---|---|---|---|
| 298 | 10c. Type **60** | 10 | 10 |
| 299 | 15c. Blunderbuss and Pouch | 20 | 20 |
| 300 | 20c. Crossed Lances and Sash | 30 | 30 |
| 301 | 30c. Sword, Shield and Sash | 40 | 75 |
| 302 | 50c. Forked Lance | 60 | 2·50 |
| 303 | 75c. Royal Drum (29×45 mm) | 80 | 4·50 |

**61** Prince Charles as Colonel of the Welsh Guards

**1981.** Royal Wedding. Multicoloured.

| No. | Description | Mint | Used |
|---|---|---|---|
| 304 | 10c. Wedding bouquet from Brunei | 15 | 15 |
| 305 | $1 Type **61** | 35 | 1·50 |
| 306 | $2 Prince Charles and Lady Diana Spencer | 50 | 2·50 |

**62** Fishing

**1981.** World Food Day. Multicoloured.

| No. | Description | Mint | Used |
|---|---|---|---|
| 307 | 10c. Type **62** | 50 | 15 |
| 308 | $1 Farm produce and machinery | 4·50 | 7·50 |

**63** Blind Man and Braille Alphabet

**1981.** International Year for Disabled Persons. Multicoloured.

| No. | Description | Mint | Used |
|---|---|---|---|
| 309 | 10c. Type **63** | 65 | 20 |
| 310 | 20c. Deaf people and sign language | 1·50 | 80 |
| 311 | 75c. Disabled person and wheelchairs | 3·00 | 6·75 |

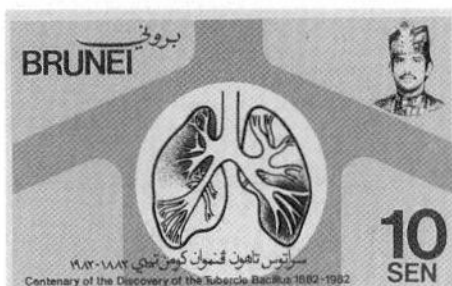


64 Drawing of Infected Lungs

**1982.** Centenary of Robert Koch's Discovery of Tubercle Bacillus. Multicoloured.

| | | | |
|---|---|---|---|
| 312 | 10c. Type **64** | 50 | 25 |
| 313 | 75c. Magnified tubercle bacillus and microscope | 3·00 | 6·50 |

**1982.** Royal Regalia (3rd series). As T 60. Mult.

| | | | |
|---|---|---|---|
| 314 | 10c. Ceremonial Ornament | 10 | 10 |
| 315 | 15c. Silver Betel Caddy | 20 | 20 |
| 316 | 20c. Traditional Flowerpot | 25 | 30 |
| 317 | 30c. Solitary Candle | 50 | 90 |
| 318 | 50c. Golden Pipe | 70 | 2·50 |
| 319 | 75c. Royal Chin Support (28×45 mm) | 90 | 4·00 |

**1982.** Royal Regalia (4th series). As T 60. Mult.

| | | | |
|---|---|---|---|
| 320 | 10c. Royal Mace | 25 | 10 |
| 321 | 15c. Ceremonial Shield and Spears | 35 | 30 |
| 322 | 20c. Embroidered Ornament | 45 | 40 |
| 323 | 30c. Golden-tasseled Cushion | 75 | 1·50 |
| 324 | 50c. Ceremonial Dagger and Sheath | 1·25 | 3·50 |
| 325 | 75c. Religious Mace (28×45 mm) | 1·60 | 4·50 |

65 Brunei Flag

**1983.** Commonwealth Day.

| | | | | |
|---|---|---|---|---|
| 326 | 65 | 10c. multicoloured | 15 | 80 |
| 327 | - | 20c. blue, black and buff | 20 | 90 |
| 328 | - | 75c. blue, black and green | 45 | 1·40 |
| 329 | - | $2 blue, black and yellow | 1·10 | 2·00 |

DESIGNS: 20c. Brunei Mosque; 75c. Machinery; $2 Sultan of Brunei.

66 "Postal Service"

**1983.** World Communications Year.

| | | | | |
|---|---|---|---|---|
| 330 | 66 | 10c. multicoloured | 15 | 10 |
| 331 | - | 75c. yellow, brown and black | 60 | 75 |
| 332 | - | $2 multicoloured | 1·75 | 2·25 |

DESIGNS: 75c. "Telephone Service"; $2 "Communications".

67 Football

**1983.** Official Opening of the National Hassanal Bolkiah Stadium. Multicoloured.

| | | | |
|---|---|---|---|
| 333 | 10c. Type **67** | 55 | 15 |
| 334 | 75c. Athletics | 2·25 | 1·50 |
| 335 | $1 View of stadium (44×27 mm) | 2·75 | 4·00 |

68 Fishermen and Crustacea

**1983.** Fishery Resources. Multicoloured.

| | | | |
|---|---|---|---|
| 336 | 10c. Type **68** | 1·50 | 15 |
| 337 | 50c. Fishermen with net | 3·75 | 1·50 |
| 338 | 75c. Fishing trawler | 4·00 | 4·25 |
| 339 | $1 Fishing with hook and tackle | 4·25 | 4·75 |

69 Royal Assembly Hall

**1984.** Independence.

| | | | | |
|---|---|---|---|---|
| 340 | 69 | 10c. brown and orange | 20 | 10 |
| 341 | - | 20c. pink and red | 30 | 20 |
| 342 | - | 35c. pink and purple | 60 | 60 |
| 343 | - | 50c. light blue and blue | 1·75 | 1·25 |
| 344 | - | 75c. light green and green | 1·75 | 2·00 |
| 345 | - | $1 grey and brown | 2·00 | 2·50 |
| 346 | - | $3 multicoloured | 7·00 | 10·00 |
| **MS**347 | | 150×120 mm. Nos. 340/6 | 12·00 | 16·00 |
| **MS**348 | | Two sheets, each 150×120 mm, containing 4 stamps (34×69 mm). (a) 25c. × 4 grey-black and new blue (Signing of the Brunei Constitution). (b) 25c. × 4 multicoloured (Signing of Brunei–U.K. Friendship Agreement) Set of 2 sheets | 2·25 | 4·50 |

DESIGNS—34×25 mm: 20c. Government Secretariat Building; 35c. New Supreme Court; 50c. Natural gas well; 75c. Omar Ali Saifuddin Mosque; $1 Sultan's Palace. 68×24 mm: $3 Brunei flag and map of South-East Asia.

70 Natural Forests and Enrichment Planting

**1984.** Forestry Resources. Multicoloured.

| | | | |
|---|---|---|---|
| 349 | 10c. Type **70** | 1·00 | 25 |
| 350 | 50c. Forests and water resources | 2·50 | 2·25 |
| 351 | 75c. Recreation forests | 3·25 | 4·50 |
| 352 | $1 Forests and wildlife | 4·75 | 6·00 |

71 Sultan Omar Saiffuddin 50c. Stamp of 1952

**1984.** "Philakorea" International Stamp Exhibition, Seoul. Multicoloured.

| | | | |
|---|---|---|---|
| 353 | 10c. Type **71** | 50 | 15 |
| 354 | 75c. Brunei River view 10c. stamp of 1907 | 1·50 | 2·25 |
| 355 | $2 Star and view ½c. stamp of 1895 | 2·50 | 6·50 |
| **MS**356 | Three sheets, 117×100 mm, each containing one stamp as Nos. 353/5 Set of 3 sheets | 3·75 | 7·00 |

72 United Nations Emblem

**1985.** Admission of Brunei to World Organizations (1st issue).

| | | | | |
|---|---|---|---|---|
| 357 | 72 | 50c. black, gold and blue | 50 | 70 |
| 358 | - | 50c. multicoloured | 50 | 70 |
| 359 | - | 50c. multicoloured | 50 | 70 |
| 360 | - | 50c. multicoloured | 50 | 70 |
| **MS**361 | | 110×151 mm. Nos. 357/60 | 4·00 | 4·00 |

DESIGNS: No. 358, Islamic Conference Organization logo; 359, Commonwealth logo; 360, A.S.E.A.N. emblem.

See also Nos. 383/7.

73 Young People and Brunei Flag

**1985.** International Youth Year. Multicoloured.

| | | | |
|---|---|---|---|
| 362 | 10c. Type **73** | 2·00 | 30 |
| 363 | 75c. Young people at work | 5·50 | 7·00 |
| 364 | $1 Young people serving the community | 6·00 | 7·50 |

74 Palestinian Emblem

**1985.** International Palestinian Solidarity Day.

| | | | | |
|---|---|---|---|---|
| 365 | 74 | 10c. multicoloured | 2·25 | 20 |
| 366 | 74 | 50c. multicoloured | 4·75 | 1·50 |
| 367 | 74 | $1 multicoloured | 6·50 | 3·75 |

75 Early and Modern Scout Uniforms

**1985.** National Scout Jamboree. Multicoloured.

| | | | |
|---|---|---|---|
| 368 | 10c. Type **75** | 60 | 10 |
| 369 | 20c. Scout on tower signalling with flag | 90 | 40 |
| 370 | $2 Jamboree emblem | 2·75 | 3·25 |

76 Sultan Sir Hassanal Bolkiah Mu'izzaddin Waddaulah

**1985**

| | | | | |
|---|---|---|---|---|
| 371 | 76 | 10c. multicoloured | 30 | 10 |
| 372 | 76 | 15c. multicoloured | 30 | 10 |
| 373 | 76 | 20c. multicoloured | 40 | 10 |
| 374 | 76 | 25c. multicoloured | 40 | 15 |
| 375 | 76 | 35c. multicoloured | 55 | 20 |
| 376 | 76 | 40c. multicoloured | 60 | 25 |
| 377 | 76 | 50c. multicoloured | 70 | 35 |
| 378 | 76 | 75c. multicoloured | 90 | 50 |
| 379 | 76 | $1 multicoloured | 1·25 | 70 |
| 380 | 76 | $2 multicoloured | 2·75 | 1·75 |
| 381 | 76 | $5 multicoloured | 4·25 | 5·00 |
| 382 | 76 | $10 multicoloured | 8·00 | 11·00 |

Nos. 379/82 are larger, size 32×39 mm.

**1986.** Admission of Brunei to World Organizations (2nd issue). As T 72.

| | | | |
|---|---|---|---|
| 383 | 50c. black, gold and green | 50 | 60 |
| 384 | 50c. black, gold and mauve | 50 | 60 |
| 385 | 50c. black, gold and red | 50 | 60 |
| 386 | 50c. black, gold and blue | 50 | 60 |
| **MS**387 | 105×155 mm. Nos. 383/6 | 1·50 | 4·00 |

DESIGNS: No. 383, World Meteorological Organ-ization emblem; 384, International Tele-communication Union emblem; 385, Universal Postal Union emblem; 386, International Civil Aviation Organization emblem.

78 Soldiers on Assault Course and Bell 205 UH-1H Iroquois Helicopter

**1986.** 25th Anniv of Brunei Armed Forces. Multicoloured.

| | | | |
|---|---|---|---|
| 388 | 10c. Type **78** | 4·25 | 4·25 |
| 389 | 20c. Operating computer | 4·50 | 4·50 |
| 390 | 50c. Anti-aircraft missile, MBB-Bolkow Bo 150L helicopter and missile boat | 6·00 | 6·00 |
| 391 | 75c. Army, commanders and parade | 6·50 | 6·50 |

Nos. 388/91 were printed together, se-tenant, forming a composite design.

79 Tunggul Charok Buritan, Alam Bernaga (Alam Besar), Pisang-Pisang and Sandaran

**1986.** Royal Ensigns (1st series).

| | | | | |
|---|---|---|---|---|
| 392 | 79 | 10c. black, yellow and red | 30 | 10 |
| 393 | - | 75c. multicoloured | 1·10 | 1·10 |
| 394 | - | $2 black, yellow and green | 2·25 | 2·75 |

DESIGNS: 75c. Ula-Ula Besar, Sumbu Layang and Payong Haram; $2 Panji-Panji, Chogan Istiadat (Chogan Di-Raja) and Chogan Ugama.

**1986.** Royal Ensigns (2nd series). As T 79.

| | | | |
|---|---|---|---|
| 395 | 10c. multicoloured | 30 | 10 |
| 396 | 75c. black, red and yellow | 1·10 | 1·10 |
| 397 | $2 multicoloured | 2·25 | 2·75 |

DESIGNS: 10c. Dadap, Tunggul Kawan, Ambal, Payong Ubor-Ubor, Sapu-Sapu Ayeng and Rawai Lidah; 75c. Payong Tinggi and Payong Ubor-Ubor Tiga Ringkat; $2 Lambang Duli Yang Maha Mulia and Mahligai.

80 Stylized Peace Doves

**1986.** International Peace Year. Multicoloured.

| | | | |
|---|---|---|---|
| 398 | 50c. Type **80** | 75 | 75 |
| 399 | 75c. Stylized hands and "1986" | 1·00 | 1·10 |
| 400 | $1 International Peace Year emblem and arms of Brunei | 1·25 | 1·50 |

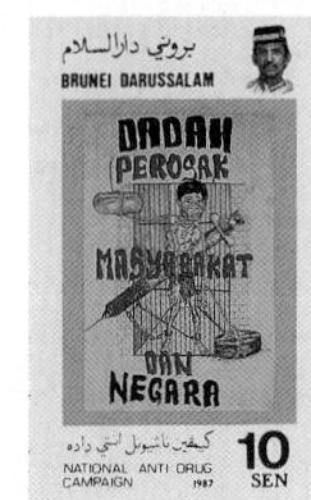


81 Drug Addict in Cage and Syringe (poster by Othman bin Ramboh)

**1987.** National Anti-drug Campaign. Children's Posters. Multicoloured.

| | | | |
|---|---|---|---|
| 401 | 10c. Type **81** | 1·50 | 35 |
| 402 | 75c. Drug addict and noose (Arman bin Mohd. Zaman) | 3·00 | 4·25 |
| 403 | $1 Blindfolded drug addict and noose (Abidin bin Hj. Rashid) | 3·50 | 5·50 |

82 Cannon ("badil")

**1987.** Brassware (1st series). Multicoloured.

| | | | |
|---|---|---|---|
| 404 | 50c. Type **82** | 50 | 50 |
| 405 | 50c. Lamp ("pelita") | 50 | 50 |
| 406 | 50c. Betel container ("langguai") | 50 | 50 |
| 407 | 50c. Water jug ("kiri") | 50 | 50 |

See also Nos. 434/7.

**83** Map showing Member Countries

**1987.** 20th Anniv of Association of South East Asian Nations. Multicoloured.

| | | | |
|---|---|---|---|
| 408 | 20c. Type **83** | 35 | 20 |
| 409 | 50c. Dates and figures "20" | 60 | 50 |
| 410 | $1 Flags of member states | 1·25 | 1·25 |

**84** Brunei Citizens

**1987.** 25th Anniv (1986) of Language and Literature Bureau. Multicoloured.

| | | | |
|---|---|---|---|
| 411 | 10c. Type **84** | 50 | 40 |
| 412 | 50c. Flame emblem and hands holding open book | 1·00 | 75 |
| 413 | $2 Scenes of village life | 1·75 | 2·00 |

Nos. 411/13 were printed together, se-tenant, forming a composite design taken from a mural.

**85** "Artocarpus odoratissima"

**1987.** Local Fruits (1st series). Multicoloured.

| | | | |
|---|---|---|---|
| 414 | 50c. Type **85** | 75 | 70 |
| 415 | 50c. "Canarium odontophyllum mig" | 75 | 70 |
| 416 | 50c. "Litsea garciae" | 75 | 70 |
| 417 | 50c. "Mangifera foetida lour" | 75 | 70 |

See also Nos. 421/4, 459/62, 480/2 and 525/8.

**86** Modern House

**1987.** International Year of Shelter for the Homeless.

| | | | | |
|---|---|---|---|---|
| 418 | **86** | 50c. multicoloured | 40 | 50 |
| 419 | - | 75c. multicoloured | 55 | 65 |
| 420 | - | $1 multicoloured | 80 | 90 |

DESIGNS: 75c., $1 Modern Brunei housing projects.

**1988.** Local Fruits (2nd series). As T 85. Mult.

| | | | |
|---|---|---|---|
| 421 | 50c. "Durio spp" | 95 | 1·25 |
| 422 | 50c. "Durio oxleyanus" | 95 | 1·25 |
| 423 | 50c. "Durio graveolens" (blue background) | 95 | 1·25 |
| 424 | 50c. "Durio graveolens" (white background) | 95 | 1·25 |

**87** Wooden Lathe

**1988.** Opening of Malay Technology Museum. Multicoloured.

| | | | |
|---|---|---|---|
| 425 | 10c. Type **87** | 15 | 10 |
| 426 | 75c. Crushing sugar cane | 55 | 70 |
| 427 | $1 Bird scarer | 70 | 85 |

**88** Patterned Cloth

**1988.** Handwoven Material (1st series). Mult.

| | | | |
|---|---|---|---|
| 428 | 10c. Type **88** | 10 | 10 |
| 429 | 20c. Jong Sarat cloth | 15 | 15 |
| 430 | 25c. Si Pugut cloth | 20 | 25 |
| 431 | 40c. Si Pugut Bunga Berlapis cloth | 30 | 35 |
| 432 | 75c. Si Lobang Bangsi Bunga Belitang Kipas cloth | 55 | 80 |
| **MS**433 | 105×204 mm. Nos. 428/32 | 3·00 | 4·50 |

See also Nos. 442/7.

**1988.** Brassware (2nd series). As T 82. Multicoloured.

| | | | |
|---|---|---|---|
| 434 | 50c. Lidded two-handled pot ("periok") | 60 | 75 |
| 435 | 50c. Candlestick ("lampong") | 60 | 75 |
| 436 | 50c. Shallow circular dish with stand ("gangsa") | 60 | 75 |
| 437 | 50c. Repousse box with lid ("celapa") | 60 | 75 |

**89** Sultan reading Proclamation

**1988.** 20th Anniv of Sultan's Coronation. Mult.

| | | | |
|---|---|---|---|
| 438 | 20c. Type **89** | 25 | 15 |
| 439 | 75c. Sultan reading from Koran | 1·00 | 60 |
| 440 | $2 In Coronation robes (26×63 mm) | 2·25 | 1·60 |
| **MS**441 | 164×125 mm. Nos. 438/40 | 3·00 | 2·50 |

**1988.** Handwoven Material (2nd series). As T 88. Multicoloured.

| | | | |
|---|---|---|---|
| 442 | 10c. Beragi cloth | 15 | 10 |
| 443 | 20c. Bertabur cloth | 20 | 20 |
| 444 | 25c. Sukma Indra cloth | 25 | 35 |
| 445 | 40c. Si Pugut Bunga cloth | 40 | 75 |
| 446 | 75c. Beragi Si Lobang Bangsi Bunga Cendera Kesuma cloth | 75 | 1·40 |
| **MS**447 | 150×204 mm. Nos. 442/6 | 3·50 | 4·50 |

**90** Malaria-carrying Mosquito

**1988.** 40th Anniv of WHO. Multicoloured.

| | | | |
|---|---|---|---|
| 448 | 25c. Type **90** | 1·25 | 30 |
| 449 | 35c. Man with insecticide spray and sample on slide | 1·40 | 45 |
| 450 | $2 Microscope and magnified malaria cells | 3·25 | 2·00 |

**91** Sultan and Council of Ministers

**1989.** 5th Anniv of National Day. Mult.

| | | | |
|---|---|---|---|
| 451 | 20c. Type **91** | 15 | 10 |
| 452 | 30c. Guard of honour | 20 | 15 |
| 453 | 60c. Firework display (27×55 mm) | 45 | 40 |
| 454 | $2 Congregation in mosque | 1·50 | 1·75 |
| **MS**455 | 164×124 mm. Nos. 451/4 | 2·25 | 2·75 |

**92** Dove escaping from Cage

**1989.** "Freedom of Palestine". Multicoloured.

| | | | |
|---|---|---|---|
| 456 | 20c. Type **92** | 50 | 20 |
| 457 | 75c. Map and Palestinian flag | 2·00 | 1·25 |
| 458 | $1 Dome of the Rock, Jerusalem | 2·75 | 1·50 |

**1989.** Local Fruits (3rd series). As T 85. Mult.

| | | | |
|---|---|---|---|
| 459 | 60c. "Daemonorops fissa" | 2·00 | 2·50 |
| 460 | 60c. "Eleiodoxa conferta" | 2·00 | 2·50 |
| 461 | 60c. "Salacca zalacca" | 2·00 | 2·50 |
| 462 | 60c. "Calamus ornatus" | 2·00 | 2·50 |

**93** Oil Pump

**1989.** 60th Anniv of Brunei Oil and Gas Industry. Multicoloured.

| | | | |
|---|---|---|---|
| 463 | 20c. Type **93** | 2·50 | 30 |
| 464 | 60c. Loading tanker | 4·00 | 2·25 |
| 465 | 90c. Oil well at sunset | 4·50 | 3·00 |
| 466 | $1 Pipe laying | 4·75 | 3·00 |
| 467 | $2 Oil terminal | 8·00 | 9·00 |

**94** Museum Building and Exhibits

**1990.** 25th Anniv of Brunei Museum. Multicoloured.

| | | | |
|---|---|---|---|
| 468 | 30c. Type **94** | 1·50 | 70 |
| 469 | 60c. Official opening, 1965 | 2·25 | 2·25 |
| 470 | $1 Brunei Museum | 3·00 | 4·00 |

**95** Letters from Malay Alphabet

**1990.** International Literacy Year. Multicoloured.

| | | | |
|---|---|---|---|
| 471 | 15c. Type **95** | 80 | 40 |
| 472 | 90c. English alphabet | 3·50 | 4·25 |
| 473 | $1 Literacy Year emblem and letters | 3·50 | 4·25 |

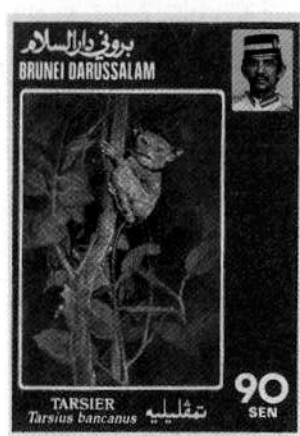


**96** Tarsier in Tree

**1990.** Endangered Species. Western Tarsier. Multicoloured.

| | | | |
|---|---|---|---|
| 474 | 20c. Western Tarsier on branch | 1·25 | 45 |
| 475 | 60c. Western Tarsier feeding | 2·50 | 3·00 |
| 476 | 90c. Type **96** | 3·50 | 4·50 |

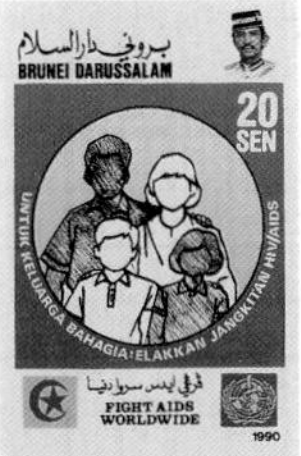


**97** Symbolic Family

**1990.** Worldwide Campaign against AIDS. Multicoloured.

| | | | |
|---|---|---|---|
| 477 | 20c. Type **97** | 3·00 | 60 |
| 478 | 30c. Sources of infection | 4·00 | 2·00 |
| 479 | 90c. "AIDS" headstone surrounded by skulls | 9·50 | 8·50 |

**1990.** Local Fruits (4th series). As T 85. Mult.

| | | | |
|---|---|---|---|
| 480 | 60c. "Willoughbea sp." (brown fruit) | 3·00 | 3·75 |
| 481 | 60c. Ripe "Willoughbea sp." (yellow fruit) | 3·00 | 3·75 |
| 482 | 60c. "Willoughbea angustifolia" | 3·00 | 3·75 |

**98** Proboscis Monkey on Ground

**1991.** Endangered Species. Proboscis Monkey. Multicoloured.

| | | | |
|---|---|---|---|
| 483 | 15c. Type **98** | 1·50 | 60 |
| 484 | 20c. Head of monkey | 1·60 | 70 |
| 485 | 50c. Monkey sitting on branch | 3·00 | 3·25 |
| 486 | 60c. Female monkey with baby climbing tree | 3·25 | 3·75 |

**99** Junior School Classes

**1991.** Teachers' Day. Multicoloured.

| | | | |
|---|---|---|---|
| 487 | 60c. Type **99** | 2·25 | 2·50 |
| 488 | 90c. Secondary school class | 2·75 | 3·50 |

**100** Young Brunei Beauty

**1991.** Fishes. Brunei Beauty. Multicoloured.

| | | | |
|---|---|---|---|
| 489 | 30c. Type **100** | 1·50 | 85 |
| 490 | 60c. Female fish | 2·50 | 4·00 |
| 491 | $1 Male fish | 3·00 | 4·75 |

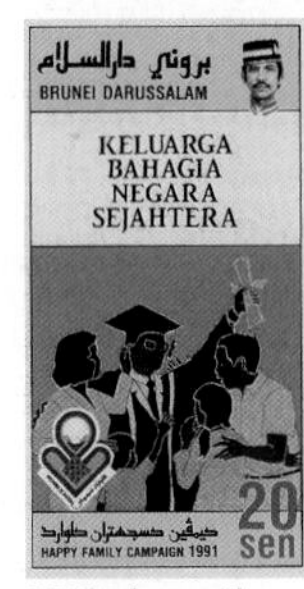


**101** Graduate with Family

**1991.** Happy Family Campaign. Multicoloured.

| | | | |
|---|---|---|---|
| 492 | 20c. Type **101** | 70 | 50 |
| 493 | 60c. Mothers with children | 1·75 | 2·00 |
| 494 | 90c. Family | 2·00 | 3·25 |

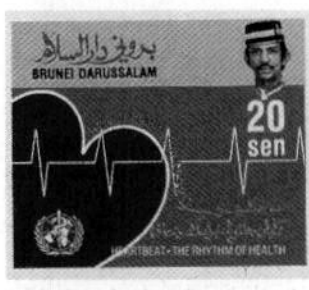


**102** Symbolic Heart and Trace

**1992.** World Health Day.

| | | | | |
|---|---|---|---|---|
| 495 | **102** | 20c. multicoloured | 2·25 | 50 |
| 496 | - | 50c. multicoloured | 4·00 | 2·50 |
| 497 | - | 75c. multicoloured | 6·00 | 6·50 |

DESIGNS: 50c., 70c. (48×27 mm) Heart and heartbeat trace.

**103** Map of Cable System

**1992.** Launching of Singapore–Borneo–Philippines Fibre Optic Submarine Cable System. Mult.

| | | | |
|---|---|---|---|
| 498 | 20c. Type **103** | 3·00 | 50 |
| 499 | 30c. Diagram of Brunei connection | 3·00 | 1·50 |
| 500 | 90c. Submarine cable | 6·00 | 6·50 |

**104** Modern Sculptures

**1992.** Visit ASEAN Year. Multicoloured.

501 20c. Type **104** 2·75 3·00
502 60c. Traditional martial arts 3·00 3·25
503 $1 Modern sculptures (different) 3·25 3·50

Nos. 501/3 were printed together, se-tenant, the backgrounds forming a composite design.

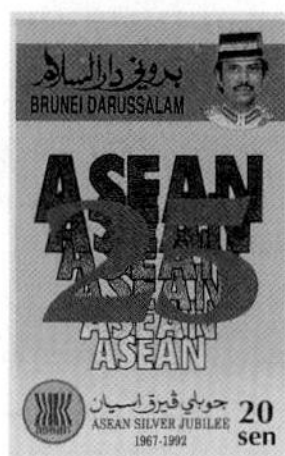


**105** "ASEAN 25" and Logo

**1992.** 25th Anniv of ASEAN (Association of South East Asian Nations). Multicoloured.

504 20c. Type **105** 1·25 65
505 60c. Headquarters building 2·75 2·75
506 90c. National landmarks 3·50 4·50

**106** Sultan in Procession

**1992.** 25th Anniv of Sultan's Accession. Mult.

507 25c. Type **106** 1·50 2·00
508 25c. Brunei International Airport 1·50 2·00
509 25c. Sultan's Palace 1·50 2·00
510 25c. Docks and Brunei University 1·50 2·00
511 25c. Mosque 1·50 2·00

Nos. 507/11 were printed together, se-tenant, forming a composite design.

**107** Crested Wood Partridge

**1992.** Birds (1st series). Multicoloured.

512 30c. Type **107** 1·00 50
513 60c. Asiatic paradise flycatcher ("Asian Paradise Flycatcher") 2·00 2·25
514 $1 Great argus pheasant 2·25 3·00

See also Nos. 515/17, 518/20, 575/7 and 602/5.

**1993.** Birds (2nd series). As T 107. Multicoloured.

515 30c. Long-tailed parakeet 1·00 50
516 60c. Magpie robin 2·00 2·25
517 $1 Blue-crowned hanging parrot ("Malay Lorikeet") 2·50 3·00

**1993.** Birds (3rd series). As T 107. Multicoloured.

518 30c. Chesnut-breasted malkoha 1·25 50
519 60c. White-rumped shama 2·25 2·50
520 $1 Black and red broadbill (vert) 3·00 3·50

**108** National Flag and "10"

**1994.** 10th Anniv of National Day. Multicoloured.

521 10c. Type **108** 1·25 1·25
522 20c. Symbolic hands 1·25 1·40
523 30c. Previous National Day symbols 1·40 1·50
524 60c. Coat of arms 1·75 1·90

**1994.** Local Fruits (5th issue). As T 85, but each 36×26 mm. Multicoloured.

525 60c. "Nephelium mutabile" 85 1·40
526 60c. "Nephelium xerospermoides" 85 1·40
527 60c. "Nephelium spp" 85 1·40
528 60c. "Nephelium macrophyllum" 85 1·40

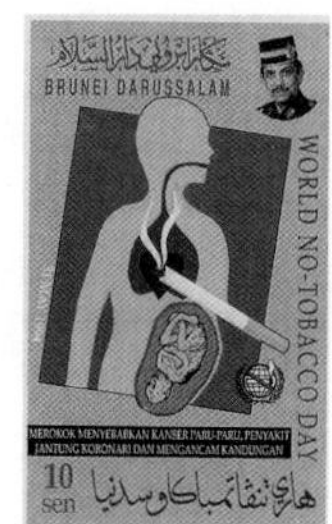


**109** Cigarette burning Heart and Deformed Baby in Womb

**1994.** World No Tobacco Day. Multicoloured.

529 10c. Type **109** 40 20
530 15c. Symbols of smoking over crowd of people 40 20
531 $2 Globe crushing cigarettes 3·00 5·00

**110** Raja Isteri (wife of Sultan in Guide uniform)

**1994.** 40th Anniv of Brunei Girl Guides' Association. Multicoloured.

532 40c. Type **110** 2·00 2·00
533 40c. Guide receiving award 2·00 2·00
534 40c. Guide reading 2·00 2·00
535 40c. Group of guides 2·00 2·00
536 40c. Guides erecting tent 2·00 2·00

**111** Fokker F-27 Friendship on Runway

**1994.** 20th Anniv of Royal Brunei Airlines. Multicoloured.

537 10c. Type **111** 1·00 45
538 20c. Boeing 757 on runway 1·50 45
539 $1 Boeing 757 in the air 3·50 4·50

**112** Malay Family

**1994.** International Day against Drug Abuse and Trafficking. Multicoloured.

540 20c. Type **112** 1·10 1·60
541 60c. Chinese family 1·40 1·90
542 $1 Doctor, police officers and members of youth organizations 1·75 2·50

Nos. 540/2 were printed together, se-tenant, forming a composite design.

**113** Aerial View of City, 1970

**1995.** 25th Anniv of Bandar Seri Begawan. Mult.

543 30c. Type **113** 1·50 45
544 50c. City in 1980 2·00 1·50
545 $1 City in 1990 2·75 4·00

**114** United Nations General Assembly

**1995.** 50th Anniv of United Nations. Multicoloured.

546 20c. Type **114** 50 25
547 60c. Security Council in session 1·00 90
548 90c. United Nations Building, New York (27×44 mm) 1·50 2·50

**115** Students in Laboratory

**1995.** 10th Anniv of University of Brunei. Mult.

549 30c. Type **115** 45 35
550 50c. University building 70 70
551 90c. Sultan visiting University 1·25 2·25

**116** Police Officers

**1996.** 75th Anniv of Royal Brunei Police Force. Multicoloured.

552 25c. Type **116** 1·50 60
553 50c. Aspects of police work 2·00 1·50
554 75c. Sultan inspecting parade 2·50 3·50

**117** Telephones

**1996.** World Telecommunications Day. Children's Paintings. Multicoloured.

555 20c. Type **117** 85 40
556 35c. Telephone dial and aspects of telecommunications 1·40 60
557 $1 Globe and aspects of telecommunications 3·50 4·00

**118** Sultan and Crowd

**1996.** 50th Birthday of Sultan Hassanal Bolkiah Mu'izzaddin Waddaulah. Multicoloured.

558 50c. Type **118** 1·40 1·75
559 50c. Sultan in ceremonial dress 1·40 1·75
560 50c. Sultan receiving dignitaries at mosque 1·40 1·75
561 50c. Sultan with subjects 1·40 1·75
**MS**562 152×100 mm. $1 Sultan in ceremonial dress (different) 2·25 3·00

**119** Sultan Hassanal Bolkiah Mu'izzaddin Waddaulah

**1996**

563 **119** 10c. multicoloured 20 10
564 **119** 15c. multicoloured 25 25
565 **119** 20c. multicoloured 30 25
566 **119** 30c. multicoloured 40 35
567 **119** 50c. multicoloured 70 50
568 **119** 60c. multicoloured 80 60
569 **119** 75c. multicoloured 1·00 70
570 **119** 90c. multicoloured 1·25 90
571 - $1 multicoloured 1·50 1·00
572 - $2 multicoloured 2·75 2·25
573 - $5 multicoloured 6·50 6·50
574 - $10 multicoloured 12·00 12·00

DESIGN—27×39 mm: $1 to $10 Sultan in ceremonial robes.

**121** Black-naped Tern

**1996.** Birds (4th series). Sea Birds. Multicoloured.

575 20c. Type **121** 75 50
576 30c. Roseate tern 75 50
577 $1 Bridled tern 1·75 2·75

No. 576 is inscr "ROSLATE TERN" in error.

**122** "Acanthus ebracteatus"

**1997.** Mangrove Flowers. Multicoloured.

578 20c. Type **122** 45 25
579 30c. "Lumnitzera littorea" 50 35
580 $1 "Nypa fruticans" 1·40 2·50

**123** "Heterocentrotus mammillatus"

**1997.** Marine Life. Multicoloured.

| | | | |
|---|---|---|---|
| 581 | 60c. Type **123** | 70 | 1·00 |
| 582 | 60c. "Linckia laevigata" (starfish) | 70 | 1·00 |
| 583 | 60c. "Oxycomanthus bennetti" (plant) | 70 | 1·00 |
| 584 | 60c. "Bohadschia argus" (sea slug) | 70 | 1·00 |

**124** Children and Sign Language

**1998.** Asian and Pacific Decade of Disabled Persons, 1993–2002. Multicoloured.

| | | | |
|---|---|---|---|
| 585 | 20c. Type **124** | 55 | 25 |
| 586 | 50c. Woman typing and firework display | 1·00 | 1·00 |
| 587 | $1 Disabled athletes | 1·75 | 2·50 |

**125** Sultan performing Ceremonial Duties

**1998.** 30th Anniv of Coronation of Sultan Hassanal Bolkiah Mu'izzaddin Waddaulah. Multicoloured.

| | | | |
|---|---|---|---|
| 588 | 60c. Type **125** | 1·00 | 50 |
| 589 | 90c. Sultan on Coronation throne | 1·40 | 1·60 |
| 590 | $1 Coronation parade | 1·50 | 1·60 |
| **MS**591 | 150×180 mm. Nos. 588/90 | 3·50 | 4·00 |

**126** A.S.E.A.N. Architecture and Transport

**1998.** 30th Anniv of Association of South-east Asian Nations. Multicoloured.

| | | | |
|---|---|---|---|
| 592 | 30c. Type **126** | 1·25 | 1·25 |
| 593 | 30c. Map of Brunei and city scenes | 1·25 | 1·25 |
| 594 | 30c. Flags of member nations | 1·25 | 1·25 |

**127** Crown Prince at Desk

**1998.** Proclamation of Prince Al-Muhtadee Billah as Crown Prince. Multicoloured.

| | | | |
|---|---|---|---|
| 595 | $1 Type **127** | 1·00 | 1·00 |
| 596 | $2 Crown Prince in military uniform | 1·75 | 2·75 |
| 597 | $3 Crown Prince's emblem | 2·25 | 3·75 |
| **MS**598 | 175×153 mm. Nos. 595/7. | 5·50 | 7·00 |

**128** Koran, Civil Servants and Handshake

**1998.** 5th Anniv of Civil Service Day. Multicoloured.

| | | | |
|---|---|---|---|
| 599 | 30c. Type **128** | 60 | 30 |
| 600 | 60c. Symbols of progress | 1·00 | 75 |
| 601 | 90c. Civil servants at work | 1·50 | 2·00 |

**129** Blue-eared Kingfisher

**1998.** Birds (5th series). Kingfishers. Multicoloured.

| | | | |
|---|---|---|---|
| 602 | 20c. Type **129** | 1·00 | 60 |
| 603 | 30c. River kingfisher ("Common Kingfisher") | 1·25 | 60 |
| 604 | 60c. White-collared kingfisher | 2·00 | 1·50 |
| 605 | $1 Stork-billed kingfisher | 2·50 | 3·00 |

**130** Water Village, Bandar Seri Begawan

**1999.** 15th Anniv of National Day. Multicoloured.

| | | | |
|---|---|---|---|
| 606 | 20c. Type **130** | 50 | 20 |
| 607 | 60c. Modern telecommunications and Boeing 757 | 1·50 | 1·10 |
| 608 | 90c. Aspects of modern Brunei | 2·00 | 2·25 |
| **MS**609 | 118×85 mm. Nos. 606/8 | 3·50 | 4·00 |

**131** Rifle-shooting

**1999.** 20th South-east Asia Games, Brunei. Mult.

| | | | |
|---|---|---|---|
| 610 | 20c. Type **131** | 65 | 75 |
| 611 | 20c. Golf and tennis | 65 | 75 |
| 612 | 20c. Boxing and judo | 65 | 75 |
| 613 | 20c. Squash and table tennis | 65 | 75 |
| 614 | 20c. Swimming and canoe racing | 65 | 75 |
| 615 | 20c. Hockey and cycling | 65 | 75 |
| 616 | 20c. Basketball and football | 65 | 75 |
| 617 | 20c. High jumping, shot putting and running | 65 | 75 |
| 618 | 20c. Snooker | 65 | 75 |
| 619 | 20c. Bowling | 65 | 75 |
| **MS**620 | 110×73 mm. $1 Various sports | 2·00 | 3·25 |

**132** Clasped Hands and Globe

**1999.** 125th Anniv of Universal Postal Union. Multicoloured.

| | | | |
|---|---|---|---|
| 621 | 20c. Type **132** | 60 | 25 |
| 622 | 30c. "125" and logos | 70 | 30 |
| 623 | 75c. Aspects of postal service | 1·50 | 2·25 |

**133** Modern Building and Children using Computer

**2000.** New Millennium. Multicoloured.

| | | | |
|---|---|---|---|
| 624 | 20c. Type **133** | 75 | 75 |
| 625 | 20c. Royal Palace, tree and people using computer | 75 | 75 |
| 626 | 20c. Aerial view of mosque and factory | 75 | 75 |
| 627 | 20c. Plan of Parterre Gardens | 75 | 75 |
| 628 | 20c. Container ships and Boeing 757 | 75 | 75 |
| 629 | 20c. Satellite dish aerials | 75 | 75 |
| **MS**630 | 221×121 mm. Nos. 624/9 | 4·00 | 4·00 |

Nos. 624/9 were printed together, se-tenant, with the backgrounds forming a composite design.

**134** Sultan Mohamed Jemal-ul-Alam and Traditional Buildings, 1901–20

**2000.** Brunei in the 20th Century. Multicoloured.

| | | | |
|---|---|---|---|
| 631 | 30c. Type **134** | 1·00 | 1·00 |
| 632 | 30c. Sultan Ahmed Tajudin, oil well and Brunei police, 1921–40 | 1·00 | 1·00 |
| 633 | 30c. Signing of the Constitution and Brunei Mosque, 1941–60 | 1·00 | 1·00 |
| 634 | 30c. Oil installation, satellite dish, Boeing 757 of Royal Brunei Airlines and bank note, 1961–80 | 1·00 | 1·00 |
| 635 | 30c. Sultan on throne, international organisation emblems and crowd with trophy, 1981–99 | 1·00 | 1·00 |

**135** Sultan Hashim Jalil-ul-Alam, 1885–1906

**2000.** The Sultans of Brunei. Multicoloured.

| | | | |
|---|---|---|---|
| 636 | 60c. Type **135** | 1·40 | 1·40 |
| 637 | 60c. Sultan Mohamed Jemal-ul-Alam, 1906–24 | 1·40 | 1·40 |
| 638 | 60c. Sultan Ahmed Tajudin, 1924–50 | 1·40 | 1·40 |
| 639 | 60c. Sultan Omar Ali Saifuddin, 1950–67 | 1·40 | 1·40 |
| 640 | 60c. Sultan Hassanal Bolkiah, 1967 | 1·40 | 1·40 |
| **MS**641 | 190×99 mm. Nos. 636/40 | 4·50 | 6·00 |

**136** *Rafflesia pricei*

**2000.** Local Flowers. Multicoloured.

| | | | |
|---|---|---|---|
| 642 | 30c. Type **136** | 75 | 30 |
| 643 | 50c. *Rhizanthes lowi* | 1·25 | 1·25 |
| 644 | 60c. *Nepenthes rafflesiana* | 1·40 | 1·40 |

**137** Information Technology

**2000.** Asia–Pacific Economic Cooperation. Heads of Government Meeting. Multicoloured.

| | | | |
|---|---|---|---|
| 645 | 20c. Type **137** | 70 | 70 |
| 646 | 30c. Small and medium businesses | 70 | 95 |
| 647 | 60c. Tourism | 1·75 | 1·75 |
| **MS**648 | 150×108 mm. Nos. 645/7 | 3·00 | 3·50 |

**138** Green Turtle

**2000.** Turtles. Multicoloured.

| | | | |
|---|---|---|---|
| 649 | 30c. Type **138** | 1·00 | 1·00 |
| 650 | 30c. Hawksbill turtle | 1·00 | 1·00 |
| 651 | 30c. Olive Ridley turtle | 1·00 | 1·00 |

**139** Tourist Canoe on River

**2001.** "Visit Brunei Year" (1st series). Multicoloured.

| | | | |
|---|---|---|---|
| 652 | 20c. Type **139** | 1·25 | 75 |
| 653 | 30c. Traditional water village | 1·25 | 75 |
| 654 | 60c. Carved building facade | 2·25 | 2·75 |

See also Nos. 669/72.

**140** Sultan in Army Uniform

**2001.** 55th Birthday of Sultan Hassanal Bolkiah Muizzaddin Waddaulah. Multicoloured.

| | | | |
|---|---|---|---|
| 655 | 55c. Type **140** | 1·40 | 1·40 |
| 656 | 55c. Sultan in Air Force uniform | 1·40 | 1·40 |
| 657 | 55c. Sultan in traditional dress | 1·40 | 1·40 |
| 658 | 55c. Sultan in Army camouflage jacket | 1·40 | 1·40 |
| 659 | 55c. Sultan in Navy uniform | 1·40 | 1·40 |
| **MS**660 | 100×75 mm. 55c. Sultan and Bandar Seri Begawan (40×71 mm) | 2·25 | 2·50 |

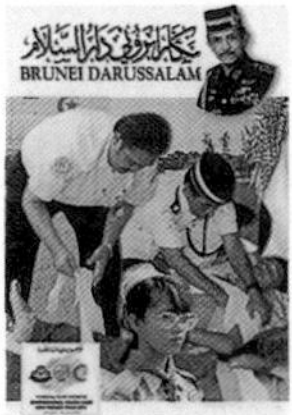


**141** First Aid Demonstration

**2001.** International Youth Camp. Multicoloured.

| | | | |
|---|---|---|---|
| 661 | 30c. Type **141** | 1·00 | 1·00 |
| 662 | 30c. Brunei guides and tent demonstration | 1·00 | 1·00 |
| 663 | 30c. Scouts with cooking pot | 1·00 | 1·00 |
| **MS**664 | 110×77 mm. Nos. 661/3 | 2·75 | 3·25 |

Nos. 661/3 were printed together, se-tenant, forming a composite design.

**142** Islamic Regalia

**2001.** 1st Islamic International Exhibition, Brunei. Multicoloured.

| | | | |
|---|---|---|---|
| 665 | 20c. Type **142** | 80 | 80 |
| 666 | 20c. Exhibition centre | 80 | 80 |
| 667 | 20c. Computer communications | 80 | 80 |
| 668 | 20c. Opening ceremony | 80 | 80 |

**143** Forest Walkway

**2001.** Visit Brunei (2nd series). Multicoloured.

| | | | |
|---|---|---|---|
| 669 | 20c. Type **143** | 85 | 85 |
| 670 | 20c. Waterfall | 85 | 85 |
| 671 | 20c. Jerudong Theme Park | 85 | 85 |
| 672 | 20c. Footbridges across lake | 85 | 85 |

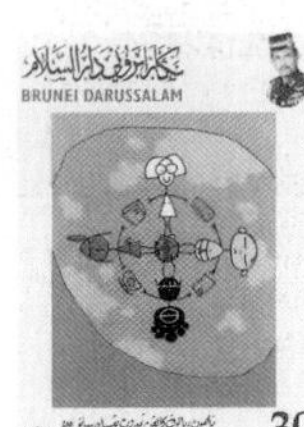


**144** "Children encircling Globe" (Urska Golob)

**2001.** U.N. Year of Dialogue among Civilisations. Multicoloured.

| | | | |
|---|---|---|---|
| 673 | 30c. Type **144** | 1·00 | 1·00 |
| 674 | 30c. Quotation marks illustrated with faces | 1·00 | 1·00 |
| 675 | 30c. Cubist portrait and Japanese girl | 1·00 | 1·00 |
| 676 | 30c. Coloured leaves | 1·00 | 1·00 |

**145** Male and Female Bulwer's Pheasants

**2001.** Endangered Species. Bulwer's Pheasant. Mult.

| | | | |
|---|---|---|---|
| 677 | 30c. Type **145** | 1·10 | 1·10 |
| 678 | 30c. Male pheasant | 1·10 | 1·10 |
| 679 | 30c. Female pheasant with chicks | 1·10 | 1·10 |
| 680 | 30c. Female pheasant | 1·10 | 1·10 |

**146** Early and Modern Telephone Systems

**2002.** 50th Anniv of Department of Telecommunications (JTB). Multicoloured.

| | | | |
|---|---|---|---|
| 681 | 50c. Type **146** | 1·40 | 1·40 |
| 682 | 50c. JTB Golden Jubilee emblem | 1·40 | 1·40 |
| 683 | 50c. Computer networks | 1·40 | 1·40 |

**147** 50th Anniversary Logo

**2002.** 50th Anniv of Survey Department. Mult.

| | | | |
|---|---|---|---|
| 684 | 50c. Type **147** | 1·40 | 1·40 |
| 685 | 50c. Survey Department Offices | 1·40 | 1·40 |
| 686 | 50c. Theodolite and thermal map | 1·40 | 1·40 |

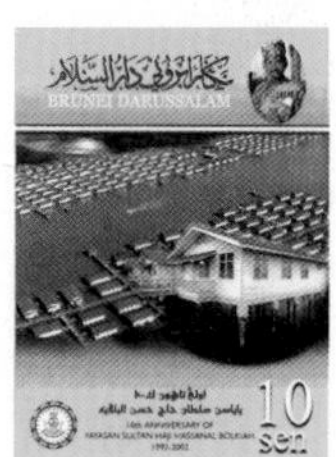


**148** Modern Housing, Water Village

**2002.** 10th Anniv of Yayasan Sultan Haji Hassanal Bolkiah Foundation. Multicoloured.

| | | | |
|---|---|---|---|
| 687 | 10c. Type **148** | 50 | 50 |
| 688 | 10c. Mosque and interior | 50 | 50 |
| 689 | 10c. School and computer class | 50 | 50 |
| 690 | 10c. University of Brunei | 50 | 50 |

**149** Anti-Corruption Bureau Headquarters

**2002.** 20th Anniv of Anti-Corruption Bureau. Multicoloured.

| | | | |
|---|---|---|---|
| 691 | 20c. Type **149** | 85 | 85 |
| 692 | 20c. Skyscrapers and mosque | 85 | 85 |
| 693 | 20c. Anti-Corruption Bureau posters | 85 | 85 |

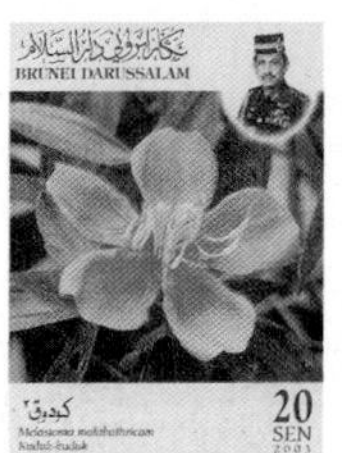


**150** *Melastoma malabathricum*

**2003.** Flowering Medicinal Plants. Multicoloured.

| | | | |
|---|---|---|---|
| 694 | 20c. Type **150** | 80 | 80 |
| 695 | 20c. *Etlingera solaris* | 80 | 80 |
| 696 | 20c. *Dillenia suffruticosa* | 80 | 80 |
| 697 | 20c. *Costus speciosus* | 80 | 80 |

**151** Drums and Musicians

**2003.** ASEAN—Japan Exchange Year. Multicoloured.

| | | | |
|---|---|---|---|
| 698 | 20c. Type **151** | 70 | 70 |
| 699 | 20c. Woodworker and handicrafts | 70 | 70 |
| 700 | 20c. Exchange Year logo | 70 | 70 |

**152** Sultan of Brunei and UN Emblem

**2004.** 20th Anniv of National Day. Multicoloured.

| | | | |
|---|---|---|---|
| 701 | 20c. Type **152** | 70 | 70 |
| 702 | 20c. In military uniform | 70 | 70 |
| 703 | 20c. Reading speech at National Day celebration | 70 | 70 |
| 704 | 20c. Emblem | 70 | 70 |
| **MS**705 | 185×140 mm. Nos. 701/4 | 2·75 | 3·00 |

**153** Brunei 1895 ½c. Stamp

**2004.** Brunei Darussalam National Philatelic Society. Multicoloured.

| | | | |
|---|---|---|---|
| 706 | 25c. Type **153** | 75 | 75 |
| 707 | 25c. Magnifying glass, perforation gauge, tweezers and stamps | 75 | 75 |
| 708 | 25c. Postmarks, stamp catalogue and first day covers | 75 | 75 |

**154** Crown Prince Al-Muhtadee Billah Bolkiah and Sarah Salleh

**2004.** Royal Wedding.

| | | | | |
|---|---|---|---|---|
| 709 | 154 | 99c. multicoloured | 1·60 | 1·75 |

**155** Sultan of Brunei and Jame'Asr Hassanal Bolkiah Mosque

**2006.** 60th Birthday of Sultan Hassanal Bolkiah Muizzaddin Waddaulah. Designs showing montage of images, all with portrait of Sultan at top right. Multicoloured (except $60), panel colours given.

| | | | |
|---|---|---|---|
| 710 | 60c. Type **155** (mauve) | 1·00 | 1·00 |
| 711 | 60c. Sultan, palace and crowd with flags (red) | 1·00 | 1·00 |
| 712 | 60c. Sultan and urban and agricultural scenes (yellow) | 1·00 | 1·00 |
| 713 | 60c. Sultan speaking at 9th ASEAN–Japan Summit and at APEC 2000 (salmon) | 1·00 | 1·00 |
| 714 | 60c. Sultan meeting woman (green) | 1·00 | 1·00 |
| 715 | 60c. Sultan in military uniform (blue) | 1·00 | 1·00 |
| **MS**716 | 166×120 mm. Nos. 710/15 | 5·50 | 6·00 |
| **MS**717 | 148×137 mm. $60 Montage of five black and white photographs of Sultan as young man, at Coronation, seated on throne and wearing crown and military uniform (black and grey) (99×90 mm) | 42·00 | 48·00 |

**156** General Post Office, Bandar Seri Begawan

**157** Parcels and Letters travelling around Globe

**2006.** Centenary of Postal Services Department. Multicoloured. Litho. (a) T 156.

| | | | |
|---|---|---|---|
| 718 | 100c. Type **156** | 1·40 | 1·60 |
| 719 | 100c. Kuala Belait Post Office | 1·40 | 1·60 |
| 720 | 100c. Tutong Post Office at the District Office, Tutong | 1·40 | 1·60 |
| 721 | 100c. Bangar Post Office at the District Office, Temburong | 1·40 | 1·60 |
| **MS**722 | 115×115 mm. Nos. 718/21 | 5·00 | 5·75 |

(b) T 157 and similar vert designs showing children's drawings.

| | | | |
|---|---|---|---|
| **MS**723 | 95×145 mm. 100s.×6 Type **157**; Postman; Globe, letter, house and aircraft; Air mail letters, postbox and post office; Letters, globe and families in Brunei and China; Globe and national flags ('EVERYONE REACHING EVERYWHERE') | 7·00 | 8·00 |

**158** *Balistapus undulates* (orangestriped triggerfish)

**2007.** Marine Life. Multicoloured.

| | | | |
|---|---|---|---|
| 724 | 60c. Type **158** | 1·25 | 1·25 |
| 725 | 60c. *Taenionotis triacanthus* (leaf scorpionfish) | 1·25 | 1·25 |
| **MS**726 | 100×70 mm. $1 *Nautilus pompilus* (chambered nautilus); $1 *Ostracion meleagris* (spotted boxfish) | 3·50 | 3·50 |

Stamps in similar designs were issued by Malaysia.

**159** Sultan Hassanal Bolkiah Mu'izzaddin Waddaulah

**2007.** Multicoloured.. Multicoloured..

| | | | | |
|---|---|---|---|---|
| 727 | **159** | 10c. multicoloured | 10 | 10 |
| 728 | **159** | 15c. multicoloured | 20 | 20 |
| 729 | **159** | 20c. multicoloured | 25 | 25 |
| 730 | **159** | 30c. multicoloured | 35 | 35 |
| 731 | **159** | 50c. multicoloured | 60 | 60 |
| 732 | **159** | 60c. multicoloured | 70 | 70 |
| 733 | **159** | 75c. multicoloured | 90 | 90 |
| 734 | **159** | 90c. multicoloured | 1·10 | 1·10 |
| 735 | – | $1 multicoloured | 1·25 | 1·25 |
| 736 | – | $2 multicoloured | 2·40 | 2·40 |
| 737 | – | $5 multicoloured | 6·00 | 6·00 |
| 738 | – | $10 multicoloured | 12·00 | 12·00 |

Nos. 735/8 are as Type **159** but larger, 27×40 mm.

**160** Bubungan Dua Belas

**2007.** Centenary of Bubungan Dua Belas, Bukit Subok. Multicoloured.

| | | | |
|---|---|---|---|
| 739 | 30s. Type **160** | 90 | 35 |
| 740 | 60s. Bubungan Dua Belas (seen from above) | 1·60 | 1·25 |

| | | | |
|---|---|---|---|
| 741 | $1 Bubungan Dua Belas, 1907 | 2·50 | 3·00 |
| **MS**742 | 150×90 mm. Nos. 739/41 | 4·50 | 4·75 |

Bubungan Dua Belas—House of 12 Roofs was the British High Commissioner's Residence.

Nos. 739/**MS**742, T **160** are left for 100 Years of Bubangan, issued 23 July 2007, not yet received.

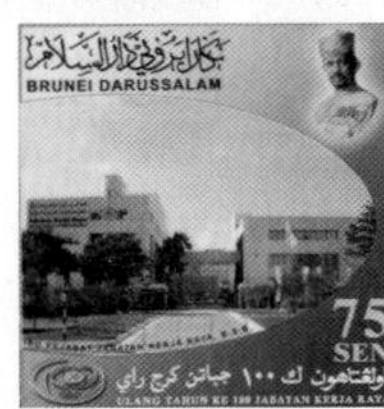

**161** Public Works Department Headquarters

**2007.** Centenary (2006) of Public Works Department. Multicoloured.

| | | | |
|---|---|---|---|
| 743 | 75c. Type **161** | 1·00 | 1·25 |
| 744 | 75c. Engineers Office, (PWD Headquarters), Subok, 1906 | 1·00 | 1·25 |
| 745 | 75c. 100 | 1·00 | 1·25 |

**162** Secretariat Building, Brunei

**2007.** 40th Anniv of ASEAN (Association of South-east Asian Nations). Ancient and Modern Architecture. Multicoloured.

| | | | |
|---|---|---|---|
| 746 | 20c. Type **162** | 1·10 | 1·10 |
| 747 | 20c. Yangon Post Office, Myanmar | 1·10 | 1·10 |
| 748 | 20c. National Museum of Cambodia | 1·10 | 1·10 |
| 749 | 20c. Malacañang Palace, Philippines | 1·10 | 1·10 |
| 750 | 20c. Fatahillah Museum, Jakarta, Indonesia | 1·10 | 1·10 |
| 751 | 20c. National Museum of Singapore | 1·10 | 1·10 |
| 752 | 20c. Lao Typical House | 1·10 | 1·10 |
| 753 | 20c. Vimanmek Mansion, Bangkok, Thailand | 1·10 | 1·10 |
| 754 | 20c. Malayan Railway Headquarters Building, Kuala Lumpur, Malaysia | 1·10 | 1·10 |
| 755 | 20c. Presidential Palace, Hanoi, Vietnam | 1·10 | 1·10 |

Similar designs were issued by the ten member countries, Indonesia, Malaysia, Philippines, Singapore, Thailand, Vietnam, Laos, Myanmar and Cambodia.

**163** Istana Majlis

**2008.** Centenary of Transition of the Capital City from Kampung Air to Mainland. Multicoloured.

| | | | |
|---|---|---|---|
| 756 | 20c. Type **163** | 60 | 40 |
| 757 | 30c. Istana Kota | 70 | 40 |
| 758 | 60c. Bandar Brunei Mula-Mula Dirona di Darat, 1906 | 1·40 | 1·25 |
| 759 | 100c. Modern city of Bandar Seri Begawan | 2·25 | 2·75 |
| **MS**760 | 130×130 mm. Nos. 756/9 | 4·50 | 4·50 |

**164** Sultan saluting

**2008.** 40th Anniv of Coronation of Sultan Hassanal Bolkiah Mu'izzadin Waddaulah. Multicoloured.

| | | | |
|---|---|---|---|
| 761 | 40s. Type **164** | 60 | 60 |
| 762 | 40s. Coronation ceremony | 60 | 60 |
| 763 | 40s. Crowning of Sultan | 60 | 60 |
| 764 | 40s. Crowned Sultan seated in chair | 60 | 60 |
| **MS**765 | 160×100 mm. Nos. 761/4 | 3·25 | 3·75 |
| **MS**766 | 159×100 mm. $40 Crowned Sultan on throne and courtiers (44×69 mm) | 35·00 | 40·00 |

**165** Sultan Omar Ali Saifuddin outside Mosque, 1958

**2008.** 50th Anniv of Omar Ali Saifuddien Mosque. Multicoloured.

| | | | |
|---|---|---|---|
| 767 | 50c. Type **165** | 85 | 85 |
| 768 | 50c. Sultan Hassanal Bolkiah Mu'izzadin Waddaulah | 85 | 85 |
| 769 | 50c. Sultan and courtiers inside Mosque | 85 | 85 |
| 770 | 50c. Aerial view of Mosque | 85 | 85 |
| **MS**771 | 150×80 mm. Noc. 767/70 | 3·00 | 3·50 |
| **MS**772 | 199×110 mm. $50 Omar Ali Saifuddin Mosque (44×71 mm) | 40·00 | 45·00 |

**166** Scanner and Medical Staff

**2009.** Centenary of Health Services in Brunei. Multicoloured.

| | | | |
|---|---|---|---|
| 773 | 10c. Type **166** | 25 | 25 |
| 774 | 10c. Nurse with mother and baby | 25 | 25 |
| 775 | $1 First government hospital in Brunei town | 1·75 | 2·00 |

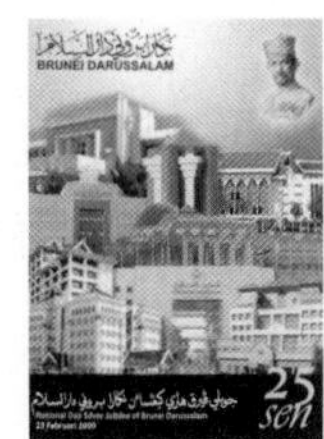

**167** Montage of Buildings

**2009.** National Day Silver Jubilee (25th Anniv of Independence). Multicoloured, background colours given.

| | | | |
|---|---|---|---|
| 776 | 25c. Type **167** | 55 | 55 |
| 777 | 25c. Montage of buildings (different) (bright green) | 55 | 55 |
| 778 | 25c. Military parade, helicopter (on ground) and buildings (cerise) | 55 | 55 |
| 779 | 25c. Montage of buildings (different) (pale yellow) | 55 | 55 |
| 780 | 25c. Oil refinery, oil well, storage tanks and docks (lavender) | 55 | 55 |
| 781 | 25c. Dancers and processions with national flags (bright purple) | 55 | 55 |
| 782 | 25c. Women using mobile phone and laptop computer, modern buildings and airliner (reddish-brown) | 55 | 55 |
| 783 | 25c. Anniversary emblem | 55 | 55 |
| 784 | 25c. As Type **167** but blue border | 55 | 55 |
| 785 | 25c. As No. 777 but blue border | 55 | 55 |
| 786 | 25c. As No. 778 but blue border | 55 | 55 |
| 787 | 25c. As No. 779 but blue border | 55 | 55 |
| 788 | 25c. As No. 780 but blue border | 55 | 55 |
| 789 | 25c. As No. 781 but blue border | 55 | 55 |
| 790 | 25c. As No. 782 but blue border | 55 | 55 |
| 791 | 25c. As No. 783 but blue border | 55 | 55 |
| **MS**792 | 180×140 mm. $25 Sultan Hassanal Bolkiah Mu'izzadin Waddaulah, Sultan Omar Ali Saifuddin and Bandar Seri Begawan city (101×71 mm) | 27·00 | 29·00 |

**2008.** 40th Anniv of Coronation of Sultan Hassanal Bolkiah Mu'izzadin Waddaulah. As T 164. Multicoloured.

| | | | |
|---|---|---|---|
| 761 | 40c. Type **164** | 60 | 60 |
| 762 | 40c. Coronation ceremony | 60 | 60 |
| 763 | 40c. Crowning of Sultan | 60 | 60 |
| 764 | 40c. Crowned Sultan seated in chair | 60 | 60 |

## JAPANESE OCCUPATION OF BRUNEI

These stamps were valid throughout British Borneo (i.e. in Brunei, Labuan, North Borneo and Sarawak).

**(1)** ("Imperial Japanese Government")

**1942.** Stamps of Brunei optd with T **1**.

| | | | | |
|---|---|---|---|---|
| J1 | **5** | 1c. black | 8·50 | 23·00 |
| J2 | **5** | 2c. green | 50·00 | £110 |
| J3 | **5** | 2c. orange | 5·50 | 9·00 |
| J4 | **5** | 3c. green | 28·00 | 75·00 |
| J5 | **5** | 4c. orange | 3·75 | 13·00 |
| J6 | **5** | 5c. brown | 4·75 | 13·00 |
| J7 | **7** | 6c. grey | 40·00 | £250 |
| J8 | **7** | 6c. red | £550 | £550 |
| J9 | **5** | 8c. black | £700 | £850 |
| J10 | **7** | 8c. red | 7·50 | 12·00 |
| J11 | **5** | 10c. purple on yellow | 9·50 | 26·00 |
| J12 | **7** | 12c. blue | 29·00 | 26·00 |
| J13 | **7** | 15c. blue | 22·00 | 26·00 |
| J14 | **5** | 25c. lilac | 26·00 | 50·00 |
| J15 | **5** | 30c. purple and orange | 95·00 | £180 |
| J16 | **5** | 50c. black on green | 38·00 | 60·00 |
| J17 | **5** | $1 black and red on blue | 55·00 | 70·00 |
| J18 | **5** | $5 red on green | £900 | £2750 |
| J19 | **5** | $25 black on red | £900 | £2750 |

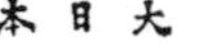

便 郵 國 帝

**(2)** ("Imperial Japanese Postal Service $3")

**1944.** No. J1 surch with T 2.

| | | | |
|---|---|---|---|
| J20 | $3 on 1c. black | £8000 | £8500 |

Pt. 7

## BRUNSWICK

Formerly a duchy of N. Germany. Joined North German Confederation in 1868.

30 silbergroschen = 1 thaler.

**1**

**1852.** Imperf.

| | | | | |
|---|---|---|---|---|
| 1 | **1** | 1sg. red | £2750 | £400 |
| 2 | **1** | 2sg. blue | £1900 | £350 |
| 3 | **1** | 3sg. red | £1900 | £350 |

**1853.** Imperf.

| | | | |
|---|---|---|---|
| 4 | 1/4gg. black on brown | £1100 | £350 |
| 5 | 1/3gg. black | £190 | £425 |
| 15 | 1/2sg. black on green | 32·00 | £325 |
| 7 | 1sg. black on buff | £550 | 85·00 |
| 8 | 2sg. black on blue | £425 | 85·00 |
| 11 | 3sg. black on red | £750 | £225 |

**3**

**1857.** Imperf.

| | | | | |
|---|---|---|---|---|
| 12 | **3** | 4/4gg. black on brown | 55·00 | £130 |

**1864.** Rouletted.

| | | | | |
|---|---|---|---|---|
| 22 | **1** | 1/3gg. black | £650 | £3000 |
| 23 | **1** | 1/2sg. black on green | £275 | £4250 |
| 24 | **1** | 1sg. black on yellow | £4250 | £2000 |
| 25 | **1** | 1sg. yellow | £550 | £190 |
| 26 | **1** | 2sg. black on blue | £550 | £450 |
| 27 | **1** | 3sg. pink | £1100 | £700 |

**4**

**1865.** Roul.

| | | | | |
|---|---|---|---|---|
| 28 | **4** | 1/3g. black | 37·00 | £475 |
| 29 | **4** | 1g. red | 3·25 | 70·00 |
| 32 | **4** | 2g. blue | 11·50 | £170 |
| 34 | **4** | 3g. brown | 9·50 | £200 |

Pt. 20

## BUENOS AIRES

A province of the Argentine Republic. Issued its own stamps from 1858 to 1862.

8 reales = 1 peso.

**P1** Paddle Steamer

**1858.** Imperf.

| | | | | |
|---|---|---|---|---|
| P13 | **P1** | 4r. brown | £225 | £170 |
| P17 | **P1** | 1 (IN) p. brown | £300 | £250 |
| P20 | **P1** | 1 (IN) p. blue | £120 | £100 |
| P25 | **P1** | 1 (TO) p. blue | £500 | £250 |
| P1 | **P1** | 2p. blue | £180 | £100 |
| P4 | **P1** | 3p. green | £1200 | £650 |
| P7 | **P1** | 4p. red | £3250 | £1700 |
| P10 | **P1** | 5p. yellow | £2500 | £1100 |

**P2** Head of Liberty

**1859.** Imperf.

| | | | | |
|---|---|---|---|---|
| P37 | **P2** | 4r. green on blue | £180 | £100 |
| P38 | **P2** | 1p. blue | 15·00 | 9·00 |
| P45 | **P2** | 1p. red | £140 | 65·00 |
| P43 | **P2** | 2p. red | £200 | £120 |
| P48 | **P2** | 2p. blue | £225 | 55·00 |

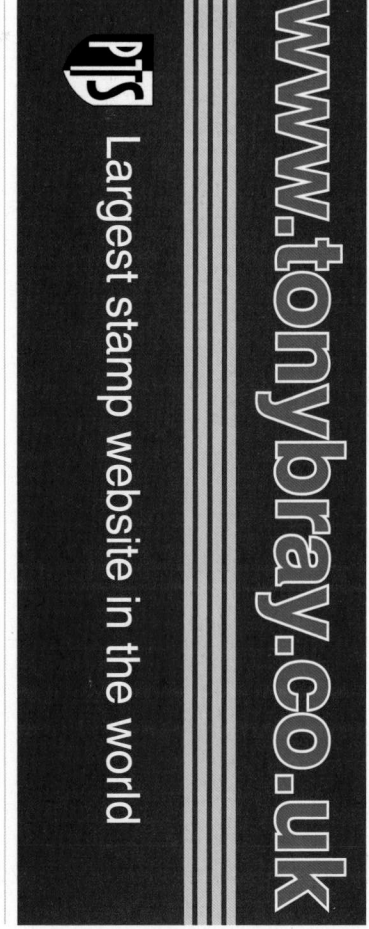

Pt. 3

# BULGARIA

Formerly a Turkish province; a principality under Turkish suzerainty from 1878 to 1908, when an independent kingdom was proclaimed. A People's Republic since 1946.

1879. 100 centimes = 1 franc.
1881. 100 stotinki = 1 lev.

**1** Large Lion

**1879.** Value in centimes and franc.

| | | | | |
|---|---|---|---|---|
| 1 | **1** | 5c. black and yellow | £225 | 75·00 |
| 3 | **1** | 10c. black and green | £1000 | £200 |
| 5 | **1** | 25c. black and purple | £600 | 50·00 |
| 7 | **1** | 50c. black and blue | £850 | £170 |
| 8 | **1** | 1f. black and red | £130 | 50·00 |

**2** Large Lion

**1881.** Value in stotinki.

| | | | | |
|---|---|---|---|---|
| 10 | **2** | 3s. red and grey | 43·00 | 8·25 |
| 11 | **2** | 5s. black and yellow | 43·00 | 8·25 |
| 14 | **2** | 10s. black and green | £250 | 26·00 |
| 15 | **2** | 15s. red and green | £250 | 26·00 |
| 18 | **2** | 25s. black and purple | £1000 | £130 |
| 19 | **2** | 30s. blue and brown | 43·00 | 21·00 |

See also No. 275/9.

**A**

**B**

**C**

**D**

**1882**

| | | | |
|---|---|---|---|
| 46 | 1s. violet (Type A) | 38·00 | 12·50 |
| 48 | 1s. violet (Type C) | 2·75 | 50 |
| 47 | 2s. green (Type B) | 37·00 | 11·50 |
| 49 | 2s. green (Type D) | 2·75 | 50 |
| 21 | 3s. orange and yellow | 2·20 | 1·00 |
| 23 | 5s. green | 16·00 | 1·60 |
| 26 | 10s. red | 22·00 | 1·60 |
| 28 | 15s. purple and mauve | 22·00 | 1·30 |
| 31 | 25s. blue | 20·00 | 2·10 |
| 33 | 30s. lilac and green | 21·00 | 1·90 |
| 34 | 50s. blue and red | 21·00 | 1·90 |
| 50 | 1l. black and red | 75·00 | 9·50 |

**1884.** Surch with large figure of value.

| | | | |
|---|---|---|---|
| 38 | 3 on 10s. red | £110 | £100 |
| 43 | 5 on 30s. blue and brown | £110 | £100 |
| 45 | 15 on 25s. blue | £200 | £140 |
| 40 | 50 on 1f. black and red | £750 | £475 |

**7**

**1889**

| | | | | |
|---|---|---|---|---|
| 85 | **7** | 1s. mauve | 20 | 20 |
| 88 | **7** | 2s. grey | 1·30 | 1·00 |
| 89 | **7** | 3s. brown | 55 | 50 |
| 90 | **7** | 5s. green | 20 | 20 |
| 94 | **7** | 10s. red | 1·60 | 1·00 |
| 96 | **7** | 15s. orange | 1·10 | 50 |
| 100 | **7** | 25s. blue | 1·10 | 50 |
| 58 | **7** | 30s. brown | 18·00 | 1·00 |
| 59 | **7** | 50s. green | 1·10 | 50 |
| 60 | **7** | 1l. red | 1·10 | 1·00 |
| 83 | **7** | 2l. red and pink | 4·25 | 3·25 |
| 84 | **7** | 3l. black and buff | 6·50 | 7·25 |

**1892.** Surch 15.

| | | | |
|---|---|---|---|
| 61 | 15 on 30s. brown | 55·00 | 2·10 |

**1895.** Surch 01.

| | | | | |
|---|---|---|---|---|
| 74 | **2a** | 01 on 2s. green (No. 49) | 1·60 | 50 |

**11** Arms of Bulgaria

**1896.** Baptism of Prince Boris.

| | | | | |
|---|---|---|---|---|
| 78 | **11** | 1s. green | 55 | 30 |
| 79 | **11** | 5s. blue | 55 | 30 |
| 81 | **11** | 15s. violet | 65 | 50 |
| 82 | **11** | 25s. red | 9·25 | 3·25 |

**1901.** Surch in figures.

| | | | | |
|---|---|---|---|---|
| 101 | **7** | 5 on 3s. brown | 2·75 | 2·10 |
| 103 | **7** | 10 on 50s. green | 2·75 | 2·30 |

**13** Cherry wood Cannon used against the Turks

**1901.** 25th Anniv of Uprising against Turkey.

| | | | | |
|---|---|---|---|---|
| 104 | **13** | 5s. red | 2·20 | 1·60 |
| 105 | **13** | 15s. green | 2·20 | 1·60 |

**14** Prince Ferdinand

**1901**

| | | | | |
|---|---|---|---|---|
| 106 | **14** | 1s. black and purple | 35 | 15 |
| 107 | **14** | 2s. blue and green | 55 | 15 |
| 108 | **14** | 3s. black and orange | 55 | 15 |
| 109 | **14** | 5s. brown and green | 2·20 | 20 |
| 110 | **14** | 10s. brown and red | 3·25 | 20 |
| 113 | **14** | 15s. black and lake | 1·60 | 30 |
| 114 | **14** | 25s. black and blue | 1·60 | 15 |
| 116 | **14** | 30s. black and brown | 49·00 | 1·00 |
| 117 | **14** | 50s. brown and blue | 2·20 | 30 |
| 118 | **14** | 1l. green and red | 5·50 | 40 |
| 120 | **14** | 2l. black and red | 11·00 | 1·60 |
| 123 | **14** | 3l. red and grey | 16·00 | 7·25 |

**16** Fighting at Shipka Pass

**1902.** 25th Anniv of Battle of Shipka Pass.

| | | | | |
|---|---|---|---|---|
| 124 | **16** | 5s. red | 3·25 | 1·00 |
| 125 | **16** | 10s. green | 3·25 | 1·00 |
| 126 | **16** | 15s. blue | 13·00 | 5·25 |

**1903.** Surch.

| | | | | |
|---|---|---|---|---|
| 140 | **15** | 5 on 15s. black and red | 3·25 | 2·10 |
| 141 | **15** | 10 on 15s. black and red | 5·50 | 1·00 |
| 143 | **15** | 25 on 30s. black & brown | 18·00 | 2·10 |

**18** Ferdinand I in 1887 and 1907

**1907.** 20th Anniv of Prince Ferdinand's Accession.

| | | | | |
|---|---|---|---|---|
| 132 | **18** | 5s. green | 22·00 | 2·10 |
| 134 | **18** | 10s. brown | 33·00 | 2·30 |
| 137 | **18** | 25s. blue | 75·00 | 4·25 |

**1909.** Optd 1909.

| | | | | |
|---|---|---|---|---|
| 146 | **7** | 1s. mauve | 2·20 | 95 |
| 149 | **7** | 5s. green | 2·20 | 95 |

**1909.** Surch 1909 and new value.

| | | | |
|---|---|---|---|
| 151 | 5 on 30s. brown | 3·75 | 65 |
| 153 | 10 on 15s. orange | 3·75 | 1·30 |
| 156 | 10 on 50s. green | 3·75 | 1·30 |

**1910.** Surch 1910 and new value.

| | | | | |
|---|---|---|---|---|
| 157 | **14** | 1 on 3s. black and orange | 8·75 | 2·10 |
| 158 | **14** | 5 on 15s. black and lake | 2·20 | 1·60 |

**23** King Asen Tower

**24** Tsar in General's Uniform

**25** Veliko Turnovo

**1911**

| | | | | |
|---|---|---|---|---|
| 159 | **23** | 1s. green | 35 | 15 |
| 182a | **23** | 1s. slate | 20 | 15 |
| 160 | **24** | 2s. black and red | 35 | 15 |
| 161 | **25** | 3s. black and lake | 85 | 15 |
| 162 | - | 5s. black and green | 1·60 | 15 |
| 181 | - | 5s. purple and green | 4·25 | 20 |
| 163 | - | 10s. black and red | 2·75 | 20 |
| 181a | - | 10s. sepia and brown | 20 | 15 |
| 164 | - | 15s. bistre | 8·25 | 30 |
| 183 | - | 15s. olive | 70 | 15 |
| 165 | - | 25s. black and blue | 55 | 15 |
| 166 | - | 30s. black and blue | 8·25 | 30 |
| 182 | - | 30s. brown and olive | 55 | 20 |
| 167 | - | 50s. black and yellow | 43·00 | 50 |
| 168 | - | 1l. brown | 20·00 | 30 |
| 169 | - | 2l. black and purple | 3·75 | 1·30 |
| 170 | - | 3l. black and violet | 22·00 | 7·75 |

DESIGNS—VERT: 5, 10, 25s., 1l. Portraits of Tsar Ferdinand. HORIZ: 15s. R. Isker; 30s. Rila Monastery; 50s. Tsars and Princes (after Ya. Veshin); 2l. Monastery of the Holy Trinity, Veliko Turnovo; 3l. Varna.

See also Nos. 229/30 and 236/7.

**35** Tsar Ferdinand

**1912.** Tsar's Silver Jubilee.

| | | | | |
|---|---|---|---|---|
| 171 | **35** | 5s. grey | 5·50 | 2·10 |
| 172 | **35** | 10s. red | 7·50 | 3·75 |
| 173 | **35** | 25s. blue | 11·00 | 5·75 |

**ОСВОБ. ВОЙНА**

**1912-1913**

**(36)** "War of Liberation" 1912–13

**1913.** Victory over Turks. Stamps of 1911 optd as T 36.

| | | | | |
|---|---|---|---|---|
| 174 | **23** | 1s. green | 55 | 20 |
| 175 | **24** | 2s. black and red | 55 | 20 |
| 176 | **25** | 3s. black and lake | 2·20 | 50 |
| 177 | - | 5s. black and green | 55 | 20 |
| 178 | - | 10s. black and red | 55 | 20 |
| 179 | - | 15s. bistre | 3·25 | 1·60 |
| 180 | - | 25s. black and blue | 8·75 | 2·50 |

**1915.** No. 165 surch 10 CT. and bar.

| | | | |
|---|---|---|---|
| 180a | 10s. on 25s. blk & blue | 1·30 | 30 |

**3**
**СТОТИНКИ**
**(37a)**

**1916.** Red Cross Fund. Surch with T 37a.

| | | | | |
|---|---|---|---|---|
| 185 | **7** | 3s. on 1s. mauve | 13·00 | 12·50 |

**38**

**39** Bulgarian Peasant

**45** Veles

**46** Bulgarian Ploughman

**1917.** Liberation of Macedonia.

| | | | | |
|---|---|---|---|---|
| 193 | **45** | 1s. grey | 20 | 10 |
| 194 | **46** | 1s. green | 20 | 10 |
| 186 | **38** | 5s. green | 55 | 40 |
| 195 | - | 5s. green | 20 | 10 |
| 187 | **39** | 15s. grey | 20 | 20 |
| 188 | - | 25s. blue | 20 | 20 |
| 189 | - | 30s. orange | 20 | 30 |
| 190 | - | 50s. violet | 1·10 | 85 |
| 191 | - | 2l. brown | 1·10 | 85 |
| 192 | - | 3l. red | 1·60 | 1·40 |

DESIGNS—As Type **45**: 5s. Monastery of St. John, Ohrid. As Type **38**: 25s. Soldier and Mt. Sonichka; 50s. Ohrid and Lake. As Type **39**: 30s. Nish. 2l. Demir Kapija; 3l. Gevgeli.

**48** Tsar Ferdinand

**1918.** 30th Anniv of Tsar's Accession.

| | | | | |
|---|---|---|---|---|
| 196 | **48** | 1s. slate | 20 | 15 |
| 197 | **48** | 2s. brown | 20 | 15 |
| 198 | **48** | 3s. blue | 55 | 50 |
| 199 | **48** | 10s. red | 55 | 50 |

**49** Parliament Building

**1919**

| | | | | |
|---|---|---|---|---|
| 201 | **49** | 1s. black | 20 | 15 |
| 202 | **49** | 2s. olive | 20 | 15 |

**50** King Boris III

**1919.** 1st Anniv of Enthronement of King Boris III.

| | | | | |
|---|---|---|---|---|
| 203 | **50** | 3s. red | 20 | 15 |
| 204 | **50** | 5s. green | 20 | 15 |
| 205 | **50** | 10s. red | 20 | 15 |
| 206 | **50** | 15s. violet | 20 | 15 |
| 207 | **50** | 25s. blue | 20 | 15 |
| 208 | **50** | 30s. brown | 20 | 15 |
| 209 | **50** | 50s. brown | 20 | 15 |

**(52)** **(53)**

**1920.** Prisoners of War Fund. Surch as T 52/53.

| | | | | |
|---|---|---|---|---|
| 210 | **49** | 1 on 2s. olive | 20 | 15 |
| 211 | **50** | 2½ on 5s. green | 20 | 15 |
| 212 | **50** | 5 on 10s. red | 20 | 15 |
| 213 | **50** | 7½ on 15s. violet | 20 | 15 |
| 214 | **50** | 12½ on 25s. blue | 20 | 15 |
| 215 | **50** | 15 on 30s. brown | 20 | 15 |
| 216 | **50** | 25 on 50s. brown | 20 | 15 |
| 217 | - | 50 on 1l. brown (No. 168) | 55 | 30 |
| 218 | - | 1 on 2l. brown (No. 191) | 55 | 50 |
| 219 | - | 1½ on 3l. red (No. 192) | 1·60 | 1·00 |

**54** Vazov's Birthplace at Sopot and Cherry-wood Cannon

**55** "The Bear-fighter", character from "Under the Yoke"

**1920.** 70th Birth Anniv of Ivan Vazov (writer).

| | | | | |
|---|---|---|---|---|
| 220 | **54** | 30s. red | 20 | 15 |
| 221 | **55** | 50s. green | 45 | 20 |
| 222 | - | 1l. sepia | 75 | 50 |
| 223 | - | 2l. brown | 2·20 | 1·30 |
| 224 | - | 3l. violet | 2·75 | 1·80 |
| 225 | - | 5l. blue | 3·75 | 2·30 |

DESIGNS—HORIZ: 1l. Ivan Vazov in 1870 and 1920; 3l. Vazov's Houses in Plovdiv and Sofia. VERT: 2l. Vazov; 5l. Father Paisii Khilendarski (historian).

**59** Aleksandr Nevski Cathedral, Sofia

**62** King Boris III

**1921**

| | | | | |
|---|---|---|---|---|
| 226 | **59** | 10s. violet | 20 | 15 |
| 227 | - | 20s. green | 20 | 15 |
| 228 | **62** | 25s. blue | 20 | 15 |
| 229 | **25** | 50s. orange | 45 | 20 |
| 230 | **25** | 50s. blue | 9·25 | 3·50 |
| 231 | - | 75s. violet | 20 | 15 |
| 232 | - | 75s. blue | 55 | 20 |
| 233 | **62** | 1l. red | 55 | 20 |
| 234 | **62** | 1l. blue | 45 | 15 |
| 235 | - | 2l. brown | 1·60 | 20 |
| 236 | - | 3l. purple | 1·60 | 20 |
| 237 | - | 5l. blue | 8·75 | 40 |
| 238 | **62** | 10l. red | 22·00 | 4·75 |

DESIGNS—HORIZ: 20s. Alexander II "The Liberator" Monument, Sofia; 75s. Shipka Pass Monastery; 5l. Rila Monastery. VERT: 2l. Harvester; 3l. King Asen Tower.

**66** Tsar Ferdinand and Map

**68** Mt. Shar

**1921**

| | | | | |
|---|---|---|---|---|
| 239 | **66** | 10s. red | 20 | 15 |
| 240 | - | 10s. red | 20 | 15 |
| 241 | **68** | 10s. red | 20 | 15 |
| 242 | - | 10s. mauve | 20 | 15 |
| 243 | - | 20s. blue | 85 | 20 |

DESIGNS—VERT: No. 240, Tsar Ferdinand. HORIZ: No. 242, Bridge over Vardar, at Skopje; 243, St. Clement's Monastery, Ohrid.

**71** Bourchier in Bulgarian Costume

**72** J. D. Bourchier

**73** Rila Monastery, Bourchier's Resting-place

**1921.** James Bourchier ("Times" Correspondent) Commemoration.

| | | | | |
|---|---|---|---|---|
| 244 | **71** | 10s. red | 20 | 20 |
| 245 | **71** | 20s. orange | 20 | 20 |
| 246 | **72** | 30s. grey | 20 | 20 |
| 247 | **72** | 50s. lilac | 20 | 20 |
| 248 | **72** | 1l. purple | 55 | 20 |
| 249 | **73** | 1½l. green | 55 | 40 |
| 250 | **73** | 2l. green | 55 | 30 |
| 251 | **73** | 3l. blue | 1·30 | 50 |
| 252 | **73** | 5l. red | 2·40 | 1·20 |

**1924.** Surch.

| | | | | |
|---|---|---|---|---|
| 253 | **49** | 10s. on 1s. black | 20 | 15 |
| 254 | **D 37** | 10s. on 20s. orange | 20 | 15 |
| 255 | **D 37** | 20s. on 5s. green | 27·00 | 26·00 |
| 256 | **D 37** | 20s. on 10s. violet | 8·25 | 7·75 |
| 257 | **D 37** | 20s. on 30s. orange | 20 | 15 |
| 258 | **50** | 1l. on 5s. green | 35 | 15 |
| 259 | **25** | 3l. on 50s. blue | 1·10 | 30 |
| 260 | **62** | 6l. on 1l. red | 2·20 | 65 |

**77** **78** **79** King Boris III

**81** Aleksandr Nevski Cathedral, Sofia

**82** Harvesters

**1925**

| | | | | |
|---|---|---|---|---|
| 261 | **77** | 10s. blue & red on rose | 35 | 20 |
| 262 | **77** | 15s. orange & red on blue | 35 | 20 |
| 263 | **77** | 30s. buff and black | 35 | 20 |
| 264 | **78** | 50s. brown on green | 35 | 20 |
| 265 | **79** | 1l. olive | 1·00 | 20 |
| 266 | **79** | 1l. green | 1·20 | 20 |
| 267 | **81** | 2l. green and buff | 4·25 | 20 |
| 267a | **79** | 2l. brown | 1·60 | 20 |
| 268 | **82** | 4l. red and yellow | 4·25 | 20 |

**83** Proposed Rest-home, Verona

**1925.** Sunday Delivery Stamps.

| | | | | |
|---|---|---|---|---|
| 268b | **83** | 1l. black on green | 11·00 | 30 |
| 268c | **83** | 1l. brown | 11·00 | 30 |
| 268d | **83** | 1l. orange | 16·00 | 50 |
| 268e | **83** | 1l. pink | 14·00 | 50 |
| 268f | **83** | 1l. violet on red | 16·00 | 50 |
| 268g | - | 2l. green | 1·60 | 30 |
| 268h | - | 2l. violet | 1·60 | 30 |
| 268i | - | 5l. blue | 17·00 | 1·30 |
| 268j | - | 5l. red | 17·00 | 1·30 |

DESIGN: 2, 5l., Proposed Sanatorium, Bankya.

**85** St. Nedelya's Cathedral, Sofia after Bomb Outrage

**1926**

| | | | | |
|---|---|---|---|---|
| 269 | **85** | 50s. black | 35 | 20 |

**86** C. Botev (poet)

**1926.** Botev Commemoration.

| | | | | |
|---|---|---|---|---|
| 270 | **86** | 1l. green | 1·30 | 50 |
| 271 | **86** | 2l. blue | 2·75 | 50 |
| 272 | **86** | 4l. red | 3·75 | 2·50 |

**87**

**1926**

| | | | | |
|---|---|---|---|---|
| 273 | **87** | 6l. olive and blue | 2·20 | 30 |
| 274 | **87** | 10l. brown and sepia | 16·00 | 4·00 |

**1927.** As T 2 in new colours.

| | | | | |
|---|---|---|---|---|
| 275 | | 10s. red and green | 20 | 20 |
| 276 | | 15s. black and yellow | 20 | 20 |
| 277 | | 30s. slate and buff | 20 | 20 |
| 278 | | 30s. blue and buff | 20 | 20 |
| 279 | | 50s. black and red | 20 | 20 |

**1927.** Air. Various stamps optd with Albatros biplane and No. 281 surch 1l also.

| | | | | |
|---|---|---|---|---|
| 281 | | 1l. on 6l. green and blue | 2·20 | 2·10 |
| 282 | **79** | 2l. brown | 2·20 | 2·10 |
| 283 | **82** | 4l. red and yellow | 3·25 | 2·10 |
| 284 | **87** | 10l. orange and brown | 85·00 | 50·00 |

**89** King Boris III

**1928**

| | | | | |
|---|---|---|---|---|
| 285 | **89** | 1l. green | 3·25 | 20 |
| 286 | **89** | 2l. brown | 4·25 | 20 |

**90** Saint Clement of Ohrid

**1929.** 50th Anniv of Liberation of Bulgaria and Millenary of Tsar Simeon.

| | | | | |
|---|---|---|---|---|
| 287 | **90** | 10s. violet | 30 | 10 |
| 288 | - | 15a. purple | 30 | 10 |
| 289 | - | 30s. red | 30 | 10 |
| 290 | - | 50s. green | 75 | 20 |
| 291 | - | 1l. red | 1·90 | 20 |
| 292 | - | 2l. blue | 2·10 | 20 |
| 293 | - | 3l. green | 5·25 | 1·00 |
| 294 | - | 4l. brown | 9·50 | 40 |
| 295 | - | 5l. brown | 7·25 | 1·00 |
| 296 | - | 6l. blue | 9·25 | 2·50 |

PORTRAITS—23½×33½ mm: 15s. Konstantin Miladinov (poet and folklorist); 1l. Father Paisii Khilendarski (historian); 2l. Tsar Simeon; 4l. Vasil Levski (revolutionary); 5l. Georgi Benkovski (revolutionary); 6l. Tsar Alexander II of Russia, "The Liberator". 19×28½ mm: 30s. Georgi Rakovski (writer). 19×26 mm: 3l. Lyuben Karavelov (journalist).

**98** Convalescent Home, Varna

**1930.** Sunday Delivery stamps.

| | | | | |
|---|---|---|---|---|
| 297 | **98** | 1l. green and purple | 18·00 | 30 |
| 298 | **98** | 1l. yellow and green | 2·10 | 30 |
| 299 | **98** | 1l. brown and red | 2·10 | 30 |

**99**

**1930.** Wedding of King Boris and Princess Giovanna of Italy.

| | | | | |
|---|---|---|---|---|
| 300 | **99** | 1l. green | 50 | 40 |
| 301 | - | 2l. purple | 85 | 50 |
| 302 | **99** | 4l. red | 85 | 50 |
| 303 | - | 6l. blue | 1·00 | 55 |

DESIGN: 2, 6l. Portraits in separate ovals.

**101** King Boris III

**1931**

| | | | | |
|---|---|---|---|---|
| 304a | **101** | 1l. green (A) | 1·30 | 20 |
| 305 | **101** | 2l. red (A) | 1·30 | 20 |
| 306 | **101** | 4l. orange (A) | 1·80 | 20 |
| 308a | **101** | 4l. orange (B) | 1·00 | 20 |
| 307 | **101** | 6l. blue (A) | 1·30 | 20 |
| 308b | **101** | 6l. blue (B) | 2·75 | 20 |
| 308c | **101** | 7l. blue (B) | 40 | 20 |
| 308d | **101** | 10l. slate (B) | 42·00 | 2·50 |
| 308 | **101** | 12l. brown (A) | 1·00 | 30 |
| 308e | **101** | 14l. brown (B) | 95 | 50 |
| 308f | - | 20l. brown & pur (B) | 2·50 | 1·00 |

(A) Without coloured frame-lines at top and bottom; (B) with frame-lines.

The 20l. is 24½×33½ mm.

**103** Gymnastics

**1931.** Balkan Olympic Games.

| | | | | |
|---|---|---|---|---|
| 309 | **103** | 1l. green | 3·25 | 1·50 |
| 326 | **103** | 1l. turquoise | 4·25 | 4·00 |
| 310 | - | 2l. red | 4·25 | 2·00 |
| 327 | - | 2l. blue | 6·25 | 4·50 |
| 311 | - | 4l. red | 9·50 | 2·50 |
| 328 | - | 4l. purple | 10·50 | 5·50 |
| 312 | - | 6l. green | 21·00 | 6·00 |
| 329 | - | 6l. red | 21·00 | 10·00 |
| 313 | - | 10l. orange | 42·00 | 15·00 |
| 330 | - | 10l. brown | £160 | 65·00 |
| 314 | - | 12l. blue | £130 | 40·00 |
| 331 | - | 12l. orange | £250 | £100 |
| 315 | - | 50l. brown | £140 | 85·00 |
| 332 | - | 50l. red | £750 | £750 |

DESIGNS—VERT (23×28 mm): 2l. Footballer; 4l. Horse-riding. As Type **103**—HORIZ: 6l. Fencing; 10l. Cycling. VERT: 12l. Diving; 50l. Spirit of Victory.

**108**

**1931.** Air.

| | | | | |
|---|---|---|---|---|
| 316 | **108** | 1l. green | 85 | 30 |
| 316a | **108** | 1l. purple | 50 | 20 |
| 317 | **108** | 2l. purple | 85 | 30 |
| 317a | **108** | 2l. green | 65 | 30 |
| 318 | **108** | 6l. blue | 1·00 | 50 |
| 318a | **108** | 6l. red | 1·60 | 60 |
| 319 | **108** | 12l. red | 2·10 | 50 |
| 319a | **108** | 12l. blue | 1·80 | 70 |
| 320 | **108** | 20l. violet | 2·10 | 1·00 |
| 321 | **108** | 30l. orange | 4·25 | 2·00 |
| 322 | **108** | 50l. brown | 5·75 | 3·50 |

**109** Rila Monastery

**1932.** Air.

| | | | | |
|---|---|---|---|---|
| 323 | **109** | 18l. green | £140 | 70·00 |
| 324 | **109** | 24l. red | 95·00 | 45·00 |
| 325 | **109** | 28l. blue | 50·00 | 35·00 |

**1934.** Surch 2.

| | | | | |
|---|---|---|---|---|
| 333 | **101** | 2 on 3l. olive | 13·50 | 1·00 |

**111** Defending the Pass

**1934.** Unveiling of Shipka Pass Memorial.

| | | | | |
|---|---|---|---|---|
| 334A | **111** | 1l. green | 2·10 | 1·00 |
| 340A | **111** | 1l. green | 2·10 | 1·00 |
| 335A | - | 2l. red | 1·60 | 50 |
| 341A | - | 2l. orange | 1·60 | 50 |
| 336A | - | 3l. brown | 5·25 | 3·00 |
| 342A | - | 3l. yellow | 5·25 | 3·00 |
| 337A | - | 4l. red | 3·75 | 1·00 |
| 343A | - | 4l. red | 3·75 | 1·00 |

| | | | | |
|---|---|---|---|---|
| 338A | - | 7l. blue | 7·25 | 3·50 |
| 344A | - | 7l. light blue | 7·25 | 3·50 |
| 339A | - | 14l. purple | 27·00 | 18·00 |
| 345 | - | 14l. bistre | 27·00 | 18·00 |

DESIGNS—VERT: 2l. Shipka Memorial; 3, 7l. Veteran standard-bearer; 14l. Widow showing memorial to orphans. HORIZ: 4l. Bulgarian veteran.

**113** Convalescent Home, Troyan

**1935.** Sunday Delivery stamps.

| | | | | |
|---|---|---|---|---|
| 346 | **113** | 1l. red and brown | 2·10 | 30 |
| 347 | **113** | 1l. blue and green | 2·10 | 30 |
| 348 | - | 5l. blue and red | 6·75 | 1·50 |

DESIGN: 5l. Convalescent Home, Bakya.

**114** Capt. Georgi Mamarchef

**1935.** Centenary of Turnovo Insurrection.

| | | | | |
|---|---|---|---|---|
| 349 | | 1l. blue | 3·25 | 80 |
| 350 | **114** | 2l. purple | 3·25 | 1·20 |

DESIGN: 1l. Velcho Atanasov Dzhamdzhiyata.

**115** Aleksandr Nevski Cathedral, Sofia

**1935.** 5th Balkan Football Tournament.

| | | | | |
|---|---|---|---|---|
| 351 | - | 1l. green | 8·25 | 6·00 |
| 352 | **115** | 2l. grey | 12·50 | 8·00 |
| 353 | - | 4l. red | 16·00 | 10·00 |
| 354 | - | 7l. blue | 29·00 | 20·00 |
| 355 | - | 14l. orange | 26·00 | 20·00 |
| 356 | - | 50l. brown | £475 | £400 |

DESIGNS—HORIZ: 1l. Match in progress at Yunak Stadium, Sofia; 4l. Footballers. VERT: 7l. Herald and Balkan map; 14l. Footballer and trophy; 50l. Trophy.

**116** Girl Gymnast

**1935.** 8th Bulgarian Gymnastic Tournament. Dated "12–14. VII. 1935".

| | | | | |
|---|---|---|---|---|
| 357 | | 1l. green | 9·50 | 8·00 |
| 358 | | 2l. blue | 10·50 | 9·00 |
| 359 | **116** | 4l. red | 13·50 | 11·00 |
| 360 | - | 7l. blue | 16·00 | 16·00 |
| 361 | - | 14l. brown | 16·00 | 15·00 |
| 362 | - | 50l. orange | £325 | £250 |

DESIGNS—VERT: 1l. Parallel bars; 2l. Male gymnast in uniform; 7l. Pole vault; 50l. Athlete and lion. HORIZ: 14l. Yunak Stadium, Sofia.

**117** Janos Hunyadi

**1935.** Unveiling of Monument to Ladislas III of Poland at Varna. Inscr "WARNEN CZYK(A)", etc.

| | | | | |
|---|---|---|---|---|
| 363A | **117** | 1l. orange | 3·25 | 1·00 |
| 364B | - | 2l. red | 5·00 | 1·50 |
| 365A | - | 4l. red | 26·00 | 7·00 |
| 366A | - | 7l. blue | 4·75 | 1·90 |
| 367A | - | 14l. green | 4·75 | 1·80 |

DESIGNS—VERT: 2l. King Ladislas of Hungary enthroned (22×32 mm); 7l. King Ladislas in armour (20×31 mm). HORIZ: 4l. Varna Memorial (33×24 mm); 14l. Battle scene (30×25 mm).

**118** Dimitur

**1935.** 67th Death Anniv of Khadzhi Dimitur (revolutionary).

| | | | | |
|---|---|---|---|---|
| 368A | | 1l. green | 3·25 | 1·00 |
| 369A | **118** | 2l. brown | 5·25 | 2·00 |
| 370A | - | 4l. red | 14·50 | 5·00 |
| 371A | - | 7l. blue | 21·00 | 9·00 |
| 372A | - | 14l. orange | 26·00 | 10·00 |

DESIGNS—VERT: 1l. Dimitur's monument at Sliven; 7l. Revolutionary group (dated 1868). HORIZ: 4l. Dimitur and Stefan Karadzha (revolutionary); 14l. Dimitur's birthplace at Sliven.

**119**

**120**

**1936**

| | | | | |
|---|---|---|---|---|
| 373 | **119** | 10s. red | 20 | 15 |
| 373a | **119** | 15s. green | 20 | 15 |
| 374 | **120** | 30s. red | 30 | 15 |
| 374a | **120** | 30s. brown | 20 | 15 |
| 374b | **120** | 30s. blue | 20 | 15 |
| 375 | **120** | 50s. blue | 30 | 15 |
| 375a | **120** | 50s. red | 30 | 15 |
| 375b | **120** | 50s. green | 20 | 15 |

**121** Nesebur

**1936.** Slav Geographical and Ethnographical Congress, Sofia.

| | | | | |
|---|---|---|---|---|
| 376 | - | 1l. violet | 4·25 | 2·00 |
| 377 | - | 2l. blue | 4·25 | 2·00 |
| 378 | **121** | 7l. blue | 8·25 | 4·00 |

DESIGNS—25×34 mm: 1l. Meteorological Bureau, Mt. Musala; 23×34 mm: 2l. Peasant girl.

**122** St. Cyril and St. Methodius

**1937.** Millenary of Introduction of Cyrillic Alphabet and Slavonic Liturgy.

| | | | | |
|---|---|---|---|---|
| 379 | **122** | 1l. green | 75 | 30 |
| 380 | **122** | 2l. purple | 75 | 30 |
| 381 | - | 4l. red | 85 | 30 |
| 382 | **122** | 7l. blue | 4·25 | 2·20 |
| 383 | - | 14l. red | 4·25 | 2·30 |

DESIGN: 4., 14l. The Saints Preaching.

**124** Princess Marie Louise

**1937**

| | | | | |
|---|---|---|---|---|
| 384 | **124** | 1l. green | 75 | 20 |
| 385 | **124** | 2l. red | 85 | 20 |
| 386 | **124** | 4l. red | 85 | 50 |

**125** King Boris III

**1937.** 19th Anniv of Accession.

| | | | | |
|---|---|---|---|---|
| 387 | **125** | 2l. red | 1·00 | 50 |

**MS**387a 76×115 mm. **125** 2l. (+18l.) ultramarine. Imperf. 10·50 20·00

**126** Harvesting

**1938.** Agricultural Products.

| | | | | |
|---|---|---|---|---|
| 388 | **126** | 10s. orange | 20 | 10 |
| 389 | **126** | 10s. red | 20 | 10 |
| 390 | - | 15s. red | 50 | 10 |
| 391 | - | 15s. purple | 50 | 10 |
| 392 | - | 30s. brown | 40 | 10 |
| 393 | - | 30s. brown | 45 | 10 |
| 394 | - | 50s. blue | 95 | 10 |
| 395 | - | 50s. black | 95 | 10 |
| 396 | - | 1l. green | 1·00 | 10 |
| 397 | - | 1l. green | 1·00 | 10 |
| 398 | - | 2l. red | 1·00 | 20 |
| 399 | - | 2l. brown | 1·00 | 20 |
| 400 | - | 3l. purple | 2·10 | 1·00 |
| 401 | - | 3l. purple | 2·10 | 1·00 |
| 402 | - | 4l. brown | 1·60 | 50 |
| 403 | - | 4l. purple | 1·60 | 50 |
| 404 | - | 7l. violet | 3·25 | 1·00 |
| 405 | - | 7l. blue | 3·25 | 1·00 |
| 406 | - | 14l. brown | 5·25 | 2·00 |
| 407 | - | 14l. brown | 5·25 | 2·00 |

DESIGNS—VERT: 15s. Sunflower; 30s. Wheat; 50s. Chickens and eggs; 1l. Grapes; 3l. Strawberries; 4l. Girl carrying grapes; 7l. Roses; 14l. Tobacco leaves. HORIZ: 2l. "Attar of Roses".

**129** Prince Simeon

**1938.** 1st Birthday of Heir Apparent.

| | | | | |
|---|---|---|---|---|
| 408 | **129** | 1l. green | 30 | 20 |
| 409 | **129** | 2l. red | 30 | 20 |
| 410 | - | 4l. red | 40 | 25 |
| 411 | **129** | 7l. blue | 1·60 | 80 |
| 412 | - | 14l. brown | 1·60 | 80 |

DESIGN: 4, 14l. Another portrait.

**131** King Boris III

**1938.** 20th Anniv of King's Accession. Portraits of King in various uniforms.

| | | | | |
|---|---|---|---|---|
| 413 | **131** | 1l. green | 25 | 20 |
| 414 | - | 2l. red | 1·30 | 30 |
| 415 | - | 4l. brown | 40 | 30 |
| 416 | - | 7l. blue | 65 | 50 |
| 417 | - | 14l. mauve | 65 | 50 |

**132** Class 01 Steam Locomotive

**1939.** 50th Anniv of Bulgarian State Railways. Locomotive types dated "1888–1938".

| | | | | |
|---|---|---|---|---|
| 418 | | 1l. green | 50 | 40 |
| 419 | **132** | 2l. brown | 50 | 40 |

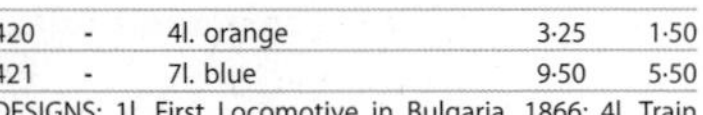

| | | | | |
|---|---|---|---|---|
| 420 | - | 4l. orange | 3·25 | 1·50 |
| 421 | - | 7l. blue | 9·50 | 5·50 |

DESIGNS: 1l. First Locomotive in Bulgaria, 1866; 4l. Train crossing viaduct; 7l. King Boris as engine-driver.

**133** P.O. Emblem

**1939.** 60th Anniv of Bulgarian P.O. Inscr "1879 1939".

| | | | | |
|---|---|---|---|---|
| 422 | **133** | 1l. green | 40 | 10 |
| 423 | - | 2l. red (G.P.O., Sofia) | 50 | 15 |

**135** Gymnast

**1939.** Yunak Gymnastic Society's Rally, Sofia.

| | | | | |
|---|---|---|---|---|
| 424 | **135** | 1l. green | 50 | 40 |
| 425 | - | 2l. red | 50 | 40 |
| 426 | - | 4l. brown | 1·00 | 50 |
| 427 | - | 7l. blue | 3·25 | 1·50 |
| 428 | - | 14l. mauve | 16·00 | 12·00 |

DESIGNS: 2l. Yunak badge; 4l. "The Discus-thrower" (statue by Miron); 7l. Rhythmic dancer; 14l. Athlete holding weight aloft.

Наводненето
1939

**1+1**

**лева**

**(136)** ("Inundation 1939")

**1939.** Sevlievo and Turnovo Floods Relief Fund. Surch as T 136 and value.

| | | | | |
|---|---|---|---|---|
| 429 | **39** | 1l.+1l. on 15s. grey | 20 | 45 |
| 430 | **73** | 2l.+1l. on 1½l. olive | 30 | 50 |
| 431 | **73** | 4l.+2l. on 2l. green | 35 | 60 |
| 432 | **73** | 7l.+4l. on 3l. blue | 1·00 | 1·50 |
| 433 | **73** | 14l.+7l. on 5l. red | 1·60 | 2·50 |

**137** Mail Plane

**1940.** Air.

| | | | | |
|---|---|---|---|---|
| 434 | **137** | 1l. green | 20 | 15 |
| 435 | - | 2l. red | 2·50 | 15 |
| 436 | - | 4l. orange | 20 | 15 |
| 437 | - | 6l. blue | 40 | 20 |
| 438 | - | 10l. brown | 75 | 30 |
| 439 | - | 12l. brown | 1·00 | 50 |
| 440 | - | 16l. violet | 1·60 | 80 |
| 441 | - | 19l. blue | 1·70 | 1·00 |
| 442 | - | 30l. mauve | 2·50 | 1·50 |
| 443 | - | 45l. violet | 6·75 | 3·75 |
| 444 | - | 70l. red | 5·25 | 4·00 |
| 445 | - | 100l. blue | 21·00 | 14·00 |

DESIGNS—VERT: Aircraft over: King Asen's Tower (2l.), Bachovo Monastery (4l.), Aleksandr Nevski Cathedral, Sofia (45l.), Shipka Pass Memorial (70l.); 10l. Airplane, mail train and express motor cycle; 30l. Airplane and swallow; 100l. Airplane and Royal cypher. HORIZ: 6l. Loading mails at aerodrome. Aircraft over: Sofia Palace (12l.), Mt. El Tepe (16l.), Rila Lakes and mountains (19l.).

**138** King Boris III

**1940**

| | | | | |
|---|---|---|---|---|
| 445a | **138** | 1l. green | 40 | 20 |
| 446 | **138** | 2l. red | 50 | 20 |

**139** First Bulgarian Postage Stamp

**1940.** Cent of 1st Adhesive Postage Stamp.

| | | | | |
|---|---|---|---|---|
| 447 | **139** | 10l. olive | 3·25 | 2·50 |
| 448 | - | 20l. blue | 3·25 | 2·50 |

DESIGN: 20l. has scroll dated "1840–1940".

**140** Grapes **141** Ploughing **142** King Boris III

**1940**

| | | | | |
|---|---|---|---|---|
| 449 | **140** | 10s. orange | 20 | 15 |
| 450 | - | 15s. blue | 20 | 15 |
| 451 | **141** | 30s. brown | 20 | 15 |
| 452 | - | 50s. violet | 20 | 15 |
| 452a | - | 50s. green | 20 | 15 |
| 453 | **142** | 1l. green | 20 | 15 |
| 454 | **142** | 2l. red | 30 | 15 |
| 455 | **142** | 4l. orange | 30 | 15 |
| 456 | **142** | 6l. violet | 50 | 20 |
| 457 | **142** | 7l. blue | 30 | 15 |
| 458 | **142** | 10l. green | 50 | 20 |

DESIGNS—VERT: 15s. Beehive. HORIZ: 50s. Shepherd and flock.

**143** Peasant Couple and King Boris **144** King Boris and Map of Dobrudja

**1940.** Recovery of Dobrudja from Rumania. Designs incorporating miniature portrait of King Boris.

| | | | | |
|---|---|---|---|---|
| 464 | **143** | 1l. green | 20 | 15 |
| 465 | - | 2l. red | 30 | 20 |
| 466 | **144** | 4l. brown | 50 | 30 |
| 467 | **144** | 7l. blue | 1·00 | 80 |

DESIGN—VERT: 2l. Bulgarian flags and wheat-field.

**145** Bee-keeping

**1940.** Agricultural Scenes.

| | | | | |
|---|---|---|---|---|
| 468 | - | 10s. purple | 20 | 15 |
| 469 | - | 10s. blue | 20 | 15 |
| 470 | - | 15s. green | 20 | 15 |
| 471 | - | 15s. olive | 20 | 15 |
| 472 | **145** | 30s. orange | 20 | 15 |
| 473 | **145** | 30s. green | 20 | 15 |
| 474 | - | 50s. violet | 20 | 15 |
| 475 | - | 50s. purple | 20 | 15 |
| 476 | - | 3l. brown | 85 | 20 |
| 477 | - | 3l. black | 1·90 | 1·00 |
| 478 | - | 5l. brown | 1·60 | 80 |
| 479 | - | 5l. blue | 2·10 | 1·50 |

DESIGNS: 10s. Threshing; 15s. Ploughing with oxen; 50s. Picking apples; 3l. Shepherd; 5l. Cattle.

**146** Pencko Slaveikov (poet) **147** St. Ivan Rilski

**1940.** National Relief.

| | | | | |
|---|---|---|---|---|
| 480 | **146** | 1l. green | 20 | 15 |
| 481 | - | 2l. red | 20 | 15 |
| 482 | **147** | 3l. brown | 25 | 20 |
| 483 | - | 4l. orange | 30 | 20 |
| 484 | - | 7l. blue | 2·10 | 1·50 |
| 485 | - | 10l. brown | 3·25 | 2·00 |

DESIGNS: 2l. Bishop Sofronii of Vratsa; 4l. Marin Drinov (historian); 7l. Chernorisets Khratur (monk); 10l. Kolo Ficheto (writer).

**148** Johannes Gutenberg **149** Nikola Karastoyanov

**1940.** 500th Anniv of Invention of Printing and Centenary of Bulgarian Printing.

| | | | | |
|---|---|---|---|---|
| 486 | **148** | 1l. green | 40 | 20 |
| 487 | **149** | 2l. brown | 50 | 20 |

**150** Botev **151** Arrival in Koslodui

**1941.** 65th Death Anniv of Khristo Botev (poet and revolutionary).

| | | | | |
|---|---|---|---|---|
| 488 | **150** | 1l. green | 20 | 20 |
| 489 | **151** | 2l. red | 50 | 30 |
| 490 | - | 3l. brown | 1·40 | 1·00 |

DESIGN—VERT: 3l. Botev Memorial Cross.

**152** National History Museum

**1941.** Buildings in Sofia.

| | | | | |
|---|---|---|---|---|
| 491 | **152** | 14l. brown | 75 | 40 |
| 492 | - | 20l. green | 85 | 50 |
| 493 | - | 50l. blue | 3·75 | 2·00 |

DESIGNS: 20l. Tsarita Icanna Workers' Hospital; 50l. National Bank.

**153** Thasos Island **154** Ohrid

**1941.** Reacquisition of Macedonia.

| | | | | |
|---|---|---|---|---|
| 494 | | 1l. green | 20 | 15 |
| 495 | **153** | 2l. orange | 20 | 15 |
| 496 | - | 2l. red | 20 | 15 |
| 497 | - | 4l. brown | 20 | 15 |
| 498 | **154** | 7l. blue | 95 | 70 |

DESIGNS—VERT: 1l. Macedonian girl. HORIZ: 2l. (No. 496) King Boris and map dated "1941"; 4l. Poganovski Monastery.

**155** Children on Beach

**1942.** Sunday Delivery. Inscr as in T 155.

| | | | | |
|---|---|---|---|---|
| 499 | - | 1l. green | 20 | 15 |
| 500 | **155** | 2l. orange | 30 | 20 |
| 501 | - | 5l. blue | 1·00 | 40 |

DESIGNS: 1l. St. Konstantin Sanatorium, Varna; 5l. Sunbathing terrace, Bankya.

**156** Bugler at Camp **157** Folk Dancers

**1942.** "Work and Joy". Inscr as at foot of T 157.

| | | | | |
|---|---|---|---|---|
| 502 | | 1l. green | 20 | 15 |
| 503 | | 2l. red | 30 | 15 |
| 504 | | 4l. black | 40 | 20 |
| 505 | **156** | 7l. blue | 50 | 30 |
| 506 | **157** | 14l. brown | 65 | 40 |

DESIGNS—VERT: 1l. Guitarist and accordion player; 2l. Camp orchestra; 4l. Hoisting the flag.

**158** Wounded Soldier **159** Queen visiting Wounded

**1942.** War Invalids. Inscr as T 158/9.

| | | | | |
|---|---|---|---|---|
| 507 | **158** | 1l. green | 20 | 15 |
| 508 | - | 2l. red | 20 | 15 |
| 509 | - | 4l. orange | 20 | 15 |
| 510 | - | 7l. blue | 20 | 15 |
| 511 | - | 14l. brown | 30 | 15 |
| 512 | **159** | 20l. black | 65 | 20 |

DESIGNS—HORIZ: 2l. Soldier and family; 4l. First aid on battlefield; 7l. Widow and orphans at grave; 14l. Unknown Soldiers Memorial.

**160** Khan Kubrat (ruled 595–642)

**1942.** Historical series.

| | | | | |
|---|---|---|---|---|
| 513 | **160** | 10s. black | 20 | 15 |
| 514 | - | 15s. blue | 20 | 15 |
| 515 | - | 30s. mauve | 20 | 15 |
| 516 | - | 50s. blue | 20 | 15 |
| 517 | - | 1l. green | 20 | 15 |
| 518 | - | 2l. red | 20 | 15 |
| 519 | - | 3l. brown | 20 | 15 |
| 520 | - | 4l. orange | 20 | 15 |
| 521 | - | 5l. green | 20 | 15 |
| 522 | - | 7l. blue | 20 | 15 |
| 523 | - | 10l. black | 20 | 15 |
| 524 | - | 14l. olive | 40 | 20 |
| 525 | - | 20l. brown | 1·00 | 70 |
| 526 | - | 30l. black | 2·10 | 1·00 |

DESIGNS: 15s. Cavalry charge (Khan as parukh, 680–701); 30s. Equestrian statue of Khan Krum (803–814); 50s. Baptism of King Boris I; 1l. St. Naum's School; 2l. King Boris crowns his son, Tsar Simeon; 3l. Golden Era of Bulgarian literature; 4l. Trial of Bogomil Vasilii; 5l. Proclamation of Second Bulgarian Empire; 7l. Ivan Asen II (1214–81) at Tebizond; 10l. Expulsion of Eutimil Patriarch of Turnovo; 14l. Wandering minstrels; 20l. Father Paisii Khilendarski (historian); 30l. Shipka Pass Memorial.

**161** King Boris III

**1944.** King Boris Mourning Issue. Portraits dated "1894–1943". Perf or imperf.

| | | | | |
|---|---|---|---|---|
| 527A | **161** | 1l. olive | 20 | 20 |
| 528A | - | 2l. brown | 25 | 25 |
| 529A | - | 4l. brown | 30 | 30 |
| 530A | - | 5l. violet | 85 | 85 |
| 531A | - | 7l. blue | 1·00 | 1·00 |

**163** King Simeon II

**1944**

| | | | | |
|---|---|---|---|---|
| 532A | **163** | 3l. orange | 20 | 10 |

ВСИЧКО
ЗА
ФРОНТА
**(164)**

**1945.** "All for the Front". Parcel Post stamps optd as T 164 or surch also.

| | | | | |
|---|---|---|---|---|
| 533 | **P163** | 1l. red | 20 | 15 |
| 534 | **P163** | 4l. on 1l. red | 20 | 15 |
| 535 | **P163** | 7l. purple | 20 | 15 |
| 536 | **P163** | 20l. brown | 30 | 15 |
| 537 | **P163** | 30l. purple | 40 | 20 |
| 538 | **P163** | 50l. orange | 75 | 50 |
| 539 | **P163** | 100l. blue | 1·80 | 1·00 |

**1945.** Air. Optd with airplane or surch also.

| | | | | |
|---|---|---|---|---|
| 540 | **142** | 1l. green | 20 | 15 |
| 541 | **142** | 4l. orange | 20 | 15 |
| 542 | **P 163** | 10l. on 100l. yellow | 30 | 15 |
| 543 | **P 163** | 45l. on 100l. yellow | 40 | 20 |
| 544 | **P 163** | 75l. on 100l. yellow | 1·00 | 60 |
| 545 | **P 163** | 100l. yellow | 1·30 | 90 |

Nos. 540/1 are perf; the rest imperf.

**167**

**1945.** Slav Congress. Perf or imperf.

| | | | | |
|---|---|---|---|---|
| 546 | **167** | 4l. red | 15 | 10 |
| 547 | **167** | 10l. blue | 15 | 10 |
| 548 | **167** | 50l. red | 40 | 30 |

СЪБИРАЙТЕ ВСЪКАКВИ ПАРЦАЛИ **(168)** "Collect All Rags"

СЪБИРАЙТЕ СТАРО ЖЕЛЪЗО **(169)** "Collect Old Iron"

СЪБИРАЙТЕ ХАРТИЕНИ ОТПАДЪЦИ **(170)** "Collect Wastepaper"

**1945.** Salvage Campaign. Nos. 457/9 optd with T 168/70.

| | | | | |
|---|---|---|---|---|
| 549B | **142** | 1l. green | 30 | 40 |
| 550C | **142** | 2l. red | 1·30 | 40 |
| 551A | **142** | 4l. orange | 1·00 | 40 |

Prices are the same for these stamps with any one of the overprints illustrated.

**171** Lion Rampant **172**

**1945.** Lion Rampant, in various frames.

| | | | | |
|---|---|---|---|---|
| 552 | - | 30s. green | 25 | 15 |
| 553 | - | 50s. blue | 25 | 15 |
| 554 | **171** | 1l. green | 25 | 15 |
| 555 | - | 2l. brown | 25 | 15 |
| 556 | - | 4l. blue | 25 | 15 |
| 557 | - | 5l. violet | 25 | 15 |
| 558 | **172** | 9l. grey | 25 | 15 |
| 559 | - | 10l. blue | 25 | 15 |
| 560 | - | 15l. brown | 25 | 15 |
| 561 | - | 20l. black | 50 | 15 |
| 562 | - | 20l. red | 50 | 15 |

**173** Chain-breaker

**1945.** Liberty Loan. Imperf.

| | | | | |
|---|---|---|---|---|
| 563 | **173** | 50l. orange | 30 | 15 |
| 564 | **173** | 50l. lake | 30 | 15 |
| 565 | - | 100l. blue | 40 | 20 |
| 566 | - | 100l. brown | 40 | 20 |
| 567 | - | 150l. red | 1·00 | 60 |
| 568 | - | 150l. green | 1·00 | 60 |
| 569 | - | 200l. olive | 1·30 | 80 |
| 570 | - | 200l. blue | 1·30 | 80 |

**MS**570a Two blocks 88×123 mm, with the four values imperf (a) in brown-red and (b) in violet. Pair 16·00 24·00

DESIGNS: 100l. Hand holding coin; 150l. Water-mill; 200l. Coin and symbols of industry and agriculture.

174 "VE Day"

1945. "Victory in Europe".

| | | | | |
|---|---|---|---|---|
| 571 | 174 | 10l. green and brown | 20 | 15 |
| 572 | 174 | 50l. green and red | 65 | 30 |

175 176

1945. 1st Anniv of Fatherland Front Coalition.

| | | | | |
|---|---|---|---|---|
| 573 | 175 | 1l. olive | 20 | 15 |
| 574 | 175 | 4l. blue | 20 | 15 |
| 575 | 175 | 5l. mauve | 20 | 15 |
| 576 | 176 | 10l. blue | 20 | 15 |
| 577 | 176 | 20l. red | 20 | 20 |
| 578 | 175 | 50l. green | 1·00 | 60 |
| 579 | 175 | 100l. brown | 1·30 | 1·00 |

177 Refugee Children 178 Red Cross Train

1946. Red Cross. Cross in red.

| | | | | |
|---|---|---|---|---|
| 580 | 177 | 2l. olive | 20 | 15 |
| 645d | 177 | 2l. brown | 15 | 15 |
| 581 | - | 4l. violet | 20 | 15 |
| 645e | - | 4l. black | 15 | 15 |
| 582 | 177 | 10l. purple | 20 | 15 |
| 645f | 177 | 10l. green | 20 | 20 |
| 583 | - | 20l. dark blue | 20 | 15 |
| 645g | - | 20l. light blue | 50 | 50 |
| 584 | - | 30l. brown | 30 | 20 |
| 645h | - | 30l. green | 65 | 60 |
| 585 | 178 | 35l. black | 50 | 40 |
| 645i | 178 | 35l. green | 75 | 70 |
| 586 | - | 50l. purple | 65 | 50 |
| 645j | - | 50l. lake | 1·00 | 1·00 |
| 587 | 178 | 100l. brown | 2·10 | 1·80 |
| 645k | 178 | 100l. blue | 1·70 | 1·60 |

DESIGNS—HORIZ: 4l., 20l. Soldier on stretcher. VERT: 30l., 50l. Nurse and wounded soldier.

179 Postal Savings Emblem 180 Savings Bank-Note

1946. 50th Anniv of Savings Bank.

| | | | | |
|---|---|---|---|---|
| 588 | 179 | 4l. red | 20 | 15 |
| 589 | 180 | 10l. olive | 20 | 15 |
| 590 | - | 20l. blue | 20 | 15 |
| 591 | - | 50l. black | 1·60 | 1·40 |

DESIGNS—VERT: 20l. Child filling money-box; 50l. Postal Savings Bank.

181 Arms of Russia and Bulgaria and Spray of Oak

1946. Bulgo-Russian Congress.

| | | | | |
|---|---|---|---|---|
| 592 | 181 | 4l. red | 10·00 | 10·00 |
| 593 | 181 | 4l. orange | 20 | 20 |
| 594 | 181 | 20l. blue | 10·00 | 10·00 |
| 595 | 181 | 20l. green | 40 | 40 |

182 Lion Rampant

1946. Stamp Day. Imperf.

| | | | | |
|---|---|---|---|---|
| 596 | 182 | 20l. blue | 85 | 40 |

183 190

1946. Air. Inscr "PAR AVION".

| | | | | |
|---|---|---|---|---|
| 597 | 183 | 1l. purple | 25 | 15 |
| 598 | 183 | 2l. grey | 25 | 15 |
| 599 | - | 4l. black | 25 | 15 |
| 600 | - | 6l. blue | 25 | 15 |
| 601 | - | 10l. green | 25 | 15 |
| 602 | - | 12l. brown | 25 | 15 |
| 603 | - | 16l. purple | 25 | 15 |
| 604 | - | 19l. red | 25 | 15 |
| 605 | - | 30l. orange | 30 | 20 |
| 606 | - | 45l. green | 65 | 25 |
| 607 | - | 75l. brown | 95 | 30 |
| 608 | 190 | 100l. red | 1·70 | 50 |
| 609 | - | 100l. grey | 1·70 | 50 |

DESIGNS—23×18 mm: 4l. Bird carrying envelope; 100l. (No. 609), Airplane. 18×23 mm: 6l. Airplane and envelope; 10, 12, 19l. Wings and posthorn; 16l. Wings and envelope; 30l. Airplane; 45, 75l. Dove and posthorn.

192 Stamboliiski

1946. 23rd Death Anniv of Aleksandur Stamboliiski (Prime Minister 1919–23).

| | | | | |
|---|---|---|---|---|
| 610 | 192 | 100l. orange | 9·50 | 9·50 |

193 Flags of Albania, Bulgaria, Yugoslavia and Rumania

1946. Balkan Games.

| | | | | |
|---|---|---|---|---|
| 611 | 193 | 100l. brown | 1·80 | 1·80 |

195 Junkers Ju87B "Stuka" Dive Bombers 196 Artillery

1946. Military and Air Services.

| | | | | |
|---|---|---|---|---|
| 612 | - | 2l. red | 20 | 15 |
| 613 | - | 4l. grey | 20 | 15 |
| 614 | 196 | 5l. red | 20 | 15 |
| 615 | 195 | 6l. brown | 20 | 15 |
| 616 | - | 9l. mauve | 20 | 15 |
| 617 | - | 10l. violet | 20 | 15 |
| 618 | - | 20l. blue | 50 | 20 |
| 619 | - | 30l. orange | 65 | 30 |
| 620 | - | 40l. olive | 75 | 40 |
| 621 | - | 50l. green | 95 | 70 |
| 622 | - | 60l. brown | 1·30 | 80 |

DESIGNS—HORIZ: 2, 20l. Grenade thrower and machine-gunner; 9l. Building pontoon-bridge; 10, 30l. Cavalry charge; 40l. Supply column; 50l. Motor convoy; 60l. Tanks. VERT: 4l. Grenade thrower.

203 St. Ivan Rilski

1946. Death Millenary of St. Ivan Rilski.

| | | | | |
|---|---|---|---|---|
| 623 | 203 | 1l. brown | 20 | 15 |
| 624 | - | 4l. sepia | 20 | 15 |
| 625 | - | 10l. green | 30 | 20 |
| 626 | - | 20l. blue | 50 | 25 |
| 627 | - | 50l. red | 2·10 | 1·10 |

DESIGNS—HORIZ: 4l. Rila Monastery; 10l. Monastery entrance; 50l. Cloistered courtyard. VERT: 20l. Aerial view of Monastery.

208 "New Republic"

1946. Referendum.

| | | | | |
|---|---|---|---|---|
| 628 | 208 | 4l. red | 20 | 15 |
| 629 | 208 | 20l. blue | 20 | 15 |
| 630 | 208 | 50l. brown | 50 | 40 |

209 Assault 210 Ambuscade

1946. Partisan Activities.

| | | | | |
|---|---|---|---|---|
| 631 | 209 | 1l. purple | 20 | 15 |
| 632 | 210 | 4l. green | 20 | 15 |
| 633 | - | 5l. brown | 20 | 15 |
| 634 | 210 | 10l. red | 20 | 15 |
| 635 | 209 | 20l. blue | 50 | 20 |
| 636 | - | 30l. brown | 65 | 30 |
| 637 | - | 50l. black | 85 | 70 |

DESIGNS—VERT: 5l., 50l. Partisan riflemen; 30l. Partisan leader.

211 Nurse and Children

1947. Winter Relief.

| | | | | |
|---|---|---|---|---|
| 638 | 211 | 1l. violet | 20 | 15 |
| 639 | - | 4l. red | 20 | 15 |
| 640 | - | 9l. olive | 20 | 15 |
| 641 | 211 | 10l. grey | 20 | 15 |
| 642 | - | 20l. blue | 20 | 15 |
| 643 | - | 30l. brown | 40 | 20 |
| 644 | - | 40l. red | 50 | 40 |
| 645 | 211 | 50l. green | 95 | 70 |

DESIGNS: 4l., 9l. Child carrying gifts; 20l., 40l. Hungry child; 30l. Destitute mother and child.

212a Partisans

1947. Anti-fascists of 1923, 1941 and 1944 Commem.

| | | | | |
|---|---|---|---|---|
| 645a | - | 10l. brown and orange | 75 | 70 |
| 645b | 212a | 20l. dp blue & lt blue | 75 | 70 |
| 645c | - | 70l. brown and red | 47·00 | 45·00 |

DESIGNS—HORIZ: 10l. Group of fighters; 70l. Soldier addressing crowd.

213 Olive Branch 214 Dove of Peace

1947. Peace.

| | | | | |
|---|---|---|---|---|
| 646 | 213 | 4l. olive | 20 | 15 |
| 647 | 214 | 10l. brown | 20 | 20 |
| 648 | 214 | 20l. blue | 50 | 50 |

"BULGARIA" is in Roman characters on the 20l.

215 "U.S.A." and "Bulgaria"

1947. Air. Stamp Day and New York International Philatelic Exhibition.

| | | | | |
|---|---|---|---|---|
| 649 | 215 | 70l.+30l. brown | 2·10 | 2·00 |

216 Esperanto Emblem and Map of Bulgaria

1947. 30th Esperanto Jubilee Congress, Sofia.

| | | | | |
|---|---|---|---|---|
| 650 | 216 | 20l.+10l. purple & green | 1·00 | 1·00 |

217 G.P.O., Sofia 218 National Theatre, Sofia

219 Parliament Building 220 President's Palace

221 G.P.O., Sofia

1947. Government Buildings. (a) T 217.

| | | | |
|---|---|---|---|
| 651 | 1l. green | 20 | 15 |

(b) T 218.

| | | | |
|---|---|---|---|
| 652 | 50s. green | 20 | 15 |
| 653 | 2l. red | 20 | 15 |
| 654 | 4l. blue | 20 | 15 |
| 655 | 9l. red | 65 | 20 |

(c) T 219.

| | | | |
|---|---|---|---|
| 656 | 50s. green | 20 | 15 |
| 657 | 2l. blue | 20 | 15 |
| 658 | 4l. blue | 20 | 15 |
| 659 | 20l. blue | 1·60 | 1·00 |

(d) T 220.

| | | | |
|---|---|---|---|
| 660 | 1l. green | 20 | 15 |

(e) T 221.

| | | | |
|---|---|---|---|
| 661 | 1l. green | 20 | 15 |
| 662 | 2l. red | 20 | 15 |
| 663 | 4l. blue | 20 | 15 |

222 Hydro-electric Power Station and Dam 223 Emblem of Industry

1947. Reconstruction.

| | | | | |
|---|---|---|---|---|
| 664 | 222 | 4l. green | 20 | 15 |
| 665 | - | 9l. brown (Miner) | 30 | 25 |

| | | | | |
|---|---|---|---|---|
| 666 | 223 | 20l. blue | 40 | 35 |
| 667 | - | 40l. green (Motor plough) | 1·30 | 1·20 |

224 Exhibition Building

225 Former Residence of the French Poet Lamartine

226 Rose and Grapes

**1947.** Plovdiv Fair. (a) Postage.

| | | | | |
|---|---|---|---|---|
| 668 | 224 | 4l. red | 15 | 10 |
| 669 | 225 | 9l. red | 20 | 10 |
| 670 | 226 | 20l. blue | 40 | 40 |

227 Airplane over City

(b) Air. Imperf.

| | | | | |
|---|---|---|---|---|
| 671 | 227 | 40l. green | 1·60 | 1·50 |

228 Cycle Racing

229 Basketball

**1947.** Balkan Games.

| | | | | |
|---|---|---|---|---|
| 672 | 228 | 2l. lilac | 75 | 40 |
| 673 | 229 | 4l. green | 85 | 50 |
| 674 | - | 9l. brown | 1·60 | 60 |
| 675 | - | 20l. blue | 2·10 | 70 |
| 676 | - | 60l. red | 4·75 | 3·25 |

DESIGNS—VERT: 9l. Chess; 20l. Football; 60l. Balkan flags.

231 V. E. Aprilov

**1947.** Death Cent of Vasil Aprilov (educationist).

| | | | | |
|---|---|---|---|---|
| 677 | 231 | 40l. blue | 85 | 50 |
| 678 | - | 4l. red | 30 | 15 |

DESIGN: 4l. Another portrait of Aprilov.

233 Postman

**1947.** Postal Employees' Relief Fund.

| | | | | |
|---|---|---|---|---|
| 679 | 233 | 4l.+2l. olive | 15 | 15 |
| 680 | - | 10l.+5l. red | 20 | 20 |
| 681 | - | 20l.+10l. blue | 30 | 30 |
| 682 | - | 40l.+20l. brown | 1·60 | 1·50 |

DESIGNS: 10l. Linesman; 20l. Telephonists; 40l. Wireless masts.

235 Geno Kirov

**1947.** Theatrical Artists' Benevolent Fund.

| | | | | |
|---|---|---|---|---|
| 683 | 235 | 50s. brown | 10 | 10 |
| 684 | - | 1l. green | 10 | 10 |
| 685 | - | 2l. green | 10 | 10 |
| 686 | - | 3l. blue | 10 | 10 |
| 687 | - | 4l. red | 10 | 10 |
| 688 | - | 5l. purple | 10 | 10 |
| 689 | - | 9l.+5l. blue | 20 | 15 |
| 690 | - | 10l.+6l. red | 20 | 20 |
| 691 | - | 15l.+7l. violet | 50 | 35 |
| 692 | - | 20l.+15l. blue | 75 | 60 |
| 693 | - | 30l.+20l. purple | 1·60 | 1·30 |

PORTRAITS: 1l. Zlotina Nedeva; 2l. Ivan Popov; 3l. Atanas Kirchev; 4l. Elena Snezhina; 5l. Stoyan Buchvarov; 9l. Khristo Ganchev; 10l. Adriana Budevska; 15l. Vasil Kirkov; 20l. Save Orgnyanov; 30l. Krustyn Sarafov.

236 "Rodina" (freighter)

**1947.** National Shipping Revival.

| | | | | |
|---|---|---|---|---|
| 694 | 236 | 50l. blue | 1·00 | 80 |

237 Worker and Flag

238 Worker and Globe

**1948.** 2nd General Workers' Union Congress.

| | | | | |
|---|---|---|---|---|
| 695 | 237 | 4l. blue (postage) | 20 | 10 |
| 696 | 238 | 60l. brown (air) | 85 | 70 |

239

240

**1948.** Leisure and Culture.

| | | | | |
|---|---|---|---|---|
| 697 | 239 | 4l. red | 20 | 15 |
| 698 | 240 | 20l. blue | 40 | 20 |
| 699 | - | 40l. green | 75 | 40 |
| 700 | - | 60l. brown | 1·30 | 80 |

DESIGNS—VERT: 40l. Workers' musical interlude; 60l. Sports girl.

241 Kikola Vaptsarov

**1948.** Poets.

| | | | | |
|---|---|---|---|---|
| 701 | 241 | 4l. red on cream | 20 | 15 |
| 702 | - | 9l. brown on cream | 25 | 20 |
| 703 | - | 15l. purple on cream | 30 | 25 |
| 704 | - | 20l. blue on cream | 40 | 35 |
| 705 | - | 45l. green on cream | 1·00 | 90 |

PORTRAITS: 9l. Peya Yavorov; 15l. Khristo Smirnenski; 20l. Ivan Vazov; 45l. Petko Slaveikov.

242 Petlyakov Pe-2 Bomber over Baldwin's Tower

**1948.** Air. Stamp Day.

| | | | | |
|---|---|---|---|---|
| 706 | 242 | 50l. brown on cream | 2·10 | 2·00 |

243 Soldier

244 Peasants and Soldiers

**1948.** Soviet Army Monument.

| | | | | |
|---|---|---|---|---|
| 707 | 243 | 4l. red on cream | 20 | 15 |
| 708 | 244 | 10l. green on cream | 25 | 20 |
| 709 | - | 20l. blue on cream | 50 | 40 |
| 710 | - | 60l. olive on cream | 1·30 | 1·00 |

DESIGNS—HORIZ: 20l. Soldiers of 1878 and 1944. VERT: 60l. Stalin and Spassky Tower, Kremlin.

245 Malyovitsa Peak

**1948.** Bulgarian Health Resorts.

| | | | | |
|---|---|---|---|---|
| 711 | | 2l. red | 20 | 15 |
| 712 | | 3l. orange | 20 | 15 |
| 713 | | 4l. blue | 20 | 15 |
| 714 | | 10l. purple | 40 | 20 |
| 715 | 245 | 20l. blue | 1·60 | 30 |
| 716 | - | 20l. blue | 2·30 | 60 |
| 717 | 245 | 5l. brown | 75 | 15 |
| 718 | - | 15l. olive | 1·00 | 15 |

DESIGNS: 2l. Bath, Gorna Banya; 3, 10l. Bath, Bankya; 4, 20l. (No. 716), Mineral bath, Sofia; 15l. Malyovitsa Peak.

246 Lion Emblem

**1948**

| | | | | |
|---|---|---|---|---|
| 719 | 246 | 50s. orange | 20 | 15 |
| 719a | 246 | 50s. brown | 20 | 15 |
| 720 | 246 | 1l. green | 20 | 15 |
| 721 | 246 | 9l. black | 50 | 30 |

247 Dimitur Blagoev

248 Youths marching

**1948.** 25th Anniv of September Uprising.

| | | | | |
|---|---|---|---|---|
| 722 | 247 | 4l. brown | 20 | 15 |
| 723 | - | 9l. orange | 20 | 15 |
| 724 | - | 20l. blue | 30 | 30 |
| 725 | 248 | 60l. brown | 1·60 | 1·20 |

DESIGNS—VERT: 9l. Gabrit Genov. HORIZ: 20l. Bishop Andrei Monument.

249 Khristo Smirnenski

**1948.** 500th Birth Anniv of Smirnenski (poet and revolutionary).

| | | | | |
|---|---|---|---|---|
| 726 | 249 | 4l. blue | 20 | 15 |
| 727 | 249 | 16l. brown | 40 | 20 |

250 Miner

**1948**

| | | | | |
|---|---|---|---|---|
| 728 | 250 | 4l. blue | 40 | 20 |

251 Battle of Grivitsa

**1948.** Treaty of Friendship with Rumania.

| | | | | |
|---|---|---|---|---|
| 729 | 251 | 20l. blue (postage) | 30 | 20 |
| 730 | - | 40l. black (air) | 50 | 40 |
| 731 | - | 100l. mauve | 1·30 | 1·20 |

DESIGNS: 40l. Parliament Buildings in Sofia and Bucharest; 100l. Projected Danube Bridge.

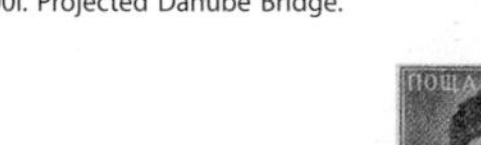

252 Botev's House, Kalofer

253 Botev

**1948.** Birth Centenary of Khristo Botev (poet and revolutionary).

| | | | | |
|---|---|---|---|---|
| 732 | 252 | 1l. green | 20 | 15 |
| 733 | 253 | 4l. brown | 20 | 15 |
| 734 | 253 | 4l. purple | 20 | 15 |
| 735 | - | 9l. violet | 20 | 15 |
| 736 | - | 15l. brown | 20 | 15 |
| 737a | - | 20l. blue | 40 | 20 |
| 738 | - | 40l. brown | 75 | 50 |
| 739 | - | 50l. black | 1·00 | 70 |

DESIGNS—HORIZ: 9l. River paddle-steamer "Radetski"; 15l. Village of Kalofer; 40l. Botev's mother and verse of poem. VERT: 20l. Botev in uniform; 50l. Quill, pistol and laurel wreath.

254 Lenin

**1949.** 25th Death Anniv of Lenin. Inscr "1924–1949".

| | | | | |
|---|---|---|---|---|
| 740 | 254 | 4l. brown | 30 | 20 |
| 741 | - | 20l. red | 75 | 60 |

DESIGN—(27×37 mm): 20l. Lenin as an orator.

255 Road Construction

**1949.** National Youth Movement.

| | | | | |
|---|---|---|---|---|
| 742 | 255 | 4l. red | 20 | 15 |
| 743 | - | 5l. brown | 40 | 20 |
| 744 | - | 9l. green | 1·00 | 50 |
| 745 | - | 10l. violet | 65 | 40 |
| 746 | - | 20l. blue | 1·30 | 1·00 |
| 747 | - | 40l. brown | 2·50 | 1·20 |

DESIGNS—HORIZ: 5l. Tunnel construction; 9l. Class 10 steam locomotive; 10l. Textile workers; 20l. Girl driving tractor; 40l. Workers in lorry.

256 Lisunov Li-2 over Pleven Mausoleum

**1949.** Air. 7th Philatelic Congress, Pleven.

| | | | | |
|---|---|---|---|---|
| 748 | **256** | 50l. bistre | 5·75 | 5·00 |

**257** G. Dimitrov **258** G. Dimitrov

**1949.** Death of Georgi Dimitrov (Prime Minister 1946–49).

| | | | | |
|---|---|---|---|---|
| 749 | **257** | 4l. red | 30 | 30 |
| 750 | **258** | 20l. blue | 1·60 | 60 |

**259** Hydro-electric Power Station **260** Symbols of Agriculture and Industry

**1949.** Five Year Industrial and Agricultural Plan.

| | | | | |
|---|---|---|---|---|
| 751 | **259** | 4l. olive (postage) | 20 | 15 |
| 752 | - | 9l. red | 30 | 25 |
| 753 | - | 15l. violet | 50 | 30 |
| 754 | - | 20l. blue | 1·60 | 90 |
| 755 | **260** | 50l. brown (air) | 4·50 | 2·00 |

DESIGNS—VERT: 9l. Cement works; 15l. Tractors in garage. HORIZ: 20l. Tractors in field.

**261** Javelin and Grenade Throwing **262** Motor-cyclist and Tractor

**1949.** Physical Culture Campaign.

| | | | | |
|---|---|---|---|---|
| 756 | **261** | 4l. red | 75 | 40 |
| 757 | - | 9l. olive | 2·10 | 90 |
| 758 | **262** | 20l. blue | 3·25 | 1·70 |
| 759 | - | 50l. red | 7·75 | 4·25 |

DESIGNS—HORIZ: 9l. Hurdling and leaping barbed-wire. VERT: 50l. Two athletes marching.

**263** Globe

**1949.** Air. 75th Anniv of Universal Postal Union.

| | | | | |
|---|---|---|---|---|
| 760 | **263** | 50l. blue | 3·25 | 1·70 |

**265** Guardsman with Dog **264** Guardsman and Peasant

**1949.** Frontier Guards.

| | | | | |
|---|---|---|---|---|
| 761 | **264** | 4l. brown (postage) | 50 | 40 |
| 762 | - | 20l. blue | 1·60 | 1·40 |
| 763 | **265** | 60l. green (air) | 4·75 | 4·00 |

DESIGN—VERT: 20l. Guardsman on coast.

**266** Georgi Dimitrov (Prime Minister 1946–49)

**267** "Unanimity"

**1949.** Fatherland Front.

| | | | | |
|---|---|---|---|---|
| 764 | **266** | 4l. brown | 20 | 15 |
| 765 | **267** | 9l. violet | 85 | 50 |
| 766 | - | 20l. blue | 95 | 60 |
| 767 | - | 50l. red | 1·30 | 1·00 |

DESIGNS: 20l. Man and woman with wheelbarrow and spade; 50l. Young people marching with banners.

**268** Zosif Stalin

**1949.** 70th Birthday of Stalin.

| | | | | |
|---|---|---|---|---|
| 768 | **268** | 4l. orange | 50 | 20 |
| 769 | - | 40l. red | 1·60 | 1·10 |

DESIGN—VERT: (25×37 mm): 40l. Stalin as an orator.

**269** Kharalampi Stoyanov

**270** Strikers and Train

**1950.** 30th Anniv of Railway Strike.

| | | | | |
|---|---|---|---|---|
| 770 | **269** | 4l. brown | 50 | 20 |
| 771 | **270** | 20l. blue | 65 | 30 |
| 772 | - | 60l. olive | 1·00 | 80 |

DESIGN—VERT: 60l. Two workers and flag.

**271** Miner

**272** Class 48 Steam Shunting Locomotive

**1950**

| | | | | |
|---|---|---|---|---|
| 773 | **271** | 1l. olive | 15 | 10 |
| 773a | **271** | 1l. violet | 30 | 10 |
| 774 | **272** | 2l. black | 1·00 | 30 |
| 774a | **272** | 2l. brown | 1·00 | 25 |
| 775 | - | 3l. blue | 50 | 10 |
| 776a | - | 4l. green | 3·25 | 1·20 |
| 777 | - | 5l. red | 65 | 10 |
| 778 | - | 9l. grey | 40 | 15 |
| 779 | - | 10l. purple | 30 | 10 |
| 780 | - | 15l. red | 1·00 | 30 |
| 781 | - | 20l. blue | 1·20 | 40 |

DESIGNS—VERT: 3l. Ship under construction; 10l. Power station; 15l., 20l. Woman in factory. HORIZ: 4l. Tractor; 5l., 9l. Threshing machines.

**273** Kolarov

**1950.** Death of Vasil Kolarov (Prime Minister 1949–50). Inscr "1877–1950".

| | | | | |
|---|---|---|---|---|
| 782 | **273** | 4l. brown | 20 | 15 |
| 783 | - | 20l. blue | 85 | 80 |

DESIGN—(27½×39½ mm): 20l. Portrait as Type **273**, but different frame.

**274** Starislas Dospevski (self-portrait)

**274a** "In the Field" (Khristo Storclev)

**1950.** Painters and paintings.

| | | | | |
|---|---|---|---|---|
| 784 | **274** | 1l. green | 65 | 40 |
| 785 | - | 4l. orange | 2·10 | 60 |
| 786 | - | 9l. brown | 3·25 | 80 |
| 787 | **274a** | 15l. brown | 4·50 | 1·00 |
| 788 | **274a** | 20l. blue | 6·75 | 3·00 |
| 789 | - | 40l. brown | 8·25 | 4·00 |
| 790 | - | 60l. orange | 9·00 | 6·00 |

DESIGNS—VERT: 4l. King Kaloyan and Desislava; 9l. Nikolai Pavlovich; 40l. Statue of Debeyanov (Ivan Lazarov); 60l. "Peasant" (Vladimir Dimitrov the Master).

**275** Ivan Vazov and Birthplace, Sopot

**1950.** Birth Centenary of Ivan Vazov (poet).

| | | | | |
|---|---|---|---|---|
| 791 | **275** | 4l. olive | 20 | 15 |

**276a** G. Dimitrov (statesman)

**1950.** 1st Death Anniv of Georgi Dimitrov.

| | | | | |
|---|---|---|---|---|
| 792 | - | 50s. brown (postage) | 40 | 15 |
| 793 | - | 50s. green | 40 | 15 |
| 794 | **276a** | 1l. brown | 50 | 20 |
| 795 | - | 2l. slate | 50 | 20 |
| 796 | - | 4l. purple | 1·00 | 30 |
| 797 | - | 9l. red | 1·80 | 90 |
| 798 | - | 10l. red | 2·50 | 1·20 |
| 799 | - | 15l. grey | 2·50 | 1·20 |
| 800 | - | 20l. blue | 4·25 | 2·50 |
| 801 | - | 40l. brown (air) | 8·25 | 4·00 |

DESIGNS—HORIZ: 50s. green, Dimitrov and birthplace, Kovachevtsi; 2l. Dimitrov's house, Sofia; 15l. Dimitrov signing new constitution; 20l. Dimitrov; 40l. Mausoleum. VERT: 50s. brown, 4, 9, 10l. Dimitrov in various poses.

**277** Runners

**1950**

| | | | | |
|---|---|---|---|---|
| 802 | **277** | 4l. green | 95 | 50 |
| 803 | - | 9l. brown (Cycling) | 1·00 | 80 |
| 804 | - | 20l. blue (Putting the shot) | 1·30 | 1·20 |
| 805 | - | 40l. purple (Volleyball) | 3·25 | 2·50 |

**278** Workers and Tractor

**1950.** 2nd National Peace Congress.

| | | | | |
|---|---|---|---|---|
| 806 | **278** | 4l. red | 20 | 15 |
| 807 | - | 20l. blue | 95 | 60 |

DESIGN—VERT: 20l. Stalin on flag and three heads.

**278b**

**1950.** Arms designs.

| | | | | |
|---|---|---|---|---|
| 807a | | 2l. brown | 20 | 15 |
| 807b | | 3l. red | 20 | 15 |
| 807c | **278b** | 5l. red | 20 | 15 |
| 807d | - | 9l. blue | 20 | 15 |

Although inscribed "OFFICIAL MAIL", the above were issued as regular postage stamps.

**279** Children on Beach

**1950.** Sunday Delivery.

| | | | | |
|---|---|---|---|---|
| 808 | | 1l. green (Sanatorium) | 20 | 15 |
| 809 | **279** | 2l. red | 30 | 15 |
| 810 | - | 5l. orange (Sunbathing) | 65 | 30 |
| 811 | **279** | 10l. blue | 1·60 | 60 |

**280** Molotov, Kolarov, Stalin and Dimitrov

**281** Russian and Bulgarian Girls

**1950.** 2nd Anniv of Soviet–Bulgarian Treaty of Friendship.

| | | | | |
|---|---|---|---|---|
| 812 | **280** | 4l. brown | 20 | 15 |
| 813 | - | 9l. red | 30 | 15 |
| 814 | **281** | 20l. blue | 65 | 50 |
| 815 | - | 50l. green | 3·25 | 1·20 |

DESIGNS—VERT: 9l. Spassky Tower and flags; 50l. Freighter and tractor.

**282** Marshal Tolbukhin

**1950.** Honouring Marshal Tolbukhin.

| | | | | |
|---|---|---|---|---|
| 816 | **282** | 4l. mauve | 30 | 20 |
| 817 | - | 20l. blue | 1·60 | 80 |

DESIGN—HORIZ: 20l. Bulgarians greeting Tolbukhin.

**284** A. S. Popov

**1951.** 45th Death Anniv of Aleksandr Popov (radio pioneer).

| | | | | |
|---|---|---|---|---|
| 818 | **284** | 4l. brown | 75 | 30 |
| 819 | **284** | 20l. blue | 1·40 | 70 |

**286** Georgi Kirkov

**1951.** Anti-fascist Heroes.

| | | | | |
|---|---|---|---|---|
| 823 | - | 1l. mauve | 40 | 20 |
| 824 | - | 2l. plum | 40 | 20 |
| 825 | **286** | 4l. red | 40 | 20 |
| 826 | - | 9l. brown | 1·20 | 60 |
| 827 | - | 15l. olive | 2·50 | 1·10 |
| 828 | - | 20l. blue | 2·50 | 1·50 |
| 829 | - | 50l. grey | 6·25 | 2·20 |

PORTRAITS: 1l. Chankova, Adalbert Antonov-Malchika, Sasho Dimitrov and Lilyana Dimitrova; 2l. Stanke Dimitrov; 9l. Anton Ivanov; 15l. Mikhailov; 20l. Georgi Dimitrov at Leipzig; 50l. Nocho Ivanov and Acram Stoyahov.

**285** First Bulgarian Truck

**1951.** National Occupations. (a) As T 285.

| | | | | |
|---|---|---|---|---|
| 820 | | 1l. violet (Tractor) | 20 | 10 |
| 821 | | 2l. green (Steam-roller) | 25 | 10 |
| 822 | **285** | 4l. brown | 30 | 10 |

**289** Embroidery

(b) As T 289.

| | | | | |
|---|---|---|---|---|
| 830 | - | 1l. brown (Tractor) | 30 | 20 |
| 831 | - | 2l. violet (Steam-roller) | 40 | 30 |
| 832 | - | 4l. brown (Truck) | 75 | 60 |
| 833 | **289** | 9l. violet | 1·30 | 80 |
| 834 | - | 15l. purple (Carpets) | 2·30 | 1·50 |
| 835 | - | 20l. blue (Roses and Tobacco) | 5·25 | 2·20 |
| 836 | - | 40l. green (Fruit) | 7·75 | 3·25 |

The 9l. and 20l. are vert, the remainder horiz.

**290** Turkish Attack

**1951.** 75th Anniv of April Uprising.

| | | | | |
|---|---|---|---|---|
| 837 | **290** | 1l. brown | 75 | 35 |
| 838 | - | 4l. green | 85 | 40 |
| 839 | - | 9l. purple | 1·30 | 1·00 |
| 840 | - | 20l. blue | 1·90 | 1·50 |
| 841 | - | 40l. lake | 2·50 | 2·00 |

DESIGNS—HORIZ: 4l. Proclamation of Uprising; 9l. Cannon and cavalry; 20l. Patriots in 1876 and 1944; 40l. Georgi Benkovsky and Georgi Dimitrov.

**291** Dimitur Blagoev as Orator

**1951.** 60th Anniv of First Bulgarian Social Democratic Party Congress, Buzludzha.

| | | | | |
|---|---|---|---|---|
| 842 | **291** | 1l. violet | 30 | 20 |
| 843 | **291** | 4l. green | 1·00 | 40 |
| 844 | **291** | 9l. purple | 1·80 | 1·20 |

**292** Babies in Creche

**1951.** Children's Day.

| | | | | |
|---|---|---|---|---|
| 845 | **292** | 1l. brown | 30 | 20 |
| 846 | - | 4l. purple | 75 | 30 |
| 847 | - | 9l. green | 1·60 | 60 |
| 848 | - | 20l. blue | 3·25 | 2·00 |

DESIGNS: 4l. Children building models; 9l. Girl and children's play ground; 20l. Boy bugler and children marching.

**293** Workers

**1951.** 3rd General Workers' Union Congress.

| | | | | |
|---|---|---|---|---|
| 849 | **293** | 1l. black | 20 | 15 |
| 850 | - | 4l. brown | 30 | 20 |

DESIGN inscr "16 XII 1951"; 4l. Georgi Dimitrov and Valdo Chervenkov (Prime minister).

**294** Labour medal (Obverse)

**295** Labour medal (Reverse)

**1952.** Order of Labour.

| | | | | |
|---|---|---|---|---|
| 851 | **294** | 1l. red | 20 | 15 |
| 852 | **295** | 1l. brown | 20 | 15 |
| 853 | **294** | 4l. green | 20 | 15 |
| 854 | **295** | 4l. green | 20 | 15 |
| 855 | **294** | 9l. violet | 75 | 20 |
| 856 | **295** | 9l. blue | 75 | 20 |

**296** Vasil Kolarov Dam

**1952**

| | | | | |
|---|---|---|---|---|
| 857 | **296** | 4s. green | 20 | 15 |
| 858 | **296** | 12s. violet | 30 | 15 |
| 859 | **296** | 16s. brown | 40 | 15 |
| 860 | **296** | 44s. red | 1·00 | 20 |
| 861 | **296** | 80s. blue | 4·50 | 50 |

**297** G. Dimitrov and Chemical Works

**1952.** 70th Birth Anniv of Georgi Dimitrov (statesman). Dated "1882–1952".

| | | | | |
|---|---|---|---|---|
| 862 | **297** | 16s. brown | 95 | 50 |
| 863 | - | 44s. brown | 1·60 | 1·00 |
| 864 | - | 80s. blue | 2·75 | 1·50 |

DESIGNS—HORIZ: 44s. Georgi Dimitrov (Prime minister 1946–49) and Prime minister Vulko Chervenkov. VERT: 80s. Full-face portrait of Georgi Dimitrov.

**298** Republika Power Station

**1952**

| | | | | |
|---|---|---|---|---|
| 866 | **298** | 16s. sepia | 65 | 20 |
| 867 | **298** | 44s. purple | 2·10 | 30 |

**299** N. Vaptsarov (revolutionary)

**1952.** 10th Death Anniv of Nikola Vaptsarov (poet and revolutionary).

| | | | | |
|---|---|---|---|---|
| 869 | **299** | 16s. lake | 95 | 70 |
| 870 | - | 44s. brown | 1·90 | 1·70 |
| 871 | - | 80s. sepia | 4·00 | 1·90 |

PORTRAITS: 44s. Facing bayonets; 80s. Full-face.

**300** Congress Delegates

**1952.** 40th Anniv of First Workers' Social Democratic Youth League Congress.

| | | | | |
|---|---|---|---|---|
| 872 | **300** | 2s. lake | 20 | 15 |
| 873 | - | 16s. violet | 40 | 30 |
| 874 | - | 44s. green | 1·60 | 85 |
| 875 | - | 80s. sepia | 2·50 | 1·90 |

DESIGNS: 16s. Young partisans; 44s. Factory and guards; 80s. Dimitrov addressing young workers.

**301** Attack on Winter Palace, St. Petersburg

**1952.** 35th Anniv of Russian Revolution. Dated "1917 1952".

| | | | | |
|---|---|---|---|---|
| 876 | **301** | 4s. lake | 40 | 20 |
| 877 | - | 8s. green | 50 | 30 |
| 878 | - | 16s. blue | 1·20 | 40 |
| 879 | - | 44s. sepia | 1·50 | 50 |
| 880 | - | 80s. olive | 3·00 | 2·40 |

DESIGNS: 8s. Volga–Don canal; 16s. Dove and globe; 44s. Lenin and Stalin; 80s. Lenin, Stalin and Himlay hydro-electric station.

**302**

**303** Vintagers and Grapes

**1952.** Wood Carvings depicting National Products.

| | | | | |
|---|---|---|---|---|
| 881 | | 2s. brown | 20 | 15 |
| 882 | | 8s. green | 20 | 15 |
| 883 | | 12s. brown | 40 | 15 |
| 884 | | 16s. purple | 80 | 15 |
| 885 | **302** | 28s. green | 1·10 | 20 |
| 886 | - | 44s. brown | 1·50 | 30 |
| 887 | **303** | 80s. blue | 1·70 | 40 |
| 888 | **303** | 1l. violet | 4·00 | 60 |
| 889 | **303** | 4l. red | 4·75 | 3·50 |

DESIGNS—VERT: 2s. Numeral in carved frame. HORIZ: 8s. Gift-offering to idol; 12s. Birds and grapes; 16s. Rose-gathering; 44s. "Attar of Roses".

**304** V. Levski

**1953.** 80th Anniv of Execution of Vasil Levski (revolutionary).

| | | | | |
|---|---|---|---|---|
| 890 | **304** | 16s. brown on cream | 20 | 15 |
| 891 | - | 44s. brown on cream | 60 | 30 |

DESIGN: 44s. Levski addressing crowd.

**305** Russian Army Crossing R. Danube

**1953.** 75th Anniv of Liberation from Turkey.

| | | | | |
|---|---|---|---|---|
| 892 | **305** | 8s. blue | 30 | 20 |
| 893 | - | 16s. brown | 40 | 20 |
| 894 | - | 44s. green | 95 | 30 |
| 895 | - | 80s. lake | 3·00 | 1·50 |
| 896 | - | 1l. black | 3·50 | 3·00 |

DESIGNS—VERT: 16s. Battle of Shipka Pass. HORIZ: 44s. Peasants welcoming Russian soldiers; 80s. Bulgarians and Russians embracing; 1l. Shipka Pass memorial and Dimitrovgrad.

**306** Mother and Children

**1953.** International Women's Day.

| | | | | |
|---|---|---|---|---|
| 897 | **306** | 16s. blue | 30 | 10 |
| 898 | **306** | 16s. green | 30 | 10 |

**307** Karl Marx

**1953.** 70th Death Anniv of Karl Marx.

| | | | | |
|---|---|---|---|---|
| 899 | **307** | 16s. blue | 30 | 20 |
| 900 | - | 44s. brown | 70 | 50 |

DESIGN—VERT: 44s. Book "Das Kapital".

**308** May Day Parade

**1953.** Labour Day.

| | | | | |
|---|---|---|---|---|
| 901 | **308** | 16s. red | 40 | 20 |

**309** Stalin

**1953.** Death of Stalin.

| | | | | |
|---|---|---|---|---|
| 902 | **309** | 16s. brown | 80 | 30 |
| 903 | **309** | 16s. black | 80 | 30 |

**310** Goce Delcev (Macedonian revolutionary)

**1953.** 50th Anniv of Ilinden–Preobrazhenie Rising.

| | | | | |
|---|---|---|---|---|
| 904 | **310** | 16s. brown | 20 | 15 |
| 905 | - | 44s. violet | 80 | 50 |
| 906 | - | 1l. purple | 1·10 | 80 |

DESIGNS. 44s. Insurgents and flag facing left. HORIZ: 1l. Insurgents and flag facing right.

**311** Soldier and Insurgents

**1953.** Army Day.

| | | | | |
|---|---|---|---|---|
| 907 | **311** | 16s. red | 50 | 20 |
| 908 | - | 44s. blue | 95 | 30 |

DESIGN: 44s. Soldier, factories and combine-harvester.

**312** Dimitur Blagoev

**1953.** 50th Anniv of Bulgarian Workers' Social Democratic Party.

| | | | | |
|---|---|---|---|---|
| 909 | **312** | 16s. brown | 50 | 30 |
| 910 | - | 44s. red | 95 | 30 |

DESIGN: 44s. Dimitrov and Blagoev.

**313** Georgi Dimitrov and Vasil Kolarov

**1953.** 30th Anniv of September Uprising.

| | | | | |
|---|---|---|---|---|
| 911 | **313** | 8s. black | 30 | 15 |
| 912 | - | 16s. brown | 40 | 20 |
| 913 | - | 44s. red | 1·30 | 60 |

DESIGNS: 16s. Insurgent and flag; 44s. Crowd of Insurgents.

**314** Railway Viaduct

**1953.** Bulgarian–Russian Friendship.

| | | | | |
|---|---|---|---|---|
| 914 | **314** | 8s. blue | 20 | 15 |
| 915 | - | 16s. slate | 30 | 20 |
| 916 | - | 44s. brown | 80 | 40 |
| 917 | - | 80s. orange | 95 | 70 |

DESIGNS—HORIZ: 16s. Welder and industrial plant; 80s. Combine-harvester. VERT: 44s. Iron foundry.

**315** Dog Rose

**1953.** Medicinal Flowers.

| | | | | |
|---|---|---|---|---|
| 918 | | 2s. blue | 20 | 15 |
| 919 | | 4s. orange | 20 | 15 |
| 920 | | 8s. turquoise | 20 | 15 |
| 921 | **315** | 12s. green | 20 | 15 |
| 922 | - | 12s. red | 20 | 15 |
| 923 | - | 16s. blue | 50 | 20 |
| 924 | - | 16s. brown | 50 | 20 |
| 925 | - | 20s. red | 80 | 25 |
| 926 | - | 28s. green | 85 | 30 |
| 927 | - | 40s. blue | 95 | 50 |
| 928 | - | 44s. brown | 1·50 | 60 |
| 929 | - | 80s. brown | 2·40 | 1·10 |
| 930 | - | 1l. brown | 6·75 | 1·90 |
| 931 | - | 2l. purple | 9·75 | 4·00 |
| **MS**931a 161×172 mm. Twelve values as above in green (sold at 6l.) | | | 70·00 | 70·00 |

FLOWERS: 2s. Deadly nightshade; 4s. Thorn-apple; 8s. Sage; 16s. Great yellow gentian; 20s. Opium poppy; 28s. Peppermint; 40s. Bear-berry; 44s. Coltsfoot; 80s. Primula; 1l. Dandelion; 2l. Foxglove.

**316** Vasil Kolarov Library

**1953.** 75th Anniv of Kolarov Library, Sofia.

| | | | | |
|---|---|---|---|---|
| 932 | **316** | 44s. brown | 60 | 40 |

**317** Singer and Musician

**1953.** Amateur Theatricals.

| | | | | |
|---|---|---|---|---|
| 933 | **317** | 16s. brown | 30 | 15 |
| 934 | - | 44s. green | 70 | 40 |

DESIGN: 44s. Folk-dancers.

**318** Airplane over Mountains

**1954.** Air.

| | | | | |
|---|---|---|---|---|
| 935 | **318** | 8s. green | 20 | 15 |
| 936 | - | 12s. lake | 20 | 15 |
| 937 | - | 16s. brown | 20 | 15 |
| 938 | - | 20s. salmon | 20 | 15 |
| 939 | - | 28s. blue | 40 | 20 |
| 940 | - | 44s. purple | 50 | 20 |
| 941 | - | 60s. brown | 85 | 30 |
| 942 | - | 80s. green | 95 | 40 |
| 943 | - | 1l. green | 3·00 | 85 |
| 944 | - | 4l. blue | 5·25 | 2·40 |

DESIGNS—VERT: 12s. Exhibition buildings, Plovdiv; 80s. Tirnovo; 4l. Partisans' Monument. HORIZ: 16s. Seaside promenade, Varna; 20s. Combine-harvester in cornfield; 28s. Rila Monastery; 44s. Studena hydro-electric barrage; 60s. Dimitrovgrad; 1l. Sofia University and equestrian statue.

**319** Lenin and Stalin

**1954.** 30th Death Anniv of Lenin.

| | | | | |
|---|---|---|---|---|
| 945 | **319** | 16s. brown | 30 | 15 |
| 946 | - | 44s. lake | 70 | 20 |
| 947 | - | 80s. blue | 95 | 40 |
| 948 | - | 1l. green | 1·90 | 1·20 |

DESIGNS—VERT: 44s. Lenin statue; 80s. Lenin–Stalin Mausoleum and Kremlin; 1l. Lenin.

**320** Dimitur Blagoev and Crowd

**1954.** 30th Death Anniv of Blagoev.

| | | | | |
|---|---|---|---|---|
| 949 | **320** | 16s. brown | 20 | 10 |
| 950 | - | 44s. sepia | 80 | 30 |

DESIGN: 44s. Blagoev writing at desk.

**321** Dimitrov Speaking

**1954.** 5th Death Anniv of Dimitrov.

| | | | | |
|---|---|---|---|---|
| 951 | **321** | 44s. lake | 50 | 30 |
| 952 | - | 80s. brown | 95 | 70 |

DESIGN—HORIZ: 80s. Dimitrov and blast-furnace.

**322** Class 10 Steam Locomotive

**1954.** Railway Workers' Day.

| | | | | |
|---|---|---|---|---|
| 953 | **322** | 44s. turquoise | 1·70 | 80 |
| 954 | **322** | 44s. black | 1·70 | 80 |

**323** Miner Operating Machinery

**1954.** Miners' Day.

| | | | | |
|---|---|---|---|---|
| 955 | **323** | 44s. green | 50 | 20 |

**324** Marching Soldiers

**1954.** 10th Anniv of Fatherland Front Government.

| | | | | |
|---|---|---|---|---|
| 956 | **324** | 12s. lake | 20 | 15 |
| 957 | - | 16s. red | 20 | 15 |
| 958 | - | 28s. slate | 30 | 20 |
| 959 | - | 44s. brown | 60 | 25 |
| 960 | - | 80s. blue | 1·30 | 50 |
| 961 | - | 1l. green | 1·50 | 60 |

DESIGNS—VERT: 16s. Soldier and parents; 80s. Girl and boy pioneers; 1l. Dimitrov. HORIZ: 28s. Industrial plant; 44s. Dimitrov and workers.

**325** Academy Building

**1954.** 85th Anniv of Academy of Sciences.

| | | | | |
|---|---|---|---|---|
| 962 | **325** | 80s. black | 1·50 | 80 |

**326** Gymnast

**1954.** Sports. Cream paper.

| | | | | |
|---|---|---|---|---|
| 963 | **326** | 16s. green | 1·50 | 50 |
| 964 | - | 44s. red | 1·60 | 95 |
| 965 | - | 80s. brown | 3·50 | 1·90 |
| 966 | - | 2l. blue | 5·25 | 4·00 |

DESIGNS—VERT: 44s. Wrestlers; 2l. Ski-jumper. HORIZ: 80s. Horse-jumper.

**327** Velingrad Rest Home

**1954.** 50th Anniv of Trade Union Movement.

| | | | | |
|---|---|---|---|---|
| 967 | **327** | 16s. green | 30 | 20 |
| 968 | - | 44s. red | 50 | 30 |
| 969 | - | 80s. blue | 1·20 | 95 |

DESIGNS—VERT: 44s. Foundryman. HORIZ: 80s. Georgi Dimitrov, Dimitur Blagoev and Georgi Kirkov.

**328** Geese

**329** Communist Party Building

**1955**

| | | | | |
|---|---|---|---|---|
| 970 | **328** | 2s. green | 20 | 10 |
| 971 | - | 4s. olive | 30 | 10 |
| 972 | - | 12s. brown | 60 | 20 |
| 973 | - | 16s. brown | 95 | 30 |
| 974 | - | 28s. blue | 60 | 20 |
| 975 | **329** | 44s. red | 11·50 | 3·50 |
| 976 | - | 80s. brown | 1·50 | 50 |
| 977 | - | 1l. green | 2·40 | 95 |

DESIGNS: 4s. Rooster and hens; 12s. Sow and piglets; 16s. Ewe and lambs; 28s. Telephone exchange; 80s. Flats; 1l. Cellulose factory.

**330** Mill Girl

**1955.** International Women's Day.

| | | | | |
|---|---|---|---|---|
| 978 | **330** | 12s. brown | 10 | 10 |
| 979 | - | 16s. green | 30 | 15 |
| 980 | - | 44s. blue | 1·10 | 20 |
| 981 | - | 44s. red | 1·10 | 20 |

DESIGNS—HORIZ: 16s. Girl feeding cattle. VERT: 44s. Mother and baby.

**1955.** As Nos. 820 and 822 surch 16 CT.

| | | | | |
|---|---|---|---|---|
| 981a | | 16s. on 1l. violet | 20 | 10 |
| 982 | **285** | 16s. on 4l. brown | 1·90 | 50 |

**332** Rejoicing Crowds

**1955.** Labour Day.

| | | | | |
|---|---|---|---|---|
| 983 | **332** | 16s. red | 30 | 20 |
| 984 | - | 44s. blue | 70 | 30 |

DESIGN: 44s. Three workers and globe.

**333** St. Cyril and St. Methodius

**1955.** 1100th Anniv of 1st Bulgarian Literature. On cream paper.

| | | | | |
|---|---|---|---|---|
| 985 | **333** | 4s. blue | 20 | 15 |
| 986 | - | 8s. olive | 20 | 15 |
| 987 | - | 16s. black | 20 | 15 |
| 988 | - | 28s. red | 50 | 40 |
| 989 | - | 44s. brown | 80 | 50 |
| 990 | - | 80s. red | 1·40 | 95 |
| 991 | - | 2l. black | 3·50 | 2·10 |

DESIGNS: 8s. Monk writing; 16s. Early printing press; 28s. Khristo Botev (poet); 44s. Ivan Vazov (poet and novelist); 80s. Dimitur Blagoev (writer and editor) and books; 2l. Dimitur Blagoev Polygraphic Complex, Sofia.

**334** Sergei Rumyantsev

**1955.** 30th Death Annivs of Bulgarian Poets. On cream paper.

| | | | | |
|---|---|---|---|---|
| 992 | **334** | 12s. brown | 40 | 20 |
| 993 | - | 16s. brown | 50 | 30 |
| 994 | - | 44s. green | 1·50 | 95 |

DESIGNS: 16s. Khristo Yusenov; 44s. Geo Milev.

**335** F. Engels and Book

**1955.** 60th Death Anniv of Engels.

| | | | | |
|---|---|---|---|---|
| 995 | **335** | 44s. brown on cream | 95 | 80 |

**336** Mother and Children

**1955.** World Mothers' Congress, Lausanne.

| | | | | |
|---|---|---|---|---|
| 996 | **336** | 44s. lake on cream | 95 | 80 |

**337** "Youth of the World"

**1955.** 5th World Youth Festival, Warsaw.

| | | | | |
|---|---|---|---|---|
| 997 | **337** | 44s. blue on cream | 95 | 80 |

**338** Main Entrance in 1892

**1955.** 16th International Fair, Plovdiv.

| | | | | |
|---|---|---|---|---|
| 998 | **338** | 4s. brown on cream | 20 | 15 |
| 999 | - | 16s. red on cream | 25 | 15 |
| 1000 | - | 44s. green on cream | 50 | 20 |
| 1001 | - | 80s. cream | 1·20 | 40 |

DESIGNS—VERT: 16s. Sculptured group; 80s. Fair poster. HORIZ: 44s. Fruit.

**339** Friedrich Schiller (dramatist) (150th death anniv)

**1955.** Cultural Annivs. Writers. On cream paper.

| | | | | |
|---|---|---|---|---|
| 1002 | **339** | 16s. brown | 50 | 20 |
| 1003 | - | 44s. red | 1·10 | 30 |
| 1004 | - | 60s. blue | 1·40 | 40 |
| 1005 | - | 80s. black | 1·70 | 60 |
| 1006 | - | 1l. purple | 3·50 | 1·50 |
| 1007 | - | 2l. olive | 4·50 | 3·00 |

PORTRAITS: 44s. Adam Mickiewicz (poet, death centenary); 60s. Hans Christian Andersen (150th birth anniv); 80s. Baron de Montesquieu (philosopher, death bicentenary); 1l. Miguel de Cervantes (350th anniv of publication of "Don Quixote"); 2l. Walt Whitman (poet) (centenary of publication of "Leaves of Grass").

**340** Industrial Plant

**1955.** Bulgarian–Russian Friendship. On cream paper.

| | | | | |
|---|---|---|---|---|
| 1008 | **340** | 2s. slate | 20 | 15 |
| 1009 | - | 4s. blue | 20 | 15 |
| 1010 | - | 16s. green | 60 | 20 |
| 1011 | - | 44s. brown | 80 | 20 |
| 1012 | - | 80s. green | 1·20 | 30 |
| 1013 | - | 1l. black | 1·30 | 70 |

DESIGNS—HORIZ: 4s. Dam; 16s. Friendship railway bridge over River Danube between Ruse and Giurgiu (Rumania). VERT: 44s. Monument; 80s. Ivan-Michurin (botanist); 1l. Vladimir Mayakovsky (writer).

**341** Emblem

**1956.** Centenary of Library Reading Rooms. On cream paper.

| | | | | |
|---|---|---|---|---|
| 1014 | **341** | 12s. red | 20 | 15 |
| 1015 | - | 16s. brown | 30 | 20 |
| 1016 | - | 44s. myrtle | 1·20 | 50 |

DESIGNS: 16s. K. Pshourka writing; 44s. B. Kiro reading.

**342** Quinces

**1956.** Fruits.

| | | | | |
|---|---|---|---|---|
| 1017 | **342** | 4s. red | 2·10 | 30 |
| 1017a | **342** | 4s. green | 20 | 10 |
| 1018 | - | 8s. green (Pears) | 95 | 30 |
| 1018a | - | 8s. brown (Pears) | 20 | 10 |
| 1019 | - | 16s. dark red (Apples) | 1·70 | 40 |
| 1019a | - | 16s. red (Apples) | 60 | 20 |
| 1020 | - | 44s. violet (Grapes) | 1·90 | 60 |
| 1020a | - | 44s. ochre (Grapes) | 1·20 | 30 |

**343** Artillerymen

**1956.** 80th Anniv of April Uprising.

| | | | | |
|---|---|---|---|---|
| 1021 | **343** | 16s. brown | 40 | 40 |
| 1022 | - | 44s. green (Cavalry charge) | 50 | 50 |

**344** Blagoev and Birthplace at Zagovichane

**1956.** Birth Centenary of Dimitur Blagoev (socialist writer).

| | | | | |
|---|---|---|---|---|
| 1023 | **344** | 44s. turquoise | 1·50 | 95 |

**345** Cherries

**1956.** Fruits.

| | | | | |
|---|---|---|---|---|
| 1024 | **345** | 2s. lake | 15 | 10 |
| 1025 | - | 12s. blue (Plums) | 20 | 10 |
| 1026 | - | 28s. buff (Greengages) | 40 | 30 |
| 1027 | - | 80s. red (Strawberries) | 1·20 | 60 |

**346** Football

**1956.** Olympic Games.

| | | | | |
|---|---|---|---|---|
| 1028 | | 4s. blue | 60 | 20 |
| 1029 | | 12s. red | 70 | 25 |
| 1030 | | 16s. brown | 80 | 30 |
| 1031 | **346** | 44s. green | 1·50 | 60 |
| 1032 | - | 80s. brown | 2·40 | 1·30 |
| 1033 | - | 1l. lake | 3·50 | 1·50 |

DESIGNS—VERT: 4s. Gymnastics; 12s. Throwing the discus; 80s. Basketball. HORIZ: 16s. Pole vaulting; 1l. Boxing.

**347** Tobacco and Rose

**1956.** 17th International Fair, Plovdiv.

| | | | | |
|---|---|---|---|---|
| 1034 | **347** | 44s. red | 1·50 | 60 |
| 1035 | **347** | 44s. green | 1·50 | 60 |

**348** Gliders

**1956.** Air. 30th Anniv of Gliding Club.

| | | | | |
|---|---|---|---|---|
| 1036 | - | 44s. blue | 40 | 20 |
| 1037 | - | 60s. violet | 50 | 30 |
| 1038 | **348** | 80s. green | 1·50 | 95 |

DESIGNS: 44s. Launching glider; 60s. Glider over hangar.

**349** National Theatre

**1956.** Centenary of National Theatre.

| | | | | |
|---|---|---|---|---|
| 1039 | **349** | 16s. brown | 30 | 20 |
| 1040 | - | 44s. turquoise | 70 | 60 |

DESIGN: 44s. Dobri Voinikov and Sava Dobroplodni (dramatist).

**350** Wolfgang Mozart (composer, birth bicent)

**1956.** Cultural Anniversaries.

| | | | | |
|---|---|---|---|---|
| 1041 | | 16s. olive | 30 | 20 |
| 1042 | | 20s. brown | 50 | 20 |
| 1043 | **350** | 40s. red | 70 | 25 |
| 1044 | - | 44s. brown | 80 | 30 |
| 1045 | - | 60s. slate | 95 | 35 |
| 1046 | - | 80s. brown | 1·50 | 80 |
| 1047 | - | 1l. green | 2·40 | 95 |
| 1048 | - | 2l. green | 4·75 | 3·00 |

PORTRAITS: 16s. Benjamin Franklin (journalist and statesman, 150th birth anniv); 20s. Rembrandt (artist, 350th birth anniv); 44s. Heinrich Heine (poet, death centenary); 60s. George Bernard Shaw (dramatist, birth centenary); 80s. Fyodor Dostoevsky (novelist, 75th death anniv); 1l. Henrik Ibsen (dramatist, 50th death anniv); 2l. Pierre Curie (physicist, 50th death anniv).

**351** Cyclists

**1957.** Tour of Egypt Cycle Race.

| | | | | |
|---|---|---|---|---|
| 1049 | **351** | 80s. brown | 1·50 | 70 |
| 1050 | **351** | 80s. turquoise | 1·50 | 70 |

**352** Woman with Microscope

**1957.** International Women's Day. Inscr as in T 352.

| | | | | |
|---|---|---|---|---|
| 1051 | **352** | 12s. blue | 10 | 10 |
| 1052 | - | 16s. brown | 30 | 15 |
| 1053 | - | 44s. green | 60 | 30 |

DESIGNS: 16s. Woman and children; 44s. Woman feeding poultry.

**353** "New Times"

**1957.** 60th Anniv of "New Times" (book).

| | | | | |
|---|---|---|---|---|
| 1054 | **353** | 16s. red | 40 | 20 |

**354** Lisunov Li-2 Airliner

**1957.** Air. 10th Anniv of Bulgarian Airways.

| | | | | |
|---|---|---|---|---|
| 1055 | **354** | 80s. blue | 1·50 | 50 |

**355** St. Cyril and St. Methodius

**1957.** Centenary of Canonization of Saints Cyril and Methodius (founders of Cyrillic alphabet).

| | | | | |
|---|---|---|---|---|
| 1056 | **355** | 44s. olive and buff | 1·50 | 60 |

**356** Basketball

**1957.** 10th European Basketball Championships.

| | | | | |
|---|---|---|---|---|
| 1057 | **356** | 44s. green | 2·40 | 70 |

**357** Girl in National Costume

**1957.** 6th World Youth Festival, Moscow.

| | | | | |
|---|---|---|---|---|
| 1058 | **357** | 44s. blue | 80 | 30 |

**358** G. Dimitrov

**1957.** 75th Birth Anniv of Georgi Dimitrov (statesman).

| | | | | |
|---|---|---|---|---|
| 1059 | **358** | 44s. red | 1·50 | 50 |

**359** V. Levski

**1957.** 120th Birth Anniv of Vasil Levski (revolutionary).

| | | | | |
|---|---|---|---|---|
| 1060 | **359** | 44s. green | 95 | 30 |

**360** View of Turnovo and Ludwig Zamenhof (inventor)

**1957.** 70th Anniv of Esperanto (invented language) and 50th Anniv of Bulgarian Esperanto Association.

| | | | | |
|---|---|---|---|---|
| 1061 | **360** | 44s. green | 1·50 | 50 |

**361** Soldiers in Battle

**1957.** 80th Anniv of Liberation from Turkey.

| | | | | |
|---|---|---|---|---|
| 1062 | - | 16s. green | 20 | 10 |
| 1063 | **361** | 44s. brown | 80 | 25 |

DESIGN: 16s. Old and young soldiers.

**362** Woman Planting Tree

**1957.** Reafforestation Campaign.

| | | | | |
|---|---|---|---|---|
| 1064 | **362** | 2s. green | 20 | 15 |
| 1065 | - | 12s. brown | 20 | 15 |
| 1066 | - | 16s. blue | 20 | 15 |
| 1067 | - | 44s. turquoise | 70 | 30 |
| 1068 | - | 80s. green | 1·20 | 60 |

DESIGNS—HORIZ: 12s. Red deer in forest; 16s. Dam and trees; 44s. Polikarpov Po-2 biplane over forest; 80s. Trees and cornfield.

**363** Two Hemispheres

**1957.** 4th World TUC, Leipzig.

| | | | | |
|---|---|---|---|---|
| 1069 | **363** | 44s. blue | 80 | 30 |

**364** Lenin

**1957.** 40th Anniv of Russian Revolution. Inscr "1917–1957".

| | | | | |
|---|---|---|---|---|
| 1070 | **364** | 12s. brown | 60 | 30 |
| 1071 | - | 16s. turquoise | 1·30 | 80 |
| 1072 | - | 44s. blue | 2·75 | 95 |

| | | | | |
|---|---|---|---|---|
| 1073 | - | 60s. red | 3·00 | 1·50 |
| 1074 | - | 80s. green | 9·75 | 3·50 |

DESIGNS: 16s. Cruiser "Aurora"; 44s. Dove of Peace over Europe; 60s. Revolutionaries; 80s. Oil refinery.

**365** Youth and Girl

**1957.** 10th Anniv of Dimitrov National Youth Movement.

| | | | | |
|---|---|---|---|---|
| 1075 | **365** | 16s. red | 30 | 20 |

**366** Partisans

**1957.** 15th Anniv of Fatherland Front.

| | | | | |
|---|---|---|---|---|
| 1076 | **366** | 16s. brown | 30 | 20 |

**367** Mikhail Glinka (composer, death centenary)

**1957.** Cultural Celebrities.

| | | | | |
|---|---|---|---|---|
| 1077 | **367** | 12s. brown | 60 | 20 |
| 1078 | - | 16s. green | 70 | 25 |
| 1079 | - | 40s. blue | 1·60 | 30 |
| 1080 | - | 44s. brown | 1·70 | 40 |
| 1081 | - | 60s. brown | 1·90 | 80 |
| 1082 | - | 80s. purple | 3·00 | 2·75 |

DESIGNS: 16s. Ion Comenius (educationist) (300th anniv of publication of "Didoetica Opera Omria"); 40s. Carl Linnaeus (botanist, 250th birth anniv); 44s. William Blake (writer, birth bicent); 60s. Carlo Goldoni (dramatist, 250th birth anniv); 80s. Auguste Comte (philosopher, death centenary).

**368** Hotel Vasil, Kolarov

**1958.** Holiday Resorts.

| | | | | |
|---|---|---|---|---|
| 1083 | | 4s. blue | 20 | 15 |
| 1084 | | 8s. brown | 20 | 15 |
| 1085 | | 12s. green | 20 | 15 |
| 1086 | **368** | 16s. green | 20 | 15 |
| 1087 | - | 44s. turquoise | 50 | 20 |
| 1088 | - | 60s. blue | 80 | 30 |
| 1089 | - | 80s. brown | 95 | 40 |
| 1090 | - | 1l. brown | 1·20 | 50 |

DESIGNS—HORIZ: 4s. Skis and Pirin Mts; 8s. Old house in Koprivshtita; 12s. Hostel at Yelingrad; 44s. Hotel at Momin-Prokhod; 60s. Seaside hotel and peninsula, Nesebur; 80s. Beach scene, Varna; 1l. Modern hotels, Varna.

**369** Brown Hare

**1958.** Forest Animals.

| | | | | |
|---|---|---|---|---|
| 1091 | **369** | 2s. deep green & green | 70 | 20 |
| 1092 | - | 12s. brown and green | 1·20 | 30 |
| 1093 | - | 16s. brown and green | 1·60 | 40 |
| 1094 | - | 44s. brown and blue | 1·90 | 60 |
| 1095 | - | 80s. brown and ochre | 2·40 | 80 |
| 1096 | - | 1l. brown and blue | 3·00 | 1·20 |

DESIGNS—VERT: 12s. Roe doe. HORIZ: 16s. Red deer; 44s. Chamois; 80s. Brown bear; 1l. Wild boar.

**370** Marx and Lenin

**1958.** 7th Bulgarian Communist Party Congress. Inscr as in T 370.

| | | | | |
|---|---|---|---|---|
| 1097 | **370** | 12s. brown | 50 | 20 |
| 1098 | - | 16s. red | 80 | 30 |
| 1099 | - | 44s. blue | 1·60 | 95 |

DESIGNS: 16s. Workers marching with banners; 44s. Lenin blast furnaces.

**371** Wrestlers

**1958.** Wrestling Championships.

| | | | | |
|---|---|---|---|---|
| 1100 | **371** | 60s. lake | 2·10 | 1·50 |
| 1101 | **371** | 80s. sepia | 2·40 | 1·90 |

**372** Chessmen and "Oval Chessboard"

**1958.** 5th World Students' Team Chess Championship, Varna.

| | | | | |
|---|---|---|---|---|
| 1102 | **372** | 80s. green | 11·50 | 10·50 |

**373** Russian Pavilion

**1958.** 18th International Fair, Plovdiv.

| | | | | |
|---|---|---|---|---|
| 1103 | **373** | 44s. red | 95 | 70 |

**374** Swimmer

**1958.** Bulgarian Students' Games.

| | | | | |
|---|---|---|---|---|
| 1104 | **374** | 16s. blue | 30 | 15 |
| 1105 | - | 28s. brown | 60 | 20 |
| 1106 | - | 44s. green | 85 | 50 |

DESIGNS: 28s. Dancer; 44s. Volleyball players at net.

**375** Onions

**1958.** "Agricultural Propaganda".

| | | | | |
|---|---|---|---|---|
| 1107 | **375** | 2s. brown | 20 | 15 |
| 1108 | - | 12s. lake (Garlic) | 20 | 15 |
| 1109 | - | 16s. myrtle (Peppers) | 30 | 20 |
| 1110 | - | 44s. red (Tomatoes) | 50 | 25 |
| 1111 | - | 80s. green (Cucumbers) | 1·20 | 40 |
| 1112 | - | 1l. violet (Aubergines) | 1·60 | 50 |

**376** Insurgent with Rifle

**1958.** 35th Anniv of September Uprising.

| | | | | |
|---|---|---|---|---|
| 1113 | **376** | 16s. orange | 50 | 30 |
| 1114 | - | 44s. lake | 95 | 70 |

DESIGN—HORIZ: 44s. Insurgent helping wounded comrade.

**377** Conference Emblem

**1958.** 1st World Trade Union's Young Workers' Conference, Prague.

| | | | | |
|---|---|---|---|---|
| 1115 | **377** | 44s. blue | 95 | 70 |

**378** Exhibition Emblem

**1958.** Brussels International Exhibition.

| | | | | |
|---|---|---|---|---|
| 1116 | **378** | 1l. blue and black | 9·75 | 9·75 |

**379** Sputnik over Globe

**1958.** Air. IGY.

| | | | | |
|---|---|---|---|---|
| 1117 | **379** | 80s. turquoise | 6·75 | 5·75 |

**380** Running

**1958.** Balkan Games. Inscr "1958".

| | | | | |
|---|---|---|---|---|
| 1118 | **380** | 16s. brown | 85 | 40 |
| 1119 | - | 44s. olive | 95 | 60 |
| 1120 | - | 60s. blue | 1·60 | 70 |
| 1121 | - | 80s. green | 1·90 | 95 |
| 1122 | - | 4l. lake | 11·50 | 7·25 |

DESIGNS—HORIZ: 44s. Throwing the javelin; 60s. High-jumping; 80s. Hurdling. VERT: 4l. Putting the shot.

**381** Young Gardeners

**1958.** 4th Dimitrov National Youth Movement Congress. Inscr as in T 381.

| | | | | |
|---|---|---|---|---|
| 1123 | **381** | 8s. green | 20 | 15 |
| 1124 | - | 12s. brown | 20 | 15 |
| 1125 | - | 16s. purple | 20 | 15 |
| 1126 | - | 40s. blue | 80 | 20 |
| 1127 | - | 44s. red | 1·20 | 50 |

DESIGNS—HORIZ: 12s. Farm girl with cattle; 40s. Youth with wheel-barrow. VERT: 16s. Youth with pickaxe and girl with spade; 44s. Communist Party Building.

**382** Smirnenski

**1958.** 60th Birth Anniv of Khristo Smirnenski (poet and revolutionary).

| | | | | |
|---|---|---|---|---|
| 1128 | **382** | 16s. red | 40 | 20 |

**383** First Cosmic Rockets

**1959.** Air. Launching of First Cosmic Rocket.

| | | | | |
|---|---|---|---|---|
| 1129 | **383** | 2l. brown and blue | 9·75 | 9·75 |

**384** Footballers

**1959.** Youth Football Games, Sofia.

| | | | | |
|---|---|---|---|---|
| 1130 | **384** | 2l. brown on cream | 3·50 | 2·40 |

**385** UNESCO Headquarters, Paris

**1959.** Inauguration of UNESCO Headquarters Building.

| | | | | |
|---|---|---|---|---|
| 1131 | **385** | 2l. purple on cream | 3·50 | 2·40 |

**386** Skier

**1959.** 40 Years of Skiing in Bulgaria.

| | | | | |
|---|---|---|---|---|
| 1132 | **386** | 1l. blue on cream | 2·40 | 95 |

**1959.** No. 1110 surch 45 CT.

| | | | | |
|---|---|---|---|---|
| 1133 | | 45s. on 44s. red | 1·50 | 50 |

**388** Military Telegraph Linesman

**1959.** 80th Anniv of 1st Bulgarian Postage Stamps.

| | | | | |
|---|---|---|---|---|
| 1134 | **388** | 12s. yellow and green | 20 | 15 |
| 1135 | - | 16s. mauve and purple | 50 | 20 |
| 1136 | - | 60s. yellow and brown | 85 | 40 |
| 1137 | - | 80s. salmon and red | 95 | 50 |
| 1138 | - | 1l. blue | 2·40 | 60 |
| 1139 | - | 2l. brown | 4·75 | 2·40 |

**MS**1139a 91×121 mm. 60s. (+4l.40) yellow and black (as 1136). Imperf — 75·00 — 75·00

**MS**1139b 125×125 mm. Remaining values in different colours (sold at 5l.) Imperf — 75·00 — 75·00

DESIGNS—HORIZ: 16s. 19th-century mail-coach; 80s. Early postal car; 2l. Striking railway workers. VERT: 60s. Bulgarian 1879 stamp; 1l. Radio tower.

**389** Great Tits

**1959.** Birds.

| | | | | |
|---|---|---|---|---|
| 1140 | **389** | 2s. slate and yellow | 40 | 20 |
| 1141 | - | 8s. green and brown | 70 | 30 |
| 1142 | - | 16s. sepia and brown | 80 | 35 |
| 1143 | - | 45s. myrtle and brown | 1·80 | 70 |
| 1144 | - | 60s. grey and blue | 3·50 | 1·20 |

| | | | | |
|---|---|---|---|---|
| 1145 | - | 80s. drab and turquoise | 4·75 | 1·90 |

DESIGNS—HORIZ: 8s. Hoopoe; 60s. Rock partridge; 80s. European cuckoo. VERT: 16s. Great spotted woodpecker; 45s. Grey partridge.

**390** Cotton-picking

**1959.** Five Year Plan.

| | | | | |
|---|---|---|---|---|
| 1146 | | 2s. brown | 20 | 15 |
| 1147 | | 4s. bistre | 20 | 15 |
| 1148 | 390 | 5s. green | 20 | 15 |
| 1149 | - | 10s. brown | 20 | 15 |
| 1150 | - | 12s. brown | 20 | 15 |
| 1151 | - | 15s. mauve | 20 | 15 |
| 1152 | - | 16s. violet | 20 | 15 |
| 1153 | - | 20s. orange | 30 | 20 |
| 1154 | - | 25s. blue | 30 | 20 |
| 1155 | - | 28s. green | 40 | 20 |
| 1156 | - | 40s. blue | 50 | 20 |
| 1157 | - | 45s. brown | 50 | 20 |
| 1158 | - | 60s. red | 95 | 40 |
| 1159 | - | 80s. olive | 1·70 | 30 |
| 1160 | - | 1l. lake | 95 | 50 |
| 1161 | - | 1l.25 blue | 3·00 | 95 |
| 1162 | - | 2l. red | 1·80 | 60 |

DESIGNS—HORIZ: 2s. Children at play; 10s. Dairymaid milking cow; 16s. Industrial plant; 20s. Combine-harvester; 40s. Hydro-electric barrage; 60s. Furnaceman; 1l.25, Machinist. VERT: 4s. Woman doctor examining child; 12s. Tobacco harvesting; 15s. Machinist; 25s. Power linesman; 28s. Tending sunflowers; 45s. Miner; 80s. Fruit-picker; 1l. Workers with symbols of agriculture and industry; 2l. Worker with banner.

**391** Patriots

**1959.** 300th Anniv of Batak.

| | | | | |
|---|---|---|---|---|
| 1163 | 391 | 16s. brown | 50 | 20 |

**392** Piper

**1959.** Spartacist Games. Inscr "1958–1959".

| | | | | |
|---|---|---|---|---|
| 1164 | 392 | 4s. olive on cream | 20 | 15 |
| 1165 | - | 12s. red on yellow | 20 | 15 |
| 1166 | - | 16s. lake on salmon | 30 | 20 |
| 1167 | - | 20s. blue on blue | 50 | 25 |
| 1168 | - | 80s. green on green | 1·50 | 60 |
| 1169 | - | 1l. brown on orange | 1·60 | 1·10 |

DESIGNS—VERT: 12s. Gymnastics; 1l. Urn. HORIZ: 16s. Girls exercising with hoops; 20s. Dancers leaping; 80s. Ballet dancers.

**393** Soldiers in Lorry

**1959.** 15th Anniv of Fatherland Front Government.

| | | | | |
|---|---|---|---|---|
| 1170 | 393 | 12s. blue and red | 20 | 15 |
| 1171 | - | 16s. black and red | 20 | 15 |
| 1172 | - | 45s. blue and red | 40 | 20 |
| 1173 | - | 60s. green and red | 50 | 30 |
| 1174 | - | 80s. brown and red | 80 | 40 |
| 1175 | - | 1l.25 brown and red | 1·60 | 70 |

DESIGNS—HORIZ: 16s. Partisans meeting Red Army soldiers; 45s. Blast furnaces; 60s. Tanks; 80s. Combine-harvester in cornfield. VERT: 1l.25, Pioneers with banner.

**394** Footballer

**1959.** 50th Anniv of Football in Bulgaria.

| | | | | |
|---|---|---|---|---|
| 1176 | 394 | 1l.25 green on yellow | 7·75 | 7·75 |

**395** Tupolev Tu-104A Jetliner and Statue of Liberty

**1959.** Air. Visit of Nikita Khrushchev (Russian Prime Minister) to U.S.A.

| | | | | |
|---|---|---|---|---|
| 1177 | 395 | 1l. pink and blue | 4·00 | 4·00 |

**396** Globe and Letter

**1959.** International Correspondence Week.

| | | | | |
|---|---|---|---|---|
| 1178 | 396 | 45s. black and green | 70 | 20 |
| 1179 | - | 1l.25 red, black & blue | 1·30 | 50 |

DESIGN: 1l.25, Pigeon and letter.

**397** Parachutist

**1960.** 3rd Voluntary Defence Congress.

| | | | | |
|---|---|---|---|---|
| 1180 | 397 | 1l.25 cream & turquoise | 3·50 | 1·60 |

**398** N. Vaptsarov

**1960.** 50th Birth Anniv of Nikola Vaptsarov (poet and revolutionary).

| | | | | |
|---|---|---|---|---|
| 1181 | 398 | 80s. brown and green | 95 | 50 |

**399** Dr. L. Zamenhof

**1960.** Birth Centenary of Dr. Ludwig Zamenhof (inventor of Esperanto).

| | | | | |
|---|---|---|---|---|
| 1182 | 399 | 1l.25 green & lt green | 1·50 | 95 |

**400**

**1960.** 50th Anniv of State Opera.

| | | | | |
|---|---|---|---|---|
| 1183 | 400 | 80s. black and green | 95 | 60 |
| 1184 | - | 1l.25 black and red | 1·50 | 85 |

DESIGN: 1l.25, Lyre.

**401** Track of Trajectory of "Lunik 3" around the Moon

**1960.** Flight of "Lunik 3".

| | | | | |
|---|---|---|---|---|
| 1185 | 401 | 1l.25 green, yellow & bl | 7·25 | 5·75 |

**402** Skier

**1960.** Winter Olympic Games.

| | | | | |
|---|---|---|---|---|
| 1186 | 402 | 2l. brown, blue & black | 1·50 | 1·50 |

**403** Vela Blagoeva

**1960.** 50th Anniv of International Women's Day. Inscr "1910–1960".

| | | | | |
|---|---|---|---|---|
| 1187 | 403 | 16s. brown and pink | 20 | 15 |
| 1188 | - | 28s. olive and yellow | 20 | 15 |
| 1189 | - | 45s. green and olive | 40 | 20 |
| 1190 | - | 60s. blue and light blue | 50 | 30 |
| 1191 | - | 80s. brown and red | 80 | 40 |
| 1192 | - | 1l.25 olive and ochre | 95 | 80 |

PORTRAITS: 28s. Anna Maimunkowa; 45s. Vela Piskova; 60s. Rosa Luxemburg; 80s. Clara Zetkin; 1l.25, Nadezhda Krupskaya.

**404** Lenin

**1960.** 90th Birth Anniv of Lenin.

| | | | | |
|---|---|---|---|---|
| 1193 | 404 | 16s. flesh and brown | 1·90 | 80 |
| 1194 | - | 45s. black and pink | 3·50 | 1·60 |

DESIGN: 45s. "Lenin at Smolny" (writing in chair).

**406** Basketball Players

**1960.** 7th European Women's Basketball Championships.

| | | | | |
|---|---|---|---|---|
| 1195 | 406 | 1l.25 black and yellow | 1·90 | 95 |

**407** Moon Rocket

**1960.** Air. Landing of Russian Rocket on Moon.

| | | | | |
|---|---|---|---|---|
| 1196 | 407 | 1l.25 black, yellow & bl | 7·25 | 5·75 |

**408** Parachutist

**1960.** World Parachuting Championships, 1960.

| | | | | |
|---|---|---|---|---|
| 1197 | 408 | 16s. blue and lilac | 60 | 55 |
| 1198 | - | 1l.25 red and blue | 3·00 | 1·20 |

DESIGN: 1l.25, Parachutes descending.

**409** "Gentiana lutea"

**1960.** Flowers.

| | | | | |
|---|---|---|---|---|
| 1199 | 409 | 2s. orange, grn & drab | 20 | 15 |
| 1200 | - | 5s. red, green and yellow | 80 | 20 |
| 1201 | - | 25s. orge, grn & salmon | 85 | 25 |
| 1202 | - | 45s. mauve, grn & lilac | 95 | 30 |
| 1203 | - | 60s. red, green and buff | 1·50 | 40 |
| 1204 | - | 80s. blue, green & drab | 1·90 | 1·50 |

FLOWERS: 5s. "Tulipa rhodopea"; 25s. "Lilium jankae"; 45s. "Rhododendron ponticum"; 60s. "Cypripedium calceolus"; 80s. "Haberlea rhodopenis".

**410** Football

**1960.** Olympic Games.

| | | | | |
|---|---|---|---|---|
| 1205 | 410 | 8s. pink and brown | 20 | 15 |
| 1206 | - | 12s. pink and violet | 20 | 15 |
| 1207 | - | 16s. pink & turquoise | 40 | 20 |
| 1208 | - | 45s. pink and purple | 50 | 25 |
| 1209 | - | 80s. pink and blue | 1·10 | 70 |
| 1210 | - | 2l. pink and green | 1·50 | 95 |

DESIGNS: 12s. Wrestling; 16s. Weightlifting; 45s. Gymnastics; 80s. Canoeing; 2l. Running.

**411** Racing Cyclists

**1960.** Tour of Bulgaria Cycle Race.

| | | | | |
|---|---|---|---|---|
| 1211 | 411 | 1l. black, yellow & red | 1·90 | 1·50 |

**412** Globes

**1960.** 15th Anniv of WFTU.

| | | | | |
|---|---|---|---|---|
| 1212 | 412 | 1l.25 cobalt and blue | 95 | 60 |

**413** Popov

**1960.** Birth Centenary of Alexsandr Popov (Russian radio pioneer).

| | | | | |
|---|---|---|---|---|
| 1213 | 413 | 90s. black and blue | 1·50 | 95 |

**414** Y. Veshin

**1960.** Birth Centenary of Yavoslav Veshin (painter).

| | | | | |
|---|---|---|---|---|
| 1214 | 414 | 1l. olive and yellow | 5·75 | 3·00 |

**415** U.N. Headquarters, New York

**1961.** 15th Anniv of UNO.

| | | | | |
|---|---|---|---|---|
| 1215 | **415** | 1l. cream and brown | 2·40 | 2·40 |
| **MS**1215a 74×57 mm. **415** 1l. (+1l.) pink and green. Imperf | | | 13·50 | 13·50 |

**416** Boyana Church

**1961.** 700th Anniv of Boyana Murals (1959).

| | | | | |
|---|---|---|---|---|
| 1216 | **416** | 60s. black, emer & grn | 95 | 40 |
| 1217 | - | 80s. grn, cream & orange | 1·50 | 50 |
| 1218 | - | 1l.25 red, cream & green | 1·90 | 95 |

DESIGNS (Frescoes of): 80s. Theodor Tiron; 1l.25, Desislava.

**417** Cosmic Rocket and Dogs Belda and Strelka

**1961.** Russian Cosmic Rocket Flight of August, 1960.

| | | | | |
|---|---|---|---|---|
| 1219 | **417** | 1l.25 blue and red | 6·75 | 6·75 |

**419** Pleven Costume

**1961.** Provincial Costumes.

| | | | | |
|---|---|---|---|---|
| 1220 | - | 12s. yellow, green & orge | 20 | 10 |
| 1221 | **419** | 16s. brown, buff & lilac | 20 | 10 |
| 1222 | - | 28s. red, black, & green | 40 | 15 |
| 1223 | - | 45s. blue and red | 80 | 20 |
| 1224 | - | 60s. yellow, blue & turq | 1·10 | 30 |
| 1225 | - | 80s. red, green & yellow | 1·30 | 70 |

COSTUMES: 12s. Kyustendil; 28s. Sliven; 45s. Sofia; 60s. Rhodope; 80c. Karnobat.

**420** Clock Tower, Vratsa

**1961.** Museums and Monuments. Values and star in red.

| | | | | |
|---|---|---|---|---|
| 1226 | **420** | 8s. green | 20 | 15 |
| 1227 | - | 12s. violet | 20 | 15 |
| 1228 | - | 16s. brown | 20 | 15 |
| 1229 | - | 20s. blue | 20 | 15 |
| 1230 | - | 28s. turquoise | 30 | 20 |
| 1231 | - | 40s. brown | 40 | 25 |
| 1232 | - | 45s. olive | 50 | 30 |
| 1233 | - | 60s. slate | 70 | 40 |
| 1234 | - | 80s. brown | 1·20 | 50 |
| 1235 | - | 1l. turquoise | 1·90 | 95 |

DESIGNS—As Type **420**. VERT: 12s. Clock Tower, Bansko; 20s. "Agushev" building, Mogilitsa (Smolensk). HORIZ: 28s. Oslekoff House, Koprivshtitsa; 40s. Pasha's House, Melnik. SQUARE (27×27 mm): 16s. Wine jug; 45s. Lion (bas-relief); 60s. "Horseman of Madara"; 80s. Fresco, Bachkovo Monastery; 1l. Coin of Tsar Konstantin-Asen (13th cent).

**421** Dalmatian Pelican

**1961.** Birds.

| | | | | |
|---|---|---|---|---|
| 1236 | | 2s. turquoise, blk & red | 25 | 15 |
| 1237 | **421** | 4s. orange, blk & grn | 30 | 20 |
| 1238 | - | 16s. orange, brn & grn | 40 | 30 |
| 1239 | - | 80s. yellow, brn & turq | 3·00 | 1·10 |
| 1240 | - | 1l. yellow, sepia and blue | 3·50 | 1·70 |
| 1241 | - | 2l. yellow, brown & blue | 4·75 | 1·90 |

DESIGNS: 2s. White capercaillie; 16s. Common pheasant; 80s. Great bustard; 1l. Lammergeier; 2l. Hazel grouse.

**422** "Communications and Transport"

**1961.** 50th Anniv of Transport Workers' Union.

| | | | | |
|---|---|---|---|---|
| 1242 | **422** | 80s. green and black | 95 | 50 |

**423** Gagarin and Rocket

**1961.** World's First Manned Space Flight.

| | | | | |
|---|---|---|---|---|
| 1243 | **423** | 4l. turquoise, blk & red | 6·75 | 4·25 |

**424** Shevchenko (Ukrainian poet)

**1961.** Death Centenary of Taras Shevchenko.

| | | | | |
|---|---|---|---|---|
| 1244 | **424** | 1l. brown and green | 6·25 | 4·25 |

**425** Throwing the Discus

**1961.** World Students' Games. Values and inscr in black.

| | | | | |
|---|---|---|---|---|
| 1245 | - | 4s. blue | 20 | 15 |
| 1246 | - | 5s. red | 20 | 15 |
| 1247 | - | 16s. olive | 30 | 20 |
| 1248 | **425** | 45s. blue | 50 | 30 |
| 1249 | - | 1l.25 brown | 1·70 | 50 |
| 1250 | - | 2l. mauve | 1·90 | 1·30 |
| **MS**1250a 66×66 mm. 5l. blue, yellow and green (Sports Palace and inscriptions). Imperf | | | 19·00 | 19·00 |

DESIGNS—VERT: 4s. Water polo; 2l. Basketball. HORIZ: 5s. Tennis; 16s. Fencing; 1l.25, Sports Palace, Sofia.

**426** Short-snouted Seahorse

**1961.** Black Sea Fauna.

| | | | | |
|---|---|---|---|---|
| 1251 | | 2s. sepia and green | 20 | 15 |
| 1252 | | 12s. pink and blue | 20 | 15 |
| 1253 | | 16s. violet and blue | 25 | 20 |
| 1254 | **426** | 45s. brown and blue | 1·50 | 95 |
| 1255 | - | 1l. blue and green | 4·00 | 1·50 |
| 1256 | - | 1l.25 brown and blue | 4·75 | 2·40 |

DESIGNS—HORIZ: 2s. Mediterranean monk seal; 12s. Lung jellyfish; 16s. Common dolphins; 1l. Stellate sturgeons; 1l.25, Thorn-backed ray.

**427** "Space" Dogs

**1961.** Air. Space Exploration.

| | | | | |
|---|---|---|---|---|
| 1257 | **427** | 2l. slate and purple | 5·75 | 4·25 |
| 1258 | - | 2l. blue, yellow & orange | 10·50 | 6·75 |

DESIGN: No. 1258, "Venus" rocket in flight (24×41½ mm).

**428** Dimitur Blagoev as Orator

**1961.** 70th Anniv of First Bulgarian Social Democratic Party Congress, Buzludzha.

| | | | | |
|---|---|---|---|---|
| 1259 | **428** | 45s. red and cream | 30 | 20 |
| 1260 | **428** | 80s. blue and pink | 70 | 50 |
| 1261 | **428** | 2l. sepia and green | 1·50 | 1·20 |

**429** Hotel

**1961.** Tourist issue. Inscr in black; designs green. Background colours given.

| | | | | |
|---|---|---|---|---|
| 1262 | **429** | 4s. green | 10 | 10 |
| 1263 | - | 12s. blue (Hikers) | 10 | 10 |
| 1264 | - | 16s. green (Tents) | 20 | 15 |
| 1265 | - | 1l.25 bistre (Climber) | 1·20 | 30 |

Nos. 1263/5 are vert.

**430** "The Golden Girl"

**1961.** Bulgarian Fables.

| | | | | |
|---|---|---|---|---|
| 1266 | **430** | 2s. multicoloured | 20 | 15 |
| 1267 | - | 8s. grey, black & purple | 20 | 15 |
| 1268 | - | 12s. pink, black & green | 25 | 20 |
| 1269 | - | 16s. multicoloured | 95 | 50 |
| 1270 | - | 45s. multicoloured | 1·90 | 80 |
| 1271 | - | 80s. multicoloured | 2·40 | 95 |

DESIGNS: 8s. Man and woman ("The Living Water"); 12s. Archer and dragon ("The Golden Apple"); 16s. Horseman ("Krali Marko", national hero); 45s. Female archer on stag ("Samovila-Vila", fairy); 80s. "Tom Thumb" and cockerel.

**431** Major Titov in Space-suit

**1961.** Air. 2nd Russian Manned Space Flight.

| | | | | |
|---|---|---|---|---|
| 1272 | **431** | 75s. flesh, blue & olive | 4·00 | 3·00 |
| 1273 | - | 1l.25 pink, bl & violet | 4·75 | 4·00 |

DESIGN: 1l.25, "Vostok-2" in flight.

**432** "Amanita caesarea"

**1961.** Mushrooms.

| | | | | |
|---|---|---|---|---|
| 1274 | **432** | 2s. red, bistre & black | 20 | 15 |
| 1275 | - | 4s. brown, grn & blk | 20 | 15 |
| 1276 | - | 12s. brown, bistre & blk | 20 | 15 |
| 1277 | - | 16s. brown, mve & blk | 20 | 20 |
| 1278 | - | 45s. multicoloured | 30 | 30 |
| 1279 | - | 80s. orange, sepia & blk | 80 | 60 |
| 1280 | - | 1l.25 lav, brn & blk | 1·60 | 80 |
| 1281 | - | 2l. brown, bistre & black | 2·10 | 1·90 |

MUSHROOMS: 4s. "Psalliota silvatica"; 12s. "Boletus elegans"; 16s. "Boletus edulis"; 45s. "Lactarius deliciosus"; 80s. "Lepiota procera"; 1l.25, "Pleurotus ostreatus"; 2l. "Armillariella mellea".

**433** Dimitur and Konstantin Miladinov (authors)

**1961.** Publication Centenary of "Bulgarian Popular Songs".

| | | | | |
|---|---|---|---|---|
| 1282 | **433** | 1l.25 black and olive | 1·50 | 95 |

**1962.** Surch. (A) Surch in one line; (B) in two lines.

| | | | |
|---|---|---|---|
| 1283 | 1s. on 10s. brown (1149) | 20 | 15 |
| 1284 | 1s. on 12s. brown (1150) | 20 | 15 |
| 1285 | 2s. on 15s. mauve (1151) | 20 | 15 |
| 1286 | 2s. on 16s. violet (1152) | 20 | 15 |
| 1287 | 2s. on 20s. orange (1153) (A) | 20 | 15 |
| 1288 | 2s. on 20s. orange (1153) (B) | 30 | 15 |
| 1289 | 3s. on 25s. blue (1154) | 20 | 15 |
| 1290 | 3s. on 28s. green (1155) | 20 | 15 |
| 1291 | 5s. on 44s. green (1087) | 30 | 15 |
| 1292 | 5s. on 44s. red (1110) | 30 | 15 |
| 1293 | 5s. on 45s. brown (1157) | 40 | 20 |
| 1294 | 10s. on 1l. red (1160) | 60 | 30 |
| 1295 | 20s. on 2l. red (1162) | 1·20 | 70 |
| 1296 | 40s. on 4l. red (889) | 3·00 | 1·50 |

**436** Isker River

**1962.** Air.

| | | | | |
|---|---|---|---|---|
| 1297 | **436** | 1s. blue and violet | 20 | 15 |
| 1298 | - | 2s. blue and pink | 20 | 15 |
| 1299 | - | 3s. brown and chestnut | 20 | 20 |
| 1300 | - | 10s. black and bistre | 60 | 25 |
| 1301 | - | 40s. black and green | 2·30 | 1·10 |

DESIGNS: 2s. Yacht at Varna; 3s. Melnik; 10s. Turnovo; 40s. Pirin Mountains.

**437** Freighter "Varna"

**1962.** Bulgarian Merchant Navy.

| | | | | |
|---|---|---|---|---|
| 1302 | **437** | 1s. green and blue | 20 | 10 |
| 1303 | - | 5s. light blue and green | 50 | 15 |
| 1304 | - | 20s. violet and blue | 1·30 | 50 |

SHIPS: 5s. Tanker "Komsomols"; 20s. Liner "Georgi Dimitrov".

**438** Rila Mountains

**1962.** Views.

| | | | | |
|---|---|---|---|---|
| 1305 | **438** | 1s. turquoise | 20 | 15 |
| 1306 | - | 2s. blue | 20 | 15 |
| 1307 | - | 6s. turquoise | 40 | 20 |
| 1308 | - | 8s. purple | 60 | 30 |
| 1309 | - | 13s. green | 1·20 | 70 |
| 1310 | - | 1l. deep green | 6·75 | 1·90 |

VIEWS: 2s. Pirin Mts; 6s. Fishing boats, Nesebur; 8s. Danube shipping; 13s. Viden Castle; 1l. Rhodope Mts.

**439** Georgi Dimitrov as Typesetter

**1962.** 80th Anniv of State Printing Office.

| | | | | |
|---|---|---|---|---|
| 1311 | **439** | 2s. red, black & yellow | 20 | 15 |
| 1312 | - | 13s. black, orange & yell | 80 | 40 |

DESIGN: 13s. Emblem of Printing Office.

**440** Pink Roses

**1962.** Bulgarian Roses. T 440 and similar designs.

| | | | | |
|---|---|---|---|---|
| 1313 | | 1s. pink, green and violet | 20 | 15 |
| 1314 | | 2s. red, green and buff | 20 | 15 |
| 1315 | | 3s. red, green and blue | 40 | 20 |
| 1316 | | 4s. yellow, turquoise & grn | 60 | 25 |
| 1317 | | 5s. pink, green and blue | 95 | 30 |
| 1318 | | 6s. red, green and turquoise | 1·30 | 70 |
| 1319 | | 8s. red, green and yellow | 3·00 | 1·30 |
| 1320 | | 13s. yellow, green and blue | 5·25 | 3·75 |

**441** "The World United against Malaria"

**1962.** Malaria Eradication.

| | | | | |
|---|---|---|---|---|
| 1321 | **441** | 5s. yellow, black & brn | 60 | 20 |
| 1322 | - | 20s. yellow, green & blk | 1·80 | 80 |

DESIGN: 20s. Campaign emblem.

**442** Lenin and Front Page of "Pravda"

**1962.** 50th Anniv of "Pravda" Newspaper.

| | | | | |
|---|---|---|---|---|
| 1323 | **442** | 5s. blue, red and black | 1·90 | 1·20 |

**443** Text-book and Blackboard

**1962.** Bulgarian Teachers' Congress.

| | | | | |
|---|---|---|---|---|
| 1324 | **443** | 5s. black, yellow & blue | 50 | 20 |

**444** Footballer

**1962.** World Football Championship, Chile.

| | | | | |
|---|---|---|---|---|
| 1325 | **444** | 13s. brown, green & blk | 1·90 | 95 |

**445** Dimitrov

**1962.** 80th Birth Anniv of Georgi Dimitrov (Prime Minister 1946–49).

| | | | | |
|---|---|---|---|---|
| 1326 | **445** | 2s. green | 50 | 20 |
| 1327 | **445** | 5s. blue | 95 | 40 |

**446** Bishop

**1962.** 15th Chess Olympiad, Varna. Inscr "1962". Inscr in black.

| | | | | |
|---|---|---|---|---|
| 1328 | **446** | 1s. green and grey | 20 | 15 |
| 1329 | - | 2s. bistre and grey | 30 | 20 |
| 1330 | - | 3s. purple and grey | 40 | 25 |
| 1331 | - | 13s. orange and grey | 1·90 | 80 |
| 1332 | - | 20s. blue and grey | 2·50 | 1·50 |
| **MS**1332a | | 76×66 mm. 20s. (+30s.) red and green (Chess pieces). Imperf | 14·50 | 14·50 |

CHESS PIECES: 2s. Rook; 3s. Queen; 13s. Knight; 20s. Pawn.

XXXV КОНГРЕС
1962

13 =

(447)

**1962.** 35th Esperanto Congress, Burgas. Surch as T 447.

| | | | | |
|---|---|---|---|---|
| 1333 | **360** | 13s. on 44s. green | 4·75 | 3·50 |

**448** Festival Emblem

**1962.** World Youth Festival, Helsinki. Inscr "1962".

| | | | | |
|---|---|---|---|---|
| 1334 | **448** | 5s. blue, pink and green | 40 | 20 |
| 1335 | - | 13s. blue, purple & grey | 1·10 | 30 |

DESIGN: 13s. Girl and emblem.

**449** Ilyushin Il-18 Airliner

**1962.** Air. 13th Anniv of TABSO Airline.

| | | | | |
|---|---|---|---|---|
| 1336 | **449** | 13s. blue, ultram & blk | 1·50 | 50 |

**450** Apollo

**1962.** Butterflies and Moths. Multicoloured.

| | | | |
|---|---|---|---|
| 1337 | 1s. Type **450** | 20 | 15 |
| 1338 | 2s. Eastern festoon | 25 | 15 |
| 1339 | 3s. Meleager's blue | 30 | 15 |
| 1340 | 4s. Camberwell beauty | 40 | 20 |
| 1341 | 5s. Crimson underwing | 50 | 30 |
| 1342 | 6s. Hebe tiger moth | 95 | 40 |
| 1343 | 10s. Danube clouded | 3·50 | 1·30 |
| 1344 | 13s. Cardinal | 4·75 | 2·40 |

**451** K. E. Tsiolkovsky (scientist)

**1962.** Air. 13th International Astronautics Congress. Inscr "1962".

| | | | | |
|---|---|---|---|---|
| 1345 | **451** | 5s. drab and green | 4·75 | 1·90 |
| 1346 | - | 13s. blue and yellow | 1·90 | 95 |

DESIGN: 13s. Moon rocket.

**452** Combine Harvester

**1962.** 8th Bulgarian Communist Party Congress.

| | | | | |
|---|---|---|---|---|
| 1347 | **452** | 1s. olive and turquoise | 20 | 15 |
| 1348 | - | 2s. turquoise and blue | 25 | 20 |
| 1349 | - | 3s. brown and red | 30 | 20 |
| 1350 | - | 13s. sepia, red & purple | 1·20 | 60 |

DESIGNS: 2s. Electric train; 3s. Steel furnace; 13s. Blagoev and Dimitrov.

**453** Cover of "History of Bulgaria"

**1962.** Bicentenary of Paisii Khilendarski's "History of Bulgaria".

| | | | | |
|---|---|---|---|---|
| 1351 | **453** | 2s. black and olive | 20 | 15 |
| 1352 | - | 5s. sepia and brown | 50 | 20 |

DESIGN—HORIZ: 5s. Father Paisii at work on book.

**454** Andrian Nikolaev and "Vostok 3"

**1962.** Air. 1st "Team" Manned Space Flight.

| | | | | |
|---|---|---|---|---|
| 1353 | **454** | 1s. olive, blue and black | 30 | 20 |
| 1354 | - | 2s. olive, green & black | 70 | 30 |
| 1355 | - | 40s. pink, turquoise & blk | 4·00 | 2·10 |

DESIGNS: 2s. Pavel Ropovich and "Vostok 4"; 40s. "Vostoks 3" and "4" in flight.

**455** Parachutist

**1963**

| | | | | |
|---|---|---|---|---|
| 1356A | | 1s. lake | 20 | 10 |
| 1357A | | 1s. brown | 20 | 10 |
| 1358A | | 1s. turquoise | 20 | 10 |
| 1359A | | 1s. green | 20 | 10 |
| 1360A | **455** | 1s. blue | 20 | 10 |

DESIGNS—VERT: No. 1356, State crest. HORIZ: No. 1357, Sofia University; 1358, "Vasil Levski" Stadium, Sofia; 1359, "The Camels" (archway), Hisar.

**456** Aleko Konstantinov

**1963.** Birth Cent of Konstantinov (author).

| | | | | |
|---|---|---|---|---|
| 1361 | **456** | 5s. green and red | 50 | 30 |

**457** Mars and "Mars 1" Space Probe

**1963.** Air. Launching of Soviet Space Station "Mars 1".

| | | | | |
|---|---|---|---|---|
| 1362 | **457** | 5s. multicoloured | 95 | 50 |
| 1363 | - | 13s. turquoise, red & blk | 1·90 | 95 |

DESIGN: 13s. Release of probe from rocket.

**458** Orpheus Restaurant, "Sunny Beach"

**1963.** Black Sea Coast Resorts.

| | | | | |
|---|---|---|---|---|
| 1364 | **458** | 1s. blue | 20 | 15 |
| 1365a | - | 2s. red | 7·25 | 20 |
| 1366 | - | 3s. bistre | 30 | 20 |
| 1367 | - | 5s. purple | 50 | 20 |
| 1368 | - | 13s. turquoise | 1·50 | 40 |
| 1369 | - | 20s. green | 1·90 | 50 |

VIEWS "Sunny Beach": 5s. The Dunes Restaurant; 20s. Hotel. "Golden Sands"; 2s., 3s., 13s. Various hotels.

**459** V. Levski

**1963.** 90th Anniv of Execution of Vasil Levski (revolutionary).

| | | | | |
|---|---|---|---|---|
| 1370 | **459** | 13s. blue and yellow | 1·90 | 75 |

**460** Dimitrov, Boy and Girl

**1963.** 10th Dimitrov Communist Youth League Congress, Sofia.

| | | | | |
|---|---|---|---|---|
| 1371 | **460** | 2s. brown, red & black | 20 | 15 |
| 1372 | - | 13s. brown, turq & blk | 80 | 45 |

DESIGN: 13s. Girl and youth holding book and hammer aloft.

**461** Eurasian Red Squirrel

**1963.** Woodland Animals.

| | | | | |
|---|---|---|---|---|
| 1373 | **461** | 1s. brown, red and green on turquoise | 20 | 15 |
| 1374 | - | 2s. blk, red & grn on yell | 25 | 15 |
| 1375 | - | 3s. sep, red & ol on drab | 30 | 20 |
| 1376 | - | 5s. brown, red and blue on violet | 95 | 35 |
| 1377 | - | 13s. black, red and brown on pink | 3·50 | 65 |
| 1378 | - | 20s. sepia, red and blue on blue | 4·75 | 1·10 |

ANIMALS—HORIZ: 2s. East European hedgehog; 3s. Marbled polecat; 5s. Beech marten; 13s. Eurasian badger. VERT: 20s. European otter.

**462** Wrestling

**1963.** 15th International Open Wrestling Championships, Sofia.

| | | | | |
|---|---|---|---|---|
| 1379 | **462** | 5s. bistre and black | 50 | 20 |
| 1380 | - | 20s. brown and black | 1·50 | 85 |

DESIGN—HORIZ: 20s. As Type **462** but different hold.

**463** Congress Emblem and Allegory

**1963.** World Women's Congress, Moscow.

| | | | | |
|---|---|---|---|---|
| 1381 | **463** | 20s. blue and black | 1·50 | 55 |

**464** Esperanto Star and Sofia Arms

**1963.** 48th World Esperanto Congress, Sofia.

| | | | | |
|---|---|---|---|---|
| 1382 | **464** | 13s. multicoloured | 1·50 | 55 |

**465** Rocket, Globe and Moon

**1963.** Launching of Soviet Moon Rocket "Luna 4". Inscr "2.IV.1963".

| | | | | |
|---|---|---|---|---|
| 1383 | **465** | 1s. blue | 20 | 10 |
| 1384 | - | 2s. purple | 20 | 10 |
| 1385 | - | 3s. turquoise | 20 | 10 |

DESIGNS: 2s. Tracking equipment; 3s. Sputniks.

**466** Valery Bykovsky in Spacesuit

**1963.** Air. 2nd "Team" Manned Space Flights. Inscr "14. VI.1963".

| | | | | |
|---|---|---|---|---|
| 1386 | **466** | 1s. turquoise and lilac | 20 | 10 |
| 1387 | - | 2s. brown and yellow | 30 | 15 |
| 1388 | - | 5s. red and light red | 50 | 20 |
| 1389 | - | 20s.+10s. grn & lt bl | 2·40 | 1·10 |
| **MS**1389a 79×68 mm. 50s. purple and brown (Spassk Tower and Globe). Imperf | | | 4·75 | 4·25 |

DESIGNS: 2s. Valentina Tereshkova in spacesuit; 5s. Globe; 20s. Bykovsky and Tereshkova.

**1963.** Europa Fair, Riccione. Nos. 1314/5 and 1318 (Roses) optd MOSTRA EUROPEISTICA.1963 RICCIONE and sailing boat motif or additionally surch.

| | | | |
|---|---|---|---|
| 1390 | 2s. red, green and buff | 50 | 20 |
| 1391 | 5s. on 3s. red, green and blue | 70 | 35 |
| 1392 | 13s. on 6s. red, green & turq | 1·70 | 55 |

**468** Relay-racing

**1963.** Balkan Games. Flags in red, yellow, blue, green and black.

| | | | | |
|---|---|---|---|---|
| 1393 | **468** | 1s. green | 10 | 10 |
| 1394 | - | 2s. violet | 15 | 10 |
| 1395 | - | 3s. turquoise | 20 | 15 |
| 1396 | - | 5s. red | 95 | 20 |
| 1397 | - | 13s. brown | 4·00 | 3·00 |
| **MS**1397a 74×69 mm. 50s. black and green (as T **468**). Imperf | | | 7·00 | 7·00 |

DESIGNS: 2s. Throwing the hammer; 3s. Long jumping; 5s. High jumping; 13s. Throwing the discus. Each design includes the flags of the competing countries.

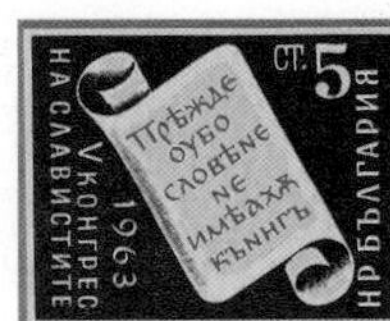


**469** Slavonic Scroll

**1963.** 5th International Slav Congress, Sofia.

| | | | | |
|---|---|---|---|---|
| 1398 | **469** | 5s. red, yellow & dp grn | 50 | 20 |

**470** Insurgents

**1963.** 40th Anniv of September Uprising.

| | | | | |
|---|---|---|---|---|
| 1399 | **470** | 2s. black and red | 30 | 15 |

**471** "Aquilegia aurea"

**1963.** Nature Protection. Flowers in natural colours; background colours given.

| | | | | |
|---|---|---|---|---|
| 1400 | **471** | 1s. turquoise | 20 | 15 |
| 1401 | - | 2s. olive | 20 | 15 |
| 1402 | - | 3s. yellow | 20 | 15 |
| 1403 | - | 5s. blue | 40 | 20 |
| 1404 | - | 6s. purple | 50 | 35 |
| 1405 | - | 8s. light grey | 95 | 45 |
| 1406 | - | 10s. mauve | 1·90 | 85 |
| 1407 | - | 13s. olive | 3·50 | 1·10 |

FLOWERS: 2s. Edelweiss; 3s. "Primula deorum"; 5s. White water-lily; 6s. Tulip; 8s. "Viola delphinantha"; 10s. Alpine clematis; 13s. "Anemone narcissiflora".

**472** Khristo Smirnenski

**1963.** 65th Birth Anniv of Smirnenski (poet and revolutionary).

| | | | | |
|---|---|---|---|---|
| 1408 | **472** | 13s. black and lilac | 95 | 45 |

**473** Chariot Horses (wall-painting)

**1963.** Thracian Tombs, Kazanilk.

| | | | | |
|---|---|---|---|---|
| 1409 | **473** | 1s. red, yellow and grey | 20 | 15 |
| 1410 | - | 2s. violet, yellow & grey | 20 | 15 |
| 1411 | - | 3s. turquoise, yell & grey | 20 | 15 |
| 1412 | - | 5s. brown, yellow & grn | 40 | 35 |
| 1413 | - | 13s. black, yellow & grn | 1·10 | 55 |
| 1414 | - | 20s. red, yellow & green | 1·90 | 85 |

DESIGNS (wall paintings on tombs): 2s. Chariot race; 3s. Flautists; 5s. Tray-bearer; 13s. Funeral feast; 20s. Seated woman.

**474** Hemispheres and Centenary Emblem

**1964.** Centenary of Red Cross.

| | | | | |
|---|---|---|---|---|
| 1415 | **474** | 1s. yellow, red & black | 20 | 15 |
| 1416 | - | 2s. blue, red and black | 20 | 15 |
| 1417 | - | 3s. multicoloured | 20 | 15 |
| 1418 | - | 5s. turq, red & black | 30 | 20 |
| 1419 | - | 13s. black, red & orange | 1·30 | 55 |

DESIGNS: 2s. Blood donation; 3s. Bandaging wrist; 5s. Nurse; 13s. Henri Dunant.

**475** Speed-skating

**1964.** Winter Olympic Games, Innsbruck.

| | | | | |
|---|---|---|---|---|
| 1420 | **475** | 1s. indigo, brown & blue | 20 | 15 |
| 1421 | - | 2s. olive, mauve & black | 20 | 15 |
| 1422 | - | 3s. green, brown & blk | 20 | 15 |
| 1423 | - | 5s. multicoloured | 40 | 20 |
| 1424 | - | 10s. orange, blk & grey | 80 | 45 |
| 1425 | - | 13s. mauve, violet & blk | 95 | 55 |
| **MS**1425a 64×67 mm. 50s. red, blue and grey (Girl skater). Imperf | | | 6·50 | 6·50 |

DESIGNS: 2s. Figure skating; 3s. Cross-country skiing; 5s. Ski jumping. Ice hockey—10s. Goalkeeper; 13s. Players.

**476** Head (2nd cent)

**1964.** 2500 Years of Bulgarian Art. Borders in grey.

| | | | | |
|---|---|---|---|---|
| 1426 | **476** | 1s. turquoise and red | 20 | 15 |
| 1427 | - | 2s. sepia and red | 20 | 15 |
| 1428 | - | 3s. bistre and red | 20 | 15 |
| 1429 | - | 5s. blue and red | 30 | 20 |
| 1430 | - | 6s. brown and red | 60 | 25 |
| 1431 | - | 8s. brown and red | 85 | 35 |
| 1432 | - | 10s. olive and red | 95 | 40 |
| 1433 | - | 13s. olive and red | 1·20 | 1·00 |

DESIGNS: 2s. Horseman (1st to 4th cent); 3s. Jug (19th cent); 5s. Buckle (19th cent); 6s. Pot (19th cent); 8s. Angel (17th cent); 10s. Animals (8th to 10th cent); 13s. Peasant woman (20th cent).

**477** "The Unborn Maid"

**1964.** Folk Tales. Multicoloured.

| | | | |
|---|---|---|---|
| 1434 | 1s. Type **477** | 20 | 15 |
| 1435 | 2s. "Grandfather's Glove" | 20 | 15 |
| 1436 | 3s. "The Big Turnip" | 20 | 15 |
| 1437 | 5s. "The Wolf and the Seven Kids" | 30 | 20 |
| 1438 | 8s. "Cunning Peter" | 60 | 35 |
| 1439 | 13s. "The Loaf of Corn" | 1·60 | 55 |

**478** Turkish Lacewing ("Ascalaphus ottomanus")

**1964.** Insects.

| | | | | |
|---|---|---|---|---|
| 1440 | **478** | 1s. black, yellow & brn | 20 | 15 |
| 1441 | - | 2s. black, ochre & turq | 20 | 15 |
| 1442 | - | 3s. green, black & drab | 25 | 20 |
| 1443 | - | 5s. violet, black & green | 90 | 35 |
| 1444 | - | 13s. brown, black & vio | 1·80 | 55 |
| 1445 | - | 20s. yellow, black & bl | 3·00 | 75 |

DESIGNS—VERT: 2s. Thread lacewing fly ("Nemoptera coa"); 5s. Alpine longhorn beetle ("Rosalia alpina"); 13s. Cockchafer ("Anisoplia austriaca"). HORIZ: 3s. Cricket ("Saga natalia"); 20s. Hunting wasp ("Scolia flavitrons").

**479** Football

**1964.** 50th Anniv of Levski Physical Culture Association.

| | | | |
|---|---|---|---|
| 1446 | 2s. Type **479** | 20 | 10 |
| 1447 | 13s. Handball | 1·20 | 55 |
| **MS**1447a 60×60 mm. 60s. green and yellow (Cup and Map of Europe). Imperf | | 4·50 | 4·25 |

**480** Title Page and Petar Beron (author)

**1964.** 40th Anniv of First Bulgarian Primer.

| | | | | |
|---|---|---|---|---|
| 1448 | **480** | 20s. black and brown | 2·20 | 2·20 |

**481** Stephenson's "Rocket", 1829

**1964.** Railway Transport. Multicoloured.

| | | | |
|---|---|---|---|
| 1449 | 1s. Type **481** | 20 | 15 |
| 1450 | 2s. Class 05 steam locomotive | 20 | 15 |
| 1451 | 3s. German V.320.001 diesel locomotive | 20 | 15 |
| 1452 | 5s. Electric locomotive | 35 | 20 |
| 1453 | 8s. Class 05 steam locomotive and train on bridge | 90 | 45 |
| 1454 | 13s. Class E41 electric train emerging from tunnel | 1·30 | 1·10 |

**482** Alsatian

**1964.** Dogs. Multicoloured.

| | | | |
|---|---|---|---|
| 1455 | 1s. Type **482** | 20 | 15 |
| 1456 | 2s. Setter | 25 | 15 |
| 1457 | 3s. Poodle | 35 | 20 |
| 1458 | 4s. Pomeranian | 45 | 25 |
| 1459 | 5s. St. Bernard | 60 | 35 |
| 1460 | 6s. Fox terrier | 90 | 55 |
| 1461 | 10s. Pointer | 3·50 | 1·60 |
| 1462 | 13s. Dachshund | 4·50 | 3·25 |

**(483)**

**1964.** Air. International Cosmic Exhibition, Riccione. No. 1386 surch with T 483 and No. 1387 surch as T 483, but in Italian.

| | | | | |
|---|---|---|---|---|
| 1463 | **466** | 10s. on 1s. turquoise and lilac | 45 | 45 |
| 1464 | - | 20s. on 2s. brown & yell | 1·30 | 65 |

**484** Partisans and Flag

**1964.** 20th Anniv of Fatherland. Front Government. Flag in red.

| | | | | |
|---|---|---|---|---|
| 1465 | **484** | 1s. blue and light blue | 20 | 15 |
| 1466 | - | 2s. olive and bistre | 20 | 15 |
| 1467 | - | 3s. lake and mauve | 20 | 15 |
| 1468 | - | 4s. violet and lavender | 20 | 15 |
| 1469 | - | 5s. brown and orange | 20 | 15 |
| 1470 | - | 6s. blue and light blue | 35 | 20 |
| 1471 | - | 8s. green and light green | 70 | 35 |
| 1472 | - | 13s. brown and salmon | 90 | 55 |

DESIGNS: 2s. Greeting Soviet troops; 3s. Soviet aid—arrival of goods; 4s. Industrial plant, Kremikovtsi; 5s. Combine-harvester; 6s. "Peace" campaigners; 8s. Soldier of National Guard; 3s. Blagoev and Dimitrov. All with flag as Type **484**.

М М панаир
ПЛОВДИВ - 1964
ST 20

**(485)**

**1964.** 21st Int Fair, Plovdiv. Surch with T 485.

| | | | |
|---|---|---|---|
| 1473 | 20s. on 44s. ochre (No. 1020a) | 1·80 | 75 |

**486** Transport

**1964.** 1st National Stamp Exn, Sofia.

| | | | | |
|---|---|---|---|---|
| 1474 | **486** | 20s. blue | 1·60 | 1·10 |

**487** Gymnastics

**1964.** Olympic Games, Tokyo. Rings and values in red.

| | | | | |
|---|---|---|---|---|
| 1475 | **487** | 1s. green and light green | 20 | 15 |
| 1476 | - | 2s. blue and lavender | 20 | 15 |
| 1477 | - | 3s. blue and turquoise | 20 | 15 |
| 1478 | - | 5s. violet and red | 35 | 20 |
| 1479 | - | 13s. blue and light blue | 1·20 | 35 |
| 1480 | - | 20s. green and buff | 1·30 | 75 |

**MS**1480a 61×67 mm. 40s.+20s. ochre, red and blue (Rings, tracks etc.). Imperf 5·75 5·50

DESIGNS: 2s. Long-jump; 3s. Swimmer on starting block; 5s. Football; 13s. Volleyball; 20s. Wrestling.

**488** Vratsata

**1964.** Landscapes.

| | | | | |
|---|---|---|---|---|
| 1481 | **488** | 1s. green | 20 | 15 |
| 1482 | - | 2s. brown | 20 | 15 |
| 1483 | - | 3s. blue | 20 | 15 |
| 1484 | - | 4s. brown | 25 | 15 |
| 1485 | - | 5s. green | 45 | 20 |
| 1486 | - | 6s. violet | 70 | 35 |

DESIGNS: 2s. The Ritli; 3s. Maliovitsa; 4s. Broken Rocks; 5s. Erkyupria; 6s. Rhodope mountain pass.

**489** Paper and Cellulose Factory, Bukovtsi

**1964.** Air. Industrial Buildings.

| | | | | |
|---|---|---|---|---|
| 1487 | **489** | 8s. turquoise | 45 | 15 |
| 1488 | - | 10s. purple | 60 | 20 |
| 1489 | - | 13s. violet | 70 | 25 |
| 1490 | - | 20s. blue | 1·30 | 55 |
| 1491 | - | 40s. green | 2·20 | 75 |

DESIGNS: 10s. Metal works, Plovdiv; 13s. Metallurgical works, Kremikovtzi; 20s. Petrol refinery, Burgas; 40s. Fertiliser factory, Stara-Zagora.

**490** Rila Monastery

**1964.** Philatelic Exn for Franco–Bulgarian Amity.

| | | | | |
|---|---|---|---|---|
| 1492 | **490** | 5s. black and drab | 55 | 25 |
| 1493 | - | 13s. black and blue | 1·30 | 65 |

DESIGN: 13s. Notre-Dame, Paris (inscr in French).

**491** 500-year-old Walnut

**1964.** Ancient Trees. Values and inscr in black.

| | | | | |
|---|---|---|---|---|
| 1494 | **491** | 1s. brown | 20 | 15 |
| 1495 | - | 2s. purple | 20 | 15 |
| 1496 | - | 3s. sepia | 20 | 15 |
| 1497 | - | 4s. blue | 20 | 15 |
| 1498 | - | 10s. green | 90 | 35 |
| 1499 | - | 13s. olive | 1·30 | 45 |

TREES: 2s. Plane (1000 yrs.); 3s. Plane (600 yrs.); 4s. Poplar (800 yrs.); 10s. Oak (800 yrs.); 13s. Fir (1200 yrs.).

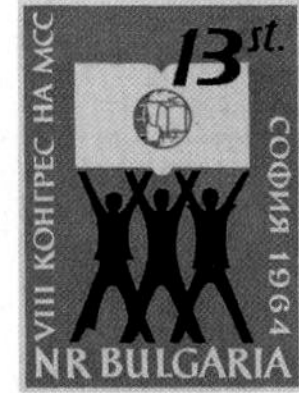

**492**

**1964.** 8th Congress of Int Union of Students, Sofia.

| | | | | |
|---|---|---|---|---|
| 1500 | **492** | 13s. black and blue | 90 | 55 |

**493** Bulgarian Veteran and Soviet Soldier (Sculpture by T. Zlatarev)

**1965.** 30 Years of Bulgarian–Russian Friendship.

| | | | | |
|---|---|---|---|---|
| 1501 | **493** | 2s. red and black | 45 | 20 |

**494** "Gold Medal"

**1965.** Olympic Games, Tokyo (1964).

| | | | | |
|---|---|---|---|---|
| 1502 | **494** | 20s. black, gold & brown | 1·30 | 75 |

**495** Vladimir Komarov

**1965.** Flight of "Voskhod 1". Multicoloured.

| | | | | |
|---|---|---|---|---|
| 1503 | | 1s. Type **495** | 20 | 15 |
| 1504 | | 2s. Konstantin Feoktistov | 20 | 15 |
| 1505 | | 5s. Boris Yegorov | 25 | 20 |
| 1506 | | 13s. The three astronauts | 1·10 | 35 |
| 1507 | | 20s. "Voskhod I" | 1·30 | 55 |

**496** Corn-cob

**1965.** Agricultural Products.

| | | | | |
|---|---|---|---|---|
| 1508 | **496** | 1s. yellow | 15 | 10 |
| 1509 | - | 2s. green | 20 | 10 |
| 1510 | - | 3s. orange | 25 | 10 |
| 1511 | - | 4s. olive | 35 | 15 |
| 1512 | - | 5s. red | 40 | 15 |
| 1513 | - | 10s. blue | 45 | 20 |
| 1514 | - | 13s. bistre | 1·30 | 35 |

DESIGNS: 2s. Ears of Wheat; 3s. Sunflowers; 4s. Sugar beet; 5s. Clover; 10s. Cotton; 13s. Tobacco.

**497** "Victory against Fascism"

**1965.** 20th Anniv of "Victory of 9 May, 1945".

| | | | | |
|---|---|---|---|---|
| 1515 | **497** | 5s. black, bistre & grey | 20 | 10 |
| 1516 | - | 13s. blue, black & grey | 70 | 45 |

DESIGN: 13s. Globes on dove ("Peace").

**498** Northern Bullfinch

**1965.** Song Birds. Multicoloured.

| | | | | |
|---|---|---|---|---|
| 1517 | | 1s. Type **498** | 20 | 15 |
| 1518 | | 2s. Golden oriole | 25 | 15 |
| 1519 | | 3s. Rock thrush | 35 | 15 |
| 1520 | | 5s. Barn swallows | 60 | 20 |
| 1521 | | 8s. European roller | 70 | 55 |
| 1522 | | 10s. Eurasian goldfinch | 2·50 | 90 |
| 1523 | | 13s. Rose-coloured starling | 2·75 | 1·70 |
| 1524 | | 20s. Nightingale | 3·75 | 3·50 |

**499** Transport, Globe and Whale

**1965.** 4th International Transport Conf, Sofia.

| | | | | |
|---|---|---|---|---|
| 1525 | **499** | 13s. multicoloured | 1·90 | 1·10 |

**500** ICY Emblem

**1965.** International Co-operation Year.

| | | | | |
|---|---|---|---|---|
| 1526 | **500** | 20s. orange, olive & blk | 1·40 | 80 |

**501** ITU Emblem and Symbols

**1965.** Centenary of ITU.

| | | | | |
|---|---|---|---|---|
| 1527 | **501** | 20s. yellow, green & bl | 1·40 | 80 |

**502** Pavel Belyaev and Aleksei Leonov

**1965.** "Voskhod 2" Space Flight.

| | | | | |
|---|---|---|---|---|
| 1528 | **502** | 2s. purple, grn & drab | 45 | 20 |
| 1529 | - | 20s. multicoloured | 3·75 | 1·50 |

DESIGN: 20s. Leonov on space.

**503** Common Stingray

**1965.** Fishes. Borders in grey.

| | | | | |
|---|---|---|---|---|
| 1530 | **503** | 1s. gold, black & orange | 10 | 10 |
| 1531 | - | 2s. silver, indigo & blue | 20 | 10 |
| 1532 | - | 3s. gold, black & green | 30 | 15 |
| 1533 | - | 5s. gold, black and red | 45 | 20 |
| 1534 | - | 10s. silver, blue & turq | 2·00 | 1·00 |
| 1535 | - | 13s. gold, black & brown | 2·50 | 1·30 |

FISHES: 2s. Atlantic bonito; 3s. Brown scorpionfish; 5s. Tub gurnard; 10s. Mediterranean horse-mackerel; 13s. Black Sea turbot.

**504** Marx and Lenin

**1965.** Organization of Socialist Countries' Postal Ministers' Conference, Peking.

| | | | | |
|---|---|---|---|---|
| 1536 | **504** | 13s. brown and red | 1·40 | 90 |


**505** Film and Screen

**1965.** Balkan Film Festival. Varna.

| | | | | |
|---|---|---|---|---|
| 1537 | **505** | 13s. black, silver & blue | 95 | 35 |

**506** Quinces

**1965.** Fruits.

| | | | | |
|---|---|---|---|---|
| 1538 | **506** | 1s. orange | 10 | 10 |
| 1539 | - | 2s. olive (Grapes) | 10 | 10 |
| 1540 | - | 3s. bistre (Pears) | 20 | 10 |
| 1541 | - | 4s. orange (Plums) | 30 | 10 |
| 1542 | - | 5s. red (Strawberries) | 35 | 20 |
| 1543 | - | 6s. brown (Walnuts) | 45 | 35 |

**507** Ballerina

**1965.** Ballet Competitions, Varna.

| | | | | |
|---|---|---|---|---|
| 1544 | **507** | 5s. black and mauve | 1·90 | 1·10 |

**508** Dove, Emblem and Map

**1965.** "Balkanphila" Stamp Exhibition, Varna.

| | | | | |
|---|---|---|---|---|
| 1545 | **508** | 1s. silver, blue & yellow | 10 | 10 |
| 1546 | - | 2s. silver, violet & yellow | 15 | 10 |
| 1547 | - | 3s. gold, green & yellow | 30 | 20 |
| 1548 | - | 13s. gold, red & yellow | 1·40 | 1·30 |
| 1549 | - | 20s. brown, blue & silver | 1·90 | 1·70 |

**MS**1550 71×62 mm. 40s. gold and blue (T **508**). Imperf 4·25 4·00

DESIGNS: 2s. Yacht emblem; 3s. Stylised fish and flowers; 13s. Stylised sun, planet and rocket. LARGER (45×25½ mm): 20s. Cosmonauts Pavel Belyaev and Aleksei Leonov.

**509** Escapers in Boat

**1965.** 40th Anniv of Political Prisoners' Escape from "Bolshevik Island".

| | | | | |
|---|---|---|---|---|
| 1551 | **509** | 2s. black and slate | 45 | 20 |

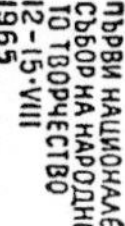

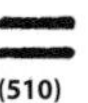
**(510)**

**1965.** National Folklore Competition. No. 1084 surch with T 510.

| | | | | |
|---|---|---|---|---|
| 1552 | | 2s. on 8s. brown | 2·20 | 2·20 |

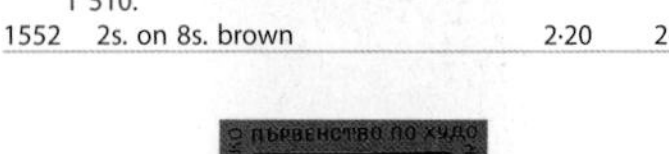

**511** Gymnast

**1965.** Balkan Games.

| | | | | |
|---|---|---|---|---|
| 1553 | **511** | 1s. black and red | 20 | 15 |
| 1554 | - | 2s. purple and black | 20 | 15 |
| 1555 | - | 3s. purple, black & red | 20 | 15 |
| 1556 | - | 5s. brown, black & red | 30 | 20 |
| 1557 | - | 10s. purple, black & mve | 1·00 | 45 |
| 1558 | - | 13s. purple and black | 1·10 | 55 |

DESIGNS: 2s. Gymnastics on bars; 3s. Weight-lifting; 5s. Rally car and building; 10s. Basketball; 13s. Rally car and map.

**512** Dressage

**1965.** Horsemanship.

| | | | | |
|---|---|---|---|---|
| 1559 | **512** | 1s. plum, black & blue | 20 | 15 |
| 1560 | - | 2s. brown, black & ochre | 20 | 15 |
| 1561 | - | 3s. red, black and purple | 20 | 15 |
| 1562 | - | 5s. brown and green | 65 | 20 |
| 1563 | - | 10s. brown, blk & grey | 2·75 | 1·30 |
| 1564 | - | 13s. brown, grn & buff | 3·25 | 1·70 |
| **MS**1565 | | 80×80 mm. 40s.+20s. plum and grey (as 13s.). Imperf | 6·00 | 5·50 |

DESIGNS: 5s. Horse-racing. Others, Horse-jumping (various).

**513** Young Pioneers

**1965.** Dimitrov Septembrist Pioneers Organization.

| | | | | |
|---|---|---|---|---|
| 1566 | **513** | 1s. green and turquoise | 20 | 15 |
| 1567 | - | 2s. mauve and violet | 20 | 15 |
| 1568 | - | 3s. bistre and olive | 20 | 15 |
| 1569 | - | 5s. ochre and blue | 30 | 20 |
| 1570 | - | 8s. orange and brown | 95 | 45 |
| 1571 | - | 13s. violet and red | 1·40 | 80 |

DESIGNS: 2s. Admitting recruit; 3s. Camp bugler; 5s. Flying model airplane; 8s. Girls singing; 13s. Young athlete.

**514** Junkers Ju 52/3m over Turnovo

**1965.** Bulgarian Civil Aviation. Multicoloured.

| | | | |
|---|---|---|---|
| 1572 | 1s. Type **514** | 20 | 15 |
| 1573 | 2s. Ilyushin Il-14M over Plovdiv | 20 | 15 |
| 1574 | 3s. Mil Mi-4 helicopter over Dimitrovgrad | 20 | 15 |
| 1575 | 5s. Tupolev Tu-104A over Ruse | 35 | 20 |
| 1576 | 13s. Ilyushin Il-18 over Varna | 1·10 | 45 |
| 1577 | 20s. Tupolev Tu-114 over Sofia | 1·90 | 80 |

**515** Women of N. and S. Bulgaria

**1965.** 80th Anniv of Union of North and South Bulgaria.

| | | | | |
|---|---|---|---|---|
| 1578 | **515** | 13s. black and green | 95 | 80 |

**516** I.Q.S.Y. Emblem and Earth's Radiation Zones

**1965.** International Quiet Sun Year.

| | | | | |
|---|---|---|---|---|
| 1579 | **516** | 1s. yellow, green & blue | 20 | 15 |
| 1580 | - | 2s. multicoloured | 20 | 15 |
| 1581 | - | 13s. multicoloured | 1·20 | 45 |

DESIGNS (I.Q.S.Y. emblem and): 2s. Sun and solar flares; 13s. Total eclipse of the Sun.

**517** "Spring Greetings"

**1966.** "Spring". National Folklore.

| | | | | |
|---|---|---|---|---|
| 1582 | **517** | 1s. mauve, blue & drab | 20 | 15 |
| 1583 | - | 2s. red, black and drab | 20 | 15 |
| 1584 | - | 3s. violet, red and grey | 20 | 15 |
| 1585 | - | 5s. red, violet and black | 30 | 20 |
| 1586 | - | 8s. purple, brown & mve | 55 | 30 |
| 1587 | - | 13s. mauve, black & bl | 1·10 | 35 |

DESIGNS: 2s. Drummer; 3s. "Birds" (stylised); 5s. Folk dancer; 8s. Vase of flowers; 13s. Bagpiper.

**518** Byala Bridge

**1966.** Ancient Monuments.

| | | | | |
|---|---|---|---|---|
| 1588 | **518** | 1s. turquoise | 20 | 15 |
| 1589 | - | 1s. green | 20 | 15 |
| 1590 | - | 2s. green | 20 | 15 |
| 1591 | - | 2s. purple | 20 | 15 |
| 1592 | - | 8s. brown | 55 | 20 |
| 1593 | - | 13s. blue | 95 | 45 |

DESIGNS: No. 1589, Svilengrand Bridge; 1590, Fountain, Samokov; 1591, Ruins of Matochina Castle, Khaskovo; 1592, Cherven Castle, Ruse; 1593, Cafe, Bozhentsi, Gabrovo.

**519** "Christ" (from fresco Boyana Church)

**1966.** "2,500 Years of Culture". Multicoloured.

| | | | |
|---|---|---|---|
| 1594 | 1s. Type **519** | 3·75 | 3·25 |
| 1595 | 2s. "Destruction of the Idols" (from fresco, Boyana Church) (horiz) | 35 | 35 |
| 1596 | 3s. Bachkovo Monastery | 45 | 40 |
| 1597 | 4s. Zemen Monastery (horiz) | 55 | 45 |
| 1598 | 5s. John the Baptist Church, Nesebur | 65 | 55 |
| 1599 | 13s. "Nativity" (icon, Aleksandr Nevski Cathedral, Sofia) | 95 | 1·00 |
| 1600 | 20s. "Virgin and Child" (icon, Archaeological Museum, Sofia) | 1·40 | 1·10 |

**520** "The First Gunshot" at Koprivshtitsa

**1966.** 90th Anniv of April Uprising.

| | | | | |
|---|---|---|---|---|
| 1601 | **520** | 1s. black, brown & gold | 20 | 15 |
| 1602 | - | 2s. black, red and gold | 20 | 15 |
| 1603 | - | 3s. black, green & gold | 20 | 15 |
| 1604 | - | 5s. black, blue & gold | 25 | 15 |
| 1605 | - | 10s. black, purple & gold | 65 | 20 |
| 1606 | - | 13s. black, violet & gold | 75 | 55 |

DESIGNS: 2s. Georgi Benkovski and Todor Kableskov; 3s. "Showing the Flag" at Panagyurishte; 5s. Vasil Petleshkov and Tsanko Dyustabanov; 10s. Landing of Khristo Botev's detachment at Kozlodui; 13s. Panyot Volov and Zlarion Dragostinov.

**521** Luna reaching for the Moon (image scaled to 75% of original size)

**1966.** Moon Landing of "Luna 9". Sheet 70×50 mm.

| | | | | |
|---|---|---|---|---|
| **MS**1607 | **521** | 60s. silver, black and red | 5·50 | 5·50 |

**522** W.H.O. Building

**1966.** Inaug of W.H.O. Headquarters, Geneva.

| | | | | |
|---|---|---|---|---|
| 1608 | **522** | 13s. blue and silver | 1·10 | 55 |

**523** Worker

**1966.** 6th Trades Union Congress, Sofia.

| | | | | |
|---|---|---|---|---|
| 1609 | **523** | 20s. black and pink | 1·40 | 80 |

**524** Indian Elephant

**1966.** Sofia Zoo Animals. Multicoloured.

| | | | |
|---|---|---|---|
| 1610 | 1s. Type **524** | 20 | 15 |
| 1611 | 2s. Tiger | 20 | 15 |
| 1612 | 3s. Chimpanzee | 20 | 15 |
| 1613 | 4s. Ibex | 30 | 20 |
| 1614 | 5s. Polar bear | 95 | 35 |
| 1615 | 8s. Lion | 1·10 | 55 |
| 1616 | 13s. American bison | 3·25 | 1·70 |
| 1617 | 20s. Eastern grey kangaroo | 4·25 | 2·20 |

**525** Boy and Girl holding Banners

**1966.** 3rd Congress of Bulgarian Sports Federation.

| | | | | |
|---|---|---|---|---|
| 1618 | **525** | 13s. blue, orge & cobalt | 95 | 55 |

**526** "Radetski" and Pioneer

**1966.** 90th Anniv of Khristo Botev's Seizure of River Paddle-steamer "Radetski".

| | | | | |
|---|---|---|---|---|
| 1619 | **526** | 2s. multicoloured | 30 | 20 |

**527** Standard-bearer Simov-Kuruto

**1966.** 90th Death Anniv of Nikola Simov-Kuruto (hero of the Uprising against Turkey).

| | | | | |
|---|---|---|---|---|
| 1620 | **527** | 5s. multicoloured | 45 | 20 |

**528** Federation Emblem

**1966.** 7th Int Youth Federation Assembly, Sofia.

| | | | | |
|---|---|---|---|---|
| 1621 | **528** | 13s. blue and black | 95 | 35 |

**529** UNESCO Emblem

**1966.** 20th Anniv of UNESCO.

| | | | | |
|---|---|---|---|---|
| 1622 | **529** | 20s. ochre, red & black | 1·10 | 55 |

**530** Footballer with Ball

**531** Jules Rimet Cup

**1966.** World Cup Football Championships, London. (a) Showing players in action. Borders in grey.

| | | | | |
|---|---|---|---|---|
| 1623 | **530** | 1s. black and brown | 20 | 15 |
| 1624 | - | 2s. black and red | 20 | 15 |
| 1625 | - | 5s. black and bistre | 30 | 20 |
| 1626 | - | 13s. black and blue | 85 | 45 |
| 1627 | - | 20s. black and blue | 95 | 55 |

(b) Sheet 60×65½ mm. T 531.

| | | | |
|---|---|---|---|
| **MS**1628 | 50s. gold, cerise and grey | 4·25 | 3·75 |

**532** Wrestling

**1966.** 3rd Int Wrestling Championships, Sofia.

| | | | | |
|---|---|---|---|---|
| 1629 | **532** | 13s. sepia, green & brn | 95 | 55 |

**533** Throwing the Javelin

**1966.** 3rd Republican Spartakiade.

| | | | | |
|---|---|---|---|---|
| 1630 | **533** | 2s. green, red & yellow | 20 | 15 |
| 1631 | - | 13s. green, red & yellow | 75 | 40 |

DESIGN: 13s. Running.

**534** Map of Balkans, Globe and UNESCO Emblem

**1966.** Int Balkan Studies Congress, Sofia.

| | | | | |
|---|---|---|---|---|
| 1632 | **534** | 13s. green, pink & blue | 95 | 55 |

**535** Children with Construction Toy

**1966.** Children's Day.

| | | | | |
|---|---|---|---|---|
| 1633 | **535** | 1s. black, yellow & red | 10 | 10 |
| 1634 | - | 2s. black, brown & grn | 10 | 10 |
| 1635 | - | 3s. black, yellow & blue | 20 | 15 |
| 1636 | - | 13s. black, mauve & bl | 1·50 | 35 |

DESIGNS: 2s. Rabbit and Teddy Bear; 3s. Children as astronauts; 13s. Children with gardening equipment.

**536** Yuri Gagarin and "Vostok 1"

**1966.** Russian Space Exploration.

| | | | | |
|---|---|---|---|---|
| 1637 | **536** | 1s. slate and grey | 10 | 10 |
| 1638 | - | 2s. purple and grey | 10 | 10 |
| 1639 | - | 3s. brown and grey | 10 | 10 |
| 1640 | - | 5s. lake and grey | 20 | 10 |
| 1641 | - | 8s. blue and grey | 35 | 20 |
| 1642 | - | 13s. turquoise and grey | 1·10 | 35 |
| 1643 | - | 20s.+10s. vio & grey | 1·90 | 65 |
| **MS**1644 | | 70×62½ mm. 30s.+10s. black, red and grey. Imperf | 4·25 | 3·75 |

DESIGNS: 2s. German Titov and "Vostok 2"; 3s. Andrian Nikolaev, Povel Popovich and "Vostok 3" and "4"; 5s. Valentina Tereshkova, Vallery Bykovsky and "Vostok 5" and "6"; 8s. Vladimir Komarov, Boris Yegorov, Konstantin Feoktistov and "Voskhod 1"; 13s. Povel Belyaev, Aleksei Leonov and "Voskhod 2"; 20s. Gagarin, Leonov and Tereshkova; 30s. Rocket and globe.

**537** St. Clement (14th-cent wood-carving)

**1966.** 1050th Death Anniv of St. Clement of Ohrid.

| | | | | |
|---|---|---|---|---|
| 1645 | **537** | 5s. brown, red & drab | 95 | 55 |

**538** Metodi Shatorov

**1966.** Anti-fascist Fighters. Frames in gold; value in black.

| | | | | |
|---|---|---|---|---|
| 1646 | **538** | 2s. violet and red | 10 | 10 |
| 1647 | - | 3s. brown and mauve | 20 | 10 |
| 1648 | - | 5s. blue and red | 30 | 15 |
| 1649 | - | 10s. brown and orange | 65 | 20 |
| 1650 | - | 13s. brown and red | 75 | 35 |

PORTRAITS: 3s. Vladno Trichkov; 5s. Vulcho Ivanov; 10s. Rasko Daskalov; 13s. Gen. Vladimir Zaimov.

**539** Georgi Dimitrov (statesman)

**1966.** 9th Bulgarian Communist Party Congress, Sofia.

| | | | | |
|---|---|---|---|---|
| 1651 | **539** | 2s. black and red | 20 | 10 |
| 1652 | - | 20s. black, red and grey | 1·70 | 45 |

DESIGN: 20s. Furnaceman and steelworks.

**540** Deer's Head Vessel

**1966.** The Gold Treasures of Panagyurishte. Multicoloured.

| | | | |
|---|---|---|---|
| 1653 | 1s. Type **540** | 20 | 15 |
| 1654 | 2s. Amazon | 25 | 15 |
| 1655 | 3s. Ram | 30 | 15 |
| 1656 | 5s. Plate | 35 | 15 |
| 1657 | 6s. Venus | 45 | 20 |
| 1658 | 8s. Roe-buck | 95 | 35 |
| 1659 | 10s. Amazon (different) | 1·10 | 45 |
| 1660 | 13s. Amphora | 1·40 | 55 |
| 1661 | 20s. Goat | 2·30 | 1·10 |

Except for the 5s. and 13s. the designs show vessels with animal heads.

**541** Bansko Hotel

**1966.** Tourist Resorts.

| | | | | |
|---|---|---|---|---|
| 1662 | **541** | 1s. blue | 20 | 15 |
| 1663 | - | 2s. green (Belogradchik) | 20 | 15 |
| 1664 | - | 2s. lake (Tryavna) | 20 | 15 |
| 1665 | - | 20s. pur (Malovitsa, Rila) | 1·10 | 45 |

**542** Christmas Tree

**1966.** New Year. Multicoloured.

| | | | |
|---|---|---|---|
| 1666 | 2s. Type **542** | 20 | 15 |
| 1667 | 13s. Money-box | 85 | 45 |

**543** Percho Slaveikov (poet)

**1966.** Cultural Celebrities.

| | | | | |
|---|---|---|---|---|
| 1668 | **543** | 1s. bistre, blue & orange | 20 | 15 |
| 1669 | - | 2s. brown, orge & grey | 20 | 15 |
| 1670 | - | 3s. blue, bistre & orange | 20 | 15 |
| 1671 | - | 5s. purple, drab & orge | 30 | 20 |
| 1672 | - | 8s. grey, purple & blue | 65 | 30 |
| 1673 | - | 13s. violet, blue & purple | 75 | 35 |

CELEBRITIES. Writers (with pen emblem): 2s. Dimcho Debelyanov (poet); 3s. Petko Todorov. Painters (with brush emblem): 5s. Dimitur Dobrovich; 8s. Ivan Murkvichka; 13s. Iliya Beshkov.

**544** Dahlias

**1966.** Flowers. Multicoloured.

| | | | |
|---|---|---|---|
| 1674 | 1s. Type **544** | 15 | 10 |
| 1675 | 1s. Clematis | 20 | 10 |
| 1676 | 2s. Poet's narcissus | 25 | 10 |
| 1677 | 2s. Foxgloves | 30 | 15 |
| 1678 | 3s. Snowdrops | 45 | 20 |
| 1679 | 5s. Petunias | 55 | 30 |
| 1680 | 13s. Tiger lilies | 1·10 | 35 |
| 1681 | 20s. Canterbury bells | 1·40 | 55 |

**545** Common Pheasant

**1967.** Hunting. Multicoloured.

| | | | |
|---|---|---|---|
| 1682 | 1s. Type **545** | 30 | 20 |
| 1683 | 2s. Chukar partridge | 30 | 20 |
| 1684 | 3s. Grey partridge | 35 | 20 |
| 1685 | 5s. Brown hare | 95 | 45 |
| 1686 | 8s. Roe deer | 2·50 | 90 |
| 1687 | 13s. Red deer | 2·75 | 1·60 |

**546** "Philately"

**1967.** 10th Bulgarian Philatelic Federation Congress, Sofia.

| | | | | |
|---|---|---|---|---|
| 1688 | **546** | 10s. yellow, black & grn | 2·30 | 1·70 |

**547** 6th-cent B.C. Coin of Thrace

**1967.** Ancient Bulgarian Coins. Coins in silver on black background except 13s. (gold on black). Frame colours given.

| | | | | |
|---|---|---|---|---|
| 1689 | **547** | 1s. brown | 20 | 15 |
| 1690 | - | 2s. purple | 20 | 15 |
| 1691 | - | 3s. green | 20 | 15 |
| 1692 | - | 5s. brown | 45 | 35 |
| 1693 | - | 13s. turquoise | 1·40 | 90 |
| 1694 | - | 20s. violet | 2·30 | 1·70 |

COINS—SQUARE: 2s. 2nd-cent B.C. Macedonian tetradrachm; 3s. 2nd-cent B.C. Odessos (Varna) tetradrachm; 5s. 4th-cent B.C. Macedonian coin of Philip II. HORIZ: (38×25 mm): 13s. Obverse and reverse of 4th cent B.C. coin of King Sevt (Thrace); 20s. Obverse and reverse of 5th-cent B.C. coin of Apollonia (Sozopol).

**548** Partisans listening to radio

**1967.** 25th Anniv of Fatherland Front. Mult.

| | | | |
|---|---|---|---|
| 1695 | 1s. Type **548** | 20 | 15 |
| 1696 | 20s. Dimitrov speaking at rally | 1·30 | 45 |

**549** Nikola Kofardzhiev

**1967.** Anti-fascist Fighters.

| | | | | |
|---|---|---|---|---|
| 1697 | **549** | 1s. red, black & blue | 20 | 15 |
| 1698 | - | 2s. green, black & blue | 20 | 15 |
| 1699 | - | 5s. brown, black & blue | 20 | 15 |
| 1700 | - | 10s. blue, black & lilac | 65 | 30 |
| 1701 | - | 13s. purple, black & grey | 95 | 35 |

PORTRAITS: 2s. Petko Napetov; 5s. Petko Petkov; 10s. Emil Markov; 13s. Traicho Kostov.

**550** "Cultural Development"

**1967.** 1st Cultural Conference, Sofia.

| | | | | |
|---|---|---|---|---|
| 1702 | **550** | 13s. yellow, grn & gold | 95 | 55 |

**551** Angora Kitten

**1967.** Cats. Multicoloured.

| | | | |
|---|---|---|---|
| 1703 | 1s. Type **551** | 20 | 15 |
| 1704 | 2s. Siamese (horiz) | 30 | 15 |
| 1705 | 3s. Abyssinian | 45 | 20 |
| 1706 | 5s. European black and white | 1·50 | 35 |
| 1707 | 13s. Persian (horiz) | 1·90 | 65 |
| 1708 | 20s. European tabby | 2·30 | 1·70 |

**552** "Golden Sands" Resort

**1967.** International Tourist Year. Multicoloured.

| | | | |
|---|---|---|---|
| 1709 | 13s. Type **552** | 45 | 20 |
| 1710 | 20s. Pamporovo | 95 | 45 |
| 1711 | 40s. Old Church, Nesebur | 2·30 | 1·00 |

**553** Scene from Iliev's Opera "The Master of Boyana"

**1967.** 3rd International Young Opera Singers' Competition, Sofia.

| | | | | |
|---|---|---|---|---|
| 1712 | **553** | 5s. red, blue and grey | 20 | 15 |
| 1713 | - | 13s. red, blue and grey | 75 | 45 |

DESIGN—VERT: 13s. "Vocal Art" (song-bird on piano-keys).

**554** G. Kirkov

**1967.** Birth Cent of Georgi Kirkov (patriot).

| | | | | |
|---|---|---|---|---|
| 1714 | **554** | 2s. bistre and red | 20 | 15 |

**555** Roses and Distillery

**1967.** Economic Achievements. Multicoloured.

| | | | |
|---|---|---|---|
| 1715 | 1s. Type **555** | 20 | 15 |
| 1716 | 1s. Chick and incubator | 20 | 15 |
| 1717 | 2s. Cucumber and glass-houses | 20 | 15 |
| 1718 | 2s. Lamb and farm building | 20 | 15 |
| 1719 | 3s. Sunflower and oil-extraction plant | 20 | 15 |
| 1720 | 4s. Pigs and piggery | 25 | 15 |
| 1721 | 5s. Hops and vines | 30 | 15 |
| 1722 | 6s. Grain and irrigation canals | 35 | 15 |
| 1723 | 8s. Grapes and "Bulgar" tractor | 40 | 15 |
| 1724 | 10s. Apples and tree | 45 | 20 |
| 1725 | 13s. Honey bees and honey | 95 | 45 |
| 1726 | 20s. Honey bee on flower, and hives | 1·20 | 55 |

**556** DKMS Emblem

**1967.** 11th Anniv of Dimitrov Communist Youth League.

| | | | | |
|---|---|---|---|---|
| 1727 | **556** | 13s. black, red and blue | 95 | 35 |

**557** Map and Spassky Tower, Moscow Kremlin

**1967.** 50th Anniv of October Revolution.

| | | | | |
|---|---|---|---|---|
| 1728 | **557** | 1s. multicoloured | 20 | 15 |
| 1729 | - | 2s. olive and purple | 20 | 15 |
| 1730 | - | 3s. violet and purple | 20 | 15 |
| 1731 | - | 5s. red and purple | 20 | 15 |
| 1732 | - | 13s. blue and purple | 65 | 35 |
| 1733 | - | 20s. blue and purple | 1·40 | 55 |

DESIGNS: 2s. Lenin directing revolutionaries; 3s. Revolutionaries; 5s. Marx, Engels and Lenin; 13s. Soviet oil refinery; 20s. "Molniya" satellite and Moon (Soviet space research).

**558** Scenic "Fish" and Rod

**1967.** 7th World Angling Championships, Varna.

| | | | | |
|---|---|---|---|---|
| 1734 | **558** | 10s. multicoloured | 75 | 45 |

**559** Cross-country Skiing

**1967.** Winter Olympic Games, Grenoble (1968).

| | | | | |
|---|---|---|---|---|
| 1735 | **559** | 1s. black, red & turq | 20 | 15 |
| 1736 | - | 2s. black, bistre & blue | 20 | 15 |
| 1737 | - | 3s. black, blue & purple | 20 | 15 |
| 1738 | - | 5s. black, yellow & grn | 30 | 20 |
| 1739 | - | 13s. black, buff & blue | 1·40 | 45 |
| 1740 | - | 20s.+10s. mult | 2·40 | 90 |

**MS**1741 98× 98 mm. (diamond) 40s.+10s. black, ochre and blue. Imperf — 3·75 — 3·25

DESIGNS: 2s. Ski jumping; 3s. Biathlon; 5s. Ice hockey; 13, 40s. Ice skating (pairs); 20s. Men's slalom.

**560** Bogdan Peak, Sredna Mts

**1967.** Tourism. Mountain Peaks.

| | | | | |
|---|---|---|---|---|
| 1742 | **560** | 1s. green and yellow | 20 | 15 |
| 1743 | - | 2s. sepia and blue | 20 | 15 |
| 1744 | - | 3s. indigo and blue | 20 | 15 |
| 1745 | - | 5s. green and blue | 30 | 15 |
| 1746 | - | 10s. brown and blue | 40 | 20 |
| 1747 | - | 13s. black and blue | 45 | 40 |
| 1748 | - | 20s. blue and purple | 95 | 80 |

DESIGNS—HORIZ: 2s. Cherni Vruh, Vitosha; 5s. Persenk, Rhodopes; 10s. Botev, Stara-Planina; 20s. Vikhren, Pirin. VERT: 3s. Ruen, Osogovska Planina; 13s. Musala, Rila.

**561** G. Rakovski

**1967.** Death Cent of G. Rakovski (revolutionary).

| | | | | |
|---|---|---|---|---|
| 1749 | **561** | 13s. black and green | 95 | 55 |

**562** Yuri Gagarin, Valentina Tereshkova and Aleksei Leonov

**1967.** Space Exploration. Multicoloured.

| | | | | |
|---|---|---|---|---|
| 1750 | 1s. Type **562** | | 20 | 15 |
| 1751 | 2s. John Glenn and Edward White | | 20 | 15 |
| 1752 | 5s. "Molniya 1" | | 30 | 20 |
| 1753 | 10s. "Gemini 6" and "7" | | 95 | 35 |
| 1754 | 13s. "Luna 13" | | 1·00 | 55 |
| 1755 | 20s. "Gemini 10" docking with "Agena" | | 1·20 | 1·10 |

**563** Railway Bridge over Yantra River

**1967.** Views of Turnovo (ancient capital).

| | | | | |
|---|---|---|---|---|
| 1756 | **563** | 1s. black, drab and blue | 20 | 15 |
| 1757 | - | 2s. multicoloured | 20 | 15 |
| 1758 | - | 3s. multicoloured | 20 | 15 |
| 1759 | - | 5s. black, slate and red | 45 | 25 |
| 1760 | - | 13s. multicoloured | 75 | 35 |
| 1761 | - | 20s. black, orange & lav | 95 | 55 |

DESIGNS: 2s. Hadji Nikola's Inn; 3s. Houses on hillside; 5s. Town and river; 13s. "House of the Monkeys"; 20s. Gurko street.

**564** "The Ruchenitsa" (folk dance, from painting by Murkvichka)

**1967.** Belgian–Bulgarian "Painting and Philately" Exhibition, Brussels.

| | | | | |
|---|---|---|---|---|
| 1762 | **564** | 20s. green and gold | 1·90 | 1·70 |

**565** "The Shepherd" (Zlatko Boyadzhiev)

**1967.** Paintings in the National Gallery, Sofia. Multicoloured.

| | | | | |
|---|---|---|---|---|
| 1763 | 1s. Type **565** | | 10 | 10 |
| 1764 | 2s. "The Wedding" (Vladimir Dimitrov) (vert) | | 10 | 10 |
| 1765 | 3s. "The Partisans" Ilya Petrov (55×35 mm) | | 45 | 20 |
| 1766 | 5s. "Anastasia Penchovich" (Nikolai Pavlovich) (vert) | | 95 | 35 |
| 1767 | 13s. "Self-portrait" (Zakharii Zograf) (vert) | | 1·90 | 1·00 |
| 1768 | 20s. "Old Town of Plovdiv" (Tsanko Lavrenov) | | 2·30 | 1·10 |

**MS**1769 65×85 mm. 60s. "St. Clement of Ohrid" (Anton Mitov) — 6·75 — 6·75

**566** Linked Satellites "Cosmos 186" and "188"

**1968.** "Cosmic Activities". Multicoloured.

| | | | | |
|---|---|---|---|---|
| 1770 | 20s. Type **566** | | 95 | 55 |
| 1771 | 40s. "Venus 4" and orbital diagram (horiz) | | 2·30 | 1·10 |

**567** "Crossing the Danube" (Orenburgski)

**1968.** 90th Anniv of Liberation from Turkey. Paintings. Inscr and frames in black and gold; centre colours below.

| | | | | |
|---|---|---|---|---|
| 1772 | **567** | 1s. green | 20 | 15 |
| 1773 | - | 2s. blue | 20 | 15 |
| 1774 | - | 3s. brown | 20 | 15 |
| 1775 | - | 13s. blue | 1·10 | 55 |
| 1776 | - | 20s. turquoise | 1·40 | 65 |

DESIGNS—VERT: 2s. "Flag of Samara" (Veschin); 13s. "Battle of Orlovo Gnezdo" (Popov). HORIZ: 3s. "Battle of Pleven" (Orenburgski); 20s. "Greeting Russian Soldiers" (Goudienov).

**568** Karl Marx

**1968.** 150th Birth Anniv of Karl Marx.

| | | | | |
|---|---|---|---|---|
| 1777 | **568** | 13s. grey, red & black | 95 | 35 |

**569** Gorky

**1968.** Birth Cent of Maksim Gorky (writer).

| | | | | |
|---|---|---|---|---|
| 1778 | **569** | 13s. green, orange & blk | 95 | 35 |

**570** Dancers

**1968.** 9th World Youth and Students' Festival. Sofia. Multicoloured.

| | | | | |
|---|---|---|---|---|
| 1779 | 2s. Type **570** | | 20 | 15 |
| 1780 | 5s. Running | | 20 | 15 |
| 1781 | 13s. "Doves" | | 85 | 35 |
| 1782 | 20s. "Youth" (symbolic design) | | 95 | 55 |
| 1783 | 40s. Bulgarian 5c. stamp of 1879 under magnifier and Globe | | 1·60 | 1·30 |

**571** "Campanula alpina"

**1968.** Wild Flowers. Multicoloured.

| | | | | |
|---|---|---|---|---|
| 1784 | 1s. Type **571** | | 20 | 15 |
| 1785 | 2s. Trumpet gentian | | 20 | 15 |
| 1786 | 3s. "Crocus veluchensis" | | 20 | 15 |
| 1787 | 5s. Siberian iris | | 45 | 20 |
| 1788 | 10s. Dog's-tooth violet | | 65 | 20 |
| 1789 | 13s. House leek | | 1·10 | 35 |
| 1790 | 20s. Burning bush | | 1·40 | 55 |

**572** "The Unknown Hero" (Ran Bosilek)

**1968.** Bulgarian–Danish Stamp Exhibition. Fairy Tales. Multicoloured.

| | | | | |
|---|---|---|---|---|
| 1791 | 13s. Type **572** | | 45 | 35 |
| 1792 | 20s. "The Witch and the Young Men" (Hans Andersen) | | 95 | 80 |

**573** Memorial Temple, Shipka

**1968.** Bulgarian–West Berlin Stamp Exn.

| | | | | |
|---|---|---|---|---|
| 1793 | **573** | 13s. multicoloured | 95 | 55 |

**574** Copper Rolling-mill, Medet

**1968.** Air.

| | | | | |
|---|---|---|---|---|
| 1794 | **574** | 1l. red | 3·25 | 80 |

**575** Lake Smolyan

**1968**

| | | | | |
|---|---|---|---|---|
| 1795 | **575** | 1s. green | 20 | 15 |
| 1796 | - | 2s. myrtle | 20 | 15 |
| 1797 | - | 3s. sepia | 20 | 15 |
| 1798 | - | 8s. green | 35 | 15 |
| 1799 | - | 10s. brown | 40 | 20 |
| 1800 | - | 13s. olive | 45 | 30 |
| 1801 | - | 40s. blue | 1·40 | 35 |
| 1802 | - | 2l. brown | 6·50 | 2·20 |

DESIGNS: 2s. River Ropotamo; 3s. Lomnitza Gorge, Erma River; 8s. River Isker; 10s. Cruise ship "Die Fregatte"; 13s. Cape Kaliakra; 40s. Sozopol; 2l. Mountain road, Kamchia River.

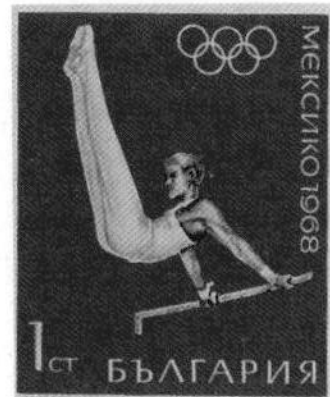

**576** Gymnastics

**1968.** Olympic Games, Mexico.

| | | | | |
|---|---|---|---|---|
| 1803 | **576** | 1s. black and red | 20 | 15 |
| 1804 | - | 2s. black, brown & grey | 20 | 15 |
| 1805 | - | 3s. black and mauve | 20 | 15 |
| 1806 | - | 10s. black, yell & turq | 65 | 20 |
| 1807 | - | 13s. black, pink & blue | 1·40 | 55 |
| 1808 | - | 20s.+10s. grey, pk & bl | 1·90 | 65 |
| **MS**1809 | | 74×76 mm. 50s.+10s. black, grey and blue. Imperf | 4·75 | 4·50 |

DESIGNS: 2s. Horse-jumping; 3s. Fencing; 10s. Boxing; 13s. Throwing the discus; 20s. Rowing; 50s. Stadium and communications satellite.

**577** Dimitur on Mt. Buzludzha, 1868

**1968.** Centenary of Exploits of Khadzhi Dimitur and Stefan Karadzha (revolutionaries).

| | | | | |
|---|---|---|---|---|
| 1810 | **577** | 2s. brown and silver | 20 | 10 |
| 1811 | - | 13s. green and gold | 75 | 45 |

DESIGN: 13s. Dimitur and Karadzha.

**578** Human Rights Emblem

**1968.** Human Rights Year.

| | | | | |
|---|---|---|---|---|
| 1812 | **578** | 20s. gold and blue | 1·10 | 55 |

**579** Cinereous Black Vulture

**1968.** 80th Anniv of Sofia Zoo.

| | | | | |
|---|---|---|---|---|
| 1813 | **579** | 1s. black, brown & blue | 20 | 20 |
| 1814 | - | 2s. black, yellow & brn | 25 | 20 |
| 1815 | - | 3s. black and green | 30 | 20 |
| 1816 | - | 5s. black, yellow & red | 65 | 35 |
| 1817 | - | 13s. black, bistre & grn | 2·40 | 1·10 |
| 1818 | - | 20s. black, green & blue | 3·25 | 1·70 |

DESIGNS: 2s. South African crowned crane; 3s. Common zebra; 5s. Leopard; 13s. Python; 20s. Crocodile.

**580** Battle Scene

**1968.** 280th Anniv of Chiprovtsi Rising.

| | | | | |
|---|---|---|---|---|
| 1819 | **580** | 13s. multicoloured | 95 | 20 |

**581** Caterpillar-hunter

**1968.** Insects.

| | | | | |
|---|---|---|---|---|
| 1820 | **581** | 1s. green | 30 | 10 |
| 1821 | - | 1s. brown | 30 | 10 |
| 1822 | - | 1s. blue | 30 | 10 |
| 1823 | - | 1s. brown | 30 | 10 |
| 1824 | - | 1s. purple | 30 | 10 |

DESIGNS—VERT: No. 1821, Stag beetle ("Lucanus cervus"); 1822, "Procerus scabrosus" (ground beetle). HORIZ: No. 1823, European rhinoceros beetle ("Oryctes nasicornis"); 1824, "Perisomena caecigena" (moth).

**582** Flying Swans

**1968.** "Co-operation with Scandinavia".

| | | | | |
|---|---|---|---|---|
| 1825 | | 2s. ochre and green | 1·90 | 1·70 |
| 1826 | **582** | 5s. blue, grey & black | 1·90 | 1·70 |
| 1827 | - | 13s. purple and maroon | 1·90 | 1·70 |
| 1828 | - | 20s. grey and violet | 1·90 | 1·70 |

DESIGNS: 2s. Wooden flask; 13s. Rose; 20s. "Viking ship".

**583** Congress Building and Emblem

**1968.** International Dental Congress, Varna.

| | | | | |
|---|---|---|---|---|
| 1829 | **583** | 20s. gold, green and red | 95 | 35 |

**584** Smirnenski and Verse from "Red Squadrons"

**1968.** 70th Birth Anniv of Khristo Smirnenski (poet).

| | | | | |
|---|---|---|---|---|
| 1830 | **584** | 13s. black, orange & gold | 95 | 35 |

**585** Dove with Letter

**1968.** National Stamp Exhibition, Sofia and 75th Anniv of "National Philately".

| | | | | |
|---|---|---|---|---|
| 1831 | **585** | 20s. green | 1·90 | 1·70 |

**586** Dalmatian Pelican

**1968.** Srebirna Wildlife Reservation. Birds. Mult.

| | | | | |
|---|---|---|---|---|
| 1832 | | 1s. Type **586** | 35 | 20 |
| 1833 | | 2s. Little egret | 45 | 30 |
| 1834 | | 3s. Great crested grebe | 55 | 35 |
| 1835 | | 5s. Common tern | 65 | 45 |
| 1836 | | 13s. White spoonbill | 2·00 | 1·50 |
| 1837 | | 20s. Glossy ibis | 4·25 | 2·20 |

**587** Silistra Costume

**1968.** Provincial Costumes. Multicoloured.

| | | | | |
|---|---|---|---|---|
| 1838 | | 1s. Type **587** | 20 | 15 |
| 1839 | | 2s. Lovech | 20 | 15 |
| 1840 | | 3s. Yamboi | 20 | 15 |
| 1841 | | 13s. Chirpan | 75 | 35 |
| 1842 | | 20s. Razgrad | 1·10 | 65 |
| 1843 | | 40s. Ikhtiman | 2·40 | 90 |

**588** "St. Arsenius" (icon)

**1968.** Rila Monastery. Icons and murals. Mult.

| | | | | |
|---|---|---|---|---|
| 1844 | | 1s. Type **588** | 20 | 15 |
| 1845 | | 2s. "Carrying St. Ivan Rilski's Relics" (horiz) | 20 | 15 |
| 1846 | | 3s. "St. Michael torments the Rich Man's Soul" | 30 | 20 |
| 1847 | | 13s. "St. Ivan Rilski" | 1·10 | 65 |
| 1848 | | 20s. "Prophet Joel" | 1·70 | 90 |
| 1849 | | 40s. "St. George" | 2·75 | 1·50 |
| **MS**1850 | | 100×74 mm. 1l. "Arrival of Relics at Rila Monastery". Imperf | 7·50 | 7·25 |

**589** "Matricaria chamomilla"

**1968.** Medicinal Plants. Multicoloured.

| | | | | |
|---|---|---|---|---|
| 1851 | | 1s. Type **589** | 20 | 15 |
| 1852 | | 1s. "Mespilus oxyacantha" | 20 | 15 |
| 1853 | | 2s. Lily of the valley | 20 | 15 |
| 1854 | | 3s. Deadly nightshade | 20 | 15 |
| 1855 | | 5s. Common mallow | 30 | 15 |
| 1856 | | 10s. Yellow peasant's eye | 65 | 20 |
| 1857 | | 13s. Common poppy | 75 | 35 |
| 1858 | | 20s. Wild thyme | 1·10 | 55 |

**590** Silkworms and Spindles

**1969.** Silk Industry. Multicoloured.

| | | | | |
|---|---|---|---|---|
| 1859 | | 1s. Type **590** | 20 | 15 |
| 1860 | | 2s. Worm, cocoons and pattern | 20 | 15 |
| 1861 | | 3s. Cocoons and spinning wheel | 20 | 15 |
| 1862 | | 5s. Cocoons and pattern | 20 | 15 |
| 1863 | | 13s. Moth, cocoon and spindles | 75 | 20 |
| 1864 | | 20s. Moth, eggs and shuttle | 1·10 | 35 |

**591** "Death of Ivan Asen"

**1969.** Manasses Chronicle (1st series). Mult.

| | | | | |
|---|---|---|---|---|
| 1865 | | 1s. Type **591** | 20 | 15 |
| 1866 | | 2s. "Emperor Nicephorus invading Bulgaria" | 20 | 15 |
| 1867 | | 3s. "Khan Krum's Feast" | 20 | 15 |
| 1868 | | 13s. "Prince Sviatoslav invading Bulgaria" | 1·10 | 45 |
| 1869 | | 20s. "The Russian invasion" | 1·60 | 55 |
| 1870 | | 40s. "Jesus Christ, Tsar Ivan Alexander and Constantine Manasses" | 2·30 | 1·10 |

See also Nos. 1911/16.

**592** "Saints Cyril and Methodius" (mural, Troyan Monastery)

**1969.** Saints Cyril and Methodius Commem.

| | | | | |
|---|---|---|---|---|
| 1871 | **592** | 28s. multicoloured | 1·90 | 1·10 |

**593** Galleon

**1969.** Air. "SOFIA 1969" International Stamp Exhibition. Transport. Multicoloured.

| | | | | |
|---|---|---|---|---|
| 1872 | | 1s. Type **593** | 20 | 15 |
| 1873 | | 2s. Mail coach | 20 | 15 |
| 1874 | | 3s. Steam locomotive | 20 | 15 |
| 1875 | | 5s. Early motor-car | 20 | 15 |
| 1876 | | 10s. Montgolfier's balloon and Henri Giffard's steam-powered dirigible airship | 35 | 20 |
| 1877 | | 13s. Early flying machines | 65 | 35 |
| 1878 | | 20s. Modern aircraft | 1·10 | 45 |
| 1879 | | 40s. Rocket and planets | 2·00 | 1·10 |
| **MS**1880 | | 57×55 mm. 1l. gold and orange. Imperf | 4·75 | 4·50 |

DESIGN: 1l. Postal courier.

**594** Posthorn Emblem

**1969.** 90th Anniv of Bulgarian Postal Services.

| | | | | |
|---|---|---|---|---|
| 1881 | **594** | 2s. yellow and green | 20 | 15 |
| 1882 | - | 13s. multicoloured | 65 | 20 |
| 1883 | - | 20s. blue | 1·10 | 55 |

DESIGNS: 13s. Bulgarian Stamps of 1879 and 1946; 20s. Post Office workers' strike, 1919.

**595** I.L.O. Emblem

**1969.** 50th Anniv of I.L.O.

| | | | | |
|---|---|---|---|---|
| 1884 | **595** | 13s. black and green | 65 | 35 |

**596** "Fox" and "Rabbit"

**1969.** Children's Book Week.

| | | | | |
|---|---|---|---|---|
| 1885 | **596** | 1s. black, orange & grn | 20 | 15 |
| 1886 | - | 2s. black, blue and red | 20 | 15 |
| 1887 | - | 13s. black, olive & blue | 75 | 35 |

DESIGNS: 2s. Boy with "hedgehog" and "squirrel"; 13s. "The Singing Lesson".

**597** Hand with Seedling

**1969.** "10,000,000 Hectares of New Forests".

1888 **597** 2s. black, green & purple 20 10

**598** "St. George" (14th Century)

**1969.** Religious Art. Multicoloured.

1889 1s. Type **598** 20 15

1890 2s. "The Virgin and St. John Bogoslov" (14th century) 20 15

1891 3s. "Archangel Michael" (17th century) 20 15

1892 5s. "Three Saints" (17th century) 30 15

1893 8s. "Jesus Christ" (17th century) 35 15

1894 13s. "St. George and St. Dimitr" (19th century) 75 20

1895 20s. "Christ the Universal" (19th century) 95 45

1896 60s. "The Forty Martyrs" (19th century) 2·75 1·70

1897 80s. "The Transfiguration" (19th century) 3·75 2·20

**MS**1898 103×165 mm. 40s. ×4, "St. Dimitur" (17th-century) 9·25 9·00

**599** Roman Coin

**1969.** "SOFIA 1969" International Stamp Exhibition. "Sofia Through the Ages".

1899 **599** 1s. silver, blue and gold 10 10

1900 - 2s. silver, green & gold 10 10

1901 - 3s. silver, lake and gold 10 10

1902 - 4s. silver, violet & gold 15 10

1903 - 5s. silver, purple & gold 20 10

1904 - 13s. silver, green & gold 45 15

1905 - 20s. silver, blue & gold 75 35

1906 - 40s. silver, red & gold 1·40 65

**MS**1907 78×72 mm. 1l. multicoloured. Imperf 6·50 5·50

DESIGNS: 2s. Roman coin showing Temple of Asculapius; 3s. Church of St. Sophia; 4s. Boyana Church; 5s. Parliament Building; 13s. National Theatre; 20s. Aleksandr Nevski Cathedral; 40s. Sofia University. 44×44 mm. 1l. Arms.

**600** St. George and the Dragon

**1969.** Int Philatelic Federation Congress, Sofia.

1908 **600** 40s. black, orange & sil 2·30 1·10

**601** St. Cyril

**1969.** 1,100th Death Anniv of St. Cyril.

1909 **601** 2s. green & red on silver 20 10

1910 - 28s. blue & red on silver 1·60 65

DESIGN: 28s. St. Cyril and procession.

**1969.** Manasses Chronicle (2nd series). Designs as T 591, but all horiz. Multicoloured.

1911 1s. "Nebuchadnezzar II and Balthasar of Babylon, Cyrus and Darius of Persia" 10 10

1912 2s. "Cambyses, Gyges and Darius of Persia" 10 10

1913 5s. "Prophet David and Tsar Ivan Alexander" 30 10

1914 13s. "Rout of the Byzantine Army, 811" 95 35

1915 20s. "Christening of Khan Boris" 1·90 45

1916 60s. "Tsar Simeon's attack on Constantinople" 2·75 1·90

**602** Partisans

**1969.** 25th Anniv of Fatherland Front Government.

1917 **602** 1s. lilac, red and black 20 15

1918 - 2s. brown, red & black 20 15

1919 - 3s. green, red and black 20 15

1920 - 5s. brown, red & black 20 15

1921 - 13s. blue, red & black 65 20

1922 - 20s. multicoloured 1·20 55

DESIGNS: 2s. Combine-harvester; 3s. Dam; 5s. Folk singers; 13s. Petroleum refinery; 20s. Lenin, Dimitrov and flags.

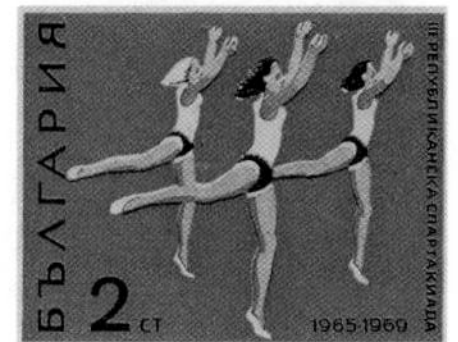


**603** Gymnastics

**1969.** 3rd Republican Spartakiad. Multicoloured.

1923 2s. Type **603** 20 10

1924 20s. Wrestling 95 65

**604** "Construction" and soldier

**1969.** 25th Anniv of Army Engineers.

1925 **604** 6s. black and blue 30 15

**605** T. Tserkovski

**1969.** Birth Cent of Tsanke Tserkovski (poet).

1926 **605** 13s. multicoloured 75 35

**606** "Woman" (Roman Statue)

**1969.** 1,800th Anniv of Silistra.

1927 **606** 2s. grey, blue and silver 20 15

1928 - 13s. brown, grn & silver 1·00 45

DESIGN—HORIZ: 13s. "Wolf" (bronze statue).

**607** Skipping-rope Exercise

**1969.** World Gymnastics Competition, Varna.

1929 **607** 1s. grey, blue and green 20 15

1930 - 2s. grey and blue 20 15

1931 - 3s. grey, green and emerald 20 15

1932 - 5s. grey, purple and red 20 15

1933 - 13s.+5s. grey, bl & red 1·10 55

1934 - 20s.+10s. grey, green and yellow 1·40 65

DESIGNS: 2s. Hoop exercise (pair); 3s. Hoop exercise (solo); 5s. Ball exercise (pair); 13s. Ball exercise (solo); 20s. Solo gymnast.

**608** Marin Drinov (founder)

**1969.** Cent of Bulgarian Academy of Sciences.

1935 **608** 20s. black and red 95 45

**609** "Neophit Rilski" (Zakharii Zograf)

**1969.** Paintings in National Gallery, Sofia. Mult.

1936 1s. Type **609** 10 10

1937 2s. "German's Mother" (Vasil Stoilov) 20 10

1938 3s. "Workers' Family" (Neuko Balkanski) (horiz) 30 10

1939 4s. "Woman Dressing" (Ivan Nenov) 35 10

1940 5s. "Portrait of a Woman" (Nikolai Pavlovich) 45 20

1941 13s. "Krustyn Sarafov as Falstaff" (Dechko Uzunov) 95 30

1942 20s. "Artist's Wife" (N. Mikhailov) (horiz) 1·30 45

1943 20s. "Worker's Lunch" (Stoyan Sotirov) (horiz) 1·40 55

1944 40s. "Self-portrait" (Tseno Todorov) (horiz) 1·90 80

**610** Pavel Banya

**1969.** Sanatoria.

1945 **610** 2s. blue 20 10

1946 - 5s. blue 20 10

1947 - 6s. green 35 10

1948 - 20s. green 75 35

SANATORIA: 5s. Khisar; 6s. Kotel; 20s. Narechen Polyclinic.

**611** Deep-sea Trawler

**1969.** Ocean Fisheries.

1949 **611** 1s. grey and blue 20 15

1950 - 1s. green and black 20 15

1951 - 2s. violet and black 20 15

1952 - 3s. blue and black 20 15

1953 - 5s. mauve and black 30 20

1954 - 10s. grey and black 1·50 45

1955 - 13s. flesh, orange & blk 2·30 80

1956 - 20s. brown, ochre & blk 3·00 1·10

DESIGNS: 1s. (No. 1950), Cape hake; 2s. Atlantic horse-mackerel; 3s. South African pilchard; 5s. Large-eyed dentex; 10s. Chub mackerel; 13s. Senegal croaker; 20s. Vadigo.

**612** Trapeze Act

**1969.** Circus. Multicoloured.

1957 1s. Type **612** 10 10

1958 2s. Acrobats 10 10

1959 3s. Balancing act with hoops 10 10

1960 5s. Juggler, and bear on cycle 20 10

1961 13s. Equestrian act 65 35

1962 20s. Clowns 1·40 55

**613** V. Kubasov, Georgi Shonin and "Soyuz 6"

**1970.** Space Flights of "Soyuz 6, 7 and 8".

1963 **613** 1s. multicoloured 10 10

1964 - 2s. multicoloured 10 10

1965 - 3s. multicoloured 20 15

1966 - 28s. pink and blue 1·50 55

DESIGNS: 2s. Viktor Gorbacko, Vladislav Volkov, Anatoly Filipchenko and "Soyuz 7"; 3s. Aleksei Elseev, Vladimir Shatalov and "Soyuz 8"; 28s. Three "Soyuz" spacecraft in orbit.

**614** Khan Asparerch and "Old-Bulgars" crossing the Danube, 679

**1970.** History of Bulgaria. Multicoloured.

1967 1s. Type **614** 20 15

1968 2s. Khan Krum and defeat of Emperor Nicephorus, 811 20 15

1969 3s. Conversion of Khan Boris I to Christianity, 865 20 15

1970 5s. Tsar Simeon and Battle of Akhelo, 917 30 15

1971 8s. Tsar Samuel and defeat of Byzantines, 976 35 15

1972 10s. Tsar Kaloyan and victory over Emperor Baldwin, 1205 55 20

1973 13s. Tsar Ivan Assen II and defeat of Komnine of Epirus, 1230 95 35

1974 20s. Coronation of Tsar Ivailo, 1277 1·40 55

**615** Bulgarian Pavilion

**1970.** "Expo 70" World's Fair, Osaka, Japan (1st issue).

1975 **615** 20s. silver, yellow & brn 1·90 1·10

See Nos. 2009/12.

**616** Footballers

**1970.** World Football Cup, Mexico.

1976 **616** 1s. multicoloured 10 10

1977 - 2s. multicoloured 10 10

1978 - 3s. multicoloured 10 10

| | | | | |
|---|---|---|---|---|
| 1979 | - | 5s. multicoloured | 20 | 15 |
| 1980 | - | 20s. multicoloured | 1·60 | 55 |
| 1981 | - | 40s. multicoloured | 2·00 | 75 |

**MS**1982 55×99 mm. 80s.+20s. multicoloured. Imperf 4·75 4·50

DESIGNS—HORIZ: 2s. to 40s. Various football scenes. VERT (45×69 mm.) 80s. Football and inscription.

**617** Lenin

**1970.** Birth Cent of Lenin. Multicoloured.

| | | | |
|---|---|---|---|
| 1983 | 2s. Type **617** | 20 | 15 |
| 1984 | 13s. Full-face portrait | 75 | 35 |
| 1985 | 20s. Lenin writing | 1·60 | 65 |

**618** "Tephrocactus Alexanderi v. bruchi"

**1970.** Flowering Cacti. Multicoloured.

| | | | |
|---|---|---|---|
| 1986 | 1s. Type **618** | 20 | 15 |
| 1987 | 2s. "Opuntia drummondii" | 20 | 15 |
| 1988 | 3s. "Hatiora cilindrica" | 20 | 15 |
| 1989 | 5s. "Gymnocalycium vatteri" | 30 | 20 |
| 1990 | 8s. "Heliantho cereus grandiflorus" | 45 | 35 |
| 1991 | 10s. "Neochilenia andreaeana" | 2·20 | 80 |
| 1992 | 13s. "Peireskia vargasii v. longispina" | 2·30 | 90 |
| 1993 | 20s. "Neobesseya rosiflora" | 2·75 | 1·10 |

**619** Rose

**1970.** Bulgarian Roses.

| | | | | |
|---|---|---|---|---|
| 1994 | **619** | 1s. multicoloured | 20 | 15 |
| 1995 | - | 2s. multicoloured | 20 | 15 |
| 1996 | - | 3s. multicoloured | 30 | 15 |
| 1997 | - | 4s. multicoloured | 40 | 15 |
| 1998 | - | 5s. multicoloured | 45 | 20 |
| 1999 | - | 13s. multicoloured | 95 | 45 |
| 2000 | - | 20s. multicoloured | 1·90 | 1·10 |
| 2001 | - | 28s. multicoloured | 3·25 | 1·90 |

DESIGNS: 2s. to 28s. Various roses.

**620** Union Badge

**1970.** 70th Anniv of Agricultural Union.

| | | | | |
|---|---|---|---|---|
| 2002 | **620** | 20s. black, gold and red | 1·40 | 45 |

**621** Gold Bowl

**1970.** Gold Treasures of Thrace.

| | | | | |
|---|---|---|---|---|
| 2003 | **621** | 1s. black, blue and gold | 20 | 15 |
| 2004 | - | 2s. black, lilac and gold | 20 | 15 |
| 2005 | - | 3s. black, red and gold | 20 | 15 |
| 2006 | - | 5s. black, green & gold | 30 | 20 |
| 2007 | - | 13s. black, orge & gold | 1·40 | 55 |
| 2008 | - | 20s. black, violet & gold | 1·90 | 1·10 |

DESIGNS: 2s. Three small bowls; 3s. Plain lid; 5s. Pear shaped ornaments; 13s. Large lid with pattern; 20s. Vase.

**622** Rose and Woman with Baskets of Produce

**1970.** "Expo 70" World's Fair, Osaka, Japan (2nd issue). Multicoloured.

| | | | |
|---|---|---|---|
| 2009 | 1s. Type **622** | 20 | 15 |
| 2010 | 2s. Three Dancers | 20 | 15 |
| 2011 | 3s. Girl in National costume | 20 | 15 |
| 2012 | 28s. Dancing couples | 1·70 | 80 |

**MS**2013 75×90 mm. 40s. Bulgarian pavilion 1·90 1·90

**623** UN Emblem (image scaled to 75% of original size)

**1970.** 25th Anniv of United Nations.

| | | | | |
|---|---|---|---|---|
| 2014 | **623** | 20s. gold and blue | 95 | 55 |

**624** I. Vasov

**1970.** 120th Birth Anniv of Ivan Vasov (poet).

| | | | | |
|---|---|---|---|---|
| 2015 | **624** | 13s. blue | 85 | 35 |

**625** Edelweiss Sanatorium, Borovets

**1970.** Health Resorts.

| | | | | |
|---|---|---|---|---|
| 2016 | **625** | 1s. green | 20 | 15 |
| 2017 | - | 2s. olive | 20 | 15 |
| 2018 | - | 4s. blue | 20 | 15 |
| 2019 | - | 8s. blue | 45 | 15 |
| 2020 | - | 10s. blue | 65 | 20 |

DESIGNS: 2s. Panorama Hotel, Pamporovo; 4s. Yachts, Albena; 8s. Harbour scene, Rousalka; 10s. Shtastlivetsa Hotel, Mt. Vitosha.

**626** Hungarian Retriever

**1970.** Dogs. Multicoloured.

| | | | |
|---|---|---|---|
| 2021 | 1s. Type **626** | 20 | 15 |
| 2022 | 2s. Retriever (vert) | 30 | 15 |
| 2023 | 3s. Great Dane (vert) | 35 | 15 |
| 2024 | 4s. Boxer (vert) | 45 | 20 |
| 2025 | 5s. Cocker spaniel (vert) | 55 | 30 |
| 2026 | 13s. Dobermann pinscher (vert) | 1·40 | 80 |
| 2027 | 20s. Scottish terrier (vert) | 2·75 | 1·20 |
| 2028 | 28s. Russian hound | 3·25 | 1·70 |

**627** Fireman with Hose

**1970.** Fire Protection.

| | | | | |
|---|---|---|---|---|
| 2029 | **627** | 1s. grey, yellow & black | 20 | 10 |
| 2030 | - | 3s. red, grey and black | 30 | 20 |

DESIGN. 3s. Fire-engine.

**628** Congress Emblem

**1970.** 7th World Sociological Congress, Varna.

| | | | | |
|---|---|---|---|---|
| 2031 | **628** | 13s. multicoloured | 75 | 20 |

**629** Two Male Players

**1970.** World Volleyball Championships.

| | | | | |
|---|---|---|---|---|
| 2032 | **629** | 2s. black and brown | 20 | 15 |
| 2033 | - | 2s. orange, black & blue | 20 | 15 |
| 2034 | - | 20s. yellow, black & grn | 1·20 | 55 |
| 2035 | - | 20s. multicoloured | 1·40 | 65 |

DESIGNS: No. 2033, Two female players; 2034, Male player; 2035, Female player.

**630** Cyclists

**1970.** 20th Round-Bulgaria Cycle Race.

| | | | | |
|---|---|---|---|---|
| 2036 | **630** | 20s. mauve, yellow & grn | 95 | 55 |

**631** Enrico Caruso and Scene from "Il Pagliacci"

**1970.** Opera Singers. Multicoloured.

| | | | |
|---|---|---|---|
| 2037 | 1s. Type **631** | 20 | 15 |
| 2038 | 2s. Khristina Morfova and "The Bartered Bride" | 20 | 15 |
| 2039 | 3s. Petur Raichev and "Tosca" | 20 | 15 |
| 2040 | 10s. Tsvetana Tabakova and "The Flying Dutchman" | 35 | 25 |
| 2041 | 13s. Katya Popova and "The Masters of Nuremberg" | 45 | 35 |
| 2042 | 20s. Fyodor Chaliapin and "Boris Godunov" | 2·30 | 1·30 |

**632** Beethoven

**1970.** Birth Bicentenary of Ludwig von Beethoven (composer).

| | | | | |
|---|---|---|---|---|
| 2043 | **632** | 28s. blue and purple | 2·75 | 2·20 |

**633** Ivan Asen II Coin

**1970.** Bulgarian Coins of the 14th century. Multicoloured.

| | | | |
|---|---|---|---|
| 2044 | 1s. Type **633** | 20 | 15 |
| 2045 | 2s. Theodor Svetoslav | 20 | 15 |
| 2046 | 3s. Mikhail Shishman | 20 | 15 |
| 2047 | 13s. Ivan Alexander and Mikhail Asen | 45 | 20 |
| 2048 | 20s. Ivan Sratsimir | 1·40 | 45 |
| 2049 | 28s. Ivan Shishman (initials) | 1·90 | 65 |

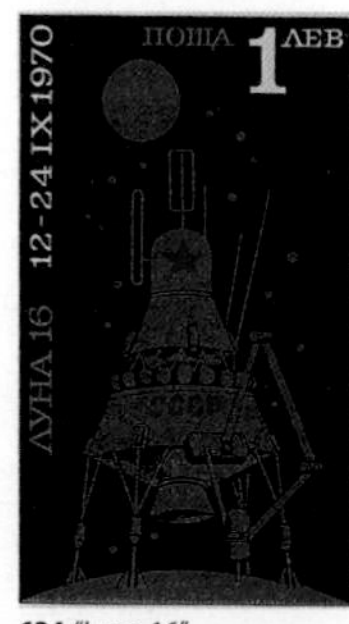


**634** "Luna 16"

**1970.** Moon Mission of "Luna 16". Sheet 51×70 mm.

**MS**2050 **634** 1l. red, silver and blue 7·50 7·25

**635** Engels

**1970.** 150th Birth Anniv of Friedrich Engels.

| | | | | |
|---|---|---|---|---|
| 2051 | **635** | 13s. brown and red | 95 | 55 |

**636** Snow Crystal

**1970.** New Year.

| | | | | |
|---|---|---|---|---|
| 2052 | **636** | 2s. multicoloured | 20 | 10 |

**637** "Lunokhod 1" on Moon

**1970.** Moon Mission of "Lunokhod 1". Sheet 60×72 mm.

**MS**2053 **637** 80s. silver, purple and blue 7·25 5·50

**638** "Girl's Head" (Zheko Spiridonov)

**1971.** Modern Bulgarian Sculpture.

| | | | | |
|---|---|---|---|---|
| 2054 | **638** | 1s. violet and gold | 20 | 15 |
| 2055 | - | 2s. green and gold | 20 | 15 |
| 2056 | - | 3s. brown and gold | 20 | 15 |
| 2057 | - | 13s. green and gold | 65 | 20 |
| 2058 | - | 20s. red and gold | 1·30 | 45 |
| 2059 | - | 28s. brown and gold | 1·40 | 65 |

**MS**2060 61×72 mm. 1l. chestnut and gold 4·75 4·75

SCULPTURES: 2s. "Third Class Carriage" (Ivan Funev); 3s. "Elin Pelin" (Marko Markov); 13s. "Nina" (Andrei Nikolov); 20s. "Kneeling Woman" (Yavorov monument, Ivan Lazarov); 28s. "Engineer" (Ivan Funev). 36½×41 mm. 1l. "Refugees" (Sekul Knimov).

**639** Birds and Flowers

**1971.** Spring.

| | | | | |
|---|---|---|---|---|
| 2061 | **639** | 1s. multicoloured | 10 | 10 |
| 2062 | - | 2s. multicoloured | 10 | 10 |
| 2063 | - | 3s. multicoloured | 10 | 10 |
| 2064 | - | 5s. multicoloured | 10 | 10 |
| 2065 | - | 13s. multicoloured | 45 | 20 |
| 2066 | - | 20s. multicoloured | 1·00 | 45 |

DESIGNS: 2s. to 20s. Various designs of birds and flowers similar to Type **639**.

**640** "Khan Asparuch crossing Danube" (Boris Angelushev)

**1971.** Bulgarian History. Paintings. Mult.

| | | | |
|---|---|---|---|
| 2067 | 2s. Type **640** | 20 | 15 |
| 2068 | 3s. "Ivajlo in Turnovo" (Ilya Petrov) | 20 | 15 |
| 2069 | 5s. "Cavalry Charge, Benkovski" (P. Morosov) | 45 | 20 |
| 2070 | 8s. "Gen. Gzrko entering Sofia, 1878" (D. Gyudzhenov) | 95 | 30 |
| 2071 | 28s. "Greeting Red Army" (Stefan Venev) | 3·75 | 2·00 |
| **MS**2072 | 137×131 mm. Nos. 2067/70 | 1·90 | 1·70 |

**641** Running

**1971.** 2nd European Indoor Track and Field Championships. Multicoloured.

| | | | |
|---|---|---|---|
| 2073 | 2s. Type **641** | 20 | 15 |
| 2074 | 20s. Putting the shot | 1·90 | 55 |

**642** School Building

**1971.** Foundation of First Bulgarian Secondary School, Bolgrad.

| | | | | |
|---|---|---|---|---|
| 2075 | **642** | 2s. green, brown & sil | 20 | 15 |
| 2076 | - | 20s. violet, brown & sil | 1·30 | 45 |

DESIGN: 20s. Dimitur Mutev, Prince Bogoridi and Sava Radulov (founders).

**643** Communards

**1971.** Centenary of Paris Commune.

| | | | | |
|---|---|---|---|---|
| 2077 | **643** | 20s. black and red | 95 | 55 |

**644** Georgi Dimitrov challenging Hermann Goering

**1971.** 20th Anniv of "Federation Internationale des Resistants".

| | | | | |
|---|---|---|---|---|
| 2078 | **644** | 2s. multicoloured | 20 | 15 |
| 2079 | **644** | 13s. multicoloured | 1·40 | 55 |

**645** Gagarin and Space Scenes (image scaled to 69% of original size)

**1971.** 10th Anniv of First Manned Space Flight. Sheet 80×53 mm.

| | | | |
|---|---|---|---|
| **MS**2080 | **645** 40s.+20s. multicoloured | 4·75 | 4·00 |

**646** G. Rakovski

**1971.** 150th Birth Anniv of Georgi Rakovski (politician and Revolutionary).

| | | | | |
|---|---|---|---|---|
| 2081 | **646** | 13s. brown, cream & grn | 75 | 20 |

**647** Worker and Banner ("People's Progress")

**1971.** 10th Bulgarian Communist Party Congress. Multicoloured.

| | | | |
|---|---|---|---|
| 2082 | 1s. Type **647** | 20 | 15 |
| 2083 | 2s. Symbols of "Technical Progress" (horiz) | 20 | 15 |
| 2084 | 12s. Men clasping hands ("Bulgarian-Soviet Friendship") | 1·40 | 45 |

**648** Pipkov and Music

**1971.** Birth Centenary of Panaiot Pipokov.

| | | | | |
|---|---|---|---|---|
| 2085 | **648** | 13s. black, green & silver | 95 | 55 |

**649** "Three Races"

**1971.** Racial Equality Year.

| | | | | |
|---|---|---|---|---|
| 2086 | **649** | 13s. multicoloured | 95 | 55 |

**650** Mammoth

**1971.** Prehistoric Animals. Multicoloured.

| | | | |
|---|---|---|---|
| 2087 | 1s. Type **650** | 20 | 20 |
| 2088 | 2s. Bear (vert) | 20 | 20 |
| 2089 | 3s. Hipparion | 20 | 20 |
| 2090 | 13s. Mastodon | 1·90 | 65 |
| 2091 | 20s. Dinotherium (vert) | 2·75 | 1·70 |
| 2092 | 28s. Sabre-toothed tiger | 3·25 | 2·20 |

**651** Facade of Ancient Building

**1971.** Ancient Buildings of Koprivshitsa.

| | | | | |
|---|---|---|---|---|
| 2093 | **651** | 1s. green, brown & grn | 10 | 10 |
| 2094 | - | 2s. brown, green & buff | 10 | 10 |
| 2095 | - | 6s. violet, brown & blue | 35 | 15 |
| 2096 | - | 13s. red, blue & orange | 95 | 45 |

DESIGNS: 1s. to 13s. Different facades.

**652** Weights Emblem on Map of Europe

**1971.** 30th European Weightlifting Championships, Sofia. Multicoloured.

| | | | |
|---|---|---|---|
| 2097 | 2s. Type **652** | 20 | 15 |
| 2098 | 13s. Figures supporting weights | 1·40 | 45 |

**653** Frontier Guard and Dog

**1971.** 25th Anniv of Frontier Guards.

| | | | | |
|---|---|---|---|---|
| 2099 | **653** | 2s. olive, green & turq | 20 | 10 |

**654** Tweezers, Magnifying Glass and "Stamp"

**1971.** 9th Congress of Bulgarian Philatelic Federation.

| | | | | |
|---|---|---|---|---|
| 2100 | **654** | 20s.+10s. brown, black and red | 1·90 | 80 |

**655** Congress Meeting (sculpture)

**1971.** 80th Anniv of Bulgarian Social Democratic Party Congress, Buzludzha.

| | | | | |
|---|---|---|---|---|
| 2101 | **655** | 2s. green, cream and red | 20 | 10 |

**656** "Mother" (Ivan Nenov)

**1971.** Paintings from the National Art Gallery (1st series). Multicoloured.

| | | | |
|---|---|---|---|
| 2102 | 1s. Type **656** | 20 | 15 |
| 2103 | 2s. "Lazorova" (Stefan Ivanov) | 20 | 15 |
| 2104 | 3s. "Portrait of Yu. Kh." (Kiril Tsonev) | 35 | 20 |
| 2105 | 13s. "Portrait of a Lady" (Dechko Uzunov) | 95 | 35 |
| 2106 | 30s. "Young Woman from Kalotina" (Vladimir Dimitrov) | 1·40 | 80 |
| 2107 | 40s. "Goryanin" (Stryan Venev) | 1·90 | 1·30 |

See also Nos. 2145/50.

**657** Factory Botevgrad

**1971.** Industrial Buildings.

| | | | | |
|---|---|---|---|---|
| 2108 | **657** | 1s. violet | 10 | 10 |
| 2109 | - | 2s. red | 10 | 10 |
| 2110 | - | 10s. violet | 35 | 15 |
| 2111 | - | 13s. red | 55 | 20 |
| 2112 | - | 40s. brown | 1·90 | 45 |

DESIGNS—VERT: 2s. Petro-chemical plant, Pleven. HORIZ: 10s. Chemical works, Vratsa; 13s. "Maritsa-Istok" plant, Dimitrovgrad; 40s. Electronics factory, Sofia.

**658** Free Style Wrestling

**1971.** European Wrestling Championships, Sofia.

| | | | | |
|---|---|---|---|---|
| 2113 | **658** | 2s. green, black and blue | 10 | 10 |
| 2114 | - | 13s. black, red and blue | 95 | 45 |

DESIGN: 13s. Greco-Roman wrestling.

**659** Posthorn Emblem

**1971.** Organization of Socialist Countries' Postal Administrations Congress.

| | | | | |
|---|---|---|---|---|
| 2115 | **659** | 20s. gold and green | 95 | 55 |

**660** Entwined Ribbons

**1971.** 7th European Biochemical Congress, Varna.

| | | | | |
|---|---|---|---|---|
| 2116 | **660** | 13s. red, brown & black | 95 | 55 |

**661** "New Republic" Statue

**1971.** 25th Anniv of People's Republic.

| | | | | |
|---|---|---|---|---|
| 2117 | **661** | 2s. red, yellow and gold | 10 | 10 |
| 2118 | - | 13s. green, red and gold | 95 | 45 |

DESIGN: 13s. Bulgarian flag.

**662** Cross-country Skiing

**1971.** Winter Olympic Games, Sapporo, Japan. Multicoloured.

| | | | |
|---|---|---|---|
| 2119 | 1s. Type **662** | 20 | 15 |
| 2120 | 2s. Downhill skiing | 20 | 15 |

| | | | |
|---|---|---|---|
| 2121 | 3s. Ski jumping | 20 | 15 |
| 2122 | 4s. Figure skating | 20 | 15 |
| 2123 | 13s. Ice hockey | 95 | 65 |
| 2124 | 28s. Slalom skiing | 1·90 | 1·10 |
| **MS**2125 | 60×70 mm. 1l. Olympic flame and stadium | 4·75 | 3·00 |

**663** Brigade Members

**1971.** 25th Anniv of Youth Brigades Movement.

| | | | | |
|---|---|---|---|---|
| 2126 | **663** | 2s. blue | 20 | 10 |

**664** UNESCO Emblem and Wreath

**1971.** 25th Anniv of UNESCO.

| | | | | |
|---|---|---|---|---|
| 2127 | **664** | 20s. multicoloured | 95 | 55 |

**665** "The Footballer"

**1971.** Paintings by Kiril Tsonev. Multicoloured.

| | | | |
|---|---|---|---|
| 2128 | 1s. Type **665** | 20 | 15 |
| 2129 | 2s. "Landscape" (horiz) | 20 | 15 |
| 2130 | 3s. Self-portrait | 30 | 20 |
| 2131 | 13s. "Lilies" | 95 | 35 |
| 2132 | 20s. "Woodland Scene" (horiz) | 1·40 | 65 |
| 2133 | 40s. "Portrait of a Young Woman" | 1·90 | 90 |

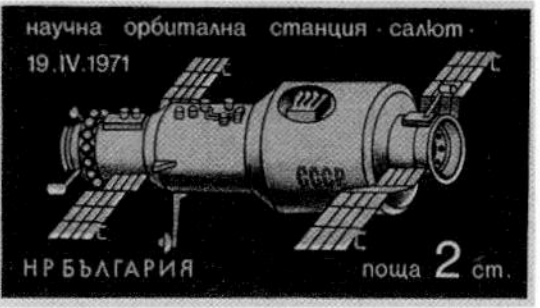


**666** "Salyut" Space-station

**1971.** Space Flights of "Salyut" and "Soyuz 11". Multicoloured.

| | | | |
|---|---|---|---|
| 2134 | 2s. Type **666** | 20 | 15 |
| 2135 | 13s. "Soyuz 11" | 45 | 30 |
| 2136 | 40s. "Salyut" and "Soyuz 11" joined together | 2·30 | 80 |
| **MS**2137 | 70×74 mm. 80s. Cosmonauts G. Dobrovolsky, Vladislav Volkov and V. Patsaev (victims of "Soyuz 11" disaster). Imperf | 3·25 | 2·75 |

**667** "Vikhren" (ore carrier)

**1972.** "One Million Tons of Bulgarian Shipping".

| | | | | |
|---|---|---|---|---|
| 2138 | **667** | 18s. lilac, red and black | 1·40 | 55 |

**668** Goce Delcev

**1972.** Birth Centenaries of Macedonian Revolutionaries.

| | | | | |
|---|---|---|---|---|
| 2139 | **668** | 2s. black and red | 10 | 10 |
| 2140 | - | 5s. black and green | 20 | 10 |
| 2141 | - | 13s. black and yellow | 65 | 35 |

PATRIOTS: 5s. Jan Sandanski (1972); 13s. Dume Gruev (1971).

**669** Gymnast with Ball

**1972.** World Gymnastics Championships, Havana (Cuba). Multicoloured.

| | | | |
|---|---|---|---|
| 2142 | 13s. Type **669** | 95 | 35 |
| 2143 | 18s. Gymnast with hoop | 1·40 | 65 |
| **MS**2144 | 61×74 mm. 70s. Team with hoops. Imperf | 4·75 | 4·50 |

**1972.** Paintings in Bulgarian National Gallery (2nd series). As T 656 but horiz. Multicoloured.

| | | | |
|---|---|---|---|
| 2145 | 1s. "Melnik" (Petur Mladenov) | 20 | 15 |
| 2146 | 2s. "Ploughman" (Pencho Georgiev) | 20 | 15 |
| 2147 | 3s. "By the Death-bed" (Aleksandur Zhendov) | 30 | 20 |
| 2148 | 13s. "Family" (Vladimir Dimitrov) | 1·20 | 35 |
| 2149 | 20s. "Family" (Neuko Balkanski) | 1·50 | 45 |
| 2150 | 40s. "Father Paisii" (Koyu Denchev) | 1·70 | 55 |

**670** Bulgarian Worker

**1972.** 7th Bulgarian Trade Unions Congress.

| | | | | |
|---|---|---|---|---|
| 2151 | **670** | 13s. multicoloured | 65 | 20 |

**671** "Singing Harvesters"

**1972.** 90th Birth Anniv of Vladimir Dimitrov, the Master (painter). Multicoloured.

| | | | |
|---|---|---|---|
| 2152 | 1s. Type **671** | 20 | 15 |
| 2153 | 2s. "Farm Worker" | 20 | 15 |
| 2154 | 3s. "Women Cultivators" (horiz) | 30 | 15 |
| 2155 | 13s. "Peasant Girl" (horiz) | 45 | 20 |
| 2156 | 20s. "My Mother" | 1·40 | 90 |
| 2157 | 40s. Self-portrait | 1·90 | 1·30 |

**672** Heart and Tree Emblem

**1972.** World Heart Month.

| | | | | |
|---|---|---|---|---|
| 2158 | **672** | 13s. multicoloured | 1·40 | 80 |

**673** St. Mark's Cathedral

**1972.** UNESCO "Save Venice" Campaign.

| | | | | |
|---|---|---|---|---|
| 2159 | **673** | 2s. green, turquoise & bl | 30 | 20 |
| 2160 | - | 13s. brown, violet & grn | 1·20 | 55 |

DESIGN: 13s. Doge's Palace.

**674** Dimitrov at Typesetting Desk

**1972.** 90th Birth Anniv of Georgi Dimitrov (statesman). Multicoloured.

| | | | |
|---|---|---|---|
| 2161 | 1s. Type **674** | 20 | 15 |
| 2162 | 2s. Dimitrov leading uprising of 1923 | 20 | 15 |
| 2163 | 3s. Dimitrov at Leipzig Trial | 20 | 15 |
| 2164 | 5s. Dimitrov addressing workers | 20 | 15 |
| 2165 | 13s. Dimitrov with Bulgarian crowd | 35 | 35 |
| 2166 | 18s. Addressing young people | 45 | 45 |
| 2167 | 28s. Dimitrov with children | 95 | 65 |
| 2168 | 40s. Dimitrov's mausoleum | 1·90 | 1·00 |
| 2169 | 80s. Portrait head (green and gold) | 5·50 | 2·10 |
| **MS**2170 | 87×84 mm. As No. 2169, but centre in red and gold. Imperf | 8·25 | 7·75 |
| 2173 | 80s. As No. 2169 | 11·00 | 11·00 |

No. 2173 has the centre in red and gold, and is imperforate.

**675** "Lamp of Learning" and Quotation

**1972.** 250th Birth Anniv of Father Paisii Khilendurski (historian).

| | | | | |
|---|---|---|---|---|
| 2171 | **675** | 2s. brown, green & gold | 20 | 10 |
| 2172 | - | 13s. brown, grn & gold | 1·20 | 45 |

DESIGN: 13s. Paisii writing.

**676** Canoeing

**1972.** Olympic Games, Munich. Multicoloured.

| | | | |
|---|---|---|---|
| 2174 | 1s. Type **676** | 20 | 15 |
| 2175 | 2s. Gymnastics | 20 | 15 |
| 2176 | 3s. Swimming | 20 | 15 |
| 2177 | 13s. Volleyball | 45 | 35 |
| 2178 | 18s. Hurdling | 95 | 55 |
| 2179 | 40s. Wrestling | 1·90 | 1·10 |
| **MS**2180 | 64×60 mm. 80s. Running track and sports. Imperf | 4·75 | 4·50 |

**677** Angel Kunchev

**1972.** Death Cent of Angel Kunchev (patriot).

| | | | | |
|---|---|---|---|---|
| 2181 | **677** | 2s. mauve, gold & purple | 20 | 15 |

**678** "Golden Sands"

**1972.** Black Sea Resorts. Hotels. Multicoloured.

| | | | |
|---|---|---|---|
| 2182 | 1s. Type **678** | 20 | 15 |
| 2183 | 2s. Druzhba | 20 | 15 |
| 2184 | 3s. "Sunny Beach" | 20 | 15 |
| 2185 | 13s. Primorsko | 65 | 20 |
| 2186 | 28s. Rusalka | 1·20 | 45 |
| 2187 | 40s. Albena | 1·40 | 55 |

**679** Canoeing (Bronze Medal)

**1972.** Bulgarian Medal Winners, Olympic Games, Munich. Multicoloured.

| | | | |
|---|---|---|---|
| 2188 | 1s. Type **679** | 20 | 15 |
| 2189 | 2s. Long jumping (Silver Medal) | 20 | 15 |
| 2190 | 3s. Boxing (Gold Medal) | 20 | 15 |
| 2191 | 18s. Wrestling (Gold Medal) | 1·40 | 45 |
| 2192 | 40s. Weightlifting (Gold Medal) | 1·70 | 90 |

**680** Subi Dimitrov

**1972.** Resistance Heroes. Multicoloured.

| | | | |
|---|---|---|---|
| 2193 | 1s. Type **680** | 10 | 10 |
| 2194 | 2s. Tsvyatko Radoinov | 10 | 10 |
| 2195 | 3s. Iordan Lyutibrodski | 10 | 10 |
| 2196 | 5s. Mito Ganev | 30 | 15 |
| 2197 | 13s. Nedelcho Nikolov | 95 | 35 |

**681** Commemorative Text

**1972.** 50th Anniv of U.S.S.R.

| | | | | |
|---|---|---|---|---|
| 2198 | **681** | 13s. red, yellow & gold | 75 | 35 |

**682** "Lilium rhodopaeum"

**1972.** Protected Flowers. Multicoloured.

| | | | |
|---|---|---|---|
| 2199 | 1s. Type **682** | 20 | 15 |
| 2200 | 2s. Marsh gentian | 20 | 15 |
| 2201 | 3s. Sea lily | 20 | 15 |
| 2202 | 4s. Globe flower | 30 | 20 |
| 2203 | 18s. "Primula frondosa" | 95 | 45 |
| 2204 | 23s. Pale pasque flower | 1·40 | 65 |
| 2205 | 40s. "Fritillaria stribrnyi" | 1·90 | 1·00 |

**СВЕТОВЕН ПЪРВЕНЕЦ**
**(683)**

**1972.** "Bulgaria, World Weightlifting Champions". No. 2192 optd with T 683.

| | | | |
|---|---|---|---|
| 2206 | 40s. multicoloured | 2·30 | 1·10 |

**684** Dobri Chintulov

**1972.** 150th Birth Anniv of Dobri Chintulov (poet).

| | | | | |
|---|---|---|---|---|
| 2207 | **684** | 2s. multicoloured | 35 | 20 |

**685** Forehead Ornament (19th-century)

**1972.** Antique Ornaments.

| | | | | |
|---|---|---|---|---|
| 2208 | **685** | 1s. black and brown | 20 | 15 |

| 2209 | - | 2s. black and green | 20 | 15 |
|---|---|---|---|---|
| 2210 | - | 3s. black and blue | 20 | 15 |
| 2211 | - | 8s. black and red | 45 | 20 |
| 2212 | - | 23s. black and brown | 1·20 | 55 |
| 2213 | - | 40s. black and violet | 1·90 | 1·30 |

DESIGNS: 2s. Belt-buckle (19th-century); 3s. Amulet (18th-century); 8s. Pendant (18th-century); 23s. Earrings (14th-century); 40s. Necklace (18th-century).

**686** Divers with Cameras

**1973.** Underwater Research in the Black Sea.

| 2214 | **686** | 1s. black, yellow & blue | 20 | 20 |
|---|---|---|---|---|
| 2215 | - | 2s. black, yellow & blue | 20 | 20 |
| 2216 | - | 18s. black, yellow & blue | 95 | 65 |
| 2217 | - | 40s. black, yellow & blue | 1·90 | 80 |
| **MS**2218 | | 118×98 mm. 20s. ×4. Designs as Nos. 2214/17, but background colours changed (sold at 11l.) | 8·75 | 8·50 |

DESIGNS—HORIZ: 2s. Divers with underwater research vessel "Shelf 1". VERT: 18s. Diver and "NIV 100" diving bell; 40s. Lifting balloon.

**687** "The Hanging of Vasil Levski" (Boris Angelushev)

**1973.** Death Cent of Vasil Levski (patriot).

| 2219 | **687** | 2s. green and red | 20 | 10 |
|---|---|---|---|---|
| 2220 | - | 20s. brown, cream & grn | 1·70 | 80 |

DESIGN: 20s. "Vasil Levski" (Georgi Danchov).

**688** Elhovo Mask

**1973.** Kukeris' Festival Masks. Mult.

| 2221 | 1a. Type **688** | 20 | 15 |
|---|---|---|---|
| 2222 | 2s. Breznik | 20 | 15 |
| 2223 | 3s. Khisar | 20 | 15 |
| 2224 | 13s. Radomir | 65 | 35 |
| 2225 | 20s. Karnobat | 95 | 65 |
| 2226 | 40s. Pernik | 4·75 | 4·25 |

**689** Copernicus

**1973.** 500th Birth Anniv of Copernicus.

| 2227 | **689** | 28s. purple, black & brn | 2·30 | 1·60 |
|---|---|---|---|---|

**1973.** "Visit Bulgaria by Air". No. MS2072 surch with various airline emblems and new sheet value.

| **MS**2228 | 137×131 mm. Nos. 2067/70 surch with new sheet value 1l. | 30·00 | 30·00 |
|---|---|---|---|

**690** Vietnamese "Girl"

**1973.** Vietnam Peace Treaty.

| 2229 | **690** | 18s. multicoloured | 75 | 55 |
|---|---|---|---|---|

**1973.** "IBRA 73" Stamp Exhibition, Munich. No. MS1907 optd with "IBRA" and Olympic symbols in green.

| **MS**2230 | 78×72 mm. 1l. multicoloured | £140 | £140 |
|---|---|---|---|

**691** Common Poppy

**1973.** Wild Flowers. Multicoloured.

| 2231 | 1s. Type **691** | 20 | 15 |
|---|---|---|---|
| 2232 | 2s. Ox-eye daisy | 20 | 15 |
| 2233 | 3s. Peony | 20 | 15 |
| 2234 | 13s. Cornflower | 65 | 35 |
| 2235 | 18s. Corn cockle | 6·50 | 4·50 |
| 2236 | 28s. Meadow buttercup | 1·90 | 1·20 |

**692** C. Botev (after T. Todorov)

**1973.** 125th Birth Anniv of Khristo Botev (poet and revolutionary).

| 2237 | **692** | 2s. yellow, brown & grn | 20 | 15 |
|---|---|---|---|---|
| 2238 | **692** | 18s. grn, lt grn & bronze | 1·40 | 1·10 |

**693** Asen Khalachev and Insurgents

**1973.** 50th Anniv of June Uprising.

| 2239 | **693** | 1s. black, red and gold | 10 | 10 |
|---|---|---|---|---|
| 2240 | - | 2s. black, orange & gold | 10 | 10 |

DESIGN: 2s. "Wounded Worker" (illustration by Boris Angelushev to the poem "September" by Geo Milev).

**694** Stamboliiski (from sculpture by A. Nikolov)

**1973.** 50th Death Anniv of Aleksandur Stamboliiski (Prime Minister 1919–23).

| 2241 | **694** | 18s. lt brn, brn & orge | 65 | 55 |
|---|---|---|---|---|
| 2242 | **694** | 18s. orange | 5·00 | 4·25 |

**695** Muskrat

**1973.** Bulgarian Fauna. Multicoloured.

| 2243 | 1s. Type **695** | 20 | 15 |
|---|---|---|---|
| 2244 | 2s. Racoon-dog | 20 | 15 |
| 2245 | 3s. Mouflon (vert) | 20 | 15 |
| 2246 | 12s. Fallow deer (vert) | 65 | 45 |
| 2247 | 18s. European bison | 1·90 | 1·10 |
| 2248 | 40s. Elk | 6·50 | 4·25 |

**696** Turnovo

**1973.** Air. Tourism. Views of Bulgarian Towns and Cities. Multicoloured.

| 2249 | 2s. Type **696** | 20 | 15 |
|---|---|---|---|
| 2250 | 13s. Rusalka | 65 | 25 |
| 2251 | 20s. Plovdiv | 3·75 | 3·25 |
| 2252 | 28s. Sofia | 95 | 85 |

**697** Insurgents on the March (Boris Angelushev)

**1973.** 50th Anniv of September Uprising.

| 2253 | **697** | 2s. multicoloured | 20 | 15 |
|---|---|---|---|---|
| 2254 | - | 5s. violet, pink & red | 30 | 20 |
| 2255 | - | 13s. multicoloured | 65 | 35 |
| 2256 | - | 18s. olive, cream & red | 1·40 | 1·10 |

DESIGNS—HORIZ: 5s. "Armed Train" (Boris Angelushev). VERT: 13s. Patriotic poster by N. Mirchev. HORIZ: 18s. Georgi Dimitrov and Vasil Kolarov.

**698** Congress Emblem

**1973.** 8th World Trade Union Congress, Varna.

| 2257 | **698** | 2s. multicoloured | 20 | 20 |
|---|---|---|---|---|

**699** "Sun" Emblem and Olympic Rings

**1973.** Olympic Congress, Varna. Multicoloured.

| 2258 | 13s. Type **699** | 1·90 | 75 |
|---|---|---|---|
| 2259 | 28s. Lion Emblem of Bulgarian Olympic Committee (vert) | 2·30 | 1·60 |
| **MS**2260 | 61×77 mm. 80s. Footballers (40×25 mm) | 6·00 | 5·50 |

**700** "Prince Kaloyan"

**1973.** Fresco Portraits, Boyana Church. Mult.

| 2261 | 1s. Type **700** | 20 | 15 |
|---|---|---|---|
| 2262 | 2s. "Desislava" | 20 | 15 |
| 2263 | 3s. "Saint" | 30 | 20 |
| 2264 | 5s. "St. Eustratius" | 55 | 25 |
| 2265 | 10s. "Tsar Constantine-Asen" | 95 | 55 |
| 2266 | 13s. "Deacon Laurentius" | 1·10 | 65 |
| 2267 | 18s. "Virgin Mary" | 1·30 | 85 |
| 2268 | 20s. "St. Ephraim" | 1·50 | 1·10 |
| 2269 | 28s. "Jesus Christ" | 4·75 | 1·60 |
| **MS**2270 | 56×76 mm. 80s. "Scribes". Imperf | 8·75 | 8·75 |

**701** Smirnenski and Cavalry Charge

**1973.** 75th Birth Anniv of Khristo Smirnenski (poet and revolutionary).

| 2271 | **701** | 1s. blue, red and gold | 20 | 10 |
|---|---|---|---|---|
| 2272 | **701** | 2s. blue, red and gold | 45 | 20 |

**702** Human Rights Emblem

**1973.** 25th Anniv of Declaration of Human Rights.

| 2273 | **702** | 13s. gold, red and blue | 65 | 55 |
|---|---|---|---|---|

**703** Tsar Todor Svetoslav meeting the Byzantine Embassy, 1307

**1973.** Bulgarian History. Multicoloured.

| 2274 | 1s. Type **703** | 20 | 15 |
|---|---|---|---|
| 2275 | 2s. Tsar Mikhail Shishman in battle against Byzantines, 1328 | 20 | 15 |
| 2276 | 3s. Battle of Rosokastro, 1332 and Tsar Ivan Aleksandur | 20 | 15 |
| 2277 | 4s. Defence of Turnovo, 1393 and Patriarch Evtimii | 20 | 15 |
| 2278 | 5s. Tsar Ivan Shisman's attack on the Turks | 30 | 20 |
| 2279 | 13s. Momchil attacks Turkish ships at Umur, 1344 | 65 | 35 |
| 2280 | 18s. Meeting of Tsar Ivan Sratsimir and Crusaders, 1396 | 95 | 45 |
| 2281 | 28s. Embassy of Empress Anne of Savoy meets Boyars Balik, Teodor and Dobrotitsa | 2·30 | 1·60 |

**704** "Finn" One-man Dinghy

**1973.** Sailing. Various Yachts. Multicoloured.

| 2282 | 1s. Type **704** | 20 | 15 |
|---|---|---|---|
| 2283 | 2s. "Flying Dutchman" two-man dinghy | 20 | 15 |
| 2284 | 3s. "Soling" yacht | 20 | 15 |
| 2285 | 13s. "Tempest" dinghy | 65 | 35 |
| 2286 | 20s. "470" two-man dinghy | 95 | 65 |
| 2287 | 40s. "Tornado" catamaran | 4·75 | 4·25 |

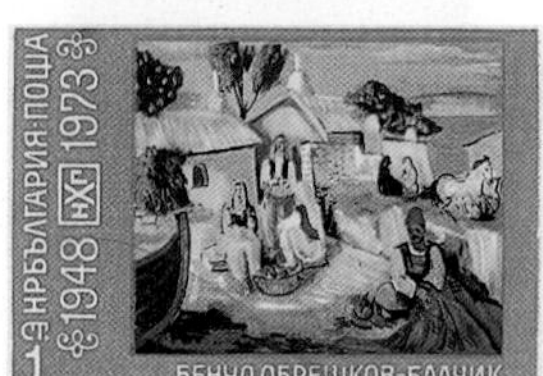


**705** "Balchik" (Bercho Obreshkov)

**1973.** 25th Anniv of National Art Gallery, Sofia and 150th Birth Anniv of Stanislav Dospevski (painter). Multicoloured.

| | | | |
|---|---|---|---|
| 2288 | 1s. Type **705** | 20 | 20 |
| 2289 | 2s. "Mother and Child" (Stryan Venev) | 20 | 20 |
| 2290 | 3s. "Rest" (Tsenko Boyadzhiev) | 20 | 20 |
| 2291 | 13s. "Vase with Flowers" (Siruk Skitnik) (vert) | 75 | 35 |
| 2292 | 18s. "Mary Kuneva" (Iliya Petrov) (vert) | 95 | 45 |
| 2293 | 40s. "Winter in Plovdiv" (Zlatyn Boyadzhiev) (vert) | 4·25 | 3·75 |
| **MS**2294 | 100×95 mm. 50s. "Domnika Lambreva" (S. Dospevski) (vert); 50s. "Self-portrait" (S. Dospevski) (vert) | 6·00 | 4·25 |

**706** Footballers and Emblem

**1973.** World Cup Football Championship, Munich (1974). Sheet 62×94 mm.

| | | | |
|---|---|---|---|
| **MS**2295 | **706** 28s. multicoloured (sold at 1l.) | 6·50 | 6·50 |

**707** Old Testament Scene (Wood-carving)

**1974.** Wood-Carvings from Rozhen Monastery.

| | | | | |
|---|---|---|---|---|
| 2296 | **707** | 1s. dk brn, cream & brn | 20 | 15 |
| 2297 | - | 2s. dk brn, cream & brn | 20 | 15 |
| 2298 | - | 3s. dk brn, cream & brn | 20 | 15 |
| 2299 | - | 5s. olive, cream & green | 30 | 15 |
| 2300 | - | 8s. olive, cream & green | 35 | 20 |
| 2301 | - | 13s. brown, cream and chestnut | 55 | 40 |
| 2302 | - | 28s. brown, cream and chestnut | 1·10 | 65 |

DESIGNS: Nos. 2296/8, "Passover Table"; 2299/2300, "Abraham and the Angel"; 2301/2, "The Expulsion from Eden".

Nos. 2296/8, 2299/300 and 2301/2 form three composite designs.

**708** "Lenin" (N. Mirchev)

**1974.** 50th Death Anniv of Lenin. Mult.

| | | | |
|---|---|---|---|
| 2303 | 2s. Type **708** | 20 | 15 |
| 2304 | 18s. "Lenin with Workers" (W. A. Serov) | 95 | 65 |

**709** "Blagoev addressing Meeting" (G. Kovachev)

**1974.** 50th Death Anniv of D. Blagoev (founder of Bulgarian Social Democratic Party).

| | | | | |
|---|---|---|---|---|
| 2305 | **709** | 2s. multicoloured | 20 | 15 |

**710** Sheep

**1974.** Domestic Animals.

| | | | | |
|---|---|---|---|---|
| 2306 | **710** | 1s. brown, buff & green | 20 | 15 |
| 2307 | - | 2s. purple, violet & red | 20 | 15 |
| 2308 | - | 3s. brown, pink & green | 20 | 15 |
| 2309 | - | 5s. brown, buff & blue | 20 | 15 |
| 2310 | - | 13s. black, blue and brown | 1·10 | 35 |
| 2311 | - | 20s. brown, pink & blue | 3·00 | 1·80 |

DESIGNS: 2s. Goat; 3s. Pig; 5s. Cow; 13s. Buffalo; 20s. Horse.

**711** Social Economic Integration Emblem

**1974.** 25th Anniv of Council for Mutual Economic Aid.

| | | | | |
|---|---|---|---|---|
| 2312 | **711** | 13s. multicoloured | 75 | 55 |

**712** Footballers

**1974.** World Cup Football Championship.

| | | | | |
|---|---|---|---|---|
| 2313 | **712** | 1s. multicoloured | 20 | 15 |
| 2314 | - | 2s. multicoloured | 20 | 15 |
| 2315 | - | 3s. multicoloured | 20 | 15 |
| 2316 | - | 13s. multicoloured | 55 | 20 |
| 2317 | - | 28s. multicoloured | 95 | 55 |
| 2318 | - | 40s. multicoloured | 2·30 | 1·60 |
| **MS**2319 | | 66×78 mm. 1l. multicoloured (55×30 mm) | 4·75 | 4·25 |

DESIGNS: Nos. 2314/19, Various designs similar to Type **712**.

**713** Folk-singers

**1974.** Amateur Arts and Sports Festival. Multicoloured.

| | | | |
|---|---|---|---|
| 2320 | 1s. Type **713** | 20 | 15 |
| 2321 | 2s. Folk-dancers | 20 | 15 |
| 2322 | 3s. Piper and drummer | 20 | 15 |
| 2323 | 5s. Wrestling | 20 | 15 |
| 2324 | 13s. Athletics | 95 | 85 |
| 2325 | 18s. Gymnastics | 1·10 | 55 |

**714** "Cosmic Research" (Penko Barnbov)

**1974.** "Mladost '74" Youth Stamp Exhibition, Sofia. Multicoloured.

| | | | |
|---|---|---|---|
| 2326 | 1s. Type **714** | 15 | 10 |
| 2327 | 2s. "Salt Production" (Mariana Bliznakaa) | 20 | 10 |
| 2328 | 3s. "Fire-dancer" (Detelina Lalova) | 55 | 10 |
| 2329 | 28s. "Friendship Train" (Vanya Boyanova) | 2·75 | 2·40 |
| **MS**2330 | 70×70 mm. 60s. "Spring" (Vladimir Kunchev) (40×40 mm) | 4·25 | 4·25 |

**715** Motor-cars

**1974.** World Automobile Federation's Spring Congress, Sofia.

| | | | | |
|---|---|---|---|---|
| 2331 | **715** | 13s. multicoloured | 65 | 45 |

**716** Period Architecture

**1974.** UNESCO Executive Council's 94th Session, Varna.

| | | | | |
|---|---|---|---|---|
| 2332 | **716** | 18s. multicoloured | 65 | 45 |

**717** Chinese Aster

**1974.** Bulgarian Flowers. Multicoloured.

| | | | |
|---|---|---|---|
| 2333 | 1s. Type **717** | 20 | 20 |
| 2334 | 2s. Mallow | 20 | 20 |
| 2335 | 3s. Columbine | 20 | 20 |
| 2336 | 18s. Tulip | 95 | 35 |
| 2337 | 20s. Marigold | 1·10 | 45 |
| 2338 | 28s. Pansy | 2·75 | 1·80 |
| **MS**2339 | 80×60 mm. 80s. Gaillarde (44×33 mm) | 3·75 | 3·25 |

**718** 19th Century Post-boy

**1974.** Centenary of UPU.

| | | | | |
|---|---|---|---|---|
| 2340 | **718** | 2s. violet & blk on orge | 20 | 15 |
| 2341 | - | 18s. green & blk on orge | 95 | 45 |
| **MS**2342 | | 80×58 mm. 28s. blue and orange (sold at 80st.) | 3·25 | 3·25 |

DESIGN: 18s. First Bulgarian mail-coach; 20s. UPU emblem.

**719** Young Pioneer and Komsomol Girl

**1974.** 30th Anniv of Dimitrov's Septembrist Pioneers Organization. Multicoloured.

| | | | |
|---|---|---|---|
| 2343 | 1s. Type **719** | 15 | 10 |
| 2344 | 2s. Pioneer with doves | 15 | 10 |
| **MS**2345 | 60×84 mm. 60s. Emblem with portrait of Dimitrov (34×44 mm) | 2·50 | 2·20 |

**720** Communist Soldiers with Flag

**1974.** 30th Anniv of Fatherland Front Government. Multicoloured.

| | | | |
|---|---|---|---|
| 2346 | 1s. Type **720** | 20 | 15 |
| 2347 | 2s. "Soviet Liberators" | 20 | 15 |
| 2348 | 5s. "Industrialisation" | 20 | 15 |
| 2349 | 13s. "Modern Agriculture" | 55 | 20 |
| 2350 | 18s. "Science and Technology" | 1·00 | 65 |

**721** Stockholm and Emblems

**1974.** "Stockholm '74" International Stamp Exhibition. Sheet 65×72 mm.

| | | | |
|---|---|---|---|
| **MS**2351 | **721** 40s. blue, green and yellow | 7·50 | 7·50 |

**722** Gymnast on Beam

**1974.** 18th World Gymnastic Championships, Varna. Multicoloured.

| | | | |
|---|---|---|---|
| 2352 | 2s. Type **722** | 15 | 10 |
| 2353 | 13s. Gymnast on horse | 65 | 55 |

**723** Doves on Script

**1974.** European Security and Co-operation Conference. Sheet 97×117 mm containing T 723 and similar vert designs.

| | | | |
|---|---|---|---|
| **MS**2354 | 13s. yellow, blue and chestnut (T **723**); 13s. blue, mauve and chestnut (Map of Europe and script); 13s. green, blue and chestnut (Leaves on script); 13s. multicoloured (Commemorative text) (sold at 60s.) | 3·50 | 3·50 |

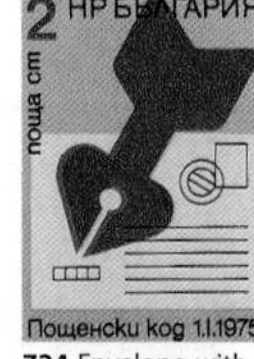


**724** Envelope with Arrow pointing to Postal Code

**1974.** Introduction of Postal Coding System (1 January 1975).

| | | | | |
|---|---|---|---|---|
| 2355 | **724** | 2s. green, orange & blk | 20 | 15 |

**725** "Sourovachka" (twig decorated with coloured ribbons)

**1974.** New Year.

| | | | | |
|---|---|---|---|---|
| 2356 | **725** | 2s. multicoloured | 20 | 15 |

**726** Icon of St. Theodor Stratilar

**1974.** Bulgarian History.

| | | | | |
|---|---|---|---|---|
| 2357 | **726** | 1s. multicoloured | 20 | 15 |
| 2358 | - | 2s. grey, mauve & black | 20 | 15 |
| 2359 | - | 3s. grey, blue and black | 20 | 15 |
| 2360 | - | 5s. grey, lilac and black | 20 | 15 |
| 2361 | - | 8s. black, buff and brown | 30 | 15 |
| 2362 | - | 13s. grey, green & black | 45 | 20 |
| 2363 | - | 18s. black, gold & red | 75 | 35 |
| 2364 | - | 28s. grey, blue & black | 2·20 | 1·10 |

DESIGNS: 2s. Bronze medallion; 3s. Carved capital; 5s. Silver bowl of Sivin Jupan; 8s. Clay goblet; 13s. Lioness (torso); 18s. Gold tray; 28s. Double-headed eagle.

**727** Apricot

**1975.** Fruit-tree Blossoms. Multicoloured.

| | | | |
|---|---|---|---|
| 2365 | 1s. Type **727** | 20 | 15 |
| 2366 | 2s. Apple | 20 | 15 |
| 2367 | 3s. Cherry | 20 | 15 |
| 2368 | 19s. Pear | 65 | 35 |
| 2369 | 28s. Peach | 1·60 | 55 |

**728** Peasant with Flag

**1975.** 75th Anniv of Bulgarian People's Agrarian Union. Sheet 104×95 mm containing T 728 and similar vert designs.

| | | |
|---|---|---|
| **MS**2370 2s. brown, orange and green; 5s. brown, orange and green; 13s. sepia, orange and green; 18s. chestnut, orange and green | 1·60 | 1·60 |

DESIGNS: 5s. Rebels keeping watch during 1923 September uprising; 13s. Dancing; 18s. Woman harvesting fruit.

**729** Spanish 6c. Stamp of 1850 and "Espana" Emblem

**1975.** "Espana 1975" International Stamp Exhibition, Madrid. Sheet 68×100 mm.

| | | |
|---|---|---|
| **MS**2371 **729** 40s. multicoloured | 8·00 | 7·50 |

**730** Star and Arrow

**1975.** 30th Anniv of "Victory in Europe" Day.

| | | | | |
|---|---|---|---|---|
| 2372 | **730** | 2s. red, black & brown | 20 | 15 |
| 2373 | - | 13s. black, brown & bl | 75 | 35 |

DESIGNS: 13s. Peace dove and broken sword.

**731** "Weights and Measures"

**1975.** Centenary of Metre Convention.

| | | | | |
|---|---|---|---|---|
| 2374 | **731** | 13s. violet, black & silver | 30 | 20 |

**732** Tree and open Book

**1975.** 50th Anniv of Forestry School.

| | | | | |
|---|---|---|---|---|
| 2375 | **732** | 2s. multicoloured | 20 | 15 |

**733** Michelangelo

**1975.** 500th Birth Anniv of Michelangelo.

| | | | | |
|---|---|---|---|---|
| 2376 | **733** | 2s. purple and blue | 20 | 15 |
| 2377 | - | 13s. violet and purple | 55 | 35 |
| 2378 | - | 18s. brown and green | 1·10 | 65 |

| | | |
|---|---|---|
| **MS**2379 70×84 mm. **733** 2s. green and red (sold at 60s.) | 2·20 | 2·20 |

DESIGNS—HORIZ: Sculptures from Giuliano de Medici's tomb: 13s. "Night"; 18s. "Day".

**734** Festival Emblem

**1975.** Festival of Humour and Satire, Gabrovo.

| | | | | |
|---|---|---|---|---|
| 2380 | **734** | 2s. multicoloured | 20 | 15 |

**735** Women's Head and Emblem

**1975.** International Women's Year.

| | | | | |
|---|---|---|---|---|
| 2381 | **735** | 13s. multicoloured | 45 | 20 |

**736** Vasil and Sava Kokareshkov

**1975.** "Young Martyrs to Fascism".

| | | | | |
|---|---|---|---|---|
| 2382 | **736** | 1s. black, green & gold | 10 | 10 |
| 2383 | - | 2s. black, mauve & gold | 10 | 10 |
| 2384 | - | 5s. black, red and gold | 15 | 10 |
| 2385 | - | 13s. black, blue & gold | 55 | 45 |

DESIGNS—HORIZ: 2s. Mitko Palauzov and Ivan Vasilev; 5s. Nikola Nakev and Stefcho Kraichev; 13s. Ivanka Pashkolouva and Detelina Mincheva.

**737** "Mother feeding Child" (Jean Millet)

**1975.** World Graphics Exhibition, Sofia. Celebrated Drawings and Engravings. Multicoloured.

| | | | |
|---|---|---|---|
| 2386 | 1s. Type **737** | 20 | 15 |
| 2387 | 2s. "Mourning a Dead Daughter" (Goya) | 20 | 15 |
| 2388 | 3s. "The Reunion" (Iliya Beshkov) | 20 | 15 |
| 2389 | 13s. "Seated Nude" (Auguste Renoir) | 45 | 20 |
| 2390 | 20s. "Man in a Fur Hat" (Rembrandt) | 65 | 55 |
| 2391 | 40s. "The Dream" (Horore Daumier) (horiz) | 2·30 | 1·20 |

| | | |
|---|---|---|
| **MS**2392 80×95 mm. 1l. "Temptation" (Albrecht Durer) (37×53 mm) | 3·75 | 3·25 |

**738** Gabrovo Costume

**1975.** Women's Regional Costumes. Mult.

| | | | |
|---|---|---|---|
| 2393 | 2s. Type **738** | 20 | 15 |
| 2394 | 3s. Trun costume | 20 | 15 |
| 2395 | 5s. Vidin costume | 20 | 15 |
| 2396 | 13s. Goce Delcev costume | 75 | 35 |
| 2397 | 18s. Ruse costume | 1·70 | 55 |

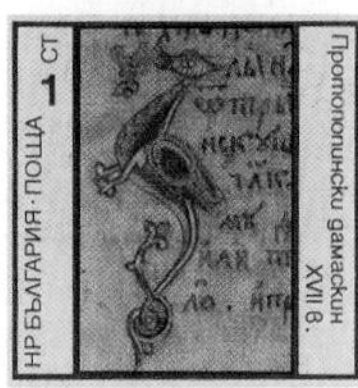

**739** "Bird" (manuscript illumination)

**1975.** Original Bulgarian Manuscripts. Mult.

| | | | |
|---|---|---|---|
| 2398 | 1s. Type **739** | 20 | 15 |
| 2399 | 2s. "Head" | 20 | 15 |
| 2400 | 3s. Abstract design | 20 | 15 |
| 2401 | 8s. "Pointing finger" | 35 | 20 |
| 2402 | 13s. "Imaginary creature" | 75 | 35 |
| 2403 | 18s. Abstract design | 1·30 | 45 |

**740** Ivan Vasov

**1975.** 125th Anniv of Ivan Vasov (writer). Multicoloured.

| | | | |
|---|---|---|---|
| 2404 | 2s. Type **740** | 20 | 10 |
| 2405 | 13s. Vasov seated | 55 | 20 |

**741** "Soyuz" and Aleksei Leonov

**1975.** "Apollo"–"Soyuz" Space Link.

| | | | | |
|---|---|---|---|---|
| 2406 | **741** | 13s. multicoloured | 45 | 20 |
| 2407 | - | 18s. multicoloured | 95 | 35 |
| 2408 | - | 28s. multicoloured | 1·90 | 65 |

| | | |
|---|---|---|
| **MS**2409 76×84 mm. 1l. blue, grey and red | 4·25 | 3·25 |

DESIGNS: 18s. "Apollo" and Thomas Stafford; 28s. The Link-up; 1l. "Apollo" and "Soyuz" after docking.

**742** Ryukyu Sailing Boat, Map and Emblems

**1975.** International Exposition, Okinawa.

| | | | | |
|---|---|---|---|---|
| 2410 | **742** | 13s. multicoloured | 45 | 20 |

**743** St. Cyril and St. Methodius

**1975.** "Balkanphila V" Stamp Exhibition, Sofia.

| | | | | |
|---|---|---|---|---|
| 2411 | **743** | 2s. brown, lt brn & red | 20 | 10 |
| 2412 | - | 13s. brown, lt brn & grn | 55 | 20 |

| | | |
|---|---|---|
| **MS**2413 90×86 mm. 50s. sepia, brown and orange | 2·20 | 2·20 |

DESIGNS—VERT: 13s. St. Constantine and St. Helene. HORIZ: 50s. Sophia Church, Sofia (53×43 mm.).

**744** Footballer

**1975.** 8th Inter-Toto (Football Pools) Congress, Varna.

| | | | | |
|---|---|---|---|---|
| 2414 | **744** | 2s. multicoloured | 20 | 15 |

**745** Deaths-head Hawk Moth

**1975.** Hawk Moths. Multicoloured.

| | | | |
|---|---|---|---|
| 2415 | 1s. Type **745** | 20 | 15 |
| 2416 | 2s. Oleander hawk moth | 20 | 15 |
| 2417 | 3s. Eyed hawk moth | 20 | 15 |
| 2418 | 10s. Mediterranean hawk moth | 55 | 20 |
| 2419 | 13s. Elephant hawk moth | 95 | 45 |
| 2420 | 18s. Broad-bordered bee hawk moth | 1·90 | 75 |

**746** UN Emblem

**1975.** 30th Anniv of UNO.

| | | | | |
|---|---|---|---|---|
| 2421 | **746** | 13s. red, brown & black | 45 | 20 |

**747** Map of Europe on Peace Dove

**1975.** European Security and Co-operation Conference, Helsinki.

| | | | | |
|---|---|---|---|---|
| 2422 | **747** | 18s. lilac, blue & yellow | 85 | 85 |

**748** D. Khristov

**1975.** Birth Cent of Dobri Khristov (composer).

| | | | | |
|---|---|---|---|---|
| 2423 | **748** | 5s. brown, yellow & grn | 20 | 10 |

**749** Constantine's Rebellion against the Turks

**1975.** Bulgarian History. Multicoloured.

| | | | |
|---|---|---|---|
| 2424 | 1s. Type **749** | 20 | 15 |
| 2425 | 2s. Vladislav III's campaign | 20 | 15 |
| 2426 | 3s. Battle of Turnovo | 20 | 15 |
| 2427 | 10s. Battle of Chiprovtsi | 30 | 20 |
| 2428 | 13s. 17 th-century partisans | 75 | 35 |
| 2429 | 18s. Return of banished peasants | 1·00 | 55 |

**750** "First Aid"

**1975.** 90th Anniv of Bulgarian Red Cross.

| | | | | |
|---|---|---|---|---|
| 2430 | **750** | 2s. brown, black and red | 15 | 10 |
| 2431 | - | 13s. green, black and red | 55 | 20 |

DESIGN: 13s. "Peace and international Co-operation".

**751** Ethnographical Museum, Plovdiv

**1975.** European Architectural Heritage Year.

| | | | | |
|---|---|---|---|---|
| 2432 | **751** | 80s. brown, yellow & grn | 2·75 | 2·75 |

**752** Christmas Lanterns

**1975.** Christmas and New Year. Multicoloured.

| | | | |
|---|---|---|---|
| 2433 | 2s. Type **752** | 20 | 10 |
| 2434 | 13s. Stylized peace dove | 45 | 35 |

**753** Egyptian Galley

**1975.** Historic Ships (1st series). Multicoloured.

| | | | |
|---|---|---|---|
| 2435 | 1s. Type **753** | 10 | 10 |
| 2436 | 2s. Phoenician galley | 10 | 10 |
| 2437 | 3s. Greek trireme | 10 | 10 |
| 2438 | 5s. Roman galley | 20 | 10 |
| 2439 | 13s. "Mora" (Norman ship) | 55 | 35 |
| 2440 | 18s. Venetian galley | 1·10 | 55 |

See also Nos. 2597/2602, 2864/9, 3286/91 and 3372/7.

**754** Modern Articulated Tramcar

**1976.** 75th Anniv of Sofia Tramways. Mult.

| | | | |
|---|---|---|---|
| 2441 | 2s. Type **754** | 20 | 10 |
| 2442 | 13s. Early 20th-century tramcar | 85 | 40 |

**755** Skiing

**1976.** Winter Olympic Games, Innsbruck. Mult.

| | | | |
|---|---|---|---|
| 2443 | 1s. Type **755** | 20 | 15 |
| 2444 | 2s. Cross-country skiing (vert) | 20 | 15 |
| 2445 | 2s. Ski jumping | 20 | 15 |
| 2446 | 13s. Biathlon (vert) | 55 | 35 |
| 2447 | 18s. Ice hockey (vert) | 65 | 55 |
| 2448 | 18s. Speed skating (vert) | 1·90 | 75 |
| **MS**2449 | 70×80 mm. 80s. Ice skating (pairs) (30×55 mm) | 3·25 | 2·75 |

**756** Stylized Bird

**1976.** 11th Bulgarian Communists Party Congress. Multicoloured.

| | | | |
|---|---|---|---|
| 2450 | 2s. Type **756** | 10 | 10 |
| 2451 | 5s. "1956–1976, Fulfilment of the Five Year Plans" | 20 | 15 |
| 2452 | 13s. Hammer and Sickle | 45 | 20 |
| **MS**2453 | 55×65 mm. 50s. Georgi Dimitrov (Prime Minister and Party secretary-general, 1945–49) (33×43 mm) | 1·90 | 1·60 |

**757** Alexander Graham Bell and early Telephone

**1976.** Telephone Centenary.

| | | | | |
|---|---|---|---|---|
| 2454 | **757** | 18s. lt brown, brn & pur | 65 | 35 |

**758** Mute Swan

**1976.** Waterfowl. Multicoloured.

| | | | |
|---|---|---|---|
| 2455 | 1s. Type **758** | 20 | 15 |
| 2456 | 2s. Ruddy shelduck | 20 | 15 |
| 2457 | 3s. Common shelduck | 30 | 20 |
| 2458 | 5s. Garganey | 1·10 | 35 |
| 2459 | 13s. Mallard | 1·40 | 85 |
| 2460 | 18s. Red-crested pochard | 3·75 | 2·75 |

**759** Guerillas' Briefing

**1976.** Cent of April Uprising (1st issue). Mult.

| | | | |
|---|---|---|---|
| 2461 | 1s. Type **759** | 10 | 10 |
| 2462 | 2s. Peasants' briefing | 10 | 10 |
| 2463 | 5s. Krishina, horse and guard | 20 | 10 |
| 2464 | 13s. Rebels with cannon | 55 | 35 |

See also Nos. 2529/33.

**760** Kozlodui Atomic Energy Centre

**1976.** Modern Industrial Installations.

| | | | | |
|---|---|---|---|---|
| 2465 | **760** | 5s. green | 20 | 15 |
| 2466 | - | 8s. red | 30 | 20 |
| 2467 | - | 10s. green | 45 | 25 |
| 2468 | - | 13s. violet | 55 | 30 |
| 2469 | - | 20s. green | 75 | 35 |

DESIGNS: 8s. Bobaudol plant; 10s. Sviloza chemical works; 13s. Devaya chemical works; 20s. Sestvitro dam.

**761** Guard with Patrol-dog

**1976.** 30th Anniv of Frontier Guards. Mult.

| | | | |
|---|---|---|---|
| 2470 | 2s. Type **761** | 20 | 15 |
| 2471 | 13s. Mounted guards | 45 | 20 |

**762** Worker with Spade

**1976.** 30th Anniv of Youth Brigades Movement.

| | | | | |
|---|---|---|---|---|
| 2472 | **762** | 2s. multicoloured | 20 | 15 |

**763** Botev

**1976.** Death Cent of Khristo Botev (poet).

| | | | | |
|---|---|---|---|---|
| 2473 | **763** | 13s. green and brown | 65 | 35 |

**764** "Martyrs of First Congress" (relief)

**1976.** 85th Anniv of 1st Bulgarian Social Democratic Party Congress, Buzludzha. Multicoloured.

| | | | |
|---|---|---|---|
| 2474 | 2s. Type **764** | 15 | 10 |
| 2475 | 5s. Modern memorial, Buzludzha Peak | 20 | 10 |

**765** Dimitur Blagoev

**1976.** 120th Birth Anniv of Dimitur Blagoev (founder of Bulgarian Social Democratic Party).

| | | | | |
|---|---|---|---|---|
| 2476 | **765** | 13s. black, red and gold | 65 | 20 |

**766** "Thematic Stamps"

**1976.** 12th Bulgarian Philatelic Federation Congress. Sheet 73×103 mm.

| | | | | |
|---|---|---|---|---|
| **MS**2477 | **766** | 50s. multicoloured | 3·25 | 2·75 |

**767** Children Playing

**1976.** Child Welfare.

| | | | | |
|---|---|---|---|---|
| 2478 | **767** | 1s. multicoloured | 20 | 15 |
| 2479 | - | 2s. multicoloured | 20 | 15 |
| 2480 | - | 5s. multicoloured | 20 | 15 |
| 2481 | - | 23s. multicoloured | 95 | 55 |

DESIGNS: 2s. Girls with pram and boy on rocking horse; 5s. Playing ball; 23s. Dancing.

**768** Wrestling

**1976.** Olympic Games, Montreal. Multicoloured.

| | | | |
|---|---|---|---|
| 2482 | 1s. Type **768** | 20 | 15 |
| 2483 | 2s. Boxing (vert) | 20 | 15 |
| 2484 | 3s. Weight-lifting (vert) | 20 | 15 |
| 2485 | 13s. Canoeing (vert) | 45 | 20 |
| 2486 | 18s. Gymnastics (vert) | 65 | 35 |
| 2487 | 28s. Diving (vert) | 1·00 | 55 |
| 2488 | 40s. Athletics (vert) | 1·40 | 65 |
| **MS**2489 | 70×80 mm. 1l. Weightlifting (vert) | 3·25 | 3·25 |

**769** Belt Buckle, Vidin

**1976.** Thracian Art (8th–4th Centuries B.C.). Mult.

| | | | |
|---|---|---|---|
| 2490 | 1s. Type **769** | 20 | 15 |
| 2491 | 2s. Brooch, Durzhanitsa | 20 | 15 |
| 2492 | 3s. Mirror handle, Chukarka | 20 | 15 |
| 2493 | 5s. Helmet cheek guard, Gurlo | 20 | 15 |
| 2494 | 13s. Gold decoration, Orizovo | 45 | 20 |
| 2495 | 18s. Decorated horse-harness, Brezovo | 65 | 30 |
| 2496 | 20s. Greave, Mogilanska Mogila | 85 | 35 |
| 2497 | 28s. Pendant, Bukovtsi | 95 | 55 |

**770** "Partisans at Night" (Petrov)

**1976.** Paintings by Iliya Petrov and Tsanko Lavrenov from the National Gallery. Multicoloured.

| No. | Description | Unused | Used |
|---|---|---|---|
| 2498 | 2s. Type **770** | 20 | 15 |
| 2499 | 5s. "Kurshum-Khan" (Lavrenov) | 20 | 15 |
| 2500 | 13s. "Seated Woman" (Petrov) | 45 | 20 |
| 2501 | 18s. "Boy seated in chair" (Petrov) (vert) | 95 | 35 |
| 2502 | 28s. "Old Plovdiv" (Lavrenov) (vert) | 1·10 | 45 |
| **MS**2503 | 60×82 mm. 80s. "Self-portrait" (Petrov) (vert) | 2·75 | 2·75 |

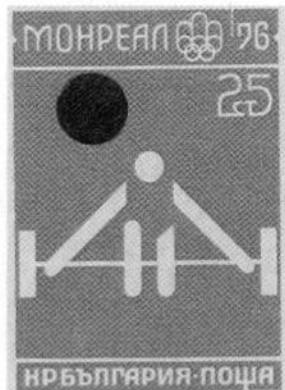

**771** Weightlifting

**1976.** Gold Medal Winners, Montreal Olympic Games. Sheet 98×116 mm containing vert designs as T 771, each with medal in red and gold.

| No. | Description | Unused | Used |
|---|---|---|---|
| **MS**2504 | 25s. yellow (T **771**); 25s. blue (rowing); 25s. green (running); 25s. red (wrestling) | 3·25 | 3·25 |

**772** Fish on line

**1976.** World Sports Fishing Congress, Varna.

| No. | Type | Description | Unused | Used |
|---|---|---|---|---|
| 2505 | **772** | 5s. multicoloured | 30 | 20 |

**773** "The Pianist"

**1976.** 75th Birth Anniv of Alex Jhendov (caricaturist).

| No. | Type | Description | Unused | Used |
|---|---|---|---|---|
| 2506 | **773** | 2s. dp grn, cream & grn | 10 | 10 |
| 2507 | - | 5s. dp violet, vio & lilac | 30 | 15 |
| 2508 | - | 13s. black, pink & red | 45 | 20 |

DESIGNS: 5s. "Trick or Treat"; 13s. "The Leader".

**774** St. Theodor

**1976.** Zemen Monastery. Frescoes. Multicoloured.

| No. | Description | Unused | Used |
|---|---|---|---|
| 2509 | 2s. Type **774** | 20 | 15 |
| 2510 | 3s. St. Paul and Apostle | 20 | 15 |
| 2511 | 5s. St. Joachim | 30 | 15 |
| 2512 | 13s. Prophet Melchisadek | 55 | 20 |
| 2513 | 19s. St. Porphyrus | 75 | 35 |
| 2514 | 28s. Queen Doya | 95 | 45 |
| **MS**2515 | 60×76 mm. 1l. Holy Communion | 3·25 | 3·25 |

**775** Legal Document

**1976.** 25th Anniv of State Archives.

| No. | Type | Description | Unused | Used |
|---|---|---|---|---|
| 2516 | **775** | 5s. multicoloured | 30 | 20 |

**776** Horse Chestnut

**1976.** Plants. Multicoloured.

| No. | Description | Unused | Used |
|---|---|---|---|
| 2517 | 1s. Type **776** | 20 | 15 |
| 2518 | 2s. Shrubby cinquefoil | 20 | 15 |
| 2519 | 5s. Holly | 20 | 15 |
| 2520 | 8s. Yew | 30 | 20 |
| 2521 | 13s. "Daphne pontica" | 45 | 35 |
| 2522 | 23s. Judas tree | 1·20 | 55 |

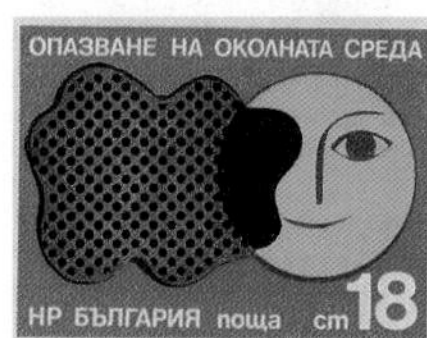

**777** Cloud over Sun

**1976.** Protection of the Environment. Mult.

| No. | Description | Unused | Used |
|---|---|---|---|
| 2523 | 2s. Cloud over tree | 20 | 15 |
| 2524 | 18s. Type **777** | 65 | 35 |

**778** Dimitur Polyanov

**1976.** Birth Cent of Dimitur Polyanov (poet).

| No. | Type | Description | Unused | Used |
|---|---|---|---|---|
| 2525 | **778** | 2s. lilac and orange | 20 | 15 |

**779** Congress Emblem

**1976.** 33rd Bulgarian People's Agrarian Union Congress. Multicoloured.

| No. | Description | Unused | Used |
|---|---|---|---|
| 2526 | 2s. Type **779** | 20 | 10 |
| 2527 | 13s. Flags | 55 | 35 |

**780** Warrior with Horses (vase painting)

**1976.** 30th Anniv of United Nations Educational Scientific and Cultural Organization. Sheet 71×81 mm.

| No. | Type | Description | Unused | Used |
|---|---|---|---|---|
| **MS**2528 | **780** | 50s. multicoloured | 2·75 | 2·75 |

**781** "Khristo Botev" (Zlatyu Boyadzhiev)

**1976.** Centenary of April Uprising (2nd issue). Multicoloured.

| No. | Description | Unused | Used |
|---|---|---|---|
| 2529 | 1s. Type **781** | 20 | 15 |
| 2530 | 2s. "Partisan carrying Cherry-wood Cannon" (Iliya Petrov) | 20 | 15 |
| 2531 | 3s. "Necklace of Immortality" (Dechko Uzunov) | 20 | 15 |
| 2532 | 13s. "April 1876" (Georgi Popov) | 45 | 20 |
| 2533 | 18s. "Partisans" (Stoyan Venev) | 75 | 45 |
| **MS**2534 | 45×82 mm. 60s. "The Oath" (Svetlin Rusev) | 2·20 | 2·20 |

**782** Tobacco Workers

**1976.** 70th Birth Anniv of Veselin Staikov (artist). Multicoloured.

| No. | Description | Unused | Used |
|---|---|---|---|
| 2535 | 1s. Type **782** | 10 | 10 |
| 2536 | 2s. "Melnik" | 15 | 10 |
| 2537 | 13s. "Boat Builders" | 55 | 25 |

**783** "Snowflake"

**1976.** New Year.

| No. | Type | Description | Unused | Used |
|---|---|---|---|---|
| 2538 | **783** | 2s. multicoloured | 20 | 10 |

**784** Zakhari Stojanov

**1976.** 125th Birth Anniv of Zakhari Stojanov (writer).

| No. | Type | Description | Unused | Used |
|---|---|---|---|---|
| 2539 | **784** | 2s. brown, red and gold | 20 | 10 |

**785** Bronze Coin of Septimus Severus

**1977.** Roman Coins struck in Serdica. Mult.

| No. | Description | Unused | Used |
|---|---|---|---|
| 2540 | 1s. Type **785** | 20 | 15 |
| 2541 | 2s. Bronze coin of Caracalla | 20 | 15 |
| 2542 | 13s. Bronze coin of Caracalla (diff.) | 30 | 20 |
| 2543 | 18s. Bronze coin of Caracalla (diff.) | 55 | 35 |
| 2544 | 23s. Copper coin of Diocletian | 95 | 55 |

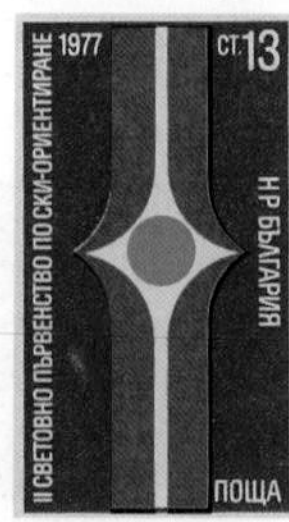

**786** Championships Emblem

**1977.** World Ski-orienteering Championships.

| No. | Type | Description | Unused | Used |
|---|---|---|---|---|
| 2545 | **786** | 13s. blue, red & ultram | 55 | 20 |

**787** Congress Emblem

**1977.** 5th Congress of Bulgarian Tourist Associations.

| No. | Type | Description | Unused | Used |
|---|---|---|---|---|
| 2546 | **787** | 2s. multicoloured | 20 | 10 |

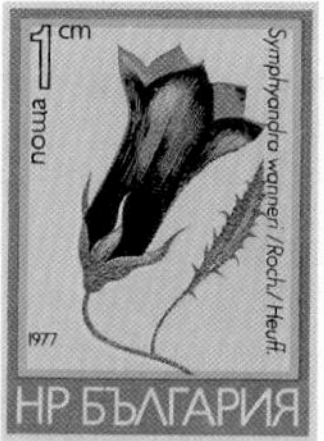

**788** "Symphyandra wanneri"

**1977.** Mountain Flowers. Multicoloured.

| No. | Description | Unused | Used |
|---|---|---|---|
| 2547 | 1s. Type **788** | 20 | 15 |
| 2548 | 2s. "Petcovia orphanidea" | 20 | 15 |
| 2549 | 3s. "Campanula lanatre" | 20 | 15 |
| 2550 | 13s. "Campanula scutellata" | 55 | 35 |
| 2551 | 43s. Nettle-leaved bellflower | 1·90 | 75 |

**789** V. Kolarov

**1977.** Birth Centenary of Vasil Kolarov (Prime Minister 1949–50).

| No. | Type | Description | Unused | Used |
|---|---|---|---|---|
| 2552 | **789** | 2s. grey, black & blue | 20 | 10 |

**790** Congress Emblem

**1977.** 8th Bulgarian Trade Unions Congress.

| No. | Type | Description | Unused | Used |
|---|---|---|---|---|
| 2553 | **790** | 2s. multicoloured | 20 | 10 |

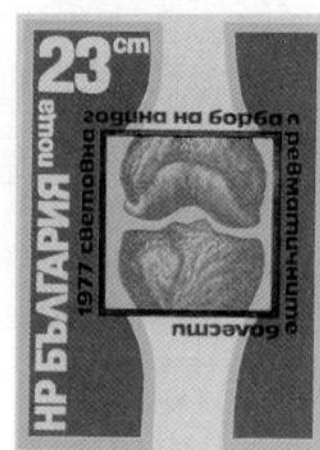

**791** Joint

**1977.** World Rheumatism Year.

| No. | Type | Description | Unused | Used |
|---|---|---|---|---|
| 2554 | **791** | 23s. multicoloured | 95 | 55 |

**792** Wrestling

**1977.** World University Games, Sofia. Mult.

| No. | Description | Unused | Used |
|---|---|---|---|
| 2555 | 2s. Type **792** | 20 | 20 |
| 2556 | 13s. Running | 45 | 25 |
| 2557 | 23s. Handball | 85 | 45 |

| | | | | |
|---|---|---|---|---|
| 2558 | | 43s. Gymnastics | 1·40 | 85 |

**793** Ivan Vazov National Theatre

**1977.** Buildings in Sofia. Pale brown backgrounds.

| | | | | |
|---|---|---|---|---|
| 2559 | **793** | 12s. red | 35 | 20 |
| 2560 | - | 13s. brown | 45 | 25 |
| 2561 | - | 23s. blue | 75 | 35 |
| 2562 | - | 30s. green | 1·10 | 45 |
| 2563 | - | 80s. violet | 1·90 | 1·20 |
| 2564 | - | 1l. brown | 2·40 | 1·50 |

DESIGNS: 13s. Party Building; 23s. People's Army Building; 30s. Clement of Ohrid University; 80s. National Art Gallery; 1l. National Assembly Building.

**794** Congress Emblem

**1977.** 13th Dimitrov Communist Youth League Congress.

| | | | | |
|---|---|---|---|---|
| 2565 | **794** | 2s. red, green and gold | 20 | 10 |

**795** "St. Nicholas" Nesebur

**1977.** Bulgarian Icons. Multicoloured.

| | | | | |
|---|---|---|---|---|
| 2566 | | 1s. Type **795** | 20 | 15 |
| 2567 | | 2s. "Old Testament Trinity", Sofia | 20 | 15 |
| 2568 | | 3s. "The Royal Gates", Veliko Turnovo | 20 | 15 |
| 2569 | | 5s. "Deisis", Nesebur | 20 | 15 |
| 2570 | | 13s. "St. Nicholas", Elena | 45 | 20 |
| 2571 | | 23s. "The Presentation of the Blessed Virgin", Rila Monastery | 75 | 35 |
| 2572 | | 35s. "The Virgin Mary with Infant", Varna | 1·10 | 75 |
| 2573 | | 40s. "St. Demetrius on Horse-back", Provadya | 2·40 | 1·10 |
| **MS**2574 | | 100×99 mm. 1l. "The Twelve Festival Days", Rila Monastery. Imperf | 4·25 | 3·25 |

**796** Wolf

**1977.** Wild Animals. Multicoloured.

| | | | | |
|---|---|---|---|---|
| 2575 | | 1s. Type **796** | 20 | 15 |
| 2576 | | 2s. Red fox | 20 | 15 |
| 2577 | | 10s. Weasel | 45 | 20 |
| 2578 | | 13s. Wild cat | 65 | 55 |
| 2579 | | 23s. Golden jackal | 1·90 | 1·10 |

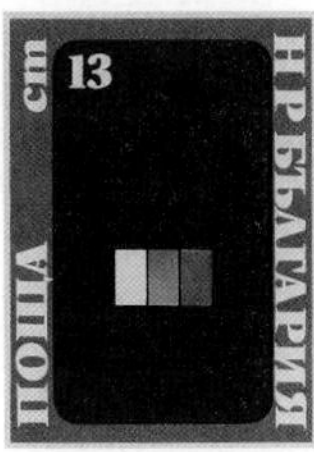

**797** Congress Emblem

**1977.** 3rd Bulgarian Culture Congress.

| | | | | |
|---|---|---|---|---|
| 2580 | **797** | 13s. multicoloured | 45 | 20 |

**798** "Crafty Peter riding a Donkey" (drawing by Iliya Beshkov)

**1977.** 11th Festival of Humour and Satire, Gabrovo.

| | | | | |
|---|---|---|---|---|
| 2581 | **798** | 2s. multicoloured | 20 | 10 |

**799** Congress Emblem

**1977.** 8th Congress of the Popular Front, Sofia.

| | | | | |
|---|---|---|---|---|
| 2582 | **799** | 2s. multicoloured | 20 | 10 |

**800** Newspaper Masthead

**1977.** Centenary of Bulgarian Daily Press.

| | | | | |
|---|---|---|---|---|
| 2583 | **800** | 2s. multicoloured | 20 | 10 |

**801** St. Cyril

**1977.** 1150th Birth Anniv of St. Cyril. Sheet 106×87 mm.

| | | | | |
|---|---|---|---|---|
| **MS**2584 | **801** | 1l. multicoloured | 3·75 | 3·75 |

**802** Conference Emblem

**1977.** International Writers Conference, Sofia.

| | | | | |
|---|---|---|---|---|
| 2585 | **802** | 23s. blue, lt blue & grn | 1·40 | 1·10 |

**803** Map of Europe

**1977.** 21st Congress of European Organization for Quality Control, Varna.

| | | | | |
|---|---|---|---|---|
| 2586 | **803** | 23s. multicoloured | 95 | 55 |

**804** Basketball

**1977.** Women's European Basketball Championships.

| | | | | |
|---|---|---|---|---|
| 2587 | **804** | 23s. multicoloured | 95 | 55 |

**805** Weightlifter

**1977.** World Junior Weightlifting Championships.

| | | | | |
|---|---|---|---|---|
| 2588 | **805** | 13s. multicoloured | 45 | 20 |

**806** Georgi Dimitrov

**1977.** 95th Birth Anniv of Georgi Dimitrov (statesman).

| | | | | |
|---|---|---|---|---|
| 2589 | **806** | 13s. brown and red | 65 | 35 |

**807** Tail Section of Tupolev Tu-154

**1977.** Air. 30th Anniv of Bulgarian Airline "Balkanair".

| | | | | |
|---|---|---|---|---|
| 2590 | **807** | 35s. multicoloured | 1·70 | 85 |

**808** Games Emblem

**1977.** World University Games, Sofia (2nd issue). Sheet 84×76 mm.

| | | | | |
|---|---|---|---|---|
| **MS**2591 | **808** | 1l. multicoloured | 3·25 | 2·75 |

**809** T.V. Towers, Berlin and Sofia

**1977.** "Sozphilex 77" Stamp Exhibition, East Berlin.

| | | | | |
|---|---|---|---|---|
| 2592 | **809** | 25s. blue and deep blue | 95 | 55 |

**810** Elin Pelin alias Dimitur Stoyanov (writer)

**1977.** Writers and Painters.

| | | | | |
|---|---|---|---|---|
| 2593 | **810** | 2s. brown and gold | 20 | 20 |
| 2594 | - | 5s. olive and gold | 20 | 20 |
| 2595 | - | 13s. red and gold | 35 | 25 |
| 2596 | - | 23s. blue and gold | 1·10 | 55 |

DESIGNS: 5s. Peyu Yavorov (poet); 13s. Boris Angelushev (painter and illustrator); 23s. Iseno Todorov (painter).

**1977.** Historic Ships (2nd series). As T 753. Multicoloured.

| | | | | |
|---|---|---|---|---|
| 2597 | | 1s. Hansa Kogge | 20 | 15 |
| 2598 | | 2s. "Santa Maria" | 20 | 15 |
| 2599 | | 3s. Drake's "Golden Hind" | 20 | 15 |
| 2600 | | 12s. Carrack "Santa Catherina" | 40 | 20 |
| 2601 | | 13s. "La Couronne" (French galleon) | 45 | 25 |
| 2602 | | 43s. Mediterranean galley | 1·90 | 65 |

**811** Women Canoeists

**1977.** World Canoe Championships.

| | | | | |
|---|---|---|---|---|
| 2603 | **811** | 2s. blue and yellow | 20 | 15 |
| 2604 | - | 23s. blue and turquoise | 95 | 45 |

DESIGN: 23s. Men canoeists.

**812** Balloon over Plovdiv

**1977.** Air. 85th Anniv "Panair". International Aviation Exhibition, Plovdiv.

| | | | | |
|---|---|---|---|---|
| 2605 | **812** | 25s. orange, yell & brn | 95 | 55 |

**813** Presidents Zhivkov and Brezhnev

**1977.** Soviet–Bulgarian Friendship.

| | | | | |
|---|---|---|---|---|
| 2606 | **813** | 18s. brown, red & gold | 55 | 45 |

**814** Conference Building

**1977.** 64th International Parliamentary Conference, Sofia.

| | | | | |
|---|---|---|---|---|
| 2607 | **814** | 23s. green, pink and red | 95 | 45 |

**815** Newspaper Mastheads

**1977.** 50th Anniv of Official Newspaper "Rabotnichesko Delo" (Workers' Press).
2608 **815** 2s. red, green and grey 20 10

**816** "The Union of Earth and Water"

**1977.** 400th Birth Anniv of Rubens. Mult.
2609 13s. Type **816** 55 20
2610 23s. "Venus and Adonis" (detail) 1·10 1·10
2611 40s. "Amorous Shepherd" (detail) 2·20 1·60
**MS**2612 71×87 mm. 1l. "Portrait of a Chambermaid" 4·75 3·75

**817** Cossack with Bulgarian Child (Angelushev)

**1977.** Centenary of Liberation from Turkey. (1978). Posters.
2613 **817** 2s. multicoloured 30 15
2614 - 13s. green, blue & red 45 20
2615 - 23s. blue, red & green 85 45
2616 - 25s. multicoloured 95 50
DESIGNS: 13s. Bugler (Cheklarov); 23s. Mars (god of war) and Russian soldiers (Petrov); 25s. Flag of Russian Imperial Army.

**818** Albena, Black Sea

**1977.** Tourism.
2617 **818** 35s. blue, turq & brn 1·30 55
2618 - 43s. yellow, grn & blue 1·40 65
DESIGN: 43s. Rila Monastery.

**819** Dr. Nikolai Pirogov (Russian surgeon)

**1977.** Cent of Dr. Pirogov's Visit to Bulgaria.
2619 **819** 13s. brown, buff & grn 45 35

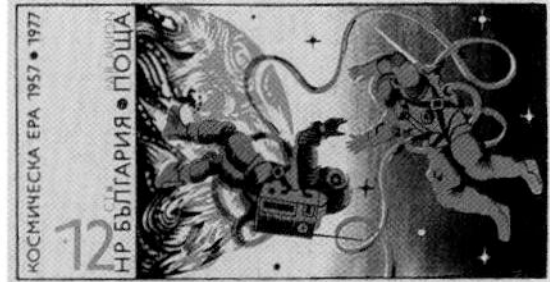
**820** Space walking

**1977.** Air. 20th Anniv of First Artificial Satellite. Multicoloured.
2620 12s. Type **820** 45 20
2621 25s. Space probe over Mars 95 45
2622 35s. Space probe "Venus-4" over Venus 1·40 55

**821** Soviet Emblems and Decree

**1977.** 60th Anniv of Russian Revolution.
2623 **821** 2s. red, black & stone 30 20
2624 - 13s. red and purple 55 25
2625 - 23s. red and violet 1·00 35
DESIGNS: 13s. Lenin; 23s. "1977" as flame.

**822** Diesel Train on Bridge

**1977.** 50th Anniv of Transport, Bridges and Highways Organization.
2626 **822** 13s. yellow, green & olive 75 55

**1977.** 150th Birth Anniv of Petko Ratshev Slaveikov (poet). As T 810.
2627 8s. brown and gold 30 20

**824** Decorative Initials of New Year Greeting

**1977.** New Year. Multicoloured.
2628 2s. Type **824** 20 10
2629 13s. "Fireworks" 45 15

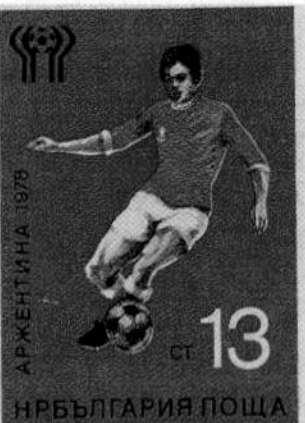

**825** Footballer

**1978.** World Cup Football Championship, Argentina. Multicoloured.
2630 13s. Type **825** 45 35
2631 23s. Shooting the ball 1·40 85
**MS**2632 77×61 mm. 50s. Tackle for ball 2·50 2·20

**826** Baba Vida Fortress, Vidin

**1977.** Air. "The Danube – European River". Mult.
2633 25s. Type **826** 75 55
2634 35s. Friendship Bridge 1·40 1·20

**827** Television Mast, Moscow

**1978.** 20th Anniv of Organization of Socialist Postal Administrations (O.S.S.).
2635 **827** 13s. multicoloured 45 20

**828** Shipka Monument

**1978.** Centenary of Liberation from Turkey (2nd issue). Sheet 55×73 mm.
**MS**2636 **828** 50s. multicoloured 1·60 1·60

**829** Red Cross in Laurel Wreath

**1978.** Centenary of Bulgarian Red Cross.
2637 **829** 25s. red, brown & blue 95 55

**830** "XXX" formed from Bulgarian and Russian National Colours

**1978.** 30th Anniv of Bulgarian–Soviet Friendship.
2638 **830** 2s. multicoloured 20 15

**831** Leo Tolstoy (Russian writer)

**1978.** Famous Personalities.
2639 **831** 2s. green and yellow 30 15
2640 - 5s. brown and bistre 30 15
2641 - 13s. green and mauve 35 20
2642 - 23s. brown and grey 40 35
2643 - 25s. brown and green 45 40
2644 - 35s. violet and blue 1·40 55
DESIGNS: 5s. Fyodor Dostoevsky (Russian writer); 13s. Ivan Turgenev (Russian writer); 23s. Vassily Vereshchagin (Russian artist); 25s. Giuseppe Garibaldi (Italian patriot); 35s. Victor Hugo (French writer).

**832** Nikolai Roerich (artist)

**1978.** Nikolai Roerich Exhibition, Sofia.
2645 **832** 8s. brown, green & red 45 20

**833** Bulgarian Flag and Red Star

**1978.** Communist Party National Conference, Sofia.
2646 **833** 2s. multicoloured 20 10

**834** Goddess

**1978.** "Philaserdica 79" International Stamp Exhibition (1st issue). Ancient Ceramics. Mult.
2647 2s. Type **834** 20 15
2648 5s. Mask with beard 20 15
2649 13s. Decorated vase 45 20
2650 23s. Vase with scallop design 75 65
2651 35s. Head of Silenus 1·10 1·10
2652 53s. Cockerel 4·00 1·60
See also Nos. 2674/9, 2714/18, 2721/5 and 2753/4.

**835** "Spirit of Nature"

**1978.** Birth Cent of Andrei Nikolov (sculptor).
2653 **835** 13s. blue, mauve & vio 45 20

**836** Heart and Arrows

**1978.** World Hypertension Month.
2654 **836** 23s. red, orange & grey 95 45

**837** "Kor Karoli" and Map of Route

**1978.** Georgi Georgiev's World Voyage.
2655 **837** 23s. blue, mauve & grn 1·90 85

**838** Doves

**1978.** 11th World Youth and Students' Festival, Havana.
2656 **838** 13s. multicoloured 45 20

**839** "Portrait of a Young Man" (Durer)

**1978.** Paintings. Multicoloured.
2657 13s. Type **839** 30 20
2658 23s. "Bathsheba at the Fountain" (Rubens) 45 35
2659 25s. "Signor de Moret" (Hans Holbein the Younger) 55 40
2660 35s. "Self portrait with Saskia" (Rembrandt) 75 45

2661 43s. "Lady in Mourning" (Tintoretto) 95 55
2662 60s. "Old Man with a Beard" (Rembrandt) 1·20 75
2663 80s. "Man in Armour" (Van Dyck) 2·75 1·80

**840** "Fritillaria stribrnyi"

**1978.** Flowers. Multicoloured.
2664 1s. Type **840** 20 15
2665 2s. "Fritillaria drenovskyi" 20 15
2666 3s. "Lilium rhodopaeum" 20 15
2667 13s. "Tulipa urumoffii" 45 20
2668 23s. "Lilium jankae" 55 35
2669 43s. "Tulipa rhodopaea" 1·90 1·10

**841** Varna

**1978.** 63rd Esperanto Congress, Varna.
2670 **841** 13s. orange, red & green 75 45

**842** Delcev

**1978.** 75th Death Anniv of Goce Delcev (Macedonian revolutionary).
2671 **842** 13s. multicoloured 55 20

**843** Freedom Fighters

**1978.** 75th Anniv of Ilinden-Preobrazhenie Rising.
2672 **843** 5s. black and red 20 10

**844** "The Sleeping Venus"

**1978.** World Masters of Art. Sheet 71×71 mm. Imperf.
**MS**2673 **844** 1l. multicoloured 2·20 2·20

**845** "Market" (Noiden Petkov)

**1978.** "Philaserdica 79" International Stamp Exhibition (2nd issue). Paintings of Sofia. Multicoloured.
2674 2s. Type **845** 20 20
2675 5s. "View of Sofia" (Euril Stoichev) 20 20
2676 13s. "View of Sofia" (Boris Ivanov) 30 20
2677 23s. "Tolbukhin Boulevard" (Nikola Tanev) 75 35
2678 35s. "National Theatre" (Nikola Petrov) 85 45
2679 53s. "Market" (Anton Mitov) 95 85
**MS**2679a 186×106 mm. Nos. 2674/9 7·00 7·00

**846** Black Woodpecker

**1978.** Woodpeckers. Multicoloured.
2680 1s. Type **846** 20 15
2681 2s. Syrian woodpecker 20 15
2682 3s. Three-toed woodpecker 20 15
2683 13s. Middle-spotted woodpecker 95 55
2684 23s. Lesser spotted woodpecker 1·40 75
2685 43s. Green woodpecker 3·75 2·40

**847** Ivan Vazov National Theatre, Sofia

**1978.** "Praga 78" and "Philaserdica 79" International Stamp Exhibitions. Sheet 153×110 mm containing T 847 and similar horiz designs. Multicoloured.
**MS**2686 (a) 40s. Type **847**; (b) 40s. Festival Hall, Sofia; (c) 40s. Charles Bridge, Prague; (d) 40s. Belvedere Palace, Prague 3·25 3·25

**848** "Elka 55" Computer

**1978.** Plovdiv International Fair.
2687 **848** 2s. multicoloured 20 10

**849** "September 1923" (Boris Angelushev)

**1978.** 55th Anniv of September Uprising.
2688 **849** 2s. red and brown 20 10

**850** Khristo Danov

**1978.** 150th Birth Anniv of Khristo Danov (first Bulgarian publisher).
2689 **850** 2s. orange and lake 20 10

**851** "The People of Vladaya" (Todor Panayotov)

**1978.** 60th Anniv of Vladaya Mutiny.
2690 **851** 2s. lilac, brown and red 20 10

**852** Hands supporting Rainbow

**1978.** International Anti-apartheid Year.
2691 **852** 13s. multicoloured 45 20

**853** Pipeline and Flags

**1978.** Inauguration of Orenburg–U.S.S.R. Natural Gas Pipeline.
2692 **853** 13s. multicoloured 45 20

**854** Acrobats

**1978.** 3rd World Sports Acrobatics Championships, Sofia.
2693 **854** 13s. multicoloured 45 20

**855** Salvador Allende

**1978.** 70th Birth Anniv of Salvador Allende (Chilean politician).
2694 **855** 13s. brown and red 45 20

**856** Human Rights Emblem

**1978.** 30th Anniv of Declaration of Human Rights.
2695 **856** 23s. yellow, red & blue 95 55

**857** "Levski and Matei Mitkaloto" (Kalina Taseva)

**1978.** History of Bulgaria. Paintings. Multicoloured.
2696 1s. Type **857** 20 15
2697 2s. "Give Strength to my Arm" (Zlatyu Boyadzhiev) 20 15
2698 3s. "Rumena Voevoda" (Nikola Mirchev) (horiz) 20 15
2699 13s. "Kolya Ficheto" (Elza Goeva) 45 35
2700 23s. "A Family of the National Revival Period" (Naiden Petkov) 1·00 65

**858** Tourist Home, Plovdiv

**1978.** European Architectural Heritage. Mult.
2701 43s. Type **858** 1·50 55
2702 43s. Tower of the Prince, Rila Monastery 1·50 55

**859** "Geroi Plevny" and Route Map

**1978.** Opening of the Varna–Ilichovsk Ferry Service.
2703 **859** 13s. blue, red & green 45 35

**860** Mosaic Bird (Santa Sofia Church)

**1978.** "Bulgaria 78" National Stamp Exhibition, Sofia.
2704 **860** 5s. multicoloured 35 20

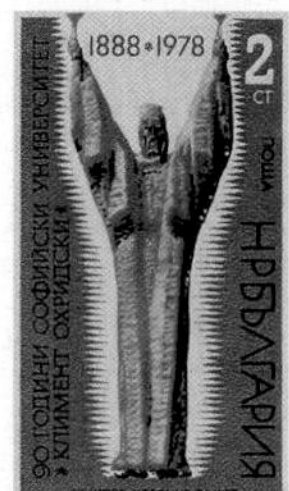

**861** Monument to St. Clement of Ohrid (university patron) (Lyubemir Dalcher)

**1978.** 90th Anniv of Sofia University.
2705 **861** 2s. lilac, black & green 20 10

**862** Nikola Karastoyanov

**1978.** Birth Bicentenary of Nikola Karastoyanov (first Bulgarian printer).
2706 **862** 2s. brn, yell & chestnut 35 20

**863** Initial from 13th Century Bible Manuscript

**1978.** Centenary of Cyril and Methodius People's Library. Multicoloured.
2707 2s. Type **863** 20 15
2708 13s. Monk writing (from a 1567 manuscript) 45 20
2709 23s. Decorated page from 16th-century manuscript Bible 85 45
**MS**2710 63×94 mm. 80s. Seated saint with attendant (from 13th century manuscript Bible) 2·20 2·20

**864** Ballet Dancers

**1978.** 50th Anniv of Bulgarian Ballet.
2711 **864** 13s. green, mauve & lav 45 35

**865** Tree of Birds

**1978.** New Year. Multicoloured.
2712 2s. Type **865** 20 10
2713 13s. Posthorn 30 15

**866** 1961 Communist Congress Stamp

**1978.** "Philaserdica 79" International Stamp Exhibition (3rd issue) and Bulgarian Stamp Centenary (1st issue).
2714 - 2s. red and green 20 15
2715 - 13s. claret and blue 20 15
2716 - 23s. green and mauve 30 20
2717 **866** 35s. grey and blue 95 45
2718 - 53s. green and red 1·70 65
**MS**2719 62×87 mm. 1l. black, yellow and green 2·20 2·20

DESIGNS—HORIZ: 2s. 1901 "Cherrywood Cannon" stamp; 13s. 1946 "New Republic" stamp; 23s. 1957 Canonisation of St. Cyril and St. Methodius stamp; 1l. First Bulgarian stamp. VERT: 53s. 1962 Dimitrov stamp.

See also Nos. 2721/5 and **MS**2755.

**867** Council Building, Moscow and Flags

**1979.** 30th Anniv of Council of Mutual Economic Aid.
2720 **867** 13s. multicoloured 45 20

**1979.** "Philaserdica 79" Int Stamp Exn (4th issue) and Bulgarian Stamp Cent (2nd issue). As Nos. 2714/18 but inscr "1979" and colours changed.
2721 - 2s. red and blue 20 15
2722 - 13s. claret and green 45 20
2723 - 23s. green, yellow & red 55 35
2724 **866** 35s. grey and red 95 45
2725 - 53s. brown and violet 1·20 65

**868** National Bank

**1979.** Centenary of Bulgarian National Bank.
2726 **868** 2s. grey and yellow 20 10

**868a**

**1979.** Coil stamps.
2726a **868a** 2s. blue 10 10
2726b **868a** 5s. red 20 10
The 5s. is as T **868a** but different pattern.

**869** Stamboliiski

**1979.** Birth Centenary of Alexandur Stamboliiski (Prime Minister 1919–23).
2727 **869** 2s. brown and yellow 20 10

**870** Child's Head as Flower

**1979.** International Year of the Child.
2728 **870** 23s. multicoloured 95 45

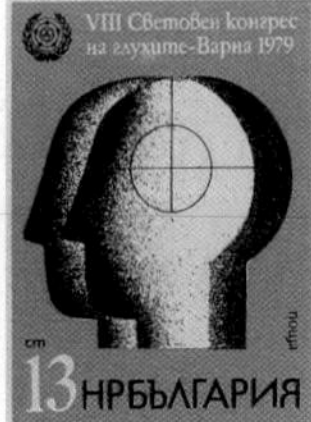

**871** Profiles

**1979.** 8th World Congress for the Deaf, Varna.
2729 **871** 13s. green and blue 45 20

**872** "75" and Emblem

**1979.** 75th Anniv of Bulgarian Trade Unions.
2730 **872** 2s. green and orange 20 10

**873** Soviet War Memorial

**1979.** Centenary of Sofia as Capital of Bulgaria. Sheet 106×105 mm containing T 873 and similar vert designs. Multicoloured.
**MS**2731 2s. Type **873**, 5s. Mother and child (sculpture); 13, 23, 25s. Bas-relief from monument to the Liberators of 1876 2·20 2·20
The 13, 23 and 25s. values form a composite design.

**874** Rocket

**1979.** Soviet–Bulgarian Space Flight. Multicoloured.
2732 2s. Georgi Ivanov (horiz) 20 15
2733 12s. Type **874** 35 20
2734 13s. Nikolai Rukavishnikov and Ivanov (horiz) 75 25
2735 25s. Link-up with "Salyut" space station (horiz) 95 45
2736 35s. Capsule descending by parachute 1·10 55
**MS**2737 67×86 mm. 1l. Globe and orbiting space craft (horiz) 2·75 2·75

**875** Carrier Pigeon and Tupolev Tu-154 Jet

**1979.** Centenary of Bulgarian Post and Telegraph Services. Multicoloured.
2738 2s. Type **875** 20 15
2739 5s. Old and new telephones 20 15
2740 13s. Morse key and teleprinter 45 20
2741 23s. Old radio transmitter and aerials 65 35
2742 35s. T.V. tower and satellite 95 45
**MS**2743 64×69 mm. 50s. Ground receiving station (38×28 mm) 2·75 2·75

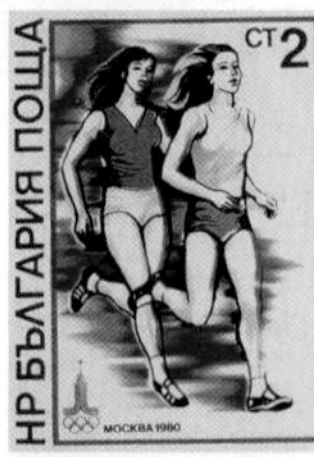

**876** Running

**1979.** Olympic Games. Moscow (1980) (1st issue). Athletics. Multicoloured.
2744 2s. Type **876** 30 25
2745 13s. Pole vault (horiz) 65 55
2746 25s. Discus 1·10 75
2747 35s. Hurdles (horiz) 1·40 1·10
2748 43s. High jump (horiz) 1·90 1·30
2749 1l. Long jump 2·75 2·20
**MS**2750 90×65 mm. 2l. Shot put 9·75 9·75

See also Nos. 2773/**MS**2779, 2803/**MS**2809, 2816/**MS**2822, 2834/**MS**2840 and 2851/**MS**2857.

**877** Thracian Gold Leaf Collar

**1979.** 48th International Philatelic Federation Congress, Sofia. Sheet 77×86 mm.
**MS**2751 **877** 1l. multicoloured 4·50 4·50

**878** First Bulgarian Stamp and 1975 European Security Conference Stamp

**1979.** "Philaserdica 79" International Exhibition, Sofia (5th issue). Sheet 63×61 mm.
**MS**2752 **878** 1l. multicoloured 7·50 7·50

**879** Hotel Vitosha-New Otani

**1979.** "Philaserdica 79" International Stamp Exhibition, Sofia (5th issue) and Bulgaria Day.
2753 **879** 2s. pink and blue 20 10

**880** "Good Morning, Little Brother" (illus by Kukuliev of folktale)

**1979.** "Philaserdica 79" International Stamp Exhibition, Sofia (6th issue) and Bulgarian–Russian Friendship Day.
2754 **880** 2s. multicoloured 20 10

**881** First Bulgarian Stamp

**1979.** Centenary of First Bulgarian Stamp (3rd issue). Sheet 91×121 mm.
**MS**2755 **881** 5s. multicoloured 60·00 60·00

**882** "Man on Donkey" (Boris Angelushev)

**1979.** 12th Festival of Humour and Satire, Grabovo.
2756 **882** 2s. multicoloured 20 15

**883** "Four Women"

**1979.** 450th Death Anniv of Albrecht Durer (artist). Multicoloured.

| | | | |
|---|---|---|---|
| 2757 | 13s. Type **883** | 20 | 20 |
| 2758 | 23s. "Three Peasants Talking" | 55 | 35 |
| 2759 | 25s. "The Cook and his Wife" | 75 | 45 |
| 2760 | 35s. "Portrait of Eobanus Hessus" | 1·10 | 65 |
| **MS**2761 | 80×81 mm. 80s. "Rhinoceros" (horiz). Imperf | 2·20 | 2·20 |

**884** Clocktower, Byala Cherkva

**1979.** Air. Clocktowers (1st series). Mult.

| | | | |
|---|---|---|---|
| 2762 | 13s. Type **884** | 35 | 20 |
| 2763 | 23s. Botevgrad | 45 | 35 |
| 2764 | 25s. Pazardzhik | 55 | 45 |
| 2765 | 35s. Gabrovo | 65 | 65 |
| 2766 | 53s. Tryavna | 1·40 | 1·10 |

See also Nos. 2891/5.

**885** Petko Todorov (birth centenary)

**1979.** Bulgarian Writers.

| | | | | |
|---|---|---|---|---|
| 2767 | **885** | 2s. black, brown & yell | 25 | 20 |
| 2768 | - | 2s. green and yellow | 25 | 20 |
| 2769 | - | 2s. red and yellow | 25 | 20 |

DESIGNS: No. 2768, Dimitur Dimov (70th birth anniv); 2769, Stefan Kostov (birth cent).

**886** Congress Emblem

**1979.** 18th Congress of International Theatrical Institute, Sofia.

| | | | | |
|---|---|---|---|---|
| 2770 | **886** | 13s. cobalt, blue & black | 35 | 20 |

**887** House of Journalists, Varna

**1979.** 20th Anniv of House of Journalists (holiday home), Varna.

| | | | | |
|---|---|---|---|---|
| 2771 | **887** | 8s. orange, black & blue | 20 | 10 |

**888** Children of Different Races

**1979.** "Banners for Peace" Children's Meeting, Sofia.

| | | | | |
|---|---|---|---|---|
| 2772 | **888** | 2s. multicoloured | 20 | 10 |

**889** Parallel Bars

**1979.** Olympic Games, Moscow (1980) (2nd issue). Gymnastics. Multicoloured.

| | | | |
|---|---|---|---|
| 2773 | 2s. Type **889** | 30 | 25 |
| 2774 | 13s. Horse exercise (horiz) | 55 | 35 |
| 2775 | 25s. Rings exercise | 75 | 55 |
| 2776 | 35s. Beam exercise | 95 | 85 |
| 2777 | 43s. Uneven bars | 1·40 | 1·20 |
| 2778 | 1l. Floor exercise | 2·75 | 2·40 |
| **MS**2779 | 65×88 mm. 2l. Horizontal bars | 9·75 | 9·75 |

**890** "Virgin and Child" (Nesebur)

**1979.** Icons of the Virgin and Child. Mult.

| | | | |
|---|---|---|---|
| 2780 | 13s. Type **890** | 45 | 20 |
| 2781 | 23s. Nesebur (diff) | 55 | 35 |
| 2782 | 35s. Sozopol | 65 | 45 |
| 2783 | 43s. Sozopol (diff) | 75 | 65 |
| 2784 | 53s. Samokov | 1·40 | 1·10 |

**891** Anton Bezenshek

**1979.** Centenary of Bulgarian Stenography.

| | | | | |
|---|---|---|---|---|
| 2785 | **891** | 2s. yellow and grey | 20 | 10 |

**892** Mountaineer

**1979.** 50th Anniv of Bulgarian Alpine Club.

| | | | | |
|---|---|---|---|---|
| 2786 | **892** | 2s. multicoloured | 20 | 10 |

**893** Commemorative Inscription

**1979.** Centenary of Bulgarian Public Health Services.

| | | | | |
|---|---|---|---|---|
| 2787 | **893** | 2s. black, silver & green | 20 | 20 |

**894** Rocket and Flowers

**1979.** 35th Anniv of Fatherland Front Government. Multicoloured.

| | | | |
|---|---|---|---|
| 2788 | 2s. Type **894** | 10 | 10 |
| 2789 | 5s. Russian and Bulgarian flags | 15 | 10 |
| 2790 | 13s. "35" in national colours | 35 | 20 |

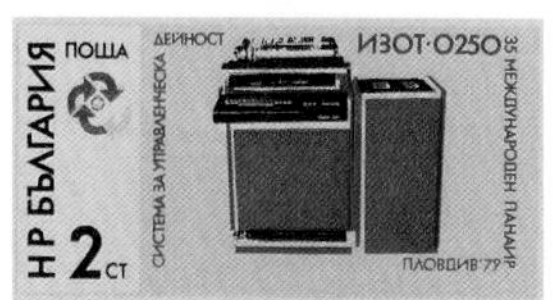


**895** "IZOT–0250" Computer

**1979.** 35th Plovdiv Fair.

| | | | | |
|---|---|---|---|---|
| 2791 | **895** | 2s. multicoloured | 20 | 10 |

**896** Games Emblem

**1979.** World University Games, Mexico.

| | | | | |
|---|---|---|---|---|
| 2792 | **896** | 5s. red, yellow and blue | 20 | 10 |

**897** Footballer

**1979.** 50th Anniv of DFS Lokomotiv Football Team.

| | | | | |
|---|---|---|---|---|
| 2793 | **897** | 2s. red and black | 20 | 10 |

**898** Lyuben Karavelov

**1979.** Death Centenary of Lyuben Karavelov (newspaper editor and President of Bulgarian Revolutionary Committee).

| | | | | |
|---|---|---|---|---|
| 2794 | **898** | 2s. green and blue | 20 | 10 |

**899** Cross-country Skiing

**1979.** Winter Olympic Games, Lake Placid (1980).

| | | | | |
|---|---|---|---|---|
| 2795 | **899** | 2s. red, purple and black | 20 | 15 |
| 2796 | - | 13s. orange, blue & blk | 35 | 20 |
| 2797 | - | 23s. turquoise, blue and black | 65 | 35 |
| 2798 | - | 43s. purple, turq & blk | 1·70 | 55 |
| **MS**2799 | | 68×77 mm. 1l. green, blue and black. Imperf | 3·25 | 3·25 |

DESIGNS: 13s. Speed skating; 23s. Skiing; 43s. Luge; 1l. Skiing (different).

**900** "Woman from Thrace"

**1979.** 80th Birth Anniv of Dechko Uzunov (artist). Multicoloured.

| | | | |
|---|---|---|---|
| 2800 | 12s. "Figure in Red" | 35 | 15 |
| 2801 | 13s. Type **900** | 35 | 20 |
| 2802 | 23s. "Composition II" | 1·10 | 65 |

**901** Canoeing (Canadian pairs)

**1979.** Olympic Games, Moscow (1980) (3rd issue). Water Sports. Multicoloured.

| | | | |
|---|---|---|---|
| 2803 | 2s. Type **901** | 35 | 35 |
| 2804 | 13s. Swimming (freestyle) | 65 | 55 |
| 2805 | 25s. Swimming (backstroke) (horiz) | 1·10 | 75 |
| 2806 | 35s. Kayak (horiz) | 1·40 | 1·10 |
| 2807 | 43s. Diving | 1·90 | 1·30 |
| 2808 | 1l. Springboard diving | 2·75 | 2·20 |
| **MS**2809 | 64×88 mm. 2l. Water polo | 9·75 | 9·75 |

**902** Nikola Vaptsarov

**1979.** 70th Birth Anniv of Nikola Vaptsarov (writer).

| | | | | |
|---|---|---|---|---|
| 2810 | **902** | 2s. pink and red | 30 | 20 |

903 "Dawn in Plovdiv" (Ioan Leviev)

**1979.** History of Bulgaria. Paintings. Mult.

| | | | |
|---|---|---|---|
| 2811 | 2s. "The First Socialists" (Boyan Petrov) (horiz) | 20 | 15 |
| 2812 | 13s. "Dimitur Blagoev as Editor of "Rabotnik" (Dimitur Gyvdzhenov) (horiz) | 35 | 20 |
| 2813 | 25s. "Workers' Party March" (Stoyan Sotirov) (horiz) | 75 | 45 |
| 2814 | 35s. Type **903** | 1·10 | 85 |

904 Doves in a Girl's Hair

**1979.** New Year.

| | | | | |
|---|---|---|---|---|
| 2815 | **904** | 13s. multicoloured | 35 | 20 |

905 Shooting

**1979.** Olympic Games, Moscow (1980) (4th issue). Multicoloured.

| | | | |
|---|---|---|---|
| 2816 | 2s. Type **905** | 35 | 25 |
| 2817 | 13s. Judo (horiz) | 65 | 55 |
| 2818 | 25s. Wrestling (horiz) | 1·10 | 85 |
| 2819 | 35s. Archery | 1·40 | 1·10 |
| 2820 | 43s. Fencing (horiz) | 1·90 | 1·20 |
| 2821 | 1l. Fencing (different) | 2·75 | 2·20 |
| **MS**2822 | 65×89 mm. 2l. Boxing | 9·75 | 9·75 |

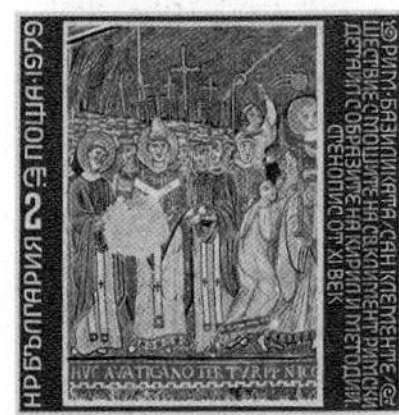
906 Procession with Relics of Saints

**1979.** Frescoes of Saints Cyril and Methodius in St. Clement's Basilica, Rome. Multicoloured.

| | | | |
|---|---|---|---|
| 2823 | 2s. Type **906** | 20 | 15 |
| 2824 | 13s. Cyril and Methodius received by Pope Adrian II | 30 | 20 |
| 2825 | 23s. Burial of Cyril the Philosopher | 55 | 35 |
| 2826 | 25s. St. Cyril | 75 | 45 |
| 2827 | 35s. St. Methodius | 1·10 | 65 |

907 Television Screen showing Emblem

**1979.** 25th Anniv of Bulgarian Television.

| | | | | |
|---|---|---|---|---|
| 2828 | **907** | 5s. blue and deep blue | 30 | 20 |

908 Puppet of Krali Marko (national hero)

**1980.** 50th Anniv of International Puppet Theatre Organization (UNIMA).

| | | | | |
|---|---|---|---|---|
| 2829 | **908** | 2s. multicoloured | 20 | 10 |

909 Thracian Rider (3rd-cent votive tablet)

**1980.** Centenary of National Archaeological Museum, Sofia.

| | | | | |
|---|---|---|---|---|
| 2830 | **909** | 2s. brown, gold & purple | 20 | 10 |
| 2831 | - | 13s. brown, gold & grn | 35 | 20 |

DESIGN: 13s. Grave stele of Deines (5th–6th cent).

910 "Meeting of Lenin and Dimitrov" (Aleksandur Poplilov)

**1980.** 110th Birth Anniv of Lenin.

| | | | | |
|---|---|---|---|---|
| 2832 | **910** | 13s. multicoloured | 35 | 20 |

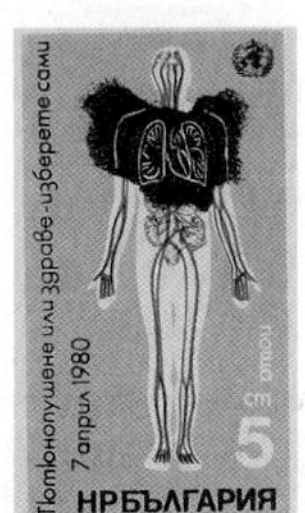
911 Diagram of Blood Circulation and Lungs obscured by Smoke

**1980.** World Health Day. Anti-smoking Campaign.

| | | | | |
|---|---|---|---|---|
| 2833 | **911** | 5s. multicoloured | 20 | 10 |

912 Basketball

**1980.** Olympic Games, Moscow (5th issue). Multicoloured.

| | | | |
|---|---|---|---|
| 2834 | 2s. Type **912** | 35 | 25 |
| 2835 | 13s. Football | 65 | 55 |
| 2836 | 25s. Hockey | 1·10 | 75 |
| 2837 | 35s. Cycling | 1·40 | 1·10 |
| 2838 | 43s. Handball | 1·90 | 1·30 |
| 2839 | 1l. Volleyball | 2·75 | 2·20 |
| **MS**2840 | 66×90 mm. 2s. Weightlifting | 9·75 | 9·75 |

913 Emblem, Cosmonauts and Space Station

**1980.** "Intercosmos" Space Programme. Sheet 111×102 mm.

| | | | | |
|---|---|---|---|---|
| **MS**2841 | **913** | 50s. multicoloured | 2·20 | 2·20 |

914 Penyo Penev

**1980.** 50th Birth Anniv of Penyo Penev (poet).

| | | | | |
|---|---|---|---|---|
| 2842 | **914** | 5s. brown, red & turq | 30 | 20 |

915 Penny Black

**1980.** "London 1980" International Stamp Exhibition.

| | | | | |
|---|---|---|---|---|
| 2843 | **915** | 25s. black and red | 1·10 | 75 |

916 Dimitur Khv. Chorbadzhuski-Chudomir (self-portrait)

**1980.** 90th Birth Anniv of Dimitur Khv. Chorbadzhusk-Chudomir (artist).

| | | | | |
|---|---|---|---|---|
| 2844 | **916** | 5s. pink, brown & turq | 20 | 10 |
| 2845 | - | 13s. black, blue & turq | 35 | 35 |

DESIGN: 13s. "Our People".

917 Nikolai Gyaurov

**1980.** 50th Birth Anniv of Nikolai Gyaurov (opera singer).

| | | | | |
|---|---|---|---|---|
| 2846 | **917** | 5s. yellow, brown & grn | 30 | 20 |

918 Soviet Soldiers raising Flag on Berlin Reichstag

**1980.** 35th Anniv of "Victory in Europe" Day.

| | | | | |
|---|---|---|---|---|
| 2847 | **918** | 5s. gold, brown & black | 20 | 10 |
| 2848 | - | 13s. gold, brown & black | 35 | 20 |

DESIGN: 13s. Soviet Army memorial, Berlin–Treptow.

919 Open Book and Sun

**1980.** 75th Anniv Bulgarian Teachers' Union.

| | | | | |
|---|---|---|---|---|
| 2849 | **919** | 5s. purple and yellow | 20 | 10 |

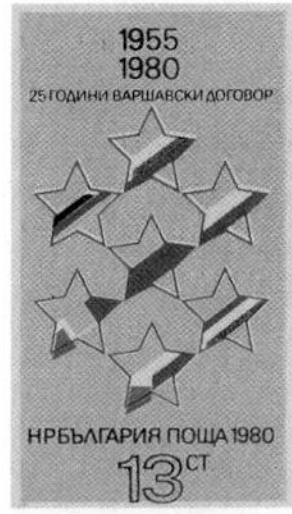
920 Stars representing Member Countries

**1980.** 25th Anniv of Warsaw Pact.

| | | | | |
|---|---|---|---|---|
| 2850 | **920** | 13s. multicoloured | 45 | 20 |

921 Greek Girl with Olympic Flame

**1980.** Olympic Games, Moscow (6th issue). Multicoloured.

| | | | |
|---|---|---|---|
| 2851 | 2s. Type **921** | 35 | 25 |
| 2852 | 13s. Spartacus monument, Sandanski | 65 | 55 |
| 2853 | 25s. Liberation monument, Sofia (detail) | 1·10 | 85 |
| 2854 | 35s. Liberation monument, Plovdiv | 1·40 | 1·00 |
| 2855 | 43s. Liberation monument, Shipka Pass | 1·90 | 1·30 |
| 2856 | 1l. Liberation monument, Ruse | 2·75 | 2·20 |
| **MS**2857 | 66×92 mm. 2l. Athlete with Olympic flame, Moscow | 9·75 | 9·75 |

922 Ballerina

**1980.** 10th International Ballet Competition, Varna.

| | | | | |
|---|---|---|---|---|
| 2858 | **922** | 13s. multicoloured | 45 | 20 |

923 Europa Hotel, Sofia

**1980.** Hotels. Multicoloured.

| | | | |
|---|---|---|---|
| 2859 | 23s. Type **923** | 55 | 35 |
| 2860 | 23s. Bulgaria Hotel, Burgas (vert) | 55 | 35 |
| 2861 | 23s. Plovdiv Hotel, Plovdiv | 55 | 35 |
| 2862 | 23s. Riga Hotel, Ruse (vert) | 55 | 35 |
| 2863 | 23s. Varna Hotel, Prazhba | 55 | 35 |

**1980.** Historic Ships (3rd series). As T 753. Multicoloured.

| | | | |
|---|---|---|---|
| 2864 | 5s. Hansa kogge "Jesus of Lubeck" | 20 | 15 |
| 2865 | 8s. Roman galley | 30 | 15 |
| 2866 | 13s. Galleon "Eagle" | 35 | 20 |
| 2867 | 23s. "Mayflower" | 55 | 35 |
| 2868 | 35s. Maltese galleon | 1·00 | 45 |
| 2869 | 53s. Galleon "Royal Louis" | 1·50 | 1·10 |

**924** Parachute Descent

**1980.** 15th World Parachute Championships, Kazanluk. Multicoloured.

2870 13s. Type **924** 35 20

2871 25s. Parachutist in free fall 75 35

**925** Clown and Children

**1980.** 1st Anniv of "Banners for Peace" Children's Meeting. Multicoloured.

2872 3s. Type **925** 20 15

2873 5s. "Cosmonauts in Spaceship" (vert) 20 15

2874 8s. "Picnic" 20 15

2875 13s. "Children with Ices" 30 20

2876 25s. "Children with Cat" (vert) 45 35

2877 35s. "Crowd" 1·00 45

2878 43s. "Banners for Peace" monument (vert) 1·50 65

**926** Assembly Emblem

**1980.** Assembly of Peoples' Parliament for Peace, Sofia.

2879 **926** 25s. multicoloured 55 45

**927** Iordan Iovkov

**1980.** Birth Centenary of Iordan Iovkov (writer).

2880 **927** 5s. multicoloured 30 25

**928** Yakovlev Yak-24 Helicopter, Missile Launcher and Tank

**1980.** Bulgarian Armed Forces. Multicoloured.

2881 3s. Type **928** 10 10

2882 5s. Mikoyan Gurevich MiG-21 bomber, radar antennae and missile transporter 20 15

2883 8s. Mil Mi-24 helicopter, missile boat and landing ship "Ropucha" 35 20

**929** Computer

**1980.** 36th Plovdiv Fair.

2884 **929** 5s. multicoloured 20 10

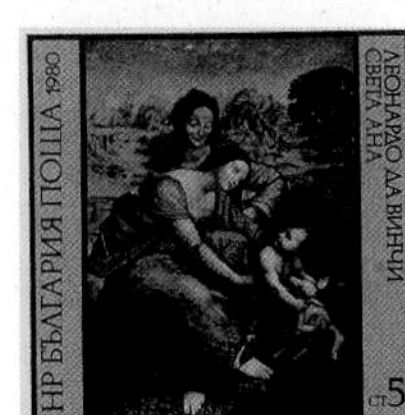

**930** "Virgin and Child with St. Anne"

**1980.** Paintings by Leonardo da Vinci. Mult.

2885 5s. Type **930** 20 15

2886 8s. Angel (detail, "The Annunciation") 20 15

2887 13s. Virgin (detail, "The Annunciation") 35 20

2888 25s. "Adoration of the Kings" (detail) 65 45

2889 35s. "Woman with Ermine" 1·10 55

**MS**2890 57×80 mm. 50s. "Mona Lisa". Imperf 1·60 1·60

**1980.** Air. Clocktowers (2nd series). As T 884. Multicoloured.

2891 13s. Byala 35 20

2892 23s. Razgrad 45 35

2893 25s. Karnobat 55 45

2894 35s. Sevlievo 95 55

2895 53s. Berkovitsa 1·90 85

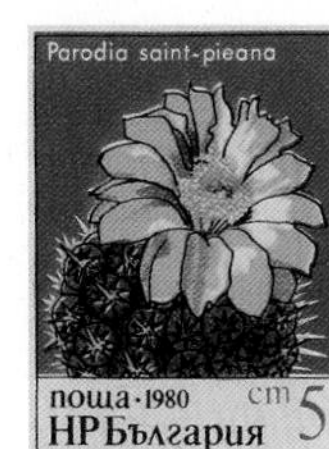

**931** "Parodia saint-pieana"

**1980.** Cacti. Multicoloured.

2896 5s. Type **931** 20 15

2897 13s. "Echinopsis bridgesii" 35 20

2898 25s. "Echinocereus purpureus" 75 45

2899 35s. "Opuntia bispinosa" 1·10 85

2900 53s. "Mamillopsis senilis" 2·30 1·10

**932** UN Building and Bulgarian Arms

**1980.** 25th Anniv of United Nations Membership. Sheet 64×86 mm.

**MS**2901 **932** 60s. multicoloured 4·25 4·25

**933** Wild Horse

**1980.** Horses. Multicoloured.

2902 3s. Type **933** 20 35

2903 5s. Tarpan 20 35

2904 13s. Arabian 55 55

2905 23s. Anglo-Arabian 1·50 1·10

2906 35s. Draught horse 3·25 2·75

**934** Vasil Stoin

**1980.** Birth Centenary of Vasil Stoin (collector of folk songs).

2907 **934** 5s. violet, yellow & gold 20 10

**935** Armorial Lion

**1980.** New Year. 1300th Anniv of Bulgarian State. Multicoloured.

2908 5s. Type **935** 20 10

2909 13s. Dish and dates "681–1981" 35 15

**936** Red Star

**1980.** 12th Bulgarian Communist Party Congress (1st issue).

2910 **936** 5s. yellow and red 20 10

See also Nos. 2920/2.

**937** Cross-country Skier

**1981.** World Ski-racing Championship, Velingrad.

2911 **937** 43s. orange, blue & blk 1·10 65

**938** Midland Hawthorn ("Crataegus oxpacantha")

**1981.** Useful Plants. Multicoloured.

2912 3s. Type **938** 20 15

2913 5s. Perforate St. John's wort ("Hypericum perforatum") 20 15

2914 13s. Elder ("Sambucus nigra") 45 20

2915 25s. Dewberry ("Rubus caesius") 85 35

2916 35s. Lime ("Tilia argentea") 1·00 55

2917 43s. Dog rose ("Rosa canina") 1·60 1·10

**939** Skier

**1981.** Alpine Skiing World Championships, Borovets.

2918 **939** 43s. yellow, black & blue 1·10 65

**940** Nuclear Traces

**1981.** 25th Anniv of Nuclear Research Institute, Dubna, U.S.S.R.

2919 **940** 13s. black and silver 35 15

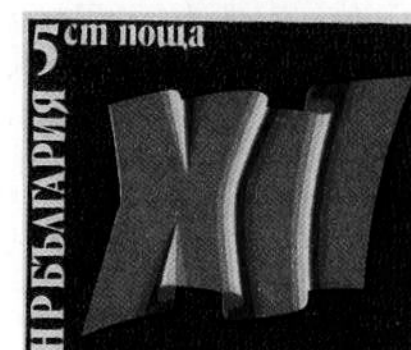

**941** "XII" formed from Flag

**1981.** 12th Bulgarian Communist Party Congress (2nd issue).

2920 **941** 5s. multicoloured 20 15

2921 - 13s. red, black and blue 35 20

2922 - 23s. red, black and blue 65 55

**MS**2923 68×86 mm. 50s. multicoloured 1·60 1·60

DESIGNS: 13s. Stars; 23s. Computer tape; 50s. Georgi Dimitrov and Dimitur Blagoev.

**942** Palace of Culture

**1981.** Opening of Palace of Culture, Sofia.

2924 **942** 5s. dp green, grn & red 20 10

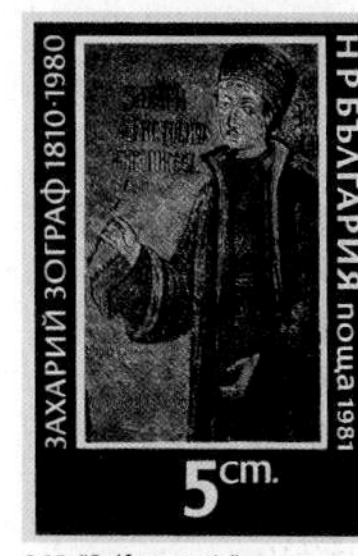

**943** "Self-portrait"

**1981.** 170th Birth Anniv (1980) of Zakharu Zograf (artist). Multicoloured.

2925 5s. Type **943** 20 15

2926 13s. "Portrait of Khristionia Zografska" 45 20

2927 23s. "The Transfiguration" (icon from Preobrazhenie Monastery) 75 35

2928 25s. "Doomsday" (detail) (horiz) 95 55

2929 35s. "Doomsday" (detail – different) (horiz) 1·40 1·10

**944** Squacco Heron

**1981.** Birds. Multicoloured.

2930 5s. Type **944** 20 15

2931 8s. Eurasian bittern 45 20

2932 13s. Cattle egret 65 35

2933 25s. Great egret 1·50 65

2934 53s. Black stork 2·75 1·60

**945** Liner "Georgi Dimitrov"

**1981.** Centenary of Bulgarian Shipbuilding. Mult.

2935 35s. Type **945** 95 35

2936 43s. Freighter "Petimata of RMS" 1·40 55

2937 53s. Tanker "Khan Asparuch" 1·90 85

**946** Hofburg Palace, Vienna

**1981.** "WIPA 1981" International Stamp Exhibition, Vienna.

| | | | | |
|---|---|---|---|---|
| 2938 | **946** | 35s. crimson, red & green | 95 | 65 |

**947** "XXXIV"

**1981.** 34th Bulgarian People's Agrarian Union Congress.

| | | | | |
|---|---|---|---|---|
| 2939 | **947** | 5s. multicoloured | 20 | 15 |
| 2940 | - | 8s. orange, black & blue | 30 | 20 |
| 2941 | - | 13s. multicoloured | 55 | 35 |

DESIGNS: 8s. Flags; 13s. Bulgarian Communist Party and Agrarian Union flags.

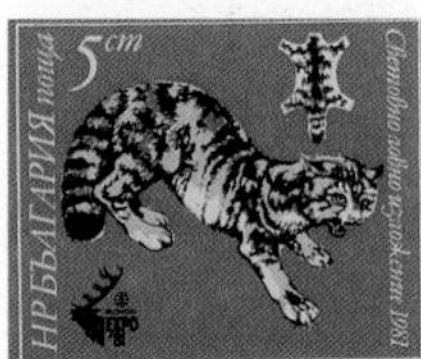
**948** Wild Cat

**1981.** International Hunting Exhibition, Plovdiv.

| | | | | |
|---|---|---|---|---|
| 2942 | **948** | 5s. stone, black & brown | 20 | 15 |
| 2943 | - | 13s. black, brn & stone | 45 | 20 |
| 2944 | - | 23s. brown, blk & orge | 95 | 45 |
| 2945 | - | 25s. black, brown & mve | 1·10 | 55 |
| 2946 | - | 35s. lt brown, blk & brn | 1·50 | 65 |
| 2947 | - | 53s. brown, blk & grn | 2·30 | 1·10 |

**MS**2948 78×103 mm. 1l. brown, black and green (52×42 mm) 3·25 3·25

DESIGNS: 13s. Wild boar; 23s. Mouflon; 25s. Chamois; 35s. Roebuck; 53s. Fallow deer; 1l. Red deer.

**949** "Crafty Peter" (sculpture, Georgi Chapkanov)

**1981.** Festival of Humour and Satire, Gabrovo.

| | | | | |
|---|---|---|---|---|
| 2949 | **949** | 5s. multicoloured | 20 | 10 |

**950** Bulgarian Arms and UNESCO Emblem

**1981.** 25th Anniv of UNESCO Membership.

| | | | | |
|---|---|---|---|---|
| 2950 | **950** | 13s. multicoloured | 35 | 20 |

**951** Deutsche Flugzeugwerke D.F.W. C.V. Biplane

**1981.** Air. Aircraft. Multicoloured.

| | | | |
|---|---|---|---|
| 2951 | 5s. Type **951** | 20 | 15 |
| 2952 | 12s. LAS-7 monoplane | 30 | 15 |
| 2953 | 25s. LAS-8 monoplane | 75 | 45 |
| 2954 | 35s. DAR-1 biplane | 95 | 55 |
| 2955 | 45s. DAR-3 biplane | 1·10 | 85 |
| 2956 | 55s. DAR-9 biplane | 1·40 | 1·10 |

**952** "Eye"

**1981.** Centenary of State Statistical Office.

| | | | | |
|---|---|---|---|---|
| 2957 | **952** | 5s. multicoloured | 20 | 10 |

**953** Veliko Tirnovo Hotel

**1981.** Hotels.

| | | | | |
|---|---|---|---|---|
| 2958 | **953** | 23s. multicoloured | 55 | 35 |

**954** "Flying Figure"

**1981.** 90th Anniv of First Bulgarian Social Democratic Party Congress, Buzludzha. Sculptures by Velichko Minekov.

| | | | | |
|---|---|---|---|---|
| 2959 | **954** | 5s. blue, black and green | 20 | 15 |
| 2960 | - | 13s. brown, blk & orge | 35 | 20 |

DESIGN: 13s. "Advancing Female".

**955** Animal-shaped Dish

**1981.** Golden Treasure of Old St. Nicholas. Multicoloured.

| | | | |
|---|---|---|---|
| 2961 | 5s. Type **955** | 20 | 15 |
| 2962 | 13s. Jug with decorated neck | 35 | 20 |
| 2963 | 23s. Jug with loop pattern | 55 | 45 |
| 2964 | 25s. Jug with bird pattern | 75 | 55 |
| 2965 | 35s. Decorated vase | 95 | 75 |
| 2966 | 53s. Decorated dish | 1·90 | 1·30 |

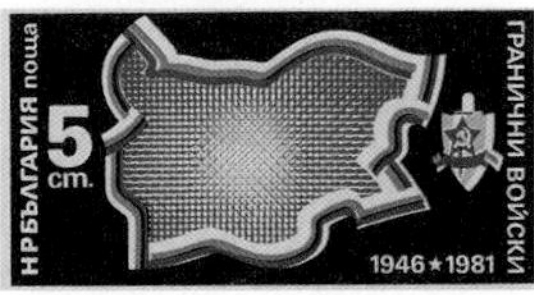

**956** Badge and Map of Bulgaria

**1981.** 35th Anniv of Frontier Guards.

| | | | | |
|---|---|---|---|---|
| 2967 | **956** | 5s. multicoloured | 20 | 10 |

**957** Saints Cyril and Methodius (9th century)

**1981.** 1300th Anniv of Bulgarian State.

| | | | | |
|---|---|---|---|---|
| 2968 | - | 5s. green and grey | 20 | 15 |
| 2969 | **957** | 5s. brown and yellow | 20 | 15 |
| 2970 | - | 8s. violet and lilac | 20 | 15 |
| 2971 | - | 12s. mauve and purple | 30 | 15 |
| 2972 | - | 13s. purple and brown | 35 | 15 |
| 2973 | - | 13s. green and black | 35 | 15 |
| 2974 | - | 16s. green & deep green | 45 | 20 |
| 2975 | - | 23s. black and blue | 65 | 35 |
| 2976 | - | 25s. green and light green | 75 | 45 |
| 2977 | - | 35s. brown and light brown | 1·00 | 55 |
| 2978 | - | 41s. red and pink | 1·20 | 65 |
| 2979 | - | 43s. red and pink | 1·20 | 65 |
| 2980 | - | 53s. dp brown and brown | 1·30 | 70 |
| 2981 | - | 55s. dp green and green | 1·40 | 75 |

**MS**2982 Two sheets, each 83×74 mm. (a) 50s. grey and green; (b) 1l. brown, black and brown 5·00 5·00

DESIGNS: No. 2968, Madara horsemen (8th century); 2970, Plan of Round Church at Veliki Preslav (10th century); 2971, Four Evangelists of King Ivan, 1356; 2972, Column of Ivan Asen II (13th century); 2973, Manasiev Chronicle (14th century); 2974, Rising of April 1876; 2975, Arrival of Russian liberation troops; 2976, Foundation ceremony of Bulgarian Social Democratic Party, 1891; 2977, Rising of September 1923; 2978, Formation of Fatherland Front Government, 9 September 1944; 2979, Bulgarian Communist Party Congress, 1948; 50s. Bas-relief of lion at Stara Zagora (10th century); 2980, 10th Communist Party Congress, 1971; 2981, Kremikovski metallurgical combine; 1l. Leonid Brezhnev and Todor Yovkov.

**958** Volleyball Players

**1981.** European Volleyball Championships.

| | | | | |
|---|---|---|---|---|
| 2983 | **958** | 13s. red, blue and black | 35 | 20 |

**959** "Pegasus" (bronze sculpture)

**1981.** Day of the Word.

| | | | | |
|---|---|---|---|---|
| 2984 | **959** | 5s. green | 20 | 10 |

**960** Loaf of Bread

**1981.** World Food Day.

| | | | | |
|---|---|---|---|---|
| 2985 | **960** | 13s. brown, black & grn | 35 | 20 |

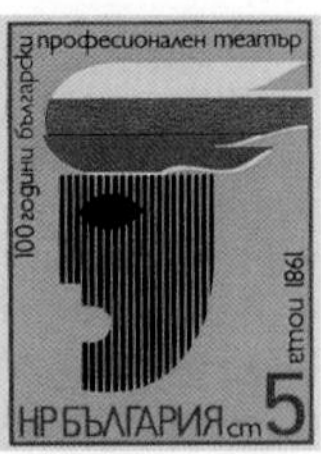

**961** Mask

**1981.** Cent of Bulgarian Professional Theatre.

| | | | | |
|---|---|---|---|---|
| 2986 | **961** | 5s. multicoloured | 20 | 15 |

**962** Examples of Bulgarian Art

**1981.** Cultural Heritage Day.

| | | | | |
|---|---|---|---|---|
| 2987 | **962** | 13s. green and brown | 95 | 20 |

**963** Footballer

**1981.** World Cup Football Championship, Spain (1982). Multicoloured.

| | | | |
|---|---|---|---|
| 2988 | 5s. Type **963** | 20 | 15 |
| 2989 | 13s. Heading ball | 30 | 20 |
| 2990 | 43s. Saving a goal | 95 | 65 |
| 2991 | 53s. Running with ball | 1·10 | 1·00 |

**964** Dove encircled by Barbed Wire

**1981.** Anti-apartheid Campaign.

| | | | | |
|---|---|---|---|---|
| 2992 | **964** | 5s. red, black and yellow | 20 | 10 |

**1981.** 13th Bulgarian Philatelic Federation Congress. Sheet 51×72 mm containing design as T 962 but inscr "XIII KONGRES NA SBF SOFIYA" at foot.

**MS**2993 60s. blue and red 9·25 8·25

**965** "Mother" (Lilyann Ruseva)

**1981.** 35th Anniv of UNICEF. Various designs showing mother and child paintings by named artists. Multicoloured.

| | | | |
|---|---|---|---|
| 2994 | 53s. Type **965** | 1·70 | 55 |
| 2995 | 53s. "Bulgarian Madonna" (Vasil Stoilov) | 1·70 | 55 |
| 2996 | 53s. "Village Madonna" (Ivan Milev) | 1·70 | 55 |
| 2997 | 53s. "Mother" (Vladimir Dimitrov) | 1·70 | 55 |

**966** 8th Century Ceramic from Pliska

**1981.** New Year. Multicoloured.

| | | | |
|---|---|---|---|
| 2998 | 5s. Armorial lion | 20 | 10 |
| 2999 | 13s. Type **966** | 35 | 15 |

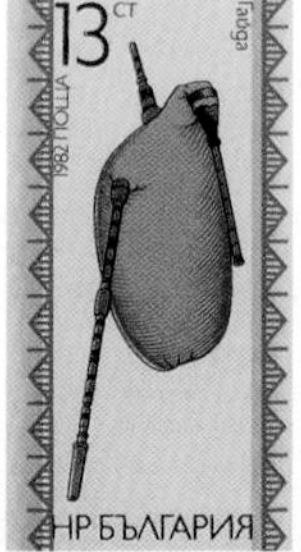

**967** Bagpipes

**1982.** Musical Instruments. Multicoloured.

| | | | |
|---|---|---|---|
| 3000 | 13s. Type **967** | 30 | 20 |
| 3001 | 25s. Single and double flutes | 55 | 25 |
| 3002 | 30s. Rebec | 65 | 35 |
| 3003 | 35s. Flute and pipe | 75 | 45 |
| 3004 | 44s. Mandolin | 1·50 | 55 |

**968** Open Book

**1982.** 125th Anniv of Public Libraries.

| | | | | |
|---|---|---|---|---|
| 3005 | **968** | 5s. green | 20 | 10 |

**969** "Sofia Plains"

**1982.** Birth Centenary of Nikola Petrov (artist).

| | | | |
|---|---|---|---|
| 3006 | 5s. Type **969** | 20 | 15 |
| 3007 | 13s. "Girl Embroidering" | 35 | 20 |
| 3008 | 30s. "Fields of Peshtera" | 1·00 | 55 |

**970** Womans' Head and Dove

**1982.** International Decade for Women. Sheet 66×76 mm.

| | | | |
|---|---|---|---|
| **MS**3009 | 1l. multicoloured | 2·75 | 2·75 |

**971** "Peasant Woman"

**1982.** Birth Centenary of Valadimir Dimitrov (artist). Multicoloured.

| | | | |
|---|---|---|---|
| 3010 | 5s. Figures in a landscape (horiz) | 20 | 15 |
| 3011 | 8s. Town and harbour (horiz) | 20 | 15 |
| 3012 | 13s. Town scene (horiz) | 45 | 20 |
| 3013 | 25s. "Reapers" | 55 | 35 |
| 3014 | 30s. Woman and child | 65 | 45 |
| 3015 | 35s. Type **971** | 95 | 50 |
| **MS**3016 | 65×58 mm. 50s. "Self-portrait" (horiz) | 1·60 | 1·60 |

**972** Georgi Dimitrov

**1982.** 9th Bulgarian Trade Unions Congress, Sofia.

| | | | | |
|---|---|---|---|---|
| 3017 | **972** | 5s. lt brn, dp brn & brn | 10 | 10 |
| 3018 | - | 5s. brown and blue | 20 | 10 |

DESIGN: No. 3018, Palace of Culture, Sofia.

**973** Summer Snowflake

**1982.** Medicinal Plants. Multicoloured.

| | | | |
|---|---|---|---|
| 3019 | 3s. Type **973** | 20 | 15 |
| 3020 | 5s. Chicory | 20 | 15 |
| 3021 | 8s. Rosebay willowherb | 30 | 15 |
| 3022 | 13s. Solomon's seal | 45 | 20 |
| 3023 | 25s. Sweet violet | 85 | 35 |
| 3024 | 35s. "Ficaria verna" | 1·40 | 55 |

**974** Russian Space Station

**1982.** 25th Anniv of First Soviet Artificial Satellite.

| | | | | |
|---|---|---|---|---|
| 3025 | **974** | 13s. multicoloured | 35 | 20 |

**975** Georgi Dimitrov

**1982.** "Sozphilex '82" Stamp Exhibition, Veliko, Tirnovo. Sheet 61×82 mm.

| | | | | |
|---|---|---|---|---|
| **MS**3026 | **975** | 50s. red and black | 3·25 | 3·25 |

**976** Dimitrov and Congress Emblem

**1982.** 14th Dimitrov Communist Youth League Congress, Sofia.

| | | | | |
|---|---|---|---|---|
| 3027 | **976** | 5s. blue, red & yellow | 20 | 10 |

**977** First French and Bulgarian Stamps

**1982.** "Philexfrance 82" International Stamp Exhibition, Paris.

| | | | | |
|---|---|---|---|---|
| 3028 | **977** | 42s. multicoloured | 95 | 55 |

**978** Abstract with Birds

**1982.** Alafrangi Frescoes from 19th-century Houses.

| | | | | |
|---|---|---|---|---|
| 3029 | **978** | 5s. multicoloured | 20 | 15 |
| 3030 | - | 13s. multicoloured | 30 | 20 |
| 3031 | - | 25s. multicoloured | 45 | 35 |
| 3032 | - | 30s. multicoloured | 55 | 45 |
| 3033 | - | 42s. multicoloured | 95 | 55 |
| 3034 | - | 60s. multicoloured | 1·90 | 65 |

DESIGNS: 13s. to 60s. Various flower and bird patterns.

During 1982 sets were issued for World Cup Football Championship, Spain (5, 13, 30s.), Tenth Anniv of First European Security and Co-operation Conference (5, 13, 25, 30s.), World Cup Results (5, 13, 30s.) and 10th Anniv (1983) of European Security and Co-operation Conference, Helsinki (5, 13, 25, 30s.). Supplies and distribution of these stamps were restricted and it is understood they were not available at face value.

**979** Georgi Dimitrov

**1982.** Birth Centenary of Georgi Dimitrov (statesman). Sheet 76×52 mm.

| | | | | |
|---|---|---|---|---|
| **MS**3035 | **979** | 50s. multicoloured | 1·60 | 1·60 |

**980** Georgi Dimitrov

**1982.** 9th Fatherland Front Congress, Sofia.

| | | | | |
|---|---|---|---|---|
| 3036 | **980** | 5s. multicoloured | 20 | 10 |

**981** Airplane

**1982.** 35th Anniv of Balkanair (state airline).

| | | | | |
|---|---|---|---|---|
| 3037 | **981** | 42s. blue, green & red | 1·00 | 65 |

**982** Atomic Bomb Mushroom-cloud

**1982.** Nuclear Disarmament Campaign.

| | | | | |
|---|---|---|---|---|
| 3038 | **982** | 13s. multicoloured | 45 | 20 |

**983** Lyudmila Zhivkova

**1982.** 40th Birth Anniv of Lyudmila Zhivkova (founder of "Banners for Peace" Children's Meetings).

| | | | | |
|---|---|---|---|---|
| 3039 | **983** | 5s. multicoloured | 20 | 10 |
| 3040 | **983** | 13s. multicoloured | 35 | 15 |
| **MS**3041 | | 62×67 mm. **983** 1l. multicoloured | 2·20 | 2·20 |

**984** Emblem

**1982.** 10th Anniv of U.N. Environment Programme.

| | | | | |
|---|---|---|---|---|
| 3042 | **984** | 13s. green and blue | 35 | 20 |

**985** Wave Pattern

**1982.** 5th Bulgarian Painters' Association Congress.

| | | | | |
|---|---|---|---|---|
| 3043 | **985** | 5s. multicoloured | 25 | 20 |

**986** Child Musicians

**1982.** 2nd "Banners for Peace" Children's Meeting (1st issue). Children's Paintings. Multicoloured.

| | | | |
|---|---|---|---|
| 3044 | 3s. Type **986** | 10 | 10 |
| 3045 | 5s. Children skating | 20 | 10 |
| 3046 | 8s. Adults, children and flowers | 30 | 15 |
| 3047 | 13s. Children with flags | 35 | 20 |
| **MS**3048 | 70×110 mm. 50s. Children in "Sun" balloon (vert) | 2·20 | 2·20 |

See also Nos. 3057/**MS**3063.

**987** Moscow Park Hotel, Sofia

**1982.** Hotels. Multicoloured.

| | | | |
|---|---|---|---|
| 3049 | 32s. Type **987** | 85 | 45 |
| 3050 | 32s. Black Sea Hotel, Varna | 85 | 45 |

**988** Cruiser "Aurora" and Satellite

**1982.** 65th Anniv of Russian October Revolution.

| | | | | |
|---|---|---|---|---|
| 3051 | **988** | 13s. red and blue | 35 | 25 |

**989** Hammer and Sickle

**1982.** 60th Anniv of U.S.S.R.

| | | | | |
|---|---|---|---|---|
| 3052 | **989** | 13s. red, gold & violet | 35 | 20 |

**990** "The Piano"

**1982.** Birth Cent of Pablo Picasso (artist). Mult.

| | | | |
|---|---|---|---|
| 3053 | 13s. Type **990** | 45 | 25 |
| 3054 | 30s. "Portrait of Jacqueline" | 65 | 55 |
| 3055 | 42s. "Maternity" | 1·40 | 85 |
| **MS**3056 | 61×79 mm. 1l. "Self-portrait" | 2·75 | 2·75 |

**991** Boy and Girl

**1982.** 2nd "Banners for Peace" Children's Meeting (2nd issue). Multicoloured.

| | | | |
|---|---|---|---|
| 3057 | 3s. Type **991** | 20 | 15 |
| 3058 | 5s. Market place | 20 | 15 |
| 3059 | 8s. Children in fancy dress (vert) | 20 | 15 |
| 3060 | 13s. Chickens (vert) | 35 | 20 |
| 3061 | 25s. Interlocking heads | 75 | 35 |
| 3062 | 30s. Lion | 85 | 45 |
| **MS**3063 | 70×109 mm. 50s. Boy and girl in garden (vert). Perf or imperf | 2·20 | 2·20 |

**992** Lions

**1982.** New Year. Multicoloured.

| | | | |
|---|---|---|---|
| 3064 | 5s. Type **992** | 20 | 10 |
| 3065 | 13s. Decorated letters | 35 | 15 |

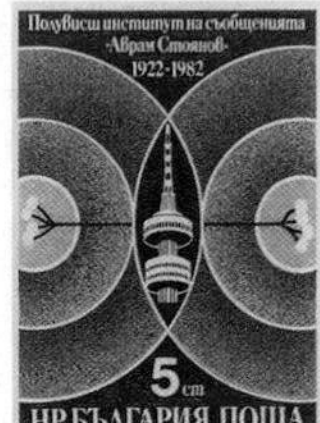

**993** Broadcasting Tower

**1982.** 60th Anniv of Avram Stoyanov Broadcasting Institute.

| | | | |
|---|---|---|---|
| 3066 | **993** 5s. blue | 20 | 15 |

**994** Dr. Robert Koch

**1982.** Cent of Discovery of Tubercle Bacillus.

| | | | |
|---|---|---|---|
| 3067 | **994** 25s. brown and green | 65 | 35 |

**995** Simon Bolivar

**1982.** Birth Anniversaries.

| | | | |
|---|---|---|---|
| 3068 | **995** 30s. green and grey | 75 | 45 |
| 3069 | - 30s. yellow and brown | 75 | 45 |

DESIGN: No. 3068, Type **995** (bicent); 3069, Rabindranath Tagore (philosopher, 120th anniv).

**996** Vasil Levski

**1983.** 110th Death Anniv of Vasil Levski (revolutionary).

| | | | |
|---|---|---|---|
| 3070 | **996** 5s. brown & green | 20 | 10 |

**997** Skier

**1983.** "Universiade 83" University Games, Sofia.

| | | | |
|---|---|---|---|
| 3071 | **997** 30s. multicoloured | 75 | 45 |

**998** Northern Pike

**1983.** Freshwater Fishes. Multicoloured.

| | | | |
|---|---|---|---|
| 3072 | 3s. Type **998** | 20 | 15 |
| 3073 | 5s. Beluga sturgeon | 20 | 15 |
| 3074 | 13s. Chub | 35 | 20 |
| 3075 | 25s. Zander | 75 | 35 |
| 3076 | 30s. Wels | 85 | 45 |
| 3077 | 42s. Brown trout | 2·40 | 55 |

**999** Karl Marx

**1983.** Death Centenary of Karl Marx.

| | | | |
|---|---|---|---|
| 3078 | **999** 13s. red, purple & yellow | 45 | 20 |

**1000** Hasek and Illustrations from "The Good Soldier Schweik"

**1983.** Birth Centenary of Jaroslav Hasek (Czech writer).

| | | | |
|---|---|---|---|
| 3079 | **1000** 13s. brown, grey & grn | 35 | 20 |

**1001** Martin Luther

**1983.** 500th Birth Anniv of Martin Luther (Protestant reformer).

| | | | |
|---|---|---|---|
| 3080 | **1001** 13s. grey, black & brn | 45 | 20 |

**1002** Figures forming Initials

**1983.** 55th Anniv of Young Workers' Union.

| | | | |
|---|---|---|---|
| 3081 | **1002** 5s. red, black & orange | 20 | 15 |

**1003** Khaskovo Costume

**1983.** Folk Costumes. Multicoloured.

| | | | |
|---|---|---|---|
| 3082 | 5s. Type **1003** | 25 | 15 |
| 3083 | 8s. Pernik | 30 | 15 |
| 3084 | 13s. Burgas | 35 | 20 |
| 3085 | 25s. Tolbukhin | 75 | 35 |
| 3086 | 30s. Blagoevgrad | 85 | 45 |
| 3087 | 42s. Topolovgrad | 2·40 | 55 |

**1004** Old Man feeding a Chicken

**1983.** 6th International Festival of Humour and Satire, Gabrovo.

| | | | |
|---|---|---|---|
| 3088 | **1004** 5s. multicoloured | 20 | 10 |

During 1983 sets were issued for European Security and Co-operation Conference, Budapest (5, 13, 25, 30s.), Olympic Games, Los Angeles (5, 13, 30, 42s.), Winter Olympic Games, Sarajevo (horiz designs, 5, 13, 30, 42s.) and European Security and Co-operation Conference, Madrid (5, 13, 30, 42s.). Supplies and distribution of these stamps were restricted, and it is understood they were not available at face value.

**1005** Smirnenski

**1983.** 85th Birth Anniv of Khristo Smirnenski (poet).

| | | | |
|---|---|---|---|
| 3089 | **1005** 5s. red, brown & yellow | 20 | 20 |

**1006** Emblem

**1983.** 17th Int Geodesy Federation Congress.

| | | | |
|---|---|---|---|
| 3090 | **1006** 30s. green, blue & yell | 65 | 45 |

**1007** Stylized Houses

**1983.** "Interarch 83" World Architecture Biennale, Sofia.

| | | | |
|---|---|---|---|
| 3091 | **1007** 30s. multicoloured | 75 | 45 |

**1008** Staunton Chessmen on Map of Europe

**1983.** 8th European Chess Team Championship, Plovdiv.

| | | | |
|---|---|---|---|
| 3092 | **1008** 13s. multicoloured | 45 | 20 |

**1009** Brazilian and Bulgarian Football Stamps

**1983.** "Brasiliana 83" International Stamp Exhibition, Rio de Janeiro. Sheet 73×103 mm.

| | | | |
|---|---|---|---|
| **MS**3093 | **1009** 1l. green, brown and gold | 2·75 | 2·75 |

**1010** Valentina Tereshkova

**1983.** Air. 20th Anniv of First Woman in Space. Sheet 121×75 mm containing T 1010 and similar vert design, each blue and brown.

| | | | |
|---|---|---|---|
| **MS**3094 | 50s. Type **1010**; 50s. Svetlana Savitskaya, 1982, cosmonaut | 3·25 | 3·25 |

**1011** Television Mast, Tolbukhin

**1983.** Air. World Communications Year.

| | | | |
|---|---|---|---|
| 3095 | **1011** 5s. blue and red | 20 | 15 |
| 3096 | - 13s. mauve and red | 35 | 20 |
| 3097 | - 30s. yellow and red | 55 | 35 |

DESIGNS: 13s. Postwoman; 30s. Radio tower, Mount Botev.

**1012** Lenin addressing Congress

**1983.** 80th Anniv of 2nd Russian Social Democratic Workers' Party Congress.

| | | | |
|---|---|---|---|
| 3098 | **1012** 5s. pur, dp pur & yell | 20 | 10 |

**1013** Pistol and Dagger on Book

**1983.** 80th Anniv of Ilinden-Preobrazhenie Rising.

| | | | |
|---|---|---|---|
| 3099 | **1013** 5s. yellow and green | 20 | 10 |

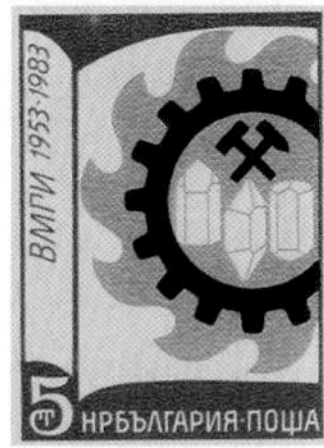

**1014** Crystals and Hammers within Gearwheels

**1983.** 30th Anniv of Mining and Geology Institute, Sofia.

| | | | |
|---|---|---|---|
| 3100 | **1014** 5s. grey, purple & blue | 20 | 10 |

**1015** Georgi Dimitrov and Revolution Scenes

**1983.** 60th Anniv of September Uprising. Mult.

| | | | |
|---|---|---|---|
| 3101 | 5s. Type **1015** | 20 | 10 |
| 3102 | 13s. Wreath and revolution scenes | 35 | 15 |

**1016** Animated Drawings

**1983.** 3rd Animated Film Festival, Varna.

| | | | | |
|---|---|---|---|---|
| 3103 | **1016** | 5s. multicoloured | 20 | 10 |

**1017** Angora

**1983.** Cats. Multicoloured.

| | | | |
|---|---|---|---|
| 3104 | 5s. Type **1017** | 25 | 20 |
| 3105 | 13s. Siamese | 45 | 20 |
| 3106 | 20s. Abyssinian (vert) | 65 | 35 |
| 3107 | 25s. European | 95 | 45 |
| 3108 | 30s. Persian (vert) | 1·10 | 65 |
| 3109 | 42s. Khmer | 1·90 | 1·10 |

**1018** Richard Trevithick's Locomotive, 1803

**1983.** Locomotives (1st series). Multicoloured.

| | | | |
|---|---|---|---|
| 3110 | 5s. Type **1018** | 20 | 10 |
| 3111 | 13s. John Blenkinsop's rack locomotive "Prince Royal", 1810 | 45 | 35 |
| 3112 | 42s. William Hedley's "Puffing Billy", 1813–14 | 2·00 | 1·10 |
| 3113 | 60s. Stephenson locomotive "Adler", 1835, Germany | 3·25 | 1·60 |

See also Nos. 3159/63.

**1019** Liberation Monument, Plovdiv

**1983.** 90th Anniv of Bulgarian Philatelic Federation and Fourth National Stamp Exhibition, Plovdiv. Sheet 65×79 mm.

| | | | |
|---|---|---|---|
| **MS**3114 | **1019** 50s. grey, blue and red | 1·60 | 1·60 |

**1020** Mask and Laurel as Lyre

**1983.** 75th Anniv of National Opera, Sofia.

| | | | | |
|---|---|---|---|---|
| 3115 | **1020** | 5s. red, black & gold | 20 | 10 |

**1021** Ioan Kukuzel

**1983.** Bulgarian Composers.

| | | | | |
|---|---|---|---|---|
| 3116 | **1021** | 5s. yellow, brown & grn | 20 | 15 |
| 3117 | - | 8s. yellow, brown & red | 20 | 15 |
| 3118 | - | 13s. yellow, brown and green | 30 | 20 |
| 3119 | - | 20s. yellow, brown & bl | 35 | 25 |
| 3120 | - | 25s. yellow, brn & grey | 45 | 35 |
| 3121 | - | 30s. yell, dp brn & brn | 55 | 45 |

DESIGNS: 8s. Georgi Atanasov; 13s. Petko Stainov; 20s. Veselin Stoyanov; 25s. Lyubomir Pipkov; 30s. Pancho Vladigerov.

**1022** Snowflake

**1983.** New Year.

| | | | | |
|---|---|---|---|---|
| 3122 | **1022** | 5s. green, blue & gold | 20 | 10 |

**1023** "Angelo Donni"

**1983.** 500th Birth Anniv of Raphael (artist). Multicoloured.

| | | | |
|---|---|---|---|
| 3123 | 5s. Type **1023** | 20 | 15 |
| 3124 | 13s. "Portrait of a Cardinal" | 35 | 20 |
| 3125 | 30s. "Baldassare Castiglioni" | 45 | 45 |
| 3126 | 42s. "Woman with a Veil" | 95 | 55 |
| **MS**3127 | 59×98 mm. 1l. "Sistine Madonna" | 2·40 | 2·40 |

**1024** Eurasian Common Shrew

**1983.** Protected Mammals. Multicoloured.

| | | | |
|---|---|---|---|
| 3128 | 12s. Type **1024** | 45 | 35 |
| 3129 | 13s. Greater horseshoe bat | 65 | 35 |
| 3130 | 20s. Common long-eared bat | 1·00 | 45 |
| 3131 | 30s. Forest dormouse | 1·60 | 65 |
| 3132 | 42s. Fat dormouse | 3·25 | 1·10 |

**1025** Karavelov

**1984.** 150th Birth Anniv of Lyuben Karavelov (poet).

| | | | | |
|---|---|---|---|---|
| 3133 | **1025** | 5s. blue, bistre & brn | 20 | 10 |

During 1984 sets were issued for European Confidence- and Security-building Measures and Disarmament Conference, Stockholm (5, 13, 30, 42s.) and Winter Olympic Games, Sarajevo (vert designs, 5, 13, 30, 42s.). Supplies and distribution of these stamps were restricted and it is understood that they were not available at face value.

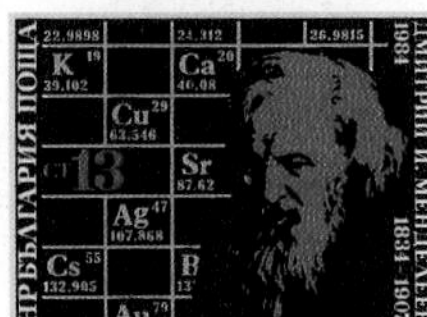


**1026** Mendeleev and Formulae

**1984.** 150th Birth Anniv of Dmitry Mendeleev (chemist).

| | | | | |
|---|---|---|---|---|
| 3134 | **1026** | 13s. multicoloured | 35 | 20 |

**1027** Bulk Carrier "Gen. Vl. Zaimov"

**1984.** Ships. Multicoloured.

| | | | |
|---|---|---|---|
| 3135 | 5s. Type **1027** | 20 | 10 |
| 3136 | 13s. Tanker "Mesta" | 35 | 15 |
| 3137 | 25s. Tanker "Veleka" | 65 | 35 |
| 3138 | 32s. Train ferry "Geroite na Odesa" | 80 | 45 |
| 3139 | 42s. Bulk carrier "Rozhen" | 1·40 | 55 |

**1028** World Cup Stamps

**1984.** "Espana 84" International Stamp Exhibition, Madrid. Sheet 89×110 mm.

| | | | |
|---|---|---|---|
| **MS**3140 | **1028** 2l. multicoloured | 8·25 | 8·25 |

**1029** Pigeon with Letter over Globe

**1984.** "Mladost '84" Youth Stamp Exhibition, Pleven (1st issue).

| | | | | |
|---|---|---|---|---|
| 3141 | **1029** | 5s. multicoloured | 20 | 10 |

See also Nos. 3171/2.

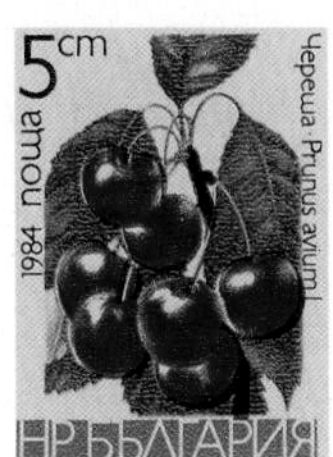


**1030** Wild Cherries

**1984.** Fruits. Multicoloured.

| | | | |
|---|---|---|---|
| 3142 | 5s. Type **1030** | 20 | 15 |
| 3143 | 8s. Wild strawberries | 20 | 15 |
| 3144 | 13s. Dewberries | 35 | 20 |
| 3145 | 20s. Raspberries | 55 | 35 |
| 3146 | 42s. Medlars | 1·70 | 55 |

**1031** "Vitosha Conference" (K. Buyukliiski and P. Petrov)

**1984.** 60th Anniv of Bulgarian Communist Party Conference, Vitosha.

| | | | | |
|---|---|---|---|---|
| 3147 | **1031** | 5s. purple, brn & red | 20 | 10 |

**1032** Security Conference 1980 13s. Stamp

**1984.** 5th International Stamp Fair, Essen. Sheet 94×147 mm containing T 1032 and similar horiz design. Multicoloured.

| | | | |
|---|---|---|---|
| **MS**3148 | 1l.50, Type **1032**; 1l.50, Security Conference 35s. stamp | 8·75 | 8·75 |

**1033** Athletes and Doves

**1984.** 6th Republican Spartakiad.

| | | | | |
|---|---|---|---|---|
| 3149 | **1033** | 13s. multicoloured | 35 | 20 |

**1034** Mt. Everest

**1984.** Bulgarian Expedition to Mt. Everest.

| | | | | |
|---|---|---|---|---|
| 3150 | **1034** | 5s. multicoloured | 20 | 10 |

**1035** Kogge

**1984.** Universal Postal Union Congress Philatelic Salon, Hamburg. Sheet 100×107 mm.

| | | | |
|---|---|---|---|
| **MS**3151 | **1035** 3l. multicoloured | 7·50 | 7·50 |

**1036** Drummer

**1984.** 6th Amateur Performers Festival.

| | | | | |
|---|---|---|---|---|
| 3152 | **1036** | 5s. multicoloured | 20 | 10 |

**1037** Seal

**1984.** 50 Years of Bulgarian–U.S.S.R. Diplomatic Relations.

| | | | | |
|---|---|---|---|---|
| 3153 | **1037** | 13s. multicoloured | 35 | 20 |

**1038** Feral Rock Pigeon

**1984.** Pigeons and Doves. Multicoloured.

| | | | |
|---|---|---|---|
| 3154 | 5s. Type **1038** | 20 | 10 |
| 3155 | 13s. Stock pigeon | 35 | 20 |
| 3156 | 20s. Wood pigeon | 55 | 35 |
| 3157 | 30s. Turtle dove | 95 | 45 |
| 3158 | 42s. Domestic pigeon | 1·20 | 55 |

**1984.** Locomotives (2nd series). As T 1018. Multicoloured.

| | | | |
|---|---|---|---|
| 3159 | 13s. "Best Friend of Charleston", 1830, U.S.A. | 35 | 20 |
| 3160 | 25s. "Saxonia", 1836, Saxony | 65 | 35 |
| 3161 | 30s. "Lafayette", 1837, U.S.A. | 85 | 45 |
| 3162 | 42s. "Borsig", 1841, Germany | 1·20 | 60 |

| | | | | |
|---|---|---|---|---|
| 3163 | | 60s. "Philadelphia", 1843, U.S.A. | 2·00 | 85 |

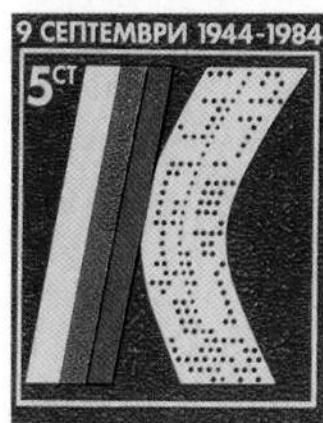


**1039** Production Quality Emblem

**1984.** 40th Anniv of Fatherland Front Government.

| | | | | |
|---|---|---|---|---|
| 3164 | **1039** | 5s. red, lt green & green | 20 | 15 |
| 3165 | - | 20s. red and violet | 55 | 25 |
| 3166 | - | 30s. red and blue | 85 | 45 |

DESIGNS: 20s. Monument to Soviet Army, Sofia; 30s. Figure nine and star.

**1040** "Boy with Harmonica"

**1984.** Paintings by Nenko Balkanski. Multicoloured.

| | | | |
|---|---|---|---|
| 3167 | 5s. Type **1040** | 20 | 15 |
| 3168 | 30s. "Window in Paris" | 85 | 45 |
| 3169 | 42s. "Portrait of Two Women" (horiz) | 1·60 | 55 |
| **MS**3170 | 65×110 mm. 1l. "Self-portrait" | 2·75 | 2·75 |

**1041** Mausoleum of Russian Soldiers

**1984.** "Mladost '84" Youth Stamp Exhibition, Pleven (2nd issue).

| | | | | |
|---|---|---|---|---|
| 3171 | **1041** | 5s. multicoloured | 20 | 10 |
| 3172 | - | 13s. black, grn & red | 35 | 15 |

DESIGN: 13s. Panorama building.

**1042** Pioneers saluting

**1984.** 40th Anniv of Dimitrov Septembrist Pioneers Organization.

| | | | | |
|---|---|---|---|---|
| 3173 | **1042** | 5s. multicoloured | 20 | 10 |

**1043** Vaptsarov (after D. Nikolov)

**1984.** 75th Birth Anniv of Nikola I. Vaptsarov (poet).

| | | | | |
|---|---|---|---|---|
| 3174 | **1043** | 5s. yellow and red | 20 | 10 |

**1044** Goalkeeper saving Goal

**1984.** 75th Anniv of Bulgarian Football.

| | | | | |
|---|---|---|---|---|
| 3175 | **1044** | 42s. multicoloured | 95 | 55 |

**1045** Profiles

**1984.** "Miadost '84" Youth Stamp Exhibition, Pleven (3rd issue). Sheet 50×76 mm.

| | | | | |
|---|---|---|---|---|
| **MS**3176 | **1045** | 50s. multicoloured | 1·60 | 1·60 |

**1046** Devil's Bridge, R. Arda

**1984.** Bridges. Multicoloured.

| | | | |
|---|---|---|---|
| 3177 | 5s. Type **1046** | 30 | 20 |
| 3178 | 13s. Kolo Ficheto Bridge, Byala | 55 | 45 |
| 3179 | 30s. Asparukhov Bridge, Varna | 95 | 85 |
| 3180 | 42s. Bebresh Bridge, Botevgrad | 2·00 | 1·50 |

**1047** Olympic Emblem

**1984.** 90th Anniv of International Olympic Committee.

| | | | | |
|---|---|---|---|---|
| 3181 | **1047** | 13s. multicoloured | 35 | 20 |

**1048** Moon and "Luna I", "II" and "III"

**1984.** 25th Anniv of First Moon Rocket. Sheet 79×57 mm.

| | | | | |
|---|---|---|---|---|
| **MS**3182 | **1048** | 1l. multicoloured | 3·25 | 3·25 |

**1049** Dalmatian Pelican with Chicks

**1984.** Wildlife Protection. Dalmatian Pelican.

| | | | | |
|---|---|---|---|---|
| 3183 | **1049** | 5s. multicoloured | 45 | 20 |
| 3184 | - | 13s. lav, blk & brn | 95 | 45 |
| 3185 | - | 20s. multicoloured | 1·40 | 1·10 |
| 3186 | - | 32s. multicoloured | 3·25 | 1·60 |

DESIGNS: 13s. Two pelicans; 20s. Pelican on water; 32s. Pelican in flight.

**1050** Anton Ivanov

**1984.** Birth Cent of Anton Ivanov (revolutionary).

| | | | | |
|---|---|---|---|---|
| 3187 | **1050** | 5s. yell, brn & red | 20 | 10 |

**1051** Girl's Profile with Text as Hair

**1984.** 70th Anniv of Bulgarian Women's Socialist Movement.

| | | | | |
|---|---|---|---|---|
| 3188 | **1051** | 5s. multicoloured | 20 | 10 |

**1052** Snezhanka Television Tower

**1984.** Television Towers.

| | | | | |
|---|---|---|---|---|
| 3189 | **1052** | 5s. blue, green & mve | 20 | 15 |
| 3190 | - | 1l. brown, mauve & bis | 2·30 | 1·10 |

DESIGN: 1l. Orelek television tower.

**1053** Birds and Posthorns

**1984.** New Year. Multicoloured.

| | | | |
|---|---|---|---|
| 3191 | 5s. Type **1053** | 20 | 10 |
| 3192 | 13s. Decorative pattern | 35 | 15 |

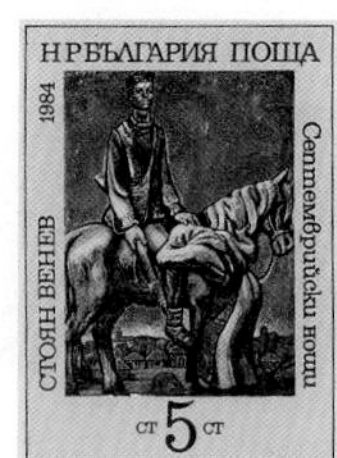


**1054** "September Nights"

**1984.** 80th Birth Anniv of Stoyan Venev (artist). Multicoloured.

| | | | |
|---|---|---|---|
| 3193 | 5s. Type **1054** | 20 | 15 |
| 3194 | 30s. "Man with Three Orders" | 85 | 45 |
| 3195 | 42s. "The Hero" | 1·40 | 55 |

**1055** Peacock (butterfly)

**1984.** Butterflies. Multicoloured.

| | | | |
|---|---|---|---|
| 3196 | 13s. Type **1055** | 35 | 20 |
| 3197 | 25s. Swallowtail | 65 | 35 |
| 3198 | 30s. Great banded grayling | 85 | 45 |
| 3199 | 42s. Orange-tip | 1·20 | 55 |
| 3200 | 60s. Red admiral | 2·00 | 75 |
| **MS**3201 | 75×60 mm. 1l. Poplar admiral (*Limenitis populi*) | 2·75 | 2·75 |

**1056** Augusto Sandino

**1984.** 50th Death Anniv of Augusto Sandino (Nicaraguan revolutionary).

| | | | | |
|---|---|---|---|---|
| 3202 | **1056** | 13s. black, red & yell | 35 | 20 |

**1057** Tupolev Tu-154 Jetliner

**1984.** 40th Anniv of ICAO.

| | | | | |
|---|---|---|---|---|
| 3203 | **1057** | 42s. multicoloured | 95 | 55 |

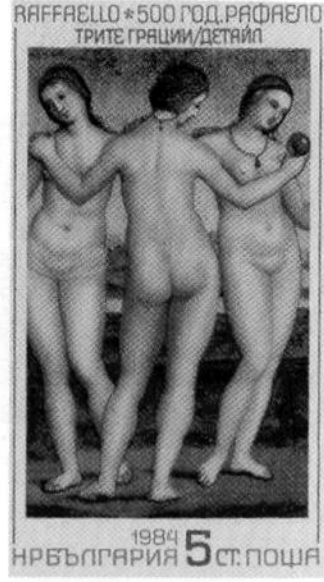


**1058** "The Three Graces" (detail)

**1984.** 500th Birth Anniv (1983) of Raphael (artist) (2nd issue). Multicoloured.

| | | | |
|---|---|---|---|
| 3204 | 5s. Type **1058** | 25 | 20 |
| 3205 | 13s. "Cupid and the Three Graces" (detail) | 30 | 25 |
| 3206 | 30s. "Original Sin" (detail) | 65 | 45 |
| 3207 | 42s. "La Fornarina" | 1·30 | 50 |
| **MS**3208 | 106×95 mm. 1l. "Galatea" (detail) | 2·50 | 2·50 |

**1059** "Sofia"

**1984.** Maiden Voyage of Danube Cruise Ship "Sofia".

| | | | | |
|---|---|---|---|---|
| 3209 | **1059** | 13s. dp blue, blue & yell | 35 | 20 |

**1060** Eastern Hog-nosed Skunk

**1985.** Mammals.

| | | | | |
|---|---|---|---|---|
| 3210 | **1060** | 13s. black, blue & orge | 30 | 15 |
| 3211 | - | 25s. black, brown & grn | 65 | 35 |
| 3212 | - | 30s. black, brown & yell | 75 | 40 |
| 3213 | - | 42s. multicoloured | 1·10 | 55 |
| 3214 | - | 60s. multicoloured | 1·90 | 85 |

DESIGNS: 25s. Banded linsang; 30s. Zorilla; 42s. Banded palm civet; 60s. Broad-striped galidia.

**1061** Nikolai Liliev

**1985.** Birth Centenary of Nikolai Liliev (poet).

| | | | | |
|---|---|---|---|---|
| 3215 | **1061** | 30s. lt brn, brn & gold | 65 | 45 |

**1062** Tsvyatko Radoinov

**1985.** 90th Birth Anniv of Tsvyatko Radoinov (resistance fighter).

| | | | | |
|---|---|---|---|---|
| 3216 | **1062** | 5s. brown and red | 20 | 10 |

**1063** Asen Zlatarov

**1985.** Birth Cent. of Asen Zlatarov (biochemist).

3217 **1063** 5s. purple, yellow & grn 20 10

**1064** Research Ship "Akademik"

**1985.** 13th General Assembley and 125th Anniv of Intergovernmental Oceanographic Commission. Sheet 90×60 mm.

**MS**3218 **1064** 80s. multicoloured 2·20 2·20

**1065** Lenin Monument, Sofia

**1985.** 115th Birth Anniv of Lenin. Sheet 55×87 mm.

**MS**3219 **1065** 50s. multicoloured 1·30 1·30

**1066** Olive Branch and Sword Blade

**1985.** 30th Anniv of Warsaw Pact.

3220 **1066** 13s. multicoloured 30 20

**1067** Bach

**1985.** Composers.

3221 **1067** 42s. blue and red 1·40 65

3222 - 42s. violet and green 1·40 65

3223 - 42s. yellow, brn & orge 1·40 65

3224 - 42s. yellow, brn & red 1·40 65

3225 - 42s. yellow, grn & blue 1·40 65

3226 - 42s. yellow, red & grn 1·40 65

DESIGNS: No. 3222, Mozart; 3223, Tchaikovsky; 3224, Modest Petrovich Musorgsky; 3225, Giuseppe Verdi; 3226, Filip Kutev.

**1068** Girl with Birds

**1985.** 3rd "Banners for Peace" Children's Meeting, Sofia. Multicoloured.

3227 5s. Type **1068** 20 15

3228 8s. Children painting 20 15

3229 13s. Girl among flowers 30 20

3230 20s. Children at market stall 45 25

3231 25s. Circle of children 55 35

3232 30s. Nurse 65 45

**MS**3233 70×110 mm. 50st. Children dancing (vert). Perf or imperf 2·20 2·20

**1069** St. Methodius

**1985.** 1100th Death Anniv of St. Methodius.

3234 **1069** 13s. multicoloured 65 35

**1070** Soldiers and Nazi Flags

**1985.** 40th Anniv of V.E. ("Victory in Europe") Day. Multicoloured.

3235 5s. Type **1070** 20 15

3236 13s. 11th Infantry parade, Sofia 35 25

3237 30s. Soviet soldier with orphan 75 35

**MS**3238 90×123 mm. 50s. Soldier raising Soviet flag 1·60 1·60

**1071** Woman carrying Child and Man on Donkey

**1985.** 7th International Festival of Humour and Satire, Gabrovo.

3239 **1071** 13s. black, yell & red 30 20

**1072** Profiles and Flowers

**1985.** International Youth Year.

3240 **1072** 13s. multicoloured 30 20

**1073** Ivan Vazov

**1985.** 135th Birth Anniv of Ivan Vazov (poet).

3241 **1073** 5s. brown and stone 20 10

**1074** Monument to Unknown Soldiers and City Arms

**1985.** Millenary of Khaskovo.

3242 **1074** 5s. multicoloured 20 10

**1075** Festival Emblem

**1985.** 12th World Youth and Students' Festival, Moscow.

3243 **1075** 13s. multicoloured 30 20

**1076** Indira Gandhi

**1985.** Indira Gandhi (Indian Prime Minister) Commemoration.

3244 **1076** 30s. brown, orge & yell 65 35

**1077** Vasil E. Aprilov (founder)

**1985.** 150th Anniv of New Bulgarian School, Gabrovo.

3245 **1077** 5s. blue, purple & grn 20 10

**1078** Congress Emblem

**1985.** 36th International Shorthand and Typing Federation Congress ("Intersteno"), Sofia.

3246 **1078** 13s. multicoloured 30 20

**1079** Alexandr Nevski Cathedral, Sofia

**1985.** Sixth General Assembly of World Tourism Organization, Sofia.

3247 **1079** 42s. green, blue & orge 95 55

**1080** State Arms and UN Flag

**1985.** 40th Anniv of UNO (3248) and 30th Anniv of Bulgaria's Membership (3249). Multicoloured.

3248 13s. Dove around UN emblem 30 20

3249 13s. Type **1080** 30 20

**1081** Rosa "Trakijka"

**1985.** Roses. Multicoloured.

3250 5s. "Rosa damascena" 20 15

3251 13s. Type **1081** 30 20

3252 20s. "Radiman" 45 25

3253 30s. "Marista" 55 35

3254 42s. "Valentina" 95 45

3255 60s. "Maria" 1·40 55

**1082** Peace Dove

**1985.** 10th Anniv of European Security and Co-operation Conference, Helsinki.

3256 **1082** 13s. multicoloured 30 20

**1083** Water Polo

**1985.** European Swimming Championships, Sofia. Multicoloured.

3257 5s. Butterfly stroke (horiz) 20 15

3258 13s. Type **1083** 30 20

3259 42s. Diving 1·10 55

3260 60s. Synchronized swimming (horiz) 1·90 75

**1084** Edelweiss

**1985.** 90th Anniv of Bulgarian Tourist Organization.

3261 **1084** 5s. multicoloured 20 10

**1085** State Arms

**1985.** Cent of Union of E. Roumelia and Bulgaria.

3262 **1085** 5s. black, orge & green 20 10

**1086** Footballers

**1985.** World Cup Football Championship, Mexico (1986) (1st issue).

3263 **1086** 5s. multicoloured 20 15

3264 - 13s. multicoloured 30 20

3265 - 30s. multicoloured 65 45
3266 - 42s. multicoloured 1·40 55
**MS**3267 54×76 mm. 1l. multicoloured (horiz) 2·30 2·30
DESIGNS: 13s. to 1l. Various footballers.
See also Nos. 3346/**MS**3352.

**1087** Computer Picture of Boy

**1985.** International Young Inventors' Exhibition, Plovdiv. Multicoloured.
3268 5s. Type **1087** 20 15
3269 13s. Computer picture of youth 30 20
3270 30s. Computer picture of cosmonaut 75 35

**1088** St. John's Church, Nesebur

**1985.** 40th Anniv of UNESCO. Mult.
3271 5s. Type **1088** 20 15
3272 13s. Rila Monastery 30 20
3273 35s. Soldier (fresco, Ivanovo Rock Church) 95 45
3274 42s. Archangel Gabriel (fresco, Boyana Church) 1·10 55
3275 60s. Thracian woman (fresco, Kazanlak tomb) 1·90 75
**MS**3276 100×83 mm. 1l. Madara horseman (horiz). Imperf 2·20 2·20

**1089** Lyudmila Zhivkova Palace of Culture

**1985.** 23rd United Nations Educational, Scientific and Cultural Organization General Session, Sofia. Sheet 62×95 mm.
**MS**3277 **1089** 1l. multicoloured 2·20 2·20

**1090** Colosseum, Rome

**1985.** "Italia '85" International Stamp Exhibition, Rome.
3278 **1090** 42s. multicoloured 95 55

**1091** "Gladiolus"

**1985.** Flowers.
3279 **1091** 5s. pink and red 20 15
3280 - 5s. blue and light blue 20 15
3281 - 5s. lt violet & violet 20 15
3282 - 8s. light blue and blue 20 15
3283 - 8s. orange and red 20 15
3284 - 32s. orange and brown 65 35
DESIGNS: No. 3280, Garden iris; 3281, Dwarf morning glory; 3282, Morning glory; 3283, "Anemone coronaria"; 3284, Golden-rayed lily.

**1092** St. Methodius

**1985.** Cultural Congress of European Security and Cooperation Conference, Budapest. Sheet 105×93 mm containing T 1092 and similar vert designs. Multicoloured.
**MS**3285 50s. St. Cyril; 50s. Map of Europe; 50s. Type **1092** 4·25 4·25

**1985.** Historic Ships (4th series). As T 753. Multicoloured.
3286 5s. 17th-century Dutch fly 20 10
3287 12s. "Sovereign of the Seas" (English galleon) 30 15
3288 20s. Mediterranean polacca 45 20
3289 25s. "Prince Royal" (English warship) 55 35
3290 42s. Xebec 1·00 65
3291 60s. 17th-century English warship 1·90 75

**1093** Cologne Cathedral

**1985.** "Philatelia '85" International Stamp Exhibition, Cologne. Sheet 109×56 mm containing T 1093 and similar vert design, each black, blue and red.
**MS**3292 30s. Type **1093**; 30s. Alexandr Nevski Cathedral, Sofia 1·60 1·60

**1094** Bacho Kiro

**1985.** Revolutionaries.
3293 **1094** 5s. light brown, brown and blue 20 10
3294 - 5s. green, purple & brown 20 10
DESIGN: No. 3294, Georgi S. Rakovski.

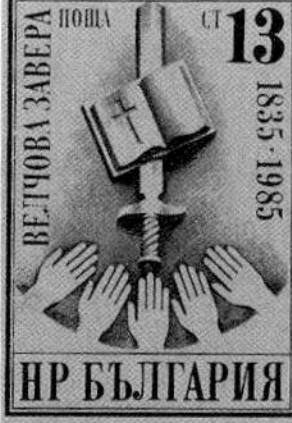

**1095** Hands, Sword and Bible

**1985.** 150th Anniv of Turnovo Uprising.
3295 **1095** 13s. brown, blue & pur 30 20

**1096** "1185 Revolution" (G. Bogdanov)

**1985.** 800th Anniv of Liberation from Byzantine Empire. Multicoloured.
3296 5s. Type **1096** 20 15
3297 13s. "1185 Revolution" (Al. Terziev) 35 20
3298 30s. "Battle of Klakotnitsa, 1230" (B. Grigorov and M. Ganovski) 45 35
3299 42s. "Veliko Turnovo" (Ts. Lavrenov) 1·40 55
**MS**3300 74×80 mm. 1l. Church of St. Dimitrius, Veliko Turnovo (38×28 mm). Imperf 2·20 2·20

**1097** Emblem

**1985.** "Bralkanfila '85" Stamp Exhibition, Vratsa. Sheet 55×80 mm.
**MS**3301 **1097** 40s. blue, black and deep blue 1·10 1·10

**1098** Emblem and Globe

**1985.** International Development Programme for Posts and Telecommunications.
3302 **1098** 13s. multicoloured 30 20

**1099** Popov

**1985.** 70th Birth Anniv of Anton Popov (revolutionary).
3303 **1099** 5s. red 20 10

**1100** Doves around Snowflake

**1985.** New Year. Multicoloured.
3304 5s. Type **1100** 20 10
3305 13s. Circle of stylized doves 30 15

**1101** Pointer and Chukar Partridge

**1985.** Hunting Dogs. Multicoloured.
3306 5s. Type **1101** 20 20
3307 8s. Irish setter and common pochard 25 20
3308 13s. English setter and mallard 30 20
3309 20s. Cocker spaniel and Eurasian woodcock 35 25
3310 25s. German pointer and rabbit 55 35
3311 30s. Bulgarian bloodhound and boar 75 40
3312 42s. Dachshund and fox 1·50 55

**1102** Person in Wheelchair and Runners

**1985.** International Year of Disabled Persons (1984).
3313 **1102** 5s. multicoloured 20 10

**1103** Georgi Dimitrov (statesman)

**1985.** 50th Anniv of 7th Communist International Congress, Moscow.
3314 **1103** 13s. red 35 20

**1104** Emblem within "40"

**1986.** 40th Anniv of UNICEF.
3315 **1104** 13s. blue, gold & black 35 20

**1105** Blagoev

**1986.** 130th Birth Anniv of Dimitur Blagoev (founder of Bulgarian Social Democratic Party).
3316 **1105** 5s. purple and orange 20 10

**1106** Hands and Dove within Laurel Wreath

**1986.** International Peace Year.
3317 **1106** 5s. multicoloured 20 10

**1107** "Dactylorhiza romana"

**1986.** Orchids. Multicoloured.
3318 5s. Type **1107** 20 15
3319 13s. "Epipactis palustris" 30 20
3320 30s. "Ophrys cornuta" 40 25
3321 32s. "Limodorum abrotivum" 45 35
3322 42s. "Cypripedium calceolus" 85 45
3323 60s. "Orchis papilionacea" 1·40 55

**1108** Angora Rabbit

**1986.** Rabbits.
3324 - 5s. grey, black & brown 20 15
3325 **1108** 25s. red and black 45 20
3326 - 30s. brown, yell & blk 55 25
3327 - 32s. orange and black 65 35
3328 - 42s. red and black 85 45
3329 - 60s. blue and black 1·40 55
DESIGNS: 5s. French grey; 30s. English lop-eared; 32s. Belgian; 42s. English spotted; 60s. Dutch black and white rabbit.

**1109** Front Page and Ivan Bogorov

**1986.** 140th Anniv of "Bulgarian Eagle".

| | | | | |
|---|---|---|---|---|
| 3330 | **1109** | 5s. multicoloured | 20 | 10 |

**1110** Neptune and Comet Position, 1980

**1986.** Appearance of Halley's Comet. Sheet 120×114 mm containing T 1110 and similar horiz designs, each violet, blue and yellow.

**MS**3331 25s. Type **1110**; 25s. Sun, Earth, Mars, Saturn and comet positions, 1985 and 1910/86; 25s. Uranus and comet positions, 1960, 1926, 1948 and 1970; 25s. Jupiter and comet position, 1911 — 2·20 2·20

**1111** Bashev

**1986.** 50th Birth Anniv (1985) of Vladimir Bashev (poet).

| | | | | |
|---|---|---|---|---|
| 3332 | **1111** | 5s. blue & light blue | 20 | 10 |

**1112** Wave Pattern

**1986.** 13th Bulgarian Communist Party Congress.

| | | | | |
|---|---|---|---|---|
| 3333 | **1112** | 5s. blue, green and red | 10 | 15 |
| 3334 | - | 8s. blue and red | 25 | 15 |
| 3335 | - | 13s. blue, red & lt blue | 30 | 20 |
| **MS**3336 60×77 mm. 50s. multicoloured | | | 1·00 | 1·10 |

DESIGNS: 8s. Printed circuit as tail of shooting star; 13s. Computer picture of man; 50s. Steel construction tower.

**1113** "Vostok I"

**1986.** 25th Anniv of First Man in Space. Sheet 105×100 mm containing T 1113 and similar horiz design, each deep blue and blue.

**MS**3337 50s. Type **1113**; 50s. Yuri Gagarin — 2·20 2·20

**1114** Monument, Panagyurishte

**1986.** 110th Anniv of April Uprising.

| | | | | |
|---|---|---|---|---|
| 3338 | **1114** | 5s. black, stone and green | 20 | 10 |
| 3339 | - | 13s. black, stone & red | 30 | 15 |

DESIGN: 13s. Statue of Khristo Botev, Vratsa.

**1115** Gymnast

**1986.** 75th Anniv of Levski-Spartak Sports Club. Sheet 81×65 mm. Imperf.

**MS**3340 **1115** 50s. multicoloured — 1·00 1·10

**1116** Stylized Ear of Wheat

**1986.** 35th Bulgarian People's Agrarian Union Congress.

| | | | | |
|---|---|---|---|---|
| 3341 | **1116** | 5s. gold, orange & blk | 10 | 10 |
| 3342 | - | 8s. gold, blue and black | 20 | 10 |
| 3343 | - | 13s. multicoloured | 30 | 15 |

DESIGNS: 8s. Stylized ear of wheat on globe; 13s. Flags.

**1117** Transport Systems

**1986.** Socialist Countries' Transport Ministers Conference.

| | | | | |
|---|---|---|---|---|
| 3344 | **1117** | 13s. multicoloured | 30 | 20 |

**1118** Emblem

**1986.** 17th International Book Fair, Sofia.

| | | | | |
|---|---|---|---|---|
| 3345 | **1118** | 13s. grey, red and black | 30 | 20 |

**1119** Player with Ball

**1986.** World Cup Football Championship, Mexico (2nd issue). Multicoloured.

| | | | |
|---|---|---|---|
| 3346 | 5s. Type **1119** | 20 | 15 |
| 3347 | 13s. Player tackling (horiz) | 30 | 20 |
| 3348 | 20s. Player heading ball (horiz) | 35 | 25 |
| 3349 | 30s. Player kicking ball (horiz) | 65 | 35 |
| 3350 | 42s. Goalkeeper (horiz) | 95 | 45 |
| 3351 | 60s. Player with trophy | 1·50 | 65 |
| **MS**3352 | 95×75 mm. 1l. Azteca Stadium (42×31 mm) | 2·20 | 2·20 |

**1120** Square Brooch

**1986.** Treasures of Preslav. Multicoloured.

| | | | |
|---|---|---|---|
| 3353 | 5s. Type **1120** | 20 | 15 |
| 3354 | 13s. Pendant (vert) | 30 | 20 |
| 3355 | 20s. Wheel-shaped pendant | 35 | 25 |
| 3356 | 30s. Breast plate decorated with birds and chalice | 65 | 35 |
| 3357 | 42s. Pear-shaped pendant (vert) | 95 | 45 |
| 3358 | 60s. Enamelled cockerel on gold base | 1·40 | 55 |

**1121** Fencers with Sabres

**1986.** World Fencing Championships, Sofia. Mult.

| | | | |
|---|---|---|---|
| 3359 | 5s. Type **1121** | 20 | 10 |
| 3360 | 13s. Fencers | 30 | 15 |
| 3361 | 25s. Fencers with rapiers | 55 | 35 |

**1122** Stockholm Town Hall

**1986.** "Stockholmia 86" International Stamp Exn.

| | | | | |
|---|---|---|---|---|
| 3362 | **1122** | 42s. brn, red & dp red | 75 | 65 |

**1123** White Stork (*Ciconia ciconia*)

**1986.** Nature Protection. Sheet 138×90 mm containing T 1123 and similar vert designs. Multicoloured.

**MS**3363 30s. Type **1132**; 30s. Yellow water-lily (*Nuphar lutea*); 30s. Fire salamander (*Salamandra salamandra*); 30s. White water-lily (*Nymphaea alba*) — 5·00 4·25

**1124** Arms and Parliament Building, Sofia

**1986.** 40th Anniv of People's Republic.

| | | | | |
|---|---|---|---|---|
| 3364 | **1124** | 5s. green, red & lt grn | 20 | 10 |

**1125** Posthorn

**1986.** 15th Organization of Socialist Countries' Postal Administrations Session, Sofia.

| | | | | |
|---|---|---|---|---|
| 3365 | **1125** | 13s. multicoloured | 30 | 20 |

**1126** "All Pull Together"

**1986.** 40th Anniv of Voluntary Brigades.

| | | | | |
|---|---|---|---|---|
| 3366 | **1126** | 5s. multicoloured | 20 | 10 |

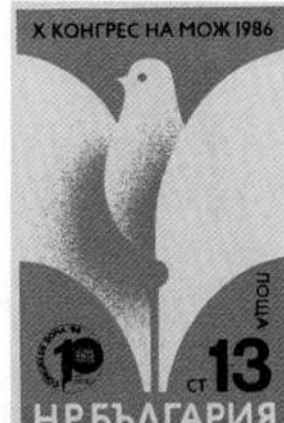
**1127** Dove and Book as Pen Nib

**1986.** 10th International Journalists Association Congress, Sofia.

| | | | | |
|---|---|---|---|---|
| 3367 | **1127** | 13s. blue & deep blue | 30 | 20 |

**1128** Wrestlers

**1986.** 75th Anniv of Levski-Spartak Sports Club.

| | | | | |
|---|---|---|---|---|
| 3368 | **1128** | 5s. multicoloured | 20 | 10 |

**1129** Saints Cyril and Methodius with Disciples (fresco)

**1986.** 1100th Anniv of Arrival in Bulgaria of Pupils of Saints Cyril and Methodius.

| | | | | |
|---|---|---|---|---|
| 3369 | **1129** | 13s. brown and buff | 30 | 20 |

**1130** Old and Modern Telephones

**1986.** Centenary of Telephone in Bulgaria.

| | | | | |
|---|---|---|---|---|
| 3370 | **1130** | 5s. multicoloured | 20 | 10 |

**1131** Weightlifter

**1986.** World Weightlifting Championships, Sofia.

| | | | | |
|---|---|---|---|---|
| 3371 | **1131** | 13s. multicoloured | 30 | 20 |

**1986.** Historic Ships (5th series). 18th-century ships. As T 753. Multicoloured.

| | | | |
|---|---|---|---|
| 3372 | 5s. "King of Prussia" | 10 | 10 |
| 3373 | 13s. Indiaman | 20 | 15 |
| 3374 | 25s. Xebec | 45 | 25 |
| 3375 | 30s. "Sv. Paul" | 55 | 35 |
| 3376 | 32s. Topsail schooner | 65 | 45 |
| 3377 | 42s. "Victory" | 1·40 | 55 |

**1132 (image scaled to 47% of original size)**

**1986.** European Security and Co-operation Conference Review Meeting, Vienna. Sheet 109×86 mm containing T 1132 and similar vert designs.

**MS**3378 50s. olive, orange and green; 50s. green, orange and blue (Vienna Town Hall); 50s. multicoloured (United Nations Centre, Vienna) — 4·25 4·25

**1133** Silver Jug decorated with Seated Woman

**1986.** 14th Congress of Bulgarian Philatelic Federation and 60th Anniv of International Philatelic Federation. Repousse work found at Rogozen.

| | | | | |
|---|---|---|---|---|
| 3379 | **1133** | 10s. grey, black & bl | 30 | 20 |
| 3380 | - | 10s. green, blk & red | 30 | 20 |

DESIGN: No. 3380, Silver jug decorated with sphinx.

**1134** Doves between Pine Branches

**1986.** New Year.

| | | | | |
|---|---|---|---|---|
| 3381 | **1134** | 5s. red, green and blue | 20 | 10 |
| 3382 | - | 13s. mauve, blue & vio | 30 | 20 |

DESIGN: 13s. Fireworks and snowflakes.

**1135** Earphones as "60" on Globe

**1986.** 60th Anniv of Bulgarian Amateur Radio.

| | | | | |
|---|---|---|---|---|
| 3383 | **1135** | 13s. multicoloured | 30 | 20 |

**1136** "The Walnut Tree" (Danail Dechev)

**1986.** 90th Anniv of Sofia Art Academy. Modern Paintings. Sheet 146×102 mm containing T 1136 and similar horiz designs. Multicoloured.

| | | |
|---|---|---|
| **MS**3384 25s. Type **1136**; 25s. "Resistance Fighters and Soldiers" (Iliya Beshkov); 30s. "Melnik" (Veselin Staikov); 30s. "The Olive Grove" (Kiril Tsonev) | 3·25 | 3·25 |

**1137** Gen. Augusto Sandino and Flag

**1988.** 25th Anniv of Sandinista National Liberation Front of Nicaragua.

| | | | | |
|---|---|---|---|---|
| 3385 | **1137** | 13s. multicoloured | 30 | 20 |

**1138** Dimitur and Konstantin Miladinov (authors)

**1986.** 125th Anniv of "Bulgarian Popular Songs".

| | | | | |
|---|---|---|---|---|
| 3386 | **1138** | 10s. blue, brn & red | 20 | 10 |

**1139** Pencho Slaveikov (poet)

**1986.** Writers' Birth Annivs. Multicoloured.

| | | | | |
|---|---|---|---|---|
| 3387 | | 5s. Type **1139** (125th anniv) | 20 | 10 |
| 3388 | | 5s. Stoyan Mikhailovski (130th anniv) | 20 | 10 |
| 3389 | | 8s. Nikola Atanasov (dramatist) (centenary) | 20 | 10 |
| 3390 | | 8s. Ran Bosilek (children's author) (centenary) | 20 | 10 |

**1140** Raiko Daskalov

**1986.** Birth Cent of Raiko Daskalov (politician).

| | | | | |
|---|---|---|---|---|
| 3391 | **1140** | 5s. brown | 20 | 10 |

**1141** "Girl with Fruit"

**1986.** 500th Birth Anniv of Titian (painter). Multicoloured.

| | | | | |
|---|---|---|---|---|
| 3392 | | 5s. Type **1141** | 20 | 15 |
| 3393 | | 13s. "Flora" | 30 | 15 |
| 3394 | | 20s. "Lucretia and Tarquin" | 35 | 20 |
| 3395 | | 30s. Caiphas and Mary Magdalene | 50 | 25 |
| 3396 | | 32s. "Toilette of Venus" (detail) | 55 | 35 |
| 3397 | | 42s. "Self-portrait" | 1·10 | 45 |
| **MS**3398 | | 105×75 mm. 1l. "Danae" (32×54 mm) | 3·00 | 2·75 |

**1142** Fiat, 1905

**1986.** Racing Cars.

| | | | | |
|---|---|---|---|---|
| 3399 | **1142** | 5s. brown, red & black | 20 | 15 |
| 3400 | - | 10s. red, orange & blk | 20 | 15 |
| 3401 | - | 25s. green, red & black | 45 | 20 |
| 3402 | - | 32s. brown, red & blk | 55 | 35 |
| 3403 | - | 40s. violet, red & black | 95 | 40 |
| 3404 | - | 42s. grey, black and red | 1·20 | 45 |

DESIGNS: 10s. Bugatti, 1928; 25s. Mercedes, 1936; 32s. Ferrari, 1952; 40s. Lotus, 1985; 42s. Maclaren, 1986.

**1143** Steam Locomotive

**1987.** 120th Anniv of Ruse–Varna Railway.

| | | | | |
|---|---|---|---|---|
| 3405 | **1143** | 5s. multicoloured | 20 | 20 |

**1144** Debelyanov

**1987.** Birth Cent of Dimcho Debelyanov (poet).

| | | | | |
|---|---|---|---|---|
| 3406 | **1144** | 5s. dp blue, yellow & bl | 20 | 10 |

**1145** Lazarus Ludwig Zamenhof (inventor)

**1987.** Centenary of Esperanto (invented language).

| | | | | |
|---|---|---|---|---|
| 3407 | **1145** | 13s. blue, yellow & grn | 30 | 20 |

**1146** The Blusher

**1987.** Edible Fungi. Multicoloured.

| | | | | |
|---|---|---|---|---|
| 3408 | | 5s. Type **1146** | 20 | 15 |
| 3409 | | 20s. Royal boletus | 30 | 20 |
| 3410 | | 30s. Red-capped scaber stalk | 45 | 35 |
| 3411 | | 32s. Shaggy ink cap | 65 | 40 |
| 3412 | | 40s. Bare-toothed russula | 75 | 45 |
| 3413 | | 60s. Chanterelle | 85 | 55 |

**1147** Worker

**1987.** 10th Trade Unions Congress, Sofia.

| | | | | |
|---|---|---|---|---|
| 3414 | **1147** | 5s. violet and red | 20 | 10 |

**1148** Silver-gilt Plate with Design of Hercules and Auge

**1987.** Treasure of Rogozen. Multicoloured.

| | | | | |
|---|---|---|---|---|
| 3415 | | 5s. Type **1148** | 20 | 15 |
| 3416 | | 8s. Silver-gilt jug with design of lioness attacking stag | 20 | 15 |
| 3417 | | 20s. Silver-gilt plate with quatrefoil design | 30 | 20 |
| 3418 | | 30s. Silver-gilt jug with design of horse rider | 35 | 25 |
| 3419 | | 32s. Silver-gilt pot with palm design | 45 | 30 |
| 3420 | | 42s. Silver jug with chariot and horses design | 55 | 35 |

**1149** Ludmila Zhivkova Featival Complex, Varna

**1987.** Modern Architecture. Sheet 107×100 mm containing T 1149 and similar horiz designs. Multicoloured.

| | | |
|---|---|---|
| **MS**3421 30s. Type **1149**; 30s. Ministry of Foreign Affairs building, Sofia; 30s. Interpred building, Sofia; 30s. Hotel, Sandanski | 2·20 | 2·20 |

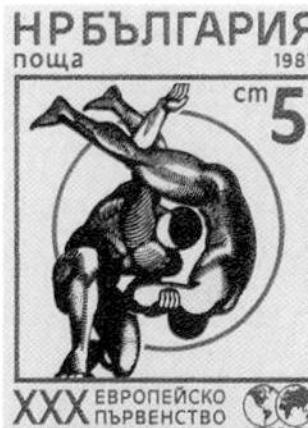


**1150** Wrestlers

**1987.** 30th European Freestyle Wrestling Championships, Turnovo.

| | | | | |
|---|---|---|---|---|
| 3422 | **1150** | 5s. lilac, red and violet | 10 | 10 |
| 3423 | - | 13s. dp blue, red & blue | 20 | 10 |

DESIGNS: 13st. Wrestlers (different).

**1151** Totem Pole

**1987.** "Capex '87" International Stamp Exhibition, Toronto.

| | | | | |
|---|---|---|---|---|
| 3424 | **1151** | 42s. multicoloured | 75 | 45 |

**1152** "X" and Flags

**1987.** 10th Fatherland Front Congress.

| | | | | |
|---|---|---|---|---|
| 3425 | **1152** | 5s. green, orange & bl | 20 | 10 |

**1153** Georgi Dimitrov and Profiles

**1987.** 15th Dimitrov Communist Youth League Congress.

| | | | | |
|---|---|---|---|---|
| 3426 | **1153** | 5s. purple, green & red | 20 | 10 |

**1154** Mask

**1987.** 8th International Festival of Humour and Satire, Gabrovo.

| | | | | |
|---|---|---|---|---|
| 3427 | **1154** | 13s. multicoloured | 30 | 20 |

**1155** Mastheads

**1987.** 60th Anniv of "Rabotnichesko Delo" (newspaper).

| | | | | |
|---|---|---|---|---|
| 3428 | **1155** | 5s. red and black | 20 | 10 |

**1156** Mariya Gigova

**1987.** 13th World Rhythmic Gymnastics Championships, Varna.

3429 **1156** 5s. blue and yellow 20 15
3430 - 8s. red and yellow 20 15
3431 - 13s. blue and stone 30 20
3432 - 25s. red and yellow 45 25
3433 - 30s. black and yellow 55 30
3434 - 42s. mauve and yellow 75 35
**MS**3435 78×87 mm. 1l. violet and ochre 2·20 2·20

DESIGNS: 8s. Iliana Raeva; 13s. Aneliya Ralenkova; 25s. Dilyana Georgieva; 30s. Liliya Ignatova; 42s. Bianka Panova; 1l. Neshka Robeva.

**1157** Man breaking Chains around Globe and Kolarov

**1987.** 110th Birth Anniv of Vasil Kolarov (Prime Minister 1949–50).

3436 **1157** 5s. multicoloured 20 10

**1158** Stela Blagoeva

**1987.** Birth Centenary of Stela Blagoeva.

3437 **1158** 5s. brown and pink 20 20

**1159** Levski

**1987.** 150th Birth Anniv of Vasil Levski (revolutionary).

3438 **1159** 5s. brown and green 10 10
3439 - 13s. green and brown 20 10

DESIGN: 13s. Levski and Bulgarian Revolutionary Central Committee emblem.

**1160** Roe Deer

**1987.** Stags. Multicoloured.

3440 5s. Type **1160** 20 15
3441 10s. Elk (horiz) 20 15
3442 32s. Fallow deer 55 25
3443 40s. Sika deer 65 35
3444 42s. Red deer (horiz) 75 45
3445 60s. Reindeer 1·00 55
**MS**3445a 145×131 mm. Nos. 3340/5. Imperf 3·75 3·75

**1161** Barbed Wire as Dove

**1987.** International Namibia Day.

3446 **1161** 13s. black, red & orge 25 10

**1162** Kirkov

**1987.** 120th Birth Anniv of Georgi Kirkov (pseudonym Maistora) (politician).

3447 **1162** 5s. red and pink 20 10

**1163** "Phacelia tanacetifolia"

**1987.** Flowers. Multicoloured.

3448 5s. Type **1163** 20 15
3449 10s. Sunflower 20 15
3450 30s. False acacia 50 30
3451 32s. Dutch lavender 55 35
3452 42s. Small-leaved lime 75 45
3453 60s. "Onobrychis sativa" 1·10 55

**1164** Mil Mi-8 Helicopter, Tupolev Tu-154 and Antonov An-12 Aircraft

**1987.** 40th Anniv of Balkanair.

3454 **1164** 25s. multicoloured 55 20

**1165** 1879 5c. Stamp

**1987.** "Bulgaria '89" International Stamp Exhibition, Sofia (1st issue).

3455 **1165** 13s. multicoloured 20 10

See also Nos. 3569, 3579/82 and 3602/5.

**1166** Copenhagen Town Hall

**1987.** "Hafnia '87" International Stamp Exhibition, Copenhagen.

3456 **1166** 42s. multicoloured 75 55

**1167** "Portrait of Girl" (Stefan Ivanov)

**1987.** Paintings in Sofia National Gallery. Mult.

3457 5s. Type **1167** 20 15
3458 8s. "Woman carrying Grapes" (Bencho Obreshkov) 20 15
3459 20s. "Portrait of a Woman wearing a Straw Hat" (David Perez) 35 20
3460 25s. "Women listening to Marimba" (Kiril Tsonev) 45 30
3461 32s. "Boy with Harmonica" (Nenko Balkanski) 65 35
3462 60s. "Rumyana" (Vasil Stoilov) 1·20 55

**1168** Battle Scene

**1987.** 75th Anniv of Balkan War.

3463 **1168** 5s. black, stone and red 20 10

**1169** Emblem

**1987.** 30th Anniv of International Atomic Energy Agency.

3464 **1169** 13s. blue, green and red 35 20

**1170** Mastheads

**1987.** 95th Anniv of "Rabotnik", 90th Anniv of "Rabotnicheski Vestnik" and 60th Anniv of "Rabotnichesko Delo" (newspapers).

3465 **1170** 5s. red, blue and gold 20 10

**1171** Winter Wren

**1987.** Birds. Multicoloured.

3466 5s. Type **1171** 20 15
3467 13s. Yellowhammer 20 15
3468 20s. Eurasian nuthatch 45 20
3469 30s. Blackbird 65 35
3470 42s. Hawfinch 1·00 45
3471 60s. White-throated dipper 1·40 55

**1172** "Vega" Automatic Space Station

**1987.** 30th Anniv of Soviet Space Exploration. Sheet 98×98 mm containing T 1172 and similar horiz design.

**MS**3472 50s. blue, orange and purple (Type **1172**); 50s. deep blue, blue and purple ("Soyuz" spacecraft docking with "Mir" space station) 2·75 2·75

**1173** Lenin and Revolutionary

**1987.** 70th Anniv of Russian Revolution.

3473 **1173** 5s. purple and red 10 10
3474 - 13s. blue and red 20 10

DESIGN: 13s. Lenin and cosmonaut.

**1174** Biathlon

**1987.** Winter Olympic Games, Calgary. Mult.

3475 5s. Type **1174** 20 15
3476 13s. Slalom 20 15
3477 30s. Figure skating (women's) 55 35
3478 42s. Four-man bobsleigh 85 55
**MS**3479 65×87 mm. 1l. Ice hockey 2·20 2·20

**1175** "Socfilex" Emblem within Folk-design Ornament

**1987.** New Year. Multicoloured.

3480 5s. Type **1175** 10 10
3481 13s. Emblem within flower ornament 20 10

**1176** Helsinki Conference Centre

**1987.** European Security and Co-operation Conference Review Meeting, Vienna. Sheet 140×100 mm containing T 1176 and similar vert designs.

**MS**3482 50s. lavender, brown and red; 50s. multicoloured (Map of Europe); 50s. multicoloured (Vienna Conference Centre) 5·00 5·00

**1177** Kabakchiev

**1988.** 110th Birth Anniv of Khristo Kabakchiev (Communist Party official).

3483 **1177** 5s. multicoloured 20 10

**1178** "Scilla bythynica"

**1988.** Marsh Flowers. Multicoloured.

3484 5s. Type **1178** 10 10
3485 10s. "Geum rhodopaeum" 15 10
3486 13s. "Caltha polypetala" 20 10
3487 25s. Fringed water-lily 45 20
3488 30s. "Cortusa matthioli" 55 30
3489 42s. Water soldier 65 45

**1179** Commander on Horseback

**1988.** 110th Anniv of Liberation from Turkey. Multicoloured.

| | | | |
|---|---|---|---|
| 3490 | 5s. Type **1179** | 10 | 10 |
| 3491 | 13s. Soldiers | 20 | 10 |

**1180** Emblem

**1988.** Public Sector Workers' 8th International Congress, Sofia.

| | | | | |
|---|---|---|---|---|
| 3492 | **1180** | 13s. multicoloured | 20 | 10 |

**1181** "Yantra", 1888

**1988.** Centenary of State Railways. Locomotives. Multicoloured.

| | | | |
|---|---|---|---|
| 3493 | 5s. Type **1181** | 15 | 10 |
| 3494 | 13s. "Khristo Botev", 1905 | 20 | 15 |
| 3495 | 25s. Steam locomotive No. 807, 1918 | 55 | 20 |
| 3496 | 32s. Class 46 steam locomotive, 1943 | 65 | 35 |
| 3497 | 42s. Diesel locomotive, 1964 | 85 | 45 |
| 3498 | 60s. Electric locomotive, 1979 | 1·40 | 55 |

**1182** Ivan Nedyalkov (Shablin)

**1988.** Post Office Anti-fascist Heroes.

| | | | | |
|---|---|---|---|---|
| 3499 | **1182** | 5s. light brown and brown | 10 | 10 |
| 3500 | - | 8s. grey and blue | 10 | 10 |
| 3501 | - | 10s. green and olive | 15 | 10 |
| 3502 | - | 13s. pink and red | 20 | 10 |

DESIGNS: 8s. Delcho Spasov; 10s. Nikola Ganchev (Gudzho); 13s. Ganka Rasheva (Boika).

**1183** Traikov

**1988.** 90th Birth Anniv of Georgi Traikov (politician).

| | | | | |
|---|---|---|---|---|
| 3503 | **1183** | 5s. orange and brown | 20 | 10 |

**1184** Red Cross, Red Crescent and Globe

**1988.** 125th Anniv of International Red Cross.

| | | | | |
|---|---|---|---|---|
| 3504 | **1184** | 13s. multicoloured | 20 | 10 |

**1185** Girl

**1988.** 4th "Banners for Peace" Children's Meeting, Sofia. Children's paintings. Multicoloured.

| | | | |
|---|---|---|---|
| 3505 | 5s. Type **1185** | 10 | 10 |
| 3506 | 8s. Artist at work | 20 | 10 |
| 3507 | 13s. Circus (horiz) | 35 | 15 |
| 3508 | 20s. Kite flying (horiz) | 45 | 20 |
| 3509 | 32s. Accordion player | 55 | 30 |
| 3510 | 42s. Cosmonaut | 65 | 35 |
| **MS**3511 | 86×90 mm. 50s. Emblem with film frame (Youth Film Festival) (horiz) | 1·10 | 1·10 |

**1186** Marx

**1988.** 170th Birth Anniv of Karl Marx.

| | | | | |
|---|---|---|---|---|
| 3512 | **1186** | 13s. red, black & yellow | 20 | 10 |

**1187** Herring Gull

**1988.** Birds. Multicoloured.

| | | | |
|---|---|---|---|
| 3513 | 5s. Type **1187** | 20 | 10 |
| 3514 | 5s. White stork | 20 | 10 |
| 3515 | 8s. Grey heron | 40 | 15 |
| 3516 | 8s. Carrion crow | 40 | 15 |
| 3517 | 10s. Northern goshawk | 55 | 20 |
| 3518 | 42s. Eagle owl | 1·60 | 45 |

**1188** African Elephant

**1988.** Centenary of Sofia Zoo. Multicoloured.

| | | | |
|---|---|---|---|
| 3519 | 5s. Type **1188** | 10 | 10 |
| 3520 | 13s. White rhinoceros | 20 | 10 |
| 3521 | 25s. Hunting dog | 55 | 20 |
| 3522 | 30s. Eastern white pelican | 65 | 35 |
| 3523 | 32s. Abyssinian ground hornbill | 75 | 45 |
| 3524 | 42s. Snowy owl | 1·00 | 65 |

**1189** "Soyuz TM" Spacecraft, Flags and Globe

**1988.** 2nd Soviet–Bulgarian Space Flight. Mult.

| | | | |
|---|---|---|---|
| 3525 | 5s. Type **1189** | 10 | 10 |
| 3526 | 13s. Rocket on globe | 20 | 10 |

**1190** Young Inventor

**1988.** International Young Inventors' Exhibition, Plovdiv.

| | | | | |
|---|---|---|---|---|
| 3527 | **1190** | 13s. multicoloured | 20 | 10 |

**1191** 1856 Handstamp of Russian Duchy of Finland

**1988.** "Finlandia '88" International Stamp Exhibition, Helsinki.

| | | | | |
|---|---|---|---|---|
| 3528 | **1191** | 30s. blue and red | 45 | 35 |

**1192** Player taking Corner Kick

**1988.** 8th European Football Championship, West Germany. Multicoloured.

| | | | |
|---|---|---|---|
| 3529 | 5s. Type **1192** | 10 | 10 |
| 3530 | 13s. Goalkeeper and player | 20 | 15 |
| 3531 | 30s. Referee and player | 65 | 35 |
| 3532 | 42s. Player with trophy | 85 | 45 |
| **MS**3533 | 90×69 mm. 1l. Stadium (horiz) | 2·20 | 2·20 |

**1193** "Portrait of Child"

**1988.** 2nd Death Anniv of Dechko Uzunov (painter). Multicoloured.

| | | | |
|---|---|---|---|
| 3534 | 5s. Type **1193** | 10 | 10 |
| 3535 | 13s. "Portrait of Mariya Vasileva" | 35 | 15 |
| 3536 | 30s. "Self-portrait" | 65 | 20 |

**1194** Valentina Tereshkova

**1988.** 25th Anniv of First Woman in Space. Sheet 87×56 mm.

| | | | | |
|---|---|---|---|---|
| **MS**3537 | **1194** | 1l. pink and blue | 2·20 | 2·20 |

**1195** "St. John"

**1988.** Icons from Kurdzhali. Multicoloured.

| | | | |
|---|---|---|---|
| 3538 | 5s. Type **1195** | 20 | 10 |
| 3539 | 8s. "St. George and Dragon" | 20 | 10 |

**1196** High Jumping

**1988.** Olympic Games, Seoul. Multicoloured.

| | | | |
|---|---|---|---|
| 3540 | 5s. Type **1196** | 10 | 10 |
| 3541 | 13s. Weightlifting | 20 | 10 |
| 3542 | 30s. Wrestling | 55 | 30 |
| 3543 | 42s. Gymnastics | 85 | 35 |
| **MS**3544 | 115×75 mm. 1l. Volleyball | 2·20 | 2·20 |

**1197** Dimitur and Karadzha

**1988.** 120th Death Anniv of Khadzhi Dimitur and Stefan Karadzha (revolutionaries).

| | | | | |
|---|---|---|---|---|
| 3545 | **1197** | 5s. green, black & brn | 20 | 10 |

**1198** Magazines

**1988.** 30th Anniv of "Problems of Peace and Socialism" (magazine).

| | | | | |
|---|---|---|---|---|
| 3546 | **1198** | 13s. multicoloured | 20 | 10 |

**1199** "The Dead Tree" (Roland Udo)

**1988.** Paintings in Lyudmila Zhivkova Art Gallery. Multicoloured.

| | | | |
|---|---|---|---|
| 3547 | 30s. Type **1199** | 55 | 35 |
| 3548 | 30s. "Algiers Harbour" (Albert Marque) | 55 | 35 |
| 3549 | 30s. "Portrait of Hermine David" (Jule Pasquin) | 55 | 35 |
| 3550 | 30s. "Madonna and Child with two Saints" (Giovanni Rosso) | 55 | 35 |

**1200** University Building

**1988.** Centenary of St. Clement of Ohrid University, Sofia.

| | | | | |
|---|---|---|---|---|
| 3551 | **1200** | 5s. black, yellow & grn | 20 | 10 |

**1201** Czechoslovakia 1918 Stamp Design

**1988.** "Praga '88" International Stamp Exhibition, Prague.

| | | | | |
|---|---|---|---|---|
| 3552 | **1201** | 25s. red and blue | 45 | 35 |

**1202** Korea 1884 5m. Stamp

**1988.** "Olymphilex '88" Olympic Stamps Exhibition, Seoul.
3553 **1202** 62s. red and green 1·30 1·10

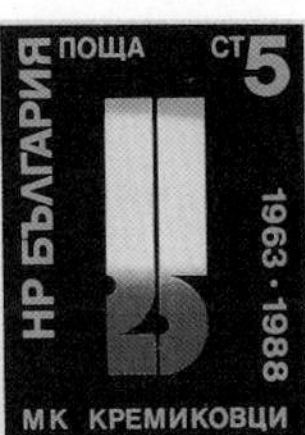


**1203** Anniversary Emblem

**1988.** 25th Anniv of Kremikovtsi Steel Mills.
3554 **1203** 5s. violet, red and blue 20 10

**1204** Parliament Building, Sofia, and Map

**1988.** 80th Interparliamentary Conference, Sofia.
3555 **1204** 13s. blue and red 35 15

**1205** Chalice, Glinena

**1988.** Kurdzhali Culture. Multicoloured.
3556 5s. Type **1205** 20 10
3557 8s. Part of ruined fortifications, Perperikon (vert) 20 10

**1206** Soldiers

**1988.** 300th Anniv of Chiprovtsi Rising.
3558 **1206** 5s. multicoloured 20 10

**1207** Brown Bear

**1988.** Bears. Multicoloured.
3559 5s. Type **1207** 10 10
3560 8s. Polar bear 10 10
3561 13s. Sloth bear 20 10
3562 20s. Sun bear 45 20
3563 32s. Asiatic black bear 65 30
3564 42s. Spectacled bear 1·10 35

**1208** Emblem

**1988.** 80th Council of Mutual Economic Aid Transport Commission Meeting, Sofia.
3565 **1208** 13s. red and black 35 15

**1209** Emblem

**1988.** World Ecoforum.
3566 **1209** 20s. multicoloured 45 20

**1210** Amphitheatre, Plovdiv

**1988.** "Plovdiv '88" National Stamp Exhibition.
3567 **1210** 5s. multicoloured 20 10

**1211** Transmission Towers

**1988.** 25th Anniv of Radio and Television.
3568 **1211** 5s. green, blue & brown 20 10

**1212** 1879 5c. Stamp

**1988.** "Bulgaria '89" International Stamp Exhibition (2nd issue).
3569 **1212** 42s. orange, blk & mve 65 55

**1213** "Ruse" (river boat)

**1988.** 40th Anniv of Danube Commission. Sheet 104×124 mm containing T 1213 and similar horiz design. Multicoloured.
**MS**3570 1l. Type **1213**; 1l. *Al. Stamboliiski* (river cruiser) 4·25 4·50

**1214** Children and Cars

**1988.** Road Safety Campaign.
3571 **1214** 5s. multicoloured 20 10

**1215** Rila Hotel, Borovets

**1988.** Hotels. Multicoloured.
3572 5s. Type **1215** 20 15
3573 8s. Pirin Hotel, Bansko 20 15
3574 13s. Shtastlivetsa Hotel, Vitosha 35 20
3575 30s. Perelik Hotel, Pamporovo 55 30

**1216** Tree Decoration

**1988.** New Year. Multicoloured.
3576 5s. Type **1216** 10 10
3577 13s. "Bulgaria '89" emblem, tree and decorations 20 10

**1217** Space Shuttle "Buran"

**1988.** Energiya–Buran Space Flight. Sheet 102×67 mm.
**MS**3578 **1217** 1l. blue 2·20 2·00

**1218** Mail Coach

**1988.** "Bulgaria '89" International Stamp Exhibition, Sofia (3rd issue). Mail Transport. Multicoloured.
3579 25s. Type **1218** 55 20
3580 25s. Paddle-steamer 55 20
3581 25s. Lorry 55 20
3582 25s. Biplane 55 20

**1219** India 1947 1½a. Independence Stamp

**1989.** "India 89" International Stamp Exhibition, New Delhi.
3583 **1219** 62s. green and orange 1·10 90

**1220** France 1850 10c. Ceres Stamp

**1989.** "Philexfrance '89" International Stamp Exhibition, Paris.
3584 **1220** 42s. brown and blue 65 55

**1221** Slalom

**1989.** "Sofia '89" University Winter Games, Sofia. Sheet 84×142 mm containing T 1221 and similar vert designs. Multicoloured. Imperf.
**MS**3585 25s. Type **1221**; 25s. Ice hockey; 25s. Biathlon; 25s. Speed skating 2·20 2·20

**1222** Don Quixote (sculpture, House of Humour and Satire)

**1989.** International Festival of Humour and Satire, Gabrovo.
3586 **1222** 13s. multicoloured 35 15

**1223** "Ramonda serbica"

**1989.** Flowers. Multicoloured.
3587 5s. Type **1223** 10 10
3588 10s. "Paeonia maskula" 20 10
3589 25s. "Viola perinensis" 45 20
3590 30s. "Dracunculus vulgaris" 55 35
3591 42s. "Tulipa splendens" 85 45
3592 60s. "Rindera umbellata" 1·10 55

**1224** Common Noctule Bat

**1989.** Bats. Multicoloured.
3593 5s. Type **1224** 20 15
3594 13s. Greater horseshoe bat 35 20
3595 30s. Large mouse-eared bat 1·10 45
3596 42s. Particoloured frosted bat 1·60 1·30

**1225** Stamboliiski

**1989.** 110th Birth Anniv of Aleksandur Stamboliiski (Prime Minister 1919–23).
3597 **1225** 5s. black and orange 20 10

**1226** Launch of "Soyuz 33"

**1989.** 10th Anniv of Soviet–Bulgarian Space Flight. Sheet 130×90 mm containing T 1226 and similar vert design. Multicoloured.
**MS**3598 50s. Type **1226**; 50s. Cosmonauts Nicolai Rukavishnikov and Georgi Ivanov 2·20 2·20

**1227** Young Inventor

**1989.** International Young Inventors' Exhibition, Plovdiv.
3599 **1227** 5s. multicoloured 20 10

**1228** Stanke Dimitrov-Marek (Party activist)

**1989.** Birth Centenaries.
3600 **1228** 5s. red and black 20 10
3601 - 5s. red and black 20 10
DESIGN: No. 3601, Petko Yenev (revolutionary).

**1229** "John the Baptist" (Toma Vishanov)

**1989.** "Bulgaria '89" International Stamp Exhibition, Sofia (4th issue). Icons. Multicoloured.
3602 30s. Type **1229** 55 20
3603 30s. "St. Dimitur" (Ivan Terziev) 55 20
3604 30s. "Archangel Michael" (Dimitur Molerov) 55 20
3605 30s. "Madonna and Child" (Toma Vishanov) 55 20

**1230** Fax Machine and Woman reading letter

**1989.** 110th Anniv of Bulgarian Post and Telegraph Services. Multicoloured.
3606 5s. Type **1230** 20 15
3607 8s. Telex machine and old telegraph machine 20 15
3608 35s. Modern and old telephones 65 45
3609 42s. Dish aerial and old radio 85 55

**1231** "Nike in Quadriga" (relief)

**1989.** 58th International Philatelic Federation Congress, Sofia. Sheet 87×120 mm.
**MS**3610 **1231** 1l. multicoloured 2·20 2·20

**1232** A. P. Aleksandrov, A. Ya. Solovov and V. P. Savinikh

**1989.** Air. "Soyuz TM5" Soviet-Bulgarian Space Flight.
3611 **1232** 13s. multicoloured 35 20

**1233** Party Programme

**1989.** 70th Anniv of First Bulgarian Communist Party Congress, Sofia.
3612 **1233** 5s. blk, red & dp red 20 10

**1234** Sofronii Vrachanski (250th anniv)

**1989.** Writers' Birth Anniversaries.
3613 **1234** 5s. green, brown & blk 20 10
3614 - 5s. green, brown & blk 20 10
DESIGN: No. 3614, Iliya Bluskov (150th anniv).

**1235** Birds

**1989.** Bicentenary of French Revolution. Each black, red and blue.
3615 13s. Type **1235** 35 15
3616 30s. Jean-Paul Marat 55 20
3617 42s. Robespierre 75 35

**1236** Gymnastics

**1989.** 7th Friendly Armies Summer Spartakiad. Multicoloured.
3618 5s. Type **1236** 10 10
3619 13s. Show jumping 35 15
3620 30s. Long jumping 55 20
3621 42s. Shooting 75 45

**1237** Aprilov

**1989.** Birth Bicent of Vasil Aprilov (educationist).
3622 **1237** 8s. lt blue, blue & blk 20 10

**1238** Zagorchinov

**1989.** Birth Centenary of Stoyan Zagorchinov (writer).
3623 **1238** 10s. turq, brown & blk 20 10

**1239** Woman in Kayak

**1989.** Canoeing and Kayak Championships, Plovdiv. Multicoloured.
3624 13s. Type **1239** 35 20
3625 30s. Man in kayak 75 35

**1240** Felix Nadar taking Photograph from his Balloon "Le Geant" (1863) and Airship "Graf Zeppelin" over Alexsandr Nevski Cathedral, Sofia

**1989.** 150th Anniv of Photography.
3626 **1240** 42s. black, stone & yell 1·10 45

**1241** Lammergeier and Lynx

**1989.** Centenary of Natural History Museum.
3627 **1241** 13s. multicoloured 35 30

**1242** Soldiers

**1989.** 45th Anniv of Fatherland Front Government. Multicoloured.
3628 5s. Type **1242** 10 10
3629 8s. Welcoming officers 10 10
3630 13s. Crowd of youths 35 15

**1243** Lyubomir Dardzhikov

**1989.** 48th Death Anniversaries of Post Office War Heroes. Multicoloured.
3631 5s. Type **1243** 10 10
3632 8s. Ivan Bankov Dobrev 10 10
3633 13s. Nestor Antonov 35 15

**1244** Yasenov

**1989.** Birth Cent of Khisto Yasenov (writer).
3634 **1244** 8s. grey, brown & blk 20 10

**1245** Lorry leaving Weighbridge

**1989.** 21st Transport Congress, Sofia.
3635 **1245** 42s. blue & deep blue 1·10 65

**1246** Nehru

**1989.** Birth Centenary of Jawaharlal Nehru (Indian statesman).
3636 **1246** 13s. yellow, brn & blk 35 20

**1247** Cranes flying

**1989.** Ecology Congress of European Security and Co-operation Conference, Sofia. Sheet 130×85 mm containing T 1247 and similar vert design. Multicoloured.
**MS**3637 50s. Type **1247**; 1l. Cranes flying (different) 4·25 4·50

**1248** Javelin Sand Boa

**1989.** Snakes. Multicoloured.
3638 5s. Type **1248** 10 10
3639 10s. Aesculapian snake 20 15
3640 25s. Leopard snake 55 35
3641 30s. Four-lined rat snake 65 45
3642 42s. Cat snake 1·00 55
3643 60s. Whip snake 1·30 65

**1249** Tiger and Balloon of Flags

**1989.** Young Inventors' Exhibition, Plovdiv.
3644 **1249** 13s. multicoloured 35 20

**1250** Boy on Skateboard

**1989.** Children's Games. Sheet 100×120 mm containing T 1250 and similar vert designs. Multicoloured.
**MS**3645 30s.+15s. Type **1250**; 30s.+15s. Girl with ball and doll; 30s.+15s. Girl jumping over ropes; 30s.+15s. Boy with toy train 3·75 4·00

**1251** Goalkeeper saving Ball

**1989.** World Cup Football Championship, Italy (1990) (1st issue). Multicoloured.

| | | | |
|---|---|---|---|
| 3646 | 5s. Type **1251** | 10 | 10 |
| 3647 | 13s. Player tackling | 20 | 10 |
| 3648 | 30s. Player heading ball | 55 | 35 |
| 3649 | 42s. Player kicking ball | 1·30 | 55 |
| **MS**3650 | 109×54 mm. 50s. Player tackling; 50s. Players | 2·20 | 2·00 |

See also Nos. 3675/**MS**3679.

**1252** Gliders

**1989.** 82nd International Airsports Federation General Conference, Varna. Aerial Sports. Mult.

| | | | |
|---|---|---|---|
| 3651 | 5s. Type **1252** | 10 | 10 |
| 3652 | 13s. Hang gliding | 35 | 20 |
| 3653 | 30s. Parachutist landing | 75 | 40 |
| 3654 | 42s. Free falling parachutist | 85 | 45 |

**1253** Children on Road Crossing

**1989.** Road Safety.

| | | | | |
|---|---|---|---|---|
| 3655 | **1253** | 5s. multicoloured | 20 | 10 |

**1254** Santa Claus's Sleigh

**1989.** New Year. Multicoloured.

| | | | |
|---|---|---|---|
| 3656 | 5s. Type **1254** | 20 | 15 |
| 3657 | 13s. Snowman | 35 | 20 |

**1255** European Shorthair

**1989.** Cats.

| | | | | |
|---|---|---|---|---|
| 3658 | **1255** | 5s. black and yellow | 20 | 15 |
| 3659 | - | 5s. black and grey | 20 | 15 |
| 3660 | - | 8s. black and yellow | 20 | 15 |
| 3661 | - | 10s. black & brown | 35 | 20 |
| 3662 | - | 10s. black and blue | 35 | 20 |
| 3663 | - | 13s. black and red | 45 | 25 |

DESIGNS—HORIZ: No. 3659, Persian; 3660, European shorthair (different); 3662, Persian (different). VERT: No. 3661, Persian (different); 3663, Siamese.

**1256** Christopher Columbus and "Santa Maria"

**1990.** Navigators and their Ships. Multicoloured.

| | | | |
|---|---|---|---|
| 3664 | 5s. Type **1256** | 20 | 20 |
| 3665 | 8s. Vasco da Gama and "Sao Gabriel" | 20 | 20 |
| 3666 | 13s. Ferdinand Magellan and "Vitoria" | 25 | 20 |
| 3667 | 32s. Francis Drake and "Golden Hind" | 65 | 45 |
| 3668 | 42s. Henry Hudson and "Discoverie" | 1·00 | 55 |
| 3669 | 60s. James Cook and H.M.S. "Endeavour" | 1·30 | 65 |

**1257** Banner

**1990.** Centenary of Esperanto (invented language) in Bulgaria.

| | | | | |
|---|---|---|---|---|
| 3670 | **1257** | 10s. stone, green & blk | 20 | 10 |

**1258** "Portrait of Madeleine Rono" (Maurice Brianchon)

**1990.** Paintings. Multicoloured.

| | | | |
|---|---|---|---|
| 3671 | 30s. Type **1258** | 75 | 45 |
| 3672 | 30s. "Still Life" (Suzanne Valadon) | 75 | 45 |
| 3673 | 30s. "Portrait of a Woman" (Moise Kisling) | 75 | 45 |
| 3674 | 30s. "Portrait of a Woman" (Giovanni Boltraffio) | 75 | 45 |

**1259** Players

**1990.** World Cup Football Championship, Italy.

| | | | | |
|---|---|---|---|---|
| 3675 | **1259** | 5s. multicoloured | 20 | 15 |
| 3676 | - | 13s. multicoloured | 35 | 20 |
| 3677 | - | 30s. multicoloured | 65 | 35 |
| 3678 | - | 42s. multicoloured | 1·10 | 45 |
| **MS**3679 | | 80×125 mm. 2×50s. multi-coloured | 2·75 | 2·50 |

DESIGNS: 13 to 50s. Various match scenes.

**1260** Bavaria 1849 1k. Stamp

**1990.** "Essen 90" International Stamp Fair.

| | | | | |
|---|---|---|---|---|
| 3680 | **1260** | 42s. black and red | 85 | 80 |

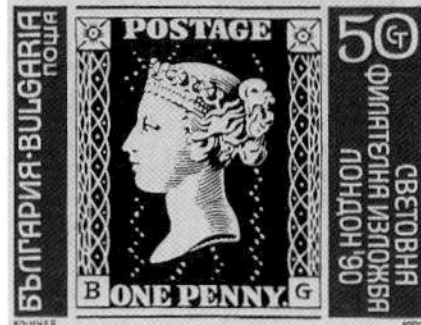

**1261** Penny Black

**1990.** "Stamp World London 90" International Stamp Exhibition. Sheet 90×140 mm containing T 1261 and similar horiz design.

| | | | |
|---|---|---|---|
| **MS**3681 | 50s. black and blue (Type **1261**); 50s. black and red (Sir Rowland Hill (instigator of postage stamps)) | 2·20 | 2·10 |

**1262** "100" and Rainbow

**1990.** Centenary of Co-operative Farming.

| | | | | |
|---|---|---|---|---|
| 3682 | **1262** | 5s. multicoloured | 20 | 10 |

**1263** "Elderly Couple at Rest"

**1990.** Birth Centenary of Dimitur Chorbadzhiiski-Chudomir (artist).

| | | | | |
|---|---|---|---|---|
| 3683 | **1263** | 5s. multicoloured | 20 | 10 |

**1264** Map

**1990.** Centenary of Labour Day.

| | | | | |
|---|---|---|---|---|
| 3684 | **1264** | 10s. multicoloured | 20 | 15 |

**1265** Emblem

**1990.** 125th Anniv of ITU.

| | | | | |
|---|---|---|---|---|
| 3685 | **1265** | 20s. blue, red & black | 55 | 35 |

**1266** Belgium 1849 10c. "Epaulettes" Stamp

**1990.** "Belgica 90" International Stamp Exhibition, Brussels.

| | | | | |
|---|---|---|---|---|
| 3686 | **1266** | 30s. brown and green | 65 | 55 |

**1267** Lamartine and his House

**1990.** Birth Bicentenary of Alphonse de Lamartine (poet).

| | | | | |
|---|---|---|---|---|
| 3687 | **1267** | 20s. multicoloured | 55 | 35 |

**1268** Brontosaurus

**1990.** Prehistoric Animals. Multicoloured.

| | | | |
|---|---|---|---|
| 3688 | 5s. Type **1268** | 20 | 15 |
| 3689 | 8s. Stegosaurus | 20 | 15 |
| 3690 | 13s. Edaphosaurus | 35 | 20 |
| 3691 | 25s. Rhamphorhynchus | 65 | 45 |
| 3692 | 32s. Protoceratops | 85 | 55 |
| 3693 | 42s. Triceratops | 1·30 | 65 |

**1269** Swimming

**1990.** Olympic Games, Barcelona (1992) (1st issue). Multicoloured.

| | | | |
|---|---|---|---|
| 3694 | 5s. Type **1269** | 10 | 10 |
| 3695 | 13s. Handball | 35 | 20 |
| 3696 | 30s. Hurdling | 65 | 40 |
| 3697 | 42s. Cycling | 1·10 | 45 |
| **MS**3698 | 77×117 mm. 50s. Tennis player serving; 50s. Tennis player waiting to receive ball | 2·75 | 2·20 |

See also Nos. 3840/**MS**3844.

**1270** Southern Festoon

**1990.** Butterflies and Moths. Multicoloured.

| | | | |
|---|---|---|---|
| 3699 | 5s. Type **1270** | 20 | 15 |
| 3700 | 10s. Jersey tiger moth | 20 | 15 |
| 3701 | 20s. Willow-herb hawk moth | 45 | 20 |
| 3702 | 30s. Striped hawk moth | 65 | 45 |
| 3703 | 42s. "Thecla betulae" | 75 | 65 |
| 3704 | 60s. Cynthia's fritillary | 1·30 | 90 |

**1271** Airbus Industrie A310 Jetliner

**1990.** Aircraft. Multicoloured.

| | | | |
|---|---|---|---|
| 3705 | 5s. Type **1271** | 20 | 15 |
| 3706 | 10s. Tupolev Tu-204 | 20 | 15 |
| 3707 | 25s. Concorde | 55 | 35 |
| 3708 | 30s. Douglas DC-9 | 60 | 40 |
| 3709 | 42s. Ilyushin Il-86 | 75 | 55 |
| 3710 | 60s. Boeing 747-300/400 | 1·30 | 90 |

No. 3705 is wrongly inscribed Airbus "A300".

**1272** Iosif I

**1990.** 150th Birth Anniv of Exarch Iosif I.

| | | | | |
|---|---|---|---|---|
| 3711 | **1272** | 5s. mauve, black & grn | 20 | 10 |

1273 Road and UN Emblem within Triangles

1990. International Road Safety Year.

| | | | | |
|---|---|---|---|---|
| 3712 | 1273 | 5s. multicoloured | 20 | 10 |

1274 Putting the Shot

1990. "Olymphilex '90" Olympic Stamps Exhibition, Varna. Multicoloured.

| | | | |
|---|---|---|---|
| 3713 | 5s. Type 1274 | 20 | 15 |
| 3714 | 13s. Throwing the discus | 20 | 15 |
| 3715 | 42s. Throwing the hammer | 75 | 55 |
| 3716 | 60s. Throwing the javelin | 1·10 | 90 |

1275 "Sputnik" (first artificial satellite, 1957)

1990. Space Research. Multicoloured.

| | | | |
|---|---|---|---|
| 3717 | 5s. Type 1275 | 10 | 10 |
| 3718 | 8s. "Vostok" and Yuri Gagarin (first manned flight, 1961) | 20 | 15 |
| 3719 | 10s. Aleksei Leonov spacewalking from "Voskhod 2" (first spacewalk, 1965) | 25 | 20 |
| 3720 | 20s. "Soyuz"–"Apollo" link, 1975 | 45 | 35 |
| 3721 | 42s. Space shuttle "Columbia", 1981 | 1·10 | 55 |
| 3722 | 60s. Space probe "Galileo" | 1·30 | 90 |
| MS3723 | 90×71 mm. 1l. Neil Armstrong from "Apollo 11" on lunar surface (first manned moon landing, 1969) (28×53 mm) | 2·20 | 2·20 |

1276 St. Clement of Ohrid

1990. 1150th Birth Anniv of St. Clement of Ohrid.

| | | | | |
|---|---|---|---|---|
| 3724 | 1276 | 5s. brown, black & grn | 20 | 10 |

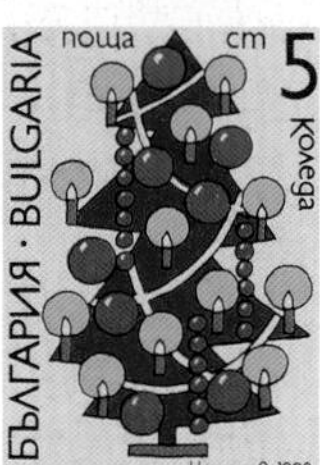
1277 Tree

1990. Christmas. Multicoloured.

| | | | |
|---|---|---|---|
| 3725 | 5s. Type 1277 | 20 | 10 |
| 3726 | 20s. Father Christmas | 45 | 20 |

1278 Skaters

1991. European Figure Skating Championships, Sofia.

| | | | | |
|---|---|---|---|---|
| 3727 | 1278 | 15s. multicoloured | 35 | 20 |

1279 Chicken

1991. Farm Animals.

| | | | | |
|---|---|---|---|---|
| 3728 | - | 20s. brown and black | 20 | 10 |
| 3729 | - | 25s. blue and black | 20 | 10 |
| 3730 | 1279 | 30s. brown and black | 20 | 10 |
| 3731 | - | 40s. brown and black | 35 | 20 |
| 3732 | - | 62s. green and black | 55 | 45 |
| 3733 | - | 86s. red and black | 75 | 45 |
| 3734 | - | 95s. mauve and black | 80 | 50 |
| 3735 | - | 1l. brown and black | 85 | 55 |
| 3736 | - | 2l. green and black | 1·60 | 1·10 |
| 3737 | - | 5l. violet and black | 2·75 | 2·00 |
| 3738 | - | 10l. blue and black | 5·00 | 2·75 |

DESIGNS: 20s. Sheep; 25s. Goose; 40s. Horse; 62, 95s. Billy goat; 86s. Sow; 1l. Donkey; 2l. Bull; 5l. Common turkey; 10l. Cow.

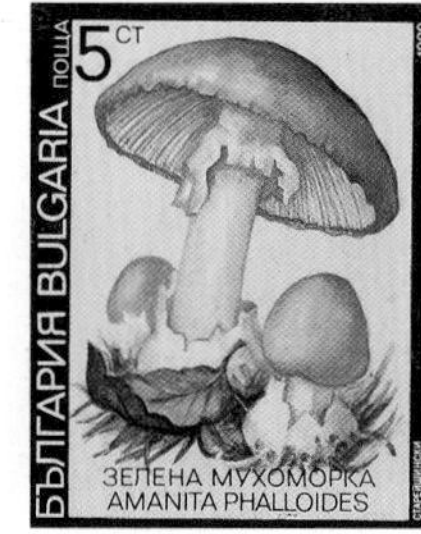
1280 Death Cap

1991. Fungi. Multicoloured.

| | | | |
|---|---|---|---|
| 3746 | 5s. Type 1280 | 10 | 10 |
| 3747 | 10s. "Amanita verna" | 25 | 20 |
| 3748 | 20s. Panther cap | 25 | 20 |
| 3749 | 32s. Fly agaric | 35 | 25 |
| 3750 | 42s. Beefsteak morel | 45 | 35 |
| 3751 | 60s. Satan's mushroom | 1·20 | 50 |

1281 "Good Day" (Paul Gauguin)

1991. Paintings. Multicoloured.

| | | | |
|---|---|---|---|
| 3752 | 20s. Type 1281 | 25 | 20 |
| 3753 | 43s. "Madame Dobini" (Edgar Degas) | 35 | 25 |
| 3754 | 62s. "Peasant Woman" (Camille Pissarro) | 60 | 35 |
| 3755 | 67s. "Woman with Black hair" (Edouard Manet) | 70 | 50 |
| 3756 | 80s. "Blue Vase" (Paul Cezanne) | 1·00 | 70 |
| 3757 | 2l. "Madame Samari" (Pierre Auguste Renoir) | 2·00 | 1·10 |
| MS3758 | 65×90 mm. 3l. "Self-portrait" (Vincent van Gogh) | 3·00 | 3·00 |

1282 Map

1991. 700th Anniv of Swiss Confederation.

| | | | | |
|---|---|---|---|---|
| 3759 | 1282 | 62s. red and violet | 70 | 50 |

1283 Postman on Bicycle, Envelopes and Paper

1991. 100 Years of Philatelic Publications in Bulgaria.

| | | | | |
|---|---|---|---|---|
| 3760 | 1283 | 30s. multicoloured | 35 | 25 |

1284 "Meteosat" Weather Satellite

1991. Europa. Europe in Space. Multicoloured.

| | | | |
|---|---|---|---|
| 3761 | 43s. Type 1284 | 1·20 | 60 |
| 3762 | 62s. "Ariane" rocket | 1·70 | 85 |

1285 Przewalski's Horse

1991. Horses. Multicoloured.

| | | | |
|---|---|---|---|
| 3763 | 5s. Type 1285 | 25 | 20 |
| 3764 | 10s. Tarpan | 25 | 20 |
| 3765 | 25s. Black arab | 30 | 25 |
| 3766 | 35s. White arab | 35 | 30 |
| 3767 | 42s. Shetland pony | 45 | 35 |
| 3768 | 60s. Draught horse | 1·20 | 60 |

1286 "Expo '91"

1991. "Expo '91" Exhibition, Plovdiv.

| | | | | |
|---|---|---|---|---|
| 3769 | 1286 | 30s. multicoloured | 35 | 25 |

1287 Mozart

1991. Death Bicentenary of Wolfgang Amadeus Mozart (composer).

| | | | | |
|---|---|---|---|---|
| 3770 | 1287 | 62s. multicoloured | 70 | 50 |

1288 Astronaut and Rear of Space Shuttle "Columbia"

1991. Space Shuttles. Multicoloured.

| | | | |
|---|---|---|---|
| 3771 | 12s. Type 1288 | 15 | 10 |
| 3772 | 32s. Satellite and "Challenger" | 25 | 20 |
| 3773 | 50s. "Discovery" and satellite | 45 | 25 |
| 3774 | 86s. Satellite and "Atlantis" (vert) | 60 | 35 |
| 3775 | 1l.50 Launch of "Buran" (vert) | 1·40 | 60 |
| 3776 | 2l. Satellite and "Atlantis" (vert) | 1·70 | 60 |
| MS3777 | 86×74 mm. 3l. Earth, "Atlantis" and Moon | 3·00 | 3·00 |

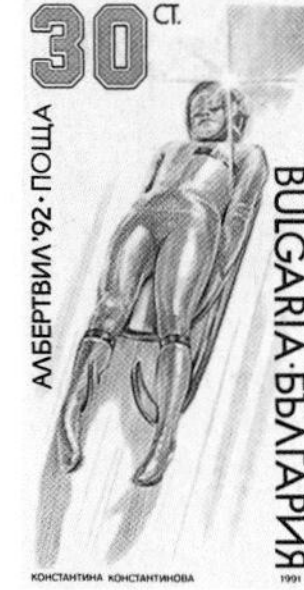
1289 Luge

1991. Winter Olympic Games, Albertville (1992). Multicoloured.

| | | | |
|---|---|---|---|
| 3778 | 30s. Type 1289 | 35 | 25 |
| 3779 | 43s. Skiing | 45 | 30 |
| 3780 | 67s. Ski jumping | 70 | 50 |
| 3781 | 2l. Biathlon | 2·30 | 1·40 |
| MS3782 | 128×86 mm. 3l. Two-man bobsleigh | 3·00 | 3·00 |

1290 Sheraton Hotel Balkan, Sofia

1991

| | | | | |
|---|---|---|---|---|
| 3783 | 1290 | 62s. multicoloured | 60 | 50 |

1291 Japanese Chin

1991. Dogs. Multicoloured.

| | | | |
|---|---|---|---|
| 3784 | 30s. Type 1291 | 25 | 25 |
| 3785 | 43s. Chihuahua | 35 | 25 |
| 3786 | 62s. Miniature pinscher | 45 | 30 |
| 3787 | 80s. Yorkshire terrier | 60 | 35 |
| 3788 | 1l. Mexican hairless | 80 | 60 |
| 3789 | 3l. Pug | 2·30 | 1·20 |

1292 Arms

1991. "Philatelia '91" Stamp Fair, Cologne.

| | | | | |
|---|---|---|---|---|
| 3790 | 1292 | 86s. multicoloured | 70 | 60 |

1293 Brandenburg Gate

1991. Bicentenary of Brandenburg Gate, Berlin. Sheet 90×70 mm.

| | | | | |
|---|---|---|---|---|
| MS3791 | 1293 | 4l. green and blue | 3·00 | 2·75 |

1294 Japan 1871 48mon "Dragon" Stamp

1991. "Phila Nippon '91" International Stamp Exhibition, Tokyo.

| | | | | |
|---|---|---|---|---|
| 3792 | 1294 | 62s. black, brown & bl | 45 | 35 |

**1295** Early Steam Locomotive and Tender

**1991.** 125th Anniv of the Railway in Bulgaria. Multicoloured.

| | | | |
|---|---|---|---|
| 3793 | 30s. Type **1295** | 35 | 25 |
| 3794 | 30s. Early six-wheeled carriage | 35 | 25 |

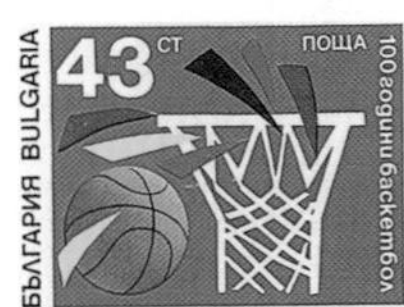

**1296** Ball ascending to Basket

**1991.** Centenary of Basketball. Multicoloured.

| | | | |
|---|---|---|---|
| 3795 | 43s. Type **1296** | 35 | 20 |
| 3796 | 62s. Ball level with basket mouth | 45 | 25 |
| 3797 | 90s. Ball entering basket | 60 | 35 |
| 3798 | 1l. Ball in basket | 70 | 50 |

**1297** "Christ carrying the Cross"

**1991.** 450th Birth Anniv of El Greco (painter). Multicoloured.

| | | | |
|---|---|---|---|
| 3799 | 43s. Type **1297** | 25 | 15 |
| 3800 | 50s. "Holy Family with St. Anna" | 30 | 20 |
| 3801 | 60s. "St. John of the Cross and St. John the Evangelist" | 45 | 25 |
| 3802 | 62s. "St. Andrew and St. Francis" | 60 | 30 |
| 3803 | 1l. "Holy Family with Magdalene" | 70 | 35 |
| 3804 | 2l. "Cardinal Fernando Nino de Guevara" | 1·20 | 50 |
| **MS**3805 | 68×86 mm. 3l. Detail of "Holy Family with St. Anna" (different) (39×50 mm) | 2·10 | 1·40 |

**1298** Snowman, Moon, Candle, Bell and Heart

**1991.** Christmas. Multicoloured.

| | | | |
|---|---|---|---|
| 3806 | 30s. Type **1298** | 25 | 15 |
| 3807 | 62s. Star, clover, angel, house and Christmas tree | 45 | 25 |

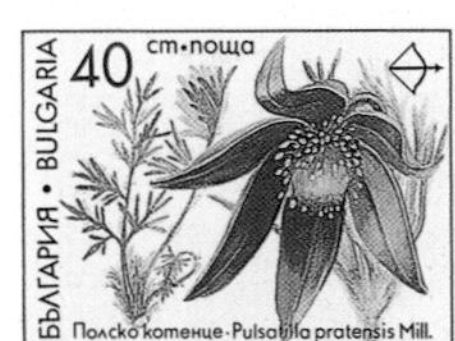

**1299** Small Pasque Flower

**1991.** Medicinal Plants. Multicoloured.

| | | | |
|---|---|---|---|
| 3808 | 30s.(+15s.) Pale pasque flower | 15 | 10 |
| 3809 | 40s. Type **1299** | 25 | 10 |
| 3810 | 55s. "Pulsatilla halleri" | 30 | 15 |
| 3811 | 60s. "Aquilegia nigricans" | 35 | 20 |
| 3812 | 1l. Sea buckthorn | 60 | 25 |
| 3813 | 2l. Blackcurrant | 1·20 | 50 |

No. 3808 includes a se-tenant premium-carrying label for 15s. inscribed "ACTION 2000. For Environment Protection".

**1300** Greenland Seals

**1991.** Marine Mammals. Multicoloured.

| | | | |
|---|---|---|---|
| 3814 | 30s. Type **1300** | 15 | 10 |
| 3815 | 43s. Killer whales | 25 | 15 |
| 3816 | 62s. Walruses | 30 | 20 |
| 3817 | 68s. Bottle-nosed dolphins | 35 | 25 |
| 3818 | 1l. Mediterranean monk seals | 60 | 35 |
| 3819 | 2l. Common porpoises | 1·20 | 50 |

**1301** Synagogue

**1992.** 500th Anniv of Jewish Settlement in Bulgaria.

| | | | | |
|---|---|---|---|---|
| 3820 | **1301** | 1l. multicoloured | 60 | 25 |

**1302** Rossini, "The Barber of Seville" and Figaro

**1992.** Birth Bicentenary of Gioacchino Rossini (composer).

| | | | | |
|---|---|---|---|---|
| 3821 | **1302** | 50s. multicoloured | 35 | 20 |

**1303** Plan of Fair

**1992.** Centenary of Plovdiv Fair.

| | | | | |
|---|---|---|---|---|
| 3822 | **1303** | 1l. black and stone | 60 | 25 |

**1304** Volvo "740"

**1992.** Motor Cars. Multicoloured.

| | | | |
|---|---|---|---|
| 3823 | 30s. Type **1304** | 25 | 10 |
| 3824 | 45s. Ford "Escort" | 30 | 15 |
| 3825 | 50s. Fiat "Croma" | 35 | 20 |
| 3826 | 50s. Mercedes Benz "600" | 35 | 20 |
| 3827 | 1l. Peugeot "605" | 80 | 25 |
| 3828 | 2l. B.M.W. "316" | 1·40 | 50 |

**1305** Amerigo Vespucci

**1992.** Explorers. Multicoloured.

| | | | |
|---|---|---|---|
| 3829 | 50s. Type **1305** | 25 | 20 |
| 3830 | 50s. Francisco de Orellana | 25 | 20 |
| 3831 | 1l. Ferdinand Magellan | 70 | 35 |
| 3832 | 1l. Jimenez de Quesada | 70 | 35 |
| 3833 | 2l. Sir Francis Drake | 1·20 | 55 |
| 3834 | 3l. Pedro de Valdivia | 1·70 | 60 |
| **MS**3835 | 121×83 mm. 4l. Christopher Columbus | 3·00 | 2·50 |

**1306** Granada

**1992.** "Granada '92" Int Stamp Exhibition.

| | | | | |
|---|---|---|---|---|
| 3836 | **1306** | 62s. multicoloured | 35 | 25 |

**1307** "Santa Maria"

**1992.** Europa. 500th Anniv of Discovery of America by Columbus. Multicoloured.

| | | | |
|---|---|---|---|
| 3837 | 1l. Type **1307** | 1·70 | 60 |
| 3838 | 2l. Christopher Columbus | 3·00 | 85 |

Nos. 3837/8 were issued together, se-tenant, forming a composite design.

**1308** House

**1992.** S.O.S. Children's Village.

| | | | | |
|---|---|---|---|---|
| 3839 | **1308** | 1l. multicoloured | 70 | 25 |

**1309** Long Jumping

**1992.** Olympic Games, Barcelona (2nd issue). Multicoloured.

| | | | |
|---|---|---|---|
| 3840 | 50s. Type **1309** | 35 | 20 |
| 3841 | 50s. Swimming | 35 | 20 |
| 3842 | 1l. High jumping | 60 | 35 |
| 3843 | 3l. Gymnastics | 1·90 | 60 |
| **MS**3844 | 52×75 mm. 4l. Olympic Torch (vert) | 2·30 | 1·80 |

**1310** 1902 Laurin and Klement Motor Cycle

**1992.** Motor Cycles. Multicoloured.

| | | | |
|---|---|---|---|
| 3845 | 30s. Type **1310** | 25 | 10 |
| 3846 | 50s. 1928 Puch "200 Luxus" | 35 | 15 |
| 3847 | 50s. 1931 Norton "CS 1" | 35 | 15 |
| 3848 | 70s. 1950 Harley Davidson | 45 | 20 |
| 3849 | 1l. 1986 Gilera "SP 01" | 70 | 25 |
| 3850 | 2l. 1990 BMW "K 1" | 1·40 | 50 |

**1311** Genoa

**1992.** "Genova '92" International Thematic Stamp Exhibition.

| | | | | |
|---|---|---|---|---|
| 3851 | **1311** | 1l. multicoloured | 70 | 25 |

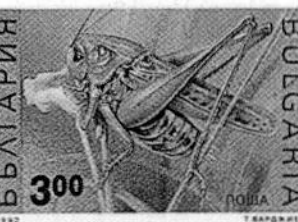

**1312** Grasshopper

**1992.** Insects. Multicoloured.

| | | | |
|---|---|---|---|
| 3852 | 1l. Four-spotted libellula | 10 | 10 |
| 3853 | 2l. "Raphidia notata" | 35 | 20 |
| 3854 | 3l. Type **1312** | 80 | 25 |
| 3855 | 4l. Stag beetle | 1·20 | 35 |
| 3856 | 5l. Fire bug | 1·40 | 50 |
| 3857 | 7l. Ant | 2·30 | 1·20 |
| 3858 | 20l. Wasp | 5·75 | 1·80 |
| 3859 | 50l. Praying mantis | 14·00 | 3·50 |

**1313** Silhouette of Head on Town Plan

**1992.** 50th Anniv of Institute of Architecture and Building.

| | | | | |
|---|---|---|---|---|
| 3862 | **1313** | 1l. red and black | 70 | 25 |

**1314** Oak

**1992.** Trees. Multicoloured.

| | | | |
|---|---|---|---|
| 3863 | 50s. Type **1314** | 20 | 15 |
| 3864 | 50s. Horse chestnut | 20 | 15 |
| 3865 | 1l. Oak | 60 | 25 |
| 3866 | 1l. Macedonian pine | 60 | 25 |
| 3867 | 2l. Maple | 1·40 | 35 |
| 3868 | 3l. Pear | 1·70 | 60 |

**1315** Embroidered Flower

**1992.** Centenary of Folk Museum, Sofia.

| | | | | |
|---|---|---|---|---|
| 3869 | **1315** | 1l. multicoloured | 70 | 25 |

**1316** "Bulgaria" (freighter)

**1992.** Centenary of National Shipping Fleet. Multicoloured.

| | | | |
|---|---|---|---|
| 3870 | 30s. Type **1316** | 10 | 10 |
| 3871 | 50s. "Kastor" (tanker) | 25 | 15 |
| 3872 | 1l. "Geroite na Sebastopol" (train ferry) | 70 | 25 |
| 3873 | 2l. "Aleko Konstantinov" (tanker) | 1·20 | 50 |
| 3874 | 2l. "Bulgaria" (tanker) | 1·20 | 50 |
| 3875 | 3l. "Varna" (container ship) | 1·90 | 70 |

**1317** Council Emblem

**1992.** Admission to Council of Europe.

| | | | | |
|---|---|---|---|---|
| 3876 | **1317** | 7l. multicoloured | 4·75 | 2·40 |

1318 Family exercising on Beach

1992. 4th World Sport for All Congress, Varna. Sheet 58×75 mm.

| | | | |
|---|---|---|---|
| MS3877 | 4l. multicoloured | 2·50 | 2·50 |

1319 "Santa Claus" (Ani Bacheva)

1992. Christmas. Children's Drawings. Mult.

| | | | |
|---|---|---|---|
| 3878 | 1l. Type 1319 | 60 | 25 |
| 3879 | 7l. "Madonna and Child" (Georgi Petkov) | 3·75 | 1·60 |

1320 Leopard

1992. Big Cats. Multicoloured.

| | | | |
|---|---|---|---|
| 3880 | 50s. Type 1320 | 35 | 10 |
| 3881 | 50s. Cheetah | 35 | 10 |
| 3882 | 1l. Jaguar | 70 | 25 |
| 3883 | 2l. Puma | 1·40 | 60 |
| 3884 | 2l. Tiger | 1·40 | 60 |
| 3885 | 3l. Lion | 1·70 | 70 |

1321 Cricket

1992. Sport. Multicoloured.

| | | | |
|---|---|---|---|
| 3886 | 50s. Type 1321 | 35 | 15 |
| 3887 | 50s. Baseball | 35 | 15 |
| 3888 | 1l. Pony and trap racing | 70 | 25 |
| 3889 | 1l. Polo | 70 | 25 |
| 3890 | 2l. Hockey | 1·40 | 60 |
| 3891 | 3l. American football | 1·70 | 70 |

1322 Tengmalm's Owl

1992. Owls. Multicoloured.

| | | | |
|---|---|---|---|
| 3892 | 30s. Type 1322 | 25 | 15 |
| 3893 | 50s. Tawny owl (horiz) | 35 | 15 |
| 3894 | 1l. Long-eared owl | 70 | 25 |
| 3895 | 2l. Short-eared owl | 1·40 | 60 |
| 3896 | 2l. Eurasian scops owl (horiz) | 1·40 | 60 |
| 3897 | 3l. Barn owl | 2·10 | 70 |

1323 "Khan Kubrat" (Dimitur Gyudzhenov)

1992. Historical Paintings. Multicoloured.

| | | | |
|---|---|---|---|
| 3898 | 50s. Type 1323 | 35 | 15 |
| 3899 | 1l. "Khan Asparukh (Nikolai Pavlovich) | 70 | 25 |
| 3900 | 2l. "Khan Terval at Tsarigrad" (Dimitur Panchev) | 1·20 | 60 |
| 3901 | 3l. "Prince Boris" (Nikolai Pavlovich) | 1·90 | 95 |
| MS3902 | 75×90 mm. 4l. "The Warrior" (Mito Ganovski) (vert) | 2·50 | 2·50 |

1324 Sculpted Head

1993. Centenary of National Archaeological Museum, Sofia.

| | | | | |
|---|---|---|---|---|
| 3903 | 1324 | 1l. multicoloured | 70 | 25 |

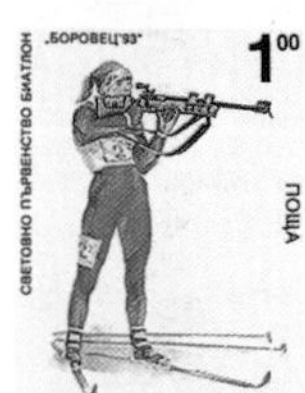
1325 Shooting

1993. "Borovets '93" Biathlon Championship. Multicoloured.

| | | | |
|---|---|---|---|
| 3904 | 1l. Type 1325 | 70 | 35 |
| 3905 | 7l. Cross-country skiing | 4·75 | 2·00 |

1326 Rilski

1993. Birth Bicentenary of Neofit Rilski (compiler of Bulgarian grammar and dictionary).

| | | | | |
|---|---|---|---|---|
| 3906 | 1326 | 1l. bistre and red | 70 | 25 |

1327 "Morning" (sculpture, Georgi Chapkunov)

1993. Europa. Contemporary Art. Multicoloured.

| | | | |
|---|---|---|---|
| 3907 | 3l. Type 1327 | 1·70 | 60 |
| 3908 | 8l. "Composition" (D. Buyukliiski) | 3·00 | 1·80 |

1328 Veil-tailed Goldfish

1993. Fishes. Multicoloured.

| | | | |
|---|---|---|---|
| 3909 | 1l. Type 1328 | 25 | 15 |
| 3910 | 2l. Yucatan sail-finned molly | 45 | 20 |
| 3911 | 3l. Two-striped lyretail | 70 | 25 |
| 3912 | 3l. Freshwater angelfish | 70 | 25 |
| 3913 | 4l. Red discus | 1·00 | 35 |
| 3914 | 8l. Pearl gourami | 2·10 | 70 |

1329 Apple

1993. Fruits. Multicoloured.

| | | | |
|---|---|---|---|
| 3915 | 1l. Type 1329 | 25 | 10 |
| 3916 | 2l. Peach | 45 | 15 |
| 3917 | 2l. Pear | 45 | 15 |
| 3918 | 3l. Quince | 70 | 25 |
| 3919 | 5l. Pomegranate | 1·40 | 35 |
| 3920 | 7l. Fig | 2·10 | 60 |

1330 Monteverdi

1993. 350th Death Anniv of Claudio Monteverdi (composer).

| | | | | |
|---|---|---|---|---|
| 3921 | 1330 | 1l. green, yellow & red | 25 | 15 |

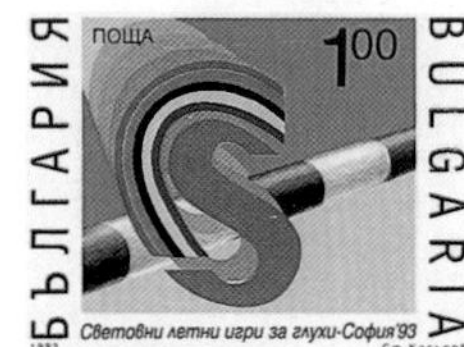
1331 High Jumping

1993. Int Games for the Deaf, Sofia. Mult.

| | | | |
|---|---|---|---|
| 3922 | 1l. Type 1331 | 25 | 15 |
| 3923 | 2l. Swimming | 45 | 20 |
| 3924 | 3l. Cycling | 80 | 25 |
| 3925 | 4l. Tennis | 85 | 35 |
| MS3926 | 86×75 mm. 5l. Football | 1·20 | 1·20 |

1332 Baptism (from Manasses Chronicle)

1993. 1100th Anniv of Preslav and Introduction of Cyrillic Script. Sheet 113×110 mm containing T 1332 and similar horiz designs. Multicoloured.

| | | | |
|---|---|---|---|
| MS3927 | 5l. Type 1332; 5l. Prince Boris I (after Dimitur Gyudzhenov); 5l. Tsar Simeon I (after Dimitur Gyudzhenov); 5l. Cavalry charge (after Manasses Chronicle) | 4·75 | 4·75 |

1333 Prince Alexander

1993. Death Centenary of Prince Alexander I.

| | | | | |
|---|---|---|---|---|
| 3928 | 1333 | 3l. multicoloured | 70 | 25 |

1334 Tchaikovsky

1993. Death Centenary of Pyotr Tchaikovsky (composer).

| | | | | |
|---|---|---|---|---|
| 3929 | 1334 | 3l. multicoloured | 70 | 25 |

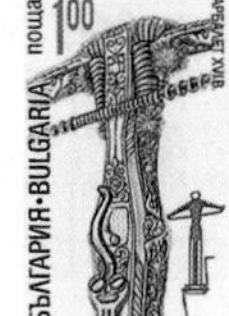
1335 Crossbow

1993. Weapons. Multicoloured.

| | | | |
|---|---|---|---|
| 3930 | 1l. Type 1335 | 25 | 15 |
| 3931 | 2l. 18th-century flintlock pistol | 45 | 20 |
| 3932 | 3l. Revolver | 70 | 25 |
| 3933 | 3l. Luger pistol | 70 | 25 |
| 3934 | 5l. Mauser rifle | 1·30 | 40 |
| 3935 | 7l. Kalashnikov assault rifle | 1·90 | 70 |

1336 Newton

1993. 350th Birth Anniv of Sir Isaac Newton (mathematician).

| | | | | |
|---|---|---|---|---|
| 3936 | 1336 | 1l. multicoloured | 25 | 15 |

1337 "100" on Stamps and Globe

1993. Centenary of Bulgarian Philately.

| | | | | |
|---|---|---|---|---|
| 3937 | 1337 | 1l. multicoloured | 25 | 15 |

1338 "Ecology" in Cyrillic Script

1993. Ecology. Multicoloured.

| | | | |
|---|---|---|---|
| 3938 | 1l. Type 1338 | 25 | 15 |
| 3939 | 7l. "Ecology" in English | 1·90 | 60 |

1339 Mallard

1993. Hunting. Multicoloured.

| | | | |
|---|---|---|---|
| 3940 | 1l. Type 1339 | 15 | 10 |
| 3941 | 1l. Common pheasant | 15 | 10 |
| 3942 | 2l. Red fox | 35 | 20 |
| 3943 | 3l. Roe deer | 60 | 25 |
| 3944 | 6l. European brown hare | 1·20 | 50 |
| 3945 | 8l. Wild boar | 1·70 | 70 |

1340 "Taurus", "Gemini" and "Cancer"

1993. Christmas. Signs of the Zodiac. Mult.

| | | | |
|---|---|---|---|
| 3946 | 1l. Type 1340 | 10 | 10 |
| 3947 | 1l. "Leo", "Virgo" and "Libra" | 10 | 10 |
| 3948 | 7l. "Aquarius", "Pisces" and "Aries" | 1·40 | 50 |
| 3949 | 7l. "Scorpio", "Sagittarius" and "Capricorn" | 1·40 | 50 |

Nos. 3946/7 and 3948/9 were each issued together, se-tenant; when placed together the four stamps form a composite design.

**1341** Sofia Costume

**1993.** Costumes. Multicoloured.

3950 1l. Type **1341** 25 10
3951 1l. Plovdiv 25 10
3952 2l. Belograd 35 15
3953 3l. Oryakhovo 45 20
3954 3l. Shumen 45 20
3955 8l. Kurdzhali 1·40 60

**1342** Freestyle Skiing

**1994.** Winter Olympic Games, Lillehammer, Norway. Multicoloured.

3956 1l. Type **1342** 10 10
3957 2l. Speed skating 35 15
3958 3l. Two-man luge 60 20
3959 4l. Ice hockey 95 25
**MS**3960 59×90 mm. 3l. multicoloured 95 95

**1343** "Self-portrait" and "Tsar Simeon"

**1994.** Death Centenary of Nikolai Pavlovich (artist).

3961 **1343** 3l. multicoloured 60 25

**1344** Plesiosaurus

**1994.** Prehistoric Animals. Multicoloured.

3962 2l. Type **1344** 35 10
3963 3l. Archaeopteryx 60 20
3964 3l. Iguanodon 60 20
3965 4l. Edmontonia 80 25
3966 5l. Styracosaurus 95 35
3967 7l. Tyrannosaurus 1·40 50

**1345** Players (Chile, 1962)

**1994.** World Cup Football Championship, U.S.A. Multicoloured.

3968 3l. Type **1345** 60 25
3969 6l. Players (England, 1966) 1·20 35
3970 7l. Goalkeeper making save (Mexico, 1970) 1·30 50
3971 9l. Player kicking (West Germany, 1974) 1·60 70
**MS**3972 90×123 mm. 5l. Player punching air (Mexico, 1986) (vert); 5l. Player tackling (U.S.A., 1994) 2·50 2·50

**1346** Photoelectric Analysis (Georgi Nadzhakov)

**1994.** Europa. Discoveries. Multicoloured.

3973 3l. Type **1346** 1·20 60
3974 15l. Cardiogram and heart (Prof. Ivan Mitev) 4·00 1·80

**1347** Khristov

**1994.** 80th Birth Anniv of Boris Khristov (actor).

3975 **1347** 3l. multicoloured 60 25

**1348** Sleeping Hamster

**1994.** The Common Hamster. Multicoloured.

3976 3l. Type **1348** 60 25
3977 7l. Hamster looking out of burrow 1·00 60
3978 10l. Hamster sitting up in grass 1·70 85
3979 15l. Hamster approaching berry 2·50 1·30

**1349** Space Shuttle, Satellite and Dish Aerial

**1994.** North Atlantic Co-operation Council (North Atlantic Treaty Organization and Warsaw Pact members).

3980 **1349** 3l. multicoloured 60 35

**1350** Baron Pierre de Coubertin (founder of modern games)

**1994.** Cent of International Olympic Committee.

3981 **1350** 3l. multicoloured 60 35

**1351** "Christ Pantocrator"

**1994.** Icons. Multicoloured.

3982 2l. Type **1351** 25 10
3983 3l. "Raising of Lazarus" 45 20
3984 5l. "Passion of Christ" 60 25
3985 7l. "Archangel Michael" 1·20 50
3986 8l. "Sts. Cyril and Methodius" 1·40 60
3987 15l. "Madonna Enthroned" 3·00 70

**1352** Vechernik

**1994.** Christmas. Breads. Multicoloured.

3988 3l. Type **1352** 60 25
3989 15l. Bogovitsa 3·00 1·60

**1353** "Golden Showers"

**1994.** Roses. Multicoloured.

3990 2l. Type **1353** 35 10
3991 3l. "Caen Peace Monument" 60 25
3992 5l. "Theresa of Lisieux" 95 35
3993 7l. "Zambra 93" 1·40 60
3994 10l. "Gustave Courbet" 2·00 65
3995 15l. "Honore de Balzac" 3·00 1·20

БЪЛГАРИЯ - С БРОНЗОВИ МЕДАЛИ

**(1354)**

**1994.** Bulgaria's Fourth Place in World Cup Football Championship. No. MS3972 overprinted with T 1354 in margin.

**MS**3996 90×123 mm. 5l. multicoloured; 5l. multicoloured 22·00 22·00

**1355** "AM/ASES", 1912

**1994.** Trams. Multicoloured.

3997 1l. Type **1355** 10 10
3998 2l. "AM/ASES", 1928 35 15
3999 3l. "M.A.N./AEG", 1931 60 25
4000 5l. "D.T.O.", 1942 95 35
4001 8l. Republika, 1951 1·70 70
4002 10l. Kosmonavt articulated tramcar set, 1961 2·10 85

**1356** Petleshkov and Flag

**1995.** 150th Birth Anniv of Vasil Petleshkov (leader of 1876 April uprising).

4003 **1356** 3l. multicoloured 60 35

**1357** Daisy growing through Cracked Helmet

**1995.** Europa. Peace and Freedom. Mult.

4004 3l. Type **1357** 1·20 60
4005 15l. Dove with olive branch on rifle barrel 4·00 1·80

**1358** Player

**1995.** Centenary of Volleyball. Sheet 92×75 mm containing T 1358 and similar multicoloured design.

**MS**4006 10l. Type **1358**; 15l. Player hitting ball (vert) 4·25 4·25

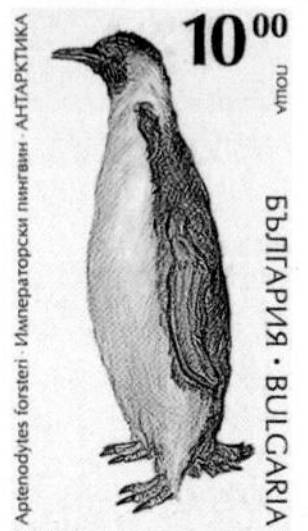

**1359** Sea Lily (*Pancratium martimum*)

**1995.** European Nature Conservation Year. Sheet 70×99 mm containing T 1359 and similar horiz design. Multicoloured.

**MS**4007 10l. Type **1359**; 15l. Imperial Eagle (*Aquila heliaca*) 5·50 5·50

**1360** Emperor Penguin

**1995.** Antarctic Animals. Multicoloured.

4008 1l. Shrimp (horiz) 15 10
4009 2l. Ice fish (horiz) 35 15
4010 3l. Sperm whale (horiz) 45 25
4011 5l. Weddell's seal (horiz) 80 35
4012 8l. South polar skua (horiz) 1·40 70
4013 10l. Type **1360** 1·70 85

**1361** Stambolov

**1995.** Death Cent of Stefan Stambolov (politician).

4014 **1361** 3l. multicoloured 60 35

BULGARIA
3.00
ПОЩА БЪЛГАРИЯ

**1362** Pole Vaulting

**1995.** Olympic Games, Atlanta (1996) (1st issue). Multicoloured.

4015 3l. Type **1362** 45 15

| | | | |
|---|---|---|---|
| 4016 | 7l. High jumping | 1·20 | 50 |
| 4017 | 10l. Long jumping | 1·70 | 60 |
| 4018 | 15l. Triple jumping | 2·50 | 85 |

See also Nos. 4083/6.

**1363** Pea

**1995.** Food Plants. Multicoloured.

| | | | |
|---|---|---|---|
| 4019 | 2l. Type **1363** | 25 | 15 |
| 4020 | 3l. Chickpea | 45 | 25 |
| 4021 | 3l. Soya bean | 45 | 25 |
| 4022 | 4l. Spinach | 70 | 35 |
| 4023 | 5l. Peanut | 80 | 50 |
| 4024 | 15l. Lentil | 2·30 | 85 |

**1364** "100"

**1995.** Centenary of Organized Tourism.

| | | | | |
|---|---|---|---|---|
| 4025 | **1364** | 1l. multicoloured | 60 | 25 |

**1365** "Ivan Nikolov-Zograf"

**1995.** Birth Centenary of Vasil Zakhariev (painter).

| | | | | |
|---|---|---|---|---|
| 4026 | **1365** | 2l. multicoloured | 35 | 15 |
| 4027 | - | 3l. multicoloured | 60 | 25 |
| 4028 | - | 5l. black, brown & grn | 95 | 50 |
| 4029 | - | 10l. multicoloured | 1·70 | 95 |

DESIGNS: 3l. "Rila Monastery"; 5l. "Self-portrait"; 10l. "Raspberry Collectors".

**1366** "Dove-Hands" holding Globe

**1995.** 50th Anniv of UNO.

| | | | | |
|---|---|---|---|---|
| 4030 | **1366** | 3l. multicoloured | 60 | 25 |

**1367** Polikarpov Po-2 Biplane

**1995.** Aircraft. Multicoloured.

| | | | |
|---|---|---|---|
| 4031 | 3l. Type **1367** | 45 | 25 |
| 4032 | 5l. Lisunov Li-2 airliner | 80 | 35 |
| 4033 | 7l. Junkers Ju 52 | 1·20 | 60 |
| 4034 | 10l. Focke Wulf FW58 | 1·70 | 70 |

**1368** Charlie Chaplin and Mickey Mouse

**1995.** Centenary of Motion Pictures. Mult.

| | | | |
|---|---|---|---|
| 4035 | 2l. Type **1368** | 35 | 15 |
| 4036 | 3l. Marilyn Monroe and Marlene Dietrich | 45 | 25 |
| 4037 | 5l. Nikolai Cherkasov and Humphrey Bogart | 60 | 30 |
| 4038 | 8l. Sophia Loren and Liza Minelli | 1·50 | 35 |
| 4039 | 10l. Gerard Philipe and Toshiro Mifune | 1·70 | 50 |
| 4040 | 15l. Katya Paskaleva and Nevena Kokanova | 2·30 | 85 |

**1369** Agate

**1995.** Minerals. Multicoloured.

| | | | |
|---|---|---|---|
| 4041 | 1l. Type **1369** | 15 | 10 |
| 4042 | 2l. Sphalerite | 35 | 15 |
| 4043 | 5l. Calcite | 95 | 25 |
| 4044 | 7l. Quartz | 1·20 | 30 |
| 4045 | 8l. Pyromorphite | 1·40 | 35 |
| 4046 | 10l. Almandine | 1·90 | 60 |

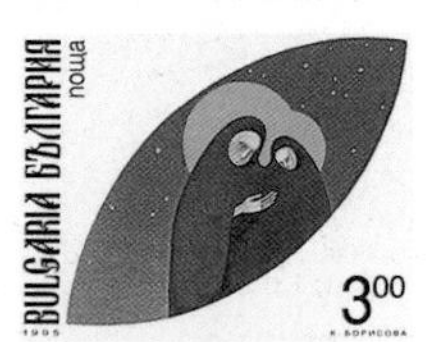


**1370** Mary and Joseph

**1995.** Christmas. Multicoloured.

| | | | |
|---|---|---|---|
| 4047 | 3l. Type **1370** | 60 | 25 |
| 4048 | 15l. Three wise men approaching stable | 2·30 | 1·30 |

**1371** "Polynesian Woman with Fruit"

**1996.** Birth Centenary of Kiril Tsonev (painter).

| | | | | |
|---|---|---|---|---|
| 4049 | **1371** | 3l. multicoloured | 60 | 25 |

**1372** Luther (after Lucas Cranach the elder)

**1996.** 450th Death Anniv of Martin Luther (Protestant reformer).

| | | | | |
|---|---|---|---|---|
| 4050 | **1372** | 3l. multicoloured | 60 | 25 |

**1373** Preobrazhenie

**1996.** Monasteries.

| | | | | |
|---|---|---|---|---|
| 4051 | **1373** | 3l. green | 15 | 10 |
| 4052 | - | 5l. red | 35 | 20 |
| 4053 | - | 10l. blue | 45 | 25 |
| 4054 | - | 20l. orange | 1·20 | 50 |
| 4055 | - | 25l. brown | 1·40 | 70 |
| 4056 | - | 40l. purple | 2·30 | 1·20 |

DESIGNS: 5l. Arapov; 10l. Dryanovo; 20l. Bachkov; 25l. Troyan; 40l. Zograf.

**1374** Bulgarian National Bank

**1996.** 5th Anniv of European Reconstruction and Development Bank.

| | | | | |
|---|---|---|---|---|
| 4063 | **1374** | 7l. green, red and blue | 60 | 35 |
| 4064 | - | 30l. blue, red & purple | 2·30 | 85 |

DESIGN: 30l. Palace of Culture, Sofia.

**1375** Yew

**1996.** Conifers. Multicoloured.

| | | | |
|---|---|---|---|
| 4065 | 5l. Type **1375** | 25 | 10 |
| 4066 | 8l. Silver fir | 45 | 20 |
| 4067 | 10l. Norway spruce | 60 | 25 |
| 4068 | 20l. Scots pine | 1·20 | 35 |
| 4069 | 25l. "Pinus heldreichii" | 1·40 | 50 |
| 4070 | 40l. Juniper | 2·30 | 1·20 |

**1376** Battle Scene and Mourning Women

**1996.** 120th Anniversaries. Multicoloured.

| | | | |
|---|---|---|---|
| 4071 | 10l. Type **1376** (April uprising) | 60 | 25 |
| 4072 | 40l. Khristo Botev and script (poet, death anniv) (horiz) | 2·30 | 1·20 |

**1377** Modern Officer's Parade Uniform

**1996.** Military Uniforms. Multicoloured.

| | | | |
|---|---|---|---|
| 4073 | 5l. Type **1377** | 20 | 10 |
| 4074 | 8l. Second World War combat uniform | 30 | 15 |
| 4075 | 10l. Balkan War uniform | 40 | 20 |
| 4076 | 20l. Guard officer's ceremonial uniform | 95 | 50 |
| 4077 | 25l. Serbo-Bulgarian War officer's uniform | 1·20 | 60 |
| 4078 | 40l. Russo-Turkish War soldier's uniform | 1·70 | 1·20 |

**1378** Monument

**1996.** 50th Anniv of the Republic.

| | | | | |
|---|---|---|---|---|
| 4079 | **1378** | 10l. multicoloured | 60 | 35 |

**1379** Elisaveta Bagryana (poet)

**1996.** Europa. Famous Women. Multicoloured.

| | | | |
|---|---|---|---|
| 4080 | 10l. Type **1379** | 2·30 | 1·20 |
| 4081 | 40l. Katya Popova (opera singer) | 3·00 | 1·80 |

**1380** Player

**1996.** European Football Championship, England. Sheet 71×86 mm containing T 1380 and similar vert design. Multicoloured.

| | | | |
|---|---|---|---|
| **MS**4082 | 10l. Type **1380**; 15l. Player (different) | 2·50 | 2·50 |

**1381** Nikola Stanchev (wrestling, Melbourne 1956)

**1996.** Olympic Games, Atlanta (2nd issue). Bulgarian Medal Winners. Multicoloured.

| | | | |
|---|---|---|---|
| 4083 | 5l. Type **1381** | 20 | 10 |
| 4084 | 8l. Boris Georgiev (boxing, Helsinki 1952) | 45 | 20 |
| 4085 | 10l. Ivanka Khristova (putting the shot, Montreal 1976) | 70 | 25 |
| 4086 | 25l. Z. Iordanova and S. Otsetova (double sculls, Montreal 1976) | 1·50 | 60 |
| **MS**4087 | 89×68 mm. 15l. Olympic Stadium, Athens, 1896 | 1·70 | 1·70 |

**1382** "The Letter" (detail)

**1996.** 250th Birth Anniv of Francisco Goya (painter). Multicoloured.

| | | | |
|---|---|---|---|
| 4088 | 5l. Detail of fresco | 20 | 10 |
| 4089 | 8l. Type **1382** | 60 | 35 |
| 4090 | 26l. "3rd of May 1808 in Madrid" (detail) | 1·50 | 70 |
| 4091 | 40l. "Neighbours on a Balcony" (detail) | 2·30 | 1·20 |
| **MS**4092 | 99×73 mm. 10l. "Clothed Maja" (50×26 mm); 15l. "Naked Maja" (50×26 mm) | 1·70 | 1·70 |

**1383** Water Flea

**1996.** Aquatic Life. Multicoloured.

| | | | |
|---|---|---|---|
| 4093 | 5l. Type **1383** | 20 | 10 |
| 4094 | 10l. Common water louse | 45 | 20 |
| 4095 | 12l. European river crayfish | 60 | 25 |
| 4096 | 25l. Prawn | 1·00 | 35 |
| 4097 | 30l. "Cumella limicola" | 1·20 | 60 |

| | | | | |
|---|---|---|---|---|
| 4098 | | 40l. Mediterranean shore crab | 3·00 | 1·20 |

**1384** St. Ivan

**1996.** 1050th Death Anniv of Ivan Rilski (founder of Rila Monastery). Sheet 56×87 mm.

| | | | | |
|---|---|---|---|---|
| **MS**4099 | **1384** | 10l. multicoloured | 1·00 | 1·00 |

**1385** Tryavna

**1996.** Houses.

| | | | | |
|---|---|---|---|---|
| 4100 | **1385** | 10l. brown and stone | 35 | 15 |
| 4101 | - | 15l. red and yellow | 45 | 20 |
| 4102 | - | 30l. green and yellow | 95 | 50 |
| 4103 | - | 50l. violet and mauve | 1·60 | 85 |
| 4104 | - | 60l. green and lt green | 2·10 | 1·20 |
| 4105 | - | 100l. ultramarine & bl | 3·25 | 1·80 |

DESIGNS: 15l. Nesebur; 30l. Tryavna (different); 50l. Koprivshtitsa; 60l. Plovdiv; 100l. Koprivshtitsa (different).

**1386** "Philadelphia", 1836

**1996.** Steam Locomotives. Multicoloured.

| | | | | |
|---|---|---|---|---|
| 4106 | | 5l. Type **1386** | 25 | 20 |
| 4107 | | 10l. "Jenny Lind", 1847 | 60 | 25 |
| 4108 | | 12l. "Liverpool", 1848 | 70 | 35 |
| 4109 | | 26l. "Anglet", 1876 | 1·50 | 70 |

**1387** Anniversary Emblem and Academy

**1996.** Centenary of National Arts Academy.

| | | | | |
|---|---|---|---|---|
| 4110 | **1387** | 15l. black and yellow | 95 | 35 |

**1388** Sword and Miniature from "Chronicle of Ivan Skilitsa"

**1996.** 1100th Anniv of Tsar Simeon's Victory over the Turks. Multicoloured.

| | | | | |
|---|---|---|---|---|
| 4111 | | 10l. Type **1388** | 60 | 25 |
| 4112 | | 40l. Dagger and right-hand detail of miniature | 2·30 | 1·20 |

Nos. 4111/12 were issued together, se-tenant, forming a composite design.

**1389** Fishes and Diver (Dilyana Lokmadzhieva)

**1996.** 50th Anniv of UNICEF. Children's Paintings. Multicoloured.

| | | | | |
|---|---|---|---|---|
| 4113 | | 7l. Type **1389** | 45 | 25 |
| 4114 | | 15l. Circus (Velislava Dimitrova) | 95 | 50 |
| 4115 | | 20l. Man and artist's pallet (Miglena Nikolova) | 1·30 | 60 |
| 4116 | | 60l. Family meal (Darena Dencheva) | 3·75 | 1·90 |

**1390** Christmas Tree

**1996.** Christmas. Multicoloured.

| | | | | |
|---|---|---|---|---|
| 4117 | | 15l. Type **1390** | 80 | 35 |
| 4118 | | 60l. Star over basilica and Christmas tree | 3·50 | 1·80 |

**1391** "Zograf Monastery"

**1996.** Birth Centenary of Tsanko Lavrenov (painter).

| | | | | |
|---|---|---|---|---|
| 4119 | **1391** | 15l. multicoloured | 80 | 35 |

**1392** Pointer

**1997.** Puppies. Multicoloured.

| | | | | |
|---|---|---|---|---|
| 4120 | | 5l. Type **1392** | 25 | 25 |
| 4121 | | 7l. Chow chow | 35 | 20 |
| 4122 | | 25l. Carakachan dog | 1·20 | 60 |
| 4123 | | 50l. Basset hound | 2·30 | 1·20 |

**1393** Bell

**1997.** 150th Birth Anniv of Alexander Graham Bell (telephone pioneer).

| | | | | |
|---|---|---|---|---|
| 4124 | **1393** | 30l. multicoloured | 95 | 50 |

**1394** Man drinking

**1997.** Birth Centenary of Ivan Milev (painter). Murals from Kazaluk. Multicoloured.

| | | | | |
|---|---|---|---|---|
| 4125 | | 5l. Type **1394** | 20 | 15 |
| 4126 | | 15l. Woman praying | 45 | 25 |
| 4127 | | 30l. Reaper | 60 | 50 |
| 4128 | | 60l. Mother and child | 1·70 | 95 |

**1395** Lady March (symbol of spring)

**1997.** Europa. Tales and Legends. Mult.

| | | | | |
|---|---|---|---|---|
| 4129 | | 120l. Type **1395** | 3·00 | 1·20 |
| 4130 | | 600l. St. George (national symbol) | 2·30 | 1·20 |

**1396** Kisimov in Character

**1997.** Birth Cent of Konstantin Kisimov (actor).

| | | | | |
|---|---|---|---|---|
| 4131 | **1396** | 120l. multicoloured | 25 | 25 |

**1397** Von Stephan

**1997.** Death Centenary of Heinrich von Stephan (founder of U.P.U.).

| | | | | |
|---|---|---|---|---|
| 4132 | **1397** | 60l. multicoloured | 25 | 25 |

**1398** Old Town, Nesebur

**1997.** Historic Sights.

| | | | | |
|---|---|---|---|---|
| 4133 | **1398** | 80l. brown and black | 10 | 10 |
| 4134 | - | 200l. violet and black | 25 | 10 |
| 4135 | - | 300l. yellow and black | 35 | 25 |
| 4136 | - | 500l. green and black | 60 | 35 |
| 4137 | - | 600l. yellow and black | 80 | 50 |
| 4138 | - | 1000l. orange and black | 1·40 | 85 |

DESIGNS: 200l. Sculpture, Ivanovski Church; 300l. Christ (detail of icon), Boyana Church; 500l. Horseman (stone relief), Madara; 600l. Figure of woman (carving from sarcophagus), Sveshary; 1000l. Tomb decoration, Kazanlak.

**1399** Gaetano Donizetti

**1997.** Composers' Anniversaries. Multicoloured.

| | | | | |
|---|---|---|---|---|
| 4139 | | 120l. Type **1399** (birth bicentenary) | 45 | 35 |
| 4140 | | 120l. Franz Schubert (birth bicentenary) | 45 | 35 |
| 4141 | | 120l. Felix Mendelssohn-Bartholdy (150th death anniv) | 45 | 35 |
| 4142 | | 120l. Johannes Brahms (death centenary) | 45 | 35 |

**1400** "Trifolium rubens"

**1997.** Flowers in the Red Book. Multicoloured.

| | | | | |
|---|---|---|---|---|
| 4143 | | 80l. Type **1400** | 25 | 10 |
| 4144 | | 100l. "Tulipa hageri" | 35 | 10 |
| 4145 | | 120l. "Inula spiraeifolia" | 35 | 25 |
| 4146 | | 200l. Thin-leafed peony | 80 | 35 |

**1401** Anniversary Emblem

**1997.** 50th Anniv of Civil Aviation.

| | | | | |
|---|---|---|---|---|
| 4147 | **1401** | 120l. multicoloured | 35 | 25 |

**1402** Georgiev

**1997.** Death Centenary of Evlogii Georgiev.

| | | | | |
|---|---|---|---|---|
| 4148 | **1402** | 120l. multicoloured | 35 | 25 |

**1403** Show Jumping and Running

**1997.** World Modern Pentathlon Championship, Sofia. Multicoloured.

| | | | | |
|---|---|---|---|---|
| 4149 | | 60l. Type **1403** | 35 | 10 |
| 4150 | | 80l. Fencing and swimming | 35 | 25 |
| 4151 | | 100l. Running and fencing | 45 | 25 |
| 4152 | | 120l. Shooting and swimming | 60 | 35 |
| 4153 | | 200l. Show jumping and shooting | 70 | 50 |

**1404** St. Basil's Cathedral

**1997.** 850th Anniv of Moscow and "Moskva 97" International Stamp Exhibition. Sheet 87×96 mm.

| | | | | |
|---|---|---|---|---|
| **MS**4154 | **1404** | 120l. multicoloured | 80 | 60 |

**1405** D 2500 M Boat Engine

**1997.** Centenary of Diesel Engine. Multicoloured.

| | | | | |
|---|---|---|---|---|
| 4155 | | 80l. Type **1405** | 35 | 10 |
| 4156 | | 100l. D 2900 T tractor engine | 50 | 25 |
| 4157 | | 120l. D 3900 A truck engine | 60 | 35 |
| 4158 | | 200l. D 2500 K fork-lift truck engine | 1·00 | 50 |

**1406** Goddess with Mural Crown

**1997.** 43rd General Assembly of Atlantic Club, Sofia.

| | | | | |
|---|---|---|---|---|
| 4159 | **1406** | 120l. mve, bl & ultram | 50 | 35 |
| 4160 | - | 120l. grn, bl & ultram | 50 | 35 |
| 4161 | - | 120l. brn, bl & ultram | 50 | 35 |
| 4162 | - | 120l. vio, bl & ultram | 50 | 35 |

DESIGNS: No. 4160, Eagle on globe; 4161, Venue; 4162, Venue (different).

**1407** Cervantes and Don Quixote with Sancho

**1997.** 450th Birth Anniv of Miguel de Cervantes (writer).

| | | | | |
|---|---|---|---|---|
| 4163 | **1407** | 120l. multicoloured | 50 | 25 |

**1408** Raztsvetnikov

**1997.** Birth Centenary of Asen Raztsvetnikov (writer and translator).

| | | | | |
|---|---|---|---|---|
| 4164 | **1408** | 120l. multicoloured | 50 | 25 |

**1409** Fragment of Tombstone

**1997.** Millenary of Coronation of Tsar Samuel. Multicoloured.

| | | | |
|---|---|---|---|
| 4165 | 120l. Type **1409** | 50 | 25 |
| 4166 | 600l. Tsar Samuel and knights in battle | 2·40 | 1·20 |

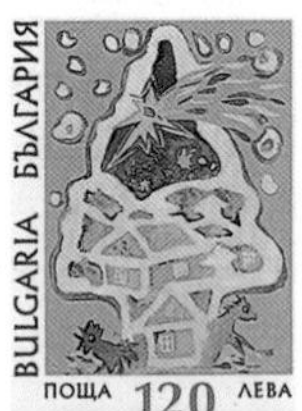


**1410** Star and Houses forming Christmas Tree

**1997.** Christmas. Multicoloured.

| | | | |
|---|---|---|---|
| 4167 | 120l. Type **1410** | 50 | 25 |
| 4168 | 600l. Stable with Christmas tree roof | 2·20 | 1·20 |

**1411** Speed Skating

**1997.** Winter Olympic Games, Nagano, Japan (1998). Multicoloured.

| | | | |
|---|---|---|---|
| 4169 | 60l. Type **1411** | 25 | 10 |
| 4170 | 80l. Skiing | 35 | 20 |
| 4171 | 120l. Shooting (biathlon) | 50 | 25 |
| 4172 | 600l. Ice skating | 3·00 | 1·90 |

**1412** Radiometric System R-400

**1997.** 25th Anniv of Bulgarian Space Experiments. Sheet 87×68 mm.

| | | | |
|---|---|---|---|
| **MS**4173 **1412** | 120l. multicoloured | 1·20 | 1·20 |

**1413** State Arms

**1997**

| | | | | |
|---|---|---|---|---|
| 4174 | **1413** | 120l. multicoloured | 40 | 25 |

**1414** Botev (after B. Petrov)

**1998.** 150th Birth and 120th Death (1996) Anniv of Khristo Botev (poet and revolutionary).

| | | | | |
|---|---|---|---|---|
| 4175 | **1414** | 120l. multicoloured | 40 | 25 |

**1415** Brecht

**1998.** Birth Cent of Bertolt Brecht (playwright).

| | | | | |
|---|---|---|---|---|
| 4176 | **1415** | 120l. multicoloured | 40 | 25 |

**1416** Arrows

**1998.** Cent of Bulgarian Telegraph Agency.

| | | | | |
|---|---|---|---|---|
| 4177 | **1416** | 120l. multicoloured | 40 | 25 |

**1417** Barn Swallow at Window

**1998.** 120th Birth Anniv of Aleksandur Bozhinov (children's illustrator). Multicoloured.

| | | | |
|---|---|---|---|
| 4178 | 120l. Type **1417** | 40 | 15 |
| 4179 | 120l. Blackbird with backpack on branch | 40 | 15 |
| 4180 | 120l. Father Frost and children | 40 | 15 |
| 4181 | 120l. Maiden Rositsa in field holding hands up to rain | 40 | 15 |

**1418** Tsar Alexander II

**1998.** 120th Anniv of Liberation from Turkey. Multicoloured.

| | | | |
|---|---|---|---|
| 4182 | 120l. Type **1418** | 40 | 15 |
| 4183 | 600l. Independence monument, Ruse | 2·00 | 95 |

**1419** Christ ascending and Hare pulling Cart of Eggs

**1998.** Easter.

| | | | | |
|---|---|---|---|---|
| 4184 | **1419** | 120l. multicoloured | 40 | 25 |

**1420** Torch Bearer

**1998.** 75th Anniv of Bulgarian Olympic Committee.

| | | | | |
|---|---|---|---|---|
| 4185 | **1420** | 120l. multicoloured | 40 | 25 |

**1421** Map of Participating Countries

**1998.** Phare International Programme for Telecommunications and Post.

| | | | | |
|---|---|---|---|---|
| 4186 | **1421** | 120l. multicoloured | 40 | 25 |

**1422** Girls in Folk Costumes

**1998.** Europa. National Festivals. Multicoloured.

| | | | |
|---|---|---|---|
| 4187 | 120l. Type **1422** | 1·40 | 70 |
| 4188 | 600l. Boys wearing dance masks | 3·50 | 2·75 |

ПЪРВИ
ЗЛАТЕН МЕДАЛ
ЗА БЪЛГАРИЯ

Е. ДАФОВСКА

**(1423)**

**1998.** Winning of Gold Medal in 15km Biathlon by Ekaterina Dafovska at Winter Olympic Games, Nagano. No. 4171 optd with T 1423.

| | | | |
|---|---|---|---|
| 4189 | 120l. multicoloured | 4·00 | 4·00 |

**1424** "Dante and Virgil in Hell"

**1998.** Birth Bicentenary of Eugene Delacroix (artist).

| | | | | |
|---|---|---|---|---|
| 4190 | **1424** | 120l. multicoloured | 40 | 25 |

**1425** Footballer and Club Badge

**1998.** 50th Anniv of TsSKA Football Club.

| | | | | |
|---|---|---|---|---|
| 4191 | **1425** | 120l. multicoloured | 40 | 25 |

**1426** European Tabby

**1998.** Cats. Multicoloured.

| | | | |
|---|---|---|---|
| 4192 | 60l. Type **1426** | 15 | 10 |
| 4193 | 80l. Siamese | 25 | 15 |
| 4194 | 120l. Exotic shorthair | 40 | 25 |
| 4195 | 600l. Birman | 2·20 | 1·10 |

**1427** "Oh, You are Jealous!"

**1998.** 150th Birth Anniv of Paul Gauguin (artist).

| | | | | |
|---|---|---|---|---|
| 4196 | **1427** | 120l. multicoloured | 40 | 25 |

**1428** Khilendarski-Bozveli

**1998.** 150th Death Anniv of Neofit Khilendarski-Bozveli (priest and writer).

| | | | | |
|---|---|---|---|---|
| 4197 | **1428** | 120l. multicoloured | 40 | 25 |

**1429** Tackling

**1998.** World Cup Football Championship, France. Multicoloured.

| | | | |
|---|---|---|---|
| 4198 | 60l. Type **1429** | 15 | 10 |
| 4199 | 80l. Players competing for ball | 25 | 15 |
| 4200 | 120l. Players and ball | 40 | 25 |
| 4201 | 600l. Goalkeeper | 2·20 | 1·10 |
| **MS**4202 | 68 ×91 mm. 120l. Lion, ball and Eiffel Tower | 1·40 | 1·40 |

**1430** A. Aleksandrov

**1998.** 10th Anniv of Second Soviet–Bulgarian Space Flight.

| | | | | |
|---|---|---|---|---|
| 4203 | **1430** | 120l. multicoloured | 55 | 25 |

**1431** Vasco da Gama

**1998.** "Expo '98" World's Fair, Lisbon. 500th Anniv of Vasco da Gama's Voyage to India. Multicoloured.

| | | | |
|---|---|---|---|
| 4204 | 600l. Type **1431** | 2·30 | 70 |
| 4205 | 600l. "Sao Gabriel" (Vasco da Gama's ship) | 2·30 | 70 |

Nos. 4204/5 were issued together, se-tenant, forming a composite design.

**1432** Focke Wolf FW 61, 1937

**1998.** Helicopters. Multicoloured.

| | | | |
|---|---|---|---|
| 4206 | 80l. Type **1432** | 25 | 10 |
| 4207 | 100l. Sikorsky R-4, 1943 | 40 | 15 |
| 4208 | 120l. Mil Mi-V12, 1970 | 55 | 25 |
| 4209 | 200l. McDonnell-Douglas MD-900, 1995 | 80 | 40 |

**1433** Mediterranean Monk Seal (*Monachus monachus*)

**1998.** International Year of the Ocean. Sheet 67×88 mm.

| | | | |
|---|---|---|---|
| **MS**4210 **1433** | 120l. multicoloured | 4·75 | 4·75 |

**1434** Talev

**1998.** Birth Centenary of Dimitur Talev (writer).

| | | | | |
|---|---|---|---|---|
| 4211 | **1434** | 180l. multicoloured | 70 | 40 |

**1435** Aleksandur Malinov (Prime Minister, 1931)

**1998.** 90th Anniv of Independence.

| | | | | |
|---|---|---|---|---|
| 4212 | **1435** | 180l. black, blue & yell | 70 | 40 |

**1436** "Limenitis redukta" and "Ligularia sibirica"

**1998.** Butterflies and Flowers. Multicoloured.

| | | | | |
|---|---|---|---|---|
| 4213 | | 60l. Type **1436** | 10 | 10 |
| 4214 | | 180l. Painted lady and "Anthemis macrantha" | 70 | 25 |
| 4215 | | 200l. Red admiral and "Trachelium jacquinii" | 80 | 40 |
| 4216 | | 600l. "Anthocharis gruneri" and "Geranium tuberosum" | 2·20 | 1·20 |

**1437** Smirnenski

**1998.** Birth Cent of Khristo Smirnenski (writer).

| | | | | |
|---|---|---|---|---|
| 4217 | **1437** | 180l. multicoloured | 70 | 40 |

**1438** Silhouette of Man

**1998.** 50th Anniv of Universal Declaration of Human Rights.

| | | | | |
|---|---|---|---|---|
| 4218 | **1438** | 180l. multicoloured | 70 | 40 |

**1439** Bruno

**1998.** 450th Birth Anniv of Giordano Bruno (scholar).

| | | | | |
|---|---|---|---|---|
| 4219 | **1439** | 180l. multicoloured | 70 | 40 |

**1440** Man diving through Heart ("I Love You")

**1998.** Greetings Stamps. Multicoloured.

| | | | | |
|---|---|---|---|---|
| 4220 | | 180l. Type **1440** | 70 | 40 |
| 4221 | | 180l. Making wine (holiday) (vert) | 70 | 40 |
| 4222 | | 180l. Man in chalice (birthday) (vert) | 70 | 40 |
| 4223 | | 180l. Waiter serving wine (name day) (vert) | 70 | 40 |

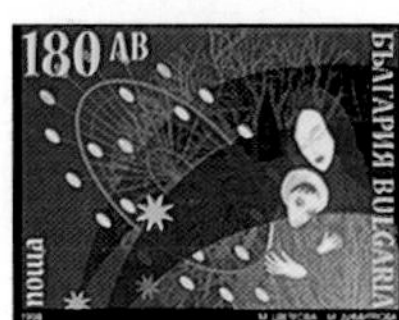


**1441** Madonna and Child

**1998.** Christmas.

| | | | | |
|---|---|---|---|---|
| 4224 | **1441** | 180l. multicoloured | 70 | 40 |

**1442** Geshov

**1999.** 150th Birth Anniv of Ivan Evstratiev Geshov (politician).

| | | | | |
|---|---|---|---|---|
| 4225 | **1442** | 180l. multicoloured | 70 | 40 |

**1443** National Assembly Building, Sofia

**1999.** 120th Anniv of Third Bulgarian State. Mult.

| | | | | |
|---|---|---|---|---|
| 4226 | | 180l. Type **1443** | 70 | 40 |
| 4227 | | 180l. Council of Ministers | 70 | 40 |
| 4228 | | 180l. Statue of Justice (Supreme Court of Appeal) | 70 | 40 |
| 4229 | | 180l. Coins (National Bank) | 70 | 40 |
| 4230 | | 180l. Army | 70 | 40 |
| 4231 | | 180l. Lion emblem of Sofia and lamp post | 70 | 40 |

**1444** Georgi Karakashev (stage designer) and Set of "Kismet"

**1999.** Birth Centenaries. Multicoloured.

| | | | | |
|---|---|---|---|---|
| 4232 | | 180l. Type **1444** | 55 | 25 |
| 4233 | | 200l. Bencho Obreshkov (artist) and "Lodki" | 70 | 35 |
| 4234 | | 300l. Score and Asen Naidenov (conductor of Sofia Opera) | 80 | 40 |
| 4235 | | 600l. Pancho Vladigerov (composer) and score of "Vardar" | 1·90 | 95 |

**1445** Rainbow Lory (*Trichoglossus haematodus*)

**1999.** "Bulgaria '99" European Stamp Exhibition. Parrots. Sheet 100×110 mm containing T **1445** and similar vert designs. Multicoloured.

**MS**4236 600l. Type **1445**; 600l. Eastern rosella; 600l. Budgerigar; 600l. Green-winged macaw 12·00 12·00

**1446** Sun and Emblem

**1999.** 50th Anniv of North Atlantic Treaty Organization.

| | | | | |
|---|---|---|---|---|
| 4237 | **1446** | 180l. multicoloured | 55 | 25 |

**1447** Decorated Eggs

**1999.** Easter.

| | | | | |
|---|---|---|---|---|
| 4238 | **1447** | 180l. multicoloured | 55 | 25 |

**1448** Red-crested Pochard and Ropotamo Reserve

**1999.** Europa. Parks and Gardens. Multicoloured.

| | | | | |
|---|---|---|---|---|
| 4239 | | 180l. Type **1448** | 95 | 40 |
| 4240 | | 600l. Central Balkan National Park | 2·40 | 2·00 |

**1449** Albrecht Durer (self-portrait) and Nuremberg

**1999.** "iBRA '99" International Stamp Exhibition, Nuremberg, Germany.

| | | | | |
|---|---|---|---|---|
| 4241 | **1449** | 600l. multicoloured | 2·00 | 95 |

**1450** Anniversary Emblem

**1999.** 50th Anniv of Council of Europe.

| | | | | |
|---|---|---|---|---|
| 4242 | **1450** | 180l. multicoloured | 1·40 | 70 |

**1451** Honore de Balzac (novelist)

**1999.** Birth Anniversaries. Multicoloured.

| | | | | |
|---|---|---|---|---|
| 4243 | | 180l. Type **1451** (bicentenary) | 55 | 15 |
| 4244 | | 200l. Johann Wolfgang von Goethe (poet and playwright) (250th anniv) | 95 | 25 |
| 4245 | | 300l. Aleksandr Pushkin (poet) (bicentenary) | 1·10 | 55 |
| 4246 | | 600l. Diego de Silva Velazquez (painter) (400th anniv) | 2·00 | 95 |

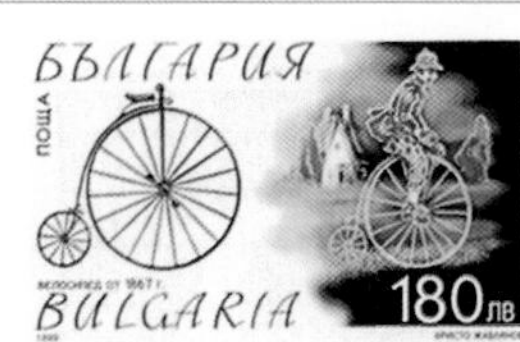


**1452** Penny Farthing

**1999.** Bicycles. Multicoloured.

| | | | | |
|---|---|---|---|---|
| 4247 | | 180l. Type **1452** | 55 | 10 |
| 4248 | | 200l. Road racing bicycles | 70 | 15 |
| 4249 | | 300l. Track racing bicycles | 1·10 | 40 |
| 4250 | | 600l. Mountain bike | 2·00 | 70 |

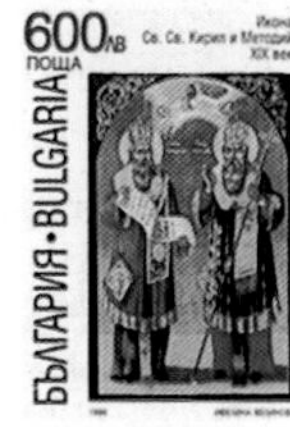


**1453** St. Cyril and Methodius

**1999.** "Bulgaria '99" European Stamp Exhibition, Sofia. 19th-century Icons of Sts. Cyril and Methodius. Sheet 100×110 mm containing T **1453** and similar vert designs. Multicoloured.

**MS**4251 600l. Type **1453**; 600l. St. Cyril with scroll and staff and St. Methodius; 600l. Sts. Cyril and Methodius with scrolls; 600l. St. Cyril with crucifix, St. Methodius and Christ 11·00 11·00

**1454** Sopot Monastery Fountain

**1999.** Fountains.

| | | | | |
|---|---|---|---|---|
| 4252 | **1454** | 1st. light brown | 15 | 10 |
| 4254 | - | 8st. green and black | 15 | 10 |
| 4255 | - | 10st. deep brown | 40 | 10 |
| 4257 | - | 18st. light blue | 55 | 15 |
| 4258 | - | 20st. bright blue | 55 | 25 |
| 4260 | - | 60st. brown and black | 1·80 | 40 |

DESIGNS: 8st. Peacock Fountain, Karlovo; 10st. Peev Fountain, Kopivshtitsa; 18st. Sandanski Fountain; 20st. Eagle Owl Fountain, Karlovo; 60st. Fountain, Sokolski Monastery.

**1455** *Oxytropis urumovii*

**1999.** "Bulgaria '99" European Stamp Exhibition, Sofia (2nd issue). Flowers in Pirin National Park. Sheet 109×100 mm containing T **1455** and similar horiz designs. Multicoloured.

**MS**4265 60st. Type **1455**; 60st. Bellflower; 60st. Iris; 60st. Spotted gentian 13·50 13·50

**1456** Cracked Green Russula

**1999.** Fungi. Multicoloured.

| | | | | |
|---|---|---|---|---|
| 4266 | | 10st. Type **1456** | 40 | 10 |
| 4267 | | 18st. Field mushroom | 55 | 15 |
| 4268 | | 20st. "Hygrophorus russula" | 80 | 25 |
| 4269 | | 60st. Wood blewit | 2·20 | 55 |

**1457** Diagram of path of Eclipse

**1999.** Solar Eclipse (11 Aug 1999). Sheet 90×90 mm.

**MS**4270 **1457** 20st. multicoloured 2·00 2·00

**1458** Four-leaved Clover

**1999.** Centenary of Organized Peasant Movement.

| | | | | |
|---|---|---|---|---|
| 4271 | **1458** | 18st. multicoloured | 40 | 25 |

**1459** 1884 25st. Postage Due Stamp

**1999.** "Bulgaria '99" European Stamp Exhibition, Sofia (3rd issue). 125th Anniv of Universal Postal Union. Sheet 110×102 mm containing T 1459 and similar vert deisgns. Multicoloured.

**MS**4272 60st. Type **1459**; 60st. Dove and hand with letter; 60st. Globe and left half of messenger; 60st. Right half of messenger with letter and globe — 11·00 — 11·00

**1460** Lesser Grey Shrike

**1999.** Song Birds and their Eggs. Multicoloured.

| | | | |
|---|---|---|---|
| 4273 | 8st. Type **1460** | 25 | 10 |
| 4274 | 18st. Mistle thrush | 55 | 15 |
| 4275 | 20st. Dunnock | 70 | 25 |
| 4276 | 60st. Ortolan bunting | 1·90 | 80 |

**1461** Greek Tortoise

**1999.** Reptiles. Multicoloured.

| | | | |
|---|---|---|---|
| 4277 | 10st. Type **1461** | 40 | 10 |
| 4278 | 18st. Swamp turtle | 55 | 15 |
| 4279 | 30st. Hermann's tortoise | 95 | 40 |
| 4280 | 60st. Caspian turtle | 1·90 | 80 |

**1462** Boxing (16 medals)

**1999.** Bulgarian Olympic Medal Winning Sports. Multicoloured.

| | | | |
|---|---|---|---|
| 4281 | 10st. Type **1462** | 40 | 10 |
| 4282 | 20st. High jumping (17 medals) | 70 | 25 |
| 4283 | 30st. Weightlifting (31 medals) | 95 | 40 |
| 4284 | 60st. Wrestling (60 medals) | 1·90 | 80 |

**1463** Police Light and Emblem

**1999.** 10th European Police Conference.

| | | | | |
|---|---|---|---|---|
| 4285 | **1463** | 18st. multicoloured | 40 | 25 |

**1464** Jug

**1999.** Gold Artefacts from Panagyurishte.

| | | | | |
|---|---|---|---|---|
| 4286 | **1464** | 2st. brown and green | 10 | 10 |
| 4287 | - | 3st. brown and green | 10 | 10 |
| 4288 | - | 5st. brown and blue | 10 | 10 |
| 4289 | - | 30st. brown and violet | 70 | 25 |
| 4290 | - | 1l. brown and red | 2·40 | 1·40 |

DESIGNS: 3st. Human figures around top of drinking horn; 5st. Bottom of chamois-shaped drinking horn; 30st. Decorated handle and spout; 1l. Head-shaped jug.

**1465** Virgin and Child

**1999.** Christmas. Religious Icons. Multicoloured.

| | | | |
|---|---|---|---|
| 4291 | 18st. Type **1465** | 40 | 25 |
| 4292 | 60st. Jesus Christ | 1·80 | 80 |

**1466** Scout beside Fire

**1999.** Scouts. Multicoloured.

| | | | |
|---|---|---|---|
| 4293 | 10st. Type **1466** | 40 | 15 |
| 4294 | 18st. Scout helping child | 55 | 25 |
| 4295 | 30st. Scout saluting | 80 | 40 |
| 4296 | 60st. Girl and boy scouts | 1·60 | 80 |

**1467** Emblem

**1999.** "Expo 2005" World's Fair, Aichi, Japan.

| | | | | |
|---|---|---|---|---|
| 4297 | **1467** | 18st. multicoloured | 55 | 25 |

**1468** Emblem and Flag

**2000.** Bulgarian Membership of European Union.

| | | | | |
|---|---|---|---|---|
| 4298 | **1468** | 18st. multicoloured | 1·40 | 70 |

**1469** White Stork (*Ciconia ciconia*)

**2000.** Endangered Species. Sheet 80×60 mm.

**MS**4299 **1469** 60st. multicoloured — 2·75 — 2·75

**1470** Peter Beron and Scientific Instruments

**2000.** Birth Anniversaries. Multicoloured.

| | | | |
|---|---|---|---|
| 4300 | 10st. Type **1470** (scientist, bicentenary) | 40 | 15 |
| 4301 | 20st. Zakhari Stoyanov (writer, 150th anniv) | 70 | 25 |
| 4302 | 50st. Kolyo Ficheto (architect, bicentenary) | 1·40 | 55 |

**1471** Madonna and Child with Circuit Board

**2000.** Europa. Multicoloured.

| | | | |
|---|---|---|---|
| 4303 | 18st. Type **1471** | 1·40 | 70 |
| 4304 | 60st. Madonna and Child (Leonardo da Vinci) with circuit board | 2·75 | 2·50 |

**1472** Judo

**2000.** Olympic Games, Sydney. Multicoloured.

| | | | |
|---|---|---|---|
| 4305 | 10st. Type **1472** | 25 | 10 |
| 4306 | 18st. Tennis | 40 | 15 |
| 4307 | 20st. Pistol shooting | 55 | 25 |
| 4308 | 60st. Long jump | 1·60 | 80 |

**1473** *Puss in Boots* (Charles Perrault)

**2000.** Children's Fairytales. Multicoloured.

| | | | |
|---|---|---|---|
| 4309 | 18st. Type **1473** | 55 | 40 |
| 4310 | 18st. *Little Red Riding Hood* (Brothers Grimm) | 55 | 40 |
| 4311 | 18st. *Thumbelina* (Hans Christian Andersen) | 55 | 40 |

**1474** "Friends" (detail) (Assen Vasiliev)

**2000.** Artists Birth Centenaries. Art. Multicoloured.

| | | | |
|---|---|---|---|
| 4312 | 18st. Type **1474** | 55 | 25 |
| 4313 | 18st. "All Soul's Day" (detail) (Pencho Georgiev) | 55 | 25 |
| 4314 | 18st. "Veliko Tunovo" (detail) (Ivan Khristov) | 55 | 25 |
| 4315 | 18st. "At the Fountain" (sculpture) (detail) (Ivan Funev) | 55 | 25 |

**1475** Roman Mosaic (detail), Stara Zagora

**2000.** "EXPO 2000" World's Fair, Hanover, Germany.

| | | | | |
|---|---|---|---|---|
| 4316 | **1475** | 60st. multicoloured | 1·80 | 70 |

**1476** Johannes Gutenberg (inventor of printing) and Printed Characters

**2000.** Anniversaries. Multicoloured.

| | | | |
|---|---|---|---|
| 4317 | 10st. Type **1476** (600th birth anniv) | 25 | 10 |
| 4318 | 18st. Johann Sebastian Bach (composer, 250th death anniv) | 40 | 15 |
| 4319 | 20st. Guy de Maupassant (writer, 150th birth anniv) | 70 | 25 |
| 4320 | 60st. Antoine de Saint-Exupery (writer and aviator, birth centenary) | 2·00 | 55 |

**1477** *La Jeune* (Lebardy-Juillot airship) and Eiffel Tower, 1903

**2000.** Centenary of First Zeppelin Flight. Airship Development. Multicoloured.

| | | | |
|---|---|---|---|
| 4321 | 10st. Type **1477** | 25 | 10 |
| 4322 | 18st. LZ-13 *Hansa* (Zeppelin airship) over Cologne | 40 | 15 |
| 4323 | 20st. N-1 *Norge* over Rome | 70 | 25 |
| 4324 | 60st. *Graf Zeppelin* over Sofia | 2·00 | 80 |

**1478** Vazov and Text

**2000.** 150th Birth Anniv of Ivan Vazov (writer).

| | | | | |
|---|---|---|---|---|
| 4325 | **1478** | 18st. multicoloured | 55 | 25 |

**1479** Letter "e" with Hands

**2000.** 25th Anniv of Organization for Security and Co-operation in Europe. Helsinki Final Act (establishing governing principles). Sheet 68×72 mm containing T 1479 and similar horiz design. Multicoloured.

**MS**4326 20st. Type **1479**; 20st. Three "e's" — 2·75 — 2·00

**1480** St. Atanasii Church, Startsevo

**2000.** Churches.

| | | | | |
|---|---|---|---|---|
| 4327 | **1480** | 22st. black and blue | 55 | 10 |
| 4328 | - | 24st. black and mauve | 70 | 15 |
| 4329 | - | 50st. black and yellow | 1·40 | 40 |
| 4330 | - | 65st. black and green | 1·80 | 70 |
| 4331 | - | 3l. black and orange | 6·75 | 2·75 |
| 4332 | - | 5l. black and rose | 11·00 | 4·75 |

DESIGNS: 24st. St. Clement of Orhid, Sofia; 50st. Mary of the Ascension, Sofia; 65st. St. Nedelya, Nedelino; 3l. Mary of the Ascension, Sofia (different), Sofia; 5l. Mary of the Ascension, Pamporovo.

**1481** Ibex (*Capra ibex*)

**2000.** Animals. Multicoloured.

| | | | |
|---|---|---|---|
| 4333 | 10st. Type **1481** | 25 | 10 |
| 4334 | 22st. Argali (*Ovis ammon*) | 55 | 20 |
| 4335 | 30st. European bison (*Bison bonasus*) | 70 | 25 |
| 4336 | 65st. Yak (*Bos grunniens*) | 1·90 | 55 |

**1482** Field Gladiolus (*Gladiolus segetum*)

**2000.** Spring Flowers. Multicoloured.

| | | | |
|---|---|---|---|
| 4337 | 10st. Type **1482** | 25 | 10 |
| 4338 | 22st. Liverwort (*Hepatica nobilis*) | 55 | 20 |
| 4339 | 30st. Pheasant's eye (*Adonis vernalis*) | 80 | 25 |
| 4340 | 65st. Peacock anemone (*Anemone pavonina*) | 1·90 | 55 |

**1483** Crowd and Emblem

**2000.** 50th Anniv of European Convention on Human Rights.

| | | | | |
|---|---|---|---|---|
| 4341 | **1483** | 65st. multicoloured | 2·00 | 1·40 |

**1484** Order of Gallantry, 1880

**2000.** Medals. Multicoloured.

| | | | |
|---|---|---|---|
| 4342 | 12st. Type **1484** | 25 | 10 |
| 4343 | 22st. Order of St. Aleksandu, 1882 | 70 | 20 |
| 4344 | 30st. Order of Merit, 1891 | 80 | 25 |
| 4345 | 65st. Order of Cyril and Methodius, 1909 | 2·00 | 55 |

**1485** Prince Boris-Mihail

**2000.** Bimillenary of Christianity. Multicoloured.

| | | | |
|---|---|---|---|
| 4346 | 22st. Type **1485** | 70 | 25 |
| 4347 | 22st. St. Sofroni Vrachanski | 70 | 25 |
| 4348 | 65st. Mary and Child (detail) | 2·00 | 55 |
| 4349 | 65st. Antim I | 2·00 | 55 |

**1486** Seal

**2000.** 120th Anniv of Supreme Audit Office.

| | | | | |
|---|---|---|---|---|
| 4350 | **1486** | 22st. multicoloured | 70 | 25 |

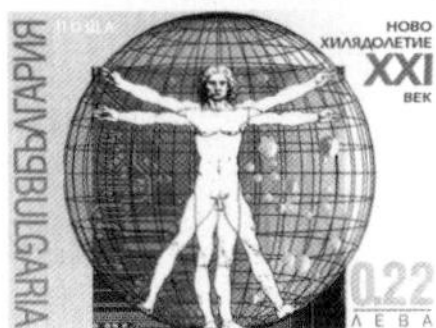

**1487** Microchip, Planets and "The Proportions of Man" (Leonardo DaVinci)

**2001.** New Millennium.

| | | | | |
|---|---|---|---|---|
| 4351 | **1487** | 22st. multicoloured | 70 | 25 |

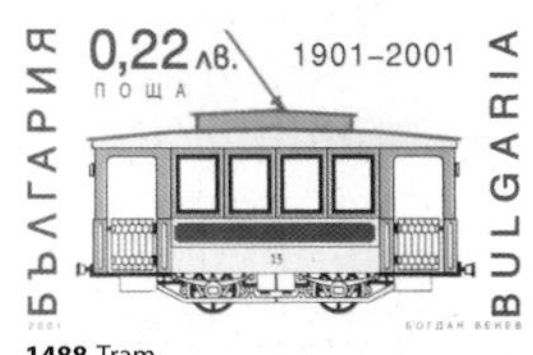

**1488** Tram

**2001.** Centenary of the Electrification of Bulgarian Transport. Multicoloured.

| | | | |
|---|---|---|---|
| 4352 | 22st. Type **1488** | 70 | 25 |
| 4353 | 65st. Train carriages | 2·00 | 55 |

**1489** Muscat Grapes and Evsinograd Palace

**2001.** Viticulture. Multicoloured.

| | | | |
|---|---|---|---|
| 4354 | 12st. Type **1489** | 25 | 10 |
| 4355 | 22st. Gumza grapes and Baba Vida Fortress | 70 | 20 |
| 4356 | 30st. Shiroka Melnishka Loza grapes and Melnik Winery | 80 | 25 |
| 4357 | 65st. Mavrud grapes and Asenova Krepost Fortress | 2·00 | 55 |

**1490** "@" and Microcircuits

**2001.** Information Technology. Sheet 82×95 mm containing T 1490 and similar horiz design. Multicoloured.

| | | | |
|---|---|---|---|
| MS4358 | Type **1490**; 65st. John Atanasoff (computer pioneer) and ABC | 34·00 | 34·00 |

**1491** Southern Europe and Emblem

**2001.** 10th Anniv of the Atlantic Club of Bulgaria. Sheet 87×67 mm.

| | | | | |
|---|---|---|---|---|
| MS4359 | **1491** | 65st. multicoloured | 5·50 | 4·00 |

**1492** Eagle and Lakes, Rila

**2001.** Europa. Water Resources. Multicoloured.

| | | | |
|---|---|---|---|
| 4360 | 22st. Type **1492** | 1·40 | 1·10 |
| 4361 | 65st. Cave and waterfall, Rhodope | 26·00 | 23·00 |

**1493** Building, Bridge and Kableschkov

**2001.** 125th Anniv of the April Uprising and 150th Birth Anniv of Todor Kableschkov (revolutionary leader).

| | | | | |
|---|---|---|---|---|
| 4362 | **1493** | 22st. multicoloured | 70 | 40 |

**1494** Juvenile Egyptian Vulture in Flight

**2001.** Endangered Species. Egyptian Vulture (Neophron perconpterus). Multicoloured.

| | | | |
|---|---|---|---|
| 4363 | 12st. Type **1494** | 40 | 10 |
| 4364 | 22st. Juvenile landing | 70 | 25 |
| 4365 | 30st. Adult and chick | 80 | 40 |
| 4366 | 65st. Adult and eggs | 1·90 | 55 |

**1495** Georgi (Gundy) Asparuchov (footballer)

**2001.** Sportsmen. Multicoloured.

| | | | |
|---|---|---|---|
| 4367 | 22st. Type **1495** | 70 | 40 |
| 4368 | 30st. Dancho (Dan) Kolev (wrestler) | 80 | 50 |
| 4369 | 65st. Gen. Krum Lekarski (equestrian) | 1·90 | 1·10 |

**1496** Rainbow and People

**2001.** 50th Anniv United Nations High Commissioner for Refugees.

| | | | | |
|---|---|---|---|---|
| 4370 | **1496** | 65st. multicoloured | 1·90 | 65 |

**1497** Alexander Zhendov

**2001.** Artists Birth Centenaries. Multicoloured.

| | | | |
|---|---|---|---|
| 4371 | 22st. Type **1497** | 70 | 40 |
| 4372 | 65st. Ilya Beshkov | 2·00 | 1·20 |

**1498** Court Seal

**2001.** 10th Anniv of Constitutional Court.

| | | | | |
|---|---|---|---|---|
| 4373 | **1498** | 25st. multicoloured | 70 | 40 |

**1499** Flags

**2001.** North Atlantic Treaty Organization Summit, Sofia. Sheet 116×111 mm containing T 1499 and similar horiz designs.

| | | | |
|---|---|---|---|
| MS4374 | 12st. Type **1499**; 24st. Streamer of flags; 25st. Flags in upper right semi-circle; 65st. Flags in upper left semi-circle | 3·00 | 2·00 |

**1500** Children encircling Globe

**2001.** United Nations Year of Dialogue among Civilizations.

| | | | | |
|---|---|---|---|---|
| 4375 | **1500** | 65st. multicoloured | 1·80 | 80 |

**1501** Black Sea Turbot (*Scopthalmus maeoticus*)

**2001.** International Day for the Protection of the Black Sea. Sheet 73×91 mm.

| | | | | |
|---|---|---|---|---|
| MS4376 | **1501** | 65st. multicoloured | 1·30 | 1·10 |

**1502** The Nativity

**2001.** Christmas.

| | | | | |
|---|---|---|---|---|
| 4377 | **1502** | 25st. multicoloured | 70 | 40 |

**1503** Cape Shabla Lighthouse

**2001.** Lighthouses.

| | | | | |
|---|---|---|---|---|
| 4378 | **1503** | 25st. red and green | 70 | 40 |
| 4379 | - | 32st. blue and yellow | 80 | 50 |

DESIGN: 32st. Kaliakra Cape lighthouse.

**1504** Monastery Buildings

**2001.** Zographu Monastery, Mount Athos. Sheet 85×105 mm containing T 1504 and similar horiz design. Multicoloured.

**MS**4380 25st. Type **1504**; 65st. Icon 2·75 2·00

**1505** Father Christmas (from film by Al. Zahariev)

**2001.** Bulgarian Animation.

4381 **1505** 25c. multicoloured 80 50

**1506** Vincenzo Bellini

**2001.** Birth Bicentenary of Vincenzo Bellini (composer).

4382 **1506** 25st. multicoloured 80 50

**1507** Crowd and Ancient Calendar

**2001.** Founders of Bulgarian State (1st series). Multicoloured.

4383 10st. Type **1507** 25 10

4384 25st. Khans, Kubrat and Asparuh 80 50

4385 30st. Khans, Krum and Omurtag 95 55

4386 65st. King Boris and Tsar Simeon 2·00 1·20

See also Nos. 4427/7, 4456/9, 4511/14, 4559/62 and 4610/13.

**1508** "€" Symbol and Stars

**2002.** The Euro (European currency).

4387 **1508** 65st. multicoloured 2·00 1·20

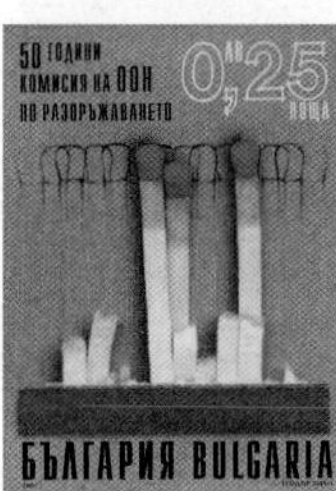


**1509** Matches

**2002.** 50th Anniv of United Nations Disarmament Commission.

4388 **1509** 25st. multicoloured 80 50

**1510** Limestone Arch

**2002.** "BALKANMAX '02" International Stamp Exhibition. Sheet 95×87 mm containing T 1510 and similar vert design. Multicoloured.

**MS**4389 25st. Type **1510**; 65st. Long-legged buzzard (*Buteo rufinus*) 34·00 33·00

**1511** Figure Skater

**2002.** Winter Olympic Games, Salt Lake City. Multicoloured.

4390 25st. Type **1511** 80 50

4391 65st. Speed skater 2·00 1·20

**1512** Station Building and Bearded Penguins

**2002.** 10th National Antarctic Expedition.

4392 **1512** 25st. multicoloured 80 50

**1513** Performing Elephant

**2002.** Europa. Circus. Multicoloured.

4393 25st. Type **1513** 95 55

4394 65st. Clown 2·40 1·50

**1514** Veselin Stojano

**2002.** Birth Centenaries. Multicoloured.

4395 25st. Type **514** (composer) 80 50

4396 65st. Angel Karaliechev (writer) 95 55

**1515** "Illustrated Landscape" (Vasil Barakov)

**2002.** Art. Multicoloured.

4397 10st. Type **1515** 25 10

4398 25st. Book illustration from "Under the Yoke" (novel by Ivan Vazov) (Boris Angulshev) (horiz) 80 50

4399 65st. "The Balcony and Canary" (Ivan Nenov) 2·00 1·20

**1516** Stefan Kanchev

**2002.** 1st Death Annivs of Stamp Designers. Multicoloured.

4400 25st. Type **1516** 80 50

4401 65st. Alex Popilov 2·00 1·20

**1517** Melon (*Cucumis melo*)

**2002.** Fruits. Multicoloured.

4402 10st. Type **1517** 40 25

4403 25st. Watermelon (*Citrullus lanatus*) 80 50

4404 27st. Pumpkin (*Cucurbita pepo*) 90 55

4405 65st. Calabash (*Lagenaria siceraria*) 2·00 1·20

**1518** Cock Bird

**2002.** Poultry. Multicoloured.

4406 10st. Type **1518** 40 25

4407 20st. Leghorn pair (horiz) 70 40

4408 25st. Two cocks fighting (horiz) 80 50

4409 65st. Plymouth rock pair (inscr "Plimouth Rock") 2·00 1·20

**1519** Pope John Paul II and Monument to Cyril & Methodius

**2002.** Pope John Paul II's Visit to Bulgaria.

4410 **1519** 65st. multicoloured 2·00 1·20

**1520** Chess Pieces

**2002.** Sheet 91×71 mm containing T 1520 and similar vert design.

**MS**4411 25st. brown, cinnamon and black (Type **1520**); 65st. multicoloured (Hand holding pawn) 2·75 2·00

**1521** Flag and Stars

**2002.** 10th Anniv of Bulgaria's Admission to Council of Europe.

4412 **1521** 25st. multicoloured 80 50

**1522** Rabbit

**2002.** Woodcarvings by Peter Kuschlev.

4413 **1522** 6st. brown and black 15 10

4414 - 12st. orange and black 40 25

4415 - 36st. green and black 1·10 65

4416 - 44st. pink and black 1·40 80

DESIGNS: 12st. Deer; 36st. Bird; 44st. Boar.

**1523** *Marie-Luisa* (1st ocean-going liner)

**2002.** Merchant Ships. Multicoloured.

4417 12st. Type **1523** 40 25

4418 36st. *Persenk* (cargo ship) 1·10 65

4419 49st. *Kaliakra* (sail training ship) 1·60 1·00

4420 65st. *Sofia* (container ship) 2·00 1·20

**1524** Father Christmas and Sun

**2002.** Christmas.

4421 **1524** 36st. multicoloured 1·10 65

**1525** Flag and NATO Emblem

**2002.** Bulgaria's Participation in NATO Conference, Prague. Sheet 85×65 mm.

**MS**4422 **1525** 65st. multicoloured 4·00 3·00

**1526** Paper Bird

**2002.** 30th Anniv of Security and Co-operation in Europe Conference. Sheet 85×60 mm.

**MS**4423 **1526** 65st. multicoloured 3·50 2·75

**1527** Tsar Samuil

**2002.** Founders of Bulgarian State (2nd series). Multicoloured.

4424 18st. Type **1527** 55 35

4425 36st. Tsars Peter II and Assen 1·10 65

4426 49st. Tsar Kaloyan 1·40 80

4427 65st. Tsar Ivan Assen II 1·90 1·10

**1528** Exhibition Emblem

**2003.** Europalia Cultural Exhibition, Belgium.

4428 **1528** 65st. multicoloured 2·00 1·20

**1529** "Rose Pickers" (Stoyan Sotirov)

**2003.** Artists' Birth Centenaries. Multicoloured.

4429 18st. Type **1529** 55 35

4430 36st. "The Blind Fiddler" (Illya Petrov) 1·10 65

4431 65st. "Swineherd" (Zlatyo Boyadjiev) 1·90 1·10

**1530** Space Construction surrounding Earth

**2003.** Space Exploration. Sheet 104×85 mm.

| | | | |
|---|---|---|---|
| **MS**4432 **1530** 65st. multicoloured | | 2·75 | 2·00 |

**1531** Statue of Russian and Bulgarian Soldiers

**2003.** 125th Anniv of Bulgarian State.

| | | | | |
|---|---|---|---|---|
| 4433 | **1531** | 36st. multicoloured | 1·10 | 65 |

**1532** Exarch Stefan I, Menorah Candlestick and Dimitar Peshev

**2003.** 60th Anniv of Rescue of Bulgarian Jews.

| | | | | |
|---|---|---|---|---|
| 4434 | **1532** | 36st. multicoloured | 1·10 | 65 |

**1533** Silhouettes of Birds and Woman

**2003.** Europa. Poster Art. Multicoloured.

| | | | |
|---|---|---|---|
| 4435 | 36st. Type **1533** | 1·10 | 65 |
| 4436 | 65st. Chicken, legs and farm animals | 1·90 | 1·10 |

**1534** "Vase with Fifteen Sunflowers"

**2003.** 150th Birth Anniv of Vincent van Gogh (artist). Sheet 70×90 mm.

| | | | |
|---|---|---|---|
| **MS**4437 **1534** 65st. multicoloured | | 1·90 | 1·50 |

**1535** Pterodactylus

**2003.** Dinosaurs. Multicoloured.

| | | | |
|---|---|---|---|
| 4438 | 30st. Type **1535** | 80 | 50 |
| 4439 | 36st. Gorgosaurus | 1·10 | 65 |
| 4440 | 49st. Mesosaurus | 1·50 | 90 |
| 4441 | 65st. Monoclonius | 1·90 | 1·10 |

**1536** *Nymphoides Peltata*

**2003.** Water Plants (1st issue). Multicoloured.

| | | | | |
|---|---|---|---|---|
| 4442 | **1536** | 36st. multicoloured | 1·10 | 65 |

See also Nos. 4447/50.

**1537** Honey Bee (*Apis mellifera*)

**2003.** Bees. Multicoloured.

| | | | |
|---|---|---|---|
| 4443 | 20st. Type **1537** | 55 | 35 |
| 4444 | 30st. *Anthidium manicatum* | 80 | 50 |
| 4445 | 36st. Bumble bee (*Bombus subterraneus*) | 95 | 55 |
| 4446 | 65st. Blue carpenter bee (*Xylocopa violacea*) | 1·80 | 1·10 |

**1538** *Butomus umbellatus*

**2003.** Water Plants (2nd issue). Multicoloured.

| | | | |
|---|---|---|---|
| 4447 | 20st. Type **1538** | 55 | 35 |
| 4448 | 36st. *Sagirraria sagittifolia* | 1·10 | 65 |
| 4449 | 50st. *Menyanthes trifoliate* | 1·50 | 90 |
| 4450 | 65st. *Iris pseudoacorus* | 1·90 | 1·10 |

**1539** Gotze Delchev

**2003.** Death Centenary of Gotze Delchev (revolutionary). Centenary of Macedonian Uprising.

| | | | | |
|---|---|---|---|---|
| 4451 | **1539** | 36st. multicoloured | 1·10 | 65 |

**1540** Mountains

**2003.** International Year of Mountains.

| | | | | |
|---|---|---|---|---|
| 4452 | **1540** | 65st. multicoloured | 6·00 | 4·50 |

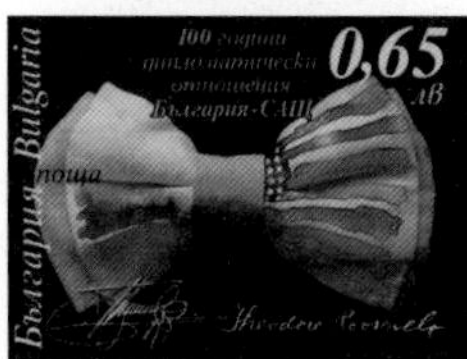

**1541** Bulgarian and USA Flags as Bowtie

**2003.** Centenary of Bulgaria—USA Diplomatic Relations.

| | | | | |
|---|---|---|---|---|
| 4453 | **1541** | 65st. multicoloured | 1·90 | 1·10 |

**1542** John Atanasoff

**2003.** Birth Centenary of John Atanasoff (computer pioneer).

| | | | | |
|---|---|---|---|---|
| 4454 | **1542** | 65st. multicoloured | 1·90 | 1·10 |

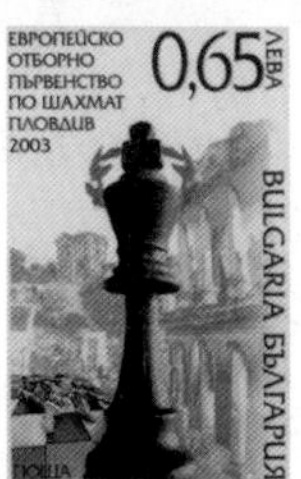

**1543** Pawn and Buildings

**2003.** European Chess Championship, Plovdiv.

| | | | | |
|---|---|---|---|---|
| 4455 | **1543** | 65st. multicoloured | 1·90 | 1·10 |

**1544** Tsar Ivan Alexander

**2003.** Founders of Bulgarian State (3rd series). Multicoloured.

| | | | |
|---|---|---|---|
| 4456 | 30st. Type **1544** | 80 | 50 |
| 4457 | 45st. Despot Dobrotitsa | 1·20 | 75 |
| 4458 | 65st. Tsar Ivan Shishman | 1·90 | 1·10 |
| 4459 | 89st. Tsar Ivan Sratsimir | 2·20 | 1·30 |

**1545** Taekwondo

**2003.** 80th Anniv of National Olympic Committee. Multicoloured.

| | | | |
|---|---|---|---|
| 4460 | 20st. Type **1545** | 55 | 35 |
| 4461 | 36st. Mountain biking | 1·10 | 65 |
| 4462 | 50st. Softball | 1·50 | 90 |
| 4463 | 65st. Canoe slalom | 1·90 | 1·10 |

**1546** Father Christmas

**2003.** Christmas.

| | | | | |
|---|---|---|---|---|
| 4464 | **1546** | 65st. multicoloured | 1·90 | 1·10 |

**1547** Carriage and Man wearing Top Hat

**2003.** Carriages. Multicoloured.

| | | | |
|---|---|---|---|
| 4465 | 30st. Type **1547** | 80 | 50 |
| 4466 | 36st. Closed carriage with woman passenger | 1·10 | 65 |
| 4467 | 50st. State coach, woman and dog | 1·50 | 90 |
| 4468 | 65st. Couple and large carriage | 1·90 | 1·10 |

**1548** FIFA Centenary Emblem

**2003.** Centenary of FIFA (Federation Internationale de Football Association). Multicoloured.

| | | | |
|---|---|---|---|
| 4469 | 20st. Type **1548** | 55 | 35 |
| 4470 | 25st. Early players | 70 | 40 |
| 4471 | 36st. Early players and rules | 1·10 | 65 |
| 4472 | 50st. FIFA fair play trophy (vert) | 1·40 | 80 |
| 4473 | 65st. FIFA world player trophy (vert) | 1·90 | 1·10 |

**1549** Eye, Square, Compass and Statue

**2003.** 10th Anniv of Re-establishment of Masonic Activity in Bulgaria.

| | | | | |
|---|---|---|---|---|
| 4474 | **1549** | 80st. multicoloured | 2·20 | 1·30 |

**1550** *Noctua tertia*

**2004.** Moths. Multicoloured.

| | | | |
|---|---|---|---|
| 4475 | 40st. Type **1550** | 1·10 | 65 |
| 4476 | 45st. *Rethera komarovi* | 1·20 | 75 |
| 4477 | 55st. *Symtomis marjana* | 1·50 | 90 |
| 4478 | 80st. *Arctia caja* | 2·20 | 1·30 |

**1551** Mask

**2004.** SERVA, International Masquerade Festival, Pernik.

| | | | | |
|---|---|---|---|---|
| 4479 | **1551** | 80st. multicoloured | 2·20 | 1·40 |

**1552** OSCE Emblem and Bridge

**2004.** Bulgaria, Chair of Organization for Security and Co-operation in Europe.

| | | | | |
|---|---|---|---|---|
| 4480 | **1552** | 80st. multicoloured | 2·10 | 1·30 |

**1553** Theatre Facade

**2004.** Centenary of Ivan Vazov National Theatre, Sofia.

| | | | | |
|---|---|---|---|---|
| 4481 | **1553** | 45st. multicoloured | 1·30 | 80 |

**1554** Atanas Dalchev

**2004.** Birth Centenaries. Multicoloured.

| | | | |
|---|---|---|---|
| 4482 | 45st. Type **1554** (poet) | 1·30 | 80 |

| | | | |
|---|---|---|---|
| 4483 | 80st. Lubomir Pipkov (composer) | 2·20 | 1·40 |

**1555** NATO Emblem and National Colours

**2004.** Accession to Full Membership of NATO.

| | | | | |
|---|---|---|---|---|
| 4484 | **1555** | 80st. multicoloured | 2·75 | 1·80 |

**1556** Georgi Ivanov

**2004.** 25th Anniv of First Bulgarian in Space. Sheet 84×68 mm.

| | | | |
|---|---|---|---|
| **MS**4485 | **1556** 80st. multicoloured | 2·20 | 1·90 |

**1557** Cover of Document

**2004.** 125th Anniv of Turnovska Constitution and Restoration of Bulgarian State. Sheet 86×67 mm.

| | | | |
|---|---|---|---|
| **MS**4486 | **1557** 45st. multicoloured | 7·00 | 5·25 |

**1558** Globe surmounted by Mortar Board

**2004.** "Bulgarian Dream" (graduate assistance) Programme.

| | | | | |
|---|---|---|---|---|
| 4487 | **1558** | 45st. multicoloured | 1·30 | 80 |

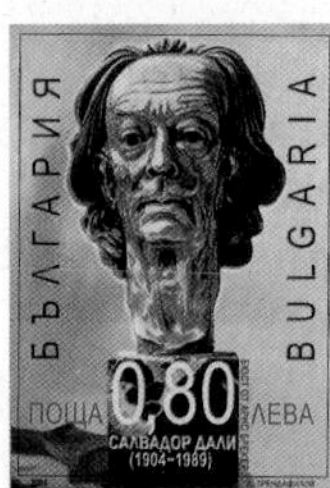


**1559** Salvador Dali (sculpture)

**2004.** Birth Centenary of Salvador Dali (artist). Sheet 85×65 mm.

| | | | |
|---|---|---|---|
| **MS**4488 | **1559** 80st. multicoloured | 4·25 | 3·50 |

**1560** Luben Dimitrov (sculptor) and Boris Ivanov (cinema director)

**2004.** Birth Centenaries. Multicoloured.

| | | | |
|---|---|---|---|
| 4489 | 45st. Type **1560** | 1·40 | 90 |
| 4490 | 80st. Vassil Stoilov and Stoyan Venev (artists) | 2·20 | 1·40 |

**1561** Mountains and Skiers

**2004.** Europa. Holidays. Multicoloured.

| | | | |
|---|---|---|---|
| 4491 | 45st. Type **1561** | 1·40 | 90 |
| 4492 | 80st. Beach scene | 2·20 | 1·40 |

**1562** Christo Stoychkov

**2004.** Bulgarian Footballers. Multicoloured.

| | | | |
|---|---|---|---|
| 4493 | 45st. Type **1562** | 1·40 | 90 |
| 4494 | 45st. Georgi Asparuchov | 1·40 | 90 |
| 4495 | 45st. Krassimir Balakov | 1·40 | 90 |
| 4496 | 45st. Nikola Kotkov | 1·40 | 90 |

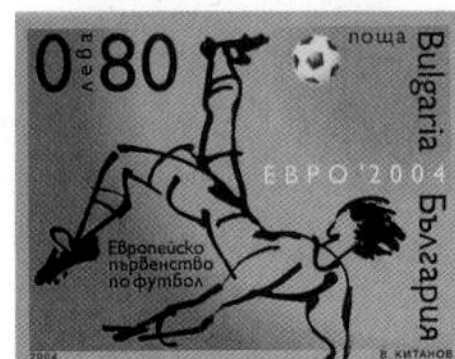


**1563** Footballer and Ball

**2004.** European Football Championship 2004, Portugal. Sheet 85×67 mm.

| | | | |
|---|---|---|---|
| **MS**4497 | 80st. multicoloured | 2·20 | 1·90 |

**1564** Seal

**2004.** 125th Anniv of Bulgaria—Austria Diplomatic Relations.

| | | | | |
|---|---|---|---|---|
| 4498 | **1564** | 80st. multicoloured | 2·20 | 1·40 |

**1565** Lion (statue), Flag and Document

**2004.** 125th Anniv of Ministry of Interior.

| | | | | |
|---|---|---|---|---|
| 4499 | **1565** | 45st. multicoloured | 1·40 | 90 |

**1566a** De Dion Button Post Car (1905)

**2004.** 125th Anniv of Postal Service. Sheet 93×80 mm.

| | | | |
|---|---|---|---|
| **MS**4500 | 45st. multicoloured | 7·00 | 5·75 |

No. **MS**4500 contains a se-tenant stamps size label, which with the stamp forms a composite design.

**1567** Red Kite (*Milvus milvus*)

**2004.** Endangered Species. Preservation of the Black Sea. Sheet 86×86 mm containing T 1567 and similar horiz design. Multicoloured.

| | | | |
|---|---|---|---|
| **MS**4501 | 45st. Type **1567**; 80st. *Blennius ocellaris* | 3·75 | 3·00 |

**1568** Runner holding Torch and Olympic Flame (Berlin, 1936)

**2004.** Olympic Games, Athens 2004. Designs showing runner and Olympic flame. Multicoloured.

| | | | |
|---|---|---|---|
| 4502 | 10st. Type **1568** | 30 | 20 |
| 4503 | 20st. Munich, 1972 | 55 | 35 |
| 4504 | 45st. Moscow, 1980 | 1·40 | 90 |
| 4505 | 80st. Athens, 2004 | 2·20 | 1·40 |

**1569** *Krum* (steamer)

**2004.** 125th Anniv of Bulgarian Navy. Multicoloured.

| | | | |
|---|---|---|---|
| 4506 | 10st. Type **1569** | 30 | 20 |
| 4507 | 25st. *Druski* (torpedo boat) | 70 | 45 |
| 4508 | 45st. *Christo Botev* (mine-sweeper) | 1·40 | 90 |
| 4509 | 80st. *Smeli* (frigate) | 2·20 | 1·40 |

**1570** Square and Compass

**2004.** 125th Anniv of Bulgarian Masonic Movement.

| | | | | |
|---|---|---|---|---|
| 4510 | **1570** | 45st. multicoloured | 7·00 | 5·25 |

**1571** Patriarch Ephtimius Turnovski

**2004.** Founders of Bulgarian State (4th series). Multicoloured.

| | | | |
|---|---|---|---|
| 4511 | 10st. Type **1571** | 30 | 20 |
| 4512 | 20st. Kniaz Fruzhin and Kniaz Constantine | 70 | 45 |
| 4513 | 45st. Georgi Peyachevich and Peter Partchevich | 1·40 | 90 |
| 4514 | 80st. Piessii Hilendarski | 2·50 | 1·60 |

**1572** *Polyporus squamosus*

**2004.** Fungi. Sheet 125×93 mm containing T 1572 and similar horiz designs. Multicoloured.

| | | | |
|---|---|---|---|
| **MS**4515 | 10st. Type **1572**; 20st. *Fomes fomentarius*; 45st. *Piptoporus betulinus*; 80st. *Laetiporus sulphurous* | 5·00 | 3·75 |

**1573** Two Sturgeon

**2004.** Sturgeon (Huso huso). Multicoloured.

| | | | |
|---|---|---|---|
| 4516 | 80st. Type **1573** | 2·50 | 1·60 |
| 4517 | 80st. From below | 2·50 | 1·60 |
| 4518 | 80st. Looking down | 2·50 | 1·60 |
| 4519 | 80st. Eating | 2·50 | 1·60 |

**1574** Father Christmas

**2004.** Christmas.

| | | | | |
|---|---|---|---|---|
| 4520 | **1574** | 45st. multicoloured | 1·40 | 90 |

**1575** Hands

**2004.** 12th Organization for Security and Co-operation in Europe (OSCE) Council, Sofia. Sheet 84×67 mm.

| | | | |
|---|---|---|---|
| **MS**4521 | 80st. multicoloured | 2·10 | 1·90 |

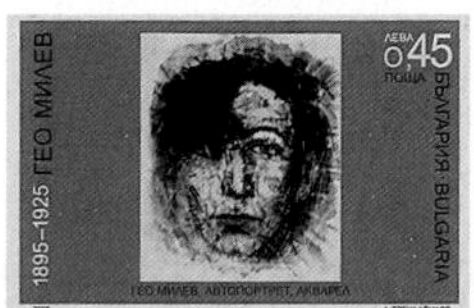


**1576** Geo Milev

**2005.** Birth Centenary of Georghi Milev Kassabov (Geo Milev) (writer and revolutionary).

| | | | | |
|---|---|---|---|---|
| 4522 | **1576** | 45st. multicoloured | 1·50 | 1·10 |

**1577** Emblem

**2005.** Centenary of Rotary International (charitable organization).

| | | | | |
|---|---|---|---|---|
| 4523 | **1577** | 80st. multicoloured | 2·40 | 1·70 |

**1578** Charlie Chaplin in "Gold Rush" (1925)

**2005.** History of Cinema. Sheet 88×118 mm containing T 1578 and similar vert designs. Multicoloured.

| | | | |
|---|---|---|---|
| **MS**4524 | 10st. Type **1578**; 20st. Scene from "Battleship Potemkin (Bronenoset Potemkin)" (1925); 45st. Marlene Dietrich in "Blue Angel (Der Blaue Engel)" (1930); 80st. Vassil Ghendov in "Bulgarian is a Gallant Man" (first Bulgarian film) | 4·75 | 4·25 |

**1579** "The Monument" (lithograph) (Nickolai Pavlovitch)

**2005.** 135th Anniv of Exarchate (independent Bulgarian ecclesiastical organisation). Sheet 68×88 mm.

**MS**4525 45st. multicoloured 2·20 1·80

**1580** European Stars and Bulgarian Flag

**2005.** Volunteers for Europe (educational campaign).

| | | | | |
|---|---|---|---|---|
| 4526 | **1580** | 80st. multicoloured | 2·40 | 1·70 |

**1581** Panayot Hitov and Philip Totyo

**2005.** 175th Birth Anniv of Panayot Hitov and Philip Totyo (revolutionaries).

| | | | | |
|---|---|---|---|---|
| 4527 | **1581** | 45st. multicoloured | 1·50 | 1·10 |

**1582** Robert Peary

**2005.** Polar Explorers. Sheet 64×95 mm containing T 1582 and similar horiz design. Multicoloured.

**MS**4528 45st. Type **1582** (American) (North Pole, 1909); 80st. Rual Admundsen (Norwegian) (South Pole, 1911) 3·75 3·25

**1583** Peugeot (1936)

**2005.** Fire Engines. Sheet 136×77 mm containing T 1583 and similar horiz design. Multicoloured.

**MS**4529 10st. Type **1583**; 20st. Mercedes (1935); 45st. Magirus (1934); 80st. Renault (1925) 4·75 4·00

**1584** Hans Christian Andersen

**2005.** Birth Bicentenary of Hans Christian Andersen (writer). Sheet 87×78 mm.

**MS**4530 **1584** 80st. multicoloured 2·40 2·00

**1585** Hand holding Scroll

**2005.** Cyrillic Alphabet. Sheet 88×59 mm.

**MS**4531 **1585** 80st. multicoloured 2·40 2·00

**1586** Electric Locomotive 46

**2005.** Railways. Multicoloured.

| | | | |
|---|---|---|---|
| 4532 | 45st. Type **1586** | 1·50 | 1·10 |
| 4533 | 80st. Modern locomotive DMV 10 | 7·25 | 5·50 |

**1587** *Radetski* (revolutionary ship) (Georgi Dimov)

**2005.** Children's Painting.

| | | | | |
|---|---|---|---|---|
| 4534 | **1587** | 45st. multicoloured | 1·50 | 1·10 |

**1588** Blinis

**2005.** Europa. Gastronomy. Multicoloured.

| | | | |
|---|---|---|---|
| 4535 | 45st. Type **1588** | 1·50 | 1·10 |
| 4536 | 80st. Bread, kebab and tomatoes | 2·40 | 1·70 |

**1589** Stylized Figures

**2005.** 50th Anniv of Europa—CEPT Postage Stamps.

| | | | | |
|---|---|---|---|---|
| 4537 | **1589** | 45st. violet, green and black | 1·50 | 1·10 |
| 4538 | - | 80st. blue, magenta and black | 2·40 | 1·70 |

DESIGNS: 45st. Type **1589**; 80st. Square of figures.

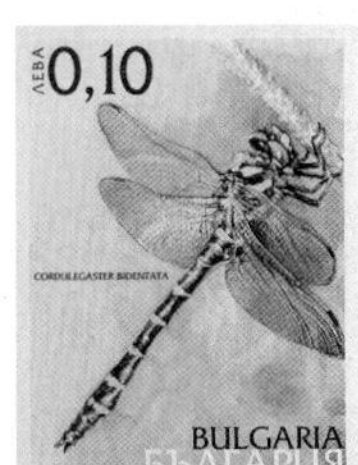

**1590** *Cordulegaster bidentata*

**2005.** Dragonflies. Multicoloured.

| | | | |
|---|---|---|---|
| 4539 | 10st. Type **1590** | 30 | 20 |
| 4540 | 20st. *Erythromma najas* (horiz) | 60 | 45 |
| 4541 | 45st. *Sympetrum pedemontanum* (horiz) | 1·30 | 1·00 |
| 4542 | 80st. *Brachytron pratense* | 2·50 | 1·80 |

**1591** Elias Canetti

**2005.** Birth Centenary of Elias Canetti (writer).

| | | | | |
|---|---|---|---|---|
| 4543 | **1591** | 80st. multicoloured | 2·50 | 1·80 |

**1592** *Synema globosum*

**2005.** Spiders. Multicoloured.

| | | | |
|---|---|---|---|
| 4544 | 10st. Type **1592** | 30 | 20 |
| 4545 | 20st. *Argiope bruennichi* | 60 | 45 |
| 4546 | 45st. *Eresus cinnaberinus* | 1·30 | 1·00 |
| 4547 | 80st. *Araneus diadematus* | 2·50 | 1·80 |

**1593** Flag as Tree Bark

**2005.** 110th Anniv of Organized Tourism.

| | | | | |
|---|---|---|---|---|
| 4548 | **1593** | 45st. multicoloured | 1·20 | 90 |

**1594** Map

**2005.** 120th Anniv of Unification of Bulgaria.

| | | | | |
|---|---|---|---|---|
| 4549 | **1594** | 45st. multicoloured | 1·20 | 90 |

**1595** Girl wearing Traditional Costume, Sofia

**2005.** Women's Traditional Costumes. Mult.

| | | | |
|---|---|---|---|
| 4550 | 20st. Type **1595** | 50 | 40 |
| 4551 | 25st. Pleven | 70 | 55 |
| 4552 | 45st. Sliven | 1·20 | 90 |
| 4553 | 80st. Stara Zagora | 2·00 | 1·60 |

**1596** Stamen Grigoroff (discoverer)

**2005.** Centenary of Discovery of Lactobacillus bulgaricus Grigoroff (yoghurt bacilli) (1st issue). Sheet 94×81 mm.

**MS**4554 **1596** 80st. multicoloured 2·20 1·70

See also **MS**4557.

**1597** Chess Board and Antoaneta Steffanova (Women's World Chess Champion)

**2005.** Chess.

| | | | | |
|---|---|---|---|---|
| 4555 | **1597** | 80st. multicoloured | 2·00 | 1·60 |

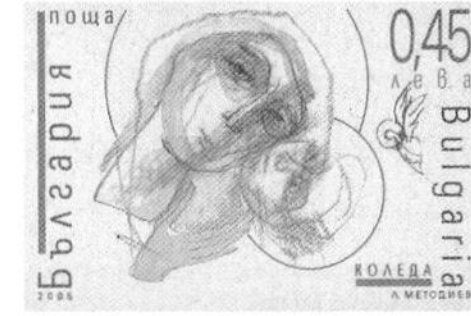

**1598** Virgin and Child

**2005.** Christmas.

| | | | | |
|---|---|---|---|---|
| 4556 | **1598** | 45st. multicoloured | 1·20 | 90 |

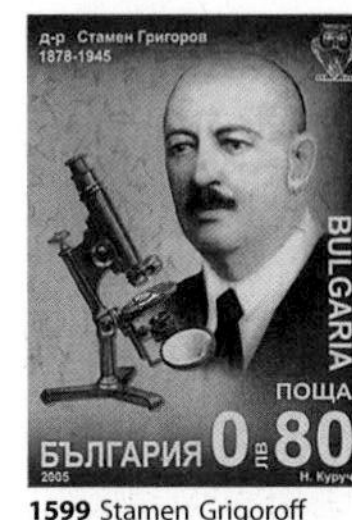

**1599** Stamen Grigoroff (discoverer)

**2005.** Centenary of Discovery of Lactobacillus bulgaricus Grigoroff (yoghurt bacilli) (2nd issue). Sheet 94×81 mm. Imperf.

**MS**4557 **1599** 80st. multicoloured 20·00 18·00

The design of **MS**4557 is as Type **1596** with the addition of an owl in the top right corner. The sheets include a perforated number.

**1600** Stylized Couple

**2005.** 50th Anniv of Membership of United Nations. Sheet 86×68 mm.

| | | | | |
|---|---|---|---|---|
| 4558 | **1600** | 80st. multicoloured | 2·20 | 1·70 |

**1601** Patriarchs Illarion Makariopolski and Antim I

**2005.** Founders of Bulgarian State (5th series).

| | | | | |
|---|---|---|---|---|
| 4559 | **1601** | 10st. chocolate and green | 35 | 25 |
| 4560 | - | 20st. brown and green | 50 | 40 |
| 4561 | - | 45st. claret and green | 1·20 | 90 |
| 4562 | - | 80st. purple and green | 2·00 | 1·60 |

DESIGNS: 10st. Type **1601**; 20st. Georgi Rakovski and Vassil Levski; 45st. Luben Karavelov and Christo Botev; 80st. Panayot Volov and Pavel Bobekov.

**1602** *Rosa pendulina*

**2006.** Roses. Multicoloured.

| | | | |
|---|---|---|---|
| 4563 | 54st. Type **1602** | 1·40 | 1·10 |
| 4564 | 1l.50 *Rosa gallica* | 3·75 | 3·00 |
| 4565 | 2l. *Rosa spinosissima* | 5·00 | 4·00 |

| | | | |
|---|---|---|---|
| 4566 | 10l. *Rosa arvensis* | 24·00 | 18·00 |

**1603** Mozart

**2006.** 250th Birth Anniv of Wolfgang Amadeus Mozart.

| | | | | |
|---|---|---|---|---|
| 4567 | **1603** | 1l. multicoloured | 8·50 | 8·00 |

**1604** Ellin Pellin (writer)

**2006.** 115th Anniv of National Philatelic Press. Bulgarian Philatelists. Multicoloured.

| | | | |
|---|---|---|---|
| 4568 | 35st. Type **1604** | 85 | 80 |
| 4569 | 55st. Lazar Dobritch (circus artiste) | 1·40 | 1·20 |
| 4570 | 60st. Boris Christov (opera singer) | 1·50 | 1·30 |
| 4571 | 1l. Bogomil Nonev (writer) | 2·50 | 2·10 |

**1605** Snowboarder

**2006.** Winter Olympic Games, Turin. Sheet 86×118 mm containing T 1605 and similar vert design. Multicoloured.

| | | |
|---|---|---|
| **MS**4572 55st. Type **1605**; 1l. Ice dancers | 4·00 | 3·75 |

**1606** Sextant

**2006.** 10th Anniv of Bulgarian Antarctic Cartography. Sheet 86×69 mm.

| | | |
|---|---|---|
| **MS**4573 **1606** 1l. multicoloured | 2·50 | 2·20 |

**1607** Ship (15th Century manuscript)

**2006.** 610th Anniv of Battle at Nikopol.

| | | | | |
|---|---|---|---|---|
| 4574 | **1607** | 1l.50 multicoloured | 3·50 | 2·75 |

**1608** *Martes martes*

**2006.** Ecology. Sheet 86×118 mm containing T 1608 and similar horiz design. Multicoloured.

| | | |
|---|---|---|
| **MS**4575 55st. Type **1608**; 1l.50 *Ursus arctos* | 4·75 | 4·25 |

**1609** Stylized Figure and Stars

**2006.** Europa. Integration. Multicoloured.

| | | | |
|---|---|---|---|
| 4576 | 55st. Type **1609** | 1·70 | 1·30 |
| 4577 | 1l. Star as flower | 3·50 | 2·75 |

**1610** Emblem

**2006.** Meeting of NATO Foreign Ministers, Sofia. Sheet 87×70 mm.

| | | |
|---|---|---|
| **MS**4578 **1610** 1l.50 multicoloured | 3·50 | 3·25 |

**1611** Mastheads

**2006.** 70th Anniv of "Trud" Newspaper.

| | | | | |
|---|---|---|---|---|
| 4579 | **1611** | 55st. multicoloured | 2·50 | 2·00 |

**1612** Vesselin Topalov

**2006.** Vesselin Topalov—World Chess Champion. Sheet 87×71 mm.

| | | |
|---|---|---|
| **MS**4580 **1612** 1l.50 multicoloured | 3·50 | 3·25 |

No. **MS**4580 also exist imperforate.

**1613** Building Facade

**2006.** 25th Anniv of National Palace of Culture.

| | | | | |
|---|---|---|---|---|
| 4581 | **1613** | 55st. multicoloured | 1·70 | 1·50 |

**1614** *Circus aeruginosus*

**2006.** Raptors. Multicoloured.

| | | | |
|---|---|---|---|
| 4582 | 10st. Type **1614** | 35 | 25 |
| 4583 | 35st. *Circus cyaneus* | 85 | 65 |
| 4584 | 55st. *Circus macrourus* | 1·20 | 90 |
| 4585 | 1l. *Circus pygargus* | 2·75 | 2·10 |

**1615** Building Facade, Ship and Sailor

**2006.** 125th Anniv of Nikola Vaptsarov Naval Academy, Varna.

| | | | | |
|---|---|---|---|---|
| 4586 | **1615** | 55st. multicoloured | 1·20 | 90 |

**1616** Players

**2006.** World Cup Football Championship, Germany. Sheet 87×87 mm.

| | | |
|---|---|---|
| **MS**4587 **1616** 1l. multicoloured | 2·20 | 2·00 |

**1617** Emblem

**2006.** 50th Anniv of Bulgaria in UNESCO.

| | | | | |
|---|---|---|---|---|
| 4588 | **1617** | 1l. multicoloured | 2·20 | 1·70 |

**1618** Gena Dimitrova

**2006.** 65th Birth Anniv and First Death Anniv of Gena Dimitrova (opera singer).

| | | | | |
|---|---|---|---|---|
| 4589 | **1618** | 1l. multicoloured | 2·20 | 1·70 |

**1619** *Saponaria strajensis*

**2006.** Flora. Multicoloured.

| | | | |
|---|---|---|---|
| 4590 | 10st. Type **1619** | 35 | 25 |
| 4591 | 35st. *Trachystemon orientalis* | 85 | 65 |
| 4592 | 55st. *Hypericum calycinum* | 1·20 | 90 |
| 4593 | 1l. *Rhododendron ponticum* | 2·75 | 2·10 |

**1620** Rover Maestro

**2006.** Bulgaria Automobile Industry. Multicoloured.

| | | | |
|---|---|---|---|
| 4594 | 10st. Type **1620** | 35 | 25 |
| 4595 | 35st. Moskovitch | 85 | 65 |
| 4596 | 55st. Bulgaralpine | 1·20 | 90 |
| 4597 | 1l. Bulgarrnault | 2·75 | 2·10 |

**1621** "Return of the Prodigal Son"

**2006.** 400th Birth Anniv of Rembrandt Harmenszoon van Rijn. Sheet 65×84 mm.

| | | |
|---|---|---|
| **MS**4598 **1621** 1l. multicoloured | 2·75 | 2·40 |

**1622** "All Soul's Day" (Ivan Murkvitchka)

**2006.** Art Anniversaries. Multicoloured.

| | | | |
|---|---|---|---|
| 4599 | 10st. Type **1622** (150th birth anniv) | 35 | 25 |
| 4600 | 35st. "Sozopol—Houses" (Vesselin Statkov) (birth centenary) | 1·00 | 80 |
| 4601 | 55st. "Sofia in Winter" (Nikola Petrov) (90th death anniv) | 1·50 | 1·20 |
| 4602 | 1l. "T. Popova" (John Popov) (birth centenary) | 2·75 | 2·10 |

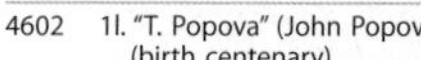

**1623** Competitors

**2006.** World Sambo Championship, Sofia.

| | | | | |
|---|---|---|---|---|
| 4603 | **1623** | 55st. multicoloured | 1·50 | 1·20 |

**1624** Post Van

**2006.** Post Europ. Sheet 85×75 mm.

| | | |
|---|---|---|
| **MS**4604 **1624** 1l. multicoloured | 15·00 | 14·50 |

**1625** Angel

**2006.** Christmas.

| | | | | |
|---|---|---|---|---|
| 4605 | **1625** | 55st. multicoloured | 1·50 | 1·20 |

**1626** Ballot Box and Flags

**2006.** Bulgaria and Romania's Membership of European Union. Multicoloured.

| | | | |
|---|---|---|---|
| 4606 | 55st. Type **1626** | 1·50 | 1·20 |
| 4607 | 1l.50 "EU" | 4·00 | 3·25 |
| **MS**4608 | 97×87 mm. Nos. 4606/7 | 5·75 | 5·50 |

Stamps of a similar design were issued by Romania.

**1627** Peter Dimkov

**2006.** 120th Birth Anniv of Peter Dimkov (naturopath).

| | | | | |
|---|---|---|---|---|
| 4609 | **1627** | 55st. multicoloured | 1·50 | 1·20 |

**1628** Generals Danail Nikolaev and Racho Petrov

**2006.** Founders of Bulgarian State (6th series). Multicoloured.

| | | | |
|---|---|---|---|
| 4610 | 10st. Type **1628** | 35 | 25 |
| 4611 | 35st. Petko Karavelov and Marin Drinov | 1·00 | 80 |
| 4612 | 55st. Konstantin Stoylov and Stephan Stambolov | 1·50 | 1·20 |
| 4613 | 1l. Prince Albert I of Bulgaria | 2·75 | 2·10 |

**1629** Boeing 737 and Terminal Building

**2006.** New Airport Terminal, Sofia. Sheet 87×72 mm.

**MS**4614 **1629** 55st. multicoloured 1·50 1·30

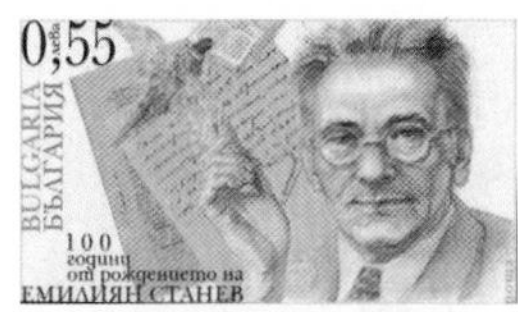


**1631** Emilian Stanev

**2007.** Birth Centenary of Nikola Stoyanov Stanev (Emilian Stanev) (writer).

4616 **1631** 55st. multicoloured 1·40 1·10

**1632** Flags as Stars

**2007.** 50th Anniv of Treaty of Rome.

4617 **1632** 1l. multicoloured 2·50 2·00

**1633** Ivan Dimov

**2007.** Theatre Personalities. Multicoloured.

4618 10st. Type **1633** 35 25

4619 55st. Sava Ognyanov 1·40 1·10

4620 1l. Krustyo Sarfov 2·50 2·00

**1634** Sputnik

**2007.** 50th Anniv of First Manmade Satellite. Sheet 87×56 mm.

**MS**4621 **1634** 1l. multicoloured 2·50 2·40

**1635** Campfire

**2007.** Europa. Centenary of Scouting. Multicoloured. (a) Size 39×28 mm.

4622 55st. Type **1635** 1·40 1·10

4623 1l.50 Route finding 3·75 3·00

(b) Size 31×23 mm.

4624 1l. As Type **1635** 1·40 1·10

4625 1l. As No. 4623 3·75 3·00

**1636** DAR-3 Garvan II (1937)

**2007.** Military Aircraft. Multicoloured.

4626 10st. Type **1636** 35 25

4627 35st. DAR-9 Siniger (1939) 85 65

4628 55st. Kaproni Bulgarski KB-6 Papagal (1939) 1·40 1·10

4629 1l. Kaproni Bulgarski KB-11A Fanzan 2·50 2·00

**1637** Boris I

**2007.** 1100th Death Anniv of Knyaz (Prince) Boris I (Michael).

4630 **1637** 55st. multicoloured 1·40 1·10

**1637a** Basilica and Saint Cyril

**2007.** 150th Anniv of Excavation of San Clement Basilica, Rome.

4630a **1637a** 1l. multicoloured 2·75 2·10

**1638** Dimcho Debelyanov

**2007.** Birth Anniversaries. Multicoloured.

4631 10st. Type **1638** (poet) (120th) 35 25

4632 35st. Nenko Balkanski (artist) (centenary) 85 65

4633 55st. Vera Lukova (artist) (centenary) 1·20 90

4634 1l. Theodor Trayanov (poet) (125th) 2·75 2·10

**1639** St. Spass Monastery, Lozenski

**2007.** Monasteries. Multicoloured.

4635 63st. Type **1639** 1·70 1·30

4636 75st. St. Mina, Obradovski 2·00 1·60

4637 1l.20 St. George the Victor, Kremikovski 3·25 2·50

4638 2l.20 Three Saints, Chepinski 6·00 4·50

**1640** Symbols of Transport

**2007.** International Transport Forum, Sofia.

4639 **1640** 1l. multicoloured 2·75 2·10

**1641** Presidents of Bulgaria and Azerbaijan

**2007.** 15th Anniv of Bulgaria–Azerbaijan Diplomatic Relations. Sheet 86×64 mm.

**MS**4640 1l. multicoloured 2·75 2·50

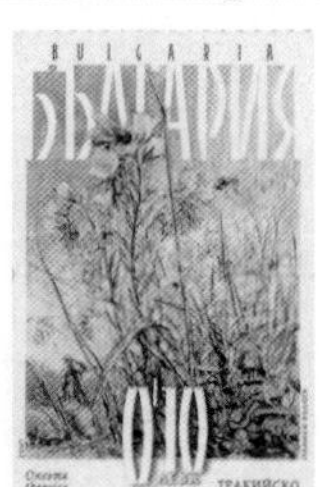


**1642** *Onosma thracica*

**2007.** Flora. Multicoloured.

4641 10st. Type **1642** 35 25

4642 45st. *Astracantha aitosensis* 1·20 90

4643 55st. *Veronica krumovii* 1·50 1·20

4644 1l. *Verbascum adrianopolitanum* 2·75 2·10

**1643** Vassal Levski

**2007.** 170th Birth Anniv of Vassal Levski (revolutionary leader).

4645 **1643** 55st. multicoloured 1·50 1·20

**1644** Sailor

**2007.** Junior World Sailing Championship–Olympian Class 470, Burgas.

4646 **1644** 1l. multicoloured 2·75 2·10

**1645** Lt. Colonel Pavel Kalitin (painting) and 'Battle at Stara Zagora' (Nikola Kozhuharov)

**2007.** 130th Anniv of Battle at Stara Zagora.

4647 **1645** 55st. multicoloured 1·50 1·20

**1646** Players

**2007.** Rugby. 50th (2005) Anniv of Locomotiv Rugby Club, Sofia. World Rugby Championship–2007, France.

4648 **1646** 55st. multicoloured 1·50 1·20

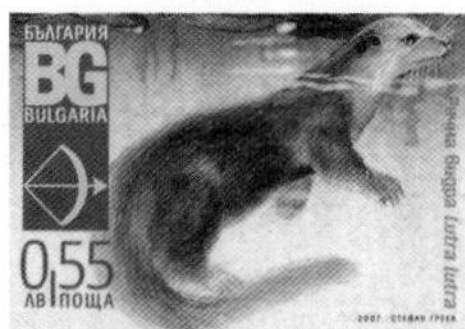


**1647** *Lutra lutra* (otter)

**2007.** Ecology. 15th Anniv of Ropotamo Reserve. Sheet 85×85 mm containing T 1647 and similar horiz design. Multicoloured.

**MS**4649 55st. Type **1647**; 1l. *Haliaeetus albicilla* (white tailed eagle) 4·25 4·00

The stamps and margins of **MS**4549 form a composite design.

**1648** *Alcedo atthis* (kingfisher)

**2007.** Endangered Species. Birds. Sheet 97×130 mm containing T 1648 and similar horiz design. Multicoloured.

**MS**4650 10st. Type **1648**; 35st. *Tichodroma muraria* (wall creeper); 55st. *Bombycilla garrulous* (waxwing); 1l. *Phoenicopterus ruber* (flamingo) 5·50 5·25

**1649** Emblem

**2007.** 10th Anniv Grand Lodge of the Ancient Freemasons.

4651 **1649** 55st. multicoloured 1·50 1·20

**1650** Centre Building

**2007.** Inauguration of Exchange and Sorting Centre, Sofia. Sheet 87×63 mm.

**MS**4652 55st. multicoloured 1·50 1·40

**1651** Ivan Hadjiski

**2007.** Birth Centenary of Ivan Hadjiski (social psychologist).

4653 **1651** 55st. multicoloured 1·50 1·20

**1652** Woman holding Offerings

**2007.** Christmas.

4654 **1652** 55st. multicoloured 1·50 1·20

**1653** Rumyana Neykova (European 2000m. skiff rowing champion)

**2007.** Women Sports Personalities. Multicoloured.

4655 10st. Type **1653** 35 25

4656 35st. Stanka Zlateva (World freestyle wrestling champion) 85 65

4657 1l. Stefka Kostadinova (World record high jump (30.8.1987)) 2·75 2·10

**1654** '100' and Soldier

**2007.** Centenary of Military Reconnaissance.
4658 **1654** 55st. multicoloured 1·50 1·20

**1655** Hristo Botev

**2008.** Birth Centenary of Hristo Botev (poet and revolutionary).
4659 **1655** 55st. multicoloured 1·50 1·20

**1656** Polar Bear

**2008.** International Polar Year. 20th Anniv of Bulgarian Antarctic Expedition. Sheet 115×85 mm containing T 1656 and similar horiz design. Multicoloured.
**MS**4660 55st. Type **1656**; 1l. Skua stealing penguin chick 4·25 4·00

The stamps and margins of **MS**4660 form a composite design.

**1657** Volleyball Player

**2008.** Olympic Games, Beijing. Sheet 88×109 mm containing T 1657 and similar vert design. Multicoloured.
**MS**4661 55st. Type **1657**; 1l. Two players 4·25 4·00

The stamps of **MS**4661 form a composite design of a volley ball match.

**1658** Arms of Bulgaria

**2008.** 130th Anniv of San Stefano Peace Treaty (treaty between Russia and the Ottoman Empire at the end of the Russo-Turkish War (setting up an autonomous self-governing tributary principality of Bulgaria)).
4662 **1658** 55st. multicoloured 1·50 1·20

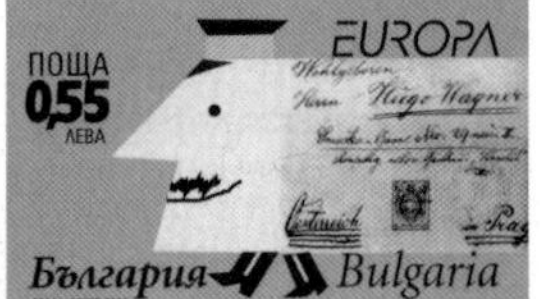


**1659** Envelope as Postman

**2008.** Europa. The Letter. Multicoloured (background colour given).
4663 55st. Type **1659** 1·50 1·20
4664 55st. As Type **1659** (purple) 1·50 1·20
4665 1l. Envelope as pigeon (blue) 2·75 2·10
4666 1l. As No. 4665 (yellow) 2·75 2·10

**1660** Captain Dimiter Spissarevski

**2008.** History of Military Aviation. Pilots' Birth Anniversaries. Multicoloured.
4667 55st. Type **1660** (90th birth anniv) 1·50 1·20
4668 1l. General Stoyan Stoyanov (95th birth anniv) 2·75 2·10

Nos. 4667/8 were issued together, se-tenant, forming a composite design.

**1661** *Women from the Rhodopes* (Boris Kotsev)

**2008.** Artists' Birth Centenaries. Multicoloured.
4669 10st. Type **1661** 35 25
4670 35st. *Nude* (Eliezer Alsheh) 85 65
4671 55st. *Nude* (Vera Nedova) 1·50 1·20
4672 1l. *Maritsa* (Assen Peykov) 2·75 2·10

**1662** Club Members

**2008.** 60th Anniv of CSKA Central Sports Club. Sheet 90×58 mm.
**MS**4673 multicoloured 1·70 1·60

**1663** White-headed Marmoset (*Callithrix geoffroyi*)

**2008.** 120th Anniv of Zoological Gardens, Sofia. Two sheets containing T 1663 and similar vert designs. Multicoloured.
**MS**4674 (a) 126×130 mm. 10st. Type **1663**; 20st. Hippopotamus (*Hippopotamus amphibius*); 35st. Bactrian camel (*Camelus bactrianus*); 55st. Meerkat (*Suricata suricatta*); 60st. Blue-and-yellow macaw (*Ara ararauna*); 1l. Eurasian lynx (*Lynx lynx*); (b) 66×85 mm. 55st. Merrkat (*Suricata suricatta*). Imperf 7·25 7·25

**1664** Alexander Alexandrov

**2008.** 20th Anniv of Alexander Alexandrov's Flight in Orbital Space Station MIR. Sheet 85×61 mm.
**MS**4675 multicoloured 2·75 2·75

**1665** BMW R12 Single Carb, 1935

**2008.** 70th Anniv of Union of Bulgarian Philatelists.
4676 **1665** 60st. multicoloured 1·70 1·30
**MS**4677 106×92 mm. 60st. As Type **1665**. Imperf 1·90 1·90

**1666** *Canis aureus* (golden jackal)

**2008.** Strandja Nature Park. Sheet 104×79 mm containing T 1666 and similar multicoloured design.
**MS**4678 60st. Type **1666**; 1l.50 *Aquila pomarina* (lesser spotted eagle) (vert) 5·50 5·50

The stamps and margins of **MS**4678 form a composite design.

**1667**

**2008.** 20th Anniv of Bulgaria—European Economic Community.
4679 **1667** 1l. black and yellow 2·75 2·10

**1668** Wagons Lits (sleeping car)

**2008.** 125th Anniv of Orient Express. Multicoloured.
4680 60st. Type **1668** 1·70 1·30
4681 1l.50 Steg Wien locomotive No. 5 3·75 3·00

The stamps also show the arms of cities enroute and the emblems of the Orient Express (60st.) or the Bulgarian State Railways (1l.50).

**1669** Nikola and Dimitar Petkov

**2008.** Birth Anniversaries of Dimitar Petkov (Prime Minister 1906–1907) (150th) and Nikola Petkov (politician, son of Dimitar Petkov and leader of Bulgarian Agrarian National Union) (115th).
4682 **1669** 60st. multicoloured 1·70 1·30

**1670** Tsar Ferdinand

**2008.** Centenary of Proclamation of Independence. Sheet 48×87 mm.
**MS**4683 multicoloured 1·90 1·90

**1671** Arms of the Templars

**2008.** 700th Anniv (2007) of Disbanding of Knights Templar (Order of the Temple) by King Philip IV of France.
4684 **1671** 1l. multicoloured 2·75 2·10

**1672** Race Car (2008)

**2008.** Ferrari Racing Cars. Multicoloured.
4685 60st. Type **1672** 1·70 1·30
4686 1l. Race car (1952) 2·75 2·10
**MS**4687 As No. 4685. Imperf 1·90 1·90

**1673** Arms

**2008.** 130th Anniv of Bulgarian Red Cross Societies.
4688 **1673** 60st. multicoloured 1·70 1·30

**1674** Virgin Mary, Rila Monastery (12th-century)

**2008.** Bulgarian Icons. Multicoloured.
4689 50st. Type **1674** 1·40 1·10
4690 60st. Virgin and Child, Troyan Monastery (18th–century) 1·70 1·30
4691 1l. Virgin and Child, Bachkovo Monastery (14th–century) 2·75 2·10
**MS**4691a 112×73 mm. As No. 4690. Imperf 1·70 1·70

**1675** Virgin and Child

**2008.** Christmas.
4692 **1675** 60st. multicoloured 1·70 1·30

**1676** Saint Clement of Ohrid (St. Kliment Ohridski)

**2008.** 120th Anniv of Sofia University St. Kliment Ohridski.
4693 **1676** 60st multicoloured 1·70 1·30

**1677** Andranik Ozanyan (Armenian general in Balkan Wars of Independence)

**2008.** Nationalist Liberation Movements of Bulgaria and Armenia. Multicoloured.

| | | | |
|---|---|---|---|
| 4694 | 60st. Type **1677** | 1·70 | 1·30 |
| 4695 | 1l.50 Peyo Yavorov (Bulgarian poet and revolutionary) | 2·75 | 2·10 |

**1678** Emblem

**2009.** Bulgaria 2009–European Philatelic Exhibition.

| | | | | |
|---|---|---|---|---|
| 4696 | **1678** | 60st. multicoloured | 1·70 | 1·30 |

**1679** Abraham Lincoln

**2009.** Birth Bicentenaries. T 1679 and similar horiz designs. Each green,olive and brown-olive.

| | | | |
|---|---|---|---|
| 4697 | 10st. Type **1679** (pres of USA) | 35 | 25 |
| 4698 | 50st. Nikolai Gogol (writer) | 1·40 | 1·10 |
| 4699 | 60st. Charles Darwin (naturalist) | 1·70 | 1·30 |
| 4700 | 1l. Edgar Allan Poe (writer) | 2·75 | 2·10 |
| **MS**4701 | 55x105mm. 60st. Charles Darwin (different). Imperf | 1·70 | 1·70 |

**1680** *Scolopax rusticola* (Eurasian woodcock)

**2009.** Ecology–Balkan Mountains. Multicoloured.

| | | | |
|---|---|---|---|
| 4702 | 60st. Type **1680** | 1·70 | 1·30 |
| 4703 | 1l. *Monticola saxatilis* (rufous-tailed rock thrush) | 2·75 | 2·10 |
| **MS**4704 | 106×85 mm. As Nos. 4702/3. Imperf | 5·50 | 5·50 |

Nos. 4702/3 were printed together, se-tenant, forming a composite design.

Stamps of a similar design were issued by Serbia.

**1681** Amethyst

**2009.** 120th Anniv of National Natural Science Museum.

| | | | | |
|---|---|---|---|---|
| 4705 | **1681** | 60st. multicoloured | 1·70 | 1·30 |
| **MS**4706 | | 87x61mm. 60st As Type **1681.** Imperf | 1·70 | 1·70 |

**1682** Hagia Sofia Church and St. Alexander Nevsky Cathedral

**2009.** 130th Anniv of Sofia as Capital of Bulgaria.

| | | | | |
|---|---|---|---|---|
| 4707 | **1682** | 60st. multicoloured | 1·70 | 1·30 |

**1683** Penguins and Narwhal

**2009.** Preserve Polar Regions and Glaciers. Sheet 127×63 mm containing T 1683 and similar horiz design. Multicoloured.

| | | | |
|---|---|---|---|
| **MS**4708 | 60st. Type **1683**; 1l.50 Polar bear, elephant seal and white-tailed eagle | 5·50 | 5·50 |

**1684** Flags as '60'

**2009.** 60th Anniv of NATO (4708). 5th Anniv of Bulgaria's Membership of NATO (4709). Multicoloured.

| | | | |
|---|---|---|---|
| 4709 | 60st. Type **1684** | 1·70 | 1·30 |
| 4710 | 1l.50 Bulgarian flag as '5' | 2·75 | 2·10 |

**1685** Bicycle

**2009.** Bicycles. Multicoloured.

| | | | |
|---|---|---|---|
| **MS**4175 | 130x71mm 60st As No. 4714. Imperf 170170 | 1·70 | 1·70 |
| 4711 | 10st. Type **1685** | 35 | 25 |
| 4712 | 50st. Purple cycle | 1·40 | 1·10 |
| 4713 | 60st. Penny farthing cycles | 1·70 | 1·30 |
| 4714 | 1l. Early pedal-less cycle | 2·75 | 2·10 |

Nos. 4711/14 were printed together, se-tenant, forming a composite design.

**1686** Georgi Ivanov

**2009.** 30th Anniv of Space Flight of First Bulgarian Cosmonaut. Sheet 93×93 mm.

| | | | |
|---|---|---|---|
| **MS**4716 | multicoloured | 1·70 | 1·30 |

**1687** Arms (1879)

**2009.** 130th Anniv of Restoration of State. Sheet 105×84 mm containing T 1687 and similar horiz design. Multicoloured.

| | | | |
|---|---|---|---|
| **MS**4717 | 60st. Type **1687**; 1l. Arms (1997) | 4·50 | 4·50 |

**1688** *Rathbunia alamosensis*

**2009.** Cacti. Multicoloured.

| | | | |
|---|---|---|---|
| 4718 | 10st. Type **1688** | 35 | 25 |
| 4719 | 50st. *Mammillaria pseudoperbella* | 1·40 | 1·10 |
| 4720 | 60st. *Obregonia degenerii* | 1·70 | 1·30 |
| 4721 | 1l.50 Inscr 'Astrophitum mayas' | 2·75 | 2·10 |
| **MS**4722 | 71×108 mm. 60t. As No. 4720. Imperf | 1·70 | 1·70 |

**1689** Spiral Galaxy IC 342

**2009.** Europa. Astronomy. Multicoloured.

| | | | |
|---|---|---|---|
| 4723 | 60st. Type **1689** | 1·70 | 1·30 |
| 4724 | 1l.50 Andromeda Galaxy (M 31) | 2·75 | 2·10 |
| **MS**4725 | 112×90 mm. Size 29×39 mm. 60st.×2, As 4725×2; 1l.50×2, As No. 4726×2 | 9·00 | 9·00 |
| 4726 | 60st. As Type **1689** | 1·70 | 1·30 |
| 4727 | 1l.50 As No. 4724 (Andromeda Galaxy (M 31)) | 2·75 | 2·10 |

**1690** Members Flags surrounding Euro

**2009.** 10th Anniv of Euro Currency.

| | | | | |
|---|---|---|---|---|
| 4728 | **1690** | 1l. multicoloured | 2·75 | 2·10 |

**1691** *Landscape* (Vassil Ivanov) (birth centenary)

**2009.** Artists' Anniversaries. Multicoloured.

| | | | |
|---|---|---|---|
| 4729 | 10st. Type **1691** | 35 | 25 |
| 4730 | 50st. *Three Vases* (Georgi Kolarov) (birth centenary) | 1·40 | 1·10 |
| 4731 | 60st *The Black Sea* (Alexander Mutaffov) (130th birth anniv) | 1·70 | 1·30 |
| 4732 | 1l. *Cast Shadows* (Konstantine Sturkelov) (120th birth anniv) | 2·75 | 2·10 |

**1692** Fan

**2009.** 80th Anniv of Locomotive Sofia Sports Club.

| | | | | |
|---|---|---|---|---|
| 4733 | **1692** | 60st. multicoloured | 1·70 | 1·30 |

**1693** *Bubo bubo* (Eurasian eagle owl )

**2009.** Owls. Multicoloured.

| | | | |
|---|---|---|---|
| 4734 | 10st. Type **1693** | 35 | 25 |
| 4735 | 50st. *Athene noctua* (Little owl ) | 1·40 | 1·10 |
| 4736 | 60st. *Strix uralensis* (Ural owl) | 1·70 | 1·30 |
| 4737 | 1l.50 *Glaucidium passerinum* (Eurasian pygmy owl ) | 2·75 | 2·10 |

**1694** Motorcycle and Rider

**2009.** SuperMoto European Championship. Sheet 96×85 mm.

| | | | |
|---|---|---|---|
| **MS**4738 | multicoloured | 1·70 | 1·70 |

**1695** Petko Voivoda

**2009.** 165th Birth Anniv of Petko Voivoda (nationalist).

| | | | | |
|---|---|---|---|---|
| 4739 | **1695** | 60st. multicoloured | 1·70 | 1·30 |

**1696** Todor Burmov (first Minister for Internal Affairs)

**2009.** 130th Anniv of Ministry of Internal Affairs.

| | | | | |
|---|---|---|---|---|
| 4740 | **1696** | 60st. multicoloured | 1·70 | 1·30 |

**1697** Airmail Envelope

**2009.** 130th Anniv of Bulgarian Communications. Sheet 97×117 mm containing T 1697 and similar horiz design. Multicoloured.

| | | | |
|---|---|---|---|
| **MS**4741 | 60st. Type **1697**; 1l. Telephone | 4·50 | 4·50 |

**1698** Neil Armstrong and Lunar Module

**2009.** 40th Anniv of First Moon Landing. Sheet 101×84 mm.

| | | | |
|---|---|---|---|
| **MS**4742 | multicoloured | 1·70 | 1·70 |

No. **MS**4742 was also issued overprinted for Bulgaria 2009.

**1699** Symbols of Science

**2009.** 140th of National Academy of Science.

| | | | | |
|---|---|---|---|---|
| 4743 | **1699** | 60st. multicoloured | 1·70 | 1·30 |

**1700** Flags as Pen and Ink

**2009.** 130th Anniv of Bulgaria–Italy Diplomatic Relations. Sheet 101×71 mm.
**MS**4744 multicoloured 2·75 2·10

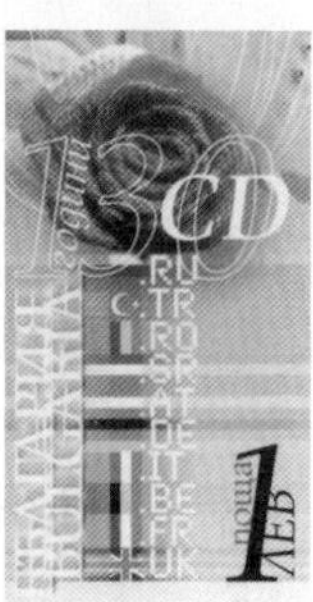

**1701** Flags and Rose

**2009.** 130th Anniv of First Bulgarian Diplomatic Relations. Sheet 113×113 mm.
**MS**4745 multicoloured 2·75 2·10

**1702** Anniversary Cake enclosed in TV Screen

**2009.** 50th Anniv of National Television.
4746 **1702** 60st. multicoloured 2·75 2·10

**1703** Fokker E. III Monoplane and Marko Parvanov (Bulgarian gunner)

**2009.** History of Bulgarian Military Aviation. Multicoloured.
4747 60st. Type **1703** 1·70 1·30
4748 1l. Assen Jordanoff (aircraft designer) and Jordanov-1 2·75 2·10

Nos. 4747/8 were printed, se-tenant, forming a composite design.

**1704** Virgin and Child

**2009.** Christmas.
4749 **1704** 60st. multicoloured 1·70 1·30

**1705** Nikola Vaptsarov

**2009.** Birth Centenary of Nikola Vaptsarov (poet, communist and revolutionary).
4750 **1705** 60st. multicoloured 1·70 1·30

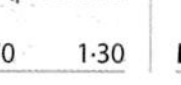


**1706** Dimitar Milandinov

**2010.** Birth Bicentenary of Dimitar Milandinov (poet and folklorist).
4751 **1706** 60st. multicoloured 1·70 1·30

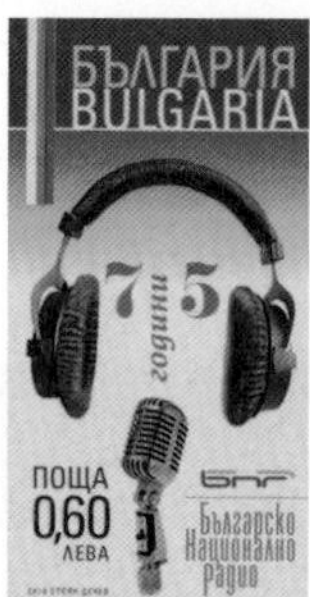


**1707** Headset and Microphone

**2010.** 75th Anniv of Bulgarian National Radio.
4752 **1707** 60st. multicoloured 1·70 1·30

**1708** Luge

**2010.** Winter Olympic Games, Vancouver. Sheet 98×90 mm containing T 1708 and similar horiz design. Multicoloured.
**MS**4753 60st. Type **1708**; 1l. Snowboarder 4·50 4·50

**1709** Frederic Chopin

**2010.** Birth Bicentenary of Frederic Chopin (composer).
4754 **1709** 1l. multicoloured 2·75 2·10

**1710** *Paeonia suffruticosa var. rockii*

**2010.** Peonies. Sheet 80×86 mm containing T 1710 and similar vert design. Multicoloured.
**MS**4755 60st×2, Type **1710**; *Paeonia officinalis 'Rubra Plena'* 3·50 3·50

**1711** General Georgi Vazov (1860-1934)

**2010.** 150th Birth Annivs of Bulgarian Commanders. Sheet 113×102 mm containing T 1711 and similar horiz designs. Multicoloured.
**MS**4756 60st.×5, Type **1711**; General Ivan Fichev (1860-1931); General Stilian Kovachev (1860-1939); Colonel Vladimir Serafimov (1860-1934); General Dimitar Geshev (1860-1922) 8·50 8·50

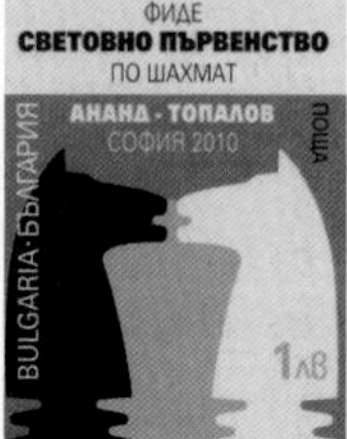


**1712** Chess Pieces

**2010.** World Chess Championship Match 2010 between Viswanathan Anand (winner) and Veselin Topalov. Sheet 69×85 mm.
**MS**4757 ochre, black and light grey 2·75 2·10

**1713** House and Hedgehog

**2010.** Europa. Multicoloured.
4758 60st Type **1713** 1·80 1·40
4759 60st. As Type **1713** (29×39 mm) 1·80 1·40
4760 Hare and fairy carrying lantern 3·00 2·40
4761 1l.50 Hare and fairy carrying lantern 3·00 2·40
**MS**4762 106×85 mm. 60st. As Type **1713**; 1l.50 As No. 4760 4·75 4·75

The stamps of No. **MS**4762 have no white borders and, with the margins form a composite design.

**1714** Dragon and Shanghai Skyline

**2010.** Expo 2010, Shanghai. Sheet 113×74 mm.
4762a 1l.40 multicoloured 1·80 1·40
**MS**4763 1l.40×4, Type **1714**×4 9·50 9·50

**1714a** Flag

**2010.** Centenary of Bulgaria–Spain Diplomatic Relations
4764 **1714a** 1l. multicoloured 1·80 1·40

**1715** Bird, Mouse and Whale

**2010.** International Year of Biodiversity
**MS**4765 78x60 mm. **1715** 1l.50 multicoloured 2·75 2·75

**1715a** Bulgarian Shepherd Dog

**2010.** Balkan Dogs
**MS**4765a **1715a** 60st. multicoloured 1·80 1·40

**1716** Emanuil Manolov

**2010.** Composers Anniversaries. Multicoloured.
4766 1l. Type **1716** (150th birth anniv) 2·75 2·10
4767 1l. Robert Schumann (birth bicentenary) 2·75 2·10

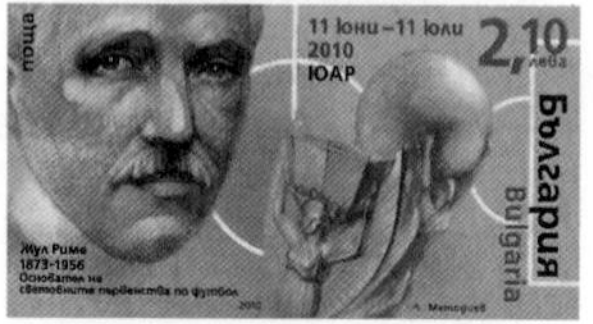


**1717** Jules Rimet and Trophies

**2010.** World Cup Football Championships, South Africa
**MS**4768 79x55 mm. 2l.10 multicoloured 5·50 5·50

**1718** St. Procopius

**2010.** Death Bicentenary of St. Procopius of Varna
4769 **1718** 60st. multicoloured 1·80 1·40

**1719** Manoeuvres (1899)

**2010.** 150th Birth Anniv of Yaroslav Veshin (Czech artist). Multicoloured.
4770 1l. Type **1719** 2·75 2·10
4771 1l. *Return from Market*(1898) 2·75 2·10

**1720** Summer and Autumn (Les Saisons (1900))

**2010.** 150th Birth Anniv of Alphonse (Alfons) Maria Mucha (Czech artist). Multicoloured.
**MS**4772 1l.×2, Type **1720**; Winter and Spring (*Les Saisons* (1900)) 5·50 5·50

**1721** Athletes, Emblem and Book

**2010.** Youth Olympic Games, Singapore 2010
4773 **1721** 1l.40 multicoloured 3·00 2·40

**1722** Entwined Tree Trunks

**2010.** 125th Anniv of Bulgaria's Reunification
4774 **1722** 60st. multicoloured 1·80 1·40

**1723** Magirus Feuerwehrwerke Fire-fighting Appliance

**2010.** History of the Fire Fighting
**MS**4775 **1723** 102x71 mm. 65st. multicoloured 1·90 1·90

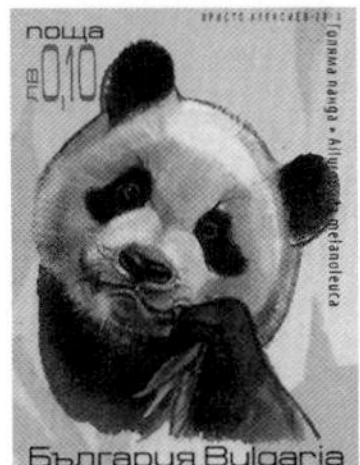
**1724** Giant Panda (Ailuropoda melanoleuca)

**2010.** Pandas. Multicoloured.
**MS**4776 95x126 mm. 10st. Type **1724**; 60st. Giant panda seated; 1l. Red panda (*Ailurus fulgens*); 1l.50 Red panda, head and shoulders 6·00 6·00

**1725** Jak-23

**2010.** 60th Anniv of Military Jet Aviation. Multicoloured.

| | | | |
|---|---|---|---|
| 4777 | 50st. Type **1725** | 1·60 | 1·10 |
| 4778 | 65st. Mikoyan-Gurevich type MiG-15 | 1·90 | 1·50 |
| 4779 | 1l. Mikoyan MiG-29 | 2·75 | 2·10 |

**1726** Santa wearing Spectacles

**2010.** Christmas

| | | | | |
|---|---|---|---|---|
| 4780 | **1726** | 65st. multicoloured | 1·90 | 1·50 |

**1727** Female Figures from Thracian Tomb of Svestari

**2010.** Regions. Multicoloured.
**MS**4781 85x113 mm. 10st. Type **1727**; 50st. Balchik Palace; 65st. Srebarna Nature Reserve; 1l. Pobiti Kamani rock formations 4·75 4·75

**1728** Self-Portrait

**2010.** Birth Bicentenary of Zahari Hristovich Dimitrov (Zahari Zograf) (artist)
**MS**4782 61x70 mm. **1728** 1l.50 multicoloured 3·00 3·00

**1729** San Cristobal Cathedral, Havana

**2010.** 50th Anniv of Bulgaria–Cuba Diplomatic Relations. Multicoloured.

| | | | |
|---|---|---|---|
| 4783 | 65c. Type **1729** | 1·90 | 1·50 |
| 4784 | 1l.40 St. Alexander Nevsky Cathedral, Sofia | 3·00 | 2·40 |

Stamps of a similar design were issued by Cuba

**1730** Griffon Vulture

**2010.** Balkanfila 2010 International Stamp Exhibition, Plovdiv
**MS**4785 88x78 mm. **1730** 65st. multicoloured 1·90 1·90

**1731** *Hydurga leptonyx* (leopard seal)

**2011.** Antarctica

| | | | | |
|---|---|---|---|---|
| 4786 | **1731** | 58st. black and scarlet-vermilion | 1·80 | 1·40 |

**1732** Princess Clementine and Soldiers

**2011.** 125th Anniv of 9th Plovdiv Infantry Regiment

| | | | | |
|---|---|---|---|---|
| 4787 | **1732** | 65st. multicoloured | 1·90 | 1·50 |

**1733** Vanga

**2011.** Birth Centenary of Vangelia Pandeva Dimitrova (Vanga) (blind mystic, healer and herbalist)

| | | | | |
|---|---|---|---|---|
| 4788 | **1733** | 65st. multicoloured | 1·90 | 1·50 |

**1734** Space and Haricot Bean

**2011.** Day of Humor and Joke (April Fool's Day)

| | | | | |
|---|---|---|---|---|
| 4789 | **1734** | 65st. multicoloured | 1·90 | 1·50 |

No. 4789 has a *se-tenant* stamp size label attached at right which, with the stamp forms a composite design of planets and space.

**1735** Politicians

**2011.** 20th Anniv of Atlantic Club of Bulgaria
**MS**2790 87x78 mm. **1735** 1l. multicoloured 2·75 2·75

**1736** Yuri Gagarin

**2011.** 50th Anniv of First Manned Space Flight. Multicoloured.
**MS**4791 83x103 mm. 65st. Type **1736**; 1l.50 *Venera 1* 5·25 5·25

### EXPRESS STAMPS

**E137** Express Delivery Van

**1939**

| | | | | |
|---|---|---|---|---|
| E429 | - | 5l. blue | 1·80 | 45 |
| E430 | **E137** | 6l. brown | 85 | 40 |
| E431 | - | 7l. brown | 1·30 | 40 |
| E432 | **E137** | 8l. red | 1·60 | 50 |
| E433 | - | 20l. red | 2·50 | 1·20 |

DESIGNS—VERT: 5l., 20l. Bicycle messenger; 7l. Motor-cyclist and sidecar.

### OFFICIAL STAMPS

**O158**

**1942**

| | | | | |
|---|---|---|---|---|
| O507 | **O158** | 10s. green | 10 | 10 |
| O508 | **O158** | 30s. orange | 10 | 10 |
| O509 | **O158** | 50s. brown | 10 | 10 |
| O510 | - | 1l. blue | 10 | 10 |
| O511 | - | 2l. green | 15 | 10 |
| O534 | - | 2l. red | 1·40 | 50 |
| O512 | - | 3l. mauve | 20 | 10 |
| O513 | - | 4l. pink | 30 | 15 |
| O514 | - | 5l. red | 50 | 20 |

The 1l. to 5l. are larger (19x23 mm).

**O177**

**1945.** Arms designs. Imperf or perf.

| | | | | |
|---|---|---|---|---|
| O580B | | 1l. mauve | 10 | 10 |
| O581B | **O 177** | 2l. green | 10 | 10 |
| O582B | - | 3l. brown | 10 | 10 |
| O583B | - | 4l. blue | 10 | 10 |
| O584B | - | 5l. red | 10 | 10 |

### PARCEL POST STAMPS

**P153** Weighing Machine

**P154** Loading Motor Lorry

**1941**

| | | | | |
|---|---|---|---|---|
| P494 | **P153** | 1l. green | 15 | 10 |
| P495 | **A** | 2l. red | 15 | 10 |
| P496 | **P 154** | 3l. brown | 15 | 10 |
| P497 | **B** | 4l. orange | 15 | 10 |
| P498 | **P 153** | 5l. blue | 15 | 10 |
| P506 | **P 153** | 5l. green | 20 | 15 |
| P499 | **B** | 6l. purple | 15 | 10 |
| P507 | **B** | 6l. brown | 20 | 15 |
| P500 | **P 153** | 7l. blue | 15 | 15 |

| | | | | |
|---|---|---|---|---|
| P508 | **P 153** | 7l. sepia | 20 | 15 |
| P501 | **P 154** | 8l. turquoise | 20 | 10 |
| P509 | **P 154** | 8l. green | 20 | 15 |
| P502 | **A** | 9l. olive | 30 | 15 |
| P503 | **B** | 10l. orange | 40 | 15 |
| P504 | **P 154** | 20l. violet | 65 | 20 |
| P505 | **A** | 30l. black | 1·50 | 30 |

DESIGNS—HORIZ: A, Loading mall coach; B, Motor-cycle combination.

**P163**

**1944.** Imperf.

| | | | | |
|---|---|---|---|---|
| P532 | **P163** | 1l. red | 20 | 15 |
| P533 | **P163** | 3l. green | 20 | 15 |
| P534 | **P163** | 5l. green | 20 | 15 |
| P535 | **P163** | 7l. mauve | 20 | 15 |
| P536 | **P163** | 10l. blue | 20 | 15 |
| P537 | **P163** | 20l. brown | 20 | 15 |
| P538 | **P163** | 30l. purple | 40 | 20 |
| P539 | **P163** | 50l. orange | 75 | 50 |
| P540 | **P163** | 100l. blue | 1·40 | 80 |

### POSTAGE DUE STAMPS

**D7**

**1884.** Perf.

| | | | | |
|---|---|---|---|---|
| D75 | **D7** | 5s. orange | 55·00 | 7·75 |
| D54 | **D7** | 25s. lake | 27·00 | 7·75 |
| D55 | **D7** | 50s. blue | 27·00 | 23·00 |

**1886.** Imperf.

| | | | |
|---|---|---|---|
| D50 | 5s. orange | £550 | 26·00 |
| D51 | 25s. lake | £800 | 23·00 |
| D52a | 50s. blue | 33·00 | 26·00 |

**1893.** Surch with bar and 30.

| | | | |
|---|---|---|---|
| D78d | 30s. on 50s. blue (perf) | 49·00 | 16·00 |
| D79 | 30s. on 50s. blue (imperf) | 43·00 | 16·00 |

**D12**

**1896.** Perf.

| | | | | |
|---|---|---|---|---|
| D83 | **D12** | 5s. orange | 27·00 | 4·25 |
| D84 | **D12** | 10s. violet | 16·00 | 3·75 |
| D85 | **D12** | 30s. green | 13·00 | 3·25 |

**D16**

**1901**

| | | | | |
|---|---|---|---|---|
| D124 | **D16** | 5s. red | 1·10 | 50 |
| D125 | **D16** | 10s. green | 2·20 | 65 |
| D126 | **D16** | 20s. blue | 16·00 | 65 |
| D127 | **D16** | 30s. red | 5·50 | 70 |
| D128 | **D16** | 50s. orange | 14·00 | 12·50 |

**D37**

**1915**

| | | | | |
|---|---|---|---|---|
| D200 | **D37** | 5s. green | 55 | 10 |
| D240 | **D37** | 10s. violet | 20 | 10 |
| D202 | **D37** | 20s. red | 55 | 20 |
| D241 | **D37** | 20s. orange | 20 | 10 |
| D203a | **D37** | 30s. red | 55 | 20 |
| D242 | **D37** | 50s. blue | 20 | 10 |
| D243 | **D37** | 1l. green | 55 | 10 |
| D244 | **D37** | 2l. red | 55 | 20 |
| D245 | **D37** | 3l. brown | 1·10 | 40 |

D110

**1932**

| | | | | |
|---|---|---|---|---|
| D326 | **D110** | 1l. bistre | 2·10 | 1·30 |
| D327 | **D110** | 2l. red | 2·10 | 1·30 |
| D328 | **D110** | 6l. purple | 4·75 | 1·50 |

D111 D112

**1933**

| | | | | |
|---|---|---|---|---|
| D333 | **D111** | 20s. sepia | 20 | 10 |
| D334 | **D111** | 40s. blue | 20 | 10 |
| D335 | **D111** | 80s. red | 20 | 10 |
| D336 | **D 112** | 1l. brown | 1·00 | 60 |
| D337 | **D 112** | 2l. olive | 1·00 | 90 |
| D338 | **D 112** | 6l. violet | 50 | 40 |
| D339 | **D 112** | 14l. blue | 75 | 60 |

**1947.** As Type D 112, but larger (18×24 mm).

| | | | |
|---|---|---|---|
| D646 | 1l. brown | 20 | 20 |
| D647 | 2l. red | 30 | 30 |
| D648 | 8l. orange | 20 | 20 |
| D649 | 20l. blue | 75 | 30 |

D293

**1951**

| | | | | |
|---|---|---|---|---|
| D849 | **D293** | 1l. brown | 20 | 15 |
| D850 | **D293** | 2l. purple | 30 | 15 |
| D851 | **D293** | 8l. orange | 65 | 50 |
| D852 | **D293** | 20l. blue | 1·70 | 1·30 |

Pt. 3

# BULGARIAN OCCUPATION OF ROMANIA

100 stotinki = 1 leva.

**(DOBRUJA DISTRICT)**

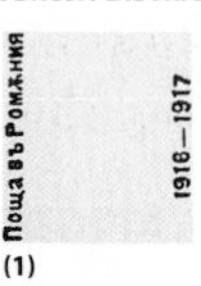
(1)

**1916.** Bulgarian stamps of 1911 optd with T 1.

| | | | | |
|---|---|---|---|---|
| 1 | **23** | 1s. grey | 25 | 25 |
| 2 | - | 5s. brown and green | 4·75 | 3·00 |
| 3 | - | 10s. sepia and brown | 45 | 35 |
| 4 | - | 25s. black and blue | 45 | 35 |

Pt. 1

# BUNDI

A state of Rajasthan, India. Now uses Indian stamps.

12 pies = 1 anna; 16 annas = 1 rupee.

3 Native Dagger

**1894.** Imperf.

| | | | | |
|---|---|---|---|---|
| 12 | **3** | ½a. grey | 6·00 | 5·00 |
| 13 | **3** | 1a. red | 5·00 | 4·75 |
| 14 | **3** | 2a. green | 17·00 | 20·00 |
| 8 | **3** | 4a. green | 85·00 | £120 |
| 15 | **3** | 8a. red | 21·00 | 24·00 |
| 16a | **3** | 1r. yellow on blue | 22·00 | 32·00 |

**1898.** As T 3, but with dagger point to left.

| | | | |
|---|---|---|---|
| 17a | 4a. green | 25·00 | 30·00 |

11 Raja protecting Sacred Cows

**1914.** Roul or perf.

| | | | | |
|---|---|---|---|---|
| 26 | **11** | ¼a. blue | 1·90 | 4·25 |
| 38 | **11** | ½a. black | 2·75 | 4·75 |
| 28 | **11** | 1a. red | 3·75 | 14·00 |
| 20a | **11** | 2a. green | 5·00 | 9·00 |
| 30 | **11** | 2½a. yellow | 10·00 | 30·00 |
| 31 | **11** | 3a. brown | 10·00 | 55·00 |
| 32 | **11** | 4a. green | 3·50 | 50·00 |
| 33a | **11** | 6a. blue | 7·00 | £130 |
| 42 | **11** | 8a. orange | 9·00 | 80·00 |
| 43 | **11** | 10a. olive | 17·00 | £130 |
| 44 | **11** | 12a. green | 16·00 | £120 |
| 25 | **11** | 1r. lilac | 32·00 | £140 |
| 46 | **11** | 2r. brown and black | 95·00 | £225 |
| 47 | **11** | 3r. blue and brown | £160 | £300 |
| 48 | **11** | 4r. green and red | £325 | £400 |
| 49 | **11** | 5r. red and green | £325 | £400 |

20

**1941.** Perf.

| | | | | |
|---|---|---|---|---|
| 79 | **20** | 3p. blue | 3·00 | 6·00 |
| 80 | **20** | 6p. blue | 6·00 | 10·00 |
| 81 | **20** | 1a. red | 8·00 | 12·00 |
| 82 | **20** | 2a. brown | 9·00 | 22·00 |
| 83 | **20** | 4a. green | 16·00 | 70·00 |
| 84 | **20** | 8a. green | 21·00 | £275 |
| 85 | **20** | 1r. blue | 45·00 | £375 |

21 Maharao Rajah Bahadur Singh

**1947**

| | | | | |
|---|---|---|---|---|
| 86 | **21** | ¼a. green | 2·25 | 45·00 |
| 87 | **21** | ½a. violet | 2·00 | 35·00 |
| 88 | **21** | 1a. green | 2·00 | 38·00 |
| 89 | - | 2a. red | 1·90 | 80·00 |
| 90 | - | 4a. orange | 2·25 | £100 |
| 91 | - | 8a. blue | 3·25 | |
| 92 | - | 1r. brown | 17·00 | |

DESIGNS: 2, 4a. Rajah in Indian dress; 8a., 1r. View of Bundi.

**OFFICIAL STAMPS**

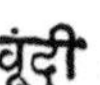

सरविस
(O1)

**1915.** Optd as Type O 1.

| | | |
|---|---|---|
| O6A | ¼a. blue | 1·60 |
| O16Aa | ½a. black | 75 |
| O8A | 1a. red | 4·50 |
| O18A | 2a. green | 11·00 |
| O2A | 2½a. yellow | 5·50 |
| O3A | 3a. brown | 5·00 |
| O19A | 4a. green | 14·00 |
| O11A | 6a. blue | 15·00 |
| O20A | 8a. orange | 15·00 |
| O21A | 10a. olive | 80·00 |
| O22A | 12a. green | 60·00 |
| O5A | 1r. lilac | 70·00 |
| O24A | 2r. brown and black | £400 |
| O25A | 3r. blue and brown | £375 |
| O26A | 4r green and red | £300 |
| O27A | 5r. red and green | £325 |

**1915.** Optd BUNDI SERVICE.

| | | | |
|---|---|---|---|
| O6B | **11** | ¼a. blue | 2·00 |
| O16B | **11** | ½a. black | 3·00 |
| O8Bb | **11** | 1a. red | 16·00 |
| O18B | **11** | 2a. green | 24·00 |
| O2B | **11** | 2½a. yellow | 20·00 |
| O3B | **11** | 3a. brown | 23·00 |
| O19B | **11** | 4a. green | 95·00 |
| O11B | **11** | 6a. blue | £300 |
| O20B | **11** | 8a. orange | 40·00 |
| O21B | **11** | 10a. olive | £120 |
| O22B | **11** | 12a. green | £140 |
| O5B | **11** | 1r. lilac | 75·00 |
| O24B | **11** | 2r. brown and black | £200 |
| O25B | **11** | 3r. blue and brown | £225 |
| O26B | **11** | 4r. green and red | £300 |
| O27B | **11** | 5r. red and green | £325 |

Prices for Nos. O2/27 are for unused examples. Used examples are generally worth a small premium over the prices quoted.

**1941.** Optd SERVICE.

| | | | | |
|---|---|---|---|---|
| O53 | **20** | 3p. blue | 8·00 | 19·00 |
| O54 | **20** | 6p. blue | 19·00 | 19·00 |
| O55 | **20** | 1a. red | 16·00 | 16·00 |
| O56 | **20** | 2a. brown | 22·00 | 15·00 |
| O57 | **20** | 4a. green | 65·00 | £150 |
| O58 | **20** | 8a. green | £225 | £700 |
| O59 | **20** | 1r. blue | £300 | £800 |

For later issues see **RAJASTHAN**.

Pt. 12

# BURKINA FASO

A country in W. Africa, formerly known as Upper Volta. The name was changed in August 1984.

100 centimes = 1 franc.

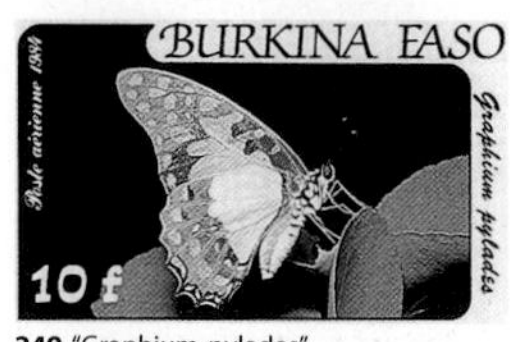

249 "Graphium pylades"

**1984.** Air. Butterflies. Multicoloured.

| | | | |
|---|---|---|---|
| 738 | 10f. Type **249** | 30 | 10 |
| 739 | 120f. "Hyploimnas misippus" | 1·30 | 55 |
| 740 | 400f. "Danaus chrysippus" | 4·25 | 2·10 |
| 741 | 450f. "Papilio demodocus" | 5·00 | 2·30 |

250 Soldier with Gun

**1984.** 1st Anniv of Captain Thomas Sankara's Presidency. Multicoloured.

| | | |
|---|---|---|
| 742 | 90f. Type **250** | 39·00 |
| 743 | 120f. Capt. Sankara and crowd | 55·00 |

**1984.** Aid for the Sahel. No. 682 of Upper Volta optd BURKINA FASO Aide au Sahel 84.

| | |
|---|---|
| 743a | 100f. multicoloured |

**1985.** Nos. 716/21 of Upper Volta optd BURKINA FASO.

| | | | |
|---|---|---|---|
| 744 | 25f. Type **246** (postage) | 45 | 20 |
| 745 | 185f. "Pterocarpus lucens" | 2·75 | 1·50 |
| 746 | 200f. "Phlebopus colossus sudanicus" | 3·75 | 1·70 |
| 747 | 250f. "Cosmos sulphureus" | 4·50 | 2·10 |
| 748 | 300f. "Trametes versicolor" (air) | 4·75 | 2·40 |
| 749 | 400f. "Ganoderma lucidum" | 6·50 | 3·25 |

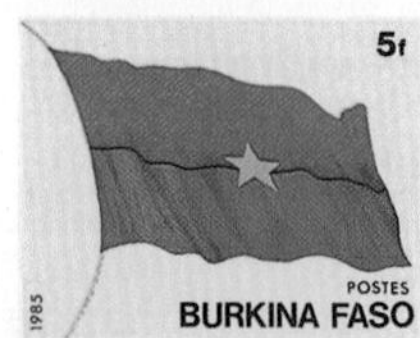

252 National Flag

**1985.** National Symbols. Multicoloured.

| | | | |
|---|---|---|---|
| 750 | 5f. Type **252** (postage) | 40 | 20 |
| 751 | 15f. National arms (vert) | 45 | 25 |
| 752 | 90f. Maps of Africa and Burkina Faso | 1·80 | 90 |
| 753 | 120f. Type **252** (air) | 1·60 | 80 |
| 754 | 150f. As No. 751 | 2·20 | 1·00 |
| 755 | 185f. As No. 752 | 2·50 | 1·20 |

253 Footballers and Statue

**1985.** World Cup Football Championship, Mexico.

| | | | | |
|---|---|---|---|---|
| 756 | **253** | 25f. mult. (postage) | 40 | 10 |
| 757 | - | 45f. multicoloured | 55 | 20 |
| 758 | - | 90f. multicoloured | 1·10 | 35 |
| 759 | - | 100f. multicoloured (air) | 1·20 | 30 |
| 760 | - | 150f. multicoloured | 1·40 | 55 |
| 761 | - | 200f. mult (horiz) | 1·90 | 85 |
| 762 | - | 250f. mult (horiz) | 2·50 | 1·10 |
| **MS**763 | | 78×77 mm. 500f. multicoloured (horiz) | 5·50 | 1·30 |

DESIGNS: 45f. to 500f. Mexican statues and various footballing scenes.

254 Children playing and Boy

**1985.** Air "Philexafrique" International Stamp Exhibition, Lome, Togo (1st issue). Multicoloured.

| | | | |
|---|---|---|---|
| 764 | 200f. Type **254** | 2·00 | 1·20 |
| 765 | 200f. Solar panels, transmission mast, windmill, dish aerial and tree | 2·00 | 1·20 |

See also Nos. 839/40.

255 G. A. Long's Steam Tricycle

**1985.** Centenary of Motor Cycle. Multicoloured.

| | | | |
|---|---|---|---|
| 766 | 50f. Type **255** (postage) | 90 | 20 |
| 767 | 75f. Pope | 1·10 | 25 |
| 768 | 80f. Manet | 1·60 | 35 |
| 769 | 100f. Ducati (air) | 95 | 30 |
| 770 | 150f. Jawa | 1·60 | 55 |
| 771 | 200f. Honda | 2·20 | 85 |
| 772 | 250f. B.M.W. | 2·75 | 1·10 |

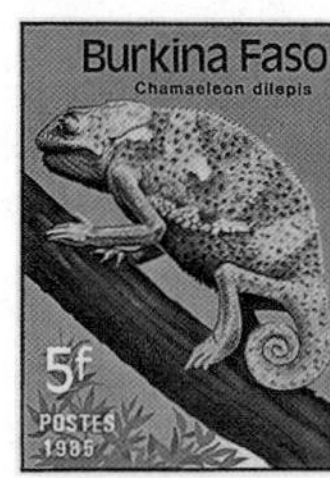

256 "Chamaeleon dilepis"

**1985.** Reptiles and Amphibians. Multicoloured.

| | | | |
|---|---|---|---|
| 773 | 5f. Type **256** (postage) | 25 | 15 |
| 774 | 15f. "Agama stellio" | 70 | 15 |
| 775 | 33f. "Lacerta lepida" (horiz) | 1·10 | 15 |
| 776 | 85f. "Hiperolius marmoratus" (horiz) | 1·70 | 30 |
| 777 | 100f. "Echis leucogaster" (horiz) (air) | 1·40 | 30 |
| 778 | 150f. "Kinixys erosa" (horiz) | 2·10 | 50 |
| 779 | 250f. "Python regius" (horiz) | 3·25 | 70 |

257 Benz "Victoria", 1893

**1985.** Motor Cars and Aircraft. Multicoloured.

| | | | |
|---|---|---|---|
| 780 | 5f. Type **257** (postage) | 20 | 10 |
| 781 | 25f. Peugeot "174", 1927 | 45 | 10 |

| | | | |
|---|---|---|---|
| 782 | 45f. Bleriot XI airplane | 60 | 10 |
| 783 | 50f. Breguet 14T biplane | 60 | 10 |
| 784 | 500f. Bugatti "Napoleon T41 Royale" (air) | 5·25 | 1·30 |
| 785 | 500f. Airbus Industrie A300 | 4·25 | 1·30 |
| 786 | 600f. Mercedes-Benz "540 K", 1938 | 5·25 | 1·70 |
| 787 | 600f. Airbus Industrie A300 | 5·25 | 1·70 |
| **MS**788 | 100×68 mm. 1000f. Louis Bleriot and Bleriot XI, Karl Benz and early Benz motor car | 8·50 | 3·50 |

**258** Wood Duck

**1985.** Birth Bicentenary of John J. Audubon (ornithologist). Multicoloured.

| | | | |
|---|---|---|---|
| 789 | 60f. Type **258** (postage) | 60 | 20 |
| 790 | 100f. Northern mockingbird | 90 | 40 |
| 791 | 300f. Northern oriole | 3·00 | 90 |
| 792 | 400f. White-breasted nuthatch | 3·50 | 1·20 |
| 793 | 500f. Common flicker (air) | 4·25 | 1·30 |
| 794 | 600f. Rough-legged buzzard | 5·25 | 1·60 |
| **MS**795 | 73×83 mm. 1000f. White-crowned pigeon | 9·00 | 3·50 |

**259** Young Lady Elizabeth Bowes-Lyon on Pony

**1985.** 85th Birthday of Queen Elizabeth the Queen Mother. Multicoloured.

| | | | |
|---|---|---|---|
| 796 | 75f. Type **259** (postage) | 80 | 35 |
| 797 | 85f. Marriage of Lady Elizabeth Bowes-Lyon and Albert, Duke of York | 80 | 35 |
| 798 | 500f. Duke and Duchess of York with Princess Elizabeth (air) | 4·00 | 1·30 |
| 799 | 600f. Royal family in Coronation robes | 5·25 | 1·60 |
| **MS**800 | 104×64 mm. 1000f. Queen Elizabeth the Queen Mother at christening of Prince William of Wales | 8·50 | 3·50 |

**260** Gaucho on Piebald Horse

**1985.** "Argentina '85" International Stamp Exhibition, Buenos Aires. Horses. Multicoloured.

| | | | |
|---|---|---|---|
| 801 | 25f. Type **260** (postage) | 45 | 10 |
| 802 | 45f. Gaucho on horse | 75 | 25 |
| 803 | 90f. Rodeo rider | 1·30 | 40 |
| 804 | 100f. Rider hunting gazelle (air) | 1·00 | 35 |
| 805 | 150f. Horses and gauchos at camp fire | 1·50 | 55 |
| 806 | 200f. Horse and man sitting on steps | 2·10 | 85 |
| 807 | 250f. Riding contest | 2·75 | 1·10 |
| **MS**808 | 100×89 mm. 500f. Foal (39×31 mm) | 7·50 | 3·00 |

**261** Electric Locomotive No. 105-30 and Tank Wagon

**1985.** Trains. Multicoloured.

| | | | |
|---|---|---|---|
| 809 | 50f. Type **261** (postage) | 80 | 10 |
| 810 | 75f. Diesel shunting locomotive | 1·00 | 25 |
| 811 | 80f. Diesel passenger locomotive | 1·30 | 25 |
| 812 | 100f. Diesel railcar (air) | 1·10 | 10 |
| 813 | 150f. Diesel locomotive No. 6093 | 1·60 | 30 |
| 814 | 200f. Diesel railcar No. 105 | 2·10 | 40 |
| 815 | 250f. Diesel locomotive pulling passenger train | 2·75 | 55 |

**262** Pot (Tikare)

**1985.** Handicrafts. Multicoloured.

| | | | |
|---|---|---|---|
| 816 | 10f. Type **262** (postage) | 25 | 10 |
| 817 | 40f. Pot with lid decorated with birds (P. Bazega) | 70 | 20 |
| 818 | 90f. Bronze statuette of mother with child (Ouagadougou) | 1·40 | 35 |
| 819 | 120f. Bronze statuette of drummer (Ouagadougou) (air) | 2·10 | 50 |

**263** "Pholiota mutabilis"

**1985.** Fungi. Multicoloured.

| | | | |
|---|---|---|---|
| 820 | 15f. Type **263** (postage) | 20 | 10 |
| 821 | 20f. "Hypholoma (nematoloma) fasciculare" | 20 | 10 |
| 822 | 30f. "Ixocomus granulatus" | 40 | 20 |
| 823 | 60f. "Agaricus campestris" | 90 | 15 |
| 824 | 80f. "Trachypus scaber" | 1·40 | 50 |
| 825 | 250f. "Marasmius scorodonius" | 3·75 | 1·50 |
| 826 | 150f. "Armillaria mellea" (air) | 2·75 | 70 |

**264** "Virgin and Child"

**1985.** "Italia '85" International Stamp Exhibition, Rome. Paintings by Botticelli.

| | | | |
|---|---|---|---|
| 827 | 25f. Type **264** (postage) | 50 | 10 |
| 828 | 45f. "Portrait of an Unknown Man" | 90 | 20 |
| 829 | 90f. "Mars and Venus" | 1·60 | 40 |
| 830 | 100f. "Birth of Venus" (air) | 1·20 | 50 |
| 831 | 150f. "Allegory of Calumny" | 1·40 | 65 |
| 832 | 200f. "Pallas and the Centaur" | 2·50 | 85 |
| 833 | 250f. "Allegory of Spring" | 3·25 | 1·10 |
| **MS**834 | 71×91 mm. 500f. "Virgin of the Pomegranate" (31×39 mm) | 5·00 | 2·00 |

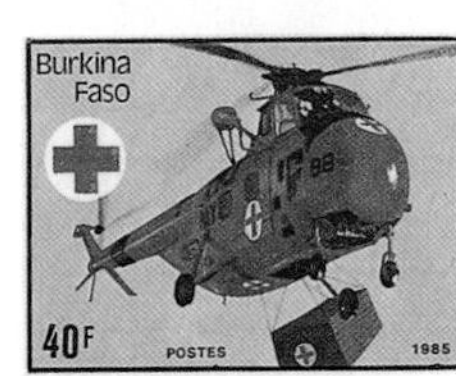

**265** Sikorsky S-55 Helicopter

**1985.** Red Cross. Multicoloured.

| | | | |
|---|---|---|---|
| 835 | 40f. Type **265** (postage) | 1·70 | 35 |
| 836 | 85f. Ambulance | 3·00 | 50 |
| 837 | 150f. Henri Dunant (founder) (vert) (air) | 2·30 | 65 |
| 838 | 250f. Nurse attending patient (vert) | 3·75 | 1·10 |

**266** Transport and Communications (development)

**1985.** Air. "Philexafrique" International Stamp Exhibition, Lome, Togo (2nd issue). Mult.

| | | | |
|---|---|---|---|
| 839 | 250f. Type **266** | 3·50 | 1·50 |
| 840 | 250f. Youth activities (youth) | 3·50 | 1·50 |

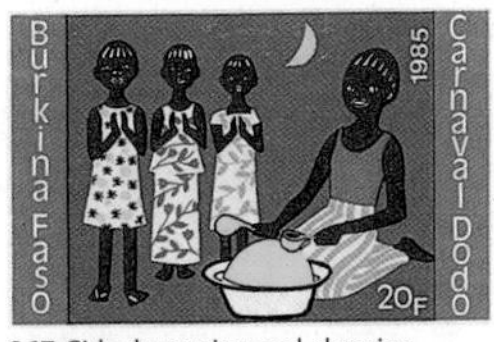

**267** Girls drumming and clapping

**1986.** Dodo Carnival. Multicoloured.

| | | | |
|---|---|---|---|
| 841 | 20f. Type **267** | 10 | 10 |
| 842 | 25f. Masked lion dancers | 25 | 10 |
| 843 | 40f. Masked stick dancers and drummers | 45 | 15 |
| 844 | 45f. Stick dancers with elaborate headdresses | 55 | 20 |
| 845 | 90f. Masked elephant dancer | 1·20 | 45 |
| 846 | 90f. Animal dancers | 1·20 | 45 |

**268** Mother breast-feeding Baby

**1986.** Child Survival Campaign.

| | | | | |
|---|---|---|---|---|
| 847 | **268** | 90f. multicoloured | 1·10 | 50 |

**269** Couple carrying Rail

**1986.** Railway Construction. Multicoloured.

| | | | |
|---|---|---|---|
| 848 | 90f. Type **269** (postage) | 85 | 35 |
| 849 | 120f. Laying tracks | 1·00 | 45 |
| 850 | 185f. Workers waving to passing train | 1·50 | 65 |
| 851 | 500f. "Inauguration of First German Railway" (Heim) (air) | 4·25 | 2·00 |
| **MS**852 | 90×68 mm. 1000f. Experimental inter-city train and diesel locomotive series 290 | 8·50 | 3·50 |

Nos. 851/**MS**852 commemorate the 150th Anniv of German railways.

**270** Columbus before King of Portugal, and "Nina"

**1986.** 480th Death Anniv of Christopher Columbus (explorer). Multicoloured.

| | | | |
|---|---|---|---|
| 853 | 250f. Type **270** (postage) | 2·50 | 70 |
| 854 | 300f. "Santa Maria" and Columbus with astrolabe | 2·75 | 90 |
| 855 | 400f. Columbus imprisoned and "Santa Maria" | 3·75 | 1·10 |
| 856 | 450f. Landing at San Salvador and "Pinta" (air) | 4·25 | 1·80 |
| **MS**857 | 90×68 mm. 1000f. Fleet leaving Palos | 8·50 | 2·10 |

**271** Village and First Aid Post

**1986.** "Health For All by Year 2000". Mult.

| | | | |
|---|---|---|---|
| 858 | 90f. Type **271** | 95 | 35 |
| 859 | 100f. Man receiving first aid (26×36 mm) | 95 | 45 |
| 860 | 120f. People queuing for vaccinations (26×36 mm) | 1·30 | 50 |

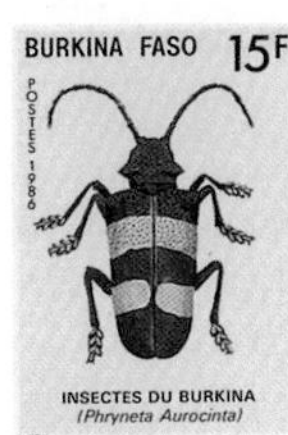

**272** "Phryneta aurocinta"

**1986.** Insects. Multicoloured.

| | | | |
|---|---|---|---|
| 861 | 15f. Type **272** | 25 | 10 |
| 862 | 20f. "Sternocera interrupta" | 35 | 10 |
| 863 | 40f. "Prosoprocera lactator" | 80 | 30 |
| 864 | 45f. "Gonimbrasia hecate" | 90 | 35 |
| 865 | 85f. "Charaxes epijasius" | 1·40 | 60 |

**273** Woman feeding Child and Fresh Foods

**1986.** Gobi Health Strategy. Multicoloured.

| | | | |
|---|---|---|---|
| 866 | 30f. Type **273** | 40 | 10 |
| 867 | 60f. Ingredients of oral rehydration therapy | 70 | 30 |
| 868 | 90f. Mother holding child for vaccination | 1·00 | 45 |
| 869 | 120f. Doctor weighing child | 1·50 | 55 |

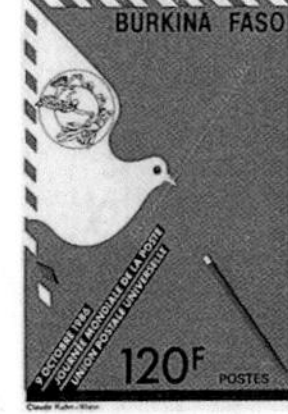

**274** UPU Emblem on Dove

**1986.** World Post Day.

| | | | | |
|---|---|---|---|---|
| 870 | **274** | 120f. multicoloured | 1·30 | 55 |

**275** Emblem

**1986.** International Peace Year.

| | | | | |
|---|---|---|---|---|
| 871 | **275** | 90f. blue | 1·20 | 55 |

**276** Namende Dancers

**1986.** National Bobo Culture Week. Mult.

| | | | |
|---|---|---|---|
| 872 | 10f. Type **276** | 25 | 10 |
| 873 | 25f. Mouhoun dancers | 50 | 10 |
| 874 | 90f. Houet dancer | 1·10 | 45 |
| 875 | 105f. Seno musicians | 1·10 | 50 |
| 876 | 120f. Ganzourgou dancers | 1·70 | 60 |

**277** Warthog

**1986.** Wildlife. Multicoloured.

| | | | |
|---|---|---|---|
| 877 | 50f. Type **277** | 70 | 20 |
| 878 | 65f. Spotted hyena | 80 | 30 |
| 879 | 90f. Antelope | 1·20 | 35 |
| 880 | 100f. Red-fronted gazelle | 1·20 | 45 |
| 881 | 120f. Harnessed antelope | 1·30 | 55 |
| 882 | 145f. Hartebeest | 1·80 | 65 |
| 883 | 500f. Kob | 5·75 | 2·20 |

**278** Peul

**1986.** Traditional Hairstyles. Multicoloured.

| | | | |
|---|---|---|---|
| 884 | 35f. Type **278** | 35 | 10 |
| 885 | 75f. Dafing | 80 | 35 |
| 886 | 90f. Peul (different) | 1·30 | 45 |
| 887 | 120f. Mossi | 1·60 | 60 |
| 888 | 185f. Peul (different) | 2·30 | 90 |

**279** Charlie Chaplin within Film Frame (10th death anniv)

**1987.** 10th Fespaco Film Festival.

| | | | | |
|---|---|---|---|---|
| 889 | - | 90f. mauve, black & brn | 1·10 | 60 |
| 890 | - | 120f. multicoloured | 2·20 | 85 |
| 891 | 279 | 185f. multicoloured | 3·25 | 1·40 |

DESIGNS: 90f. Camera on map in film frame; 120f. Cameraman and soundman (60th anniv of first talking film "The Jazz Singer").

**280** Woman trimming Rug

**1987.** International Women's Day.

| | | | | |
|---|---|---|---|---|
| 892 | 280 | 90f. multicoloured | 1·00 | 45 |

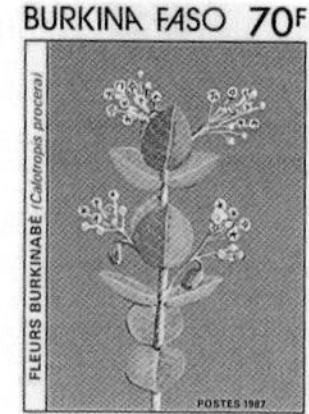

**281** "Calotripis procera"

**1987.** Flowers. Multicoloured.

| | | | |
|---|---|---|---|
| 893 | 70f. Type **281** | 80 | 30 |
| 894 | 75f. "Acacia seyal" | 80 | 30 |
| 895 | 85f. "Parkia biglobosa" | 1·00 | 50 |
| 896 | 90f. "Sterospernum kunthianum" | 1·00 | 50 |
| 897 | 100f. "Dichrostachys cinerea" | 1·40 | 55 |
| 898 | 300f. "Combretum paniculatum" | 3·50 | 1·30 |

**282** High Jumping

**1987.** Olympic Games, Seoul (1988). 50th Death Anniv of Pierre de Coubertin (founder of modern Olympic Games). Multicoloured.

| | | | |
|---|---|---|---|
| 899 | 75f. Type **282** | 80 | 40 |
| 900 | 85f. Tennis (vert) | 90 | 40 |
| 901 | 90f. Ski jumping | 95 | 55 |
| 902 | 100f. Football | 1·00 | 55 |
| 903 | 145f. Running | 1·40 | 70 |
| 904 | 350f. Pierre de Coubertin and tennis game (vert) | 3·50 | 1·70 |

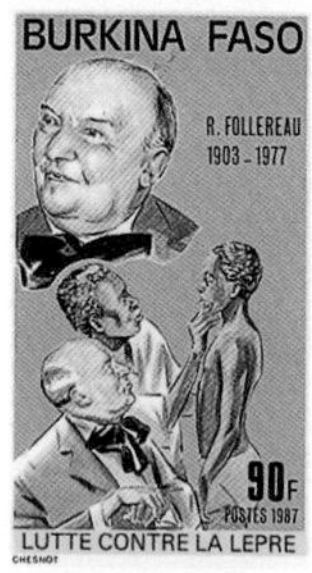

**283** Follereau and Doctor treating Patient

**1987.** Anti-leprosy Campaign. 10th Death Anniv of Raoul Follereau (pioneer). Multicoloured.

| | | | |
|---|---|---|---|
| 905 | 90f. Type **283** | 1·10 | 45 |
| 906 | 100f. Laboratory technicians | 1·30 | 45 |
| 907 | 120f. Gerhard Hansen (discoverer of bacillus) | 1·50 | 55 |
| 908 | 300f. Follereau kissing patient | 3·50 | 1·50 |

**284** Woman sweeping

**1987.** World Environment Day. Multicoloured.

| | | | |
|---|---|---|---|
| 909 | 90f. Type **284** | 1·00 | 60 |
| 910 | 145f. Emblem | 1·50 | 75 |

**285** Globe in Envelope

**1987.** World Post Day.

| | | | | |
|---|---|---|---|---|
| 911 | 285 | 90f. multicoloured | 1·00 | 55 |

**286** Luthuli and Open Book

**1987.** Anti-Apartheid Campaign. 20th Death Anniv of Albert John Luthuli (anti-apartheid campaigner). Multicoloured.

| | | | |
|---|---|---|---|
| 912 | 90f. Barbed wire and apartheid victims | 1·00 | 45 |
| 913 | 100f. Type **286** | 1·10 | 45 |

**287** Dagari

**1987.** Traditional Costumes. Multicoloured.

| | | | |
|---|---|---|---|
| 914 | 10f. Type **287** | 10 | 10 |
| 915 | 30f. Peul | 25 | 10 |
| 916 | 90f. Mossi (female) | 85 | 45 |
| 917 | 200f. Senoufo | 1·60 | 90 |
| 918 | 500f. Mossi (male) | 5·00 | 2·30 |

**288** Balafon (16 key xylophone)

**1987.** Traditional Music Instruments. Multicoloured.

| | | | |
|---|---|---|---|
| 919 | 20f. Type **288** | 25 | 10 |
| 920 | 25f. Kunde en more (3 stringed lute) (vert) | 25 | 20 |
| 921 | 35f. Tiahoun en bwaba (zither) | 40 | 25 |
| 922 | 90f. Jembe en dioula (conical drum) | 90 | 45 |
| 923 | 1000f. Bendre en more (calabash drum) (vert) | 9·75 | 4·50 |

**289** Dwellings

**1987.** International Year of Shelter for the Homeless.

| | | | | |
|---|---|---|---|---|
| 924 | 289 | 90f. multicoloured | 1·00 | 45 |

**290** Small Industrial Units

**1987.** Five Year Plan for Popular Development. Multicoloured.

| | | | |
|---|---|---|---|
| 925 | 40f. Type **290** | 35 | 10 |
| 926 | 55f. Management of dams | 60 | 25 |
| 927 | 60f. Village community building primary school | 60 | 25 |
| 928 | 90f. Bus (Transport and communications) | 1·00 | 35 |
| 929 | 100f. National education: literacy campaign | 1·00 | 55 |
| 930 | 120f. Intensive cattle farming | 1·30 | 55 |

**291** People with Candles

**1988.** 40th Anniv of WHO.

| | | | | |
|---|---|---|---|---|
| 931 | 291 | 120f. multicoloured | 1·30 | 45 |

**292** Exhibition Emblem and Games Mascot

**1988.** Olympic Games, Seoul, and "Olymphilex '88" Olympic Stamps Exhibition, Rome (932). Multicoloured.

| | | | |
|---|---|---|---|
| 932 | 30f. Type **292** | 30 | 10 |
| 933 | 160f. Olympic flame (vert) | 1·50 | 60 |
| 934 | 175f. Football | 1·70 | 70 |
| 935 | 235f. Volleyball (vert) | 2·30 | 1·10 |
| 936 | 450f. Basketball (vert) | 4·25 | 2·00 |
| **MS**937 | 115×100 mm. 500f. 1500 metres race (36×48 mm) | 5·75 | 5·25 |

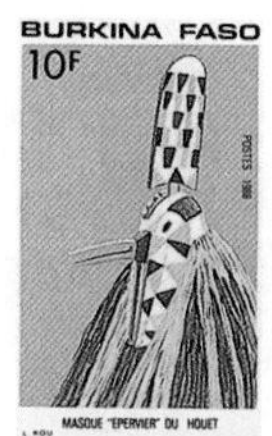

**293** Houet "Sparrow Hawk" Mask

**1988.** Masks. Multicoloured.

| | | | |
|---|---|---|---|
| 938 | 10f. Type **293** | 10 | 10 |
| 939 | 20f. Ouillo "Young Girls" mask | 30 | 25 |
| 940 | 30f. Houet "Hartebeest" mask | 40 | 25 |
| 941 | 40f. Mouhoun "Blacksmith" mask | 45 | 25 |
| 942 | 120f. Ouri "Nanny" mask | 1·30 | 45 |
| 943 | 175f. Ouri "Bat" mask (horiz) | 1·80 | 75 |

**294** Kieribа Jug

**1988.** Handicrafts. Multicoloured.

| | | | |
|---|---|---|---|
| 944 | 5f. Type **294** | 10 | 10 |
| 945 | 15f. Mossi basket (horiz) | 10 | 10 |
| 946 | 25f. Gurunsi chair (horiz) | 25 | 10 |
| 947 | 30f. Bissa basket (horiz) | 25 | 20 |
| 948 | 45f. Ouagadougou hide box (horiz) | 45 | 20 |
| 949 | 85f. Ouagadougou bronze statuette | 75 | 40 |
| 950 | 120f. Ouagadougou hide travelling bag (horiz) | 1·10 | 55 |

**295** Envelopes forming Map

**1988.** World Post Day.

| | | | | |
|---|---|---|---|---|
| 951 | 295 | 120f. blue, black & yellow | 1·10 | 45 |

**296** White-collared Kingfisher

**1988.** Aquatic Wildlife. Multicoloured.

| | | | |
|---|---|---|---|
| 952 | 70f. Type **296** | 60 | 25 |
| 953 | 100f. Elephantfish | 1·00 | 40 |
| 954 | 120f. Frog | 1·40 | 45 |
| 955 | 160f. White-faced whistling duck | 1·60 | 70 |

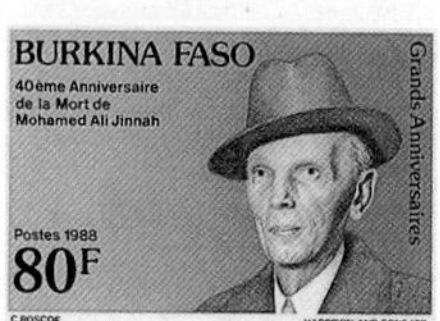

**297** Mohammed Ali Jinnah (first Pakistan Governor-General)

**1988.** Death Anniversaries. Multicoloured.

| | | | |
|---|---|---|---|
| 956 | 80f. Type **297** (40th anniv) (postage) | 75 | 40 |
| 957 | 120f. Mahatma Gandhi (Indian human rights activist, 40th anniv) | 1·10 | 55 |
| 958 | 160f. John Fitzgerald Kennedy (U.S. President, 25th anniv) | 1·70 | 70 |
| 959 | 235f. Martin Luther King (human rights activist, 20th anniv) (air) | 2·10 | 1·10 |

**298** Shepherds adoring Child

**1988.** Christmas. Stained Glass Windows. Mult.

| | | | |
|---|---|---|---|
| 960 | 120f. Type **298** | 1·20 | 40 |
| 961 | 160f. Wise men presenting gifts to Child | 1·40 | 70 |
| 962 | 450f. Virgin and Child | 4·00 | 1·80 |
| 963 | 1000f. Flight into Egypt | 8·50 | 4·50 |

**299** Satellite and Globe

**1989.** 20th Anniv of FESPACO Film Festival. Multicoloured.

| | | | |
|---|---|---|---|
| 964 | 75f. Type **299** (postage) | 1·70 | 40 |
| 965 | 500f. Ababacar Samb Makharam (air) | 6·25 | 2·75 |
| 966 | 500f. Jean Michel Tchissoukou | 6·25 | 2·75 |
| 967 | 500f. Paulin Soumanou Vieyra | 6·25 | 2·75 |
| **MS**968 | 114×85 mm. As Nos. 965/7 but with anniversary inscriptions and values in gold | 21·00 | 19·00 |

**300** WHO and Aids Emblems

**1989.** Campaign against AIDS.

| | | | |
|---|---|---|---|
| 969 | **300** 120f. multicoloured | 1·10 | 55 |

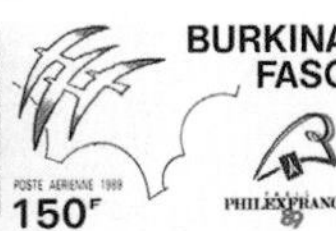

**301** "Oath of the Tennis Court" (Jacques Louis David) (½-size illustration) (image scaled to 62% of original size)

**1989.** Air. "Philexfrance 89" International Stamp Exhibition, Paris, and Bicentenary of French Revolution. Multicoloured.

| | | | |
|---|---|---|---|
| 970 | 150f. Type **301** | 1·40 | 80 |
| 971 | 200f. "Storming of the Bastille" (Thevenin) | 2·00 | 1·20 |
| 972 | 600f. "Rouget de Lisle singing La Marseillaise" (Pils) | 6·25 | 3·50 |

**302** Map and Tractor

**1989.** 30th Anniv of Council of Unity.

| | | | |
|---|---|---|---|
| 973 | **302** 75f. multicoloured | 75 | 40 |

**303** "Striga generioides"

**1989.** Parasitic Plants. Multicoloured.

| | | | |
|---|---|---|---|
| 974 | 20f. Type **303** | 25 | 10 |
| 975 | 50f. "Striga hermonthica" | 45 | 25 |
| 976 | 235f. "Striga aspera" | 2·10 | 1·10 |
| 977 | 450f. "Alectra vogelii" | 4·00 | 1·80 |

**304** Sahel Dog

**1989.** Dogs. Multicoloured.

| | | | |
|---|---|---|---|
| 978 | 35f. Type **304** | 45 | 25 |
| 979 | 50f. Young dog | 55 | 25 |
| 980 | 60f. Hunting dog | 80 | 35 |
| 981 | 350f. Guard dog | 3·50 | 1·80 |

**305** Statue

**1989.** Solidarity with Palestinian People.

| | | | |
|---|---|---|---|
| 982 | **305** 120f. multicoloured | 1·20 | 45 |

**1989.** Nos. 647/9 of Upper Volta optd BURKINA FASO.

| | | | |
|---|---|---|---|
| 983 | **229** 90f. multicoloured | 80 | 30 |
| 984 | **229** 120f. multicoloured | 1·00 | 40 |
| 985 | **229** 170f. multicoloured | 1·50 | 60 |

**307** Pilgrims at Shrine of Our Lady of Yagma

**1990.** Visit of Pope John Paul II. Multicoloured.

| | | | |
|---|---|---|---|
| 986 | 120f. Type **307** | 1·20 | 55 |
| 987 | 160f. Pope and crowd | 1·70 | 90 |

**308** Mail Steamer, Globe and Penny Black

**1990.** 150th Anniv of Penny Black and "Stamp World London 90" International Stamp exhibition. Multicoloured.

| | | | |
|---|---|---|---|
| 988 | 120f. Type **308** | 1·20 | 55 |
| **MS**989 | 70×80 mm. 500f. Penny Black and early mail steamers (vert) | 4·25 | 4·00 |

**309** Goalkeeper catching Ball

**1990.** World Cup Football Championship, Italy. Multicoloured.

| | | | |
|---|---|---|---|
| 990 | 30f. Type **309** | 35 | 25 |
| 991 | 150f. Footballers | 1·60 | 70 |
| **MS**992 | 72×65 mm. 1000f. Footballers and "1990" | 8·50 | 8·25 |

**310** "Cantharellus cibarius"

**1990.** Fungi. Multicoloured.

| | | | |
|---|---|---|---|
| 993 | 10f. Type **310** | 20 | 20 |
| 994 | 15f. "Psalliota bispora" | 25 | 20 |
| 995 | 60f. "Amanita caesarea" | 85 | 60 |
| 996 | 190f. "Boletus badius" | 2·75 | 1·50 |
| **MS**997 | 77×108 mm. 75f.×4 As Nos. 993/6 | 4·75 | 4·00 |

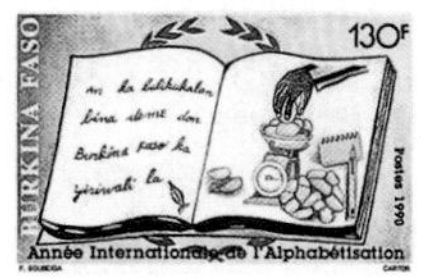

**311** Open Book

**1990.** International Literacy Year.

| | | | |
|---|---|---|---|
| 998 | **311** 40f. multicoloured | 45 | 20 |
| 999 | **311** 130f. multicoloured | 1·20 | 55 |

**312** Maps, Emblem and Native Artefacts

**1990.** 2nd International Salon of Arts and Crafts, Ouagadougou. Multicoloured.

| | | | |
|---|---|---|---|
| 1000 | 35f. Type **312** | 25 | 20 |
| 1001 | 45f. Pottery (horiz) | 40 | 20 |
| 1002 | 270f. Cane chair | 2·20 | 1·10 |

**313** De Gaulle

**1990.** Birth Centenary of Charles de Gaulle (French statesman).

| | | | |
|---|---|---|---|
| 1003 | **313** 200f. multicoloured | 2·00 | 90 |

**314** Quartz

**1991.** Rocks. Multicoloured.

| | | | |
|---|---|---|---|
| 1004 | 20f. Type **314** | 25 | 10 |
| 1005 | 50f. Granite | 70 | 40 |
| 1006 | 280f. Amphibolite | 2·75 | 1·70 |

**315** Hand Holding Cigarette, Syringe and Tablets

**1991.** Anti-drugs Campaign.

| | | | |
|---|---|---|---|
| 1007 | **315** 130f. multicoloured | 1·10 | 65 |

**316** Film and Landscape

**1991.** 12th "Fepaco 91" Pan-African Cinema and Television Festival. Multicoloured.

| | | | |
|---|---|---|---|
| 1008 | 150f. Type **316** | 1·70 | 90 |
| **MS**1009 | 77×108 mm. 1000f. "Stallion of Yennenga" (Festival Grand Prix statuette) | 12·00 | 12·00 |

**317** Morse and Key

**1991.** Birth Bicentenary of Samuel Morse (inventor of signalling system).

| | | | |
|---|---|---|---|
| 1010 | **317** 200f. multicoloured | 1·80 | 1·10 |

**318** Traditional Hairstyle

**1991**

| | | | |
|---|---|---|---|
| 1011 | **318** 5f. multicoloured | 10 | 10 |
| 1012 | **318** 10f. multicoloured | 10 | 10 |
| 1013 | **318** 25f. multicoloured | 10 | 10 |
| 1014 | **318** 50f. multicoloured | 20 | 10 |
| 1018 | **318** 130f. multicoloured | 1·10 | 25 |
| 1019 | **318** 150f. multicoloured | 1·40 | 60 |
| 1020 | **318** 200f. multicoloured | 1·70 | 85 |
| 1021 | **318** 330f. multicoloured | 2·20 | 75 |

**319** "Grewia tenax"

**1991.** Flowers. Multicoloured.

| | | | |
|---|---|---|---|
| 1025 | 5f. Type **319** | 10 | 10 |
| 1026 | 15f. "Hymenocardia acide" | 10 | 10 |
| 1027 | 60f. "Cassia sieberiana" (vert) | 70 | 30 |
| 1028 | 100f. "Adenium obesum" | 90 | 55 |
| 1029 | 300f. "Mitragyna inermis" | 2·75 | 1·60 |

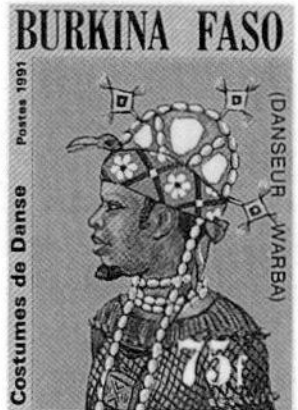

**320** Warba

**1991.** Dance Costumes. Multicoloured.

| | | | |
|---|---|---|---|
| 1030 | 75f. Type **320** | 85 | 40 |
| 1031 | 130f. Wiskamba | 1·20 | 70 |
| 1032 | 280f. Pa-Zenin | 3·00 | 1·60 |

**321** Pillar Box and Globe

**1991.** World Post Day.

| | | | | |
|---|---|---|---|---|
| 1033 | **321** | 130f. multicoloured | 1·20 | 55 |

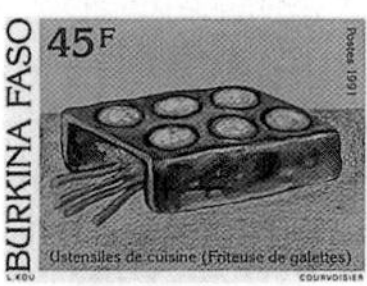

**322** Cake Tin

**1992.** Cooking Utensils.

| | | | |
|---|---|---|---|
| 1034 | 45f. Type **322** | 70 | 65 |
| 1035 | 130f. Cooking pot (vert) | 1·40 | 70 |
| 1036 | 310f. Pestle and mortar (vert) | 2·75 | 1·40 |
| 1037 | 500f. Ladle and bowl | 4·75 | 2·10 |

**323** Yousouf Fofana

**1992.** African Nations Cup Football Championship, Senegal. Multicoloured.

| | | | |
|---|---|---|---|
| 1038 | 50f. Type **323** | 50 | 30 |
| 1039 | 100f. Francois-Jules Bocande | 1·00 | 70 |
| **MS**1040 | 98×93 mm. 500f. Stadium and trophy | 4·75 | 4·50 |

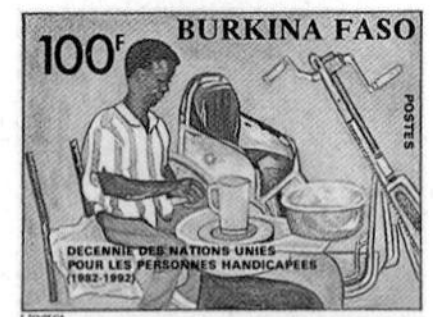

**324** Disabled Man at Potter's Wheel

**1992.** U.N. Decade of the Handicapped.

| | | | | |
|---|---|---|---|---|
| 1041 | **324** | 100f. multicoloured | 90 | 55 |

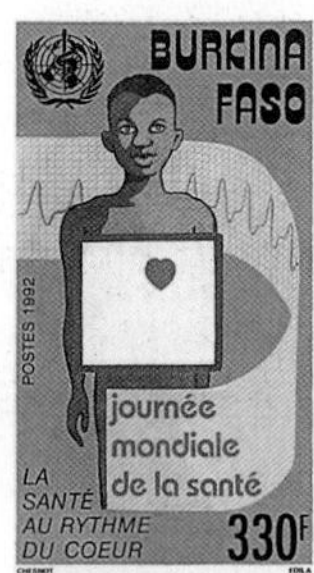

**325** Child and Cardiograph

**1992.** World Health Day. "Health in Rhythm with the Heart".

| | | | | |
|---|---|---|---|---|
| 1042 | **325** | 330f. multicoloured | 3·50 | 1·80 |

**326** Columbus and "Santa Maria"

**1992.** "Genova '92" International Thematic Stamp Exhibition and 500th Anniv of Discovery of America by Columbus. Multicoloured.

| | | | |
|---|---|---|---|
| 1043 | 50f. Type **326** | 70 | 30 |
| 1044 | 150f. Amerindians watching Columbus's fleet off San Salvador | 2·10 | 90 |
| **MS**1045 | 129×91 mm. 350f. Route map of first voyage (51×30 mm) | 4·75 | 3·50 |

**327** "Dysdercus voelkeri" (fire bug) on Cotton Boll

**1992.** Insects. Multicoloured.

| | | | |
|---|---|---|---|
| 1046 | 20f. Type **327** | 25 | 10 |
| 1047 | 40f. "Rhizopertha dominica" (beetle) on leaf | 50 | 30 |
| 1048 | 85f. "Orthetrum microstigma" (dragonfly) on stem | 1·20 | 50 |
| 1049 | 500f. Honey bee on flower | 5·25 | 2·50 |

**328** Crib

**1992.** Christmas. Multicoloured.

| | | | |
|---|---|---|---|
| 1050 | 10f. Type **328** | 10 | 10 |
| 1051 | 130f. Children decorating crib | 1·30 | 65 |
| 1052 | 1000f. Boy with Christmas card | 9·50 | 5·25 |

**329** Film Makers' Monument

**1993.** 13th "Fespaco" Pan-African Film Festival, Ouagadougou. Multicoloured.

| | | | |
|---|---|---|---|
| 1053 | 250f. Type **329** | 2·50 | 1·50 |
| 1054 | 750f. Douta Seck (comedian) (horiz) | 7·50 | 4·50 |

**330** Yellow-billed Stork

**1993.** Birds. Multicoloured.

| | | | |
|---|---|---|---|
| 1055 | 100f. Type **330** | 95 | 60 |
| 1056 | 200f. Marabou stork | 2·00 | 1·20 |
| 1057 | 500f. Saddle-bill stork | 5·00 | 2·75 |
| **MS**1058 | 120×82 mm. Nos. 1046/8 (sold at 1200f.) | 14·50 | 11·00 |

**331** Statue of Liberty, Globe and Ball

**1993.** World Cup Football Championship, U.S.A. (1994). Multicoloured.

| | | | |
|---|---|---|---|
| 1059 | 500f. Type **331** | 5·00 | 2·50 |
| 1060 | 1000f. Players, map of world and U.S. flag | 9·75 | 5·50 |

**332** Peterbilt Canadian Hauler and Diesel Locomotive Type BB 852, France

**1993.** Centenary of Invention of Diesel Engine.

| | | | | |
|---|---|---|---|---|
| 1061 | **332** | 1000f. multicoloured | 9·50 | 5·25 |

**333** "Saba senegalensis"

**1993.** Wild Fruits. Multicoloured.

| | | | |
|---|---|---|---|
| 1062 | 150f. Type **333** | 1·60 | 80 |
| 1063 | 300f. Karite (horiz) | 3·00 | 1·60 |
| 1064 | 600f. Baobab | 6·50 | 3·25 |

**334** Flowers, "Stamps" and Sights of Paris

**1993.** 1st European Stamp Salon, Flower Gardens, Paris (1994). Multicoloured.

| | | | |
|---|---|---|---|
| 1065 | 400f. Type **334** | 4·50 | 2·30 |
| 1066 | 650f. "Stamps", sights of Paris, daffodils and irises | 5·75 | 3·75 |

**335** Peulh Copper Hair Ornament

**1993.** Jewellery. Multicoloured.

| | | | |
|---|---|---|---|
| 1067 | 200f. Type **335** | 1·80 | 1·10 |
| 1068 | 250f. Mossi agate necklace (vert) | 2·20 | 1·30 |
| 1069 | 500f. Gourounsi copper bracelet | 4·50 | 2·50 |

**336** Gazelle

**1993.** The Red-fronted Gazelle. Multicoloured.

| | | | |
|---|---|---|---|
| 1070 | 30f. Type **336** | 1·00 | 35 |
| 1071 | 40f. Two gazelle | 1·00 | 40 |
| 1072 | 60f. Two gazelle (different) | 2·00 | 75 |
| 1073 | 100f. Gazelle | 4·00 | 1·30 |
| **MS**1074 | 110×89 mm. Nos. 1061/4 (sold at 400f.) | 6·25 | 6·00 |

**337** Woodland Kingfisher

**1994.** Kingfishers.

| | | | |
|---|---|---|---|
| 1075 | 600f. Type **337** | 4·75 | 2·75 |
| 1076 | 1200f. Striped kingfisher | 9·50 | 5·50 |
| **MS**1077 | 84×72 mm. 2000f. African pygmy kingfisher | 15·00 | 13·50 |

**338** Players

**1994.** World Cup Football Championship, United States. Multicoloured.

| | | | |
|---|---|---|---|
| 1078 | 1000f. Type **338** | 6·00 | 2·75 |
| 1079 | 1800f. Goalkeeper saving ball | 9·00 | 4·50 |
| **MS**1080 | 84×72 mm. No. 1079 (sold at 2000f.) | 9·75 | 9·25 |

**339** Dog with Puppy

**1994.** 1st European Stamp Salon, Flower Gardens, Paris, France.

| | | | | |
|---|---|---|---|---|
| 1081 | **339** | 1500f. multicoloured | 6·75 | 4·00 |
| **MS**1082 | | 82×80 mm. No. 1081 (sold at 2000f.) | 9·75 | 9·25 |

**340** Astronaut planting Flag on Moon

**1994.** 25th Anniv of First Manned Moon Landing. Multicoloured.

| | | | |
|---|---|---|---|
| 1083 | 750f. Type **340** | 3·75 | 2·10 |
| 1084 | 750f. Landing module on Moon | 3·75 | 2·10 |

Nos. 1083/4 were issued together, se-tenant, forming a composite design.

**341** Guinea Sorrel

**1994.** Vegetables. Multicoloured.

| | | | |
|---|---|---|---|
| 1085 | 40f. Type **341** | 35 | 10 |
| 1086 | 45f. Aubergine | 35 | 10 |
| 1087 | 75f. Aubergine | 35 | 20 |
| 1088 | 100f. Okra | 60 | 30 |

**342** Pig

**1994.** Domestic Animals. Multicoloured.

| | | | |
|---|---|---|---|
| 1089 | 150f. Type **342** | 80 | 45 |
| 1090 | 1000f. Goat (vert) | 4·75 | 2·75 |
| 1091 | 1500f. Sheep | 7·00 | 3·00 |

**343** Pierre de Coubertin (founder) and Anniversary Emblem

**1994.** Centenary of Int Olympic Committee.

| | | | | |
|---|---|---|---|---|
| 1092 | **343** | 320f. multicoloured | 1·60 | 90 |

**344** Donkey Rider

**1995.** 20th Anniv of World Tourism Organization. Multicoloured.

| | | | |
|---|---|---|---|
| 1093 | 150f. Type **344** | 80 | 65 |
| 1094 | 350f. Bobo-Dioulasso railway station (horiz) | 1·50 | 90 |
| 1095 | 450f. Great Mosque, Bani (horiz) | 2·00 | 1·20 |
| 1096 | 650f. Roan antelope and map (horiz) | 2·75 | 1·70 |

**345** Crocodile

**1995.** Multicoloured, colour of frame given.

| | | | | |
|---|---|---|---|---|
| 1097 | **345** | 10f. brown | 10 | 10 |
| 1098 | **345** | 20f. mauve | 10 | 10 |
| 1099 | **345** | 25f. brown | 10 | 10 |
| 1100 | **345** | 30f. green | 10 | 10 |
| 1101 | **345** | 40f. purple | 10 | 10 |
| 1102 | **345** | 50f. grey | 10 | 10 |
| 1103 | **345** | 75f. purple | 25 | 10 |
| 1104 | **345** | 100f. brown | 40 | 10 |
| 1105 | **345** | 150f. green | 55 | 35 |
| 1106 | **345** | 175f. blue | 75 | 40 |
| 1107 | **345** | 250f. brown | 90 | 60 |
| 1108 | **345** | 400f. green | 1·40 | 1·00 |

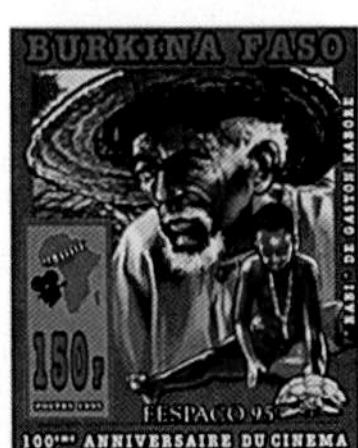


**346** "Rabi" (dir. Gaston Kabore)

**1995.** "Fespaco 95" Pan-African Film Festival and Centenary of Motion Pictures. Multicoloured.

| | | | |
|---|---|---|---|
| 1109 | 150f. Type **346** | 80 | 50 |
| 1110 | 250f. "Tila" (Idrissa Ouedraogo) | 95 | 65 |

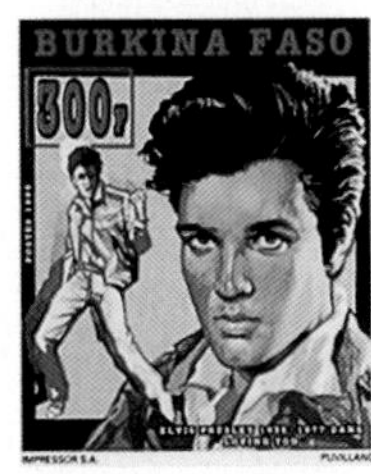


**347** Elvis Presley in "Loving You"

**1995.** Entertainers. Multicoloured.

| | | | |
|---|---|---|---|
| 1111 | 300f. Type **347** | 1·40 | 80 |
| 1112 | 400f. Marilyn Monroe | 1·80 | 1·10 |
| 1113 | 500f. Elvis Presley in "Jailhouse Rock" | 2·30 | 1·40 |
| 1114 | 650f. Marilyn Monroe in "Asphalt Jungle" | 2·75 | 1·80 |
| 1115 | 750f. Marilyn Monroe in "Niagara" | 3·00 | 2·10 |
| 1116 | 1000f. Elvis Presley in "Blue Hawaii" | 4·50 | 3·00 |
| **MS**1117 | Two sheets. (a) 123×95 mm. 1500f. Marilyn Monroe in "The Seven Year Itch" (41×48 mm). (b) 137×89 mm. 1500f. Marilyn Monroe and Elvis Presley (60th birth anniv of Presley (50×41 mm)) Set of 2 sheets | 13·00 | 12·50 |

**348** Common Gonolek

**1995.** Birds. Multicoloured.

| | | | |
|---|---|---|---|
| 1118 | 450f. Type **348** | 2·00 | 1·00 |
| 1119 | 600f. Red-cheeked cordon-bleu | 3·00 | 1·50 |
| 1120 | 750f. Golden bishop | 3·50 | 2·10 |
| **MS**1121 | 80×120 mm. Nos. 1118/20 (sold at 2000f.) | 8·75 | 8·25 |

**349** Hissing Sand Snake

**1995.** Reptiles. Multicoloured.

| | | | |
|---|---|---|---|
| 1122 | 450f. Type **349** | 2·50 | 1·50 |
| 1123 | 500f. Sand python | 2·50 | 1·60 |
| 1124 | 1500f. Tortoise | 7·50 | 4·50 |

**350** Basketball

**1995.** Olympic Games, Atlanta (1996). Mult.

| | | | |
|---|---|---|---|
| 1125 | 150f. Type **350** | 55 | 30 |
| 1126 | 250f. Baseball | 95 | 55 |
| 1127 | 650f. Tennis | 2·20 | 1·40 |
| 1128 | 750f. Table tennis | 3·25 | 1·80 |
| **MS**1129 | 127×89 mm. 1500f. Dressage (35×50 mm) | 6·50 | 6·25 |

**351** Juan Manuel Fangio (racing driver)

**1995.** Sportsmen. Multicoloured.

| | | | |
|---|---|---|---|
| 1130 | 300f. Type **351** | 3·75 | 95 |
| 1131 | 400f. Andre Agassi (tennis player) | 1·40 | 90 |
| 1132 | 500f. Ayrton Senna (racing driver) | 2·00 | 1·10 |
| 1133 | 1000f. Michael Schumacher (racing driver) | 3·75 | 2·10 |
| **MS**1134 | 146×112 mm. 1500f. Enzo Ferrari, Formula 1 racing car and Ferrari F40 sports car (56×48 mm) | 13·00 | 8·75 |

**352** Children and Christmas Tree

**1995.** Christmas. Multicoloured.

| | | | |
|---|---|---|---|
| 1135 | 150f. Type **352** | 75 | 55 |
| 1136 | 450f. Grotto, Yagma | 2·20 | 1·50 |
| 1137 | 500f. Flight into Egypt | 2·50 | 1·60 |
| 1138 | 1000f. Adoration of the Wise Men | 4·50 | 3·00 |

**353** Headquarters Building, New York

**1995.** 50th Anniv of United Nations. Multicoloured.

| | | | |
|---|---|---|---|
| 1139 | 500f. Type **353** | 2·20 | 1·70 |
| 1140 | 1000f. Village council under tree with superimposed U.N. emblem (vert) | 4·25 | 3·00 |

**354** Mossi Type

**1995.** Traditional Houses. Multicoloured.

| | | | |
|---|---|---|---|
| 1141 | 70f. Type **354** | 25 | 10 |
| 1142 | 100f. Kassena type | 45 | 25 |
| 1143 | 200f. Roro type | 90 | 35 |
| 1144 | 250f. Peulh type | 1·10 | 55 |

Nos.1145/8 and Type **355** are left for Christmas, issued on 18 Dec 1995, not yet received.

Nos.1149/50 and Type **356** are left for 50th Anniv of UN, issued on 20 Dec 1995, not yet received.

**357** Les Etalons (national team) Emblem

**1996.** African Cup of Nations Football Championships. Multicoloured.

| | | | |
|---|---|---|---|
| 1151 | 150f.+25f. Type **357** | 80 | 35 |
| 1152 | 250f.+25f. Player and map of Africa | 1·40 | 65 |
| **MS**1153 | 90×84mm. 150f. + 25f. As Type **357** | 2·75 | 1·30 |

The premium was for the benefit of national sport

**358** *Panthera leo* (lions) (image scaled to 68% of original size)

**1996.** Big Cats. Multicoloured.

| | | | |
|---|---|---|---|
| 1154 | 100f. Type **358** | 60 | 25 |
| 1155 | 150f. *Acinonyx jubatus* (cheetah) | 85 | 30 |
| 1156 | 175f. *Lynx caracal* (caracal) | 1·00 | 40 |
| 1157 | 250f. *Panthera pardus* (leopard) | 1·60 | 70 |

Nos.1158/9 and Type **359** are left for France–Africa Summit, issued 1996, not yet received.

**360** Orchid

**1996.** Orchids. Multicoloured.

| | | | |
|---|---|---|---|
| 1160 | 100f. Type **360** | 85 | 45 |
| 1161 | 175f. Yellow orchid | 1·30 | 70 |
| 1162 | 250f. Red and pink orchid | 1·90 | 90 |
| 1163 | 300f. Lime green and dark pink orchid | 2·30 | 1·10 |

Nos. 1164/5 and Type **361** are left for FESPACO Film Festival, issued 5 February 1997, not yet received.

Nos. 1166/9 and Type **362** are left for Fauna, issued 20 March 1997, not yet received.

No. 1170 and Type **363** are left for Death Centenary of H. von Stephan, issued 8 April 1997, not yet received.

Nos. 1171/4 and Type **364** are left for Masks, issued 20 May 1997, not yet received.

Nos. 1175/8 and Type **365** are left for Ceramics, issued 11 September 1997, not yet received.

Nos. 1179/83 and Type **366** are left for Fish, issued 20 November 1997, not yet received.

Nos. 1184/7 and Type **367** are left for African Football, issued 20 January 1998, not yet received.

Nos. 1188/91 and Type **368** are left for Traditional Costumes, issued 20 February 1998, not yet received.

Nos. 1192/3 and Type **369** are left for 20th Anniv of Agricultural Development Fund, issued 20 March 1998, not yet received.

Nos. 1194/7 and Type **370** are left for Endangered Species, issued 20 May 1998, not yet received.

Nos. 1198/9 and Type **371** are left for Organization for African Unity Summit, issued 20 May 1998, not yet received.

**372** White-winged Triller

**1998.** Birds. Multicoloured.

| | | | |
|---|---|---|---|
| 1200 | 5f. Type **372** | 15 | 10 |
| 1201 | 10f. (Arabian) Golden sparrow | 15 | 10 |
| 1202 | 100f. American goldfinch | 55 | 30 |
| 1203 | 170f. Red-legged thrush | 95 | 45 |
| 1204 | 260f. Willow warbler | 1·70 | 85 |
| 1205 | 425f. Blue grosbeak | 2·75 | 1·90 |
| **MS**1206 | 106×152 mm. 260f.×9, Bank swallow (sand martin); Kirtland's warbler; Long-tailed minivet; Blue-grey gnatcatcher; Reed bunting; Black-collared apalis; American robin; Cape longclaw; Wood thrush | 11·50 | 3·35 |
| **MS**1207 | 106×152 mm. 425f.×9, Song sparrow; Dartford warbler; Eastern bluebird; Rock thrush; Northern mockingbird; Northern cardinal; Eurasian goldfinch; Varied thrush; Northern oriole | 17·00 | 5·75 |
| **MS**1208 | 84×110 mm. 1500f. Golden whistler (horiz) | 7·25 | 2·50 |
| **MS**1209 | 110×84 mm. 1500f. Swallow | 7·25 | 2·50 |

Nos.1210 and Type **373** are left for 40th Anniv of Council of Entente, issued 5 May 1999, not yet received.

**374** Family of Lions

**1999.** Lions

| | | | | |
|---|---|---|---|---|
| 1211 | **374** | 170f. multicoloured | 75 | 30 |
| 1212 | **374** | 260f. multicoloured | 95 | 40 |
| 1213 | **374** | 425f. multicoloured | 2·00 | 85 |
| 1214 | **374** | 530f. multicoloured | 2·30 | 1·10 |
| 1215 | **374** | 590f. multicoloured | 4·25 | 2·00 |

**375** Kitten and Butterfly

**1999.** Pets. Multicoloured.

| | | | |
|---|---|---|---|
| 1216 | 5f. Type **375** | 10 | 10 |
| 1217 | 10f. Two chinchilla kittens (horiz) | 15 | 10 |
| 1218 | 20f. Yorkshire terriers (horiz) | 25 | 15 |
| 1219 | 25f. Cocker spaniels (horiz) | 35 | 25 |
| **MS**1220 | 105×110 mm. Vert: 260f.×6, Afghan hound puppy; Wire fox terrier; Pug; Dalmatian; Boston terrier; Cocker spaniel | 5·75 | 2·30 |
| **MS**1221 | 157×88 mm. Horiz: 530f.×6, American wire-haired kitten; Tabby; Burmese blue and frog; Abyssian; Burmese lilac lying down; Siamese playing with string | 13·00 | 8·00 |
| **MS**1222 | 97×79 mm. 1000f. Flowers and two labrador retriever puppies | 4·25 | 2·60 |
| **MS**1223 | 105×80 mm. 1000f. Labrador retriever puppy | 4·25 | 2·60 |
| **MS**1224 | 110×85 mm. 1000f. Persian tabby (horiz) | 4·25 | 2·60 |
| **MS**1225 | 82×110 mm. 1000f. Japanese bobtail kitten | 4·25 | 2·60 |

**376** Gelderlander

**1999.** Domestic Animals. Multicoloured.

| | | | |
|---|---|---|---|
| 1226 | 170f. Type **376** | 60 | 25 |
| 1227 | 170f. Trait lourd horse | 60 | 25 |
| 1228 | 170f. Vladimir heavy draft horse | 60 | 25 |
| 1229 | 170f. Percheron horse | 60 | 25 |
| 1230 | 170f. Sumba pony | 60 | 25 |
| 1231 | 170f. Dartmoor pony | 60 | 25 |
| 1232 | 425f. French bulldog | 2·10 | 60 |
| 1233 | 425f. Bernese dog | 2·10 | 60 |
| 1234 | 425f. Griffon dog | 2·10 | 60 |
| 1235 | 425f. King Charles spaniel | 2·10 | 60 |
| 1236 | 425f. Miniature Spitz dog | 2·10 | 60 |
| 1237 | 425f. Yorkshire terrier | 2·10 | 60 |
| 1238 | 590f. American wire-haired cat | 3·00 | 1·20 |
| 1239 | 590f. Japanese bob-tail cats | 3·00 | 1·20 |
| 1240 | 590f. Himalayan cat | 3·00 | 1·20 |
| 1241 | 590f. LaPerm cat | 3·00 | 1·20 |
| 1242 | 590f. Lilac point Siamese cat and kitten | 3·00 | 1·20 |
| 1243 | 590f. Norwegian forest cat | 3·00 | 1·20 |
| **MS**1244 | 76×106 mm. 1000f. Shetland pony leaning over stable door (vert) | 4·25 | 3·00 |
| **MS**1245 | 106×78 mm. 1000f. Japanese bobtail cat (vert) | 4·25 | 3·00 |
| **MS**1246 | 107×77 mm. 1000f. Basset hound (vert) | 4·00 | 3·25 |

**377** *Portland*

**1999.** Historic Ships. Multicoloured.

| | | | |
|---|---|---|---|
| **MS**1247 135×97 mm. 170f.×3, Type **377**; *Goethe*; *Fulton* | | 2·25 | 1·10 |
| **MS**1248 104×76 mm. 1000f. *Grand Voiler* | | 4·25 | 2·00 |
| **MS**1249 104×76 mm. 1000f. *Batavia* | | 8·25 | 4·25 |

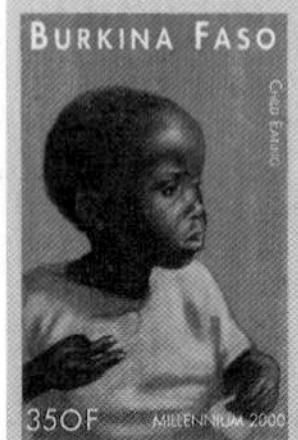


**378** Sukhoi Su-24

**1999.** Aviation. Multicoloured.

| | | | |
|---|---|---|---|
| **MS**1250 145×95 mm. 425f.×6, Type **378**; Yakolev Yak-38; Tupolev *Blackjack*; Antonov An-26; Antonov An-22 Antheus (inscr 'Anteus'); Antonov An-124 | | 10·50 | 6·00 |
| **MS**1251 76×105 mm. 1000f. Ilyushin Il-76 T (57×42 mm) | | 4·25 | 2·75 |

**379** Child holding Food

**1999.** Millennium 2000

| | | | |
|---|---|---|---|
| 1252 | 350f. multicoloured | 1·40 | 80 |

### APPENDIX

The following stamps have either been issued in excess of postal needs or have not been available to the public in reasonable quantities at face value. Such stamps may later be given full listing if there is evidence of regular postal use.

**1985**

85th Birthday of Queen Elizabeth the Queen Mother. 1500f.

**1996**

Fungi. 150f., 250f., 300f., 400f., 500f., 650f., 1000f.
Fungi. 175f., 250f., 300f., 450f.
Entertainers. 150f., 250f., 300f., 400f., 500f., 650f., 1000f.
Butterflies and Insects. 100f., 150f., 175f., 250f.
Butterflies. 150f., 250f., 450f., 600f.
Insects. 25f., 75f., 300f., 400f.
Andre Agassi Olympic Gold Medal. 400f.
Endangered Birds. 500f., 750f., 1000f., 1500f.

**1997**

Princess Diana. 260f., 425f.×2, 590f.
Mother Teresa. 260f.

**1998**

Butterflies. 170f.×9
Christmas. 100f., 170f., 260f., 425f., 530f.
Football World Cup. 50f., 150f., 250f., 450f.

Pt. 1, Pt. 21

# BURMA

A territory in the east of India, which was granted independence by the British in 1948. From May 1990 it was known as Myanmar.

Burma.
1937. 12 pies = 1 anna; 16 annas = 1 rupee.
1953. 100 pyas = 1 kyat.

Japanese Occupation of Burma.
1942. 12 pies = 1 anna; 16 annas = 1 rupee.
1942. 100 cents = 1 rupee.

**1937.** Stamps of India (King George V) optd BURMA.

| | | | | |
|---|---|---|---|---|
| 1 | **55** | 3p. grey | 1·75 | 10 |
| 3 | **80** | 9p. green | 1·00 | 10 |
| 2 | **79** | ½a. green | 1·00 | 10 |
| 4 | **81** | 1a. brown | 3·50 | 10 |
| 5 | **59** | 2a. red | 1·00 | 10 |
| 6 | **61** | 2½a. orange | 75 | 10 |
| 7 | **62** | 3a. red | 3·50 | 30 |
| 8 | **83** | 3½a. blue | 5·00 | 10 |
| 9 | **63** | 4a. olive | 1·00 | 10 |
| 10 | **64** | 6a. bistre | 1·00 | 35 |
| 11 | **65** | 8a. mauve | 3·25 | 10 |
| 12 | **66** | 12a. red | 11·00 | 2·75 |
| 13 | **67** | 1r. brown and green | 50·00 | 4·50 |
| 14 | **67** | 2r. red and orange | 40·00 | 25·00 |
| 15 | **67** | 5r. blue and violet | 48·00 | 26·00 |
| 16 | **67** | 10r. green and red | £180 | 85·00 |
| 17 | **67** | 15r. blue and olive | £650 | £180 |
| 18 | **67** | 25r. orange and blue | £1100 | £450 |

**2** King George VI and "Chinthes"

**3** King George VI and "Nagas"

**4** "Karaweik" (royal barge)

**8** King George VI and Peacock

**1938.** King George VI.

| | | | | |
|---|---|---|---|---|
| 18b | **2** | 1p. orange | 3·00 | 1·50 |
| 19 | **2** | 3p. violet | 30 | 2·75 |
| 20 | **2** | 6p. blue | 30 | 10 |
| 21 | **2** | 9p. green | 1·25 | 1·50 |
| 22 | **3** | 1a. brown | 30 | 10 |
| 23 | **3** | 1½a. green | 35 | 3·25 |
| 24 | **3** | 2a. red | 2·75 | 1·00 |
| 25 | **4** | 2a.6p. red | 14·00 | 3·25 |
| 26 | - | 3a. mauve | 14·00 | 3·25 |
| 27 | - | 3a.6p. blue | 3·50 | 8·50 |
| 28 | **3** | 4a. blue | 3·25 | 20 |
| 29 | - | 8a. green | 4·00 | 55 |
| 30 | **8** | 1r. purple and blue | 4·00 | 1·00 |
| 31 | **8** | 2r. brown and purple | 22·00 | 4·75 |
| 32 | - | 5r. violet and red | 70·00 | 50·00 |
| 33 | - | 10r. brown and green | 75·00 | 80·00 |

DESIGNS—HORIZ: As Type **4**: 3a. Burma teak; 3a.6p. Burma rice; 8a. River Irrawaddy. VERT: As Type **3**: 5, 10r. King George VI and "Nats".

**1940.** Cent of First Adhesive Postage Stamp. Surch COMMEMORATION POSTAGE STAMP 6th MAY 1840 ONE ANNA 1A and value in native characters.

| | | | | |
|---|---|---|---|---|
| 34 | **4** | 1a. on 2a.6p. red | 4·00 | 2·00 |

For Japanese issues see "Japanese Occupation of Burma".

**1945.** British Military Administration. Stamps of 1938 optd MILY ADMN.

| | | | | |
|---|---|---|---|---|
| 35 | **2** | 1p. orange | 10 | 10 |
| 36 | **2** | 3p. violet | 20 | 1·75 |
| 37 | **2** | 6p. blue | 20 | 30 |
| 38 | **2** | 9p. green | 30 | 1·50 |
| 39 | **3** | 1a. brown | 20 | 10 |
| 40 | **3** | 1½a. green | 20 | 15 |
| 41 | **3** | 2a. red | 20 | 15 |
| 42 | **4** | 2a.6p. red | 2·25 | 3·00 |
| 43 | - | 3a. mauve | 1·50 | 20 |
| 44 | - | 3a.6p. blue | 20 | 70 |
| 45 | **3** | 4a. blue | 20 | 70 |
| 46 | - | 8a. green | 20 | 1·50 |
| 47 | **8** | 1r. purple and blue | 50 | 50 |
| 48 | **8** | 2r. brown and purple | 50 | 1·50 |
| 49 | - | 5r. violet and red | 50 | 1·50 |
| 50 | - | 10r. brown and green | 50 | 1·50 |

**1946.** British Civil Administration. As 1938, but colours changed.

| | | | | |
|---|---|---|---|---|
| 51 | **2** | 3p. brown | 10 | 3·75 |
| 52 | **2** | 6p. violet | 10 | 30 |
| 53 | **2** | 9p. green | 1·00 | 6·00 |
| 54 | **3** | 1a. blue | 40 | 20 |
| 55 | **3** | 1½a. orange | 20 | 10 |
| 56 | **3** | 2a. red | 20 | 50 |
| 57 | **4** | 2a.6p. blue | 2·75 | 7·00 |
| 57a | - | 3a. blue | 6·50 | 9·50 |
| 57b | - | 3a.6p. black and blue | 2·75 | 4·50 |
| 58 | **3** | 4a. purple | 50 | 1·25 |
| 59 | - | 8a. mauve | 1·75 | 6·50 |
| 60 | **8** | 1r. violet and mauve | 2·50 | 3·25 |
| 61 | **8** | 2r. brown and orange | 8·00 | 6·50 |
| 62 | - | 5r. green and brown | 9·00 | 26·00 |
| 63 | - | 10r. red and violet | 21·00 | 38·00 |

**14** Burman

**1946.** Victory.

| | | | | |
|---|---|---|---|---|
| 64 | **14** | 9p. green | 20 | 20 |
| 65 | - | 1½a. violet (Burmese woman) | 20 | 10 |
| 66 | - | 2a. red (Chinthe) | 20 | 10 |
| 67 | - | 3a.6p. (Elephant) | 50 | 20 |

**(18)** Trans. "Interim Government"

**1947.** Stamps of 1946 opt with T 18 or with larger opt on large stamps.

| | | | | |
|---|---|---|---|---|
| 68 | **2** | 3p. brown | 1·75 | 70 |
| 69 | **2** | 6p. violet | 10 | 30 |
| 70 | **2** | 9p. green | 10 | 30 |
| 71 | **3** | 1a. blue | 10 | 30 |
| 72 | **3** | 1½a. orange | 2·50 | 10 |
| 73 | **3** | 2a. red | 30 | 15 |
| 74 | **4** | 2a.6p. blue | 1·75 | 1·00 |
| 75 | - | 3a. blue | 2·50 | 1·75 |
| 76 | - | 3a.6p. black and blue | 2·00 | 2·75 |
| 77 | **3** | 4a. purple | 1·75 | 30 |
| 78 | - | 8a. mauve | 1·75 | 3·00 |
| 79 | **8** | 1r. violet and mauve | 8·00 | 3·00 |
| 80 | **8** | 2r. brown and orange | 8·00 | 8·50 |
| 81 | - | 5r. green and brown | 8·00 | 6·50 |
| 82 | - | 10r. red and violet | 5·50 | 6·50 |

**20** Gen. Aung San, Chinthe and Map of Burma

**1948.** Independence Day.

| | | | | |
|---|---|---|---|---|
| 83 | **20** | ½a. green | 10 | 10 |
| 84 | **20** | 1a. pink | 10 | 10 |
| 85 | **20** | 2a. red | 20 | 15 |
| 86 | **20** | 3½a. blue | 25 | 15 |
| 87 | **20** | 8a. brown | 25 | 25 |

**21** Martyrs' Memorial

**1948.** 1st Anniv of Murder of Aung San and his Ministers.

| | | | | |
|---|---|---|---|---|
| 88 | **21** | 3p. blue | 10 | 10 |
| 89 | **21** | 6p. green | 10 | 10 |
| 90 | **21** | 9p. red | 10 | 10 |
| 91 | **21** | 1a. violet | 10 | 10 |
| 92 | **21** | 2a. mauve | 10 | 10 |
| 93 | **21** | 3½a. green | 10 | 10 |
| 94 | **21** | 4a. brown | 20 | 10 |
| 95 | **21** | 8a. red | 20 | 15 |
| 96 | **21** | 12a. purple | 25 | 15 |
| 97 | **21** | 1r. green | 45 | 25 |
| 98 | **21** | 2r. blue | 90 | 50 |
| 99 | **21** | 5r. brown | 2·00 | 1·30 |

**22** Playing Cane-ball

**25** Bell, Mingun Pagoda

**27** Transplanting Rice

**28** Lion Throne

**1949.** 1st Anniv of Independence.

| | | | | |
|---|---|---|---|---|
| 100 | **22** | 3p. blue | 1·10 | 25 |
| 120 | **22** | 3p. orange | 20 | 10 |
| 101 | - | 6p. green | 20 | 10 |
| 121 | - | 6p. purple | 10 | 10 |
| 102 | - | 9p. red | 20 | 10 |
| 122 | - | 9p. blue | 10 | 10 |
| 103 | **25** | 1a. red | 20 | 10 |
| 123 | **25** | 1a. blue | 10 | 10 |
| 104 | - | 2a. orange | 20 | 10 |
| 124 | - | 2a. green | 35 | 15 |
| 105 | **27** | 2a.6p. mauve | 20 | 15 |
| 125 | **27** | 2a.6p. green | 35 | 15 |
| 106 | - | 3a. violet | 20 | 15 |
| 126 | - | 3a. red | 20 | 15 |
| 107 | - | 3a.6p. green | 25 | 15 |
| 127 | - | 3a.6p. orange | 20 | 15 |
| 108 | - | 4a. brown | 25 | 15 |
| 128 | - | 4a. red | 20 | 15 |
| 109 | - | 8a. red | 35 | 15 |
| 129 | - | 8a. blue | 35 | 20 |
| 110 | **28** | 1r. green | 65 | 15 |
| 130 | **28** | 1r. violet | 50 | 55 |
| 111 | **28** | 2r. blue | 1·50 | 45 |
| 131 | **28** | 2r. green | 1·10 | 60 |
| 112 | **28** | 5r. brown | 3·00 | 1·40 |
| 132 | **28** | 5r. blue | 3·25 | 1·70 |
| 113 | **28** | 10r. orange | 5·50 | 2·20 |
| 133 | **28** | 10r. blue | 6·25 | 4·25 |

DESIGNS—As Type **22**: 6p. Dancer; 9p. Girl playing saung-gaut (string instrument); 2a. Hintha (legendary bird). As Type **25**: 4a. Elephant hauling log. As Type **27**: 3a. Girl weaving; 3a.6p. Royal Palace; 8a. Ploughing paddy field with oxen.

See also Nos. 137/50.

**29** UPU Monument, Berne

**1949.** 75th Anniv of UPU.

| | | | | |
|---|---|---|---|---|
| 114 | **29** | 2a. orange | 25 | 25 |
| 115 | **29** | 3½a. green | 25 | 15 |
| 116 | **29** | 6a. violet | 35 | 25 |
| 117 | **29** | 8a. red | 45 | 45 |
| 118 | **29** | 12½a. blue | 90 | 60 |
| 119 | **29** | 1r. green | 1·10 | 85 |

**30** Independence Monument, Rangoon, and Map

**1953.** 5th Anniv of Independence.

| | | | | |
|---|---|---|---|---|
| 134 | **30** | 14p. green (22×18 mm) | 20 | 10 |
| 135 | **30** | 20p. red (36½×26½ mm) | 25 | 15 |
| 136 | **30** | 25p. blue (36½×26½ mm) | 45 | 15 |

**1954.** New Currency. As 1949 issue but values in pyas and kyats.

| | | | | |
|---|---|---|---|---|
| 137 | **22** | 1p. orange | 70 | 10 |
| 138 | - | 2p. purple (as 6p.) | 10 | 10 |
| 139 | - | 3p. blue (as 9p.) | 10 | 10 |
| 140 | **25** | 5p. blue | 10 | 10 |
| 141 | **27** | 10p. green | 10 | 10 |
| 142 | - | 15p. green (as 2a.) | 25 | 10 |
| 143 | - | 20p. red (as 3a.) | 20 | 10 |
| 144 | - | 25p. orange (as 3a.6p.) | 20 | 15 |
| 145 | - | 30p. red (as 4a.) | 25 | 15 |
| 146 | - | 50p. blue (as 8a.) | 25 | 15 |

| | | | | |
|---|---|---|---|---|
| 147 | **28** | 1k. violet | 80 | 25 |
| 148 | **28** | 2k. green | 1·50 | 45 |
| 149 | **28** | 5k. blue | 4·25 | 80 |
| 150 | **28** | 10k. blue | 7·75 | 1·40 |

**31** Sangiti Mahapasana Rock Cave in Grounds of Kaba-Aye Pagoda

**1954.** 6th Buddhist Council, Rangoon.

| | | | | |
|---|---|---|---|---|
| 151 | - | 10p. blue | 10 | 10 |
| 152 | - | 15p. purple | 15 | 15 |
| 153 | **31** | 35p. brown | 25 | 25 |
| 154 | - | 50p. green | 45 | 25 |
| 155 | - | 1k. red | 95 | 50 |
| 156 | - | 2k. violet | 1·60 | 1·10 |

DESIGNS: 10p. Rock caves and Songha of Cambodia; 15p. Buddhist priests and Kuthodaw Pagoda, Mandalay; 50p. Rock cave and Songha of Thailand; 1k. Rock cave and Songha of Ceylon; 2k. Rock cave and Songha of Laos.

**32** Fifth Buddhist Council Monuments

**1956.** Buddha Jayanti.

| | | | | |
|---|---|---|---|---|
| 157 | **32** | 20p. green and blue | 15 | 15 |
| 158 | - | 40p. green and blue | 35 | 25 |
| 159 | - | 60p. yellow and green | 45 | 35 |
| 160 | - | 1k.25 blue and yellow | 95 | 80 |

DESIGNS: 40p. Thatbyinnyu Pagoda, Pagan; 60p. Shwedagan Pagoda, Rangoon; 1k.25, Sangiti Mahapasana Rock Cave and Kaba-Aye Pagoda, Rangoon (venue of 6th Buddhist Council).

မြို့မန္တလာ-နှစ်တရာ
၁၂၂၁-၁၃၂၁
15P ၁၅ပြား

**(33)** "Mandalay Town—100 Years/1221–1321"

**1959.** Centenary of Mandalay. No. 144 surch with T 33 and Nos. 147/8 with two-line opt only.

| | | | | |
|---|---|---|---|---|
| 161 | | 15p. on 25p. orange | 25 | 15 |
| 162 | **28** | 1k. violet | 85 | 80 |
| 163 | **28** | 2k. green | 1·70 | 1·20 |

**1961.** No. 134 surch as right-hand characters in third line of T 33.

| | | | | |
|---|---|---|---|---|
| 164 | **30** | 15p. on 14p. green | 60 | 25 |

**35** Torch-bearer in Rangoon

**1961.** 2nd South-East Asia Peninsula Games, Rangoon.

| | | | | |
|---|---|---|---|---|
| 165 | **35** | 15p. blue and red | 40 | 25 |
| 166 | - | 25p. green and brown | 1·50 | 50 |
| 167 | - | 50p. mauve and blue | 1·60 | 1·00 |
| 168 | - | 1k. yellow and green | 3·50 | 2·00 |

DESIGNS—VERT: 25p. Contestants; 50p. Women sprinting in Aung San Stadium, Rangoon. HORIZ: 1k. Contestants.

**36** Children at Play

**1961.** 15th Anniv of UNICEF.

| | | | | |
|---|---|---|---|---|
| 169 | **36** | 15p. red and pink | 1·50 | 40 |

**37** Flag and Map

**1963.** 1st Anniv of Military Coup by General Ne Win.

| | | | | |
|---|---|---|---|---|
| 170 | **37** | 15p. red | 1·50 | 65 |

**1963.** Freedom from Hunger. Nos. 141 and 146 optd FREEDOM FROM HUNGER.

| | | | | |
|---|---|---|---|---|
| 171 | **27** | 10p. green | 1·00 | 80 |
| 172 | - | 50p. blue | 3·00 | 2·00 |

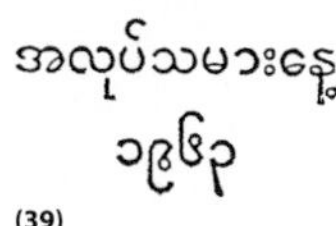

အလုပ်သမားနေ့
၁၉၆၃

**(39)**

**1963.** Labour Day. No. 143 optd with T 39.

| | | | | |
|---|---|---|---|---|
| 173 | | 20p. red | 65 | 35 |

**40** White-browed Fantail

**1964.** Burmese Birds (1st series).

| | | | | |
|---|---|---|---|---|
| 174 | **40** | 1p. black | 25 | 15 |
| 175 | **40** | 2p. red | 75 | 30 |
| 176 | **40** | 3p. green | 75 | 30 |
| 177 | - | 5p. blue | 75 | 30 |
| 178 | - | 10p. brown | 80 | 35 |
| 179 | - | 15p. green | 1·20 | 50 |
| 180 | - | 20p. brown and red | 1·60 | 60 |
| 181 | - | 25p. brown and yellow | 2·00 | 75 |
| 182 | - | 50p. blue and red | 4·00 | 1·50 |
| 183 | - | 1k. blue, yellow & grey | 7·50 | 2·00 |
| 184 | - | 2k. blue, green and red | 16·00 | 4·00 |
| 185 | - | 5k. multicoloured | 35·00 | 10·00 |

BIRDS—22×26 mm: 5 to 15p. Indian roller. 27×37 mm: 25p. Crested serpent eagle. 50p. Sarus crane. 1k. Indian pied hornbill. 5k. Green peafowl. 35½×25 mm: 20p. Red-whiskered bulbul. 37×27 mm: 2k. Kalij pheasant.
See also Nos. 195/206.

**41** ITU Emblem and Symbols

**1965.** Centenary of ITU.

| | | | | |
|---|---|---|---|---|
| 186 | **41** | 20p. mauve | 90 | 40 |
| 187 | **41** | 50p. green (34×24½ mm) | 1·10 | 80 |

**42** ICY Emblem

**1965.** International Co-operation Year.

| | | | | |
|---|---|---|---|---|
| 188 | **42** | 5p. blue | 25 | 15 |
| 189 | **42** | 10p. brown | 45 | 25 |
| 190 | **42** | 15p. olive | 1·40 | 60 |

**43** Harvesting

**1966.** Peasants' Day.

| | | | | |
|---|---|---|---|---|
| 191 | **43** | 15p. multicoloured | 1·50 | 40 |

**44** Cogwheel and Hammer

**1967.** May Day.

| | | | | |
|---|---|---|---|---|
| 192 | **44** | 15p. yellow, black & blue | 1·75 | 40 |

**45** Aung San and Agricultural Cultivation

**1968.** 20th Anniv of Independence.

| | | | | |
|---|---|---|---|---|
| 193 | **45** | 15p. multicoloured | 2·20 | 50 |

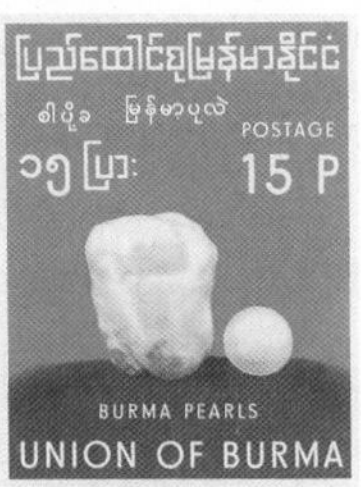

**46** Burma Pearls

**1968.** Burmese Gems, Jades and Pearls Emporium, Rangoon.

| | | | | |
|---|---|---|---|---|
| 194 | **46** | 15p. ultram, blue & yell | 3·00 | 1·00 |

**1968.** Burmese Birds (2nd series). Designs and colours as Nos. 174/85 but formats and sizes changed.

| | | | | |
|---|---|---|---|---|
| 195 | **40** | 1p. black | 80 | 35 |
| 196 | **40** | 2p. red | 75 | 35 |
| 197 | **40** | 3p. green | 75 | 35 |
| 198 | - | 5p. blue | 75 | 35 |
| 199 | - | 10p. brown | 1·00 | 45 |
| 200 | - | 15p. yellow | 1·50 | 50 |
| 201 | - | 20p. brown and red | 2·20 | 75 |
| 202 | - | 25p. brown and yellow | 2·60 | 95 |
| 203 | - | 50p. blue and red | 4·50 | 1·40 |
| 204 | - | 1k. blue, yellow & grey | 10·00 | 3·00 |
| 205 | - | 2k. blue, green and red | 20·00 | 6·00 |
| 206 | - | 5k. multicoloured | 45·00 | 18·00 |

NEW SIZES—21×17 mm: 1, 2, 3p. 39×21 mm: 20p., 2k. 23×28 mm: 5, 10, 15p. 21×39 mm: 25, 50p., 1, 5k.

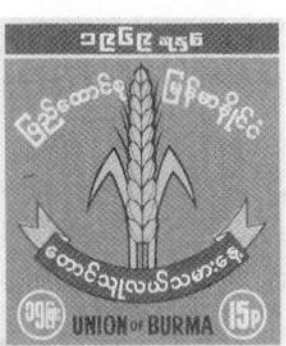

**47** Spike of Paddy

**1969.** Peasants' Day.

| | | | | |
|---|---|---|---|---|
| 218 | **47** | 15p. yellow, blue & green | 2·00 | 40 |

**48** ILO Emblem

**1969.** 50th Anniv of ILO.

| | | | | |
|---|---|---|---|---|
| 219 | **48** | 15p. gold and green | 40 | 30 |
| 220 | **48** | 50p. gold and red | 1·90 | 80 |

**49** Football

**1969.** 5th South-East Asian Peninsula Games, Rangoon.

| | | | | |
|---|---|---|---|---|
| 221 | **49** | 15p. multicoloured | 80 | 40 |
| 222 | - | 25p. multicoloured | 90 | 40 |
| 223 | - | 50p. multicoloured | 1·80 | 80 |
| 224 | - | 1k. black, green & blue | 3·50 | 1·50 |

DESIGNS—HORIZ: 25p. Running. VERT: 50p. Weightlifting; 1k. Volleyball.

**50** Marchers with Independence, Resistance and Union Flags

**1970.** 25th Anniv of Burmese Armed Forces.

| | | | | |
|---|---|---|---|---|
| 225 | **50** | 15p. multicoloured | 2·00 | 40 |

**51** "Peace and Progress"

**1970.** 25th Anniv of United Nations.

| | | | | |
|---|---|---|---|---|
| 226 | **51** | 15p. multicoloured | 2·00 | 40 |

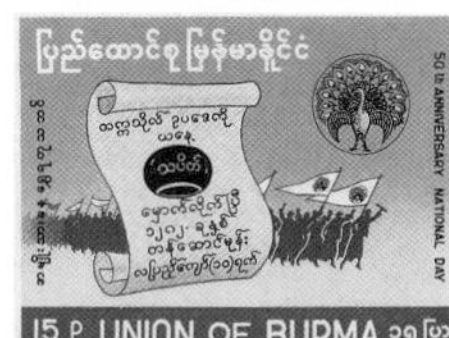

**52** Boycott Declaration and Marchers

**1970.** National Day and 50th Anniv of University Boycott. Multicoloured.

| | | | | |
|---|---|---|---|---|
| 227 | | 15p. Type **52** | 45 | 25 |
| 228 | | 25p. Students on boycott march | 85 | 50 |
| 229 | | 50p. Banner and demonstrators | 2·00 | 75 |

**53** Burmese Workers

**1971.** 1st Burmese Socialist Programme Party Congress. Multicoloured.

| | | | | |
|---|---|---|---|---|
| 230 | | 5p. Type **53** | 25 | 20 |
| 231 | | 15p. Burmese races and flags | 45 | 50 |
| 232 | | 25p. Hands holding scroll | 1·25 | 65 |
| 233 | | 50p. Party flag | 1·75 | 85 |
| **MS**234 | | 179×127 mm. Nos. 230/3. Imperf | 18·00 | 18·00 |

**54** Child drinking Milk

**1971.** 25th Anniv of UNICEF. Multicoloured.

| | | | | |
|---|---|---|---|---|
| 235 | | 15p. Type **54** | 1·00 | 35 |
| 236 | | 50p. Marionettes | 2·75 | 1·30 |

**55** Aung San and Independence Monument, Panglong

**1972.** 25th Anniv of Independence. Multicoloured.

| | | | | |
|---|---|---|---|---|
| 237 | | 15p. Type **55** | 45 | 30 |
| 238 | | 50p. Aung San and Burmese in national costumes | 1·40 | 45 |
| 239 | | 1k. Flag and map (vert) | 2·75 | 1·20 |

**56** Burmese and Stars

**1972.** 10th Anniv of Revolutionary Council.

| | | | | |
|---|---|---|---|---|
| 240 | **56** | 15p. multicoloured | 1·00 | 45 |

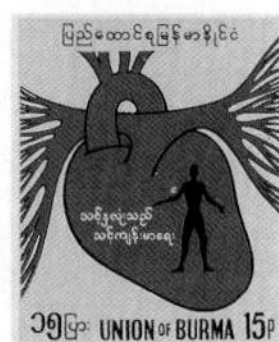

**57** Human Heart

**1972.** World Health Day.
241 **57** 15p. red, black & yellow 2·00 65

**58** Ethnic Groups

**1973.** National Census.
242 **58** 15p. multicoloured 80 40

**59** Casting Vote

**1973.** National Constitutional Referendum.
243 **59** 5p. red and black 15 10
244 - 10p. multicoloured 15 10
245 - 15p. multicoloured 15 10
DESIGNS—HORIZ: 10p. Voter supporting map. VERT: 15p. Burmese with ballot papers.

**60** Open-air Meeting

**1974.** Opening of 1st Pyithu Hluttaw (People's Assembly). Multicoloured.
246 15p. Burmese flags, 1752–1974 (80×26 mm) 40 25
247 50p. Type **60** 1·00 45
248 1k. Burmese badge 1·80 1·00

**61** UPU Emblem and Carrier Pigeon

**1974.** Centenary of Universal Postal Union. Mult.
249 15p. Type **61** 60 35
250 20p. Woman reading letter (vert) 70 35
251 50p. UPU emblem on "stamps" (vert) 1·20 65
252 1k. Stylized doll (vert) 2·50 1·20
253 2k. Postman delivering letter to family 5·00 1·80

**62** Kachin Couple

**63** Bamar Couple

**1974.** Burmese Costumes. Inscr "SOCIALIST REPUBLIC OF THE UNION OF BURMA".
254 **62** 1p. mauve 25 25
255 **62** 3p. brown and mauve 30 20
256 **62** 5p. violet and mauve 35 20
257 **62** 10p. blue 45 20
258 **62** 15p. green and light green 55 20
259 **63** 20p. black, brown & blue 95 35
260 - 50p. violet, brown & ochre 2·40 80
261 - 1k. violet, mauve & black 4·75 1·80
262 - 5k. multicoloured 20·00 8·00

DESIGNS—As Type **62**: 3p. Kayah girl; 5p. Kayin couple and bronze drum; 15p. Chin couple. As Type **63**: 50p. Mon woman; 1k. Rakhine woman; 5k. Musician.

For 15, 50p. and 1k. stamps in these designs, but inscr "UNION OF BURMA", see Nos. 309/11.

**64** Woman on Globe and IWY Emblem

**1975.** International Women's Year.
263 **64** 50p. black and green 1·25 60
264 - 2k. black and blue 4·50 2·30
DESIGN—VERT: 2k. Globe on flower and IWY emblem.

**65** Burmese and Flag

**1976.** Constitution Day.
265 **65** 20p. black and blue 60 30
266 - 50p. brown and blue 1·10 70
267 - 1k. multicoloured 2·20 1·20
DESIGNS—As Type **65**: 50p. Burmese with banners and flag. 57×21 mm: 1k. Map of Burma, Burmese and flag.

**66** Emblem and Burmese Learning Alphabet

**1976.** International Literacy Year.
268 **66** 10p. brown and red 35 30
269 - 15p. turquoise, grn & blk 55 30
270 - 50p. blue, orange & black 2·00 90
271 - 1k. multicoloured 3·60 2·00
DESIGNS—HORIZ: 15p. Abacus and open books. 50p. Emblem. VERT: 1k. Emblem, open book and globe.

**67** Early Train and Ox-cart

**1977.** Centenary of Railway.
272 15p. green, black & mauve 7·25 1·50
273 **67** 20p. multicoloured 2·00 80
274 - 25p. multicoloured 3·00 1·00
275 - 50p. multicoloured 4·75 1·90
276 - 1k. multicoloured 11·00 3·50
DESIGNS—26×17 mm: 15p. Early steam locomotive. As Type **67**—HORIZ: 25p. Diesel locomotive DD1517, steam train and railway station; 50p. Ava railway bridge over River Irrawaddy. VERT: Diesel train emerging from tunnel.

**68** Karaweik Hall

**1978**
277 **68** 50p. brown 2·60 1·60
278 - 1k. multicoloured 85 60
DESIGN—79½×25 mm: 1k. Side view of Karaweik Hall.

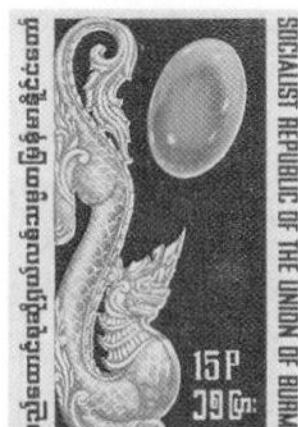

**69** Jade Naga and Gem

**1979.** 16th Gem Emporium.
279 **69** 15p. green and turquoise 15 10
280 - 20p. blue, yellow & mauve 1·40 40
281 - 50p. blue, brown & green 3·75 1·00
282 - 1k. multicoloured 7·50 1·75
DESIGNS—As T **69**: 20p. Hintha (legendary bird) holding pearl in beak; 50p. Hand holding pearl and amethyst pendant. 55×20 mm: 1k. Gold jewel-studded dragon.

**70** "Intelsat IV" Satellite over Burma

**1979.** Introduction of Satellite Communications System.
283 **70** 25p. multicoloured 25 15

**71** IYC Emblem on Map of Burma

**1979.** International Year of the Child.
284 **71** 25p. orange and blue 1·25 50
285 **71** 50p. red and violet 2·50 1·00

**72** Weather Balloon

**1980.** World Meteorological Day.
286 **72** 25p. blue, yellow & black 1·00 40
287 - 50p. green, black and red 2·00 80
DESIGN: 50p. Meteorological satellite and WMO emblem.

**73** Weightlifting

**1980.** Olympic Games, Moscow.
288 **73** 20p. green, orange & blk 45 25
289 - 50p. black, orange and red 1·20 50
290 - 1k. black, orange and blue 2·75 1·20
DESIGNS: 50p. Boxing; 1k. Football.

**74** ITU and WHO Emblems with Ribbons forming Caduceus

**1981.** World Telecommunications Day.
291 **74** 25p. orange and black 1·50 35

**75** Livestock and Vegetables

**1981.** World Food Day. Multicoloured.
292 25p. Type **75** 70 35
293 50p. Farm produce and farmer holding wheat 1·60 55
294 1k. Globe and stylized bird 2·60 90

**76** Athletes and Person in Wheelchair

**1981.** International Year of Disabled Persons.
295 **76** 25p. multicoloured 2·00 60

**77** Telephone, Satellite and Antenna

**1983.** World Communications Year.
296 **77** 15p. blue and black 60 30
297 **77** 25p. mauve and black 1·00 40
298 **77** 50p. green, black and red 2·30 90
299 **77** 1k. brown, black & green 4·50 1·80

**78** Fish and Globe

**1983.** World Food Day.
300 **78** 15p. yellow, blue & black 65 45
301 **78** 25p. orange, green & black 1·30 75
302 **78** 50p. green, yellow & black 2·60 1·50
303 **78** 1k. blue, yellow and black 5·00 3·00

**79** Globe and Log

**1984.** World Food Day.
304 **79** 15p. blue, yellow & black 50 35
305 **79** 25p. violet, yellow & black 1·00 60
306 **79** 50p. green, pink and black 2·00 1·20
307 **79** 1k. mauve, yellow & black 4·50 3·00

**80** Potted Plant

**1985.** International Youth Year.
308 **80** 15p. multicoloured 1·40 35

**1989.** As Nos. 258/9 and 260/1 but inscr "UNION OF BURMA".
309 **62** 15p. dp green & green 40 35

| | | | | |
|---|---|---|---|---|
| 310 | - | 50p. violet and brown | 90 | 70 |
| 311 | - | 1k. violet, mauve & black | 1·70 | 1·40 |

Examples of No. 309a, which have been prepared several years earlier but not issued, were inadvertently supplied to Shan State post office in July 1995. Subsequently a limited quantity were sold to philatelists in Yangon.

### OFFICIAL STAMPS

**1937.** Stamps of India (King George V) optd BURMA SERVICE.

| | | | | |
|---|---|---|---|---|
| O1 | **55** | 3p. grey | 4·00 | 10 |
| O3 | **80** | 9p. green | 5·00 | 1·75 |
| O2 | **79** | ½a. green | 16·00 | 10 |
| O4 | **81** | 1a. brown | 8·50 | 10 |
| O5 | **59** | 2a. red | 17·00 | 45 |
| O6 | **61** | 2½a. orange | 8·00 | 3·25 |
| O7 | **63** | 4a. olive | 8·50 | 10 |
| O8 | **64** | 6a. bistre | 9·00 | 16·00 |
| O9 | **65** | 8a. mauve | 8·00 | 3·25 |
| O10 | **66** | 12a. red | 8·50 | 13·00 |
| O11 | **67** | 1r. brown and green | 24·00 | 10·00 |
| O12 | **67** | 2r. red and orange | 48·00 | 70·00 |
| O13 | **67** | 5r. blue and violet | £170 | 70·00 |
| O14 | **67** | 10r. green and red | £450 | £250 |

**1939.** Stamps of 1938 optd SERVICE.

| | | | | |
|---|---|---|---|---|
| O15 | **2** | 3p. violet | 15 | 20 |
| O16 | **2** | 6p. blue | 15 | 20 |
| O17 | **2** | 9p. green | 4·00 | 6·50 |
| O18 | **3** | 1a. brown | 15 | 15 |
| O19 | **3** | 1½a. green | 3·50 | 3·00 |
| O20 | **3** | 2a. red | 1·25 | 20 |
| O21 | **4** | 2a.6p. red | 24·00 | 20·00 |
| O22 | **3** | 4a. blue | 4·50 | 2·00 |
| O23 | - | 8a. green (No. 29) | 16·00 | 4·00 |
| O24 | **8** | 1r. purple and blue | 16·00 | 5·50 |
| O25 | **8** | 2r. brown and purple | 30·00 | 17·00 |
| O26 | - | 5r. violet and red (No. 32) | 25·00 | 40·00 |
| O27 | - | 10r. brown and green (No. 33) | £130 | 45·00 |

**1946.** Stamps of 1946 optd SERVICE.

| | | | | |
|---|---|---|---|---|
| O28 | **2** | 3p. brown | 3·50 | 5·00 |
| O29 | **2** | 6p. violet | 2·50 | 2·25 |
| O30 | **2** | 9p. green | 1·00 | 6·00 |
| O31 | **3** | 1a. blue | 30 | 2·00 |
| O32 | **3** | 1½a. orange | 1·00 | 20 |
| O33 | **3** | 2a. red | 30 | 2·00 |
| O34 | **4** | 2a.6p. blue | 2·75 | 11·00 |
| O35 | **3** | 4a. purple | 1·00 | 70 |
| O36 | - | 8a. mauve (No. 59) | 4·50 | 6·50 |
| O37 | **8** | 1r. violet and mauve | 2·50 | 9·50 |
| O38 | **8** | 2r. brown and orange | 8·00 | 48·00 |
| O39 | - | 5r. green and brown (No. 62) | 18·00 | 60·00 |
| O40 | - | 10r. red and violet (No. 63) | 18·00 | 70·00 |

**1947.** Interim Government. Nos. O28 etc., optd with T 18 or with large overprint on larger stamps.

| | | | | |
|---|---|---|---|---|
| O41 | **2** | 3p. brown | 2·50 | 40 |
| O42 | **2** | 6p. violet | 4·75 | 10 |
| O43 | **2** | 9p. green | 6·50 | 90 |
| O44 | **3** | 1a. blue | 6·50 | 80 |
| O45 | **3** | 1½a. orange | 11·00 | 30 |
| O46 | **3** | 2a. red | 6·50 | 15 |
| O47 | **4** | 2a.6p. blue | 30·00 | 18·00 |
| O48 | **3** | 4a. purple | 24·00 | 40 |
| O49 | - | 8a. mauve | 24·00 | 4·00 |
| O50 | **8** | 1r. violet and mauve | 17·00 | 3·00 |
| O51 | **8** | 2r. brown and orange | 17·00 | 20·00 |
| O52 | - | 5r. green and brown | 18·00 | 20·00 |
| O53 | - | 10r. red and violet | 18·00 | 32·00 |

အစိုးရကိစ္စ

**(O29)** (size of opt varies)

**1949.** 1st Anniv of Independence. Nos. 100/4 and 107/113 optd as Type O 29.

| | | | | |
|---|---|---|---|---|
| O114 | **22** | 3p. blue | 55 | 15 |
| O115 | - | 6p. green | 10 | 10 |
| O116 | - | 9p. red | 10 | 10 |
| O117 | **25** | 1a. red | 10 | 10 |
| O118 | - | 2a. orange | 20 | 15 |
| O119 | - | 3a.6p. green | 20 | 15 |
| O120 | - | 4a. brown | 20 | 15 |
| O121 | - | 8a. red | 20 | 15 |
| O122 | **28** | 1r. green | 55 | 25 |
| O123 | **28** | 2r. blue | 90 | 45 |
| O124 | **28** | 5r. brown | 2·40 | 1·70 |
| O125 | **28** | 10r. orange | 6·00 | 4·25 |

**1954.** Nos. 137/40 and 142/50 optd as Type O 29.

| | | | | |
|---|---|---|---|---|
| O151 | **22** | 1p. orange | 55 | 15 |
| O152 | - | 2p. purple | 20 | 15 |
| O153 | - | 3p. blue | 20 | 15 |
| O154 | **25** | 5p. blue | 20 | 15 |
| O155 | - | 15p. green | 20 | 15 |
| O156 | - | 20p. red | 20 | 15 |
| O157 | - | 25p. orange | 20 | 15 |
| O158 | - | 30p. red | 20 | 15 |
| O159 | - | 50p. blue | 20 | 15 |
| O160 | **28** | 1k. violet | 65 | 15 |
| O161 | **28** | 2k. green | 1·50 | 35 |
| O162 | **28** | 5k. blue | 3·00 | 95 |
| O163 | **28** | 10k. blue | 6·50 | 3·00 |

**1964.** No. 139 optd Service.

| | | | |
|---|---|---|---|
| O174 | 3p. blue | 12·00 | 8·50 |

**1965.** Nos. 174/7 and 179/85 optd as Type O 29.

| | | | | |
|---|---|---|---|---|
| O196 | **40** | 1p. black | 15 | 15 |
| O197 | **40** | 2p. red | 25 | 25 |
| O198 | **40** | 3p. green | 25 | 25 |
| O199 | - | 5p. blue | 35 | 25 |
| O200 | - | 15p. green | 35 | 25 |
| O201 | - | 20p. brown and red | 70 | 60 |
| O202 | - | 25p. brown and yellow | 80 | 70 |
| O203 | - | 50p. blue and red | 1·40 | 85 |
| O204 | - | 1k. blue, yellow & grey | 4·00 | 1·10 |
| O205 | - | 2k. blue, green & red | 5·25 | 1·90 |
| O206 | - | 5k. multicoloured | 15·00 | 13·00 |

**1968.** Nos. 195/8 and 200/6 optd as Type O 29.

| | | | |
|---|---|---|---|
| O207 | 1p. black | 15 | 15 |
| O208 | 2p. red | 15 | 15 |
| O209 | 3p. green | 15 | 15 |
| O210 | 5p. blue | 25 | 15 |
| O211 | 15p. green | 25 | 15 |
| O212 | 20p. brown and red | 25 | 15 |
| O213 | 25p. brown and yellow | 45 | 15 |
| O214 | 50p. blue and red | 85 | 45 |
| O215 | 1k. blue, yellow and grey | 1·30 | 1·10 |
| O216 | 2k. blue, green and red | 2·75 | 2·30 |
| O217 | 5k. multicoloured | 6·50 | 5·75 |

For later issues see **MYANMAR**.

### JAPANESE OCCUPATION OF BURMA

Note.—There are various types of the Peacock overprint. Our prices, as usual in this Catalogue, are for the cheapest type.

**(1)**

**(3)**

**1942.** Postage stamps of Burma of 1937 (India types) optd as T 1.

| | | | | |
|---|---|---|---|---|
| J22 | **55** | 3p. grey | 4·00 | 23·00 |
| J23 | **80** | 9p. green | 27·00 | 70·00 |
| J24 | **59** | 2a. red | £120 | £200 |
| J2 | **83** | 3½a. blue | 80·00 | |

**1942.** Official stamp of Burma of 1937 (India type) optd as T 1.

| | | | | |
|---|---|---|---|---|
| J3 | **64** | 6a. bistre | 80·00 | |

**1942.** Postage stamps of Burma, 1938, optd as T 1 or with T 3 (rupee values).

| | | | | |
|---|---|---|---|---|
| J25 | **1** | 1p. orange | £225 | £350 |
| J12 | **1** | 3p. violet | 19·00 | 75·00 |
| J27 | **1** | 6p. blue | 25·00 | 55·00 |
| J14 | **1** | 9p. green | 24·00 | 70·00 |
| J29 | **3** | 1a. brown | 9·00 | 42·00 |
| J30 | **3** | 1½a. green | 23·00 | 70·00 |
| J16 | **3** | 2a. red | 26·00 | 85·00 |
| J17 | **3** | 4a. blue | 50·00 | £110 |
| J18 | **8** | 1r. purple and blue | £400 | £650 |
| J19 | **8** | 2r. brown and purple | £225 | £450 |

**1942.** Official stamps of Burma of 1939 optd with T 1.

| | | | | |
|---|---|---|---|---|
| J7 | **1** | 3p. violet | 35·00 | 90·00 |
| J8 | **1** | 6p. blue | 24·00 | 65·00 |
| J9 | **3** | 1a. brown | 25·00 | 55·00 |
| J35 | **3** | 1½a. green | £180 | £325 |
| J10 | **3** | 2a. red | 32·00 | £100 |
| J11 | **3** | 4a. blue | 32·00 | 80·00 |

**(6a)** ("Yon Thon" = "Office Use")

**1942.** Official stamp of Burma of 1939 optd with T 6a.

| | | | |
|---|---|---|---|
| J44 | 8a. green (No. O23) | £100 | £225 |

**7**

**1942.** Yano Seal.

| | | | | |
|---|---|---|---|---|
| J45 | **7** | (1a.) red | 48·00 | 70·00 |

**8** Farmer

**1942**

| | | | | |
|---|---|---|---|---|
| J46 | **8** | 1a. red | 21·00 | 23·00 |

**1942.** Stamps of Japan surch in annas or rupees.

| | | | | |
|---|---|---|---|---|
| J47 | - | ¼a. on 1s. brown (No. 314) | 45·00 | 50·00 |
| J48 | **83** | ½a. on 2s. red | 55·00 | 50·00 |
| J49 | - | ¾a. on 3s. green (No. 316) | 80·00 | 80·00 |
| J50 | - | 1a. on 5s. purple (No. 396) | 80·00 | 70·00 |
| J51 | - | 3a. on 7s. green (No. 320) | £130 | £150 |
| J52 | - | 4a. on 4s. green (No. 317) | 60·00 | 65·00 |
| J53 | - | 8a. on 8s. violet (No. 321) | £150 | £150 |
| J54 | - | 1r. on 10s. red (No. 322) | 26·00 | 30·00 |
| J55 | - | 2r. on 20s. blue (No. 325) | 55·00 | 55·00 |
| J56 | - | 5r. on 30s. blue (No. 327) | 16·00 | 27·00 |

**1942.** No. 386 of Japan commemorating the fall of Singapore, surch in figures.

| | | | |
|---|---|---|---|
| J56g | 4a. on 4s.+2s. green and red | £180 | £190 |

**1942.** Handstamped 5 C.

| | | | | |
|---|---|---|---|---|
| J57 | **5** | 5c. on 1a. red (No. J46) | 22·00 | 26·00 |

**1942.** Nos. J47/53 with anna surcharges obliterated, and handstamped with new values in figures.

| | | | | |
|---|---|---|---|---|
| J58 | - | 1c. on ¼a. on 1s. brown | 55·00 | 55·00 |
| J59 | **84** | 2c. on ½a. on 2s. red | 55·00 | 55·00 |
| J60 | - | 3c. on ¾a. on 3s. green | 60·00 | 60·00 |
| J61 | - | 5c. on 1a. on 5s. red | 80·00 | 65·00 |
| J62 | - | 10c. on 3a. on 7s. green | £150 | £140 |
| J63 | - | 15c. on 4a. on 4s. green | 50·00 | 55·00 |
| J64 | - | 20c. on 8a. on 8s. violet | £800 | £650 |

**1942.** Stamps of Japan surch in cents.

| | | | | |
|---|---|---|---|---|
| J65 | - | 1c. on 1s. brown (No. 314) | 32·00 | 20·00 |
| J66 | **83** | 2c. on 2s. red | 60·00 | 40·00 |
| J67 | - | 3c. on 3s. green (No. 316) | 90·00 | 65·00 |
| J68 | - | 5c. on 5s. purple (No. 396) | 90·00 | 55·00 |
| J69 | - | 10c. on 7s. green (No. 320) | £120 | 80·00 |
| J70 | - | 15c. on 4s. green (No. 317) | 26·00 | 26·00 |
| J71 | - | 20c. on 8s. violet (No. 321) | £190 | 90·00 |

**14** Burma State Crest

**1943.** Perf or imperf.

| | | | | |
|---|---|---|---|---|
| J72 | **14** | 5c. red | 25·00 | 30·00 |

**15** Farmer

**1943**

| | | | | |
|---|---|---|---|---|
| J73a | **15** | 1c. orange | 4·00 | 8·00 |
| J74 | **15** | 2c. green | 60 | 1·00 |
| J75 | **15** | 3c. blue | 4·00 | 1·00 |
| J77 | **15** | 5c. red | 3·50 | 6·50 |
| J78 | **15** | 10c. brown | 8·00 | 8·00 |
| J79 | **15** | 15c. mauve | 30 | 3·75 |
| J80 | **15** | 20c. lilac | 30 | 1·00 |
| J81 | **15** | 30c. green | 30 | 2·25 |

**16** Soldier carving word "Independence"

**17** Rejoicing Peasant

**(18)** Boy with National Flag

**1943.** Independence Day. Perf or roul.

| | | | | |
|---|---|---|---|---|
| J85 | **16** | 1c. orange | 1·25 | 1·75 |
| J86 | **17** | 3c. blue | 2·50 | 3·25 |
| J87 | **18** | 5c. red | 3·00 | 3·50 |

**19** Burmese Woman

**20** Elephant carrying Log

**21** Watch Tower Mandalay

**1943**

| | | | | |
|---|---|---|---|---|
| J88 | **19** | 1c. orange | 20·00 | 15·00 |
| J89 | **19** | 2c. green | 50 | 2·00 |
| J90 | **19** | 3c. violet | 50 | 2·25 |
| J91 | **20** | 5c. red | 65 | 60 |
| J92 | **20** | 10c. blue | 1·75 | 1·10 |
| J93 | **20** | 15c. orange | 1·00 | 3·00 |
| J94 | **20** | 20c. green | 1·00 | 1·75 |
| J95 | **20** | 30c. brown | 1·00 | 2·00 |
| J96 | **21** | 1r. orange | 30 | 2·00 |
| J97 | **21** | 2r. violet | 30 | 2·25 |

**22** Playing Cane-ball

**23** Shan Woman

**1943.** Shan States issue.

| | | | | |
|---|---|---|---|---|
| J98 | **22** | 1c. brown | 38·00 | 45·00 |
| J99 | **22** | 2c. green | 42·00 | 45·00 |
| J100 | **22** | 3c. violet | 6·00 | 13·00 |
| J101 | **22** | 5c. blue | 2·50 | 8·00 |
| J102 | **23** | 10c. blue | 15·00 | 18·00 |
| J103 | **23** | 20c. red | 40·00 | 21·00 |
| J104 | **23** | 30c. brown | 24·00 | 60·00 |

ဗမာနိုင်ငံတော်

၂၀ ဆင့်။

**(24)** "Burma State" and value

**1944.** Optd with T 24.

| | | | | |
|---|---|---|---|---|
| J105 | **22** | 1c. brown | 4·00 | 8·00 |
| J106 | **22** | 2c. green | 50 | 4·75 |
| J107 | **22** | 3c. violet | 2·25 | 7·00 |
| J108 | **22** | 5c. blue | 2·25 | 3·00 |
| J109 | **23** | 10c. blue | 3·25 | 2·00 |
| J110 | **23** | 20c. red | 50 | 1·50 |
| J111 | **23** | 30c. brown | 50 | 1·75 |

Pt. 12

# BURUNDI

Once part of the Belgian territory, Ruanda-Urundi. Independent on 1 July 1962, when a monarchy was established. After a revolution in 1967 Burundi became a republic.

100 centimes = 1 franc.

**1962.** Stamps of Ruanda-Urundi optd Royaume du Burundi and bar or surch also. (a) Flowers. (Nos. 178 etc.).

| | | | | |
|---|---|---|---|---|
| 1 | | 25c. multicoloured | 25 | 20 |
| 2 | | 40c. multicoloured | 25 | 20 |
| 3 | | 60c. multicoloured | 35 | 35 |
| 4 | | 1f.25 multicoloured | 16·00 | 16·00 |
| 5 | | 1f.50 multicoloured | 60 | 60 |
| 6 | | 5f. multicoloured | 1·10 | 90 |
| 7 | | 7f. multicoloured | 1·75 | 1·40 |
| 8 | | 10f. multicoloured | 2·50 | 2·25 |

(b) Animals (Nos. 203/14).

| | | | | |
|---|---|---|---|---|
| 9 | | 10c. black, red and brown | 10 | 10 |
| 10 | | 20c. black and green | 10 | 10 |
| 11 | | 40c. black, olive and mauve | 10 | 10 |
| 12 | | 50c. brown, yellow & green | 10 | 10 |
| 13 | | 1f. black, blue and brown | 10 | 10 |
| 14 | | 1f.50 black and orange | 10 | 10 |
| 15 | | 2f. black, brown and turq | 10 | 10 |
| 16 | | 3f. black, red and brown | 10 | 10 |
| 17 | | 3f.50 on 3f. black, red & brn | 10 | 10 |
| 18a | | 4f. on 10f. multicoloured | 20 | 20 |
| 19 | | 5f. multicoloured | 20 | 20 |
| 20 | | 6f.50 brown, yellow and red | 20 | 20 |
| 21 | | 8f. black, mauve and blue | 35 | 25 |
| 23 | | 10f. multicoloured | 50 | 30 |

(c) Animals (Nos. 229/30).

| | | | | |
|---|---|---|---|---|
| 24 | **25** | 20f. multicoloured | 1·60 | 60 |
| 25 | - | 50f. multicoloured | 1·90 | 1·10 |

**10** King Mwambutsa IV and Royal Drummers

**1962.** Independence. Inscr "1.7.1962".

| | | | | |
|---|---|---|---|---|
| 26 | **10** | 50c. sepia and lake | 10 | 10 |
| 27 | **A** | 1f. green, red & deep green | 10 | 10 |
| 28 | **B** | 2f. sepia and olive | 10 | 10 |
| 29 | **10** | 3f. sepia and red | 10 | 10 |
| 30 | **A** | 4f. green, red and blue | 15 | 10 |
| 31 | **B** | 8f. sepia and violet | 30 | 15 |
| 32 | **10** | 10f. sepia and green | 40 | 15 |
| 33 | **A** | 20f. green, red and sepia | 45 | 20 |
| 34 | **B** | 50f. sepia and mauve | 1·25 | 45 |

DESIGNS—VERT: A, Burundi flag and arms. HORIZ: B, King and outline map of Burundi.

**1962.** Dag Hammarskjold Commem. No. 222 of Ruanda-Urundi surch HOMMAGE A DAG HAMMARSKJOLD ROYAUME DU BURUNDI and new value. U.N. emblem and wavy pattern at foot. Inscr in French or Flemish.

| | | | | |
|---|---|---|---|---|
| 35 | | 3f.50 on 3f. salmon and blue | 35 | 35 |
| 36 | | 6f.50 on 3f. salmon and blue | 65 | 45 |
| 37 | | 10f. on 3f. salmon and blue | 1·25 | 1·10 |

**1962.** Malaria Eradication. As Nos. 31 and 34 but colours changed and with campaign emblem superimposed on map.

| | | | | |
|---|---|---|---|---|
| 38 | | 8f. sepia, turquoise & bistre | 55 | 35 |
| 39 | | 50f. sepia, turquoise & olive | 1·40 | 35 |

**12** Prince Louis Rwagasore

**1963.** Prince Rwagasore Memorial and Stadium Fund.

| | | | | |
|---|---|---|---|---|
| 40 | **12** | 50c.+25c. violet | 10 | 10 |
| 41 | - | 1f.+50c. blue and orange | 10 | 10 |
| 42 | - | 1f.50+75c. vio & bistre | 10 | 10 |
| 43 | **12** | 3f.50+1f.50 mauve | 20 | 10 |
| 44 | - | 5f.+2f. blue and pink | 20 | 10 |
| 45 | - | 6f.50+3f. violet & olive | 25 | 10 |

DESIGNS—HORIZ: 1f., 5f. Prince and stadium; 1f.50, 6f.50 Prince and memorial.

**13** "Sowing"

**1963.** Freedom from Hunger.

| | | | | |
|---|---|---|---|---|
| 46 | **13** | 4f. purple and olive | 15 | 15 |
| 47 | **13** | 8f. purple and olive | 20 | 15 |
| 48 | **13** | 15f. purple and green | 35 | 15 |

**1963.** "Peaceful Uses of Outer Space" Nos. 28 and 34 optd UTILISATIONS PACIFIQUES DE L'ESPACE around globe encircled by rocket.

| | | | | |
|---|---|---|---|---|
| 49 | **B** | 2f. sepia and olive | 2·25 | 2·25 |
| 50 | **B** | 50f. sepia and mauve | 3·50 | 3·50 |

**1963.** 1st Anniv of Independence. Nos. 30/3 but with colours changed and optd Premier Anniversaire.

| | | | | |
|---|---|---|---|---|
| 51 | **A** | 4f. green, red and olive | 20 | 10 |
| 52 | **B** | 8f. sepia and orange | 30 | 10 |
| 53 | **10** | 10f. sepia and mauve | 40 | 20 |
| 54 | **A** | 20f. green, red and grey | 90 | 30 |

**1963.** Nos. 27 and 33 surch.

| | | | | |
|---|---|---|---|---|
| 55 | | 6f.50 on 1f. green, red and deep green | 55 | 10 |
| 56 | | 15f. on 20f. grn, red & sepia | 85 | 35 |

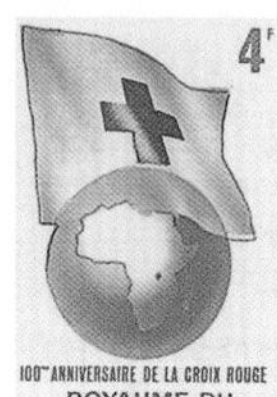


**17** Globe and Red Cross Flag

**1963.** Centenary of Red Cross.

| | | | | |
|---|---|---|---|---|
| 57 | **17** | 4f. green, red and grey | 20 | 10 |
| 58 | **17** | 8f. brown, red and grey | 40 | 20 |
| 59 | **17** | 10f. blue, red and grey | 50 | 20 |
| 60 | **17** | 20f. violet, red and grey | 1·10 | 40 |
| **MS**60a | | 90×140 mm. Nos. 57/60 in new colours, each with +2f. surcharge in black. Imperf | 3·50 | 3·50 |

**IMPERF STAMPS.** Many Burundi stamps from No. 61 onwards exist imperf from limited printings and/or miniature sheets.

**18** "1962" and UNESCO Emblem

**1963.** 1st Anniv of Admission to UNO. Emblems and values in black.

| | | | | |
|---|---|---|---|---|
| 61 | **18** | 4f. olive and yellow | 15 | 10 |
| 62 | - | 8f. blue and lilac | 25 | 10 |
| 63 | - | 10f. violet and blue | 40 | 10 |
| 64 | - | 20f. green and yellow | 65 | 20 |
| 65 | - | 50f. brown and ochre | 1·75 | 35 |
| **MS**65a | | 111×74 mm. Nos. 64/5 but with emblems changed. Imperf | 4·25 | 4·25 |

EMBLEMS: 8f. ITU; 10f. WMO; 20f. UPU, 50f. FAO; **MS**65a 20f. FAO; 50f. WMO.

**19** UNESCO Emblem and Scales of Justice

**1963.** 15th Anniv of Declaration of Human Rights.

| | | | | |
|---|---|---|---|---|
| 66 | **19** | 50c. blk, blue and pink | 10 | 10 |
| 67 | - | 1f.50 black, blue & orange | 10 | 10 |
| 68 | - | 3f.50 black, green & brown | 15 | 10 |
| 69 | - | 6f.50 black, green and lilac | 25 | 10 |
| 70 | - | 10f. black, bistre and blue | 40 | 15 |
| 71 | - | 20f. multicoloured | 70 | 25 |

DESIGNS: 3f.50, 6f.50, Scroll; 10f., 20f. Lincoln.

**20** Ice-hockey

**1964.** Winter Olympic Games, Innsbruck.

| | | | | |
|---|---|---|---|---|
| 72 | **20** | 50c. black, gold and olive | 15 | 10 |
| 73 | - | 3f.50 black, gold & brown | 20 | 10 |
| 74 | - | 6f.50 black, gold and grey | 45 | 20 |
| 75 | - | 10f. black, gold and grey | 90 | 35 |
| 76 | - | 20f. black, gold and bistre | 2·10 | 65 |
| **MS**76a | | 122×85 mm. 10f.+5f. and 20f.+5f. (as Nos. 75/6 but in new colours). Perf or imperf | 4·25 | 1·30 |

DESIGNS: 3f.50, Figure-skating; 6f.50, Olympic flame; 10f. Speed-skating; 20f. Skiing (slalom).

**21** Hippopotamus

**1964.** Burundi Animals. Multicoloured. (i) Postage. (a) Size as T 21.

| | | | | |
|---|---|---|---|---|
| 77 | | 50c. Impala | 10 | 10 |
| 78 | | 1f. Type **21** | 10 | 10 |
| 79 | | 1f.50 Giraffe | 10 | 10 |
| 80 | | 2f. African buffalo | 20 | 10 |
| 81 | | 3f. Common zebra | 20 | 10 |
| 82 | | 3f.50 Waterbuck | 20 | 10 |

(b) Size 16×42½ mm or 42½×26 mm.

| | | | | |
|---|---|---|---|---|
| 83 | | 4f. Impala | 25 | 10 |
| 84 | | 5f. Hippopotamus | 30 | 10 |
| 85 | | 6f.50 Common zebra | 30 | 10 |
| 86 | | 8f. African buffalo | 55 | 20 |
| 87 | | 10f. Giraffe | 60 | 20 |
| 88 | | 15f. Waterbuck | 85 | 30 |

(c) Size 53½×33½ mm.

| | | | | |
|---|---|---|---|---|
| 89 | | 20f. Cheetah | 1·50 | 40 |
| 90 | | 50f. African elephant | 4·00 | 65 |
| 91 | | 100f. Lion | 6·50 | 1·10 |

(ii) Air. Inscr "POSTE AERIENNE" and optd with gold border. (a) Size 26×42½ mm or 42½×26 mm.

| | | | | |
|---|---|---|---|---|
| 92 | | 6f. Common zebra | 35 | 10 |
| 93 | | 8f. African buffalo | 60 | 10 |
| 94 | | 10f. Impala | 70 | 10 |
| 95 | | 14f. Hippopotamus | 85 | 15 |
| 96 | | 15f. Waterbuck | 1·40 | 35 |

(b) Size 53½×33½ mm.

| | | | | |
|---|---|---|---|---|
| 97 | | 20f. Cheetah | 1·75 | 40 |
| 98 | | 50f. African elephant | 4·00 | 90 |

The impala, giraffe and waterbuck stamps are all vert. designs, and the remainder are horiz.

**22** Burundi Dancer

**1964.** World's Fair, New York (1st series). Gold backgrounds.

| | | | | |
|---|---|---|---|---|
| 99 | **22** | 50c. multicoloured | 10 | 10 |
| 100 | - | 1f. multicoloured | 10 | 10 |
| 101 | - | 4f. multicoloured | 15 | 10 |
| 102 | - | 6f.50 multicoloured | 20 | 10 |
| 103 | - | 10f. multicoloured | 40 | 15 |
| 104 | - | 15f. multicoloured | 70 | 20 |
| 105 | - | 20f. multicoloured | 90 | 30 |
| **MS**105a | | 120×100 mm. Nos. 103/5. Perf or imperf | 3·50 | 3·50 |

DESIGNS: 1f. to 20f. Various dancers and drummers as Type **22**.

See also Nos. 175/**MS**81a.

**23** Pope Paul and King Mwambutsa IV

**1964.** Canonization of 22 African Martyrs. Inscriptions in gold.

| | | | | |
|---|---|---|---|---|
| 106 | **23** | 50c. lake and blue | 15 | 10 |
| 107 | - | 1f. blue and purple | 15 | 10 |
| 108 | - | 4f. sepia and mauve | 25 | 10 |
| 109 | - | 8f. brown and red | 40 | 15 |
| 110 | - | 14f. brown and turquoise | 40 | 20 |
| 111 | **23** | 20f. green and red | 65 | 40 |

DESIGNS—VERT: 1f., 8f. Group of martyrs. HORIZ: 4f., 14f., Pope John XXIII and King Mwambutsa IV.

**24** Putting the Shot

**1964.** Olympic Games, Tokyo. Inscr "TOKYO 1964". Multicoloured.

| | | | | |
|---|---|---|---|---|
| 112 | | 50c. Type **24** | 10 | 10 |
| 113 | | 1f. Throwing the discus | 10 | 10 |
| 114 | | 3f. Swimming (horiz) | 10 | 10 |
| 115 | | 4f. Relay-racing | 10 | 10 |
| 116 | | 6f.50 Throwing the javelin | 30 | 20 |
| 117 | | 8f. Hurdling (horiz) | 35 | 20 |
| 118 | | 10f. Long-jumping (horiz) | 40 | 20 |
| 119 | | 14f. High-diving | 55 | 20 |
| 120 | | 18f. High-jumping (horiz) | 65 | 35 |
| 121 | | 20f. Gymnastics (horiz) | 85 | 35 |
| **MS**121a | | 115×71 mm. 18f.+2f. and 20f.+5f. (as Nos. 120/1). Perf or imperf | 3·25 | 3·25 |

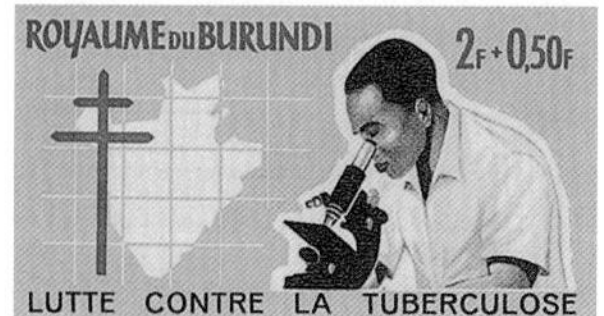


**25** Scientist, Map and Emblem

**1965.** Anti-T.B. Campaign. Country name, values and Lorraine Cross in red.

| | | | | |
|---|---|---|---|---|
| 122 | **25** | 2f.+50c. sepia and drab | 10 | 10 |
| 123 | **25** | 4f.+1f.50 green & pink | 25 | 10 |
| 124 | **25** | 5f.+2f.50 violet & buff | 30 | 15 |
| 125 | **25** | 8f.+3f. blue and grey | 40 | 20 |
| 126 | **25** | 10f.+5f. red and green | 55 | 30 |
| **MS**126a | | 100×71 mm. 10f.+10f. sepia and olive. Perf or imperf | 1·10 | 1·10 |

**26** Purple Swamphen

**1965.** Birds. Multicoloured. (i) Postage. (a) Size as T 26.

| | | | |
|---|---|---|---|
| 127 | 50c. Type **26** | 10 | 10 |
| 128 | 1f. Little bee eater | 10 | 10 |
| 129 | 1f.50 Secretary bird | 10 | 10 |
| 130 | 2f. Painted stork | 20 | 10 |
| 131 | 3f. Congo peafowl | 25 | 10 |
| 132 | 3f.50 African darter | 30 | 10 |

(b) Size 26×42½ mm.

| | | | |
|---|---|---|---|
| 133 | 4f. Type **26** | 40 | 10 |
| 134 | 5f. Little bee eater | 50 | 15 |
| 135 | 6f.50 Secretary bird | 60 | 15 |
| 136 | 8f. Painted stork | 60 | 15 |
| 137 | 10f. Congo peafowl | 70 | 15 |
| 138 | 15f. African darter | 85 | 25 |

(c) Size 33½×53 mm.

| | | | |
|---|---|---|---|
| 139 | 20f. Saddle-bill stork | 1·25 | 25 |
| 140 | 50f. Abyssinian ground hornbill | 2·40 | 50 |
| 141 | 100f. South African crowned crane | 4·00 | 90 |

(ii) Air. Inscr "POSTE AERIENNE". Optd with gold border. (a) Size 26×42½ mm.

| | | | |
|---|---|---|---|
| 142 | 6f. Secretary bird | 50 | 10 |
| 143 | 8f. African darter | 60 | 15 |
| 144 | 10f. Congo peafowl | 70 | 15 |
| 145 | 14f. Little bee eater | 75 | 20 |
| 146 | 15f. Painted stork | 85 | 20 |

(b) Size 33½×53 mm.

| | | | |
|---|---|---|---|
| 147 | 20f. Saddle-bill stork | 1·25 | 30 |
| 148 | 50f. Abyssinian ground hornbill | 2·25 | 80 |
| 149 | 75f. Martial eagle | 2·50 | 1·00 |
| 150 | 130f. Lesser flamingo | 4·75 | 1·60 |

**27** "Relay" Satellite and Telegraph Key

**1965.** Centenary of ITU. Multicoloured.

| | | | |
|---|---|---|---|
| 151 | 1f. Type **27** | 10 | 10 |
| 152 | 3f. "Telstar 1" and hand telephone | 10 | 10 |
| 153 | 4f. "Lunik 3" and wall telephone | 10 | 10 |
| 154 | 6f.50 Weather satellite and tracking station | 15 | 10 |
| 155 | 8f. "Telstar 2" and headphones | 15 | 15 |
| 156 | 10f. "Sputnik" and radar scanner | 20 | 15 |
| 157 | 14f. "Syncom" and aerial | 30 | 20 |
| 158 | 20f. "Pioneer 5" space probe and radio aerial | 35 | 30 |
| **MS**158a | 121×85 mm. Nos. 156 and 158. Perf or imperf | 2·50 | 2·50 |

**28** Arms (reverse of 10f. coin)

**1965.** 1st Independence Anniv Gold Coinage Commem. Circular designs on gold foil, backed with multicoloured patterned paper. Imperf. (i) Postage. (a) 10f. coin. Diameter 1½ in.

| | | | | |
|---|---|---|---|---|
| 159 | 28 | 2f.+50c. red & yellow | 15 | 15 |
| 160 | - | 4f.+50c. blue & red | 20 | 20 |

(b) 25f. coin. Diameter 1¾ in.

| | | | | |
|---|---|---|---|---|
| 161 | 28 | 6f.+50c. orange & grey | 50 | 30 |
| 162 | - | 8f.+50c. blue & purple | 60 | 60 |

(c) 50f. coin. Diameter 2½ in.

| | | | | |
|---|---|---|---|---|
| 163 | 28 | 12f.+50c. green & purple | 60 | 60 |
| 164 | - | 15f.+50c. green & lilac | 65 | 65 |

(d) 100f. coin. Diameter 258in.

| | | | | |
|---|---|---|---|---|
| 165 | 28 | 25f.+50c. blue and flesh | 1·25 | 1·25 |
| 166 | - | 40f.+50c. mauve & brn | 1·75 | 1·75 |

(ii) Air. (a) 10f. coin. Diameter 1½ in.

| | | | | |
|---|---|---|---|---|
| 167 | 28 | 3f.+1f. violet & lavender | 30 | 30 |
| 168 | - | 5f.+1f. red & turquoise | 40 | 40 |

(b) 25f. coin. Diameter 1¾ in.

| | | | | |
|---|---|---|---|---|
| 169 | 28 | 11f.+1f. purple & yellow | 60 | 60 |
| 170 | - | 14f.+1f. green and red | 60 | 60 |

(c) 50f. coin. Diameter 2½ in.

| | | | | |
|---|---|---|---|---|
| 171 | 28 | 20f.+1f. black and blue | 85 | 85 |
| 172 | - | 30f.+1f. red and orange | 1·10 | 1·10 |

(d) 100f. coin. Diameter 2¾ in.

| | | | | |
|---|---|---|---|---|
| 173 | 28 | 50f.+1f. violet and blue | 1·25 | 1·25 |
| 174 | - | 100f.+1f. purple & mve | 3·00 | 3·00 |

DESIGNS: The 4, 5, 8, 14, 15, 30, 40 and 100f. each show the obverse side of the coin (King Mwambutsa IV).

**1965.** Worlds Fair, New York (2nd series). As Nos. 99/105, but with silver backgrounds.

| | | | | |
|---|---|---|---|---|
| 175 | 22 | 50c. multicoloured | 10 | 10 |
| 176 | - | 1f. multicoloured | 10 | 10 |
| 177 | - | 4f. multicoloured | 15 | 10 |
| 178 | - | 6f.50 multicoloured | 25 | 10 |
| 179 | - | 10f. multicoloured | 45 | 20 |
| 180 | - | 15f. multicoloured | 55 | 30 |
| 181 | - | 20f. multicoloured | 70 | 35 |
| **MS**181a | | 120×100 mm. Nos. 179/81. perf or imperf | 2·50 | 2·50 |

**29** Globe and ICY Emblem

**1965.** International Co-operation Year. Mult.

| | | | |
|---|---|---|---|
| 182 | 1f. Type **29** | 10 | 10 |
| 183 | 4f. Map of Africa and cogwheel emblem of UN Science and Technology Conference | 15 | 10 |
| 184 | 8f. Map of South-East Asia and Colombo Plan emblem | 20 | 10 |
| 185 | 10f. Globe and UN emblem | 25 | 10 |
| 186 | 18f. Map of Americas and "Alliance for Progress" emblem | 40 | 10 |
| 187 | 25f. Map of Europe and CEPT emblems | 60 | 30 |
| 188 | 40f. Space map and satellite (UN—"Peaceful Uses of Outer Space") | 1·00 | 50 |
| **MS**188a | 100×100 mm. 18f. (Map of Africa and UN emblem); 25f. and 40f. (similar to Nos. 187/8). Perf or imperf | 2·60 | 2·60 |

**30** Prince Rwagasore and Memorial

**1966.** Prince Rwagasore and Pres. Kennedy Commemoration.

| | | | | |
|---|---|---|---|---|
| 189 | 30 | 4f.+1f. brown and blue | 20 | 10 |
| 190 | - | 10f.+1f. blue, brn & grn | 30 | 10 |
| 191 | - | 20f.+2f. green and lilac | 65 | 15 |
| 192 | - | 40f.+2f. brown & green | 75 | 30 |
| **MS**193 | | 75×90 mm. 20f.+5f. and 40f.+5f. (as Nos. 189 and 191). Perf or imperf | 2·25 | 2·50 |

DESIGNS—HORIZ: 10f. Prince Rwagasore and Pres. Kennedy; 20f. Pres. Kennedy and memorial library. VERT: 40f. King Mwambutsa at Pres. Kennedy's grave.

**31** Protea

**1966.** Flowers. Multicoloured. (i) Postage. (a) Size as T 31.

| | | | |
|---|---|---|---|
| 194 | 50c. Type **31** | 15 | 10 |
| 195 | 1f. Crossandra | 15 | 10 |
| 196 | 1f.50 Ansellia | 15 | 10 |
| 197 | 2f. Thunbergia | 15 | 10 |
| 198 | 3f. Schizoglossum | 25 | 10 |
| 199 | 3f.50 Dissotis | 25 | 10 |

(b) Size 41×41 mm.

| | | | |
|---|---|---|---|
| 200 | 4f. Type **31** | 25 | 10 |
| 201 | 5f. Crossandra | 35 | 10 |
| 202 | 6f.50 Ansellia | 45 | 10 |
| 203 | 8f. Thunbergia | 65 | 10 |
| 204 | 10f. Schizoglossum | 70 | 10 |
| 205 | 15f. Dissotis | 85 | 10 |

(c) Size 50×50 mm.

| | | | |
|---|---|---|---|
| 206 | 20f. Type **31** | 1·10 | 15 |
| 207 | 50f. Gazania | 2·50 | 35 |
| 208 | 100f. Hibiscus | 4·00 | 55 |
| 209 | 150f. Markhamia | 6·25 | 75 |

(ii) Air. (a) Size 41×41 mm.

| | | | |
|---|---|---|---|
| 210 | 6f. Dissotis | 25 | 15 |
| 211 | 8f. Crossandra | 35 | 15 |
| 212 | 10f. Ansellia | 35 | 15 |
| 213 | 14f. Thunbergia | 40 | 15 |
| 214 | 15f. Schizoglossum | 40 | 15 |

(b) Size 50×50 mm.

| | | | |
|---|---|---|---|
| 215 | 20f. Gazania | 65 | 20 |
| 216 | 50f. Type **31** | 1·75 | 40 |
| 217 | 75f. Hibiscus | 2·50 | 1·00 |
| 218 | 130f. Markhamia | 3·75 | 1·40 |

**32** UNESCO

**33**

**1966.** 20th Anniv of UNESCO.

**MS**219 Three sheets, each 201×127 mm, each containing single stamps (Type **32**) with se-tenant label inscribed in English or French and an adjoining block of six stamps (3×2) as Type **33**, forming a composite design of the mural tapestry hanging in the U.N. General Assembly building, New York. (a) Postage: Two sheets 1f.50×7 and 4f.×7. (b) Air. One sheet 14f.×7 multicoloured Set of 3 sheets 6·00

**1967.** 4th Anniv of Independence (1966).

**MS**220 Four unissued sheets, diamond-shaped, 200×200 mm, each containing eight "Flower" stamps as Type **31** but with values and corresponding designs changed, and centre se-tenant label showing "Flag", "Map", "Arms" or "Flower" emblem. Values: 6, 7, 8, 10, 14, 15, 20 and 50f. Multicoloured. Stamps and sheet margins have the original inscriptions obliterated by the overprint **REPUBLIQUE DU BURUNDI** in black on gold panels Set of 4 sheets 11·00

**1967.** Various stamps optd. (i) Nos. 127, etc. (Birds) optd REPUBLIQUE DU BURUNDI and bar. (a) Postage.

| | | | |
|---|---|---|---|
| 221 | 50c. multicoloured | 1·60 | 25 |
| 222 | 1f.50 multicoloured | 35 | 25 |
| 223 | 3f.50 multicoloured | 45 | 35 |
| 224 | 5f. multicoloured | 60 | 45 |
| 225 | 6f.50 multicoloured | 60 | 65 |
| 226 | 8f. multicoloured | 70 | 80 |
| 227 | 10f. multicoloured | 80 | 80 |
| 228 | 15f. multicoloured | 1·10 | 1·25 |
| 229 | 20f. multicoloured | 2·75 | 1·75 |
| 230 | 50f. multicoloured | 5·25 | 3·75 |
| 231 | 100f. multicoloured | 8·50 | 7·00 |

(b) Air.

| | | | |
|---|---|---|---|
| 232 | 6f. multicoloured | 55 | 25 |
| 233 | 8f. multicoloured | 70 | 40 |
| 234 | 10f. multicoloured | 85 | 65 |
| 235 | 14f. multicoloured | 1·10 | 65 |
| 236 | 15f. multicoloured | 1·25 | 80 |
| 237 | 20f. multicoloured | 1·75 | 95 |
| 238 | 50f. multicoloured | 6·25 | 2·75 |
| 239 | 75f. multicoloured | 8·50 | 3·50 |
| 240 | 130f. multicoloured | 12·00 | 5·75 |

(ii) Nos. 194, etc. (Flowers) optd as Nos. 221, etc., but with two bars. (a) Postage.

| | | | |
|---|---|---|---|
| 241 | 50c. multicoloured | 15 | 15 |
| 242 | 1f. multicoloured | 15 | 15 |
| 243 | 1f.50 multicoloured | 15 | 15 |
| 244 | 2f. multicoloured | 15 | 15 |
| 245 | 3f. multicoloured | 20 | 15 |
| 246 | 3f.50 multicoloured | 30 | 15 |
| 247 | 4f. multicoloured | 1·90 | 15 |
| 248 | 5f. multicoloured | 50 | 20 |
| 249 | 6f.50 multicoloured | 45 | 30 |
| 250 | 8f. multicoloured | 45 | 30 |
| 251 | 10f. multicoloured | 60 | 40 |
| 252 | 15f. multicoloured | 75 | 45 |
| 253 | 50f. multicoloured | 3·75 | 65 |
| 254 | 100f. multicoloured | 9·00 | 2·50 |
| 255 | 150f. multicoloured | 8·50 | 9·25 |

(b) Air.

| | | | |
|---|---|---|---|
| 256 | 6f. multicoloured | 20 | 15 |
| 257 | 8f. multicoloured | 30 | 15 |
| 258 | 10f. multicoloured | 35 | 15 |
| 259 | 14f. multicoloured | 45 | 30 |
| 260 | 15f. multicoloured | 55 | 30 |
| 261 | 20f. multicoloured | 1·75 | 40 |
| 262 | 50f. multicoloured | 3·75 | 65 |
| 263 | 75f. multicoloured | 5·75 | 90 |
| 264 | 130f. multicoloured | 5·75 | 1·50 |

**35** Sir Winston Churchill and St. Paul's Cathedral

**1967.** Churchill Commemoration. Multicoloured.

| | | | |
|---|---|---|---|
| 265 | 4f.+1f. Type **35** (postage) | 30 | 10 |
| 266 | 15f.+2f. Churchill and Tower of London | 50 | 25 |
| 267 | 20f.+3f. Big Ben and Boadicea Statue, Westminster | 60 | 35 |
| **MS**268 | 80×80 mm. 50f.+5f. Sir Winston Churchill (57×57 mm) (air). Perf or imperf | 3·00 | 3·00 |

**36** Egyptian Mouthbrooder

**1967.** Fish. Multicoloured. (a) Postage. (i) Size as T 36.

| | | | |
|---|---|---|---|
| 269 | 50c. Type **36** | 15 | 20 |
| 270 | 1f. Spotted climbing-perch | 15 | 20 |
| 271 | 1f.50 Six-banded lyretail | 15 | 20 |
| 272 | 2f. Congo tetra | 15 | 20 |
| 273 | 3f. Jewel cichlid | 15 | 20 |
| 274 | 3f.50 Spotted mouthbrooder | 15 | 20 |

(ii) Size 53½×27 mm.

| | | | |
|---|---|---|---|
| 275 | 4f. Type **36** | 50 | 20 |
| 276 | 5f. As 1f. | 50 | 20 |
| 277 | 6f.50. As 1f.50 | 65 | 20 |
| 278 | 8f. As 2f. | 65 | 20 |
| 279 | 10f. As 3f. | 1·00 | 20 |
| 280 | 15f. As 3f.50 | 1·10 | 20 |

(iii) Size 63½×31½ mm.

| | | | |
|---|---|---|---|
| 281 | 20f. Type **36** | 1·90 | 30 |
| 282 | 50f. Dusky snakehead | 3·50 | 50 |
| 283 | 100f. Red-tailed notho | 7·50 | 75 |
| 284 | 150f. African tetra | 7·50 | 1·10 |

(b) Air. (i) Size 50×23 mm.

| | | | |
|---|---|---|---|
| 285 | 6f. Type **36** | 30 | 20 |
| 286 | 8f. As 1f. | 45 | 20 |
| 287 | 10f. As 1f.50 | 55 | 20 |
| 288 | 14f. As 2f. | 65 | 20 |
| 289 | 15f. As 3f. | 80 | 20 |

(ii) Size 59×27 mm.

| | | | |
|---|---|---|---|
| 290 | 20f. As 3f.50 | 95 | 20 |
| 291 | 50f. As 50f. (No. 282) | 4·75 | 30 |
| 292 | 75f. As 100f. | 6·00 | 50 |
| 293 | 130f. As 150f. | 11·00 | 1·00 |

**37** Baule Ancestral Figures

**1967.** "African Art". Multicoloured.

| | | | |
|---|---|---|---|
| 294 | 50c. Type **37** (postage) | 10 | 10 |
| 295 | 1f. "Master of Buli's" carved seat | 10 | 10 |
| 296 | 1f.50 Karumba antelope's head | 10 | 10 |
| 297 | 2f. Bobo buffalo's head | 10 | 10 |
| 298 | 4f. Guma-Goffa funeral figures | 15 | 10 |
| 299 | 10f. Bakoutou "spirit" (carving) (air) | 30 | 20 |
| 300 | 14f. Bamum sultan's throne | 40 | 20 |
| 301 | 17f. Bebin bronze head | 45 | 20 |
| 302 | 24f. Statue of 109th Bakouba king | 55 | 30 |
| 303 | 26f. Burundi basketwork and lances | 60 | 35 |

**1967.** 50th Anniv of Lions International. Nos. 265/MS268 optd 1917 1967 and emblem.

| | | | |
|---|---|---|---|
| 304 | 4f.+1f. multicoloured | 50 | 20 |
| 305 | 15f.+2f. multicoloured | 80 | 35 |
| 306 | 20f.+3f. multicoloured | 95 | 35 |
| **MS**307 | 80×80 mm. 50f.+5f. multicoloured (air) Perf or imperf | 4·25 | 4·25 |

**39** Lord Baden-Powell (founder)

**1967.** 60th Anniv of Scout Movement and World Scout Jamboree, Idaho.

| | | | |
|---|---|---|---|
| 308 | 50c. Scouts climbing (postage) | 20 | 10 |
| 309 | 1f. Scouts preparing meal | 20 | 10 |
| 310 | 1f.50 Type **39** | 20 | 10 |
| 311 | 2f. Two scouts | 20 | 10 |
| 312 | 4f. Giving first aid | 30 | 10 |
| 313 | 10f. As 50c. (air) | 60 | 15 |
| 314 | 14f. As 1f. | 70 | 15 |
| 315 | 17f. Type **39** | 85 | 15 |
| 316 | 24f. As 2f. | 1·10 | 35 |
| 317 | 26f. As 4f. | 1·25 | 40 |

**40** "The Gleaners" (Millet)

**1967.** World Fair, Montreal. Multicoloured.

| | | | |
|---|---|---|---|
| 318 | 4f. Type **40** | 15 | 10 |
| 319 | 8f. "The Water-carrier of Seville" (Velasquez) | 15 | 10 |
| 320 | 14f. "The Triumph of Neptune and Amphitrite" (Poussin) | 35 | 15 |
| 321 | 18f. "Acrobat with a ball" (Picasso) | 35 | 15 |
| 322 | 25f. "Margaret van Eyck" (Van Eyck) | 95 | 25 |
| 323 | 40f. "St. Peter denying Christ" (Rembrandt) | 1·10 | 50 |
| **MS**324 | 105×105 mm. Nos. 322/3. Perf or imperf | 3·25 | 3·25 |

**41** Boeing 707

**1967.** Air. Opening of Bujumbura Airport. Aircraft and inscr in black and silver.

| | | | | |
|---|---|---|---|---|
| 325 | **41** | 10f. green | 40 | 10 |
| 326 | - | 14f. yellow | 65 | 20 |
| 327 | - | 17f. blue | 95 | 20 |
| 328 | - | 26f. purple | 1·60 | 30 |

AIRCRAFT: 14f. Boeing 727-100 over lakes. 17f. Vickers Super VC-10 over lake. 26f. Boeing 727 over Bujumbura Airport.

**42** Pres. Micombero and Flag

**1967.** 1st Anniv of Republic. Multicoloured.

| | | | |
|---|---|---|---|
| 329 | 5f. Type **42** | 25 | 10 |
| 330 | 14f. Memorial and Arms | 35 | 15 |
| 331 | 20f. View of Bujumbura and Arms | 50 | 20 |
| 332 | 30f. "Place de la Revolution" and President Micombero | 90 | 30 |

**43** "The Adoration of the Shepherds" (J. B. Mayno)

**1967.** Christmas. Religious Paintings. Mult.

| | | | |
|---|---|---|---|
| 333 | 1f. Type **43** | 10 | 10 |
| 334 | 4f. "The Holy Family" (A. van Dyck) | 15 | 10 |
| 335 | 14f. "The Nativity" (Maitre de Moulins) | 40 | 20 |
| 336 | 26f. "Madonna and Child" (C. Crivelli) | 75 | 30 |
| **MS**337 | 120×120 mm. Nos. 333/6 | 4·25 | 4·25 |

**44** Burundi Scouts

**1968.** Air. 20th Anniv of Burundi Scouts and 60th Anniv of Scout Movement. Diamond-shaped sheet containing T 44 and similar design. Multicoloured.

| | | | |
|---|---|---|---|
| **MS**338 | 142×142 mm. 24f. and 26f. with two se-tenant labels depicting Lord Baden-Powell and scouting activities | 2·25 | 2·25 |

DESIGN: 26f. Burundi scouts practising first-aid.

**45** Downhill Skiing

**1968.** Winter Olympic Games, Grenoble. Mult.

| | | | |
|---|---|---|---|
| 339 | 5f. Type **45** | 20 | 10 |
| 340 | 10f. Ice-hockey | 25 | 10 |
| 341 | 14f. Figure-skating | 40 | 10 |
| 342 | 17f. Bobsleighing | 50 | 10 |
| 343 | 26f. Ski-jumping | 65 | 10 |
| 344 | 40f. Speed-skating | 1·10 | 25 |
| 345 | 60f. Olympic torch | 1·75 | 30 |
| **MS**346 | 129×82 mm. Nos. 344/5. Perf or imperf | 2·75 | 2·75 |

**46** "Portrait of a Young Man" (Botticelli)

**1968.** Famous Paintings. Multicoloured.

| | | | |
|---|---|---|---|
| 347 | 1f.50 Type **46** (postage) | 10 | 10 |
| 348 | 2f. "La Maja Vestida" (Goya) (horiz) | 10 | 10 |
| 349 | 4f. "The Lacemaker" (Vermeer) | 15 | 10 |
| 350 | 17f. "Woman and Cat" (Renoir) (air) | 40 | 20 |
| 351 | 24f. "The Jewish Bride" (Rembrandt) (horiz) | 55 | 30 |
| 352 | 26f. "Pope Innocent X" (Velasquez) | 80 | 40 |

**47** Module landing on Moon

**1968.** Space Exploration. Multicoloured.

| | | | |
|---|---|---|---|
| 353 | 4f. Type **47** (postage) | 20 | 10 |
| 354 | 6f. Russian cosmonaut in Space | 30 | 10 |
| 355 | 8f. Weather satellite | 30 | 10 |
| 356 | 10f. American astronaut in Space | 45 | 15 |
| 357 | 14f. Type **47** (air) | 40 | 15 |
| 358 | 18f. As 6f. | 50 | 15 |
| 359 | 25f. As 8f. | 80 | 25 |
| 360 | 40f. As 10f. | 1·10 | 40 |
| **MS**361 | 109×82 mm. 25f. Type **47**; 40f. Weather satellite. Perf or imperf | 2·40 | 2·40 |

**48** "Salamis aethiops"

**1968.** Butterflies. Multicoloured. (a) Postage. (i) Size 30½×34 mm.

| | | | |
|---|---|---|---|
| 362 | 50c. Type **48** | 15 | 15 |
| 363 | 1f. "Graphium ridleyanus" | 20 | 15 |
| 364 | 1f.50 "Cymothoe" | 25 | 15 |
| 365 | 2f. "Charaxes eupale" | 35 | 15 |
| 366 | 3f. "Papilio bromius" | 40 | 15 |
| 367 | 3f.50 "Teracolus annae" | 50 | 15 |

(ii) Size 34×38 mm.

| | | | |
|---|---|---|---|
| 368 | 4f. Type **48** | 50 | 15 |
| 369 | 5f. As 1f. | 50 | 15 |
| 370 | 6f.50 As 1f.50 | 60 | 15 |
| 371 | 8f. As 2f. | 90 | 20 |
| 372 | 10f. As 3f. | 1·10 | 20 |
| 373 | 15f. As 3f.50 | 1·40 | 25 |

(iii) Size 41×46 mm.

| | | | |
|---|---|---|---|
| 374 | 20f. Type **48** | 2·50 | 30 |
| 375 | 50f. "Papilio zenobia" | 4·50 | 75 |
| 376 | 100f. "Danais chrysippus" | 8·25 | 1·25 |
| 377 | 150f. "Salamis temora" | 14·00 | 2·10 |

(b) Air. With gold frames. (i) Size 33×37 mm.

| | | | |
|---|---|---|---|
| 378 | 6f. As 3f.50 | 50 | 15 |
| 379 | 8f. As 1f. | 55 | 15 |
| 380 | 10f. As 1f.50 | 60 | 15 |
| 381 | 14f. As 2f. | 70 | 20 |
| 382 | 15f. As 3f. | 1·00 | 20 |

(ii) Size 39×44 mm.

| | | | |
|---|---|---|---|
| 383 | 20f. As 50f. (No. 375) | 2·40 | 25 |
| 384 | 50f. Type **48** | 5·50 | 50 |
| 385 | 75f. As 100f. | 6·75 | 90 |
| 386 | 130f. As 150f. | 12·50 | 1·10 |

**49** "Woman by the Manzanares" (Goya)

**1968.** International Letter-writing Week. Mult.

| | | | |
|---|---|---|---|
| 387 | 4f. Type **49** (postage) | 25 | 10 |
| 388 | 7f. "Reading a Letter" (De Hooch) | 35 | 10 |
| 389 | 11f. "Woman reading a Letter" (Terborch) | 40 | 10 |
| 390 | 14f. "Man writing a Letter" (Metsu) | 45 | 10 |
| 391 | 17f. "The Letter" (Fragonard) (air) | 60 | 10 |
| 392 | 26f. "Young Woman reading Letter" (Vermeer) | 80 | 20 |
| 393 | 40f. "Folding a Letter" (Vigee-Lebrun) | 90 | 25 |
| 394 | 50f. "Mademoiselle Lavergne" (Liotard) | 95 | 35 |
| **MS**395 | 103×120 mm. Nos. 393/4 (without "POSTE AERIENNE" inscr). Perf or imperf | 2·00 | 2·00 |

**50** Football

**1968.** Olympic Games, Mexico. Multicoloured.

| | | | |
|---|---|---|---|
| 396 | 4f. Type **50** (postage) | 25 | 10 |
| 397 | 7f. Basketball | 30 | 10 |
| 398 | 13f. High jumping | 35 | 10 |
| 399 | 24f. Relay racing | 55 | 20 |
| 400 | 40f. Throwing the javelin | 1·25 | 40 |
| 401 | 10f. Putting the shot (air) | 25 | 15 |
| 402 | 17f. Running | 45 | 15 |
| 403 | 26f. Throwing the hammer | 70 | 25 |
| 404 | 50f. Hurdling | 1·40 | 45 |
| 405 | 75f. Long jumping | 2·25 | 60 |
| **MS**406 | 95×85 mm. Nos. 404/5 (without "POSTE AERIENNE" inscr). Perf or imperf | 6·00 | 6·00 |

51 "Virgin and Child" (Lippi)

**1968.** Christmas. Paintings. Multicoloured.

| | | | |
|---|---|---|---|
| 407 | 3f. Type **51** (postage) | 20 | 10 |
| 408 | 5f. "The Magnificat" (Botticelli) | 25 | 10 |
| 409 | 6f. "Virgin and Child" (Durer) | 40 | 10 |
| 410 | 11f. "Virgin and Child" (Raphael) | 40 | 10 |
| 411 | 10f. "Madonna" (Correggio) (air) | 25 | 10 |
| 412 | 14f. "The Nativity" (Baroccio) | 35 | 15 |
| 413 | 17f. "The Holy Family" (El Greco) | 55 | 20 |
| 414 | 26f. "Adoration of the Magi" (Maino) | 75 | 35 |
| **MS**415 | Two sheets each 120×120 mm. (a) Nos. 407/10; (b) Nos. 411/14. Perf or imperf | 2·75 | 2·75 |

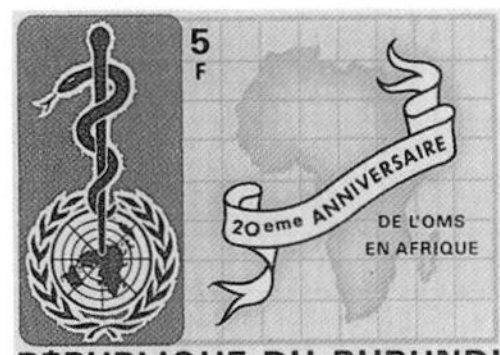


**52** WHO Emblem and Map

**1969.** 20th Anniv of World Health Organization Operation in Africa.

| | | | | |
|---|---|---|---|---|
| 416 | **52** | 5f. multicoloured | 15 | 10 |
| 417 | **52** | 6f. multicoloured | 20 | 10 |
| 418 | **52** | 11f. multicoloured | 25 | 15 |

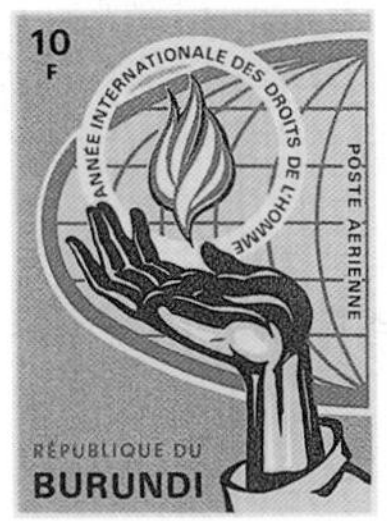


**53** Hand holding Flame

**1969.** Air. Human Rights Year.

| | | | | |
|---|---|---|---|---|
| 419 | **53** | 10f. multicoloured | 35 | 10 |
| 420 | **53** | 14f. multicoloured | 45 | 10 |
| 421 | **53** | 26f. multicoloured | 65 | 25 |

**1969.** Space Flight of "Apollo 8". Nos. 407/14 optd *VOL DE NOEL APOLLO 8* and space module.

| | | | |
|---|---|---|---|
| 422 | 3f. multicoloured (postage) | 15 | 10 |
| 423 | 5f. multicoloured | 25 | 10 |
| 424 | 6f. multicoloured | 40 | 10 |
| 425 | 11f. multicoloured | 50 | 20 |
| 426 | 10f. multicoloured (air) | 30 | 15 |
| 427 | 14f. multicoloured | 35 | 20 |
| 428 | 17f. multicoloured | 55 | 25 |
| 429 | 26f. multicoloured | 70 | 35 |

**55** Map showing African Members

**1969.** 5th Anniv of Yaounde Agreement between Common Market Countries and African-Malagasy Economic Community. Multicoloured.

| | | | |
|---|---|---|---|
| 430 | 5f. Type **55** | 20 | 10 |
| 431 | 14f. Ploughing with tractor | 40 | 15 |
| 432 | 17f. Teacher and pupil | 55 | 20 |
| 433 | 26f. Maps of Africa and Europe (horiz) | 75 | 25 |

**56** "Resurrection" (Isenmann)

**1969.** Easter. Multicoloured.

| | | | |
|---|---|---|---|
| 434 | 11f. Type **56** | 30 | 10 |
| 435 | 14f. "Resurrection" (Caron) | 40 | 15 |
| 436 | 17f. "Noli me Tangere" (Schongauer) | 45 | 20 |
| 437 | 26f. "Resurrection" (El Greco) | 75 | 30 |
| **MS**438 | 102×125 mm. Nos. 434/7. Perf or imperf | 1·50 | 1·60 |

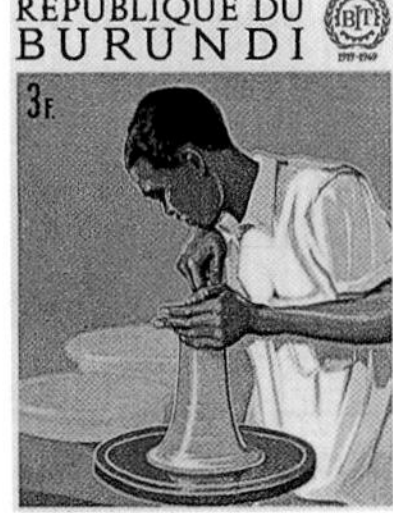


**57** Potter

**1969.** 50th Anniv of ILO. Multicoloured.

| | | | |
|---|---|---|---|
| 439 | 3f. Type **57** | 10 | 10 |
| 440 | 5f. Farm workers | 10 | 10 |
| 441 | 7f. Foundry worker | 25 | 10 |
| 442 | 10f. Harvester | 25 | 15 |

**58** Nurse and Patient

**1969.** 50th Anniv of League of Red Cross Societies. Multicoloured.

| | | | |
|---|---|---|---|
| 443 | 4f.+1f. Type **58** (postage) | 15 | 10 |
| 444 | 7f.+1f. Stretcher bearers | 35 | 10 |
| 445 | 11f.+1f. Operating theatre | 50 | 15 |
| 446 | 17f.+1f. Blood bank | 60 | 25 |
| 447 | 26f.+3f. Laboratory (air) | 75 | 25 |
| 448 | 40f.+3f. Red Cross truck in African village | 1·10 | 45 |
| 449 | 50f.+3f. Nurse and woman patient | 1·60 | 50 |
| **MS**450 | 90×97 mm. Nos. 447/9 (without "POSTE AERIENNE" inscr). Perf or imperf | 3·50 | 3·50 |

**59** Steel Works

**1969.** 5th Anniv of African Development Bank. Multicoloured.

| | | | |
|---|---|---|---|
| 451 | 10f. Type **59** | 30 | 30 |
| 452 | 17f. Broadcaster | 50 | 50 |
| 453 | 30f. Language laboratory | 70 | 70 |
| 454 | 50f. Tractor and harrow | 1·25 | 1·25 |
| **MS**455 | 103×125 mm. Nos. 451/4. Perf or imperf | 2·50 | 2·50 |

**60** Pope Paul VI

**1969.** 1st Papal Visit to Africa. Multicoloured.

| | | | |
|---|---|---|---|
| 456 | 3f.+2f. Type **60** | 15 | 10 |
| 457 | 5f.+2f. Pope Paul and map of Africa (horiz) | 30 | 10 |
| 458 | 10f.+2f. Pope Paul and African flags (horiz) | 30 | 10 |
| 459 | 14f.+2f. Pope Paul and the Vatican (horiz) | 55 | 10 |
| 460 | 17f.+2f. Type **60** | 60 | 10 |
| 461 | 40f.+2f. Pope Paul and Uganda Martyrs (horiz) | 1·25 | 30 |
| 462 | 50f.+2f. Pope Paul enthroned (horiz) | 1·60 | 35 |
| **MS**463 | 80×103 mm. As Nos. 461/2 but face values 40f.+5f. and 50f.+5f. Perf or imperf | 2·75 | 2·75 |

**61** "Girl reading Letter" (Vermeer)

**1969.** International Letter-writing Week. Mult.

| | | | |
|---|---|---|---|
| 464 | 4f. Type **61** | 15 | 10 |
| 465 | 7f. "Graziella" (Renoir) | 20 | 10 |
| 466 | 14f. "Woman writing a Letter" (Terborch) | 30 | 10 |
| 467 | 26f. "Galileo" (unknown painter) | 55 | 15 |
| 468 | 40f. "Beethoven" (unknown painter) | 1·10 | 35 |
| **MS**469 | 133×75 mm. Nos. 467/8. Perf or imperf | 2·10 | 2·10 |

**62** Blast-off

**1969.** 1st Man on the Moon. Multicoloured.

| | | | |
|---|---|---|---|
| 470 | 4f. Type **62** (postage) | 30 | 10 |
| 471 | 6f.50 Rocket in Space | 40 | 10 |
| 472 | 7f. Separation of lunar module | 50 | 10 |
| 473 | 14f. Module landing on Moon | 80 | 15 |
| 474 | 17f. Command module in orbit | 1·10 | 25 |
| 475 | 26f. Astronaut descending ladder (air) | 1·25 | 20 |
| 476 | 40f. Astronaut on Moon's surface | 2·00 | 25 |
| 477 | 50f. Module in sea | 3·00 | 45 |
| **MS**478 | 140×90 mm. 26f. As 14f.; 40f. As 26f.; 50f. As 40f. Perf or imperf | 6·25 | 6·25 |

**63** "Adoration of the Magi" (detail, Rubens)

**1969.** Christmas. Multicoloured.

| | | | |
|---|---|---|---|
| 479 | 5f. Type **63** (postage) | 15 | 10 |
| 480 | 6f. "Virgin and Child with St. John" (Romano) | 15 | 10 |
| 481 | 10f. "Madonna of the Magnificat" (Botticelli) | 40 | 15 |
| 482 | 17f. "Virgin and Child" (Garofalo) (horiz) (air) | 60 | 15 |
| 483 | 26f. "Madonna and Child" (Negretti) (horiz) | 80 | 20 |
| 484 | 50f. "Virgin and Child" (Barbarelli) (horiz) | 1·60 | 35 |
| **MS**485 | Two sheets (a) 110×85 mm. Nos. 479/81; (b) 85×110 mm. Nos. 482/4. Perf or imperf Set of 2 sheets | 3·75 | 1·10 |

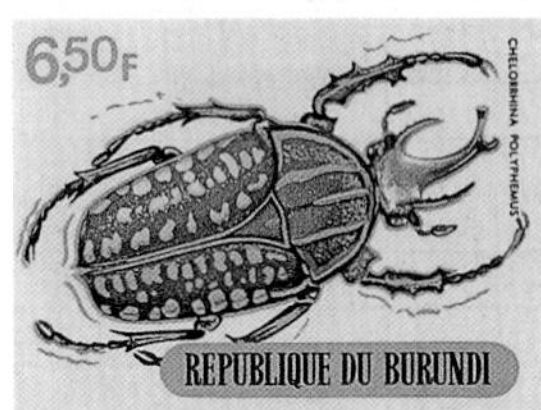


**64** "Chelorrhina polyphemus"

**1970.** Beetles. Multicoloured. (a) Postage. (i) Size 39×28 mm.

| | | | |
|---|---|---|---|
| 486 | 50c. "Sternotomis bohemani" | 20 | 10 |
| 487 | 1f. "Tetralobus flabellicornis" | 20 | 10 |
| 488 | 1f.50 Type **64** | 20 | 10 |
| 489 | 2f. "Brachytritus hieroglyphicus" | 20 | 10 |
| 490 | 3f. "Goliathus goliathus" | 20 | 10 |
| 491 | 3f.50 "Homoderus mellyi" | 30 | 10 |

(ii) Size 46×32 mm.

| | | | |
|---|---|---|---|
| 492 | 4f. As 50c. | 45 | 10 |
| 493 | 5f. As 1f. | 65 | 10 |
| 494 | 6f. Type **64** | 65 | 10 |
| 495 | 8f. As 2f. | 65 | 10 |
| 496 | 10f. As 3f. | 70 | 10 |
| 497 | 15f. As 3f.50 | 1·10 | 15 |

(iii) Size 62×36 mm.

| | | | |
|---|---|---|---|
| 498 | 20f. As 50c. | 1·50 | 30 |
| 499 | 50f. "Stephanorrhina guttata" | 4·00 | 40 |
| 500 | 100f. "Phyllocnema viridocostata" | 6·75 | 85 |
| 501 | 150f. "Mecynorrhina oberthueri" | 8·25 | 1·60 |

(b) Air. (i) Size 46×32 mm.

| | | | |
|---|---|---|---|
| 502 | 6f. As 3f.50 | 35 | 10 |
| 503 | 8f. As 1f. | 45 | 10 |
| 504 | 10f. Type **64** | 60 | 15 |
| 505 | 14f. As 2f. | 70 | 15 |
| 506 | 15f. As 3f. | 75 | 20 |

(ii) Size 52×36 mm.

| | | | |
|---|---|---|---|
| 507 | 20f. As 50f. (No. 499) | 1·25 | 25 |
| 508 | 50f. As 50c. | 4·00 | 35 |
| 509 | 75f. As 100f. | 5·00 | 55 |
| 510 | 130f. As 150f. | 8·00 | 80 |

**65** "Jesus Condemned to Death"

**1970.** Easter. "The Stations of the Cross" (Carredano). Multicoloured.

| | | | |
|---|---|---|---|
| 511 | 1f. Type **65** (postage) | 10 | 10 |
| 512 | 1f.50 "Carrying the Cross" | 10 | 10 |
| 513 | 2f. "Jesus falls for the First Time" | 10 | 10 |
| 514 | 3f. "Jesus meets His Mother" | 10 | 10 |

| | | | |
|---|---|---|---|
| 515 | 3f.50 "Simon of Cyrene takes the Cross" | 15 | 10 |
| 516 | 4f. "Veronica wipes the face of Christ" | 15 | 10 |
| 517 | 5f. "Jesus falls for the Second Time" | 15 | 10 |
| 518 | 8f. "The Women of Jerusalem" (air) | 20 | 10 |
| 519 | 10f. "Jesus falls for the Third Time" | 25 | 15 |
| 520 | 14f. "Christ stripped" | 30 | 25 |
| 521 | 15f. "Jesus nailed to the Cross" | 40 | 25 |
| 522 | 18f. "The Crucifixion" | 40 | 30 |
| 523 | 20f. "Descent from the Cross" | 50 | 30 |
| 524 | 50f. "Christ laid in the Tomb" | 1·25 | 45 |
| **MS**525 | Two sheets each 155×125 mm. (a) Nos. 511/17; (b) Nos. 518/24 | 4·00 | 2·50 |

**66** Japanese Parade

**1970.** World Fair, Osaka, Japan (EXPO '70). Multicoloured.

| | | | |
|---|---|---|---|
| 526 | 4f. Type **66** | 15 | 10 |
| 527 | 6f.50 Exhibition site from the air | 75 | 15 |
| 528 | 7f. African pavilions | 20 | 10 |
| 529 | 14f. Pagoda (vert) | 30 | 10 |
| 530 | 26f. Recording pavilion and pool | 60 | 15 |
| 531 | 40f. Tower of the Sun (vert) | 1·00 | 30 |
| 532 | 50f. National flags (vert) | 1·25 | 35 |
| **MS**533 | 105×80 mm. As Nos. 531/2 with additional "POSTE AERIENNE" inscr. Perf or imperf | 2·25 | 65 |

**67** Burundi Cow

**1970.** Source of the Nile. Multicoloured.

| | | | |
|---|---|---|---|
| 534 | 7f. Any design (postage) | 95 | 30 |
| 535 | 14f. Any design (air) | 1·25 | 30 |

Nos. 534 and 535 were each issued in se-tenant sheets of 18 stamps as Type **67**, showing map sections, animals and birds, forming a map of the Nile from Cairo to Burundi.

**68** Common Redstart

**1970.** Birds. Multicoloured. (a) Postage. Size 44×33 mm or 33×44 mm.

| | | | |
|---|---|---|---|
| 536 | 2f. Great grey shrike (vert) | 25 | 10 |
| 537 | 2f. Common starling (vert) | 25 | 10 |
| 538 | 2f. Yellow wagtail (vert) | 25 | 10 |
| 539 | 2f. Sand martin (vert) | 25 | 10 |
| 540 | 3f. Winter wren | 60 | 10 |
| 541 | 3f. Firecrest | 60 | 10 |
| 542 | 3f. Eurasian sky lark | 60 | 10 |
| 543 | 3f. Crested lark | 60 | 10 |
| 544 | 3f.50 Woodchat shrike (vert) | 65 | 10 |
| 545 | 3f.50 Rock thrush (vert) | 65 | 10 |
| 546 | 3f.50 Black redstarts (vert) | 65 | 10 |
| 547 | 3f.50 Ring ousel (vert) | 65 | 10 |
| 548 | 4f. Type **68** | 95 | 10 |
| 549 | 4f. Dunnock | 95 | 10 |
| 550 | 4f. Grey wagtail | 95 | 10 |
| 551 | 4f. Meadow pipit | 95 | 10 |
| 552 | 5f. Hoopoe (vert) | 1·25 | 15 |
| 553 | 5f. Pied flycatcher (vert) | 1·25 | 15 |
| 554 | 5f. Great reed warbler (vert) | 1·25 | 15 |
| 555 | 5f. River kingfisher (vert) | 1·25 | 15 |
| 556 | 6f.50 House martin | 1·40 | 20 |
| 557 | 6f.50 Sedge warbler | 1·40 | 20 |
| 558 | 6f.50 Fieldfare | 1·40 | 20 |
| 559 | 6f.50 Golden oriole | 1·40 | 20 |

(b) Air. Size 52×44 mm or 44×52 mm.

| | | | |
|---|---|---|---|
| 560 | 8f. As No. 536 | 1·50 | 20 |
| 561 | 8f. As No. 537 | 1·50 | 20 |
| 562 | 8f. As No. 538 | 1·50 | 20 |
| 563 | 8f. As No. 539 | 1·50 | 20 |
| 564 | 10f. As No. 540 | 1·75 | 25 |
| 565 | 10f. As No. 541 | 1·75 | 25 |
| 566 | 10f. As No. 542 | 1·75 | 25 |
| 567 | 10f. As No. 543 | 1·75 | 25 |
| 568 | 14f. As No. 544 | 1·75 | 25 |
| 569 | 14f. As No. 545 | 1·75 | 25 |
| 570 | 14f. As No. 546 | 1·75 | 25 |
| 571 | 14f. As No. 547 | 1·75 | 25 |
| 572 | 20f. Type **68** | 2·10 | 30 |
| 573 | 20f. As No. 549 | 2·10 | 30 |
| 574 | 20f. As No. 550 | 2·10 | 30 |
| 575 | 20f. As No. 551 | 2·10 | 30 |
| 576 | 30f. As No. 552 | 2·25 | 30 |
| 577 | 30f. As No. 553 | 2·25 | 30 |
| 578 | 30f. As No. 554 | 2·25 | 30 |
| 579 | 30f. As No. 555 | 2·25 | 30 |
| 580 | 50f. As No. 556 | 3·75 | 30 |
| 581 | 50f. As No. 557 | 3·75 | 30 |
| 582 | 50f. As No. 558 | 3·75 | 30 |
| 583 | 50f. As No. 559 | 3·75 | 30 |

**69** Library

**1970.** International Educational Year. Mult.

| | | | |
|---|---|---|---|
| 584 | 3f. Type **69** | 10 | 10 |
| 585 | 5f. Examination | 15 | 10 |
| 586 | 7f. Experiments in the laboratory | 25 | 10 |
| 587 | 10f. Students with electron microscope | 30 | 10 |

**70** United Nations Building, New York

**1970.** Air. 25th Anniv of United Nations. Mult.

| | | | |
|---|---|---|---|
| 588 | 7f. Type **70** | 25 | 10 |
| 589 | 11f. Security Council in session | 30 | 10 |
| 590 | 26f. Paul VI and U Thant | 70 | 20 |
| 591 | 40f. U.N. and National flags | 1·00 | 30 |
| **MS**592 | 125×80 mm. As Nos. 590/1 but without "POSTE AERIENNE" inscr. Perf or imperf | 1·70 | 50 |

**71** Pres. Micombero and Wife

**1970.** 4th Anniv of Republic.

| | | | |
|---|---|---|---|
| 593 | 4f. Type **71** | 10 | 10 |
| 594 | 7f. Pres. Micombero and flag | 25 | 10 |
| 595 | 11f. Revolution Memorial | 35 | 15 |
| **MS**596 | 125×142 mm. Nos. 593/5 (air). Perf or imperf | 70 | 35 |

**72** King Baudouin and Queen Fabiola

**1970.** Air. Visit of King and Queen of the Belgians. Each brown, purple and gold.

| | | | |
|---|---|---|---|
| 597 | 6f. Type **72** | 65 | 15 |
| 598 | 20f. Pres. Micombero and King Baudouin | 1·50 | 40 |
| 599 | 40f. Pres. Micombero in evening dress | 3·00 | 70 |
| **MS**600 | 143×117 mm. As Nos. 597/9 but with "POSTE AERIENNE" inscr omitted. Perf or imperf | 5·00 | 1·25 |

**73** "Adoration of the Magi" (Durer)

**1970.** Christmas. Multicoloured.

| | | | |
|---|---|---|---|
| 601 | 6f.50+1f. Type **73** (postage) | 50 | 15 |
| 602 | 11f.+1f. "The Virgin of the Eucharist" (Botticelli) | 60 | 25 |
| 603 | 20f.+1f. "The Holy Family" (El Greco) | 90 | 30 |
| 604 | 14f.+3f. "The Adoration of the Magi" (Velasquez) (air) | 50 | 25 |
| 605 | 26f.+3f. "The Holy Family" (Van Cleve) | 85 | 40 |
| 606 | 40f.+3f. "Virgin and Child" (Van der Weyden) | 1·40 | 60 |
| **MS**607 | Two sheets each 135×75 mm. (a) Nos. 601/3; (b) Nos. 604/6. Perf or imperf | 4·75 | 2·00 |

**74** Lenin in Discussion

**1970.** Birth Cent of Lenin. Each brown and gold.

| | | | |
|---|---|---|---|
| 608 | 3f.50 Type **74** | 20 | 15 |
| 609 | 5f. Lenin addressing Soviet | 30 | 15 |
| 610 | 6f.50 Lenin with soldier and sailor | 40 | 15 |
| 611 | 15f. Lenin speaking to crowd | 60 | 25 |
| 612 | 50f. Lenin | 2·00 | 55 |

**75** Lion

**1971.** African Animals (1st series). Multicoloured. (a) Postage. Size 38×38 mm.

| | | | |
|---|---|---|---|
| 613 | 1f. Type **75** | 35 | 10 |
| 614 | 1f. African buffalo | 35 | 10 |
| 615 | 1f. Hippopotamus | 35 | 10 |
| 616 | 1f. Giraffe | 35 | 10 |
| 617 | 2f. Topi | 50 | 15 |
| 618 | 2f. Black rhinoceros | 50 | 15 |
| 619 | 2f. Common zebra | 50 | 15 |
| 620 | 2f. Leopard | 50 | 15 |
| 621 | 3f. Grant's gazelle | 85 | 25 |
| 622 | 3f. Cheetah | 85 | 25 |
| 623 | 3f. African white-backed vultures | 85 | 25 |
| 624 | 3f. Okapi | 85 | 25 |
| 625 | 5f. Chimpanzee | 1·00 | 25 |
| 626 | 5f. African elephant | 1·00 | 25 |
| 627 | 5f. Spotted hyena | 1·00 | 25 |
| 628 | 5f. Gemsbok | 1·00 | 25 |
| 629 | 6f. Gorilla | 1·40 | 25 |
| 630 | 6f. Blue wildebeest | 1·40 | 25 |
| 631 | 6f. Warthog | 1·40 | 25 |
| 632 | 6f. Hunting dog | 1·40 | 25 |
| 633 | 11f. Sable antelope | 2·25 | 30 |
| 634 | 11f. Caracal | 2·25 | 30 |
| 635 | 11f. Ostriches | 2·25 | 30 |
| 636 | 11f. Bongo | 2·25 | 30 |

(b) Air. Size 44×44 mm.

| | | | |
|---|---|---|---|
| 637 | 10f. Type **75** | 70 | 35 |
| 638 | 10f. As No. 614 | 70 | 35 |
| 639 | 10f. As No. 615 | 70 | 35 |
| 640 | 10f. As No. 616 | 70 | 35 |
| 641 | 14f. As No. 617 | 80 | 40 |
| 642 | 14f. As No. 618 | 80 | 40 |
| 643 | 14f. As No. 619 | 80 | 40 |
| 644 | 14f. As No. 620 | 80 | 40 |
| 645 | 17f. As No. 621 | 90 | 40 |
| 646 | 17f. As No. 622 | 90 | 40 |
| 647 | 17f. As No. 623 | 90 | 40 |
| 648 | 17f. As No. 624 | 90 | 40 |
| 649 | 24f. As No. 625 | 1·50 | 55 |
| 650 | 24f. As No. 626 | 1·50 | 55 |
| 651 | 24f. As No. 627 | 1·50 | 55 |
| 652 | 24f. As No. 628 | 1·50 | 55 |
| 653 | 26f. As No. 629 | 1·50 | 55 |
| 654 | 26f. As No. 630 | 1·50 | 55 |
| 655 | 26f. As No. 631 | 1·50 | 55 |
| 656 | 26f. As No. 632 | 1·50 | 55 |
| 657 | 31f. As No. 633 | 1·60 | 70 |
| 658 | 31f. As No. 634 | 1·60 | 70 |
| 659 | 31f. As No. 635 | 1·60 | 70 |
| 660 | 31f. As No. 636 | 1·60 | 70 |

See also Nos. 1028/75, 1178/1225 and 1385/97.

**76** "The Resurrection" (Il Sodoma)

**1971.** Easter. Multicoloured.

| | | | |
|---|---|---|---|
| 661 | 3f. Type **76** (postage) | 15 | 10 |
| 662 | 6f. "The Resurrection" (Del Castagno) | 30 | 10 |
| 663 | 11f. "Noli Me Tangere" (Correggio) | 45 | 15 |
| 664 | 14f. "The Resurrection" (Borrassa) (air) | 50 | 20 |
| 665 | 17f. "The Resurrection" (Della Francesca) | 65 | 20 |
| 666 | 26f. "The Resurrection" (Pleydenwyurff) | 85 | 30 |
| **MS**667 | Two sheets each 117×84 mm. (a) Nos. 661/3; (b) Nos. 664/6. Colours changed. Perf or imperf | 3·00 | 1·10 |

**1971.** Air. United Nations Campaigns. Nos. 637/48 optd or surch. (a) Optd LUTTE CONTRE LE RACISME ET LA DISCRIMINATION RACIALE and Racial Equality Year emblem.

| | | | |
|---|---|---|---|
| 668 | 10f. multicoloured | 90 | 15 |
| 669 | 10f. multicoloured | 90 | 15 |
| 670 | 10f. multicoloured | 90 | 15 |
| 671 | 10f. multicoloured | 90 | 15 |

(b) Surch LUTTE CONTRE L'ANALPHABETISME, UNESCO emblem and premium (Campaign against Illiteracy).

| | | | |
|---|---|---|---|
| 672 | 14f.+2f. multicoloured | 1·40 | 25 |
| 673 | 14f.+2f. multicoloured | 1·40 | 25 |
| 674 | 14f.+2f. multicoloured | 1·40 | 25 |
| 675 | 14f.+2f. multicoloured | 1·40 | 25 |

(c) Surch AIDE INTERNATIONALE AUX REFUGIES, emblem and premium (Int Help for Refugees).

| | | | |
|---|---|---|---|
| 676 | 17f.+1f. multicoloured | 2·25 | 40 |
| 677 | 17f.+1f. multicoloured | 2·25 | 40 |
| 678 | 17f.+1f. multicoloured | 2·25 | 40 |
| 679 | 17f.+1f. multicoloured | 2·25 | 40 |

**1971.** Air. Olympic Commems. Nos. 653/56 surch. (a) Surch 75eme ANNIVERSAIRE DES JEUX OLYMPIQUES MODERNES (1896–1971), Olympic rings and premium.

| | | | |
|---|---|---|---|
| 680 | 26f.+1f. multicoloured | 1·25 | 35 |
| 681 | 26f.+1f. multicoloured | 1·25 | 35 |
| 682 | 26f.+1f. multicoloured | 1·25 | 35 |
| 683 | 26f.+1f. multicoloured | 1·25 | 35 |

(b) Surch JEUX PRE-OLYMPIQUES MUNICH 1972, rings and premium (Olympic Games, Munich (1972)).

| | | | |
|---|---|---|---|
| 684 | 31f.+1f. multicoloured | 2·25 | 1·10 |
| 685 | 31f.+1f. multicoloured | 2·25 | 1·10 |
| 686 | 31f.+1f. multicoloured | 2·25 | 1·10 |
| 687 | 31f.+1f. multicoloured | 2·25 | 1·10 |

**79** "Venetian Girl"

**1971.** International Letter-writing Week. Paintings by Durer. Multicoloured.

| | | | |
|---|---|---|---|
| 688 | 6f. Type **79** | 30 | 30 |
| 689 | 11f. "Jerome Holzschuhers" | 35 | 35 |
| 690 | 14f. "Emperor Maximilian" | 40 | 40 |
| 691 | 17f. Altar painting, Paumgartner | 65 | 65 |
| 692 | 26f. "The Halle Madonna" | 80 | 80 |
| 693 | 31f. Self-portrait | 1·00 | 1·00 |
| **MS**694 | 137×80 mm. As Nos. 692/3 (air). Perf or imperf | 1·80 | 1·80 |

**1971.** 6th Congress of International Institute of French Law, Bujumbura. Nos. 668/693 optd VIeme CONGRES DE L'INSTITUT INTERNATIONAL DE DROIT D'EXPRESSION FRANCAISE.

| | | | |
|---|---|---|---|
| 695 | 6f. multicoloured | 30 | 10 |
| 696 | 11f. multicoloured | 35 | 10 |
| 697 | 14f. multicoloured | 45 | 20 |
| 698 | 17f. multicoloured | 65 | 20 |
| 699 | 26f. multicoloured | 75 | 25 |
| 700 | 31f. multicoloured | 1·00 | 25 |
| **MS**701 | 137×80 mm. No. **MS**694. Perf or imperf | 1·50 | 1·50 |

**81** "The Virgin and Child" (Il Perugino)

**1971.** Christmas. Paintings of "Virgin and Child" by following artists. Multicoloured.

| | | | |
|---|---|---|---|
| 702 | 3f. Type **81** (postage) | 15 | 10 |
| 703 | 5f. Del Sarto | 25 | 10 |
| 704 | 6f. Morales | 50 | 10 |
| 705 | 14f. Da Conegliano (air) | 55 | 15 |
| 706 | 17f. Lippi | 60 | 20 |
| 707 | 31f. Leonardo da Vinci | 1·10 | 45 |
| **MS**708 | Two sheets each 125×80 mm. (a) Nos. 702/4; (b) Nos. 705/7 | 3·00 | 1·10 |

**1971.** 25th Anniv of UNICEF. Nos. 702/7 surch UNICEF XXVe ANNIVERSAIRE 1946–1971, emblem and premium.

| | | | |
|---|---|---|---|
| 709 | 3f.+1f. mult (postage) | 30 | 10 |
| 710 | 5f.+1f. multicoloured | 50 | 20 |
| 711 | 6f.+1f. multicoloured | 60 | 30 |
| 712 | 14f.+1f. mult (air) | 40 | 20 |
| 713 | 17f.+1f. multicoloured | 95 | 25 |
| 714 | 31f.+1f. multicoloured | 1·50 | 45 |
| **MS**715 | Two sheets each 125×80 mm. No. **MS**708 surch with 2f. premium on each stamp in the sheets | 3·00 | 3·00 |

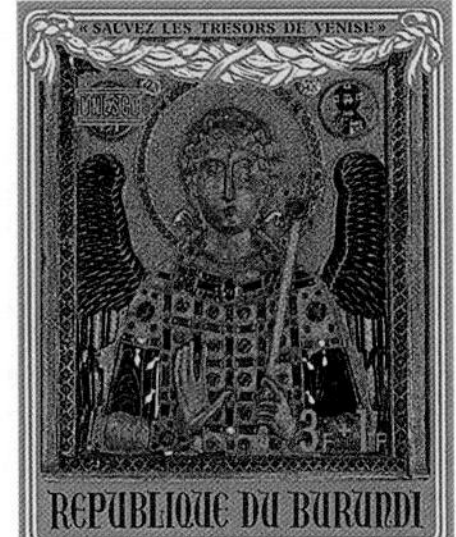

**83** "Archangel Michael" (icon, St. Mark's)

**1971.** UNESCO "Save Venice" Campaign. Multicoloured.

| | | | |
|---|---|---|---|
| 716 | 3f.+1f. Type **83** (postage) | 25 | 10 |
| 717 | 5f.+1f. "La Polenta" (Longhi) | 35 | 15 |
| 718 | 6f.+1f. "Gossip" (Longhi) | 35 | 15 |
| 719 | 11f.+1f. "Diana's Bath" (Pittoni) | 45 | 25 |
| 720 | 10f.+1f. Casa d'Oro (air) | 45 | 10 |
| 721 | 17f.+1f. Doge's Palace | 65 | 15 |
| 722 | 24f.+1f. St. John and St. Paul Church | 90 | 25 |
| 723 | 31f.+1f. "Doge's Palace and Piazzetta" (Canaletto) | 2·00 | 40 |
| **MS**724 | Two sheets each 115×132 mm. (a) Nos. 716/19; (b) Nos. 720/3. Each design in sheet has a 2f. premium. Perf or imperf | 5·25 | 1·50 |

**84** "Lunar Orbiter"

**1972.** Conquest of Space. Multicoloured.

| | | | |
|---|---|---|---|
| 725 | 6f. Type **84** | 15 | 15 |
| 726 | 11f. "Vostok" spaceship | 40 | 15 |
| 727 | 14f. "Luna 1" | 45 | 30 |
| 728 | 17f. First Man on Moon | 65 | 30 |
| 729 | 26f. "Soyuz 11" space flight | 80 | 40 |
| 730 | 40f. "Lunar Rover" | 1·60 | 95 |
| **MS**731 | 135×135 mm. Nos. 725/30 with additional inscr (air) | 4·00 | 2·25 |

**85** Slalom skiing

**1972.** Winter Olympic Games, Sapporo, Japan. Multicoloured.

| | | | |
|---|---|---|---|
| 732 | 5f. Type **85** | 15 | 10 |
| 733 | 6f. Pair skating | 20 | 10 |
| 734 | 11f. Figure-skating | 35 | 10 |
| 735 | 14f. Ski-jumping | 35 | 20 |
| 736 | 17f. Ice-hockey | 50 | 20 |
| 737 | 24f. Speed skating | 60 | 25 |
| 738 | 26f. Ski-bobbing | 60 | 25 |
| 739 | 31f. Downhill skiing | 75 | 25 |
| 740 | 50f. Bobsleighing | 1·50 | 35 |
| **MS**741 | 107×127 mm. As Nos. 738/40. Perf or imperf (air) | 2·75 | 85 |

**86** "Ecce Homo" (Metzys)

**1972.** Easter. Paintings. Multicoloured.

| | | | |
|---|---|---|---|
| 742 | 3f.50 Type **86** | 20 | 10 |
| 743 | 6f.50 "The Crucifixion" (Rubens) | 30 | 10 |
| 744 | 10f. "The Descent from the Cross" (Portormo) | 40 | 10 |
| 745 | 18f. "Pieta" (Gallegos) | 70 | 15 |
| 746 | 27f. "The Trinity" (El Greco) | 1·40 | 30 |
| **MS**747 | 111×160 mm. Nos. 742/6. Perf or imperf | 3·00 | 75 |

**87** Gymnastics

**1972.** Olympic Games. Munich. Multicoloured.

| | | | |
|---|---|---|---|
| 748 | 5f. Type **87** (postage) | 20 | 10 |
| 749 | 6f. Throwing the javelin | 20 | 10 |
| 750 | 11f. Fencing | 35 | 15 |
| 751 | 14f. Cycling | 50 | 20 |
| 752 | 17f. Pole-vaulting | 75 | 20 |
| 753 | 24f. Weightlifting (air) | 65 | 25 |
| 754 | 26f. Hurdling | 90 | 25 |
| 755 | 31f. Throwing the discus | 1·40 | 40 |
| 756 | 40f. Football | 1·50 | 50 |
| **MS**757 | 123×75 mm. Nos. 755/6 without "POSTE AERIENNE" inscr | 3·00 | 90 |

**88** Prince Rwagasore, Pres. Micombero and Drummers

**1972.** 10th Anniv of Independence. Multicoloured.

| | | | |
|---|---|---|---|
| 758 | 5f. Type **88** (postage) | 15 | 10 |
| 759 | 7f. Rwagasore, Micombero and map | 25 | 10 |
| 760 | 13f. Pres. Micombero and Burundi flag | 40 | 15 |
| 761 | 15f. Type **65** (air) | 30 | 15 |
| 762 | 18f. As 7f. | 35 | 15 |
| 763 | 27f. As 13f. | 60 | 30 |
| **MS**764 | Two sheets each 147×80 mm. (a) Nos. 758/60; (b) Nos. 761/3 | 2·10 | 95 |

**1972.** Christmas. "Madonna and Child" paintings by artists given below. Multicoloured.

| | | | |
|---|---|---|---|
| 765 | 5f. Type **89** (postage) | 30 | 10 |
| 766 | 10f. Raphael | 50 | 10 |
| 767 | 15f. Botticelli | 75 | 15 |
| 768 | 18f. S. Mainardi (air) | 50 | 15 |
| 769 | 27f. H. Memling | 1·00 | 25 |
| 770 | 40f. Lotto | 1·50 | 40 |
| **MS**771 | Two sheets each 128×82 mm. (a) Nos. 765/7; (b) Nos. 768/70 | 4·50 | 1·10 |

**90** "Platycoryne crocea"

**1972.** Orchids. Multicoloured.

| | | | |
|---|---|---|---|
| 772 | 50c. Type **90** (postage) | 30 | 15 |
| 773 | 1f. "Cattleya trianaei" | 30 | 15 |
| 774 | 2f. "Eulophia cucullata" | 30 | 15 |
| 775 | 3f. "Cymbidium hamsey" | 30 | 15 |
| 776 | 4f. "Thelymitra pauciflora" | 30 | 15 |
| 777 | 5f. "Miltassia" | 30 | 15 |
| 778 | 6f. "Miltonia" | 1·25 | 15 |
| 779 | 7f. Type **90** | 1·25 | 15 |
| 780 | 8f. As 1f. | 1·40 | 15 |
| 781 | 9f. As 2f. | 1·40 | 20 |
| 782 | 10f. As 3f. | 1·90 | 20 |
| 783 | 13f. As 4f. (air) | 1·25 | 15 |
| 784 | 14f. As 5f. | 1·25 | 15 |
| 785 | 15f. As 6f. | 1·60 | 20 |
| 786 | 18f. Type **90** | 1·60 | 20 |
| 787 | 20f. As 1f. | 1·60 | 25 |
| 788 | 27f. As 2f. | 2·75 | 30 |
| 789 | 36f. As 3f. | 4·50 | 40 |

Nos. 779/89 are size 53×53 mm.

**1972.** Christmas Charity. Nos. 765/770 surch.

| | | | |
|---|---|---|---|
| 790 | 5f.+1f. mult (postage) | 35 | 15 |
| 791 | 10f.+1f. multicoloured | 65 | 20 |
| 792 | 15f.+1f. multicoloured | 75 | 25 |
| 793 | 18f.+1f. multicoloured (air) | 60 | 20 |
| 794 | 27f.+1f. multicoloured | 90 | 25 |
| 795 | 40f.+1f. multicoloured | 1·50 | 45 |
| **MS**796 | Two sheets as **MS**771 with 2f. premium surch on each stamp | 4·50 | 1·10 |

**92** H. M. Stanley

**1973.** Centenary of Stanley/Livingstone African Exploration. Multicoloured.

| | | | |
|---|---|---|---|
| 797 | 5f. Type **92** (postage) | 20 | 10 |
| 798 | 7f. Expedition bearers | 25 | 10 |
| 799 | 13f. Stanley directing foray | 45 | 15 |
| 800 | 15f. Dr. Livingstone (air) | 35 | 20 |
| 801 | 18f. Stanley meets Livingstone | 55 | 20 |
| 802 | 27f. Stanley conferring with Livingstone | 1·00 | 30 |
| **MS**803 | 100×141 mm. Nos. 800/2. Perf or imperf | 1·90 | 70 |

**93** "The Scourging" (Caravaggio)

**1973.** Easter. Multicoloured.

| | | | |
|---|---|---|---|
| 804 | 5f. Type **93** (postage) | 15 | 10 |
| 805 | 7f. "Crucifixion" (Van der Weyden) | 25 | 10 |
| 806 | 13f. "The Deposition" (Raphael) | 50 | 15 |
| 807 | 15f. "Christ bound to the Pillar" (Guido Reni) (air) | 45 | 25 |
| 808 | 18f. "Crucifixion" (M. Grunewald) | 70 | 25 |
| 809 | 27f. "The Descent from the Cross" (Caravaggio) | 1·10 | 30 |
| **MS**810 | Two sheets each 121×74 mm. (a) Nos. 804/6; (b) Nos. 807/9 | 3·00 | 1·10 |

**94** Interpol Emblem

**1973.** 50th Anniv of Interpol. Multicoloured.

| | | | |
|---|---|---|---|
| 811 | 5f. Type **94** (postage) | 25 | 10 |
| 812 | 10f. Burundi flag | 40 | 10 |
| 813 | 18f. Interpol H.Q., Paris | 60 | 15 |
| 814 | 27f. As 5f. (air) | 75 | 25 |
| 815 | 40f. As 10f. | 1·25 | 35 |

**95** Capricorn, Aquarius and Pisces

**1973.** 500th Birth Anniv of Copernicus.

| | | | | |
|---|---|---|---|---|
| 816 | **95** | 3f. gold, red and black (postage) | 20 | 10 |
| 817 | - | 3f. gold, red and black | 20 | 10 |
| 818 | - | 3f. gold, red and black | 20 | 10 |
| 819 | - | 3f. gold, red and black | 20 | 10 |
| 820 | - | 5f. multicoloured | 30 | 10 |
| 821 | - | 5f. multicoloured | 30 | 10 |
| 822 | - | 5f. multicoloured | 30 | 10 |
| 823 | - | 5f. multicoloured | 30 | 10 |
| 824 | - | 7f. multicoloured | 40 | 10 |
| 825 | - | 7f. multicoloured | 40 | 10 |
| 826 | - | 7f. multicoloured | 40 | 10 |
| 827 | - | 7f. multicoloured | 40 | 10 |
| 828 | - | 13f. multicoloured | 60 | 10 |
| 829 | - | 13f. multicoloured | 60 | 10 |
| 830 | - | 13f. multicoloured | 60 | 10 |
| 831 | - | 13f. multicoloured | 60 | 10 |
| 832 | - | 15f. multicoloured (air) | 40 | 15 |
| 833 | - | 15f. multicoloured | 40 | 15 |
| 834 | - | 15f. multicoloured | 40 | 15 |
| 835 | - | 15f. multicoloured | 40 | 15 |
| 836 | - | 18f. multicoloured | 55 | 15 |
| 837 | - | 18f. multicoloured | 55 | 15 |

| | | | | |
|---|---|---|---|---|
| 838 | - | 18f. multicoloured | 55 | 15 |
| 839 | - | 18f. multicoloured | 55 | 15 |
| 840 | - | 27f. multicoloured | 95 | 25 |
| 841 | - | 27f. multicoloured | 95 | 25 |
| 842 | - | 27f. multicoloured | 95 | 25 |
| 843 | - | 27f. multicoloured | 95 | 25 |
| 844 | - | 36f. multicoloured | 2·10 | 40 |
| 845 | - | 36f. multicoloured | 2·10 | 40 |
| 846 | - | 36f. multicoloured | 2·10 | 40 |
| 847 | - | 36f. multicoloured | 2·10 | 40 |

**MS**848 Two sheets each 137×147 mm. (a) Nos. 816/31; (b) Nos. 832/47 20·00 10·00

DESIGNS: No. 816, Type **95**; 817, Aries, Taurus and Gemini; 818, Cancer, Leo and Virgo; 819, Libra, Scorpio and Sagittarius; 820/23, Greek and Roman Gods; 824/7, Ptolemy and Ptolemaic System; 828/31, Copernicus and Solar System; 823/5, Copernicus, Earth, Pluto and Jupiter; 836/39, Copernicus, Venus, Saturn and Mars; 840/43, Copernicus, Uranus, Neptune and Mercury; 844/7, Earth and spacecraft.

The four designs of each value were issued se-tenant in blocks of four within the sheet, forming composite designs.

**96** "Protea cynaroides"

**1973.** Flora and Butterflies. Multicoloured.

| | | | |
|---|---|---|---|
| 849 | 1f. Type **96** (postage) | 70 | 15 |
| 850 | 1f. "Precis octavia" | 70 | 15 |
| 851 | 1f. "Epiphora bauhiniae" | 70 | 15 |
| 852 | 1f. "Gazania longiscapa" | 70 | 15 |
| 853 | 2f. "Kniphofia" – "Royal Standard" | 70 | 15 |
| 854 | 2f. "Cymothoe coccinata hew" | 1·00 | 20 |
| 855 | 2f. "Nudaurelia zambesina" | 1·00 | 20 |
| 856 | 2f. "Freesia refracta" | 1·00 | 15 |
| 857 | 3f. "Calotis eupompe" | 1·00 | 20 |
| 858 | 3f. Narcissus | 1·00 | 15 |
| 859 | 3f. "Cineraria hybrida" | 1·00 | 15 |
| 860 | 3f. "Cyrestis camillus" | 1·00 | 20 |
| 861 | 5f. "Iris tingitana" | 1·40 | 15 |
| 862 | 5f. "Papilio demodocus" | 2·10 | 20 |
| 863 | 5f. "Catopsilia avelaneda" | 2·10 | 20 |
| 864 | 5f. "Nerine sarniensis" | 1·40 | 15 |
| 865 | 6f. "Hypolimnas dexithea" | 2·10 | 20 |
| 866 | 6f. "Zantedeschia tropicalis" | 1·40 | 15 |
| 867 | 6f. "Sandersonia aurantiaca" | 1·40 | 15 |
| 868 | 6f. "Drurya antimachus" | 2·10 | 20 |
| 869 | 11f. "Nymphaea capensis" | 1·75 | 20 |
| 870 | 11f. "Pandoriana pandora" | 2·75 | 25 |
| 871 | 11f. "Precis orythia" | 2·75 | 25 |
| 872 | 11f. "Pelargonium domesticum"–"Aztec" | 1·75 | 20 |
| 873 | 10f. Type **96** (air) | 50 | 10 |
| 874 | 10f. As No. 850 | 90 | 10 |
| 875 | 10f. As No. 851 | 90 | 10 |
| 876 | 10f. As No. 852 | 50 | 10 |
| 877 | 14f. As No. 853 | 60 | 10 |
| 878 | 14f. As No. 854 | 1·00 | 20 |
| 879 | 14f. As No. 855 | 1·00 | 20 |
| 880 | 14f. As No. 856 | 40 | 15 |
| 881 | 17f. As No. 857 | 1·25 | 25 |
| 882 | 17f. As No. 858 | 90 | 20 |
| 883 | 17f. As No. 859 | 90 | 20 |
| 884 | 17f. As No. 860 | 1·25 | 25 |
| 885 | 24f. As No. 861 | 1·40 | 25 |
| 886 | 24f. As No. 862 | 1·75 | 30 |
| 887 | 24f. As No. 863 | 1·75 | 30 |
| 888 | 24f. As No. 864 | 1·10 | 25 |
| 889 | 26f. As No. 865 | 1·75 | 30 |
| 890 | 26f. As No. 866 | 1·10 | 30 |
| 891 | 26f. As No. 867 | 1·10 | 30 |
| 892 | 26f. As No. 868 | 1·75 | 30 |
| 893 | 31f. As No. 869 | 1·25 | 35 |
| 894 | 31f. As No. 870 | 1·90 | 45 |
| 895 | 31f. As No. 871 | 1·90 | 45 |
| 896 | 31f. As No. 872 | 1·25 | 35 |

Nos. 849, 852/3, 856, 858/9, 861, 864, 866/7, 869, 872, 876/7, 880, 882/3, 885, 888, 890/1, 893 and 896 depict flora and the remainder butterflies.

The four designs of each value were issued se-tenant in blocks of four within the sheet, forming composite designs.

**97** "Virgin and Child" (G. Bellini)

**1973.** Christmas. Various paintings of "The Virgin and Child" by artists listed below. Multicoloured.

| | | | |
|---|---|---|---|
| 897 | 5f. Type **97** (postage) | 45 | 10 |
| 898 | 10f. Van Eyck | 55 | 15 |
| 899 | 15f. G. A. Boltraffio | 75 | 20 |
| 900 | 18f. Raphael (air) | 35 | 10 |
| 901 | 27f. P. Perugino | 1·10 | 30 |
| 902 | 40f. Titian | 1·60 | 40 |

**MS**903 Two sheets each 144×78 mm. (a) Nos. 897/9; (b) Nos. 900/2 4·75 1·25

**1973.** Christmas Charity. Nos. 897/902 surch.

| | | | | |
|---|---|---|---|---|
| 904 | **97** | 5f.+1f. mult (postage) | 50 | 15 |
| 905 | - | 10f.+1f. multicoloured | 80 | 20 |
| 906 | - | 15f.+1f. multicoloured | 95 | 25 |
| 907 | - | 18f.+1f. mult (air) | 70 | 15 |
| 908 | - | 27f.+1f. multicoloured | 1·10 | 35 |
| 909 | - | 40f.+1f. multicoloured | 1·60 | 50 |

**MS**910 Two sheets as **MS**903 with 2f. premium surch on each stamp 4·75 1·25

**98** "The Pieta" (Veronese)

**1974.** Easter. Religious Paintings. Multicoloured.

| | | | |
|---|---|---|---|
| 911 | 5f. Type **98** | 15 | 10 |
| 912 | 10f. "The Virgin and St. John" (Van der Weyden) | 30 | 15 |
| 913 | 18f. "The Crucifixion" (Van der Weyden) | 60 | 20 |
| 914 | 27f. "The Entombment" (Titian) | 85 | 30 |
| 915 | 40f. "The Pieta" (El Greco) | 2·10 | 50 |

**MS**916 145×120 mm. Nos. 911/15 4·00 1·25

**99** Egyptian Mouthbrooder ("Haplochromis multicolor")

**1974.** Fishes. Multicoloured.

| | | | |
|---|---|---|---|
| 917 | 1f. Type **99** (postage) | 55 | 10 |
| 918 | 1f. Spotted mouthbrooder ("Tropheus duboisi") | 55 | 10 |
| 919 | 1f. Freshwater butterfly-fish ("Pantodon buchholzi") | 55 | 10 |
| 920 | 1f. Six-banded distichodus ("Distichodus sexfasciatus") | 55 | 10 |
| 921 | 2f. Rainbow krib ("Pelmatochromis kribensis") | 55 | 10 |
| 922 | 2f. African leaf-fish ("Polycentropsis abbreviata") | 55 | 10 |
| 923 | 2f. Three-lined tetra ("Nannaethiops tritaeniatus") | 55 | 10 |
| 924 | 2f. Jewel cichlid ("Hemichromis bimaculatus") | 55 | 10 |
| 925 | 3f. Spotted climbing-perch ("Ctenopoma acutirostre") | 55 | 10 |
| 926 | 3f. African mouthbrooder ("Tilapia melanopleura") | 55 | 10 |
| 927 | 3f. Angel squeaker ("Synodontis angelicus") | 55 | 10 |
| 928 | 3f. Two-striped lyretail ("Aphyosemion bivittatum") | 55 | 10 |
| 929 | 5f. Diamond fingerfish ("Monodactylus argenteus") | 90 | 10 |
| 930 | 5f. Regal angelfish ("Pygoplites diacanthus") | 90 | 10 |
| 931 | 5f. Moorish idol ("Zanclus canescens") | 90 | 10 |
| 932 | 5f. Peacock hind ("Cephalopholis argus") and surgeonfish | 90 | 10 |
| 933 | 6f. Bigeye ("Priacanthus arenatus") | 2·75 | 10 |
| 934 | 6f. Rainbow parrotfish ("Scarus guacamaia") and French angelfish | 2·75 | 10 |
| 935 | 6f. French angelfish ("Pomacanthus arcuatus") | 2·75 | 10 |
| 936 | 6f. John dory ("Zeus faber") | 2·75 | 10 |
| 937 | 11f. Scribbled cowfish ("Lactophrys quadricornis") | 3·00 | 20 |
| 938 | 11f. Ocean surgeonfish ("Acanthurus bahianus") | 3·00 | 20 |
| 939 | 11f. Queen triggerfish ("Balistes vetula") | 3·00 | 20 |
| 940 | 11f. Queen angelfish ("Holocanthus ciliaris") | 3·00 | 20 |
| 941 | 10f. Type **99** (air) | 45 | 10 |
| 942 | 10f. As No. 918 | 45 | 10 |
| 943 | 10f. As No. 919 | 45 | 10 |
| 944 | 10f. As No. 920 | 45 | 10 |
| 945 | 14f. As No. 921 | 95 | 10 |
| 946 | 14f. As No. 922 | 95 | 10 |
| 947 | 14f. As No. 923 | 95 | 10 |
| 948 | 14f. As No. 924 | 95 | 10 |
| 949 | 17f. As No. 925 | 95 | 10 |
| 950 | 17f. As No. 926 | 95 | 10 |
| 951 | 17f. As No. 927 | 95 | 10 |
| 952 | 17f. As No. 928 | 95 | 10 |
| 953 | 24f. As No. 929 | 2·10 | 10 |
| 954 | 24f. As No. 930 | 2·10 | 10 |
| 955 | 24f. As No. 931 | 2·10 | 10 |
| 956 | 24f. As No. 932 | 2·10 | 10 |
| 957 | 26f. As No. 933 | 3·00 | 20 |
| 958 | 26f. As No. 934 | 3·00 | 20 |
| 959 | 26f. As No. 935 | 3·00 | 20 |
| 960 | 26f. As No. 936 | 3·00 | 20 |
| 961 | 31f. As No. 937 | 3·75 | 30 |
| 962 | 31f. As No. 938 | 3·75 | 30 |
| 963 | 31f. As No. 939 | 3·75 | 30 |
| 964 | 31f. As No. 940 | 3·75 | 30 |

The four designs of each value are arranged together in se-tenant blocks of four within the sheet, forming composite designs.

**100** Footballers and World Cup Trophy

**1974.** World Cup Football Championships.

| | | | | |
|---|---|---|---|---|
| 965 | **100** | 5f. mult (postage) | 25 | 10 |
| 966 | - | 6f. multicoloured | 30 | 10 |
| 967 | - | 11f. multicoloured | 40 | 20 |
| 968 | - | 14f. multicoloured | 50 | 25 |
| 969 | - | 17f. multicoloured | 55 | 25 |
| 970 | - | 20f. multicoloured (air) | 70 | 35 |
| 971 | - | 26f. multicoloured | 90 | 45 |
| 972 | - | 40f. multicoloured | 1·40 | 60 |

**MS**973 88×142 mm. As Nos. 970/2 but without airmail inscriptions 3·00 1·40

DESIGNS: Nos. 966/72, Football scenes as Type **100**.

**101** Burundi Flag

**1974.** Centenary of UPU. Multicoloured.

| | | | |
|---|---|---|---|
| 974 | 6f. Type **101** (postage) | 20 | 10 |
| 975 | 6f. Burundi P.T.T. Building | 20 | 10 |
| 976 | 11f. Postmen carrying letters | 30 | 10 |
| 977 | 11f. Postmen carrying letters | 30 | 10 |
| 978 | 14f. UPU Monument | 1·25 | 70 |
| 979 | 14f. Mail transport | 1·25 | 70 |
| 980 | 17f. Burundi on map | 55 | 10 |
| 981 | 17f. Dove and letter | 55 | 10 |
| 982 | 24f. Type **101** (air) | 80 | 20 |
| 983 | 24f. As No. 975 | 80 | 20 |
| 984 | 26f. As No. 976 | 1·10 | 30 |
| 985 | 26f. As No. 977 | 1·10 | 30 |
| 986 | 31f. As No. 978 | 2·75 | 1·10 |
| 987 | 31f. As No. 979 | 2·75 | 1·10 |
| 988 | 40f. As No. 980 | 3·50 | 45 |
| 989 | 40f. As No. 981 | 3·50 | 45 |

**MS**990 Two sheets each 96×164 mm. (a) Nos. 974/81; (b) Nos. 982/9 20·00 6·00

The two designs in each denomination were arranged together in se-tenant pairs within the sheet, each pair forming a composite design.

**102** "St. Ildefonse writing a letter" (El Greco)

**1974.** International Letter-writing Week. Mult.

| | | | |
|---|---|---|---|
| 991 | 6f. Type **102** | 30 | 15 |
| 992 | 11f. "Lady sealing a letter" (Chardin) | 50 | 20 |
| 993 | 14f. "Titus at desk" (Rembrandt) | 55 | 30 |
| 994 | 17f. "The Love-letter" (Vermeer) | 60 | 30 |
| 995 | 26f. "The Merchant G. Gisze" (Holbein) | 65 | 50 |
| 996 | 31f. "A. Lenoir" (David) | 90 | 55 |

**MS**997 95×105 mm. Nos. 955/6 1·50 1·00

**103** "Virgin and Child". (Van Orley)

**1974.** Christmas. Showing "Virgin and Child" paintings by artists named. Multicoloured.

| | | | |
|---|---|---|---|
| 998 | 5f. Type **103** (postage) | 25 | 10 |
| 999 | 10f. Hans Memling | 45 | 15 |
| 1000 | 15f. Botticelli | 1·00 | 20 |
| 1001 | 18f. Hans Memling (different) (air) | 35 | 20 |
| 1002 | 27f. F. Lippi | 1·10 | 35 |
| 1003 | 40f. L. di Gredi | 1·50 | 45 |

**MS**1004 Two sheets each 126×89 mm. (a) Nos. 998/1000; (b) Nos. 1001/3 4·50 1·50

**1974.** Christmas Charity. Nos. 998/1003 surch.

| | | | | |
|---|---|---|---|---|
| 1005 | **103** | 5f.+1f. mult (postage) | 30 | 10 |
| 1006 | - | 10f.+1f. multicoloured | 40 | 25 |
| 1007 | - | 15f.+1f. multicoloured | 1·10 | 30 |
| 1008 | - | 18f.+1f. mult (air) | 55 | 20 |
| 1009 | - | 27f.+1f. multicoloured | 85 | 35 |
| 1010 | - | 40f.+1f. multicoloured | 1·60 | 45 |

**MS**1011 Two sheets as **MS**1004 with 2f. premium on each stamp 4·50 1·50

**104** "Apollo" Spacecraft with Docking Tunnel

**1975.** "Apollo–Soyuz" Space Project.

| | | | |
|---|---|---|---|
| 1012 | 26f. Type **104** (postage) | 45 | 30 |
| 1013 | 26f. Leonov and Kubasov | 45 | 30 |
| 1014 | 26f. "Soyuz" Spacecraft | 45 | 30 |
| 1015 | 26f. Slayton, Brand and Stafford | 45 | 30 |
| 1016 | 31f. "Soyuz" launch | 55 | 40 |
| 1017 | 31f. "Apollo" and "Soyuz" spacecraft | 55 | 40 |
| 1018 | 31f. "Apollo" third stage separation | 55 | 40 |
| 1019 | 31f. Slayton, Brand, Stafford, Leonov and Kubasov | 55 | 40 |
| 1020 | 27f. Type **104** (air) | 60 | 45 |
| 1021 | 27f. As No. 1012 | 60 | 45 |
| 1022 | 27f. As No. 1013 | 60 | 45 |
| 1023 | 27f. As No. 1014 | 60 | 45 |
| 1024 | 40f. As No. 1015 | 80 | 60 |
| 1025 | 40f. As No. 1016 | 80 | 60 |
| 1026 | 40f. As No. 1017 | 80 | 60 |
| 1027 | 40f. As No. 1018 | 80 | 60 |

The four designs in each value were issued together in se-tenant blocks of four within the sheet.

**105** Addax

**1975.** African Animals (2nd series). Multicoloured.

| | | | |
|---|---|---|---|
| 1028 | 1f. Type **105** (postage) | 40 | 15 |
| 1029 | 1f. Roan antelope | 40 | 15 |
| 1030 | 1f. Nyala | 40 | 15 |
| 1031 | 1f. White rhinoceros | 40 | 15 |
| 1032 | 2f. Mandrill | 40 | 15 |
| 1033 | 2f. Eland | 40 | 15 |
| 1034 | 2f. Salt's dik-dik | 40 | 15 |
| 1035 | 2f. Thomson's gazelles | 40 | 15 |
| 1036 | 3f. African claw-less otter | 55 | 15 |
| 1037 | 3f. Bohar reedbuck | 55 | 15 |
| 1038 | 3f. African civet | 55 | 15 |
| 1039 | 3f. African buffalo | 55 | 15 |
| 1040 | 5f. Black wildebeest | 55 | 15 |
| 1041 | 5f. African asses | 55 | 15 |
| 1042 | 5f. Angolan black and white colobus | 55 | 15 |
| 1043 | 5f. Gerenuk | 55 | 15 |
| 1044 | 6f. Addra gazelle | 95 | 20 |
| 1045 | 6f. Black-backed jackal | 95 | 20 |
| 1046 | 6f. Sitatungas | 95 | 20 |
| 1047 | 6f. Banded duiker | 95 | 20 |
| 1048 | 11f. Fennec fox | 1·40 | 20 |
| 1049 | 11f. Lesser kudus | 1·40 | 20 |
| 1050 | 11f. Blesbok | 1·40 | 20 |
| 1051 | 11f. Serval | 1·40 | 20 |
| 1052 | 10f. Type **105** (air) | 60 | 10 |
| 1053 | 10f. As No. 1029 | 60 | 10 |
| 1054 | 10f. As No. 1030 | 60 | 10 |
| 1055 | 10f. As No. 1031 | 60 | 10 |
| 1056 | 14f. As No. 1032 | 70 | 15 |
| 1057 | 14f. As No. 1033 | 70 | 15 |
| 1058 | 14f. As No. 1034 | 70 | 15 |
| 1059 | 14f. As No. 1035 | 70 | 15 |
| 1060 | 17f. As No. 1036 | 1·10 | 15 |
| 1061 | 17f. As No. 1037 | 1·10 | 15 |
| 1062 | 17f. As No. 1038 | 1·10 | 15 |
| 1063 | 17f. As No. 1039 | 1·10 | 15 |
| 1064 | 24f. As No. 1040 | 1·75 | 20 |
| 1065 | 24f. As No. 1041 | 1·75 | 20 |
| 1066 | 24f. As No. 1042 | 1·75 | 20 |
| 1067 | 24f. As No. 1043 | 1·75 | 20 |
| 1068 | 26f. As No. 1044 | 1·90 | 20 |
| 1069 | 26f. As No. 1045 | 1·90 | 20 |
| 1070 | 26f. As No. 1046 | 1·90 | 20 |
| 1071 | 26f. As No. 1047 | 1·90 | 20 |
| 1072 | 31f. As No. 1048 | 2·25 | 25 |
| 1073 | 31f. As No. 1049 | 2·25 | 25 |
| 1074 | 31f. As No. 1050 | 2·25 | 25 |
| 1075 | 31f. As No. 1051 | 2·25 | 25 |

The four designs in each value were issued together in horiz. se-tenant strips within the sheet, forming composite designs.

**1975.** Air. International Women's Year. Nos. 1052/9 optd ANNEE INTERNATIONALE DE LA FEMME.

| | | | | |
|---|---|---|---|---|
| 1076 | **105** | 10f. multicoloured | 80 | 50 |
| 1077 | - | 10f. multicoloured | 80 | 50 |
| 1078 | - | 10f. multicoloured | 80 | 50 |
| 1079 | - | 10f. multicoloured | 80 | 50 |
| 1080 | - | 14f. multicoloured | 1·40 | 60 |
| 1081 | - | 14f. multicoloured | 1·40 | 60 |
| 1082 | - | 14f. multicoloured | 1·40 | 60 |
| 1083 | - | 14f. multicoloured | 1·40 | 60 |

**1975.** Air. 30th Anniv of United Nations. Nos. 1068/75 optd 30eme ANNIVERSAIRE DES NATIONS UNIES.

| | | | |
|---|---|---|---|
| 1084 | 26f. multicoloured | 1·40 | 1·25 |
| 1085 | 26f. multicoloured | 1·40 | 1·25 |
| 1086 | 26f. multicoloured | 1·40 | 1·25 |
| 1087 | 26f. multicoloured | 1·40 | 1·25 |
| 1088 | 31f. multicoloured | 2·25 | 2·00 |
| 1089 | 31f. multicoloured | 2·25 | 2·00 |
| 1090 | 31f. multicoloured | 2·25 | 2·00 |
| 1091 | 31f. multicoloured | 2·25 | 2·00 |

**108** "Jonah"

**1975.** Christmas. 500th Birth Anniv of Michaelangelo. Multicoloured.

| | | | |
|---|---|---|---|
| 1092 | 5f. Type **108** (postage) | 25 | 10 |
| 1093 | 5f. "Libyan Sibyl" | 25 | 10 |
| 1094 | 13f. "Daniel" | 90 | 10 |
| 1095 | 13f. "Cumaean Sybil" | 90 | 10 |
| 1096 | 27f. "Isaiah" | 1·25 | 15 |
| 1097 | 27f. "Delphic Sybil" (different) | 1·25 | 15 |
| 1098 | 18f. "Zachariah" (air) | 90 | 10 |
| 1099 | 18f. "Joel" | 90 | 10 |
| 1100 | 31f. "Erythraean Sybil" | 1·60 | 30 |
| 1101 | 31f. "Ezekiel" | 1·60 | 30 |
| 1102 | 40f. "Persian Sybil" | 2·00 | 35 |
| 1103 | 40f. "Jeremiah" | 2·00 | 35 |
| **MS**1104 | Two sheets each 138×111 mm. (a) Nos. 1092/7; (b) Nos. 1098/1103 | 14·00 | 2·25 |

**1975.** Christmas Charity. Nos. 1092/1103 surch +1F.

| | | | | |
|---|---|---|---|---|
| 1105 | **108** | 5f.+1f. mult (postage) | 45 | 10 |
| 1106 | - | 5f.+1f. multicoloured | 45 | 10 |
| 1107 | - | 13f.+1f. multicoloured | 75 | 10 |
| 1108 | - | 13f.+1f. multicoloured | 75 | 10 |
| 1109 | - | 27f.+1f. multicoloured | 1·25 | 15 |
| 1110 | - | 27f.+1f. multicoloured | 1·25 | 15 |
| 1111 | - | 18f.+1f. mult (air) | 1·00 | 10 |
| 1112 | - | 18f.+1f. multicoloured | 1·00 | 10 |
| 1113 | - | 31f.+1f. multicoloured | 1·60 | 30 |
| 1114 | - | 31f.+1f. multicoloured | 1·60 | 30 |
| 1115 | - | 40f.+1f. multicoloured | 1·90 | 35 |
| 1116 | - | 40f.+1f. multicoloured | 1·90 | 35 |
| **MS**1117 | | Two sheets as **MS**1104 with 2f. premium on each stamp | 14·00 | 2·25 |

**110** Speed Skating

**1976.** Winter Olympic Games, Innsbruck. Mult.

| | | | |
|---|---|---|---|
| 1118 | 17f. Type **110** (postage) | 45 | 20 |
| 1119 | 24f. Figure-skating | 50 | 20 |
| 1120 | 26f. Two-man bobsleigh | 60 | 20 |
| 1121 | 31f. Cross-country skiing | 70 | 30 |
| 1122 | 18f. Ski-jumping (air) | 40 | 25 |
| 1123 | 36f. Skiing (slalom) | 1·50 | 40 |
| 1124 | 50f. Ice-hockey | 1·60 | 60 |
| **MS**1125 | Two sheets (a) 101×101 mm. Nos. 1118/21; (b) 131×131 mm. Nos. 1122/4 | 5·75 | 2·10 |

**111** Basketball

**1976.** Olympic Games, Montreal. Multicoloured.

| | | | |
|---|---|---|---|
| 1126 | 14f. Type **111** (postage) | 40 | 30 |
| 1127 | 14f. Pole-vaulting | 40 | 30 |
| 1128 | 17f. Running | 60 | 45 |
| 1129 | 17f. Football | 60 | 45 |
| 1130 | 28f. As No. 1127 | 90 | 65 |
| 1131 | 28f. As No. 1128 | 90 | 65 |
| 1132 | 40f. As No. 1129 | 1·50 | 1·10 |
| 1133 | 40f. Type **111** | 1·50 | 1·10 |
| 1134 | 27f. Hurdling (air) | 90 | 65 |
| 1135 | 27f. High-jumping (horiz) | 90 | 65 |
| 1136 | 31f. Gymnastics (horiz) | 1·25 | 90 |
| 1137 | 31f. As No. 1134 (horiz) | 1·25 | 90 |
| 1138 | 50f. As No. 1135 (horiz) | 1·90 | 1·40 |
| 1139 | 50f. As No. 1136 (horiz) | 1·90 | 1·40 |
| **MS**1140 | Two sheets. (a) 115×120 mm. 14f. Football; 17f. Pole vault; 28f. Basketball; 40f. Running (postage). (b) 99×120 mm. 27f. Gymnastics; 31f. High jump; 50f. Hurdles (air) | 7·00 | 5·50 |

**112** "Battle of Bunker Hill" (detail, John Trumbull)

**1976.** Air. Bicent of American Revolution. Mult.

| | | | |
|---|---|---|---|
| 1141 | 18f. Type **112** | 55 | 15 |
| 1142 | 18f. As Type **112** | 55 | 15 |
| 1143 | 26f. Franklin, Jefferson and John Adams | 75 | 25 |
| 1144 | 26f. As No. 1143 | 75 | 25 |
| 1145 | 36f. "Signing of Declaration of Independence" (Trumbull) | 1·25 | 35 |
| 1146 | 36f. As No. 1145 | 1·25 | 35 |
| **MS**1147 | 101×148 mm. Nos. 1141/6 | 5·00 | 1·50 |

The two designs of each value form composite pictures. Type **112** is the left-hand portion of the painting.

**113** "Virgin and Child" (Dirk Bouts)

**1976.** Christmas. Multicoloured.

| | | | |
|---|---|---|---|
| 1148 | 5f. Type **113** (postage) | 35 | 10 |
| 1149 | 13f. "Virgin of the Trees" (Bellini) | 65 | 10 |
| 1150 | 27f. "Virgin and Child" (C. Crivelli) | 1·00 | 25 |
| 1151 | 18f. "Virgin and Child" with St. Anne" (Leonardo) (air) | 80 | 30 |
| 1152 | 31f. "Holy Family with Lamb" (Raphael) | 1·10 | 60 |
| 1153 | 40f. "Virgin with Basket" (Correggio) | 1·60 | 70 |
| **MS**1154 | Two sheets each 122×80 mm. (a) Nos. 1148/50; (b) Nos. 1151/3 | 5·50 | 2·00 |

**1976.** Christmas Charity. Nos. 1148/53 surch +1F.

| | | | | |
|---|---|---|---|---|
| 1155 | **113** | 5f.+1f. mult (postage) | 25 | 10 |
| 1156 | - | 13f.+1f. multicoloured | 70 | 30 |
| 1157 | - | 27f.+1f. multicoloured | 1·10 | 50 |
| 1158 | - | 18f.+1f. mult (air) | 60 | 30 |
| 1159 | - | 31f.+1f. multicoloured | 1·00 | 45 |
| 1160 | - | 40f.+1f. multicoloured | 1·90 | 65 |
| **MS**1161 | | Two sheets as **MS**1154 with 2f. premium on each stamp | 5·50 | 2·00 |

**115** "The Ascent of Calvary" (Rubens)

**1977.** Easter. 400th Birth Anniv of Peter Paul Rubens. Multicoloured.

| | | | |
|---|---|---|---|
| 1162 | 10f. Type **115** | 35 | 25 |
| 1163 | 21f. "Christ Crucified" | 95 | 70 |
| 1164 | 27f. "The Descent from the Cross" | 1·10 | 80 |
| 1165 | 35f. "The Deposition" | 1·50 | 1·10 |
| **MS**1166 | 111×85 mm. As Nos. 1162/5 (air) | 4·00 | 2·70 |

**116** Alexander Graham Bell

**1977.** Telephone Centenary and World Telecommunications Day. Multicoloured.

| | | | |
|---|---|---|---|
| 1167 | 10f. Type **116** (postage) | 25 | 15 |
| 1168 | 10f. Satellite, Globe and telephones | 25 | 15 |
| 1169 | 17f. Switchboard operator and wall telephone | 45 | 30 |
| 1170 | 17f. Satellite transmitting to Earth | 45 | 30 |
| 1171 | 26f. A. G. Bell and first telephone | 80 | 60 |
| 1172 | 26f. Satellites circling Globe, and videophone | 80 | 60 |
| 1173 | 18f. Type **116** (air) | 40 | 30 |
| 1174 | 18f. As No. 1172 | 40 | 30 |
| 1175 | 36f. As No. 1169 | 1·10 | 80 |
| 1176 | 36f. As No. 1168 | 1·10 | 80 |
| **MS**1177 | 120×135 mm. 10f. As No. 1171; 17f. Type **116**; 26f. As No. 1168; 18f. As No. 1170; 36f. As No. 1172 | 3·25 | 2·00 |

**117** Kobs

**1977.** African Animals (3rd series). Multicoloured.

| | | | |
|---|---|---|---|
| 1178 | 2f. Type **117** (postage) | 75 | 20 |
| 1179 | 2f. Marabou storks | 75 | 20 |
| 1180 | 2f. Blue wildebeest | 75 | 20 |
| 1181 | 2f. Bush pig | 75 | 20 |
| 1182 | 5f. Grevy's zebras | 85 | 20 |
| 1183 | 5f. Whale-headed stork | 85 | 20 |
| 1184 | 5f. Striped hyenas | 85 | 20 |
| 1185 | 5f. Pygmy chimpanzee | 85 | 20 |
| 1186 | 8f. Greater flamingoes | 95 | 20 |
| 1187 | 8f. Nile crocodiles | 95 | 20 |
| 1188 | 8f. Green tree snake | 95 | 20 |
| 1189 | 8f. Greater kudus | 95 | 20 |
| 1190 | 11f. Large-toothed rock hyrax | 1·00 | 20 |
| 1191 | 11f. Cobra | 1·00 | 20 |
| 1192 | 11f. Golden jackals | 1·00 | 20 |
| 1193 | 11f. Verreaux eagles | 1·00 | 20 |
| 1194 | 21f. Ratel | 1·25 | 30 |
| 1195 | 21f. Bushbuck | 1·25 | 30 |
| 1196 | 21f. Secretary bird | 1·25 | 30 |
| 1197 | 21f. Klipspringer | 1·25 | 30 |
| 1198 | 27f. Bat-eared fox | 1·60 | 30 |
| 1199 | 27f. African elephants | 1·60 | 30 |
| 1200 | 27f. Vulturine guineafowl | 1·60 | 30 |
| 1201 | 27f. Impalas | 1·60 | 30 |
| 1202 | 9f. Type **117** (air) | 60 | 25 |
| 1203 | 9f. As No. 1179 | 60 | 25 |
| 1204 | 9f. As No. 1180 | 60 | 25 |
| 1205 | 9f. As No. 1181 | 60 | 25 |
| 1206 | 13f. As No. 1182 | 85 | 30 |
| 1207 | 13f. As No. 1183 | 85 | 30 |
| 1208 | 13f. As No. 1184 | 85 | 30 |
| 1209 | 13f. As No. 1185 | 85 | 30 |
| 1210 | 30f. As No. 1186 | 1·25 | 50 |
| 1211 | 30f. As No. 1187 | 1·25 | 50 |
| 1212 | 30f. As No. 1188 | 1·25 | 50 |
| 1213 | 30f. As No. 1189 | 1·25 | 50 |
| 1214 | 35f. As No. 1190 | 1·40 | 60 |
| 1215 | 35f. As No. 1191 | 1·40 | 60 |
| 1216 | 35f. As No. 1192 | 1·40 | 60 |
| 1217 | 35f. As No. 1193 | 1·40 | 60 |
| 1218 | 54f. As No. 1194 | 2·40 | 70 |
| 1219 | 54f. As No. 1195 | 2·40 | 70 |
| 1220 | 54f. As No. 1196 | 2·40 | 70 |
| 1221 | 54f. As No. 1197 | 2·40 | 70 |
| 1222 | 70f. As No. 1198 | 3·25 | 85 |
| 1223 | 70f. As No. 1199 | 3·25 | 85 |
| 1224 | 70f. As No. 1200 | 3·25 | 85 |
| 1225 | 70f. As No. 1201 | 3·25 | 85 |

The four designs in each value were issued together se-tenant in horizontal strips within the sheet, forming composite designs.

**118** "The Man of Iron" (Grimm)

**1977.** Fairy Tales. Multicoloured.

| | | | |
|---|---|---|---|
| 1226 | 5f. Type **118** | 20 | 10 |
| 1227 | 5f. "Snow White and Rose Red" (Grimm) | 20 | 10 |
| 1228 | 5f. "The Goose Girl" (Grimm) | 20 | 10 |
| 1229 | 5f. "The Two Wanderers" (Grimm) | 20 | 10 |

| | | | |
|---|---|---|---|
| 1230 | 11f. "The Hermit and the Bear" (Aesop) | 60 | 10 |
| 1231 | 11f. "The Fox and the Stork" (Aesop) | 60 | 10 |
| 1232 | 11f. "The Litigious Cats" (Aesop) | 60 | 10 |
| 1233 | 11f. "The Blind and the Lame" (Aesop) | 60 | 10 |
| 1234 | 14f. "The Ice Maiden" (Andersen) | 70 | 10 |
| 1235 | 14f. "The Old House" (Andersen) | 70 | 10 |
| 1236 | 14f. "The Princess and the Pea" (Andersen) | 70 | 10 |
| 1237 | 14f. "The Elder Tree Mother" (Andersen) | 70 | 10 |
| 1238 | 17f. "Hen with the Golden Eggs" (La Fontaine) | 80 | 15 |
| 1239 | 17f. "The Wolf Turned Shepherd" (La Fontaine) | 80 | 15 |
| 1240 | 17f. "The Oyster and Litigants" (La Fontaine) | 80 | 15 |
| 1241 | 17f. "The Wolf and the Lamb" (La Fontaine) | 80 | 15 |
| 1242 | 26f. "Jack and the Beanstalk" (traditional) | 1·60 | 25 |
| 1243 | 26f. "Alice in Wonderland) (Lewis Carroll) | 1·60 | 25 |
| 1244 | 26f. "Three Heads in the Well" (traditional) | 1·60 | 25 |
| 1245 | 26f. "Tales of Mother Goose" (traditional) | 1·60 | 25 |

**119** UN General Assembly and UN 3c. Stamp, 1954

**1977.** 25th Anniv of United Nations Postal Administration. Multicoloured.

| | | | |
|---|---|---|---|
| 1246 | 8f. Type **119** (postage) | 40 | 30 |
| 1247 | 8f. UN 4c. stamp, 1957 | 40 | 30 |
| 1248 | 8f. UN 3c. stamp, 1954 (FAO) | 40 | 30 |
| 1249 | 8f. UN 1½c. stamp, 1951 | 40 | 30 |
| 1250 | 10f. Security Council and UN 8c. red, 1954 | 50 | 35 |
| 1251 | 10f. UN 8c. green, 1956 | 50 | 35 |
| 1252 | 10f. UN 8c. black, 1955 | 50 | 35 |
| 1253 | 10f. UN 7c. stamp, 1959 | 50 | 35 |
| 1254 | 21f. Meeting hall and UN 3c. grey, 1956 | 80 | 60 |
| 1255 | 21f. UN 8c. stamp, 1956 | 80 | 60 |
| 1256 | 21f. UN 3c. brown, 1953 | 80 | 60 |
| 1257 | 21f. UN 3c. green, 1952 | 80 | 60 |
| 1258 | 24f. Building by night and UN 4c. red, 1957 (air) | 80 | 60 |
| 1259 | 24f. UN 8c. brn & grn, 1960 | 80 | 60 |
| 1260 | 24f. UN 8c. green, 1955 | 80 | 60 |
| 1261 | 24f. UN 8c. red, 1955 | 80 | 60 |
| 1262 | 27f. Aerial view of UN 8c. red, 1957 | 90 | 65 |
| 1263 | 27f. UN 3c. stamp, 1953 | 90 | 65 |
| 1264 | 27f. UN 8c. green, 1954 | 90 | 65 |
| 1265 | 27f. UN 8c. brown, 1956 | 90 | 65 |
| 1266 | 35f. UN Building by day and UN 5c. stamp, 1959 | 1·40 | 1·00 |
| 1267 | 35f. UN 3c. stamp, 1962 | 1·40 | 1·00 |
| 1268 | 35f. UN 3c. bl & pur, 1951 | 1·40 | 1·00 |
| 1269 | 35f. UN 1c. stamp, 1951 | 1·40 | 1·00 |
| **MS**1270 | Two sheets each 127×76 mm. (a) 8f. As No. 1253; 10f. As No. 1255; 21f. As No. 1248. (b) 24f. As No. 1263; 27f. As No. 1266; 35f. As No. 1260 | 4·75 | 3·30 |

The four designs in each value were issued together in se-tenant blocks of four, each design in the block having the same background.

**120** "Virgin and Child" (Jean Lambardos)

**1977.** Christmas. Paintings of Virgin and Child by artists named. Multicoloured.

| | | | |
|---|---|---|---|
| 1271 | 5f. Type **120** (postage) | 15 | 10 |
| 1272 | 13f. Melides Toscano | 65 | 50 |
| 1273 | 27f. Emmanuel Tzanes | 95 | 70 |
| 1274 | 18f. Master of Moulins (air) | 50 | 35 |
| 1275 | 31f. Lorenzo di Credi | 1·00 | 75 |
| 1276 | 40f. Palma the Elder | 1·25 | 90 |
| **MS**1277 | Two sheets each 130×72 mm. (a) Nos. 1271/3. (b) Nos. 1274/6 | 4·50 | 3·25 |

**121** Cruiser "Aurora" and Russian 5r. Stamp, 1922

**1977.** 60th Anniv of Russian Revolution. Mult.

| | | | |
|---|---|---|---|
| 1278 | 5f. Type **121** | 40 | 10 |
| 1279 | 5f. Russia S.G. 455 | 40 | 10 |
| 1280 | 5f. Russia S.G. 1392 | 40 | 10 |
| 1281 | 5f. Russia S.G. 199 | 40 | 10 |
| 1282 | 8f. Decemberists' Square, Leningrad and Russia S.G. 983 | 25 | 10 |
| 1283 | 8f. Russia S.G. 2122 | 25 | 10 |
| 1284 | 8f. Russia S.G. 1041 | 25 | 10 |
| 1285 | 8f. Russia S.G. 2653 | 25 | 10 |
| 1286 | 11f. Pokrovski Cathedral, Moscow and Russia S.G. 3929 | 45 | 10 |
| 1287 | 11f. Russia S.G. 3540 | 45 | 10 |
| 1288 | 11f. Russia S.G. 3468 | 45 | 10 |
| 1289 | 11f. Russia S.G. 3921 | 45 | 10 |
| 1290 | 13f. May Day celebrations, Moscow and Russia S.G. 4518 | 60 | 15 |
| 1291 | 13f. Russia S.G. 3585 | 60 | 15 |
| 1292 | 13f. Russia S.G. 3024 | 60 | 15 |
| 1293 | 13f. Russia S.G. 2471 | 60 | 15 |

The four designs in each value were issued in se-tenant blocks of four, each design in the block having the same background.

**122** Tanker Unloading (Commerce)

**1977.** 15th Anniv of Independence. Mult.

| | | | |
|---|---|---|---|
| 1294 | 1f. Type **122** | 20 | 15 |
| 1295 | 5f. Assembling electric armatures (Economy) | 20 | 15 |
| 1296 | 11f. Native dancers (Tourism) | 30 | 20 |
| 1297 | 14f. Picking coffee (Agriculture) | 45 | 30 |
| 1298 | 17f. National Palace, Bujumbura | 55 | 40 |

**1977.** Christmas Charity. Nos. 1271/6 surch +1F.

| | | | | |
|---|---|---|---|---|
| 1299 | **120** | 5f.+1f. mult (postage) | 30 | 15 |
| 1300 | - | 13f.+1f. multicoloured | 65 | 20 |
| 1301 | - | 27f.+1f. multicoloured | 95 | 45 |
| 1302 | - | 18f.+1f. mult (air) | 65 | 25 |
| 1303 | - | 31f.+1f. multicoloured | 1·00 | 45 |
| 1304 | - | 40f.+1f. multicoloured | 1·60 | 60 |
| **MS**1305 | | Two sheets as **MS**1277 with 2f. premium on each stamp | 4·75 | 3·50 |

**123** "Madonna and Child" (Solario)

**1979.** Christmas (1978). Paintings of Virgin and Child by named artists. Multicoloured.

| | | | |
|---|---|---|---|
| 1306 | 13f. Rubens | 85 | 85 |
| 1307 | 17f. Type **123** | 90 | 90 |
| 1308 | 27f. Tiepolo | 1·40 | 1·40 |
| 1309 | 31f. Gerard David | 1·60 | 1·60 |
| 1310 | 40f. Bellini | 2·00 | 2·00 |
| **MS**1311 | 114×120 mm. Nos. 1306/10 (air) | 6·75 | 6·75 |

**1979.** Christmas Charity. Nos. 1306/10 surch +1F.

| | | | | |
|---|---|---|---|---|
| 1312 | - | 13f.+1f. multicoloured | 85 | 85 |
| 1313 | **123** | 17f.+1f. multicoloured | 90 | 90 |
| 1314 | - | 27f.+1f. multicoloured | 1·40 | 1·40 |
| 1315 | - | 31f.+1f. multicoloured | 1·60 | 1·60 |
| 1316 | - | 40f.+1f. multicoloured | 2·00 | 2·00 |
| **MS**1317 | | As **MS**1311 with 2f. premium on each stamp | 6·75 | 6·75 |

**124** Abyssinian Ground Hornbill

**1979.** Birds. Multicoloured.

| | | | |
|---|---|---|---|
| 1318 | 1f. Type **124** (postage) | 1·10 | 60 |
| 1319 | 2f. African darter | 1·10 | 60 |
| 1320 | 3f. Little bee eater | 1·10 | 60 |
| 1321 | 5f. Lesser flamingo | 1·50 | 80 |
| 1322 | 8f. Congo peafowl | 1·90 | 1·10 |
| 1323 | 10f. Purple swamphen | 2·10 | 1·25 |
| 1324 | 20f. Martial eagle | 2·40 | 1·40 |
| 1325 | 27f. Painted stork | 3·00 | 1·75 |
| 1326 | 50f. Saddle-bill stork | 4·75 | 2·50 |
| 1327 | 6f. Type **124** (air) | 1·75 | 1·00 |
| 1328 | 13f. As No. 1319 | 2·10 | 1·25 |
| 1329 | 18f. As No. 1320 | 2·40 | 1·40 |
| 1330 | 26f. As No. 1321 | 2·75 | 1·60 |
| 1331 | 31f. As No. 1322 | 3·00 | 1·60 |
| 1332 | 36f. As No. 1323 | 3·00 | 1·75 |
| 1333 | 40f. As No. 1324 | 3·75 | 2·10 |
| 1334 | 54f. As No. 1325 | 4·00 | 2·40 |
| 1335 | 70f. As No. 1326 | 5·25 | 3·00 |

**125** Mother and Child

**1979.** International Year of the Child. Mult.

| | | | |
|---|---|---|---|
| 1336 | 10f. Type **125** | 90 | 90 |
| 1337 | 20f. Baby | 1·40 | 1·40 |
| 1338 | 27f. Child with doll | 1·50 | 1·50 |
| 1339 | 50f. S.O.S. village, Gitega | 2·00 | 2·00 |
| **MS**1340 | 131×85 mm. Nos. 1336/9 additionally inscr "+ 2f." | 6·25 | 6·25 |

**126** "Virgin and Child" (Raffaellino Del Garbo)

**1979.** Christmas. "Virgin and Child" paintings by named artists. Multicoloured.

| | | | |
|---|---|---|---|
| 1341 | 20f. Type **126** | 90 | 90 |
| 1342 | 27f. Giovanni Penni | 1·10 | 1·10 |
| 1343 | 31f. Giulio Romano | 1·25 | 1·25 |
| 1344 | 50f. Detail of "Adoration of the Shepherds" (Jacopo Bassano) | 1·75 | 1·75 |
| **MS**1345 | 85×110 mm. Nos. 1341/4 (air) | 5·00 | 5·00 |

**127** Sir Rowland Hill and Penny Black

**1979.** Death Centenary of Sir Rowland Hill. Mult.

| | | | |
|---|---|---|---|
| 1346 | 20f. Type **127** | 80 | 80 |
| 1347 | 27f. German East Africa 25p. stamp and Ruanda-Urundi 5c. stamp | 95 | 95 |
| 1348 | 31f. Burundi 1f.25 and 50f. stamps of 1962 | 1·10 | 1·10 |
| 1349 | 40f. 4f. (1962) and 14f. (1969) stamps of Burundi | 1·25 | 1·25 |
| 1350 | 60f. Heinrich von Stephan (founder of UPU) and Burundi 14f. UPU stamps of 1974 | 6·75 | 3·00 |
| **MS**1351 | 110×105 mm. Nos. 1346/50 | 11·00 | 7·00 |

**1979.** Christmas Charity. Nos. 1341/4 additionally inscr with premium.

| | | | |
|---|---|---|---|
| 1352 | 20f.+1f. multicoloured | 65 | 65 |
| 1353 | 27f.+1f. multicoloured | 1·40 | 1·40 |
| 1354 | 31f.+1f. multicoloured | 1·60 | 1·60 |
| 1355 | 50f.+1f. multicoloured | 2·10 | 2·10 |
| **MS**1356 | 85×110 mm. As **MS**1345 with 2f. premium on each stamp (air) | 11·00 | 7·00 |

**1980.** As Nos. 1318/19 and 1321/3 but new values. (a) With copper frames.

| | |
|---|---|
| 1356a | 5f. Abyssinian ground hornbill |
| 1356b | 10f. African darter |
| 1356c | 40f. Lesser flamingo |
| 1356d | 45f. Congo peafowl |
| 1356e | 50f. Purple swamphen |

(b) With grey-green frames.

| | |
|---|---|
| 1356f | 5f. As No. 1356a |
| 1356g | 10f. As No. 1356b |
| 1356h | 40f. As No. 1356c |
| 1356i | 45f. As No. 1356d |
| 1356j | 50f. As No. 1356e |

**128** Approaching Hurdle (110 m Hurdles, Thomas Munkelt)

**1980.** Olympic Medal Winners. Multicoloured.

| | | | |
|---|---|---|---|
| 1357 | 20f. Type **128** | 95 | 95 |
| 1358 | 20f. Jumping hurdle | 95 | 95 |
| 1359 | 20f. Completing jump | 95 | 95 |
| 1360 | 30f. Discus—beginning to throw | 1·40 | 1·40 |
| 1361 | 30f. Continuing throw | 1·40 | 1·40 |
| 1362 | 30f. Releasing discus | 1·40 | 1·40 |
| 1363 | 40f. Football—running for goal (Czechoslovakia) | 1·50 | 1·50 |
| 1364 | 40f. Kicking ball | 1·50 | 1·50 |
| 1365 | 40f. Saving ball | 1·50 | 1·50 |
| **MS**1366 | 145×111 mm. As Nos. 1357/65 | 8·75 | 8·75 |

**129** "The Virgin and Child" (Sebastiano Mainardi)

**1980.** Christmas. Multicoloured.

| | | | |
|---|---|---|---|
| 1367 | 10f. Type **129** | 90 | 90 |
| 1368 | 30f. "Doni Tondo" (Michelangelo) | 1·50 | 1·50 |
| 1369 | 40f. "The Virgin and Child" (Piero di Cosimo) | 2·10 | 2·10 |
| 1370 | 45f. "The Holy Family" (Fra Bartolomeo) | 2·25 | 2·25 |
| **MS**1371 | 134×103 mm. As Nos. 1367/70 (air) | 6·75 | 6·75 |

**130** Congress Emblem

**1980.** 1st National Party Congress, Uprona.

| | | | | |
|---|---|---|---|---|
| 1372 | **130** | 10f. multicoloured | 30 | 30 |
| 1373 | **130** | 40f. multicoloured | 1·50 | 1·50 |
| 1374 | **130** | 45f. multicoloured | 1·60 | 1·60 |
| **MS**1375 | | 108×68 mm. As Nos. 1372/4 (air) | 3·25 | 3·25 |

**1981.** Christmas Charity. Nos. 1367/70 additionally inscr with premium.

| | | | |
|---|---|---|---|
| 1376 | 10f.+1f. multicoloured | 75 | 75 |
| 1377 | 30f.+1f. multicoloured | 1·75 | 1·75 |
| 1378 | 40f.+1f. multicoloured | 2·25 | 2·25 |
| 1379 | 50f.+1f. multicoloured | 2·50 | 2·50 |
| **MS**1380 | 134×103 mm. As Nos. 1376/9 but each stamp with 2f. premium (air) | 7·25 | 7·25 |

**131** Kepler and Dish Aerial

**1981.** 350th Death Anniv of Johannes Kepler (astronomer). First Earth Satellite Station in Burundi. Multicoloured.

| | | | |
|---|---|---|---|
| 1381 | 10f. Type **131** | 60 | 60 |
| 1382 | 40f. Satellite and antenna | 1·50 | 1·50 |
| 1383 | 45f. Satellite (different) and antenna | 1·90 | 1·90 |
| **MS**1384 | 78×108 mm. Nos. 1381/3 | 3·50 | 3·50 |

**132** Giraffes

**1982.** African Animals (4th series). Multicoloured.

| | | | |
|---|---|---|---|
| 1385 | 2f. Lion | 4·75 | 2·10 |
| 1386 | 3f. Type **132** | 4·75 | 2·10 |
| 1387 | 5f. Black rhinoceros | 4·75 | 2·10 |
| 1388 | 10f. African buffalo | 15·00 | 6·75 |
| 1389 | 20f. African elephant | 23·00 | 11·50 |
| 1390 | 25f. Hippopotamus | 26·00 | 12·50 |
| 1391 | 30f. Common zebra | 30·00 | 14·50 |
| 1392 | 50f. Warthog | 55·00 | 26·00 |
| 1393 | 60f. Eland | 70·00 | 32·00 |
| 1394 | 65f. Black-backed jackal | 85·00 | 40·00 |
| 1395 | 70f. Cheetah | 95·00 | 45·00 |
| 1396 | 75f. Blue Wildebeest | £100 | 48·00 |
| 1397 | 85f. Spotted hyena | £120 | 60·00 |

**1983.** Animal Protection Year. Nos. 1385/97 optd with World Wildlife Fund Emblem.

| | | | |
|---|---|---|---|
| 1398 | 2f. Type **131** | 5·00 | 4·25 |
| 1399 | 3f. Giraffe | 5·00 | 4·25 |
| 1400 | 5f. Black rhinoceros | 5·00 | 4·25 |
| 1401 | 10f. African buffalo | 14·00 | 13·00 |
| 1402 | 20f. African elephant | 23·00 | 20·00 |
| 1403 | 25f. Hippopotamus | 26·00 | 24·00 |
| 1404 | 30f. Common zebra | 28·00 | 25·00 |
| 1405 | 50f. Warthog | 55·00 | 48·00 |
| 1406 | 60f. Eland | 70·00 | 60·00 |
| 1407 | 65f. Jackal ("Canis mesomelas") | 80·00 | 75·00 |
| 1408 | 70f. Cheetah | 95·00 | 80·00 |
| 1409 | 75f. Blue wildebeest | £100 | 90·00 |
| 1410 | 85f. Spotted Hyena | £120 | £110 |

**133** Flag and National Party Emblem

**1983.** 20th Anniv (1982) of Independence. Multicoloured.

| | | | |
|---|---|---|---|
| 1411 | 10f. Type **133** | 65 | 65 |
| 1412 | 25f. Flag and arms | 1·00 | 1·00 |
| 1413 | 30f. Flag and map of Africa | 1·10 | 1·10 |
| 1414 | 50f. Flag and emblem | 1·50 | 1·50 |
| 1415 | 65f. Flag and President Bagaza | 2·00 | 2·00 |

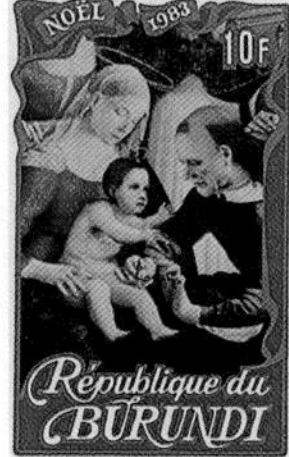

**134** "Virgin and Child" (Lucas Signorelli)

**1983.** Christmas. Multicoloured.

| | | | |
|---|---|---|---|
| 1416 | 10f. Type **134** | 1·10 | 1·10 |
| 1417 | 25f. E. Murillo | 1·50 | 1·50 |
| 1418 | 30f. Carlo Crivelli | 1·75 | 1·75 |
| 1419 | 50f. Nicolas Poussin | 2·40 | 2·40 |
| **MS**1420 | 106×151 mm. As Nos. 1416/19, but with green backgrounds | 6·75 | 6·75 |

DESIGNS: Virgin and Child paintings by named artists.

**1983.** Christmas Charity. Nos. 1416/19 additionally inscr with premium.

| | | | |
|---|---|---|---|
| 1421 | 10f.+1f. multicoloured | 1·10 | 1·10 |
| 1422 | 25f.+1f. multicoloured | 1·50 | 1·50 |
| 1423 | 30f.+1f. multicoloured | 1·75 | 1·75 |
| 1424 | 50f.+1f. multicoloured | 2·40 | 2·40 |
| **MS**1425 | 106×151 mm. As **MS**1420 with 2f. premium on each stamp (air) | 6·75 | 6·75 |

Nos. 1421/4 have green backgrounds; stamps on **MS**1425 have carmine backgrounds.

**135** "Papilio zalmoxis"

**1984.** Butterflies. Multicoloured.

| | | | |
|---|---|---|---|
| 1426 | 5f. Type **135** | 2·00 | 85 |
| 1427 | 5f. "Cymothoe coccinata" | 2·00 | 85 |
| 1428 | 10f. "Papilio antimachus" | 4·75 | 2·10 |
| 1429 | 10f. "Asterope pechueli" | 4·75 | 2·10 |
| 1430 | 30f. "Bebearia mardania" | 9·25 | 4·00 |
| 1431 | 30f. "Papilio hesperus" | 9·25 | 4·00 |
| 1432 | 35f. "Euphaedra perseis" | 12·00 | 5·25 |
| 1433 | 35f. "Euphaedra neophron" | 12·00 | 5·25 |
| 1434 | 65f. "Pseudacraea striata" | 22·00 | 9·75 |
| 1435 | 65f. "Euphaedra imperialis" | 22·00 | 9·75 |

**136** Stamps of German East Africa and Belgian Occupation

**1984.** 19th U.P.U. Congress, Hamburg. Mult.

| | | | |
|---|---|---|---|
| 1436 | 10f. Type **136** | 65 | 65 |
| 1437 | 30f. 1962 Burundi overprinted stamps | 1·10 | 1·10 |
| 1438 | 35f. 1969 14f. Letter-writing Week and 1982 30f. Zebra stamps | 1·25 | 1·25 |
| 1439 | 65f. Heinrich von Stephan (founder of UPU) and 1974 14f. UPU Centenary stamps | 18·00 | 11·50 |
| **MS**1440 | 147×84 mm. As Nos. 1436/9 but each 39×31 mm (air) | 21·00 | 15·00 |

**137** Jesse Owens (runner)

**1984.** Olympic Games, Los Angeles. Mult.

| | | | |
|---|---|---|---|
| 1441 | 10f. Type **137** | 1·10 | 1·10 |
| 1442 | 30f. Rafer Johnson (discus thrower) | 1·60 | 1·60 |
| 1443 | 35f. Bob Beamon (long jumper) | 1·75 | 1·75 |
| 1444 | 65f. K. Keino (sprinter) | 2·25 | 2·25 |
| **MS**1445 | 119×99 mm. As Nos. 1441/4 but some colours changed (air) | 6·75 | 6·75 |

**138** "Virgin and Child" (Botticelli)

**1984.** Christmas. Multicoloured.

| | | | |
|---|---|---|---|
| 1446 | 10f. "Rest on the Flight into Egypt" (Murillo) | 30 | 30 |
| 1447 | 25f. "Virgin and Child" (R. del Garbo) | 1·10 | 1·10 |
| 1448 | 30f. Type **138** | 1·60 | 1·60 |
| 1449 | 50f. "Adoration of the Shepherds" (J. Bassano) | 2·00 | 2·00 |
| **MS**1450 | 125×92 mm. As Nos. 1446/9 but some colours changed. Olive border | 5·00 | 5·00 |

**1984.** Christmas Charity. As Nos. 1446/49 but with additional premium.

| | | | |
|---|---|---|---|
| 1451 | 10f.+1f. multicoloured | 30 | 30 |
| 1452 | 25f.+1f. multicoloured | 1·10 | 1·10 |
| 1453 | 30f.+1f. multicoloured | 1·60 | 1·60 |
| 1454 | 50f.+1f. multicoloured | 2·00 | 2·00 |
| **MS**1455 | 125×92 mm. As No. **MS**1450 with 2f. premium on each stamp (air) | 5·00 | 5·00 |

**139** Thunbergia

**1986.** Flowers. Multicoloured.

| | | | |
|---|---|---|---|
| 1456 | 2f. Type **139** (postage) | 1·40 | 80 |
| 1457 | 3f. African violets | 1·40 | 80 |
| 1458 | 5f. "Clivia" | 1·40 | 80 |
| 1459 | 10f. "Cassia" | 1·40 | 80 |
| 1460 | 20f. Bird of Paradise flower | 2·50 | 1·60 |
| 1461 | 35f. "Gloriosa" | 4·50 | 3·00 |
| 1462 | 70f. Type **139** (air) | 2·50 | 2·10 |
| 1463 | 75f. As No. 1457 | 2·75 | 2·25 |
| 1464 | 80f. As No. 1458 | 2·75 | 2·40 |
| 1465 | 85f. As No. 1459 | 3·25 | 2·75 |
| 1466 | 100f. As No. 1460 | 3·50 | 2·75 |
| 1467 | 150f. As No. 1461 | 6·00 | 5·00 |

**140** Bombs as Flats

**1987.** International Peace Year (1986). Mult.

| | | | |
|---|---|---|---|
| 1468 | 10f. Type **140** | 20 | 20 |
| 1469 | 20f. Molecular diagrams as flower | 40 | 40 |
| 1470 | 30f. Clasped hands across globe | 1·10 | 1·10 |
| 1471 | 40f. Chicks in split globe | 1·25 | 1·25 |
| **MS**1472 | 85×120 mm. Nos. 1468/71 | 3·00 | 3·00 |

**141** Map, Airplane and Emblem

**1987.** 10th Anniv of Great Lakes Countries Economic Community. Multicoloured.

| | | | |
|---|---|---|---|
| 1473 | 5f. Type **141** | 55 | 55 |
| 1474 | 10f. Map, ear of wheat, cog-wheel and emblem | 65 | 65 |
| 1475 | 15f. Map, factory and emblem | 75 | 75 |
| 1476 | 25f. Map, electricity pylons and emblem | 1·60 | 1·60 |
| 1477 | 35f. Map, flags and emblem | 2·25 | 2·25 |
| **MS**1478 | 117×114 mm. Nos. 1473/7 plus label | 5·75 | 5·75 |

**142** Leaves and Sticks Shelter

**1988.** International Year of Shelter for the Homeless (1987). Multicoloured.

| | | | |
|---|---|---|---|
| 1479 | 10f. Type **142** | 55 | 55 |
| 1480 | 20f. People living in concrete pipes | 70 | 70 |
| 1481 | 80f. Boys mixing mortar | 1·50 | 1·50 |
| 1482 | 150f. Boys with model house | 3·00 | 3·00 |
| **MS**1483 | 124×100 mm. Nos. 1479/82 | 5·75 | 5·75 |

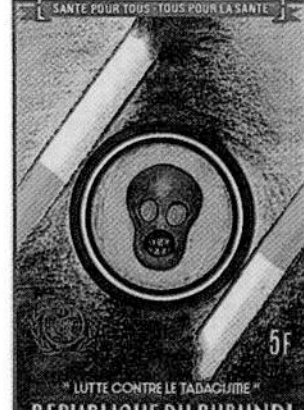

**143** Skull between Cigarettes

**1989.** Anti-smoking Campaign. Multicoloured.

| | | | |
|---|---|---|---|
| 1484 | 5f. Type **143** | 70 | 70 |
| 1485 | 20f. Cigarettes, lungs and skull | 1·40 | 1·40 |
| 1486 | 80f. Cigarettes piercing skull | 2·25 | 2·25 |
| **MS**1487 | 120×80 mm. Nos. 1484/6 | 4·25 | 4·25 |

No. **MS**1487 also shows World Health Organization 40th Anniv emblem.

**1989.** Various stamps surch.

| | | | |
|---|---|---|---|
| 1487b | 20f. on 3f. mult (No. 1457) | 70 | 70 |
| 1487c | 80f. on 30f. mult (No. 1430) | 2·00 | 2·00 |
| 1487d | 80f. on 30f. mult (No. 1431) | 2·00 | 2·00 |
| 1487e | 80f. on 35f. mult (No. 1432) | 2·00 | 2·00 |
| 1487f | 80f. on 35f. mult (No. 1433) | 2·00 | 2·00 |
| 1487g | 85f. on 65f. mult (No. 1435) | | |

**144** Pope John Paul II

**1990.** Papal Visit.

| | | | | |
|---|---|---|---|---|
| 1488 | **144** | 5f. multicoloured | 45 | 45 |
| 1489 | **144** | 10f. multicoloured | 45 | 45 |
| 1490 | **144** | 20f. multicoloured | 70 | 70 |
| 1491 | **144** | 30f. multicoloured | 70 | 70 |
| 1492 | **144** | 50f. multicoloured | 1·40 | 1·40 |
| 1493 | **144** | 80f. multicoloured | 2·00 | 2·00 |

**145** Hippopotamus

**1991.** Animals. Multicoloured.

| | | | |
|---|---|---|---|
| 1495 | 5f. Type **145** | 1·10 | 75 |
| 1496 | 10f. Hen and cockerel | 1·10 | 75 |
| 1497 | 20f. Lion | 1·10 | 75 |
| 1498 | 30f. Elephant | 1·10 | 1·10 |
| 1499 | 50f. Helmet guineafowl ("Pintade") | 3·00 | 2·25 |
| 1500 | 80f. Crocodile | 4·50 | 3·25 |
| **MS**1501 | 109×123 mm. Nos. 1495/1500 | 16·00 | 8·75 |

**146** Drummer

**1992.** Traditional Dancing. Multicoloured.

| | | | |
|---|---|---|---|
| 1502 | 15f. Type **146** | 25 | 25 |
| 1503 | 30f. Men dancing | 40 | 40 |
| 1504 | 115f. Group of drummers (horiz) | 1·90 | 1·90 |
| 1505 | 200f. Men dancing in fields (horiz) | 3·25 | 3·25 |
| **MS**1506 | 120×105 mm. Nos. 1502/5 | 5·75 | 5·75 |

**147** "Impatiens petersiana"

**1992.** Flowers. Multicoloured.

| | | | |
|---|---|---|---|
| 1507 | 15f. Type **147** | 90 | 65 |
| 1508 | 20f. "Lachenalia aloides" "Nelsonii" | 90 | 65 |
| 1509 | 30f. Egyptian lotus | 1·40 | 1·00 |
| 1510 | 50f. Kaffir lily | 3·00 | 2·25 |
| **MS**1511 | 105×120 mm. Nos. 1507/10 | 6·25 | 4·50 |

**148** Pigtail Macaque

**1992.** Air. Animals. Multicoloured.

| | | | |
|---|---|---|---|
| 1512 | 100f. Type **148** | 2·40 | 1·75 |
| 1513 | 115f. Grevy's zebra | 2·75 | 2·10 |
| 1514 | 200f. Ox | 4·00 | 3·00 |
| 1515 | 220f. Eastern white pelican | 5·00 | 3·75 |
| **MS**1516 | 105×120 mm. Nos. 1512/15 | 14·00 | 10·00 |

**149** People holding Hands and Flag

**1992.** 30th Anniv of Independence. Multicoloured.

| | | | |
|---|---|---|---|
| 1517 | 30f. Type **149** | 20 | 20 |
| 1518 | 85f. State flag | 80 | 80 |
| 1519 | 110f. Independence monument (vert) | 1·10 | 1·10 |
| 1520 | 115f. As No. 1518 | 1·10 | 1·10 |
| 1521 | 120f. Map (vert) | 1·40 | 1·40 |
| 1522 | 140f. Type **149** | 1·50 | 1·50 |
| 1523 | 200f. As No. 1519 | 2·10 | 2·10 |
| 1524 | 250f. As No. 1521 | 2·75 | 2·75 |

**150** "Russula ingens"

**1992.** Fungi. Multicoloured.

| | | | |
|---|---|---|---|
| 1525 | 10f. Type **150** | 15 | 15 |
| 1526 | 15f. "Russula brunneorigida" | 20 | 20 |
| 1527 | 20f. "Amanita zambiana" | 25 | 30 |
| 1528 | 30f. "Russula subfistulosa" | 40 | 45 |
| 1529 | 75f. "Russula meleagris" | 90 | 95 |
| 1530 | 85f. As No. 1529 | 1·00 | 1·10 |
| 1531 | 100f. "Russula immaculata" | 1·25 | 1·25 |
| 1532 | 110f. Type **150** | 1·40 | 1·40 |
| 1533 | 115f. As No. 1526 | 1·40 | 1·40 |
| 1534 | 120f. "Russula sejuncta" | 1·40 | 1·60 |
| 1535 | 130f. As No. 1534 | 1·50 | 1·60 |
| 1536 | 250f. "Afroboletus luteolus" | 3·00 | 3·25 |

**151** Columbus's Fleet, Treasure and Globes

**1992.** 500th Anniv of Discovery of America by Columbus. Multicoloured.

| | | | |
|---|---|---|---|
| 1541 | 200f. Type **151** | 2·00 | 2·00 |
| 1542 | 400f. American produce, globes and Columbus's fleet | 4·25 | 4·25 |

**152** Serval

**1992.** The Serval. Multicoloured.

| | | | |
|---|---|---|---|
| 1543 | 30f. Type **152** | 60 | 50 |
| 1544 | 130f. Pair sitting and crouching | 2·40 | 2·00 |
| 1545 | 200f. Pair, one standing over the other | 3·75 | 3·00 |
| 1546 | 220f. Heads of pair | 4·00 | 3·50 |

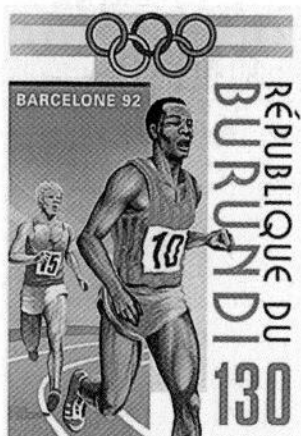

**153** Running

**1992.** Olympic Games, Barcelona. Multicoloured.

| | | | |
|---|---|---|---|
| 1547 | 130f. Type **153** | 1·50 | 1·50 |
| 1548 | 500f. Hurdling | 5·25 | 5·25 |

**154** Emblems

**1992.** International Nutrition Conference, Rome. Multicoloured.

| | | | |
|---|---|---|---|
| 1549 | 200f. Type **154** | 2·00 | 2·00 |
| 1550 | 220f. Woman's face made from vegetables (G. Arcimbolo) | 2·40 | 2·40 |

**155** Horsemen

**1992.** Christmas. Details of "Adoration of the Magi" by Gentile da Fabriano. Multicoloured.

| | | | |
|---|---|---|---|
| 1551 | 100f. Type **155** | 90 | 90 |
| 1552 | 130f. Three Kings | 1·10 | 1·10 |
| 1553 | 250f. Holy family | 2·50 | 2·50 |
| **MS**1554 | 109×91 mm. Nos. 1551/3 (sold at 580f.) | 4·50 | 4·50 |

**156** Flags of Member Countries and European Community Emblem

**1993.** European Single Market. Multicoloured.

| | | | |
|---|---|---|---|
| 1555 | 130f. Type **156** | 1·25 | 1·25 |
| 1556 | 500f. Europe shaking hands with Africa | 5·00 | 5·00 |

**157** Indonongo

**1993.** Musical Instruments. Multicoloured.

| | | | |
|---|---|---|---|
| 1557 | 200f. Type **157** | 2·00 | 2·00 |
| 1558 | 220f. Ingoma (drum) | 2·25 | 2·25 |
| 1559 | 250f. Ikembe (xylophone) | 2·50 | 2·50 |
| 1560 | 300f. Umuduri (musical bow) | 3·25 | 3·25 |

**158** Broad Blue-banded Swallowtail

**1993.** Butterflies. Multicoloured.

| | | | |
|---|---|---|---|
| 1561 | 130f. Type **158** | 1·50 | 1·25 |
| 1562 | 200f. Green charaxes | 2·40 | 2·10 |
| 1563 | 250f. Migratory glider | 3·00 | 2·50 |
| 1564 | 300f. Red swallowtail | 3·75 | 3·50 |
| **MS**1565 | 84×123 mm. Nos. 1561/4 (sold at 980f.) | 10·00 | 9·00 |

**159** Players, Stadium, United States Flag and Statue of Liberty

**1993.** World Cup Football Championship, U.S.A. (1994). Multicoloured.

| | | | |
|---|---|---|---|
| 1566 | 130f. Type **159** | 1·25 | 1·25 |
| 1567 | 200f. Players, stadium, United States flag and Golden Gate Bridge | 2·50 | 2·50 |

**160** Cattle

**1993.** Domestic Animals. Multicoloured.

| | | | |
|---|---|---|---|
| 1568 | 100f. Type **160** | 1·00 | 1·00 |
| 1569 | 120f. Sheep | 1·10 | 1·10 |
| 1570 | 130f. Pigs | 1·25 | 1·25 |
| 1571 | 250f. Goats | 2·50 | 2·50 |

**161** Woman with Baby and Two Men

**1993.** Christmas. Each orange and black.

| | | | |
|---|---|---|---|
| 1572 | 100f. Type **161** | 1·25 | 1·25 |
| 1573 | 130f. Nativity | 1·50 | 1·50 |
| 1574 | 250f. Woman with baby and three men | 3·00 | 3·00 |
| **MS**1575 | 127×82 mm. Nos. 1572/4 (sold at 580f.) | 5·75 | 5·75 |

**162** Elvis Presley

**1994.** Entertainers. Multicoloured.

| | | | |
|---|---|---|---|
| 1576 | 60f. Type **162** | 30 | 30 |
| 1577 | 115f. Mick Jagger | 55 | 55 |
| 1578 | 120f. John Lennon | 60 | 60 |
| 1579 | 200f. Michael Jackson | 1·00 | 1·00 |
| **MS**1580 | 80×114 mm. Nos. 1576/9 | 2·40 | 2·40 |

**163** "The Discus Thrower" (statue)

**1994.** Cent of International Olympic Committee.

| | | | |
|---|---|---|---|
| 1581 | **163** 150f. multicoloured | 75 | 75 |

**164** Pres. Buyoya handing over Baton of Power to Pres. Ndadaye

**1994.** 1st Anniv of First Multi-party Elections in Burundi. Multicoloured.

| | | | |
|---|---|---|---|
| 1582 | 30f.+10f. Type **164** | 20 | 20 |
| 1583 | 110f.+10f. Pres. Ndadaye (first elected President) giving inauguration speech | 60 | 60 |
| 1584 | 115f.+10f. Arms on map | 60 | 60 |
| 1585 | 120f.+10f. Warrior on map | 65 | 65 |

**165** Madonna, China

**1994.** Christmas. Multicoloured.

| | | | |
|---|---|---|---|
| 1586 | 115f. Type **165** | 55 | 55 |
| 1587 | 120f. Madonna, Japan | 60 | 60 |
| 1588 | 250f. Black Virgin, Poland | 1·25 | 1·25 |
| **MS**1589 | 80×118 mm. No. 1588 | 1·25 | 1·25 |

**166** Emblem and Earth

**1995.** 50th Anniversaries. Multicoloured.

| | | | |
|---|---|---|---|
| 1590 | 115f. Type **166** (FAO) | 55 | 55 |
| 1591 | 120f. UNO emblems and dove | 60 | 60 |

**167** "Cassia didymobotrya"

**1995.** Flowers. Multicoloured.

| | | | |
|---|---|---|---|
| 1592 | 15f. Type **167** | 15 | 15 |
| 1593 | 20f. "Mitragyna rubrostipulosa" | 15 | 15 |
| 1594 | 30f. "Phytolacca dodecandra" | 25 | 20 |
| 1595 | 85f. "Acanthus pubescens" | 65 | 60 |
| 1596 | 100f. "Bulbophyllum comatum" | 80 | 75 |
| 1597 | 110f. "Angraecum evrardianum" | 90 | 80 |
| 1598 | 115f. "Eulophia burundiensis" | 90 | 80 |
| 1599 | 120f. "Habenaria adolphii" | 1·00 | 90 |

**168** Otraca Bus

**1995.** Transport. Multicoloured.

| | | | |
|---|---|---|---|
| 1600 | 30f. Type **168** | 15 | 15 |
| 1601 | 115f. Transintra lorry | 65 | 65 |
| 1602 | 120f. Lake ferry | 90 | 70 |
| 1603 | 250f. Air Burundi Beeck King Air | 1·40 | 1·40 |

**169** Boy with Panga

**1995.** Christmas. Multicoloured.

| | | | |
|---|---|---|---|
| 1604 | 100f. Type **169** | 55 | 55 |
| 1605 | 130f. Boy with sheaf of wheat | 75 | 75 |
| 1606 | 250f. Mother and children | 1·40 | 1·40 |
| **MS**1607 | 126×82 mm. Nos. 1604/6 (sold at 580f.) | 5·75 | 5·75 |

**170** Venuste Niyongabo

**1996.** Olympic Games, Atlanta. Runners. Mult.

| | | | |
|---|---|---|---|
| 1608 | 130f. Type **170** (5000 m gold medal winner) | 40 | 40 |
| 1609 | 500f. Arthemon Hatungimana | 1·50 | 1·50 |

**171** Hadada Ibis

**1996.** Birds. Multicoloured.

| | | | |
|---|---|---|---|
| 1610 | 15f. Type **171** | 25 | 25 |
| 1611 | 20f. Egyptian goose | 25 | 25 |
| 1612 | 30f. African fish eagle | 25 | 25 |
| 1613 | 120f. Goliath heron | 75 | 75 |
| 1614 | 165f. South African crowned crane | 1·00 | 1·00 |
| 1615 | 220f. African jacana | 1·40 | 1·40 |

**172** Marlier's Julie

**1996.** Fishes of Lake Tanganyika. Multicoloured.

| | | | |
|---|---|---|---|
| 1616 | 30f. Type **172** | 25 | 20 |
| 1617 | 115f. "Cyphotilapia frontosa" | 75 | 60 |
| 1618 | 120f. "Lamprologus brichardi" | 75 | 60 |
| 1619 | 250f. Stone squeaker | 1·50 | 1·25 |
| **MS**1620 | 108×108 mm. Nos. 1616/19 (sold at 615f.) | 6·00 | 6·00 |

**173** Children

**1998.** 50th Anniv of S.O.S Children's Villages. Multicoloured.

| | | | |
|---|---|---|---|
| 1621 | 100f. Type **173** | 25 | 25 |
| 1622 | 250f. Flags, "50" and children waving | 65 | 65 |
| 1623 | 270f. Children dancing around flag | 70 | 70 |

**174** Madonna and Child

**1999.** Christmas (1996–98). Multicoloured.

| | | | |
|---|---|---|---|
| 1624 | 100f. Type **174** (1996) | 25 | 25 |
| 1625 | 130f. Madonna and Child (different) (1997) | 30 | 30 |
| 1626 | 250f. Madonna and Child (different) (1998) | 65 | 65 |
| **MS**1627 | 125×82 mm. Nos. 1624/6 (sold at 580f.) | 5·75 | 5·75 |

**175** Diana, Princess of Wales

**1999.** 2nd Death Anniv of Diana, Princess of Wales.

| | | | | |
|---|---|---|---|---|
| 1628 | **175** | 100f. multicoloured | 20 | 20 |
| 1629 | **175** | 250f. multicoloured | 20 | 20 |
| 1630 | **175** | 300f. multicoloured | 50 | 50 |

**176** Danny Kaye (entertainer) holding African Baby

**2000.** New Millennium. "A World Free from Hunger".

| | | | | |
|---|---|---|---|---|
| 1631 | **176** | 350f. multicoloured | 60 | 60 |

Pt. 1

## BUSHIRE

An Iranina seaport. Stamps issued during the British occupation in the 1914-18 War.

20 chahis = 1 kran, 10 krans = 1 toman

**1915.** Portrait stamps of Iran (1911) optd **BUSHIRE Under British Occupation**.

| | | | | |
|---|---|---|---|---|
| 1 | **57** | 1ch. orange and green | 65·00 | 70·00 |
| 2 | **57** | 2ch. brown and red | 65·00 | 60·00 |
| 3 | **57** | 3ch. green and grey | 80·00 | 80·00 |
| 4 | **57** | 5ch. red and brown | £450 | £400 |
| 5 | **57** | 6ch. lake and green | 65·00 | 45·00 |
| 6 | **57** | 9ch. lilac and brown | 60·00 | 75·00 |
| 7 | **57** | 10ch. brown and red | 65·00 | 75·00 |
| 8 | **57** | 12ch. blue and green | 85·00 | 80·00 |
| 9 | **57** | 24ch. green and purple | £150 | 90·00 |
| 10 | **57** | 1kr. red and blue | £140 | 50·00 |
| 11 | **57** | 2kr. red and green | £400 | £275 |
| 12 | **57** | 3kr. black and lilac | £325 | £325 |
| 13 | **57** | 5kr. blue and red | £250 | £200 |
| 14 | **57** | 10kr. red and brown | £225 | £180 |

**1915.** Coronation issue of Iran optd **BUSHIRE Under British Occupation**.

| | | | | |
|---|---|---|---|---|
| 15 | **66** | 1ch. blue and red | £650 | £500 |
| 16 | **66** | 2ch. red and blue | £10000 | £10000 |
| 17 | **66** | 3ch. green | £750 | £750 |
| 18 | **66** | 5ch. red | £9000 | £9000 |
| 19 | **66** | 6ch. red and green | £8000 | £8000 |
| 20 | **66** | 9ch. violet and brown | £1200 | £950 |
| 21 | **66** | 10ch. brown and green | £1700 | £1700 |
| 22 | **66** | 12ch. blue | £2000 | £2000 |
| 23 | **66** | 24ch. black and brown | £850 | £650 |
| 24 | **67** | 1kr. black, brown and silver | £850 | £800 |
| 25 | **67** | 2kr. red, blue and silver | £800 | £850 |
| 26 | **67** | 3kr. black, lilac and silver | £900 | £900 |
| 27 | **67** | 5kr. slate, brown and silver | £850 | £900 |
| 28 | - | 1t. black, violet and gold | £750 | £750 |
| 29 | - | 3t. red, lake and gold | £6000 | £6000 |

Pt. 1

## BUSSAHIR (BASHAHR)

A state in the Punjab, India. Now uses Indian stamps.

12 pies = 1 anna; 16 annas = 1 rupee.

**1**

**1895.** Various frames. Imperf, perf or roul.

| | | | | |
|---|---|---|---|---|
| 9 | **1** | ¼a. pink | 90·00 | £130 |
| 10 | **1** | ½a. grey | 24·00 | £160 |
| 11 | **1** | 1a. red | 24·00 | £100 |
| 12 | **1** | 2a. yellow | 32·00 | £100 |
| 13 | **1** | 4a. violet | 30·00 | £100 |
| 14 | **1** | 8a. brown | 24·00 | £120 |
| 15 | **1** | 12a. green | 85·00 | £140 |
| 16 | **1** | 1r. blue | 55·00 | £130 |

**1896.** Similar types, but inscriptions on white ground and inscr "POSTAGE" instead of "STAMP".

| | | | |
|---|---|---|---|
| 27 | ¼a. violet | 22·00 | 22·00 |
| 37 | ¼a. red | 4·50 | 14·00 |
| 25 | ½a. blue | 14·00 | 23·00 |
| 26 | 1a. olive | 21·00 | 50·00 |
| 32 | 1a. red | 5·00 | 18·00 |
| 41 | 2a. yellow | 70·00 | 95·00 |
| 36 | 4a. red | 70·00 | £150 |

Pt. 1

## CAICOS ISLANDS

Separate issues for these islands, part of the Turks and Caicos Islands group, appeared from 1981 to 1985.

100 cents = 1 dollar.

**1981.** Nos. 514, 518, 520, 523 and 525/7 of Turks and Caicos Islands optd **CAICOS ISLANDS**.

| | | | |
|---|---|---|---|
| 1 | 1c. Indigo hamlet | 15 | 15 |
| 2 | 5c. Spanish grunt | 20 | 20 |
| 3 | 8c. Four-eyed butterflyfish | 20 | 20 |
| 4 | 20c. Queen angelfish | 35 | 30 |
| 5 | 50c. Royal gramma ("Fairy Basslet") | 40 | 1·00 |
| 6 | $1 Fin-spot wrasse | 60 | 1·75 |
| 7 | $2 Stoplight parrotfish | 1·10 | 3·25 |

**1981.** Royal Wedding. Nos. 653/6 of Turks and Caicos Islands optd. (A) **Caicos Islands**.

| | | | |
|---|---|---|---|
| 8A | 35c. Prince Charles and Lady Diana Spencer | 20 | 25 |
| 9A | 65c. Kensington Palace | 30 | 40 |
| 10A | 90c. Prince Charles as Colonel of the Welsh Guards | 40 | 50 |
| **MS**11A | 96×82 mm. $2 Glass Coach | 1·00 | 2·00 |

(B) **CAICOS ISLANDS**.

| | | | |
|---|---|---|---|
| 8B | 35c. Prince Charles and Lady Diana Spencer | 30 | 70 |
| 9B | 65c. Kensington Palace | 40 | 1·00 |
| 10B | 90c. Prince Charles as Colonel of the Welsh Guards | 50 | 1·50 |
| **MS**11B | 96×82 mm. $2 Glass Coach | 1·00 | 2·50 |

**1981.** Royal Wedding. As Nos. 657/9 of Turks and Caicos Islands, but each inscr "Caicos Islands". Mult. Self-adhesive.

| | | | |
|---|---|---|---|
| 12 | 20c. Lady Diana Spencer | 30 | 40 |
| 13 | $1 Prince Charles | 80 | 1·25 |
| 14 | $2 Prince Charles and Lady Diana Spencer | 4·00 | 5·50 |

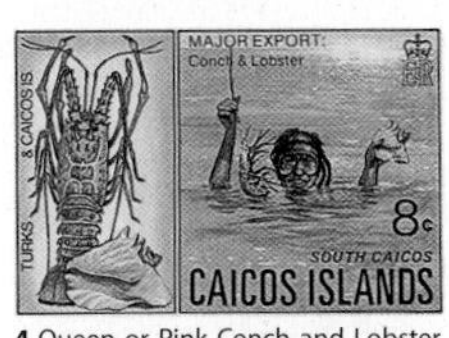

**4** Queen or Pink Conch and Lobster Fishing, South Caicos

**1983.** Multicoloured.. Multicoloured..

| | | | |
|---|---|---|---|
| 15 | 8c. Type **4** | 1·50 | 85 |
| 16 | 10c. Hawksbill turtle, East Caicos | 1·75 | 1·00 |
| 17 | 20c. Arawak Indians and idol, Middle Caicos | 1·75 | 1·00 |
| 18 | 35c. Boat-building, North Caicos | 2·00 | 1·50 |
| 19 | 50c. Marine biologist at work, Pine Cay | 3·00 | 2·25 |
| 20 | 95c. Boeing 707 airliner at new airport, Providenciales | 5·50 | 3·00 |
| 21 | $1.10 Columbus's "Pinta", West Caicos | 5·50 | 3·00 |
| 22 | $2 Fort George Cay | 3·75 | 4·75 |
| 23 | $3 Pirates Anne Bonny and Calico Jack at Parrot Cay | 6·00 | 4·75 |

**5** Goofy and Patch

**1983.** Christmas. Multicoloured.

| | | | |
|---|---|---|---|
| 30 | 1c. Type **5** | 10 | 30 |
| 31 | 1c. Chip and Dale | 10 | 30 |
| 32 | 2c. Morty | 10 | 30 |
| 33 | 2c. Morty and Ferdie | 10 | 30 |
| 34 | 3c. Goofy and Louie | 10 | 30 |
| 35 | 3c. Donald Duck, Huey, Dewey and Louie | 10 | 30 |
| 36 | 50c. Uncle Scrooge | 4·00 | 3·25 |
| 37 | 70c. Mickey Mouse and Ferdie | 4·25 | 3·75 |
| 38 | $1.10 Pinocchio, Jiminy Cricket and Figaro | 5·00 | 4·50 |
| **MS**39 | 126×101 mm. $2 Morty and Ferdie | 3·75 | 3·50 |

**6** "Leda and the Swan"

**1984.** 500th Birth Anniv of Raphael. Mult.

| | | | |
|---|---|---|---|
| 40 | 35c. Type **6** | 75 | 50 |
| 41 | 50c. "Study of Apollo for Parnassus" | 1·00 | 70 |
| 42 | 95c. "Study of two figures for the battle of Ostia" | 2·00 | 1·25 |
| 43 | $1.10 "Study for the Madonna of the Goldfinch" | 2·00 | 1·50 |
| **MS**44 | 71×100 mm. $2.50, "The Garvagh Madonna" | 3·00 | 3·25 |

**7** High Jumping

**1984.** Olympic Games, Los Angeles.

| | | | | |
|---|---|---|---|---|
| 45 | **7** | 4c. multicoloured | 10 | 10 |
| 46 | - | 25c. multicoloured | 30 | 20 |
| 47 | - | 65c. black, deep blue and blue | 1·75 | 50 |
| 48 | - | $1.10 multicoloured | 1·25 | 85 |
| **MS**49 | | 105×75 mm. $2 multicoloured | 2·25 | 3·00 |

DESIGNS—VERT: 25c. Archery; 65c. Cycling; $1.10, Football. HORIZ: $2.50, Show jumping.

**8** Horace Horsecollar and Clarabelle Cow

**1984.** Easter. Walt Disney Cartoon Characters. Multicoloured.

| | | | |
|---|---|---|---|
| 50 | 35c. Type **8** | 1·40 | 60 |
| 51 | 45c. Mickey and Minnie Mouse, and Chip | 1·50 | 75 |
| 52 | 75c. Gyro Gearloose, Chip 'n Dale | 1·90 | 1·25 |
| 53 | 85c. Mickey Mouse, Chip 'n Dale | 1·90 | 1·40 |

| | | |
|---|---|---|
| MS54 127×101 mm. $2.20, Donald Duck | 5·50 | 3·75 |

**1984.** Universal Postal Union Congress Hamburg. Nos. 20/1 optd **UNIVERSAL POSTAL UNION 1874-1984** and emblem.

| | | | |
|---|---|---|---|
| 55 | 95c. Boeing 707 airliner at new airport, Providenciales | 1·00 | 1·25 |
| 56 | $1.10 Columbus's "Pinta", West Caicos | 1·25 | 1·50 |

**1984.** "Ausipex" International Stamp Exhibition, Melbourne. No. 22 optd **AUSIPEX 1984**.

| | | | |
|---|---|---|---|
| 57 | $2 Fort George Cay | 2·40 | 2·50 |

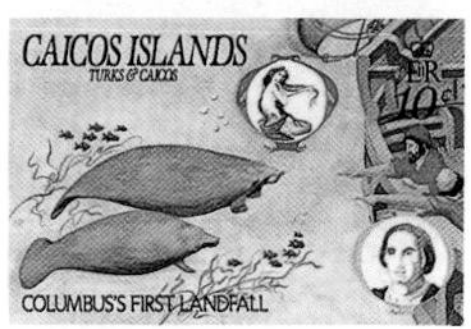


**11** Seamen sighting American Manatees

**1984.** 492nd Anniv of Columbus's First Landfall. Multicoloured.

| | | | |
|---|---|---|---|
| 58 | 10c. Type **11** | 1·00 | 80 |
| 59 | 70c. Columbus's fleet | 3·75 | 3·25 |
| 60 | $1 First landing in the West Indies | 4·25 | 3·75 |
| MS61 | 99×69 mm. $2 Fleet of Columbus (different) | 2·75 | 3·00 |

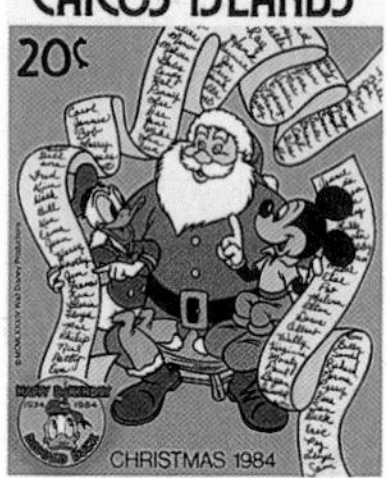


**12** Donald Duck and Mickey Mouse with Father Christmas

**1984.** Christmas. Walt Disney Cartoon Characters. Multicoloured.

| | | | |
|---|---|---|---|
| 62 | 20c. Type **12** | 1·50 | 85 |
| 63 | 35c. Donald Duck opening refrigerator | 1·75 | 1·00 |
| 64 | 50c. Mickey Mouse, Donald Duck and toy train | 2·50 | 2·25 |
| 65 | 75c. Donald Duck and parcels | 3·00 | 3·00 |
| 66 | $1.10 Donald Duck and carol singers | 3·25 | 3·25 |
| MS67 | 127×102 mm. $2 Donald Duck as Christmas tree | 3·75 | 4·00 |

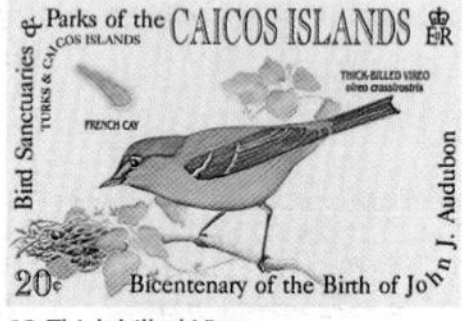


**13** Thick-billed Vireo

**1985.** Birth Bicentenary of John J. Audubon (ornithologist). Multicoloured.

| | | | |
|---|---|---|---|
| 68 | 20c. Type **13** | 1·75 | 70 |
| 69 | 35c. Black-faced grassquit | 2·00 | 95 |
| 70 | 50c. Pearly-eyed thrasher | 2·25 | 1·50 |
| 71 | $1 Greater Antillean bullfinch | 2·75 | 2·50 |
| MS72 | 100×70 mm. $2 Striped-headed tanager | 3·50 | 3·50 |

**14** Two Children learning to Read and Write (Education)

**1985.** International Youth Year. 40th Anniv of United Nations. Multicoloured.

| | | | |
|---|---|---|---|
| 73 | 16c. Type **14** | 20 | 25 |
| 74 | 35c. Two children on play-ground swings (Health) | 50 | 55 |
| 75 | 70c. Boy and girl (Love) | 1·00 | 1·10 |
| 76 | 90c. Three children (Peace) | 1·25 | 1·40 |
| MS77 | 101×71 mm. $2 Child, dove carrying ears of wheat and map of the Americas | 2·75 | 3·25 |

**15** Douglas DC-3 on Ground

**1985.** 40th Anniv of International Civil Aviation Organization. Multicoloured.

| | | | |
|---|---|---|---|
| 78 | 35c. Type **15** | 3·00 | 55 |
| 79 | 75c. Convair CV 440 Metropolitan | 4·00 | 1·40 |
| 80 | 90c. Britten Norman Islander | 4·00 | 1·60 |
| MS81 | 100×70 mm. $2.20, Hand-gliding over the Caicos Islands | 3·00 | 3·25 |

**16** The Queen Mother visiting Foundation for the Disabled, Leatherhead

**1985.** Life and Times of Queen Elizabeth the Queen Mother. Multicoloured.

| | | | |
|---|---|---|---|
| 82 | 35c. Type **16** | 1·25 | 55 |
| 83 | 65c. With Princess Anne (horiz) | 1·75 | 95 |
| 84 | 95c. At Epsom, 1961 | 2·25 | 1·60 |
| MS85 | 56×85 mm. $2 Visiting Royal Hospital, Chelsea | 4·75 | 3·00 |

**1985.** 150th Birth Anniv of Mark Twain (author). Designs as T **118** of Anguilla, showing Walt Disney cartoon characters in scenes from "Tom Sawyer, Detective". Multicoloured.

| | | | |
|---|---|---|---|
| 86 | 8c. Huckleberry Finn (Goofy) and Tom Sawyer (Mickey Mouse) reading reward notice | 60 | 20 |
| 87 | 35c. Huck and Tom meeting Jake Dunlap | 1·75 | 65 |
| 88 | 95c. Huck and Tom spying on Jubiter Dunlap | 3·25 | 2·00 |
| 89 | $1.10 Huck and Tom with hound (Pluto) | 3·25 | 2·25 |
| MS90 | 127×101 mm. Tom unmasking Jubiter Dunlap | 4·75 | 4·25 |

**1985.** Birth Bicentenaries of Grimm Brothers (folklorists). Designs as T **119** of Anguilla, showing Walt Disney cartoon characters in scenes from "Six Soldiers of Fortune". Multicoloured.

| | | | |
|---|---|---|---|
| 91 | 16c. The Soldier (Donald Duck) with his meagre pay | 1·75 | 30 |
| 92 | 25c. The Soldier meeting the Strong Man (Horace Horsecollar) | 2·00 | 45 |
| 93 | 65c. The Soldier meeting the Marksman (Mickey Mouse) | 3·50 | 1·25 |
| 94 | $1.35 The Fast Runner (Goofy) winning the race against the Princess (Daisy Duck) | 4·25 | 2·25 |
| MS95 | 126×101 mm. $2 The Soldier and the Strong Man with sack of gold | 4·75 | 4·00 |

Pt. 21

# CAMBODIA

A kingdom in south-east Asia.

From 1887 Cambodia was part of the Union of Indo-China. In 1949 it became an Associated State of the French Union, in 1953 it attained sovereign independence and in 1955 it left the Union.

Following the introduction of a republican constitution in 1970 the name of the country was changed to Khmer Republic and in 1975 to Kampuchea.

In 1989 it reverted to the name of Cambodia. Under a new constitution in 1993 it became a parliamentary monarchy.

1951. 100 cents = 1 piastre.
1955. 100 cents = 1 riel.

**1** "Apsara" or Dancing Nymph

**2** Throne Room, Phnom-Penh

**3** King Norodom Sihanouk

**1951**

| | | | | |
|---|---|---|---|---|
| 1 | 1 | 10c. green and deep green | 50 | 3·50 |
| 2 | 1 | 20c. brown and red | 45 | 1·50 |
| 3 | 1 | 30c. blue and violet | 55 | 60 |
| 4 | 1 | 40c. blue and ultramarine | 1·10 | 90 |
| 5 | 2 | 50c. green and deep green | 95 | 85 |
| 6 | 3 | 80c. green and blue | 1·70 | 4·25 |
| 7 | 2 | 1p. violet and blue | 1·30 | 45 |
| 8 | 3 | 1p.10 red and lake | 2·10 | 4·25 |
| 9 | 1 | 1p.50 red and lake | 2·00 | 1·40 |
| 10 | 2 | 1p.50 blue and indigo | 2·10 | 2·30 |
| 11 | 3 | 1p.50 brown and chocolate | 2·10 | 1·80 |
| 12 | 3 | 1p.90 blue and indigo | 3·75 | 6·00 |
| 13 | 2 | 2p. brown and red | 2·75 | 75 |
| 14 | 3 | 3p. brown and red | 4·25 | 2·30 |
| 15 | 1 | 5p. violet and blue | 12·50 | 5·75 |
| 16 | 2 | 10p. blue and violet | 13·50 | 10·50 |
| 17 | 3 | 15p. violet and deep violet | 28·00 | 45·00 |
| MS17a | | Three sheets, each 130×90 mm. Nos. 15/17. Price for 3 sheets | £120 | £100 |

**1952.** Students' Aid Fund. Surch AIDE A L'ETUDIANT and premium.

| | | | | |
|---|---|---|---|---|
| 18 | | 1p.10+40c. red and lake | 3·50 | 13·00 |
| 19 | | 1p.90+60c. blue & indigo | 3·50 | 13·00 |
| 20 | | 3p.+1p. brown and red | 3·50 | 13·00 |
| 21 | 1 | 5p.+2p. violet and blue | 3·75 | 13·00 |

**5** "Kinnari"

**1953.** Air.

| | | | | |
|---|---|---|---|---|
| 22 | 5 | 50c. green | 1·10 | 2·10 |
| 23 | 5 | 3p. red | 2·00 | 1·80 |
| 24 | 5 | 3p.30 violet | 2·50 | 5·25 |
| 25 | 5 | 4p. blue and brown | 2·75 | 1·20 |
| 26 | 5 | 5p.10 ochre, red and brown | 4·00 | 6·75 |
| 27 | 5 | 6p.50 purple and brown | 3·75 | 8·75 |
| 28 | 5 | 9p. green and mauve | 5·00 | 13·00 |
| 29 | 5 | 11p.50 multicoloured | 9·75 | 18·00 |
| 30 | 5 | 30p. ochre, brown and green | 16·00 | 26·00 |
| MS30a | | Three sheets, each 129×100 mm. Nos. 22, 24, 26 and 30 (sold at 50p.); Nos. 23, 25 and 29 (sold at 25p.); Nos. 27/8 (sold at 20p.) Price for 3 sheets | £180 | £160 |

**6** Arms of Cambodia

**7** "Postal Transport"

**1954**

| | | | | |
|---|---|---|---|---|
| 31 | - | 10c. red | 1·20 | 1·80 |
| 32 | - | 20c. green | 1·40 | 50 |
| 33 | - | 30c. blue | 1·40 | 2·10 |
| 34 | - | 40c. violet | 1·40 | 85 |
| 35 | - | 50c. purple | 1·40 | 25 |
| 36 | - | 70c. brown | 1·60 | 3·25 |
| 37 | - | 1p. violet | 1·70 | 1·80 |
| 38 | - | 1p.50 red | 1·70 | 60 |
| 39 | 6 | 2p. red | 1·30 | 45 |
| 40 | 6 | 2p.50 green | 1·60 | 60 |
| 41 | 7 | 2p.50 green | 2·50 | 2·10 |
| 42 | 6 | 3p. blue | 2·10 | 1·70 |
| 43 | 7 | 4p. sepia | 3·25 | 2·75 |
| 44 | 6 | 4p.50 violet | 2·75 | 1·80 |
| 45 | 7 | 5p. red | 3·50 | 2·50 |
| 46 | 6 | 6p. brown | 3·00 | 2·50 |
| 47 | 7 | 10p. violet | 4·00 | 2·75 |
| 48 | 7 | 15p. blue | 5·00 | 5·00 |
| 49 | - | 20p. blue | 11·50 | 5·75 |
| 50 | - | 30p. green | 18·00 | 9·75 |
| MS50a | | Three sheets, each 120×20 mm. Nos. 31/5 (sold at 2p.); Nos. 39/40, 42, 44 and 46 (sold at 20p.); Nos. 41, 43, 45 and 47/8 (sold at 40p.) and one sheet 160×92 mm containing Nos. 36/8 and 49/50 (sold at 60p.) Price for 4 sheets | £150 | £140 |

DESIGNS—VERT: 10c. to 50c. View of Phnom Daun Penah. HORIZ: 70c. 1, 1p.50, 20, 30p. East Gate, Temple of Angkor.

**8** King Norodom Suramarit

**1955**

| | | | | |
|---|---|---|---|---|
| 51 | | 50c. blue | 25 | 20 |
| 52 | 8 | 50c. violet | 35 | 30 |
| 53 | 8 | 1r. red | 40 | 30 |
| 54 | 8 | 2r. blue | 70 | 45 |
| 55 | - | 2r.50 brown | 1·00 | 35 |
| 56 | - | 4r. green | 1·40 | 45 |
| 57 | - | 6r. lake | 1·90 | 1·20 |
| 58 | 8 | 7r. brown | 2·30 | 1·40 |
| 59 | - | 15r. lilac | 3·25 | 1·20 |
| 60 | 8 | 20r. green | 4·75 | 4·25 |

PORTRAIT: Nos. 51, 55/7 and 59, Queen Kossamak.

For stamps as Nos. 58 and 60, but with black border, see Nos. 101/2.

**9** King and Queen of Cambodia

**1955.** Coronation (1st issue).

| | | | | |
|---|---|---|---|---|
| 61 | 9 | 1r.50 sepia and brown | 75 | 45 |
| 62 | 9 | 2r. black and blue | 75 | 55 |
| 63 | 9 | 3r. red and orange | 95 | 30 |
| 64 | 9 | 5r. black and green | 1·50 | 55 |
| 65 | 9 | 10r. purple and violet | 2·50 | 55 |

See Nos. 66/71.

**10** King Norodom Suramarit

**1956.** Coronation (2nd issue).

| | | | | |
|---|---|---|---|---|
| 66 | 10 | 2r. red | 1·10 | 2·30 |
| 67 | - | 3r. blue | 1·60 | 3·25 |
| 68 | - | 5r. green | 2·40 | 4·50 |
| 69 | 10 | 10r. green | 6·25 | 9·25 |
| 70 | 10 | 30r. violet | 13·00 | 22·00 |
| 71 | - | 50r. purple | 25·00 | 25·00 |

PORTRAIT—VERT: 3, 5, 50r. Queen of Cambodia.

**11** Prince Sihanouk, Flags and Globe

**1957.** 1st Anniv of Admission of Cambodia to UNO.

| | | | | |
|---|---|---|---|---|
| 72 | 11 | 2r. red, blue and green | 1·20 | 90 |
| 73 | 11 | 4r.50 blue | 1·20 | 90 |
| 74 | 11 | 8r.50 red | 1·20 | 90 |

12

**1957.** 2,500th Anniv of Buddhism. (a) With premiums.

| | | | | |
|---|---|---|---|---|
| 75 | **12** | 1r.50+50c. bis, red & bl | 1·40 | 1·80 |
| 76 | **12** | 6r.50+1r.50 bis, red & pur | 2·10 | 2·75 |
| 77 | **12** | 8r.+2r. bistre, red & blue | 3·50 | 4·50 |

(b) Colours changed and premiums omitted.

| | | | |
|---|---|---|---|
| 78 | 1r.50 red | 1·30 | 1·00 |
| 79 | 6r.50 violet | 1·50 | 1·20 |
| 80 | 8r. green | 1·50 | 1·50 |

**13** Mythological Bird

**1957.** Air.

| | | | | |
|---|---|---|---|---|
| 81 | **13** | 50c. lake | 35 | 10 |
| 82 | **13** | 1r. green | 60 | 10 |
| 83 | **13** | 4r. blue | 1·80 | 45 |
| 84 | **13** | 50r. red | 7·50 | 2·75 |
| 85 | **13** | 100r. red, green and blue | 13·00 | 5·00 |
| **MS**85a | | 160×92 mm. Nos. 81/5 (sold at 160r.) | 13·00 | 28·00 |

**14** King Ang Duong

**1958.** King Ang Duong Commemoration.

| | | | | |
|---|---|---|---|---|
| 86 | **14** | 1r.50 brown and violet | 55 | 45 |
| 87 | **14** | 5r. bistre and black | 70 | 65 |
| 88 | **14** | 10r. sepia and purple | 1·40 | 90 |
| **MS**88a | | 156×92 mm. Nos. 86/8 (sold at 25r.) | 6·00 | 5·00 |

**15** King Norodom I

**1958.** King Norodom I Commemoration.

| | | | | |
|---|---|---|---|---|
| 89 | **15** | 2r. brown and blue | 60 | 35 |
| 90 | **15** | 6r. green and orange | 85 | 55 |
| 91 | **15** | 15r. brown and green | 1·70 | 1·10 |
| **MS**91a | | 156×92 mm. Nos. 89/91 (sold at 32r.) | 6·00 | 4·50 |

**16** Children

**1959.** Children's World Friendship.

| | | | | |
|---|---|---|---|---|
| 92 | **16** | 20c. purple | 25 | 35 |
| 93 | **16** | 50c. blue | 45 | 45 |
| 94 | **16** | 80c. red | 90 | 85 |

**1959.** Red Cross Fund. Nos. 92/4 surch with red cross and premium.

| | | | |
|---|---|---|---|
| 95 | 20c.+20c. purple | 30 | 45 |
| 96 | 50c.+30c. blue | 65 | 65 |
| 97 | 80c.+50c. red | 1·30 | 1·20 |

**18** Prince Sihanouk, Plan of Port and Freighter

**1960.** Inauguration of Sihanoukville Port.

| | | | | |
|---|---|---|---|---|
| 98 | **18** | 2r. sepia and red | 55 | 55 |
| 99 | **18** | 5r. brown and blue | 55 | 65 |
| 100 | **18** | 20r. blue and violet | 2·00 | 2·00 |

**1960.** King Norodom Suramarit Mourning issue. Nos. 58 and 60 reissued with black border.

| | | | | |
|---|---|---|---|---|
| 101 | **8** | 7r. brown and black | 3·00 | 4·25 |
| 102 | **8** | 20r. green and black | 3·00 | 4·25 |

**19** Sacred Plough in Procession

**1960.** Festival of the Sacred Furrow.

| | | | | |
|---|---|---|---|---|
| 103 | **19** | 1r. purple | 60 | 45 |
| 104 | **19** | 2r. brown | 75 | 65 |
| 105 | **19** | 3r. green | 1·20 | 90 |

**20** Child and Book ("Education")

**1960.** "Works of the Five Year Plan".

| | | | | |
|---|---|---|---|---|
| 106 | **20** | 2r. brown, blue and green | 50 | 30 |
| 107 | - | 3r. green and brown | 65 | 35 |
| 108 | - | 4r. violet, green and pink | 65 | 45 |
| 109 | - | 6r. brown, orange & green | 75 | 55 |
| 110 | - | 10r. blue, green and bistre | 1·80 | 1·10 |
| 111 | - | 25r. red and lake | 3·75 | 2·20 |
| **MS**111a | | Two sheets, each 150×100 mm. Nos. 106, 109 and 111 (sold at 42r.); Nos. 107/8 and 110 (sold at 23r.) Price for 2 sheets | 5·25 | 6·50 |

DESIGNS—HORIZ: 3r. Chhouksar Barrage ("Irrigation"); 6r. Carpenter and huts ("Construction"); 10r. Rice-field ("Agriculture"). VERT: 4r. Industrial scene and books ("National balance-sheet"); 25r. Anointing children ("Child welfare").

**21** Flag and Dove of Peace

**1961.** Peace. Flag in red and blue.

| | | | | |
|---|---|---|---|---|
| 112 | **21** | 1r.50 green and brown | 30 | 45 |
| 113 | **21** | 5r. red | 45 | 65 |
| 114 | **21** | 7r. blue and green | 60 | 90 |
| **MS**114a | | 147×93 mm. Nos. 112/14 (sold at 16r.) | 20·00 | 11·00 |
| **MS**114b | | as **MS**114a but stamps in new colours (sold at 20r.) | 4·00 | 11·00 |

**23** Frangipani

**1961.** Cambodian Flowers.

| | | | | |
|---|---|---|---|---|
| 115 | **23** | 2r. yellow, green & mauve | 50 | 55 |
| 116 | - | 5r. mauve, green and blue | 80 | 1·10 |
| 117 | - | 10r. red, green and blue | 2·30 | 2·00 |
| **MS**117a | | 130×100 mm. Nos. 115/17 (sold at 20r.) | 7·00 | 7·00 |

FLOWERS: 5r. Oleander. 10r. Amaryllis.

**24** "Rama" (from temple door, Baphoun)

**1961.** Cambodian Soldiers Commemoration.

| | | | | |
|---|---|---|---|---|
| 118 | **24** | 1r. mauve | 50 | 20 |
| 118a | **24** | 2r. blue | 1·90 | 1·80 |
| 119 | **24** | 3r. green | 85 | 30 |
| 120 | **24** | 6r. orange | 1·00 | 45 |
| **MS**120a | | 150×85 mm. Nos. 118/20 (sold at 12r.) | 3·25 | 3·25 |

**25** Prince Norodom Sihanouk and Independence Monument

**1961.** Independence Monument.

| | | | | |
|---|---|---|---|---|
| 121 | **25** | 2r. green (postage) | 80 | 35 |
| 122 | **25** | 4r. sepia | 80 | 45 |
| 123 | **25** | 7r. multicoloured (air) | 75 | 75 |
| 124 | **25** | 30r. red, blue and green | 2·30 | 2·30 |
| 125 | **25** | 50r. multicoloured | 3·50 | 3·75 |
| **MS**125a | | Two sheets, each 150×85 mm. Nos. 121/2 (sold at 10r.); Nos. 123/5 (sold at 100r.). Price for 2 sheets | 15·00 | 11·00 |

**1961.** 6th World Buddhist Conference. Optd VIe CONFERENCE MONDIALE BOUDDHIQUE 12-11-1961.

| | | | | |
|---|---|---|---|---|
| 126 | **6** | 2p.50 (2r.50) green | 90 | 55 |
| 127 | **6** | 4p.50 (4r.50) violet | 1·40 | 85 |

**27** Power Station (Czech Aid)

**1962.** Foreign Aid Programme.

| | | | | |
|---|---|---|---|---|
| 128 | **27** | 2r. lake and red | 30 | 20 |
| 129 | - | 3r. brown, green and blue | 35 | 20 |
| 130 | - | 4r. brown, red and blue | 35 | 30 |
| 131 | - | 5r. purple and green | 55 | 35 |
| 132 | - | 6r. brown and blue | 1·00 | 35 |
| **MS**132a | | 150×85 mm. Nos. 128/32 (sold at 25r.) | 7·50 | 5·00 |

DESIGNS: 3r. Motorway (American Aid); 4r. Textile Factory (Chinese Aid); 5r. Friendship Hospital (Soviet Aid); 6r. Airport (French Aid).

**28** Campaign Emblem

**1962.** Malaria Eradication.

| | | | | |
|---|---|---|---|---|
| 133 | **28** | 2r. purple and brown | 35 | 30 |
| 134 | **28** | 4r. green and brown | 40 | 35 |
| 135 | **28** | 6r. violet and bistre | 35 | 45 |

**29** Curucmas

**1962.** Cambodian Fruits (1st issue).

| | | | | |
|---|---|---|---|---|
| 136 | **29** | 2r. yellow and brown | 45 | 45 |
| 137 | - | 4r. green and turquoise | 65 | 55 |
| 138 | - | 6r. red, green and blue | 75 | 85 |
| **MS**138a | | 150×85 mm. Nos. 136/8 (sold at 15r.) | 6·00 | 3·75 |

FRUITS: 4r. Lychees. 6r. Mangosteens.

**1962.** Cambodian Fruits (2nd issue).

| | | | |
|---|---|---|---|
| 139 | 2r. brown and green | 75 | 35 |
| 140 | 5r. green and brown | 1·10 | 55 |
| 141 | 9r. brown and green | 1·30 | 75 |

DESIGNS—VERT: 2r. Pineapples. 5r. Sugar-cane. 9r. "Bread" trees.

**1962.** Surch.

| | | | | |
|---|---|---|---|---|
| 142 | **16** | 50c. on 80c. red | 55 | 35 |
| 150 | - | 3r. on 2r.50 brn (No. 55) | 75 | 45 |

**1962.** Inauguration of Independence Monument. Surch INAUGURATION DU MONUMENT and new value.

| | | | | |
|---|---|---|---|---|
| 143 | **25** | 3r. on 2r. green (postage) | 55 | 35 |
| 144 | **25** | 12r. on 7r. mult (air) | 1·50 | 1·00 |

**32** Campaign Emblem, Corn and Maize

**1963.** Freedom from Hunger.

| | | | | |
|---|---|---|---|---|
| 145 | **32** | 3r. chestnut, brown & blue | 50 | 45 |
| 146 | **32** | 6r. chestnut, brown & blue | 50 | 45 |

**33** Temple Preah Vihear

**1963.** Reunification of Preah Vihear Temple with Cambodia.

| | | | | |
|---|---|---|---|---|
| 147 | **33** | 3r. brown, purple & green | 40 | 35 |
| 148 | **33** | 6r. green, orange and blue | 70 | 55 |
| 149 | **33** | 15r. brown, blue & green | 1·10 | 90 |

**35** Kep sur Mer

**1963.** Cambodian Resorts. Multicoloured.

| | | | |
|---|---|---|---|
| 151 | 3r. Koh Tonsay (vert) | 40 | 30 |
| 152 | 7r. Popokvil (waterfall) (vert) | 65 | 35 |
| 153 | 20r. Type **35** | 2·10 | 90 |

**1963.** Red Cross Centenary. Surch 1863 1963 CENTENAIRE DE LA CROIX-ROUGE and premium.

| | | | | |
|---|---|---|---|---|
| 154 | **28** | 4r.+40c. green & brown | 65 | 75 |
| 155 | **28** | 6r.+60c. violet & bistre | 1·00 | 1·10 |

**37** Scales of Justice

**1963.** 15th Anniv of Declaration of Human Rights.

| | | | | |
|---|---|---|---|---|
| 156 | **37** | 1r. green, red and blue | 40 | 45 |
| 157 | **37** | 3r. red, blue and green | 70 | 55 |
| 158 | **37** | 12r. blue, green and red | 1·30 | 1·30 |

**38** Kouprey

**1964.** Wild Animal Protection.

| | | | | |
|---|---|---|---|---|
| 159 | **38** | 50c. brown, green & chest | 85 | 35 |
| 160 | **38** | 3r. brown, chestnut & grn | 1·20 | 55 |
| 161 | **38** | 6r. brown, blue and green | 1·80 | 1·10 |

**39** Black-billed Magpie

**1964.** Birds.

| | | | | |
|---|---|---|---|---|
| 162 | **39** | 3r. blue, green and indigo | 1·10 | 65 |
| 163 | - | 6r. orange, purple & blue | 1·80 | 1·00 |
| 164 | - | 12r. green and purple | 3·25 | 2·00 |

BIRDS: 6r. River kingfisher. 12r. Grey heron.

**40** "Hanuman"

**1964.** Air.

| | | | | |
|---|---|---|---|---|
| 165 | **40** | 5r. mauve, brown & blue | 65 | 45 |
| 166 | **40** | 10r. bistre, mauve & green | 1·00 | 55 |
| 167 | **40** | 20r. bistre, violet and blue | 1·70 | 1·10 |
| 168 | **40** | 40r. bistre, blue and red | 3·75 | 2·00 |
| 169 | **40** | 80r. orange, green & purple | 6·00 | 5·00 |

**1964.** Air Olympic Games, Tokyo. Surch JEUX OLYMPIQUES TOKYO-1964, Olympic rings and value.

| | | | |
|---|---|---|---|
| 170 | 3r. on 5r. mve, brn and bl | 60 | 35 |
| 171 | 6r. on 10r. bis, mve & grn | 1·00 | 55 |
| 172 | 9r. on 20r. bistre, vio & bl | 1·10 | 90 |
| 173 | 12r. on 40r. bis, bl & red | 2·30 | 1·40 |

**42** Airline Emblem

**1964.** 8th Anniv of Royal Air Cambodia.

| | | | | |
|---|---|---|---|---|
| 174 | **42** | 1r.50 red and violet | 25 | 20 |
| 175 | **42** | 3r. red and blue | 45 | 30 |
| 176 | **42** | 7r.50 red and blue | 90 | 45 |

**43** Prince Norodom Sihanouk

**1964.** 10th Anniv of Foundation of Sangkum (Popular Socialist Community).

| | | | | |
|---|---|---|---|---|
| 177 | **43** | 2r. violet | 45 | 30 |
| 178 | **43** | 3r. brown | 60 | 35 |
| 179 | **43** | 10r. blue | 1·20 | 75 |

**44** Weaving

**1965.** Native Handicrafts.

| | | | | |
|---|---|---|---|---|
| 180 | **44** | 1r. violet, brown & bistre | 30 | 30 |
| 181 | - | 3r. brown, green & purple | 55 | 35 |
| 182 | - | 5r. red, purple and green | 85 | 75 |

DESIGNS: 3r. Engraving. 5r. Basket-making.

**1965.** Indo-Chinese People's Conference. Nos. 178/9 optd CONFERENCE DES PEUPLES INDOCHINOIS.

| | | | | |
|---|---|---|---|---|
| 183 | **43** | 3r. brown | 45 | 45 |
| 184 | **43** | 10r. blue | 70 | 65 |

**46** ITU Emblem and Symbols

**1965.** Centenary of ITU.

| | | | | |
|---|---|---|---|---|
| 185 | **46** | 3r. bistre and green | 35 | 35 |
| 186 | **46** | 4r. blue and red | 45 | 55 |
| 187 | **46** | 10r. purple and violet | 75 | 75 |

**47** Cotton

**1965.** Industrial Plants. Multicoloured.

| | | | |
|---|---|---|---|
| 188 | 1r.50 Type **47** | 45 | 30 |
| 189 | 3r. Groundnuts | 70 | 35 |
| 190 | 7r.50 Coconut palms | 1·10 | 75 |

**48** Preah Ko

**1966.** Cambodian Temples.

| | | | | |
|---|---|---|---|---|
| 191 | **48** | 3r. green, turquoise & brn | 75 | 45 |
| 192 | - | 5r. brown, green & purple | 95 | 55 |
| 193 | - | 7r. brown, green & ochre | 1·30 | 65 |
| 194 | - | 9r. purple, green and blue | 2·20 | 90 |
| 195 | - | 12r. red, green & verm | 2·75 | 1·60 |

TEMPLES: 5r. Baksei Chamkrong, 7r. Banteay Srei, 9r. Angkor Vat. 12r. Bayon.

**49** WHO Building

**1966.** Inaug of WHO Headquarters, Geneva.

| | | | | |
|---|---|---|---|---|
| 196 | **49** | 2r. multicoloured | 30 | 20 |
| 197 | **49** | 3r. multicoloured | 35 | 30 |
| 198 | **49** | 5r. multicoloured | 60 | 45 |

**50** Tree-planting

**1966.** Tree Day.

| | | | | |
|---|---|---|---|---|
| 199 | **50** | 1r. brown, green & dp brn | 25 | 30 |
| 200 | **50** | 3r. brown, green & orange | 40 | 35 |
| 201 | **50** | 7r. brown, green and grey | 70 | 45 |

**51** UNESCO Emblem

**1966.** 20th Anniv of UNESCO.

| | | | | |
|---|---|---|---|---|
| 202 | **51** | 3r. multicoloured | 35 | 30 |
| 203 | **51** | 7r. multicoloured | 45 | 55 |

**52** Stadium

**1966.** "Ganefo" Games, Phnom Penh.

| | | | | |
|---|---|---|---|---|
| 204 | **52** | 3r. blue | 15 | 20 |
| 205 | - | 4r. green | 20 | 35 |
| 206 | - | 7r. red | 30 | 55 |
| 207 | - | 10r. brown | 40 | 75 |

DESIGNS: 4r., 7r., 10r. Various bas-reliefs of ancient sports from Angkor Vat.

**53** Wild Boar

**1967.** Fauna.

| | | | | |
|---|---|---|---|---|
| 208 | **53** | 3r. black, green and blue | 70 | 45 |
| 209 | - | 5r. multicoloured | 80 | 75 |
| 210 | - | 7r. multicoloured | 1·30 | 1·10 |

FAUNA—VERT: 5r. Hog-deer. HORIZ: 7r. Indian elephant.

**1967.** International Tourist Year. Nos. 191/2, 194/5 and 149 optd ANNEE INTERNATIONALE DU TOURISME 1967.

| | | | | |
|---|---|---|---|---|
| 211 | **48** | 3r. green, turquoise & brn | 65 | 45 |
| 212 | **48** | 5r. brown, green & purple | 75 | 45 |
| 213 | - | 9r. purple, green and blue | 1·10 | 75 |
| 214 | - | 12r. red, green & verm | 1·30 | 90 |
| 215 | **33** | 15r. brown, blue & green | 1·60 | 1·10 |

**1967.** Millenary of Banteay Srei Temple. No. 193 optd MILLENAIRE DE BANTEAY SREI 967–1967.

| | | | |
|---|---|---|---|
| 216 | 7r. brown, green and ochre | 1·10 | 45 |

**56** Ballet Dancer

**1967.** Cambodian Royal Ballet. Designs showing ballet dancers.

| | | | | |
|---|---|---|---|---|
| 217 | **56** | 1r. orange | 30 | 35 |
| 218 | - | 3r. blue | 65 | 35 |
| 219 | - | 5r. blue | 85 | 45 |
| 220 | - | 7r. red | 1·30 | 65 |
| 221 | - | 10r. multicoloured | 1·70 | 90 |

**1967.** Int Literacy Day. Surch Journee Internationale de l'Alphabetisation 8-9-67 and new value.

| | | | | |
|---|---|---|---|---|
| 222 | **37** | 6r. on 12r. blue, grn & red | 70 | 35 |
| 223 | **15** | 7r. on 15r. brown & green | 85 | 55 |

**58** Decade Emblem

**1967.** International Hydrological Decade.

| | | | | |
|---|---|---|---|---|
| 224 | **58** | 1r. orange, blue and black | 20 | 20 |
| 225 | **58** | 6r. orange, blue and violet | 40 | 35 |
| 226 | **58** | 10r. orange, lt green & grn | 60 | 55 |

**59** Royal University of Kompong-Cham

**1968.** Cambodian Universities and Institutes.

| | | | | |
|---|---|---|---|---|
| 227 | **59** | 4r. purple, blue & brown | 40 | 30 |
| 228 | - | 6r. brown, green and blue | 55 | 35 |
| 229 | - | 9r. brown, green and blue | 75 | 45 |

DESIGNS: 6r. "Khmero-Soviet Friendship" Higher Technical Institute; 9r. Sangkum Reaster Niyum University Centre.

**60** Doctor tending child

**1968.** 20th Anniv of WHO.

| | | | | |
|---|---|---|---|---|
| 230 | **60** | 3r. blue | 45 | 30 |
| 231 | - | 7r. blue | 65 | 45 |

DESIGN: 7r. Man using insecticide.

**61** Stadium

**1968.** Olympic Games, Mexico.

| | | | | |
|---|---|---|---|---|
| 232 | **61** | 1r. brown, green and red | 40 | 30 |
| 233 | - | 2r. brown, red and blue | 45 | 35 |
| 234 | - | 3r. brown, blue and purple | 55 | 35 |
| 235 | - | 5r. violet | 60 | 35 |
| 236 | - | 7r.50 brown, green & red | 85 | 45 |

DESIGNS—HORIZ: 2r. Wrestling; 3r. Cycling. VERT: 5r. Boxing; 7r.50, Runner with torch.

**62** Stretcher-party

**1968.** Cambodian Red Cross Fortnight.

| | | | | |
|---|---|---|---|---|
| 237 | **62** | 3r. red, green and blue | 70 | 30 |

**63** Prince Norodom Sihanouk

**1968.** 15th Anniv of Independence.

| | | | | |
|---|---|---|---|---|
| 238 | **63** | 7r. violet, green and blue | 45 | 45 |
| 239 | - | 8r. brown, green and blue | 45 | 65 |

DESIGN: 8r. Soldiers wading through stream.

**64** Human Rights Emblem and Prince Norodom Sihanouk

**1968.** Human Rights Year.

| | | | | |
|---|---|---|---|---|
| 240 | **64** | 3r. blue | 30 | 20 |
| 241 | **64** | 5r. purple | 65 | 30 |
| 242 | **64** | 7r. black, orange & green | 95 | 45 |

**65** ILO Emblem

**1969.** 50th Anniv of ILO.

| | | | | |
|---|---|---|---|---|
| 243 | **65** | 3r. blue | 25 | 20 |
| 244 | **65** | 6r. red | 40 | 30 |
| 245 | **65** | 9r. green | 65 | 45 |

**66** Red Cross Emblems around Globe

**1969.** 50th Anniv of League of Red Cross Societies.

| | | | | |
|---|---|---|---|---|
| 246 | **66** | 1r. multicoloured | 30 | 20 |
| 247 | **66** | 3r. multicoloured | 40 | 30 |
| 248 | **66** | 10r. multicoloured | 85 | 45 |

**67** Golden Birdwing

**1969.** Butterflies.

| | | | | |
|---|---|---|---|---|
| 249 | **67** | 3r. black, yellow & violet | 1·40 | 55 |
| 250 | - | 4r. black, green & verm | 1·40 | 85 |
| 251 | - | 8r. black, orange & green | 1·80 | 1·40 |

DESIGNS: 4r. Tailed jay. 8r. Orange tiger.

**68** Diesel Train and Route Map

**1969.** Opening of Phnom Penh–Sihanoukville Railway.

| | | | | |
|---|---|---|---|---|
| 252 | **68** | 3r. multicoloured | 30 | 30 |
| 253 | - | 6r. brown, black & green | 45 | 30 |
| 254 | - | 8r. black | 75 | 35 |
| 255 | - | 9r. blue, turquoise & grn | 85 | 45 |

DESIGNS: 6r. Phnom Penh Station; 8r. Diesel locomotive and Kampor Station; 9r. Steam locomotive at Sihanoukville Station.

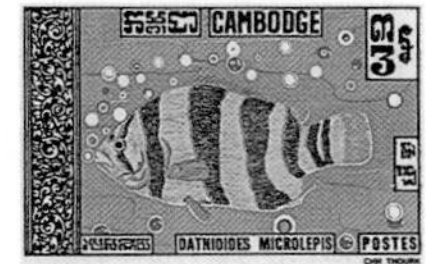


**69** Siamese Tigerfish

**1970.** Fishes. Multicoloured.

| | | | |
|---|---|---|---|
| 256 | 3r. Type **69** | 75 | 65 |
| 257 | 7r. Marbled sleeper | 1·50 | 1·10 |
| 258 | 9r. Chevron snakehead | 2·40 | 1·50 |

**70** Vat Tepthidaram

**1970.** Buddhist Monasteries in Cambodia. Mult.

| | | | |
|---|---|---|---|
| 259 | 2r. Type **70** | 40 | 30 |
| 260 | 3r. Vat Maniratanaram (horiz) | 45 | 30 |
| 261 | 6r. Vat Patumavati (horiz) | 85 | 35 |
| 262 | 8r. Vat Unnalom (horiz) | 1·60 | 45 |

**71** Dish Aerial and Open Book

**1970.** World Telecommunications Day.

| | | | | |
|---|---|---|---|---|
| 263 | **71** | 3r. multicoloured | 15 | 20 |
| 264 | **71** | 4r. multicoloured | 25 | 20 |
| 265 | **71** | 9r. multicoloured | 40 | 35 |

**72** New Headquarters Building

**1970.** Opening of New UPU Headquarters Building, Berne.

| | | | | |
|---|---|---|---|---|
| 266 | **72** | 1r. multicoloured | 20 | 10 |
| 267 | **72** | 3r. multicoloured | 30 | 10 |
| 268 | **72** | 4r. multicoloured | 55 | 10 |
| 269 | **72** | 10r. multicoloured | 1·10 | 35 |

**73** "Nelumbium speciosum"

**1970.** Aquatic Plants. Multicoloured.

| | | | |
|---|---|---|---|
| 270 | 3r. Type **73** | 40 | 55 |
| 271 | 4r. "Eichhornia crassipes" | 60 | 55 |
| 272 | 13r. "Nymphea lotus" | 1·10 | 85 |

**74** "Banteay-srei" (bas-relief)

**1970.** World Meteorological Day.

| | | | | |
|---|---|---|---|---|
| 273 | **74** | 3r. red and green | 30 | 10 |
| 274 | **74** | 4r. red, green and blue | 45 | 30 |
| 275 | **74** | 7r. green, blue and black | 60 | 55 |

**75** Rocket, Dove and Globe

**1970.** 25th Anniv of United Nations.

| | | | | |
|---|---|---|---|---|
| 276 | **75** | 3r. multicoloured | 25 | 20 |
| 277 | **75** | 5r. multicoloured | 45 | 35 |
| 278 | **75** | 10r. multicoloured | 65 | 55 |

**76** IEY Emblem

**1970.** International Education Year.

| | | | | |
|---|---|---|---|---|
| 279 | **76** | 1r. blue | 15 | 10 |
| 280 | **76** | 3r. purple | 20 | 10 |
| 281 | **76** | 8r. green | 50 | 35 |

**77** Samdech Chuon Nath

**1971.** 2nd Death Anniv of Samdech Chuon-Nath (Khmer language scholar).

| | | | | |
|---|---|---|---|---|
| 282 | **77** | 3r. multicoloured | 25 | 10 |
| 283 | **77** | 8r. multicoloured | 60 | 30 |
| 284 | **77** | 9r. multicoloured | 75 | 45 |

For issues between 1971 and 1989 see under KHMER REPUBLIC and KAMPUCHEA in volume 3.

**203** 17th-century Coach

**1989.** Coaches. Multicoloured.

| | | | |
|---|---|---|---|
| 1020 | 2r. Type **203** | 10 | 10 |
| 1021 | 3r. Paris–Lyon coach, 1720 | 15 | 10 |
| 1022 | 5r. Mail coach, 1793 | 25 | 10 |
| 1023 | 10r. Light mail coach, 1805 | 55 | 20 |
| 1024 | 15r. Royal mail coach | 80 | 30 |
| 1025 | 20r. Russian mail coach | 95 | 35 |
| 1026 | 35r. Paris–Lille coupe, 1837 (vert) | 1·90 | 55 |
| **MS**1027 | 60×84 mm. 45r. Royal messenger coach, 1815 (31×39 mm) | 4·25 | 90 |

No. **MS**1027 commemorates "Philexfrance '89" International Stamp Exhibition, Paris.

**204** "Papilio zagreus"

**1989.** "Brasiliana 89" International Stamp Exhibition, Rio de Janeiro. Butterflies. Multicoloured.

| | | | |
|---|---|---|---|
| 1028 | 2r. Type **204** | 10 | 10 |
| 1029 | 3r. "Morpho catenarius" | 15 | 10 |
| 1030 | 5r. "Morpho aega" | 25 | 10 |
| 1031 | 10r. "Callithea sapphira" ("wrongly inscr "saphhira") | 50 | 10 |
| 1032 | 15r. "Catagramma sorana" | 75 | 20 |
| 1033 | 20r. "Pierella nereis" | 95 | 20 |
| 1034 | 35r. "Papilio brasiliensis" | 1·90 | 20 |
| **MS**1035 | 100×66 mm. 45r. *Thecla marsyas* (39×31 mm) | 5·25 | 90 |

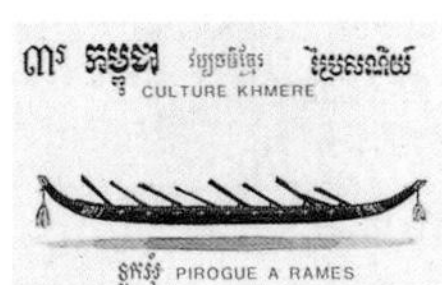


**205** Pirogue

**1989.** Khmer Culture. Multicoloured.

| | | | |
|---|---|---|---|
| 1036 | 3r. Type **205** | 20 | 10 |
| 1037 | 12r. Pirogue (two sets of oars) | 80 | 35 |
| 1038 | 30r. Pirogue with cabin | 2·10 | 90 |

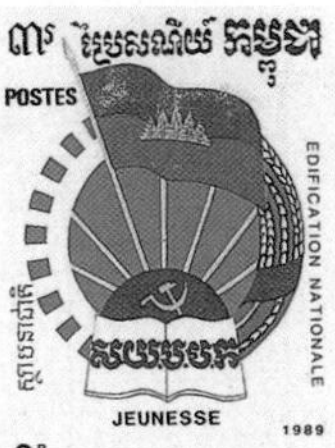


**206** Youth

**1989.** National Development. Multicoloured.

| | | | |
|---|---|---|---|
| 1039 | 3r. Type **206** | 20 | 10 |
| 1040 | 12r. Trade unions emblem (horiz) | 60 | 20 |
| 1041 | 30r. National Front emblem (horiz) | 1·70 | 75 |

**207** Goalkeeper

**1990.** World Cup Football Championship, Italy. Multicoloured.

| | | | |
|---|---|---|---|
| 1042 | 2r. Type **207** | 10 | 10 |
| 1043 | 3r. Dribbling ball | 15 | 10 |
| 1044 | 5r. Controlling ball with thigh | 25 | 10 |
| 1045 | 10r. Running with ball | 55 | 10 |
| 1046 | 15r. Shooting | 80 | 20 |
| 1047 | 20r. Tackling | 95 | 20 |
| 1048 | 35r. Tackling (different) | 1·90 | 20 |
| **MS**1049 | 94×75 mm. 45r. Players (31×39 mm) | 4·25 | 90 |

**208** Two-horse Postal Van

**1990.** "Stamp World London 90" International Stamp Exhibition. Royal Mail Horse-drawn Transport. Multicoloured.

| | | | |
|---|---|---|---|
| 1050 | 2r. Type **208** | 10 | 10 |
| 1051 | 3r. One-horse cart | 10 | 10 |
| 1052 | 5r. Rural post office cart | 15 | 10 |
| 1053 | 10r. Rural post office van | 25 | 10 |
| 1054 | 15r. Local post office van | 40 | 20 |
| 1055 | 20r. Parcel-post cart | 55 | 20 |
| 1056 | 35r. Two-horse wagon | 1·10 | 20 |
| **MS**1057 | 69×80 mm. 45r. Rural one-horse van (39×31 mm) | 4·25 | 90 |

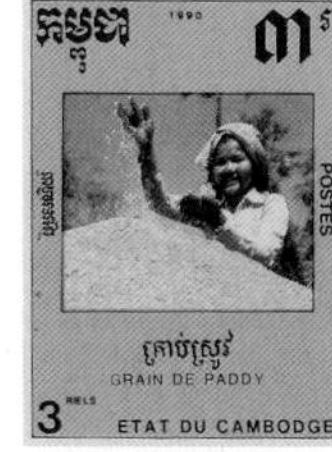


**209** Rice Grains

**1990.** Cultivation of Rice. Multicoloured.

| | | | |
|---|---|---|---|
| 1058 | 3r. Type **209** | 20 | 10 |
| 1059 | 12r. Transporting rice (horiz) | 80 | 35 |
| 1060 | 30r. Threshing rice | 2·10 | 90 |

**210** Shooting

**1990.** Olympic Games, Barcelona (1992) (1st issue). Multicoloured.

| | | | |
|---|---|---|---|
| 1061 | 2r. Type **210** | 10 | 10 |
| 1062 | 3r. Putting the shot | 15 | 10 |
| 1063 | 5r. Weightlifting | 25 | 10 |
| 1064 | 10r. Boxing | 55 | 10 |
| 1065 | 15r. Pole vaulting | 80 | 20 |
| 1066 | 20r. Basketball | 1·10 | 20 |
| 1067 | 35r. Fencing | 1·90 | 20 |
| **MS**1068 | 83×70 mm. 45r. Gymnastics (31×37 mm) | 4·25 | 90 |

See also Nos. 1163/**MS**1170, 1208/**MS**1213 and 1241/**MS**1246.

**211** Four-man Bobsleighing

**1990.** Winter Olympic Games, Albertville (1992) (1st issue). Multicoloured.

| | | | |
|---|---|---|---|
| 1069 | 2r. Type **211** | 10 | 10 |
| 1070 | 3r. Speed skating | 15 | 10 |
| 1071 | 5r. Figure skating | 20 | 10 |
| 1072 | 10r. Ice hockey | 45 | 10 |
| 1073 | 15r. Biathlon | 70 | 20 |
| 1074 | 20r. Lugeing | 90 | 20 |
| 1075 | 35r. Ski jumping | 1·70 | 20 |
| **MS**1076 | 64×104 mm. Ice hockey goalkeeper (31×38 mm) | 4·25 | 90 |

See also Nos. 1152/**MS**1159.

**212** Facade of Banteay Srei

**1990.** Khmer Culture. Multicoloured.

| | | | |
|---|---|---|---|
| 1077 | 3r. Type **212** | 20 | 10 |
| 1078 | 12r. Ox-carts (12th-century relief) | 80 | 35 |
| 1079 | 30r. Banon ruins (36×21 mm) | 2·10 | 90 |

**213** "Zizina oxleyi"

**1990.** "New Zealand 1990" International Stamp Exhibition, Auckland. Butterflies. Multicoloured.

| | | | |
|---|---|---|---|
| 1080 | 2r. Type **213** | 10 | 10 |
| 1081 | 3r. "Cupha prosope" | 10 | 10 |
| 1082 | 5r. "Heteronympha merope" | 15 | 10 |
| 1083 | 10r. "Dodonidia helmsi" | 30 | 20 |
| 1084 | 15r. "Argiropjenga antipodum" | 55 | 20 |
| 1085 | 20r. "Tysonotis danis" | 80 | 20 |
| 1086 | 35r. "Pyrameis gonnarilla" | 1·20 | 30 |
| **MS**1087 | 76×65 mm. 45r. "Pyrameis itea" (39×31 mm) | 5·75 | 1·10 |

**214** "Vostok"

**1990.** Spacecraft. Multicoloured.

| | | | |
|---|---|---|---|
| 1088 | 2r. Type **214** | 10 | 10 |
| 1089 | 3r. "Soyuz" | 10 | 10 |
| 1090 | 5r. Satellite | 15 | 10 |
| 1091 | 10r. "Luna 10" | 35 | 20 |
| 1092 | 15r. "Mars 1" | 55 | 30 |
| 1093 | 20r. "Venus 3" | 70 | 35 |
| 1094 | 35r. "Mir" space station | 1·10 | 75 |
| **MS**1095 | 92×72 mm. 45r. "Energiya" and space shuttle "Burn" (31×39 mm) | 5·25 | 90 |

**215** Poodle

**1990.** Dogs. Multicoloured.

| | | | |
|---|---|---|---|
| 1096 | 20c. Type **215** | 20 | 10 |
| 1097 | 80c. Shetland sheepdog | 20 | 10 |
| 1098 | 3r. Samoyede | 45 | 10 |
| 1099 | 6r. Springer spaniel | 85 | 10 |
| 1100 | 10r. Wire-haired fox terrier | 1·10 | 20 |
| 1101 | 15r. Afghan hound | 1·70 | 20 |
| 1102 | 25r. Dalmatian | 2·30 | 20 |
| **MS**1103 | 95×83 mm. Burmese mountain dog (39×31 mm) | 4·25 | 90 |

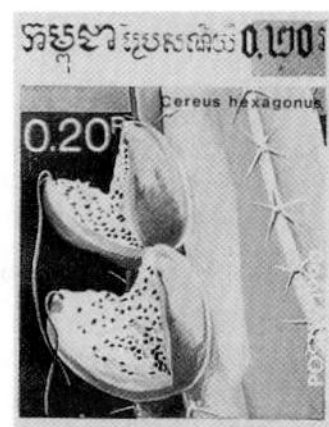


**216** "Cereus hexagonus"

**1990.** Cacti. Multicoloured.

| | | | |
|---|---|---|---|
| 1104 | 20c. Type **216** | 10 | 10 |
| 1105 | 80c. "Arthrocereus rondonianus" | 10 | 10 |
| 1106 | 3r. "Matucana multicolor" | 15 | 10 |
| 1107 | 6r. "Hildewintera aureispina" | 25 | 10 |
| 1108 | 10r. "Opuntia retrosa" | 50 | 20 |
| 1109 | 15r. "Erdisia tenuicula" | 75 | 20 |
| 1110 | 25r. "Mamillaria yaquensis" | 1·10 | 20 |

**217** Learning to Write

**1990.** International Literacy Year.

| | | | | |
|---|---|---|---|---|
| 1111 | **217** | 3r. black and blue | 15 | 10 |
| 1112 | **217** | 12r. black and yellow | 1·10 | 35 |
| 1113 | **217** | 30r. black and pink | 3·50 | 90 |

**218** English Nef, 1200

**1990.** Ships. Multicoloured.

| | | | |
|---|---|---|---|
| 1114 | 20c. Type **218** | 20 | 10 |
| 1115 | 80c. 16th-century Spanish galleon | 30 | 10 |
| 1116 | 3r. Dutch jacht, 1627 | 45 | 10 |
| 1117 | 6r. "La Couronne" (French galleon), 1638 | 85 | 10 |
| 1118 | 10r. Dumont d'Urville's ship "L'Astrolabe", 1826 | 1·10 | 20 |
| 1119 | 15r. "Louisiane" (steamer), 1864 | 1·90 | 20 |
| 1120 | 25r. Clipper, 1900 (vert) | 2·30 | 20 |
| **MS**1121 | 97×80 mm. 45r. 19th-century merchant brig (31×39 mm) | 4·75 | 90 |

No. 1118 is wrongly inscribed "d'Uville".

**219** Phnom-Penh–Kampong Som Railway

**1990.** National Development. Multicoloured.

| | | | |
|---|---|---|---|
| 1122 | 3r. Type **219** | 30 | 10 |
| 1123 | 12r. Port, Kampong Som | 1·30 | 35 |
| 1124 | 30r. Fishing boats, Kampong Som | 3·75 | 90 |

**220** Sacre-Coeur de Montmartre and White Bishop

**1990.** "Paris '90" World Chess Championship, Paris. Multicoloured.

| | | | |
|---|---|---|---|
| 1125 | 2r. Type **220** | 20 | 10 |
| 1126 | 3r. "The Horse Trainer" (statue) and white knight | 30 | 10 |
| 1127 | 5r. "Victory of Samothrace" (statue) and white queen | 45 | 10 |
| 1128 | 10r. Azay-le-Rideau Chateau and white rook | 95 | 20 |
| 1129 | 15r. "The Dance" (statue) and white pawn | 1·40 | 30 |
| 1130 | 20r. Eiffel Tower and white king | 1·90 | 35 |
| 1131 | 35r. Arc de Triomphe and black chessmen | 3·25 | 55 |
| **MS**1132 | 91×58 mm. 45r. White chessmen (39×31 mm) | 5·25 | 1·10 |

**221** Columbus

**1990.** 500th Anniv (1992) of Discovery of America by Columbus (1st issue). Multicoloured.

| | | | |
|---|---|---|---|
| 1133 | 2r. Type **221** | 30 | 10 |
| 1134 | 3r. Queen Isabella's jewel-chest | 45 | 10 |
| 1135 | 5r. Queen Isabella the Catholic | 55 | 10 |
| 1136 | 10r. "Santa Maria" (flagship) | 95 | 10 |
| 1137 | 15r. Juan de la Cosa | 1·40 | 10 |
| 1138 | 20r. Monument to Columbus | 1·90 | 20 |
| 1139 | 35r. Devin Pyramid, Yucatan | 3·50 | 20 |
| **MS**1140 | 79×60 mm. 45r. Christopher Columbus (31×39 mm) | 5·25 | 90 |

See also Nos. 1186/**MS**1193.

**222** Tyre Factory

**1991.** National Festival. Multicoloured.

| | | | |
|---|---|---|---|
| 1141 | 100r. Type **222** | 55 | 20 |
| 1142 | 300r. Rural hospital | 2·10 | 90 |
| 1143 | 500r. Freshwater fishing (27×40 mm) | 3·25 | 1·20 |

**223** Tackle

**1991.** World Cup Football Championship, U.S.A. (1994) (1st issue).

| | | | | |
|---|---|---|---|---|
| 1144 | **223** | 5r. multicoloured | 15 | 10 |
| 1145 | - | 25r. multicoloured | 15 | 10 |
| 1146 | - | 70r. multicoloured | 35 | 10 |
| 1147 | - | 100r. multicoloured | 40 | 10 |
| 1148 | - | 200r. multicoloured | 75 | 20 |
| 1149 | - | 400r. multicoloured | 1·50 | 20 |
| 1150 | - | 1000r. multicoloured | 3·50 | 20 |
| **MS**1151 | | 85×93 mm. 900r. multicoloured | 5·25 | 90 |

DESIGNS: 25r. to 1000r. Different footballing scenes.

See also Nos. 1220/**MS**1225, 1317/**MS**1322 and 1381/**MS**1386.

**224** Speed Skating

**1991.** Winter Olympic Games, Albertville (1992) (2nd issue). Multicoloured.

| | | | |
|---|---|---|---|
| 1152 | 5r. Type **224** | 20 | 10 |
| 1153 | 25r. Slalom skiing | 30 | 10 |
| 1154 | 70r. Ice hockey | 55 | 10 |
| 1155 | 100r. Bobsleighing | 65 | 10 |
| 1156 | 200r. Freestyle skiing | 1·30 | 20 |
| 1157 | 400r. Ice skating | 2·50 | 20 |
| 1158 | 1000r. Downhill skiing | 3·75 | 20 |
| **MS**1159 | 87×62 mm. 900r. Ski jumping (31×39 mm) | 5·25 | 90 |

**225** "Torso of Vishnu Reclining" (11th cent)

**1991.** Sculpture. Multicoloured.

| | | | |
|---|---|---|---|
| 1160 | 100r. "Garuda" (Koh Ker, 10th century) | 35 | 20 |
| 1161 | 300r. Type **225** | 1·10 | 90 |
| 1162 | 500r. "Reclining Nandin" (7th century) | 1·90 | 1·10 |

**226** Pole Vaulting

**1991.** Olympic Games, Barcelona (1992) (2nd issue). Multicoloured.

| | | | |
|---|---|---|---|
| 1163 | 5r. Type **226** | 20 | 10 |
| 1164 | 25r. Table tennis | 30 | 10 |
| 1165 | 70r. Running | 45 | 10 |
| 1166 | 100r. Wrestling | 55 | 10 |
| 1167 | 200r. Gymnastics (bars) | 95 | 20 |
| 1168 | 400r. Tennis | 1·80 | 20 |
| 1169 | 1000r. Boxing | 4·25 | 20 |
| **MS**1170 | 78×73 mm. 900r. Gymnastics (beam) (31×39 mm) | 5·25 | 90 |

**227** Douglas DC-10-30

**1991.** Airplanes. Multicoloured.

| | | | |
|---|---|---|---|
| 1171 | 5r. Type **227** | 15 | 10 |
| 1172 | 25r. McDonnell Douglas MD-11 | 20 | 10 |
| 1173 | 70r. Ilyushin Il-96-300 | 30 | 10 |
| 1174 | 100r. Airbus Industrie A310 | 40 | 10 |
| 1175 | 200r. Yakovlev Yak-42 | 80 | 20 |
| 1176 | 400r. Tupolev Tu-154 | 1·50 | 20 |
| 1177 | 1000r. Douglas DC-9 | 3·75 | 20 |

**228** Diaguita Funerary Urn, Catamarca

**1991.** "Espamer '91" Iberia–Latin America Stamp Exhibition, Buenos Aires. Multicoloured.

| | | | |
|---|---|---|---|
| 1178 | 5r. Bareales glass pot, Catamarca (horiz) | 15 | 10 |
| 1179 | 25r. Type **228** | 20 | 10 |
| 1180 | 70r. Quiroga urn, Tucuman | 30 | 10 |
| 1181 | 100r. Round glass pot, Santiago del Estero (horiz) | 45 | 10 |
| 1182 | 200r. Pitcher, Santiago del Estero (horiz) | 85 | 20 |
| 1183 | 400r. Diaguita funerary urn, Tucuman | 1·60 | 20 |
| 1184 | 1000r. Bareales funerary urn, Catamarca (horiz) | 4·00 | 20 |
| **MS**1185 | 80×65 mm. 900r. Funerary urn, Catamarce (36×27 mm) | 5·25 | 90 |

229 "Pinta"

**1991.** 500th Anniv (1992) of Discovery of America by Columbus (2nd issue). Each brown, stone and black.

| | | | |
|---|---|---|---|
| 1186 | 5r. Type **229** | 20 | 10 |
| 1187 | 25r. "Nina" | 30 | 10 |
| 1188 | 70r. "Santa Maria" | 55 | 10 |
| 1189 | 100r. Landing at Guanahani, 1492 (horiz) | 65 | 10 |
| 1190 | 200r. Meeting of two cultures (horiz) | 1·30 | 20 |
| 1191 | 400r. La Navidad (first European settlement in America) (horiz) | 2·50 | 20 |
| 1192 | 1000r. Amerindian village (horiz) | 5·75 | 20 |
| **MS**1193 | 84×59 mm. Columbus (39×31 mm) | 5·75 | 90 |

230 "Neptis pryeri"

**1991.** "Phila Nippon '91" International Stamp Exhibition, Tokyo. Butterflies. Multicoloured.

| | | | |
|---|---|---|---|
| 1194 | 5r. Type **230** | 15 | 10 |
| 1195 | 25r. "Papilio xuthus" | 15 | 10 |
| 1196 | 70r. Common map butterfly | 10 | 10 |
| 1197 | 100r. "Argynnis anadiomene" | 40 | 10 |
| 1198 | 200r. "Lethe marginalis" | 75 | 20 |
| 1199 | 400r. "Artopoetes pryeri" | 95 | 20 |
| 1200 | 1000r. African monarch | 3·50 | 20 |
| **MS**1201 | 73×57 mm 900r. "Ochlodes subhyalina" (39×31 mm) | 5·25 | 1·10 |

231 Coastal Fishing Port

**1991.** National Development. Food Industry. Multicoloured.

| | | | |
|---|---|---|---|
| 1202 | 100r. Type **231** | 50 | 45 |
| 1203 | 300r. Preparing palm sugar (29×40 mm) | 1·40 | 90 |
| 1204 | 500r. Picking peppers | 2·40 | 1·20 |

232 Chakdomuk Costumes

**1992.** National Festival. Traditional Costumes. Multicoloured.

| | | | |
|---|---|---|---|
| 1205 | 150r. Type **232** | 50 | 20 |
| 1206 | 350r. Longvek | 1·40 | 30 |
| 1207 | 1000r. Angkor | 2·50 | 45 |

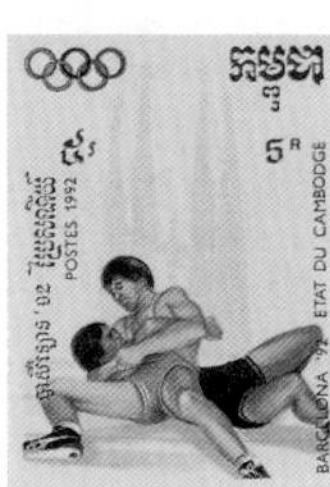
233 Wrestling

**1992.** Olympic Games, Barcelona (3rd issue). Multicoloured.

| | | | |
|---|---|---|---|
| 1208 | 5r. Type **233** | 15 | 10 |
| 1209 | 15r. Football | 15 | 10 |
| 1210 | 80r. Weightlifting | 20 | 10 |
| 1211 | 400r. Archery | 1·00 | 30 |
| 1212 | 1500r. Gymnastics | 3·50 | 35 |
| **MS**1213 | 79×59 mm. 1000r. show jumping (31×39 mm) | 4·25 | 90 |

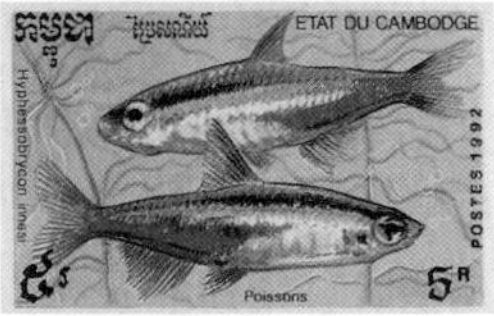
234 Neon Tetra

**1992.** Fishes. Multicoloured.

| | | | |
|---|---|---|---|
| 1214 | 5r. Type **234** | 15 | 10 |
| 1215 | 15r. Siamese fighting fish | 15 | 10 |
| 1216 | 80r. Kaiser tetra | 20 | 10 |
| 1217 | 400r. Dwarf gourami | 1·00 | 30 |
| 1218 | 1500r. Port hoplo | 3·50 | 35 |
| **MS**1219 | 80×65 mm. 1000r. Freshwater angelfish (39×31 mm) | 4·25 | 90 |

235 Germany v. Columbia

**1992.** World Cup Football Championship, U.S.A. (1994) (2nd issue). Multicoloured.

| | | | |
|---|---|---|---|
| 1220 | 5r. Type **235** | 15 | 10 |
| 1221 | 15r. Netherlands player (horiz) | 15 | 10 |
| 1222 | 80r. Uruguay v. C.I.S. (ex-Soviet states) | 20 | 10 |
| 1223 | 400r. Cameroun v. Yugoslavia | 1·00 | 30 |
| 1224 | 1500r. Italy v. Sweden | 3·50 | 35 |
| **MS**1225 | 75×51 mm. 1000r. Shot at goal (39×31 mm) | 4·25 | 90 |

236 Monument

**1992.** Khmer Culture. 19th-century Architecture. Multicoloured.

| | | | |
|---|---|---|---|
| 1226 | 150r. Type **236** | 55 | 35 |
| 1227 | 350r. Stupa | 1·30 | 85 |
| 1228 | 1000r. Mandapa library | 3·50 | 2·00 |

237 Motor Car

**1992.** 540th Birth Anniv (1992) of Leonardo da Vinci (artist and inventor). Multicoloured.

| | | | |
|---|---|---|---|
| 1229 | 5r. Type **237** | 20 | 10 |
| 1230 | 15r. Container ship | 20 | 10 |
| 1231 | 80r. Helicopter | 30 | 10 |
| 1232 | 400r. Scuba diver | 1·50 | 30 |
| 1233 | 1500r. Parachutists (vert) | 4·75 | 35 |
| **MS**1234 | 79×59 mm. 1000r. Da Vinci and drawing of "Flying Man" (31×39 mm) | 4·75 | 90 |

238 Juan de la Cierva and Autogyro

**1992.** "Expo '92" World's Fair, Seville. Inventors. Multicoloured (except MS1240).

| | | | |
|---|---|---|---|
| 1235 | 5r. Type **238** | 20 | 10 |
| 1236 | 15r. Thomas Edison and electric light bulb | 20 | 10 |
| 1237 | 80r. Samuel Morse and Morse telegraph | 30 | 10 |
| 1238 | 400r. Narciso Monturiol and "Ictineo" (early submarine) | 1·40 | 30 |
| 1239 | 1500r. Alexander Graham Bell and early telephone | 2·75 | 35 |
| **MS**1240 | 83×62 mm.1000r. pink and black (Robert Fulton (steamship)) (31×39 mm) | 4·75 | 90 |

239 Weightlifting

**1992.** Olympic Games, Barcelona (4th issue). Multicoloured.

| | | | |
|---|---|---|---|
| 1241 | 5r. Type **239** | 20 | 10 |
| 1242 | 15r. Boxing | 20 | 10 |
| 1243 | 80r. Basketball | 30 | 10 |
| 1244 | 400r. Running | 1·40 | 30 |
| 1245 | 1500r. Water polo | 4·75 | 35 |
| **MS**1246 | 71×75 mm. 1000r. Gymnastics (39×31 mm) | 4·50 | 90 |

240 Palm Trees

**1992.** Environmental Protection. Multicoloured.

| | | | |
|---|---|---|---|
| 1247 | 5r. Couple on riverside | 20 | 10 |
| 1248 | 15r. Pagoda | 20 | 10 |
| 1249 | 80r. Type **240** | 30 | 10 |
| 1250 | 400r. Boy riding water buffalo | 1·40 | 30 |
| 1251 | 1500r. Swimming in river | 4·75 | 35 |
| **MS**1252 | 100×71 mm. 1000r. Angkor Wat (39×31 mm) | 4·50 | 90 |

241 Louis de Bougainville and "La Boudeuse"

**1992.** "Genova '92" International Thematic Stamp Exhibition, Genoa. Multicoloured.

| | | | |
|---|---|---|---|
| 1253 | 5r. Type **241** | 20 | 10 |
| 1254 | 15r. James Cook and H.M.S. "Endeavour" | 30 | 10 |
| 1255 | 80r. Charles Darwin and H.M.S. "Beagle" | 45 | 10 |
| 1256 | 400r. Jacques Cousteau and "Calypso" | 1·50 | 30 |
| 1257 | 1500r. "Kon Tiki" (replica of balsa raft) | 5·25 | 35 |
| **MS**1258 | 80×65 mm. 1000r. Christopher Columbus (28×36 mm) | 4·50 | 90 |

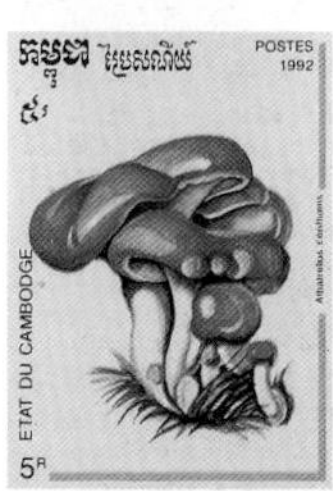
242 "Albatrellus confluens"

**1992.** Fungi. Multicoloured.

| | | | |
|---|---|---|---|
| 1259 | 5r. Type **242** | 15 | 10 |
| 1260 | 15r. Scarlet-stemmed boletus | 20 | 10 |
| 1261 | 80r. Verdigris agaric | 25 | 10 |
| 1262 | 400r. "Telamonia armillata" | 1·00 | 30 |
| 1263 | 1500r. Goaty smell cortinarius | 3·75 | 35 |

243 Bellanca Pacemaker Seaplane, 1930

**1992.** Aircraft. Multicoloured.

| | | | |
|---|---|---|---|
| 1264 | 5r. Type **243** | 20 | 10 |
| 1265 | 15r. Canadair CL-215 fire-fighting amphibian, 1965 | 20 | 10 |
| 1266 | 80r. Grumman G-21 Goose amphibian, 1937 | 30 | 10 |
| 1267 | 400r. Grumman SA-6 Sealand flying boat, 1947 | 1·30 | 30 |
| 1268 | 1500r. Short S.23 Empire "C" Class flying boat, 1936 | 4·50 | 35 |
| **MS**1269 | 80×60 mm. Grumman G-44 Widgeon, 1940 (31×39 mm) | 4·50 | 90 |

244 Dish Aerial

**1992.** National Development. Multicoloured.

| | | | |
|---|---|---|---|
| 1270 | 150r. Type **244** | 55 | 20 |
| 1271 | 350r. Dish aerial, flags and satellite | 1·30 | 30 |
| 1272 | 1000r. Hotel Cambodiana | 4·00 | 45 |

245 Sociological Institute

**1993.** National Festival. Multicoloured.

| | | | |
|---|---|---|---|
| 1273 | 50r. Type **245** | 45 | 20 |
| 1274 | 450r. Motel Cambodiana | 1·40 | 30 |
| 1275 | 1000r. Theatre, Bassac | 4·00 | 45 |

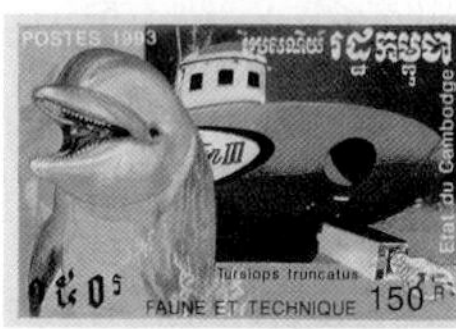
246 Bottle-nosed Dolphin and Submarine

**1993.** Wildlife and Technology. Multicoloured.

| | | | |
|---|---|---|---|
| 1276 | 150r. Type **246** | 55 | 10 |
| 1277 | 200r. Supersonic jet airplane and peregrine falcon | 65 | 20 |
| 1278 | 250r. Eurasian beaver and dam | 75 | 20 |
| 1279 | 500r. Satellite and natterer's bat | 2·00 | 20 |
| 1280 | 900r. Rufous humming-bird and helicopter | 3·00 | 30 |

247 "Datura suaveolens"

**1993.** Wild Flowers. Multicoloured.

| | | | |
|---|---|---|---|
| 1281 | 150r. Type **247** | 55 | 10 |
| 1282 | 200r. "Convolvulus tricolor" | 65 | 20 |
| 1283 | 250r. "Hippeastrum" hybrid | 75 | 20 |
| 1284 | 500r. "Camellia" hybrid | 1·90 | 20 |
| 1285 | 900r. "Lilium speciosum" | 3·00 | 30 |
| **MS**1286 | 75×50 mm. 1000t. Various flowers (31×39 mm) | 4·50 | 1·10 |

**248** Vihear Temple

**1993.** Khmer Culture. Multicoloured.

| | | | |
|---|---|---|---|
| 1287 | 50r. Sculpture of ox | 45 | 20 |
| 1288 | 450r. Type **248** | 1·30 | 75 |
| 1289 | 1000r. Offering to Buddha | 3·75 | 1·70 |

**249** Philippine Flying Lemur

**1993.** Animals. Multicoloured.

| | | | |
|---|---|---|---|
| 1290 | 150r. Type **249** | 55 | 20 |
| 1291 | 200r. Red giant flying squirrel | 65 | 20 |
| 1292 | 250r. Fringed gecko | 75 | 30 |
| 1293 | 500r. Wallace's flying frog | 2·00 | 35 |
| 1294 | 900r. Flying lizard | 3·00 | 65 |

**250** "Symbrenthia hypselis"

**1993.** "Brasiliana '93" International Stamp Exhibition, Rio de Janeiro. Butterflies. Mult.

| | | | |
|---|---|---|---|
| 1295 | 250r. Type **250** | 75 | 20 |
| 1296 | 350r. "Sithon nedymond" | 1·30 | 20 |
| 1297 | 600r. "Geitoneura minyas" | 1·90 | 30 |
| 1298 | 800r. "Argyreus hyperbius" | 2·40 | 35 |
| 1299 | 1000r. "Argyrophenga antipodum" | 3·25 | 65 |
| MS1300 | 82×52 mm. 1500r. "Parage schakra" (39×31 mm) | 5·75 | 1·10 |

**251** Armed Cambodians reporting to U.N. Base

**1993.** United Nations Transitional Authority in Cambodia Pacification Programme. Each black and blue.

| | | | |
|---|---|---|---|
| 1301 | 150r. Type **251** | 55 | 10 |
| 1302 | 200r. Military camp | 65 | 20 |
| 1303 | 250r. Surrender of arms | 75 | 20 |
| 1304 | 500r. Vocational training | 1·70 | 20 |
| 1305 | 900r. Liberation | 2·75 | 30 |
| MS1306 | 54×84 mm. 1000r. Return to homes (31×39 mm) | 4·75 | 1·10 |

**252** Venetian Felucca

**1993.** Sailing Ships. Multicoloured.

| | | | |
|---|---|---|---|
| 1307 | 150r. Type **252** | 40 | 10 |
| 1308 | 200r. Phoenician galley | 50 | 20 |
| 1309 | 250r. Egyptian merchantman | 65 | 20 |
| 1310 | 500r. Genoese merchantman | 1·50 | 20 |
| 1311 | 900r. English merchantman | 2·40 | 30 |

**253** Santos-Dumont, Eiffel Tower and "Ballon No. 6", 1901

**1993.** 120th Birth Anniv of Alberto Santos-Dumont (aviator). Multicoloured.

| | | | |
|---|---|---|---|
| 1312 | 150r. Type **253** | 55 | 10 |
| 1313 | 200r. "14 bis" (biplane), 1906 (horiz) | 65 | 20 |
| 1314 | 250r. "Demoiselle" (monoplane), 1909 (horiz) | 75 | 20 |
| 1315 | 500r. Embraer EMB-201 A (horiz) | 2·00 | 20 |
| 1316 | 900r. Embraer EMB-111 (horiz) | 3·00 | 30 |

**254** Footballer

**1993.** World Cup Football Championship, U.S.A. (1994) (3rd issue).

| | | | | |
|---|---|---|---|---|
| 1317 | **254** | 250r. multicoloured | 75 | 10 |
| 1318 | - | 350r. multicoloured | 1·30 | 20 |
| 1319 | - | 600r. multicoloured | 1·90 | 20 |
| 1320 | - | 800r. multicoloured | 2·40 | 20 |
| 1321 | - | 1000r. mult (vert) | 3·25 | 30 |
| MS1322 | | 60×85 mm. 1500r. multicoloured (39×31 mm) | 5·75 | 1·10 |

DESIGNS: 350r. to 1500r. Various footballing scenes.

**255** European Wigeon

**1993.** "Bangkok 1993" International Stamp Exhibition, Thailand. Ducks. Multicoloured.

| | | | |
|---|---|---|---|
| 1323 | 250r. Type **255** | 75 | 20 |
| 1324 | 350r. Baikal teal | 1·30 | 30 |
| 1325 | 600r. Mandarin | 1·90 | 35 |
| 1326 | 800r. Wood duck | 2·40 | 65 |
| 1327 | 1000r. Harlequin duck | 3·25 | 85 |
| MS1328 | 63×89 mm. 1500tr. Head of mandarin (39×31 mm) | 5·75 | 90 |

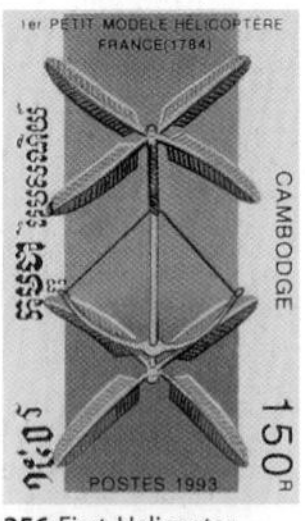


**256** First Helicopter Model, France, 1784

**1993.** Vertical Take-off Aircraft. Multicoloured.

| | | | |
|---|---|---|---|
| 1329 | 150r. Type **256** | 55 | 10 |
| 1330 | 200r. Model of steam helicopter, 1863 | 65 | 20 |
| 1331 | 250r. New York–Atlanta–Miami autogyro flight, 1927 (horiz) | 75 | 20 |
| 1332 | 500r. Sikorsky helicopter, 1943 (horiz) | 1·70 | 20 |
| 1333 | 900r. French vertical take-off jet | 3·00 | 30 |
| MS1334 | 90×49 mm. 1000r. Juan de la Clerva's C.4, 1923 (first practical autogyro) | 4·75 | 90 |

**257** "Cnaphalocrosis medinalis"

**1993.** National Development. Harmful Insects. Multicoloured.

| | | | |
|---|---|---|---|
| 1335 | 50r. Type **257** | 30 | 20 |
| 1336 | 450r. Brown leaf-hopper | 1·50 | 20 |
| 1337 | 500r. "Scirpophaga incertulas" | 1·70 | 30 |
| 1338 | 1000r. Stalk-eyed fly | 3·50 | 30 |
| MS1339 | 89×90 mm. 1000r. "Leptocorisa oratorius" (31×39 mm) | 4·75 | 90 |

**258** Ministry of Posts and Telecommunications

**1993.** 40th Anniv of Independence.

| | | | | |
|---|---|---|---|---|
| 1340 | **258** | 300r. multicoloured | 1·10 | 30 |
| 1341 | - | 500r. multicoloured | 1·70 | 65 |
| 1342 | - | 700r. blue. red & black | 2·50 | 90 |

DESIGNS—VERT: 500r. Independence monument. HORIZ: 700r. National flag.

**259** Boy with Pony

**1993.** Figurines by M. J. Hummel. Multicoloured.

| | | | |
|---|---|---|---|
| 1343 | 50r. Type **259** | 20 | 10 |
| 1344 | 100r. Girl and pram | 55 | 10 |
| 1345 | 150r. Girl bathing doll | 75 | 10 |
| 1346 | 200r. Girl holding doll | 95 | 20 |
| 1347 | 250r. Boys playing | 1·20 | 20 |
| 1348 | 300r. Girls pulling boy in cart | 1·50 | 30 |
| 1349 | 350r. Girls playing ring-o-roses | 1·70 | 35 |
| 1350 | 600r. Boys with stick and drum | 2·75 | 55 |

**260** Figure Skating

**1994.** Winter Olympic Games, Lillehammer, Norway. Multicoloured.

| | | | |
|---|---|---|---|
| 1351 | 150r. Type **260** | 45 | 10 |
| 1352 | 250r. Two-man luge (horiz) | 75 | 20 |
| 1353 | 400r. Skiing (horiz) | 1·30 | 20 |
| 1354 | 700r. Biathlon (horiz) | 2·30 | 20 |
| 1355 | 1000r. Speed skating | 3·25 | 30 |
| MS1356 | 85×60 mm. 1500r. Curling (31×39 mm) | 5·75 | 90 |

**261** Opel 4/12 Laubfrosch two-seater, 1924

**1994.** Motor Cars. Multicoloured.

| | | | |
|---|---|---|---|
| 1357 | 150r. Type **261** | 55 | 10 |
| 1358 | 200r. Mercedes 35 h.p. four-seater, 1901 | 65 | 20 |
| 1359 | 250r. Ford Model "T" Tudor sedan, 1927 | 75 | 20 |
| 1360 | 500r. Rolls Royce 40/50 Silver Ghost tourer, 1907 | 1·70 | 20 |
| 1361 | 900r. Hutton racing car, 1908 | 2·75 | 30 |
| MS1362 | 80×60 mm 1000r. Duesenberg model J phaeton, 1931 (31×39 mm) | 4·50 | 90 |

**262** Gymnastics

**1994.** Olympic Games, Atlanta (1996) (1st issue). Multicoloured.

| | | | |
|---|---|---|---|
| 1363 | 150r. Type **262** | 45 | 10 |
| 1364 | 200r. Football | 65 | 10 |
| 1365 | 250r. Throwing the javelin | 75 | 20 |
| 1366 | 300r. Canoeing | 85 | 20 |
| 1367 | 600r. Running | 1·90 | 20 |
| 1368 | 1000r. Diving (horiz) | 3·50 | 20 |
| MS1369 | 79×63 mm. 1500r. Show jumping (31×39 mm) | 5·75 | 90 |

See also Nos. 1437/**MS**1442 and 1495/**MS**1501.

**263** Siva and Uma (10th century, Banteay Srei)

**1994.** Khmer Culture. Statues. Multicoloured.

| | | | |
|---|---|---|---|
| 1370 | 300r. Type **263** | 1·10 | 55 |
| 1371 | 500r. Vishnu (6th cent, Tvol Dai-Buon) | 1·90 | 90 |
| 1372 | 700r. King Jayavarman VII (12th–13th century, Krol Romeas Angkor) | 2·75 | 1·30 |

**264** Olympic Flag

**1994.** Centenary of International Olympic Committee. Multicoloured.

| | | | |
|---|---|---|---|
| 1373 | 100r. Type **264** | 30 | 10 |
| 1374 | 300r. Flag and torch | 1·10 | 45 |
| 1375 | 600r. Flag and Pierre de Coubertin (reviver of modern Olympic Games) | 2·30 | 85 |

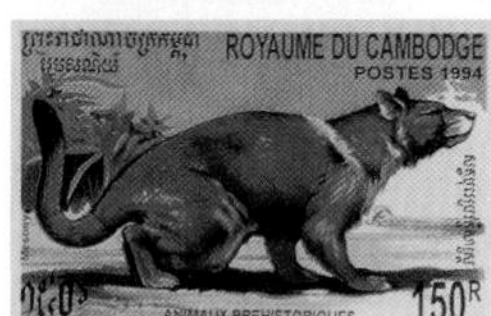


**265** Mesonyx

**1994.** Prehistoric Animals. Multicoloured.

| | | | |
|---|---|---|---|
| 1376 | 150r. Type **265** | 55 | 20 |
| 1377 | 250r. Doedicurus | 85 | 30 |
| 1378 | 400r. Mylodon | 1·50 | 45 |
| 1379 | 700r. Uintatherium | 2·50 | 55 |
| 1380 | 1000r. Hyrachyus | 3·50 | 85 |

**266** Players

**1994.** World Cup Football Championship, U.S.A. (4th issue).

| | | | | |
|---|---|---|---|---|
| 1381 | **266** | 150r. multicoloured | 45 | 10 |
| 1382 | - | 250r. multicoloured | 75 | 20 |
| 1383 | - | 400r. multicoloured | 1·30 | 20 |
| 1384 | - | 700r. multicoloured | 2·30 | 20 |
| 1385 | - | 1000r. multicoloured | 3·25 | 30 |
| **MS**1386 | | 58×78 mm. 1500r. multicoloured | 5·75 | 90 |

DESIGNS: 250r. to 1500r. Various footballing scenes.

**267** "Soldiers in Combat"

**1994.** Tourism. Statues in Public Gardens. Mult.

| | | | |
|---|---|---|---|
| 1387 | 300r. "Stag and Hind" | 1·30 | 45 |
| 1388 | 500r. Type **267** | 1·90 | 90 |
| 1389 | 700r. "Lions" | 2·75 | 1·40 |

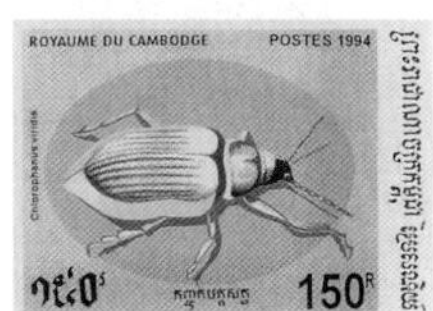
**268** "Chlorophanus viridis"

**1994.** Beetles. Multicoloured.

| | | | |
|---|---|---|---|
| 1390 | 150r. Type **268** | 55 | 10 |
| 1391 | 200r. "Chrysochroa fulgidissima" | 65 | 20 |
| 1392 | 250r. "Lytta vesicatoria" | 75 | 20 |
| 1393 | 500r. "Purpuricenus kaehleri" | 2·00 | 45 |
| 1394 | 900r. Herculese beetle | 3·00 | 75 |
| **MS**1395 | 69×50 mm. "Timarcha tenebricosa" (31×39 mm) | 4·75 | 90 |

**269** Halley's Diving-bell, 1690

**1994.** Submarines. Multicoloured.

| | | | |
|---|---|---|---|
| 1396 | 150r. Type **269** | 55 | 10 |
| 1397 | 200r. "Gimnote", 1886 (horiz) | 65 | 20 |
| 1398 | 250r. "Peral" (Spain), 1888 (horiz) | 75 | 20 |
| 1399 | 500r. "Nautilus" (first nuclear-powered submarine), 1954 (horiz) | 2·00 | 20 |
| 1400 | 900r. "Trieste" (bathyscaphe), 1953 (horiz) | 3·00 | 30 |
| **MS**1401 | 80×70 mm. 1000r. Narciso Monturiol's submarine "Ictineo", 1885 (39×31 mm) | 4·75 | 90 |

**270** Francois-Andre Philidor, 1795

**1994.** Chess Champions. Multicoloured.

| | | | |
|---|---|---|---|
| 1402 | 150r. Type **270** | 55 | 10 |
| 1403 | 200r. Mahe de la Bourdonnais, 1821 | 65 | 20 |
| 1404 | 250r. Karl Anderssen, 1851 | 75 | 20 |
| 1405 | 500r. Paul Morphy, 1858 | 2·00 | 45 |
| 1406 | 900r. Wilhelm Steinitz, 1866 | 3·00 | 75 |
| **MS**1407 | 90×50 mm. 1000r. Emanual Lasker, 1894 (31×38 mm) | 4·50 | 1·10 |

**271** Sikorsky S-42 Flying Boat

**1994.** Aircraft. Multicoloured.

| | | | |
|---|---|---|---|
| 1408 | 150r. Type **271** | 55 | 10 |
| 1409 | 200r. Vought-Sikorsky VS-300A helicopter prototype | 65 | 20 |
| 1410 | 250r. Sikorsky S-37 biplane | 75 | 20 |
| 1411 | 500r. Sikorsky S-35 biplane | 2·00 | 20 |
| 1412 | 900r. Sikorsky S-43 amphibian | 3·00 | 30 |
| **MS**1413 | 80×50 mm. 1500r. Sikorsky Ilya Muroments (80th Anniv of first multi-engined airplane) (39×31 mm) | 4·50 | 90 |

**272** Penduline Tit

**1994.** Birds. Multicoloured.

| | | | |
|---|---|---|---|
| 1414 | 150r. Type **272** | 45 | 10 |
| 1415 | 250r. Bearded reedling | 75 | 20 |
| 1416 | 400r. Little bunting | 1·40 | 20 |
| 1417 | 700r. Cirl bunting | 2·40 | 45 |
| 1418 | 1000r. Goldcrest | 3·50 | 75 |
| **MS**1419 | 60×90 mm. 1500r. African pitta (31×39) | 5·75 | 1·40 |

**273** Postal Service Float

**1994.** National Independence Festival. Mult.

| | | | |
|---|---|---|---|
| 1420 | 300r. Type **273** | 1·10 | 45 |
| 1421 | 500r. Soldiers marching | 1·60 | 90 |
| 1422 | 700r. Women's army units on parade | 2·50 | 1·40 |

**274** Chruoi Changwar Bridge

**1994.** National Development. Multicoloured.

| | | | |
|---|---|---|---|
| 1423 | 300r. Type **274** | 85 | 30 |
| 1424 | 500r. Olympique Commercial Centre | 1·50 | 45 |
| 1425 | 700r. Sakyamony Chedei Temple | 1·90 | 65 |

**275** Psittacosaurus

**1995.** Prehistoric Animals. Multicoloured.

| | | | |
|---|---|---|---|
| 1426 | 100r. Type **275** | 20 | 10 |
| 1427 | 200r. Protoceratops | 45 | 20 |
| 1428 | 300r. Montanoceraptors | 65 | 20 |
| 1429 | 400r. Centrosaurus | 1·40 | 30 |
| 1430 | 700r. Styracosaurus | 2·30 | 35 |
| 1431 | 800r. Triceratops | 3·00 | 55 |

**276** Orange-tip

**1995.** Butterflies. Multicoloured.

| | | | |
|---|---|---|---|
| 1432 | 100r. Type **276** | 20 | 10 |
| 1433 | 200r. Scarce swallowtail | 65 | 20 |
| 1434 | 300r. Dark green fritillary | 95 | 20 |
| 1435 | 600r. Red admiral | 1·40 | 20 |
| 1436 | 800r. Peacock | 2·10 | 30 |

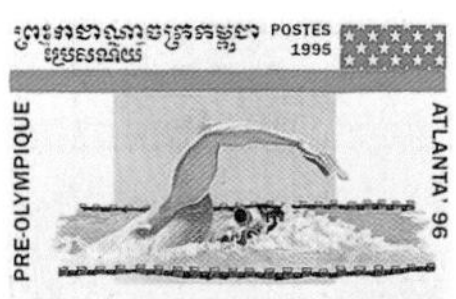
**277** Swimming

**1995.** Olympic Games, Atlanta (1996) (2nd issue). Multicoloured.

| | | | |
|---|---|---|---|
| 1437 | 100r. Type **277** | 30 | 10 |
| 1438 | 200r. Callisthenics (vert) | 65 | 20 |
| 1439 | 400r. Basketball (vert) | 1·20 | 20 |
| 1440 | 800r. Football (vert) | 2·75 | 20 |
| 1441 | 1000r. Cycling (vert) | 3·25 | 30 |
| **MS**1442 | 48×69 mm. 1500r. Running (31×39 mm) | 3·75 | 90 |

**278** Death Cap

**1995.** Fungi. Multicoloured.

| | | | |
|---|---|---|---|
| 1443 | 100r. Type **278** | 30 | 10 |
| 1444 | 200r. Chanterelle | 75 | 20 |
| 1445 | 300r. Honey fungus | 1·10 | 20 |
| 1446 | 600r. Field mushroom | 1·80 | 20 |
| 1447 | 800r. Fly agaric | 2·40 | 30 |

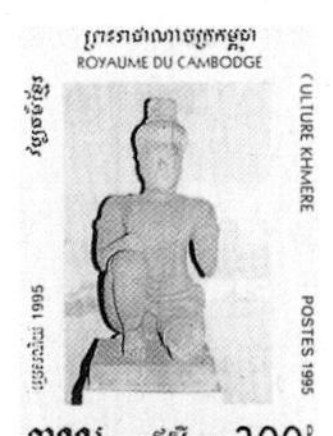
**279** Kneeling Ascetic

**1995.** Khmer Culture. Statues. Multicoloured.

| | | | |
|---|---|---|---|
| 1448 | 300r. Type **279** | 85 | 30 |
| 1449 | 500r. Parasurama | 1·50 | 45 |
| 1450 | 700r. Shiva | 1·90 | 65 |

**280** Gaur

**1995.** Protected Animals. Multicoloured.

| | | | |
|---|---|---|---|
| 1451 | 300r. Type **280** | 85 | 20 |
| 1452 | 500r. Kouprey (vert) | 1·50 | 30 |
| 1453 | 700r. Saurus crane (vert) | 1·90 | 45 |

**281** Black-capped Lory

**1995.** Parrot Family. Multicoloured.

| | | | |
|---|---|---|---|
| 1454 | 100r. Type **281** | 30 | 10 |
| 1455 | 200r. Princess parrot | 65 | 20 |
| 1456 | 400r. Eclectus parrot | 1·20 | 20 |
| 1457 | 800r. Scarlet macaw | 2·75 | 20 |
| 1458 | 1000r. Budgerigar | 3·25 | 30 |
| **MS**1459 | 52×81 mm. 1500r. Yellow-headed amazon (30×38 mm) | 4·75 | 90 |

**282** Bird (sculpture)

**1995.** Tourism. Public Gardens. Multicoloured.

| | | | |
|---|---|---|---|
| 1460 | 300r. Type **282** | 85 | 30 |
| 1461 | 500r. Water feature | 1·50 | 45 |
| 1462 | 700r. Mythical figures (sculpture) | 1·60 | 65 |

**283** Richard Trevithick's Locomotive, 1804

**1995.** Steam Locomotives. Multicoloured.

| | | | |
|---|---|---|---|
| 1463 | 100r. Type **283** | 20 | 10 |
| 1464 | 200r. G. and R. Stephenson's "Rocket", 1829 | 75 | 20 |
| 1465 | 300r. George Stephenson's "Locomotion", 1825 | 1·10 | 20 |
| 1466 | 600r. "Lafayette", 1837 | 1·70 | 45 |
| 1467 | 800r. "Best Friend of Charleston", 1830 | 2·10 | 75 |
| **MS**1468 | 74×59 mm. 1000r. George Stephenson (inventor of steam locomotive) (31×38 mm) | 3·25 | 1·50 |

**284** Bristol Type 142 Blenheim Mk II Bomber

**1995.** Second World War Planes. Multicoloured.

| | | | |
|---|---|---|---|
| 1469 | 100r. Type **284** | 20 | 10 |
| 1470 | 200r. North American B-25B Mitchell bomber (horiz) | 75 | 20 |
| 1471 | 300r. Avro Type 652 Anson Mk I general purpose plane (horiz) | 1·10 | 20 |
| 1472 | 600r. Avro Manchester bomber (horiz) | 1·70 | 20 |
| 1473 | 800r. Consolidated B-24 Liberator bomber (horiz) | 2·10 | 30 |
| **MS**1474 | 81×49 mm. 1000r. Boeing B-17 Flying Fortress bomber (31×38 mm) | 3·25 | 90 |

**285** Gathering Crops

**1995.** 50th Anniv of FAO. Multicoloured.

| | | | |
|---|---|---|---|
| 1475 | 300r. Type **285** | 55 | 30 |
| 1476 | 500r. Transplanting crops | 1·10 | 45 |
| 1477 | 700r. Paddy field | 1·60 | 65 |

286 Bridge

**1995.** 50th Anniv of UNO. Preah Kunlorng Bridge. Multicoloured.

| | | | |
|---|---|---|---|
| 1478 | 300r. Type **286** | 55 | 30 |
| 1479 | 500r. People on bridge | 1·10 | 45 |
| 1480 | 700r. Closer view of bridge | 1·60 | 65 |

287 Queen Monineath

**1995.** National Independence. Multicoloured.

| | | | |
|---|---|---|---|
| 1481 | 700r. Type **287** | 2·10 | 65 |
| 1482 | 800r. King Norodom Sihanouk | 2·75 | 75 |

288 Pennant Coralfish

**1995.** Fishes. Multicoloured.

| | | | |
|---|---|---|---|
| 1483 | 100r. Type **288** | 30 | 10 |
| 1484 | 200r. Copper-banded butterflyfish | 65 | 20 |
| 1485 | 400r. Crown anemonefish | 1·20 | 20 |
| 1486 | 800r. Palette surgeonfish | 2·75 | 20 |
| 1487 | 1000r. Queen angelfish | 2·10 | 30 |
| **MS**1488 | 85×50 mm. win-spotted wrasse | 4·75 | 90 |

289 Post Office Building

**1995.** Cent of Head Post Office, Phnom Penh.

| | | | | |
|---|---|---|---|---|
| 1489 | **289** | 300r. multicoloured | 85 | 30 |
| 1490 | **289** | 500r. multicoloured | 1·60 | 45 |
| 1491 | **289** | 700r. multicoloured | 2·30 | 65 |

290 Independence Monument

**1995.** 40th Anniv of Admission of Cambodia to United Nations Organization. Multicoloured.

| | | | |
|---|---|---|---|
| 1492 | 300r. Type **290** | 55 | 30 |
| 1493 | 400r. Angkor Wat | 1·10 | 45 |
| 1494 | 800r. U.N. emblem and national flag (vert) | 1·60 | 65 |

291 Tennis

**1996.** Olympic Games, Atlanta (3rd issue). Mult.

| | | | |
|---|---|---|---|
| 1495 | 100r. Type **291** | 10 | 10 |
| 1496 | 200r. Volleyball | 25 | 10 |
| 1497 | 300r. Football | 45 | 20 |
| 1498 | 500r. Running | 60 | 20 |
| 1499 | 900r. Baseball | 1·10 | 20 |
| 1500 | 1000r. Basketball | 1·10 | 20 |
| **MS**1501 | 64×94 mm. 1500r. Windsurfing (28×38 mm) | 3·25 | 90 |

292 Kep State Chalet

**1996**

| | | | | |
|---|---|---|---|---|
| 1502 | **292** | 50r. blue and black | 20 | 10 |
| 1503 | - | 100r. red and black | 20 | 10 |
| 1504 | - | 200r. yellow and black | 20 | 10 |
| 1505 | - | 500r. blue and black | 55 | 20 |
| 1506 | - | 800r. mauve and black | 95 | 30 |
| 1507 | - | 1000r. yellow and black | 1·30 | 45 |
| 1508 | - | 1500r. green and black | 1·90 | 65 |

DESIGNS—HORIZ: 100r. Power station; 200r. Wheelchair; 500r. Handicapped basketball team; 1000r. Kep beach; 1500r. Serpent Island. VERT: 800r. Man making crutches.

293 European Wild Cat

**1996.** Wild Cats. Multicoloured.

| | | | |
|---|---|---|---|
| 1509 | 100r. "Felis libyca" (vert) | 20 | 10 |
| 1510 | 200r. Type **293** | 35 | 10 |
| 1511 | 300r. Caracal | 50 | 20 |
| 1512 | 500r. Geoffroy's cat | 80 | 20 |
| 1513 | 900r. Black-footed cat | 1·20 | 20 |
| 1514 | 1000r. Flat-headed cat | 1·40 | 20 |

294 Player dribbling Ball

**1996.** World Cup Football Championship, France (1998) (1st issue). Multicoloured.

| | | | | |
|---|---|---|---|---|
| 1515 | **294** | 100r. multicoloured | 30 | 10 |
| 1516 | - | 200r. multicoloured | 45 | 10 |
| 1517 | - | 300r. multicoloured | 75 | 20 |
| 1518 | - | 500r. multicoloured | 1·30 | 20 |
| 1519 | - | 900r. multicoloured | 2·30 | 20 |
| 1520 | - | 1000r. mult (horiz) | 2·75 | 20 |
| **MS**1521 | | 65×79 mm. 1500r. multicoloured (31×38 mm) | 4·75 | 90 |

DESIGNS: 200r. to 1500r. Different players.
See also Nos. 1613/**MS**1619 and 1726/**MS**1732.

295 Tusmukh

**1996.** Khmer Culture. Multicoloured.

| | | | |
|---|---|---|---|
| 1522 | 100r. Type **295** | 20 | 10 |
| 1523 | 300r. Ream Iso | 1·30 | 45 |
| 1524 | 900r. Isei | 2·20 | 85 |

296 Pacific Steam Locomotive No. 620, Finland

**1996.** Railway Locomotives. Multicoloured.

| | | | |
|---|---|---|---|
| 1525 | 100r. Type **296** | 10 | 10 |
| 1526 | 200r. GNR steam locomotive No. 261, Great Britain | 10 | 10 |
| 1527 | 300r. Steam tank locomotive, 1930 | 30 | 20 |
| 1528 | 500r. Steam tank locomotive No. 1362, 1914 | 40 | 20 |
| 1529 | 900r. LMS Turbomotive No. 6202, 1930, Great Britain | 55 | 20 |
| 1530 | 1000r. Locomotive "Snake", 1884, New Zealand | 75 | 20 |
| **MS**1531 | 80×55 mm. 1500r. Canadian Pacific train with Vistadome observation car (39×31 mm) | 4·75 | 90 |

No. **MS**1531 commemorates "CEPEX '96" International Stamp Exhibition, Toronto.

297 White-rumped Shama

**1996.** Birds. Multicoloured.

| | | | |
|---|---|---|---|
| 1532 | 100r. Type **297** | 30 | 10 |
| 1533 | 200r. Pekin robin | 45 | 10 |
| 1534 | 300r. Varied tit | 75 | 20 |
| 1535 | 500r. Black-naped oriole | 1·30 | 20 |
| 1536 | 900r. Japanese bush warbler | 2·30 | 20 |
| 1537 | 1000r. Blue and white flycatcher | 2·75 | 20 |

298 Rhythmic Gymnastics

**1996.** "Olymphilex '96" Olympic Stamps Exhibition, Atlanta, U.S.A. Multicoloured.

| | | | |
|---|---|---|---|
| 1538 | 100r. Type **298** | 20 | 10 |
| 1539 | 200r. Judo | 30 | 10 |
| 1540 | 300r. High jumping | 55 | 20 |
| 1541 | 500r. Wrestling | 1·10 | 20 |
| 1542 | 900r. Weightlifting | 1·90 | 20 |
| 1543 | 1000r. Football | 2·30 | 20 |
| **MS**1544 | 84×55 mm. 1500r. Diving (31×39 mm) | 3·75 | 90 |

299 Douglas M-2, 1926

**1996.** Biplanes. Multicoloured.

| | | | |
|---|---|---|---|
| 1545 | 100r. Type **299** | 30 | 10 |
| 1546 | 200r. Pitcairn PS-5 Mailwing, 1926 | 45 | 10 |
| 1547 | 300r. Boeing 40-B, 1928 | 75 | 20 |
| 1548 | 500r. Potez 25. 1925 | 1·30 | 20 |
| 1549 | 900r. Stearman C-3MB, 1927 | 2·30 | 20 |
| 1550 | 1000r. De Havilland D.H.4. 1918 | 2·75 | 20 |
| **MS**1551 | 80×60 mm. 1500r. Standar JR-1B, 1918 (39×30 mm) | 4·75 | 90 |

300 Aspara

**1996.** Tonle Bati Temple Ruins.

| | | | | |
|---|---|---|---|---|
| 1552 | **300** | 50r. black and yellow | 20 | 10 |
| 1553 | - | 100r. black and blue | 20 | 10 |
| 1554 | - | 200r. black and brown | 45 | 10 |
| 1555 | - | 500r. black and blue | 75 | 20 |
| 1556 | - | 800r. black and green | 1·10 | 30 |
| 1557 | - | 1000r. black and green | 1·40 | 45 |
| 1558 | - | 1500r. black and bistre | 2·30 | 65 |

DESIGNS—VERT: 100r. Aspara (different); 200r. Aspara (different); 800r. Taprum Temple; 1000r. Grandmother Peou Temple. HORIZ: 500r. Reliefs on wall; 1500r. Overall view of Tonle Bati.

301 Coelophysis

**1996.** Prehistoric Animals. Multicoloured.

| | | | |
|---|---|---|---|
| 1559 | 50r. Type **301** | 10 | 10 |
| 1560 | 100r. Euparkeria | 10 | 10 |
| 1561 | 150r. Plateosaurus | 30 | 10 |
| 1562 | 200r. Herrerasaurus | 50 | 10 |
| 1563 | 250r. Dilophosaurus | 55 | 10 |
| 1564 | 300r. Tuojiangosaurus | 70 | 10 |
| 1565 | 350r. Camarasaurus | 1·10 | 20 |
| 1566 | 400r. Ceratosaurus | 1·30 | 20 |
| 1567 | 500r. Espinosaurio | 1·50 | 30 |
| 1568 | 700r. Ouranosaurus | 2·00 | 35 |
| 1569 | 800r. Avimimus | 2·50 | 55 |
| 1570 | 1200r. Deinonychus | 3·50 | 65 |

Nos. 1559/62, 1563/6 and 1567/70 respectively were issued together, se-tenant, each sheetlet containing a composite design of a globe.

302 Jose Raul Capablanca (1921–27)

**1996.** World Chess Champions. Multicoloured.

| | | | |
|---|---|---|---|
| 1571 | 100r. Type **302** | 30 | 10 |
| 1572 | 200r. Aleksandr Alekhine (1927–35, 1937–46) | 45 | 10 |
| 1573 | 300r. Vasily Vasilevich Smyslov (1957–58) | 75 | 20 |
| 1574 | 500r. Mikhail Nekhemyevich Tal (1960–61) | 1·30 | 20 |
| 1575 | 900r. Robert Fischer (1972–75) | 2·30 | 20 |
| 1576 | 1000r. Anatoly Karpov (1975–85) | 2·75 | 20 |
| **MS**1577 | 70×87 mm. 1500r. Garry Kasparov (1985–2000) (31×38 mm) | 4·75 | 90 |

303 Brown Bear

**1996.** Mammals and their Young. Multicoloured.

| | | | |
|---|---|---|---|
| 1578 | 100r. Type **303** | 30 | 10 |
| 1579 | 200r. Lion | 45 | 10 |
| 1580 | 300r. Malayan tapir | 65 | 20 |
| 1581 | 500r. Bactrian camel | 1·30 | 20 |
| 1582 | 900r. Ibex (vert) | 2·10 | 20 |
| 1583 | 1000r. Californian sealion (vert) | 2·75 | 20 |

304 Rough Collie

**1996.** Dogs. Multicoloured.

| | | | |
|---|---|---|---|
| 1584 | 200r. Type **304** | 45 | 10 |
| 1585 | 300r. Labrador retriever | 65 | 20 |
| 1586 | 500r. Dobermann pinscher | 1·30 | 20 |
| 1587 | 900r. German shepherd | 2·10 | 20 |
| 1588 | 1000r. Boxer | 2·40 | 30 |

**305** Chinese Junk

**1996.** Ships. Multicoloured.

| | | | |
|---|---|---|---|
| 1589 | 200r. Type **305** | 45 | 10 |
| 1590 | 300r. Phoenician warship, 1500–1000 B.C. | 65 | 20 |
| 1591 | 500r. Roman war galley, 264–241 B.C. | 1·30 | 20 |
| 1592 | 900r. 19th-century full-rigged ship | 2·10 | 20 |
| 1593 | 1000r. "Sirius" (paddle- steamer), 1838 | 2·40 | 30 |
| **MS**1594 | 90×60 mm. 1500r. "Great Eastern" (cable ship and paddle-steamer), 1858 (39×31 mm) | 4·75 | 90 |

**306** Silver Pagoda, Phnom Penh

**1996.** 45th Anniv of Cambodian Membership of Universal Postal Union.

| | | | | |
|---|---|---|---|---|
| 1595 | **306** | 200r. multicoloured | 55 | 20 |
| 1596 | **306** | 400r. multicoloured | 1·10 | 35 |
| 1597 | **306** | 900r. multicoloured | 2·10 | 85 |

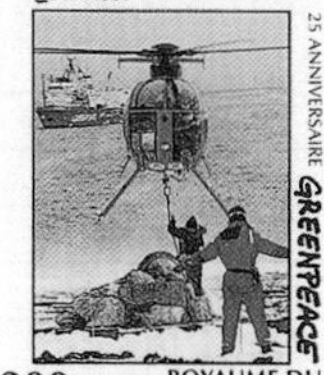

**307** Environmental Vessel and Helicopter

**1996.** 25th Anniv of Greenpeace (environmental organization). Multicoloured.

| | | | |
|---|---|---|---|
| 1598 | 200r. Type **307** | 75 | 10 |
| 1599 | 300r. Float-helicopter hovering over motor launch | 1·40 | 20 |
| 1600 | 500r. Helicopter on deck and motor launches | 2·10 | 30 |
| 1601 | 900r. Helicopter with two bar-rels suspended beneath | 3·75 | 35 |
| **MS**1602 | 111×90 mm. 10000r. Float-helicopter (31×39 mm) | 4·75 | 90 |

**308** Ox

**1996.** New Year. Year of the Ox. Details of painting by Han Huang. Multicoloured.

| | | | |
|---|---|---|---|
| 1603 | 500r. Type **308** | 65 | 20 |
| 1604 | 500r. Ox with head turned to right (upright horns) | 65 | 20 |
| 1605 | 500r. Brown and white ox with head up ("handlebar" horns) | 65 | 20 |
| 1606 | 500r. Ox with head in bush ("ram's" horns) | 65 | 20 |

**309** Dam, Phnom Kaun Sat

**1996.** 10th International United Nations Volunteers Day. Multicoloured.

| | | | |
|---|---|---|---|
| 1607 | 100r. Type **309** | 30 | 10 |
| 1608 | 500r. Canal, O Angkrung | 1·40 | 45 |
| 1609 | 900r. Canal, Chrey Krem | 2·50 | 85 |

**310** Architect's Model of Reservoir

**1996.** 43rd Anniv of Independence. Water Management. Multicoloured.

| | | | |
|---|---|---|---|
| 1610 | 100r. Type **310** | 30 | 10 |
| 1611 | 500r. Reservoir | 1·40 | 45 |
| 1612 | 900r. Reservoir (different) | 2·50 | 85 |

**311** Players

**1997.** World Cup Football Championship, France (1998) (2nd issue).

| | | | | |
|---|---|---|---|---|
| 1613 | **311** | 100r. multicoloured | 30 | 10 |
| 1614 | - | 200r. multicoloured | 45 | 10 |
| 1615 | - | 300r. multicoloured | 75 | 20 |
| 1616 | - | 500r. multicoloured | 1·30 | 20 |
| 1617 | - | 900r. multicoloured | 2·30 | 20 |
| 1618 | - | 1000r. multicoloured | 2·75 | 20 |
| **MS**1619 | | 99×68 mm. 2000r. multicol-oured (39×31 mm) | 4·75 | 90 |

DESIGNS: 200r. to 2000r. Different footballing scenes.

**312** Two Elephants

**1997.** The Indian Elephant. Multicoloured.

| | | | |
|---|---|---|---|
| 1620 | 300r. Type **312** | 30 | 10 |
| 1621 | 500r. Group of three | 55 | 20 |
| 1622 | 900r. Elephants fighting | 1·10 | 30 |
| 1623 | 1000r. Adult and calf | 1·30 | 35 |

**314** Horse-drawn Water Pump, 1731

**1997.** Fire Engines. Multicoloured.

| | | | |
|---|---|---|---|
| 1630 | 200r. Type **314** | 30 | 10 |
| 1631 | 500r. Putnam horse-drawn water pump, 1863 | 45 | 10 |
| 1632 | 900r. Merryweather horse-drawn engine, 1894 | 65 | 20 |
| 1633 | 1000r. Shand Mason Co horse-drawn water pump, 1901 | 85 | 20 |
| 1634 | 1500r. Maxin Motor Co auto-matic pump, 1949 | 1·30 | 20 |
| 1635 | 4000r. Merryweather exhaust pump, 1950 | 3·50 | 20 |
| **MS**1636 | 106×87 mm. 5400r. Mack Truck Co. mechanical ladder, 1953 (39×31 mm) | 4·75 | 90 |

**315** Statue on Plinth

**1997.** Angkor Wat.

| | | | | |
|---|---|---|---|---|
| 1637 | **315** | 300r. black and red | 30 | 10 |
| 1638 | - | 300r. black and blue | 30 | 10 |
| 1639 | - | 800r. black and green | 65 | 10 |
| 1640 | - | 1500r. black & brown | 1·30 | 10 |
| 1641 | - | 1700r. black & orange | 1·50 | 20 |
| 1642 | - | 2500r. black and blue | 1·90 | 20 |
| 1643 | - | 3000r. black & green | 2·50 | 20 |

DESIGNS—VERT: No. 1638, Statue in wall recess; 1639, Walled courtyard; 1640, Decorative panel with two figures. HORIZ: No. 1641, Rectangular gateway; 1642, Statues and arched gateway; 1643, Stupa and ruins.

**316** Steller's Eider

**1997.** Aquatic Birds. Multicoloured.

| | | | |
|---|---|---|---|
| 1644 | 200r. Type **316** | 10 | 10 |
| 1645 | 500r. Egyptian goose | 25 | 10 |
| 1646 | 900r. American wigeon | 40 | 20 |
| 1647 | 1000r. Falcated teal | 45 | 20 |
| 1648 | 1500r. Surf scoter | 65 | 20 |
| 1649 | 4000r. Blue-winged teal | 1·90 | 20 |
| **MS**1650 | 95×75 mm. 5400r. Baikal teal (31×39 mm) | 4·75 | 90 |

**317** Von Stephan

**1997.** Death Centenary of Heinrich von Stephan (founder of UPU).

| | | | | |
|---|---|---|---|---|
| 1651 | **317** | 500r. blue & dp blue | 45 | 20 |
| 1652 | **317** | 1500r. green and olive | 1·30 | 30 |
| 1653 | **317** | 2000r. yellow & green | 1·80 | 45 |

**318** Main Entrance

**1997.** Khmer Culture. Banteay Srei Temple. Multicoloured.

| | | | |
|---|---|---|---|
| 1654 | 500r. Type **318** | 45 | 20 |
| 1655 | 1500r. Main and side entrances | 1·30 | 30 |
| 1656 | 2000r. Courtyard | 1·80 | 45 |

**319** Birman

**1997.** Cats. Multicoloured.

| | | | |
|---|---|---|---|
| 1657 | 200r. Type **319** | 30 | 10 |
| 1658 | 500r. Exotic shorthair | 45 | 10 |
| 1659 | 900r. Persian | 65 | 20 |
| 1660 | 1000r. Turkish van | 85 | 20 |
| 1661 | 1500r. American shorthair | 1·30 | 20 |
| 1662 | 4000r. Scottish fold | 3·50 | 20 |
| **MS**1663 | 90×70 mm. 5400r. Sphinx (31×39 mm) | 3·75 | 90 |

**320** No. 488 S.W.R. Loco British Rail No. 30583

**1997.** Steam Railway Locomotives. Multicoloured.

| | | | |
|---|---|---|---|
| 1664 | 200r. Type **320** | 30 | 10 |
| 1665 | 500r. "Frederick Smith" | 45 | 10 |
| 1666 | 900r. No. 3131 | 65 | 20 |
| 1667 | 1000r. London Transport No. L44, Great Britain | 85 | 20 |
| 1668 | 1500r. LNER No. 1711, Great Britain | 1·30 | 20 |
| 1669 | 4000r. No. 60523 "Chateau du Soleil" | 3·50 | 20 |
| **MS**1670 | 76×60 mm. 5400r. LNER No. 2006, Great Britain | 4·25 | 90 |

**321** Shar-pei

**1997.** Dogs. Multicoloured.

| | | | |
|---|---|---|---|
| 1671 | 200r. Type **321** | 30 | 10 |
| 1672 | 500r. Chin-chin | 45 | 10 |
| 1673 | 900r. Pekingese | 55 | 20 |
| 1674 | 1000r. Chow-chow (vert) | 65 | 20 |
| 1675 | 1500r. Pug (vert) | 1·30 | 20 |
| 1676 | 4000r. Akita (vert) | 3·50 | 20 |
| **MS**1677 | 111×88 mm. 5400r. Chinese crested (vert) | 3·75 | 90 |

**322** Qunalom Temple

**1997.** 30th Anniv of Association of South East Asian Nations. Multicoloured.

| | | | |
|---|---|---|---|
| 1678 | 500r. Type **322** | 45 | 20 |
| 1679 | 1500r. Royal Palace | 1·30 | 30 |
| 1680 | 2000r. National Museum | 1·80 | 45 |

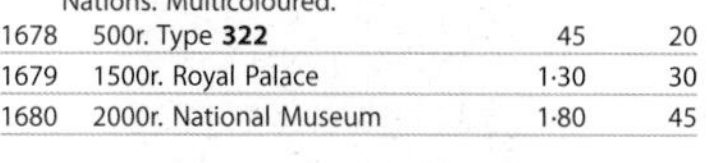

**323** 15th-century Caravelle

**1997.** Sailing Ships. Multicoloured.

| | | | |
|---|---|---|---|
| 1681 | 200r. Type **323** | 30 | 10 |
| 1682 | 500r. Spanish galleon | 45 | 10 |
| 1683 | 900r. "Great Harry" (British galleon) | 65 | 20 |
| 1684 | 1000r. "La Couronne" (French galleon) | 85 | 20 |
| 1685 | 1500r. 18th-century East Indiaman | 1·30 | 20 |
| 1686 | 4000r. 19th-century clipper | 3·50 | 20 |
| **MS**1687 | 94×68 mm. 5400r. H.M.S. "Victory" (Nelson) | 4·25 | 90 |

**324** Public Garden

**1997.** Public Gardens (Nos. 1688/91) and Tuk Chha Canal (others).

| | | | | |
|---|---|---|---|---|
| 1688 | **324** | 300r. green and black | 30 | 10 |
| 1689 | - | 300r. red and black | 30 | 10 |
| 1690 | - | 800r. yellow and black | 65 | 10 |
| 1691 | - | 1500r. orange and black | 1·30 | 10 |
| 1692 | - | 1700r. pink and black | 1·50 | 20 |
| 1693 | - | 2500r. blue and black | 1·90 | 20 |
| 1694 | - | 3000r. blue and black | 2·50 | 20 |

DESIGNS—HORIZ: 300r. Statue at intersection of paths; 300r. Hedging in triangular bed; 1500r. Tree and statue of lion; 1700r. View along canal; 2500r. View across canal; 3000r. Closed lock gates. VERT: 800r. Mounted bowl.

**325** Satan's Mushroom

**1997.** Fungi. Multicoloured.

| | | | |
|---|---|---|---|
| 1695 | 200r. Type **325** | 30 | 10 |
| 1696 | 500r. "Amanita regalis" | 45 | 10 |
| 1697 | 900r. "Morchella semilibera" | 65 | 20 |

| | | | |
|---|---|---|---|
| 1698 | 1000r. "Gomphus clavatus" | 85 | 20 |
| 1699 | 1500r. "Hygrophorus hypothejus" | 1·30 | 20 |
| 1700 | 4000r. "Albatrellus confluens" | 3·50 | 20 |
| **MS**1701 | 110×89 mm. 5400r. Red-cracked boletus | 4·75 | 90 |

**326** Peaceful Fightingfish ("Betta imbellis") and Siamese Fightingfish ("Betta splendens")

**1997.** Fishes. Multicoloured.

| | | | |
|---|---|---|---|
| 1702 | 200r. Type **326** | 20 | 10 |
| 1703 | 500r. Banded gourami | 25 | 10 |
| 1704 | 900r. Rosy barbs | 40 | 20 |
| 1705 | 1000r. Paradise fish | 55 | 20 |
| 1706 | 1500r. "Epalzeorhynchos frenatus" | 1·00 | 20 |
| 1707 | 4000r. "Capoeta tetrazona" | 2·10 | 20 |
| **MS**1708 | 96×72 mm. 5400r. Harlequin fish | 4·75 | 90 |

**327** Kampot Post Office

**1997.** 44th Anniv of Independence. Multicoloured.

| | | | |
|---|---|---|---|
| 1709 | 1000r. Type **327** | 85 | 30 |
| 1710 | 3000r. Prey Veng Post Office | 2·75 | 65 |

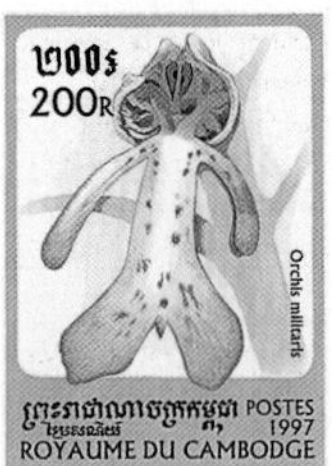


**328** "Orchis militaris"

**1997.** Orchids. Multicoloured.

| | | | |
|---|---|---|---|
| 1711 | 200r. Type **328** | 20 | 10 |
| 1712 | 500r. "Orchiaceras bivonae" | 30 | 10 |
| 1713 | 900r. "Orchiaceras spuria" | 50 | 20 |
| 1714 | 1000r. "Gymnadenia conopsea" | 60 | 20 |
| 1715 | 1500r. "Serapias neglecta" | 1·30 | 20 |
| 1716 | 4000r. "Pseudorhiza bruniana" | 2·75 | 20 |
| **MS**1717 | 70×90 mm. 5400r. "Dactylodenia wintonii" | 4·75 | 90 |

**329** In black Jacket

**1997.** Diana, Princess of Wales Commemoration. Multicoloured.

| | | | |
|---|---|---|---|
| 1718 | 100r. Type **329** | 15 | 10 |
| 1719 | 200r. In black dress | 15 | 10 |
| 1720 | 300r. In blue jacket | 15 | 10 |
| 1721 | 500r. Close-up of Princess in visor | 30 | 10 |
| 1722 | 1000r. In mine-protection clothing | 50 | 10 |
| 1723 | 1500r. With Elizabeth Dole | 85 | 10 |
| 1724 | 2000r. Holding landmine | 1·20 | 20 |
| 1725 | 2500r. With Mother Teresa and Sisters of Charity | 1·40 | 20 |

**330** Player with Ball

**1998.** World Cup Football Championship, France (3rd issue).

| | | | | |
|---|---|---|---|---|
| 1726 | **330** | 200r. multicoloured | 15 | 10 |
| 1727 | - | 500r. multicoloured | 25 | 10 |
| 1728 | - | 900r. multicoloured | 45 | 20 |
| 1729 | - | 1000r. multicoloured | 55 | 20 |
| 1730 | - | 1500r. multicoloured | 80 | 20 |
| 1731 | - | 4000r. multicoloured | 2·30 | 20 |
| **MS**1732 | | 110×90 mm. 5400r. multicoloured (39×31 mm) | 3·25 | 90 |

DESIGNS: 500r. to 5400r. Different footballing scenes.

**331** Suorprat Gateway

**1998.** Temple Ruins.

| | | | | |
|---|---|---|---|---|
| 1733 | **331** | 300r. orange and black | 20 | 10 |
| 1734 | - | 500r. pink and black | 30 | 10 |
| 1735 | - | 1200r. orange and black | 45 | 10 |
| 1736 | - | 1500r. orange and black | 65 | 10 |
| 1737 | - | 1700r. blue and black | 75 | 20 |
| 1738 | - | 2000r. green and black | 95 | 20 |
| 1739 | - | 3000r. lilac and black | 1·50 | 20 |

DESIGNS—HORIZ: No. 1734, Kumlung wall; 1735, Bapuon entrance; 1737, Prerup; 1738, Preah Khan. VERT: No. 1736, Palilai; 1739, Bayon.

**332** Tiger Cub

**1998.** New Year. Year of the Tiger. Multicoloured.

| | | | |
|---|---|---|---|
| 1740 | 200r. Type **332** | 20 | 10 |
| 1741 | 500r. Tiger and cubs | 30 | 10 |
| 1742 | 990r. Tiger on alert | 45 | 20 |
| 1743 | 1000r. Tiger washing itself (horiz) | 55 | 20 |
| 1744 | 1500r. Tiger lying in grass (horiz) | 80 | 20 |
| 1745 | 4000r. Tiger snarling (horiz) | 2·30 | 20 |
| **MS**1746 | 120×90 mm. 5400r. Tiger on rock (31×30 mm) | 3·25 | 90 |

**333** Oakland, Antioch and Eastern Electric Locomotive No. 105

**1998.** Railway Locomotives. Multicoloured.

| | | | |
|---|---|---|---|
| 1747 | 200r. Type **333** | 20 | 10 |
| 1748 | 500r. New York, Westchester and electric locomotive No. 1 | 45 | 10 |
| 1749 | 900r. Spokane and Inland electric locomotive No. MII | 55 | 20 |
| 1750 | 1000r. International Railway electric locomotive | 75 | 20 |
| 1751 | 1500r. British Columbia Electric Railway locomotive No. 823 | 1·10 | 20 |
| 1752 | 4000r. Southern Pacific electric locomotive No. 200 | 3·00 | 20 |
| **MS**1753 | 88×94 mm. Storage battery locomotive (vert triangle) | 3·75 | 90 |

**334** Rottweiler

**1998.** Dogs. Multicoloured.

| | | | |
|---|---|---|---|
| 1754 | 200r. Type **334** | 15 | 10 |
| 1755 | 500r. Beauceron | 35 | 10 |
| 1756 | 900r. Boxer | 50 | 20 |
| 1757 | 1000r. Siberian husky | 60 | 20 |
| 1758 | 1500r. Welsh Pembroke corgi | 85 | 20 |
| 1759 | 4000r. Basset hound | 2·30 | 20 |
| **MS**1760 | 110×89 mm. Schnauzer (28×37½ mm) | 3·75 | 90 |

**335** Stag Beetle

**1998.** Beetles. Multicoloured.

| | | | |
|---|---|---|---|
| 1761 | 200r. Type **335** | 20 | 10 |
| 1762 | 500r. "Carabus auronitens" (ground beetle) | 45 | 10 |
| 1763 | 900r. Alpine longhorn beetle | 65 | 20 |
| 1764 | 1000r. "Geotrupes" (dor beetle) | 75 | 20 |
| 1765 | 1500r. "Megasoma elephas" | 1·10 | 20 |
| 1766 | 4000r. "Chalcosoma" | 2·75 | 20 |
| **MS**1767 | 110×90 mm. 5400r. "Leptura rubra" (longhorn beetle) | 3·75 | 90 |

**336** Prerup Temple

**1998.** Khmer Culture. Multicoloured.

| | | | |
|---|---|---|---|
| 1768 | 500r. Type **336** | 30 | 20 |
| 1769 | 1500r. Bayon Temple | 75 | 30 |
| 1770 | 2000r. Angkor Vat | 1·10 | 45 |

**337** Cutter

**1998.** Ships. Multicoloured.

| | | | |
|---|---|---|---|
| 1771 | 200r. Type **337** | 20 | 10 |
| 1772 | 500r. "Britannia" (mail paddle-steamer, 1840) | 45 | 10 |
| 1773 | 900r. Viking longship, Gokstad | 65 | 20 |
| 1774 | 1000r. "Great Britain" (steam/sail) | 75 | 20 |
| 1775 | 1500r. Medieval coasting nau | 1·10 | 20 |
| 1776 | 4000r. Full-rigged ship (inscr "Fregate") | 2·75 | 20 |
| **MS**1777 | 110×91 mm. 5400r. "Tartane" (fishing boat) (39×31 mm) | 3·75 | 90 |

**338** Scottish Fold

**1998.** Domestic Cats. Multicoloured.

| | | | |
|---|---|---|---|
| 1778 | 200r. Type **338** | 15 | 10 |
| 1779 | 500r. Ragdoll | 35 | 10 |
| 1780 | 900r. Cymric | 50 | 20 |
| 1781 | 1000r. Devon rex | 60 | 20 |
| 1782 | 1500r. American curl | 85 | 20 |
| 1783 | 4000r. Sphinx | 2·30 | 20 |
| **MS**1784 | 90×108 mm. 5400r. Japanese bobtail (39×31 mm) | 3·75 | 90 |

**339** "Petasites japonica"

**1998.** Flowers. Multicoloured.

| | | | |
|---|---|---|---|
| 1785 | 200r. Type **339** | 15 | 10 |
| 1786 | 500r. "Gentiana triflora" | 30 | 10 |
| 1787 | 900r. "Doronicum cordatum" | 50 | 20 |
| 1788 | 1000r. "Scabiosa japonica" | 55 | 20 |
| 1789 | 1500r. "Magnolia sieboldii" | 75 | 20 |
| 1790 | 4000r. "Erythronium japonica" | 2·30 | 20 |
| **MS**1791 | 90×101 mm. China aster (30×36 mm) | 3·25 | 90 |

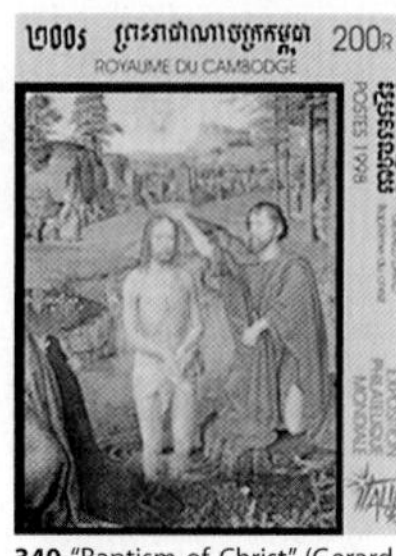


**340** "Baptism of Christ" (Gerard David)

**1998.** "Italia 98" International Stamp Exhibition, Milan. Paintings. Multicoloured.

| | | | |
|---|---|---|---|
| 1792 | 200r. Type **340** | 20 | 10 |
| 1793 | 500r. "Madonna of Martin van Niuwenhoven" (Hans Memling) | 30 | 10 |
| 1794 | 900r. "Baptism of Christ" (Hendrich Holtzius) | 55 | 20 |
| 1795 | 1000r. "Christ with the Cross" (Luis de Morales) | 65 | 20 |
| 1796 | 1500r. "Elias in the Desert" (Dirk Bouts) | 95 | 20 |
| 1797 | 4000r. "The Virgin" (Petrus Christus) | 2·75 | 20 |
| **MS**1798 | 87×107 mm. "The Immaculate Conception" (Bartolome Murillo) (39×31 mm) | 3·75 | 90 |

There are errors of spelling in some of the inscriptions.

**341** "Phyciodes tharos"

**1998.** Butterflies. Multicoloured.

| | | | |
|---|---|---|---|
| 1799 | 200r. Type **341** | 20 | 10 |
| 1800 | 500r. "Pararge megera" | 30 | 10 |
| 1801 | 900r. Monarch | 55 | 20 |
| 1802 | 1000r. Apollo | 65 | 20 |
| 1803 | 1500r. Swallowtail | 95 | 20 |
| 1804 | 4000r. "Eumenis semele" | 2·75 | 20 |
| **MS**1805 | 91×110 mm. 5400r. Blue morpho (39×31 mm) | 3·75 | 90 |

**342** Post Box, 1997

**1998.** World Post Day. Multicoloured.

| | | | |
|---|---|---|---|
| 1806 | 1000r. Type **342** | 55 | 30 |
| 1807 | 3000r. Wall-mounted post box, 1951 | 1·40 | 65 |

343 Big-Headed Turtle

**1998.** Tortoise and Turtles. Multicoloured.

| | | | |
|---|---|---|---|
| 1808 | 200r. Type **343** | 15 | 10 |
| 1809 | 500r. Green turtle | 25 | 10 |
| 1810 | 900r. American soft-shelled turtle | 40 | 20 |
| 1811 | 1000r. Hawksbill turtle | 50 | 20 |
| 1812 | 1500r. Aldabra tortoise | 70 | 20 |
| 1813 | 4000r. Leatherback sea turtle | 2·00 | 20 |
| **MS**1814 | 5400r. Matamata turtle (39×31 mm) | 3·25 | 90 |

344 Bayon Dance

**1998.** 45th Anniv of Independence. Multicoloured.

| | | | |
|---|---|---|---|
| 1815 | 500r. Type **344** | 35 | 20 |
| 1816 | 1500r. Bayon dance (different) | 85 | 30 |
| 1817 | 2000r. Bayon dance (different) | 1·20 | 45 |

345 Cheetah

**1998.** Big Cats. Multicoloured.

| | | | |
|---|---|---|---|
| 1818 | 200r. Type **345** | 15 | 10 |
| 1819 | 500r. Snow leopard | 25 | 10 |
| 1820 | 900r. Ocelot | 40 | 20 |
| 1821 | 1000r. Leopard | 50 | 20 |
| 1822 | 1500r. Serval | 70 | 20 |
| 1823 | 4000r. Jaguar | 2·00 | 20 |
| **MS**1824 | 90×109 mm. 5400r. Tiger (31×39 mm) | 3·25 | 90 |

346 Rabbit

**1999.** New Year. Year of the Rabbit. Multicoloured. Showing rabbits.

| | | | |
|---|---|---|---|
| 1825 | 200r. Type **346** | 30 | 10 |
| 1826 | 500r. Facing left | 45 | 10 |
| 1827 | 900r. Sitting in bush | 75 | 20 |
| 1828 | 1000r. Sitting on rock | 85 | 20 |
| 1829 | 1500r. Sitting upright | 1·40 | 20 |
| 1830 | 4000r. Head looking out from grass (vert) | 3·75 | 20 |
| **MS**1831 | 110×84 mm. 5400r. Rabbit (39×31 mm) | 3·75 | 90 |

347 Foster and Rastik's "Stourbridge Lion", 1829, U.S.A.

**1999.** Steam Railway Locomotives. Multicoloured.

| | | | |
|---|---|---|---|
| 1832 | 200r. Type **347** | 20 | 10 |
| 1833 | 500r. "Atlantic", 1832 | 30 | 10 |
| 1834 | 900r. No. O35, 1934 | 45 | 20 |
| 1835 | 1000r. Daniel Gooch's "Iron Duke", 1847, Great Britain | 60 | 20 |
| 1836 | 1500r. "4-6-0" | 95 | 20 |
| 1837 | 4000r. "4-4-2" | 2·50 | 20 |
| **MS**1838 | 84×109 mm. 5400r. "Fire Fly", 1840, "Great Britain" (39×31 mm) | 3·75 | 90 |

348 Aquamarine

**1999.** Minerals. Multicoloured.

| | | | |
|---|---|---|---|
| 1839 | 200r. Type **348** | 10 | 10 |
| 1840 | 500r. Cat's eye | 20 | 10 |
| 1841 | 900r. Malachite | 35 | 20 |
| 1842 | 1000r. Emerald | 45 | 20 |
| 1843 | 1500r. Turquoise | 65 | 20 |
| 1844 | 4000r. Ruby | 1·80 | 20 |
| **MS**1845 | 107×88 mm. 5400r. Diamond (39×31 mm) | 3·75 | 90 |

349 Alsatian

**1999.** Dogs. Multicoloured.

| | | | |
|---|---|---|---|
| 1846 | 200r. Type **349** | 20 | 10 |
| 1847 | 500r. Shih tzu (horiz) | 30 | 10 |
| 1848 | 900r. Tibetan spaniel (horiz) | 50 | 20 |
| 1849 | 1000r. Ainu-ken | 55 | 20 |
| 1850 | 1500r. Lhassa apso (horiz) | 90 | 20 |
| 1851 | 4000r. Tibetan terrier (horiz) | 2·50 | 20 |
| **MS**1852 | 109×88 mm. 5400r. Tosa inu (31×39 mm) | 3·75 | 90 |

350 La Rapide steam carriage, 1881

**1999.** Cars. Multicoloured.

| | | | |
|---|---|---|---|
| 1853 | 200r. Type **350** | 15 | 10 |
| 1854 | 500r. Duryea motor buggy, 1895 | 25 | 10 |
| 1855 | 900r. Marius Barbarou voiturette, 1898 | 40 | 20 |
| 1856 | 1000r. Panhard and Levassor voiturette, 1898 | 50 | 20 |
| 1857 | 1500r. Mercedes-Benz Tonneau, 1901 | 70 | 20 |
| 1858 | 4000r. Ford model sedan, 1915 | 2·00 | 20 |
| **MS**1859 | 108×86 mm. 5400r. Marcus, 1875 (39×31 mm) | 3·75 | 90 |

351 Ragdoll

**1999.** Cats. Multicoloured.

| | | | |
|---|---|---|---|
| 1860 | 200r. Type **351** | 20 | 10 |
| 1861 | 500r. Russian blue | 25 | 10 |
| 1862 | 900r. Bombay | 50 | 20 |
| 1863 | 1000r. Siamese | 55 | 20 |
| 1864 | 1500r. Oriental shorthair | 95 | 20 |
| 1865 | 4000r. Somali | 2·50 | 20 |
| **MS**1866 | 84×109 mm. 5400r. Egyptian mau (31×38 mm) | 3·75 | 90 |

352 Dragon Bridge

**1999.** Khmer Culture. Multicoloured.

| | | | |
|---|---|---|---|
| 1867 | 500r. Type **352** | 25 | 20 |
| 1868 | 1500r. Temple of 100 Columns, Kratie | 80 | 30 |
| 1869 | 2000r. Krapum Chhouk, Kratie | 1·20 | 45 |

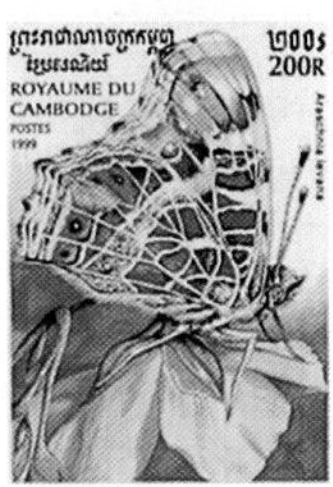
353 *Araschnia levana*

**1999.** Butterflies. Multicoloured.

| | | | |
|---|---|---|---|
| 1870 | 200r. Type **353** | 20 | 10 |
| 1871 | 500r. Painted lady (horiz) | 25 | 10 |
| 1872 | 900r. *Clossiana euphrosyne* | 50 | 20 |
| 1873 | 1000r. *Coenonympha hero* | 55 | 20 |
| 1874 | 1500r. Apollo (horiz) | 90 | 20 |
| 1875 | 4000r. *Plebejus argus* | 2·50 | 20 |
| **MS**1876 | 109×90 mm. 5400r. Purple-edged copper (31×39 mm) | 3·75 | 90 |

354 Saurornitholestes

**1999.** Prehistoric Animals. Multicoloured.

| | | | |
|---|---|---|---|
| 1877 | 200r. Type **354** | 15 | 10 |
| 1878 | 500r. Prenocephale | 20 | 10 |
| 1879 | 900r. Wuerhosaurus | 40 | 20 |
| 1880 | 1000r. Muttaburrasaurus | 45 | 20 |
| 1881 | 1500r. Shantungosaurus | 70 | 20 |
| 1882 | 4000r. Microceratops | 2·10 | 20 |
| **MS**1883 | 111×84 mm. 5400r. Dasplетosaurus | 3·75 | 90 |

355 *Flabellina affinis*

**1999.** Molluscs. Multicoloured.

| | | | |
|---|---|---|---|
| 1884 | 200r. Type **355** | 20 | 10 |
| 1885 | 500r. *Octopus macropus* | 30 | 10 |
| 1886 | 900r. *Helix hortensis* | 55 | 20 |
| 1887 | 1000r. *Lima hians* | 65 | 20 |
| 1888 | 1500r. *Arion empiricorum* | 95 | 20 |
| 1889 | 4000r. Swan mussel | 2·75 | 20 |
| **MS**1890 | 110×84 mm. 5400r. *Eledone aldrovandii* | 3·75 | 90 |

356 "Flowers in a Vase" (Henri Fantin-Latour)

**1999.** "Philexfrance 99" International Stamp Exhibition, Paris. Paintings. Multicoloured.

| | | | |
|---|---|---|---|
| 1891 | 200r. Type **356** | 30 | 10 |
| 1892 | 500r. "Fruit" (Paul Cezanne) | 45 | 10 |
| 1893 | 900r. "Table and Chairs" (Andre Derain) | 75 | 20 |
| 1894 | 1000r. "Vase on a Table" (Henri Matisse) | 85 | 20 |
| 1895 | 1500r. "Tulips and Marquerites" (Othon Friesz) | 1·40 | 20 |
| 1896 | 4000r. "Still Life with Tapestry" (Matisse) | 3·75 | 20 |
| **MS**1897 | 107×84 mm. 5400r. "Still Life with Tapestry" (detail) (Cezanne) | 3·75 | 90 |

357 Prasat Neak Poan

**1999.** Temples.

| | | | | |
|---|---|---|---|---|
| 1898 | **357** | 100r. blue and black | 20 | 10 |
| 1899 | - | 300r. red and black | 20 | 10 |
| 1900 | - | 500r. grn & blk (vert) | 30 | 10 |
| 1901 | - | 1400r. green and black | 85 | 10 |
| 1902 | - | 1600r. mauve and black | 95 | 20 |
| 1903 | - | 1800r. vio & blk (vert) | 1·10 | 20 |
| 1904 | - | 1900r. brown and black | 1·20 | 20 |

DESIGNS: 300r. Statue, Neak Poan; 500r. Banteay Srey; 1400r. Banteay Samre; 1600r. Banteay Srey; 1800r. Bas-relief, Angkor Vat; 1900r. Brasat Takeo.

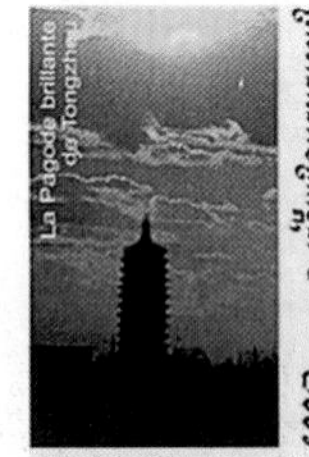

358 Pagoda, Tongzhou

**1999.** "China 1999" International Stamp Exhibition, Peking. Multicoloured.

| | | | |
|---|---|---|---|
| 1905 | 200r. Type **358** | 20 | 10 |
| 1906 | 500r. Pagoda, Tianning Temple | 30 | 10 |
| 1907 | 900r. Pagoda, Summer Palace | 75 | 10 |
| 1908 | 900r. Pagoda, Blue Cloud Temple | 75 | 10 |
| 1909 | 1000r. White pagoda, Bei Hai | 75 | 10 |
| 1910 | 1000r. Pagoda, Scented Hill | 75 | 10 |
| 1911 | 1500r. Pagoda, Yunju Temple | 1·30 | 20 |
| 1912 | 4000r. White pagoda, Miaoying Temple | 3·25 | 20 |

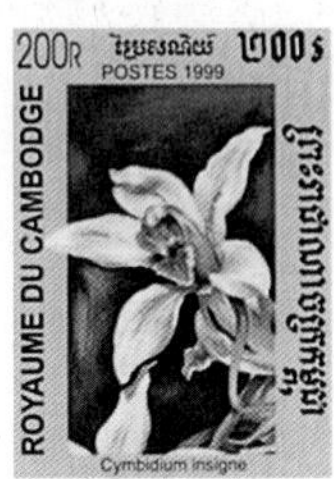
359 *Cymbidium insigne*

**1999.** Orchids. Multicoloured.

| | | | |
|---|---|---|---|
| 1913 | 200r. Type **359** | 20 | 10 |
| 1914 | 500r. *Papilionanthe teres* | 30 | 10 |
| 1915 | 900r. *Panisea uniflora* | 55 | 20 |
| 1916 | 1000r. *Euanthe sanderiana* | 65 | 20 |
| 1917 | 1500r. *Dendrobium trigonopus* | 95 | 20 |
| 1918 | 4000r. *Vanda coerulea* | 2·75 | 20 |
| **MS**1919 | 109×80 mm. 5400r. *Paphiopedilum callosum* (26×36 mm) | 3·75 | 90 |

360 Northern Bullfinch

**1999.** Birds. Multicoloured.

| | | | |
|---|---|---|---|
| 1920 | 200r. Type **360** | 30 | 10 |
| 1921 | 500r. Hawfinch | 45 | 10 |
| 1922 | 900r. Western greenfinch | 75 | 20 |
| 1923 | 1000r. Yellow warbler | 85 | 20 |
| 1924 | 1500r. Great grey shrike | 1·40 | 20 |
| 1925 | 4000r. Blue tit | 3·75 | 20 |
| **MS**1926 | 109×85 mm. 5400r. European robin (39×30 mm) | 3·75 | 90 |

**361** Emblem

**1999.** 46th Anniv of Independence. Multicoloured.

| | | | |
|---|---|---|---|
| 1927 | 500r. Type **361** | 30 | 20 |
| 1928 | 1500r. People with symbols of transport and industry | 75 | 30 |
| 1929 | 2000r. People queueing to vote | 1·10 | 45 |

**362** Tiger Barbs

**1999.** Fishes. Multicoloured.

| | | | |
|---|---|---|---|
| 1930 | 200r. Type **362** | 30 | 10 |
| 1931 | 500r. Rainbow shark minnow | 45 | 10 |
| 1932 | 900r. Clown rasbora | 75 | 20 |
| 1933 | 1000r. Orange-spotted cichlid | 85 | 20 |
| 1934 | 1500r. Crescent betta | 1·40 | 20 |
| 1935 | 4000r. Honey gourami | 3·75 | 20 |
| **MS**1936 | 109×84 mm. Eyespot puffer-fish (39×31 mm) | 3·75 | 90 |

**363** Harpy Eagle

**1999.** Birds of Prey. Multicoloured.

| | | | |
|---|---|---|---|
| 1937 | 200r. Type **363** | 30 | 10 |
| 1938 | 500r. Bateleur (vert) | 45 | 10 |
| 1939 | 900r. Egyptian vulture (vert) | 75 | 20 |
| 1940 | 1000r. Peregrine falcon (vert) | 85 | 20 |
| 1941 | 1500r. Red-tailed hawk (vert) | 1·40 | 20 |
| 1942 | 4000r. American bald eagle | 3·75 | 20 |
| **MS**1943 | 109×85 mm. 5400r. Red kite (31×39 mm) | 3·75 | 90 |

**364** Mail Carriage and Globe

**1999.** 125th Anniv of Universal Postal Union.

| | | | | |
|---|---|---|---|---|
| 1944 | **364** | 1600r. multicoloured | 1·60 | 90 |

**365** Giant Panda

**1999.** Mammals. Multicoloured.

| | | | |
|---|---|---|---|
| 1945 | 200r. Type **365** | 20 | 10 |
| 1946 | 500r. Yak | 30 | 10 |
| 1947 | 900r. Chinese water deer | 55 | 20 |
| 1948 | 1000r. Eurasian water shrew (horiz) | 65 | 20 |
| 1949 | 1500r. European otter (horiz) | 95 | 20 |
| 1950 | 4000r. Tiger (horiz) | 2·75 | 20 |
| **MS**1951 | 110×81 mm. 5400r. Pere David's deer (39×31 mm) | 3·75 | 90 |

**366** Coral Snake

**1999.** Snakes. Multicoloured.

| | | | |
|---|---|---|---|
| 1952 | 200r. Type **366** | 30 | 10 |
| 1953 | 500r. Rainbow boa | 45 | 10 |
| 1954 | 900r. Yellow anaconda | 75 | 20 |
| 1955 | 1000r. Southern ring-necked snake | 85 | 20 |
| 1956 | 1500r. Harlequin snake | 1·40 | 20 |
| 1957 | 4000r. Eastern tiger snake | 3·75 | 20 |
| **MS**1958 | 107×81 mm. 5400r. Green python (36×28 mm) | 3·75 | 90 |

**367** Dragon

**2000.** New Year. Year of the Dragon.

| | | | | |
|---|---|---|---|---|
| 1959 | **367** | 200r. multicoloured | 30 | 10 |
| 1960 | - | 500r. red, buff and black | 45 | 10 |
| 1961 | - | 900r. multicoloured | 75 | 20 |
| 1962 | - | 1000r. multicoloured | 85 | 20 |
| 1963 | - | 1500r. multicoloured | 1·40 | 20 |
| 1964 | - | 4000r. multicoloured | 3·75 | 20 |
| **MS**1965 | | 86×110 mm. 4500r. multi-coloured | 3·25 | 90 |

DESIGNS: 500r. Dragon enclosed in circle; 900r. Green dragon with red flames; 1000r. Heraldic dragon; 1500r. Red dragon with blue extremities; 4000r. Blue dragon with yellow flames; 4500r. Dragon's head (32×40 mm).

**368** Iguanodon (image scaled to 71% of original size)

**2000.** Dinosaurs. Multicoloured.

| | | | |
|---|---|---|---|
| 1966 | 200r. Type **368** | 20 | 10 |
| 1967 | 500r. Euoplocepalus | 30 | 10 |
| 1968 | 900r. Diplosaurus | 55 | 20 |
| 1969 | 1000r. Diplodocus | 65 | 20 |
| 1970 | 1500r. Stegoceras | 95 | 20 |
| 1971 | 4000r. Stegosaurus | 2·75 | 20 |
| **MS**1972 | 110×85 mm. 4500r. Brachio-saurus (32×40 mm) | 3·75 | 90 |

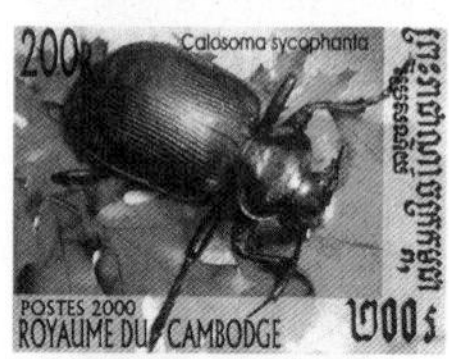

**369** Ground Beetle (*Calosoma sycophanta*)

**2000.** Insects. Multicoloured.

| | | | |
|---|---|---|---|
| 1973 | 200r. Type **369** | 30 | 10 |
| 1974 | 500r. European rhinoceros beetle (*Oryctes nasicornis*) | 45 | 10 |
| 1975 | 900r. *Diochrysa fastuosa* | 75 | 20 |
| 1976 | 1000r. *Blaps gigas* | 85 | 20 |
| 1977 | 1500r. Green tiger beetle (*Cincindela campestris*) | 1·40 | 20 |
| 1978 | 4000r. *Cissistes cephalotes* | 3·75 | 20 |
| **MS**1979 | 107×85 mm. 4500r. Scarab beetle (*Scarabaeus aegyptiorum*) (40×32 mm) | 3·25 | 90 |

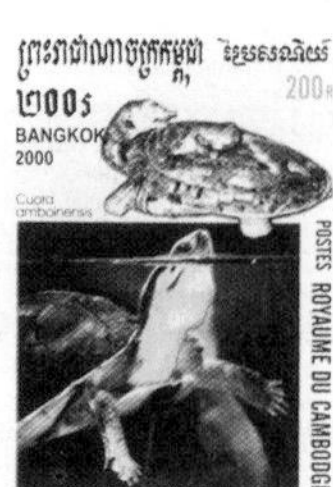

**370** Box Turtle (*Cuora amboinensis*)

**2000.** "Bangkok 2000" International Stamp Exhibition. Turtles and Tortoise. Multicoloured.

| | | | |
|---|---|---|---|
| 1980 | 200r. Type **370** | 30 | 10 |
| 1981 | 500r. Yellow box turtle (*Cuora flavomarginata*) | 45 | 10 |
| 1982 | 900r. Black-breasted leaf turtle (*Geoemyda spengleri*) (horiz) | 75 | 20 |
| 1983 | 1000r. Impressed tortoise (*Manouria (Geochelone) impressa*) (horiz) | 85 | 20 |
| 1984 | 1500r. Reeves' turtle (*Chinemys reevesi*) (horiz) | 1·40 | 20 |
| 1985 | 4000r. Spiny turtle (*Heosemys spinosa*) (horiz) | 3·75 | 20 |
| **MS**1986 | 111×86 mm. 4500r. Annadal's turtle (*Hieremys annandalei*) (horiz) (40×32 mm) | 3·25 | 90 |

**371** Ox-cart carrying Rice

**2000.** Rice Cultivation.

| | | | | |
|---|---|---|---|---|
| 1987 | **371** | 100r. green and black | 20 | 10 |
| 1988 | - | 300r. blue and black | 30 | 10 |
| 1989 | - | 500r. mauve and black | 45 | 10 |
| 1990 | - | 1400r. blue and black | 1·10 | 10 |
| 1991 | - | 1600r. brown and black | 1·50 | 20 |
| 1992 | - | 1900r. brown and black | 1·80 | 20 |
| 1993 | - | 2200r. red and black | 2·10 | 20 |

DESIGNS: 300r. Harrowing; 500r. Threshing; 1400r. Winnowing; 1600r. Planting; 1900r. Ploughing; 2200r. Binding sheaves.

**372** *Jules Petiet* Steam Locomotive

**2000.** Locomotives. "WIPA 2000" International Stamp Exhibition, Vienna (MS2000). Multicoloured.

| | | | |
|---|---|---|---|
| 1994 | 200r. Type **372** | 30 | 10 |
| 1995 | 500r. *Longue Chaudiere* steam locomotive, 1891 | 45 | 10 |
| 1996 | 900r. *Le Grand Chocolats* steam locomotive | 65 | 20 |
| 1997 | 1000r. *Glehn du Busquet* steam locomotive, 1891 | 85 | 20 |
| 1998 | 1500r. *Le Pendule Francais* diesel locomotive | 1·30 | 20 |
| 1999 | 4000r. TGV 001 locomotive, 1976 | 3·50 | 20 |
| **MS**2000 | 110×86 mm. 4500r. "Le Shuttle" in tunnel (80×32 mm) | 3·25 | 90 |

**373** Fly Agaric (*Amanita muscaria*)

**2000.** Fungi. Multicoloured.

| | | | |
|---|---|---|---|
| 2001 | 200r. Type **373** | 20 | 10 |
| 2002 | 500r. Panther cap (*Amanita pantherina*) | 30 | 10 |
| 2003 | 900r. *Clitocybe olearia* | 55 | 20 |
| 2004 | 1000r. *Lactarius scrobiculatus* | 65 | 20 |
| 2005 | 1500r. *Scleroderma vulgare* | 95 | 20 |
| 2006 | 4000r. *Amanita verna* | 2·75 | 20 |
| **MS**2007 | 110×86 mm. 4500r. Death cap (*Amanita phalloides*) (32×40 mm) | 3·75 | 90 |

**374** *Betta unimaculata* and *Betta pugnax* (*image scaled to 70% of original size*)

**2000.** Fighting Fish. Multicoloured.

| | | | |
|---|---|---|---|
| 2008 | 200r. Type **374** | 10 | 10 |
| 2009 | 500r. *Betta macrostoma* and *Betta taeniata* | 30 | 10 |
| 2010 | 900r. *Betta foerschi* and *Betta imbellis* | 65 | 20 |
| 2011 | 1000r. *Betta tessyae* and *Betta picta* | 65 | 20 |
| 2012 | 1500r. *Betta edithae* and *Betta bellica* | 95 | 20 |
| 2013 | 4000r. *Betta smaragdina* | 2·75 | 20 |
| **MS**2014 | 110×85 mm. 4500r. Siamese fighting fish (*Betta splendens*) (40×32 mm) | 3·25 | 90 |

**375** Woman in Arched Alcove (stone carving)

**2000.** Khmer Cultural Heritage. Each brown and black.

| | | | |
|---|---|---|---|
| 2015 | 500r. Type **375** | 30 | 20 |
| 2016 | 1000r. Woman in flowered head-dress in rectangula bas-relief | 75 | 30 |
| 2017 | 2000r. Woman with right arm raised in arche bas-relief | 1·10 | 45 |

**376** Galapagos Albatross (*Diomedea irrorata*)

**2000.** Sea Birds. Multicoloured.

| | | | |
|---|---|---|---|
| 2018 | 200r. Type **376** | 30 | 10 |
| 2019 | 500r. Kentish plover (*Charadrius alexandrinus*) (*vert*) | 45 | 10 |
| 2020 | 900r. Blue-footed booby (*Sula nebouxii*) | 65 | 20 |
| 2021 | 1000r. Common tern (*Sterna hirundo*) | 85 | 20 |
| 2022 | 1500r. Herring gull (*Larus argentatus*) (*vert*) | 1·30 | 20 |
| 2023 | 4000r. Whiskered tern (*Chlidonias hybrida*) | 3·50 | 20 |
| **MS**2024 | 108×83 mm. 4500r. Gannet (*Sula (Morus) bassana*) | 3·25 | 90 |

**377** *Cypripedium macranthum*

**2000.** Orchids. Multicoloured.

| | | | |
|---|---|---|---|
| 2025 | 200r. Type **377** | 30 | 10 |
| 2026 | 500r. *Vandopsis gigantean* | 45 | 10 |
| 2027 | 900r. *Calypso bulbosa* | 65 | 20 |
| 2028 | 1000r. *Vanda luzonica* | 85 | 20 |
| 2029 | 1500r. *Paphiopedilum villosum* | 1·30 | 20 |
| 2030 | 4000r. *Vanda merrillii* | 3·50 | 20 |
| **MS**2031 | 81×107 mm. 4500r. *Paphiopedilum Victoria* | 3·25 | 90 |

**378** Rowers in Large Canoe

**2000.** Tourism. Multicoloured.

| | | | |
|---|---|---|---|
| 2032 | 500r. Type **378** | 30 | 20 |
| 2033 | 1500r. Front of decorated canoe | 75 | 30 |
| 2034 | 2000r. Temple, elephant and dancer | 1·10 | 45 |

**379** Weightlifting

**2000.** Sports. Multicoloured.

| | | | |
|---|---|---|---|
| 2035 | 200r. Type **379** | 20 | 10 |
| 2036 | 500r. Gymnastics | 45 | 10 |

| | | | |
|---|---|---|---|
| 2037 | 900r. Baseball | 55 | 20 |
| 2038 | 1000r. Tennis | 65 | 20 |
| 2039 | 1500r. Basketball | 1·10 | 20 |
| 2040 | 4000r. High jump | 2·75 | 20 |
| **MS**2041 | 110×85 mm. 4500r. Running | 3·00 | 90 |

**380** Metz DLK 23-6

**2000.** Fire Engines. Multicoloured.

| | | | |
|---|---|---|---|
| 2042 | 200r. Type **380** | 20 | 20 |
| 2043 | 500r. Iveco-Magirus SLF 24/100 | 45 | 35 |
| 2044 | 900r. Metz SLF 7000 WS | 55 | 45 |
| 2045 | 1000r. Iveco-Magirus TLF 24/50 | 65 | 55 |
| 2046 | 1500r. Saval-Konenburg RFF-11.000 | 1·10 | 90 |
| 2047 | 4000r. Metz TLF 24/50 | 2·75 | 2·30 |
| **MS**2048 | 110×85 mm. 4500r. Metz TLF 16/25 | 6·50 | 5·50 |

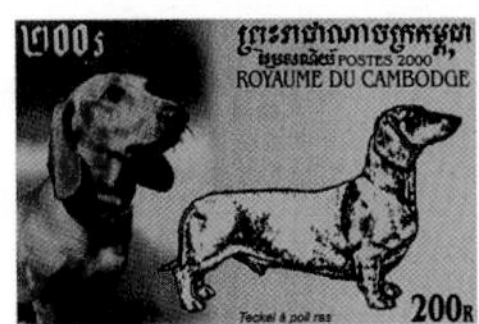


**381** Smooth Haired Dachshund

**2000.** Dachshunds. Multicoloured.

| | | | |
|---|---|---|---|
| 2049 | 200r. Type **381** | 20 | 10 |
| 2050 | 500r. Wire haired | 45 | 10 |
| 2051 | 900r. Long haired | 55 | 20 |
| 2052 | 1000r. Two smooth haired | 65 | 20 |
| 2053 | 1500r. Mother and pups | 1·10 | 20 |
| 2054 | 4000r. Two puppies | 2·75 | 20 |
| **MS**2055 | 117×86 mm. 4500r. Head of wire haired (32×40 mm) | 3·00 | 90 |

**382** Rover 12 C (1912)

**2000.** Cars. Espana 2000 International Stamp Exhibition, Madrid. Multicoloured.

| | | | |
|---|---|---|---|
| 2056 | 200r. Type **382** | 20 | 10 |
| 2057 | 500r. Austin 30 CV (1907) | 45 | 10 |
| 2058 | 900r. Rolls-Royce Silver Ghost (1909) | 55 | 20 |
| 2059 | 1000r. Graham Paige (1929) | 65 | 20 |
| 2060 | 1500r. Austin 12 (1937) | 1·10 | 20 |
| 2061 | 4000r. Mercedes-Benz 300SL (1957) | 2·75 | 20 |
| **MS**2062 | 110×86 mm. 4500r. MG (1936) (40×32 mm) | 3·00 | 90 |

**383** 18th-century Korean Painting and Two Kittens

**2000.** Cats. Multicoloured.

| | | | |
|---|---|---|---|
| 2063 | 200r. Type **383** | 20 | 10 |
| 2064 | 500r. 18th-century Portuguese tiles and tabby cat | 45 | 10 |
| 2065 | 900r. Satsuma ceramic cat and two cats | 55 | 20 |
| 2066 | 1000r. Goddess Basset (Egyptian) and mother cat and kittens | 65 | 20 |
| 2067 | 1500r. Goddess Freya (engraving) and tortoiseshell cat | 1·10 | 20 |
| 2068 | 4000r. Japanese painting and Manx cat | 2·75 | 20 |
| **MS**2069 | 110×86 mm. 4500r. Leaping cat (40×32 mm) | 3·00 | 90 |

**384** Flowers, Monument and Flag

**2000.** 47th Anniv of Independence. Multicoloured.

| | | | |
|---|---|---|---|
| 2070 | 500r. Type **384** | 30 | 20 |
| 2071 | 1500r. Dove, monument and flag | 75 | 30 |
| 2072 | 2000r. Flag, monument and crowd | 1·10 | 45 |

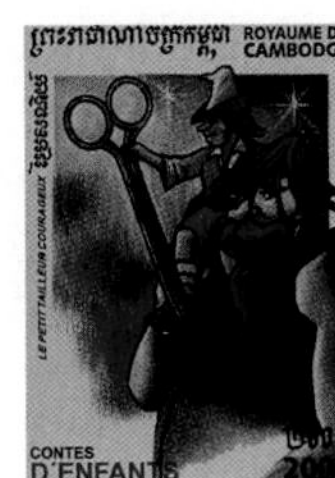


**385** The Courageous Little Tailor

**2000.** Children's Stories. Multicoloured.

| | | | |
|---|---|---|---|
| 2073 | 200r. Type **385** | 20 | 10 |
| 2074 | 500r. Tom Thumb | 45 | 10 |
| 2075 | 900r. Thumbelina | 50 | 20 |
| 2076 | 1000r. Pinocchio (*horiz*) | 65 | 20 |
| 2077 | 1500r. The Crayfish (*horiz*) | 1·10 | 20 |
| 2078 | 4000r. Peter Pan (*horiz*) | 2·75 | 20 |
| **MS**2079 | 110×85 mm. 4500r. Pied Piper of Hamelin (32×40 mm) | 3·00 | 90 |

**386** Wattled Starling (*Creatophora cinera*)

**2000.** Birds. Multicoloured.

| | | | |
|---|---|---|---|
| 2080 | 200r. Type **386** | 20 | 10 |
| 2081 | 500r. Common starling (*Sturnus vulgaris*) | 45 | 10 |
| 2082 | 900r. Pekin robin (*Leiothrix lutea*) | 55 | 20 |
| 2083 | 1000r. Guianian cock of the rock (*Rupicola rupicola*) | 85 | 20 |
| 2084 | 1500r. Alpine accentor (*Prunella collaris*) | 1·10 | 20 |
| 2085 | 4000r. Bearded reedling (*Panurus biarmicus*) (inscr "biarnicus") | 2·75 | 20 |
| **MS**2086 | 85×110 mm. 4500r. Inscr "Muscicapula pallipes" (32×40 mm) | 3·00 | 90 |

**387** Johannes Gutenberg (invention of printing press)

**2001.** Millennium. Multicoloured.

| | | | |
|---|---|---|---|
| 2087 | 200r. Type **387** | 20 | 10 |
| 2088 | 500r. Michael Faraday (discovery of electricity) | 45 | 10 |
| 2089 | 900r. Samuel Morse (invention of Morse code) | 55 | 20 |
| 2090 | 1000r. Alexander Bell (invention of telephone) | 65 | 20 |
| 2091 | 1500r. Enrico Fermi (discovery of nuclear fission) | 1·10 | 20 |
| 2092 | 4000r. Edward Roberts (invention of personal computer) | 2·75 | 20 |
| **MS**2093 | 86×112 mm. 5400r. Christopher Columbus (discovery of America) (40×32 mm); 5400r. Neil Armstrong (first moon walk) (40×32 mm) | 7·50 | 90 |

**388** Snake Head

**2001.** Year of the Snake. Multicoloured.

| | | | |
|---|---|---|---|
| 2094 | 200r. Type **388** | 20 | 10 |
| 2095 | 500r. Two snakes entwined | 45 | 10 |
| 2096 | 900r. Snake entwined with moon | 55 | 20 |
| 2097 | 1000r. Entwined snakes (*different*) | 65 | 20 |
| 2098 | 1500r. Snake encircling moon | 1·10 | 20 |
| 2099 | 4000r. Three snakes' heads | 2·75 | 20 |
| **MS**2100 | 110×86 mm. 5400r. Snake head (*different*) (40×32 mm) | 3·75 | 90 |

**389** Sandou Ladder Transport (1910)

**2001.** Fire Engines. Multicoloured.

| | | | |
|---|---|---|---|
| 2101 | 200r. Type **389** | 20 | 10 |
| 2102 | 500r. Gallo ladder transport (1899) | 45 | 10 |
| 2103 | 900r. Merry Weather appliance (1950) | 55 | 20 |
| 2104 | 1000r. Merry Weather ambulance (1940) | 65 | 20 |
| 2105 | 1500r. Man-Metz appliance (1972) | 1·10 | 20 |
| 2106 | 4000r. Roman diesel appliance (1970) | 2·75 | 20 |
| **MS**2107 | 111×87 mm. 5400r. Metropolitan steam engine (1898) (40×32 mm). | 3·75 | 90 |

**390** Puff Ball (*Lycoperdon perlatum*)

**2001.** Fungi. Multicoloured.

| | | | |
|---|---|---|---|
| 2108 | 200r. Type **390** | 20 | 10 |
| 2109 | 500r. *Trametes versicolor* | 45 | 10 |
| 2110 | 900r. *Hypholoma sublaterium* (inscr "Hipholoma") | 55 | 20 |
| 2111 | 1000r. Fly agaric (*Amanita muscaria*) | 65 | 20 |
| 2112 | 1500r. *Lycoperdon umbrinum* | 1·10 | 20 |
| 2113 | 4000r. *Cortinarius orellanus* | 2·75 | 20 |
| **MS**2114 | 111×84 mm. 5400r. Death cap (*Amanita phalloides*) (32×40 mm) | 3·75 | 90 |

**391** Preah Vihear

**2001.** Temples.

| | | | | |
|---|---|---|---|---|
| 2115 | 391 | 200r. blue and black | 20 | 10 |
| 2116 | - | 300r. red and black | 30 | 10 |
| 2117 | - | 600r. green and black | 45 | 10 |
| 2118 | - | 1000r. orange and black | 65 | 10 |
| 2119 | - | 1500r. green and black | 95 | 20 |
| 2120 | - | 1700r. violet and black | 1·20 | 20 |
| 2121 | - | 2200r. brown and black | 1·40 | 20 |

DESIGNS: 300r. Thonmanom; 600r. Tasom; 1000r. Kravan; 1500r. Takeo; 1700r. Mebon; 2200r. Banteay Kdei.

**392** Angkor Wat

**2001.** 3rd Anniv of Day of Khmer Culture. Showing bas-reliefs. Multicoloured.

| | | | |
|---|---|---|---|
| 2122 | 500r. Type **392** | 30 | 20 |
| 2123 | 1500r. Bayon Temple | 1·10 | 30 |
| 2124 | 2000r. Bayon Temple (different) | 1·40 | 45 |

**393** Large Tortoiseshell (*Nymphalis polychloros*)

**2001.** Butterflies. Belgica 2001 International Stamp Exhibition, Brussels. Multicoloured.

| | | | |
|---|---|---|---|
| 2125 | 200r. Type **393** | 20 | 10 |
| 2126 | 500r. *Cethosia hypsea* | 45 | 10 |
| 2127 | 900r. *Papilio palinurus* | 55 | 20 |
| 2128 | 1000r. Lesser purple emperor (*Apatua ilia*) | 65 | 20 |
| 2129 | 1500r. Clipper (*Parthenos Sylvia*) | 1·10 | 20 |
| 2130 | 4000r. *Morpho grandensis* | 2·75 | 20 |
| **MS**2131 | 111×85 mm. 5400r. *Heliconius melpomene* (40×32 mm) | 3·75 | 90 |

**394** Gary Cooper

**2001.** Cinema Actors. Multicoloured.

| | | | |
|---|---|---|---|
| 2132 | 200r. Type **394** | 20 | 10 |
| 2133 | 500r. Marlene Dietrich | 45 | 10 |
| 2134 | 900r. Walt Disney | 55 | 20 |
| 2135 | 1000r. Clark Gable | 65 | 20 |
| 2136 | 1500r. Jeanette Macdonald | 1·10 | 20 |
| 2137 | 4000r. Melvyn Douglas | 2·75 | 20 |
| **MS**2138 | 86×111 mm. 5400r. Rudolf Valentino (32×40 mm); 5400r. Marilyn Monroe (32×40 mm) | 7·50 | 90 |

**395** TVR M series (1972)

**2001.** Cars. Multicoloured.

| | | | |
|---|---|---|---|
| 2139 | 200r. Type **395** | 20 | 10 |
| 2140 | 500r. Ferrari 410 (1956) | 45 | 10 |
| 2141 | 900r. Peugeot 405 (1995) | 55 | 20 |
| 2142 | 1000r. Fiat 8VZ (1953) | 65 | 20 |
| 2143 | 1500r. Citroen Xsara (1997) | 1·10 | 20 |
| 2144 | 4000r. Renault Espace (1997) | 2·75 | 20 |
| **MS**2145 | 111×85 mm. 5400r. Ferrari 250 GT (1963) (40×32 mm) | 3·75 | 90 |

**396** Bayon Temple

**2001.** Tourism. Bayon Temple. Multicoloured.

| | | | |
|---|---|---|---|
| 2146 | 500r. Type **396** | 30 | 30 |
| 2147 | 1500r. Faces and monument | 1·10 | 90 |
| 2148 | 2000r. Face and trees | 1·40 | 1·20 |

**397** Steam Locomotive 4-6-0

**2001.** Trains. Philanippon '01 International Stamp Exhibition, Tokyo. Multicoloured.

| | | | |
|---|---|---|---|
| 2149 | 200r. Type **397** | 20 | 20 |
| 2150 | 500r. Steam locomotive 4-6-4 | 45 | 35 |
| 2151 | 900r. Steam locomotive 4-4-0 | 55 | 45 |
| 2152 | 1000r. Steam locomotive 4-6-4 | 65 | 55 |
| 2153 | 1500r. Locomotive 4-6-2 | 1·10 | 90 |

| | | | |
|---|---|---|---|
| 2154 | 4000r. Locomotive 4-8-2 | 2·75 | 2·30 |
| MS2155 | 110×84 mm. 5400r. Steam locomotive 2-8-2 (40×32 mm). | 3·75 | 3·25 |

**398** Emperor Penguin (*Aptenodytes forsteri*)

**2001.** Penguins. Multicoloured.

| | | | |
|---|---|---|---|
| 2156 | 200r. Type **398** | 20 | 20 |
| 2157 | 500r. Jackass penguin (*Spheniscus demersus*) | 45 | 35 |
| 2158 | 900r. Humboldt penguin (*Spheniscus humboldti*) | 55 | 45 |
| 2159 | 1000r. Rockhopper penguin (*Eudypes crestatus*) (inscr "cristatus") | 65 | 55 |
| 2160 | 1500r. King penguin (*Aptenodytes patagonica*) | 1·10 | 90 |
| 2161 | 4000r. Bearded penguin (*Pygocelis Antarctica*) | 2·75 | 2·30 |
| MS2162 | 108×83 mm. 5400r. Gentoo penguin (*Pygoscelis papua*) (40×32 mm) | 3·75 | 3·25 |

**399** Singapura

**2001.** Cats. Multicoloured.

| | | | |
|---|---|---|---|
| 2163 | 200r. Type **399** | 10 | 10 |
| 2164 | 500r. Cymric | 30 | 30 |
| 2165 | 900r. Exotic short haired (inscr "shirthair") | 65 | 55 |
| 2166 | 1000r. Ragdoll | 65 | 55 |
| 2167 | 1500r. Manx | 1·10 | 90 |
| 2168 | 4000r. Somali | 2·75 | 2·40 |
| MS2169 | 110×85 mm. 5400r. Egyptian mau (40×32 mm) | 3·75 | 3·25 |

**400** Khleng Chak

**2001.** Traditional Kites. Multicoloured.

| | | | |
|---|---|---|---|
| 2170 | 300r. Type **400** | 20 | 20 |
| 2171 | 500r. Khleng Kanton | 30 | 30 |
| 2172 | 1000r. Khleng Phnong | 55 | 45 |
| 2173 | 1500r. Khleng KaunMorn | 1·10 | 90 |
| 2174 | 3000r. Khleng Me Ambao | 2·10 | 1·80 |

**401** *Parodia cintiensis*

**2001.** Cacti. Multicoloured.

| | | | |
|---|---|---|---|
| 2175 | 200r. Type **401** | 10 | 10 |
| 2176 | 500r. *Astrophytum asterias* | 30 | 30 |
| 2177 | 900r. *Parodia faustiana* | 65 | 55 |
| 2178 | 1000r. *Coryphantha sulcolanata* | 65 | 55 |
| 2179 | 1500r. *Neochilenia hankena* | 1·10 | 90 |
| 2180 | 4000r. *Mammillaria boolii* (inscr "Mamillaria") | 2·75 | 2·40 |
| MS2181 | 110×85 mm. 5400r. *Mammillaria* inscr "Mamilleria swinglei" (32×40 mm) | 3·75 | 3·25 |

**402** Fishing Dance

**2001.** Dances. Multicoloured.

| | | | |
|---|---|---|---|
| 2182 | 500r. Type **402** | 30 | 30 |
| 2183 | 1500r. Red fish dance | 1·10 | 90 |
| 2184 | 2000r. Dance of Apsara | 1·50 | 1·30 |

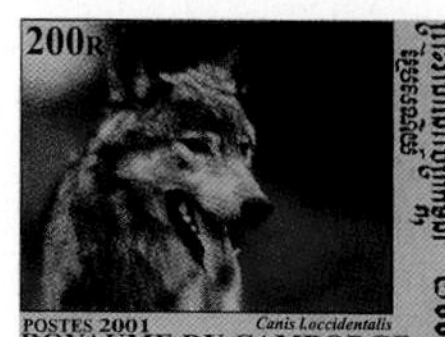


**403** Timber Wolf (*Canis occidentalis*)

**2001.** Wolves and Foxes. Multicoloured.

| | | | |
|---|---|---|---|
| 2185 | 200r. Type **403** | 20 | 20 |
| 2186 | 500r. Alaska tundra wolf (*Canis tundrorum*) | 45 | 30 |
| 2187 | 900r. Fox (inscr "Vulpes fulvas") | 55 | 45 |
| 2188 | 1000r. Coyote (*Canis latrans*) | 65 | 55 |
| 2189 | 1500r. Fennec fox (*Vulpes zerda*) | 1·10 | 90 |
| 2190 | 4000r. Arctic fox (*Alopex lagopus*) | 2·75 | 2·30 |
| MS2191 | 112×87 mm. 5400r. Iberian wolf (*Canis signatus*) (40×32 mm) | 3·75 | 3·25 |

**404** *Australopithecus anamensis*

**2001.** Prehistoric Man. Multicoloured.

| | | | |
|---|---|---|---|
| 2192 | 100r. Type **404** | 10 | 10 |
| 2193 | 200r. *Australopithecus afarensis* | 20 | 20 |
| 2194 | 300r. *Australopithecus africanus* | 20 | 20 |
| 2195 | 500r. *Australopithecus rudolfensis* | 30 | 30 |
| 2196 | 500r. *Australopithecus boisei* | 30 | 30 |
| 2197 | 1000r. *Homo habilis* | 65 | 55 |
| 2198 | 1500r. *Homo erectus* | 1·10 | 90 |
| 2199 | 4000r. *Homo sapiens neanderthalensis* (inscr "nesnderthalensis") | 2·75 | 2·40 |
| MS2200 | 110×85 mm. 5400r. *Homo sapiens sapiens* (40×32 mm) | 3·75 | 3·25 |

**404a** World Cup Champions (1934)

**2001.** Italian Football. Multicoloured.

| | | | |
|---|---|---|---|
| 2200a | 200r. Type **404a** | 20 | 15 |
| 2200b | 500r. World Cup champions (1938) | 30 | 25 |
| 2200c | 900r. European Cup champions (1968) | 55 | 45 |
| 2200d | 1000r. World Cup champions (1982) | 65 | 50 |
| 2200e | 1500r. World Cup qualifying team (2002) | 1·10 | 90 |
| 2200f | 4000r. Federazione Italiana Giuoco Calcio emblem | 2·75 | 2·40 |

**404b** Castle (18th-century)

**2001.** Chess. Multicoloured.

| | | | |
|---|---|---|---|
| 2200g | 200r. Type **404b** | 20 | 15 |
| 2200h | 500r. Pawn (19th-century) | 30 | 25 |
| 2200i | 900r. King (19th-century) | 55 | 45 |
| 2200j | 1000r. Bishop (17th-century) | 65 | 50 |
| 2200k | 1500r. Queen (17th-century) | 1·10 | 90 |
| 2200l | 4000r. Knight (20th-century) 2.74 | | 2·40 |

| | | | |
|---|---|---|---|
| MS2200m | 112×87 mm. 5400r. King (16th-century) (40×32 mm) | 3·75 | 3·25 |

**405** Preah Vihear Temple

**2002.** 10th Anniv of ASEAN (Association of South East Asian Nations) Post. Temples. Multicoloured.

| | | | |
|---|---|---|---|
| 2201 | 500r. Type **405** | 30 | 25 |
| 2202 | 1000r. Preah Ko | 55 | 40 |
| 2203 | 1500r. Banteay Srei | 1·10 | 85 |
| 2204 | 2500r. Bayon | 1·80 | 1·40 |
| 2205 | 3500r. Ankor Wat | 2·20 | 1·70 |

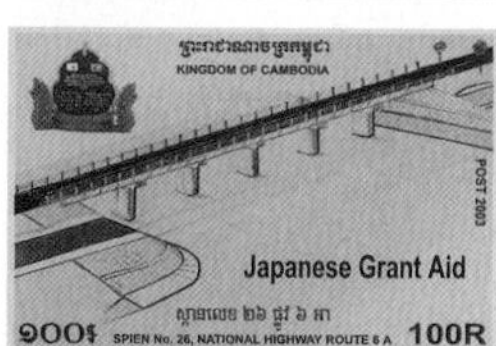


**406** Bridge No. 26, Route 6A

**2003.** Japanese Grant Aid. Multicoloured.

| | | | |
|---|---|---|---|
| 2206 | 100r. Type **406** | 15 | 10 |
| 2207 | 200r. Bridge No. 25, Route 6A | 30 | 25 |
| 2208 | 400r. Chroy Changvar bridge | 45 | 35 |
| 2209 | 800r. Kazuna bridge | 60 | 45 |
| 2210 | 3500r. Monument | 3·00 | 2·40 |

**407** Ox Cart carrying supplies

**2003.** 140th Anniv of Red Cross and Red Crescent. Multicoloured.

| | | | |
|---|---|---|---|
| 2211 | 100r. Type **407** | 25 | 20 |
| 2212 | 200r. Red Cross worker (vert) | 25 | 20 |
| 2213 | 300r. Queen Norodom Monineath Sihanouk and young men | 30 | 25 |
| 2214 | 400r. Queen greeting young woman in crowd | 30 | 25 |
| 2215 | 500r. Queen and man | 30 | 25 |
| 2216 | 700r. Queen greeting older woman in crowd | 40 | 30 |
| 2217 | 800r. Queen presenting cloth | 65 | 45 |
| 2218 | 1000r. Woman with shaved head and Queen | 65 | 45 |
| 2219 | 1900r. Queen and M. Bun Rany Hun Sen (pres. of Cambodian Red Cross) (vert) | 1·20 | 95 |
| 2220 | 2100r. M. Bun Rany Hun Sen and Red Cross worker (vert) | 1·20 | 95 |
| 2221 | 4000r. Queen and M. Bun Rany Hun Sen holding baby | 2·50 | 2·00 |

**408** Sugar Palm Tree

**2003.** Sugar Palm. Multicoloured.

| | | | |
|---|---|---|---|
| 2222 | 300r. Type **408** | 30 | 25 |
| 2223 | 500r. Female flower | 30 | 25 |
| 2224 | 700r. Male flower | 40 | 30 |
| 2225 | 1500r. Fruit | 1·10 | 85 |

**409** Ankor Wat, Cambodia

**2003.** 50th Anniv of China–Cambodia Diplomatic Relations. Multicoloured.

| | | | |
|---|---|---|---|
| 2226 | 2000r. Type **409** | 1·20 | 95 |
| 2227 | 2000r. Great Wall, China | 1·20 | 95 |

**410** Conference Emblem

**2003.** 36th ASEAN Ministerial Meeting and Tenth ASEAN Regional Forum, Phnom Penh. Multicoloured.

| | | | |
|---|---|---|---|
| 2228 | 400r. Type **410** | 40 | 30 |
| 2229 | 500r. Dancer (Apsara dance) | 50 | 40 |
| 2230 | 600r. Seated dancer | 55 | 45 |
| 2231 | 1600r. Two seated dancers | 1·30 | 1·00 |
| 2232 | 1900r. Two dancers (Temono-rom dance) | 1·50 | 1·20 |

**411** King Norodom Sihanouk and Map

**2003.** 50th Anniv of Independence. King Norodom Sihanouk. Multicoloured.

| | | | |
|---|---|---|---|
| 2233 | 200r. Type **411** | 25 | 20 |
| 2234 | 400r. With soldiers (vert) | 40 | 30 |
| 2235 | 500r. Seated (vert) | 50 | 40 |
| 2236 | 800r. With arm extended (vert) | 55 | 45 |
| 2237 | 1000r. Saluting (vert) | 65 | 50 |
| 2238 | 2000r. Independence monument and King Norodom Sihanouk (vert) | 1·20 | 95 |
| 2239 | 5000r. Wearing suit | 3·50 | 2·70 |

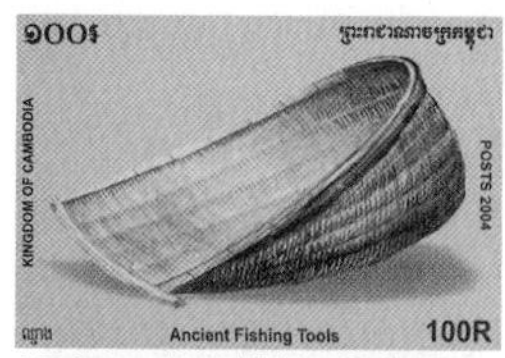


**412** Scoop-shaped Fishing Basket

**2004.** Fishing Tools. Multicoloured.

| | | | |
|---|---|---|---|
| 2240 | 100r. Type **412** | 20 | 10 |
| 2241 | 200r. Narrow basket | 30 | 20 |
| 2242 | 800r. Cylindrical basket | 40 | 25 |
| 2243 | 1700r. Goblet-shaped basket (vert) | 90 | 55 |
| 2244 | 2200r. Cylindrical basket with baffles (vert) | 1·10 | 70 |
| MS2245 | 85×110 mm. 2000r. Child and basket (vert) | 1·10 | 1·10 |

**413** Bayon Sculpture

**2004.** Day of Khmer Culture. Multicoloured.

| | | | |
|---|---|---|---|
| 2246 | 100r. Type **413** | 20 | 10 |
| 2247 | 200r. Banteay Srei sculpture | 30 | 20 |
| 2248 | 400r. Banteay Srei sculpture (detail) | 40 | 25 |
| 2249 | 800r. Bayon sculpture (different) (vert) | 55 | 35 |
| 2250 | 3500r. Banteay Srei sculpture (detail) (different) (vert) | 1·50 | 90 |
| MS2251 | 110×85 mm. 2000r. As No. 2250 with design enlarged (vert) | 1·10 | 1·10 |

**414** Waterwheel

**2004.** Tourism. Landscapes. Multicoloured.

| | | | |
|---|---|---|---|
| 2252 | 600r. Type **414** | 30 | 20 |
| 2253 | 900r. Paddy fields | 50 | 30 |
| 2254 | 2000r. River and palms | 1·10 | 70 |
| MS2255 | 110×85 mm. 2000r. Ox cart | 1·10 | 1·10 |

**415** Two Dancers

**2004.** Tepmonorum Dance. Multicoloured.

| | | | |
|---|---|---|---|
| 2256 | 400r. Type **415** | 40 | 30 |
| 2257 | 1000r. Two dancers wearing blue outfits | 65 | 50 |
| 2258 | 2100r. Two female dancers | 1·30 | 1·00 |
| **MS**2259 | 110×85 mm. 2000r. As No. 2259 with design enlarged | 1·20 | 1·20 |

**416** *Cassia fistula*

**2004.** Flowers. Multicoloured.

| | | | |
|---|---|---|---|
| 2260 | 600r. Type **416** | 35 | 25 |
| 2261 | 700r. *Butea monosperma* | 40 | 30 |
| 2262 | 900r. *Couroupita quianensis* | 55 | 40 |
| 2263 | 1000r. *Delonix regia* (horiz) | 65 | 50 |
| 2264 | 1800r. *Lagerstroemia floribunda* | 1·00 | 80 |
| **MS**2265 | 110×85 mm. 2000r. *Lagerstroemia floribunda* (horiz) | 1·20 | 1·20 |

**417** Preah Khan

**2004.** Tourism. Temples. Multicoloured.

| | | | |
|---|---|---|---|
| 2266 | 200r. Type **417** | 20 | 10 |
| 2267 | 500r. Pre Rup | 25 | 15 |
| 2268 | 600r. Banteay Samre | 30 | 20 |
| 2269 | 1600r. Bayon | 80 | 50 |
| 2270 | 1900r. Ankor Wat | 90 | 55 |
| **MS**2271 | 110×85 mm. 2000r. Stone head, Bayon (vert) | 1·10 | 1·10 |

**418** King Norodom Sihamoni

**2004.** Coronation of King Norodom Sihamoni. Multicoloured.

| | | | |
|---|---|---|---|
| 2272 | 100r. Type **418** | 20 | 10 |
| 2273 | 400r. With monks | 30 | 20 |
| 2274 | 500r. Planting tree | 35 | 20 |
| 2275 | 600r. King Norodom Sihamoni (portrait) | 40 | 25 |
| 2276 | 700r. With crowd, greeting child (horiz) | 45 | 30 |
| 2277 | 900r. Greeting men in uniform (horiz) | 50 | 35 |
| 2278 | 2100r. Releasing dove (horiz) | 95 | 55 |
| 2279 | 2200r. With young men (horiz) | 1·10 | 70 |
| 2280 | 4000r. King Norodom Sihamoni and temple (horiz) | 1·70 | 1·10 |

**419** Anniversary Emblem

**2005.** 50th Anniv of Cambodian Red Cross Society. Multicoloured.

| | | | |
|---|---|---|---|
| 2281 | 400r. Type **419** | 15 | 10 |
| 2282 | 700r. Signing book (horiz) | 30 | 20 |
| 2283 | 800r. Lok Chumteav Bun Rany Hun Sen (president) dispensing aid (horiz) | 35 | 20 |
| 2284 | 1900r. Queen Mother Norodom Monineath Sihanouk dispensing aid (horiz) | 1·00 | 60 |
| 2285 | 2100r. Lok Chumteav Bun Rany Hun Sen presenting certificate to volunteer (horiz) | 1·10 | 65 |
| 2286 | 2200r. King Norodom Sihamoni and Queen Mother Norodom Monineath Sihanouk on dais (horiz) | 1·20 | 70 |

**420** Aspara Dance

**2005.** Traditional Dance. Aspara Dance. Mult.

| | | | |
|---|---|---|---|
| 2287 | 800r. Type **420** | 35 | 20 |
| 2288 | 900r. Gold skirt, facing right | 40 | 30 |
| 2289 | 1400r. Blue skirt, facing left | 55 | 35 |
| 2290 | 1600r. Cream skirt, leg raised | 95 | 55 |
| 2291 | 2000r. Chequered skirt, facing left | 1·10 | 65 |

**421** Banteay Kdei

**2005.** Cultural Heritage. Multicoloured.

| | | | |
|---|---|---|---|
| 2292 | 500r. Type **421** | 20 | 10 |
| 2293 | 700r. Elephant terrace, Angkor Thom | 30 | 20 |
| 2294 | 1000r. Thommanon temple, Angkor | 50 | 30 |
| 2295 | 2000r. Ta Prohm temple, Angkor | 1·10 | 65 |
| 2296 | 2500r. Angkor Wat | 1·30 | 80 |

## EXPRESS MAIL STAMPS

**E313** Bohemian Waxwing

**1997.** Birds. Multicoloured.

| | | | |
|---|---|---|---|
| E1624 | 600r. Type E **313** | 1·10 | 45 |
| E1625 | 900r. Great grey shrike | 1·30 | 65 |
| E1626 | 1000r. Eurasian tree sparrow | 1·80 | 75 |
| E1627 | 2000r. Black redstart | 3·50 | 1·70 |
| E1628 | 2500r. Reed bunting | 4·75 | 2·00 |
| E1629 | 3000r. Ortolan bunting | 5·25 | 2·50 |

## POSTAGE DUE STAMPS

**D13**

**1957**

| | | | | |
|---|---|---|---|---|
| D81 | **D13** | 10c. red, blue & black | 20 | 20 |
| D82 | **D13** | 50c. red, blue & black | 55 | 45 |
| D83 | **D13** | 1r. red, blue & black | 85 | 75 |
| D84 | **D13** | 3r. red, blue & black | 1·10 | 90 |
| D85 | **D13** | 5r. red, blue & black | 1·80 | 1·60 |

Pt. 1

# CAMEROON

Former German colony occupied by British and French troops during 1914–16. The territory was divided between them and the two areas were administered under League of Nations mandates from 1922, converted into United Nations trusteeships in 1946.

The British section was administered as part of Nigeria until 1960, when a plebiscite was held. The northern area voted to join Nigeria and the southern part joined the newly-independent Cameroun Republic (formerly the French trust territory). In November 1995 this republic joined the Commonwealth.

12 pence = 1 shilling;
20 shillings = 1 pound.

### I. CAMEROONS EXPEDITIONARY FORCE

**1915.** "Yacht" key-types of German Kamerun surch C.E.F. and value in English currency.

| | | | | |
|---|---|---|---|---|
| B1 | N | ½d. on 3pf. brown | 13·00 | 50·00 |
| B2 | N | ½d. on 5pf. green | 5·00 | 9·50 |
| B3 | N | 1d. on 10pf. red | 1·25 | 9·50 |
| B4 | N | 2d. on 20pf. blue | 3·50 | 22·00 |
| B5 | N | 2½d. on 25pf. black and red on yellow | 14·00 | 55·00 |
| B6 | N | 3d. on 30pf. black and orange on buff | 12·00 | 60·00 |
| B7 | N | 4d. on 40pf. black and red | 12·00 | 60·00 |
| B8 | N | 6d. on 50pf. black and purple on buff | 12·00 | 60·00 |
| B9 | N | 8d. on 80pf. black and red on rose | 12·00 | 60·00 |
| B10 | O | 1s. on 1m. red | £180 | £800 |
| B11 | O | 2s. on 2m. blue | £180 | £800 |
| B12 | O | 3s. on 3m. black | £180 | £800 |
| B13 | O | 5s. on 5m. red and black | £250 | £850 |

### II. CAMEROONS TRUST TERRITORY

Issue used in the British trusteeship from October 1960 to June 1961 in the northern are and until Spetember 1961 in the southern area, when they joined with Nigeria nad the Cameroun Republic respectively.

**1960.** Stamps of Nigeria of 1953 optd CAMEROONS U.K.T.T.

| | | | | |
|---|---|---|---|---|
| T1 | **18** | ½d. black and orange | 10 | 1·50 |
| T2 | - | 1d. black and green | 10 | 70 |
| T3 | - | 1½d. green | 10 | 20 |
| T4c | - | 2d. grey | 2·25 | 2·50 |
| T5 | - | 3d. black and lilac | 20 | 10 |
| T6 | - | 4d. black and blue | 20 | 2·25 |
| T7 | - | 6d. brown and black | 30 | 20 |
| T8 | - | 1s. black and purple | 30 | 10 |
| T9 | **26** | 2s.6d. black and green | 1·50 | 1·00 |
| T10 | - | 5s. black and orange | 2·00 | 3·50 |
| T11 | - | 10s. black and brown | 3·00 | 7·00 |
| T12 | **29** | £1 black and violet | 12·00 | 27·00 |

### III. REPUBLIC OF CAMEROON

The Republic of Cameroon joined the Commonwealth on 1 November 1995 and issues from that date will be listed below, when examples and information have been received.

**PRICES:** Prices shown for used stamps of Cameroon are somewhat tentative, but have been compiled with the assistance of collectors of these issues. Unused stamps for this period are scarce to rare and, when offered, can command very high prices. Under the cirumstances it has been decided not to quote unused prices at the present time, but we hope to be able to add these in a future edition of this catalogue.

**418** Athlete holding Olympic Rings ('Records du monde')

**1996.** Olympic Games, Atlanta. Multicoloured.

| | | | |
|---|---|---|---|
| 1186 | 125f. Type **418** | | 65 |
| 1187 | 250f. As No. 1186 but inscr 'Records olympiques' (vert) | | 1·40 |

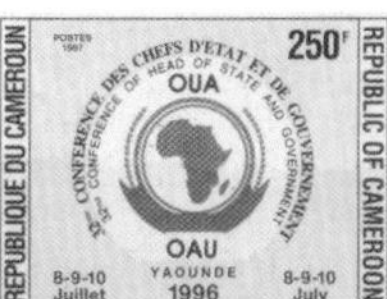


**419** Conference Emblem

**1996.** 32nd Conference of Heads of State of Organisation of African Unity, Yaounde.

| | | | | |
|---|---|---|---|---|
| 1188 | **419** | 125f. multicoloured | | 1·25 |
| 1189 | **419** | 200f. multicoloured (1997) | | 1·10 |
| 1190 | **419** | 250f. multicoloured (1997) | | 1·40 |
| 1191 | – | 410f. multicoloured (vert) | | 1·90 |

Imprint dates: '1996' Nos. 1188, 1191; '1997' Nos. 1188a, 1189, 1190.

**420** Emblem

**1997**

| | | | | |
|---|---|---|---|---|
| 1192 | **420** | 500f. multicoloured | | 15·00 |

No. 1192 was originally produced to pay fees for opening a Cameroon Postal Savings Bank account, but has been found used on mail.

**421** Pineapple

**1998.** Tourism. Multicoloured.

| | | | |
|---|---|---|---|
| 1193 | 100f. Type **421** | | 2·50 |
| 1194 | 125f. Type **421** | | 2·50 |
| 1195 | 150f. Coffee | | 3·00 |
| 1196 | 175f. Crowned crane | | 6·00 |
| 1197 | 200f. Mandrill | | 1·10 |
| 1198 | 250f. As No. 1195 | | 1·40 |
| 1199 | 410f. As No. 1196 | | 1·90 |

**422** *Lanius* sp. (bird)

**1998**

| | | | | |
|---|---|---|---|---|
| 1200 | **422** | 125f. multicoloured | | 65 |

**423** World Cup Trophy, Emblem and Cameroon Flag

**1998.** 4th Participation of Cameroon in World Cup Football, France. Multicoloured.

| | | | |
|---|---|---|---|
| 1201 | 125f. Type **423** | | 2·50 |
| 1202 | 250f. Football and map containing national colours (horiz) | | 2·75 |

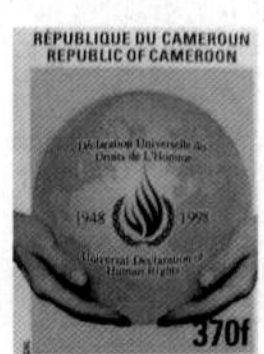


**424** Emblem

**1998.** 50th Anniv of Declaration of Human Rights.

| | | | | |
|---|---|---|---|---|
| 1203 | **424** | 370f. multicoloured | | 3·50 |

**425** Flags and Africa on Globe

**1999.** CEMAC Conference, Yaounde. Multicoloured.

| | | | |
|---|---|---|---|
| 1204 | 125f. Flags (different) and Africa on globe | 8·00 | |
| 1205 | 225f. Type **425** | 2·50 | |

**426** National Symbols

**2000.** National Symbols. Multicoloured.

| | | | |
|---|---|---|---|
| 1206 | 125f. Type **426** | 65 | |
| 1207 | 200f. Outline map enclosing Cameroon scenes (vert) | 1·10 | |
| 1208 | 250f. Airplane over landscape with wild animals (vert) | 1·40 | |

**427** Congress Centre, Yaounde

**2001.** 30th Anniv of Co-operation between Cameroon and People's Republic of China.

| | | | | |
|---|---|---|---|---|
| 1209 | **427** | 125f. multicoloured | 1·25 | |

**428** Chantal Biya with Baby

**2001.** Chantal Biya Foundation. Multicoloured.

| | | | |
|---|---|---|---|
| 1210 | 125f. Type **428** | 2·50 | |
| 1211 | 250f. Baby in uterus and emblems | 1·25 | |

**MS**1212 110×90 mm. Nos. 1210/11

**429** Lion, National Flags and Football

**2002.** World Cup Football, Japan and South Korea. Multicoloured.

| | | | |
|---|---|---|---|
| 1213 | 125f. Type **429** | 1·25 | |
| 1214 | 250f. Pres. Paul Biya, lion and Africa Cup (horiz) | 2·75 | |

**MS**1215 Circular 96×96 mm. No. 1213; As No. 1214 but square

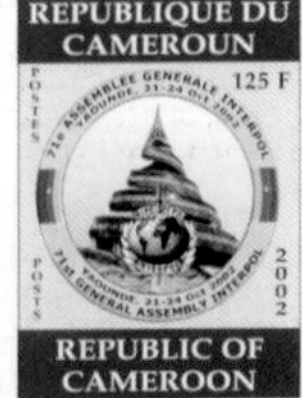


**430** Emblem

**2002.** 71st General Assembly of Interpol, Yaounde.

| | | | | |
|---|---|---|---|---|
| 1216 | **430** | 125f. multicoloured | 1·25 | |

**MS**1217 91×120 mm. No. 1216

**431** Pres. Biya, Japanese Prime Minister Koizumi and Primary School Mfandena 2, Yaoundé)

**2005.** Co-operation between Cameroon and Japan.

| | | | | |
|---|---|---|---|---|
| 1218 | **431** | 100f. multicoloured | 1·25 | |
| 1219 | **431** | 125f. multicoloured | 1·25 | |
| 1220 | **431** | 200f. multicoloured | 2·25 | |
| 1221 | **431** | 250f. multicoloured | 2·75 | |
| 1222 | **431** | 370f. multicoloured | 3·50 | |
| 1223 | **431** | 410f. multicoloured | 3·75 | |
| 1224 | **431** | 500f. multicoloured | 4·50 | |
| 1225 | **431** | 1000f. multicoloured | 7·50 | |

Pt. 6, Pt. 7, Pt. 12

# CAMEROUN

Territory in western Africa which became a German Protectorate in 1884. During 1914-16 it was occupied by Allied troops and in 1922 Britain and France were granted separate United Nations mandates.

In 1960 the French trust territory became an independent republic and, following a plebiscite, in September 1961 the southern part of the area under British control joined the Cameroun Republic. In November 1995 the republic joined the Commonwealth.

A. German Colony of Kamerun.
100 pfennig = 1 mark.

B. French Administration of Cameroun.
100 centimes = 1 franc.

## A. GERMAN COLONY OF KAMERUN

**1897.** Stamps of Germany optd **Kamerun**.

| | | | | |
|---|---|---|---|---|
| K1a | **8** | 3pf. brown | 12·50 | 21·00 |
| K2 | **8** | 5pf. green | 7·50 | 10·50 |
| K3 | **9** | 10pf. red | 5·25 | 6·25 |
| K4 | **9** | 20pf. blue | 5·25 | 9·50 |
| K5 | **9** | 25pf. orange | 23·00 | 55·00 |
| K6a | **9** | 50pf. brown | 18·00 | 34·00 |

**1900.** "Yacht" key-types inscr "KAMERUN".

| | | | | |
|---|---|---|---|---|
| K7 | **N** | 3pf. brown | 1·70 | 2·10 |
| K21 | **N** | 5pf. green | 1·10 | 2·10 |
| K22 | **N** | 10pf. red | 3·25 | 2·10 |
| K10 | **N** | 20pf. blue | 30·00 | 3·00 |
| K11 | **N** | 25pf. black & red on yell | 1·90 | 6·75 |
| K12 | **N** | 30pf. black & orge on buff | 2·50 | 5·75 |
| K13 | **N** | 40pf. black and red | 2·50 | 5·25 |
| K14 | **N** | 50pf. black & pur on buff | 2·50 | 8·00 |
| K15 | **N** | 80pf. black & red on rose | 3·25 | 13·50 |
| K16 | **O** | 1m. red | 85·00 | 95·00 |
| K17 | **O** | 2m. blue | 6·75 | 95·00 |
| K18 | **O** | 3m. black | 6·75 | £150 |
| K19 | **O** | 5m. red and black | £200 | £650 |

## B. FRENCH ADMINISTRATION OF CAMEROUN

**1915.** Stamps of Gabon with inscription "AFRIQUE EQUATORIALE-GABON" optd **Corps Expeditionnaire Franco-Anglais CAMEROUN.**

| | | | | |
|---|---|---|---|---|
| 1 | **7** | 1c. brown and orange | £100 | 60·00 |
| 2 | **7** | 2c. black and brown | £170 | £170 |
| 3 | **7** | 4c. violet and blue | £170 | £170 |
| 4 | **7** | 5c. olive and green | 37·00 | 33·00 |
| 5 | **7** | 10c. red and lake (on No. 37 of Gabon) | 39·00 | 22·00 |
| 6 | **7** | 20c. brown and violet | £170 | £190 |
| 7 | **8** | 25c. brown and blue | 70·00 | 60·00 |
| 8 | **8** | 30c. red and grey | £170 | £190 |
| 9 | **8** | 35c. green and violet | 70·00 | 55·00 |
| 10 | **8** | 40c. blue and brown | £170 | £190 |
| 11 | **8** | 45c. violet and red | £170 | £190 |
| 12 | **8** | 50c. grey and green | £170 | £190 |
| 13 | **8** | 75c. brown and orange | £180 | £200 |
| 14 | **9** | 1f. yellow and brown | £190 | £200 |
| 15 | **9** | 2f. brown and red | £200 | £225 |

**1916.** Optd **Occupation Francaise du Cameroun**. (a) On stamps of Middle Congo.

| | | | | |
|---|---|---|---|---|
| 16 | **1** | 1c. olive and brown | £100 | £110 |
| 17 | **1** | 2c. violet and brown | £100 | £110 |
| 18 | **1** | 4c. blue and brown | £100 | £110 |
| 19 | **1** | 5c. green and blue | 50·00 | 50·00 |
| 20 | **2** | 35c. brown and blue | £120 | 90·00 |
| 21 | **2** | 45c. violet and orange | £100 | £100 |

(b) On stamps of French Congo.

| | | | | |
|---|---|---|---|---|
| 22 | **6** | 15c. violet and green | £110 | £110 |
| 23 | **8** | 20c. green and red | £120 | £110 |
| 24 | **8** | 30c. red and yellow | £100 | 90·00 |
| 25 | **8** | 40c. brown and green | 70·00 | £100 |
| 26 | **8** | 50c. violet and lilac | £110 | £100 |
| 27 | **8** | 75c. purple and orange | £100 | 80·00 |
| 28 | - | 1f. drab and grey (48) | £120 | £120 |
| 29 | - | 2f. red and brown (49) | £120 | £120 |

**1916.** Stamps of Middle Congo optd **CAMEROUN Occupation Francaise**.

| | | | | |
|---|---|---|---|---|
| 30 | **1** | 1c. olive and brown | 35 | 3·25 |
| 31 | **1** | 2c. violet and brown | 65 | 3·25 |
| 32 | **1** | 4c. blue and brown | 75 | 3·25 |
| 33 | **1** | 5c. green and blue | 90 | 2·40 |
| 34 | **1** | 10c. red and blue | 1·20 | 2·75 |
| 34a | **1** | 15c. purple and red | 3·00 | 4·50 |
| 35 | **1** | 20c. brown and blue | 1·70 | 3·50 |
| 36 | **2** | 25c. blue and green | 1·00 | 1·30 |
| 37 | **2** | 30c. pink and green | 2·00 | 2·75 |
| 38 | **2** | 35c. brown and blue | 1·70 | 3·50 |
| 39 | **2** | 40c. green and brown | 2·00 | 4·75 |
| 40 | **2** | 45c. violet and orange | 2·75 | 5·50 |
| 41 | **2** | 50c. green and orange | 2·75 | 4·50 |
| 42 | **2** | 75c. brown and blue | 2·50 | 6·00 |
| 43 | **3** | 1f. green and violet | 2·30 | 3·50 |
| 44 | **3** | 2f. violet and green | 8·75 | 16·00 |
| 45 | **3** | 5f. blue and pink | 13·00 | 33·00 |

**1921.** Stamps of Middle Congo (colours changed) optd CAMEROUN.

| | | | | |
|---|---|---|---|---|
| 46 | **1** | 1c. orange and green | 20 | 5·50 |
| 47 | **1** | 2c. red and brown | 20 | 5·75 |
| 48 | **1** | 4c. green and grey | 45 | 6·25 |
| 49 | **1** | 5c. orange and red | 45 | 3·25 |
| 50 | **1** | 10c. light green and green | 90 | 3·75 |
| 51 | **1** | 15c. orange and blue | 1·50 | 6·25 |
| 52 | **1** | 20c. grey and purple | 2·00 | 5·00 |
| 53 | **2** | 25c. orange and grey | 1·90 | 2·00 |
| 54 | **2** | 30c. red and carmine | 1·50 | 5·50 |
| 55 | **2** | 35c. blue and grey | 2·00 | 5·50 |
| 56 | **2** | 40c. orange and green | 1·90 | 5·50 |
| 57 | **2** | 45c. red and brown | 1·30 | 5·00 |
| 58 | **2** | 50c. ultramarine and blue | 1·10 | 3·50 |
| 59 | **2** | 75c. green and purple | 1·30 | 6·00 |
| 60 | **3** | 1f. orange and grey | 3·25 | 6·50 |
| 61 | **3** | 2f. red and green | 7·75 | 18·00 |
| 62 | **3** | 5f. grey and red | 8·75 | 33·00 |

**1924.** Stamps of 1921 surch.

| | | | | |
|---|---|---|---|---|
| 63 | **1** | 25c. on 15c. orange & blue | 1·20 | 7·75 |
| 64 | **3** | 25c. on 2f. red and green | 1·80 | 7·75 |
| 65 | **3** | 25c. on 5f. grey and red | 1·50 | 8·25 |
| 66 | **2** | "65" on 45c. red and brown | 2·20 | 8·75 |
| 67 | **2** | "85" on 75c. green & red | 3·25 | 9·00 |

**5** Cattle fording River

**1925**

| | | | | |
|---|---|---|---|---|
| 68 | **5** | 1c. mauve and olive | 20 | 3·75 |
| 69 | **5** | 2c. green & red on green | 35 | 2·50 |
| 70 | **5** | 4c. black and blue | 45 | 3·25 |
| 71 | **5** | 5c. mauve and yellow | 40 | 40 |
| 72 | **5** | 10c. orange & pur on yell | 1·30 | 90 |
| 73 | **5** | 15c. green | 2·75 | 5·50 |
| 88 | **5** | 15c. red and lilac | 1·00 | 3·00 |
| 74 | **A** | 20c. brown and olive | 1·70 | 5·75 |
| 89 | **A** | 20c. green | 1·10 | 3·25 |
| 90 | **A** | 20c. brown and red | 65 | 25 |
| 75 | **A** | 25c. black and green | 1·40 | 55 |
| 76 | **A** | 30c. red and green | 1·30 | 1·20 |
| 91 | **A** | 30c. green and olive | 1·10 | 1·30 |
| 77 | **A** | 35c. black and brown | 1·80 | 7·00 |
| 91a | **A** | 35c. green | 4·50 | 5·75 |
| 78 | **A** | 40c. violet and orange | 4·00 | 3·25 |
| 79 | **A** | 45c. red | 1·00 | 5·50 |
| 92 | **A** | 45c. brown and mauve | 3·25 | 3·50 |
| 80 | **A** | 50c. red and green | 3·00 | 45 |
| 93 | **A** | 55c. red and blue | 5·00 | 8·25 |
| 81 | **A** | 60c. black and mauve | 2·50 | 5·25 |
| 94 | **A** | 60c. red | 1·30 | 6·00 |
| 82 | **A** | 65c. brown and blue | 3·00 | 90 |
| 83 | **A** | 75c. blue | 1·70 | 3·00 |
| 95 | **A** | 75c. mauve and brown | 1·30 | 1·40 |
| 95a | **A** | 80c. brown and red | 2·00 | 7·75 |
| 84 | **A** | 85c. blue and red | 1·40 | 3·25 |
| 96 | **A** | 90c. red | 3·50 | 3·50 |
| 85 | **B** | 1f. brown and blue | 2·20 | 6·50 |
| 97 | **B** | 1f. blue | 1·70 | 1·40 |
| 98 | **B** | 1f. mauve and brown | 2·00 | 2·75 |
| 99 | **B** | 1f. brown and green | 4·00 | 2·10 |
| 100 | **B** | 1f.10 brown and red | 4·50 | 11·50 |
| 100a | **B** | 1f.25 blue and brown | 12·00 | 11·50 |
| 101 | **B** | 1f.50 blue | 3·00 | 95 |
| 101a | **B** | 1f.75 red and brown | 2·30 | 1·90 |
| 101b | **B** | 1f.75 blue | 11·50 | 16·00 |
| 86 | **B** | 2f. orange and olive | 4·50 | 1·10 |
| 102 | **B** | 3f. mauve and brown | 5·00 | 2·50 |
| 87 | **B** | 5f. black & brown on bl | 5·25 | 1·50 |
| 103 | **B** | 10f. mauve and orange | 12·00 | 9·00 |
| 104 | **B** | 20f. green and red | 30·00 | 21·00 |

DESIGNS—VERT: A, Tapping rubber-trees. HORIZ: B, Liana suspension bridge.

**1926.** Surch with new value.

| | | | | |
|---|---|---|---|---|
| 105 | | 1f.25 on 1f. blue | 1·80 | 6·00 |

**1931.** "Colonial Exhibition" key-types inscribed "CAMEROUN".

| | | | | |
|---|---|---|---|---|
| 106 | **E** | 40c. green | 5·25 | 9·25 |
| 107 | **F** | 50c. mauve | 5·50 | 9·00 |
| 108 | **G** | 90c. orange | 6·25 | 8·75 |
| 109 | **H** | 1f.50 blue | 6·25 | 6·75 |

**14** Sailing Ships

**1937.** Paris International Exhibition. Inscr "EXPOSITION INTERNATIONALE PARIS 1937".

| | | | | |
|---|---|---|---|---|
| 110 | - | 20c. violet | 2·30 | 6·75 |
| 111 | **14** | 30c. green | 2·50 | 6·50 |
| 112 | - | 40c. red | 1·80 | 6·25 |
| 113 | - | 50c. brown & deep brown | 2·30 | 3·50 |
| 114 | - | 90c. red | 2·10 | 5·50 |
| 115 | - | 1f.50 blue | 2·00 | 6·25 |

**MS**115a 120×100 mm. 163f. red and agate 10·50 31·00

DESIGNS—VERT: 20c. Allegory of Commerce; 50c. Allegory of Agriculture. HORIZ: 40c. Berber, Negress and Annamite; 90c. France extends torch of Civilization; 1f.50, Diane de Poitiers.

**19** Pierre and Marie Curie

**1938.** International Anti-cancer Fund.

| | | | | |
|---|---|---|---|---|
| 116 | **19** | 1f.75+50c. blue | 10·50 | 33·00 |

**20**

**1939.** New York World's Fair.

| | | | | |
|---|---|---|---|---|
| 117 | **20** | 1f.25 red | 2·30 | 6·75 |
| 118 | **20** | 2f.25 blue | 2·75 | 6·75 |

**21** Lamido Woman

**1939**

| | | | | |
|---|---|---|---|---|
| 119 | **21** | 2c. black | 30 | 5·25 |
| 120 | **21** | 3c. mauve | 40 | 5·25 |
| 121 | **21** | 4c. blue | 75 | 5·25 |
| 122 | **21** | 5c. brown | 60 | 5·25 |
| 123 | **21** | 10c. green | 65 | 4·75 |
| 124 | **21** | 15c. red | 90 | 6·50 |
| 125 | **21** | 20c. purple | 95 | 6·50 |
| 126 | **A** | 25c. black | 1·40 | 4·75 |
| 127 | **A** | 30c. orange | 85 | 6·50 |
| 128 | **A** | 40c. blue | 85 | 5·25 |
| 129 | **A** | 45c. green | 2·10 | 8·50 |
| 130 | **A** | 50c. brown | 1·10 | 4·00 |
| 131 | **A** | 60c. blue | 1·50 | 7·25 |
| 132 | **A** | 70c. purple | 3·00 | 8·75 |
| 133 | **B** | 80c. blue | 3·50 | 10·50 |
| 134 | **B** | 90c. blue | 2·10 | 2·30 |
| 135 | **B** | 1f. red | 3·25 | 4·25 |
| 135a | **B** | 1f. brown | 1·90 | 3·25 |
| 136 | **B** | 1f.25 red | 4·50 | 16·00 |
| 137 | **B** | 1f.40 orange | 2·75 | 8·00 |
| 138 | **B** | 1f.50 brown | 1·70 | 3·00 |
| 139 | **B** | 1f.60 brown | 2·75 | 8·25 |
| 140 | **B** | 1f.75 blue | 2·20 | 4·00 |
| 141 | **B** | 2f. green | 1·90 | 2·30 |
| 142 | **B** | 2f.25 blue | 2·50 | 4·75 |

| | | | | |
|---|---|---|---|---|
| 143 | B | 2f.50 purple | 3·25 | 4·00 |
| 144 | B | 3f. violet | 1·70 | 2·50 |
| 145 | C | 5f. brown | 2·40 | 2·75 |
| 146 | C | 10f. purple | 2·40 | 5·75 |
| 147 | C | 20f. green | 4·00 | 6·50 |

DESIGNS—VERT: A, Banyo Waterfall; C, African boatman. HORIZ: B, African elephants.

**25** Storming the Bastille

**1939.** 150th Anniv of Revolution.

| | | | | |
|---|---|---|---|---|
| 148 | 25 | 45c.+25c. green | 10·00 | 22·00 |
| 149 | 25 | 70c.+30c. brown | 10·00 | 22·00 |
| 150 | 25 | 90c.+35c. orange | 10·00 | 27·00 |
| 151 | 25 | 1f.25+1f. red | 10·00 | 28·00 |
| 152 | 25 | 2f.25+2f. blue | 12·00 | 33·00 |

**1940.** Adherence to General de Gaulle. Optd **CAMEROUN FRANCAIS 27-8-40.**

| | | | | |
|---|---|---|---|---|
| 153 | 21 | 2c. black | 90 | 1·60 |
| 154 | 21 | 3c. mauve | 90 | 3·25 |
| 155 | 21 | 4c. blue | 55 | 1·70 |
| 156 | 21 | 5c. brown | 7·75 | 7·50 |
| 157 | 21 | 10c. green | 75 | 1·60 |
| 158 | 21 | 15c. red | 1·40 | 5·50 |
| 159 | 21 | 20c. purple | 26·00 | 23·00 |
| 160 | A | 25c. black | 1·10 | 95 |
| 161 | A | 30c. orange | 22·00 | 23·00 |
| 162 | A | 40c. blue | 6·00 | 4·75 |
| 163 | A | 45c. green | 1·80 | 2·00 |
| 164 | - | 50c. red & green (No. 80) | 90 | 1·20 |
| 165 | A | 60c. blue | 6·75 | 9·75 |
| 166 | A | 70c. purple | 1·80 | 1·90 |
| 167 | B | 80c. blue | 7·25 | 4·00 |
| 168 | B | 90c. blue | 55 | 80 |
| 169 | 20 | 1f.25 red | 4·50 | 5·00 |
| 170 | B | 1f.25 red | 85 | 90 |
| 171 | B | 1f.40 orange | 1·40 | 2·20 |
| 172 | B | 1f.50 brown | 70 | 1·00 |
| 173 | B | 1f.60 brown | 1·00 | 1·40 |
| 174 | B | 1f.75 blue | 85 | 1·30 |
| 175 | 20 | 2f.25 blue | 3·50 | 3·50 |
| 176 | B | 2f.25 blue | 70 | 1·10 |
| 177 | B | 2f.50 purple | 70 | 55 |
| 178 | - | 5f. black and brown on blue (No. 87) | 19·00 | 6·50 |
| 179 | C | 5f. brown | 24·00 | 5·50 |
| 180 | - | 10f. mve & orge (No. 103) | 28·00 | 7·75 |
| 181 | C | 10f. purple | 80·00 | 75·00 |
| 182 | - | 20f. green & red (No. 104) | 65·00 | 11·00 |
| 183 | C | 20f. green | £160 | £200 |

**1940.** War Relief Fund. Nos. 100a, 101a and 86 surch **OEUVRES DE GUERRE** and premium.

| | | | |
|---|---|---|---|
| 184 | 1f.25+2f. blue and brown | 37·00 | 46·00 |
| 185 | 1f.75+3f. red and brown | 37·00 | 46·00 |
| 186 | 2f.+5f. orange and olive | 27·00 | 30·00 |

**1940.** Spitfire Fund. Nos. 126, 129, 131/2 surch **+5 Frs. SPITFIRE.**

| | | | | |
|---|---|---|---|---|
| 187 | A | 25c.+5f. black | £120 | £120 |
| 188 | A | 45c.+5f. green | £120 | £120 |
| 189 | A | 60c.+5f. blue | £130 | £130 |
| 190 | A | 70c.+5f. purple | £130 | £130 |

**1941.** Spitfire Fund. Surch **SPITFIRE+10 fr. General de GAULLE.**

| | | | | |
|---|---|---|---|---|
| 190a | 20 | 1f.25+10f. red | £120 | £130 |
| 190b | 20 | 2f.25+10f. blue | £120 | £130 |

**29b** Sikorsky S-43 over Map

**29c** Sikorsky S-43 Amphibian

**1941.** Air.

| | | | | |
|---|---|---|---|---|
| 190c | 29b | 25c. red | 1·00 | 7·00 |
| 190d | 29b | 50c. green | 75 | 7·00 |
| 190e | 29b | 1f. purple | 2·50 | 7·00 |
| 190f | 29c | 2f. olive | 1·50 | 4·75 |
| 190g | 29c | 3f. brown | 1·70 | 5·00 |
| 190h | 29c | 4f. blue | 1·30 | 5·00 |
| 190i | 29c | 6f. myrtle | 1·50 | 4·25 |
| 190j | 29c | 7f. purple | 1·40 | 4·25 |
| 190k | 29c | 12f. orange | 7·25 | 16·00 |
| 190l | 29c | 20f. red | 4·50 | 8·50 |
| 190m | - | 50f. blue | 4·75 | 8·50 |

DESIGN: 50f. Latecoere 631 flying boat over harbour.

**1941.** Laquintinie Hospital Fund. Surch **+10 Frs. AMBULANCE LAQUINTINIE.**

| | | | | |
|---|---|---|---|---|
| 191 | 20 | 1f.25+10f. red | 41·00 | 47·00 |
| 192 | 20 | 2f.25+10f. blue | 50·00 | 47·00 |

**31** Cross of Lorraine, Sword and Shield

**32** Fairey FC-1

**1942.** Free French Issue.

| | | | | |
|---|---|---|---|---|
| 193 | 31 | 5c. brown (postage) | 15 | 1·90 |
| 194 | 31 | 10c. blue | 15 | 60 |
| 195 | 31 | 25c. green | 15 | 70 |
| 196 | 31 | 30c. red | 40 | 70 |
| 197 | 31 | 40c. green | 50 | 60 |
| 198 | 31 | 80c. purple | 60 | 95 |
| 199 | 31 | 1f. mauve | 90 | 55 |
| 200 | 31 | 1f.50 red | 80 | 45 |
| 201 | 31 | 2f. black | 85 | 55 |
| 202 | 31 | 2f.50 blue | 60 | 70 |
| 203 | 31 | 4f. violet | 60 | 1·20 |
| 204 | 31 | 5f. yellow | 90 | 1·40 |
| 205 | 31 | 10f. brown | 65 | 45 |
| 206 | 31 | 20f. green | 95 | 1·20 |
| 207 | 32 | 1f. orange (air) | 1·30 | 5·50 |
| 208 | 32 | 1f.50 red | 2·00 | 6·25 |
| 209 | 32 | 5f. purple | 1·20 | 6·25 |
| 210 | 32 | 10f. black | 1·40 | 6·75 |
| 211 | 32 | 25f. blue | 2·00 | 6·75 |
| 212 | 32 | 50f. green | 2·75 | 4·00 |
| 213 | 32 | 100f. red | 2·30 | 4·25 |

**1943.** Surch **Valmy+100 frs.**

| | | | | |
|---|---|---|---|---|
| 213a | - | 1f.25+100f. blue and brown (No. 100a) | 13·00 | 65·00 |
| 213b | 20 | 1f.25+100f. red | 10·50 | 65·00 |
| 213c | - | 1f.25+100f. red (No. 136) | 33·00 | 65·00 |
| 213d | - | 1f.50+100f. brown (No. 138) | 20·00 | 65·00 |
| 213e | 20 | 2f.25+100f. blue | 18·00 | 65·00 |

**33**

**1944.** Mutual Aid and Red Cross Funds.

| | | | | |
|---|---|---|---|---|
| 214 | 33 | 5f.+20f. red | 85 | 11·00 |

**1945.** Surch.

| | | | | |
|---|---|---|---|---|
| 215 | 31 | 50c. on 5c. brown | 1·30 | 7·00 |
| 216 | 31 | 60c. on 5c. brown | 55 | 7·00 |
| 217 | 31 | 70c. on 5c. brown | 65 | 7·25 |
| 218 | 31 | 1f.20 on 5c. brown | 1·00 | 7·25 |
| 219 | 31 | 2f.40 on 25c. green | 1·00 | 2·75 |
| 220 | 31 | 3f. on 25c. green | 1·10 | 3·25 |
| 221 | 31 | 4f.50 on 25c. green | 1·70 | 8·75 |
| 222 | 31 | 15f. on 2f.50 blue | 1·40 | 8·25 |

**34** Felix Eboue

**1945**

| | | | | |
|---|---|---|---|---|
| 223 | 34 | 2f. black | 45 | 2·30 |
| 224 | 34 | 25f. green | 90 | 5·50 |

**35** "Victory"

**1946.** Air. Victory.

| | | | | |
|---|---|---|---|---|
| 225 | 35 | 8f. purple | 70 | 2·30 |

**36** Chad

**1946.** Air. From Chad to the Rhine. Inscr "DU TCHAD AU RHIN".

| | | | | |
|---|---|---|---|---|
| 226 | 36 | 5f. blue | 2·50 | 8·25 |
| 227 | - | 10f. purple | 1·70 | 8·25 |
| 228 | - | 15f. red | 2·00 | 8·25 |
| 229 | - | 20f. blue | 2·10 | 8·25 |
| 230 | - | 25f. brown | 3·00 | 8·25 |
| 231 | - | 50f. black | 2·75 | 8·50 |

DESIGNS: 10f. Koufra; 15f. Mareth; 20f. Normandy; 25f. Paris; 50f. Strasbourg.

**37** Zebu and Herdsman

**45** Aeroplane, African and Mask

**1946**

| | | | | |
|---|---|---|---|---|
| 232 | 37 | 10c. green (postage) | 25 | 2·10 |
| 233 | 37 | 30c. orange | 25 | 4·00 |
| 234 | 37 | 40c. blue | 25 | 5·75 |
| 235 | - | 50c. sepia | 70 | 1·40 |
| 236 | - | 60c. purple | 90 | 5·50 |
| 237 | - | 80c. brown | 90 | 6·00 |
| 238 | - | 1f. orange | 1·10 | 30 |
| 239 | - | 1f.20 green | 1·50 | 6·50 |
| 240 | - | 1f.50 red | 2·75 | 3·25 |
| 241 | - | 2f. black | 90 | 30 |
| 242 | - | 3f. red | 2·40 | 35 |
| 243 | - | 3f.60 red | 2·30 | 6·75 |
| 244 | - | 4f. blue | 1·10 | 30 |
| 245 | - | 5f. red | 2·20 | 70 |
| 246 | - | 6f. blue | 2·20 | 55 |
| 247 | - | 10f. green | 1·60 | 30 |
| 248 | - | 15f. blue | 2·75 | 85 |
| 249 | - | 20f. green | 3·25 | 1·00 |
| 250 | - | 25f. black | 2·75 | 1·80 |
| 251 | - | 50f. green (air) | 2·75 | 1·30 |
| 252 | - | 100f. brown | 3·50 | 2·50 |
| 253 | 45 | 200f. olive | 6·25 | 5·00 |

DESIGNS—VERT: 50c. to 80c. Tikar women; 1f. to 1f.50, Africans carrying bananas; 2f. to 4f. Bowman; 5f. to 10f. Lamido horsemen; 15f. to 25f. Native head. HORIZ: 50f. Birds over mountains; 100f. African horsemen and Dewoitine D-333 trimotor airplane.

**46** People of Five Races, Lockheed Constellation Airplane and Globe

**1949.** Air. 75th Anniv of UPU.

| | | | | |
|---|---|---|---|---|
| 254 | 46 | 25f. multicoloured | 4·00 | 7·50 |

**47** Doctor and Patient

**1950.** Colonial Welfare Fund.

| | | | | |
|---|---|---|---|---|
| 255 | 47 | 10f.+2f. green & turq | 5·25 | 15·00 |

**48** Military Medal

**1952.** Military Medal Centenary.

| | | | | |
|---|---|---|---|---|
| 256 | 48 | 15f. red, yellow and green | 5·50 | 5·00 |

**49** Porters Carrying Bananas

**50** Transporting Logs

**1953**

| | | | | |
|---|---|---|---|---|
| 257 | 49 | 8f. violet, orange and purple (postage) | 65 | 25 |
| 258 | 49 | 15f. brown, yellow & red | 2·50 | 55 |
| 259 | - | 40f. brown, pink & choc | 2·00 | 70 |
| 260 | 50 | 50f. ol, brn & sep (air) | 5·00 | 90 |
| 261 | - | 100f. sepia, brown & turq | 13·00 | 1·80 |
| 262 | - | 200f. brown, blue & grn | 15·00 | 7·00 |
| 262a | - | 500f. indigo, blue and lilac | 28·00 | 17·00 |

DESIGNS—As Type **49**: 40f. Woman gathering coffee. As Type **50**: HORIZ: 100f. Airplane over giraffes; 200f. Freighters, Douala Port. VERT: 500f. Sud Ouest Corse II over Piton d'Humsiki.

**51** Edea Barrage

**1953.** Air. Opening of Edea Barrage.

| | | | | |
|---|---|---|---|---|
| 263 | 51 | 15f. blue, lake and brown | 2·75 | 1·00 |

**52** "D-Day"

**1954.** Air. 10th Anniv of Liberation.

| | | | | |
|---|---|---|---|---|
| 264 | 52 | 15f. green and turquoise | 7·75 | 6·50 |

**53** Dr. Jamot and Students

**1954.** Air. 75th Birthday of Dr. Jamot (physician).

| | | | | |
|---|---|---|---|---|
| 265 | 53 | 15f. brown, blue & green | 5·25 | 7·25 |

**54** Native Cattle

**1956.** Economic and Social Development Fund. Inscr "F.I.D.E.S.".

| | | | | |
|---|---|---|---|---|
| 266 | **54** | 5f. brown and sepia | 55 | 30 |
| 267 | - | 15f. turq, blue & black | 1·40 | 45 |
| 268 | - | 20f. turquoise and blue | 1·20 | 75 |
| 269 | - | 25f. blue | 1·80 | 90 |

DESIGNS: 15f. R. Wouri bridge; 20f. Technical education; 25f. Mobile medical unit.

**55** Coffee

**1956**

| | | | | |
|---|---|---|---|---|
| 270 | **55** | 15f. vermilion and red | 50 | 30 |

**56** Woman, Child and Flag

**1958.** 1st Anniv of First Cameroun Govt.

| | | | | |
|---|---|---|---|---|
| 271 | **56** | 20f. multicoloured | 55 | 35 |

**57** "Human Rights"

**1958.** 30th Anniv of Declaration of Human Rights.

| | | | | |
|---|---|---|---|---|
| 272 | **57** | 20f. brown and red | 1·20 | 2·50 |

**58** "Randia malleifera"

**1958.** Tropical Flora.

| | | | | |
|---|---|---|---|---|
| 273 | **58** | 20f. multicoloured | 1·10 | 55 |

**59** Loading Bananas on Ship at Douala

**1959**

| | | | | |
|---|---|---|---|---|
| 274 | **59** | 20f. multicoloured | 1·00 | 35 |
| 275 | - | 25f. green, brn & pur | 1·20 | 90 |

DESIGN—VERT: 25f. Bunch of bananas and native bearers in jungle path.

**C. INDEPENDENT REPUBLIC**

**60** Prime Minister A. Ahidjo

**1960.** Proclamation of Independence. Inscr "1 ER JANVIER 1960".

| | | | | |
|---|---|---|---|---|
| 276 | | 20f. multicoloured | 80 | 25 |
| 277 | **60** | 25f. green, bistre & black | 80 | 25 |

DESIGN: 20f. Cameroun flag and map.

**61** "Uprooted Tree"

**1960.** World Refugee Year.

| | | | | |
|---|---|---|---|---|
| 278 | **61** | 30f. green, blue and brown | 1·10 | 55 |

**62** CCTA Emblem

**1960.** 10th Anniv of African Technical Co-operation Commission.

| | | | | |
|---|---|---|---|---|
| 279 | **62** | 50f. black and purple | 1·60 | 80 |

**63** Map and Flag

**1961.** Red Cross Fund. Flag in green, red and yellow; cross in red; background colours given.

| | | | | |
|---|---|---|---|---|
| 280 | **63** | 20f.+5f. green and red | 1·20 | 95 |
| 281 | **63** | 25f.+10f. red and green | 1·50 | 1·20 |
| 282 | **63** | 30f.+15f. red and green | 2·10 | 1·60 |

**64** U.N. Headquarters, Emblem and Cameroun Flag

**1961.** Admission to UNO. Flag in green, red and yellow; emblem in blue, buildings and inscr in colours given.

| | | | | |
|---|---|---|---|---|
| 283 | **64** | 15f. brown and green | 50 | 30 |
| 284 | **64** | 25f. green and blue | 75 | 40 |
| 285 | **64** | 85f. purple, blue and red | 2·30 | 1·40 |

**1961.** Surch **REPUBLIQUE FEDERALE** and value in Sterling currency.

| | | | | |
|---|---|---|---|---|
| 286 | - | ½d. on 1f. orange (238) (postage) | 45 | 25 |
| 287 | - | 1d. on 2f. black (241) | 45 | 40 |
| 288 | **54** | 1½d. on 5f. brown & sepia | 55 | 45 |
| 289 | - | 2d. on 10f. green (247) | 1·00 | 70 |
| 290 | - | 3d. on 15f. turquoise, indigo and black (267) | 1·30 | 70 |
| 291 | - | 4d. on 15f. vermilion and red (270) | 1·50 | 90 |
| 292 | - | 6d. on 20f. mult (274) | 2·10 | 1·30 |
| 293 | **60** | 1s. on 25f. grn, bis & blk | 3·00 | 2·20 |
| 294a | **61** | 2s.6d. on 30f. green, blue and brown | 5·50 | 5·00 |
| 295a | - | 5s. on 100r. sepia, brown and turquoise (264) (air) | 10·00 | 9·50 |
| 296a | - | 10s. on 200f. brown, blue and green (265) | 20·00 | 19·00 |
| 297a | - | £1 on 500f. indigo, blue and lilac (253a) | 34·00 | 32·00 |

The above were for use in the former British Cameroon Trust Territory pending the introduction of the Cameroun franc.

**66** Pres. Ahidjo and Prime Minister Foncha

**1962.** Reunification. (a) T **66**.

| | |
|---|---|
| 298 | 20f. brown and violet |
| 299 | 25f. brown and green |
| 300 | 60f. green and red |

(b) T **66** surch in Sterling currency.

| | |
|---|---|
| 301 | 3d. on 20f. brown & violet |
| 302 | 6d. on 25f. brown and green |
| 303 | 2s.6d. on 60f. green and red |

**68** Lions International Badge, Doctor and Leper

**1962.** World Leprosy Day. Lions International Relief Fund.

| | | | | |
|---|---|---|---|---|
| 304 | **68** | 20f.+5f. purple & brown | 75 | 70 |
| 305 | **68** | 25f.+10f. purple & blue | 95 | 90 |
| 306 | **68** | 50f.+15f. purple & green | 1·80 | 1·60 |

**69** European, African and Boeing 707 Airliners

**1962.** Air. Foundation of "Air Afrique" Airline.

| | | | | |
|---|---|---|---|---|
| 307 | **69** | 25f. purple, violet & grn | 1·00 | 50 |

**70** Campaign Emblem

**1962.** Malaria Eradication.

| | | | | |
|---|---|---|---|---|
| 308 | **70** | 25f.+5f. mauve | 1·00 | 80 |

**71** Giraffes and Waza Camp

**1962.** (a) Postage. Animals.

| | | | | |
|---|---|---|---|---|
| 309 | **A** | 50c. sepia, blue & turquoise | 10 | 10 |
| 310 | **B** | 1f. black, turquoise & orge | 10 | 10 |
| 311 | **C** | 1f.50 brown, sage & blk | 20 | 10 |
| 312 | **D** | 2f. black, blue and green | 20 | 20 |
| 313 | **C** | 3f. brown, orange & purple | 20 | 20 |
| 314 | **B** | 4f. sepia, green & turq | 25 | 20 |
| 315 | **D** | 5f. purple, green & brown | 35 | 20 |
| 316 | **A** | 6f. sepia, blue and lemon | 45 | 25 |
| 317 | **E** | 8f. blue, red and green | 95 | 70 |
| 318 | **F** | 10f. black, orange & blue | 75 | 25 |
| 319 | **A** | 15f. brown, blue & turq | 1·40 | 45 |
| 320 | **71** | 20f. brown and grey | 95 | 45 |
| 321 | **F** | 25f. brown, yellow & grn | 2·75 | 1·00 |
| 322 | **E** | 30f. black, blue & brown | 3·00 | 1·10 |
| 323 | **71** | 40f. lake and green | 6·50 | 2·10 |

(b) Air.

| | | | |
|---|---|---|---|
| 324 | 50f. brown, myrtle & blue | 95 | 70 |
| 325 | 100f. multicoloured | 4·75 | 1·50 |
| 326 | 200f. black, brn & turq | 8·00 | 2·40 |
| 327 | 500f. buff, purple and blue | 11·00 | 3·75 |

DESIGNS—HORIZ: As Type **71**: A, Moustached monkey; B, African elephant and Ntem Falls; C, Kob, Dschang; D, Hippopotamus, Hippo Camp; E, African manatee, Lake Ossa; F, Buffalo, Batoun Region. (48×27 mm): 50f. Cocotiers Hotel, Douala; 100f. "Cymothoe sangaris" (butterfly); 200f. Ostriches; 500f. Kapsikis, Mokolo (landscape).

**72** Union Flag

**1962.** 1st Anniv of Union of African and Malagasy States. Flag in green, red and gold.

| | | | | |
|---|---|---|---|---|
| 328 | **72** | 30f. brown | 2·00 | 90 |

**73** Map and View

**1962.** 1st Anniv of Reunification.

| | | | | |
|---|---|---|---|---|
| 329 | **73** | 9f. bistre, violet & brown | 35 | 25 |
| 330 | **73** | 18f. red, green and blue | 45 | 40 |
| 331 | - | 20f. bistre, blue and purple | 60 | 40 |
| 332 | - | 25f. orange, sepia & blue | 60 | 45 |
| 333 | - | 50f. blue, sepia and red | 1·50 | 90 |

DESIGNS: 20f., 25f. Sunrise over Cameroun; 50f. Commemorative scroll.

**74** "The School Under the Tree"

**1962.** Literacy and Popular Education Plan.

| | | | | |
|---|---|---|---|---|
| 334 | **74** | 20f. red, yellow and green | 1·00 | 50 |

**75** Globe and "Telstar"

**1963.** 1st Trans-Atlantic Television Satellite Link.

| | | | | |
|---|---|---|---|---|
| 335 | **75** | 1f. ol, vio & blue (postage) | 20 | 10 |
| 336 | **75** | 2f. lake, green and blue | 30 | 25 |
| 337 | **75** | 3f. olive, purple and green | 30 | 25 |
| 338 | **75** | 25f. blue and green | 1·00 | 1·00 |
| 339 | **75** | 100f. brown and green (air) (48×27 mm) | 2·30 | 1·40 |

**76** Globe and Emblem

**1963.** Freedom from Hunger.

| | | | | |
|---|---|---|---|---|
| 340 | **76** | 18f.+5f. blue, brn & grn | 90 | 50 |
| 341 | **76** | 25f.+5f. green & brown | 1·30 | 60 |

**77** VHF Station, Mt. Bankolo, Yaounde

**1963.** Inauguration of Doala–Yaounde VHF Radio Service.

| | | | | |
|---|---|---|---|---|
| 342 | **77** | 15f. mult (postage) | 45 | 30 |
| 343 | - | 20f. multicoloured | 60 | 45 |
| 344 | - | 100f. multicoloured (air) | 2·30 | 1·40 |

DESIGNS: 20f. Aerials and control panel; 100f. Edea relay station (26×44 mm).

**78** "Centre regional ..."

**1963.** Inauguration of UNESCO Regional Schoolbooks Production Centre, Yaounde.

| | | | | |
|---|---|---|---|---|
| 345 | **78** | 20f. red, black and green | 45 | 25 |
| 346 | **78** | 25f. red, black and orange | 55 | 25 |

| | | | | |
|---|---|---|---|---|
| 347 | 78 | 100f. red, black and gold | 2·00 | 1·10 |

**1963.** Air. African and Malagasian Posts and Telecommunications Union. As T **18** of Central African Republic.

| | | | | |
|---|---|---|---|---|
| 348 | | 85f. multicoloured | 2·20 | 1·50 |

**80** Pres. Ahidjo

**1963.** 2nd Anniv of Reunification. Multicoloured.

| | | | | |
|---|---|---|---|---|
| 349 | | 9f. Type **80** | 40 | 30 |
| 350 | | 18f. Map and flag | 60 | 30 |
| 351 | | 20f. Type **80** | 75 | 40 |

**1963.** Air. Inauguration of "DC-8" Service. As T **11** of Congo Republic.

| | | | | |
|---|---|---|---|---|
| 352 | | 50f. multicoloured | 1·30 | 60 |

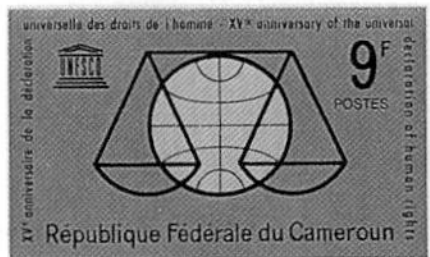

**82** Globe and Scales of Justice

**1963.** 15th Anniv of Declaration of Human Rights.

| | | | | |
|---|---|---|---|---|
| 353 | **82** | 9f. brown, black and blue | 40 | 25 |
| 354 | **82** | 18f. red, black and green | 55 | 25 |
| 355 | **82** | 25f. green, black & red | 75 | 35 |
| 356 | **82** | 75f. blue, black & yellow | 1·80 | 95 |

**83** Lion

**1964.** Waza National Park.

| | | | | |
|---|---|---|---|---|
| 357 | **83** | 10f. bistre green & brown | 1·40 | 45 |
| 358 | **83** | 25f. bistre and green | 2·00 | 85 |

**84** Football Stadium, Yaounde

**1964.** Tropics Cup. Inscr as in T **84**.

| | | | | |
|---|---|---|---|---|
| 359 | **84** | 10f. brown, turquoise & grn | 45 | 25 |
| 360 | - | 18f. green, red and violet | 60 | 40 |
| 361 | - | 30f. blue, brown and black | 1·00 | 60 |

DESIGNS: 18f. Sports Equipment; 30f. Stadium Entrance. Yaounde.

**85** Palace of Justice, Yaounde

**1964.** 1st Anniv of European–African Economic Convention. Multicoloured.

| | | | | |
|---|---|---|---|---|
| 362 | | 15f. Type **85** | 1·20 | 70 |
| 363 | | 40f. Sun, moon and economic emblems (vert) | 2·30 | 1·40 |

**86** Olympic Flame and Hurdling

**1964.** Olympic Games, Toyko.

| | | | | |
|---|---|---|---|---|
| 364 | **86** | 9f. red, blk & grn (postage) | 1·70 | 1·40 |
| 365 | - | 10f. brown, violet and red | 2·20 | 1·40 |
| 366 | - | 300f. turquoise, brown and red (air) | 8·25 | 4·75 |
| **MS**366a | | 168×100 mm. Nos. 364/66 (air) | 14·50 | 14·50 |

DESIGNS—VERT: 10f. Running. HORIZ: 300f. Wrestling.

**87** Ntem Falls

**1964.** Folklore and Tourism.

| | | | | |
|---|---|---|---|---|
| 367 | | 9f. red, blue & grn (postage) | 55 | 25 |
| 368 | | 18f. blue, brown and red | 75 | 45 |
| 369 | **87** | 20f. drab, green and red | 90 | 45 |
| 370 | - | 25f. red, brown & orange | 1·40 | 75 |
| 371 | - | 50f. brown, grn & bl (air) | 1·20 | 70 |
| 372 | - | 250f. sepia, grn & brn | 11·00 | 3·75 |

DESIGNS—As Type **87**. VERT: 9f. Bamileke dance costume; 18f. Bamenda dance mask. HORIZ: 25f. Fulani horseman. LARGER (43×27½ mm): 50f. View of Kribi and Longji; 250f. Black rhinoceros.

**88** Co-operation

**1964.** French, African and Malagasy Co-operation.

| | | | | |
|---|---|---|---|---|
| 373 | **88** | 18f. brown, green and blue | 95 | 40 |
| 374 | **88** | 30f. brown, turq & brn | 1·40 | 55 |

**89** Pres. Kennedy

**1964.** Air. Pres. Kennedy Commem.

| | | | | |
|---|---|---|---|---|
| 375 | **89** | 100f. sepia, grn & apple | 2·30 | 2·20 |
| **MS**375a | **89** | 129×90 mm. Block of four | 9·00 | 9·00 |

**90** Inscription recording laying of First Rail

**1965.** Opening of Mbanga–Kumba Railway.

| | | | | |
|---|---|---|---|---|
| 376 | **90** | 12f. indigo, green and blue | 95 | 50 |
| 377 | - | 20f. yellow, green and red | 2·50 | 1·00 |

DESIGN—HORIZ: (36×22 mm): 20f. Series BB500 diesel locomotive.

**91** Abraham Lincoln

**1965.** Air. Death Centenary of Abraham Lincoln.

| | | | | |
|---|---|---|---|---|
| 378 | **91** | 100f. multicoloured | 2·30 | 1·60 |

**92** Ambulance and First Aid Post

**1965.** Cameroun Red Cross.

| | | | | |
|---|---|---|---|---|
| 379 | **92** | 25f. yellow, green and red | 75 | 30 |
| 380 | - | 50f. brown, red and grey | 1·50 | 55 |

DESIGN—VERT: 50f. Nurse and child.

**93** "Syncom" and ITU Emblem

**1965.** Air. Centenary of ITU.

| | | | | |
|---|---|---|---|---|
| 381 | **93** | 70f. black, blue and red | 1·60 | 85 |

**94** Churchill giving "V" Sign

**1965.** Air. Churchill Commem. Multicoloured.

| | | | | |
|---|---|---|---|---|
| 382 | | 12f. Type **94** | 1·20 | 70 |
| 383 | | 18f. Churchill, oak spray and cruiser "De Grasse" | 1·20 | 70 |

**95** "Map" Savings Bank

**1965.** Federal Postal Savings Bank.

| | | | | |
|---|---|---|---|---|
| 384 | **95** | 9f. yellow, red and green | 40 | 25 |
| 385 | - | 15f. brown, green & blue | 55 | 25 |
| 386 | - | 20f. brown, chest & turq | 60 | 40 |

DESIGNS—HORIZ: (48×27 mm): 15f. Savings Bank building. VERT: (27×48 mm): 20f. "Cocoa-bean" savings bank.

**96** Africa Cup and Players

**1965.** Winning of Africa Cup by Oryx Football Club.

| | | | | |
|---|---|---|---|---|
| 387 | **96** | 9f. brown, yellow and red | 75 | 35 |
| 388 | **96** | 20f. blue, yellow and red | 1·50 | 55 |

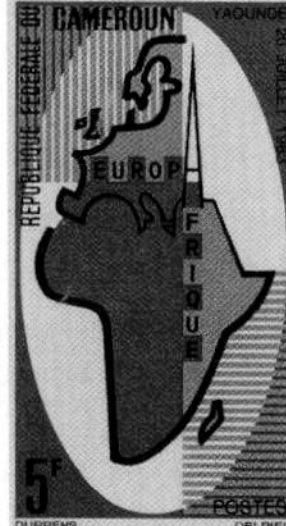

**97** Map of Europe and Africa

**1965.** "Europafrique".

| | | | | |
|---|---|---|---|---|
| 389 | **97** | 5f. red, lilac and black | 30 | 25 |
| 390 | - | 40f. multicoloured | 1·30 | 80 |

DESIGN: 40f. Yaounde Conference.

**98** UPU Monument, Berne and Doves

**1965.** 5th Anniv of Admission to UPU.

| | | | | |
|---|---|---|---|---|
| 391 | **98** | 30f. purple and red | 80 | 60 |

**99** ICY Emblem

**1965.** International Co-operation Year.

| | | | | |
|---|---|---|---|---|
| 392 | **99** | 10f. red & blue (postage) | 45 | 35 |
| 393 | **99** | 100f. blue and red (air) | 2·30 | 1·00 |

**100** Pres. Ahidjo and Government House

**1965.** Re-election of Pres. Ahidjo. Multicoloured.

| | | | | |
|---|---|---|---|---|
| 394 | | 9f. Pres. Ahidjo wearing hat, and Government House (vert) | 30 | 10 |
| 395 | | 18f. Type **100** | 45 | 20 |
| 396 | | 20f. As 9f. | 55 | 25 |
| 397 | | 25f. Type **100** | 85 | 45 |

**101** Musgum Huts, Pouss

**1965.** Folklore and Tourism.

| | | | | |
|---|---|---|---|---|
| 398 | **101** | 9f. green, brown and red (postage) | 40 | 25 |
| 399 | - | 18f. brown, green & blue | 45 | 25 |
| 400 | - | 20f. brown and blue | 95 | 40 |
| 401 | - | 25f. grey, lake and green | 95 | 40 |
| 402 | - | 50f. brown, blue and green (48×27 mm) (air) | 2·20 | 80 |

DESIGNS—HORIZ: 18f. Great Calao's dance (N. Cameroons); 25f. National Tourist office, Yaounde; 50f. Racing pirogue on Sanaga River, Edea. VERT: 20f. Sultan's palace gate Foumban.

**102** "Vostok 6"

**1966.** Air. Spacecraft.

| | | | | |
|---|---|---|---|---|
| 403 | **102** | 50f. green and red | 95 | 55 |
| 404 | - | 100f. blue and purple | 2·10 | 90 |
| 405 | - | 200f. violet and blue | 3·75 | 2·20 |
| 406 | - | 500f. blue and indigo | 8·75 | 4·50 |

DESIGNS: 100f. "Gemini 4", and White in space; 200f. "Gemini 5"; 500f. "Gemini 6" and "Gemini 7" making rendezvous.

**103** Mountain's Hotel, Buea

**1966.** Cameroun Hotels.

| | | | | |
|---|---|---|---|---|
| 407 | **103** | 9f. bistre, green and red (postage) | 35 | 25 |
| 408 | - | 20f. black, green & blue | 45 | 25 |
| 409 | - | 35f. red, brown & green | 95 | 55 |
| 410 | **103** | 18f. black, grn & bl (air) | 45 | 25 |
| 411 | - | 25f. indigo, red and blue | 65 | 45 |
| 412 | - | 50f. brown, orange & grn | 2·40 | 1·10 |
| 413 | - | 60f. brown, green & blue | 1·40 | 75 |
| 414 | - | 85f. blue, red and green | 1·80 | 85 |
| 415 | - | 100f. purple, blue & grn | 2·75 | 1·20 |
| 416 | - | 150f. orange, brn & blue | 3·50 | 1·60 |

HOTELS—HORIZ: 20f. Deputies, Yaounde. 25f. Akwa Palace, Douala. 35f. Dschang. 50f. Terminus, Yaounde. 60f. Imperial, Yaounde. 85f. Independence, Yaounde. 150f. Huts, Waza Camp. VERT: 100f. Hunting Lodge, Mora.

**104** Foumban Bas-relief

**1966.** World Festival of Negro Arts, Dakar.

| | | | | |
|---|---|---|---|---|
| 417 | **104** | 9f. black and red | 75 | 25 |
| 418 | - | 18f. purple, brn and grn | 75 | 30 |
| 419 | - | 20f. brown, blue & violet | 1·00 | 40 |
| 420 | - | 25f. brown and plum | 1·20 | 40 |

DESIGNS—VERT: 18f. Ekoi mask; 20f. Bamileke statue. HORIZ: 25f. Bamoun stool.

**105** WHO Headquarters, Geneva

**1966.** U.N. Agency Buildings.

| | | | | |
|---|---|---|---|---|
| 421 | **105** | 50f. lake, blue and yellow | 1·20 | 70 |
| 422 | - | 50f. yellow, blue & green | 55 | 25 |

DESIGN: No. 422, ITU Headquarters, Geneva.

**106** "Phaeomeria magnifica"

**1966.** Flowers. Multicoloured. (a) Postage. Size as T **106**.

| | | | | |
|---|---|---|---|---|
| 423 | | 9f. Type **106** | 60 | 25 |
| 424 | | 15f. "Strelitzia reginae" | 95 | 25 |
| 425 | | 18f. "Hibiscus schizopetalus x rosa-sinensis" | 75 | 25 |
| 426 | | 20f. "Antigonon leptopus" | 75 | 25 |

(b) Air. Size 26×45½ mm.

| | | | | |
|---|---|---|---|---|
| 427 | | 25f. "Hibiscus mutabilis" ("Ca-price des dames") | 75 | 25 |
| 428 | | 50f. "Delonix regia" | 1·50 | 30 |
| 429 | | 100f. "Bougainvillea glabra" | 3·00 | 60 |
| 430 | | 200f. "Thevetia peruviana" | 4·50 | 1·60 |
| 431 | | 250f. "Hippeastrum equestre" | 5·50 | 2·10 |

For stamps as Type **106** but showing fruits, see Nos. 463/71.

**107** Mobile Gendarmerie

**1966.** Air. Cameroun Armed Forces.

| | | | | |
|---|---|---|---|---|
| 432 | **107** | 20f. blue, brown & plum | 55 | 25 |
| 433 | - | 25f. green, violet & brown | 55 | 25 |
| 434 | - | 60f. indigo, green & blue | 1·80 | 80 |
| 435 | - | 100f. blue, red & purple | 2·75 | 1·20 |

DESIGNS: 25f. Paratrooper; 60f. Gunboat "Vigilant"; 100f. Dassault MD-315 Flamant airplane.

**108** Wembley Stadium

**1966.** Air. World Cup Football Championship.

| | | | | |
|---|---|---|---|---|
| 436 | **108** | 50f. green, blue and red | 1·40 | 55 |
| 437 | - | 200f. red, blue and green | 4·50 | 2·20 |

DESIGN: 200f. Footballers.

**109** Douglas DC-8F Jet Trader and "Air Afrique" Emblem

**1966.** Air. Inauguration of DC-8 Air Service.

| | | | | |
|---|---|---|---|---|
| 438 | **109** | 25f. grey, black & purple | 80 | 45 |

**110** U.N. General Assembly

**1966.** 6th Anniv of Admission to U.N.

| | | | | |
|---|---|---|---|---|
| 439 | **110** | 50f. purple, green & blue | 90 | 25 |
| 440 | - | 100f. blue, brown & green | 1·90 | 85 |

DESIGN—VERT: 100f. Africans encircling U.N. emblem within figure "6".

**111** 1st Minister's Residency, Buea (side view)

**1966.** 5th Anniv of Cameroun's Reunification. Multicoloured.

| | | | | |
|---|---|---|---|---|
| 441 | | 9f. Type **111** | 40 | 25 |
| 442 | | 18f. Prime Minister's Residency, Yaounde (front view) | 50 | 25 |
| 443 | | 20f. As 18f. but side view | 55 | 45 |
| 444 | | 25f. As Type **111** but front view | 85 | 45 |

**112** Learning to Write

**1966.** 20th Anniv of UNESCO and UNICEF.

| | | | | |
|---|---|---|---|---|
| 445 | **112** | 50f. brown, purple & blue | 1·30 | 60 |
| 446 | - | 50f. black, blue & purple | 1·30 | 60 |

DESIGN: No. 446. Cameroun children.

**113** Buea Cathedral

**1966.** Air. Religious Buildings.

| | | | | |
|---|---|---|---|---|
| 447 | **113** | 18f. purple, blue & green | 45 | 25 |
| 448 | - | 25f. violet, brown & green | 55 | 25 |
| 449 | - | 30f. lake, green & purple | 75 | 40 |
| 450 | - | 60f. green, red & turquoise | 1·40 | 70 |

BUILDINGS: 25f. Yaounde Cathedral. 30f. Orthodox Church, Yaounde. 60f. Garoua Mosque.

**114** Proclamation

**1967.** 7th Anniv of Independence.

| | | | | |
|---|---|---|---|---|
| 451 | **114** | 20f. red, green & yellow | 2·00 | 1·10 |

**115** Map of Africa, Railway Lines and Signals

**1967.** 5th African and Malagasy Railway Technicians Conference, Yaounde. Multicoloured.

| | | | | |
|---|---|---|---|---|
| 452 | | 20f. Type **115** | 2·30 | 1·00 |
| 453 | | 20f. Map of Africa and diesel train | 3·25 | 1·40 |

**116** Lions Emblem and Jungle

**1967.** 50th Anniv of Lions International. Mult.

| | | | | |
|---|---|---|---|---|
| 454 | | 50f. Type **116** | 95 | 55 |
| 455 | | 100f. Lions emblem and palms | 2·00 | 1·20 |

**117** Aircraft and ICAO Emblem

**1967.** International Civil Aviation Organization.

| | | | | |
|---|---|---|---|---|
| 456 | **117** | 50f. multicoloured | 1·30 | 60 |

**118** Dove and IAEA Emblem

**1967.** International Atomic Energy Agency.

| | | | | |
|---|---|---|---|---|
| 457 | **118** | 50f. blue and green | 1·30 | 60 |

**119** Rotary Banner and Emblem

**1967.** 10th Anniv of Cameroun Branch, Rotary Int.

| | | | | |
|---|---|---|---|---|
| 458 | **119** | 25f. red, gold and blue | 1·20 | 55 |

**120** "Pioneer A"

**1967.** Air. "Conquest of the Moon".

| | | | | |
|---|---|---|---|---|
| 459 | **120** | 25f. green, brown & blue | 45 | 25 |
| 460 | - | 50f. violet, purple & grn | 90 | 40 |
| 461 | - | 100f. purple, brown & bl | 2·30 | 90 |
| 462 | - | 250f. purple, grey and brown | 5·00 | 2·75 |

DESIGNS: 50f. "Ranger 6"; 100f. "Luna 9"; 250f. "Luna 10".

**121** Grapefruit

**1967.** Fruits. Multicoloured.

| | | | | |
|---|---|---|---|---|
| 463 | | 1f. Type **121** | 10 | 10 |
| 464 | | 2f. Papaw | 10 | 10 |
| 465 | | 3f. Custard-apple | 25 | 25 |
| 466 | | 4f. Breadfruit | 25 | 25 |
| 467 | | 5f. Coconut | 35 | 25 |
| 468 | | 6f. Mango | 45 | 25 |
| 469 | | 8f. Avocado | 95 | 30 |
| 470 | | 10f. Pineapple | 1·50 | 45 |
| 471 | | 30f. Bananas | 3·50 | 1·50 |

**122** Sanaga Waterfalls

**1967.** International Tourist Year.

| | | | | |
|---|---|---|---|---|
| 472 | **122** | 30f. multicoloured | 80 | 35 |

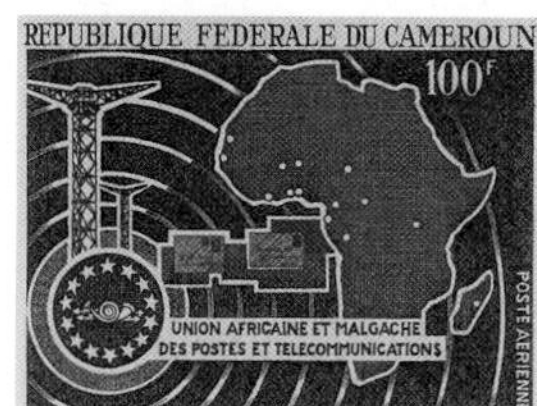


**123** Map, Letters and Pylons

**1967.** Air. 5th Anniv of African and Malagasy Posts and Telecommunications Union (UAMPT).

| | | | | |
|---|---|---|---|---|
| 473 | **123** | 100f. pur, lake & turq | 2·20 | 95 |

**124** Harvesting Coconuts (carved box)

**1967.** Cameroun Art.

| | | | | |
|---|---|---|---|---|
| 474 | **124** | 10f. brown, red and blue | 35 | 25 |
| 475 | - | 20f. brown, green & yell | 50 | 30 |
| 476 | - | 30f. brown, red & green | 90 | 45 |
| 477 | - | 100f. brown, red & grn | 2·30 | 95 |

DESIGNS (Carved boxes): 20f. Lion-hunting; 30f. Harvesting coconuts (different); 100f. Carved chest.

**125** Crossed Skis

**1967.** Air. Winter Olympic Games, Grenoble.

| | | | | |
|---|---|---|---|---|
| 478 | **125** | 30f. brown and blue | 1·50 | 85 |

**126** Cameroun Exhibit

**1967.** Air. World Fair, Montreal.

| | | | | |
|---|---|---|---|---|
| 479 | **126** | 50f. brown, chest & pur | 95 | 40 |
| 480 | - | 100f. brown, purple & grn | 3·00 | 1·10 |
| 481 | - | 200f. green, purple & brn | 4·25 | 2·20 |

DESIGNS: 100f. Totem poles; 200f. African pavilion.

For No. 481 optd **PREMIER HOMME SUR LA LUNE 20 JUILLET 1969/FIRST MAN LANDING ON MOON 20 JULY 1969** see note below Nos. 512/17.

**127** Chancellor Adenauer and Cologne Cathedral

**1967.** Air. Adenauer Commem. Multicoloured.

| | | | |
|---|---|---|---|
| 482 | 30f. Type **127** | 95 | 40 |
| 483 | 70f. Adenauer and Chancellor's residence, Bonn | 2·00 | 70 |

**128** Arms of the Republic

**1968.** 8th Anniv of Independence.

| | | | | |
|---|---|---|---|---|
| 484 | **128** | 30f. multicoloured | 1·00 | 50 |

**129** Pres. Ahidjo and King Faisal of Saudi Arabia

**1968.** Air. Pres. Ahidjo's Pilgrimage to Mecca and Visit to the Vatican. Multicoloured.

| | | | |
|---|---|---|---|
| 485 | 30f. Type **129** | 85 | 45 |
| 486 | 60f. Pope Paul VI greeting Pres. Ahidjo | 2·10 | 70 |

**130** "Explorer VI" (televised picture of Earth)

**1968.** Air. Telecommunications Satellites.

| | | | | |
|---|---|---|---|---|
| 487 | **130** | 20f. grey, red and blue | 50 | 25 |
| 488 | - | 30f. blue, indigo and red | 80 | 45 |
| 489 | - | 40f. green, red & plum | 1·10 | 50 |

DESIGNS: 30f. "Molnya"; 40f. "Molnya" (televised picture of Earth).

**131** Douala Port

**1968.** Air. Five-year Development Plan.

| | | | | |
|---|---|---|---|---|
| 490 | | 20f. blue, red and green | 55 | 30 |
| 491 | | 30f. blue, green & brown | 4·50 | 1·80 |
| 492 | | 30f. blue, brown & green | 1·00 | 50 |
| 493 | | 40f. brown, green & turq | 1·00 | 40 |
| 494 | **131** | 60f. purple, indigo & blue | 2·50 | 1·00 |

DESIGNS—VERT: 20f. Steel forge; 30f. (No. 491), "Transcamerounais" express train leaving tunnel; 30f. (No. 492), Tea-harvesting; 40f. Rubber-tapping.

**132** Spiny Lobster

**1968.** Fishes and Crustaceans.

| | | | | |
|---|---|---|---|---|
| 495 | **132** | 5f. green, brown & violet | 20 | 20 |
| 496 | - | 10f. slate, brown & blue | 30 | 20 |
| 497 | - | 15f. brown, chest & pur | 65 | 20 |
| 498 | - | 20f. brown and blue | 75 | 20 |
| 499 | - | 25f. blue, brown and green | 1·10 | 55 |
| 500 | - | 30f. brown, blue and red | 1·50 | 55 |
| 501 | - | 40f. blue, brown & orge | 1·70 | 70 |
| 502 | - | 50f. red, slate and green | 2·50 | 85 |
| 503 | - | 55f. purple, brown & blue | 3·25 | 1·20 |
| 504 | - | 60f. blue, purple & green | 5·25 | 1·60 |

DESIGNS—HORIZ: 10f. Freshwater crayfish; 15f. Nile mouthbrooder; 20f. Sole. 25f. Northern pike; 30f. Swimming crab; 55f. Dusky snakehead; 60f. Capitaine threadfin. VERT: 40f. African spadefish; 50f. Prawn.

**133** Refinery and Tanker

**1968.** Inauguration of Petroleum Refinery, Port Gentil, Gabon.

| | | | | |
|---|---|---|---|---|
| 505 | **133** | 30f. multicoloured | 1·20 | 45 |

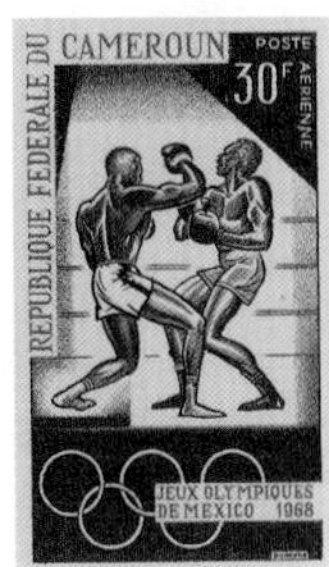

**134** Boxing

**1968.** Air. Olympic Games, Mexico.

| | | | | |
|---|---|---|---|---|
| 506 | **134** | 30f. brown, green & emer | 75 | 35 |
| 507 | - | 50f. brown, red & green | 1·30 | 60 |
| 508 | - | 60f. brown, blue & green | 1·50 | 70 |
| **MS**509 | | 131×101 mm. Nos. 506/8 | 4·50 | 4·50 |

DESIGNS: 50f. Long-jumping; 60f. Gymnastics.

**135** Human Rights Emblem

**1968.** Human Rights Year.

| | | | | |
|---|---|---|---|---|
| 510 | **135** | 15f. blue & orge (postage) | 60 | 25 |
| 511 | **135** | 30f. green & purple (air) | 75 | 40 |

**136** Mahatma Gandhi and Map of India

**1968.** Air. "Apostles of Peace".

| | | | | |
|---|---|---|---|---|
| 512 | **136** | 30f. black, yellow & blue | 55 | 45 |
| 513 | - | 30f. black and blue | 55 | 45 |
| 514 | - | 40f. black and pink | 95 | 75 |
| 515 | - | 60f. black and lilac | 1·20 | 75 |
| 516 | - | 70f. black, blue & buff | 1·30 | 90 |
| 517 | - | 70f. black and green | 1·30 | 90 |
| **MS**518 | | 122×162 mm. Nos. 512, 514/15 and 517 | 7·50 | 7·50 |

PORTRAITS: No. 513, Martin Luther King. No. 514, J. F. Kennedy. No. 515, R. F. Kennedy. No. 516, Gandhi (full-face). No. 517, Martin Luther King (half-length).

During 1969, Nos. 481 and 512/17 were issued optd **PREMIER HOMME SUR LA LUNE 20 JUILLET 1969/ FIRST MAN LANDING ON MOON 20 JULY 1969** in very limited quantities.

**137** "The Letter" (A. Cambon)

**1968.** Air. "Philexafrique" Stamp Exhibition, Abidjan (in 1969). (1st issue).

| | | | | |
|---|---|---|---|---|
| 519 | **137** | 100f. multicoloured | 3·25 | 2·50 |

**138** Wouri Bridge and 1f. stamp of 1925

**1969.** Air. "Philexafrique" Stamp Exhibition, Abidjan, Ivory Coast (2nd issue).

| | | | | |
|---|---|---|---|---|
| 520 | **138** | 50f. blue, olive and green | 3·25 | 2·10 |

**139** President Ahidjo

**1969.** 9th Anniv of Independence.

| | | | | |
|---|---|---|---|---|
| 521 | **139** | 30f. multicoloured | 80 | 30 |

**140** Vat of Chocolate

**1969.** Chocolate Industry Development.

| | | | | |
|---|---|---|---|---|
| 522 | **140** | 15f. blue, brown and red | 45 | 25 |
| 523 | - | 30f. brown, choc & grn | 75 | 40 |
| 524 | - | 50f. red, green & bistre | 1·00 | 55 |

DESIGNS—HORIZ: 30f. Chocolate factory. VERT: 50f. Making confectionery.

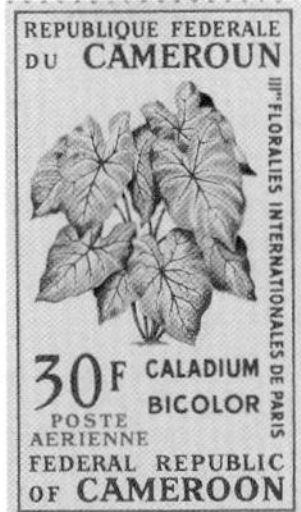

**141** "Caladium bicolor"

**1969.** Air. 3rd Int Flower Show, Paris. Mult.

| | | | |
|---|---|---|---|
| 525 | 30f. Type **141** | 80 | 55 |
| 526 | 50f. "Aristolochia elegans" | 1·70 | 80 |
| 527 | 100f. "Gloriosa simplex" | 3·50 | 1·50 |

**142** Reproduction Symbol

**1969.** Abbia Arts and Folklore.

| | | | | |
|---|---|---|---|---|
| 528 | **142** | 5f. purple, turq & blue | 30 | 20 |
| 529 | - | 10f. orange, olive & blue | 45 | 20 |
| 530 | - | 15f. indigo, red & blue | 45 | 25 |
| 531 | - | 30f. green, brown & blue | 95 | 40 |
| 532 | - | 70f. red, green and blue | 1·70 | 85 |

DESIGNS—HORIZ: 10f. "Two Toucans"; 30f. "Vulture attacking Monkey". VERT: 15f. Forest Symbol; 70f. Oliphant-player.

**143** Post Office, Douala

**1969.** Air. New Post Office Buildings.

| | | | | |
|---|---|---|---|---|
| 533 | **143** | 30f. brown, blue & green | 55 | 25 |
| 534 | - | 50f. red, slate & turquoise | 95 | 45 |
| 535 | - | 100f. brown and turquoise | 1·80 | 85 |

DESIGNS: 50f. G.P.O., Buea; 100f. G.P.O., Bafoussam.

**144** "Coronation of Napoleon" (David)

**1969.** Air. Birth Bicent of Napoleon Bonaparte.

| | | | | |
|---|---|---|---|---|
| 536 | **144** | 30f. multicoloured | 1·20 | 70 |
| 537 | - | 1,000f. gold | 42·00 | 40·00 |

DESIGN: 1,000f. "Napoleon crossing the Alps". No. 537 is embossed on gold foil.

**145** Kumba Station

**1969.** Opening of Mbanga–Kumba Railway. Mult.

| | | | |
|---|---|---|---|
| 538 | 30f. Type **145** | 1·10 | 55 |
| 539 | 50f. Diesel train on bridge over River Mungo (vert) | 2·75 | 1·00 |

**146** Bank Emblem

**1969.** 5th Anniv of African Development Bank.

| | | | | |
|---|---|---|---|---|
| 540 | **146** | 30f. brown, green & vio | 80 | 40 |

**1969.** Air. Negro Writers. Portrait designs as T 136.

| | | | |
|---|---|---|---|
| 541 | 15f. brown and blue | 45 | 25 |
| 542 | 30f. brown and purple | 75 | 25 |
| 543 | 30f. brown and yellow | 75 | 25 |
| 544 | 50f. brown and green | 95 | 45 |
| 545 | 50f. brown and agate | 95 | 45 |
| 546 | 100f. brown and yellow | 1·90 | 1·10 |
| **MS**547 | 115×125 mm. Nos. 541/6 | 7·25 | 7·25 |

DESIGNS—VERT: No. 541, Dr. P. Mars (Haiti); No. 542, W. Dubois (U.S.A.); No. 543, A. Cesaire (Martinique); No. 544, M. Garvey (Jamaica); No. 545, L. Hughes (U.S.A.); No. 546, R. Maran (Martinique).

**148** I.L.O. Emblem

**1969.** Air. 50th Anniv of I.L.O.

| | | | | |
|---|---|---|---|---|
| 548 | **148** | 30f. black and turquoise | 70 | 40 |
| 549 | **148** | 50f. black and mauve | 1·30 | 60 |

**149** Astronauts and "Apollo 11" in Sea

**1969.** Air. 1st Man on the Moon. Multicoloured.

| | | | |
|---|---|---|---|
| 550 | 200f. Type **149** | 4·75 | 2·20 |
| 551 | 500f. Astronaut and module on Moon | 11·50 | 4·50 |

**150** Airplane, Map and Airport

**1969.** 10th Anniv of Aerial Navigation Security Agency for Africa and Madagascar (ASECNA).

| | | | | |
|---|---|---|---|---|
| 552 | **150** | 100f. green | 1·80 | 85 |

**151** President Ahidjo, Arms and Map

**1970.** Air. 10th Anniv of Independence.

| | | | | |
|---|---|---|---|---|
| 553 | **151** | 1,000f. gold & mult | 25·00 | 23·00 |

No. 553 is embossed on gold foil.

**152** Mont Febe Hotel, Yaounde

**1970.** Air. Tourism.

| | | | | |
|---|---|---|---|---|
| 554 | **152** | 30f. grey, green & brn | 80 | 30 |

**153** Lenin

**1970.** Air. Birth Centenary of Lenin.

| | | | | |
|---|---|---|---|---|
| 555 | **153** | 50f. brown and yellow | 1·90 | 75 |

**154** "Lantana camara"

**1970.** African Climbing Plants. Multicoloured.

| | | | |
|---|---|---|---|
| 556 | 15f. Type **154** (postage) | 45 | 25 |
| 557 | 30f. "Passiflora quadrangularis" | 1·00 | 40 |
| 558 | 50f. "Cleome speciosa" (air) | 1·50 | 70 |
| 559 | 100f. "Mussaenda erythrophylla" | 3·00 | 1·40 |

**155** Lions' Emblem and Map of Africa

**1970.** Air. 13th Congress of Lions International District 403, Yaounde.

| | | | | |
|---|---|---|---|---|
| 560 | **155** | 100f. multicoloured | 2·20 | 95 |

**156** New UPU HQ.

**1970.** New UPU Headquarters Building, Berne.

| | | | | |
|---|---|---|---|---|
| 561 | **156** | 30f. green, violet & blue | 90 | 25 |
| 562 | **156** | 50f. blue, red and grey | 1·30 | 40 |

**157** U.N. Emblem and Stylized Doves

**1970.** Air. 25th Anniv of United Nations.

| | | | | |
|---|---|---|---|---|
| 563 | **157** | 30f. brown and orange | 90 | 45 |
| 564 | - | 50f. indigo and blue | 1·30 | 65 |

DESIGN—VERT: 50f. U.N. emblem and stylized dove.

**158** Fermenting Vats

**1970.** Brewing Industry.

| | | | | |
|---|---|---|---|---|
| 565 | **158** | 15f. brown, green & grey | 45 | 25 |
| 566 | - | 30f. red, brown and blue | 90 | 40 |

DESIGN: 30f. Storage tanks.

**159** Japanese Pavilion

**1970.** Air. Expo 70.

| | | | | |
|---|---|---|---|---|
| 567 | **159** | 50f. blue, red and green | 95 | 55 |
| 568 | - | 100f. red, blue and green | 2·00 | 90 |
| 569 | - | 150f. brown, slate & blue | 3·50 | 1·60 |

DESIGNS—VERT: 100f. Expo Emblem and Map of Japan. HORIZ: 150f. Australian Pavilion.

**160** Gen. De Gaulle in Tropical Kit

**1970.** Air. "Homage to General De Gaulle".

| | | | | |
|---|---|---|---|---|
| 570 | **160** | 100f. brown, blue & grn | 3·00 | 1·60 |
| 571 | - | 200f. blue, green & brn | 5·50 | 2·50 |

DESIGN: 200f. Gen. De Gaulle in military uniform.

Nos. 570/1 were issued together as a triptych, separated by a stamp-size label showing maps of France and Cameroun.

**161** Aztec Stadium, Mexico City

**1970.** Air. World Cup Football Championship, Mexico. Multicoloured.

| | | | |
|---|---|---|---|
| 572 | 50f. Type **161** | 95 | 55 |
| 573 | 100f. Mexican team | 2·00 | 1·10 |
| 574 | 200f. Pele and Brazilian team with World Cup (vert) | 3·50 | 1·90 |

**162** Dancers

**1970.** Ozila Dancers.

| | | | | |
|---|---|---|---|---|
| 575 | **162** | 30f. red, orange & grn | 1·20 | 45 |
| 576 | **162** | 50f. red, brown & scar | 2·40 | 95 |

**163** Doll in National Costume

**1970.** Cameroun Dolls.

| | | | | |
|---|---|---|---|---|
| 577 | **163** | 10f. green, black & red | 65 | 45 |
| 578 | **163** | 15f. red, green & yellow | 75 | 55 |
| 579 | **163** | 30f. brown, green & blk | 1·60 | 70 |

**164** Beethoven (after Stieler)

**1970.** Air. Birth Bicent of Beethoven.

| | | | | |
|---|---|---|---|---|
| 580 | **164** | 250f. multicoloured | 5·25 | 2·75 |

**1970.** Air. Rembrandt Paintings. As T **144**. Mult.

| | | | |
|---|---|---|---|
| 581 | 70f. "Christ at Emmaus" | 1·50 | 60 |
| 582 | 150f. "The Anatomy Lesson" | 2·50 | 1·30 |

**166** "Industry and Agriculture"

**1970.** "Europafrique" Economic Community.

| | | | | |
|---|---|---|---|---|
| 583 | **166** | 30f. multicoloured | 80 | 40 |

**167** Bust of Dickens

**1970.** Air. Death Centenary of Charles Dickens.

| | | | | |
|---|---|---|---|---|
| 584 | **167** | 40f. brown and red | 95 | 35 |
| 585 | - | 50f. multicoloured | 1·10 | 55 |
| 586 | - | 100f. multicoloured | 1·90 | 1·10 |

DESIGNS: 50f. Characters from David Copperfield; 100f. Dickens writing.

**1971.** Air. De Gaulle Memorial Issue. Nos. 570/1 optd **IN MEMORIAM 1890-1970**.

| | | | | |
|---|---|---|---|---|
| 587 | **160** | 100f. brown, blue & grn | 3·00 | 1·40 |
| 588 | - | 200f. blue, green & brn | 5·50 | 2·30 |

**169** University Buildings

**1971.** Inauguration of Federal University, Yaounde.

| | | | | |
|---|---|---|---|---|
| 589 | **169** | 50f. green, blue & brown | 1·00 | 45 |

**170** Presidents Ahidjo and Pompidou

**1971.** Visit of Pres. Pompidou of France.

| | | | | |
|---|---|---|---|---|
| 590 | **170** | 30f. multicoloured | 1·50 | 70 |

**171** "Cameroun Youth"

**1971.** 5th National Youth Festival.

| | | | | |
|---|---|---|---|---|
| 591 | **171** | 30f. multicoloured | 80 | 45 |

**172** Timber Yard, Douala

**1971.** Air. Industrial Expansion.

| | | | | |
|---|---|---|---|---|
| 592 | **172** | 40f. brown, green & red | 55 | 25 |
| 593 | - | 70f. brown, green and blue | 1·20 | 50 |
| 594 | - | 100f. red, blue & green | 1·60 | 70 |

DESIGNS—VERT: 70f. "Alucam" aluminium plant, Edea. HORIZ: 100f. Mbakaou Dam.

**173** "Gerbera hybrida"

**1971.** Flowers. Multicoloured.

| | | | | |
|---|---|---|---|---|
| 595 | | 20f. Type **173** | 65 | 40 |
| 596 | | 40f. "Opuntia polyantha" | 1·50 | 55 |
| 597 | | 50f. "Hemerocallis hybrida" | 1·90 | 70 |

For similar designs inscr "United Republic of Cameroon" etc., see Nos. 648/52.

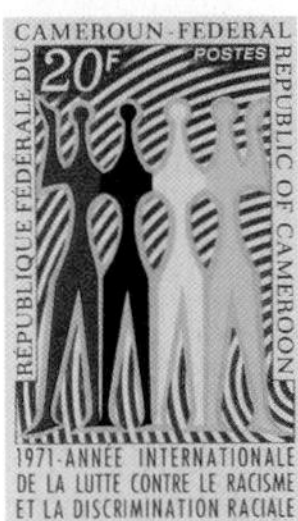

**174** "World Races"

**1971.** Racial Equality Year. Multicoloured.

| | | | | |
|---|---|---|---|---|
| 598 | | 20f. Type **174** | 50 | 25 |
| 599 | | 30f. Hands of four races clasping globe | 75 | 25 |

**175** Crowned Cranes, Camp de Waza

**1971.** Landscapes.

| | | | | |
|---|---|---|---|---|
| 600 | **175** | 10f. blue, red and green | 1·70 | 45 |
| 601 | - | 20f. red, brown & green | 1·10 | 45 |
| 602 | - | 30f. green, blue & brown | 1·10 | 45 |

DESIGNS: 20f. African pirogue; 30f. Sanaga River.

**176** Relay-racing

**1971.** Air. 75th Anniv of Modern Olympic Games.

| | | | | |
|---|---|---|---|---|
| 603 | **176** | 30f. blue, red and brown | 60 | 30 |
| 604 | - | 50f. purple and blue | 85 | 40 |
| 605 | - | 100f. black, green & red | 1·70 | 70 |

DESIGNS—VERT: 50f. Olympic runner with torch. HORIZ: 100f. Throwing the discus.

**177** "Villalba" (deep-sea trawler)

**1971.** Air. Fishing Industry.

| | | | | |
|---|---|---|---|---|
| 606 | **177** | 30f. brown, green & blue | 95 | 50 |
| 607 | - | 40f. purple, blue & green | 1·00 | 70 |
| 608 | - | 70f. brown, red and blue | 1·90 | 90 |
| 609 | - | 150f. multicoloured | 4·75 | 1·90 |

DESIGNS: 40f. Traditional fishing method, Northern Cameroun; 70f. Fish quay, Douala; 150f. Shrimp-boats, Douala.

**178** Peace Palace, The Hague

**1971.** 25th Anniv of International Court of Justice, The Hague.

| | | | | |
|---|---|---|---|---|
| 610 | **178** | 50f. brown, blue & green | 90 | 35 |

**179** 1916 French Occupation 20c. and 1914–18 War Memorial, Yaounde

**1971.** Air. "Philatecam 71" Stamp Exhibition, Yaounde (1st issue).

| | | | | |
|---|---|---|---|---|
| 611 | **179** | 20f. brown, ochre & grn | 50 | 25 |
| 612 | - | 25f. brown, green & blue | 60 | 25 |
| 613 | - | 40f. green, grey & brown | 95 | 25 |
| 614 | - | 50f. multicoloured | 1·10 | 45 |
| 615 | - | 100f. green, brown & orge | 2·10 | 85 |

DESIGNS: 25f. 1954 15f. Jamot stamp and memorial; 40f. 1965 25f. Tourist Office stamp and public buildings, Yaounde; 50f. German stamp and Imperial German postal emblem; 100f. 1915 Expeditionary Force optd, error, and Expeditionary Force memorial.

See also No. 620.

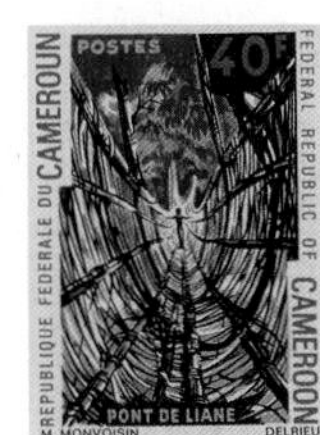

**180** Rope Bridge

**1971.** "Rural Life". Multicoloured.

| | | | | |
|---|---|---|---|---|
| 616 | | 40f. Type **180** | 1·40 | 45 |
| 617 | | 45f. Local market (horiz) | 1·40 | 45 |

**181** Bamoun Horseman (carving)

**1971.** Cameroun Carving.

| | | | | |
|---|---|---|---|---|
| 618 | **181** | 10f. brown and yellow | 45 | 20 |
| 619 | - | 15f. brown and yellow | 45 | 25 |

DESIGN: 15f. Fetish statuette.

**182** Pres. Ahidjo, Flag and "Reunification" Road

**1971.** Air. "Philatecam 71" Stamp Exhibition, Yaounde (2nd issue).

| | | | | |
|---|---|---|---|---|
| 620 | **182** | 250f. multicoloured | 6·00 | 4·25 |

**183** Satellite and Globe

**1971.** Pan-African Telecommunications Network.

| | | | | |
|---|---|---|---|---|
| 621 | **183** | 40f. multicoloured | 80 | 50 |

**184** UAMPT Headquarters, Brazzaville and Carved Stool

**1971.** Air. 10th Anniv of African and Malagasy Posts and Telecommunications Union.

| | | | | |
|---|---|---|---|---|
| 622 | **184** | 100f. multicoloured | 1·90 | 85 |

**185** Children acclaiming Emblem

**1971.** 25th Anniv of UNICEF.

| | | | | |
|---|---|---|---|---|
| 623 | **185** | 40f. purple, blue & slate | 85 | 25 |
| 624 | - | 50f. red, green and blue | 1·00 | 50 |

DESIGN—VERT: 50f. Ear of Wheat and Emblem.

**186** "The Annunciation" (Fra Angelico)

**1971.** Air. Christmas. Paintings. Multicoloured.

| | | | | |
|---|---|---|---|---|
| 625 | | 40f. Type **186** | 55 | 25 |
| 626 | | 45f. "Virgin and Child" (Del Sarto) | 80 | 45 |
| 627 | | 150f. "The Holy Family with the Lamb" (detail Raphael) (vert) | 3·25 | 1·20 |

**187** Cabin, South-Central Region

**1972.** Traditional Cameroun Houses. Mult.

| | | | | |
|---|---|---|---|---|
| 628 | | 10f. Type **187** | 30 | 25 |
| 629 | | 15f. Adamaoua round house | 50 | 25 |

**188** Airline Emblem

**1972.** Air. Cameroun Airlines' Inaugural Flight.

| | | | | |
|---|---|---|---|---|
| 630 | **188** | 50f. multicoloured | 80 | 25 |

**189** Giraffe and Palm Tree

**1972.** Festival of Youth. Multicoloured.

| | | | | |
|---|---|---|---|---|
| 631 | | 2f. Type **189** | 30 | 10 |
| 632 | | 5f. Domestic scene | 30 | 10 |
| 633 | | 10f. Blacksmith (horiz) | 30 | 20 |
| 634 | | 15f. Women | 30 | 20 |

**190** Africa Cup

**1972.** African Football Cup Championship. Mult.

| | | | | |
|---|---|---|---|---|
| 635 | | 20f. Type **190** | 65 | 25 |
| 636 | | 40f. Players with ball (horiz) | 85 | 40 |
| 637 | | 45f. Team captains | 1·40 | 55 |

**191** "St. Mark's Square and Doge's Palace" (detail-Caffi)

**1972.** Air. UNESCO "Save Venice" Campaign. Multicoloured.

| | | | | |
|---|---|---|---|---|
| 638 | | 40f. Type **191** | 75 | 40 |
| 639 | | 100f. "Regatta on the Grand Canal" (detail – Canaletto) | 2·00 | 70 |
| 640 | | 200f. "Regatta on the Grand Canal" (detail – Canaletto) (different) | 4·00 | 1·40 |

**192** Assembly Building, Yaounde

**1972.** 110th Session of Inter-Parliamentary Council, Yaounde.

| | | | | |
|---|---|---|---|---|
| 641 | **192** | 40f. multicoloured | 80 | 40 |

**193** Horseman, North Cameroun

**1972.** Traditional Life and Folklore. Mult.

| | | | | |
|---|---|---|---|---|
| 642 | | 15f. Type **193** | 40 | 20 |
| 643 | | 20f. Bororo woman (vert) | 50 | 20 |
| 644 | | 40f. Wouri River and Mt. Cameroun | 1·80 | 55 |

**194** Pataiev, Dobrovolsky and Volkov

**1972.** Air. "Soyuz 11" Cosmonauts. Memorial Issue.

| | | | | |
|---|---|---|---|---|
| 645 | **194** | 50f. multicoloured | 90 | 50 |

**195** U.N. Building, New York, Gate of Heavenly Peace, Peking and Chinese Flag

**1972.** Air. Admission of Chinese People's Republic to U.N.

| | | | | |
|---|---|---|---|---|
| 646 | **195** | 50f. multicoloured | 2·75 | 70 |

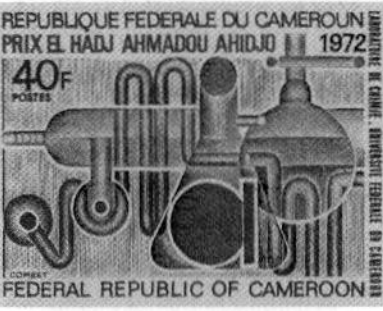

**196** Chemistry Laboratory, Federal University

**1972.** Pres. Ahidjo Prize.

| | | | | |
|---|---|---|---|---|
| 647 | **196** | 40f. red, green & purple | 80 | 50 |

**1972.** Flowers. As T 173, but inscr "UNITED REPUBLIC OF CAMEROON", etc. Mult.

| | | | | |
|---|---|---|---|---|
| 648 | | 40f. "Solanum macranthum" | 85 | 30 |
| 649 | | 40f. "Kaempferia aethiopica" | 1·00 | 25 |
| 650 | | 45f. "Hoya carnosa" | 1·00 | 50 |
| 651 | | 45f. "Cassia alata" | 1·20 | 30 |
| 652 | | 50f. "Crinum sanderianum" | 1·50 | 40 |

**197** Swimming

**1972.** Air. Olympic Games, Munich.

| | | | | |
|---|---|---|---|---|
| 653 | **197** | 50f. green, brown & lake | 95 | 45 |
| 654 | - | 50f. brown, blue and sepia | 95 | 45 |
| 655 | - | 200f. lake, grey & purple | 3·75 | 1·70 |

**MS**656 140×100 mm. As Nos. 653/5 but colours changed; 50f. brown, violet and blue; 50f. brown, blue and purple; 200f. brown and blue 6·50 6·50

DESIGNS—HORIZ: No. 655, Horse-jumping. VERT: No. 654, Boxing.

**198** "Charaxes ameliae"

**1972.** Butterflies. Multicoloured.

| | | | |
|---|---|---|---|
| 657 | 40f. Type **198** | 3·00 | 90 |
| 658 | 45f. "Papiliotynderaeus" | 4·25 | 1·30 |

**1972.** No. 471 surch.

| | | | |
|---|---|---|---|
| 659 | 40f. on 30f. multicoloured | 1·00 | 50 |

**1972.** Air. Olympic Gold Medal Winners. Nos. 653/5 optd as listed below.

| | | | |
|---|---|---|---|
| 660 | 50f. green, brown and red | 95 | 45 |
| 661 | 50f. brown, blue and sepia | 95 | 45 |
| 662 | 200f. lake, grey and purple | 3·75 | 1·70 |

OVERPRINTS: No. 660, **NATATION MARK SPITZ 7 MEDAILLES D'OR**. No. 661, **SUPER-WELTER KOTTYSCH MEDAILLE D'OR**. No. 662, **CONCOURS COMPLET MEADE MEDAILLE D'OR**.

**201** Great Blue Turacos

**1972.** Birds. Multicoloured.

| | | | |
|---|---|---|---|
| 663 | 10f. Type **201** | 1·20 | 45 |
| 664 | 45f. Red-faced lovebirds (horiz) | 2·75 | 1·10 |

**202** "The Virgin with Angels" (Cimabue)

**1972.** Air. Christmas. Multicoloured.

| | | | |
|---|---|---|---|
| 665 | 45f. Type **202** | 1·00 | 45 |
| 666 | 140f. "The Madonna of the Rose Arbour" (S. Lochner) | 2·75 | 1·60 |

**203** St. Theresa

**1973.** Air. Birth Centenary of St. Theresa of Lisieux.

| | | | | |
|---|---|---|---|---|
| 667 | **203** | 45f. blue, brown & violet | 75 | 25 |
| 668 | - | 100f. mauve, brown, & bl | 1·70 | 70 |

DESIGN: 100f. Lisieux Basilica.

**204** Emperor Haile Selassie and "Africa Hall", Addis Ababa

**1973.** Air. 80th Birthday of Emperor Haile Selassie of Ethiopia.

| | | | | |
|---|---|---|---|---|
| 669 | **204** | 45f. multicoloured | 90 | 50 |

**205** Cotton Cultivation, North Cameroun

**1973.** 3rd Five Year Plan. Multicoloured.

| | | | |
|---|---|---|---|
| 670 | 5f. Type **205** | 20 | 10 |
| 671 | 10f. Cacao pods, South-central region | 30 | 10 |
| 672 | 15f. Forestry, South-eastern area | 50 | 20 |
| 673 | 20f. Coffee plant, West Cameroun | 1·00 | 25 |
| 674 | 45f. Tea-picking, West Cameroun | 2·20 | 40 |

**206** "Food for All"

**1973.** Air. 10th Anniv of World Food Programme.

| | | | | |
|---|---|---|---|---|
| 675 | **206** | 45f. multicoloured | 80 | 45 |

**207** Human Hearts

**1973.** Air. 25th Anniv of W.H.O.

| | | | | |
|---|---|---|---|---|
| 676 | **207** | 50f. red and blue | 90 | 45 |

**208** Pres. Ahidjo, Map, Flag and Cameroun Stamp

**1973.** 1st Anniv of United Republic. Mult.

| | | | |
|---|---|---|---|
| 677 | 10f. Type **208** (postage) | 65 | 25 |
| 678 | 20f. Pres. Ahidjo, proclamation and stamp | 1·00 | 50 |
| 679 | 45f. Pres. Ahidjo, map of Cameroun rivers and stamp (air) | 85 | 25 |
| 680 | 70f. Significant dates on Cameroun flag | 1·10 | 65 |

**209** Mask

**1973.** Bamoun Masks.

| | | | | |
|---|---|---|---|---|
| 681 | **209** | 5f. black, brown & green | 10 | 10 |
| 682 | - | 10f. brown, black & purple | 30 | 10 |
| 683 | - | 45f. brown, black & red | 75 | 40 |
| 684 | - | 100f. brown, black & blue | 1·90 | 70 |

DESIGNS: 10f., 45f., 100f., as Type **209**, but different masks.

**210** Dr. G. A. Hansen

**1973.** Centenary of Hansen's Identification of Leprosy Bacillus.

| | | | | |
|---|---|---|---|---|
| 685 | **210** | 45f. blue, lt blue & brown | 1·70 | 70 |

**211** Scout Emblem and Flags

**1973.** Air. Admission of Cameroun to 24th World Scout Conference.

| | | | | |
|---|---|---|---|---|
| 686 | **211** | 40f. multicoloured | 85 | 35 |
| 687 | **211** | 45f. multicoloured | 1·20 | 50 |
| 688 | **211** | 100f. multicoloured | 2·50 | 80 |

**1973.** African Solidarity "Drought Relief". No. 670 surch 100F. SECHERESSE SOLIDARITE AFRICAINE.

| | | | | |
|---|---|---|---|---|
| 689 | **205** | 100f. on 5f. multicoloured | 1·70 | 1·20 |

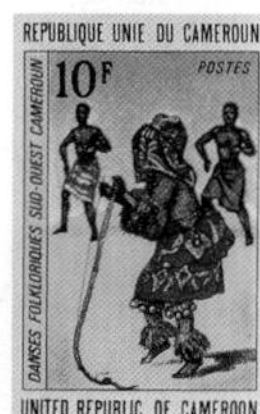

**213** Folk-dancers

**1973.** Folklore Dances of South-west Cameroun. Multicoloured.

| | | | |
|---|---|---|---|
| 690 | 10f. Type **213** | 20 | 10 |
| 691 | 25f. Dancer in plumed hat | 55 | 20 |
| 692 | 45f. Dancers with "totem" | 1·10 | 30 |

**214** WMO Emblem

**1973.** Centenary of WMO.

| | | | | |
|---|---|---|---|---|
| 693 | **214** | 45f. blue and green | 1·50 | 40 |

**215** Garoua Party H.Q. Building

**1973.** 7th Anniv of Cameroun National Union.

| | | | | |
|---|---|---|---|---|
| 694 | **215** | 40f. multicoloured | 80 | 45 |

**216** Crane with Letter and Telecommunications Emblem

**1973.** 12th Anniv of UAMPT.

| | | | | |
|---|---|---|---|---|
| 695 | **216** | 100f. blue, lt blue & green | 1·70 | 75 |

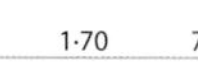

**217** African Mask and Old Town Hall, Brussels

**1973.** Air. African Fortnight, Brussels.

| | | | | |
|---|---|---|---|---|
| 696 | **217** | 40f. brown and purple | 80 | 45 |

**218** Avocado

**1973.** Cameroun Fruits. Multicoloured.

| | | | |
|---|---|---|---|
| 697 | 10f. Type **218** | 60 | 25 |
| 698 | 20f. Mango | 75 | 30 |
| 699 | 45f. Plum | 1·70 | 65 |
| 700 | 50f. Custard-apple | 2·10 | 80 |

**219** Map of Africa

**1973.** Air. Aid for Handicapped Children.

| | | | | |
|---|---|---|---|---|
| 701 | **219** | 40f. red, brown & green | 80 | 50 |

**220** Kirdi Village

**1973.** Cameroun Villages.

| | | | | |
|---|---|---|---|---|
| 702 | **220** | 15f. black, green & brown | 35 | 20 |
| 703 | - | 45f. brown, red & orange | 85 | 45 |
| 704 | - | 50f. black, green & orange | 1·00 | 55 |

DESIGNS: 45f. Mabas village. 50f. Fishing village.

**221** Earth Station

**1973.** Air. Inauguration of Satellite Earth Station, Zamengoe.

| | | | | |
|---|---|---|---|---|
| 705 | **221** | 100f. brown, blue & grn | 1·40 | 75 |

222 "The Madonna with Chancellor Rolin" (Van Eyck)

**1973.** Air. Christmas. Multicoloured.
706 45f. Type **222** 1·00 55
707 140f. "The Nativity" (Federico Fiori–Il Barocci) 2·75 1·70

223 Handclasp on Map of Africa

**1974.** 10th Anniv of Organization of African Unity.
708 **223** 40f. blue, red and green 55 25
709 **223** 45f. green, blue and red 65 25

224 Mill-worker

**1974.** C.I.C.A.M. Industrial Complex.
710 **224** 45f. brown, green & red 80 25

225 Bilinga Carved Panel (detail)

**1974.** Cameroun Art.
711 **225** 10f. brown and green 30 25
712 - 40f. brown and red 85 25
713 - 45f. red and blue 1·00 45
DESIGNS: 40f. Tubinga carving (detail); 45f. Acajou Ngollon carved panel (detail).

**1974.** No. 469 surch.
714 40f. on 8f. multicoloured 80 35

227 Cameroun Cow

**1974.** Cattle-raising in North Cameroun. Mult.
715 40f. Type **227** (postage) 1·20 50
716 45f. Cattle in pen (air) 1·20 50

228 Route-map and Track

**1974.** Trans-Cameroun Railway. Inauguration of Yaounde–Ngaoundere Line.
717 **228** 5f. brown, blue & green 45 25
718 - 20f. brown, blue & violet 95 40
719 - 40f. red, blue & green 1·80 80
720 - 100f. green, blue & brown 3·00 1·40
DESIGNS—HORIZ: 20f. Laying track; 100f. Railway bridge over Djerem River. VERT: 40f. Welding rails.

**229** Sir Winston Churchill

**1974.** Air. Birth Cent of Sir Winston Churchill.
721 **229** 100f. black, red & blue 1·60 75

**230** Footballer and City Crests

**1974.** Air. World Cup Football Championship.
722 **230** 45f. orange, slate & grey 80 25
723 - 100f. orange, slate & grey 1·40 70
724 - 200f. blue, orange & blk 3·00 1·70
DESIGNS: 100f. Goalkeeper and city crests; 200f. World Cup.

**1974.** Air. West Germany's Victory in World Cup Football Championship. Nos. 722/4 optd **7th JULY 1974 R.F.A. 2 HOLLANDE 1 7 JUILLET 1974**.
725 **230** 45f. orange, slate & grey 75 25
726 - 100f. orange, slate & grey 1·30 70
727 - 200f. blue, orange & blk 2·75 1·70

**232** UPU Emblem and Hands with Letters

**1974.** Centenary of Universal Postal Union.
728 **232** 40f. red, blue and green (postage) 90 45
729 - 100f. green, vio & bl (air) 1·70 85
730 - 200f. green, red and blue 2·75 1·70
DESIGNS: 100f. Cameroun UPU headquarters stamps of 1970; 200f. Cameroun UPU 75th anniv stamps of 1949.

**233** Copernicus and Solar System

**1974.** Air. 500th Birth Anniv (1973) of Copernicus.
731 **233** 250f. blue, red & brown 4·00 2·30

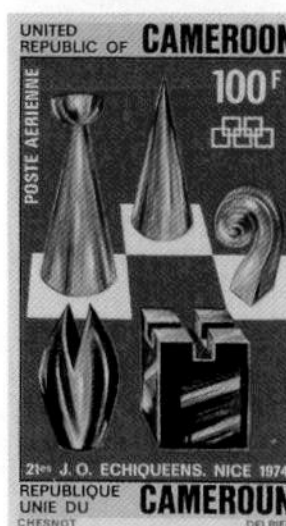

**234** Modern Chess Pieces

**1974.** Air. Chess Olympics, Nice.
732 **234** 100f. multicoloured 4·00 1·60

**235** African Mask and "Arphila" Emblem

**1974.** Air. "Arphila 75" Stamp Exhibition, Paris.
733 **235** 50f. brown and red 60 45

**236** African Leaders, UDEAC HQ and Flags

**1974.** 10th Anniv of Central African Customs and Economics Union.
734 **236** 40f. mult (postage) 1·40 70
735 - 100f. multicoloured (air) 1·80 75
DESIGN: 100f. Similar to Type **236**.

**1974.** No. 717 surch **100F 10 DECEMBRE 1974**.
736 **228** 100f. on 5f. brn, bl & grn 1·90 1·10

**238** "Apollo" Emblem, Astronaut, Module and Astronaut's Boots

**1974.** Air. 5th Anniv of 1st Landing on Moon.
737 **238** 200f. brown, red & blue 3·25 1·70

**1974.** Christmas. As T **222**. Multicoloured.
738 40f. "Virgin of Autumn" (15th-century sculpture) 95 45
739 45f. "Virgin and Child" (Luis de Morales) 1·20 60

**239** De Gaulle and Eboue

**1975.** Air. 30th Anniv of Felix Eboue ("Free French" leader).
740 **239** 45f. multicoloured 1·70 70
741 **239** 200f. multicoloured 6·00 2·75

**240** "Celosia cristata"

**1975.** Flowers of North Cameroun. Mult.
742 5f. Type **240** 20 20
743 40f. "Costus spectabilis" 1·20 40
744 45f. "Mussaenda erythrophylla" 1·40 50

**241** Fish and Fishing-boat

**1975.** Offshore Fishing.
745 **241** 40f. brown, blue & choc 1·90 70
746 - 45f. brown, bistre & blue 1·90 70
DESIGN: 45f. Fishing-boat and fish in net.

**242** Afo Akom Statue

**1975**
747 **242** 40f. multicoloured 50 25
748 **242** 45f. multicoloured 75 45
749 **242** 200f. multicoloured 2·50 1·60

**243** "Polypore" (fungus)

**1975.** Natural History. Multicoloured.
750 15f. Type **243** 75·00 2·10
751 40f. "Nymphalis Chrysalis" 45·00 95

**244** View of Building

**1975.** Inaug of New Ministry of Posts Building.
752 **244** 40f. blue, green & brown 65 25
753 **244** 45f. brown, green & blue 90 50

**245** Presbyterian Church, Elat

**1975.** Churches and Mosque.
754 **245** 40f. brown, blue & black 45 25
755 - 40f. brown, blue & slate 45 25
756 - 45f. brown, green & blk 55 25
DESIGNS: No. 755, Foumban Mosque; No. 756, Catholic Church, Ngaoundere.

**246** Marquis de Lafayette (after Chappel) and Naval Battle

**1975.** Air. Bicent (1976) of American Revolution.
757 **246** 100f. blue, turq & brn 2·10 1·10
758 - 140f. blue, brown & green 2·30 1·10
759 - 500f. green, brown & blue 7·25 2·50
DESIGNS: 140f. George Washington (after Stuart) and Continental Infantry (after Ogden); 500f. Benjamin Franklin (after Peale and Nee) and Boston.

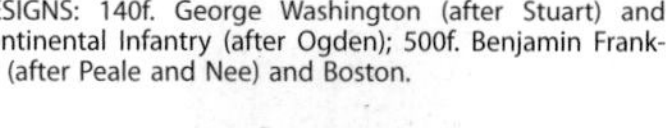

**247** Harvesting Maize

**1975.** "Green Revolution". Multicoloured.
760 40f. Type **247** 75 25
761 40f. Ploughing with oxen (horiz) 75 25

248 "The Burning Bush" (N. Froment)

1975. Air. Christmas. Multicoloured.

| | | | |
|---|---|---|---|
| 762 | 50f. Type **248** | 85 | 50 |
| 763 | 500f. "Adoration of the Magi" (Gentile da Fabriano) (horiz) | 7·25 | 5·25 |

249 Tracking Aerial

1976. Inauguration of Satellite Monitoring Station, Zamengoe. Multicoloured.

| | | | |
|---|---|---|---|
| 764 | 40f. Type **249** | 50 | 25 |
| 765 | 100f. Close-up of tracking aerial (vert) | 1·20 | 50 |

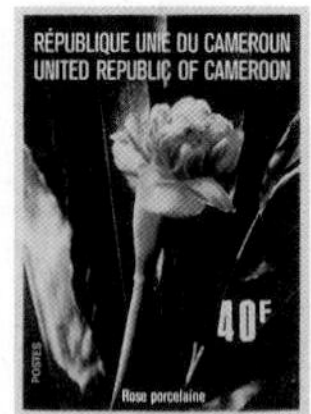
250 Porcelain Rose

1976. Flowers. Multicoloured.

| | | | |
|---|---|---|---|
| 766 | 40f. Type **250** | 90 | 25 |
| 767 | 50f. Flower of North Cameroun | 1·40 | 35 |

251 Concorde

1976. Air. Concorde's First Commercial Flight, Paris to Rio de Janeiro.

| | | | | |
|---|---|---|---|---|
| 768 | **251** | 500f. multicoloured | 5·25 | 2·75 |
| **MS**769 | | 130×93 mm. No. 768 | 7·75 | 7·75 |

252 Masked Dancer

1976. Cameroun Dances. Multicoloured.

| | | | |
|---|---|---|---|
| 770 | 40f. Type **252** (postage) | 80 | 50 |
| 771 | 50f. Drummers and two dancers (air) | 60 | 25 |
| 772 | 100f. Female dancer | 1·20 | 50 |

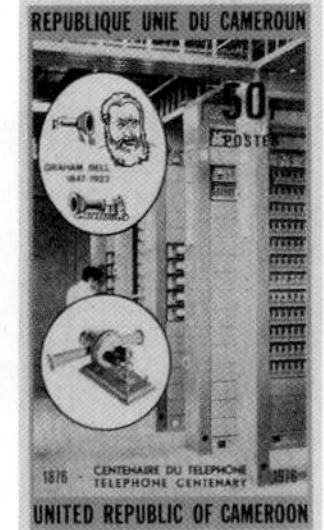
253 Telephone Exchange

1976. Air. Telephone Centenary.

| | | | | |
|---|---|---|---|---|
| 773 | **253** | 50f. multicoloured | 85 | 55 |

254 Young Men Building House

1976. 10th Anniv of National Youth Day. Multicoloured.

| | | | |
|---|---|---|---|
| 774 | 40f. Type **254** | 45 | 25 |
| 775 | 45f. Gathering palm leaves | 50 | 25 |

255 Dr. Adenauer and Cologne Cathedral

1976. Birth Centenary of Dr. Konrad Adenauer (Statesman).

| | | | | |
|---|---|---|---|---|
| 776 | **255** | 100f. multicoloured | 95 | 45 |

256 "Adoration of the Shepherds" (Charles Le Brun)

1976. Air. Christmas.

| | | | |
|---|---|---|---|
| 777 | 30f. Type **256** | 80 | 35 |
| 778 | 60f. "Adoration of the Magi" (Rubens) | 1·00 | 45 |
| 779 | 70f. "Virgin and Child" (Bellini) | 1·30 | 60 |
| 780 | 500f. "The New-born" (G. de la Tour) | 8·50 | 4·75 |
| **MS**781 | 149×119 mm. Nos. 777/80 | 12·50 | 12·50 |

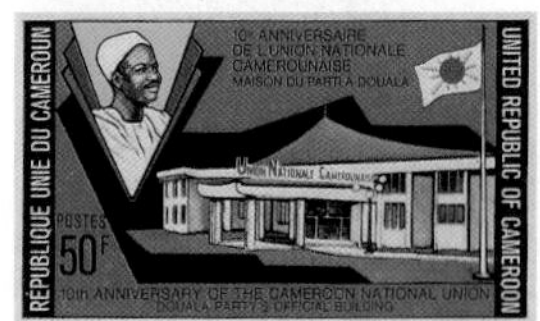
257 Pres. Ahidjo and Douala Party H.Q.

1976. 10th Anniv of Cameroun National Union. Multicoloured.

| | | | |
|---|---|---|---|
| 782 | 50f. Type **257** | 45 | 20 |
| 783 | 50f. Pres. Ahidjo and Yaounde Party H.Q. | 45 | 20 |

258 Bamoun Copper Pipe

1977. 2nd World Festival of Negro Arts, Nigeria. Multicoloured.

| | | | |
|---|---|---|---|
| 784 | 50f. Type **258** (postage) | 75 | 30 |
| 785 | 60f. Traditional chief on throne (sculpture) (air) | 1·10 | 45 |

259 Crowned Cranes ("Crown-Cranes")

1977. Cameroun Birds. Multicoloured.

| | | | |
|---|---|---|---|
| 786 | 30f. Ostrich | 2·50 | 70 |
| 787 | 50f. Type **259** | 2·75 | 80 |

260 "Christ on the Cross" (Issenheim Altarpiece, Mathias Grunewald)

1977. Air. Easter. Multicoloured.

| | | | |
|---|---|---|---|
| 788 | 50f. Type **260** | 95 | 30 |
| 789 | 125f. "Christ on the Cross" (Veslasquez) (vert) | 1·50 | 75 |
| 790 | 150f. "The Entombment" (Titian) | 2·50 | 1·10 |
| **MS**791 | 210×115 mm. Nos. 788/90 | 7·00 | 7·00 |

261 Lions Club Emblem

1977. Air. 19th Congress of Douala Lions Club.

| | | | | |
|---|---|---|---|---|
| 792 | **261** | 250f. multicoloured | 3·50 | 2·10 |

262 Rotary Club Emblem, Mountain and Road

1977. Air. 20th Anniv of Douala Rotary Club.

| | | | | |
|---|---|---|---|---|
| 793 | **262** | 60f. red and blue | 75 | 45 |

263 Jean Mermoz and Seaplane "Comte de la Vaulx"

1977. Air. History of Aviation.

| | | | | |
|---|---|---|---|---|
| 794 | **263** | 50f. blue, orange & brown | 95 | 40 |
| 795 | - | 60f. purple and orange | 95 | 55 |
| 796 | - | 80f. lake and blue | 1·20 | 55 |
| 797 | - | 100f. green and yellow | 1·60 | 80 |
| 798 | - | 300f. blue, red & purple | 5·25 | 2·50 |
| 799 | - | 500f. purple, grn & plum | 7·75 | 4·50 |
| **MS**800 | | Two sheets (a) 170×100 mm. Nos. 794/6; (b) 190×100 mm. Nos. 797/9 | 20·00 | 20·00 |

DESIGNS—VERT: 60f. Antoine de Saint-Exupery and Latecoere 2b. HORIZ: 80f. Maryse Bastie and Caudron C-635 Simoun; 100f. Sikorski S-43 amphibian (1st airmail, Marignane–Douala, 1937); 300f. Concorde; 500f. Charles Lindbergh and "Spirit of St. Louis".

1977. Air. 10th Anniv of International French Language Council. As T **204** of Benin.

| | | | |
|---|---|---|---|
| 801 | 70f. multicoloured | 1·40 | 1·10 |

264 Cameroun 40f. and Basle 2½r. Stamps

1977. "Jufilex" Stamp Exhibition, Berne.

| | | | | |
|---|---|---|---|---|
| 802 | **264** | 50f. multicoloured | 95 | 45 |
| 803 | - | 70f. green, black & brown | 1·30 | 60 |
| 804 | - | 100f. multicoloured | 2·10 | 95 |

DESIGNS: 70f. Zurich 4r. and Kamerun 1m. stamps; 100f. Geneva 5+5c. and Cameroun 20f. stamps.

265 Stafford and "Apollo" Rocket

1977. U.S.A.–U.S.S.R. Space Co-operation. Mult.

| | | | |
|---|---|---|---|
| 805 | 40f. Type **265** (postage) | 45 | 25 |
| 806 | 60f. Leonov and "Soyuz" rocket | 65 | 25 |
| 807 | 100f. Brand and "Apollo" space vehicle (air) | 95 | 45 |
| 808 | 250f. "Apollo–Soyuz" link-up | 2·30 | 1·10 |
| 809 | 350f. Kubasov and "Soyuz" vehicle | 3·25 | 1·50 |
| **MS**810 | 120×81 mm. 500f. Slayton and space handshake | 5·00 | 5·00 |

266 Luge Sledging

1977. Winter Olympics. Innsbruck. Multicoloured.

| | | | |
|---|---|---|---|
| 811 | 40f. Type **266** (postage) | 1·10 | 45 |
| 812 | 50f. Ski-jumping | 1·70 | 45 |
| 813 | 140f. Ski-marathon (air) | 1·20 | 60 |
| 814 | 200f. Ice-hockey | 1·80 | 85 |
| 815 | 350f. Figure-skating | 3·25 | 1·50 |
| **MS**816 | 116×77 mm. 500f. Slalom | 5·00 | 5·00 |

1977. Palestinian Welfare. No. 765 optd **Au bien-etre des familles des martyrs et des combattants pour la liberte de la Palestine. To the Welfare of the families of martyrs and freedom fighters of Palestine.**

| | | | |
|---|---|---|---|
| 817 | 100f. multicoloured | 95 | 55 |

268 Mao Tse-tung and Great Wall of China

1977. 1st Death Anniv of Mao Tse-tung.

| | | | | |
|---|---|---|---|---|
| 818 | **268** | 100f. brown and green | 2·75 | 90 |

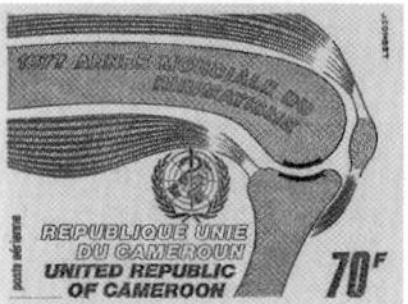
269 Knee Joint

1977. Air. World Rheumatism Year.

| | | | | |
|---|---|---|---|---|
| 819 | **269** | 70f. brown, red & blue | 75 | 30 |

**1977.** Air. 1st Paris–New York Commercial Flight of Concorde. Nos. 798 and 768 optd **PREMIER VOL PARIS-NEW YORK FIRST FLIGHT PARIS-NEW YORK 22 nov. 1977 — 22nd Nov. 1977.**

| | | | | |
|---|---|---|---|---|
| 820 | - | 300f. blue, red & purple | 3·25 | 1·60 |
| 821 | **251** | 500f. multicoloured | 5·00 | 2·50 |

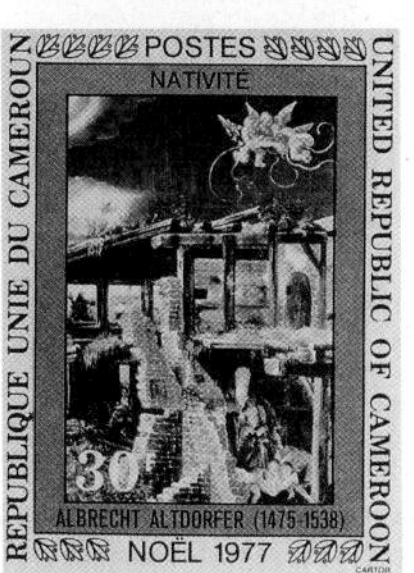


**271** "The Nativity" (Albrecht Altdorfer)

**1977.** Christmas. Multicoloured.

| | | | |
|---|---|---|---|
| 822 | 30f. Type **271** (postage) | 55 | 25 |
| 823 | 50f. "Madonna of the Grand Duke" (Raphael) | 1·10 | 40 |
| 824 | 60f. "Virgin and Child with Four Saints" (Bellini) (horiz) (air) | 1·00 | 45 |
| 825 | 400f. "Adoration of the Shepherds" (G. de la Tour) (horiz) | 5·00 | 2·50 |

**272** Club Flag and Rotary Emblem

**1978.** 20th Anniv of Yaounde Rotary Club.

| | | | | |
|---|---|---|---|---|
| 826 | **272** | 50f. multicoloured | 75 | 30 |

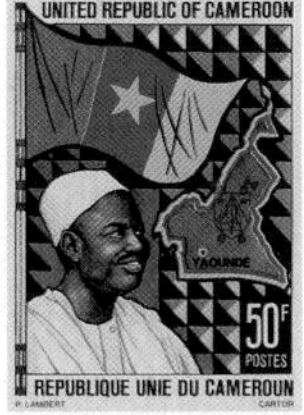


**273** Pres. Ahidjo, Flag and Map

**1978.** New Cameroun Flag. Multicoloured.

| | | | |
|---|---|---|---|
| 827 | 50f. Type **273** (postage) | 90 | 30 |
| 828 | 60f. President, Flag and arms (air) | 75 | 30 |

**274** "Cardioglossa escalerae"

**1978.** Cameroun Frogs. Multicoloured.

| | | | |
|---|---|---|---|
| 829 | 50f. Type **274** (postage) | 1·40 | 55 |
| 830 | 60f. "Cardioglossa elegans" | 2·10 | 80 |
| 831 | 100f. "Cardioglossa trifasciata" (air) | 3·00 | 1·20 |

**275** "L'Arlesienne" (Van Gogh)

**1978.** Air. Paintings. Multicoloured.

| | | | |
|---|---|---|---|
| 832 | 200f. Type **275** | 4·50 | 1·80 |
| 833 | 200f. "Deposition of Christ" (Durer) | 3·50 | 1·10 |

**276** Raoul Follereau and Leprosy Distribution Map

**1978.** Air. World Leprosy Day.

| | | | | |
|---|---|---|---|---|
| 834 | **276** | 100f. multicoloured | 1·20 | 55 |

**277** Capt. Cook and the Siege of Quebec

**1978.** Air. 250th Birth Anniv of Capt. James Cook.

| | | | | |
|---|---|---|---|---|
| 835 | **277** | 100f. green, blue & lilac | 2·10 | 90 |
| 836 | - | 250f. brown, red and lilac | 4·75 | 2·00 |

DESIGN: 250f. Capt. Cook, H.M.S. "Adventure" and H.M.S. "Resolution".

**278** Footballers

**1978.** Air. World Cup Football Championship, Argentina. Multicoloured.

| | | | |
|---|---|---|---|
| 837 | 100f. Argentinian Team (horiz) | 1·00 | 45 |
| 838 | 200f. Type **278** | 2·00 | 95 |
| 839 | 1000f. Football illuminating globe | 10·00 | 5·50 |

**279** Jules Verne and scene from "From the Earth to the Moon"

**1978.** 150th Birth Anniv of Jules Verne (novelist). Multicoloured.

| | | | |
|---|---|---|---|
| 840 | 250f. Type **279** (postage) | 2·30 | 80 |
| 841 | 400f. Portrait and "20,000 Leagues under the Sea" (horiz) (air) | 4·00 | 1·60 |

**280** "Hypolimnas salmacis"

**1978.** Butterflies. Multicoloured.

| | | | |
|---|---|---|---|
| 842 | 20f. Type **280** | 1·40 | 65 |
| 843 | 25f. "Euxanthe trajanus" | 1·80 | 65 |
| 844 | 30f. "Euphaedra cyparissa" | 2·50 | 65 |

**281** Planting Trees

**1978.** Protection against Saharan Encroachment.

| | | | | |
|---|---|---|---|---|
| 845 | **281** | 10f. multicoloured | 30 | 10 |
| 846 | **281** | 15f. multicoloured | 35 | 10 |

**282** Carved Bamoun Drum

**1978.** Musical Instruments. Multicoloured.

| | | | |
|---|---|---|---|
| 847 | 50f. Type **282** (postage) | 45 | 25 |
| 848 | 60f. Gueguerou (horiz) | 80 | 40 |
| 849 | 100f. Mvet Zither (air) | 1·20 | 50 |

**283** Presidents of Cameroun and France with Independence Monument, Douala

**1978.** Visit of President Giscard d'Estaing.

| | | | | |
|---|---|---|---|---|
| 850 | **283** | 60f. multicoloured | 1·40 | 80 |

**284** African, Human Rights Charter and Emblem

**1979.** 30th Anniv of Declaration of Human Rights.

| | | | | |
|---|---|---|---|---|
| 851 | **284** | 5f. mult (postage) | 30 | 10 |
| 852 | **284** | 500f. multicoloured (air) | 6·00 | 2·75 |

See also No. 1070.

**285** Lions Emblem and Map of Cameroon

**1979.** Air. Lions International Congress.

| | | | | |
|---|---|---|---|---|
| 853 | **285** | 60f. multicoloured | 75 | 40 |

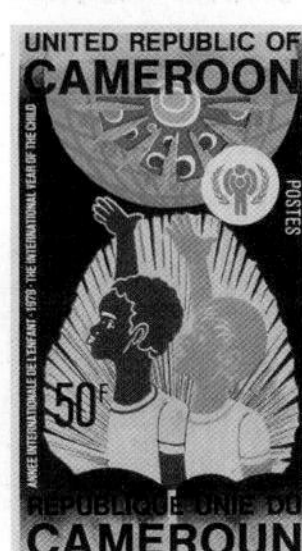


**286** Globe, Emblem and Waving Children

**1979.** International Year of the Child.

| | | | | |
|---|---|---|---|---|
| 854 | **286** | 50f. multicoloured | 75 | 25 |

**287** Penny Black, Rowland Hill and German Cameroun 10pf. Stamp

**1979.** Air. Death Cent of Sir Rowland Hill.

| | | | | |
|---|---|---|---|---|
| 855 | **287** | 100f. black, red & turq | 1·20 | 60 |

**288** Black Rhinoceros

**1979.** Endangered Animals (1st series). Mult.

| | | | |
|---|---|---|---|
| 856 | 50f. Type **288** | 1·30 | 35 |
| 857 | 60f. Giraffe (vert) | 1·70 | 45 |
| 858 | 60f. Gorilla | 1·70 | 45 |
| 859 | 100f. African elephant (vert) | 2·75 | 65 |
| 860 | 100f. Leopard | 2·75 | 65 |

See also Nos. 891/2, 904/6, 975/7, 939/40 and 1007/8.

**289** "Telecom 79"

**1979.** Air. 3rd World Telecommunications Exhibition, Geneva.

| | | | | |
|---|---|---|---|---|
| 861 | **289** | 100f. orange, blue & grey | 1·20 | 60 |

**290** Pope John Paul II

**1979.** Air. Popes.

| | | | | |
|---|---|---|---|---|
| 862 | **290** | 100f. blue, violet & grn | 2·30 | 80 |
| 863 | - | 100f. brown, red & green | 2·30 | 80 |
| 864 | - | 100f. chestnut, olive & grn | 2·30 | 80 |

DESIGNS: No. 863, Pope John Paul I. No. 864, Pope Paul VI.

**291** Dr. Jamot, Map and "Glossina palpalis"

**1979.** Birth Centenary of Dr. Eugene Jamot (discoverer of sleeping sickness cure).

| | | | | |
|---|---|---|---|---|
| 865 | **291** | 50f. brown, blue and red | 2·75 | 70 |

**292** "The Annunciation" (Fra Filippo Lippi)

**1979.** Christmas. Multicoloured.

| | | | |
|---|---|---|---|
| 866 | 10f. Type **292** | 10 | 10 |
| 867 | 50f. "Rest during the Flight into Egypt" (Antwerp Master) | 45 | 10 |
| 868 | 60f. "The Nativity" (Kalkar) | 80 | 25 |
| 869 | 60f. "The Flight into Egypt" (Kalkar) | 80 | 25 |

870 100f. "The Nativity" (Boticelli) 1·60 45

**293** "Double Eagle II" and Balloonists

**1979.** Air. 1st Atlantic Crossing by Balloon. Multicoloured.
871 500f. Type **293** 5·25 2·00
872 500f. "Double Eagle II" over Atlantic and balloonists in basket 5·25 2·00

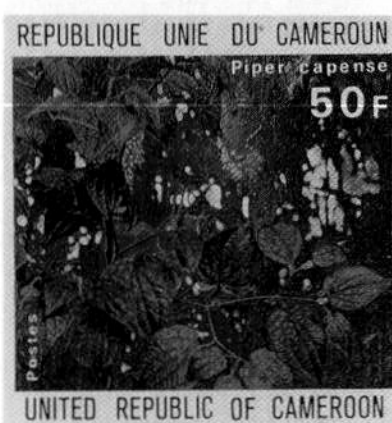

**294** "Piper capense"

**1979.** Medicinal Plants. Multicoloured.
873 50f. Type **294** 1·10 25
874 60f. "Pteridium aquilinum" 1·30 25

**295** Pres. Ahidjo, Map, Independence Stamp and Arms

**1980.** 20th Anniv of Independence.
875 **295** 50f. multicoloured 60 25

**296** Congress Building

**1980.** 3rd Ordinary Congress of Cameroun National Union, Bafoussam.
876 **296** 50f. multicoloured 60 25

**297** Globe

**1980.** 75th Anniv of Rotary International. Mult.
877 200f. Type **297** 2·20 90
878 200f. Map of Cameroun 2·20 90
**MS**879 179×140 mm. Nos. 877/8 plus 8 labels 5·00 5·00

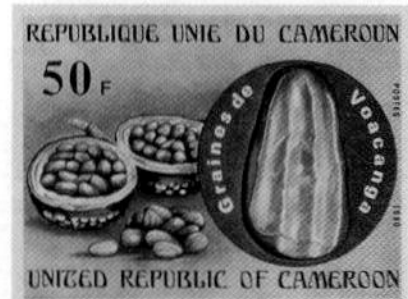

**298** Voacanga Fruit and Seeds

**1980.** Medicinal Plants. Multicoloured.
880 50f. Type **298** 65 10
881 60f. Voacanga tree 75 10
882 100f. Voacanga flowers 1·10 25

**299** "Dissotis perkinsiae"

**1980.** Flowers. Multicoloured.
883 50f. Type **299** 70 10
884 60f. "Brillantaisia" sp. 1·00 20
885 100f. "Clerodendron splendens" 1·70 45

**300** Ka'aba, Mecca

**1980.** 1350th Anniv of Mohammed's Occupation of Mecca.
886 **300** 50f. multicoloured 95 40

**301** Ice Skating

**1980.** Air. Olympic Games, Moscow and Lake Placid.
887 - 100f. brown and ochre 95 45
888 **301** 150f. brown and blue 1·30 60
889 - 200f. brown and green 2·00 75
890 - 300f. brown and red 2·50 1·30
DESIGNS: 100f. Running; 200f. Throwing the Javelin; 300f. Wrestling.

**302** Crocodile

**1980.** Endangered Animals (2nd series). Mult.
891 200f. Type **302** 3·00 80
892 300f. Kob 4·00 1·30

**303** Bororo Girls and Roumsiki Peak

**1980.** Tourism. Multicoloured.
893 50f. Type **303** 55 25
894 60f. Dschang tourist centre 55 25

**304** Banana Trees

**1981.** Bertona Agricultural Research Station. Multicoloured.
895 50f. Type **304** 65 10
896 60f. Cattle in watering hole 85 25

**305** Girl on Crutches

**1981.** Int Year of Disabled People. Multicoloured.
897 60f. Type **305** 55 25
898 150f. Boy in wheelchair 1·40 65

**306** Camair Headquarters, Douala

**1981.** 10th Anniv of Cameroun Airlines. Mult.
899 100f. Type **306** 95 35
900 200f. Boeing 747 "Mount Cameroun" 2·00 75
901 300f. Douala International Airport 3·00 1·10

**307** Presentation African Club Champions Cup

**1981.** Football Victories of Cameroun Clubs. Multicoloured.
902 60f. Type **307** 95 45
903 60f. Cup presentation (African Cup Winner's Cup) 95 45

**308** African Buffalo

**1981.** Endangered Animals (3rd series). Mult.
904 50f. Type **308** 1·50 45
905 50f. Cameroun tortoise 1·50 45
906 100f. Long-tailed pangolin 3·00 50

**309** Prince Charles, Lady Diana Spencer and St. Paul's Cathedral

**1981.** Wedding of Prince of Wales. Multicoloured.
907 500f. Type **309** 4·50 1·90
908 500f. Prince Charles, Lady Diana and Royal Coach 4·50 1·90
**MS**909 145×94 mm. Nos. 907/8 10·00 10·00

**310** Bafoussam–Bamenda Road

**1981.** Tourism.
910 **310** 50f. multicoloured 55 25

**311** Yuri Gagarin and "Vostok 1"

**1981.** 20th Anniv of 1st Men in Space. Mult.
911 500f. Type **311** 5·00 1·70
912 500f. Alan Shepard and "Freedom 7" 5·00 1·70

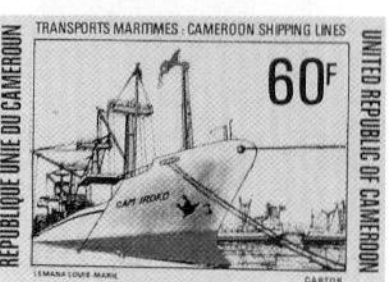

**312** "Cam Iroko" (freighter) in Harbour

**1981.** Cameroun Shipping Lines.
913 **312** 60f. multicoloured 95 40

**313** Scout Salute and Badge within Knotted Rope, and National Flag

**1981.** Air. 4th African Scouting Conference, Abidjan. Multicoloured.
914 100f. Type **313** 95 40
915 500f. Saluting Girl Guide 4·50 1·80

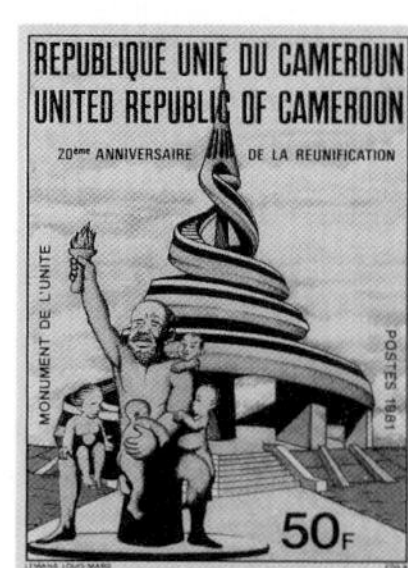

**314** Unity Monument

**1981.** 20th Anniv of Reunification.
916 **314** 50f. multicoloured 60 25

**315** "L'Estaque" (Cezanne)

**1981.** Air. Paintings. Multicoloured.
917 500f. Type **315** 6·00 1·80
918 500f. "Guernica" (detail) (Picasso) 6·00 1·80

**316** "Virgin and Child" (detail of San Zeno altarpiece, Mantegna)

**1981.** Air. Christmas. Paintings. Multicoloured.

| | | | |
|---|---|---|---|
| 919 | 50f. "Virgin and Child" (detail, "The Burning Bush") (Nicholas Froment) | 45 | 10 |
| 920 | 60f. Type **316** | 60 | 25 |
| 921 | 400f. "The Flight into Egypt" (Giotto) (horiz) | 3·50 | 1·30 |
| **MS**922 | 190×111 mm. Nos. 919/21 | 7·75 | 7·75 |

**317** "Voacanga thouarsii"

**1981.** Medicinal Plants. Multicoloured.

| | | | |
|---|---|---|---|
| 923 | 60f. Type **317** | 1·00 | 35 |
| 924 | 70f. "Cassia alata" | 1·30 | 50 |

**318** "Descent from the Cross" (detail, Giotto)

**1982.** Easter. Paintings. Multicoloured.

| | | | |
|---|---|---|---|
| 925 | 100f. "Christ in the Garden of Olives" (Eugene Delacroix) | 1·00 | 30 |
| 926 | 200f. Type **318** | 1·90 | 70 |
| 927 | 250f. "Pieta in the Countryside" (Bellini) | 2·30 | 80 |

**319** Carving, Giraffes and Map

**1982.** "Philexfrance 82" International Stamp Exhibition, Paris.

| | | | | |
|---|---|---|---|---|
| 928 | **319** | 90f. multicoloured | 1·50 | 35 |

**320** Clay Water Jug

**1982.** Local Handicrafts. Multicoloured.

| | | | |
|---|---|---|---|
| 929 | 60f. Python-skin handbag | 60 | 25 |
| 930 | 70f. Type **320** | 80 | 25 |

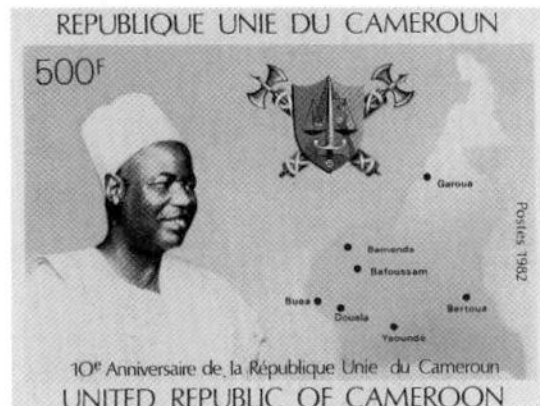


**321** Pres. Ahidjo, Map and Arms

**1982.** 10th Anniv of United Republic.

| | | | | |
|---|---|---|---|---|
| 931 | **321** | 500f. multicoloured | 5·25 | 1·70 |

**322** Douala Town Hall

**1982.** Town Halls. Multicoloured.

| | | | |
|---|---|---|---|
| 932 | 40f. Type **322** | 45 | 10 |
| 933 | 60f. Yaounde town hall | 60 | 25 |

See also No. 1139.

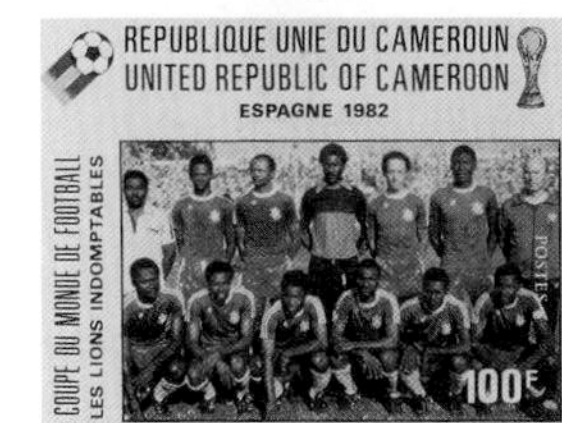


**323** Cameroun Football Team

**1982.** World Cup Football Championship, Spain. Multicoloured.

| | | | |
|---|---|---|---|
| 934 | 100f. Type **323** | 1·50 | 45 |
| 935 | 200f. Cameroun and Algerian teams | 3·00 | 75 |
| 936 | 300f. Nkono Thomas, Cameroun goalkeeper | 4·50 | 1·00 |
| 937 | 400f. Cameroun team (different) | 6·00 | 1·50 |
| **MS**938 | 216×95 mm. No. 937×2 | 15·00 | 15·00 |

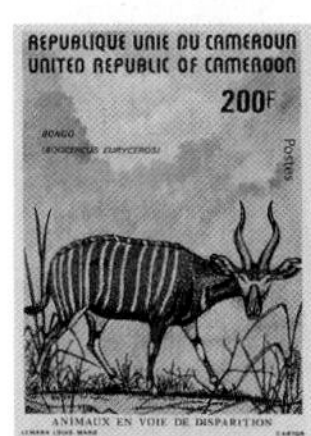


**324** Bongo

**1982.** Endangered Animals (4th series). Mult.

| | | | |
|---|---|---|---|
| 939 | 200f. Type **324** | 3·00 | 80 |
| 940 | 300f. Black colobus | 4·25 | 1·30 |

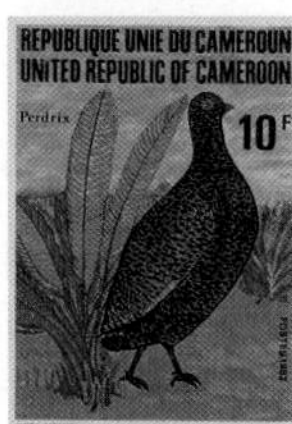


**325** Cameroun Mountain Francolin ("Perdrix")

**1982.** Birds. Multicoloured.

| | | | |
|---|---|---|---|
| 941 | 10f. Type **325** | 1·80 | 35 |
| 942 | 15f. Red-eyed dove ("Tourterelle") | 2·10 | 60 |
| 943 | 20f. Barn swallow ("Hirondelle") | 3·00 | 80 |

See also No. 1071.

**326** Scouts round Campfire

**1982.** 75th Anniv of Boy Scout Movement. Multicoloured.

| | | | |
|---|---|---|---|
| 944 | 200f. Type **326** | 2·30 | 80 |
| 945 | 400f. Lord Baden-Powell | 4·00 | 1·60 |

**327** ITU Emblem

**1982.** ITU Delegates' Conference, Nairobi.

| | | | | |
|---|---|---|---|---|
| 946 | **327** | 70f. multicoloured | 75 | 25 |

**328** Nyasoso Chapel

**1982.** 25th Anniv of Presbyterian Church. Multicoloured.

| | | | |
|---|---|---|---|
| 947 | 45f. Buea Chapel | 50 | 25 |
| 948 | 60f. Type **328** | 75 | 25 |

**329** World Cup, Footballers and Globe

**1982.** World Cup Football Championship Result.

| | | | | |
|---|---|---|---|---|
| 949 | **329** | 500f. multicoloured | 5·25 | 2·20 |
| 950 | **329** | 1000f. multicoloured | 10·50 | 3·50 |

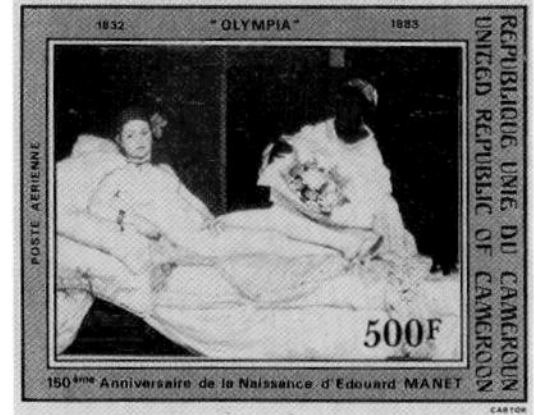


**330** "Olympia" (Edouard Manet)

**1982.** Air. Artists' Anniversaries. Multicoloured.

| | | | |
|---|---|---|---|
| 951 | 500f. Type **330** (150th birth anniv) | 5·50 | 2·10 |
| 952 | 500f. "Still-life" (Georges Braque, birth centenary) | 5·50 | 2·10 |

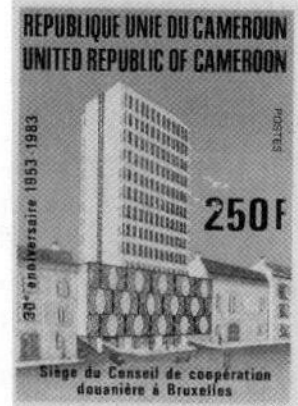


**331** Council Headquarters, Brussels

**1983.** 30th Anniv of Customs Co-operation Council. Multicoloured.

| | | | |
|---|---|---|---|
| 953 | 250f. Type **331** | 2·30 | 1·10 |
| 954 | 250f. Council emblem | 2·30 | 1·10 |

**332** Yaounde University Hospital

**1983.** Second Yaounde Medical Days.

| | | | | |
|---|---|---|---|---|
| 955 | **332** | 60f. multicoloured | 75 | 25 |
| 956 | **332** | 70f. multicoloured | 95 | 25 |

**333** Pres. Kennedy

**1983.** Air. 20th Death Anniv of John F. Kennedy (U.S. President).

| | | | | |
|---|---|---|---|---|
| 957 | **333** | 500f. multicoloured | 5·00 | 2·20 |

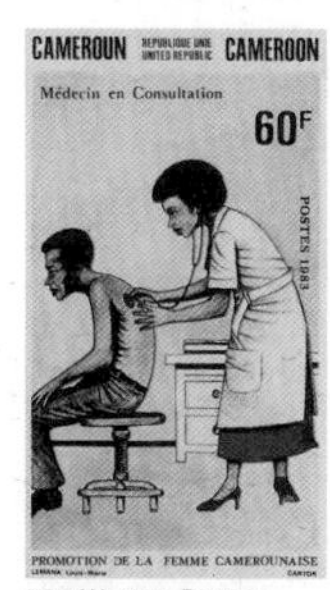


**334** Woman Doctor

**1983.** Cameroun Women. Multicoloured.

| | | | |
|---|---|---|---|
| 958 | 60f. Type **334** | 75 | 25 |
| 959 | 70f. Woman lawyer | 75 | 25 |

**335** Lions Emblem and Map

**1983.** Air. District 403 of Lions International Convention, Douala.

| | | | | |
|---|---|---|---|---|
| 960 | **335** | 70f. multicoloured | 65 | 25 |
| 961 | **335** | 150f. multicoloured | 1·10 | 65 |

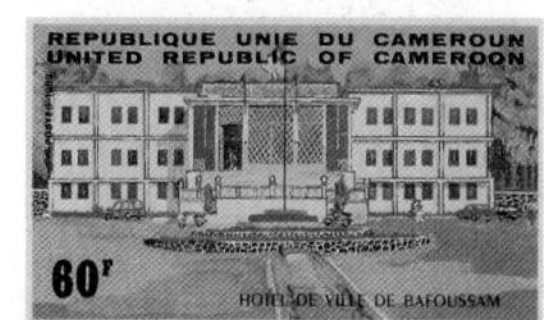


**336** Bafoussam Town Hall

**1983.** Town Halls. Multicoloured.

| | | | |
|---|---|---|---|
| 962 | 60f. Type **336** | 65 | 25 |
| 963 | 70f. Garoua town hall | 75 | 25 |

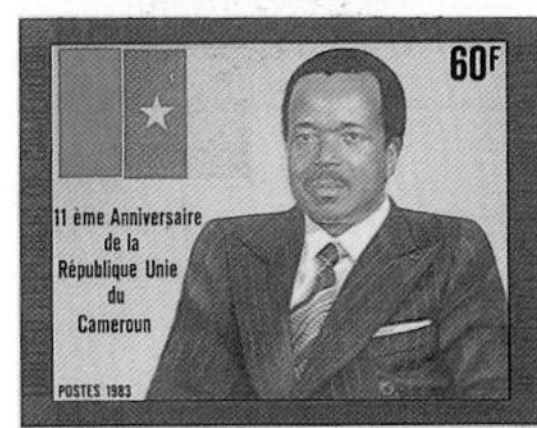


**337** President Biya and National Flag

**1983.** 11th Anniv of United Republic. Mult.

| | | | |
|---|---|---|---|
| 964 | 60f. Type **337** | 55 | 20 |
| 965 | 70f. Pres. Biya and national arms | 75 | 25 |

**338** Container Ship and Buoy

**1983.** 25th Anniv of IMO.

| | | | | |
|---|---|---|---|---|
| 966 | **338** | 500f. multicoloured | 5·00 | 2·10 |

**339** Martial Eagle ("L'Aigle Martial")

**1983.** Birds. Multicoloured.

| | | | |
|---|---|---|---|
| 967 | 25f. Type **339** | 1·10 | 45 |
| 968 | 30f. Rufous-breasted sparrow hawk ("L'Epervier") | 1·50 | 60 |
| 969 | 50f. Purple heron ("Le Heron Pourpre") | 2·75 | 80 |

See also Nos. 1157 and 1169.

**340** Bread Mask ("Wery-Nwen-Nto")

**1983.** Cameroun Artists. Multicoloured.

| | | | |
|---|---|---|---|
| 970 | 60f. Type **340** | 75 | 20 |
| 971 | 70f. Basket with lid ("Chechia Bamoun") | 95 | 25 |

**341** Mobile Rural Post Office

**1983.** World Communications Year. Multicoloured.

| | | | |
|---|---|---|---|
| 972 | 90f. Type **341** | 95 | 30 |
| 973 | 150f. Radio operator with morse key | 1·50 | 50 |
| 974 | 250f. Tom-tom drums | 2·75 | 85 |

**342** African Civet

**1983.** Endangered Animals (5th series). Mult.

| | | | |
|---|---|---|---|
| 975 | 200f. Type **342** | 2·75 | 75 |
| 976 | 200f. Gorilla | 2·75 | 75 |
| 977 | 350f. Guinea-pig (vert) | 4·50 | 1·50 |

See also No. 1170.

**343** "Jeanne d'Aragon" (Raphael)

**1983.** Air. Paintings. Multicoloured.

| | | | |
|---|---|---|---|
| 978 | 500f. Type **343** | 5·50 | 1·90 |
| 979 | 500f. "Massacre of Scio" (Delacroix) | 5·50 | 1·90 |

**344** Lake Tizon

**1983.** Landscapes. Multicoloured.

| | | | |
|---|---|---|---|
| 980 | 60f. Type **344** | 55 | 20 |
| 981 | 70f. Mount Cameroun in eruption | 75 | 25 |

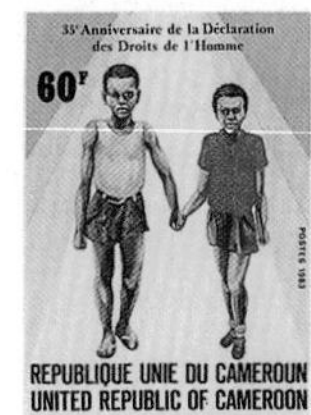

**345** Boy and Girl holding Hands

**1983.** 35th Anniv of Declaration of Human Rights.

| | | | | |
|---|---|---|---|---|
| 982 | **345** | 60f. multicoloured | 55 | 20 |
| 983 | **345** | 70f. multicoloured | 75 | 20 |

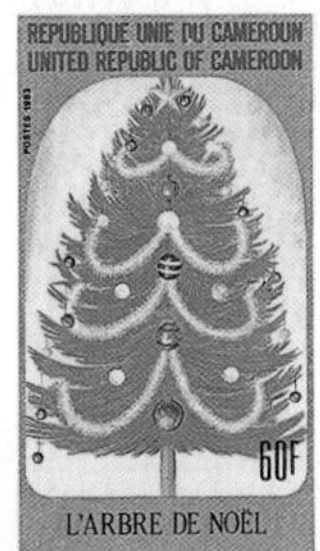

**346** Christmas Tree

**1983.** Christmas. Multicoloured.

| | | | |
|---|---|---|---|
| 984 | 60f. Type **346** | 50 | 20 |
| 985 | 200f. Stained-glass window, Yaounde Cathedral | 1·80 | 75 |
| 986 | 500f. Statue of angel, Reims Cathedral | 4·75 | 1·70 |
| 987 | 500f. "The Rest on the Flight into Egypt" (Philipp Otto Runge) (horiz) | 4·75 | 1·70 |
| **MS**988 | 140×89 mm. Nos. 985/7 | 12·00 | 12·00 |

**348** "Pieta" (G. Hernandez)

**1984.** Air. Easter. Multicoloured.

| | | | |
|---|---|---|---|
| 992 | 200f. Type **348** | 2·00 | 75 |
| 993 | 500f. "Martyrdom of St. John the Evangelist" (C. le Brun) | 5·00 | 2·20 |
| **MS**994 | 160×104 mm. Nos. 992/3 | 8·25 | 8·25 |

**349** Urban Council Building, Bamenda

**1984.** Town Halls. Multicoloured.

| | | | |
|---|---|---|---|
| 995 | 60f. Type **349** | 60 | 25 |
| 996 | 70f. Mbalmayo | 75 | 35 |

**350** High Jump

**1984.** Air. Olympic Games, Los Angeles. Mult.

| | | | |
|---|---|---|---|
| 997 | 100f. Type **350** | 95 | 40 |
| 998 | 150f. Volleyball | 1·40 | 60 |
| 999 | 250f. Basketball | 2·30 | 90 |
| 1000 | 500f. Cycling | 4·50 | 1·80 |

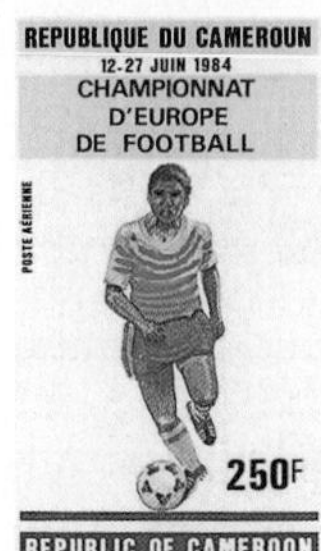

**351** Running with Ball

**1984.** Air. European Football Championship. Multicoloured.

| | | | |
|---|---|---|---|
| 1001 | 250f. Type **351** | 2·30 | 90 |
| 1002 | 250f. Heading ball | 2·30 | 45 |
| 1003 | 500f. Tackle | 4·50 | 1·80 |
| **MS**1004 | 130×85 mm. As Nos. 1001/3, but with the background colours different | 11·00 | 11·00 |

**352** Catholic Church, Zoetele

**1984.** Churches. Multicoloured.

| | | | |
|---|---|---|---|
| 1005 | 60f. Type **352** | 55 | 25 |
| 1006 | 70f. Marie Gocker Protestant Church, Yaounde | 75 | 40 |

**353** Antelope

**1984.** Endangered Animals (6th series). Mult.

| | | | |
|---|---|---|---|
| 1007 | 250f. Type **353** | 3·50 | 1·10 |
| 1008 | 250f. Wild boar | 3·50 | 1·10 |

**354** Pres. Biya and Arms

**1984.** Air. President's Oath-taking Ceremony. (a) Inscr in French.

| | | | | |
|---|---|---|---|---|
| 1009 | **354** | 60f. multicoloured | 45 | 25 |
| 1010 | **354** | 70f. multicoloured | 55 | 25 |
| 1011 | **354** | 200f. multicoloured | 2·00 | 70 |

(b) Inscr in English.

| | | | |
|---|---|---|---|
| 1012 | 60f. multicoloured | 50 | 25 |
| 1013 | 70f. multicoloured | 75 | 25 |
| 1014 | 200f. multicoloured | 2·00 | 70 |

**355** "Diana Bathing" (Watteau)

**1984.** Air. Anniversaries. Multicoloured.

| | | | |
|---|---|---|---|
| 1015 | 500f. Type **355** (300th birth anniv) (wrongly inscr "1624") | 5·75 | 1·90 |
| 1016 | 500f. Diderot (encyclopaedist, death bicentenary) | 5·75 | 1·90 |

**1984.** Air. Olympic Games Medal Winners. Nos. 997/1000 optd.

| | | | |
|---|---|---|---|
| 1017 | 100f. **MOEGENBURG (R.F.A.) 11-08-84** | 95 | 50 |
| 1018 | 150f. **U.S.A. 11-08-84** | 1·40 | 70 |
| 1019 | 250f. **YOUGOSLAVIE 9-08-84** | 2·30 | 1·10 |
| 1020 | 500f. **GORSKI (U.S.A.) 3-08-84** | 4·50 | 2·20 |

**357** Nightingale ("Le Rossignol")

**1984.** Birds. Multicoloured.

| | | | |
|---|---|---|---|
| 1021 | 60f. Type **357** | 3·00 | 80 |
| 1022 | 60f. Ruppell's griffon ("Le Vautour") | 3·00 | 80 |

See also No. 1158.

**358** Neil Armstrong

**1984.** Air. 15th Anniv of 1st Man on the Moon. Multicoloured.

| | | | |
|---|---|---|---|
| 1023 | 500f. Type **358** | 5·00 | 1·90 |
| 1024 | 500f. Launching of "Apollo 12" | 5·00 | 1·90 |

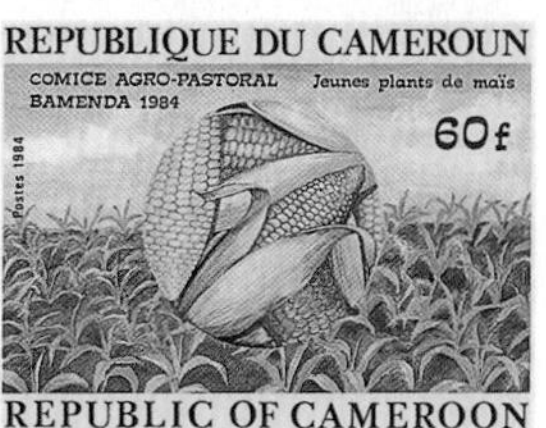

**359** Maize and Young Plants

**1984.** Agro-pastoral Fair. Bamenda. Mult.

| | | | |
|---|---|---|---|
| 1025 | 60f. Type **359** | 65 | 25 |
| 1026 | 70f. Zebus | 75 | 30 |
| 1027 | 300f. Potatoes | 3·50 | 1·30 |

**360** Anniversary Emblem

**1984.** 40th Anniv of ICAO.

| | | | | |
|---|---|---|---|---|
| 1028 | - | 200f. multicoloured | 1·90 | 90 |
| 1029 | **360** | 200f. blue & deep blue | 1·90 | 90 |
| 1030 | - | 300f. multicoloured | 2·75 | 1·40 |

1031 - 300f. multicoloured 3·50 1·50

DESIGNS: No. 1028, "Icarus" (Hans Herni); 1030, Cameroun Airlines Boeing 737; 1031, "Solar Princess" (Sadiou Diouf).

**361** Wrestling

**1985.** "Olymphilex '85" International Thematic Stamps Exhibition, Lausanne.

1032 **361** 150f. multicoloured 1·50 70

**362** Balafons (xylophone)

**1985.** Musical Instruments. Multicoloured.

| | | | |
|---|---|---|---|
| 1033 | 60f. Type **362** | 65 | 20 |
| 1034 | 70f. Mvet (stringed instrument) | 85 | 30 |
| 1035 | 100f. Flute | 1·40 | 40 |

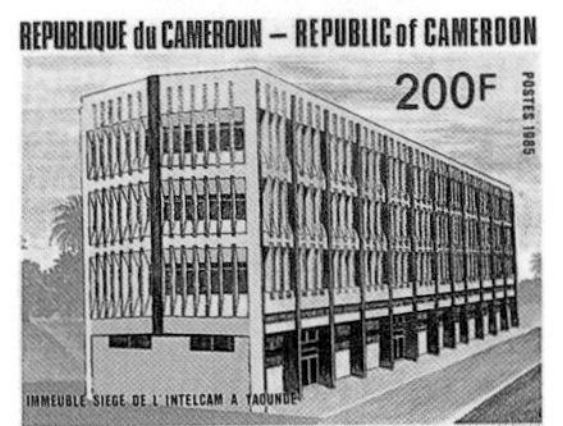


**363** Intelcam Headquarters, Yaounde

**1985.** 20th Anniv of Int Telecommunications Satellite Consortium.

| | | | | |
|---|---|---|---|---|
| 1036 | - | 125f. black, orange & bl | 1·70 | 60 |
| 1037 | **363** | 200f. multicoloured | 2·20 | 90 |

DESIGN: 125f. "Intelsat V" satellite.

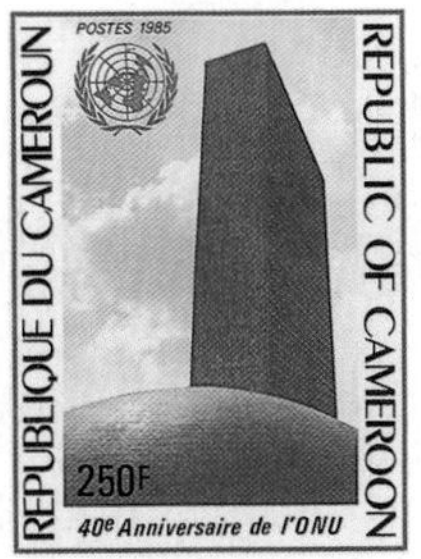


**365** U.N. Emblem and Headquarters

**1985.** 40th Anniv of UNO.

| | | | | |
|---|---|---|---|---|
| 1038 | **365** | 250f. multicoloured | 2·50 | 1·00 |
| 1039 | **365** | 500f. multicoloured | 5·00 | 2·00 |

**366** French and Cameroun Flags and Presidents

**1985.** President Mitterrand of France's Visit to Cameroun.

(a) Inscr "Mitterand" in error.

| | | |
|---|---|---|
| 1040 | **366** | 60f. multicoloured |
| 1041 | **366** | 70f. multicoloured |

(b) Inscr corrected to "Mitterrand".

| | | | |
|---|---|---|---|
| 1041a | 60f. multicoloured | 1·40 | 45 |
| 1041b | 70f. multicoloured | 1·40 | 45 |

**367** UNICEF Emblem

**1985.** Child Survival Campaign.

| | | | | |
|---|---|---|---|---|
| 1042 | **367** | 60f. black, blue & yell | 65 | 25 |
| 1043 | - | 300f. multicoloured | 3·00 | 1·30 |

DESIGN: Doctor inoculating babies.

**368** Lake Barumbi, Kumba

**1985.** Landscapes. Multicoloured.

| | | | |
|---|---|---|---|
| 1044 | 60f. Type **368** | 80 | 25 |
| 1045 | 70f. Pygmy village, Bonando | 80 | 30 |
| 1046 | 150f. River Cameroun | 1·60 | 65 |

**369** Ebolowa Town Hall

**1985.** Town Halls. Multicoloured.

| | | | |
|---|---|---|---|
| 1047 | 60f. Type **369** | 55 | 25 |
| 1048 | 60f. Ngaoundere town hall | 55 | 25 |

**370** Pope John Paul II

**1985.** Papal Visit to Cameroun. Multicoloured.

| | | | |
|---|---|---|---|
| 1049 | 60f. Type **370** | 1·00 | 40 |
| 1050 | 70f. Pope John Paul II holding crucifix | 1·30 | 70 |
| 1051 | 200f. Pres. Biya and Pope John Paul II | 3·50 | 1·70 |
| **MS**1052 | 137×100 mm. Nos. 1049/51 | 6·75 | 6·75 |

**371** Porcupine

**1985.** Animals. Multicoloured.

| | | | |
|---|---|---|---|
| 1053 | 125f. Type **371** | 1·40 | 55 |
| 1054 | 200f. Squirrel | 2·20 | 90 |
| 1055 | 350f. Greater cane rat | 3·75 | 1·60 |

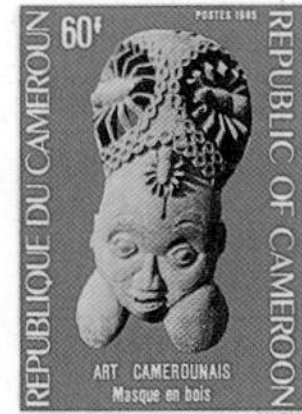


**372** Wooden Mask

**1985.** Cameroun Art (1st series). Multicoloured.

| | | | |
|---|---|---|---|
| 1056 | 60f. Type **372** | 65 | 20 |
| 1057 | 70f. Wooden mask (different) | 80 | 30 |
| 1058 | 100f. Men using pestle and mortar (wooden bas-relief) | 1·40 | 75 |

See also Nos. 1081/3.

**373** "Tomb of Henri Claude d'Harcourt" (detail)

**1985.** Air. Death Anniversaries. Multicoloured.

| | | | |
|---|---|---|---|
| 1059 | 500f. Type **373** (bicentenary Jean Baptiste Pigalle (sculptor)) | 5·75 | 2·30 |
| 1060 | 500f. Louis Pasteur (bacteriologist, 90th anniv) (after Edelfelt) | 5·75 | 2·30 |

**374** Yellow-casqued Hornbill ("Le Toucan")

**1985.** Birds. Multicoloured.

| | | | |
|---|---|---|---|
| 1061 | 140f. Type **374** | 2·00 | 70 |
| 1062 | 150f. Cock | 2·10 | 70 |
| 1063 | 200f. European robins ("Le Rouge-gorge") | 3·00 | 1·10 |

See also No. 1156.

**375** Child's Toys

**1985.** Air. Christmas. Multicoloured.

| | | | |
|---|---|---|---|
| 1064 | 250f. Type **375** | 2·30 | 1·00 |
| 1065 | 300f. Akono church | 2·75 | 1·30 |
| 1066 | 400f. Christmas crib | 3·25 | 1·70 |
| 1067 | 500f. "The Virgin of the Blue Diadem" (Raphael) | 5·00 | 2·30 |

**376** Emblem, Flag and Volunteers

**1986.** 25th Anniv of American Peace Corps in Cameroun.

| | | | | |
|---|---|---|---|---|
| 1068 | **376** | 70f. multicoloured | 75 | 30 |
| 1069 | **376** | 100f. multicoloured | 1·00 | 45 |

**1986.** As Nos. 851 and 941 but inscr "Republique du Cameroun/Republic of Cameroon".

| | | | | |
|---|---|---|---|---|
| 1070 | **284** | 5f. multicoloured | 25 | 10 |
| 1071 | **325** | 10f. multicoloured | 45 | 10 |

**377** "Virgin Mary" (Pierre Prud'hon)

**1986.** Easter. Multicoloured.

| | | | |
|---|---|---|---|
| 1072 | 210f. Type **377** | 2·00 | 95 |
| 1073 | 350f. "Stoning of St. Stephen" (Van Scorel) | 3·00 | 1·50 |

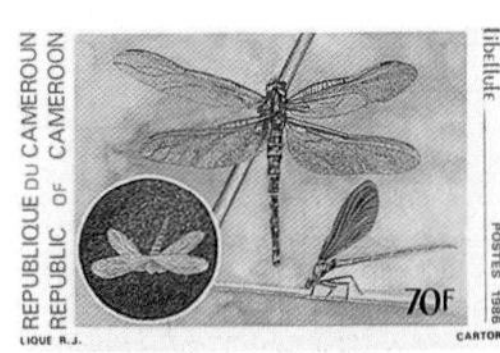


**378** "Anax sp."

**1986.** Insects. Multicoloured.

| | | | |
|---|---|---|---|
| 1074 | 70f. Type **378** | 1·20 | 45 |
| 1075 | 70f. Bee on flower (vert) | 1·30 | 50 |
| 1076 | 100f. Grasshopper | 1·90 | 70 |

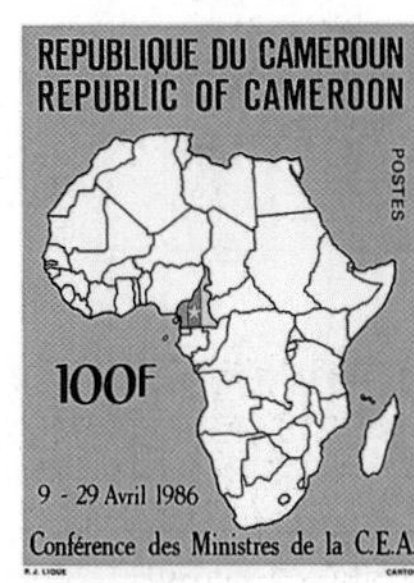


**379** Map of Africa

**1986.** Economic Commission for Africa Ministers' Conference. Multicoloured.

| | | | |
|---|---|---|---|
| 1077 | 100f. Type **379** | 1·00 | 55 |
| 1078 | 175f. Members' flags | 2·10 | 85 |

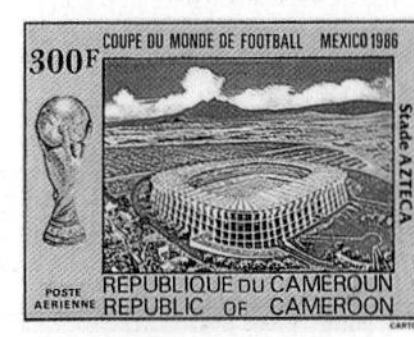


**380** Azteca Stadium

**1986.** Air. World Cup Football Championship, Mexico. Multicoloured.

| | | | |
|---|---|---|---|
| 1079 | 300f. Type **380** | 2·75 | 1·40 |
| 1080 | 400f. Mexico team | 3·75 | 1·70 |

**1986.** Cameroun Art (2nd series). As T 372. Multicoloured.

| | | | |
|---|---|---|---|
| 1081 | 70f. Copper Statuette | 65 | 30 |
| 1082 | 100f. Wooden ash-tray | 95 | 35 |
| 1083 | 130f. Wooden horseman | 1·70 | 55 |

**381** Queen Elizabeth

**1986.** 60th Birthday of Queen Elizabeth II. Multicoloured.

| | | | |
|---|---|---|---|
| 1084 | 100f. Type **381** | 1·10 | 50 |
| 1085 | 175f. Queen and President Biya | 1·60 | 80 |
| 1086 | 210f. Queen Elizabeth (different) | 2·10 | 1·00 |

**382** President Biya

**1986.** 1st Anniv of Cameroun Republic Democratic Party. Multicoloured.

| No. | Description | Unused | Used |
|---|---|---|---|
| 1087 | 70f. Type **382** | 80 | 30 |
| 1088 | 70f. Bamenda Party headquarters (horiz) | 80 | 30 |
| 1089 | 100f. President Biya making speech | 1·00 | 40 |

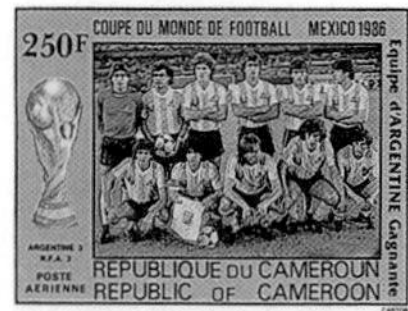

**383** Argentine Team

**1986.** Air. World Cup Football Championship Winners.

| No. | Type | Description | Unused | Used |
|---|---|---|---|---|
| 1090 | **383** | 250f. multicoloured | 3·00 | 1·40 |

**384** Mask Dancer with Sword

**1986.** Traditional Dances of North-west Kwem. Multicoloured.

| No. | Description | Unused | Used |
|---|---|---|---|
| 1091 | 100f. Type **384** | 1·00 | 55 |
| 1092 | 130f. Mask dancer with rattle | 1·40 | 70 |

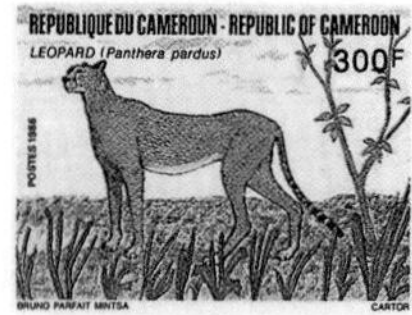

**385** Cheetah

**1986.** Endangered Animals (7th series). Mult.

| No. | Description | Unused | Used |
|---|---|---|---|
| 1093 | 300f. Type **385** | 3·25 | 1·50 |
| 1094 | 300f. Varan | 3·25 | 1·50 |

**386** Bishop Desmond Tutu (Nobel Peace Prize Winner)

**1986.** International Peace Year. Multicoloured.

| No. | Description | Unused | Used |
|---|---|---|---|
| 1095 | 175f. Type **386** | 1·90 | 80 |
| 1096 | 200f. Type **386** | 2·10 | 95 |
| 1097 | 250f. I.P.Y. and U.N. emblems | 2·40 | 1·20 |

**387** Pierre Curie (physicist)

**1986.** Air. Death Anniversaries. Multicoloured.

| No. | Description | Unused | Used |
|---|---|---|---|
| 1098 | 500f. Type **387** (80th anniv) | 6·75 | 2·50 |
| 1099 | 500f. Jean Mermoz and "Arc en Ciel" (aviation pioneer, 50th anniv) | 6·75 | 2·50 |

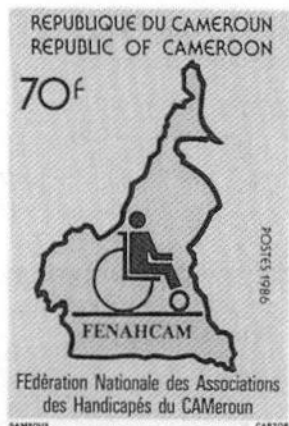

**388** Emblem

**1986.** National Federation of Cameroun Handicapped Associations.

| No. | Type | Description | Unused | Used |
|---|---|---|---|---|
| 1100 | **388** | 70f. yellow and red | 70 | 25 |

**389** Man holding Syringe and National Flag "Umbrella" over Woman and Child

**1986.** African Vaccination Year.

| No. | Description | Unused | Used |
|---|---|---|---|
| 1101 | 70f. Type **389** | 85 | 30 |
| 1102 | 100f. Flag behind woman holding child being immunised | 1·00 | 45 |

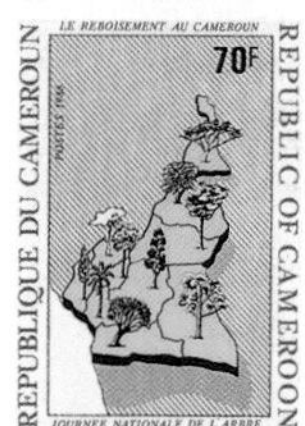

**390** Trees on Map

**1986.** National Tree Day.

| No. | Description | Unused | Used |
|---|---|---|---|
| 1103 | 70f. Type **390** | 85 | 30 |
| 1104 | 100f. Hands holding clump of earth and seedling | 1·00 | 45 |

**391** Loading Palm Nuts onto Trailer at Dibombari

**1986.** Agricultural Development. Multicoloured.

| No. | Description | Unused | Used |
|---|---|---|---|
| 1105 | 70f. Type **391** | 85 | 30 |
| 1106 | 70f. Payment for produce harvested | 85 | 30 |
| 1107 | 200f. Pineapple plantation | 1·90 | 90 |

**392** "Antestiopsis lineaticollis intricata"

**1987.** Harmful Insects. Multicoloured.

| No. | Description | Unused | Used |
|---|---|---|---|
| 1108 | 70f. Type **392** | 1·10 | 45 |
| 1109 | 100f. "Distantiella theobroma" | 1·60 | 65 |

**393** Millet

**1987.** Agricultural Show, Maroua. Multicoloured.

| No. | Description | Unused | Used |
|---|---|---|---|
| 1110 | 70f. Type **393** | 85 | 30 |
| 1111 | 100f. Cotton | 1·00 | 45 |
| 1112 | 150f. Cattle | 1·50 | 80 |

**394** Shot-putting

**1987.** 4th All-Africa Games, Kenya. Mult.

| No. | Description | Unused | Used |
|---|---|---|---|
| 1113 | 100f. Type **394** | 95 | 40 |
| 1114 | 140f. Pole-vaulting | 1·40 | 60 |

**395** Drill Baboon

**1988.** Endangered Mammals. Drill Baboon. Multicoloured.

| No. | Description | Unused | Used |
|---|---|---|---|
| 1115 | 30f. Type **395** | 1·80 | 80 |
| 1116 | 40f. Adult baboons | 2·00 | 90 |
| 1117 | 70f. Young baboon | 2·50 | 1·50 |
| 1118 | 100f. Mother with baby | 4·75 | 2·10 |

**396** National Assembly Building

**1989.** Centenary of Interparliamentary Union.

| No. | Type | Description | Unused | Used |
|---|---|---|---|---|
| 1119 | **396** | 50f. multicoloured | 55 | 15 |

**397** Cameroun and Argentine Players

**1990.** World Cup Football Championship, Italy. Multicoloured.

| No. | Description | Unused | Used |
|---|---|---|---|
| 1120 | 200f. Type **397** | 1·80 | 75 |
| 1121 | 250f. Cameroun player and match scene | 2·20 | 1·10 |
| 1122 | 250f. Cameroun winning goal | 2·20 | 1·10 |
| 1123 | 300f. Cameroun first eleven | 2·75 | 1·40 |
| **MS**1124 | 108×77 mm. Nos. 1120/3 | 10·00 | 10·00 |

**1990.** Nos. 1062 and 1093 surch.

| No. | Type | Description | Unused | Used |
|---|---|---|---|---|
| 1125 | - | 20f. on 150f. mult | 1·90 | 20 |
| 1126 | **385** | 70f. on 300f. mult | 6·25 | 35 |

**399** Milla and Match Scene

**1990.** Roger Milla, 4th Best Player in World Cup.

| No. | Type | Description | Unused | Used |
|---|---|---|---|---|
| 1127 | **399** | 500f. multicoloured | 5·25 | 2·75 |
| **MS**1128 | | 108×76 mm. No. 1125 | 8·50 | 8·50 |

**400** Anniversary Emblem

**1990.** 40th Anniv of United Nations Development Programme.

| No. | Type | Description | Unused | Used |
|---|---|---|---|---|
| 1129 | **400** | 50f. multicoloured | 55 | 25 |

**401** UNESCO and ILY Emblems

**1990.** International Literacy Year.

| No. | Type | Description | Unused | Used |
|---|---|---|---|---|
| 1130 | **401** | 200f. black, lt blue & bl | 1·90 | 80 |

**402** Arms and Pres. Paul Biya

**1991.** 30th Anniv (1990) of Independence. Multicoloured.

| No. | Description | Unused | Used |
|---|---|---|---|
| 1131 | 150f. Type **402** | 1·60 | 70 |
| 1132 | 1000f. Flag, city and 1960 20f. Independence stamp | 9·75 | 4·50 |
| **MS**1133 | 164×99 mm. Nos. 1131/2 | 12·00 | 12·00 |

**403** Treating Cacao Plantation

**1991.** Unissued stamps (for Ebolowa Agricultural Show) with bars over inscr and surch 125F. Multicoloured.

| No. | Description | Unused | Used |
|---|---|---|---|
| 1134 | 125f. on 70f. Type **403** | 95 | 45 |
| 1135 | 125f. on 100f. Sheep | 1·30 | 75 |

The stamps without surcharge were sold only by the Paris agency.

**405** Snake on National Colours and Map

**1991.** Anti-AIDS Campaign. Multicoloured.

| No. | Description | Unused | Used |
|---|---|---|---|
| 1137 | 15f. Type **405** | 10 | 10 |
| 1138 | 25f. Youth pushing back "AIDS" in French and English (horiz) | 40 | 10 |

See also Nos. 1171/2.

**1991.** As No. 932 but inscr "Republic du Cameroun / Republic of Cameroun".

| No. | Type | Description | Unused | Used |
|---|---|---|---|---|
| 1139 | **322** | 40f. multicoloured | 45 | 10 |

**406** Oribi

**1991.** Sovereign Military Order of Malta Child Survival Project. Antelopes. Multicoloured.

| No. | Description | Unused | Used |
|---|---|---|---|
| 1140 | 125f.+10f. Type **406** | 1·80 | 1·10 |
| 1141 | 250f.+20f. Waterbucks | 2·75 | 2·20 |
| **MS**1142 | 144×90 mm. Nos. 1140/1 | 6·25 | 6·25 |

**407** Serle's Bush Shrike ("La Pie Grieche du Mont-kupe")

**1991.** Birds. Multicoloured.

| No. | Description | Unused | Used |
|---|---|---|---|
| 1143 | 70f. Type **407** | 75 | 45 |
| 1144 | 70f. Grey-necked bald crow ("Le Picathartes Chauve ") (horiz) | 75 | 45 |
| 1145 | 300f. As No. 1144 | 2·75 | 1·60 |
| 1146 | 350f. Type **407** | 3·50 | 1·60 |
| **MS**1147 | 108×80 mm. Nos. 144/5 | 7·75 | 7·75 |

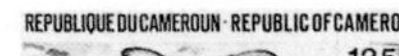

**408** African Elephant

**1991.** Animals. Multicoloured.

| | | | | |
|---|---|---|---|---|
| 1148 | | 125f. Type **408** | 1·50 | 70 |
| 1149 | | 250f. Buffalo | 2·75 | 1·60 |
| **MS**1150 | | 120×80 mm. Nos. 1148/9 | 6·25 | 6·25 |

**409** Mvolye Church

**1991.** Centenary (1990) of Catholic Church in Cameroun. Multicoloured.

| | | | | |
|---|---|---|---|---|
| 1151 | | 125f. Type **409** | 1·40 | 70 |
| 1152 | | 250f. Akono church | 2·40 | 1·50 |
| **MS**1153 | | 108×80 mm. Nos. 1151/2 | 4·00 | 4·00 |

**410** Emblems

**1991.** 7th African Group Meeting of Int Savings Banks Institute, Yaounde.

| | | | | |
|---|---|---|---|---|
| 1154 | **410** | 250f. multicoloured | 2·40 | 1·20 |
| **MS**1155 | | 107×80 mm. No. 1154 | 2·75 | 2·75 |

**1992.** Birds. As previous designs but with values changed. Multicoloured.

| | | | | |
|---|---|---|---|---|
| 1156 | | 125f. As No. 1063 | 1·40 | 50 |
| 1157 | | 200f. As No. 968 | 2·00 | 85 |
| 1158 | | 350f. Type **357** | 3·50 | 1·50 |

**411** Columbus's Fleet

**1992.** 500th Anniv of Discovery of America by Columbus. Multicoloured.

| | | | | |
|---|---|---|---|---|
| 1159 | | 125f. Type **411** | 1·40 | 70 |
| 1160 | | 250f. Columbus kneeling on beach | 2·50 | 1·40 |
| 1161 | | 400f. Meeting Amerindians | 3·75 | 2·10 |
| 1162 | | 500f. Fleet crossing the Atlantic | 5·25 | 3·00 |

**412** Mbappe Lepe (footballer)

**1992.** Cameroun Football. Multicoloured.

| | | | | |
|---|---|---|---|---|
| 1163 | | 125f. Type **412** | 1·30 | 70 |
| 1164 | | 250f. League emblem | 2·50 | 1·50 |
| 1165 | | 400f. National Football Federation emblem (horiz) | 3·75 | 2·10 |
| 1166 | | 500f. Ahmadou Ahidjo Stadium, Yaounde (horiz) | 5·50 | 3·00 |

See also Nos. 1173/5.

**413** Crocodile

**1993.** Endangered Animals. Mult. Self-adhesive.

| | | | | |
|---|---|---|---|---|
| 1167 | | 125f. Type **413** | 1·40 | 70 |
| 1168 | | 250f. Kob (vert) | 2·40 | 1·40 |

**1993.** As Nos. 967 and 975 but inscr "REPUBLIQUE DU CAMEROUN REPUBLIC OF CAMEROON" and with values changed.

| | | | | |
|---|---|---|---|---|
| 1169 | **339** | 370f. multicoloured | 3·50 | 1·80 |
| 1170 | **342** | 410f. multicoloured | 4·25 | 2·10 |

**1993.** Anti-AIDS Campaign. As Nos. 1137/8 but values changed. Multicoloured.

| | | | | |
|---|---|---|---|---|
| 1171 | | 100f. Type **405** | 1·00 | 60 |
| 1172 | | 175f. As No. 1138 | 1·90 | 1·00 |

**1993.** As Nos. 1163/5 but values changed.

| | | | | |
|---|---|---|---|---|
| 1173 | | 10f. As No. 1165 | | |
| 1174 | | 25f. As No. 1164 | | |
| 1175 | | 50f. Type **412** | | |

**414** President Biya holding Football and Lion (national team mascot)

**1994.** World Cup Football Championship, United States. Multicoloured.

| | | | | |
|---|---|---|---|---|
| 1176 | | 125f. Type **414** | 85 | 45 |
| 1177 | | 250f. Emblem, lion, player and map of Cameroun | 1·40 | 75 |
| 1178 | | 450f. Players, ball showing world map, national flag and trophy | 2·50 | 1·50 |
| 1179 | | 500f. Eagle and lion supporting ball | 3·00 | 1·70 |
| **MS**1180 | | 120×100 mm. Nos. 1176/9 | 13·00 | 13·00 |

**415** Grey Parrot

**1995**

| | | | | |
|---|---|---|---|---|
| 1181 | **415** | 125f. multicoloured | 1·30 | 45 |

**416** Chi-rho, Cross and Pope John Paul II

**1995.** 2nd Papal Visit.

| | | | | |
|---|---|---|---|---|
| 1182 | **416** | 55f. black, pink & yell | 35 | 25 |
| 1183 | - | 125f. multicoloured | 85 | 35 |

DESIGN: 125f. Pope and open book.

**417** Anniversary Emblem and Dove carrying Branch

**1995.** 50th Anniv of UNO Multicoloured.

| | | | | |
|---|---|---|---|---|
| 1184 | | 200f. Type **417** | 1·20 | 55 |
| 1185 | | 250f. Anniversary emblem and figures joining hands | 1·50 | 75 |

## MILITARY FRANK STAMP

Cameroun joined the Commonwealth on 1 November 1995.

**M78** Arms and Crossed Swords

**1963.** No value indicated.

| | | | | |
|---|---|---|---|---|
| M1 | **M78** | (-) lake | 3·00 | 3·25 |

## POSTAGE DUE STAMPS

**D8** Felling Mahogany Tree

**1925**

| | | | | |
|---|---|---|---|---|
| D88 | **D8** | 2c. black and blue | 40 | 3·75 |
| D89 | **D8** | 4c. purple and olive | 40 | 3·00 |
| D90 | **D8** | 5c. black and lilac | 80 | 3·75 |
| D91 | **D8** | 10c. black and red | 80 | 4·50 |
| D92 | **D8** | 15c. black and grey | 1·00 | 4·25 |
| D93 | **D8** | 20c. black and olive | 1·70 | 4·75 |
| D94 | **D8** | 25c. black and yellow | 1·60 | 5·75 |
| D95 | **D8** | 30c. orange and blue | 1·60 | 5·75 |
| D96 | **D8** | 50c. black and brown | 1·90 | 5·75 |
| D97 | **D8** | 60c. red and green | 2·00 | 6·50 |
| D98 | **D8** | 1f. green & red on grn | 2·30 | 1·70 |
| D99 | **D8** | 2f. mauve and red | 4·00 | 8·25 |
| D100 | **D8** | 3f. blue and brown | 7·25 | 10·50 |

**D25** African Idols

**1939**

| | | | | |
|---|---|---|---|---|
| D148 | **D25** | 5c. purple | 45 | 4·50 |
| D149 | **D25** | 10c. blue | 55 | 5·00 |
| D150 | **D25** | 15c. red | 35 | 4·50 |
| D151 | **D25** | 20c. brown | 35 | 4·50 |
| D152 | **D25** | 30c. blue | 35 | 3·25 |
| D153 | **D25** | 50c. green | 40 | 4·50 |
| D154 | **D25** | 60c. purple | 55 | 4·50 |
| D155 | **D25** | 1f. violet | 90 | 3·25 |
| D156 | **D25** | 2f. orange | 1·00 | 5·00 |
| D157 | **D25** | 3f. blue | 1·10 | 6·00 |

**D46**

**1947**

| | | | | |
|---|---|---|---|---|
| D254 | **D46** | 10c. red | 25 | 4·50 |
| D255 | **D46** | 30c. orange | 25 | 4·75 |
| D256 | **D46** | 50c. black | 25 | 4·75 |
| D257 | **D46** | 1f. red | 70 | 4·50 |
| D258 | **D46** | 2f. green | 2·10 | 5·00 |
| D259 | **D46** | 3f. mauve | 2·10 | 5·25 |
| D260 | **D46** | 4f. blue | 1·80 | 4·25 |
| D261 | **D46** | 5f. brown | 1·70 | 4·75 |
| D262 | **D46** | 10f. blue | 2·10 | 3·00 |
| D263 | **D46** | 20f. sepia | 2·75 | 4·50 |

**D77** "Hibiscus rosa sinensis"

**1963.** Flowers. Multicoloured.

| | | | | |
|---|---|---|---|---|
| D342 | | 50c. Type D **77** | 10 | 50 |
| D343 | | 50c. "Erythrine" | 10 | 50 |
| D344 | | 1f. "Plumeria lutea | 10 | 50 |
| D345 | | 1f. "Ipomoea sp." | 10 | 50 |
| D346 | | 1f.50 "Grinum sp." | 10 | 50 |
| D347 | | 1f.50 "Hoodia gordonii" | 10 | 50 |
| D348 | | 2f. "Ochna" | 20 | 60 |
| D349 | | 2f. "Gloriosa" | 20 | 60 |
| D350 | | 5f. "Costus spectabilis" | 20 | 60 |
| D351 | | 5f. "Bougainvillea spectabilis" | 20 | 60 |
| D352 | | 10f. "Delonix regia" | 55 | 55 |
| D353 | | 10f. "Haemanthus" | 55 | 55 |
| D354 | | 20f. "Titanopsis" | 1·30 | 1·20 |
| D355 | | 20f. "Ophthalmophyllum" | 1·30 | 1·20 |
| D356 | | 40f. "Zingiberacee" | 2·00 | 1·80 |
| D357 | | 40f. "Amorphophalus" | 2·00 | 1·80 |

Cameroun joined the Commonwealth on 1 November 1995.

Pt. 1

# CANADA

A British dominion consisting of the former province of Canada with British Columbia, New Brunswick, Newfoundland, Nova Scotia and Prince Edward Island.

1851. 12 pence = 1 shilling (Canadian).
1859. 100 cents = 1 dollar.

## COLONY OF CANADA

1 Beaver 2 Prince Albert 3

4 5 6 Jacques Cartier

**1851.** Imperf.

| | | | | |
|---|---|---|---|---|
| 17 | 4 | ½d. red | £900 | £550 |
| 5 | 1 | 3d. red | £2000 | £200 |
| 9 | 2 | 6d. purple | £35000 | £1000 |
| 12 | 5 | 7½d. green | £10000 | £2250 |
| 14 | 6 | 10d. blue | £10000 | £1500 |
| 4 | 3 | 12d. black | £170000 | £95000 |

**1858.** Perf.

| | | | | |
|---|---|---|---|---|
| 25 | | ½d. red | £4000 | £900 |
| 26 | 1 | 3d. red | £9500 | £350 |
| 27a | 2 | 6d. purple | £15000 | £3500 |

**1859.** Values in cents. Perf.

| | | | | |
|---|---|---|---|---|
| 29 | 4 | 1c. red | £400 | 45·00 |
| 44 | 4 | 2c. red | £600 | £170 |
| 31 | 1 | 5c. red | £425 | 17·00 |
| 36 | 2 | 10c. brown | £1200 | 75·00 |
| 38 | 2 | 10c. purple | £1300 | 75·00 |
| 40 | 5 | 12½c. green | £1000 | 70·00 |
| 42 | 6 | 17c. blue | £1400 | 90·00 |

## DOMINION OF CANADA

13

14

**1868.** Various frames.

| | | | | |
|---|---|---|---|---|
| 54 | 13 | ½c. black | 75·00 | 60·00 |
| 55 | 14 | 1c. brown | £450 | 55·00 |
| 56a | 14 | 1c. yellow | £1000 | 90·00 |
| 57 | 14 | 2c. green | £600 | 45·00 |
| 49 | 14 | 3c. red | £1300 | 32·00 |
| 63 | 14 | 5c. green | £850 | 85·00 |
| 59b | 14 | 6c. brown | £1100 | 55·00 |
| 60 | 14 | 12½c. blue | £850 | 60·00 |
| 69 | 14 | 15c. blue | £170 | 32·00 |
| 70 | 14 | 15c. purple | 70·00 | 19·00 |

21

27

**1870.** Various frames.

| | | | | |
|---|---|---|---|---|
| 101 | 27 | ½c. black | 18·00 | 11·00 |
| 75 | 21 | 1c. yellow | 38·00 | 2·00 |
| 104 | 21 | 2c. green | 50·00 | 3·25 |
| 105 | 21 | 3c. red | 45·00 | 1·25 |
| 106 | 21 | 5c. grey | 90·00 | 1·75 |
| 107 | 21 | 6c. brown | 45·00 | 14·00 |
| 117 | - | 8c. grey | £160 | 8·00 |
| 120 | - | 8c. purple | £110 | 8·00 |
| 111 | 21 | 10c. pink | £250 | 32·00 |

On 8c. head is to left.

28

**1893**

| | | | | |
|---|---|---|---|---|
| 115 | 28 | 20c. red | £225 | 60·00 |
| 116 | 28 | 50c. blue | £250 | 45·00 |

30

**1897.** Jubilee.

| | | | | |
|---|---|---|---|---|
| 121 | 30 | ½c. black | 65·00 | 65·00 |
| 122 | 30 | 1c. orange | 11·00 | 5·50 |
| 124 | 30 | 2c. green | 21·00 | 9·00 |
| 126 | 30 | 3c. red | 12·00 | 2·25 |
| 128 | 30 | 5c. blue | 45·00 | 14·00 |
| 129 | 30 | 6c. brown | £110 | £100 |
| 130 | 30 | 8c. violet | 42·00 | 32·00 |
| 131 | 30 | 10c. purple | 70·00 | 60·00 |
| 132 | 30 | 15c. slate | £120 | £100 |
| 133 | 30 | 20c. red | £130 | £100 |
| 134 | 30 | 50c. blue | £170 | £110 |
| 136 | 30 | $1 lake | £500 | £475 |
| 137 | 30 | $2 violet | £900 | £400 |
| 138 | 30 | $3 bistre | £1200 | £750 |
| 139 | 30 | $4 violet | £1100 | £650 |
| 140 | 30 | $5 green | £1100 | £650 |

31

**1897.** Maple-leaves in four corners.

| | | | | |
|---|---|---|---|---|
| 141 | 31 | ½c. black | 12·00 | 6·50 |
| 143 | 31 | 1c. green | 23·00 | 90 |
| 144 | 31 | 2c. violet | 21·00 | 1·50 |
| 145 | 31 | 3c. red | 40·00 | 2·25 |
| 146 | 31 | 5c. blue | 70·00 | 2·75 |
| 147 | 31 | 6c. brown | 60·00 | 29·00 |
| 148 | 31 | 8c. orange | 85·00 | 7·50 |
| 149 | 31 | 10c. purple | £140 | 55·00 |

**1898.** As T 31 but figures in lower corners.

| | | | |
|---|---|---|---|
| 150 | ½c. black | 6·50 | 1·10 |
| 151 | 1c. green | 27·00 | 60 |
| 154 | 2c. purple | 26·00 | 30 |
| 155 | 2c. red | 38·00 | 30 |
| 156 | 3c. red | 70·00 | 1·00 |
| 157 | 5c. blue | £110 | 3·75 |
| 159 | 6c. brown | £100 | 65·00 |
| 160 | 7c. yellow | 70·00 | 22·00 |
| 162 | 8c. orange | £120 | 40·00 |
| 163 | 10c. purple | £170 | 14·00 |
| 165 | 20c. green | £300 | 50·00 |

33

**1898.** Imperial Penny Postage.

| | | | | |
|---|---|---|---|---|
| 168 | 33 | 2c. black, red and blue | 35·00 | 7·00 |

**1899.** Surch 2 CENTS.

| | | | |
|---|---|---|---|
| 171 | 2c. on 3c. red (No. 145) | 20·00 | 8·00 |
| 172 | 2c. on 3c. red (No. 156) | 19·00 | 4·25 |

**35** King Edward VII

**1903**

| | | | | |
|---|---|---|---|---|
| 175 | 35 | 1c. green | 28·00 | 50 |
| 176 | 35 | 2c. red | 20·00 | 50 |
| 178 | 35 | 5c. blue | 85·00 | 2·50 |
| 180 | 35 | 7c. olive | 70·00 | 2·75 |
| 182 | 35 | 10c. purple | £150 | 20·00 |
| 185 | 35 | 20c. olive | £275 | 28·00 |
| 187 | 35 | 50c. violet | £425 | £100 |

**36** King George V and Queen Mary, when Prince and Princess of Wales

**1908.** Tercententary of Quebec. Dated "1608 1908".

| | | | | |
|---|---|---|---|---|
| 188 | 36 | ½c. brown | 4·50 | 3·50 |
| 189 | - | 1c. green | 23·00 | 2·75 |
| 190 | - | 2c. red | 23·00 | 1·00 |
| 191 | - | 5c. blue | 60·00 | 30·00 |
| 192 | - | 7c. olive | 85·00 | 65·00 |
| 193 | - | 10c. violet | 95·00 | 80·00 |
| 194 | - | 15c. orange | £110 | 80·00 |
| 195 | - | 20c. brown | £150 | £120 |

DESIGNS: 1c. Cartier and Champlain; 2c. King Edward VII and Queen Alexandra; 5c. Champlain's House in Quebec; 7c. Generals Montcalm and Wolfe; 10c. Quebec in 1700; 15c. Champlain's departure for the West; 20c. Cartier's arrival before Quebec.

44

**1912**

| | | | | |
|---|---|---|---|---|
| 196 | 44 | 1c. green | 8·50 | 50 |
| 200 | 44 | 2c. red | 7·50 | 50 |
| 205 | 44 | 3c. brown | 5·50 | 50 |
| 205b | 44 | 5c. blue | 60·00 | 75 |
| 209 | 44 | 7c. yellow | 22·00 | 3·00 |
| 210 | 44 | 10c. purple | 90·00 | 2·75 |
| 212 | 44 | 20c. olive | 40·00 | 1·50 |
| 215 | 44 | 50c. sepia | 50·00 | 3·75 |

See also Nos. 246/55.

**1915.** Optd WAR TAX diagonally.

| | | | |
|---|---|---|---|
| 225 | 5c. blue | £120 | £200 |
| 226 | 20c. olive | 60·00 | £100 |
| 227 | 50c. sepia | £120 | £160 |

46

**1915**

| | | | | |
|---|---|---|---|---|
| 228 | 46 | 1c. green | 8·00 | 50 |
| 229 | 46 | 2c. red | 24·00 | 2·50 |

47

**1916**

| | | | | |
|---|---|---|---|---|
| 233 | 47 | 2c.+1c. red | 45·00 | 2·00 |
| 239 | 47 | 2c.+1c. brown | 5·00 | 50 |

**48** Quebec Conference, 1864, from painting "The Fathers of the Confederation" by Robert Harris

**1917.** 50th Anniv of Confederation.

| | | | | |
|---|---|---|---|---|
| 244 | 48 | 3c. brown | 21·00 | 3·25 |

**1922**

| | | | | |
|---|---|---|---|---|
| 246 | 44 | 1c. yellow | 2·75 | 60 |
| 247 | 44 | 2c. green | 2·25 | 10 |
| 248 | 44 | 3c. red | 3·75 | 10 |
| 249 | 44 | 4c. yellow | 8·00 | 3·50 |
| 250 | 44 | 5c. violet | 5·00 | 1·75 |
| 251 | 44 | 7c. brown | 12·00 | 9·00 |
| 252 | 44 | 8c. blue | 21·00 | 11·00 |
| 253 | 44 | 10c. blue | 15·00 | 3·25 |
| 254 | 44 | 10c. brown | 23·00 | 4·00 |
| 255 | 44 | $1 orange | 55·00 | 9·50 |

**1926.** Surch 2 CENTS in one line.

| | | | |
|---|---|---|---|
| 264 | 2c. on 3c. red | 50·00 | 60·00 |

**1926.** Surch 2 CENTS in two lines.

| | | | |
|---|---|---|---|
| 265 | 2c. on 3c. red | 16·00 | 26·00 |

**51** Sir J. A. Macdonald

**52** "The Fathers of the Confederation"

**1927.** 60th Anniv of Confederation. I. Commemoration Issue. Dated "1867–1927".

| | | | | |
|---|---|---|---|---|
| 266 | 51 | 1c. orange | 2·50 | 1·50 |
| 267 | 52 | 2c. green | 2·25 | 30 |
| 268 | - | 3c. red | 8·50 | 5·00 |
| 269 | - | 5c. violet | 5·50 | 4·25 |
| 270 | - | 12c. blue | 27·00 | 7·00 |

DESIGNS—HORIZ: As Type **52**: 3c. Parliament Buildings, Ottawa; 12c. Map of Canada, 1867–1927. VERT: As Type **51**: 5c. Sir W. Laurier.

**56** Darcy McGee

**57** Sir W. Laurier and Sir J. A. Macdonald

II. Historical Issue.

| | | | | |
|---|---|---|---|---|
| 271 | 56 | 5c. violet | 3·00 | 2·50 |
| 272 | 57 | 12c. green | 17·00 | 4·50 |
| 273 | - | 20c. red | 17·00 | 13·00 |

DESIGN—As Type **57**: 20c. R. Baldwin and L. H. Lafontaine.

59

**1928.** Air.

| | | | | |
|---|---|---|---|---|
| 274 | 59 | 5c. brown | 7·50 | 5·00 |

**60** King George V

**61** Mount Hurd and Indian Totem Poles

**1928**

| | | | | |
|---|---|---|---|---|
| 275 | 60 | 1c. orange | 2·75 | 2·25 |
| 276 | 60 | 2c. green | 1·25 | 20 |
| 277 | 60 | 3c. lake | 19·00 | 21·00 |
| 278 | 60 | 4c. bistre | 13·00 | 9·50 |
| 279 | 60 | 5c. violet | 6·50 | 5·50 |
| 280 | 60 | 8c. blue | 7·50 | 7·50 |
| 281 | 61 | 10c. green | 8·50 | 2·25 |
| 282 | - | 12c. black | 26·00 | 16·00 |
| 283 | - | 20c. lake | 32·00 | 16·00 |
| 284 | - | 50c. blue | £150 | 50·00 |
| 285 | - | $1 olive | £140 | 80·00 |

DESIGNS—HORIZ: 12c. Quebec Bridge; 20c. Harvesting with horses; 50c. "Bluenose" (fishing schooner); $1 Parliament Buildings, Ottawa.

66

**67** Parliamentary Library, Ottawa

**68** The Old Citadel, Quebec

**1930**

| | | | | |
|---|---|---|---|---|
| 288 | 66 | 1c. orange | 1·75 | 1·25 |
| 289 | 66 | 1c. green | 2·00 | 10 |
| 290 | 66 | 2c. green | 1·75 | 10 |
| 291 | 66 | 2c. red | 2·25 | 3·00 |
| 292b | 66 | 2c. brown | 1·50 | 10 |
| 293 | 66 | 3c. red | 1·50 | 10 |
| 294 | 66 | 4c. yellow | 9·00 | 4·50 |
| 295 | 66 | 5c. violet | 2·75 | 6·50 |
| 296 | 66 | 5c. blue | 5·50 | 20 |
| 297 | 66 | 8c. blue | 11·00 | 16·00 |
| 298 | 66 | 8c. orange | 7·50 | 5·50 |
| 299 | 67 | 10c. olive | 20·00 | 1·25 |
| 300 | 68 | 12c. black | 14·00 | 5·50 |
| 325 | 68 | 13c. violet | 65·00 | 2·25 |
| 301 | - | 20c. red | 22·00 | 1·75 |
| 302 | - | 50c. blue | 90·00 | 17·00 |
| 303 | - | $1 olive | £120 | 30·00 |

DESIGNS—HORIZ: 20c. Harvesting with tractor; 50c. Acadian Memorial Church, Grand Pre, Nova Scotia; $1 Mount Edith Cavell.

**72** Mercury and Western Hemisphere

**1930.** Air.

| | | | | |
|---|---|---|---|---|
| 310 | **72** | 5c. brown | 23·00 | 23·00 |

**73** Sir Georges Etienne Cartier

**1931**

| | | | | |
|---|---|---|---|---|
| 312 | **73** | 10c. green | 12·00 | 20 |

**1932.** Air. Surch 6 and bars.

| | | | | |
|---|---|---|---|---|
| 313 | **59** | 6c. on 5c. brown | 3·00 | 2·50 |

**1932.** Surch 3 between bars.

| | | | | |
|---|---|---|---|---|
| 314a | **66** | 3c. on 2c. red | 1·00 | 60 |

**76** King George V

**77** Duke of Windsor when Prince of Wales

**78** Allegory of British Empire

**1932.** Ottawa Conference. (a) Postage.

| | | | | |
|---|---|---|---|---|
| 315 | **76** | 3c. red | 70 | 80 |
| 316 | **77** | 5c. blue | 12·00 | 5·00 |
| 317 | **78** | 13c. green | 12·00 | 6·00 |

(b) Air. Surch 6 6 OTTAWA CONFERENCE 1932.

| | | | | |
|---|---|---|---|---|
| 318 | **72** | 6c. on 5c. brown | 12·00 | 20·00 |

**80** King George V

**1932**

| | | | | |
|---|---|---|---|---|
| 319 | **80** | 1c. green | 60 | 10 |
| 320 | **80** | 2c. brown | 70 | 10 |
| 321b | **80** | 3c. red | 85 | 10 |
| 322 | **80** | 4c. brown | 42·00 | 11·00 |
| 323 | **80** | 5c. blue | 11·00 | 10 |
| 324 | **80** | 8c. orange | 32·00 | 4·25 |

**81** Parliament Buildings, Ottawa

**1933.** UPU Congress (Preliminary Meeting).

| | | | | |
|---|---|---|---|---|
| 329 | **81** | 5c. blue | 9·50 | 3·00 |

**1933.** Optd WORLD'S GRAIN EXHIBITION & CONFERENCE REGINA 1933.

| | | | |
|---|---|---|---|
| 330 | 20c. red (No. 295) | 19·00 | 8·50 |

**83** S.S. "Royal William" (after S. Skillett)

**1933.** Cent of 1st Transatlantic Steamboat Crossing.

| | | | | |
|---|---|---|---|---|
| 331 | **83** | 5c. blue | 19·00 | 3·75 |

**84** Jacques Cartier approaching Land

**1934.** 4th-century of Discovery of Canada.

| | | | | |
|---|---|---|---|---|
| 332 | **84** | 3c. blue | 5·50 | 1·50 |

**85** U.E.L. Statue, Hamilton

**1934.** 150th Anniv of Arrival of United Empire Loyalists.

| | | | | |
|---|---|---|---|---|
| 333 | **85** | 10c. olive | 10·00 | 7·50 |

**86** Seal of New Brunswick

**1934.** 150th Anniv of New Brunswick.

| | | | | |
|---|---|---|---|---|
| 334 | **86** | 2c. brown | 1·50 | 3·25 |

**87** Queen Elizabeth II when Princess

**88** King George VI when Duke of York

**89** King George V and Queen Mary

**1935.** Silver Jubilee. Dated "1910–1935".

| | | | | |
|---|---|---|---|---|
| 335 | **87** | 1c. green | 70 | 80 |
| 336 | **88** | 2c. brown | 70 | 80 |
| 337 | **89** | 3c. red | 3·00 | 1·25 |
| 338 | - | 5c. blue | 5·50 | 7·50 |
| 339 | - | 10c. green | 9·00 | 9·50 |
| 340 | - | 13c. blue | 9·50 | 9·50 |

DESIGNS—VERT: 5c. Duke of Windsor when Prince of Wales. HORIZ: 10c. Windsor Castle; 13c. Royal Yacht "Britannia".

**93** King George V

**94** Royal Canadian Mounted Policeman

**1935**

| | | | | |
|---|---|---|---|---|
| 341 | **93** | 1c. green | 1·75 | 10 |
| 342 | **93** | 2c. brown | 1·75 | 10 |
| 343 | **93** | 3c. red | 1·75 | 10 |
| 344 | **93** | 4c. yellow | 3·50 | 2·75 |
| 345 | **93** | 5c. blue | 3·50 | 10 |
| 346 | **93** | 8c. orange | 4·25 | 5·00 |
| 347 | **94** | 10c. red | 6·50 | 50 |
| 348 | - | 13c. purple | 7·50 | 65 |
| 349 | - | 20c. green | 25·00 | 1·50 |
| 350 | - | 50c. violet | 25·00 | 7·00 |
| 351 | - | $1 blue | 40·00 | 11·00 |

DESIGNS—HORIZ: 13c. Confederation, Charlottetown, 1864; 20c. Niagara Falls; 50c. Parliament Buildings, Victoria, B.C.; $1 Champlain Monument, Quebec.

**99** Daedalus

**1935.** Air.

| | | | | |
|---|---|---|---|---|
| 355 | **99** | 6c. brown | 3·25 | 1·00 |

**100** King George VI and Queen Elizabeth

**1937.** Coronation.

| | | | | |
|---|---|---|---|---|
| 356 | **100** | 3c. red | 1·75 | 1·50 |

**101** King George VI

**102** Memorial Chamber Parliament Buildings, Ottawa

**104** Fort Garry Gate, Winnipeg

**1937**

| | | | | |
|---|---|---|---|---|
| 357 | **101** | 1c. green | 2·00 | 10 |
| 358 | **101** | 2c. brown | 2·50 | 10 |
| 359 | **101** | 3c. red | 1·75 | 10 |
| 360 | **101** | 4c. yellow | 5·50 | 1·75 |
| 361 | **101** | 5c. blue | 6·50 | 10 |
| 362 | **101** | 8c. orange | 6·50 | 3·75 |
| 363 | **102** | 10c. red | 5·00 | 60 |
| 364 | - | 13c. blue | 28·00 | 2·75 |
| 365 | **104** | 20c. brown | 24·00 | 2·75 |
| 366 | - | 50c. green | 48·00 | 16·00 |
| 367 | - | $1 violet | 60·00 | 16·00 |

DESIGNS—HORIZ: 13c. Halifax Harbour; 50c. Vancouver Harbour; $1 Chateau de Ramezay, Montreal.

**107** Fairchild 45-80 Sekani Seaplane over "Distributor" on Mackenzie River

**1938.** Air.

| | | | | |
|---|---|---|---|---|
| 371 | **107** | 6c. blue | 17·00 | 2·25 |

**108** Queen Elizabeth II when Princess and Princess Margaret

**1939.** Royal Visit.

| | | | | |
|---|---|---|---|---|
| 372 | **108** | 1c. black and green | 2·50 | 25 |
| 373 | - | 2c. black and brown | 2·75 | 2·00 |
| 374 | - | 3c. black and red | 2·00 | 25 |

DESIGNS—HORIZ: 3c. King George VI and Queen Elizabeth. VERT: 2c. National War Memorial, Ottawa.

**111** King George VI in Naval Uniform

**112** King George VI in Military Uniform

**114** Grain Elevator

**115** Farm Scene

**121** Air Training Camp

**1942.** War Effort.

| | | | | |
|---|---|---|---|---|
| 375 | **111** | 1c. green (postage) | 1·50 | 10 |
| 376 | **112** | 2c. brown | 1·75 | 10 |
| 377 | - | 3c. red | 1·25 | 60 |
| 378 | - | 3c. purple | 1·25 | 10 |
| 379 | **114** | 4c. grey | 5·50 | 2·50 |
| 380 | **112** | 4c. red | 70 | 10 |
| 381 | **111** | 5c. blue | 3·00 | 10 |
| 382 | **115** | 8c. brown | 5·50 | 1·00 |
| 383 | - | 10c. brown | 12·00 | 10 |
| 384 | - | 13c. green | 9·00 | 9·50 |
| 385 | - | 14c. green | 26·00 | 1·00 |
| 386 | - | 20c. brown | 21·00 | 45 |
| 387 | - | 50c. violet | 26·00 | 7·00 |
| 388 | - | $1 blue | 45·00 | 9·50 |
| 399 | **121** | 6c. blue (air) | 30·00 | 13·00 |
| 400 | **121** | 7c. blue | 4·50 | 50 |

DESIGNS—As Type **112**: 3c. King George VI. As Type **121**. VERT: 10c. Parliament Buildings. HORIZ: 13, 14c. Ram tank; 20c. Corvette; 50c. Munitions factory; $1 H.M.S. "Cossack" (destroyer).

**122** Ontario Farm Scene

**1946.** Re-conversion to Peace.

| | | | | |
|---|---|---|---|---|
| 401 | **122** | 8c. brown (postage) | 1·75 | 2·75 |
| 402 | - | 10c. green | 2·75 | 10 |
| 403 | - | 14c. sepia | 5·00 | 3·25 |
| 404 | - | 20c. grey | 3·25 | 10 |
| 405 | - | 50c. green | 16·00 | 6·50 |
| 406 | - | $1 purple | 26·00 | 6·50 |
| 407 | - | 7c. blue (air) | 5·50 | 40 |

DESIGNS: 10c. Great Bear Lake; 14c. St. Maurice River power station; 20c. Combine harvester; 50c. Lumbering in British Columbia; $1 "Abegweit" (train ferry); 7c. Canada geese in flight.

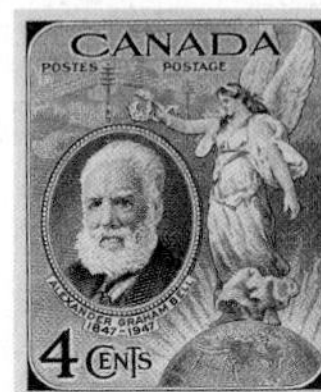

**129** Alexander Graham Bell and "Fame"

**1947.** Birth Centenary of Graham Bell (inventor of the telephone).

| | | | | |
|---|---|---|---|---|
| 408 | **129** | 4c. blue | 15 | 50 |

**130** "Canadian Citizenship"

**1947.** Advent of Canadian Citizenship and 80th Anniv of Confederation.

| | | | | |
|---|---|---|---|---|
| 409 | **130** | 4c. blue | 10 | 40 |

**131** Queen Elizabeth II when Princess

**1948.** Princess Elizabeth's Wedding.

| | | | | |
|---|---|---|---|---|
| 410 | **131** | 4c. blue | 10 | 15 |

**132** Queen Victoria. Parliament Building, Ottawa, and King George VI

**1948.** Centenary of Responsible Government.

| | | | | |
|---|---|---|---|---|
| 411 | 132 | 4c. grey | 10 | 10 |

**133** Cabot's Ship "Matthew"

**1949.** Entry of Newfoundland into Canadian Confederation.

| | | | | |
|---|---|---|---|---|
| 412 | 133 | 4c. green | 30 | 10 |

**134** "Founding of Halifax, 1749" (after C. W. Jeffries)

**1949.** Halifax Bicentenary.

| | | | | |
|---|---|---|---|---|
| 413 | 134 | 4c. violet | 45 | 10 |

**135** King George VI

**1949.** Portraits of King George VI.

| | | | | |
|---|---|---|---|---|
| 414 | 135 | 1c. green | 50 | 10 |
| 415 | - | 2c. sepia | 2·25 | 45 |
| 415a | - | 2c. green | 2·25 | 10 |
| 416 | - | 3c. purple | 30 | 10 |
| 417 | - | 4c. red | 20 | 10 |
| 418 | - | 5c. blue | 2·50 | 60 |

**1950.** As Nos. 414 and 416/18 but without "POSTES POSTAGE".

| | | | |
|---|---|---|---|
| 424 | 1c. green | 70 | 1·00 |
| 425 | 2c. sepia | 70 | 4·25 |
| 426 | 3c. purple | 70 | 65 |
| 427 | 4c. red | 70 | 20 |
| 428 | 5c. blue | 70 | 2·25 |

**141** Oil Wells in Alberta

**142** Drying Furs

**1950**

| | | | | |
|---|---|---|---|---|
| 432 | 142 | 10c. purple | 4·50 | 10 |
| 441 | - | 20c. grey | 2·25 | 10 |
| 431 | 141 | 50c. green | 6·00 | 1·00 |
| 433 | - | $1 blue | 42·00 | 5·50 |

DESIGNS: 20c. Forestry products; $1 Fisherman.

**145** Mackenzie King

**1951.** Canadian Prime Ministers.

| | | | | |
|---|---|---|---|---|
| 434 | | 3c. green (Borden) | 20 | 1·50 |
| 444 | - | 3c. purple (Abbott) | 35 | 75 |
| 435 | 145 | 4c. red | 60 | 15 |
| 445 | - | 4c. red (A. Mackenzie) | 25 | 35 |
| 475 | - | 4c. violet (Thompson) | 15 | 75 |
| 483 | - | 4c. violet (Bennett) | 20 | 60 |
| 476 | - | 5c. blue (Bowell) | 15 | 40 |
| 484 | - | 5c. blue (Tupper) | 20 | 10 |

**146** Mail Trains, 1851 and 1951

**149** Reproduction of 3d., 1851

**1951.** Centenary of First Canadian Postage Stamp. Dated "1851 1951".

| | | | | |
|---|---|---|---|---|
| 436 | 146 | 4c. black | 75 | 10 |
| 437 | - | 5c. violet | 2·00 | 2·75 |
| 438 | - | 7c. blue | 75 | 1·75 |
| 439 | 149 | 15c. red | 1·60 | 10 |

DESIGNS—As Type **146**: 5c. "City of Toronto" and S.S. "Prince George"; 7c. Mail coach and Canadair DC-4M North Star airplane.

**150** Queen Elizabeth II when Princess and Duke of Edinburgh

**1951.** Royal Visit.

| | | | | |
|---|---|---|---|---|
| 440 | 150 | 4c. violet | 20 | 20 |

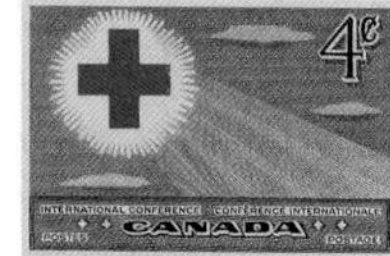
**152** Red Cross Emblem

**1952.** 18th Int Red Cross Conf, Toronto.

| | | | | |
|---|---|---|---|---|
| 442 | 152 | 4c. red and blue | 15 | 10 |

**153** Canada Goose

**1952**

| | | | | |
|---|---|---|---|---|
| 443 | 153 | 7c. blue | 1·25 | 10 |

**154** Pacific Coast Indian House and Totem Pole

**160** Textile Industry

**164** Northern Gannet

**165** Eskimo Hunter

**1953**

| | | | | |
|---|---|---|---|---|
| 477 | 165 | 10c. brown | 1·25 | 10 |
| 474 | 164 | 15c. black | 1·25 | 10 |
| 488 | - | 20c. green | 60 | 10 |
| 489 | - | 25c. red | 70 | 10 |
| 462 | 160 | 50c. green | 1·75 | 10 |
| 446 | 154 | $1 black | 3·25 | 20 |

DESIGNS (As Type **160**)—HORIZ: 20c. Pulp and paper industry. VERT: 25c. Chemical industry.

**155** Polar Bear

**1953.** National Wild Life Week.

| | | | | |
|---|---|---|---|---|
| 447 | 155 | 2c. blue | 10 | 10 |
| 448 | - | 3c. sepia (Elk) | 10 | 70 |
| 449 | - | 4c. slate (American bighorn) | 15 | 10 |

**158** Queen Elizabeth II

**1953**

| | | | | |
|---|---|---|---|---|
| 450 | 158 | 1c. brown | 10 | 10 |
| 451 | 158 | 2c. green | 15 | 10 |
| 452 | 158 | 3c. red | 15 | 15 |
| 453 | 158 | 4c. violet | 20 | 10 |
| 454 | 158 | 5c. blue | 25 | 10 |

**159** Queen Elizabeth II

**1953.** Coronation.

| | | | | |
|---|---|---|---|---|
| 461 | 159 | 4c. violet | 10 | 10 |

**161**

**1954**

| | | | | |
|---|---|---|---|---|
| 463 | 161 | 1c. brown | 10 | 10 |
| 464 | 161 | 2c. green | 20 | 10 |
| 465 | 161 | 3c. red | 1·00 | 10 |
| 466 | 161 | 4c. violet | 30 | 10 |
| 467 | 161 | 5c. blue | 30 | 10 |
| 468 | 161 | 6c. orange | 1·75 | 55 |

**1954.** National Wild Life Week. As T 155.

| | | | |
|---|---|---|---|
| 472 | 4c. slate (Walrus) | 35 | 20 |
| 473 | 5c. blue (American beaver) | 35 | 10 |

**166** Musk-ox

**167** Whooping Cranes

**1955.** National Wild Life Week.

| | | | | |
|---|---|---|---|---|
| 478 | 166 | 4c. violet | 30 | 10 |
| 479 | 167 | 5c. blue | 1·00 | 20 |

**168** Dove and Torch

**1955.** 10th Anniv of ICAO.

| | | | | |
|---|---|---|---|---|
| 480 | 168 | 5c. blue | 30 | 20 |

**169** Pioneer Settlers

**1955.** 50th Anniv of Alberta and Saskatchewan Provinces.

| | | | | |
|---|---|---|---|---|
| 481 | 169 | 5c. blue | 20 | 25 |

**170** Scout Badge and Globe

**1955.** 8th World Scout Jamboree.

| | | | | |
|---|---|---|---|---|
| 482 | 170 | 5c. brown and green | 30 | 10 |

**173** Ice-hockey Players

**1956.** Ice-hockey Commemoration.

| | | | | |
|---|---|---|---|---|
| 485 | 173 | 5c. blue | 20 | 20 |

**1956.** National Wild Life Week. As T 155.

| | | | |
|---|---|---|---|
| 486 | 4c. violet (Reindeer) | 20 | 15 |
| 487 | 5c. blue (Mountain goat) | 20 | 10 |

**178**

**1956.** Fire Prevention Week.

| | | | | |
|---|---|---|---|---|
| 490 | 178 | 5c. red and black | 30 | 10 |

**179** Fishing

**1957.** Outdoor Recreation.

| | | | | |
|---|---|---|---|---|
| 491 | 179 | 5c. blue | 25 | 10 |
| 492 | - | 5c. blue | 25 | 10 |
| 493 | - | 5c. blue | 25 | 10 |
| 494 | - | 5c. blue | 25 | 10 |

DESIGNS: No. 492, Swimming; 493, Hunting; 494, Skiing.

**183** White-billed Diver

**1957.** National Wild Life Week.

| | | | | |
|---|---|---|---|---|
| 495 | 183 | 5c. black | 50 | 20 |

**184** Thompson with Sextant, and North American Map

**1957.** Death Cent of David Thompson (explorer).

| | | | | |
|---|---|---|---|---|
| 496 | 184 | 5c. blue | 45 | 30 |

**185** Parliament Buildings, Ottawa

**1957.** 14th UPU Congress, Ottawa.

| | | | | |
|---|---|---|---|---|
| 497 | 185 | 5c. slate | 15 | 10 |
| 498 | - | 15c. slate | 55 | 1·75 |

DESIGNS—HORIZ (33½×22 mm): 15c. Globe within posthorn.

**187** Miner

**1957.** Mining Industry.

| | | | | |
|---|---|---|---|---|
| 499 | 187 | 5c. black | 35 | 20 |

**188** Queen Elizabeth II and Duke of Edinburgh

**1957.** Royal Visit.

| | | | | |
|---|---|---|---|---|
| 500 | 188 | 5c. black | 30 | 10 |

**189** "A Free Press"

**1958.** The Canadian Press.

| | | | | |
|---|---|---|---|---|
| 501 | **189** | 5c. black | 15 | 70 |

**190** Microscope

**1958.** International Geophysical Year.

| | | | | |
|---|---|---|---|---|
| 502 | **190** | 5c. blue | 20 | 10 |

**191** Miner panning for Gold

**1958.** Centenary of British Columbia.

| | | | | |
|---|---|---|---|---|
| 503 | **191** | 5c. turquoise | 20 | 10 |

**192** La Verendrye statue

**1958.** La Verendrye (explorer) Commemoration.

| | | | | |
|---|---|---|---|---|
| 504 | **192** | 5c. blue | 15 | 10 |

**193** Samuel de Champlain and Heights of Quebec

**1958.** 350th Anniv of Founding of Quebec by Samuel de Champlain.

| | | | | |
|---|---|---|---|---|
| 505 | **193** | 5c. brown and green | 30 | 10 |

**194** Nurse

**1958.** National Health.

| | | | | |
|---|---|---|---|---|
| 506 | **194** | 5c. purple | 30 | 10 |

**195** "Petroleum 1858–1958"

**1958.** Centenary of Canadian Oil Industry.

| | | | | |
|---|---|---|---|---|
| 507 | **195** | 5c. red and olive | 30 | 10 |


**196** Speaker's Chair and Mace

**1958.** Bicentenary of First Elected Assembly.

| | | | | |
|---|---|---|---|---|
| 508 | **196** | 5c. slate | 30 | 10 |

**197** John McCurdy's Biplane "Silver Dart"

**1959.** 50th Anniv of First Flight of the "Silver Dart" in Canada.

| | | | | |
|---|---|---|---|---|
| 509 | **197** | 5c. black and blue | 30 | 10 |

**198** Globe showing NATO Countries

**1959.** 10th Anniv of NATO.

| | | | | |
|---|---|---|---|---|
| 510 | **198** | 5c. blue | 40 | 10 |

**199**

**1959.** "Associated Country Women of the World" Commemoration.

| | | | | |
|---|---|---|---|---|
| 511 | **199** | 5c. black and olive | 15 | 10 |

**200** Queen Elizabeth II

**1959.** Royal Visit.

| | | | | |
|---|---|---|---|---|
| 512 | **200** | 5c. red | 30 | 10 |

**201** Maple Leaf linked with American Eagle

**1959.** Opening of St. Lawrence Seaway.

| | | | | |
|---|---|---|---|---|
| 513 | **201** | 5c. blue and red | 20 | 10 |

**202** Maple Leaves

**1959.** Bicentenary of Battle of Quebec.

| | | | | |
|---|---|---|---|---|
| 514 | **202** | 5c. green and red | 30 | 10 |

**203** Girl Guides Badge

**1960.** Golden Jubilee of Canadian Girl Guides Movement.

| | | | | |
|---|---|---|---|---|
| 515 | **203** | 5c. blue and brown | 20 | 10 |

**204** Dollard des Ormeaux

**1960.** Tercent of Battle of Long Sault.

| | | | | |
|---|---|---|---|---|
| 516 | **204** | 5c. blue and brown | 20 | 10 |


**205** Surveyor, Bulldozer and Compass Rose

**1961.** Northern Development.

| | | | | |
|---|---|---|---|---|
| 517 | **205** | 5c. green and red | 15 | 10 |

**206** E. Pauline Johnson

**1961.** Birth Centenary of E. Pauline Johnson (Mohawk poetess).

| | | | | |
|---|---|---|---|---|
| 518 | **206** | 5c. green and red | 15 | 10 |

**207** Arthur Meighen (statesman)

**1961.** Arthur Meighen Commemoration.

| | | | | |
|---|---|---|---|---|
| 519 | **207** | 5c. blue | 15 | 10 |


**208** Engineers and Dam

**1961.** Colombo Plan.

| | | | | |
|---|---|---|---|---|
| 520 | **208** | 5c. brown and blue | 30 | 10 |

**209** "Resources for Tomorrow"

**1961.** Natural Resources.

| | | | | |
|---|---|---|---|---|
| 521 | **209** | 5c. green and brown | 15 | 10 |

**210** "Education"

**1962.** Education Year.

| | | | | |
|---|---|---|---|---|
| 522 | **210** | 5c. black and brown | 15 | 10 |

**211** Lord Selkirk and Farmer

**1962.** 150th Anniv of Red River Settlement.

| | | | | |
|---|---|---|---|---|
| 523 | **211** | 5c. brown and green | 20 | 10 |

**212** Talon bestowing Gifts on Married Couple

**1962.** Jean Talon Commemoration.

| | | | | |
|---|---|---|---|---|
| 524 | **212** | 5c. blue | 20 | 10 |

**213** British Columbia and Vancouver Island 2½d. Stamp of 1860, and Parliament Buildings, B.C.

**1962.** Centenary of Victoria, B.C.

| | | | | |
|---|---|---|---|---|
| 525 | **213** | 5c. red and black | 30 | 10 |

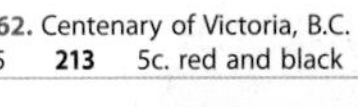

**214** Highway (map version) and Provincial Arms

**1962.** Opening of Trans-Canada Highway.

| | | | | |
|---|---|---|---|---|
| 526 | **214** | 5c. black and brown | 15 | 20 |

**215** Queen Elizabeth II and Wheat (agriculture) Symbol

**1962.** Different symbols in top left corner.

| | | | | |
|---|---|---|---|---|
| 527 | **215** | 1c. brown | 10 | 10 |
| 528 | - | 2c. green | 15 | 10 |
| 529 | - | 3c. violet | 15 | 10 |
| 530 | - | 4c. red | 20 | 10 |
| 531 | - | 5c. blue | 50 | 10 |

SYMBOLS: 1c. Crystals (Mining); 2c. Tree (Forestry); 3c. Fish (Fisheries); 4c. Electricity pylon (Industrial power); 5c. Wheat (Agriculture).

**216** Sir Casimir Gzowski

**1963.** 150th Birth Anniv of Sir Casimir Gzowski (engineer).

| | | | | |
|---|---|---|---|---|
| 535 | **216** | 5c. purple | 10 | 10 |

**217** "Export Trade"

**1963**

| | | | | |
|---|---|---|---|---|
| 536 | **217** | $1 red | 4·75 | 2·00 |

**218** Frobisher and barque "Gabriel"

**1963.** Sir Martin Frobisher Commemoration.

| | | | | |
|---|---|---|---|---|
| 537 | **218** | 5c. blue | 20 | 10 |

**219** Horseman and Map

**1963.** Bicent of Quebec–Trois-Rivieres–Montreal Postal Service.

| | | | | |
|---|---|---|---|---|
| 538 | **219** | 5c. brown and green | 15 | 25 |

**220** Canada Geese

**221** Douglas DC-9 Airliner and Uplands Airport, Ottawa

**1963**

| | | | | |
|---|---|---|---|---|
| 540 | **221** | 7c. blue | 35 | 70 |
| 540a | **221** | 8c. blue | 50 | 50 |
| 539 | **220** | 15c. blue | 1·00 | 10 |

**222** "Peace on Earth"

**1964.** "Peace".
541 **222** 5c. ochre, blue & turq 15 10

**223** Maple Leaves

**1964.** "Canadian Unity".
542 **223** 5c. lake and blue 10 10

**224** White Trillium and Arms of Ontario

**1964.** Provincial Badges.
543 **224** 5c. green, brown and orange 40 20
544 - 5c. green, brown and yellow 40 20
545 - 5c. red, green and violet 30 20
546 - 5c. blue, red and green 30 20
547 - 5c. purple, green and brown 30 20
548 - 5c. brown, green and mauve 30 20
549 - 5c. lilac, green and purple 50 20
550 - 5c. green, yellow and red 30 20
551 - 5c. sepia, orange and green 30 20
552 - 5c. black, red and green 30 20
553 - 5c. drab, green and yellow 30 20
554 - 5c. blue, green and red 30 20
555 - 5c. red and blue 30 20

FLOWERS AND ARMS OF: No. 544, Madonna Lily, Quebec; 545, Purple Violet, New Brunswick; 546, Mayflower, Nova Scotia; 547, Dogwood, British Columbia; 548, Prairie Crocus, Manitoba; 549, Lady's Slipper, Prince Edward Island; 550, Wild Rose, Alberta; 551, Prairie Lily, Saskatchewan; 552, Pitcher Plant, Newfoundland; 553, Mountain Avens, Northwest Territories; 554, Fireweed, Yukon Territory; 555, Maple Leaf, Canada.

**1964.** Surch 8.
556 **221** 8c. on 7c. blue 15 15

**238** Fathers of the Confederation Memorial, Charlottetown

**1964.** Centenary of Charlottetown Conference.
557 **238** 5c. black 10 10

**239** Maple Leaf and Hand with Quill Pen

**1964.** Centenary of Quebec Conference.
558 **239** 5c. red and brown 15 10

**240** Queen Elizabeth II

**1964.** Royal Visit.
559 **240** 5c. purple 15 10

**241** "Canadian Family"

**1964.** Christmas.
560 **241** 3c. red 10 10
561 **241** 5c. blue 10 10

**242** "Co-operation"

**1965.** International Co-operation Year.
562 **242** 5c. green 35 10

**243** Sir W. Grenfell

**1965.** Birth Centenary of Sir Wilfred Grenfell (missionary).
563 **243** 5c. green 20 10

**244** National Flag

**1965.** Inauguration of National Flag.
564 **244** 5c. red and blue 15 10

**245** Sir Winston Churchill

**1965.** Churchill Commemoration.
565 **245** 5c. brown 15 10

**246** Peace Tower, Parliament Buildings, Ottawa

**1965.** Inter-Parliamentary Union Conference, Ottawa.
566 **246** 5c. green 10 10

**247** Parliament Buildings, Ottawa, 1865

**1965.** Centenary of Proclamation of Ottawa as Capital.
567 **247** 5c. brown 10 10

**248** "Gold, Frankincense and Myrrh"

**1965.** Christmas.
568 **248** 3c. green 10 10
569 **248** 5c. blue 10 10

**249** "Alouette 2" over Canada

**1966.** Launching of Canadian Satellite, "Alouette 2".
570 **249** 5c. blue 15 10

**250** La Salle

**1966.** 300th Anniv of La Salle's Arrival in Canada.
571 **250** 5c. green 15 10

**251** Road Signs

**1966.** Highway Safety.
572 **251** 5c. yellow, blue and black 15 10

**252** Canadian Delegation and Houses of Parliament

**1966.** Centenary of London Conference.
573 **252** 5c. brown 10 10

**253** Douglas Point Nuclear Power Station

**1966.** Peaceful Uses of Atomic Energy.
574 **253** 5c. blue 10 10

**254** Parliamentary Library, Ottawa

**1966.** Commonwealth Parliamentary Association Conference, Ottawa.
575 **254** 5c. purple 10 10

**255** "Praying Hands", after Durer

**1966.** Christmas.
576 **255** 3c. red 10 10
577 **255** 5c. orange 10 10

**256** Flags and Canada on Globe

**1967.** Canadian Centennial.
578 **256** 5c. red and blue 10 10

**257** Queen Elizabeth, Northern Lights and Dog-team

**262** "Alaska Highway" (A. Y. Jackson)

**1967**
579 **257** 1c. brown 10 10
580 - 2c. green 10 10
581 - 3c. purple 30 40
582 - 4c. red 20 10
583 - 5c. blue 20 10
601 - 6c. red 45 10
607 - 6c. black 30 10
609 - 7c. green 30 60
584 **262** 8c. purple 25 1·00
610 - 8c. black 30 10
585 - 10c. olive 25 10
586 - 15c. purple 30 10
587 - 20c. blue 1·60 10
588 - 25c. green 1·50 10
589 - 50c. brown 1·50 10
590 - $1 red 1·50 1·00

DESIGNS—As Type **257**: 2c. Totem pole; 3c. Combine-harvester and oil derrick; 4c. Ship in lock; 5c., Harbour scene; 6c., 7c. "Transport"; 8c. (No. 610), Library of Parliament. As Type **262**: 10c. "The Jack Pine" (T. Thomson); 15c. "Bylot Island" (L. Harris); 20c. "Quebec Ferry" (J. W. Morrice); 25c. "The Solemn Land" (J. E. H. MacDonald); 50c. "Summer's Stores" (Grain elevators, J. Ensor); $1 "Oilfield" (near Edmonton, H. G. Glyde).

**269** Canadian Pavilion

**1967.** World Fair, Montreal.
611 **269** 5c. blue and red 10 10

**270** Allegory of "Womanhood" on Ballot-box

**1967.** 50th Anniv of Women's Franchise.
612 **270** 5c. purple and black 10 10

**271** Queen Elizabeth II and Centennial Emblem

**1967.** Royal Visit.
613 **271** 5c. plum and brown 15 10

**272** Athlete

**1967.** Pan-American Games, Winnipeg.
614 **272** 5c. red 10 10

**273** "World News"

**1967.** 50th Anniv of Canadian Press.
615 **273** 5c. blue 10 10

**274** Governor-General Vanier

**1967.** Vanier Commemoration.
616 **274** 5c. black 10 10

**275** People of 1867, and Toronto, 1967

**1967.** Cent of Toronto as Capital City of Ontario.
617 **275** 5c. green and red 10 10

**276** Carol Singers

**1967.** Christmas.
618 **276** 3c. red 10 10
619 **276** 5c. green 10 10

**277** Grey Jays

**1968.** Wild Life.
620 **277** 5c. multicoloured 30 10
See also Nos. 638/40.

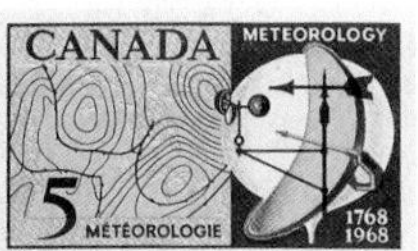


**278** Weather Map and Instruments

**1968.** 20th Anniv of First Meteorological Readings.
621 **278** 5c. multicoloured 15 10

**279** Narwhal

**1968.** Wild Life.
622 **279** 5c. multicoloured 15 10

**280** Globe, Maple Leaf and Rain Gauge

**1968.** International Hydrological Decade.
623 **280** 5c. multicoloured 15 10

**281** The "Nonsuch"

**1968.** 300th Anniv of Voyage of the "Nonsuch".
624 **281** 5c. multicoloured 20 10

**282** Lacrosse Players

**1968.** Lacrosse.
625 **282** 5c. multicoloured 15 10

**283** Front Page of "The Globe", George Brown and Legislative Building

**1968.** 150th Birth Anniv of George Brown (politician and journalist).
626 **283** 5c. multicoloured 10 10

**284** H. Bourassa (politician and journalist)

**1968.** Birth Centenary of Henri Bourassa.
627 **284** 5c. black, red and cream 10 10

**285** John McCrae, Battlefield and First Lines of "In Flanders Fields"

**1968.** 50th Death Anniv of John McCrae (soldier and poet).
628 **285** 5c. multicoloured 10 10

**286** Armistice Monument, Vimy

**1968.** 50th Anniv of 1918 Armistice.
629 **286** 15c. black 30 40

**287** Eskimo Family (carving)

**1968.** Christmas.
630 **287** 5c. black and blue 10 10
631 - 6c. black and ochre 10 10
DESIGN: 6c. "Mother and Child" (carving).

**289** Curling

**1969.** Curling.
632 **289** 6c. black, blue and red 15 15

**290** Vincent Massey

**1969.** Vincent Massey, First Canadian-born Governor-General.
633 **290** 6c. sepia and ochre 10 10

**291** "Return from the Harvest Field" (Suzor-Cote)

**1969.** Birth Centenary of Marc Aurele de Foy Suzor-Cote (painter).
634 **291** 50c. multicoloured 1·50 2·75

**292** Globe and Tools

**1969.** 50th Anniv of I.L.O.
635 **292** 6c. green 10 10

**293** Vickers Vimy Aircraft over Atlantic Ocean

**1969.** 50th Anniv of 1st Non-stop Transatlantic Flight.
636 **293** 15c. brown, green and blue 40 55

**294** "Sir William Osler" (J. S. Sargent)

**1969.** 50th Death Anniv of Sir William Osler (physician).
637 **294** 6c. blue and brown 20 10

**295** White-throated Sparrow

**1969.** Birds. Multicoloured.
638 6c. Type **295** 25 10
639 10c. Savannah sparrow ("Ipswich Sparrow") (horiz) 35 1·10
640 25c. Hermit thrush (horiz) 1·10 3·75

**298** Flags of Winter and Summer Games

**1969.** Canadian Games.
641 **298** 6c. green, red and blue 10 10

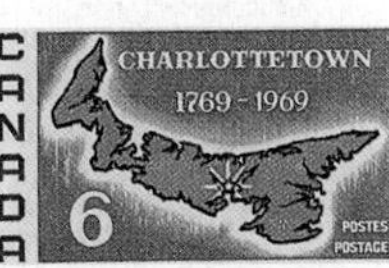


**299** Outline of Prince Edward Island showing Charlottetown

**1969.** Bicentenary of Charlottetown as Capital of Prince Edward Island.
642 **299** 6c. brown, black and blue 20 20

**300** Sir Isaac Brock and Memorial Column

**1969.** Birth Bicentenary of Sir Isaac Brock.
643 **300** 6c. orange, bistre and brown 10 10

**301** Children of the World in Prayer

**1969.** Christmas.
644 **301** 5c. multicoloured 10 10
645 **301** 6c. multicoloured 10 10

**302** Stephen Butler Leacock, Mask and "Mariposa"

**1969.** Birth Centenary of Stephen Butler Leacock (humorist).
646 **302** 6c. multicoloured 10 10

**303** Symbolic Cross-roads

**1970.** Centenary of Manitoba.
647 **303** 6c. blue, yellow and red 15 10

**304** "Enchanted Owl" (Kenojuak)

**1970.** Centenary of Northwest Territories.
648 **304** 6c. red and black 10 10

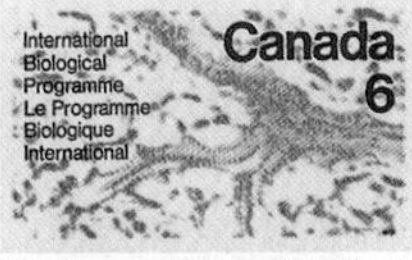


**305** Microscopic View of Inside of Leaf

**1970.** International Biological Programme.
649 **305** 6c. green, yellow and blue 15 10

**306** Expo 67 Emblem and stylized Cherry Blossom

**1970.** World Fair, Osaka. Multicoloured.
650 25c. Type **306** (red) 1·50 2·25
651 25c. Dogwood (violet) 1·50 2·25
652 25c. White trillium (green) 1·50 2·25
653 25c. White garden lily (blue) 1·50 2·25
NOTE: Each stamp shows a stylized cherry blossom, in a different colour, given above in brackets.

**310** Henry Kelsey

**1970.** 300th Birth Anniv of Henry Kelsey (explorer).

| | | | | |
|---|---|---|---|---|
| 654 | **310** | 6c. multicoloured | 10 | 10 |

**311** "Towards Unification"

**1970.** 25th Anniv of UNO.

| | | | | |
|---|---|---|---|---|
| 655 | **311** | 10c. blue | 75 | 1·50 |
| 656 | **311** | 15c. mauve and lilac | 75 | 50 |

**312** Louis Riel (Metis leader)

**1970.** Louis Riel Commemoration.

| | | | | |
|---|---|---|---|---|
| 657 | **312** | 6c. blue and red | 10 | 10 |

**313** Mackenzie's Inscription, Dean Channel

**1970.** Sir Alexander Mackenzie (explorer).

| | | | | |
|---|---|---|---|---|
| 658 | **313** | 6c. brown | 15 | 10 |

**314** Sir Oliver Mowat (statesman)

**1970.** Sir Oliver Mowat Commemoration.

| | | | | |
|---|---|---|---|---|
| 659 | **314** | 6c. red and black | 10 | 10 |

**315** "Isles of Spruce" (A. Lismer)

**1970.** 50th Anniv of "Group of Seven" (artists).

| | | | | |
|---|---|---|---|---|
| 660 | **315** | 6c. multicoloured | 10 | 10 |

**316** "Horse-drawn Sleigh" (D. Niskala)

**1970.** Christmas. Children's Drawings. Mult.

| | | | |
|---|---|---|---|
| 661 | 5c. Type **316** | 40 | 20 |
| 662 | 5c. "Stable and Star of Bethlehem" (L. Wilson) | 40 | 20 |
| 663 | 5c. "Snowmen" (M. Lecompte) | 40 | 20 |
| 664 | 5c. "Skiing" (D. Durham) | 40 | 20 |
| 665 | 5c. "Santa Claus" (A. Martin) | 40 | 20 |
| 666 | 6c. "Santa Claus" (E. Bhattacharya) | 40 | 20 |
| 667 | 6c. "Christ in Manger" (J. McKinney) | 40 | 20 |
| 668 | 6c. "Toy Shop" (N. Whateley) | 40 | 20 |
| 669 | 6c. "Christmas Tree" (J. Pomperleau) | 40 | 20 |
| 670 | 6c. "Church" (J. McMillan) | 40 | 20 |
| 671 | 10c. "Christ in Manger" (C. Fortier) (37×20 mm) | 25 | 30 |
| 672 | 15c. "Trees and Sledge" (J. Dojcak) (37×20 mm) | 35 | 60 |

**328** Sir Donald A. Smith

**1970.** 150th Birth Anniv of Sir Donald Alexander Smith.

| | | | | |
|---|---|---|---|---|
| 673 | **328** | 6c. yellow, brown and green | 15 | 10 |

**329** "Big Raven" (E. Carr)

**1971.** Birth Centenary of Emily Carr (painter).

| | | | | |
|---|---|---|---|---|
| 674 | **329** | 6c. multicoloured | 20 | 30 |

**330** Laboratory Equipment

**1971.** 50th Anniv of Discovery of Insulin.

| | | | | |
|---|---|---|---|---|
| 675 | **330** | 6c. multicoloured | 30 | 30 |

**331** "The Atom"

**1971.** Birth Centenary of Lord Rutherford (scientist).

| | | | | |
|---|---|---|---|---|
| 676 | **331** | 6c. yellow, red and brown | 20 | 20 |

**332** Maple "Keys"

**1971.** "The Maple Leaf in Four Seasons". Mult.

| | | | |
|---|---|---|---|
| 677 | 6c. Type **332** (spring) | 20 | 20 |
| 678 | 6c. Green leaves (summer) | 20 | 20 |
| 679 | 7c. Autumn leaves | 20 | 20 |
| 680 | 7c. Withered leaves and snow (winter) | 20 | 20 |

**333** Louis Papineau

**1971.** Death Centenary of Louis-Joseph Papineau (politician).

| | | | | |
|---|---|---|---|---|
| 681 | **333** | 6c. multicoloured | 15 | 25 |

**334** Chart of Coppermine River

**1971.** Bicentenary of Samuel Hearne's Expedition to the Coppermine River.

| | | | | |
|---|---|---|---|---|
| 682 | **334** | 6c. red, brown and buff | 40 | 40 |

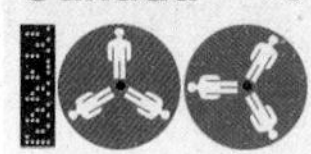

**335** "People" and Computer Tapes

**1971.** Centenary of 1st Canadian Census.

| | | | | |
|---|---|---|---|---|
| 683 | **335** | 6c. blue, red and black | 30 | 20 |

**336** Maple Leaves

**1971.** Radio Canada International.

| | | | | |
|---|---|---|---|---|
| 684 | **336** | 15c. red, yellow and black | 50 | 1·50 |

**337** "B. C."

**1971.** Centenary of British Columbia's Entry into the Confederation.

| | | | | |
|---|---|---|---|---|
| 685 | **337** | 7c. multicoloured | 15 | 10 |

**338** "Indian Encampment on Lake Huron" (Kane)

**1971.** Death Centenary of Paul Kane (painter).

| | | | | |
|---|---|---|---|---|
| 686 | **338** | 7c. multicoloured | 20 | 10 |

**339** "Snowflake"

**1971.** Christmas.

| | | | | |
|---|---|---|---|---|
| 687 | **339** | 6c. blue | 10 | 10 |
| 688 | **339** | 7c. green | 15 | 10 |
| 689 | - | 10c. silver and red | 50 | 1·25 |
| 690 | - | 15c. silver, purple and lavender | 65 | 2·00 |

DESIGN: 10c., 15c. "Snowflake" design similar to Type **339** but square (26×26 mm).

**340** Pierre Laporte (Quebec Cabinet Minister)

**1971.** 1st Anniv of Assassination of Pierre Laporte.

| | | | | |
|---|---|---|---|---|
| 691 | **340** | 7c. black on buff | 15 | 10 |

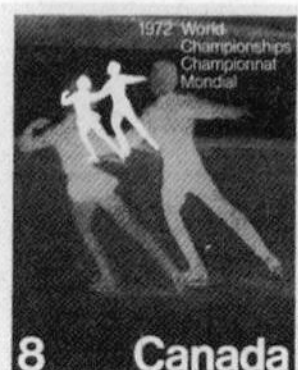

**341** Skaters

**1972.** World Figure Skating Championships, Calgary.

| | | | | |
|---|---|---|---|---|
| 692 | **341** | 8c. purple | 15 | 20 |

**342** J. A. MacDonald

**343** Forest, Central Canada

**344** Vancouver

**1972**

| | | | | |
|---|---|---|---|---|
| 693 | **342** | 1c. orange | 10 | 30 |
| 694 | - | 2c. green | 10 | 10 |
| 695 | - | 3c. brown | 10 | 50 |
| 696 | - | 4c. black | 10 | 50 |
| 697 | - | 5c. mauve | 10 | 10 |
| 698 | - | 6c. red | 10 | 50 |
| 699 | - | 7c. brown | 40 | 50 |
| 700 | - | 8c. blue | 15 | 10 |
| 701 | - | 10c. red | 75 | 10 |
| 702a | **343** | 10c. green, turquoise and orange | 40 | 15 |
| 703b | - | 15c. blue and brown | 1·25 | 10 |
| 704a | - | 20c. orange, violet and blue | 1·50 | 10 |
| 705b | - | 25c. ultram and blue | 1·00 | 10 |
| 706 | - | 50c. green, blue and brown | 1·00 | 30 |
| 709a | **344** | $1 multicoloured | 85 | 70 |
| 708 | - | $2 multicoloured | 1·50 | 2·00 |

DESIGNS—As Type **342** (1 to 7c. show Canadian Prime Ministers): 2c. W. Laurier; 3c. R. Borden; 4c. W. L. Mackenzie King; 5c. R. B. Bennett; 6c. L. B. Pearson; 7c. Louis St. Laurent; 8, 10c. Queen Elizabeth II. As Type **343**: 15c. American bighorn; 20c. Prairie landscape from the air; 25c. Polar bears; 50c. Seashore, Eastern Canada. As Type **344**: $2 Quebec.

**345** Heart

**1972.** World Health Day.

| | | | | |
|---|---|---|---|---|
| 719 | **345** | 8c. red | 30 | 10 |

**346** Frontenac and Fort Saint-Louis, Quebec

**1972.** 300th Anniv of Governor Frontenac's Appointment to New France.

| | | | | |
|---|---|---|---|---|
| 720 | **346** | 8c. red, brown and blue | 15 | 15 |

**347** Plains Indians' Artefacts

**347a** Buffalo Chase

**1972.** Canadian Indians. (a) Horiz designs showing Artefacts as T 347 or Scenes from Indian Life as T 347a.

| | | | | |
|---|---|---|---|---|
| 721 | **347** | 8c. multicoloured | 40 | 10 |
| 722 | **347a** | 8c. brown, yellow & blk | 40 | 10 |
| 723 | - | 8c. multicoloured | 40 | 10 |
| 724 | - | 8c. multicoloured | 40 | 10 |
| 725 | - | 8c. multicoloured | 40 | 10 |
| 726 | - | 8c. brown, yellow & blk | 40 | 10 |
| 727 | - | 8c. multicoloured | 40 | 10 |
| 728 | - | 8c. multicoloured | 40 | 10 |
| 729 | - | 10c. multicoloured | 40 | 20 |
| 730 | - | 10c. red, brown and black | 40 | 20 |

TRIBES: Nos. 721/2, Plains Indians; Nos. 723/4, Algonkians; Nos. 725/6, Pacific Coast Indians; Nos. 727/8, Subarctic Indians; Nos. 729/30, Iroquoians.

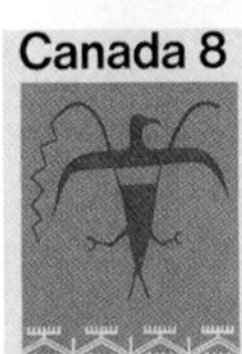


348 Thunderbird and Tribal Pattern

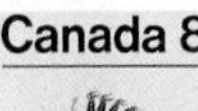

348a Dancer in Ceremonial Costume

(b) Vert designs showing Thunderbird and pattern as T 348 or Costumes as T 348a.

| | | | | |
|---|---|---|---|---|
| 731 | 348 | 8c. orange, red and black | 40 | 15 |
| 732 | 348a | 8c. multicoloured | 40 | 15 |
| 733 | - | 8c. red, violet and black | 40 | 10 |
| 734 | - | 8c. green, brown and black | 40 | 10 |
| 735 | - | 8c. red and black | 40 | 10 |
| 736 | - | 8c. multicoloured | 40 | 10 |
| 737 | - | 8c. green, brown and black | 40 | 10 |
| 738 | - | 8c. multicoloured | 40 | 10 |
| 739 | - | 10c. brown, orange & blk | 40 | 20 |
| 740 | - | 10c. multicoloured | 40 | 20 |

TRIBES: Nos. 731/2, Plains Indians; Nos. 733/4, Algonkians; Nos. 735/6, Pacific Coast Indians; Nos. 737/8, Subarctic Indians; Nos. 739/40, Iroquoians.

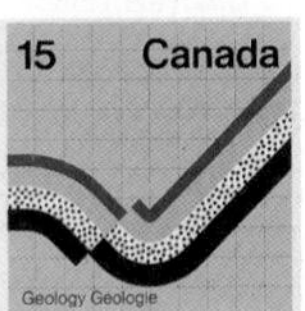


349 Earth's Crust

**1972.** Earth Sciences.

| | | | | |
|---|---|---|---|---|
| 741 | | 15c. multicoloured | 1·10 | 1·90 |
| 742 | | 15c. grey, blue and black | 1·10 | 1·90 |
| 743 | 349 | 15c. multicoloured | 1·10 | 1·90 |
| 744 | - | 15c. green, orange and black | 1·10 | 1·90 |

DESIGNS AND EVENTS: No. 741 Photogrammetric surveying (12th Congress of International Society of Photogrammetry); No. 742 "Siegfried" lines (6th Conference of Int Cartographic Association); No. 743 (24th International Geological Congress); No. 744 Diagram of village at road-intersection (22nd Int Geographical Congress).

350 Candles

**1972.** Christmas. Multicoloured.

| | | | |
|---|---|---|---|
| 745 | 6c. Type **350** | 15 | 10 |
| 746 | 8c. Type **350** | 15 | 10 |
| 747 | 10c. Candles with fruits and pine boughs (horiz) | 50 | 1·25 |
| 748 | 15c. Candles with prayer-book, caskets and vase (horiz) | 60 | 2·00 |

Nos. 747/8 are size 36×20 mm.

351 "The Blacksmith's Shop" (Krieghoff)

**1972.** Death Centenary of Cornelius Krieghoff (painter).

| | | | | |
|---|---|---|---|---|
| 749 | 351 | 8c. multicoloured | 30 | 15 |

352 F. de Montmorency-Laval

**1973.** 350th Birth Anniv of Monsignor de Laval (1st Bishop of Quebec).

| | | | | |
|---|---|---|---|---|
| 750 | 352 | 8c. blue, gold and silver | 20 | 40 |

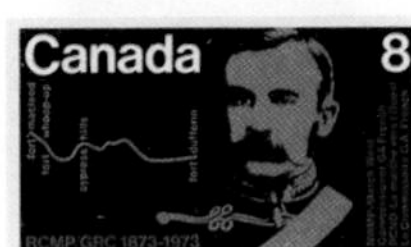


353 Commissioner French and Route of the March West

**1973.** Centenary of Royal Canadian Mounted Police.

| | | | | |
|---|---|---|---|---|
| 751 | 353 | 8c. brown, orange and red | 35 | 20 |
| 752 | - | 10c. multicoloured | 1·00 | 1·25 |
| 753 | - | 15c. multicoloured | 2·25 | 2·00 |

DESIGNS: 10c. Spectrograph; 15c. Mounted policeman.

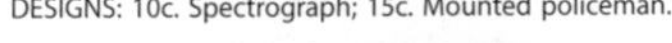

354 Jeanne Mance

**1973.** 300th Death Anniv of Jeanne Mance (nurse).

| | | | | |
|---|---|---|---|---|
| 754 | 354 | 8c. multicoloured | 20 | 40 |

355 Joseph Howe

**1973.** Death Centenary of Joseph Howe (Nova Scotian politician).

| | | | | |
|---|---|---|---|---|
| 755 | 355 | 8c. gold and black | 20 | 40 |

356 "Mist Fantasy" (MacDonald)

**1973.** Birth Cent of J. E. H. MacDonald (artist).

| | | | | |
|---|---|---|---|---|
| 756 | 356 | 15c. multicoloured | 30 | 55 |

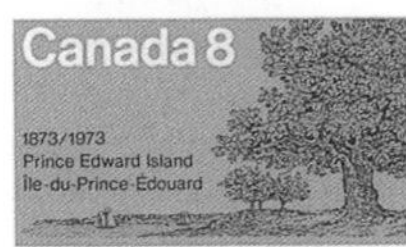


357 Oaks and Harbour

**1973.** Centenary of Prince Edward Island's Entry into the Confederation.

| | | | | |
|---|---|---|---|---|
| 757 | 357 | 8c. orange and red | 20 | 30 |

358 Scottish Settlers

**1973.** Bicentenary of Arrival of Scottish Settlers at Pictou, Nova Scotia.

| | | | | |
|---|---|---|---|---|
| 758 | 358 | 8c. multicoloured | 25 | 20 |

359 Queen Elizabeth II

**1973.** Royal Visit and Commonwealth Heads of Government Meeting, Ottawa.

| | | | | |
|---|---|---|---|---|
| 759 | 359 | 8c. multicoloured | 25 | 20 |
| 760 | 359 | 15c. multicoloured | 80 | 1·50 |

360 Nellie McClung

**1973.** Birth Centenary of Nellie McClung (feminist).

| | | | | |
|---|---|---|---|---|
| 761 | 360 | 8c. multicoloured | 20 | 50 |

361 Emblem of 1976 Olympics

**1973.** 1976 Olympic Games, Montreal (1st issue).

| | | | | |
|---|---|---|---|---|
| 762 | 361 | 8c. multicoloured | 25 | 15 |
| 763 | 361 | 15c. multicoloured | 45 | 1·25 |

See also Nos. 768/71, 772/4, 786/9, 798/802, 809/11, 814/16, 829/32, 833/7 and 842/4.

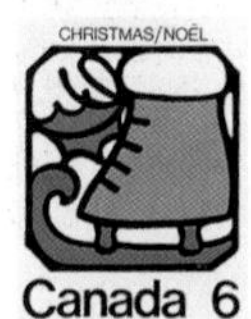


362 Ice-skate

**1973.** Christmas. Multicoloured.

| | | | |
|---|---|---|---|
| 764 | 6c. Type **362** | 15 | 10 |
| 765 | 8c. Bird decoration | 15 | 10 |
| 766 | 10c. Santa Claus (20×36 mm) | 50 | 1·10 |
| 767 | 15c. Shepherd (20×36 mm) | 60 | 1·50 |

363 Diving

**1974.** 1976 Olympic Games, Montreal. (2nd issue). "Summer Activities". Each blue.

| | | | |
|---|---|---|---|
| 768 | 8c. Type **363** | 30 | 50 |
| 769 | 8c. "Jogging" | 30 | 50 |
| 770 | 8c. Cycling | 30 | 50 |
| 771 | 8c. Hiking | 30 | 50 |

**1974.** 1976 Olympic Games, Montreal. (3rd issue). As T 361 but smaller (20×36½ mm).

| | | | |
|---|---|---|---|
| 772 | 8c.+2c. multicoloured | 25 | 45 |
| 773 | 10c.+5c. multicoloured | 40 | 1·00 |
| 774 | 15c.+5c. multicoloured | 45 | 1·40 |

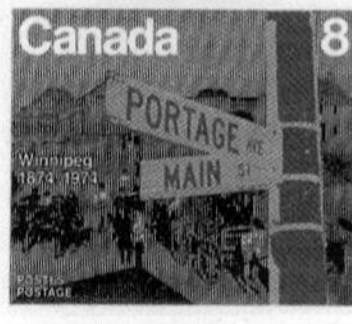


364 Winnipeg Signpost, 1872

**1974.** Winnipeg Centennial.

| | | | | |
|---|---|---|---|---|
| 775 | 364 | 8c. multicoloured | 20 | 15 |

365 Postmaster and Customer

**1974.** Centenary of Canadian Letter Carrier Delivery Service. Multicoloured.

| | | | |
|---|---|---|---|
| 776 | 8c. Type **365** | 50 | 80 |
| 777 | 8c. Postman collecting mail | 50 | 80 |
| 778 | 8c. Mail handler | 50 | 80 |
| 779 | 8c. Mail sorters | 50 | 80 |
| 780 | 8c. Postman making delivery | 50 | 80 |
| 781 | 8c. Rural delivery by car | 50 | 80 |

366 "Canada's Contribution to Agriculture"

**1974.** Centenary of "Agricultural Education". Ontario Agricultural College.

| | | | | |
|---|---|---|---|---|
| 782 | 366 | 8c. multicoloured | 20 | 20 |

367 Telephone Development

**1974.** Centenary of Invention of Telephone by Alexander Graham Bell.

| | | | | |
|---|---|---|---|---|
| 783 | 367 | 8c. multicoloured | 20 | 20 |

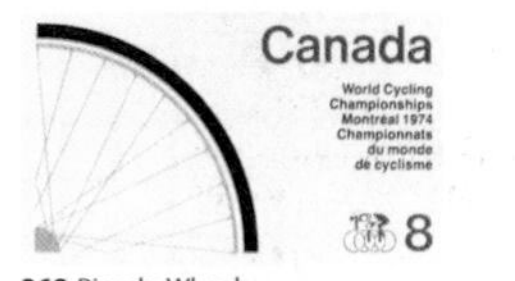


368 Bicycle Wheel

**1974.** World Cycling Championships, Montreal.

| | | | | |
|---|---|---|---|---|
| 784 | 368 | 8c. black, red and silver | 20 | 30 |

369 Mennonite Settlers

**1974.** Centenary of Arrival of Mennonites in Manitoba.

| | | | | |
|---|---|---|---|---|
| 785 | 369 | 8c. multicoloured | 20 | 20 |

**1974.** 1976 Olympic Games, Montreal (4th issue). "Winter Activities". As T 363. Each red.

| | | | |
|---|---|---|---|
| 786 | 8c. Snow-shoeing | 55 | 60 |
| 787 | 8c. Skiing | 55 | 60 |
| 788 | 8c. Skating | 55 | 60 |
| 789 | 8c. Curling | 55 | 60 |

370 Mercury, Winged Horses and UPU Emblem

**1974.** Centenary of UPU.

| | | | | |
|---|---|---|---|---|
| 790 | 370 | 8c. violet, red and blue | 15 | 15 |
| 791 | 370 | 15c. red, violet and blue | 50 | 1·50 |

371 "The Nativity" (J. P. Lemieux)

**1974.** Christmas. Multicoloured.

| | | | |
|---|---|---|---|
| 792 | 6c. Type **371** | 10 | 10 |
| 793 | 8c. "Skaters in Hull" (H. Masson) (34×31 mm) | 10 | 10 |
| 794 | 10c. "The Ice Cone, Montmorency Falls" (R. C. Todd) | 30 | 75 |
| 795 | 15c. "Village in the Laurentian Mountains" (C. A. Gagnon) | 35 | 1·10 |

372 Marconi and St. John's Harbour, Newfoundland

**1974.** Birth Centenary of Guglielmo Marconi (radio pioneer).

| | | | | |
|---|---|---|---|---|
| 796 | **372** | 8c. multicoloured | 20 | 20 |

**373** Merritt and Welland Canal

**1974.** William Merritt Commemoration.

| | | | | |
|---|---|---|---|---|
| 797 | **373** | 8c. multicoloured | 20 | 30 |

**374** Swimming

**1975.** 1976 Olympic Games, Montreal (5th issue). Multicoloured.

| | | | |
|---|---|---|---|
| 798 | 8c.+2c. Type **374** | 45 | 65 |
| 799 | 10c.+5c. Rowing | 60 | 1·25 |
| 800 | 15c.+5c. Sailing | 70 | 1·40 |

**375** "The Sprinter"

**1975.** 1976 Olympic Games, Montreal (6th issue). Multicoloured.

| | | | |
|---|---|---|---|
| 801 | $1 Type **375** | 1·25 | 2·00 |
| 802 | $2 "The Diver" (vert) | 1·75 | 3·50 |

**376** "Anne of Green Gables" (Lucy Maud Montgomery)

**1975.** Canadian Writers (1st series). Multicoloured.

| | | | |
|---|---|---|---|
| 803 | 8c. Type **376** | 30 | 10 |
| 804 | 8c. "Maria Chapdelaine" (Louis Hemon) | 30 | 10 |

See also Nos. 846/7, 940/1 and 1085/6.

**377** Marguerite Bourgeoys (founder of the Order of Notre Dame)

**378** S. D. Chown (founder of United Church of Canada)

**1975.** Canadian Celebrities.

| | | | | |
|---|---|---|---|---|
| 805 | **377** | 8c. multicoloured | 60 | 40 |
| 806 | - | 8c. multicoloured | 60 | 40 |
| 807 | **378** | 8c. multicoloured | 30 | 75 |
| 808 | - | 8c. multicoloured | 30 | 75 |

DESIGNS—As Type **377**: No. 806, Alphonse Desjardins (leader of Credit Union movement). As Type **378**: No. 808, Dr. J. Cook (first moderator of Presbyterian Church in Canada).

**379** Pole-vaulting

**1975.** 1976 Olympics (7th issue). Multicoloured.

| | | | |
|---|---|---|---|
| 809 | 20c. Type **379** | 40 | 50 |
| 810 | 25c. Marathon-running | 55 | 80 |
| 811 | 50c. Hurdling | 70 | 1·25 |

**380** "Untamed" (photo by Walt Petrigo)

**1975.** Centenary of Calgary.

| | | | | |
|---|---|---|---|---|
| 812 | **380** | 8c. multicoloured | 30 | 30 |

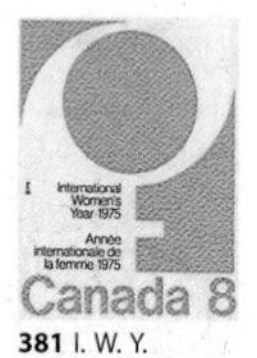


**381** I. W. Y. Symbol

**1975.** International Women's Year.

| | | | | |
|---|---|---|---|---|
| 813 | **381** | 8c. grey, brown and black | 30 | 30 |

**382** Fencing

**1975.** Olympic Games, Montreal (1976) (8th issue). Multicoloured.

| | | | |
|---|---|---|---|
| 814 | 8c.+2c. Type **382** | 35 | 75 |
| 815 | 10c.+5c. Boxing | 45 | 1·50 |
| 816 | 15c.+5c. Judo | 55 | 1·75 |

**383** "Justice-Justitia" (statue by W. S. Allward)

**1975.** Centenary of Canadian Supreme Court.

| | | | | |
|---|---|---|---|---|
| 817 | **383** | 8c. multicoloured | 20 | 30 |

**384** "William D. Lawrence" (full-rigged ship)

**1975.** Canadian Ships (1st series). Coastal Vessels.

| | | | | |
|---|---|---|---|---|
| 818 | **384** | 8c. brown and black | 70 | 75 |
| 819 | - | 8c. green and black | 70 | 75 |
| 820 | - | 8c. green and black | 70 | 75 |
| 821 | - | 8c. brown and black | 70 | 75 |

DESIGNS: No. 819, "Neptune" (steamer); 820, "Beaver" (paddle-steamer); 821, "Quadra" (steamer).

See also Nos. 851/4, 902/5 and 931/4.

**385** "Santa Claus" (G. Kelly)

**1975.** Christmas. Multicoloured.

| | | | |
|---|---|---|---|
| 822 | 6c. Type **385** | 15 | 10 |
| 823 | 6c. "Skater" (B. Cawsey) | 15 | 10 |
| 824 | 8c. "Child" (D. Hebert) | 15 | 10 |
| 825 | 8c. "Family" (L. Caldwell) | 15 | 10 |
| 826 | 10c. "Gift" (D. Lovely) | 30 | 50 |
| 827 | 15c. "Trees" (R. Kowalski) (horiz) | 40 | 75 |

**386** Text, Badge and Bugle

**1975.** 50th Anniv of Royal Canadian Legion.

| | | | | |
|---|---|---|---|---|
| 828 | **386** | 8c. multicoloured | 20 | 20 |

**387** Basketball

**1976.** Olympic Games, Montreal (9th issue). Mult.

| | | | |
|---|---|---|---|
| 829 | 8c.+2c. Type **387** | 1·50 | 1·00 |
| 830 | 10c.+5c. Gymnastics | 60 | 1·40 |
| 831 | 20c.+5c. Soccer | 70 | 1·60 |

**388** Games Symbol and Snow Crystal

**1976.** 12th Winter Olympic Games, Innsbruck.

| | | | | |
|---|---|---|---|---|
| 832 | **388** | 20c. multicoloured | 20 | 40 |

**389** "Communications Arts"

**1976.** Olympic Games, Montreal (10th issue). Multicoloured.

| | | | |
|---|---|---|---|
| 833 | 20c. Type **389** | 40 | 25 |
| 834 | 25c. Handicrafts | 65 | 75 |
| 835 | 50c. Performing Arts | 95 | 1·60 |

**390** Place Ville Marie and Notre-Dame Church

**1976.** Olympic Games, Montreal (11th issue). Multicoloured.

| | | | |
|---|---|---|---|
| 836 | $1 Type **390** | 2·25 | 4·50 |
| 837 | $2 Olympic stadium and flags | 2·75 | 5·50 |

**391** Flower and Urban Sprawl

**1976.** HABITAT. U.N. Conference on Human Settlements, Vancouver.

| | | | | |
|---|---|---|---|---|
| 838 | **391** | 20c. multicoloured | 20 | 30 |

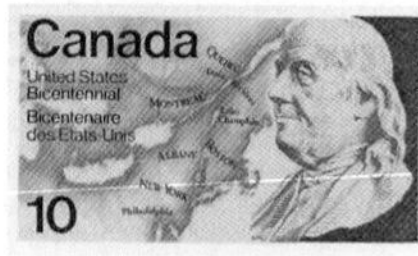


**392** Benjamin Franklin and Map

**1976.** Bicentenary of American Revolution.

| | | | | |
|---|---|---|---|---|
| 839 | **392** | 10c. multicoloured | 20 | 35 |

**393** Wing Parade before Mackenzie Building

**1976.** Centenary of Royal Military College. Mult.

| | | | |
|---|---|---|---|
| 840 | 8c. Colour party and Memorial Arch | 25 | 30 |
| 841 | 8c. Type **393** | 25 | 30 |

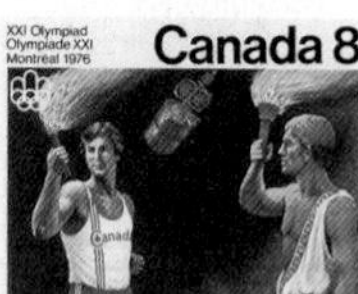


**394** Transfer of Olympic Flame by Satellite

**1976.** Olympic Games, Montreal (12th issue). Multicoloured.

| | | | |
|---|---|---|---|
| 842 | 8c. Type **394** | 20 | 10 |
| 843 | 20c. Carrying the Olympic flag | 45 | 60 |
| 844 | 25c. Athletes with medals | 45 | 85 |

**395** Archer

**1976.** Disabled Olympics.

| | | | | |
|---|---|---|---|---|
| 845 | **395** | 20c. multicoloured | 20 | 30 |

**396** "Sam McGee" (Robert W. Service)

**1976.** Canadian Writers (2nd series). Mult.

| | | | |
|---|---|---|---|
| 846 | 8c. Type **396** | 15 | 40 |
| 847 | 8c. "Le Survenant" (Germaine Guevremont) | 15 | 40 |

**397** "Nativity" (F. Mayer)

**1976.** Christmas. Stained-glass Windows. Mult.

| | | | |
|---|---|---|---|
| 848 | 8c. Type **397** | 10 | 10 |
| 849 | 10c. "Nativity" (G. Maile & Son) | 10 | 10 |

| | | | | |
|---|---|---|---|---|
| 850 | | 20c. "Nativity" (Yvonne Williams) | 20 | 60 |

**398** "Northcote" (paddle-steamer)

**1976.** Canadian Ships (2nd series). Inland Vessels.

| | | | | |
|---|---|---|---|---|
| 851 | **398** | 10c. lt brown, brn & blk | 45 | 60 |
| 852 | - | 10c. blue and black | 45 | 60 |
| 853 | - | 10c. blue and black | 45 | 60 |
| 854 | - | 10c. lt green, green & blk | 45 | 60 |

DESIGNS: No. 852, "Passport" (paddle-steamer); 853, "Chicora" (paddle-steamer); 854, "Athabasca" (steamer).

**399** Queen Elizabeth II

**1977.** Silver Jubilee.

| | | | | |
|---|---|---|---|---|
| 855 | **399** | 25c. multicoloured | 30 | 50 |

**400** Bottle Gentian

**401** Queen Elizabeth II (bas-relief by J. Huta)

**402** Houses of Parliament

**403** Trembling Aspen

**404** Prairie Town Main Street

**405** Fundy National Park

**1977**

| | | | | |
|---|---|---|---|---|
| 856 | **400** | 1c. multicoloured | 10 | 20 |
| 870 | **402** | 1c. blue | 1·25 | 3·25 |
| 857 | - | 2c. multicoloured | 10 | 10 |
| 858 | - | 3c. multicoloured | 10 | 10 |
| 859 | - | 4c. multicoloured | 10 | 10 |
| 860 | - | 5c. multicoloured | 10 | 10 |
| 871 | **402** | 5c. lilac | 50 | 1·25 |
| 861 | - | 10c. multicoloured | 15 | 10 |
| 866 | - | 12c. multicoloured | 15 | 60 |
| 867 | **401** | 12c. blue, grey and black | 15 | 10 |
| 872 | **402** | 12c. blue | 70 | 30 |
| 868 | **401** | 14c. red, grey and black | 20 | 10 |
| 873 | **402** | 14c. red | 15 | 10 |
| 866a | - | 15c. multicoloured | 15 | 15 |
| 875 | **403** | 15c. multicoloured | 15 | 10 |
| 869 | **401** | 17c. black, grey and green | 50 | 10 |
| 874 | **402** | 17c. green | 30 | 10 |
| 876 | - | 20c. multicoloured | 15 | 10 |
| 877 | - | 25c. multicoloured | 15 | 10 |
| 869b | **401** | 30c. dp pur, grey & pur | 70 | 1·25 |
| 878 | - | 30c. multicoloured | 20 | 10 |
| 869c | **401** | 32c. black, grey and blue | 50 | 1·25 |
| 879 | - | 35c. multicoloured | 25 | 10 |
| 883 | **404** | 50c. multicoloured | 85 | 1·00 |
| 883b | - | 60c. multicoloured | 65 | 80 |
| 881 | - | 75c. multicoloured | 1·00 | 1·50 |
| 882 | - | 80c. multicoloured | 85 | 1·25 |
| 884 | **405** | $1 multicoloured | 70 | 50 |
| 884b | - | $1 multicoloured | 85 | 45 |
| 884c | - | $1.50 multicoloured | 1·75 | 2·75 |
| 885 | - | $2 multicoloured | 1·00 | 45 |
| 885c | - | $2 multicoloured | 4·75 | 2·00 |
| 885d | - | $5 multicoloured | 3·00 | 3·00 |
| 885e | - | $5 multicoloured | 8·00 | 4·50 |

DESIGN—As Type **400**: 2c. Red columbine; 3c. Canada lily; 4c. Hepatica; 5c. Shooting star; 10c. Franklin's lady's slipper orchid. 12c. Jewel-weed; 15c. (No. 866a) Canada violet. As Type **403**: 20c. Douglas fir; 25c. Sugar maple; 30c. Red oak; 35c. White pine. As Type **404**: 60c. Ontario City street; 75c. Eastern City street; 80c. Maritimes street. As Type **405**: $1 Glacier; $1.50, Waterton Lakes; $2 (No. 885) Kluane; $2 (No. 885c) Banff; $5 (No. 885d) Point Pelee; $5 (No. 885e) La Maurice.

**406** Puma

**1977.** Endangered Wildlife (1st series).

| | | | | |
|---|---|---|---|---|
| 886 | **406** | 12c. multicoloured | 20 | 20 |

See also Nos. 906, 936/7, 976/7 and 1006/7.

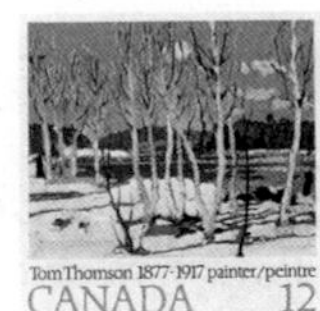


**407** "April in Algonquin Park"

**1977.** Birth Centenary of Tom Thomson (painter). Multicoloured.

| | | | |
|---|---|---|---|
| 887 | 12c. Type **407** | 15 | 20 |
| 888 | 12c. "Autumn Birches" | 15 | 20 |

**408** Crown and Lion

**1977.** Anniversaries. Multicoloured.

| | | | |
|---|---|---|---|
| 889 | 12c. Type **408** | 15 | 25 |
| 890 | 12c. Order of Canada | 15 | 25 |

EVENTS: No. 889, 25th anniv of First Canadian-born Governor-General; No. 890, 10th anniv of Order of Canada.

**409** Peace Bridge, Niagara River

**1977.** 50th Anniv of Opening of Peace Bridge.

| | | | | |
|---|---|---|---|---|
| 891 | **409** | 12c. multicoloured | 15 | 15 |

**410** Sir Sandford Fleming (engineer)

**1977.** Famous Canadians.

| | | | | |
|---|---|---|---|---|
| 892 | **410** | 12c. blue | 30 | 30 |
| 893 | - | 12c. brown | 30 | 30 |

DESIGN: No. 893, Joseph E. Bernier (explorer) and "Arctic" (survey ship).

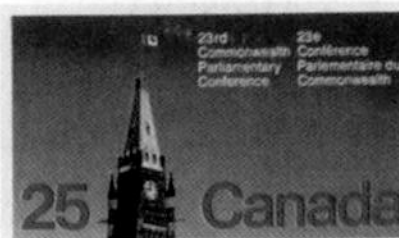


**411** Peace Tower, Parliament Buildings, Ottawa

**1977.** 23rd Commonwealth Parliamentary Conference.

| | | | | |
|---|---|---|---|---|
| 894 | **411** | 25c. multicoloured | 20 | 30 |

**412** Hunter Braves following Star

**1977.** Christmas. Canada's first carol "Jesous Ahatonhia". Multicoloured.

| | | | |
|---|---|---|---|
| 895 | 10c. Type **412** | 10 | 10 |
| 896 | 12c. Angelic choir | 10 | 10 |
| 897 | 25c. Christ Child and "Chiefs from afar" | 20 | 45 |

**413** Seal Hunter (soapstone sculpture)

**1977.** Canadian Eskimos ("Inuits") (1st series). Hunting. Multicoloured.

| | | | |
|---|---|---|---|
| 898 | 12c. Type **413** | 35 | 35 |
| 899 | 12c. Fishing with spear | 35 | 35 |
| 900 | 12c. Disguised archer | 35 | 35 |
| 901 | 12c. Walrus hunting | 35 | 35 |

See also Nos. 924/7, 958/61 and 989/92.

**414** Pinky (fishing boat)

**1977.** Canadian Ships (3rd series). Sailing Craft. Multicoloured.

| | | | |
|---|---|---|---|
| 902 | 12c. Type **414** | 20 | 35 |
| 903 | 12c. "Malahat" (schooner) | 20 | 35 |
| 904 | 12c. Tern schooner | 20 | 35 |
| 905 | 12c. Mackinaw boat | 20 | 35 |

**415** Peregrine Falcon

**1978.** Endangered Wildlife (2nd series).

| | | | | |
|---|---|---|---|---|
| 906 | **415** | 12c. multicoloured | 30 | 20 |

**416** Pair of 1851 12d. Black Stamps

**1978.** "CAPEX '78" International Philatelic Exhibition, Toronto.

| | | | | |
|---|---|---|---|---|
| 907 | **416** | 12c. black and sepia | 10 | 10 |
| 914 | - | 14c. blue, lt grey & grey | 15 | 10 |
| 915 | - | 30c. red, lt grey and grey | 25 | 40 |
| 916 | - | $1.25 violet, lt grey & grey | 70 | 1·50 |
| **MS**917 | | 101×96 mm. Nos. 914/16 | 1·25 | 2·50 |

DESIGNS: 14c. Pair of 1855 10d. Cartier stamps; 30c. Pair of 1857 ½d. red stamps; $1.25, Pair of 1851 6d. Prince Albert stamps.

**417** Games Emblem

**1978.** 11th Commonwealth Games, Edmonton (1st issue). Multicoloured.

| | | | |
|---|---|---|---|
| 908 | 14c. Type **417** | 10 | 10 |
| 909 | 30c. Badminton | 20 | 60 |

See also Nos. 918/21.

**418** "Captain Cook" (Nathaniel Dance)

**1978.** Bicentenary of Cook's 3rd Voyage. Mult.

| | | | |
|---|---|---|---|
| 910 | 14c. Type **418** | 20 | 20 |
| 911 | 14c. "Nootka Sound" (J. Webber) | 20 | 20 |

**419** Hardrock Silver Mine, Cobalt, Ontario

**1978.** Resources Development. Multicoloured.

| | | | |
|---|---|---|---|
| 912 | 14c. Type **419** | 15 | 20 |
| 913 | 14c. Giant excavators, Athabasca Tar Sands | 15 | 20 |

**1978.** 11th Commonwealth Games, Edmonton (2nd issue). As T 417. Multicoloured.

| | | | |
|---|---|---|---|
| 918 | 14c. Games stadium | 20 | 20 |
| 919 | 14c. Running | 20 | 20 |
| 920 | 30c. Alberta legislature building | 50 | 50 |
| 921 | 30c. Bowls | 50 | 50 |

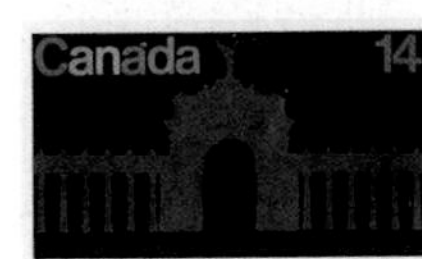


**420** Princes' Gate (Exhibition entrance)

**1978.** Centenary of National Exhibition.

| | | | | |
|---|---|---|---|---|
| 922 | **420** | 14c. multicoloured | 15 | 30 |

**421** Marguerite d'Youville

**1978.** Marguerite d'Youville (founder of Grey Nuns) Commemoration.

| | | | | |
|---|---|---|---|---|
| 923 | **421** | 14c. multicoloured | 15 | 30 |

**1978.** Canadian Eskimos ("Inuits") (2nd series). Travel. As T 413. Multicoloured.

| | | | |
|---|---|---|---|
| 924 | 14c. Woman on foot (painting by Pitseolak) | 30 | 40 |
| 925 | 14c. "Migration" (soapstone sculpture of sailing umiak by Joe Talurinili) | 30 | 40 |
| 926 | 14c. Aeroplane (stonecut and stencil print by Pudlo) | 30 | 40 |
| 927 | 14c. Dogteam and dogsled (ivory sculpture by Abraham Kingmeatook) | 30 | 40 |

**422** "Madonna of the Flowering Pea" (Cologne School)

**1978.** Christmas. Paintings. Multicoloured.

| | | | |
|---|---|---|---|
| 928 | 12c. Type **422** | 10 | 10 |
| 929 | 14c. "The Virgin and Child with St. Anthony and Donor" (detail, Hans Memling) | 10 | 10 |
| 930 | 30c. "The Virgin and Child" (Jacopo di Cione) | 25 | 90 |

**423** "Chief Justice Robinson" (paddle-steamer)

**1978.** Canadian Ships (4th series). Ice Vessels. Multicoloured.

| | | | |
|---|---|---|---|
| 931 | 14c. Type **423** | 45 | 65 |
| 932 | 14c. "St. Roch" (steamer) | 45 | 65 |
| 933 | 14c. "Northern Light" (steamer) | 45 | 65 |
| 934 | 14c. "Labrador" (steamer) | 45 | 65 |

**424** Carnival Revellers

**1978.** Quebec Carnival.

| | | | | |
|---|---|---|---|---|
| 935 | **424** | 14c. multicoloured | 20 | 20 |

**425** Eastern Spiny Soft-shelled Turtle

**1979.** Endangered Wildlife (3rd series). Multicoloured.

| | | | |
|---|---|---|---|
| 936 | 17c. Type **425** | 20 | 10 |
| 937 | 35c. Bowhead whale | 90 | 90 |

**426** Knotted Ribbon round Woman's Finger

**1979.** Postal Code Publicity. Multicoloured.

| | | | |
|---|---|---|---|
| 938 | 17c. Type **426** | 20 | 15 |
| 939 | 17c. Knotted string around man's finger | 20 | 15 |

**427** Scene from "Fruits of the Earth" by Frederick Philip Grove

**1979.** Canadian Writers (3rd series). Multicoloured.

| | | | |
|---|---|---|---|
| 940 | 17c. Type **427** | 15 | 15 |
| 941 | 17c. Scene from "Le Vaisseau d'Or" by Emile Nelligan | 15 | 15 |

**428** Charles-Michel de Salaberry (military hero)

**1979.** Famous Canadians. Multicoloured.

| | | | |
|---|---|---|---|
| 942 | 17c. Type **428** | 25 | 15 |
| 943 | 17c. John By (engineer) | 25 | 15 |

**429** Ontario

**1979.** Canada Day. Flags. Multicoloured.

| | | | |
|---|---|---|---|
| 944a | 17c. Type **429** | 25 | 40 |
| 944b | 17c. Quebec | 25 | 40 |
| 944c | 17c. Nova Scotia | 25 | 40 |
| 944d | 17c. New Brunswick | 25 | 40 |
| 944e | 17c. Manitoba | 25 | 40 |
| 944f | 17c. British Columbia | 25 | 40 |
| 944g | 17c. Prince Edward Island | 25 | 40 |
| 944h | 17c. Saskatchewan | 25 | 40 |
| 944i | 17c. Alberta | 25 | 40 |
| 944j | 17c. Newfoundland | 25 | 40 |
| 944k | 17c. Northwest Territories | 25 | 40 |
| 944l | 17c. Yukon Territory | 25 | 40 |

**430** Paddling Kayak

**1979.** Canoe-Kayak Championships.

| | | | | |
|---|---|---|---|---|
| 956 | **430** | 17c. multicoloured | 15 | 30 |

**431** Hockey Players

**1979.** Women's Field Hockey Championships, Vancouver.

| | | | | |
|---|---|---|---|---|
| 957 | **431** | 17c. black, yellow and green | 15 | 30 |

**1979.** Canadian Eskimos (3rd series). Shelter and the Community. As T 413. Multicoloured.

| | | | |
|---|---|---|---|
| 958 | 17c. "Summer Tent" (print by Kiakshuk) | 15 | 40 |
| 959 | 17c. "Five Eskimos building an Igloo" (soapstone sculpture by Abraham) | 15 | 40 |
| 960 | 17c. "The Dance" (print by Kalvak) | 15 | 40 |
| 961 | 17c. "Inuit drum dance" (soapstone sculptures by Madeleine Isserkut and Jean Mapsalak) | 15 | 40 |

**432** Toy Train

**1979.** Christmas. Multicoloured.

| | | | |
|---|---|---|---|
| 962 | 15c. Type **432** | 10 | 10 |
| 963 | 17c. Hobby-horse | 10 | 10 |
| 964 | 35c. Rag doll (vert) | 25 | 1·00 |

**433** Child watering Tree of Life (painting by Marie-Annick Viatour)

**1979.** International Year of the Child.

| | | | | |
|---|---|---|---|---|
| 965 | **433** | 17c. multicoloured | 15 | 30 |

**434** Canadair CL-215

**1979.** Canadian Aircraft (1st series). Flying Boats. Multicoloured.

| | | | |
|---|---|---|---|
| 966 | 17c. Type **434** | 25 | 20 |
| 967 | 17c. Curtiss HS-2L | 25 | 20 |
| 968 | 35c. Vickers Vedette | 65 | 65 |
| 969 | 35c. Consolidated Canso | 65 | 65 |

See also Nos. 996/9, 1026/9 and 1050/3.

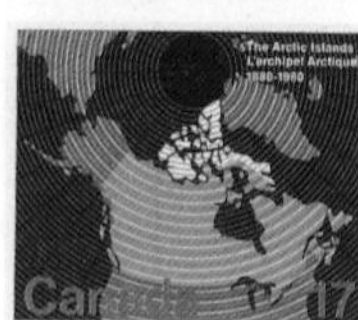
**435** Map of Arctic Islands

**1980.** Centenary of Arctic Islands Acquisition.

| | | | | |
|---|---|---|---|---|
| 970 | **435** | 17c. multicoloured | 15 | 30 |

**436** Skier

**1980.** Winter Olympic Games, Lake Placid.

| | | | | |
|---|---|---|---|---|
| 971 | **436** | 35c. multicoloured | 55 | 85 |

**437** "A Meeting of the School Trustees" (Robert Harris)

**1980.** Centenary of Royal Canadian Academy of Arts. Multicoloured.

| | | | |
|---|---|---|---|
| 972 | 17c. Type **437** | 25 | 20 |
| 973 | 17c. "Inspiration" (Philippe Hebert) | 25 | 20 |
| 974 | 35c. "Sunrise on the Saguenay" (Lucius O'Brien) | 50 | 55 |
| 975 | 35c. Thomas Fuller's design sketch for the original Parliament Buildings | 50 | 55 |

**438** Canadian Whitefish

**1980.** Endangered Wildlife (4th series). Multicoloured.

| | | | |
|---|---|---|---|
| 976 | 17c. Type **438** | 30 | 15 |
| 977 | 17c. Prairie chicken | 30 | 15 |

**439** Garden Flowers

**1980.** International Flower Show, Montreal.

| | | | | |
|---|---|---|---|---|
| 978 | **439** | 17c. multicoloured | 15 | 20 |

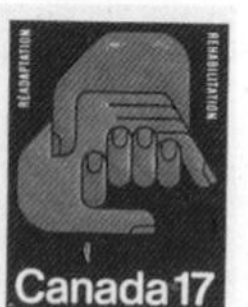

**440** "Helping Hand"

**1980.** Rehabilitation.

| | | | | |
|---|---|---|---|---|
| 979 | **440** | 17c. gold and blue | 15 | 20 |

**441** Opening Bars of "O Canada"

**1980.** Centenary of "O Canada" (national song). Multicoloured.

| | | | |
|---|---|---|---|
| 980 | 17c. Type **441** | 15 | 15 |
| 981 | 17c. Calixa Lavallee (composer), Adolphe-Basile Routhier (original writer) and Robert Stanley Weir (writer of English version) | 15 | 15 |

**442** John G. Diefenbaker (statesman)

**1980.** John G. Diefenbaker Commemoration.

| | | | | |
|---|---|---|---|---|
| 982 | **442** | 17c. blue | 15 | 20 |

**443** Emma Albani (singer)

**1980.** Famous Canadians. Multicoloured.

| | | | |
|---|---|---|---|
| 983 | 17c. Type **443** | 15 | 25 |
| 984 | 17c. Healey Willan (composer) | 15 | 25 |
| 985 | 17c. Ned Hanlan (oarsman) (horiz) | 15 | 15 |

**444** Alberta

**1980.** 75th Anniv of Alberta and Saskatchewan Provinces. Multicoloured.

| | | | |
|---|---|---|---|
| 986 | 17c. Type **444** | 15 | 15 |
| 987 | 17c. Saskatchewan | 15 | 15 |

**445** Uraninite Molecular Structure

**1980.** Uranium Resources.

| | | | | |
|---|---|---|---|---|
| 988 | **445** | 35c. multicoloured | 30 | 30 |

**1980.** Canadian Eskimos ("Inuits") (4th series). Spirits. As T 413. Multicoloured.

| | | | |
|---|---|---|---|
| 989 | 17c. "Return of the Sun" (print, Kenojouak) | 20 | 15 |
| 990 | 17c. "Sedna" (sculpture, Ashoona Kiawak) | 20 | 15 |
| 991 | 35c. "Shaman" (print, Simon Tookoome) | 35 | 55 |
| 992 | 35c. "Bird Spirit" (sculpture, Doris Hagiolok) | 35 | 55 |

**446** "Christmas Morning" (J. S. Hallam)

**1980.** Christmas. Multicoloured.

| | | | |
|---|---|---|---|
| 993 | 15c. Type **446** | 10 | 10 |
| 994 | 17c. "Sleigh Ride" (Frank Hennessy) | 15 | 10 |
| 995 | 35c. "McGill Cab Stand" (Kathleen Morris) | 30 | 1·40 |

**447** Avro (Canada) CF-100 Canuck Mk 5

**1980.** Canadian Aircraft (2nd series). Multicoloured.

| | | | |
|---|---|---|---|
| 996 | 17c. Type **447** | 40 | 20 |
| 997 | 17c. Avro Type 683 Lancaster | 40 | 20 |
| 998 | 35c. Curtiss JN-4 Canuck biplane | 60 | 65 |
| 999 | 35c. Hawker Hurricane Mk I | 60 | 65 |

**448** Emmanuel-Persillier Lachapelle

**1980.** Dr. E.-P. Lachapelle (founder, Notre-Dame Hospital, Montreal) Commemoration.

| | | | | |
|---|---|---|---|---|
| 1000 | **448** | 17c. brown, deep brown and blue | 15 | 15 |

**449** Mandora (18th century)

**1981.** "The Look of Music" Exhibition, Vancouver.

| | | | | |
|---|---|---|---|---|
| 1001 | **449** | 17c. multicoloured | 15 | 15 |

**450** Henrietta Edwards

**1981.** Feminists. Multicoloured.

| | | | |
|---|---|---|---|
| 1002 | 17c. Type **450** | 30 | 30 |
| 1003 | 17c. Louise McKinney | 30 | 30 |
| 1004 | 17c. Idola Saint-Jean | 30 | 30 |
| 1005 | 17c. Emily Stowe | 30 | 30 |

**451** Vancouver Marmot

**1981.** Endangered Wildlife (5th series). Multicoloured.

| | | | |
|---|---|---|---|
| 1006 | 17c. Type **451** | 15 | 10 |
| 1007 | 35c. American bison | 35 | 30 |

**452** Kateri Tekakwitha

**1981.** 17th-century Canadian Women. Statues by Emile Brunet.

| | | | | |
|---|---|---|---|---|
| 1008 | **452** | 17c. brown and green | 15 | 20 |
| 1009 | - | 17c. deep blue and blue | 15 | 20 |

DESIGN: No. 1009, Marie de l'Incarnation.

**453** "Self Portrait" (Frederick H. Varley)

**1981.** Canadian Paintings. Multicoloured.

| | | | |
|---|---|---|---|
| 1010 | 17c. Type **453** | 20 | 10 |
| 1011 | 17c. "At Baie Saint-Paul" (Marc-Aurele Fortin) (horiz) | 20 | 10 |
| 1012 | 35c. "Untitled No 6" (Paul-Emile Borduas) | 40 | 45 |

**454** Canada in 1867

**1981.** Canada Day. Maps showing evolution of Canada from Confederation to present day. Multicoloured.

| | | | |
|---|---|---|---|
| 1013 | 17c. Type **454** | 15 | 20 |
| 1014 | 17c. Canada in 1873 | 15 | 20 |
| 1015 | 17c. Canada in 1905 | 15 | 20 |
| 1016 | 17c. Canada since 1949 | 15 | 20 |

**455** Frere Marie-Victorin

**1981.** Canadian Botanists. Multicoloured.

| | | | |
|---|---|---|---|
| 1017 | 17c. Type **455** | 20 | 30 |
| 1018 | 17c. John Macoun | 20 | 30 |

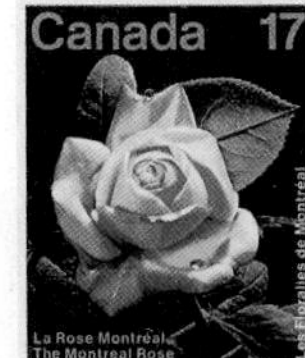


**456** The Montreal Rose

**1981.** Montreal Flower Show.

| | | | | |
|---|---|---|---|---|
| 1019 | **456** | 17c. multicoloured | 15 | 20 |

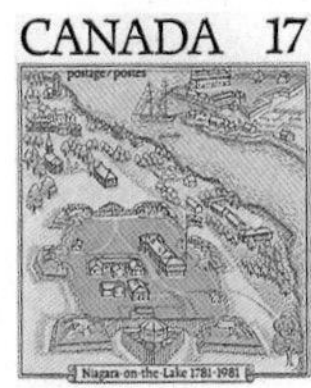


**457** Drawing of Niagara-on-the-Lake

**1981.** Bicentenary of Niagara-on-the-Lake (town).

| | | | | |
|---|---|---|---|---|
| 1020 | **457** | 17c. multicoloured | 15 | 20 |

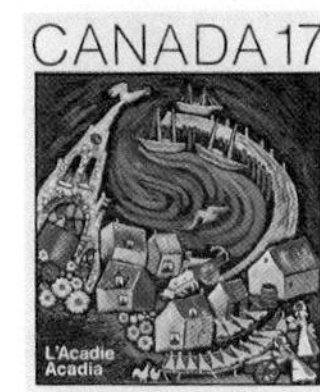


**458** Acadian Community

**1981.** Centenary of First Acadia (community) Convention.

| | | | | |
|---|---|---|---|---|
| 1021 | **458** | 17c. multicoloured | 15 | 20 |

**459** Aaron R. Mosher

**1981.** Birth Centenary of Aaron R. Mosher (founder of Canadian Labour Congress).

| | | | | |
|---|---|---|---|---|
| 1022 | **459** | 17c. multicoloured | 15 | 20 |

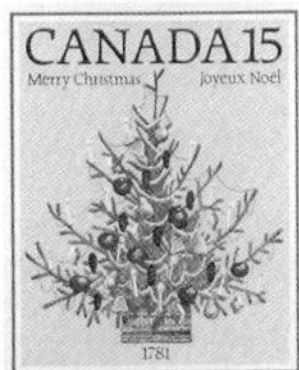


**460** Christmas Tree, 1781

**1981.** Christmas. Bicentenary of First Illuminated Christmas Tree in Canada.

| | | | |
|---|---|---|---|
| 1023 | 15c. Type **460** | 20 | 15 |
| 1024 | 15c. Christmas Tree, 1881 | 20 | 15 |
| 1025 | 15c. Christmas Tree, 1981 | 20 | 15 |

**461** De Havilland Tiger Moth

**1981.** Canadian Aircraft (3rd series). Multicoloured.

| | | | |
|---|---|---|---|
| 1026 | 17c. Type **461** | 25 | 15 |
| 1027 | 17c. Canadair CL-41 Tutor jet trainer | 25 | 15 |
| 1028 | 35c. Avro (Canada) CF-102 jet airliner | 45 | 40 |
| 1029 | 35c. de Havilland DHC-7 Dash 7 | 45 | 40 |

**462** Canadian Maple Leaf Emblem

**1981**

| | | | | |
|---|---|---|---|---|
| 1030a | **462** | A (30c.) red | 20 | 45 |

No. 1030a was printed before a new first class domestic letter rate had been agreed, "A" representing the face value of the stamp, later decided to be 30c.

**1982.** As T 462 but including face values.

| | | | |
|---|---|---|---|
| 1033 | 5c. purple | 10 | 20 |
| 1033d | 8c. blue | 1·75 | 2·50 |
| 1034 | 10c. green | 1·50 | 2·25 |
| 1032 | 30c. red, grey and blue | 30 | 60 |
| 1036 | 30c. red | 35 | 40 |
| 1032b | 32c. red, brown and stone | 45 | 45 |
| 1036b | 32c. red | 1·50 | 2·50 |

**463** 1851 3d. Stamp

**1982.** "Canada 82" International Philatelic Youth Exhibition, Toronto. Stamps on Stamps. Mult.

| | | | |
|---|---|---|---|
| 1037 | 30c. Type **463** | 30 | 30 |
| 1038 | 30c. 1908 Centenary of Quebec 15c. commemorative | 30 | 30 |
| 1039 | 35c. 1935 10c. R.C.M.P | 30 | 50 |
| 1040 | 35c. 1928 10c. | 30 | 50 |
| 1041 | 60c. 1929 50c. | 60 | 1·00 |
| **MS**1042 | 159×108 mm. Nos. 1037/41 | 2·25 | 3·75 |

**464** Jules Leger

**1982.** Jules Leger (politician) Commemoration.

| | | | | |
|---|---|---|---|---|
| 1043 | **464** | 30c. multicoloured | 20 | 20 |

**465** Stylized drawing of Terry Fox

**1982.** Cancer victim Terry Fox's "Marathon of Hope" (Trans-Canada fund-raising run) Commemoration.

| | | | | |
|---|---|---|---|---|
| 1044 | **465** | 30c. multicoloured | 20 | 20 |

**466** Stylized Open Book

**1982.** Patriation of Constitution.

| | | | | |
|---|---|---|---|---|
| 1045 | **466** | 30c. multicoloured | 20 | 20 |

**467** Male and Female Salvationists with Street Scene

**1982.** Centenary of Salvation Army in Canada.

| | | | | |
|---|---|---|---|---|
| 1046 | **467** | 30c. multicoloured | 20 | 20 |

**468** "The Highway near Kluane Lake" (Yukon Territory) (Jackson)

**1982.** Canada Day. Paintings of Canadian Landscapes. Multicoloured.

| | | | |
|---|---|---|---|
| 1047a | 30c. Type **468** | 35 | 40 |
| 1047b | 30c. "Street Scene, Montreal" (Quebec) (Hebert) | 35 | 40 |
| 1047c | 30c. "Breakwater" (Newfoundland) (Pratt) | 35 | 40 |
| 1047d | 30c. "Along Great Slave Lake" (Northwest Territories) (Richard) | 35 | 40 |
| 1047e | 30c. "Till Hill" (Prince Edward Island) (Lamb) | 35 | 40 |
| 1047f | 30c. "Family and Rainstorm" (Nova Scotia) (Colville) | 35 | 40 |
| 1047g | 30c. "Brown Shadows" (Saskatchewan) (Knowles) | 35 | 40 |
| 1047h | 30c. "The Red Brick House" (Ontario) (Milne) | 35 | 40 |
| 1047i | 30c. "Campus Gates" (New Brunswick) (Bobak) | 35 | 40 |
| 1047j | 30c. "Prairie Town—Early Morning" (Alberta) (Kerr) | 35 | 40 |
| 1047k | 30c. "Totems at Ninstints" (British Columbia) (Plaskett) | 35 | 40 |
| 1047l | 30c. "Doc Snider's House" (Manitoba) (Fitzgerald) | 35 | 40 |

**469** Regina Legislative Building

**1982.** Centenary of Regina.

| | | | | |
|---|---|---|---|---|
| 1048 | **469** | 30c. multicoloured | 20 | 20 |

**470** Finish of Race

**1982.** Centenary of Royal Canadian Henley Regatta.

| | | | | |
|---|---|---|---|---|
| 1049 | **470** | 30c. multicoloured | 20 | 25 |

**471** Fairchild FC-2W1

**1982.** Canadian Aircraft (4th series). Bush Aircraft. Multicoloured.

| | | | |
|---|---|---|---|
| 1050 | 30c. Type **471** | 35 | 20 |
| 1051 | 30c. de Havilland DHC-2 Beaver | 35 | 20 |
| 1052 | 60c. Fokker Super Universal | 65 | 85 |
| 1053 | 60c. Noorduyn Norseman | 65 | 85 |

**472** Decoy

**1982.** Heritage Artefacts.

| | | | | |
|---|---|---|---|---|
| 1054 | **472** | 1c. black, lt brn and brn | 10 | 10 |
| 1055 | - | 2c. black, blue and green | 10 | 10 |
| 1056 | - | 3c. black and deep blue | 10 | 10 |
| 1057 | - | 5c. black, pink and brown | 10 | 10 |
| 1058 | - | 10c. black, blue & turq | 10 | 10 |
| 1059 | - | 20c. black, lt brn & brn | 20 | 10 |
| 1060 | - | 25c. multicoloured | 1·25 | 10 |
| 1061 | - | 37c. black, grn & dp grn | 45 | 70 |
| 1062 | - | 39c. black, grey and violet | 1·75 | 2·00 |
| 1063 | - | 42c. multicoloured | 2·25 | 1·00 |
| 1064 | - | 48c. dp brn, brn & pink | 50 | 40 |
| 1065 | - | 50c. black, lt blue & blue | 1·75 | 20 |
| 1066 | - | 55c. multicoloured | 2·00 | 30 |
| 1067 | - | 64c. dp grey, blk & grey | 60 | 35 |
| 1068 | - | 68c. black, lt brn & brn | 1·75 | 50 |
| 1069 | - | 72c. multicoloured | 2·00 | 35 |

DESIGNS—VERT: 2c. Fishing spear; 3c. Stable lantern; 5c. Bucket; 10c. Weathercock; 20c. Skates; 25c. Butter stamp. HORIZ: 37c. Plough; 39c. Settle-bed; 42c. Linen chest; 48c. Cradle; 50c. Sleigh; 55c. Iron kettle; 64c. Kitchen stove; 68c. Spinning wheel; 72c. Hand-drawn cart.

**475** Mary, Joseph and Baby Jesus

**1982.** Christmas. Nativity Scenes.

| | | | |
|---|---|---|---|
| 1080 | 30c. Type **475** | 20 | 10 |
| 1081 | 35c. The Shepherds | 25 | 60 |
| 1082 | 60c. The Three Wise Men | 45 | 1·50 |

**476** Globes forming Symbolic Designs

**1983.** World Communications Year.

| | | | | |
|---|---|---|---|---|
| 1083 | **476** | 32c. multicoloured | 30 | 30 |

**477** Map of World showing Canada

**1983.** Commonwealth Day.

| | | | | |
|---|---|---|---|---|
| 1084 | **477** | $2 multicoloured | 2·00 | 3·25 |

**478** Scene from Novel "Angeline de Montbrun" by "Laure Conan" (Felicite Angers)

**1983.** Canadian Writers (4th series).

| | | | |
|---|---|---|---|
| 1085 | 32c. Type **478** | 40 | 90 |
| 1086 | 32c. Woodcut illustrating "Sea-gulls" (poem by E. J. Pratt) | 40 | 90 |

**479** St. John Ambulance Badge and "100"

**1983.** Centenary of St. John Ambulance in Canada.

| | | | | |
|---|---|---|---|---|
| 1087 | **479** | 32c. red, yellow and brown | 30 | 30 |

**480** Victory Pictogram

**1983.** "Universiade 83" World University Games, Edmonton.

| | | | | |
|---|---|---|---|---|
| 1088 | **480** | 32c. multicoloured | 25 | 15 |
| 1089 | **480** | 64c. multicoloured | 50 | 70 |

**481** Fort William, Ontario

**1983.** Canada Day. Forts (1st series). Multicoloured.

| | | | |
|---|---|---|---|
| 1090 | 32c. Fort Henry, Ontario (44×22 mm) | 55 | 80 |
| 1091 | 32c. Type **481** | 55 | 80 |
| 1092 | 32c. Fort Rodd Hill, British Columbia | 55 | 80 |
| 1093 | 32c. Fort Wellington, Ontario (28×22 mm) | 55 | 80 |
| 1094 | 32c. Fort Prince of Wales, Manitoba (28×22 mm) | 55 | 80 |
| 1095 | 32c. Halifax Citadel, Nova Scotia (44×22 mm) | 55 | 80 |
| 1096 | 32c. Fort Chambly, Quebec | 55 | 80 |
| 1097 | 32c. Fort No. 1, Point Levis, Quebec | 55 | 80 |
| 1098 | 32c. Coteau-du-Lac Fort, Quebec (28×22 mm) | 55 | 80 |
| 1099 | 32c. Fort Beausejour, New Brunswick (28×22 mm) | 55 | 80 |

See also Nos. 1163/72.

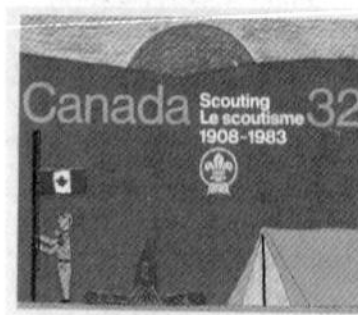


**482** Scouting Poster by Marc Fournier (aged 21)

**1983.** Scouting in Canada (75th Anniv) and 15th World Scout Jamboree, Alberta.

| | | | | |
|---|---|---|---|---|
| 1100 | **482** | 32c. multicoloured | 30 | 30 |

**483** Cross Symbol

**1983.** 6th Assembly of the World Council of Churches, Vancouver.

| | | | | |
|---|---|---|---|---|
| 1101 | **483** | 32c. green and lilac | 30 | 20 |

**484** Sir Humphrey Gilbert (founder)

**1983.** 400th Anniv of Newfoundland.

| | | | | |
|---|---|---|---|---|
| 1102 | **484** | 32c. multicoloured | 30 | 30 |

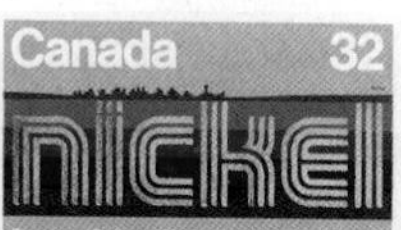


**485** "NICKEL" Deposits

**1983.** Cent of Discovery of Sudbury Nickel Deposits.

| | | | | |
|---|---|---|---|---|
| 1103 | **485** | 32c. multicoloured | 30 | 30 |

**486** Josiah Henson and Escaping Slaves

**1983.** 19th-century Social Reformers. Multicoloured.

| | | | |
|---|---|---|---|
| 1104 | 32c. Type **486** | 35 | 50 |
| 1105 | 32c. Father Antoine Labelle and rural village (32×26 mm) | 35 | 50 |

**487** Robert Stephenson's Locomotive "Dorchester", 1836

**1983.** Railway Locomotives (1st series). Mult.

| | | | |
|---|---|---|---|
| 1106 | 32c. Type **487** | 1·00 | 1·00 |
| 1107 | 32c. Locomotive "Toronto", 1853 | 1·00 | 1·00 |
| 1108 | 37c. Timothy Hackworth's locomotive "Samson", 1838 | 1·00 | 1·00 |
| 1109 | 64c. Western Canadian Railway locomotive "Adam Brown", 1855 | 1·60 | 2·50 |

See also Nos. 1132/5, 1185/8 and 1223/6.

**488** School Coat of Arms

**1983.** Centenary of Dalhousie Law School.

| | | | | |
|---|---|---|---|---|
| 1110 | **488** | 32c. multicoloured | 30 | 40 |

**489** City Church

**1983.** Christmas. Churches. Multicoloured.

| | | | |
|---|---|---|---|
| 1111 | 32c. Type **489** | 30 | 10 |
| 1112 | 37c. Family walking to church | 40 | 90 |
| 1113 | 64c. Country chapel | 1·00 | 2·00 |

**490** Royal Canadian Regiment and British Columbia Regiment

**1983.** Canadian Army Regiments. Multicoloured.

| | | | |
|---|---|---|---|
| 1114 | 32c. Type **490** | 75 | 1·25 |
| 1115 | 32c. Royal Winnipeg Rifles and Royal Canadian Dragoons | 75 | 1·25 |

**491** Gold Mine in Prospecting Pan

**1984.** 50th Anniv of Yellowknife.

| | | | | |
|---|---|---|---|---|
| 1116 | **491** | 32c. multicoloured | 30 | 30 |

**492** Montreal Symphony Orchestra

**1983.** 50th Anniv of Montreal Symphony Orchestra.

| | | | | |
|---|---|---|---|---|
| 1117 | **492** | 32c. multicoloured | 35 | 30 |

**493** Jacques Cartier

**1984.** 450th Anniv of Jacques Cartier's Voyage to Canada.

| | | | | |
|---|---|---|---|---|
| 1118 | **493** | 32c. multicoloured | 40 | 30 |

**494** U.S.C.S. "Eagle"

**1984.** Tall Ships Visit.

| | | | | |
|---|---|---|---|---|
| 1119 | **494** | 32c. multicoloured | 35 | 30 |

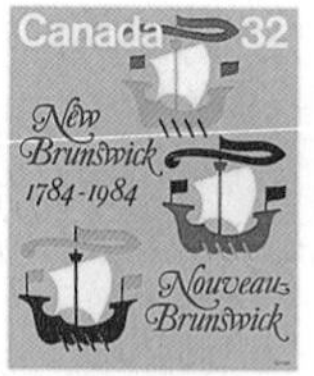


**495** Service Medal

**1984.** 75th Anniv of Canadian Red Cross Society.

| | | | | |
|---|---|---|---|---|
| 1120 | **495** | 32c. multicoloured | 35 | 40 |

**496** Oared Galleys

**1984.** Bicentenary of New Brunswick.

| | | | | |
|---|---|---|---|---|
| 1121 | **496** | 32c. multicoloured | 35 | 30 |

**497** St. Lawrence Seaway

**1984.** 25th Anniv of St. Lawrence Seaway.

| | | | | |
|---|---|---|---|---|
| 1122 | **497** | 32c. multicoloured | 45 | 30 |

**498** New Brunswick

**1984.** Canada Day. Paintings by Jean Paul Lemieux. Multicoloured.

| | | | |
|---|---|---|---|
| 1123a | 32c. Type **498** | 50 | 60 |
| 1123b | 32c. British Columbia | 50 | 60 |
| 1123c | 32c. Northwest Territories | 50 | 60 |
| 1123d | 32c. Quebec | 50 | 60 |
| 1123e | 32c. Manitoba | 50 | 60 |
| 1123f | 32c. Alberta | 50 | 60 |
| 1123g | 32c. Prince Edward Island | 50 | 60 |
| 1123h | 32c. Saskatchewan | 50 | 60 |
| 1123i | 32c. Nova Scotia (vert) | 50 | 60 |
| 1123j | 32c. Yukon Territory | 50 | 60 |
| 1123k | 32c. Newfoundland | 50 | 60 |
| 1123l | 32c. Ontario (vert) | 50 | 60 |

The captions on the Northwest Territories and Yukon Territory paintings were transposed at the design stage.

**499** Loyalists of 1784

**1984.** Bicentenary of Arrival of United Empire Loyalists.

| | | | | |
|---|---|---|---|---|
| 1124 | **499** | 32c. multicoloured | 30 | 30 |

**500** St. John's Basilica

**1984.** Bicentenary of Roman Catholic Church in Newfoundland.

| | | | | |
|---|---|---|---|---|
| 1125 | **500** | 32c. multicoloured | 30 | 25 |

**501** Coat of Arms of Pope John Paul II

**1984.** Papal Visit.

| | | | | |
|---|---|---|---|---|
| 1126 | **501** | 32c. multicoloured | 40 | 20 |
| 1127 | **501** | 64c. multicoloured | 85 | 1·10 |

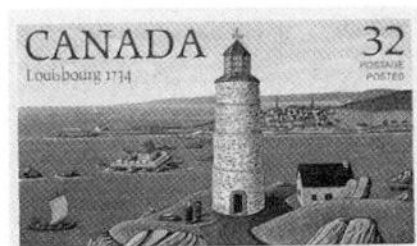


**502** Louisbourg Lighthouse, 1734

**1984.** Canadian Lighthouse (1st series). Mult.

| | | | |
|---|---|---|---|
| 1128 | 32c. Type **502** | 1·75 | 1·75 |
| 1129 | 32c. Fisgard Lighthouse, 1860 | 1·75 | 1·75 |
| 1130 | 32c. Ile Verte Lighthouse, 1809 | 1·75 | 1·75 |
| 1131 | 32c. Gibraltar Point Lighthouse, 1808 | 1·75 | 1·75 |

See also Nos. 1176/9.

**503** Great Western Railway Locomotive "Scotia", 1860

**1984.** Railway Locomotives (2nd series). Mult.

| | | | |
|---|---|---|---|
| 1132 | 32c. Type **503** | 1·40 | 1·40 |
| 1133 | 32c. Northern Pacific Railroad locomotive "Countess of Dufferin", 1872 | 1·40 | 1·40 |
| 1134 | 37c. Grand Trunk Railway Class E3 locomotive, 1886 | 1·40 | 1·60 |
| 1135 | 64c. Canadian Pacific Class D10a steam locomotive | 2·00 | 2·75 |
| **MS**1136 | 153×104 mm. As Nos. 1132/5, but with background colour changed from green to blue | 5·50 | 6·50 |

No. **MS**1136 commemorates "CANADA '84" National Stamp Exhibition, Montreal.

See also Nos. 1185/8 and 1223/6.

**504** "The Annunciation" (Jean Dallaire)

**1984.** Christmas. Religious Paintings. Multicoloured.

| | | | |
|---|---|---|---|
| 1137 | 32c. Type **504** | 40 | 10 |
| 1138 | 37c. "The Three Kings" (Simone Bouchard) | 70 | 1·00 |
| 1139 | 64c. "Snow in Bethlehem" (David Milne) | 90 | 1·75 |

**505** Pilots of 1914–18, 1939–45 and 1984

**1984.** 60th Anniv of Royal Canadian Air Force.

| | | | | |
|---|---|---|---|---|
| 1140 | **505** | 32c. multicoloured | 35 | 30 |

**506** Treffle Berthiaume (editor)

**1984.** Centenary of "La Presse" (newspaper).

| | | | | |
|---|---|---|---|---|
| 1141 | **506** | 32c. brown, red & lt brn | 35 | 30 |

**507** Heart and Arrow

**1985.** International Youth Year.

| | | | | |
|---|---|---|---|---|
| 1142 | **507** | 32c. multicoloured | 30 | 30 |

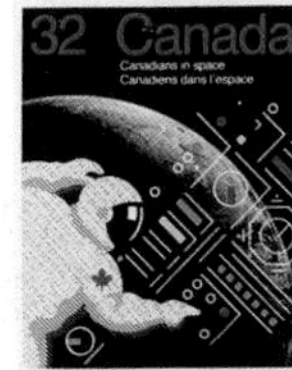


**508** Astronaut in Space, and Planet Earth

**1985.** Canadian Space Programme.

| | | | | |
|---|---|---|---|---|
| 1143 | **508** | 32c. multicoloured | 40 | 30 |

**509** Emily Murphy

**1985.** Women's Rights Activists. Multicoloured.

| | | | |
|---|---|---|---|
| 1144 | 32c. Type **509** | 40 | 90 |
| 1145 | 32c. Therese Casgrain | 40 | 90 |

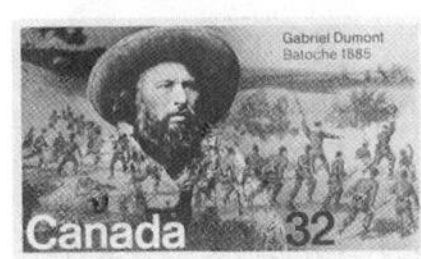


**510** Gabriel Dumont (Metis leader) and Battle of Batoche, 1885

**1985.** Centenary of the North-West Rebellion.

| | | | | |
|---|---|---|---|---|
| 1146 | **510** | 32c. blue, red and grey | 30 | 30 |

**511** Rear View, Parliament Building, Ottawa

**512** Queen Elizabeth II

**512a** Queen Elizabeth II in 1984 (from photo by Karsh)

**1985**

| | | | | |
|---|---|---|---|---|
| 1147b | - | 1c. green | 1·00 | 80 |
| 1148 | - | 2c. green | 25 | 1·50 |
| 1149 | - | 5c. brown | 75 | 1·75 |
| 1150a | - | 6c. brown | 70 | 50 |
| 1150b | - | 6c. purple | 2·50 | 1·00 |
| 1151 | **511** | 34c. black | 2·25 | 2·75 |
| 1155 | **511** | 34c. multicoloured | 60 | 10 |
| 1158 | **511** | 34c. brown | 2·25 | 3·00 |
| 1161 | **512** | 34c. black and blue | 1·40 | 30 |
| 1152 | **511** | 36c. purple | 4·00 | 5·00 |
| 1156a | **511** | 36c. multicoloured | 30 | 45 |
| 1159 | **511** | 36c. red | 2·25 | 55 |
| 1162 | **512** | 36c. purple | 2·75 | 1·10 |
| 1153 | **511** | 37c. blue | 1·75 | 30 |
| 1157 | - | 37c. multicoloured | 85 | 10 |
| 1162a | **512a** | 37c. multicoloured | 3·50 | 10 |
| 1154 | **511** | 38c. blue | 2·75 | 1·25 |
| 1157c | - | 38c. multicoloured | 65 | 10 |
| 1160b | **511** | 38c. green | 50 | 30 |
| 1162b | **512a** | 38c. multicoloured | 1·50 | 20 |
| 1162c | **512a** | 39c. multicoloured | 1·00 | 20 |
| 1162d | **512a** | 40c. multicoloured | 1·00 | 20 |
| 1162e | **512a** | 42c. multicoloured | 1·00 | 40 |
| 1162f | **512a** | 43c. multicoloured | 1·25 | 80 |
| 1162g | **512a** | 45c. multicoloured | 2·50 | 80 |
| 1162h | **512a** | 46c. multicoloured | 1·00 | 45 |
| 1162i | **512a** | 47c. multicoloured | 1·00 | 60 |

DESIGNS: 1, 5, 6c. (1150b) East Block, Parliament Building; 2, 6c. (1150a) West Block, Parliament Building; 37c. (1157) Front view, Parliament Building; 38c. (1157c) Side view, Parliament Building.

**1985.** Canada Day. Forts (2nd series). As T 481. Multicoloured.

| | | | |
|---|---|---|---|
| 1163 | 34c. Lower Fort Garry, Manitoba | 50 | 60 |
| 1164 | 34c. Fort Anne, Nova Scotia | 50 | 60 |
| 1165 | 34c. Fort York, Ontario | 50 | 60 |
| 1166 | 34c. Castle Hill, Newfoundland | 50 | 60 |
| 1167 | 34c. Fort Whoop Up, Alberta | 50 | 60 |
| 1168 | 34c. Fort Erie, Ontario | 50 | 60 |
| 1169 | 34c. Fort Walsh, Saskatchewan | 50 | 60 |
| 1170 | 34c. Fort Lennox, Quebec | 50 | 60 |
| 1171 | 34c. York Redoubt, Nova Scotia | 50 | 60 |
| 1172 | 34c. Fort Frederick, Ontario | 50 | 60 |

Nos. 1163 and 1168 measure 44×22 mm and Nos. 1166/7 and 1171/2 28×22 mm.

**513** Louis Hebert (apothecary)

**1985.** 45th International Pharmaceutical Sciences Congress of Pharmaceutical Federation, Montreal.

| | | | | |
|---|---|---|---|---|
| 1173 | **513** | 34c. multicoloured | 45 | 45 |

**514** Parliament Buildings and Map of World

**1985.** 74th Conference of Inter-Parliamentary Union, Ottawa.

| | | | | |
|---|---|---|---|---|
| 1174 | **514** | 34c. multicoloured | 45 | 45 |

**515** Guide and Brownie Saluting

**1985.** 75th Anniv of Girl Guide Movement.

| | | | | |
|---|---|---|---|---|
| 1175 | **515** | 34c. multicoloured | 45 | 35 |

**516** Sisters Islets Lighthouse

**1985.** Canadian Lighthouses (2nd series). Multicoloured.

| | | | |
|---|---|---|---|
| 1176 | 34c. Type **516** | 2·00 | 2·00 |
| 1177 | 34c. Pelee Passage Lighthouse | 2·00 | 2·00 |
| 1178 | 34c. Haut-fond Prince Lighthouse | 2·00 | 2·00 |
| 1179 | 34c. Rose Blanche Lighthouse, Cains Island | 2·00 | 2·00 |
| **MS**1180 | 190×90 mm. Nos. 1176/9 | 7·50 | 8·00 |

No. **MS**1180 publicises "Capex 87" International Stamp Exhibition, Toronto.

**517** Santa Claus in Reindeer-drawn Sleigh

**1985.** Christmas. Santa Claus Parade. Multicoloured.

| | | | |
|---|---|---|---|
| 1181 | 32c. Canada Post's parade float | 60 | 85 |
| 1182 | 34c. Type **517** | 70 | 20 |
| 1183 | 39c. Acrobats and horse-drawn carriage | 1·00 | 1·25 |
| 1184 | 68c. Christmas tree, pudding and goose on float | 1·90 | 2·50 |

**1985.** Steam Railway Locomotives (3rd series). As T 503. Multicoloured.

| | | | |
|---|---|---|---|
| 1185 | 34c. Grand Trunk Railway Class K2 | 1·25 | 1·75 |
| 1186 | 34c. Canadian Pacific Class P2a | 1·25 | 1·75 |
| 1187 | 39c. Canadian Northern Class O10a | 1·25 | 1·50 |
| 1188 | 68c. Canadian Govt Railway Class H4D | 2·00 | 2·75 |

**518** Naval Personnel of 1910, 1939–45 and 1985

**1985.** 75th Anniv of Royal Canadian Navy.

| | | | | |
|---|---|---|---|---|
| 1189 | **518** | 34c. multicoloured | 65 | 65 |

**519** "The Old Holton House, Montreal" (James Wilson Morrice)

**1985.** 125th Anniv of Montreal Museum of Fine Arts.

| | | | | |
|---|---|---|---|---|
| 1190 | **519** | 34c. multicoloured | 40 | 50 |

**520** Map of Alberta showing Olympic Sites

**1986.** Winter Olympic Games, Calgary (1988) (1st issue).

| | | | | |
|---|---|---|---|---|
| 1191 | **520** | 34c. multicoloured | 40 | 50 |

See also Nos. 1216/17, 1236/7, 1258/9 and 1281/4.

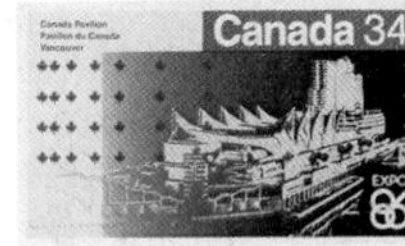


**521** Canada Pavilion

**1986.** "Expo '86" World Fair, Vancouver (1st issue). Multicoloured.

| | | | |
|---|---|---|---|
| 1192 | 34p. Type **521** | 1·25 | 50 |
| 1193 | 39p. Early telephone, dish aerial and satellite | 2·00 | 3·25 |

See also Nos. 1196/7.

**522** Molly Brant

**1986.** 250th Birth Anniv of Molly Brant (Iroquois leader).

| | | | | |
|---|---|---|---|---|
| 1194 | **522** | 34c. multicoloured | 40 | 50 |

**523** Aubert de Gaspe and Scene from "Les Anciens Canadiens"

**1986.** Birth Bicentenary of Philippe Aubert de Gaspe (author).

| | | | | |
|---|---|---|---|---|
| 1195 | **523** | 34c. multicoloured | 40 | 50 |

**1986.** "Expo '86" World Fair, Vancouver (2nd issue). As T 521. Multicoloured.

| | | | |
|---|---|---|---|
| 1196 | 34c. Expo Centre, Vancouver (vert) | 70 | 50 |
| 1197 | 68c. Early and modern trains | 1·40 | 3·25 |

**524** Canadian Field Post Office and Cancellation, 1944

**1986.** 75th Anniv of Canadian Forces Postal Service.

| | | | | |
|---|---|---|---|---|
| 1198 | **524** | 34c. multicoloured | 60 | 60 |

**525** Great Blue Heron

**1986.** Birds of Canada. Multicoloured.

| | | | |
|---|---|---|---|
| 1199 | 34c. Type **525** | 1·75 | 2·25 |
| 1200 | 34c. Snow goose | 1·75 | 2·25 |
| 1201 | 34c. Great horned owl | 1·75 | 2·25 |
| 1202 | 34c. Spruce grouse | 1·75 | 2·25 |

**526** Railway Rotary Snowplough

**1986.** Canada Day. Science and Technology. Canadian Inventions (1st series). Multicoloured.

| | | | |
|---|---|---|---|
| 1203 | 34c. Type **526** | 1·75 | 2·25 |
| 1204 | 34c. Space shuttle "Challenger" launching satellite with Canadarm | 1·75 | 2·25 |
| 1205 | 34c. Pilot wearing anti-gravity flight suit and Supermarine Spitfire | 1·75 | 2·25 |
| 1206 | 34c. Variable-pitch propeller and Avro 504 airplane | 1·75 | 2·25 |

See also Nos. 1241/4 and 1292/5.

**527** C.B.C. Logos over Map of Canada

**1986.** 50th Anniv of Canadian Broadcasting Corporation.

| | | | | |
|---|---|---|---|---|
| 1207 | **527** | 34c. multicoloured | 40 | 50 |

**528** Ice Age Artefacts, Tools and Settlement

**1986.** Exploration of Canada (1st series). Discoverers. Multicoloured.

| | | | |
|---|---|---|---|
| 1208 | 34c. Type **528** | 1·50 | 2·00 |
| 1209 | 34c. Viking ships | 1·50 | 2·00 |
| 1210 | 34c. John Cabot's "Matthew", 1497, compass and Arctic char (fish) | 1·50 | 2·00 |
| 1211 | 34c. Henry Hudson cast adrift, 1611 | 1·50 | 2·00 |
| **MS**1212 | 119×84 mm. Nos. 1208/11 | 5·50 | 7·50 |

No. **MS**1212 publicises "Capex '87" International Stamp Exhibition, Toronto.

See also Nos. 1232/5, 1285/8 and 1319/22.

**529** Crowfoot (Blackfoot Chief) and Indian Village

**1986.** Founders of the Canadian West. Multicoloured.

| | | | |
|---|---|---|---|
| 1213 | 34c. Type **529** | 80 | 1·00 |
| 1214 | 34c. James Macleod of the North West Mounted Police and Fort Macleod | 80 | 1·00 |

**530** Peace Dove and Globe

**1986.** International Peace Year.

| | | | | |
|---|---|---|---|---|
| 1215 | **530** | 34c. multicoloured | 60 | 60 |

**531** Ice Hockey

**1986.** Winter Olympic Games, Calgary (1988) (2nd issue). Multicoloured.

| | | | |
|---|---|---|---|
| 1216 | 34c. Type **531** | 1·75 | 1·75 |
| 1217 | 34c. Biathlon | 1·75 | 1·75 |

**532** Angel with Crown

**1986.** Christmas. Multicoloured.

| | | | |
|---|---|---|---|
| 1218 | 29c. Angel singing carol (36×22 mm) | 65 | 35 |
| 1219 | 34c. Type **532** | 60 | 25 |
| 1220 | 39c. Angel playing lute | 1·00 | 1·60 |
| 1221 | 68c. Angel with ribbon | 1·75 | 3·00 |

**533** John Molson with Theatre Royal, Montreal, "Accomodation" (paddle-steamer) and Railway Train

**1986.** 150th Death Anniv of John Molson (businessman).

| | | | | |
|---|---|---|---|---|
| 1222 | **533** | 34c. multicoloured | 1·25 | 75 |

**1986.** Railway Locomotives (4th series). As T 503 but size 60×22 mm. Multicoloured.

| | | | |
|---|---|---|---|
| 1223 | 34c. Canadian National Class V-1-a diesel locomotive No. 9000 | 1·90 | 1·90 |
| 1224 | 34c. Canadian Pacific Class T1a steam locomotive No. 9000 | 1·90 | 1·90 |
| 1225 | 39c. Canadian National Class U-2-a steam locomotive | 1·90 | 1·00 |
| 1226 | 68c. Canadian Pacific Class H1c steam locomotive No. 2850 | 2·50 | 3·50 |

**534** Toronto's First Post Office

**1987.** "Capex '87" International Stamp Exhibition, Toronto. Post Offices.

| | | | |
|---|---|---|---|
| 1227 | 34c. Type **534** | 60 | 20 |
| 1228 | 36c. Nelson-Miramichi, New Brunswick | 65 | 45 |
| 1229 | 42c. Saint-Ours, Quebec | 70 | 65 |
| 1230 | 72c. Battleford, Saskatchewan | 1·00 | 1·25 |
| **MS**1231 | 155×92 mm. 36c. As No. 1227 and Nos. 1228/30, but main inscr in green | 3·25 | 2·75 |

**535** Etienne Brule exploring Lake Superior

**1987.** Exploration of Canada (2nd series). Pioneers of New France. Multicoloured.

| | | | |
|---|---|---|---|
| 1232 | 34c. Type **535** | 1·75 | 2·00 |
| 1233 | 34c. Radisson and Des Groseilliers with British and French flags | 1·75 | 2·00 |
| 1234 | 34c. Jolliet and Father Marquette on the Mississippi | 1·75 | 2·00 |
| 1235 | 34c. Jesuit missionary preaching to Indians | 1·75 | 2·00 |

**1987.** Winter Olympic Games, Calgary (1988) (3rd issue). As T 531. Multicoloured.

| | | | |
|---|---|---|---|
| 1236 | 36c. Speed skating | 50 | 40 |
| 1237 | 42c. Bobsleighing | 75 | 60 |

**536** Volunteer Activities

**1987.** National Volunteer Week.

| | | | | |
|---|---|---|---|---|
| 1238 | **536** | 36c. multicoloured | 30 | 35 |

**537** Canadian Coat of Arms

**1987.** 5th Anniv of Canadian Charter of Rights and Freedoms.

| | | | | |
|---|---|---|---|---|
| 1239 | **537** | 36c. multicoloured | 75 | 35 |

**538** Steel Girder, Gear Wheel and Microchip

**1987.** Centenary of Engineering Institute of Canada.

| | | | | |
|---|---|---|---|---|
| 1240 | **538** | 36c. multicoloured | 75 | 40 |

**539** R. A. Fessenden (AM Radio)

**1987.** Canada Day. Science and Technology. Canadian Inventors (2nd series). Multicoloured.

| | | | |
|---|---|---|---|
| 1241 | 36c. Type **539** | 1·25 | 1·75 |
| 1242 | 36c. C. Fenerty (newsprint pulp) | 1·25 | 1·75 |
| 1243 | 36c. G.-E. Desbarats and W. Leggo (half-tone engraving) | 1·25 | 1·75 |
| 1244 | 36c. F. N. Gisborne (first North American undersea telegraph) | 1·25 | 1·75 |

**540** "Segwun"

**1987.** Canadian Steamships. Multicoloured.

| | | | |
|---|---|---|---|
| 1245 | 36c. Type **540** | 1·75 | 2·50 |
| 1246 | 36c. "Princess Marguerite" (52×22 mm) | 1·75 | 2·50 |

**541** Figurehead from "Hamilton", 1813

**1987.** Historic Shipwrecks. Multicoloured.

| | | | |
|---|---|---|---|
| 1247 | 36c. Type **541** | 1·50 | 2·00 |
| 1248 | 36c. Hull of "San Juan", 1565 | 1·50 | 2·00 |
| 1249 | 36c. Wheel from "Breadalbane", 1853 | 1·50 | 2·00 |
| 1250 | 36c. Bell from "Ericsson", 1892 | 1·50 | 2·00 |

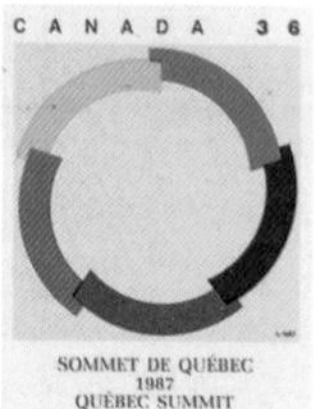


**542** Air Canada Boeing 767-200 and Globe

**1987.** 50th Anniv of Air Canada.

| | | | | |
|---|---|---|---|---|
| 1251 | **542** | 36c. multicoloured | 1·00 | 35 |

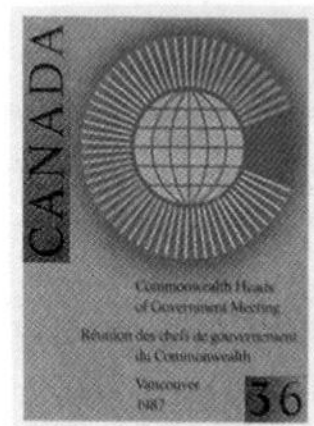


**543** Summit Symbol

**1987.** 2nd Int Francophone Summit, Quebec.

| | | | | |
|---|---|---|---|---|
| 1252 | **543** | 36c. multicoloured | 30 | 35 |

**544** Commonwealth Symbol

**1987.** Commonwealth Heads of Government Meeting, Vancouver.

| | | | | |
|---|---|---|---|---|
| 1253 | **544** | 36c. multicoloured | 35 | 40 |

**545** Poinsettia

**1987.** Christmas. Christmas Plants. Multicoloured.

| | | | |
|---|---|---|---|
| 1254 | 31c. Decorated Christmas tree and presents (36×20 mm) | 90 | 50 |
| 1255 | 36c. Type **545** | 40 | 20 |
| 1256 | 42c. Holly wreath | 1·25 | 50 |
| 1257 | 72c. Mistletoe and decorated tree | 1·75 | 80 |

**1987.** Winter Olympic Games, Calgary (1988) (4th issue). As T 531. Multicoloured.

| | | | |
|---|---|---|---|
| 1258 | 36c. Cross-country skiing | 90 | 75 |
| 1259 | 36c. Ski-jumping | 90 | 75 |

**546** Football, Grey Cup and Spectators

**1987.** 75th Grey Cup Final (Canadian football championship), Vancouver.

| | | | | |
|---|---|---|---|---|
| 1260 | **546** | 36c. multicoloured | 35 | 40 |



**547** Flying Squirrel

**1988.** Canadian Mammals and Architecture. Multicoloured. (a) As T 547.

| | | | |
|---|---|---|---|
| 1261 | 1c. Type **547** | 10 | 10 |
| 1262 | 2c. Porcupine | 10 | 10 |

| | | | |
|---|---|---|---|
| 1263 | 3c. Muskrat | 10 | 10 |
| 1264 | 5c. Varying hare | 10 | 10 |
| 1265 | 6c. Red fox | 10 | 10 |
| 1266 | 10c. Striped skunk | 10 | 10 |
| 1267 | 25c. American beaver | 30 | 15 |
| 1268 | 43c. Lynx (26×20 mm) | 1·40 | 1·25 |
| 1269 | 44c. Walrus (27×21 mm) | 1·40 | 20 |
| 1270 | 45c. Pronghorn (27×21 mm) | 50 | 40 |
| 1270c | 46c. Wolverine (27×21 mm) | 1·50 | 1·50 |
| 1271 | 57c. Killer whale (26×20 mm) | 2·00 | 55 |
| 1272 | 59c. Musk ox (27×21 mm) | 3·50 | 2·75 |
| 1273 | 61c. Wolf (27×21 mm) | 70 | 1·25 |
| 1273b | 63c. Harbour porpoise (27×21 mm) | 2·00 | 2·50 |
| 1274 | 74c. Wapiti (26×20 mm) | 1·60 | 50 |
| 1275 | 76c. Brown bear (27×21 mm) | 2·50 | 50 |
| 1276 | 78c. White whale (27×21 mm) | 1·00 | 55 |
| 1276c | 80c. Peary caribou (27×21 mm) | 1·00 | 60 |

**548a** Runnymede Library, Toronto

(b) As T 548a.

| | | | |
|---|---|---|---|
| 1277 | $1 Type **548a** | 1·50 | 30 |
| 1278 | $2 McAdam Railway Station, New Brunswick | 2·25 | 50 |
| 1279 | $5 Bonsecours Market, Montreal | 4·75 | 4·00 |

**1988.** Winter Olympic Games, Calgary (5th issue). As T 531. Multicoloured.

| | | | |
|---|---|---|---|
| 1281 | 37c. Slalom skiing | 85 | 50 |
| 1282 | 37c. Curling | 85 | 50 |
| 1283 | 43c. Figure skating | 85 | 45 |
| 1284 | 74c. Luge | 1·40 | 80 |

**549** Trade Goods, Blackfoot Encampment and Page from Anthony Henday's Journal

**1988.** Exploration of Canada (3rd series). Explorers of the West. Multicoloured.

| | | | |
|---|---|---|---|
| 1285 | 37c. Type **549** | 1·00 | 70 |
| 1286 | 37c. Discovery and map of George Vancouver's voyage | 1·00 | 70 |
| 1287 | 37c. Simon Fraser's expedition portaging canoes | 1·00 | 70 |
| 1288 | 37c. John Palliser's surveying equipment and view of prairie | 1·00 | 70 |

**550** "The Young Reader" (Ozias Leduc)

**1988.** Canadian Art (1st series).

| | | | | |
|---|---|---|---|---|
| 1289 | **550** | 50c. multicoloured | 70 | 70 |

See also Nos. 1327, 1384, 1421, 1504, 1539, 1589, 1629, 1681, 1721, 1825, 1912, 2011, 2097 and 2133.

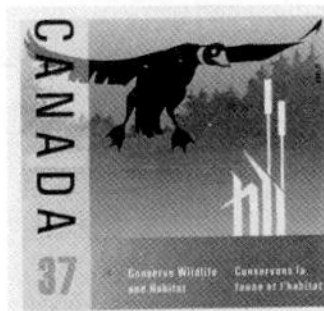


**551** Mallard landing on Marsh

**1988.** Wildlife and Habitat Conservation. Mult.

| | | | |
|---|---|---|---|
| 1290 | 37c. Type **551** | 1·00 | 50 |
| 1291 | 37c. Moose feeding in marsh | 1·00 | 50 |

**552** Kerosene Lamp and Diagram of Distillation Plant

**1988.** Canada Day. Science and Technology. Canadian Inventions (3rd series). Multicoloured.

| | | | |
|---|---|---|---|
| 1292 | 37c. Type **552** | 1·00 | 1·00 |
| 1293 | 37c. Ears of Marquis wheat | 1·00 | 1·00 |
| 1294 | 37c. Electron microscope and magnified image | 1·00 | 1·00 |
| 1295 | 37c. Patient under "Cobalt 60" cancer therapy | 1·00 | 1·00 |

**553** "Papilio brevicauda"

**1988.** Canadian Butterflies. Multicoloured.

| | | | |
|---|---|---|---|
| 1296 | 37c. Type **553** | 80 | 1·00 |
| 1297 | 37c. "Lycaeides idas" | 80 | 1·00 |
| 1298 | 37c. "Oeneis macounii" | 80 | 1·00 |
| 1299 | 37c. "Papilio glaucus" | 80 | 1·00 |

**554** St. John's Harbour Entrance and Skyline

**1988.** Centenary of Incorporation of St. John's, Newfoundland.

| | | | | |
|---|---|---|---|---|
| 1300 | **554** | 37c. multicoloured | 35 | 40 |

**555** Club Members working on Forestry Project and Rural Scene

**1988.** 75th Anniv of 4-H Clubs.

| | | | | |
|---|---|---|---|---|
| 1301 | **555** | 37c. multicoloured | 35 | 40 |

**556** Saint-Maurice Ironworks

**1988.** 250th Anniv of Saint-Maurice Ironworks, Quebec.

| | | | | |
|---|---|---|---|---|
| 1302 | **556** | 37c. black, orange & brn | 40 | 40 |

**557** Tahltan Bear Dog

**1988.** Canadian Dogs. Multicoloured.

| | | | |
|---|---|---|---|
| 1303 | 37c. Type **557** | 1·25 | 1·40 |
| 1304 | 37c. Nova Scotia duck tolling retriever | 1·25 | 1·40 |
| 1305 | 37c. Canadian eskimo dog | 1·25 | 1·40 |
| 1306 | 37c. Newfoundland | 1·25 | 1·40 |

**558** Baseball, Glove and Pitch

**1988.** 150th Anniv of Baseball in Canada. Multicoloured.

| | | | | |
|---|---|---|---|---|
| 1307 | **558** | 37c. multicoloured | 35 | 40 |

**559** Virgin with Inset of Holy Child

**1988.** Christmas. Icons. Multicoloured.

| | | | |
|---|---|---|---|
| 1308 | 32c. Holy Family (36×21 mm) | 45 | 55 |
| 1309 | 37c. Type **559** | 45 | 20 |
| 1310 | 43c. Virgin and Child | 50 | 45 |
| 1311 | 74c. Virgin and Child (different) | 90 | 75 |

On No. 1308 the left-hand third of the design area is taken up by the bar code.

No. 1309 also commemorates the millennium of Ukrainian Christianity.

**560** Bishop Inglis and Nova Scotia Church

**1988.** Bicentenary of Consecration of Charles Inglis (first Canadian Anglican bishop) (1987).

| | | | | |
|---|---|---|---|---|
| 1312 | **560** | 37c. multicoloured | 35 | 40 |

**561** Frances Ann Hopkins and "Canoe manned by Voyageurs"

**1988.** 150th Birth Anniv of Frances Anne Hopkins (artist).

| | | | | |
|---|---|---|---|---|
| 1313 | **561** | 37c. multicoloured | 35 | 40 |

**562** Angus Walters and "Bluenose" (yacht)

**1988.** 20th Death Anniv of Angus Walters (yachtsman).

| | | | | |
|---|---|---|---|---|
| 1314 | **562** | 37c. multicoloured | 40 | 40 |

**563** Chipewyan Canoe

**1989.** Small Craft of Canada (1st series). Native Canoes. Multicoloured.

| | | | |
|---|---|---|---|
| 1315 | 38c. Type **563** | 90 | 70 |
| 1316 | 38c. Haida canoe | 90 | 70 |
| 1317 | 38c. Inuit kayak | 90 | 70 |
| 1318 | 38c. Micmac canoe | 90 | 70 |

See also Nos. 1377/80 and 1428/31.

**564** Matonabbee and Hearne's Expedition

**1989.** Exploration of Canada (4th issue). Explorers of the North. Multicoloured.

| | | | |
|---|---|---|---|
| 1319 | 38c. Type **564** | 1·25 | 75 |
| 1320 | 38c. Relics of Franklin's expedition and White Ensign | 1·25 | 75 |
| 1321 | 38c. Joseph Tyrell's compass, hammer and fossil | 1·25 | 75 |
| 1322 | 38c. Vilhjalmur Stefansson, camera on tripod and sledge dog team | 1·25 | 75 |

**565** Construction of Victoria Bridge, Montreal and William Notman

**1989.** Canada Day. "150 Years of Canadian Photography". Designs showing early photographs and photographers. Multicoloured.

| | | | |
|---|---|---|---|
| 1323 | 38c. Type **565** | 85 | 85 |
| 1324 | 38c. Plains Indian village and W. Hanson Boorne | 85 | 85 |
| 1325 | 38c. Horse-drawn sleigh and Alexander Henderson | 85 | 85 |
| 1326 | 38c. Quebec street scene and Jules-Ernest Livernois | 85 | 85 |

**566** Tsimshian Ceremonial Frontlet, c. 1900

**1989.** Canadian Art (2nd series).

| | | | | |
|---|---|---|---|---|
| 1327 | **566** | 50c. multicoloured | 1·00 | 60 |

**567** Canadian Flag and Forest

**1989.** Self-adhesive. Multicoloured.

| | | | |
|---|---|---|---|
| 1328 | 38c. Type **567** | 1·50 | 2·75 |
| 1328b | 39c. Canadian flag and prairie | 1·50 | 2·75 |
| 1328c | 40c. Canadian flag and sea | 1·75 | 1·75 |
| 1328d | 42c. Canadian flag over mountains | 2·00 | 3·00 |
| 1328e | 43c. Canadian flag over lake | 1·75 | 2·50 |

**568** Archibald Lampman

**1989.** Canadian Poets. Multicoloured.

| | | | |
|---|---|---|---|
| 1329 | 38c. Type **568** | 1·25 | 1·40 |
| 1330 | 38c. Louis-Honore Frechette | 1·25 | 1·40 |

**569** "Clavulinopsis fusiformis"

**1989.** Mushrooms. Multicoloured.

| | | | |
|---|---|---|---|
| 1331 | 38c. Type **569** | 70 | 1·00 |
| 1332 | 38c. "Boletus mirabilis" | 70 | 1·00 |
| 1333 | 38c. "Cantharellus cinnabarinus" | 70 | 1·00 |
| 1334 | 38c. "Morchella esculenta" | 70 | 1·00 |

**570** Night Patrol, Korea

**1989.** 75th Anniv of Canadian Regiments. Mult.

| | | | |
|---|---|---|---|
| 1335 | 38c. Type **570** (Princess Patricia's Canadian Light Infantry) | 1·75 | 1·75 |
| 1336 | 38c. Trench raid, France, 1914–18 (Royal 22e Regiment) | 1·75 | 1·75 |

**571** Globe in Box

**1989.** Canada Export Trade Month.

| | | | | |
|---|---|---|---|---|
| 1337 | **571** | 38c. multicoloured | 40 | 45 |

**572** Film Director

**1989.** Arts and Entertainment.

| | | | | |
|---|---|---|---|---|
| 1338 | **572** | 38c. brown, dp brn & vio | 1·00 | 1·25 |
| 1339 | - | 38c. brown, dp brn & grn | 1·00 | 1·25 |
| 1340 | - | 38c. brown, dp brn & mve | 1·00 | 1·25 |
| 1341 | - | 38c. brown, dp brn & bl | 1·00 | 1·25 |

DESIGNS: No. 1339, Actors; No. 1340, Dancers; No. 1341, Musicians.

**573** "Snow II" (Lawren S. Harris)

**1989.** Christmas. Paintings of Winter Landscapes. Multicoloured.

| | | | |
|---|---|---|---|
| 1342 | 33c. "Champ-de-Mars, Winter" (William Brymner) (35×21 mm) | 1·00 | 65 |
| 1343 | 38c. "Bend in the Gosselin River" (Marc-Aurele Suzor-Cote) (21×35 mm) | 40 | 25 |
| 1344 | 44c. Type **573** | 65 | 50 |
| 1345 | 76c. "Ste. Agnes" (A. H. Robinson) | 1·40 | 85 |

On No. 1342 the left-hand third of the design area is taken up by a bar code.

**574** Canadians listening to Declaration of War, 1939

**1989.** 50th Anniv of Outbreak of Second World War (1st issue).

| | | | | |
|---|---|---|---|---|
| 1346 | **574** | 38c. black, silver & pur | 1·10 | 1·25 |
| 1347 | - | 38c. black, silver and grey | 1·10 | 1·25 |
| 1348 | - | 38c. black, silver and green | 1·10 | 1·25 |
| 1349 | - | 38c. black, silver and blue | 1·10 | 1·25 |

DESIGNS: No. 1347, Army mobilization; No. 1348, British Commonwealth air crew training; No. 1349, North Atlantic convoy.

See also Nos. 1409/12, 1456/9, 1521/4, 1576/9, 1621/4, and 1625/8.

**575** Canadian Flag **576**

**1989**

| | | | | |
|---|---|---|---|---|
| 1350 | **575** | 1c. multicoloured | 20 | 1·00 |
| 1351 | - | 5c. multicoloured | 40 | 30 |
| 1352 | - | 39c. multicoloured | 1·40 | 2·25 |
| 1354 | **576** | 39c. multicoloured | 70 | 10 |
| 1360 | - | 39c. purple | 60 | 75 |
| 1353 | - | 40c. multicoloured | 2·00 | 2·75 |
| 1355 | - | 40c. multicoloured | 80 | 10 |
| 1361 | - | 40c. blue | 40 | 60 |
| 1356 | - | 42c. multicoloured | 1·00 | 15 |
| 1362 | - | 42c. red | 40 | 60 |
| 1357 | - | 43c. multicoloured | 1·00 | 1·50 |
| 1363 | - | 43c. green | 1·50 | 2·25 |
| 1358d | - | 45c. multicoloured | 1·00 | 1·00 |
| 1364 | - | 45c. green | 65 | 1·50 |
| 1359 | - | 46c. multicoloured | 1·10 | 65 |
| 1365 | - | 46c. red | 60 | 1·25 |
| 1367 | - | 47c. multicoloured | 1·00 | 75 |
| 1368 | - | 48c. multicoloured | 80 | 1·50 |
| 1369 | - | 49c. multicoloured | 1·10 | 1·50 |
| 1370 | - | 50c. multicoloured | 1·10 | 1·25 |
| 1371 | - | 50c. multicoloured | 1·10 | 1·25 |
| 1372 | - | 50c. multicoloured | 1·10 | 1·25 |
| 1373 | - | 50c. multicoloured | 1·10 | 1·25 |
| 1374 | - | 50c. multicoloured | 1·10 | 1·25 |
| 1374a | - | 51c. multicoloured | 1·00 | 1·25 |
| 1374b | - | 51c. multicoloured | 1·00 | 1·25 |
| 1374c | - | 51c. multicoloured | 1·00 | 1·25 |
| 1374d | - | 51c. multicoloured | 1·00 | 1·25 |
| 1374e | - | 51c. multicoloured | 1·00 | 1·25 |

DESIGNS: Nos. 1351/3, 1360/5, As T **575** but different folds in flag. As T **576**: No. 1355, Flag over forest; 1356, Flag over mountains; 1357, Flag over prairie; 1358d, Flag and skyscraper; 1359, Flag and iceberg; 1367, Flag and inukshuk (Inuit cairn); 1368, Flag in front of Canada Post Headquarters, Ottawa, Flag and Edmonton; 1370, Broadway Bridge, Saskatoon; 1371, Durrell, South Twillingate Island; 1372, Shannon Falls, Squamish; 1373, Church of Saint-Hilaire, Quebec; 1374, Cruise boat and skyline, Toronto; 1374a, Winter scene near New Glasgow, Prince Edward Island; 1374b, Bridge, Bouctouche, New Brunswick; 1374c, Wind turbines, Pincher Creek, Alberta; 1374d, Southwest bastion, Lower Fort Garry National Historic Site, Manitoba; 1374e, Dogsled, St. Elias Mountains, Yukon.

No. 1359 comes with ordinary or self-adhesive gum and 1367/9 and 1370/4e are self-adhesive.

**577** Norman Bethune in 1937 and performing Operation, Montreal

**1990.** Birth Centenary of Dr. Norman Bethune (surgeon). Multicoloured.

| | | | |
|---|---|---|---|
| 1375 | 39c. Type **577** | 1·75 | 2·25 |
| 1376 | 39c. Bethune in 1939, and treating wounded Chinese soldiers | 1·75 | 2·25 |

**1990.** Small Craft of Canada (2nd series). Early Work Boats. As T 563. Multicoloured.

| | | | |
|---|---|---|---|
| 1377 | 39c. Fishing dory | 1·10 | 1·50 |
| 1378 | 39c. Logging pointer | 1·10 | 1·50 |
| 1379 | 39c. York boat | 1·10 | 1·50 |
| 1380 | 39c. North canoe | 1·10 | 1·50 |

**578** Maple Leaf Mosaic

**1990.** Multiculturalism.

| | | | | |
|---|---|---|---|---|
| 1381 | **578** | 39c. multicoloured | 35 | 40 |

**579** Mail Van (facing left)

**1990.** "Moving the Mail". Multicoloured.

| | | | |
|---|---|---|---|
| 1382 | 39c. Type **579** | 75 | 75 |
| 1383 | 39c. Mail van (facing right) | 75 | 75 |

**1990.** Canadian Art (3rd series). As T 550. Multicoloured.

| | | | |
|---|---|---|---|
| 1384 | 50c. "The West Wind" (Tom Thomson) | 1·00 | 1·00 |

**580** Amerindian and Inuit Dolls

**1990.** Dolls. Multicoloured.

| | | | |
|---|---|---|---|
| 1385 | 39c. Type **580** | 1·25 | 1·50 |
| 1386 | 39c. 19th-century settlers' dolls | 1·25 | 1·50 |
| 1387 | 39c. Commerical dolls, 1917–36 | 1·25 | 1·50 |
| 1388 | 39c. Commercial dolls, 1940–60 | 1·25 | 1·50 |

**581** Canadian Flag and Fireworks

**1990.** Canada Day.

| | | | | |
|---|---|---|---|---|
| 1389 | **581** | 39c. multicoloured | 50 | 50 |

**582** "Stromatolites" (fossil algae)

**1990.** Prehistoric Canada (1st series). Primitive Life. Multicoloured.

| | | | |
|---|---|---|---|
| 1390 | 39c. Type **582** | 1·25 | 1·50 |
| 1391 | 39c. "Opabinia regalis" (soft invertebrate) | 1·25 | 1·50 |
| 1392 | 39c. "Paradoxides davidis" (trilobite) | 1·25 | 1·50 |
| 1393 | 39c. "Eurypterus remipes" (sea scorpion) | 1·25 | 1·50 |

See also Nos. 1417/20, 1568/71 and 1613/16.

**583** Acadian Forest

**1990.** Canadian Forests. Multicoloured.

| | | | |
|---|---|---|---|
| 1394 | 39c. Type **583** | 80 | 70 |
| 1395 | 39c. Great Lakes–St. Lawrence forest | 80 | 70 |
| 1396 | 39c. Pacific Coast forest | 80 | 70 |
| 1397 | 39c. Boreal forest | 80 | 70 |

**584** Clouds and Rainbow

**1990.** 150th Anniv of Weather Observing in Canada.

| | | | | |
|---|---|---|---|---|
| 1398 | **584** | 39c. multicoloured | 60 | 50 |

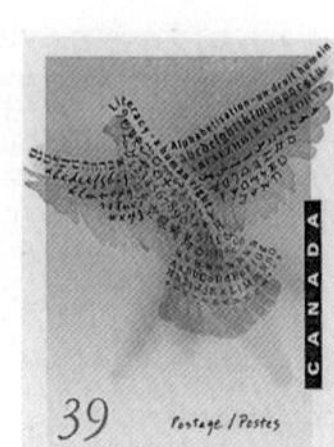


**585** "Alphabet" Bird

**1990.** International Literacy Year.

| | | | | |
|---|---|---|---|---|
| 1399 | **585** | 39c. multicoloured | 40 | 50 |

**586** Sasquatch

**1990.** Legendary Creatures. Multicoloured.

| | | | |
|---|---|---|---|
| 1400 | 39c. Type **586** | 1·25 | 1·50 |
| 1401 | 39c. Kraken | 1·25 | 1·50 |
| 1402 | 39c. Werewolf | 1·25 | 1·50 |
| 1403 | 39c. Ogopogo | 1·25 | 1·50 |

**587** Agnes Macphail

**1990.** Birth Centenary of Agnes Macphail (first woman elected to Parliament).

| | | | | |
|---|---|---|---|---|
| 1404 | **587** | 39c. multicoloured | 40 | 50 |

**588** "Virgin Mary with Christ Child and St. John the Baptist" (Norval Morrisseau)

**1990.** Christmas. Native Art.

| | | | | |
|---|---|---|---|---|
| 1405 | - | 34c. multicoloured | 65 | 55 |
| 1406 | **588** | 39c. multicoloured | 30 | 20 |
| 1407 | - | 45c. multicoloured | 35 | 45 |
| 1408 | - | 78c. black, red and grey | 70 | 75 |

DESIGNS—35×21 mm: 34c. "Rebirth" (Jackson Beardy). As T **588**: 45c. "Mother and Child" (Inuit sculpture, Cape Dorset); 78c. "Children of the Raven" (Bill Reid).

No. 1405 includes a bar code in the design.

**1990.** 50th Anniv of Second World War (2nd issue). As T 574.

| | | | |
|---|---|---|---|
| 1409 | 39c. black, silver and green | 2·00 | 2·00 |
| 1410 | 39c. black, silver and brown | 2·00 | 2·00 |
| 1411 | 39c. black, silver and brown | 2·00 | 2·00 |
| 1412 | 39c. black, silver and mauve | 2·00 | 2·00 |

DESIGNS: No. 1409, Canadian family at home, 1940; 1410, Packing parcels for the troops; 1411, Harvesting; 1412, Testing anti-gravity flying suit.

**589** Jennie Trout (first woman physician) and Women's Medical College, Kingston

**1991.** Medical Pioneers. Multicoloured.

| | | | |
|---|---|---|---|
| 1413 | 40c. Type **589** | 1·10 | 90 |
| 1414 | 40c. Wilder Penfield (neurosurgeon) and Montreal Neurological Institute | 1·10 | 90 |
| 1415 | 40c. Frederick Banting (discoverer of insulin) and University of Toronto medical faculty | 1·10 | 90 |
| 1416 | 40c. Harold Griffith (anesthesiologist) and Queen Elizabeth Hospital, Montreal | 1·10 | 90 |

**1991.** Prehistoric Canada (2nd series). Primitive Vertebrates. As T 582. Multicoloured.

| | | | |
|---|---|---|---|
| 1417 | 40c. Foord's crossopt ("Eusthenopteron foordi") (fish fossil) | 2·25 | 2·50 |
| 1418 | 40c. "Hylonomus lyelli" (land reptile) | 2·25 | 2·50 |
| 1419 | 40c. Fossil conodonts (fossil teeth) | 2·25 | 2·50 |
| 1420 | 40c. "Archaeopteris halliana" (early tree) | 2·25 | 2·50 |

**1991.** Canadian Art (4th series). As T 550. Multicoloured.

| | | | |
|---|---|---|---|
| 1421 | 50c. "Forest, British Columbia" (Emily Carr) | 1·25 | 1·75 |

**590** Blue Poppies and Butchart Gardens, Victoria

**1991.** Public Gardens. Multicoloured.

| | | | |
|---|---|---|---|
| 1422 | 40c. Type **590** | 70 | 70 |
| 1423 | 40c. Marigolds and International Peace Garden, Boissevain | 70 | 70 |
| 1424 | 40c. Lilac and Royal Botanical Gardens, Hamilton | 70 | 70 |
| 1425 | 40c. Roses and Montreal Botanical Gardens | 70 | 70 |
| 1426 | 40c. Rhododendrons and Halifax Public Gardens | 70 | 70 |

**591** Maple Leaf

**1991.** Canada Day.

| | | | | |
|---|---|---|---|---|
| 1427 | **591** | 40c. multicoloured | 50 | 60 |

**1991.** Small Craft of Canada (3rd series). As T 563. Multicoloured.

| | | | |
|---|---|---|---|
| 1428 | 40c. Verchere rowboat | 1·40 | 1·40 |
| 1429 | 40c. Touring kayak | 1·40 | 1·40 |
| 1430 | 40c. Sailing dinghy | 1·40 | 1·40 |
| 1431 | 40c. Cedar strip canoe | 1·40 | 1·40 |

**592** South Nahanni River

**1991.** Canadian Rivers (1st series). Multicoloured.

| | | | |
|---|---|---|---|
| 1432 | 40c. Type **592** | 1·00 | 1·40 |
| 1433 | 40c. Athabasca River | 1·00 | 1·40 |
| 1434 | 40c. Boundary Waters, Voyageur Waterway | 1·00 | 1·40 |
| 1435 | 40c. Jacques-Cartier River | 1·00 | 1·40 |
| 1436 | 40c. Main River | 1·00 | 1·40 |

See also Nos. 1492/6, 1558/62 and 1584/8.

**593** "Leaving Europe"

**1991.** Centenary of Ukrainian Immigration. Panels from "The Ukrainian Pioneer" by William Kurelek. Multicoloured.

| | | | |
|---|---|---|---|
| 1437 | 40c. Type **593** | 80 | 85 |
| 1438 | 40c. "Canadian Winter" | 80 | 85 |
| 1439 | 40c. "Clearing the Land" | 80 | 85 |
| 1440 | 40c. "Harvest" | 80 | 85 |

**594** Ski Patrol rescuing Climber

**1991.** Emergency Services. Multicoloured.

| | | | |
|---|---|---|---|
| 1441 | 40c. Type **594** | 2·25 | 2·25 |
| 1442 | 40c. Police at road traffic accident | 2·25 | 2·25 |
| 1443 | 40c. Firemen on extending ladder | 2·25 | 2·25 |
| 1444 | 40c. Boeing-Vertol Chinook rescue helicopter and "Spindrift" (lifeboat) | 2·25 | 2·25 |

**595** "The Witched Canoe"

**1991.** Canadian Folktales. Multicoloured.

| | | | |
|---|---|---|---|
| 1445 | 40c. Type **595** | 1·40 | 95 |
| 1446 | 40c. "The Orphan Boy" | 1·40 | 95 |
| 1447 | 40c. "Chinook" | 1·40 | 95 |
| 1448 | 40c. "Buried Treasure" | 1·40 | 95 |

**596** Grant Hall Tower

**1991.** 150th Anniv of Queen's University, Kingston.

| | | | | |
|---|---|---|---|---|
| 1449 | **596** | 40c. multicoloured | 1·10 | 1·00 |

**597** North American Santa Claus

**1991.** Christmas. Multicoloured.

| | | | |
|---|---|---|---|
| 1450 | 35c. British Father Christmas (35×21 mm) | 1·00 | 1·00 |
| 1451 | 40c. Type **597** | 1·00 | 20 |
| 1452 | 46c. French Bonhomme Noel | 1·25 | 1·60 |
| 1453 | 80c. Dutch Sinterklaas | 2·00 | 3·75 |

**598** Players jumping for Ball

**1991.** Basketball Centenary. Multicoloured.

| | | | |
|---|---|---|---|
| 1454 | 40c. Type **598** | 1·50 | 75 |
| **MS**1455 | 155×90 mm. 40c. Type **598**, but with shorter inscr below face value; 46c. Player taking shot; 80c. Player challenging opponent | 6·50 | 6·00 |

**1991.** 50th Anniv of Second World War (3rd issue). As T 574.

| | | | |
|---|---|---|---|
| 1456 | 40c. black, silver and blue | 2·00 | 2·00 |
| 1457 | 40c. black, silver and brown | 2·00 | 2·00 |
| 1458 | 40c. black, silver and lilac | 2·00 | 2·00 |
| 1459 | 40c. black, silver and brown | 2·00 | 2·00 |

DESIGNS: No. 1456, Women's services, 1941; 1457, Armament factory; 1458, Cadets and veterans, 1459, Defence of Hong Kong.

**599** Blueberry **600** McIntosh Apple

**600a** Court House, Yorktown

**1991.** Multicoloured. (a) Edible Berries. As T 599.

| | | | |
|---|---|---|---|
| 1460 | 1c. Type **599** | 10 | 10 |
| 1461 | 2c. Wild strawberry | 10 | 10 |
| 1462 | 3c. Black crowberry | 50 | 10 |
| 1463 | 5c. Rose hip | 10 | 10 |
| 1464 | 6c. Black raspberry | 10 | 10 |
| 1465 | 10c. Kinnikinnick | 10 | 10 |
| 1466 | 25c. Saskatoon berry | 25 | 25 |

(b) Fruit and Nut Trees. As T 600.

| | | | |
|---|---|---|---|
| 1467 | 48c. Type **600** | 50 | 35 |
| 1468 | 49c. Delicious apple | 2·50 | 1·00 |
| 1469 | 50c. Snow apple | 1·50 | 1·00 |
| 1470 | 52c. Grauenstein apple | 1·60 | 50 |
| 1471 | 65c. Black walnut | 1·75 | 50 |
| 1472 | 67c. Beaked hazelnut | 1·75 | 1·25 |
| 1473 | 69c. Shagbark hickory | 2·75 | 1·25 |
| 1474 | 71c. American chestnut | 3·00 | 1·00 |
| 1475 | 84c. Stanley plum | 1·00 | 75 |
| 1476 | 86c. Bartlett pear | 2·75 | 1·00 |
| 1477 | 88c. Westcot apricot | 1·75 | 1·60 |
| 1478 | 90c. Elberta peach | 1·60 | 1·00 |

(c) Architecture. As T 600a.

| | | | |
|---|---|---|---|
| 1479b | $1 Type **600a** | 2·75 | 1·00 |
| 1480b | $2 Provincial Normal School, Truro | 3·50 | 1·60 |
| 1481 | $5 Public Library, Victoria | 7·00 | 4·75 |

**601** Ski Jumping

**1992.** Winter Olympic Games, Albertville. Mult.

| | | | |
|---|---|---|---|
| 1482 | 42c. Type **601** | 1·25 | 1·25 |
| 1483 | 42c. Figure skating | 1·25 | 1·25 |
| 1484 | 42c. Ice hockey | 1·25 | 1·25 |
| 1485 | 42c. Bobsleighing | 1·25 | 1·25 |
| 1486 | 42c. Alpine skiing | 1·25 | 1·25 |

**602** Ville-Marie in 17th Century

**1992.** "CANADA 92" International Youth Stamp Exhibition, Montreal. Multicoloured.

| | | | |
|---|---|---|---|
| 1487 | 42c. Type **602** | 1·50 | 1·50 |
| 1488 | 42c. Modern Montreal | 1·50 | 1·50 |
| 1489 | 48c. Compass rose, snow shoe and crow's nest of Cartier's ship "Grande Hermine" | 2·25 | 1·25 |
| 1490 | 84c. Atlantic map, Aztec "calendar stone" and navigational instrument | 3·50 | 4·50 |
| **MS**1491 | 181×120 mm. Nos. 1487/90 | 8·00 | 8·00 |

**1992.** Canadian Rivers (2nd series). As T 592 but horiz. Multicoloured.

| | | | |
|---|---|---|---|
| 1492 | 42c. Margaree River | 1·50 | 1·50 |
| 1493 | 42c. West (Eliot) River | 1·50 | 1·50 |
| 1494 | 42c. Ottawa River | 1·50 | 1·50 |
| 1495 | 42c. Niagara River | 1·50 | 1·50 |
| 1496 | 42c. South Saskatchewan River | 1·50 | 1·50 |

**603** Road Bed Construction and Route Map

**1992.** 50th Anniv of Alaska Highway.

| | | | | |
|---|---|---|---|---|
| 1497 | **603** | 42c. multicoloured | 1·50 | 70 |

**1992.** Olympic Games, Barcelona. As T 601. Multicoloured.

| | | | |
|---|---|---|---|
| 1498 | 42c. Gymnastics | 1·10 | 1·25 |
| 1499 | 42c. Athletics | 1·10 | 1·25 |
| 1500 | 42c. Diving | 1·10 | 1·25 |
| 1501 | 42c. Cycling | 1·10 | 1·25 |
| 1502 | 42c. Swimming | 1·10 | 1·25 |

**604** "Quebec, Patrimoine Mondial" (A. Dumas)

**1992.** Canada Day. Paintings. Multicoloured.

| | | | |
|---|---|---|---|
| 1503a | 42c. Type **604** | 1·50 | 1·75 |
| 1503b | 42c. "Christie Passage, Hurst Island, British Columbia" (E. J. Hughes) | 1·50 | 1·75 |
| 1503c | 42c. "Toronto, Landmarks of Time" (Ontario) (V. McIndoe) | 1·50 | 1·75 |
| 1503d | 42c. "Near the Forks" (Manitoba) (S. Gouthro) | 1·50 | 1·75 |
| 1503e | 42c. "Off Cape St. Francis" (Newfoundland) (R. Shepherd) | 1·50 | 1·75 |
| 1503f | 42c. "Crowd at City Hall" (New Brunswick) (Molly Bobak) | 1·50 | 1·75 |
| 1503g | 42c. "Across the Tracks to Shop" (Alberta) (Janet Mitchell) | 1·50 | 1·75 |
| 1503h | 42c. "Cove Scene" (Nova Scotia) (J. Norris) | 1·50 | 1·75 |
| 1503i | 42c. "Untitled" (Saskatchewan) (D. Thauberger) | 1·50 | 1·75 |
| 1503j | 42c. "Town Life" (Yukon) (T. Harrison) | 1·50 | 1·75 |
| 1503k | 42c. "Country Scene" (Prince Edward Island) (Erica Rutherford) | 1·50 | 1·75 |
| 1503l | 42c. "Playing on an Igloo" (Northwest Territories) (Agnes Nanogak) | 1·50 | 1·75 |

**1992.** Canadian Art (5th series). As T 550. Multicoloured.

| | | | |
|---|---|---|---|
| 1504 | 50c. "Red Nasturtiums" (David Milne) | 1·25 | 1·40 |

**605** Jerry Potts (scout)

**1992.** Folk Heroes. Multicoloured.

| | | | |
|---|---|---|---|
| 1505 | 42c. Type **605** | 1·25 | 1·50 |
| 1506 | 42c. Capt. William Jackman and wreck of "Sea Clipper", 1867 | 1·25 | 1·50 |
| 1507 | 42c. Laura Secord (messenger) | 1·25 | 1·50 |
| 1508 | 42c. Jos Montferrand (lumberjack) | 1·25 | 1·50 |

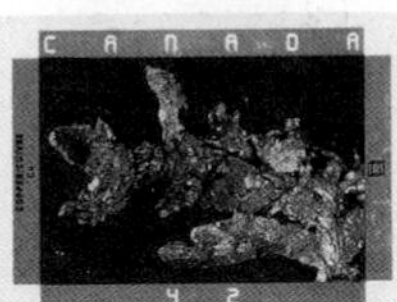


**606** Copper

**1992.** 150th Anniv of Geological Survey of Canada. Minerals. Multicoloured.

| | | | |
|---|---|---|---|
| 1509 | 42c. Type **606** | 1·75 | 2·00 |
| 1510 | 42c. Sodalite | 1·75 | 2·00 |
| 1511 | 42c. Gold | 1·75 | 2·00 |

| | | | |
|---|---|---|---|
| 1512 | 42c. Galena | 1·75 | 2·00 |
| 1513 | 42c. Grossular | 1·75 | 2·00 |

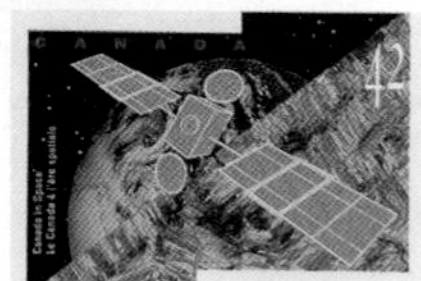


**607** Satellite and Photographs from Space

**1992.** Canadian Space Programme. Multicoloured.

| | | | |
|---|---|---|---|
| 1514 | 42c. Type **607** | 1·25 | 1·75 |
| 1515 | 42c. Space shuttle over Canada (hologram) (32×26 mm) | 1·25 | 1·75 |

**608** Babe Siebert, Skates and Stick

**1992.** 75th Anniv of National Ice Hockey League. Multicoloured.

| | | | |
|---|---|---|---|
| 1516 | 42c. Type **608** | 1·60 | 1·75 |
| 1517 | 42c. Claude Provost, Terry Sawchuck and team badges | 1·60 | 1·75 |
| 1518 | 42c. Hockey mask, gloves and modern player | 1·60 | 1·75 |

**609** Companion of the Order of Canada Insignia

**1992.** 25th Anniv of the Order of Canada and Daniel Roland Michener (former Governor-General) Commermoration. Multicoloured.

| | | | |
|---|---|---|---|
| 1519 | 42c. Type **609** | 1·40 | 1·75 |
| 1520 | 42c. Daniel Roland Michener | 1·40 | 1·75 |

**1992.** 50th Anniv of Second World War (4th issue). As T 574.

| | | | |
|---|---|---|---|
| 1521 | 42c. black, silver & brown | 2·25 | 2·50 |
| 1522 | 42c. black, silver & green | 2·25 | 2·50 |
| 1523 | 42c. black, silver & brown | 2·25 | 2·50 |
| 1524 | 42c. black, silver and blue | 2·25 | 2·50 |

DESIGNS: No. 1521, Reporters and soldier, 1942; 1522, Consolidated Liberator bombers over Newfoundland; 1523 Dieppe raid; 1524, U-boat sinking merchant ship.

**610** Estonian Jouluvana

**1992.** Christmas. Multicoloured.

| | | | |
|---|---|---|---|
| 1525 | 37c. North American Santa Claus (35×21 mm) | 1·10 | 80 |
| 1526 | 42c. Type **610** | 40 | 20 |
| 1527 | 48c. Italian La Befana | 1·50 | 2·25 |
| 1528 | 84c. German Weihnachtsmann | 2·25 | 3·25 |

**611** Adelaide Hoodless (women's movement pioneer)

**1993.** Prominent Canadian Women. Multicoloured.

| | | | |
|---|---|---|---|
| 1529 | 43c. Type **611** | 1·10 | 1·50 |
| 1530 | 43c. Marie-Josephine Gerin-Lajoie (social reformer) | 1·10 | 1·50 |
| 1531 | 43c. Pitseolak Ashoona (Inuit artist) | 1·10 | 1·50 |
| 1532 | 43c. Helen Kinnear (lawyer) | 1·10 | 1·50 |

**612** Ice Hockey Players with Cup

**1993.** Centenary of Stanley Cup.

| | | | |
|---|---|---|---|
| 1533 | **612** 43c. multicoloured | 1·00 | 60 |

**613** Coverlet, New Brunswick

**1993.** Hand-crafted Textiles. Multicoloured.

| | | | |
|---|---|---|---|
| 1534 | 43c. Type **613** | 1·50 | 2·00 |
| 1535 | 43c. Pieced quilt, Ontario | 1·50 | 2·00 |
| 1536 | 43c. Doukhobor bedcover, Saskatchewan | 1·50 | 2·00 |
| 1537 | 43c. Ceremonial robe, Kwakwaka'wakw | 1·50 | 2·00 |
| 1538 | 43c. Boutonne coverlet, Quebec | 1·50 | 2·00 |

**1993.** Canadian Art (6th series). As T 550. Multicoloured.

| | | | |
|---|---|---|---|
| 1539 | 86c. "The Owl" (Kenojuak Ashevak) | 2·25 | 3·25 |

**614** Empress Hotel, Victoria

**1993.** Historic Hotels. Multicoloured.

| | | | |
|---|---|---|---|
| 1540 | 43c. Type **614** | 60 | 1·10 |
| 1541 | 43c. Banff Springs Hotel | 60 | 1·10 |
| 1542 | 43c. Royal York Hotel, Toronto | 60 | 1·10 |
| 1543 | 43c. Le Chateau Frontenac, Quebec | 60 | 1·10 |
| 1544 | 43c. Algonquin Hotel, St. Andrews | 60 | 1·10 |

**615** Algonquin Park, Ontario

**1993.** Canada Day. Provincial and Territorial Parks. Multicoloured.

| | | | |
|---|---|---|---|
| 1545 | 43c. Type **615** | 70 | 80 |
| 1546 | 43c. De La Gaspesie Park, Quebec | 70 | 80 |
| 1547 | 43c. Cedar Dunes Park, Prince Edward Island | 70 | 80 |
| 1548 | 43c. Cape St. Mary's Seabird Reserve, Newfoundland | 70 | 80 |
| 1549 | 43c. Mount Robson Park, British Columbia | 70 | 80 |
| 1550 | 43c. Writing-on-Stone Park, Alberta | 70 | 80 |
| 1551 | 43c. Spruce Woods Park, Manitoba | 70 | 80 |
| 1552 | 43c. Herschel Island Park, Yukon | 70 | 80 |
| 1553 | 43c. Cypress Hills Park, Saskatchewan | 70 | 80 |
| 1554 | 43c. The Rocks Park, New Brunswick | 70 | 80 |
| 1555 | 43c. Blomidon Park, Nova Scotia | 70 | 80 |
| 1556 | 43c. Katannilik Park, Northwest Territories | 70 | 80 |

**616** Toronto Skyscrapers

**1993.** Bicentenary of Toronto.

| | | | |
|---|---|---|---|
| 1557 | **616** 43c. multicoloured | 1·00 | 70 |

**1993.** Canadian Rivers (3rd series). As T 592. Multicoloured.

| | | | |
|---|---|---|---|
| 1558 | 43c. Fraser River | 80 | 1·10 |
| 1559 | 43c. Yukon River | 80 | 1·10 |
| 1560 | 43c. Red River | 80 | 1·10 |
| 1561 | 43c. St. Lawrence River | 80 | 1·10 |
| 1562 | 43c. St. John River | 80 | 1·10 |

**617** Taylor's Steam Buggy, 1867

**1993.** Historic Automobiles (1st issue). Sheet 177×125 mm, containing T 617 and similar horiz designs. Multicoloured.

| | | | |
|---|---|---|---|
| **MS**1563 | 43c. Type **617**; 43c. Russel Model L touring car, 1908; 49c. Ford Model T touring car, 1914 (43×22 mm); 49c. Studebaker Champion Deluxe Starlight coupe, 1950 (43×22 mm); 86c. McLaughlin-Buick 28–496 special, 1928 (43×22 mm); 86c. Gray-Dort 25 SM luxury sedan, 1923 (43×22 mm) | 7·50 | 8·00 |

See also Nos. **MS**1611, **MS**1636 and **MS**1683/4.

**618** "The Alberta Homesteader"

**1993.** Folk Songs. Multicoloured.

| | | | |
|---|---|---|---|
| 1564 | 43c. Type **618** | 70 | 1·00 |
| 1565 | 43c. "Les Raftmans" (Quebec) | 70 | 1·00 |
| 1566 | 43c. "I'se the B'y that Builds the Boat" (Newfoundland) | 70 | 1·00 |
| 1567 | 43c. "Onkwa:ri Tenhanonniahkwe" (Mohawk Indian) | 70 | 1·00 |

**1993.** Prehistoric Canada (3rd series). Dinosaurs. As T 582 but 40×28 mm. Multicoloured.

| | | | |
|---|---|---|---|
| 1568 | 43c. Massospondylus | 80 | 80 |
| 1569 | 43c. Stryacosaurus | 80 | 80 |
| 1570 | 43c. Albertosaurus | 80 | 80 |
| 1571 | 43c. Platecarpus | 80 | 80 |

**619** Polish Swiety Mikolaj

**1993.** Christmas. Multicoloured.

| | | | |
|---|---|---|---|
| 1572 | 38c. North American Santa Claus (35×22 mm) | 90 | 90 |
| 1573 | 43c. Type **619** | 55 | 20 |
| 1574 | 49c. Russian Ded Moroz | 1·10 | 1·40 |
| 1575 | 86c. Australian Father Christmas | 1·90 | 2·75 |

**1993.** 50th Anniv of Second World War (5th issue). As T 574.

| | | | |
|---|---|---|---|
| 1576 | 43c. black, silver and green | 2·25 | 2·25 |
| 1577 | 43c. black, silver and blue | 2·25 | 2·25 |
| 1578 | 43c. black, silver and blue | 2·25 | 2·25 |
| 1579 | 43c. black, silver and brown | 2·25 | 2·25 |

DESIGNS: No. 1576, Loading munitions for Russia, 1943; No. 1577, Loading bombs on Avro Lancaster; No. 1578, Escorts attacking U-boat; No. 1579, Infantry advancing, Italy.

**620** (face value at right)

**1994.** Self-adhesive Greetings stamps. Mult.

| | | | |
|---|---|---|---|
| 1580 | 43c. Type **620** | 1·00 | 1·00 |
| 1581 | 43c. As Type **620** but face value at left | 1·00 | 1·00 |

It was intended that the sender should insert an appropriate greetings label into the circular space on each stamp before use.

For 45c. values in this design see Nos. 1654/5.

**621** Jeanne Sauve

**1994.** Jeanne Sauve (former Governor-General) Commemoration.

| | | | |
|---|---|---|---|
| 1582 | **621** 43c. multicoloured | 60 | 60 |

**622** Timothy Eaton, Toronto Store of 1869 and Merchandise

**1994.** 125th Anniv of T. Eaton Company Ltd (department store group).

| | | | |
|---|---|---|---|
| 1583 | **622** 43c. multicoloured | 55 | 75 |

**1994.** Canadian Rivers (4th series). As T 592, but horiz. Multicoloured.

| | | | |
|---|---|---|---|
| 1584 | 43c. Saguenay River | 80 | 90 |
| 1585 | 43c. French River | 80 | 90 |
| 1586 | 43c. Mackenzie River | 80 | 90 |
| 1587 | 43c. Churchill River | 80 | 90 |
| 1588 | 43c. Columbia River | 80 | 90 |

**1994.** Canadian Art (7th series). As T 550. Multicoloured.

| | | | |
|---|---|---|---|
| 1589 | 88c. "Vera" (detail) (Frederick Varley) | 1·50 | 2·00 |

**623** Lawn Bowls

**1994.** 15th Commonwealth Games, Victoria. Multicoloured.

| | | | |
|---|---|---|---|
| 1590 | 43c. Type **623** | 50 | 70 |
| 1591 | 43c. Lacrosse | 50 | 70 |
| 1592 | 43c. Wheelchair race | 50 | 70 |
| 1593 | 43c. High jumping | 50 | 70 |
| 1594 | 50c. Diving | 50 | 55 |
| 1595 | 88c. Cycling | 2·25 | 2·00 |

**624** Mother and Baby

**1994.** International Year of the Family. Sheet 178×134 mm, containing T 624 and similar vert designs. Multicoloured.

| | | | |
|---|---|---|---|
| **MS**1596 | 43c. Type **624**; 43c. Family outing; 43c. Grandmother and granddaughter; 43c. Computer class; 43c. Play group, nurse with patient and female lawyer | 3·00 | 3·50 |

**625** Big Leaf Maple Tree

**1994.** Canada Day. Maple Trees. Multicoloured.

| | | | |
|---|---|---|---|
| 1597 | 43c. Type **625** | 80 | 90 |
| 1598 | 43c. Sugar maple | 80 | 90 |
| 1599 | 43c. Silver maple | 80 | 90 |
| 1600 | 43c. Striped maple | 80 | 90 |
| 1601 | 43c. Norway maple | 80 | 90 |
| 1602 | 43c. Manitoba maple | 80 | 90 |
| 1603 | 43c. Black maple | 80 | 90 |

| | | | |
|---|---|---|---|
| 1604 | 43c. Douglas maple | 80 | 90 |
| 1605 | 43c. Mountain maple | 80 | 90 |
| 1606 | 43c. Vine maple | 80 | 90 |
| 1607 | 43c. Hedge maple | 80 | 90 |
| 1608 | 43c. Red maple | 80 | 90 |

**626** Billy Bishop (fighter ace) and Nieuport 17

**1994.** Birth Centenaries. Multicoloured.

| | | | |
|---|---|---|---|
| 1609 | 43c. Type **626** | 1·00 | 1·25 |
| 1610 | 43c. Mary Travers ("La Bolduc") (singer) and musicians | 1·00 | 1·25 |

**1994.** Historic Automobiles (2nd issue). Sheet 177×125 mm, containing horiz designs as T 617. Multicoloured.

| | | | |
|---|---|---|---|
| **MS**1611 | 43c. Ford Model F60L-AMB military ambulance, 1942–43; 43c. Winnipeg police wagon, 1925; 50c. Sicard snowblower, 1927 (43×22 mm); 50c. Bickle Chieftain fire engine, 1936 (43×22 mm); 88c. St. John Railway Company tramcar No. 40, 1894 (51×22 mm), 88c. Motor Coach Industries Courier 50 Skyview coach, 1950 (51×22 mm) | 10·00 | 10·00 |

No. **MS**1611 was sold in a protective pack.

**627** Symbolic Aircraft, Radar Screen and Clouds

**1994.** 50th Anniv of ICAO.

| | | | | |
|---|---|---|---|---|
| 1612 | **627** | 43c. multicoloured | 1·00 | 70 |

**1994.** Prehistoric Canada (4th series). Mammals. As T 582, but 40×28 mm. Multicoloured.

| | | | |
|---|---|---|---|
| 1613 | 43c. Coryphodon | 2·00 | 2·00 |
| 1614 | 43c. Megacerops | 2·00 | 2·00 |
| 1615 | 43c. Arctodus simus (bear) | 2·00 | 2·00 |
| 1616 | 43c. Mammuthus primigenius (mammoth) | 2·00 | 2·00 |

**628** Carol Singing around Christmas Tree

**1994.** Christmas. Multicoloured.

| | | | |
|---|---|---|---|
| 1617 | (–)c. Carol singer (35×21 mm) | 65 | 75 |
| 1618 | 43c. Type **628** | 50 | 20 |
| 1619 | 50c. Choir (vert) | 1·00 | 1·40 |
| 1620 | 88c. Couple carol singing in snow (vert) | 2·25 | 3·25 |

No. 1617 is without face value, but was intended for use as a 38c. on internal greetings cards posted before 31 January 1995. The design shows a barcode at left.

**1994.** 50th Anniv of Second World War (6th issue). As T 574.

| | | | |
|---|---|---|---|
| 1621 | 43c. black, silver and green | 2·25 | 2·25 |
| 1622 | 43c. black, silver and red | 2·25 | 2·25 |
| 1623 | 43c. black, silver and blue | 2·25 | 2·25 |
| 1624 | 43c. black, silver and grey | 2·25 | 2·25 |

DESIGNS: No. 1621, D-Day landings, Normandy; No. 1622, Canadian artillery, Normandy; No. 1623, Hawker Typhoons on patrol; No. 1624, Canadian infantry and disabled German self-propelled gun, Walcheren.

**1995.** 50th Anniv of Second World War (7th issue). As T 574.

| | | | |
|---|---|---|---|
| 1625 | 43c. black, silver and purple | 2·25 | 2·25 |
| 1626 | 43c. black, silver and brown | 2·25 | 2·25 |
| 1627 | 43c. black, silver and green | 2·25 | 2·25 |
| 1628 | 43c. black, silver and blue | 2·25 | 2·25 |

DESIGNS: No. 1625, Returning troop ship; 1626, Canadian P.O.W.s celebrating freedom; 1627, Canadian tank liberating Dutch town; 1628, Parachute drop in support of Rhine Crossing.

**1995.** Canadian Art (8th series). As T 550. Multicoloured.

| | | | |
|---|---|---|---|
| 1629 | 88c. "Floraison" (Alfred Pellan) | 1·50 | 2·25 |

**629** Flag and Lake

**1995.** 30th Anniv of National Flag. No face value.

| | | | | |
|---|---|---|---|---|
| 1630 | **629** | (43c.) multicoloured | 1·00 | 50 |

**630** Louisbourg Harbour

**1995.** 275th Anniv of Fortress of Louisbourg. Multicoloured.

| | | | |
|---|---|---|---|
| 1631 | (43c.) Type **630** | 70 | 80 |
| 1632 | (43c.) Barracks (32×29 mm) | 70 | 80 |
| 1633 | (43c.) King's Bastion (40×29 mm) | 70 | 80 |
| 1634 | (43c.) Site of King's Garden, convent and hospital (56×29 mm) | 70 | 80 |
| 1635 | (43c.) Site of coastal fortifications | 70 | 80 |

**1995.** Historic Automobiles (3rd issue). Sheet 177×125 mm, containing horiz designs as T 617. Multicoloured.

| | | | |
|---|---|---|---|
| **MS**1636 | 43c. Cockshutt "30" farm tractor, 1950; 43c. Bombadier "Ski-Doo Olympique 335" snowmobile, 1970; 50c. Bombadier "B-12 CS" multi-passenger snowmobile, 1948 (43×22 mm); 50c. Gotfredson "Model 20" farm truck, 1924 (43×22 mm); 88c. Robin-Nodwell "RN 110" tracked carrier, 1962 (43×22 mm); 88c. Massey-Harris "No. 21" self-propelled combine-harvester, 1942 (43×22 mm) | 7·00 | 7·50 |

No. **MS**1636 was sold in a protective pack.

**631** Banff Springs Golf Club, Alberta

**1995.** Centenaries of Canadian Amateur Golf Championship and of the Royal Canadian Golf Association. Multicoloured.

| | | | |
|---|---|---|---|
| 1637 | 43c. Type **631** | 80 | 80 |
| 1638 | 43c. Riverside Country Club, New Brunswick | 80 | 80 |
| 1639 | 43c. Glen Abbey Golf Club, Ontario | 80 | 80 |
| 1640 | 43c. Victoria Golf Club, British Columbia | 80 | 80 |
| 1641 | 43c. Royal Montreal Golf Club, Quebec | 80 | 80 |

**632** "October Gold" (Franklin Carmichael)

**1995.** Canada Day. 75th Anniv of "Group of Seven" (artists). Miniature sheets, each 180×80 mm, containing square designs as T 632. Multicoloured.

| | | | |
|---|---|---|---|
| **MS**1642a | 43c. Type **632**; 43c. "From the North Shore, Lake Superior" (Lawren Harris); 43c. "Evening, Les Eboulements, Quebec" (A. Jackson) | 3·00 | 3·50 |
| **MS**1642b | 43c. "Serenity, Lake of the Woods" (Frank Johnston); 43c. "A September Gale, Georgian Bay" (Arthur Lismer); 43c. "Falls, Montreal River" (J. E. H. MacDonald); 43c. "Open Window" (Frederick Varley) | 3·00 | 3·50 |
| **MS**1642c | 43c. "Mill Houses" (Alfred Casson); 43c. "Pembina Valley" (Lionel FitzGerald); 43c. "The Lumberjack" (Edwin Holgate) | 3·00 | 3·50 |

The three sheets were sold together in an envelope which also includes a small descriptive booklet.

**633** Academy Building and Ship Plan

**1995.** Centenary of Lunenburg Academy.

| | | | | |
|---|---|---|---|---|
| 1643 | **633** | 43c. multicoloured | 50 | 45 |

**634** Aspects of Manitoba

**1995.** 125th Anniv of Manitoba as Canadian Province.

| | | | | |
|---|---|---|---|---|
| 1644 | **634** | 43c. multicoloured | 50 | 45 |

**635** Monarch Butterfly

**1995.** Migratory Wildlife. Multicoloured.

| | | | |
|---|---|---|---|
| 1645 | 45c. Type **635** | 1·10 | 1·40 |
| 1646 | 45c. Belted kingfisher* | 1·10 | 1·40 |
| 1647 | 45c. Belted kingfisher* | 1·10 | 1·40 |
| 1648 | 45c. Pintail | 1·10 | 1·40 |
| 1649 | 45c. Hoary bat | 1·10 | 1·40 |

*No. 1646: Inscr "aune migratrice" in error. No. 1647: Inscr corrected to "faune migratrice".

**636** Quebec Railway Bridge

**1995.** 20th World Road Congress, Montreal. Bridges. Multicoloured.

| | | | |
|---|---|---|---|
| 1650 | 45c. Type **636** | 2·25 | 2·25 |
| 1651 | 45c. 401-403-410 Interchange, Mississauga | 2·25 | 2·25 |
| 1652 | 45c. Hartland Bridge, New Brunswick | 2·25 | 2·25 |
| 1653 | 45c. Alex Fraser Bridge, British Columbia | 2·25 | 2·25 |

**1995.** Self-adhesive Greetings stamps. As T 620. Multicoloured. Imperf.

| | | | |
|---|---|---|---|
| 1654 | 45c. Face value at right | 60 | 75 |
| 1655 | 45c. Face value at left | 60 | 75 |

It is intended the sender should insert an appropriate greetings label into the circular space on each stamp before use.

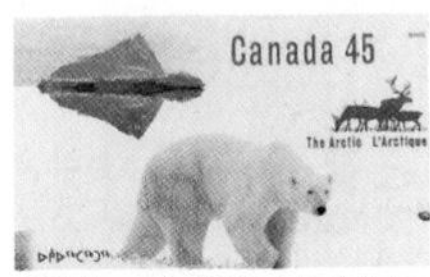

**637** Mountain, Baffin Island, Polar Bear and Caribou

**1995.** 50th Anniv of Arctic Institute of North America. Multicoloured.

| | | | |
|---|---|---|---|
| 1656 | 45c. Type **637** | 1·00 | 1·25 |
| 1657 | 45c. Arctic poppy, Auyuittuq National Park and cargo canoe | 1·00 | 1·25 |
| 1658 | 45c. Inuk man and igloo | 1·00 | 1·25 |
| 1659 | 45c. Ogilvie Mountains, dog team and ski-equipped airplane | 1·00 | 1·25 |
| 1660 | 45c. Inuit children | 1·00 | 1·25 |

**638** Superman

**1995.** Comic Book Superheroes. Multicoloured.

| | | | |
|---|---|---|---|
| 1661 | 45c. Type **638** | 80 | 90 |
| 1662 | 45c. Johnny Canuck | 80 | 90 |
| 1663 | 45c. Nelvana | 80 | 90 |
| 1664 | 45c. Captain Canuck | 80 | 90 |
| 1665 | 45c. Fleur de Lys | 80 | 90 |

**639** Prime Minister MacKenzie King signing U.N. Charter, 1945

**1995.** 50th Anniv of United Nations.

| | | | | |
|---|---|---|---|---|
| 1666 | **639** | 45c. multicoloured | 75 | 50 |

**640** "The Nativity"

**1995.** Christmas. Sculptured Capitals from Ste.-Anne-de-Beaupre Basilica designed by Emile Brunet (Nos. 1668/70). Multicoloured.

| | | | |
|---|---|---|---|
| 1667 | 40c. Sprig of holly (35×22 mm) | 85 | 70 |
| 1668 | 45c. Type **640** | 50 | 20 |
| 1669 | 52c. "The Annunciation" | 1·60 | 1·60 |
| 1670 | 90c. "The Flight to Egypt" | 2·25 | 2·75 |

**641** World Map and Emblem

**1995.** 25th Anniv of La Francophonie and The Agency for Cultural and Technical Co-operation.

| | | | | |
|---|---|---|---|---|
| 1671 | **641** | 45c. multicoloured | 60 | 50 |

**642** Concentration Camp Victims, Uniform and Identity Card

**1995.** 50th Anniv of the End of The Holocaust.

| | | | | |
|---|---|---|---|---|
| 1672 | **642** | 45c. multicoloured | 70 | 50 |

**643** American Kestrel

**1996.** Birds (1st series). Multicoloured.

| | | | |
|---|---|---|---|
| 1673 | 45c. Type **643** | 1·90 | 1·75 |
| 1674 | 45c. Atlantic puffin | 1·90 | 1·75 |
| 1675 | 45c. Pileated woodpecker | 1·90 | 1·75 |
| 1676 | 45c. Ruby-throated hummingbird | 1·90 | 1·75 |

See also Nos. 1717/20, 1779/82, 1865/8, 1974/7 and 2058/61.

**644** "Louis R. Desmarais" (tanker), Three-dimensional Map and Radar Screen

**1996.** High Technology Industries. Multicoloured.

| | | | |
|---|---|---|---|
| 1677 | 45c. Type **644** | 65 | 1·00 |
| 1678 | 45c. Canadair Challenger 601-3R, jet engine and navigational aid | 65 | 1·00 |
| 1679 | 45c. Map of North America and eye | 65 | 1·00 |
| 1680 | 45c. Genetic engineering experiment and Canola (plant) | 65 | 1·00 |

**1996.** Canadian Art (9th series). As T 550. Multicoloured.

| | | | |
|---|---|---|---|
| 1681 | 90c. "The Spirit of Haida Gwaii" (sculpture) (Bill Reid) | 1·40 | 2·25 |

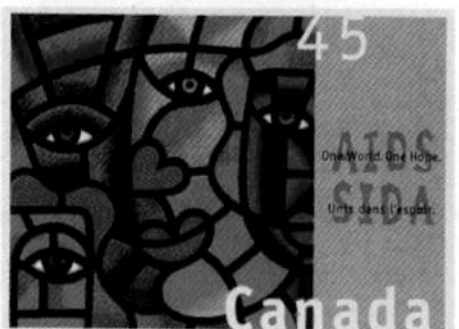


**645** "One World, One Hope" (Joe Average)

**1996.** 11th International Conference on AIDS, Vancouver.

| | | | | |
|---|---|---|---|---|
| 1682 | **645** | 45c. multicoloured | 70 | 70 |

**1996.** Historic Automobiles (4th issue). Sheet 177×125 mm, containing horiz designs as T 617. Multicoloured.

**MS**1683 45c. Still Motor Co electric van, 1899; 45c. Waterous Engine Works steam roller, 1914; 52c. International D.35 delivery truck, 1938; 52c. Champion road grader, 1936; 90c. White Model WA 122 articulated lorry, 1947 (51×22 mm); 90c. Hayes HDX 45-115 logging truck, 1975 (51×22 mm) 7·50 8·00

No. **MS**1683 also includes the "CAPEX '96" International Stamp Exhibition logo on the sheet margin and was sold in a protective pack.

**1996.** "CAPEX '96" International Stamp Exhibitiion, Toronto. Sheet 368×182 mm, containing horiz designs as Nos. MS1563, MS1611, MS1636 and MS1683, but with different face values, and one new design (45c.).

**MS**1684 5c. Bombadier "Ski-Doo Olympique 335" snowmobile, 1970; 5c. Cockshutt "30" farm tractor, 1950; 5c. Type **617**; 5c. Ford "Model F160L-AMB" military ambulance, 1942; 5c. Still Motor Co electric van, 1895; 5c. International "D.35" delivery truck, 1936; 5c. Russel "Model L" touring car, 1908; 5c. Winnipeg police wagon, 1925; 5c. Waterous Engine Works steam roller, 1914; 5c. Champion road grader, 1936; 10c. White "Model WA 122" articulated lorry, 1947 (51×22 mm); 10c. St. John Railway Company tramcar, 1894 (51×22 mm); 10c. Hayes "HDX 45-115" logging truck, 1975 (51×22 mm); 10c. Motor Couch Industries "Courier 50 Skyview" coach, 1950 (51×22 mm); 20c. Ford "Model T" touring car, 1914 (43×22 mm); 20c. McLaughlin-Buick "28-496 special", 1928 (43×22 mm); 20c. Bombadier "B-12 CS" multi-passenger snowmobile, 1948 (43×22 mm); 20c. Robin-Nodwell "RN 110" tracked carrier, 1962 (43×22 mm); 20c. Studebaker "Champion Deluxe Starlight" coupe, 1950 (43×22 mm); 20c. Gray-Dort "25 SM" luxury sedan, 1923 (43×22 mm); 20c. Gotfredson "Model 20" farm truck, 1924 (43×22 mm); 20c. Massey-Harris "No. 21" self-propelled combine-harvester, 1942 (43×22 mm); 20c. Bickle "Chieftain" fire engine, 1936 (43×22 mm); 20c. Sicard snowblower, 1927 (43×22 mm); 45c. Bricklin "SV-1" sports car, 1975 (51×22 mm) 8·00 9·00

The price quoted for No. **MS**1684 is for a folded example.

**646** Skookum Jim Mason and Bonanza Creek

**1996.** Centenary of Yukon Gold Rush. Multicoloured.

| | | | |
|---|---|---|---|
| 1685 | 45c. Type **646** | 80 | 1·00 |
| 1686 | 45c. Prospector and boats on Lake Laberge | 80 | 1·00 |
| 1687 | 45c. Superintendent Sam Steele (N.W.M.P.) and U.S.A.–Canada border | 80 | 1·00 |
| 1688 | 45c. Dawson saloon | 80 | 1·00 |
| 1689 | 45c. Miner with rocker box and sluice | 80 | 1·00 |

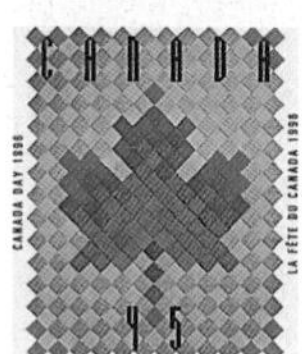


**647** Patchwork Quilt Maple Leaf

**1996.** Canada Day. Self-adhesive. Imperf.

| | | | | |
|---|---|---|---|---|
| 1690 | **647** | 45c. multicoloured | 1·00 | 60 |

**648** Ethel Catherwood (high jump), 1928

**1996.** Canadian Olympic Gold Medal Winners. Multicoloured.

| | | | |
|---|---|---|---|
| 1691 | 45c. Type **648** | 70 | 85 |
| 1692 | 45c. Etienne Desmarteau (56lb weight throw), 1904 | 70 | 85 |
| 1693 | 45c. Fanny Rosenfeld (400 m relay), 1928 | 70 | 85 |
| 1694 | 45c. Gerald Ouellette (small bore rifle, prone), 1956 | 70 | 85 |
| 1695 | 45c. Percy Williams (100 and 200 m), 1928 | 70 | 85 |

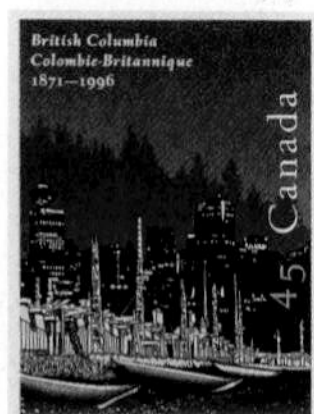


**649** Indian Totems, City Skyline, Forest and Mountains

**1996.** 125th Anniv of British Columbia.

| | | | | |
|---|---|---|---|---|
| 1696 | **649** | 45c. multicoloured | 50 | 50 |

**650** Canadian Heraldic Symbols

**1996.** 22nd International Congress of Genealogical and Heraldic Sciences, Ottawa.

| | | | | |
|---|---|---|---|---|
| 1697 | **650** | 45c. multicoloured | 50 | 50 |

**651** "L'Arivee d'un Train en Gare" (1896)

**1996.** Centenary of Cinema. Two sheets, each 180×100 mm, containing T 651 and similar vert designs. Multicoloured. Self-adhesive.

**MS**1698a 45c. Type **651**; 45c. "God's Country" (1919); 45c. "Hen Hop" (1942); 45c."Pour la Suite du Monde" (1963); 45c. "Goin' Down the Road" (1970). 4·25 4·75

**MS**1698b 45c. "Mon Oncle Antoine" (1971); 45c. "The Apprenticeship of Duddy Kravitz" (1974); 45c. "Les Ordres" (1974); 45c. "Les Bons Debarras" (1980); 45c. "The Grey Fox" (1982) 4·25 4·75

The two sheets were sold together in an envelope with a descriptive booklet.

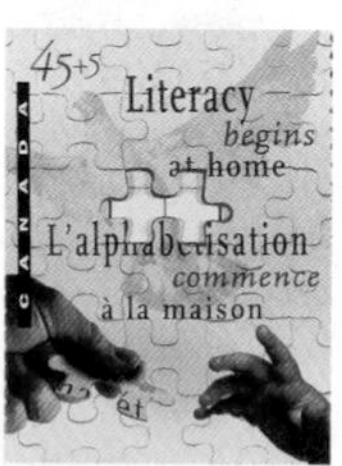


**652** Interlocking Jigsaw Pieces and Hands

**1996.** Literacy Campaign.

| | | | | |
|---|---|---|---|---|
| 1699 | **652** | 45c.+5c. mult | 85 | 1·00 |

**653** Edouard Montpetit and Montreal University

**1996.** Edouard Montpetit (academic) Commem.

| | | | | |
|---|---|---|---|---|
| 1700 | **653** | 45c. multicoloured | 50 | 50 |

**654** Winnie and Lt. Colebourn, 1914

**1996.** Stamp Collecting Month. Winnie the Pooh. Multicoloured.

| | | | |
|---|---|---|---|
| 1701 | 45c. Type **654** | 1·75 | 1·50 |
| 1702 | 45c. Christopher Robin Milne and teddy bear, 1925 | 1·75 | 1·50 |
| 1703 | 45c. Illustration from "Winnie the Pooh", 1926 | 1·75 | 1·50 |
| 1704 | 45c. Winnie the Pooh at Walt Disney World, 1996 | 1·75 | 1·50 |
| **MS**1705 | 152×112 mm. Nos 1701/4 | 6·25 | 6·50 |

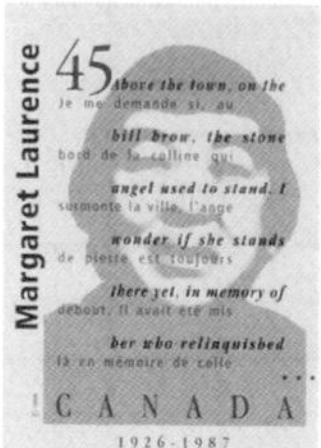


**655** Margaret Laurence

**1996.** Canadian Authors.

| | | | | |
|---|---|---|---|---|
| 1706 | **655** | 45c. multicoloured | 80 | 1·40 |
| 1707 | - | 45c. black, grey and red | 80 | 1·40 |
| 1708 | - | 45c. multicoloured | 80 | 1·40 |
| 1709 | - | 45c. multicoloured | 80 | 1·40 |
| 1710 | - | 45c. multicoloured | 80 | 1·40 |

DESIGNS: No. 1707, Donald G. Creighton; 1708, Gabrielle Roy; 1709, Felix-Antoine Savard; 1710, Thomas C. Haliburton.

**656** Children tobogganing

**1996.** Christmas. 50th Anniv of UNICEF. Multicoloured.

| | | | |
|---|---|---|---|
| 1711 | 45c. Type **656** | 50 | 20 |
| 1712 | 52c. Father Christmas skiing | 70 | 1·00 |
| 1713a | 90c. Couple ice-skating | 1·25 | 2·00 |

**657** Head of Ox

**1997.** Chinese New Year ("Year of the Ox").

| | | | | |
|---|---|---|---|---|
| 1714 | **657** | 45c. multicoloured | 85 | 90 |
| **MS**1715 | | 155×75 mm. Nos. 1714×2 | 2·00 | 2·50 |

No. **MS**1715 is an extended fan shape with overall measurements as quoted.

**1997.** "HONG KONG '97" International Stamp Exhibition. As No. MS1715, but with exhibition logo added to the sheet margin in gold.

| | | | |
|---|---|---|---|
| **MS**1716 | 155×75 mm. No. 1714×2 | 6·50 | 7·50 |

**1997.** Birds (2nd series). As T 643. Multicoloured.

| | | | |
|---|---|---|---|
| 1717 | 45c. Mountain bluebird | 1·25 | 1·40 |
| 1718 | 45c. Western grebe | 1·25 | 1·40 |
| 1719 | 45c. Northern gannet | 1·25 | 1·40 |
| 1720 | 45c. Scarlet tanager | 1·25 | 1·40 |

**1997.** Canadian Art (10th series). As T 550. Multicoloured.

| | | | |
|---|---|---|---|
| 1721 | 90c. "York Boat on Lake Winnipeg, 1930" (Walter Phillips) | 1·50 | 2·25 |

**658** Man and Boy with Bike, and A. J. and J. W. Billes (company founders)

**1997.** 75th Anniv of the Canadian Tire Corporation.

| | | | | |
|---|---|---|---|---|
| 1722 | **658** | 45c. multicoloured | 80 | 70 |

**659** Abbe Charles-Emile Gadbois

**1997.** Abbe Charles-Emile Gadbois (musicologist) Commemoration.

| | | | | |
|---|---|---|---|---|
| 1723 | **659** | 45c. multicoloured | 60 | 50 |

**660** Blue Poppy

**1997.** "Quebec in Bloom" International Floral Festival.

| | | | | |
|---|---|---|---|---|
| 1724 | **660** | 45c. multicoloured | 75 | 55 |

**661** Nurse attending Patient

**1997.** Centenary of Victorian Order of Nurses.

| | | | | |
|---|---|---|---|---|
| 1725 | **661** | 45c. multicoloured | 1·25 | 50 |

**662** Osgoode Hall and Seal of Law School

**1997.** Bicentenary of Law Society of Upper Canada.

| | | | | |
|---|---|---|---|---|
| 1726 | **662** | 45c. multicoloured | 75 | 50 |

**663** Great White Shark

**1997.** Ocean Fishes. Multicoloured.

| | | | |
|---|---|---|---|
| 1727 | 45c. Type **663** | 1·00 | 1·25 |
| 1728 | 45c. Pacific halibut | 1·00 | 1·25 |
| 1729 | 45c. Common sturgeon | 1·00 | 1·25 |
| 1730 | 45c. Blue-finned tuna | 1·00 | 1·25 |

**664** Lighthouse and Confederation Bridge

**1997.** Opening of Confederation Bridge, Northumberland Strait. Multicoloured.

| | | | |
|---|---|---|---|
| 1731 | 45c. Type **664** | 1·40 | 1·00 |
| 1732 | 45c. Confederation Bridge and great blue heron | 1·40 | 1·00 |

**665** Gilles Villeneuve in Ferrari T-3

**1997.** 15th Death Anniv of Gilles Villeneuve (racing car driver). Multicoloured.

| | | | |
|---|---|---|---|
| 1733 | 45c. Type **665** | 1·00 | 60 |
| 1734 | 90c. Villeneuve in Ferrari T-4 | 2·00 | 2·25 |
| **MS**1735 | 203×115 mm. Nos. 1733/4 each × 4 | 8·00 | 8·00 |

**666** Globe and the "Matthew"

**1997.** 500th Anniv of John Cabot's Discovery of North America.

| | | | | |
|---|---|---|---|---|
| 1736 | **666** | 45c. multicoloured | 1·00 | 55 |

**667** Sea to Sky Highway, British Columbia, and Skier

**1997.** Scenic Highways (1st series). Multicoloured.

| | | | |
|---|---|---|---|
| 1737 | 45c. Type **667** | 1·25 | 1·40 |
| 1738 | 45c. Cabot Trail, Nova Scotia, and rug-making | 1·25 | 1·40 |
| 1739 | 45c. Wine route, Ontario, and glasses of wine | 1·25 | 1·40 |
| 1740 | 45c. Highway 34, Saskatchewan, and cowboy | 1·25 | 1·40 |

See also Nos. 1810/13 and 1876/9.

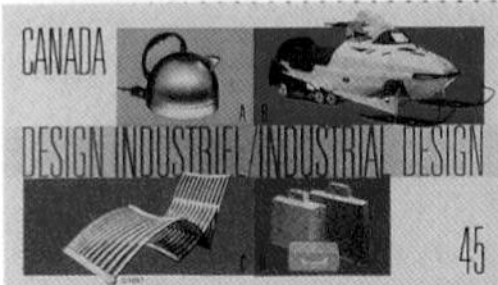


**668** Kettle, Ski-bike, Lounger and Plastic Cases

**1997.** 20th Congress of International Council of Societies for Industrial Design.

| | | | | |
|---|---|---|---|---|
| 1741 | **668** | 45c. multicoloured | 60 | 50 |

**669** Caber Thrower, Bagpiper, Drummer and Highland Dancer

**1997.** 50th Anniv of Glengarry Highland Games, Ontario.

| | | | | |
|---|---|---|---|---|
| 1742 | **669** | 45c. multicoloured | 1·00 | 50 |

**670** Knights of Columbus Emblem

**1997.** Centenary of Knights of Columbus (welfare charity) in Canada.

| | | | | |
|---|---|---|---|---|
| 1743 | **670** | 45c. multicoloured | 50 | 50 |

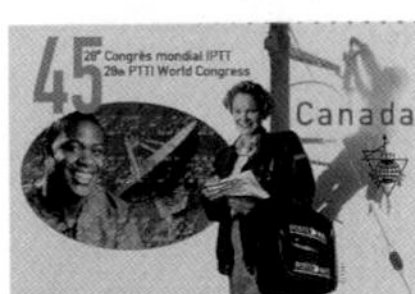


**671** Postal and Telephone Workers with PTTI Emblem

**1997.** 28th World Congress of Postal, Telegraph and Telephone International Staff Federation, Montreal.

| | | | | |
|---|---|---|---|---|
| 1744 | **671** | 45c. multicoloured | 50 | 50 |

**672** CYAP Logo

**1997.** Canada's Year of Asia Pacific.

| | | | | |
|---|---|---|---|---|
| 1745 | **672** | 45c. multicoloured | 1·00 | 50 |

**673** Paul Henderson celebrating Goal

**1997.** 25th Anniv of Canada–U.S.S.R. Ice Hockey Series. Multicoloured.

| | | | |
|---|---|---|---|
| 1746 | 45c. Type **673** | 1·25 | 1·25 |
| 1747 | 45c. Canadian team celebrating | 1·25 | 1·25 |

**674** Martha Black

**1997.** Federal Politicians. Multicoloured.

| | | | |
|---|---|---|---|
| 1748 | 45c. Type **674** | 70 | 1·00 |
| 1749 | 45c. Lionel Chevrier | 70 | 1·00 |
| 1750 | 45c. Judy LaMarsh | 70 | 1·00 |
| 1751 | 45c. Real Caouette | 70 | 1·00 |

**675** Vampire and Bat

**1997.** The Supernatural. Centenary of Publication of Bram Stoker's "Dracula". Multicoloured.

| | | | |
|---|---|---|---|
| 1752 | 45c. Type **675** | 65 | 85 |
| 1753 | 45c. Werewolf | 65 | 85 |
| 1754 | 45c. Ghost | 65 | 85 |
| 1755 | 45c. Goblin | 65 | 85 |

**676** Grizzly Bear

**1997.** Fauna . Multicoloured.

| | | | |
|---|---|---|---|
| 1756 | $1 Great northern diver ("Loon") (47×39 mm) (27.10.98) | 1·00 | 90 |
| 1757 | $1 White-tailed deer (47×39 mm) (20.10.05) | 1·50 | 1·50 |
| 1758 | $1 Atlantic walrus (47×39 mm) (20.10.05) | 1·50 | 1·50 |
| 1759 | $2 Polar bear (47×39 mm) (27.10.98) | 2·25 | 1·75 |
| 1760 | $2 Peregrine falcon (47×39 mm) (19.12.05) | 2·25 | 2·50 |
| 1761 | $2 Sable Island horse (mare and foal) (47×39 mm) (19.12.05) | 2·25 | 2·50 |
| 1762 | $5 Moose (19.12.03) | 8·00 | 7·00 |
| 1762b | $8 Type **676** | 9·00 | 9·00 |
| 1762c | $10 Blue whale (128×49 mm) (4.10.2010) | 9·00 | 9·00 |
| **MS**1762d | Two sheets, each 155×130 mm. (a) Nos. 1757/8, each ×2. (b) Nos. 1760/1, each ×2 | 15·00 | 17·00 |

**677** "Our Lady of the Rosary" (detail, Holy Rosary Cathedral, Vancouver)

**1997.** Christmas. Stained Glass Windows. Multicoloured.

| | | | |
|---|---|---|---|
| 1763a | 45c. Type **677** | 50 | 40 |
| 1764 | 52c. "Nativity" (detail, Leith United Church, Ontario) | 60 | 65 |
| 1765 | 90c. "Life of the Blessed Virgin" (detail, St. Stephen's Ukrainian Catholic Church, Calgary) | 1·00 | 1·40 |

**678** Livestock and Produce

**1997.** 75th Anniv of Royal Agricultural Winter Fair, Toronto.

| | | | | |
|---|---|---|---|---|
| 1766 | **678** | 45c. multicoloured | 1·50 | 55 |

**679** Tiger

**1998.** Chinese New Year ("Year of the Tiger").

| | | | | |
|---|---|---|---|---|
| 1767 | **679** | 45c. multicoloured | 60 | 50 |
| **MS**1768 | | 130×110 mm. As No. 1767×2 | 1·25 | 1·50 |

No. **MS**1768 is diamond-shaped with overall measurements as quoted.

**680** John Robarts (Ontario, 1961–71)

**1998.** Canadian Provincial Premiers. Multicoloured.

| | | | |
|---|---|---|---|
| 1769 | 45c. Type **680** | 65 | 75 |
| 1770 | 45c. Jean Lesage (Quebec, 1960–66) | 65 | 75 |
| 1771 | 45c. John McNair (New Brunswick, 1940–52) | 65 | 75 |
| 1772 | 45c. Tommy Douglas (Saskatchewan, 1944–61) | 65 | 75 |
| 1773 | 45c. Joseph Smallwood (Newfoundland, 1949–72) | 65 | 75 |
| 1774 | 45c. Angus MacDonald (Nova Scotia, 1933–40, 1945–54) | 65 | 75 |
| 1775 | 45c. W. A. C. Bennett (British Columbia, 1960–66) | 65 | 75 |
| 1776 | 45c. Ernest Manning (Alberta, 1943–68) | 65 | 75 |
| 1777 | 45c. John Bracken (Manitoba, 1922–43) | 65 | 75 |
| 1778 | 45c. J. Walter Jones (Prince Edward Island, 1943–53) | 65 | 75 |

**1998.** Birds (3rd series). As T 643. Multicoloured.

| | | | |
|---|---|---|---|
| 1779 | 45c. Hairy woodpecker | 1·40 | 1·25 |
| 1780 | 45c. Great crested flycatcher | 1·40 | 1·25 |
| 1781 | 45c. Eastern screech owl | 1·40 | 1·25 |
| 1782 | 45c. Rosy finch ("Gray-crowned Rosy-finch") | 1·40 | 1·25 |

**681** Maple Leaf

**1998.** Self-adhesive Automatic Cash Machine Stamps. Imperf.

| | | | | |
|---|---|---|---|---|
| 1783 | **681** | 45c. multicoloured | 45 | 40 |

For stamps in this design, but without "POSTAGE POSTES" at top left see Nos. 1836/40.

**682** Coquihalla Orange Fly

**1998.** Fishing Flies. Multicoloured.

| | | | |
|---|---|---|---|
| 1784 | 45c. Type **682** | 90 | 90 |
| 1785 | 45c. Steelhead Bee | 90 | 90 |
| 1786 | 45c. Dark Montreal | 90 | 90 |
| 1787 | 45c. Lady Amherst | 90 | 90 |
| 1788 | 45c. Coho Blue | 90 | 90 |
| 1789 | 45c. Cosseboom Special | 90 | 90 |

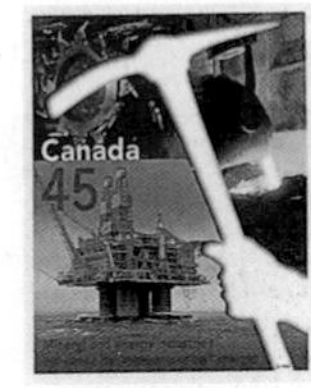


**683** Mineral Excavation, Oil Rig and Pickaxe

**1998.** Centenary of Canadian Institute of Mining, Metallurgy and Petroleum.

| | | | | |
|---|---|---|---|---|
| 1790 | **683** | 45c. multicoloured | 70 | 50 |

**684** 1898 2c. Imperial Penny Postage Stamp and Postmaster General Sir William Mulock

**1998.** Centenary of Imperial Penny Postage.

| | | | | |
|---|---|---|---|---|
| 1791 | **684** | 45c. multicoloured | 1·00 | 55 |

**685** Two Sumo Wrestlers

**1998.** 1st Canadian Sumo Basho (tournament), Vancouver. Multicoloured.

| | | | |
|---|---|---|---|
| 1792 | 45c. Type **685** | 65 | 75 |
| 1793 | 45c. Sumo wrestler in ceremonial ritual | 65 | 75 |
| **MS**1794 | 84×152 mm. Nos. 1792/3 | 1·25 | 1·50 |

**686** St. Peters Canal, Nova Scotia

**1998.** Canadian Canals. Multicoloured.

| | | | |
|---|---|---|---|
| 1795 | 45c. Type **686** | 1·10 | 1·25 |
| 1796 | 45c. St. Ours Canal, Quebec | 1·10 | 1·25 |
| 1797 | 45c. Port Carling Lock, Ontario | 1·10 | 1·25 |
| 1798 | 45c. Lock on Rideau Canal, Ontario | 1·10 | 1·25 |
| 1799 | 45c. Towers and platform of Peterborough Lift Lock, Trent–Severn Waterway, Ontario | 1·10 | 1·25 |
| 1800 | 45c. Chambly Canal, Quebec | 1·10 | 1·25 |
| 1801 | 45c. Lachine Canal, Quebec | 1·10 | 1·25 |
| 1802 | 45c. Rideau Canal in winter, Ontario | 1·10 | 1·25 |
| 1803 | 45c. Boat on Big Chute incline railway, Trent–Severn Waterway, Ontario | 1·10 | 1·25 |
| 1804 | 45c. Sault Ste. Marie Canal, Ontario | 1·10 | 1·25 |

**687** Staff of Aesculapius and Cross

**1998.** Canadian Health Professionals.

| | | | |
|---|---|---|---|
| 1805 | **687** 45c. multicoloured | 1·00 | 55 |

**688** Policeman of 1873 and Visit to Indian Village

**1998.** 125th Anniv of Royal Canadian Mounted Police. Multicoloured.

| | | | |
|---|---|---|---|
| 1806 | 45c. Type **688** | 90 | 75 |
| 1807 | 45c. Policewoman of 1998 and aspects of modern law enforcement | 90 | 75 |
| **MS**1808 | 160×102 mm. Nos. 1806/7 | 1·75 | 1·90 |

**689** William J. Roue (designer) and "Bluenose" (schooner)

**1998.** William James Roue (naval architect) Commemoration.

| | | | |
|---|---|---|---|
| 1809 | **689** 45c. multicoloured | 70 | 50 |

**1998.** Scenic Highways (2nd series). As T 667. Multicoloured.

| | | | |
|---|---|---|---|
| 1810 | 45c. Dempster Highway, Yukon, and caribou | 65 | 75 |
| 1811 | 45c. Dinosaur Trail, Alberta, and skeleton | 65 | 75 |
| 1812 | 45c. River Valley Drive, New Brunswick, and fern | 65 | 75 |
| 1813 | 45c. Blue Heron Route, Prince Edward Island, and lobster | 65 | 75 |

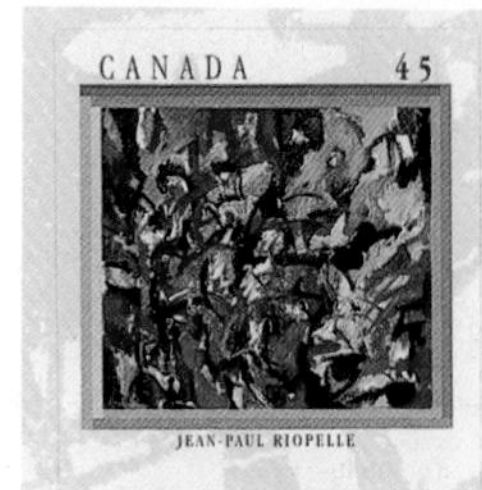


**690** "Painting" (Jean-Paul Riopelle)

**1998.** 50th Anniv of "Refus Global" (manifesto of The Automatistes group of artists). Multicoloured. Self-adhesive. Imperf.

| | | | |
|---|---|---|---|
| 1814 | 45c. Type **690** | 1·10 | 1·10 |
| 1815 | 45c. "La derniere campagne de Napoleon" (Fernand Leduc) (37×31½ mm) | 1·10 | 1·10 |
| 1816 | 45c. "Jet fuligineux sur noir torture" (Jean-Paul Mousseau) | 1·10 | 1·10 |
| 1817 | 45c. "Le fond du garde-robe" (Pierre Gauvreau) (29½×42 mm) | 1·10 | 1·10 |
| 1818 | 45c. "Joie lacustre" (Paul-Emile Borduas) | 1·10 | 1·10 |
| 1819 | 45c. "Seafarers Union" (Marcelle Ferron) (36×34 mm) | 1·10 | 1·10 |
| 1820 | 45c. "Le tumulte a la machoire crispee" (Marcel Barbeau) (36×34 mm) | 1·10 | 1·10 |

**691** Napoleon-Alexandre Comeau (naturalist)

**1998.** Legendary Canadians. Multicoloured.

| | | | |
|---|---|---|---|
| 1821 | 45c. Type **691** | 55 | 75 |
| 1822 | 45c. Phyllis Munday (mountaineer) | 55 | 75 |
| 1823 | 45c. Bill Mason (film-maker) | 55 | 75 |
| 1824 | 45c. Harry Red Foster (sports commentator) | 55 | 75 |

**1998.** Canadian Art (11th series). As T 550. Multicoloured.

| | | | |
|---|---|---|---|
| 1825 | 90c. "The Farmer's Family" (Bruno Bobak) | 1·00 | 1·60 |

**692** Indian Wigwam

**1998.** Canadian Houses. Multicoloured.

| | | | |
|---|---|---|---|
| 1826 | 45c. Type **692** | 50 | 70 |
| 1827 | 45c. Settler sod hut | 50 | 70 |
| 1828 | 45c. Maison Saint-Gabriel (17th-century farmhouse), Quebec | 50 | 70 |
| 1829 | 45c. Queen Anne style brick house, Ontario | 50 | 70 |
| 1830 | 45c. Terrace of town houses | 50 | 70 |
| 1831 | 45c. Prefabricated house | 50 | 70 |
| 1832 | 45c. Veterans' houses | 50 | 70 |
| 1833 | 45c. Modern bungalow | 50 | 70 |
| 1834 | 45c. Healthy House, Toronto | 50 | 70 |

**693** University of Ottawa

**1998.** 150th Anniv of University of Ottawa.

| | | | |
|---|---|---|---|
| 1835 | **693** 45c. multicoloured | 50 | 50 |

**1998.** As T 681, but without "POSTAGE POSTES" at top left. Self-adhesive gum, imperf (46c.) or ordinary gum, perf (others).

| | | | |
|---|---|---|---|
| 1839 | **681** 45c. multicoloured | 1·25 | 1·25 |
| 1840 | **681** 46c. multicoloured | 1·00 | 1·25 |
| 1836 | **681** 55c. multicoloured | 1·75 | 1·75 |
| 1837 | **681** 73c. multicoloured | 1·25 | 1·40 |
| 1838 | **681** 95c. multicoloured | 2·25 | 2·25 |

**694** Performing Animals

**1998.** Canadian Circus. Multicoloured.

| | | | |
|---|---|---|---|
| 1851 | 45c. Type **694** | 1·25 | 1·25 |
| 1852 | 45c. Flying trapeze and acrobat on horseback | 1·25 | 1·25 |
| 1853 | 45c. Lion tamer | 1·25 | 1·25 |
| 1854 | 45c. Acrobats and trapeze artists | 1·25 | 1·25 |
| **MS**1855 | 133×133 mm. Nos. 1851/4 | 4·00 | 4·50 |

**695** John Peters Humphrey (author of original Declaration draft)

**1998.** 50th Anniv of Universal Declaration of Human Rights.

| | | | |
|---|---|---|---|
| 1856 | **695** 45c. multicoloured | 50 | 50 |

**696** H.M.C.S. "Sackville" (corvette)

**1998.** 75th Anniv of Canadian Naval Reserve. Multicoloured.

| | | | |
|---|---|---|---|
| 1857 | 45c. Type **696** | 80 | 90 |
| 1858 | 45c. H.M.C.S. "Shawinigan" (coastal defence vessel) | 80 | 90 |

**697** Angel blowing Trumpet

**1998.** Christmas. Statues of Angels. Multicoloured.

| | | | |
|---|---|---|---|
| 1859 | 45c. Type **697** | 50 | 20 |
| 1860b | 52c. Adoring Angel | 85 | 75 |
| 1861b | 90c. Angel at prayer | 1·60 | 2·00 |

**698** Rabbit

**1999.** Chinese New Year ("Year of the Rabbit").

| | | | |
|---|---|---|---|
| 1862 | **698** 46c. multicoloured | 50 | 50 |
| **MS**1863 | Circular 100 mm diam. **698** 95c. mult (40×40 mm) | 1·75 | 2·25 |

No. **MS**1863 also exists with the "CHINA '99" World Stamp Exhibition, Beijing, logo overprinted in gold on the top of the margin.

**699** Stylized Mask and Curtain

**1999.** 50th Anniv of Le Theatre du Rideau Vert.

| | | | |
|---|---|---|---|
| 1864 | **699** 46c. multicoloured | 50 | 50 |

**1999.** Birds (4th series). As T 643. Multicoloured. Ordinary or self-adhesive gum.

| | | | |
|---|---|---|---|
| 1865 | 46c. Northern goshawk | 85 | 85 |
| 1866 | 46c. Red-winged blackbird | 85 | 85 |
| 1867 | 46c. American goldfinch | 85 | 85 |
| 1868 | 46c. Sandhill crane | 85 | 85 |

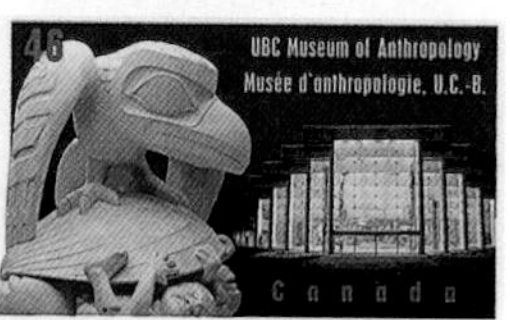


**700** "The Raven and the First Men" (B. Reid) and The Great Hall

**1999.** 50th Anniv of University of British Columbia Museum of Anthropology.

| | | | |
|---|---|---|---|
| 1873 | **700** 46c. multicoloured | 50 | 50 |

**701** "Marco Polo" (full-rigged ship)

**1999.** Canada–Australia Joint Issue. "Marco Polo" (emigrant ship).

| | | | |
|---|---|---|---|
| 1874 | **701** 46c. multicoloured | 50 | 50 |
| **MS**1875 | 160×95 mm. 85c. As No. 1728 of Australia. 46c. Type **701**. (No. **MS**1875 was sold at $1.25 in Canada) | 1·75 | 2·00 |

No. **MS**1875 includes the "Australia '99" emblem on the sheet margin and was postally valid in Canada to the value of 46c.

The same miniature sheet was also available in Australia.

**1999.** Scenic Highways (3rd series). As T 667. Multicoloured.

| | | | |
|---|---|---|---|
| 1876 | 46c. Route 132, Quebec, and hang-glider | 75 | 85 |
| 1877 | 46c. Yellowhead Highway, Manitoba, and bison | 75 | 85 |
| 1878 | 46c. Dempster Highway, Northwest Territories, and Indian village elder | 75 | 85 |
| 1879 | 46c. The Discovery Trail, Newfoundland, and whale's tailfin | 75 | 85 |

**702** Inuit Children and Landscape

**1999.** Creation of Nunavut Territory.

| | | | |
|---|---|---|---|
| 1880 | **702** 46c. multicoloured | 50 | 50 |

**703** Elderly Couple on Country Path

**1999.** International Year of Older Persons.

| | | | |
|---|---|---|---|
| 1881 | **703** 46c. multicoloured | 50 | 50 |

**704** Khanda (Sikh symbol)

**1999.** Centenary of Sikhs in Canada.

| | | | |
|---|---|---|---|
| 1882 | **704** 46c. multicoloured | 50 | 50 |

705 "Arethusa bulbosa" (orchid)

**1999.** 16th World Orchid Conference, Vancouver. Multicoloured.

| | | | |
|---|---|---|---|
| 1883 | 46c. Type **705** | 75 | 75 |
| 1884 | 46c. "Amerorchis rotundifolia" | 75 | 75 |
| 1885 | 46c. "Cypripedium pubescens" | 75 | 75 |
| 1886 | 46c. "Platanthera psycodes" | 75 | 75 |

**706** Bookbinding

**1999.** Traditional Trades. Multicoloured. (a) Ordinary gum.

| | | | |
|---|---|---|---|
| 1887 | 1c. Type **706** | 10 | 10 |
| 1888 | 2c. Decorative ironwork | 10 | 10 |
| 1889 | 3c. Glass-blowing | 10 | 10 |
| 1890 | 4c. Oyster farming | 10 | 10 |
| 1891 | 5c. Weaving | 10 | 10 |
| 1892 | 9c. Quilting | 10 | 10 |
| 1893 | 10c. Wood carving | 10 | 15 |
| 1894 | 25c. Leatherworking | 20 | 25 |

(b) Self-adhesive.

| | | | |
|---|---|---|---|
| 1895 | 65c. Jewellery making (horiz) | 50 | 55 |
| 1896 | 77c. Basket weaving (horiz) | 1·50 | 1·50 |
| 1897 | $1.25 Wood-carving (horiz) | 1·00 | 1·10 |

**707** "Northern Dancer" (racehorse)

**1999.** Canadian Horses. Multicoloured. Ordinary or self-adhesive gum.

| | | | |
|---|---|---|---|
| 1903 | 46c. Type **707** | 80 | 80 |
| 1904 | 46c. "Kingsway Skoal" (rodeo horse) | 80 | 80 |
| 1905 | 46c. "Big Ben" (show jumper) | 80 | 80 |
| 1906 | 46c. "Armbro Flight" (trotter) | 80 | 80 |

**708** Logo engraved on Limestone

**1999.** 150th Anniv of Barreau du Quebec (Quebec lawyers' association).

| | | | |
|---|---|---|---|
| 1911 | **708** 46c. multicoloured | 50 | 50 |

**1999.** Canadian Art (12th series). As T 550. Mult.

| | | | |
|---|---|---|---|
| 1912 | 95c. "Coq licorne" (Jean Dallaire) | 1·25 | 1·75 |

**709** Athletics

**1999.** 13th Pan-American Games, Winnipeg. Mult.

| | | | |
|---|---|---|---|
| 1913 | 46c. Type **709** | 85 | 90 |
| 1914 | 46c. Cycling | 85 | 90 |
| 1915 | 46c. Swimming | 85 | 90 |
| 1916 | 46c. Football | 85 | 90 |

**1999.** "China '99" International Stamp Exhibition, Beijing. Sheet 78×133 mm, containing Nos. 1883/6. Multicoloured.

**MS**1917 46c. Type **705**; 46c. Amerorchis rotundifolia; 46c. Cypripedium pubescens; 46c. Platanthera psycodes 2·25 2·75

**710** Female Rower

**1999.** 23rd World Rowing Championships, St. Catharines.

| | | | |
|---|---|---|---|
| 1918 | **710** 46c. multicoloured | 50 | 50 |

**711** UPU Emblem and World Map

**1999.** 125th Anniv of Universal Postal Union.

| | | | |
|---|---|---|---|
| 1919 | **711** 46c. multicoloured | 75 | 50 |

**712** De Havilland Mosquito F.B. VI

**1999.** 75th Anniv of Canadian Air Force. Mult.

| | | | |
|---|---|---|---|
| 1920 | 46c. Type **712** | 75 | 85 |
| 1921 | 46c. Sopwith F.1 Camel | 75 | 85 |
| 1922 | 46c. De Havilland Canada DHC-3 Otter | 75 | 85 |
| 1923 | 46c. De Havilland Canada CC-108 Caribou | 75 | 85 |
| 1924 | 46c. Canadair CL-28 Argus Mk 2 | 75 | 85 |
| 1925 | 46c. Canadair (North American) F-86 Sabre 6 | 75 | 85 |
| 1926 | 46c. McDonnell Douglas CF-18 | 75 | 85 |
| 1927 | 46c. Sopwith 5.F.1 Dolphin | 75 | 85 |
| 1928 | 46c. Armstrong Whitworth Siskin IIIA | 75 | 85 |
| 1929 | 46c. Canadian Vickers (Northrop) Delta II | 75 | 85 |
| 1930 | 46c. Sikorsky CH-124A Sea King helicopter | 75 | 85 |
| 1931 | 46c. Vickers-Armstrong Wellington Mk II | 75 | 85 |
| 1932 | 46c. Avro Anson Mk I | 75 | 85 |
| 1933 | 46c. Canadair (Lockheed) CF-104G Starfighter | 75 | 85 |
| 1934 | 46c. Burgess-Dunne | 75 | 85 |
| 1935 | 46c. Avro 504K | 75 | 85 |

**713** Fokker DR-1

**1999.** 50th Anniv of Canadian International Air Show. Multicoloured.

| | | | |
|---|---|---|---|
| 1936 | 46c. Type **713** | 85 | 90 |
| 1937 | 46c. H101 Salto glider | 85 | 90 |
| 1938 | 46c. De Havilland DH100 Vampire Mk III | 85 | 90 |
| 1939 | 46c. Wing walker on Stearman A-75 | 85 | 90 |

Nos. 1936/9 were printed together, se-tenant, forming a composite design which includes a nine-plane Snowbird formation of Canadair CT114 Tutor in the background.

**714** NATO Emblem and National Flags

**1999.** 50th Anniv of North Atlantic Treaty Organization.

| | | | |
|---|---|---|---|
| 1940 | **714** 46c. multicoloured | 1·00 | 50 |

**715** Man ploughing on Book

**1999.** Centenary of Frontier College (workers' education organization).

| | | | |
|---|---|---|---|
| 1941 | **715** 46c. multicoloured | 50 | 50 |

**716** Master Control Sports Kite

**1999.** Stamp Collecting Month. Kites. Mult.

| | | | |
|---|---|---|---|
| 1942 | 46c. Type **716** | 55 | 65 |
| 1943 | 46c. Indian Garden Flying Carpet (irregular rectangle, 35½×32 mm) | 55 | 65 |
| 1944 | 46c. Gibson Girl box kite (horiz, 38½×25 mm) | 55 | 65 |
| 1945 | 46c. Dragon Centipede (oval, 39×29 mm) | 55 | 65 |

**717** Boy holding Dove

**1999.** New Millennium. Three sheets, each 108×108 mm, containing T 717 and similar square designs in blocks of 4. Self-adhesive.

| | | | |
|---|---|---|---|
| **MS**1946 | – 46c.×4 multicoloured | 2·00 | 2·50 |
| **MS**1947 | **717** 55c.×4 multicoloured | 4·50 | 4·75 |
| **MS**1948 | – 95c.×4 brown | 3·75 | 4·50 |

DESIGNS: 46c. Holographic image of dove in flight; 95c. Dove with olive branch.

**718** Angel playing Drum

**1999.** Christmas. Victorian Angels. Multicoloured.

| | | | |
|---|---|---|---|
| 1949 | 46c. Type **718** | 60 | 20 |
| 1950 | 55c. Angel with toys | 80 | 50 |
| 1951 | 95c. Angel with star | 1·40 | 2·25 |

**719** Portia White (singer)

**1999.** Millennium Collection (1st series). Entertainment and Arts. Miniature sheets, each 108×112 mm, containing T 719 and similar vert designs. Multicoloured.

**MS**1952 46c. Type **719**; 46c. Glenn Gould (pianist); 46c. Guy Lombardo (conductor of "Royal Canadians"); 46c. Félix Leclerc (musician, playwright and actor) 2·25 2·75

**MS**1952/5 Set of 4 sheets 8·00 10·00

**MS**1953 46c. Artists looking at painting (Royal Canadian Academy of Arts); 46c. Cloud, stave and pencil marks (The Canada Council); 46c. Man with video camera (National Film Board of Canada); 46c. Newsreader (Canadian Broadcasting Corporation) 2·25 2·75

**MS**1954 46c. Calgary Stampede; 46c. Circus performers; 46c. Ice hockey (Hockey Night); 46c. Goalkeeper (Ice hockey live from The Forum) 2·25 2·75

**MS**1955 46c. IMAX cinema; 46c. Computer image (Softimage); 46c. Ted Rogers Sr ("Plugging in the Radio"); 46c. Sir William Stephenson (inventor of radio facsimile system) 2·25 2·75

See also Nos. **MS**1959/62, **MS**1969/73 and **MS**1982/5.

**720** Millennium Partnership Programme Logo

**2000.** Canada Millennium Partnership Programme.

| | | | |
|---|---|---|---|
| 1956 | **720** 46c. red, green and blue | 50 | 50 |

**721** Chinese Dragon

**2000.** Chinese New Year ("Year of the Dragon").

| | | | |
|---|---|---|---|
| 1957 | **721** 46c. multicoloured | 50 | 50 |
| **MS**1958 | 150×85 mm. **721** 90c. multicoloured | 1·25 | 1·50 |

**2000.** Millennium Collection (2nd series). Charities, Medical Pioneers, Peacekeepers and Social Reforms. Miniature sheets, each 108×112 mm, containing vert designs as T 719. Multicoloured.

**MS**1959 46c. Providing equipment (Canadian International Development Agency); 46c. Dr. Lucille Teasdale (medical missionary); 46c. Terry Fox (Marathon of Hope); 46c. Delivering meal (Meals on Wheels) 2·25 2·50

**MS**1959/62 Set of 4 sheets 8·00 9·00

**MS**1960 46c. Sir Frederick Banting (discovery of insulin); 46c. Armand Frappier (developer of BCG vaccine); 46c. Dr. Hans Selye (research into stress); 46c. "Dr. Maude Abbott" (pathologist) (M. Bell Eastlake) 2·25 2·50

**MS**1961 46c. Senator Raoul Dandurand (diplomat); 46c. Pauline Vanier and Elizabeth Smellie (nursing pioneers); 46c. Lester B. Pearson (diplomat); 46c. One-legged man (Ottawa Convention on Banning Landmines) 2·25 2·50

**MS**1962 46c. Nun and surgeon (medical care); 46c. "Women are persons" (sculpture by Barbara Paterson) (Appointment of women senators); 46c. Alphonse and Dorimène Desjardins (People's bank movement); 46c. Father Moses Coady (Adult education pioneer) 2·25 2·50

**722** Wayne Gretzky (ice-hockey player)

**2000.** 50th National Hockey League All-Star Game. Multicoloured.

| | | | |
|---|---|---|---|
| 1963 | 46c. Type **722** | 80 | 80 |
| 1964 | 46c. Gordie Howe (No. 9 in white jersey) | 80 | 80 |
| 1965 | 46c. Maurice Richard (No. 9 in blue and red jersey) | 80 | 80 |
| 1966 | 46c. Doug Harvey (No. 2) | 80 | 80 |
| 1967 | 46c. Bobby Orr (No. 4) | 80 | 80 |
| 1968 | 46c. Jacques Plante (No. 1) | 80 | 80 |

See also Nos. 2052/7, 2118/23, 2178/3, 2250/5 and 2316/27.

**2000.** Millennium Collection (3rd series). First Inhabitants, Great Thinkers, Culture and Literary Legends, and Charitable Foundations. Miniature sheets, each 108×112 mm, containing vert designs as T 719. Multicoloured.

**MS**1969 46c. Pontiac (Ottawa chief); 46c. Tom Longboat (long-distance runner); 46c. "Inuit Shaman" (sculpture by Paul Toolooktook); 46c. Shaman and patient (Indian medicine) 2·25 2·50

**MS**1969/73 Set of 5 sheets 10·00 11·00

**MS**1970 46c. Prof. Marshall McLuhan (media philosopher); 46c. Northrop Frye (literary critic); 46c. Roger Lemelin (novelist); 46c. Prof. Hilda Marion Neatby (educator) 2·25 2·50

**MS**1971 46c. Bow of Viking longship (L'Anse aux Meadows World Heritage Site); 46c. Immigrant family (Pier 21 monument); 46c. Neptune mask (Neptune Theatre, Halifax); 46c. Auditorium and actor (The Stratford Festival) 2·25 2·50

**MS**1972 46c. W. O. Mitchell (writer); 46c. Gratien Gélinas (actor, producer and playwright); 46c. Text and fountain pen (Cercle du Livre de France); 46c. Harlequin and roses (Harlequin Books) 2·25 2·50

**MS**1973 46c. Hart Massey (Massey Foundation); 46c. Izaak Walton Killam and Dorothy Killam; 46f. Eric Lafferty Harvie (Glenbow Foundation); 46c. Macdonald Stewart Foundation 2·25 2·50

**2000.** Birds (5th series). As T 643. Multicoloured. Ordinary or self-adhesive gum.

1974 46c. Canadian warbler 85 90
1975 46c. Osprey 85 90
1976 46c. Pacific diver ("Pacific Loon") 85 90
1977 46c. Blue jay 85 90

**2000.** Millennium Collection (4th series). Canadian Agriculture, Commerce and Technology. Miniature sheets, each 108×112 mm, containing vert designs as T 719. Multicoloured.

**MS**1982 46c. Sir Charles Saunders (developer of Marquis wheat); 46c. Baby (Pablum baby food); 46c. Dr. Archibald Gowanlock Huntsman (frozen fish pioneer); 46c. Oven chips and field of potatoes (McCain Frozen Foods) 2·25 2·50

**MS**1982/5 Set of 4 sheets 8·00 9·00

**MS**1983 46c. Early trader and Indian (Hudson's Bay Company); 46c. Satellite over earth (Bell Canada Enterprises); 46c. Jos. Louis biscuits and Vachon family (Vachon Family Bakery); 46c. Bread and eggs (George Weston Limited) 2·25 2·50

**MS**1984 46c. George Klein and cog wheels (inventor of electric wheelchair and micro-surgical staple gun); 46c. Abraham Gesner (developer of kerosene); 46c. Alexander Graham Bell (inventor of telephone); 46c. Joseph-Armand Bombadier (inventor of snowmobile) 2·25 2·50

**MS**1985 46c. Workers and steam locomotive (Rogers Pass rail tunnel); 46c. Manic 5 dam (Manicouagan River hydro-electric project); 46c. Mobile Servicing System for International Space Station (Canadian Space Program); 46c. CN Tower (World's tallest building) 2·25 2·50

**723** Judges and Supreme Court Building

**2000.** 125th Anniv of Supreme Court of Canada.

1986 **723** 46c. multicoloured 50 50

**724** Lethbridge Bridge, Synthetic Rubber Plant, X-ray of Heart Pacemaker and Microwave Radio System

**2000.** 75th Anniv of Ceremony for Calling of an Engineer.

1987 **724** 46c. multicoloured 50 50

Each vertical pair completes the engineer's ring as shown on Type **274**.

**725**

**2000.** "Picture Postage" Greetings Stamps. Self-adhesive.

1988 **725** 46c. multicoloured 50 50

No. 1988 was issued to include appropriate greetings labels which could be inserted into the rectangular space on each stamp.

See also Nos. 2045 and 2099.

**726** Coastal-style Mailboxes in Autumn

**2000.** Traditional Rural Mailboxes. Multicoloured.

1989 46c. Type **726** 75 75
1990 46c. House and cow-shaped mailboxes in springtime 75 75
1991 46c. Tractor-shaped mailbox in summertime 75 75
1992 46c. Barn and duck-shaped mailboxes in winter 75 75

**727** Gorge and Fir Tree

**2000.** Canadian Rivers and Lakes. Multicoloured. Self-adhesive.

1993 55c. Type **727** 60 65
1994 55c. Lake and water lilies 60 65
1995 55c. Glacier and reflected mountains 60 65
1996 55c. Estuary and aerial view 60 65
1997 55c. Waterfall and forest edge 60 65
1998 95c. Iceberg and mountain river 95 1·10
1999 95c. Rapids and waterfall 95 1·10
2000 95c. Moraine and river 95 1·10
2001 95c. Shallows and waves on lake 95 1·10
2002 95c. Forest sloping to waters edge and tree 95 1·10

**728** Queen Elizabeth the Queen Mother with Roses

**2000.** Queen Elizabeth the Queen Mother's 100th Birthday.

2003 **728** 95c. multicoloured 1·40 1·40

**729** Teenager with Two Children

**2000.** Centenary of Boys and Girls Clubs of Canada.

2004 **729** 46c. multicoloured 50 50

**730** Clouds over Rockies and Symbol

**2000.** 57th General Conference Session of Seventh-day Adventist Church, Toronto.

2005 **730** 46c. multicoloured 50 50

**731** "Space Travellers and Canadian Flag" (Rosalie Anne Nardelli)

**2000.** "Stampin' the Future" (children's stamp design competition). Multicoloured.

2006 46c. Type **731** 60 70
2007 46c. "Travelling to the Moon" (Sarah Lutgen) 60 70
2008 46c. "Astronauts in shuttle" (Andrew Wright) 60 70
2009 46c. "Children completing Canada as jigsaw" (Christine Weera) 60 70

**MS**2010 114×90 mm. Nos. 2006/9 2·40 3·00

**2000.** Canadian Art (13th series). As T 550. Mult.

2011 95c. "The Artist at Niagara, 1858" (Cornelius Krieghoff) 1·25 1·75

**732** Tall Ships, Halifax Harbour

**2000.** Tall Ships Race. Multicoloured. Self-adhesive.

2012 46c. Type **732** 75 85
2013 46c. Tall ships, Halifax Harbour (face value top right) 75 85

Nos. 2012/13 are arranged as five se-tenant pairs on a background photograph of Halifax Harbour.

**733** Workers, Factory and Transport

**2000.** Centenary of Department of Labour.

2014 **733** 46c. multicoloured 50 50

**734** Petro-Canada Sign, Oil Rig and Consumers

**2000.** 25th Anniv of Petro-Canada (oil company). Self-adhesive.

2015 **734** 46c. multicoloured 75 50

**735** Narwhal

**2000.** Whales. Multicoloured.

2016 46c. Type **735** 1·40 1·40
2017 46c. Blue whale (*Balaenoptera musculus*) 1·40 1·40
2018 46c. Bowhead whale (*Balaena mysticetus*) 1·40 1·40
2019 46c. White whales (*Delphinapterus leucas*) 1·40 1·40

Nos. 2016/19 were printed together, se-tenant, with the backgrounds forming an overall composite design.

**736**

**2000.** "Picture Postage" Christmas Greetings. Self-adhesive.

2020 **736** 46c. multicoloured 50 50

See also Nos. 2045/9 and 2099/103.

**737** "The Nativity" (Susie Matthias)

**2000.** Christmas. Religious Paintings by Mouth and Foot Artists. Multicoloured.

2021 46c. Type **737** 50 20
2022 55c. "The Nativity and Christmas Star" (Michael Guillemette) 65 60
2023 95c. "Mary and Joseph journeying to Bethlehem" (David Allan Carter) 1·25 1·90

**738** Lieut.-Col. Sam Steele, Lord Strathcona's Horse

**2000.** Canadian Regiments. Multicoloured.

2024 46c. Type **738** 75 75
2025 46c. Drummer, Voltigeurs de Quebec 75 75

**739** Red Fox

**2000.** Wildlife. Multicoloured.

2026 60c. Type **739** 65 75
2027 75c. Grey wolf 1·25 1·25
2028 $1.05 White-tailed deer 1·10 1·25

**740** Maple Leaves

**740a** Maple Leaves and Key

**740b** Red Maple Leaf and Stem

**2000.** Self-adhesive coil stamp.

2029 **740** 47c. multicoloured 1·00 1·00
2030 **740** 48c. multicoloured 1·00 1·00
2031 **740a** 49c. multicoloured 1·00 1·00
2032 **740b** 80c. multicoloured 1·10 1·10
2036 **740b** $1.40 multicoloured (green leaf) 1·90 1·90

**2000.** "Picture Postage" Greetings Stamps. As T 725 and 736. Multicoloured. Self-adhesive.

2045 47c. Type **725** 55 60
2046 47c. Type **736** 55 60
2047 47c. Roses frame 55 60
2048 47c. Mahogany frame 55 60
2049 47c. Silver frame 55 60

**741** Green Jade Snake

**2001.** Chinese New Year. ("Year of the Snake").

2050 **741** 47c. multicoloured 50 50

**MS**2051 112×75 mm. $1.05, Brown jade snake 1·25 1·60

**2001.** National Hockey League. All-Star Game Players (2nd series). As T 722. Multicoloured.

2052 47c. Jean Beliveau (wearing No. 4) 75 75
2053 47c. Terry Sawchuk (on one knee) 75 75
2054 47c. Eddie Shore (wearing No. 2) 75 75
2055 47c. Denis Potvin (wearing No. 5) 75 75
2056 47c. Bobby Hull (wearing No. 9) 75 75
2057 47c. Syl Apps (in Toronto jersey) 75 75

See also Nos. 2118/23 and 2178/83.

**2001.** Birds (6th series). As T 643. Multicoloured. Ordinary or self-adhesive gum.

2058 47c. Golden eagle 75 75
2059 47c. Arctic tern 75 75
2060 47c. Rock ptarmigan 75 75
2061 47c. Lapland bunting ("Lapland Longspur") 75 75

742 Highjumping

2001. 4th Francophonie Games. Multicoloured.

| | | | |
|---|---|---|---|
| 2066 | 47c. Type **742** | 70 | 70 |
| 2067 | 47c. Folk dancing | 70 | 70 |

743 Ice Dancing

2001. World Figure Skating Championships, Vancouver. Multicoloured.

| | | | |
|---|---|---|---|
| 2068 | 47c. Type **743** | 80 | 80 |
| 2069 | 47c. Pairs | 80 | 80 |
| 2070 | 47c. Men's singles | 80 | 80 |
| 2071 | 47c. Women's singles | 80 | 80 |

744 3d. Beaver Stamp of 1851

2001. 150th Anniv of the Canadian Postal Service.

| | | | | |
|---|---|---|---|---|
| 2072 | **744** | 47c. multicoloured | 1·00 | 1·00 |

745 Toronto Blue Jay Emblem, Maple Leaf and Baseball

2001. 25th Season of the Toronto Blue Jays (baseball team). Self-adhesive.

| | | | | |
|---|---|---|---|---|
| 2073 | **745** | 47c. multicoloured | 60 | 70 |

746 North and South America on Globe

2001. Summit of the Americas, Quebec.

| | | | | |
|---|---|---|---|---|
| 2074 | **746** | 47c. multicoloured | 1·00 | 50 |

747 Butchart Gardens, British Columbia

2001. Tourist Attractions (1st series). Multicoloured. Self-adhesive.

| | | | |
|---|---|---|---|
| 2075 | 60c. Type **747** | 95 | 1·10 |
| 2076 | 60c. Apple Blossom Festival, Nova Scotia | 95 | 1·10 |
| 2077 | 60c. White Pass and Yukon Route | 95 | 1·10 |
| 2078 | 60c. Sugar Bushes, Quebec | 95 | 1·10 |
| 2079 | 60c. Court House, Niagra-on-the-Lake, Ontario | 95 | 1·10 |
| 2080 | $1.05 The Forks, Winnipeg, Manitoba | 1·40 | 1·60 |
| 2081 | $1.05 Barkerville, British Colombia | 1·40 | 1·60 |
| 2082 | $1.05 Canadian Tulip Festival, Ontario | 1·40 | 1·60 |
| 2083 | $1.05 Auyuittuq National Park, Nunavut | 1·40 | 1·60 |
| 2084 | $1.05 Signal Hill, St. John's, Newfoundland | 1·40 | 1·60 |

See also Nos. 2143/52, 2205/14 and 2257/61.

748 Christ on Palm Sunday and Khachkar (stone cross)

2001. 1700th Anniv of Armenian Church.

| | | | | |
|---|---|---|---|---|
| 2085 | **748** | 47c. multicoloured | 60 | 70 |

749 Cadets, Mackenzie Building and Military Equipment

2001. 125th Anniv of Royal Military College of Canada.

| | | | | |
|---|---|---|---|---|
| 2086 | **749** | 47c. multicoloured | 70 | 45 |

750 Pole-vaulting

2001. 8th International Amateur Athletic Federation World Championships, Edmonton. Multicoloured.

| | | | |
|---|---|---|---|
| 2087 | 47c. Type **750** | 80 | 1·00 |
| 2088 | 47c. Sprinting | 80 | 1·00 |

751 "Pierre Trudeau" (Myfanwy Pavelic)

2001. Pierre Trudeau (former Prime Minister) Commemoration.

| | | | | |
|---|---|---|---|---|
| 2089 | **751** | 47c. multicoloured | 60 | 45 |
| **MS**2090 | | 128×155 mm. No. 2090×4 | 2·00 | 2·25 |

752 "Morden Centennial" Rose (image scaled to 71% of original size)

2001. Canadian Roses. Multicoloured. Self-adhesive.

| | | | |
|---|---|---|---|
| 2091 | 47c. Type **752** | 1·00 | 1·10 |
| 2092 | 47c. "Agnes" | 1·00 | 1·10 |
| 2093 | 47c. "Champlain" | 1·00 | 1·10 |
| 2094 | 47c. "Canadian White Star" | 1·00 | 1·10 |
| **MS**2095 | 145×90 mm. Nos. 2091/4 | 3·50 | 4·00 |

753 Ottawa Chief Hassaki addressing Peace Delegates

2001. 300th Anniv of Great Peace Treaty of Montreal between American Indians and New France.

| | | | | |
|---|---|---|---|---|
| 2096 | **753** | 47c. multicoloured | 60 | 70 |

2001. Canadian Art (14th series). As T 550. Multicoloured.

| | | | |
|---|---|---|---|
| 2097 | $1.05 "The Space Between Columns 21 (Italian)" (Jack Shadbolt) | 1·40 | 1·75 |

754 Clown juggling with Crutches and Handicapped Boy

2001. The Shriners (charitable organization) Commemoration.

| | | | | |
|---|---|---|---|---|
| 2098 | **754** | 47c. multicoloured | 60 | 45 |

755 Toys and Flowers

2001. "Picture Postage" Greetings Stamps. Frames as Nos. 2045/7 and 2049, but each inscr "Domestic Lettermail Postes-lettres du regime interieur". Multicoloured. Self-adhesive.

| | | | |
|---|---|---|---|
| 2099 | As Type **725** | 60 | 60 |
| 2100 | As Type **736** | 60 | 60 |
| 2101 | Type **755** | 60 | 60 |
| 2102 | Roses frame | 60 | 60 |
| 2103 | Silver frame | 60 | 60 |

756 Jean Gascon and Jean-Louis Roux (founders of Theatre du Nouveau Monde, Montreal)

2001. Theatre Anniversaries. Multicoloured.

| | | | |
|---|---|---|---|
| 2104 | 47c. Type **756** (50th anniv) | 65 | 80 |
| 2105 | 47c. Ambrose Small (founder of Grand Theatre, London, Ontario) (centenary) | 65 | 80 |

757 Hot Air Balloons

2001. Stamp Collecting Month. Hot Air Balloons. Multicoloured, background colours given below. Self-adhesive.

| | | | |
|---|---|---|---|
| 2106 | 47c. Type **757** (green background) | 80 | 90 |
| 2107 | 47c. Balloons with lavender background | 80 | 90 |
| 2108 | 47c. Balloons with mauve background | 80 | 90 |
| 2109 | 47c. Balloons with bistre background | 80 | 90 |

758 Horse-drawn Sleigh and Christmas Lights

2001. Christmas. Festive Lights. Multicoloured.

| | | | |
|---|---|---|---|
| 2110 | 47c. Type **758** | 70 | 20 |
| 2111 | 60c. Ice skaters and Christmas lights | 1·00 | 1·00 |
| 2112 | $1.05 Children with snowman and Christmas lights | 1·40 | 1·90 |

759 Pattern of Ys Logo

2001. 150th Anniv of YMCA in Canada.

| | | | | |
|---|---|---|---|---|
| 2113 | **759** | 47c. multicoloured | 70 | 45 |

760 Statues from Canadian War Memorial, Ottawa and Badge

2001. 75th Anniv of Royal Canadian Legion.

| | | | | |
|---|---|---|---|---|
| 2114 | **760** | 47c. multicoloured | 70 | 45 |

761 Queen Elizabeth II and Maple Leaf

2002. Golden Jubilee.

| | | | | |
|---|---|---|---|---|
| 2115 | **761** | 48c. multicoloured | 70 | 45 |

762 Horse and Bamboo Leaves

2002. Chinese New Year ("Year of the Horse"). Multicoloured.

| | | | |
|---|---|---|---|
| 2116 | **762** 48c. multicoloured | 60 | 45 |
| **MS**2117 | 102×102 mm. $1.25, Horse and peach blossom | 1·40 | 1·75 |

2002. National Hockey League. All-Star Game Players (3rd series). As T 722. Multicoloured.

| | | | |
|---|---|---|---|
| 2118 | 48c. Tim Horton (wearing Maple Leaf No. 7 jersey) | 1·00 | 1·00 |
| 2119 | 48c. Guy Lafleur (wearing Canadiens No. 10 jersey) | 1·00 | 1·00 |
| 2120 | 48c. Howie Morenz (wearing Canadiens jersey and brown gloves) | 1·00 | 1·00 |
| 2121 | 48c. Glenn Hall (wearing Chicago Blackhawks jersey) | 1·00 | 1·00 |
| 2122 | 48c. Red Kelly (wearing Maple Leaf No. 4 jersey) | 1·00 | 1·00 |
| 2123 | 48c. Phil Esposito (wearing Boston Bruins No. 7 jersey) | 1·00 | 1·00 |

763 Speed Skating

2002. Winter Olympic Games, Salt Lake City. Multicoloured.

| | | | |
|---|---|---|---|
| 2124 | 48c. Type **763** | 75 | 85 |
| 2125 | 48c. Curling | 75 | 85 |
| 2126 | 48c. Aerial skiing | 75 | 85 |
| 2127 | 48c. Women's ice hockey | 75 | 85 |

764 Lion Symbol of Governor General and Rideau Hall, Ottawa

**2002.** 50th Anniv of First Canadian Governor-General.
2128 **764** 48c. multicoloured 60 45

**765** University of Manitoba (125th Anniv)

**2002.** Canadian Universities' Anniversaries (1st issue). Multicoloured.
2129 48c. Type **765** 85 85
2130 48c. Universite Laval, Quebec (150th anniv of charter) 85 85
2131 48c. Trinity College, Toronto (150th anniv of foundation) 85 85
2132 48c. Saint Mary's University, Halifax (bicent) 85 85
See also Nos. 2190/1, 2271/2, 2333/7, 2419, 2487 and 2544/5.

**2002.** Canadian Art (15th series). As T 550. Multicoloured.
2133 $1.25 "Church and Horse" (Alex Colville) 1·40 1·60

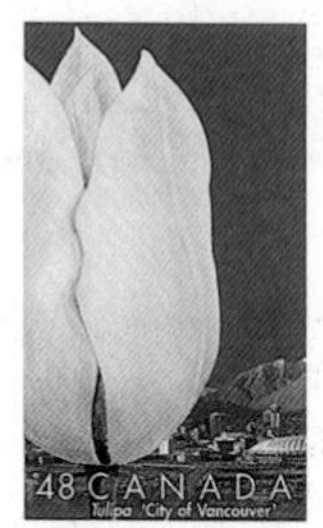

**766** "City of Vancouver" Tulip and Vancouver Skyline

**2002.** 50th Canadian Tulip Festival, Ottawa. Tulips. Multicoloured. Self-adhesive.
2134 48c. Type **766** 70 85
2135 48c. "Monte Carlo" and Dows Lake tulip beds 70 85
2136 48c. "Ottawa" and National War Memorial 70 85
2137 48c. "The Bishop" and Ottawa Hospital 70 85

**767** *Dendronepthea gigantea* and *Dendronepthea* (coral)

**2002.** Canada–Hong Kong Joint Issue. Corals. Multicoloured.
2138 48c. Type **767** 70 85
2139 48c. *Tubastrea, Echinogorgia* and island 70 85
2140 48c. North Atlantic pink tree coral, Pacific orange cup and North Pacific horn coral 70 85
2141 48c. North Atlantic giant orange tree coral and black coral 70 85
**MS**2142 161×87 mm. Nos. 2138/41 2·25 3·00

**2002.** Tourist Attractions (2nd series). As T 747. Multicoloured. Self-adhesive.
2143 65c. Yukon Quest Sled Dog Race 1·00 1·10
2144 65c. Icefields Parkway, Alberta 1·00 1·10
2145 65c. Train in Agawa Canyon, Northern Ontario 1·00 1·10
2146 65c. Old Port, Montreal 1·00 1·10
2147 65c. Saw mill, Kings Landing, New Brunswick 1·00 1·10
2148 $1.25 Northern Lights, North-west Territories 1·75 2·00
2149 $1.25 Stanley Park, British Columbia 1·75 2·00
2150 $1.25 Head-Smashed-In Buffalo Jump, Alberta 1·75 2·00
2151 $1.25 Saguenay Fjord, Quebec 1·75 2·00
2152 $1.25 Lighthouse, Peggy's Cove, Nova Scotia 1·75 2·00

**768** "Embacle" (Charles Daudelin)

**2002.** Sculptures. Multicoloured.
2153 48c. Type **768** 60 70
2154 48c. "Lumberjacks" (Leo Mol) 60 70

**769** 1899 Queen Victoria 2c. Stamp, Stonewall Post Office and Postmark

**2002.** Centenary of Canadian Postmasters and Assistants Association.
2155 **769** 48c. multicoloured 60 70

**770** World Youth Day Logo

**2002.** 17th World Youth Day, Toronto. Self-adhesive.
2156 **770** 48c. multicoloured 60 70

**2002.** "Amphilex 2002" International Stamp Exhibition, Amsterdam. Ordinary gum.
**MS**2157 160×97 mm. As Nos. 2134/7 2·25 2·75

**771** Hands gripping Rope and P.S.I. Logo

**2002.** Public Services International World Congress, Ottawa.
2158 **771** 48c. multicoloured 60 45

**772** Tree in Four Seasons

**2002.** 75th Anniv of Public Pensions.
2159 **772** 48c. multicoloured 60 45

**773** Mount Elbrus, Russia

**2002.** International Year of Mountains. Multicoloured. Self-adhesive.
2160 48c. Type **773** 70 85
2161 48c. Puncak Jaya, Indonesia 70 85
2162 48c. Mount Everest, Nepal 70 85
2163 48c. Mount Kilimanjaro, Tanzania 70 85
2164 48c. Vinson Massif, Antarctica 70 85
2165 48c. Mount Aconcagua, Argentina 70 85
2166 48c. Mount McKinley, U.S.A. 70 85
2167 48c. Mount Logan, Canada 70 85

**774** Teacher writing on Board

**2002.** World Teachers' Day.
2168 **774** 48c. multicoloured 60 45

**775** Frieze from Toronto Stock Exchange and Globe

**2002.** 150th Anniv of Toronto Stock Exchange.
2169 **775** 48c. multicoloured 60 45

**776** Sir Sandford Fleming, Map of Canada and *Iris* (cable ship)

**2002.** Communications Centenaries. Multicoloured.
2170 48c. Type **776** (opening of Pacific Cable) 65 75
2171 48c. Guglielmo Marconi, Map of Canada and wireless equipment (first Transatlantic radio message) 65 75

**777** "Genesis" (painting by Daphne Odjig)

**2002.** Christmas. Aboriginal Art. Multicoloured.
2172 48c. Type **777** 55 20
2173 65c. "Winter Travel" (painting by Cecil Youngfox) 70 70
2174 $1.25 "Mary and Child" (sculpture by Irene Katak Angutitaq) 1·25 1·75

**778** Conductor's Hands and Original Orchestra

**2002.** Centenary of Quebec Symphony Orchestra.
2175 **778** 48c. multicoloured 1·00 45

**779** Sculpture of Ram's Head

**2003.** Chinese New Year ("Year of the Ram"). Multicoloured.
2176 48c. Type **779** 60 45
**MS**2177 125×103 mm. $1.25 Sculpture of goat's head (33×57 mm) 1·25 1·50

**2003.** National Hockey League. All-Star Game Players (4th series). As T 722. Multicoloured. Ordinary or self-adhesive.
2178 48c. Frank Mahovlich (wearing Maple Leaf No. 27 jersey) 80 90
2179 48c. Raymond Bourque (wearing Boston Bruins No. 77 jersey) 80 90
2180 48c. Serge Savard (wearing Canadiens No. 18 jersey) 80 90
2181 48c. Stan Mikita (wearing Chicago Blackhawks No. 21 jersey) 80 90
2182 48c. Mike Bossy (wearing New York Islanders No. 22 jersey) 80 90
2183 48c. Bill Durnan (wearing Canadiens jersey and brown gloves) 80 90

**779a** Bishop's University, Quebec (150th anniv of university status)

**2003.** Canadian Universities' Anniversaries (2nd issue). Multicoloured.
2190 48c. Bishop's University, Quebec (150th anniv of university status) 70 75
2191 48c. University of Western Ontario, London (125th anniv) 70 75
2192 48c. St. Francis Xavier University, Nova Scotia (150th Anniv) 70 75
2193 48c. Macdonald Institute, University of Guelph, Ontana (centenary) 70 75
2194 48c. Universite de Montreal (125th anniv) 70 75

**780** Leach's Storm Petrel

**2003.** Bird Paintings by John Audubon (1st series). Multicoloured. Ordinary gum.
2195 48c. Type **780** 85 85
2196 48c. Brent goose ("Brant") 85 85
2197 48c. Great cormorant 85 85
2198 48c. Common murre 85 85

(b) Self-adhesive.
2199 65c. Gyrfalcon (vert) 2·00 2·50
See also Nos. 2274/8 and 2340/4.

**781** Ranger looking through Binoculars

**2003.** 60th Anniv of Canadian Rangers.
2200 **781** 48c. multicoloured 70 45

**782** Greek Figure with Dove

**2003.** 75th Anniv of American Hellenic Educational Progressive Association in Canada.
2201 **782** 48c. multicoloured 70 45

**783** Firefighter carrying Boy and Burning Buildings

**2003.** Volunteer Firefighters.
2202 **783** 48c. multicoloured 1·25 65

784 Queen Elizabeth II

**2003.** 50th Anniv of Coronation.

| | | | | |
|---|---|---|---|---|
| 2203 | **784** | 48c. multicoloured | 1·00 | 55 |

785 Quebec City (c. 1703) Seal and Excerpt from Letter

**2003.** Pedro da Silva (first official courier of New France).

| | | | | |
|---|---|---|---|---|
| 2204 | **785** | 48c. multicoloured | 70 | 55 |

**2003.** Tourist Attractions (3rd series). As T 747. Multicoloured. Self-adhesive.

| | | | |
|---|---|---|---|
| 2205 | 65c. Wilberforce Falls, Nunavut | 1·10 | 1·40 |
| 2206 | 65c. Inside Passage, British Columbia | 1·10 | 1·40 |
| 2207 | 65c. Royal Canadian Mounted Police Depot Division, Regina, Saskatchewan | 1·10 | 1·40 |
| 2208 | 65c. Casa Loma, Toronto | 1·10 | 1·40 |
| 2209 | 65c. Gatineau Park, Quebec | 1·10 | 1·40 |
| 2210 | $1.25 Dragon boat race, Vancouver | 1·75 | 1·90 |
| 2211 | $1.25 Polar bear, Churchill, Manitoba | 1·75 | 1·90 |
| 2212 | $1.25 Niagara Falls, Ontario | 1·75 | 1·90 |
| 2213 | $1.25 Magdalen Islands, Quebec | 1·75 | 1·90 |
| 2214 | $1.25 Province House, Charlottetown, Prince Edward Island | 1·75 | 1·90 |

**2003.** Vancouver's Successful Bid for Winter Olympic Games, 2010. No. 1368 (Canadian flag definitive) optd VANCOUVER 2010.

| | | | |
|---|---|---|---|
| 2215 | 48c. multicoloured | 80 | 80 |

787 Mountains and Sea

**2003.** Canada–Alaska Cruise "Picture Postage". Multicoloured. Self-adhesive.

| | | | |
|---|---|---|---|
| 2216 | (-) Type **787** | 3·75 | 4·50 |
| 2217 | (-) Tail fin of whale, mountains and sea | 3·75 | 4·50 |

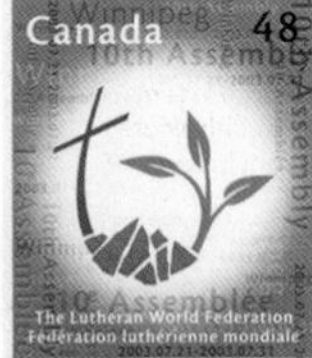
788 Assembly Logo

**2003.** 10th Lutheran World Federation Assembly, Winnipeg.

| | | | | |
|---|---|---|---|---|
| 2218 | **788** | 48c. multicoloured | 70 | 55 |

789 Canadian F-86 Sabre Fighter Plane, Sailors and Infantrymen

**2003.** 50th Anniv of Signing of Korea Armistice.

| | | | | |
|---|---|---|---|---|
| 2219 | **789** | 48c. multicoloured | 70 | 55 |

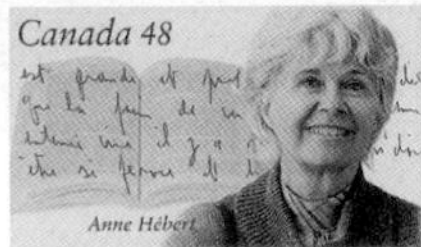
790 Anne Hebert

**2003.** 50th Anniv of National Library of Canada. Showing authors and portions of their handwritten text. Multicoloured.

| | | | |
|---|---|---|---|
| 2220 | 48c. Type **790** | 80 | 85 |
| 2221 | 48c. Hector de Saint-Denys Garneau | 80 | 85 |
| 2222 | 48c. Morley Callaghan | 80 | 85 |
| 2223 | 48c. Susanna Moodie and Catharine Parr Traill | 80 | 85 |

791 Cyclists in Road Race

**2003.** World Road Cycling Championships, Hamilton, Ontario.

| | | | | |
|---|---|---|---|---|
| 2224 | **791** | 48c. multicoloured | 1·10 | 70 |

792 Marc Garneau

**2003.** Stamp Collecting Month. Canadian Astronauts. Multicoloured. Self-adhesive.

| | | | |
|---|---|---|---|
| 2225 | 48c. Type **792** | 85 | 1·00 |
| 2226 | 48c. Roberta Bondar | 85 | 1·00 |
| 2227 | 48c. Steve MacLean | 85 | 1·00 |
| 2228 | 48c. Chris Hadfield | 85 | 1·00 |
| 2229 | 48c. Robert Thirsk | 85 | 1·00 |
| 2230 | 48c. Bjarni Tryggvason | 85 | 1·00 |
| 2231 | 48c. Dave Williams | 85 | 1·00 |
| 2232 | 48c. Julie Payette | 85 | 1·00 |

793 Maple Leaves, Canada

**2003.** National Emblems. Multicoloured.

| | | | |
|---|---|---|---|
| 2233 | 48c. Type **793** | 1·00 | 1·00 |
| 2234 | 48c. Cassis fistula flowers, Thailand | 1·00 | 1·00 |
| **MS**2235 | 120×96 mm. Nos. 2233/4 | 2·00 | 2·25 |

No. **MS**2235 commemorates Bangkok 2003 International Stamp Exhibition, Thailand.

Stamps of the same designs were issued by Thailand.

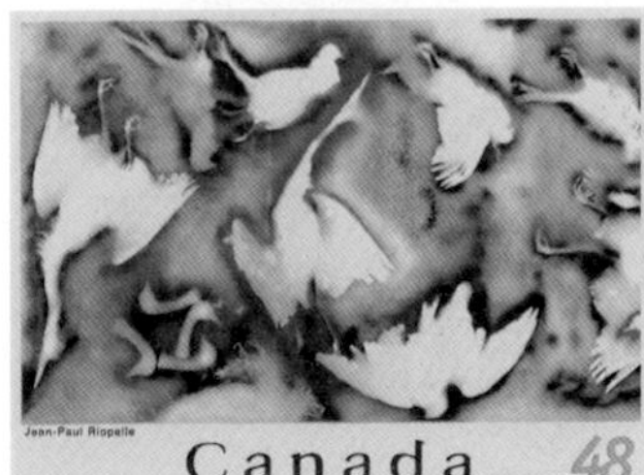
794 White Birds

**2003.** 80th Birth Anniv of Jean-Paul Riopelle (painter and sculptor). T 794 and similar horiz designs showing details from fresco "L'Hommage a Rosa Luxemburg". Multicoloured.

| | | | |
|---|---|---|---|
| **MS**2236 | 178×244 mm. 48c. Type **794**; 48c. Two white herons and white birds; 48c. Flying bird, flower and three white birds in cameo; 48c. Grouse on moor, white bird and sun; 48c. Two flying white birds in cameo and silhouette of falcon; 48c. Two white birds and cameo of flying duck | 4·00 | 5·00 |
| **MS**2237 | 159×95 mm. $1.25 Eggs and bird silhouette | 2·00 | 2·50 |

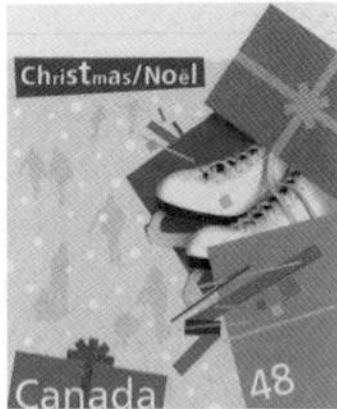
795 Ice Skates and Wrapped Presents

**2003.** Christmas. Multicoloured.

| | | | |
|---|---|---|---|
| 2238 | 48c. Type **795** | 70 | 55 |
| 2239 | 65c. Teddy bear and wrapped presents | 1·25 | 1·50 |
| 2240 | $1.25 Toy duck on wheels and wrapped presents | 1·90 | 2·50 |

796 Queen Elizabeth II, 2002

**2003.** Self-adhesive.

| | | | | |
|---|---|---|---|---|
| 2241 | **796** | 49c. black, mauve and scarlet | 1·10 | 80 |
| 2242 | **796** | 50c. multicoloured | 70 | 80 |

797 Monkey King on Cloud

**2004.** Chinese New Year ("Year of the Monkey"). Showing scenes from "Journey to the West" by Wu Ch'eng-en. Multicoloured.

| | | | |
|---|---|---|---|
| 2247 | 49c. Type **797** | 1·00 | 70 |
| **MS**2248 | 115×82 mm. $1.40 Monkey on road to India | 1·90 | 2·25 |

**2004.** Hong Kong 2004 International Stamp Exhibition. No. MS2248 optd Hong Kong Stamp Expo 2004 and exhibition emblem in gold on sheet margin.

| | | | |
|---|---|---|---|
| **MS**2249 | 115×82 mm. $1.40 Monkey on road to India | 1·90 | 2·25 |

**2004.** National Hockey League. All-Star Players (5th series). As T 722. Multicoloured. Ordinary or self-adhesive gum.

| | | | |
|---|---|---|---|
| 2250 | 49c. Larry Robinson (wearing Canadiens jersey) | 1·40 | 1·40 |
| 2251 | 49c. Marcel Dionne (wearing Los Angeles Kings jersey) | 1·40 | 1·40 |
| 2252 | 49c. Ted Lindsay (wearing Detroit Red Wings jersey) | 1·40 | 1·40 |
| 2253 | 49c. Johnny Bower (wearing Toronto Maple Leafs goal keeper kit) | 1·40 | 1·40 |
| 2254 | 49c. Brad Park (wearing New York Rangers jersey) | 1·40 | 1·40 |
| 2255 | 49c. Milt Schmidt (wearing Boston Bruins jersey) | 1·40 | 1·40 |

798 Bonhomme (Snowman), Quebec Winter Carnival

**2004.** Tourist Attractions (4th series). Multicoloured. Self-adhesive. Imperf.

| | | | |
|---|---|---|---|
| 2257 | 49c. Type **798** | 1·25 | 1·40 |
| 2258 | 49c. St. Joseph's Oratory | 1·25 | 1·40 |
| 2259 | 49c. Audience at International Jazz Festival, Montreal | 1·25 | 1·40 |
| 2260 | 49c. People watching Traversee Internationale du Lac St-Jean | 1·25 | 1·40 |
| 2261 | 49c. People at Canadian National Exhibition and Prince's Gate | 1·25 | 1·40 |

799 Governor General Ramon Hnatyshyn

**2004.** 70th Birth Anniv of Governor General Ramon Hnatyshyn.

| | | | | |
|---|---|---|---|---|
| 2262 | **799** | 49c. multicoloured | 70 | 70 |

800 *Fram* (polar research ship)

**2004.** 150th Birth Anniv of Otto Sverdrup (polar explorer). Each purple and buff.

| | | | |
|---|---|---|---|
| 2263 | 49c. Type **800** | 1·50 | 70 |
| **MS**2264 | 166×60 mm. $1.40 As No. 2263 plus two labels | 2·25 | 2·50 |

Stamps of similar designs were issued by Greenland and Norway.

801 Silhouettes of Cadets

**2004.** 125th Anniv of Royal Canadian Army Cadets. Self-adhesive. Imperf.

| | | | | |
|---|---|---|---|---|
| 2265 | **801** | 49c. multicoloured | 1·25 | 1·00 |

802 Subway Train, Toronto

**2004.** Light Rail Urban Transit. Multicoloured.

| | | | |
|---|---|---|---|
| 2266 | 49c. Type **802** | 1·50 | 1·50 |
| 2267 | 49c. TransLink SkyTrain, Vancouver | 1·50 | 1·50 |
| 2268 | 49c. Metro train, Montreal | 1·50 | 1·50 |
| 2269 | 49c. CTrain, Calgary | 1·50 | 1·50 |

803 Canadian Map and Employee

**2004.** 40th Anniv of Home Hardware (co-operative business). Self-adhesive.

| | | | | |
|---|---|---|---|---|
| 2270 | **803** | 49c. multicoloured | 90 | 90 |

**2004.** Canadian Universities Anniversaries (3rd series). As T 779a. Multicoloured.

| | | | |
|---|---|---|---|
| 2271 | 49c. University of Sherbrooke (50th anniv) | 90 | 90 |
| 2272 | 49c. University of Prince Edward Island (bicent) | 90 | 90 |

804 Teddy Bears

**2004.** Centenary of Montreal Children's Hospital. Self-adhesive.

| | | | | |
|---|---|---|---|---|
| 2273 | **804** | 49c. multicoloured | 90 | 90 |

**805** Ruby-crowned kinglet

**2004.** Bird Paintings by John Audubon (2nd series). Multicoloured. (a) Ordinary gum.

| | | | |
|---|---|---|---|
| 2274 | 49c. Type **805** | 85 | 85 |
| 2275 | 49c. White-winged crossbill | 85 | 85 |
| 2276 | 49c. Bohemian waxwing | 85 | 85 |
| 2277 | 49c. Boreal chickadee | 85 | 85 |

(b) Self-adhesive. Imperf.

| | | | |
|---|---|---|---|
| 2278 | 80c. Lincoln's sparrow | 2·00 | 2·25 |

**806** Sir Samuel Cunard

**2004.** Sir Samuel Cunard and Sir Hugh Allan (founders of transatlantic mail service) Commemorations. Multicoloured. Self-adhesive.

| | | | |
|---|---|---|---|
| 2279 | 49c. Type **806** | 80 | 1·00 |
| 2280 | 49c. Sir Hugh Allan | 80 | 1·00 |

Nos. 2279/80 were printed together, se-tenant, forming a composite design.

**806a** Butterfly on Flower

**2004.** "Write me...Ring me" Greetings Stamps. Multicoloured.

| | | | |
|---|---|---|---|
| 2280a | Type **806a** | 2·00 | 2·00 |
| 2280b | Two young children at beach | 2·00 | 2·00 |
| 2280c | Red rose | 2·00 | 2·00 |
| 2280d | Pug (dog) | 2·00 | 2·00 |

Nos. 2280a/d are inscribed "Domestic Lettermail" (initial value was 49c.).

**807** Soldiers storming Juno Beach, Normandy

**2004.** 60th Anniv of D-Day Landings.

| | | | | |
|---|---|---|---|---|
| 2281 | **807** | 49c. multicoloured | 1·25 | 80 |

**808** Pierre Dugua de Mons

**2004.** 400th Anniv of First French Settlement in Acadia, St. Croix Island (1st issue).

| | | | | |
|---|---|---|---|---|
| 2282 | **808** | 49c. ochre, blue and orange | 80 | 70 |

See also No. 2361, 2400 and 2508.

**809** Spyros Louis (Greek athlete) and Marathon Runner

**2004.** Olympic Games, Athens, Greece. Multicoloured.

| | | | |
|---|---|---|---|
| 2283 | 49c. Type **809** | 1·50 | 1·50 |
| 2284 | 49c. Girls playing football | 1·50 | 1·50 |

**810** Golfer and Trophy from Early Tournament

**2004.** Canadian Open Golf Championship. Multicoloured. Self-adhesive.

| | | | |
|---|---|---|---|
| 2285 | 49c. Type **810** | 1·00 | 1·25 |
| 2286 | 49c. Golfer and trophy from modern tournament | 1·00 | 1·25 |

**811** Segmented Heart

**2004.** 50th Anniv of Montreal Heart Institute. Self-adhesive.

| | | | | |
|---|---|---|---|---|
| 2287 | **811** | 49c. multicoloured | 80 | 1·00 |

**812** Goldfish in Bowl

**2004.** Pets. Multicoloured. Self-adhesive. Imperf.

| | | | |
|---|---|---|---|
| 2288 | 49c. Type **812** | 1·10 | 1·25 |
| 2289 | 49c. Two cats on chair | 1·10 | 1·25 |
| 2290 | 49c. Child with rabbit | 1·10 | 1·25 |
| 2291 | 49c. Child with dog | 1·10 | 1·25 |

**813** Gerhard Herzberg (Chemistry, 1971)

**2004.** Nobel Chemistry Prize Winners. Mult.

| | | | |
|---|---|---|---|
| 2292 | 49c. Type **813** | 90 | 1·00 |
| 2293 | 49c. Michael Smith (Chemistry, 1993) | 90 | 1·00 |

**814** Maple Leaf in Photo Album Frame

**2004.** Picture Postage. Multicoloured. Self-adhesive.

| | | | |
|---|---|---|---|
| 2294 | (49c.) Type **814** | 90 | 1·00 |
| 2295 | (49c.) Maple leaf in silver frame | 90 | 1·00 |

Nos. 2294/2295 were both inscribed "Domestic Postage Paid" and sold for 49c.

**815** Victoria Cross (embossed)

**2004.** 150th Anniv of First Canadian Recipient of the Victoria Cross. Multicoloured.

| | | | |
|---|---|---|---|
| 2296 | 49c. Type **815** | 1·10 | 1·25 |
| 2297 | 49c. Victoria Cross and signature of Queen Elizabeth II | 1·10 | 1·25 |

Nos. 2296/7 were printed together as sheetlets of 16 around a central illustration and the names of 94 Canadians who have received the Victoria Cross.

**816** "Self-portrait", 1974

**2004.** "Art Canada". Birth Centenary of Jean Paul Lemieux (artist). Multicoloured.

| | | | |
|---|---|---|---|
| 2298 | 49c. Type **816** | 1·00 | 85 |
| **MS**2299 | 150×86 mm. 49c. Type **815**; 80c. "A June Wedding", 1972 (53×34 mm); $1.40 "Summer", 1959 (64×31 mm) | 4·50 | 5·00 |

**817** Santa in his Sleigh and Reindeer

**2004.** Christmas. Multicoloured. Self-adhesive.

| | | | |
|---|---|---|---|
| 2300 | 49c. Type **817** | 1·00 | 45 |
| 2301 | 80c. Santa sitting in a Cadillac and towing a house | 1·60 | 2·00 |
| 2302 | $1.40 Santa driving a train | 2·50 | 3·00 |

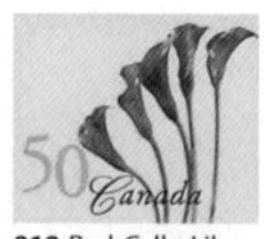

**818** Red Calla Lily

**2004.** Flowers. Multicoloured. (1st series) Self-adhesive.

| | | | |
|---|---|---|---|
| 2303 | 50c. Type **818** | 70 | 80 |
| 2304 | 51c. Red bergamot | 70 | 55 |
| 2305 | 85c. Yellow calla lily | 1·00 | 1·25 |
| 2306 | 89c. Lady's slipper orchids | 1·25 | 1·25 |
| 2307 | $1.05 Pink fairy slipper orchids | 1·50 | 1·60 |
| 2308 | $1.45 purple Dutch iris | 1·90 | 2·00 |
| 2309 | $1.49 Himalayan blue poppies | 1·90 | 2·00 |

Nos. 2305/9 come imperf.

See also Nos. 2470/**MS**2477 and 2530/**MS**2537.

**819** Rooster facing East (right)

**2005.** Chinese New Year ("Year of the Rooster"). 35th Anniv of Diplomatic Relations with China (MS2315b). T 819 and similar multicoloured designs.

| | | | |
|---|---|---|---|
| 2314 | 50c. Type **819** | 1·00 | 60 |
| **MS**2315 | Two sheets, each 105×82 mm. (a) $1.45 Rooster facing west (left) (40×41 mm). (b) $1.45 As No. **MS**2315a. | 2·50 | 3·00 |

Nos. **MS**2315a/b both have a barcode tab attached at foot.

**2004.** National Hockey League. All-Star Game Players (6th series). As T 722. Multicoloured. Ordinary or self-adhesive gum.

| | | | |
|---|---|---|---|
| 2316 | 50c. Henri Richard (wearing Habs jersey) | 1·40 | 1·40 |
| 2317 | 50c. Grant Fuhr (wearing Oilers goal keeper kit) | 1·40 | 1·40 |
| 2318 | 50c. Allan Stanley (wearing Toronto Maple Leafs jersey) | 1·40 | 1·40 |
| 2319 | 50c. Pierre Pilote (wearing Chicago Black Hawks jersey) | 1·40 | 1·40 |
| 2320 | 50c. Bryan Trottier (wearing New York Islanders jersey) | 1·40 | 1·40 |
| 2321 | 50c. John Bucyk (wearing Boston Bruins jersey) | 1·40 | 1·40 |

**820** Alevin Fishing Fly

**2005.** Fishing Flies. Multicoloured. (a) Ordinary gum.

| | | | |
|---|---|---|---|
| **MS**2328 | 190×112 mm. 50c.×4 Type **820**; Jock Scott; P.E.I. Fly; Mickey Finn | 3·00 | 3·25 |

(b) Self-adhesive.

| | | | |
|---|---|---|---|
| 2329 | 50c. Type **820** | 1·25 | 1·25 |
| 2330 | 50c. Jock Scott | 1·25 | 1·25 |
| 2331 | 50c. Mickey Finn | 1·25 | 1·25 |
| 2332 | 50c. P.E.I. Fly | 1·25 | 1·25 |

**2005.** Canadian Universities Anniversaries (4th series). As T 779a (No. 2190). Multicoloured.

| | | | |
|---|---|---|---|
| 2333 | 50c. Nova Scotia Agricultural College | 80 | 75 |

**821** Inukshuk of Five Rocks

**2005.** Expo 2005 International Exhibition, Aichi, Japan.

| | | | | |
|---|---|---|---|---|
| 2335 | **821** | 50c. multicoloured | 70 | 50 |

**822** Yellow Daffodils

**2005.** Daffodils. Multicoloured. (a) Self-adhesive.

| | | | |
|---|---|---|---|
| 2336 | 50c. Type **822** | 90 | 90 |
| 2337 | 50c. White daffodils with yellow trumpets | 90 | 90 |

(b) Ordinary gum.

| | | | |
|---|---|---|---|
| **MS**2338 | 120×80 mm. Nos. 2336/7 | 1·25 | 1·60 |

No. **MS**2338 also commemorates Pacific Explorer 2005 World Stamp Expo Exhibition, Sydney, Australia.

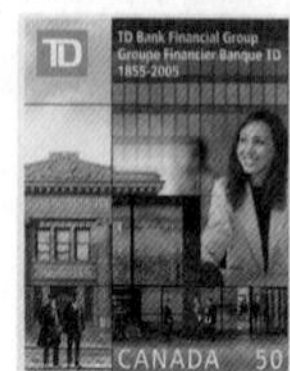

**823** TD Bank Building of c.1900, Cashier and TD Tower, Toronto

**2005.** 150th Anniv of TD Bank Financial Group. Self-adhesive.

| | | | | |
|---|---|---|---|---|
| 2339 | **823** | 50c. multicoloured | 80 | 80 |

**824** Horned Lark

**2005.** Bird Paintings by John Audubon (3rd series). Multicoloured. (a) Ordinary gum.

| | | | |
|---|---|---|---|
| 2340 | 50c. Type **824** | 1·25 | 1·25 |
| 2341 | 50c. Piping plover | 1·25 | 1·25 |
| 2342 | 50c. Stilt sandpiper | 1·25 | 1·25 |
| 2343 | 50c. Willow ptarmigan | 1·25 | 1·25 |

(b) Size 45×35 mm. Self-adhesive. Imperf.

| | | | |
|---|---|---|---|
| 2344 | 85c. Double-crested cormorant | 1·90 | 2·25 |

**825** Jacques Cartier Bridge, Montreal, Quebec

**2005.** Bridges. Multicoloured. Self-adhesive.

| | | | |
|---|---|---|---|
| 2345 | 50c. Type **825** | 75 | 1·00 |
| 2346 | 50c. Souris Swinging Bridge, Manitoba | 75 | 1·00 |

2347 50c. Angus L. Macdonald Bridge, Halifax, Nova Scotia 75 1·00

2348 50c. Canso Causeway, Nova Scotia 75 1·00

**826** Magazine Covers of 1911, 1954, 1962 and 1917

**2005.** Centenary of Maclean's Magazine.

2349 **826** 50c. multicoloured 60 50

**827** Saskatoon Berries and Osprey, Waterton Lakes National Park, Alberta, Canada

**2005.** Biosphere Reserves. Multicoloured.

2350 50c. Type **827** 1·10 1·10

2351 50c. Red Deer stags, Killarney National Park, Ireland 1·10 1·10

**MS**2352 120×70 mm. Nos. 2350/1 2·10 2·40

Stamps in similar designs were issued by Ireland.

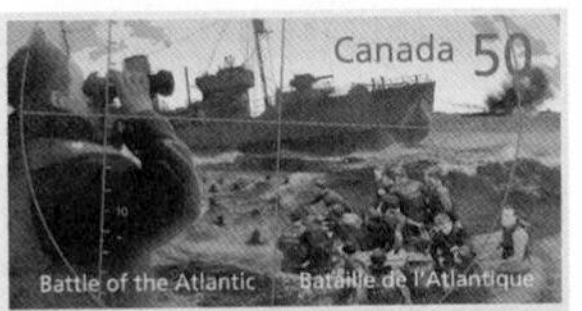


**828** Sailor Lookout, Canadian Navy Corvette and Survivors in Lifeboat

**2005.** 60th Anniv of Battle of the Atlantic.

2353 **828** 50c. multicoloured 1·00 60

**829** Candle, Silhouettes, Memorial Cross GRV and New Museum Building

**2005.** Opening of New Canadian War Museum Building, Ottawa. Self-adhesive.

2354 **829** 50c. multicoloured 70 70

**830** "Down in the Laurentides"

**2005.** "Art Canada". 150th Birth Anniv of Homer Watson (artist). Paintings. Multicoloured.

2355 50c. Type **830** 70 50

**MS**2356 150×87 mm. 50c. Type **830**; 85c. "The Flood Gate" (53×39 mm) 1·10 1·40

No. **MS**2356 also commemorates the 125th anniversary of the National Gallery of Canada.

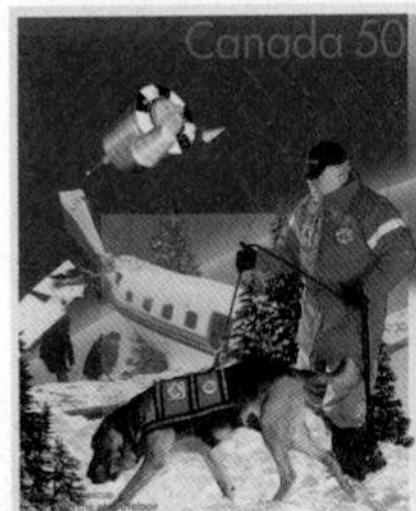


**831** Volunteer with Search Dog, Crashed Aircraft and Satellite

**2005.** Search and Rescue. Sheet 260×170 mm containing T 831 and similar vert designs. Multicoloured.

**MS**2357 50c.×2 Type **831**; 50c.×2 Rescuers, crew in life raft and sinking ship; 50c.×2 Seaman winched into helicopter and float plane; 50c.×2 Mountain rescue team with stretcher and satellite 6·50 6·50

**832** Ellen Fairclough and Parliament Buildings, Ottawa

**2005.** Birth Centenary of Ellen Fairclough (first woman federal cabinet minister).

2358 **832** 50c. multicoloured 70 50

**833** Diver spinning in mid-air

**2005.** 11th FINA (Federation Internationale de Natation) World Championships, Montreal. Multicoloured.

2359 50c. Type **833** 75 90

2360 50c. Swimmer in butterfly stroke 75 90

**834** Port-Royal, 1605 (from drawing by Samuel de Champlain)

**2005.** French Settlement in North America (2nd issue). 400th Anniv of Founding of Port-Royal, Nova Scotia.

2361 **834** 50c. multicoloured 70 55

**835** Chemicals Plant, Calgary Skyline, Mount Grassi and Railway Line

**2005.** Centenary of Alberta Province. Self-adhesive.

2362 **835** 50c. multicoloured 70 55

The backing paper is illustrated with four different scenes, each running across two stamps: Calgary Stampede; Jasper Avenue, Edmonton, 1963; Lake Minnewanka, Banff; and oil refinery of c. 1912.

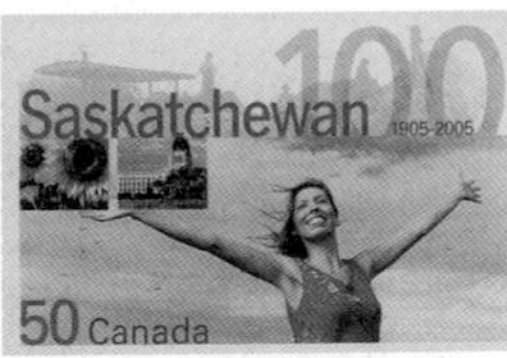


**836** Woman with Arms outstretched, Sunflowers and Legislature Building, Regina

**2005.** Centenary of Saskatchewan.

2363 **836** 50c. multicoloured 70 55

**837** 1930 50c. Acadian Memorial Church Stamp and Acadian Flag

**2005.** 250th Anniv of Deportation of French Settlers from Acadia (Nova Scotia) to British Colonies of North America.

2364 **837** 50c. multicoloured 80 60

**838** Oscar Peterson

**2005.** 80th Birthday of Oscar Peterson (jazz composer and musician).

2365 **838** 50c. multicoloured 1·00 50

**MS**2366 112×116 mm. No. 2365×4 3·50 4·25

**839** Children playing and discarded Leg Braces

**2005.** 50th Anniv of Mass Polio Vaccination in Canada.

2367 **839** 50c. multicoloured 70 50

**840** Wall climbing

**2005.** Youth Sports. Multicoloured. Self-adhesive.

2368 50c. Type **840** 60 70

2369 50c. Skateboarding 60 70

2370 50c. Mountain biking 60 70

2371 50c. Snowboarding 60 70

**841** *Puma concolor* (cougar)

**2005.** 35th Anniv of Canada—China Diplomatic Relations. Carnivores. Multicoloured.

2372 50c. Type **841** 60 70

2373 50c. *Panthera pardus orientalis* (Amur leopard) 60 70

**MS**2374 104×58 mm. Nos. 2372/3 1·25 1·60

Stamps of the same design were issued by China (People's Republic).

**842** Snowman

**2005.** Christmas (1st issue). Self-adhesive.

2375 **842** 50c. multicoloured 70 50

**843** Creche by Michel Forest

**2005.** Christmas (2nd issue). Showing Christmas creches. Multicoloured. Self-adhesive.

2376 50c. Type **843** 70 50

2377 85c. Creche with aboriginal figures by Keena (31×39 mm) 1·40 2·00

2378 $1.45 Creche by Sylvia Daoust (27×40 mm) 2·25 3·00

**844** Chow

**2006.** Chinese New Year ("Year of the Dog"). Multicoloured.

2379 51c. Type **844** 60 60

**MS**2380 129×106 mm. $1.49 Chow with puppy 2·50 3·00

**845** Queen Elizabeth II, Ottawa, 2002

**2006.** 80th Birthday of Queen Elizabeth II (1st issue). Self-adhesive.

2381 **845** 51c. multicoloured 70 70

See also No. **MS**2392.

**846** Team Pursuit Speed Skating

**2006.** Winter Olympic Games, Turin, Italy. Multicoloured.

2382 51c. Type **846** 75 75

2383 51c. Skeleton (sled) 75 75

**847** Trilliums and Black-throated Blue Warbler (Shade Garden)

**2006.** Gardens. Multicoloured. Self-adhesive.

2384 51c. Type **847** 1·25 1·25

2385 51c. Purple coneflowers and American painted lady butterfly (flower garden) 1·25 1·25

2386 51c. Water lilies and green darner dragonfly 1·25 1·25

2387 51c. Rock garden and blue-spotted salamander 1·25 1·25

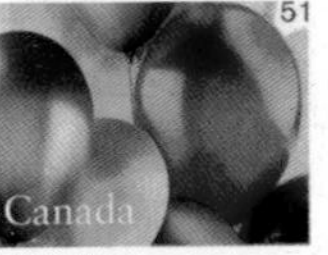


**848** Balloons

**2006.** Greetings Stamp. Self-adhesive.

2388 **848** 51c. multicoloured 75 75

**849** "The Field of Rapeseed"

**2006.** "Art Canada". Paintings by Dorothy Knowles. Multicoloured.

| | | | |
|---|---|---|---|
| 2389 | 51c. Type **849** | 75 | 50 |
| **MS**2390 | 150×87 mm. 51c. Type **849**; 89c. "North Saskatchewan River" (42×51 mm) | 2·25 | 2·75 |

**850** Hands enclosing Globe

**2006.** 50th Anniv of Canadian Labour Congress.

| | | | |
|---|---|---|---|
| 2391 | **850** 51c. multicoloured | 70 | 50 |

**2006.** 80th Birthday of Queen Elizabeth II (2nd issue). Sheet 125×75 mm. Multicoloured.

| | | | |
|---|---|---|---|
| **MS**2392 | $1.49×2 As Type **845** but 39×31 mm | 4·75 | 5·50 |

**851** Colophon emerging from Book

**2006.** Centenary of McClelland & Stewart (publishing house). Self-adhesive.

| | | | |
|---|---|---|---|
| 2393 | **851** 51c. blue and silver | 1·40 | 1·25 |

**852** Mid 19th-Century Transformation Mask and Other Exhibits

**2006.** 150th Anniv of Canadian Museum of Civilization, Gatineau, Quebec. Self-adhesive.

| | | | |
|---|---|---|---|
| 2394 | **852** 89c. multicoloured | 1·75 | 2·25 |

**853** Lorne Greene

**2006.** Canadians in Hollywood. Multicoloured. (a) Self-adhesive.

| | | | |
|---|---|---|---|
| 2395 | 51c. Type **853** | 75 | 85 |
| 2396 | 51c. Fay Wray | 75 | 85 |
| 2397 | 51c. Mary Pickford | 75 | 85 |
| 2398 | 51c. John Candy | 75 | 85 |

(b) Ordinary gum.

| | | | |
|---|---|---|---|
| **MS**2399 | 180×63 mm. As Nos. 2395/8 | 3·25 | 3·75 |

**854** Champlain's Ship

**2006.** French Settlement in North America (3rd issue). 400th Anniv of Samuel de Champlain's Survey of East Coast of North America.

| | | | |
|---|---|---|---|
| 2400 | 51c. ×2 Type **854** | 70 | 50 |
| **MS**2401 | 204×146 mm. 51c. Type **854**; 39c.×2, As Type **2879** of USA | 1·00 | 1·25 |

No. **MS**2401 also commemorates Washington 2006 International Stamp Exhibition.

A self-adhesive stamp in the same design and an identical miniature sheet were also issued by the United States.

**855** Girl watching Beluga Whale

**2006.** 50th Anniv of Vancouver Aquarium. Self-adhesive.

| | | | |
|---|---|---|---|
| 2402 | **855** 51c. multicoloured | 70 | 60 |

**856** Pilot and Snowbirds

**2006.** 35th Anniv of Snowbirds Demonstration Team (431 Squadron). Multicoloured.

| | | | |
|---|---|---|---|
| 2403 | 51c. Type **856** | 1·25 | 1·25 |
| 2404 | 51c. Snowbirds and emblem | 1·25 | 1·25 |
| **MS**2405 | 130×65 mm. Nos. 2403/4 | 2·50 | 2·50 |

**857** James White (Chief Geographer), Proportional Dividers and Modern Map

**2006.** Centenary of "The Atlas of Canada".

| | | | |
|---|---|---|---|
| 2406 | **857** 51c. multicoloured | 1·25 | 1·00 |

**858** Player and Event Tickets

**2006.** World Lacrosse Championships, London, Ontario. Self-adhesive.

| | | | |
|---|---|---|---|
| 2407 | **858** 51c. multicoloured | 70 | 70 |

**859** Early and Modern Climbers

**2006.** Centenary of the Alpine Club of Canada. Self-adhesive.

| | | | |
|---|---|---|---|
| 2408 | **859** 51c. multicoloured | 1·00 | 85 |

**860** Barrow's Goldeneye

**2006.** Duck Decoys. Multicoloured.

| | | | |
|---|---|---|---|
| 2409 | 51c. Type **860** | 1·10 | 1·10 |
| 2410 | 51c. Mallard (decoy with white ring around neck) | 1·10 | 1·10 |
| 2411 | 51c. Black duck (plain brown decoy) | 1·10 | 1·10 |
| 2412 | 51c. Red-breasted merganser (black and white decoy with red bill) | 1·10 | 1·10 |
| **MS**2413 | 130×145 mm. Nos. 2409/12 | 4·00 | 4·25 |

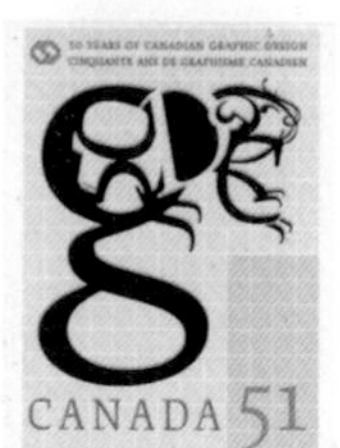


**861** "g" as Beaver enclosing "50"

**2006.** 50th Anniv of the Society of Graphic Designers of Canada.

| | | | |
|---|---|---|---|
| 2414 | **861** 51c. multicoloured | 70 | 50 |

**862** Glasses of Wine

**2006.** Canadian Wine and Cheese. Multicoloured. Self-adhesive.

| | | | |
|---|---|---|---|
| 2415 | 51c. Type **862** | 80 | 90 |
| 2416 | 51c. Wine taster (horiz as Type **862**) | 80 | 90 |
| 2417 | 51c. Canadian cheeses (wedge-shaped, 36×38 mm) | 80 | 90 |
| 2418 | 51c. Serving cheese platter at fromagerie (wedge-shaped, 36×38 mm) | 80 | 90 |

**2006.** Canadian Universities Anniversaries (5th series). Vert design as T 779a (No. 2190). Multicoloured.

| | | | |
|---|---|---|---|
| 2419 | 51c. Macdonald College, Sainte-Anne-de-Bellevue, Quebec (centenary) | 1·00 | 85 |

**863** Newfoundland Marten

**2006.** Endangered Species (1st series). Multicoloured. (a) Self-adhesive.

| | | | |
|---|---|---|---|
| 2420 | 51c. Type **863** | 1·10 | 1·10 |
| 2421 | 51c. Blotched tiger salamander | 1·10 | 1·10 |
| 2422 | 51c. Blue racer | 1·10 | 1·10 |
| 2423 | 51c. Swift fox | 1·10 | 1·10 |

(b) Ordinary gum. Size 48×24 mm.

| | | | |
|---|---|---|---|
| **MS**2424 | 160×74 mm. Nos. 2420/3 | 4·00 | 4·50 |

See also Nos. 2511/**MS**2515.

**864** Maureen Forrester and Place des Arts, Montréal

**2006.** Canadian Opera Singers. Multicoloured.

| | | | |
|---|---|---|---|
| 2425 | 51c. Type **864** | 1·10 | 1·10 |
| 2426 | 51c. Raoul Jobin and Palais Garnier, Paris | 1·10 | 1·10 |
| 2427 | 51c. Leopold Simoneau, Pierrette Alarie and Opera-Comique, France | 1·10 | 1·10 |
| 2428 | 51c. Jon Vickers and La Scala, Milan | 1·10 | 1·10 |
| 2429 | 51c. Edward Johnson and Metropolitan Opera Company, New York | 1·10 | 1·10 |

**865** "Madonna and Child" (detail) (Antoine-Sebastien Falardeau)

**2006.** Christmas (1st issue). Self-adhesive.

| | | | |
|---|---|---|---|
| 2430 | **865** 51c. multicoloured | 85 | 55 |

**866** "Snowman" (Yvonne McKague Housser)

**2006.** Christmas (2nd issue). Showing Christmas cards from 1931 "Painters of Canada" series. Multicoloured. Self-adhesive.

| | | | |
|---|---|---|---|
| 2431 | 51c. Type **866** | 85 | 55 |
| 2432 | 89c. "Winter Joys" (J. E. Sampson) | 1·75 | 2·25 |
| 2433 | $1.49 "Contemplation" (Edwin Holgate) | 2·25 | 3·25 |

**867** Ice Fields and Fjord, Sirmilik National Park, Nunavut

**2006.** (a) Self-adhesive stamps inscr "P" instead of face value. Each showing Canadian flag. Multicoloured.

| | | | |
|---|---|---|---|
| 2434 | (51c.) Type **867** | 1·10 | 1·25 |
| 2435 | (51c.) Coast and ancient trees, Chemainus, British Columbia | 1·10 | 1·25 |
| 2436 | (51c.) Polar bears, Churchill, Manitoba | 1·10 | 1·25 |
| 2437 | (51c.) Lighthouse at Bras d'Or Lake, Nova Scotia | 1·10 | 1·25 |
| 2438 | (51c.) Tuktut Nogait National Park, Northwest Territories | 1·10 | 1·25 |
| 2439 | (52c.) Sambra Island lighthouse, Nove Scotia (red and white striped) | 1·40 | 1·40 |
| 2440 | (52c.) Point Clark lighthouse, (trees at left)(above cliff) Ontario | 1·40 | 1·40 |
| 2441 | (52c.) Cap-des-Rosiers lighthouse, Quebec | 1·40 | 1·40 |
| 2442 | (52c.) Warren Landing lighthouse, Manitoba (in sandunes) | 1·40 | 1·40 |
| 2443 | (52c.) Pachena Point lighthouse, and keepers house, British Coloumbia | 1·40 | 1·40 |
| 2444 | (52c.) Pachena Point Lighthouse and part of keeper's house (at right) | 1·40 | 1·40 |
| 2445 | (57c.) Watson's Mill (three storey stone building), Manotick, Ontario | 1·40 | 1·40 |
| 2445 | (57c.) Watson's Mill (three storey stone building), Manotick, Ontario | 1·40 | 1·40 |
| 2446 | (57c.) Keremeos Grist Mill (wooden building with waterwheel at left), British Columbia | 1·40 | 1·40 |
| 2446 | (57c.) Keremeos Grist Mill (wooden building with waterwheel at left), British Columbia | 1·40 | 1·40 |
| 2447 | (57c.) Old stone Mill National Historic Site (four storey stone building with red doors), Delta, Ontario | 1·40 | 1·40 |
| 2448 | (57c.) Riordon Grist Mill (two storey stone building), Caraquet, New Brunswick | 1·40 | 1·40 |
| 2449 | (57c.) Cornell Mill (weir at right), Stanbridge East, Quebec | 1·40 | 1·40 |

Nos. 2434/8 were inscribed "P" and initially sold for 51c. each and Nos. 2439/43 were inscribed 'P' and initially sold for 52c. each and nos 2445/9 were all inscribed 'P' and initially sold for 57c.

**868** Queen Elizabeth II, 2005

**2006.** Self-adhesive. Multicoloured.

| | | | |
|---|---|---|---|
| 2464 | (51c.) Type **868** | 90 | 90 |
| 2465 | (52c.) Queen Elizabeth II, Saskatoon, 2005 | 1·00 | 1·00 |
| 2466 | (54c.) Queen Elizabeth in Canada, 19 May 2005 (red background) | 1·25 | 1·25 |
| 2467 | (57c.) Queen Elizabeth II (wearing deep blue jacket and hat) | 1·40 | 1·40 |
| 2467 | (57c.) Queen Elizabeth II (wearing deep blue jacket and hat) | 1·40 | 1·40 |

No. 2464 was inscribed 'P' and initially sold for 51c., and No. 2465 was inscribed 'P' and initially sold for 52c. No. 2466, in scribed 'P', and intially sold for 54c.No. 2467 inscribed 'P', was intiailly sold for 57c.

**869** Spotted coralroot

**2006.** Flowers (2nd series). Multicoloured. Self-adhesive.

| | | | | |
|---|---|---|---|---|
| 2470 | **869** | (51c.) Spotted coralroot | 60 | 35 |
| 2471 | **869** | 93c. Flat-leaved bladderwort | 1·10 | 1·25 |
| 2472 | **869** | $1.10 Marsh skullcap | 1·25 | 1·50 |
| 2473 | **869** | $1.55 Little larkspur | 1·75 | 2·25 |

(b) Self-adhesive.

| | | | |
|---|---|---|---|
| 2474 | 93c. Flat-leaved bladderwort | 1·10 | 1·25 |
| 2475 | $1.10 Marsh skullcap | 1·25 | 1·50 |
| 2476 | $1.55 Little larkspur | 1·75 | 2·25 |

(c) Ordinary gum.

| | | |
|---|---|---|
| **MS**2477 120×72 mm. As Nos. 2470/3 | 6·00 | 7·00 |

No. 2470 was inscribed "P" and initially sold for 51c. each.

**870** Pig

**2007.** Chinese New Year ("Year of the Pig"). Multicoloured.

| | | |
|---|---|---|
| 2478 52c. Type **870** | 1·25 | 60 |
| **MS**2479 98×97 mm. $1.55 Pig (running to right) | 2·25 | 2·75 |

No. 2479 is cut in a lantern shape.

**871** Ribbons and Confetti

**2007.** Greetings Stamp. Self-adhesive.

| | | | | |
|---|---|---|---|---|
| 2480 | **871** | 52c. multicoloured | 85 | 1·00 |

**872** King Eider (*Somateria spectabilis*)

**2007.** International Polar Year. Multicoloured.

| | | |
|---|---|---|
| 2481 52c. Type **872** | 1·50 | 1·50 |
| 2482 52c. *Crossota millsaeare* (deep-sea jellyfish) | 1·50 | 1·50 |
| **MS**2483 105×70 mm. Nos. 2481/2 | 3·00 | 3·00 |

**873** *Syringa vulgaris* "Princess Alexandra"

**2007.** Lilacs. Multicoloured. (a) Self-adhesive.

| | | |
|---|---|---|
| 2484 52c. Type **873** | 90 | 90 |
| 2485 52c. *Syringa×prestoniae* "Isabella" | 90 | 90 |

(b) Ordinary gum.

| | | |
|---|---|---|
| **MS**2486 128×80 mm. As Nos. 2484/5 | 1·75 | 2·00 |

**2007.** Canadian Universities' Anniversaries (6th issue). As T 779a (No. 2190). Multicoloured. Self-adhesive.

| | | |
|---|---|---|
| 2487 52c. HEC (Ecole des hautes etudes commerciales), Montreal (centenary) | 85 | 85 |
| 2488 52c. University of Saskatchewan | 85 | 85 |

**874** "Jelly Shelf"

**2007.** "Art Canada". Paintings by Mary Pratt. Multicoloured.

| | | |
|---|---|---|
| 2489 52c. Type **874** | 75 | 50 |
| **MS**2490 150×87 mm. 52c. Type **874**; $1.55 "Iceberg in the North Atlantic" (62×40 mm) | 3·00 | 3·50 |

**875** Parliament Buildings, Ottawa, 2007 and Lumberers Regatta, 1860

**2007.** 150th Anniv of Ottawa as Capital of Canada. Self-adhesive.

| | | | | |
|---|---|---|---|---|
| 2491 | **875** | 52c. multicoloured | 1·00 | 85 |

(b) Ordinary gum.

| | | |
|---|---|---|
| **MS**2492 102×102 mm. 52c. As No. 2491; $1.55 As No. 2491 | 3·50 | 3·75 |

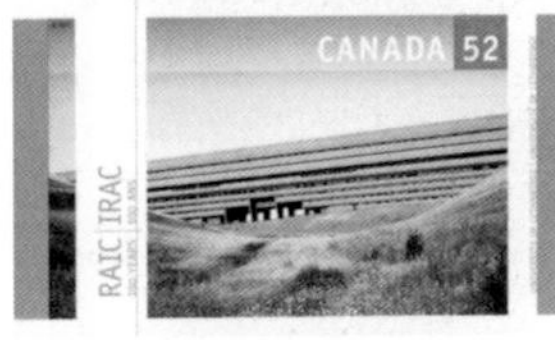

**876** University of Lethbridge (Arthur Erickson), 1971

**2007.** Centenary of Royal Architectural Institute of Canada. Multicoloured.

| | | |
|---|---|---|
| 2493 52c. Type **876** | 1·00 | 1·00 |
| 2494 52c. St. Mary's Church (Douglas Cardinal), 1969 | 1·00 | 1·00 |
| 2495 52c. Ontario Science Centre (Raymond Moriyama), 1969 | 1·00 | 1·00 |
| 2496 52c. National Gallery of Canada (Moshe Safdie), 1988 | 1·00 | 1·00 |

**877** Capt. George Vancouver

**2007.** 250th Birth Anniv of Captain George Vancouver (explorer of west coast of North America).

| | | |
|---|---|---|
| 2497 **877** $1.55 multicoloured | 2·50 | 2·50 |
| **MS**2498 70×120 mm. **877** $1.55 multicoloured | 2·50 | 3·00 |

**878** Official U-20 World Cup Football and Canadian Team in Action

**2007.** FIFA U-20 World Cup, Canada.

| | | | | |
|---|---|---|---|---|
| 2499 | **878** | 52c. multicoloured | 1·00 | 85 |

**879** Gordon Lightfoot

**2007.** Canadian Recording Artists. Multicoloured. (a) Self-adhesive.

| | | |
|---|---|---|
| 2500 52c. Type **879** | 1·00 | 1·10 |
| 2501 52c. Joni Mitchell | 1·00 | 1·10 |
| 2502 52c. Anne Murray | 1·00 | 1·10 |
| 2503 52c. Paul Anka | 1·00 | 1·10 |

(b) Ordinary gum.

| | | |
|---|---|---|
| **MS**2504 Circular 105×105 mm. As Nos. 2500/3 | 3·25 | 4·00 |

**880** Sunrise over Alexander Bay, Terra Nova National Park, Newfoundland

**2007.** 50th Anniv of Terra Nova National Park, Newfoundland. Self-adhesive.

| | | | | |
|---|---|---|---|---|
| 2505 | **880** | 52c. multicoloured | 1·00 | 1·00 |

**881** Jasper National Park

**2007.** Centenary of Jasper National Park, Alberta. Self-adhesive.

| | | | | |
|---|---|---|---|---|
| 2506 | **881** | 52c. multicoloured | 1·00 | 1·00 |

**882** Scouts forming Emblem

**2007.** Centenary of Scouting. Self-adhesive.

| | | | | |
|---|---|---|---|---|
| 2507 | **882** | 52c. multicoloured | 1·25 | 1·00 |

**883** Membertou (Grand Chief of the Mi'kmaq) and French Settlement, Port Royal

**2007.** French Settlement in North America (4th issue). Chief Membertou.

| | | | | |
|---|---|---|---|---|
| 2508 | **883** | 52c. multicoloured | 1·00 | 85 |

**884** Founding Members and Registry Roll

**2007.** Centenary of the Law Society of Saskatchewan.

| | | | | |
|---|---|---|---|---|
| 2509 | **884** | 52c. multicoloured | 1·00 | 1·00 |

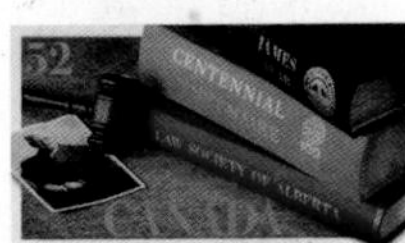

**885** Books, Photograph of James Muir Gavel (first President)

**2007.** Centenary of the Law Society of Alberta.

| | | | | |
|---|---|---|---|---|
| 2510 | **885** | 52c. multicoloured | 1·00 | 85 |

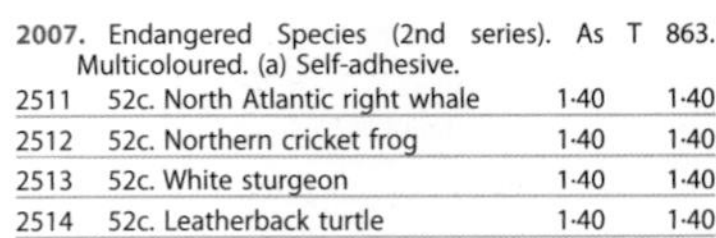

**2007.** Endangered Species (2nd series). As T 863. Multicoloured. (a) Self-adhesive.

| | | |
|---|---|---|
| 2511 52c. North Atlantic right whale | 1·40 | 1·40 |
| 2512 52c. Northern cricket frog | 1·40 | 1·40 |
| 2513 52c. White sturgeon | 1·40 | 1·40 |
| 2514 52c. Leatherback turtle | 1·40 | 1·40 |

(b) Ordinary gum. Size 48×24 mm.

| | | |
|---|---|---|
| **MS**2515 160×75 mm. As Nos. 2511/14 | 5·00 | 5·00 |

**886** *Hippodamia convergens* and (convergent lady beetle)

**2007.** Beneficial Insects. . Multicoloured.

| | | |
|---|---|---|
| 2516 1c. Type **886** | 10 | 10 |
| 2517 2c. *Danaus plexippus* (monarch butterfly caterpilliar) | 10 | 10 |
| 2518 3c. *Chrysopa oculata* (golden-eyed lacewing) | 10 | 10 |
| 2518a 4c. *Polistes fuscatus* (paper wasp) | 10 | 10 |
| 2519 5c. *Bombus polaris* (northern bumblebee) | 10 | 10 |
| 2519a 6c. *Zelus luridus* (assassin bug) | 15 | 10 |
| 2519b 7c. *Oncopeltus fasciatus* (large milkweed bug) | 20 | 15 |
| 2519c 8c. *Chauliognathus marginatus* (margined leatherwing) | 25 | 20 |
| 2519d 9c. *Chrysochus auratus* (dog-bane beetle) | 25 | 20 |
| 2520 10c. *Aeshna canadensis* (Canada darner dragonfly) | 25 | 20 |
| 2521 25c. *Hyalophora cecropia* (cecropia moth) | 50 | 40 |
| **MS**2522 133×58 mm. Nos. 2516/21 | 1·00 | 1·25 |
| **MS**2523 133×58 mm. Nos. 2518*a* and 2519*a/d* | 1·00 | 1·25 |

**887** Reindeer

**2007.** Christmas (1st issue). Self-adhesive.

| | | | | |
|---|---|---|---|---|
| 2526 | **887** | (52c.) multicoloured | 1·00 | 85 |

No. 2526 was inscribed 'P' and initially sold for 52c.

**888** Nativity ('HOPE')

**2007.** Christmas (2nd issue). Multicoloured. Self-adhesive.

| | | |
|---|---|---|
| 2527 (52c.) Type **888** | 1·00 | 85 |
| 2528 93c. Angel playing trumpet ('JOY') | 2·00 | 2·50 |
| 2529 $1.55 Dove ('PEACE') | 2·75 | 3·25 |

No. 2527 was inscribed 'P' and initially sold for 52c.

**889** *Odontioda* Island Red

**2007.** Flowers (3rd series). Canadian Hybrid Orchids. Multicoloured. (a) Self-adhesive.

| | | |
|---|---|---|
| 2530 (52c.) Type **889** | 1·00 | 85 |
| 2531 96c. *Potinara* Janet Elizabeth 'Fire Dancer' | 1·75 | 1·75 |
| 2532 $1.15 *Laeliocattleya* Memoria Evelyn Light | 1·90 | 1·90 |
| 2533 $1.60 *Masdevallia* Kaleidoscope 'Conni' | 2·75 | 3·00 |

(b) Ordinary gum.

| | | |
|---|---|---|
| **MS**2537 120×72 mm. As Nos. 2530/3 | 7·50 | 8·50 |

No. 2530 was inscribed 'P' and sold for 52c.

890 Rat Bride

2008. Chinese New Year ('Year of the Rat'). Multicoloured.

| | | | | |
|---|---|---|---|---|
| 2538 | 52c. Type **890** | | 1·25 | 1·00 |
| **MS**2539 130×100 mm. $1.60 Rat groom | | | 2·75 | 3·25 |

891 Fireworks

2008. Greetings Stamp. Self-adhesive.

| | | | | |
|---|---|---|---|---|
| 2540 | **891** | (52c.) multicoloured | 1·25 | 1·25 |

No. 2540 was inscribed 'P' and initially sold for 52c.

892 *Paeonia lactiflora* 'Elgin'

2008. Peonies. Multicoloured. (a) Self-adhesive.

| | | | |
|---|---|---|---|
| 2541 | 52c. Type **892** | 1·00 | 1·00 |
| 2542 | 52c. *Paeonia lactiflora* 'Coral 'n Gold' | 1·00 | 1·00 |

(b) Ordinary gum.

| | | |
|---|---|---|
| **MS**2543 120×84 mm. As Nos. 2541/2 | 2·00 | 2·25 |

893 Dentistry Building, University of Alberta (centenary)

2008. Canadian Universities' Anniversaries (7th issue). Multicoloured. Self-adhesive.

| | | | |
|---|---|---|---|
| 2544 | 52c. Type **893** | 1·00 | 1·00 |
| 2545 | 52c. Walter C. Koerner Library, University of British Columbia (centenary) | 1·00 | 1·00 |

894 Ice Hockey Players

2008. International Ice Hockey Federation World Championship, Halifax and Quebec. Self-adhesive.

| | | | | |
|---|---|---|---|---|
| 2546 | **894** | 52c. multicoloured | 1·00 | 1·00 |

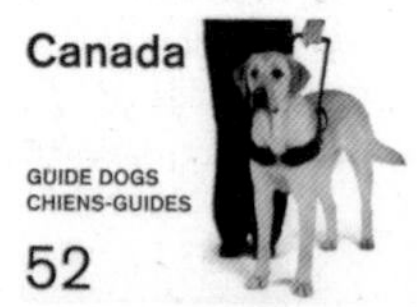

895 Guide Dog at Work

2008. Guide Dogs. Self-adhesive.

| | | | | |
|---|---|---|---|---|
| 2547 | **895** | 52c. multicoloured | 1·40 | 1·40 |

No. 2547 it has the face value in Braille.

896 Welder working on Pipeline

2008. Oil and Gas Industry. Multicoloured. Self-adhesive.

| | | | |
|---|---|---|---|
| 2548 | 52c. Type **896** | 1·10 | 1·10 |
| 2549 | 52c. James Miller Williams (drilled first Canadian oil well, 1858) and Charles Tripp (developed bitumen deposits of southwest Ontario, 1850s) | 1·10 | 1·10 |

897 Samuel de Champlain's Ship, Native Canoe and New Settlement of Quebec, 1608

2008. French Settlement in North America (5th issue). 400th Anniv of City of Quebec. Fluorescent frame.

| | | | | |
|---|---|---|---|---|
| 2550 | **897** | 52c. multicoloured | 1·00 | 90 |

A stamp in a similar design was issued by France.

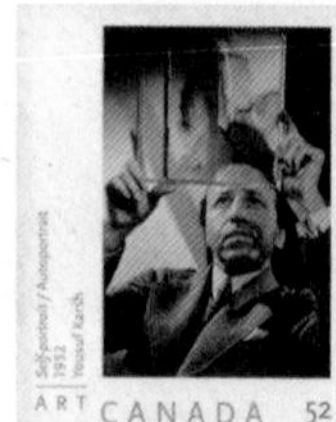
898 Self-portrait

2008. Art Canada. Birth Centenary of Yousuf Karsh (portrait photographer). Multicoloured. (a) Ordinary gum.

| | | | |
|---|---|---|---|
| 2551 | 52c. Type **898** | 1·00 | 90 |
| **MS**2552 150×87 mm. 52c. Type **898**; 96c. Audrey Hepburn; $1.60 Winston Churchill | | 5·25 | 6·00 |

(b) Self-adhesive.

| | | | |
|---|---|---|---|
| 2553 | 96c. Audrey Hepburn | 2·00 | 2·50 |
| 2554 | $1.60 Winston Churchill | 3·50 | 4·00 |

899 50 Cent Coin, 1908

2008. Centenary of the Royal Canadian Mint.

| | | | | |
|---|---|---|---|---|
| 2555 | **899** | 52c. multicoloured | 1·00 | 90 |

900 Nurse

2008. Centenary of Canadian Nurses Association. Self-adhesive.

| | | | | |
|---|---|---|---|---|
| 2556 | **900** | 52c. multicoloured | 1·10 | 1·10 |

901 Anne

2008. Centenary of Publication of Anne of Green Gables by Lucy Maud Montgomery. Multicoloured. (a) Self-adhesive.

| | | | |
|---|---|---|---|
| 2557 | 52c. Type **901** | 1·00 | 1·00 |
| 2558 | 52c. Green Gables (house), Cavendish, Prince Edward Island | 1·00 | 1·00 |

(b) Ordinary gum.

| | | |
|---|---|---|
| **MS**2559 124×72 mm. As Nos. 2557/8 | 1·75 | 2·00 |

2008. Canadians in Hollywood (2nd series). As T 853. Multicoloured. (a) Self-adhesive.

| | | | |
|---|---|---|---|
| 2560 | 52c. Norma Shearer | 1·25 | 1·25 |
| 2561 | 52c. Chief Dan George | 1·25 | 1·25 |
| 2562 | 52c. Marie Dressler | 1·25 | 1·25 |
| 2563 | 52c. Raymond Burr | 1·25 | 1·25 |

(b) Ordinary gum.

| | | |
|---|---|---|
| **MS**2564 136×77 mm. As Nos. 2560/3 | 4·00 | 4·50 |

902 Athlete and Canadian Flag

2008. Olympic Games, Beijing. Self-adhesive.

| | | | | |
|---|---|---|---|---|
| 2565 | **902** | 52c. multicoloured | 1·40 | 1·40 |

903 Lifeguard and Water Rescue

2008. Centenary of Lifesaving Society. Self-adhesive.

| | | | | |
|---|---|---|---|---|
| 2566 | **903** | 52c. multicoloured | 1·00 | 1·00 |

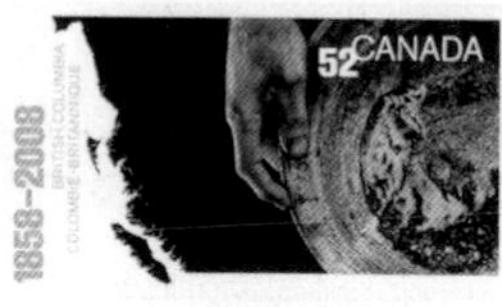
904 Panning for Gold

2008. 150th Anniv of British Columbia.

| | | | | |
|---|---|---|---|---|
| 2567 | **904** | 52c. multicoloured | 1·40 | 1·00 |

905 McLaughlin Buick, c. 1912 and Sam McLaughlin

2008. Sam McLaughlin (founder of McLaughlin Motor Car Company and philanthropist) Commemoration.

| | | | | |
|---|---|---|---|---|
| 2568 | **905** | 52c. multicoloured | 1·00 | 85 |

2008. Endangered Species (3rd series). As T 863. Multicoloured. (a) Self-adhesive.

| | | | |
|---|---|---|---|
| 2569 | 52c. Prothonotary warbler | 1·40 | 1·40 |
| 2570 | 52c. Taylor's checkerspot (butterfly) | 1·40 | 1·40 |
| 2571 | 52c. Roseate tern | 1·40 | 1·40 |
| 2572 | 52c. Burrowing owl | 1·40 | 1·40 |

(b)Ordinary gum. Size 48×24 mm.

| | | |
|---|---|---|
| **MS**2573 160×75 mm. As Nos. 2569/72 | 5·00 | 5·50 |

906 Woman with Megaphone

2008. Mental Health. Self-adhesive.

| | | | | |
|---|---|---|---|---|
| 2574 | **906** | (52c.)+10c. multicoloured | 1·25 | 1·40 |

No. 2574 was inscribed 'P+10' and initially sold for 52c. plus a 10c. surcharge for the Canada Post Foundation for Mental Health.

907 Québec City Skyline

2008. 12th Francophone Summit, Quebec.

| | | | | |
|---|---|---|---|---|
| 2575 | **907** | 52c. multicoloured | 1·00 | 85 |

908 Infant Jesus (creche figure by Antonio Caruso)

2008. Christmas (1st issue). Self-adhesive.

| | | | | |
|---|---|---|---|---|
| 2576 | **908** | (52c.) multicoloured | 1·10 | 85 |

No. 2576 was inscribed 'P' and was initially valid for 52c.

909 Child making Snow Angels

2008. Christmas (2nd issue). Winter Fun. Showing children. (a) Self-adhesive.

| | | | |
|---|---|---|---|
| 2577 | (52c.) Type **909** | 1·10 | 85 |
| 2578 | 96c. Child skiing | 1·90 | 2·25 |
| 2579 | $1.60 Child tobogganing | 3·00 | 3·50 |

(b) Ordinary gum.

| | | |
|---|---|---|
| **MS**2580 102×72 mm. As Nos. 2577/9 | 5·50 | 6·50 |

No. 2577 was inscribed 'P' and was initially valid for 52c.

910 Ox

2009. Chinese New Year. Year of the Ox. Multicoloured.

| | | | |
|---|---|---|---|
| 2581 | (54c.) Type **910** | 1·40 | 1·00 |
| **MS**2582 40×140 mm. $1.65 Earthenware cooking pot by Shu-Hwei Kao | | 3·25 | 3·75 |

No. 2581 was inscribed 'P' and initially sold for 54c. It has a background flower pattern which extends over the stamps and sheet margins.

2009. China 2009 World Stamp Exhibition. No. MS2582 optd with CHINA 2009 logo in gold on the sheet margin.

| | | |
|---|---|---|
| **MS**2583 40×140 mm. $1.65 Earthenware cooking pot by Shu-Hwei Kao | 3·25 | 3·75 |

911 Freestyle Skiing

2009. Winter Olympic Games, Vancouver, 2010 (1st issue). Olympic Sports. Multicoloured. (a) Self-adhesive.

| | | | |
|---|---|---|---|
| 2584 | (54c.) Type **911** | 1·40 | 1·40 |
| 2585 | (54c.) Snowboarding | 1·40 | 1·40 |
| 2586 | (54c.) Ice sledge hockey | 1·40 | 1·40 |
| 2587 | (54c.) Bobsleigh | 1·40 | 1·40 |
| 2588 | (54c.) Curling | 1·40 | 1·40 |

(b) Ordinary gum.

| | | |
|---|---|---|
| **MS**2589 140×82 mm. As Nos. 2584/8 | 5·75 | 6·25 |

Nos. 2584/8 and stamps from **MS**2589 were all inscribed 'P' and initially sold for 54c. each.

912 Vancouver 2010 Winter Olympic Games Emblem

2009. Winter Olympic Games, Vancouver, 2010 (2nd issue). Mascots and Emblems. Multicoloured. (a) Self-adhesive.

| | | | |
|---|---|---|---|
| 2590 | (54c.) Type **912** | 1·00 | 1·25 |
| 2591 | (54c.) Vancouver 2010 Paralympic Games emblem | 1·00 | 1·25 |
| 2592 | 98c. Miga skiing | 2·00 | 2·25 |
| 2593 | $1.18 Sumi curling (12 Feb) | 2·25 | 2·75 |
| 2594 | $1.65 Quatchi playing ice hockey | 3·25 | 3·75 |

(b) Ordinary gum.

| | | |
|---|---|---|
| **MS**2598 140×82 mm. As Nos. 2590/4 | 9·00 | 10·00 |

Nos. 2590/1 were initially sold for 54c. each.

**913** Stylized Ribbons, Fireworks and Confetti bursting from Envelope

**2009.** Greetings Stamp. 'Celebrate'. Self-adhesive.

| | | | | |
|---|---|---|---|---|
| 2599 | **913** | (54c.) multicoloured | 1·10 | 1·00 |

No. 2599, inscribed 'P', was initially sold for 54c.

**914** Rosemary Brown (civil rights campaigner) and BC Legislative Building

**2009.** Black History Month. Multicoloured.

| | | | |
|---|---|---|---|
| 2600 | 54c. Type **914** | 1·00 | 1·25 |
| 2601 | 54c. Abraham Doras Shadd (holding lantern) and runaway slaves | 1·00 | 1·25 |

**915** Flight of *Silver Dart*, Bras d'Or Lake, Nova Scotia, 23 February 1909

**2009.** Centenary of First Powered Flight in Canada. Self-adhesive.

| | | | | |
|---|---|---|---|---|
| 2602 | **915** | (54c.) multicoloured | 1·50 | 1·00 |

**916** White Rhododendron with Pink Buds

**2009.** Rhododendrons. Multicoloured. (a) Self-adhesive.

| | | | |
|---|---|---|---|
| 2603 | 54c. Type **916** | 1·10 | 1·25 |
| 2604 | 54c. Deep pink rhododendron | 1·10 | 1·25 |

(b) Ordinary gum.

| | | | |
|---|---|---|---|
| **MS**2605 | 120×74 mm. As Nos. 2603/4 | 2·00 | 2·50 |

**917** *Striped Column* (Jack Bush), 1964

**2009.** Art Canada. Birth Centenary of Jack Bush (artist). Design showing paintings. Multicoloured.

| | | | |
|---|---|---|---|
| 2606 | 54c. Type **917** | 1·00 | 85 |
| **MS**2607 | 150×87 mm. No. 2606; Chopsticks, 1977 (57×23 mm) | 4·00 | 4·50 |

**918** Horsehead Nebula and Dominion Astrophysical Observatory, Saanich, BC

**2009.** International Year of Astronomy. Multicoloured. (a) Self-adhesive.

| | | | |
|---|---|---|---|
| 2608 | 54c. Type **918** | 1·10 | 1·25 |
| 2609 | 54c. Eagle Nebula and Canada-France-Hawaii Telescope, Mauna Kea, Hawaii | 1·10 | 1·25 |

(b) Ordinary gum.

| | | | |
|---|---|---|---|
| **MS**2610 | 101×90 mm. As Nos. 2608/9 but 30×40 mm | 2·00 | 2·50 |

**919** Polar Bear

**2009.** Preserve the Polar Regions and Glaciers. Multicoloured.

| | | | |
|---|---|---|---|
| 2611 | 54c. Type **919** | 1·25 | 1·25 |
| 2612 | 54c. Arctic tern | 1·25 | 1·25 |
| **MS**2613 | 120×80 mm. Nos. 2611/12 | 2·50 | 2·50 |

**920** Canadian Horse

**2009.** Canadian Horse and Newfoundland Pony. Multicoloured. Self-adhesive.

| | | | |
|---|---|---|---|
| 2614 | 54c. Type **920** | 1·40 | 1·40 |
| 2615 | 54c. Newfoundland Pony | 1·40 | 1·40 |

Nos. 2614/2615 form a composite background design.

**921** Canadian Flag and Globe

**2009.** Centenary of Department of Foreign Affairs and International Trade.

| | | | | |
|---|---|---|---|---|
| 2616 | **921** | 54c. multicoloured | 1·25 | 1·00 |

**922** Niagara Falls in 1909 and 2009

**2009.** Centenary of the Boundary Waters Treaty.

| | | | | |
|---|---|---|---|---|
| 2617 | **922** | 54c. multicoloured | 1·00 | 85 |

**923** Robert Charlebois

**2009.** Canadian Recording Artists. Multicoloured. (a) Self-adhesive.

| | | | |
|---|---|---|---|
| 2618 | 54c. Type **923** | 80 | 90 |
| 2619 | 54c. Edith Butler | 80 | 90 |
| 2620 | 54c. Stompin' Tom Connors | 80 | 90 |
| 2621 | 54c. Bryan Adams | 80 | 90 |

(b) Ordinary gum.

| | | | |
|---|---|---|---|
| **MS**2622 | Circular 105×105 mm. As Nos. 2618/21 | 4·00 | 4·50 |

**924** Mr. PG, Prince George, British Columbia

**2009.** Roadside Attractions. Multicoloured. (a) Self-adhesive.

| | | | |
|---|---|---|---|
| 2623 | 54c. Type **924** | 1·40 | 1·50 |
| 2624 | 54c. Sign Post Forest, Watson Lake, Yukon | 1·40 | 1·50 |
| 2625 | 54c. Inukshuk (stone giant), Hay River, Northwest Territories | 1·40 | 1·50 |
| 2626 | 54c. Pysanka (giant Easter egg), Vegreville, Alberta | 1·40 | 1·50 |

(b) Ordinary gum.

| | | | |
|---|---|---|---|
| **MS**2627 | 98×109 mm. As Nos. 2623/6 | 4·00 | 5·00 |

**925** Captain Bartlett with Sextant and *Roosevelt* in the Canadian Arctic

**2009.** Captain Robert Abram 'Bob' Bartlett (Arctic explorer, ice captain and scientist) Commemoration.

| | | | | |
|---|---|---|---|---|
| 2628 | **925** | 54c. multicoloured | 1·25 | 85 |

No. 2628 commemorates the centenary of Capt. Bartlett's attempt to reach the North Pole.

**926** Five-pin Bowling

**2009.** Canadian Inventions. Sports. Multicoloured. Self-adhesive.

| | | | |
|---|---|---|---|
| 2629 | 54c. Type **926** | 1·25 | 1·40 |
| 2630 | 54c. Ringette | 1·25 | 1·40 |
| 2631 | 54c. Lacrosse | 1·25 | 1·40 |
| 2632 | 54c. Basketball | 1·25 | 1·40 |

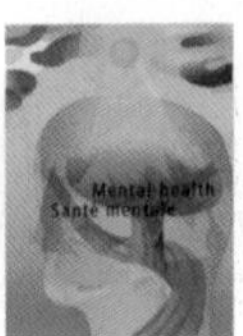


**927** Tree and River inside Human Head and Sun breaking through Clouds

**2009.** Mental Health. Self-adhesive.

| | | | | |
|---|---|---|---|---|
| 2633 | **927** | (54c.)+10c. multicoloured | 1·25 | 1·40 |

No. 2633 was inscr 'P+10' and was initially valid for 54c. plus a 10c. surcharge for the Canada Post Foundation for Mental Health.

**928** Detail from Maurice Richard's Hockey Sweater

**929** Maurice Richard, 19 October 1957

**2009.** Centenary of Montreal Canadiens (ice hockey team). Multicoloured. Self-adhesive. (a)

| | | | | |
|---|---|---|---|---|
| 2634 | **928** | (54c.) multicoloured | 1·25 | 1·25 |

(b) Sheet 130×100 mm containing T929 and similar horiz designs showing 500th goals of famous players.

| | | | |
|---|---|---|---|
| **MS**2635 | $3 Type **929**; Jean Beliveau, 11 February 1971; Guy Lafleur, 20 December 1983 | 18·00 | 20·00 |

No. 2634 was inscribed 'P' and originally valid for 54c.

The stamps within No. **MS**2635 are based on digital clips and use Motionstamp technology to show action replays of goals.

**930** Two Soldiers (detail from National War Memorial, Ottawa)

**2009.** 'Lest We Forget'. (a) Self-adhesive.

| | | | | |
|---|---|---|---|---|
| 2636 | **930** | (54c.) multicoloured | 1·10 | 1·10 |

(b) Ordinary gum.

| | | | |
|---|---|---|---|
| **MS**2637 | 108×60 mm. As Type **930**×2 | 2·50 | 3·00 |

No. 2636 and the stamps within **MS**2637 were all inscr 'P' and were originally valid for 54c.

**MS**2637 was originally sold for $1.08.

**931** Madonna and Infant Jesus

**2009.** Christmas (1st issue). Showing creche figures by Antonio Caruso. Multicoloured. (a) Self-adhesive.

| | | | |
|---|---|---|---|
| 2638 | (54c.) Type **931** | 1·25 | 95 |
| 2639 | 98c. Magi with gift | 2·00 | 2·50 |
| 2640 | $1.65 Shepherd carrying lamb | 3·25 | 4·00 |

(b) Ordinary gum.

| | | | |
|---|---|---|---|
| **MS**2641 | 150×100 mm. As Nos. 2576 and 2638/40 | 7·00 | 8·00 |

No. 2638 was inscr 'P' and was originally valid for 54c.

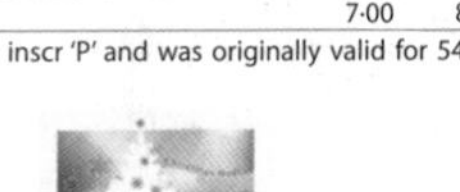

**932** Christmas Tree

**2009.** Christmas (2nd issue). Self-adhesive.

| | | | | |
|---|---|---|---|---|
| 2642 | **932** | (54c.) multicoloured | 1·10 | 85 |

No. 2642 was inscribed 'P' and was initially valid for 54c.

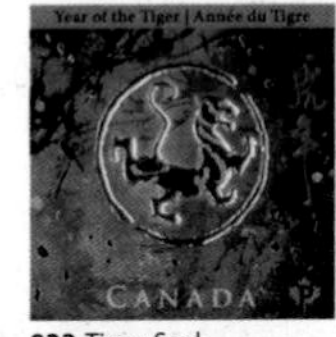


**933** Tiger Seal

**2010.** Chinese New Year. Year of the Tiger.

| | | | |
|---|---|---|---|
| 2643 | (54c.) Type **933** | 1·25 | 1·00 |
| **MS**2644 | 40×140 mm. 170c. Tiger's head seal | 3·50 | 4·00 |

**934** Striped Coralroot (*Corallorhiza striata*)

**2010.** Flowers (4th series). Wild Orchids. Multicoloured. (a) Self-adhesive coil stamps.

| | | | |
|---|---|---|---|
| 2645 | (57c.) Type **934** | 1·10 | 95 |
| 2646 | $1 Giant helleborine (*Epipactis gigantea*) | 2·25 | 2·00 |
| 2647 | $1.22 Rose pogonia (*Pogonia ophioglossoides*) | 2·40 | 2·75 |
| 2648 | $1.70 Grass pink (*Calopogon tuberosus*) | 3·50 | 3·75 |

(b) Self-adhesive.

| | | | |
|---|---|---|---|
| 2649 | $1 As No. 2646 | 2·50 | 2·75 |
| 2650 | $1.22 As No. 2647 | 2·75 | 3·25 |
| 2651 | $1.70 As No. 2648 | 4·00 | 4·50 |

(c) Ordinary gum.

| | | | |
|---|---|---|---|
| **MS**2652 | 120×72 mm. As Nos. 2645/8 | 9·25 | 9·75 |

No. 2645 was inscribed 'P' and originally sold for 57c.

**935** Whistler, British Columbia

**2010.** Olympic Winter Games, Vancouver (3rd issue). Multicoloured. (a) Self-adhesive.

2653 57c. Type **935** 1·40 1·40
2654 57c. Vancouver 1·40 1·40

(b) Ordinary gum.

**MS**2655 141×83 mm. As Nos. 2653/4 2·75 3·25

**936** William Hall, V.C. in 1900 and HMS *Shannon*

**2010.** Black History Month.

2656 **936** 57c. multicoloured 1·50 1·10

**937** *Romeo LeBlanc* (Christan Nicholson)

**2010.** Romeo LeBlanc (former Minister of Fisheries and Governor General of Canada 1995–9) Commemoration.

2657 **937** 57c. multicoloured 1·25 1·10

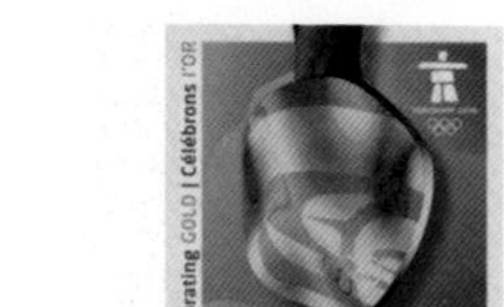


**938** Vancouver 2010 Olympic Gold Medal

**2010.** Olympic Winter Games, Vancouver (4th issue). Canada's First Olympic Gold on Canadian Soil. (a) Self-adhesive.

2658 **938** 57c. multicoloured 1·40 1·25

(b) Ordinary gum.

**MS**2659 150×60 mm. As Type **938**×2 2·50 2·75

**939** Child with Painted Face, Bobsleigh and Speed Skaters

**2010.** Olympic Winter Games, Vancouver (5th issue). Multicoloured. (a) Self-adhesive.

2660 57c. Type **939** 1·40 1·40
2661 57c. Child with painted face, Chandra Crawford with gold medal (Turin 2006) and skiers 1·40 1·40

(b) Ordinary gum.

**MS**2662 134×60 mm. As Nos. 2660/1 2·50 2·75

**940** African Violet 'Decelles' Avalanche'

**2010.** African Violets. Multicoloured. (a) Self-adhesive.

2663 (57c.) Type **940** 1·40 1·40
2664 (57c.) African violet 'Picasso' (violet and white flowers) 1·40 1·40

(b) Ordinary gum.

**MS**2665 120×82 mm. As Nos. 2663/4 2·50 2·75

Nos. 2663/4 and the stamps within **MS**2665 were all inscr 'P' and were originally valid for 57c.

**MS**2665 was originally sold for $1.14.

**941** Figures forming Maple Leaf and Star of David

**2010.** Canada–Israel, 60 Years of Friendship. Self-adhesive.

2666 **941** $1.70 rosine, new blue and brownish grey 4·25 4·50

A similar design was issued by Israel,

**942** Tee Yee Neen Ho Ga Row

**2010.** Four Indian Kings paintings by John Verelst. Multicoloured.

2667 57c. Type **942** 1·60 1·60
2668 57c. Sa Ga Yeath Qua Pieth Tow 1·60 1·60
2669 57c. Ho Nee Yeath Taw No Row 1·60 1·60
2670 57c. Etow Oh Koam 1·60 1·60
**MS**2671 168×75 mm. Nos. 2667/70 5·75 5·75

The portraits show representatives of the Iroquois and Algonquin nations who travelled to London in 1710 for an audience with Queen Anne.

**2010.** London 2010 Festival of Stamps. No. MS2671 optd with LONDON 2010 FESTIVAL OF STAMPSlogo on the sheet margin.

**MS**2672 168×75 mm. Nos. 2667/70 5·00 5·50

**943** HMCS *Niobe* and Sailor, c. 1910

**2010.** Centenary of the Canadian Navy. Multicoloured. (a) Self-adhesive.

2673 57c. Type **943** 1·40 1·40
2674 57c. HMCS *Halifax* (modern frigate) and Wren 1·40 1·40

(b) Ordinary gum.

**MS**2675 108×64 mm. As Nos. 2673/4 2·75 3·00

**944** Harbour Porpoise (Phocoena phocoena)

**2010.** . Each black, dull ultramarine and turquoise-blue.

2676 57c. Type **944** 1·40 1·40
2677 57c. Sea otter (*Enhydra lutris* 1·40 1·40
**MS**2678 105×69 mm. As Nos. 2676/7 2·50 2·75

Stamps of a similar design were issued by Sweden.

**945** *Selasphorus rufus* (hummingbird) (Wing Yan Tam)

**2010.** Canadian Geographic's Wildlife Photography of the Year

(a) Self-adhesive. Die-cut perf 13

2679 57c. Type **945** 1·40 1·40
2680 57c. *Tachycineta bicolor* (tree swallows) (Mark Bradley) 1·40 1·40
2681 57c. *Tettigoniidae* (katydid) (Julie Bazinet) (vert) 1·40 1·40
2682 57c. *Ardea herodias* (great blue heron) (Martin Cooper) (vert) 1·40 1·40
2683 57c. *Vulpes vulpes* (red fox) (Ben Boulter) (vert) 1·40 1·40

(b) Ordinary gum. P 12½×13

**MS**2684 150×100 mm. As Nos. 2679/83 6·25 6·75

**946** Man wearing Rotary Vest

**2010.** Centenary of Rotary International

2685 **946** 57c. multicoloured 1·40 1·40

**947** Rollande, 1929

**2010.** Art Canada. Multicoloured.

2686 57c. Type **947** 1·25 1·10
**MS**2687 150×87 mm. 57c. Type **947**; $1.70 *At the Theatre*, 1928 (42×40 mm) 5·50 6·00

**2010.** Roadside Attractions (2nd series)

(a) Self-adhesive

2688 (57c.) The Coffee Pot, David-son, SK 1·40 1·40
2689 (57c.) Happy Rock, Gladstone, Manitoba 1·40 1·40
2690 (57c.) Goose, Wawa, Ontario 1·40 1·40
2691 (57c.) Puffin, Longue-Pointe-de-Mingan, Quebec 1·40 1·40

(b) Ordinary gum

**MS**2692 99×109 mm. As Nos. 2688/91 5·00 5·00

Nos. 2688/91 and the stamps within **MS**2692 were all inscr 'P' and were originally valid for 57c.

**948** Guides

**2010.** Centenary of Girl Guides of Canada

2693 **948** (57c.) multicoloured 1·40 1·40

No. 2693 was inscr 'P' and was originally valid for 57c.

**949** Coins, Glass and Amber Trading Beads and 17th-century Map of Avalon Peninsula, Newfoundland

**2010.** 400th Anniv of Cupids, Newfoundland (first English settlement in Canada)

2694 **949** 57c. multicoloured 1·25 1·10

**950** Immigrant Boy, Boy ploughing and SS Sardinian

**2010.** 'Home Children' (British orphaned and abandoned children sent to Canada)

2695 **950** 57c. multicoloured 1·25 1·10

**951** Mental Health Patient on Road to Recovery

**2010.** Mental Health

2696 **951** (57c.)+10c. multicoloured 1·40 1·40

No. 2696 was inscr 'P+10' and was initially valid for 57c. plus a 10c. surcharge for the Canada Post Foundation for Mental Health.

**952** Our Lady of the Night (sculpture by Antonio Caruso)

**2010.** Christmas (1st issue)

2697 **952** (57c.) multicoloured 1·25 1·10

**953** Red Baubles

**2010.** Christmas (2nd issue). Multicoloured.

(a) Self-adhesive

2698 (57c.) Type **953** 1·25 1·10
2699 $1 Blue baubles 2·40 2·25
2700 $1.70 Pink baubles 3·75 3·50

(b) Ordinary gum

**MS**2701 116×60 mm. As Nos. 2698/700 7·50 7·75

**954** Rabbit

**2011.** Chinese New Year. Year of the Rabbit. Multicoloured.

2702 (59c.) Type **954** 1·25 1·10
**MS**2703 140x40mm. $1.75 Two rabbits (on medallion) 3·75 3·50

**955** Arctic Hares

**2011.** Young Wildlife. Multicoloured.

(a) Self-adhesive coil stamps

2704 (59c.) Type **955** 1·25 1·10
2705 $1.03 Red fox cub 2·25 2·10
2706 $1.25 Two Canada geese goslings 2·75 2·50
2707 $1.75 Polar bear cub 3·75 3·50

(b) Self-adhesive

2708 $1.03 As No. 2705 2·25 2·10
2709 $1.25 As No. 2706 2·75 2·50
2710 $1.75 As No. 2707 3·75 3·50

(c) Ordinary gum

**MS**2711 120×72 mm. As Nos. 2704/7 10·00 9·50

No. 2704 was inscribed 'P' and originally sold for 59c.

Nos. 2712/27 are left for additions to this definitive series.

**956** Canadian Flag on Soldier's Uniform and Helicopter lifting Supplies

**2011.** 'Canadian Pride'. Multicoloured.

(a) Self-adhesive booklet stamps

| | | | |
|---|---|---|---|
| 2728 | (59c.) Type **956** | 1·25 | 1·10 |
| 2729 | (59c.) Canadian flag on hot air balloon | 1·25 | 1·10 |
| 2730 | (59c.) Canadian flag on search and rescue uniform and ship | 1·25 | 1·10 |
| 2731 | (59c.) Canadian flag on Canadarm | 1·25 | 1·10 |
| 2732 | (59c.) Canadian flag on back-pack and Colosseum, Rome | 1·25 | 1·10 |

(b) Ordinary gum

| | | |
|---|---|---|
| **MS**2749 148×70 mm. As Nos. 2728/32 | 6·25 | 6·00 |

Nos. 2728/32 and the stamps within **MS**2749 were all inscr 'P' and originally valid for 59c. each.

Nos. 2733/48 are left for additions to this definitive series.

**957** Carrie Best (journalist and civil rights campaigner)

**2011.** Black History Month. Multicoloured.

| | | | |
|---|---|---|---|
| 2750 | 59c. Type **957** | 1·25 | 1·10 |
| 2751 | 59c. Fergie (Ferguson) Jenkins (baseball pitcher) | 1·25 | 1·10 |

**958** Wrapped Gift

**2011.** Greetings Stamp. 'Celebration'

| | | | | |
|---|---|---|---|---|
| 2752 | **958** | (59c.) multicoloured | 1·25 | 1·10 |

No. 2752, inscribed 'P', was initially valid for 59c.

**959** *Pow-wow Dancer*, 1978

**2011.** Art Canada. Paintings by Daphne Odjig

(a) Ordinary gum

| | | | |
|---|---|---|---|
| 2753 | 59c. Type **959** | 1·25 | 1·10 |
| **MS**2754 | 150×87 mm. 59c. Type **959**; $1.03 *Pow-wow*, 1969 (32×39 mm); $1.75 *Spiritual Renewal*, 1984 (55×39 mm) | 7·50 | 7·25 |

(b) Self-adhesive

| | | | |
|---|---|---|---|
| 2755 | $1.03 *Pow-wow*, 1969 (32×39 mm) | 2·25 | 2·10 |
| 2756 | $1.75 *Spiritual Renewal*, 1984 (55×39 mm) | 3·75 | 3·50 |

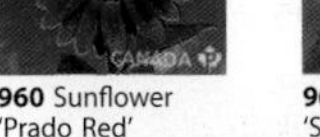

**960** Sunflower 'Prado Red' **961** Sunflower 'Sunbright'

**2011.** Sunflowers (*Helianthus annuus*)

(a) Coil stamps. Horiz designs as T **960**. Self-adhesive.

| | | | |
|---|---|---|---|
| 2757 | (59c.) Type **960** | 1·40 | 1·25 |
| 2758 | (59c.) Sunflower 'Sunbright' | 1·40 | 1·25 |

(b) Booklet stamps. Vert designs as T **961**. Self-adhesive

| | | | |
|---|---|---|---|
| 2759 | (59c.) Sunflower 'Prado Red' | 1·40 | 1·25 |
| 2760 | (59c.) Type **961** | 1·40 | 1·20 |

(c) Ordinary gum. Sheet 120×84 mm containing T **961** and similar vert design

| | | |
|---|---|---|
| **MS**2761 (59c.) Sunflower 'Prado Red'; (59c.) As Type **961** | 2·50 | 2·25 |

Nos. 2757/60 and the stamps within **MS**2761 were all inscr 'P' and were originally valid for 59c.

**962** Ram's Head

**2011.** Signs of the Zodiac (1st series). Aries

| | | | | |
|---|---|---|---|---|
| 2762 | **962** | (59c.) multicoloured | 1·40 | 1·25 |

No. 2762 was inscr P' and was originally valid for 59c.

## OFFICIAL STAMPS

**1949.** Optd O.H.M.S.

| | | | | |
|---|---|---|---|---|
| O162 | **111** | 1c. green (postage) | 4·25 | 5·00 |
| O163 | **112** | 2c. brown | 12·00 | 12·00 |
| O164 | - | 3c. purple (No. 378) | 3·25 | 3·50 |
| O165 | **112** | 4c. red | 4·25 | 4·50 |
| O171 | - | 7c. blue (No. 407) (air) | 24·00 | 10·00 |
| O166 | - | 10c. green (No. 402) | 6·00 | 15 |
| O167 | - | 14c. sepia (No. 403) | 11·00 | 5·50 |
| O168 | - | 20c. grey (No. 404) | 12·00 | 60 |
| O169 | - | 50c. green (No. 405) | £170 | £130 |
| O170 | - | $1 purple (No. 406) | 45·00 | 60·00 |

**1949.** Optd O.H.M.S.

| | | | | |
|---|---|---|---|---|
| O172 | **135** | 1c. green | 4·00 | 2·50 |
| O173 | - | 2c. sepia (No. 415) | 3·50 | 3·00 |
| O174 | - | 3c. purple (No. 416) | 2·75 | 2·50 |
| O175 | - | 4c. red (No. 417) | 2·75 | 35 |
| O176 | - | 5c. blue (No. 418) | 7·50 | 2·25 |
| O177 | **141** | 50c. green | 38·00 | 40·00 |

**1950.** Optd G.

| | | | | |
|---|---|---|---|---|
| O178 | **135** | 1c. green (postage) | 1·50 | 10 |
| O179 | - | 2c. sepia (No. 415) | 4·00 | 4·75 |
| O180 | - | 2c. green (No. 415a) | 1·75 | 10 |
| O181 | - | 3c. purple (No. 416) | 2·25 | 10 |
| O183 | - | 4c. red (No. 417) | 3·00 | 60 |
| O184 | - | 5c. blue (No. 418) | 5·50 | 2·00 |
| O190 | - | 7c. blue (No. 407) (air) | 24·00 | 15·00 |
| O193 | **153** | 7c. blue | 2·00 | 3·25 |
| O185 | - | 10c. green (No. 402) | 3·00 | 10 |
| O191 | **142** | 10c. purple | 4·00 | 1·00 |
| O186 | - | 14c. sepia (No. 403) | 23·00 | 11·00 |
| O187 | - | 20c. grey (No. 404) | 45·00 | 30 |
| O194 | - | 20c. grey (No. 441) | 2·00 | 20 |
| O188 | **141** | 50c. green | 17·00 | 21·00 |
| O189 | - | $1 purple (No. 406) | 75·00 | 75·00 |
| O192 | - | $1 blue (No. 433) | 75·00 | 80·00 |

**1953.** First Queen Elizabeth II stamps optd G.

| | | | | |
|---|---|---|---|---|
| O196 | **158** | 1c. brown | 15 | 10 |
| O197 | **158** | 2c. green | 20 | 10 |
| O198 | **158** | 3c. red | 20 | 10 |
| O199 | **158** | 4c. violet | 30 | 10 |
| O200 | **158** | 5c. blue | 30 | 10 |

**1953.** Pictorial stamps optd G.

| | | | | |
|---|---|---|---|---|
| O206 | **165** | 10c. brown | 70 | 60 |
| O207 | - | 20c. green (No. 488) | 3·25 | 30 |
| O201 | **160** | 50c. green | 3·25 | 4·00 |
| O195 | **154** | $1 black | 10·00 | 15·00 |

**1955.** Second Queen Elizabeth II stamps optd G.

| | | | | |
|---|---|---|---|---|
| O202 | **161** | 1c. brown | 65 | 20 |
| O203 | **161** | 2c. green | 15 | 20 |
| O204 | **161** | 4c. violet | 40 | 1·00 |
| O205 | **161** | 5c. blue | 15 | 10 |

**1963.** Third Queen Elizabeth II stamps optd G.

| | | | | |
|---|---|---|---|---|
| O208 | **215** | 1c. brown | 50 | 5·00 |
| O209 | **215** | 2c. green | 60 | 5·00 |
| O210 | **215** | 4c. red | 60 | 2·25 |
| O211 | **215** | 5c. blue | 50 | 2·50 |

## OFFICIAL SPECIAL DELIVERY STAMPS

**1950.** Optd O.H.M.S.

| | | | |
|---|---|---|---|
| OS20 | 10c. green (No. S15) | 17·00 | 30·00 |

**1950.** Optd G.

| | | | |
|---|---|---|---|
| OS21 | 10c. green (No. S15) | 26·00 | 30·00 |

## POSTAGE DUE STAMPS

**D1**

**1906**

| | | | | |
|---|---|---|---|---|
| D1 | **D1** | 1c. violet | 10·00 | 2·75 |
| D3 | **D1** | 2c. violet | 28·00 | 1·00 |
| D5 | **D1** | 4c. violet | 45·00 | 55·00 |
| D7 | **D1** | 5c. violet | 40·00 | 4·25 |
| D8 | **D1** | 10c. violet | 32·00 | 23·00 |

**D2**

**1930**

| | | | | |
|---|---|---|---|---|
| D9 | **D2** | 1c. violet | 8·50 | 11·00 |
| D10 | **D2** | 2c. violet | 7·50 | 1·90 |
| D11 | **D2** | 4c. violet | 15·00 | 6·50 |
| D12 | **D2** | 5c. violet | 16·00 | 38·00 |
| D13 | **D2** | 10c. violet | 65·00 | 38·00 |

**D3**

**1933**

| | | | | |
|---|---|---|---|---|
| D14 | **D3** | 1c. violet | 11·00 | 17·00 |
| D15 | **D3** | 2c. violet | 8·50 | 5·00 |
| D16 | **D3** | 4c. violet | 14·00 | 15·00 |
| D17 | **D3** | 10c. violet | 26·00 | 45·00 |

**D4**

**1935**

| | | | | |
|---|---|---|---|---|
| D18 | **D4** | 1c. violet | 80 | 10 |
| D19 | **D4** | 2c. violet | 3·75 | 10 |
| D20 | **D4** | 3c. violet | 6·00 | 5·00 |
| D21 | **D4** | 4c. violet | 1·50 | 10 |
| D22 | **D4** | 5c. violet | 6·00 | 4·75 |
| D23 | **D4** | 6c. violet | 2·00 | 3·00 |
| D24 | **D4** | 10c. violet | 70 | 10 |

**1967.** (a) Size 21×17½ mm.

| | | | | |
|---|---|---|---|---|
| D25 | **D5** | 1c. red | 1·75 | 4·50 |
| D26 | **D5** | 2c. red | 1·00 | 1·00 |
| D27 | **D5** | 3c. red | 1·75 | 5·00 |
| D28 | **D5** | 4c. red | 2·75 | 1·25 |
| D29 | **D5** | 5c. red | 4·25 | 5·50 |
| D30 | **D5** | 6c. red | 1·60 | 3·75 |
| D31 | **D5** | 10c. red | 2·00 | 2·50 |

**D5**

(b) Size 19½×16 mm.

| | | | |
|---|---|---|---|
| D32 | 1c. red | 75 | 30 |
| D33 | 2c. red | 1·00 | 3·00 |
| D34 | 3c. red | 2·75 | 4·00 |
| D35 | 4c. red | 60 | 60 |
| D36a | 5c. red | 30 | 2·00 |
| D37 | 6c. red | 2·75 | 3·75 |
| D38 | 8c. red | 30 | 45 |
| D39 | 10c. red | 40 | 45 |
| D40 | 12c. red | 30 | 50 |
| D41 | 16c. red | 4·00 | 4·75 |
| D42 | 20c. red | 30 | 1·25 |
| D43 | 24c. red | 30 | 1·50 |
| D44 | 50c. red | 40 | 2·00 |

## REGISTRATION STAMPS

**R1**

**1875**

| | | | | |
|---|---|---|---|---|
| R1 | **R1** | 2c. orange | 60·00 | 1·00 |
| R6 | **R1** | 5c. green | 85·00 | 1·25 |
| R9 | **R1** | 8c. blue | £375 | £275 |

## SPECIAL DELIVERY STAMPS

**S1**

**1898**

| | | | | |
|---|---|---|---|---|
| S2 | **S1** | 10c. green | 60·00 | 12·00 |

**S2**

**1922**

| | | | | |
|---|---|---|---|---|
| S4 | **S2** | 20c. red | 35·00 | 6·50 |

**S3** Mail-carrying, 1867 and 1927

**1927.** 60th Anniv of Confederation.

| | | | | |
|---|---|---|---|---|
| S5 | **S3** | 20c. orange | 11·00 | 13·00 |

**S4**

**1930**

| | | | | |
|---|---|---|---|---|
| S6 | **S4** | 20c. red | 42·00 | 7·00 |

**1932.** As Type S 4, but inscr "CENTS" instead of "TWENTY CENTS".

| | | | |
|---|---|---|---|
| S7 | 20c. red | 45·00 | 18·00 |

**S5** Allegory of Progress

**1935**

| | | | | |
|---|---|---|---|---|
| S8 | **S5** | 20c. red | 4·75 | 5·00 |

**S6** Canadian Coat of Arms

**1938**

| | | | | |
|---|---|---|---|---|
| S9 | **S6** | 10c. green | 21·00 | 4·00 |
| S10 | **S6** | 20c. red | 40·00 | 28·00 |

**1939.** Surch 10 10 and bars.

| | | | |
|---|---|---|---|
| S11 | 10c. on 20c. red | 10·00 | 17·00 |

**S8** Coat of Arms and Flags

**S9** Lockheed L.18 Lodestar

**1942**

| | | | | |
|---|---|---|---|---|
| S12 | **S8** | 10c. green (postage) | 9·50 | 30 |
| S13 | **S9** | 16c. blue (air) | 6·00 | 45 |
| S14 | **S9** | 17c. blue | 4·50 | 55 |

**1946**

| | | | |
|---|---|---|---|
| S15 | 10c. green (postage) | 8·50 | 60 |
| S16 | 17c. blue (air) | 4·50 | 8·00 |

DESIGNS: 10c. As Type S **8** but with wreath of leaves; 17c. As Type S **9** but with Canadair DC-4M North Star airplane.

Pt. 22

# CANAL ZONE

Territory adjacent to the Panama Canal leased by the U.S.A. from the Republic of Panama. The U.S. Canal Zone postal service closed on 30 September 1979.

1904. 100 centavos = 1 peso.
1906. 100 centesimos = 1 balboa.
1924. 100 cents = 1 dollar (U.S.).

**1904.** Stamps of Panama (with PANAMA optd twice) optd CANAL ZONE horiz in one line.

| | | | | |
|---|---|---|---|---|
| 1 | **5** | 2c. red (No. 54) | £450 | £350 |
| 2 | **5** | 5c. blue (No. 55) | £275 | £180 |
| 3 | **5** | 10c. orange (No. 56) | £375 | £225 |

**1904.** Stamps of the United States of 1902 optd CANAL ZONE PANAMA.

| | | | | |
|---|---|---|---|---|
| 4 | **103** | 1c. green | 36·00 | 20·00 |
| 5 | **117** | 2c. red | 27·00 | 25·00 |
| 6 | **107** | 5c. blue | £100 | 60·00 |
| 7 | **109** | 8c. violet | £160 | 95·00 |
| 8 | **110** | 10c. brown | £140 | 80·00 |

**1904.** 1905 stamps optd CANAL ZONE in two lines.

| | | | | |
|---|---|---|---|---|
| 9 | **38** | 1c. green | 3·25 | 2·30 |
| 10 | **38** | 2c. red | 5·00 | 3·00 |

**1904.** Stamps with PANAMA optd twice, optd CANAL ZONE in two lines or surch also.

| | | | | |
|---|---|---|---|---|
| 11 | **5** | 2c. red (No. 54) | 7·75 | 5·50 |
| 12 | **5** | 5c. blue (No. 55) | 8·75 | 4·00 |
| 14 | **5** | 8c. on 50c. brown (No. 65) | 35·00 | 25·00 |
| 13 | **5** | 10c. orange (No. 56) | 23·00 | 13·50 |

**1906.** 1892 stamps surch PANAMA on both sides and CANAL ZONE and new value in centre between bars.

| | | | |
|---|---|---|---|
| 19 | 1c. on 20c. violet (No. 64) | 2·20 | 1·70 |
| 22 | 2c. on 1p. red (No. 66) | 3·00 | 3·00 |

**1906.** 1906 stamps optd CANAL ZONE vert.

| | | | | |
|---|---|---|---|---|
| 26 | **42** | 1c. black and green | 2·75 | 1·20 |
| 27 | **43** | 2c. black and red | 3·50 | 1·50 |
| 28 | **45** | 5c. black and blue | 6·50 | 2·50 |
| 29 | **46** | 8c. black and purple | 23·00 | 8·75 |
| 30 | **47** | 10c. black and violet | 22·00 | 8·75 |

**1909.** 1909 stamps optd CANAL ZONE vert.

| | | | | |
|---|---|---|---|---|
| 35 | **48** | 1c. black and green | 4·25 | 1·40 |
| 36 | **49** | 2c. black and red | 5·00 | 1·50 |
| 37 | **51** | 5c. black and blue | 19·00 | 4·25 |
| 38 | **52** | 8c. black and purple | 13·00 | 6·50 |
| 43 | **53** | 10c. black and purple | 55·00 | 9·25 |

**1911.** Surch CANAL ZONE 10 cts.

| | | | | |
|---|---|---|---|---|
| 53 | **38** | 10c. on 13c. grey | 6·50 | 2·50 |

**1914.** Optd CANAL ZONE vert.

| | | | |
|---|---|---|---|
| 54 | 10c. grey | 55·00 | 13·50 |

**1915.** 1915 and 1918 stamps optd CANAL ZONE vert.

| | | | |
|---|---|---|---|
| 55 | 1c. black and green (No. 162) | 11·00 | 7·00 |
| 56 | 2c. black and red (No. 163) | 13·00 | 4·75 |
| 57 | 5c. black and blue (No. 166) | 12·00 | 6·25 |
| 58 | 10c. black & orange (No. 167) | 25·00 | 12·00 |
| 59 | 12c. black & violet (No. 178) | 19·00 | 5·50 |
| 60 | 15c. black & blue (No. 179) | 55·00 | 27·00 |
| 61 | 24c. black & brown (No. 180) | 46·00 | 15·00 |
| 62 | 50c. black & orange (No. 181) | £300 | £170 |
| 63 | 1b. black & violet (No. 182) | £190 | 70·00 |

**1921.** 1921 stamps optd CANAL ZONE vert.

| | | | | |
|---|---|---|---|---|
| 64 | **65** | 1c. green | 4·25 | 1·60 |
| 65 | - | 2c. red (No. 186) | 3·25 | 1·40 |
| 66 | **68** | 5c. blue | 12·00 | 3·75 |
| 67 | - | 10c. violet (No. 191) | 20·00 | 8·25 |
| 68 | - | 15c. blue (No. 192) | 55·00 | 19·00 |
| 69 | - | 24c. sepia (No. 194) | 75·00 | 25·00 |
| 70 | - | 50c. black (No. 195) | £160 | £100 |

**1924.** 1924 stamps optd CANAL ZONE vert.

| | | | | |
|---|---|---|---|---|
| 72 | **72** | 1c. green | 11·00 | 5·00 |
| 73 | **72** | 2c. red | 8·25 | 3·00 |

**1924.** Stamps of the United States of 1922 optd CANAL ZONE horiz.

| | | | |
|---|---|---|---|
| 74 | ½c. sepia (No. 559) | 1·90 | 80 |
| 75 | 1c. green (No. 602) | 2·00 | 1·10 |
| 76 | 1½c. brown (No. 603) | 2·75 | 1·90 |
| 103 | 2c. red (No. 604) | 2·75 | 1·40 |
| 87 | 3c. violet (No. 638a) | 4·00 | 3·50 |
| 88 | 5c. blue (No. 640) | 5·00 | 3·25 |
| 106 | 10c. orange (No. 645) | 19·00 | 11·00 |
| 90 | 12c. purple (No. 693) | 25·00 | 15·00 |
| 141 | 14c. blue (No. 695) | 5·00 | 3·75 |
| 92 | 15c. grey (No. 696) | 8·25 | 5·00 |
| 93 | 17c. black (No. 697) | 5·00 | 3·25 |
| 94 | 20c. red (No. 698) | 8·00 | 3·50 |
| 95 | 30c. sepia (No. 700) | 6·25 | 4·00 |
| 84 | 50c. mauve (No. 701) | 85·00 | 49·00 |
| 97 | $1 brown (No. 579) | £150 | 60·00 |

**1926.** Liberty Bell stamp of United States optd CANAL ZONE.

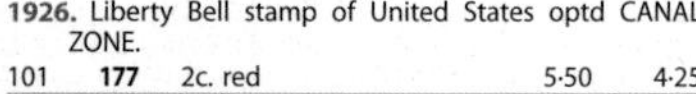

| | | | | |
|---|---|---|---|---|
| 101 | **177** | 2c. red | 5·50 | 4·25 |

**22** Gen. Gorgas **24** Panama Canal under Construction

**1928**

| | | | | |
|---|---|---|---|---|
| 107 | **22** | 1c. green | 25 | 10 |
| 108 | - | 2c. red | 25 | 10 |
| 109 | **24** | 5c. blue | 1·10 | 45 |
| 110 | - | 10c. orange | 25 | 20 |
| 111 | - | 12c. purple | 80 | 65 |
| 112 | - | 14c. blue | 95 | 75 |
| 113 | - | 15c. grey | 45 | 35 |
| 114 | - | 20c. brown | 65 | 20 |
| 115 | - | 30c. black | 95 | 75 |
| 116 | - | 50c. mauve | 1·60 | 70 |

PORTRAITS: 2c. Gen. Goethals. 10c. H. F. Hodges. 12c. Col. Gaillard. 14c. Gen. Sibert. 15c. Jackson Smith. 20c. Admiral Rousseau. 30c. Col. S. B. Williamson. 50c. Governor Blackburn.

**1929.** Air. Stamps of 1928 surch AIR MAIL and value.

| | | | | |
|---|---|---|---|---|
| 124 | - | 10c. on 50c. mauve | 9·25 | 6·50 |
| 117 | **22** | 15c. on 1c. green | 8·75 | 6·00 |
| 125 | - | 20c. on 2c. red | 5·25 | 1·60 |
| 119 | - | 25c. on 2c. red | 3·75 | 2·20 |

**36** Steamer, Panama Canal

**1931.** Air.

| | | | | |
|---|---|---|---|---|
| 126 | **36** | 4c. purple | 80 | 70 |
| 127 | **36** | 5c. green | 65 | 35 |
| 128 | **36** | 6c. brown | 80 | 40 |
| 129 | **36** | 10c. orange | 1·10 | 40 |
| 130 | **36** | 15c. blue | 1·40 | 40 |
| 131 | **36** | 20c. violet | 2·20 | 40 |
| 132 | **36** | 30c. red | 5·00 | 1·10 |
| 133 | **36** | 40c. yellow | 3·75 | 1·20 |
| 134 | **36** | $1 black | 9·75 | 1·70 |

**1933.** No. 720 of United States optd CANAL ZONE.

| | | | |
|---|---|---|---|
| 140 | 3c. violet | 3·00 | 35 |

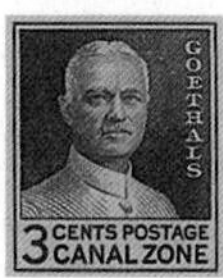


**38** Gen. Goethals

**1934.** 20th Anniv of Opening of Panama Canal.

| | | | | |
|---|---|---|---|---|
| 142 | **38** | 3c. violet | 25 | 20 |

**45** Balboa (before construction)

**1939.** 25th Anniv of Opening of Panama Canal and 10th Anniv of Canal Zone Airmail Service. (a) Postage. As T 45. Inscr "25TH ANNIVERSARY 1939 OPENING PANAMA CANAL 1914".

| | | | | |
|---|---|---|---|---|
| 149 | **45** | 1c. green | 70 | 35 |
| 150 | - | 2c. red | 75 | 40 |
| 151 | - | 3c. violet | 75 | 25 |
| 152 | - | 5c. blue | 1·70 | 1·40 |
| 153 | - | 6c. orange | 3·25 | 3·25 |
| 154 | - | 7c. black | 3·50 | 3·25 |
| 155 | - | 8c. green | 5·50 | 3·75 |
| 156 | - | 10c. blue | 3·75 | 5·50 |
| 157 | - | 11c. green | 8·75 | 8·75 |
| 158 | - | 12c. purple | 9·25 | 8·25 |
| 159 | - | 14c. violet | 9·25 | 8·25 |
| 160 | - | 15c. olive | 13·00 | 6·50 |
| 161 | - | 18c. red | 11·00 | 9·25 |
| 162 | - | 20c. brown | 16·00 | 8·25 |
| 163 | - | 25c. orange | 20·00 | 19·00 |
| 164 | - | 50c. purple | 31·00 | 6·50 |

DESIGNS: 2c. Balboa (after construction); 3c., 5c. Gaillard Cut; 6c., 7c. Bas Obispo; 8c., 10c. Gatun Locks; 11c., 12c. Canal Channel; 14c., 15c. Gamboa; 18c., 20c. Pedro Miguel Locks; 25c.50c. Gatun Spillway.

(b) Air. Inscr "TENTH ANNIVERSARY AIR MAIL" and "25TH ANNIVERSARY OPENING PANAMA CANAL".

| | | | |
|---|---|---|---|
| 143 | 5c. black | 4·25 | 2·50 |
| 144 | 10c. violet | 3·75 | 3·25 |
| 145 | 15c. brown | 5·50 | 1·10 |
| 146 | 25c. blue | 14·00 | 8·75 |
| 147 | 30c. red | 15·00 | 8·50 |
| 148 | $1 green | 38·00 | 30·00 |

DESIGNS—HORIZ: As Type **45**: 5c. Douglas DC-3 airplane over Sosa Hill; 10c. Douglas DC-3 airplane, Sikorsky S-42A flying boat and map of Central America; 15c. Sikorsky S-42A and Fort Amador; 25c. Sikorsky S-42A at Cristobal Harbour, Manzanillo Island; 30c. Sikorsky S-42A over Culebra Cut. $1 Sikorsky S-42A and palm trees.

**1939.** Stamps of United States (1938) optd CANAL ZONE.

| | | | | |
|---|---|---|---|---|
| 165 | **276** | ½c. orange | 20 | 10 |
| 166 | - | 1½c. brown (No. 801) | 20 | 10 |

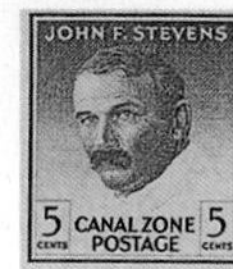


**67** John F. Stevens

**1946.** Portraits.

| | | | | |
|---|---|---|---|---|
| 188 | | ½c. red (Davis) | 45 | 25 |
| 189 | | 1½c. brown (Magoon) | 45 | 25 |
| 190 | | 2c. red (Theodore Roosevelt) | 20 | 20 |
| 191 | **67** | 5c. blue | 40 | 20 |
| 192 | - | 25c. green (Wallace) | 95 | 60 |

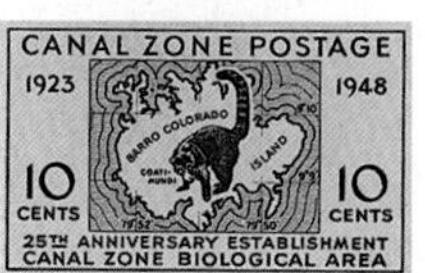


**69** Northern Coati and Barro Colorado Island

**1948.** 25th Anniv of Establishment of Canal Zone Biological Area.

| | | | | |
|---|---|---|---|---|
| 194 | **69** | 10c. black | 1·90 | 85 |

**70** "Arriving at Chagres on the Atlantic Side."

**1949.** Centenary of the Gold Rush.

| | | | | |
|---|---|---|---|---|
| 195 | **70** | 3c. blue | 70 | 25 |
| 196 | - | 6c. violet | 70 | 35 |
| 197 | - | 12c. green | 1·90 | 1·00 |
| 198 | - | 18c. mauve | 2·20 | 1·60 |

DESIGNS: 6c. "Up the Chagres River to Las Cruces"; 12c. "Las Cruces Trail to Panama"; 18c. "Leaving Panama for San Francisco".

**74** Western Hemisphere

**1951.** Air.

| | | | | |
|---|---|---|---|---|
| 199 | **74** | 4c. purple | 80 | 40 |
| 200 | **74** | 5c. green | 1·10 | 65 |
| 201 | **74** | 6c. brown | 55 | 25 |
| 202 | **74** | 7c. olive | 1·10 | 50 |
| 210 | **74** | 8c. red | 80 | 35 |
| 203 | **74** | 10c. orange | 1·00 | 40 |
| 204 | **74** | 15c. purple | 5·50 | 3·00 |
| 205 | **74** | 21c. blue | 8·25 | 4·25 |
| 206 | **74** | 25c. yellow | 13·00 | 3·00 |
| 207 | **74** | 31c. red | 8·25 | 4·00 |
| 208 | **74** | 35c. blue | 8·75 | 3·00 |
| 209 | **74** | 80c. black | 5·00 | 1·60 |

**75** Labourers in Gaillard Cut

**1951.** West Indian Panama Canal Labourers.

| | | | | |
|---|---|---|---|---|
| 211 | **75** | 10c. red | 3·25 | 1·60 |

**76** Locomotive "Nueva Granada", 1852

**1955.** Centenary of Panama Railway.

| | | | | |
|---|---|---|---|---|
| 212 | **76** | 3c. violet | 1·10 | 65 |

**77** Gorgas Hospital

**1957.** 75th Anniv of Gorgas Hospital.

| | | | | |
|---|---|---|---|---|
| 213 | **77** | 3c. black on green | 50 | 40 |

**78** "Ancon II" (liner)

**1958**

| | | | | |
|---|---|---|---|---|
| 214 | **78** | 4c. turquoise | 45 | 35 |

**79** Roosevelt Medal and Map of Canal Zone

**1958.** Birth Centenary of Theodore Roosevelt.

| | | | | |
|---|---|---|---|---|
| 215 | **79** | 4c. brown | 65 | 35 |

**80** "First Class" Scout Badge

**1960.** 50th Anniv of American Boy Scout Movement.

| | | | | |
|---|---|---|---|---|
| 216 | **80** | 4c. ochre, red and blue | 60 | 45 |

**81** Administration Building, Balboa

**1960**

| | | | | |
|---|---|---|---|---|
| 217 | **81** | 4c. purple | 20 | 20 |

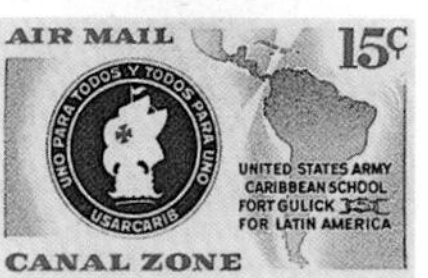


**82** U.S. Army Caribbean School Crest

**1961.** Air.

| | | | | |
|---|---|---|---|---|
| 221 | **82** | 15c. blue and red | 1·90 | 80 |

**83** Girl Scout Badge and Camp on Lake Gatun

**1962.** 50th Anniv of U.S. Girl Scout Movement.

| | | | | |
|---|---|---|---|---|
| 222 | **83** | 4c. ochre, green and blue | 45 | 35 |

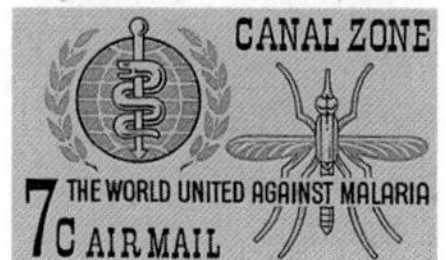


**84** Campaign Emblem and Mosquito

**1962.** Air. Malaria Eradication.

| | | | | |
|---|---|---|---|---|
| 223 | **84** | 7c. black on yellow | 55 | 45 |

**85** Thatcher Ferry Bridge

**1962.** Opening of Thatcher Ferry Bridge.

| | | | | |
|---|---|---|---|---|
| 224 | **85** | 4c. black and silver | 40 | 25 |

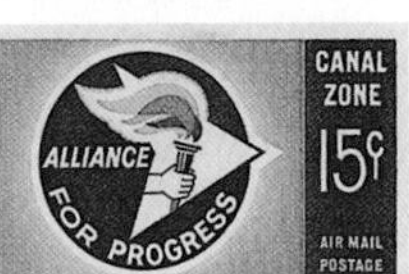

**86** Torch of Progress

**1963.** Air. "Alliance for Progress".

| | | | | |
|---|---|---|---|---|
| 225 | **86** | 15c. blue, green and black | 1·60 | 95 |

**87** Cristobal

**1964.** Air. 50th Anniv of Panama Canal.

| | | | | |
|---|---|---|---|---|
| 226 | **87** | 6c. black and green | 65 | 40 |
| 227 | - | 8c. black and red | 65 | 40 |
| 228 | - | 15c. black and blue | 1·40 | 80 |
| 229 | - | 20c. black and purple | 1·70 | 1·10 |
| 230 | - | 30c. black and brown | 3·00 | 2·50 |
| 231 | - | 80c. black and bistre | 4·75 | 3·25 |

DESIGNS: 8c. Gatun Locks; 15c. Madden Dam; 20c. Gaillard Cut; 30c. Miraflores Locks; 80c. Balboa.

**93** Seal and Jetliner

**1965.** Air.

| | | | | |
|---|---|---|---|---|
| 232 | **93** | 6c. black and green | 55 | 35 |
| 233 | **93** | 8c. black and red | 50 | 20 |
| 234 | **93** | 10c. black and orange | 40 | 20 |
| 235 | **93** | 11c. black and green | 40 | 20 |
| 236 | **93** | 13c. black and green | 95 | 25 |
| 237 | **93** | 15c. black and blue | 80 | 20 |
| 238 | **93** | 20c. black and violet | 85 | 35 |
| 239 | **93** | 22c. black and violet | 1·20 | 2·20 |
| 240 | **93** | 25c. black and green | 85 | 75 |
| 241 | **93** | 30c. black and brown | 1·20 | 35 |
| 242 | **93** | 35c. black and red | 1·40 | 2·20 |
| 243 | **93** | 80c. black and ochre | 2·75 | 80 |

**94** Goethal's Memorial, Balboa

**1968**

| | | | | |
|---|---|---|---|---|
| 244 | **94** | 6c. blue and green | 35 | 35 |
| 245 | - | 8c. multicoloured | 40 | 20 |

DESIGN: 8c. Fort San Lorenzo.

**96** Dredger "Cascadas"

**1976**

| | | | | |
|---|---|---|---|---|
| 249 | **96** | 13c. black, green & blue | 40 | 20 |

**97** Electric Towing Locomotive

**1978**

| | | | | |
|---|---|---|---|---|
| 251 | **97** | 15c. green and deep green | 45 | 20 |

**OFFICIAL STAMPS**

**1941.** Air. Optd OFFICIAL PANAMA CANAL.

| | | | | |
|---|---|---|---|---|
| O167 | **36** | 5c. green | 6·00 | 1·60 |
| O168 | **36** | 6c. brown | 13·00 | 5·50 |
| O169 | **36** | 10c. orange | 9·25 | 3·75 |
| O170 | **36** | 15c. blue | 12·00 | 4·25 |
| O171 | **36** | 20c. violet | 14·00 | 7·75 |
| O172 | **36** | 30c. red | 20·00 | 9·75 |
| O173 | **36** | 40c. yellow | 19·00 | 8·75 |
| O174 | **36** | $1 black | 22·00 | 13·00 |

**1941.** Optd OFFICIAL PANAMA CANAL.

| | | | | |
|---|---|---|---|---|
| O180 | **22** | 1c. green | 2·20 | 45 |
| O181 | **38** | 3c. violet | 4·00 | 80 |
| O182 | **24** | 5c. blue | £1100 | 55·00 |
| O183 | - | 10c. orange | 8·25 | 2·20 |
| O184 | - | 15c. grey (No. 113) | 14·00 | 3·25 |
| O185 | - | 20c. brown (No. 114) | 16·00 | 3·75 |
| O186 | - | 50c. mauve (No. 116) | 41·00 | 9·75 |

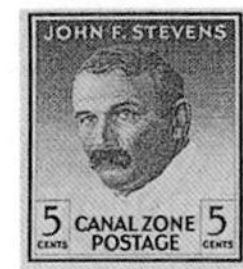

**67** John F. Stevens

**1947.** No. 192 optd OFFICIAL PANAMA CANAL.

| | | | | |
|---|---|---|---|---|
| O193 | **67** | 5c. blue | 9·75 | 3·25 |

**POSTAGE DUE STAMPS**

**1914.** Postage Due stamps of United States of 1894 optd CANAL ZONE diag.

| | | | | |
|---|---|---|---|---|
| D55 | **D87** | 1c. red | 95·00 | 22·00 |
| D56 | **D87** | 2c. red | £275 | 47·00 |
| D57 | **D87** | 10c. red | £1100 | 44·00 |

**1915.** Postage Due stamps of Panama of 1915 optd CANAL ZONE vert.

| | | | | |
|---|---|---|---|---|
| D59 | **D58** | 1c. brown | 13·50 | 5·50 |
| D60 | - | 2c. brown | £250 | 19·00 |
| D61 | - | 10c. brown | 55·00 | 11·00 |

**1915.** Postage Due stamps of Panama of 1915 surch CANAL ZONE vert and value in figures.

| | | | | |
|---|---|---|---|---|
| D62 | **D58** | 1c. on 1c. brown | £120 | 16·00 |
| D63 | - | 2c. on 2c. brown | 27·00 | 8·25 |
| D66 | - | 4c. on 4c. brown | 38·00 | 16·00 |
| D64 | - | 10c. on 10c. brown | 25·00 | 5·50 |

**1925.** Postage Due stamps of United States of 1894 optd CANAL ZONE horiz in two lines.

| | | | | |
|---|---|---|---|---|
| D92 | **D87** | 1c. red | 8·75 | 3·25 |
| D93 | **D87** | 2c. red | 16·00 | 4·25 |
| D94 | **D87** | 10c. red | £160 | 22·00 |

**1925.** Stamps of Canal Zone of 1924 optd POSTAGE DUE.

| | | | |
|---|---|---|---|
| D89 | 1c. green (No. 75) | £100 | 16·00 |
| D90 | 2c. red (No. 103) | 25·00 | 7·75 |
| D91 | 10c. orange (No. 106) | 55·00 | 12·00 |

**1929.** No. 109 surch POSTAGE DUE and value and bars.

| | | | | |
|---|---|---|---|---|
| D120 | **24** | 1c. on 5c. blue | 5·00 | 2·50 |
| D121 | **24** | 2c. on 5c. blue | 8·75 | 3·25 |
| D122 | **24** | 5c. on 5c. blue | 8·75 | 3·50 |
| D123 | **24** | 10c. on 5c. blue | 8·75 | 3·50 |

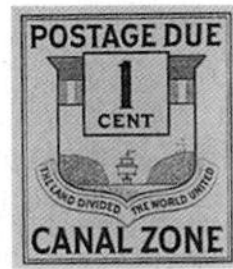

**D37** Canal Zone Shield

**1932**

| | | | | |
|---|---|---|---|---|
| D135 | **D37** | 1c. red | 20 | 20 |
| D136 | **D37** | 2c. red | 20 | 20 |
| D137 | **D37** | 5c. red | 40 | 20 |
| D138 | **D37** | 10c. red | 1·50 | 1·60 |
| D139 | **D37** | 15c. red | 1·20 | 1·10 |

Pt. 17

## CANTON

A treaty port in S. China. Stamps issued at the French Indo-Chinese P.O., which was closed in 1922.

1901. 100 centimes = 1 franc.
1919. 100 cents = 1 piastre.

**Stamps of Indo-China overprinted or surcharged.**

CANTON
州 廣
**(1)**

**1901.** "Tablet" key-type, optd with T 1. The Chinese characters represent "Canton" and are therefore the same on every value.

| | | | | |
|---|---|---|---|---|
| 1 | **D** | 1c. black and blue | 1·00 | 1·60 |
| 2 | **D** | 2c. brown on yellow | 2·00 | 2·75 |
| 3 | **D** | 4c. brown on grey | 3·00 | 3·00 |
| 4 | **D** | 5c. green | 90 | 1·70 |
| 6 | **D** | 10c. black on lilac | 4·50 | 9·25 |
| 7 | **D** | 15c. blue | 2·30 | 4·25 |
| 8 | **D** | 15c. grey | 7·00 | 4·50 |
| 9 | **D** | 20c. red on green | 18·00 | 25·00 |
| 10 | **D** | 25c. black on pink | 13·00 | 10·00 |
| 11 | **D** | 30c. brown on drab | 23·00 | 60·00 |
| 12 | **D** | 40c. red on yellow | 55·00 | 65·00 |
| 13 | **D** | 50c. red on rose | 36·00 | 65·00 |
| 14 | **D** | 75c. brown on orange | 50·00 | 95·00 |
| 15 | **D** | 1f. green | 70·00 | 75·00 |
| 16 | **D** | 5f. mauve on lilac | £225 | £225 |

**1903.** "Tablet" key-type, surch. as T 1. The Chinese characters indicate the value and therefore differ for each value.

| | | | |
|---|---|---|---|
| 17 | 1c. black on blue | 2·75 | 8·25 |
| 18 | 2c. brown on yellow | 6·00 | 8·00 |
| 19 | 4c. brown on grey | 3·75 | 9·25 |
| 20 | 5c. green | 2·50 | 9·25 |
| 21 | 10c. red | 2·75 | 8·75 |
| 22 | 15c. grey | 3·00 | 3·75 |
| 23 | 20c. red on green | 12·00 | 34·00 |
| 24 | 25c. blue | 7·50 | 14·00 |
| 25 | 25c. black on pink | 13·00 | 14·50 |
| 26 | 30c. brown on drab | 50·00 | 55·00 |
| 27 | 40c. red on yellow | 75·00 | 80·00 |
| 28 | 50c. red on rose | £325 | £300 |
| 29 | 50c. brown on blue | 85·00 | 95·00 |
| 30 | 75c. brown on orange | £110 | 95·00 |
| 31 | 1f. green | 80·00 | 90·00 |
| 32 | 5f. mauve on lilac | £100 | 95·00 |

**1906.** Surch CANTON (letters without serifs) and value in Chinese.

| | | | | |
|---|---|---|---|---|
| 33 | **8** | 1c. green | 1·70 | 4·75 |
| 34 | **8** | 2c. purple on yellow | 90 | 2·75 |
| 35 | **8** | 4c. mauve on blue | 75 | 2·30 |
| 36 | **8** | 5c. green | 1·40 | 2·50 |
| 37 | **8** | 10c. red | 4·50 | 4·75 |
| 38 | **8** | 15c. brown on blue | 3·00 | 8·50 |
| 39 | **8** | 20c. red on green | 3·00 | 6·50 |
| 40 | **8** | 25c. blue | 3·25 | 2·75 |
| 41 | **8** | 30c. brown on cream | 4·50 | 14·00 |
| 42 | **8** | 35c. black on yellow | 2·50 | 6·50 |
| 43 | **8** | 40c. black on grey | 6·25 | 16·00 |
| 44 | **8** | 50c. brown on cream | 9·25 | 18·00 |
| 45 | **D** | 75c. brown on orange | 75·00 | 95·00 |
| 46 | **8** | 1f. green | 16·00 | 36·00 |
| 47 | **8** | 2f. brown on yellow | 32·00 | 75·00 |
| 48 | **D** | 5f. mauve on lilac | £100 | £120 |
| 49 | **8** | 10f. red on green | 65·00 | £120 |

**1908.** 1907 stamps surch CANTON and value in Chinese.

| | | | | |
|---|---|---|---|---|
| 50 | **10** | 1c. black and brown | 55 | 35 |
| 51 | **10** | 2c. black and brown | 35 | 55 |
| 52 | **10** | 4c. black and blue | 75 | 1·80 |
| 53 | **10** | 5c. black and green | 90 | 35 |
| 54 | **10** | 10c. black and red | 2·50 | 45 |
| 55 | **10** | 15c. black and violet | 3·25 | 3·00 |
| 56 | **11** | 20c. black and violet | 4·50 | 5·00 |
| 57 | **11** | 25c. black and blue | 7·25 | 45 |
| 58 | **11** | 30c. black and brown | 8·00 | 7·00 |
| 59 | **11** | 35c. black and green | 10·00 | 6·50 |
| 60 | **11** | 40c. black and brown | 20·00 | 7·25 |
| 61 | **11** | 50c. black and red | 21·00 | 3·75 |
| 62 | **12** | 75c. black and orange | 19·00 | 9·25 |
| 63 | - | 1f. black and red | 40·00 | 22·00 |
| 64 | - | 2f. black and green | 60·00 | 70·00 |
| 65 | - | 5f. black and blue | 75·00 | 70·00 |
| 66 | - | 10f. black and violet | £120 | £120 |

**1919.** As last, but additionally surch.

| | | | | |
|---|---|---|---|---|
| 67 | **10** | ⅖c. on 1c. black and brown | 90 | 4·50 |
| 68 | **10** | ⅘c. on 2c. black and brown | 75 | 1·90 |
| 69 | **10** | 1⅗c. on 4c. black and blue | 1·30 | 2·75 |
| 70 | **10** | 2c. on 5c. black and green | 2·00 | 85 |
| 71 | **10** | 4c. on 10c. black and red | 1·80 | 1·40 |
| 72 | **10** | 6c. on 15c. black & violet | 2·50 | 1·40 |
| 73 | **11** | 8c. on 20c. black & violet | 2·75 | 2·50 |
| 74 | **11** | 10c. on 25c. black & blue | 6·50 | 45 |
| 75 | **11** | 12c. on 30c. black & brown | 3·75 | 1·80 |
| 76 | **11** | 14c. on 35c. black & green | 90 | 75 |
| 77 | **11** | 16c. on 40c. black & brown | 2·00 | 1·80 |
| 78 | **11** | 20c. on 50c. black and red | 4·50 | 45 |
| 79 | **12** | 30c. on 75c. black & orange | 4·00 | 75 |
| 80 | - | 40c. on 1f. black and red | 21·00 | 10·00 |
| 81 | - | 80c. on 2f. black and green | 28·00 | 21·00 |
| 82 | - | 2p. on 5f. black and blue | 16·00 | 40·00 |
| 83 | - | 4p. on 10f. black & violet | 10·00 | 46·00 |

Pt. 9

## CAPE JUBY

Former Spanish possession on the N.W. coast of Africa, ceded to Morocco in 1958.

100 centimos = 1 peseta.

**1916.** Stamps of Rio de Oro surch CABO JUBI and value.

| | | | | |
|---|---|---|---|---|
| 1 | **12** | 5c. on 4p. red | £250 | 27·00 |
| 2 | **12** | 10c. on 10p. violet | 55·00 | 27·00 |
| 3 | **12** | 15c. on 50c. brown | 55·00 | 27·00 |
| 4 | **12** | 40c. on 1p. lilac | 90·00 | 37·00 |

**1919.** Stamps of Spain optd CABO JUBY.

| | | | | |
|---|---|---|---|---|
| 5 | **38a** | ¼c. green | 20 | 20 |
| 18 | **66** | 1c. green (imperf) | 28·00 | 18·00 |
| 6 | **64** | 2c. brown | 20 | 20 |
| 7 | **64** | 5c. green | 70 | 45 |
| 8 | **64** | 10c. red | 90 | 65 |
| 9 | **64** | 15c. yellow | 3·75 | 3·50 |
| 10 | **64** | 20c. green | 24·00 | 23·00 |
| 19 | **64** | 20c. violet | £140 | 47·00 |
| 11 | **64** | 25c. blue | 3·50 | 1·80 |
| 12 | **64** | 30c. green | 3·50 | 1·80 |
| 13 | **64** | 40c. orange | 3·50 | 1·40 |
| 14 | **64** | 50c. blue | 4·50 | 3·50 |
| 15 | **64** | 1p. red | 12·00 | 11·00 |
| 16 | **64** | 4p. purple | 50·00 | 50·00 |
| 17 | **64** | 10p. orange | 70·00 | 70·00 |

**1925.** Stamps of Spain optd CABO JUBY.

| | | | | |
|---|---|---|---|---|
| 19a | **68** | 2c. green | £375 | |
| 20 | **68** | 5c. purple | 5·50 | 4·25 |
| 21 | **68** | 10c. green | 16·00 | 4·25 |
| 22 | **68** | 20c. violet | 32·00 | 14·50 |

**1926.** As Red Cross stamps of Spain of 1926 optd CABO-JUBY.

| | | | | |
|---|---|---|---|---|
| 23 | **70** | 1c. orange | 17·00 | 17·00 |
| 24 | - | 2c. red | 17·00 | 17·00 |
| 25 | - | 5c. brown | 4·25 | 4·25 |
| 26 | - | 10c. green | 2·10 | 2·10 |
| 27 | **70** | 15c. violet | 1·50 | 1·50 |
| 28 | - | 20c. purple | 1·50 | 1·50 |
| 29 | **71** | 25c. red | 1·50 | 1·50 |
| 30 | **70** | 30c. green | 1·50 | 1·50 |
| 31 | - | 40c. blue | 50 | 50 |
| 32 | - | 50c. red | 50 | 50 |
| 33 | - | 1p. red | 50 | 50 |
| 34 | - | 4p. bistre | 1·90 | 1·90 |
| 35 | **71** | 10p. violet | 4·50 | 4·50 |

**1929.** Seville and Barcelona Exhibition stamps of Spain (Nos. 504/14) optd CABO JUBY.

| | | | | |
|---|---|---|---|---|
| 36 | - | 5c. red | 50 | 70 |
| 37 | - | 10c. green | 50 | 70 |
| 38 | **83** | 15c. blue | 50 | 70 |
| 39 | **84** | 20c. violet | 50 | 70 |
| 40 | **83** | 25c. red | 50 | 70 |
| 41 | - | 30c. brown | 50 | 70 |
| 42 | - | 40c. blue | 50 | 70 |
| 43 | **84** | 50c. orange | 60 | 90 |
| 44 | - | 1p. grey | 24·00 | 34·00 |
| 45 | - | 4p. red | 35·00 | 55·00 |
| 46 | - | 10p. brown | 35·00 | 55·00 |

**1934.** Stamps of Spanish Morocco optd Cabo Juby. (a) Stamps of 1928.

| | | | | |
|---|---|---|---|---|
| 47 | **11** | 1c. red | 1·90 | 1·40 |
| 48 | **11** | 2c. violet | 4·25 | 2·75 |
| 49 | **11** | 5c. blue | 4·25 | 2·75 |
| 50 | **11** | 10c. green | 10·50 | 8·25 |
| 51 | **11** | 15c. brown | 25·00 | 18·00 |
| 52 | **12** | 25c. red | 4·25 | 2·75 |
| 53 | - | 1p. green | 42·00 | 33·00 |
| 54 | - | 2p.50 purple | £100 | 70·00 |
| 55 | - | 4p. blue | £120 | 95·00 |

(b) Stamps of 1933.

| | | | | |
|---|---|---|---|---|
| 56 | **14** | 1c. red | 45 | 35 |
| 57 | - | 10c. green | 2·75 | 2·10 |
| 58 | **14** | 20c. black | 9·50 | 6·25 |
| 59 | - | 30c. red | 9·50 | 6·25 |
| 60 | **15** | 40c. blue | 31·00 | 25·00 |
| 61 | **15** | 50c. orange | 60·00 | 47·00 |

**1935.** Stamps of Spanish Morocco of 1933 optd CABO JUBY.

| | | | | |
|---|---|---|---|---|
| 62 | **14** | 1c. red | 20 | 10 |
| 63 | - | 2c. green | 60 | 50 |
| 64 | - | 5c. mauve | 2·40 | 1·70 |
| 65 | - | 10c. green | 16·00 | 11·00 |
| 66 | - | 15c. yellow | 5·50 | 4·25 |
| 67 | **14** | 20c. black | 5·50 | 4·25 |
| 68 | - | 25c. red | 70·00 | 47·00 |
| 73 | - | 25c. violet | 5·25 | 5·25 |
| 74 | - | 30c. red | 5·25 | 5·25 |
| 75 | - | 40c. orange | 7·50 | 7·50 |
| 76 | - | 50c. blue | 15·00 | 15·00 |
| 77 | - | 60c. green | 20·00 | 20·00 |
| 69 | - | 1p. grey | 10·50 | 7·00 |
| 78 | - | 2p. brown | £110 | £110 |
| 70 | - | 2p.50 brown | 37·00 | 27·00 |

| | | | | |
|---|---|---|---|---|
| 71 | - | 4p. green | 60·00 | 45·00 |
| 72 | - | 5p. black | 50·00 | 36·00 |

**1937.** 1st Anniv of Civil War. Nos. 184/99 of Spanish Morocco optd CABO JUBY.

| | | | |
|---|---|---|---|
| 79 | 1c. blue | 50 | 50 |
| 80 | 2c. brown | 50 | 50 |
| 81 | 5c. mauve | 50 | 50 |
| 82 | 10c. green | 50 | 50 |
| 83 | 15c. blue | 50 | 50 |
| 84 | 20c. purple | 50 | 50 |
| 85 | 25c. mauve | 50 | 50 |
| 86 | 30c. red | 50 | 50 |
| 87 | 40c. orange | 1·50 | 1·50 |
| 88 | 50c. blue | 1·50 | 1·50 |
| 89 | 60c. green | 1·50 | 1·50 |
| 90 | 1p. violet | 1·50 | 1·50 |
| 91 | 2p. blue | £110 | £110 |
| 92 | 2p.50 black | £110 | £110 |
| 93 | 4p. brown | £110 | £110 |
| 94 | 10p. black | £110 | £110 |

**1938.** Air. Nos. 203/12 of Spanish Morocco optd CABO JUBY.

| | | | |
|---|---|---|---|
| 95 | 5c. brown | 20 | 20 |
| 96 | 10c. green | 20 | 20 |
| 97 | 25c. red | 20 | 20 |
| 98 | 40c. blue | 3·75 | 3·75 |
| 99 | 50c. mauve | 20 | 20 |
| 100 | 75c. blue | 20 | 20 |
| 101 | 1p. brown | 20 | 20 |
| 102 | 1p.50 violet | 2·50 | 2·50 |
| 103 | 2p. red | 5·50 | 5·50 |
| 104 | 3p. black | 15·00 | 15·00 |

**1939.** As Nos. 213/16 of Spanish Morocco optd CABO JUBY.

| | | | |
|---|---|---|---|
| 105 | 5c. red | 55 | 55 |
| 106 | 10c. green | 55 | 55 |
| 107 | 15c. purple | 55 | 55 |
| 108 | 20c. blue | 55 | 55 |

**1940.** Nos. 217/32 of Spanish Morocco, but without "ZONA" on back, optd CABO JUBY.

| | | | |
|---|---|---|---|
| 109 | 1c. brown | 15 | 15 |
| 110 | 2c. green | 15 | 15 |
| 111 | 5c. blue | 15 | 15 |
| 112 | 10c. mauve | 15 | 15 |
| 113 | 15c. green | 15 | 15 |
| 114 | 20c. violet | 15 | 15 |
| 115 | 25c. brown | 15 | 15 |
| 116 | 30c. green | 15 | 15 |
| 117 | 40c. green | 60 | 60 |
| 118 | 45c. red | 60 | 60 |
| 119 | 50c. brown | 60 | 60 |
| 120 | 75c. blue | 2·00 | 2·00 |
| 121 | 1p. brown and blue | 4·25 | 4·25 |
| 122 | 2p.50 green and brown | 12·50 | 12·50 |
| 123 | 5p. brown and purple | 12·50 | 12·50 |
| 124 | 10p. brown & deep brown | 35·00 | 35·00 |

**1942.** Air. Nos. 258/62 of Spanish Morocco, but without "Z" opt and inscr "CABO JUBY".

| | | | |
|---|---|---|---|
| 125 | 5c. blue | 15 | 15 |
| 126 | 10c. brown | 15 | 15 |
| 127 | 15c. green | 15 | 15 |
| 128 | 90c. pink | 55 | 55 |
| 129 | 5p. black | 1·80 | 1·80 |

**1944.** Nos. 269/82 (agricultural scenes) of Spanish Morocco optd CABO JUBY.

| | | | | |
|---|---|---|---|---|
| 130 | - | 1c. blue and brown | 15 | 15 |
| 131 | - | 2c. light green & green | 15 | 15 |
| 132 | 26 | 5c. green and brown | 15 | 15 |
| 133 | - | 10c. orange and blue | 15 | 15 |
| 134 | - | 15c. light green & green | 15 | 15 |
| 135 | - | 20c. black and purple | 15 | 15 |
| 136 | - | 25c. brown and blue | 15 | 15 |
| 137 | - | 30c. blue and green | 15 | 15 |
| 138 | - | 40c. purple and brown | 15 | 15 |
| 139 | 26 | 50c. brown and blue | 15 | 15 |
| 140 | - | 75c. blue and green | 1·40 | 1·40 |
| 141 | - | 1p. brown and blue | 1·40 | 1·40 |
| 142 | - | 2p.50 blue and black | 4·00 | 4·00 |
| 143 | - | 10p. black and orange | 27·00 | 27·00 |

**1946.** Nos. 285/94 (craftsmen) of Spanish Morocco optd CABO JUBY.

| | | | | |
|---|---|---|---|---|
| 144 | | 1c. brown and purple | 25 | 25 |
| 145 | 27 | 2c. violet and green | 25 | 25 |
| 146 | - | 10c. blue and orange | 25 | 25 |
| 147 | 27 | 15c. green and blue | 25 | 25 |
| 148 | - | 25c. blue and green | 25 | 25 |
| 149 | - | 40c. brown and blue | 25 | 25 |
| 150 | 27 | 45c. red and black | 30 | 30 |
| 151 | - | 1p. blue and green | 2·20 | 2·20 |
| 152 | - | 2p.50 green and orange | 6·50 | 6·50 |
| 153 | - | 10p. grey and blue | 20·00 | 20·00 |

**1948.** Nos. 307/17 (transport and commerce) of Spanish Morocco, but without "Z" on back, optd CABO JUBY.

| | | | | |
|---|---|---|---|---|
| 154 | 30 | 2c. brown and violet | 25 | 25 |
| 155 | - | 5c. violet and purple | 25 | 25 |
| 156 | - | 15c. green and blue | 25 | 25 |
| 157 | - | 25c. green and black | 25 | 25 |
| 158 | - | 35c. black and blue | 25 | 25 |
| 159 | - | 50c. violet and red | 25 | 25 |
| 160 | - | 70c. blue and green | 25 | 25 |
| 161 | - | 90c. green and mauve | 25 | 25 |
| 162 | - | 1p. violet and blue | 35 | 35 |
| 163 | 30 | 2p.50 green and purple | 2·00 | 2·00 |
| 164 | - | 10p. blue and black | 6·00 | 6·00 |

**EXPRESS LETTER STAMPS**

**1919.** Express letter stamp of Spain optd CABO JUBY.

| | | | | |
|---|---|---|---|---|
| E18 | E53 | 20c. red | 3·50 | 3·50 |

**1926.** Red Cross stamp. As Express letter stamp of Spain optd CABO-JUBY.

| | | | | |
|---|---|---|---|---|
| E36 | E77 | 20c. black and blue | 4·50 | 4·50 |

**1934.** Stamp of Spanish Morocco optd Cabo Juby.

| | | | | |
|---|---|---|---|---|
| E62 | E12 | 20c. black | 10·50 | 10·50 |

**1935.** Stamp of Spanish Morocco optd CABO JUBY.

| | | | | |
|---|---|---|---|---|
| E79 | E16 | 20c. red | 5·25 | 5·25 |

**1937.** No. E200 of Spanish Morocco optd CABO JUBY.

| | | | | |
|---|---|---|---|---|
| E95 | E19 | 20c. red | 1·50 | 1·50 |

**1940.** No. E233 of Spanish Morocco optd CABO JUBY.

| | | | | |
|---|---|---|---|---|
| E125 | E21 | 25c. red | 55 | 55 |

Pt. 1

# CAPE OF GOOD HOPE

Formerly a British Colony, later the southern-most province of the Union of South Africa.

12 pence = 1 shilling;
20 shillings = 1 pound.

1 'Hope'

**1853.** Imperf.

| | | | | |
|---|---|---|---|---|
| 18 | 1 | 1d. red | £225 | £250 |
| 19 | 1 | 4d. blue | £200 | 90·00 |
| 20 | 1 | 6d. lilac | £325 | £450 |
| 8b | 1 | 1s. green | £375 | £500 |

3

**1861.** Imperf.

| | | | | |
|---|---|---|---|---|
| 13 | 3 | 1d. red | £16000 | £2500 |
| 14 | 3 | 4d. blue | £24000 | £1800 |

4 'Hope' seated with vine and ram (with outer frame)

**1864.** With outer frame line. Perf.

| | | | | |
|---|---|---|---|---|
| 23a | 4 | 1d. red | £100 | 30·00 |
| 24 | 4 | 4d. blue | £150 | 4·25 |
| 52a | 4 | 6d. purple | 16·00 | 20 |
| 53a | 4 | 1s. green | £140 | 50 |

6 (no outer frame line)

**1868.** Surch.

| | | | | |
|---|---|---|---|---|
| 32 | | 1d. on 6d. violet | £600 | £120 |
| 33 | | 1d. on 1s. green | £110 | 65·00 |
| 34 | 6 | 3d. on 4d. blue | £140 | 2·00 |
| 27 | | 4d. on 6d. violet | £400 | 17·00 |

**1880.** No outer frame line.

| | | | |
|---|---|---|---|
| 48 | ½d. black | 8·00 | 10 |
| 49 | 1d. red | 10·00 | 10 |
| 36 | 3d. pink | £275 | 32·00 |
| 43 | 3d. purple | 9·50 | 1·50 |
| 51 | 4d. blue | 19·00 | 50 |
| 54 | 5s. orange | £130 | 8·00 |

**1880.** Surch THREEPENCE.

| | | | |
|---|---|---|---|
| 35 | 3d. on 4d. pink | 90·00 | 2·75 |

**1880.** Surch 3.

| | | | |
|---|---|---|---|
| 37 | "3" on 3d. pink | £110 | 1·75 |

**1882.** Surch One Half-penny.

| | | | |
|---|---|---|---|
| 47 | ½d. on 3d. purple | 45·00 | 5·00 |

**1882**

| | | | |
|---|---|---|---|
| 61 | ½d. green | 1·50 | 50 |
| 62 | 2d. brown | 2·50 | 2·25 |
| 56 | 2½d. olive | 18·00 | 10 |
| 63a | 2½d. blue | 9·00 | 10 |
| 64 | 3d. mauve | 15·00 | 1·00 |
| 65 | 4d. olive | 8·00 | 3·50 |
| 66 | 1s. green | 85·00 | 7·00 |
| 67 | 1s. yellow | 15·00 | 2·75 |

On the 2½d. stamps the value is in a white square at upper right-hand corner as well as at foot.

**1891.** Surch 2½d.

| | | | |
|---|---|---|---|
| 55a | 2½d. on 3d. mauve | 6·00 | 20 |

**1893.** Surch ONE PENNY.

| | | | |
|---|---|---|---|
| 57a | 1d. on 2d. brown | 4·75 | 50 |

17 'Hope' standing. Table Bay in background

**1893**

| | | | | |
|---|---|---|---|---|
| 58 | 17 | ½d. green | 6·50 | 20 |
| 59a | 17 | 1d. red | 2·50 | 10 |
| 60 | 17 | 3d. mauve | 5·50 | 2·50 |

18 Table Mountain and Bay and Arms of the colony

**1900**

| | | | | |
|---|---|---|---|---|
| 69 | 18 | 1d. red | 6·00 | 10 |

19

**1902.** Various frames.

| | | | | |
|---|---|---|---|---|
| 70 | 19 | ½d. green | 2·50 | 10 |
| 71 | 19 | 1d. red | 2·50 | 10 |
| 72 | 19 | 2d. brown | 18·00 | 80 |
| 73 | 19 | 2½d. blue | 4·00 | 9·00 |
| 74 | 19 | 3d. purple | 13·00 | 1·25 |
| 75 | 19 | 4d. green | 16·00 | 65 |
| 76 | 19 | 6d. mauve | 24·00 | 30 |
| 77 | 19 | 1s. yellow | 17·00 | 1·25 |
| 78 | 19 | 5s. orange | £130 | 24·00 |

Pt. 9, Pt. 12

# CAPE VERDE ISLANDS

Islands in the Atlantic. Formerly Portuguese; became independent on 5 July 1975.

1877. 1000 reis = 1 milreis.
1913. 100 centavos = 1 escudo.

**1877.** "Crown" key-type inscr "CABO VERDE".

| | | | | |
|---|---|---|---|---|
| 1 | P | 5r. black | 2·50 | 1·70 |
| 2a | P | 10r. yellow | 15·00 | 10·50 |
| 18 | P | 10r. green | 2·20 | 1·70 |
| 3 | P | 20r. bistre | 1·50 | 1·20 |
| 19 | P | 20r. red | 4·50 | 3·00 |
| 4 | P | 25r. pink | 1·90 | 80 |
| 20 | P | 25r. lilac | 3·25 | 2·40 |
| 5 | P | 40r. blue | 75·00 | 45·00 |
| 21 | P | 40r. yellow | 1·90 | 1·40 |
| 15 | P | 50r. green | £120 | 65·00 |
| 22 | P | 50r. blue | 5·50 | 3·50 |
| 7b | P | 100r. lilac | 6·75 | 2·75 |
| 8 | P | 200r. orange | 4·00 | 3·00 |
| 9b | P | 300r. brown | 4·75 | 4·25 |

**1886.** "Embossed" key-type inscr "PROVINCIA DE CABO-VERDE".

| | | | | |
|---|---|---|---|---|
| 33 | Q | 5r. black | 3·75 | 2·50 |
| 34 | Q | 10r. green | 5·50 | 2·40 |
| 35 | Q | 20r. red | 6·75 | 4·25 |
| 26 | Q | 25r. mauve | 6·75 | 4·50 |
| 27 | Q | 40r. brown | 6·75 | 2·75 |
| 28 | Q | 50r. blue | 6·75 | 2·75 |
| 29 | Q | 100r. brown | 6·75 | 3·75 |
| 30 | Q | 200r. lilac | 15·00 | 8·50 |
| 31 | Q | 300r. orange | 17·00 | 3·50 |

**1894.** "Figures" key-type inscr "CABO-VERDE".

| | | | | |
|---|---|---|---|---|
| 37 | R | 5r. orange | 1·30 | 1·00 |
| 38 | R | 10r. mauve | 1·30 | 1·00 |
| 39 | R | 15r. brown | 3·25 | 2·10 |
| 40 | R | 20r. lilac | 3·25 | 2·10 |
| 41 | R | 25r. green | 2·75 | 1·70 |
| 42 | R | 50r. blue | 2·75 | 1·70 |
| 51 | R | 75r. red | 9·25 | 4·75 |
| 43 | R | 80r. green | 10·00 | 5·25 |
| 44 | R | 100r. brown on buff | 7·50 | 4·25 |
| 58 | R | 150r. red on rose | 26·00 | 22·00 |
| 59 | R | 200r. blue on blue | 26·00 | 22·00 |
| 46 | R | 300r. blue on buff | 30·00 | 14·00 |

**1898.** "King Carlos" key-type inscr "CABO VERDE".

| | | | | |
|---|---|---|---|---|
| 60 | S | 2½r. grey | 30 | 25 |
| 61 | S | 5r. orange | 40 | 25 |
| 62 | S | 10r. green | 40 | 25 |
| 63 | S | 15r. brown | 4·50 | 1·60 |
| 111 | S | 15r. green | 1·50 | 1·00 |
| 64 | S | 20r. lilac | 1·30 | 75 |
| 65 | S | 25r. green | 2·75 | 1·00 |
| 112 | S | 25r. red | 80 | 30 |
| 66 | S | 50r. blue | 2·75 | 1·20 |
| 113 | S | 50r. brown | 3·00 | 1·90 |
| 114 | S | 65r. blue | 19·00 | 12·00 |
| 67 | S | 75r. red | 7·00 | 2·75 |
| 115 | S | 75r. purple | 2·75 | 1·70 |
| 68 | S | 80r. mauve | 7·00 | 2·75 |
| 69 | S | 100r. blue on blue | 2·75 | 1·50 |
| 116 | S | 115r. brown on pink | 12·00 | 8·00 |
| 117 | S | 130r. brown on yellow | 12·50 | 8·00 |
| 70 | S | 150r. brown on yellow | 2·20 | 1·20 |
| 71 | S | 200r. purple on pink | 3·25 | 2·40 |
| 72 | S | 300r. blue on pink | 8·25 | 4·00 |
| 118 | S | 400r. blue on yellow | 13·00 | 8·50 |
| 73 | S | 500r. black on blue | 8·25 | 4·00 |
| 74 | S | 700r. mauve on yellow | 23·00 | 14·50 |

**1902.** Key-types of Cape Verde Is. surch.

| | | | | |
|---|---|---|---|---|
| 119 | S | 50r. on 65r. blue | 3·25 | 2·40 |
| 75 | Q | 65r. on 5r. black | 4·50 | 3·00 |
| 78 | R | 65r. on 10r. mauve | 5·50 | 3·00 |
| 79 | R | 65r. on 20r. lilac | 5·50 | 3·00 |
| 80 | R | 65r. on 100r. brn on buff | 7·00 | 4·25 |
| 76 | Q | 65r. on 200r. lilac | 4·50 | 3·00 |
| 77 | Q | 65r. on 300r. orange | 4·50 | 3·00 |
| 85 | R | 115r. on 5r. orange | 3·25 | 2·40 |
| 82 | Q | 115r. on 10r. green | 4·50 | 3·00 |
| 83 | Q | 115r. on 20r. red | 4·50 | 3·00 |
| 87 | R | 115r. on 25r. green | 2·30 | 1·70 |
| 88 | R | 115r. on 150r. red on rose | 6·75 | 5·25 |
| 90 | Q | 130r. on 50r. blue | 4·50 | 3·00 |
| 93 | R | 130r. on 75r. red | 3·25 | 2·40 |
| 96 | R | 130r. on 80r. green | 2·75 | 1·60 |
| 92 | Q | 130r. on 100r. brown | 4·50 | 3·00 |
| 97 | R | 130r. on 200r. blue on blue | 3·00 | 2·10 |
| 106 | V | 400r. on 2½r. brown | 1·30 | 1·20 |
| 98 | Q | 400r. on 25r. mauve | 2·20 | 2·10 |
| 99 | Q | 400r. on 40r. brown | 4·50 | 3·00 |
| 101 | R | 400r. on 50r. blue | 4·50 | 2·40 |
| 103 | R | 400r. on 300r. blue on buff | 2·00 | 1·40 |

**1902.** "King Carlos" key-type of Cape Verde Is. optd PROVISORIO.

| | | | |
|---|---|---|---|
| 107 | 15r. brown | 1·50 | 1·00 |
| 108 | 25r. green | 1·50 | 1·00 |
| 109 | 50r. blue | 1·50 | 1·00 |
| 110 | 75r. red | 3·00 | 2·10 |

**1911.** "King Carlos" key-type of Cape Verde Is. optd REPUBLICA.

| | | | |
|---|---|---|---|
| 120 | 2½r. grey | 20 | 20 |
| 121 | 5r. orange | 20 | 20 |
| 122 | 10r. green | 80 | 65 |
| 123 | 15r. green | 70 | 35 |
| 124 | 20r. lilac | 1·20 | 65 |
| 125 | 25r. red | 70 | 35 |
| 126 | 50r. brown | 7·00 | 4·75 |
| 127 | 75r. purple | 1·10 | 65 |
| 128 | 100r. blue on blue | 1·10 | 65 |
| 129 | 115r. brown on pink | 1·10 | 65 |
| 130 | 130r. brown on yellow | 1·10 | 65 |
| 131 | 200r. purple on pink | 5·25 | 3·25 |
| 132 | 400r. blue on yellow | 2·75 | 95 |
| 133 | 500r. black on blue | 2·75 | 95 |
| 134 | 700r. mauve on yellow | 2·75 | 1·10 |

**1912.** "King Manoel" key-type inscr "CABO VERDE" and optd REPUBLICA.

| | | | | |
|---|---|---|---|---|
| 135 | T | 2½r. lilac | 15 | 15 |
| 136 | T | 5r. black | 15 | 15 |
| 137 | T | 10r. green | 35 | 30 |
| 138 | T | 20r. red | 1·90 | 1·10 |
| 139 | T | 25r. brown | 35 | 15 |
| 140 | T | 50r. blue | 3·75 | 2·75 |
| 141 | T | 75r. brown | 90 | 80 |
| 142 | T | 100r. brown on green | 90 | 80 |
| 143 | T | 200r. green on pink | 1·40 | 80 |
| 144 | T | 300r. black on blue | 1·40 | 80 |
| 145 | T | 400r. blue and black | 3·00 | 2·40 |
| 146 | T | 500r. brown and olive | 3·00 | 2·40 |

**1913.** Surch. REPUBLICA CABO VERDE and new value on "Vasco da Gama" issues of (a) Portuguese Colonies.

| | | | |
|---|---|---|---|
| 147 | ¼c. on 2½r. green | 1·10 | 50 |
| 148 | ½c. on 5r. red | 1·10 | 50 |
| 149 | 1c. on 10r. purple | 1·10 | 50 |
| 150 | 2½c. on 25r. green | 1·10 | 50 |
| 151 | 5c. on 50r. blue | 1·50 | 1·20 |
| 152 | 7½c. on 75r. brown | 3·00 | 2·30 |
| 153 | 10c. on 100r. brown | 1·50 | 1·50 |
| 154 | 15c. on 150r. bistre | 2·00 | 2·00 |

(b) Macao.

| | | | |
|---|---|---|---|
| 155 | ¼c. on ½a. green | 1·10 | 70 |
| 156 | ½c. on 1a. red | 1·10 | 70 |
| 157 | 1c. on 2a. purple | 1·10 | 70 |
| 158 | 2½c. on 4a. green | 1·10 | 70 |
| 159 | 5c. on 8a. blue | 5·75 | 5·00 |
| 160 | 7½c. on 12a. brown | 4·75 | 2·00 |
| 161 | 10c. on 16a. brown | 1·70 | 1·30 |
| 162 | 15c. on 24a. bistre | 4·75 | 2·75 |

(c) Timor.

| | | | |
|---|---|---|---|
| 163 | ¼c. on ½a. green | 1·10 | 70 |
| 164 | ½c. on 1a. red | 1·10 | 70 |
| 165 | 1c. on 2a. purple | 1·10 | 70 |
| 166 | 2½c. on 4a. green | 1·00 | 70 |
| 167 | 5c. on 8a. blue | 5·75 | 4·50 |
| 168 | 7½c. on 12a. brown | 4·50 | 2·50 |
| 169 | 10c. on 16a. brown | 1·80 | 1·50 |
| 170 | 15c. on 24a. bistre | 3·75 | 1·90 |

**1913.** Stamps of 1902 optd REPUBLICA.

| | | | | |
|---|---|---|---|---|
| 171 | S | 75r. red (No. 110) | 4·50 | 3·00 |
| 192 | R | 115r. on 5r. (No. 85) | 1·10 | 60 |
| 193 | Q | 115r. on 10r. (No. 82) | 2·00 | 1·20 |
| 195 | Q | 115r. on 20r. (No. 83) | 2·20 | 1·40 |
| 198 | R | 115r. on 25r. (No. 87) | 2·00 | 1·40 |
| 200 | R | 115r. on 150r. (No. 88) | 65 | 60 |
| 201 | Q | 130r. on 50r. (No. 90) | 2·00 | 1·00 |
| 202 | R | 130r. on 75r. (No. 93) | 2·00 | 80 |
| 204 | R | 130r. on 80r. (No. 96) | 2·00 | 80 |
| 206 | Q | 130r. on 100r. (No. 92) | 1·30 | 80 |
| 208 | R | 130r. on 200r. (No. 97) | 1·30 | 80 |

**1914.** "Ceres" key-type inscr "CABO VERDE". Name and value in black.

| | | | | |
|---|---|---|---|---|
| 219 | U | ¼c. green | 60 | 45 |
| 220 | U | ½c. black | 60 | 45 |
| 221 | U | 1c. green | 60 | 45 |
| 222 | U | 1½c. brown | 60 | 45 |
| 223 | U | 2c. red | 1·00 | 55 |
| 224 | U | 2c. grey | 25 | 20 |
| 180 | U | 2½c. violet | 50 | 45 |
| 214 | U | 2½c. mauve | 20 | 20 |
| 215 | U | 3c. orange | 2·10 | 1·90 |
| 216 | U | 4c. red | 20 | 15 |
| 228 | U | 4½c. grey | 30 | 30 |
| 229 | U | 5c. blue | 75 | 65 |
| 230 | U | 6c. mauve | 30 | 30 |
| 231 | U | 7c. blue | 30 | 30 |
| 232 | U | 7½c. brown | 30 | 25 |
| 233 | U | 8c. grey | 50 | 40 |
| 234 | U | 10c. red | 30 | 30 |
| 235 | U | 12c. green | 50 | 45 |
| 236 | U | 15c. pink | 30 | 25 |
| 237 | U | 20c. green | 30 | 25 |
| 238 | U | 24c. blue | 90 | 70 |
| 239 | U | 25c. brown | 90 | 70 |
| 188 | U | 30c. brown on green | 3·75 | 2·50 |
| 240 | U | 30c. green | 40 | 40 |
| 189 | U | 40c. brown on pink | 2·20 | 1·90 |
| 241 | U | 40c. turquoise | 40 | 40 |
| 190 | U | 50c. orange on orange | 2·75 | 1·90 |
| 242 | U | 50c. mauve | 75 | 60 |
| 243 | U | 60c. blue | 1·00 | 70 |
| 244 | U | 60c. red | 1·10 | 70 |
| 245 | U | 80c. red | 3·50 | 1·00 |
| 191 | U | 1e. green on blue | 2·75 | 2·10 |
| 246 | U | 1e. pink | 4·25 | 2·20 |
| 247 | U | 1e. blue | 4·50 | 2·75 |
| 248 | U | 2e. purple | 4·25 | 2·20 |
| 249 | U | 5e. brown | 7·50 | 5·25 |
| 250 | U | 10e. pink | 17·00 | 10·50 |
| 251 | U | 20e. green | 48·00 | 35·00 |

**1921.** Nos. 153/4 surch.

| | | | |
|---|---|---|---|
| 252 | 2c. on 15c. on 150r. brown | 1·80 | 1·20 |
| 253 | 4c. on 10c. on 100r. brown | 2·20 | 2·10 |

**1921.** No. 69 surch 6 c. REPUBLICA.

| | | | | |
|---|---|---|---|---|
| 254 | S | 6c. on 100r. blue on blue | 2·20 | 1·70 |

**1921.** Charity Tax stamp of Portuguese Colonies (General issues) optd CABO VERDE CORREIOS or surch also.

| | | | |
|---|---|---|---|
| 255 | ¼ on 1c. green | 45 | 30 |
| 256 | ½c. on 1c. green | 55 | 40 |
| 257 | 1c. green | 50 | 40 |

**1922.** Provisionals of 1913 surch $04.

| | | | | |
|---|---|---|---|---|
| 260 | R | 4c. on 130r. on 75r. red (No. 202) | 80 | 60 |
| 262 | R | 4c. on 130r. on 80r. green (No. 204) | 80 | 60 |
| 265 | R | 4c. on 130r. on 200r. blue (No. 208) | 80 | 65 |

**1925.** Provisional stamps of 1902 surch Republica 40 C.

| | | | | |
|---|---|---|---|---|
| 267 | V | 40c. on 400r. on 2½r. brown (No. 106) | 80 | 65 |
| 268 | R | 40c. on 400r. on 300r. blue on buff (No. 103) | 80 | 60 |

**1931.** No. 245 surch 70 C.

| | | | | |
|---|---|---|---|---|
| 269 | U | 70c. on 80c. red | 21·00 | 8·25 |

**1934.** As T 17 of Angola (new "Ceres" type).

| | | | | |
|---|---|---|---|---|
| 270 | 17 | 1c. brown | 15 | 10 |
| 271 | 17 | 5c. sepia | 15 | 10 |
| 272 | 17 | 10c. mauve | 15 | 10 |
| 273 | 17 | 15c. black | 20 | 20 |
| 274 | 17 | 20c. grey | 20 | 20 |
| 275 | 17 | 30c. green | 20 | 20 |
| 276 | 17 | 40c. red | 20 | 20 |
| 277 | 17 | 45c. blue | 1·60 | 70 |
| 278 | 17 | 50c. brown | 75 | 45 |
| 279 | 17 | 60c. olive | 75 | 45 |
| 280 | 17 | 70c. brown | 75 | 45 |
| 281 | 17 | 80c. green | 75 | 45 |
| 282 | 17 | 85c. red | 3·25 | 2·10 |
| 283 | 17 | 1e. red | 2·20 | 40 |
| 284 | 17 | 1e.40 blue | 3·00 | 2·50 |
| 285 | 17 | 2e. mauve | 3·75 | 2·10 |
| 286 | 17 | 5e. green | 17·00 | 4·00 |
| 287 | 17 | 10e. brown | 26·00 | 15·00 |
| 288 | 17 | 20e. orange | 50·00 | 20·00 |

**1938.** As Nos. 383/409 of Angola.

| | | | |
|---|---|---|---|
| 289 | 1c. olive (postage) | 15 | 10 |
| 290 | 5c. brown | 15 | 10 |
| 291 | 10c. red | 15 | 10 |
| 292 | 15c. purple | 80 | 70 |
| 293 | 20c. slate | 40 | 20 |
| 294 | 30c. purple | 40 | 20 |
| 295 | 35c. green | 40 | 20 |
| 296 | 40c. brown | 40 | 20 |
| 297 | 50c. mauve | 40 | 20 |
| 298 | 60c. black | 40 | 20 |
| 299 | 70c. violet | 40 | 20 |
| 300 | 80c. orange | 35 | 20 |
| 301 | 1e. red | 55 | 20 |
| 302 | 1e.75 blue | 1·50 | 55 |
| 303 | 2e. green | 2·75 | 1·60 |
| 304 | 5e. olive | 6·50 | 1·60 |
| 305 | 10e. blue | 10·50 | 2·10 |
| 306 | 20e. brown | 35·00 | 4·25 |
| 307 | 10c. red (air) | 65 | 50 |
| 308 | 20c. violet | 65 | 50 |
| 309 | 50c. orange | 65 | 50 |
| 310 | 1e. blue | 65 | 50 |
| 311 | 2e. red | 1·50 | 80 |
| 312 | 3e. green | 2·00 | 1·40 |
| 313 | 5e. brown | 5·75 | 2·00 |
| 314 | 9e. red | 9·50 | 3·50 |
| 315 | 10e. mauve | 10·50 | 4·50 |

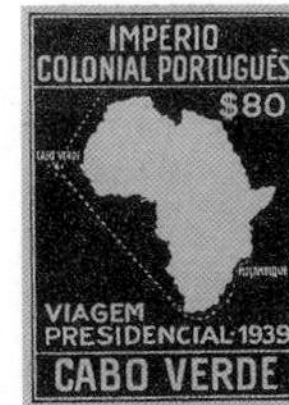


**14** Route of President's Tour

**1939.** Pres. Carmona's 2nd Colonial Tour.

| | | | | |
|---|---|---|---|---|
| 316 | 14 | 80c. violet on mauve | 4·50 | 3·00 |
| 317 | 14 | 1e.75 blue on blue | 37·00 | 27·00 |
| 318 | 14 | 20e. brown on cream | 75·00 | 25·00 |

**1948.** Nos. 276 and 294 surch.

| | | | |
|---|---|---|---|
| 319 | 10c. on 30c. purple | 1·80 | 1·00 |
| 320 | 25c. on 40c. red | 1·90 | 1·00 |

**16** Machado Point, Sao Vicente

**17** Ribeira Brava, Sao Nicolau

**1948**

| | | | | |
|---|---|---|---|---|
| 321 | 16 | 5c. purple and bistre | 40 | 30 |
| 322 | - | 10c. green and light green | 40 | 30 |
| 323 | 17 | 50c. purple and lilac | 75 | 30 |
| 324 | - | 1e. purple | 2·75 | 1·10 |
| 325 | - | 1e.75 blue and green | 3·25 | 1·70 |
| 326 | - | 2e. brown and ochre | 7·50 | 2·10 |
| 327 | - | 5e. green and yellow | 15·00 | 4·00 |
| 328 | - | 10e. red and orange | 24·00 | 14·00 |
| 329 | - | 20e. violet and buff | 60·00 | 26·00 |

DESIGNS—VERT: 10c. Ribeira Grande. HORIZ: 1e. Porto Grande, Sao Vicente; 1e.75, 5e. Mindelo, Sao Vicente; 2e. Joao de Evora beach, Sao Vicente; 10e. Volcano, Fogo; 20e. Paul.

**1948.** Honouring the Statue of Our Lady of Fatima. As T 33 of Angola.

| | | | |
|---|---|---|---|
| 330 | 50c. blue | 8·75 | 3·75 |

**1949.** 75th Anniv of U.P.U. As T 39 of Angola.

| | | | |
|---|---|---|---|
| 331 | 1e. mauve | 7·00 | 3·50 |

**1950.** Holy Year. As T 41/2 of Angola.

| | | | |
|---|---|---|---|
| 332 | 1e. brown | 85 | 45 |
| 333 | 2e. blue | 3·50 | 1·70 |

**1951.** Surch with figures and bars over old value.

| | | | |
|---|---|---|---|
| 334 | 10c. on 35c. (No. 295) | 45 | 40 |
| 335 | 20c. on 70c. (No. 299) | 60 | 45 |
| 336 | 40c. on 70c. (No. 299) | 70 | 45 |
| 337 | 50c. on 80c. (No. 300) | 70 | 45 |
| 338 | 1e. on 1e.75 (No. 302) | 75 | 45 |
| 339 | 2e. on 10e. (No. 305) | 1·40 | 1·50 |

**1951.** Termination of Holy Year. As T 44 of Angola.

| | | | |
|---|---|---|---|
| 340 | 2e. violet and mauve | 1·00 | 80 |

**1952.** No. 302 surch with figures and cross over old values.

| | | | |
|---|---|---|---|
| 341 | 10c. on 1e.75 blue | 1·10 | 95 |
| 342 | 20c. on 1e.75 blue | 1·10 | 95 |
| 343 | 50c. on 1e.75 blue | 4·75 | 4·25 |
| 344 | 1e. on 1e.75 blue | 60 | 15 |
| 345 | 1e.50 on 1e.75 blue | 60 | 15 |

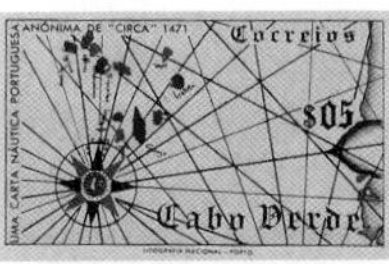


**20** Map, c. 1471

**21** V. Dias and G. de Cintra

**1952.** Portuguese Navigators as T 20/21. Mult.

| | | | |
|---|---|---|---|
| 346 | 5c. Type **20** | 10 | 10 |
| 347 | 10c. Type **21** | 10 | 10 |
| 348 | 30c. D. Afonso and A. Fernandes | 15 | 10 |
| 349 | 50c. Lancarote and S. da Costa | 15 | 10 |
| 350 | 1e. D. Gomes and A. da Nola | 15 | 10 |
| 351 | 2e. Princes Fernando and Henry the Navigator | 1·10 | 10 |
| 352 | 3e. A. Goncalves and D. Dias | 9·50 | 1·30 |
| 353 | 5e. A. Goncalves Baldaia and J. Fernandes | 3·25 | 65 |
| 354 | 10e. D. Eanes da Gra and A. de Freitas | 6·25 | 1·60 |
| 355 | 20e. Map, 1502 | 11·50 | 2·10 |

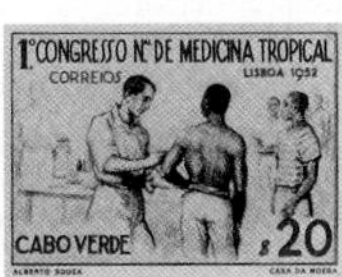


**22** Doctor giving Injection

**1952.** 1st Tropical Medicine Congress, Lisbon.

| | | | | |
|---|---|---|---|---|
| 356 | 22 | 20c. black and green | 55 | 40 |

**23** Facade of Monastery

**1953.** Missionary Art Exhibition.

| | | | | |
|---|---|---|---|---|
| 357 | 23 | 10c. brown and olive | 10 | 10 |
| 358 | 23 | 50c. violet and salmon | 70 | 35 |
| 359 | 23 | 1e. green and orange | 1·70 | 1·00 |

**1953.** Portuguese Stamp Centenary. As T 48 of Angola.

| | | | |
|---|---|---|---|
| 360 | 50c. multicoloured | 1·40 | 90 |

**1954.** 4th Cent of Sao Paulo. As T 49 of Angola.

| | | | |
|---|---|---|---|
| 361 | 1e. black, green and buff | 55 | 45 |

**24** Arms of Cape Verde Is. and Portuguese Guinea

**1955.** Presidential Visit.

| | | | | |
|---|---|---|---|---|
| 362 | 24 | 1e. multicoloured | 40 | 20 |
| 363 | 24 | 1e.60c. multicoloured | 60 | 55 |

**25** Arms of Praia

**1958.** Centenary of City of Praia. Multicoloured.

| | | | | |
|---|---|---|---|---|
| 364 | 25 | 1e. on yellow | 50 | 40 |
| 365 | 25 | 2e.50 on salmon | 1·00 | 80 |

**1958.** Brussels International Exn. As T 55 of Angola.

| | | | |
|---|---|---|---|
| 366 | 2e. multicoloured | 65 | 30 |

**1958.** 6th International Congress of Tropical Medicine. As T 56 of Angola. Multicoloured.

| | | | |
|---|---|---|---|
| 367 | 3c. "Aloe vera" (plant) | 1·70 | 1·90 |

**26** Prince Henry the Navigator

**1960.** 500th Death Anniv of Prince Henry the Navigator.

| | | | | |
|---|---|---|---|---|
| 368 | 26 | 2e. multicoloured | 40 | 20 |

**27** Antonio da Nola

**1960.** 500th Anniv of Colonization of Cape Verde Islands. Multicoloured.

| | | | |
|---|---|---|---|
| 369 | 1e. Type **27** | 60 | 40 |
| 370 | 2e.50 Diogo Gomes | 1·70 | 90 |

**28** "Education"

**1960.** 10th Anniv of African Technical Co-operation Commission.

| | | | | |
|---|---|---|---|---|
| 371 | 28 | 2e.50 multicoloured | 1·10 | 60 |

**29** Arms of Praia

**1961.** Urban Arms. As T 29. Arms multicoloured; inscriptions in red and green; background colours given.

| | | | |
|---|---|---|---|
| 372 | 5c. buff | 20 | 15 |
| 373 | 15c. blue | 20 | 15 |
| 374 | 20c. yellow | 20 | 15 |
| 375 | 30c. lilac | 20 | 15 |
| 376 | 1e. green | 65 | 15 |
| 377 | 2e. lemon | 65 | 15 |
| 378 | 2e.50 pink | 95 | 15 |
| 379 | 3e. brown | 1·50 | 45 |
| 380 | 5e. blue | 1·50 | 45 |
| 381 | 7e.50 olive | 1·60 | 80 |
| 382 | 15e. mauve | 2·30 | 80 |
| 383 | 30e. yellow | 6·00 | 2·30 |

ARMS: 15c. Nova Sintra. 20c. Ribeira Brava. 30c. Assomada. 1e. Maio. 2e. Mindelo. 2e.50 Santa Maria. 3e. Pombas. 5e. Sal-Rei. 7e.50, Tarrafal. 15e. Maria Pia. 30e. San Felipe.

**1962.** Sports. As T 62 of Angola. Multicoloured.

| | | | |
|---|---|---|---|
| 384 | 50c. Throwing the javelin | 25 | 20 |
| 385 | 1e. Discus thrower | 85 | 20 |
| 386 | 1e.50 Batsman (cricket) | 60 | 30 |
| 387 | 2e.50 Boxing | 85 | 35 |
| 388 | 4e.50 Hurdler | 1·40 | 95 |
| 389 | 12e.50 Golfers | 2·75 | 1·90 |

**1962.** Malaria Eradication. Mosquito design as T 63 of Angola. Multicoloured.

| | | | |
|---|---|---|---|
| 390 | 2e.50 "Anopheles pretoriensis" | 1·20 | 85 |

**1963.** 10th Anniv of T.A.P. Airline. As T 69 of Angola.

| | | | |
|---|---|---|---|
| 391 | 2e.50 multicoloured | 90 | 60 |

**1964.** Centenary of National Overseas Bank. As T 71 of Angola but portrait of J. da S. M. Leal.

| | | | |
|---|---|---|---|
| 392 | 1e.50 multicoloured | 85 | 65 |

**1965.** Centenary of I.T.U. As T 73 of Angola.

| | | | |
|---|---|---|---|
| 393 | 2e.50 multicoloured | 1·70 | 1·20 |

**30** Militia Regiment Drummer, 1806

**1965.** Portuguese Military Uniforms. Mult.

| | | | |
|---|---|---|---|
| 394 | 50c. Type **30** | 25 | 20 |
| 395 | 1e. Militiaman, 1806 | 45 | 20 |
| 396 | 1e.50 Infantry Grenadiers officers, 1833 | 60 | 35 |
| 397 | 2e.50 Infantry grenadier, 1833 | 1·10 | 30 |
| 398 | 3e. Cavalry officer, 1834 | 2·30 | 45 |
| 399 | 4e. Infantry grenadier, 1835 | 1·10 | 45 |
| 400 | 5e. Artillery officer, 1848 | 1·20 | 45 |
| 401 | 10e. Infantry drum-major, 1856 | 2·50 | 1·50 |

**1966.** 40th Anniv of National Revolution. As T 77 of Angola, but showing different building. Multicoloured.

| | | | |
|---|---|---|---|
| 402 | 1e. Dr A. Moreira's Academy and Public Assistance Building | 50 | 40 |

**1967.** Centenary of Military Naval Association. As T 79 of Angola. Multicoloured.

| | | | |
|---|---|---|---|
| 403 | 1e. F. da Costa and gunboat "Mandovy" | 60 | 45 |
| 404 | 1e. 50 C. Araujo and mine-sweeper "Augusto Castilho" | 1·00 | 75 |

**1967.** 50th Anniv of Fatima Apparitions. As T 80 of Angola. Multicoloured.

| | | | |
|---|---|---|---|
| 405 | 1e. Image of Virgin Mary | 25 | 20 |

**33** President Tomas

**1968.** Visit of President Tomas of Portugal.

| | | | | |
|---|---|---|---|---|
| 406 | **33** | 1e. multicoloured | 25 | 20 |

**1968.** 500th Birth Anniv of Pedro Cabral (explorer). As T 84 of Angola. Multicoloured.

| | | | |
|---|---|---|---|
| 407 | 1e. Cantino's map, 1502 | 65 | 60 |
| 408 | 1e.50 Pedro Alvares Cabral (vert) | 1·10 | 65 |

**34** Port of Sao Vicente

**1968.** "Produce of Cape Verde Islands". Mult.

| | | | |
|---|---|---|---|
| 409 | 50c. Type **34** | 20 | 15 |
| 410 | 1e. "Purgueira" (Tatrophus curcus) (vert) | 35 | 20 |
| 411 | 1e.50 Groundnuts (vert) | 35 | 20 |
| 412 | 2e.50 Castor-oil plant (vert) | 35 | 20 |
| 413 | 3e.50 "Inhame" (Dioscorea alata) (vert) | 40 | 20 |
| 414 | 4e. Date palm (vert) | 40 | 20 |
| 415 | 4e.50 "Goiabeira" (Psidium guajava) (vert) | 65 | 20 |
| 416 | 5e. Tamarind (vert) | 95 | 25 |
| 417 | 10e. Manioc (vert) | 1·20 | 50 |
| 418 | 30e. Girl of Cape Verde (vert) | 3·00 | 2·10 |

**1969.** Birth Centenary of Admiral Gago Coutinho. As T 86 of Angola. Multicoloured.

| | | | |
|---|---|---|---|
| 419 | 30c. Fairey IIID seaplane "Lusitania" and map of Lisbon-Rio flight (vert) | 15 | 15 |

**1969.** 500th Birth Anniv of Vasco da Gama (explorer). Multicoloured. As T 87 of Angola.

| | | | |
|---|---|---|---|
| 420 | 1e.50 Vasco da Gama (vert) | 30 | 25 |

**1969.** Centenary of Overseas Administrative Reforms. As T 88 of Angola.

| | | | |
|---|---|---|---|
| 421 | 2e. multicoloured | 30 | 20 |

**1969.** 500th Birth Anniv of King Manoel I. As T 89 of Angola. Multicoloured.

| | | | |
|---|---|---|---|
| 422 | 3e. Manoel I | 40 | 30 |

**1970.** Birth Centenary of Marshal Carmona. As T 91 of Angola. Multicoloured.

| | | | |
|---|---|---|---|
| 423 | 2e.50 Half-length portrait | 40 | 30 |

**35** Desalination Installation

**1971.** Inauguration of Desalination Plant, Mindelo.

| | | | | |
|---|---|---|---|---|
| 424 | **35** | 4e. multicoloured | 1·00 | 70 |

**1972.** 400th Anniv of Camoens' "Lusiad" (epic poem). As T 96 of Angola. Multicoloured.

| | | | |
|---|---|---|---|
| 425 | 5e. Galleons at Cape Verde | 50 | 25 |

**1972.** Olympic Games, Munich. As T 97 of Angola. Multicoloured.

| | | | |
|---|---|---|---|
| 426 | 4e. Basketball and boxing | 50 | 25 |

**1972.** 50th Anniv of 1st Flight Lisbon–Rio de Janeiro. As T 98 of Angola. Multicoloured.

| | | | |
|---|---|---|---|
| 427 | 3e.50 Fairey IIID seaplane "Lusitania" near Sao Vicente | 50 | 25 |

**1973.** Centenary of I.M.O./W.M.O. As Type 99 of Angola.

| | | | |
|---|---|---|---|
| 428 | 2e.50 multicoloured | 50 | 25 |

**1975.** Independence. No. 407 optd INDEPENDENCIA 5-Julho-75.

| | | | |
|---|---|---|---|
| 430 | 1e. multicoloured | 1·00 | 60 |

**37** Cabral, Flag and People

**1975.** 3rd Anniv of Amilcar Cabral's Assassination.

| | | | | |
|---|---|---|---|---|
| 431 | **37** | 5e. multicoloured | 1·25 | 75 |

**38** Islanders with Broken Shackles

**1976.** 1st Anniv of Independence.

| | | | | |
|---|---|---|---|---|
| 432 | **38** | 50c. multicoloured | 40 | 25 |
| 433 | **38** | 3e. multicoloured | 15 | 10 |
| 434 | **38** | 15e. multicoloured | 40 | 20 |
| 435 | **38** | 50e. multicoloured | 1·25 | 65 |
| **MS**436 | | 150×110 mm. Nos. 432/5 | 10·00 | 7·50 |

**1976.** Nos. 428, 424 and 415 optd REPUBLICA DE.

| | | | | |
|---|---|---|---|---|
| 437 | **38** | 2e.50 multicoloured (No. 428) | 1·00 | 50 |
| 438 | **38** | 4e. multicoloured (No. 424) | 30·00 | 10·00 |
| 439 | **38** | 4e.50 multicoloured (No. 415) | 4·50 | 2·75 |

**40** Cabral and Map

**1976.** 20th Anniv of PAIGC (Revolutionary Party).

| | | | | |
|---|---|---|---|---|
| 440 | **40** | 1e. multicoloured | 75 | 40 |

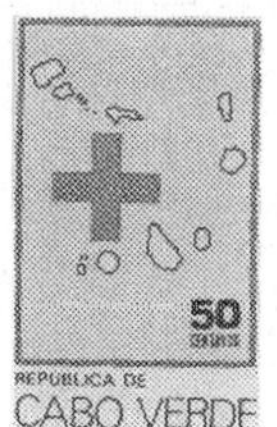

**41** Map of Islands

**1977.** Red Cross.

| | | | | |
|---|---|---|---|---|
| 441 | **41** | 50c. multicoloured | 1·00 | 60 |

**42** Printed Circuit

**1977.** International Telecommunications Day.

| | | | | |
|---|---|---|---|---|
| 442 | **42** | 5e.50 orange, brown and black | 40 | 25 |

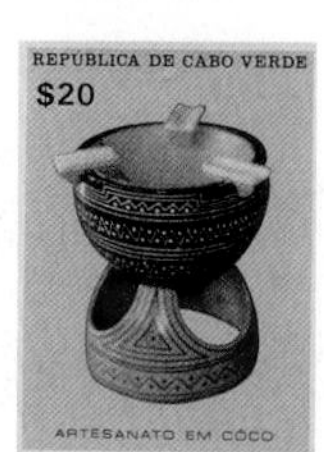

**43** Ashtray on Stand

**1977.** Craftsmanship in Coconut. Multicoloured.

| | | | |
|---|---|---|---|
| 443 | 20c. Type **43** | 10 | 10 |
| 444 | 30c. Ornamental bell | 10 | 10 |
| 445 | 50c. Lamp | 10 | 10 |
| 446 | 1e. Nativity | 10 | 10 |
| 447 | 1e.50 Desk lamp | 15 | 10 |
| 448 | 5e. Storage jar | 50 | 25 |
| 449 | 10e. Container with hinged lid | 1·00 | 50 |
| 450 | 20e. Tobacco jar | 2·00 | 1·00 |
| 451 | 30e. Stringed instrument | 3·00 | 1·50 |

**44** 5r. Stamp, 1877

**1977.** Centenary of First Cape Verde Stamps.

| | | | | |
|---|---|---|---|---|
| 452 | **44** | 4e. multicoloured | 1·00 | 60 |
| 453 | **44** | 8e. multicoloured | 2·00 | 1·20 |

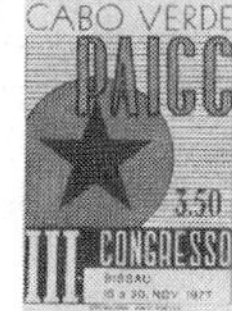

**45** Congress Emblem

**1977.** 3rd PAIGC Congress, Bissau.

| | | | | |
|---|---|---|---|---|
| 454 | **45** | 3e.50 multicoloured | 2·00 | 1·20 |

**1978.** No. 419 surch 3$00.

| | | | |
|---|---|---|---|
| 455 | 3e. on 30c. multicoloured | 4·00 | 2·00 |

**47** Microwave Antenna

**1978.** 10th World Telecommunications Day.

| | | | | |
|---|---|---|---|---|
| 456 | **47** | 3e.50 multicoloured | 40 | 20 |

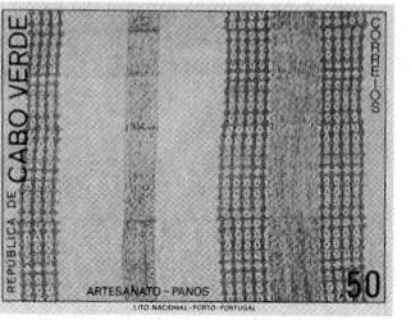

**48** Textile Pattern

**1978.** Handicrafts. Multicoloured.

| | | | |
|---|---|---|---|
| 457 | 50c. Type **48** | 10 | 10 |
| 458 | 1e.50 Carpet runner and map of Islands | 30 | 15 |
| 459 | 2e. Woven ribbon and map of Islands | 40 | 20 |
| 460 | 3e. Shoulder bag and map of Islands | 55 | 30 |
| 461 | 10e. Woven Cushions (vert) | 1·80 | 1·00 |

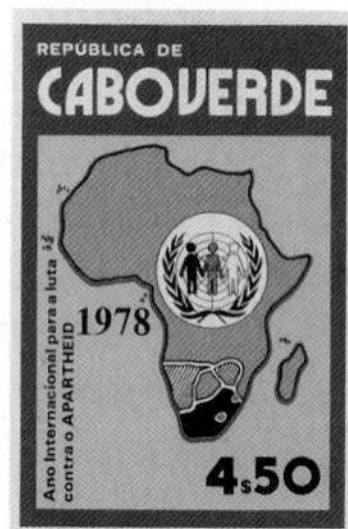

**49** Map of Africa

**1978.** International Anti-Apartheid Year.

| | | | | |
|---|---|---|---|---|
| 462 | **49** | 4e.50 multicoloured | 1·20 | 75 |

**50** Freighter "Cabo Verde"

**1978.** 1st Cape Verde Merchant Ship.

| | | | | |
|---|---|---|---|---|
| 463 | **50** | 1e. multicoloured | 80 | 30 |

**51** Human Rights Emblem

**1978.** 30th Anniv of Declaration of Human Rights.

| | | | | |
|---|---|---|---|---|
| 464 | **51** | 1e.50 multicoloured | 60 | 40 |
| 465 | **51** | 2e. multicoloured | 80 | 50 |

**52** Children with Flowers

**1979.** International Year of the Child. Mult.

| No. | Description | Mint | Used |
|---|---|---|---|
| 466 | 1e.50 Children with balloons and flags | 60 | 30 |
| 467 | 3e.50 Type **52** | 1·20 | 1·40 |

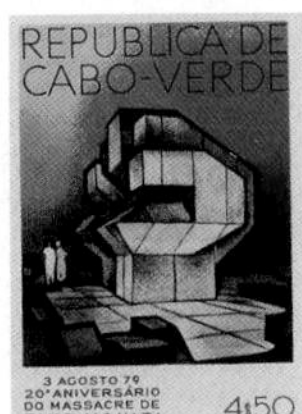


**53** Monument

**1979.** 20th Anniv of Pindjiguiti Massacre.

| No. | Type | Description | Mint | Used |
|---|---|---|---|---|
| 468 | **53** | 4e.50 multicoloured | 15 | 10 |

**54** Poster

**1979.** 1st National Youth Week.

| No. | Type | Description | Mint | Used |
|---|---|---|---|---|
| 469 | **54** | 3e.50 multicoloured | 80 | 35 |

**55** Mindelo

**1980.** Centenary of Mindelo City.

| No. | Type | Description | Mint | Used |
|---|---|---|---|---|
| 470 | **55** | 4e. multicoloured | 55 | 15 |

**56** Family, Graph and Map

**1980.** 1st Population and Housing Census.

| No. | Type | Description | Mint | Used |
|---|---|---|---|---|
| 471 | **56** | 3e.50 multicoloured | 65 | 35 |
| 472 | **56** | 4e.50 multicoloured | 80 | 45 |

**57** National Flag

**1980.** 5th Anniv of Independence (1st issue).

| No. | Type | Description | Mint | Used |
|---|---|---|---|---|
| 473 | **57** | 4e. multicoloured | 75 | 40 |

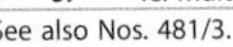
See also Nos. 481/3.

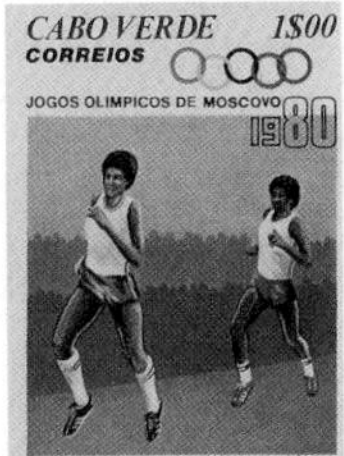


**58** Running

**1980.** Olympic Games, Moscow. Multicoloured.

| No. | Description | Mint | Used |
|---|---|---|---|
| 474 | 1e. Type **58** | 10 | 10 |
| 475 | 2e.50 Boxing | 10 | 10 |
| 476 | 3e. Basketball | 10 | 10 |
| 477 | 4e. Volleyball | 30 | 15 |
| 478 | 20e. Swimming | 50 | 90 |
| 479 | 50e. Tennis | 3·75 | 2·30 |
| **MS**480 | 98×67 mm. 30e. Football (horiz) | 10·00 | 7·50 |

**59** Stylized Bird

**1980.** 5th Anniv of Independence (2nd issue).

| No. | Type | Description | Mint | Used |
|---|---|---|---|---|
| 481 | **59** | 4e. multicoloured | 40 | 25 |
| 482 | **59** | 7e. multicoloured | 75 | 45 |
| 483 | **59** | 11e. multicoloured | 1·20 | 80 |

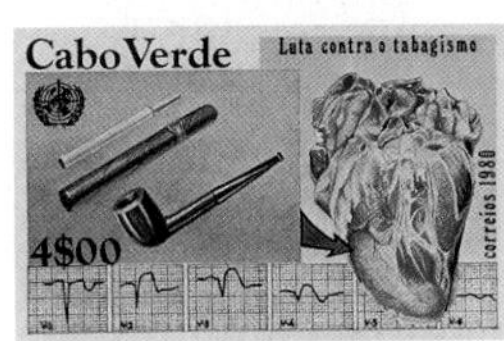


**60** Cigarette, Cigar, Pipe and Diseased Heart

**1980.** World Health Day. Anti-smoking Campaign. Multicoloured.

| No. | Description | Mint | Used |
|---|---|---|---|
| 484 | 4e. Type **60** | 1·00 | 45 |
| 485 | 7e. Healthy lungs plus smoking equals diseased lungs | 1·50 | 75 |

**61** Albacore

**1980.** Marine Life. Multicoloured.

| No. | Description | Mint | Used |
|---|---|---|---|
| 486 | 50c. Type **61** | 10 | 10 |
| 487 | 4e.50 Atlantic horse-mackerel | 30 | 15 |
| 488 | 8e. Mediterranean moray | 50 | 45 |
| 489 | 10e. Brown meagre | 70 | 35 |
| 490 | 12e. Skipjack tuna | 80 | 40 |
| 491 | 50e. Blue shark | 3·25 | 1·80 |

**62** "Area Verdel"

**1980.** Freighters. Multicoloured.

| No. | Description | Mint | Used |
|---|---|---|---|
| 492 | 3e. Type **62** | 30 | 20 |
| 493 | 5e.50 "Ilha do Maio" | 60 | 20 |
| 494 | 7e.50 "Ilha de Komo" | 80 | 40 |
| 495 | 9e. "Boa Vista" | 1·00 | 50 |
| 496 | 12e. "Santo Antao" | 1·40 | 65 |
| 497 | 30e. "Santiago" | 3·25 | 1·80 |

**63** "Lochnera rosea"

**1980.** Flowers. Multicoloured.

| No. | Description | Mint | Used |
|---|---|---|---|
| 498 | 50c. Type **63** | 10 | 10 |
| 499 | 4e.50 "Poinciana regia Bojer" | 40 | 20 |
| 500 | 8e. "Mirabilis jalapa" | 85 | 45 |
| 501 | 10e. "Nerium oleander" | 25 | 10 |
| 502 | 12e. "Bougainvillea litoralis" | 1·00 | 55 |
| 503 | 30e. "Hibiscus rosa sinenis" | 2·50 | 1·25 |

**64** Desert Scene and Hands holding plant

**1981.** Desert Erosion Prevention. Multicoloured.

| No. | Description | Mint | Used |
|---|---|---|---|
| 504 | 4e.50 Type **64** | 70 | 35 |
| 505 | 10e.50 Hands caring for plant and river scene | 1·60 | 80 |

**65** Map, Flag, and "Official Bulletin" announcing Constitution

**1981.** 6th Anniv of Constitution.

| No. | Type | Description | Mint | Used |
|---|---|---|---|---|
| 506 | **65** | 4e.50 multicoloured | 1·50 | 70 |

**66** Austrian Winter Olympics Stamps of 1975

**1981.** WIPA 1981 International Stamp Exhibition, Vienna. Sheet 107×62 mm.

| No. | Type | Description | Mint | Used |
|---|---|---|---|---|
| **MS**507 | **66** | 50e. multicoloured | 3·75 | 3·75 |

**67** Antenna

**1981.** Telecommunications. Multicoloured.

| No. | Description | Mint | Used |
|---|---|---|---|
| 508 | 4e.50 Type **67** | 40 | 20 |
| 509 | 8e. Dish antenna | 75 | 35 |
| 510 | 20e. Dish antenna and satellite | 1·80 | 90 |

**68** Disabled Person in Wheelchair and IYDP Emblem

**1981.** International Year of Disabled Persons.

| No. | Type | Description | Mint | Used |
|---|---|---|---|---|
| 511 | **68** | 4e.50 multicoloured | 75 | 30 |

**69** Moorhens

**1981.** Birds. Multicoloured.

| No. | Description | Mint | Used |
|---|---|---|---|
| 512 | 1e. Little egret (vert) | 20 | 15 |
| 513 | 4e.50 Barn owl (vert) | 40 | 20 |
| 514 | 8e. Grey-headed kingfisher (vert) | 90 | 30 |
| 515 | 10e. Type **69** | 2·30 | 1·10 |
| 516 | 12e. Helmet guineafowls | 2·50 | 1·30 |
| **MS**517 | 79×54 mm. 50e. Raza Island lark (Alauda razae) (vert) | 9·00 | 5·00 |

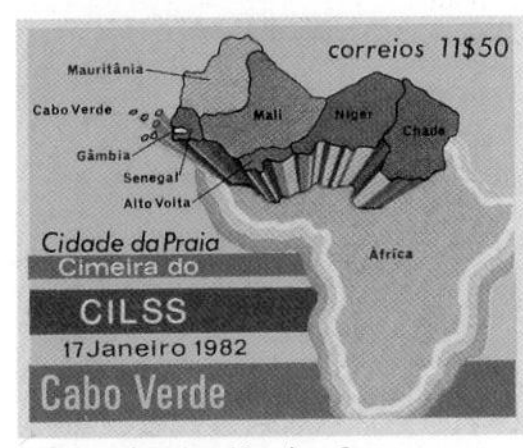


**70** Map showing Member States

**1982.** CILSS Congress, Praia.

| No. | Type | Description | Mint | Used |
|---|---|---|---|---|
| 518 | **70** | 11e.50 multicoloured | 55 | 50 |

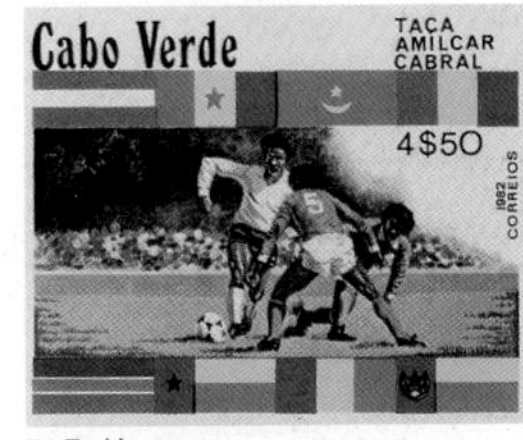


**71** Tackle

**1982.** "Amilcar Cabral" Football Cup Competition. Multicoloured.

| No. | Description | Mint | Used |
|---|---|---|---|
| 519 | 4e.50 Type **71** | 55 | 15 |
| 520 | 7e.50 Running with ball | 95 | 35 |
| 521 | 11e.50 Goalmouth scene | 1·40 | 65 |

**72** Militiawomen

**1982.** 1st Anniv of Cape Verde Women's Organization. Multicoloured.

| No. | Description | Mint | Used |
|---|---|---|---|
| 522 | 4e.50 Type **72** | 30 | 15 |
| 523 | 8e. Women farmers | 94 | 40 |
| 524 | 12e. Nursery teacher | 1·30 | 70 |

**73** Footballers

**1982.** World Cup Football Championship, Spain.

| No. | Type | Description | Mint | Used |
|---|---|---|---|---|
| 525 | **73** | 1e.50 multicoloured | 15 | 10 |
| 526 | - | 4e.50 multicoloured | 40 | 25 |
| 527 | - | 8e. multicoloured | 80 | 40 |
| 528 | - | 10e.50 multicoloured | 1·00 | 60 |
| 529 | - | 12e. multicoloured | 1·20 | 65 |
| 530 | - | 20e. multicoloured | 2·00 | 1·10 |
| **MS**531 | | 82×96 mm. 50e. multicoloured (29×37 mm) | 4·75 | 2·75 |

DESIGNS: 4e.50 to 50e. Various footballing scenes.

**74** "Morrissey-Ernestina"

**1982.** Return of Schooner "Morrissey-Ernestina".

| | | | | |
|---|---|---|---|---|
| 532 | **74** | 12e. multicoloured | 2·50 | 1·50 |

**75** San Vicente Shipyard

**1982.** 7th Anniv of Independence.

| | | | | |
|---|---|---|---|---|
| 533 | **75** | 10e.50 multicoloured | 2·00 | 1·00 |

**76** "Hypolimnas misippus"

**1982.** Butterflies. Multicoloured.

| | | | |
|---|---|---|---|
| 534 | 2e. Type **76** | 30 | 15 |
| 535 | 4e.50 "Melanitis lede" | 70 | 30 |
| 536 | 8e. "Catopsilia florella" | 1·30 | 60 |
| 537 | 10e.50 "Colias electo" | 1·60 | 75 |
| 538 | 11e.50 "Danaus chrysippus" | 1·80 | 80 |
| 539 | 12e. "Papilio demodecus" | 2·00 | 85 |

**77** Amilcar Cabral

**1983.** Amilcar Cabral Symposium.

| | | | | |
|---|---|---|---|---|
| 540 | **77** | 7e. multicoloured | 80 | 65 |
| 541 | **77** | 10e.50 multicoloured | 1·30 | 1·00 |

**78** Francisco Xavier de Cruz (composer)

**1983.** Composers and Poets. Multicoloured.

| | | | |
|---|---|---|---|
| 543 | 7e. Type **78** | 1·00 | 60 |
| 544 | 14e. Eugenio Tavares (poet) | 2·00 | 1·30 |

**79** "World Communications Network"

**1983.** World Communications Year.

| | | | | |
|---|---|---|---|---|
| 545 | **79** | 13e. multicoloured | 1·50 | 75 |

**80** Cape Verde Cone

**1983.** Shells. Multicoloured.

| | | | |
|---|---|---|---|
| 546 | 50c. Type **80** | 10 | 10 |
| 547 | 1e. "Conus decoratus" | 15 | 15 |
| 548 | 3e. "Conus salreiensis" | 40 | 25 |
| 549 | 10e. "Conus verdensis" | 1·40 | 1·40 |
| 550 | 50e. "Conus cuneolus" | 6·50 | 3·50 |

**81** Arch and Cross

**1983.** 450th Anniv of Christianity in Cape Verde Islands.

| | | | | |
|---|---|---|---|---|
| 551 | **81** | 7e. multicoloured | 1·40 | 1·30 |

**82** Auster D5/160 Husky

**1984.** 40th Anniv of ICAO. Multicoloured.

| | | | |
|---|---|---|---|
| 552 | 50c. Type **82** | 25 | 10 |
| 553 | 2e. de Havilland Dove | 30 | 15 |
| 554 | 10e. Hawker Siddeley HS748 | 90 | 60 |
| 555 | 13e. de Havilland Dragon Rapide | 1·20 | 95 |
| 556 | 20e. de Havilland Twin Otter | 1·80 | 1·50 |
| 557 | 50e. Britten-Norman Islander | 4·75 | 3·50 |

**83** Families, Houses and Emblems as Balloons

**1984.** National Solidarity Campaign.

| | | | | |
|---|---|---|---|---|
| 558 | **83** | 6e.50 multicoloured | 1·20 | 50 |
| 559 | **83** | 13e.50 multicoloured | 2·30 | 1·20 |

**84** Figure rising from Nautilus Shell

**1985.** 2nd Cape Verde Womens' Organization Conference.

| | | | | |
|---|---|---|---|---|
| 560 | **84** | 8e. multicoloured | 1·30 | 1·00 |

**85** Emblem

**1985.** 10th Anniv of Independence.

| | | | | |
|---|---|---|---|---|
| 561 | **85** | 8e. multicoloured | 1·40 | 95 |
| 562 | **85** | 12e. multicoloured | 2·00 | 1·40 |

**87** "Steamer"

**1985**

| | | | | |
|---|---|---|---|---|
| 564 | **87** | 30e. on 10c. multicoloured | 22·00 | 22·00 |

**MS**565 Three sheets, each 190×260 mm. (a) 50e. As No. 564 but ship upper structure red×4; (b) 50e. As No. 564 but ship upper structure yellow×4; (c) 50e. As No. 564 but ship upper structure green×4 £375

**88** "Mabuya vaillanti"

**1986.** Endangered Reptiles. Multicoloured.

| | | | |
|---|---|---|---|
| 566 | 8e. Type **88** | 4·50 | 2·50 |
| 567 | 10e. "Tarentola gigas brancoensis" | 5·50 | 3·25 |
| 568 | 15e. "Tarentola gigas gigas" | 8·00 | 4·75 |
| 569 | 30e. "Hemidactylus bouvieri" | 16·00 | 10·00 |
| **MS**570 | 130×60 mm. 50e. Type **88**; 50e. As No. 569 | 25·00 | 20·00 |

**89** Food in Pot over Fire

**1986.** World Food Day. Multicoloured.

| | | | |
|---|---|---|---|
| 571 | 8e. Type **89** | 45 | 35 |
| 572 | 12e. Women pounding food in mortar | 70 | 55 |
| 573 | 15e. Woman rolling flat bread with stone | 1·00 | 70 |

**90** Dove and Olive Branch

**1986.** International Peace Year.

| | | | | |
|---|---|---|---|---|
| 574 | **90** | 12e. multicoloured | 65 | 35 |
| 575 | **90** | 30e. multicoloured | 1·70 | 85 |

**91** Family Planning and Child Health Centre, Praia, and Woman breast-feeding Baby

**1987.** Child Survival Campaign. Multicoloured.

| | | | |
|---|---|---|---|
| 576 | 8e. Type **91** | 40 | 30 |
| 577 | 10e. Assomada SOS children's village | 50 | 35 |
| 578 | 12e. Family planning clinic, Mindelo, and nurse with child | 60 | 45 |
| 579 | 16e. Children's home, Mindelo, and nurse with baby | 80 | 55 |
| 580 | 100e. Calouste Gulbenkian kindergarten, Praia, and child writing | 4·75 | 3·50 |

**92** Mindelo City

**1987.** Tourism. Multicoloured.

| | | | |
|---|---|---|---|
| 581 | 1e. Type **92** | 20 | 10 |
| 582 | 2e.50 Santo Antao island | 25 | 15 |
| 583 | 5e. Fogo island | 30 | 20 |
| 584 | 8e. Pillory, Velha City | 50 | 25 |
| 585 | 10e. Boa Entrada valley, Santiago island | 60 | 30 |
| 586 | 12e. Fishing boats, Santiago | 75 | 40 |
| 587 | 100e. Furna harbour, Brava island | 6·00 | 3·00 |

**93** "Carvalho" (schooner)

**1987.** Sailing Ships. Multicoloured.

| | | | | |
|---|---|---|---|---|
| 588 | **93** | 12e. black, mauve & blue | 80 | 50 |
| 589 | - | 16e. black, blue & mauve | 1·00 | 85 |
| 590 | - | 50e. black, blue & dp blue | 3·00 | 2·50 |

**MS**591 105×105 mm 60e.×2, black, brown and violet 7·25 6·25

DESIGNS: 16e. "Nauta"; 50e. "Maria Sony"; 60e. "Madalan".

**94** Emblem

**1987.** 2nd National Development Plan.

| | | | | |
|---|---|---|---|---|
| 592 | **94** | 8e. multicoloured | 1·00 | 50 |

**95** Moths on Stem

**1988.** Crop Protection. Multicoloured.

| | | | |
|---|---|---|---|
| 593 | 50c. Type **95** | 10 | 10 |
| 594 | 2e. Caterpillars on plant treated with bio-insecticides | 20 | 15 |
| 595 | 9e. Use of imported predators | 75 | 45 |
| 596 | 13e. Use of imported predatorial insects | 1·10 | 60 |
| 597 | 16e. Locust on stem | 1·40 | 80 |
| 598 | 19e. Damaged wood | 1·60 | 90 |
| **MS**599 | 115×70 mm. 50e. Agricultural Research Institute (41×30 mm) | 4·00 | 4·50 |

**96** 17th-century Dutch Map

**1988.** Antique Maps of Cape Verde Islands. Multicoloured.

| | | | |
|---|---|---|---|
| 600 | 1e.50 Type **96** | 55 | 30 |
| 601 | 2e.50 18th-cent Belgian map | 90 | 50 |
| 602 | 4e.50 18th-cent French map | 1·10 | 65 |
| 603 | 9e.50 18th-cent English map | 1·30 | 80 |
| 604 | 19e.50 19th-cent English map | 60 | 1·00 |
| 605 | 20e. 18th-cent French map (vert) | 2·30 | 1·30 |

**97** Church of the Abbot of the Holy Shelter, Tarrafal, Santiago

**1988.** Churches. Multicoloured.

| | | | |
|---|---|---|---|
| 606 | 5e. Type **97** | 30 | 20 |
| 607 | 8e. Church of Our Lady of Light, Maio | 50 | 30 |
| 608 | 10e. Church of the Nazarene, Praia, Santiago | 65 | 35 |
| 609 | 12e. Church of Our Lady of the Rosary, Sao Nicolau | 80 | 40 |
| 610 | 15e. Church of the Nazarene, Mindelo, Sao Vicente | 1·10 | 50 |
| 611 | 20e. Church of Our Lady of Grace, Praia, Santiago | 1·40 | 1·30 |

**98** Boy filling Tin with Water

**1988.** Water Economy Campaign.

| | | | | |
|---|---|---|---|---|
| 612 | **98** | 12e. multicoloured | 80 | 50 |

**99** Red Cross Workers

**1988.** 125th Anniv of Red Cross Movement.

| | | | | |
|---|---|---|---|---|
| 613 | **99** | 7e. multicoloured | 75 | 40 |

**100** Group of Youths and Pres. Pereira

**1988.** 3rd Congress of African Party for the Independence of Cape Verde. Multicoloured.

| | | | |
|---|---|---|---|
| 614 | 7e. Type **100** | 30 | 20 |
| 615 | 10e.50 Pres. Pereira and Perez de Cuellar (U.N. Secretary-General) | 50 | 30 |
| 616 | 30e. Emblem and Pres. Pereira | 1·40 | 80 |
| **MS**617 | 130×90 mm. 100e. As No. 616 | 4·75 | 4·00 |

**101** Handball

**1988.** Olympic Games, Seoul. Multicoloured.

| | | | |
|---|---|---|---|
| 618 | 12e. Type **101** | 85 | 60 |
| 619 | 15e. Tennis | 1·10 | 80 |
| 620 | 20e. Football | 1·50 | 1·10 |
| 621 | 30e. Boxing | 2·00 | 1·70 |
| **MS**622 | 130×90 mm. 50e. Long jump | 3·00 | 3·00 |

**102** Hot-air Balloon "Pro Juventute"

**1989.** 2nd Pro Juventute Congress.

| | | | | |
|---|---|---|---|---|
| 623 | **102** | 30e. multicoloured | 1·50 | 75 |

**103** Silva

**1989.** Death Centenary of Roberto Duarte Silva (chemist).

| | | | | |
|---|---|---|---|---|
| 624 | **103** | 12e.50 multicoloured | 1·50 | 75 |

**104** "Liberty guiding the People" (Eugene Delacroix)

**1989.** Bicentenary of French Revolution.

| | | | | |
|---|---|---|---|---|
| 625 | **104** | 20e. multicoloured | 90 | 50 |
| 626 | **104** | 24e. multicoloured | 1·20 | 60 |
| 627 | **104** | 25e. multicoloured | 1·20 | 65 |
| **MS**628 | | 120×76 mm. 100e. multicoloured | 4·75 | 4·00 |

DESIGNS: 29×37 mm. 100e. Detail of Arc de Triomphe, Paris.

No. **MS**628 also commemorates "Philexfrance 89" International Stamp Exhibition.

**105** Anniversary Emblem

**1989.** Centenary of Interparliamentary Union. Mult.

| | | | |
|---|---|---|---|
| 629 | 2e. Type **105** | 20 | 10 |
| 630 | 4e. Dove | 30 | 20 |
| 631 | 13e. National Assembly building | 90 | 65 |

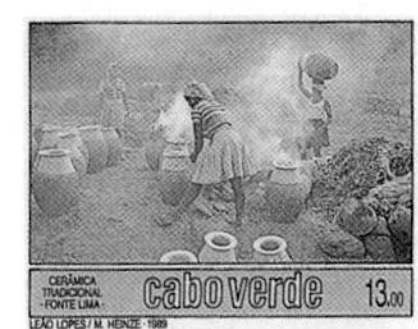


**106** Fonte Lima Women firing Pots

**1989.** Traditional Pottery. Multicoloured.

| | | | |
|---|---|---|---|
| 632 | 13e. Type **106** | 50 | 35 |
| 633 | 20e. Terra di Monti women and children arranging pots to bake in sun (vert) | 85 | 55 |
| 634 | 24e. Terra di Monti woman shaping pot | 1·00 | 65 |
| 635 | 25e. Fonte Lima women kneading clay (vert) | 1·10 | 70 |

**107** Boy and Truck

**1989.** Christmas. Home-made Toys. Mult.

| | | | |
|---|---|---|---|
| 636 | 1e. Type **107** | 25 | 25 |
| 637 | 6e. Boy with car on waste ground | 35 | 30 |
| 638 | 8e. Boy with truck on pavement | 50 | 35 |
| 639 | 11e.50 Boys with various vehicles | 1·00 | 50 |
| 640 | 18e. Boys and sit-on scooter | 1·50 | 90 |
| 641 | 100e. Boy with boat | 5·00 | 4·50 |

**108** Pope John Paul II

**1990.** Papal Visit.

| | | | | |
|---|---|---|---|---|
| 642 | **108** | 13e. multicoloured | 1·00 | 50 |
| 643 | **108** | 20e. multicoloured | 1·00 | 50 |
| **MS**644 | | 110 mm. 200e. multicoloured | 6·50 | 6·00 |

DESIGN: 200e. Pope wearing mitre.

**109** Green Turtles

**1990.** Turtles. Multicoloured.

| | | | |
|---|---|---|---|
| 645 | 50c. Type **109** | 15 | 10 |
| 646 | 1e. Leatherback turtles | 20 | 10 |
| 647 | 5e. Olive ridley turtles | 45 | 25 |
| 648 | 10e. Loggerhead turtles | 90 | 60 |
| 649 | 42e. Hawksbill turtles | 3·50 | 2·50 |

**110** Footballers

**1990.** World Cup Football Championship, Italy.

| | | | | |
|---|---|---|---|---|
| 650 | **110** | 4e. multicoloured | 15 | 10 |
| 651 | - | 7e.50 multicoloured | 20 | 10 |
| 652 | - | 8e. multicoloured | 25 | 10 |
| 653 | - | 100e. multicoloured | 3·00 | 2·00 |
| **MS**654 | | 87×54 mm. 100e. multicoloured | 4·00 | 2·50 |

DESIGNS: 7e.50 to 100e. Different footballing scenes.

**111** Face

**1990.** 1st Congress of Cape Verde Women's Movement.

| | | | | |
|---|---|---|---|---|
| 655 | **111** | 9e. multicoloured | 50 | 30 |

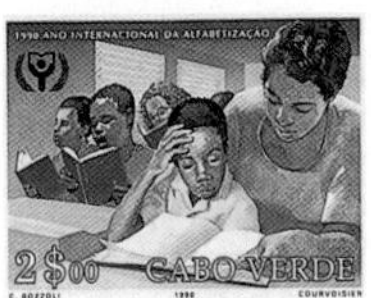


**112** Teacher helping Boy to Read

**1990.** International Literacy Year. Multicoloured.

| | | | |
|---|---|---|---|
| 656 | 2e. Type **112** | 20 | 10 |
| 657 | 3e. Teacher with adult class | 25 | 15 |
| 658 | 15e. Teacher with flash-card | 80 | 50 |
| 659 | 19e. Adult student pointing to letters on blackboard | 1·10 | 70 |

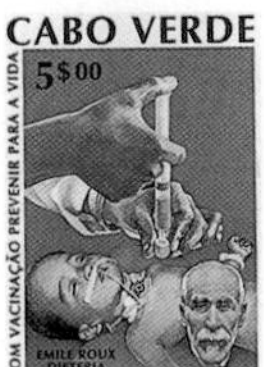


**113** Diphtheria Treatment and Emile Roux (pioneer of antitoxic method)

**1990.** Vaccination Campaign. Multicoloured.

| | | | |
|---|---|---|---|
| 660 | 5e. Type **113** | 75 | 30 |
| 661 | 13e. Tuberculosis vaccination and Robert Koch (discoverer of tubercle bacillus) | 1·40 | 75 |
| 662 | 20e. Tetanus vaccination and Gaston Ramon | 2·30 | 1·30 |
| 663 | 24e. Poliomyelitis oral vaccination and Jonas Edward Salk (discoverer of vaccine) | 2·50 | 1·50 |

**114** Musician on Bull's Back

**1990.** Traditional Stories. Multicoloured.

| | | | |
|---|---|---|---|
| 664 | 50c. Type **114** | 10 | 10 |
| 665 | 2e.50 Fisherman and mermaid ("Joao Piquinote") | 20 | 15 |
| 666 | 12e. Girl and snake | 90 | 50 |
| 667 | 25e. Couple and eggs ("Ti Lobo, Ti Lobo") | 1·80 | 1·00 |

**115** World Map and Beam destroying AIDS Virus

**1991.** Anti-AIDS Campaign. Multicoloured.

| | | | |
|---|---|---|---|
| 668 | 13e. Type **115** | 2·40 | 1·80 |
| 669 | 24e. Beam, AIDS virus and "SIDA" | 4·50 | 3·35 |

**116** Fishing Boat at Sea and Fishermen on Shore

**1991.** Fishing Industry. Multicoloured.

| | | | |
|---|---|---|---|
| 670 | 10e. Type **116** | 60 | 45 |
| 671 | 24e. Fisherman removing hook from fish | 1·50 | 1·20 |
| 672 | 25e. Fishing boats | 1·60 | 1·20 |
| 673 | 50e. Fishermen taking in lines | 3·25 | 2·30 |

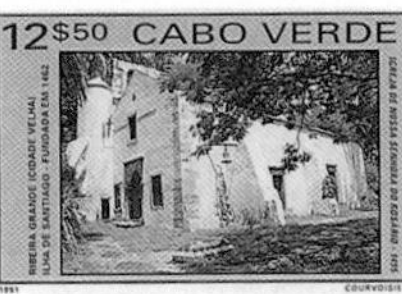


**117** Our Lady of the Rosary Church

**1991.** Tourism. Ruins of Ribeira Grande, Santiago Island. Multicoloured.

| | | | |
|---|---|---|---|
| 674 | 12e.50 Type **117** | 75 | 50 |
| 675 | 15e. Se Cathedral | 90 | 75 |
| 676 | 20e. Sao Filipe fortress | 1·30 | 1·00 |
| 677 | 30e. St. Francis's Convent | 1·80 | 1·50 |
| **MS**678 | 81×79 mm. 100e. Pillory (vert) | 5·25 | 5·25 |

**118** "Lavandula rotundifolia"

**1991.** Medicinal Plants. Multicoloured.

| | | | |
|---|---|---|---|
| 679 | 10e. Type **118** | 45 | 30 |
| 680 | 15e. "Micromeria forbesii" | 70 | 50 |
| 681 | 21e. "Sarcostemma daltonii" | 90 | 70 |
| 682 | 24e. "Periploca chevalieri" | 1·10 | 80 |
| 683 | 30e. "Echium hypertropicum" | 1·30 | 1·10 |
| 684 | 35e. "Erysimum caboverdeanum" | 1·50 | 1·20 |

**119** Guitar

**1991.** Musical Instruments. Multicoloured.

| | | | |
|---|---|---|---|
| 685 | 10e. Type **119** | 50 | 40 |
| 686 | 20e. Violin | 1·00 | 80 |
| 687 | 29e. Guitar with five double strings | 1·40 | 1·20 |
| 688 | 47e. Cimboa | 2·30 | 1·90 |
| **MS**689 | 97×82 mm. (a) 60e. Accordian (horiz) | 3·50 | 2·50 |

**120** Crib (Tito Livio Goncalves)

**1991.** Christmas. Multicoloured.

| | | | |
|---|---|---|---|
| 690 | 31e. Type **120** | 1·00 | 90 |
| 691 | 50e. Fonte-Lima crib | 1·60 | 1·50 |

**121** Rose Apples

**1992.** Tropical Fruits. Multicoloured.

| | | | |
|---|---|---|---|
| 692 | 16e. Type **121** | 80 | 60 |
| 693 | 25e. Mangoes | 1·30 | 1·10 |
| 694 | 31e. Cashews | 1·50 | 1·40 |
| 695 | 32e. Avocados | 1·60 | 1·50 |

**122** Ships anchored in Bay

**1992.** 500th Anniv of Discovery of America by Columbus. Columbus's Landings in Cape Verde Islands. Multicoloured.

696 40e. Type **122** 2·50 2·00

697 40e. Caravel 2·50 2·00

**MS**698 130×63 mm. Nos. 696/7 (sold at 150e.) 9·50 7·50

**123** Alhambra, Granada

**1992.** Granada 92 International Stamp Exhibition, Spain. Sheet 135×95 mm.

**MS**699 **123** 50e. 50e. multicoloured (sold at 150e.) 8·00 8·00

**124** Throwing the Javelin

**1992.** Olympic Games, Barcelona. Multicoloured.

700 16e. Type **124** 60 40

701 20e. Weightlifting 80 65

702 32e. Pole vaulting 1·30 1·00

703 40e. Putting the shot 1·50 1·30

**MS**704 98×71 mm. 100e. Gymnastics (26×32 m) 3·75 3·75

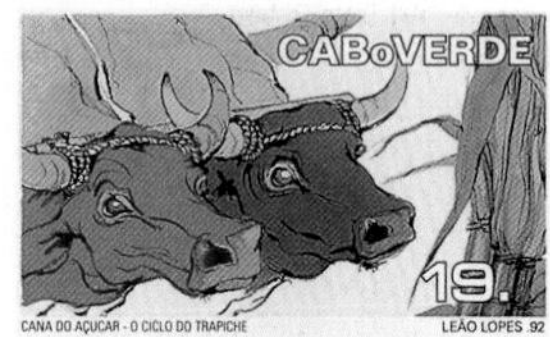


**125** Oxen and Sugar Cane

**1992.** Production of Molasses. Multicoloured.

705 19e. Type **125** 85 45

706 20e. Crushing cane 90 75

707 37e. Feeding cane into mill 1·70 1·60

708 38e. Cooking molasses 1·80 1·70

**126** Cat

**1992.** Domestic Animals. Multicoloured.

709 16e. Type **126** 75 25

710 31e. Chickens 1·50 1·30

711 32e. Dog (vert) 1·50 1·40

712 50e. Horse 2·30 2·00

**127** "Tubastrea aurea"

**1993.** Corals. Multicoloured.

713 5e. Type **127** 20 15

714 31e. "Corallium rubrum" 1·20 1·00

715 37e. "Porites porites" 1·80 1·60

716 50e. "Millepora alcicornis" £180 1·60

**128** "Praia Harbour, Santiago Island, 1806"

**1993.** Brasilliana 93 International Stamp Exhibition, Rio de Janeiro, and union of Portuguese-speaking Capital Cities. Sheet 118×75 mm.

**MS**717 **128** 100e. multicoloured 5·50 4·50

**129** King Ferdinand and Queen Isabella of Spain and Pope Alexander VI

**1993.** 500th Annivs of Pope Alexander VI's Bulls (on Portuguese and Spanish spheres of influence) and of Treaty of Tordesillas. Multicoloured.

718 37e. Type **129** 1·10 95

719 37e. King Joao II of Portugal and Pope Julius II 1·10 95

720 38e. Astrolabe, quill and left-half of globe 1·20 1·00

721 38e. Map of Iberian Peninsula and right-half of globe with Cape Verde Islands highlighted 1·20 1·00

Stamps of the same value were issued together in se-tenant pairs, each pair forming a composite design.

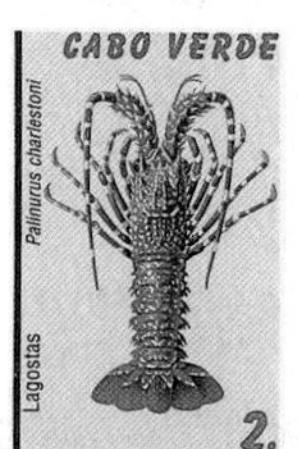


**130** "Palinurus charlestoni"

**1993.** Lobsters. Multicoloured.

722 2e. Type **130** 25 20

723 10e. Brown lobster 60 50

724 17e. Royal lobster 1·00 90

725 38e. Stone lobster 2·30 2·00

**MS**726 110×70 mm.100e. Royal lobster on seabed (51×36 mm) 5·75 5·75

**131** Cory's Shearwater

**1993.** Nature Reserves. Multicoloured.

727 10e. Type **131** (Branco and Raso Islets) 80 70

728 30e. Brown booby (De Cima and Raso Islets) 2·50 2·00

729 40e. Magnificent frigate bird (Curral Velho and Baluarte Islets) 3·50 2·50

730 41e. Red-billed tropic bird (Raso and De Cima Islets) 3·75 2·75

**132** Rose

**1993.** Flowers. Multicoloured.

731 5e. Type **132** 25 20

732 30e. Bird of Paradise flower 1·30 1·10

733 37e. Sweet William 1·60 1·40

734 50e. Cactus dahlia 1·90 1·80

**1994.** Hong Kong 94 International Stamp Exhibition,. Sheet 110×70 mm. Multicoloured.

**MS**735 No. 729 (sold at 150e.) 9·00 9·00

**133** Map and Prince Henry (image scaled to 62% of original size)

**1994.** 600th Birth Anniv of Prince Henry the Navigator.

736 **133** 37e. multicoloured 2·75 2·00

**134** Players and Giants Stadium, New York

**1994.** World Cup Football Championship, U.S.A. Multicoloured.

737 1e. Type **134** 40 10

738 20e. Referee showing red card and Rose Bowl, Los Angeles 80 55

739 37e. Scoring goal and Foxboro Stadium, Boston 1·50 1·00

740 38e. Linesman raising flag and Silverdome, Detroit 1·60 1·10

**MS**741 110×70 mm. 100e. Tackle and RFK Stadium, Washington D.C 4·50 3·00

**135** Sand Tiger

**1994.** Sharks. Multicoloured.

742 21e. Type **135** 1·30 1·20

743 27e. Black-tipped shark 1·60 1·50

744 37e. Whale shark 2·30 2·10

745 38e. Velvet belly 2·50 2·20

**136** "Prata" Bananas

**1994.** Bananas. Multicoloured.

746 12e. Type **136** 70 40

747 16e. "Pao" bananas (horiz) 90 55

748 30e. "Ana roberta" bananas 1·60 1·00

749 40e. "Roxa" bananas 2·30 1·30

**MS**750 64×82 mm. 100e. "Prata" bananas on tree (27×40 mm) (sold at 150e.) 8·00 5·00

No. **MS**750 commemorates Philakorea 1994 International and Singpex 94 stamp exhibitions.

**137** Fontes Pereira de Melo

**1994.** Lighthouses. Multicoloured.

751 2e. Type **137** 50 40

752 37e. Morro Negro 2·50 2·30

753 38e. D. Amelia (vert) 2·75 2·50

754 50e. D. Maria Pia (vert) 8·50 3·00

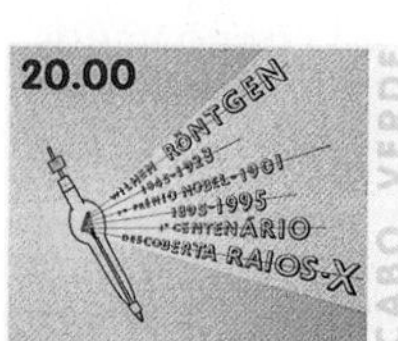


**138** X-Ray Tube and Dates

**1995.** Centenary of Discovery of X-Rays by Wilhelm Rontgen.

755 **138** 20e. multicoloured 1·50 1·30

756 **138** 37e. multicoloured 2·75 2·50

**MS**757 Sheet 142×95 mm. Nos. 755/6 (sold at 100e.) 7·00 7·00

**139** Child with Tuna

**1995.** 50th Anniv of FAO. Multicoloured.

758 37e. Type **139** 2·20 2·20

759 38e. Globe and wheat ear 2·40 2·40

**140** Wire-haired Fox Terrier and "Two Foxhounds and Fox Terrier" (John Emms)

**1995.** Dogs. Heads of dogs and paintings. Mult.

760 1e. Type **140** 20 20

761 10e. Cavalier King Charles and "Shooting Over Dogs" (Richard Ansdell) 15 10

762 40e. German shepherd and rough collies 2·30 1·60

763 50e. Bearded collie and "Hounds at Full Cry" (Thomas Blinks) 2·75 2·00

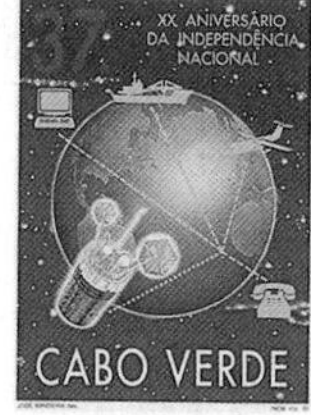


**141** Communications

**1995.** 20th Anniv of Independence.

764 **141** 37e. multicoloured 1·30 1·00

**142** Sweet William ("Dianthus barbatus")

**1995.** Singapore 95 International Stamp Exhibition. Sheet 110×70 mm.

**MS**765 **142** 37e. multicoloured (sold at 150e.) 7·00 7·00

**143** Horse Race

**1995.** St. Philip's Flag Festival, Fogo. Mult.

766 2e. Type **143** 20 20

767 10e. Preparing for horse race 25 25

768 37e. Preparing food and clapping to music 95 85

769 40e. Crowd watching final horse race 1·10 95

**144** Grasshopper playing Guitar

**1995.** Childrens' Stories. 300th Death Anniv of Jean de La Fontaine (writer). Scenes from "The Ant and the Grasshopper". Multicoloured.

770 10e. Type **144** 25 20

771 25e. Grasshopper in snowstorm looking through ants' window 60 55

772 38e. Ant laying-in supplies for winter 90 80

773 45e. Ants welcoming grasshopper into their home 1·10 1·00

**145** "Sonchus daltonii"

**1996.** Endangered Flowers. Multicoloured.
774 20e. Type **145** 65 60
775 37e. "Echium vulcanorum" 1·20 1·00
776 38e. "Nauplius smithii" 1·30 1·10
777 50e. "Campanula jacobaea" 1·60 1·40

**146** Table Tennis

**1996.** Olympic Games, Atlanta. Multicoloured.
778 1e. Type **146** 25 40
779 37e. Gymnastics 1·40 1·40
780 100e. Athletics 1·50 75

**147** Student (Education of Girls)

**1996.** 50th Anniv of UNICEF. Multicoloured.
781 20e. Type **147** 1·50 75
782 40e. Mother kissing child (Right to Love) 80 75

**148** Deep Sea Fishing

**1996.** Water Sports. Multicoloured.
783 2e.50 Type **148** 50 25
784 10e. Sailboard 5·00 45
785 22e.50 Jet skiing 1·10 1·00
786 100e. Surfing (horiz) 4·75 4·50
**MS**787 155×110 mm. 100e. Fish (scuba diving) (78×60 mm) 5·25 5·00

**1997.** Nos. 582 and 650/1 surch.
788 3e. on 2e.50 multicoloured 50 50
789 37e. on 4e. multicoloured 5·00 5·00
790 38e. on 7e.50 multicoloured 5·00 5·00

**150** State Arms

**1997.** National Symbols. Multicoloured.
791 25e. Type **150** 80 70
792 37e. National anthem 1·20 1·00
793 50e. State flag 1·50 1·30

**151** Small-toothed Sawfish

**1997.** The Small-toothed Sawfish. Multicoloured.
794 15e. Type **151** 70 70
795 15e. Underside of sawfish 70 70
796 15e. Sawfish and school of fishes 70 70
797 15e. Two sawfishes 20 10

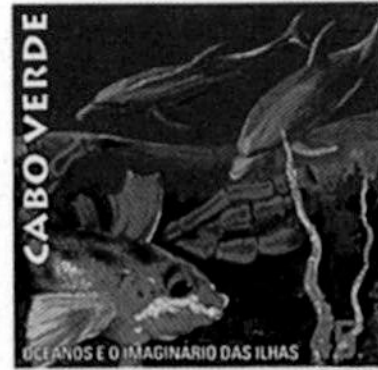

**152** Fish and Dolphins

**1997.** Oceans. Multicoloured.
798 45e. Type **152** 1·50 1·50
799 45e. Mermaid and merman 1·50 1·50
800 45e. Fishes, eel, coral and sunken gate 1·50 1·50

Nos. 798/800 were issued together, se-tenant, forming a composite design.

**153** Yellow-finned Tuna

**1997.** Tuna. Multicoloured.
801 13e. Type **153** 50 45
802 21e. Big-eyed tuna 80 75
803 41e. Little tuna 1·60 1·50
804 45e. Skipjack tuna 1·80 1·60

**154** Players chasing Ball

**1998.** World Cup Football Championship, France. Multicoloured.
805 10e. Type **154** 40 20
806 30e. Ball in net (vert) 1·10 80
807 45e. Player with ball (vert) 1·60 1·10
808 50e. Globe, football and trophy 1·80 1·30

**155** Fish Dish

**1998.** Local Cuisine.
809 **155** 5e. multicoloured 30 30
810 - 25e. multicoloured 1·30 1·30
811 - 35e. multicoloured 1·80 1·80
812 - 40e. multicoloured 2·00 2·00

DESIGNS: 25e. to 40e. Different food dishes.

**156** Navigators reading Books and Banana Tree

**1998.** 500th Anniv (1997) of Vasco da Gama's Expedition to India. Multicoloured.
813 50e. Type **156** 1·80 1·80
814 50e. Seaman with sword and couple 1·80 1·80
815 50e. Compass rose and Portuguese galleon in harbour 1·80 1·80

Nos. 813/15 were issued together, se-tenant, forming a composite design.

**157** Brava Island Costume

**1998.** Local Women's Costumes. Multicoloured.
816 10e. Type **157** 25 25
817 18e. Fogo Island 75 60
818 30e. Boa Vista Island 1·30 1·20
819 50e. Santiago Island 2·00 1·90

**158** "Byblia ilithyia"

**1999.** Butterflies and Moths. Multicoloured.
820 5e. Type **158** 25 25
821 10e. "Aganais speciosa" 30 30
822 20e. Crimson-speckled moth 80 75
823 30e. Painted lady 35 15
824 50e. Cabbage looper 1·90 1·80
825 100e. "Grammodes congenita" 3·75 3·50
**MS**826 114×68 mm. No. 822/3 3·75 3·75

**159** Concorde in Flight

**1999.** 30th Anniv of Concorde (supersonic airplane). Multicoloured.
827 30e. Type **159** 2·75 2·75
828 50e. Concorde on airport apron 4·50 4·50

**160** Alain Gerbault (solo yachtsman) and Mindelo Harbour

**1999.** "Philexfrance 99" International Stamp Exhibition, Paris, France. Multicoloured.
829 30e. Type **160** 3·00 3·00
830 50e. Roberto Duarte Silva (chemist) and Eiffel Tower, Paris 3·00 3·00
**MS**831 155×79 mm. Nos. 829/30 (sold at 100e.) 7·00 7·00

**161** Globe in Envelope and UPU Emblem

**1999.** 125th Anniv of Universal Postal Union. Mult.
832 30e. Type **161** 2·30 22·30
833 50e. Paper airplanes 3·50 3·50

Nos. 832/3 are not inscribed with the country name.

**162** Cola Sanjon Dance

**1999.** Local Dances. Multicoloured.
834 10e. Type **162** 35 35
835 30e. Contradanca 1·00 1·00
836 50e. Desfile de Tabanca (horiz) 1·80 1·70
837 100e. Batuque (horiz) 3·50 3·25

**163** Globe, Open Book and Hourglass

**2000.** New Millennium. Multicoloured.
838 40e. Type **163** 2·30 2·30
839 50e. "2000" (horiz) 2·50 2·50

**164** Baby

**2000.** 50th Anniv (1999) of S.O.S. Children's Villages. Multicoloured.
840 50e. Type **164** 1·80 1·60
841 100e. Child and emblem (horiz) 3·50 3·25

**165** "25" and Emblem

**2000.** 25th Anniv of Independence.
842 **165** 50e. multicoloured 1·50 1·50

**166** Gymnastics

**2000.** Olympic Games, Sydney. Multicoloured.
843 10e. Type **166** 35 30
844 40e. Taekwondo 1·00 90
845 50e. Athletics 1·50 1·40
**MS**846 70×120 mm. Nos. 843/5 3·00 3·00

**167** Dragon Tree

**2000.** Dragon Tree.
847 **167** 5e. green 25 25
848 **167** 40e. red 1·30 80
849 **167** 60e. brown 2·00 1·30

**168** Students (left-hand detail)

**2000.** 134th Anniv of the Liceu de Sao Nicolau Seminary. Multicoloured.
850 60e. Type **168** 2·00 1·90
851 60e. Students (right-hand detail) 2·00 1·90
852 60e. Jose Alves Feio, Jose Julio Dias (co-founders) and Antonio Jose de Oliveira Boucas (Principal) (56×26 mm) 70 35

Nos. 850/2 were issued together, se-tenant, forming a composite design.

**169** White Sea Bream (*Diplodus sargus*)

**2001.** Fish. Multicoloured.
853 10e. Type **169** 50 50
854 22e. *Diplodus prayensis* 1·10 1·00
855 28e. Marmora sea bream (*Lithognathus mormyrus*) 1·40 1·30
856 48e. *Diplodus fasciatus* 2·30 2·10
857 60e. *Diplodus puntazzo* 2·75 2·50

**170** *Thomisus onustus*

**2001.** Spiders. Multicoloured.

| | | | |
|---|---|---|---|
| 858 | 13e. Type **170** | 65 | 65 |
| 859 | 16e. *Scytodes velutina* | 75 | 70 |
| 860 | 40e. *Hersiliola simony* | 2·00 | 1·80 |
| 861 | 100e. *Loxosceles rufescens* | 4·75 | 4·50 |

**171** *Acacia albida*

**2001.** Trees. Multicoloured.

| | | | |
|---|---|---|---|
| 862 | 50e. Type **171** | 2·10 | 2·00 |
| 863 | 60e. *Ficus sycomorus* | 2·50 | 2·30 |

**172** Grand Place, Brussels and Fountain

**2001.** "Belgica 2001" International Stamp Exhibition, Brussels. Sheet 116×86 mm.

| | | | |
|---|---|---|---|
| **MS**864 | **172** 100e. multicoloured | 4·00 | 4·00 |

**173** Artemisia gorgonum (inscr "Artimisia")

**2001.** Plants (1st series). Multicoloured.

| | | | |
|---|---|---|---|
| 865 | 20e. Type **173** | 70 | 65 |
| 866 | 27e. *Globularia amygdalifolia* | 90 | 85 |
| 867 | 47e.50 *Sidereoxylon marginata* (horiz) | 1·60 | 1·50 |
| 868 | 50e. *Umbilicus schmidtii* (horiz) | 1·70 | 1·70 |
| 869 | 60e. *Verbascum cystolithicum* | 2·10 | 1·90 |
| 870 | 100e. *Limonium lobinii* | 3·50 | 3·25 |

See also Nos. 873/6.

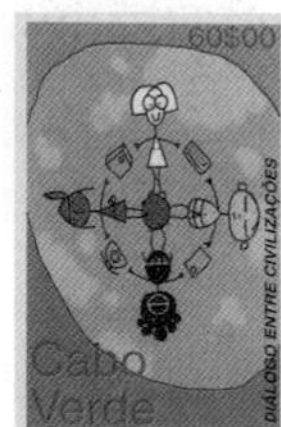

**174** Children encircling Globe

**2001.** United Nations Year of Dialogue among Civilizations.

| | | | |
|---|---|---|---|
| 871 | **174** 60e. multicoloured | 2·00 | 2·00 |

**175** Antonio Goncalves

**2001.** Birth Centenary of Antonio Aurelio Goncalves (writer).

| | | | |
|---|---|---|---|
| 872 | **175** 100e. multicoloured | 3·25 | 3·00 |

**2002.** Plants (2nd series). As T 173. Multicoloured.

| | | | |
|---|---|---|---|
| 873 | 10e. *Euphorbia tuckeyana* (inscr "tuckeyna") (horiz) | 35 | 35 |
| 874 | 50e. *Limonium* | 1·80 | 1·60 |
| 875 | 60e. *Aeonium gorgoneum* | 2·00 | 1·90 |
| 876 | 100e. *Polycarpaea gayi* | 3·50 | 3·25 |

**176** Player heading Ball into Goal

**2002.** World Cup Football Championship, Japan and South Korea. Multicoloured.

| | | | |
|---|---|---|---|
| 877 | 60e. Type **176** | 2·00 | 1·80 |
| 878 | 100e. Player kicking ball towards goal | 3·25 | 3·00 |

**177** Two Adult Turtles

**2002.** Marine Turtles (Caretta caretta). Multicoloured.

| | | | |
|---|---|---|---|
| 879 | 10e. Type **177** | 45 | 40 |
| 880 | 20e. Laying eggs | 80 | 75 |
| 881 | 30e. Young emerging from sand | 1·30 | 1·20 |
| 882 | 60e. Young crawling towards sea | 2·60 | 2·50 |
| 883 | 100e. Adult swimming | 4·25 | 4·00 |
| **MS**884 | 150×110 mm. 100e. Adult on beach (80×61 mm) | 4·25 | 4·25 |

**178** Basket from St. Nicholas Island

**2002.** Traditional Baskets. Multicoloured.

| | | | |
|---|---|---|---|
| 885 | 20e. Type **178** | 70 | 65 |
| 886 | 33e. From St. Anthony Island | 1·20 | 1·10 |
| 887 | 60e. From Santiago Island | 2·10 | 2·00 |
| 888 | 100e. From Boa Vista Island | 3·50 | 3·25 |

**179** Carlos Alberto Silva Martins (Katchass) (musician)

**2003.** Poets and Musicians. Multicoloured.

| | | | |
|---|---|---|---|
| 889 | 12e. Type **179** | 50 | 45 |
| 890 | 20e. Jorge Monteiro (Jota-monte) (composer) | 75 | 70 |
| 891 | 32e. Luís Rendall (composer) | 1·20 | 1·00 |
| 892 | 47e.50 Jorge Barbosa (poet) | 1·80 | 1·70 |
| 893 | 60e. Januario Leite (poet) | 2·20 | 2·10 |
| 894 | 100e. Jose Lopes (poet) | 3·75 | 3·50 |

**180** Cesaria Evora

**2003.** Cesaria Evora (singer) Commemoration. Multicoloured.

| | | | |
|---|---|---|---|
| 895 | 60e. Type **180** | 2·30 | 2·00 |
| 896 | 100e. Cesaria Evora (different) | 3·75 | 3·50 |
| **MS**897 | 85×115 mm. 200e. Cesaria Evora's legs (51×38 mm) | 7·75 | 7·25 |

**MS**897 forms a composite design of Cesaria Evora singing.

**181** Purple Heron (*Ardea purpurea bournei*)

**2003.** Herons and Egrets. Multicoloured.

| | | | |
|---|---|---|---|
| 898 | 10e. Type **181** | 80 | 70 |
| 899 | 27e. Grey heron (*Ardea cinerea*) | 1·10 | 1·00 |
| 900 | 42e. Cattle egret (*Bubulcus ibis*) | 1·80 | 1·60 |
| 901 | 60e. Little egret (*Egretta garzeta*) | 2·50 | 2·25 |

**182** Scout

**2003.** Scouting. Multicoloured.

| | | | |
|---|---|---|---|
| 902 | 60e. Type **182** (13th anniv of Scouts Association) | 2·30 | 2·00 |
| 903 | 100e. Scout with raised hand (3rd anniv of Catholic Scouts Corps) | 3·50 | 3·25 |

**183** Blue Whale (Balaenoptera musculus)

**2003.** Marine Mammals. Multicoloured.

| | | | |
|---|---|---|---|
| 904 | 10e. Type **183** | 65 | 60 |
| 905 | 20e. Sperm whale (Physeter macrocephalus) | 1·30 | 1·30 |
| 906 | 50e. Humpback whale (Megaptera novaeangliae) | 3·25 | 3·00 |
| 907 | 60e. Pilot whale (Globicephala macrorhynchus) | 4·00 | 3·75 |

**184** CAMS 51-F (biplane flying boat) at Calheta de Sao Martinho

**2003.** 75th Anniv of First Postal Hydroplane Base, Calheta de Sao Martinho. Multicoloured.

| | | | |
|---|---|---|---|
| 908 | 10e. Type **184** | 65 | 60 |
| 909 | 42e. Paulin Paris (1st pilot) and route | 2·75 | 2·50 |
| 910 | 60e. Route and CAMS 51-F | 3·75 | 3·50 |
| **MS**911 | 100×54 mm. 100e. As No. 908 but with design enlarged (57×33 mm) | 4·75 | 4·50 |

**185** Pope John Paul II and Child

**2003.** 25th Anniv of the Pontificate of Pope John Paul II. Multicoloured.

| | | | |
|---|---|---|---|
| 912 | 30e. Type **185** | 1·90 | 1·50 |
| 913 | 60e. Pope John Paul II and ships (horiz) | 3·50 | 3·50 |
| **MS**914 | 83×64 mm. 100e. Pope John Paul II blessing crucifix | 6·00 | 6·00 |

**186** Mahogany (*Khaya senegalensis*)

**2004.** Trees. Multicoloured.

| | | | |
|---|---|---|---|
| 915 | 20e. Type **186** | 90 | 80 |
| 916 | 27e. Black thorn (*Acacia nilotica*) | 1·30 | 1·10 |
| 917 | 60e. Ceiba (*Ceiba pentandra*) | 2·50 | 2·40 |
| 918 | 100e. Palm (*Phoenix atlantica*) | 4·25 | 4·00 |

**187** Windmill

**2004.** Ecological Energy Production.

| | | | |
|---|---|---|---|
| 919 | **187** 20e. blue | 80 | 70 |
| 920 | **187** 60e. magenta | 2·50 | 2·20 |
| 921 | **187** 100e. green | 4·00 | 3·75 |

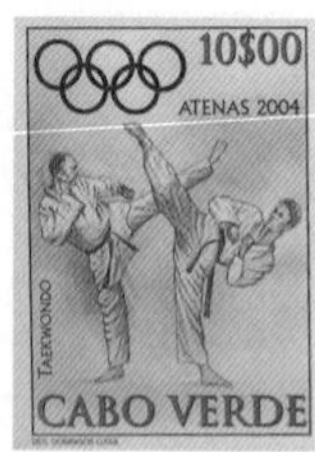

**188** Taekwondo

**2004.** Olympic Games, Athens. Multicoloured.

| | | | |
|---|---|---|---|
| 922 | 10e. Type **188** | 60 | 50 |
| 923 | 60e. Gymnastics | 2·50 | 2·30 |
| 924 | 100e. Boxing (horiz) | 4·00 | 3·75 |

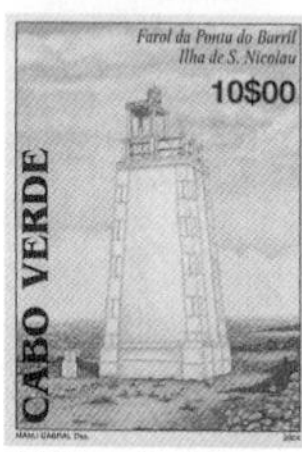

**189** Ponta Barril, Sao Nicolau

**2004.** Lighthouses. Multicoloured.

| | | | |
|---|---|---|---|
| 925 | 10e. Type **189** | 60 | 50 |
| 926 | 30e. Ponta Jalunga, Brava | 1·80 | 1·50 |
| 927 | 40e. Dom Luis, Sao Vicente (horiz) | 2·25 | 2·00 |
| 928 | 50e. Ponta Preta, Santiago (horiz) | 3·00 | 2·75 |

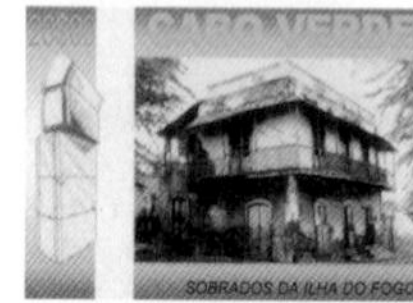

**190** House with Veranda

**2004.** Fogo Island's Historic Houses. Multicoloured.

| | | | |
|---|---|---|---|
| 929 | 20e. Type **190** | 80 | 75 |
| 930 | 40e. House with veranda, bay window and wall with gate | 2·00 | 1·75 |
| 931 | 50e. Three storied house | 2·50 | 2·25 |
| 932 | 60e. Pink house | 3·25 | 3·73 |

**191** Wall-mounted Telephone

**2004.** Twentieth-century Telephones. Multicoloured.

| | | | |
|---|---|---|---|
| 933 | 10e. Type **191** | 1·00 | 75 |
| 934 | 40e. Early windup handset | 1·50 | 1·50 |
| 935 | 60e. Candlestick telephone | 2·30 | 2·00 |
| 936 | 100e. Bakelite telephone | 3·75 | 3·00 |

**192** "storia storia"

**2005.** Stories. Multicoloured.

| | | | |
|---|---|---|---|
| 937 | 10e. Type **192** | 75 | 35 |
| 938 | 20e. "era um vez!" | 1·30 | 60 |
| 939 | 30e. "sapatinha ribera baxu" | 1·50 | 1·00 |
| 940 | 60e. "Quem ki sabi mas conta midjor" | 75 | 45 |

**193** Amilcar Cabral (freedom fighter)

**2005.** 30th Anniv of Independence.

| | | | | |
|---|---|---|---|---|
| 941 | **193** | 60e. multicoloured | 3·50 | 3·00 |

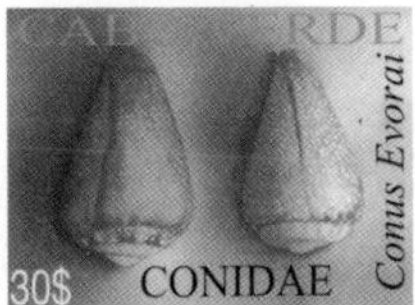

**194** *Conus evorai*

**2005.** Shells. Multicoloured.

| | | | |
|---|---|---|---|
| 942 | 30e. Type **194** | 1·30 | 90 |
| 943 | 40e. *Harpa doris* | 2·00 | 1·80 |
| 944 | 50e. Strombus lotus | 2·50 | 2·25 |
| 945 | 60e. *Phyllonotus duplex* | 3·00 | 2·75 |

**195** *Passer iagoensis*

**2005.** Birds. Multicoloured.

| | | | |
|---|---|---|---|
| 946 | 19e. Type **195** | 1·40 | 1·00 |
| 947 | 42e. *Estrilda astrid* | 1·80 | 1·50 |
| 948 | 44e. *Passer domesticus* | 2·00 | 1·80 |
| 949 | 55e. *Acrocephalus brevipennis* | 2·50 | 2·25 |

**196** Emblem

**2005.** World Information Society Summit, Tunis.

| | | | | |
|---|---|---|---|---|
| 950 | **196** | 60e. multicoloured | 4·00 | 3·50 |

**197** Tobacco Pipes

**2005.** Artefacts. Multicoloured.

| | | | |
|---|---|---|---|
| 951 | 5e. Type **197** | 50 | 50 |
| 952 | 10e. Spy glass, ornate stand and decorated box | 75 | 75 |
| 953 | 30e. Cannon | 2·75 | 2·50 |
| 954 | 60e. Astrolabe | 5·50 | 2·25 |
| **MS**955 115×85 mm. 100e. Shackles (80×60 mm) | | 7·50 | 7·50 |

**CHARITY TAX STAMPS**

Used on certain days of the year as an additional postal tax on internal letters. Other values in some of the types were for use on telegrams only. The proceeds were devoted to public charities. If one was not affixed in addition to the ordinary postage, special postage due stamps were used to collect the deficiency and the fine.

**1925.** As Marquis de Pombal issue of Portugal but inscr "CABO VERDE".

| | | | | |
|---|---|---|---|---|
| C266 | **C73** | 15c. violet | 1·10 | 1·10 |
| C267 | - | 15c. violet | 1·10 | 1·10 |
| C268 | **C 75** | 15c. violet | 1·10 | 1·10 |

**C16** St. Isabel

**1948**

| | | | | |
|---|---|---|---|---|
| C321 | **C16** | 50c. green | 2·30 | 1·40 |
| C322 | **C16** | 1e. red | 3·25 | 1·60 |

**1959.** Surch.

| | | | |
|---|---|---|---|
| C368 | 50c. on 1e. red | 90 | 70 |

**1959.** Colours changed.

| | | | |
|---|---|---|---|
| C369 | 50c. mauve | 1·60 | 90 |
| C370 | 1e. blue | 1·60 | 90 |

**C31**

**1967**

| | | | | |
|---|---|---|---|---|
| C406 | **C31** | 30c. multicoloured | 35 | 35 |
| C407 | **C31** | 50c. mult (purple panel) | 70 | 70 |
| C408 | **C31** | 50c. mult (red panel) | 30 | 30 |
| C409 | **C31** | 1e. mult (brown panel) | 70 | 70 |
| C410 | **C31** | 1e. mult (purple panel) | 70 | 70 |

**C32**

**1968.** Pharmaceutical Tax stamps surch as in Type C 32.

| | | | | |
|---|---|---|---|---|
| C411a | **C32** | 50c. on 1c. black, orange and green | 1·20 | 90 |
| C412c | **C32** | 50c. on 2c. black, orange and green | 70 | 40 |
| C413 | **C32** | 50c. on 3c. black, orange and green | 85 | 60 |
| C414 | **C32** | 50c. on 5c. black, orange and green | 85 | 60 |
| C415 | **C32** | 50c. on 10c. black, orange and green | 90 | 80 |
| C416 | **C32** | 1e. on 1c. black, orange and green | 1·80 | 1·40 |
| C417a | **C32** | 1e. on 2c. black, orange and green | 1·40 | 1·10 |

**NEWSPAPER STAMP**

**1893.** "Newspaper" key-type inscr "CABO VERDE".

| | | | | |
|---|---|---|---|---|
| N37 | **V** | 2½r. brown | 75 | 50 |

**POSTAGE DUE STAMPS**

**1904.** "Due" key-type inscr "CABO VERDE".

| | | | | |
|---|---|---|---|---|
| D119 | **W** | 5r. green | 30 | 30 |
| D120 | **W** | 10r. grey | 30 | 30 |
| D121 | **W** | 20r. brown | 30 | 30 |
| D122 | **W** | 30r. orange | 65 | 35 |
| D123 | **W** | 50r. brown | 40 | 30 |
| D124 | **W** | 60r. brown | 3·75 | 2·40 |
| D125 | **W** | 100r. mauve | 1·10 | 80 |
| D126 | **W** | 130r. blue | 1·10 | 80 |
| D127 | **W** | 200r. red | 1·00 | 85 |
| D128 | **W** | 500r. lilac | 2·40 | 1·80 |

**1911.** Nos. D119/28 optd REPUBLICA.

| | | | |
|---|---|---|---|
| D135 | 5r. green | 20 | 20 |
| D136 | 10r. grey | 20 | 20 |
| D137 | 20r. brown | 20 | 20 |
| D138 | 30r. orange | 20 | 20 |
| D139 | 50r. brown | 20 | 20 |
| D140 | 60r. brown | 40 | 30 |
| D141 | 100r. mauve | 40 | 30 |
| D142 | 130r. blue | 50 | 40 |
| D143 | 200r. red | 1·00 | 85 |
| D144 | 500r. lilac | 1·30 | 1·00 |

**1921.** "Due" key-type inscr "CABO VERDE" with currency in centavos.

| | | | |
|---|---|---|---|
| D252 | ½c. green | 15 | 15 |
| D253 | 1c. slate | 15 | 15 |
| D254 | 2c. brown | 15 | 15 |
| D255 | 3c. orange | 15 | 15 |
| D256 | 5c. brown | 15 | 15 |
| D257 | 6c. brown | 15 | 15 |
| D258 | 10c. mauve | 15 | 15 |
| D259 | 13c. blue | 55 | 40 |
| D260 | 20c. red | 55 | 40 |
| D261 | 50c. grey | 75 | 55 |

**1925.** As Nos. C266/8, optd MULTA.

| | | | | |
|---|---|---|---|---|
| D266 | **C73** | 30c. violet | 45 | 45 |
| D267 | - | 30c. violet | 45 | 45 |
| D268 | **C75** | 30c. violet | 45 | 45 |

**1952.** As Type D 45 of Angola, but inscr "CABO VERDE". Numerals in red; name in black.

| | | | |
|---|---|---|---|
| D356 | 10c. brown and grey | 15 | 15 |
| D357 | 30c. black, blue & mauve | 15 | 15 |
| D358 | 50c. blue, green & yellow | 15 | 15 |
| D359 | 1e. blue and pale blue | 15 | 15 |
| D360 | 2e. brown and orange | 30 | 30 |
| D361 | 5e. green and grey | 60 | 60 |

Pt. 7

## CAROLINE ISLANDS

A group of islands in the Pacific Ocean, formerly a German protectorate; under Japanese mandate after 1918. Now under United States trusteeship.

100 pfennig = 1 mark.

**1899.** Stamps of Germany optd **Karolinen**.

| | | | | |
|---|---|---|---|---|
| 7 | **8** | 3pf. brown | 15·00 | 17·00 |
| 8 | **8** | 5pf. green | 21·00 | 21·00 |
| 9 | **9** | 10pf. red | 21·00 | 23·00 |
| 10 | **9** | 20pf. blue | 27·00 | 34·00 |
| 11 | **9** | 25pf. orange | 65·00 | 75·00 |
| 12 | **9** | 50pf. brown | 65·00 | 75·00 |

**1901.** "Yacht" key-types inscr "KAROLINEN".

| | | | | |
|---|---|---|---|---|
| 13 | **N** | 3pf. brown | 1·30 | 2·10 |
| 14 | **N** | 5pf. green | 1·30 | 2·50 |
| 15 | **N** | 10pf. red | 1·30 | 5·75 |
| 16 | **N** | 20pf. blue | 1·50 | 10·50 |
| 17 | **N** | 25f. black & red on yellow | 1·80 | 17·00 |
| 18 | **N** | 30pf. black & orge on buff | 1·80 | 17·00 |
| 19 | **N** | 40pf. black and red | 1·80 | 19·00 |
| 20 | **N** | 50pf. black & pur on buff | 2·30 | 26·00 |
| 21 | **N** | 80pf. black & red on rose | 3·50 | 30·00 |
| 22 | **O** | 1m. red | 5·25 | 75·00 |
| 23 | **O** | 2m. blue | 8·50 | £110 |
| 24 | **O** | 3m. black | 11·50 | £180 |
| 25 | **O** | 5m. red and black | £190 | £650 |

**1910.** No. 13 surch **5 Pf.**

| | | | | |
|---|---|---|---|---|
| 26 | **N** | 5pf. on 3pf. brown | | £7500 |

Pt. 3

## CASTELROSSO

One of the Aegean Is. Occupied by the French Navy on 27 December 1915. The French withdrew in August 1921 and, after a period of Italian Naval administration, the island was included in the Dodecanese territory.

A. French Occupation.
100 centimes = 1 franc = 4 piastres.

B. Italian Occupation.
100 centesimi = 1 lira.

**A. FRENCH OCCUPATION**

**1920.** Stamps of 1902–20 of French Post Offices in Turkish Empire optd B. N. F. CASTELLORIZO.

| | | | | |
|---|---|---|---|---|
| F1 | **A** | 1c. grey | 60·00 | 60·00 |
| F2 | **A** | 2c. purple | 60·00 | 60·00 |
| F3 | **A** | 3c. red | 60·00 | 60·00 |
| F4 | **A** | 5c. green | 75·00 | 70·00 |
| F5 | **B** | 10c. red | 75·00 | 70·00 |
| F6 | **B** | 15c. red | £110 | £100 |
| F7 | **B** | 20c. brown | £120 | £120 |
| F9 | **B** | 30c. lilac | £130 | £130 |
| F10 | **C** | 40c. red and blue | £225 | £225 |
| F8 | **B** | 1pi. on 20c. blue | £120 | £120 |
| F11 | **C** | 2pi. on 50c. brown & lilac | £250 | £250 |
| F12 | **C** | 4pi. on 1f. red & green | £325 | £325 |
| F13 | **C** | 20pi. on 5f. blue & brown | £900 | £850 |

**1920.** Optd O. N. F. Castellorizo. (a) On stamps of 1902–20 of French Post Offices in Turkish Empire.

| | | | | |
|---|---|---|---|---|
| F14 | **A** | 1c. grey | 50·00 | 50·00 |
| F15 | **A** | 2c. purple | 50·00 | 50·00 |
| F16 | **A** | 3c. red | 50·00 | 50·00 |
| F17 | **A** | 5c. green | 50·00 | 50·00 |
| F18 | **B** | 10c. red | 55·00 | 55·00 |
| F19 | **B** | 15c. red | 65·00 | 65·00 |
| F20 | **B** | 20c. brown | £130 | £130 |
| F22 | **B** | 30c. lilac | £120 | £120 |
| F23 | **C** | 40c. red and blue | £120 | £120 |
| F21 | **B** | 1pi. on 25c. blue | £130 | £120 |
| F24 | **C** | 2pi. on 50c. brown & lilac | £120 | £120 |
| F25 | **C** | 4pi. on 1f. red and green | £150 | £150 |
| F26 | **C** | 20pi. on 5f. blue & brown | £550 | £500 |

(b) On Nos. 334 and 341 of France.

| | | | | |
|---|---|---|---|---|
| F27 | **18** | 10c. red | 55·00 | 32·00 |
| F28 | **18** | 25c. blue | 55·00 | 32·00 |

**1920.** Stamps of France optd O F CASTELLORISO.

| | | | | |
|---|---|---|---|---|
| F29 | | 5c. green | £300 | £275 |
| F30 | | 10c. red | £300 | £275 |
| F31 | | 20c. red | £300 | £275 |
| F32 | | 25c. blue | £300 | £275 |
| F33 | **13** | 50c. brown and lilac | £1600 | £1600 |
| F34 | **13** | 1f. red and green | £1600 | £1600 |

**B. ITALIAN OCCUPATION**

**1922.** Stamps of Italy optd CASTELROSSO.

| | | | | |
|---|---|---|---|---|
| 15 | **37** | 5c. green | 2·20 | 27·00 |
| 16 | **37** | 10c. red | 2·20 | 27·00 |
| 17 | **37** | 15c. grey | 2·20 | 38·00 |
| 18 | **41** | 20c. orange | 2·20 | 38·00 |
| 19 | **39** | 25c. blue | 2·20 | 30·00 |
| 20 | **39** | 40c. brown | 2·20 | 30·00 |
| 21 | **39** | 50c. violet | 2·20 | 38·00 |
| 22 | **39** | 60c. red | 2·20 | 43·00 |
| 23 | **39** | 85c. brown | 2·75 | 55·00 |
| 24 | **34** | 1l. brown and green | 2·75 | 55·00 |

**2**

**1923**

| | | | | |
|---|---|---|---|---|
| 10 | **2** | 5c. green | 4·00 | 18·00 |
| 11 | **2** | 10c. red | 4·00 | 18·00 |
| 12 | **2** | 25c. blue | 4·00 | 18·00 |
| 13 | **2** | 50c. purple | 4·00 | 18·00 |
| 14 | **2** | 1l. brown | 4·00 | 18·00 |

**1930.** Ferrucci stamps of Italy optd CASTELROSSO.

| | | | | |
|---|---|---|---|---|
| 25 | **114** | 20c. violet | 8·50 | 7·50 |
| 26 | - | 25c. green (No. 283) | 8·50 | 13·00 |
| 27 | - | 50c. black (as No. 284) | 8·50 | 7·50 |
| 28 | - | 1l.25 blue (No. 285) | 8·50 | 15·00 |
| 29 | - | 5l.+2l. red (as No. 286) | 39·00 | 75·00 |

**1932.** Garibaldi stamps of Italy optd CASTELROSSO.

| | | | | |
|---|---|---|---|---|
| 30 | | 10c. brown | 34·00 | 55·00 |
| 31 | **128** | 20c. brown | 34·00 | 55·00 |
| 32 | - | 25c. green | 34·00 | 55·00 |
| 33 | **128** | 30c. blue | 34·00 | 55·00 |
| 34 | - | 50c. purple | 34·00 | 55·00 |
| 35 | - | 75c. red | 34·00 | 55·00 |
| 36 | - | 1l.25 blue | 34·00 | 55·00 |
| 37 | - | 1l.75+25c. brown | 34·00 | 55·00 |
| 38 | - | 2l.55+50c. red | 34·00 | 55·00 |
| 39 | - | 5l.+1l. violet | 34·00 | 55·00 |

Pt. 20

## CAUCA

A State of Colombia, reduced to a Department in 1886, now uses Colombian stamps.

100 centavos = 1 peso.

**2**

**1902.** Imperf.

| | | | | |
|---|---|---|---|---|
| 2 | **2** | 10c. black on red | 6·00 | 5·75 |
| 3 | **2** | 20c. black on orange | 4·00 | 3·75 |

Pt. 16

## CAVALLA (KAVALLA)

French P.O. in a former Turkish port, now closed.

100 centimes = 1 franc.
40 paras = 1 piastre.

**1893.** Stamps of France optd **Cavalle** or surch also in figures and words.

| | | | | |
|---|---|---|---|---|
| 41 | **10** | 5c. green | 19·00 | 36·00 |
| 43 | **10** | 10c. black on lilac | 12·00 | 13·00 |
| 45 | **10** | 15c. blue | 50·00 | 28·00 |
| 46 | **10** | 1pi. on 25c. black on pink | 21·00 | 4·50 |
| 47 | **10** | 2pi. on 50c. red | 80·00 | 46·00 |
| 48 | **10** | 4pi. on 1f. green | £110 | 70·00 |
| 49 | **10** | 8pi. on 2f. brown on blue | £120 | £13 |

**1902.** "Blanc", "Mouchon" and "Merson" key-type "CAVALLE". The four higher values surch also

| | | | | |
|---|---|---|---|---|
| 50 | **A** | 5c. green | 2·7 | |
| 51 | **B** | 10c. red | | |
| 52 | **B** | 15c. red | | |
| 53 | **B** | 15c. orange | | |

| | | | | |
|---|---|---|---|---|
| 54 | B | 1pi. on 25c. blue | 4·25 | 2·50 |
| 55 | C | 2pi. on 50c. brown & lilac | 6·00 | 4·00 |
| 56 | C | 4pi. on 1f. red and green | 7·25 | 5·50 |
| 57 | C | 8pi. on 2f. lilac and brown | 22·00 | 13·00 |

Pt. 1

# CAYES OF BELIZE

A chain of several hundred islands, coral atolls, reefs and sandbanks stretching along the eastern seaboard of Belize. The following issues for the Cayes of Belize fall outside the criteria for full listing as detailed on page viii.

100 cents = 1 dollar

### APPENDIX

**1984**

Marine Life, Map and Views, 1, 2, 5, 10, 15, 25, 75c., $3, $5.
250th Anniv of "Lloyd's List" (newspaper). 25, 75c., $1, $2.
Olympic Games, Los Angeles. 10, 15, 75c., $2.
90th Anniv of "Caye Service" Local Stamps. 10, 15, 75c., $2.

Marine Life, Map and Views, 1, 2, 5, 10, 15, 25, 75c., $3, $5.
250th Anniv of "Lloyd's List" (newspaper). 25, 75c., $1, $2.
Olympic Games, Los Angeles. 10, 15, 75c., $2.
90th Anniv of "Caye Service" Local Stamps. 10, 15, 75c., $2.

**1985**

Birth Bicent of John J. Audubon (ornithologist). 25, 75c., $1, $3.
Shipwrecks. $1×4.

Pt. 1

# CAYMAN ISLANDS

A group of islands in the British West Indies. A dependency of Jamaica until August 1962, when it became a Crown Colony.

1900. 12 pence = 1 shilling; 20 shillings = 1 pound.
1969. 100 cents = 1 Jamaican dollar.

1

**1900**

| | | | | |
|---|---|---|---|---|
| 1a | 1 | ½d. green | 11·00 | 20·00 |
| 2 | 1 | 1d. red | 11·00 | 3·25 |

2

**1902**

| | | | | |
|---|---|---|---|---|
| 8 | 2 | ½d. green | 9·00 | 12·00 |
| 4 | 2 | 1d. red | 10·00 | 9·00 |
| 10 | 2 | 2½d. blue | 9·00 | 4·25 |
| 13 | 2 | 4d. brown and blue | 32·00 | 60·00 |
| 11 | 2 | 6d. brown | 17·00 | 38·00 |
| 14 | 2 | 6d. olive and red | 35·00 | 70·00 |
| 12 | 2 | 1s. orange | 28·00 | 48·00 |
| 15 | 2 | 1s. violet and green | 60·00 | 80·00 |
| 16 | 2 | 5s. orange and green | £200 | £325 |

**1907.** Surch One Halfpenny.

| | | | | |
|---|---|---|---|---|
| 17 | | ½d. on 1d. red | 55·00 | 85·00 |

**1907.** Surch.

| | | | | |
|---|---|---|---|---|
| 18 | | ½d. on 5s. orange and green | £300 | £450 |
| 19 | | 1d. on 5s. orange and green | £275 | £400 |
| 35 | | 2½d. on 4d. brown and blue | £1800 | £3500 |

11

8

**1907**

| | | | | |
|---|---|---|---|---|
| 38 | 11 | ¼d. brown | 3·75 | 50 |
| 25 | 8 | ½d. green | 3·25 | 4·00 |
| 26 | 8 | 1d. red | 1·75 | 75 |
| 27 | 8 | 2½d. blue | 4·50 | 2·50 |
| 28 | 8 | 3d. purple on yellow | 3·25 | 3·50 |
| 29 | 8 | 4d. black and red on yellow | 60·00 | 75·00 |
| 30 | 8 | 6d. purple | 19·00 | 35·00 |
| 31 | 8 | 1s. black on green | 8·50 | 22·00 |
| 32 | 8 | 5s. green and red on yellow | 38·00 | 70·00 |
| 34 | 8 | 10s. green and red on green | £180 | £225 |

12

**1912**

| | | | | |
|---|---|---|---|---|
| 40 | 12 | ¼d. brown | 1·00 | 40 |
| 41 | 12 | ½d. green | 2·75 | 5·00 |
| 42 | 12 | 1d. red | 3·25 | 2·50 |
| 43 | 12 | 2d. grey | 1·00 | 10·00 |
| 44 | 12 | 2½d. blue | 6·00 | 9·50 |
| 45a | 12 | 3d. purple on yellow | 3·50 | 8·00 |
| 46 | 12 | 4d. black and red on yellow | 1·00 | 10·00 |
| 47 | 12 | 6d. purple | 3·75 | 7·50 |
| 48b | 12 | 1s. black on green | 3·50 | 3·50 |
| 49 | 12 | 2s. purple and blue on blue | 12·00 | 65·00 |
| 50 | 12 | 3s. green and violet | 19·00 | 75·00 |
| 51 | 12 | 5s. green and red on yellow | 80·00 | £170 |
| 52b | 12 | 10s. green and red on green | £110 | £170 |

**1917.** Surch 1½d with WAR STAMP. in two lines.

| | | | | |
|---|---|---|---|---|
| 54 | | 1½d. on 2½d. blue | 1·75 | 6·00 |

**1917.** Optd or surch as last, but with WAR STAMP in one line and without full point.

| | | | | |
|---|---|---|---|---|
| 57 | | ½d. green | 60 | 2·50 |
| 58 | | 1½d. on 2d. grey | 4·00 | 7·00 |
| 56 | | 1½d. on 2½d. blue | 30 | 60 |
| 59 | | 1½d. on 2½d. orange | 80 | 1·25 |

19

**1921**

| | | | | |
|---|---|---|---|---|
| 69 | 19 | ¼d. brown | 50 | 1·50 |
| 70 | 19 | ½d. green | 50 | 30 |
| 71 | 19 | 1d. red | 1·40 | 85 |
| 72 | 19 | 1½d. brown | 1·75 | 30 |
| 73 | 19 | 2d. grey | 1·75 | 4·00 |
| 74 | 19 | 2½d. blue | 50 | 50 |
| 75 | 19 | 3d. purple on yellow | 1·75 | 4·00 |
| 62 | 19 | 4d. red on yellow | 1·00 | 4·00 |
| 76 | 19 | 4½d. green | 3·00 | 3·00 |
| 77 | 19 | 6d. red | 5·50 | 32·00 |
| 63 | 19 | 1s. black on green | 1·25 | 9·50 |
| 80 | 19 | 2s. violet on blue | 14·00 | 26·00 |
| 81 | 19 | 3s. violet | 23·00 | 16·00 |
| 82 | 19 | 5s. green on yellow | 24·00 | 50·00 |
| 83 | 19 | 10s. red on green | 65·00 | £100 |

20 Kings William IV and George V

**1932.** Centenary of "Assembly of Justices and Vestry".

| | | | | |
|---|---|---|---|---|
| 84 | 20 | ¼d. brown | 1·50 | 1·00 |
| 85 | 20 | ½d. green | 2·75 | 8·50 |
| 86 | 20 | 1d. red | 2·75 | 13·00 |
| 87 | 20 | 1½d. orange | 2·75 | 2·75 |
| 88 | 20 | 2d. grey | 2·75 | 3·50 |
| 89 | 20 | 2½d. blue | 2·75 | 1·50 |
| 90 | 20 | 3d. green | 6·00 | 5·00 |
| 91 | 20 | 6d. purple | 9·50 | 23·00 |
| 92 | 20 | 1s. black and brown | 17·00 | 32·00 |
| 93 | 20 | 2s. black and blue | 48·00 | 80·00 |
| 94 | 20 | 5s. black and green | 95·00 | £140 |
| 95 | 20 | 10s. black and red | £300 | £400 |

21 Cayman Islands

**1935**

| | | | | |
|---|---|---|---|---|
| 96 | 21 | ¼d. black and brown | 50 | 1·00 |
| 97 | - | ½d. blue and green | 1·00 | 1·00 |
| 98 | - | 1d. blue and red | 4·00 | 2·25 |
| 99 | - | 1½d. black and orange | 1·50 | 1·75 |
| 100 | - | 2d. blue and purple | 3·75 | 1·10 |
| 101 | - | 2½d. blue and black | 3·25 | 1·25 |
| 102 | 21 | 3d. black and green | 2·50 | 3·00 |
| 103 | - | 6d. purple and black | 8·50 | 4·00 |
| 104 | - | 1s. blue and orange | 6·00 | 6·50 |
| 105 | - | 2s. blue and black | 48·00 | 35·00 |
| 106 | - | 5s. green and black | 60·00 | 60·00 |
| 107 | - | 10s. black and red | 95·00 | £100 |

DESIGNS—HORIZ: ½, 2d., 1s. Cat boat; 1d., 2s. Red-footed boobys ("Booby-birds"); 2½, 6d., 5s. Hawksbill turtles. VERT: 1½d., 10s. Queen or pink conch shells and coconut palms.

**1935.** Silver Jubilee. As T 13 of Antigua.

| | | | | |
|---|---|---|---|---|
| 108 | | ½d. black and green | 15 | 1·00 |
| 109 | | 2½d. brown and blue | 4·00 | 1·00 |
| 110 | | 6d. blue and olive | 1·50 | 6·50 |
| 111 | | 1s. grey and purple | 10·00 | 9·00 |

**1937.** Coronation. As T 2 of Aden.

| | | | | |
|---|---|---|---|---|
| 112 | | ½d. green | 30 | 1·90 |
| 113 | | 1d. red | 50 | 20 |
| 114 | | 2½d. blue | 95 | 40 |

26 Beach View

29 Hawksbill Turtles

**1938**

| | | | | |
|---|---|---|---|---|
| 115a | 26 | ¼d. orange | 10 | 65 |
| 116 | - | ½d. green | 1·00 | 55 |
| 117 | - | 1d. red | 30 | 75 |
| 118 | 26 | 1½d. black | 30 | 10 |
| 119a | 29 | 2d. violet | 60 | 30 |
| 120 | - | 2½d. blue | 40 | 20 |
| 120a | - | 2½d. orange | 3·50 | 50 |
| 121 | - | 3d. orange | 40 | 15 |
| 121a | - | 3d. blue | 3·00 | 30 |
| 122a | 29 | 6d. olive | 3·25 | 1·25 |
| 123a | - | 1s. brown | 6·50 | 2·00 |
| 124a | 26 | 2s. green | 25·00 | 9·00 |
| 125 | - | 5s. red | 35·00 | 15·00 |
| 126 | 29 | 10s. brown | 28·00 | 9·00 |

DESIGNS—HORIZ: ½d., 1s. Caribbean dolphin; 1d., 3d. Map of Islands; 2½d., 5s. "Rembro" (schooner).

**1946.** Victory. As T 9 of Aden.

| | | | | |
|---|---|---|---|---|
| 127 | | 1½d. black | 30 | 40 |
| 128 | | 3d. yellow | 30 | 40 |

**1948.** Silver Wedding. As T 10/11 of Aden.

| | | | | |
|---|---|---|---|---|
| 129 | | ½d. green | 10 | 1·00 |
| 130 | | 10s. blue | 23·00 | 28·00 |

**1949.** U.P.U. As T 20/25 of Antigua.

| | | | | |
|---|---|---|---|---|
| 131 | | 2½d. orange | 30 | 1·00 |
| 132 | | 3d. blue | 1·50 | 2·25 |
| 133 | | 6d. olive | 60 | 2·25 |
| 134 | | 1s. brown | 60 | 50 |

31 Cat Boat

**1950**

| | | | | |
|---|---|---|---|---|
| 135 | 31 | ¼d. blue and red | 15 | 60 |
| 136 | - | ½d. violet and green | 15 | 1·25 |
| 137 | - | 1d. olive and blue | 60 | 75 |
| 138 | - | 1½d. green and brown | 40 | 75 |
| 139 | - | 2d. violet and red | 1·25 | 1·50 |
| 140 | - | 2½d. blue and black | 1·25 | 60 |
| 141 | - | 3d. green and blue | 1·40 | 1·50 |
| 142 | - | 6d. brown and blue | 2·00 | 1·25 |
| 143 | - | 9d. red and green | 12·00 | 2·00 |
| 144 | - | 1s. brown and orange | 3·25 | 2·75 |
| 145 | - | 2s. violet and purple | 13·00 | 11·00 |
| 146 | - | 5s. olive and violet | 23·00 | 7·00 |
| 147 | - | 10s. black and red | 27·00 | 20·00 |

DESIGNS: ½d. Coconut grove, Cayman Brac; 1d. Green turtle; 1½d. Making thatch rope; 2d. Cayman seamen; 2½d. Map; 3d. Parrotfish; 6d. Bluff, Cayman Brac; 9d. Georgetown Harbour. 1s. Turtle in "crawl"; 2s. "Ziroma" (schooner); 5s. Boat-building; 10s. Government offices, Grand Cayman.

44 South Sound Lighthouse, Grand Cayman

**1953.** As 1950 issue but with portrait of Queen Elizabeth II as in T 44.

| | | | | |
|---|---|---|---|---|
| 148 | | ¼d. blue and red | 1·00 | 50 |
| 149 | | ½d. violet and green | 75 | 50 |
| 150 | | 1d. olive and blue | 70 | 40 |
| 151 | | 1½d. green and brown | 60 | 20 |
| 152 | | 2d. violet and red | 3·00 | 85 |
| 153 | | 2½d. blue and black | 3·50 | 80 |
| 154 | | 3d. green and blue | 4·00 | 60 |
| 155 | | 4d. black and blue | 2·00 | 40 |
| 156 | | 6d. brown and blue | 1·75 | 30 |
| 157 | | 9d. red and green | 7·50 | 30 |
| 158 | | 1s. brown and orange | 3·75 | 20 |
| 159 | | 2s. violet and purple | 13·00 | 9·00 |
| 160 | | 5s. olive and violet | 15·00 | 8·00 |
| 161 | | 10s. black and red | 21·00 | 8·00 |
| 161a | | £1 blue | 40·00 | 10·00 |

Portrait faces right on ¼d., 2d., 2½d., 4d., 1s. and 10s. values and left on others. The £1 shows a larger portrait of the Queen (vert).

**1953.** Coronation. As T 13 of Aden.

| | | | | |
|---|---|---|---|---|
| 162 | | 1d. black and green | 30 | 2·00 |

46 Arms of the Cayman Islands

**1959.** New Constitution.

| | | | | |
|---|---|---|---|---|
| 163 | 46 | 2½d. black and blue | 45 | 2·50 |
| 164 | 46 | 1s. black and orange | 55 | 50 |

48 Cat Boat

**1962.** Portraits as in T 48.

| | | | | |
|---|---|---|---|---|
| 165 | - | ¼d. green and red | 55 | 1·00 |
| 166 | 48 | 1d. black and olive | 80 | 20 |
| 167 | - | 1½d. yellow and purple | 2·75 | 80 |
| 168 | - | 2d. blue and brown | 1·00 | 30 |
| 169 | - | 2½d. violet and turquoise | 85 | 1·00 |
| 170 | - | 3d. blue and red | 30 | 10 |
| 171 | - | 4d. green and purple | 3·25 | 60 |
| 172 | - | 6d. turquoise and sepia | 3·25 | 30 |
| 173 | 48 | 9d. blue and purple | 3·50 | 40 |
| 174 | - | 1s. sepia and red | 1·25 | 10 |
| 175 | - | 1s.3d. turquoise and brown | 5·00 | 2·25 |
| 176 | - | 1s.9d. turquoise and violet | 18·00 | 1·25 |
| 177 | - | 5s. plum and green | 11·00 | 13·00 |
| 178 | - | 10s. olive and blue | 20·00 | 13·00 |
| 179 | - | £1 red and black | 20·00 | 25·00 |

DESIGNS—VERT: ¼d. Cuban amazon ("Cayman Parrot"); 9d. Angler with king mackerel; 10s. Arms; £1 Queen Elizabeth II. HORIZ: 1½d. "Schomburgkia thomsoniana" (orchid); 2d. Cayman Islands map; 2½d. Fisherman casting net; 3d. West Bay Beach; 4d. Green turtle; 6d. "Lydia E. Wilson" (schooner), 1s Iguana; 1s.3d. Swimming pool, Cayman Brac; 1s.9d. Water sports; 5s. Fort George.

**1963.** Freedom from Hunger. As T 28 of Aden.

| | | | | |
|---|---|---|---|---|
| 180 | | 1s.9d. red | 30 | 15 |

**1963.** Centenary of Red Cross. As T 33 of Antigua.

| | | | | |
|---|---|---|---|---|
| 181 | | 1d. red and black | 30 | 75 |
| 182 | | 1s.9d. red and blue | 70 | 1·75 |

**1964.** 400th Birth Anniv of Shakespeare. As T 34 of Antigua.

| | | | | |
|---|---|---|---|---|
| 183 | | 6d. purple | 20 | 10 |

**1965.** Centenary of ITU. As T 36 of Antigua.

| | | | | |
|---|---|---|---|---|
| 184 | | 1d. blue and purple | 15 | 10 |
| 185 | | 1s.3d. purple and green | 55 | 45 |

**1965.** ICY. As T 37 of Antigua.

| | | | | |
|---|---|---|---|---|
| 186 | | 1d. purple and turquoise | 20 | 10 |
| 187 | | 1s. green and lavender | 60 | 25 |

**1966.** Churchill Commemoration. As T 38 of Antigua.

| | | | |
|---|---|---|---|
| 188 | ¼d. blue | 10 | 2·25 |
| 189 | 1d. green | 60 | 15 |
| 190 | 1s. brown | 1·50 | 15 |
| 191 | 1s.9d. violet | 1·60 | 75 |

**1966.** Royal Visit. As T 39 of Antigua.

| | | | |
|---|---|---|---|
| 192 | 1d. black and blue | 75 | 35 |
| 193 | 1s.9d. black and mauve | 2·75 | 1·50 |

**1966.** World Cup Football Championship. As T 40 of Antigua.

| | | | |
|---|---|---|---|
| 194 | 1½d. multicoloured | 15 | 10 |
| 195 | 1s.9d. multicoloured | 50 | 25 |

**1966.** Inauguration of WHO Headquarters, Geneva. As T 41 of Antigua.

| | | | |
|---|---|---|---|
| 196 | 2d. black, green and blue | 65 | 15 |
| 197 | 1s.3d. black, purple and ochre | 1·60 | 60 |

**62** Telephone and Map

**1966.** International Telephone Links.

| | | | | |
|---|---|---|---|---|
| 198 | **62** | 4d. multicoloured | 20 | 20 |
| 199 | **62** | 9d. multicoloured | 20 | 30 |

**1966.** 20th Anniv of UNESCO. As T 54/6 of Antigua.

| | | | |
|---|---|---|---|
| 200 | 1d. multicoloured | 15 | 10 |
| 201 | 1s.9d. yellow, violet and olive | 60 | 10 |
| 202 | 5s. black, purple and orange | 1·50 | 70 |

**63** B.A.C One Eleven 200/400 Airliner over "Ziroma" (Cayman schooner)

**1966.** Opening of Cayman Jet Service.

| | | | | |
|---|---|---|---|---|
| 203 | **63** | 1s. black, blue and green | 35 | 30 |
| 204 | **63** | 1s.9d. purple, blue and green | 40 | 35 |

**64** Water-skiing

**1967.** International Tourist Year. Multicoloured.

| | | | |
|---|---|---|---|
| 205 | 4d. Type **64** | 35 | 10 |
| 206 | 6d. Skin diving | 35 | 30 |
| 207 | 1s. Sport fishing | 35 | 30 |
| 208 | 1s.9d. Sailing | 40 | 75 |

**68** Former Slaves and Emblem

**1968.** Human Rights Year.

| | | | | |
|---|---|---|---|---|
| 209 | **68** | 3d. green, black and gold | 10 | 10 |
| 210 | **68** | 9d. brown, gold and green | 10 | 10 |
| 211 | **68** | 5s. ultram, gold and green | 30 | 90 |

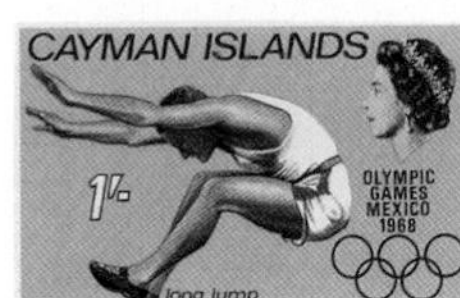


**69** Long-jumping

**1968.** Olympic Games, Mexico. Multicoloured.

| | | | |
|---|---|---|---|
| 212 | 1s. Type **69** | 15 | 10 |
| 213 | 1s.3d. High-jumping | 20 | 25 |
| 214 | 2s. Pole-vaulting | 20 | 75 |

**72** "The Adoration of the Shepherds" (Fabritius)

**1968.** Christmas. Multicoloured.

| | | | |
|---|---|---|---|
| 215 | ¼d. Type **72*** | 10 | 20 |
| 221 | ¼d. Type **72*** | 10 | 20 |
| 216 | 1d. "The Adoration of the Shepherds" (Rembrandt) | 10 | 10 |
| 217 | 6d. Type **72** | 15 | 10 |
| 218 | 8d. As 1d. | 15 | 15 |
| 219 | 1s.3d. Type **72** | 20 | 25 |
| 220 | 2s. As 1d. | 25 | 35 |

*No. 215 has a brown background and No. 221 a bright purple one.

**74** Grand Cayman Thrush ("Cayman Thrush")

**1969.** Multicoloured.. Multicoloured..

| | | | |
|---|---|---|---|
| 222 | ¼d. Type **74** | 10 | 75 |
| 223 | 1d. Brahmin cattle | 10 | 10 |
| 224 | 2d. Blowholes on the coast | 10 | 10 |
| 225 | 2½d. Map of Grand Cayman | 15 | 10 |
| 226 | 3d. Georgetown scene | 10 | 10 |
| 227 | 4d. Royal "Poinciana" | 15 | 10 |
| 228 | 6d. Cayman Brac and Little Cayman on chart | 20 | 10 |
| 229 | 8d. Motor vessels at berth | 25 | 10 |
| 230 | 1s. Basket-making | 15 | 10 |
| 231 | 1s.3d. Beach scene | 35 | 1·00 |
| 232 | 1s.6d. Straw-rope making | 35 | 1·00 |
| 233 | 2s. Great barracuda | 1·25 | 80 |
| 234 | 4s. Government House | 35 | 80 |
| 235 | 10s. Arms of the Cayman Islands (vert) | 1·00 | 1·50 |
| 236 | £1 black, ochre and red (Queen Elizabeth II) (vert) | 1·25 | 2·00 |

**1969.** Decimal Currency. Nos. 222/36 surch C-DAY 8th September 1969. Multicoloured.

| | | | | |
|---|---|---|---|---|
| 238 | **74** | ¼c. on ¼d. | 10 | 75 |
| 239 | - | 1c. on 1d. | 10 | 10 |
| 240 | - | 2c. on 2d. | 10 | 10 |
| 241 | - | 3c. on 4d. | 10 | 10 |
| 242 | - | 4c. on 2½d. | 10 | 10 |
| 243 | - | 5c. on 6d. | 10 | 10 |
| 244 | - | 7c. on 8d. | 10 | 10 |
| 245 | - | 8c. on 3d. | 15 | 10 |
| 246 | - | 10c. on 1s. | 25 | 10 |
| 247 | - | 12c. on 1s.3d. | 35 | 1·75 |
| 248 | - | 15c. on 1s.6d. | 45 | 1·50 |
| 249 | - | 20c. on 2s. | 1·25 | 1·75 |
| 250 | - | 40c. on 4s. | 45 | 85 |
| 251 | - | $1 on 10s. | 1·00 | 2·50 |
| 252 | - | $2 on £1 | 1·50 | 3·25 |

**90** "Madonna and Child" (Vivarini)

**1969.** Christmas. Multicoloured. Background colours given.

| | | | | |
|---|---|---|---|---|
| 253 | **90** | ¼c. red | 10 | 10 |
| 254 | **90** | ¼c. mauve | 10 | 10 |
| 255 | **90** | ¼c. green | 10 | 10 |
| 256 | **90** | ¼c. blue | 10 | 10 |
| 257 | - | 1c. blue | 10 | 10 |
| 258 | **90** | 5c. red | 10 | 10 |
| 259 | - | 7c. green | 10 | 10 |
| 260 | **90** | 12c. green | 15 | 15 |
| 261 | - | 20c. purple | 20 | 25 |

DESIGNS: 1c., 7c., 20c. "The Adoration of the Kings" (Gossaert).

**92** "Noli me tangere" (Titian)

**1970.** Easter. Multicoloured; frame colours given.

| | | | | |
|---|---|---|---|---|
| 262 | **92** | ¼c. red | 10 | 10 |
| 263 | **92** | ¼c. green | 10 | 10 |
| 264 | **92** | ¼c. brown | 10 | 10 |
| 265 | **92** | ¼c. violet | 10 | 10 |
| 266 | **92** | 10c. blue | 35 | 10 |
| 267 | **92** | 12c. brown | 40 | 10 |
| 268 | **92** | 40c. plum | 55 | 60 |

**93** Barnaby (*Barnaby Rudge*)

**1970.** Death Centenary of Charles Dickens.

| | | | | |
|---|---|---|---|---|
| 269 | **93** | 1c. black, green and yellow | 10 | 10 |
| 270 | - | 12c. black, brown and red | 35 | 10 |
| 271 | - | 20c. black, brown and gold | 40 | 10 |
| 272 | - | 40c. black, ultram & blue | 45 | 25 |

DESIGNS: 12c. Sairey Gamp ("Martin Chuzzlewit"); 20c. Mr. Micawber and David ("David Copperfield"); 40c. The "Marchioness" ("The Old Curiosity Shop").

**97** Grand Cayman Thrush ("Cayman Thrush")

**1970.** Decimal Currency. Designs as Nos. 222/36, but with values inscribed in decimal currency as in T 97.

| | | | |
|---|---|---|---|
| 273 | ¼c. multicoloured | 65 | 30 |
| 274 | 1c. multicoloured | 10 | 10 |
| 275 | 2c. multicoloured | 10 | 10 |
| 276 | 3c. multicoloured | 20 | 10 |
| 277 | 4c. multicoloured | 20 | 10 |
| 278 | 5c. multicoloured | 35 | 10 |
| 279 | 7c. multicoloured | 30 | 10 |
| 280 | 8c. multicoloured | 30 | 10 |
| 281 | 10c. multicoloured | 30 | 10 |
| 282 | 12c. multicoloured | 90 | 1·00 |
| 283 | 15c. multicoloured | 1·25 | 4·00 |
| 284 | 20c. multicoloured | 3·25 | 1·25 |
| 285 | 40c. multicoloured | 85 | 75 |
| 286 | $1 multicoloured | 1·25 | 4·75 |
| 287 | $2 black, ochre and red | 2·00 | 4·75 |

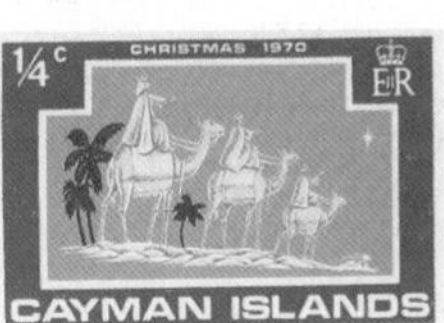


**98** The Three Wise Men

**1970.** Christmas.

| | | | | |
|---|---|---|---|---|
| 288 | **98** | ¼c. green, grey and emerald | 10 | 10 |
| 289 | - | 1c. black, yellow and green | 10 | 10 |
| 290 | **98** | 5c. grey, orange and red | 10 | 10 |
| 291 | - | 10c. black, yellow and red | 10 | 10 |
| 292 | **98** | 12c. grey, green and blue | 15 | 10 |
| 293 | - | 20c. black, yellow and green | 20 | 15 |

DESIGN: 1, 10, 20c. Nativity scene and Globe.

**100** Grand Cayman Terrapin

**1971.** Turtles. Multicoloured.

| | | | |
|---|---|---|---|
| 294 | 5c. Type **100** | 30 | 25 |
| 295 | 7c. Green turtle | 35 | 25 |
| 296 | 12c. Hawksbill turtle | 55 | 30 |
| 297 | 20c. Turtle farm | 1·00 | 1·40 |

**101** "Dendrophylax fawcettii"

**1971.** Orchids. Multicoloured.

| | | | |
|---|---|---|---|
| 298 | ¼c. Type **101** | 10 | 1·25 |
| 299 | 2c. "Schomburgkia thomsoniana" | 60 | 90 |
| 300 | 10c. "Vanilla claviculata" | 2·25 | 50 |
| 301 | 40c. "Oncidium variegatum" | 4·50 | 3·50 |

**102** "Adoration of the Kings" (French 15th century)

**1971.** Christmas. Multicoloured.

| | | | |
|---|---|---|---|
| 302 | ¼c. Type **102** | 10 | 10 |
| 303 | 1c. "The Nativity" (Parisian, 14th century) | 10 | 10 |
| 304 | 5c. "Adoration of the Magi" (Burgundian, 15th century) | 10 | 10 |
| 305 | 12c. Type **102** | 20 | 15 |
| 306 | 15c. As 1c. | 20 | 25 |
| 307 | 20c. As 5c. | 25 | 35 |
| **MS**308 | 113×115 mm. Nos. 302/7 | 1·25 | 2·25 |

**103** Turtle and Telephone Cable

**1972.** Co-axial Telephone Cable.

| | | | | |
|---|---|---|---|---|
| 309 | **103** | 2c. multicoloured | 10 | 10 |
| 310 | **103** | 10c. multicoloured | 15 | 10 |
| 311 | **103** | 40c. multicoloured | 30 | 40 |

**104** Court House Building

**1972.** New Government Buildings. Multicoloured.

| | | | |
|---|---|---|---|
| 312 | 5c. Type **104** | 10 | 10 |
| 313 | 15c. Legislative Assembly Building | 10 | 10 |
| 314 | 25c. Type **104** | 15 | 15 |
| 315 | 40c. As 15c. | 20 | 30 |
| **MS**316 | 121×108 mm. Nos. 312/15 | 50 | 2·00 |

**1972.** Royal Silver Wedding. As T 52 of Ascension but with Hawksbill Turtle and Queen or Pink Conch in background.

| | | | |
|---|---|---|---|
| 317 | 12c. violet | 15 | 10 |
| 318 | 30c. green | 15 | 20 |

**106** $1 Coin and Note

**1972.** First Issue of Currency. Multicoloured.

| No. | Description | Mint | Used |
|---|---|---|---|
| 319 | 3c. Type **106** | 20 | 10 |
| 320 | 6c. $5 Coin and note | 20 | 70 |
| 321 | 15c. $10 Coin and note | 60 | 30 |
| 322 | 25c. $25 Coin and note | 80 | 45 |
| **MS**323 | 128×107 mm. Nos. 319/22 | 3·50 | 3·25 |

**107** "The Way of Sorrow"

**1973.** Easter. Stained-glass Windows. Multicoloured.

| No. | Description | Mint | Used |
|---|---|---|---|
| 324 | 10c. Type **107** | 15 | 10 |
| 325 | 12c. "Christ Resurrected" | 20 | 10 |
| 326 | 20c. "The Last Supper" (horiz) | 25 | 15 |
| 327 | 30c. "Christ on the Cross" (horiz) | 30 | 25 |
| **MS**328 | 122×105 mm. Nos. 324/7 (imperf) | 1·00 | 1·60 |

**108** "The Nativity" (Sforza Book of Hours)

**1973.** Christmas.

| No. | Type | Description | Mint | Used |
|---|---|---|---|---|
| 329 | **108** | 3c. multicoloured | 10 | 10 |
| 330 | - | 5c. multicoloured | 10 | 10 |
| 331 | **108** | 9c. multicoloured | 15 | 10 |
| 332 | - | 12c. multicoloured | 15 | 10 |
| 333 | **108** | 15c. multicoloured | 15 | 15 |
| 334 | - | 25c. multicoloured | 20 | 25 |

DESIGN: 5, 12, 25c. "The Adoration of the Magi" (Breviary of Queen Isabella).

**1973.** Royal Wedding. As T 47 of Anguilla. Background colour given. Multicoloured.

| No. | Description | Mint | Used |
|---|---|---|---|
| 335 | 10c. green | 10 | 10 |
| 336 | 30c. mauve | 15 | 10 |

**109** White-winged Dove

**1974.** Birds (1st series). Multicoloured.

| No. | Description | Mint | Used |
|---|---|---|---|
| 337 | 3c. Type **109** | 2·00 | 30 |
| 338 | 10c. Vitelline warbler | 2·75 | 30 |
| 339 | 12c. Antillean grackle ("Greater Antiliean Grackle") | 2·75 | 30 |
| 340 | 20c. Great red-bellied woodpecker ("West Indian Red-bellied Woodpecker") | 4·25 | 80 |
| 341 | 30c. Stripe-headed tanager | 5·50 | 1·50 |
| 342 | 50c. Yucatan vireo | 7·00 | 5·50 |

See also Nos. 383/8.

**110** Old School Building

**1974.** 25th Anniv of University of West Indies. Multicoloured.

| No. | Description | Mint | Used |
|---|---|---|---|
| 343 | 12c. Type **110** | 10 | 10 |
| 344 | 20c. New Comprehensive School | 15 | 20 |
| 345 | 30c. Creative Arts Centre, Mona | 15 | 60 |

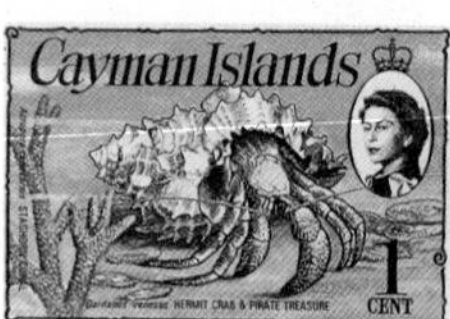


**111** Hermit Crab and Staghorn Coral

**1974.** Size 41½×27 mm or 27×41½ mm. Mult.

| No. | Description | Mint | Used |
|---|---|---|---|
| 346 | 1c. Type **111** | 3·50 | 1·25 |
| 347 | 3c. Treasure-chest and lion's paw | 3·50 | 75 |
| 348 | 4c. Treasure and spotted scorpionfish | 50 | 70 |
| 349 | 5c. Flintlock pistol and brain coral | 3·00 | 75 |
| 350 | 6c. Blackbeard and green turtle | 35 | 2·25 |
| 366 | 8c. As 9c. | 2·50 | 8·50 |
| 351 | 9c. Jewelled pomander and porkfish | 4·00 | 11·00 |
| 352 | 10c. Spiny lobster and treasure | 4·50 | 80 |
| 353 | 12c. Jewelled sword and dagger and sea-fan | 35 | 2·00 |
| 354 | 15c. Cabrit's murex and treasure | 45 | 1·25 |
| 417 | 20c. Queen or pink conch and treasure | 3·50 | 3·00 |
| 356 | 25c. Hogfish and treasure | 45 | 70 |
| 357 | 40c. Gold chalice and seawhip | 4·00 | 1·25 |
| 358 | $1 Coat of arms (vert) | 2·75 | 3·25 |
| 419 | $2 Queen Elizabeth II (vert) | 8·50 | 6·50 |

For smaller designs see Nos. 445/52.

**112** Sea Captain and Ship (Shipbuilding)

**1974.** Local Industries. Multicoloured.

| No. | Description | Mint | Used |
|---|---|---|---|
| 360 | 8c. Type **112** | 30 | 10 |
| 361 | 12c. Thatcher and cottage | 25 | 10 |
| 362 | 20c. Farmer and plantation | 25 | 20 |
| **MS**363 | 92×132 mm. Nos. 360/2 | 1·50 | 3·25 |

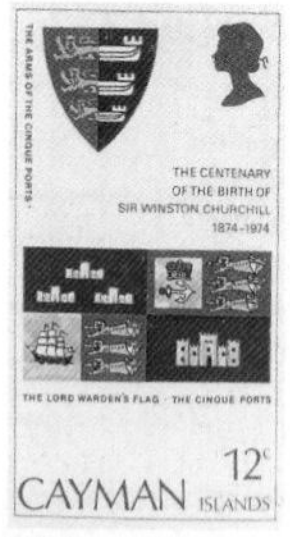


**113** Arms of Cinque Ports and Lord Warden's Flag

**1974.** Birth Centenary of Sir Winston Churchill. Multicoloured.

| No. | Description | Mint | Used |
|---|---|---|---|
| 380 | 12c. Type **113** | 15 | 10 |
| 381 | 50c. Churchill's coat of arms | 45 | 70 |
| **MS**382 | 98×86 mm. Nos. 380/1 | 60 | 1·60 |

**1975.** Birds (2nd series). As T 109. Multicoloured.

| No. | Description | Mint | Used |
|---|---|---|---|
| 383 | 3c. Common flicker ("Yellow-shafted Flicker") | 70 | 50 |
| 384 | 10c. Black-billed whistling duck ("West Indian Tree Duck") | 1·25 | 50 |
| 385 | 12c. Yellow warbler | 1·40 | 65 |
| 386 | 20c. White-bellied dove | 2·00 | 2·00 |
| 387 | 30c. Magnificent frigate bird | 3·25 | 4·25 |
| 388 | 50c. Cuban amazon ("Cayman Amazon") | 3·75 | 12·00 |

**114** "The Crucifixion"

**1975.** Easter. French Pastoral Staffs.

| No. | Type | Description | Mint | Used |
|---|---|---|---|---|
| 389 | **114** | 15c. multicoloured | 10 | 20 |
| 390 | - | 35c. multicoloured | 20 | 45 |
| **MS**391 | | 128×98 mm. Nos. 389/90 | 65 | 2·75 |

DESIGN: 35c. Pastoral staff similar to Type **114**.

**115** Israel Hands

**1975.** Pirates. Multicoloured.

| No. | Description | Mint | Used |
|---|---|---|---|
| 392 | 10c. Type **115** | 35 | 15 |
| 393 | 12c. John Fenn | 35 | 30 |
| 394 | 20c. Thomas Anstis | 60 | 50 |
| 395 | 30c. Edward Low | 65 | 1·50 |

**1975.** Christmas. "Virgin and Child with Angels". As T 114.

| No. | Description | Mint | Used |
|---|---|---|---|
| 396 | 12c. multicoloured | 10 | 10 |
| 397 | 50c. multicoloured | 30 | 30 |
| **MS**398 | 113×85 mm. Nos. 396/7 | 1·00 | 3·00 |

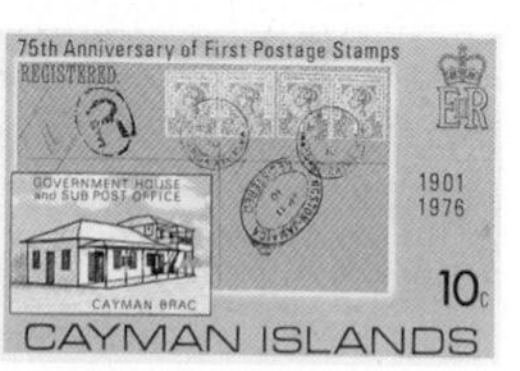


**116** Registered Cover, Government House and Sub-Post Office

**1975.** 75th Anniv of First Cayman Islands Postage Stamp. Multicoloured.

| No. | Description | Mint | Used |
|---|---|---|---|
| 399 | 10c. Type **116** | 15 | 10 |
| 400 | 20c. ½d. stamp and 1890–94 postmark | 20 | 15 |
| 401 | 30c. 1d. stamp and 1908 surcharge | 30 | 25 |
| 402 | 50c. ½d. and 1d. stamps | 45 | 65 |
| **MS**403 | 117×147 mm. Nos. 399/402 | 2·50 | 3·00 |

**117** Seals of Georgia, Delaware and New Hampshire

**1976.** Bicentenary of American Revolution. Mult.

| No. | Description | Mint | Used |
|---|---|---|---|
| 404 | 10c. Type **117** | 40 | 15 |
| 405 | 15c. Carolina, New Jersey and Maryland seals | 55 | 20 |
| 406 | 20c. Virginia, Rhode Island and Massachusetts seals | 65 | 25 |
| 407 | 25c. New York, Connecticut and North Carolina seals | 65 | 35 |
| 408 | 30c. Pennsylvania seal, Liberty Bell and U.S. Great Seal | 70 | 40 |
| **MS**409 | 166×124 mm. Nos. 404/8 | 4·00 | 8·50 |

**118** "470" Dinghies

**1976.** Olympic Games, Montreal. Multicoloured.

| No. | Description | Mint | Used |
|---|---|---|---|
| 410 | 20c. Type **118** | 40 | 10 |
| 411 | 50c. Racing dinghy | 70 | 50 |

**119** Queen Elizabeth II and Westminster Abbey

**1977.** Silver Jubilee. Multicoloured.

| No. | Description | Mint | Used |
|---|---|---|---|
| 427 | 8c. The Prince of Wales' visit, 1973 | 10 | 20 |
| 428 | 30c. Type **119** | 15 | 40 |
| 429 | 50c. Preparation for the Anointing (horiz) | 30 | 75 |

**120** Scuba Diving

**1977.** Tourism. Multicoloured.

| No. | Description | Mint | Used |
|---|---|---|---|
| 430 | 5c. Type **120** | 15 | 10 |
| 431 | 10c. Exploring a wreck | 20 | 10 |
| 432 | 20c. Royal gramma ("Fairy basslet") (fish) | 55 | 20 |
| 433 | 25c. Sergeant major (fish) | 65 | 35 |
| **MS**434 | 146×89 mm. Nos. 430/3 | 2·00 | 4·50 |

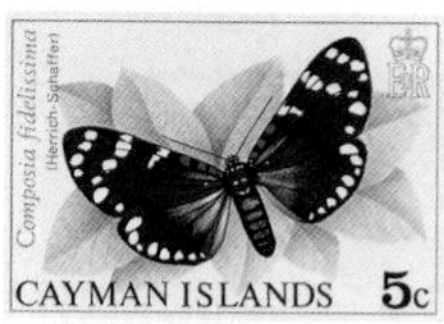


**121** "Composia fidelissima" (moth)

**1977.** Butterflies and Moth. Multicoloured.

| No. | Description | Mint | Used |
|---|---|---|---|
| 435 | 5c. Type **121** | 75 | 20 |
| 436 | 8c. "Heliconius charithonia" | 85 | 20 |
| 437 | 10c. "Danaus gilippus" | 85 | 20 |
| 438 | 15c. "Agraulis vanillae" | 1·25 | 45 |
| 439 | 20c. "Junonia evarete" | 1·25 | 45 |
| 440 | 30c. "Anartia jatrophae" | 1·50 | 70 |

**122** Cruise Liner "Southward"

**1978.** New Harbour and Cruise Ships. Multicoloured.

| No. | Description | Mint | Used |
|---|---|---|---|
| 441 | 3c. Type **122** | 40 | 10 |
| 442 | 5c. Cruise liner "Renaissance" | 40 | 10 |
| 443 | 30c. New harbour (vert) | 90 | 25 |
| 444 | 50c. Cruise liner "Daphne" (vert) | 1·25 | 65 |

**1978.** As Nos. 346/7, 349, 352, 417, 357/8 and 419, but designs smaller, 40×26 mm or 26×40 mm.

| No. | Description | Mint | Used |
|---|---|---|---|
| 445 | 1c. Type **111** | 1·00 | 1·25 |
| 446 | 3c. Treasure chest and lion's paw | 80 | 50 |
| 447 | 5c. Flintlock pistol and brain coral | 1·50 | 2·00 |
| 448 | 10c. Spiny lobster and treasure | 1·25 | 60 |
| 449 | 20c. Queen or pink conch and treasure | 2·25 | 1·00 |
| 450 | 40c. Gold chalice and seawhip | 13·00 | 18·00 |
| 451 | $1 Coat of arms (vert) | 20·00 | 5·50 |
| 452 | $2 Queen Elizabeth II (vert) | 4·00 | 20·00 |

**123** "The Crucifixion" (Durer)

**1978.** Easter and 450th Death Anniv of Durer.

| | | | | |
|---|---|---|---|---|
| 459 | **123** | 10c. mauve and black | 30 | 10 |
| 460 | - | 15c. yellow and black | 40 | 15 |
| 461 | - | 20c. turquoise and black | 50 | 20 |
| 462 | - | 30c. lilac and black | 60 | 35 |
| **MS**463 | | 120×108 mm. Nos. 459/62 | 4·25 | 6·50 |

DESIGNS: 15c. "Christ at Emmaus"; 20c. "The Entry into Jerusalem"; 30c. "Christ washing Peter's Feet".

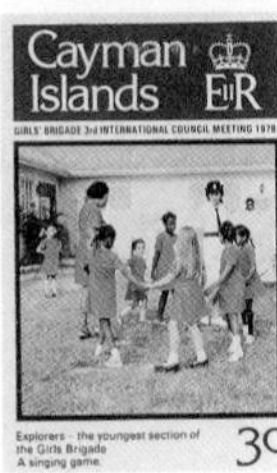

**124** "Explorers" Singing Game

**1978.** 3rd International Council Meeting of Girls' Brigade. Multicoloured.

| | | | |
|---|---|---|---|
| 464 | 3c. Type **124** | 20 | 10 |
| 465 | 10c. Colour party | 25 | 10 |
| 466 | 20c. Girls and Duke of Edinburgh Award interests | 40 | 20 |
| 467 | 50c. Girls using domestic skills | 70 | 80 |

**125** Yale of Beaufort

**1978.** 25th Anniv of Coronation.

| | | | | |
|---|---|---|---|---|
| 468 | **125** | 30c. green, mauve and silver | 20 | 25 |
| 469 | - | 30c. multicoloured | 20 | 25 |
| 470 | - | 30c. green, mauve and silver | 20 | 25 |

DESIGNS: No. 469, Queen Elizabeth II; 470, Barn owl.

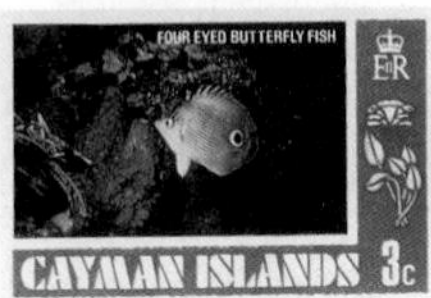

**126** Four-eyed Butterflyfish

**1978.** Fish (1st series). Multicoloured.

| | | | |
|---|---|---|---|
| 471 | 3c. Type **126** | 25 | 10 |
| 472 | 5c. Grey angelfish | 30 | 10 |
| 473 | 10c. Squirrelfish | 45 | 10 |
| 474 | 15c. Queen parrotfish | 60 | 30 |
| 475 | 20c. Spanish hogfish | 70 | 35 |
| 476 | 30c. Queen angelfish | 80 | 50 |

**127** Lockheed L.18 Lodestar

**1979.** 25th Anniv of Owen Roberts Airfield. Mult.

| | | | |
|---|---|---|---|
| 477 | 3c. Type **127** | 30 | 15 |
| 478 | 5c. Consolidated PBY-5A Catalina amphibian | 30 | 15 |
| 479 | 10c. Vickers Viking 1B | 35 | 15 |
| 480 | 15c. B.A.C. One Eleven 455 on tarmac | 65 | 25 |
| 481 | 20c. Piper PA-31 Cheyenne II, Bell 47G Trooper helicopter and Hawker Siddeley H.S.125 | 75 | 35 |
| 482 | 30c. B.A.C. One Eleven 475 over airfield | 1·00 | 50 |

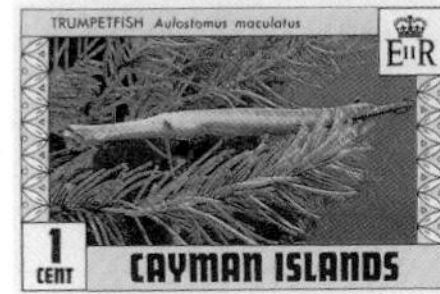

**128** Trumpetfish

**1979.** Fishes (2nd series). Multicoloured.

| | | | |
|---|---|---|---|
| 483 | 1c. Type **128** | 10 | 10 |
| 484 | 3c. Nassau grouper | 25 | 10 |
| 485 | 5c. French angelfish | 25 | 10 |
| 486 | 10c. Schoolmaster snapper | 35 | 10 |
| 487 | 20c. Banded butterflyfish | 55 | 25 |
| 488 | 50c. Black-barred soldierfish | 1·00 | 70 |

**129** 1900 1d. Stamp

**1979.** Death Centenary of Sir Rowland Hill.

| | | | | |
|---|---|---|---|---|
| 489 | **129** | 5c. black, carmine and blue | 10 | 10 |
| 490 | - | 10c. multicoloured | 15 | 10 |
| 491 | - | 20c. multicoloured | 20 | 25 |
| **MS**492 | | 138×90 mm. 50c. mult | 55 | 65 |

DESIGNS: 10c. Great Britain 1902 3d. purple on lemon; 20c. 1955 £1 blue.

**130** The Holy Family and Angels

**1979.** Christmas. Multicoloured.

| | | | |
|---|---|---|---|
| 493 | 10c. Type **130** | 15 | 10 |
| 494 | 20c. Angels appearing to Shepherds | 25 | 10 |
| 495 | 30c. Nativity | 30 | 20 |
| 496 | 40c. The Magi | 40 | 30 |

**131** Local Rotary Project

**1980.** 75th Anniv of Rotary International.

| | | | | |
|---|---|---|---|---|
| 497 | **131** | 20c. blue, black and yellow | 20 | 15 |
| 498 | - | 30c. blue, black and yellow | 25 | 20 |
| 499 | - | 50c. blue, yellow and black | 35 | 30 |

DESIGNS—VERT: 30c. Paul P. Harris (founder); 50c. Rotary anniversary emblem.

**132** Walking Mail Carrier

**1980.** "London 1980" International Stamp Exhibition. Multicoloured.

| | | | |
|---|---|---|---|
| 500 | 5c. Type **132** | 10 | 10 |
| 501 | 10c. Delivering mail by cat boat | 15 | 10 |
| 502 | 15c. Mounted mail carrier | 20 | 10 |
| 503 | 30c. Horse-drawn wagonette | 25 | 15 |
| 504 | 40c. Postman on bicycle | 35 | 15 |
| 505 | $1 Motor transport | 45 | 55 |

**133** Queen Elizabeth the Queen Mother at the Derby, 1976

**1980.** 80th Birthday of the Queen Mother.

| | | | | |
|---|---|---|---|---|
| 506 | **133** | 20c. multicoloured | 20 | 25 |

**134** American Thorny Oyster

**1980.** Shells (1st series). Multicoloured.

| | | | |
|---|---|---|---|
| 507 | 5c. Type **134** | 25 | 10 |
| 508 | 10c. West Indian murex | 30 | 10 |
| 509 | 30c. Angular triton | 45 | 40 |
| 510 | 50c. Caribbean vase | 70 | 80 |

See also Nos. 565/8 and 582/5.

**135** Lantana

**1980.** Flowers (1st series). Multicoloured.

| | | | |
|---|---|---|---|
| 511 | 5c. Type **135** | 15 | 10 |
| 512 | 15c. "Bauhinia" | 20 | 10 |
| 513 | 30c. "Hibiscus Rosa" | 25 | 10 |
| 514 | $1 "Milk and Wine Lily" | 50 | 90 |

See also Nos. 541/4.

**136** Juvenile Tarpon and Fire Sponge

**1980.** Multicoloured.. Multicoloured..

| | | | |
|---|---|---|---|
| 515A | 3c. Type **136** | 1·00 | 2·50 |
| 516B | 5c. Flat tree or mangrove-root oyster | 1·25 | 80 |
| 517A | 10c. Mangrove crab | 50 | 1·50 |
| 518A | 15c. Lizard and "Phyciodes phaon" (butterfly) | 1·00 | 1·75 |
| 519A | 20c. Louisiana heron ("Tricoloured Heron") | 1·50 | 2·25 |
| 520A | 30c. Red mangrove flower | 70 | 1·00 |
| 521A | 40c. Red mangrove seeds | 75 | 1·00 |
| 522A | 50c. Waterhouse's leaf-nosed bat | 1·25 | 1·50 |
| 523A | $1 Black-crowned night heron | 4·50 | 5·00 |
| 524A | $2 Coat of arms | 1·25 | 3·75 |
| 525A | $4 Queen Elizabeth II | 2·00 | 4·25 |

**137** Eucharist

**1981.** Easter. Multicoloured.

| | | | |
|---|---|---|---|
| 526 | 3c. Type **137** | 10 | 10 |
| 527 | 10c. Crown of thorns | 10 | 10 |
| 528 | 20c. Crucifix | 15 | 10 |
| 529 | $1 Lord Jesus Christ | 50 | 60 |

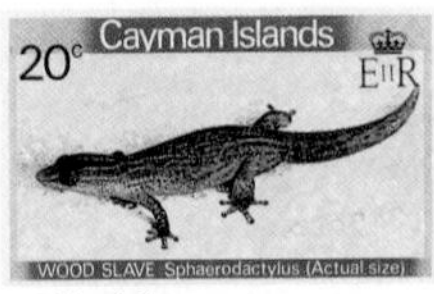

**138** Wood Slave

**1981.** Reptiles and Amphibians. Multicoloured.

| | | | |
|---|---|---|---|
| 530 | 20c. Type **138** | 25 | 20 |
| 531 | 30c. Cayman iguana | 30 | 35 |
| 532 | 40c. Lion lizard | 40 | 45 |
| 533 | 50c. Terrapin ("Hickatee") | 45 | 55 |

**139** Prince Charles

**1981.** Royal Wedding. Multicoloured.

| | | | |
|---|---|---|---|
| 534 | 20c. Wedding bouquet from Cayman Islands | 15 | 10 |
| 535 | 30c. Type **139** | 20 | 10 |
| 536 | $1 Prince Charles and Lady Diana Spencer | 50 | 75 |

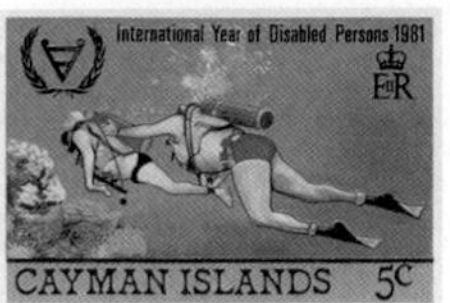

**140** Disabled Scuba Divers

**1981.** Int Year for Disabled Persons. Mult.

| | | | |
|---|---|---|---|
| 537 | 5c. Type **140** | 10 | 10 |
| 538 | 15c. Old school for the handicapped | 25 | 20 |
| 539 | 20c. New school for the handicapped | 30 | 25 |
| 540 | $1 Disabled people in wheelchairs by the sea | 1·25 | 85 |

**1981.** Flowers (2nd series). As T 135. Multicoloured.

| | | | |
|---|---|---|---|
| 541 | 3c. Bougainvillea | 10 | 10 |
| 542 | 10c. Morning Glory | 15 | 10 |
| 543 | 20c. Wild amaryllis | 25 | 25 |
| 544 | $1 Cordia | 1·00 | 1·75 |

**141** Dr. Robert Koch and Microscope

**1982.** Centenary of Robert Koch's Discovery of Tubercle Bacillus. Multicoloured.

| | | | |
|---|---|---|---|
| 545 | 15c. Type **141** | 25 | 25 |
| 546 | 30c. Koch looking through microscope (vert) | 45 | 45 |
| 547 | 40c. Microscope (vert) | 70 | 70 |
| 548 | 50c. Dr. Robert Koch (vert) | 80 | 80 |

**142** Bride and Groom walking down Aisle

**1982.** 21st Birthday of Princess of Wales. Mult.

| | | | |
|---|---|---|---|
| 549 | 20c. Cayman Islands coat of arms | 20 | 25 |
| 550 | 30c. Lady Diana Spencer in London, June, 1981 | 60 | 45 |
| 551 | 40c. Type **142** | 60 | 65 |
| 552 | 50c. Formal portrait | 2·25 | 1·00 |

**143** Pitching Tent

**1982.** 75th Anniv of Boy Scout Movement. Mult.

| | | | |
|---|---|---|---|
| 553 | 3c. Type **143** | 15 | 10 |
| 554 | 20c. Scouts camping | 40 | 40 |
| 555 | 30c. Cub Scouts and Leaders | 60 | 55 |
| 556 | 50c. Boating skills | 80 | 85 |

**144** "Madonna and Child with the Infant Baptist"

**1982.** Christmas. Raphael Paintings. Multicoloured.

| | | | |
|---|---|---|---|
| 557 | 3c. Type **144** | 10 | 10 |
| 558 | 10c. "Madonna of the Tower" | 20 | 20 |
| 559 | 20c. "Ansidei Madonna" | 35 | 35 |
| 560 | 30c. "Madonna and Child" | 50 | 50 |

**145** Mace

**1982.** 150th Anniv of Representative Government. Multicoloured.
561 3c. Type **145** 10 20
562 10c. Old Courthouse 20 20
563 20c. Commonwealth Parliamentary Association coat of arms 35 45
564 30c. Legislative Assembly building 50 90

**1983.** Shells (2nd series). As T 134. Multicoloured.
565 5c. Colourful Atlantic moon 15 30
566 10c. King helmet 25 30
567 20c. Rooster-tail conch 30 40
568 $1 Reticulated cowrie-helmet 50 4·00

**146** Legislative Building, Cayman Brac

**1983.** Royal Visit. Multicoloured.
569 20c. Type **146** 45 35
570 30c. Legislative Building, Grand Cayman 60 50
571 50c. Duke of Edinburgh (vert) 1·25 90
572 $1 Queen Elizabeth II (vert) 2·00 2·00
**MS**573 113×94 mm. Nos. 569/72 6·50 4·25

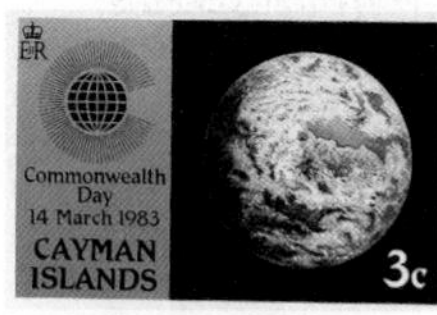

**147** Satellite View of Earth

**1983.** Commonwealth Day. Multicoloured.
574 3c. Type **147** 20 15
575 15c. Cayman Islands and Commonwealth flags 50 40
576 20c. Fishing 50 40
577 40c. Portrait of Queen Elizabeth II 75 80

**148** MRCU Cessna Ag Wagon

**1983.** Bicentenary of Manned Flight. Multicoloured.
578 3c. Type **148** 60 50
579 10c. Consolidated PBY-5A Catalina amphibian 65 50
580 20c. Boeing 727-200 1·25 1·50
581 40c. Hawker Siddeley H.S.748 1·75 3·75

**1984.** Shells (3rd series). As T 134. Multicoloured.
582 3c. Florida moon 70 40
583 10c. Austin's cone 80 40
584 30c. Leaning dwarf triton 2·25 2·75
585 50c. Filose or threaded turban 2·50 4·25

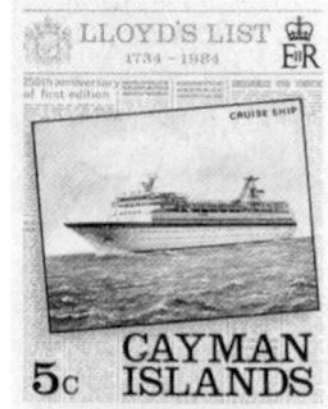

**149** "Song of Norway" (cruise liner)

**1984.** 250th Anniv of "Lloyd's List" (newspaper). Multicoloured.
586 5c. Type **149** 55 20
587 10c. View of old harbour 55 25
588 25c. Wreck of "Ridgefield" (freighter) 1·10 1·00
589 50c. "Goldfield" (schooner) 2·00 2·75
**MS**590 105×75 mm. $1 "Goldfield" (schooner) (different) 2·10 2·25

**1984.** Universal Postal Union Congress, Hamburg. No. 589 optd UPU CONGRESS HAMBURG 1984.
591 50c. Schooner "Goldfield" 1·50 2·00

**151** Snowy Egret

**1984.** Birds of the Cayman Islands (1st series). Multicoloured.
592 5c. Type **151** 1·00 75
593 10c. Bananaquit 1·00 75
594 35c. Belted kingfisher ("Kingfisher") 3·25 2·50
595 $1 Brown booby 6·00 11·00
See also Nos. 627/30.

**152** Couple on Beach at Sunset

**1984.** Christmas. Local Festivities. Multicoloured.
596 5c. Type **152** 85 1·50
597 5c. Family and schooner 85 1·50
598 5c. Carol singers 85 1·50
599 5c. East End bonfire 85 1·50
600 25c. Yachts 1·25 1·50
601 25c. Father Christmas in power-boat 1·25 1·50
602 25c. Children on beach 1·25 1·50
603 25c. Beach party 1·25 1·50
**MS**604 59×79 mm. $1 As No. 599, but larger 27×41 mm 4·00 4·50

Nos. 596/9 and 600/3 were each printed together, se-tenant, the four designs of each value forming a composite picture of a beach scene at night (5c.) or in the daytime (25c.).

**153** "Schomburgkia thomsoniana" (var. minor)

**1985.** Orchids. Multicoloured.
605 5c. Type **153** 1·00 30
606 10c. "Schomburgkia thomsoniana" 1·00 30
607 25c. "Encyclia plicata" 2·50 1·00
608 50c. "Dendrophylax fawcettii" 3·75 3·00

**154** Freighter Aground

**1985.** Shipwrecks. Multicoloured.
609 5c. Type **154** 90 50
610 25c. Submerged sailing ship 2·75 1·25
611 35c. Wrecked trawler 3·00 2·50
612 40c. Submerged wreck on its side 3·25 3·50

**155** Athletics

**1985.** International Youth Year. Multicoloured.
613 5c. Type **155** 25 25
614 15c. Students in library 40 30
615 25c. Football (vert) 75 55
616 50c. Netball (vert) 1·75 2·50

**156** Morse Key (1935)

**1985.** 50th Anniv of Telecommunications System. Multicoloured.
617 5c. Type **156** 45 70
618 10c. Hand cranked telephone 50 70
619 25c. Tropospheric scatter dish (1966) 1·50 80
620 50c. Earth station dish aerial (1979) 2·50 5·00

**1986.** 60th Birthday of Queen Elizabeth II. As T 110 of Ascension. Multicoloured.
621 5c. Princess Elizabeth at wedding of Lady May Cambridge, 1931 10 30
622 10c. In Norway, 1955 15 30
623 25c. Queen inspecting Royal Cayman Islands Police, 1983 1·50 75
624 50c. During Gulf tour, 1979 75 2·00
625 $1 At Crown Agents Head Office, London, 1983 1·10 2·75

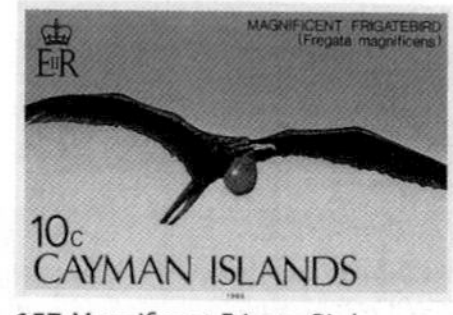

**157** Magnificent Frigate Bird

**1986.** Birds of the Cayman Islands (2nd series). Multicoloured.
627 10c. Type **157** 1·75 1·00
628 25c. Black-billed whistling duck ("West Indian Whistling Duck") (vert) 2·25 1·40
629 35c. La Sagra's flycatcher (vert) 2·50 2·50
630 40c. Yellow-faced grassquit 3·00 5·00

**1986.** Royal Wedding. As T 112 of Ascension. Multicoloured.
633 5c. Prince Andrew and Miss Sarah Ferguson 40 25
634 50c. Prince Andrew aboard H.M.S. "Brazen" 1·60 2·25

**158** Red Coral Shrimp

**1986.** Marine Life. Multicoloured.
635 5c. Type **158** 40 1·00
636 10c. Yellow crinoid 40 50
637 15c. Hermit crab 35 60
638 20c. Tube dwelling anemone 35 1·75
639 25c. Christmas tree worm 45 2·50
640 35c. Porcupinefish 70 2·75
641 50c. Orangeball anenome 80 4·50
642 60c. Basket starfish 3·50 9·00
643 75c. Flamingo tongue 10·00 11·00
644 $1 Sea anenome 1·10 2·50
645 $2 Diamond blenny 1·25 4·75
646 $4 Rough file shell 2·00 6·50

**159** Golf

**1987.** Tourism. Multicoloured.
647 10c. Type **159** 2·50 1·25
648 15c. Sailing 2·50 1·25
649 25c. Snorkelling 2·50 1·25
650 35c. Paragliding 2·75 2·00
651 $1 Game fishing 5·50 11·00

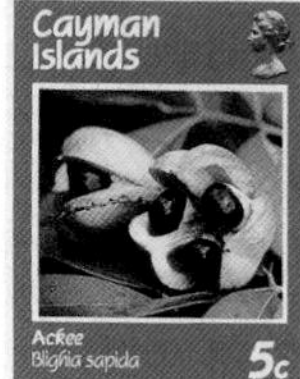

**160** Ackee

**1987.** Cayman Islands Fruits. Multicoloured.
652 5c. Type **160** 75 1·25
653 25c. Breadfruit 2·00 55
654 35c. Pawpaw 2·00 70
655 $1 Soursop 4·50 8·00

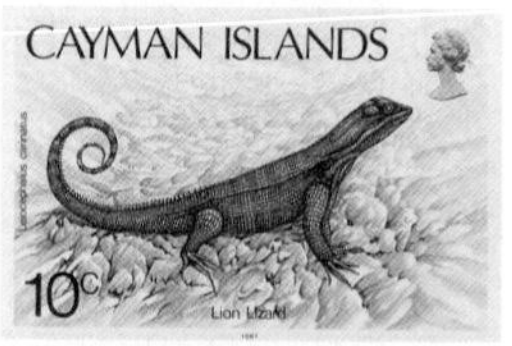

**161** Lion Lizard

**1987.** Lizards. Multicoloured.
656 10c. Type **161** 2·25 65
657 50c. Iguana 4·50 3·50
658 $1 Anole 5·50 7·00

**162** Poinsettia

**1987.** Flowers. Multicoloured.
659 5c. Type **162** 65 45
660 25c. Periwinkle 1·75 75
661 35c. Yellow allamanda 1·90 1·10
662 75c. Blood lily 3·50 4·50

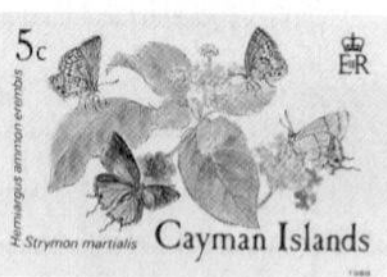

**163** "Hemiargus ammon" and "Strymon martialis"

**1988.** Butterflies. Multicoloured.
663 5c. Type **163** 1·25 65
664 25c. "Phocides pigmalion" 2·50 85
665 50c. "Anaea troglodyta" 4·00 3·75
666 $1 "Papilio andraemon" 5·00 5·00

**164** Green-backed Heron

**1988.** Herons. Multicoloured.
667 5c. Type **164** 1·25 65
668 25c. Louisiana heron 2·25 85
669 50c. Yellow-crowned night heron 3·00 3·00
670 $1 Little blue heron 3·50 4·25

**165** Cycling

**1988.** Olympic Games, Seoul. Multicoloured.
671 10c. Type **165** 3·00 1·00
672 50c. Cayman Airways Boeing 727 airliner and national team 4·00 3·25
673 $1 "470" dinghy 4·00 4·25
**MS**674 53×60 mm. $1 Tennis 4·00 3·00

**166** Princess Alexandra

**1988.** Visit of Princess Alexandra. Multicoloured.

| | | | |
|---|---|---|---|
| 675 | 5c. Type **166** | 1·75 | 1·00 |
| 676 | $1 Princess Alexandra in evening dress | 7·50 | 6·50 |

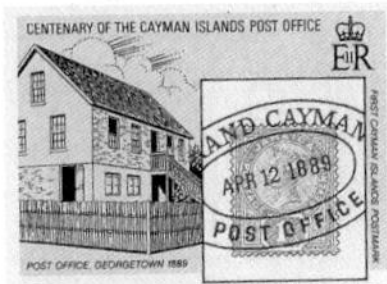

**167** George Town Post Office, and Cayman Postmark on Jamaica 1d., 1889

**1989.** Centenary of Cayman Islands Postal Service. Multicoloured.

| | | | | |
|---|---|---|---|---|
| 677 | **167** | 5c. multicoloured | 85 | 1·00 |
| 678 | - | 25c. green, black and blue | 2·00 | 1·00 |
| 679 | - | 35c. multicoloured | 2·00 | 1·25 |
| 680 | - | $1 multicoloured | 8·00 | 9·50 |

DESIGNS: 25c. "Orinoco" (mail steamer) and 1900 ½d. stamp; 35c. G.P.O., Grand Cayman and "London 1980" $1 stamp; $1 Cayman Airways B.A.C. One Eleven 200/400 airplane and 1966 1s. Jet Service stamp.

**168** Captain Bligh ashore in West Indies

**1989.** Captain Bligh's Second Breadfruit Voyage, 1791–93. Multicoloured.

| | | | |
|---|---|---|---|
| 681 | 50c. Type **168** | 5·00 | 5·00 |
| 682 | 50c. H.M.S. "Providence" (sloop) at anchor | 5·00 | 5·00 |
| 683 | 50c. Breadfruit in tubs and H.M.S. "Assistant" (transport) | 5·00 | 5·00 |
| 684 | 50c. Sailors moving tubs of breadfruit | 5·00 | 5·00 |
| 685 | 50c. Midshipman and stores | 5·00 | 5·00 |

Nos. 681/5 were printed together, se-tenant, forming a composite design.

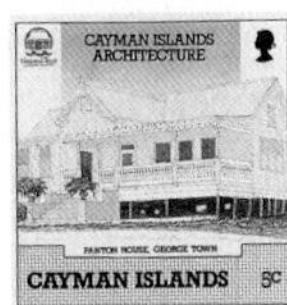

**169** Panton House

**1989.** Architecture. Designs showing George Town buildings. Multicoloured.

| | | | |
|---|---|---|---|
| 686 | 5c. Type **169** | 75 | 1·00 |
| 687 | 10c. Town hall and clock tower | 75 | 1·00 |
| 688 | 25c. Old Court House | 1·40 | 60 |
| 689 | 35c. Elmslie Memorial Church | 1·60 | 75 |
| 690 | $1 Post Office | 3·50 | 6·50 |

**170** Map of Grand Cayman, 1773, and Surveying Instruments

**1989.** Island Maps and Survey Ships. Multicoloured.

| | | | |
|---|---|---|---|
| 691 | 5c. Type **170** | 2·00 | 1·50 |
| 692 | 25c. Map of Cayman Islands, 1956, and surveying instruments | 4·25 | 1·25 |
| 693 | 50c. H.M.S. "Mutine", 1914 | 6·00 | 5·50 |
| 694 | $1 H.M.S. "Vidal", 1956 | 9·00 | 11·00 |

**171** French Angelfish

**1990.** Angelfishes. Multicoloured.

| | | | |
|---|---|---|---|
| 707 | 10c. Type **171** | 1·25 | 70 |
| 708 | 25c. Grey angelfish | 2·25 | 90 |
| 709 | 50c. Queen angelfish | 3·50 | 4·25 |
| 710 | $1 Rock beauty | 5·50 | 8·00 |

**1990.** 90th Birthday of Queen Elizabeth the Queen Mother. As T 134 of Ascension.

| | | | |
|---|---|---|---|
| 711 | 50c. multicoloured | 1·25 | 2·25 |
| 712 | $1 black and blue | 2·75 | 4·00 |

DESIGNS—21×36 mm: 50c. Silver Wedding photograph, 1948. 29×37 mm: $1 King George VI and Queen Elizabeth with Winston Churchill, 1940.

**172** "Danaus eresimus"

**1990.** "Expo 90" International Garden and Greenery Exhibition, Osaka. Butterflies. Multicoloured.

| | | | |
|---|---|---|---|
| 713 | 5c. Type **172** | 65 | 60 |
| 714 | 25c. "Brephidium exilis" | 1·50 | 1·10 |
| 715 | 35c. "Phyciodes phaon" | 1·75 | 1·25 |
| 716 | $1 "Agraulis vanillae" | 4·00 | 6·50 |

**173** Goes Weather Satellite

**1991.** International Decade for Natural Disaster Reduction. Multicoloured.

| | | | |
|---|---|---|---|
| 717 | 5c. Type **173** | 80 | 70 |
| 718 | 30c. Meteorologist tracking hurricane | 2·00 | 1·10 |
| 719 | 40c. Damaged buildings | 2·25 | 1·25 |
| 720 | $1 U.S. Dept of Commerce weather reconnaisance Lockheed WP-3D Orion | 5·00 | 8·00 |

**174** Angels and "Datura candida"

**1991.** Christmas. Multicoloured.

| | | | |
|---|---|---|---|
| 721 | 5c. Type **174** | 80 | 80 |
| 722 | 30c. Mary and Joseph going to Bethlehem and "Allamanda cathartica" | 2·00 | 60 |
| 723 | 40c. Adoration of the Kings and "Euphorbia pulcherrima" | 2·25 | 1·10 |
| 724 | 60c. Holy Family and "Guaiacum officinale" | 3·25 | 6·00 |

**175** Coconut Palm

**1991.** Island Scenes. Multicoloured.

| | | | |
|---|---|---|---|
| 725 | 5c. Type **175** | 50 | 50 |
| 726 | 15c. Beach scene (horiz) | 1·75 | 50 |
| 727 | 20c. Poincianas in bloom (horiz) | 70 | 35 |
| 728 | 30c. Blowholes (horiz) | 1·75 | 50 |
| 729 | 40c. Police band (horiz) | 2·50 | 1·40 |
| 730 | 50c. "Song of Norway" (liner) at George Town | 2·00 | 1·40 |
| 731 | 60c. The Bluff, Cayman Brac (horiz) | 1·75 | 2·25 |
| 732 | 80c. Coat of arms | 1·50 | 2·50 |
| 733 | 90c. View of Hell (horiz) | 1·60 | 2·50 |
| 734 | $1 Game fishing (horiz) | 3·25 | 2·50 |
| 735 | $2 "Nieuw Amsterdam" (1983) and "Holiday" (liners) in harbour | 8·00 | 7·50 |
| 736 | $8 Queen Elizabeth II | 16·00 | 19·00 |

**1992.** 40th Anniv of Queen Elizabeth II's Accession. As T 143 of Ascension. Multicoloured.

| | | | |
|---|---|---|---|
| 737 | 5c. Caymans' house | 30 | 30 |
| 738 | 20c. Sunset over islands | 1·00 | 50 |
| 739 | 30c. Beach | 1·10 | 65 |
| 740 | 40c. Three portraits of Queen Elizabeth | 1·10 | 1·00 |
| 741 | $1 Queen Elizabeth II | 2·00 | 3·50 |

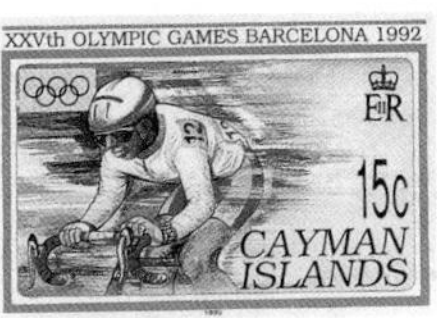

**176** Single Cyclist

**1992.** Olympic Games, Barcelona. Cycling. Mult.

| | | | |
|---|---|---|---|
| 742 | 15c. Type **176** | 1·75 | 65 |
| 743 | 40c. Two cyclists | 2·50 | 1·50 |
| 744 | 60c. Cyclist's legs | 3·00 | 3·25 |
| 745 | $1 Two pursuit cyclists | 3·75 | 4·50 |

**177** Woman and Donkey with Panniers

**1992.** Island Heritage. Multicoloured.

| | | | |
|---|---|---|---|
| 746 | 5c. Type **177** | 50 | 50 |
| 747 | 30c. Fisherman weaving net | 1·25 | 85 |
| 748 | 40c. Maypole dancing | 1·50 | 1·10 |
| 749 | 60c. Basket making | 2·50 | 3·50 |
| 750 | $1 Cooking on caboose | 3·00 | 4·50 |

**178** Yellow Stingray

**1993.** Rays. Multicoloured.

| | | | |
|---|---|---|---|
| 751 | 5c. Type **178** | 70 | 60 |
| 752 | 30c. Southern stingray | 1·75 | 1·25 |
| 753 | 40c. Spotted eagle-ray | 2·00 | 1·50 |
| 754 | $1 Manta | 4·25 | 5·50 |

**179** Turtle and Sailing Dinghies

**1993.** Tourism. Multicoloured.

| | | | |
|---|---|---|---|
| 755 | 15c. Type **179** | 1·50 | 1·75 |
| 756 | 15c. Tourist boat, fishing launch and scuba diver | 1·50 | 1·75 |
| 757 | 15c. Golf | 1·50 | 1·75 |
| 758 | 15c. Tennis | 1·50 | 1·75 |
| 759 | 15c. Pirates and ship | 1·50 | 1·75 |
| 760 | 30c. Liner, tourist launch and yacht | 1·75 | 1·90 |
| 761 | 30c. George Town street | 1·75 | 1·90 |
| 762 | 30c. Tourist submarine | 1·75 | 1·90 |
| 763 | 30c. Motor scooter riders and cyclist | 1·75 | 1·90 |
| 764 | 30c. Cayman Airways Boeing 737 airliners | 1·75 | 1·90 |

**180** Cuban Amazon with Wings spread

**1993.** Endangered Species. Cuban Amazon ("Grand Cayman Parrot"). Multicoloured.

| | | | |
|---|---|---|---|
| 765 | 5c. Type **180** | 85 | 1·50 |
| 766 | 5c. On branch with wings folded | 85 | 1·50 |
| 767 | 30c. Head of parrot | 2·25 | 2·50 |
| 768 | 30c. Pair of parrots | 2·25 | 2·50 |

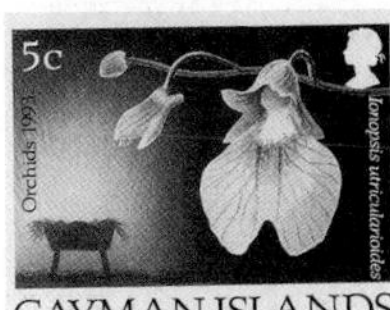

**181** "Ionopsis utricularioides" and Manger

**1993.** Christmas. Orchids. Multicoloured.

| | | | |
|---|---|---|---|
| 769 | 5c. Type **181** | 1·25 | 75 |
| 770 | 40c. "Encyclia cochleata" and shepherd | 2·75 | 85 |
| 771 | 60c. "Vanilla pompona" and wise men | 3·75 | 4·00 |
| 772 | $1 "Oncidium caymanense" and Virgin Mary | 4·75 | 7·00 |

**182** Queen Angelfish

**1994.** "Hong Kong '94" International Stamp Exhibition. Reef Life. Sheet 121×85 mm, containing T 182 and similar vert designs. Multicoloured.

| | | | |
|---|---|---|---|
| **MS**773 | 60c. Type **182**; 60c. Diver with porkfish and short-finned hogfish; 60c. Rock beauty and Royal gramma; 60c. French angelfish and Banded butterflyfish | 8·50 | 9·50 |

**183** Flags of Great Britain and Cayman Islands

**1994.** Royal Visit. Multicoloured.

| | | | |
|---|---|---|---|
| 774 | 5c. Type **183** | 2·00 | 1·25 |
| 775 | 15c. Royal Yacht "Britannia" | 3·00 | 1·00 |
| 776 | 30c. Queen Elizabeth II | 3·00 | 1·25 |
| 777 | $2 Queen Elizabeth and Prince Philip disembarking | 9·00 | 12·00 |

**184** Black-billed Whistling Duck

**1994.** Black-billed Whistling Duck ("West Indian Whistling Duck"). Multicoloured.

| | | | |
|---|---|---|---|
| 778 | 5c. Type **184** | 1·50 | 1·00 |
| 779 | 15c. Duck landing on water (horiz) | 2·25 | 75 |
| 780 | 20c. Duck preening (horiz) | 2·25 | 80 |
| 781 | 80c. Duck flapping wings | 4·50 | 5·50 |
| 782 | $1 Adult and duckling | 5·00 | 6·50 |
| **MS**783 | 71×45 mm. $1 As No. 782, but including Cayman Islands National Trust symbol | 7·00 | 8·00 |

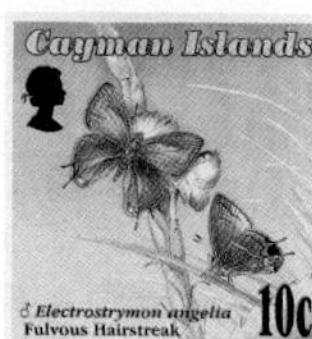

**185** "Electrostrymon angelia"

**1994.** Butterflies. Multicoloured.

| | | | |
|---|---|---|---|
| 784 | 10c. Type **185** | 1·00 | 1·50 |
| 785 | 10c. "Eumaeus atala" | 1·00 | 1·50 |
| 786 | $1 "Eurema daira" | 4·75 | 5·00 |
| 787 | $1 "Urbanus dorantes" | 4·75 | 5·00 |

**186** H.M.S. "Convert" (frigate)

**1994.** Bicentenary of Wreck of Ten Sail off Grand Cayman. Multicoloured.

| | | | |
|---|---|---|---|
| 788 | 10c. Type **186** | 55 | 55 |
| 789 | 10c. Merchant brig and full-rigged ship | 55 | 55 |
| 790 | 15c. Full-rigged ship near rock | 75 | 50 |
| 791 | 20c. Long boat leaving full-rigged ship | 85 | 55 |
| 792 | $2 Merchant brig | 4·50 | 7·50 |

**187** Young Green Turtles

**1995.** Sea Turtles. Multicoloured.

| | | | |
|---|---|---|---|
| 793 | 10c. Type **187** | 55 | 45 |
| 794 | 20c. Kemp's ridley turtle | 80 | 55 |
| 795 | 25c. Hawksbill turtle | 90 | 60 |
| 796 | 30c. Leatherback turtle | 95 | 70 |
| 797 | $1.30 Loggerhead turtle | 3·50 | 4·75 |
| 798 | $2 Pacific ridley turtles | 4·50 | 6·00 |
| **MS**799 | 167×94 mm. Nos. 793/8 | 10·00 | 11·50 |

**188** Running

**1995.** CARIFTA and IAAF Games, George Town. Multicoloured.

| | | | |
|---|---|---|---|
| 800 | 10c. Type **188** | 60 | 40 |
| 801 | 20c. High jumping | 90 | 70 |
| 802 | 30c. Javelin throwing | 1·25 | 80 |
| 803 | $1.30 Yachting | 4·25 | 6·00 |
| **MS**804 | 100×70 mm. $2 Athletes with medals | 6·50 | 7·50 |

**1995.** 50th Anniv of End of Second World War. As T 161 of Ascension. Multicoloured.

| | | | |
|---|---|---|---|
| 805 | 10c. Members of Cayman Home Guard | 70 | 55 |
| 806 | 25c. "Comayagua" (freighter) | 1·75 | 85 |
| 807 | 40c. U-boat "U125" | 2·00 | 1·50 |
| 808 | $1 U.S. Navy L-3 airship | 3·75 | 6·00 |
| **MS**809 | 75×85 mm. $1.30, Reverse of 1939–45 War Medal (vert) | 2·50 | 3·00 |

**189** Queen Elizabeth the Queen Mother

**1995.** 95th Birthday of Queen Elizabeth the Queen Mother. Sheet 70×90 mm.

| | | | |
|---|---|---|---|
| **MS**810 | **189** $4 multicoloured | 8·50 | 9·50 |

**190** Ox and Christ Child

**1995.** Christmas. Nativity Animals. Multicoloured.

| | | | |
|---|---|---|---|
| 811 | 10c. Type **190** | 70 | 30 |
| 812 | 20c. Sheep and lamb | 1·25 | 45 |
| 813 | 30c. Donkey | 2·00 | 60 |
| 814 | $2 Camels | 8·00 | 10·00 |
| **MS**815 | 160×75 mm. Nos. 811/14 | 11·00 | 11·00 |

**191** Sea Grape

**1996.** Wild Fruit. Multicoloured.

| | | | |
|---|---|---|---|
| 816 | 10c. Type **191** | 50 | 40 |
| 817 | 25c. Guava | 1·00 | 50 |
| 818 | 40c. West Indian cherry | 1·50 | 80 |
| 819 | $1 Tamarind | 2·75 | 4·50 |

**192** "Laser" Dinghy

**1996.** Centenary of Modern Olympic Games. Multicoloured.

| | | | |
|---|---|---|---|
| 820 | 10c. Type **192** | 55 | 40 |
| 821 | 20c. Sailboarding | 85 | 60 |
| 822 | 30c. "Finn" dinghy | 1·00 | 80 |
| 823 | $2 Running | 4·25 | 7·00 |

**193** Guitar and Score of National Song

**1996.** National Identity. Multicoloured.

| | | | |
|---|---|---|---|
| 824 | 10c. Type **193** | 35 | 40 |
| 825 | 20c. Cayman Airways Boeing 737-200 | 1·25 | 40 |
| 826 | 25c. Queen Elizabeth opening Legislative Assembly | 75 | 50 |
| 827 | 30c. Seven Mile Beach | 75 | 55 |
| 828 | 40c. Scuba diver and stingrays | 1·00 | 75 |
| 829 | 60c. Children at turtle farm | 2·00 | 1·10 |
| 830 | 80c. Cuban amazon ("Cayman Parrot") (national bird) | 3·00 | 2·25 |
| 831 | 90c. Silver thatch palm (national tree) | 1·75 | 2·25 |
| 832 | $1 Cayman Islands flag | 3·75 | 2·50 |
| 833 | $2 Wild Banana Orchid (national flower) | 5·50 | 5·50 |
| 834 | $4 Cayman Islands coat of arms | 9·00 | 13·00 |
| 835 | $6 Cayman Islands currency | 11·00 | 15·00 |

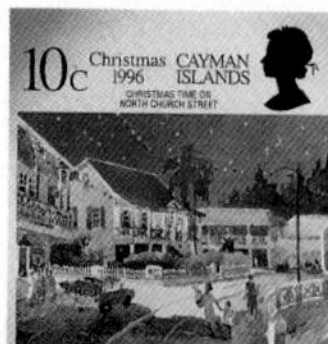

**194** "Christmas Time on North Church Street" (Joanne Sibley)

**1996.** Christmas. Paintings. Multicoloured.

| | | | |
|---|---|---|---|
| 836 | 10c. Type **194** | 40 | 30 |
| 837 | 25c. "Gone Fishing" (Lois Brezinsky) | 70 | 50 |
| 838 | 30c. "Claus Encounters" (John Doak) | 80 | 70 |
| 839 | $2 "A Caymanian Christmas" (Debbie van der Bol) | 4·00 | 6·50 |

**1997.** "HONG KONG '97" International Stamp Exhibition. Sheet 130×90 mm, containing design as No. 830 with "1997" imprint date. Multicoloured.

| | | | |
|---|---|---|---|
| **MS**840 | 80c. Cuban amazon ("Cayman Parrot") | 1·75 | 2·00 |

**1997.** Golden Wedding of Queen Elizabeth and Prince Philip. As T 173 of Ascension. Multicoloured.

| | | | |
|---|---|---|---|
| 841 | 10c. Queen Elizabeth | 1·10 | 1·40 |
| 842 | 10c. Prince Philip and Prince Charles at Trooping the Colour | 1·10 | 1·40 |
| 843 | 30c. Prince William horse riding, 1989 | 1·75 | 1·90 |
| 844 | 30c. Queen Elizabeth and Prince Philip at Royal Ascot | 1·75 | 1·90 |
| 845 | 40c. Prince Philip at the Brighton Driving Trials | 1·90 | 2·00 |
| 846 | 40c. Queen Elizabeth at Windsor Horse Show, 1993 | 1·90 | 2·00 |
| **MS**847 | 110×70 mm. $1 Queen Elizabeth and Prince Philip in landau (horiz) | 5·50 | 5·50 |

**195** Children accessing Internet

**1997.** Telecommunications. Multicoloured.

| | | | |
|---|---|---|---|
| 848 | 10c. Type **195** | 35 | 25 |
| 849 | 25c. Cable & Wireless cable ship | 70 | 45 |
| 850 | 30c. New area code "345" on children's T-shirts | 75 | 60 |
| 851 | 60c. Satellite dish | 1·50 | 2·50 |

**196** Santa in Hammock

**1997.** Christmas. Multicoloured.

| | | | |
|---|---|---|---|
| 852 | 10c. Type **196** | 35 | 25 |
| 853 | 30c. Santa with children on the Bluff | 65 | 45 |
| 854 | 40c. Santa playing golf | 1·50 | 80 |
| 855 | $1 Santa scuba diving | 2·00 | 3·50 |

**1998.** Diana, Princess of Wales Commemoration. As T177 of Ascension. Multicoloured.

| | | | |
|---|---|---|---|
| 856 | 10c. Wearing gold earrings, 1997 | 40 | 30 |
| 857 | 20c. Wearing black hat | 70 | 90 |
| **MS**858 | 145×70 mm. 10c. As No. 856; 20c. As No. 857; 40c. With bouquet, 1995; $1 Wearing black and white blouse, 1983 (sold at $1.70 + 30c. charity premium) | 2·75 | 4·00 |

**1998.** 80th Anniv of the Royal Air Force. As T 178 of Ascension. Multicoloured.

| | | | |
|---|---|---|---|
| 859 | 10c. Hawker Horsley | 60 | 70 |
| 860 | 20c. Fairey Hendon | 75 | 80 |
| 861 | 25c. Hawker Siddeley Gnat | 85 | 90 |
| 862 | 30c. Hawker Siddeley Dominie | 95 | 1·00 |
| **MS**863 | 110×77 mm. 40c. Airco D.H.9; 60c. Spad 13 Scout; 80c. Airspeed Oxford; $1 Martin Baltimore | 5·50 | 6·50 |

**197** Black-billed Whistling Duck ("West Indian Whistling Duck")

**1998.** Birds. Multicoloured.

| | | | |
|---|---|---|---|
| 864 | 10c. Type **197** | 1·25 | 60 |
| 865 | 20c. Magnificent frigate bird ("Magnificent Frigatbird") | 1·75 | 60 |
| 866 | 60c. Red-footed booby | 2·75 | 3·00 |
| 867 | $1 Cuban amazon ("Grand Cayman Parrot") | 3·50 | 4·25 |

**198** Santa at the Blowholes

**1998.** Christmas. Multicoloured.

| | | | |
|---|---|---|---|
| 868 | 10c. Type **198** | 30 | 30 |
| 869 | 30c. Santa diving on wreck of "Capt. Keith Tibbetts" | 75 | 60 |
| 870 | 40c. Santa at Pedro Castle | 90 | 75 |
| 871 | 60c. Santa arriving on Little Cayman | 1·75 | 2·50 |

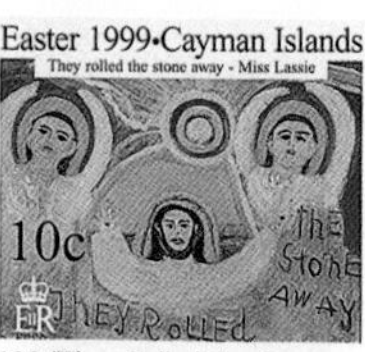

**199** "They Rolled the Stone Away" (Miss Lassie)

**1999.** Easter. Paintings by Miss Lassie (Gladwyn Bush). Multicoloured.

| | | | |
|---|---|---|---|
| 884 | 10c. Type **199** | 30 | 35 |
| 885 | 20c. "Ascension" (vert) | 60 | 70 |
| 886 | 30c. "The World Praying for Peace" | 75 | 85 |
| 887 | 40c. "Calvary" (vert) | 95 | 1·10 |

**200** "Cayman House" (Jessica Cranston)

**1999.** Vision 2008 Project. Children's Paintings. Multicoloured.

| | | | |
|---|---|---|---|
| 888 | 10c. Type **200** | 40 | 20 |
| 889 | 30c. "Coral Reef" (Sarah Hetley) | 1·00 | 55 |
| 890 | 40c. "Fisherman on North Sound" (Sarah Cuff) | 1·10 | 70 |
| 891 | $2 "Three Fish and a Turtle" (Ryan Martinez) | 4·25 | 6·50 |

**1999.** Royal Wedding. As T 185 of Ascension. Multicoloured.

| | | | |
|---|---|---|---|
| 892 | 10c. Photographs of Prince Edward and Miss Sophie Rhys-Jones | 50 | 30 |
| 893 | $2 Engagement photograph | 3·75 | 4·75 |

**1999.** 30th Anniv of First Manned Landing on Moon. As T 186 of Ascension. Multicoloured.

| | | | |
|---|---|---|---|
| 894 | 10c. Coastguard cutter on patrol during launch | 45 | 35 |
| 895 | 25c. Firing of third stage rockets | 80 | 60 |
| 896 | 30c. Buzz Aldrin descending to Moon's surface | 85 | 65 |
| 897 | 60c. Jettisoning of lunar module | 1·40 | 2·25 |
| **MS**898 | 90×80 mm. $1.50, Earth as seen from Moon (circular, 40 mm diam) | 3·25 | 3·50 |

**1999.** "Queen Elizabeth the Queen Mother's Century". As T 187 of Ascension. Multicoloured.

| | | | |
|---|---|---|---|
| 899 | 10c. Visiting anti-aircraft battery, London, 1940 | 45 | 40 |
| 900 | 20c. With children on her 94th birthday, 1994 | 65 | 65 |
| 901 | 30c. With Prince Charles and Prince William, 1997 | 80 | 90 |

| | | | |
|---|---|---|---|
| 902 | 40c. Reviewing Chelsea Pensioners, 1986 | 90 | 1·00 |
| MS903 | 145×70 mm. $1.50, Duchess of York with Princess Elizabeth, 1926, and Royal Wedding, 1923 | 2·50 | 3·00 |

**201** 1969 Christmas ¼c. Stamp

**1999.** Christmas. Designs showing previous Christmas stamps. Multicoloured.

| | | | |
|---|---|---|---|
| 904 | 10c. Type **201** | 40 | 25 |
| 905 | 30c. 1984 Christmas 5c. | 70 | 50 |
| 906 | 40c. 1997 Christmas 10c. | 85 | 65 |
| 907 | $1 1979 Christmas 20c. (horiz) | 1·90 | 2·50 |
| **MS**908 | 111×100 mm. Nos. 904/7 | 3·50 | 3·50 |

**2000.** "Stamp Show 2000" International Stamp Exhibition, London. Kings and Queens of England. As T 223 of British Virgin Islands. Multicoloured.

| | | | |
|---|---|---|---|
| 909 | 10c. King Henry VII | 60 | 70 |
| 910 | 40c. King Henry VIII | 1·40 | 1·75 |
| 911 | 40c. Queen Mary I | 1·40 | 1·75 |
| 912 | 40c. King Charles II | 1·40 | 1·75 |
| 913 | 40c. Queen Anne | 1·40 | 1·75 |
| 914 | 40c. King George IV | 1·40 | 1·75 |
| 915 | 40c. King George V | 1·40 | 1·75 |

**202** Ernie fishing from Rubber Ring

**2000.** "Sesame Street" (children's T.V. programme). Multicoloured.

| | | | |
|---|---|---|---|
| 916 | 10c. Type **202** | 25 | 35 |
| 917 | 20c. Grover flying | 40 | 50 |
| 918 | 20c. Zoe in airplane | 40 | 50 |
| 919 | 20c. Oscar the Grouch in balloon | 40 | 50 |
| 920 | 20c. The Count on motorbike | 40 | 50 |
| 921 | 20c. Big Bird rollerskating | 40 | 50 |
| 922 | 20c. Cookie Monster heading for Cookie Factory | 40 | 50 |
| 923 | 20c. Type **202** | 40 | 50 |
| 924 | 20c. Bert in rowing boat | 40 | 50 |
| 925 | 20c. Elmo snorkeling | 40 | 50 |
| 926 | 30c. As No. 920 | 55 | 55 |
| **MS**927 | 139×86 mm. 20c. Elmo with stamps | 1·00 | 1·00 |

Nos. 917/25 were printed together, se-tenant, with the backgrounds forming a composite design.

**2000.** 18th Birthday of Prince William. As T 191 of Ascension. Multicoloured.

| | | | |
|---|---|---|---|
| 928 | 10c. Prince William in 1999 (horiz) | 50 | 40 |
| 929 | 20c. In evening dress, 1997 (horiz) | 75 | 60 |
| 930 | 30c. At Muick Falls, 1997 | 90 | 80 |
| 931 | 40c. In uniform of Parachute Regiment, 1986 | 1·25 | 1·25 |
| **MS**932 | 175×95 mm. $1 As baby with toy mouse (horiz) and Nos. 928/31 | 7·50 | 7·50 |

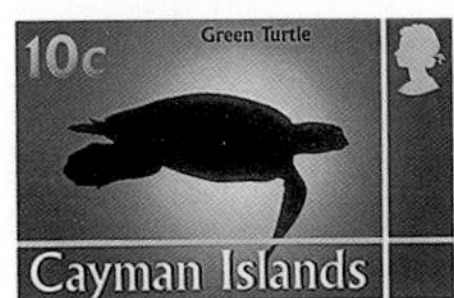

**203** Green Turtle

**2000.** Marine Life. Multicoloured.

| | | | |
|---|---|---|---|
| 933 | 10c. Type **203** | 55 | 45 |
| 934 | 20c. Queen angel fish | 80 | 50 |
| 935 | 30c. Sleeping parrotfish | 1·10 | 65 |
| 936 | $1 Green moray eel | 3·50 | 4·50 |

**204** Boy thinking about Drugs and Fitness

**2000.** National Drugs Council. Multicoloured.

| | | | |
|---|---|---|---|
| 937 | 10c. Type **204** | 60 | 35 |
| 938 | 15c. Rainbow, sun, clouds and "ez2B Drug Free" | 85 | 35 |
| 939 | 30c. Musicians dancing | 1·40 | 65 |
| 940 | $2 Hammock between two palm trees | 5·00 | 8·00 |

**205** Children on Beach ("Backing Sand")

**2000.** Christmas. Traditional Customs. Mult.

| | | | |
|---|---|---|---|
| 941 | 10c. Type **205** | 85 | 50 |
| 942 | 30c. Christmas dinner | 2·00 | 80 |
| 943 | 40c. Yard dance | 2·25 | 85 |
| 944 | 60c. Conch shell borders | 2·75 | 3·25 |

**206** Woman on Beach

**2001.** United Nations Women's Human Rights Campaign.

| | | | |
|---|---|---|---|
| 945 | **206** 10c. multicoloured | 60 | 60 |

**207** Red Mangrove Cay

**2001.** Cayman Brac Tourism Project. Mult.

| | | | |
|---|---|---|---|
| 946 | 15c. Type **207** | 1·10 | 75 |
| 947 | 20c. Peter's Cave (vert) | 1·25 | 80 |
| 948 | 25c. Bight Road steps (vert) | 1·40 | 90 |
| 949 | 30c. Westerly Ponds | 1·50 | 1·00 |
| 950 | 40c. Aerial view of Spot Bay | 1·75 | 1·40 |
| 951 | 60c. The Marshes | 2·75 | 3·50 |

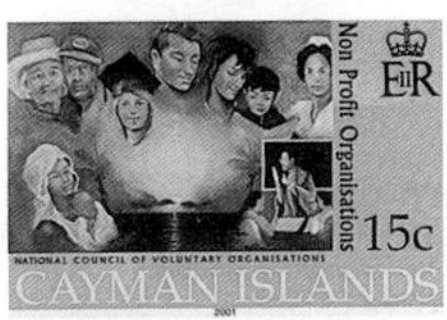

**208** Work of National Council of Voluntary Organizations

**2001.** Non-Profit Organizations. Multicoloured.

| | | | |
|---|---|---|---|
| 952 | 15c. Type **208** | 80 | 65 |
| 953 | 20c. Pet welfare (Cayman Humane Society) | 1·75 | 1·00 |
| 954 | 25c. Stick figures (Red Cross and Red Crescent) | 1·75 | 1·50 |
| 955 | 30c. Pink flowers (Cayman Islands Cancer Society) (vert) | 1·75 | 1·50 |
| 956 | 40c. Women's silhouettes and insignia (Lions Club Breast Cancer Awareness Campaign) (vert) | 1·90 | 1·75 |
| **MS**957 | 145×95 mm. Nos. 952/6 (sold at $1.80) | 7·50 | 8·00 |

No. **MS**957 was sold at $1.80 which included a 50c. donation to the featured organisations.

**209** Children walking Home

**2001.** Transportation. Multicoloured.

| | | | |
|---|---|---|---|
| 958 | 15c. Type **209** | 70 | 60 |
| 959 | 15c. Boy on donkey | 70 | 60 |
| 960 | 20c. Bananas by canoe | 70 | 45 |
| 961 | 25c. Horse and buggy | 1·00 | 55 |
| 962 | 30c. Catboats fishing | 1·00 | 55 |
| 963 | 40c. Schooner | 1·25 | 65 |
| 964 | 60c. Police cyclist (vert) | 2·50 | 1·50 |
| 965 | 80c. Lady drivers | 2·00 | 1·75 |
| 966 | 90c. Launching *Cimboco* (motor coaster) (vert) | 2·50 | 2·00 |
| 967 | $1 Amphibian aircraft | 2·75 | 2·25 |
| 968 | $4 Container ship | 8·50 | 9·00 |
| 969 | $10 Boeing 767 airliner | 18·00 | 20·00 |

**210** Father Christmas on Scooter with Children, Cayman Brac

**2001.** Christmas. Multicoloured.

| | | | |
|---|---|---|---|
| 970 | 15c. Type **210** | 1·00 | 55 |
| 971 | 30c. Father Christmas on eagle ray, Little Cayman | 1·40 | 80 |
| 972 | 40c. Father Christmas in catboat, Grand Cayman | 1·60 | 1·10 |
| 973 | 60c. Father Christmas parasailing over Grand Cayman | 2·40 | 3·00 |

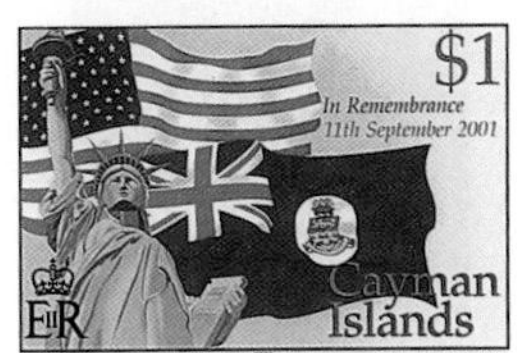

**211** Statue of Liberty, U.S. and Cayman Flags

**2002.** In Remembrance. Victims of Terrorist Attacks on U.S.A. (11 September 2001).

| | | | |
|---|---|---|---|
| 974 | **211** $1 multicoloured | 3·00 | 3·50 |

**2002.** Golden Jubilee. As T 200 of Ascension.

| | | | |
|---|---|---|---|
| 975 | 15c. grey, blue and gold | 50 | 40 |
| 976 | 20c. multicoloured | 65 | 40 |
| 977 | 30c. black, blue and gold | 80 | 60 |
| 978 | 80c. multicoloured | 2·00 | 2·25 |
| **MS**979 | 162×95 mm. Nos. 975/8 and $1 multicoloured | 7·00 | 7·00 |

DESIGNS—HORIZ: 15c. Princess Elizabeth as young child; 20c. Queen Elizabeth in evening dress, 1976; 30c. Princess Elizabeth and Princess Margaret as Girl Guides, 1942; 80c. Queen Elizabeth at Newbury, 1996. VERT (38×51 mm)—$1 Queen Elizabeth after Annigoni.

Designs as Nos. 975/8 in No. **MS**979 omit the gold frame around each stamp and the "Golden Jubilee 1952–2002" inscription.

**212** Snoopy painting Woodstock at Cayman Brac Bluff

**2002.** "A Cayman Vacation". Peanuts (cartoon characters by Charles Schulz). Multicoloured.

| | | | |
|---|---|---|---|
| 980 | 15c. Type **212** | 75 | 65 |
| 981 | 20c. Charlie Brown and Sally at Hell Post Office, Grand Cayman | 80 | 65 |
| 982 | 25c. Peppermint Patty and Marcie on beach, Little Cayman | 85 | 75 |
| 983 | 30c. Snoopy as Red Baron and Boeing 737-200 over Grand Cayman | 1·10 | 85 |
| 984 | 40c. Linus and Snoopy at Point of Sand, Little Cayman | 1·40 | 1·10 |
| 985 | 60c. Charlie Brown playing golf at The Links, Grand Cayman | 2·25 | 3·00 |
| **MS**986 | 230×160 mm. Nos. 980/5 | 6·50 | 7·00 |

No. **MS**986 is die-cut in the shape of a suitcase.

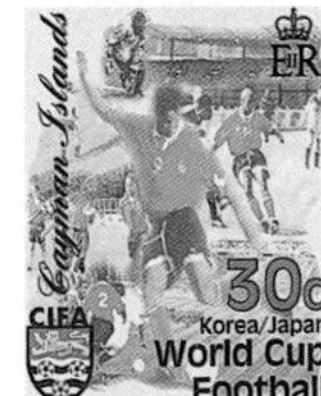

**213** Cayman Islands Footballers

**2002.** World Cup Football Championship, Japan and Korea and 35th Anniv of Cayman Islands Football Association.

| | | | |
|---|---|---|---|
| 987 | **213** 30c. multicoloured | 1·50 | 1·25 |
| 988 | **213** 40c. multicoloured | 1·50 | 1·25 |

**2002.** Queen Elizabeth the Queen Mother Commemoration. As T 202 of Ascension.

| | | | |
|---|---|---|---|
| 989 | 15c. black, gold and purple | 80 | 30 |
| 990 | 30c. multicoloured | 1·25 | 60 |
| 991 | 40c. black, gold and purple | 1·50 | 1·00 |
| 992 | $1 multicoloured | 2·75 | 3·75 |
| **MS**993 | 145×70 mm. Nos. 991/2 | 5·00 | 6·00 |

DESIGNS: 15c. Queen Elizabeth at Red Corss and St. John's summer fair, London, 1943; 30c. Queen Mother at Royal Caledonian School, Bushey; 40c. Duchess of York in 1936; $1 Queen Mother at film premiere in 1989.

Designs in No. **MS**993 omit the "1900–2002" inscription and the coloured frame.

**214** Angel Gabriel appearing to Virgin Mary

**2002.** Christmas. Multicoloured.

| | | | |
|---|---|---|---|
| 994 | 15c. Type **214** | 60 | 55 |
| 995 | 20c. Mary and Joseph travelling to Bethlehem | 70 | 55 |
| 996 | 30c. The Holy Family | 85 | 60 |
| 997 | 40c. Angel appearing to shepherds | 1·00 | 90 |
| 998 | 60c. Three Wise Men | 1·60 | 2·50 |
| **MS**999 | 234×195 mm. Nos. 994/8 | 4·25 | 5·00 |

**215** Catalina Flying Boat, North Sound, Grand Cayman

**2002.** 50th Anniv of Cayman Islands. Aviation. Multicoloured.

| | | | |
|---|---|---|---|
| 1000 | 15c. Type **215** | 1·10 | 75 |
| 1001 | 20c. Grand Cayman Airport, 1952 | 1·25 | 75 |
| 1002 | 25c. Cayman Brac Airways AC 50 | 1·25 | 80 |
| 1003 | 30c. Cayman Airways Boeing 737 | 1·40 | 85 |
| 1004 | 40c. British Airways Concorde at Grand Cayman, 1984 | 2·00 | 1·50 |
| 1005 | $1.30 Island Air DHC 6 Twin Otter on Little Cayman | 4·50 | 5·50 |

**216** Skipping

**2003.** Children's Games. Multicoloured.

| | | | |
|---|---|---|---|
| 1006 | 15c. Type **216** | 80 | 60 |
| 1007 | 20c. Maypole dancing | 90 | 60 |
| 1008 | 25c. Gig | 1·00 | 70 |
| 1009 | 30c. Hopscotch | 1·10 | 70 |
| 1010 | $1 Marbles | 3·00 | 4·00 |

**2003.** 50th Anniv of Coronation. As T 206 of Ascension. Multicoloured.

| | | | |
|---|---|---|---|
| 1011 | 15c. Queen Elizabeth II wearing Imperial State Crown | 75 | 35 |
| 1012 | $2 Newly crowned Queen flanked by Bishops of Durham and Bath & Wells | 4·25 | 5·00 |
| **MS**1013 | 95×115 mm. 20c. As 15c.; $4 As $2 | 9·00 | 10·00 |

Nos. 1011/12 have red frames; stamps from **MS**1013 have no frame and country name in mauve panel.

**2003.** As T 207 of Ascension.

| | | | |
|---|---|---|---|
| 1014 | $4 black, red and violet | 8·00 | 8·50 |

**2003.** 21st Birthday of Prince William of Wales. As T 208 of Ascension. Multicoloured.

| | | | |
|---|---|---|---|
| 1015 | 15c. Prince William at Tidworth Polo Club, 2002 and on Raleigh International Expedition, 2000 | 70 | 35 |
| 1016 | 40c. At Golden Jubilee church service, 2002 and Queen Mother's 101st birthday, 2001 | 1·25 | 60 |
| 1017 | 80c. At Queen Mother's 101st birthday and at Holyrood House, 2001 | 2·25 | 3·00 |
| 1018 | $1 At Eton College and at Christmas Day church service in 2000 | 2·25 | 3·00 |

**217** Turtles hatching

**2003.** 500th Anniv of Discovery of Cayman Islands. Multicoloured.

| | | | |
|---|---|---|---|
| 1019 | 15c. Type **217** | 80 | 65 |
| 1020 | 20c. Old waterfront, George Town, 1975 | 1·00 | 75 |
| 1021 | 20c. *Santa Maria* (Columbus) and turtle | 1·25 | 80 |
| 1022 | 25c. Nassau grouper (fish) and corals | 1·25 | 80 |
| 1023 | 30c. *Kirk-B* (Cayman Brac schooner) | 1·40 | 80 |
| 1024 | 40c. George Town harbour | 1·40 | 85 |
| 1025 | 60c. Musical instruments | 1·50 | 1·40 |
| 1026 | 80c. Smokewood tree and ghost orchids | 2·25 | 2·25 |
| 1027 | 90c. Little Cayman Baptist Church | 2·25 | 2·50 |
| 1028 | $1 Loading thatch rope onto *Caymania* | 2·75 | 3·00 |
| 1029 | $1.30 Children's dance troupe | 3·25 | 4·50 |
| 1030 | $2 Cayman Parliament in session | 4·25 | 6·00 |
| **MS**1031 | 216×151 mm. Nos. 1019/30 | 21·00 | 23·00 |

**218** Bell and "Merry Christmas"

**2003.** Christmas. Multicoloured.

| | | | |
|---|---|---|---|
| 1032 | 15c. Type **218** | 85 | 55 |
| 1033 | 20c. Christmas wreath and "Celebrate with Family" | 95 | 55 |
| 1034 | 30c. Gold star, angel and "Happy New Year" | 1·25 | 60 |
| 1035 | 40c. Christmas lights and "Happy Holidays" | 1·50 | 70 |
| 1036 | 60c. Poinsettias and "Seasons Greetings" | 2·00 | 2·75 |

**219** Female and Calf

**2003.** Endangered Species. Short-finned Pilot Whale. Multicoloured.

| | | | |
|---|---|---|---|
| 1037 | 15c. Type **219** | 1·40 | 75 |
| 1038 | 20c. Four pilot whales | 1·50 | 90 |
| 1039 | 30c. Two pilot whales at surface | 1·75 | 1·10 |
| 1040 | 40c. Short-finned pilot whale | 2·50 | 1·90 |

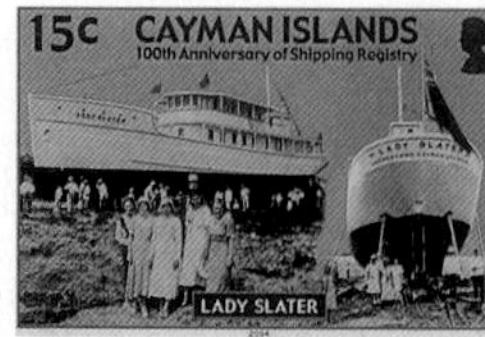


**220** *Lady Slater*

**2004.** Centenary of Shipping Registry. Multicoloured.

| | | | |
|---|---|---|---|
| 1041 | 15c. Type **220** | 85 | 55 |
| 1042 | 20c. *Seanostrum* | 95 | 70 |
| 1043 | 30c. *Kirk Pride* | 1·40 | 1·00 |
| 1044 | $1 *Boadicea* | 4·25 | 5·50 |

**221** "Jesus carrying His Cross" (Carole Mayer) **222** Swimming

**2004.** Easter. Multicoloured.

| | | | |
|---|---|---|---|
| 1045 | 15c. Type **221** | 75 | 40 |
| 1046 | 30c. "The Ascension" (Natasha Claire Kozaily) | 1·25 | 1·00 |

**222** Swimming

**2004.** Olympic Games, Athens, Greece. Multicoloured.

| | | | |
|---|---|---|---|
| 1047 | 15c. Type **222** | 75 | 40 |
| 1048 | 40c. Sprinting | 1·25 | 75 |
| 1049 | 60c. Long jump | 1·90 | 1·60 |
| 1050 | 80c. Two Cayman Islands swimmers | 2·40 | 3·00 |

**223** Blue Iguana

**2004.** Blue Iguana. Multicoloured.

| | | | |
|---|---|---|---|
| 1051 | 15c. Type **223** | 75 | 60 |
| 1052 | 20c. Baby iguana hatching from egg | 85 | 60 |
| 1053 | 25c. Four iguanas | 95 | 70 |
| 1054 | 30c. Baby iguana on finger | 1·10 | 70 |
| 1055 | 40c. Iguana with open mouth | 1·25 | 80 |
| 1056 | 90c. Eye of iguana | 2·75 | 3·50 |
| **MS**1057 | 104×58 mm. 60c. Iguana on rock facing right; 80c. Iguana on rock facing left | 4·50 | 5·00 |

**2005.** Bicentenary of Battle of Trafalgar. As T 216 of Ascension. Multicoloured.

| | | | |
|---|---|---|---|
| 1058 | 15c. HMS *Victory* (horiz) | 1·00 | 70 |
| 1059 | 20c. HMS *Tonnant* tangling into bow of *Algesiras* (horiz) | 1·10 | 70 |
| 1060 | 25c. Flint cannon lock and linstock (horiz) | 1·10 | 80 |
| 1061 | 60c. Boatswain's Mate RN (horiz) | 1·75 | 1·25 |
| 1062 | $1 Portrait of Admiral Nelson | 2·75 | 3·00 |
| 1063 | $2 HMS *Orion* in action against *Intrepide* (horiz) | 5·00 | 6·00 |
| **MS**1064 | 120×79 mm. 60c. Pluton; $2 HMS *Tonnant* | 6·00 | 7·00 |

No. 1058 contains traces of powdered wood from HMS *Victory*.

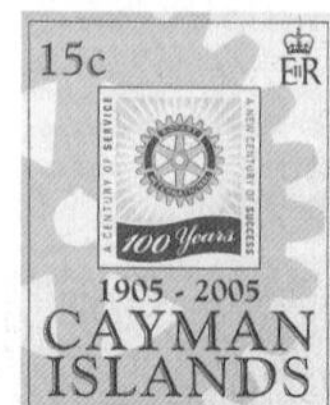


**224** Rotary Emblem

**2005.** Centenary of Rotary International.

| | | | | |
|---|---|---|---|---|
| 1065 | **224** | 15c. multicoloured | 70 | 60 |
| 1066 | - | 30c. ultramarine, black and grey | 1·10 | 1·00 |

DESIGN: 30c. Polio Plus and Rotary emblems.

**225** *Myrmecophila purpurea*

**2005.** Orchids. Multicoloured.

| | | | |
|---|---|---|---|
| 1067 | 15c. Type **225** | 75 | 55 |
| 1068 | 20c. *Prosthechea boothiana* | 80 | 55 |
| 1069 | 30c. *Tolumnia calochila* (vert) | 90 | 60 |
| 1070 | 40c. *Encyclia Phoenicia* | 1·10 | 80 |
| 1071 | 80c. *Prosthechea cochleata* (vert) | 2·00 | 2·50 |
| **MS**1072 | 80×52 mm. $1.50 *Encyclia kingsii* | 4·00 | 4·50 |

**2005.** Pope John Paul II Commemoration. As T 219 of Ascension.

| | | | |
|---|---|---|---|
| 1073 | 30c. multicoloured | 1·75 | 1·25 |

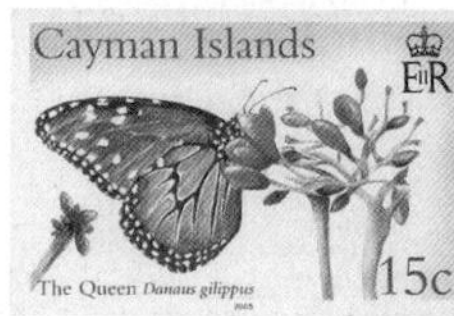


**226** The Queen (butterfly)

**2005.** Butterflies. Multicoloured. (a) Ordinary gum.

| | | | |
|---|---|---|---|
| 1074 | 15c. Type **226** | 70 | 60 |
| 1075 | 20c. Mexican fritillary | 75 | 65 |
| 1076 | 25c. Malachite | 80 | 70 |
| 1077 | 30c. Cayman crescent spot | 85 | 70 |
| 1078 | 40c. Cloudless sulphur | 1·10 | 80 |
| 1079 | 90c. Swallowtail | 2·25 | 3·00 |

(b) Self-adhesive. Size 29×24 mm.

| | | | |
|---|---|---|---|
| 1080 | 15c. Type **226** | 70 | 80 |
| 1081 | 20c. Mexican fritillary | 75 | 85 |
| 1082 | 30c. Cayman crescent spot | 90 | 1·10 |

**227** Angels

**2005.** Christmas. Multicoloured.

| | | | |
|---|---|---|---|
| 1083 | 15c. Type **227** | 60 | 40 |
| 1084 | 30c. Three Wise Men (horiz) | 80 | 50 |
| 1085 | 40c. Holy Family | 1·00 | 75 |
| 1086 | 60c. Shepherds (horiz) | 1·40 | 1·75 |
| **MS**1087 | 156×106 mm. Nos. 1083/6 | 3·50 | 3·50 |

**228** Wash Wood (*Jacquinia keyensis*)

**2006.** Trees. Multicoloured.

| | | | |
|---|---|---|---|
| 1088 | 15c. Type **228** | 70 | 50 |
| 1089 | 20c. Red mangrove (*Rhizophora mangle*) | 80 | 60 |
| 1090 | 30c. Ironwood (*Chionanthus caymanensis*) | 90 | 60 |
| 1091 | 60c. West Indian cedar (*Cedrela odorata*) | 1·75 | 1·40 |
| 1092 | $2 Spanish elm (*Cordia gerascanthus*) | 4·50 | 5·50 |

**2006.** 80th Birthday of Queen Elizabeth II. As T 223 of Ascension. Multicoloured.

| | | | |
|---|---|---|---|
| 1093 | 15c. Princess Elizabeth as young child | 80 | 50 |
| 1094 | 40c. Queen Elizabeth in uniform, c. 1952 | 1·50 | 80 |
| 1095 | $1 Wearing tiara | 2·25 | 2·50 |
| 1096 | $2 Wearing white blouse | 4·25 | 4·75 |
| **MS**1097 | 144×75 mm. As Nos. 1094/5, but without white borders | 8·00 | 8·50 |

**229** Hawksbill Turtle

**2006.** Cayman's Aquatic Treasures. Multicoloured. (a) Ordinary gum.

| | | | |
|---|---|---|---|
| 1098 | 25c. Type **229** | 1·00 | 90 |
| 1099 | 25c. Grey angelfish | 1·00 | 90 |
| 1100 | 60c. Queen angelfish (vert) | 2·00 | 1·75 |
| 1101 | 75c. Diamond blenny | 2·25 | 2·50 |
| 1102 | $1 Spotted drum (juvenile) (vert) | 3·00 | 3·50 |
| **MS**1103 | 145×95 mm. As Nos. 1098/102 | 8·00 | 8·50 |

(b) Size 29×24 mm. Self-adhesive.

| | | | |
|---|---|---|---|
| 1104 | 25c. As Type **229** | 90 | 1·10 |
| 1105 | 25c. As No. 1099 | 90 | 1·10 |
| 1106 | 60c. As No. 1100 | 1·75 | 2·00 |
| 1107 | 75c. As No. 1101 | 1·90 | 2·50 |

Stamps from **MS**1103 do not have white borders.

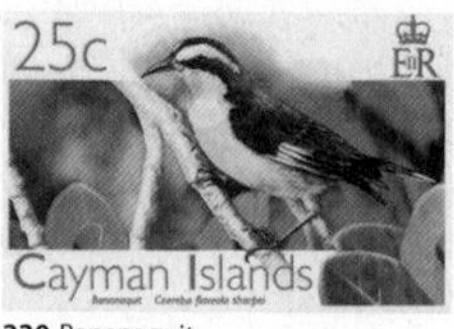


**230** Bananaquit

**2006.** Birds (1st series). Multicoloured.

| | | | |
|---|---|---|---|
| 1108 | 25c. Type **230** | 75 | 15 |
| 1109 | 50c. Vitelline warbler | 1·40 | 90 |
| 1110 | 75c. Cuban Amazon ("Grand Cayman Parrot") | 1·75 | 1·25 |
| 1111 | 80c. White-bellied dove ("Caribbean Dove") | 1·75 | 1·25 |
| 1112 | $1 Caribbean elaenia | 2·00 | 1·75 |
| 1113 | $1.50 Great red-bellied woodpecker ("West Indian Woodpecker") | 3·00 | 3·00 |
| 1114 | $1.60 Thick-billed vireo | 3·25 | 3·25 |
| 1115 | $2 Common flicker ("Northern Flicker") | 4·00 | 4·25 |
| 1116 | $4 Cuban bullfinch | 8·00 | 8·50 |
| 1117 | $5 Stripe-headed tanager ("Western spindalis") | 9·00 | 9·50 |
| 1118 | $10 Loggerhead kingbird | 17·00 | 18·00 |
| 1119 | $20 Red-legged thrush | 30·00 | 32·00 |

See also Nos. 1124/6.

**231** "Faith" and the Three Magi

**2006.** Christmas. Multicoloured.

| | | | |
|---|---|---|---|
| 1120 | 25c. Type **231** | 75 | 30 |
| 1121 | 75c. "Hope" and prophet speaking of the Messiah | 1·90 | 1·75 |
| 1122 | 80c. "Joy" and angel | 1·90 | 1·75 |
| 1123 | $1 "Love" and Mary with baby Jesus | 2·00 | 2·50 |

**232** Bananaquit

**2007.** Birds (2nd series). Designs as Nos. 1108, and 1110/11 but each 30×25 mm with redrawn inscriptions. Self-adhesive.

| | | | |
|---|---|---|---|
| 1124 | 25c. Type **232** | 1·10 | 1·40 |
| 1125 | 75c. Cuban amazon ('GRAND CAYMAN PARROT') | 2·25 | 2·75 |
| 1126 | 80c. White-bellied dove ('CARIBBEAN DOVE') | 2·25 | 2·75 |

**233** Brac Reef Dock

**2007.** Cayman Islands Scenes. Multicoloured.

| | | | |
|---|---|---|---|
| 1127 | 20c. Type **233** | 70 | 50 |
| 1128 | 25c. Waterfront, Hog Sty Bay, George Town, Grand Cayman | 75 | 60 |

1129 30c. East End blowholes, Grand Cayman Island (vert) 80 60
1130 40c. Man lying in hammock on beach at sunset (vert) 1·10 75
1131 75c. Poinciana flowers 2·00 2·50
1132 $1 Driftwood on shore, Little Cayman Island 2·25 2·75

**2007.** Centenary of Scouting. As T 281 of Bahamas. Multicoloured.
1133 25c. Early Wolf Cubs with their flag 75 50
1134 75c. Modern Cub Scouts after Remembrance Day Parade, 2006 2·00 2·00
1135 80c. Scouts camping 2·00 2·00
1136 $1 Drill team, Remembrance Day Parade, 2005 2·25 2·50
**MS**1137 90×65 mm. 50c. Cayman Islands scouts in opening ceremony of 13th Caribbean Scout Jamboree, Jamaica, 2006 (vert); $1.50 Lord Baden-Powell (vert) 3·75 4·00

**2007.** Diamond Wedding of Queen Elizabeth II and Duke of Edinburgh. As T 58 of British Indian Ocean Territory. Multicoloured.
1138 50c. Princess Elizabeth alighting from car and Lt. Philip Mountbatten, c. 1949 1·40 1·10
1139 75c. Princess Elizabeth wearing tiara and wedding veil, 1949 2·00 2·00
1140 80c. Queen Elizabeth the Queen Mother and Princesses Elizabeth and Margaret 2·00 2·00
1141 $1 Princess Elizabeth and Duke of Edinburgh in procession down Westminster Abbey aisle on wedding day, 1949 2·25 2·50
**MS**1142 125×85 mm. $2 Princess Elizabeth and Lt. Philip Mountbatten, c. 1949 (42×56 mm) 4·25 4·75

**234** Nativity

**2007.** Christmas. Stained glass windows. Mult.
1143 25c. Type **234** 75 50
1144 50c. Jesus Christ 1·40 1·00
1145 75c. Jesus with disciples 1·75 1·40
1146 80c. Peace dove 1·75 1·75
1147 $1 The Cross 2·25 2·25
1148 $1.50 Shepherd with lamb 3·25 4·00

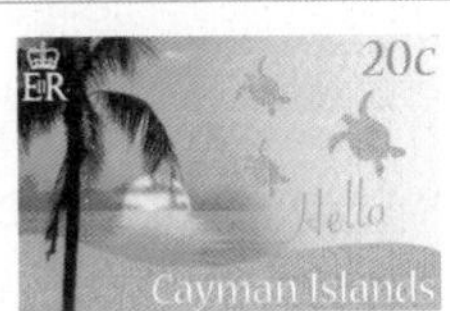

**235** Beach at Sunset and Turtles ('Hello')

**2008.** Greetings Stamps. Multicoloured. (a) Ordinary gum.
1149 20c. Type **235** 60 65
1150 20c. Crossed fingers and horseshoes ('Good Luck') 60 65
1151 20c. Balloons and stars ('Congratulations') 60 65
1152 20c. Invitation and fireworks ('You're Invited') 60 65
1153 20c. Fountain pen and flowers ('Best Wishes') 60 65
1154 20c. Cupid and hearts ('Love') 60 65
1155 25c. Type **235** 60 65
1156 25c. As No. 1150 60 65
1157 25c. As No. 1151 60 65
1158 25c. As No. 1152 60 65
1159 25c. As No. 1153 60 65
1160 25c. As No. 1154 60 65
1161 50c. Type **235** 1·00 1·25
1162 50c. As No. 1150 1·00 1·25
1163 50c. As No. 1151 1·00 1·25
1164 50c. As No. 1152 1·00 1·25
1165 50c. As No. 1153 1·00 1·25
1166 50c. As No. 1154 1·00 1·25
1167 75c. Type **235** 1·50 1·60
1168 75c. As No. 1150 1·50 1·60
1169 75c. As No. 1151 1·50 1·60
1170 75c. As No. 1152 1·50 1·60
1171 75c. As No. 1153 1·50 1·60
1172 75c. As No. 1154 1·50 1·60
1173 80c. Type **235** 1·60 1·75
1174 80c. As No. 1150 1·60 1·75
1175 80c. As No. 1151 1·60 1·75
1176 80c. As No. 1152 1·60 1·75
1177 80c. As No. 1153 1·60 1·75
1178 80c. As No. 1154 1·60 1·75
1179 $1 Type **235** 1·75 1·90
1180 $1 As No. 1150 1·75 1·90
1181 $1 As No. 1151 1·75 1·90
1182 $1 As No. 1152 1·75 1·90
1183 $1 As No. 1153 1·75 1·90
1184 $1 As No. 1154 1·75 1·90

(b) Self-adhesive. Size 30×25 mm.
1185 20c. As Type **235** 55 65
1186 25c. As No. 1151 55 65
1187 25c. As No. 1152 55 65
1188 25c. As No. 1154 55 65

**236** Land Crab

**2008.** Darwin Initiative. Indigenous Creatures. Multicoloured.
1189 20c. Type **236** 70 50
1190 25c. Needlecase Freshwater Pools 75 55
1191 75c. Little Cayman green anole 2·00 2·00
1192 80c. Cayman Brac ground boa 2·00 2·00
1193 $1 White-shouldered bat 2·25 2·50
**MS**1194 110×78 mm. $2 Caribbean reef squid 4·25 4·75

**2008.** Olympic Games, Beijing. As T 287 of Bahamas. Multicoloured.
1195 20c. Swimming – backstroke 70 55
1196 25c. Swimming – butterfly 75 60
1197 50c. Running 1·50 1·50
1198 75c. Hurdling 2·00 2·50

**238** Father Christmas on board Sailing Ship

**2008.** Christmas. Unique Transportation. Multicoloured.
1202 25c. Type **238** 75 60
1203 75c. Father Christmas with horse and carriage laden with presents 2·25 2·00
1204 80c. Father Christmas in helicopter dropping presents by parachute 2·25 2·00
1205 $1 Father Christmas with racing car 2·75 2·75

**239** Silver Thatch Palm

**2009.** Silver Thatch Palm. Multicoloured.
1206 25c. Type **239** 90 95
1207 25c. Rope strands 90 95
1208 25c. Twisting the three strands into rope ('Cobbing rope') 90 95
1209 25c. Basketware ('Thatch products') 90 95
1210 25c. Traditional home with silver thatch roof 90 95

Nos. 1206/10 were printed together, se-tenant, forming a composite design.

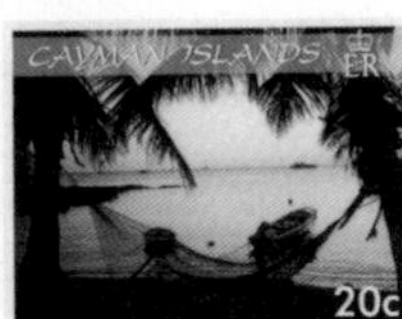

**240** Hammock at Sunset

**2009.** Cayman Islands Scenes (2nd series). Multicoloured. (a) Ordinary gum.
1211 20c. Type **240** 45 55
1212 25c. Cayman Islands houses 55 60
1213 75c. Palm trees on beach (vert) 2·00 2·00
1214 80c. Cruise ships off Cayman Islands 2·00 2·00
1215 $1 Street with signpost (vert) 2·25 2·50
1216 $1.50 Inland landscape of rocks and scrub 4·25 4·50
**MS**1217 80×65 mm. $2 Iguana in road, Little Cayman 5·25 5·25

(b) Self-adhesive. Size 30×25 mm.
1218 20c. As Type **240** 55 60
1219 25c. As No. 1212 65 70

**2009.** International Year of Astronomy. 40th Anniv of First Moon Landing. A T 214 of Bermuda. Multicoloured.
1220 20c. Mars Rover, 2004 45 50
1221 25c. Space Transportation System 71 launch, 1995 50 55
1222 75c. Hubble Telescope 1·50 1·75
1223 $1 Apollo 11, 1969 2·25 2·50
1224 $1.50 International Space Station 3·25 3·50
**MS**1225 100×80 mm. $2 *Hadley Rille* (astronaut Jim Irwin and Lunar Rover) (Alan Bean) (39×59 mm). Wmk upright 3·75 4·00

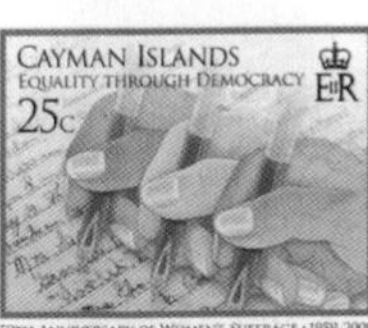

**241** Women's Hands signing Petition

**2009.** 'Equality through Democracy'. 50th Anniv of the Constitution and Women's Suffrage. Multicoloured.
1226 25c. Type **241** 60 60
1227 25c. Town Hall, George Town 60 60
1228 50c. Woman casting vote 1·25 1·25
**MS**1229 135×86 mm. Nos. 1226/8 2·50 2·50

**242** 10c. Santa in Hammock Stamp

**2009.** Christmas. Showing 1997 Christmas stamps. Multicoloured.
1230 25c. Type **242** 60 60
1231 75c. 30c. Santa with children on the Bluff stamp 1·50 1·75
1232 80c. 40c. Santa playing golf 1·60 2·00
1233 $1 $1 Santa scuba diving stamp 2·25 2·50

**243** Hawk-wing Conch (Strombus raninus)

**2010.** Shells

(a) Ordinary gum
1234 20c. Type **243** 60 65
1235 25c. Ornate scallop (*Chlamys ornata*) 80 85
1236 60c. Chestnut turban (*Turbo castanea*) 1·50 1·60
1237 75c. Beautiful mitre (*Vexillum pulchellum*) 1·90 2·00
1238 80c. Four-toothed nerite (*Nerita versicolor gmelin*) 2·00 2·10
1239 $1.60 White-spotted marginella (*Marginella guttata*) 4·25 4·50
**MS**1240 94×64 mm. $3 Queen conch (*Strombus gigas*) 7·75 8·00

(b) Self-adhesive
1241 25c. As No. 1235 80 85
1242 75c. As No. 1237 1·90 2·00

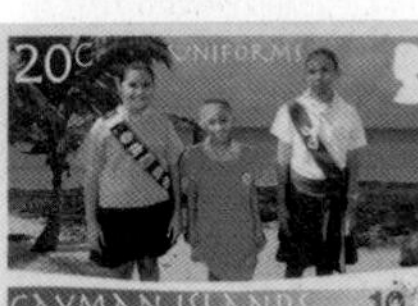

**244** Brownie, Rainbow and Guide Uniforms

**2010.** Centenary of Girlguiding. Multicoloured.
1243 20c. Type **244** 55 60
1244 25c. Camping 65 70
1245 50c. Parade of guides, 1930s 1·20 1·40
1246 80c. Badges of rainbows, brownies and guides 2·00 2·10

Pt. 12

# CENTRAL AFRICAN EMPIRE

Central African Republic was renamed Central African Empire on 4 December 1976, when Pres. Bokassa became Emperor.

The country reverted to Central African Republic on his overthrow in 1979.

100 centimes = 1 franc.

**1977.** Various stamps of Central African Republic optd EMPIRE CENTRAFRICAIN.

| | | | | |
|---|---|---|---|---|
| 439 | 150 | 3f. mult (postage) | 55 | 50 |
| 444 | 167 | 10f. multicoloured | 30 | 25 |
| 457 | - | 10f. red and blue (386) | 30 | 25 |
| 459 | 172 | 10f. multicoloured | 45 | 40 |
| 460 | - | 15f. multicoloured (391) | 75 | 75 |
| 465 | - | 15f. brown, grn & bl (397) | 30 | 25 |
| 445 | - | 20f. multicoloured (366) | 45 | 40 |
| 461 | - | 20f. multicoloured (392) | 55 | 55 |
| 446 | - | 25f. multicoloured (367) | 35 | 30 |
| 451 | - | 25f. multicoloured (376) | 35 | 30 |
| 449 | 168 | 30f. multicoloured | 30 | 25 |
| 452 | - | 30f. multicoloured (377) | 55 | 55 |
| 462 | - | 30f. multicoloured (393) | 30 | 25 |
| 447 | - | 40f. multicoloured (370) | 45 | 40 |
| 450 | - | 40f. multicoloured (373) | 45 | 40 |
| 453 | - | 40f. multicoloured (378) | 45 | 40 |
| 454 | - | 40f. multicoloured (380) | 55 | 55 |
| 455 | 170 | 40f. multicoloured | 45 | 40 |
| 456 | - | 40f. multicoloured (384) | 40 | 25 |
| 458 | - | 40f. multicoloured (389) | 75 | 75 |
| 482 | - | 40f. multicoloured (423) | 40 | 25 |
| 466 | - | 50f. blue, brn & grn (398) | 75 | 75 |
| 483 | - | 50f. mult (424) (air) | 45 | 25 |
| 440 | 163 | 100f. multicoloured | 1·70 | 1·60 |
| 441 | 164 | 100f. grn, red & brn | 1·80 | 1·80 |
| 442 | 165 | 100f. brn, grn & blue | 1·70 | 1·60 |
| 448 | - | 100f. multicoloured (371) | 95 | 90 |
| 463 | 173 | 100f. red and blue | 95 | 90 |
| 467 | 178 | 100f. multicoloured | 95 | 90 |
| 468 | 179 | 100f. black and yellow | 1·70 | 1·60 |
| 469 | 180 | 100f. purple, blue & grn | 1·80 | 1·90 |
| 484 | - | 100f. multicoloured (425) | 95 | 90 |
| 491 | 185 | 100f. multicoloured | 1·80 | 1·90 |
| 464 | 174 | 200f. multicoloured | 4·25 | 2·10 |
| 443 | 166 | 500f. red, green & brown | 8·50 | 8·25 |

**1977.** "Apollo–Soyuz" Space Link. Nos. 410/MS415 of Central African Republic optd EMPIRE CENTRAFRICAIN.

| | | | | |
|---|---|---|---|---|
| 470 | 181 | 40f. mult (postage) | 50 | 25 |
| 471 | - | 50f. multicoloured | 75 | 40 |
| 472 | - | 100f. multicoloured (air) | 95 | 55 |
| 473 | - | 200f. multicoloured | 1·90 | 90 |
| 474 | - | 300f. multicoloured | 3·00 | 1·30 |

**MS**475 103×78 mm. 500f. multicoloured 5·25 3·50

**1977.** Air. Bicentenary of American Revolution. Nos. 416/MS421 of Central African Republic optd EMPIRE CENTRAFRICAIN.

| | | | | |
|---|---|---|---|---|
| 476 | 182 | 100f. multicoloured | 1·00 | 70 |
| 477 | - | 125f. multicoloured | 1·40 | 1·10 |
| 478 | - | 150f. multicoloured | 1·60 | 1·30 |
| 479 | - | 200f. multicoloured | 2·30 | 1·80 |
| 480 | - | 250f. multicoloured | 2·50 | 2·00 |

**MS**481 119×81 mm. 450f. multicoloured 5·25 5·25

**1977.** Winners of Winter Olympic Games, Innsbruck. Nos. 426/MS430 of Central African Republic optd EMPIRE CENTRAFRICAIN.

| | | | | |
|---|---|---|---|---|
| 485 | | 40f. mult (postage) | 55 | 50 |
| 486 | | 60f. multicoloured | 75 | 65 |
| 487 | 184 | 100f. multicoloured (air) | 1·00 | 80 |
| 488 | - | 200f. multicoloured | 2·20 | 1·70 |
| 489 | - | 300f. multicoloured | 3·25 | 2·40 |

**MS**490 103×78 mm. 500f. multicoloured 5·25 5·00

**1977.** "Viking" Space Mission. Nos. 433/MS438 of Central African Republic optd EMPIRE CENTRAFRICAIN.

| | | | | |
|---|---|---|---|---|
| 492 | 186 | 40f. mult (postage) | 55 | 50 |
| 493 | - | 60f. multicoloured | 75 | 65 |
| 494 | - | 100f. multicoloured (air) | 1·00 | 1·00 |
| 495 | - | 200f. multicoloured | 2·30 | 2·20 |
| 496 | - | 300f. multicoloured | 3·50 | 3·50 |

**MS**497 102×78 mm. 500f. multicoloured 5·25 5·00

**189** Pierre and Marie Curie (Physics, 1903)

**1977.** Nobel Prize-winners. Multicoloured.
503 40f. Type **189** (postage) 1·00 40
504 60f. W. C. Rontgen (Physics, 1901) 90 45
505 100f. Rudyard Kipling (Literature, 1907) (air) 1·80 50
506 200f. Ernest Hemingway (Literature, 1954) 3·50 85
507 300f. L. Pirandello (Literature, 1934) 3·50 1·00
**MS**508 118×80 mm. 500f. Rabindranath Tagore (Literature, 1913) 5·25 1·90

**190** Roman Temple and Italy 1933 3l. stamp

**1977.** "Graf Zeppelin" Flights. Multicoloured.
509 40f. Type **190** (postage) 85 25
510 60f. St. Basil's Cathedral, Moscow, and Russia 1930 40k. stamp 1·00 45
511 100f. North Pole and Germany 1931 "Polarfahrt" stamp (air) 1·40 40
512 200f. Museum of Science and Industry, Chicago, and Germany 1933 "Chicagofahrt" stamp 2·50 75
513 300f. Brandenburg Gate, Berlin, and German 1931 stamp 3·75 1·00
**MS**514 129×90 mm. 500f. Capitol, Washington, and US $1.30 stamp, 1930 5·50 2·20

**191** Charles Lindbergh and "Spirit of St. Louis"

**1977.** History of Aviation. Multicoloured.
515 50f. Type **191** 50 25
516 60f. Alberto Santos-Dumont and "14 bis" biplane 75 25
517 100f. Louis Bleriot and Bleriot XI 1·40 45
518 200f. Roald Amundsen and Dornier Wal flying boat 2·10 60
519 300f. Concorde 4·00 1·40
**MS**520 117×91 mm. 500f. Lindbergh and his arrival in Paris 5·00 1·80

**192** Lily

**1977.** Flowers. Multicoloured.
521 5f. Type **192** 45 30
522 10f. Hibiscus 90 70

**193** Group of Africans and Rotary Emblem

**1977.** 20th Anniv of Bangui Rotary Club.
523 **193** 60f. multicoloured 3·50 1·80

**194** Africans queueing beside Bible

**1977.** Bible Week.
524 **194** 40f. multicoloured 5·75 1·40

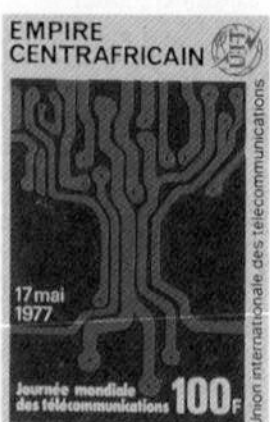

**195** Printed Circuit

**1977.** World Telecommunications Day.
525 **195** 100f. orange, brown & blk 3·00 2·10

**196** Doctor inoculating Child

**1977.** Air. World Health Day.
526 **196** 150f. multicoloured 3·50 1·80

**197** Goalkeeper

**1977.** World Cup Football Championship (1978). Multicoloured.
527 50f. Type **197** 50 25
528 60f. Goalmouth melee 60 25
529 100f. Mid-field play 1·00 30
530 200f. World Cup poster 2·10 60
531 300f. Mario Jorge Lobo Zagalo (Argentine trainer) and Buenos Aires stadium 3·75 1·30
**MS**532 120×81 mm. 500f. Ferenc Puskas (Hungarian player) 6·25 2·20

**198** Emperor Bokassa I

**1977.** Coronation of Emperor Bokassa.
533 **198** 40f. mult (postage) 35 15
534 **198** 60f. multicoloured 50 25
535 **198** 100f. multicoloured 1·00 55
536 **198** 150f. multicoloured 1·40 70
537 **198** 200f. mult (air) 1·90 85
538 **198** 300f. multicoloured 2·50 1·40
**MS**539 102×80 mm. 500f. Emperor Bokassa, inscription and furled flag (48×39 mm) 5·25 2·50

**199** Bangui Telephone Exchange

**1978.** Opening of Automatic Telephone Exchange, Bangui. Multicoloured.
541 40f. Type **199** 45 25
542 60f. Bangui Telephone Exchange (different) 60 35

**200** Bokassa Sports Palace

**1978.** Bokassa Sports Palace. Multicoloured.
543 40f. Type **200** 45 25
544 60f. Sports Palace (different) 60 35

**201** "The Holy Family"

**1978.** 400th Birth Anniv of Rubens. Mult.
545 60f. Type **201** 75 25
546 150f. "Marie de Medici" 1·30 45
547 200f. "The Artist's Sons" 2·00 65
548 300f. "Neptune" (horiz) 3·25 85
**MS**549 90×116 mm. 500f. "Marie de Medici" (different) (37×49 mm) 5·75 2·00

**202** Black Rhinoceros

**1978.** Endangered Animals. Multicoloured.
550 40f. Type **202** 1·10 25
551 50f. Crocodile 1·70 30
552 60f. Leopard (vert) 1·90 45
553 100f. Giraffe (vert) 3·00 65
554 200f. African elephant 7·75 90
555 300f. Gorilla (vert) 9·25 1·50

**203** Mail Coach and Satellite

**1978.** 100 Years of Progress in Posts and Telecommunications. Multicoloured.
556 40f. Type **203** (postage) 45 25
557 50f. Steam locomotive and space communications 1·80 85
558 60f. Paddle-steamer and ship-to-shore communications 55 25
559 80f. Renault car and "Pioneer" satellite 75 25
560 100f. Mail balloon and "Apollo"–"Soyuz" link-up (air) 1·00 40
561 200f. Seaplane "Comte da la Vaulx" and Concorde 1·80 70
**MS**562 104×70 mm. 500f. Tom-toms and Zeppelin (53×35 mm) 6·75 1·90

**205** H.M.S. "Endeavour" under Repair (after W. Byrne)

**1978.** 250th Birth Anniv of Captain Cook. Mult.
578 60f. Type **205** 75 25
579 80f. Cook on board "Endeavour" (vert) 1·00 40
580 200f. Landing party in New Hebrides 2·75 75
581 350f. Masked paddlers in canoe (after Webber) 4·50 1·50

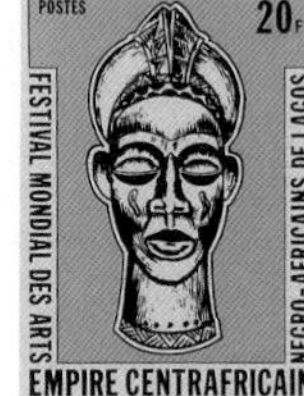

**206** Ife Bronze Head

**1978.** 2nd World Festival of Negro Arts, Lagos.
582 **206** 20f. black and yellow 30 25
583 - 30f. black and blue 30 25
584 - 60f. multicoloured 70 40
585 - 100f. multicoloured 1·20 70
DESIGNS—VERT: 30f. Carved mask. HORIZ: 60f. Dancers; 100f. Dancers with musical instruments.

**207** Clement Ader and "Avion III"

**1978.** Air. Aviation Pioneers. Multicoloured.
586 40f. Type **207** 50 25
587 50f. Wright Brothers and glider No. III 50 25
588 60f. Alcock, Brown and Vickers Vimy 60 40
589 100f. Sir Alan Cobham and De Havilland D.H.50 1·20 40
590 150f. Dr. Claude Dornier and Dornier Gs1 flying boat 1·80 70
**MS**591 117×80 mm. 500f. Wright Brothers and "Flyer" 5·50 1·80

**208** "Self-portrait"

**1978.** 450th Death Anniv of Albrecht Durer (artist). Multicoloured.
592 60f. Type **208** 60 25
593 80f. "The Four Apostles" 1·00 25
594 200f. "The Virgin and Child" 2·40 90
595 350f. "The Emperor Maximilian I" 4·00 1·50

**1978.** Air. "Philexafrique" Stamp Exhibition, Gabon (1st issue) and International Stamp Fair, Essen. As T 237 of Benin. Multicoloured.
596 100f. Red crossbills and Mecklenberg-Schwerin 1856 ¼s. stamp 2·20 1·40
597 100f. Crocodile and Central African Republic 1960 500f. stamp 2·20 1·40
See also Nos. 647/8.

**209** Third Mummiform Coffin

**1978.** Treasures of Tutankhamun. Mult.
598 40f. Type **209** 70 30
599 60f. Tutankhamun and Ankhesenamun (back of gilt throne) 95 35
600 80f. Ecclesiastical throne 1·40 50
601 100f. Head of Tutankhamun (wooden statuette) 1·50 50
602 120f. Lion's head (funerary bedhead) 2·00 65
603 150f. Life-size statue of Tutankhamun 2·50 70

604 180f. Gilt throne 3·25 85
605 250f. Canopic coffin 4·00 1·10

210 Lenin speaking at the Smolny Institute

**1978.** 60th Anniv of Russian Revolution.
606 **210** 40f. multicoloured 50 30
607 - 60f. multicoloured 60 45
608 - 100f. black, grey and gold 1·00 50
609 - 150f. red, black and gold 1·90 80
610 - 200f. multicoloured 2·50 1·00
611 - 300f. multicoloured 3·25 1·50
**MS**612 78×110 mm. 500f. multicoloured 5·25 4·00
DESIGNS—VERT: 60f. Lenin addressing crowd in Red Square; 200f. Lenin in Smolny Institute; 300f. Lenin and banner; 500f. Cruiser "Aurora" and Order of Lenin. HORIZ: 100f. Lenin, Kurpskaya and family; 150f. Lenin, cruiser "Aurora", banner and revolutionaries.

211 Catherine Bokassa

**1978.** 1st Anniv of Emperor Bokassa's Coronation. Multicoloured.
613 40f. Type **211** (postage) 50 25
614 60f. Emperor Bokassa 70 30
615 150f. The Emperor and Empress (horiz) (air) 1·70 75
**MS**616 Two sheets. (a) 101×82 mm. 250f. Coronation ceremony (horiz); (b) 76×100 mm. 1000f. Emperor and eagle 12·00 5·50

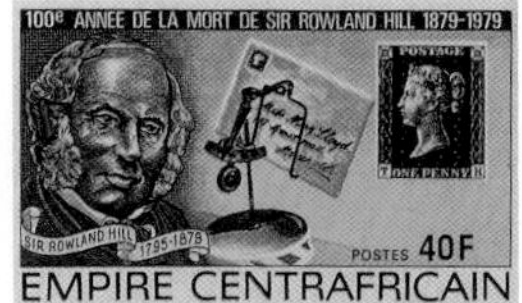

212 Rowland Hill, Letter-weighing Scale and Penny Black

**1978.** Death Centenary of Sir Rowland Hill (1st issue). Multicoloured.
617 40f. Type **212** (postage) 55 25
618 50f. Postman on bicycle and U.S. 5c. stamp, 1847 55 25
619 60f. Danish postman and Austrian newspaper stamp, 1856 80 35
620 80f. Postilion, mail coach and Geneva 5+5c. stamp, 1843 95 45
621 100f. Postman, mail train and Tuscan 3l. stamp, 1860 (air) 2·40 1·00
622 200f. Mail balloon and French 10c. stamp, 1850 1·70 70
**MS**623 81×85 mm. 500f. First Central African Republic stamps, 1959 (37×38 mm) 5·50 1·80
See also Nos. 671/**MS**675.

**1978.** Argentina's Victory in World Cup Football Championship. Nos. 527/31 optd VAINQUEUR ARGENTINE.
625 50f. Type **197** 55 35
626 60f. Goalmouth melee 60 40
627 100f. Midfield play 95 60
628 200f. World Cup poster 2·00 1·10
629 300f. Mario Jorge Lobo Zagalo and Buenos Aires Stadium 3·00 1·40
**MS**630 120×81 mm. 500f. multicoloured, optd **ARGENTINE-PAYS BAS 3-1/25 juin 1978** 5·25 5·25

**214** Children painting and Dutch Master

**1979.** International Year of the Child (1st issue). Multicoloured.
631 40f. Type **214** (postage) 50 10
632 50f. Eskimo children and skier 65 20
633 60f. Benz automobile and children with toy car 85 25
634 80f. Satellite and children launching rocket 1·20 25
635 100f. Dornier Do-X flying boat and Chinese child flying kite (air) 1·30 45
636 200f. Hurdler and children playing leap-frog 2·50 70
**MS**637 109×79 mm. 500f. Albert Einstein and child with abacus (55×32 mm) 5·50 1·80
See also Nos. 666/70.

**215** High Jump

**1979.** Pre-Olympic Year (1st issue). Mult.
639 40f. Type **215** (postage) 50 10
640 50f. Cycling 55 20
641 60f. Weightlifting 65 25
642 80f. Judo 90 30
643 100f. Hurdles (air) 1·00 40
644 200f. Long jump 1·90 70
**MS**645 110×79 mm. 500f. Pole vault (55×37 mm) 5·00 1·70
See also Nos. 676/80 and 700/**MS**706.

**216** Co-operation Monument, "Aurivillius arata" and Hibiscus

**1979.** "Philexafrique" Exhibition (2nd issue). Mult.
647 60f. Type **216** 2·40 1·20
648 150f. Envelopes, van, canoeist and UPU emblem 4·25 2·30

**217** School Teacher

**1979.** 50th Anniv of International Bureau of Education.
649 **217** 70f. multicoloured 85 45

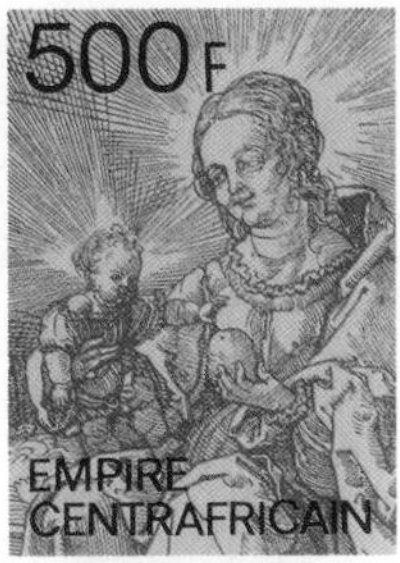

**218** "Madonna seated on a Bench" (woodcut)

**1979.** 450th Death Anniv (1978) of Albrecht Durer (artist) (2nd issue). Sheet 90×115 mm.
**MS**650 **218** 500f. green and lake 5·50 1·80

**219** Chicken

**1979.** National Association of Farmers. Mult.
651 10f. Type **219** (postage) 1·80 1·10
652 20f. Bullock 1·80 1·10
653 40f. Sheep 3·75 2·20
654 60f. Horse (air) 5·50 2·10

### OFFICIAL STAMPS

**1977.** Official stamps of Central African Republic optd EMPIRE CENTRAFRICAIN.
O498 **O109** 5f. multicoloured 25 10
O499 **O109** 40f. multicoloured 45 25
O500 **O109** 100f. multicoloured 1·20 40
O501 **O109** 140f. multicoloured 1·50 80
O502 **O109** 200f. multicoloured 2·50 1·10

**O204** Coat of Arms

**1978**
O564 **O204** 1f. multicoloured 10 10
O565 **O204** 2f. multicoloured 10 10
O566 **O204** 5f. multicoloured 10 10
O567 **O204** 10f. multicoloured 25 10
O568 **O204** 15f. multicoloured 25 10
O569 **O204** 20f. multicoloured 25 10
O570 **O204** 30f. multicoloured 45 25
O571 **O204** 40f. multicoloured 45 25
O572 **O204** 50f. multicoloured 70 55
O673 **O204** 60f. multicoloured 65 45
O574 **O204** 100f. multicoloured 1·10 90
O575 **O204** 130f. multicoloured 1·40 1·50
O576 **O204** 140f. multicoloured 1·70 1·30
O577 **O204** 200f. multicoloured 3·25 1·60

Pt. 12

# CENTRAL AFRICAN REPUBLIC

Formerly Ubangi-Shari. An independent republic within the French Community.

100 centimes = 1 franc.

**1** President Boganda

**1959.** Republic. 1st Anniv. Centres multicoloured. Frame colours given.
1 **1** 15f. blue 55 25
2 - 25f. red 55 25
DESIGN—HORIZ: 25f. As Type **1** but flag behind portrait.

**1960.** 10th Anniv of African Technical Co-operation Commission. As T **62** of Cameroun.
3 50f. blue and green 1·80 95

**3** "Dactyloceras widenmanni"

**4** Abyssinian Roller

**1960**
4 - 50c. brn, red & turq (postage) 10 10
5 - 1f. myrtle, brown & violet 10 10
6 - 2f. myrtle, brown and green 10 20
7 - 3f. brown, red and olive 45 20
8 **3** 5f. brown and green 45 25
9 - 10f. blue, black and green 95 55
10 - 20f. red, black and green 2·30 80
12 - 50f. turq, red & green (air) 1·90 60
11 - 85f. red, black and green 7·25 1·70
13 **4** 100f. violet, brown & green 2·40 90
14 - 200f. multicoloured 4·50 2·20
15 - 250f. multicoloured 6·75 2·50
16 - 500f. brown, blue and green 13·00 5·25
BUTTERFLIES—As Type **3**: 50c., 3f. "Cymothoe sangaris"; 1f., 2f. "Charaxe mobilis"; 10f. "Charaxes ameliae"; 20f. "Charaxes zingha"; 85f. "Drurya antimachus". BIRDS—As Type **4**: 50f. Great blue turaco; 200f. Green turaco; 250f. Red-faced lovebirds; 500f. African fish eagle.
See also Nos. 42/5.

**1960.** National Festival. No. 2 optd **FETE NATIONALE 1-12-1960.**
17 25f. multicoloured 1·40 1·30

**1960.** Air. Olympic Games. No. 276 of French Equatorial Africa optd with Olympic rings, **XVIIe OLYMPIADE 1960 REPUBLIQUE CENTRAFRICAINE** and surch 250F and bars.
18 250f. on 500f. blue, blk & grn 8·75 8·25

**7** Pasteur Institute, Bangui

**1961.** Opening of Pasteur Institute, Bangui.
19 **7** 20f. multicoloured 1·00 80

**8** U.N. Emblem, Map and Flag

**1961.** Admission into UNO.
20 **8** 15f. multicoloured 40 30
21 **8** 25f. multicoloured 50 30
22 **8** 85f. multicoloured 1·50 1·00

**1961.** National Festival. Optd with star and **FETE NATIONALE 1-12-01.**
23 25f. multicoloured 2·00 1·90

**1962.** Air. "Air Afrique" Airline. As T **69** of Cameroun.
24 50f. violet, brown and green 95 70

**1962.** Union of African States and Madagascar Conference, Bangui. Surch **U.A.M. CONFERENCE DE BANGUI 25-27 MARS 1962 50F.**
25 50f. on 85f. multicoloured 1·70 1·60

**1962.** Malaria Eradication. As T **70** of Cameroun.
26 25f.+5f. slate 1·10 1·10

**12** Hurdling

**1962.** Sports.

| | | | | |
|---|---|---|---|---|
| 27 | 12 | 20f. sep, yell & grn (postage) | 45 | 30 |
| 28 | - | 50f. sepia, yellow and green | 1·30 | 80 |
| 29 | - | 100f. sep, yell & grn (air) | 2·20 | 1·50 |

DESIGNS—As Type **12**: 50f. Cycling. VERT: (26×47 mm): 100f. Pole-vaulting.

**13** Pres. Dacko

**1962**

| | | | | |
|---|---|---|---|---|
| 30 | 13 | 20f. multicoloured | 35 | 20 |
| 31 | 13 | 25f. multicoloured | 45 | 25 |

**1962.** 1st Anniv of Union of African and Malagasy States. As T 72 of Cameroun.

| | | | |
|---|---|---|---|
| 32 | 30f. green | 1·20 | 95 |

**15** Athlete

**1962.** Air. "Coupe des Tropiques" Games, Bangui.

| | | | | |
|---|---|---|---|---|
| 33 | 15 | 100f. brown, turquoise & red | 2·40 | 1·60 |

**1963.** Freedom from Hunger. As T **76** of Cameroun.

| | | | |
|---|---|---|---|
| 34 | 25f.+5f. turquoise, brn & bis | 1·00 | 1·00 |

**17** "National Army"

**1963.** 3rd Anniv of Proclamation of Republic.

| | | | | |
|---|---|---|---|---|
| 35 | 17 | 20f. multicoloured | 65 | 45 |

**18** "Posts and Telecommunications"

**1963.** Air. African and Malagasy Posts and Telecommunications Union.

| | | | | |
|---|---|---|---|---|
| 36 | 18 | 85f. multicoloured | 1·80 | 90 |

**19** "Telecommunications"

**1963.** Space Telecommunications.

| | | | | |
|---|---|---|---|---|
| 37 | 19 | 25f. green and purple | 75 | 60 |
| 38 | - | 100f. green, orange & blue | 1·80 | 1·60 |

DESIGN: 100f. Radio waves and globe.

**20** "Young Pioneers"

**1963.** Young Pioneers.

| | | | | |
|---|---|---|---|---|
| 39 | 20 | 30f. brown, blue & turquoise | 85 | 50 |

**21** Boali Falls

**1963**

| | | | | |
|---|---|---|---|---|
| 40 | 21 | 30f. purple, green and blue | 85 | 50 |

**22** Map of Africa and Sun

**1963.** Air. "African Unity".

| | | | | |
|---|---|---|---|---|
| 41 | 22 | 25f. ultramarine, yellow & bl | 65 | 45 |

**23** "Colotis evippe"

**1963.** Butterflies. Multicoloured.

| | | | |
|---|---|---|---|
| 42 | 1f. Type **23** | 20 | 20 |
| 43 | 3f. "Papilio dardanus" | 55 | 25 |
| 44 | 4f. "Papilio lormieri" | 80 | 35 |
| 45 | 60f. "Papilio zalmoxis" | 5·00 | 3·00 |

**24** "Europafrique"

**1963.** Air. European–African Economic Convention.

| | | | | |
|---|---|---|---|---|
| 46 | 24 | 50f. multicoloured | 2·75 | 2·10 |

**25** ABJ-6 Diesel Railcar

**1963.** Air. Bangui–Douala Railway Project.

| | | | | |
|---|---|---|---|---|
| 47 | - | 20f. green, purple & brown | 65 | 50 |
| 48 | 25 | 25f. chocolate, blue & brn | 95 | 60 |
| 49 | - | 50f. violet, purple & brown | 2·50 | 1·90 |
| 50 | - | 100f. purple, turquoise and brown | 3·75 | 2·75 |
| **MS**50a | | 190×98 mm. Nos. 47/50 | 8·00 | 8·00 |

DESIGNS: (Diesel rolling stock)—HORIZ: 20f. ABJ-6 railcar; 100f. Diesel locomotive. VERT: 50f. Series BB500 diesel shunter.

**26** UNESCO Emblem, Scales of Justice and Tree

**1963.** 15th Anniv of Declaration of Human Rights.

| | | | | |
|---|---|---|---|---|
| 51 | 26 | 25f. bistre, green and brown | 85 | 60 |

**27** Bangui Cathedral

**1964.** Air.

| | | | | |
|---|---|---|---|---|
| 52 | 27 | 100f. brown, green & blue | 2·00 | 1·10 |

**28** Cleopatra, Temple of Kalabsha

**1964.** Air. Nubian Monuments Preservation.

| | | | | |
|---|---|---|---|---|
| 53 | 28 | 25f.+10f. mauve, bl & grn | 1·30 | 1·20 |
| 54 | 28 | 50f.+10f. brn, grn & turq | 2·20 | 2·10 |
| 55 | 28 | 100f.+10f. pur, vio & grn | 3·50 | 3·25 |

**29** Radar Scanner

**1964.** Air. World Meteorological Day.

| | | | | |
|---|---|---|---|---|
| 56 | 29 | 50f. violet, brown and blue | 1·00 | 1·00 |

**30** "Tree" and Sun Emblem

**1964.** International Quiet Sun Years.

| | | | | |
|---|---|---|---|---|
| 57 | 30 | 25f. orange, ochre & turq | 1·30 | 85 |

**31** Map and African Heads of State

**1964.** Air. 5th Anniv of Equatorial African Heads of State Conference.

| | | | | |
|---|---|---|---|---|
| 58 | 31 | 100f. multicoloured | 1·80 | 90 |

**32** Throwing the Javelin

**1964.** Air. Olympic Games, Tokyo.

| | | | | |
|---|---|---|---|---|
| 59 | 32 | 25f. brown, green and blue | 45 | 30 |
| 60 | - | 50f. red, black and green | 95 | 55 |
| 61 | - | 100f. brown, blue and green | 2·20 | 1·30 |
| 62 | - | 250f. black, green and red | 6·50 | 3·00 |
| **MS**62a | | 130×100 mm. Nos. 59/62 | 16·00 | 15·00 |

DESIGNS: 50f. Basketball; 100f. Running; 250f. Diving and swimming.

**33** Pres. Kennedy

**1964.** Air. Pres. Kennedy Memorial Issue.

| | | | | |
|---|---|---|---|---|
| 63 | 33 | 100f. brown, black & violet | 2·40 | 1·70 |
| **MS**63a | | 90×130 mm. No. 63 in block of four | 10·50 | 10·00 |

**34** African Child

**1964.** Child Welfare. Different portraits of children. As T **34**.

| | | | | |
|---|---|---|---|---|
| 64 | 34 | 20f. brown, green & purple | 45 | 25 |
| 65 | - | 25f. brown, blue and red | 45 | 30 |
| 66 | - | 40f. brown, purple & green | 60 | 45 |
| 67 | - | 50f. brown, green and red | 80 | 60 |
| **MS**67a | | 144×100 mm. Nos. 64/7 | 3·25 | 3·00 |

**1964.** French, African and Malagasy Co-operation. As T **88** of Cameroun.

| | | | |
|---|---|---|---|
| 68 | 25f. brown, red and green | 85 | 50 |

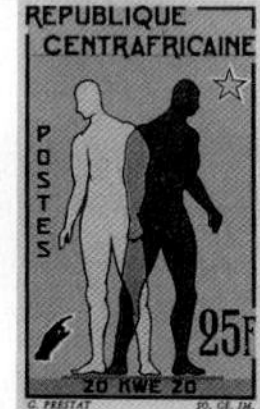


**35** Silhouettes of European and African

**1964.** National Unity.

| | | | | |
|---|---|---|---|---|
| 69 | 35 | 25f. multicoloured | 85 | 50 |

**36** "Economic Co-operation"

**1964.** Air. "Europafrique".

| | | | | |
|---|---|---|---|---|
| 70 | 36 | 50f. green, red and yellow | 1·20 | 85 |

**37** Handclasp

**1965.** Air. International Co-operation Year.

| | | | | |
|---|---|---|---|---|
| 71 | 37 | 100f. multicoloured | 1·80 | 90 |

**38** Weather Satellite

**1965.** Air. World Meteorological Day.

| | | | | |
|---|---|---|---|---|
| 72 | **38** | 100f. blue and brown | 1·80 | 90 |

**39** Abraham Lincoln

**1965.** Air. Death Centenary of Abraham Lincoln.

| | | | | |
|---|---|---|---|---|
| 73 | **39** | 100f. flesh, blue & green | 1·80 | 90 |

**40** Team of Oxen

**1965.** Harnessed Animals in Agriculture.

| | | | | |
|---|---|---|---|---|
| 74 | **40** | 25f. red, brown and green | 50 | 30 |
| 75 | - | 50f. purple, green and blue | 95 | 55 |
| 76 | - | 85f. brown, green and blue | 1·30 | 80 |
| 77 | - | 100f. multicoloured | 1·70 | 90 |

DESIGNS: 50f. Ploughing with bullock; 85f. Ploughing with oxen; 100f. Oxen with hay cart.

**41** Pouget-Maisonneuve Telegraph Instrument

**1965.** Centenary of ITU.

| | | | | |
|---|---|---|---|---|
| 78 | **41** | 25f. blue, red & grn (post) | 55 | 45 |
| 79 | - | 30f. lake and green | 60 | 55 |
| 80 | - | 50f. red and violet | 1·00 | 70 |
| 81 | - | 85f. blue and purple | 1·80 | 1·20 |
| 82 | - | 100f. brown, blue & green (48½×27 mm) (air) | 2·00 | 1·20 |

DESIGNS—VERT: 30f. Chappe's telegraph instrument; 50f. Doignon regulator for Hughes telegraph. HORIZ: 85f. Pouillet's telegraph apparatus; 100f. "Relay" satellite and ITU emblem.

**42** Women and Loom ("To Clothe")

**1965.** "MESAN" Welfare Campaign. Designs depicting "Five Aims".

| | | | | |
|---|---|---|---|---|
| 83 | **42** | 25f. green, brown and blue (postage) | 45 | 30 |
| 84 | - | 50f. brown, blue and green | 80 | 55 |
| 85 | - | 60f. brown, blue and green | 1·00 | 65 |
| 86 | - | 85f. multicoloured | 1·40 | 70 |
| 87 | - | 100f. blue, brown and green (48×27 mm) (air) | 1·80 | 1·10 |

DESIGNS: 50f. Doctor examining child, and hospital ("To care for"); 60f. Student and school ("To instruct"); 85f. Women and child, and harvesting scene ("To nourish"); 100f. Village houses ("To house"). "MESAN—Mouvement Evolution Social Afrique Noire".

**43** Coffee Plant, Hammer Grubs and "Epicampoptera strandi"

**1965.** Plant Protection.

| | | | | |
|---|---|---|---|---|
| 88 | **43** | 2f. purple, red and green | 30 | 10 |
| 89 | - | 3f. red, green and black | 75 | 20 |
| 90 | - | 30f. purple, green and red | 4·50 | 90 |

DESIGNS—HORIZ: 3f. Coffee plant, caterpillar and hawk-moth. VERT: 30f. Cotton plant caterpillar and rose-moth.

**1965.** Surch.

| | | | | |
|---|---|---|---|---|
| 91 | | 2f. on 3f. (No. 43) | 4·25 | 4·00 |
| 92 | **1** | 5f. on 15f. | 3·75 | 3·00 |
| 93 | - | 5f. on 85f. (No. 76) | 35 | 30 |
| 94 | **13** | 10f. on 20f. | 4·50 | 4·25 |
| 95 | - | 10f. on 100f. (No. 77) | 55 | 55 |

**45** Camp Fire

**1965.** Scouting.

| | | | | |
|---|---|---|---|---|
| 96 | **45** | 25f. red, purple and blue | 75 | 25 |
| 97 | - | 50f. brown and blue (Boy Scout) | 1·30 | 65 |

**46** U.N. and Campaign Emblems

**1965.** Freedom from Hunger.

| | | | | |
|---|---|---|---|---|
| 98 | **46** | 50f. brown, blue and green | 1·10 | 75 |

**47** "Industry and Agriculture"

**1965.** Air. "Europafrique".

| | | | | |
|---|---|---|---|---|
| 99 | **47** | 50f. multicoloured | 1·00 | 75 |

**48** Mercury (statue after Coysevox)

**1965.** Air. 5th Anniv of Admission to UPU.

| | | | | |
|---|---|---|---|---|
| 100 | **48** | 100f. black, blue & red | 2·30 | 1·30 |

**49** Father and Child

**1965.** Air. Red Cross.

| | | | | |
|---|---|---|---|---|
| 101 | **49** | 50f. black, blue and red | 1·20 | 55 |
| 102 | - | 100f. brown, green and red (Mother and Child) | 2·50 | 1·20 |

**50** Grading Diamonds

**1966.** National Diamond Industry.

| | | | | |
|---|---|---|---|---|
| 103 | **50** | 25f. brown, violet and red | 1·00 | 50 |

**51** Mbaka Porter

**1966.** World Festival of Negro Arts, Dakar.

| | | | | |
|---|---|---|---|---|
| 104 | **51** | 25f. multicoloured | 85 | 50 |

**52** WHO Building

**1966.** WHO Headquarters, Geneva. Inaug.

| | | | | |
|---|---|---|---|---|
| 105 | **52** | 25f. violet, blue & yellow | 85 | 50 |

**53** "Eulophia cucullata"

**1966.** Flowers. Multicoloured.

| | | | |
|---|---|---|---|
| 106 | 2f. Type **53** | 25 | 10 |
| 107 | 5f. "Lissochilus horsfalii" | 45 | 10 |
| 108 | 10f. "Tridactyle bicaudata" | 45 | 25 |
| 109 | 15f. "Polystachya" | 95 | 50 |
| 110 | 20f. "Eulophia alta" | 1·40 | 60 |
| 111 | 25f. "Microcelia macrorrhynchium" | 2·00 | 95 |

**54** Douglas DC-8F Aircraft and "Air Afrique" Emblem

**1966.** Air. Inaug of "DC-8" Air Services.

| | | | | |
|---|---|---|---|---|
| 112 | **54** | 25f. multicoloured | 85 | 45 |

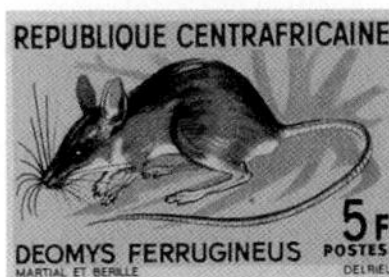


**55** Congo Forest Mouse

**1966.** Rodents. Multicoloured.

| | | | |
|---|---|---|---|
| 113 | 5f. Type **55** | 55 | 30 |
| 114 | 10f. Black-striped mouse | 1·00 | 50 |
| 115 | 20f. Dollman's tree mouse | 1·70 | 80 |

**56** "Luna 9"

**1966.** Air. "Conquest of the Moon". Mult.

| | | | |
|---|---|---|---|
| 116 | 130f. Type **56** | 1·70 | 1·00 |
| 117 | 130f. "Surveyor" | 1·70 | 1·00 |
| 118 | 200f. "From the Earth to the Moon" (Jules Verne) | 3·25 | 1·80 |
| **MS**119 | 132×160 mm. Nos. 116/18 | 8·25 | 7·75 |

**57** Cernan

**1966.** Air. Astronauts. Multicoloured.

| | | | |
|---|---|---|---|
| 120 | 50f. Type **57** | 1·10 | 60 |
| 121 | 50f. Popovich | 1·10 | 60 |

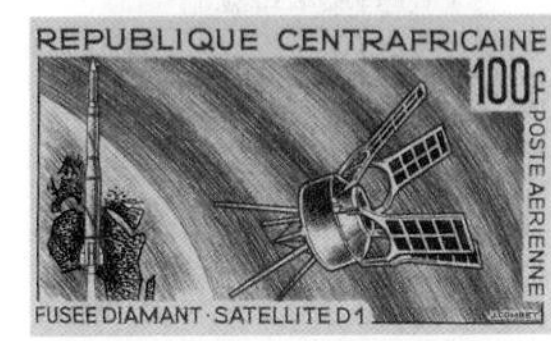


**58** Satellite "D 1" and Rocket "Diamant"

**1966.** Air. Launching of Satellite "D 1".

| | | | | |
|---|---|---|---|---|
| 122 | **58** | 100f. purple and brown | 1·80 | 95 |

**59** UNESCO Emblem

**1966.** 20th Anniv of UNESCO.

| | | | | |
|---|---|---|---|---|
| 123 | **59** | 30f. multicoloured | 60 | 45 |

**60** Symbols of Industry and Agriculture

**1966.** Air. Europafrique.

| | | | | |
|---|---|---|---|---|
| 124 | **60** | 50f. multicoloured | 1·20 | 95 |

**61** Pres. Bokassa

**1967**

| | | | | |
|---|---|---|---|---|
| 125 | **61** | 30f. black, ochre & green | 60 | 35 |

**1967.** Provisional Stamps. (a) Postage. No. 111 surch **XX** and value.

| | | | |
|---|---|---|---|
| 126 | 10f. on 25f. multicoloured | 50 | 25 |

(b) Air. No. 112 with face value altered by obliteration of figure "2" in "25".

| | | | | |
|---|---|---|---|---|
| 127 | **54** | 5f. multicoloured | 45 | 25 |

**63** Douglas DC-8 over Bangui M'Poko Airport

**1967.** Air.

| | | | | |
|---|---|---|---|---|
| 128 | **63** | 100f. blue, green & brown | 2·30 | 1·10 |

**64** Aerial View of Fair

**1967.** Air. World Fair, Montreal.

| | | | | |
|---|---|---|---|---|
| 129 | **64** | 100f. brown, ultram & bl | 2·00 | 80 |

**65** Central Market, Bangui

**1967.** Multicoloured.. Multicoloured..

| | | | |
|---|---|---|---|
| 130 | 30f. Type **65** | 85 | 45 |
| 131 | 30f. Safari Hotel, Bangui | 85 | 35 |

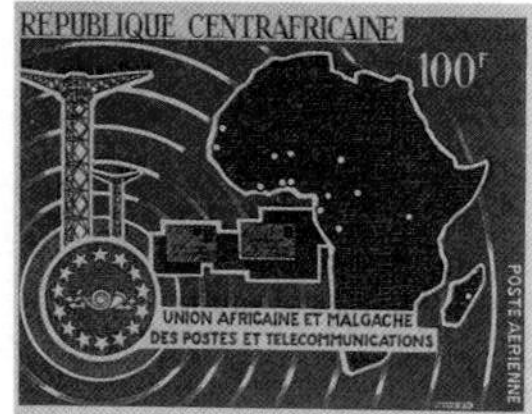


**66** Map, Letters and Pylons

**1967.** Air. 5th Anniv of African and Malagasy Posts and Telecommunications Union (UAMPT).

| | | | | |
|---|---|---|---|---|
| 132 | **66** | 100f. purple, grn & red | 2·00 | 85 |

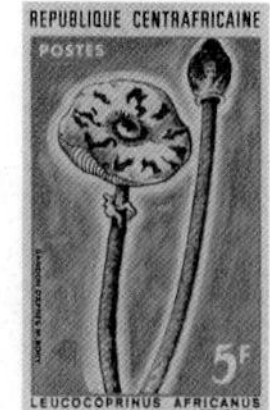


**67** "Leucocoprinus africanus"

**1967.** Mushrooms. Multicoloured.

| | | | |
|---|---|---|---|
| 133 | 5f. Type **67** | 5·25 | 60 |
| 134 | 10f. "Synpodia arborescens" | 8·25 | 1·00 |
| 135 | 15f. "Phlebopus sudanicus" | 9·25 | 1·30 |
| 136 | 30f. "Termitomyces schimperi" | 26·00 | 3·25 |
| 137 | 50f. "Psalliota sebedulis" | 42·00 | 5·00 |

**68** Projector, Africans and Map

**1967.** "Radiovision" Service.

| | | | | |
|---|---|---|---|---|
| 138 | **68** | 30f. blue, green and brown | 85 | 50 |

**69** Coiffure

**1967.** Female Coiffures. Showing different hairstyles.

| | | | | |
|---|---|---|---|---|
| 139 | **69** | 5f. brown and blue | 30 | 15 |
| 140 | - | 10f. brown, choc & red | 45 | 25 |
| 141 | - | 15f. brown, choc & grn | 75 | 45 |
| 142 | - | 20f. brown, choc & orge | 95 | 55 |
| 143 | - | 30f. brown, choc & purple | 1·30 | 70 |

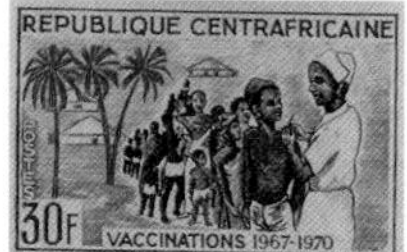


**70** Inoculation Session

**1967.** Vaccination Programme, 1967–70.

| | | | | |
|---|---|---|---|---|
| 144 | **70** | 30f. brown, green & red | 85 | 60 |

**71** Douglas DC-3

**1967.** Aircraft.

| | | | | |
|---|---|---|---|---|
| 145 | **71** | 1f. grey, grn & brn (post) | 10 | 10 |
| 146 | - | 2f. black, blue and purple | 10 | 10 |
| 147 | - | 5f. black, green and blue | 30 | 10 |
| 148 | - | 100f. brown, grn & bl (air) | 2·00 | 85 |
| 149 | - | 200f. blue, brown and green | 4·75 | 1·80 |
| 150 | - | 500f. slate, red and blue | 12·50 | 4·75 |

DESIGNS—As T **71**: 2f. Beechcraft Baron; 5f. Douglas DC-4. 48×27 mm: 100f. Potez 25-TOE; 200f. Junkers 52/3m; 500f. Sud Aviation Caravelle.

**72** Presidents Boganda and Bokassa

**1967.** Air. 9th Anniv of Republic.

| | | | | |
|---|---|---|---|---|
| 151 | **72** | 130f. multicoloured | 2·00 | 1·30 |

**73** Primitive Shelter, Toulou

**1967.** 6th Pan-African Prehistory Congress, Dakar.

| | | | | |
|---|---|---|---|---|
| 152 | **73** | 30f. blue, purple and red | 75 | 40 |
| 153 | - | 50f. bistre, ochre & green | 1·50 | 80 |
| 154 | - | 100f. purple, brown & blue | 2·75 | 1·10 |
| 155 | - | 130f. red, green & brown | 3·00 | 1·10 |

DESIGNS—VERT: 50f. Kwe perforated stone; 100f. Megaliths, Bouar. HORIZ: 130f. Rock drawings, Toulou.

**74** Pres. Bokassa

**1968.** Air.

| | | | | |
|---|---|---|---|---|
| 156 | **74** | 30f. multicoloured | 85 | 50 |

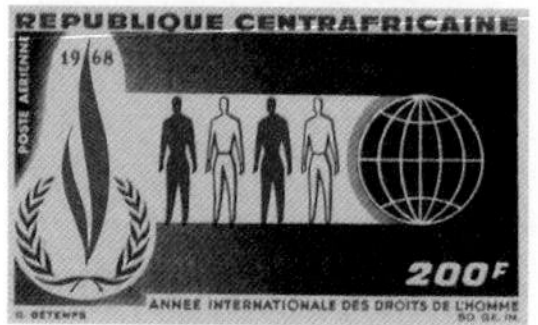


**75** Human Rights Emblem, Human Figures and Globe

**1968.** Air. Human Rights Year.

| | | | | |
|---|---|---|---|---|
| 157 | **75** | 200f. red, green and violet | 3·50 | 1·70 |

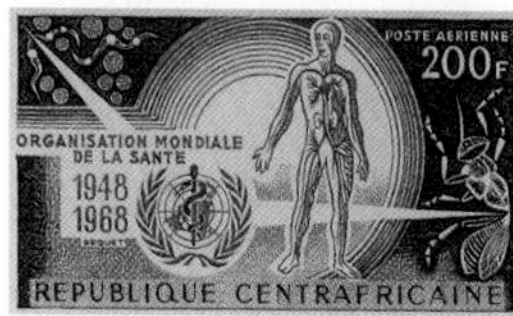


**76** Human Figure and WHO Emblem

**1968.** Air. 20th Anniv of WHO.

| | | | | |
|---|---|---|---|---|
| 158 | **76** | 200f. red, blue & brown | 3·75 | 2·10 |

**77** Alpine Skiing

**1968.** Air. Olympic Games, Grenoble and Mexico.

| | | | | |
|---|---|---|---|---|
| 159 | **77** | 200f. brown, blue and red | 5·00 | 3·25 |
| 160 | - | 200f. brown, blue and red | 5·00 | 3·25 |

DESIGN: No. 160, Throwing the javelin.

**78** Parachute-landing on Venus

**1968.** Air. "Venus 4". Exploration of planet Venus.

| | | | | |
|---|---|---|---|---|
| 161 | **78** | 100f. blue, turquoise & grn | 1·80 | 95 |

**79** Marie Curie and impaled Crab (of Cancer)

**1968.** Air. Marie Curie Commem.

| | | | | |
|---|---|---|---|---|
| 162 | **79** | 100f. brown, violet & blue | 2·40 | 1·20 |

**80** Refinery and Tanker

**1968.** Inauguration of Petroleum Refinery, Port Gentil, Gabon.

| | | | | |
|---|---|---|---|---|
| 163 | **80** | 30f. multicoloured | 85 | 40 |

**1968.** Air. Surch. Nos. 165/6 are obliterated with digit.

| | | | | |
|---|---|---|---|---|
| 164 | **56** | 5f. on 130f. (No. 116) | 10 | 10 |
| 165 | - | 10f. (100f. No. 148) | 30 | 10 |
| 166 | - | 20f. (200f. No. 149) | 45 | 30 |
| 167 | - | 50f. on 130f. (No. 117) | 1·00 | 60 |

**82** "CD-8" Bulldozer

**1968.** Bokassa Project.

| | | | | |
|---|---|---|---|---|
| 168 | **82** | 5f. brown, black & green | 35 | 15 |
| 169 | - | 10f. black, brown & green | 65 | 30 |
| 170 | - | 20f. green, yellow & brown | 75 | 40 |
| 171 | - | 30f. blue, drab and brown | 1·20 | 55 |
| 172 | - | 30f. red, blue and green | 1·20 | 60 |

DESIGNS: 10f. Baoule cattle; 20f. Spinning-machine; 30f. (No. 171), Automatic looms; 30f. (No. 172), "D4-C" bulldozer.

**83** Bangui Mosque

**1968.** 2nd Anniv of Bangui Mosque.

| | | | | |
|---|---|---|---|---|
| 173 | **83** | 30f. flesh, green and blue | 80 | 45 |

**84** Za Throwing-knife

**1968.** Hunting Weapons.

| | | | | |
|---|---|---|---|---|
| 174 | **84** | 10f. blue and bistre | 45 | 25 |
| 175 | - | 20f. green, brown & blue | 60 | 40 |
| 176 | - | 30f. green, orange & blue | 95 | 45 |

DESIGNS: 20f. Kpinga-Gbengue throwing-knife; 30f. Mbano cross-bow.

**85** "Ville de Bangui" (1958)

**1968.** River Craft.

| | | | | |
|---|---|---|---|---|
| 177 | **85** | 10f. blue, green and purple (postage) | 60 | 40 |
| 178 | - | 30f. brown, blue & green | 1·10 | 55 |
| 179 | - | 50f. black, brown & grn | 1·90 | 90 |
| 180 | - | 100f. brown, grn & bl (air) | 2·40 | 1·10 |
| 181 | - | 130f. blue, green & purple | 2·75 | 1·40 |

DESIGNS: 30f. "J. B. Gouandjia" (1968); 50f. "Lamblin" (1944). LARGER (48×27 mm): 100f. "Pie X" (Bangui, 1894); 130f. "Ballay" (Bangui, 1891).

**86** "Madame de Sevigne" (French School, 17th century)

**1968.** Air. "Philexafrique" Stamp Exhibition, Abidjan, Ivory Coast (1969) (1st issue).

| | | | | |
|---|---|---|---|---|
| 182 | **86** | 100f. multicoloured | 3·00 | 2·50 |

**87** President Bokassa, Cotton Plantation, and Ubangui Chari stamp of 1930

**1969.** Air. "Philexafrique" Stamp Exhibition, Abidjan, Ivory Coast (2nd issue).

| | | | | |
|---|---|---|---|---|
| 183 | **87** | 50f. black, green & brown | 1·80 | 1·70 |

**88** "Holocerina angulata"

**1969.** Air. Butterflies. Multicoloured.

| | | | |
|---|---|---|---|
| 184 | 10f. Type **88** | 75 | 30 |
| 185 | 20f. "Nudaurelia dione" | 1·20 | 55 |
| 186 | 30f. "Eustera troglophylla" (vert) | 2·75 | 85 |
| 187 | 50f. "Aurivillius aratus" | 4·50 | 2·20 |
| 188 | 100f. "Epiphora albida" | 7·50 | 3·50 |

**89** Throwing the Javelin

**1969.** Sports. Multicoloured.

| | | | |
|---|---|---|---|
| 189 | 5f. Type **89** (postage) | 20 | 10 |
| 190 | 10f. Start of race | 30 | 15 |
| 191 | 15f. Football | 45 | 20 |
| 192 | 50f. Boxing (air) | 1·00 | 40 |
| 193 | 100f. Basketball | 2·10 | 70 |

Nos. 192/3 are 48×28 mm.

**90** Miner and Emblems

**1969.** 50th Anniv of I.L.O.

| | | | | |
|---|---|---|---|---|
| 194 | **90** | 30f. multicoloured | 90 | 40 |
| 195 | **90** | 50f. multicoloured | 1·40 | 65 |

**91** "Apollo 8" over Moon's Surface

**1969.** Air. Flight of "Apollo 8" Around Moon.

| | | | | |
|---|---|---|---|---|
| 196 | **91** | 200f. multicoloured | 3·50 | 1·80 |

**92** Nuremberg Spire and Toys

**1969.** Air. International Toy Fair, Nuremberg.

| | | | | |
|---|---|---|---|---|
| 197 | **92** | 100f. black, purple & grn | 1·90 | 1·10 |

**1969.** Air. Birth Bicentenary of Napoleon Bonaparte. As T **144** of Cameroun. Multicoloured.

| | | | |
|---|---|---|---|
| 198 | 100f. "Napoleon as First Consul" (Girodet-Trioson) (vert) | 2·30 | 1·40 |
| 199 | 130f. "Meeting of Napoleon and Francis II of Austria" (Gros) | 3·25 | 1·60 |
| 200 | 200f. "Marriage of Napoleon and Marie-Louise" (Rouget) | 4·75 | 3·00 |

**93** President Bokassa in Military Uniform

**1969**

| | | | | |
|---|---|---|---|---|
| 201 | **93** | 30f. multicoloured | 60 | 30 |

**1969.** 10th Anniv of ASECNA. As T 151 of Cameroun.

| | | | |
|---|---|---|---|
| 202 | 100f. blue | 1·80 | 85 |

**94** Pres. Bokassa, Flag and Map

**1970.** Air. Die-stamped on gold foil.

| | | | | |
|---|---|---|---|---|
| 203 | **94** | 2000f. gold | 37·00 | 35·00 |

**95** Garayah

**1970.** Musical Instruments.

| | | | | |
|---|---|---|---|---|
| 204 | **95** | 10f. brown, sepia & green | 60 | 25 |
| 205 | - | 15f. brown and green | 65 | 25 |
| 206 | - | 30f. brown, lake & yellow | 1·00 | 50 |
| 207 | - | 50f. blue and red | 1·50 | 55 |
| 208 | - | 130f. brown, olive & blue | 5·00 | 1·30 |

DESIGNS—VERT: 130f. Gatta and Babylon. HORIZ: 15f. Ngombi; 30f. Xylophone; 50f. Nadla.

**96** Flour Storage Depot

**1970.** Societie Industrielle Centrafricaine des Produits Alimentaires et Derives (SICPAD) Project. Multicoloured.

| | | | |
|---|---|---|---|
| 209 | 25f. Type **96** | 11·50 | 80 |
| 210 | 50f. Mill machinery | 24·00 | 1·60 |
| 211 | 100f. View of flour mill | 36·00 | 2·50 |

**97** F. D. Roosevelt (25th Death Anniv)

**1970.** Air. World Leaders. Multicoloured.

| | | | |
|---|---|---|---|
| 212 | 100f. Lenin (birth centenary) | 3·50 | 1·50 |
| 213 | 100f. Type **97** | 1·90 | 1·00 |

**1970.** New UPU Headquarters Building, Berne. As T 156 of Cameroun.

| | | | |
|---|---|---|---|
| 214 | 100f. vermilion, red and blue | 1·70 | 75 |

**1970.** Air. Moon Landing of "Apollo 12". No. 196 optd **ATTERRISSAGE d'APOLLO 12 19 novembre 1969**.

| | | | | |
|---|---|---|---|---|
| 215 | **91** | 200f. multicoloured | 15·00 | 10·50 |

**99** Pres. Bokassa

**1970**

| | | | | |
|---|---|---|---|---|
| 216 | **99** | 30f. multicoloured | 7·25 | 4·50 |
| 217 | **99** | 40f. multicoloured | 8·25 | 4·75 |

**100** Cheese Factory, Sarki

**101** Silkworm

**1970.** "Operation Bokassa" Development Projects. Multicoloured.

| | | | |
|---|---|---|---|
| 218 | 5f. Type **100** (postage) | 45 | 25 |
| 219 | 10f. M'Bali Ranch | 5·50 | 4·00 |
| 220 | 20f. Zebu bull and herdsman (vert) | 75 | 40 |
| 221 | 40f. Type **101** | 2·20 | 70 |
| 222 | 140f. Type **101** (air) | 2·20 | 90 |

**102** African Dancer

**1970.** Air. "Knokphila 70" Stamp Exhibition, Knokke, Belgium. Multicoloured.

| | | | |
|---|---|---|---|
| 223 | 100f. Type **102** | 1·80 | 60 |
| 224 | 100f. African produce | 2·00 | 60 |

**103** Footballer

**1970.** Air. World Cup Football Championship, Mexico.

| | | | | |
|---|---|---|---|---|
| 225 | **103** | 200f. multicoloured | 3·75 | 1·70 |

**104** Central African Republic's Pavilion

**1970.** Air. "EXPO 70", Osaka, Japan.

| | | | | |
|---|---|---|---|---|
| 226 | **104** | 200f. multicoloured | 4·00 | 1·90 |

**105** Dove and Cogwheel

**1970.** Air. 25th Anniv of UNO.

| | | | | |
|---|---|---|---|---|
| 227 | **105** | 200f. black, yellow & bl | 3·75 | 1·70 |

**106** Presidents Mobutu, Bokassa and Tombalbaye

**1970.** Air. Reconciliation with Chad and Zaire.

| | | | | |
|---|---|---|---|---|
| 228 | **106** | 140f. multicoloured | 2·75 | 1·10 |

**107** Scaly Francolin and Helmeted Guineafowl

**1971.** Wildlife. Multicoloured.

| | | | |
|---|---|---|---|
| 229 | 5f.+5f. Type **107** | 4·75 | 2·20 |
| 230 | 10f.+5f. Common duiker and true achatina (snail) | 6·25 | 3·00 |
| 231 | 20f.+5f. Hippopotamus, African elephant and tortoise in tug-of-war | 7·75 | 3·25 |
| 232 | 30f.+10f. Tortoise and Senegal coucal | 10·50 | 7·75 |
| 233 | 50f.+20f. Monkey and leopard | 18·00 | 12·50 |

**108** Lengue Dancer

**1971.** Traditional Dances. Multicoloured.

| | | | |
|---|---|---|---|
| 234 | 20f.+5f. Type **108** | 55 | 25 |
| 235 | 40f.+10f. Lengue (diff) | 95 | 45 |
| 236 | 100f.+40f. Teke | 2·75 | 1·30 |
| 237 | 140f.+40f. Englabolo | 3·25 | 1·60 |

**110** Monteir's Mormyrid

**1971.** Fishes. Multicoloured.

| | | | |
|---|---|---|---|
| 244 | 10f. Type **110** | 35 | 25 |
| 245 | 20f. Trunk-nosed mormyrid | 75 | 30 |
| 246 | 30f. Wilverth's mormyrid | 1·20 | 65 |
| 247 | 40f. Elephant-nosed mormyrid | 2·30 | 75 |
| 248 | 50f. Curve-nosed mormyrid | 3·00 | 1·30 |

**111** Satellite and Globe

**1971.** Air. World Telecommunications Day.

| | | | | |
|---|---|---|---|---|
| 249 | **111** | 100f. multicoloured | 1·90 | 90 |

**112** Berberati Cathedral

**1971.** Consecration of Roman Catholic Cathedral, Berberati.

| | | | | |
|---|---|---|---|---|
| 250 | **112** | 5f. multicoloured | 45 | 20 |

**113** Gen. De Gaulle

**1971.** 1st Death Anniv of De Gaulle.

| | | | | |
|---|---|---|---|---|
| 251 | **113** | 100f. multicoloured | 3·50 | 2·10 |

**114** Lesser Bushbaby

**1971.** Animals: Primates. Multicoloured.

| | | | |
|---|---|---|---|
| 252 | 30f. Type **114** | 85 | 65 |
| 253 | 40f. Western needle-clawed bushbaby | 1·20 | 75 |
| 254 | 100f. Angwantibo (horiz) | 2·75 | 1·70 |
| 255 | 150f. Potto (horiz) | 4·75 | 2·50 |
| 256 | 200f. Red colobus (horiz) | 6·50 | 3·75 |

**1971.** Air. 10th Anniv of African and Malagasy Posts and Telecommunications Union. Similar to T 184 of Cameroun. Multicoloured.

| | | | |
|---|---|---|---|
| 257 | 100f. Headquarters and carved head | 1·90 | 90 |

**115** Shepard in Capsule

**1971.** Space Achievements. Multicoloured.

| | | | |
|---|---|---|---|
| 258 | 40f. Type **115** | 55 | 40 |
| 259 | 40f. Gagarin in helmet | 55 | 40 |
| 260 | 100f. Aldrin in Space | 1·40 | 55 |
| 261 | 100f. Leonov in Space | 1·40 | 55 |
| 262 | 200f. Armstrong on Moon | 2·50 | 1·20 |
| 263 | 200f. "Lunokhod 1" on Moon | 2·50 | 1·20 |

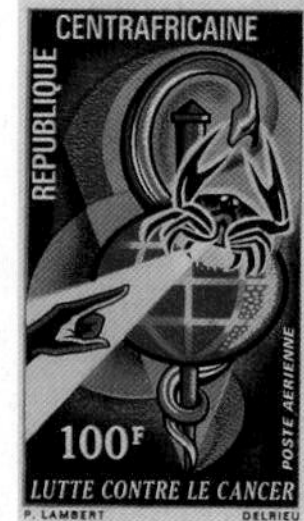


**116** Crab Emblem

**1971.** Air. Anti-cancer Campaign.

| | | | | |
|---|---|---|---|---|
| 264 | **116** | 100f. multicoloured | 2·40 | 1·20 |

**117** "Operation Bokassa"

**1971.** 12th Year of Independence.

| | | | | |
|---|---|---|---|---|
| 265 | **117** | 40f. multicoloured | 80 | 50 |

**118** Racial Equality Year Emblem

**1971.** Racial Equality Year.

| | | | | |
|---|---|---|---|---|
| 266 | **118** | 50f. multicoloured | 80 | 50 |

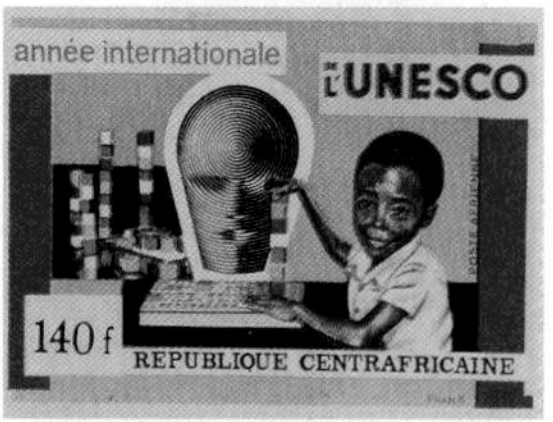


**119** IEY Emblem and Child with Toy Bricks

**1971.** Air. 25th Anniv of UNESCO.

| | | | | |
|---|---|---|---|---|
| 267 | **119** | 140f. multicoloured | 1·90 | 85 |

**120** African Children

**1971.** Air. 25th Anniv of UNICEF.

| | | | | |
|---|---|---|---|---|
| 268 | **120** | 140f.+50f. mult | 3·00 | 1·80 |

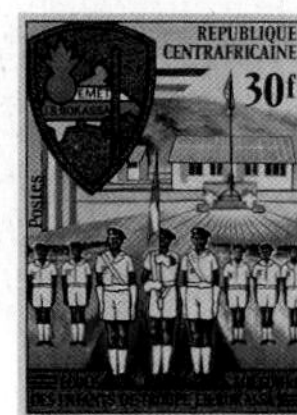


**121** Arms and Parade

**1972.** Bokassa Military School.

| | | | | |
|---|---|---|---|---|
| 269 | **121** | 30f. multicoloured | 80 | 50 |

**122** Pres. G. Nasser

**1972.** Air. Nasser Commemoration.

| | | | | |
|---|---|---|---|---|
| 270 | **122** | 100f. ochre, brown & red | 2·10 | 95 |

**123** Book Year Emblem

**1972.** International Book Year.

| | | | | |
|---|---|---|---|---|
| 271 | **123** | 100f. gold, yellow & brn | 3·00 | 1·30 |

**124** Heart Emblem

**1972.** World Heart Month.

| | | | | |
|---|---|---|---|---|
| 272 | **124** | 100f. red, black & yellow | 1·80 | 95 |

**125** First-Aid Post

**1972.** Red Cross Day.

| | | | | |
|---|---|---|---|---|
| 273 | **125** | 150f. multicoloured | 3·25 | 1·60 |

**126** Global Emblem

**1972.** World Telecommunications Day.

| | | | | |
|---|---|---|---|---|
| 274 | **126** | 50f. black, yellow & red | 95 | 60 |

**127** Boxing

**1972.** Air. Olympic Games, Munich.

| | | | | |
|---|---|---|---|---|
| 275 | **127** | 100f. bistre and brown | 1·70 | 1·10 |
| 276 | - | 100f. violet and green | 1·70 | 1·10 |

**MS**277 130×100 mm. Designs as Nos. 275/6, but colours changed: 100f. emerald and purple; 100f. purple and brown — 4·50 — 4·25

DESIGN—VERT: No. 276 Long jump.

**128** Pres. Bokassa and Family

**1972.** Mothers' Day.

| | | | | |
|---|---|---|---|---|
| 278 | **128** | 30f. multicoloured | 60 | 40 |

**129** Pres. Bokassa planting Cotton Bush

**1972.** "Operation Bokassa" Cotton Development.

| | | | | |
|---|---|---|---|---|
| 279 | **129** | 40f. multicoloured | 95 | 45 |

**130** Savings Bank Building

**1972.** Opening of New Postal Cheques and Savings Bank Building.

| | | | | |
|---|---|---|---|---|
| 280 | **130** | 30f. multicoloured | 95 | 45 |

**131** "Le Pacifique" Hotel

**1972.** "Operation Bokassa" Completion of "Le Pacifique" Hotel.

| | | | | |
|---|---|---|---|---|
| 281 | **131** | 30f. blue, red and green | 55 | 25 |

**132** Giraffe and Monkeys

**1972.** Clock-faces from Central African HORCEN Factory. Multicoloured.

| | | | |
|---|---|---|---|
| 282 | 5f. Rhinoceros chasing African | 30 | 25 |
| 283 | 10f. Camp fire and Native warriors | 45 | 25 |
| 284 | 20f. Fishermen | 45 | 30 |
| 285 | 30f. Type **132** | 75 | 55 |
| 286 | 40f. Warriors fighting | 1·20 | 70 |

**133** Postal Runner

**134** Tiling's Postal Rocket, 1931

**1972.** "CENTRAPHILEX" Stamp Exhibition, Bangui.

| | | | | |
|---|---|---|---|---|
| 287 | **133** | 10f. mult (postage) | 30 | 20 |
| 288 | - | 20f. multicoloured | 45 | 25 |
| 289 | **134** | 40f. orange, blue and slate (air) | 70 | 45 |
| 290 | - | 50f. blue, slate & orange | 80 | 70 |
| 291 | - | 150f. grey, orange & brn | 2·30 | 1·50 |
| 292 | - | 200f. blue, orange & brn | 3·25 | 2·30 |
| **MS**293 | | 201×100 mm. Nos. 289/92 | 8·75 | 8·50 |

DESIGNS—AS Type **133**: HORIZ: Protestant Youth Centre. As Type **134**: VERT: 50f. Douglas DC-3 and camel postman; 150f. "Sirio" satellite and rocket. HORIZ: 200f. "Intelsat 4" satellite and rocket.

**135** University Buildings

**1972.** Inauguration of Bokassa University.

| | | | | |
|---|---|---|---|---|
| 294 | **135** | 40f. grey, blue and red | 80 | 45 |

**136** Mail Van

**1972.** World UPU Day.

| | | | | |
|---|---|---|---|---|
| 295 | **136** | 100f. multicoloured | 2·00 | 80 |

**137** Paddy Field

**1972.** Bokassa Plan. State Farms. Multicoloured.

| | | | |
|---|---|---|---|
| 296 | 5f. Type **137** | 65 | 20 |
| 297 | 25f. Rice cultivation | 1·30 | 25 |

**138** Four Linked Arrows

**1972.** Air. "Europafrique".

| | | | | |
|---|---|---|---|---|
| 298 | **138** | 100f. multicoloured | 1·60 | 85 |

**1972.** Air. Munich Olympic Gold Medal Winners. Nos. 275/6 optd as listed below.

| | | | | |
|---|---|---|---|---|
| 299 | **127** | 100f. bistre and brown | 1·60 | 95 |
| 300 | - | 100f. violet and green | 1·60 | 95 |
| **MS**301 | | 130×100 mm. **MS**277 with opts as Nos. 299/300 | 3·75 | 3·50 |

OVERPRINTS: No. 299, **POIDS-MOYEN LEMECHEV MEDAILLE D'OR**. No. 300, **LONGUEUR WILLIAMS MEDAILLE D'OR**.

**140** Hotel Swimming Pool

**1972.** Opening of Hotel St. Sylvestre.

| | | | | |
|---|---|---|---|---|
| 302 | **140** | 30f. brown, turq & grn | 45 | 30 |
| 303 | - | 40f. purple, green & blue | 50 | 35 |

DESIGN: 40f. Facade of Hotel.

**141** Landing Module and Lunar Rover on Moon

**1972.** Air. Moon Flight of "Apollo 16".

| | | | | |
|---|---|---|---|---|
| 304 | **141** | 100f. green, blue & grey | 1·60 | 80 |

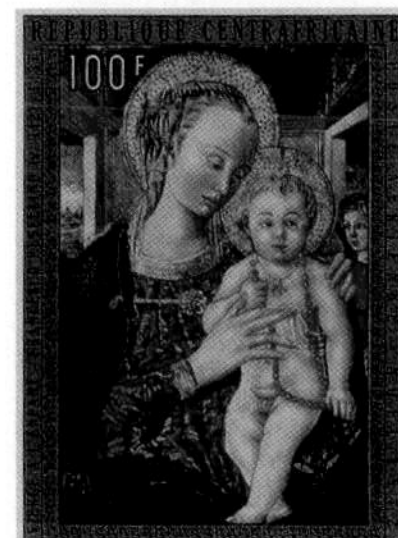

**142** "Virgin and Child" (F. Pesellino)

**1972.** Air. Christmas. Multicoloured.

| | | | |
|---|---|---|---|
| 305 | 100f. Type **142** | 1·80 | 1·10 |
| 306 | 150f. "Adoration of the Child" (F. Lippi) | 2·75 | 1·50 |

**143** Learning to Write

**1972.** "Central African Mothers". Multicoloured.

| | | | |
|---|---|---|---|
| 307 | 5f. Type **143** | 10 | 10 |
| 308 | 10f. Baby-care | 30 | 10 |
| 309 | 15f. Dressing hair | 40 | 25 |
| 310 | 20f. Learning to read | 45 | 25 |
| 311 | 180f. Suckling baby | 2·50 | 1·30 |
| 312 | 190f. Learning to walk | 2·50 | 1·50 |

**144** Louys (marathon), Athens, 1896

**1972.** Air. 75th Anniv of Revival of Olympic Games.

| | | | | |
|---|---|---|---|---|
| 313 | **144** | 30f. purple, brown & grn | 35 | 25 |
| 314 | - | 40f. green, blue & brown | 45 | 25 |
| 315 | - | 50f. violet, blue and red | 55 | 45 |
| 316 | - | 100f. purple, brn & grey | 1·20 | 55 |
| 317 | - | 150f. black, blue & purple | 1·70 | 1·30 |

DESIGNS: 40f. Barrelet (sculling), Paris, 1900; 50f. Prinstein (triple-jump), St. Louis, U.S.A., 1904; 100f. Taylor (400 m freestyle swimming), London, 1908; 150f. Johansson (Greco-Roman wrestling), Stockholm, 1912.

**145** WHO Emblem, Doctor and Nurse

**1973.** Air. 25th Anniv of WHO.

| | | | | |
|---|---|---|---|---|
| 318 | **145** | 100f. multicoloured | 1·60 | 85 |

**146** "Telecommunications"

**1973.** World Telecommunications Day.

| | | | | |
|---|---|---|---|---|
| 319 | **146** | 200f. orange, blue & black | 2·40 | 1·20 |

**147** Harvesting

**1973.** 10th Anniv of World Food Programme.

| | | | | |
|---|---|---|---|---|
| 320 | **147** | 50f. multicoloured | 80 | 50 |

**148** "Garcinia punctata"

**1973.** "Flora". Multicoloured.

| | | | |
|---|---|---|---|
| 321 | 10f. Type **148** | 45 | 20 |
| 322 | 20f. "Bertiera racemosa" | 65 | 25 |
| 323 | 30f. "Coryanthe pachyceras" | 90 | 50 |
| 324 | 40f. "Combretodendron africanum" | 1·30 | 60 |
| 325 | 50f. "Xylopia villosa" | 1·70 | 25 |

**149** Pygmy Chameleon

**1973**

| | | | | |
|---|---|---|---|---|
| 326 | **149** | 15f. multicoloured | 1·50 | 40 |

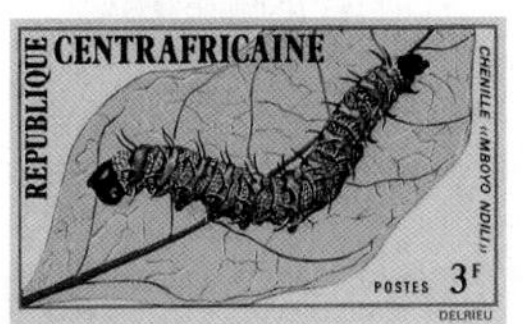

**150** "Mboyo Ndili"

**1973.** Caterpillars. Multicoloured.

| | | | |
|---|---|---|---|
| 327 | 3f. Type **150** | 75 | 25 |
| 328 | 5f. "Piwili" | 1·20 | 45 |
| 329 | 25f. "Loulia Konga" | 2·50 | 65 |

**1973.** African Solidarity "Drought Relief". No. 321 surch **SECHERESSE SOLIDARITE AFRICAINE** and value.

| | | | | |
|---|---|---|---|---|
| 330 | **148** | 100f. on 10f. mult | 1·60 | 1·10 |

**1973.** UAMPT. As Type **216** of Cameroun.

| | | | |
|---|---|---|---|
| 331 | 100f. red, brown and olive | 1·10 | 70 |

**1973.** Air. African Fortnight, Brussels. As T **217** of Cameroun.

| | | | |
|---|---|---|---|
| 332 | 100f. brown and violet | 1·30 | 75 |

**152** African and Symbolic Map

**1973.** Air. Europafrique.

| | | | | |
|---|---|---|---|---|
| 333 | **152** | 100f. red, green & brown | 1·60 | 85 |

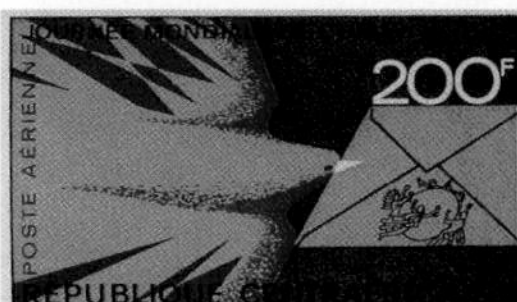

**153** Bird with Letter

**1973.** Air. World UPU Day.

| | | | | |
|---|---|---|---|---|
| 334 | **153** | 200f. multicoloured | 2·30 | 1·40 |

**154** Weather Map

**1973.** Air. Centenary of IMO/WMO.

| | | | | |
|---|---|---|---|---|
| 335 | **154** | 150f. multicoloured | 2·40 | 1·00 |

**155** Copernicus

**1973.** Air. 500th Birth Anniv of Copernicus.

| | | | | |
|---|---|---|---|---|
| 336 | **155** | 100f. multicoloured | 2·75 | 1·80 |

**156** Pres. Bokassa

**1973**

| | | | | |
|---|---|---|---|---|
| 337 | **156** | 1f. mult (postage) | 10 | 10 |
| 338 | **156** | 2f. multicoloured | 10 | 10 |
| 339 | **156** | 3f. multicoloured | 10 | 10 |
| 340 | **156** | 5f. multicoloured | 10 | 10 |
| 341 | **156** | 10f. multicoloured | 35 | 10 |
| 342 | **156** | 15f. multicoloured | 35 | 20 |
| 343 | **156** | 20f. multicoloured | 45 | 25 |
| 344 | **156** | 30f. multicoloured | 45 | 30 |
| 345 | **156** | 40f. multicoloured | 60 | 35 |
| 346 | - | 50f. multicoloured (air) | 65 | 35 |
| 347 | - | 100f. multicoloured | 1·30 | 70 |

DESIGNS—SQUARE (35×35 mm): 50f. Pres. Bokassa facing left. VERT (26×47 mm): 100f. Pres. Bokassa in military uniform.

**158** Launch

**1973.** Air. Moon Flight of "Apollo 17".

| | | | | |
|---|---|---|---|---|
| 348 | **158** | 50f. red, green & brown | 55 | 30 |
| 349 | - | 65f. green, red & purple | 75 | 45 |
| 350 | - | 100f. blue, brown & red | 1·20 | 70 |
| 351 | - | 150f. green, brown & red | 1·70 | 85 |
| 352 | - | 200f. green, red and blue | 2·20 | 1·30 |

DESIGNS—HORIZ: 65f. Surveying lunar surfaces; 100f. Descent on Moon. VERT: 150f. Astronauts on Moon's surface; 200f. Splashdown.

**159** Interpol Emblem within "Eye"

**1973.** 50th Anniv of Interpol.

| | | | | |
|---|---|---|---|---|
| 353 | **159** | 50f. multicoloured | 80 | 55 |

**160** St. Theresa

**1973.** Air. Birth Centenary of St. Theresa of Lisieux.

354 **160** 500f. blue and light blue 6·25 4·00

**161** Main Entrance

**1974.** Opening of "Catherine Bokassa" Mother-and-Child Centre.

355 **161** 30f. brown, red and blue 35 25
356 - 40f. brown, blue and red 45 40

DESIGN: 40f. General view of Centre.

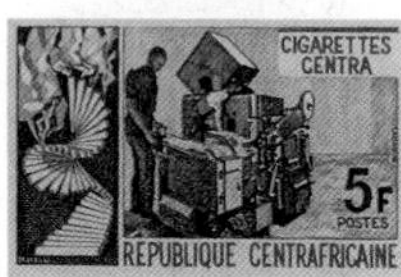


**162** Cigarette-packing Machine

**1974.** "Centra" Cigarette Factory.

357 **162** 5f. purple, green & red 10 10
358 - 10f. blue, green & brown 35 20
359 - 30f. blue, green and red 45 25

DESIGNS: 10f. Administration block and factory building; 30f. Tobacco warehouse.

**163** "Telecommunications"

**1974.** World Telecommunications Day.

360 **163** 100f. multicoloured 1·50 85

**164** "Peoples of the World"

**1974.** World Population Year.

361 **164** 100f. green, red & brown 1·20 70

**165** Mother and Baby

**1974.** 26th Anniv of WHO.

362 **165** 100f. brown, blue & grn 1·70 75

**166** Letter and UPU Emblem

**1974.** Centenary of UPU.

363 **166** 500f. red, green & brown 7·00 4·25

**167** Battle Scene

**1974.** "Activities of Forces' Veterans". Mult.

364 10f. Type **167** 10 10
365 15f. "Today" (Peace-time activities) 20 10
366 20f. Planting rice 30 10
367 25f. Cattle-shed 35 20
368 30f. Workers hoeing 35 25
369 40f. Veterans' houses 55 25

**1974.** 10th Anniv of Central African Customs and Economics Union. As Nos. 734/5 of Cameroun.

370 40f. multicoloured (postage) 60 35
371 100f. multicoloured (air) 1·30 80

**168** Modern Building

**1975.** "OCAM City" Project.

372 **168** 30f. multicoloured 35 10
373 - 40f. multicoloured 45 25
374 - 50f. multicoloured 55 40
375 - 100f. multicoloured 1·00 55

DESIGNS: Nos. 373/5, Various views similar to Type **150**.

**1975.** "J. B. Bokassa Pilot Village Project". As T **168**, but inscr "VILLAGE PILOTE J. B. BOKASSA".

376 25f. multicoloured 30 10
377 30f. multicoloured 35 25
378 40f. multicoloured 45 30

DESIGNS: Nos. 376/8, Various views similar to Type **168**.

**169** President Bokassa's Sword

**1975.** "Homage to President Bokassa". Mult.

379 30f. Type **169** (postage) 45 30
380 40f. President Bokassa's baton 55 25
381 50f. Pres. Bokassa in uniform (vert, 36×49 mm) (air) 60 35
382 100f. Pres. Bokassa in cap and cape (vert, 36×49 mm) 1·30 55

**170** Foreign Minister and Ministry

**1975.** Government Buildings. Multicoloured.

383 40f. Type **170** 55 35
384 40f. Television Centre (36×23 mm) 55 35

**171** "No Entry"

**1975.** Road Signs.

385 **171** 5f. red and blue 10 10
386 - 10f. red and blue 10 10
387 - 20f. red and blue 30 10
388 - 30f. multicoloured 45 25
389 - 40f. multicoloured 75 30

SIGNS: 10f. "Stop"; 20f. "No stopping"; 30f. "School"; 40f. "Crossroads".

**172** Kob

**1975.** Wild Animals. Multicoloured.

390 10f. Type **172** 45 10
391 15f. Warthog 90 25
392 20f. Waterbuck 1·20 25
393 30f. Lion 1·30 40

**173** Carved Wooden Mask

**1975.** Air. "Arphila" International Stamp Exhibition. Paris.

394 **173** 100f. red, rose and blue 1·30 70

**174** Dr. Schweitzer and Dug-out Canoe

**1975.** Air. Birth Centenary of Dr. Albert Schweitzer.

395 **174** 200f. black, blue & brown 3·75 2·00

**175** Forest Scene

**1975.** Central African Woods.

396 **175** 10f. brown, green & red 10 10
397 - 15f. brown, green & blue 30 10
398 - 50f. blue, brown & green 55 25
399 - 100f. brown, blue & grn 1·20 60
400 - 150f. blue, brown & grn 1·60 1·00
401 - 200f. brown, red & green 2·10 1·40

DESIGNS—VERT: 15f. Cutting sapeles. HORIZ: 50f. Mobile crane; 100f. Log stack; 150f. Floating logs; 200f. Timber-sorting yard.

**176** Women's Heads and Women Working

**1975.** International Women's Year.

402 **176** 40f. multicoloured 45 25
403 **176** 100f. multicoloured 1·30 65

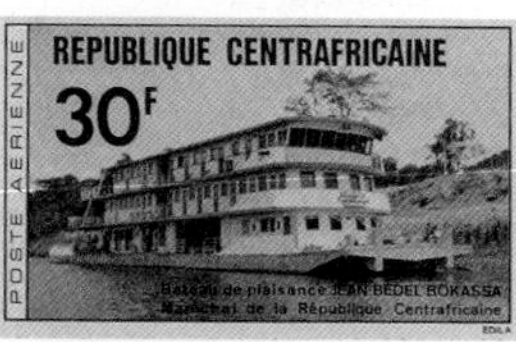


**177** River Vessel "Jean Bedel Bokassa"

**1976.** Air. Multicoloured.

404 30f. Type **177** 60 30
405 40f. Frontal view of "Jean Bedel Bokassa" 85 50

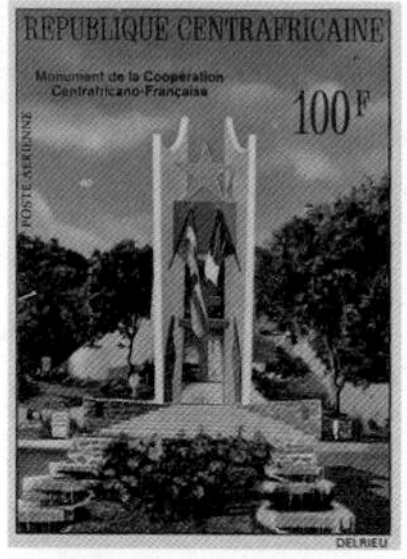


**178** Co-operation Monument

**1976.** Air. Central African–French Co-operation and Visit of President Giscard d'Estaing. Mult.

406 100f. Type **178** 1·30 85
407 200f. Flags and Presidents Giscard d'Estaing and Bokassa 2·75 1·40

**179** Alexander Graham Bell

**1976.** Telephone Centenary.

408 **179** 100f. black and yellow 1·70 1·00

**180** Telecommunications Satellite

**1976.** World Telecommunications Day.

409 **180** 100f. purple, blue & grn 1·70 1·10

**181** Rocket on Launch-pad

**1976.** Apollo–Soyuz Space Link. Multicoloured.

410 40f. Type **181** (postage) 60 30
411 50f. Blast-off 75 40
412 100f. "Soyuz" in flight (air) 1·00 25
413 200f. "Apollo" in flight 1·90 65
414 300f. Crew meeting in space 3·00 1·00
**MS**415 103×78 mm. 500f. Space link 5·00 1·90

**182** French Hussar

**1976.** Air. American Revolution Bicent. Mult.

| No. | Description | Unused | Used |
|---|---|---|---|
| 416 | 100f. Type **182** | 85 | 40 |
| 417 | 125f. Black Watch soldier | 1·20 | 50 |
| 418 | 150f. German Dragoons' officer | 1·20 | 55 |
| 419 | 200f. British Grenadiers' officer | 2·20 | 60 |
| 420 | 250f. American Ranger | 2·50 | 95 |
| **MS**421 | 119×81 mm. 450f. American dragoon | 7·25 | 2·10 |

**183** "Drurya antimachus"

**1976.** Butterflies. Multicoloured.

| No. | Description | Unused | Used |
|---|---|---|---|
| 422 | 30f. Type **183** (postage) | 5·25 | 1·10 |
| 423 | 40f. "Argema mittrei" (vert) | 7·50 | 1·10 |
| 424 | 50f. "Acherontia atropos" and "Saturnia pyri" (air) | 4·75 | 1·10 |
| 425 | 100f. "Papilio nireus" and "Heniocha marnois" | 9·50 | 1·60 |

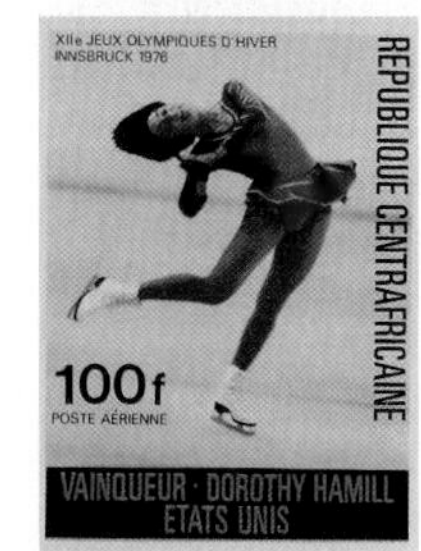


**184** Dorothy Hamill of U.S.A. (figure skating)

**1976.** Medal Winners, Winter Olympic Games, Innsbruck. Multicoloured.

| No. | Description | Unused | Used |
|---|---|---|---|
| 426 | 40f. Piero Gros of Italy (slalom) (horiz) (postage) | 50 | 25 |
| 427 | 60f. Karl Schnabl and Toni Innauer of Austria (ski- jumping) (horiz) | 75 | 40 |
| 428 | 100f. Type **184** (air) | 95 | 45 |
| 429 | 200f. Alexandre Gorshkov and Ludmilla Pakhomova (figure-skating, pairs) (horiz) | 1·90 | 75 |
| 430 | 300f. John Curry of Great Britain (figure-skating) | 3·00 | 1·10 |
| **MS**431 | 103×78 mm. 500f. Rosi Mittermaier of West Germany (skiing) | 6·00 | 1·90 |

**185** UPU Emblem, Letters, and Types of Mail Transport

**1976.** World UPU Day.

| No. | Type | Description | Unused | Used |
|---|---|---|---|---|
| 432 | **185** | 100f. multicoloured | 1·60 | 90 |

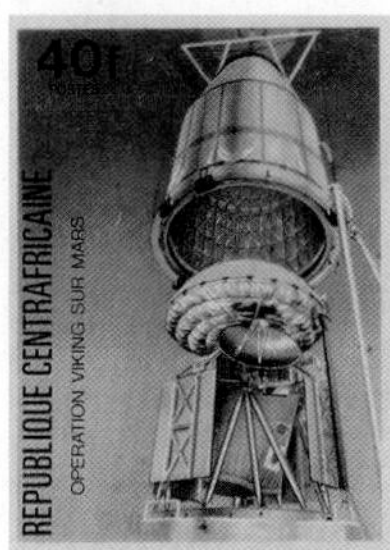


**186** Assembly of "Viking"

**1976.** "Viking" Space Mission to Mars. Multicoloured.

| No. | Description | Unused | Used |
|---|---|---|---|
| 433 | 40f. Type **186** (postage) | 50 | 25 |
| 434 | 60f. Launch of "Viking" | 75 | 40 |
| 435 | 100f. Parachute descent on Mars (air) | 95 | 45 |
| 436 | 200f. "Viking" on Mars (horiz) | 1·90 | 70 |
| 437 | 300f. "Viking" operating gravel scoop | 3·00 | 1·00 |
| **MS**438 | 102×78 mm. 500f. "Viking" in flight (horiz) | 5·00 | 1·90 |

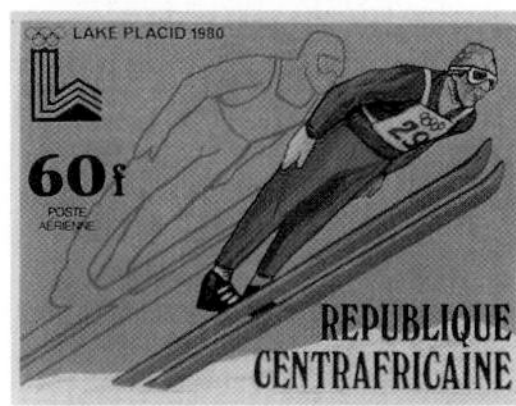


**220** Ski Jump

**1979.** Air. Winter Olympic Games, Lake Placid (1980). Multicoloured.

| No. | Description | Unused | Used |
|---|---|---|---|
| 655 | 60f. Type **220** | 60 | 25 |
| 656 | 100f. Downhill skiing | 1·00 | 45 |
| 657 | 200f. Ice hockey | 2·10 | 90 |
| 658 | 300f. Skiing (slalom) | 3·00 | 1·40 |
| **MS**659 | 103×77 mm. 500f. Two-man bobsleigh | 5·50 | 1·80 |

Issues between 1977 and 1979 are listed under **CENTRAL AFRICAN EMPIRE**.

**1979.** "Apollo 11" Moon Landing. 10th Anniv. Nos. 433/7 optd **ALUNISSAGE APOLLO XI JUILLET 1969** and lunar module.

| No. | Type | Description | Unused | Used |
|---|---|---|---|---|
| 660 | **186** | 40f. mult (postage) | 50 | 30 |
| 661 | - | 60f. multicoloured | 65 | 45 |
| 662 | - | 100f. multicoloured (air) | 95 | 60 |
| 663 | - | 200f. multicoloured | 1·80 | 95 |
| 664 | - | 300f. multicoloured | 2·75 | 1·40 |
| **MS**665 | | 102×78 mm. 500f. multicoloured | 5·50 | 5·00 |

**222** Thumbellina (Andersen)

**1979.** International Year of the Child (2nd issue). Multicoloured.

| No. | Description | Unused | Used |
|---|---|---|---|
| 666 | 30f. Type **222** | 30 | 10 |
| 667 | 40f. Sleeping Beauty (horiz) | 40 | 10 |
| 668 | 60f. Hansel and Gretel | 55 | 25 |
| 669 | 200f. The Match Girl (horiz) | 2·10 | 75 |
| 670 | 250f. The Little Mermaid | 2·50 | 85 |

**223** Steam Locomotive, U.S.A. Stamp and Hill

**1979.** Death Centenary of Sir Rowland Hill (2nd issue). Multicoloured.

| No. | Description | Unused | Used |
|---|---|---|---|
| 671 | 60f. Type **223** | 55 | 25 |
| 672 | 100f. Locomotive "Champion" (1882, U.S.A.), French stamp and Hill | 1·00 | 35 |
| 673 | 150f. Steam locomotive, German stamp and Hill | 1·70 | 55 |
| 674 | 250f. Steam locomotive, British stamp and Hill | 2·75 | 1·10 |
| **MS**675 | 115×78 mm. 500f. Locomotive, Central African Republic stamps and Hill | 6·00 | 2·10 |

**224** Basketball

**1979.** Olympic Games, Moscow (2nd issue). Basketball.

| No. | Type | Description | Unused | Used |
|---|---|---|---|---|
| 676 | **224** | 50f. multicoloured | 45 | 10 |
| 677 | - | 125f. multicoloured | 1·20 | 45 |
| 678 | - | 200f. multicoloured | 2·00 | 60 |
| 679 | - | 300f. multicoloured | 3·00 | 95 |
| 680 | - | 500f. multicoloured | 4·50 | 1·50 |

DESIGNS: 125f. to 500f. Views of different basketball matches.

**1980.** Various stamps, including one unissued, of Central African Empire optd **REPUBLIQUE CENTRAFRICAINE**.

| No. | Type | Description | Unused | Used |
|---|---|---|---|---|
| 681 | **192** | 5f. multicoloured | 20 | 20 |
| 682 | - | 10f. mult (No. 522) | 20 | 25 |
| 683 | - | 20f. multicoloured (Balambo (stand)) | 20 | 10 |
| 684 | **206** | 20f. black and yellow | 20 | 10 |
| 685 | - | 30f. black and blue (No. 583) | 40 | 20 |

**226** "Viking"

**1980.** Space Exploration. Multicoloured.

| No. | Description | Unused | Used |
|---|---|---|---|
| 686 | 40f. Type **226** (postage) | 45 | 10 |
| 687 | 50f. "Apollo"–"Soyuz" link | 55 | 15 |
| 688 | 60f. "Voyager" | 65 | 20 |
| 689 | 100f. European Space Agency | 1·10 | 30 |
| 690 | 150f. Early satellites (air) | 1·50 | 40 |
| 691 | 200f. Space shuttle | 2·00 | 55 |
| **MS**692 | 85×58 mm. 500f. Neil Armstrong (50×41 mm) | 5·25 | 1·60 |

**1980.** Air. Winter Olympic Medal Winners. Nos. 655/8 optd as listed below.

| No. | Type | Description | Unused | Used |
|---|---|---|---|---|
| 693 | **220** | 60f. multicoloured | 55 | 25 |
| 694 | - | 100f. multicoloured | 95 | 45 |
| 695 | - | 200f. multicoloured | 1·80 | 90 |
| 696 | - | 300f. multicoloured | 2·75 | 1·40 |
| **MS**697 | | 103×77 mm. 500f. multicoloured | 5·50 | 3·25 |

DESIGNS: 60f. **VAINQUEUR INNAVER AUTRICHE**; 100f. **VAINQUEUR MOSER-PROELL AUTRICHE**; 200f. **VAINQUEUR ETATS-UNIS**; 300f. **VAINQUEUR STENMARK SUEDE**; 500f. **VAINQUEURS / SCHAERER-BENZ / SUISSE**.

**228** Telephone and Sun

**1980.** World Telecommunications Day. Mult.

| No. | Description | Unused | Used |
|---|---|---|---|
| 698 | 100f. Type **228** | 1·00 | 60 |
| 699 | 150f. Telephone and sun (different) | 1·50 | 85 |

**229** Walking

**1980.** Olympic Games, Moscow (3rd issue). Mult.

| No. | Description | Unused | Used |
|---|---|---|---|
| 700 | 30f. Type **229** (postage) | 40 | 10 |
| 701 | 40f. Women's relay | 50 | 10 |
| 702 | 70f. Running | 75 | 25 |
| 703 | 80f. Women's high jump | 75 | 25 |
| 704 | 100f. Boxing (air) | 95 | 25 |
| 705 | 150f. Hurdles | 1·50 | 45 |
| **MS**706 | 87×84 mm. 250f. Long jump (39×36 mm) | 5·25 | 1·60 |

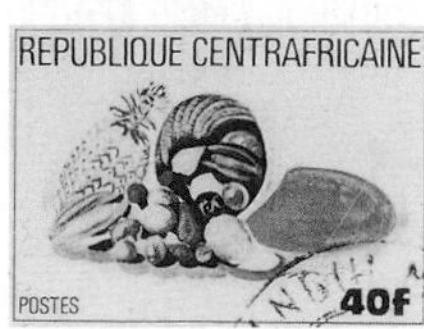


**229a** Fruit

**1980**

| No. | Type | Description | Unused | Used |
|---|---|---|---|---|
| 706a | **229a** | 40f. multicoloured | | |

**230** Agriculture

**1980.** European-African Co-operation. Mult.

| No. | Description | Unused | Used |
|---|---|---|---|
| 707 | 30f. Type **230** (postage) | 35 | 10 |
| 708 | 40f. Industry | 45 | 10 |
| 709 | 70f. Communications | 80 | 25 |
| 710 | 100f. Building construction and rocket | 1·40 | 40 |
| 711 | 150f. Meteorological satellite (air) | 1·50 | 50 |
| 712 | 200f. Space shuttle | 1·80 | 65 |
| **MS**713 | 89×64 mm. 500f. Concorde (41×29 mm) | 5·25 | 1·70 |

**1980.** Olympic Medal Winners. Nos. 676/80 optd.

| No. | Description | Unused | Used |
|---|---|---|---|
| 717 | 50f. **MEDAILLE OR YOUGOSLAVIE** | 50 | 25 |
| 718 | 125f. **MEDAILLE OR URSS** | 1·20 | 45 |
| 719 | 200f. **MEDAILLE OR URSS** | 1·80 | 70 |
| 720 | 300f. **MEDAILLE ARGEN TITALIE** | 3·00 | 1·10 |
| 721 | 500f. **MEDAILLE BRONZE URSS** | 4·50 | 1·70 |

**232** "Foligne Madonna" (detail)

**1980.** Christmas. Multicoloured.

| No. | Description | Unused | Used |
|---|---|---|---|
| 722 | 60f. Type **232** | 60 | 25 |
| 723 | 150f. "Virgin and Saints" | 1·50 | 65 |
| 724 | 250f. "Conestabile Madonna" | 2·75 | 1·10 |

**1980.** 5th Anniv of African Posts and Telecommunications Union. As T 269 of Benin.

| No. | Description | Unused | Used |
|---|---|---|---|
| 725 | 70f. multicoloured | 75 | 40 |

**233** Peruvian Football Team

**1981.** World Cup Football Championship, Spain (1982). Multicoloured.

| No. | Description | Unused | Used |
|---|---|---|---|
| 726 | 10f. Type **233** (postage) | 10 | 10 |
| 727 | 15f. Scottish team | 20 | 10 |
| 728 | 20f. Mexican team | 30 | 10 |
| 729 | 25f. Swedish team | 30 | 10 |
| 730 | 30f. Austrian team | 45 | 10 |
| 731 | 40f. Polish team | 45 | 25 |
| 732 | 50f. French team | 75 | 25 |
| 733 | 60f. Italian team | 75 | 25 |
| 734 | 70f. West German team | 95 | 35 |
| 735 | 80f. Brazilian team | 95 | 40 |
| 736 | 100f. Dutch team (air) | 95 | 25 |
| 737 | 200f. Spanish team | 1·80 | 45 |
| **MS**738 | 119×87 mm. 500f. Argentina team | 6·00 | 1·70 |

**234** "Fight between Jacob and the Angel"

**1981.** Air. 375th Birth Anniv of Rembrandt. Multicoloured.

739 60f. Type **234** 55 25
740 90f. "Christ in the Tempest" 95 25
741 150f. "Jeremiah mourning the Destruction of Jerusalem" 1·70 70
742 250f. "Anna accused by Tobit of Theft of a Goat" 2·75 80
**MS**743 104×80 mm. 500f. "Belshazzar's Feast" (horiz) 5·50 1·80

**1981.** Olympic Games Medal Winners. Nos. 700/MS706 optd.

744 30f. **50 K.M. MARCHE HARTWIG GAUDER–G.D.R.** (postage) 30 10
745 40f. **4×400 M. DAMES–U.R.S.S** 45 25
746 70f. **100 M. COURSE HOMMES ALAN WELLS–G.B.R** 75 30
747 80f. **SAUT EN HAUTEUR DAMES SARA SIMEONI–ITALIE** 75 45
748 100f. **BOXE–71 KG ARMANDO MARTINEZ–CUBA** (air) 1·00 35
749 150f. **110 M. HAIES HOMMES THOMAS MUNKELT–G.D.R** 1·50 65
**MS**750 87×84 mm. 250f. **SAUT LONGUEUR / LUTZ DOMBROWSKI–G.D.R** 5·50 5·00

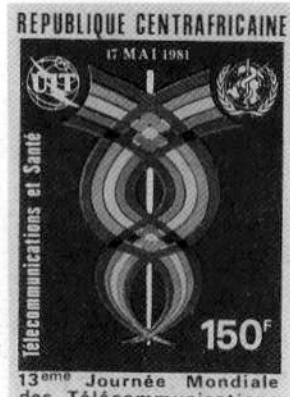

**236** ITU and WHO Emblems and Ribbons forming Caduceus

**1981.** World Telecommunications Day.

751 **236** 150f. multicoloured 1·40 75

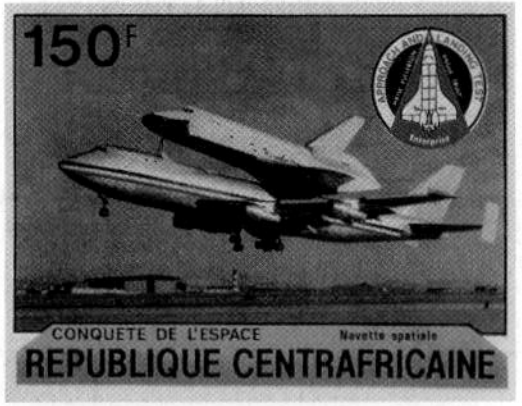

**237** Boeing 747 carrying Space Shuttle "Enterprise"

**1981.** Conquest of Space. Multicoloured.

752 100f. "Apollo 15" and jeep on the Moon 95 40
753 150f. Type **237** 1·40 45
754 200f. Space Shuttle launch 1·80 65
755 300f. Space Shuttle performing experiment in space 3·00 1·00
**MS**756 103×78 mm. 500f. Space shuttle approaching landing strip 6·00 1·70

**238** "Family of Acrobats with a Monkey"

**1981.** Birth Bicentenary of Pablo Picasso. Mult.

757 40f. Type **238** (postage) 45 10
758 50f. "The Balcony" 75 25
759 80f. "The Artist's Son as Pierrot" 1·20 40
760 100f. "The Three Dancers" 1·70 45
761 150f. "Woman and Mirror with Self-portrait" (air) 2·10 50
762 200f. "Sleeping Woman, the Dream" 5·00 1·40
**MS**763 78×113 mm. 500f. "Portrait of Maria" (40×50 mm) 5·50 1·60

**239** Tractor and Plough breaking Chain

**1981.** 1st Anniv of Zimbabwe's Independence.

764 **239** 100f. multicoloured 1·00 45
765 **239** 150f. multicoloured 1·40 60
766 **239** 200f. multicoloured 2·00 80

**240** Prince Charles

**1981.** Royal Wedding (1st issue). Multicoloured.

767 75f. Type **240** 55 25
768 100f. Lady Diana Spencer 95 30
769 150f. St. Paul's Cathedral 1·40 65
770 175f. Couple and Prince's personal Standard 1·80 65
**MS**771 69×91 mm. 500f. Prince and Lady Diana 7·75 1·80

See also Nos. 772/**MS**778.

**241** Lady Diana Spencer with Children

**1981.** Royal Wedding (2nd issue). Multicoloured.

772 40f. Type **241** (postage) 45 10
773 50f. Investiture of the Prince of Wales 55 25
774 80f. Lady Diana Spencer at Althorp House 75 25
775 100f. Prince Charles in naval uniform 1·20 40
776 150f. Prince of Wales's feathers (air) 2·30 55
777 200f. Highgrove House 3·50 1·00
**MS**778 120×70 mm. 500f. St. Paul's Cathedral (57×33 mm) 5·25 1·80

**242** C. V. Rietschoten

**1981.** Navigators. Multicoloured.

779 40f. Type **242** (postage) 45 25
780 50f. M. Pajot 45 30
781 60f. L. Jaworski 65 45
782 80f. M. Birch 85 55
783 100f. O. Kersauson (air) 1·20 60
784 200f. Sir Francis Chichester 2·20 1·10
**MS**785 100×80 mm. 500f. A. Colas 6·00 1·60

**243** Renault, 1906

**1981.** 75th Anniv of French Grand Prix Motor Race. Multicoloured.

786 20f. Type **243** 45 10
787 40f. Mercedes-Benz, 1937 45 10
788 50f. Matra-Ford, 1969 65 25
789 110f. Tazio Nuvolari 1·40 45
790 150f. Jackie Stewart 2·00 70
**MS**791 104×80 mm. 450f. Racing car, 1914 7·75 4·00

**244** Emperor's Crown pierced by Bayonet

**1981.** Overthrow of the Empire. Multicoloured.

792 5f. Type **244** 10 10
793 10f. Type **244** 25 10
794 25f. Axe splitting crown, and angel holding map 30 10
795 60f. As 25f. 65 25
796 90f. Emperor Bokassa's statue being toppled and map of Republic 1·00 45
797 500f. As 90f. 4·50 2·00

**245** FAO Emblem

**1981.** World Food Day.

798 **245** 90f. green, brown & yell 95 30
799 **245** 110f. green, brown & bl 1·10 45

**246** Lizard

**1981.** Air. Reptiles. Multicoloured.

800 30f. Type **246** 80 20
801 60f. Snake 1·00 30
802 110f. Crocodile 1·80 50

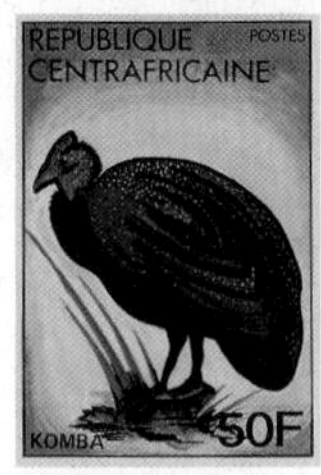

**247** Plumed Guineafowl ("Komba")

**1981.** Birds. Multicoloured.

803 50f. Type **247** 65 25
804 90f. Schlegel's francolin ("Dodoro") 1·30 25
805 140f. Black-headed bunting and ortolan bunting ("Kaya") 2·10 40

**248** Bank Building

**1981.** Central African States' Bank.

806 **248** 90f. multicoloured 95 30
807 **248** 110f. multicoloured 1·10 45

**249** "Madonna and Child" (Fra Angelico)

**1981.** Christmas. Various paintings showing Virgin and Child by named artists. Multicoloured.

808 50f. Type **249** (postage) 65 25
809 60f. Cosme-Tura 85 35
810 90f. Bramantino 1·30 50
811 110f. Memling 1·70 70
812 140f. Corrège (air) 1·80 45
813 200f. Gentileschi 3·00 70
**MS**814 81×98 mm. 500f. "The Holy Family" (Cranach) (41×50 mm) 6·25 1·90

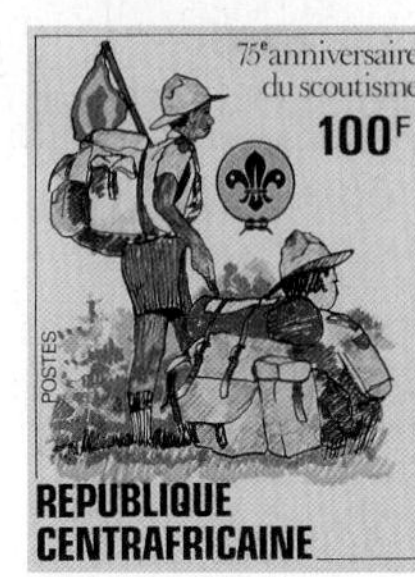

**250** Scouts with Packs

**1982.** 75th Anniv of Boy Scout Movement. Mult.

815 100f. Type **250** 1·10 45
816 150f. Three scouts (horiz) 1·60 60
817 200f. Scouts admiring mountain view (horiz) 2·30 85
818 300f. Scouts taking oath 3·25 1·40
**MS**819 84×113 mm. 500f. Lord Baden-Powell, scout and totem 5·75 1·70

**251** African Elephant

**1982.** Animals. Multicoloured.

820 60f. Type **251** (postage) 70 10
821 90f. Giraffe 1·00 30
822 100f. Addax 1·20 40
823 110f. Okapi 1·40 55
824 300f. Mandrill (air) 3·00 70
825 500f. Lion 5·00 1·50
**MS**826 100×80 mm. 600f. Nile crocodile (47×38 mm) 6·50 1·80

**252** "Grandfather Snowman"

**1982.** Norman Rockwell Illustrations. Mult.

827 30f. Type **252** 30 10
828 60f. "Croquet Players" 80 25
829 110f. "Women talking" 1·20 45
830 150f. "Searching" 1·70 60

**253** Vickers Valentia biplane, 1928

**1982.** Transport. Multicoloured.

| | | | |
|---|---|---|---|
| 831 | 5f. Astra Torres AT-16 airship, 1919 (postage) | 10 | 10 |
| 832 | 10f. Beyer-Garratt 1 locomotive | 10 | 10 |
| 833 | 20f. Bugatti "Royale" car, 1926 | 30 | 25 |
| 834 | 110f. Type **253** | 1·30 | 45 |
| 835 | 300f. Nuclear-powered freighter "Savannah" (air) | 3·75 | 70 |
| 836 | 500f. Space shuttle | 5·25 | 1·50 |
| **MS**837 | 100×81 mm. 600f. Man with winged horse (38×48 mm) | 5·25 | 1·60 |

**254** George Washington

**1982.** Anniversaries. Multicoloured.

| | | | |
|---|---|---|---|
| 838 | 200f. "Le Jardin de Bellevue" (E. Manet) (150th birth anniv) (horiz) | 3·00 | 90 |
| 839 | 300f. Type **254** (250th birth anniv) | 2·75 | 1·00 |
| 840 | 400f. Goethe (150th death anniv) | 3·75 | 1·50 |
| 841 | 500f. Princess of Wales (21st Birthday) | 4·50 | 2·30 |
| **MS**842 | 80×104 mm. 500f. Princess of Wales (different) | 5·25 | 1·60 |

**255** Edward VII and Lady Diana Spencer with her Brother

**1982.** 21st Birthday of Princess of Wales. Mult.

| | | | |
|---|---|---|---|
| 843 | 5f. George II and portrait of Lady Diana as child (postage) | 10 | 10 |
| 844 | 10f. Type **255** | 10 | 10 |
| 845 | 20f. Charles I and Lady Diana with guinea pig | 30 | 10 |
| 846 | 110f. George V and Lady Diana as student in Switzerland | 1·20 | 25 |
| 847 | 300f. Charles II and Lady Diana in skiing clothes (air) | 3·00 | 70 |
| 848 | 500f. George IV and Lady Diana as nursery teacher | 4·75 | 1·50 |
| **MS**849 | 120×74 mm. 600f. Prince and Princess of Wales on wedding day (56×33 mm) | 5·75 | 1·60 |

**256** Football

**1982.** Olympic Games, Los Angeles. (1984). Multicoloured.

| | | | |
|---|---|---|---|
| 850 | 5f. Type **256** (postage) | 10 | 10 |
| 851 | 10f. Boxing | 10 | 10 |
| 852 | 20f. Running | 30 | 10 |
| 853 | 110f. Hurdling | 1·00 | 25 |
| 854 | 300f. Diving (air) | 2·75 | 70 |
| 855 | 500f. Show jumping | 4·50 | 1·50 |
| **MS**856 | 80×108 mm. 600f. Basketball (38×56 mm) | 5·50 | 1·70 |

**257** Weather Satellite

**1982.** Space Resources. Multicoloured.

| | | | |
|---|---|---|---|
| 857 | 5f. Space shuttle and scientist (Food resources) (postage) | 10 | 10 |
| 858 | 10f. Type **257** | 10 | 10 |
| 859 | 20f. Space laboratory (Industrial use) | 30 | 10 |
| 860 | 110f. Astronaut on Moon (Lunar resources) | 1·00 | 25 |
| 861 | 300f. Satellite and energy map (Planetary energy) (air) | 2·75 | 75 |
| 862 | 500f. Satellite and solar panels (Solar energy) | 4·50 | 1·50 |
| **MS**863 | 104×67 mm. 600f. Kohoutek, Halley's comet and satellites (Energy from comets) | 5·50 | 1·60 |

**1982.** Birth of Prince William of Wales. Nos. 767/70 optd **NAISSANCE ROYALE 1982**.

| | | | | |
|---|---|---|---|---|
| 864 | **240** | 75f. multicoloured | 55 | 25 |
| 865 | - | 100f. multicoloured | 75 | 45 |
| 866 | - | 150f. multicoloured | 1·30 | 60 |
| 867 | - | 175f. multicoloured | 1·90 | 85 |
| **MS**868 | | 69×91 mm. 500f. multicoloured | 4·75 | 3·75 |

**259** Pestle and Mortar, Chopping Board and Dish

**1982.** Utensils. Multicoloured.

| | | | |
|---|---|---|---|
| 869 | 5f. Basket of vegetables (horiz) | 10 | 10 |
| 870 | 10f. As. No. 869 | 10 | 10 |
| 871 | 25f. Flagon made from decorated gourd | 30 | 10 |
| 872 | 60f. As No. 871 | 75 | 25 |
| 873 | 120f. Clay jars (horiz) | 1·40 | 45 |
| 874 | 175f. Decorated bowls (horiz) | 1·80 | 65 |
| 875 | 300f. Type **259** | 3·75 | 1·30 |

**260** Footballers

**1982.** World Cup Football Championship Results. Unissued stamps optd as T **260**. Multicoloured.

| | | | |
|---|---|---|---|
| 876 | 60f. **ITALIE 1er ALLEMAGNE 2e (R.F.A.)** | 80 | 25 |
| 877 | 150f. **POLOGNE 3e** | 1·60 | 60 |
| 878 | 300f. **FRANCE 4e** | 3·25 | 1·30 |
| **MS**879 | 104×81 mm. 500f. **ITALIE 1er** | 5·25 | 1·60 |

**261** Jean Tubind

**1982.** Painters. Multicoloured.

| | | | |
|---|---|---|---|
| 880 | 40f. Type **261** | 55 | 25 |
| 881 | 70f. Pierre Ndarata and 10f. stamp | 85 | 35 |
| 882 | 90f. As No. 881 | 1·10 | 45 |
| 883 | 140f. Type **261** | 1·70 | 75 |

**262** Globe and UPU Emblem

**1982.** UPU Day.

| | | | | |
|---|---|---|---|---|
| 884 | **262** | 60f. violet, blue and red | 55 | 25 |
| 885 | **262** | 120f. violet, yellow & red | 1·20 | 50 |

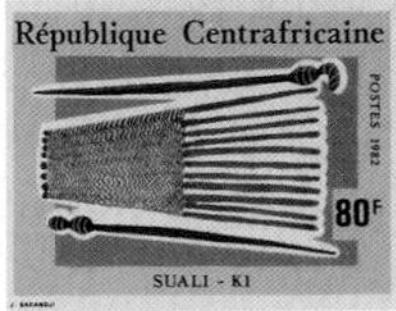

**263** Hairpins and Comb

**1983.** Hair Accessories.

| | | | | |
|---|---|---|---|---|
| 886 | **263** | 20f. multicoloured | 10 | 10 |
| 887 | **263** | 30f. multicoloured | 35 | 20 |
| 888 | **263** | 70f. multicoloured | 65 | 30 |
| 889 | **263** | 80f. multicoloured | 95 | 45 |
| 890 | **263** | 120f. multicoloured | 1·30 | 50 |

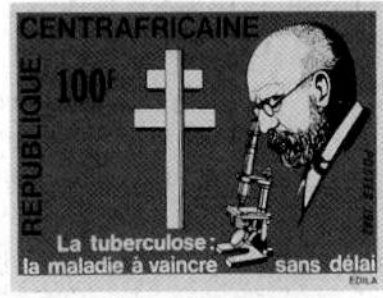

**264** Koch and Microscope

**1982.** Centenary of Discovery of Tubercle Bacillus by Dr. Robert Koch.

| | | | | |
|---|---|---|---|---|
| 891 | **264** | 100f. mauve and black | 1·20 | 30 |
| 892 | **264** | 120f. red and black | 1·50 | 50 |
| 893 | **264** | 175f. blue and black | 2·00 | 80 |

**265** Emblem

**1982.** 10th Anniv of United Nations Environment Programme.

| | | | | |
|---|---|---|---|---|
| 894 | **265** | 120f. blue, orange & blk | 1·20 | 35 |
| 895 | **265** | 150f. blue, yellow & blk | 1·30 | 55 |
| 896 | **265** | 300f. blue, green & black | 2·75 | 1·10 |

**266** Granary

**1982**

| | | | | |
|---|---|---|---|---|
| 897 | **266** | 60f. multicoloured | 55 | 25 |
| 898 | **266** | 80f. multicoloured | 95 | 40 |
| 899 | **266** | 120f. multicoloured | 1·30 | 60 |
| 900 | **266** | 200f. multicoloured | 2·20 | 1·10 |

**267** "The Beautiful Gardener"

**1982.** Air. Christmas. Paintings by Raphael. Multicoloured.

| | | | |
|---|---|---|---|
| 901 | 150f. Type **267** | 2·00 | 45 |
| 902 | 500f. "The Holy Family" | 5·00 | 1·50 |

**268** Stylized Transmitter

**1983.** I.T.U. Delegates' Conference, Nairobi (1982).

| | | | | |
|---|---|---|---|---|
| 903 | **268** | 100f. multicoloured | 95 | 40 |
| 904 | **268** | 120f. multicoloured | 1·30 | 55 |

**269** Steinitz

**1983.** Chess Masters. Multicoloured.

| | | | |
|---|---|---|---|
| 905 | 5f. Type **269** (postage) | 10 | 10 |
| 906 | 10f. Aaron Niemsovich | 10 | 10 |
| 907 | 20f. Aleksandr Alekhine | 30 | 10 |
| 908 | 110f. Botvinnik | 1·40 | 25 |
| 909 | 300f. Boris Spassky (air) | 3·50 | 80 |
| 910 | 500f. Bobby Fischer | 5·00 | 1·40 |
| **MS**911 | 116×72 mm. 600f. Korchnoi and Karpov (55×52 mm) | 6·75 | 2·10 |

**270** George Washington

**1983.** Celebrities. Multicoloured.

| | | | |
|---|---|---|---|
| 912 | 20f. Type **270** (postage) | 10 | 10 |
| 913 | 110f. Pres. Tito of Yugoslavia | 1·10 | 30 |
| 914 | 500f. Princess of Wales with Prince William (air) | 5·00 | 1·60 |
| **MS**915 | 120×70 mm. 600f. Prince and Princess of Wales with Prince William | 5·00 | 3·00 |

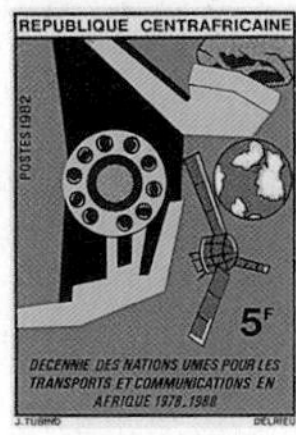

**271** Telephone, Satellite and Globe

**1983.** U.N. Decade for African Transport and Communications. Multicoloured.

| | | | |
|---|---|---|---|
| 916 | 5f. Type **271** | 10 | 10 |
| 917 | 60f. Type **271** | 75 | 25 |
| 918 | 120f. Radar screen and map of Africa | 1·20 | 45 |
| 919 | 175f. As No. 918 | 1·70 | 60 |

**272** Billy Hamilton and Bruno Pezzey

**1983.** World Cup Football Championship, Spain. Multicoloured.

| | | | |
|---|---|---|---|
| 920 | 5f. Type **272** (postage) | 10 | 10 |
| 921 | 10f. Sergeij Borovski and Zbigniew Boniek | 10 | 10 |

| | | | |
|---|---|---|---|
| 922 | 20f. Pierre Littbarski and Jesus Maria Zamora | 35 | 25 |
| 923 | 110f. Zico and Alberto Pajsarella | 1·30 | 30 |
| 924 | 300f. Paolo Rossi and Smolarek (air) | 2·75 | 75 |
| 925 | 500f. Rummenigge and Alain Giresse | 5·00 | 1·30 |
| **MS**926 | 101×81 mm. 600f. Paolo Rossi and Karl Heinz Rummenigge | 5·50 | 3·00 |

**273** "Entombment"

**1983.** Easter. Paintings by Rembrandt. Mult.

| | | | |
|---|---|---|---|
| 927 | 100f. Type **273** | 95 | 45 |
| 928 | 300f. "Christ on the Cross" | 2·75 | 1·30 |
| 929 | 400f. "Descent from the Cross" | 3·75 | 1·80 |

**274** J. and L. Robert and Colin Hullin's Balloon, 1784

**1983.** Air. Bicentenary of Manned Flight. Mult.

| | | | |
|---|---|---|---|
| 930 | 65f. Type **274** | 85 | 25 |
| 931 | 130f. John Wise and "Atlantic", 1859 | 1·40 | 35 |
| 932 | 350f. "Ville d'Orleans", Paris, 1870 | 3·75 | 1·10 |
| 933 | 400f. Modern advertising balloon | 4·25 | 1·40 |
| **MS**934 | 116×91 mm. 500f. Montgolfier balloon, 1783 | 6·00 | 1·60 |

**275** Emile Levassor, Rene Panhard and Panhard-Levassor Car, 1895

**1983.** Car Manufacturers. Multicoloured.

| | | | |
|---|---|---|---|
| 935 | 10f. Type **275** (postage) | 10 | 10 |
| 936 | 20f. Henry Ford and first Ford car, 1896 | 10 | 10 |
| 937 | 30f. Louis Renault and first Renault car, 1899 | 30 | 25 |
| 938 | 80f. Ettore Bugatti and Bugatti "Type 37", 1925 | 95 | 30 |
| 939 | 400f. Enzo Ferrari and Ferrari "815 Sport", 1940 (air) | 4·25 | 1·00 |
| 940 | 500f. Ferdinand Porsche and Porsche "356 Coupe", 1951 | 4·75 | 1·20 |
| **MS**941 | 77×88 mm. 600f. Karl Benz and first petrol-driven car, 1886 | 5·75 | 1·60 |

**276** IMO Emblem

**1983.** 25th Anniv of Int Maritime Organization.

| | | | | |
|---|---|---|---|---|
| 942 | **276** | 40f. blue, lt blue & turq | 45 | 10 |
| 943 | **276** | 100f. multicoloured | 95 | 45 |

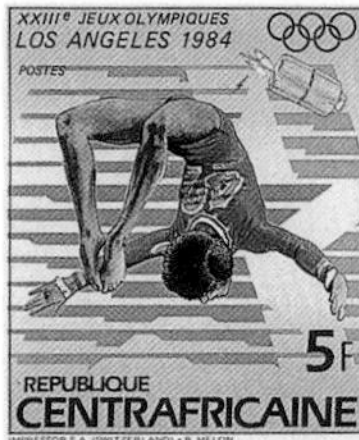


**277** Gymnastics

**1983.** Olympic Games, Los Angeles. Mult.

| | | | |
|---|---|---|---|
| 944 | 5f. Type **277** (postage) | 10 | 10 |
| 945 | 40f. Javelin | 45 | 10 |
| 946 | 60f. High jump | 60 | 25 |
| 947 | 120f. Fencing | 1·50 | 30 |
| 948 | 200f. Cycling (air) | 2·00 | 45 |
| 949 | 300f. Sailing | 3·00 | 75 |
| **MS**950 | 108×80 mm. 600f. Ball games (horiz 50×41 mm) | 5·50 | 1·60 |

**278** WCY Emblem and Satellite

**1983.** World Communications Year. Mult.

| | | | |
|---|---|---|---|
| 951 | 50f. Type **278** | 40 | 25 |
| 952 | 130f. WCY emblem and satellite (different) | 1·30 | 50 |

**279** Horse Jumping

**1983.** Air. Pre-Olympic Year. Multicoloured.

| | | | |
|---|---|---|---|
| 953 | 100f. Type **279** | 95 | 40 |
| 954 | 200f. Dressage | 2·00 | 80 |
| 955 | 300f. Jumping double jump | 3·00 | 90 |
| 956 | 400f. Trotting | 4·00 | 1·30 |
| **MS**957 | 104×79 mm. 500f. Horse jumping (different) | 5·75 | 1·60 |

**280** Andre Kolingba

**1983.** 2nd Anniv of Military Committee for National Recovery.

| | | | | |
|---|---|---|---|---|
| 958 | **280** | 65f. multicoloured | 55 | 25 |
| 959 | **280** | 130f. multicoloured | 1·40 | 40 |

**281** Antenna, Bangui M'Poko Earth Station

**1983.** Bangui M'Poko Earth Station.

| | | | | |
|---|---|---|---|---|
| 960 | **281** | 130f. multicoloured | 1·40 | 60 |

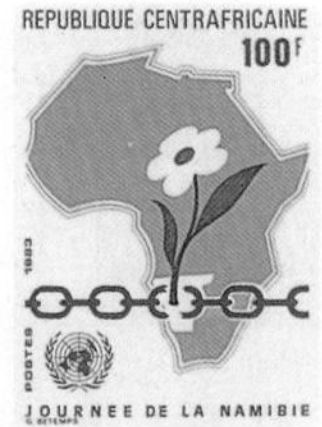


**282** Flower and Broken Chain on Map of Africa

**1983.** Namibia Day.

| | | | | |
|---|---|---|---|---|
| 961 | **282** | 100f. green, lt grn & red | 1·30 | 45 |
| 962 | **282** | 200f. multicoloured | 1·80 | 85 |

**283** J. Montgolfier and Balloon

**1983.** Bicentenary of Manned Flight. Mult.

| | | | |
|---|---|---|---|
| 963 | 50f. Type **283** (postage) | 45 | 10 |
| 964 | 100f. J. Blanchard and Channel crossing, 1785 | 1·00 | 25 |
| 965 | 200f. Joseph Gay-Lussac and ascent to 4000 m, 1804 | 2·20 | 65 |
| 966 | 300f. Henri Giffard and steam-powered dirigible airship, 1852 | 3·00 | 1·00 |
| 967 | 400f. Santos-Dumont and airship "Ballon No. 6", Paris, 1901 (air) | 4·00 | 1·30 |
| 968 | 500f. A. Laquot and captive observation balloon, 1914 | 5·00 | 1·70 |
| **MS**969 | 79×85 mm. 600f. J. Charles and hydrogen balloon and G. Tissandier and dirigible | 6·00 | 1·60 |

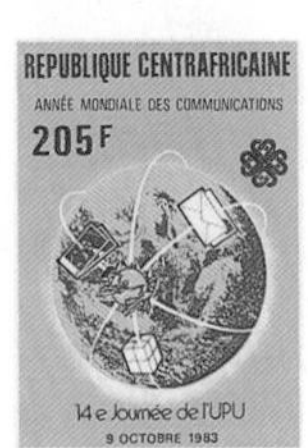


**284** "Global Communications"

**1983.** World Communications Year. UPU Day.

| | | | | |
|---|---|---|---|---|
| 970 | **284** | 205f. multicoloured | 2·00 | 1·00 |

**285** Black Rhinoceros

**1983.** Endangered Animals. Multicoloured.

| | | | |
|---|---|---|---|
| 971 | 10f. Type **285** (postage) | 40 | 10 |
| 972 | 40f. Two rhinoceros | 1·10 | 20 |
| 973 | 70f. Black rhinoceros (different) | 1·80 | 35 |
| 974 | 180f. Black rhinoceros and young | 5·00 | 65 |
| 975 | 400f. Rangers attending sick rhinoceros (air) | 5·25 | 1·20 |
| 976 | 500f. Wild animals and flag | 6·50 | 1·40 |
| **MS**977 | 111×75 mm. 600f. Cheetah (47×32 mm) | 5·75 | 1·70 |

**286** Handicapped Person and Old Man

**1983.** National Day of the Handicapped and Old.

| | | | | |
|---|---|---|---|---|
| 978 | **286** | 65f. orange and mauve | 55 | 30 |
| 979 | **286** | 130f. orange and blue | 1·20 | 55 |
| 980 | **286** | 250f. orange and green | 1·80 | 85 |

**287** Fish Pond

**1983.** Fishery Resources. Multicoloured.

| | | | |
|---|---|---|---|
| 981 | 25f. Type **287** | 20 | 10 |
| 982 | 65f. Net fishing | 80 | 25 |
| 983 | 100f. Traditional fishing | 1·00 | 45 |
| 984 | 130f. Butter catfish, eel and cichlids on plate | 2·00 | 70 |
| 985 | 205f. Weir basket | 2·40 | 75 |

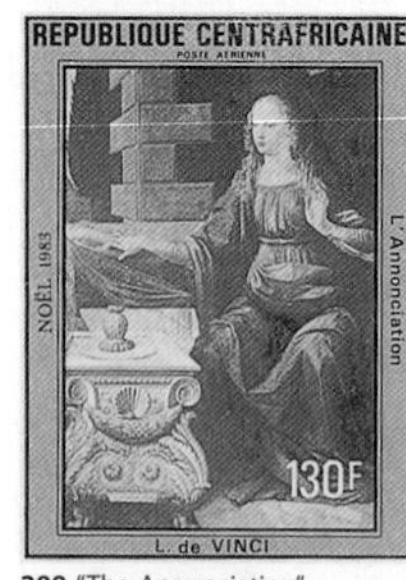


**288** "The Annunciation" (Leonardo da Vinci)

**1984.** Air. Christmas. Multicoloured.

| | | | |
|---|---|---|---|
| 986 | 130f. Type **288** | 1·20 | 40 |
| 987 | 205f. "The Virgin of the Rocks" (Leonardo da Vinci) | 2·00 | 55 |
| 988 | 350f. "Adoration of the Shepherds" (Rubens) | 3·50 | 1·10 |
| 989 | 500f. "A. Goubeau before the Virgin" (Rubens) | 4·75 | 1·40 |

**289** Bush Fire

**1984.** Nature Protection. Multicoloured.

| | | | |
|---|---|---|---|
| 990 | 30f. Type **289** | 2·10 | 40 |
| 991 | 130f. Soldiers protecting wildlife from hunters | 3·00 | 1·00 |

**290** Goethe and Scene from "Faust"

**1984.** Celebrities. Multicoloured.

| | | | |
|---|---|---|---|
| 992 | 50f. Type **290** (postage) | 45 | 10 |
| 993 | 100f. Henri Dunant and battle scene | 95 | 10 |
| 994 | 200f. Alfred Nobel | 1·60 | 40 |
| 995 | 300f. Lord Baden-Powell and scout camp | 2·50 | 70 |
| 996 | 400f. President Kennedy and first foot-print on Moon (air) | 4·25 | 1·10 |
| 997 | 500f. Prince and Princess of Wales | 4·75 | 1·30 |
| **MS**998 | 101×72 mm. 600f. Prince and Princess of Wales | 5·25 | 1·60 |

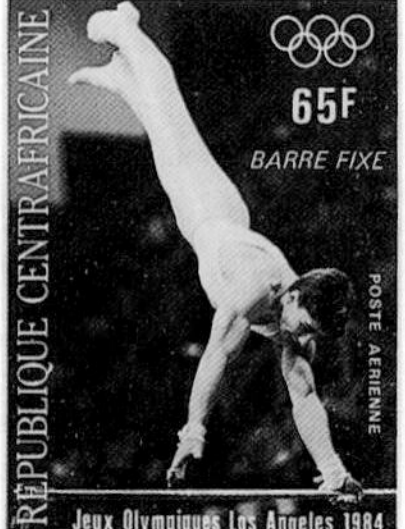


**291** Fixed Bar

**1984.** Air. Olympic Games, Los Angeles. Gymnastics. Multicoloured.

| | | | |
|---|---|---|---|
| 999 | 65f. Type **291** | 55 | 25 |
| 1000 | 100f. Parallel bars | 1·00 | 25 |

| | | | |
|---|---|---|---|
| 1001 | 130f. Ribbon (horiz) | 1·40 | 40 |
| 1002 | 205f. Cord | 2·20 | 70 |
| 1003 | 350f. Hoop | 3·75 | 1·10 |
| **MS**1004 | 102×78 mm. 500f. Rhythmic team gymnastics (horiz) | 5·25 | 1·60 |

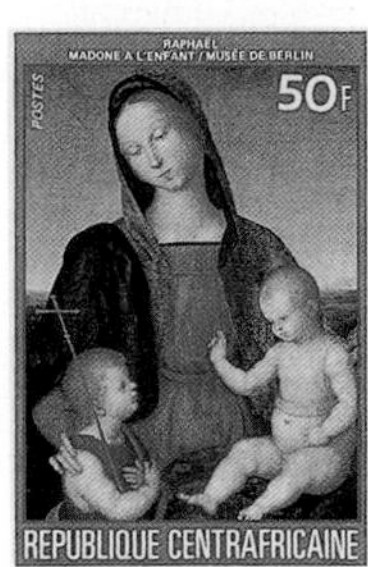


**292** "Madonna and Child" (Raphael)

**1984.** Paintings. Multicoloured.

| | | | |
|---|---|---|---|
| 1005 | 50f. Type **292** (postage) | 50 | 10 |
| 1006 | 100f. "The Madonna of the Pear" (Durer) | 1·00 | 20 |
| 1007 | 200f. "Aldobrandini Madonna" (Raphael) | 2·20 | 50 |
| 1008 | 300f. "Madonna of the Pink" (Durer) | 3·00 | 85 |
| 1009 | 400f. "Virgin and Child" (Correggio) (air) | 4·00 | 1·60 |
| 1010 | 500f. "The Bohemian" (Modigliani) | 5·50 | 2·10 |
| **MS**1011 | 80×111 mm. 600f. "Madonna and Child on the Throne" (Raphael) (vert 29×58 mm) | 6·00 | 1·60 |

**293** "Le Pericles" (mail ship)

**1984.** Transport. Multicoloured. (a) Ships.

| | | | |
|---|---|---|---|
| 1012 | 65f. Type **293** | 80 | 30 |
| 1013 | 120f. "Pereire" (steamer) | 1·30 | 55 |
| 1014 | 250f. "Admella" (passenger steamer) | 2·50 | 1·10 |
| 1015 | 400f. "Royal William" (paddle-steamer) | 4·50 | 1·90 |
| 1016 | 500f. "Great Britain" (steam/sail) | 5·50 | 2·50 |

(b) Locomotives.

| | | | |
|---|---|---|---|
| 1017 | 110f. CC-1500 ch | 1·20 | 45 |
| 1018 | 240f. Series 210, 1968 | 2·50 | 95 |
| 1019 | 350f. 231-726, 1937 | 3·75 | 1·30 |
| 1020 | 440f. Pacific Series S3/6, 1908 | 5·00 | 1·50 |
| 1021 | 500f. Henschel 151 Series 45, 1937 | 5·75 | 3·25 |

Nos. 1017/21 each include an inset portrait of George Stephenson in the design.

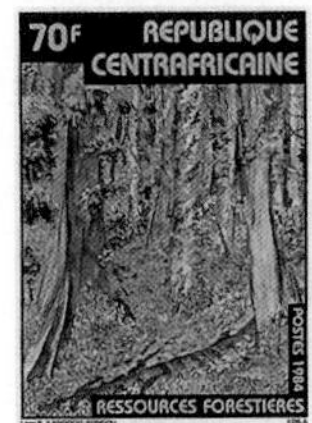


**294** Forest

**1984.** Forest Resources. Multicoloured.

| | | | |
|---|---|---|---|
| 1022 | 70f. Type **294** | 85 | 30 |
| 1023 | 130f. Log cabin and timber | 1·70 | 65 |

**295** Weighing Baby and Emblem

**1984.** Infant Survival Campaign. Multicoloured.

| | | | |
|---|---|---|---|
| 1024 | 10f. Type **295** | 10 | 10 |
| 1025 | 30f. Vaccinating baby | 45 | 25 |
| 1026 | 65f. Feeding dehydrated baby | 55 | 40 |
| 1027 | 100f. Mother, healthy baby and foodstuffs | 1·10 | 60 |

**296** Bangui-Kette Conical Trap

**1984.** Fish Traps. Multicoloured.

| | | | |
|---|---|---|---|
| 1028 | 50f. Type **296** | 75 | 30 |
| 1029 | 80f. Mbres fish trap | 1·00 | 60 |
| 1030 | 150f. Bangui-Kette round fish trap | 2·20 | 80 |

**297** Galileo and "Ariane" Rocket

**1984.** Space Technology. Multicoloured.

| | | | |
|---|---|---|---|
| 1031 | 20f. Type **297** (postage) | 30 | 10 |
| 1032 | 70f. Auguste Piccard and stratosphere balloon "F.N.R.S." | 70 | 25 |
| 1033 | 150f. Hermann Oberth and satellite | 1·50 | 50 |
| 1034 | 205f. Albert Einstein and "Giotto" satellite | 2·00 | 65 |
| 1035 | 300f. Marie Curie and "Viking I" and "II" (air) | 3·50 | 90 |
| 1036 | 500f. Dr. U. Merbold and "Navette" space laboratory | 4·50 | 1·10 |
| **MS**1037 | 75×59 mm. 600f. Neil Armstrong and "Apollo II" (41×34 mm) | 5·25 | 1·60 |

**298** "Leptoporus lignosus"

**1984.** Fungi. Multicoloured.

| | | | |
|---|---|---|---|
| 1038 | 5f. Type **298** (postage) | 10 | 10 |
| 1039 | 10f. "Phlebopus sudanicus" | 10 | 10 |
| 1040 | 40f. "Termitomyces letestui" | 60 | 25 |
| 1041 | 130f. "Lepiota esculenta" | 1·50 | 30 |
| 1042 | 300f. "Termitomyces aurantiacus" (air) | 3·25 | 85 |
| 1043 | 500f. "Termitomyces robustus" | 6·00 | 1·30 |
| **MS**1044 | 68×90 mm. 600f. "Tricholoma lobayensis" (34×40 mm) | 6·00 | 1·80 |

**299** Hibiscus

**1984.** Flowers. Multicoloured.

| | | | |
|---|---|---|---|
| 1045 | 65f. Type **299** | 90 | 45 |
| 1046 | 130f. Canna | 1·60 | 75 |
| 1047 | 205f. Water Hyacinth | 2·50 | 1·00 |

**300** G. Boucher (speed skating)

**1984.** Winter Olympic Gold Medallists. Mult.

| | | | |
|---|---|---|---|
| 1048 | 30f. Type **300** (postage) | 30 | 10 |
| 1049 | 90f. W. Hoppe, R. Wetzig, D. Schauerhammer and A. Kirchner (bobsleigh) | 95 | 30 |
| 1050 | 140f. P. Magoni (ladies' slalom) | 1·40 | 45 |
| 1051 | 200f. J. Torvill and C. Dean (ice skating) | 2·00 | 60 |
| 1052 | 400f. M. Nykanen (90 m ski jump) (air) | 4·00 | 1·00 |
| 1053 | 400f. Russia (ice hockey) | 4·75 | 1·30 |
| **MS**1054 | 79×58 mm. 600f. W.D. Johnson (men's downhill skiing) | 5·50 | 1·60 |

**301** Workers sowing Cotton Seeds

**1984.** Economic Campaign. Multicoloured.

| | | | |
|---|---|---|---|
| 1055 | 25f. Type **301** | 35 | 20 |
| 1056 | 40f. Selling cotton | 55 | 45 |
| 1057 | 130f. Cotton market | 1·60 | 65 |

**302** Woman picking corn

**1984.** World Food Day.

| | | | | |
|---|---|---|---|---|
| 1058 | **302** | 205f. multicoloured | 2·50 | 1·00 |

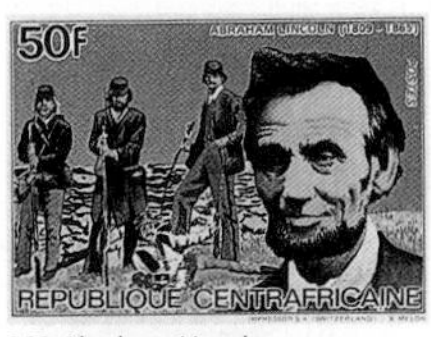


**303** Abraham Lincoln

**1984.** Celebrities. Multicoloured.

| | | | |
|---|---|---|---|
| 1059 | 50f. Type **303** (postage) | 50 | 90 |
| 1060 | 90f. Auguste Piccard (undersea explorer) | 95 | 30 |
| 1061 | 120f. Gottlieb Daimler (automobile designer) | 1·50 | 45 |
| 1062 | 200f. Louis Bleriot (pilot) | 2·30 | 60 |
| 1063 | 350f. A. Karpov (chess champion) (air) | 3·75 | 90 |
| 1064 | 400f. Henri Dunant (founder of Red Cross) | 4·25 | 1·10 |
| **MS**1065 | 79×114 mm. 600f. Queen Elizabeth, the Queen Mother (85th birthday, 1985) (35×50 mm) | 5·25 | 1·60 |

**304** Profile, Water and Emblem

**1984.** Bangui Rotary Club and Water.

| | | | | |
|---|---|---|---|---|
| 1066 | **304** | 130f. multicoloured | 1·70 | 50 |
| 1067 | **304** | 205f. multicoloured | 2·50 | 80 |

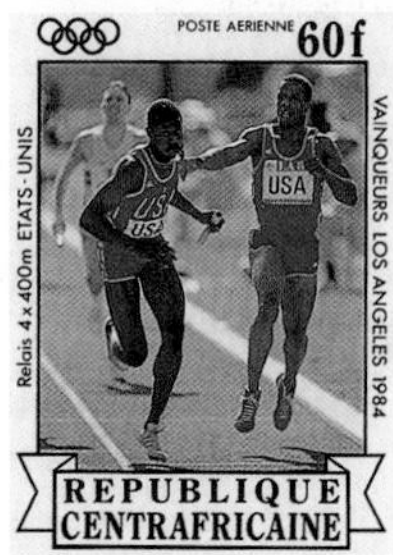


**305** United States (4×400 m relay)

**1985.** Air Olympic Games Gold Medallists. Multicoloured.

| | | | |
|---|---|---|---|
| 1068 | 60f. Type **305** | 55 | 20 |
| 1069 | 140f. E. Moses (400 m hurdles) | 1·60 | 45 |
| 1070 | 300f. S. Aouita (5000 m) | 3·50 | 90 |
| 1071 | 440f. D. Thompson (decathlon) | 4·25 | 1·20 |
| **MS**1072 | 102×76 mm. 500f. J. Cruz (800 metres) (horiz) | 5·50 | 3·00 |

**306** "Virgin and Infant Jesus" (Titian)

**1985.** Air. Christmas (1984). Multicoloured.

| | | | |
|---|---|---|---|
| 1073 | 130f. Type **306** | 1·20 | 60 |
| 1074 | 350f. "Virgin with Rabbit" (Titian) | 3·25 | 1·30 |
| 1075 | 400f. "Virgin and Child" (Titian) | 3·75 | 1·50 |

**307** Eastern Screech Owls

**1985.** Air. Birth Bicentenary of John J. Audubon (ornithologist) (1st issue). Multicoloured.

| | | | |
|---|---|---|---|
| 1076 | 60f. Type **307** | 60 | 20 |
| 1077 | 110f. Mangrove cuckoo (vert) | 1·20 | 50 |
| 1078 | 200f. Mourning doves (vert) | 2·00 | 1·00 |
| 1079 | 500f. Wood ducks | 5·25 | 2·20 |

See also Nos. 1099/1104.

**1985.** International Exhibitions. Nos. 1014/15, 1019/20 and MS1004 optd.

| | | | |
|---|---|---|---|
| 1083 | 250f. multicoloured (postage) | 2·40 | 1·50 |
| 1084 | 350f. multicoloured | 3·50 | 1·80 |
| 1085 | 400f. multicoloured | 4·25 | 2·30 |
| 1086 | 440f. multicoloured | 5·25 | 2·75 |
| **MS**1087 | 102×78 mm. 500f. multicoloured (air) | 4·75 | 4·50 |

DESIGNS: 250f. **ARGENTINA '85 BUENOS AIRES**; 350f. **TSUKUBA EXPO '85**; 400f **Italia '85 ROME** and emblem; 440f. **MOPHILA '85 HAMBOURG**; 500f. **OLYMPICPHILEX '85 LUSANNE** and emblem.

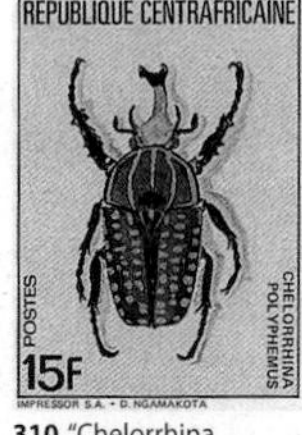


**310** "Chelorrhina polyphemus"

**1985.** Beetles. Multicoloured.

| | | | |
|---|---|---|---|
| 1088 | 15f. Type **310** | 1·70 | 25 |
| 1089 | 20f. "Fornasinius russus" | 2·10 | 35 |
| 1090 | 25f. "Goliathus giganteus" | 2·50 | 45 |
| 1091 | 65f. "Goliathus meleagris" | 6·25 | 75 |

**311** Olympic Games Poster and Stockholm

**1985.** "Olymphilex '85" Olympic Stamps Exhibition, Lausanne. Multicoloured.

| | | | |
|---|---|---|---|
| 1092 | 5f. Type **311** (postage) | 15 | 10 |
| 1093 | 10f. Olympic Games poster and Paris | 15 | 10 |
| 1094 | 20f. Olympic Games poster and London | 30 | 15 |
| 1095 | 100f. Olympic Games poster and Tokyo | 3·00 | 75 |
| 1096 | 400f. Olympic Games poster and Mexico (air) | 4·00 | 90 |
| 1097 | 500f. Olympic Games poster and Munich | 4·50 | 1·10 |
| **MS**1098 | 107×68 mm. 600f. Baron Pierre de Coubertin (55×25 mm) | 5·50 | 1·60 |

**312** Blue Jay

**1985.** Birth Bicentenary of John J. Audubon (ornithologist) (2nd issue). Multicoloured.

| | | | |
|---|---|---|---|
| 1099 | 40f. Type **312** (postage) | 65 | 15 |
| 1100 | 80f. Chuck Will's widow | 1·00 | 20 |
| 1101 | 130f. Ivory-billed woodpecker | 1·70 | 40 |
| 1102 | 250f. Collie's magpie-jay | 2·75 | 60 |
| 1103 | 300f. Mangrove cuckoo (horiz) (air) | 3·00 | 70 |
| 1104 | 500f. Barn swallow (horiz) | 5·25 | 1·30 |
| **MS**1105 | 69×103 mm. 600f. Pileated woodpeckers | 6·25 | 1·70 |

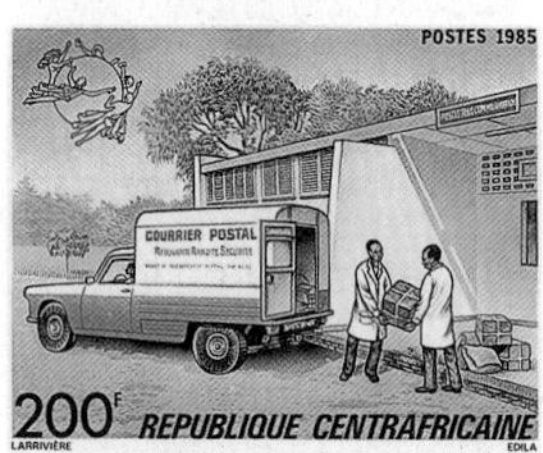

**313** Delivering Post by Van

**1985.** "Philexafrique" Stamp Exhibition, Lome, Togo (1st issue). Multicoloured.

| | | | |
|---|---|---|---|
| 1106 | 200f. Type **313** | 2·30 | 1·10 |
| 1107 | 200f. Scouts and flag | 2·30 | 1·10 |

See also Nos. 1154/5.

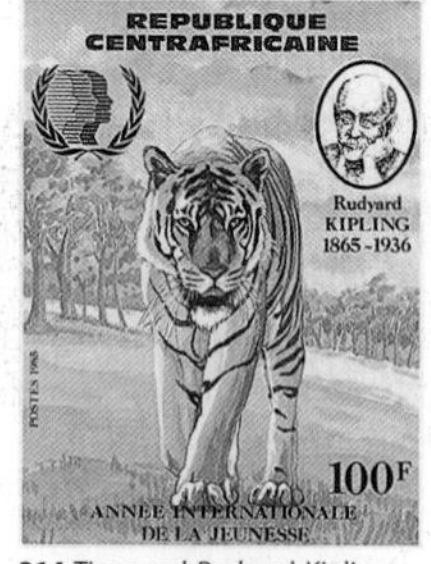

**314** Tiger and Rudyard Kipling

**1985.** Int Youth Year (1st issue). Multicoloured.

| | | | |
|---|---|---|---|
| 1108 | 100f. Type **314** | 1·20 | 40 |
| 1109 | 200f. Men on horseback and Joseph Kessel | 2·20 | 80 |
| 1110 | 300f. Submarine gripped by octopus and Jules Verne | 2·75 | 1·20 |
| 1111 | 400f. Mississippi stern-wheeler, Huckleberry Finn and Mark Twain | 3·75 | 1·70 |

See also Nos. 1163/**MS**1169.

**315** Louis Pasteur

**1985.** Anniversaries. Multicoloured.

| | | | |
|---|---|---|---|
| 1112 | 150f. Type **315** (centenary of discovery of anti-rabies vaccine) (postage) | 2·20 | 60 |
| 1113 | 200f. Henri Dunant (founder of Red Cross) and 125th anniv of Battle of Solferino (horiz) | 2·50 | 80 |
| 1114 | 300f. Girl guides (75th anniv of Girl Guide Movement) (air) | 2·20 | 1·20 |
| 1115 | 450f. Queen Elizabeth the Queen Mother (85th birthday) | 4·00 | 2·00 |
| 1116 | 500f. Statue of Liberty (cent) | 5·00 | 2·40 |

**316** Pele and Footballers

**1985.** World Cup Football Championship, Mexico. Multicoloured.

| | | | |
|---|---|---|---|
| 1117 | 5f. Type **316** (postage) | 10 | 10 |
| 1118 | 10f. Harald "Tony" Schumacher | 10 | 10 |
| 1119 | 20f. Paolo Rossi | 10 | 15 |
| 1120 | 350f. Kevin Keegan (wrongly inscr "Kervin") | 3·25 | 1·00 |
| 1121 | 400f. Michel Platini (air) | 4·00 | 1·00 |
| 1122 | 500f. Karl Heinz Rummenigge | 4·50 | 1·20 |
| **MS**1123 | 94×64 mm. 600f. Diego Armando Maradona | 5·25 | 1·50 |

**317** La Kotto Waterfalls

**1985**

| | | | | |
|---|---|---|---|---|
| 1124 | **317** | 65f. multicoloured | 95 | 35 |
| 1125 | **317** | 90f. multicoloured | 1·10 | 45 |
| 1126 | **317** | 130f. multicoloured | 1·70 | 75 |

**318** Pope with Hand raised in Blessing

**1985.** Papal Visit. Multicoloured.

| | | | |
|---|---|---|---|
| 1127 | 65f. Type **318** | 1·00 | 35 |
| 1128 | 130f. Pope John Paul II in Communion robes | 1·90 | 75 |

**319** Soldier using Ox-drawn Plough

**1985.** Economic Campaign. Multicoloured.

| | | | |
|---|---|---|---|
| 1129 | 5f. Type **319** | 15 | 10 |
| 1130 | 60f. Soldier sowing cotton | 60 | 30 |
| 1131 | 130f. Soldier sowing cotton (different) | 1·30 | 50 |

**320** As Young Girl with her Brother

**1985.** 85th Birthday of Queen Elizabeth the Queen Mother. Multicoloured.

| | | | |
|---|---|---|---|
| 1132 | 100f. Type **320** (postage) | 80 | 25 |
| 1133 | 200f. Queen Mary with Duke and Duchess of York | 1·90 | 45 |
| 1134 | 300f. Duchess of York inspecting Irish Guards | 3·00 | 85 |
| 1135 | 350f. Duke and Duchess of York with the young Princesses | 3·25 | 95 |
| 1136 | 400f. In the Golden State Coach at Coronation of King George VI (air) | 4·00 | 1·00 |
| 1137 | 500f. At the service for her Silver Wedding | 5·00 | 1·30 |
| **MS**1138 | 75×87 mm. 600f. Holding Prince Charles at his christening | 5·25 | 1·50 |

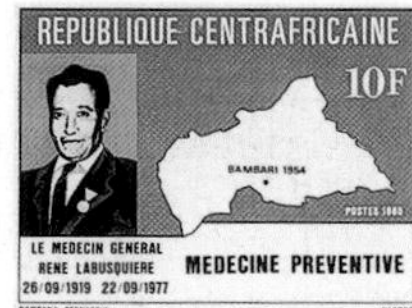

**321** Dr. Labusquiere and Map of Republic

**1985.** 8th Death Anniv of General Doctor Labusquiere. Multicoloured.

| | | | | |
|---|---|---|---|---|
| 1139 | **321** | 10f. multicoloured | 15 | 10 |
| 1140 | **321** | 45f. multicoloured | 45 | 25 |
| 1141 | **321** | 110f. multicoloured | 95 | 50 |

**322** Mail Van delivering Parcels to Local Post Office

**1985.** Postal Service. Multicoloured.

| | | | |
|---|---|---|---|
| 1142 | 15f. Type **322** | 15 | 10 |
| 1143 | 60f. Van collecting mail from local post office | 60 | 25 |
| 1144 | 150f. Vans at main post office | 1·50 | 75 |

**323** Gagarin, Korolev and Space Station Complex

**1985.** Space Research. Multicoloured.

| | | | |
|---|---|---|---|
| 1145 | 40f. Type **323** (postage) | 30 | 10 |
| 1146 | 110f. Copernicus and "Cassini" space probe | 1·00 | 40 |
| 1147 | 240f. Galileo and "Viking" orbiter | 2·20 | 70 |
| 1148 | 300f. T. von Karman and astronaut recovering satellite | 2·75 | 80 |
| 1149 | 450f. Percival Lowell and "Viking" space probe (air) | 4·75 | 1·00 |
| 1150 | 500f. Dr. U. Merbold and "Columbus" space station | 5·00 | 1·20 |
| **MS**1151 | 96×68 mm. 600f. "Apollo II" capsule and astronaut | 5·50 | 1·50 |

**324** Damara Solar Energy Plant

**1985**

| | | | | |
|---|---|---|---|---|
| 1152 | **324** | 65f. multicoloured | 80 | 30 |
| 1153 | **324** | 130f. multicoloured | 1·40 | 65 |

**325** Ouaka Sugar Refinery

**1985.** "Philexafrique" Stamp Exhibition, Lome, Togo (2nd issue). Multicoloured.

| | | | |
|---|---|---|---|
| 1154 | 250f. Nature studies | 3·50 | 1·60 |
| 1155 | 250f. Type **325** | 3·50 | 1·60 |

**326** Pres. Mitterrand, Gen. Kolingba and Flags

**1985.** Visit of President Mitterrand of France.

| | | | | |
|---|---|---|---|---|
| 1156 | **326** | 65f. multicoloured | 65 | 25 |
| 1157 | **326** | 130f. multicoloured | 1·30 | 50 |
| 1158 | **326** | 160f. multicoloured | 1·90 | 80 |

**327** Map and U.N. Emblem

**1985.** 40th Anniv of UNO and 25th Anniv of Central African Republic Membership.

| | | | | |
|---|---|---|---|---|
| 1159 | **327** | 140f. multicoloured | 1·30 | 60 |

**328** "Virgin and Angels" (Master of Burgo de Osma)

**1985.** Air. Christmas. Multicoloured.

| | | | |
|---|---|---|---|
| 1160 | 100f. Type **328** | 1·00 | 35 |
| 1161 | 200f. "Nativity" (Louis Le Nain) | 2·20 | 85 |
| 1162 | 400f. "Virgin and Child with Dove" (Piero di Cosimo) | 4·00 | 1·60 |

**329** Leonardo da Vinci and "Madonna of the Eyelet"

**1985.** Int Youth Year (2nd issue). Multicoloured.

| | | | |
|---|---|---|---|
| 1163 | 40f. Type **329** (postage) | 55 | 10 |
| 1164 | 80f. Johann Sebastian Bach | 95 | 25 |
| 1165 | 100f. Diego Velasquez and "St. John of Patmos" | 1·20 | 40 |
| 1166 | 250f. Franz Schubert and illustration of "King of Aulnes" | 2·50 | 60 |
| 1167 | 400f. Francisco Goya and "Vicente Osario de Moscoso" (air) | 4·25 | 1·00 |
| 1168 | 500f. Wolfang Amadeus Mozart | 4·75 | 1·20 |
| **MS**1169 | 79×79 mm. 600f. Pablo Picasso and "Woman in Plumed Hat" | 6·50 | 1·80 |

**330** Halley and "Comet"

**1985.** Appearance of Halley's Comet (1st issue). Multicoloured.

| | | | |
|---|---|---|---|
| 1170 | 100f. Type **330** (postage) | 75 | 25 |
| 1171 | 200f. Newton's telescope | 1·80 | 45 |
| 1172 | 300f. Halley and Newton observing comet | 2·75 | 80 |
| 1173 | 350f. American space probe and comet | 3·25 | 1·00 |
| 1174 | 400f. Sun, Russian space probe and diagram of comet trajectory (air) | 3·75 | 95 |
| 1175 | 500f. Infra-red picture of comet | 4·75 | 1·20 |
| **MS**1176 | 70×100 mm. 600f. American space probe, Earth, sun and comet | 5·50 | 1·60 |

See also No. 1184/8.

**331** Columbus with Globe

**1986.** 480th Death Anniv of Christopher Columbus (explorer). Multicoloured.
1177 90f. Type **331** (postage) 95 25
1178 110f. Receiving blessing 1·20 40
1179 240f. Crew going ashore in rowing boat 2·40 1·00
1180 300f. Columbus with American Indians 3·00 80
1181 400f. Ships at sea in storm (air) 4·25 1·60
1182 500f. Sun breaking through clouds over fleet 5·00 1·90
**MS**1183 71×100 mm. 600f. Columbus 5·25 1·50

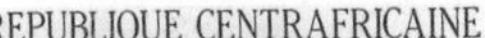

**332** Halley and Comet

**1986.** Air. Appearance of Halley's Comet (2nd issue). Multicoloured.
1184 110f. Type **332** 95 25
1185 130f. "Giotto" space probe 1·30 25
1186 200f. Comet and globe 2·00 55
1187 300f. "Vega" space probe 2·75 75
1188 400f. Space shuttle 4·00 1·00

**1986.** Nos. 874/5 surch.
1188a - 30f. on 175f. mult
1188b **259** 65f. on 300f. mult

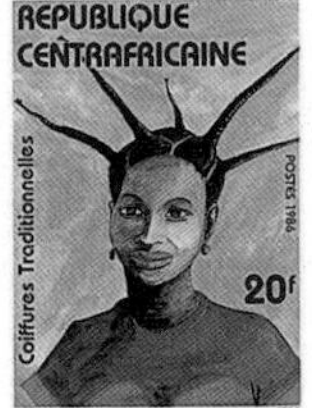

**333** Spiky Hair Style

**1986.** Traditional Hair Styles. Multicoloured.
1189 20f. Type **333** 35 10
1190 30f. Braids around head 40 20
1191 65f. Plaits 55 35
1192 160f. Braids from front to back of head 2·20 70

**334** Communications

**1986.** Franco-Central African Week. Mult.
1193 40f. Type **334** 45 15
1194 60f. Youth 55 25
1195 100f. Basket weaver (craft) 1·20 45
1196 130f. Cyclists (sport) 1·70 60

**335** "Allamanda neriifolia"

**1986.** Flora and Fauna. Multicoloured.
1197 25f. Type **335** (postage) 30 15
1198 65f. Bongo (horiz) 85 25
1199 160f. "Plumieria acuminata" 1·80 40
1200 300f. Cheetah (horiz) 3·50 85
1201 400f. "Eulophia erthoplata" (air) 4·00 1·00
1202 500f. Leopard (horiz) 5·25 1·20
**MS**1203 100×69 mm. 600f. Giant eland and "Eulophia cucllata" (50×29) 5·50 1·70

**336** Palm Tree and Bossongo Oil Refinery

**1986.** Centrapalm. Multicoloured.
1204 25f. Type **336** 30 20
1205 65f. Type **336** 75 45
1206 120f. Palm tree and Bossongo agro-industrial complex 1·30 75
1207 160f. As No. 1206 1·70 90

**337** Pointer

**1986.** Dogs and Cats. Multicoloured.
1208 10f. Type **337** (postage) 20 15
1209 20f. Egyptian mau 45 25
1210 200f. Newfoundland 2·50 70
1211 300f. Borzoi (air) 3·25 70
1212 400f. Persian red 4·75 1·10
**MS**1213 95×60 mm. 500f. Spaniel and Burmese 5·50 1·60

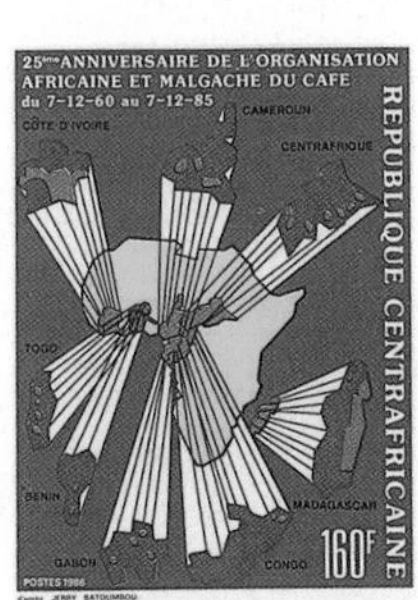

**338** Map of Africa showing Member Countries

**1986.** 25th Anniv of African and Malagasy Coffee Producers Organization.
1214 **338** 160f. multicoloured 1·70 70

**339** Trophy, Brazilian flag, L.-A. Muller and Socrates

**1986.** World Cup Football Championship, Mexico. Multicoloured.
1215 30f. Type **339** (postage) 30 15
1216 110f. Trophy, Belgian flag, V. Scifo and F. Ceulemans 1·00 45
1217 160f. Trophy, French flag. Y. Stopyra and M. Platini 1·50 55
1218 350f. Trophy, West German flag, A. Brehme and H. Schumacher 3·25 90
1219 450f. Trophy, Argentinian flag and Diego Maradona (air) 4·25 1·20
**MS**1220 110×68 mm. 500f. Hands holding trophy, H. Schumacher and J. L. Burruehaga (50×35 mm) 5·25 1·70

**340** Judith Resnik and Astronaut

**1986.** Anniversaries and "Challenger" Astronauts Commemoration. Multicoloured.
**MS**1227 86×86 mm. 500f. "Challenger" crew (50×41 mm) 4·50 1·50
1221 15f. Type **340** (postage) 20 10
1222 25f. Frederic Bartholdi and torch (centenary of Statue of Liberty) 35 10
1223 70f. Elvis Presley (9th death anniv) 1·30 25
1224 300f. Ronald MacNair and man watching astronaut on screen 3·00 80
1226 450f. Christa McAulife and Shuttle lifting off (air) 4·25 1·50
1225 485f. on 70f. No. 1223 6·75 1·40

**341** People around Globe within Emblem

**1986.** International Peace Year.
1228 **341** 160f. multicoloured 1·60 65

**342** Globe, Douglas DC-10 and "25"

**1986.** 25th Anniv of Air Afrique.
1229 **342** 200f. multicoloured 1·80 85

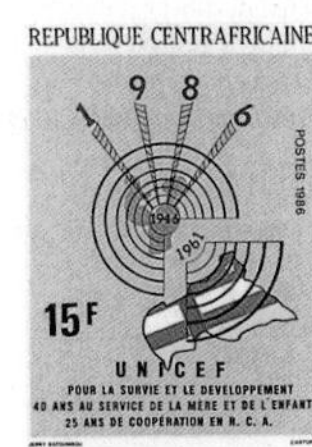

**343** Emblem and Flag as Map

**1986.** UNICEF Child Survival Campaign. Multicoloured.
1230 15f. Type **343** 10 10
1231 130f. Doctor vaccinating child 1·30 60
1232 160f. Basket of fruit and boy holding fish on map 1·50 75

**344** "Nativity" (detail, Giotto)

**1986.** Air. Christmas. Multicoloured.
1233 250f. Type **344** 2·30 1·10
1234 440f. "Adoration of the Magi" (detail, Sandro Botticelli) (vert) 4·25 1·60
1235 500f. "Nativity" (detail, Giotto) (different) 5·00 2·00

**345** Transmission Mast, People with Radios and Baskets of Produce

**1986.** African Telecommunications Day. Telecommunications and Agriculture. Mult.
1236 170f. Type **345** (Rural Radio Agriculture Project) 1·90 95
1237 265f. Lorry, satellite, men using telephones and sacks of produce 2·75 1·40

**346** Steam Locomotive Class "DH 2 Green Elephant" and Alfred de Glehn

**1986.** 150th Anniv of German Railways. Mult.
1238 40f. Type **346** (postage) 50 10
1239 70f. Rudolf Diesel (engineer) and steam locomotive No. 1829 Rheingold 75 45
1240 160f. Electric locomotive Type 103 Rapide and Carl Golsdorf 1·90 55
1241 300f. Wilhelm Schmidt and Beyer-Garratt type steam locomotive 3·25 90
1242 400f. De Bousquet and compound locomotive Class 3500 (air) 4·00 1·20
**MS**1243 83×67 mm. 500f. Werner von Siemens (electrical engineer) and electric locomotive 5·00 1·50

**347** Player returning Ball

**1986.** Air. Olympic Games, Seoul (1988) (1st issue). Tennis. Multicoloured.
1244 150f. Type **347** 1·70 55
1245 250f. Player serving (vert) 2·75 75
1246 440f. Right-handed player returning to left-handed player (vert) 4·25 1·40
1247 600f. Left-handed player returning to right-handed player 6·00 1·60

See also Nos. 1261/4, 1310/13 and 1315/18.

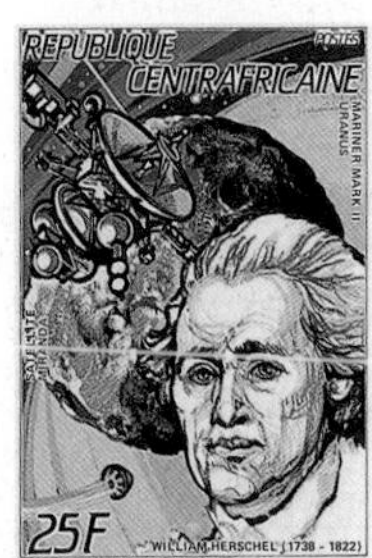

**348** "Miranda" Satellite, Uranus, "Mariner II" and William Herschel (astronomer)

**1987.** Space Research. Multicoloured.
1248 25f. Type **348** (postage) 30 10
1249 65f. Mars Rover vehicle and Werner von Braun (rocket pioneer) 70 20
1250 160f. "Mariner II", Titan and Rudolf Hanel 1·50 40
1251 300f. Space ship "Hermes", space platform "Eureka" and Patrick Baudry 2·75 80
1252 400f. Halley's Comet, "Giotto" space probe and Dr. U. Keller (air) 3·50 1·10
1253 500f. European space station "Columbus", Wubbo Ockels and Ulf Merbold 4·50 1·20

**349** Footballer and "Woman with Umbrella" Fountain

**1987.** Olympic Games, Barcelona (1992). Mult.

| | | | |
|---|---|---|---|
| 1255 | 30f. Type **349** (postage) | 35 | 15 |
| 1256 | 150f. Judo competitors and Barcelona Cathedral | 1·30 | 50 |
| 1257 | 265f. Cyclist and Church of the Holy Family | 2·50 | 80 |
| 1258 | 350f. Diver and Christopher Columbus's tomb (air) | 3·25 | 1·00 |
| 1259 | 495f. Runner and human tower | 4·75 | 1·50 |

**350** Triple Jumping

**1987.** Air. Olympic Games, Seoul (1988) (2nd issue). Multicoloured.

| | | | |
|---|---|---|---|
| 1261 | 100f. Type **350** | 95 | 35 |
| 1262 | 200f. High jumping (horiz) | 1·80 | 75 |
| 1263 | 300f. Long jumping (horiz) | 2·75 | 1·10 |
| 1264 | 400f. Pole vaulting | 3·50 | 1·50 |
| **MS**1265 | 104×86 mm. 500f. High jumping (different) (horiz) | 4·50 | 2·50 |

**351** Two-man Luge

**1987.** Winter Olympic Games, Calgary (1988) (1st issue). Multicoloured.

| | | | |
|---|---|---|---|
| 1266 | 20f. Type **351** (postage) | 30 | 10 |
| 1267 | 140f. Cross-country skiing | 1·40 | 55 |
| 1268 | 250f. Figure skating | 2·30 | 70 |
| 1269 | 300f. Ice hockey (air) | 2·75 | 90 |
| 1270 | 400f. Slalom | 3·75 | 1·20 |
| **MS**1271 | 130×77 mm. 500f. Downhill skiing | 4·50 | 1·50 |

See also Nos. 1320/**MS**1324.

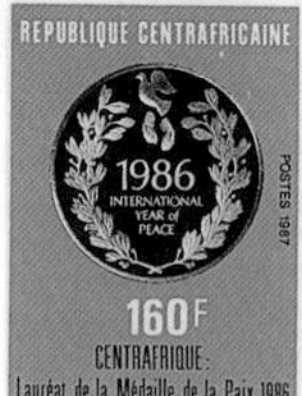

**352** Peace Medal

**1987.** International Peace Year (1986).

| | | | | |
|---|---|---|---|---|
| 1272 | **352** | 50f. brown, blue & blk | 45 | 25 |
| 1273 | **352** | 160f. brown, grn & blk | 1·50 | 1·30 |

**1987.** 10th Death Anniv of Elvis Presley (singer). Nos. 1223 and 1225 optd **Elvis Presley 1977–1987**.

| | | | |
|---|---|---|---|
| 1274 | 70f. multicoloured | 95 | 25 |
| 1275 | 485f. on 70f. multicoloured | 5·75 | 1·70 |

**354** Woman at Village Pump

**1987.** International Decade of Drinkable Water. Multicoloured.

| | | | |
|---|---|---|---|
| 1276 | 5f. Type **354** | 33·00 | |
| 1277 | 10f. Woman at village pump (different) | 33·00 | |
| 1278 | 200f. Three women at village pump | 38·00 | |

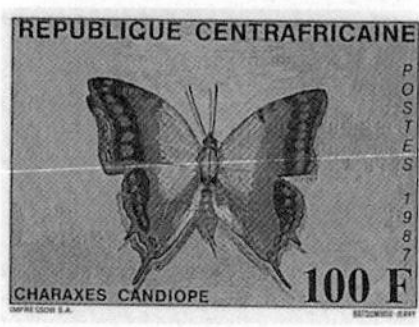

**355** "Charaxes candiope"

**1987.** Butterflies. Multicoloured.

| | | | |
|---|---|---|---|
| 1279 | 100f. Type **355** | 1·50 | 65 |
| 1280 | 120f. "Graphium leonidas" | 2·00 | 75 |
| 1281 | 130f. "Charaxes brutus" | 2·20 | 80 |
| 1282 | 160f. "Salamis aetiops" | 2·50 | 1·00 |

**356** Nola Football Team

**1987.** Campaign for Integration of Pygmies.

| | | | | |
|---|---|---|---|---|
| 1283 | **356** | 90f. multicoloured | 1·50 | 80 |
| 1284 | **356** | 160f. multicoloured | 2·00 | 1·20 |

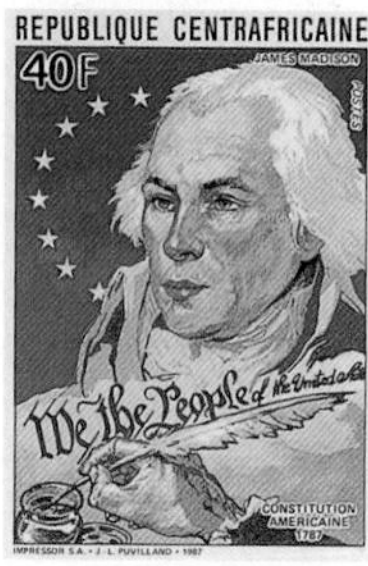

**357** James Madison (U.S. President, 1809–17)

**1987.** Anniversaries and Celebrities. Mult.

| | | | |
|---|---|---|---|
| 1285 | 40f. Type **357** (bicent of U.S. constitution) (postage) | 45 | 15 |
| 1286 | 160f. Queen Elizabeth II and Prince Philip (40th wedding anniv) | 1·50 | 25 |
| 1287 | 200f. Steffi Graf (tennis player) | 2·00 | 55 |
| 1288 | 300f. Gary Kasparov (chess champion) and "The Chess Players" (after Honore Daumier) (air) | 3·00 | 85 |
| 1289 | 400f. Boris Becker (tennis player) | 3·75 | 1·30 |
| **MS**1290 | 86×86 mm. 500f. Scene from "Orpheus" (opera) and Christoph Wilibald Gluck (composer, death bicent) (50×35 mm) | 5·50 | 1·50 |

**358** Brontosaurus

**1988.** Prehistoric Animals. Multicoloured.

| | | | |
|---|---|---|---|
| 1291 | 50f. Type **358** | 50 | 15 |
| 1292 | 65f. Triceratops | 65 | 20 |
| 1293 | 100f. Ankylosaurus | 1·00 | 35 |
| 1294 | 160f. Stegosaurus | 1·60 | 55 |
| 1295 | 200f. Tyrannosaurus rex (vert) | 2·00 | 75 |
| 1296 | 240f. Corythosaurus (vert) | 2·40 | 85 |
| 1297 | 300f. Allosaurus (vert) | 3·00 | 1·10 |
| 1298 | 350f. Brachiosaurus (vert) | 3·75 | 1·40 |

**359** Pres. Kolingba vaccinating Baby

**1988.** 40th Anniv of WHO.

| | | | | |
|---|---|---|---|---|
| 1299 | **359** | 70f. multicoloured | 75 | 45 |
| 1300 | **359** | 120f. multicoloured | 1·20 | 65 |

**360** Carmine Bee Eater

**1988.** Scouts and Birds. Multicoloured.

| | | | |
|---|---|---|---|
| 1301 | 25f. Type **360** (postage) | 30 | 15 |
| 1302 | 170f. Red-crowned bishop | 1·50 | 60 |
| 1303 | 300f. Lesser pied kingfisher | 3·00 | 1·40 |
| 1304 | 400f. Red-cheeked cordon-bleu (air) | 2·75 | 1·60 |
| 1305 | 450f. Lizard buzzard | 3·25 | 2·10 |
| **MS**1306 | 90×70 mm. 500f. Splendid glossy starling | 5·25 | 1·70 |

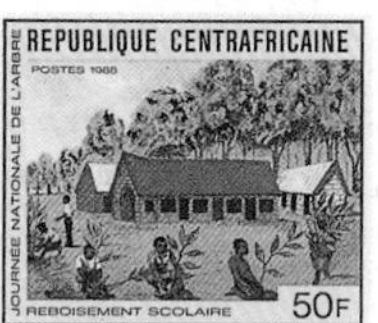

**361** Schools replanting Campaign

**1988.** National Tree Day. Multicoloured.

| | | | |
|---|---|---|---|
| 1307 | 50f. Type **361** | 45 | 25 |
| 1308 | 100f. Type **361** | 95 | 60 |
| 1309 | 130f. Felling tree and planting saplings | 1·50 | 75 |

**362** 1972 100f. Stamp and Beam Exercise

**1988.** Air. Olympic Games, Seoul (3rd issue). Gymnastics. Multicoloured.

| | | | |
|---|---|---|---|
| 1310 | 90f. Type **362** | 95 | 35 |
| 1311 | 200f. 1964 50f. stamp and beam exercise (horiz) | 1·80 | 65 |
| 1312 | 300f. 1964 100f. stamp and vault exercise (horiz) | 2·75 | 1·10 |
| 1313 | 400f. 1964 250f. stamp and parallel bars exercise (horiz) | 3·50 | 1·50 |
| **MS**1314 | 105×85 mm. 500f. 1972 100f. stamp and ring exercise (horiz) | 4·50 | 2·30 |

**363** Running

**1988.** Olympic Games, Seoul (4th issue). Mult.

| | | | |
|---|---|---|---|
| 1315 | 150f. Type **363** (postage) | 1·50 | 25 |
| 1316 | 300f. Judo | 2·75 | 80 |
| 1317 | 400f. Football (air) | 3·00 | 1·00 |
| 1318 | 450f. Tennis | 4·50 | 1·40 |
| **MS**1319 | 70×100 mm. 500f. Boxing (horiz) | 4·50 | 1·50 |

**364** Cross-country Skiing

**1988.** Winter Olympic Games, Calgary (2nd issue). Multicoloured.

| | | | |
|---|---|---|---|
| 1320 | 170f. Type **364** (postage) | 1·50 | 45 |
| 1321 | 350f. Ice hockey | 3·00 | 80 |
| 1322 | 400f. Downhill skiing (air) | 2·75 | 80 |
| 1323 | 450f. Slalom | 3·75 | 1·20 |
| **MS**1324 | 122×85 mm. 500f. Slalom (horiz) | 4·50 | 1·40 |

**1988.** Nos. 1302/5 surch.

| | | | |
|---|---|---|---|
| 1325 | 30f. on 170f. mult (postage) | 40 | 20 |
| 1326 | 70f. on 300f. mult | 1·10 | 65 |
| 1327 | 160f. on 400f. mult (air) | 1·90 | 1·00 |
| 1328 | 200f. on 450f. mult | 2·75 | 1·40 |

**366** Hospital and Grounds

**1988.** 1st Anniv of L'Amitie Hospital. Mult.

| | | | |
|---|---|---|---|
| 1329 | 5f. Type **366** | 45 | 25 |
| 1330 | 60f. Aerial view of hospital complex | 95 | 55 |
| 1331 | 160f. Hospital entrance | 1·50 | 80 |

**367** Buildings Complex

**1988.** 30th Anniv of Republic. Multicoloured.

| | | | |
|---|---|---|---|
| 1332 | 65f. Family on map, flags and dove | 50·00 | |
| 1334 | 240f. Type **367** | 50·00 | |

**368** Kristine Otto (East Germany)

**1989.** Olympic Games, Seoul, Gold Medal Winners. Multicoloured.

| | | | |
|---|---|---|---|
| 1335 | 150f. Type **368** (100 m butterfly and 100 m backstroke) (postage) | 1·80 | 55 |
| 1336 | 240f. Matt Biondi (100 m freestyle) | 2·75 | 80 |
| 1337 | 300f. Florence Griffith-Joyner (U.S.A.) (100 and 200 m sprints) | 3·50 | 90 |
| 1338 | 450f. Pierre Durand (France) (show jumping) (air) | 5·50 | 1·30 |
| **MS**1339 | 98×68 mm. 600f. Carl Lewis (USA) (100m., 200m., long jump relay) | 6·25 | 1·80 |

**369** Hebmuller and Volkswagen Cabriolet, 1953

**1989.** Transport. Multicoloured.

| | | | |
|---|---|---|---|
| 1340 | 20f. Type **369** (postage) | 30 | 10 |
| 1341 | 205f. Werner von Siemens and his first electric locomotive, 1879 | 2·00 | 70 |
| 1342 | 300f. Dennis Conner and "Stars and Stripes" (winner of Americas Cup yacht races) | 2·75 | 80 |
| 1343 | 400f. Andre Citroen and "16 Six" car, 1955 | 3·75 | 1·40 |
| 1344 | 450f. Mare Seguin and Decauville Mallet locomotive, 1895 (air) | 4·00 | 1·40 |
| **MS**1345 | 80×75 mm. 750f. Duesenberg brothers and "J" Phaeton, 1929 (41×29 mm) | 6·75 | 2·10 |

**370** Allegory in Honour of Liberty

**1989.** Bicentenary of French Revolution and "Philexfrance 89" International Stamp Exhibition, Paris (1st issue). Multicoloured.

| | | | |
|---|---|---|---|
| 1346 | 200f. Type **370** | 2·50 | 80 |
| 1347 | 300f. Declaration of Rights of Man | 3·00 | 1·50 |
| **MS**1348 | 113×80 mm. 500f. Demolition of the Bastille (51×40 mm) | 5·00 | 3·25 |

See also Nos. 1366/**MS**1370.

**371** Statue of Liberty at Night

**1989.** Centenary of Statue of Liberty. Mult.

| | | | |
|---|---|---|---|
| 1349 | 150f. Type **371** | 1·50 | 70 |
| 1350 | 150f. Maintenance worker | 1·50 | 70 |
| 1351 | 150f. Close-up of face | 1·50 | 80 |
| 1352 | 200f. Maintenance worker (different) | 1·80 | 1·10 |
| 1353 | 200f. Colour party in front of statue | 1·80 | 1·10 |
| 1354 | 200f. Close-up of head at night | 1·80 | 1·10 |

**373** "Apollo 11" Astronaut on Moon

**1989.** Air. 20th Anniv of First Manned Landing on Moon. Multicoloured.

| | | | |
|---|---|---|---|
| 1355 | 40f. Type **373** | 35 | 20 |
| 1356 | 80f. "Apollo 15" astronaut and moon buggy | 75 | 30 |
| 1357 | 130f. "Apollo 16" module landing in sea | 1·50 | 55 |
| 1358 | 1000f. "Apollo 17" astronaut on Moon | 9·00 | 2·75 |

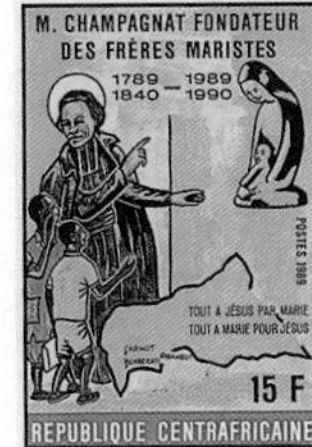


**374** Champagnat, Map and "Madonna and Child"

**1989.** Birth Bicentenary of Marcelino Champagnat (founder of Marist Brothers). Multicoloured.

| | | | |
|---|---|---|---|
| 1359 | 15f. Type **374** | 10 | 10 |
| 1360 | 50f. Champagnat, cross, globe and emblem | 45 | 25 |
| 1361 | 160f. Champagnat and flags (horiz) | 1·60 | 1·20 |

**375** Food Products

**1989.** Bambari Harvest Festival. Multicoloured.

| | | | |
|---|---|---|---|
| 1362 | 100f. Type **375** | 1·00 | 60 |
| 1363 | 160f. Ploughing with oxen | 1·60 | 75 |

**376** Raising of Livestock

**1989.** World Food Day. Multicoloured.

| | | | |
|---|---|---|---|
| 1364 | 60f. Type **376** | 55 | 40 |
| 1365 | 240f. Soldiers catching poachers | 2·40 | 1·20 |

**377** Gen. Kellermann and Battle of Valmy

**1989.** Bicentenary of French Revolution and "Philexfrance 89" International Stamp Exhibition, Paris (2nd issue). Multicoloured.

| | | | |
|---|---|---|---|
| 1366 | 160f. Type **377** (postage) | 1·80 | 40 |
| 1367 | 200f. Gen. Dumouriez and Battle of Jemappes (wrongly inscr "JEMMAPES") | 2·40 | 60 |
| 1368 | 500f. Gen. Pichegru and capture of Dutch fleet (air) | 5·50 | 1·30 |
| 1369 | 600f. Gen. Hoche and Royalist landing at Quiberon | 6·50 | 1·20 |
| **MS**1370 | 160×107 mm. 1000f. Napoleon Bonaparte and Battle of Rivoli (60×50 mm) | 14·50 | 3·75 |

**378** Players and Trophy

**1989.** Victory in 1987 African Basketball Championships, Tunis (1st issue). Multicoloured.

| | | | |
|---|---|---|---|
| 1371 | 160f. Type **378** | 1·50 | 70 |
| 1372 | 240f. National team with medals and trophy (horiz) | 2·00 | 95 |
| 1373 | 500f. Type **378** | 5·00 | 2·10 |

See also Nos. 1383/4.

**379** Governor's Palace, 1906

**1989.** Centenary of Bangui. Multicoloured.

| | | | |
|---|---|---|---|
| 1374 | 100f. Type **379** | 1·00 | 45 |
| 1375 | 160f. Bangui post office | 1·70 | 95 |
| 1376 | 200f. A. Dosilie (founder of Bangui post office) (vert) | 2·10 | 1·00 |
| 1377 | 1000f. Michel Dolisie and Chief Gbembo agreeing peace pact (vert) | 9·75 | 4·50 |

**380** Footballer and Palermo Cathedral Belltower

**1989.** World Cup Football Championship, Italy (1990) (1st issue). Multicoloured.

| | | | |
|---|---|---|---|
| 1378 | 20f. Type **380** (postage) | 15 | 20 |
| 1379 | 160f. Footballer and St. Francis's church, Bologna | 1·50 | 45 |
| 1380 | 200f. Footballer and Old Palace, Florence | 2·00 | 70 |
| 1381 | 120f. Footballer and Church of Trinita dei Monti, Rome (air) | 1·20 | 55 |
| **MS**1382 | 83×84 mm. 1000f. Footballer and Milan cathedral (30×42 mm) | 10·00 | 2·30 |

See also Nos. 1405/8.

**381** Trophy and Map of Africa

**1990.** Victory in 1987 African Basketball Championships, Tunis (2nd issue).

| | | | | |
|---|---|---|---|---|
| 1383 | **381** | 100f. multicoloured | 95 | 45 |
| 1384 | **381** | 130f. multicoloured | 1·30 | 70 |

**382** Tree with Map as Foliage

**1990.** Inauguration (1989) of Forest Conservation Organization.

| | | | | |
|---|---|---|---|---|
| 1385 | **382** | 160f. multicoloured | 1·70 | 70 |

**383** Speed Skating

**1990.** Winter Olympic Games, Albertville (1992). Multicoloured.

| | | | |
|---|---|---|---|
| 1386 | 10f. Type **383** (postage) | 15 | 15 |
| 1387 | 60f. Cross-country skiing | 55 | 40 |
| 1388 | 500f. Slalom skiing (air) | 4·50 | 1·10 |
| 1389 | 750f. Ice dancing | 6·75 | 1·60 |
| **MS**1390 | 105×71 mm. 1000f. Skiing | 8·75 | 2·10 |

**384** "Euphaera eusemoides"

**1990.** Scouts and Butterflies. Multicoloured.

| | | | |
|---|---|---|---|
| 1391 | 25f. Type **384** | 30 | 15 |
| 1392 | 65f. Becker's glider | 55 | 25 |
| 1393 | 160f. "Pseudacraea clarki" | 1·50 | 40 |
| 1394 | 250f. Giant charaxes | 2·40 | 70 |
| 1395 | 300f. "Euphaedra gausape" | 2·75 | 75 |
| 1396 | 500f. Red swallowtail | 4·50 | 1·10 |
| **MS**1397 | 131×103 mm. 1000f. "Euphaedra edwardsi" | 9·50 | 2·20 |

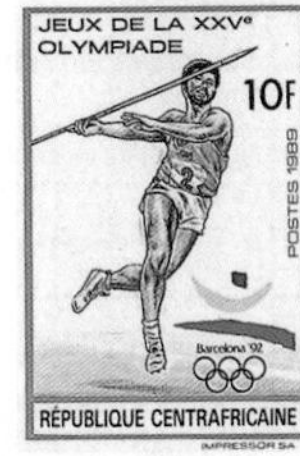


**385** Throwing the Javelin

**1990.** Olympic Games, Barcelona (1992). Mult.

| | | | |
|---|---|---|---|
| 1398 | 10f. Type **385** (postage) | 15 | 15 |
| 1399 | 40f. Running | 40 | 25 |
| 1400 | 130f. Tennis | 1·20 | 40 |
| 1401 | 240f. Hurdling (horiz) | 2·20 | 55 |
| 1402 | 400f. Yachting (horiz) (air) | 3·75 | 1·00 |
| 1403 | 500f. Football (horiz) | 4·75 | 1·30 |
| **MS**1404 | 95×68 mm. 1000f. Boxing (38×27 mm) | 8·75 | 2·10 |

**386** Footballers and Globe

**1990.** Air. World Cup Football Championship, Italy (2nd issue).

| | | | | |
|---|---|---|---|---|
| 1405 | **386** | 5f. multicoloured | 20 | 10 |
| 1406 | - | 30f. multicoloured | 30 | 15 |
| 1407 | - | 500f. multicoloured | 5·00 | 1·10 |
| 1408 | - | 1000f. multicoloured | 8·75 | 2·10 |

DESIGNS: 30 to 1000f. Various footballing scenes.

**387** Pres. Gorbachev of U.S.S.R., Map of Malta and Pres. Bush of U.S.A.

**1990.** Anniversaries and Events. Multicoloured.

| | | | |
|---|---|---|---|
| 1409 | 120f. Type **387** (summit conference, Malta) (postage) | 95 | 25 |
| 1410 | 130f. Sir Rowland Hill and Penny Black (150th anniv of first postage stamps) | 1·20 | 25 |
| 1411 | 160f. Galileo space probe and planet Jupiter | 1·30 | 25 |
| 1412 | 200f. Pres. Gorbachev meeting Pope John Paul II, statue of Saturn and dove | 1·80 | 40 |
| 1413 | 240f. Neil Armstrong and eagle (21st anniv of first manned landing on Moon) | 2·20 | 55 |
| 1414 | 250f. Concorde, German experimental Maglev train and Rotary International emblem | 2·40 | 70 |
| 1415 | 300f. Don Mattingly (baseball player) and New York Yankees club badge (air) | 2·75 | 70 |

| | | | |
|---|---|---|---|
| 1416 | 500f. Charles de Gaulle (French statesman, birth centenary) | 4·75 | 1·10 |
| MS1417 | 82×112 mm. 1000f. Astronauts and rocket (35×50 mm) | 8·75 | 2·10 |

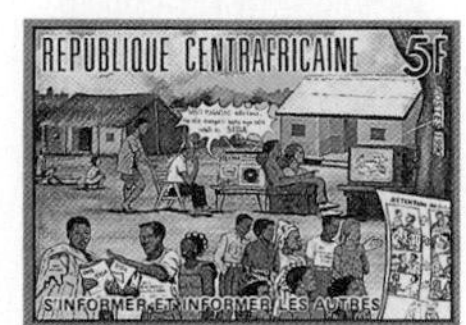

**388** AIDS Information on Radio, Television and Leaflets

**1991.** Anti-AIDS Campaign. Multicoloured.

| | | | |
|---|---|---|---|
| 1418 | 5f. Type **388** | 25 | 10 |
| 1419 | 70f. Type **388** | 1·00 | 50 |
| 1420 | 120f. Lecture on AIDS (vert) | 1·50 | 75 |

**389** Demonstrators

**1991.** Protection of Animals. Multicoloured.

| | | | |
|---|---|---|---|
| 1421 | 15f. Type **389** | 40 | 10 |
| 1422 | 60f. Type **389** | 1·50 | 35 |
| 1423 | 100f. Decrease in elephant population, 1945–2045 (vert) | 2·20 | 50 |

**390** Butter Catfish

**1991.** Fishes. Multicoloured.

| | | | |
|---|---|---|---|
| 1424 | 50f. Type **390** | 85 | 25 |
| 1425 | 160f. Type **390** | 2·00 | 80 |
| 1426 | 240f. Distichodus | 3·00 | 1·40 |

**391** President Kolingba

**1992.** 10th Anniv (1991) of Assumption of Power by Military Committee under Andre Kolingba.

| | | | | |
|---|---|---|---|---|
| 1427 | **391** | 160f. multicoloured | 1·50 | 65 |

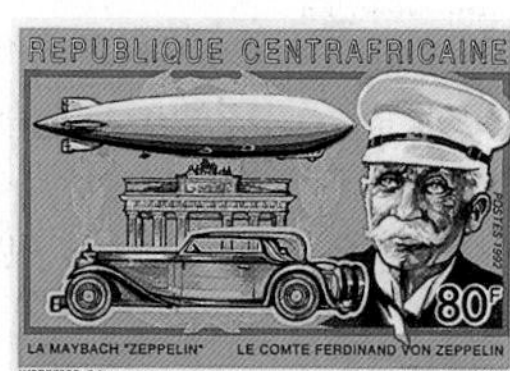

**392** Count Ferdinand von Zeppelin (airship pioneer)

**1992.** Celebrities, Anniversaries and Events. Multicoloured.

| | | | |
|---|---|---|---|
| 1428 | 80f. Type **392** (75th death anniv) (postage) | 80 | 20 |
| 1429 | 140f. Henri Dunant (founder of Red Cross) | 1·50 | 45 |
| 1430 | 160f. Michael Schumacher (racing driver) | 1·80 | 70 |
| 1431 | 350f. Brandenburg Gate (bicent) and Konrad Adenauer (German Federal Republic Chancellor) signing 1949 constitution | 4·25 | 1·20 |
| 1432 | 500f. Pope John Paul II (tour of West Africa) (air) | 5·50 | 1·20 |
| 1433 | 600f. Wolfgang Amadeus Mozart (composer, death bicent (1991)) | 6·50 | 1·40 |
| MS1434 | 81×105 mm. 1000f. Christopher Columbus, "Santa Maria" and 15th-cent view of La Cartuja de las Cuevas (Expo' 92 World's Fair, Seville) | 9·50 | 2·10 |

**393** Dam

**1993.** River M'Bali Dam. Multicoloured.

| | | | |
|---|---|---|---|
| 1435 | 160f. Type **393** | 1·50 | 70 |
| 1436 | 200f. People fishing near dam (self-sufficiency in food) | 2·00 | 90 |

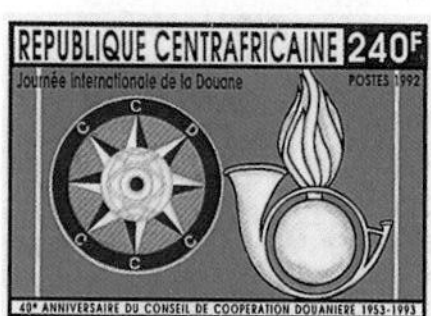

**394** Compass Rose and Organization Emblem

**1993.** International Customs Day and 40th Anniv of Customs Co-operation Council.

| | | | | |
|---|---|---|---|---|
| 1437 | **394** | 240f. multicoloured | 2·30 | 1·40 |

**395** Breastfeeding

**1993.** International Nutrition Conference, Rome (1992). Multicoloured.

| | | | |
|---|---|---|---|
| 1438 | 90f. Type **395** | 75 | 40 |
| 1439 | 140f. Foodstuffs | 1·30 | 70 |

**396** Bangui University

**1993**

| | | | | |
|---|---|---|---|---|
| 1440 | **396** | 100f. multicoloured | 95 | 40 |

**397** Masako Owada as Baby

**1993.** Wedding of Crown Prince Naruhito of Japan and Masako Owada. Multicoloured.

| | | | |
|---|---|---|---|
| 1441 | 50f. Type **397** (postage) | 40 | 25 |
| 1442 | 65f. Prince Naruhito as child with parents | 60 | 25 |
| 1443 | 160f. Masako Owada at Harvard University, U.S.A. | 1·60 | 55 |
| 1444 | 450f. Prince Naruhito at Oxford University (air) | 4·25 | 1·20 |
| MS1445 | 184×83 mm. 750f. Prince Naruhito and Masako Owada | 6·75 | 1·80 |

**398** Presley singing "Heartbreak Hotel" (1956)

**1993.** 16th Death Anniv of Elvis Presley (entertainer). Multicoloured.

| | | | |
|---|---|---|---|
| 1446 | 200f. Type **398** | 2·10 | 55 |
| 1447 | 300f. "Love Me Tender", 1957 | 3·00 | 80 |
| 1448 | 400f. "Jailhouse Rock", 1957 | 3·75 | 1·40 |
| 1449 | 600f. "Harum Scarum", 1965 (air) | 5·50 | 1·40 |
| MS1450 | 98×69 mm. 1000f. Elvis performing (35×50 mm) | 8·75 | 2·30 |

**399** First World Cup Final, 1928, and Uruguay v. Argentina, 1930

**1993.** World Cup Football Championship, U.S.A. (1994). History of the World Cup. Multicoloured.

| | | | |
|---|---|---|---|
| 1451 | 40f. Type **399** | 35 | 10 |
| 1452 | 50f. Italy v. Czechoslovakia, 1934, and Italy v. Hungary, 1938 | 45 | 10 |
| 1453 | 60f. Uruguay v. Brazil, 1950, and Germany v. Hungary, 1954 | 55 | 25 |
| 1454 | 80f. Brazil v. Sweden, 1958, and Brazil v. Czechoslovakia, 1962 | 75 | 25 |
| 1455 | 160f. England v. West Germany, 1966, and Brazil v. Italy, 1970 | 1·50 | 25 |
| 1456 | 200f. West Germany v. The Netherlands, 1974, and Argentina v. The Netherlands, 1978 | 1·80 | 40 |
| 1457 | 400f. Italy v. West Germany, 1982, and Argentina v. West Germany, 1986 | 3·50 | 70 |
| 1458 | 500f. West Germany v. Argentina, 1990, and 1994 Championship emblem and player | 4·50 | 1·20 |
| MS1459 | 101×85 mm. 1000f. West Germany and Argentina teams (59×29 mm) | 8·75 | 2·10 |

**400** Baron Pierre de Coubertin (founder of modern games)

**1993.** Centenary (1996) of Modern Olympic Games. Multicoloured.

| | | | |
|---|---|---|---|
| 1460 | 90f. Ancient Greek athlete | 75 | 30 |
| 1461 | 90f. Type **400** | 75 | 30 |
| 1462 | 90f. Charles Bennett (running), Paris, 1900 | 75 | 30 |
| 1463 | 90f. Etienne Desmarteau (stone throwing), St. Louis, 1904 | 75 | 30 |
| 1464 | 90f. Harry Porter (high jump), London, 1908 | 75 | 30 |
| 1465 | 90f. Patrick MacDonald (putting the shot), Stockholm, 1912 | 75 | 30 |
| 1466 | 90f. Coloured and black Olympic rings (1916) | 75 | 30 |
| 1467 | 90f. Frank Loomis (400 m hurdles), Antwerp, 1920 | 75 | 30 |
| 1468 | 90f. Albert White (diving), Paris, 1924 | 95 | 35 |
| 1469 | 100f. El Ouafi (marathon), Amsterdam, 1928 | 95 | 35 |
| 1470 | 100f. Eddie Tolan (100 m), Los Angeles, 1932 | 95 | 35 |
| 1471 | 100f. Jesse Owens (100 m, long jump and 200 m hurdles), Berlin, 1936 | 95 | 35 |
| 1472 | 100f. Coloured and black Olympic rings (1940) | 95 | 35 |
| 1473 | 100f. Coloured and black Olympic rings (1944) | 95 | 35 |
| 1474 | 100f. Tapio Rautavaara (throwing the javelin), London, 1948 | 95 | 35 |
| 1475 | 100f. Jean Boiteux (400 m freestyle swimming), Helsinki, 1952 | 95 | 35 |
| 1476 | 100f. Petrus Kasterman (three-day equestrian event), Melbourne, 1956 | 95 | 35 |
| 1477 | 100f. Sante Gaiardoni (cycling), Rome, 1960 | 95 | 35 |
| 1478 | 160f. Anton Geesink (judo), Tokyo, 1964 | 1·50 | 45 |
| 1479 | 160f. Bob Beamon (long jump), Mexico, 1968 | 1·50 | 45 |
| 1480 | 160f. Mark Spitz (swimming), Munich, 1972 | 1·50 | 45 |
| 1481 | 160f. Nadia Comaneci (gymnastics (beam)), Montreal, 1976 | 1·50 | 45 |
| 1482 | 160f. Aleksandre Ditjatin (gymnastics (rings) and dressage), Moscow, 1980 | 1·50 | 45 |
| 1483 | 160f. J. F. Lamour (sabre), Los Angeles, 1984 | 1·50 | 45 |
| 1484 | 160f. Pierre Durand (show jumping), Seoul, 1988 | 1·50 | 45 |
| 1485 | 160f. Michael Jordan (basketball), Barcelona, 1992 | 1·50 | 45 |
| 1486 | 160f. Footballer and Games emblem, Atlanta, 1996 | 1·50 | 45 |

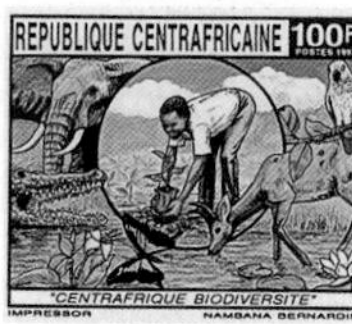

**401** Man planting Sapling, and Animals

**1993.** Biodiversity. Multicoloured.

| | | | |
|---|---|---|---|
| 1487 | 100f. Type **401** | 1·50 | 70 |
| 1488 | 130f. Man amongst flora and fauna (vert) | 2·10 | 90 |

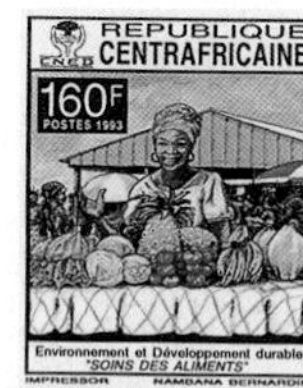

**402** Woman selling Foodstuffs

**1993.** The Environment and Sustainable Development. Multicoloured.

| | | | |
|---|---|---|---|
| 1489 | 160f. Type **402** | 1·50 | 70 |
| 1490 | 240f. Woman tending cooking pot | 2·50 | 1·40 |

**403** Saltoposuchus

**1993.** Prehistoric Animals. Multicoloured.

| | | | |
|---|---|---|---|
| 1491 | 25f. Type **403** | 35 | 10 |
| 1492 | 25f. Rhamphorhynchus | 35 | 10 |
| 1493 | 25f. Dimorphodon | 35 | 10 |
| 1494 | 25f. Archaeopteryx | 35 | 10 |
| 1495 | 30f. "Compsognathos longipes" | 35 | 10 |
| 1496 | 30f. "Cryptocleidus oxoniensis" | 35 | 10 |
| 1497 | 30f. Stegosaurus | 35 | 10 |
| 1498 | 30f. Cetiosaurus | 35 | 10 |
| 1499 | 50f. Brontosaurus | 45 | 20 |
| 1500 | 50f. "Corythosaurus casuarius" | 45 | 20 |
| 1501 | 50f. Styracosaurus | 45 | 20 |
| 1502 | 50f. Gorgosaurus | 45 | 20 |
| 1503 | 500f. Scolosaurus | 4·75 | 1·00 |
| 1504 | 500f. Trachodon | 4·75 | 1·00 |
| 1505 | 500f. Struthiomimus | 4·75 | 1·00 |
| 1506 | 500f. "Tarbosaurus bataar" | 4·75 | 1·00 |
| MS1507 | 120×170 mm. 1000f. Tylosaur (50×59 mm) (air) | 10·00 | 2·30 |

Nos. 1491/1506 were issued together, se-tenant, forming a composite design of a volcanic landscape.

**404** Th. Haug (combined skiing, Chamonix, 1924)

**1994.** Winter Olympic Games, Lillehammer, Norway. Previous Medal Winners. Multicoloured.

| | | | |
|---|---|---|---|
| 1508 | 100f. Type **404** | 1·00 | 25 |
| 1509 | 100f. J. Heaton (luge, St. Moritz, 1928) | 1·00 | 25 |
| 1510 | 100f. B. Ruud (ski jumping, Lake Placid, 1932) | 1·00 | 25 |
| 1511 | 100f. I. Ballangrud (speed skating, Garmisch-Partenkirchen, 1936) | 1·00 | 25 |
| 1512 | 100f. G. Fraser (slalom, St. Moritz, 1948) | 1·00 | 25 |
| 1513 | 100f. West German 4-man bob-sleigh team (Oslo, 1952) | 1·00 | 25 |
| 1514 | 100f. U.S.S.R. ice hockey team (Cortina d'Ampezzo, 1956) | 1·00 | 25 |
| 1515 | 100f. J. Vuarnet (downhill skiing, Squaw Valley, 1960) | 1·00 | 25 |
| 1516 | 200f. M. Goitschel (giant slalom, Innsbruck, 1964) | 1·70 | 45 |
| 1517 | 200f. Jean-Claud Killy (special slalom, Grenoble, 1968) | 1·70 | 45 |
| 1518 | 200f. U. Wehling (cross- country skiing, Sapporo, 1972) | 1·70 | 45 |
| 1519 | 200f. Irina Rodnina and Aleksandr Zaitsev (figure skating, Innsbruck, 1976) | 1·70 | 45 |
| 1520 | 200f. E. Heiden (speed skating, Lake Placid, 1980) | 1·70 | 45 |
| 1521 | 200f. Katarina Witt (figure skating, Sarajevo, 1984) | 1·70 | 45 |
| 1522 | 200f. J. Mueller (single luge, Calgary, 1988) | 1·70 | 45 |
| 1523 | 200f. E. Grospiron (acrobatic skiing, Albertville, 1992) | 1·70 | 45 |
| 1524 | 200f. Speed skiing, Lillehammer, 1994 | 1·70 | 45 |

**405** "Ansellia africa"

**1994.** Flowers, Vegetables, Fruit and Fungi. Multicoloured.

| | | | |
|---|---|---|---|
| 1525 | 25f. Type **405** | 10 | 10 |
| 1526 | 30f. Yams | 30 | 10 |
| 1527 | 40f. Oranges | 30 | 10 |
| 1528 | 50f. Termite mushroom | 40 | 10 |
| 1529 | 60f. "Polystachia bella" (flower) | 45 | 10 |
| 1530 | 65f. Manioc | 55 | 10 |
| 1531 | 70f. Banana | 55 | 10 |
| 1532 | 80f. "Synpodia arborescens" (wrongly inscr "Sympodia") (fungi) | 75 | 10 |
| 1533 | 90f. "Aerangis rhodosticta" (flower) | 75 | 10 |
| 1534 | 100f. Maize | 85 | 10 |
| 1535 | 160f. Mango | 1·40 | 25 |
| 1536 | 200f. "Phlebopus sudanicus" (fungi) | 1·70 | 25 |
| 1537 | 300f. Coffee beans | 2·75 | 45 |
| 1538 | 400f. Sweet potato | 3·75 | 55 |
| 1539 | 500f. "Angraecum eburneum" (flower) | 4·50 | 75 |
| 1540 | 600f. "Leucocoprinus africanus" (fungi) | 5·25 | 90 |

Nos. 1525/40 were issued together, se-tenant, the backgrounds forming a composite design.

### MILITARY FRANK STAMPS

**1963.** Optd FM. No. M1 also has the value obliterated with two bars. Centre multicoloured; frame colour given.

| | | | |
|---|---|---|---|
| M35 | **1** | (-) on 15f. blue | 14·50 |
| M36 | **1** | 15f. blue | 15·00 |

### OFFICIAL STAMPS

**O41** Arms

**1965**

| | | | | |
|---|---|---|---|---|
| O78 | **O41** | 1f. multicoloured | 10 | 10 |
| O79 | **O41** | 2f. multicoloured | 10 | 10 |
| O80 | **O41** | 5f. multicoloured | 10 | 10 |
| O81 | **O41** | 10f. multicoloured | 30 | 10 |
| O82 | **O41** | 20f. multicoloured | 50 | 25 |
| O83 | **O41** | 30f. multicoloured | 90 | 55 |
| O84 | **O41** | 50f. multicoloured | 1·00 | 80 |
| O85 | **O41** | 100f. multicoloured | 2·50 | 1·20 |
| O86 | **O41** | 130f. multicoloured | 4·00 | 2·30 |
| O87 | **O41** | 200f. multicoloured | 6·00 | 3·00 |

**O109** Arms

**1971**

| | | | | |
|---|---|---|---|---|
| O238 | **O109** | 5f. multicoloured | 10 | 10 |
| O239 | **O109** | 30f. multicoloured | 50 | 25 |
| O240 | **O109** | 40f. multicoloured | 85 | 25 |
| O241 | **O109** | 100f. multicoloured | 1·50 | 55 |
| O242 | **O109** | 140f. multicoloured | 2·20 | 80 |
| O243 | **O109** | 200f. multicoloured | 3·50 | 1·40 |

### POSTAGE DUE STAMPS

**D15** "Sternotomis gama" (Beetle)

**1962.** Beetles.

| | | | |
|---|---|---|---|
| D33 | 50c. brown and turquoise | 10 | 10 |
| D34 | 50c. turquoise and brown | 10 | 10 |
| D35 | 1f. brown and green | 20 | 20 |
| D36 | 1f. green and brown | 20 | 20 |
| D37 | 2f. pink and black | 25 | 25 |
| D38 | 2f. green, black and pink | 25 | 25 |
| D39 | 5f. green and brown | 45 | 40 |
| D40 | 5f. green and brown | 45 | 40 |
| D41 | 10f. green, black and drab | 75 | 75 |
| D42 | 10f. drab, black and green | 75 | 75 |
| D43 | 25f. brown, black and green | 2·00 | 1·90 |
| D44 | 25f. brown, green and black | 2·00 | 1·90 |

DESIGNS: No. D33, Type D **15**; D34, "Sternotomis virescens"; D35, "Augosoma centaurus"; D36, "Phosphorus virescens" and "Ceroplesis carabarica"; D37, "Ceroplesis S.P."; D38, "Cetoine scaraboidae"; D39, "Cetoine scaraboidae"; D40, "Macrorhina S.P."; D41, "Taurina longiceps"; D42, "Phryneta leprosa"; D43, "Monohamus griseoplagiatus"; D44, "Jambonus trifasciatus".

**D308** Giant Pangolin ("Manis gigantea")

**1985**

| | | | | |
|---|---|---|---|---|
| D1080 | **D308** | 5f. multicoloured | 40 | 35 |
| D1081 | **D308** | 20f. multicoloured | 70 | 70 |
| D1082 | **D308** | 30f. multicoloured | 80 | 80 |

### APPENDIX

The following stamps have either been issued in excess of postal needs or have not been availble to the public in reasonable quantities at face value. Such stamps may later be given full listing if there is evidence of regular postal use.

All the stamps listed below are embossed on gold foil.

**1977**

Coronation of Emperor Bokassa. Air 2500f.

**1978**

100 Years of Progress in Posts and Telecommunications. Air 1500f.
Death Centenary of Sir Rowland Hill. Air 1500f.

**1979**

International Year of the Child. Air 1500f.
Olympic Games, Moscow. Air 1500f. ("The Discus-thrower")
Space Exploration. Air 1500f.

**1980**

Olympic Games, Moscow. Air 1500f. (Relay)
European-African Co-operation. Air 1500f.
World Cup Football Championship, Spain. Air 1500f.

**1981**

Olympic Games Medal Winners. 1980 Olympic Games issue optd. Air 1500f.
Birth Centenary of Pablo Picasso. Air 1500f.
Wedding of Prince of Wales. Air 1500f.
Navigators. Air 1500f.
Christmas. Air 1500f.

**1982**

Animals and Rotary International. Air 1500f.
Transport. Air 1500f.
21st Birthday of Princess of Wales. Air 1500f.
Olympic Games, Los Angeles.Air 1500f. (horiz)
Space Resources. Air 1500f.

**1983**

Chess Masters. Air 1500f.
World Cup Football Championship, Spain. Air 1500f.
Car Manufacturers. Air 1500f.
Olympic Games, Los Angeles. Air 1500f. (vert)
Bicentenary of manned flight. Air 1500f.

**1984**

Winter Olympic Gold Medalists. Air 1500f.
Celebrities. Air 1500f.

**1985**

85th Birthday of Queen Elizabeth the Queen Mother. Air 1500f.
Appearence of Halley's Comet. Air 1500f.
480th Death Anniv of Christopher Columbus. Air 1500f.

**1988**

Olympic Games, Seoul. Air 1500f.
Scouts and Birds. Air 1500f.

**1989**

Olympic Games, Seoul, Gold Medal Winner. Air 1500f.
Bicentenary of French Revolution. Air 1500f.
World Cup Football Championship, Italy. Air 1500f.

**1990**

Winter Olympic Games, Albertville (1992). Air 1500f.
Scouts and Butterflies. Air 1500f.
Birth Centenary of Charles de Gaulle. Air 1500f.

**1993**

Wedding of Crown Prince Naruhito of Japan and Masako Owada. Air 1500f.
16th Death Anniv of Elvis Presley. Air 1500f.
World Cup Football Championship, U.S.A. (1994). Air 1500f.
Visit of Pope John Paul II to Africa. Air 1500f.

**1994**

Winter Olympic Games, Lillehammer. Air 1500f.

Pt. 10

# CENTRAL LITHUANIA

Became temporarily independent in 1918 and was subsequently absorbed by Poland.

100 fenigi = 1 mark.

### POLISH OCCUPATION

**1**

**1920.** Imperf or perf.

| | | | | |
|---|---|---|---|---|
| 1 | **1** | 25f. red | 10 | 10 |
| 20 | **1** | 25f. green | 20 | 30 |
| 2 | **1** | 1m. blue | 10 | 10 |
| 21 | **1** | 1m. brown | 20 | 30 |
| 3 | **1** | 2m. violet | 15 | 15 |
| 22 | **1** | 2m. yellow | 20 | 30 |

**1920.** Stamps of Lithuania of 1919 surch SRODKOWA LITWA POCZTA, new value and Arms of Poland and Lithuania. Perf.

| | | | | |
|---|---|---|---|---|
| 4 | **5** | 2m. on 15s. violet | 6·50 | 8·00 |
| 5 | **5** | 4m. on 10s. red | 4·00 | 5·00 |
| 6 | **5** | 4m. on 20s. blue | 6·00 | 8·00 |
| 7 | **5** | 4m. on 30s. orange | 5·00 | 6·00 |
| 8 | **6** | 6m. on 50s. green | 6·00 | 7·00 |
| 9 | **6** | 6m. on 60s. red and violet | 6·00 | 8·00 |
| 10 | **6** | 6m. on 75s. red & yellow | 6·00 | 8·00 |
| 11 | **7** | 10m. on 1a. red & grey | 12·00 | 14·00 |
| 12 | **7** | 10m. on 3a. red & brown | £450 | £550 |
| 13 | **7** | 10m. on 5a. red and green | £450 | £550 |

**3** Girl

**1920.** Imperf or perf. Inscr "LITWA SRODKOWA".

| | | | | |
|---|---|---|---|---|
| 14 | **3** | 25f. grey | 15 | 15 |
| 15 | - | 1m. orange | 20 | 15 |
| 16 | - | 2m. red | 40 | 50 |
| 17 | - | 4m. olive and yellow | 60 | 75 |
| 18 | - | 6m. grey and red | 1·00 | 1·25 |
| 19 | - | 10m. yellow and brown | 1·50 | 2·00 |

DESIGNS: 1m. Warrior; 2m. Ostrabrama Gate, Vilnius; 4m. St. Stanislaus Cathedral and Tower, Vilnius; 6m. Rector's insignia; 10m. Gen. Zeligowski.

**1921.** Fund for Polish Participation in Plebiscite for Upper Silesia. Surch NA SLASK and new value. Imperf or perf.

| | | | | |
|---|---|---|---|---|
| 23 | **1** | 25f.+2m. red | 50 | 60 |
| 24 | **1** | 25f.+2m. green | 50 | 60 |
| 25 | **1** | 1m.+2m. blue | 60 | 80 |
| 26 | **1** | 1m.+2m. brown | 60 | 80 |
| 27 | **1** | 2m.+2m. violet | 70 | 1·10 |
| 28 | **1** | 2m.+2m. yellow | 70 | 1·10 |

**1921.** Red Cross Fund. Nos. 16/17 surch with cross and value. Imperf or perf.

| | | | |
|---|---|---|---|
| 29 | 2m.+1m. red | 50 | 65 |
| 30 | 4m.+1m. green and yellow | 50 | 65 |

**1921.** White Cross Fund. As Nos. 16, 17 and 19, but with cross and value in white added. Imperf or perf.

| | | | |
|---|---|---|---|
| 31 | 2m.+1m. purple | 30 | 30 |
| 32 | 4m.+1m. green and buff | 30 | 30 |
| 33 | 10m.+2m. yellow and brown | 30 | 30 |

**13** St. Nicholas Cathedral

**14** St. Stanislaus Cathedral

**1921.** Imperf or perf.

| | | | | |
|---|---|---|---|---|
| 34 | **13** | 1m. yellow and slate | 30 | 40 |
| 35 | **14** | 2m. green and red | 30 | 40 |
| 36 | - | 3m. green | 40 | 50 |
| 37 | - | 4m. brown | 40 | 60 |
| 38 | - | 5m. brown | 40 | 60 |
| 39 | - | 6m. buff and green | 40 | 60 |
| 40 | - | 10m. buff and purple | 60 | 80 |
| 41 | - | 20m. buff and brown | 60 | 90 |

DESIGNS—HORIZ: 4m. Queen Jadwiga and King Wladislaw Jagiello; 6m. Poczobut Observatory, Vilnius University; 10m. Union of Lithuania and Poland, 1569; 20m. Kosciuszko and Mickiewicz. VERT: 3m. Arms (Eagle); 5m. Arms (Shield).

**21** Entry into Vilnius

**22** General Zeligowski

**1921.** Ist Anniv of Entry of Gen. Zeligowski into Vilnius. Imperf or perf.

| | | | | |
|---|---|---|---|---|
| 42 | **21** | 100m. blue and bistre | 1·75 | 1·75 |
| 43 | **22** | 150m. green and brown | 2·25 | 2·25 |

**24** Arms

**1922.** Opening of National Parliament. Inscr "SEJM—WILNIE". Imperf or perf.

| | | | | |
|---|---|---|---|---|
| 44 | - | 10m. brown | 1·50 | 1·75 |
| 45 | **24** | 25m. red and buff | 1·75 | 1·90 |
| 46 | - | 50m. blue | 2·75 | 3·00 |
| 47 | - | 75m. lilac | 4·00 | 4·50 |

DESIGNS—HORIZ: 50m. National Assembly, Vilnius. VERT: 10m. Agriculture; 75m. Industry.

### POSTAGE DUE STAMPS

D9 Government Offices

**1921.** Inscr "DOPLATA". Imperf or perf.

| | | | | |
|---|---|---|---|---|
| D23 | D9 | 50f. red | 50 | 60 |
| D24 | - | 1m. green | 50 | 60 |
| D25 | - | 2m. purple | 50 | 60 |
| D26 | - | 3m. purple | 75 | 90 |
| D27 | - | 5m. purple | 75 | 90 |
| D28 | - | 20m. red | 1·00 | 1·25 |

DESIGNS—HORIZ: 2m. Castle on Troki Island. VERT: 1m. Castle Hill, Vilnius; 3m. Ostrabrama Gate, Vilnius; 5m. St. Stanislaus Cathedral; 20m. (larger) St. Nicholas Cathedral.

Pt. 1

# CEYLON

An island to the south of India formerly under British administration, then a self-governing Dominion. The island became a Republic within the Commonwealth on 22 May 1972 and was renamed Sri Lanka (q.v.).

1857. 12 pence = 1 shilling; 20 shillings = 1 pound.
1872. 100 cents = 1 rupee.

1 2 4

**1857.** Imperf.

| | | | | |
|---|---|---|---|---|
| 17 | 4 | ½d. lilac | £180 | £225 |
| 2 | 1 | 1d. blue | £1100 | 45·00 |
| 3 | 1 | 2d. green | £200 | 65·00 |
| 4 | 2 | 4d. red | £70000 | £4500 |
| 5 | 1 | 5d. brown | £1600 | £150 |
| 6 | 1 | 6d. brown | £2750 | £140 |
| 7 | 2 | 8d. brown | £28000 | £1500 |
| 8 | 2 | 9d. brown | £60000 | £900 |
| 9 | 1 | 10d. orange | £900 | £325 |
| 10 | 1 | 1s. violet | £5500 | £200 |
| 11 | 2 | 1s.9d. green | £800 | £800 |
| 12 | 2 | 2s. blue | £6500 | £1300 |

The prices of these imperf stamps vary greatly according to condition. The above prices are for fine copies with four margins. Poor to medium specimens are worth much less.

**1861.** Perf.

| | | | | |
|---|---|---|---|---|
| 48c | 4 | ½d. lilac | 48·00 | 48·00 |
| 49 | 1 | 1d. blue | £160 | 8·00 |
| 50 | 1 | 2d. green | 95·00 | 14·00 |
| 64b | 1 | 2d. yellow | 85·00 | 9·00 |
| 65b | 2 | 4d. red | 80·00 | 20·00 |
| 22 | 1 | 5d. brown | £110 | 8·00 |
| 66c | 1 | 5d. green | 50·00 | 50·00 |
| 67b | 1 | 6d. brown | £150 | 8·50 |
| 56 | 2 | 8d. brown | £130 | 60·00 |
| 69b | 2 | 9d. brown | 65·00 | 6·00 |
| 70b | 1 | 10d. orange | 80·00 | 17·00 |
| 71b | 1 | 1s. violet | £130 | 10·00 |
| 72b | 2 | 2s. blue | £150 | 14·00 |

8

**1866.** The 3d. has portrait in circle.

| | | | | |
|---|---|---|---|---|
| 61 | 8 | 1d. blue | 25·00 | 11·00 |
| 62 | - | 3d. red | 90·00 | 50·00 |

9

10

30

**1872.** Various frames.

| | | | | |
|---|---|---|---|---|
| 147 | 9 | 2c. green | 2·50 | 15 |
| 256 | 9 | 2c. brown | 4·50 | 30 |
| 122 | 10 | 4c. grey | 42·00 | 1·50 |
| 148 | 10 | 4c. purple | 5·00 | 30 |
| 149 | 10 | 4c. red | 6·00 | 13·00 |
| 258 | 10 | 4c. yellow | 3·50 | 3·50 |
| 150a | - | 8c. yellow | 4·50 | 10·00 |
| 126 | - | 16c. violet | £120 | 2·75 |
| 127 | - | 24c. green | 70·00 | 2·00 |
| 128 | - | 32c. grey | £170 | 15·00 |
| 129 | - | 36c. blue | £190 | 27·00 |
| 130 | - | 48c. red | 90·00 | 9·00 |
| 131 | - | 64c. brown | £300 | 75·00 |
| 132 | - | 96c. grey | £275 | 28·00 |
| 201 | 30 | 1r.12 red | 29·00 | 29·00 |
| 138 | 30 | 2r.50 red | £750 | £400 |
| 249 | 30 | 2r.50 purple on red | 35·00 | 55·00 |

**1882.** Nos. 127 and 131 surch in words and figures.

| | | | | |
|---|---|---|---|---|
| 142 | 30 | 16c. on 24c. green | 35·00 | 8·50 |
| 143 | 30 | 20c. on 64c. brown | 12·00 | 8·50 |

**1885.** As Nos. 148/132 surch Postage & Revenue and value in words.

| | | | |
|---|---|---|---|
| 178 | 5c. on 4c. red | 25·00 | 4·75 |
| 179 | 5c. on 8c. yellow | 85·00 | 11·00 |
| 180 | 5c. on 16c. violet | £150 | 16·00 |
| 154 | 5c. on 24c. green | £5000 | £110 |
| 182 | 5c. on 24c. purple | | £500 |
| 155 | 5c. on 32c. grey | 65·00 | 15·00 |
| 156 | 5c. on 36c. blue | £300 | 13·00 |
| 157 | 5c. on 48c. red | £2000 | 60·00 |
| 158 | 5c. on 64c. brown | £130 | 11·00 |
| 159 | 5c. on 96c. grey | £550 | 70·00 |

**1885.** As Nos. 126/249 surch with new value in words.

| | | | |
|---|---|---|---|
| 184 | 10c. on 16c. violet | £11000 | £1700 |
| 162 | 10c. on 24c. green | £500 | £120 |
| 185 | 10c. on 24c. purple | 16·00 | 9·00 |
| 163 | 10c. on 36c. blue | £425 | £225 |
| 174 | 10c. on 64c. brown | 85·00 | £150 |
| 186 | 15c. on 16c. violet | 14·00 | 11·00 |
| 165 | 20c. on 24c. green | 75·00 | 24·00 |
| 166 | 20c. on 32c. grey | 80·00 | 60·00 |
| 167 | 25c. on 32c. grey | 23·00 | 6·50 |
| 168 | 28c. on 48c. red | 40·00 | 9·50 |
| 169x | 30c. on 36c. blue | 15·00 | 10·00 |
| 170 | 56c. on 96c. grey | 30·00 | 25·00 |
| 176 | 1r.12 on 2r.50 red | £110 | 45·00 |

**1885.** Surch REVENUE AND POSTAGE 5 CENTS.

| | | | |
|---|---|---|---|
| 187 | 5c. on 8c. lilac (as No. 150a) | 25·00 | 1·50 |

**1885.** As Nos. 126/32 surch in words and figures.

| | | | |
|---|---|---|---|
| 188 | 10c. on 24c. purple | 12·00 | 8·50 |
| 189 | 15c. on 16c. yellow | 60·00 | 15·00 |
| 190 | 28c. on 32c. grey | 27·00 | 2·50 |
| 191 | 30c. on 36c. olive | 29·00 | 15·00 |
| 192 | 56c. on 96c. grey | 50·00 | 17·00 |

**1885.** Surch 1 R. 12 C.

| | | | |
|---|---|---|---|
| 193 | 1r.12 on 2r.50 red | 60·00 | £130 |

28

39

43

**1886**

| | | | | |
|---|---|---|---|---|
| 245 | 39 | 3c. brown and green | 5·50 | 45 |
| 257 | 39 | 3c. green | 4·50 | 55 |
| 195 | 28 | 5c. purple | 3·50 | 10 |
| 259 | 39 | 6c. red and black | 2·50 | 45 |
| 260 | 39 | 12c. olive and red | 4·50 | 8·50 |
| 196 | 39 | 15c. olive | 8·50 | 2·25 |
| 261 | 39 | 15c. blue | 7·50 | 1·25 |
| 198 | 39 | 25c. brown | 5·50 | 1·75 |
| 199 | 39 | 28c. grey | 24·00 | 1·40 |
| 247 | 39 | 30c. mauve and brown | 4·50 | 3·25 |
| 262 | 39 | 75c. black and brown | 9·00 | 9·00 |
| 263 | 43 | 1r.50 red | 32·00 | 50·00 |
| 264 | 43 | 2r.25 blue | 35·00 | 50·00 |

**1887.** Nos. 148/9 surch. A. Surch TWO CENTS.

| | | | | |
|---|---|---|---|---|
| 202 | 10 | 2c. on 4c. purple | 1·40 | 80 |
| 203 | 10 | 2c. on 4c. red | 2·50 | 30 |

B. Surch TWO.

| | | | |
|---|---|---|---|
| 204 | 2c. on 4c. purple | 1·00 | 30 |
| 205 | 2c. on 4c. red | 7·50 | 20 |

C. Surch 2 Cents and bar.

| | | | |
|---|---|---|---|
| 206 | 2c. on 4c. purple | 75·00 | 32·00 |
| 207 | 2c. on 4c. red | 3·75 | 75 |

D. Surch Two Cents and bar.

| | | | |
|---|---|---|---|
| 208 | 2c. on 4c. purple | 65·00 | 28·00 |
| 209 | 2c. on 4c. red | 2·50 | 1·10 |

E. Surch 2 Cents without bar.

| | | | |
|---|---|---|---|
| 210 | 2c. on 4c. purple | 65·00 | 35·00 |
| 211 | 2c. on 4c. red | 13·00 | 1·00 |

**1890.** Surch POSTAGE Five Cents REVENUE.

| | | | | |
|---|---|---|---|---|
| 233 | 39 | 5c. on 15c. olive | 3·75 | 2·50 |

**1891.** Surch FIFTEEN CENTS.

| | | | |
|---|---|---|---|
| 239 | 15c. on 25c. brown | 18·00 | 17·00 |
| 240 | 15c. on 28c. grey | 19·00 | 9·00 |

**1892.** Surch 3 Cents and bar.

| | | | | |
|---|---|---|---|---|
| 241 | 10 | 3c. on 4c. purple | 1·00 | 3·25 |
| 242 | 10 | 3c. on 4c. red | 7·00 | 10·00 |
| 243 | 39 | 3c. on 28c. grey | 6·00 | 5·50 |

**1898.** Surch Six Cents.

| | | | |
|---|---|---|---|
| 250 | 6c. on 15c. green | 1·25 | 75 |

**1898.** Surch with new value.

| | | | | |
|---|---|---|---|---|
| 254 | 30 | 1r.50 on 2r.50 grey | 20·00 | 50·00 |
| 255 | 30 | 2r.25 on 2r.50 yellow | 45·00 | 80·00 |

44

45

**1903.** Various frames.

| | | | | |
|---|---|---|---|---|
| 277 | 44 | 2c. brown | 1·50 | 10 |
| 278 | 45 | 3c. green (A) | 1·50 | 15 |
| 293 | 45 | 3c. green (B) | 1·00 | 75 |
| 279 | 45 | 4c. orange and blue | 2·50 | 1·50 |
| 268 | - | 5c. purple | 2·00 | 60 |
| 289 | - | 5c. purple | 5·00 | 10 |
| 281 | - | 6c. red | 3·75 | 15 |
| 291 | - | 6c. red | 1·75 | 10 |
| 294 | 45 | 10c. olive and red | 2·50 | 3·25 |
| 282 | 45 | 12c. olive and red | 1·50 | 1·75 |
| 283 | 45 | 15c. blue | 3·00 | 60 |
| 284 | 45 | 25c. brown | 6·00 | 3·75 |
| 295 | 45 | 25c. grey | 2·50 | 2·75 |
| 285 | 45 | 30c. violet and green | 2·50 | 3·00 |
| 296 | 45 | 50c. brown | 4·00 | 7·50 |
| 286 | 45 | 75c. blue and orange | 5·25 | 8·00 |
| 297 | 45 | 1r. purple on yellow | 8·00 | 11·00 |
| 287 | 45 | 1r.50 grey | 28·00 | 11·00 |
| 298 | 45 | 2r. red on yellow | 15·00 | 28·00 |
| 288 | 45 | 2r.25 brown and green | 22·00 | 30·00 |
| 299 | 45 | 5r. black on green | 40·00 | 80·00 |
| 300 | 45 | 10r. black on red | £110 | £225 |

(A) has value in shaded tablet; (B) in white tablet as in Type **45**.

Nos. 268 and 281 have the value in words; Nos. 289 and 291 in figures.

52

**1912**

| | | | | |
|---|---|---|---|---|
| 301 | 52 | 1c. brown | 1·00 | 10 |
| 307a | 52 | 2c. orange | 30 | 20 |
| 339 | 52 | 3c. green | 4·50 | 75 |
| 340 | 52 | 3c. grey | 75 | 20 |
| 341 | 52 | 5c. purple | 60 | 15 |
| 342 | 52 | 6c. red | 2·50 | 75 |
| 343 | 52 | 6c. violet | 2·00 | 15 |
| 345 | 52 | 9c. red on yellow | 2·25 | 30 |
| 346 | 52 | 10c. olive | 1·40 | 40 |
| 347a | 52 | 12c. red | 1·00 | 2·25 |
| 311a | 52 | 15c. blue | 1·75 | 1·25 |
| 349a | 52 | 15c. green on yellow | 4·00 | 1·00 |
| 350b | 52 | 20c. blue | 3·50 | 45 |
| 351 | 52 | 25c. yellow and blue | 2·50 | 1·90 |
| 352a | 52 | 30c. green and violet | 5·50 | 1·25 |
| 353 | 52 | 50c. black and red | 1·75 | 80 |
| 315 | 52 | 1r. purple on yellow | 5·00 | 4·00 |
| 355 | 52 | 2r. black and red on yellow | 7·00 | 11·00 |
| 317 | 52 | 5r. black on green | 19·00 | 38·00 |
| 318 | 52 | 10r. purple & blk on red | 70·00 | 90·00 |
| 319 | 52 | 20r. black and red on blue | £150 | £160 |

Large type, As Bermuda T 15.

| | | | |
|---|---|---|---|
| 358 | 50r. purple | £600 | £1000 |
| 359 | 100r. black | £2250 | |
| 360 | 100r. purple and blue | £1600 | |

**1918.** Optd WAR STAMP, No. 335 surch ONE CENT and bar also.

| | | | |
|---|---|---|---|
| 335 | 1c. on 5c. purple | 50 | 40 |
| 330 | 2c. orange | 20 | 40 |
| 332 | 3c. green | 20 | 50 |
| 333 | 5c. purple | 50 | 30 |

**1918.** Surch ONE CENT and bar.

| | | | |
|---|---|---|---|
| 337 | 1c. on 5c. purple | 15 | 25 |

**1926.** Surch with new value and bar.

| | | | |
|---|---|---|---|
| 361 | 2c. on 3c. grey | 2·25 | 1·00 |
| 362 | 5c. on 6c. violet | 60 | 40 |

57

**1927**

| | | | | |
|---|---|---|---|---|
| 363 | 57 | 1r. purple | 2·50 | 1·25 |
| 364 | 57 | 2r. green and red | 3·75 | 2·75 |
| 365 | 57 | 5r. green and purple | 15·00 | 24·00 |
| 366 | 57 | 10r. green and orange | 50·00 | £110 |
| 367 | 57 | 20r. purple and blue | £180 | £325 |

59 Adam's Peak

**1935.** King George V.

| | | | | |
|---|---|---|---|---|
| 368 | - | 2c. black and red | 30 | 40 |
| 369 | 59 | 3c. black and green | 35 | 40 |
| 370 | - | 6c. black and blue | 30 | 30 |
| 371 | - | 9c. green and orange | 1·00 | 65 |
| 372 | - | 10c. black and purple | 1·25 | 3·00 |
| 373 | - | 15c. brown and green | 1·00 | 50 |
| 374 | - | 20c. black and blue | 2·50 | 3·25 |
| 375 | - | 25c. blue and brown | 1·40 | 1·25 |
| 376 | - | 30c. red and green | 2·25 | 3·50 |
| 377 | - | 50c. black and violet | 14·00 | 1·75 |
| 378 | - | 1r. violet and brown | 32·00 | 23·00 |

DESIGNS—VERT: 2c. Tapping rubber; 6c. Colombo Harbour; 9c. Plucking tea; 20c. Coconut palms. HORIZ: 10c. Hill paddy (rice); 15c. River scene; 25c. Temple of the Tooth, Kandy; 30c. Ancient irrigation tank; 50c. Indian elephants; 1r. Trincomalee.

**1935.** Silver Jubilee. As T 13 of Antigua.

| | | | |
|---|---|---|---|
| 379 | 6c. blue and grey | 75 | 30 |
| 380 | 9c. green and blue | 75 | 2·75 |
| 381 | 20c. brown and blue | 4·25 | 2·75 |
| 382 | 50c. grey and purple | 5·25 | 16·00 |

**1937.** Coronation. As T 2 of Aden.

| | | | |
|---|---|---|---|
| 383 | 6c. red | 65 | 1·00 |
| 384 | 9c. green | 2·50 | 4·50 |
| 385 | 20c. blue | 3·50 | 4·00 |

70 Sigiriya (Lion Rock)

**1938.** As 1935 issue but with portrait of King George VI, and "POSTAGE & REVENUE" omitted.

| | | | | |
|---|---|---|---|---|
| 386b | - | 2c. black and red | 2·00 | 10 |
| 387d | 59 | 3c. black and green | 80 | 10 |
| 387f | - | 5c. green and orange | 30 | 10 |
| 388 | - | 6c. black and blue | 30 | 10 |
| 389 | 70 | 10c. black and blue | 3·25 | 20 |
| 390 | - | 15c. green and brown | 2·00 | 20 |
| 391 | - | 20c. black and blue | 3·25 | 20 |
| 392a | - | 25c. blue and brown | 4·25 | 20 |
| 393 | - | 30c. red and green | 12·00 | 3·50 |
| 394e | - | 50c. black and violet | 5·00 | 20 |
| 395 | - | 1r. blue and brown | 17·00 | 1·50 |
| 396 | - | 2r. black and red | 14·00 | 3·75 |
| 396b | - | 2r. black and violet | 2·75 | 3·00 |

DESIGNS—VERT: 5c. Coconut palms; 20c. Plucking tea; 2r. Ancient guard-stone, Anuradhapura. Others, same as for corresponding values of 1935 issue.

**1938.** As T 57, but head of King George VI to right.

| | | | | |
|---|---|---|---|---|
| 397a | | 5r. green and purple | 27·00 | 8·50 |

**1940.** Surch with new value and bars.

| | | | | |
|---|---|---|---|---|
| 398 | | 3c. on 6c. blk & bl (No. 388) | 65 | 10 |
| 399 | | 3c. on 20c. blk & bl (No. 391) | 4·50 | 2·75 |

**1946.** Victory. As T 9 of Aden.

| | | | | |
|---|---|---|---|---|
| 400 | | 6c. blue | 30 | 35 |
| 401 | | 15c. brown | 30 | 1·75 |

**75** Parliament Building

**1947.** New Constitution.

| | | | | |
|---|---|---|---|---|
| 402 | **75** | 6c. black and blue | 20 | 15 |
| 403 | - | 10c. black, orange and red | 25 | 40 |
| 404 | - | 15c. green and purple | 25 | 80 |
| 405 | - | 25c. yellow and green | 25 | 1·75 |

DESIGNS—VERT: 10c. Adam's Peak; 25c. Anuradhapura. HORIZ: 15c. Temple of the Tooth.

**79** Lion Flag of Dominion

**80** D. S. Senanayake

**1949.** 1st Anniv of Independence.

| | | | | |
|---|---|---|---|---|
| 406 | **79** | 4c. red, yellow and brown | 20 | 20 |
| 407 | **80** | 5c. brown and green | 10 | 10 |
| 408 | **79** | 15c. red, yellow and orange | 1·00 | 40 |
| 409 | **80** | 25c. brown and blue | 15 | 1·00 |

No. 408 is larger, 28×22 mm.

**82** Globe and Forms of Transport

**1949.** 75th Anniv of UPU. Inscr as in T 82. Designs showing globe.

| | | | | |
|---|---|---|---|---|
| 410 | **82** | 5c. brown and green | 75 | 10 |
| 411 | - | 15c. black and red (horiz) | 1·10 | 2·75 |
| 412 | - | 25c. black and blue (vert) | 1·10 | 1·10 |

**85** Kandyan Dancer

**88** Sigiriya (Lion Rock)

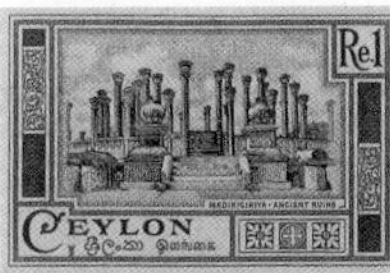

**90** Ruins at Madirigiriya

**1950**

| | | | | |
|---|---|---|---|---|
| 413 | **85** | 4c. purple and red | 15 | 10 |
| 414 | - | 5c. green | 15 | 10 |
| 415 | - | 15c. green and violet | 2·50 | 50 |
| 416 | **88** | 30c. red and yellow | 30 | 70 |
| 417 | - | 75c. blue and orange | 8·50 | 20 |
| 418 | **90** | 1r. blue and brown | 1·75 | 30 |

DESIGNS—VERT (As Types **85** and **88**): 5c. Kiri Vehera, Polonnaruwa; 15c. Vesak orchid. (As Type **90**): 75c. Octagon Library, Temple of the Tooth.

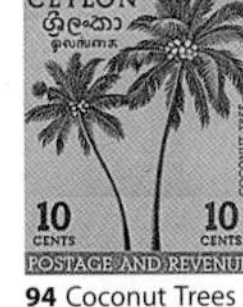

**94** Coconut Trees

**99** Tea Plantation

**1951**

| | | | | |
|---|---|---|---|---|
| 419 | - | 2c. brown and turquoise | 10 | 1·25 |
| 420 | - | 3c. black and violet | 10 | 1·00 |
| 421 | - | 6c. sepia and green | 15 | 30 |
| 422 | **94** | 10c. green and grey | 1·00 | 65 |
| 423 | - | 25c. orange and blue | 20 | 20 |
| 424 | - | 35c. red and green | 1·50 | 1·50 |
| 425 | - | 40c. brown | 5·00 | 1·00 |
| 426 | - | 50c. slate | 30 | 10 |
| 427 | **99** | 85c. black and turquoise | 1·50 | 30 |
| 428 | - | 2r. blue and brown | 9·00 | 1·25 |
| 429 | - | 5r. brown and orange | 9·00 | 1·40 |
| 430 | - | 10r. brown and buff | 60·00 | 22·00 |

DESIGNS—VERT (As Type **94**): 2c. Sambars, Ruhuna National Park; 3c. Ancient guardstone, Anuradhapura; 6c. Harvesting rice; 25c. Sigiriya fresco; 35c. Star orchid. (As Type **99**): 5r. Bas-relief, Anuradhapura; 10r. Harvesting rice. HORIZ (As Type **94**): 40c. Rubber plantation; 50c. Outrigger canoe. (As Type **99**): 2r. River Gal Dam.

**103** Ceylon, Mace and Symbols of Progress

**1952.** Colombo Plan Exhibition.

| | | | | |
|---|---|---|---|---|
| 431 | **103** | 5c. green | 10 | 30 |
| 432 | **103** | 15c. blue | 20 | 60 |

**104** Queen Elizabeth II

**1953.** Coronation.

| | | | | |
|---|---|---|---|---|
| 433 | **104** | 5c. green | 1·25 | 10 |

**105** Ceremonial Procession

**1954.** Royal Visit.

| | | | | |
|---|---|---|---|---|
| 434 | **105** | 10c. blue | 1·00 | 10 |

**106** King Coconuts

**1954**

| | | | | |
|---|---|---|---|---|
| 435 | **106** | 10c. orange, brown and buff | 10 | 10 |

**107** Farm Produce

**1955.** Royal Agricultural and Food Exhibition.

| | | | | |
|---|---|---|---|---|
| 436 | **107** | 10c. brown and orange | 10 | 10 |

**108** Sir John Kotelawala and House of Representatives

**1956.** Prime Minister's 25 Years of Public Service.

| | | | | |
|---|---|---|---|---|
| 437 | **108** | 10c. green | 10 | 10 |

**109** Arrival of Vijaya in Ceylon

**110** Lampstand and Dharmachakra

**1956.** Buddha Jayanti. Inscr "2500".

| | | | | |
|---|---|---|---|---|
| 438 | **109** | 3c. blue and grey | 15 | 15 |
| 439 | **110** | 4c.+2c. yellow and blue | 20 | 75 |
| 440 | - | 10c.+5c. red, yell & grey | 20 | 1·00 |
| 441 | - | 15c. blue | 25 | 10 |

DESIGNS—VERT: 10c. Hand of Peace and Dharmachakra. HORIZ: 15c. Dharmachakra encircling the globe.

**113** Mail Transport

**114** Stamp of 1857

**1957.** Stamp Centenary.

| | | | | |
|---|---|---|---|---|
| 442 | **113** | 4c. red and turquoise | 75 | 50 |
| 443 | **113** | 10c. red and blue | 75 | 10 |
| 444 | **114** | 35c. brown, yellow and blue | 30 | 50 |
| 445 | **114** | 85c. brown, yellow & grn | 80 | 1·60 |

**1958.** Nos. 439/40 with premium obliterated with bars.

| | | | | |
|---|---|---|---|---|
| 446 | **110** | 4c. yellow and blue | 10 | 10 |
| 447 | - | 10c. red, yellow and grey | 10 | 10 |

**117** Kandyan Dancer

**1958.** As Nos. 413 and 419 etc, and 435, but with inscriptions changed as in T 117.

| | | | | |
|---|---|---|---|---|
| 448 | | 2c. brown and turquoise | 10 | 50 |
| 449 | | 3c. black and violet | 10 | 70 |
| 450 | | 4c. purple and red | 10 | 10 |
| 451 | | 5c. green | 10 | 1·60 |
| 452 | | 6c. sepia and green | 10 | 65 |
| 453 | | 10c. orange, brown and buff | 10 | 10 |
| 454 | | 15c. green and violet | 3·50 | 1·00 |
| 455 | | 25c. orange and blue | 20 | 10 |
| 456 | | 30c. red and yellow | 20 | 1·40 |
| 457 | | 35c. red and green | 5·00 | 30 |
| 459 | | 50c. slate | 30 | 10 |
| 460a | | 75c. blue and orange | 9·50 | 2·75 |
| 461 | | 85c. black and turquoise | 3·75 | 9·00 |
| 462 | | 1r. blue and brown | 60 | 10 |
| 463 | | 2r. blue and brown | 2·00 | 30 |
| 464 | | 5r. brown and orange | 12·00 | 30 |
| 465 | | 10r. brown and buff | 13·00 | 1·00 |

**118** "Human Rights"

**1958.** 10th Anniv of Declaration of Human Rights.

| | | | | |
|---|---|---|---|---|
| 466 | **118** | 10c. red, brown and purple | 10 | 10 |
| 467 | **118** | 85c. red, turq & grn | 30 | 55 |

**119** Portraits of Founders and University Buildings

**1959.** Institution of Pirivena Universities.

| | | | | |
|---|---|---|---|---|
| 468 | **119** | 10c. orange and blue | 10 | 10 |

**120** "Uprooted Tree"

**1960.** World Refugee Year.

| | | | | |
|---|---|---|---|---|
| 469 | **120** | 4c. brown and gold | 10 | 85 |
| 470 | **120** | 25c. violet and gold | 10 | 15 |

**121** S. W. R. D. Bandaranaike

**1961.** Prime Minister Bandaranaike Commemoration.

| | | | | |
|---|---|---|---|---|
| 471 | **121** | 10c. blue and turquoise | 10 | 10 |

See also Nos. 479 and 481.

**122** Ceylon Scout Badge

**1962.** Golden Jubilee of Ceylon Boy Scouts Association.

| | | | | |
|---|---|---|---|---|
| 472 | **122** | 35c. buff and blue | 15 | 10 |

**123** Campaign Emblem

**1962.** Malaria Eradication.

| | | | | |
|---|---|---|---|---|
| 473 | **123** | 25c. red and drab | 10 | 10 |

**124** De Havilland Leopard Moth and Hawker Siddeley Comet 4

**1963.** 25th Anniv of Airmail Services.

| | | | | |
|---|---|---|---|---|
| 474 | **124** | 50c. black and blue | 50 | 50 |

**125** "Produce" and Campaign Emblem

**1963.** Freedom from Hunger.

| | | | | |
|---|---|---|---|---|
| 475 | **125** | 5c. red and blue | 75 | 2·00 |
| 476 | **125** | 25c. brown and olive | 3·00 | 30 |

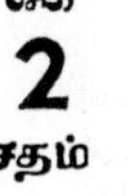

**(126)**

**1963.** No. 450 surch with T 126.

| | | | | |
|---|---|---|---|---|
| 477 | | 2c. on 4c. purple and red | 10 | 10 |

**127** "Rural Life"

**1963.** Golden Jubilee of Ceylon Co-operative Movement (1962).

| | | | | |
|---|---|---|---|---|
| 478 | **127** | 60c. red and black | 2·00 | 50 |

**1963.** Design as T 121, but smaller (21×26 mm) and with inscription rearranged at top.

| | | | | |
|---|---|---|---|---|
| 479 | | 10c. blue | 10 | 10 |
| 481 | | 10c. violet and grey | 10 | 10 |

No. 481 has a decorative pattern at foot instead of the inscription.

**129** Terrain, Indian Elephant and Tree

**1963.** National Conservation Week.

| | | | | |
|---|---|---|---|---|
| 480 | **129** | 5c. sepia and blue | 60 | 40 |

**131** Anagarika Dharmapala (Buddhist missionary)

**1964.** Birth Centenary of A. Dharmapala (founder of Maha Bodhi Society).

| | | | | |
|---|---|---|---|---|
| 482 | **131** | 25c. sepia and yellow | 10 | 10 |

**135** D. S. Senanayake

**143** Ceylon Jungle Fowl

**138** Ruins at Madirigiriya

**1964**

| | | | | |
|---|---|---|---|---|
| 485 | - | 5c. multicoloured | 2·00 | 1·00 |
| 486 | **135** | 10c. green | 80 | 10 |
| 487 | - | 10c. green | 10 | 10 |
| 488 | - | 15c. multicoloured | 4·25 | 30 |
| 489 | **138** | 20c. purple and buff | 20 | 25 |
| 494 | **143** | 60c. multicoloured | 4·00 | 1·25 |
| 495 | - | 75c. multicoloured | 3·00 | 70 |
| 497 | - | 1r. brown and green | 1·00 | 30 |
| 499 | - | 5r. multicoloured | 8·50 | 8·50 |
| 500 | - | 10r. multicoloured | 25·00 | 3·00 |
| **MS**500a 148×174 mm. As Nos. 485, 488, 494 and 495 (imperf) | | | 7·00 | 14·00 |

DESIGNS—HORIZ (As Type **143**): 5c. Southern grackle ("Grackle"); 15c. Common peafowl ("Peacock"); 75c. Asian black-headed oriole ("Oriole"). (As Type **138**): 5r. Girls transplanting rice. VERT (As Type **135**): 10c. (No. 487) Similar portrait, but large head and smaller inscriptions. (21×35 mm): 1r. Tea plantation. (23×36 mm): 10r. Map of Ceylon.

**150** Exhibition Buildings and Cogwheels

**1964.** Industrial Exhibition.

| | | | | |
|---|---|---|---|---|
| 501 | | 5c. multicoloured | 10 | 75 |
| 502 | **150** | 5c. multicoloured | 10 | 75 |

No. 501 is inscribed "INDUSTRIAL EXHIBITION" in Sinhala and Tamil, No. 502 in Sinhala and English.

**151** Trains of 1864 and 1964

**1964.** Centenary of Ceylon Railways.

| | | | | |
|---|---|---|---|---|
| 503 | - | 60c. blue, purple and green | 2·75 | 40 |
| 504 | **151** | 60c. blue, purple and green | 2·75 | 40 |

No. 503 is inscribed "RAILWAY CENTENARY" in Sinhala and Tamil, No. 504 in Sinhala and English.

**152** ITU Emblem and Symbols

**1965.** Centenary of ITU.

| | | | | |
|---|---|---|---|---|
| 505 | **152** | 2c. blue and red | 1·00 | 1·10 |
| 506 | **152** | 30c. brown and red | 3·00 | 45 |

**153** ICY Emblem

**1965.** International Co-operation Year.

| | | | | |
|---|---|---|---|---|
| 507 | **153** | 3c. blue and red | 1·25 | 1·00 |
| 508 | **153** | 50c. black, red and gold | 3·25 | 50 |

**154** Town Hall, Colombo

**1965.** Centenary of Colombo Municipal Council.

| | | | | |
|---|---|---|---|---|
| 509 | **154** | 25c. green and sepia | 20 | 20 |

**1965.** No. 481 surch 5.

| | | | | |
|---|---|---|---|---|
| 510 | | 5c. on 10c. violet and grey | 10 | 1·75 |

**157** Kandy and Council Crest

**1966.** Centenary of Kandy Municipal Council.

| | | | | |
|---|---|---|---|---|
| 512 | **157** | 25c. multicoloured | 20 | 20 |

**158** WHO Building

**1966.** Inauguration of WHO Headquarters, Geneva.

| | | | | |
|---|---|---|---|---|
| 513 | **158** | 4c. multicoloured | 2·75 | 3·00 |
| 514 | **158** | 1r. multicoloured | 7·00 | 1·50 |

**159** Rice Paddy and Map of Ceylon

**1966.** International Rice Year. Multicoloured.

| | | | | |
|---|---|---|---|---|
| 515 | | 6c. Type **159** | 20 | 75 |
| 516 | | 30c. Rice paddy and globe | 30 | 15 |

**161** UNESCO Emblem

**1966.** 20th Anniv of UNESCO.

| | | | | |
|---|---|---|---|---|
| 517 | **161** | 3c. multicoloured | 2·75 | 3·75 |
| 518 | **161** | 50c. multicoloured | 8·00 | 50 |

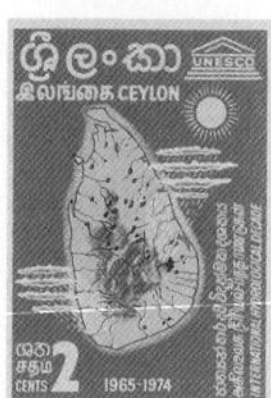


**162** Water-resources Map

**1966.** International Hydrological Decade.

| | | | | |
|---|---|---|---|---|
| 519 | **162** | 2c. brown, yellow and blue | 30 | 85 |
| 520 | **162** | 2r. multicoloured | 1·50 | 2·25 |

**163** Devotees at Buddhist Temple

**1967.** Poya Holiday System. Multicoloured.

| | | | | |
|---|---|---|---|---|
| 521 | | 5c. Type **163** | 15 | 60 |
| 522 | | 20c. Mihintale | 15 | 10 |
| 523 | | 35c. Sacred Bo-tree, Anuradhapura | 15 | 15 |
| 524 | | 60c. Adam's Peak | 15 | 10 |

**167** Galle Fort and Clock Tower

**1967.** Centenary of Galle Municipal Council.

| | | | | |
|---|---|---|---|---|
| 525 | **167** | 25c. multicoloured | 70 | 20 |

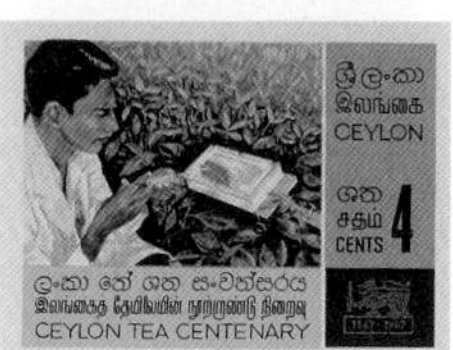


**168** Field Research

**1967.** Centenary of Ceylon Tea Industry. Mult.

| | | | | |
|---|---|---|---|---|
| 526 | | 4c. Type **168** | 60 | 80 |
| 527 | | 40c. Tea-tasting equipment | 1·75 | 1·50 |
| 528 | | 50c. Leaves and bud | 1·75 | 20 |
| 529 | | 1r. Shipping tea | 1·75 | 10 |

**169** Elephant Ride

**1967.** International Tourist Year.

| | | | | |
|---|---|---|---|---|
| 530 | **169** | 45c. multicoloured | 2·25 | 80 |

**1967.** 1st National Stamp Exhibition. No. **MS**500a optd "FIRST NATIONAL STAMP EXHIBITION 1967".

| | | | | |
|---|---|---|---|---|
| **MS**531 148×174 mm. Nos. 485, 488, 494/5. Imperf | | | 8·50 | 9·00 |

**170** Ranger, Jubilee Emblem and Flag

**1967.** Golden Jubilee of Ceylon Girl Guides' Association.

| | | | | |
|---|---|---|---|---|
| 532 | **170** | 3c. multicoloured | 50 | 20 |
| 533 | **170** | 25c. multicoloured | 75 | 10 |

**171** Colonel Olcott and Buddhist Flag

**1967.** 60th Death Anniv of Colonel Olcott (theosophist).

| | | | | |
|---|---|---|---|---|
| 534 | **171** | 15c. multicoloured | 30 | 20 |

**172** Independence Hall

**1968.** 20th Anniv of Independence. Multicoloured.

| | | | | |
|---|---|---|---|---|
| 535 | | 5c. Type **172** | 10 | 55 |
| 536 | | 1r. Lion flag and sceptre | 50 | 10 |

**174** Sir D. B. Jayatilleke

**1968.** Birth Centenary of Sir Baron Jayatilleke (scholar and statesman).

| | | | | |
|---|---|---|---|---|
| 537 | **174** | 25c. brown | 10 | 10 |

**175** Institute of Hygiene

**1968.** 20th Anniv of World Health Organization.

| | | | | |
|---|---|---|---|---|
| 538 | **175** | 50c. multicoloured | 10 | 10 |

**176** Vickers Super VC-10 over Terminal Building

**1968.** Opening of Colombo Airport.

| | | | | |
|---|---|---|---|---|
| 539 | **176** | 60c. multicoloured | 1·00 | 10 |

**177** Open Koran and "1400"

**1968.** 1400th Anniv of Koran.

| | | | | |
|---|---|---|---|---|
| 541 | **177** | 25c. multicoloured | 10 | 10 |

**178** Human Rights Emblem

**1968.** Human Rights Year.

| | | | | |
|---|---|---|---|---|
| 542 | **178** | 2c. multicoloured | 10 | 30 |
| 543 | **178** | 20c. multicoloured | 10 | 10 |
| 544 | **178** | 40c. multicoloured | 10 | 10 |
| 545 | **178** | 2r. multicoloured | 80 | 4·75 |

**179** All-Ceylon Buddhist Congress Headquarters

**1968.** Golden Jubilee of All-Ceylon Buddhist Congress.

| | | | | |
|---|---|---|---|---|
| 546 | **179** | 5c. multicoloured | 10 | 50 |

**180** E. W. Perera (patriot)

**1969.** Perera Commemoration.

| | | | | |
|---|---|---|---|---|
| 547 | **180** | 60c. brown | 10 | 30 |

**181** Symbols of Strength in Savings

**1969.** Silver Jubilee of National Savings Movement.

| | | | | |
|---|---|---|---|---|
| 548 | **181** | 3c. multicoloured | 10 | 30 |

**182** Seat of Enlightenment under Sacred Bodhi Tree

**1969.** Vesak Day. Inscr "Wesak".

| | | | | |
|---|---|---|---|---|
| 549 | **182** | 4c. multicoloured | 10 | 50 |
| 550 | - | 6c. multicoloured | 10 | 50 |
| 551 | **182** | 35c. multicoloured | 10 | 10 |

DESIGN: 6c. Buduresmala (six-fold Buddha-rays).

**184** A. E. Goonesinghe

**1969.** Goonesinghe Commemoration.

| | | | | |
|---|---|---|---|---|
| 552 | **184** | 15c. multicoloured | 10 | 10 |

**185** ILO Emblem

**1969.** 50th Anniv of ILO.

| | | | | |
|---|---|---|---|---|
| 553 | **185** | 5c. black and blue | 10 | 10 |
| 554 | **185** | 25c. black and red | 10 | 10 |

**186** Convocation Hall, University of Ceylon

**1969.** Educational Centenary. Multicoloured.

| | | | | |
|---|---|---|---|---|
| 555 | | 4c. Type **186** | 10 | 80 |
| 556 | | 35c. Lamp of learning, globe and flags (horiz) | 20 | 10 |
| 557 | | 50c. Uranium atom | 20 | 10 |
| 558 | | 60c. Symbols of scientific education | 30 | 10 |

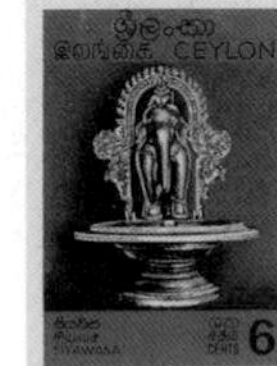

**188** Ath Pana (Elephant Lamp)

**1969.** Archaeological Centenary. Multicoloured.

| | | | | |
|---|---|---|---|---|
| 559 | | 6c. Type **188** | 25 | 1·50 |
| 560 | | 1r. Rock fortress of Sigiriya | 25 | 10 |

**190** Leopard

**1970.** Wild Life Conservation. Multicoloured.

| | | | | |
|---|---|---|---|---|
| 561 | | 5c. Water buffalo | 1·25 | 1·25 |
| 562 | | 15c. Slender loris | 2·00 | 1·25 |
| 563 | | 50c. Spotted deer | 1·40 | 1·25 |
| 564 | | 1r. Type **190** | 1·40 | 1·75 |

**191** Emblem and Symbols

**1970.** Asian Productivity Year.

| | | | | |
|---|---|---|---|---|
| 565 | **191** | 60c. multicoloured | 10 | 10 |

**192** New UPU HQ Building

**1970.** New UPU Headquarters Building.

| | | | | |
|---|---|---|---|---|
| 566 | **192** | 50c. orange, black and blue | 50 | 10 |
| 567 | **192** | 1r.10 red, black and blue | 4·50 | 40 |

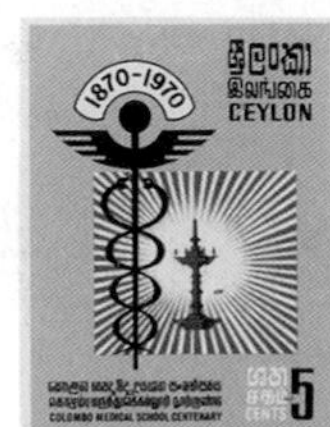

**193** Oil Lamp and Caduceus

**1970.** Centenary of Colombo Medical School.

| | | | | |
|---|---|---|---|---|
| 568 | **193** | 5c. multicoloured | 1·25 | 80 |
| 569 | **193** | 45c. multicoloured | 1·50 | 60 |

**194** Victory March and S. W. R. D. Bandaranaike

**1970.** Establishment of United Front Government.

| | | | | |
|---|---|---|---|---|
| 570 | **194** | 10c. multicoloured | 10 | 10 |

**195** U.N. Emblem and Dove of Peace

**1970.** 25th Anniv of United Nations.

| | | | | |
|---|---|---|---|---|
| 571 | **195** | 2r. multicoloured | 2·00 | 3·75 |

**196** Keppetipola Dissawa

**1970.** 152nd Death Anniv of Keppetipola Dissawa (Kandyan patriot).

| | | | | |
|---|---|---|---|---|
| 572 | **196** | 25c. multicoloured | 10 | 10 |

**197** Ola Leaf Manuscript

**1970.** International Education Year.

| | | | | |
|---|---|---|---|---|
| 573 | **197** | 15c. multicoloured | 2·75 | 1·25 |

**198** C. H. de Soysa

**1971.** 135th Birth Anniv of C. H. de Soysa (philanthropist).

| | | | | |
|---|---|---|---|---|
| 574 | **198** | 20c. multicoloured | 15 | 50 |

**199** D. E. H. Pedris (patriot)

**1971.** D. E. H. Pedris Commemoration.

| | | | | |
|---|---|---|---|---|
| 575 | **199** | 25c. multicoloured | 15 | 50 |

**200** Lenin

**1971.** Lenin Commemoration.

| | | | | |
|---|---|---|---|---|
| 576 | **200** | 40c. multicoloured | 15 | 50 |

**201** Ananda Rajakaruna

**1971.** Poets and Philosophers.

| | | | | |
|---|---|---|---|---|
| 577 | **201** | 5c. blue | 10 | 15 |
| 578 | - | 5c. brown | 10 | 15 |
| 579 | - | 5c. orange | 10 | 15 |
| 580 | - | 5c. blue | 10 | 15 |
| 581 | - | 5c. brown | 10 | 15 |

PORTRAITS: No. 578, Arumuga Navalar; 579, Rev. S. Mahinda; 580, Ananda Coomaraswamy; 581, Cumaratunga Munidasa.

**1971.** Surch in figures.

| | | | | |
|---|---|---|---|---|
| 582 | **182** | 5c. on 4c. multicoloured | 6·50 | 1·75 |
| 583 | **186** | 5c. on 4c. multicoloured | 10 | 1·25 |
| 584 | **194** | 15c. on 10c. multicoloured | 10 | 30 |
| 585 | - | 25c. on 6c. mult (No. 550) | 30 | 60 |
| 586 | **188** | 25c. on 6c. multicoloured | 30 | 2·25 |

**203** Colombo Plan Emblem and Ceylon

**1971.** 20th Anniv of Colombo Plan.

| | | | | |
|---|---|---|---|---|
| 587 | **203** | 20c. multicoloured | 15 | 30 |

**204** Globe and CARE Package

**1971.** 20th Anniv of Co-operative for American Relief Everywhere.

| | | | | |
|---|---|---|---|---|
| 588 | **204** | 50c. blue, violet and lilac | 35 | 30 |

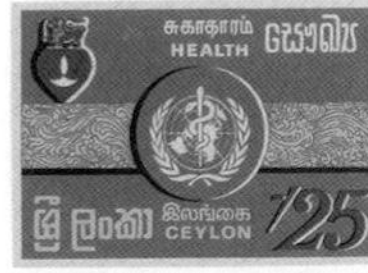

**205** WHO Emblem and Heart

**1972.** World Health Day.

| | | | | |
|---|---|---|---|---|
| 589 | **205** | 25c. multicoloured | 2·50 | 60 |

**206** Map of Asia and U.N. Emblem

**1972.** 25th Anniv of ECAFE.

| | | | | |
|---|---|---|---|---|
| 590 | **206** | 85c. multicoloured | 4·75 | 2·75 |

## OFFICIAL STAMPS

**1895.** Stamps of Queen Victoria optd On Service.

| | | | | |
|---|---|---|---|---|
| O11 | **9** | 2c. green | 16·00 | 70 |
| O18 | **9** | 2c. brown | 10·00 | 60 |
| O12 | **39** | 3c. brown and green | 10·00 | 2·25 |
| O19 | **39** | 3c. green | 12·00 | 4·25 |
| O13 | **28** | 5c. purple | 5·00 | 30 |
| O14 | **39** | 15c. olive | 19·00 | 50 |
| O20 | **39** | 15c. blue | 24·00 | 60 |
| O15 | **39** | 25c. brown | 13·00 | 2·75 |
| O16 | **39** | 30c. mauve and brown | 13·00 | 60 |
| O21 | **39** | 75c. black and brown | 8·00 | 8·00 |
| O17 | **30** | 1r.12 red | 95·00 | 60·00 |

**1903.** Stamps of King Edward VII optd On Service.

| | | | | |
|---|---|---|---|---|
| O22 | **44** | 2c. brown | 19·00 | 1·00 |
| O23 | **45** | 3c. green | 13·00 | 2·00 |
| O24 | - | 5c. purple (No. 268) | 27·00 | 1·50 |
| O25 | **45** | 15c. blue | 38·00 | 2·50 |
| O26 | **45** | 25c. brown | 32·00 | 18·00 |
| O27 | **45** | 30c. violet and green | 19·00 | 1·50 |

For later issues see **SRI LANKA**.

Pt. 6, Pt. 12

# CHAD

Formerly a dependency of Ubangi-Shari. Became one of the separate colonies of Fr. Equatorial Africa in 1937. In 1958 became a republic within the French Community.

100 centimes = 1 franc.

**1922.** Stamps of Middle Congo, colours changed, optd TCHAD.

| | | | | |
|---|---|---|---|---|
| 1 | 1 | 1c. pink and violet | 60 | 6·75 |
| 2 | 1 | 2c. brown and pink | 1·50 | 6·75 |
| 3 | 1 | 4c. blue and violet | 2·10 | 7·25 |
| 4 | 1 | 5c. brown and green | 3·00 | 7·75 |
| 5 | 1 | 10c. green and turquoise | 5·25 | 8·50 |
| 6 | 1 | 15c. violet and pink | 4·50 | 9·00 |
| 7 | 1 | 20c. green and violet | 8·75 | 18·00 |
| 8 | 2 | 25c. brown and chocolate | 10·50 | 34·00 |
| 9 | 2 | 30c. red | 3·25 | 8·25 |
| 10 | 2 | 35c. blue and pink | 3·75 | 11·00 |
| 11 | 2 | 40c. brown and green | 3·75 | 11·50 |
| 12 | 2 | 45c. violet and green | 3·75 | 11·00 |
| 13 | 2 | 50c. blue and light blue | 3·00 | 11·00 |
| 14 | 2 | 60 on 75c. violet on pink | 5·00 | 16·00 |
| 15 | 2 | 75c. pink and violet | 4·00 | 10·50 |
| 16 | 3 | 1f. blue and pink | 19·00 | 37·00 |
| 17 | 3 | 2f. blue and violet | 24·00 | 60·00 |
| 18 | 3 | 5f. blue and brown | 20·00 | 55·00 |

**1924.** Stamps of 1922 and similar stamps further optd AFRIQUE EQUATORIALE FRANCAISE.

| | | | | |
|---|---|---|---|---|
| 19 | 1 | 1c. pink and violet | 35 | 6·00 |
| 20 | 1 | 2c. brown and pink | 25 | 6·25 |
| 21 | 1 | 4c. blue and violet | 70 | 6·50 |
| 22 | 1 | 5c. brown and green | 75 | 6·25 |
| 23 | 1 | 10c. green and turquoise | 2·50 | 7·75 |
| 24 | 1 | 10c. red and grey | 1·10 | 6·25 |
| 25 | 1 | 15c. violet and red | 1·10 | 6·50 |
| 26 | 1 | 20c. green and violet | 2·10 | 6·75 |
| 27 | 2 | 25c. brown and chocolate | 2·10 | 6·75 |
| 28 | 2 | 30c. red | 1·40 | 6·75 |
| 29 | 2 | 30c. grey and blue | 95 | 6·25 |
| 30 | 2 | 30c. olive and green | 2·10 | 8·25 |
| 31 | 2 | 35c. blue and pink | 1·10 | 7·00 |
| 32 | 2 | 40c. brown and green | 2·10 | 6·75 |
| 33 | 2 | 45c. violet and green | 1·90 | 7·75 |
| 34 | 2 | 50c. blue and light blue | 1·20 | 7·00 |
| 35 | 2 | 50c. green and purple | 2·40 | 2·30 |
| 36 | 2 | 60 on 75c. violet on pink | 85 | 7·25 |
| 37 | 2 | 65c. brown and blue | 3·50 | 10·00 |
| 38 | 2 | 75c. pink and violet | 1·40 | 5·50 |
| 39 | 2 | 75c. blue and light blue | 2·20 | 5·75 |
| 40 | 2 | 75c. purple and brown | 3·75 | 9·75 |
| 41 | 2 | 90c. carmine and red | 6·25 | 25·00 |
| 42 | 3 | 1f. blue and pink | 3·00 | 4·75 |
| 43 | 3 | 1f.10 green and blue | 3·75 | 11·50 |
| 44 | 3 | 1f.25 brown and blue | 13·50 | 28·00 |
| 45 | 3 | 1f.50 ultramarine and blue | 6·00 | 28·00 |
| 46 | 3 | 1f.75 brown and mauve | 55·00 | 95·00 |
| 47 | 3 | 2f. blue and violet | 3·25 | 5·50 |
| 48 | 3 | 3f. mauve on pink | 8·75 | 39·00 |
| 49 | 3 | 5f. blue and brown | 3·75 | 7·25 |

**1925.** Stamps of Middle Congo optd TCHAD and AFRIQUE EQUATORIALE FRANCAISE and surch also.

| | | | | |
|---|---|---|---|---|
| 50 | | 65 on 1f. brown and green | 2·75 | 8·50 |
| 51 | | 85 on 1f. brown and green | 2·75 | 8·50 |
| 52 | 2 | 90 on 75c. red and pink | 2·30 | 8·75 |
| 53 | 3 | 1f.25 on 1f. blue & ultram | 1·40 | 6·25 |
| 54 | 3 | 1f.50 on 1f. blue & ultram | 3·00 | 8·75 |
| 55 | 3 | 3f. on 5f. brown and red | 5·25 | 14·50 |
| 56 | 3 | 10f. on 5f. green and red | 15·00 | 34·00 |
| 57a | 3 | 20f. on 5f. violet & orange | 24·00 | 43·00 |

**1931.** "Colonial Exhibition" key-types inscr "TCHAD".

| | | | | |
|---|---|---|---|---|
| 58 | E | 40c. green | 5·00 | 15·00 |
| 59 | F | 50c. mauve | 5·00 | 15·00 |
| 60 | G | 90c. red | 5·00 | 15·00 |
| 61 | H | 1f.50 blue | 5·00 | 15·00 |

**2** "Birth of the Republic"

**1959.** 1st Anniv of Republic.

| | | | | |
|---|---|---|---|---|
| 62 | 2 | 15f. multicoloured | 3·50 | 3·25 |
| 63 | - | 25f. lake and myrtle | 75 | 50 |

DESIGN: 25f. Map and birds.

**1960.** 10th African Technical Co-operation Commission. As T 62 of Cameroun.

| | | | |
|---|---|---|---|
| 64 | 50f. violet and purple | 2·75 | 4·75 |

**1960.** Air. Olympic Games. No. 276 of French Equatorial Africa surch with Olympic rings and XVIIe OLYMPIADE 1960 REPUBLIQUE DU TCHAD 250F.

| | | | |
|---|---|---|---|
| 65 | 250f. on 500f. blue, black & grn | 13·50 | 13·00 |

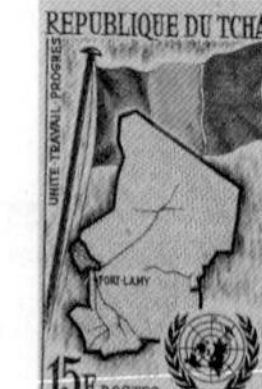


**3** Flag, Map and U.N. Emblem

**1961.** Admission into U.N.

| | | | | |
|---|---|---|---|---|
| 66 | 3 | 15f. multicoloured | 65 | 25 |
| 67 | 3 | 25f. multicoloured | 80 | 40 |
| 68 | 3 | 85f. multicoloured | 2·40 | 1·10 |

**4** Shari Bridge and Hippopotamus

**1961**

| | | | | |
|---|---|---|---|---|
| 69 | - | 50c. green and black | 10 | 10 |
| 70 | - | 1f. green and black | 10 | 10 |
| 71 | - | 2f. brown and black | 10 | 10 |
| 72 | - | 3f. orange and green | 10 | 10 |
| 73 | - | 4f. red and black | 20 | 10 |
| 74 | 4 | 5f. lemon and black | 20 | 20 |
| 75 | - | 10f. pink and black | 40 | 25 |
| 76 | - | 15f. violet and black | 80 | 30 |
| 77 | - | 20f. red and black | 90 | 45 |
| 78 | - | 25f. blue and black | 1·00 | 50 |
| 79 | - | 30f. blue and black | 1·20 | 65 |
| 80 | - | 60f. yellow and black | 2·30 | 1·00 |
| 81 | - | 85f. orange and black | 2·50 | 1·20 |

DESIGNS (with animal silhouettes)—VERT: 50c. Biltine and Dorcas gazelle; 1f. Logone and elephant; 2f. Batha and lion; 3f. Salamat and buffalo; 4f. Ouaddai and greater kudu; 10f. Abtouyour and bullock; 15f. Bessada and Derby's eland; 20f. Tibesti and moufflon; 25f. Tikem Rocks and hartebeest; 30f. Kanem and cheetah; 60f. Borkou and oryx; 85f. Guelta D'Archei and addax.

**5** Red Bishops

**1961.** Air.

| | | | | |
|---|---|---|---|---|
| 82 | 5 | 50f. black, red and green | 1·50 | 55 |
| 83 | - | 100f. multicoloured | 4·50 | 1·30 |
| 84 | - | 200f. multicoloured | 4·75 | 2·40 |
| 85 | - | 250f. blue, orange and green | 10·00 | 4·25 |
| 86 | - | 500f. multicoloured | 22·00 | 13·00 |

BIRDS: 100f. Scarlet-chested sunbird; 200f. African paradise flycatcher; 250f. Malachite kingfisher; 500f. Carmine bee eater.

**1962.** Air. "Air Afrique" Airline. As T 69 of Cameroun.

| | | | |
|---|---|---|---|
| 87 | 25f. blue, brown and black | 1·00 | 40 |

**1962.** Malaria Eradication. As T 70 of Cameroun.

| | | | |
|---|---|---|---|
| 88 | 25f.+5f. orange | 1·30 | 1·10 |

**1962.** Sports. As T 12 of Central African Republic. Multicoloured.

| | | | |
|---|---|---|---|
| 89 | 20f. Relay-racing (horiz) (postage) | 75 | 60 |
| 90 | 50f. High-jumping (horiz) | 1·80 | 95 |
| 91 | 100f. Throwing the discus (air) | 3·75 | 1·90 |

The 100f. is 26×47 mm.

**1962.** 1st Anniv of Union of African and Malagasy States. As No. 328 of Cameroun.

| | | | | |
|---|---|---|---|---|
| 92 | 72 | 30f. blue | 1·30 | 70 |

**1963.** Freedom from Hunger. As T 76 of Cameroun.

| | | | |
|---|---|---|---|
| 93 | 25f.+5f. blue, brown & green | 1·30 | 1·10 |

**6** Pres. Tombalbaye

**1963**

| | | | | |
|---|---|---|---|---|
| 94 | 6 | 20f. multicoloured | 65 | 30 |
| 95 | 6 | 85f. multicoloured | 1·70 | 80 |

**1963.** Air. African and Malagasy Posts and Telecommunications Union. As T 11 of Central African Republic.

| | | | |
|---|---|---|---|
| 96 | 85f. multicoloured | 2·20 | 1·10 |

**1963.** Space Telecommunications, As Nos. 37/8 of Central African Republic.

| | | | |
|---|---|---|---|
| 97 | 25f. violet, emerald and green | 85 | 55 |
| 98 | 100f. blue and pink | 3·25 | 1·60 |

**1963.** Air. 1st Anniv of "Air Afrique" and Inauguration of "DC-8" Service. As T 11 of Congo Republic.

| | | | |
|---|---|---|---|
| 99 | 50f. multicoloured | 2·40 | 1·10 |

**1963.** Air. European–African Economic Convention. As T 24 of Central African Republic.

| | | | |
|---|---|---|---|
| 100 | 50f. multicoloured | 1·70 | 95 |

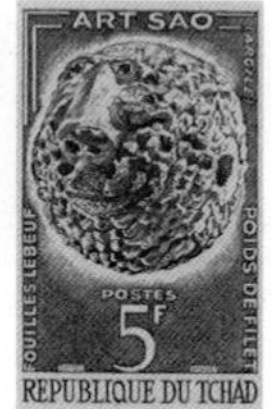


**7** Carved Thread-weight

**1963.** Sao Art.

| | | | | |
|---|---|---|---|---|
| 101 | 7 | 5f. orange and turquoise | 20 | 10 |
| 102 | - | 15f. purple, slate and red | 50 | 25 |
| 103 | - | 25f. brown and blue | 1·00 | 70 |
| 104 | - | 60f. bronze and brown | 2·50 | 1·00 |
| 105 | - | 80f. bronze and brown | 3·00 | 1·30 |

DESIGNS: 15f. Ancestral mask; 25f. Ancestral statuette; 60f. Gazelle's-head pendant; 80f. Pectoral.

**1963.** 15th Anniv of Declaration of Human Rights. As Central African Republic T 26.

| | | | |
|---|---|---|---|
| 106 | 25f. purple and green | 1·00 | 55 |

**8** Broussard Monoplane

**1963.** Air.

| | | | | |
|---|---|---|---|---|
| 107 | 8 | 100f. blue, green & brown | 3·75 | 1·80 |

**9** Pottery

**1964.** Sao Handicrafts.

| | | | | |
|---|---|---|---|---|
| 108 | 9 | 10f. black, orange & blue | 40 | 25 |
| 109 | - | 30f. red, black and yellow | 95 | 50 |
| 110 | - | 50f. black, red and green | 1·50 | 75 |
| 111 | - | 85f. black, yellow & purple | 2·30 | 1·10 |

DESIGNS: 30f. Canoe-building; 50f. Carpet-weaving; 85f. Blacksmith working iron.

**10** Rameses II in War Chariot, Abu Simbel

**1964.** Air. Nubian Monuments Preservation Fund.

| | | | | |
|---|---|---|---|---|
| 112 | 10 | 10f.+5f. violet, grn & red | 90 | 55 |
| 113 | 10 | 25f.+5f. purple, grn & red | 1·50 | 85 |
| 114 | 10 | 50f.+5f. turq, grn & red | 3·00 | 1·90 |

**1964.** World Meteorological Day. As T 14 of Congo Republic.

| | | | |
|---|---|---|---|
| 115 | 50f. violet, blue and purple | 1·30 | 75 |

**11** Cotton

**1964.** Multicoloured.. Multicoloured..

| | | | |
|---|---|---|---|
| 116 | 20f. Type **11** | 1·70 | 70 |
| 117 | 25f. Flamboyant tree | 1·80 | 85 |

**1964.** Air. 5th Anniv of Equatorial African Heads of State Conf. As T 31 of Central African Republic.

| | | | |
|---|---|---|---|
| 118 | 100f. multicoloured | 2·40 | 1·10 |

**12** Globe, Chimneys and Ears of Wheat

**1964.** Air. Europafrique.

| | | | | |
|---|---|---|---|---|
| 119 | 12 | 50f. orange, purple & brn | 1·70 | 85 |

**13** Football

**1964.** Air. Olympic Games. Tokyo.

| | | | | |
|---|---|---|---|---|
| 120 | 13 | 25f. green, lt green & brn | 1·00 | 60 |
| 121 | - | 50f. brown, indigo & blue | 1·80 | 1·00 |
| 122 | - | 100f. black, green and red | 3·50 | 1·90 |
| 123 | - | 200f. black, bistre and red | 6·25 | 3·50 |
| **MS**123a | | 191×100 mm. Nos. 120/3 | 17·00 | 13·50 |

DESIGNS—VERT: 50f. Throwing the javelin; 100f. High-jumping. HORIZ: 200f. Running.

**1964.** Air. Pan-African and Malagasy Post and Telecommunications Congress, Cairo. As T 23 of Congo Republic.

| | | | |
|---|---|---|---|
| 124 | 25f. sepia, red and mauve | 1·00 | 40 |

**1964.** French, African and Malagasy Co-operation. As T 88 of Cameroun.

| | | | |
|---|---|---|---|
| 125 | 25f. brown, blue and red | 1·50 | 80 |

**14** Pres. Kennedy

**1964.** Air. Pres. Kennedy Commem.

| | | | | |
|---|---|---|---|---|
| 126 | 14 | 100f. multicoloured | 2·50 | 1·80 |
| **MS**126a | | 90×129 mm. No. 126 (×4) | 12·00 | 9·75 |

**15** National Guard

**1964.** Chad Army. Multicoloured.

| | | | |
|---|---|---|---|
| 127 | 20f. Type **15** | 80 | 40 |
| 128 | 25f. Standard-bearer and troops of Land Forces | 1·10 | 40 |

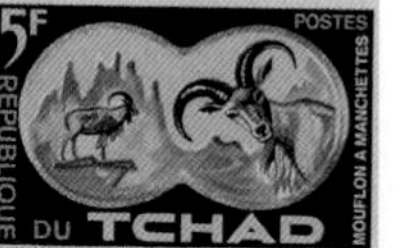


**16** Barbary Sheep

**1964.** Fauna. Protection. Multicoloured.

| | | | |
|---|---|---|---|
| 129 | 5f. Type **16** | 40 | 10 |
| 130 | 10f. Addax | 70 | 30 |
| 131 | 20f. Scimitar oryx | 1·30 | 45 |
| 132 | 25f. Giant eland (vert) | 1·70 | 60 |
| 133 | 30f. Giraffe, African buffalo and lion (Zakouma Park)(vert) | 2·30 | 75 |
| 134 | 85f. Greater kudu (vert) | 5·00 | 1·50 |

**17** Perforator of Olsen's Telegraph Apparatus

**1965.** I.T.U. Centenary.

| | | | | |
|---|---|---|---|---|
| 135 | **17** | 30f. brown, red and green | 90 | 40 |
| 136 | - | 60f. green, red and brown | 1·50 | 75 |
| 137 | - | 100f. green, brown & red | 2·40 | 1·10 |

DESIGNS—VERT: 60f. Milde's telephone. HORIZ: 100f. Distributor of Baudot's telegraph apparatus.

**18** Badge and Mobile Gendarmes

**1965.** National Gendarmerie.

| | | | | |
|---|---|---|---|---|
| 138 | **18** | 25f. multicoloured | 90 | 50 |

**19** ICY Emblem

**1965.** Air. International Co-operation Year.

| | | | | |
|---|---|---|---|---|
| 139 | **19** | 100f. multicoloured | 1·80 | 1·10 |

**20** Abraham Lincoln

**1965.** Air. Death Centenary of Abraham Lincoln.

| | | | | |
|---|---|---|---|---|
| 140 | **20** | 100f. multicoloured | 2·50 | 1·30 |

**21** Guitar

**1965.** Native Musical Instruments.

| | | | | |
|---|---|---|---|---|
| 141 | - | 1f. brown & grn (postage) | 10 | 10 |
| 142 | **21** | 2f. brown, purple and red | 10 | 10 |
| 143 | - | 3f. lake, black and brown | 10 | 10 |
| 144 | - | 15f. green, orange and red | 1·00 | 30 |
| 145 | - | 60f. green and lake | 2·00 | 1·40 |
| 146 | - | 100f. ultram, brn & bl (48½×27 mm) (air) | 3·00 | 1·90 |

DESIGNS—VERT: 1f. Drum and seat; 3f. Shoulder drum; 60f. Harp. HORIZ: 15f. Viol; 100f. Xylophone.

**22** Sir Winston Churchill

**1965.** Air. Churchill Commemoration.

| | | | | |
|---|---|---|---|---|
| 147 | **22** | 50f. black and green | 1·50 | 85 |

**23** Dr. Albert Schweitzer (philosopher and missionary) and "Appealing Hands"

**1966.** Air. Schweitzer Commemoration.

| | | | | |
|---|---|---|---|---|
| 148 | **23** | 100f. multicoloured | 3·00 | 1·50 |

**24** Mask in Mortar

**1966.** World Festival of Negro Arts, Dakar.

| | | | | |
|---|---|---|---|---|
| 149 | **24** | 15f. purple, bistre & blue | 50 | 20 |
| 150 | - | 20f. brown, red and green | 80 | 40 |
| 151 | - | 60f. purple, blue and red | 1·90 | 90 |
| 152 | - | 80f. green, brown & violet | 3·00 | 1·20 |

DESIGNS—Sao Art: 20f. Mask; 60f. Mask (different) (All from J. Courtin's excavations at Bouta Kebira); 80f. Armband (from INTSH excavations, Gawi).

**1966.** No. 94 surch.

| | | | | |
|---|---|---|---|---|
| 153 | **6** | 25f. on 20f. multicoloured | 90 | 55 |

**26** WHO Building

**1966.** Inaug of WHO Headquarters, Geneva.

| | | | | |
|---|---|---|---|---|
| 154 | **26** | 25f. blue, yellow and red | 65 | 30 |
| 155 | **26** | 32f. blue, yellow & green | 85 | 40 |

**27** Caduceus and Map of Africa

**1966.** Central African Customs and Economic Union.

| | | | | |
|---|---|---|---|---|
| 156 | **27** | 30f. multicoloured | 90 | 50 |

**28** Footballer

**1966.** World Cup Football Championship.

| | | | | |
|---|---|---|---|---|
| 157 | **28** | 30f. red, green and emerald | 80 | 40 |
| 158 | - | 60f. red, black and blue | 1·60 | 75 |

DESIGN—VERT: 60f. Footballer (different).

**29** Youths, Flag and Arms

**1966.** Youth Movement.

| | | | | |
|---|---|---|---|---|
| 159 | **29** | 25f. multicoloured | 90 | 50 |

**30** Columns

**1966.** 20th Anniv of UNESCO.

| | | | | |
|---|---|---|---|---|
| 160 | **30** | 32f. blue, violet and red | 90 | 50 |

**1966.** Air. Inauguration of "DC-8" Air Services. As T 54 of Central African Republic.

| | | | |
|---|---|---|---|
| 161 | 30f. grey, black and green | 90 | 40 |

**31** Skull of Lake Chad Man ("Tchadanthropus uxoris")

**1966.** Archaeological Excavation.

| | | | | |
|---|---|---|---|---|
| 162 | **31** | 30f. slate, yellow and red | 2·40 | 1·10 |

**32** White-throated Bee Eater

**1966.** Air. Birds. Multicoloured.

| | | | |
|---|---|---|---|
| 163 | 50f. Greater blue-eared glossy starling | 1·60 | 70 |
| 164 | 100f. Type **32** | 3·50 | 1·70 |
| 165 | 200f. African pigmy kingfisher | 6·00 | 2·75 |
| 166 | 250f. Red-throated bee eater | 7·75 | 3·00 |
| 167 | 500f. Little green bee eater | 14·00 | 6·00 |

**33** Battle-axe

**1966.** Prehistoric Implements.

| | | | | |
|---|---|---|---|---|
| 168 | **33** | 25f. brown, blue and red | 75 | 30 |
| 169 | - | 30f. black, brown & blue | 1·00 | 50 |
| 170 | - | 85f. brown, red and blue | 2·75 | 95 |
| 171 | - | 100f. brown, turq & sepia | 3·25 | 1·40 |
| **MS**172 | | 129×99 mm. Nos. 168/71 | 13·00 | 9·25 |

DESIGNS: 30f. Arrowhead; 85f. Harpoon; 100f. Sandstone grindstone and pounder. From Tchad National Museum.

**34** Congress Palace

**1967.** Air.

| | | | | |
|---|---|---|---|---|
| 173 | **34** | 25f. multicoloured | 90 | 40 |

**35** Sportsmen and Dais on Map

**1967.** Sports Day.

| | | | | |
|---|---|---|---|---|
| 174 | **35** | 25f. multicoloured | 90 | 55 |

**36** "Colotis protomedia klug"

**1967.** Butterflies. Multicoloured.

| | | | |
|---|---|---|---|
| 175 | 5f. Type **36** | 1·40 | 40 |
| 176 | 10f. "Charaxes jasius epijasius L" | 2·75 | 95 |
| 177 | 20f. "Junonia cebrene trim" | 6·00 | 2·00 |
| 178 | 130f. "Danaida petiverana H.D." | 13·00 | 3·50 |

**37** Lions Emblem

**1967.** Air. 50th Anniv of Lions International.

| | | | | |
|---|---|---|---|---|
| 179 | **37** | 50f.+10f. multicoloured | 1·80 | 95 |

**38** Dagnaux's Breguet "19" Aircraft

**1967.** Air. 1st Anniv of Air Chad Airline.

| | | | | |
|---|---|---|---|---|
| 180 | **38** | 25f. green, blue & brown | 90 | 40 |
| 181 | - | 30f. indigo, green and blue | 1·10 | 55 |
| 182 | - | 50f. brown, green & blue | 2·10 | 1·20 |
| 183 | - | 100f. red, blue and green | 3·75 | 1·60 |

DESIGNS: 30f. Latecoere "631" flying-boat; 50f. Douglas "DC-3"; 100f. Piper Cherokee "6".

**1967.** Air. 5th Anniv of UAMPT. As T 66 of Central African Republic.

| | | | |
|---|---|---|---|
| 184 | 100f. brown, bistre & mve | 2·40 | 1·10 |

**39** H.Q. Building

**1967.** Opening of WHO Regional Headquarters, Brazzaville.

| | | | | |
|---|---|---|---|---|
| 185 | **39** | 30f. multicoloured | 90 | 50 |

**40** Scouts and Jamboree Emblem

**1967.** World Scout Jamboree, Idaho. Multicoloured.

| | | | |
|---|---|---|---|
| 186 | 25f. Type **40** | 80 | 30 |
| 187 | 32f. Scout and Jamboree emblem | 1·10 | 40 |

**41** Flour Mills

**1967.** Economic Development.

| | | | | |
|---|---|---|---|---|
| 188 | **41** | 25f. slate, brown and blue | 70 | 30 |
| 189 | - | 30f. blue, brown & green | 90 | 50 |

DESIGN: 30f. Land reclamation, Lake Bol.

**42** Woman and Harpist

**1967.** Bailloud Mission in the Ennedi. Rock paintings.

| | | | | |
|---|---|---|---|---|
| 190 | | 2f. choc, brn & red (post) | 50 | 15 |
| 191 | | 10f. red, brown and violet | 1·20 | 40 |
| 192 | **42** | 15f. lake, brown and blue | 1·60 | 40 |
| 193 | - | 20f. red, brown and green | 3·00 | 1·10 |
| 194 | - | 25f. red, brown and blue | 3·25 | 1·20 |
| 195 | - | 30f. lake, brown and blue | 1·50 | 75 |

196 - 50f. lake, brown and green 2·40 1·20
197 - 100f. red, brn & grn (air) 6·75 2·10
198 - 125f. lake, brown & blue 8·00 3·00

DESIGNS: 2f. Archers; 10f. Male and female costumes; 20f. Funeral vigil; 25f. "Dispute"; 30f. Giraffes; 50f. Cameleer pursuing ostrich. (48×27 mm): 100f. Masked dancers; 125f. Hunters and hare.

43 Emblem of Rotary International

**1968.** 10th Anniv of Rotary Club, Fort Lamy.
199 43 50f. multicoloured 1·30 75

44 Downhill Skiing

**1968.** Air. Winter Olympic Games, Grenoble.
200 44 30f. brown, green & purple 1·20 60
201 - 100f. blue, green & turq 3·75 1·60

DESIGN—VERT: 100f. Ski-jumping.

45 Chancellor Adenauer

**1968.** Air. Adenauer Commemoration.
202 45 52f. brown, lilac and green 1·50 75
**MS**203 120×170 mm. No. 202×4 6·50 6·00

46 "Health Services"

**1968.** Air. Anniv of WHO.
204 46 25f. multicoloured 70 45
205 46 32f. multicoloured 90 45

47 Allegory of Irrigation

**1968.** International Hydrological Decade.
206 47 50f. blue, brown & green 1·20 50

48 "The Snake-charmer"

**1968.** Air. Paintings by Henri Rousseau. Mult.
207 100f. Type **48** 3·75 2·10
208 130f. "The War" (49×35 mm) 5·75 3·00

49 College Building, Student and Emblem

**1968.** National College of Administration.
209 49 25f. purple, blue and red 75 30

50 Child writing and Blackboard

**1968.** Literacy Day.
210 50 60f. black, blue & brown 1·20 55

51 Harvesting Cotton

**1968.** Cotton Industry.
211 51 25f. purple, green & blue 80 30
212 - 30f. brown, blue & green 85 40

DESIGN—VERT: 30f. Loom, Fort Archambault Mill.

52 "Utetheisa pulchella"

**1968.** Butterflies and Moths. Multicoloured.
213 25f. Type **52** 4·00 90
214 30f. "Ophideres materna" 4·75 1·00
215 50f. "Gynanisa maja" 7·75 1·20
216 100f. "Epiphora bauhiniae" 9·50 2·40

53 Hurdling

**1968.** Air. Olympic Games, Mexico.
217 53 32f. chocolate, grn & brn 1·20 75
218 - 80f. purple, blue and red 3·00 1·40

DESIGN: 80f. Relay-racing.

54 Human Rights Emblem within Man

**1968.** Human Rights Year.
219 54 32f. red, green and blue 90 40

**1969.** Air. "Philexafrique" Stamp Exn, Abidjan, Ivory Coast (1st issue). As T 137 of Cameroun. Multicoloured.
220 100f. "The actor Wolf, called Bernard" (J. L. David) 4·25 3·75

**1969.** Air. "Philexafrique" Stamp Exn, Abidjan, Ivory Coast (2nd issue). As T 138 of Cameroun. Multicoloured.
221 50f. Moundangs dancers and Chad postage due stamp of 1930 2·75 2·50

55 G. Nachtigal and Tibesti landscape, 1869

**1969.** Air. Chad Explorers.
222 - 100f. violet, green & blue 2·75 1·10
223 55 100f. purple, blue & brown 2·75 1·10

DESIGN: No. 222, H. Barth (portrait) and aboard canoe, Lake Region, 1851.

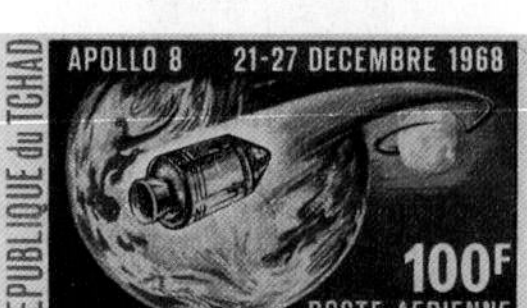

56 "Apollo 8" circling Moon

**1969.** Air. Flight of "Apollo 8" around the Moon.
224 56 100f. black, blue & orange 2·40 1·10

57 St. Bartholomew

**1969.** Jubilee Year of Catholic Church. Mult.
225 50c. St. Paul 10 10
226 1f. St. Peter 10 10
227 2f. St. Thomas 10 10
228 5f. St. John the Evangelist 10 10
229 10f. Type **57** 15 10
230 20f. St. Matthew 35 15
231 25f. St. James the Less 40 20
232 30f. St. Andrew 55 30
233 40f. St. Jude 60 40
234 50f. St. James the Greater 75 40
235 85f. St. Philip 1·20 70
236 100f. St. Simon 1·20 80

58 Mahatma Gandhi

**1969.** Air. "Apostles of Peace".
237 58 50f. brown and green 1·50 75
238 - 50f. sepia and agate 1·50 75
239 - 50f. brown and pink 1·50 75
240 - 50f. brown and blue 1·50 75
**MS**241 120×160 mm. Nos. 237/40 6·75 6·50

DESIGNS: No. 238, President Kennedy; No. 239, Martin Luther King; No. 240, Robert F. Kennedy.

59 Motor Vehicles and ILO Emblem

**1969.** 50th Anniv of ILO.
242 59 32f. blue, purple & green 90 50

60 Cipolla, Baran and Sambo (pair with cox)

61 "African Woman" (Bezombes)

**1969.** "World Solidarity". Multicoloured. (a) Gold Medal Winners, Mexico Olympics.
243 1f. Type **60** 50 45
244 1f. R. Beamon (long-jump) 40 40
245 1f. I. Becker (women's pentathlon) 40 40
246 1f. C. Besson (women's 400 m) 40 40
247 1f. W. Davenport (110 m hurdles) 40 40
248 1f. K. Dibiasi (diving) 40 40
249 1f. R. Fosbury (high-jump) 40 40
250 1f. M. Gamoudi (5000 m) 40 40
251 1f. Great Britain (sailing) 40 40
252 1f. J. Guyon (cross-country riding) 40 40
253 1f. D. Hemery (400 m hurdles) 40 40
254 1f. S. Kato (gymnastics) 40 40
255 1f. B. Klinger (small bore rifle shooting) 40 40
256 1f. R. Matson (shot put) 40 40
257 1f. R. Matthes (100 m backstroke) 40 40
258 1f. D. Meyer (women's 200 m freestyle) 40 40
259 1f. Morelon and Trentin (tandem cycle) 40 40
260 1f. D. Rebillard (4000 m cycle pursuit) 40 40
261 1f. T. Smith (200 m) 40 40
262 1f. P. Trentin (1000 m cycle) 40 40
263 1f. F. Vianelli (196 km cycle race) 40 40
264 1f. West Germany (dressage) 40 40
265 1f. M. Wolke (welterweight boxing) 40 40
266 1f. Zimmermann and Esser (women's kayak pair) 40 40

(b) Paintings.
267 1f. Type **61** 40 40
268 1f. "Mother and Child" (Gauguin) 40 40
269 1f. "Holy Family" (Murillo) (horiz) 40 40
270 1f. "Adoration of the Kings" (Rubens) 40 40
271 1f. "Three Negroes" (Rubens) 40 40
272 1f. "Woman with Flowers" (Veneto) 40 40

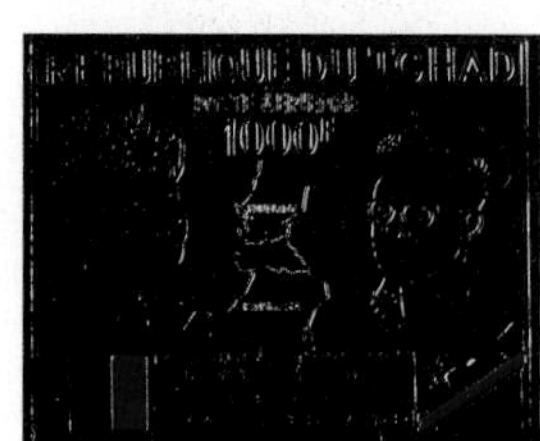

62 Presidents Tombalbaye and Mobutu

**1969.** Air. 1st Anniv of Central African States Union.
273 62 1000f. gold, red and blue 30·00 29·00

This stamp is embossed in gold foil; colours of flags enamelled.

63 "Cochlospermum tinctorium"

**1969.** Flowers. Multicoloured.
274 1f. Type **63** 40 10
275 4f. "Parkia biglobosa" 65 20
276 10f. "Pancratium trianthum" 90 40
277 15f. "Ipomoea aquatica" 1·50 50

**1969.** Air. Birth Bicentenary of Napoleon Bonaparte. Multicoloured. As T 144 of Cameroun.
278 30f. "Napoleon visiting the Hotel des Invalides" (Veron-Bellecourt) 1·50 1·10
279 85f. "The Battle of Wagram" (H. Vernet) 3·00 1·50
280 130f. "The Battle of Austerlitz" (Gerard) 5·00 2·50

**64** Frozen Carcases

**1969.** Frozen Meat Industry.

281 **64** 25f. red, green and orange 60 30

282 - 30f. brown, slate & green 75 40

DESIGN: 30f. Cattle and refrigerated abattoir, Farcha.

**1969.** 5th Anniv of African Development Bank. As T 146 of Cameroun.

283 30f. brown, green and red 75 40

**66** Astronaut and Lunar Module

**1969.** Air. 1st Man on the Moon. Embossed on gold foil.

289 **66** 1000f. gold 30·00 29·00

**67** Nile Mouthbrooder

**1969.** Fishes.

290 **67** 2f. purple, grey and green 50 15

291 - 3f. grey, red and blue 75 25

292 - 5f. blue, yellow and ochre 1·10 35

293 - 20f. blue, green and red 3·50 90

FISHES: 3f. Deep-sided citharinid; 5f. Nile pufferfish; 20f. Lesser tigerfish.

**1969.** 10th Anniv of ASECNA. As T 150 of Cameroun.

294 30f. orange 90 50

**68** President Tombalbaye

**1970.** President Tombalbaye.

295 **68** 25f. multicoloured 75 30

**69** "Village Life" (G. Narcisse)

**1970.** Air. African Paintings. Multicoloured.

296 100f. Type **69** 3·50 1·50

297 250f. "Market Woman" (I. N'Diaye) 5·50 2·20

298 250f. "Flower-seller" (I. N'Diaye) (vert) 5·50 2·20

**70** Lenin

**1970.** Birth Centenary of Lenin.

299 **70** 150f. black, cream & gold 4·25 1·90

**1970.** New U.P.U. Headquarters Building, Berne, As T 156 of Cameroun.

300 30f. brown, violet and red 90 50

**71** Class and Torchbearers

**1970.** International Education Year.

301 **71** 100f. multicoloured 2·10 1·20

**72** Osaka Print

**1970.** Air. World Fair "EXPO 70", Osaka, Japan.

302 **72** 50f. green, blue and red 90 55

303 - 100f. blue, green and red 1·50 75

304 - 125f. slate, brown & red 2·20 1·10

DESIGNS: 100f. Tower of the Sun; 125f. Osaka print (different).

**1970.** Air. "Apollo" Moon Flights. Nos. 164/6 surch with new value, and optd with various inscriptions and diagrams concerning space flights.

305 **32** 50f. on 100f. mult ("Apollo 11") 1·50 55

306 - 100f. on 200f. mult ("Apollo 12") 3·00 90

307 - 125f. on 250f. mult ("Apollo 13") 3·75 1·10

**74** Meteorological Equipment and "Agriculture"

**1970.** World Meteorological Day.

308 **74** 50f. grey, green & orange 1·10 45

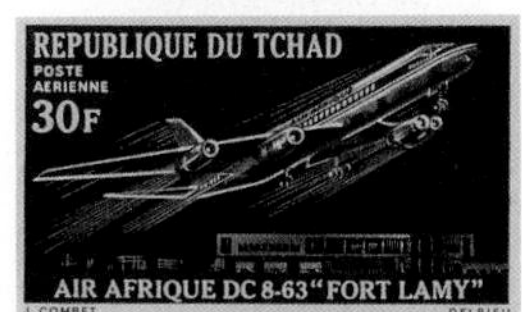


**75** "DC-8-63" over Airport

**1970.** Air. "Air Afrique" DC-8 "Fort Lamy".

309 **75** 30f. multicoloured 1·20 60

**76** Ahmed Mangue (Minister of Education)

**1970.** Ahmed Mangue (air crash victim) Commem.

310 **76** 100f. black, red and gold 1·80 75

**77** Tanning

**1970.** Trades and Handicrafts.

311 **77** 1f. bistre, brown and blue 15 10

312 - 2f. brown, blue and green 20 10

313 - 3f. violet, brown & mauve 35 15

314 - 4f. brown, bistre & green 40 15

315 - 5f. brown, green and red 80 50

DESIGNS—VERT: 2f. Dyeing; 4f. Water-carrying. HORIZ: 3f. Milling palm-nuts for oil; 5f. Copper-founding.

**78** U.N. Emblem and Dove

**1970.** 25th Anniv of United Nations.

316 **78** 32f. multicoloured 90 55

**79** "The Visitation" (Venetian School, 15th cent)

**1970.** Air. Christmas. Multicoloured.

317 20f. Type **79** 80 50

318 25f. "The Nativity" (Venetian School, 15th cent) 1·20 55

319 30f. "Virgin and Child" (Veneziano) 1·40 75

**80** Map and OCAM Building

**1971.** OCAM (Organization Commune Africane et Malgache) Conference, Fort Lamy.

320 **80** 30f. multicoloured 90 50

**81** Maritius "Post Office" 2d. of 1847

**1971.** Air. "PHILEXOCAM" Stamp Exhibition, Fort-Lamy.

321 **81** 10f. slate, brown & turq 55 30

322 - 20f. brown, black & turq 55 30

323 - 30f. brown, black and red 75 50

324 - 60f. black, brown & purple 1·20 60

325 - 80f. slate, brown and blue 1·80 1·10

326 - 100f. brown, slate & blue 2·20 1·50

**MS**327 160×130 mm. Nos. 321/6 8·75 8·25

DESIGNS—20f. Tuscany 3 lire of 1860; 30f. France 1f. of 1849; 30f., 60f. U.S.A. 10c. of 1847; 80f. Japan 5 sen of 1872; 100f. Saxony 3pf. of 1850.

**82** Pres. Nasser

**1971.** Air. 1st Death Anniv of Gamal Abdel Nasser (Egypt).

328 **82** 75f. multicoloured 1·20 55

**83** "Racial Harmony" Tree

**1971.** Racial Equality Year.

329 **83** 40f. red, green and blue 1·10 60

**1971.** Air. Reconciliation with Central African Republic and Zaire. As T 106 of Central African Republic.

330 100f. multicoloured 2·10 1·10

**84** Map and Dish Aerial

**1971.** World Telecommunications Day.

331 **84** 5f. orge, red & bl (postage) 35 10

332 - 40f. green, brown & pur 95 40

333 - 50f. black, brown & red 1·10 60

334 - 125f. red, green & blue (air) 2·75 1·40

DESIGNS: 40f. Map and communications tower; 50f. Map and satellite. (48×27 mm): 125f. Map and telecommunications symbols.

**85** Scouts by Camp-fire

**1971.** Air. World Scout Jamboree, Asagiri, Japan.

335 **85** 250f. multicoloured 5·75 2·75

**86** Great Egret

**1971.** Air.

336 **86** 1000f. multicoloured 60·00 22·00

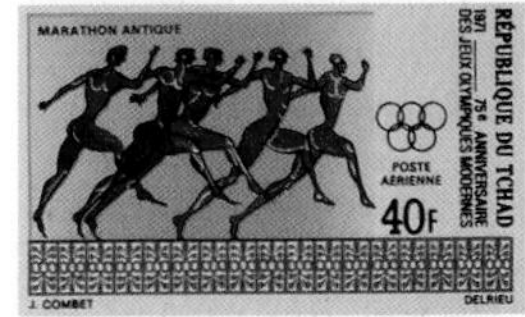


**87** Ancient Marathon Race

**1971.** Air. 75th Anniv of Modern Olympic Games. Multicoloured.

337 40f. Type **87** 95 50

338 45f. Ancient stadium, Olympia 1·30 50

339 75f. Ancient wrestling 1·60 75

340 130f. Athens Stadium, 1896 Games 2·50 1·10

**88** Sidney Bechet

**1971.** Air. Famous American Black Musicians. Multicoloured.

| | | | | |
|---|---|---|---|---|
| 341 | | 50f. Type **88** | 2·00 | 85 |
| 342 | | 75f. Duke Ellington | 3·00 | 1·20 |
| 343 | | 100f. Louis Armstrong | 4·75 | 1·70 |

**89** Gen. de Gaulle

**1971.** Air. 1st Death Anniv of De Gaulle.

| | | | | |
|---|---|---|---|---|
| 344 | - | 200f. gold, blue and light blue | 9·00 | 8·75 |
| 345 | **89** | 200f. gold, green & yellow | 8·75 | 8·25 |
| **MS**346 | | 110×70 mm. Nos. 344/5 and central stamp-sized label with inscr | 22·00 | 22·00 |

DESIGN: No. 344, Governor-General Felix Eboue.

**1971.** Air. 10th Anniv of African and Malagasy Posts and Telecommunications Union. As T 184 of Cameroun. Multicoloured.

| | | | |
|---|---|---|---|
| 347 | 100f. Headquarters building and Sao carved animal head | 1·80 | 1·10 |

**90** Children's Heads

**1971.** 25th Anniv of UNICEF.

| | | | | |
|---|---|---|---|---|
| 348 | **90** | 50f. blue, green & purple | 1·20 | 55 |

On the above stamp, "24e" has been obliterated and "25e" inserted in the commemorative inscription.

**91** Gorane Nangara Dancers

**1971.** Chad Dancers. Multicoloured.

| | | | |
|---|---|---|---|
| 349 | 10f. Type **91** | 75 | 30 |
| 350 | 15f. Yondo initiates | 1·10 | 45 |
| 351 | 30f. M'Boum (vert) | 1·60 | 65 |
| 352 | 40f. Sara Kaba (vert) | 2·40 | 90 |

**93** Presidents Pompidou and Tombalbaye

**1972.** Visit of French President.

| | | | | |
|---|---|---|---|---|
| 354 | **93** | 40f. multicoloured | 1·90 | 85 |

**94** Bobsleighing

**1972.** Air. Winter Olympic Games, Sapporo, Japan.

| | | | | |
|---|---|---|---|---|
| 355 | **94** | 50f. red and blue | 1·10 | 70 |
| 356 | - | 100f. green and purple | 2·20 | 95 |

DESIGN: 100f. Slalom.

**95** Human Heart

**1972.** World Heart Month.

| | | | | |
|---|---|---|---|---|
| 357 | **95** | 100f. red, blue and violet | 2·10 | 1·10 |

**96** "Gorrizia dubiosa"

**1972.** Insects. Multicoloured.

| | | | |
|---|---|---|---|
| 358 | 1f. Type **96** | 85 | 25 |
| 359 | 2f. "Argiope sector" | 1·40 | 30 |
| 360 | 3f. "Nephila senegalense" | 1·60 | 40 |
| 361 | 4f. "Oryctes boas" | 2·75 | 55 |
| 362 | 5f. "Hemistigma albipunctata" | 3·50 | 55 |
| 363 | 25f. "Dinothrombium tinctorium" | 1·10 | 40 |
| 364 | 30f. "Bupreste sternocera H." | 1·70 | 45 |
| 365 | 40f. "Hyperechia bomboides" | 2·10 | 50 |
| 366 | 50f. "Chrysis" (Hymenoptere) | 2·50 | 70 |
| 367 | 100f. "Tithoes confinis" (Longicore) | 4·25 | 1·20 |
| 368 | 130f. "Galeodes araba" (Solifuge) | 7·00 | 1·90 |

**1972.** Air. UNESCO "Save Venice" Campaign. As T 191 of Cameroun. Multicoloured.

| | | | |
|---|---|---|---|
| 369 | 40f. "Harbour Panorama" (detail, Caffi) | 1·80 | 70 |
| 370 | 45f. "Venice Panorama" (detail, Caffi) (horiz) | 2·40 | 1·10 |
| 371 | 140f. "Grand Canal" (detail, Caffi) | 4·75 | 2·10 |

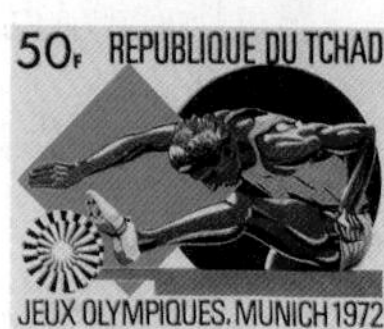

**97** Hurdling

**1972.** Olympic Games, Munich. Multicoloured.

| | | | |
|---|---|---|---|
| 372 | 50f. Type **97** | 90 | 45 |
| 373 | 130f. Gymnastics | 2·20 | 1·10 |
| 374 | 150f. Swimming | 3·00 | 1·40 |
| **MS**375 | 102×86 mm. 300f. Cycling | 7·75 | 3·25 |

**98** Alphonse Daudet and Scene from "Tartarin de Tarascon"

**1972.** Air. International Book Year.

| | | | | |
|---|---|---|---|---|
| 376 | **98** | 100f. brown, red & purple | 2·20 | 1·10 |

**99** Dromedary

**1972.** Domestic Animals.

| | | | | |
|---|---|---|---|---|
| 377 | **99** | 25f. brown and violet | 1·30 | 30 |
| 378 | - | 30f. blue and mauve | 1·70 | 40 |
| 379 | - | 40f. brown and green | 2·40 | 55 |
| 380 | - | 45f. brown and blue | 2·75 | 60 |

DESIGNS: 30f. Horse; 40f. Saluki hound; 45f. Goat.

**100** "Luna 16" and Moon Probe

**1972.** Air. Russian Moon Exploration.

| | | | | |
|---|---|---|---|---|
| 381 | **100** | 100f. violet, brown & blue | 2·20 | 95 |
| 382 | - | 150f. brown, blue & purple | 3·00 | 1·50 |

DESIGN—HORIZ: 150f. "Lunokhod 1" Moon vehicle.

**101** Tobacco Production

**1972.** Economic Development.

| | | | | |
|---|---|---|---|---|
| 383 | **101** | 40f. green, red & brown | 80 | 40 |
| 384 | - | 50f. brown, green & blue | 1·20 | 55 |

DESIGN: 50f. Ploughing with oxen.

**102** Microscope, Cattle and Laboratory

**1972.** Air. 20th Anniv of Farcha Veterinary Laboratory.

| | | | | |
|---|---|---|---|---|
| 385 | **102** | 75f. multicoloured | 1·50 | 60 |

**103** Massa Warrior

**1972.** Chad Warriors. Multicoloured.

| | | | |
|---|---|---|---|
| 386 | 15f. Type **103** | 85 | 30 |
| 387 | 20f. Moudang archer | 1·00 | 55 |

**104** King Faisal and Pres. Tombalbaye

**1972.** Visit of King Faisal of Saudi Arabia. Multicoloured.

| | | | |
|---|---|---|---|
| 389 | 75f. King Faisal and Ka'aba, Mecca (air) | 1·50 | 75 |
| 388 | 100f. Type **104** (postage) | 2·75 | 1·30 |

**105** Gen. Gowon, Pres. Tombalbaye and Map

**1972.** Visit of Gen. Gowon, Nigerian Head-of-State.

| | | | | |
|---|---|---|---|---|
| 390 | **105** | 70f. multicoloured | 1·10 | 50 |

**106** "Madonna and Child" (G. Bellini)

**1972.** Air. Christmas. Paintings. Multicoloured.

| | | | |
|---|---|---|---|
| 391 | 40f. Type **106** | 90 | 40 |
| 392 | 75f. "Virgin and Child" (bas-relief, Da Santivo, Dall' Occhio) | 1·40 | 65 |
| 393 | 80f. "Nativity" (B. Angelico) (horiz) | 2·10 | 80 |
| 394 | 90f. "Adoration of the Magi" (P. Perugino) | 2·40 | 1·40 |

**107** Commemorative Scroll

**1972.** 50th Anniv of U.S.S.R.

| | | | | |
|---|---|---|---|---|
| 395 | **107** | 150f. multicoloured | 2·20 | 85 |

**108** High-jumping

**1973.** 2nd African Games, Lagos. Multicoloured.

| | | | |
|---|---|---|---|
| 396 | 50f. Type **108** | 1·10 | 55 |
| 397 | 125f. Running | 1·90 | 80 |
| 398 | 200f. Putting the shot | 3·00 | 1·40 |
| **MS**399 | 103×86 mm. 250f. Throwing the discus | 4·25 | 2·75 |

**109** Copernicus and Planetary System Diagram

**1973.** Air. 500th Birth Anniv of Nicholas Copernicus.

| | | | | |
|---|---|---|---|---|
| 400 | **109** | 250f. grey, brown & mve | 6·00 | 2·50 |

**1973.** African Solidarity. "Drought Relief". No. 377 surch SECHERESSE SOLIDARITE AFRICAINE 100F.

| | | | | |
|---|---|---|---|---|
| 401 | **99** | 100f. on 25f. brown & vio | 2·40 | 1·10 |

**1973.** UAMPT. As Type 216 of Cameroun.

| | | | |
|---|---|---|---|
| 402 | 100f. green, red & brown | 2·10 | 95 |

**111** "Skylab" over Globe

**1974.** Air. "Skylab" Exploits.

| | | | | |
|---|---|---|---|---|
| 403 | **111** | 100f. brown, red & blue | 1·80 | 80 |
| 404 | - | 150f. turquoise, blue & brn | 3·00 | 1·20 |

DESIGN: 150f. Close-up of "Skylab".

**112** Chad Mother and Children

**1974.** 1st Anniv of Chad Red Cross.

| | | | | |
|---|---|---|---|---|
| 405 | **112** | 30f.+10f. multicoloured | 1·00 | 85 |

**113** Football Players

**1974.** Air. World Cup Football Championship, West Germany.

| | | | | |
|---|---|---|---|---|
| 406 | **113** | 50f. brown and red | 75 | 60 |
| 407 | - | 125f. green and red (vert) | 2·10 | 95 |
| 408 | - | 150f. red and green | 2·75 | 1·50 |

DESIGNS: Nos. 407/8, Footballers in action similar to Type **113**.

**114** Chad Family

**1974.** Air. World Population Year.

| | | | | |
|---|---|---|---|---|
| 409 | **114** | 250f. brown, green & bl | 4·50 | 2·40 |

**115** U.P.C. Emblem and Mail Canoe

**1974.** Air. Centenary of U.P.U.

| | | | | |
|---|---|---|---|---|
| 410 | **115** | 30f. brown, red & green | 75 | 30 |
| 411 | - | 40f. black and blue | 1·10 | 50 |
| 412 | - | 100f. blue, brown & blk | 2·20 | 75 |
| 413 | - | 150f. violet, green & turq | 3·00 | 1·10 |

DESIGNS—U.P.U. Emblem and: 40f. Electric train; 100f. Jet airliner; 150f. Satellite.

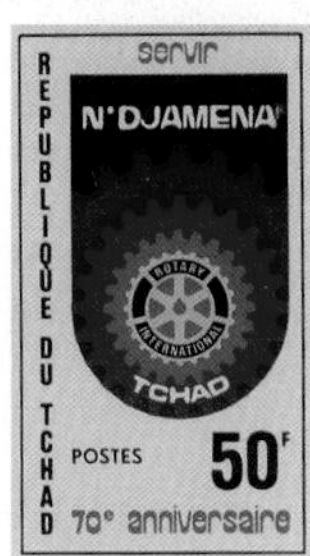


**116** Rotary Emblem

**1975.** 70th Anniv of Rotary International.

| | | | | |
|---|---|---|---|---|
| 414 | **116** | 50f. multicoloured | 1·10 | 55 |

**117** Heads of Women of Four Races

**1975.** Air. International Women's Year.

| | | | | |
|---|---|---|---|---|
| 415 | **117** | 250f. multicoloured | 5·25 | 2·50 |

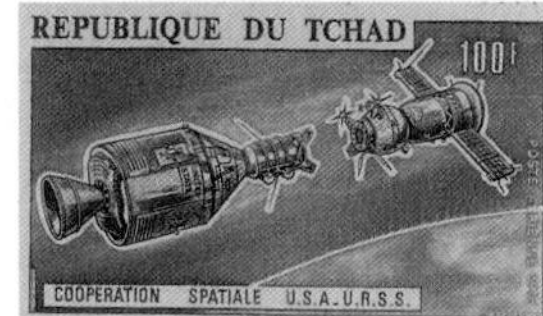


**118** "Apollo" and "Soyuz" Spacecraft about to dock

**1975.** Air. "Apollo–Soyuz" Test Project.

| | | | | |
|---|---|---|---|---|
| 416 | **118** | 100f. brown, blue & green | 1·60 | 75 |
| 417 | - | 130f. brown, blue & green | 2·10 | 1·00 |

DESIGN: 130f. "Apollo" and "Soyuz" spacecraft docked.

**119** "Craterostigma plantagineum"

**1975.** Flowers. Multicoloured.

| | | | |
|---|---|---|---|
| 418 | 5f. Type **119** | 30 | 10 |
| 419 | 10f. "Tapinanthus globiferus" | 50 | 15 |
| 420 | 15f. "Commelina forsalaei" (vert) | 75 | 20 |
| 421 | 20f. "Adenium obasum" | 90 | 25 |
| 422 | 25f. "Hibiscus esulenus" | 1·50 | 30 |
| 423 | 30f. "Hibiscus sabdariffa" | 1·70 | 50 |
| 424 | 40f. "Kigelia africana" | 2·40 | 75 |

**120** Football

**1975.** Air. Olympic Games, Montreal (1976).

| | | | | |
|---|---|---|---|---|
| 425 | **120** | 75f. green and red | 1·10 | 55 |
| 426 | - | 100f. brown, blue & red | 1·80 | 80 |
| 427 | - | 125f. blue and brown | 2·10 | 1·20 |

DESIGNS: 100f. Throwing the discus; 125f. Running.

**1975.** Air. Successful Rendezvous of "Apollo–Soyuz" Mission. Optd JONCTION 17 JUILLET 1975.

| | | | | |
|---|---|---|---|---|
| 428 | **118** | 100f. brown, blue & grn | 1·70 | 95 |
| 429 | - | 130f. brown, blue & grn | 2·30 | 1·50 |

**122** Stylized British and American Flags

**1975.** Air. Bicentenary of American Revolution.

| | | | | |
|---|---|---|---|---|
| 430 | **122** | 150f. blue, red & brown | 2·75 | 1·20 |

**123** "Adoration of the Shepherds" (Murillo)

**1975.** Air. Christmas. Religious Paintings. Mult.

| | | | |
|---|---|---|---|
| 431 | 40f. Type **123** | 85 | 55 |
| 432 | 75f. "Adoration of the Shepherds" (G. de la Tour) | 1·60 | 80 |
| 433 | 80f. "Virgin of the Bible" (R. van der Weyden) (vert) | 1·80 | 80 |
| 434 | 100f. "Holy Family with the Lamb" (attrib. Raphael) (vert) | 2·75 | 1·40 |

**124** Alexander Graham Bell and Satellite

**1976.** Telephone Centenary.

| | | | | |
|---|---|---|---|---|
| 435 | **124** | 100f. multicoloured | 1·70 | 75 |
| 436 | **124** | 125f. multicoloured | 2·50 | 1·10 |

**125** U.S.S.R. (ice hockey)

**1976.** Winter Olympics. Medal-winners, Innsbruck. Multicoloured.

| | | | |
|---|---|---|---|
| 437 | 60f. Type **125** (postage) | 95 | 50 |
| 438 | 90f. Ski-jumping (K. Schnabl, Austria) | 1·40 | 50 |
| 439 | 250f. Bobsleighing (West Germany) (air) | 3·25 | 1·10 |
| 440 | 300f. Speed-skating (J. E. Storholt, Norway) | 4·00 | 1·50 |
| **MS**441 | 103×78 mm. 500f. F. Klamner of Austria (downhill skiing) | 6·50 | 2·75 |

These stamps were not issued without overprints.

**126** Paul Revere (after Copley) and his Night Ride

**1976.** Air. Bicentenary of American Revolution.

| | | | |
|---|---|---|---|
| 442 | 100f. Type **126** | 1·20 | 30 |
| 443 | 125f. Washington (after Stuart) and "Washington crossing the Delaware" (detail, Leutze) | 1·50 | 50 |
| 444 | 150f. Lafayette offering his services to America | 2·10 | 65 |
| 445 | 200f. Rochambeau and detail "Siege of Yorktown" (Couder) | 2·40 | 95 |
| 446 | 250f. Franklin (after Duplessis) and "Declaration of Independence" (detail, Trumball) | 3·75 | 1·10 |
| **MS**447 | 103×78 mm. 400f. De Grasse (after Mauzaisse) and "Battle of Virginia Capes" (detail, Zveg) | 6·50 | 2·75 |

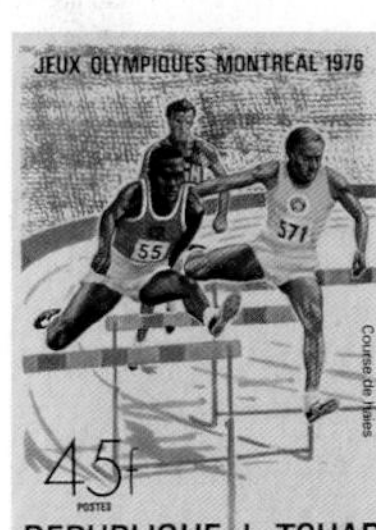


**127** Hurdles

**1976.** Olympic Games, Montreal. Multicoloured.

| | | | |
|---|---|---|---|
| 448 | 45f. Type **127** (postage) | 90 | 30 |
| 449 | 100f. Boxing (air) | 1·50 | 60 |
| 450 | 200f. Pole vaulting | 2·75 | 90 |
| 451 | 300f. Putting the shot | 3·75 | 1·20 |
| **MS**452 | 103×77 mm. 500f. Sprint | 6·50 | 2·75 |

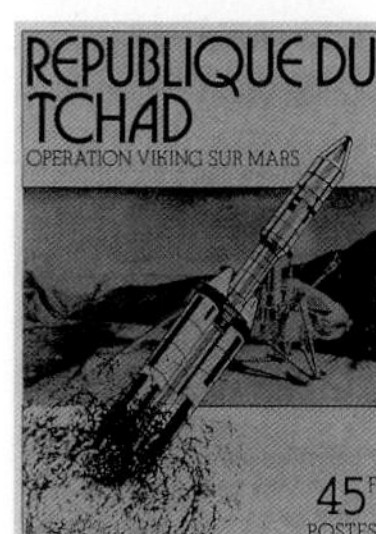


**128** Launch of "Viking"

**1976.** "Viking" landing on Mars. Mult.

| | | | |
|---|---|---|---|
| 453 | 45f. Type **128** (postage) | 60 | 30 |
| 454 | 90f. Trajectory of flight | 1·50 | 50 |
| 455 | 100f. Descent to Mars (air) | 1·10 | 45 |
| 456 | 200f. "Viking" in flight | 2·40 | 65 |
| 457 | 250f. "Viking" on landing approach | 3·00 | 1·10 |
| **MS**458 | 114×89 mm. 450f. "Viking" on Mars | 5·00 | 1·90 |

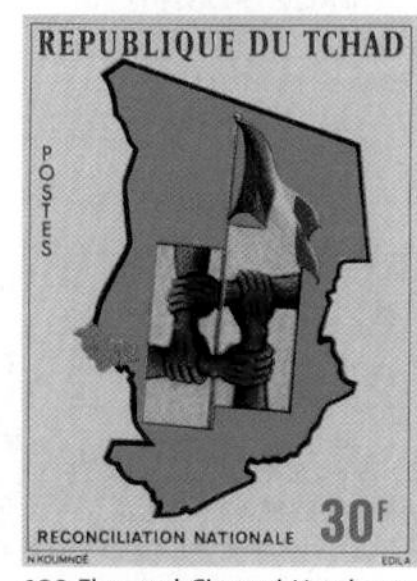


**129** Flag and Clasped Hands on Map of Chad

**1976.** National Reconciliation. Mult.

| | | | |
|---|---|---|---|
| 459 | 30f. Type **129** | 65 | 30 |
| 460 | 60f. Type **129** | 1·20 | 60 |
| 461 | 120f. Map, people and various occupations | 2·75 | 1·20 |

**130** Release of Political Prisoners

**1976.** 1st Anniv of April 1st Revolution. Mult.

| | | | |
|---|---|---|---|
| 462 | 30f. Type **130** | 35 | 20 |
| 463 | 60f. Officer-cadets on parade | 85 | 55 |
| 464 | 120f. Type **130** | 1·80 | 85 |

**131** Concorde

**1976.** Air. Concorde's First Commercial Flight.

| | | | | |
|---|---|---|---|---|
| 465 | **131** | 250f. blue, red & black | 6·50 | 3·75 |

**132** Gourd and Ladle

**1976.** Pyrograved Gourds.

| | | | | |
|---|---|---|---|---|
| 466 | **132** | 30f. multicoloured | 60 | 30 |
| 467 | - | 60f. multicoloured | 95 | 45 |
| 468 | - | 120f. multicoloured | 1·90 | 95 |

DESIGNS: 60f., 120f. Gourds with different decorations.

**1976.** Nobel Prizewinners. As T 189 of Central African Empire. Multicoloured.

| | | | |
|---|---|---|---|
| 469 | 45f. Robert Koch (Medicine, 1905) | 1·50 | 55 |
| 470 | 90f. Anatole France (Literature, 1921) | 1·80 | 80 |
| 471 | 100f. Albert Einstein (Physics, 1921) (air) | 2·20 | 55 |
| 472 | 200f. Dag Hammarskjold (Peace, 1961) | 2·75 | 80 |

473 300f. Dr. S. Tomonaga (Physics, 1965) 4·25 1·10
MS474 116×79 mm. 500f. Alexander Fleming (Medicine, 1945) 9·00 3·00

**133** "The Nativity" (Hans Holbein)

**1976.** Air. Christmas. Multicoloured.
475 30f. "The Nativity" (Altdorfer) 60 30
476 60f. Type **133** 90 50
477 120f. "Adoration of the Shepherds" (Honthorst) (horiz) 1·60 95
478 150f. "Adoration of the Magi" (David) (horiz) 2·40 1·40

**134** "Lesdiguieres Bridge"

**1976.** Air. Centenary of Impressionism. Paintings by Johan Bathold Jongkind. Multicoloured.
479 100f. Type **134** 1·90 1·10
480 120f. "Warship" 2·20 1·10

**1977.** Zeppelin Flights. As T 190 of Central African Empire. Multicoloured.
481 100f. Friedrichshafen and German 50pf. stamp, 1936 (postage) 2·10 1·70
482 125f. Polar scene and German 1m. stamp, 1931 (air) 2·00 60
483 150f. Chicago store and German 4m. stamp, 1933 3·25 75
484 175f. New York, London and German 2m. stamp, 1928 3·75 90
485 200f. New York and U.S. $2.60 stamp, 1930 4·00 1·40
MS486 130×92 mm. 500f. As No. 485 8·75 2·75

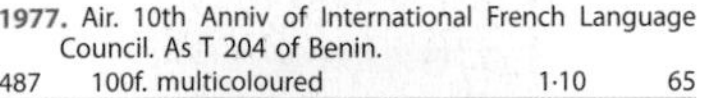

**1977.** Air. 10th Anniv of International French Language Council. As T 204 of Benin.
487 100f. multicoloured 1·10 65

**135** Simon Bolivar

**1977.** Great Personalities. Multicoloured.
488 150f. Type **135** 1·70 65
489 175f. Joseph J. Roberts 2·30 80
490 200f. Queen Wilhelmina 3·00 1·10
491 200f. General de Gaulle 3·50 1·30
493 250f. Coronation of Queen Elizabeth II (horiz) 3·75 1·50
492 325f. King Baudouin and Queen Fabiola 4·25 1·60

**136** Queen Elizabeth II

**1977.** 25th Anniv of Queen Elizabeth II's Accession to Throne Multicoloured.
493a 250f. Type **136** 2·50 90

MS494 110×91 mm. 450f. Queen Elizabeth and Prince Philip 6·50 2·40

**137** Lafayette and Arrival in America

**1977.** Air. Bicentenary of American Independence. Multicoloured.
495 100f. Type **137** 1·50 65
496 120f. Abraham Lincoln 1·90 80
497 150f. F. J. Madison 2·50 1·10

**138** Radio Aerial, Sound Waves and Map

**1977.** Posts and Telecommunications Emblems.
498 - 30f. black and yellow 60 30
499 **138** 60f. multicoloured 90 40
500 - 120f. multicoloured 1·70 95
DESIGNS—HORIZ (47×26 mm): 30f. Posthorn and initials "ONPT". VERT (26×36 mm): 120f. Telecommunications skyline and initials "TIT".

**139** Concorde

**1977.** Air. "North Atlantic"—Concorde and Lindbergh Commemorations.
501 **139** 100f. blue, red & lt blue 2·30 1·20
502 - 120f. brown, blue & grn 1·40 75
503 - 150f. violet, red & green 1·80 1·10
504 - 200f. orange, pur & brn 2·40 1·20
505 - 300f. blue, purple & blk 3·50 1·80
DESIGNS: 120f. to 300f. Various portraits of Lindbergh with "Spirit of St. Louis" against different backgrounds.

**140** "Mariner 10"

**1977.** Air. Space Research.
506 **140** 100f. blue, olive & green 1·20 85
507 - 200f. brown, green & red 2·40 1·40
508 - 300f. brown, grn & bistre 3·50 1·80
DESIGNS: 200f. "Luna 21"; 300f. "Viking".

**141** Running

**1977.** Air. Sports.
509 **141** 30f. brown, red & blue 40 25
510 - 60f. brown, blue & orge 90 50
511 - 120f. multicoloured 1·50 80
512 - 125f. mauve, violet & grn 2·10 1·00
DESIGNS: 60f. Volleyball; 120f. Football; 125f. Basketball.

**142** "Back Pain"

**1977.** World Rheumatism Year.
513 **142** 30f. red, green and violet 60 30
514 - 60f. red, violet and green 1·00 50
515 - 120f. blue, red & lt blue 1·70 1·00
DESIGNS—HORIZ: 60f. "Neck pain". VERT: 120f. "Knee pain".

**1977.** Air. 1st Commercial Paris–New York Flight of Concorde. Optd PARIS NEW-YORK 22.11.77.
516 **139** 100f. blue, red & lt blue 3·50 1·80

**144** Saving a Goal

**1977.** World Football Cup Championship. Mult.
517 40f. Type **144** 55 15
518 60f. Heading the ball 80 30
519 100f. Referee 1·50 50
520 200f. Foot kicking ball 3·00 95
521 300f. Pele (Brazilian player) 4·50 1·30
MS522 118×80 mm. 500f. Helmut Schoen and stadium 6·50 2·75

**145** "Christ in the Manger" (detail)

**1977.** Air. Christmas. Paintings by Rubens. Mult.
523 30f. Type **145** 75 35
524 60f. "Virgin and Child with Two Donors" 1·50 60
525 100f. "The Adoration of the Shepherds" 2·10 85
526 125f. "The Adoration of the Magi" (detail) 2·30 1·20

**1978.** Coronation of Queen Elizabeth II. No. 493 MS494 optd ANNIVERSAIRE DU COURONNEMENT 1953–1978.
527 250f. multicoloured 3·25 1·90
MS528 111×92 mm. 450f. multicoloured 6·75 4·00

**147** Antoine de Saint-Exupery

**1978.** Air. History of Aviation. Multicoloured.
529 40f. Type **147** 75 30
530 50f. Wright Brothers and aircraft in flight 90 50
531 80f. Hugo Junkers 1·20 65
532 100f. Italo Balbo 1·70 85
533 120f. "Concorde" 2·00 1·00
MS534 104×98 mm. 500f. Wright Brothers and aircraft on ground 7·50 2·75

**1978.** Air. "Philexafrique" Stamp Exhibition, Gabon (1st issue), and International Stamp Fair, Essen. As T 237 of Benin. Multicoloured.
535 100f. Grey heron and Mecklenburg-Strelitz, ¼sgr. stamp, 1864 3·75 2·40
536 100f. Black rhinoceros and Chad 500f. stamp, 1961 3·75 2·40

**148** "Portrait"

**1978.** 450th Death Anniv of Albrecht Durer (artist). Multicoloured.
537 60f. Type **148** 65 20
538 150f. "Jacob Muffel" 2·10 50
539 250f. "Young Girl" 3·25 95
540 350f. "Oswolt Krel" 5·00 1·20

**149** "Helene Fourment"

**1978.** 400th Birth Anniv of Peter Paul Rubens (artist). Multicoloured.
541 60f. "Abraham and Melchisedek" (horiz) 95 20
542 120f. Type **149** 2·00 40
543 200f. "David and the Elders of Israel" (horiz) 3·00 95
544 300f. "Anne of Austria" 5·25 1·20
MS545 78×104 mm. 500f. "Marie de Medici" 7·25 2·75

**150** Head and Unhealthy and Healthy Villages

**1978.** National Health Day.
546 **150** 60f. multicoloured 1·10 55

**1978.** World Cup Football Championship Finalists. Nos. 517/21 optd with teams and scores of past finals.
547 **144** 40f. multicoloured 55 30
548 - 60f. multicoloured 80 45
549 - 100f. multicoloured 1·60 75
550 - 200f. multicoloured 3·00 1·40
551 - 300f. multicoloured 4·50 2·20
MS552 118×80 mm. 500f. multicoloured 6·50 6·00
OPTS: 40f. **1962 BRESIL-TCHECOSLOVAQUE 3-1**; 60f. **1966 GRANDE BRETAGNE ALLEMAGNE (RFA) 4-2**; 100f. **1970 BRESIL-ITALIE 4-1**; 200f. **1974 ALLEMAGNE (RFA)-PAYS BAS 2-1**; 300f. **1978 ARGENTINE-PAYS BAS 3-1**; 500f. **ARGENTINE-PAYS BAS 3-1**.

**152** Camel Riders, Satellites and UPU Emblem

**1978.** "Philexafrique 2" Exhibition, Libreville, Gabon (2nd issue).
553 **152** 60f. red, mauve & blue 3·00 1·70
554 - 150f. multicoloured 5·00 3·00
DESIGN: 150f. Mother and child, native village and hibiscus.

**153** Sand Gazelle

**1979.** Endangered Animals. Multicoloured.

| | | | |
|---|---|---|---|
| 555 | 40f. Type **153** | 1·40 | 25 |
| 556 | 50f. Addax | 1·50 | 45 |
| 557 | 60f. Scimitar oryx | 1·80 | 70 |
| 558 | 100f. Cheetah | 3·00 | 1·20 |
| 559 | 150f. African ass | 4·50 | 1·60 |
| 560 | 300f. Black rhinoceros | 8·75 | 2·00 |

**154** African Boy and Wall Painting

**1979.** International Year of the Child. Mult.

| | | | |
|---|---|---|---|
| 561 | 65f. Type **154** | 75 | 20 |
| 562 | 75f. Asian girl | 90 | 40 |
| 563 | 100f. European child and doves | 1·10 | 50 |
| 564 | 150f. African boys and drawing of boats | 1·80 | 75 |
| **MS**565 | 103×77 mm. 250f. Pencil and drawing of hands | 3·50 | 1·70 |

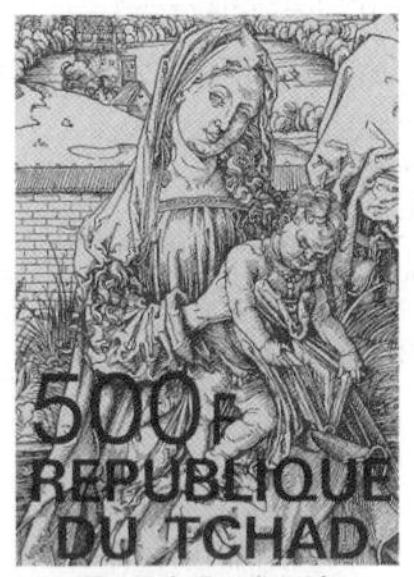


**155** "The Holy Family with There Hares" (woodcut)

**1979.** 450th Death Anniv (1978) of Albrecht Durer (artist). Sheet 90×115 mm.

| | | | |
|---|---|---|---|
| **MS**566 | **155** 500f. lake and brown | 7·75 | 2·40 |

**1979.** 10th Anniv of "Apollo 11" Moon Landing. Nos. 453/7 optd with lunar module and ALUNISSAGE APOLLO XI JUILLET 1969.

| | | | |
|---|---|---|---|
| 567 | 45f. Type **128** (postage) | 65 | 30 |
| 568 | 90f. Trajectory of flight | 1·20 | 50 |
| 569 | 100f. Descent on Mars (air) | 1·20 | 70 |
| 570 | 200f. "Viking" in flight | 2·30 | 1·20 |
| 571 | 250f. "Viking" on landing approach | 3·00 | 1·60 |
| **MS**572 | 114×89 mm. 450f. multicoloured | 5·50 | 5·25 |

**157** Hurdles

**1979.** Air. Olympic Games, Moscow 1980. Mult.

| | | | |
|---|---|---|---|
| 573 | 15f. Type **157** | 15 | 10 |
| 574 | 30f. Hockey | 35 | 25 |
| 575 | 250f. Swimming | 2·75 | 95 |
| 576 | 350f. Running | 3·75 | 1·20 |
| **MS**577 | 117×80 mm. 500f. Yachting | 6·75 | 2·75 |

**158** Reed Canoe and Austrian 10k. stamp, 1910

**1979.** Air. Death Centenary of Sir Rowland Hill. Multicoloured.

| | | | |
|---|---|---|---|
| 578 | 65f. Type **158** | 90 | 10 |
| 579 | 100f. Sailing canoe and U.S. $1 stamp of 1894 | 1·50 | 50 |
| 580 | 200f. "Curacao" (paddle- steamer) and French 1f. stamp of 1853 | 2·75 | 85 |
| 581 | 300f. "Calypso" (liner) and Holstein 1¼s. stamp of 1864 | 3·25 | 1·10 |
| **MS**582 | 103×91 mm. 500f. Liner and Chad 10c. Postage Due stamps of 1930 | 7·25 | 2·75 |

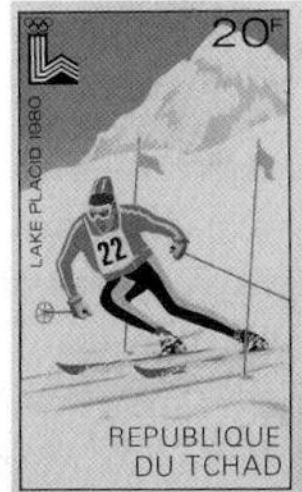


**159** Slalom

**1979.** Winter Olympic Games, Lake Placid (1980). Multicoloured.

| | | | |
|---|---|---|---|
| 583 | 20f. Type **159** | 35 | 10 |
| 584 | 40f. Biathlon | 60 | 10 |
| 585 | 60f. Ski jump (horiz) | 90 | 20 |
| 586 | 150f. Women's giant slalom | 1·80 | 50 |
| 587 | 350f. Cross-country skiing (horiz) | 3·50 | 1·20 |
| 588 | 500f. Downhill skiing (horiz) | 5·25 | 1·80 |

**160** "Concorde" and Map of Africa

**1980.** 20th Anniv of African Air Safety Organization (ASECNA).

| | | | | |
|---|---|---|---|---|
| 589 | **160** | 15f. multicoloured | 15 | 10 |
| 590 | **160** | 30f. multicoloured | 35 | 15 |
| 591 | **160** | 60f. multicoloured | 65 | 30 |

**1981.** Various stamps optd POSTES 1981 or surch also.

| | | | | |
|---|---|---|---|---|
| 592 | **157** | 30f. on 15f. multicoloured | 1·30 | 85 |
| 593 | - | 30f. mult (No. 574) | 1·30 | 85 |
| 594 | **158** | 60f. on 65f. multicoloured | 2·40 | 1·60 |
| 595 | - | 60f. on 100f. mult (No. 579) | 2·40 | 1·60 |

**162** Footballer

**1982.** World Cup Football Championship, Spain. Multicoloured.

| | | | |
|---|---|---|---|
| 596 | 30f. Hungary (postage) | 35 | 10 |
| 597 | 40f. Type **162** | 55 | 10 |
| 598 | 50f. Algeria | 55 | 30 |
| 599 | 60f. Argentina | 65 | 40 |
| 600 | 80f. Brazil (air) | 1·00 | 45 |
| 601 | 300f. West Germany | 3·50 | 1·00 |
| **MS**602 | 77×100 mm. 500f. Spain (38×48 mm) | 6·50 | 2·20 |

DESIGNS: As T **162** but each value showing different team's footballer.

**163** Lady Diana and her Brother (1967)

**1982.** 21st Birthday of Princess of Wales. Mult.

| | | | |
|---|---|---|---|
| 603 | 30f. Lady Diana in christening robe (1961) (postage) | 45 | 10 |
| 604 | 40f. Portrait of Lady Diana (1965) | 50 | 15 |
| 605 | 50f. Type **163** | 75 | 30 |
| 606 | 60f. Lady Diana and her pony (1975) | 80 | 40 |
| 607 | 80f. Lady Diana in Switzerland (1977) (air) | 1·00 | 40 |
| 608 | 300f. Lady Diana as nursery teacher (1980) | 3·50 | 1·10 |
| **MS**609 | 78×75 mm. 500f. Princess of Wales (39×36 mm) | 6·00 | 1·90 |

**164** West German Scouts

**1982.** 75th Anniv of Scout Movement. Mult.

| | | | |
|---|---|---|---|
| 610 | 30f. Type **164** (postage) | 55 | 10 |
| 611 | 40f. Upper Volta scouts | 55 | 15 |
| 612 | 50f. Mali scouts and African dancers | 75 | 30 |
| 613 | 60f. Scottish scout, piper and dancer | 80 | 40 |
| 614 | 80f. Kuwait scouts (air) | 1·00 | 40 |
| 615 | 300f. Chad cub scout | 3·50 | 1·10 |
| **MS**616 | 110×74 mm. 500f. Chad scouts (53×35 mm) | 5·50 | 1·90 |

**165** Judo

**1982.** Olympic Games, Los Angeles (1984) (1st issue). Multicoloured.

| | | | |
|---|---|---|---|
| 617 | 30f. Gymnastics (horse exercise) (postage) | 35 | 10 |
| 618 | 40f. Show jumping | 55 | 15 |
| 619 | 50f. Type **165** | 55 | 30 |
| 620 | 60f. High jumping | 65 | 40 |
| 621 | 80f. Hurdling (air) | 1·00 | 40 |
| 622 | 300f. Gymnastics (floor exercise) | 3·50 | 1·10 |
| **MS**623 | 110×82 mm. 500f. Relay (56×38 mm) | 5·50 | 1·90 |

See also Nos. 678/**MS**684 and 735/**MS**739.

**1982.** Birth of Prince William of Wales. Nos. 603/8 optd 21 JUIN 1982 WILLIAM ARTHUR PHILIP LOUIS PRINCE DE GALLES.

| | | | |
|---|---|---|---|
| 624 | 30f. Type **163** (postage) | 55 | 10 |
| 625 | 40f. Portrait of Lady Diana as a young girl | 55 | 10 |
| 626 | 50f. Lady Diana and her brother | 75 | 30 |
| 627 | 60f. Lady Diana with her pony | 80 | 30 |
| 628 | 80f. Lady Diana in Switzerland (air) | 90 | 30 |
| 629 | 300f. Lady Diana with children | 3·50 | 1·30 |
| **MS**630 | 78×75 mm. 500f. Portrait (39×36 mm) | 5·50 | 2·75 |

**167** Marco Tardelli (Italy) and Passarella (Argentine)

**1983.** World Cup Football Championship Results. Multicoloured.

| | | | |
|---|---|---|---|
| 631 | 30f. Type **167** (postage) | 55 | 10 |
| 632 | 40f. Paolo Rossi (Italy) and Zico (Brazil) | 55 | 15 |
| 633 | 50f. Pierre Littbarski (West Germany) and Platini (France) | 75 | 30 |
| 634 | 60f. Gabriele Oriali (Italy) and Smolarek (Poland) | 80 | 40 |
| 635 | 70f. Boniek (Poland) and Alain Giresse (France) (air) | 90 | 40 |
| 636 | 300f. Bruno Conti (Italy) and Paul Breitner (West Germany) | 3·25 | 1·10 |
| **MS**637 | 110×79 mm. 500f. Rummenigge (West Germany) and Paolo Rossi (Italy) (56×32 mm) | 6·25 | 2·30 |

**168** Philidor and 19th-century European Rook

**1982.** Chess Grand Masters. Multicoloured.

| | | | |
|---|---|---|---|
| 638 | 30f. Type **168** (postage) | 85 | 10 |
| 639 | 40f. Paul Morphy and 19th-century Chinese knight | 1·00 | 15 |
| 640 | 50f. Howard Staunton and Lewis knight | 1·30 | 30 |
| 641 | 60f. Jean-Paul Capablanca and African knight | 1·40 | 40 |
| 642 | 80f. Boris Spassky and Staunton knight (air) | 2·10 | 55 |
| 643 | 300f. Anatoly Karpov and 19th-century Chinese knight | 4·25 | 1·10 |
| **MS**644 | 98×80 mm. 500f. Victor Kortschnoi and modern chess pieces (53×35 mm) | 9·50 | 2·75 |

**169** K. E. Tsiolkovski and "Soyuz"

**1983.** Exploitation of Space. Multicoloured.

| | | | |
|---|---|---|---|
| 645 | 30f. Type **169** (postage) | 55 | 10 |
| 646 | 40f. R. H. Goddard and space telescope | 55 | 15 |
| 647 | 50f. Korolev and ultra-violet telescope | 75 | 30 |
| 648 | 60f. Von Braun and Space Shuttle | 60 | 30 |
| 649 | 80f. Esnault Pelterie and "Ariane" rocket and "Symphonie" satellite (air) | 1·00 | 40 |
| 650 | 300f. H. Oberth and construction of orbiting space station | 3·50 | 1·10 |
| **MS**651 | 85×85 mm. 500f. J.F.Kennedy and first man on the Moon (vert 41×50 mm) | 6·25 | 2·30 |

**170** Charles and Robert Balloon, 1783

**1983.** Air. Balloons. Multicoloured.

| | | | |
|---|---|---|---|
| 652 | 100f. Type **170** | 85 | 25 |
| 653 | 200f. Blanchard balloon, Berlin, 1788 | 1·80 | 50 |
| 654 | 300f. Charles Green balloon, London, 1837 (horiz) | 2·40 | 80 |
| 655 | 400f. Modern advertising airship (horiz) | 3·00 | 1·00 |
| **MS**656 | 79×98 mm. 500f. Montgolfiere balloon, 1783 | 6·50 | 2·30 |

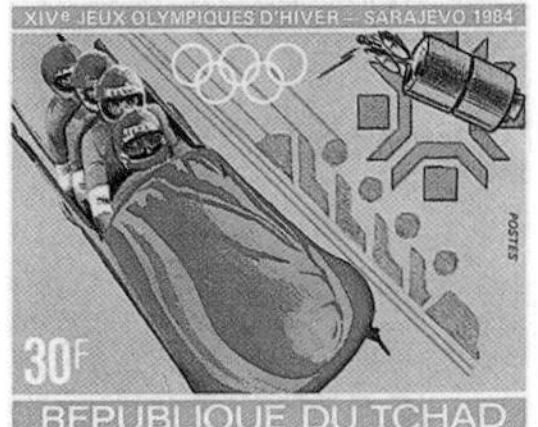


**171** Bobsleigh

**1983.** Winter Olympic Games, Sarajevo. Mult.

| | | | |
|---|---|---|---|
| 657 | 30f. Type **171** (postage) | 55 | 10 |
| 658 | 40f. Speed skating | 55 | 15 |
| 659 | 50f. Cross-country skiing | 75 | 30 |
| 660 | 60f. Ice hockey | 80 | 40 |
| 661 | 80f. Ski jump (air) | 1·00 | 40 |
| 662 | 300f. Downhill skiing | 3·50 | 1·10 |
| **MS**663 | 100×80 mm. 500f. Ice dancing | 5·50 | 2·20 |

**172** Montgolfier Brothers and "Le Martial" Balloon, 1783

**1983.** Bicentenary of Manned Flight. Multicoloured.

| | | | |
|---|---|---|---|
| 664 | 25f. Type **172** (postage) | 35 | 10 |
| 665 | 45f. Pilatre de Rozier and first manned flight, 1783 | 75 | 25 |
| 666 | 50f. Jacques Garnerin and balloon (first parachute descent, 1797) | 75 | 30 |
| 667 | 60f. J. P. Blanchard and balloon at Chelsea, 1784 | 85 | 70 |
| 668 | 80f. H. Giffard and steam- powered dirigible, 1852 (air) | 1·10 | 40 |
| 669 | 250f. Zeppelin and airship "L 21", 1900 | 3·25 | 1·10 |
| **MS**670 | 57×95 mm. 300f. Montgolfier Brothers and ascent of La Flesselles (41×38 mm) | 6·25 | 1·90 |

**173** Gottlieb Daimler, Karl Benz and Mercedes "Type S," 1927

**1983.** Car Manufacturers. Multicoloured.

| | | | |
|---|---|---|---|
| 671 | 25f. Type **173** (postage) | 40 | 10 |
| 672 | 35f. Friedrich von Martini and Torpedo, Martini "Type GC 32", 1913 | 75 | 15 |
| 673 | 50f. Walter P. Chrysler and Chrysler "70", 1926 | 75 | 30 |
| 674 | 60f. Nicola Romeo and Alfa Romeo "6 C 1750 Grand Sport", 1929 | 85 | 40 |
| 675 | 80f. Stewart Rolls, Henry Royce and "Phantom II Continental", 1934 (air) | 1·50 | 40 |
| 676 | 250f. Lord Shrewsbury and Talbot-Lago "Record", 1948 | 3·75 | 1·10 |
| **MS**677 | 109×68 mm. 300f. Ettore Bugatti and Royale Coupe de Ville "41", 1926–33 | 4·25 | 1·60 |

**174** Kayak

**1983.** Olympic Games, Los Angeles (2nd issue). Multicoloured.

| | | | |
|---|---|---|---|
| 678 | 25f. Type **174** (postage) | 35 | 10 |
| 679 | 45f. Long jumping | 75 | 15 |
| 680 | 50f. Boxing | 75 | 30 |
| 681 | 60f. Discus-throwing | 85 | 40 |
| 682 | 80f. Relay race (air) | 1·10 | 40 |
| 683 | 350f. Horse jumping | 3·75 | 1·10 |
| **MS**684 | 90×93 mm. 500f. Gymnastics (horiz 50×41 mm) | 5·00 | 1·60 |

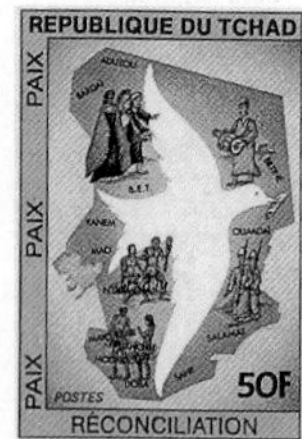

**175** Dove on Map

**1983.** Peace and Reconciliation. Multicoloured.

| | | | |
|---|---|---|---|
| 685 | 50f. Type **175** (postage) | 60 | 15 |
| 686 | 50f. Foodstuffs on map | 60 | 15 |
| 687 | 50f. President Habre | 80 | 20 |
| 688 | 60f. As No. 687 | 75 | 15 |
| 689 | 80f. Type **175** | 85 | 30 |
| 690 | 80f. As No. 686 | 90 | 30 |
| 691 | 80f. As No. 687 | 1·20 | 30 |
| 692 | 100f. As No. 687 | 1·00 | 30 |
| 693 | 150f. Type **175** (air) | 1·80 | 55 |
| 694 | 150f. As No. 686 | 1·80 | 55 |
| 695 | 200f. Type **175** | 2·50 | 80 |
| 696 | 200f. As No. 686 | 2·50 | 80 |

**1983.** 15th World Scout Jamboree, Canada. Nos. 610/15 optd XV WORLD JAMBOREE MONDIAL ALBERTA CANADA 1983.

| | | | |
|---|---|---|---|
| 697 | 30f. multicoloured (postage) | 35 | 10 |
| 698 | 40f. multicoloured | 45 | 10 |
| 699 | 50f. multicoloured | 55 | 20 |
| 700 | 60f. multicoloured | 65 | 20 |
| 701 | 80f. multicoloured (air) | 80 | 45 |
| 702 | 300f. multicoloured | 3·25 | 1·60 |

**1983.** 60th Anniv of Int Chess Federation. Nos. 638/43 optd 60e ANNIVERSAIRE FEDERATION MONDIAL D'ECHECS 1924–1984.

| | | | |
|---|---|---|---|
| 704 | 30f. multicoloured (postage) | 1·00 | 10 |
| 705 | 40f. multicoloured | 1·30 | 20 |
| 706 | 50f. multicoloured | 1·70 | 30 |
| 707 | 60f. multicoloured | 2·00 | 45 |
| 708 | 80f. multicoloured (air) | 2·50 | 65 |
| 709 | 300f. multicoloured | 5·00 | 2·20 |
| **MS**710 | 98×80 mm. 500f. multicoloured | 9·00 | 4·00 |

**178** Chad Martyrs

**1984.** Celebrities. Multicoloured.

| | | | |
|---|---|---|---|
| 711 | 50f. Type **178** (postage) | 60 | 15 |
| 712 | 200f. P. Harris and Rotary Headquarters, U.S.A. | 2·20 | 50 |
| 713 | 300f. Alfred Nobel and will | 3·75 | 90 |
| 714 | 350f. Raphael and "Virgin with the Infant and St. John the Baptist" | 5·25 | 1·10 |
| 715 | 400f. Rembrandt and "The Holy Family" (air) | 5·25 | 1·10 |
| 716 | 500f. Goethe and Scenes from "Faust" | 6·50 | 1·40 |
| **MS**717 | 78×86 mm. 600f. Rubens and "Helene Fourment and two of her Children" | 7·75 | 2·40 |

**179** Martyrs Memorial

**1984.** Martyrs Memorial.

| | | | | |
|---|---|---|---|---|
| 718 | **179** | 50f. mult (postage) | 60 | 10 |
| 719 | **179** | 80f. multicoloured | 90 | 25 |
| 720 | **179** | 120f. multicoloured | 1·20 | 40 |
| 721 | **179** | 200f. multicoloured (air) | 2·40 | 75 |
| 722 | **179** | 250f. multicoloured | 3·00 | 1·00 |

**180** Durer and Painting

**1984.** Celebrities and Events. Multicoloured.

| | | | |
|---|---|---|---|
| 723 | 50f. Type **180** (postage) | 1·10 | 10 |
| 724 | 200f. Henri Dunant and battle scene | 2·40 | 50 |
| 725 | 300f. Early telephone and satellite receiving station, Goonhilly Downs | 3·25 | 80 |
| 726 | 350f. President Kennedy and first foot-print on Moon | 4·00 | 95 |
| 727 | 400f. Infra-red satellite picture (Europe–Africa co-operation) (air) | 4·75 | 1·10 |
| 728 | 500f. Prince and Princess of Wales | 5·50 | 1·40 |
| **MS**729 | 60×110 mm. 600f. Wedding of Prince and Princess of Wales | 6·50 | 1·90 |

**181** "Communications"

**1984.** World Communications Year.

| | | | | |
|---|---|---|---|---|
| 730 | **181** | 50f. mult (postage) | 55 | 10 |
| 731 | **181** | 60f. multicoloured | 75 | 15 |
| 732 | **181** | 70f. multicoloured | 90 | 30 |
| 733 | **181** | 125f. multicoloured (air) | 1·50 | 35 |
| 734 | **181** | 250f. multicoloured | 2·75 | 1·10 |

**182** Two-man Kayak

**1984.** Air. Olympic Games, Los Angeles (3rd issue). Multicoloured.

| | | | |
|---|---|---|---|
| 735 | 100f. Type **182** | 1·10 | 45 |
| 736 | 200f. Kayaks (close-up) | 2·20 | 85 |
| 737 | 300f. One-man kayak | 2·75 | 1·30 |
| 738 | 400f. Coxed fours | 3·75 | 1·70 |
| **MS**739 | 104×80 mm. 500f. Coxless four | 5·25 | 2·75 |

**183** Class 13 Kitson Steam Locomotive

**1984.** Historic Transport. Multicoloured.

| | | | |
|---|---|---|---|
| 740 | 50f. Type **183** (postage) | 95 | 25 |
| 741 | 200f. Sailing boat on Lake Chad | 2·50 | 90 |
| 742 | 300f. Graf Zeppelin (airship) | 4·75 | 1·40 |
| 743 | 350f. Six-wheel Renault automobile, 1930 | 4·50 | 1·70 |
| 744 | 400f. Bloch "120" airplane (air) | 4·75 | 1·90 |
| 745 | 500f. Douglas "DC-8" airplane | 5·75 | 2·30 |
| **MS**746 | 84×109 mm. 600f. Ariane space rocket and "Intelsat V" communications satellite | 6·75 | 4·00 |

**184** African with broken Manacles

**1984.** 2nd Anniv of Entrance of Government Forces in N'Djamena.

| | | | | |
|---|---|---|---|---|
| 747 | **184** | 50f. multicoloured | 75 | 40 |

**185** Pres. Hissein Habre

**1984**

| | | | | |
|---|---|---|---|---|
| 748 | **185** | 125f. black, blue & yellow | 1·80 | 75 |

**186** British East Indiaman

**1984.** Transport. Multicoloured. (a) Ships.

| | | | |
|---|---|---|---|
| 749 | 90f. Type **186** | 1·20 | 50 |
| 750 | 125f. "Vera Cruz" (steamer) | 1·90 | 75 |
| 751 | 200f. "Carlisle Castle" (sail merchantman) | 3·25 | 1·20 |
| 752 | 300f. "Britannia" (steamer) | 4·50 | 1·60 |

(b) Locomotives.

| | | | |
|---|---|---|---|
| 753 | 100f. Series 701, 1885, France | 1·60 | 45 |
| 754 | 150f. "Columbia", 1888, Belgium | 1·90 | 75 |
| 755 | 250f. Mediterranean locomotive, 1900, Italy | 3·25 | 1·10 |
| 756 | 350f. MAV 114 | 4·50 | 1·70 |

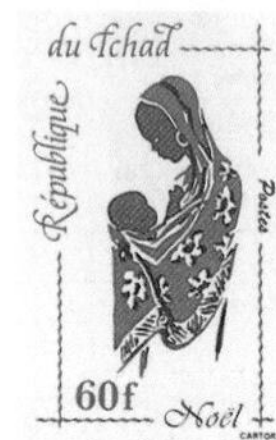

**187** Virgin and Child

**1984.** Christmas.

| | | | | |
|---|---|---|---|---|
| 757 | **187** | 50f. brown and blue | 60 | 20 |
| 758 | **187** | 60f. brown and orange | 70 | 30 |
| 759 | **187** | 80f. brown and green | 90 | 45 |
| 760 | **187** | 85f. brown and purple | 60 | 40 |
| 761 | **187** | 100f. brown and orange | 1·50 | 55 |
| 762 | **187** | 135f. brown and blue | 1·60 | 85 |

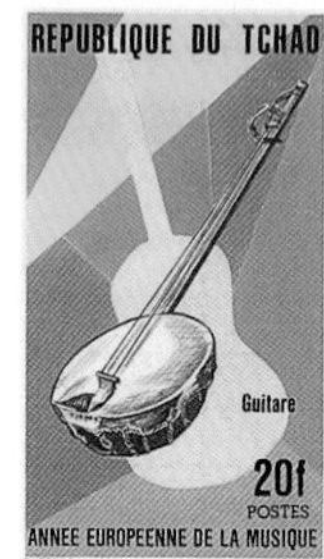

**188** Guitars

**1985.** European Music Year. Multicoloured.

| | | | |
|---|---|---|---|
| 763 | 20f. Type **188** | 30 | 10 |
| 764 | 25f. Harps | 35 | 10 |
| 765 | 30f. Xylophones | 40 | 20 |
| 766 | 50f. Drums | 55 | 40 |
| 767 | 70f. As No. 766 | 90 | 45 |
| 768 | 80f. As No. 764 | 1·10 | 50 |
| 769 | 100f. Type **188** | 1·50 | 70 |
| 770 | 250f. As No. 765 | 3·00 | 1·40 |

**189** "Chlorophyllum molybdites"

**1985.** Fungi. Multicoloured.

| | | | |
|---|---|---|---|
| 771 | 25f. Type **189** | 50 | 10 |
| 772 | 30f. "Tulostoma volvulatum" | 70 | 10 |
| 773 | 50f. "Lentinus tuberregium" | 90 | 40 |
| 774 | 70f. As No. 773 | 1·30 | 50 |
| 775 | 80f. "Podaxis pistillaris" | 1·50 | 55 |
| 776 | 100f. Type **189** | 2·20 | 85 |

**190** Stylized Tree and Scout

**1985.** Air. "Philexafrique" Stamp Exhibition, Lome, Togo (1st issue). Multicoloured.

| | | | |
|---|---|---|---|
| 777 | 200f. Type **190** | 3·00 | 2·30 |
| 778 | 200f. Fokker "27" airplane | 3·00 | 2·30 |

See also Nos. 808/9.

**191** Abraham Lincoln

**1985.** Celebrities. Multicoloured.

| | | | |
|---|---|---|---|
| 779 | 25f. Type **191** (postage) | 35 | 10 |
| 780 | 45f. Henri Dunant (founder of Red Cross) | 80 | 10 |
| 781 | 50f. Gottlieb Daimler (automobile designer) | 85 | 20 |
| 782 | 60f. Louis Bleriot (pilot) (air) | 1·00 | 30 |
| 783 | 80f. Paul Harris (founder of Rotary International) | 1·10 | 50 |
| 784 | 350f. Auguste Piccard (undersea explorer) | 5·00 | 1·70 |
| **MS**785 | 78×75 mm. 600f. Anatoly Karpov (chess champion) | 7·75 | 4·25 |

**192** Figures within Geometric Pattern

**1985.** International Youth Year. Multicoloured.

| | | | |
|---|---|---|---|
| 786 | 70f. Type **192** | 80 | 35 |
| 787 | 200f. Figures on ribbon around globe | 2·00 | 1·20 |

**193** Sun and Hands breaking through Darkness

**1985.** 3rd Anniv of Entrance of Government Forces in N'DJamena. Multicoloured.

| | | | |
|---|---|---|---|
| 788 | 70f. Type **193** | 85 | 40 |
| 789 | 70f. Claw attacking hand | 85 | 40 |
| 790 | 70f. Pres. Hissein Habre (36×48 mm) | 85 | 40 |
| 791 | 110f. Type **193** | 1·50 | 85 |
| 792 | 110f. As No. 789 | 1·50 | 85 |
| 793 | 110f. As No. 790 | 1·50 | 85 |

**194** Saddle-bill Stork ("Jabiru")

**1985.** Birth Bicentenary of John J. Audubon (ornithologist).

| | | | | |
|---|---|---|---|---|
| 794 | **194** | 70f. black, blue & brown | 1·20 | 60 |
| 795 | - | 110f. olive, green & brown | 1·70 | 85 |
| 796 | - | 150f. blue, red and olive | 2·40 | 1·20 |
| 797 | - | 200f. dp blue, mauve & bl | 3·25 | 1·80 |
| **MS**798 | | 129×100 mm. 500f. sepia, brown and olive | 7·25 | 6·75 |

DESIGNS: 110f. Ostrich; 150f. Marabou stork; 200, 500f. Crested serpent eagle.

**195** Fokker Friendship, Farman M.F.11 and Emblem

**1985.** Air. 25th Anniv of ASECNA (navigation agency). Multicoloured.

| | | | |
|---|---|---|---|
| 799 | 70f. Type **195** | 90 | 45 |
| 800 | 110f. Fokker "F.27" "Friendship" and "Spirit of St. Louis" | 1·50 | 65 |
| 801 | 250f. Fokker "F.27" "Friendship" and Vickers Vimy | 2·75 | 1·60 |

**196** Sitatunga

**1985.** Mammals.

| | | | | |
|---|---|---|---|---|
| 802 | **196** | 50f. brown, bl & dp brn | 85 | 50 |
| 803 | - | 70f. brown, green and red | 1·10 | 75 |
| 804 | - | 250f. multicoloured | 3·75 | 2·30 |
| **MS**805 | | 130×100 mm. 500f. black, red and turquoise | 6·50 | 5·75 |

DESIGNS—HORIZ:70f. Greater kudus; 500f. White rhinoceros. VERT: 250f. Bearded mouflons.

**197** U.N. Emblem on Peace Dove and Girl with Flowers

**1985.** 40th Anniv of UNO and 25th Anniv of U.N. Membership.

| | | | | |
|---|---|---|---|---|
| 806 | **197** | 200f. blue, red & brown | 2·20 | 1·50 |
| 807 | - | 300f. blue, red & yellow | 3·50 | 2·10 |

DESIGN: 300f. U.N. emblem as flower with peace doves forming stalk.

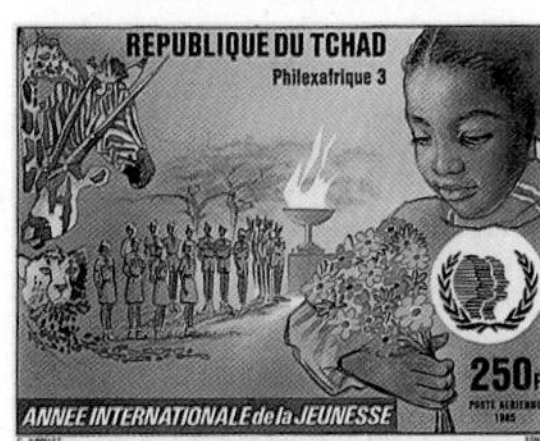

**198** Girl with Posy, Youth Ceremony and IYY Emblem

**1985.** Air. "Philexafrique" Stamp Exhibition, Lome, Togo (2nd issue). Multicoloured.

| | | | |
|---|---|---|---|
| 808 | 250f. Type **198** (International Youth Year) | 4·00 | 2·50 |
| 809 | 250f. Computer terminal, liner, airplane, diesel freight train, rocket and UPU emblem | 4·00 | 2·50 |

**199** Hugo

**1985.** Air. Death Centenary of Victor Hugo (writer).

| | | | | |
|---|---|---|---|---|
| 810 | **199** | 70f. blue, sepia and brown | 90 | 45 |
| 811 | **199** | 110f. brown, green & red | 1·50 | 65 |
| 812 | **199** | 250f. black, red & orange | 2·75 | 1·50 |
| 813 | **199** | 300f. purple, blue and red | 4·25 | 1·80 |

**200** Nativity

**1985.** Air. Christmas.

| | | | | |
|---|---|---|---|---|
| 814 | **200** | 250f. multicoloured | 3·00 | 1·20 |

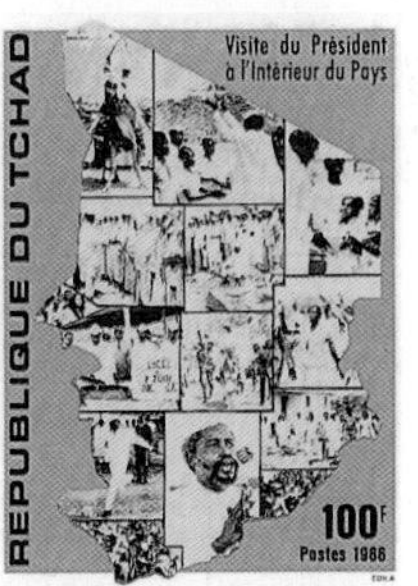

**201** Pictures of Visit on Map

**1986.** Visit of President to Interior.

| | | | | |
|---|---|---|---|---|
| 815 | **201** | 100f. yellow, black & grn | 1·40 | 70 |
| 816 | **201** | 170f. yellow, black & pink | 2·50 | 1·10 |
| 817 | **201** | 200f. yellow, black & grn | 2·75 | 1·70 |

**1987.** Various stamps surch.

| | | | | |
|---|---|---|---|---|
| 822 | **175** | 100f. on 200f. mult (air) | 70 | 55 |
| 823 | - | 100f. on 200f. mult (696) | 60 | 60 |
| 824 | - | 100f. on 250f. mult (669) | 70 | 55 |
| 825 | - | 100f. on 300f. mult (643) | 40 | 30 |
| 826 | - | 100f. on 300f. mult (662) | 40 | 30 |
| 827 | **179** | 170f. on 200f. mult | 70 | 60 |
| 828 | **181** | 170f. on 250f. mult | 1·10 | 90 |
| 818 | - | 170f. on 300f. mult (725) (postage) | 70 | 60 |
| 829 | - | 170f. on 300f. mult (601) | 70 | 60 |
| 830 | - | 170f. on 300f. mult (622) | 70 | 60 |
| 819 | - | 230f. on 300f. blue, red and yellow (807) | 1·00 | 85 |
| 820 | - | 240f. on 300f. mult (742) | 1·00 | 85 |
| 831 | - | 240f. on 300f. mult (636) | 1·00 | 90 |

**203** Fada

**1987.** Liberation of Fada.

| | | | | |
|---|---|---|---|---|
| 832 | **203** | 40f. multicoloured | | |

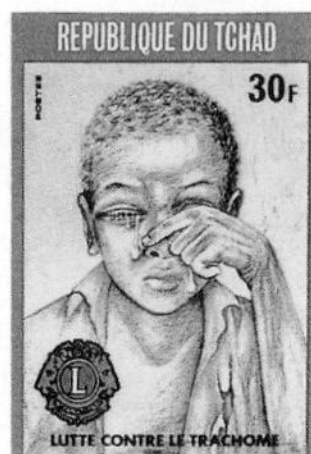

**204** Boy suffering from Trachoma

**1987.** Lions Club Anti-trachoma Campaign. Mult.

| | | | |
|---|---|---|---|
| 835 | 30f. Type **204** | | |
| 837 | 100f. Type **204** | | |
| 838 | 120f. Healthy boy and afflicted boys (horiz) | | |
| 840 | 200f. Doctor examining boy (horiz) | | |

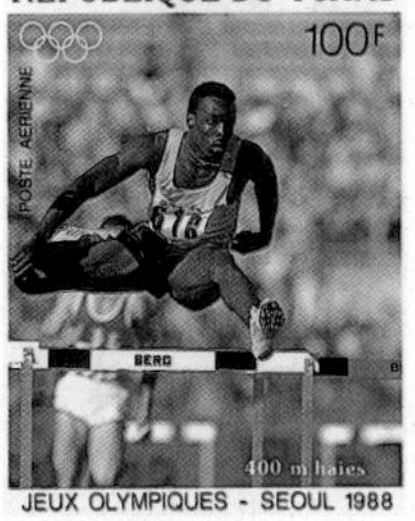

**205** 400 m Hurdles

**1988.** Air. Olympic Games, Seoul. Multicoloured.

| | | | |
|---|---|---|---|
| 841 | 100f. Type **205** | 1·20 | 45 |
| 842 | 170f. 5000 m (horiz) | 1·90 | 80 |
| 843 | 200f. Long jump (horiz) | 2·40 | 85 |
| 844 | 600f. Triple jump | 6·50 | 2·75 |
| **MS**845 | 105×80 mm. 750f. 10,000 metres | 8·50 | 4·50 |

**206** Barbary Sheep

**1988.** Endangered Animals. Barbary Sheep. Mult.

| | | | |
|---|---|---|---|
| 846 | 25f. Type **206** | 2·00 | 75 |
| 847 | 45f. Mother and lamb | 2·50 | 85 |
| 848 | 70f. Two sheep | 3·00 | 1·00 |
| 849 | 100f. Two adults with lamb | 4·50 | 1·70 |

**207** President and Crowd on Map

**1989.** "Liberation".

| | | | | |
|---|---|---|---|---|
| 850 | **207** | 20f. multicoloured | 30 | 10 |
| 851 | **207** | 25f. multicoloured | 35 | 10 |
| 852 | **207** | 40f. multicoloured | 55 | 20 |
| 853 | **207** | 100f. multicoloured | 1·60 | 50 |
| 854 | **207** | 170f. multicoloured | 2·20 | 1·10 |

**208** Boy posting Letter

**1989.** World Post Day.

| | | | | |
|---|---|---|---|---|
| 855 | **208** | 100f. multicoloured | | |
| 856 | **208** | 120f. multicoloured | | |
| 857 | **208** | 170f. multicoloured | | |
| 858 | **208** | 250f. multicoloured | | |

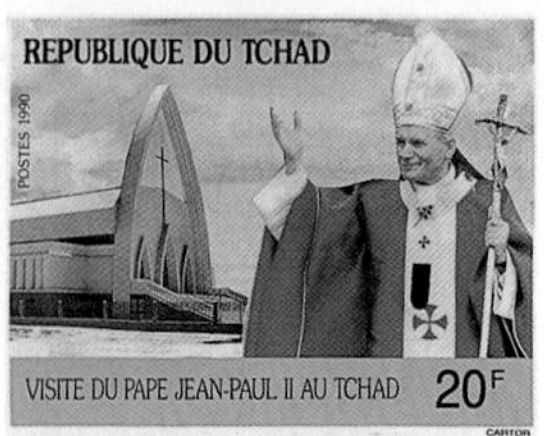


**209** N'Djamena Cathedral and Pope with Crucifix

**1990.** Visit of Pope John Paul II. Multicoloured.

| No. | Description | Unused | Used |
|---|---|---|---|
| 859 | 20f. Type **209** | 45 | 10 |
| 860 | 80f. Cathedral and Pope (different) | 1·10 | 55 |
| 861 | 100f. Type **209** | 1·30 | 85 |
| 862 | 170f. As No. 860 | 2·20 | 1·60 |

**210** Traditional Hairstyle

**1990**

| No. | Type | Description | Unused | Used |
|---|---|---|---|---|
| 863 | **210** | 100f. multicoloured | 24·00 | |
| 864 | **210** | 120f. multicoloured | 24·00 | |
| 865 | **210** | 170f. multicoloured | 25·00 | |
| 866 | **210** | 250f. multicoloured | 26·00 | |

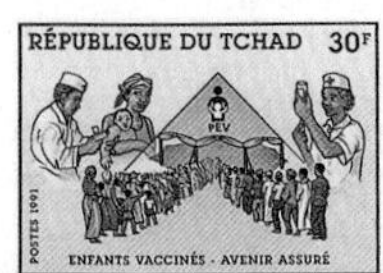


**215** Queues and Nurse vaccinating Child

**1991.** "Child Vaccination—Assured Future".

| No. | Type | Description | Unused | Used |
|---|---|---|---|---|
| 880 | **215** | 30f. multicoloured | 40 | 10 |
| 881 | **215** | 100f. multicoloured | 1·10 | 75 |
| 882 | **215** | 170f. multicoloured | 1·80 | 1·20 |
| 883 | **215** | 180f. multicoloured | 2·00 | 1·30 |
| 884 | **215** | 200f. multicoloured | 2·20 | 1·50 |

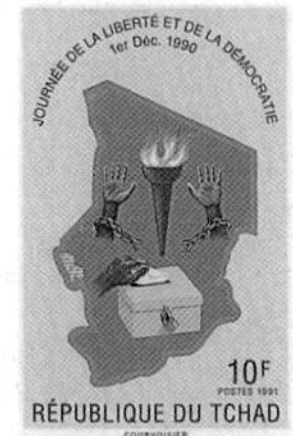


**216** Torch, Hands with Broken Manacles and Ballot Box

**1991.** Day of Freedom and Democracy.

| No. | Type | Description | Unused | Used |
|---|---|---|---|---|
| 885 | **216** | 10f. multicoloured | 10 | 10 |
| 886 | **216** | 20f. multicoloured | 30 | 10 |
| 887 | **216** | 40f. multicoloured | 50 | 30 |
| 888 | **216** | 70f. multicoloured | 65 | 55 |
| 889 | **216** | 130f. multicoloured | 1·40 | 1·20 |
| 890 | **216** | 200f. multicoloured | 2·10 | 1·40 |

**217** Mother and Child

**1992.** 20th Anniv of Medecins sans Frontieres (medical relief organization).

| No. | Type | Description | Unused | Used |
|---|---|---|---|---|
| 891 | **217** | 20f. multicoloured | 30 | 10 |
| 892 | **217** | 45f. multicoloured | 50 | 20 |
| 893 | **217** | 85f. multicoloured | 1·10 | 60 |
| 894 | **217** | 170f. multicoloured | 2·00 | 1·20 |
| 895 | **217** | 300f. multicoloured | 3·25 | 2·10 |

**218** Class

**1992.** Literacy Campaign.

| No. | Type | Description | Unused | Used |
|---|---|---|---|---|
| 896 | **218** | 25f. multicoloured | 30 | 10 |
| 897 | **218** | 40f. multicoloured | 50 | 20 |
| 898 | **218** | 70f. multicoloured | 65 | 50 |
| 899 | **218** | 100f. multicoloured | 1·00 | 70 |
| 900 | **218** | 180f. multicoloured | 1·80 | 1·20 |
| 901 | **218** | 200f. multicoloured | 2·20 | 1·50 |

**219** Mother and Child, Globe and Cereals

**1992.** International Nutrition Conference, Rome.

| No. | Type | Description | Unused | Used |
|---|---|---|---|---|
| 902 | **219** | 10f. multicoloured | 35 | 10 |
| 903 | **219** | 60f. multicoloured | 80 | 45 |
| 904 | **219** | 120f. multicoloured | 1·80 | 80 |
| 905 | **219** | 500f. multicoloured | 5·00 | 3·00 |

**219a** Symbols of Literacy

**1997.** Development of Literacy.

| No. | Type | Description | Unused | Used |
|---|---|---|---|---|
| 905a | **219a** | 150f. multicoloured | 90 | 60 |
| 905b | **219a** | 300f. multicoloured | 1·80 | 1·20 |
| 905c | **219a** | 475f. multicoloured | 2·75 | 1·80 |

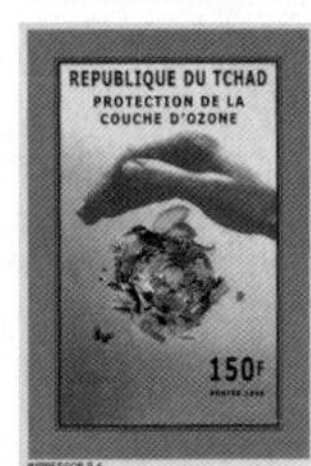


**219b** Hand over Symbols of Environment

**1998.** Protection of Ozone Layer.

| No. | Type | Description | Unused | Used |
|---|---|---|---|---|
| 905d | **219b** | 150f. multicoloured | 75 | 60 |
| 905e | **219b** | 300f. multicoloured | 1·80 | 1·20 |
| 905f | **219b** | 475f. multicoloured | 2·75 | 1·80 |
| 905g | **219b** | 500f. multicoloured | 3·00 | 2·00 |

**220** Stone Heads, Easter Island

**2000.** Wonders of the World. Multicoloured.

| No. | Description | Unused | Used |
|---|---|---|---|
| 906 | 50f. Type **220** | 10 | 10 |
| 907 | 150f. Stonehenge | 65 | 50 |
| 908 | 300f. Jericho | 1·30 | 1·00 |
| 909 | 400f. Machu Picchu | 1·80 | 1·40 |
| 910 | 500f. Valley of statues | 2·20 | 1·70 |
| 911 | 700f. Chichen Itza | 3·25 | 3·00 |
| 912 | 900f. Persepolis | 4·00 | 3·00 |

**221** Mastiff ("Matin Espagnol")

**2000.** Dogs. Multicoloured.

| No. | Description | Unused | Used |
|---|---|---|---|
| 915 | 400f. Type **221** | 1·40 | 55 |
| 916 | 500f. Kuvasz | 1·70 | 65 |
| 917 | 700f. Beauceron | 2·40 | 85 |
| 918 | 900f. Rough collie | 3·00 | 1·20 |

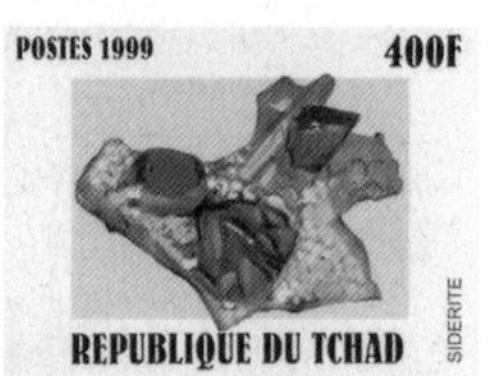


**222** Siderite

**2000.** Minerals. Multicoloured.

| No. | Description | Unused | Used |
|---|---|---|---|
| 921 | 400f. Type **222** | 1·80 | 1·40 |
| 922 | 500f. Dolomite and quartz | 2·20 | 1·70 |
| 923 | 700f. Azurite | 3·25 | 2·30 |
| 924 | 900f. Calcite | 4·00 | 3·00 |

**223** Renault (1906)

**2000.** Vintage Cars. Multicoloured.

| No. | Description | Unused | Used |
|---|---|---|---|
| 927 | 400f. Type **223** | 1·80 | 1·40 |
| 928 | 500f. Pierce Arrow (1919) | 2·20 | 1·70 |
| 929 | 700f. Citroen (1919) | 3·25 | 2·30 |
| 930 | 900f. Ford (1928) | 4·00 | 3·00 |

**224** Green Locomotive 0-6-0

**2000.** Trains. Multicoloured.

| No. | Description | Unused | Used |
|---|---|---|---|
| 933 | 400f. Type **224** | 1·80 | 1·40 |
| 934 | 500f. Brown locomotive | 2·20 | 1·70 |
| 935 | 700f. Blue locomotive | 3·25 | 2·30 |
| 936 | 900f. Purple locomotive with red stripe | 4·00 | 3·00 |

**225** Betty Boop

**2000.** Betty Boop (cartoon character). Multicoloured.

| No. | Description | Unused | Used |
|---|---|---|---|
| 937 | 250f. Type **225** | 1·10 | 85 |
| 938 | 250f. As cheer leader | 1·10 | 85 |
| 939 | 250f. Wearing fur coat | 1·10 | 85 |
| 940 | 250f. At soda bar | 1·10 | 85 |
| 941 | 250f. Wearing short leotard and leggings | 1·10 | 85 |
| 942 | 250f. Wearing cap and shorts | 1·10 | 85 |
| 943 | 250f. Wearing cap and leggings | 1·10 | 85 |
| 944 | 250f. Seated | 1·10 | 85 |
| 945 | 250f. Wearing ragged shorts and boots | 1·10 | 85 |
| **MS**946 | 89×140 mm. 1500f. Riding bicycle | 7·00 | 5·25 |
| **MS**947 | 140×94 mm. 2000f. Roller skating | 8·75 | 6·50 |

Nos. 937/8 and 940/5 have a composite background design.

**226** Larry and Curly

**2000.** Three Stooges (comedy act) (1st issue). Multicoloured.

| No. | Description | Unused | Used |
|---|---|---|---|
| 948 | 250f. Type **226** | 1·10 | 85 |
| 949 | 250f. As cowboys | 1·10 | 85 |
| 950 | 250f. As cowboys on horseback | 1·10 | 85 |
| 951 | 250f. Larry with raised arm | 1·10 | 85 |
| 952 | 250f. Moe having hair pulled | 1·10 | 85 |
| 953 | 250f. Moe holding hammer | 1·10 | 85 |
| 954 | 250f. As cowboys, Curly kneeling | 1·10 | 85 |
| 955 | 250f. Larry and Moe leading man by nose | 1·10 | 85 |
| 956 | 250f. Moe and patient | 1·10 | 85 |
| **MS**957 | 130×92 mm. 1500f. As No. 956 (42×51 mm) | 7·00 | 4·75 |
| **MS**958 | 122×92 mm. 2000f. As No. 954 (42×51 mm) | 8·75 | 6·50 |

See also Nos. 969/**MS**978.

**227** Lucy

**2000.** "I love Lucy" (TV show starring Lucille Ball). Multicoloured.

| No. | Description | Unused | Used |
|---|---|---|---|
| 959 | 225f. Type **227** | 1·00 | 70 |
| 960 | 225f. Crouched wearing tutu | 1·00 | 70 |
| 961 | 225f. Dressed as clown | 1·00 | 70 |
| 962 | 225f. Wearing tutu and wings | 1·00 | 70 |
| 963 | 225f. With leg raised | 1·00 | 70 |
| 964 | 225f. Falling backwards | 1·00 | 70 |
| 965 | 225f. With bent knees | 1·00 | 70 |
| 966 | 225f. Wearing clown outfit being sprayed with water | 1·00 | 70 |
| 967 | 225f. Wearing tutu with leg on barre | 1·00 | 70 |
| **MS**968 | Two sheets, each 122×88 mm. (a) 1500f. As clown (51×36 mm). (b) 2000f. As clown jumping | 17·00 | 12·50 |

**228** Larry and Moe

**2000.** Three Stooges (comedy act) (2nd issue). Multicoloured.

| No. | Description | Unused | Used |
|---|---|---|---|
| 969 | 300f. Type **228** | 1·50 | 1·00 |
| 970 | 300f. Larry and Moe wearing suits holding diplomas | 1·50 | 1·00 |
| 971 | 300f. Moe | 1·50 | 1·00 |
| 972 | 300f. Larry | 1·50 | 1·00 |
| 973 | 300f. Three Stooges | 1·50 | 1·00 |
| 974 | 300f. Shemp facing left | 1·50 | 1·00 |
| 975 | 300f. Shemp facing right | 1·50 | 1·00 |
| 976 | 300f. Shemp and Larry | 1·50 | 1·00 |
| 977 | 300f. Moe and Larry | 1·50 | 1·00 |
| **MS**978 | Two sheets, each 130×92 mm. (a) 1500f. Moe as troubadour (42×51 mm). (b) 2000f. Larry holding fiddle (42×51 mm) | 18·00 | 11·50 |

**229** Emblem

**2000.** Centenary of Fort Lamy N'Djamena.

| | | | | |
|---|---|---|---|---|
| 980 | **229** | 300f. multicoloured | | |
| 981 | **229** | 475f. multicoloured | | |

**230** Giraffes (*Giraffa camelopardalis*)

**2000.** Fauna. Multicoloured.

| | | | |
|---|---|---|---|
| 982 | 150f. Type **230** | 95 | 60 |
| 983 | 150f. Two giraffes | 95 | 60 |
| 984 | 150f. Three giraffes | 95 | 60 |
| 985 | 150f. Two giraffes (different) | 95 | 60 |
| 986 | 200f. Gazelle (*Gazella granti*) | 1·20 | 75 |
| 987 | 200f. Facing right | 1·20 | 75 |
| 988 | 200f. Eating | 1·20 | 75 |
| 989 | 200f. Drinking | 1·20 | 75 |
| 990 | 250f. Addax (*Addax nasomaculatus*) | 1·50 | 90 |
| 991 | 250f. Laying down | 1·50 | 90 |
| 992 | 250f. Facing left | 1·50 | 90 |
| 993 | 250f. Grazing | 1·50 | 90 |
| 994 | 300f. Barbary sheep(*Ammotragus lervia*) | 1·80 | 1·10 |
| 995 | 300f. Barbary sheep's head | 1·80 | 1·10 |
| 996 | 300f. Facing left | 1·80 | 1·10 |
| 997 | 300f. Facing front | 1·80 | 1·10 |
| 998 | 375f. Black rhinoceros (*Diceros bicornis*) | 2·10 | 1·40 |
| 999 | 375f. Facing right | 2·10 | 1·40 |
| 1000 | 375f. Facing left | 2·10 | 1·40 |
| 1001 | 375f. Amongst herbage | 2·10 | 1·40 |
| 1002 | 400f. Leopard (*Panthera pardus*) | 2·10 | 1·40 |
| 1003 | 400f. Laying down | 2·10 | 1·40 |
| 1004 | 400f. Facing left | 2·10 | 1·40 |
| 1005 | 400f. Leopard's head | 2·10 | 1·40 |
| 1006 | 450f. Hippopotamus (*Hippopotamus amphibius*) | 2·40 | 1·70 |
| 1007 | 450f. Two laying down | 2·40 | 1·70 |
| 1008 | 450f. Group | 2·40 | 1·70 |
| 1009 | 450f. Drinking | 2·40 | 1·70 |
| 1010 | 450f. Gelada baboon (*Theropithecus gelada*) | 2·40 | 1·70 |
| 1011 | 450f. Vervet monkey (*Cercopithecus aethiops*) | 2·40 | 1·70 |
| 1012 | 450f. Olive baboon (Papio anubis) | 2·40 | 1·70 |
| 1013 | 450f. Gelada baboon mother and baby | 2·40 | 1·70 |
| 1014 | 475f. Scimitar-horned oryx (*Oryx dammah*) | 2·75 | 1·90 |
| 1015 | 475f. Facing right | 2·75 | 1·90 |
| 1016 | 475f. Grazing | 2·75 | 1·90 |
| 1017 | 475f. Two scimitar-horned oryx | 2·75 | 1·90 |
| 1018 | 500f. Two lions (*Panthera leo*) | 2·75 | 1·90 |
| 1019 | 500f. Drinking | 2·75 | 1·90 |
| 1020 | 500f. Mother and cub | 2·75 | 1·90 |
| 1021 | 500f. Laying down | 2·75 | 1·90 |
| 1022 | 600f. Elephant (Loxodonta africana) | 3·25 | 2·10 |
| 1023 | 600f. Grazing | 3·25 | 2·10 |
| 1024 | 600f. Facing front | 3·25 | 2·10 |
| 1025 | 600f. Elephant's head | 3·25 | 2·10 |
| 1026 | 750f. African buffalo cow and calf (*Syncerus caffer*) | 4·00 | 2·50 |
| 1027 | 750f. African buffalo | 4·00 | 2·50 |
| 1028 | 750f. Laying down | 4·00 | 2·50 |
| 1029 | 750f. African buffalo's head | 4·00 | 2·50 |
| **MS**1030 | Three sheets, each 130×90 mm. (a) 1000f. Two hippopotami (42×51 mm). (b) 1000f. Two rhinoceros (42×51 mm). (b) 1500f. Lion eating (42×51 mm) | 19·00 | 14·50 |

Nos. 1031/50 and Types **231/40** are left for possible issues not yet seen.

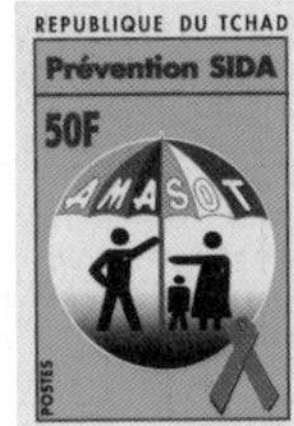

**241** Family under Umbrella

**2004.** AIDS Prevention Campaign. Multicoloured.

| | | | |
|---|---|---|---|
| 1051 | 50f. Type **241** | 40 | 25 |
| 1052 | 100f. Couple and 'PRUDENCE' | 80 | 50 |
| 1053 | 150f. Doctor holding medicines | 1·20 | 75 |
| 1054 | 300f. 'Prudence', 'Abstinence' and 'Fidelite' | 2·30 | 2·00 |

Nos. 1055/1060 and Types **242/5** are left for possible issues not yet seen.

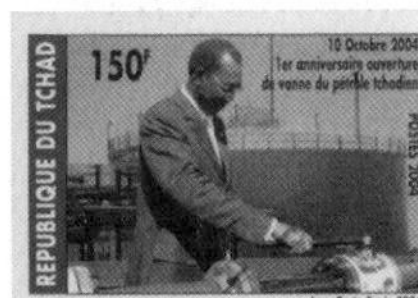

**246** Opening the Valuve and Storage Tank

**2004.** First Anniv of Chad Oil Pipeline. Multicoloured.

| | | | |
|---|---|---|---|
| 1061 | 150f. Type **246** | 80 | 40 |
| 1062 | 350f. Opening valve and two storage tanks | 1·70 | 80 |
| 1063 | 400f. Opening valve and refinery | 2·20 | 1·00 |
| 1064 | 500f. Opening valve and well head (vert) | 2·75 | 1·30 |

Nos. 1065/70 and Types **247/50** are left for possible issues not yet seen.

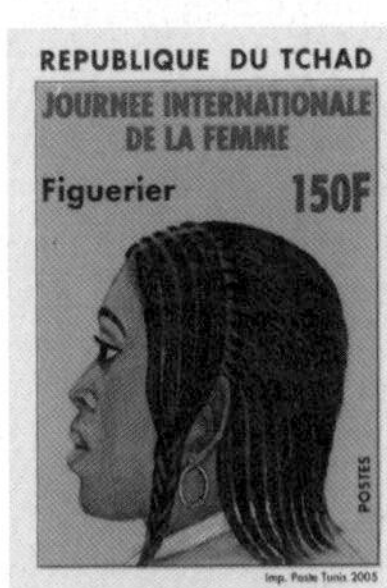

**251** Figuerier

**2005.** International Women's Day Women's Hairstyles. Multicoloured.

| | | | |
|---|---|---|---|
| 1071 | 150f. Type **251** | 90 | 45 |
| 1072 | 350f. Sakkindjala | 1·80 | 80 |
| 1073 | 550f. Kileskou | 2·40 | 1·20 |
| 1074 | 575f. Dabbou | 3·00 | 1·50 |

## MILITARY FRANK STAMPS

**1965.** No. 77 optd F.M.

| | | | |
|---|---|---|---|
| M148 | 20f. red and black | £325 | £325 |

**M 24** Soldier with Standard

**1966.** No value indicated.

| | | | | |
|---|---|---|---|---|
| M149 | **M 24** | (–) multicoloured | 2·00 | 3·50 |

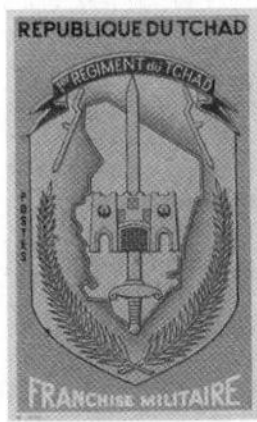

**M 92** Shoulder Flash of 1st Regiment

**1972.** No value indicated.

| | | | | |
|---|---|---|---|---|
| M353 | **M 92** | (–) multicoloured | 1·10 | 1·40 |

## OFFICIAL STAMPS

**O23** Flag and Map

**1966.** Flag in blue, yellow and red.

| | | | | |
|---|---|---|---|---|
| O148 | **O23** | 1f. blue | 10 | 10 |
| O149 | **O23** | 2f. grey | 10 | 10 |
| O150 | **O23** | 5f. black | 10 | 10 |
| O151 | **O23** | 10f. blue | 10 | 10 |
| O152 | **O23** | 25f. orange | 35 | 10 |
| O153 | **O23** | 30f. turquoise | 45 | 30 |
| O154 | **O23** | 40f. red | 90 | 40 |
| O155 | **O23** | 50f. purple | 45 | 30 |
| O156 | **O23** | 85f. green | 1·10 | 50 |
| O157 | **O23** | 100f. brown | 2·00 | 65 |
| O158 | **O23** | 200f. red | 3·25 | 1·10 |

## POSTAGE DUE STAMPS

**1928.** Postage Due type of France optd TCHAD A. E. F.

| | | | | |
|---|---|---|---|---|
| D58 | **D11** | 5c. blue | 45 | 6·50 |
| D59 | **D11** | 10c. brown | 45 | 6·50 |
| D60 | **D11** | 20c. olive | 1·00 | 7·00 |
| D61 | **D11** | 25c. red | 1·60 | 7·25 |
| D62 | **D11** | 30c. red | 1·60 | 7·25 |
| D63 | **D11** | 45c. green | 1·60 | 8·50 |
| D64 | **D11** | 50c. purple | 1·70 | 8·75 |
| D65 | **D11** | 60c. brown on cream | 1·80 | 9·50 |
| D66 | **D11** | 1f. red on cream | 2·00 | 9·50 |
| D67 | **D11** | 2f. red | 2·75 | 15·00 |
| D68 | **D11** | 3f. violet | 2·30 | 10·50 |

**D3** Village of Straw Huts

**D 4** Pirogue on Lake Chad

**1930**

| | | | | |
|---|---|---|---|---|
| D69 | **D3** | 5c. olive and blue | 60 | 7·25 |
| D70 | **D3** | 10c. brown and red | 1·00 | 7·50 |
| D71 | **D3** | 20c. brown and green | 2·30 | 8·00 |
| D72 | **D3** | 25c. brown and blue | 2·75 | 8·25 |
| D73 | **D3** | 30c. green and brown | 2·75 | 8·25 |
| D74 | **D3** | 45c. olive and green | 2·75 | 9·00 |
| D75 | **D3** | 50c. brown & mauve | 3·25 | 10·00 |
| D76 | **D3** | 60c. black and lilac | 3·75 | 13·00 |
| D77 | **D 4** | 1f. black and brown | 5·50 | 13·50 |
| D78 | **D 4** | 2f. brown and mauve | 5·25 | 21·00 |
| D79 | **D 4** | 3f. brown and red | 21·00 | 80·00 |

**D6** Gonoa Hippopotamus

**1962**

| | | | |
|---|---|---|---|
| D89 | 50c. bistre | 10 | 10 |
| D90 | 50c. brown | 10 | 10 |
| D91 | 1f. blue | 10 | 10 |
| D92 | 1f. green | 10 | 10 |
| D93 | 2f. red | 10 | 10 |
| D94 | 2f. red | 10 | 10 |
| D95 | 5f. myrtle | 60 | 60 |
| D96 | 5f. violet | 60 | 60 |
| D97 | 10f. brown | 1·10 | 1·10 |
| D98 | 10f. brown | 1·10 | 1·10 |
| D99 | 25f. purple | 2·75 | 2·75 |
| D100 | 25f. violet | 2·75 | 2·75 |

DESIGNS (rock-paintings): No. D89, Type D **6**; D90, Gonoa kudu; D91, Two Gonoa antelopes; D92, Three Gonoa antelopes; D93, Gonoa antelope; D94, Tibestiram; D95, Tibestiox; D96, Oudingueur boar; D97, Gonoa elephant; D98, Gira-Gira rhinoceros; D99, Bardai warrior; D100, Gonoa masked archer. The two designs in each value are arranged in tete-beche pairs throughout the sheet.

**D65** Kanem Puppet

**1969.** Native Puppets.

| | | | | |
|---|---|---|---|---|
| D284 | **D65** | 1f. brown, red & grn | 10 | 10 |
| D285 | - | 2f. brown, grn & red | 10 | 10 |
| D286 | - | 5f. green and brown | 10 | 10 |
| D287 | - | 10f. brown, pur & grn | 20 | 20 |
| D288 | - | 25f. brown, pur & grn | 45 | 25 |

DESIGNS: 2f. Kotoko doll; 5f. Copper doll; 10f. Kotoko (diff); 25f. Guera doll.

## APPENDIX

The following stamps have either been issued in excess of postal needs or have not been available to the public in reasonable quantities at face value. Such stamps may later be given full listing if there is evidence of regular postal use.

**1970**

"Apollo programme". Postage 40f.; Air 15, 25f.
Birth Bicent of Napoleon. Air. 10, 25, 32f.
World Cup Football Championship, Mexico. Air 5f.
World Cup. Previous Winners. 1, 4f., 5f.×2.
"Expo 70" World Fair, Osaka, Japan. Japanese Paintings. 50c., 1, 2f.
Christmas. Paintings. Postage 3, 25f.; Air 32f.
Past Olympic Venues. Postage 3, 8, 20f.; Air 10, 35f.

**1971**

Space Exploration. 8, 10, 35f.
Winter Olympic Games, Sapporo, Japan. Japanese Paintings. 50c., 1, 2f.
Kings and Queens of France. Postage 25f.×2, 30, 32, 35f., 40f.×2, 50f.×4, 60f.; Air 40, 50, 60, 70, 75, 80f., 100f.×5, 150f., 200f.×4.
150th Death Anniv of Napoleon. Air. 10f.
Famous Paintings. 1, 4, 5f.
Past Olympic Venues. Postage 15, 20f.; Air 25, 50f.
Winter Olympic Games, Sapporo, Japan. Optd on 1970 "Expo 70" issue 50c., 1, 2f.
Olympic Games Munich. World Cup Previous Winners issue (1970) optd **1f.**

**1972**

Moon Flight of "Apollo 15". Air 40, 80, 150, 250, 300, 500f.
"Soyuz 11" Disaster. Air 30, 50, 100, 200, 300, 400f.
Pres. Tombalbaye. Postage 30, 40f.; Air 70, 80f.
Winter Olympic Games, Sapporo, Japan. Postage 25, 75, 150f.; Air 130, 200f.
13th World Scout Jamboree, Asagiri, Japan (1971). Postage 30, 70, 80f.; Air 100, 200f.
Medal Winners, Sapporo Winter Olympics. Postage 25, 75, 100, 130f.; Air 150, 200f.
Olympic Games, Munich. Postage 20, 40, 60f.; Air 100, 120, 150f.
African Animals. Air 20, 30, 100, 130, 150f.
Medal Winners, Munich Olympics (1st series). Postage 10, 20, 40, 60f.; Air 150, 250f.
Medal Winners, Munich Olympics (2nd series). Gold frames, Postage 20, 30, 50f.; Air 150, 250f.

**1973**

Locomotives. 10, 40, 50, 150, 200f.
Domestic Animals (2nd issue). Postage 20, 30f.; Air 100, 130, 150f.
Horses. 20, 60, 100, 120f.
Airplanes. Air 5, 25, 70, 150, 200f.
Christmas. Postage 30, 40, 55f.; Air 60, 250f.

Other issues exist which were prepared by various agencies, but it is uncertain whether these were placed on sale in Chad. They include further values in the "Kings and Queens of France" series.

All the stamps below are on gold foil.

**1982**

World Cup Football Championship, Spain. Air 1500f.
21st Birthday of Princess of Wales. Air 1500f.
75th Anniv of Scout Movement. Air 1500f.
Olympic Games, Los Angeles. Air 1500f.
Birth of Prince William of Wales. 21st Birthday of Princess of Wales stamp optd. Air 1500f.

**1983**

World Cup Football Championship Results. Air 1500f.
Chess Grand Masters. Air 1500f.
Exploitation of Space. Air 1500f.
Winter Olympic Games, Sarajevo. Air 1500f.
Bicentary of Manned Flight. Air 1500f.
Olympic Games, Los Angeles. Air 1500f.

**1993**

30th Anniv of the Organisation for African Unity. 15f.; 30f.; 110f.; 190f.
Death Centenary of Victor Schoelcher. 55; 105; 125; 300f.

**1994**

Inauguration of Bank of Central African States 20; 30; 105; 190f.

**1995**

Traditional Grain Stores. 75; 150; 300; 450f.

**1996**

Fungi. 150; 170; 200; 350; 450; 800f.
Marilyn Monroe Commemoration. 170; 200; 300; 1000f.
Singers and Entertainers. 170; 350; 500; 700f.
The Beatles. 300f.×9.

John Lennon Commemoration. 100f.×9.
Elvis Presley Commemoration. 500f.×9.
Jacqueline Kennedy Commemoration. 200f.×9.
Marilyn Monroe Commemoration. 250f.×9.
Olympic Games, Nagano. 250f.×4; 300f.×4.
Sumo Wrestlers. 400f.×4.
Michael Schumacher. 700f.×4.
Rotary International. Ungulates. 170; 350; 500; 600f.
Rotary International. Ungulates. Overprinted for Calgary '96. 170; 350; 500; 600f.
World Cup Football Championships. 150f.; 250f.; 300f.; 600f.
Scouting. 200f.; 250f.; 300f.; 400f.; 450f.; 500f.
UNICEF. 150f.; 170f.; 400f.; 500f.;
Red Cross. 100f.; 350f.
Lions. 200f.; 800f.
Rotary International. 300f.; 700f.
Scouting. 250f.; 1000f.
John Lennon Commemoration. 400f.; 600f.
Elvis presley commemoration.200f.; 350f.; 500f.; 800f.

**1997**

Deng Xiaoping Commemoration. 75f.×6
Bruce Lee commemoration. 125f.×6.
Jacqueline Kennedy Commemoration. 150f.×9.
Traditional Housework. 50f.; 100f.; 150; 300; 450; 500f.
Diana, Princess of Wales. 250f.×9; 300f.×9; 450f.×9.
John f. Kennedy Commemoration. 250f.×9.
20th Death Anniv of Elvis Presley. 600f.×9.
Marilyn Monroe Commemoration. 500f.×9.
Aircraft. 150f.×6; 200f.×6; 250f.×6; 475f.×6.
150th Anniv of Swiss Railways. 350f.×6.
Trains. 600f.×6.

**1998**

Personalities. 100; 150; 300; 450; 475; 500; 600; 800; 1000f.
50th Anniv of Diplomatic relations with India. 150f.×3.
Dogs and Cats. 330f.×2; 450f.×2; 475f.×2; 500f.×2.
Wild Animals. 150f.×2; 550f.×2; 600f.×2.
Traditional Hairstyles. 50; 100; 150; 300; 400f.
Fauna. 150f.×6; 250f.×6; 300f.×12; 350f.×6.
Butterflies. 660f.×6
Ostrich. Surcharged. 300f.×4 on 220f.×4
Kofi Annan. 150f.×9.
American Railway Pioneers. 200f.×9.
Bela Lugosi Commemoration. 250f.×9.
Pope John Paul II. 300f.×9.
Ronald Reagan. 450f.×9.
John Glenn. 500f.×9.
Fossils and Pre-History. 150f.×9.
Dinosaurs. 400f.×6; 450f.×6.
Historical Vehicles. 50; 150; 200; 300; 400; 500f.
Winter Olympic Games, Nagano. 100f.; 170f.; 350f.; 750f.

**1999**

African Birds. 75; 150; 200; 300; 400; 475f.
Diana, Princess of Wales Commemoration. 250f.×9.
Football. 300f.×4; 400f.×4; 500f.×4.
Chess. 375f.×6; 500f.×6.
Betty Boop. 450f.×9.
Carl Benz Commemoration. 250f.×6.
Elvis Presley Commemoration. 300f.×9.
Napoleon Bonaparte. 300×6.
Pope John Paul II. 475f.×6.
Space Exploration. 500f.×6.

**2001**

Personalities. 200f.; 250f.; 300f.; 400f.; 500f.; 550f.; 600f.; 750f.; 800f.; 1000f.

**2002**

Tomb of Tutankamun. 3000f.×8

**2003**

Eagle. 3000f.
Yugi Gagarin Commemoration. 3000f.

**2004**

Personalities.300f.; 350f.; 400f.×2; 750f.×2; 1000f.×2

Pt. 1

## CHAMBA

An Indian "convention" state of the Punjab.

12 pies = 1 anna; 16 annas = 1 rupee.

**Stamps of India overprinted.**

**1886.** Queen Victoria. Optd CHAMBA STATE in two lines.

| | | | | |
|---|---|---|---|---|
| 1 | **23** | ½a. turquoise | 1·75 | 1·75 |
| 2 | - | 1a. purple | 3·25 | 3·25 |
| 4 | - | 1a.6p. brown | 4·00 | 17·00 |
| 6 | - | 2a. blue | 2·25 | 2·75 |
| 7 | - | 2a.6p. green | 42·00 | £130 |
| 9 | - | 3a. orange | 3·00 | 7·00 |
| 11 | - | 4a. green (No. 96) | 6·00 | 12·00 |
| 12 | - | 6a. brown (No. 80) | 8·00 | 27·00 |
| 14 | - | 8a. mauve | 9·50 | 15·00 |
| 16 | - | 12a. purple on red | 7·50 | 19·00 |
| 17 | - | 1r. grey (No. 101) | 60·00 | £180 |
| 18 | **37** | 1r. green and red | 12·00 | 22·00 |
| 19 | **38** | 2r. red and brown | £130 | £475 |
| 20 | **38** | 3r. brown and green | £140 | £425 |
| 21 | **38** | 5r. blue and violet | £160 | £700 |

**1900.** Queen Victoria. Optd CHAMBA STATE in two lines.

| | | | | |
|---|---|---|---|---|
| 22 | **40** | 3p. red | 75 | 1·50 |
| 23 | **40** | 3p. grey | 60 | 3·00 |
| 25 | **23** | ½a. green | 75 | 2·50 |
| 26 | - | 1a. red | 1·25 | 50 |
| 27 | - | 2a. lilac | 14·00 | 42·00 |

**1903.** King Edward VII. Optd CHAMBA STATE in two lines.

| | | | | |
|---|---|---|---|---|
| 28 | **41** | 3p. grey | 25 | 1·75 |
| 30 | - | ½a. green (No. 122) | 1·25 | 1·25 |
| 31 | - | 1a. red (No. 123) | 2·50 | 1·50 |
| 33 | - | 2a. lilac | 2·50 | 4·25 |
| 34 | - | 3a. orange | 7·00 | 7·50 |
| 35 | - | 4a. olive | 8·50 | 27·00 |
| 36 | - | 6a. bistre | 5·00 | 29·00 |
| 37 | - | 8a. mauve | 7·50 | 27·00 |
| 39 | - | 12a. purple on red | 9·50 | 48·00 |
| 40 | - | 1r. green and red | 10·00 | 27·00 |

**1907.** King Edward VII. Optd CHAMBA STATE in two lines.

| | | | |
|---|---|---|---|
| 41 | ½a. green (No. 149) | 2·50 | 4·00 |
| 42 | 1a. red (No. 150) | 2·50 | 4·50 |

**1913.** King George V. Optd CHAMBA STATE in two lines.

| | | | | |
|---|---|---|---|---|
| 43 | **55** | 3p. grey | 40 | 1·50 |
| 44 | **56** | ½a. green | 2·00 | 2·25 |
| 45a | **57** | 1a. red | 2·50 | 4·75 |
| 55 | **57** | 1a. brown | 3·50 | 7·00 |
| 56 | **58** | 1½a. brown (No. 163) | 32·00 | £160 |
| 57 | **58** | 1½a. brown (No. 165) | 3·00 | 8·00 |
| 58 | **58** | 1½a. red | 1·00 | 27·00 |
| 47 | **59** | 2a. purple | 5·00 | 16·00 |
| 59 | **61** | 2a.6p. blue | 75 | 5·50 |
| 60 | **61** | 2a.6p. orange | 4·00 | 30·00 |
| 48 | **62** | 3a. orange | 6·00 | 11·00 |
| 61 | **62** | 3a. blue | 4·50 | 27·00 |
| 49 | **63** | 4a. olive | 4·25 | 7·00 |
| 50 | **64** | 6a. bistre | 6·00 | 10·00 |
| 51 | **65** | 8a. mauve | 7·00 | 20·00 |
| 52 | **66** | 12a. red | 5·50 | 16·00 |
| 53b | **67** | 1r. brown and green | 21·00 | 38·00 |

**1921.** No. 192 of India optd CHAMBA.

| | | | | |
|---|---|---|---|---|
| 54 | **57** | 9p. on 1a. red | 1·00 | 19·00 |

**1927.** Stamps of India (King George V) optd CHAMBA STATE in one line.

| | | | | |
|---|---|---|---|---|
| 62 | **55** | 3p. grey | 20 | 2·50 |
| 64 | **80** | 9p. green | 8·00 | 28·00 |
| 63 | **56** | ½a. green | 30 | 3·25 |
| 76 | **79** | ½a. green | 1·10 | 14·00 |
| 65 | **57** | 1a. brown | 2·25 | 2·25 |
| 77 | **81** | 1a. brown | 2·75 | 1·50 |
| 66 | **82** | 1a.3p. mauve | 2·00 | 7·50 |
| 67 | **58** | 1½a. red | 8·00 | 9·00 |
| 68 | **70** | 2a. lilac | 2·50 | 4·75 |
| 78 | **59** | 2a. red | 1·40 | 27·00 |
| 69 | **61** | 2a.6p. orange | 4·00 | 23·00 |
| 70 | **62** | 3a. blue | 1·25 | 25·00 |
| 80 | **62** | 3a. red | 3·00 | 16·00 |
| 71 | **71** | 4a. green | 1·25 | 8·50 |
| 81 | **63** | 4a. olive | 7·00 | 21·00 |
| 72 | **64** | 6a. bistre | 29·00 | £200 |
| 73 | **65** | 8a. mauve | 1·60 | 13·00 |
| 74 | **66** | 12a. red | 1·60 | 17·00 |
| 75 | **67** | 1r. brown and green | 16·00 | 38·00 |

**1938.** Stamps of India (King George VI Nos. 247/64) optd CHAMBA STATE.

| | | | | |
|---|---|---|---|---|
| 82 | **91** | 3p. slate | 17·00 | 28·00 |
| 84 | **91** | 9p. green | 13·00 | 45·00 |
| 83 | **91** | ½a. brown | 2·25 | 20·00 |
| 85 | **91** | 1a. red | 4·00 | 5·00 |
| 86 | **92** | 2a. red | 11·00 | 25·00 |
| 87 | - | 2a.6p. violet | 11·00 | 40·00 |
| 88 | - | 3a. green | 12·00 | 35·00 |
| 89 | - | 3a.6p. blue | 12·00 | 38·00 |
| 90 | - | 4a. brown | 28·00 | 42·00 |
| 91 | - | 6a. green | 35·00 | 90·00 |
| 92 | - | 8a. violet | 30·00 | 75·00 |
| 93 | - | 12a. red | 24·00 | 80·00 |
| 94 | **93** | 1r. slate and brown | 42·00 | 95·00 |
| 95 | **93** | 2r. purple and brown | 80·00 | £400 |
| 96 | **93** | 5r. green and blue | £120 | £600 |
| 97 | **93** | 10r. purple and red | £170 | £900 |
| 98 | **93** | 15r. brown and green | £160 | £1300 |
| 99 | **93** | 25r. slate and purple | £250 | £1400 |

**1942.** Stamps of India (King George VI) optd CHAMBA. (a) On issue of 1938.

| | | | | |
|---|---|---|---|---|
| 100 | **91** | ½a. brown | 80·00 | 65·00 |
| 101 | **91** | 1a. red | £120 | 75·00 |
| 102 | **93** | 1r. slate and brown | 24·00 | 70·00 |
| 103 | **93** | 2r. purple and brown | 24·00 | £300 |
| 104 | **93** | 5r. green and blue | 45·00 | £325 |
| 105 | **93** | 10r. purple and red | 80·00 | £550 |
| 106 | **93** | 15r. brown and green | £180 | £1000 |
| 107 | **93** | 25r. slate and purple | £150 | £1000 |

(b) On issue of 1940.

| | | | | |
|---|---|---|---|---|
| 108 | **100a** | 3p. slate | 2·25 | 8·00 |
| 110 | **100a** | 9p. green | 1·25 | 25·00 |
| 109 | **100a** | ½a. mauve | 1·00 | 8·00 |
| 111 | **100a** | 1a. red | 2·75 | 6·00 |
| 112 | **101** | 1½a. violet | 3·50 | 17·00 |
| 113 | **101** | 2a. red | 13·00 | 20·00 |
| 114 | **101** | 3a. violet | 27·00 | 65·00 |
| 115 | **101** | 3½a. blue | 14·00 | 50·00 |
| 116 | **102** | 4a. brown | 20·00 | 18·00 |
| 117 | **102** | 6a. green | 21·00 | 48·00 |
| 118 | **102** | 8a. violet | 24·00 | 65·00 |
| 119 | **102** | 12a. purple | 27·00 | 75·00 |
| 120 | - | 14a. purple (No. 277) | 18·00 | 3·00 |

**OFFICIAL STAMPS**

**Stamps of India overprinted**

**1886.** Queen Victoria. Optd SERVICE CHAMBA STATE.

| | | | | |
|---|---|---|---|---|
| O1 | **23** | ½a. turquoise | 1·00 | 20 |
| O3 | - | 1a. purple | 3·25 | 20 |
| O5 | - | 2a. blue | 3·25 | 3·00 |
| O7 | - | 3a. orange | 2·50 | 16·00 |
| O8 | - | 4a. green (No. 96) | 4·50 | 9·50 |
| O10 | - | 6a. brown (No. 80) | 6·00 | 18·00 |
| O13 | - | 8a. mauve | 4·50 | 4·50 |
| O14 | - | 12a. purple on red | 12·00 | 55·00 |
| O15 | - | 1r. grey (No. 101) | 20·00 | £200 |
| O16 | **37** | 1r. green and red | 6·50 | 50·00 |

**1902.** Queen Victoria. Optd SERVICE CHAMBA STATE.

| | | | | |
|---|---|---|---|---|
| O17 | **40** | 3p. grey | 60 | 1·00 |
| O18 | **23** | ½a. green | 2·00 | 4·75 |
| O20 | - | 1a. red | 2·00 | 75 |
| O21 | - | 2a. lilac | 13·00 | 42·00 |

**1903.** King Edward VII. Optd SERVICE CHAMBA STATE.

| | | | | |
|---|---|---|---|---|
| O22 | **41** | 3p. grey | 35 | 15 |
| O24 | **41** | ½a. green (No. 122) | 25 | 10 |
| O25 | **41** | 1a. red (No. 123) | 1·25 | 30 |
| O27 | - | 2a. lilac | 1·25 | 2·00 |
| O28 | - | 4a. olive | 3·50 | 22·00 |
| O29 | - | 8a. mauve | 10·00 | 23·00 |
| O31 | - | 1r. green and red | 1·75 | 17·00 |

**1907.** King Edward VII. Optd SERVICE CHAMBA STATE.

| | | | |
|---|---|---|---|
| O32 | ½a. green (No. 149) | 40 | 75 |
| O33 | 1a. red (No. 150) | 2·25 | 3·00 |

**1913.** King George V Official stamps optd CHAMBA STATE.

| | | | | |
|---|---|---|---|---|
| O34 | **55** | 3p. grey | 20 | 40 |
| O36 | **56** | ½a. green | 20 | 60 |
| O38 | **57** | 1a. red | 20 | 10 |
| O47 | **57** | 1a. brown | 5·50 | 1·25 |
| O40 | **59** | 2a. lilac (No. O83) | 1·10 | 18·00 |
| O41 | **63** | 4a. olive (No. O86) | 1·10 | 23·00 |
| O42 | **65** | 8a. mauve | 1·75 | 26·00 |
| O43 | **67** | 1r. brown and green | 7·00 | 42·00 |

**1914.** King George V Postage stamps optd SERVICE CHAMBA STATE.

| | | | | |
|---|---|---|---|---|
| O44 | **59** | 2a. lilac (No. 166) | 15·00 | |
| O45 | **63** | 4a. olive (No. 210) | 13·00 | |

**1921.** No O97 of India optd CHAMBA.

| | | | | |
|---|---|---|---|---|
| O46 | **57** | 9p. on 1a. red | 20 | 10·00 |

**1927.** King George V Postage stamps optd CHAMBA STATE SERVICE.

| | | | | |
|---|---|---|---|---|
| O48 | **55** | 3p. grey | 50 | 40 |
| O50 | **80** | 9p. green | 6·00 | 14·00 |
| O49 | **56** | ½a. green | 35 | 15 |
| O61 | **79** | ½a. green | 7·50 | 50 |
| O51 | **57** | 1a. brown | 20 | 10 |
| O62 | **81** | 1a. brown | 4·00 | 45 |
| O52 | **82** | 1¼a. mauve | 7·50 | 1·00 |
| O53 | **70** | 2a. lilac | 3·50 | 75 |
| O63 | **59** | 2a. red | 6·50 | 1·25 |
| O54 | **71** | 4a. olive | 2·00 | 3·50 |
| O65 | **63** | 4a. green | 9·50 | 9·00 |
| O55 | **65** | 8a. mauve | 11·00 | 14·00 |
| O56 | **66** | 12a. red | 6·50 | 30·00 |
| O57 | **67** | 1r. brown and green | 16·00 | 55·00 |
| O60 | **67** | 1r. green and red | 70·00 | £350 |
| O58 | **67** | 2r. red and orange | 25·00 | £300 |
| O59 | **67** | 5r. blue and violet | 45·00 | £350 |

**1938.** King George VI Postage stamps of India optd CHAMBA STATE SERVICE.

| | | | | |
|---|---|---|---|---|
| O66 | **91** | 9p. green | 40·00 | 80·00 |
| O67 | **91** | 1a. red | 45·00 | 8·50 |
| O68 | **93** | 1r. slate and brown | £200 | £750 |
| O69 | **93** | 2r. purple and brown | 42·00 | £475 |
| O70 | **93** | 5r. green and blue | 60·00 | £550 |
| O71 | **93** | 10r. purple and red | 85·00 | £950 |

**1940.** Official stamps of India optd CHAMBA.

| | | | | |
|---|---|---|---|---|
| O72 | **O20** | 3p. grey | 70 | 1·40 |
| O75 | **O20** | 9p. green | 10·00 | 16·00 |
| O73 | **O20** | ½a. brown | 60·00 | 5·00 |
| O74 | **O20** | ½a. purple | 70 | 4·50 |
| O76 | **O20** | 1a. red | 2·00 | 3·25 |
| O77 | **O20** | 1a.3p. brown | £120 | 24·00 |
| O78 | **O20** | 1½a. violet | 13·00 | 11·00 |
| O79 | **O20** | 2a. orange | 11·00 | 11·00 |
| O80 | **O20** | 2½a. violet | 7·00 | 29·00 |
| O81 | **O20** | 4a. brown | 11·00 | 24·00 |
| O82w | **O20** | 8a. violet | 22·00 | 95·00 |

**1942.** King George VI Postage stamps of India optd CHAMBA SERVICE.

| | | | | |
|---|---|---|---|---|
| O83 | **93** | 1r. slate and brown | 20·00 | £250 |
| O84 | **93** | 2r. purple and brown | 35·00 | £325 |
| O85 | **93** | 5r. green and blue | 70·00 | £550 |
| O86 | **93** | 10r. purple and red | 75·00 | £900 |

Pt. 1

## CHARKHARI

A state of Central India. Now uses Indian stamps.

12 pies = 1 anna; 16 annas = 1 rupee.

1

**1894.** Imperf. No gum.

| | | | | |
|---|---|---|---|---|
| 10 | **1** | ¼a. purple | 1·75 | 2·50 |
| 6a | **1** | ½a. purple | 2·50 | 3·00 |
| 7a | **1** | 1a. green | 4·50 | 7·00 |
| 8a | **1** | 2a. green | 7·00 | 9·00 |
| 9a | **1** | 4a. green | 7·50 | 17·00 |

2

**1909.** Perf or imperf.

| | | | | |
|---|---|---|---|---|
| 15a | **2** | 1p. brown | 5·00 | 38·00 |
| 16 | **2** | 1p. blue | 75 | 45 |
| 32 | **2** | 1p. green | 70·00 | £300 |
| 33 | **2** | 1p. violet | 22·00 | £190 |
| 25 | **2** | ½a. red | 2·75 | 1·60 |
| 34 | **2** | ½a. olive | 2·50 | 15·00 |
| 35 | **2** | ½a. brown | 6·00 | 26·00 |
| 36 | **2** | ½a. black | 70·00 | £250 |
| 18a | **2** | 1a. green | 3·25 | 1·75 |
| 40 | **2** | 1a. brown | 13·00 | 27·00 |
| 41 | **2** | 1a. red | £160 | 85·00 |
| 19 | **2** | 2a. blue | 3·25 | 3·25 |
| 43 | **2** | 2a. grey | 70·00 | 95·00 |
| 20 | **2** | 4a. green | 4·25 | 5·50 |
| 44 | **2** | 4a. red | 3·00 | 21·00 |
| 21 | **2** | 8a. red | 7·50 | 23·00 |
| 22 | **2** | 1r. brown | 13·00 | 48·00 |

4

**1912.** Imperf.

| | | | | |
|---|---|---|---|---|
| 28 | **4** | 1p. violet | 7·00 | 5·00 |

5

**1922.** Imperf.

| | | | | |
|---|---|---|---|---|
| 29 | **5** | 1a. violet | 90·00 | £100 |

7 The Lake

**1931.** Perf.

| | | | | |
|---|---|---|---|---|
| 45 | - | ½a. green | 2·50 | 10 |
| 46 | **7** | 1a. sepia | 1·60 | 10 |
| 47 | - | 2a. violet | 1·75 | 10 |
| 48 | - | 4a. olive | 1·75 | 15 |
| 49 | - | 8a. mauve | 2·75 | 10 |
| 50 | - | 1r. green and red | 3·50 | 20 |
| 51 | - | 2r. red and brown | 5·50 | 25 |
| 52 | - | 3r. brown and green | 20·00 | 40 |
| 53 | - | 5r. blue and lilac | 9·50 | 50 |

DESIGNS—HORIZ: ½a. The Lake; 2a. Industrial school; 4a. Bird's-eye view of city; 8a. Fort; 1r. Guest House; 2r. Palace Gate; 3r. Temples at Rainpur; 5r. Goverdhan Temple.

**1940.** Nos. 21/2 surch.

| | | | | |
|---|---|---|---|---|
| 54 | **2** | ½a. on 8a. red | 42·00 | £160 |
| 55 | **2** | 1a. on 1r. brown | £150 | £500 |
| 56 | **2** | "1 ANNA" on 1r. brown | £1500 | £1200 |

# Index